POULTNEY HIGH SCHOOL LIBRARY
154 E. Main Street
Poultney, VT 05764

THE AUTHORITY SINCE 1868

THE WORLD ALMANAC
ALMANAC®
AND BOOK OF FACTS
2010

WORLD ALMANAC BOOKS

THE WORLD ALMANAC®
AND BOOK OF FACTS
2010

Senior Editor: Sarah Janssen
Desktop Production Manager: Elizabeth J. Lazzara **Editor:** M. L. Liu
Consulting Editor: C. Alan Joyce **Index Editor:** Nan Badgett
Contributors: Jeremy Eagle, Brian Fitzgerald, Marshall Gerometta, Barbara Gottfried Hollander, Geoffrey M. Horn, Michael J. Kaufman, William A. McGeveran Jr., John Mastroberardino, Joyce A. Ober, Lisa Renaud, Shmuel Ross, Clayton Simmons, George W. Smith, Vincent G. Spadafora, Andrew Steinitz, Edward A. Thomas, Lori Wiesenthal, Dale Williams

Design, Year in Pictures: Bill Smith Group
Design, Cover: Takeshi Takahashi
Photo Research: Edward A. Thomas

For Infobase Publishing:
Editorial Director: Laurie Likoff
Project Editor: Edward A. Thomas
Production Director: T. J. Mancini

Photos are from AP Images unless otherwise noted. **Back Cover.** Polar bear & auto worker: Shutterstock. **Tabs.** Shutterstock: Stock market; Photodisc/BSS image: gold bars, circuit board; ©2007 JupiterImages: vials, movie reels, flag, golf tee; Corel Stock Photo Library/BSS Image: crowd, UN flag. **Text Pages. 60:** Dollar bill: ©2008 The United States Treasury Bureau of Engraving and Printing. **193, 809:** Afghanistan: U.S. Army photo by Sgt. Teddy Wade/Released. **193, 812:** Hubble: NASA. **195:** Bankers: Getty Images. **197:** Blagojevich: Getty Images. **198:** Cronkite: Everett Collection. **199:** Gosselins: WireImage/Getty Images. **200:** Boyle: Photo by Ken McKay/Rex USA, courtesy Everett Collection; Slumdog: ©Fox Searchlight/courtesy Everett Collection; Abdul: Getty Images. **317:** NOAA. **478, 479 (t), 480, 483 (t), 484 (b), 485-87, 652, 661-62, 664, 666-67:** Library of Congress. **491:** Nixon Presidential Materials Project. **492, 675:** Ronald Reagan Presidential Library. **496:** U.S. Navy Photo by Photographer's Mate 2nd Class Jim Watson. **497:** United States Coast Guard. **501, 503, 669:** NARA. **523-32:** Library of Congress, unless otherwise indicated; ©1967 by Dover Publications: J. Adams, Jackson, Harrison, Arthur, Harrison, McKinley, Harding, Hoover, Eisenhower; Lyndon B. Johnson Library: L. Johnson; Gerald R. Ford Museum: Ford; Jimmy Carter Library & Museum: Carter; Eric Draper-The White House: G. W. Bush; Pete Souza-The White House: Obama. **670, 678:** Getty Images. **812:** Fossil: Press Association via AP Images. **816:** Fawcett: Photo by Richard Young/Rex USA, Courtesy Everett Collection; Kitt: Getty Images; McNamara: DoD photo by Oscar Porter, U.S. Army (Released); Odetta: Getty Images; Wyeth: Time & Life Pictures/Getty Images.

Copyright © 2010 by Infobase Publishing
The World Almanac® and The World Almanac and Book of Facts® are registered trademarks of Infobase Publishing. All rights reserved. No part of this book may be reproduced or utilized in any form or by any means, electronic or mechanical, including photocopying, recording, or by any information storage or retrieval systems, without permission in writing from the publisher. For information contact:

World Almanac® Books
An imprint of Infobase Publishing
132 West 31st Street
New York, NY 10001

Hardcover	Paperback
ISBN-13: 978-1-60057-126-8	ISBN-13: 978-1-60057-123-7
ISBN-10: 1-60057-126-3	ISBN-10: 1-60057-123-9

Library of Congress Catalog Card Number 4-378
International Standard Serial Number (ISSN): 0084-1382

The World Almanac® and Book of Facts is available at special discounts when purchased in bulk quantities for businesses, associations, institutions, or sales promotions. Please call our Special Sales Department in New York at (212) 967-8800 or (800) 322-8755.

You can find The World Almanac® and Book of Facts on the Internet at www.worldalmanac.com.
Email: almanac@factsonfile.com

The World Almanac® and Book of Facts 2010
Book printed and bound by Hamilton Printing Company, Castleton, NY
Date printed: November 2009
Printed in the United States of America
HPC 10 9 8 7 6 5 4 3 2 1

CONTENTS

SPECIAL FEATURES

2009: YEAR IN REVIEW

2009: YEAR IN PICTURES 193, 809

ECONOMY, BUSINESS, & ENERGY

CRIME

MILITARY AFFAIRS

HEALTH & VITAL STATISTICS

PERSONALITIES, ARTS, & MEDIA

SCIENCE & TECHNOLOGY

CONSUMER INFORMATION

U.S. GOVERNMENT

U.S. FACTS, HISTORY, & ELECTIONS

U.S. CITIES, STATES, & POPULATION

WORLD HISTORY & CULTURE

SPORTS

GENERAL INDEX

THE WORLD ALMANAC
AND BOOK OF FACTS 2010

Top Ten News Topics of 2009

1. Obama Presidency Begins. With the U.S. at war in Iraq and Afghanistan, and facing its worst economic crisis since the Great Depression, Barack Obama was sworn in as the nation's 44th president Jan. 20 in Washington, DC. The inauguration of Obama and Vice Pres. Joe Biden, both Democrats, and the departure of a Republican administration headed by Pres. George W. Bush and Vice Pres. Dick Cheney heralded a major political as well as cultural shift, with Obama becoming the nation's first black president.

Pres. Obama assembled a cabinet that included Sec. of State Hillary Clinton, his principal 2008 Democratic campaign rival; Sec. of Defense Robert Gates, a Bush administration holdover; Eric Holder Jr., the first African American attorney general; and Treasury Sec. Tim Geithner. Later, Obama filled his first Supreme Court vacancy when Associate Justice David Souter stepped down in late June. Sonia Sotomayor, an experienced prosecutor and litigator with a long judicial record, was confirmed Aug. 6 by the Senate, becoming the first Hispanic to join the court.

2. Recession in U.S. Ends, but Jobless Rate Rises. The American Recovery and Reinvestment Act, a $787 bil stimulus measure that became law Feb. 17, was the largest legislative piece of the year-long effort to revive the ailing U.S. economy. Federal programs eased credit markets, aided first-time home buyers, and helped some mortgage holders avert foreclosure. Two of Detroit's "Big 3" automakers, General Motors and Chrysler, were restructured through government-managed bankruptcies, and "cash for clunkers" tax credits subsidized trade-ins of gas-guzzling vehicles.

Results were mixed. The economy emerged from recession as indicated by the U.S. gross domestic product, which grew at an annual rate of 3.5% during July-Sept., and the Dow Jones Industrial Average, which closed above the 10,000 mark Oct. 14 for the first time in a year. But the annual U.S. budget deficit soared to a record $1.4 tril, and employers continued to slash jobs. The unemployment rate rose to 10.2% in Oct., and 17.5% of Americans were either unemployed or underemployed.

3. Pullout from Iraq, Buildup in Afghanistan. The U.S. military withdrew from Iraq's cities and towns June 30, and America's coalition partners removed their last remaining combat forces in July, but around 130,000 U.S. troops remained in bases on Iraqi soil. Insurgents exploited security gaps, launching bloody attacks Aug. 19 and Oct. 25 against the government of Prime Min. Nouri al-Maliki in Baghdad.

Pres. Obama announced Feb. 17 that the U.S. would raise its troop strength in Afghanistan by 17,000, for a projected total of 68,000. Seven months later, with coalition and civilian casualties mounting, U.S. commanders requested another 40,000 or more troops. Afghanistan held a presidential election Aug. 20, but international monitors found the balloting riddled with fraud. A runoff election was scheduled Nov. 7 between incumbent Pres. Hamid Karzai and former Foreign Min. Abdullah Abdullah, but the challenger pulled out, saying a fair vote could not be held. Meanwhile, militants stepped up activities in neighboring Pakistan, where the government launched major offensives to dislodge the Taliban and al-Qaeda from the Swat Valley and South Waziristan.

4. U.S. Launches Diplomatic Outreach. Emphasizing collective diplomacy over unilateral action, the Obama administration shifted U.S. foreign policy. Obama ordered the closure of the U.S. military prison at Guantánamo Bay, barred the use of torture in the interrogation of suspected terrorist detainees, encouraged negotiations on nuclear disarmament and global warming, and made conciliatory gestures toward Cuba, Iran, and Russia. In a major speech June 4 at Cairo University in Egypt, Pres. Obama called for "a new beginning" in relations between the U.S. and the Muslim world. Obama had been in office less than 9 months when the Norwegian Nobel Committee Oct. 9 surprised the world (and outraged some of Obama's U.S. critics) by awarding him the 2009 Nobel Peace Prize.

5. Protests Follow Iran Election. Iran's Islamic regime faced its most serious crisis in decades following elections June 12. Defying expectations of a close result, official tallies gave Pres. Mahmoud Ahmadinejad a landslide win over former Prime Min. Mir Hussein Moussavi, a conservative reformer. Protests by hundreds of thousands of Iranians in Tehran and other cities were crushed by police and paramilitary groups. Under Ahmadinejad, Iran continued to pursue its nuclear program. Accused Sept. 25 of building a secret uranium enrichment facility near Qom, Iran agreed Oct. 1 to open the facility to international inspection.

6. Democrats Push Agenda; Conservatives Push Back. In control of the White House and both houses of Congress, Democrats acted on an agenda that included challenging workplace pay discrimination, expanding national service programs, and regulating tobacco products and greenhouse gases. Republicans and their conservative allies denounced the growth of federal power and deficit spending. They held anti-tax "tea party" protests Apr. 15, disrupted town hall meetings convened by some lawmakers in Aug., and organized a protest march Sept. 12 in Washington, DC. During months of rancorous debate over health insurance reform, they blasted legislation backed by Democrats as a dangerous "government takeover" of the U.S. health care system.

7. Global Swine Flu Pandemic. An outbreak of swine flu—officially called influenza A (H1N1)—triggered worldwide alerts by public health authorities. The World Health Organization (WHO) June 11 raised its H1N1 pandemic warning to the highest level. In late Oct., WHO reported more than 440,000 confirmed H1N1 cases and at least 5,700 deaths. Between Aug. 30 and Oct. 31, U.S. authorities said 17,838 Americans had been hospitalized with H1N1, and 672 had died from it. Pres. Obama declared the outbreak a national emergency Oct. 24, giving hospitals greater latitude in dealing with an influx of new patients. Because of manufacturing delays, deliveries of swine flu vaccine in the U.S. were behind schedule.

8. Worldwide Economic Picture Brightens. Countries around the world battled a severe recession through economic stimulus programs and international financial reforms. In a series of summit meetings the Group of 20 (G-20), which includes developed nations and emerging economies such as China and India, agreed on ways to strengthen oversight of multinational financial institutions, boost resources for emergency lending by the International Monetary Fund (IMF), and ensure that national policies promoted international economic stability. On Oct. 1 the IMF forecasted that world economic activity would increase about 3.1% in 2010.

9. North Korea Policy Shifts. Responding to UN condemnation of its Apr. 5 rocket launch over the Pacific, North Korea said Apr. 14 that it would restart its nuclear weapons program. In late May the nation carried out an underground nuclear test and test-fired several short-range missiles, drawing an immediate UN rebuke. North Korea's tone changed, however, after a visit Aug. 4-5 by former U.S. Pres. Bill Clinton, who succeeded in winning the release of 2 American journalists who had been held by North Korea since Mar. 17. Following the Clinton mission, North Korea made several conciliatory gestures toward South Korea, including an easing of restrictions on family visits and commercial traffic.

10. Israelis Elect Netanyahu After Gaza War. A truce Jan. 18 ended a 3-week Israeli assault against Hamas militants in the Gaza Strip. The offensive, which also killed hundreds of Palestinian civilians, sought to halt years of Hamas rocket attacks against southern Israel. Elections in Israel Feb. 10 brought former Prime Min. Benjamin Netanyahu back to power, heading a government dominated by his conservative Likud bloc and another right-wing party, Yisrael Beitenu. Former Labor Prime Min. Ehud Barak retained the defense post from which, as a member of the previous government, he had overseen the Gaza war. A UN panel concluded Sept. 15 that both Hamas and Israel had committed war crimes.

THE WORLD
AT A GLANCE

Top-selling **light truck** in the U.S. . . . . Ford F-Series, 476,469 sold in 2008 (157,480 fewer than in 2007) *(p. 88)*

Top-selling **passenger car** in the U.S. . . . . Toyota Camry, 436,617 sold in 2008 (36,491 fewer than in 2007) *(p. 88)*

Most popular **compact/sports car color** in the U.S. . . . . Silver, 20% of 2008 model year cars *(p. 88)*

Most popular **light truck color** in the U.S. White/white pearl, 30% of 2008 model year trucks *(p. 88)*

Most popular **luxury car color** in the U.S. . . . . Black/black effect, 26% of 2008 model year cars *(p. 88)*

Nation hosting the most **refugees** . . . . Pakistan, 1.8 million, mostly from Afghanistan, in 2008 *(p. 740)*

Biggest U.S. **defense contractor** . . . . Lockheed Martin, $21.0 billion in contracts in 2008 *(p. 138)*

Nation with largest **crude oil reserves** . . . . Saudi Arabia, 262.3 billion barrels (U.S. reserves, 21.0 billion barrels) *(p. 119)*

U.S. state with highest **crude oil production** . . . . Texas, 398.0 million barrels in 2008 *(p. 118)*

U.S. state with highest **energy consumption per capita** . . . . Alaska, 1.1 billion Btu in 2007 *(p. 118)*

Nation most dependent on **nuclear energy** . . . . France, 76.2% of electricity was nuclear-generated in 2008 *(p. 121)*

Largest U.S. **bank company** . . . . Bank of America, $2.3 trillion in assets in 2009 *(p. 66)*

Fastest **roller coaster** in the world . . . . Kingda Ka, 128 mph (Six Flags Great Adventure, Jackson, NJ) *(p. 95)*

Top U.S. state by domestic **traveler spending** . . . . California, $96.2 billion in 2007 *(p. 93)*

Airline that carried the most passengers. . . . . Delta, 120.4 million in 2008 *(p. 94)*

Busiest **U.S. airport** by passenger traffic . . . . . . .Hartsfield-Jackson Airport (Atlanta, GA), 90.0 million passengers in 2008 *(p. 94)*

Most-visited **social networking website** . . . . .Facebook.com, 92.2 million unique visitors in Aug. 2009 *(p. 367)*

Most-visited **online search engine**. . . . . Google, 140.0 million unique visitors in Aug. 2009 *(p. 367)*

U.S. sales of compact discs totalled $384.7 million in 2008, **less than half the value of sales in 2000**. Digital music sales increased from $143.9 million in 2004 to more than $1.1 billion in 2008. *(pp. 254-55)*

U.S. farmers grew **800.5 million pounds of tobacco** in 2008—less than half the quantity of tobacco grown in 1990 *(p. 102)*. Yet Americans spent $77.1 billion on tobacco products in 2008—almost twice the $41.0 billion they spent in 1990 *(p. 55)*.

The U.S. produces 15% of the world's **total energy**, but consumes more than 20% of it. *(p. 117)*

Americans paid an average of **24.7% of their total income** in income tax and Social Security payments in 2008; Germans paid 42.7%. *(p. 739)*

If all circulating U.S. dollars and coins were equally distributed among the nation's population, **everyone would receive $2,963**. *(p. 61)*

Harvard University Library holds 16.0 million volumes, second in the U.S. only to the Library of Congress (32.3 million volumes). *(p. 396)*

54,043: number of U.S. military personnel stationed in Germany in 2009, the highest number for any foreign country after Iraq and Afghanistan. *(p. 134)*

24.9%: percentage of the population of Texas without health insurance, the highest percentage of any U.S. state. *(p. 146)*

59.7%: increase in the prison population of Minnesota between 2000 and 2008, the greatest increase of any U.S. state. *(p. 127)*

55.8%: high school graduation rate of Nevada, the lowest in the U.S. *(p. 387)*

27.6: median age at first marriage for U.S. men in 2008 (25.9 for women). *(p. 168)*

47: average total hours of television viewed per week by U.S. women over age 55. *(p. 256)*

24: average total hours of television viewed per week by U.S. men age 18-24. *(p. 256)*

135,932,930: number of registered cars in the U.S. in 2007, down from a high of 137.6 million in 2001. *(p. 89)*

$33,161: median income for U.S. men in 2008. *(p. 52)*

$20,867: median income for U.S. women in 2008. *(p. 52)*

1,000%: change in U.S. annual per capita consumption of broccoli since 1970. *(p. 100)*

–16%: change in U.S. annual per capita consumption of red meat since 1970. *(p. 101)*

66.9%: percentage of U.S. population that was overweight or obese between 2003 and 2006. *(p. 166)*

26%: percentage of all U.S. deaths due to heart disease, the leading cause of death. *(p. 172)*

NASA's Deep Impact space probe is scheduled to rendezvous with comet Hartley 2 in Oct. and examine its surface features and composition. *(p. 327)*

Aug. 12-13: Approximate peak of the Perseid meteor shower; viewing should be good due to proximity to New Moon. *(p. 333)*

September: Launch of Space Shuttle *Discovery* (STS-133), the final scheduled U.S. shuttle flight before the fleet is retired. *(p. 326)*

December 21: A total lunar eclipse will be visible from the entire U.S. and Canada. *(p. 338)*

Money in America (pp. 51-52)

Amount of money that Americans put in savings . . . . in 1990: $276.7 bil . . . . in 2008: $286.4 bil

Percent of disposable income that Americans put in savings. . . . . in 1990: 6.5% . . . . in 2008: 2.7%

Revolving consumer credit outstanding from commercial banks. . . . . in 2008: $390.6 bil

Personal expenditures, 2007-08 (p. 55)

	2007	2008
Health	$1,790.4 bil	$1,878.2 bil
Housing	$1,480.0 bil	$1,543.1 bil
Food and beverages	$740.1 bil	$784.3 bil
Gasoline and oil	$368.0 bil	$413.0 bil
Clothing and shoes	$359.1 bil	$355.6 bil
New automobiles	$233.3 bil	$184.5 bil
Casino gambling	$109.6 bil	$113.7 bil
Tobacco products	$75.1 bil	$77.1 bil
Books	$33.2 bil	$33.9 bil

Spending on selected food products, 2008-09 (p. 77)

	Sales	Change
Beer	$9.4 bil	5.4%
Soft drinks	$8.6 bil	2.9%
Cereal	$6.6 bil	1.7%
Ice cream	$4.5 bil	0.5%
Bottled water	$3.8 bil	−6.7%
Ground coffee	$2.4 bil	6.5%
Dog food (dry)	$2.1 bil	12.9%
Chocolate candy	$2.0 bil	1.5%
Cat food (dry)	$1.2 bil	6.9%

Wealthiest American, 2009 (p. 53)
Bill Gates, $50 billion net worth

Corporation with largest revenues, 2009 (p. 58)
Exxon Mobil, $442.9 billion

The Economic Crisis: By the Numbers

15.1 million: number of U.S. adults unemployed in Sept. 2009.

6 to 1: ratio of people looking for jobs to job openings in July 2009.

10: number of financial institutions (out of 19) that failed the "stress test" in May 2009, meaning that they would need more money to survive an even worse economic downturn. (p. 23)

$1.5 trillion: value of U.S. Treasury securities held by China and Japan in July 2009.

4.17%: percentage of single-family mortgages held by Fannie Mae that were seriously delinquent in July 2009.

$962 billion: amount of revolving debt held by Americans in June 2009.

98: number of bank closings in 2009 as of Oct. (there were none in 2005 and 2006). (p. 66)

Top of the World, 2008

Top U.S. trade partners
(millions, p. 80)

Canada	$600,641
China	$407,505
Mexico	$367,162
Japan	$204,404
Germany	$152,002

Top U.S. exports
(millions, p. 81)

Vehicles	$98,871
Electrical machinery	$82,049
Airplanes	$80,206
Gen. industrial machines	$55,192
Spec. industrial machines	$51,928

Top U.S. imports
(millions, p. 81)

Crude oil	$353,537
Vehicles	$190,799
Televisions, VCRs, etc.	$133,187
Electrical machinery	$112,623
Data/office equip.	$96,526

Top tourist destinations
(millions of visitors, p. 92)

France	79.3
United States	58.0
Spain	57.3
China	53.0
Italy	42.7

Top cell phone users
(thousands of subscriptions, p. 369)

China	634,000
India	346,890
United States	270,500
Russia	187,500
Brazil	150,641

Top emitters of CO_2, 2007
(billion metric tons, p. 295)

China	6.3
United States	6.0
Russia	1.7
India	1.4
Japan	1.3

Top motor vehicle producers
(thousands of vehicles, p. 86)

Japan	10,969
United States	8,503
China	8,185
Germany	5,778
South Korea	3,736

Top countries for U.S. foreign adoptions (p. 169)

Guatemala	4,082
China	3,852
Russia	1,859
Ethiopia	1,666
South Korea	1,038

Top world airports
(millions of total passengers, p. 94)

London Heathrow	67.1
Tokyo Haneda	66.8
Paris Charles de Gaulle	60.9
Beijing Capital	55.9
Frankfurt, Germany	53.5

Award Winners, Then and Now (pp. 258-78)

	1959	2009
Highest-rated TV show	Gunsmoke (1958-59)	American Idol (2008-09)
Best Picture Oscar[1]	Gigi	Slumdog Millionaire
Emmy Awards		
Comedy	The Jack Benny Show	30 Rock
Drama	Playhouse 90 and Alcoa-Goodyear Theatre	Mad Men
Album of the Year Grammy[1]	The Music From Peter Gunn Show, Henry Mancini	Raising Sand, Robert Plant and Alison Krauss
Tony Awards		
Play	J.B.	God of Carnage
Musical	Redhead	Billy Elliot, The Musical
Pulitzer Prizes		
Fiction	The Travels of Jaimie McPheeters, Robert Lewis Taylor	Olive Kitteridge, Elizabeth Strout
Drama	J.B., Archibald MacLeish	Ruined, Lynn Nottage

Thespians of the Year, 2008-09 (pp. 272-76)

	Best Actor	Best Actress
Academy Awards	Sean Penn, Milk	Kate Winslet, The Reader
Golden Globes		
Drama (Film)	Mickey Rourke, The Wrestler	Kate Winslet, Revolutionary Road
Comedy/Musical (Film)	Colin Farrell, In Bruges	Sally Hawkins, Happy-Go-Lucky
Drama (TV)	Gabriel Byrne, In Treatment	Anna Paquin, True Blood
Comedy (TV)	Alec Baldwin, 30 Rock	Tina Fey, 30 Rock
Emmy Awards		
Drama	Bryan Cranston, Breaking Bad	Glenn Close, Damages
Comedy	Alec Baldwin, 30 Rock	Toni Collette, United States of Tara
Tony Awards		
Play	Geoffrey Rush, Exit the King	Marcia Gay Harden, God of Carnage
Musical	David Alvarez, Trent Kowalik, and Kiril Kulish, Billy Elliot, The Musical	Alice Ripley, Next to Normal

Best Sellers, 2008 (pp. 246-51, 364)

DVD	The Dark Knight
Video game	Wii Play
PC game[2]	World of Warcraft: Wrath of the Lich King
PC software[2]	MS Office 2007 (Home & Student)
Newspaper	USA Today
Magazine	AARP Bulletin
Fiction book	The Appeal, John Grisham
Nonfiction book	The Last Lecture, Randy Pausch

Moviegoing in the U.S. (p. 246)

	1975	2008	% Change
Total box office	$2.1 bil	$9.8 bil	366.7%
Screens	15,030	40,194	167.4%
Avg. ticket price	$2.05	$7.18	250.2%
Films produced	258	520	101.6%
Films released	233	610	161.8%

Number Ones (pp. 244-57)

Top-grossing U.S. movie, 2008	The Dark Knight, $530.9 mil
All-time top-grossing U.S. movie	Titanic (1997), $600.8 mil
#1 syndicated TV program, 2008-09	ESPN NFL Regular Season, 7.8% of TV households
All-time most watched TV program	M*A*S*H finale, Feb. 28, 1983, 50.2 mil households
#1 commercial radio format in U.S., 2009	Country, 1,997 stations
#1 recorded music genre in U.S., 2008	Rock, 31.8% of all music sold
All-time top-selling U.S. album	Eagles/Their Greatest Hits 1971-75, Eagles, 29 mil copies
Longest-running Broadway play	The Phantom of the Opera (1988-), 9,003 performances[3]

Milestone Birthdays in 2010 (pp. 175-242)

100	70	50	30
Gloria Stuart, July 4	Tom Brokaw, Feb. 6	Michael Stipe, Jan. 4	Chelsea Clinton, Feb. 27
	Ted Koppel, Feb. 8	Bono, May 10	Jessica Simpson, July 10
90	Peter Fonda, Feb. 23	Sean Penn, Aug. 17	Gisele Bündchen, July 20
Helen Thomas, Aug. 4	Al Pacino, Apr. 25	Damon Wayans, Sept. 4	
Ray Bradbury, Aug. 22	Ringo Starr, July 7	Allison Janney, Nov. 19	**21**
Mickey Rooney, Sept. 23	Alex Trebek, July 22	Julianne Moore, Dec. 3	Joe Jonas, Aug. 15
Dave Brubeck, Dec. 6	Raquel Welch, Sept. 5		Taylor Swift, Dec. 13
80	**60**	**40**	**18**
Edwin "Buzz" Aldrin, Jan. 20	Jay Leno, Apr. 28	Mariah Carey, Mar. 27	Nick Jonas, Sept. 16
Clint Eastwood, May 31	Stevie Wonder, May 13	Vince Vaughn, Mar. 28	Miley Cyrus, Nov. 23
Neil Armstrong, Aug. 5	Bill Murray, Sept. 21	Tina Fey, May 18	
Sean Connery, Aug. 25	Tom Petty, Oct. 20	Matt Damon, Oct. 8	
Warren Buffett, Aug. 30			

(1) Awards for 1958 (Then) and 2008 (Now). (2) July 2008-June 2009. (3) Through Sept. 2009; play was still running.

The 2009 Swine Flu Pandemic

Source: Facts on File News Digest; World Almanac research. As of Oct. 2009.

In Apr. 2009, the first cases of a previously unknown strain of influenza were detected in U.S. citizens near the Mexican border. Over the next few weeks the outbreak in Mexico, at first considered the epicenter of the disease, appeared to taper off, while continuing to spread in the Americas, Europe, and the Asia-Pacific area. By May 27, the influenza A (H1N1) "swine flu" virus had been confirmed in 13,398 people in 48 countries, and 95 deaths had been linked to the disease. The U.S. had reported 6,764 cases of the disease, the highest of any country, and had linked 10 deaths to the virus. Mexico had the highest number of fatalities linked to the initial outbreak, with 83, and had reported 4,541 confirmed cases.

Despite initial fears that the virus had a high mortality rate, health officials reported that most confirmed cases of the disease were relatively mild. They warned, however, that there remained significant concern that the swine flu virus could become more deadly after mixing with other flu virus strains circulating during the flu season that was about to begin in the Southern Hemisphere.

U.S. Health and Human Services Sec. Kathleen Sebelius said May 22 that the U.S. government would provide $1 bil to fund the development and production of a swine flu vaccine. Officials with the U.S. Centers for Disease Control and Prevention (CDC) June 1 reported that the swine flu virus had been confirmed in all 50 U.S. states. It also said the number of confirmed cases likely only represented 5% of the country's total number of cases. As of June 11, there were 13,217 cases of confirmed swine flu in the U.S., with 27 deaths from the disease.

The World Health Organization (WHO) June 11 declared the virus a pandemic—as it does when a new strain emerges against which the population has little or no immunity—raising its alert system to phase six, the highest level, for the first time since 1968, when the so-called Hong Kong flu emerged. Under the organization's guidelines, a pandemic has reached stage six when there is widespread person-to-person transmission of an infectious disease in two distinct geographical regions of the world.

The World Health Organization (WHO) Aug. 28 reported that a severe form of infection by the A (H1N1) virus had been increasingly found worldwide. According to the WHO, the severe form of the disease directly infected the lungs, a circumstance that could lead to respiratory failure and required that patients be treated in hospital intensive-care units. Some cities had reported that almost 15% of patients hospitalized with swine flu had required

intensive care. The WHO also noted that the severe form of the disease had been found in "young and otherwise healthy people," something rarely seen during normal seasonal flu infections.

The President's Council of Advisors on Science and Technology Aug. 24 released a report detailing a "plausible scenario" in which 60 mil-120 mil people in the U.S. contracted swine flu in the upcoming fall and winter, resulting in 30,000-90,000 deaths. (The seasonal flu causes about 36,000 deaths in the U.S. annually.) The council said its estimates were not a prediction, but a model to aid officials in their planning efforts. The scenario nonetheless was widely reported by news media.

CDC health officials announced Oct. 9 that 76 children had died from swine flu in the U.S. since the virus first appeared in Apr., and they expected that number to rise during the 2009-10 flu season. While most of these children had underlying conditions that made them more vulnerable, 20%-30% of deaths occurred in otherwise healthy children.

In early Oct., the CDC released the first batch of swine flu vaccines, to be administered in private doctors' offices and public settings such as schools and city clinics. The CDC also began an early campaign to encourage regular flu vaccinations. According to Dr. Anthony Fauci of the U.S. National Institute of Allergy and Infectious Diseases, studies indicated that both vaccines could be given together without increased risk for side effects, protecting most people within 8 to 10 days.

In the last week of Sept., the final week of the official 2008-09 flu season, 6.1% of U.S. deaths were due to influenza and pneumonia, according to the CDC, just below the 6.4% that officially indicates an epidemic. Swine flu represented more than 99% of confirmed flu cases.

Previous Influenza Pandemics

Since the 16th century, more than 30 influenza pandemics have been described. The most destructive pandemic of modern times, the so-called Spanish flu of 1918-20, is estimated to have caused more than 20 mil deaths. More than 500,000 persons died in the U.S., generally following complications from bacterial pneumonia. A 1957-58 pandemic of "Asian flu," first detected in China, resulted in some 70,000 deaths in the U.S. A 1968-69 pandemic caused by a virus strain known as "Hong Kong flu" (it was first identified in Hong Kong) was responsible for about 34,000 deaths in the U.S.

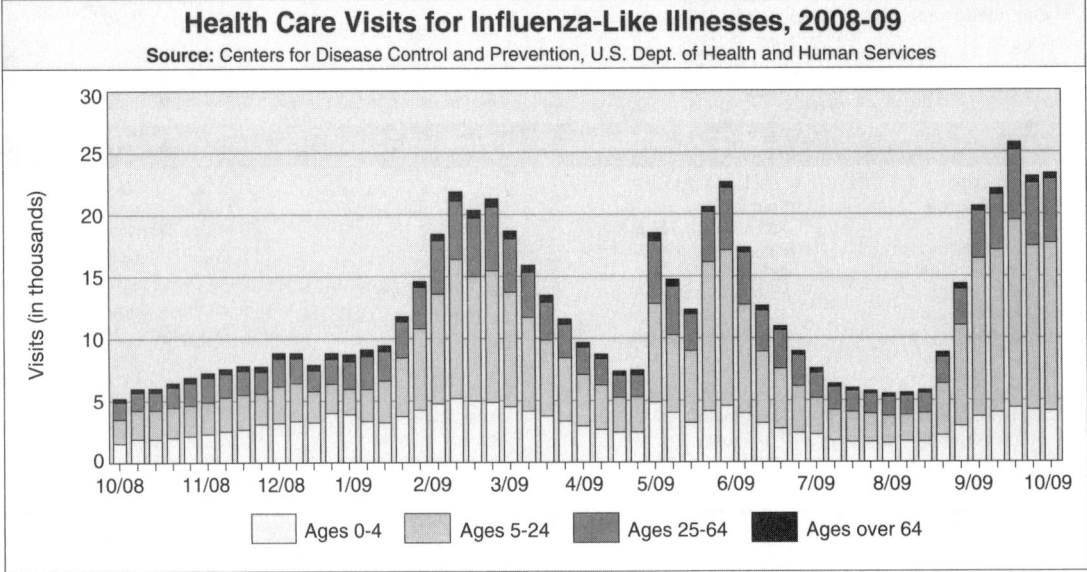

Health Care Visits for Influenza-Like Illnesses, 2008-09

Source: Centers for Disease Control and Prevention, U.S. Dept. of Health and Human Services

Visits (in thousands)

Ages 0-4   Ages 5-24   Ages 25-64   Ages over 64

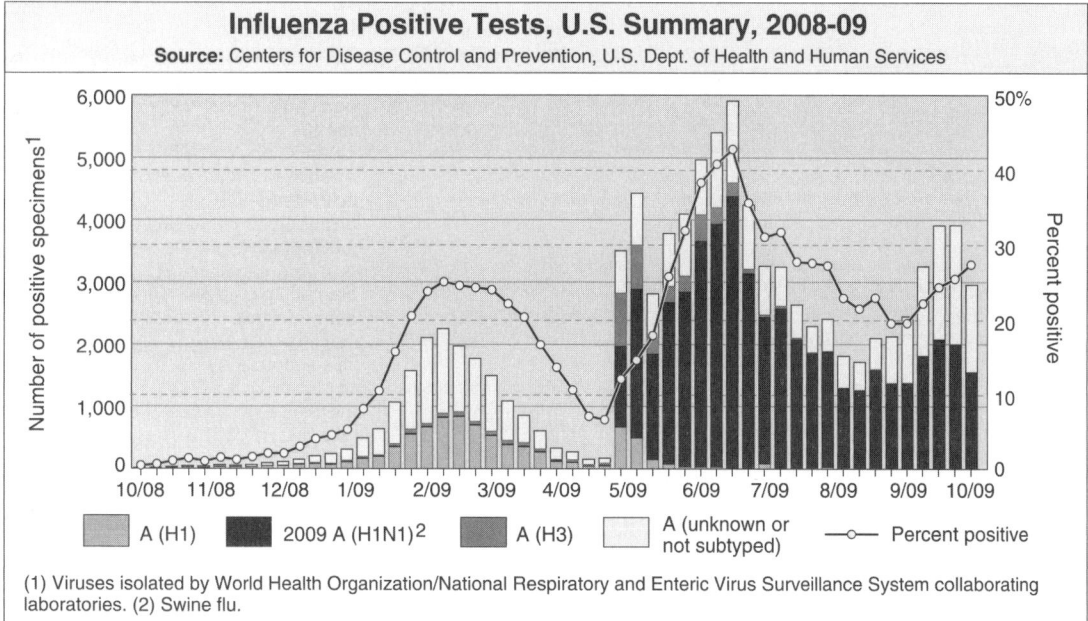

Influenza Positive Tests, U.S. Summary, 2008-09
Source: Centers for Disease Control and Prevention, U.S. Dept. of Health and Human Services

Legend: A (H1) | 2009 A (H1N1)[2] | A (H3) | A (unknown or not subtyped) | —o— Percent positive

(1) Viruses isolated by World Health Organization/National Respiratory and Enteric Virus Surveillance System collaborating laboratories. (2) Swine flu.

Seasonal Influenza and Swine Flu FAQs
Source: Centers for Disease Control and Prevention, U.S. Dept. of Health and Human Services
Additional details available at www.cdc.gov/h1n1flu/

Influenza is caused by single-stranded RNA viruses that are commonly spread via droplets released into the air when an infected individual coughs or sneezes, or through contact with surfaces that have been contaminated by such droplets. Influenza viruses may also be transmittable to humans through contact with an infected animal. There are three main types that are known to infect humans: influenza A, B, and C. Type A viruses are most frequently responsible for disease epidemics in humans; 2009 H1N1 ("swine flu") is a type A influenza strain.

Why is 2009 A (H1N1) called "swine flu"?

2009 H1N1 became known as "swine flu" because initial testing indicated that the virus had some genes in common with influenza viruses common to North American swine. Further testing showed that the strain actually contains a combination of swine, bird, and human genes. However, the virus appears to spread in the same way as regular seasonal influenza. It cannot be transmitted through the handling or eating of pork products.

What are the symptoms of H1N1?

In many people, the symptoms are no different from a regular case of mild seasonal influenza. However, some people—mainly people 65 years and older, children younger than five years old, pregnant women, and people with certain chronic medical conditions—are at special risk for more severe, or even life-threatening complications. Common symptoms include fever, cough, sore throat, runny or stuffy nose, body aches, headache, chills, and fatigue. But as with those with seasonal influenza, some people may be infected with H1N1 and have only respiratory symptoms without a fever.

How does H1N1 flu compare to typical seasonal influenza?

In a typical year, an estimated 5%-20% of Americans are infected with seasonal (non-H1N1) influenza viruses; more than 200,000 are hospitalized, and 36,000 may die from influenza-associated causes. Of those hospitalized, 20,000 are under age 5, and more than 90% of deaths occur in people over age 65. Initial testing indicates that H1N1-related hospitalizations and deaths have been proportionally higher among people under age 25, but other conditions—including asthma, diabetes, suppressed immune systems, heart disease, kidney disease, neurocogni-

tive and neuromuscular disorders, and pregnancy—also seem to be associated with an increased risk of complications from 2009 H1N1 influenza.

How can I protect myself?

Standard flu-prevention precautions will also help in preventing H1N1 infection. Washing your hands with soap and water, avoiding close contact with sick people, and avoiding touching your eyes, nose, and mouth are all effective. Starting in Oct. 2009, a vaccine to protect against the 2009 H1N1 virus was made available. The CDC provides information about H1N1 and other flu vaccines at www.cdc.gov/h1n1flu/vaccination/.

Emergency Warning Signs
If you notice any of the following warning signs, you should seek medical care immediately:

In children:
Fast breathing or trouble breathing
Bluish skin color
Not drinking enough fluids
Not waking up or not interacting
Being so irritable that the child does not want to be held
Flu-like symptoms improving but then returning with fever and worse cough
Fever with a rash

In adults:
Difficulty breathing or shortness of breath
Pain or pressure in the chest or abdomen
Sudden dizziness
Confusion
Severe or persistent vomiting

Decade in Review:

Even though we still don't know what to call these years ("the Aughts" never quite caught on), the first decade of the 21st century the new millennium so far, from politics to pop culture—as well as some of the moments you may have already forgotten.

	U.S. News	Business & Economy	International
2000	Six-year-old Elián González is taken from his U.S. relatives by federal agents Apr. 22 and returned to his father in Cuba. Vermont becomes the first state to authorize same-sex civil unions Apr. 26. Pres. Clinton signs legislation Oct. 10 granting China permanent normal trade relations. George W. Bush wins the presidency after the U.S. Supreme Court calls a halt to the Florida recount Dec. 12.	America Online announces the $165 bil purchase of Time Warner Inc. Jan. 20—the largest corporate merger in U.S. history. A U.S. district court judge June 7 orders that Microsoft be split into 2 companies. Tire maker Bridgestone/Firestone recalls 6.5 million SUV and truck tires Aug. 9. Chase Manhattan Corp., the nation's third-largest bank, announces Sept. 13 a $35-billion takeover of the fifth largest, J. P. Morgan & Co. Inc.	Vladimir Putin is elected president of Russia Mar. 26. Israel ends its 22-year occupation of southern Lebanon May 24. South and North Korean leaders hold the first-ever summit between the 2 countries June 13-15. Seventeen U.S. sailors are killed and 39 wounded Oct. 12 in a terrorist bombing attack on the USS *Cole* in Aden, Yemen.
2001	Pres. Bush signs a 10-year, $1.35 tril tax cut bill June 7. Oklahoma City bomber Timothy McVeigh is executed June 11 by lethal injection. Hijackers Sept. 11 crash 2 airliners into New York City's World Trade Center, 1 into Pentagon; another crashes in a field near Shanksville, PA. Anthrax-laced letters, mailed to several Senate and news media offices, kill 5 and sicken 14 Oct. 4-Nov. 21.	The U.S. enters a prolonged economic slowdown; by Aug., the Federal Reserve has lowered interest rates 7 times, to their lowest level since 1994. A U.S. appeals court June 28 reverses an order that Microsoft split, and the company announces a settlement with the Justice Dept. Enron Inc. files for bankruptcy Dec. 2; it is the largest Chapter 11 filing in U.S. history.	Ariel Sharon is elected prime minister of Israel Feb. 6, amid violent clashes between Israeli and Palestinian forces. Former Yugoslavian Pres. Milosevic is arrested Apr. 1 and later charged with war crimes and crimes against humanity. Russian Pres. Vladimir Putin and Chinese Pres. Jiang Zemin sign the first friendship treaty between the 2 countries since the Cold War July 16. The Irish Republican Army begins decommissioning its arsenal Oct. 23.
2002	The U.S. Roman Catholic Church is engulfed by a scandal over its handling of cases of sexual abuse of minors by priests. Pres. Bush signs McCain-Feingold campaign finance reform bill Mar. 27. The federal government takes control of security at commercial airports Sept. 28. Suburbs of Washington, DC, are terrorized in Oct. by a series of sniper attacks.	Kmart becomes the largest American retailer to file for bankruptcy Jan. 22; WorldCom Inc. files the largest-ever bankruptcy in the U.S. July 21. Congressional hearings into Enron's business practices lead to the June 15 conviction of auditing firm Arthur Andersen LLP on obstruction charges. Pres. Bush signs legislation July 30 creating an accounting oversight board and establishing strict penalties for corporate fraud.	The euro begins circulating in cash form in 12 European nations Jan. 1. A treaty establishing the International Criminal Court takes effect July 1. The government of North Korea admits Oct. 17 that it has been pursuing a secret nuclear weapons program. NATO offers full membership to 7 Central and Eastern European countries Nov. 21 and grants Russia a partnership without full membership.
2003	U.S.-led coalition invades Iraq Mar. 19. Pres. Bush signs a new round of tax cuts totaling $330 mil over 10 years May 28. On Aug. 14, the largest blackout in North American history affects 50 mil in 8 U.S. states and Ontario. California voters recall Gov. Gray Davis Oct. 7 and elect Arnold Schwarzenegger to replace him.	After forcing out 3 top executives over accounting irregularities, govt.-sponsored mortgage finance company Freddie Mac admits Nov. 21 that it understated profits from 2000 to 2002 to smooth out results in future years. The U.S., Honduras, Guatemala, El Salvador, and Nicaragua sign the Central American Free Trade Agreement (CAFTA) Dec. 7, phasing out industrial and agricultural tariffs and trade barriers over the next 18 years.	An outbreak of a new disease, severe acute respiratory syndrome (SARS), hits China in early 2003 and spreads around the world. A heat wave in Europe kills an estimated 35,000 people, 11,000 in France alone. North Korean officials announce July 14 that the country has produced enough weapons-grade plutonium to make 6 nuclear bombs.
2004	Anti-gay marriage ballot initiatives are approved in 11 states Nov. 2, passing with more than 60% of votes in 10 states; Massachusetts becomes the first state to issue marriage licenses to same-sex couples Feb. 12. The U.S. Senate Select Committee on Intelligence blames the CIA July 7 for incorrect, unsupported, and misleading pre-war claims about Iraq's supposed weapons of mass destruction. Pres. Bush wins a second term in office Nov. 2, and the GOP adds a seat to its majorities in both houses of Congress.	The U.S. dollar falls against all major world currencies, ending the year against the euro at its lowest value since 1999, and hitting a 12-year low against the British pound. Martha Stewart and her former stockbroker are found guilty Mar. 5 of obstructing an investigation into a sale of her personal stock. Crude oil prices top $50 a barrel for the first time Sept. 27.	U.S. Sec. of State Colin Powell declares the conflict in Sudan's Darfur region "genocide" Sept. 9. Afghanistan holds its first presidential election Oct. 9; interim Pres. Hamid Karzai defeats 17 challengers. Palestinian Authority leader Yasir Arafat dies Nov. 11 in a French hospital. A massive earthquake in the Indian Ocean triggers a tsunami Dec. 26 that kills more than 225,000, most of them in coastal regions of Indonesia, Sri Lanka, and India.

2000-2009 at a Glance

was unquestionably a time of great change. The following timeline highlights some of the most memorable events and trends of

Science, Health, & Technology	Sports	Media & Pop Culture	
Despite widespread concern, the Y2K computer bug fails to cause any major problems.

Scientists announce June 26 that they have deciphered the structure of the human genome.

The first crash of a Concorde jet, near Paris, France, kills 113 people July 25.

The International Space Station welcomes its first crew Sept. 11.

The FDA approves RU-486, the so-called "abortion pill," Sept. 28. | Tiger Woods wins the U.S. Open by a record 15 strokes June 19; at British Open he becomes the youngest golfer, and only the fifth in history, to win all 4 of golf's majors.

At the Sydney Olympics, American Marion Jones becomes the first woman to win 5 track and field medals in a single Olympic Games Oct. 1.

The New York Yankees win their third straight World Series Oct. 26. | *American Beauty* wins the Oscar for Best Picture; the highest-grossing movie in the U.S. is *How the Grinch Stole Christmas*.

Britney Spears's *Oops!... I Did It Again* is released May 16, selling more than 1 million copies in its first week.

Survivor premieres on American TV May 31; corporate trainer Richard Hatch wins $1 mil in a 4-3 vote by fellow "castaways" Aug. 23. | 2000 |
| A midyear outbreak of foot-and-mouth disease leads to the destruction of 3.8 mil livestock animals in Great Britain, Ireland, France, and the Netherlands.

The Netherlands becomes the first country to legalize and regulate euthanasia Apr. 11.

Inventor and engineer Dean Kamen introduces the Segway Human Transporter Dec. 3, which he claims will bring about a transformation in travel and reductions in pollution. | Racing legend Dale Earnhardt dies in a crash on the final lap at the Daytona 500 Feb. 21.

Tiger Woods becomes the first golfer to win 4 consecutive major titles Apr. 9.

After 2 years of retirement, Michael Jordan returns to the NBA Sept. 26.

Barry Bonds sets a new single-season record for home runs, with 73. | Apple introduces iTunes, an application for storing and playing digital media Jan. 9, and the first iPod, featuring a 5-gigabyte hard drive, Oct. 23.

Punk legend Joey Ramone, Apr. 15, and former Beatle George Harrison, Dec. 1, both die of cancer.

Harry Potter and the Sorcerer's Stone, the first Harry Potter film adaptation, is released Nov. 16 and goes on to gross $318 mil in North America. | 2001 |
| Scientists discover 11 new moons orbiting Jupiter May 22.

U.S. scientists create the first synthetic virus July 11.

Pres. Bush announces Aug. 9 he will allow federal funding for limited stem-cell research using human embryos. | Lennox Lewis defeats Mike Tyson to retain his IBF and WBC heavyweight titles June 9.

The L.A. Lakers win their third straight NBA title, defeating the New Jersey Nets June 13.

Brazil wins the World Cup for a record fifth time June 30.

Annika Sorenstam finishes the LPGA Tour season Nov. 25 with a record $2.86 mil in prize money. | Canadian company Research in Motion (RIM) releases the first BlackBerry smartphone Mar. 4, based on a line of 2-way pagers it first introduced in 1999.

American Idol debuts on American television June 11; Kelly Clarkson becomes the first winner Sept. 4. | 2002 |
| Space Shuttle *Columbia* breaks apart on reentry Feb. 2, killing all aboard, as a result of damage sustained during liftoff.

Dolly the sheep, the first animal to be cloned from an adult somatic cell, dies Feb. 14 at the relatively young age of 6.

China becomes the third nation to launch a manned spacecraft Oct. 15.

The USDA announces the first suspected U.S. case of "mad cow" disease Dec. 23. | High-school basketball player LeBron James is the number-one pick in the NBA draft June 26.

Roger Federer wins his first Grand Slam title July 7 at age 21.

The underdog Florida Marlins defeat the New York Yankees to win their second World Series title Oct. 25. | The *New York Times* reveals a history of plagiarism, dateline falsification, and factual error by 27-year-old reporter Jayson Blair May 11.

Myspace.com launches in Aug.

The Return of the King, the final chapter in filmmaker Peter Jackson's adaptation of J.R.R. Tolkien's *Lord of the Rings* trilogy, is released Dec. 17; it goes on to tie *Ben-Hur* and *Titanic* for most Academy Awards won (11). | 2003 |
| *SpaceShipOne* becomes the first privately sponsored craft to carry a human into space.

Pres. Bush announces a plan Jan. 14 to resume manned lunar exploration between 2015 and 2020.

The FDA rules May 17 that Plan B, commonly known as the "morning after" pill, could not be sold without a prescription.

Contamination at a British drug plant results in a severe shortage in the U.S. of the flu vaccine in the fall. | At the Olympic Games in Athens Aug. 14, Michael Phelps wins his first gold medal, breaking his own world record in the 400m individual medley. A record 24 athletes are expelled from the games for doping violations.

The NHL Board of Governors votes to lock out the league's players Sept. 16, leading to the cancellation of the 2004-05 professional hockey season.

The Boston Red Sox defeat the St. Louis Cardinals in 4 games to win their first World Series in 86 years Oct. 27. | Facebook.com is founded by Mark Zuckerberg and fellow students at Harvard Univ. Feb. 4.

The FCC fines 20 CBS TV stations a total of $550,000 Sept. 22, for an incident in which singer Janet Jackson's breast was bared during the Super Bowl halftime show.

Version 1.0 of the Firefox Internet browser is released Nov. 9. | 2004 |

U.S. News	Business & Economy	International

2005

After a drawn-out legal battle involving Pres. Bush and congressional intervention, severely brain-damaged Terri Schiavo dies Mar. 31, 13 days after her feeding tube is removed.

Hurricane Katrina and subsequent flooding devastates the Mississippi, Louisiana, and Alabama Gulf Coast in Aug.; hundreds of thousands are left homeless.

Vice Pres. Dick Cheney's chief of staff I. Lewis "Scooter" Libby is indicted Oct. 28 on 5 felony counts related to the leak of a CIA agent's identity to the press.

General Motors announces June 7 plans to cut 25,000 jobs by the end of 2008 in a bid to stay competitive with foreign automakers.

WorldCom ex-CEO Bernard Ebbers is sentenced July 13 to 25 years in prison for the fraud that led to the company's $11 bil bankruptcy filing in 2002.

Burdened by record-high fuel prices, airlines Delta and Northwest file for bankruptcy Sept. 14.

The Kyoto Protocol takes effect Feb. 16, requiring participating nations to collectively reduce emissions of heat-trapping gases by 2012.

Pope John Paul II dies Apr. 2 after more than 26 years as leader of the Roman Catholic Church; Cardinal Joseph Ratzinger succeeds him Apr. 20, taking the name Benedict XVI.

Suicide bombings kill 56 and injure 700 in the London transit system July 7.

Israel evacuates settlements in the Gaza Strip, surrendering control to the Palestinian Authority Aug. 23.

2006

Zacarias Moussaoui is sentenced to life in prison May 3 for his role in the Sept. 11, 2001, terrorist attacks.

A massive, secret NSA program to collect the telephone records of millions of Americans and conduct warrantless wiretaps is revealed May 11.

Pres. Bush signs a measure calling for construction of a 700-mile fence along the U.S.-Mexico border Oct. 26.

Defense Sec. Donald Rumsfeld resigns Nov. 8 following midterm elections in which Democrats gain control of the House and Senate.

Bill Gates announces June 15 he will stop running day-to-day operations at Microsoft within 2 years, and will begin focusing on his charitable foundation.

Dell issues the largest-ever consumer electronic product recall, of 4.1 mil notebook computer batteries, Aug. 14 due to the risk of fire.

The U.S. stock market booms late in the year, with the Dow Jones Industrial Average setting record highs on 22 separate occasions.

North Korea test-fires ballistic missiles July 5 and later in the year conducts its first nuclear test.

Fidel Castro July 31 hands over power to his brother, Raúl Castro, while he undergoes gastrointestinal surgery.

British authorities announce Aug. 10 they have thwarted a terrorist plot to use liquid explosives on board transatlantic passenger flights; the U.S. implements new security regulations, restricting liquids in carry-on luggage.

Former Iraqi President Saddam Hussein is hanged Dec. 30 for crimes against humanity.

2007

Millions of products imported from China—from pet food to toothpaste to toys—are recalled over concerns with design flaws and tainted ingredients.

Thirty-three people are killed at Virginia Tech in Blacksburg, VA, in the worst school shooting in U.S. history Apr. 16.

A highway bridge over the Mississippi River in Minneapolis, MN, collapses Aug. 1 during evening rush hour, killing 13 people and dropping more than 50 cars into the river.

A "surge" of additional troops is added to U.S. forces in Iraq to contain violence; Gen. Petraeus calls the surge effective Sept. 10.

The first minimum wage increase in nearly 10 years takes effect July 24, rising to $5.85 per hour in 2007 with further increases over the next 2 years.

In response to record numbers of mortgage defaults and foreclosures, Pres. Bush announces a plan to help homeowners refinance Aug. 31.

The Labor Dept. reports Sept. 7 that the U.S. suffered its first decline in employment since 2003.

North Korea agrees Feb. 13 to shut down its main nuclear facility and admit weapons inspectors in exchange for foreign fuel and economic aid.

British Prime Min. Tony Blair steps down June 27 after 10 years in power and is succeeded by Gordon Brown.

British police thwart two terrorist car bombs set to go off in London June 29; the next day, 2 men ram an SUV into the main terminal of Glasgow Airport.

The Myanmar military cracks down violently Sept. 27 on protests led by Buddhist monks.

2008

Heavy rains cause severe flooding in the Midwest June 9-19, forcing tens of thousands from their homes.

Pres. Bush signs an update of the 1978 Foreign Intelligence Service Act (FISA) into law July 10, granting the government expanded powers to gather data on U.S. citizens.

Sen. Barack Obama defeats Sen. John McCain to become the nation's first black president-elect Nov. 4.

The U.S. deficit hits a record high of $454.8 bil in fiscal 2008; 2.5 million jobs are lost—the largest yearly job loss since 1945.

Oil prices pass $100 a barrel for the first time Jan. 2 and top $140 in July.

Investment giant Lehman Bros. files for bankruptcy Sept. 15, sending the stock market spiraling. The Federal Reserve moves to prop up other financial institutions, but the economy continues a downward slide.

Tens of thousands are killed May 2-3 when tropical cyclone Nargis hits southern Myanmar.

An earthquake in China's Sichuan province May 12 kills nearly 70,000 and leaves nearly 5 million homeless.

Clashes between separatist forces and Georgian military troops prompt Russia to dispatch its own troops to the breakaway region of South Ossetia Aug. 7.

2009

Former Pres. Clinton visits N. Korea Aug. 4 and secures the release of 2 journalists accused of illegally entering the country.

After contentious confirmation hearings, federal judge Sonia Sotomayor is confirmed Aug. 6 as the 111th Supreme Court justice, the first Hispanic in the court's history.

Sen. Edward Kennedy dies of brain cancer at age 77 Aug. 26.

Pres. Obama wins the Nobel Peace Prize Oct. 9 for creating "a new climate in international politics."

At the G-20 summit in London Apr. 2, world leaders agree to increase funding for the International Monetary Fund (IMF) to $1.1 tril to boost global trade and combat the global economic crisis.

U.S. automaker General Motors declares bankruptcy June 1; the federal government announces it will assume a 60% market share in the restructured company.

U.S. unemployment stands at 9.8% (as of Oct.).

Israel declares a unilateral cease-fire in the Gaza Strip Jan. 17, ending a 22-day war in which about 1,300 Palestinians were killed and 5,000 were wounded.

In violation of recent agreements, North Korea conducts its second successful nuclear test May 25.

The World Health Organization declares a pandemic June 11 of influenza A (H1N1) "swine flu," the first such declaration since 1968.

Science, Health, & Technology	Sports	Media & Pop Culture
The unmanned U.S. spacecraft Deep Impact collides (intentionally) July 4 with comet Tempel 1, in an attempt to learn more about the comet's makeup. Astronomers July 29 announce the discovery of the most distant known object in the solar system, UB313, later named Eris. Open enrollment for Medicare Part D begins Nov. 15, with new prescription benefits. French surgeons perform the world's first partial face transplant Nov. 27.	The New England Patriots win their third Super Bowl in 4 years Feb. 6. Curt Schilling, Rafael Palmeiro, Mark McGwire, and Sammy Sosa testify before a House committee investigating steroid abuse in baseball Mar. 17. Lance Armstrong wins his seventh straight Tour de France July 24 and announces his retirement from competitive cycling. The Chicago White Sox sweep the Houston Astros to win their first World Series in 88 years Oct. 26.	*The Gates*, a public art project by husband-and-wife team Christo and Jeanne-Claude, takes over New York City's Central Park in Feb. The identity of Watergate source "Deep Throat" is revealed by *Vanity Fair* May 31 to be FBI official W. Mark Felt. Pop star Michael Jackson is acquitted June 13 on criminal charges of child molestation after a 14-week trial. The first episode of *The Colbert Report* airs on Comedy Central Oct. 17. Microsoft releases the Xbox 360 gaming console Nov. 22.
E. coli-tainted spinach kills 3 and sickens about 200 in the western U.S. The U.S. announces a plan to deal with a potential influenza A (H5N1) "bird flu" pandemic May 3. Pres. Bush issues the first veto of his presidency July 19, rejecting a bill that would have opened up federal funding for human embryonic stem cell research. Pluto is downgraded to "dwarf planet" status by the International Astronomical Union Aug. 24.	Speed skater Shani Davis becomes the first black athlete to win an individual gold at the Winter Olympic games Feb. 18 in Turin, Italy. A colt named Barbaro, favored to win the first Triple Crown since 1978, falls at the Preakness Stakes May 20 with broken bones in one leg. Thirteen cyclists are banned from the Tour de France over doping allegations before the race begins; U.S. cyclist Floyd Landis wins the race July 23, but his title is revoked when he is found to have taken a banned substance.	Apple Inc. Feb. 23 announces the sale of its 1 billionth song through iTunes. Pres. Bush signs a bill June 15 increasing indecency fines for radio and TV stations to a maximum of $325,000 per incident. Katie Couric becomes the first solo female evening news anchor for CBS Sept. 5. Google purchases YouTube for $1.65 bil Oct. 9.
The USDA rules Jan. 31 that meat from cloned animals cannot be labeled "organic." The Intergovernmental Panel on Climate Change issues its latest review of climate-related research Feb. 2, calling evidence supporting global warming "unequivocal" and placing the blame primarily on human activities. Pres. Bush vetoes a bill Oct. 3 that would have expanded funding for the state Children's Health Insurance Program (CHIP or SCHIP) by $35 bil over the next 5 years.	Barry Bonds hits his 756th career home run, breaking Hank Aaron's all-time record Aug. 7; he is later indicted on charges of perjury and obstruction of justice in a steroids case. Sprinter Marion Jones admits performance-enhancing drug use Oct. 5, returns her 5 medals from the 2000 Olympics in Sydney, and is charged with lying to federal investigators. The New England Patriots finish the regular NFL season Dec. 29 with 16 wins and no losses, the first team to go undefeated since 1972.	Talk show host Don Imus is fired Apr. 12 by CBS Radio over sexist and racist references to members of the Rutgers Univ. women's basketball team. Bob Barker retires from *The Price Is Right* after a 35-year run June 15. Apple Inc. releases the iPhone June 29, priced at $499–$599. *Harry Potter and the Deathly Hallows*, the final book in the Harry Potter series, becomes the fastest-selling book ever, with 15 mil copies sold within the first 24 hours of its July 21 release.
NASA's Phoenix Mars Lander confirms the presence of water ice on Mars June 20. An estimated 1.2 million pounds of beef are recalled in the U.S. Aug. 11. China conducts its first space walk Sept. 27 during the country's third manned space mission. Scientists report Oct. 2 that the area of Arctic ice has hit its second-lowest measurement on record.	The New York Giants defeat the heavily-favored Patriots in Super Bowl XLII Feb. 4, ending New England's drive to achieve the NFL's first 19-0 season. The Boston Celtics rack up a record 17th NBA championship, defeating longtime rivals the L.A. Lakers for the ninth time June 17. At the Beijing Summer Olympics, U.S. swimmer Michael Phelps wins 8 gold medals, a record for a single Olympic Games.	Starring the recently deceased Heath Ledger, *The Dark Knight* becomes the second highest grossing film of all time. A 14-week writers' strike that brought film and TV production to a halt ends Feb. 12. Pop star Madonna turns 50 Aug. 16. O. J. Simpson is convicted Oct. 3 of 12 charges stemming from a 2007 theft of Simpson-related memorabilia from a Las Vegas hotel room.
Pres. Obama signs an order lifting restrictions on federal funds for human embryonic stem cell research Mar. 9. People in China, India, and other parts of Asia view the longest solar eclipse of the 21st century June 22. Three teams of scientists report evidence of "widespread" ice on the moon Sept. 24.	The Pittsburgh Steelers become the first NFL team to win 6 Super Bowl titles Feb. 1. Mark Buehrle pitches the 18th perfect game in Major League Baseball history July 23. Lance Armstrong returns to the Tour de France after a 3-year absence and places third July 26.	Conan O'Brien takes the reins of NBC's long-running *Tonight Show* June 1. Pop star Michael Jackson dies June 25 at age 50. *American Idol* judge Paula Abdul announces Aug. 4 she is leaving the show.

2005

2006

2007

2008

2009

The Bush Presidency

Source: Issues and Controversies On File; Facts On File World News Digest; World Almanac research

George W. Bush (R), the 43rd president of the U.S., left office in Jan. 2009 after presiding over what was arguably one of the most turbulent periods in U.S. history. Below is a summary of issues, bills, and policy decisions introduced by Pres. Bush that continue to influence American (and global) politics, the economy, and society.

War on Terror

Afghanistan

Although Pres. Bush decried the practice of "nation building" during his first election campaign, he spent much of his presidency pursuing that goal in Afghanistan and Iraq. In Oct. 2001, a U.S.-led coalition began bombing Afghanistan, whose ruling Taliban regime had been harboring Osama bin Laden and members of terrorist group Al Qaeda, which perpetrated the Sept. 11, 2001, terrorist attacks. The Taliban regime was overthrown by the end of the year, but establishing a stable government in Afghanistan proved a significant challenge. In Dec. 2001, a council of Afghan leaders appointed Hamid Karzai, an opposition leader who had been living in exile, as interim president; in Oct. 2004, Karzai won the country's first democratic elections. Karzai's general outlook was considered to be pro-Western and pro-U.S., but by the end of Bush's presidency in Jan. 2009, there were still around 60,000 international troops—roughly half of them from the U.S.—engaged in fighting insurgents and providing basic security for reconstruction. Pentagon officials announced that Oct. 2009 was the deadliest month for U.S. troops in Afghanistan, and at month's end, Pres. Barack Obama was weighing a recommendation by top commander in Afghanistan, Gen. Stanley McChrystal, to deploy 40,000 more troops to the region.

Iraq

A U.S.-led coalition invaded Iraq in Mar. 2003. Though Saddam Hussein's government fell within weeks, the nation remained in chaos throughout much of Pres. Bush's second term. A so-called "surge" in U.S. troops in 2007 was credited with prompting a decline in violence, touted by Pres. Bush as one of his major foreign policy successes. Pres. Obama set a deadline of Aug. 31, 2010, for the end of all combat operations in Iraq, and a U.S.-Iraq security pact signed in 2008 called for the withdrawal of all troops by the end of 2011. U.S. troops withdrew from Iraqi cities in June 2009, but as of Oct. 30, 2009, nearly 120,000 troops remained in Iraq, and possible complications with Iraq elections scheduled for Jan. 2010 threatened to delay the withdrawal timetable.

Dept. of Homeland Security

The war on terror led Bush to significantly alter the structure of the federal government. Shortly after the terrorist attacks of Sept. 11, 2001, Bush introduced the Office of Homeland Security, which was created with the overarching goal of protecting the U.S. from future terrorist attacks. In Mar. 2003, that office became an official cabinet-level department; its secretary was to oversee a wide range of functions, from airport security to immigration enforcement and disaster relief. During the first half of the Bush presidency, the DHS made frequent use of a system of color-coded alerts to signal a potential terrorist attack, but critics argued that the alert system accomplished little. (See p. 132 for a record of changes in the system's status.)

USA PATRIOT Act

Pres. Bush was a driving force behind enactment of the Uniting and Strengthening America by Providing Appropriate Tools Required to Intercept and Obstruct Terrorism (USA PATRIOT) Act, which passed Congress by a large margin in Oct. 2001 in response to the Sept. 11 attacks. Among other changes, the Patriot Act expanded the power of law enforcement authorities to search homes, monitor phone calls and electronic communications, and access the records of people under investigation. In 2006, Pres. Bush signed a bill that made permanent 14 of 16 Patriot Act provisions that were set to expire that year. In Sept. 2009, Pres. Obama indicated that he might support reauthorization of several provisions—dealing primarily with the government's ability to conduct surveillance within the U.S.—that were set to expire at the end of 2009.

NSA Wiretapping and FISA

In late 2001, the National Security Agency (NSA) began monitoring international phone calls made by U.S. citizens without obtaining a warrant to do so. The program's existence was unknown until the *New York Times* published an article on it in 2005, and the Bush administration later admitted the story was accurate. Critics said the surveillance violated the Foreign Intelligence Surveillance Act (FISA), a

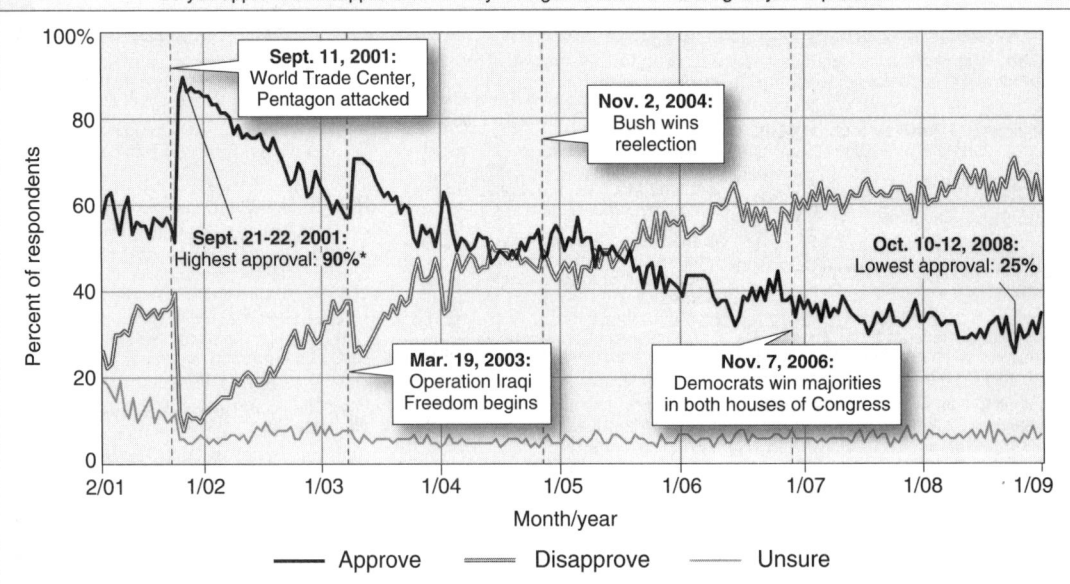

Approval Ratings of President George W. Bush, 2001-09

Source: Gallup Poll and *USA Today*/Gallup Poll of adults nationwide, for the question "Do you approve or disapprove of the way George W. Bush is handling his job as president?"

Sept. 11, 2001: World Trade Center, Pentagon attacked

Nov. 2, 2004: Bush wins reelection

Sept. 21-22, 2001: Highest approval: 90%*

Oct. 10-12, 2008: Lowest approval: 25%

Mar. 19, 2003: Operation Iraqi Freedom begins

Nov. 7, 2006: Democrats win majorities in both houses of Congress

Percent of respondents — 100%, 80, 60, 40, 20, 0

Month/year — 2/01, 1/02, 1/03, 1/04, 1/05, 1/06, 1/07, 1/08, 1/09

—— Approve   ==== Disapprove   —— Unsure

* The highest approval rating recorded for any president by the Gallup Organization, which began asking the question when Franklin D. Roosevelt was in the White House.

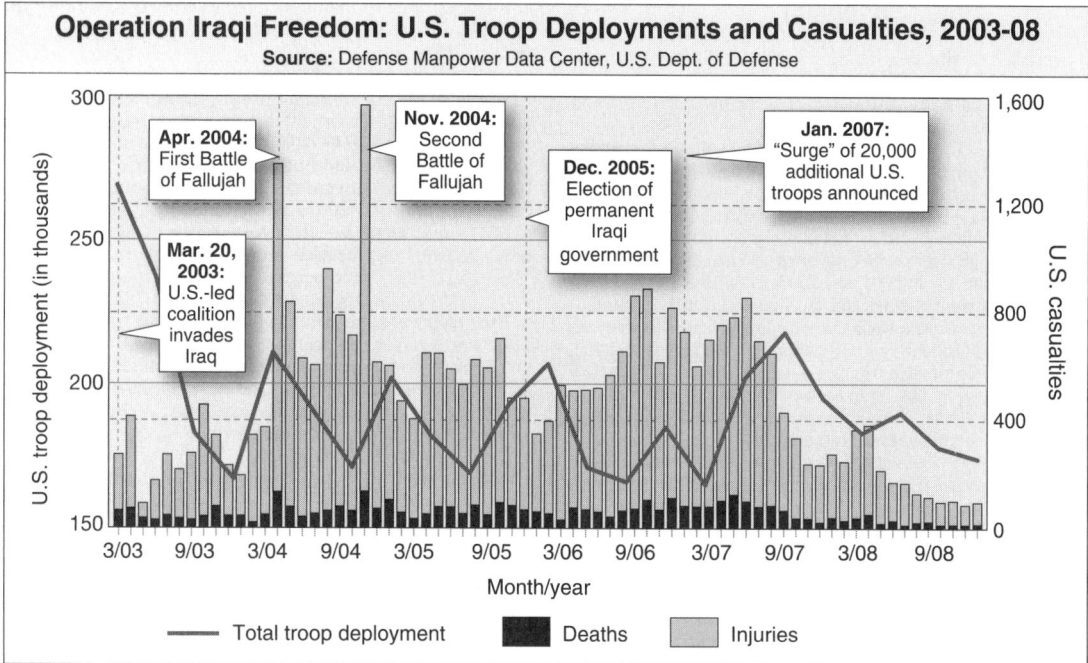

Operation Iraqi Freedom: U.S. Troop Deployments and Casualties, 2003-08

Source: Defense Manpower Data Center, U.S. Dept. of Defense

Callouts on chart:
- **Mar. 20, 2003:** U.S.-led coalition invades Iraq
- **Apr. 2004:** First Battle of Fallujah
- **Nov. 2004:** Second Battle of Fallujah
- **Dec. 2005:** Election of permanent Iraqi government
- **Jan. 2007:** "Surge" of 20,000 additional U.S. troops announced

Y-axis (left): U.S. troop deployment (in thousands) — 150, 200, 250, 300
Y-axis (right): U.S. casualties — 0, 400, 800, 1,200, 1,600
X-axis: Month/year — 3/03, 9/03, 3/04, 9/04, 3/05, 9/05, 3/06, 9/06, 3/07, 9/07, 3/08, 9/08

Legend: —— Total troop deployment   ■ Deaths   ▨ Injuries

1978 law meant to curtail government spying in the U.S. In response, the Bush administration pushed for legislation that would make the program legal. Laws passed by Congress in 2007 and 2008—with the support of then-Sen. Obama—amended FISA to legalize the program and grant retroactive immunity from prosecution to telecommunications companies that had gone along with the wiretapping.

Guantánamo

Terrorism suspects have been detained at the U.S. military base at Guantánamo Bay, Cuba, since Jan. 2002, just months after the U.S. invasion of Afghanistan. According to Bush administration lawyers, the detainees were "enemy combatants" and therefore not entitled either to the rights afforded criminal suspects in the U.S. or to the rights guaranteed prisoners of war under the international Geneva Conventions. The Supreme Court ruled repeatedly—in *Rasul v. Bush* and *Al Odah v. U.S.* (June 2004), *Hamdan v. Rumsfeld* (June 2006), and *Boumediene v. Bush* (June 2008)—in support of Guantánamo prisoners' right to challenge their detention in the court system. Many of the prisoners were released after being cleared of connections to terrorism; others, however, could not be released because their home countries either did not want them returned or would likely treat them inhumanely. Other detainees were more strongly suspected of being involved in terrorist activity. Although Bush expressed a desire to close the Guantánamo detention facilities, he argued that the U.S. first needed to find a way to deal with the detainees. At its peak, the number of detainees stood at around 700, but as of Oct. 2009 more than 220 detainees remained and Congress had not yet authorized funds required to release the remaining prisoners and complete the shutdown of the facility.

Aid to Africa
Public Health

In 2003, Pres. Bush announced the President's Emergency Plan for AIDS Relief (PEPFAR), which provided $15 bil over the course of five years to 12 African countries (as well as Haiti, Guyana, and Vietnam). That money was expressly intended to fund AIDS treatment measures—particularly the provision of expensive antiretroviral drugs, which can keep the ravages of HIV and AIDS in check. Bush administration officials said that PEPFAR enabled nearly 2 mil Africans to receive antiretroviral drugs. In 2005, Bush also initiated a five-year, $1.2 billion effort to combat malaria by providing mosquito nets, medicine,

and other anti-malaria measures to especially vulnerable African countries. Critics argued that much of the aid money given to Africa during the Bush presidency came with significant strings attached, such as requiring countries to open up their markets to foreign investment before they become eligible for U.S. aid.

Darfur

Bush has been criticized for his actions regarding the humanitarian crisis in Darfur, a region of Sudan which is said by many—including Bush himself—to be the site of ongoing genocide. The ethnic conflict there has resulted in some 300,000 deaths, according to the UN, with an additional 2.7 mil forced to leave their homes. Pres. Bush declined to send peacekeeping troops to the region, despite many calls from international organizations, but he did support the efforts of the International Criminal Court to prosecute Sudanese president Omar al-Bashir for genocide and related war crimes.

United States Africa Command

Another controversial aspect of Pres. Bush's Africa policy was the creation of a new unified combat command to oversee the continent. The goal of U.S. Africa Command, or AFRICOM, was immediately questioned by some African leaders. They expressed concerns that the U.S. was attempting to establish a permanent military presence in Africa. Bush, however, maintained that AFRICOM would be used primarily for regional stabilization and anti-terrorism purposes. AFRICOM launched in Oct. 2008, but is still viewed skeptically by many African heads of state. As of Oct. 2009, it remained provisionally based in Stuttgart, Germany.

Education

Bush signed the No Child Left Behind Act (NCLB) into law Jan. 2002. Under the law, all public school students between third and eighth grades must perform at grade level in reading and math by the year 2014. Until then, students are required to improve gradually, according to state-set standards. Schools whose students consistently fall short of state standards must be taken over by the state or a private company, or face other types of restructuring, such as being divided into smaller schools. Pres. Obama campaigned in part on a promise to overhaul, but not dismantle, NCLB.

Economy

When Pres. Bush entered office in 2001, the economy was in a precarious situation. Starting in the late 1990s, Congress had allowed investment and commercial banks to merge, creating new financial institutions that were big enough to imperil the entire economy if they failed. Laws were also passed that liberalized the use of derivatives, which allowed financial institutions to make investments based on predictions of the future prices of assets (such as home values). Economic growth during Pres. Bill Clinton's term had been fueled in part by a bubble in Internet-related stocks, which burst and led to an economic decline that was exacerbated by the terrorist attacks of Sept. 11. In 2001 and 2003, Pres. Bush signed a series of extensive tax cuts, and the Federal Reserve dramatically cut interest rates. Banks lent large amounts of money to businesses, individuals, and other banks. Unemployment fell, and the economy began to grow again. But much of the new growth was tied to a boom in the housing market, where "subprime" loans (loans made to borrowers traditionally considered high risk) increased rapidly. Many borrowers paid excessively high prices and within a few years were unable to make their mortgage payments, causing their homes to go into foreclosure. The housing market began to slump in late 2006 or early 2007, and real estate prices fell.

Many of the world's largest financial institutions, however, had bet large sums of money that real estate prices would continue to rise. When prices began to fall, those banks lost billions of dollars. In Sept. 2008, Lehman Brothers, one of the oldest and largest investment banks in the world, filed for bankruptcy. Other large financial institutions collapsed as well, prompting the stock market to go into a free fall, triggering a global credit freeze and a sustained economic downturn into 2009.

Environment

In Mar. 2001, Bush pulled the U.S. out of the Kyoto Protocol, an international agreement that would have legally bound the U.S. to reduce its emissions of carbon dioxide, nitrous oxide, and other gases that contribute to climate change. The U.S. is the world's leading producer of such gases, but as of Oct. 2009, it remained one of the only countries in the world not to have signed the Kyoto Proto-

col—though Pres. Obama pledged that the U.S. would participate in renewal discussions set to begin in Copenhagen in Dec. 2009.

Although the Bush administration's policies came under fire by many environmental groups, the administration initiated several environmentally friendly programs: under Pres. Bush, the EPA passed regulations cutting diesel emissions from construction vehicles, trains, and school buses by 90%, expanded the federal Energy Star program (which promotes the use of energy-efficient consumer goods), and launched the WaterSense program (which helps households conserve water).

Trade

Bush achieved one of his most important trade goals in 2002 when Congress granted him "fast track" negotiating authority, expanding his power to negotiate trade deals with other countries. Prior to 2002, the office of the president had not possessed that power for eight years, since Congress stripped it from Pres. Bill Clinton in 1994; the fast track authority expired in 2007. In 2005, Bush signed the Central American Free Trade Agreement (CAFTA), which removed most trade barriers between the U.S., El Salvador, Guatemala, Honduras, Nicaragua, Costa Rica, and the Dominican Republic. CAFTA was opposed by many lawmakers over concerns about labor conditions in the Latin American countries involved, as well as concerns about the threat that increased trade with Central America could pose to certain U.S. industries, such as sugar and textiles, whose commodities can be produced more cheaply abroad.

Health Care

Medicare

When Bush took office, approximately 40 mil Americans were uninsured; by 2008, that number had increased to 47 mil. The most significant health-care reform signed by Bush was the Medicare Prescription Drug Modernization Act, in 2003. The new law, which took effect in 2006 and will last until 2015, provides prescription-drug benefits for Medicare recipients. Under the drug-benefit plan, which is voluntary, senior citizens can elect to pay a small monthly fee, plus a larger annual fee, in order to purchase prescription drugs at a

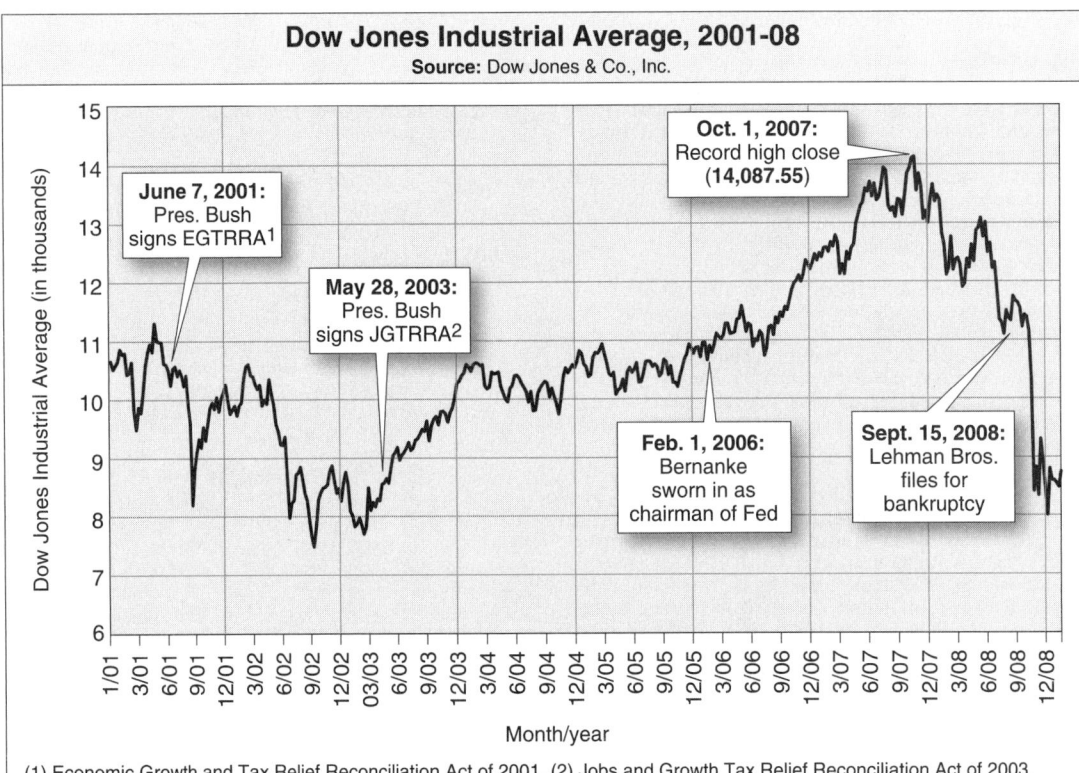

Dow Jones Industrial Average, 2001-08
Source: Dow Jones & Co., Inc.

June 7, 2001:
Pres. Bush signs EGTRRA[1]

May 28, 2003:
Pres. Bush signs JGTRRA[2]

Oct. 1, 2007:
Record high close
(14,087.55)

Feb. 1, 2006:
Bernanke sworn in as chairman of Fed

Sept. 15, 2008:
Lehman Bros. files for bankruptcy

Dow Jones Industrial Average (in thousands)

Month/year

(1) Economic Growth and Tax Relief Reconciliation Act of 2001. (2) Jobs and Growth Tax Relief Reconciliation Act of 2003.

reduced cost. Under Bush, the U.S. also reduced its federal Medicaid spending. In 2006, future spending on Medicaid was cut by $34 bil over the course of five years. Bush argued that if the federal government contributed too much to Medicaid, it would run the risk of creating a universal health care system.

Children's Health Care

Perhaps Bush's most controversial act concerning health care was his veto of an expansion of the government-sponsored state Children's Health Insurance Program (CHIP or SCHIP). Jointly funded by states and the federal government (much like Medicaid), SCHIP was established in the mid-1990s. It provided health insurance for more than 6 mil children from low-income families in 2006. The program was scheduled to expire in Oct. 2007. Bush, along with most congressional Republicans, wanted to renew SCHIP for five years at a cost of $6 bil per year—an increase over its current annual budget of roughly $4 bil. Democrats in Congress, meanwhile, favored more drastic action. They wanted to allot $12 bil a year to SCHIP for the next five years, an expansion funded by a proposed 61-cent increase in the federal tax on cigarettes. Democrats, who had won a majority in Congress in the 2006 midterm elections, pushed their plan for SCHIP through Congress. Bush, however, vetoed the bill, arguing that it would expand the program too greatly.

Abortion

In 2003, Bush signed into law a bill banning "intact dilation and extraction," referred to by some as "partial-birth abortion." The procedure, which had been rare before the ban, involves removing a fetus intact from the mother's uterus. The technique is used only when the mother has been pregnant longer than 12 weeks. The bill that Bush signed, the Partial-Birth Abortion Ban Act, was first overturned in 2005 by the U.S. Eighth Circuit Court of Appeals in St. Louis, MO. The court found the law unconstitutional because, while it included an exemption for mothers whose lives would be directly threatened if they gave birth, it did not contain an exemption to preserve the mother's health in a more general sense. In 2007, however, the U.S. Supreme Court overturned the Eighth Circuit Court's ruling with a 5-4 decision in which both of Bush's Supreme Court appointees, Chief Justice John Roberts and Associate Justice Samuel Alito, voted with the majority. Bush praised the Supreme Court for upholding the ban.

Thwarted Reforms
Social Security

After winning reelection in 2004, Pres. Bush's first significant attempt to assert his authority during his second term came in an attempt to partially privatize Social Security. Bush proposed allowing workers to divert a portion of their pay into personal retirement accounts. Rather than paying into the existing Social Security system, they would be able to invest their money privately in the stock market. Resistance to Bush's plan prompted him to quietly cease his calls for Social Security reform. At the end of Bush's presidency, some critics pointed out that, had the government allowed individuals to divert their Social Security payments into private accounts, much of that money would have been lost during the stock market crash of 2008.

Immigration

In 2006, Bush promoted comprehensive immigration policy reform, though members of Congress were ultimately unable to reconcile their differences to produce a cohesive bill. Bush favored allowing illegal immigrants currently living in the U.S. to stay in the country as "guest workers," putting them on an eventual path to citizenship. House Republicans bristled at the plan, drafting their own legislation that differed radically from Bush's vision. The House bill drastically increased penalties against illegal immigrants, and classified anyone who assisted them as felons. The proposed legislation prompted large protests throughout the U.S. on behalf of immigrants. Bush, meanwhile, pushed for a bill that would ease penalties imposed on illegal immigrants. He said at the time, "There are people in our country doing work that Americans will not do, and those people ought to be given a chance to have a tamper-proof card that enables them to work in our country legally for a period of time." The Senate drafted an immigration bill more in keeping with Bush's vision, but the two houses of Congress were unable to reconcile their proposals. Rather than continuing to pursue comprehensive immigration reform, Congress agreed to focus on preventing undocumented immigrants from entering the country by constructing a fence and increasing patrols along the Mexican-American border. In Dec. 2008, Bush authorized changes to the existing H-2A guest worker program. The program allows farmers to hire immigrant workers to fill temporary farm jobs for which no willing American workers can be found.

U.S. Home Price Index and Unemployment Rate, 2001-08
Source: S&P/Case-Shiller Home Price Index; Bureau of Labor Statistics, U.S. Dept. of Labor

June 7, 2001: Pres. Bush signs EGTRRA[1]

May 28, 2003: Pres. Bush signs JGTRRA[2]

2nd quarter 2006: All-time high (**189.93**)

7.6%

4.2%

139.18

109.27

—■— Case-Shiller Home Price Index   Unemployed

(1) Economic Growth and Tax Relief Reconciliation Act of 2001. (2) Jobs and Growth Tax Relief Reconciliation Act of 2003.

November 2008

National

Obama Wins Presidential Election, as Democrats Expand Control of Congress—Sen. Barack Obama of Illinois, the Democratic presidential nominee, and his vice-presidential running mate, Sen. Joe Biden of Delaware, swept to victory Nov. 4 over the Republican ticket of Arizona Sen. John McCain and Alaska Gov. Sarah Palin. Obama, the 47-year-old son of a black father from Kenya and a white mother from Kansas, was the first African American to win the U.S. presidency. "If there is anyone out there who still doubts that America is a place where all things are possible ... tonight is your answer," said Obama on election night.

When the 538 members of the Electoral College met in their respective states Dec. 15, Obama won 365 electoral votes to McCain's 173; the results were certified in a joint session of Congress Jan. 8, 2009. Tabulations released in July 2009 by the Federal Election Commission showed that Obama had won 69,498,516 popular votes, or 52.93% of the total, while McCain had received 59,948,323 votes, or 45.65%. Candidates of other parties received a combined total of less than 1.5% of the 131,313,820 ballots cast.

Democratic gains of at least 6 seats in the Senate and more than 20 seats in the House (pending recounts, runoffs, and special elections) left the party in command of the White House and both chambers of Congress for the first time in 14 years. Several close contests took 2 weeks or more to decide. In Alaska, Anchorage Mayor Mark Begich (D) claimed victory Nov. 18 after a recount showed him with an insurmountable lead over Ted Stevens, the longest-serving Republican in the Senate. Stevens had been convicted by a federal jury Oct. 27 of accepting and then failing to report more than $250,000 in gifts he received between 1999 and 2006. (The criminal charges against Stevens were dismissed Apr. 7, 2009, on grounds of prosecutorial misconduct.) Georgia's Senate race was not decided until a Dec. 2 runoff election, in which incumbent Sen. Saxby Chambliss (R) turned back a challenge from Jim Martin (D). In Minnesota, a tight race between incumbent Sen. Norm Coleman (R) and former comedian Al Franken (D) led to an extended recount and legal battle that remained unresolved until the Minnesota Supreme Court ruled in Franken's favor, June 30, 2009.

Democrats won 7 of 11 state governorships and made modest gains in state legislatures. The election left Democrats in control of 29 of the 50 state governor's offices and 55% of all state legislative seats, their highest share since 1994.

Same-Sex Marriage Rescinded in California, Allowed in Connecticut—By a margin of 52.3% to 47.7%, California voters Nov. 4 passed a ballot measure, known as Proposition 8, which abolished the right of same-sex couples to marry. Voters in Arizona and Florida also enacted bans on same-sex marriage, and Arkansans approved a measure prohibiting unmarried couples living together, regardless of sexual orientation, from adopting children or becoming foster parents. Passage of Proposition 8 overturned a May 2008 ruling by the California Supreme Court that had opened the way for some 18,000 same-sex couples to obtain marriage licenses in the state. On May 26, 2009, California's highest court turned down a challenge to the constitutionality of Proposition 8, while ruling that the same-sex marriages authorized before Election Day were still legally valid.

A 4-year legal battle in Connecticut ended Nov. 12, 2008, when that state began issuing marriage licenses to same-sex couples. The action followed the issuance of a court order implementing an Oct. 10 decision by the Connecticut Supreme Court, which held that the state's civil union law, enacted in 2005, violated equal-protection provisions of Connecticut's constitution. The 2005 law had explicitly defined marriage as "the union of one man and one woman," but had authorized homosexual couples to form civil unions that conferred the same "benefits, protections and responsibilities" as heterosexual marriage.

President-Elect Appoints Top Staff, Economic Team—One day after he was elected president, Barack Obama Nov. 5 designated John Podesta, Valerie Jarrett, and Pete Rouse to lead his transition team. Podesta had extensive White House experience as chief of staff (1998-2001) under Pres. Bill Clinton. Jarrett was a longtime Obama friend and adviser, and Rouse had served as Obama's Senate chief of staff. On Nov. 6, another former Clinton aide, Rep. Rahm Emanuel (D, IL), agreed to become Obama's White House chief of staff. Greg Craig, a lawyer who had defended Clinton during his 1999 impeachment trial, was named White House counsel Nov. 19, and Robert Gibbs, who had been Obama's chief campaign spokesman, was chosen Nov. 22 to become White House press secretary.

Promising to "act swiftly and boldly" to deal with "an economic crisis of historic dimensions," Obama began unveiling his economic policy team Nov. 24. Selected for Treasury secretary was Tim Geithner, who as president of the Federal Reserve Bank of New York had worked closely with Federal Reserve Chairman Ben Bernanke, Treasury Sec. Henry Paulson, and other Bush administration officials on a $700 bil bank bailout plan enacted the previous month. Other economic policy makers selected by Obama Nov. 24-26 included former Treasury Sec. Lawrence Summers to direct the National Economic Council, Christina Romer to head the Council of Economic Advisers, and Peter Orszag to direct the Office of Management and Budget.

Economic Downturn Deepens, as Bush Administration Revamps Bailout Efforts—Housing sales slumped, retail sales plummeted, personal and corporate bankruptcy filings rose, and employers slashed payrolls at the fastest pace in 34 years, as the U.S. unemployment rate rose to 6.7%, the highest since 1993. After months of shrinking sales, Circuit City, one of the nation's largest consumer electronics retailers, filed for bankruptcy protection Nov. 10. (The 60-year-old company, based in Richmond, VA, shut down its 567 remaining stores Mar. 8, 2009.) Also on Nov. 10, the insurance giant American International Group (AIG) disclosed that it had lost $24.5 bil during July-Sept. 2008, and Bush administration officials announced that the AIG rescue package, already raised from $85 bil in Sept. to $123 bil in Oct., would be increased to $150 bil. The ailing New York City-based Citigroup, reached agreement Nov. 23 with the Treasury Dept., the Federal Reserve, and the Federal Deposit Insurance Corp. (FDIC) on a rescue plan under which the government would invest $20 bil in the bank and partially guarantee more than $300 bil of Citigroup's assets.

Treasury Sec. Paulson revealed Nov. 12 that the $700 bil bank bailout, known as the Troubled Asset Relief Program (TARP) and originally intended to remove troubled (or "toxic") assets from bank balance sheets, would instead be used to stabilize and stimulate credit markets by bolstering the consumer finance industry and purchasing shares in ailing banks. (The Treasury Dept. also allocated $40 bil of the TARP money to the expanded AIG rescue.) To assist struggling mortgage holders, the FDIC proposed Nov. 14 to use $24 bil to help some 1.5 mil U.S. households avoid foreclosure. On Nov. 25 the Federal Reserve and Treasury announced an $800 bil program to ease frozen credit markets; $600 bil would be allocated to purchase debt from Fannie Mae, Freddie Mac, and other mortgage-financiers, and $200 bil would be used to encourage investors to buy securities tied to car and student loans, and other forms of consumer credit.

Detroit's "Big 3" auto companies—General Motors, Chrysler, and Ford—asked Congress Nov. 18-19 for a taxpayer-financed rescue. Many legislators were critical of the firms' business plans and management practices, repeatedly citing the fact that the executives had flown to DC in separate private jets to give testimony before Congress.

Despite a final-week rally, the Dow Jones Industrial Average declined 5.3% during the month, closing Nov. 28 at 8,829.04. The S&P 500 finished at 896.24, a drop of 7.5%, and the Nasdaq Composite Index closed at 1,535.57, down 10.8%.

International
Industrialized Nations Take Steps to Combat Global Recession—With output and private investment shrinking and unemployment rising in much of the world, leading industrialized countries sought, individually and collectively, to slow the economic downslide. On Nov. 3 the South Korean government proposed a stimulus program of new spending and tax cuts amounting to about $11 bil. Two days later, the German cabinet approved a 4-year, $30 bil plan to fund infrastructure projects, stimulate bank lending, and provide tax breaks for companies, homeowners, and car buyers. Chinese authorities said Nov. 9 they expected to spend about $586 bil during 2009-10 on railways, airports, mass transit, and other construction projects, including rebuilding efforts in Sichuan Province, parts of which were devastated by an earthquake in May 2008. In his budget speech Nov. 24, UK Chancellor of the Exchequer Alistair Darling said the British government would implement nearly $30 bil in tax reductions, spending increases, and debt guarantees for small businesses.

At an emergency meeting of the Group of 20 (G-20), which includes a consortium of developed nations and emerging economies, conferees reached agreement in principle on measures to strengthen oversight of multinational financial institutions, credit-rating agencies, and the types of highly speculative investments that had driven the global financial system to the brink of collapse. The G-20 leaders, who met Nov. 14-15 in Washington, DC, also agreed not to impose protectionist barriers that might interfere with international investment and trade for at least 12 months.

Haiti School Cave-In Kills 91—The Collège La Promesse Évangélique, a church-run school on the outskirts of Port-au-Prince, Haiti, collapsed Nov. 7, killing 94 students and teachers and injuring another 162 people. Rescuers were still clearing the rubble from the disaster site Nov. 12 when another school in the Haitian capital partially collapsed, injuring 9 people. The cave-ins were blamed on shoddy, unregulated construction practices, a problem throughout the poverty-stricken island nation.

Conservatives Win in New Zealand—In parliamentary elections Nov. 8, the center-right National Party won 59 of 122 seats, 16 more than the Labour Party, which had governed New Zealand for nearly 9 years. Helen Clark, prime min. since 1999, announced that she would step down as Labour Party leader. On Nov. 19 the 47-year-old John Key, a former investment banker, was sworn in as head of a government that included the free market-oriented Association of Consumers and Taxpayers (ACT) and the Maori Party, both of which won 5 seats in Parliament.

Iraq and U.S. Approve Security Accord—A long-debated Status of Forces Agreement (SOFA) between the U.S. and Iraq won approval from Iraq's cabinet Nov. 16 and was signed by Iraqi Foreign Min. Hoshyar Zebari and U.S. Ambassador Ryan Crocker the following day. Endorsed by the Iraqi Parliament Nov. 27 and by Iraq's Presidential Council Dec. 4, the SOFA provided a legal basis for the continued presence of U.S. military forces and contractors in Iraq when the UN Security Council resolution authorizing U.S. military operations expired Dec. 31. Included in the accord was a timetable calling for U.S. combat troops to pull out of Iraq's major cities and towns by June 30, 2009, and to leave the country by Dec. 31, 2011. The U.S. still had 148,000 troops in Iraq as of Nov. 2008. U.S. military deaths numbered 16 for the month.

Terrorists Strike Mumbai, India—Ten heavily armed Pakistanis Nov. 26 penetrated the heart of Mumbai, India, killing at least 172 people and injuring more than 300 at multiple locations before Indian Army commandos took control of the Taj Mahal Palace and Tower Hotel 3 days later. The young militants, linked to the banned Pakistani terror group Lashkar-e-Taiba, had set out by boat from Karachi, in southern Pakistan. They commandeered an Indian fishing trawler, murdered its captain and crew, and landed at Mumbai's southern tip. Splitting up, the men assaulted downtown sites including 2 luxury hotels (the Oberoi Trident and the Taj Mahal Palace and Tower), a railway station, a Jewish center, a hospital, and a cafe. A dossier compiled by Indian authorities revealed the attackers had been in telephone contact with their handlers. According to the transcript of one phone conversation, the Oberoi gunmen were told, "Everything is being recorded by the media. Inflict maximum damage. Keep fighting. Don't be taken alive."

Nine of the attackers were killed; the tenth, Ajmal Kasab, was captured in a shootout. The 21-year-old Kasab confessed in open court July 20, 2009, that he had been recruited by Lashkar-e-Taiba in Rawalpindi, and that he and the other attackers had been trained in Karachi.

Hundreds Die in Nigeria Riots—Anger over a disputed local election Nov. 27 triggered sectarian rioting Nov. 28-29 in Jos, the capital of Plateau State in central Nigeria. The death toll reached 200 according to early official estimates, but a July 20 report by Human Rights Watch put it far higher, at over 700. Mosques, churches, shops, and homes were looted and burned in clashes between rival Muslim and Christian gangs. A week later, according to the Nigerian Red Cross, 7,070 people who fled the fighting were living in 10 displaced-persons camps throughout the city.

General
First Photographs of Distant Planets Published—The first direct optical images of planets orbiting stars outside our solar system appeared Nov. 13 in the online journal *Science Express*, published by the American Association for the Advancement of Science. A team led by Dr. Christian Marois of the Herzberg Institute of Astrophysics, Victoria, BC, Canada, used the Gemini North and Keck telescopes at Mauna Kea, HI, to photograph 3 planets circling the star HR 8799, about 130 light-years from Earth, in the constellation Pegasus. (One light-year equals the distance that light travels in a year, or nearly 6 tril miles.) A second team, directed by Dr. Paul Kalas of the Univ. of California, Berkeley, used images from the Hubble Space Telescope to find optical evidence of a planet orbiting the star Fomalhaut, 25 light-years from Earth. Previously, scientists had offered only indirect evidence for the existence of extrasolar planets.

Dunwoody Becomes First Woman to Achieve Rank of 4-Star General—In ceremonies at the Pentagon Nov. 14, the U.S. Army awarded a fourth star to Gen. Ann Dunwoody, making her the first female officer in the history of the U.S. military to attain that rank. Later that same day, at Fort Belvoir, VA—the base where she was born in 1953—Dunwoody was sworn in to head the Army Materiel Command, which provides supplies and services for U.S. soldiers around the world. Commissioned in 1975, she had been nominated for promotion by Pres. George W. Bush in June 2008 and confirmed by the U.S. Senate in July.

December 2008
National
Obama Picks Hillary Clinton as Sec. of State; Other Cabinet Choices Named—At a news conference in Chicago Dec. 1, Pres.-elect Barack Obama announced his choice of New York Sen. Hillary Clinton (D) to become sec. of state. The former first lady had been Obama's principal rival for the 2008 Democratic presidential nomination. Other prospective cabinet members and high-ranking national security officials named Dec. 1 included Robert Gates, a Bush appointee who agreed to remain in office as sec. of defense; retired Marine Gen. James L. Jones, former supreme allied commander of NATO, selected as White House national security adviser; Eric Holder Jr., a former Justice Dept. official, who would become the first African American to serve as attorney general; and Arizona Gov. Janet Napolitano (D), chosen as homeland security sec. Designated as the new U.S. ambassador to the UN was Susan Rice, a former State Dept. official.

Obama continued to fill out his cabinet Dec. 7, choosing retired Army Gen. Eric K. Shinseki to head the Dept. of Veterans Affairs. Twice awarded the Purple Heart for injuries sustained during the Vietnam War, Shinseki was Army chief of staff in 2003 when he publicly disputed the Bush administration's Iraq war strategy. On Dec. 15 Obama introduced his "green" team, including Nobel Prize-winning physicist Steven Chu as sec. of energy; Lisa Jackson, a former New

Jersey environmental official, to head the Environmental Protection Agency (EPA); and Carol Browner, a former EPA chief, to coordinate White House policy on energy and climate change. Other cabinet members named during the month included New York City Housing Comm. Shaun Donovan as sec. of housing and urban development, reform-minded Chicago school chief Arne Duncan as sec. of education, Sen. Ken Salazar (D) of Colorado as sec. of the interior, former Iowa Gov. Tom Vilsack (D) as agriculture sec., Rep. Ray LaHood (R) of Illinois as transportation sec., and Rep. Hilda Solis (D) of California as sec. of labor.

Most of Obama's prominent cabinet choices easily endured the nomination and Senate confirmation process. Two who did not were New Mexico Gov. Bill Richardson (D), who was nominated to be commerce sec. Dec. 3, and former Sen. Tom Daschle (D, SD), who was officially introduced Dec. 11 as both health and human services sec. and head of a new White House Office of Health Reform. Richardson withdrew his name Jan. 4, 2009, because of an ongoing federal probe into dealings between the New Mexico state government and a company headed by one of his foremost campaign contributors. Daschle pulled out Feb. 3 after revealing that he had paid more than $140,000 in back taxes and interest Jan. 2. The debt stemmed mostly from Daschle's use of a chauffeur and limousine provided to him while he was a consultant, 2005-07, to InterMedia Advisors, a private equity firm.

Illinois Gov. Blagojevich Accused of Trying to Sell Obama's Senate Seat—Federal prosecutors Dec. 9 accused Gov. Rod Blagojevich (D) of attempting to use his authority to fill the Senate seat vacated by Pres.-elect Obama as a means of extorting campaign contributions and other favors. The arrest of Blagojevich (along with his chief of staff, John Harris) accompanied the release of a 76-page FBI affidavit that detailed the governor's alleged role in "pay-to-play" schemes" involving kickbacks and influence peddling.

The arrests marked the culmination of a 5-year-long probe known as Operation Board Games, which had accelerated after court-approved wiretaps detected Blagojevich discussing ways to profit from the sale of Obama's Senate seat and other illicit fund raising efforts. U.S. Attorney Patrick J. Fitzgerald stated Dec. 9 that the case made "no allegations about the president-elect whatsoever." Federal investigators interviewed Obama Dec. 18. A report released 5 days later on behalf of the Obama transition team stated that neither Obama nor his staff had had inappropriate contact with Blagojevich, although Rep. Rahm Emanuel (D, IL)—the incoming White House chief of staff—had discussed both his and Obama's departures from Congress with the governor.

On Dec. 15, by a vote of 113-0, the Illinois state House of Representatives launched impeachment proceedings against the governor. On Dec. 30 the defiant Blagojevich appointed former state Atty. Gen. Roland W. Burris, a 71-year-old African American, as Obama's successor.

Madoff Arrested for Multibillion-Dollar Ponzi Scheme—One of the largest frauds in U.S. history was exposed Dec. 11 when Bernard Madoff, a well-known Wall Street investment adviser, was arrested by federal agents in New York City and charged with swindling his clients out of more than $50 bil. Separate criminal and civil complaints accused Madoff of operating a giant Ponzi scheme in which some investors, lured by the promise of consistently high returns, had been repaid with funds generated not from Madoff's purported investment strategy but from capital pumped in from other investors. His empire collapsed during the autumn financial crisis, when investors' demands for withdrawals far exceeded the available supply of new capital. Madoff, a former chairman of the Nasdaq Stock Exchange, told senior employees Dec. 10 that his investment scheme was "all just one big lie."

Madoff pleaded guilty Mar. 12, 2009, to 11 counts of fraud, money laundering, perjury, and theft. By that time, federal investigators calculated that he had defrauded some 4,800 clients out of nearly $65 bil. Among the victims were international banks, hedge funds, Hollywood and sports celebrities, and Jewish schools and charitable foundations. Madoff, 71, was sentenced June 29 to 150 years in prison by U.S. District Judge Denny Chin. An internal investigation completed Aug. 31 by the Securities and Exchange Commission (SEC) concluded the agency had failed to act on substantive complaints that "raised significant red flags" about Madoff's investment operations as early as 1992.

Tennessee Coal Ash Spill Causes Pollution Disaster—An earthen retaining wall at a Kingston, TN, power plant ruptured Dec. 22, allowing 5.4 mil cu yards of coal ash sludge to spill from a storage pond. The sludge blocked roads and rail lines, polluted 300 acres of land, and contaminated the Emory River. The ash, laced with toxins, was a by-product of combustion at the coal-fired Kingston Fossil Plant, managed by the federally owned Tennessee Valley Authority (TVA). The cleanup operation, taken over in May 2009 by the EPA, included the transfer of up to 3 mil cu yards of ash to a landfill about 350 mi away, in an impoverished region of rural Alabama.

Five Convicted in Fort Dix Terror Plot—Five men accused of plotting to kill American soldiers at the Fort Dix, NJ, military base were convicted by a federal jury in Camden Dec. 22 on conspiracy charges, but acquitted of attempted murder. The men, all foreign-born Muslims living in near Philadelphia, were arrested in an FBI sting operation after 2 of the men attempted to buy weapons from a federal informant. On Apr. 28, 2009, U.S. District Judge Robert B. Kugler sentenced 3 of the defendants—brothers Eljvir, Dritan, and Shain Duka—to life in prison, with Dritan and Shain also sentenced to an additional 30 years on gun charges. The following day, Mohamad Ibrahim Shnewer received a life sentence plus 30 years, and Serdar Tatar got a 33-year sentence. A sixth defendant, Agron Abdullahu, had pleaded guilty to weapons charges in Oct. 2007.

Markets End Dismal Year, as Signs of Painful Recession Grow; Auto Industry Gets Reprieve—U.S. stock exchanges finished Dec. 31, 2008, with major indexes recording their worst single-year performance since the Great Depression. The Dow Jones Industrial Average closed at 8,776.39, for a decline in 2008 of 33.8%—the Dow's steepest one-year drop since 1931. The S&P 500 plunged 38.5% in 2008, closing at 903.25, and the Nasdaq Composite Index showed a one-year slide of 40.5%, ending at 1,577.03. In all, shareholders lost about $7 tril in wealth in 2008, erasing the gains of the previous 6 years.

The month's relentless drumbeat of negative economic news began Dec. 1, when the Business Cycle Dating Committee of the National Bureau of Economic Research announced that the U.S. had been in recession since Dec. 2007. The Bureau of Labor Statistics reported Dec. 5 that employers cut 533,000 jobs in Nov.—the largest one-month loss since 1974. Despite efforts by retailers to attract holiday shoppers with steep discounts, same-store sales at leading retail outlets in Dec. 2008 were 1.7% below those of Dec. 2007, according to the International Council of Shopping Centers. The Conference Board reported that its Consumer Confidence Index plummeted from 44.7 in Nov. to an all-time low of 38.0 in late Dec.

The banking industry continued to stagger. As Citigroup implemented job cuts that would shrink the company's work force by 52,000 between Sept. 2008 and early 2009, Bank of America revealed Dec. 11 that it planned to slash up to 35,000 jobs over a 3-year period. Newspapers, another ailing industry, were further weakened by the loss of advertising revenue because of the recession. On Dec. 8 the Tribune Co., with holdings that included the *Los Angeles Times* and *Chicago Tribune*, filed for bankruptcy, although the papers continued to publish.

Rebuffed by Congress in Nov., Detroit's "Big 3" auto companies resubmitted their bailout requests and restructuring plans Dec. 4, but Congress again refused to provide assistance. With both General Motors and Chrysler claiming they were in immediate danger of running out of cash, Pres. George W. Bush announced Dec. 19 that the Treasury Dept. would use some of the funds from the $700 bil bank bailout to finance up to $17.4 bil in loans to the auto industry. The third Detroit auto giant, Ford, chose not to accept federal bailout money and the restrictions that went along with it.

International
Thai Court Disbands Ruling Party—Thailand's Constitutional Court Dec. 2 ordered the dissolution of the ruling People Power Party (PPP) and barred Prime Min. Somchai Wongsawat from politics. The decision, which found the PPP and 2 of its coalition partners guilty of fraud in the run-up to Dec. 2007 elections, marked the second time in 3 months that the court had ousted a prime min. Somchai was the brother-in-law of former Prime Min. Thaksin Shinawatra, who in Oct. 2008 was convicted in absentia on charges of corruption and abuse of power. Supporters and opponents of Thaksin were involved in a continuing power struggle that had paralyzed Thai politics. On Dec. 15, Parliament chose as prime min. Abhisit Vejjajiva of the opposition Democrat Party, defeating a Thaksin ally, Pracha Promnok of the Puea Thai (For Thais) Party, the successor to the PPP.

Canadian Parliament Shuts Down, as Harper Avoids Ouster—At the request of Prime Min. Stephen Harper, who was facing a no-confidence vote he was virtually guaranteed to lose, Gov.-Gen. Michaëlle Jean took the extraordinary step Dec. 4 of agreeing to suspend, or prorogue, Parliament until late Jan. 2009. Harper, whose Conservatives had fallen short of a majority in Oct. 14 elections, angered opponents by proposing to end public financing of political parties. Three opposition groups—the Liberals, Bloc Québécois, and New Democratic Party—agreed Dec. 1 to form an alliance to replace the Conservative prime min. with a Liberal, Stéphane Dion, but Harper's parliamentary maneuver thwarted their strategy. Dion, who had earlier pledged to give up the Liberal leadership post after his party's disappointing election performance, was succeeded Dec. 10 by Michael Ignatieff as leader of the opposition.

Oil Prices Fall, as Recession Impact Spreads—Nations throughout the world continued to confront the deepening economic downturn. France Dec. 4 unveiled a $33 bil stimulus plan that included bonuses for car owners who traded in their old models for newer, more fuel-efficient vehicles. Japan's central bank Dec. 19 slashed its benchmark interest rate to near zero, and Canada Dec. 20 offered emergency loans to its struggling auto industry.

Revenues of petroleum-exporting countries declined, as manufacturing slowed and energy demand dropped in most industrialized countries. Hurt by falling oil exports, Russia spent more than $160 bil to prop up its sagging currency against the dollar and euro, but the ruble declined from mid-Nov. through the close of the year. OPEC member countries, meeting Dec. 17 in Oran, Algeria, agreed to cut their combined oil output by 2.2 mil barrels per day, the greatest output cut in its history. Oil was trading below $45 a barrel as the year ended, down from a peak of more than $145 in July.

Bush Visits Iraq, Afghanistan—Pres. George W. Bush made surprise visits Dec. 14-15 to Iraq and Afghanistan, meeting with officials and troops on a farewell tour. A press conference with Iraqi Prime Min. Nouri al-Maliki in Baghdad's Green Zone was marred when an Iraqi journalist, Muntader al-Zaidi, threw his shoes at Bush in protest. Arrested, beaten, and imprisoned for 9 months in Iraq, Zaidi was hailed as a hero in parts of the Arab world.

U.S. troop deaths in Iraq numbered 14 during the month; the U.S. casualty total for 2008 was 314, far fewer than the 904 fatalities recorded in 2007. According to U.S. military estimates, overall violence in Iraq declined 40% to 80% during 2007-08. In Afghanistan, 27 coalition troops died in Dec.; the death toll for 2008 was 294, including 155 from the U.S., 51 from the UK, and 32 from Canada.

Coup Follows Death of Pres. Conté in Guinea—Authoritarian Pres. Lansana Conté, who had ruled the West African nation of Guinea for more than 24 years, died Dec. 22 after a long illness. The following day, a military junta led by Capt. Moussa Dadis Camara seized power, calling itself the National Council for Democracy and Development. Camara, who joined the army in 1990, had reportedly been involved in military uprisings in 2007-08. The coup was for the most part condemned by the international community— Guinea was suspended from the African Union (AU) Dec. 29 and the Economic Community of West African States (ECOWAS) Jan. 10, 2009, as a result.

Awami League Wins Election in Bangladesh—Nearly 2 years of emergency rule by a military-dominated caretaker government ended Dec. 29, as the Awami League swept to victory in Bangladesh legislative elections. Final results showed the Awami League, led by former Prime Min. Sheikh Hasina Wazed, with 231 of the 300 seats in Parliament. The Bangladesh Nationalist Party, headed by Hasina's longtime rival, former Prime Min. Begum Khaleda Zia, had only 29. While it held power, the caretaker government had sought to prosecute or exile both women.

Sheikh Hasina took office as prime min. Jan. 6, 2009. Her government survived its first major test Feb. 25-26 when a mutiny at the Dhaka headquarters of the paramilitary Bangladesh Rifles was suppressed; the rebellion left 74 people dead, according to official figures.

General
Kirill I Succeeds Aleksy II as Russian Orthodox Patriarch—Aleksy II, patriarch since 1990 of the world's largest Orthodox church, died of heart failure Dec. 5 at the age of 79. The Estonian-born spiritual leader of more than 140 mil Russian Orthodox Christians was succeeded by Metropolitan Kirill of Smolensk and Kaliningrad, who as interim patriarch presided over Aleksy II's funeral Dec. 9. Kirill, a 62-year-old native of Leningrad (now St. Petersburg), became the 16th patriarch of Moscow and All Russia following his election Jan. 27, 2009, and his enthronement Feb. 1 as Kirill I. Russian Pres. Dmitri Medvedev and Prime Min. Vladimir Putin attended Aleksy II's funeral and Kirill's installation.

January 2009
National
111th Congress Convenes—With large Democratic majorities in both the House and the Senate, the 111th Congress convened Jan. 6. House Speaker Nancy Pelosi (D, CA), House Majority Leader Steny Hoyer (D, MD), House Minority Leader John Boehner (R, OH), Senate Majority Leader Harry Reid (D, NV), and Senate Minority Leader Mitch McConnell (R, KY) all retained the same positions they had held in the 110th Congress. A newcomer to the top Republican ranks was House Minority Whip Eric Cantor (VA), who won his post in Nov. 2008.

Major changes in Senate membership during the month included the seating Jan. 15 of Roland Burris (D, IL) (see below) and the swearing-in Jan. 16 of Edward Kaufman (D, DE) to replace Vice Pres.-elect Joe Biden. On Jan. 22, Michael Bennet (D, CO) replaced Ken Salazar (D), who had been confirmed by the Senate as sec. of the interior, and on Jan. 27 Kirsten Gillibrand (D, NY) replaced Hillary Clinton, who had been confirmed as sec. of state.

Confirmation hearings took up much of the Senate's attention during the month. Among the most contentious were hearings on the nominations of Treasury Sec. Tim Geithner, who acknowledged failing to pay $34,000 in self-employment taxes in 2001-04, when he was employed by the International Monetary Fund. Atty. Gen. Eric Holder was criticized for his role in a series of pardons issued in Jan. 2001 by Pres. Bill Clinton, when Holder was deputy attorney general. The Senate confirmed Geithner by a vote of 60-34 on Jan. 26, and Holder was approved, 75-21, on Feb. 2.

Obama Inaugurated as 44th President; First Actions in Office—With the U.S. at war in Iraq and Afghanistan, and the nation facing its worst economic crisis since the Great Depression, Barack Hussein Obama was inaugurated Jan. 20 in Washington, DC, becoming the nation's 44th president. He took the oath of office at about noon, shortly after Joe Biden was sworn in as vice president. (Because the words of the presidential oath, administered by Chief Justice John Roberts, were somewhat garbled, Obama and Roberts repeated the oath-taking ceremony at the White House Jan. 21.) In an 18-minute inaugural address delivered to more than 1 mil people in attendance in below-freezing temperatures on the National Mall, Obama cited the Bible in warning that "the time has come to set aside childish things." He outlined in broad strokes an activist presidential agenda and said, "Starting today, we must pick ourselves up, dust ourselves off, and begin again the work of remaking America."

The inauguration of Obama and Biden, both Democrats, and the departure of a Republican administration headed by Pres. George W. Bush and Vice Pres. Dick Cheney heralded a major cultural as well as political shift. Obama was the nation's first black president, and in his wife Michelle the U.S. had, for the first time, a first lady who was the direct descendant of African American slaves. Their daughters Malia, 10, and Sasha, 7, were the youngest children to make their home in the White House in more than 45 years. The inauguration was preceded by a national day of service on Jan. 19, the Martin Luther King Jr. holiday.

Obama moved quickly to put his stamp on the presidency. In executive orders issued Jan. 21-22, he ordered the closure within one year of the U.S. military prison at Guantánamo Bay, Cuba; barred the use of torture in the interrogation of terrorism detainees; and tightened ethics requirements for members of his administration. On Jan. 29 he signed into law the Lilly Ledbetter Fair Pay Act, making it easier for women and minorities to challenge workplace pay discrimination; the measure had cleared the Senate Jan. 22 and the House Jan. 27.

Blagojevich Impeached, Convicted in Illinois; Senate Seats Burris—One month after his arrest on federal corruption charges, Illinois Gov. Rod Blagojevich (D) was impeached Jan. 9 by the Illinois state House of Representatives and convicted Jan. 29 by the state Senate. The House vote was 114-1, the Senate vote 59-0. The Senate also voted to bar Blagojevich from ever again holding public office in Illinois. Prosecutors at his 4-day Senate impeachment trial played and read excerpts from taped conversations purporting to show abuse of power, including an attempt to sell Obama's Senate seat. Blagojevich declined to testify at his impeachment trial, but returned from a series of media appearances to deliver a 45-minute closing statement. Immediately upon Blagojevich's conviction and removal from office, Lt. Gov. Pat Quinn (D) became governor.

Blagojevich's pick to succeed Obama in the U.S. Senate, Roland Burris, was sworn in Jan. 15, becoming the Senate's lone African American member. Senate leaders had initially refused to seat Burris because of the circumstances surrounding his appointment, but relented after Burris provided assurances that he had not behaved unethically in his contact with Blagojevich. A month later, Burris confirmed that his discussions with Blagojevich had been more extensive than previously acknowledged, and that in Nov. 2008, while seeking the Senate seat, he had tried to raise funds for Blagojevich. Burris remained in the Senate, but said July 10, 2009, that he would not seek reelection in 2010.

Salmonella Outbreak Traced to Peanut Products—Triggering one of the largest food contamination scares in U.S. history, the U.S. Food and Drug Administration and the Centers for Disease Control and Prevention issued a nationwide alert Jan. 17 linking an outbreak of salmonella that had begun in Sept. 2008 with peanut butter and peanut paste produced at a Blakely, GA, factory. The plant, owned by the Peanut Corp. of America, sold the contaminated items to institutions such as hospitals and nursing homes and to producers of cookies, snacks, and pet food. By the time the company filed for bankruptcy Feb. 13, the peanut products had been linked to at least 637 illnesses and 9 deaths.

Major Parties Choose New Leaders—Members of the Democratic National Committee Jan. 21 elected Virginia Gov. Tim Kaine to head the DNC. Kaine was Pres. Obama's choice to succeed former Vermont Gov. Howard Dean. On Jan. 30, former Maryland Lt.-Gov. Michael Steele became the first African American to win election as chairman of the Republican National Committee, replacing Mike Duncan. Steele's elevation reflected recognition that the party needed to improve outreach to minorities, who had supported Obama by overwhelming margins in Nov. 2008.

Ice Storm Blasts Kentucky, Arkansas—Ice and snow storms extending from the southern Plains to the East Coast in late Jan. were blamed for at least 55 deaths and left 1.3 mil people without electric power, some of them for more than a week. The death toll in Kentucky was at least 24. Some 700,000 people experienced power outages. Power disruptions were also widespread in northern Arkansas.

Unemployment Rises, Stock Market Falls—The U.S. economy continued to shed jobs with alarming speed, as the unemployment rate soared to 7.2% in Dec. 2008 and 7.6% in Jan. 2009. Regional and state data released Jan. 27 by the U.S. Bureau of Labor Statistics showed the unemployment rate had risen in all 50 states.

U.S. stock exchanges experienced their weakest Jan. in more than a century, as the Dow Jones Industrial Average closed Jan. 30 at 8,000.86, a one-month decline of 8.8%. The S&P 500 was down 8.6% to 825.88, and the Nasdaq Composite Index dropped 6.4% to 1,476.42.

International
3-Week War in Gaza Ends with Truce—A cease-fire Jan. 18 ended a 3-week, Israeli assault on Hamas militants in the Gaza Strip. The offensive, called Operation Cast Lead, was aimed at stopping attacks on Israeli civilians by Hamas, which had launched thousands of rockets at southern Israel since 2001. The rocket attacks, which had virtually stopped when Hamas and Israel agreed to a truce in June 2008, resumed after Israeli forces killed 6 Hamas fighters in Gaza Nov. 4. Israel began intensive aerial bombardment of Gaza Dec. 27, 2008, and launched a ground offensive Jan. 3, 2009. One of the war's most controversial attacks involved Israeli shelling Jan. 6 near a UN-run school at the Jabaliya refugee camp, which killed at least 35 people.

On Mar. 26 the Israeli military stated that 1,166 Palestinians were killed in the invasion, of whom 709 had been identified as "Hamas terror operatives." A more comprehensive analysis published Sept. 9 by the Israeli human rights organization B'Tselem concluded that Israeli forces had killed 1,387 Palestinians, of whom 773 (including 320 children) were noncombatants. Palestinians killed 5 Israeli soldiers in Gaza; 3 civilians and one member of Israel's security forces were killed by rockets in southern Israel; and 4 Israelis died from friendly fire. A report published Sept. 15 by a UN panel cited evidence that both sides in the conflict had committed war crimes.

Ukraine and Russia Resolve Gas Feud—A bitter dispute that had led to a cutoff of natural gas shipments from Russia to Ukraine and up to 20 other European countries was resolved Jan. 19, as Russian Prime Min. Vladimir Putin and Ukrainian Prime Min. Yulia Tymoshenko signed a 10-year gas supply deal. A price dispute had led Gazprom, Russia's financially troubled natural gas monopoly, to halt supplies to Ukraine Jan. 1. The dispute escalated Jan. 6 when Russia, accusing Ukraine of siphoning gas intended for other countries, slashed exports that had to pass through Ukraine. Countries throughout Europe began reporting shortages, with Bulgaria, Slovakia, and the Czech Republic among the hardest hit in the middle of a harsh winter cold spell. Russia provides Europe with about 25% of its natural gas, about 80% of which flows through pipelines in Ukraine.

UK Grapples with Worsening Recession—Signs that the British economy was continuing to weaken prompted the Bank of England to cut a key interest rate to the lowest levels in the bank's 315-year history. The rate, which had stood at 5% as recently as Sept. 2008, dropped to 1.5% by Jan. 8. (Further half-point cuts reduced the rate to 1.0% on Feb. 5 and 0.5% on Mar. 5.) On Jan. 19, Prime Min. Gordon Brown announced a $147.5 bil plan to protect banks from losses due to troubled assets in exchange for expanded credit.

Constitution Expands Rights of Indigenous Bolivians—Voters in Bolivia Jan. 25 gave approval to a new constitution expanding the rights of its indigenous people, who make up at least 55% of the population but have long held much less wealth and power than Bolivians of European or mixed ancestry. In a separate vote, a majority of Bolivians also approved limits to the size of agricultural landholdings.

The new charter, which had the backing of leftist Evo Morales, the country's first indigenous president, guarantees seats in Congress and on the Supreme Court to Bolivian Indians, protects indigenous groups' rights to their own legal and religious systems, declares natural resources to be state-owned, and diffuses limited power to regional governments. Unlike the previous constitution, the new document allows Morales to run for reelection in Dec. 2009.

General

Florida Wins College Football Championship—In a matchup of Heisman Trophy-winning quarterbacks Jan. 8, Florida's Tim Tebow outdueled Oklahoma's Sam Bradford as the Gators beat the Sooners, 24-14, to win the Bowl Championship Series title game at Dolphins Stadium in Miami Gardens, FL. (The field was renamed Land Shark Stadium in May.) Florida, which ended the season with a 13-1 record, finished first in the Associated Press Top 25 and USA Today Poll final rankings.

Pilot Lands Crippled Jet in Hudson River—All 150 passengers and 5 crew members on US Airways Flight 1549 escaped serious injury Jan. 15 when Capt. Chesley "Sully" Sullenberger III gently brought down his disabled aircraft in the middle of the Hudson River, between New York and New Jersey. The plane, an Airbus A320, lost power in both engines after it collided with a flock of Canada geese shortly following takeoff from New York City's LaGuardia Airport en route to Charlotte, NC. Sullenberger, who had more than 30 years' experience as a military and commercial pilot and aviation-safety consultant, maneuvered the jetliner past the city's skyscrapers and crowded neighborhoods before executing a smooth landing on the busy waterway. Ferries and other boats quickly converged on the scene to help evacuate the passengers and crew.

Octuplets Born in California—Doctors in Bellflower, CA, reported the birth Jan. 26 of only the second set of live octuplets in U.S. history. The babies—6 boys and 2 girls—were born to Nadya Suleman, 33, a single mother who had conceived them (and 6 previous children) through in vitro fertilization. The "Octomom" story received sensational coverage from some news organizations, especially after it became known that Suleman had been unemployed for several years and was facing financial difficulties.

Serena Williams, Rafael Nadal Win Australian Tennis Titles—Serena Williams needed just 59 minutes to dispatch the Russian-born Dinara Safina in straight sets, 6-0, 6-3, to win her fourth Australian Open women's singles title Jan. 31. The next night, Rafael Nadal of Spain captured his first Australian singles crown by defeating Switzerland's Roger Federer, 7-5, 3-6, 7-6 (3), 3-6, 6-2. To reach the 4-hour, 23-minute final, Nadal first had to vanquish fellow Spaniard Fernando Verdasco in a 5-hour, 14-minute semifinal, the longest match in Australian Open history.

February 2009

National

Obama Faces Delays in Filling Cabinet—In his first full month in office, Pres. Barack Obama stumbled in some efforts to staff his administration. To fill the commerce secretary position left open Jan. 4 when New Mexico Gov. Bill Richardson (D) withdrew from consideration, Obama Feb. 3 nominated Sen. Judd Gregg (R, NH). The bipartisan gesture backfired Feb. 12 when Gregg pulled out, citing "irresolvable conflicts" with the Obama administration on issues such as the economic stimulus package (see below). On Feb. 25, the president introduced a third choice for the commerce post, former Washington Gov. Gary Locke (D). Locke, the first Chinese American in U.S. history to serve as state governor, won Senate confirmation by voice vote Mar. 24.

More than 3 weeks after controversy over Tom Daschle's tax problems scuttled the former Senate Democratic leader's bid to head the Dept. of Health and Human Services (HHS), Obama on Feb. 28 offered the post to Kansas Gov. Kathleen Sebelius (D). Progress on the nomination was slowed by Republican objections to her support for abortion rights, along with her acknowledgment Mar. 31 that she had paid nearly $8,000 to settle tax errors. Approval Apr. 28, by a 65-31 vote, came only after Democrats said that the vacancy was impeding U.S. response to the swine flu pandemic.

In other actions, the Senate voted by unanimous consent Feb. 12 to confirm Leon Panetta as CIA director; the California Democrat was formerly budget director and chief of staff under Pres. Bill Clinton. On Feb. 24, the Senate voted 80-17 to confirm Rep. Hilda Solis (D, CA) as sec. of labor.

Congress Passes $787 Bil Stimulus Measure; Other Federal Actions—Pres. Obama on Feb. 17 signed the American Recovery and Reinvestment Act, intended to boost the nation's struggling economy by providing $212 bil in tax cuts and $575 bil in new federal spending. Congressional passage had been secured Feb. 13 by mostly party-line votes of 246-183 in the House and 60-38 in the Senate. House Republicans were united in opposing the bill; in the Senate the package received 3 GOP votes, from Olympia Snowe (ME), Susan Collins (ME), and Arlen Specter (PA). Spending provisions included $100 bil for education, $87 bil to support Medicaid payments for the poor and disabled, $61 bil for transportation and housing infrastructure, $45 bil for energy conservation and alternative-energy projects, and $43 bil to extend and increase unemployment insurance benefits and job-training. The measure raised the ceiling on the national debt from $11.3 tril to $12.1 tril.

The stimulus bill contained a provision restricting bonuses paid at financial firms receiving federal assistance under the $700 bil Troubled Asset Relief Program (TARP), enacted in Oct. 2008. Public debate over federal efforts to bail out big banks and investment companies had been inflamed by news that Merrill Lynch, which lost more than $27 bil in 2008, had nevertheless paid bonuses of $1 mil or more to 696 employees before the ailing investment giant was taken over by Bank of America on Jan. 1, 2009.

Treasury Sec. Tim Geithner on Feb. 10 outlined the Obama administration's $2 tril program to stabilize banking and ease credit markets. One part of the plan called for federal regulatory authorities to conduct "stress tests" to determine the ability of banks to withstand financial crises. Tests of 19 major banks began Feb. 25. When the tests were completed, regulators ordered 10 of the banks on May 7 to protect themselves against further losses by raising a combined $74.6 bil in new capital, with Bank of America accounting for about 45% of that figure.

A cascade of gloomy economic news continued to impact the broader economy. The U.S. unemployment rate rose to a 26-year high of 8.1%, auto sales sank, and data for Jan. showed housing starts at their lowest annual level in at least a half-century. To boost the housing market and stem a rising tide of mortgage defaults, Pres. Obama on Feb. 18 introduced a $275 bil program that provided $75 bil to help an estimated 3-4 mil homeowners avoid foreclosure, and $100 bil each to Fannie Mae and Freddie Mac so the agencies could help some 4-5 mil homeowners paying high interest rates to refinance their mortgages on more favorable terms.

Budget Deficits Grow, as Stock Market Plunge Continues—Showing the effects of stimulus spending, financial bailouts, operations in Iraq and Afghanistan, and reduced revenues because of the recession, the federal budget unveiled Feb. 26 projected fiscal-year deficits of $1.75 tril in 2009, $1.17 tril in 2010, and $912 bil in 2011. During the 2010 federal fiscal year, the Obama administration estimated government spending of $3.55 tril, 9.8% less than 2009, and expected revenues to rise 8.9% to $2.38 tril.

Despite extensive aid from the federal stimulus package, most U.S. states also battled budget shortfalls. In no state was the funding crisis more prolonged than in California, where legislators ended a 15-week deadlock with a Feb. 19 deal to close a $42 bil budget gap over a 17-month period. The accord, signed Feb. 20 by Gov. Arnold Schwarzenegger (R), relied on $13 bil in tax increases; $15 bil in spending reductions, including an $8.6 bil cut in education; up to $9 bil in federal stimulus money; and more than $5 bil in new borrowing. The deal angered many California voters, and 5 ballot measures implementing the accord were all defeated May 19, leaving the state with a $26 bil budget gap that was closed by another budget-cutting measure July 24.

Revised data released Feb. 27 by the U.S. Commerce Dept. showed that gross domestic product declined at a 6.2% annual rate during Oct.-Dec. 2008, much faster than the 3.8% initially reported and the steepest drop since 1982. The GDP report and other bleak economic news propelled the Dow Jones Industrial Average (7,062.93 at the monthly closing) and the S&P 500 (735.09) to 12-year lows. The Nasdaq Composite Index fell to 1,377.84.

International

Australian Wildfires Kill 173—The worst bushfires in Australian history claimed over 200 lives, destroyed almost 2,000 homes, and burned at least 1.1 mil acres in Victoria State. The fires reached maximum intensity Feb. 7, when more than 400 separate blazes were reported. Arsonists were blamed for starting some of the fires, which were intensified by a record heat wave and prolonged drought.

Netanyahu Forms Government After Israeli Elections—Following a campaign dominated by Israel's 3-week war against Hamas in the Gaza Strip, right-wing parties made a strong showing in Feb. 10 elections. Although the centrist Kadima party, led by Foreign Min. Tzipi Livni, won the single largest bloc (28 seats) in the 120-member Knesset, the conservative Likud (27 seats) and the ultranationalist Yisrael Beitenu (15 seats) formed the core of a governing coalition. Likud leader Benjamin Netanyahu, who had served as prime min. 1996-99, was sworn in for a second term Mar. 31, heading a cabinet that included Yisrael Beitenu leader Avigdor Lieberman as foreign min. Former Labor Prime Min. Ehud Barak was named defense min., retaining the post from which, as a member of the previous Kadima government, he had overseen the Gaza war.

Tsvangirai Joins Power-Sharing Government in Zimbabwe—With longtime Pres. Robert Mugabe administering the oath of office, opposition leader Morgan Tsvangirai was sworn in as prime min. Feb. 11, apparently resolving a political crisis that followed a contentious Mar. 2008 election. Under Mugabe's authoritarian rule, Zimbabwe's unemployment rate had soared above 90%, and inflation had reached astronomical proportions. Tsvangirai was injured and his wife Susan was killed Mar. 6 in a car crash the prime min. characterized 2 days later as "an accident," dismissing the chance of foul play as "one in a thousand."

Presidential Term Limits Abolished in Venezuela—In a referendum Feb. 15, Venezuelan voters approved, by a margin of 54% to 46%, a proposal to eliminate a constitutional provision that had restricted the president to two 6-year terms. The vote, which had been sought by Pres. Hugo Chávez, would allow the Venezuelan leader to run for re-election in 2012. Venezuelan voters narrowly rejected a similar proposal in Dec. 2007.

Truce Leaves Pakistani Taliban in Control of Strategic Swat Valley—Taliban insurgents in the Swat Valley announced Feb. 24 that they had accepted a cease-fire offered by the Pakistani military 8 days earlier. The truce allowed the militants to impose Islamic law in the region (located near the border of Afghanistan, about 100 mi from Pakistan's capital, Islamabad) where an estimated 3,000 insurgents had battled some 12,000 government troops. In an interview with CBS News made public Feb. 13, Pakistani Pres. Asif Ali Zardari said the Taliban had "a presence in huge amounts of land on our side."

Outside the Swat Valley, Pakistani and U.S. forces continued to battle the militants. On Feb. 6, Pakistani helicopter gunships reportedly killed 52 fighters in clashes near the Khyber region, where militants had sought to disrupt a supply line for U.S. and NATO troops in Afghanistan. U.S. air strikes targeting Taliban and al-Qaeda activity near the Afghan border Feb. 14-16 left more than 60 people dead.

U.S. Troop Withdrawals Planned for Iraq, Buildup in Afghanistan—In a Feb. 27 speech to Marines at Camp Lejeune, NC, Pres. Obama laid out a timetable for American troop withdrawals from Iraq. Most of the 142,000 U.S. troops would be pulled out by Aug. 2010, when the U.S. combat mission would end; a residual force of 35,000 to 50,000 troops would remain in Iraq until 2011. Announcement of the pullout schedule was made possible by continued improvements in Iraqi security. Elections to provincial councils Jan. 31 had proceeded with relatively little violence, and preliminary results announced Feb. 5 showed broad support for a strong central government under Prime Min. Nouri al-Maliki. Eighteen U.S. troops died in the Iraq war in Feb.

Signs were much less hopeful in Afghanistan, where civilian deaths increased nearly 40%, from 1,523 in 2007 to 2,118 in 2008, according to a UN survey released Feb. 17. That day, Pres. Obama announced that the U.S. would send 17,000 more troops—8,000 Marines and 9,000 Army personnel—to Afghanistan during the spring and summer of 2009. On Feb. 18, Gen. David McKiernan, senior U.S. commander in Afghanistan, said that even with the additional forces, "2009 is going to be a tough year." Coalition fatalities in Afghanistan totaled 25 in Jan. and 24 in Feb., more than double the total of the corresponding months in 2008.

General

Steelers Take Super Bowl—A 6-yard touchdown pass from Pittsburgh quarterback Ben Roethlisberger to wide receiver Santonio Holmes with 35 seconds remaining on the clock lifted the Steelers to a come-from-behind 27-23 victory over the Arizona Cardinals in Super Bowl XLIII, played Feb. 1 at Raymond James Stadium in Tampa, FL. Holmes caught 9 passes for 131 yds and was voted MVP. The Steelers won their second Super Bowl in 4 seasons and their sixth overall, the most of any NFL franchise.

Coach Pat Summitt Passes 1,000-Win Mark—Pat Summitt, the winningest coach in NCAA college basketball history, notched her 1,000th career victory Feb. 5, as the Univ. of Tennessee Lady Vols romped over Georgia's Lady Bulldogs, 73-43, at Thompson-Boling Arena, Knoxville, TN. Summitt, who became the Lady Vols' head coach in 1974, raised her NCAA career won-lost mark by the end of the 2008-09 season to 1,005-193, with 8 national championships.

Alex Rodriguez Admits Past Steroid Use; Other Baseball Violations—On Feb. 7, *Sports Illustrated* magazine reported on its website that Alex Rodriguez, Major League Baseball's highest-paid player, had tested positive in 2003 for elevated levels of testosterone and an anabolic steroid known as Primobolan. In interviews 2 days later, Rodriguez acknowledged having used performance-enhancing drugs while he played for the Texas Rangers in 2001-03 but claimed he had stopped using them by the time he joined the New York Yankees in 2004.

Houston Astros shortstop Miguel Tejada pleaded guilty Feb. 11 to having misled Congress in 2005 when he denied using performance-enhancing drugs or knowing anything about his teammates' use of them. He was sentenced Mar. 26 to one year of probation, fined $5,000, and ordered to perform 100 hours of community service. On May 7, MLB Commissioner Bud Selig issued a 50-game suspension to Los Angeles Dodgers outfielder Manny Ramirez for using human chorionic gonadotrophin, or HCG, a banned substance that stimulates testosterone production.

Grammy Awards Honor Alison Krauss and Robert Plant—*Raising Sand*, a collaboration between bluegrass star Alison Krauss, former Led Zeppelin lead singer Robert Plant, and producer-guitarist T Bone Burnett, won the Grammy Award for Album of the Year Feb. 8 at ceremonies broadcast from the Staples Center in Los Angeles. Krauss and Plant also won 4 other Grammy Awards, including Record of the Year ("Please Read the Letter"). Other big winners included Lil Wayne, whose *Tha Carter III* topped the rap album category; the rock-pop band Coldplay, which won for Song of the Year ("Viva la Vida"); and British singer-songwriter Adele, selected as best new artist.

Slumdog Millionaire Wins Best Picture Oscar—*Slumdog Millionaire* took home 8 Academy Awards Feb. 22, including Best Picture and Best Director (Danny Boyle). The rags-to-riches story, set in Mumbai, India, also earned Best Original Score and Best Song ("Jai Ho") honors for veteran Bollywood composer A. R. Rahman. Top acting awards went to Kate Winslet, for her leading role in *The Reader*, and to Sean Penn, for his portrayal of a gay rights activist in *Milk*. A posthumous Oscar was awarded to Heath Ledger for his supporting role as the Joker in the Batman blockbuster *The Dark Knight*.

March 2009

National

Supreme Court Rules on Drug Lawsuits, Indefinite Detention—In a 6-3 decision, the Supreme Court held Mar. 4 in *Wyeth v. Levine* that a federally approved warning label from the Food and Drug Administration (FDA) did not necessarily shield pharmaceutical manufacturers from state court lawsuits by individuals harmed by their products. The justices upheld a $6.7 mil verdict by a Vermont state jury in favor of Diana Levine, a musician whose arm had to be amputated after she was improperly injected with the anti-nausea drug Phenergan. Levine had sued Wyeth, the manufacturer of Phenergan, successfully contending that its warning label, although approved by the FDA, failed to satisfy state requirements on product liability.

Another important ruling involved Ali Saleh Kahlah al-Marri, a Qatari citizen who was legally studying in the U.S. when he was detained in 2001 as a terrorist suspect. On Mar. 6 the Supreme Court vacated an appellate court ruling that had affirmed the right of the U.S. president to order the indefinite detention of a lawful U.S. resident who was classified as an enemy combatant. Al-Marri, who was held for 6 years in a U.S. Navy brig near Charleston, SC, had challenged his military detention, but the Supreme Court declined to hear that case after the Obama administration filed criminal charges against al-Marri in federal court in Peoria, IL. He pleaded guilty Apr. 30 to a charge of knowingly aiding al-Qaeda operatives, including Khalid Sheikh Mohammed, the alleged mastermind of the terrorist attacks of Sept. 11, 2001.

Congress Passes $410 Bil Spending Measure, Protects Public Lands—The Senate approved by voice vote Mar. 10 a $410 bil omnibus spending measure to fund the federal government though Sept. 30, the end of the 2009 fiscal year. Final passage was made possible after the Senate voted 62-35 to cut off debate on the bill; the House had passed it Feb. 25 by a vote of 245-178. According to Taxpayers for Common Sense, a nonpartisan budget watchdog group, the legislation contained more than 8,800 separate spending items, or earmarks, providing $7.6 bil for projects in lawmakers' home states and districts. Conceding that the bill was "imperfect," Pres. Barack Obama signed it Mar. 11, while pledging to crack down on earmarks in future measures.

Pres. Obama on Mar. 30 signed the Omnibus Public Land Management Act. The ambitious measure, which protected 2 mil acres of wilderness and established 9 new National Heritage Areas, had passed the Senate Mar. 19, by a vote of 77-20, and the House Mar. 25, by a 285-140 margin.

Mass Shootings in Alabama, Other States—Gun violence claimed dozens of lives in several unrelated incidents throughout Mar. and Apr. On Mar. 10, in rural southern Alabama, a gunman identified as Michael McLendon murdered 10 people, including his mother and 4 other relatives, before killing himself. On Mar. 21, in Oakland, CA, Lovelle Mixon, who had a long criminal record and was wanted for parole violations, shot and killed 4 police officers before he was killed in a shootout in the deadliest sin-.5 gle day for U.S. law enforcement since the 2001 terrorist attacks. Eight days later, a shooting rampage at a Carthage, NC, nursing home left 8 people dead. That same day an apparent family-related murder-suicide claimed 6 in Santa Clara, CA. On Apr. 3, a Vietnamese immigrant shot and killed 13 people at an immigrant education center in Binghamton, NY, before killing himself. A day later, a gunman killed 3 police officers responding to a domestic disturbance call in Pittsburgh, PA, before he surrendered. Also on Apr. 4, a father in Graham, WA, shot 5 of his children, ages 7 to 16, before killing himself.

Army Will End Stop-Loss Policy—Defense Sec. Robert Gates announced Mar. 18 that the Army would phase out its unpopular stop-loss policy, which had compelled thousands of soldiers whose service obligations were expiring to remain in the military if their units were about to deploy to Afghanistan or Iraq. Army officials disclosed that about 120,000 soldiers had been affected by the policy since 2001, and that more than 13,000 were still being kept in the military against their will. Gates said that, barring a national emergency, the number of troops affected by stop-loss would be cut in half by June 2010, and the practice would be virtually ended by Mar. 2011.

Obama Administration Addresses Auto, Finance Industries—Speaking at the White House Mar. 30, Pres. Obama issued an ultimatum to 2 ailing U.S. automobile manufacturers, warning that both Chrysler and General Motors faced a cutoff of taxpayer funds if they failed to come up with viable restructuring plans. Chrysler was given 30 days to merge with Italian automaker Fiat or another suitable partner, and GM was given 60 days to make leadership changes and revamp its business plan. Rick Wagoner, who had led GM for 9 years, was asked to step down Mar. 27 by Obama's automobile task force, then headed by "car czar" Steven Rattner. Data disclosed in early Mar. indicated that GM sales in Feb. 2009 had been 53% below those of a year earlier, while Chrysler sales had dropped 44%, Ford 48%, Toyota 40%, and Honda 38%. On Mar. 19 the Treasury Dept. announced a $5 bil program to aid struggling auto parts manufacturers, whose fortunes had declined along with those of the big car companies.

American International Group (AIG), the insurance giant whose catastrophic failure in Sept. 2008 helped push the global financial system to the brink of collapse, reported Mar. 2 that it had lost $61.7 bil during Oct.-Dec. 2008, the largest quarterly loss ever for a U.S. firm. That day, the federal government, which had already provided AIG with more than $150 bil in exchange for a nearly 80% stake in the company, agreed to extend another $30 bil in financing to keep the firm afloat. Public anger at the continuing bailout was stoked by revelations that AIG (with the advance knowledge of federal officials) had paid retention bonuses of $165 mil to employees of the firm's financial products unit, whose reckless investment strategy was primarily responsible for the AIG failure. New York Atty. Gen. Andrew Cuomo announced Mar. 23 that employees had been persuaded to give back at least $50 mil in bonuses.

On Mar. 23, Treasury Sec. Tim Geithner formally introduced the Public-Private Investment Program (PPIP), the latest federal effort to deal with troubled, or "toxic," assets that had clogged financial institutions' balance sheets. The PPIP offered subsidies and other incentives to encourage private investors to purchase up to $1 tril in problem loans and securities. Stock markets reacted favorably to the announcement, with the Dow experiencing a one-day rise of 497.48 points. In Mar. 26 testimony before the House Financial Services Committee, Geithner urged Congress to enact comprehensive reform of financial markets, including new mechanisms to limit systemic risk; protect consumers; and regulate activities by hedge funds, venture capital companies, and private equity firms. At the close of trading Mar. 31, the Dow finished the month up 7.7% at 7,608.92, and the S&P 500 rose 8.5% to close at 797.87. After hitting a 6 1/2-year low Mar. 9, the Nasdaq Composite Index rebounded to close at 1,528.59, for a one-month gain of 11%.

International

Defense Chief and President Murdered in Guinea-Bissau—Longstanding rivalries among civilian and military leaders in the small West African nation of Guinea-Bissau culminated in the assassinations of Gen. Batista Tagme Na Waie and Pres. João Bernardo Vieira. Tagme, the army chief of staff, was killed Mar. 1 by a bomb blast at general staff headquarters in Bissau; in the early morning hours of Mar. 2, soldiers loyal to Tagme murdered Vieira at the presidential palace. Poverty, violence, and political instability have plagued Guinea-Bissau, which has become a transit point for international drug trafficking; 2 other army chiefs had been assassinated in 2000 and 2004.

National People's Assembly Speaker Raimundo Pereira was sworn in as interim president Mar. 3. Following an election campaign that was also marred by violence, Malam Bacai Sanhá, a former interim president and National People's Assembly leader who had lost to Vieira in 2005, was the top finisher in the June 28 presidential vote and won a runoff election July 26.

Mexico Drug Violence Escalates—Mexican government officials announced Mar. 2 that 1,000 more federal police personnel would be sent to Ciudad Juárez, in addition to a military buildup expected to raise the troop presence there to 7,000. Warring drug cartels were blamed for violence that had killed more than 2,000 people in Ciudad Juárez during the previous 12 months and over 10,000 people throughout Mexico since Dec. 2006. On Mar. 23 the government offered rewards of up to $2 mil apiece for information leading to the capture of 24 drug kingpins, and $1 mil each for 13 of their leading lieutenants.

The upsurge in violence in Ciudad Juárez and other border cities caught the attention of officials in the U.S., both the prime market for illegal drugs from Mexico and the main source of weapons used by drug gangs. On Mar. 24, U.S. Homeland Security Sec. Janet Napolitano said that 360 federal agents would be dispatched to the border with Mexico to beef up U.S. immigration, drug, and firearms control efforts. Sec. of State Hillary Clinton, Atty. Gen. Eric Holder, and Napolitano all visited Mexico during the next 10 days to discuss drug-related violence and other issues. At a press conference in Mexico City Apr. 16 with U.S. Pres. Obama, Mexican Pres. Felipe Calderón linked the rising power of organized crime in Mexico to the expiration of a U.S. ban on assault weapons in 2004. Obama pledged to curb illegal arms trafficking to Mexico, but acknowledged the political difficulty in persuading the U.S. Congress to renew the assault weapons ban.

International Arrest Warrant Issued for Pres. Bashir of Sudan—The International Criminal Court in The Hague, Netherlands, issued a warrant Mar. 4 calling for the arrest of Pres. Omar Hassan Ahmad al-Bashir of Sudan. The warrant, the first issued by the ICC against a sitting head of state, accused Bashir of responsibility for war crimes and other crimes against humanity in the Darfur region of western Sudan, where about 300,000 people, many of them civilians, had been killed in a 6-year-long conflict. Openly defying the court order, Bashir traveled during the month to Eritrea, Egypt, Libya, Saudi Arabia, and an Arab League summit conference in Qatar. Both the African Union and the Arab League refused to cooperate with ICC requests to extradite Bashir.

France Rejoins NATO Command—French Pres. Nicolas Sarkozy announced Mar. 11 that France would rejoin the military command structure of the North Atlantic Treaty Organization. France, a founding member of NATO in 1949, had withdrawn from its military command in 1966, during Charles de Gaulle's presidency, but had remained part of the alliance for the next 43 years. After Sarkozy's proposal won approval from the French National Assembly Mar. 17, France submitted its formal request to NATO Mar. 21. Sarkozy co-hosted NATO's 60th anniversary summit meeting in Strasbourg Apr. 3-4, during which France resumed full participation in the organization. Two French generals were appointed to high NATO command posts in July.

Recession Takes Toll on Trade; Eastern Europe Hit Hard—The World Trade Organization Mar. 23 forecast a drop in international trade of at least 9% in 2009. Data compiled by Global Trade Information Services estimated export declines in Jan. of 34% in Canada, 26% in China, and 21% in the U.S. Conditions were even worse in Japan, where exports in Feb. were valued at about half those of a year earlier. In late Feb., the European Bank for Reconstruction and Development warned that the global economic crisis threatened to reverse nearly 2 decades of economic reform in Eastern and Central Europe. Financial turmoil brought down Latvia's governing coalition Feb. 20 and toppled governments in Hungary and the Czech Republic Mar. 23-24.

U.S. Rethinks Strategy in Afghanistan and Pakistan as Casualties in Iraq Drop to New Low—Pres. Obama announced Mar. 27 a retooled U.S. strategy "to disrupt, dismantle, and defeat al-Qaeda in Pakistan and Afghanistan." The plan called for sending billions of dollars in aid to Pakistan and deploying 4,000 U.S. troops (in addition to the increase of 17,000 troops announced Feb. 17) to train and advise the Afghan army. The *New York Times* reported Mar. 19 that the Obama administration hoped to increase the size of the Afghan army and national police force to 400,000, more than double the current strength.

The U.S. strategic review came as Pakistan endured a fresh wave of terrorist attacks. In Lahore, Mar. 3, about a dozen gunmen attacked a bus carrying Sri Lanka's national cricket team—6 slain Pakistani police and 7 wounded Sri Lankan cricketers were among the victims. A suicide bombing Mar. 27 at a crowded mosque in Jamrud, in the Khyber region of northwestern Pakistan, claimed at least 50 lives, and an insurgent assault Mar. 30 at a police academy near Lahore killed at least 8 recruits and instructors and left more than 100 people injured.

NATO announced Mar. 23 that Maulawi Hassan, a senior Taliban commander in southern Afghanistan, had been killed 2 days earlier along with 9 other insurgents. Coalition casualties in Afghanistan during the month numbered 28. In Iraq, where 137,000 U.S. troops were still deployed, 9 U.S. military fatalities were recorded, the lowest monthly total since the war began.

General

Japan Wins World Baseball Classic—With a 2-out, 2-run single in the 10th inning, Seattle Mariners outfielder Ichiro Suzuki led the Japanese national team to a 5-3 victory over South Korea in the World Baseball Classic championship game, played Mar. 23 at Dodger Stadium in Los Angeles. Teams representing 15 countries plus Puerto Rico competed in the 19-day tournament. Japan had also won the championship in the inaugural World Baseball Classic in 2006, and Red Sox pitcher Daisuke Matsuzaka (who was 3-0 with a 2.45 earned run average for Japan) repeated as tournament MVP.

***Discovery* Mission Raises Space Station to Full Power**—Commanded by U.S. Air Force Col. Lee Archambault, space shuttle *Discovery* landed safely Mar. 28 at Kennedy Space Center in Florida, concluding a 13-day mission to the International Space Station (ISS). The 7-member crew successfully brought the ISS to full power by installing a 31,000-lb truss containing the station's fourth set of solar wings. The shuttle also delivered Japan Aerospace Exploration Agency astronaut Koichi Wakata to the space station and ferried home U.S. astronaut Sandra H. Magnus, who had been on the ISS for 129 days.

April 2009

National

Same-Sex Marriage Advances in Iowa and New England—Iowa's Supreme Court unanimously ruled Apr. 3 that a state law restricting marriage to one man and one woman violated the state constitution; marriage licenses were issued to same-sex couples in Iowa beginning Apr. 27. In Vermont—the first state to legalize same-sex civil unions in 2000—gay marriage became a reality after legislators Apr. 7 overrode a veto by Gov. Jim Douglas (R) of a measure providing full marriage rights for homosexuals. The new law took effect Sept. 1. Lawmakers in Maine passed and Gov. John Baldacci (D) signed a same-sex marriage bill May 6, but implementation was suspended when opponents collected enough signatures to put the measure on the Nov. 3 ballot. New Hampshire legislators also passed a same-sex marriage bill May 6, but Gov. John Lynch (D) insisted on revisions to make clear that clergy and religiously affiliated institutions could not be compelled to perform homosexual weddings. He signed the revised measure into law June 3, with an effective date of Jan. 1, 2010.

Newly Released Documents Spark Controversy Over Detainee Treatment—The *New York Review of Books* posted on its website Apr. 6 a confidential report prepared in Feb. 2007 by the International Committee of the Red Cross (ICRC), which concluded that the CIA had violated international law in its handling of 14 "high-value detainees." The report, which covered the period before the prisoners were transferred Sept. 2006 to the military facility at Guantánamo, stated that CIA interrogators had subjected the suspects to multiple forms of mistreatment that, "either singly or in combination, constituted torture." The Justice Dept. Apr. 16 made public 4 memos its Office of Legal Counsel prepared in 2002 and 2005 (and has since rescinded) that provided a detailed description of, and legal rationale for, the methods the CIA had employed, including beatings, prolonged sleep deprivation, and waterboarding, which simulates drowning. One memo noted that the CIA had waterboarded a suspected al-Qaeda operative, Abu Zubaydah, at least 83 times in Aug. 2002, and had employed waterboarding 183 times in Mar. 2003 against Khalid Sheikh Mohammed, the alleged mastermind of the Sept. 11, 2001, terrorist attacks. Waterboarding was described as torture by Atty. Gen. Eric Holder during his Senate confirmation hearings and barred, along with other harsh interrogation practices, shortly after Pres. Barack Obama took office.

Release of the documents touched off a series of controversies. On May 14, House Speaker Nancy Pelosi (D) said she had been misled about CIA interrogation methods at a briefing in Sept. 2002. CIA Director Leon Panetta, a former House colleague of Pelosi's, responded May 15 that a review of documents from that period showed that Pelosi had been "briefed truthfully" by CIA officers. Claiming that the Bush administration's detention and interrogation techniques had helped to prevent further terrorist attacks, former vice pres. Dick Cheney, on May 21, called them "legal, essential, justified, successful, and the right thing to do."

The Justice Dept. released hundreds of pages of additional CIA documents Aug. 24, the same day Holder appointed a special prosecutor, John Durham, to investigate whether CIA officials or contractors broke the law in their treatment of terrorist suspects. Durham, a federal prosecutor from Connecticut, had been chosen by the Bush administration in 2008 to investigate the CIA's destruction of 92 videotapes on which detainee interrogations had been recorded.

Defense Budget Shows Revised Pentagon Priorities; War Funding Requested—The military budget outlined by Defense Sec. Robert Gates Apr. 6 called for spending $534 bil in fiscal year 2010, a $20 bil increase over 2009. The budget increased funding for some relatively low-tech weapons systems needed for irregular warfare and counterinsurgency operations, while cutting expenditures on certain high-tech systems that already accounted for billions of dollars in cost overruns. Targeted for cutbacks were the Air Force's F-22 fighter jet, the Navy's DDG 1000 destroyer, and the lightly armored vehicles that form part of the Army's Future Combat Systems program.

On Apr. 9 the Obama administration submitted to Congress a supplemental spending request of $83.4 bil for the balance of the 2009 fiscal year; of that total, $75.8 bil would fund the Iraq and Afghanistan wars through Sept. 30. The administration expected to spend another $130 bil on the 2 wars during the 2010 fiscal year.

"Tea Parties" Protest Obama Policies—On Apr. 15, the federal income tax filing deadline, demonstrators gathered in hundreds of U.S. cities and towns to protest Obama administration spending programs and other federal policies. In addition to patriotic symbols and anti-tax, anti-government, and anti-Obama placards, some demonstrators displayed tea bags to link their protest with the 1773 Boston Tea Party against British colonial rule. The "tea parties" had been promoted by some conservative Republicans, including former House Majority Leader Dick Armey (R, TX), and by Fox News. The combined number of protesters throughout the U.S. was estimated in the hundreds of thousands.

EPA Clears Way for Regulation of Greenhouse Gases—For the first time, the U.S. EPA declared Apr. 17 that carbon dioxide, methane, and 4 other greenhouse gases (so-called because of their heat-trapping properties) "contribute to air pollution that may endanger public health or welfare." The finding, which the EPA said was based on "rigorous, peer-reviewed scientific analysis," cleared the way for the agency to use the Clean Air Act to regulate emissions of gases that contribute to global warming and other changes in the Earth's climate.

Congress Approves National Service, Budget Measures; Specter Switches Parties—Pres. Obama signed Apr. 21 the Sen. Edward M. Kennedy Serve America Act. The measure would increase the number of AmeriCorps community service volunteers from 75,000 to 250,000 by 2017. On Mar. 23, the Congressional Budget Office estimated it would cost $5.7 bil between 2010 and 2014. The bill passed

the Senate Mar. 26 by a margin of 79-19, and cleared the House Mar. 31 by a 275-149 vote.

On Apr. 29, the House (233-193) and Senate (53-43) approved the Obama administration's 2010 budget of more than $3.5 tril. No Republicans in either chamber supported the budget blueprint.

Sen. Arlen Specter (PA) announced Apr. 29 that he would leave the Republican party and join the Democratic fold. The move by Specter, who was first elected to the Senate in 1980, would potentially give the Democrats a 60th vote and with it, a so-called "supermajority" that would allow them to overcome any filibusters. Before switching parties, Specter had faced a stiff primary challenge from Pat Toomey, a conservative Republican whom he narrowly defeated in a 2004 party primary. In welcoming Specter, Pres. Barack Obama and Vice Pres. Joe Biden pledged to support him against any Democratic primary opponent.

Chrysler Files for Bankruptcy; Other Economic Developments—Kept afloat by government loans after losing $16.8 bil in 2008, U.S. automaker Chrysler LLC filed for bankruptcy protection Apr. 30. The filing was a key element in a restructuring plan, shaped by the Obama administration, under which the United Automobile Workers retirement health-care fund would gain a 55% stake in the reorganized company. Italian car manufacturer Fiat (which would share its technology with Chrysler) would hold a 35% stake, the U.S. government 8%, and Canada 2%. The U.S., which had already loaned $4 bil to Chrysler, agreed to provide another $8 bil, with Canada supplying additional financing. Chrysler operations would continue during the accelerated bankruptcy proceedings, which were required after some bondholders refused an out-of-court settlement. Announcing the plan at the White House, Pres. Obama said it would save more than 35,000 jobs.

According to U.S. government data, economic output fell 6.1% during the first 3 months of 2009, and unemployment rose in Apr. to 8.9%. Hopeful that the recession had hit bottom, investors fueled a global stock rally, with the Dow Jones Industrial Average closing Apr. 30 at 8,168.12, up 7.4% for the month. The S&P 500 (872.81) had its best month in 9 years, rising 9.4%, and the Nasdaq Composite Index (1,717.30) soared 12.4%.

International

Obama Visits Europe, Iraq, Latin America, and Caribbean; Participates in G-20, NATO, and Americas Summit Meetings—Barack Obama made his presidential debut on the world stage with an 8-day European trip, Mar. 31-Apr. 7. He began his journey in London, participating Apr. 1-2 in a summit meeting of the Group of 20 (G-20), which includes many of the world's major developed nations and emerging economies. To promote international financial stability and global trade, the G-20 leaders agreed to increase by $1.1 tril the financial resources available for lending by the International Monetary Fund. On Apr. 1, Obama also held his first face-to-face meetings with Russian Pres. Dmitri Medvedev and Chinese Pres. Hu Jintao. Discussions with Medvedev focused in part on nuclear disarmament, a goal Obama spelled out in a speech Apr. 5 in Prague, during a visit to the Czech Republic for a U.S.-European Union summit.

Honoring the 60th anniversary of the North Atlantic Treaty Organization, Obama and other NATO leaders met Apr. 3-4 in Strasbourg, France. America's NATO partners, who had already sent about 30,000 troops to Afghanistan, pledged to provide up to 5,000 more personnel, of whom 3,000 would be temporarily deployed to provide security for Aug. 2009 elections. NATO and U.S. casualties in Afghanistan in Apr. decreased to 14.

Obama visited Turkey Apr. 6-7, his first journey as president to a predominantly Muslim nation. He told the Turkish Parliament "the United States is not and will not ever be at war with Islam." From Turkey, Apr. 7, he made his first trip as commander in chief to Iraq, greeting U.S. troops in the Baghdad area and conferring with Iraqi Prime Min. Nouri al-Maliki. His Iraq stopover, followed Apr. 25 by Hillary Clinton's first visit as sec. of state, coincided with a rise in insurgent violence, much of it targeting Shiite sites. Major attacks included a truck bombing near police headquarters in Mosul Apr. 10 that killed 5 U.S. troops and 2 Iraqi police officers; a series of bombings Apr. 23-24 that killed at least 140 people in Baghdad and Diyala Province; and 6 bombings Apr. 29 that left at least 48 people dead in the Iraqi capital. U.S. combat deaths in Iraq totaled 19 in Apr., more than double the previous month's fatalities.

The president's first foray into Latin America began with a visit Apr. 16-17 to Mexico, where he discussed the illegal arms trafficking and cross-border drug-related violence with Pres. Felipe Calderón. Obama then traveled to Trinidad and Tobago, where he joined 33 other democratically elected leaders for the Summit of the Americas, held Apr. 17-19 in the capital, Port of Spain. Cuba, not represented at the conference, was a principal subject of discussion. On Apr. 13 the Obama administration had eased restrictions on family travel and on the sending of remittances to Cuba, steps that Cuba's former Pres. Fidel Castro described as "positive although minimal." At the Americas summit, Obama called for a "new beginning with Cuba."

Earthquake Strikes Italy's Abruzzo Region—A powerful earthquake Apr. 6, followed by more than 400 aftershocks, devastated the town of L'Aquila, capital of central Italy's Abruzzo region. The 6.3 magnitude quake claimed at least 295 lives, left at least 55,000 people homeless, and damaged historic buildings throughout the region. Italy's interior minister, Roberto Maroni, estimated Apr. 14 that reconstruction work would cost at least $16 bil.

North Korea Resumes Missile Testing, Nuclear Program—The Supreme People's Assembly Apr. 9 reelected North Korean leader Kim Jong Il to head the National Defense Commission, as his regime took an increasingly belligerent stance toward the world community. Responding to UN Security Council condemnation of North Korea's Apr. 5 rocket launch over the Pacific, the Pyongyang government said Apr. 14 that it would restart its Yongbyon nuclear facility and boycott multinational talks aimed at halting the nation's nuclear weapons program. On May 25, North Korea carried out an underground nuclear test and test-fired several short-range missiles, drawing an immediate rebuke from the Security Council. Hours later, Pyongyang test-fired 2 more short-range missiles. On May 27, North Korea announced that the truce that ended the Korean War was invalid and threatened to attack U.S. and South Korean warships off its coast.

Thai Protesters Force Cancellation of Asian Summit—An Asian summit meeting planned for the resort town of Pattaya, Thailand, was canceled Apr. 11 after the conference site was disrupted by supporters of former Prime Min. Thaksin Shinawatra, a wealthy former telecommunications executive who had been accused of corruption and ousted in a 2006 military coup. Mass demonstrations by Thaksin backers in Bangkok led to the proclamation of a state of emergency, Apr. 12-24, and to violent clashes between protesters and the Thai military.

Navy SEALs Rescue U.S. Captain, but Problem of Piracy Persists—A hostage drama that began Apr. 8, when Somali pirates unsuccessfully tried to hijack the merchant ship *Maersk Alabama*, ended 4 days later when U.S. Navy SEALs rescued Richard Phillips, the ship's American captain. Phillips, who had allowed himself to be taken hostage in exchange for the safety of his U.S. crew, was being held in an 18-ft lifeboat off the coast of Somalia when snipers on the USS *Bainbridge* shot and killed 3 of his captors. Pres. Obama had authorized the Navy sharpshooters to take action if they believed Phillips's life was in danger.

Somalia's lack of law and order, extreme poverty, and the willingness of shipping companies with lucrative cargoes to pay multimillion-dollar ransoms had all contributed to the rapid growth of piracy in the region. According to the International Maritime Bureau, piracy attacks rose worldwide from 114 during the first half of 2008 to 240 during Jan.-June 2009, with attacks in the Gulf of Aden and off the east coast of Somalia accounting for most of the increase.

World Health Authorities Warn of Swine Flu Pandemic—A growing outbreak of swine flu, first in Mexico and then in the U.S., triggered worldwide alerts by public health authorities. Swine flu—officially designated influenza A (H1N1)—was considered potentially very dangerous because it was caused by a new viral strain against which the population had little to no immunity. U.S. officials declared a public health emergency Apr. 26. The World Health Organization (WHO) raised the pandemic threat level to 4 (on a scale of 1 to 6) on Apr. 27 and then to 5 on Apr. 29. The following day, WHO reported 257 confirmed cases of swine flu in 11 countries. In Mexico, where the number of suspected cases had reached 1,500, schools and museums around Mexico City were closed, and Pres. Calderón called Apr. 30 for all nonessential businesses to shut down May 1-5.

In Egypt, where no cases of H1N1 had yet been reported, the government took the extreme step Apr. 29 of ordering pig herds slaughtered. WHO experts said the order had no scientific basis, and the UN called the cull "a real mistake." Egypt's minority Coptic Christians, who collect much of Cairo's trash and raise most of the hogs in the majority Muslim country, rioted in protest.

General

North Carolina Takes Men's College Basketball Title; UConn Wins Women's Crown—The Univ. of North Carolina crushed Michigan State, 89-72, in the NCAA men's basketball championship game Apr. 6 at Ford Field in Detroit, MI. The Tar Heels exploited 14 first-half turnovers by the underdog Spartans, jumping out to a 55-34 halftime lead en route to their fourth NCAA national men's basketball title. In women's basketball Apr. 7, the top-ranked Univ. of Connecticut (UConn) capped a 39-0 season by beating Louisville, 76-54, at the Scottrade Center in St. Louis, MO.

Cabrera Captures Masters—Angel Cabrera became the first South American golfer to win the Masters when he survived a 3-man sudden-death playoff Apr. 12 at Augusta (GA) National Golf Club. Two par 4s allowed the Argentine Cabrera to outlast Kenny Perry and Chad Campbell after the 3 men tied at 72 holes with a 12-under-par 276.

May 2009

National

Sotomayor Named to Replace Souter on Supreme Court—In a letter dated May 1 to Pres. Barack Obama, Associate Justice David Souter formally declared his intention to leave the Supreme Court when the 2008-09 term ended in late June. Souter, 69, had served on the Court since 1990, when he was nominated by Pres. George H. W. Bush. Initially regarded as a conservative, Souter increasingly aligned himself with the Court's liberal bloc, supporting abortion rights (see below), gay rights, affirmative action, and limitations on the death penalty and presidential power. Rumors about his intentions had circulated for weeks, because he had hired no law clerks for the fall 2009 term.

Souter's resignation offered Obama the opportunity to select his first Supreme Court justice, and on May 26 he nominated Sonia Sotomayor. Born June 25, 1954, in the Bronx, NY, she was an honors graduate of Princeton Univ. and Yale Law School, with a long record of service as a prosecuting attorney (1979-84), commercial litigator (1984-92), federal trial court judge (1992-98), and appellate court judge (1998-2009). Sotomayor, both of whose parents were Puerto Rican, was the first woman of Hispanic ancestry to be nominated for a Supreme Court judgeship.

Abortion Controversy Rekindled—The replacement of a Supreme Court justice, a new Gallup Poll, a presidential speech, and the murder of a well-known abortion provider all contributed to the resurgence of a controversy that has flourished since the Supreme Court's *Roe v. Wade* decision (1973) legalized abortion in the U.S. On May 15, Gallup released a survey showing that, for the first time since the pollster began asking the question in 1995, a majority of Americans described themselves as "pro-life" (51%) rather than "pro-choice" (42%). The pro-life position drew support from a preponderance of women (49%-44%) as well as men (54%-39%).

Pres. Obama addressed the abortion issue directly in a commencement address May 17 at the Univ. of Notre Dame in South Bend, IN. Calling for civility and compromise, he urged both sides of the abortion debate to work together to make adoption more available, improve care and support for mothers and babies, and reduce the number of unintended pregnancies along with abortions. Notre Dame, a Catholic university, had been criticized by some Catholic bishops, and Obama's campus visit drew hundreds of protesters. Pope Benedict XVI raised the issues of abortion and embryonic stem cell research, also supported by Obama, when the pontiff and president met at the Vatican July 10. Meanwhile, pro-choice groups sought reassurance from the White House that Obama's Supreme Court selection, Sonia Sotomayor, reflected pro-choice views on abortion rights.

On May 31, George Tiller, a 67-year-old abortion doctor in Wichita, KS, was shot and killed at Reformation Lutheran Church, where he was serving as an usher. Scott Roeder, a fervent opponent of abortion, was arrested and charged with first-degree murder. Tiller's clinic was one of the few medical facilities in the U.S. that performed abortions on women who were more than 21 weeks pregnant. It had been bombed in 1986, and an anti-abortion protester had shot Tiller in both arms in 1993. Tiller's family announced June 9 that the clinic would not reopen.

Auto Fuel-Efficiency Standards Raised—Pres. Obama ordered automobile manufacturers May 19 to improve the fuel efficiency of vehicles sold in the U.S. Corporate average fuel economy (CAFE) standards for cars and light trucks would rise from 25 miles per gallon in 2009 to 35.5 mpg by 2016, a target date 4 years earlier than had been established by Congress in 2007. The Obama administration estimated that the higher standards would allow the U.S. to reduce its petroleum imports by 1.8 bil barrels and cut its greenhouse gas emissions by 900 mil metric tons during 2009-16. Administration officials claimed that an average savings of $2,800 in fuel costs over the life of a vehicle would more than make up for the $1,300 the new energy-saving technology would add, on average, to each vehicle's purchase price by 2016.

Congress Approves Consumer Protection Bills, Other Measures—On May 20-22, Pres. Obama signed 3 consumer protection measures, all of which Congress had passed with large bipartisan majorities. The Fraud Enforcement and Recovery Act strengthened federal resources to crack down on predatory mortgage lending and other forms of financial fraud; the Helping Families Save Their Homes Act expanded federal efforts to help homeowners avoid foreclosure; and the Credit Card Accountability, Responsibility, and Disclosure (CARD) Act restricted the ability of credit card issuers to raise interest rates and impose fees on cardholders. Enacted along with the CARD measure was an amendment championed by Sen. Tom Coburn (R, OK) allowing visitors to national parks and wildlife refuges to carry concealed, loaded weapons, unless forbidden to do so by state law. On May 22, Pres. Obama also signed the Weapons Systems Acquisition Reform Act; the measure, which enjoyed virtually unanimous support in Congress, was intended to reduce cost overruns by increasing oversight of defense contracts and improving Pentagon weapons procurement, testing, and management procedures.

Stocks Gain as Broader Economy Struggles—Stock markets rose for the third consecutive month. The Dow Jones Industrial Average closed May 31 at 8,500.33, up 4.1% since the end of Apr. The S&P 500 finished at 919.14, a jump of 5.3%, and the Nasdaq Composite Index reached 1,774.33, for a one-month gain of 3.3%. Rising commodities prices fueled part of the May rally, with gold soaring to $980 an ounce and crude oil rebounding to $66 a barrel (its highest level since Nov. 2008).

Away from Wall Street, the economic indicators were much more negative. The retailer Filene's Basement filed for bankruptcy May 4, and the federally backed mortgage financing agency Fannie Mae reported May 8 that it would need an infusion of $19 bil from the U.S. Treasury. In mid-May, 6 major insurance firms qualified for federal bailout funds, and the bankrupt Chrysler and nearly bankrupt General Motors auto firms sent out notices terminating their relationships with nearly 2,000 car dealers. Data released in early June showed that the rate of job losses was slowing, but that unemployment in May had risen to 9.4%, the highest point since Aug. 1983.

International

U.S. Pushes More Aggressive Approach in Pakistan and Afghanistan—Seeking to increase pressure on al-Qaeda and the Taliban, Pres. Obama and other members of his administration conferred May 6 in Washington, DC, with Pres. Asif Ali Zardari of Pakistan and Pres. Hamid Karzai of Afghanistan. The discussions coincided with the launching of a new offensive by Pakistani government troops against Taliban forces in the Swat Valley, where a Feb. truce had been abandoned. On May 11, Def. Sec. Robert Gates said he had requested the resignation of Gen. David McKiernan, the top U.S. commander in Afghanistan. Gates called for "fresh eyes" and a "new approach" in announcing that McKiernan would be replaced by Lt. Gen. Stanley McChrystal, a former Green Beret with extensive experience in unconventional warfare. In an interview in late May, Gates told the *Wall Street Journal* that the Obama administration needed to achieve "a perceptible shift in momentum" to keep U.S. public support for the Afghan war from dissipating. Coalition forces in Afghanistan suffered 27 fatalities during the month, while U.S. combat deaths in Iraq numbered 25.

Iran Frees Imprisoned Journalist—A Tehran appeals court May 11 authorized the release of Iranian-American journalist Roxana Saberi, resolving a case that had drawn the personal attention of top U.S. officials, including Pres. Obama and Sec. of State Hillary Clinton, and of Iranian Pres. Mahmoud Ahmadinejad, who was up for re-election June 12. The U.S.-born Saberi, 32, a freelance reporter who had been living in Iran since 2003, was arrested in Jan. and accused of spying for the U.S.; after a closed trial Apr. 13, she was sentenced to 8 years in prison. (Saberi and the U.S. rejected the espionage charge.) The appellate court reduced her punishment to a 2-year suspended sentence, allowing her to leave the country. The U.S. had recently made several conciliatory gestures to Iran, including a videotaped message from Obama Mar. 19, marking the spring holiday of Nowruz, but the Saberi case had been widely viewed as an impediment to improved U.S.-Iranian relations.

Sri Lankan Leader Claims Victory in War Against Tamil Rebels—In an address to Parliament May 19, Pres. Mahinda Rajapaksa of Sri Lanka claimed victory over Tamil Tiger separatists, declaring an end to a civil war that since 1983 had claimed up to 80,000 lives in the South Asian island nation. During the second half of 2008, government forces had launched a major offensive against the rebels, who were seeking to establish an independent homeland for Sri Lanka's Tamil minority. The rebels, who formerly controlled up to 25% of the country, had surrendered Kilinochchi, their de facto capital, on Jan. 2. During the next 4 1/2 months they had been forced back into a small sliver of northeastern territory in fierce fighting that left some 7,000 civilians dead and forced another 265,000 to flee. Rebel leader Vellupillai Prabhakaran died in the decisive battle May 18. The army estimated that during the final 3 years of the conflict, more than 6,000 soldiers were killed and nearly 30,000 wounded; up to 22,000 Tamil Tigers were killed during the same period.

British Parliamentarians Caught in Expense Scandal—A press exposé of improper expense claims by members of Parliament brought down the speaker of the House of Commons May 19. Michael Martin, a Labour member from Glasgow, Scotland, who had led a 5-year fight to suppress the expense filings, resigned his post and gave up his seat after British newspapers, led by the *Daily Telegraph*, reported that parliamentarians of all parties had sought compensation for such items as pet food, moat cleaning at a country house, interest expenses on a mortgage that had already been paid off, and refurbishing of houses that had then been sold for a quick profit. Allegations of dubious expense claims were also lodged against several other members of Parliament as well as Labour Prime Min. Gordon Brown, who on Oct. 12 agreed to pay back more than £12,000 in cleaning and gardening bills.

Congress Party Wins Mandate in India—Prime Min. Manmohan Singh was sworn in for a second term May 22 after a coalition led by his Congress Party scored a convincing victory in parliamentary elections. More than 400 mil voters went to the polls Apr. 16-May 13, as the ruling United Progressive Alliance (UPA) won 261 seats, just 11 short of a majority in the 543-member Lok Sabha, the lower house of India's Parliament. Support for the opposition National Democratic Alliance, led by the Hindu nationalist Bharatiya Janata Party, dropped to 159 seats, according to final results. The UPA joined with smaller parties to form a stable center-left government with 322 seats.

General

Mine That Bird Wins Kentucky Derby; Rachel Alexandra Takes Preakness—After riding Mine That Bird to an unlikely victory May 2 in the Kentucky Derby, jockey Calvin Borel helped filly Rachel Alexandra make history in the Preakness May 16. Mine That Bird, a 50-1 long shot who was winless since Oct. 2008, scored the biggest upset in the Derby since 1913 on a muddy Churchill Downs track at Louisville, KY. Two weeks later at Pimlico in Baltimore, MD, Borel switched horses and rode 2-1 favorite Rachel Alexandra, who held off a late charge by Mine That Bird (ridden by Mike Smith) to become the first filly to win the Preakness in 85 years. Borel was the first rider since 1898 to win the Derby and Preakness in the same year on different mounts.

Hubble Space Telescope Repaired—The space shuttle *Atlantis* carried out a 14-day servicing mission to the 19-year-old Hubble Space Telescope (HST), taking off May 11 from Florida's Kennedy Space Center and landing May 24 at California's Edwards Air Force Base. Commanded by retired U.S. Navy Capt. Scott Altman, the 7-member crew conducted 5 technically challenging space walks, which included installation of the Cosmic Origins Spectrograph, designed to detect faint light from faraway quasars, and the new Wide Field Camera 3, capable of taking extremely detailed pictures at infrared and ultraviolet wavelengths. The crew also installed a new command and data-handling unit, repaired the Advanced Camera for Surveys, replaced worn-out gyroscopes and batteries, and upgraded the HST's thermal and radiation shielding.

Allen Beats Lambert in *American Idol* Voting—More than 100 mil votes were cast in the final round of *American Idol*, with country-flavored pop singer Kris Allen defeating Adam Lambert May 20 in the FOX's reality TV series.

Singer, dancer, and producer Paula Abdul, a celebrity judge on *American Idol* since the show debuted in 2002, disclosed (via the social networking site Twitter) Aug. 4 that she would not be returning to the show for the 2010 season. Stand-up comedienne and TV talk-show host Ellen DeGeneres was named to replace her Sept. 9.

Castroneves Captures Indy 500—At the Indianapolis (IN) Motor Speedway May 24, Helio Castroneves of Brazil won the Indianapolis 500 for the third time (his previous victories were in 2001 and 2002). Driving for Team Penske, Castroneves maintained an average speed of 150.318 mph, outpacing Dan Wheldon, the 2005 winner, and Danica Patrick, who in third place had the highest finish ever by a woman in the 500-mi race.

June 2009

National

Restructuring Plans for General Motors and Chrysler Approved; Additional Economic Developments—General Motors, the largest car manufacturer in the U.S. (and, until 2008, in the world) filed for bankruptcy June 1. The filing, which followed years of massive losses, was part of a federally mandated agreement, under which the U.S. government promised to supply $30.1 bil, in addition to the $19.4 bil it had already provided, to keep a leaner GM operating. The night before the GM filing, U.S. Bankruptcy Judge Arthur J. Gonzalez approved a plan under which Chrysler—another leading U.S. auto manufacturer, which had filed for bankruptcy protection Apr. 30—would emerge as a restructured company in partnership with the Italian automaker Fiat. The U.S. Supreme Court June 9 rejected a challenge to the restructuring plan brought by a group of Indiana pension funds, and Chrysler exited bankruptcy the following day.

The General Motors restructuring proceeded with similar dispatch. The reorganized GM that emerged July 10 included such profitable brands as Chevrolet, Buick, Cadillac,

and GMC trucks, vans, and SUVs; the U.S. government held a 60.8% stake, with a United Auto Workers retiree health care fund controlling 17.5%, carryover bondholders 10%, and Canadian authorities 11.7%. Less valuable brands such as Saturn, Hummer, Saab, and Pontiac would be sold off individually or shut down under court supervision. After a proposed deal with the Penske Automotive Group fell apart, GM announced Sept. 30 that the Saturn division, which employed about 13,000 people, would close in 2010.

The U.S. unemployment rate for June rose to 9.5%, as cumulative job losses reached 6.5 mil since the recession began in Dec. 2007. Meanwhile, 10 major financial firms, seeking to escape the government controls that accompanied their taxpayer-funded bailouts, received permission from the U.S. Treasury June 9 to return about $68 bil they had received from the Troubled Asset Relief Program (TARP). The paybacks, made June 17, included $25 bil from JPMorgan Chase, $10 bil each from Goldman Sachs and Morgan Stanley, and $6.6 billion from U.S. Bancorp. Stocks consolidated their gains for the second quarter despite a mixed performance in June, with the Dow Jones Industrial Average closing at 8,447.00 (down 0.6% for the month), the S&P 500 at 919.32 (up 0.02%), and the Nasdaq Composite at 1,835.04 (up 3.5%).

Obama, Congress Wrestle With Health Care, Other Domestic Issues—In a speech to a convention of the American Medical Association in Chicago June 15, Pres. Barack Obama made a detailed case for revamping the U.S. health care system, a top priority for his administration. "If we fail to act," he told the doctors' group, "premiums will climb higher, benefits will erode further, [and] the rolls of the uninsured will swell to include millions more Americans." Instead of submitting its own comprehensive health insurance bill to Congress, as the Clinton administration had done during its failed effort in 1993-94, the Obama administration allowed 5 separate congressional committees to work on their own versions of the bill, which differed on key questions such as how to control rising health care costs, how to finance expansion of coverage, and whether the measure would offer a government-run "public option" to compete with private insurers. Committee work on the divergent health care proposals consumed much of the summer.

On another top administration priority, Pres. Obama June 17 outlined a plan to prevent a recurrence of the crisis that had shaken many of the nation's leading financial institutions in 2008. The program—which Obama described as "a sweeping overhaul of the financial regulatory system, a transformation on a scale not seen since the reforms that followed the Great Depression"—called for tougher oversight of financial markets and expansion of federal authority to regulate financial institutions that posed a systemic risk to the economy. Detailed legislation to establish a consumer financial protection agency was submitted to Congress June 30.

On June 26 the House, by a 219-212 vote, passed landmark legislation to require increased use of renewable energy sources, such as wind and solar power, and to deal with the threat of global climate change. The measure included "cap-and-trade" provisions offering market-based incentives for companies to cut their emissions of greenhouse gases that contribute to global warming. Because "cap-and-trade" also required companies to buy federal permits to emit such gases, opponents derided the bill as a "cap-and-tax" plan that would raise costs to businesses and consumers. The Congressional Budget Office on June 22 estimated the annual cost of the plan at about $175 per household by 2020, while rebates to the poorest households would lower those energy costs by $40 per year. The Senate began working on a similar measure in Sept.

TV Broadcasters Switch to Digital Signals—U.S. television stations turned off their analog signals June 12 and began all-digital broadcasting, a transmission method mandated by Congress in 2005 to free up parts of the broadcast spectrum for police and fire emergency services, wireless broadband, and other telecommunications purposes. Satellite- and cable-TV subscribers were unaffected by the shift, but older sets receiving signals through antennas needed a special analog-to-digital converter box in order to continue receiving free over-the-air broadcasts. Congress had postponed the changeover from Feb. 17 to give viewers more time to upgrade. The Nielsen Co. estimated that, as of June 10, about 2.8 mil households were still unprepared for the switch.

Ensign, Sanford Admit Affairs—Two prominent Republican officeholders, each regarded as a possible presidential candidate in 2012, publicly acknowledged extramarital affairs. At a Las Vegas press conference June 16, Sen. John Ensign (R, NV) apologized for carrying on a 9-month affair with a former staffer later identified as Cynthia Hampton. Until Apr. 2008, Hampton had been Ensign's campaign treasurer, and her husband, Doug Hampton, was a high-ranking member of Ensign's Senate staff; in that month, both Hamptons left their jobs, and Ensign's parents wrote multiple checks totaling $96,000 to members of the Hampton family. Ensign resigned his Senate leadership post as chairman of the Republican Policy Committee on June 17, but refused to give up his Senate seat, which expires in 2013. The Senate Ethics Committee later launched an inquiry into the Ensigns' and Hamptons' tangled relationship.

Another scandal erupted when South Carolina Gov. Mark Sanford could not be found for 6 days in late June. A spokesman said the governor was hiking the Appalachian Trail, but Sanford admitted on June 24 that he had been pursuing an extramarital affair with a woman from Argentina. Sanford later repaid the state $3,300 for a June 2008 trip he had taken to Buenos Aires to visit the woman, but a South Carolina state inquiry found no other misuse of taxpayer money. Sanford resigned his chairmanship of the national Republican Governors Association, but he refused to give up the governorship, despite calls for his resignation Sept. 10 from state party leader Karen Floyd and more than two-thirds of the state GOP executive committee.

Texas Financier Charged with $7 Bil Fraud—Texas billionaire R. Allen Stanford turned himself in to the FBI June 18, hours after a federal grand jury indicted him on charges of running a Ponzi scheme that had defrauded some 30,000 investors out of $7 bil. The financier, whose holdings included the Stanford International Bank on the Caribbean island of Antigua, was accused of carrying out his fraud by paying more than $100,000 in bribes to Leroy King, who headed Antigua and Barbuda's Financial Services Regulatory Commission. King was indicted along with Stanford and several of his associates. The accusations against Stanford had first become public in Feb., when the Securities and Exchange Commission lodged a civil complaint against him and shut down his Houston-based financial operations.

FDA Gets Power to Regulate Tobacco Products—Pres. Obama signed June 22 a measure authorizing the Food and Drug Administration (FDA) to regulate the content and marketing of tobacco products for adults, banning the display of tobacco ads near schools and playgrounds, and outlawing the types of flavored cigarettes specifically designed to appeal to young people. The Family Smoking Prevention and Tobacco Control Act had passed the Senate June 11 by a vote of 79-17, and the House June 12 by 307-97.

Metrorail Crash Kills 9 in Nation's Capital—An evening rush-hour collision on the Red Line of the Washington, DC, Metrorail mass-transit system left 9 people dead and 80 injured June 22. The accident occurred when one train rear-ended another that had stopped just outside the Fort Totten station in northeast DC, near the Maryland border. An investigation by the National Transportation Safety Board focused on a faulty circuit in a computerized crash-avoidance system that had been malfunctioning for 18 months.

Supreme Court Rules on Voting Rights, Affirmative Action—The Supreme Court marked the concluding month of its 2008-09 term, and its last month with Associate Justice David Souter on the bench, by issuing a flurry of major rulings. In one of the year's most closely watched cases, an 8-1 majority on June 22 let stand, in *Northwest Austin Municipal Utility District Number One v. Holder*, a key provision of the federal Voting Rights Act that required many states and cities, mostly in the South, to seek permission from federal authorities before making any changes in voting procedures. In another highly anticipated ruling, *Ricci v. DiStefano*, the Court held June 29 that a group of mostly white firefighters in New Haven, CT, suffered discrimination when the city

threw out a promotion exam because African American firefighters had done poorly. The affirmative action case attracted attention in part because the justices' 5-4 ruling reversed an appellate court ruling in which Supreme Court nominee Sonia Sotomayor had participated.

International

Obama Reaches Out to Muslim World—Speaking June 4 at Cairo Univ. in Egypt, Pres. Obama called for "a new beginning" in relations between the U.S. and the Muslim world. Calling America's bond with Israel "unbreakable," Obama also condemned Israeli settlements in the West Bank and reaffirmed his support for a Palestinian state. He quoted frequently from the Qur'an and noted that, although he was a Christian, he had a direct connection to Islam through his father's Muslim heritage and his own boyhood experiences in Indonesia. He emphasized the need to combat violent extremism, prevent Iran from developing nuclear weapons, seek a just peace between Palestinians and Israelis, and promote democracy, religious freedom, women's rights, and economic opportunity. The Cairo address, regarded by the White House as one of the most important foreign policy speeches of Obama's young presidency, was a highlight of a 5-day trip that also included a visit to Saudi Arabia; a speech commemorating the Holocaust, delivered at the site of the Nazi death camp in Buchenwald, Germany; and remarks at ceremonies in Normandy, France, honoring the 65th anniversary of the D-Day invasion.

Two Airbus Crashes Kill 380—Air France Flight 447, traveling overnight from Rio de Janeiro, Brazil, to Paris, France, plunged into the Atlantic Ocean June 1, killing all 228 people on board. Based on automated transmissions from the Airbus A330-200, investigators concentrated on the apparent failure of the plane's airspeed sensors, known as Pitot tubes. Airbus had recommended replacement of the tubes, but the change had not been made on the plane that crashed. Air France later completed the repair on other planes in its Airbus fleet.

On June 30, Yemenia Airways Flight IY626, which had taken off from Sana'a, Yemen, plunged into the Indian Ocean while attempting to land at Moroni, capital of Comoros. The crash killed 152 of 153 people on the Airbus A310. The lone survivor was a 14-year-old girl.

Pro-Western Coalition Wins Lebanon Election—The March 14 Movement, an alliance of pro-Western and anti-Syrian parties, retained its majority in Lebanon's Parliament in June 7 elections. Led by Saad Hariri, the March 14 coalition out-polled Hezbollah, a militant Shiite Muslim group classified by the U.S. as a terrorist organization. Hezbollah was supported by Iran and Syria, which was the country many Lebanese blamed for the 2005 assassination of Hariri's father, a former prime min. Lebanese Pres. Michel Suleiman designated Hariri to form a new government June 27, a task made difficult by the complex array of factions and external forces that shape Lebanese politics.

WHO Raises Swine Flu Pandemic Warning to Highest Level—The World Health Organization announced June 11 that it had raised its swine flu pandemic warning to Level 6 (the highest level on a scale of 1 to 6). "Further spread is considered inevitable," said WHO's director general, Dr. Margaret Chan. As of June 15, 76 countries had reported 163 deaths from 35,928 confirmed cases of influenza A (H1N1), the name by which the strain of swine flu was formally known. Five U.S. companies were working to produce a swine flu vaccine; the CDC released the first doses of the vaccine to the U.S. public Oct. 5.

Ahmadinejad Claims Victory in Iran Election; Mass Protests Follow—With oil revenues falling, unemployment rising, and inflation soaring, Iranians went to the polls June 12 for a presidential election in which the incumbent, Mahmoud Ahmadinejad, faced a spirited challenge from former Prime Min. Mir Hussein Moussavi and 2 other candidates. Ahmadinejad retained support among rural, poor, and religiously conservative voters, along with hardliners from the Revolutionary Guards and Basij militia, while Moussavi relied on urban, middle-class voters, especially women, and was backed by former presidents Hashemi Rafsanjani and Mohammad Khatami.

With turnout high, a close result was anticipated, and both Ahmadinejad and Moussavi claimed victory when polls closed. But official returns, released by Iran's Interior Ministry, awarded Ahmadinejad 62.6% of the total vote, followed by Moussavi with 33.8%. Citing widespread irregularities, Moussavi called for the election to be rerun, and asked Iran's religious leader, Ayatollah Sayyed Ali Khamenei, to intervene. In a televised statement, however, Khamenei declared Ahmadinejad the winner and urged the other candidates to support him.

In the weeks that followed, protests by hundreds of thousands of Iranians in Tehran and other cities were crushed by police and Basij paramilitaries. Many protesters were wounded, and at least 2,500 were arrested. Government officials estimated that 17 people had been killed by June 25; among them was a 26-year-old woman, Neda Agha-Soltan, a video of whose death in Tehran June 20 was widely viewed in Iran and, via YouTube, throughout the world. Iran's powerful Guardian Council certified the election results June 29, and Ahmadinejad was sworn in for a second term Aug. 5.

Zelaya Ousted as President of Honduras—Storming the presidential palace at dawn June 28, Honduran soldiers forced Pres. Manuel Zelaya to leave Tegucigalpa, the Honduran capital, and fly into exile in Costa Rica. Later that same day, the Honduran National Congress chose legislative leader Roberto Micheletti to serve the remainder of Zelaya's term. The Honduran constitution had limited Zelaya to a single 4-year term, which was due to expire Jan. 2010.

The coup was the culmination of a power struggle that began when Zelaya, a leftist, pushed for a nonbinding referendum to determine popular support for revising the constitution—revisions his critics believed would include abolition of the one-term limit. Defying opposition from the Congress, military, and Supreme Court, Zelaya pressed forward and was ousted on the day it was scheduled to take place. The Micheletti government suspended basic rights and suppressed pro-Zelaya demonstrations.

The ouster was condemned by the U.S., the UN, and the Organization of American States (OAS), which suspended Honduras July 4. The U.S. refused to deem it a coup, however, which would have suspended foreign aid. Costa Rican Pres. Óscar Arias Sánchez, a former Nobel Peace Prize winner, sought to mediate a resolution of the dispute in early July, but talks between Zelaya and the de facto government deadlocked.

U.S. Pulls Forces Out of Iraqi Cities—Fulfilling its commitment under the Status of Forces Agreement (SOFA) reached in late 2008, the U.S. military completed its withdrawal from Iraq's cities and towns June 30—a milestone the Iraqi government marked by proclaiming a national holiday. Nearly 130,000 U.S. troops remained at forward-operating bases in Iraq. The U.S. redeployment was greeted by a series of insurgent attacks, including a truck bombing June 20 near a Shiite mosque at Taza, in northern Iraq, that killed at least 82 people and wounded more than 250, and a market bombing June 24 in Sadr City, a predominantly Shiite section of Baghdad, that left at least 76 people dead and more than 160 injured. U.S. military fatalities in Iraq during the month numbered 15; coalition losses in Afghanistan totaled 38 during the same period.

General

Summer Bird Takes Belmont—Riding the unheralded Summer Bird, jockey Kent Desormeaux June 6 won his first Belmont Stakes in his sixth attempt at Belmont Park in Elmont, NY. Calvin Borel, who had ridden to victory on board Mine That Bird in the Kentucky Derby and Rachel Alexandra in the Preakness Stakes, failed in his bid to become the first jockey to gain a Triple Crown sweep on different horses, finishing third in the Belmont on Mine That Bird.

Kuznetsova, Federer Win French Open Singles Titles—In an all-Russian women's final June 6 at the French Open (Roland Garros) in Paris, Svetlana Kuznetsova defeated an error-prone Dinara Safina, 6-4, 6-2. The following day, Swiss tennis master Roger Federer dominated Sweden's Robin Soderling, 6-1, 7-6 (1), 6-4. The victory, his first French Open crown, made Federer the sixth man in history to win all 4 Grand Slam events, and tied Federer with Pete Sampras's record of 14 career Grand Slam singles championships.

***Billy Elliot* and *God of Carnage* Top Tony Honors**—The Broadway production of *Billy Elliot* danced away with 10 Tony Awards June 7. The London import, with music by pop star Elton John, won for Best Musical, and 3 teenagers who shared the title role—David Alvarez, Trent Kowalik, and Kiril Kulish—took home acting honors. Yasmina Reza's comedy *God of Carnage* won 3 Tony Awards, including Best Play. For her supporting role in a revival of *Blithe Spirit*, Angela Lansbury won her fourth Tony, tying a career record held by Julie Harris.

Pittsburgh Penguins Capture Stanley Cup—Avenging their loss to Detroit in the 2008 Stanley Cup finals, the Pittsburgh Penguins beat the Red Wings, 2-1, on Detroit's home ice June 12 to take the championship series, 4 games to 3. Pittsburgh center Evgeni Malkin, who led the NHL in scoring in both the regular season and the playoffs, won the Conn Smythe Trophy as postseason MVP.

Bryant Leads Lakers to NBA Championship—Propelled by Kobe Bryant's MVP performance, the Los Angeles Lakers June 14 defeated the Orlando Magic, 99-86, to clinch the 15th NBA title in franchise history. The Lakers wrapped up the best-of-7 series in game 5 at Amway Arena in Orlando, FL. Coach Phil Jackson set a career mark of 10 NBA championships, 6 with the Michael Jordan-era Chicago Bulls and 4 with the Lakers.

Glover Is U.S. Open Golf Winner—Lucas Glover held off late charges by Phil Mickelson and David Duval to win his first U.S Open Golf championship June 22. Playing on the Bethpage Black course at Bethpage State Park, Farmingdale, NY, Glover finished a rain-delayed final round with a 72-hole total of 276, 4 under par and 2 strokes ahead of his closest competitors.

Brazil Thwarts U.S. Hopes in Confederations Cup Soccer—Four days after the American men's team upset Spain, 2-0, to score one of the greatest wins in U.S. soccer history, Brazil overcame a 2-goal U.S. halftime lead June 28 to win the FIFA Confederations Cup crown, 3-2. The final match, played at Ellis Park Stadium in Johannesburg, South Africa, gave Brazil its second consecutive championship in the prestigious international tournament, which is held every 4 years.

Pop Superstar Michael Jackson Dies—Famed singer, songwriter, and dancer Michael Jackson died suddenly June 25 at the age of 50. He was found in cardiac arrest and taken to UCLA Medical Center, where resuscitation efforts failed and he was pronounced dead. Jackson, renowned in recent years as much for his personal eccentricities and legal problems as for his talents, had been rehearsing for a comeback concert series at the time of his death. His assets, which included a 50% stake in the Beatles song catalog, and his debts, attributed to a lavish lifestyle, were each estimated in the hundreds of millions of dollars.

In death as in life, Jackson remained the subject of public fascination. A star-studded memorial service at the Staples Center in Los Angeles July 7 attracted tens of millions of viewers on television and via the Internet. On Aug. 28, after a 2-month inquiry, the Los Angeles County coroner ruled Jackson's death a homicide and that he had died of "acute propofol intoxication." The investigation had centered on the activities of Jackson's personal physician, Dr. Conrad Murray, who acknowledged that he had used the anesthetic propofol and other drugs to treat the entertainer's chronic insomnia.

July 2009

National

Palin Quits as Alaska Governor—Alaska Gov. Sarah Palin (R) unexpectedly announced July 3 that she would resign her office within 4 weeks. Palin, who had been governor for 31 months, said she had decided not to run for reelection and did not wish to serve out the remaining 17 months of her term as a lame duck. She stepped down July 26, and Lt. Gov. Sean Parnell (R) was sworn in to replace her. Palin had become a national figure as the vice presidential candidate on the Republican ticket headed by Arizona Sen. John McCain. Some speculated that leaving the governorship would provide her with greater freedom to explore a possible presidential run in 2012.

Senate Moves to Confirm Sotomayor—The Senate Judiciary Committee held confirmation hearings July 13-16 on Pres. Barack Obama's nomination of Judge Sonia Sotomayor to fill the vacancy left by Assoc. Justice David Souter's retirement from the Supreme Court. The proceedings generated little suspense, since Senate Democrats—who were united in supporting the nomination—held solid majorities on the committee and in the Senate as a whole. Republican committee members focused their criticism on a remark Sotomayor had made in a 2001 speech: "I would hope that a wise Latina woman with the richness of her experiences would more often than not reach a better conclusion than a white male who hasn't lived that life." She called the comment "a rhetorical flourish that fell flat," and said she did not believe "any ethnic, racial, or gender group has an advantage in sound judging."

On July 28 the Judiciary Committee approved her nomination, 13-6, with all Democrats and one Republican, Sen. Lindsey Graham (SC), voting in favor. She was confirmed Aug. 6 by the full Senate, 68-31, with support from 9 Republicans. Two days later she was sworn in by Chief Justice John Roberts, becoming the first Latina and the third woman to join the Supreme Court.

Gates Case Raises Racial Profiling Controversy—In an incident that exposed divergent American attitudes toward race and class, Harvard Prof. Henry Louis "Skip" Gates Jr., one of the nation's leading African American scholars, was arrested July 16 in Cambridge, MA, by Sgt. James Crowley, a white police officer. Gates was seen struggling to open his jammed front door by a neighbor who called police to report a possible break-in. An argument erupted after Crowley arrived on the scene, and he subsequently arrested Gates for "loud and tumultuous behavior," according to his police report. After Gates's friends complained he had been the victim of racial profiling, Cambridge police dropped charges July 21, calling the arrest "regrettable and unfortunate."

The next evening, near the end of a presidential press conference that dealt almost entirely with health care, Pres. Obama was asked what he thought the incident showed about race relations in the U.S. Acknowledging that he might be "a little biased" because "Skip Gates is a friend," Obama said, "Blacks and Hispanics are picked up more frequently, and often time for no cause," adding that the Cambridge police had "acted stupidly." As controversy over his remarks grew, Obama admitted he could have chosen his words differently, called Crowley to apologize, and invited Gates and Crowley to the White House July 30 to share a beer with him and Vice Pres. Joe Biden.

Corruption Probe Nets 3 New Jersey Mayors—More than 200 FBI and Internal Revenue Service agents fanned out across metropolitan New Jersey and New York July 23, enforcing warrants against 44 people charged in a probe of public corruption, bribery, money laundering, and, in at least one instance, human organ trafficking. Among those arrested were 3 New Jersey mayors, all Democrats: Dennis Elwell of Secaucus, Peter Cammarano III of Hoboken, and Anthony Suarez of Ridgefield. Elements of the case included the passing of $97,000 in cash in an Apple Jacks cereal box; the arrest of 5 rabbis accused of participating in money-laundering schemes; and the arrest of a Brooklyn, NY, man for allegedly dealing in black-market kidneys.

Profits Return to Wall Street, as Hopes for Recovery Rise—Profit reports released in July showed that major U.S. financial companies such as Goldman Sachs, JPMorgan Chase, Citigroup, and Bank of America had all gained ground in Apr.-June 2009. Job losses slowed, and the gross domestic product, which contracted at a revised rate of 6.4% during Jan.-Mar., shrank by only 1.0% during the second quarter (revised numbers released in Sept. 2009 put the GDP contraction even lower, at 0.7%). Stocks responded to the hopeful news with a new growth spurt. The Dow Jones Industrial Average jumped 8.6% for the month, closing July 31 at 9,171.61. The S&P 500 (987.47) climbed 7.4%, and the Nasdaq Composite Index (1,978.50) gained 7.8%.

International

Obama Travels to Russia, Italy, Ghana—Accompanied by First Lady Michelle Obama and daughters Malia and Sasha, Pres. Obama arrived in Russia July 6 for meetings with Pres. Dmitri Medvedev and Prime Min. Vladimir Putin. Russia and the U.S. agreed on steps to reduce their nuclear arsenals, and the U.S. received permission to fly troops and weapons into Afghanistan through Russian airspace. In Italy, July 8-10, Obama had a private audience with Pope Benedict XVI and participated in a summit meeting of the Group of 8 (G-8) leading industrialized nations. Conferring in L'Aquila, which was rebuilding from an Apr. 6 earthquake, the G-8 leaders agreed on long-term targets for curbing global warming and on a 3-year, $20 bil program to aid food production in the world's poorest countries. Obama made his first presidential trip to sub-Saharan Africa July 10-11, addressing the Ghanaian parliament and taking a tour of Ghana's Cape Coast Castle, which for many years had been a departure point for transatlantic slave shipments.

Uighurs Clash with Han Chinese in Xinjiang Region—Violence July 5-7 between Uighurs and Han Chinese in Urumqi, the capital of Xinjiang Uighur Autonomous Region in northwestern China, left at least 197 dead and more than 1,700 injured. The riots began when Uighur protest marchers in Urumqi, angered by the killing June 25-26 of 2 Uighur migrant workers in the southern city of Guangdong, began attacking Han businesses and killing Han civilians. Police cracked down, arresting hundreds of rioters, and Han vigilantes retaliated against the Uighurs. Urumqi's top Communist official was replaced Sept. 5 after renewed disturbances, including protests by Han over alleged attacks by Uighurs using hypodermic syringes as weapons; a week later, 3 Uighurs in Urumqi received prison sentences in syringe-related cases. The Turkic-speaking, predominantly Muslim Uighurs have long complained of cultural prejudice and economic discrimination against them by Han Chinese, who represent the majority of China's population and whose numbers in the Xinjiang region have grown rapidly in recent decades.

Yudhoyono Reelected in Indonesia; Bombs Hit Jakarta Hotels—Benefiting from a robust economy that was growing at a rate of 4% annually despite a global recession, Pres. Susilo Bambang Yudhoyono easily won a second 5-year term, in an election July 8 that received praise from international observers. He became the first Indonesian prime minister ever to be re-elected. Final results gave Yudhoyono 60.8% of the total vote, followed by former Pres. Megawati Sukarnoputri with 26.8% and current Vice Pres. Jusuf Kalla with 12.4%. More than 120 mil people cast ballots, and there were no reports of major incidents at some 450,000 polling stations.

On July 17, coordinated suicide bombings at 2 Jakarta luxury hotels left 9 people dead and injured more than 50. Police confirmed Sept. 17 that Noordin Muhamad Top, suspected of plotting the Jakarta attacks and earlier bombings, had been killed in a shootout. Noordin, one of Asia's most wanted terrorists, had eluded capture for 7 years.

Nigerian Forces Clash with Radical Islamist Sect—Fighting July 26-30 in northeastern Nigeria between government security forces and Boko Haram, a radical Islamist group, left up to 700 people dead. The sect's founder and spiritual leader, Mohammed Yusuf, was captured in Maiduguri and killed while in police custody July 30.

Casualties Rise in Afghanistan; Coalition Partners Leave Iraq—The widening war in Afghanistan claimed a record monthly total of 76 coalition troop fatalities in July, with 45 of the losses coming from the U.S. The number of U.S. troops reached 62,000, more than double the total a year earlier; over 34,000 additional troops were provided by NATO allies. According to a UN report released July 31, the number of Afghan civilians killed during Jan.-June 2009 totaled 1,013, a 23% increase over the corresponding period in 2008.

Australia, Romania, and the UK pulled out their last remaining forces from Iraq, leaving the U.S., with nearly 130,000 troops, as the last remnant of the multinational coalition that had invaded and occupied the country. U.S. military deaths in July numbered 8, the lowest monthly total since the Iraq war began in Mar. 2003.

General

Former Pro QB Steve McNair Shot Dead—Former pro football star Steve McNair, 36, was found dead July 4 in a Nashville, TN, condominium along with his 20-year-old girlfriend Sahel Kazemi. McNair, who was married, had met Kazemi 6 months earlier. Nashville police July 8 described the killings as a murder-suicide, concluding that Kazemi, anxious about her financial situation and convinced that McNair was cheating on her, had shot him while he slept on a couch, then fatally shot herself in the head. McNair, who retired in Apr. 2008 after 13 NFL seasons, had led the Tennessee Titans to the Super Bowl in 2000 and was honored as league co-MVP 3 years later.

Federer, Serena Williams Win Wimbledon Championships—Roger Federer of Switzerland earned his sixth Wimbledon men's singles crown by defeating Andy Roddick, 5-7, 7-6 (6), 7-6 (5), 3-6, 16-14, in an epic match played July 5 at the All England Lawn Tennis Club. The victory was Federer's 15th Grand Slam title, breaking a career record of 14, which he shared with Pete Sampras. A day earlier, Serena Williams bested her sister Venus to win the women's singles championship, 7-6 (3), 6-2; the contest was a rematch of their 2008 final, which was won by Venus. The Williams sisters also teamed up to win the women's doubles crown for a second consecutive year.

Watson Loses to Cink at British Open—Playing July 19 for his sixth British Open title, 59-year-old golfing legend Tom Watson tied Stewart Cink with a 2-under-par 278 after 72 holes at Turnberry, Ayrshire, Scotland. But Cink—who was 2 years old when Watson, the sentimental favorite, first won the British Open in 1975—easily bested the weary Watson in a 4-hole playoff to gain his first major championship.

Contador Captures Tour de France—Alberto Contador overcame an acrimonious relationship with his Astana teammate, 7-time Tour de France winner Lance Armstrong, to triumph in the 3-week, 2,175-mi cycling race which ended in Paris July 26. Armstrong finished in third place, behind the Spaniard Contador and Andy Schleck of Luxembourg.

August 2009

National

Health Care Debate Heats Up—Returning to their home districts during the Aug. congressional recess, some lawmakers ran into a barrage of anger, as protesters opposed to Obama administration plans to extend health care coverage to millions of uninsured Americans shouted down legislators at town hall meetings and other gatherings. Opponents claimed "Obamacare" meant a government takeover of the health care system, which would then lead to rationing by "death panels" of federal bureaucrats empowered to deny life-saving care to the sick, elderly, or disabled. The rumors about "death panels" stemmed from misinformation about a provision allowing Medicare to pay for end-of-life counseling, which had bipartisan support in the House. In his own Aug. town hall meetings and in a speech to a joint session of Congress Sept. 9, Pres. Barack Obama sought to dispel what he called "scare tactics" and "bogus claims" made by his critics. He said that under Democratic plans (which were still working their way through the House and Senate) insurance companies would not be allowed to deny coverage based on preexisting conditions, revoke coverage when people got sick, place an arbitrary cap on annual or lifetime reimbursements, require patients to pay high out-of-pocket costs, or exclude coverage for routine checkups and preventive care. Insisting that restructuring the health insurance system would actually reduce costs, he said he would refuse to "sign a plan that adds one dime to our deficits."

Midway through his address to Congress, Obama vehemently denied that his administration's reform plans would "set up panels of bureaucrats with the power to kill off senior citizens" or provide health insurance coverage for illegal immigrants. At that point, an audience member, Rep. Joe Wilson (R, SC), shouted out, "You lie!" Later that day, Wilson released a statement apologizing to the president for the "lack of civility." Wilson's outburst made him a lightning rod for both parties. The House voted 240-179 to rebuke

Wilson for his breach of decorum Sept. 15. By Sept. 30 his reelection campaign had received more money than any other 2010 House campaign, with nearly $2.7 mil flowing to Wilson and almost $1.7 mil raised by a Democratic challenger, Rob Miller.

Former Rep. Jefferson Convicted—A federal jury in Alexandria, VA, found former Rep. William J. Jefferson (D, LA) guilty Aug. 5 on 11 counts of conspiracy, bribery, wire fraud, money laundering, and racketeering. The 9-term congressman, who lost his reelection bid in Nov. 2008, was accused of soliciting bribes in exchange for helping U.S. firms arrange business deals in Africa. The case drew national attention when federal agents raided his Washington, DC, home in 2005 and found $90,000 wrapped in aluminum foil in his freezer.

Martinez Leaves Senate—Sen. Mel Martinez (R, FL), who declared in Dec. 2008 that he would not run for a second term in 2010, surprised his colleagues Aug. 7 by announcing that he would leave the Senate as soon as Florida Gov. Charlie Crist (R) chose a successor. Martinez, who was 15 years old when he immigrated to the U.S. from Cuba in 1962, headed the Dept. of Housing and Urban Development (2001-03) before his election to the Senate in 2004; while serving in the Senate, he became the first Hispanic to lead the Republican National Committee (2006-07). Gov. Crist, who in May had announced that he would run for Martinez's seat, on Aug. 28 named Crist's former chief of staff, George LeMieux, as the interim replacement. Martinez left the Senate Sept. 9, and LeMieux was sworn in the following day.

Indictment Alleges Massive Theft of Personal Data—In a case described by prosecutors as the largest identity theft in U.S. history, a federal indictment Aug. 17 charged Albert Gonzalez of Miami, FL, and 2 unidentified Russian co-conspirators with stealing more than 130 mil credit and debit card numbers between late 2006 and early 2008. The indictment, filed in Newark, NJ, accused the defendants of hacking into the computer systems of 5 major companies; some of the stolen card numbers were then sold online, for use in unauthorized retail and bank transactions. Court documents filed Aug. 28 in Boston, MA, indicated that Gonzalez, who had been in federal custody since May 2008, had agreed to plead guilty to earlier cyber-crime charges.

Sen. Edward Kennedy Dies—After a 15-month battle with brain cancer, Sen. Edward M. (Ted) Kennedy (R, MA), 77, died Aug. 25 at Hyannis Port, MA. Kennedy had been a leading champion of liberal causes during a Senate career that spanned more than 46 years. Among the headline events that marked his life were the assassinations of 2 older brothers, Pres. John F. Kennedy in 1963 and Sen. Robert F. (Bobby) Kennedy (D, NY) in 1968, and the drowning death of Mary Jo Kopechne, a passenger in a car he drove off a bridge in 1969 on Chappaquiddick Island, MA. In 1980 he unsuccessfully challenged incumbent Pres. Jimmy Carter for the Democratic presidential nomination.

Following a funeral Mass Aug. 29 at a Catholic church in Boston, with Pres. Obama delivering the eulogy, Kennedy's body was transported to Washington, DC, where congressional staffers and others waited at the Capitol to pay their respects. From there he was taken to Arlington National Cemetery, where he was buried near the graves of his brothers. On Sept. 24, Mass. Gov. Deval Patrick (D) appointed Paul Kirk, a longtime Kennedy associate and former Democratic National Committee Chair, to fill Kennedy's Senate seat until a special election Jan. 19, 2010.

"Cash for Clunkers" Boosts Auto Sales; Other Economic Developments—According to data released Aug. 26 by the Dept. of Transportation, U.S. consumers bought 690,114 vehicles under the "cash for clunkers" program, which offered refund vouchers of up to $4,500 on trade-ins of old, gas-guzzling cars, trucks, and SUVs for newer, more fuel-efficient vehicles. The first phase of the program, which began July 24 with funding of $1 bil, ran out of money so quickly that Congress passed a $2 bil extension that funded the program for another 17 days, which Pres. Obama signed on Aug. 7. Of the top 5 models sold, only one—the Ford Focus—was produced by a U.S.-based automaker. The trade-ins, about 84% of which were trucks, were disabled by pouring sodium silicate (known as "liquid glass") into their engines. Nearly 60% of the new vehicles were passenger cars.

Pres. Obama Aug. 25 announced that he was appointing Ben Bernanke to a second term as Federal Reserve chairman when his current term expired in Jan. 2010. Obama praised Bernanke for "bold action and out-of-the-box thinking" in expanding the powers of the Fed to deal with the severe financial crisis that began in Sept. 2008.

The Dow Jones Industrial Average closed Aug. 31 at 9,496.28, recording a one-month gain of 3.5% and its best Aug. performance in 9 years. The S&P 500 finished at 1,020.62, up 3.4% for its sixth consecutive monthly gain. The Nasdaq Composite Index (2,009.06) was 1.5% above its July close.

International

Former Pres. Clinton Visits North Korea; 2 U.S. Journalists Released—A 20-hour mission to North Korea Aug. 4-5 by Bill Clinton ended successfully when the former president returned to the U.S. accompanied by 2 American journalists who had been held since Mar. 17 by the Pyongyang regime. The reporters, Laura Ling and Euna Lee, had been researching a story for Current (a media firm headed by former Vice Pres. Al Gore) when they strayed across the Chinese border into North Korean territory; convicted in June after a secret trial, they were sentenced to 12 years of "reform through labor." Although the visit by Bill Clinton was considered unofficial, both the White House and Sec. of State Hillary Clinton had been involved in arranging the trip, during which the former president met with North Korean leader Kim Jong Il and secured a pardon for the reporters. Clinton's mission was followed by a thaw in relations between North and South Korea. Conciliatory gestures by the North included the release of several South Korean detainees, an easing of restrictions on family visits and commercial traffic, and the sending of a high-level delegation to attend the funeral in Seoul Aug. 23 of former South Korean Pres. Kim Dae Jung.

Typhoon Morakot Batters Taiwan—Typhoon Morakot dumped more than 80 inches of rain on Taiwan, Aug. 7-9, causing floods and mudslides that left at least 700 people dead or missing. The tropical storm was also blamed for the deaths of 23 people in the Philippines and at least 8 in China. Domestic criticism of the Taiwan government's handling of evacuation and rescue operations led Prime Min. Liu Chao-shiuan to submit his resignation Sept. 7. Pres. Ma Ying-jeou named Wu Den-yih, the general secretary of the ruling Kuomintang party, as the new prime minister.

Myanmar Frees Jailed American; Aung San Suu Kyi Detention Extended—Visiting Myanmar (formerly Burma) Aug. 14-16, Sen. Jim Webb (D, VA), chairman of the U.S. Senate Foreign Relations Subcommittee on East Asian and Pacific Affairs, succeeded in winning the release of a U.S. citizen, John Yettaw, who had been detained by Myanmar's military government. The episode began May 3, when Yettaw entered Myanmar's capital of Yangon, swam across a lake, and showed up uninvited at the home of Nobel Peace Prize winner and political prisoner Aung San Suu Kyi, who had been held there for years under house arrest. On Aug. 11 he received a 7-year prison sentence for breaking immigration laws and violating the terms of her detention. The same military court sentenced Aung San Suu Kyi to 3 years of hard labor, but Gen. Than Shwe, the head of Myanmar's ruling junta, almost immediately commuted the terms to house arrest for up to an additional 18 months.

Scotland Releases Lockerbie Bomber—Abdel Basset Ali al-Megrahi received a jubilant welcome Aug. 20 at Libya's Tripoli airport after Scottish authorities freed the former Libyan agent, who had been imprisoned for his role in the 1988 bombing of Pan Am Flight 103. The aircraft blew up over Lockerbie, Scotland, killing 259 people on the plane (including 189 Americans) and 11 on the ground. The ailing Megrahi, who had received a life sentence in 2001, was ostensibly freed on humanitarian grounds, although British Justice Min. Jack Straw acknowledged in a *Daily Telegraph* interview published Sept. 5 that the prospect of improved economic cooperation with Libya, a major oil and natural gas producer, had played a part in the British government's decision not to exclude Megrahi from a prisoner transfer agreement.

Ruling Party Routed in Japan—The Liberal Democratic Party (LDP), which had dominated Japanese politics almost continuously since the mid-1950s, suffered a devastating defeat in parliamentary elections Aug. 30. With the economy shrinking and unemployment rising, the Democratic Party of Japan (DPJ) increased its representation in the 480-seat lower house of the Diet from 112 to 308 seats, while the LDP plunged from 303 to 119 seats. DPJ leader Yukio Hatoyama, who had pledged to boost social welfare benefits, raise low birth rates, strengthen trade and diplomatic ties with the rest of Asia, and lessen the nation's dependence on the U.S., replaced LDP leader Taro Aso as prime min. Sept. 16. Twelve days later, the LDP chose a new leader, former Finance Min. Sadakazu Tanigaki.

Afghan Election, Iraq Bombings Challenge U.S. War Strategies—Pres. Hamid Karzai of Afghanistan sought a second term Aug. 20 in national elections that U.S. strategists hoped would produce a clear mandate for a strengthened central government in Kabul. Fragmentary tallies, announced Aug. 26 and based on ballots from 17% of polling stations, gave Karzai a lead of 45% to 35% over his main rival, former Foreign Min. Abdullah Abdullah. More worrisome than the slow count, however, were reports of massive vote rigging, most of it apparently in Karzai's favor. Preliminary results released Sept. 8 showed Karzai with more than 50% of the total vote—enough to avoid a runoff against Abdullah—but the UN-backed Electoral Complaints Commission called for a recount, citing "clear and convincing evidence of fraud" at numerous polling stations. Taliban violence escalated throughout the month, including attacks that killed at least 30 people on election day, and a car bombing in Kandahar Aug. 25 that left 43 people dead and more than 65 wounded. Coalition troop fatalities during the month numbered 77, of whom 51 came from the U.S. As of Sept. 1, the total number of U.S. and coalition fatalities in 2009 were both higher than in any previous entire year since the war began in 2001.

In Iraq, meanwhile, war-related violence rose to the highest level in more than a year, according to official figures. The Iraqi death toll of 456 (including 393 civilians) represented a 66% increase over the July total. In one attack, on Aug. 19, 2 huge truck bombs at the Foreign and Finance ministries, in the heart of Baghdad, killed at least 95 people and wounded nearly 600. With American troops no longer providing security in Iraqi cities and towns, the number of U.S. military fatalities dropped to 7, the lowest single-month total since the war began in 2003.

General

Yang Upsets Woods to Win PGA Golf Championship—In one of the most startling reversals in golf history, 110th-ranked Y. E. Yang of South Korea overtook Tiger Woods in the concluding round Aug. 16 to win the PGA Championship at Hazeltine National Golf Club in Chaska, MN. Yang's 70 strokes on the final 18-holes gave him an 8-under-par 280 for the tournament, while Woods scored a 75 on the round, including bogeys on the last 2 holes, to finish 3 strokes behind at 283. Woods's previous record in major championships had been a perfect 14-for-14 when leading after the third round. Yang became the first Asian-born male to win one of golf's 4 major championships.

Bolt Shatters Sprint Records—Jamaican sprinter Usain Bolt broke his own world marks for the 100 and 200 meters at the International Association of Athletics Federations (IAAF) World Championships, held Aug. 15-23 in Berlin, Germany. His 100-m time of 9.58 seconds on Aug. 16 sliced 0.11 second off his record-setting pace at the 2008 Olympics in Beijing, and his 200-m mark of 19.19 on Aug. 20 was also 0.11 second faster than his gold-medal-winning 2008 Olympic pace.

September 2009

National

Economic Reports Raise Fears of Jobless Recovery— Data compiled by the U.S. Bureau of Labor Statistics showed that employers cut about 216,000 jobs in Aug. and 263,000 jobs in Sept., raising the nationwide unemployment rate to 9.8%. Unemployment among Hispanics reached 12.7%, African Americans 15.4%, and teenagers of any ethnicity 25.9%. The states hardest hit were Michigan with 15.3% unemployment (much of it attributable to the ailing auto industry and reverberations in dependent industries), Nevada 13.3%, Rhode Island 13.0%, and California 12.2%. On Sept. 15, Federal Reserve Chairman Ben Bernanke said that the recession, which began in Dec. 2007, was "very likely over," but he added that "it's still going to feel like a very weak economy for some time, as many people will still find that their job security and their employment status is not what they wish it was."

Bank lending, especially to small businesses, continued to be a problem. On Sept. 29 the Federal Deposit Insurance Corp. (FDIC) called on member banks to prepay their fees for the 4th quarter of 2009 and for years 2010 through 2012, to provide the FDIC with the $45 bil cash infusion it would need to protect depositors against future bank failures. The number of insolvent banks closed by the FDIC exceeded 100 by Oct. 23, more than 4 times the total for all of 2008.

Stocks maintained their upward trend, with the Dow Jones Industrial Average closing Sept. 30 at 9,712.28, an increase of about 15% for the July-Sept. quarter. The S&P 500 (1,057.08) and Nasdaq Composite Index (2,122.42) showed similar quarterly gains.

Arson Suspected in California Wildfire—Investigators for the U.S. Forest Service and Los Angeles County determined Sept. 3 that the Station Fire, one of the largest wildfires in the modern history of southern California, had been deliberately set. The Station Fire, which began Aug. 26 near a ranger station in Angeles National Forest, spread quickly because of dry conditions and record heat. Of the more than 5,200 firefighters involved in suppressing the blaze, 2 were killed Aug. 30 when their vehicle plunged down an embankment. By Sept. 26, when the wildfire was 98% contained, it had burned 160,577 acres and destroyed 89 homes. The blaze was classified as 100% contained Oct. 16.

Undercover Videos Lead to ACORN Funding Cuts— The Association of Community Organizations for Reform Now (ACORN), long a target of conservative attacks, came under increased scrutiny after videos purportedly showing ACORN employees counseling illegal activity were widely viewed on television and online. The unfavorable publicity led the Census Bureau, Sept. 11, and Internal Revenue Service, Sept. 23, to terminate their partnerships with the group, and the House and Senate, Sept. 14-17, to pass measures barring federal funding for the organization.

The video makers, conservative activists Hannah Giles and James E. O'Keefe III, used a hidden camera to record workers at several ACORN offices providing advice on how to evade taxes, launder money, and smuggle underage, illegal immigrants from El Salvador to work in a brothel. While acknowledging that some employees had acted improperly, ACORN officials claimed that workers in other locations not shown in the circulated videos had thrown out the couple and called the police.

Founded in Little Rock, AR, in 1970, ACORN had grown into the largest community organizing group in the U.S., with some 400,000 members in 105 cities. The group drew criticism in 2008 when it became known that workers hired to register new voters had inserted fictitious names like Mickey Mouse and Donald Duck on sign-up sheets. Several major private foundations had stopped funding ACORN during 2008-09 before the video exposés surfaced.

Trumka Becomes AFL-CIO President—Richard L. Trumka, a former coal miner, was elected president of the AFL-CIO Sept. 16, replacing the retiring John Sweeney, who had headed the nation's largest labor federation since 1995. Trumka, who ran unopposed, had led the United Mine Workers from 1982 to 1995, when he was elected AFL-CIO secretary-treasurer. With Trumka's elevation to the presidency, Liz Shuler was elected secretary-treasurer, becoming the highest-ranking woman in the history of the AFL-CIO. Although union membership in the U.S. has declined in recent decades, the AFL-CIO (comprising 57 unions with some 8.5 mil members) retains considerable political muscle.

Zazi Accused in Bomb Plot—Federal prosecutors Sept. 24 charged Najibullah Zazi, a 24-year-old airport shuttle driver in Denver, CO, with plotting to turn chemicals he purchased at beauty supply stores into homemade bombs that could be used in terror attacks against buses and subways. He had been arrested in Denver along with his father Sept. 19. Prosecutors alleged that the Afghan-born Zazi, a legal U.S. resident, had learned bomb-making techniques at an al-Qaeda training camp in Pakistan in 2008 and had then conspired to use readily available chemicals to carry out mass-transit bombings similar to ones in Madrid in 2004 and London in 2005. Through an attorney, Zazi Sept. 29 pleaded not guilty in federal court in Brooklyn, NY. At a Justice Dept. press briefing Oct. 6, U.S. Atty. Gen. Eric Holder called the alleged plot "one of the most serious terrorist threats to our country since Sept. 11, 2001."

International

As Setbacks Accumulate, U.S. Reviews Afghan War Strategy—With evidence mounting of election fraud in Afghanistan's Aug. 20 presidential election, the U.S. and its NATO allies faced additional challenges in the nearly 8-year-old Afghan war. Fighting in the southern region remained intense, and the Taliban had stepped up attacks in the formerly quiet northern and western regions. NATO counterattacks contributed to a rise in civilian casualties. In the northern province of Kunduz, an official inquiry determined that a NATO air strike on 2 hijacked fuel tanker trucks Sept. 4 killed 30 civilians along with 69 Taliban fighters. On Sept. 15, Adm. Mike Mullen, chairman of the U.S. Joint Chiefs of Staff, told members of the Senate Armed Services Committee that "a properly resourced counterinsurgency probably means more forces." The White House Sept. 29 launched a full-scale strategic review of its Afghanistan strategy after the top U.S. commander there, Gen. Stanley McChrystal, reportedly submitted a request for 40,000 troops, in addition to the 68,000 U.S. troops already committed. During the month, the U.S. accounted for 59 of the 76 coalition fatalities in the Afghan war; 8 U.S. military personnel died in Iraq in the same period.

Former Taiwan President Gets Life Sentence—Jailed on corruption charges since Nov. 2008, former Pres. Chen Shui-bian of Taiwan was convicted Sept. 11 of embezzlement, bribe taking, and money laundering. Chen, who had held office from May 2000 to May 2008, received a sentence of life imprisonment as did his wife, Wu Shu-chen, who was also convicted of corruption. In addition, they were fined more than $15 mil. The former president and first lady were accused of taking more than $3 mil from a special presidential fund and accepting more than $12 mil in bribes and kickbacks.

U.S. Scraps Plans for Missile Shield in Eastern Europe—The Obama administration Sept. 17 announced it was canceling plans for a ground-based antiballistic missile system in Eastern Europe and said it would no longer seek to place 10 ballistic missile interceptors in Poland and to build a radar facility in the Czech Republic. The missile shield, favored by the Bush administration as a way to protect the U.S. and its allies against long-range missiles from Iran and other "rogue states," had aroused opposition from Russian leaders, who saw the system as a threat to Russia's own nuclear arsenal. The Obama administration's revised defense strategy relied for the most part on currently available radar and antimissile technologies based on Navy vessels to be deployed in the eastern Mediterranean and the North Sea. The deployment would target Iranian short- and medium-range missiles (see below), which the U.S. intelligence community viewed as a more immediate threat to NATO allies, Israel, and U.S. troops deployed in the Middle East.

Iran Nuclear Disclosure Overshadows G-20 Summit—
Meeting Sept. 24-25 in Pittsburgh, PA, leaders of the Group
of 20 (G-20), comprising the world's major industrialized
and emerging economies, agreed on measures intended to
enhance global economic cooperation, including a system of
"peer reviews" through which individual countries would be
encouraged to adjust their policies in ways that promoted
worldwide economic stability. Conferees also agreed on the
need to phase out government subsidies that encouraged
production and consumption of fossil fuels, but no firm
timetable was set.

The summit agenda was overshadowed by a joint televised
appearance on the morning of Sept. 25 at which Pres. Obama,
British Prime Min. Gordon Brown, and French Pres. Nicolas
Sarkozy accused Iran of building a secret uranium enrichment
facility near Qom. The nuclear site, a mountain tunnel complex about 115 mi southwest of Tehran, had reportedly been
known for years to U.S. intelligence services, but Iran had not
formally notified the International Atomic Energy Agency
(IAEA) of its existence until Sept. 21. Iranian Pres. Mahmoud
Ahmadinejad, who was in New York City for a UN summit
session, denied that Iran had violated international laws and
described the Qom complex as a "very ordinary facility in the
beginning stages."

Controversy over the nuclear site immediately preceded a
series of Iranian tests of short- and medium-range missiles
and the resumption, Oct. 1, of nuclear talks between Iran and
the West. In face-to-face negotiations, Iran agreed to open
the Qom facility to IAEA monitors, who arrived at the installation Oct. 25. Negotiators also reached tentative agreement on a proposal to ship the bulk of Iran's stockpile of
enriched uranium to Russia and France, where it would be
reprocessed into fuel, otherwise unsuitable for use in atomic
weapons, for a Tehran medical research reactor.

Typhoon, Earthquakes Strike Pacific Region—A series
of natural disasters battered Pacific nations extending from
Samoa to Vietnam. Typhoon Ketsana, Sept. 26-Oct. 1,
crossed the Philippines (where the storm was known as On-
doy) before slamming into Southeast Asia. According to
damage assessments released Oct. 30, the most casualties
were in the Philippines, with 464 confirmed dead and 37
missing, and Vietnam, with 163 killed and 11 missing. An
8.0 magnitude undersea earthquake and tsunami Sept. 29
claimed at least 143 lives in Samoa and 9 in Tonga, according to UN data compiled Oct. 22; confirmed fatalities on the
U.S. territory of American Samoa totaled 32 as of Oct. 12.
Padang, Sumatra, in Indonesia, was hit Sept. 30 by a magnitude 7.6 quake, which triggered mudslides in the region. Official estimates Oct. 28 put the numbers killed at nearly
1,200 and houses destroyed at about 119,000.

Merkel Reelected in Germany—Aided by signs that
Germany had emerged from recession, the Christian Democrats, led by Chancellor Angela Merkel, won parliamentary
elections Sept. 27. Merkel's party captured 239 seats in the
622-member Bundestag, the lower house of parliament, easily defeating the Social Democrats, who took only 146 seats,
a drop of 76 since the 2005 elections. To form a majority
government, the Christian Democrats turned to the pro-business Free Democratic Party (FDP), which won 93 seats in
the Bundestag, a gain of 32. The Christian Democrats and
the FDP agreed Oct. 24 on a legislative program that included a 24 bil euro tax cut to stimulate economic growth.
FDP leader Guido Westerwelle, the highest-ranking openly
gay man in German politics, was sworn in Oct. 28 as the
new cabinet's foreign minister.

General

Clijsters, Del Potro Take U.S. Open Tennis Titles—
Playing in only her third tournament since returning from a 2-
year hiatus, Kim Clijsters of Belgium won her second U.S.
Open women's singles championship Sept. 13, defeating Caroline Wozniacki of Denmark, 7-5, 6-3, at Arthur Ashe Stadium in Flushing, NY. Clijsters, an unseeded, wild-card entry,
reached the finals by dethroning 2008 winner Serena Williams in a tense semifinal lost by Williams when she was penalized for unsportsmanlike conduct for venting her fury at a
line judge who had called a foot fault against her. Williams,

who was fined $10,000 for the outburst (and another $500 for
angrily mangling her racket at the end of her first set against
Clijsters) posted an apology on her website Sept. 14, as she
and her sister Venus won the U.S. Open women's doubles title. Later that day, Juan Martín del Potro of Argentina won his
first Grand Slam title, snapping Roger Federer's streak of 5
consecutive U.S. Open men's crowns by overpowering the
Swiss champion, 3-6, 7-6 (5), 4-6, 7-6 (4), 6-2.

Anglo-Saxon Treasures Discovered—One of the most
important finds in British archaeological history was announced Sept. 24 at the Birmingham Museums and Art Gallery in England. The treasure hoard, including more than
1,500 finely crafted gold, silver, and copper artifacts, was
uncovered in July by an amateur, Terry Herbert, while using
a metal detector to search a Staffordshire field owned by a
friend. Experts theorized that the items may have been plundered and then buried by 7th-cent. rulers of the Anglo-Saxon
kingdom of Mercia.

Filmmaker Roman Polanski Arrested—Film director
Roman Polanski, 76, was detained by Swiss authorities Sept.
26 as he arrived in Zürich to accept a lifetime achievement
award from the Zürich Film Festival. Polanski, a Polish and
French citizen, was wanted on an international arrest warrant stemming from a 1977 U.S. case in which he was accused of drugging and raping a 13-year-old girl during a
Hollywood modeling shoot. He had pled guilty to a reduced
charge of unlawful sexual intercourse. After serving 42 days
of his 90-day jail sentence, he was released on the recommendation of a psychiatric evaluator and subsequently fled
the U.S. in Feb. 1978. Although Polanski and the victim
agreed in 1993 on a $500,000 civil settlement, L.A. law en-
forcement still considered him a fugitive from justice. Twice
nominated for Academy Awards for directing *Chinatown*
(1974) and *Tess* (1980), Polanski won the Best Director Oscar for *The Pianist* (2002), a Holocaust drama.

October 2009

National

Regulators Focus on Distracted Drivers, Pilots—
Transportation Sec. Ray LaHood announced Oct. 1 that, under an executive order signed by Pres. Barack Obama, some
4.5 mil federal employees, including military personnel,
were barred from text messaging, or texting, while driving.
LaHood said the Obama administration would also seek to
ban bus drivers and truckers on interstate routes from texting
while operating their vehicles. Concern about the problem of
distracted driving had grown since the publication in July of
a Virginia Tech Transportation Institute study showing that
truck drivers increased their collision risk 23-fold when they
took their eyes off the road while texting on their cell
phones. LaHood's announcement came at the close of a 2-
day Distracted Driving Summit sponsored by the Transportation Dept. in Washington, DC.

The problem of distracted flying came into clearer focus
Oct. 21 when Northwest Airlines Flight 188, a Minneapolis-
bound Airbus A320 carrying 149 passengers and crew, over-
shot its destination by 150 miles. The Federal Aviation Administration revoked the licenses of the jetliner's 2 pilots
Oct. 27 after the men said they had become distracted while
working on their laptop computers.

Pres. Obama Receives Nobel Peace Prize—Citing his
"extraordinary efforts to strengthen international diplomacy
and cooperation between peoples" and his "vision of and
work for a world without nuclear weapons," the Norwegian
Nobel Committee Oct. 9 awarded the Nobel Peace Prize for
2009 to Pres. Barack Obama. Obama was the third sitting
U.S. president to receive the award, following Theodore
Roosevelt (1906) and Woodrow Wilson (1919); a fourth
U.S. head of state, Jimmy Carter (2002), was honored long
after he left the White House. Obama said he was "surprised
and deeply humbled" by the award, which came after he had
been in office for less than 9 months.

Justice Dept. Eases Policy on Medical Marijuana—In a
memo to prosecutors Oct. 19, the Justice Dept. advised that
"efficient use of limited federal resources" precluded enforcement of federal anti-marijuana statutes against people

who used or provided marijuana for medical purposes where allowed by state law. (More than a dozen states have authorized use of the federally banned drug when prescribed by a doctor to patients with cancer or other serious illnesses.) The new Justice Dept. guidelines represented a reversal of a Bush administration policy under which federal agents had continued to raid state-sanctioned medical-marijuana dispensaries. The memo, signed by Deputy Atty. Gen. David W. Ogden, emphasized that enforcement of drug laws against criminal enterprises, gangs, cartels, and other commercial traffickers continued to be a federal priority. On Oct. 21-22, in raids carried out in 38 cities in 19 states, federal agents arrested more than 300 people connected with La Familia, a violent Mexican drug cartel that sold methamphetamine, cocaine, and other drugs to U.S. buyers in exchange for cash and guns.

$680 Bil Defense Measure Expands Law Against Hate Crimes—Pres. Obama signed into law Oct. 28 a bill appropriating $550 bil for Pentagon operations in the 2010 fiscal year and another $130 bil for the wars in Iraq and Afghanistan. The bill had passed the House Oct. 8 by a vote of 281-146 and cleared the Senate Oct. 22 by a margin of 68-29. Incorporated in the legislation was an expanded hate-crimes measure that, for the first time, made it a federal crime to assault someone because of that person's sexual orientation or gender identity. At the White House signing ceremony, Obama noted that during the previous 10 years more than 12,000 hate crimes based on sexual orientation had been reported. In a speech Oct. 10 at a Washington, DC, fundraising dinner for the Human Rights Campaign, an advocacy group for lesbian, gay, bisexual, and transgender equality, Obama had described his commitment to homosexual rights as "unwavering" and repeated his pledge to end the military's "don't ask, don't tell" policy prohibiting openly gay men and women from serving in the military. On Oct. 30, Obama announced that he would end long-standing U.S. travel and immigration restrictions on people infected with HIV, the virus that causes AIDS.

U.S. Emerges from Recession, but Problems Remain—The Commerce Dept.'s Bureau of Economic Analysis reported Oct. 29 that real gross domestic product increased at an annual rate of 3.5% during July-Sept. The 3rd-quarter GDP growth signaled that key sectors of the U.S. economy had emerged from recession. Much of the growth stemmed from government efforts to stimulate consumer spending, including an $8,000 federal tax credit for first-time home buyers and the "cash for clunkers" credit. With major financial firms returning to profitability, the Obama administration announced plans to cut the pay of top executives at 7 companies that had received taxpayer bailouts and to limit compensation practices that encouraged bankers to take excessive risks.

Reflecting the more optimistic investment climate, the Dow Jones Industrial Average closed above the 10,000 mark Oct. 14 for the first time in about a year. The markets retrenched during the latter half of the month, with the Dow finishing Oct. 30 at 9,712.73, the S&P 500 at 1,036.19, and the Nasdaq Composite Index at 2,045.11.

Unemployment remained a serious concern. Christina Romer, head of the White House Council of Economic Advisers, warned in congressional testimony Oct. 22 that the unemployment rate would probably be at or above 10% in early 2010 and would likely remain at a "severely elevated level" through the remainder of that year. The White House claimed Oct. 30 that the $787 bil American Recovery and Reinvestment Act, passed in Feb., had created or saved some 640,000 jobs through the end of Sept., of which about 325,000 were in education and 80,000 in construction.

International

IMF Forecasts World Economic Recovery—In its quarterly *World Economic Outlook*, issued Oct. 1, the International Monetary Fund said that after a "deep global recession," expansion of the world economy had resumed. Global economic activity, which had contracted by about 1.1% in 2009, was expected to increase about 3.1% in 2010. Asia remained the most dynamic region, with China's economy expected to grow by 9.0% and India's by 6.4% in 2010.

Recovery was expected to be sluggish in areas hit hard by the 2009 recession, including Russia, whose economy shrank by 7.5% in 2009, Japan (–5.4%), Germany (–5.3%), and Italy (–5.1%). Both Germany and Japan had returned to positive territory by the summer of 2009. On Oct. 6, Australia, where a robust recovery raised inflation fears, became the first member of the Group of 20 to raise interest rates since the onset of the world financial crisis in 2008.

Irish Vote Paves Way for Ratification of EU's Lisbon Treaty—By a margin of 67%-33%, Irish voters in a referendum Oct. 2 endorsed a plan to transform the governing structure of the European Union. The plan, known as the Lisbon Treaty, provides for the appointment of a full-time European president, strengthening of the EU's foreign ministry, and revision of voting procedures so that fewer decisions require unanimous consent from the 27 current EU member countries. Irish voters had rejected the measure 53%-47% in a previous referendum June 2008. Following Ireland's approval, Polish Pres. Lech Kaczynski signed the treaty Oct. 10. The ratification process was completed Nov. 3 when Czech Pres. Vaclav Klaus signed the EU document after his nation's Constitutional Court advised him that the Lisbon Treaty did not conflict with the Czech constitution.

Socialists Win Election in Greece—The Panhellenic Socialist Movement, known as PASOK, won a landslide victory in Greek elections Oct. 4, taking 160 seats in the 300-member parliament. The PASOK triumph ended 5 1/2 years of rule by the center-right New Democracy Party, which had been plagued by financial scandals as well as a global economic downturn that hurt Greece's tourism and shipping industries. U.S.-born George Papandreou, the PASOK leader whose father and grandfather had headed previous Greek governments, was sworn in Oct. 6 as prime min. He pledged to streamline government, crack down on tax evasion, and revive the economy with a $4.4 bil stimulus program.

Armenia and Turkey Agree to Normalize Relations—Aided by last-minute intervention from U.S. Sec. of State Hillary Clinton, officials from Armenia and Turkey, meeting Oct. 10 in Zürich, Switzerland, agreed to establish diplomatic ties between the 2 countries. Accords also called for reopening of the Turkish-Armenian border, closed since 1993, and establishing bilateral committees to work on economic, environmental, and other issues. Swiss, French, Russian, and U.S. officials had cooperated on efforts to improve Turkish-Armenian relations, which were clouded by longstanding bitterness over the killing of more than 1 mil Armenians by Ottoman Turks in 1915-18. The Oct. 10 agreements, which await parliamentary approval in both countries, provided for the establishment of an international commission to document the extent of the massacres, which most scholars regard as genocide.

Toll from Global Swine Flu Pandemic Rises—The World Health Organization reported Oct. 30 that more than 440,000 cases of "swine flu"—formally known as pandemic influenza A (H1N1)—had been confirmed through laboratory testing. WHO stated that as of Oct. 25 at least 5,700 deaths worldwide were attributable to the disease. Most countries had reported confirmed cases of H1N1. Areas where the incidence of influenza-like illnesses was especially high included Mexico, the U.S., parts of western Canada, and some countries in the Caribbean and Western Europe. Russia reported its first swine flu deaths Oct. 27.

According to the Centers for Disease Control and Prevention (CDC) in Atlanta, GA, as of Oct. 27 more than 12,400 people in the U.S. had been hospitalized for swine flu since the outbreak began. The death toll through Oct. 24 was 530, with 114 of the victims being children under 18. CDC Dir. Thomas R. Frieden said the U.S. figures were likely underestimates and that "many, many millions" of Americans had been infected with the H1N1 virus. Pres. Obama declared the H1N1 pandemic a national emergency Oct. 24, which administration officials explained would give hospitals greater flexibility in dealing with any influxes of new patients. Because of manufacturing delays, swine flu vaccine deliveries in the U.S. were behind schedule; only some 23 mil doses of the vaccine were available by Oct. 26, less than had been anticipated.

U.S. Revises Policy on Sudan—After months of internal debate, the Obama administration announced Oct. 19 a revised policy toward Sudan, where an estimated 300,000 people, many of them civilians, have been killed in a 6-year-long conflict in the western region of Darfur. The administration said it would renew sanctions against Sudan, whose president, Omar Hassan Ahmad Al-Bashir, has been charged with war crimes and other crimes against humanity by the International Criminal Court in The Hague, Netherlands. But the new U.S. policy also called for engagement with the Sudanese government to end the fighting in Darfur, combat international terrorism, and fully implement a 2005 peace accord halting a long civil war between northern and southern Sudan. Violence had been increasing in the south, where most of Sudan's oil reserves are located and where a referendum on self-determination is scheduled for 2011.

Karzai Wins by Default; Other Afghanistan, Pakistan, Iraq War Developments—While Pres. Obama considered whether to commit additional U.S. troops to Afghanistan and how rapidly to pull American forces out of Iraq, events both on and off the battlefield made the decisions increasingly difficult. In Afghanistan, the UN-backed Electoral Complaints Commission threw out hundreds of thousands of ballots from the Aug. 20 presidential election because of apparent fraud; the nation's own Independent Election Commission (IEC) ruled Oct. 20 that incumbent Pres. Hamid Karzai had won 49.7% of the vote—just under the 50% he needed to avoid a runoff. Bowing to U.S. pressure, a reluctant Karzai agreed to a Nov. 7 runoff vote against second-place finisher former Foreign Min. Abdullah Abdullah. On Nov. 1, however, Abdullah withdrew from the runoff, claiming that a "transparent election is not possible." The IEC declared Karzai the winner the following day. Afghan and U.S. views of Karzai were further complicated by an Oct. 28 *New York Times* report alleging that the president's brother, Ahmed Wali Karzai, long suspected of involvement in Afghanistan's opium trade, had received payments from the U.S. Central Intelligence Agency over the past 8 years. As the Afghan conflict entered its ninth year, Oct. became the deadliest month so far for U.S. forces, with 59 fatalities; the military death toll for other coalition members was 16.

On Oct. 14, Pres. Obama signed legislation tripling U.S. economic aid to Pakistan. Final approval of the 5-year, $7.5 bil measure came just 3 days before more than 30,000 Pakistani troops launched a full-scale ground assault against Taliban and al-Qaeda strongholds in the mountainous border region of South Waziristan. On Oct. 28, the same day U.S. Sec. of State Hillary Clinton arrived in Islamabad for talks with Pakistani leaders, insurgents in Pakistan carried out a car bombing that killed at least 118 people at a crowded market in Peshawar, and Taliban militants in Afghanistan killed 5 UN employees and 3 others in an attack on a UN guesthouse in Kabul.

Baghdad experienced its bloodiest day since 2007 as a van and a minibus, both laden with explosives, penetrated security checkpoints Oct. 25 and blew up in the heart of the Iraqi capital. The blasts killed at least 155 people, wounded more than 500, and devastated the Ministry of Justice, the Ministry of Municipalities and Public Works, and the Baghdad Provincial Council building. Nine U.S. troops were killed in the Iraq war in Oct., raising the cumulative total to more than 4,350 since the war began in Mar. 2003.

General

"Ardi" Marks Breakthrough in Study of Human Ancestry—In press conferences Oct. 1 in Washington, DC, and Addis Ababa, Ethiopia, and through 11 papers published in the online edition of *Science*, an international scientific team introduced the world to "Ardi," a nearly complete skeleton of an early human ancestor dating from about 4.4 mil years ago. Ardi—short for *Ardipithecus ramidus*—was female, stood about 4 feet tall, weighed about 110 pounds, had grasping feet (with thumb-like big toes) well suited for tree climbing, and an upper pelvis that would have allowed her to walk upright. Scientists spent more than 15 years analyzing and assembling Ardi, whose remains were found in an ancient woodland region, now an arid floodplain, of Ethiopia. Ardi predates the famed "Lucy" skeleton, also found in Ethiopia, by about 1.2 mil years.

Letterman Reports Extortion Attempt—David Letterman, host of *The Late Show* on CBS, told viewers Oct. 1 he had been the target of an extortion attempt involving his sexual liaisons with female staff members. Three weeks earlier, Letterman said, a would-be blackmailer who threatened to publicly disclose evidence of Letterman's affairs unless the TV comic paid him $2 mil. Letterman admitted to the affairs but reported the blackmail threat to New York City prosecutors and testified before a grand jury. On Oct. 2 the accused extortionist, CBS News producer Robert Joel Halderman, pleaded not guilty to a charge of attempted grand larceny.

Brazil Will Host 2016 Olympics—Meeting in Copenhagen, Denmark, the International Olympic Committee Oct. 2 chose Rio de Janeiro, Brazil, as the site of the 2016 Olympic Games. Rio, the first South American city to host the games, won out over of Madrid, Tokyo, and Chicago, whose bid had the personal support of Michelle and Barack Obama. Brazil's excitement over the Rio selection was dampened by a sudden spike in drug-related violence in the city's *favelas*, or shantytowns, which claimed 33 lives Oct. 17-21.

NASA Tests for Lunar Water; Ares I-X Rocket Launched—The National Aeronautics and Space Administration (NASA) deliberately crashed a bus-sized piece of space junk into the lunar surface Oct. 9 in an effort to determine whether permanently shadowed lunar craters held significant deposits of water ice. The Lunar CRater Observation and Sensing Satellite mission, known as LCROSS, had been launched June 18 along with NASA's Lunar Reconnaissance Orbiter. Despite initial doubts about the success of the mission, LCROSS images released Oct. 16 showed a mile-high plume of debris above the lunar surface. NASA reported it would take weeks to finish analyzing the data.

On Oct. 28 at the Kennedy Space Center in Florida, NASA made its initial launch of the Ares I-X rocket. The tall, slim Ares I-X is a prototype of the Ares I system that NASA scientists hope will carry astronauts to the International Space Station by 2014.

Criminal Charges Sought in "Balloon Boy" Hoax—Breathless reports of a 6-year-old boy adrift thousands of feet above the Colorado landscape enthralled millions of viewers Oct. 15, as emergency vehicles and TV cameras raced for nearly 3 hours in pursuit of a homemade helium balloon before it crumpled to the ground near Denver International Airport. Authorities examining the balloon's remains found no trace of the boy since, his parents later said, he had been hiding in the attic of his family's garage the whole time. Three days later, Larimer County (CO) Sheriff Jim Alderden called the entire episode a "hoax" and "publicity stunt" and said he would recommend criminal charges against the parents.

Vatican Seeks to Attract Disaffected Anglicans—At a Vatican press conference Oct. 20, Cardinal William J. Levada announced that Pope Benedict XVI had established a new path for groups of disaffected Anglicans, troubled by their church's growing acceptance of female priests and bishops and of openly gay clergy, to embrace the Roman Catholic Church. Cardinal Levada, prefect of the Congregation for the Doctrine of the Faith, said that under a new apostolic constitution, groups of Anglicans entering the Catholic fold would be allowed to preserve "elements of the distinctive Anglican spiritual and liturgical patrimony," including married men serving as priests. The new Anglican rite within the Catholic Church would allow for significant numbers of married Anglican clergy to be ordained as Catholic priests, but only unmarried clergy would be permitted to serve as bishops.

OBITUARIES

Deaths, Nov. 1, 2008-Oct. 31, 2009

A

Ackerman, Forrest J., 92, magazine editor and literary agent in the science fiction, horror, and fantasy genres, who edited the influential pulp magazine *Famous Monsters of Filmland* (1958-83); Los Angeles, CA, Dec. 4, 2008.

Adenhart, Nick, 22, starting pitcher for the Los Angeles Angels of Anaheim (2008-09) with a promising career; Fullerton, CA, Apr. 9, 2009.

Albano, Lou, 76, pro wrestler and manager who later launched an acting career; Carmel, NY, Oct. 14, 2009.

Albury, Charles Donald, 88, World War II aviator who copiloted the bomber that dropped the atom bomb on Nagasaki, Japan, on Aug. 9, 1945; Miami, FL, May 23, 2009.

Aleksy II, 79, Patriarch of the Russian Orthodox Church who restored his institution as the largest Orthodox church in the world; Peredelkino, Russia, Dec. 5, 2008.

Allingham, Henry William, 113, British veteran of WW I; last surviving original member of the Royal Air Force (RAF); Brighton, England, July 18, 2009.

Anderson, Robert Woodruff, 91, playwright and screenwriter best known for his play *Tea and Sympathy*; NYC, Feb. 9, 2009.

Annenberg, Leonore, 91, arts patron and philanthropist who briefly served as U.S. chief of protocol under Pres. Ronald Reagan; Rancho Mirage, CA, Mar. 12, 2009.

Aquino, Corazon C., 76, pres. of the Philippines, 1986-92, who withstood many coup attempts and military revolts and restored democratic institutions after the reign of Ferdinand Marcos; Makati City, Philippines, Aug. 1, 2009.

Archerd, Army (Armand Andre), 87, longtime columnist for the entertainment trade magazine *Daily Variety* (1953-2005); Los Angeles, CA, Sept. 8, 2009.

Arneson, Dave (David Lance), 61, creator, with Gary Gygax, of the role-playing game Dungeons & Dragons (1974); St. Paul, MN, Apr. 7, 2009.

Arthur, Bea(trice), 86, deep-voiced actress who starred in two long-running TV sitcoms, *Maude* (1972-78) and *The Golden Girls* (1985-92), and on Broadway in *Fiddler on the Roof* (1964) and *Mame* (1966), for which she won a Tony Award; Los Angeles, CA, Apr. 25, 2009.

Asheton, Ron(ald), 60, guitarist with the Stooges, a band which helped set the stage for the evolution of punk rock; Ann Arbor, MI, Jan. 6, 2009.

Ashley, Sir Bernard, 82, British entrepreneur who, with wife Laura Ashley, founded the international textiles, clothing, and home furnishings empire that bore her name; Elan Valley, Wales, Feb. 14, 2009.

Atkins, Susan, 61, follower of cult leader Charles Manson who had been convicted of committing 8 murders, including that of actress Sharon Tate (1969); Central California Women's Facility, Chowchilla, CA, Sept. 24, 2009.

B

Ballard, J(ames) G(raham), 78, British novelist and short story writer whose wide-ranging work included apocalyptic science fiction; best known for his novels *Crash* (1973) and *Empire of the Sun* (1984); London, England, Apr. 19, 2009.

Barnes, Clive, 81, British-born critic of dance and drama at the *NY Times* (1965-78), and *NY Post* (1978-2008); NYC, Nov. 19, 2008.

Baugh, Sammy (Samuel Adrian), 94, football player who was one of 17 charter members of the Pro Football Hall of Fame (1963); Rotan, TX, Dec. 17, 2008.

Bausch, Pina (Philippine), 68, German choreographer; Wuppertal, Germany, June 30, 2009.

Bellows, James G., 86, editor credited with invigorating 3 U.S. papers: the *NY Herald Tribune* (early 1960s), *Washington Star* (1970s), and *LA Herald Examiner* (1978-81); Santa Monica, CA, Mar. 6, 2009.

Bennett, Estelle, 67, member of the 1960s "girl group" the Ronettes; inducted into the Rock and Roll Hall of Fame (2007); Englewood, NJ, Feb. 11, 2009.

Bissinger, Karl, 94, portraitist known for his photographs of leading post-World War II figures; NYC, Nov. 19, 2008.

Blair, Betsy, 85, film actress known for her Academy Award-nominated role in *Marty* (1955); career was cut short when she was blacklisted for her leftist politics; London, England, Mar. 13, 2009.

Bohr, Aage Niels, 87, Danish physicist who was one of 3 winners of the Nobel Prize in physics (1975), honored for showing that atomic nuclei could be distorted by motion of the protons and neutrons within; Copenhagen, Denmark, Sept. 8, 2009.

Bond, J(ames) Max, Jr., 73, African American architect; his firm was responsible for such projects as NYC's Schomberg Center for Research in Black Culture, and the Martin Luther King Center for Nonviolent Social Change in Atlanta, GA; NYC, Feb. 18, 2009.

Bongo, Albert (El Hadj Omar Bongo Ondimba), 73, authoritarian ruler of the African nation of Gabon since 1967; Barcelona, Spain, June 8, 2009.

Borlaug, Norman, 95, Nobel Peace Prize-winning agricultural scientist (1970) who developed improved strains of wheat and rice credited with saving millions of lives in the developing world; Dallas, TX, Sept. 12, 2009.

Brecher, Irving, 94, comedy writer whose lengthy radio, TV, and film career included creating the radio and TV series *The Life of Riley* (1949-50, 1953-58); Los Angeles, CA, Nov. 17, 2008.

Brown, Anne Wiggins, 96, soprano best known for originating the role of Bess in the first production of George Gershwin's folk opera *Porgy and Bess* (1935); Oslo, Norway, Mar. 13, 2009.

C

Calisher, Hortense, 97, writer of complex, elusive fiction and many short stories, which first appeared in *The New Yorker* magazine; NYC, Jan. 13, 2009.

Carasso, Daniel, 103, pioneer in the yogurt business, who founded Danone brand in Europe and Dannon in the U.S.; Paris, France, May 17, 2009.

Carey, Ron(ald Robert), 72, pres. of the Intl. Brotherhood of Teamsters union (1992-97); NYC, Dec. 11, 2008.

Carradine, David (John), 72, actor known for TV series *Kung Fu* (1972-75); appeared in many films, notably Quentin Tarantino's two *Kill Bill* films (2003, 2004); Bangkok, Thailand, June 4, 2009.

Carroll, Jim (James), 60, memoirist, poet, and rock musician; best known for *The Basketball Diaries* (1978); NYC, Sept. 11, 2009.

Chambers, Marilyn (born Marilyn Ann Briggs), 56, actress best known for her work in pornographic films, notably *Behind the Green Door* (1972), which shattered taboos; Santa Clarita, CA, Apr. 12, 2009.

Cohn, Sam(uel), 79, longtime talent agent who represented a host of actors, directors, playwrights, and composers; NYC, May 6, 2009.

Cover, Jack (John), 88, physicist and aerospace scientist who in the late 1960s invented the Taser stun gun; Mission Viejo, CA, Feb. 7, 2009.

Crichton, (John) Michael, 66, best-selling novelist, screenwriter, and director who wrote *Jurassic Park* (1990); created the TV medical drama *ER* (1994); Los Angeles, CA, Nov. 4, 2008.

Cronkite, Walter, 92, TV journalist who anchored the *CBS Evening News* (1962-81); with his avuncular manner and air of trustworthiness, he became a national institution; NYC, July 17, 2009

Cunningham, Merce, 90, choreographer who created some of the most striking and innovative dance works of the 20th century; NYC, July 26, 2009.

D

Daly, Chuck (Charles), 78, basketball coach who guided the NBA's Detroit Pistons to the NBA playoffs 9 seasons in a row (1983-92) and won consecutive NBA championships (1989-90); Jupiter, FL, May 9, 2009.

Dannenberg, Konrad, 96, German-born rocket scientist who played a key role in the development of the Saturn V rockets that propelled U.S. astronauts to the moon; Huntsville, AL, Feb. 16, 2009.

Dean, Millvina, 97, youngest and last survivor of the *Titanic* disaster; 9 weeks old when the ship sank in Apr. 1912; Southampton, England, May 31, 2009.

De Larrocha, Alicia, 86, Spanish pianist known as an exponent of the keyboard music of Spanish composers Enrique Granados, Isaac Albeniz, and Federico Mompou; Barcelona, Spain, Sept. 25, 2009.

Dearie, Blossom, 84, jazz and cabaret singer and pianist known for her delicate, high-pitched voice and understated piano-playing; NYC, Feb. 7, 2009.

DeCarava, Roy, 89, photographer who was known for capturing life in Harlem and for portraits of high-profile black entertainers; NYC, Oct. 27, 2009.

DeLuise, Dom(inick), 75, zany comedian; appeared in films incl. Mel Brooks's *Blazing Saddles* (1974) and *Silent Movie* (1976); Santa Monica, CA, May 4, 2009.

DiMaggio, Dom(inic), 92, baseball player who lived in the shadow of his more famous brother, Joe; Marion, MA, May 8, 2009.

Donald, David Herbert, 88, Civil War historian whose book *Lincoln* (1995) was widely thought of as the definitive one-volume biography of Pres. Abraham Lincoln; twice won the Pulitzer Prize for biography (1961, 1988); Boston, MA, May 17, 2009.

Dreyfus, Jack, Jr., 95, creator, in the early 1950s, of the Dreyfus Fund, which became one of the U.S.'s most successful mutual funds; NYC, Mar. 27, 2009.

Dulles, Cardinal Avery, 90, only U.S. theologian appointed to the College of Cardinals (2001), largely in recognition of his spirited defense of conservative theological principles; Bronx, NY, Dec. 12, 2008.

Dunne, Dominick (John), 83, journalist and author who wrote accounts of high-profile crimes and trials; his work had been a regular feature of *Vanity Fair* magazine since the mid-1980s; NYC, Aug. 26, 2009.

F

Fawcett, Farrah, 62, model and actress whose swimsuit-clad appearance on a poster, and role as one of 3 female detectives in the TV series *Charlie's Angels* (1976-77), made her a 1970s sex symbol; Santa Monica, CA, June 25, 2009.

Felt, W(illiam) Mark, 95, one-time high-ranking FBI official who in 2005 revealed himself to have been "Deep Throat," the source who anonymously bared crucial details of the Watergate political scandal; Santa Rosa, CA, Dec. 18, 2008.

FitzGerald, Jerri Nielsen (born Jerri Lin Cahill), 57, physician who was dramatically rescued from an Antarctic research station in 1999 after 5 months of self-administered breast-cancer treatment; Southwick, MA, June 23, 2009.

Foch, Nina, 84, actress whose films included *The Ten Commandments* (1956) and *Executive Suite* (1954), for which she was nominated for an Academy Award; Los Angeles, CA, Dec. 5, 2008.

Foote, Horton, 92, playwright and screenwriter who won Academy Awards for *To Kill a Mockingbird* (1963) and *Tender Mercies* (1983); Hartford, CT, Mar. 4, 2009.

Foss, Lukas (born Lukas Fuchs), 86, German-born composer known for his experimental music; NYC, Feb. 1, 2009.

Franklin, John Hope, 94, historian who wrote *From Slavery to Freedom: A History of African Americans* (1947) and other landmark studies of blacks in U.S. history; Durham, NC, Mar. 25, 2009.

French, Marilyn (born Marilyn Edwards), 79, feminist author; semi-autobiographical first novel, *The Women's Room* (1977) became an international bestseller; NYC, May 2, 2009.

Friedman, Rose, 98, economist who collaborated with husband Milton Friedman on a number of books, including the best-selling *Free to Choose* (1980); Davis, CA, Aug. 18, 2009.

Fuller, Millard Dean, 74, co-founder of the house-building nonprofit Habitat for Humanity (1976); Albany, GA, Feb. 3, 2009.

Furchgott, Robert, 92, one of 3 scientists awarded the 1998 Nobel Prize in medicine for discovering the important role nitric oxide played in biological processes; work helped lead to the development of Viagra; Seattle, WA, May 19, 2009.

G

Gelbart, Larry, 81, playwright, screenwriter, director, and producer; helped develop the long-running American TV series *M.A.S.H.* (1972-83); wrote screenplays for *Oh, God!* (1977) and *Tootsie* (1982); won Tony Awards for *A Funny Thing Happened on the Way to the Forum* (1962) and *City of Angels* (1989); Beverly Hills, CA, Sept. 11, 2009.

Gibson, Henry, 73, actor, comedian, and writer best remembered for his roles on *Rowan and Martin's Laugh-In* (1968-71); Malibu, CA, Sept. 14, 2009.

Gibson, William, 94, playwright whose best-known work was *The Miracle Worker*; Stockbridge, MA, Nov. 25, 2008.

Goody, Jade, 27, reality show contestant in Britain, who lived out her life and death (from cervical cancer) in the public spotlight; Essex, England, Mar. 22, 2009.

Gordy, John, 73, former Detroit Lions lineman who was pres. of the NFL players' union; Orange, CA, Jan. 30, 2009.

Graham, Robert (born Robert Pena), 70, sculptor of monumental public works in bronze, including the Olympic Gateway at the entrance to the L.A. Memorial Coliseum; Santa Monica, CA, Dec. 27, 2008.

Greenwich, Ellie, 68, songwriter who wrote some of the best-known pop songs of the 1960s, including "Da Doo Ron Ron" (1963), "Be My Baby" (1963), and "Leader of the Pack" (1964); NYC, Aug. 26, 2009.

Gwathmey, Charles, 71, Modernist architect whose high-profile projects included an addition to NYC's Guggenheim Museum (1992) and the Naismith Memorial Basketball Hall of Fame (2002) in Springfield, MA; NYC, Aug. 3, 2009.

H

Halprin, Lawrence, 93, landscape architect whose works included the Franklin D. Roosevelt memorial in Wash., DC, and Ghirardelli Square in San Francisco; Kentfield, CA, Oct. 25, 2009.

Harris, E(verette) Lynn, 54, author of best-selling novels primarily featuring homosexual black men; Los Angeles, CA, July 23, 2009.

Hartigan, Grace, 86, Abstract Expressionist painter who rose to fame in the 1950s; Timonium, MD, Nov. 15, 2008.

Harvey, Paul (born Paul Harvey Aurandt), 90, Chicago-based radio commentator who reached millions of people in the U.S. via the ABC Radio Networks; Phoenix, AZ, Feb. 28, 2009.

Hewitt, Don(ald), 86, creator and executive producer of CBS's pioneering TV newsweekly *60 Minutes* (1968-2004); Bridgehampton, NY, Aug. 19, 2009.

Hubbard, Freddie, 70, jazz trumpet virtuoso in the post-bebop era; Sherman Oaks, CA, Dec. 29, 2008.

Hughes, John, 59, screenwriter, director, and producer who made films about disaffected suburban teenagers, including *Sixteen Candles* (1984), *The Breakfast Club* (1985), and *Ferris Bueller's Day Off* (1986); NYC, Aug. 6, 2009.

I

Ike, Reverend (born Frederick J. Eikerenkoetter II), 74, minister who preached the blessings of prosperity and made millions; Los Angeles, CA, Aug. 11, 2009.

J

Jacobs, Richard, 83, real estate tycoon; owner of the Cleveland Indians (1986-2001); Lakewood, OH, June 5, 2009.

Jackson, Michael, 50, one of the world's most famous entertainers, started singing in the Jackson 5 before a solo career; album *Thriller* (1982) became the all-time best-selling album and included 7 top 10 hits; nearly as famous for his personal eccentricities; Los Angeles, CA, June 25, 2009.

Jameson, Betty, 89, golfer who was one of 13 women to found the Ladies Professional Golf Assn. (1950); first woman to break 300 in a 72-hole tournament (1947); Boynton Beach, FL, Jan. 31, 2009.

Jarre, Maurice, 84, French composer who won Academy Awards for *Lawrence of Arabia* (1963), *Doctor Zhivago* (1966), and *A Passage to India* (1985); Malibu, CA, Mar. 28, 2009.

Johansson, Ingemar, 76, Swedish heavyweight boxer; world titleholder (1959-60); Kunsbacka, Sweden, Jan. 30, 2009.

Johnson, Van, 92, actor whose boyish looks helped propel him to matinee idol status in such MGM films as *State of the Union* (1948) and *The Caine Mutiny* (1954); Nyack, NY, Dec. 12, 2008.

K

Kalas, Harry, 73, longtime radio and TV broadcaster for Major League Baseball's Philadelphia Phillies; Wash., DC, Apr. 13, 2009.

Kaminsky, Stuart, 75, film scholar turned mystery writer who wrote over 60 crime novels; St. Louis, MO, Oct. 9, 2009.

Kaplan, Stanley, 90, pioneer in systematically preparing students for standardized tests; NYC, Aug. 23, 2009.

Katzir, Ephraim (born Katchalski), 93, pres. of Israel, 1973-78; also a biophysicist whose research included work on proteins that contributed to the human genome project; Rehovot, Israel, May 30, 2009.

Keith, Carl, 88, co-leader of an engineering team that invented the 3-way catalytic converter, a major advance in reducing pollution from automobiles, in the early 1970s; New Bern, NC, Nov. 9, 2008.

Kell, George, 86, Major League Baseball third baseman in the 1940s and 1950s; inducted into the Baseball Hall of Fame (1983); Swifton, AR, Mar. 24, 2009.

Kemp, Jack, 73, AFL football player and member of Congress (R, NY, 1970-88); instrumental in getting the GOP to embrace tax cuts; served as sec. of Housing and Urban Development under George H. W. Bush, and was the running mate of 1996 GOP nominee Sen. Bob Dole (KS); Bethesda, MD, May 2, 2009.

Kennedy, Ted (Edward Moore), 77, liberal senator (D, MA) since 1962 and scion of one of the country's most prominent political families; adhered to the values of liberalism and helped shape key legislation in areas ranging from civil rights to education to health care; image tarnished by a 1969 car accident on Chappaquiddick Island, MA, in which a young woman died; Hyannis Port, MA, Aug. 25, 2009.

Kerr, Johnny "Red", 76, former Chicago Bulls coach who went on to be the broadcaster for the team for over three decades; Chicago, IL, Feb. 26, 2009.

Kim Dae Jung, 85, pres. of South Korea (1998-2003), recipient of the Nobel Peace Prize (2000) for his pro-democracy efforts during military rule and for his reaching out to North Korean leader Kim Jung Il; Seoul, South Korea, Aug. 18, 2009.

Kitt, Eartha (born Eartha Mae Keith), 81, seductive singer, dancer, and actress; one of the first black women entertainers to become an international sex symbol; Weston, CT, Dec. 25, 2008.

Kolff, Willem, 97, Dutch-born physician who invented the kidney dialysis machine; he became a leader in the field of artificial-organ development; Newtown Square, PA, Feb. 11, 2009.

Kramer, Jack, 88, world's no. 1 tennis player (1946-53); won the men's singles title at Wimbledon (1947) while wearing shorts, the first Wimbledon competitor to do so; Los Angeles, CA, Sept. 12, 2009.

Kristol, Irving, 89, one of the founders of the U.S. neoconservative movement, a group of thinkers who, disenchanted with liberalism, moved to the political right; Arlington, VA, Sept. 18, 2009.

L

La Rue, Danny, 81, British drag impersonator known for his impressions of celebrities Elizabeth Taylor and Marlene Dietrich; Kent, England, May 31, 2009.

Lévi-Strauss, Claude, 100, French anthropologist and philosopher; leading proponent of the structural approach in social anthropology; Paris, France, Oct. 30, 2009.

Levitt, Helen, 95, photographer celebrated for her images of NYC streets, notably of children congregating or playing; NYC, Mar. 29, 2009.

Lusk, Jeremy, 24, freestyle motocross star who won a gold medal at the 2008 X Games; San Jose, Costa Rica, Feb. 10, 2009.

M

Makeba, Miriam Zenzi, 76, South African singer known as "Mama Africa," a powerful anti-apartheid figure; Castel Volturno, Italy, Nov. 9, 2008.

Malden, Karl (born Mladen George Sekulovich), 97, character actor best-known for his Academy Award-winning role in *A Streetcar Named Desire* (1951); Los Angeles, CA, July 1, 2009.

Maloof, Sam, 93, furniture maker and a key figure in the crafts movement; Rancho Cucamonga, CA, May 21, 2009.

Mays, Billy, 50, TV infomercial pitchman who promoted household projects and gadgets; Tampa, FL, June 28, 2009.

McCourt, Frank, 78, acclaimed memoirist of *Angela's Ashes* (1996), which dealt with growing up in a poverty-stricken Irish household; NYC, July 19, 2009.

McMahon, Ed, 86, entertainer best known for his role as the announcer and sidekick on NBC's *Tonight Show* during the 3 decades (1962-92) that Johnny Carson hosted it; Los Angeles, CA, June 23, 2009.

McNair, Steve, 36, quarterback who led the National Football League's Tennessee Titans to their first Super Bowl appearance, in Jan. 2000; Nashville, TN, July 4, 2009.

McNamara, Robert, 93, U.S. sec. of defense (1961-68), who came to be vilified for his role as chief architect of the Vietnam War; Wash., DC, July 6, 2009.

Montalban, Ricardo, 88, Mexican-born actor best remembered for the *Fantasy Island* TV series (1978-84); Los Angeles, CA, Jan. 14, 2009.

Mortimer, Sir John, 85, British barrister, novelist, and playwright who created the TV series *Rumpole of the Bailey* (1978-92); Turville Heath, England, Jan. 16, 2009.

Motwani, Rajeev, 47, Stanford Univ. computer scientist who did pioneering data-mining research; students included Larry Page and Sergey Brin, the founders of Google; Atherton, CA, June 5, 2009.

N

Naess, Arne, 96, Norwegian philosopher who founded the "deep ecology" movement; Oslo, Norway, Jan. 12, 2009.

Nolan, Christopher, 43, Irish author; mute and brain-damaged since birth; won Britain's Whitbread Award (1988) for his autobiography *Under the Eye of the Clock*; Dublin, Ireland, Feb. 20, 2009.

Novak, Robert, 78, conservative political columnist and TV commentator; wrote syndicated column "Inside Report" (1963-2008); Wash., DC, Aug. 18, 2009.

O

O'Brien, Conor Cruise, 91, Irish politician, journalist, broadcaster, historian, and playwright; gained international attention in the early 1960s as a special UN envoy to the Congo; Howth, Ireland, Dec. 18, 2008.

Odetta (Holmes), 77, singer who played a key role in the U.S. folk music revival of the 1950s and 1960s and was active in the civil rights movement; NYC, Dec. 2, 2008.

P

Page, Bettie, 85, leading pinup model of the 1950s whose revealing photos were a precursor to the sexual revolution; Los Angeles, CA, Dec. 11, 2008.

Patch, Harry, 111, last of Britain's World War I army veterans; Wells, England, July 25, 2009.

Paul, Les (born Lester William Polsfuss), 94, virtuoso guitarist and guitar designer; innovated electric guitars and introduced recording techniques, including overdubbing and multitrack recording; White Plains, NY, Aug. 13, 2009.

Pell, Claiborne, 90, senator (D, RI, 1961-97) who was known for his concern for the welfare of middle- and lower-income Americans; Newport, RI, Jan. 1, 2009.

Penn, Irving, 92, photographer who for years was a dominant force at the crossroads of fashion and art; NYC, Oct. 7, 2009.

Pinter, Harold, 78, Nobel Prize-winning British playwright of dramas *The Birthday Party* (1958), *The Caretaker* (1960), *The Homecoming* (1965), and *Betrayal* (1978); London, England, Dec. 24, 2008.

Pohlad, Carl, 93, owner of Major League Baseball's Minnesota Twins franchise since 1984; Edina, MN, Jan. 5, 2009.

Powell, Jody (Joseph Lester, Jr.), 65, White House press secretary under Pres. Jimmy Carter (1977-81); Cambridge, MD, Sept. 14, 2009.

Prosky, Robert (born Robert Joseph Porzuczek), 77, character actor known for the TV series *Hill Street Blues* (1984-87), and Tony-nominated performances in *Glengarry Glen Ross* (1984) and *A Walk in the Woods* (1988); Wash., DC, Dec. 8, 2008.

R

Richardson, Natasha, 45, British-born actress and member of Redgrave acting family who won a 1988 Tony Award for *Cabaret*; NYC, Mar. 18, 2009.

Roh Moo Hyun, 62, pres. of South Korea (2003-08); before entering politics, he had been a human rights and labor lawyer; Bongha, South Korea, May 23, 2009.

S

Saban, Lou, 87, football coach for the Boston Patriots, Buffalo Bills, and Denver Broncos; North Myrtle Beach, SC, Mar. 29, 2009.

Safire, William (born William Lewis Safir), 79, speechwriter for Pres. Richard Nixon and Pulitzer Prize-winning *NY Times* columnist (1973-2005); voiced conservative opinions from a libertarian perspective; Rockville, MD, Sept. 27, 2009.

Sales, Soupy (born Milton Supman), 83, comedian who is reputed to have thrown 19,000 pies; Bronx, NY, Oct. 22, 2009.

Schoenfeld, Gerald, 84, since 1972, chairman of Shubert Organization, the largest U.S. owner/operator of stage theaters, incl. 17 on Broadway; NYC, Nov. 25, 2008.

Schulberg, Budd, 95, novelist, journalist, and screenwriter; best-known for Academy Award-winning screenplay for *On the Waterfront* (1954); identified colleagues as communists before the House Committee on Un-American Activities; Westhampton Beach, NY, Aug. 5, 2009.

Selfridge, Oliver, 82, British-born computer scientist who did important early work in the field of artificial intelligence at MIT; Belmont, MA, Dec. 3, 2008.

Shriver, Eunice Kennedy, 88, cofounder of Special Olympics and advocate for people with developmental disabilities; sister of Pres. John F. Kennedy; Hyannis, MA, Aug. 11, 2009.

Shulman, Julius, 98, architectural photographer known for his images of Modernist houses in Southern CA; Los Angeles, CA, July 15, 2009.

Silver, Ron, 62, actor and political activist; won Tony Award as a repulsive film producer in David Mamet's *Speed-the-Plough* (1988); NYC, Mar. 15, 2009.

Sims, Naomi, 61, first black model to appear on the cover of the mainstream women's magazine *Ladies' Home Journal* (1968); considered the first black supermodel; Newark, NJ, Aug. 1, 2009.

Smith, Randy, 60, 2-time NBA All-Star who became known for his durability; played a record 906-straight NBA games (1972-83); Norwich, CT, June 4, 2009.

Sosa, Mercedes, 74, Argentine contralto; Buenos Aires, Argentina, Oct. 4, 2009.

Storm, Gale (born Josephine Owaissa Cottle), 87, actress who starred in two popular sitcoms, *My Little Margie* (1952-55) and *The Gale Storm Show* (1956-60); Danville, CA, June 27, 2009.

Sutton, Crystal Lee, 68, union organizer whose experiences inspired the Academy Award-winning movie *Norma Rae* (1979); Burlington, NC, Sept. 11, 2009.

Swayze, Patrick, 57, dancer turned actor who achieved stardom by portraying a dance instructor in *Dirty Dancing* (1987) and a slain banker in *Ghost* (1998); Los Angeles, CA, Sept. 14, 2009.

T

Tiller, George, 67, physician who performed abortions, incl. late-term abortions, at his KS clinic; assassinated in Wichita, KS, May, 31, 2009.

Travers, Mary, 72, singer who was the "Mary" in the popular 1960s folk-pop trio Peter, Paul, and Mary; Danbury, CT, Sept. 16, 2009.

U

Updike, John, 76, prolific novelist, short story writer, essayist, and literary critic hailed for his seemingly effortless mastery of the English language; best known for his "Rabbit" tetralogy and *The Witches of Eastwick* (1984); Danvers, MA, Jan. 27, 2009.

Utzon, Jørn, 90, Danish architect who created the Sydney Opera House; won his profession's highest honor, the Pritzker Prize (2003); Copenhagen, Denmark, Nov. 29, 2008.

V

Van Pelt, Brad, 57, football linebacker who was named to the Pro Bowl for 5 consecutive seasons (1976-80); Harrison, MI, Feb. 17, 2009.

Von Bulow, Martha (Sunny), 76, heiress who had been in a vegetative state since 1980; financier-husband Claus von Bulow was convicted of her attempted murder (1982), but the conviction was reversed (1985); NYC, Dec. 6, 2008.

W

Wald, Florence (born Florence Sophie Schorske), 91, dean of the Yale Univ. School of Nursing (1959-66) and force behind the first U.S. palliative-care hospice (1974); Branford, CT, Nov. 8, 2008.

Whitmore, James, 87, character actor; had major success in the 1970s with 3 one-man shows in which he impersonated humorist Will Rogers and 2 U.S. presidents; Malibu, CA, Feb. 6, 2009.

Wyeth, Andrew, 91, realist painter whose most iconic painting, *Christina's World*, showed his disabled neighbor dragging herself through a field; Chadds Ford, PA, Jan. 16, 2009.

Y

Yang, Xiangzhong (Jerry), 49, reproductive biologist, born in China, who led a team that developed the first cloned farm animal in the U.S., a calf named Amy (1999) at the Univ. of Connecticut; Boston, MA, Feb. 5, 2009.

Yow, (Sandra) Kay, 66, coach of U.S. Olympic gold medal-winning women's basketball team (1988); won 737 games over a 38-year coaching career, NC State Univ.; Cary, NC, Jan. 24, 2009.

Offbeat News Stories, 2009

When Mummies Are Actually Daddies

Brooklyn Museum curators thought they knew their mummies. On June 23, 2009, they sent two female mummies, Lady Hor and Thothirdes, to North Shore Univ. Hospital for CT scans to gather information on their health histories. What they found surprised them: both were men.

"Lady" Hor's gender identity was apparent as soon as researchers scanned the genital area. In the 1920s, Hor had been classified a woman because he was depicted without a beard on his coffin. "When we found out Hor's true sex, we did the quickest label change in the history of the Brooklyn Museum," explained curator Edward Bleiberg. "We had people asking the guards on June 30: 'Where's the woman who turned into a man?'" The discovery would "revise some of our ideas about how you can tell if a mummy is male or female," he noted. The other newly recognized man, Thothirdes, had endured 80 years of curators' comments about the homeliness of "her" portrait, but his sex-change didn't receive the same level of publicity. More than a month later, Bleiberg admitted that the museum had yet to change that label.

Pregnancy Night a Hit

How did the Brooklyn Cyclones minor league baseball team come up with the idea of a promotion for pregnant women? "It started out as a joke," admitted Cyclones communications director Dave Camapanaro. But they ran with "Bellies and Baseball" on July 19. Before the game, a dozen couples attended a "Lamaze on the Lawn" class in center field. Women in their third trimesters collectively threw out the first pitches, and for the "7th Inning Stretch Marks," moms-to-be sang "Take Me Out to the Ballgame" on the field. A "craving station" stocked with pizza, pickles, ice cream, and olives was set up behind home plate. Expectant fathers were offered a couple of activities of their own, including a "Trimester Tricycle" race and a "Water Break" water balloon race. The team offered lifetime free tickets for any mom who would agree to name her child "Brooklyn" or "Cy" or for any baby actually born at the game. That didn't happen this year, but the team's holding out hope for 2010.

The Right Stuff

If you're looking to send just a few people into space, out of a country of 1.3 billion people, you can afford to be picky. That seems to be the idea behind screenings for China's newest astronauts. Shi Bing Bing, a doctor at China's 454th Air Force Hospital, revealed some of the 100 criteria that China will use to screen candidates. Those with bad breath or body odor, which would "affect fellow colleagues in the narrow confines of a space shuttle," are out, as are applicants with scars, which "might burst and bleed when spaceships are accelerating." Chronic colds, cavities, drug allergies, or ringworm will similarly disqualify applicants, as will the occurrence of a serious illness within the last three generations of their family. Successful candidates must have "pleasant and adaptable" dispositions and the support of their spouses. The very few who make the cut "can really be called super human beings," said Shi.

Fair Doesn't Butter-Up Michael

A life-sized sculpture of a cow, made using about 600 pounds of butter molded upon a wood and metal frame, has been an annual fixture at the Iowa State Fair since 1911. Other butter sculptures often shared the cow's stage. Past additions include Elvis Presley, Tiger Woods, and even Harry Potter. This year, in honor of the 40th anniversary of the moon landing, a diorama was planned showing the lunar surface, an astronaut, and a U.S. flag made of butter.

When Michael Jackson died, fair organizers proposed adding him to the diorama, in honor of his perfection of the "moonwalk" dance. Complaints came pouring in. Some Iowans deemed Jackson's personal life too controversial, while animal activists objected to the use of animal products instead of nondairy substitutes. After a barrage of letters, e-mail messages, and phone calls, fair officials decided to put it to a vote on their website. It wasn't even close: 65% voted to leave Jackson out of the butter diorama.

Dogs Have Their Day

Since time immemorial, advocates for felines and canines have argued about the relative intelligence of their favorite quadrupeds. This year, Britta Osthaus, who teaches psychology at Canterbury Christ Church Univ. in the UK, entered into the dispute. She placed treats attached to strings under a plastic screen; the cats could see the treats but had to tug on the strings to bring the treats toward themselves. When a treat on one string was presented to the cats, they made the connection between pulling on the string and getting the snack. But when given a choice of two strings—one with a treat and one without—they proved unable to consistently choose the string with the treat. It made no difference whether the strings were parallel to each other or crossed. By contrast, similar testing conducted by Osthaus revealed that dogs would choose the string with the treat when shown two strings in parallel (though they seemed equally baffled by crossed strings).

Feline defenders suggested the cats simply didn't care about the experiment, but Osthaus insisted otherwise. "You can see them trying to figure it out," she said. "They just couldn't." She is "not trying to say cats are stupid, just they are different."

Benson Sleeps with the Fishes

When 25-year-old Benson died in Britain on July 28, 2009, it made headlines in the *Guardian* and the London *Times*. *The Economist* ran an obituary, and the mystery surrounding her death made the front page of the *Wall Street Journal*. She had died well short of her expected lifespan of 60 years—the beloved Benson was a carp.

Named after a cigarette brand (for a hole in her dorsal fin that looked like a cigarette burn), Benson weighed 64 pounds at her peak, making her the largest-known common carp in the UK. She was caught and released more than 60 times in 16 years, and in 2005, she was voted Britain's favorite carp by readers of *Angler's Mail*.

Initially, fishermen came under suspicion in her death. Traces of tiger nuts, used to lure carp to the surface but potentially poisonous to them, were found on the banks of her lake home. An autopsy, however, found no traces of nuts in the carp's digestive system but did find evidence that Benson's death resulted from pregnancy complications. While the possibility of more Bensons was a slight consolation to her admirers, she will be missed.

The Latest in Omphaloscopic Research

Why do some belly buttons collect so much lint—and what is it made out of? Austrian chemist Georg Steinhauser set out to find the answer. Over the course of three years, he collected and studied 503 pieces of lint from his own navel, and gathered additional information from family, friends, and coworkers. It turns out navel lint is primarily accumulated by abdominal hair, according to his study, published in the June 2009 issue of *Medical Hypotheses*. The hair rubs fibers off cotton clothes and moves it toward the belly button, where it collects. "Innies," or concave belly buttons, are especially prone to buildup. Newer clothes produce more lint than older clothes, but navel lint also contains bits of dead skin, fat, and dust. Navel piercings or shaving one's belly can cut down on fluff, at least until the hair grows back.

Are You There, God? It's Me, @margaret613

Love it or hate it, the website Twitter has exploded in popularity since its launch in 2006. The service allows people to use computers or cell phones to share short messages called "tweets." In the past year, it has provided timely information on a host of topics, from Iranian election protests to earthquakes. Now, it might even help you talk to God.

Jerusalem's Western Wall (or *Kotel*) is the holiest accessible prayer site in Judaism. Every year, thousands of visitors write prayers and messages to put in the wall's cracks. In July 2009, Alon Nir, a 25-year-old Israeli student, opened the @TheKotel account on Twitter, bridging the gap between time-honored practices and the newest online sensation. (The @ sign just indicates that something is being addressed to Twitter user "TheKotel.") He prints out each message, rolls it into a miniature scroll, and places it in the wall's crevices, allowing anyone in the world access to the ancient site with mere keystrokes.

Historical Anniversaries, 2010

1910 – 100 Years Ago

Cape Colony, Natal, Transvaal, and the Orange Free State unite May 31 to form the self-governing Union of **South Africa**.

Congress passes the Mann Act June 25; otherwise known as the **"white slave traffic act,"** the legislation barred international and interstate transportation of women for "immoral purposes."

Former Pres. Theodore Roosevelt calls for a **"new nationalism"** in a Kansas speech Aug. 31.

Japan annexes Korea with the Aug. 22 signing of the Japan-Korea Annexation Treaty.

The **Portuguese monarchy is overthrown** as King Manuel II flees the country

Revolution in Mexico breaks out Nov. 20 with liberal reformers rebelling against Pres. Porfirio Díaz.

Congressional midterm elections Nov. 8 handed **Democrats control of the House** of Representatives for the first time since 1895.

Eugene Ely becomes the **first pilot** to launch a naval aircraft from the deck of a U.S. warship Nov. 14.

Art. The "Younger American Painters" exhibition at Alfred Stieglitz's "291" gallery shows works by Max Weber, John Marin, and others. Pablo Picasso's *Girl With a Mandolin*; Auguste Rodin's *The Old Courtesan*; Henri Rousseau's *The Dream*.

Film. *The Jeffries-Johnson World's Championship Boxing Contest* shows the defeat of "white hope" Jim Jeffries by Jack Johnson, the first African American heavyweight champion; the outcome sparked riots and national race debate.

Literature. Florence Barclay's *The Rosary*; Winston Churchill's *A Modern Chronicle*; E. M. Forster's *Howards End*; O. Henry's *Whirligigs* and *Strictly Business*.

Music. The Metropolitan Opera in New York City produces Frederick Converse's *The Pipe of Desire*, its first American production, and Puccini's *The Girl of the Golden West*.

Nonfiction. The first volume of Bertrand Russell and Alfred North Whitehead's *Principia Mathematica* is published; Ezra Pound's *The Spirit of Romance*; Albert Schweitzer's *The Quest of the Historical Jesus* is published in English for the first time.

Pop music. "A Perfect Day," by Carrie Jacobs-Bond; tango is a popular dance craze.

Science and technology. Marie Curie publishes *Treatise on Radiography*, her principal paper on radioactivity. Halley's Comet reappears after a 76-year absence.

Sports. Ty Cobb and Napoleon Lajoie battle for an automobile awarded to the top batter in the major leagues. Lajoie is helped by the opposition in his final doubleheader, enabling him to pass Cobb, but the final standings unexpectedly place Cobb on top. Due to the controversy, the Chalmers Motor Car Company awards cars to both players.

Theater. *Get-Rich-Quick Wallingford* and *Baby Mine* are hits on Broadway.

Miscellaneous. The Boy Scouts of America is founded. Pope Pius X requires all priests and seminary professors take an oath against Modernism's reinterpretation of Catholicism.

1960 – 50 Years Ago

Four black college students ignite the **"sit-in"** movement Feb. 1 at a Woolworth lunch counter in Greensboro, NC.

The Soviet Union, May 1, shoots down a U.S. **U-2 spy plane** and captures pilot Gary Powers.

The **European Free Trade Association** forms May 3 to promote expansion of free trade between member nations.

Pres. Dwight D. Eisenhower signs the **Civil Rights Act** of 1960 into law May 6; it is the first bill addressing civil rights to survive a filibuster.

Belgian **Congo becomes independent** nation of Congo Republic June 30 but heads quickly toward crisis: Army mutinies July 5; Katanga—the richest province in resources—secedes July 11.

Iran, Iraq, Kuwait, Saudi Arabia, and Venezuela form the Organization of Oil Exporting States (**OPEC**) Sept. 14.

The U.S. state department **embargoes exports to Cuba**, Oct. 19, in response to Cuban nationalization of many private businesses.

Sen. John F. **Kennedy** (D, MA) defeats Vice Pres. Richard **Nixon** to becomes the first Catholic president-elect Nov. 8, in one of the closest elections in history.

Two **flights collide** in fog over New York Harbor Dec. 16, killing 134 in the worst air disaster to date.

Art. M.C. Escher's *Ascending and Descending*, David Hockney's *Adhesiveness*; Tony Vaccaro photographs Georgia O'Keefe.

Film. Billy Wilder's *The Apartment* starring Jack Lemmon, Shirley MacLaine, and Fred MacMurray; *Elmer Gantry*; *House of Usher* starring Vincent Price; *Inherit the Wind* starring Frederic March and Spencer Tracy; the documentary *Primary*, which follows John F. Kennedy and Hubert Humphrey during the Wisconsin presidential primary race; *The Magnificent Seven*; Alfred Hitchcock's *Psycho*; Stanley Kubrick's *Spartacus* starring Kirk Douglas and Laurence Olivier; Elia Kazan's *Wild River* starring Montgomery Clift. Michelangelo Antonioni's *L'Avventura*, Federico Fellini's *La Dolce Vita*, and Jean-Luc Godard's *Breathless* are released in Europe.

Literature. John Knowles's *A Separate Peace*; Harper Lee's *To Kill a Mockingbird*; Flannery O'Connor's *The Violent Bear It Away*; Scott O'Dell's *Island of the Blue Dolphins*; John Updike's *Rabbit, Run*.

Music. Benjamin Britten's *A Midsummer Night's Dream* (opera); Miles Davis's *Sketches of Spain*; Walter Piston's *Symphony No. 7*.

Nonfiction. Jean-Paul Sartre's *Critique of Dialectical Reason*, William L. Shirer's *The Rise and Fall of the Third Reich*; Elie Wiesel's *Night* is published in English for the first time.

Pop music. Chubby Checker's "The Twist"; The Drifters' "Save the Last Dance for Me"; Brian Hyland's "Itsy Bitsy Teenie Weenie Yellow Polka Dot Bikini"; Roy Orbison's "Only the Lonely"; Elvis Presley's "Are You Lonesome Tonight" and "It's Now or Never."

Science and technology. France detonates an atomic bomb in the Sahara Desert in Algeria, Feb. 13. The FDA approves the first birth-control pill for safe use May 9. John H. Reynolds of Univ. of California-Berkeley estimates the age of the universe at 4.95 billion years.

Sports. Floyd Patterson defeats Ingemar Johansson to regain the heavyweight boxing title; the Soviet Union dominates the Olympic Games; MLB's World Series—NY Yankees vs. Pittsburgh Pirates—ends with a home run for the first time, for a Pittsburgh victory.

Television. *The Flintstones*, *The Andy Griffith Show*, and *My Three Sons* premiere; the first televised presidential debate—between Vice Pres. Richard Nixon and Sen. John F. Kennedy—Sept. 26 broadcasts the split-screen technique for the first time.

Theater. Broadway features *Bye Bye Birdie* starring Dick Van Dyke and Chita Rivera, *An Evening With Mike Nichols and Elaine May*, and Tennessee Williams's *Period of Adjustment*. Eugène Ionesco's *Rhinoceros* and Harold Pinter's *The Caretaker* make their London debuts.

Miscellaneous. Soviet Premier Nikita Khrushchev bangs his shoe on a table at the UN to emphasize a point Oct. 13.

1985 – 25 Years Ago

Pres. Ronald **Reagan visits Bergen-Belsen** concentration camp and a German military cemetery with the graves of Nazi troops, inciting controversy May 5.

Philadelphia **police bombed** a house occupied by the radical group MOVE May 13, killing 11 people and setting off a fire that burned down 61 houses.

Lebanese **terrorists hijack** a TWA jet taking off June 14 from Athens, Greece; 39 Americans are held hostage until June 30.

Mikhail **Gorbachev** becomes general-secretary of USSR's Communist Party Mar. 11 and emphasizes redirection to *glasnost* after the death of Konstantin U. Chernenko.

House of Representatives vote for the first economic **sanctions on South Africa** June 5; many public companies begin divestment, but a bill approved by both chambers of Congress will not become law until Pres. Reagan's veto is overridden in Oct. 1986.

A Japan Air Lines flight crashes into Mt. Ogura, killing 520 in the world's **worst single-plane disaster**.

Palestinian terrorists hijack the cruise ship *Achille Lauro* in the Mediterranean Oct. 7-9; a wheelchair-bound American tourist is killed.

The **Nevado del Ruiz volcano erupts** Nov. 13, causing avalanches and flooding that overwhelm more than a dozen Colombian towns and kill more than 23,000 people.

Reagan and Gorbachev meet Nov. 19 in Geneva, Switzerland for the first **U.S.-USSR summit** in 6 years; it is the first in a series that would thaw relations between the two countries.

In the **largest corporate merger** to date outside the oil industry, General Electric agrees to acquire RCA Corp. for $6.28 bil.

Art. *Knife Ship 1* by Claes Oldenburg and Coosje van Bruggen; the Saatchi Gallery opens in London.

Film. *Back to the Future*; Terry Gilliam's *Brazil*; John Hughes's *The Breakfast Club*; Ron Howard's *Cocoon*; Steven Spielberg's *The Color Purple* starring Whoopi Goldberg and Oprah Winfrey; *The Goonies*; *Kiss of the Spider Woman*; Sydney Pollack's *Out of Africa* starring Robert Redford and Meryl Streep; John Huston's *Prizzi's Honor* starring Anjelica Huston, Jack Nicholson, and Kathleen Turner; Akira Kurosawa's *Ran*; *Witness* starring Harrison Ford.

Literature. Margaret Atwood's *The Handmaid's Tale*; Orson Scott Card's *Ender's Game*; John Irving's *The Cider House Rules*; Garrison Keillor's *Lake Wobegon Days*; Cormac McCarthy's *Blood Meridian*; Larry McMurtry's *Lonesome Dove*; Carl Sagan's *Contact*.

Music. William Schuman wins Pulitzer's Special Citation in Music.

Nonfiction. J. Anthony Lukas's *Common Ground*; Priscilla Presley's *Elvis and Me*; Random House acquires rights to Ronald Reagan's memoirs for a record $3 mil.

Pop music. Hit singles include Madonna's "Into the Groove" and "Material Girl," REO Speedwagon's "Can't Fight This Feeling," and Bruce Springsteen's "Glory Days"; albums released include Phil Collins's *No Jacket Required*, Dire Straits's *Brothers in Arms*, New Order's *Low-Life*, The Smiths' *Meat Is Murder*, Tears for Fears's *Songs from the Big Chair*, and Tom Waits's *Rain Dogs*. Johnny Cash, Waylon Jennings, Kris Kristofferson, and Willie Nelson form The Highwaymen supergroup.

Science and technology. The FDA approves the first commercial blood test for AIDS in Mar.; film star Rock Hudson becomes first well-known public figure to die from AIDS in Oct. Microsoft debuts Windows 1.0; the Nintendo Entertainment System is released in U.S.

Sports. Pete Rose breaks Ty Cobb's all-time hits record with his 4,192nd, a single; Dwight Gooden claims MLB pitching's "Triple Crown" with 24 wins, 268 strike-outs, and a 1.53 ERA. Wayne Gretzky scores an NHL-record-setting 47 points in the playoffs, leading the Edmonton Oilers to their second consecutive Stanley Cup.

Television. The U.S. cable network Discovery Channel launches. *The Cosby Show* and *Cagney and Lacey* win Best Comedy and Best Drama Emmy Awards, respectively.

Theater. Neil Simon's *Biloxi Blues*, *Big River*, and *I'm Not Rappaport* make their Broadway debuts. A revival of *The Odd Couple* features female title characters Rita Moreno and Sally Struthers.

Miscellaneous. 1985 is dubbed "The Year of the Spy" because of the large number of high-profile Cold War spies arrested on U.S. soil. Coca-Cola Co. announces July 10 that it will resume marketing its original "Classic" formula, ending the "New Coke" debacle. The marathon concert Live Aid and single "We Are the World" feature hundreds of pop artists to raise money for African famine relief.

WORLD ALMANAC EDITORS' PICKS
2009 Time Capsule

The editors of *The World Almanac* have selected the following items as representative of the year 2009.

1. Canada goose feathers, recovered from the engine of US Airways Flight 1549, which pilot Chesley "Sully" Sullenberger III safely landed in the Hudson River, NY-NJ, after a "double bird strike" took out both engines Jan. 15, 2009.

2. Pair of tickets to the Jan. 20, 2009, inauguration of Pres. Barack Obama.

3. Tea bag from anti-tax "tea party" protests that an estimated 100,000 people attended in more than 800 cities and towns Apr. 15, 2009.

4. Divorce papers filed by Jon and Kate Gosselin, who announced June 22, 2009, on their reality show *Jon & Kate Plus 8*, that they planned to end their 10-year marriage.

5. Michael Jackson's signature white glove. After the pop singer died June 25, 2009, more than 1.6 million people entered a lottery to win tickets to the star's memorial ceremonies in Los Angeles.

6. A collection of "tweets" from the web service Twitter about the Iranian election protests, at which tens of thousands gathered June-July 2009.

7. Pres. Barack Obama's birth records, whose authenticity was reaffirmed by the state of Hawaii July 27, 2009, following increasing calls for proof of Obama's birthplace.

8. The four bottles of beer served at the White House "beer summit" July 30, 2009: Bud Light for Obama, Sam Adams Light for Harvard Prof. Henry Louis Gates Jr., Blue Moon for Cambridge police Sgt. James Crowley, and a nonalcoholic Buckler beer for Vice Pres. Joe Biden.

9. A $4,500 voucher from the "cash-for-clunkers" program, which was credited with spiking Aug. 2009 automobile sales up 26% over the previous month.

10. A vial of influenza A (H1N1) "swine flu" vaccine, which was being distributed in fall 2009, in response to the new, severe strain of influenza that first emerged in Mexico in Apr. 2009.

11. Serena Williams's broken tennis racket from her Sept. 12, 2009, meltdown in a semi-final match at the U.S. Open.

12. A copy of the so-called Baucus Bill on health-care reform, formally released Sept. 16, 2009.

Supreme Court, 2008-09

The U.S. Supreme Court's 2008-09 term began Oct. 6, 2008, and concluded June 29, 2009, when the court began its summer recess. The 9 justices decided 79 cases (74 of which carried signed decisions), an increase from 71 in the 2007-08 term and 72 in 2006-07. The court issued 23 rulings (29%) by a 5-4 majority, a sharp increase from 11 (15%) in 2007-08, but more in line with an earlier term: 24 (33%) in 2006-07.

Membership. Chief Justice John G. Roberts Jr. presided over his 3rd full term on the court. The 8 associate justices, by order of seniority, were John Paul Stevens, Antonin Scalia, Anthony M. Kennedy, David H. Souter, Clarence Thomas, Ruth Bader Ginsburg, Stephen G. Breyer, and Samuel A. Alito Jr. See also the historical listing of justices on page 437.

Pres. Barack Obama nominated federal appeals court judge Sonia Sotomayor May 26, 2009, to fill the seat vacated by Justice David H. Souter, who had announced his retirement May 1, 2009. Following confirmation hearings, Sotomayor was confirmed by the Senate, 68-31, Aug. 6, 2009; she was sworn in by Chief Justice John Roberts Aug. 8.

In 2008-09, Roberts, Scalia, Thomas, and Alito tended to vote together as a conservative bloc, while Stevens, Souter, Ginsburg, and Breyer comprised the court's liberal wing. Kennedy was often the swing vote on key 5-4 rulings.

Following are summaries of major decisions issued during the 2008-09 term. Detailed information on Supreme Court activities and opinions may be accessed via the Internet at www.supremecourtus.gov. A more extensive archive of recent and historic rulings is available through Cornell Law School's Legal Information Institute: www.law.cornell.edu/supct/index.html.

Notable Supreme Court Decisions, 2008-09

Note: The columns on the right provide information on how each justice voted. Shading indicates a justice who was part of the majority. MO = justice authored majority opinion; CO = justice authored concurring opinion; DO = justice authored dissenting opinion. CD in part = justice authored opinion which contains both concurring and dissenting opinions.

Civil Rights

In *Ricci v. DeStefano*, the Supreme Court June 29, 2009, ruled 5-4 that the city of New Haven, CT, had discriminated against a group of white and Hispanic firefighters by throwing out the results of a promotion test after no blacks performed well on it.

The court June 22, 2009, ruled 8-1, in *Northwest Austin Municipal Utility District Number One v. Holder*, to uphold Section 5 of the 1965 Voting Rights Act, which required nine states, and parts of seven others, to gain federal approval before changing voting procedures.

The court Mar. 9, 2009, ruled 5-4 that protections designed to preserve a minority population's voting power were only applicable in areas where the minority-group voter population exceeded 50% of the total voter population. The case was *Bartlett v. Strickland*.

Defendants' Rights

In *Melendez-Diaz v. Massachusetts*, the court June 25, 2009, ruled 5-4 that defendants had the constitutional right at trial to cross-examine lab analysts who had submitted forensic reports as evidence.

The court June 18, 2009, ruled 5-4, in *District Attorney's Office for the Third Judicial District v. Osborne*, that convicts did not have a constitutional right to DNA testing.

Campaign Finance

The court June 8, 2009, ruled 5-4 that judges must recuse themselves from cases involving individuals who had made unusually large contributions to their election campaigns. The case was *Caperton v. A.T. Massey Coal Co.*

Criminal Law

The court May 26, 2009, ruled in *Montejo v. Louisiana*, 5-4, that police officers could initiate an interrogation of a suspect even if the suspect's lawyer was not present.

The court Jan. 14, 2009, ruled 5-4, in *Herring v. United States*, that evidence collected after an illegal arrest was sometimes admissible in court, as long as the arrest resulted from "isolated negligence," and was not part of a wider disregard for the law by police.

Federal Regulation

In *Wyeth v. Levine*, the court Mar. 4, 2009, ruled 6-3 that pharmaceutical companies could be held liable by state courts for harm done to individuals who took drugs that carried federally approved warnings.

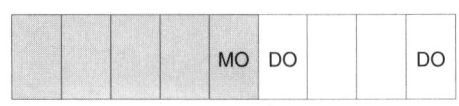

The court Dec. 15, 2008, ruled in *Altria Group Inc. v. Good*, 5-4, that a federal law regulating cigarette marketing did not preempt challenges brought in state courts.

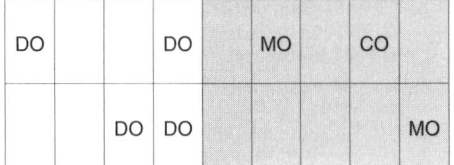

Environment

The court June 22, 2009, ruled 6-3 that Coeur Alaska Inc., a gold-mining company, could dump slurry waste in Lower Slate Lake near Juneau, Alaska. Environmentalists said the waste would kill all the life in the lake. The case was *Coeur Alaska Inc. v. Southeast Alaska Conservation Council*.

The court Apr. 1, 2009, ruled 6-3, in *Entergy Corp. v. Riverkeeper Inc.*, that the Environmental Protection Agency (EPA) could weigh cost against benefit to determine the "best" technology a power plant must use to minimize any adverse effects it may have on the environment.

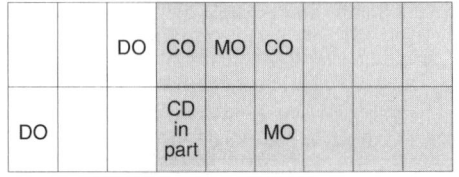

Case	Stevens	Souter	Ginsburg	Breyer	Kennedy	Scalia	Thomas	Alito	Roberts
Ricci v. DeStefano			DO		MO	CO		CO	
Northwest Austin v. Holder							CD in part		MO
Bartlett v. Strickland		DO	DO	DO	MO		CO		
Melendez-Diaz v. Massachusetts					DO	MO	CO		
Osborne	DO	DO						CO	MO
Caperton v. A.T. Massey Coal Co.					MO	DO			DO
Montejo v. Louisiana	DO			DO		MO		CO	
Herring v. United States			DO	DO					MO
Wyeth v. Levine	MO			CO			CO	DO	
Altria Group Inc. v. Good	MO						DO		
Coeur Alaska Inc.			DO	CO	MO	CO			
Entergy Corp. v. Riverkeeper Inc.	DO			CD in part		MO			

111th Congress: Committees

Congress divides its tasks among some 225 committees and subcommittees. Standing committees generally have legislative jurisdiction and operate with subcommittees that handle work in specific areas. Select and joint committees are chiefly for oversight or housekeeping. The chair of each House or Senate committee and a majority of its members come from the majority party (Democratic Party as of Oct. 2009).

Senate Standing Committees

Agriculture, Nutrition, and Forestry
Chair: Blanche L. Lincoln (D, AR)
Ranking: Saxby Chambliss (R, GA)

Appropriations
Chair: Daniel K. Inouye (D, HI)
Ranking: Thad Cochran (R, MS)

Armed Services
Chair: Carl Levin (D, MI)
Ranking: John McCain (R, AZ)

Banking, Housing, and Urban Affairs
Chair: Christopher J. Dodd (D, CT)
Ranking: Richard C. Shelby (R, AL)

Budget
Chair: Kent Conrad (D, ND)
Ranking: Judd Gregg (R, NH)

Commerce, Science, and Transportation
Chair: John D. Rockefeller IV (D, WV)
Ranking: Kay Bailey Hutchison (R, TX)

Energy and Natural Resources
Chair: Jeff Bingaman (D, NM)
Ranking: Lisa Murkowski (R, AK)

Environment and Public Works
Chair: Barbara Boxer (D, CA)
Ranking: James M. Inhofe (R, OK)

Finance
Chair: Max Baucus (D, MT)
Ranking: Chuck Grassley (R, IA)

Foreign Relations
Chair: John F. Kerry (D, MA)
Ranking: Richard G. Lugar (R, IN)

Health, Education, Labor, and Pensions
Chair: Tom Harkin (D, IA)
Ranking: Michael B. Enzi (R, WY)

Homeland Security and Governmental Affairs
Chair: Joseph I. Lieberman (I, CT)
Ranking: Susan M. Collins (R, ME)

Judiciary
Chair: Patrick J. Leahy (D, VT)
Ranking: Jeff Sessions (R, AL)

Rules and Administration
Chair: Charles E. Schumer (D, NY)
Ranking: Robert F. Bennett (R, UT)

Small Business and Entrepreneurship
Chair: Mary L. Landrieu (D, LA)
Ranking: Olympia J. Snowe (R, ME)

Veterans' Affairs
Chair: Daniel K. Akaka (D, HI)
Ranking: Richard Burr (R, NC)

Senate Special, Select, and Other Committees

Special Committee on Aging
Chair: Herb Kohl (D, WI)
Ranking: Bob Corker (R, TN)

Select Committee on Ethics
Chair: Barbara Boxer (D, CA)
Ranking: Johnny Isakson (R, GA)

Indian Affairs
Chair: Byron L. Dorgan (D, ND)
Ranking: John Barrasso (R, WY)

Select Committee on Intelligence
Chair: Dianne Feinstein (D, CA)
Vice Chair: Christopher S. Bond (R, MO)

Joint Committees of Congress

Joint Committee on the Library
Chair: Rep. Robert A. Brady (D, PA)
Vice Chair: Sen. Charles E. Schumer (D, NY)

Joint Committee on Printing
Chair: Sen. Charles E. Schumer (D, NY)
Vice Chair: Rep. Robert A. Brady (D, PA)

Joint Committee on Taxation
Chair: Rep. Charles B. Rangel (D, NY)
Vice Chair: Sen. Max Baucus (D, MT)

Joint Economic Committee
Chair: Rep. Carolyn B. Maloney (D, NY)
Vice Chair: Sen. Charles E. Schumer (D, NY)

House Standing Committees

Agriculture
Chair: Collin C. Peterson (D, MN)
Ranking: Frank D. Lewis (R, OK)

Appropriations
Chair: David R. Obey (D, WI)
Ranking: Jerry Lewis (R, CA)

Armed Services
Chair: Ike Skelton (D, MO)
Ranking: Howard P. "Buck" McKeon (R, CA)

Budget
Chair: John M. Spratt Jr. (D, SC)
Ranking: Paul Ryan (R, WI)

Education and Labor
Chair: George Miller (D, CA)
Ranking: John Kline (R, MN)

Energy and Commerce
Chair: Henry A. Waxman (D, CA)
Ranking: Joe Barton (R, TX)

Financial Services
Chair: Barney Frank (D, MA)
Ranking: Spencer Bachus (R, AL)

Foreign Affairs
Chair: Howard L. Berman (D, CA)
Ranking: Ileana Ros-Lehtinen (R, FL)

Homeland Security
Chair: Bennie G. Thompson (D, MS)
Ranking: Peter T. King (R, NY)

House Administration
Chair: Robert A. Brady (D, PA)
Ranking: Daniel E. Lungren (R, CA)

Judiciary
Chair: John Conyers Jr. (D, MI)
Ranking: Lamar Smith (R, TX)

Natural Resources
Chair: Nick J. Rahall II (D, WV)
Ranking: Doc Hastings (R, WA)

Oversight and Government Reform
Chair: Edolphus Towns (D, NY)
Ranking: Darrell E. Issa (R, CA)

Rules
Chair: Louise McIntosh Slaughter (D, NY)
Ranking: David Dreier (R, CA)

Science and Technology
Chair: Bart Gordon (D, TN)
Ranking: Ralph M. Hall (R, TX)

Small Business
Chair: Nydia M. Velázquez (D, NY)
Ranking: Sam Graves (R, MO)

Standards of Official Conduct
Chair: Zoe Lofgren (D, CA)
Ranking: Jo Bonner (R, AL)

Transportation and Infrastructure
Chair: James L. Oberstar (D, MN)
Ranking: John L. Mica (R, FL)

Veterans' Affairs
Chair: Bob Filner (D, CA)
Ranking: Steve Buyer (R, IN)

Ways and Means
Chair: Charles B. Rangel (D, NY)
Ranking: Dave Camp (R, MI)

House Select Committees

Permanent Committee on Intelligence
Chair: Silvestre Reyes (D, TX)
Ranking: Peter Hoekstra (R, MI)

Committee on Energy Independence & Global Warming
Chair: Edward J. Markey (D, MA)
Ranking: F. James Sensenbrenner Jr. (R, WI)

ECONOMICS

Index of Leading Economic Indicators

Source: The Conference Board

The index of leading economic indicators is used to project the U.S. economy's performance. The index is made up of 10 measurements of economic activity that tend to change direction in advance of the overall economy. The index has predicted economic downturns from 8 to 20 months in advance and recoveries from 1 to 10 months in advance; however, it can be inconsistent, and has occasionally shown "false signals" of recessions. The following components make up the Leading Economic Index:

- Average weekly hours of production workers in manufacturing
- Average weekly initial claims for unemployment insurance, state programs
- Manufacturers' new orders for consumer goods and materials, adjusted for inflation
- Vendor performance (slower deliveries diffusion index)
- Stock prices, 500 common stocks
- Manufacturers' new orders, nondefense capital goods industries, adjusted for inflation
- New private housing units authorized by local building permits
- Money supply: M-2, adjusted for inflation
- Interest rate spread, 10-yr Treasury bonds less federal funds
- Consumer expectations (researched by Univ. of Michigan)

U.S. Gross Domestic Product, Gross National Product, Net National Product, National Income, and Personal Income, 1970-2008

Source: Bureau of Economic Analysis, U.S. Dept. of Commerce

(in billions of current dollars, revised)

	1970	1980	1990	2000	2005	2006	2007	2008
Gross domestic product	1,038.3	2,788.1	5,800.5	9,951.5	12,638.4	13,398.9	14,077.6	14,441.4
Gross national product	1,044.7	2,822.3	5,835.0	9,989.2	12,735.5	13,471.3	14,193.3	14,583.3
Less: Consumption of fixed capital	108.3	344.1	691.2	1,184.3	1,541.4	1,660.7	1,760.0	1,847.1
Net national product	936.4	2,478.2	5,143.7	8,804.9	11,194.2	11,810.7	12,433.3	12,736.2
Less: Statistical discrepancy	6.9	45.3	84.2	−134.0	−79.7	−220.6	−14.8	101.0
Equals: National income	929.5	2,433.0	5,059.5	8,938.9	11,273.8	12,031.2	12,448.2	12,635.2
Less: Corporate profits with inventory valuation and capital consumption adjustments	82.5	201.4	434.4	819.2	1,456.1	1,608.3	1,541.7	1,360.4
Taxes on production and imports less subsidies	86.6	190.5	398.0	662.7	869.3	935.5	974.0	993.8
Contributions for government social insurance	46.4	166.2	410.1	705.8	872.7	921.8	959.3	990.6
Net interest and miscellaneous payments on assets	39.1	181.8	444.2	539.3	543.0	652.2	739.2	815.1
Business current transfer payments (net)	4.5	14.7	40.1	87.0	95.9	83.0	102.2	118.8
Current surplus of government enterprises	0.0	−5.1	1.6	9.1	−3.5	−4.2	−6.6	−6.9
Wage accruals less disbursements	0.0	0.0	0.1	0.0	5.0	1.3	−6.3	−5.0
Plus: Personal income receipts on assets	93.5	338.7	920.8	1,360.7	1,542.0	1,829.7	2,031.5	1,994.4
Personal current transfer receipts	74.7	279.5	594.9	1,083.0	1,508.6	1,605.0	1,718.0	1,875.9
Equals: Personal income	838.6	2,301.5	4,846.7	8,559.4	10,485.9	11,268.1	11,894.1	12,238.8

U.S. Gross Domestic Product, 1997-2009

Source: Bureau of Economic Analysis, U.S. Dept. of Commerce

(in billions of current dollars)

	1997	2007	4th quarter 2008	1st quarter 2009	2nd quarter 2009[1]
Gross domestic product	8,332.4	14,077.6	14,347.3	14,178.0	14,151.2
Personal consumption expenditures	5,570.6	9,826.4	10,009.8	9,987.7	9,999.3
Nondurable goods	1,291.2	2,204.5	2,207.6	2,172.4	2,182.2
Services	3,563.9	6,461.4	6,782.3	6,790.0	6,805.6
Gross private domestic investment	1,388.7	2,288.5	2,022.1	1,689.9	1,561.5
Fixed investment	1,317.7	2,269.1	2,066.6	1,817.2	1,737.7
Nonresidential	968.6	1,640.2	1,638.7	1,442.6	1,391.8
Structures	250.3	535.4	620.7	533.1	494.8
Equipment and software	718.3	1,104.8	1,018.0	909.5	897.0
Residential	349.1	629.0	427.8	374.6	345.9
Change in private inventories	71.0	19.4	−44.5	−127.4	−176.2
Net exports of goods and services	−101.4	−713.8	−590.5	−378.5	−339.1
Exports	955.4	1,655.9	1,706.2	1,509.3	1,493.7
Goods	687.7	1,139.4	1,155.7	989.5	978.1
Services	266.7	516.4	550.5	519.8	515.6
Imports	1,055.8	2,369.7	2,296.7	1,887.9	1,832.8
Goods	885.7	1,987.7	1,892.5	1,508.2	1,461.1
Services	170.1	382.1	404.2	379.6	371.7
Government consumption expenditures and gross investment	1,474.4	2,676.5	2,905.9	2,879.0	2,929.4
National defense	349.8	662.1	758.9	750.7	776.2
Nondefense	181.1	314.5	355.3	356.0	362.1
State and local	943.5	1,699.8	1,791.7	1,772.3	1,791.2

(1) Seasonally adjusted at annual rates.

U.S. Gross Domestic Product, 1930-2008

Source: Bureau of Economic Analysis, U.S. Dept. of Commerce

(in billions of current dollars)

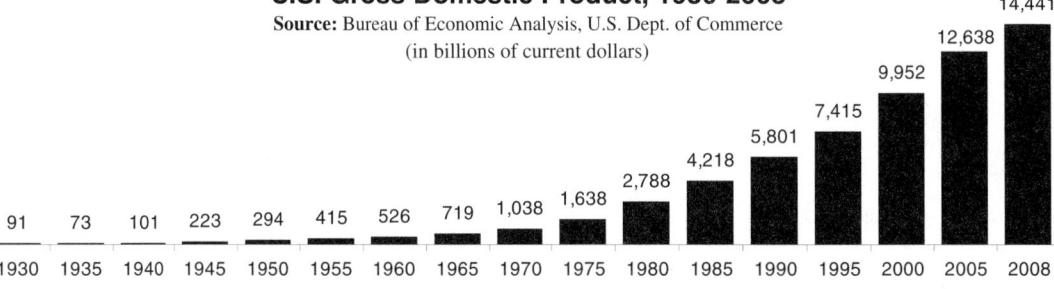

1930	1935	1940	1945	1950	1955	1960	1965	1970	1975	1980	1985	1990	1995	2000	2005	2008
91	73	101	223	294	415	526	719	1,038	1,638	2,788	4,218	5,801	7,415	9,952	12,638	14,441

Consumer Price Index

The Consumer Price Index (CPI) is a measure of the change in prices over time of one or more kinds of basic consumer goods and services.

From Jan. 1978, the Bureau of Labor Statistics began publishing CPIs for two population groups: (1) a CPI for all urban consumers (CPI-U), which covers about 87% of the total population; and (2) a CPI for urban wage earners and clerical workers (CPI-W), which covers about 32% of the total population. The CPI-U includes, in addition to wage earners and clerical workers, groups such as professional, managerial, and technical workers, the self-employed, short-term workers, the unemployed, retirees, and others not in the labor force.

The CPI is based on prices of food, clothing, shelter, and fuels; transportation fares; charges for doctors' and dentists' services; drug prices; and prices of other goods and services bought for day-to-day living. The index currently measures price changes from a designated reference period, 1982-84, which equals 100.0. Use of this reference period began in Jan. 1988.

U.S. Consumer Price Index, 2008-09

Source: Bureau of Labor Statistics, U.S. Dept. of Labor

(Data are semiannual averages of monthly figures; for all urban consumers; % change not annualized. **1982-84 = 100**, unless otherwise noted.)

	1st half 2008	% change, 2nd half 2007 to 1st half 2008	2nd half 2008	% change, 1st half 2008 to 2nd half 2008	1st half 2009	% change, 2nd half 2008 to 1st half 2009
All items	214.4	2.6%	216.2	0.8%	213.1	−1.4%
Food, beverages	210.8	2.6	217.6	3.2	218.7	0.5
Housing	214.7	1.8	217.8	1.4	217.3	−0.2
Apparel	119.1	0.8	118.7	−0.3	120.0	1.0
Transportation	198.7	6.2	192.4	−3.2	173.0	−10.1
Medical care	362.6	2.2	365.5	0.8	373.3	2.1
Recreation[1]	112.7	1.0	113.8	1.0	114.3	0.4
Education and communication[1]	122.1	1.0	125.2	2.5	126.3	0.9
Other goods, services	342.5	2.2	348.3	1.7	362.3	4.0
Services	253.3	1.8	257.7	1.8	258.5	0.3
Special indexes						
All items less food	215.1	2.6	216.0	0.4	212.3	−1.7
Commodities less food	157.2	4.3	153.4	−2.4	144.0	−6.1
Nondurables	206.0	5.2	205.8	−0.1	195.4	−5.0
Energy	240.4	12.6	233.0	−3.1	183.8	−21.1
All items less energy	213.4	1.5	216.1	1.3	217.8	0.8

(1) Dec. 1997 = 100.

U.S. Consumer Price Indexes (CPI-U)[1], Annual Percent Change, 1992-2008

Source: Bureau of Labor Statistics, U.S. Dept. of Labor

	1992	1993	1994	1995	1996	1997	1998	1999	2000	2001	2002	2003	2004	2005	2006	2007	2008
All items	3.0	3.0	2.6	2.8	3.0	2.3	1.6	2.2	3.4	2.8	1.6	2.3	2.7	3.4	3.2	2.8	3.8
Food	1.2	2.2	2.4	2.8	3.3	2.6	2.2	2.1	2.3	3.2	1.8	2.2	3.4	2.4	2.4	4.0	5.5
Shelter	3.3	3.0	3.1	3.2	3.2	3.1	3.3	2.9	3.3	3.7	3.7	2.4	2.7	2.6	3.4	3.7	2.5
Rent, residential	2.5	2.3	2.5	2.5	2.7	2.9	3.2	3.1	3.6	4.5	4.0	2.9	2.7	3.0	3.6	4.3	3.7
Fuel and other utilities	2.2	3.0	1.0	0.7	3.1	2.6	−1.8	0.2	7.1	8.9	−4.4	7.6	4.8	10.6	8.8	3.0	9.7
Apparel and upkeep	2.5	1.4	−0.2	−1.0	−0.2	0.9	0.1	−1.3	−1.3	−1.8	−2.6	−2.5	−0.4	−0.7	0.0	−0.4	−0.1
Private transportation	2.2	2.3	3.1	3.7	2.7	0.7	−2.2	1.9	6.1	0.6	−0.8	3.2	3.8	6.8	4.0	2.1	5.7
New cars	2.5	2.4	3.4	2.2	1.7	0.2	−0.6	−0.3	−0.1	−0.5	−1.2	−1.5	−0.6	0.6	−0.2	−1.0	−1.5
Gasoline	−0.2	−1.3	0.5	1.6	6.1	−0.1	−13.4	9.3	28.5	−3.6	−6.5	16.5	18.2	21.9	12.9	8.2	16.6
Public transportation	1.7	10.3	3.0	2.3	3.4	2.6	1.9	3.9	6.0	0.5	−1.5	0.9	−0.1	3.9	4.3	1.5	8.9
Medical care	7.4	5.9	4.8	4.5	3.5	2.8	3.2	3.5	4.1	4.6	4.7	4.0	4.4	4.2	4.0	4.4	3.7
Entertainment/recreation[2,3]	2.8	2.5	2.9	2.5	3.4	2.1	1.5	0.9	1.3	1.5	1.2	1.2	1.0	0.7	1.4	0.5	1.6
Education[3]	—	—	6.3	5.6	5.3	5.0	4.9	4.8	5.1	5.3	6.3	1.8	6.9	6.3	6.2	5.7	5.8
Commodities	2.0	1.9	1.7	1.9	2.6	1.4	0.1	1.8	3.3	1.0	−0.7	1.0	2.3	3.6	2.4	2.1	4.3

(1) The Consumer Price Index CPI-U measures average change in prices of goods and services purchased by all urban consumers. 1982-84 = 100 unless otherwise noted. (2) The Bureau of Labor Statistics reclassified Entertainment as Recreation in 1997. (3) Dec. 1997 = 100.

Consumer Price Index, 1915-2008

Source: Bureau of Labor Statistics, U.S. Dept. of Labor

(Annual averages of monthly figures, specified for all urban consumers. **1967 = 100**.)

Prices as measured by the U.S. Consumer Price Index have risen steadily since World War II. What cost $1.00 in 1967 cost about 30 cents in 1915, 54 cents in 1945, and $6.45 in 2008.

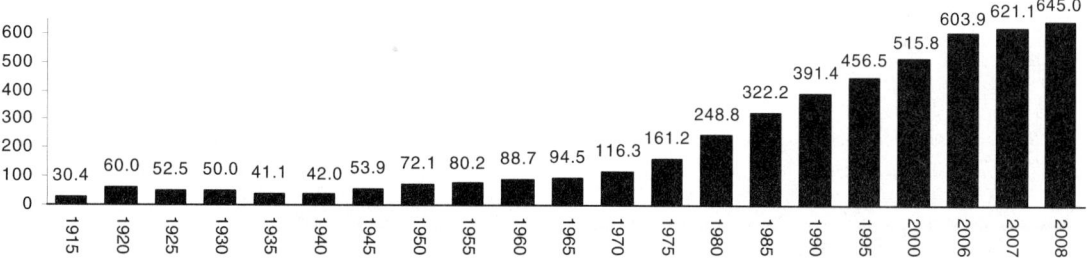

U.S. Consumer Price Indexes for Selected Items and Groups, 1970-2008

Source: Bureau of Labor Statistics, U.S. Dept. of Labor

(Annual averages of monthly figures; for all urban consumers. **1982-84 = 100**, unless otherwise noted.)

	1970	1975	1980	1985	1990	1995	2000	2005	2006	2007	2008
ALL ITEMS	38.8	53.8	82.4	107.6	130.7	152.4	172.2	195.3	201.6	207.3	215.3
Food and beverages	40.1	60.2	86.7	105.6	132.1	148.9	168.4	191.2	195.7	203.3	214.2
Food	39.2	59.8	86.8	105.6	132.4	148.4	167.8	190.7	195.2	202.9	214.1
Food at home	39.9	61.8	88.4	104.3	132.3	148.8	167.9	189.8	193.1	201.2	214.1
Cereals and bakery products	37.1	62.9	83.9	107.9	140.0	167.5	188.3	209.0	212.8	222.1	244.9
Meats, poultry, fish, and eggs	44.6	67.0	92.0	100.1	130.0	138.8	154.5	184.7	186.6	195.6	204.7
Dairy products	44.7	62.6	90.9	103.2	126.5	132.8	160.7	182.4	181.4	194.8	210.4
Fruits and vegetables	37.8	56.9	82.1	106.4	149.0	177.7	204.6	241.4	252.9	262.6	279.0
Sugar and sweets	30.5	65.3	90.5	105.8	124.7	137.5	154.0	165.2	171.5	176.8	186.6
Fats and oils	39.2	73.5	89.3	106.9	126.3	137.3	147.4	167.7	168.0	172.9	196.8
Nonalcoholic beverages	27.1	41.3	91.4	104.3	113.5	131.7	137.8	144.4	147.4	153.4	160.0
Other foods	39.6	58.9	83.6	106.4	131.2	151.1	172.2	182.5	185.0	188.2	198.1
Food away from home	37.5	54.5	83.4	108.3	133.4	149.0	169.0	193.4	199.4	206.7	215.8
Alcoholic beverages	52.1	65.9	86.4	106.4	129.3	153.9	174.7	195.9	200.7	207.0	214.5
Housing	36.4	50.7	81.1	107.7	128.5	148.5	169.6	195.7	203.2	209.6	216.3
Shelter	35.5	48.8	81.0	109.8	140.0	165.7	193.4	224.4	232.1	240.6	246.7
Rent of primary residence	46.5	58.0	80.9	111.8	138.4	157.8	183.9	217.3	225.1	234.7	243.3
Fuel and other utilities	29.1	45.4	75.4	106.5	111.6	123.7	137.9	179.0	194.7	200.6	220.0
Gas (piped) and electricity	25.4	40.1	71.4	107.1	109.3	119.2	128.0	166.5	182.1	186.3	202.2
Household furnishings and operations	46.8	63.4	86.3	103.8	113.3	123.0	128.2	126.1	127.0	126.9	127.8
Apparel	59.2	72.5	90.9	105.0	124.1	132.0	129.6	119.5	119.5	119.0	118.9
Men's and boys'	62.2	75.5	89.4	105.0	120.4	126.2	129.7	116.1	114.1	112.4	113.0
Women's and girls'	71.8	85.5	96.0	104.9	122.6	126.9	121.5	110.8	110.7	110.3	107.5
Footwear	56.8	69.6	91.8	102.3	117.4	125.4	123.8	122.6	123.5	122.4	124.2
Transportation	37.5	50.1	83.1	106.4	120.5	139.1	153.3	173.9	180.9	184.7	195.5
Private	37.5	50.6	84.2	106.2	118.8	136.3	149.1	170.2	177.0	180.8	191.0
New vehicles	53.0	62.9	88.4	106.1	121.4	139.0	142.8	137.9	137.6	136.3	134.2
Used cars and trucks	31.2	43.8	62.3	113.7	117.6	156.5	155.8	139.4	140.0	135.7	134.0
Gasoline	27.9	45.1	97.5	98.6	101.0	99.8	128.6	194.7	219.9	238.0	277.5
Public	35.2	43.5	69.0	110.5	142.6	175.9	209.6	217.3	226.6	230.0	250.5
Medical care	34.0	47.5	74.9	113.5	162.8	220.5	260.8	323.2	336.2	351.1	364.1
Entertainment/recreation[1]	47.5	62.0	83.6	107.9	132.4	153.9	103.3	109.4	110.9	111.4	113.3
Other goods and services	40.9	53.9	75.2	114.5	159.0	206.9	271.1	313.4	321.7	333.3	345.4
Tobacco products	43.1	54.7	72.0	116.7	181.5	225.7	394.9	502.8	519.9	554.2	588.7
Personal care	43.5	57.9	81.9	106.3	130.4	147.1	165.6	185.6	190.2	195.6	201.3
Personal care products	42.7	58.0	79.6	107.6	128.2	143.1	153.7	154.4	155.8	158.3	159.3
Personal care services	44.2	57.7	83.7	108.9	132.8	151.5	178.1	203.9	209.7	216.6	223.7

(1) Dec. 1997 = 100. Entertainment was reclassified as Recreation in 1997.

Consumer Price Indexes by Region and Selected Cities, 2007-08

Source: Bureau of Labor Statistics, U.S. Dept. of Labor

(For all urban consumers; % change not annualized. **1982-84 = 100**, unless otherwise noted.)

	Semiannual averages				% change from preceding semiannual average			
	1st half 2007	2nd half 2007	1st half 2008	2nd half 2008	1st half 2007	2nd half 2007	1st half 2008	2nd half 2008
U.S. CITY AVERAGE	205.7	209.0	214.4	216.2	1.5%	1.6%	2.6%	0.8%
Northeast urban	218.7	222.3	227.9	230.7	1.2	1.6	2.5	1.2
Size A—More than 1,500,000	221.3	224.8	229.9	233.1	1.1	1.6	2.3	1.4
Size B/C—50,000 to 1,500,000[1]	129.1	131.2	135.4	136.7	1.4	1.7	3.2	0.9
Midwest urban	196.6	199.6	204.8	206.0	1.6	1.5	2.6	0.6
Size A—More than 1,500,000	198.5	201.0	206.0	207.0	1.6	1.3	2.5	0.5
Size B/C—50,000 to 1,500,000[1]	125.4	127.5	131.0	132.0	1.6	1.7	2.7	0.7
Size D—Nonmetro. (less than 50,000)	190.9	195.4	200.4	202.3	1.2	2.3	2.6	0.9
South urban	198.5	202.2	207.8	209.6	1.5	1.9	2.7	0.9
Size A—More than 1,500,000	200.9	204.7	210.0	212.1	1.5	1.9	2.6	1.0
Size B/C—50,000 to 1,500,000[1]	126.2	128.6	132.2	133.1	1.5	1.9	2.7	0.7
Size D—Nonmetro. (less than 50,000)	198.8	201.6	208.6	211.6	1.0	1.4	3.5	1.4
West urban	210.9	213.6	219.0	220.3	1.9	1.3	2.5	0.6
Size A—More than 1,500,000	214.4	216.9	222.5	224.1	1.9	1.2	2.6	0.7
Size B/C—50,000 to 1,500,000[1]	128.0	130.0	133.1	133.5	1.9	1.3	2.7	0.3
SELECTED AREAS								
Atlanta, GA	198.1	202.0	206.7	206.2	1.6	1.9	2.4	−0.3
Boston-Brockton-Nashua, MA-NH-ME-CT	225.9	229.0	234.2	236.5	0.8	1.3	2.3	1.0
Chicago-Gary-Kenosha, IL-IN-WI	203.1	206.6	212.2	212.9	2.1	1.7	2.7	0.3
Cleveland-Akron, OH	194.5	197.5	203.0	203.1	1.9	1.5	2.8	0.0
Dallas-Fort Worth, TX	191.1	195.4	200.1	203.5	0.3	2.3	2.4	1.7
Detroit-Ann Arbor-Flint, MI	199.6	200.7	204.5	205.0	1.2	0.5	1.9	0.3
Houston-Galveston-Brazoria, TX	182.9	184.8	189.4	190.6	1.0	1.1	2.5	0.6
L.A.-Riverside-Orange County, CA	216.3	218.4	224.4	225.6	2.2	1.0	2.7	0.6
Miami-Fort Lauderdale, FL	210.0	214.8	221.2	223.1	2.4	2.3	3.0	0.8
New York-Northern NJ-Long Island, NY-NJ-CT-PA	225.1	228.8	233.8	237.8	1.3	1.6	2.2	1.7
Philadelphia-Wilmington-Atlantic City, PA-DE-NJ-MD	214.8	218.7	223.5	224.7	0.6	1.9	2.2	0.5
San Francisco-Oakland-San Jose, CA	214.7	217.4	221.7	223.8	2.0	1.2	2.0	0.9
Seattle-Tacoma-Bremerton, WA	213.8	217.5	223.6	225.9	2.1	1.7	2.8	1.0
Washington-Baltimore, DC-MD-VA-WV[2]	132.0	135.0	138.5	140.5	1.5	2.2	2.6	1.5

(1) Dec. 1996 = 100. (2) Nov. 1996 = 100.

U.S. National Income by Industry[1], 2002-08

Source: Bureau of Economic Analysis, U.S. Dept. of Commerce; in billions of current dollars; as of Oct. 5, 2009

	2002	2003	2004	2005	2006	2007	2008
National income without capital consumption adjustment	9,206.1	9,650.3	10,373.9	11,353.9	12,126.9	12,547.0	12,547.4
Domestic industries	9,157.0	9,581.6	10,282.7	11,256.8	12,054.4	12,431.3	12,405.4
Private industries	8,015.0	8,364.3	9,006.9	9,921.4	10,655.9	10,959.3	10,863.0
Agriculture, forestry, fishing, and hunting	67.6	83.3	104.1	92.8	91.9	109.7	116.6
Mining	81.2	103.3	125.0	163.1	198.8	194.7	231.6
Utilities	134.4	136.8	149.1	161.3	196.5	196.8	191.8
Construction	514.2	534.8	583.3	657.0	701.8	693.7	626.3
Manufacturing	1,038.1	1,074.4	1,171.6	1,304.8	1,400.9	1,424.5	1,328.0
Durable goods	595.8	613.9	659.6	744.0	791.3	806.5	742.7
Nondurable goods	442.3	460.6	512.0	560.8	609.5	618.0	585.3
Wholesale trade	561.9	582.3	634.3	688.4	741.2	770.7	753.6
Retail trade	723.2	759.8	789.2	859.6	903.8	914.0	861.2
Transportation and warehousing	262.6	275.9	301.3	332.9	360.7	362.6	338.5
Information	299.7	309.8	357.6	408.1	424.5	445.6	428.0
Finance, insurance, real estate, rental, leasing	1,643.6	1,682.1	1,785.2	1,998.5	2,140.8	2,192.4	2,239.9
Professional and business services	1,212.5	1,272.8	1,349.2	1,490.3	1,623.2	1,691.1	1,730.9
Educ. services, health care, social assistance	817.4	873.5	937.7	993.5	1,059.4	1,115.1	1,167.9
Arts, entertain., recreation, accommod., food service	362.8	377.0	406.1	434.8	460.6	482.2	475.0
Other services, except government	295.7	298.5	313.1	336.3	351.7	366.4	373.5
Government	1,142.0	1,217.3	1,275.8	1,335.3	1,398.5	1,471.9	1,542.5
Non-domestic industries	49.1	68.7	91.2	97.1	72.4	115.7	141.9

(1) Figures may not add up to totals because of rounding. Total national income also includes income from outside the U.S.

U.S. National Income by Type[1], 1930-2008

Source: Bureau of Economic Analysis, U.S. Dept. of Commerce; in billions of current dollars; as of Oct. 12, 2009

	1930	1940	1950	1960	1970	1980	1990	2000	2007	2008
NATIONAL INCOME[2]	83.1	90.9	263.9	473.9	929.5	2,433.0	5,059.5	8,938.9	12,448.2	12,635.2
Employee compensation	46.9	52.2	155.3	296.4	617.2	1,647.6	3,326.3	5,788.8	7,856.5	8,037.4
Wage and salary accruals	46.2	49.9	147.3	272.9	551.6	1,373.4	2,741.2	4,827.7	6,402.6	6,540.8
Government	5.2	8.5	22.6	49.2	117.2	261.5	519.0	779.7	1,089.1	1,141.3
Supplements to wages and salaries	0.7	2.3	8.0	23.6	65.7	274.2	585.1	961.2	1,453.8	1,496.6
Employer contributions for employee pension and insurance funds	0.6	0.9	4.7	14.3	41.8	185.2	378.6	615.9	993.0	1,023.9
Employer contributions for government social insurance	0.0	1.4	3.4	9.3	23.8	88.9	206.5	345.2	460.8	472.7
Proprietors' income with inventory valuation and capital consumption adjustments	11.1	12.3	37.5	50.7	78.5	173.5	365.1	817.5	1,096.4	1,106.3
Farm	4.0	4.1	12.9	10.6	12.9	11.7	32.2	29.6	39.4	48.7
Nonfarm	7.0	8.2	24.6	40.1	65.6	161.8	333.0	787.8	1,056.9	1,057.5
Rental income of persons with capital consumption adjustments	5.5	3.9	9.1	17.0	21.1	28.5	49.8	215.3	144.9	210.4
Corporate profits with inventory valuation and capital consumption adjustment	7.5	9.6	35.6	53.1	82.5	201.4	434.4	819.2	1,541.7	1,360.4
Taxes on corporate income	0.8	2.8	17.9	22.8	34.8	87.2	145.4	265.1	451.5	292.2
Profits after tax with inventory valuation and capital consumption adjustments	6.6	6.8	17.7	30.3	47.7	114.2	289.0	554.1	1,090.2	1,068.2
Net dividends	5.5	4.0	8.8	13.4	24.3	64.1	169.1	377.9	767.8	689.9
Undistributed profits with inventory valuation and capital consumption adjustments	1.1	2.8	8.9	16.9	23.4	50.2	120.0	176.3	322.4	378.3
Net interest and miscellaneous payments	4.8	3.3	3.2	10.6	39.1	181.8	444.2	539.3	739.2	815.1

(1) Figures may not add up to totals because of rounding and incomplete enumeration. (2) National income is the aggregate of labor and property earnings that arise in the production of goods and services. It is the sum of employee compensation, proprietors' income, rental income, adjusted corporate profits, and net interest. It measures the total factor costs of goods and services produced by the economy. Income is measured before deduction of taxes. Total national income figures include adjustments not itemized.

Distribution of U.S. Total Personal Income[1], 1930-2008

Source: Bureau of Economic Analysis, U.S. Dept. of Commerce; in billions of current dollars; as of Oct. 7, 2009

Year	Personal income	Personal taxes and nontax payments	Disposable personal income	Personal outlays	Personal savings Amount	Personal savings as % of disposable income
1930	$76.1	$1.6	$74.6	$71.6	$2.9	4.0%
1940	78.4	1.7	76.8	72.4	4.3	5.7
1950	228.0	18.9	209.9	195.0	14.9	7.1
1960	411.3	46.1	365.2	338.9	26.3	7.2
1970	838.6	103.1	735.5	666.1	69.4	9.4
1980	2,301.5	298.9	2,002.7	1,806.4	196.3	9.8
1990	4,846.7	592.7	4,254.0	3,977.3	276.7	6.5
1995	6,200.9	743.9	5,457.0	5,170.8	286.3	5.2
2000	8,559.7	1,232.3	7,327.2	7,114.1	213.1	2.9
2001	8,883.3	1,234.8	7,648.5	7,443.5	204.9	2.7
2002	9,060.1	1,050.4	8.009.7	7,727.5	282.2	3.5
2003	9,378.1	1,000.3	8,377.8	8,088.0	289.8	3.5
2004	9,937.2	1,047.8	8,889.4	8,585.7	303.7	3.4
2005	10,485.9	1,208.6	9,277.3	9,149.6	127.7	1.4
2006	11,268.1	1,352.4	9,915.7	9,680.7	235.0	2.4
2007	11,894.1	1,490.9	10,403.1	10,224.3	178.9	1.7
2008	12,238.8	1,432.4	10,806.4	10,520.0	286.4	2.7

(1) Personal income minus taxes/nontax payments = disposable income; disposable income minus outlays = savings. Figures may not add up to totals because of rounding.

Median Income by Race, Hispanic Origin, and Sex, 1947-2008[1]

Source: Bureau of the Census, U.S. Dept. of Commerce

	Year	Male No. with income (thous.)	Male Median income Current dollars	Male Median income 2008 dollars	Female No. with income (thous.)	Female Median income Current dollars	Female Median income 2008 dollars
All Races	2008	105,428	$33,161	$33,161	106,403	$20,867	$20,867
	2007	104,789	33,196	34,472	105,230	20,922	21,726
	2006	103,909	32,265	34,455	104,582	20,014	21,373
	2005	102,986	31,275	34,493	104,245	18,576	20,487
	2000	98,504	28,343	35,437	101,704	16,063	20,084
	1990	88,220	20,293	32,407	92,245	10,070	16,081
	1980	78,661	12,530	31,172	80,826	4,920	12,240
	1970	65,008	6,670	33,006	51,647	2,237	11,069
	1960	55,172	4,080	25,958	36,526	1,261	8,023
	1950	47,585	2,570	20,065	24,651	953	7,440
	1947	46,813	2,230	18,803	21,479	1,017	8,575
White	2008	87,581	35,120	35,120	86,228	20,950	20,950
	2007	87,223	35,141	36,491	85,230	21,069	21,879
	2006	86,674	33,843	36,140	84,955	20,082	21,445
	2005	85,996	32,179	35,490	84,768	18,669	20,590
	2000	83,372	29,797	37,255	84,123	16,079	20,104
	1990	76,480	21,170	33,808	78,566	10,317	16,476
	1980	69,420	13,328	33,157	70,573	4,947	12,307
	1970	58,447	7,011	34,693	45,288	2,266	11,213
	1960	49,788	4,296	27,332	32,001	1,352	8,602
	1950	NA	2,709	21,150	NA	1,060	8,276
	1948	NA	2,510	19,597	NA	1,133	8,846
White, not Hispanic	2008	73,748	37,409	37,409	75,322	21,749	21,749
	2007	73,617	37,373	38,809	74,902	21,687	22,520
	2006	73,246	36,564	39,046	74,761	20,727	22,134
	2005	73,219	35,345	38,982	75,014	19,451	21,452
	2000	72,530	31,508	39,384	75,206	16,665	20,836
	1990	69,987	21,958	35,066	72,939	10,581	16,898
	1980	65,564	13,681	34,036	67,084	4,980	12,389
Black	2008	11,183	25,118	25,118	13,616	20,203	20,203
	2007	10,981	25,792	26,783	13,427	19,712	20,469
	2006	10,738	25,075	26,777	13,172	19,065	20,359
	2005	10,651	22,609	24,935	13,237	17,595	19,405
	2000	9,905	21,343	26,685	12,461	15,881	19,856
	1990	8,820	12,868	20,550	10,687	8,328	13,300
	1980	7,387	8,009	19,925	8,596	4,580	11,394
	1970	5,844	4,157	20,570	5,844	2,063	10,208
	1960	5,384	2,260	14,379	4,525	837	5,325
	1950	NA	1,471	11,485	NA	474	3,701
Asian	2008	4,788	36,204	36,204	4,535	23,109	23,109
	2007	4,446	37,193	38,140	4,497	24,355	25,291
	2006	4,432	37,417	39,624	4,419	22,201	23,708
	2005	4,245	34,215	36,435	4,255	21,641	23,868
	2000	4,303	30,833	38,550	4,192	17,356	21,700
	1990	2,235	19,394	30,972	2,333	11,086	17,704
Hispanic	2008	14,855	24,003	24,003	11,828	16,417	16,417
	2007	14,609	24,451	25,390	11,265	16,748	17,392
	2006	14,358	23,452	25,044	11,090	15,758	16,828
	2005	13,714	22,089	24,362	10,638	15,036	16,583
	2000	11,343	19,498	24,378	9,431	12,248	15,314
	1990	6,767	13,470	21,511	5,903	7,532	12,028
	1980	3,996	9,659	24,030	3,617	4,405	10,959

NA = Not available. (1) People 15 years of age and over beginning in Mar. 1980; 14 years of age and over as of Mar. of the following year for previous years.

Consumer Credit Outstanding, 2006-08

Source: Federal Reserve System
(in billions of dollars, revised)
Estimated amounts of credit outstanding as of end of year. Not seasonally adjusted.

	2006	2007	2008		2006	2007	2008
TOTAL	$2,415.0	$2,551.9	$2,592.1	Credit unions	$27.4	$31.1	$33.4
Major holders				Fed. govt. and Sallie Mae.	NA	NA	NA
Commercial banks.	741.2	804.1	878.6	Savings institutions.	42.5	44.8	39.6
Finance companies	534.4	584.1	575.8	Nonfinancial business.	7.8	4.6	4.2
Credit unions	234.5	235.7	235.0	Pools of securitized assets[1] . .	414.4	450.0	446.0
Fed. govt. and Sallie Mae	91.7	98.4	111.0				
Savings institutions	95.5	90.8	86.3	**Nonrevolving**[2]	**1,515.8**	**1,582.1**	**1,603.9**
Nonfinancial business	56.7	55.3	55.3	Commercial banks	413.9	450.7	488.1
Pools of securitized assets[1] . .	661.1	683.6	650.0	Finance companies	454.5	498.0	501.3
				Credit unions	207.1	204.6	201.6
Major types of credit				Fed. govt. and Sallie Mae.	91.7	98.4	111.0
Revolving[2].	**899.2**	**969.9**	**988.2**	Savings institutions.	53.1	46.0	46.8
Commercial banks.	327.3	353.4	390.6	Nonfinancial business.	48.9	50.7	51.1
Finance companies	79.9	86.0	74.4	Pools of securitized assets[1] . .	246.7	233.6	204.0

NA = Not available. (1) Outstanding balances of pools upon which securities have been issued; these balances are no longer carried on the balance sheets of the loan originators. (2) Includes estimates for holders that do not separately report consumer credit holding by type.

Distribution of Financial Assets of U.S. Families, 1989-2007[1]

Source: Federal Reserve System; by type of asset, as percent of family financial assets

Type of financial asset	1989	1995	2001	2004	2007	Type of financial asset	1989	1995	2001	2004	2007
Transaction accounts........	19.0	13.9	11.5	13.2	11.0	Retirement accounts........	21.5	28.1	28.4	32.0	34.6
Certificates of deposit.......	10.2	5.6	3.1	3.7	4.1	Cash value of life insurance ..	6.0	7.2	5.3	3.0	3.2
Savings bonds	1.5	1.3	0.7	0.5	0.4	Other managed assets	6.6	5.9	10.6	8.0	6.5
Bonds....................	10.2	6.3	4.6	5.3	4.2	Other....................	4.8	3.3	2.0	2.1	2.1
Stocks	15.0	15.6	21.7	17.6	17.9	**Financial assets as % of total**					
Mutual funds (excluding money market funds).......	5.3	12.7	12.2	14.7	15.9	**assets**	**30.5**	**36.7**	**42.0**	**35.7**	**33.9**

(1) Data from the triennial Survey of Consumer Finances.

Stock Ownership of U.S. Families, by Income and Age, 1989-2007[1]

Source: Federal Reserve System

(in percent, except as noted)

		Families having direct or indirect stock holdings[2]				Median value of portfolios (thous. of 2007 dollars)				Stock holdings as share of financial assets[3]			
		1989	2001	2004	2007	1989	2001	2004	2007	1989	2001	2004	2007
All families		**31.7%**	**52.2%**	**50.2%**	**51.1%**	**$12.5**	**$40.4**	**$35.7**	**$35.0**	**27.8%**	**56.1%**	**51.3%**	**53.3%**
Percentile of income:	Less than 20....	3.3	12.9	11.7	13.6	29.3	8.8	8.2	6.5	13.6	37.4	32.0	39.0
	20-39.9........	15.2	34.1	29.6	34.0	8.8	9.1	11.0	8.8	10.0	35.6	30.9	34.3
	40-59.9........	28.6	52.5	51.7	49.5	6.8	17.5	16.5	17.7	16.7	46.8	43.4	38.3
	60-79.9........	44.0	75.7	69.9	70.5	8.5	33.5	28.7	34.1	21.8	52.0	41.7	52.5
	80-89.9........	57.6	82.0	83.8	84.4	13.9	75.6	60.9	62.0	26.1	57.3	48.8	49.3
	90-100	76.9	89.7	92.7	91.0	57.9	289.7	225.2	219.0	34.3	60.5	57.5	57.6
By age of family head (years):	Under 35.......	22.4	49.0	40.8	38.6	4.4	8.2	8.8	7.0	20.2	52.5	40.3	44.3
	35-44	39.0	59.5	54.5	53.5	7.6	32.2	22.0	26.0	29.4	57.2	53.5	53.7
	45-54	41.8	59.3	56.5	60.4	19.3	58.5	54.9	45.0	33.5	59.1	53.8	53.0
	55-64	36.2	57.4	62.8	58.9	27.0	94.2	78.0	78.0	27.7	56.2	55.0	55.0
	65-74	26.7	40.0	46.9	52.1	29.8	175.8	76.9	57.0	26.0	55.4	51.5	55.3
	75+...........	25.9	35.7	34.8	40.1	36.7	128.7	94.3	41.0	25.0	51.8	39.3	48.1

(1) Data from the triennial Survey of Consumer Finances. (2) Indirect holdings are those in mutual funds, retirement accounts, and other managed assets. (3) Among stock-holding families.

Wealthiest Americans, 2009

Source: *Forbes* magazine; as of Sept. 30, 2009

Rank	Name	Net worth (bil dollars)	Age	Residence	Source
1.	William Gates III	$50.0........	53	... Medina, WA	Microsoft
2.	Warren Buffett......................	40.0........	79	... Omaha, NE	Berkshire Hathaway
3.	Lawrence Ellison	26.0........	65	... Redwood City, CA	Oracle
4.	Christy Walton and family	21.5........	54	... Jackson, WY	Wal-Mart
5.	Jim C. Walton.......................	19.6........	61	... Bentonville, AR	Wal-Mart
6.	Alice Walton........................	19.3........	60	... Fort Worth, TX.............	Wal-Mart
7.	S. Robson Walton	19.0........	65	... Bentonville, AR	Wal-Mart
8.	Michael Bloomberg	17.5........	67	... New York, NY..............	Bloomberg
9.	Charles Koch.......................	16.0........	73	... Wichita, KS	Manufacturing, energy
	David Koch	16.0........	69	... New York, NY..............	Manufacturing, energy

Poverty Rate

Source: Bureau of the Census, U.S. Dept. of Commerce

The poverty rate is the proportion of the population whose income falls below the government's official poverty level, and is adjusted each year for inflation. The national poverty rate was 13.2% in 2008, statistically higher than the 2007 rate of 12.5%, and above the 2000 rate of 11.3%. About 39.8 million people in the U.S. were in poverty in 2008, up from 37.2 million in 2007. In 2008, 19.0% of children and 9.7% of people aged 65 and older were defined as poor.

Persons Below Poverty Level, 1960-2008

Source: Bureau of the Census, U.S. Dept. of Commerce

	Number below poverty level (millions)					% of subgroup below poverty level					Avg. income cut-offs, family of 4 at poverty level[4]
Year	All races[1]	Asian[2]	White	Black	Hispanic[3]	All races[1]	Asian[2]	White	Black	Hispanic[3]	
1960	39.9	NA	28.3	NA	NA	22.2%	NA	17.8%	NA	NA	$3,022
1970	25.4	NA	17.5	7.5	NA	12.6	NA	9.9	33.5%	NA	3,968
1980	29.3	NA	19.7	8.6	3.5	13.0	NA	10.2	32.5	25.7%	8,414
1990	33.6	0.9	22.3	9.8	6.0	13.5	12.2%	10.7	31.9	28.1	13,359
1992	38.0	1.0	25.3	10.8	7.6	14.8	12.7	11.9	33.4	29.6	14,335
1993	39.3	1.1	26.2	10.9	8.1	15.1	15.3	12.2	33.1	30.6	14,763
1994	38.1	1.0	25.4	10.2	8.4	14.5	14.6	11.7	30.6	30.7	15,141
1995	36.4	1.4	24.4	9.9	8.6	13.8	14.6	11.2	29.3	30.3	15,569
1996	36.5	1.5	24.7	9.7	8.7	13.7	14.5	11.2	28.4	29.4	16,036
1997	35.6	1.5	24.4	9.1	8.3	13.3	14.0	11.0	26.5	27.1	16,400
1998	34.5	1.4	23.5	9.1	8.1	12.7	12.5	10.5	26.1	25.6	16,660
1999	32.8	1.3	21.2	8.4	7.9	11.9	10.7	9.8	23.6	22.7	17,029
2000	31.6	1.3	21.6	8.0	7.7	11.3	9.9	9.5	22.5	21.5	17,063
2002	34.6	1.2	23.5	8.6	8.6	12.1	10.1	10.2	24.1	21.8	18,556
2003	35.9	1.4	24.3	8.8	9.1	12.5	11.8	10.5	24.4	22.5	18,979
2004	37.0	1.2	25.3	9.0	9.1	12.7	9.8	10.8	24.7	21.9	19,307
2005	37.0	1.4	24.9	9.2	9.4	12.6	11.1	10.6	24.9	21.8	19,971
2006	36.5	1.4	24.4	9.0	9.2	12.3	10.3	10.3	24.3	12.3	20,614
2007	37.2	1.3	25.1	9.2	9.9	12.5	10.2	10.5	24.5	21.5	21,203
2008	39.8	1.6	27.0	9.4	11.0	13.2	11.8	11.2	24.7	23.2	22,025

NA = Not available. **Note:** Because of a change in the definition of poverty, data prior to 1980 are not directly comparable to data since 1980. (1) Includes other races not shown separately. (2) Asian and Pacific Islander, 1990-2000. (3) Persons of Hispanic origin may be of any race. (4) Figures for 1960-80 represent only nonfarm families.

Poverty Thresholds by Family Size, 1980-2008

Source: Bureau of the Census, U.S. Dept. of Commerce. Weighted average; not used for computing poverty data.

	1980	1990	2000	2008		1980	1990	2000	2008
1 person	$4,190	$6,652	$8,794	$10,991	4 people	$8,414	$13,359	$17,603	$22,025
Under age 65	4,290	6,800	8,959	11,201	5 people	9,966	15,792	20,819	26,049
Age 65 or older	3,949	6,268	8,259	10,326	6 people	11,269	17,839	23,528	29,456
2 people	5,363	8,509	11,239	14,051	7 people	12,761	20,241	26,754	33,529
Householder under age 65	5,537	8,794	11,590	14,489	8 people	14,199	22,582	29,701	37,220
Householder age 65 or older	4,983	7,905	10,419	13,030	9 people or more	16,896	26,848	35,060	44,346
3 people	6,565	10,419	13,738	17,163					

Poverty by Family Status, Sex, and Race, 1990-2008

Source: Bureau of the Census, U.S. Dept. of Commerce
(numbers in thousands)

	1990 No.	1990 %[1]	1995 No.	1995 %[1]	2000 No.	2000 %[1]	2006 No.	2006 %[1]	2007 No.	2007 %[1]	2008 No.	2008 %[1]
TOTAL POOR	33,585	13.5	36,425	13.8	31,581	11.3	36,460	12.3	37,276	12.5	39,829	13.2
In families	25,232	12.0	27,501	12.3	22,347	9.6	25,915	10.6	26,509	10.8	28,564	11.5
Head of household	7,098	10.7	7,532	10.8	6,400	8.7	7,668	9.8	7,623	9.8	8,147	10.3
Related children	12,715	19.9	13,999	20.2	11,005	15.6	12,333	17.0	12,826	17.6	13,542	18.5
Families, female householder, no husband present	12,578	37.2	14,205	36.5	10,926	28.5	13,199	30.5	13,478	30.7	13,812	31.4
Head of household	3,768	33.4	4,057	32.4	3,278	25.4	4,087	28.3	4,078	28.3	4,163	28.7
Related children	7,363	53.4	8,364	50.3	6,300	40.0	7,360	42.0	7,558	42.9	7,609	43.5
Unrelated individuals	7,446	20.7	8,247	20.9	8,653	19.0	9,977	20.0	10,189	19.7	10,710	20.8
Unrelated female individuals	4,589	24.0	4,865	23.5	5,071	21.6	5,589	22.2	5,841	22.2	5,951	22.6
Unrelated male individuals	2,857	16.9	3,382	18.0	3,548	16.0	4,388	17.8	4,348	17.1	4,759	18.9
Total white poor[2]	22,326	10.7	24,423	11.2	21,645	9.5	24,416	10.3	25,120	10.5	26,990	11.2
In families	15,916	9.0	17,593	9.6	14,692	7.8	16,644	8.5	17,141	8.7	18,558	9.4
Head of household	4,622	8.1	4,994	8.5	4,333	7.1	5,118	8.0	5,046	7.9	5,414	8.4
Related children	7,696	15.1	8,474	15.5	6,834	12.4	7,542	13.6	8,014	14.4	8,463	15.3
Families, female householder, no husband present	6,210	29.8	7,047	29.7	5,609	23.2	7,160	26.5	7,188	26.5	7,340	27.2
Unrelated individuals	5,739	18.6	6,336	19.0	6,454	17.1	7,334	18.1	7,505	17.9	7,982	19.1
Total black poor[2]	9,837	31.9	9,872	29.3	7,982	22.5	9,048	24.3	9,237	24.5	9,379	24.7
In families	8,160	31.0	8,189	28.5	6,221	21.2	7,072	23.1	7,312	23.8	7,339	23.7
Head of household	2,193	29.3	2,127	26.4	1,686	19.3	2,007	21.6	2,045	22.1	2,055	22.0
Related children	4,412	44.2	4,644	41.5	3,495	30.9	3,699	33.1	3,848	34.4	3,791	34.4
Families, female householder, no husband present	6,005	50.6	6,553	48.2	4,774	38.6	5,180	39.1	5,459	39.7	5,533	40.5
Unrelated individuals	1,491	35.1	1,551	32.6	1,702	28.9	1,897	29.0	1,898	27.9	1,970	28.8

NA = Not available. (1) Percentage of total U.S. population in each category who fell below poverty level and are enumerated here. For example, of all persons in families in 2006, 10.6%, or 25,915,000, were poor. (2) Data are for one race only. The Census Bureau revised race categories in 2002; 2006 figures are not directly comparable with previous years.

Persons in Poverty, by State, 2004-08[1]

Source: Bureau of the Census, U.S. Dept. of Commerce
(percent of state population)

	2004-05	2005-06	2006-07	2007-08		2004-05	2005-06	2006-07	2007-08
Alabama	16.8%	15.5%	14.4%	14.4%	Montana	14.0%	13.7%	13.2%	12.9%
Alaska	9.5	9.4	8.3	7.9	Nebraska	9.5	9.9	10.1	10.3
Arizona	14.8	14.8	14.4	16.1	Nevada	10.8	10.1	9.6	10.3
Arkansas	14.5	15.8	15.8	14.5	New Hampshire	5.5	5.5	5.6	6.4
California	13.2	12.7	12.5	13.6	New Jersey	7.4	7.8	8.7	9.0
Colorado	10.7	10.6	9.8	10.4	New Mexico	17.2	17.4	15.5	16.6
Connecticut	9.7	8.7	8.4	8.5	New York	14.8	14.3	14.3	14.3
Delaware	9.1	9.3	9.3	9.4	North Carolina	13.8	13.5	14.7	14.7
Dist. of Columbia	19.1	19.8	18.1	17.3	North Dakota	10.4	11.3	10.3	10.5
Florida	11.4	11.3	12.0	12.8	Ohio	11.9	12.2	12.5	13.2
Georgia	13.7	13.5	13.1	14.6	Oklahoma	13.2	15.4	14.3	13.5
Hawaii	8.6	8.9	8.3	8.7	Oregon	11.9	11.9	12.3	11.7
Idaho	9.9	9.7	9.7	11.1	Pennsylvania	11.3	11.3	10.8	10.7
Illinois	11.9	11.0	10.3	11.1	Rhode Island	11.8	11.3	10.0	11.1
Indiana	12.1	11.6	11.2	13.1	South Carolina	15.0	13.1	12.7	14.0
Iowa	11.1	10.8	9.6	9.2	South Dakota	12.7	11.3	10.1	11.2
Kansas	12.0	12.7	12.3	12.2	Tennessee	15.4	14.9	14.8	14.9
Kentucky	16.3	15.8	16.2	16.3	Texas	16.3	16.3	16.5	16.2
Louisiana	17.6	17.6	16.5	17.1	Utah	9.6	9.2	9.4	8.6
Maine	12.1	11.4	10.5	11.4	Vermont	7.7	7.7	8.8	9.4
Maryland	9.8	9.1	8.6	8.8	Virginia	9.3	8.9	8.6	9.5
Massachusetts	9.7	11.1	11.6	11.2	Washington	10.8	9.1	9.1	10.3
Michigan	12.6	12.6	12.1	11.9	West Virginia	14.8	15.3	15.0	14.6
Minnesota	7.5	8.1	8.7	9.6	Wisconsin	11.3	10.2	10.6	10.4
Mississippi	19.4	20.4	21.6	20.4	Wyoming	10.3	10.3	10.4	10.5
Missouri	11.9	11.5	12.1	13.1	**U.S. total**	**12.7**	**12.5**	**12.4**	**12.9**

(1) 2-year average.

Selected Personal Consumption Expenditures in the U.S., 1990-2008[1]

Source: Bureau of Economic Analysis, U.S. Dept. of Commerce

(in billions of dollars)

	1990	1995	2000	2005	2006	2007	2008
Personal consumption expenditures	$3,835.5	$4,987.3	$6,830.4	$8,819.0	$9,322.7	$9,826.4	$10,129.9
Durable goods	497.1	635.7	915.8	1,105.5	1,133.0	1,160.5	1,095.2
Motor vehicles and parts.	205.1	255.7	363.2	409.6	397.1	400.3	342.3
New motor vehicles	134.7	147.5	210.7	248.9	233.0	233.3	184.5
Motor vehicle fuels, lubricants, and fluids . . .	111.4	120.4	172.9	283.8	314.7	343.9	386.4
Furniture and durable household equipment	120.9	146.7	208.1	263.9	276.5	279.8	270.1
Furniture, furnishings, and floor coverings.	65.3	78.8	114.4	143.0	149.7	150.8	143.4
Household appliances	24.8	29.0	37.6	47.6	50.0	51.0	50.4
Glassware, tableware, and household utensils	18.4	23.7	35.3	45.4	47.8	49.1	48.2
Video and audio equipment	43.7	56.8	83.1	107.8	114.6	116.6	117.7
Information processing equipment.	9.6	25.0	44.1	55.9	60.4	65.3	66.3
Therapeutic appliances and equipment	18.4	21.0	32.2	38.2	40.2	43.2	44.6
Sports and recreational goods and related services . . .	74.2	101.9	147.9	188.4	199.6	209.3	211.5
Jewelry and watches	30.3	37.8	49.1	56.2	59.6	61.6	60.0
Recreational books	10.9	16.4	24.4	29.8	31.4	33.2	33.9
Tools and equipment for house and garden.	9.7	13.0	17.1	22.3	23.4	23.5	23.2
Nondurable goods	994.2	1,179.8	1,543.4	1,968.4	2,088.7	2,204.5	2,308.0
Food and beverages purchased for off-premise consumption	391.2	443.7	537.5	665.0	698.0	740.1	784.3
Alcoholic beverages purchased for off-premise consumption	49.3	55.0	74.0	95.1	103.3	109.8	114.5
Purchased meals and beverages.	228.3	272.4	346.0	443.5	471.2	493.9	511.5
Food furnished to employees (incl. military) and food produced and consumed on farms.	7.4	8.3	9.2	12.1	13.8	14.4	14.1
Clothing, footwear, and related services	207.0	244.1	297.3	331.8	347.2	359.1	355.6
Footwear	32.1	38.1	46.9	51.5	54.3	55.2	55.4
Women's and girls' clothing	94.5	108.9	132.7	151.9	158.9	165.2	162.2
Men's and boys' clothing	57.4	72.2	85.9	93.6	97.4	100.6	99.5
Gasoline and other energy goods	124.2	133.4	188.8	304.8	336.9	368.0	413.0
Fuel oil and other fuels.	12.8	13.0	15.9	21.0	22.4	24.1	26.6
Other nondurable goods	283.6	371.4	536.2	683.0	723.7	755.2	773.2
Tobacco	41.0	49.2	68.5	71.1	72.3	75.1	77.1
Personal care products	39.3	50.2	68.5	79.5	83.5	87.4	91.3
Household supplies	54.2	70.4	86.7	103.0	108.6	111.9	114.0
Pharmaceuticals and other medical products	59.1	85.1	159.0	247.3	267.1	277.6	279.4
Magazines, newspapers, and stationery	36.5	46.1	56.6	63.2	66.8	70.2	71.7
Services	2,344.2	3,171.7	4,371.2	5,745.1	6,100.9	6,461.4	6,726.8
Housing.	570.4	756.2	1,010.5	1,328.9	1,416.3	1,480.0	1,543.1
Owner-occupied nonfarm dwellings-imputed rental. .	412.8	559.8	768.9	1,044.5	1,111.0	1,143.5	1,186.8
Tenant-occupied nonfarm dwellings-rent	150.7	186.2	227.9	264.7	283.4	311.9	330.3
Rental value of farm dwellings	6.3	9.4	12.7	18.8	20.9	23.6	24.9
Household consumption expenditures	2,264.5	3,064.6	4,205.9	5,531.0	5,860.6	6,207.9	6,448.0
Housing and utilities.	696.4	913.8	1,198.6	1,582.8	1,686.0	1,763.1	1,843.7
Electricity.	71.8	87.6	98.4	128.7	140.9	148.7	157.0
Natural gas	27.0	30.7	39.3	61.6	59.9	61.5	66.5
Water and other sanitary services.	27.1	39.3	50.4	63.6	68.8	72.9	77.1
Telecommunication services	60.7	85.2	130.2	146.1	157.8	162.0	168.0
Internet access	0.1	1.6	16.4	29.9	32.3	38.6	42.5
Transportation	442.9	554.1	798.4	979.3	1,008.7	1,051.6	1,036.5
Public transportation	39.2	48.8	73.0	76.8	80.6	83.3	86.2
Ground.	12.9	16.7	21.6	26.4	28.4	28.6	31.0
Air	25.9	31.1	49.2	47.7	49.4	51.7	52.2
Water	0.3	1.1	2.2	2.7	2.8	3.0	3.0
Health	583.7	826.0	1,109.6	1,601.5	1,688.1	1,790.4	1,878.2
Physician services	134.8	177.8	229.2	332.4	346.8	365.6	381.8
Dental services	32.4	45.4	63.6	89.0	93.5	99.3	103.5
Other professional services	40.1	62.5	84.1	127.1	132.5	142.3	153.3
Home health care.	18.4	41.6	42.8	61.2	64.1	70.9	77.9
Hospitals and nursing homes.	274.1	383.3	481.8	679.5	715.7	762.3	807.0
Health insurance	43.4	60.7	88.1	145.1	150.6	156.3	161.8
Recreation services	121.8	181.1	255.5	326.8	348.8	371.7	383.1
Admissions to specified spectator amusements	14.4	20.1	30.6	39.2	42.1	44.5	45.6
Gambling	23.7	45.4	67.6	95.6	103.9	109.6	113.7
Pets, pet products, and related services	18.8	27.3	39.7	53.1	56.9	61.6	65.1
Personal care	72.4	93.8	132.2	169.1	178.8	189.5	198.8
Personal items	40.0	48.7	63.7	72.6	77.3	80.4	78.9
Financial services and insurance.	253.2	364.7	570.0	712.6	752.4	824.2	835.6
Financial services furnished without payment	93.0	130.6	195.4	220.0	224.8	254.6	271.4
Financial service charges, fees, and commissions . .	48.5	81.9	174.6	207.2	233.0	260.5	249.5
Life insurance.	42.3	54.3	65.0	76.5	80.9	83.8	82.7
Legal services	41.0	47.4	65.4	89.7	95.2	102.1	102.9
Funeral and burial expenses	9.5	12.4	15.8	19.0	19.0	18.5	18.7
Education services	66.0	92.3	134.3	170.4	182.4	196.4	210.5
Higher education	34.7	51.9	76.8	108.8	116.6	125.0	135.0
Nursery, elementary, and secondary schools	14.8	19.2	24.1	31.8	33.8	36.6	38.5
Commercial and vocational schools.	11.1	14.4	24.3	29.8	32.0	34.7	37.0
Social services and religious activities	41.2	58.1	85.0	118.7	125.9	135.9	144.4
Net foreign travel	-10.3	-23.0	-16.5	-5.1	-1.6	-9.3	-19.8
Foreign travel by U.S. residents	42.7	54.7	84.3	99.8	108.5	114.0	118.8
Less: expenditures in the United States by nonresidents.	53.0	77.7	100.8	104.9	110.1	123.3	138.6
Final consumption expenditures of nonprofit institutions serving households.	79.6	107.2	165.4	214.1	240.4	253.5	278.7

(1) Subtotals may not add up to totals due to rounding or incomplete enumeration.

Leading U.S. Businesses, 2009

Source: *Fortune* magazine

(in millions of dollars of revenue; rank among all businesses by revenue)

Company (rank)	Revenue
Advertising, Marketing	
Omnicom (202)	$13,360
Interpublic Group (361)	6,963
Aerospace and Defense	
Boeing (34)	$60,909
United Technologies (37)	58,681
Lockheed Martin (54)	42,731
Honeywell International (63)	36,556
Northrop Grumman (69)	33,940
General Dynamics (83)	29,302
Raytheon (108)	23,174
L-3 Communications (171)	14,901
Textron (173)	14,806
Goodrich (354)	7,062
Precision Castparts (362)	6,916
Airlines	
AMR (104)	$23,766
Delta Air Lines (111)	22,697
UAL (123)	20,194
Continental Airlines (167)	15,241
US Airways Group (222)	12,118
Southwest Airlines (246)	11,023
Apparel	
Nike (136)	$18,627
VF (335)	7,643
Automotive Retailing, Services	
AutoNation (182)	$14,288
Penske Automotive Group (225)	11,918
Hertz Global Holdings (305)	8,525
CarMax (311)	8,319
Sonic Automotive (337)	7,488
Beverages	
Coca-Cola (73)	$31,944
Coca-Cola Enterprises (116) . . .	21,807
Pepsi Bottling (189)	13,796
Chemicals	
Dow Chemical (38)	$57,514
DuPont (75)	31,836
PPG Industries (161)	15,849
Monsanto (235)	11,579
Air Products & Chemicals (248) .	10,939
Praxair (249)	10,796
Huntsman (262)	10,215
Mosaic (276)	9,813
Rohm & Haas (281)	9,575
Ashland (310)	8,381
Sherwin-Williams (322)	7,980
Eastman Chemical (364)	6,895
Celanese (368)	6,823
Avery Dennison (376)	6,710
Commercial Banks	
Bank of America Corp. (11)	$113,106
Citigroup (12)	112,372
JPMorgan Chase & Co. (16)	101,491
Morgan Stanley (30)	62,262
Goldman Sachs Group (40)	53,579
Wells Fargo (41)	51,652
GMAC (66)	35,445
American Express (74)	31,877
U.S. Bancorp (129)	19,229
Capital One Financial (145)	17,869
Bank of New York Mellon Corp.	
(156)	16,355
State Street Corp. (206)	12,922
SunTrust Banks (211)	12,801
BB&T Corp. (260)	10,404
PNC Financial Services Group	
(278)	9,680
Regions Financial (280)	9,637
Fifth Third Bancorp (302)	8,554
KeyCorp (382)	6,499
CIT Group (397)	6,229
Computer Peripherals	
EMC (172)	$14,876
Western Digital (319)	8,074
Computer Software	
Microsoft (35)	$60,420
Oracle (113)	22,430

Company (rank)	Revenue
Computers, Office Equipment	
Hewlett-Packard (9)	$118,364
Dell (33)	61,101
Apple (71)	32,479
Xerox (147)	17,608
Sun Microsystems (187)	13,880
Pitney Bowes (395)	6,262
Construction and Farm Machinery	
Caterpillar (44)	$51,324
Deere (87)	28,438
Cummins (181)	14,342
Terex (275)	9,890
AGCO (306)	8,425
Diversified Financials	
General Electric (5)	$183,207
Fannie Mae (112)	22,652
International Assets Holding	
(140)	18,359
Freddie Mac (220)	12,302
Marsh & McLennan (232)	11,587
Aon (307)	8,406
SLM (331)	7,689
Ameriprise Financial (348)	7,149
Diversified Outsourcing	
Aramark (198)	$13,470
Automatic Data Processing (297)	8,777
Electronics, Electrical Equipment	
Emerson Electric (94)	$25,281
Whirlpool (133)	18,907
General Cable (396)	6,230
Energy	
Constellation Energy (125)	$19,818
AES (158)	16,170
American Electric Power (180) . .	14,442
Integrys Energy Group (185)	14,048
Reliant Energy (214)	12,553
Williams (218)	12,357
Energy Future Holdings (237) . . .	11,364
Calpine (272)	9,937
Global Partners (291)	9,019
NRG Energy (363)	6,905
UGI (377)	6,648
Engineering, Construction	
Fluor (114)	$22,326
KBR (234)	11,581
Jacobs Engineering Group (241) .	11,252
URS (264)	10,086
Peter Kiewit Sons' (321)	8,012
Shaw Group (357)	6,998
Emcor Group (370)	6,785
Entertainment	
Time Warner (48)	$46,984
Walt Disney (60)	37,843
News Corp. (70)	32,996
Viacom (177)	14,625
CBS (186)	13,950
CC Media Holdings (372)	6,765
Financial Data Services	
First Data (295)	$8,811
Discover Financial Services (352)	7,088
Visa (394)	6,263
Food and Drug Stores	
CVS Caremark (19)	$87,472
Kroger (22)	76,000
Walgreen (36)	59,034
Safeway (50)	44,104
Supervalu (51)	44,048
Rite Aid (100)	24,418
Publix Super Markets (100)	24,110
Whole Food Market (324)	7,954
Winn-Dixie Stores (340)	7,281
Great Atlantic & Pacific Tea (360)	6,964
Food	
PepsiCo (52)	$43,251
Kraft Foods (53)	42,867
ConAgra Foods (188)	13,809
General Mills (193)	13,652
Sara Lee (199)	13,450

Company (rank)	Revenue
Kellogg (210)	12,822
Dean Foods (216)	12,455
Land O'Lakes (224)	12,039
H.J. Heinz (267)	10,071
Campbell Soup (309)	8,391
Dole Food (329)	7,732
Hormel Foods (373)	6,755
Food Production	
Archer Daniels Midland (27)	$69,816
Tyson Foods (89)	28,130
Smithfield Foods (183)	14,264
Pilgrim's Pride (304)	8,525
Food Services	
McDonald's (107)	$23,522
Yum Brands (239)	11,279
Starbucks (261)	10,383
Darden Restaurants (374)	6,747
Forest and Paper Products	
International Paper (97)	$24,829
Weyerhaeuser (236)	11,401
AbitibiBowater (379)	6,645
Domtar (390)	6,394
General Merchandisers	
Wal-Mart Stores (2)	$405,607
Target (28)	64,948
Sears Holdings (49)	46,770
Macy's (96)	24,892
J.C. Penney (139)	18,486
Kohl's (155)	16,389
Dollar General (259)	10,458
Nordstrom (301)	8,573
Dillard's (358)	6,988
Family Dollar Stores (359)	6,984
Health Care: Insurance & Managed Care	
UnitedHealth Group (21)	$81,186
WellPoint (32)	61,251
Aetna (77)	30,951
Humana (85)	28,946
Cigna (132)	19,101
Health Net (165)	15,367
Coventry Health Care (226)	11,914
WellCare Health Plans (381) . . .	6,522
Health Care: Medical Facilities	
HCA (88)	$28,374
Community Health Systems (243)	11,156
Tenet Healthcare (283)	9,494
Health Care: Pharmacy and	
Other Services	
Medco Health Solutions (45) . . .	$51,258
Express Scripts (115)	22,023
Quest Diagnostics (341)	7,249
Omnicare (392)	6,311
Home Equipment, Furnishings	
Masco (277)	$9,700
Fortune Brands (351)	7,105
Newell Rubbermaid (387)	6,471
Home Builders	
Centex (308)	$8,406
D.R. Horton (378)	6,646
Pulte Homes (393)	6,290
Hotels, Casinos, Resorts	
Marriott International (208)	$12,880
Harrah's Entertainment (263) . . .	10,127
MGM Mirage (283)	7,209
Household and Personal Products	
Procter & Gamble (20)	$83,503
Kimberly-Clark (128)	19,415
Colgate-Palmolive (166)	15,330
Avon Products (255)	10,690
Estée Lauder (325)	7,911
Industrial Machinery	
Illinois Tool Works (148)	$17,218
Eaton (164)	15,376
Parker Hannifin (221)	12,146
ITT (229)	11,703
Dover (333)	7,653
Information Technology Services	
International Business Machines	
(14)	$103,630

Company (rank)	Revenue
Computer Sciences (153)	16,500
SAIC (266)	10,078
Insurance: Life, Health (Mutual)	
New York Life Insurance (76)	$31,416
TIAA-CREF (82)	29,363
Northwestern Mutual (118)	21,734
Massachusetts Mutual Life Insurance (135)	18,745
Guardian Life Ins. Co. of America (279)	9,675
Insurance: Life, Health (Stock)	
MetLife (39)	$55,085
Prudential Financial (84)	29,275
AFLAC (152)	16,554
Unum Group (270)	9,982
Genworth Financial (271)	9,948
Principal Financial (273)	9,936
Lincoln National (274)	9,905
Insurance: Property & Casualty (Mutual)	
State Farm Insurance Cos. (31)	$61,343
Insurance: Property & Casualty (Stock)	
Berkshire Hathaway (13)	$107,786
Allstate (81)	29,394
Liberty Mutual Insurance Group (86)	28,855
Travelers Cos. (99)	24,477
Nationwide (124)	19,848
Loews (174)	14,733
Chubb (203)	13,221
United Services Automobile Association (207)	12,912
Progressive (209)	12,840
American International Group (245)	11,104
Hartford Financial Services (287)	9,219
Assurant (299)	8,601
American Family Insurance Group (388)	6,431
First American Corp. (398)	6,214
Internet Services and Retailing	
Google (117)	$21,796
Amazon.com (130)	19,166
Liberty Media (265)	10,084
eBay (303)	8,541
Yahoo (345)	7,209
Mail, Package, Freight Delivery	
United Parcel Service (43)	$51,486
FedEx (59)	37,953
Medical Products and Equipment	
Medtronic (196)	$13,515
Baxter International (219)	12,348
Boston Scientific (320)	8,050
Becton Dickinson (347)	7,159
Stryker (375)	6,718
Metals	
Alcoa (90)	$28,119
United States Steel (105)	23,754
Nucor (106)	23,663
Commercial Metals (251)	10,765
Steel Dynamics (318)	8,081
AK Steel Holding (334)	7,644
Mining, Crude Oil Production	
Occidental Petroleum (98)	$24,480
Freeport-McMoRan Copper & Gold (146)	17,796
Anadarko Petroleum (162)	15,723
Devon Energy (163)	15,560
Apache (217)	12,390
Chesapeake Energy (230)	11,629
XTO Energy (330)	7,695
EOG Resources (350)	7,127
Peabody Energy (353)	7,074
Miscellaneous	
3M (95)	$25,269
Mohawk Industries (367)	6,826
Motor Vehicles and Parts	
General Motors (6)	$148,979
Ford Motor (7)	146,277
Johnson Controls (58)	38,062
Delphi (121)	20,383
Goodyear Tire & Rubber (127)	19,488
TRW Automotive Holdings (169)	14,995
Paccar (170)	14,973
Navistar International (175)	14,724

Company (rank)	Revenue
Lear (195)	13,571
Visteon (282)	9,544
Dana Holding (316)	8,101
ArvinMeritor (346)	7,174
Oshkosh (349)	7,138
Autoliv (386)	6,473
Network and Other Communications Equipment	
Cisco Systems (57)	$39,540
Motorola (78)	30,146
Qualcomm (244)	11,142
Oil and Gas Equipment Services	
Halliburton (141)	$18,279
National Oilwell Varco (200)	13,431
Baker Hughes (227)	11,864
Smith International (250)	10,771
Packaging, Containers	
Crown Holdings (312)	$8,305
Owens-Illinois (326)	7,885
Ball (336)	7,562
Smurfit-Stone Container (356)	7,042
MeadWestvaco (365)	6,890
Petroleum Refining	
Exxon Mobil (1)	$442,851
Chevron (3)	263,159
ConocoPhillips (4)	230,764
Valero Energy (10)	118,298
Marathon Oil (23)	73,504
Sunoco (41)	51,652
Hess (55)	41,094
Tesoro (91)	28,031
Murphy Oil (92)	27,513
Western Refining (253)	10,726
Frontier Oil (383)	6,499
Pharmaceuticals	
Johnson & Johnson (29)	$63,747
Pfizer (46)	48,296
Abbott Laboratories (80)	29,528
Merck (103)	23,850
Wyeth (110)	22,834
Bristol-Myers Squibb (120)	21,366
Eli Lilly (122)	20,378
Schering-Plough (138)	18,502
Amgen (168)	15,003
Pipelines	
Enterprise GP Holdings (65)	$35,470
Plains All American Pipeline (79)	30,061
Oneok (159)	16,157
Knight (223)	12,095
Enbridge Energy Partners (268)	10,060
Energy Transfer Equity (286)	9,293
Targa Resources (323)	7,970
Publishing, Printing	
R.R. Donnelley & Sons (233)	$11,582
Gannett (371)	6,768
McGraw-Hill (391)	6,355
Railroads	
Burlington Northern Santa Fe (142)	$18,018
Union Pacific (143)	17,970
CSX (240)	11,255
Norfolk Southern (256)	10,661
Scientific, Photo, Control Equipment	
Danaher (213)	$12,698
Thermo Fisher Scientific (258)	10,498
Eastman Kodak (284)	9,416
Securities	
Merrill Lynch (150)	$16,784
Semiconductors and Other Electronic Components	
Intel (61)	$37,586
Jabil Circuit (212)	12,780
Texas Instruments (215)	12,501
Sanmina-SCI (292)	9,005
Applied Materials (315)	8,129
Specialty Retailers	
Costco Wholesale (24)	$72,483
Home Depot (25)	71,288
Lowe's (47)	48,230
Best Buy (56)	40,023
Staples (109)	23,084
TJX (131)	19,148
Gap (178)	14,526

Company (rank)	Revenue
Office Depot (179)	$14,496
Toys"R"Us (192)	13,724
Circuit City Stores (228)	11,744
BJ's Wholesale Club (269)	10,027
Limited Brands (290)	9,043
GameStop (296)	8,806
OfficeMax (313)	8,267
Pantry (317)	8,089
TravelCenters of America (332)	7,658
Bed Bath & Beyond (355)	7,049
AutoZone (380)	6,523
Ross Stores (384)	6,486
Telecommunications	
AT&T (8)	$124,028
Verizon Communications (17)	97,354
Sprint Nextel (64)	35,635
Comcast (68)	34,256
DirecTV Group (126)	19,693
Qwest Communications (197)	13,475
DISH Network (231)	11,617
Liberty Global (257)	10,561
Virgin Media (338)	7,440
Cablevision Systems (342)	7,230
Charter Communications (385)	6,479
Temporary Help	
Manpower (119)	$21,553
Tobacco	
Philip Morris International (93)	$25,705
Altria Group (160)	15,957
Reynolds American (294)	8,845
Transportation and Logistics	
C.H. Robinson Worldwide (300)	$8,579
Trucking, Truck Leasing	
YRC Worldwide (293)	$8,940
Ryder System (399)	6,204
Utilities: Gas and Electric	
Exelon (134)	$18,859
Southern (149)	17,127
FPL Group (154)	16,410
Dominion Resources (157)	16,290
PG&E Corp. (176)	14,628
Edison International (184)	14,112
Public Service Enterprise Group (190)	13,741
Consolidated Edison (191)	13,726
FirstEnergy (194)	13,627
Duke Energy (204)	13,212
Entergy (205)	13,094
CenterPoint Energy (238)	11,322
Xcel Energy (242)	11,203
Sempra Energy (252)	10,758
Pepco Holdings (254)	10,700
DTE Energy (285)	9,336
Progress Energy (288)	9,186
NiSource (289)	9,070
PPL (314)	8,206
Ameren (327)	7,839
Atmos Energy (343)	7,221
CMS Energy (369)	6,821
Waste Management	
Waste Management (201)	$13,388
Wholesalers: Diversified	
World Fuel Services (137)	$18,509
Genuine Parts (247)	11,015
Reliance Steel & Aluminum (298)	8,719
W.W. Grainger (366)	6,850
Wholesalers: Electronics and Office Equipment	
Ingram Micro (67)	$34,362
Tech Data (102)	24,081
Avnet (144)	17,953
Arrow Electronics (151)	16,761
Synnex (328)	7,768
Wholesalers: Food and Grocery	
Sysco (62)	$37,522
CHS (72)	32,168
Wholesalers: Health Care	
McKesson (15)	$101,703
Cardinal Health (18)	91,091
AmerisourceBergen (26)	70,594
Owens & Minor (339)	7,338
Henry Schein (389)	6,408

75 U.S. Corporations with Largest Revenues, 2009

Source: *Fortune* magazine

(in millions of dollars)

Rank	Company (2008 rank)	Revenues	Profits	Rank	Company (2008 rank)	Revenues	Profits
1.	Exxon Mobil (2)	$442,851.0	$45,220.0	38.	Dow Chemical (42)	$57.514.0	$579.0
2.	Wal-Mart Stores (1)	405,607.0	13,400.0	39.	MetLife (43)	55,085.0	3,209.0
3.	Chevron (3)	263,159.0	23,931.0	40.	Goldman Sachs Group (20)	53,579.0	2,322.0
4.	ConocoPhillips (5)	230,764.0	−16,998.0	41.	Sunoco (56)	51,652.0	776.0
5.	General Electric (6)	183,207.0	17,410.0		Wells Fargo (41)	51,652.0	2,655.0
6.	General Motors (4)	148,979.0	−30,860.0	43.	United Parcel Service (46)	51,486.0	3,003.0
7.	Ford Motor (7)	146,277.0	−14,672.0	44.	Caterpillar (50)	51,324.0	3,557.0
8.	AT&T (10)	124,028.0	12,867.0	45.	Medco Health Solutions (51)	51,258.0	1,102.9
9.	Hewlett-Packard (14)	118,364.0	8,329.0	46.	Pfizer (47)	48,296.0	8,104.0
10.	Valero Energy (16)	118,298.0	−1,131.0	47.	Lowe's (48)	48,230.0	2,195.0
11.	Bank of America Corp. (9)	113,106.0	4,008.0	48.	Time Warner (49)	46,984.0	−13,402.0
12.	Citigroup (8)	112,372.0	−27,684.0	49.	Sears Holdings (45)	46,770.0	53.0
13.	Berkshire Hathaway (11)	107,786.0	4,994.0	50.	Safeway (55)	44,104.0	965.3
14.	International Business Machines (15)	103,630.0	12,334.0	51.	Supervalu (62)	44,048.0	593.0
15.	McKesson (18)	101,703.0	990.0	52.	PepsiCo (59)	43,251.0	5,142.0
16.	JPMorgan Chase & Co. (12)	101,491.0	5,605.0	53.	Kraft Foods (63)	42,867.0	2,901.0
17.	Verizon Communications (17)	97,354.0	6,428.0	54.	Lockheed Martin (57)	42,731.0	3,217.0
18.	Cardinal Health (19)	91,091.4	1,300.6	55.	Hess (77)	41,094.0	2,360.0
19.	CVS Caremark (24)	87,471.9	3,212.1	56.	Best Buy (66)	40,023.0	1,407.0
20.	Procter & Gamble (23)	83,503.0	12,075.0	57.	Cisco Systems (71)	39,540.0	8,052.0
21.	UnitedHealth Group (25)	81,186.0	2,977.0	58.	Johnson Controls (72)	38,062.0	979.0
22.	Kroger (26)	76,000.0	1,249.4	59.	FedEx (68)	37,953.0	1,125.0
23.	Marathon Oil (36)	73,504.0	3,528.0	60.	Walt Disney (67)	37,843.0	4,427.0
24.	Costco Wholesale (29)	72,483.0	1,282.7	61.	Intel (60)	37,586.0	5,292.0
25.	Home Depot (22)	71,288.0	2,260.0	62.	Sysco (70)	37,522.1	1,106.2
26.	AmerisourceBergen (28)	70,593.5	250.6	63.	Honeywell International (73)	36,556.0	2,792.0
27.	Archer Daniels Midland (52)	69,816.0	1,802.0	64.	Sprint Nextel (58)	35,635.0	−2,796.0
28.	Target (31)	64,948.0	2,214.0	65.	Enterprise GP Holdings (90)	35,469.6	164.1
29.	Johnson & Johnson (35)	63,747.0	12,949.0	66.	GMAC (78)	35,445.0	1,868.0
30.	Morgan Stanley (21)	62,262.0	1,707.0	67.	Ingram Micro (69)	34,362.2	−394.9
31.	State Farm Insurance Cos. (32)	61,343.4	−541.8	68.	Comcast (79)	34,256.0	2,547.0
32.	WellPoint (33)	61,251.1	2,490.7	69.	Northrop Grumman (76)	33,940.0	−1,262.0
33.	Dell (34)	61,101.0	2,478.0	70.	News Corp. (84)	32,996.0	5,387.0
34.	Boeing (27)	60,909.0	2,672.0	71.	Apple (103)	32,479.0	4,834.0
35.	Microsoft (44)	60,420.0	17,681.0	72.	CHS (145)	32,167.5	803.0
36.	Walgreen (40)	59,034.0	2,157.0	73.	Coca-Cola (83)	31,944.0	5,807.0
37.	United Technologies (39)	58,681.0	4,689.0	74.	American Express (75)	31,877.0	2,699.0
				75.	DuPont (81)	31,836.0	2,007.0

Fastest-Growing U.S. Franchises, 2009[1]

Source: *Entrepreneur* magazine

Company	Type of business	Minimum start-up cost[2]
1. Jan-Pro Franchising Intl. Inc.	Commercial cleaning	$3.3K-54.3K
2. Subway	Submarine sandwiches and salads	$78.6K-238.3K
3. Instant Tax Service	Retail tax preparation and electronic filing	$39K-89K
4. Stratus Building Solutions	Commercial cleaning	$3.5K-57.8K
5. Snap Fitness Inc.	24-hour fitness center	$77.4K-272.8K
6. Dunkin' Donuts	Coffee, doughnuts, baked goods	Varies
7. Jazzercise Inc.	Dance/exercise classes	$2.98K-38.4K
8. Bonus Building Care	Commercial cleaning	$8.8K-14.7K
9. Anytime Fitness	Fitness center	$30K-292.6K
10. Vanguard Cleaning Systems	Commercial cleaning	$8.2K-38.1K
11. Jani-King	Commercial cleaning	$11.4K-35.1K+
12. Domino's Pizza LLC	Pizza, breadsticks, buffalo wings	$119.95K-461.7K
13. Choice Hotels Intl.	Hotels, inns, suites, resorts	$2.5M-15.3M
14. McDonald's	Hamburgers, chicken, salads	$950.2K-1.8M
15. Liberty Tax Service	Income tax preparation services	$56.8K-69.9K
16. Long John Silver's Restaurants Inc.	Fish and chicken	$879.5K-1.3M
17. ExpressTax	Tax preparation and electronic filing	$15.4K-40.1K
18. System4	Commercial cleaning	$5.5K-37.8K
19. Anago Cleaning Systems	Commercial cleaning	$8.5K-55K
20. Massage Envy	Therapeutic massage services	$291.9K-469.8K
21. Edible Arrangements Intl. Inc.	Floral-like designs from sculpted fresh fruit	$154.9K-298K
22. InterContinental Hotels Group	Hotels	Varies
23. Jimmy John's Gourmet Sandwich Shops	Gourmet sandwiches	$304.5K-420.5K
24. Denny's Inc.	Full-service family restaurant	$1.2M-2.6M
25. Colbert/Ball Tax Service	Tax preparation and electronic filing	$27K-39K

(1) Ranked by number of new franchise units added. (2) "K" denotes thousands; "M" denotes millions. This number does not include franchise fee, which varies.

United States Mint

Source: United States Mint, U.S. Dept. of the Treasury

The United States Mint was created on Apr. 2, 1792, by an act of Congress, which established the U.S. national coinage system. In 1799 the mint became an independent agency reporting directly to the president. It was made a statutory bureau of the Treasury Department in 1873, with a director appointed by the president. The mint manufactures and ships all U.S. coins for circulation to Federal Reserve banks and branches, which in turn issue coins to the public and business community through depository institutions. The mint also safeguards the Treasury Department's stored gold and silver, as well as other monetary assets.

The composition of dimes, quarters, and half dollars, traditionally produced from silver, was changed by the Coinage Act of 1965, which mandated that these coins from then on be minted from a cupronickel-clad alloy and reduced the silver content of the half dollar to 40%. In 1970, legislative action mandated that the half dollar and a dollar coin be minted from the same alloy.

Mint headquarters are in Washington, DC. Mint production facilities are in Philadelphia, Denver, San Francisco, and West Point, NY. In addition, the mint is responsible for the U.S. Bullion Depository at Fort Knox, KY.

The mint offers free public tours and operates sales centers at the U.S. mints in Denver and Philadelphia. Further information is available from the U.S. Mint, Customer Care Center, 801 9th St. NW, Washington, DC 20220; (800) USA-MINT. **Website:** www.usmint.gov

History of the Dollar Coin: The Eisenhower dollar was minted 1971 through 1978, when legislation called for the minting of the smaller Susan B. Anthony dollar coin. The Anthony dollar, minted through 1981, marked the first time that a woman other than a mythical figure appeared on a generally circulated U.S. coin. It was replaced in 2000 by the Golden Dollar Coin. Golden in color, with a smooth edge and wide border, the obverse depicts Sacagawea (a Shoshone woman who helped guide explorers Lewis and Clark) and her infant son. The reverse shows an American eagle and 17 stars, one for each of the states at the time of the Lewis and Clark expedition. In 2007, the mint began issuing a series of Golden Dollar Coins featuring U.S. presidents. Each includes the president's name, likeness, and years of service. Four will be issued each year in the order in which the presidents served. Presidents serving non-consecutive terms (Grover Cleveland) will be honored twice. According to the current schedule, coins will be minted through 2016 and only presidents deceased more than two years will be honored. The reverse features the Statue of Liberty. The mint mark, "e Pluribus Unum," and "In God We Trust," are edge-incused.

New Circulating and Commemorative Coins

Source: United States Mint, U.S. Dept. of the Treasury

The 50 State Quarters program that began in 1999 ended in 2008 with the final five states to enter the union: Oklahoma, New Mexico, Arizona, Alaska, and Hawaii. An unofficial extension of the program in 2009 planned to issue six quarter-dollar coins in honor of the District of Columbia and five U.S. territories: the Commonwealth of Puerto Rico, Guam, American Samoa, the U.S. Virgin Islands, and the Commonwealth of the Northern Mariana Islands.

In 2010, the U.S. Mint begins its America the Beautiful Quarters program, an initiative to honor 56 national parks and other sites in each state, the District of Columbia, and outlying U.S. territories. Five new reverse designs will appear on the quarter-dollar each year, 2010-21, issued in the order in which the featured site was first established as a national park or site.

The 2010 America the Beautiful Quarters will be released in the following order: Hot Springs National Park, AR; Yellowstone National Park, WY; Yosemite National Park, CA; Grand Canyon National Park, AZ; and Mt. Hood National Forest, OR.

The mint produced congressionally authorized commemorative coins from 1892 to 1954, and again since 1982. Through 2009, Congress has authorized 49 commemorative coin programs. Recent congressionally authorized coins are the 2007 Jamestown 400th Anniversary gold $5 and silver $1; the 2007 Little Rock Central High School Desegregation silver $1; the 2008 American Bald Eagle Recovery and National Emblem gold $5, silver $1, and clad half dollar; the 2009 Louis Braille Bicentennial-Braille Literacy silver $1; the 2009 Lincoln Penny Series; and the 2010 American Veterans Disabled for Life silver $1.

Bureau of Engraving and Printing

Source: Bureau of Engraving and Printing, U.S. Dept. of the Treasury; www.moneyfactory.gov

The Bureau of Engraving and Printing manufactures the financial and other securities of the United States. It designs and prints a variety of products, including Federal Reserve notes (bills in various denominations), Treasury securities, identification cards, naturalization certificates, and other special security documents. Denominations of the various types of printings produced by the bureau range from a 1/5-cent wine stamp to a $100,000,000 International Monetary Fund special note. Among its products are all hand-engraved invitations issued by the White House.

The first general circulation of paper money by the federal government dates back to 1861, prior to the establishment of the bureau, when, to finance the Civil War, Congress authorized the U.S. Treasury to issue non-interest-bearing demand notes, nicknamed "greenbacks" because of their color. A portrait of Pres. Abraham Lincoln appeared on the face of the first $10 notes. By 1862, the design of U.S. currency incorporated fine-line engraving, intricate geometric lathe work patterns, a Treasury seal, and engraved signatures to aid in counterfeit deterrence. All U.S. currency issued since 1861 remain valid and redeemable at full face value.

The Bureau of Engraving and Printing began operations by 1862, originally separating and sealing bank notes that were printed by private companies. In 1877, the bureau became the sole producer of U.S. currency. In 1894, it also began producing postage stamps. On June 10, 2005, the bureau printed its last stamps, a roll of 37-cent flag stamps; stamps are now produced by private printers.

The Federal Reserve Act of 1913 created the Federal Reserve as the nation's central bank, and provided for currency called Federal Reserve notes. The first notes, issued the following year, were $10 notes bearing a portrait of Pres. Andrew Jackson. In 1929, the look of U.S. currency was standardized. The national motto, "In God We Trust," was added to paper money in 1957.

The Bureau of Engraving and Printing currently operates two facilities, one in Washington, DC, opened in 1914, and one in Fort Worth, TX, which began operations in 1991.

Denominations of U.S. Currency

Since 1969 the largest denomination of U.S. currency that has been issued is the $100 bill. As larger-denomination bills reach the Federal Reserve Bank, they are removed from circulation. Because some discontinued currency is expected to be in the hands of holders for many years, the description of the various denominations below is continued.

Amt.	Portrait	Embellishment on back	Amt.	Portrait	Embellishment on back
$1	Washington	Great Seal of U.S.	$500	McKinley	Ornate denominational marking
2	Jefferson	Signers of Declaration	1,000	Cleveland	Ornate denominational marking
5	Lincoln	Lincoln Memorial	5,000	Madison	Washington Resigning as Army Commander
10	Hamilton	U.S. Treasury			
20	Jackson	White House	10,000	Salmon Chase	Embarkation of the Pilgrims
50	Grant	U.S. Capitol	100,000*	Wilson	Ornate denominational marking
100	Franklin	Independence Hall			

*For use only in transactions between Federal Reserve System and Treasury Department.

Portraits on U.S. Treasury Bills, Bonds, Notes, and Savings Bonds

The U.S. Treasury discontinued issuing treasury bill, bond, and note certificates in 1986. Since then, all issues of marketable treasury securities have been available only in book-entry form, although some certificates remain in circulation.

Denomination	EE savings bonds	Treasury bills	Treasury bonds	Treasury notes
$50	Washington		Jefferson	
75	Adams			
100	Jefferson		Jackson	
200	Madison			
500	Hamilton		Washington	
1,000	B. Franklin	H. McCulloch	Lincoln	Lincoln
5,000	P. Revere	J. G. Carlisle	Monroe	Monroe
10,000	J. Wilson	J. Sherman	Cleveland	Cleveland
50,000	C. Glass			
100,000		A. Gallatin	Grant	Grant
1,000,000		O. Wolcott	T. Roosevelt	T. Roosevelt
100,000,000				Madison
500,000,000				McKinley

U.S. Currency Designs

On Mar. 25, 1996, the U.S. Treasury issued a redesigned $100 note incorporating many new and modified anti-counterfeiting features. A new $50 note was issued Oct. 27, 1997, a new $20 note was released into circulation Sept. 24, 1998, and new $10 and $5 notes were issued May 24, 2000. Old notes are being removed from circulation as they are returned to the Federal Reserve.

The new $100 bill has a larger portrait, moved off-center; a watermark (seen only when held up to the light) to the right of the portrait, depicting the same person (Benjamin Franklin); a security thread that glows red when exposed to ultraviolet light in a dark environment; color-shifting ink that changes from green to black when viewed at different angles, to appear in the numeral on the lower, front right-hand corner of the bill; microprinting in the numeral in the note's lower, front left-hand corner and on the portrait; and other features for security, machine authentication, and processing of the currency. The redesigned $5, $10, $20, and $50 bills incorporated the same features as the $100 bill,

with the notable addition of a low-vision feature, a large (14-mm high, as compared to 7.8-mm on the old design), dark numeral on a light background on the back of the note. (The security thread glows yellow in the $50, green in the $20, orange in the $10, and blue in the $5. There is no color-shifting ink on the $5 note.)

Beginning in 2003, the Treasury launched another major redesign of U.S. currency: on Oct. 9, 2003, the U.S. Treasury introduced a new $20 note, using background colors for the first time since 1905. The notes have a security thread running vertically up one side, with "USA TWENTY" and a small U.S. flag; the thread glows green under UV light. Other security features include color-shifting ink in the number "20" in the lower right corner on the note's face. A new $50 note with similar security features was released Sept. 28, 2004, followed by a new $10 note on Mar. 2, 2006. A new $5 bill was issued Mar. 13, 2008, followed by another redesign of the $100 note.

Website: www.moneyfactory.gov/newmoney

The U.S. $1 Bill

Plate position: Shows where on the 32-note plate this bill was printed.

Serial number Each bill has its own.

Federal Reserve District Number: Shows which district issued the bill.

Federal Reserve District Seal: The name of the Federal Reserve Bank that issued the bill is printed in the seal. The letter tells you quickly where the bill is from. Here are the letter codes for the 12 Federal Reserve Districts:

  A: Boston
  B: New York
  C: Philadelphia
  D: Cleveland
  E: Richmond
  F: Atlanta
  G: Chicago
  H: St. Louis
  I: Minneapolis
  J: Kansas City
  K: Dallas
  L: San Francisco

The Treasury Department seal: The balancing scales represent justice. The pointed stripe across the middle has 13 stars for the original 13 colonies. The key represents authority.

Plate serial number Shows which printing plate was used for the face of the bill.

Treasurer of the U.S. signature

Series indicator (year note's design was first used)

Secretary of the Treasury signature

Plate serial number Shows which plate was used for the back.

Front of the Great Seal of the United States: The bald eagle is the national bird. The shield has 13 stripes for the 13 original colonies. The eagle holds 13 arrows (symbol of war) and an olive branch (symbol of peace). Above the eagle is the motto "E Pluribus Unum," Latin for "out of many, one," and a constellation of 13 stars.

Reverse of the Great Seal of the United States: The pyramid symbolizes something that endures for ages. The eye, known as the "Eye of Providence," probably comes from an ancient Egyptian symbol. The pyramid has 13 levels; at its base are the Roman numerals for 1776, the year of American independence. "Annuit Coeptis" is Latin for "God has favored our undertaking." "Novus Ordo Seclorum" is Latin for "a new order of the ages." Both phrases are from the works of the Roman poet Virgil.

U.S. Currency and Coin

Source: Financial Management Service, U.S. Dept. of the Treasury; as of June 30, 2009

Comparative Totals of Money in Circulation—Selected Dates

Date	Dollars (in millions)	Per capita[1]	Date	Dollars (in millions)	Per capita[1]	Date	Dollars (in millions)	Per capita[1]
June 30, 2009	$909,697	$2,963	Sept. 30, 2005	$766,487	$2,578	June 30, 1975....	$81,196	$380
May 31, 2009	908,504	2,962	Sept. 30, 2000	568,614	2,061	June 30, 1970....	54,351	265
Apr. 30, 2009	903,317	2,947	Sept. 30, 1995	409,272	1,553	June 30, 1965....	39,719	204
June 30, 2008	826,314	2,712	Sept. 30, 1990	278,903	1,105	June 30, 1960....	32,064	177
May 31, 2008	822,745	2,703	Sept. 30, 1985	187,337	782	June 30, 1955....	30,229	183
Apr. 30, 2008	814,027	2,676	Sept. 30, 1980	129,916	581			

(1) Based on Census Bureau population estimates.

Amounts Outstanding and in Circulation, 2009

Currency	Total currency and coin	Total currency	Federal Reserve notes[1]	U.S. notes	Currency no longer issued
Amounts outstanding	$1,095,548,566,543	$1,053,606,706,109	$1,053,121,169,155	$240,992,566	$244,544,388
Less amounts held by:					
Treasury..............	379,169,771	16,092,613	16,046,629	7,505	38,479
Federal Reserve banks ...	185,470,808,438	183,695,818,173	183,695,787,133	—	31,040
Amounts in circulation	826,313,890,478	869,894,795,323	869,409,335,393	240,985,061	244,474,869

Coins[2]	Total	Dollars[3]	Fractional coins
Amounts outstanding.....................	$41,941,860,434	$5,247,869,008	$36,693,991,426
Less amounts held by:			
Treasury................................	363,077,158	296,208,208	66,868,950
Federal Reserve banks	1,774,990,265	703,150,715	1,071,839,550
Amounts in circulation	39,803,793,011	4,248,510,085	35,555,282,926

(1) Issued on or after July 1, 1929. (2) Excludes coins sold to collectors at premium prices. (3) Includes $481,781,898 in standard silver dollars.

Currency in Circulation by Denominations, 2009

Denomination	Total currency in circulation	Federal Reserve notes[1]	U.S. notes	Currency no longer issued
$1................................	$9,342,956,896	$9,200,224,898	$143,503	$142,588,495
$2................................	1,685,300,132	1,553,188,490	132,099,018	12,624
$5................................	10,667,172,695	10,531,768,135	108,721,310	26,683,250
$10...............................	15,512,236,200	15,491,296,180	6,300	20,933,720
$20...............................	122,731,850,400	122,711,741,240	3,840	20,105,320
$50...............................	63,596,888,850	63,585,386,050	500	11,502,300
$100..............................	646,045,213,050	646,023,211,900	NA	22,001,150
$500..............................	142,271,500	142,066,500	5,500	199,500
$1,000	165,615,000	165,382,000	5,000	228,000
$5,000	1,780,000	1,710,000	NA	70,000
$10,000	3,510,000	3,360,000	NA	150,000
Fractional notes[2]	600	NA	90	510
Total currency....................	**$869,894,795,323**	**$869,409,335,393**	**$240,985,061**	**$244,474,869**

NA = Not available. (1) Issued on or after July 1, 1929. (2) Represents the value of certain partial denominations not presented for redemption.

U.S. Budget Receipts and Outlays, Fiscal Years 2003-08

Source: Congressional Budget Office; Budget of the U.S. Government, Office of Mgt. and Budget, Exec. Office of the President

As of Sept. 2008, the estimate from the Congressional Budget Office of the total U.S. budget deficit for fiscal year 2009 was $407 mil, a $3 mil decrease from the $410 mil deficit in 2008, but a $245 million increase from the $162 million deficit in 2007.

(In millions of current dollars. Figures may not add up to totals because of independent rounding or omitted subcategories, including some subcategories with negative values.)

Function and subfunction	2003	2004	2005	2006	2007	2008
NET RECEIPTS............................	$1,782,532	$1,880,279	$2,153,859	$2,407,254	$2,568,239	$2,521,175
Individual income taxes..........................	793,699	808,959	927,222	1,043,908	1,163,472	1,219,661
Corporation income taxes........................	131,778	189,371	278,282	353,915	370,243	345,336
Social insurance and retirement receipts	712,978	733,407	794,125	837,821	869,607	910,125
Employment and general retirement	674,981	689,360	747,664	790,043	824,258	862,023
Old-age and survivors insurance	447,806	457,120	493,646	520,069	542,901	566,104
Disability insurance (off-budget)...................	76,036	77,625	83,830	88,313	92,188	96,111
Hospital insurance	147,186	150,589	166,068	177,429	184,908	195,453
Railroad retirement/pension fund:	2,333	2,297	2,284	2,338	2,309	2,359
Railroad social security equivalent account	1,620	1,729	1,836	1,894	1,952	1,996
Unemployment insurance.........................	33,366	39,453	42,002	43,420	41,091	43,382
Other retirement................................	4,631	4,594	4,459	4,358	4,258	4,720
Excise taxes.....................................	67,524	69,855	73,094	73,961	65,069	68,835
Federal funds	23,804	24,566	22,547	22,460	11,076	14,825
Alcohol	7,893	8,105	8,111	8,484	8,648	8,819
Tobacco	7,934	7,926	7,920	7,710	7,556	7,622
Telephone....................................	5,788	5,997	6,047	4,897	−2,125	586
Transportation fuels	920	1,381	−770	−2,386	−3,291	−4,261
Trust funds	43,720	45,289	50,547	51,501	53,993	54,010
Highway	33,726	34,711	37,892	38,542	39,361	39,203
Airport and airway	8,684	9,174	10,314	10,426	11,468	11,871
Black lung disability	506	566	610	607	639	638
Inland waterway	90	91	91	81	91	89
Oil spill liability	—	—	—	54	452	273
Aquatic resources	392	416	429	519	581	561
Leaking underground storage tank	184	189	189	197	226	197
Tobacco assessments	—	—	899	891	934	960
Vaccine injury compensation	138	142	123	184	241	218
Other receipts...................................	76,553	78,687	81,136	97,649	99,848	−22,782

Function and subfunction	2003	2004	2005	2006	2007	2008
OUTLAYS	$2,160,117	$2,293,006	$2,472,205	$2,655,435	$2,730,241	$2,931,222
National defense	404,778	455,847	495,326	521,840	552,568	607,263
Department of Defense—Military						
Military personnel........................	106,744	113,576	127,463	127,543	128,826	137,401
Operation and maintenance...............	151,408	174,045	188,118	203,789	216,631	225,062
Procurement............................	67,926	76,216	82,294	89,757	99,647	130,477
Research, development, test, and evaluation	53,098	60,759	65,694	68,629	73,136	74,735
Military construction	5,851	6,312	5,331	6,245	7,899	10,241
Family housing..........................	3,784	3,905	3,720	3,717	3,473	4,290
Subtotal, Department of Defense—Military	387,170	436,453	474,089	499,310	529,845	583,054
Atomic energy defense activities...............	16,029	16,625	18,042	17,468	17,050	17,775
Defense-related activities....................	1,579	2,769	3,195	5,062	5,673	6,434
International affairs	21,209	26,891	34,595	29,549	28,510	34,826
International development and humanitarian assistance...	10,332	13,825	17,711	16,720	15,542	14,253
International security assistance	8,620	8,369	7,895	7,811	7,982	9,025
Conduct of foreign affairs....................	6,683	7,897	9,149	8,568	8,389	12,202
Foreign information and exchange activities	959	1,141	1,143	1,176	1,220	1,252
International financial programs................	−5,385	−4,341	−1,303	−4,726	−4,623	−1,906
General science, space and technology	20,873	23,053	23,628	23,616	25,566	27,631
General science and basic research	7,993	8,416	8,850	9,125	10,308	10,907
Space flight, research, and supporting activities	12,880	14,637	14,778	14,491	15,258	16,724
Energy..................................	−735	−166	429	782	−860	3,005
Energy supply	−2,061	−1,555	−940	231	−1,991	865
Energy conservation	897	926	883	747	580	924
Emergency energy preparedness	182	158	162	−441	195	776
Energy information, policy, and regulation	247	305	324	245	356	440
Natural resources and environment..................	29,703	30,725	28,023	33,055	31,772	35,549
Water resources...........................	5,492	5,571	5,723	8,026	5,099	8,749
Conservation and land management..............	9,739	9,758	6,226	7,813	9,646	9,735
Recreational resources	2,872	2,963	3,018	3,069	2,983	3,377
Pollution control and abatement................	8,208	8,485	8,079	8,572	8,426	7,771
Agriculture	22,497	15,440	26,566	25,970	17,663	20,967
Farm income stabilization	18,304	11,186	22,048	21,411	13,094	16,305
Agricultural research and services..............	4,193	4,254	4,518	4,559	4,569	4,662
Commerce and housing credit	728	5,266	7,567	6,188	488	7,361
Mortgage credit	−4,551	2,659	−862	−619	−4,986	325
Postal Service	−5,169	−4,070	−1,223	−971	−3,161	−4,556
Deposit insurance	−1,430	−1,976	−1,371	−1,110	−1,492	−1,941
Transportation	67,069	64,627	67,894	70,244	72,905	80,268
Ground transportation	37,491	40,744	42,317	45,209	46,818	53,090
Air transportation	23,343	16,743	18,807	18,005	18,096	18,132
Water transportation......................	5,907	6,898	6,439	6,688	7,695	8,484
Community and regional development	18,850	15,822	26,264	54,531	29,567	27,601
Community development	6,346	6,167	5,861	5,845	11,834	12,688
Area and regional development	2,397	2,351	2,745	2,580	2,514	2,890
Disaster relief and insurance	10,107	7,304	17,658	46,106	15,219	12,023
Education, training, employment, and social services ...	82,603	87,990	97,567	118,560	91,676	93,389
Elementary, secondary, and vocational education	31,473	34,360	38,271	39,710	38,430	39,788
Higher education	22,697	25,264	31,442	50,471	24,637	24,475
Research and general education aids	3,008	3,047	3,136	3,076	3,170	3,230
Training and employment.....................	8,379	7,918	6,852	7,199	7,080	7,096
Social services..........................	15,573	15,855	16,251	16,473	16,724	17,200
Health	219,576	240,134	250,614	252,780	266,432	284,499
Health care services.......................	192,608	210,092	219,625	220,841	233,928	251,834
Health research and training	24,044	27,099	28,050	28,828	29,279	29,518
Consumer and occupational health and safety	2,924	2,943	2,939	3,111	3,225	3,147
Medicare	249,433	269,360	298,638	329,868	375,407	396,333
Income security	334,632	333,059	345,847	352,477	365,975	388,440
Retirement and disability insurance (excl. social security)..	7,047	6,573	6,976	4,592	7,829	7,923
Federal employee retirement and disability	85,154	88,729	93,351	98,296	103,916	109,086
Unemployment compensation	57,054	44,994	35,435	33,814	35,107	37,333
Housing assistance	35,525	36,790	37,899	38,295	39,715	41,041
Food and nutrition assistance	42,526	46,012	50,833	53,928	54,458	60,269
Social security	474,680	495,548	523,305	548,549	586,153	615,256
Veterans benefits and services	57,022	59,779	70,151	69,842	72,847	86,618
Income security for veterans	29,091	30,849	35,767	35,771	35,684	42,466
Veterans education, training, and rehabilitation.........	2,106	2,562	2,790	2,638	2,713	2,907
Hospital and medical care for veterans	24,082	26,859	28,754	29,888	32,294	37,810
Veterans housing	505	−1,982	860	−1,242	−868	−403
Administration of justice.....................	35,340	45,576	40,019	41,016	41,244	46,202
Federal law enforcement activities..............	15,745	19,131	19,912	20,039	19,617	24,926
Federal litigative and judicial activities............	9,085	9,685	9,641	10,051	10,954	10,953
Federal correctional activities.................	5,384	5,509	5,862	6,158	6,328	6,229
Criminal justice assistance...................	5,126	11,251	4,604	4,768	4,345	4,094
General government	23,168	22,347	17,010	18,215	17,457	19,809
Legislative functions	2,840	3,187	3,451	3,446	3,541	3,553
Executive direction and management	706	503	569	522	490	499
Central fiscal operations.....................	11,455	9,302	9,516	10,165	10,300	10,393
General property and records management	201	228	482	328	291	736
Central personnel management................	203	217	101	151	−1	261
General purpose fiscal assistance	7,464	7,675	3,333	3,798	3,543	4,026
Deductions for offsetting receipts...............	−1,745	−1,068	−2,841	−1,359	−2,343	−1,357
Net interest	153,073	160,245	183,986	226,603	237,109	243,947
Undistributed offsetting receipts	−54,382	−58,537	−65,224	−68,250	−82,238	−87,742
Employer share, employee retirement (on-budget)	−39,751	−42,100	−47,977	−49,231	−49,476	−51,355
Total surplus/deficit.........................	−377,585	−412,727	−318,346	−248,181	−162,002	−410,047

Note: Fiscal year ends Sept. 30.

Federal Receipts, Outlays, and Surpluses or Deficits, 1941-2009

Source: Financial Management Service, U.S. Dept. of the Treasury; Congressional Budget Office

(in millions of current dollars)

Fiscal year[1]	Receipts	Outlays	Surplus or deficit (−)[2]	Fiscal year[1]	Receipts	Outlays	Surplus or deficit (−)[2]
1941	$8,712	$13,653	−$4,941	1976	$298,060	$371,792	−$73,732
1942	14,634	35,137	−20,503	Transition quarter[3]	81,232	95,975	−14,744
1943	24,001	78,555	−54,554	1977	355,559	409,218	−53,659
1944	43,747	91,304	−47,557	1978	399,561	458,746	−59,185
1945	45,159	92,712	−47,553	1979	463,302	504,028	−40,726
1946	39,296	55,232	−15,936	1980	517,112	590,941	−73,830
1947	38,514	34,496	4,018	1981	599,272	678,241	−78,968
1948	41,560	29,764	11,796	1982	617,766	745,743	−127,977
1949	39,415	38,835	580	1983	600,562	808,364	−207,802
1950	39,443	42,562	−3,119	1984	666,486	851,853	−185,367
1951	51,616	45,514	6,102	1985	734,088	946,396	−212,308
1952	66,167	67,686	−1,519	1986	769,215	990,441	−221,227
1953	69,608	76,101	−6,493	1987	854,353	1,004,083	−149,730
1954	69,701	70,855	−1,154	1988	909,303	1,064,481	−155,178
1955	65,451	68,444	−2,993	1989	991,190	1,143,829	−152,639
1956	74,587	70,640	3,947	1990	1,032,094	1,253,130	−221,036
1957	79,990	76,578	3,412	1991	1,055,093	1,324,331	−269,238
1958	79,636	82,405	−2,769	1992	1,091,328	1,381,649	−290,321
1959	79,249	92,098	−12,849	1993	1,154,471	1,409,522	−255,051
1960	92,492	92,191	301	1994	1,258,721	1,461,907	−203,186
1961	94,388	97,723	−3,335	1995	1,351,932	1,515,884	−163,952
1962	99,676	106,821	−7,146	1996	1,453,177	1,560,608	−107,431
1963	106,560	111,316	−4,756	1997	1,579,423	1,601,307	−21,884
1964	112,613	118,528	−5,915	1998	1,721,955	1,652,685	69,270
1965	116,817	118,228	−1,411	1999	1,827,645	1,702,035	125,610
1966	130,835	134,532	−3,698	2000	2,025,457	1,789,216	236,241
1967	148,822	157,464	−8,643	2001	1,991,426	1,863,190	128,236
1968	152,973	178,134	−25,161	2002	1,853,395	2,011,153	−157,758
1969	186,882	183,640	3,242	2003	1,782,532	2,160,117	−377,585
1970	192,807	195,649	−2,842	2004	1,880,279	2,293,006	−412,727
1971	187,139	210,172	−23,033	2005	2,153,859	2,472,205	−318,346
1972	207,309	230,681	−23,373	2006	2,407,254	2,655,435	−248,181
1973	230,799	245,707	−14,908	2007	2,568,239	2,728,940	−160,701
1974	263,224	269,359	−6,135	2008P	2,524,326	2,982,881	−458,555
1975	279,090	332,332	−53,242	2009E	2,156,654	3,997,842	−1,841,188

P = Preliminary. E = Estimate as of Oct. 12, 2009. (1) Fiscal years 1936 to 1976 end June 30; after 1976, fiscal years end Sept. 30. (2) May not equal difference between figures shown because of rounding. (3) Transition quarter covers July 1, 1976-Sept. 30, 1976.

Budget Receipts and Outlays, 1789-1940

Source: U.S. Dept. of the Treasury

(in thousands of dollars; annual statements for years ending June 30, unless otherwise noted)

Yearly average	Receipts	Outlays	Yearly average	Receipts	Outlays
1789-1800[1]	$5,717	$5,776	1881-1885	$366,961	$257,691
1801-1810[2]	13,056	9,086	1886-1890	375,448	279,134
1811-1820[2]	21,032	23,943	1891-1895	352,891	363,599
1821-1830[2]	21,928	16,162	1896-1900	434,877	457,451
1831-1840[2]	30,461	24,495	1901-1905	559,481	535,559
1841-1850[2]	28,545	34,097	1906-1910	628,507	639,178
1851-1860	60,237	60,163	1911-1915	710,227	720,252
1861-1865	160,907	683,785	1916-1920	3,483,652	8,065,333
1866-1870	447,301	377,642	1921-1925	4,306,673	3,578,989
1871-1875	336,830	287,460	1926-1930	4,069,138	3,182,807
1876-1880	288,124	255,598	1931-1935	2,770,973	5,214,874
			1936-1940	4,960,614	10,192,367

(1) Average for period Mar. 4, 1789, to Dec. 31, 1800. (2) Years 1801-42 end Dec. 31; average for 1841-50 is for the period Jan. 1, 1841, to June 30, 1850.

Budget Deficits as Percent of GDP, Selected Countries, 1990-2008[1]

Source: Organization for Economic Cooperation and Development

Country	1990	1995	2000	2006	2007	2008	Country	1990	1995	2000	2006	2007	2008
Australia	−2.0%	−3.7%	0.9%	1.9%	1.8%	1.2%	Korea	3.1%	3.8%	5.4%	3.9%	4.7%	3.2%
Austria	−2.5	−5.9	−1.9	−1.7	−0.7	−0.5	Luxembourg	4.3	2.4	6.0	1.4	3.6	2.6
Belgium	−6.7	−4.5	0.0	0.2	−0.3	−1.2	Netherlands	−5.3	−9.2	2.0	0.6	0.3	1.0
Canada	−5.8	−5.3	2.9	1.6	1.6	0.1	New Zealand	−4.6	2.8	1.9	5.9	5.0	2.9
Czech Republic	NA	−13.4	−3.7	−2.6	−0.6	−1.4	Norway	2.2	3.2	15.4	18.5	17.7	18.8
Denmark	−1.3	−2.9	2.3	5.0	4.5	3.4	Poland	NA	−4.4	−3.0	−3.9	−1.9	−3.9
Finland	5.4	−6.2	6.9	3.9	5.2	4.1	Portugal	−6.1	−5.0	−3.0	−3.9	−2.7	−2.7
France	−2.4	−5.5	−1.5	−2.3	−2.7	−3.4	Slovak Republic	NA	−3.4	−12.3	−3.5	−1.9	−2.2
Germany	−1.9	−9.7	1.3	−1.5	−0.2	−0.1	Spain	−4.1	−6.5	−1.0	2.0	2.2	−3.8
Greece	−14.0	−9.1	−3.7	−3.1	−3.9	−5.0	Sweden	3.3	−7.3	3.7	2.4	3.8	2.5
Hungary	NA	−6.1	−3.0	−9.3	−4.9	−3.4	Switzerland	−0.1	−2.0	0.1	1.0	1.3	1.0
Iceland	−3.3	−3.0	1.7	6.3	5.4	−14.3	United Kingdom	−1.8	−5.8	3.7	−2.7	−2.7	−5.5
Ireland	−2.8	−2.1	4.8	3.0	0.2	−7.1	United States	−4.2	−3.1	1.6	−2.2	−2.9	−5.9
Italy	−11.4	−7.4	−0.9	−3.3	−1.5	−2.7	Euro area	−4.3	−7.6	0.0	−1.3	−0.7	−1.9
Japan	2.1	−5.1	−7.6	−1.6	−2.5	−2.7	**Total OECD**	**−2.9**	**−4.7**	**0.3**	**−1.3**	**−1.4**	**−3.2**

NA = Not available. (1) Financial balances include revenues from the sale of mobile telephone licenses in some years.

Public Debt of the U.S., 1870-2009

Source: Bureau of Public Debt, U.S. Dept. of the Treasury; World Almanac research

Fiscal year	Debt (bil)	Debt per cap. (dollars)	Interest paid (bil)	% of federal outlays	Fiscal year	Debt (bil)	Debt per cap. (dollars)	Interest paid (bil)	% of federal outlays
1870	$2.4	$61.06	—	—	1989	$2,857.4	$11,545	$240.9	21.0%
1880	2.0	41.60	—	—	1990	3,233.3	13,000	264.8	21.1
1890	1.1	17.80	—	—	1991	3,665.3	14,436	285.5	21.6
1900	1.2	16.60	—	—	1992	4,064.6	15,846	292.3	21.2
1910	1.1	12.41	—	—	1993	4,411.5	17,105	292.5	20.8
1920	24.2	228	—	—	1994	4,692.8	18,025	296.3	20.3
1930	16.1	131	—	—	1996	5,224.8	19,805	344.0	22.0
1940	43.0	325	$1.0	10.5%	1997	5,413.1	20,026	355.8	22.2
1950	256.1	1,688	5.7	13.4	1998	5,526.2	20,443	363.8	22.0
1960	284.1	1,572	9.2	10.0	1999	5,656.3	20,746	353.5	20.7
1970	370.1	1,814	19.3	9.9	2000	5,674.2	20,106[1]	362.0	20.2
1977	698.8	3,170	41.9	10.2	2001	5,807.5	20,361[1]	359.5	19.3
1978	771.5	3,463	48.7	10.6	2002	6,228.2	21,616[1]	332.5	16.5
1979	826.5	3,669	59.8	11.9	2003	6,783.2	23,326[1]	318.1	14.7
1980	907.7	3,985	74.9	12.7	2004	7,379.1	25,130[1]	321.6	14.0
1981	997.9	4,338	95.6	14.1	2005	7,932.7	26,754[1]	352.4	14.3
1982	1,142.0	4,913	117.4	15.7	2006	8,507.0	28,414[1]	405.9	15.3
1983	1,377.2	5,870	128.8	15.9	2007	9,007.7	29,804[1]	430.0	15.4[1]
1984	1,572.3	6,640	153.8	18.1	2008	10,025.0	33,237[1]	451.2	16.2[1]
1986	2,125.3	8,774	190.2	19.2	2009	11.956.6	38,850[1]	383.4	26.0[2]
1987	2,350.3	9,615	195.4	19.5					
1988	2,602.3	10,534	214.1	20.1					

Note: As of end of fiscal year. Through 1976, the fiscal year ended June 30. From 1977 on, the fiscal year ends Sept. 30. (1) Estimated. (2) Based on 2009 federal outlays estimate.

State Finances: Revenue, Expenditures, Debt, and Taxes, 2007

Source: Census Bureau, U.S. Dept. of Commerce

(fiscal year)

State	Revenue (thous.)	Expenditures (thous.)	Debt (thous.)	Per capita debt	Per capita taxes	Per capita expenditures
Alabama	$27,536,360	$23,192,507	$7,059,343	$1,525	$1,916	$5,012
Alaska	12,477,998	9,191,744	6,553,080	9,588	5,397	13,448
Arizona	29,875,612	28,332,841	9,546,428	1,506	2,273	4,470
Arkansas	18,175,873	14,948,566	4,508,511	1,590	2,608	5,273
California	299,948,562	233,578,021	114,701,797	3,138	3,139	6,390
Colorado	26,881,361	21,243,982	14,905,758	3,066	1,896	4,370
Connecticut	25,492,170	22.115,190	23,836,187	6,806	3,668	6,314
Delaware	7,432,535	6,751,452	5,242,613	6,062	3,360	7,807
Florida	95,044,996	72,773,050	36,331,829	1,991	2,127	3,987
Georgia	45,067,031	41,843,352	11,370,040	1,191	1,919	4,384
Hawaii	11,176,293	9,848,210	5,959,064	4,643	3,966	7,674
Idaho	9,095,154	6,895,319	2,812,655	1,876	2,359	4,599
Illinois	71,255,039	59,302,221	54,535,159	4,243	2,339	4,614
Indiana	32,429,387	28,809,586	19,180,194	3,023	2,208	4,540
Iowa	19,053,312	15,461,766	6,727,065	2,251	2,165	5,175
Kansas	14,998,530	13,183,436	5,671,144	2,043	2,483	4,749
Kentucky	25,425,381	23,680,419	10,857,128	2,560	2,333	5,583
Louisiana	33,286,017	27,855,931	14,251,968	3,320	2,556	6,488
Maine	9,434,179	7,935,673	5,326,692	4,044	2,719	6,025
Maryland	34,848,081	31,610,548	19,017,465	3,385	2,687	5,626
Massachusetts	49,425,934	44,048,424	67,938,742	10,534	3,208	6,829
Michigan	63,070,866	54,745,355	33,657,214	3,342	2,368	5,435
Minnesota	38,745,022	31,880,478	8,866,611	1,706	3,419	6,134
Mississippi	22,398,649	18,628,639	5,858,340	2,007	2,191	6,382
Missouri	32,728,288	25,318,686	18,715,821	3,184	1,821	4,307
Montana	7,129,303	5,554,244	4,649,819	4,854	2,422	5,799
Nebraska	9,986,412	7,829,584	2,196,880	1,238	2,294	4,412
Nevada	14,183,611	10,755,326	4,140,910	1,614	2,458	4,192
New Hampshire	7,171,927	6,226,121	7,690,409	5,845	1,653	4,732
New Jersey	65,495,222	56,076,165	51,384,806	5,916	3,395	6,456
New Mexico	16,781,588	14,907,060	7,323,101	3,717	2,806	7,567
New York	178,908,359	151,338,991	110,084,829	5,705	3,273	7,842
North Carolina	51,841,493	44,009,293	19,245,613	2,124	2,496	4,857
North Dakota	4,786,348	3,777,523	1,792,485	2,802	2,787	5,905
Ohio	86,429,629	66,207,138	26,065,238	2,273	2,266	5,774
Oklahoma	22,329,933	18,104,268	8,667,100	2,396	2,286	5,005
Oregon	30,587,369	20,605,597	11,303,477	3,016	2,066	5,499
Pennsylvania	83,384,773	68,292,746	37,125,118	2,986	2,480	5,493
Rhode Island	8,417,797	7,071,396	8,418,744	7,958	2,615	6,685
South Carolina	27,530,567	24,824,628	14,981,290	3,399	1,917	5,632
South Dakota	4,920,193	3,571,741	3,232,457	4,060	1,590	4,486
Tennessee	29,469,615	24,992,628	4,141,541	673	1,850	4,059
Texas	114,728,001	90,623,748	23,909,021	1,000	1,686	3,791
Utah	15,863,997	12,774,196	5,926,589	2,240	2,226	4,829
Vermont	5,437,494	4,993,860	3,052,469	4,913	4,126	8,038
Virginia	47,155,581	36,774,042	19,683,529	2,552	2,420	4,768
Washington	47,030,140	37,116,177	21,058,558	3,256	2,735	5,738
West Virginia	11,945,313	9,766,972	5,628,065	3,106	2,561	5,390
Wisconsin	40,164,298	30,895,963	21,461,270	3,831	2,585	5,516
Wyoming	5,844,703	4,536,373	1,205,067	2,305	3,873	8,677
All states[1]	$1,992,826,296	$1,634,801,176	$937,799,233	$3,109	$2,509	$5,420

(1) Figures may not add up to totals because of rounding.

State and Local Government Receipts and Current Expenditures, 2001-08

Source: Bureau of Economic Analysis, U.S. Dept. of Commerce

(in billions of current dollars; as of Oct. 2009)

	2001	2002	2003	2004	2005	2006	2007	2008
Receipts	**$1,374.0**	**$1,412.7**	**$1,496.3**	**$1,601.0**	**$1,730.4**	**$1,829.7**	**$1927.3**	**$1,974.2**
Current tax receipts	914.8	928.7	977.7	1,059.4	1,163.1	1,249.0	1,313.4	1,336.3
Personal current taxes	243.0	221.8	226.2	248.6	276.7	302.5	322.8	330.0
Income taxes	223.3	201.3	204.1	224.7	251.7	276.1	295.5	302.4
Other	19.7	20.5	22.1	23.8	25.0	26.4	27.3	27.6
Taxes on production and imports	642.4	676.0	717.5	769.1	831.4	887.4	934.0	955.3
Sales taxes	321.8	331.1	348.8	370.7	402.2	430.4	446.3	443.9
Property taxes	268.0	289.4	306.8	326.7	346.9	370.1	396.3	410.6
Other	52.6	55.5	61.9	71.7	82.3	86.9	91.5	100.9
Taxes on corporate income	28.9	30.9	34.0	41.7	54.9	59.2	56.5	51.0
Contributions for government social insurance	13.7	15.9	20.1	24.1	24.8	21.8	19.8	21.1
Income receipts on assets	90.0	79.6	74.0	77.1	88.3	103.5	114.2	113.9
Interest receipts	82.1	71.5	64.6	66.7	76.4	90.9	101.2	100.1
Dividends	1.4	1.6	1.7	2.0	2.1	2.3	2.5	2.9
Rents and royalties	6.5	6.6	7.6	8.5	9.8	10.3	10.5	11.0
Current transfer receipts	348.0	382.3	421.3	439.4	454.3	456.7	483.9	506.1
Federal grants-in-aid	276.1	304.2	338.0	349.2	361.2	359.0	378.9	391.7
From business (net)	29.8	32.6	33.8	36.5	36.5	38.4	41.3	45.6
From persons	42.0	45.6	49.5	53.7	56.5	59.2	63.7	68.8
Current surplus of government enterprises	8.0	6.1	3.3	1.0	0.1	-1.3	-3.9	-3.2
Current expenditures	**1,389.9**	**1,466.8**	**1,535.1**	**1,609.3**	**1,704.5**	**1,778.6**	**1,905.6**	**2,014.4**
Consumption expenditures	994.2	1,049.4	1,096.5	1,139.1	1,212.0	1,282.3	1,366.1	1,452.4
Government social benefit payments to persons	305.1	333.0	333.0	384.3	404.8	402.9	433.7	455.0
Interest payments	83.0	83.5	83.5	85.6	87.3	93.0	98.7	103.9
Subsidies	7.7	0.9	0.1	0.4	0.4	0.4	7.1	3.0
Less: Wage accruals less disbursements	0.0	0.0	0.0	0.0	0.0	0.0	0.0	0.0
Net state and local government saving	-15.9	-54.1	-38.8	-8.4	25.9	51.0	21.7	-40.2
Social insurance funds	2.6	1.5	3.4	6.9	7.4	4.7	1.9	2.0
Other	-18.5	-55.6	-42.2	-15.3	18.5	46.4	19.8	-42.2
Addenda:								
Total receipts	1,425.2	1,465.1	1,547.8	1,648.5	1,780.2	1,887.1	1,986.4	2,035.9
Current receipts	1,374.0	1,412.7	1,496.3	1,601.0	1,730.4	1,829.7	1,927.3	1,974.2
Capital transfer receipts	51.2	52.4	51.5	47.5	49.8	57.4	59.1	61.7
Total expenditures	1,524.5	1,609.5	1,678.9	1,752.7	1,846.2	1,931.4	2,074.6	2,184.3
Current expenditures	1,389.9	1,466.8	1,535.1	1,609.3	1,704.5	1,778.6	1,905.6	2,014.4
Gross government investment	240.5	253.3	259.6	269.1	281.6	304.4	333.7	348.2
Net purchases of nonproduced assets	10.1	11.2	11.4	11.4	10.3	11.1	13.1	12.9
Less: Consumption of fixed capital	116.0	121.8	127.3	137.1	150.1	162.7	177.9	191.2
Net lending or net borrowing (–)	**-99.3**	**-144.4**	**-131.1**	**-104.2**	**-66.0**	**-44.3**	**-88.2**	**-148.4**

Federal Deposit Insurance Corporation (FDIC)

The Federal Deposit Insurance Corporation (FDIC) is the independent deposit insurance agency created by Congress to maintain stability and public confidence in the nation's banking system. In its unique role as deposit insurer of banks and savings associations, and in cooperation with other federal and state regulatory agencies, the FDIC seeks to promote the safety and soundness of insured depository institutions in the U.S. financial system by identifying, monitoring, and addressing risks to the deposit insurance funds. The FDIC aims to promote public understanding and sound public policies by providing financial and economic information and analyses. It seeks to minimize disruptive effects from the failure of banks and savings associations, and to ensure fairness in the sale of financial products and the provision of financial services.

To maintain its insurance funds, the FDIC assesses depository institutions insurance premiums twice a year. The amount of the premium is based on the institution's balance of insured deposits for the preceding two quarters and the institution's risk to the insurance fund. In 2009, Congress permanently increased the limit that the Corporation may borrow from the U.S. Treasury from $30 bil to $100 bil, and temporarily raised this borrowing limit to $500 bil through the end of 2010. The FDIC's Bank Insurance Fund and the Savings Association Insurance Fund were merged Mar. 31, 2006, to form the Deposit Insurance Fund, which stood at $648.1 mil on Aug. 12, 2009, significantly lower than the Oct. 7, 2008, level of $45.2 bil.

U.S. Banks, 1935-2009

Source: Federal Deposit Insurance Corp.; as of June 30, 2009

Comprises all FDIC-insured commercial and savings banks, including savings and loan institutions (S&Ls).

	Total number of banks					Total deposits (millions of dollars)				
	All	Commercial banks[1]		Non-	All		Commercial banks[1]		Non-	All
Year	banks	Natl.	State	members	savings	All deposits	Natl.	State	members	savings
1935	15,295	5,386	1,001	7,735	1,173	$45,102[2]	$24,802	$13,653	$5,669	$978[2]
1940	15,772	5,144	1,342	6,956	2,330	67,494	35,787	20,642	7,040	4,025
1950	16,500	4,958	1,912	6,576	3,054	171,963	84,941	41,602	19,726	25,694
1960	17,549	4,530	1,641	6,955	4,423	310,262	120,242	65,487	34,369	90,164
1970	18,205	4,621	1,147	7,743	4,694	686,901	285,436	101,512	95,566	204,367
1980	18,763	4,425	997	9,013	4,328	1,832,716	656,752	191,183	344,311	640,470
1990	15,158	3,979	1,009	7,355	2,815	3,637,292	1,558,915	397,797	693,438	987,142
2000	9,905	2,230	991	5,094	1,590	4,914,808	2,250,464	1,032,110	894,000	738,234
2002	9,354	2,077	950	4,861	1,439	5,568,508	2,565,771	1,152,380	971,730	878,627
2003	9,182	2,001	935	4,833	1,413	5,954,288	2,786,756	1,195,914	1,046,195	925,423
2004	8,976	1,907	919	4,805	1,345	6,584,200	3,581,416	872,228	1,139,168	991,388
2005	8,832	1,818	907	4,802	1,305	7,141,178	3,850,051	936,299	1,286,983	1,067,845
2006[3]	8,767	1,780	903	4,796	1,276	6,449,864	3,190,482	818,565	1,311,720	1,118,948
2007[3]	8,605	1,676	888	4,786	1,244	6,702,212	3,273,531	831,081	1,425,607	1,165,119
2008[3]	8,441	1,585	874	4,744	1,227	7,025,790	3,596,712	857,003	1,432,609	1,132,360
2009[3]	8,185	1,505	858	4,632	1,180	7,559,616	4,141,792	962,232	1,512,703	936,101

(1) "Nonmembers" are banks that are not members of the Federal Reserve System; "National" and "State" institutions are members.
(2) Figures for 1935 do not include data for S&Ls (not available). (3) June 30.

U.S. Bank Failures, 1934-2009

Source: Federal Deposit Insurance Corp.; as of Oct. 5, 2009

Covers all FDIC-insured commercial and savings banks, including savings and loan institutions (S&Ls) 1980 and after.

Year	Closed or assisted	Year	Closed or assisted	Year	Closed or assisted	Year	Closed or assisted	Year	Closed or assisted
1934	9	1963	2	1976	17	1988	465	1998	3
1935	26	1964	7	1978	7	1989	534	1999	8
1936	69	1965	5	1979	10	1990	382	2000	7
1937	77	1966	7	1980	22	1991	271	2001	4
1938	74	1967	4	1981	40	1992	181	2002	11
1939	60	1969	9	1982	119	1993	50	2003	3
1940	43	1970	7	1983	99	1994	15	2004	4
1955	5	1971	7	1984	106	1995	8	2007	3
1959	3	1972	2	1985	180	1996	6	2008	26
1960	1	1973	6	1986	204	1997	1	2009	98
1961	5	1975	13	1987	262				

Note: There were no bank failures in 2005 or in 2006.

50 Largest U.S. Bank Holding Companies[1]

Source: Federal Reserve System; as of June 30, 2009

Company, location	Total assets[2]	Company, location	Total assets[2]
Bank of America, Charlotte, NC	$2,256,059,674	Bancwest Corporation, Honolulu, HI	$75,962,799
JPMorgan Chase & Co., New York, NY	2,026,642,000	Northern Trust Corp., Chicago, IL	75,045,238
Citigroup Inc., New York, NY	1,848,533,000	UnionBanCal Corp., San Francisco, CA	73,984,812
Wells Fargo & Co., San Francisco, CA	1,284,176,000	CIT Group, Inc., New York, NY	71,019,240
Goldman Sachs Group, Inc., The, New York, NY	890,137,000	M & T Bank Corp., Buffalo, NY	69,913,217
Morgan Stanley, New York, NY	676,957,000	Harris Financial Corp., Wilmington, DE	67,788,776
Metlife, Inc., New York, NY	509,457,014	Comerica Inc., Dallas, TX	63,859,610
HSBC North America Holdings Inc., Mettawa, IL	383,820,898	Marshall & Ilsley Corp., Milwaukee, WI	59,749,122
Taunus Corp., New York, NY	366,350,000	BBVA USA Bancshares, Inc., Houston, TX.	59,466,375
Barclays Group US Inc., Wilmington, DE	323,685,026	Zions Bancorp, Salt Lake City, UT	52,906,728
PNC Financial Services Group, Inc., Pittsburgh, PA	279,788,303	Huntington Bancshares Inc., Columbus, OH.	51,485,101
U.S. Bancorp, Minneapolis, MN	265,560,000	Discover Financial Services, Riverwoods, IL	41,250,577
Bank of New York Mellon Corp., The, New York, NY	203,246,000	Ultrecht-America Holdings, Inc., New York, NY	39,513,445
		Popular, Inc., San Juan, Puerto Rico	36,499,000
GMAC, Inc. Detroit, MI	181,250,000	Synovus Financial Corp., Columbus, GA	34,349,670
Suntrust Banks, Inc., Atlanta, GA.	176,854,034	New York Community Bancorp, Inc., Westbury, NY	32,887,597
Capital One Financial Corp., McLean, VA	171,911,307	RBC Bancorp, Raleigh, NC	29,938,139
Citizens Financial Group, Inc., Providence, RI.	153,304,291	First Horizon National Corp., Memphis, TN.	28,759,618
State Street Corp., Boston, MA	152,921,189	Associated Banc-Corp., Green Bay, WI	24,013,567
BB&T Corp., Winston-Salem, NC	152,398,410	BOK Financial Corp., Tulsa, OK	22,785,019
Regions Financial Corp. Birmingham, AL	142,824,610	First Bancorp, San Juan, Puerto Rico	20,012,887
TD Banknorth Inc., Portland, ME	131,355,762	FBOP Corp., Oak Park, IL	18,574,217
Fifth Third Bancorp, Cincinnati, OH	115,983,653	Commerce Bancshares, Inc., Kansas City, MO	17,733,266
American Express Co., New York, NY	115,975,155	City National Corporation, Los Angeles, CA	17,664,367
Keycorp, Cleveland, OH	98,389,472	TCF Financial Corp., Wayzata, MN.	17,503,325
		Webster Financial Corp., Waterbury, CT	17,471,449

(1) Includes foreign-owned banks with a strong presence in the U.S. (2) In thousands.

Top Recipients of Treasury Department "Bailout" Funds[1]

Source: Propublica; as of Oct. 2009

Automobile	Treasury funds committed
General Motors Corp., Detroit, MI	$50.4 bil
Chrysler Group LLC, Auburn Hills, MI[2]	12.5 bil
GM Supplier Receivables, LLC	2.5 bil
Chrysler Receivables SPV LLC	1.0 bil

Banking	
Citigroup Inc., New York, NY[3]	50.0 bil
Bank of America, Charlotte, NC	45.0 bil
Wells Fargo & Co, San Francisco, CA	25.0 bil
PNC Financial Services, Pittsburgh, PA	7.6 bil
SunTrust Banks, Inc. Atlanta, GA	4.9 bil
Regions Financial Corp., Birmingham, AL	3.5 bil
Fifth Third Bancorp, Cincinnati, OH	3.4 bil
KeyCorp, Cleveland, OH	2.5 bil
CIT Group, New York, NY	2.3 bil
Comerica, Inc., Dallas, TX	2.3 bil
Marshall & Ilsley, Milwaukee, WI	1.7 bil
Zions Bancorp, Salt Lake City, UT	1.4 bil
Huntington Bancshares, Columbus, OH	1.4 bil
Synovus Financial Corp., Columbus, GA	967.9 mil
Popular, Inc., San Juan, Puerto Rico	935.0 mil
First Horizon National, Memphis, TN	866.5 mil

Insurance	
American International Group, Inc. (AIG), New York, NY[4]	69.8 bil
Hartford Financial Services, CT	3.4 bil
Lincoln National Corp., Radnor, PA	950.0 mil

Financial services	Treasury funds committed
Freddie Mac, VA	$50.7 bil
Fannie Mae, Washington, DC	44.9 bil
GMAC, Detroit, MI	12.5 bil
Discover Financial Services, Riverwoods, IL	1.2 bil

Investment fund	
The TCW Group, Inc., Wilmington, DE	3.3 bil
Invesco Ltd., Wilmington, DE	3.3 bil
Wellington Management Co., Wilmington, DE	3.3 bil
BlackRock, Inc., Wilmington, DE	3.3 bil
AllianceBernstein, LP, Wilmington, DE	3.3 bil

Mortgage servicer	
Bank of America (incl. Countrywide), Simi Valley, CA	5.4 bil
GMAC Mortgage, Ft. Washington, PA	3.6 bil
JPMorgan Chase subsidiaries, Iselin, NJ[5]	3.4 bil
Wells Fargo Bank, NA, Des Moines, IA	2.5 bil
CitiMortgage, O'Fallon, MO	2.1 bil
Wachovia subsidiaries, Des Moines, IA	1.4 bil
American Home Mortgage Servicing, Inc., Coppell, TX	1.2 bil
Litton Loan Servicing, Houston, TX	1.1 bil
Saxon Mortgage Services, Irving, TX	886.4 mil
OneWest Bank, Pasadena, CA	814.2 mil

(1) Does not include companies that have completely refunded their bailout money. (2) Chrysler Financial Services returned $1.5 bil July 14, 2009. (3) Citigroup received other aid, including a $10 bil commitment from the FDIC and up to $220 bil from the Federal Reserve. (4) AIG also received aid from the Federal Reserve. The Treasury Dept. and the Federal Reserve together loaned or invested at least $134 bil in AIG. (5) JPMorgan Chase returned $25 bil on June 9, 2009.

Federal Reserve System

The Federal Reserve System is the central bank for the U.S. The system was established on Dec. 23, 1913, originally to give the country an elastic currency, provide facilities for discounting commercial paper, and improve the supervision of banking. Since then, the system's responsibilities have been broadened. Over the years, stability and growth of the economy, a high level of employment, stability in the purchasing power of the dollar, and reasonable balance in transactions with other countries have come to be recognized as primary objectives of governmental economic policy.

The Federal Reserve System consists of the Board of Governors, the 12 District Reserve Banks and their branch offices, and the Federal Open Market Committee. Several advisory councils help the board meet its varied responsibilities.

The hub of the system is the 7-member **Board of Governors** in Washington, DC. The members of the board are appointed by the president and confirmed by the Senate, to serve 14-year terms. The president also appoints the chairman and vice chairman of the board from among the board members for 4-year terms that may be renewed. As of Oct. 2009, the board members were: Ben Bernanke, chair; Donald Kohn, vice-chair; Kevin Warsh; Elizabeth Duke; and Daniel Tarullo.

The 12 **District Reserve Banks** and their branch offices serve as the decentralized portion of the system, carrying out day-to-day operations such as circulating currency and coin and providing fiscal agency functions and payments mechanism services. The 12 are in Boston, New York, Philadelphia, Cleveland, Richmond, Atlanta, Chicago, St. Louis, Minneapolis, Kansas City, Dallas, and San Francisco.

The system's principal function is monetary policy, which it controls using three tools: reserve requirements, the discount rate, and open market operations.

Uniform **reserve requirements**, set by the board, are applied to the transaction accounts and nonpersonal time deposits of all depository institutions. Responsibility for setting the **discount rate** (the interest rate at which depository institutions can borrow money from the Reserve Banks) is shared by the Board of Governors and the Reserve Banks. Changes in the discount rate are recommended by the individual boards of directors of the Reserve Banks and are subject to approval by the Board of Governors.

The most important tool of monetary policy is **open market operations** (the purchase and sale of government securities). Responsibility for influencing the cost and availability of money and credit through the purchase and sale of government securities lies with the **Federal Open Market Committee** (FOMC), which is composed of the 7 members of the Board of Governors, the president of the Federal Reserve Bank of New York, and 4 other Federal Reserve Bank presidents, who each serve 1-year terms on a rotating basis. The committee bases its decisions on economic and financial developments and outlook, setting yearly growth objectives for key measures of money supply and credit. The decisions of the committee are carried out by the Domestic Trading Desk of the Federal Reserve Bank of New York.

A Federal Advisory Council meets with the Federal Reserve Board four times a year to discuss business and financial conditions, as well as to make recommendations.

Website: www.federalreserve.gov

Federal Reserve Board Primary and Secondary Credit Rate, 1980-2008

Prior to Jan. 9, 2003, the federal reserve set a single "discount rate," the interest rate that member banks were charged when borrowing money through the Federal Reserve System. This adjustment credit rate was replaced with two rates, the primary credit rate and secondary credit rate. The primary credit rate (listed first) is available to banks in generally sound financial condition. The secondary credit (listed second) rate is given to banks that do not qualify for the primary credit rate. Both are extended for very short terms, usually overnight. On Aug. 17, 2007, this term was temporarily extended to 30 days. Under the new system, financially sound institutions are not required to exhaust all funds before borrowing from the Fed.

Effective date	Rates	Effective date	Rates	Effective date	Rates	Effective date	Rates	Effective date	Rates	Effective date	Rates
1980:		**1984:**		**1991:**		**1999:**		**2002:**		**2006:**	
Feb. 15	13	Apr. 9	9	Apr. 30	5½	Aug. 24	4¾	Nov. 6	¾	Jan. 31	5½, 6
May 30	12	Nov. 21	8½	Sept. 13	5	Nov. 16	5	**2003:**		Mar. 28	5¾, 6¼
June 13	11	Dec. 24	8	Nov. 6	4½	**2000:**		Jan. 9	2¼, 2¾	May 10	6, 6½
July 28	10	**1985:**		Dec. 20	3½	Feb. 2	5¼	June 25	2, 2½	June 29	6¼, 6¾
Sept. 26	11	May 20	7½	**1992:**		Mar. 21	5½	**2004:**		Aug. 17	5¾, 6¼
Nov. 17	12	**1986:**		July 2	3	May 16	6	June 30	2¼, 2¾	**2007:**	
Dec. 5	13	Mar. 7	7	**1994:**		**2001:**		Aug. 10	2½, 3	Aug. 17	5¾, 6¼
1981:		Apr. 21	6½	May 17	3½	Jan. 3	5¾	Sept. 21	2¾, 3¼	Sept.18	5¼, 5¾
May 5	14	July 11	6	Aug. 16	4	Jan. 31	5	Nov. 10	3, 3½	Nov. 1	5, 5½
Nov. 2	13	Aug. 21	5½	Nov. 15	4¾	Mar. 20	4½	Dec. 14	3¼, 3¾	Dec. 12	4¾, 5¼
Dec. 4	12	**1987:**		**1995:**		Apr. 18	4	**2005:**		**2008:**	
1982:		Sept. 4	6	Feb. 1	5	May 15	3½	Feb. 2	3½, 4	Jan. 22	4, 4½
July 20	11½	**1988:**		**1996:**		June 27	3¼	Mar. 22	3¾, 4¼	Jan. 30	3½, 4
Aug. 2	11	Aug. 9	6½	Jan. 31	5	Aug. 21	3	May 3	4, 4½	Mar. 17	3¼, 3¾
Aug. 16	10	**1989:**		**1998:**		Sept. 17	2½	June 30	4¼, 4¾	Mar. 18	2½, 3
Aug. 27	10	Feb. 24	7	Oct. 15	4¾	Oct. 2	2	Aug. 9	4½, 5	Apr. 30	2¼, 2¾
Oct. 12	9½	**1990:**		Nov. 17	4½	Dec. 11	1¼	Sept. 20	4¾, 5¼	Oct. 08	1¾, 2¼
Dec. 15	8½	Dec. 18	6½					Nov. 1	5, 5½	Oct. 29	1¼, 1¾
								Dec. 13	5¼, 5¾	Dec. 16	½, 1

(1) Through Oct. 31, 2008.

Standard & Poor's 500 Index, 1994-2009

Monthly closing levels; record high daily closing was 1,565.15, Oct. 30, 2009.

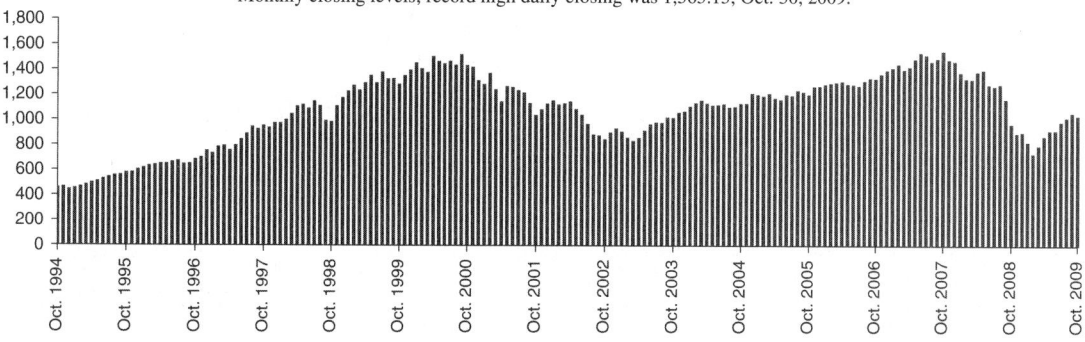

U.S. Holdings of Foreign Stocks[1], 2005-08

Source: Bureau of Economic Analysis, U.S. Dept. of Commerce

(in billions of dollars)

	2005	2006	2007	2008		2005	2006	2007	2008
Europe...............	**$1,614.0**	**$2,191.1**	**$2,569.4**	**$1,336.0**	Cayman Islands......	$102.6	$160.6	$231.9	$165.9
United Kingdom	544.5	689.1	734.7	376.8	Brazil..............	68.6	$92.0	172.6	82.8
France	205.1	306.9	347.8	196.5	Mexico.............	57.9	84.6	85.4	46.8
Switzerland.........	191.9	262.9	281.0	195.9	**Asia**................	**849.9**	**1,050.2**	**1,193.7**	**661.3**
Germany	158.0	220.4	329.2	177.0	Japan..............	493.3	543.5	529.2	355.6
Netherlands	132.8	161.5	154.0	80.1	South Korea	110.3	114.2	129.2	55.9
Spain	63.5	85.6	106.6	60.8	Taiwan.............	57.1	74.2	81.0	42.1
Italy...............	63.9	92.7	96.9	49.0	Hong Kong	44.5	85.8	119.5	48.6
Finland............	44.4	55.9	90.2	40.8	**Africa**	**39.9**	**49.4**	**65.6**	**39.5**
Canada	**247.8**	**298.1**	**379.0**	**212.5**	South Africa........	31.6	39.6	49.1	30.7
Latin America and					Other countries.......	81.7	115.1	157.9	78.5
Caribbean........	**484.4**	**625.1**	**882.4**	**523.7**	Australia	71.1	102.0	138.1	69.0
Bermuda............	173.8	191.9	256.1	145.1	**Total holdings**	**$3,317.7**	**$4,329.0**	**$5,248.0**	**$2,851.4**

(1) As of year end.

Global Stock Markets, 1960-2009

Source: The Conference Board; not seasonally adjusted (1990 = 100)

Stock price index[1]	June 1, 1960	June 1, 1970	June 1, 1980	June 1, 1990	June 1, 2000	June 1, 2004	June 1, 2005	June 1, 2006	June 1, 2007	June 1, 2008	June 1, 2009
United States	17.1	21.9	34.3	107.6	437.2	342.9	358.1	381.8	451.9	384.8	276.3
Japan...................	4.4	7.3	23.8	110.8	60.4	41.1	40.2	53.8	62.9	46.8	34.5
Germany	36.1	27.5	30.5	111.1	407.9	239.6	271.2	336.0	473.4	379.5	284.3
France	16.3	15.6	23.8	112.0	354.7	205.4	232.7	273.2	333.2	244.0	172.8
United Kingdom	8.2	11.6	24.9	108.2	279.9	205.9	236.5	274.1	314.5	263.8	200.5
Italy....................	28.9	20.6	15.9	117.3	309.0	206.5	241.1	271.5	319.9	221.0	149.1
Canada..................	14.8	25.0	60.3	103.6	298.0	249.8	289.5	339.4	406.5	422.9	303.3

(1) 12-month average.

Record One-Day Gains and Losses on the Dow Jones Industrial Average

Source: Dow Jones & Co., Inc.; as of Oct. 30, 2009

(Ranked by largest one-day losses and gains for two terms.)

Greatest % losses

Rank	Date	Close	Net chg.	% chg.
1.	10/19/1987	1738.74	−508.00	−22.61%
2.	10/28/1929	260.64	−38.33	−12.82
3.	10/29/1929	230.07	−30.57	−11.73
4.	11/6/1929	232.13	−25.55	−9.92
5.	12/18/1899	58.27	−5.57	−8.72
6.	8/12/1932	63.11	−5.79	−8.40
7.	3/14/1907	76.23	−6.89	−8.29
8.	10/26/1987	1793.93	−156.83	−8.04
9.	10/15/2008	8577.91	−733.08	−7.87
10.	7/21/1933	88.71	−7.55	−7.84

Greatest point losses

Rank	Date	Close	Net chg.	% chg.
1.	9/29/2008	10365.45	−777.68	−6.98%
2.	10/15/2008	8577.91	−733.08	−7.87
3.	9/17/2001	8920.70	−684.81	−7.13
4.	12/0/2008	8149.09	−679.95	−7.70
5.	10/9/2008	8579.19	−678.92	−7.33
6.	4/14/2000	10305.78	−617.78	−5.66
7.	10/27/1997	7161.14	−554.26	−7.18
8.	10/22/2008	8519.21	−514.45	−5.69
9.	8/31/1998	7539.06	−512.61	−6.37
10.	10/7/2008	9447.11	−508.39	−5.11

Greatest % gains

Rank	Date	Close	Net chg.	% chg.
1.	3/15/1933	62.10	8.26	15.34%
2.	10/6/1931	99.34	12.86	14.87
3.	10/30/1929	258.47	28.40	12.34
4.	9/21/1932	75.16	7.67	11.36
5.	10/13/2008	9387.61	936.42	11.08
6.	10/28/2008	9065.12	889.35	10.88
7.	10/21/1987	2027.85	186.84	10.15
8.	8/3/1932	58.22	5.06	9.52
9.	2/11/1932	78.60	6.80	9.47
10.	11/14/1929	217.28	18.59	9.36

Greatest point gains

Rank	Date	Close	Net chg.	% chg.
1.	10/13/2008	9387.61	936.42	11.08%
2.	10/28/2008	9065.12	889.35	10.88
3.	11/13/2008	8835.25	552.60	6.67
4.	3/16/2000	10630.61	499.19	4.93
5.	3/23/2009	7775.86	497.48	6.84
6.	11/21/2008	8046.42	494.14	6.54
7.	7/24/2002	8191.29	488.95	6.35
8.	9/30/2008	10850.66	485.21	4.68
9.	7/29/2002	8711.88	447.48	5.41
10.	3/18/2008	12392.66	420.40	3.51

Dow Jones Industrial Average, 1963-2009

Source: Dow Jones & Co., Inc.; as of Oct. 30, 2009

Highest close		Year	Lowest close		Highest close		Year	Lowest close	
Dec. 18	767.21	1963	Jan. 2	646.79	Dec. 31	3168.83	1991	Jan. 9	2470.30
Dec. 31	969.26	1965	June 28	840.59	June 1	3413.21	1992	Oct. 9	3136.58
Dec. 29	842.00	1970	May 6	631.16	Dec. 29	3794.33	1993	Jan. 20	3241.95
July 15	881.81	1975	Jan. 2	632.04	Jan. 31	3978.36	1994	Apr. 4	3593.35
Sept. 21	1014.79	1976	Jan. 2	858.71	Dec. 13	5216.47	1995	Jan. 30	3832.08
Jan. 3	999.75	1977	Nov. 2	800.85	Dec. 27	6560.91	1996	Jan. 10	5032.94
Sept. 8	907.74	1978	Feb. 28	742.12	Aug. 6	8259.31	1997	Apr. 11	6391.69
Oct. 5	897.61	1979	Nov. 7	796.67	Nov. 23	9374.27	1998	Aug. 31	7539.07
Nov. 20	1000.17	1980	Apr. 21	759.13	Dec. 31	11497.12	1999	Jan. 22	9120.67
Apr. 27	1024.05	1981	Sept. 25	824.01	Jan. 14	11722.98	2000	Mar. 7	9796.03
Dec. 27	1070.55	1982	Aug. 12	776.92	May 21	11337.92	2001	Sept. 21	8235.81
Nov. 29	1287.20	1983	Jan. 3	1027.04	Mar. 19	10635.25	2002	Oct. 9	7286.27
Jan. 6	1286.64	1984	July 24	1086.57	Dec. 31	10453.90	2003	Mar. 11	7524.06
Dec. 16	1553.10	1985	Jan. 4	1184.96	Dec. 28	10854.54	2004	Oct. 25	9749.99
Dec. 2	1955.57	1986	Jan. 22	1502.29	Mar. 4	10940.50	2005	Apr. 20	10012.36
Aug. 25	2722.42	1987	Oct. 19	1738.74	Dec. 27	12510.57	2006	Jan. 20	10667.39
Oct. 21	2183.50	1988	Jan. 20	1879.14	Oct. 9	14164.53*	2007	Mar. 5	12050.41
Oct. 9	2791.41	1989	Jan. 3	2144.64	Jan. 3	13056.72	2008	Nov. 20	7552.29
July 16	2999.75	1990	Oct. 11	2365.10	Oct. 19	10092.19	2009	Mar. 9	6547.05

*Record high closing.

Milestones of the Dow Jones Industrial Average
(as of Oct. 4, 2009)

First close over...	First close over...	First close over...	First close over...	First close over...
100 Jan. 12, 1906	8000 July 16, 1997	9100 Apr. 14, 1998	11000 May 3, 1999*	12600 Jan. 24, 2007
500 Mar. 12, 1956	8100 July 24, 1997	9200 May 13, 1998	11100 May 13, 1999	12700 Feb. 14, 2007
1000 Nov. 14, 1972	8200 July 30, 1997	9300 July 16, 1998	11200 July 12, 1999	12800 Apr. 18, 2007
1500 Dec. 11, 1985	8100 July 24, 1997	9500 Jan. 6, 1999*	11300 Aug. 25, 1999	12900 Apr. 20, 2007
2000 Jan. 8, 1987	8200 July 30, 1997	9600 Jan. 8, 1999	11400 Dec. 23, 1999	13000 Apr. 25, 2007
2500 July 17, 1987	8300 Feb. 12, 1998	9700 Mar. 5, 1999	11500 Jan. 7, 2000	13100 Apr. 26, 2007
3000 Apr. 17, 1991	8400 Feb. 18, 1998	9800 Mar. 11, 1999	11700 Jan. 14, 2000*	13200 May 2, 2007
3500 May 19, 1993	8300 Feb. 12, 1998	9900 Mar. 15, 1999	11800 Oct. 4, 2006	13300 May 7, 2007
4000 Feb. 23, 1995	8400 Feb. 18, 1998	10000 Mar. 29, 1999	11900 Oct. 12, 2006	13400 May 16, 2007
4500 June 16, 1995	8500 Feb. 27, 1998	10100 Apr. 8, 1999	12000 Oct. 19, 2006	13500 May 18, 2007
5000 Nov. 21, 1995	8600 Mar. 10, 1998	10300 Apr. 12, 1999*	12100 Oct. 23, 2006	13600 May 30, 2007
5500 Feb. 8, 1996	8700 Mar. 16, 1998	10400 Apr. 14, 1999	12200 Nov. 14, 2006	13800 July 12, 2007*
6000 Oct. 14, 1996	8800 Mar. 19, 1998	10500 Apr. 21, 1999	12300 Nov. 16, 2006	13900 July 13, 2007
6500 Nov. 25, 1996	8900 Mar. 20, 1998	10700 Apr. 22, 1999*	12400 Dec. 14, 2006	14000 July 19, 2007
7000 Feb. 13, 1997	9000 Apr. 6, 1998	10800 Apr. 27, 1999	12500 Dec. 27, 2006	14100 Oct. 9, 2007
7500 June 10, 1997				

*9,400; 10,200; 10,600; 10,900; 11,600; and 13,700 are not listed because the Dow had risen another 100 points or more by the time the market closed for the day.

Components of the Dow Jones Averages
(as of Oct. 4, 2009)

Dow Jones Industrial Average

Alcoa
Altria Group
American Express Co.
AT&T Inc.
Bank of America Corp.
Boeing Co.
Caterpillar Inc.
Chevron Corp.
Cisco Systems, Inc.
Citigroup Inc.
Coca-Cola Co.
E.I DuPont de Nemours & Co.

Exxon Mobil Corp.
General Electric Co.
General Motors Corp.
Hewlett-Packard Co.
Home Depot Inc.
Honeywell International Inc.
IBM
Intel Corp.
JPMorgan Chase & Co.
Johnson & Johnson
Kraft Foods Inc.

McDonald's Corp.
Merck & Co. Corp.
Microsoft Corp.
Pfizer Inc.
Procter & Gamble Co.
3M Co.
Travelers Companies, Inc.
United Technologies Corp.
Verizon Communications Inc.
Wal-Mart Stores Inc.
Walt Disney Co.

Dow Jones Utility Average

AES Corp.
American Electric Power Co. Inc.
CenterPoint Energy
Consolidated Edison Inc.
Dominion Resources Inc. (Virginia)

Duke Energy Corp.
Edison International
Exelon Corp.
FirstEnergy Corp.
FPL Group Inc.

NiSource Inc.
PG&E Corp.
Public Service Enterprise Group Inc.
Southern Co.
Williams Cos.

Dow Jones Transportation Average

Alexander & Baldwin Inc.
AMR (American Airlines) Corp.
Burlington Northern Santa Fe Corp.
C.H. Robinson Worldwide Inc.
Con-way Inc.
Continental Airlines C.I.B.
CSX Corp.

Expeditors Intl. of Washington Inc.
FedEx Corp.
GATX Corp.
J.B. Hunt Transportation Services Inc.
JetBlue Airways Corp.
Landstar System Inc.
Norfolk Southern Corp.

Overseas Shipholding Group Inc.
Ryder System Inc.
Southwest Airlines Co.
Union Pacific Corp.
United Parcel Service Inc. C.I.B.
YRC Worldwide Inc.

Record One-Day Gains and Losses on the Nasdaq Stock Market
Source: Nasdaq Stock Market; as of Oct. 5, 2009
(Ranked by largest one-day losses and gains for two terms.)

	Greatest point gains			Greatest % gains			Greatest point losses			Greatest % losses	
Rank	Date	Change	Rank	Date	% change	Rank	Date	Change	Rank	Date	% change
1.	1/3/2001	324.83	1.	1/3/2001	14.17%	1.	4/14/2000	−355.49	1.	10/19/1987	−11.35%
2.	12/5/2000	274.05	2.	10/13/2008	11.81	2.	4/3/2000	−349.15	2.	4/14/2000	−9.67
3.	4/18/2000	254.41	3.	12/5/2000	10.48	3.	4/12/2000	−286.27	3.	09/29/2008	−9.14
4.	5/30/2000	254.37	4.	10/28/2008	9.53	4.	4/10/2000	−258.25	4.	10/20/1987	−9.00
5.	10/19/2000	247.04	5.	4/5/2001	8.92	5.	1/4/2000	−229.46		10/26/1987	−9.00
6.	10/13/2000	242.09	6.	4/18/2001	8.12	6.	3/14/2000	−200.61	6.	12/1/2008	−8.95
7.	6/2/2000	230.88	7.	5/30/2000	7.94	7.	5/10/2000	−200.28	7.	8/31/1998	−8.56
8.	4/25/2000	228.75	8.	10/13/2000	7.87	8.	5/23/2000	−199.66	8.	10/15/2008	−8.47
9.	4/17/2000	217.87	9.	10/19/2000	7.79	9.	9/29/2008	−199.61	9.	4/3/2000	−7.64
10.	10/13/2008	194.74	10.	5/8/2002	7.78	10.	10/25/2000	−190.22	10.	1/2/2001	−7.23

Nasdaq Stock Market, 1971-2009

High	Year	Low	High	Year	Low	High	Year	Low	High	Year	Low
114.12	1971	99.68	223.96	1981	170.80	586.35	1991	352.85	2892.36	2001	1387.06
135.15	1972	113.65	241.63	1982	158.92	676.95	1992	545.85	2059.38	2002	1114.11
136.84	1973	88.67	329.11	1983	229.88	790.56	1993	645.02	2009.88	2003	1271.47
96.53	1974	54.87	288.41	1984	223.91	803.93	1994	691.23	2178.00	2004	1752.00
88.00	1975	60.70	325.53	1985	245.82	1072.82	1995	740.53	2273.37	2005	1904.18
97.88	1976	78.06	411.21	1986	322.14	1328.45	1996	978.17	2465.98	2006	2020.39
105.05	1977	93.66	456.27	1987	288.49	1748.62	1997	1194.39	2811.61	2007	2340.68
139.25	1978	99.09	397.54	1988	329.00	2200.63	1998	1357.09	2609.63	2008	1505.90
152.29	1979	117.84	487.60	1989	376.87	4090.61	1999	2193.13	2167.70	2009	1265.52
208.29	1980	124.09	470.30	1990	322.93	5048.62*	2000	2332.78			

*Record high closing, Mar. 10, 2000; as of Oct. 8, 2009.

Milestones of the Nasdaq Stock Market

Source: Nasdaq Stock Market; as of Oct. 31, 2009

First close over...	First close over...	First close over...	First close over...	First close over...
100 Feb. 5, 1971	400 May 30, 1986	1,500 July 11, 1997	3,000 Nov. 3, 1999	4,500 Feb. 17, 2000
200 Nov. 13, 1980	500 Apr. 12, 1991	2,000 July 16, 1998	3,500 Dec. 3, 1999	5,000 Mar. 9, 2000
300 May 6, 1983	1,000 July 17, 1995	2,500 Jan. 29, 1999	4,000 Dec. 29, 1999	

U.S. Dollar Index[1], 1995-2008

Source: Federal Reserve Bank of Atlanta

Year[2]	Dollar Index	Americas	Europe	Pacific	Pacific (excl. Japan)	Year[2]	Dollar Index	Americas	Europe	Pacific	Pacific (excl. Japan)
1995	103.505	105.454	100.340	103.663	100.498	2004	108.816	114.779	93.026	113.810	116.195
2000	125.347	124.427	134.919	121.740	123.397	2005	111.753	108.547	104.654	120.086	116.105
2001	130.183	127.373	136.137	130.685	127.266	2006	107.545	103.386	93.961	116.050	110.306
2002	127.021	133.303	119.893	126.488	124.301	2007	100.196	97.897	86.773	111.765	106.589
2003	115.066	121.124	101.702	118.428	121.136	2008	110.025	121.212	98.043	107.546	115.454

(1) A trade-weighted dollar index that shows foreign exchange movements of the U.S. dollar. (2) As of Dec.

Average Yields of Long-Term Treasury, Corporate, and Municipal Bonds

Source: Office of Market Finance, U.S. Dept. of the Treasury; Federal Reserve System

Period	Treasury 30-year bonds[1]	New Aa corporate bonds[2]	New Aa municipal bonds[3]	Period	Treasury 30-year bonds[1]	New Aa corporate bonds[2]	New Aa municipal bonds[3]	Period	Treasury 30-year bonds[1]	New Aa corporate bonds[2]	New Aa municipal bonds[3]
1986				**1994**				**2002**			
June	7.57	9.39	7.87	June	7.40	8.16	6.11	June	5.65	6.57	5.09
Dec.	7.37	8.87	6.87	Dec.	7.87	8.66	6.80	Dec.	5.01	5.93	4.85
1987				**1995**				**2003**			
June	8.57	9.64	7.79	June	6.57	7.42	5.84	June	4.34	4.97	4.33
Dec.	9.12	10.22	7.96	Dec.	6.06	7.02	5.45	Dec.	5.11	5.62	4.65
1988				**1996**				**2004**			
June	9.00	10.08	7.78	June	7.06	8.00	6.02	June	5.45	6.01	5.05
Dec.	9.01	10.05	7.61	Dec.	6.55	7.45	5.64	Dec.	4.88	5.47	4.49
1989				**1997**				**2005**			
June	8.27	9.24	7.02	June	6.77	7.71	5.53	June	4.35	4.96	4.23
Dec.	7.90	9.23	6.98	Dec.	5.99	6.68	5.19	Dec.	4.73	5.37	4.46
1990				**1998**				**2006**			
June	8.46	9.69	7.24	June	5.70	6.43	5.12	June	5.15	5.89	4.60
Dec.	8.24	9.55	7.09	Dec.	5.06	6.13	4.98	Dec.	4.68	5.32	4.11
1991				**1999**				**2007**			
June	8.47	9.37	7.13	June	6.04	7.21	5.37	June	5.20	5.79	4.60
Dec.	7.70	8.55	6.69	Dec.	6.35	7.55	5.95	Dec.	4.53	5.49	4.42
1992				**2000**				**2008**			
June	7.84	8.45	6.49	June	5.93	7.75	5.80	June	4.69	5.68	4.69
Dec.	7.44	8.12	6.22	Dec.	5.49	7.21	5.22	Dec.	2.87	5.05	5.56
1993				**2001**				**2009**			
June	6.81	7.48	5.63	June	5.67	7.11	5.20	June	4.52	5.61	4.81
Dec.	6.25	7.22	5.35	Dec.	5.48	6.80	5.25				

(1) On Feb. 18, 2002, the U.S. treasury discontinued the 30-year constant maturity yield and reintroduced it on Feb. 9, 2006; rates in the interim are for 20-year yields. (2) Treasury series based on 3-week moving average of reoffering yields of new corporate bonds rated Aa by Moody's Investors Service with an original maturity of at least 20 years. Treasury discontinued yield index after Jan. 31, 2003. Rates thereafter are for Moody's seasoned Aaa corporate bonds as listed by Federal Reserve. (3) Index of new reoffering yields on 20-year general obligations rated Aa by Moody's Investors Service; discontinued by Treasury Jan. 31, 2003; rates thereafter are from Bond Buyer Index of general obligation, 20-year-to-maturity, mixed quality state and local bonds.

U.S. Capital Gains Tax, 1960-2009

Source: George W. Smith IV, CPA, Partner, George W. Smith & Company, P.C.; as of Oct. 2009

The following shows changes in the maximum tax rate on net long-term capital gains for individuals since 1960.

Year	Max %	Year	Max %	Year	Max %	Year	Max %	Year	Max %	Year	Max %
1960	25.0	1972	35.0[1]	1981	20.0	1988	33.0[2]	1997	20.0[4]	2001	20/18[6]
1970	29.5	1978	28.0	1987	28.0	1990	28.0[3]	1999	20.0[5]	2003	20/15[7]
1971	32.5										

(1) From 1972 to 1976, the interplay of minimum tax and maximum tax resulted in a marginal rate of 49.125%. (2) Statutory maximum of 28%, but "phase-out" notch increased marginal rate to 33%; interplay of all "phase-outs" could produce an effective marginal rate to 49.5%. (3) The Budget Act of 1990 increased the statutory rate to 31% and capped the marginal rate at 28%; effective marginal rates could exceed 34% because of the phase-out of personal exemptions and itemized deductions. (4) New rate was for those who, after July 28, 1997, sell capital assets held for more than 18 mos. (12 mos. for sales after Dec. 31, 1997). A 10% capital gains rate applied to individuals in the 15% income tax bracket. (Those who, after July 28, 1997, but before Jan. 1, 1998, sold capital assets held between 12 and 18 mos. to be taxed at the old top rate of 28%. Those who sold capital assets after May 6, 1997, but before July 29, 1997, to be taxed at the 20% rate, so long as such assets were held for at least a year.) (5) The IRS Restructuring and Reform Act of 1998 repealed the more-than-18-month holding period for sales after Dec. 31, 1997. Beginning Jan. 1, 1998, capital assets needed only be held 12 months to have the 20%/10% capital gains rates apply. (6) For capital assets bought after Dec. 31, 2000, and held for more than 5 years, the 20% minimum capital gains rate was lowered to 18%. The 10% rate was lowered to 8%, regardless of when the assets were bought. This provision was repealed in 2003. (7) The maximum capital gains rate for capital assets held more than one year and sold on or after May 6, 2003, was decreased to 15%. The 10% bracket was reduced to 5%. The capital gains rate for the sale of collectibles such as antiques remained at 28%, and the sale of certain depreciable real estate was to be taxed at a maximum of 25%. A 0% rate replaced the 5% tax rate for tax years beginning after Dec. 31, 2007.

2009 Federal Corporate Tax Rates

Personal service corporations (used by incorporated professionals such as attorneys and doctors) pay a flat rate of 35%.

Taxable income amount	Tax rate	Taxable income amount	Tax rate
Not more than $50,000	15%	$335,001 to $10,000,000	34%
$50,001 to $75,000	25%	$10,000,001 to $15,000,000	35%
$75,001 to $100,000	34%	$15,000,001 to $18,333,333	38%
$100,001 to $335,000	39%	More than $18,333,333	35%

Performance of Mutual Funds by Type, 2009

Source: *Kiplinger* magazine

(as of Sept. 30, 2009)

Fund type/fund objective	Average annual return 1-year	3-year	5-year	Fund type/fund objective	Average annual return 1-year	3-year	5-year
Large-Company				**Sector**			
Growth	-2.7%	-3.26%	1.83%	Financial	-8.88%	-13.5%	-4.31%
Blend	-5.6	-5.17	1.23	Precious Metals	33.92	11.49	15.56
Value	7.14	6.68	0.94	Health	-2.53	-0.22	3.91
Midsize-Company				Natural Resources	-10.7	0.63	9.26
Growth	-3.19	-2.78	3.26	Realty	-26.12	-13.37	0.44
Blend	-3.04	-3.77	2.68	Technology	11.72	0.51	4.89
Value	-2.75	-4.22	2.95	Utilities	-3.52	-0.9	7.17
Small-Company				Hybrid	1.74	-1.14	2.79
Growth	-5.17	-3.83	2.07	**International**			
Blend	-6.76	-4.95	2.2	Diversified	1.61	-3.61	5.94
Value	-6.00	-4.52	2.37	Small/Midsize Diversified	9.28	-3.2	7.82
Taxable Government Bond				Specialized	11.21	1.15	9.96
Short-Term	5.48	4.95	3.79	**Corporate Bond**			
Intermediate-Term	8.12	5.55	4.32	High Yield	13.41	2.7	4.14
Long-Term	10.08	7.59	6.05	Short-Term	5.72	2.89	2.73
Tax-Free Government Bond				Intermediate-Term	11.81	4.43	3.79
Long-Term Municipal	13.71	3.06	3.47	Long-Term	20.85	6.17	4.53

U.S. Mutual Fund Shareholders[1]

Source: The Investment Company Institute

Shareholder characteristics, 2008

Median age[2]	49
Median annual household income	$80,000
Median household financial assets[3]	$200,000
Median mutual fund assets	$100,000
Median number of funds owned	4
Employed[2]	78%
Married or living with a partner[2]	76%
Four-year college degree or more[2]	46%
Invest to save for retirement	95%

Owning:

Equity funds	80%
Bond funds	48%
Hybrid funds	38%
Money market funds	66%

Households owning mutual funds

Year	No. (mil)[4]	Year	No. (mil)[4]	Year	No. (mil)[4]
1980	4.6	1999	48.4	2004	53.9
1984	10.2	2000	51.7	2005	53.7
1988	22.2	2001	56.3	2006	54.9
1992	25.8	2002	54.2	2007	51.0
1994	30.2	2003	53.3	2008	52.5
1996	36.8				

(1) Except where noted, data include mutual funds both inside and outside employer-sponsored retirement plans. (2) Of persons responding to survey. (3) Excluding primary residence. (4) Data from 1980-88 exclude households owning mutual funds solely through employer-sponsored retirement plans.

Chicago Board of Trade, Contracts Traded, 2007-08

Source: Chicago Board of Trade

FUTURES GROUP	2007	2008	% change 2007-08		2007	2008	% change 2007-08
Commodity	132,781,431	147,194,596	10.9%	Equity index	406,167	356,902	-12.1%
Interest rate	709,686,985	615,339,969	-13.3	Metals	116,522	28,701	-75.4
Equity index	41,648,651	56,581,806	35.9	**Total options**	**134,047,704**	**135,519,960**	**1.1**
Metals	11,323,920	5,862,554	-48.2	**COMBINED FUTURES AND OPTIONS**			
Total futures	**895,521,099**	**825,257,796**	**-7.8**	Commodity	161,616,371	184,451,243	14.1
				Interest rate	814,371,012	713,175,202	-12.4
OPTIONS GROUP				Equity index[1]	42,054,818	56,938,708	35.4
Commodity	28,834,940	37,256,647	29.2	Metals	11,440,442	5,891,255	48.5
Interest rate	104,684,027	97,835,233	-6.5	**Grand total**	**1,029,568,803**	**960,777,756**	**-6.7**

(1) Now called the Equity Index, and composed of 6 Dow Jones Indexes; not comparable to Stock Index shown for 1996.

Economic and Financial Glossary

Source: Reviewed by William M. Gentry, Graduate School of Business, Columbia University

Annuity contract: An investment vehicle sold by insurance companies. Annuity buyers can elect to receive periodic payments for the rest of their lives. Annuities provide insurance against outliving one's wealth.

Arbitrage: A form of hedged investment meant to capture slight differences in the prices of two related securities—for example, buying gold in London and selling it at a higher price in New York.

Balanced budget: A budget is balanced when receipts equal expenditures. When receipts exceed expenditures, there is a **surplus**; when they fall short of expenditures, there is a **deficit**.

Balance of payments: The difference between all payments, for some categories of transactions, made to and from foreign countries over a set period of time. A favorable balance of payments exists when more payments are coming in than going out; an unfavorable balance of payments obtains when the reverse is true. Payments may include gold, the cost of merchandise and services, interest and dividend payments, money spent by travelers, and repayment of principal on loans.

Balance of trade (trade gap): The difference between exports and imports, in both actual funds and credit. A nation's balance of trade is favorable when exports exceed imports and unfavorable when the reverse is true.

Bear market: A market in which prices are falling.

Bearer bond: A bond issued in bearer form rather than being registered in a specific owner's name. Ownership is determined by possession.

Bond: A written promise, or IOU, by the issuer to repay a fixed amount of borrowed money on a specified date and generally to pay interest at regular intervals in the interim.

Bull market: A market in which prices are on the rise.

Capital gain (loss): An increase (decrease) in the market value of an asset over some period of time. For tax purposes, capital gains are typically calculated from when an asset is bought to when it is sold.

Commercial paper: An extremely short-term corporate IOU, generally due in 270 days or less.

Consumer price index (CPI): A statistical measure of the change in the price of consumer goods.

Convertible bond: A corporate bond (see below) that may be converted into a stated number of shares of common stock. Its price tends to fluctuate along with fluctuations in the price of the stock and with changes in interest rates.

Corporate bond: A bond issued by a corporation. The bond normally has a stated life and pays a fixed rate of interest. Considered safer than the common or preferred stock of the same company.

Cost of living: The cost of maintaining a standard of living measured in terms of purchased goods and services. Inflation typically measures changes in the cost of living.

Cost-of-living adjustments: Changes in promised payments, such as retirement benefits, to account for changes in the cost of living.

Credit crunch (liquidity crisis): A situation in which cash for lending is in short supply.

Debenture: An unsecured bond backed only by the general credit of the issuing corporation.

Deficit spending: Government spending in excess of revenues, generally financed with the sale of bonds. A deficit increases the government debt.

Deflation: A decrease in the level of prices.

Depression: A long period of economic decline marked by low prices, high unemployment, and many business failures.

Derivatives: Financial contracts, such as options, whose values are based on, or derived from, the price of an underlying financial asset or indicator such as a stock or an interest rate.

Devaluation: The official lowering of a nation's currency, decreasing its value in relation to foreign currencies.

Discount rate: The rate of interest set by the Federal Reserve that member banks are charged when borrowing money through the Federal Reserve System.

Disposable income: Income after taxes that is available to persons for spending and saving.

Diversification: Investing in more than one asset in order to reduce the riskiness of the overall asset portfolio. By holding more than one asset, losses on some assets may be offset by gains realized on other assets.

Dividend: Discretionary payment by a corporation to its shareholders, usually in the form of cash or stock shares.

Dow Jones Industrial Average: An index of stock market prices, based on the prices of 30 companies, 28 of which are on the New York Stock Exchange.

Econometrics: The use of statistical methods to study economic and financial data.

Federal Deposit Insurance Corp. (FDIC): A U.S. government-sponsored corporation that insures accounts in national banks and other qualified institutions against bank failures.

Federal Reserve System: The entire banking system of the U.S., incorporating 12 Federal Reserve banks (one in each of 12 Federal Reserve districts), 25 Federal Reserve branch banks, all national banks, and state-chartered commercial banks and trust companies that have been admitted to its membership. The governors of the system greatly influence the nation's monetary and credit policies.

Full employment: The economy is said to be at full employment when everyone who wishes to work at the going wage-rate for his or her type of labor is employed, save only for the small amount of unemployment due to the time it takes to switch from one job to another.

Futures: A futures contract is an agreement to buy or sell a specific amount of a commodity or financial instrument at a particular price at a set date in the future. For example, futures based on a stock index (such as the Dow Jones Industrial Average) are bets on the future price of that group of stocks.

Golden parachute: Provisions in contracts of some high-level executives guaranteeing substantial severance benefits if they lose their position in a corporate takeover.

Government bond: A bond issued by the U.S. Treasury, considered a safe investment. These are divided into 2 categories—marketable and not marketable. Savings bonds cannot be bought and sold once the original purchase is made. Marketable bonds fall into several categories. Treasury bills are short-term U.S. obligations, maturing in 3, 6, or 12 months. Treasury notes mature in up to 10 years. Treasury bonds mature in 10 to 30 years. Indexed bonds are adjusted for inflation.

Greenmail: A company buying back its own shares for more than the going market price to avoid a threatened hostile takeover.

Gross domestic product (GDP): The market value of all goods and services that have been bought for final use during a period of time. It became the official measure of the size of the U.S. economy in 1991, replacing gross national product (GNP), in use since 1941. GDP covers workers and capital employed within the nation's borders. GNP covers production by U.S. residents regardless of where it takes place. The switch aligned U.S. terminology with that of most other industrialized countries.

Hedge fund: A flexible investment fund for a limited number of large investors (the minimum investment is typically $1 million). Hedge funds use a variety of investment techniques, including those forbidden to mutual funds, such as short-selling and heavy leveraging.

Hedging: Taking 2 positions whose gains and losses will offset each other if prices change, in order to limit risk.

Individual retirement account (IRA): A self-funded tax-advantaged retirement plan that allows employed individuals to contribute up to a maximum yearly sum. With a traditional IRA, individuals contribute pre-tax earnings and defer income taxes until retirement. With a Roth IRA, individuals contribute after-tax earnings but do not pay taxes on future withdrawals (the interest is never taxed). 401(k) plans are employer-sponsored plans similar to traditional IRAs, but having higher contribution limits.

Inflation: An increase in the level of prices.

Insider information: Important facts about the condition or plans of a corporation that have not been released to the general public.

Interest: The cost of borrowing money.

Investment bank: A financial institution that arranges the initial issuance of stocks and bonds and offers companies advice about acquisitions and divestitures.

Junk bonds: Bonds issued by companies with low credit ratings. They typically pay relatively high interest rates because of the fear of default.

Leading indicators: A series of 11 indicators from different segments of the economy used by the U.S. Commerce Department to predict when changes in the level of economic activity will occur.

Leverage: The extent to which a purchase was paid for with borrowed money. Amplifies the potential gain or loss for the purchaser.

Leveraged buyout (LBO): An acquisition of a company in which much of the purchase price is borrowed, with the debt to be repaid from future profits or by subsequently selling off company assets. A leveraged buyout is typically carried out by a small group of investors, often including incumbent management.

Liquid assets: Assets consisting of cash and/or items that are easily converted into cash.

Margin account: A brokerage account that allows a person to trade securities on credit. A **margin call** is a demand for more collateral on the account.

Money supply: The currency held by the public, plus checking accounts in commercial banks and savings institutions.

Mortgage-backed securities: Created when a bank, builder, or government agency gathers together a group of mortgages and then sells bonds to other institutions and the public. The investors receive their proportionate share of the interest payments on the loans as well as the principal payments. Usually, the mortgages in question are guaranteed by the government.

Municipal bond: Issued by governmental units such as states, cities, local taxing authorities, and other agencies. Interest is exempt from U.S.—and sometimes state and local—income tax. Municipal bond unit investment trusts offer a portfolio of many different municipal bonds chosen by professionals. The income is exempt from federal income taxes.

Mutual fund: A portfolio of professionally bought and managed financial assets in which you pool your money along with that of many other people. A share price is based on net asset value, or the value of all the investments owned by the funds, less any debt, and divided by the total number of shares. The major advantage, relative to investing individually in only a small number of stocks, is less risk—the holdings are spread out over many assets and if one or two do badly the remainder may shield you from the losses. Bond funds are mutual funds that deal in the bond market exclusively. Money market mutual funds buy in the so-called money market—institutions that need to borrow large sums of money for short terms. These funds often offer special checking account advantages.

National debt: The debt of the national government, as distinguished from the debts of political subdivisions of the nation and of private business and individuals.

National debt ceiling: Total borrowing limit set by Congress beyond which the U.S. national debt cannot rise. This limit is periodically raised by congressional vote.

Option: A type of contractual agreement between a buyer and a seller to buy or sell shares of a security. A **call** option contract gives the right to purchase shares of a specific stock at a stated price within a given period of time. A **put** option contract gives the buyer the right to sell shares of a specific stock at a stated price within a given period of time.

Per capita income: The total income of a group divided by the number of people in the group.

Prime interest rate: The rate charged by banks on short-term loans to large commercial customers with the highest credit rating.

Producer price index: A statistical measure of the change in the price of wholesale goods. It is reported for 3 different stages of the production chain: crude, intermediate, and finished goods.

Program trading: Trading techniques involving large numbers and large blocks of stocks, usually used in conjunction with computer programs. Techniques include index arbitrage, in which traders profit from price differences between stocks and futures contracts on stock indexes, and portfolio insurance, which is the use of stock-index futures to protect stock investors from potentially large losses when the market drops.

Public debt: The total of a nation's debts owed by state, local, and national government. Increases in this sum, reflected in public-sector deficits, indicate how much of the nation's spending is being financed by borrowing rather than by taxation.

Recession: A mild decrease in economic activity marked by a decline in real (inflation-adjusted) GDP, employment, and trade, usually lasting from 6 months to a year, and marked by widespread decline in many sectors of the economy.

Savings Association Insurance Fund (SAIF): Created in 1989 to insure accounts in savings and loan associations up to $100,000.

Seasonal adjustment: Statistical changes made to compensate for regular fluctuations in data that are so great they tend to distort the statistics and make comparisons meaningless. For instance, seasonal adjustments are made for a slowdown in housing construction in midwinter and for the rise in farm income in the fall after summer crops are harvested.

Short-selling: Borrowing shares of stock from a brokerage firm and selling them, hoping to buy the shares back at a lower price, return them, and realize a profit from the decline in prices.

Stagnation: Economic slowdown in which there is little growth in the GDP, capital investment, and real income.

Stock: Common stocks are shares of ownership in a corporation. For publicly held firms, the stock typically trades on an exchange, such as the New York Stock Exchange; for closely held firms, the founders and managers own most of the stock. There can be wide swings in the prices of this kind of stock. Preferred stock is a type of stock on which a fixed dividend must be paid before holders of common stock are issued their share of the issuing corporation's earnings. Preferred stock is less risky than common stock. Convertible preferred stock can be converted into the common stock of the company that issued the preferred. Over-the-counter stock is not traded on the major or regional exchanges, but rather through dealers from whom you buy directly. Blue chip stocks are so called because they have been leading stocks for a long time. Growth stocks are from companies that reinvest their earnings, rather than pay dividends, with the expectation of future stock price appreciation.

Supply-side economics: A school of thinking about economic policy holding that lowering income tax rates will inevitably lead to enhanced economic growth and general revitalization of the economy.

Takeover: Acquisition of one company by another company or group by sale or merger. A friendly takeover occurs when the acquired company's management is agreeable to the merger; when management is opposed to the merger, it is a hostile takeover.

Tender offer: A public offer to buy a company's stock; usually priced at a premium above the market.

Zero coupon bond: A corporate or government bond that is issued at a deep discount from the maturity value and pays no interest during the life of the bond. It is redeemable at face value.

Minerals

Source: U.S. Geological Survey, U.S. Dept. of the Interior; as of mid-2009; minerals.usgs.gov/minerals

Aluminum: The second most abundant metallic element in the earth's crust. Bauxite is the main source of aluminum. Guinea, Australia, Vietnam, and Jamaica have about 64% of the world's reserves. Main uses in the U.S. are transportation (33%), packaging (26%), and construction (14%).

Chromium: Most of the world's production of chromite ore is in India, Kazakhstan, and South Africa. The metallurgical industry uses about 93% of the chromite consumed in the world; the refractory and foundry industry, 4%; and the chemical industry, 3%.

Cobalt: Used in rechargeable batteries; superalloys for jet engines; cemented carbides for cutting tools; catalysts; ceramics, and other chemical applications; permanent magnets, tool steels, and other alloys. Australia, Canada, China, Congo (Kinshasa), Cuba, Russia, and Zambia account for most of the world cobalt mine production.

Construction aggregates: Construction sand and gravel and crushed stone are two of the most accessible natural resources in the world. Construction sand and gravel is produced in every U.S. state, and crushed stone is mined in every state except Delaware. They are used mostly in construction but also in agriculture, chemicals, and metallurgy and are produced worldwide.

Copper: Main uses of copper and copper alloy products in the U.S. are building construction (50%), electrical and electronic products (21%), transportation (11%), consumer and general products (10%), and industrial machinery and equipment (8%). The leading mine producers are Chile, the U.S. (mostly in Arizona, Utah, New Mexico, and Nevada), Peru, China, Australia, Indonesia, Russia, and Canada.

Gold: Used in the U.S. in jewelry and the arts (80%), dentistry and other industrial (12%), and electrical and electronics

(8%). South Africa has about one-third of the world's resources; significant quantities are also present in the U.S. (mined in most Western states and Alaska), Australia, China, Russia, Uzbekistan, Canada, and Brazil.

Gypsum: Used in wallboard and plaster products, cement production, and agriculture. Leading producers are China, the U.S., Iran, Spain, Thailand, and Japan.

Iron ore: The source of primary iron for the world's iron and steel industries. Major iron ore producers include Brazil, China, Australia, India, Russia, Ukraine, and the U.S., listed in order of iron content of ore produced in 2007.

Lead: Australia, China, the U.S. (mostly in Alaska and Missouri), Peru, Canada, and Mexico are the world's largest producers of lead. The major end use in the U.S. is in lead acid storage batteries (88%). The U.S. produces 15% and consumes about 17% of the world's lead metal. Most U.S. lead production (89%) is recycled material, and 97% of lead acid batteries (mostly automotive) are recycled.

Manganese: Essential to iron and steel production. South Africa and Ukraine have over 80% and 10%, respectively, of the world's identified resources.

Nickel: Vital to the stainless steel industry, and used to make superalloys. Leading producers are Russia, Canada, Indonesia, Australia, New Caledonia, and Colombia.

Platinum-group metals: This group consists of six metals: platinum, palladium, rhodium, ruthenium, iridium, and osmium. They commonly occur together in nature and are among the scarcest of the metallic elements. In the U.S., the automotive and chemical industries use PGMs mainly as catalysts. They also are consumed in electrical and electronics, glass, dental, and medical industries. Russia and South Africa have most of the world's reserves.

Phosphate rock: Used in fertilizers, animal feed supplements, chemicals, and food. Phosphorus is an essential element for plant and animal nutrition. China, the U.S., Morocco, Russia, and Tunisia are the world's leading producers.

Salt: Used in chemicals, highway deicing, industry, agriculture, food, and water treatment. Leading producers are the U.S., China, Germany, India, and Canada.

Silver: Used in decorative, industrial, and medical applications; coins; jewelry and silverware; and photography. Silver is mined in more than 50 countries, mainly as a by-product from gold, copper, and lead-zinc mining. Alaska and Nevada produce more than 70% of U.S. silver, and Peru and Mexico lead the world in production.

Soda ash: A raw material for glass, chemicals, and detergents, it can be mined or produced synthetically. The U.S. is the world's second leading producer of natural soda ash.

Sulfur: Used in agricultural chemicals production, oil refining, metal mining, and many other industries. It is produced as a by-product of oil refining, natural gas processing, and nonferrous metal smelting. Leading producers are the U.S., Canada, China, Russia, Japan, and Germany.

Titanium: Ilmenite and rutile are the major mineral sources of titanium. Titanium minerals are used to produce TiO_2 pigments (94%) and other uses (6%) including alloys, ceramics, chemicals, titanium metal, and welding rod coatings. Major mining operations are in Australia, Canada, China, Norway, and South Africa. U.S. mine production is in Florida and Virginia.

Zinc: Used as a protective coating on steel, as die castings, as an alloying metal with copper to make brass, and as a component of chemical compounds in rubber and paints. Leading producers of zinc ores and concentrates by zinc content are China, Peru, Australia, the U.S. (in Alaska, Idaho, Missouri, Montana, New York, Tennessee, and Washington), Canada, India, and Kazakhstan.

U.S. Reliance on Foreign Supplies of Minerals

Source: U.S. Geological Survey, U.S. Dept. of the Interior

Mineral	% imported in 2008	Major sources (2004-07)	Major uses
Arsenic (trioxide)	100%	China, Morocco, Hong Kong, Mexico	Wood preservatives, nonferrous alloys
Asbestos	100	Canada	Roofing products, gaskets, chloralkali industry
Bauxite & alumina	100	Jamaica, Guinea, Brazil, Australia	Aluminum production, refractories, abrasives, chemicals
Cesium	100	Canada	Drilling fluids, atomic clocks, DNA separation, infrared detectors, night vision devices
Fluorspar	100	China, Mexico, South Africa, Mongolia	Hydrofluoric acid, aluminum fluoride, steelmaking
Graphite (natural)	100	China, Mexico, Canada, Brazil	Refractories, batteries, foundry operations, lubricants, brake linings, steelmaking
Indium	100	China, Japan, Canada, Belgium	Coatings, electrical components, semiconductors, solders, alloys
Manganese	100	South Africa, Gabon, China, Australia	Iron and steelmaking, batteries, agricultural chemicals
Niobium	100	Brazil, Canada, Estonia	Steelmaking, superalloys
Quartz crystal (industrial)	100	China, Japan, Russia	Electronics, optical applications
Rare earths	100	China, France, Japan, Russia	Catalysts, metallurgy, glass polishing, ceramics, phosphors, magnets
Rubidium	100	Canada	DNA separation, fiber optics, inorganic chemicals, lamps, night vision devices
Strontium	100	Mexico, Germany	Television picture tubes, ferrite magnets, pyrotechnics
Tantalum	100	Australia, China, Brazil, Japan	Capacitors, superalloys, cemented carbide tools
Thallium	100	Russia, Netherlands, Belgium	Medical imaging, radiation detection, superconductors, glass, alloys
Thorium	100	United Kingdom, France	High-temperature ceramics, catalysts, welding electrodes
Vanadium	100	Czech Republic, Swaziland, Canada, Republic of Korea	Steelmaking, catalysts
Yttrium	100	China, Japan, France	Lamp and cathode ray tube phosphors, alloys
Gallium	99	China, Ukraine, Germany, Canada	Electronic components
Gemstones	99	Israel, India, Belgium, South Africa	Jewelry, carvings, gem and mineral collections
Bismuth	97	Belgium, Mexico, United Kingdom, China	Alloys, solder, ammunition, metallurgy, pharmaceuticals, chemicals
Diamond (industrial stone)	92	Botswana, South Africa, Namibia, Ireland	Abrasives, stone cutting, highway repair and construction
Platinum	91	South Africa, Germany, United Kingdom, Canada	Catalysts, jewelry, dental & medical alloys
Stone (dimension)	89	Italy, Brazil, Turkey, China	Construction, monuments
Rhenium	87	Chile, Germany, Netherlands	Petroleum-reforming catalysts, superalloys
Antimony	86	China, Mexico, Belgium	Flame retardants, transportation, chemicals, ceramics and glass
Mica, sheet (natural)	86	China, India, Belgium, Brazil	Electronic and electrical equipment
Germanium	85	Belgium, Canada, Germany, China	Fiber and infrared optics, catalysts, electronics, solar cells
Cobalt	81	Norway, Russia, China, Canada	Superalloys, cemented carbides, magnetic alloys, chemicals
Potash	81	Canada, Belarus, Russia, Germany	Fertilizers, chemicals
Tin	80	Peru, Bolivia, China, Indonesia	Chemicals, tinplate, solder, alloys
Barite	79	China, India	Oil and gas well drilling fluids, fillers and extenders, chemicals
Titanium mineral concentrates	77	South Africa, Australia, Canada, Ukraine	Pigment, metal, welding rod coatings, chemicals, ceramics
Zinc	73	Canada, Peru, Mexico, Ireland	Galvanizing, zinc-base alloys, brass and bronze
Palladium	72	Russia, South Africa, United Kingdom, Belgium	Jewelry, catalysts, dental alloys, chemicals, electronics
Tungsten	61	China, Germany, Canada, Bolivia	Cemented carbides, electrical and electronic components, tool steels, alloys
Silver	60	Mexico, Canada, Peru, Chile	Coins and medals, industrial applications, jewelry and silverware, photography
Peat	58	Canada	Horticulture, absorbents, filter media
Diamond (dust, grit, and powders)	56	China, Ireland, Russia, South Korea	Abrasives, stone cutting, highway repair and construction
Silicon (ferrosilicon)	56	China, Russia, Venezuela, Canada	Iron and steel alloys, aluminum and aluminum alloys, specialty chemicals
Chromium	54	South Africa, Kazakhstan, Russia, Zimbabwe	Steel, chemicals, refractories
Titanium (sponge)	54	Kazakhstan, Japan, Russia, China	High-strength alloys for aerospace and non-aerospace uses
Magnesium compounds	52	China, Canada, Austria, Australia	Refractories, agriculture, chemicals, construction, environment, industry
Magnesium metal	50	Canada, Russia, Israel, China	Castings and wrought products, aluminum alloys, desulfurization of iron and steel

World Mineral Reserve Base, 2008
Source: U.S. Geological Survey, U.S. Dept. of the Interior; as of year-end 2008

Mineral	Reserve base[1]	Mineral	Reserve base[1]
Aluminum	38,000 mil metric tons[2]	Nickel	150 mil metric tons
Cobalt	13 mil metric tons	Phosphate rock	47,000 mil metric tons
Copper	1,000 mil metric tons	Platinum-group metals	80,000 metric tons
Gold	100,000 metric tons	Silver	570,000 metric tons
Iron ore	350,000 mil metric tons	Soda ash (natural)	40,000 mil metric tons
Lead	170 mil metric tons	Titanium (ilmenite/rutile)	1,500 mil metric tons[3]
Manganese	5,200 mil metric tons	Zinc	480 mil metric tons

(1) Includes demonstrated resources that are currently economic or marginally economic, plus some that are currently subeconomic. (2) Bauxite. (3) Titanium dioxide (TiO_2) content of titanium minerals (ilmenite and rutile).

World Gold Production, 1980-2008[1]
Source: U.S. Geological Survey, U.S. Dept. of the Interior
(in thousands of troy ounces)

Year	World prod.	Africa South Africa	Africa Ghana	Africa Congo, Dem. Rep.	North and South America U.S.	North and South America Canada	North and South America Mexico	North and South America Colombia	Other Australia	Other China	Other Philippines	Other Russia[2]
1980	39,197	21,669	353	96	970	1,627	196	510	548	NA	753	8,425
1985	49,284	21,565	299	257	2,427	2,815	266	1,142	1,881	1,950	1,063	8,700
1990	70,207	19,454	541	299	9,458	5,447	311	944	7,849	3,215	791	9,710
1995	71,800	16,800	1,710	322	10,200	4,890	652	680	8,150	4,500	873	4,250
1996	73,600	16,000	1,580	160	10,500	5,350	787	710	9,310	4,660	970	3,960
1997	78,900	15,800	1,760	220	11,600	5,510	836	605	10,100	5,630	1,050	3,990
1998	80,300	15,000	2,330	160	11,800	5,320	817	605	10,000	5,720	1,090	3,690
1999	82,600	14,500	2,570	180	11,000	5,070	764	1,410	9,680	5,560	1,000	4,050
2000	81,700	13,900	2,320	231	11,300	5,020	848	1,190	9,530	5,790	1,170	5,000
2001	81,700	12,700	2,200	196	10,800	5,110	757	701	9,000	5,950	1,090	4,900
2002	81,300	12,800	2,230	244	9,580	4,880	686	669	8,560	6,170	1,150	5,410
2003	81,800	12,000	2,270	286	8,900	4,530	656	1,500	9,070	6,590	1,220	5,470
2004	77,800	10,800	2,030	338	8,290	4,160	701	1,210	8,330	6,910	1,140	5,250
2005	79,400	9,470	2,150	290	8,220	3,840	976	1,150	8,420	7,230	1,210	5,280
2006	76,200	8,750	2,240	322	8,100	3,330	1,250	504	7,940	7,880	1,160	5,120
2007	75,800	8,120	2,490	322	7,660	3,290	1,270	498	7,940	8,840	1,250	5,040
2008P	72,900	6,840	2,400	322	7,520	3,050	1,620	643	6,910	9,160	1,140	5,067

P = Preliminary. NA = Not available. (1) Figures are rounded. (2) 1980-94 figures for USSR as constituted prior to Dec. 1991; after 1994, Russia only.

U.S. Nonfuel Minerals Production, 1998-2008
Source: U.S. Geological Survey, U.S. Dept. of the Interior
Production as measured by mine shipments, sales, or marketable production, including consumption by producers.

Mineral	Measurement	1998	2000	2005	2006	2007	2008
Beryllium (metal equivalent)	metric tons	243	180	110	155	152	176
Copper (recoverable content of ores, etc.)	thousand metric tons	1,860	1,450	1,140	1,200	1,170	1,310
Gold (recoverable content of ores, etc.)	metric tons	366	353	256	252	238	234P
Iron ore, usable	million metric tons	62.9	63.1	54.3	52.7	52.5	53.6E
Lead (recoverable content of ores, etc.)	thousand metric tons	481	449	426	419	434	399
Molybdenum (content of ore and concentrates)	metric tons	53,300	40,900	58,000	59,800	57,000	55,900
Silver (recoverable content of ores, etc.)	metric tons	2,060	1,860	1,230	1,140	1,260	1,120
Zinc (recoverable content of ores, etc.)	thousand metric tons	722	796	720	699	769	748
Barite (sold or used)	thousand metric tons	476	392	489	589	455	648
Boron minerals (B_2O_3 equivalent)	thousand metric tons	587	546	612	W	W	W
Bromine	thousand metric tons	230	228	226	243	W	W
Cement (portland, masonry; excludes Puerto Rico)	thousand metric tons	83,931	87,846	99,319	98,167	95,464	86,500E
Clays	thousand metric tons	41,900	40,800	41,200	41,200	36,800	33,200E
Diatomite	thousand metric tons	725	677	653	799	687	764
FeldsparE	thousand metric tons	820E	790	750	760	730	650
Garnet (industrial)	metric tons	74,000	60,200	40,100	34,100	61,400	62,900
Gemstones (natural)	million dollars	14	17.2	13.4	11.3	11.9	11.5
Gypsum	thousand metric tons	19,000	19,500	18,800	18,500	17,900	14,400
Helium (extracted from natural gas)	million cubic meters	114	98	76	79	77	80
Helium (Grade A sold)	million cubic meters	114	127	133	137	138	130
Iodine	thousand kilograms	1,490	1,470	1,570	W	W	W
Lime	thousand metric tons	20,100	19,500	20,000	21,000	20,200	19,900
Mica (scrap and flake)	thousand metric tons	87	101	78	110	97	99E
Peat	thousand metric tons	685	792	685	551	635	615
Perlite (sold and used by producers)	thousand metric tons	685	672	508	454	409	434
Phosphate rock (marketable product)	thousand metric tons	44,200	38,600	36,100	30,100	29,700	30,200
Potash (K_2O equivalent)	thousand metric tons	1,300	1,300	1,200	1,100	1,100	1,200E
Pumice and pumicite	thousand metric tons	872	1,050	1,270	1,540	1,270	791
Salt	thousand metric tons	40,800	43,300	45,000	40,600	45,400	47,600
Sand and gravel (construction)	million metric tons	1,070	1,120	1,270	1,320	1,230	1,010E
Sand and gravel (industrial)	thousand metric tons	28,200	28,400	30,600	28,900	30,100	30,400
Soda ash (sodium carbonate)	thousand metric tons	10,100	10,200	11,000	11,000	11,100	11,300
Stone (crushed)	million metric tons	1,510	1,550	1,700	1,770	1,650	1,440
Stone (dimension)	thousand metric tons	1,140	1,320	1,360	1,330	1,390	1,300E
Sulfur (in all forms)	thousand metric tons	11,700	10,500	9,460	9,060	9,090	9,360
Talc	thousand metric tons	971	851	856	895	769	706
Titanium mineral concentrates (TiO_2 content)[1]	thousand metric tons	400	300	300	300	300	200
Vermiculite concentrateE	thousand metric tons	W	150	100	100	100	115

W = Withheld to avoid disclosing company proprietary data. E = Estimated. P = Preliminary. (1) Rounded to one significant digit to avoid disclosing company proprietary data.

Who Owns What: Familiar Consumer Products and Services

The following is a partial list of well-known consumer brands with their (U.S.) parent companies as of Oct. 2009. Among brands not listed are many brands whose parent companies have the same or a similar name (e.g., Colgate is a product of Colgate-Palmolive Co.). For company contact information, *see* Business Directory on p. 416.

A&W root beer: Dr Pepper Snapple Group
ABC broadcasting: Walt Disney
Admiral appliances: Whirlpool Corp.
Advil: Pfizer
Ajax cleanser: Colgate-Palmolive
Almond Joy candy bar: Hershey
American Girl: Mattel
Arm & Hammer: Church & Dwight
Arrid antiperspirant: Church & Dwight
Aunt Jemima Pancake mix: PepsiCo
Banana Republic stores: Gap Inc.
Band-Aid bandages: Johnson & Johnson
Barbie dolls: Mattel
Bengay: Johnson & Johnson
Betty Crocker prods.: General Mills
Bounty paper towels: Procter & Gamble
Brillo soap pads: Church & Dwight
Brita water systems: Clorox
Budweiser beer: Anheuser-Busch
Cap'n Crunch cereal: PepsiCo
Calphalon cookware: Newell Rubbermaid
Camel cigarettes: Reynolds American
Charmin toilet tissue: Procter & Gamble
Cheer detergent: Procter & Gamble
Cheerios cereal: General Mills
Cheez Whiz: Kraft
Chef Boyardee: ConAgra
Chips Ahoy!: Kraft
Clairol hair prods.: Procter & Gamble
Clinique: Estée Lauder
CNN: Time Warner
Combat insecticides: Henkel
Coppertone sun care prods.: Schering-Plough
Crest toothpaste: Procter & Gamble
Crisco shortening: J.M. Smucker
DC Comics: Time Warner
Dr Pepper: Dr Pepper Snapple Group
Doritos chips: PepsiCo
Dove soap: Unilever
Duracell batteries: Procter & Gamble
Dutch Boy paints: Sherwin-Williams
Efferdent dental cleanser: Johnson & Johnson
ESPN: Walt Disney
Fantastik: S.C. Johnson
Febreze: Procter & Gamble
Fisher Price toys: Mattel
Folger's coffee: J.M. Smucker
Formula 409 spray cleaner: Clorox
FOX News Channel: News Corp.
Fortune magazine: Time Warner
Friskies cat food: Nestlé
Frito-Lay's snacks: PepsiCo
Fruit of the Loom apparel: Berkshire Hathaway
Gatorade: PepsiCo
Gillette razors: Procter & Gamble
Glade air fresheners: S.C. Johnson
Glad products: Clorox
Häagen-Dazs: General Mills
Halcion: Pfizer
Halls cough drops: Cadbury Adams USA
Hamburger Helper: General Mills
HBO: Time Warner

Head and Shoulders shampoo: Procter & Gamble
Hellmann's mayonnaise: Unilever
Hi-C fruit drinks: Coca-Cola
Hidden Valley prods.: Clorox
Hillshire Farm meats: Sara Lee
Hot Wheels/Matchbox cars: Mattel
Hostess cupcakes: Interstate Bakeries
Huggies diapers: Kimberly-Clark
Irish Spring: Colgate-Palmolive
Ivory soap: Procter & Gamble
Jack Daniel's whiskey: Brown-Forman
Jell-O: Kraft
Jennie-O turkey: Hormel
Jif peanut butter: J.M. Smucker
Jim Beam bourbon: Fortune Brands
Keds footwear: Collective Brands
Kent cigarettes: Lorillard Tobacco Co.
KFC restaurants: Yum! Brands
Kibbles 'n Bits pet foods: Del Monte
KitchenAid appliances: Whirlpool
Kit Kat candy: Hershey
Kleenex: Kimberly-Clark
Kmart: Sears Holdings Corp.
Knorr soups: Unilever
Kool-Aid: Kraft
Ladies Home Journal magazine: Meredith
Lee jeans: V.F. Corp.
L'eggs hosiery: Hanesbrands
LifeSavers candy: Wm. Wrigley Jr. Co.
Lipton tea: Unilever
Listerine mouthwash: Johnson & Johnson
Marlboro cigarettes: Altria (Philip Morris)
Max Factor beauty products: Procter & Gamble
Maxwell House coffee: Kraft
Maytag appliances: Whirlpool
Metamucil: Procter & Gamble
Michelob beer: Anheuser-Busch
Miller beer: MillerCoors
Milton Bradley games: Hasbro
Minute Maid juices: Coca-Cola
Mr. Clean: Procter & Gamble
Monroe automotive parts: Tenneco Inc.
Mountain Dew soda: PepsiCo
MTV: Viacom
Nature Valley granola bars: General Mills
NBC broadcasting: General Electric
Neosporin: Johnson & Johnson
Neutrogena soap: Johnson & Johnson
Newport cigarettes: Lorillard Tobacco Co.
Newsweek magazine: Washington Post Co.
Nickelodeon TV: Viacom
9 Lives cat food: Del Monte
Olay: Procter & Gamble
Old Navy clothing: Gap Inc.
Oreo cookies: Kraft
Oscar Mayer meats: Kraft
Pampers: Procter & Gamble
Pantene shampoo: Procter & Gamble
Parker Bros. games: Hasbro
People magazine: Time Warner
Pepperidge Farm prods.: Campbell Soup
Pepto-Bismol: Procter & Gamble
Philadelphia Cream Cheese: Kraft
Pillsbury: General Mills
Pine-Sol cleaner: Clorox

Pizza Hut restaurants: Yum! Brands
Planters nuts: Kraft
Playskool toys: Hasbro
PlayStation: Sony
Playtex apparel: Hanesbrands
Post cereals: Ralcorp
Post-it notes: 3M
Prego pasta sauce: Campbell Soup
Prozac: Eli Lilly
Purina pet foods: Nestlé
Q-Tips: Unilever
Ragu sauce: Unilever
Reese's candy: Hershey
Rice-A-Roni: PepsiCo
Rice Krispies: Kellogg Co.
Right Guard deodorant: Henkel
Ritz crackers: Kraft
Robitussin: Pfizer
Rogaine hair growth aide: Johnson & Johnson
Ruffles chips: PepsiCo
Schick razors: Energizer
Scope mouthwash: Procter & Gamble
Scotch tape: 3M
Scott tissue: Kimberly-Clark
Simon & Schuster publishing: CBS Corp.
Skippy peanut butter: Unilever
SlimFast: Unilever
SnackWell's cookies: Kraft
S.O.S. cleanser: Clorox
Southern Comfort liquor: Brown-Forman
SPAM meat: Hormel Foods
Sports Illustrated magazine: Time Warner
Sprite soda: Coca-Cola
StarKist tuna: Del Monte
Sudafed: Johnson & Johnson
Swanson broth: Campbell Soup
Swiffer: Procter & Gamble
Taco Bell restaurants: Yum! Brands
Tampax tampons: Procter & Gamble
Tide detergent: Procter & Gamble
Time magazine: Time Warner
Titleist: Fortune Brands
Tombstone pizza: Kraft
Triscuit crackers: Kraft
Trojan condoms: Church & Dwight
Tropicana juice: PepsiCo
Tylenol: Johnson & Johnson
USA Today newspaper: Gannett
V8 vegetable juice: Campbell Soup
Vanity Fair apparel: Berkshire Hathaway
Vaseline: Unilever
Velveeta cheese products: Kraft
VH1: Viacom
Viagra: Pfizer
Vicks cold medicines: Procter & Gamble
Victoria's Secret stores: Limited Brands
Visine eye drops: Johnson & Johnson
Wheaties cereal: General Mills
Windex: S.C. Johnson
Windows software applications: Microsoft
Wonderbra: Hanesbrands
Wonder bread: Interstate Bakeries
Xbox: Microsoft
Zest soap: Procter & Gamble
Ziploc storage bags: S.C. Johnson

Top Brands in Selected Categories, 2008-09

Source: Information Resources, Inc., a Chicago-based marketing research company; figures for 52-week period ending Oct. 4, 2009. Sales in millions of dollars; change represents dollar sales change over 52-week period ending Oct. 4, 2008.

Beer	Sales	% change	Market share
Bud Light	$1,434.1	5.6%	19.3%
Coors Light	708.1	9.0	9.5
Miller Lite	677.5	−1.4	9.1
Budweiser	658.5	−0.2	8.9
Corona Extra	410.6	−1.5	21.4
Total sales	9,378.9	5.4	

Baby Food	Sales	% change	Market share
Gerber Second Foods	$210.1	−9.1%	24.8%
Gerber	90.9	6.4	10.7
Gerber Third Foods	63.2	−5.3	7.4
Gerber Graduates	53.9	29.7	6.4
Gerber First Foods	47.9	−8.5	5.6
Total sales	848.4	−0.3	

Batteries (Alkaline)	Sales	% change	Market share
Duracell Coppertop	$465.8	−6.2%	39.1%
Energizer Max	332.4	−1.2	27.9
Private label	224.4	6.1	18.8
Energizer	37.9	13.7	3.2
Ray O Vac	31.8	−4.2	2.7
Total sales	1,192.3	−3.1	

Bottled Water	Sales	% change	Market share
Private label	$735.9	4.6%	19.3%
Aquafina	388.1	−12.7	10.2
Dasani	353.8	−17.7	9.3
Glaceau Vitamin Water	353.3	−18.8	9.2
Poland Spring	256.9	−6.0	6.7
Total sales	3,822.0	−6.7	

Cat Food (Dry)	Sales	% change	Market share
Meow Mix	$118.0	6.0%	10.1%
Private label	102.8	15.5	8.8
Purina Cat Chow Indoor Formula	75.3	16.6	6.4
Purina Cat Chow	68.6	−19.2	5.9
Iams	59.6	−8.7	5.1
Total sales	1,169.0	6.9	

Chocolate Candies	Sales	% change	Market share
M & Ms	$262.9	4.0%	13.2%
Hershey's	193.5	3.6	9.7
Dove	109.9	−1.6	5.5
Hershey's Kisses	95.6	−16.0	4.8
Reese's	92.2	13.1	4.6
Total sales	1,993.5	1.5	

Ready-to-Eat Cold Cereals	Sales	% change	Market share
Private label	$698.9	9.0%	10.5%
General Mills Honey Nut Cheerios	342.2	10.3	5.2
General Mills Cheerios	311.6	−3.6	4.7
Post Honey Bunches of Oats	305.2	−1.3	4.6
Kellogg's Special K	245.2	12.3	3.7
Total sales	6,635.3	1.7	

Ground Coffee (excluding Decaf)	Sales	% change	Market share
Folgers	$676.6	52.9%	22.7%
Maxwell House	386.8	4.5	15.8
Private label	237.0	9.4	9.7
Starbucks	207.9	−5.7	8.5
Dunkin' Donuts	133.2	46.7	5.4
Total sales	2,445.1	6.5	

Coffee (Decaf)	Sales	% change	Market share
Folgers	$60.6	−1.6%	22.8%
Private label	42.2	4.8	15.8
Maxwell House	28.8	−13.7	10.8
Starbucks	21.0	−8.8	7.9
Dunkin Donuts	18.3	34.6	6.9
Total sales	266.2	−2.0	

Cookies	Sales	% change	Market share
Private label	$589.6	16.4%	15.8%
Nabisco Chips Ahoy	317.2	3.8	8.5
Nabisco Oreo	266.5	10.4	7.1
Nabisco Oreo Double Stuf	172.0	8.5	4.6
Lofthouse	131.9	2.4	43.6
Total sales	3,742.3	0.4	

Dog Food (Dry)	Sales	% change	Market share
Private label	$222.9	30.5%	10.6%
Iams	176.6	−2.4	8.4
Purina Beneful	152.3	35.9	7.2
Pedigree	144.8	13.9	6.9
Purina Dog Chow	144.2	20.1	6.8
Total sales	2,110.2	12.9	

Ice Cream	Sales	% change	Market share
Private label	$1,040.0	7.3%	25.1%
Breyers	463.1	−6.3	11.2
Dreyer's Edy's Slowchurned	313.2	5.1	7.6
Blue Bell	288.5	12.4	7.0
Häagen Dazs	254.7	−7.4	6.2
Total sales	4,521.8	0.5	

Paper Towels	Sales	% change	Market share
Bounty	$933.2	3.9%	38.3%
Private label	559.3	7.9	23.0
Brawny	202.7	−5.3	8.3
Kleenex Viva	173.6	18.4	7.1
Bounty Basic	161.4	23.5	6.6
Total sales	2,433.9	2.6	

Potato Chips	Sales	% change	Market share
Lay's	$787.8	0.2%	23.3%
Wavy Lay's	332.4	11.7	9.8
Ruffles	304.0	10.5	9.0
Lay's Kettle Cooked	247.1	171.1	7.3
Private label	239.7	33.6	7.1
Total sales	3,380.6	11.3	

Frozen Pizza	Sales	% change	Market share
Di Giorno	$589.2	18.1%	18.8%
Private label	313.9	30.7	10.0
Tombstone	258.4	4.2	8.3
Red Baron	249.5	5.2	8.0
California Pizza Kitchen	176.5	6.8	5.6
Total sales	3,129.0	6.5	

Salad Dressing	Sales	% change	Market share
Hidden Valley Ranch	$223.5	10.0%	16.0%
Private label	187.1	13.5	13.4
Ken's Steak House	151.8	10.0	10.9
Kraft	150.3	−4.4	10.8
Wishbone	143.8	9.5	10.3
Total sales	1,393.2	2.4	

Soft Drinks	Sales	% change	Market share
Coke Classic	$1,888.2	1.3%	22.1%
Pepsi	1,466.5	−2.3	17.1
Mountain Dew	773.3	1.9	9.0
Private label	665.1	11.9	7.8
Dr Pepper	649.9	7.7	7.6
Total sales	8,555.2	2.9	

Soft Drinks (Low Calorie)	Sales	% change	Market share
Diet Coke	$1,196.8	3.0%	24.6%
Diet Pepsi	695.3	4.1	14.3
Diet Dr Pepper	327.0	12.5	6.7
Caffeine Free Diet Coke	317.0	−0.6	6.5
Diet Mountain Dew	306.7	8.1	6.3
Total sales	4,858.9	3.1	

Toothpaste	Sales	% change	Market share
Crest Whitening plus Scope	$113.6	1.4%	8.9%
Crest	109.2	10.3	8.5
Colgate	92.0	4.2	7.2
Colgate Total	90.2	−4.7	7.0
Crest Pro Health	90.0	26.2	6.2
Total sales	1,281.4	1.2	

Note: For all categories, brands are ranked by dollar sales at supermarkets, drugstores, and mass merchandisers, excluding Wal-Mart. "Private label" represents the aggregated sales figures for store-branded products in that category. Total category sales include other brands not listed here.

Median Price of Existing Single-Family Homes, by Metropolitan Area, 2007-09

Source: National Association of REALTORS®

Median prices are in thousands of dollars and based on all transactions within time period shown. 2nd qtr. 2009 figures are preliminary.

Metropolitan area	2007	2008	2nd qtr. 2009	Metropolitan area	2007	2008	2nd qtr. 2009
Akron, OH	119.3	100.5	88.0	Lexington-Fayette, KY	147.5	144.3	142.7
Albany-Schenectady-Troy, NY	198.9	197.9	189.4	Lincoln, NE	137.5	135.2	133.1
Albuquerque, NM	198.5	192.6	182.2	Little Rock-N. Little Rock, AR	129.1	129.8	134.6
Allentown-Bethlehem-Easton, PA-NJ	260.8	243.6	225.6	Los Angeles-Long Beach-Santa Ana, CA	593.6	402.1	311.1
Amarillo, TX	118.4	124.7	127.3	Louisville, KY-IN	137.4	132.2	132.7
Anaheim-Santa Ana, CA (Orange Co.)	709.5	533.2	468.1	Madison, WI	226.5	226.6	214.2
Atlanta-Sandy Springs-Marietta, GA	172.0	149.5	121.4	Manchester-Nashua, NH	NA	242.8	222.6
Atlantic City, NJ	269.7	253.3	218.7	Memphis, TN-MS-AR	137.2	119.3	121.1
Austin-Round Rock, TX	183.7	188.6	194.0	Miami-Fort Lauderdale-Miami Beach, FL	365.5	285.1	207.4
Baltimore-Towson, MD	286.1	274.1	253.0	Milwaukee-Waukesha-West Allis, WI	223.4	212.3	218.1
Baton Rouge, LA	174.4	165.0	168.5	Minneapolis-St. Paul-Bloomington, MN-WI	225.2	202.0	184.5
Beaumont-Port Arthur, TX	123.0	127.4	138.6	Mobile, AL	136.4	134.2	128.8
Birmingham-Hoover, AL	161.3	153.9	152.3	Montgomery, AL	143.8	135.2	134.2
Bismarck, ND	152.9	155.2	157.8	New Haven-Milford, CT	286.5	263.8	236.2
Bloomington-Normal, IL	154.0	159.8	153.0	New Orleans-Metairie-Kenner, LA	160.3	160.5	165.8
Boise City-Nampa, ID	206.0	188.7	160.4	New York-Northern New Jersey-Long			
Boston-Cambridge-Quincy, MA-NH	395.6	361.1	336.1	Island, NY-NJ-PA	469.7	437.9	379.8
Boulder, CO	376.2	359.6	373.3	New York-Wayne-White Plains, NY-NJ	540.3	494.3	425.2
Bridgeport-Stamford-Norwalk, CT	486.6	437.9	442.9	New York: Nassau-Suffolk, NY	477.2	435.8	386.8
Buffalo-Niagara Falls, NY	104.0	105.4	115.4	New York: Newark-Union, NJ-PA	443.7	417.2	379.4
Cedar Rapids, IA	136.2	136.5	141.7	Ocala, FL	164.6	137.5	110.2
Champaign-Urbana, IL	144.1	141.9	141.0	Oklahoma City, OK	134.9	128.1	128.3
Charleston-North Charleston, SC	215.4	206.2	198.2	Omaha, NE-IA	138.0	135.2	134.9
Charleston, WV	122.5	126.9	131.2	Orlando, FL	261.3	208.9	149.2
Charlotte-Gastonia-Concord, NC-SC	204.3	197.8	199.7	Pensacola-Ferry Pass-Brent, FL	165.6	155.7	147.8
Chattanooga, TN-GA	130.9	129.1	125.7	Philadelphia-Camden-Wilmington, PA-NJ-			
Chicago-Naperville-Joliet, IL	276.6	245.6	204.3	DE-MD	234.9	231.4	211.0
Cincinnati-Middletown, OH-KY-IN	140.8	131.8	129.6	Phoenix-Mesa-Scottsdale, AZ	257.4	191.3	131.1
Cleveland-Elyria-Mentor, OH	130.0	108.5	106.0	Pittsburgh, PA	120.7	118.4	124.2
Colorado Springs, CO	217.5	205.5	189.0	Portland-South Portland-Biddeford, ME	242.7	229.3	209.4
Columbia, MO	147.1	146.3	144.3	Portland-Vancouver-Beaverton, OR-WA	295.2	280.1	246.2
Columbia, SC	146.6	145.0	137.9	Providence-New Bedford-Fall River, RI-MA	286.5	250.6	215.7
Columbus, OH	147.4	139.3	136.6	Raleigh-Cary, NC	224.2	223.4	211.3
Corpus Christi, TX	136.5	139.1	133.4	Reading, PA	154.7	155.7	151.9
Cumberland, MD-WV	109.4	99.5	123.5	Reno-Sparks, NV	321.4	259.1	192.1
Dallas-Fort Worth-Arlington, TX	150.9	145.8	150.7	Richmond, VA	233.7	223.5	211.2
Davenport-Moline-Rock Island, IA-IL	108.7	94.2	113.2	Riverside-San Bernardino-Ontario, CA	379.5	234.2	161.5
Dayton, OH	115.6	107.0	106.5	Rochester, NY	117.9	117.0	119.1
Decatur, IL	83.1	87.4	91.3	Sacramento–Arden-Arcade–Roseville, CA	342.8	216.7	177.5
Denver-Aurora, CO	245.4	219.3	223.7	Saginaw-Saginaw Township North, MI	82.1	62.2	55.7
Des Moines, IA	149.2	153.2	150.1	Saint Louis, MO-IL	145.4	133.2	133.6
Detroit-Warren-Livonia, MI	140.3	NA	NA	Salem, OR	228.3	208.8	191.2
Dover, DE	207.5	206.2	193.7	Salt Lake City, UT	232.0	229.6	216.5
Durham, NC	178.4	180.6	185.5	San Antonio, TX	153.2	152.8	153.1
El Paso, TX	131.9	137.5	131.8	San Diego-Carlsbad-San Marcos, CA	588.7	385.6	347.1
Erie, PA	98.1	99.5	98.1	San Francisco-Oakland-Fremont, CA	804.8	622.0	472.9
Eugene-Springfield, OR	239.6	224.7	202.4	San Jose-Sunnyvale-Santa Clara, CA	836.8	668.0	500.0
Fargo, ND-MN	140.9	139.1	141.2	Sarasota-Bradenton-Venice, FL	310.9	240.6	175.8
Farmington, NM	191.1	190.6	188.6	Seattle-Tacoma-Bellevue, WA	386.9	357.2	328.4
Ft. Wayne, IN	97.1	92.6	94.6	Shreveport-Bossier City, LA	135.6	138.5	146.8
Gainesville, FL	211.1	188.6	178.2	Sioux Falls, SD	144.5	142.3	146.0
Gary-Hammond, IN	134.2	127.7	115.1	South Bend-Mishawaka, IN	90.7	86.0	88.1
Glens Falls, NY	167.6	161.1	152.4	Spartanburg, SC	128.6	127.3	122.7
Grand Rapids, MI	129.4	100.9	86.5	Spokane, WA	193.8	191.2	177.8
Green Bay, WI	150.7	146.2	141.3	Springfield, IL	109.0	108.0	116.2
Greensboro-High Point, NC	152.0	145.3	141.8	Springfield, MA	211.9	200.6	189.5
Greenville, SC	153.6	155.7	140.0	Springfield, MO	122.6	121.1	120.9
Gulfport-Biloxi, MS	154.5	140.2	138.7	Syracuse, NY	121.8	120.2	124.6
Hartford-West Hartford-East Hartford, CT	263.2	246.2	234.1	Tallahassee, FL	179.5	179.9	149.8
Honolulu, HI	643.5	624.0	569.5	Tampa-St.Petersburg-Clearwater, FL	214.9	173.0	140.9
Houston-Baytown-Sugar Land, TX	152.5	151.6	157.4	Toledo, OH	106.6	91.2	87.1
Indianapolis, IN	120.5	111.2	121.3	Topeka, KS	111.9	108.0	113.3
Jackson, MS	139.0	128.7	140.1	Trenton-Ewing, NJ	307.1	303.2	254.3
Jacksonville, FL	189.2	174.6	152.7	Tucson, AZ	244.8	204.3	174.1
Kankakee-Bradley, IL	134.5	130.8	132.2	Tulsa, OK	NA	136.9	133.2
Kansas City, MO-KS	153.3	144.3	144.1	Virginia Beach-Norfolk-Newport News,			
Kennewick-Richland-Pasco, WA	169.2	166.1	163.9	VA-NC	226.8	220.0	216.0
Knoxville, TN	156.4	149.1	144.7	Washington-Arlington-Alexandria, DC-VA-			
Lansing-E.Lansing, MI	126.8	97.7	81.2	MD-WV	430.8	343.4	319.2
Las Vegas-Paradise, NV	297.7	220.5	141.8	Waterloo/Cedar Falls, IA	112.8	111.5	106.7

NA = Not available.

U.S. Home Ownership Rates, by Selected Characteristics[1], 2005, 2009

Source: Bureau of the Census, U.S. Dept. of Commerce

Region	2005	2009	Age	2005	2009	Race/ethnicity[2]	2005	2009	Income	2005	2009
Northeast	64.7%	64.3%	Under 35	42.8%	39.0%	White, non-			Median family		
Midwest	73.4	70.5	35-44	68.7	66.8	Hispanic	75.6%	74.9%	income or more	84.0%	82.2%
South	70.4	70.0	45-54	76.3	74.5	Black	48.0	46.5	Below median		
West	63.8	62.5	55-64	81.3	79.9	Hispanic	49.2	48.1	family income	52.7	51.5
			65+	80.3	80.4	Other	58.0	57.6	**Total U.S.**	**68.6%**	**67.4%**

(1) Figures are for 2nd quarter of the year shown. Not seasonally adjusted. (2) Hispanic householders may be of any race. "Other" includes householders reporting Asian, Native Hawaiian/Pacific Islander, and Native American/AK Native, as well as combinations of two or more races/ethnicities.

U.S. Housing Affordability, 1990-2009

Source: National Association of REALTORS®

Year	Median priced existing home	Avg. mortgage rate[1]	Monthly principal & interest payment	Payment as % of median monthly income	Year	Median priced existing home	Avg. mortgage rate[1]	Monthly principal & interest payment	Payment as % of median monthly income
1990	$92,000	10.04%	$648	22.0%	2000	$139,000	8.03%	$818	19.3%
1991	97,100	9.30	642	21.4	2001	147,800	7.03	789	18.4
1992	99,700	8.11	591	19.3	2002	158,100	6.55	804	18.3
1993	103,100	7.16	558	18.1	2003	180,200	5.74	840	19.1
1994	107,200	7.47	598	18.5	2004	195,200	5.73	909	20.2
1995	110,500	7.85	639	18.9	2005	219,000	5.91	1,040	22.4
1996	115,800	7.71	661	18.8	2006	221,900	6.58	1,131	23.2
1997	121,800	7.68	693	18.7	2007	217,900	6.52	1,104	21.6
1998	128,400	7.10	690	17.4	2008	196,600	6.15	958	18.5
1999	133,300	7.33	733	18.0	2009[2]	177,500	5.33	791	15.7

(1) All figures assume a down payment of 20% of the home price. Based on effective rate on loans closed on existing homes for the period shown. (2) Preliminary figures, as of Aug. 2009.

U.S. Foreclosure Filings by State, 2009

Source: RealtyTrac, Inc.

(Foreclosure filings, Jan.-June 2009.)

State	No. filings	Rank	% total housing units	% change[1]	State	No. filings	Rank	% total housing units	% change[1]
Alabama	9,657	30	0.45%	179.75%[2]	Montana	290	48	0.07%	−59.61%
Alaska	1,072	34	0.38	18.45	Nebraska	638	45	0.08	−69.65
Arizona	89,799	2	3.37	54.51	Nevada	68,708	1	6.23	61.33
Arkansas	8,646	25	0.67	25.69	New Hampshire	4,044	22	0.68	24.16
California	391,611	4	2.94	14.52	New Jersey	23,889	21	0.68	−30.25
Colorado	26,565	10	1.25	−18.62	New Mexico	2,631	37	0.31	11.11[2]
Connecticut	8,801	27	0.61	−31.18	New York	24,210	38	0.30	−18.87
Delaware	1,559	32	0.40	32.01	North Carolina	12,642	36	0.31	−37.91
Dist. of Columbia	1,776	NA	0.62	−31.06	North Dakota	200	49	0.06	85.19[2]
Florida	268,064	3	3.07	41.95	Ohio	58,937	12	1.16	−14.76
Georgia	56,391	6	1.42	16.06	Oklahoma	5,609	35	0.35	−27.03
Hawaii	3,603	18	0.71	296.81	Oregon	19,053	11	1.18	122.43
Idaho	7,952	9	1.26	112.90[2]	Pennsylvania	23,864	31	0.44	24.61[2]
Illinois	68,932	8	1.31	29.46	Rhode Island	3,172	19	0.70	−7.95
Indiana	24,665	13	0.89	−10.77	South Carolina	13,145	26	0.65	125.12[2]
Iowa	2,996	41	0.23	3.67	South Dakota	256	47	0.07	59.01
Kansas	4,660	33	0.38	43.61	Tennessee	20,365	16	0.75	−20.96
Kentucky	4,356	40	0.23	28.95[2]	Texas	49,144	29	0.52	−14.38
Louisiana	5,160	39	0.28	34.38[2]	Utah	13,496	5	1.46	87.65
Maine	1,540	42	0.22	10.63	Vermont	35	50	0.01	−42.62
Maryland	18,112	15	0.78	2.76	Virginia	28,368	14	0.87	3.76
Mass.	18,458	23	0.68	−43.73	Washington	19,855	17	0.72	43.01
Michigan	60,786	7	1.34	−1.28	West Virginia	663	46	0.08	73.56
Minnesota	15,537	24	0.67	52.74	Wisconsin	17,984	20	0.70	49.69[2]
Mississippi	2,175	43	0.17	94.37[2]	Wyoming	413	44	0.17	43.40
Missouri	13,880	28	0.52	−21.11[3]	**U.S.**	**1,528,364**		**1.19**	

NA = Not available. (1) Percent change over same period in 2008 (Jan.-June 2008). (2) Actual increase may not be as high due to data collection changes or improvements. (3) Collection of some records previously classified as notice-of-default in this state was discontinued starting in Jan. 2009.

Average Premiums for Homeowners and Renters Insurance by State, 2006

Source: © 2009 National Association of Insurance Commissioners (NAIC)

State	Home-owners[1]	Renters[2]	State	Home-owners[1]	Renters[2]	State	Home-owners[1]	Renters[2]
Alabama	$894	$223	Louisiana	$1,257	$245	Ohio	$530	$163
Alaska	850	182	Maine	573	145	Oklahoma	1,018	230
Arizona	640	207	Maryland	721	160	Oregon	502	162
Arkansas	802	217	Massachusetts	925	223	Pennsylvania	643	148
California[3]	937	244	Michigan	715	164	Rhode Island	919	189
Colorado	813	169	Minnesota	788	139	South Carolina	851	189
Connecticut	878	197	Mississippi	998	252	South Dakota	628	120
Delaware	530	159	Missouri	707	166	Tennessee	706	208
Dist. of Columbia	1,012	185	Montana	666	160	Texas[4]	1,409	261
Florida	1,386	201	Nebraska	783	148	Utah	494	139
Georgia	703	215	Nevada	693	205	Vermont	677	160
Hawaii	776	213	New Hampshire	669	157	Virginia	662	147
Idaho	477	153	New Jersey	726	179	Washington	603	170
Illinois	674	168	New Mexico	638	200	West Virginia	650	177
Indiana	638	173	New York	869	220	Wisconsin	490	122
Iowa	596	132	North Carolina	649	144	Wyoming	648	155
Kansas	866	170	North Dakota	742	119	**U.S.**	**804**	**189**
Kentucky	637	161						

Note: Average premium = Premiums/exposure per house years. A house year is equal to 365 days of insured coverage for a single dwelling. The NAIC does not rank state average expenditures and does not endorse any conclusions drawn from this data. (1) Based on the HO-3 homeowner package policy for owner-occupied dwellings, 1 to 4 family units. Provides "all risks" coverage (except those specifically excluded in the policy) on buildings and broad named-peril coverage on personal property, and is the most common package written. (2) Based on the HO-4 renters insurance policy for tenants. Includes broad named-peril coverage for the personal property of tenants. (3) California data were provided by the California Department of Insurance. (4) The Texas Department of Insurance developed home insurance policy forms that are similar but not identical to the standard forms.

TRADE

U.S. Trade with Selected Countries and Major Areas, 2008

Source: U.S. Census Bureau and U.S. Bureau of Economic Analysis, U.S. Dept. of Commerce
(in millions of dollars; top 26 countries as ranked by amount of total trade with U.S.)

COUNTRY	Total trade with U.S.	U.S. exports to	Rank[1]	U.S. imports from	Rank[1]	U.S. trade balance with	Rank[2]
Canada	$600,641.2	$261,149.8	1	$339,491.4	1	–$78,341.6	2
China[3]	407,505.4	69,732.8	3	337,772.6	2	–268,039.8	1
Mexico	367,161.7	151,220.1	2	215,941.6	3	–64,721.6	4
Japan	204,404.0	65,141.8	4	139,262.2	4	–74,120.4	3
Germany	152,001.9	54,505.3	5	97,496.6	5	–42,991.3	5
United Kingdom	112,186.5	53,599.1	6	58,587.4	6	–4,988.3	28
South Korea	82,737.8	34,668.7	8	48,069.1	9	–13,400.4	18
France	72,889.4	28,840.1	11	44,049.3	10	–15,209.2	16
Saudi Arabia	67,231.6	12,484.2	23	54,747.4	7	–42,263.2	6
Venezuela	64,033.6	12,610.0	22	51,423.6	8	–38,813.6	7
Brazil	62,751.6	32,298.7	9	30,452.9	16	1,845.7	214
Taiwan	61,252.4	24,926.3	13	36,326.1	12	–11,399.8	19
Netherlands	60,842.4	39,719.5	7	21,122.9	22	18,596.6	231
Italy	51,595.8	15,460.8	18	36,135.0	13	–20,674.1	10
Belgium	46,211.6	28,903.5	10	17,308.1	26	11,595.4	226
Singapore	43,738.5	27,853.6	12	15,884.9	27	11,968.7	228
Malaysia	43,685.6	12,949.5	21	30,736.1	15	–17,786.6	13
India	43,386.5	17,682.1	17	25,704.4	18	–8,022.3	22
Nigeria	42,170.4	4,102.4	44	38,068.0	11	–33,965.6	8
Switzerland	39,805.5	22,023.6	15	17,781.9	25	4,241.8	223
Ireland	38,957.3	7,610.8	31	31,346.5	14	–23,735.7	9
Israel	36,822.7	14,486.9	19	22,335.8	20	–7,849.0	23
Russia	36,117.6	9,334.6	28	26,783.0	17	–17,448.4	14
Thailand	32,604.9	9,066.6	29	23,538.3	19	–14,471.7	17
Australia	32,807.4	22,218.6	14	10,588.8	33	11,629.8	227
Hong Kong	27,982.0	21,498.6	16	6,483.4	42	15,015.2	230
MAJOR AREA/GROUP							
North America	967,802.9	412,369.9		555,433.0		–143,063.2	
Europe	760,200.5	324,997.1		435,203.4		–110,206.2	
Euro Area	477,643.8	199,985.8		277,658.0		–77,672.3	
EU	639,427.5	271,810.1		367,617.4		–95,807.4	
Africa	141,888.3	28,392.7		113,495.6		–85,102.9	
OECD	1,991,192.2	840,698.1		1,150,494.1		–309,796.0	
Pacific Rim Countries	949,893.1	295,951.4		653,941.7		–357,990.3	
Asia Near East	166,121.1	55,002.7		111,118.4		–56,115.7	
NICS	215,710.7	108,947.2		106,763.5		2,183.7	
Asia/South	56,016.8	20,841.4		35,175.4		–14,334.0	
ASEAN	177,034.3	66,893.2		110,141.1		–43,247.9	
APEC	2,032,935.7	747,245.6		1,285,690.1		–538,444.5	
South/Central America	296,925.1	136,945.7		159,979.4		–23,033.8	
Twenty Latin American Republics	632,227.3	271,422.7		360,804.6		–89,381.9	
Central American Common Market	34,174.1	18,800.5		15,373.6		3,426.9	
LAFTA	580,109.1	239,485.1		340,624.0		–101,138.9	
NATO Allies	1,187,979.4	527,170.4		660,809.0		–133,638.6	
OPEC	307,458.8	64,880.0		242,578.8		–177,698.8	
WORLD TOTAL	**3,391,082.7**	**1,287,442.0**		**2,103,640.7**		**–816,198.7**	

Note: Figures may not equal totals due to rounding. Country grouping data reflect the groups as they were at the time of reporting. (1) Rank shown is for column to the left. Ranking includes territories as well as nations. (2) Rank by size of U.S. trade deficit. Ranking includes territories as well as nations. (3) Not including Hong Kong, Macao, and Taiwan. *Definitions of major areas/groups used in table, as provided by source:* **North America**—Canada, Mexico. **Europe**—Albania, Andorra, Armenia, Austria, Azerbaijan, Belarus, Belgium, Bosnia-Herzegovina, Bulgaria, Croatia, Cyprus, Czech Republic, Denmark, Estonia, Faroe Isls., Finland, France, Georgia, Germany, Gibraltar, Greece, Hungary, Iceland, Ireland, Italy, Kazakhstan, Kyrgyzstan, Latvia, Liechtenstein, Lithuania, Luxembourg, Macedonia, Malta and Gozo, Moldova, Monaco, Montenegro, Netherlands, Norway, Poland, Portugal, Romania, Russia, San Marino, Serbia, Slovakia, Slovenia, Spain, Svalbard, Jan Mayen Isl., Sweden, Switzerland, Tajikistan, Turkey, Turkmenistan, Ukraine, United Kingdom, Uzbekistan, Vatican City. **Euro Area**—Austria, Belgium, Finland, France, Germany, Greece, Ireland, Italy, Luxembourg, Netherlands, Portugal, Slovenia, Spain. **EU (European Union)**—Euro Area plus Bulgaria, Cyprus, Czech Republic, Denmark, Estonia, Hungary, Latvia, Lithuania, Malta, Poland, Romania, Slovakia, Sweden, United Kingdom. **Africa**—Algeria, Angola, Benin, Botswana, British Indian Ocean Territories, Burkina, Burundi, Cameroon, Cape Verde, Central African Republic, Chad, Comoros, Congo (Brazzaville), Congo (Kinshasa), Djibouti, Egypt, Equatorial Guinea, Eritrea, Ethiopia, French Southern and Antarctic Lands, Gabon, Gambia, Ghana, Guinea, Guinea-Bissau, Côte d'Ivoire, Kenya, Lesotho, Liberia, Libya, Madagascar, Malawi, Mali, Mauritania, Mauritius, Mayotte, Morocco, Mozambique, Namibia, Niger, Nigeria, Réunion, Rwanda, St. Helena, São Tomé and Príncipe, Senegal, Seychelles, Sierra Leone, Somalia, South Africa, Sudan, Swaziland, Tanzania, Togo, Tunisia, Uganda, Western Sahara, Zambia, Zimbabwe. **OECD (Org. for Economic Cooperation and Development)**—Australia, Austria, Belgium, Canada, Czech Republic, Denmark, Finland, France, Germany, Greece, Hungary, Iceland, Ireland, Italy, Japan, Luxembourg, Mexico, Netherlands, New Zealand, Norway, Poland, Portugal, Slovakia, South Korea, Spain, Sweden, Switzerland, Turkey, United Kingdom. **Pacific Rim Countries**—Australia, Brunei, China, Hong Kong, Indonesia, Japan, Korea, Macao, Malaysia, New Zealand, Papua New Guinea, Philippines, Singapore, Taiwan. **Asia Near East**—Bahrain, Iran, Iraq, Israel, Jordan, Kuwait, Lebanon, Oman, Qatar, Saudi Arabia, Syria, United Arab Emirates, Yemen. **NICS (Newly Industrialized Countries)**—Hong Kong, South Korea, Singapore, Taiwan. **Asia/South**—Afghanistan, Bangladesh, India, Nepal, Pakistan, Sri Lanka. **ASEAN (Assoc. of South East Asia Nations)**—Brunei, Cambodia, Indonesia, Laos, Malaysia, Myanmar, Philippines, Singapore, Thailand, Vietnam. **APEC (Asia-Pacific Economic Cooperation)**—Australia, Brunei, Canada, Chile, China, Hong Kong, Indonesia, Japan, South Korea, Malaysia, Mexico, New Zealand, Peru, Philippines, Russia, Singapore, Taiwan, Thailand, Vietnam. **South/Central America**—Anguilla, Antigua and Barbuda, Argentina, Aruba, Bahamas, Barbados, Belize, Bermuda, Bolivia, Brazil, British Virgin Isls., Cayman Isls., Chile, Colombia, Costa Rica, Cuba, Dominica, Dominican Republic, Ecuador, El Salvador, Falkland Isls., French Guiana, Grenada, Guadeloupe, Guatemala, Guyana, Haiti, Honduras, Jamaica, Martinique, Montserrat, Netherlands Antilles, Nicaragua, Panama, Paraguay, Peru, St. Kitts and Nevis, St. Lucia, St. Vincent and the Grenadines, Suriname, Trinidad and Tobago, Turks and Caicos Isls., Uruguay, Venezuela. **Twenty Latin American Republics**—Argentina, Bolivia, Brazil, Chile, Colombia, Costa Rica, Cuba, Dominican Republic, Ecuador, El Salvador, Guatemala, Haiti, Honduras, Mexico, Nicaragua, Panama, Paraguay, Peru, Uruguay, Venezuela. **Central American Common Market**—Costa Rica, El Salvador, Guatemala, Honduras, Nicaragua. **LAFTA (Latin American Free Trade Assoc.)**—Argentina, Bolivia, Brazil, Chile, Colombia, Ecuador, Mexico, Paraguay, Peru, Uruguay, Venezuela. **NATO (North Atlantic Treaty Org.) Allies**—Belgium, Bulgaria, Canada, Czech Republic, Denmark, Estonia, France, Germany, Greece, Hungary, Iceland, Italy, Latvia, Lithuania, Luxembourg, Netherlands, Norway, Poland, Portugal, Romania, Slovakia, Slovenia, Spain, Turkey, United Kingdom. **OPEC (Org. of Petroleum Exporting Countries)**—Algeria, Angola, Ecuador (reinstated Dec. 2007), Indonesia, Iran, Iraq, Kuwait, Libya, Nigeria, Qatar, Saudi Arabia, United Arab Emirates, Venezuela.

U.S. Exports and Imports by Principal Commodity Groupings, 2008

Source: U.S. Census Bureau and U.S. Bureau of Economic Analysis, U.S. Dept. of Commerce
(in millions of dollars)

Item	Exports	Imports	Item	Exports	Imports
TOTAL CENSUS BASIS[1]	**$1,287,442**	**$2,103,641**	Liquefied propane/butane	$1,011	$4,755
Manufactured goods[2]	**912,382**	**1,490,383**	Live animals	826	2,755
Agricultural commodities[2]	**115,248**	**80,662**	Meat and preparations	12,584	5,046
Mineral fuels[2]	**76,075**	**491,885**	Metal manufactures[4].	18,743	30,403
			Metal ores; scrap.	29,431	9,309
Selected commodities[2]			Metalworking machinery	6,074	8,548
ADP equipment; office machinery	28,639	96,526	Mineral fuels, other	7,030	4,452
Airplanes, engines, and parts[3].......	80,206	25,630	Natural gas	4,879	34,423
Alcoholic bev.,distilled	1,049	5,478	Nickel.	1,567	3,430
Aluminum......................	6,204	13,429	Oils/fats, vegetable	2,693	4,796
Animal feeds	7,610	1,258	Optical goods	2,860	5,090
Artwork/antiques	5,409	7,513	Paper and paperboard	14,668	18,073
Basketware, etc..................	7,692	12,196	Petroleum preparations	51,384	87,103
Cereal flour....................	2,870	4,268	Photographic equipment	3,595	2,489
Chemicals-cosmetics	11,534	9,557	Plastic articles[4].	9,511	15,793
Chemicals-dyeing.	6,238	3,073	Platinum	1,161	7,115
Chemicals-fertilizers.	6,540	8,377	Pottery.	120	1,551
Chemicals-inorganic.	12,846	16,826	Power generating machines[3]	33,658	48,187
Chemicals-medicinal	37,379	59,212	Printed materials	6,355	5,372
Chemicals-organic.	34,256	47,802	Pulp and waste paper	7,744	4,004
Chemicals-plastics	40,281	18,912	Records/magnetic media.	5,250	6,735
Chemicals[4].	25,287	12,713	Rice	2,198	545
Cigarettes	706	180	Rubber articles[4].	1,915	3,169
Clothing	3,169	78,893	Rubber tires and tubes[3].	3,981	9,705
Coal	8,196	3,958	Scientific instruments[3].	42,588	37,275
Coffee.	3	3,804	Ships, boats.	3,114	1,675
Copper........................	3,439	10,358	Silver and bullion.	965	3,003
Cork, wood, and lumber...........	4,241	5,704	Soybeans	15,455	182
Corn	13,931	350	Spacecraft[4]	217	34
Cotton, raw and linters	4,812	12	Specialized industrial machines	51,928	35,574
Crude fertilizers	2,428	2,966	Sugar.	42	615
Crude oil......................	2,270	353,537	Televisions, VCRs, etc.[3]	24,379	133,187
Electrical machinery[3]	82,049	112,623	Textile yearn, fabric.	11,860	21,854
Fish and preparations	4,017	13,994	Tobacco, unmanufactured.	1,238	811
Footwear	673	19,545	Toys, games, and sporting goods	4,697	32,617
Furniture and bedding[3]	5,170	31,371	Travel goods	463	7,986
Gem diamonds..................	5,943	19,744	Vegetables and fruits.	14,040	19,145
General industrial machines.........	55,192	66,910	Vehicles.......................	98,871	190,799
Glass[3]	3,317	2,653	Watches, clocks, and parts	416	4,340
Glassware	990	2,519	Wheat	11,294	1,080
Gold, nonmonetary.	18,714	6,120	Wood manufactures	2,270	8,446
Hides and skins	1,801	53	**Re-exports**	**131,066**	**NA**
Iron and steel mill products	18,493	38,910	Agricultural commodities.........	2,994	NA
Jewelry.......................	4,834	9,615	Manufactured goods	126,207	NA
Lighting, plumbing	2,516	7,767	Mineral fuels	667	NA

NA = Not available. **Note:** Commodity group totals include products not listed here. Figures may not equal totals due to rounding. (1) Both domestic and foreign exports (re-exports). (2) Domestic exports. (3) Due to non-disclosure requirements, certain 10-digit Schedule B commodity classifications are subject to suppression and require a change in aggregation. For additional information see www.census.gov/ft900. (4) Not specified elsewhere.

Trends in U.S. Foreign Trade, 1790-2008

Source: U.S. Census Bureau and U.S. Bureau of Economic Analysis, U.S. Dept. of Commerce
(in millions of dollars)

In 1790, U.S. exports and imports combined came to $43 mil, and there was a $3 mil trade deficit. In 2008, U.S. exports and imports combined amounted to $3.39 tril, and the trade deficit—which has been climbing steadily since the last recorded surplus in 1975—reached more than $816 bil, just shy of the all-time high of $817 bil recorded in 2006.

Year	Exports	Imports	Trade balance	Year	Exports	Imports	Trade balance	Year	Exports	Imports	Trade balance
1790	$20	$23	–$3	1885	$742	$578	$165	1975	$107,652	$98,503	$9,149
1795	48	70	–22	1890	858	789	69	1980	220,626	244,871	–24,245
1800	71	91	–20	1895	808	732	76	1985	213,133	345,276	–132,143
1805	96	121	–25	1900	1,394	850	545	1990	394,030	495,042	–101,012
1810	67	85	–19	1905	1,519	1,118	401	1995	584,742	743,445	–158,703
1815	53	113	–60	1910	1,745	1,557	188	1996	625,075	795,289	–170,214
1820	70	74	–5	1915	2,769	1,674	1,094	1997	689,182	870,671	–181,489
1825	91	90	1	1920	8,228	5,278	2,950	1998	682,138	911,896	–229,758
1830	72	63	9	1925	4,910	4,227	683	1999	695,797	1,024,618	–328,821
1835	115	137	–22	1930	3,843	3,061	782	2000	781,918	1,218,022	–436,104
1840	124	98	25	1935	2,283	2,047	235	2001	729,100	1,140,999	–411,899
1845	106	113	–7	1940	4,021	2,625	1,396	2002	693,103	1,161,366	–468,263
1850	144	174	–29	1945	9,806	4,159	5,646	2003	724,771	1,257,121	–532,350
1855	219	258	–39	1950	9,997	8,954	1,043	2004	818,775	1,469,704	–650,930
1860	334	354	–20	1955	14,298	11,566	2,732	2005	905,978	1,673,455	–767,477
1865	166	239	–73	1960	19,659	15,073	4,586	2006	1,036,635	1,853,939	–817,304
1870	393	436	–43	1965	26,742	21,520	5,222	2007	1,162,479	1,956,962	–794,483
1875	513	533	–20	1970	42,681	40,356	2,325	2008	1,287,442	2,103,641	–816,199
1880	836	668	168								

World Trade Organization (WTO)

The World Trade Organization is an international body that seeks to promote free trade by eliminating barriers to trade. Founded in 1995, the WTO had grown to 153 member countries as of Oct. 2009, with 30 others, including Russia and Vatican City, granted observer status. International intergovernmental organizations, such as the International Monetary Fund and the World Bank, may also be granted observer status. With the exception of Vatican City, observers must start accession negotiations within five years of becoming observers.

Foreign Exchange Rates, 1970-2008

Source: Federal Reserve Board

(national currency units per U.S. dollar except as noted; annual average rates of exchange)

Year	Australia[1] (dollar)	Austria[1] (schilling; euro)	Belgium[1] (franc; euro)	Canada (dollar)	China (yuan)	Denmark (krone)	France[1] (franc; euro)	Germany[1,2] (deutsche mark; euro)	Greece[1] (drachma; euro)
1970	1.1136	25.8800	49.6800	1.0103	NA	7.4890	5.5200	3.6480	30.0000
1975	1.3077	17.4430	36.7990	1.0175	NA	5.7480	4.2876	2.4613	32.2900
1980	1.1400	12.9450	29.2370	1.1693	NA	5.6340	4.2250	1.8175	42.6200
1985	0.7003	20.6900	59.3780	1.3655	NA	10.5960	8.9852	2.9440	138.1200
1990	0.7813	11.3700	33.4180	1.1668	NA	6.1890	5.4453	1.6157	158.5100
1995	0.7415	10.0810	29.4800	1.3724	8.3700	5.6020	4.9915	1.4331	231.6600
2000	0.5815	0.9232	0.9232	1.4855	8.2784	8.0950	0.9232	0.9232	365.9200
2004	0.7365	1.2438	1.2438	1.3017	8.2768	5.9891	1.2438	1.2438	1.2438
2005	0.7627	1.2449	1.2449	1.2115	8.1936	5.9953	1.2449	1.2449	1.2449
2006	0.7535	1.2563	1.2563	1.1340	7.9723	5.9422	1.2563	1.2563	1.2563
2007	0.8391	1.3711	1.3711	1.0734	7.6058	5.4413	1.3711	1.3711	1.3711
2008	0.8537	1.4726	1.4726	1.0660	6.9477	5.0885	1.4726	1.4726	1.4726

Year	Hong Kong (dollar)	India (rupee)	Ireland[1] (pound; euro)	Italy[1] (lira; euro)	Japan (yen)	Malaysia (ringgit)	Mexico (new peso)	Netherlands[1] (guilder; euro)	Norway (krone)
1970	NA	7.576	2.3959	623.0000	357.60	3.0900	NA	3.5970	7.1400
1975	NA	8.409	2.2216	653.0000	296.78	2.4030	NA	2.5293	5.2282
1980	NA	7.887	2.0577	856.0000	226.63	2.1767	NA	1.9875	4.9381
1985	NA	12.369	1.0656	1,909.0000	238.54	2.4830	NA	3.3214	8.5972
1990	NA	17.504	1.6585	1,198.0000	144.79	2.7049	2.8126	1.8209	6.2597
1995	7.7357	32.427	1.6038	1,628.9000	94.06	2.5044	6.4194	1.6057	6.3352
2000	7.7925	45.000	0.9232	0.9232	107.80	3.8000	9.4590	0.9232	8.8131
2004	7.7891	45.260	1.2438	1.2438	108.15	3.8000	11.2900	1.2438	6.7399
2005	7.7775	44.000	1.2449	1.2449	110.11	3.7869	10.8940	1.2449	6.4412
2006	7.7681	45.190	1.2563	1.2563	116.31	3.6661	10.9060	1.2563	6.4095
2007	7.8016	41.180	1.3711	1.3711	117.76	3.4354	10.9280	1.3711	5.8557
2008	7.7862	43.390	1.4726	1.4726	103.39	3.3292	11.1430	1.4726	5.6365

Year	Portugal[1] (escudo; euro)	Singapore (dollar)	South Korea (won)	Spain[1] (peseta; euro)	Sweden (krona)	Switzerland (franc)	Taiwan (dollar)	Thailand (baht)	UK[1] (pound)
1970	28.7500	3.0800	310.57	69.7200	5.1700	4.3160	NA	21.000	2.3959
1975	25.5100	2.3713	484.00	57.4300	4.1530	2.5839	NA	20.379	2.2216
1980	50.0800	2.1412	607.43	71.7600	4.2309	1.6772	NA	20.476	2.3243
1985	170.3900	2.2002	870.02	170.0400	8.6039	2.4571	NA	27.159	1.2963
1990	142.5500	1.8125	707.76	101.9300	5.9188	1.3892	NA	25.585	1.7847
1995	151.1100	1.4174	771.27	124.6900	7.1333	1.1825	26.495	24.915	1.5785
2000	0.9232	1.7250	1,130.90	0.9232	9.1735	1.6904	31.260	40.210	1.5156
2004	1.2438	1.6902	1,145.24	1.2438	7.3480	1.2428	33.372	40.271	1.8330
2005	1.2449	1.6639	1,023.75	1.2449	7.4710	1.2459	32.131	40.252	1.8204
2006	1.2563	1.5882	54.32	1.2563	7.3718	1.2532	32.506	37.876	1.8434
2007	1.3711	1.5065	928.97	1.3711	6.7550	1.1999	32.852	32.203	2.0020
2008	1.4726	1.4140	1,098.71	1.4726	6.5846	1.0816	31.521	32.962	1.8545

NA = Not available. **Note:** The euro, the European Union's single currency, replaced the national currencies in the EU nations shown above. Exchange rates have been in euros since 1999 for the following countries: Austria, Belgium, France, Germany, Ireland, Italy, Netherlands, Portugal, Spain. For Greece, exchange rates from 2001 on are in euros. (1) U.S. dollars per unit of national currency. (2) West Germany before 1991.

North American Free Trade Agreement (NAFTA)

NAFTA, a free trade pact between the U.S., Canada, and Mexico, took effect Jan. 1, 1994. Major provisions, which were fully implemented Jan. 1, 2008, are as follows:

Agriculture: With limited exceptions, tariffs on all agricultural products to be eliminated over 15 years. Domestic price-support systems may continue provided they do not distort trade.

Automobiles: At least 62.5% of an automobile's value must have been produced in North America for it to qualify for duty-free status. Tariffs to be phased out over 10 years.

Disputes: Special judges have jurisdiction to resolve disagreements within strict timetables.

Energy: Mexico bars foreign ownership of its oil fields but, as of 2004, U.S. and Canadian companies could bid on contracts offered by Mexico's state-owned oil and electricity monopolies.

Environment: The trade agreement cannot be used to overrule national and state environmental, health, or safety laws.

Finance: Limits on ownership of banks, insurance companies, and brokerages eliminated by Jan. 1, 2000.

Immigration: Restrictions on the movement of business executives and professionals eased.

Jobs: Barriers to limit Mexican migration to U.S. remain unaffected by NAFTA.

Patent and copyright protection: Mexico strengthened its laws providing protection to intellectual property and agreed to honor pharmaceutical patents for 20 years.

Tariffs: Tariffs on 10,000 customs goods are to be eliminated over 15 years. One-half of U.S. exports to Mexico were considered duty-free by 1999.

Textiles: A "rule of origin" provision requires most garments to be made from yarn and fabric that have been produced in North America. Most tariffs phased out by 1999.

Trucking: Trucks to have free access throughout the 3 countries by 1999, but the U.S. restricted Mexican trucks to a 20-mi comm. zone at the border. In 2001, an arbitration panel ruled the restrictions were in violation of NAFTA. In 2008, the U.S. House terminated a pilot program, begun in 2007, granting limited access to some Mexican trucks.

U.S. Trade with Mexico and Canada, 1996-2008

Source: U.S. Census Bureau and U.S. Bureau of Economic Analysis, U.S. Dept. of Commerce

(in millions of dollars)

Year	WITH MEXICO Exports	Imports	U.S. trade balance[1]	Year	WITH CANADA Exports	Imports	U.S. trade balance[1]
1996	$56,792	$74,297	–$17,506	1996	$134,210	$155,893	–$21,682
1997	71,388	85,938	–14,549	1997	151,767	167,234	–15,467
1998	78,773	94,629	–15,857	1998	156,603	173,256	–16,653
1999	86,909	109,721	–22,812	1999	166,600	198,711	–32,111
2000	111,349	135,926	–24,577	2000	178,941	230,838	–51,897
2001	101,297	131,338	–30,041	2001	163,424	216,268	–52,844
2002	97,470	134,616	–37,146	2002	160,923	209,088	–48,165
2003	97,412	138,060	–40,648	2003	169,924	221,595	–51,671
2004	110,835	155,902	–45,067	2004	189,880	256,360	–66,480
2005	120,365	170,109	–49,744	2005	211,899	290,384	–78,486
2006	133,979	198,253	–64,274	2006	230,656	302,438	–71,782
2007	136,092	210,714	–74,622	2007	248,888	317,057	–68,169
2008	151,220	215,942	–64,722	2008	261,150	339,491	–78,342

(1) Figures may not equal totals due to rounding.

Central American Free Trade Agreement (CAFTA)

CAFTA (also known as CAFTA-DR) is a free trade agreement between the U.S. and Costa Rica, Dominican Republic, El Salvador, Guatemala, Honduras, and Nicaragua. The U.S. and El Salvador approved the agreement Mar. 1, 2006; Nicaragua joined a month later, and Guatemala entered into the accord July 1, 2006. The Dominican Republic approved CAFTA Mar. 1, 2007, and Costa Rica completed the treaty by signing on Jan. 1, 2009. Some highlights of the agreement:

Agriculture: Tariffs on 50% of U.S. farm goods eliminated; other goods deemed "sensitive"—including corn, milk, and potatoes—to have tariffs reduced to zero over 20 years. Sugar imports to the U.S. allowed to rise to 1.2% of annual U.S. production, up to 1.7% over 15 years.

Automobiles: Tariffs on autos and auto parts to be phased out over 5 years.

Environment and labor: Party nations agree to enforce local labor and environmental protections, although no mechanisms to monitor enforcement currently exist.

Intellectual property: Party nations agree to uphold international standards of trademark, copyright, and patent protection to which the U.S. is a signatory. This includes seizing pirated and counterfeit goods and prosecuting those who traffic in them.

Manufacturing: Tariffs eliminated on 80% of U.S. goods.

Market barriers: Barriers for services such as telecommunications, insurance, and financial services eliminated or reduced.

Pharmaceuticals: U.S. pharmaceuticals given 5-year patent protection from their date of introduction to CAFTA markets, regardless of date introduced in U.S.

Textiles and clothing: Elimination of duties on nearly all textiles and clothing instituted, retroactive to Jan. 1, 2004.

Busiest U.S. Ports, 2007

Source: U.S. Army Corps of Engineers, Dept. of the Army, U.S. Dept. of Defense

(figures in tons; ranked by tonnage handled)

Rank	Port	Total	Domestic	Foreign	Imports	Exports
1.	South Louisiana, LA	229,040,085	121,549,984	107,490,101	47,342,820	60,147,281
2.	Houston, TX	216,064,325	70,721,886	145,342,439	94,691,663	50,650,776
3.	New York, NY-NJ	157,202,043	65,780,088	91,421,955	74,958,234	16,463,721
4.	Long Beach, CA	85,939,895	15,383,519	70,556,376	49,706,082	20,850,294
5.	Beaumont, TX	81,383,531	24,339,637	57,043,894	50,456,036	6,587,858
6.	Corpus Christi, TX	81,072,509	22,707,247	58,365,262	48,025,392	10,339,870
7.	Huntington, WV-KY-OH	76,488,980	76,488,980	0	0	0
8.	New Orleans, LA	76,045,540	38,254,521	37,791,019	21,653,327	16,137,692
9.	Los Angeles, CA.	65,501,632	8,160,656	57,340,976	40,466,058	16,874,918
10.	Mobile, AL	64,494,312	29,678,698	34,815,614	22,973,267	11,842,347
11.	Lake Charles, LA	64,234,040	24,521,814	39,712,226	34,456,609	5,255,617
12.	Plaquemines, LA	58,816,539	34,820,824	23,995,715	8,467,693	15,528,022
13.	Texas City, TX	56,786,525	16,307,273	40,479,252	35,918,567	4,560,685
14.	Baton Rouge, LA	54,623,559	36,080,449	18,543,110	13,720,145	4,822,965
15.	Tampa, FL	46,857,461	31,703,325	15,154,136	8,847,566	6,306,570
16.	Duluth-Superior, MN-WI	46,497,518	31,358,729	15,138,789	258,387	14,880,402
17.	Baltimore, MD.	41,250,672	14,502,458	26,748,214	16,044,238	10,703,976
18.	Norfolk Harbor, VA	39,736,580	7,681,315	32,055,265	10,178,755	21,876,510
19.	Pittsburgh, PA	38,086,035	38,086,035	0	0	0
20.	Paulsboro, NJ	37,984,437	13,826,389	24,158,048	22,797,376	1,360,672
21.	Valdez, AK	37,774,797	37,774,797	0	0	0
22.	Savannah, GA	36,485,648	1,690,671	34,794,977	21,981,235	12,813,742
23.	Pascagoula, MS	35,195,425	11,828,497	23,366,928	18,960,956	4,405,972
24.	Philadelphia, PA.	35,148,631	13,482,738	21,665,893	21,100,666	565,227
25.	St. Louis, MO-IL	32,124,597	32,124,597	0	0	0
26.	Portland, OR.	31,118,987	12,308,514	18,810,473	4,661,239	14,149,234
27.	Freeport, TX	29,597,892	5,532,766	24,065,126	20,966,733	3,098,393
28.	Port Arthur, TX	29,261,601	11,614,436	17,647,165	11,851,472	5,795,693
29.	Seattle, WA	28,169,104	6,840,750	21,328,354	9,511,764	11,816,590
30.	Tacoma, WA.	26,943,545	7,596,877	19,346,668	6,845,029	12,501,639
31.	Richmond, CA	24,992,117	11,053,956	13,938,161	12,490,393	1,447,768
32.	Marcus Hook, PA	24,785,050	11,808,299	12,976,751	12,932,291	44,460
33.	Chicago, IL	24,482,157	21,127,722	3,354,435	2,296,537	1,057,898
34.	Portland, ME.	24,253,826	1,442,247	22,811,579	22,764,560	47,019
35.	Port Everglades, FL	24,215,781	9,930,959	14,284,822	11,062,555	3,222,267
36.	Charleston, SC	22,615,504	3,040,123	19,575,381	13,051,703	6,523,678
37.	Boston, MA.	22,370,438	8,008,814	14,361,624	13,031,902	1,329,722
38.	Jacksonville, FL	21,207,086	7,601,494	13,605,592	12,287,471	1,318,121
39.	Memphis, TN	18,825,124	18,825,124	0	0	0
40.	Honolulu, HI	17,581,912	16,427,756	1,154,156	794,852	359,304
41.	Oakland, CA.	16,911,645	2,967,382	13,944,263	6,317,303	7,626,960
42.	Indiana Harbor, IN	15,025,641	14,490,891	534,750	493,196	41,554
43.	Newport News, VA	14,968,808	4,861,751	10,107,057	1,029,046	9,078,011
44.	Detroit, MI.	14,942,973	11,412,888	3,530,085	3,090,013	440,072
45.	Anacortes, WA	14,341,218	10,857,662	3,483,556	2,322,413	1,161,143
46.	Two Harbors, MN	13,671,654	13,071,191	600,463	0	600,463
47.	Cincinnati, OH	13,220,804	13,220,804	0	0	0
48.	Cleveland, OH	12,792,544	10,374,399	2,418,145	2,247,988	170,157
49.	Toledo, OH.	12,468,072	4,480,143	7,987,929	4,145,053	3,842,876
50.	San Juan, PR	12,225,899	7,023,272	5,202,627	4,602,848	599,779

U.S. Railroad Freight and Miles, 1890-2008

Source: Association of American Railroads

(in billion ton-miles)

Year	Class I freight[1]	All freight	Miles[2]	Year	Class I freight[1]	All freight	Miles[2]	Year	Class I freight[1]	All freight	Miles[2]
1890...	NA	76	163,597	1950...	589	592	223,779	2000...	1,466	1,534	144,473
1900...	NA	142	193,346	1960...	572	575	217,552	2005...	1,696	1,765	140,810
1910...	NA	255	240,293	1970...	765	771	205,782	2006...	1,772	1,830	140,490
1920...	410	414	252,845	1980...	919	932	178,056	2007...	1,771	1,831	140,695
1930...	383	386	249,052	1990...	1,034	1,091	145,979	2008...	1,777	NA	NA
1940...	373	375	233,670								

NA = Not available. **Note:** A ton-mile equals one ton of freight transported one statute mile. (1) Largest class of freight railroad companies, determined by annual operating revenue. (2) Aggregate length of operating roadway in U.S., excluding yard tracks, sidings, and parallel tracks.

Merchant Fleets of the World, 2006

Source: Maritime Administration, U.S. Dept. of Transportation

(tonnage in thousands; self-propelled oceangoing vessels of 10,000 gross deadweight tons or more, ranked by total tons, all vessels)

	All vessels		Tanker		Dry bulk carrier		Container		Other[1]	
By flag of registry	No.	Tons	No.	Tons	No.	Tons	No.	Tons	No.	Tons
Panama	3,668	221,216	616	59,016	1,851	122,519	588	25,324	613	14,357
Liberia	1,620	100,329	585	52,270	327	19,915	537	22,975	171	5,169
Greece	567	54,966	247	32,294	262	19,501	47	2,755	11	416
Hong Kong	777	51,850	88	11,839	512	33,244	112	5,168	65	1,599
Marshall Islands	738	51,315	341	32,511	185	11,098	148	4,890	64	2,816
Bahamas	772	49,755	235	26,085	310	16,028	70	2,561	157	5,081
Singapore	760	47,411	304	26,949	182	11,931	194	5,456	80	3,076
Malta	759	38,100	187	13,782	441	21,427	49	1,316	82	1,574
Cyprus	675	30,787	98	6,520	349	18,428	148	4,431	80	1,408
China[2]	812	28,862	133	7,143	375	14,926	89	3,374	215	3,418
Norway (NIS)[3]	389	20,189	158	8,869	86	5,409	4	165	141	5,747
Isle of Man	193	14,232	108	9,400	41	3,413	16	566	28	852
India	197	12,613	101	8,443	74	3,394	4	101	18	675
Germany	271	12,368	19	791	4	456	239	10,986	9	135
United States	286	12,269	94	5,494	60	2,314	70	2,922	62	1,538
South Korea	193	11,398	17	1,231	126	8,769	37	1,150	13	247
Italy	271	11,119	124	5,180	48	3,432	27	1,017	72	1,489
Japan	125	9,752	18	3,144	48	3,920	11	519	48	2,169
United Kingdom	226	9,526	43	1,575	24	1,785	112	5,105	47	1,061
Denmark (DIS)[4]	136	9,246	40	2,856	4	322	77	5,724	15	344
All others	3,314	132,577	726	49,156	1,155	48,555	583	15,955	850	18,911
By country[5]										
Greece	2,506	171,099	795	76,865	1,347	82,124	174	7,499	190	4,611
Japan	2,259	150,308	428	44,368	1,150	85,121	225	10,118	456	10,701
China[2]	1,798	87,734	220	18,424	1,016	53,763	214	8,749	348	6,798
Germany	1,622	64,740	148	8,343	187	10,986	1,152	41,984	135	3,427
United States	684	39,632	301	23,931	203	10,157	52	1,736	128	3,808
Singapore	587	38,419	235	22,967	173	9,596	110	3,145	69	2,711
Norway	693	35,941	287	19,391	176	8,174	10	361	220	8,015
United Kingdom	500	35,583	167	18,184	158	11,246	68	2,636	107	3,517
South Korea	428	28,961	63	8,188	222	15,879	75	2,641	68	2,253
Taiwan	482	28,186	42	5,388	216	14,893	201	7,332	23	573
Denmark	385	20,655	102	6,651	41	1,822	191	11,274	51	908
Bermuda	97	19,277	79	17,620	5	153	2	47	11	1,458
India	239	14,740	103	8,795	105	5,007	3	87	28	851
Italy	334	14,551	153	7,035	79	5,023	19	728	83	1,766
Cyprus	259	11,972	86	6,729	90	3,404	50	1,247	33	591
Monaco	171	11,589	42	3,822	71	4,998	43	2,271	15	498
Saudi Arabia	72	11,136	64	10,888	—	—	—	—	8	248
Switzerland	242	10,198	13	352	26	1,195	173	8,080	30	571
Russia	222	10,061	102	7,506	73	1,633	21	419	26	503
Iran	126	9,792	35	6,272	52	2,534	11	409	28	578
All others	3,043	115,305	817	42,830	1,074	43,078	368	11,700	784	17,698
TOTAL	**16,749**	**929,880**	**4,282**	**364,549**	**6,464**	**370,785**	**3,162**	**122,462**	**2,841**	**72,083**

— = Not available. (1) Includes roll-on/roll-off, gas carriers, general cargo carriers, partial container ships, refrigerated cargo ships, barge carriers, and specialized cargo ships. (2) Excludes Hong Kong. (3) Norwegian Intl. Shipping Registry. (4) Danish Intl. Shipping Registry. (5) Based on parent company nationality.

U.S. International Transactions, 1970-2008

Source: U.S. Bureau of Economic Analysis, U.S. Dept. of Commerce

(in millions of dollars; revised as of Sept. 2009)

CURRENT ACCT.	1970	1975	1980	1985	1990	1995	2000	2008
Exports of goods & services								
and income receipts	$68,387	$157,936	$344,440	$387,612	$706,975	$1,004,631	$1,421,515	$2,591,233
Goods, BOP basis[1]	42,469	107,088	224,250	215,915	387,401	575,204	771,994	1,276,994
Services	14,171	25,497	47,584	73,155	147,832	219,183	298,603	549,602
Income receipts on U.S.-owned assets								
abroad	11,748	25,351	72,606	98,542	170,570	208,065	348,083	764,637
Imports of goods & services								
and income payments	−59,901	−132,745	−333,774	−483,769	−759,290	−1,080,124	−1,780,296	−3,168,938
Goods, BOP basis[1]	−39,866	−98,185	−249,750	−338,088	−498,438	−749,374	−1,226,684	−2,117,245
Services	−14,520	−21,996	−41,491	−72,862	−117,659	−141,397	−223,748	−405,287
Income payments on foreign-owned								
assets in U.S.	−5,515	−12,564	−42,532	−72,819	−139,728	−183,090	−322,345	−646,406
Unilateral current transfers, net	−6,156	−7,075	−8,349	−21,998	−26,654	−38,074	−58,645	−128,363
CAPITAL ACCT.: Transactions, net	NA	NA	NA	315	−6,579	−927	−1,010	953
FINANCIAL ACCT.								
U.S.-owned assets abroad								
(decrease/financial outflow [−])[2] . . .	−8,470	−39,703	−85,815	−44,752	−81,234	−352,264	−560,523	−106
U.S. official reserve assets	3,348	−849	−7,003	−3,858	−2,158	−9,742	−290	−4,848
U.S. govt. assets, other than official								
reserve assets	−1,589	−3,474	−5,162	−2,821	2,317	−984	−941	−529,615
U.S. private assets	−10,229	−35,380	−73,651	−38,074	−81,393	−341,538	−559,292	534,357
Foreign-owned assets in U.S.								
(increase/financial inflow [+])[2]	6,359	16,870	60,885	144,231	139,357	435,102	1,038,224	534,071
Stat. discrepancy (sum of above								
with sign reversed)	−219	4,717	22,613	18,362	27,425	31,656	−59,265	200,055
Memo: Balance on current acct.	2,331	18,116	2,317	−118,155	−78,968	−113,567	−417,426	−706,068

NA = Not available or applicable. (1) BOP = Balance of payments. Excl. exports of goods under U.S. military agency sales contracts identified in Census export documents, excl. imports of goods under direct defense expenditures identified in Census import documents, and reflects various other adjustments. (2) Excl. financial derivatives.

Foreign Direct Investment[1] in the U.S. by Selected Countries and Territories, 1995-2008

Source: U.S. Bureau of Economic Analysis, U.S. Dept. of Commerce
(in millions of dollars)

	2008	2000	1995		2008	2000	1995
ALL COUNTRIES[2]	$2,278,892	$1,256,867	$535,553	Other Western			
Canada	221,870	114,309	45,618	Hemisphere	$33,623	$40,307	$19,806
Europe	**1,622,911**	**887,014**	**332,374**	Bahamas	81	1,254	1,286
Austria	2,406	3,007	1,553	Bermuda	10,750	18,336	2,626
Belgium	18,580	14,787	4,397	Netherlands Antilles. .	6,266	3,807	8,044
Denmark	4,992	4,025	3,444	UK isls., Caribbean . .	21,604	15,191	7,207
Finland.	12,499	8,875	2,710	**Africa**.	**2,002**	**2,700**	**1,113**
France	163,430	125,740	36,167	South Africa	643	704	−3
Germany	211,521	122,412	46,017	**Middle East**.	**14,676**	**6,506**	**5,801**
Ireland	34,094	25,523	4,749	Israel	6,143	3,012	1,883
Italy	17,575	6,576	3,062	Kuwait	359	908	2,525
Liechtenstein	NA	319	176	Lebanon.	NA	1	−9
Luxembourg.	113,248	58,930	5,756	Saudi Arabia	NA	NA	1,211
Netherlands	259,385	138,894	65,116	United Arab Emirates . .	2,744	64	98
Norway	6,755	2,665	2,172	**Asia and Pacific**	**368,200**	**192,647**	**122,774**
Spain	38,662	5,068	3,237	Australia.	64,316	18,775	10,356
Sweden	35,020	21,991	9,584	China	1,235	NA	NA
Switzerland	165,697	64,719	27,458	Hong Kong.	3,973	1,493	1,511
United Kingdom	454,123	277,613	116,272	India.	4,527	NA	NA
Latin America and other				Japan.	259,569	159,690	104,997
Western Hemisphere	**49,233**	**53,691**	**27,873**	Malaysia	395	310	400
South and Central				New Zealand	1,062	395	149
America	**15,609**	**13,384**	**8,067**	Philippines	NA	47	75
Brazil	778	882	750	Singapore	12,718	5,087	1,637
Mexico	7,948	7,462	1,850	South Korea.	15,632	3,110	692
Panama	881	3,819	4,939	Taiwan.	3,900	3,174	2,142
Venezuela	4,563	792	−152	**EUROPEAN UNION[3]**	**1,434,060**	**814,033**	**302,193**
				OPEC[4].	**13,345**	**4,330**	**3,854**

NA = Not available. (1) In all industries. Book value of foreign direct investors' equity in, and net outstanding loans to, their U.S. affiliates. A U.S. affiliate is a U.S. business enterprise in which a single foreign direct investor owns at least 10% of the voting securities, or the equivalent. (2) Totals and subtotals include countries or territories not shown in table. (3) European Union members in 2008: Austria, Belgium, Bulgaria, Cyprus, Czech Republic, Denmark, Estonia, Finland, France, Germany, Greece, Hungary, Ireland, Italy, Latvia, Lithuania, Luxembourg, Malta, Netherlands, Poland, Portugal, Romania, Slovakia, Slovenia, Spain, Sweden, and the United Kingdom. (4) Org. of Petroleum Exporting Countries in 2008: Algeria, Angola, Ecuador, Indonesia, Iran, Iraq, Kuwait, Libya, Nigeria, Qatar, Saudi Arabia, United Arab Emirates, and Venezuela.

U.S. Direct Investment Abroad[1] in Selected Countries and Territories, 1995-2008

Source: U.S. Bureau of Economic Analysis, U.S. Dept. of Commerce
(in millions of dollars)

	2008	2000	1995		2008	2000	1995
ALL COUNTRIES[2]	$3,162,021	$1,316,247	$699,015	Honduras	$700	$399	$68
Canada	227,298	132,472	83,498	Mexico	95,618	39,352	16,873
Europe	**1,809,876**	**687,320**	**344,596**	Panama	7,243	30,758	15,123
Austria	17,518	2,872	2,829	**Other Western**			
Belgium	65,054	17,973	18,706	**Hemisphere**	**345,153**	**108,515**	**48,714**
Czech Republic	4,654	1,228	NA	Bahamas	NA	NA	1,768
Denmark	10,393	5,270	2,161	Barbados	873	2,141	698
Finland.	2,298	1,342	965	Bermuda	165,857	60,114	28,374
France	75,040	42,628	33,358	Dominican Republic. .	960	1,143	330
Germany	110,784	55,508	44,242	Jamaica	NA	NA	1,287
Greece.	2,125	795	533	Netherlands Antilles. .	NA	NA	6,835
Hungary	5,103	1,920	NA	Trinidad and Tobago. .	NA	NA	673
Ireland	146,194	35,903	7,996	UK isls., Caribbean . .	139,290	33,451	8,358
Italy	28,653	23,484	17,096	**Africa**.	**36,640**	**11,891**	**6,017**
Luxembourg.	163,167	27,849	5,929	Egypt	8,771	1,998	1,093
Netherlands	442,926	115,429	42,113	Nigeria	3,393	470	629
Norway	10,889	4,379	4,741	South Africa	4,915	3,562	1,422
Poland	15,597	3,884	NA	**Middle East**.	**32,488**	**10,863**	**7,198**
Portugal	3,397	2,664	1,413	Israel	10,153	3,735	1,831
Russia	9,157	1,147	NA	Saudi Arabia	5,382	3,661	2,741
Spain	69,649	21,236	10,856	United Arab Emirates . .	3,423	683	500
Sweden	43,391	25,959	6,816	**Asia and Pacific**	**491,910**	**207,125**	**122,711**
Switzerland	123,358	55,377	31,125	Australia.	88,549	34,838	24,328
Turkey	6,089	1,826	973	China	45,695	11,140	2,765
United Kingdom	420,873	230,762	106,332	Hong Kong.	51,505	27,447	11,768
Latin America and other				India.	16,104	2,379	1,105
Western Hemisphere	**563,809**	**266,576**	**131,377**	Indonesia	17,909	8,904	6,777
South America	**108,231**	**84,220**	**49,170**	Japan.	79,235	57,091	37,309
Argentina	15,195	17,488	7,660	South Korea.	27,673	8,968	5,557
Brazil	45,500	36,717	25,002	Malaysia	13,291	7,910	4,237
Chile	12,613	10,052	6,216	New Zealand	5,266	4,271	4,601
Colombia	6,263	3,693	3,506	Philippines	5,914	3,638	2,719
Ecuador	1,276	832	889	Singapore	106,529	24,133	12,140
Peru	8,458	3,130	1,335	Taiwan.	16,604	7,836	4,293
Venezuela	17,332	10,531	3,634	Thailand.	9,128	5,824	4,283
Central America	**110,424**	**73,841**	**33,493**	**EUROPEAN UNION[3]**	**1,630,785**	**609,674**	**301,345**
Costa Rica	2,525	1,716	921	**OPEC[4]**.	**69,299**	**28,545**	**15,546**
Guatemala	NA	NA	233				

NA = Not available. (1) In all industries. Book value of U.S. direct investors' equity in, and net outstanding loans to, their foreign affiliates. A foreign affiliate is a foreign business enterprise in which a single U.S. investor owns at least 10% of the voting securities, or the equivalent. (2) Totals and subtotals include countries or territories not shown in table. (3) European Union members in 2008: Austria, Belgium, Bulgaria, Cyprus, Czech Republic, Denmark, Estonia, Finland, France, Germany, Greece, Hungary, Ireland, Italy, Latvia, Lithuania, Luxembourg, Malta, Netherlands, Poland, Portugal, Romania, Slovakia, Slovenia, Spain, Sweden, and the United Kingdom. (4) Org. of Petroleum Exporting Countries in 2008: Algeria, Angola, Ecuador, Indonesia, Iran, Iraq, Kuwait, Libya, Nigeria, Qatar, Saudi Arabia, United Arab Emirates, and Venezuela.

TRANSPORTATION AND TRAVEL

Top Motor Vehicle Producing Nations, 2008

Source: Automotive News Data Center and R.L. Polk Marketing Systems GmbH
(numbers in thousands of units; ranked by total production)

	Total motor vehicles	Cars	Trucks[1]	% change 2007-08		Total motor vehicles	Cars	Trucks[1]	% change 2007-08
Japan	10,969	9,916	1,053	−0.35%	Belgium	680	680	NA	−13.87%
U.S.	8,503	3,775	4,728	−19.44	Argentina	588	400	189	9.13
China[2]	8,185	5,682	2,503	6.03	South Africa	545	305	240	−1.21
Germany	5,778	5,532	246	−3.06	Slovakia	514	514	NA	−2.43
South Korea	3,736	3,450	285	−6.40	Malaysia	512	420	92	19.92
Brazil	3,007	2,561	446	7.79	Indonesia	476	38	438	25.71
Spain	2,507	1,943	564	−12.15	Sweden	450	450	NA	−22.53
France	2,477	2,141	335	−15.35	Ukraine	413	413	NA	11.23
Mexico	2,098	1,277	821	3.15	Hungary	354	354	NA	0.21
Canada	2,046	1,195	851	−19.51	Romania	350	336	14	−6.99
India	1,830	1,636	194	4.14	**Asia-Pacific/**				
Russia	1,662	1,469	194	9.28	**Middle East**	28,880	23,132	5,748	2.14
UK	1,622	1,447	175	−6.24	**Western Europe**	14,860	13,188	1,672	−10.10
Iran	1,348	1,193	155	22.57	**North America**	12,647	6,247	6,400	−16.42
Thailand	1,233	325	908	2.76	**Eastern Europe**	6,748	5,932	816	6.63
Turkey	1,088	622	467	4.17	**South America**	3,807	3,114	693	5.04
Poland	991	864	127	13.82	**Africa**	660	418	242	−1.26
Italy	974	659	315	−20.91	**World[3]**	67,602	52,032	15,570	−4.19
Czech Republic	938	938	NA	1.47					

(1) Light commercial vehicles (pickup trucks and vans). (2) Not including Taiwan. (3) Total includes countries or territories not shown.

World Motor Vehicle Production, 1950-2008

Source: For 1950-97, American Automobile Manufacturers Assn.;
for 1998 and on, Automotive News Data Center and R.L. Polk Marketing Systems GmbH
(numbers in thousands of units, unless otherwise noted)

Year	United States	Canada	Western Europe[1]	Japan	Other	World total	U.S. % of world total
1950	8,006	388	1,991	32	160	10,577	75.7%
1960	7,905	398	6,837	482	866	16,488	47.9
1970	8,284	1,160	13,049	5,289	1,637	29,419	28.2
1980	8,010	1,324	15,496	11,043	2,692	38,565	20.8
1985	11,653	1,933	16,113	12,271	2,939	44,909	25.9
1990	9,783	1,928	18,866	13,487	4,496	48,554	20.1
1995	11,985	2,408	17,045	10,196	8,349	49,983	24.0
1996	11,799	2,397	17,550	10,346	9,241	51,332	23.0
1997	12,119	2,571	17,773	10,975	10,024	53,463	22.7
1998	12,047	2,568	16,332	10,050	12,844	53,841	22.4
1999	13,107	3,042	17,603	9,985	14,050	57,787	22.7
2000	12,832	2,952	17,678	10,145	16,098	59,704	21.5
2001	11,518	2,535	17,825	9,777	16,170	57,705	19.7
2002	12,328	2,624	17,419	10,240	16,975	59,587	20.7
2003	12,145	2,547	16,943	10,286	19,641	61,562	19.7
2004	12,021	2,698	20,850	10,512	16,573	65,654	18.3
2005	12,018	2,665	21,718	10,800	20,691	67,892	17.7
2006	11,351	2,545	22,430	11,486	23,180	70,992	16.0
2007	10,611	2,602	23,819	11,596	26,019	74,647	14.2
2008	8,503	2,046	14,860	10,969	31,224	67,602	12.6

Note: Data for 1998 and on not fully comparable with earlier years because derived from different source. (1) Beginning in 2004, data includes all European countries.

New and Used Passenger Cars Imported into the U.S., by Country of Origin[1], 1970-2008

Source: Foreign Trade Division, U.S. Census Bureau
(in number of units)

Year	Japan	Germany[2]	Italy	United Kingdom	Sweden	France	South Korea	Mexico	Canada	Total[3]
1970	381,338	674,945	42,523	76,257	57,844	37,114	NA	NA	692,783	2,013,420
1975	695,573	370,012	102,344	67,106	51,993	15,647	NA	0	733,766	2,074,653
1980	1,991,502	338,711	46,899	32,517	61,496	47,386	NA	1	594,770	3,116,448
1985	2,527,467	473,110	8,689	24,474	142,640	42,882	NA	13,647	1,144,805	4,397,679
1988	2,123,051	264,249	6,053	31,636	108,006	15,990	455,741	148,065	1,191,357	4,450,213
1989	2,051,525	216,881	9,319	29,378	101,571	4,885	270,609	133,049	1,151,122	4,042,728
1990	1,867,794	245,286	11,045	27,271	93,084	1,976	201,475	215,986	1,220,221	3,944,602
1995	1,114,360	204,932	1,031	42,450	82,593	14	131,718	462,800	1,552,691	3,624,428
1996	1,190,896	234,909	1,365	44,373	86,619	27	225,623	550,867	1,690,733	4,069,113
1997	1,387,812	300,489	1,912	43,691	79,780	67	222,568	544,075	1,731,209	4,378,295
1998	1,456,081	373,330	2,104	49,891	84,543	56	211,650	584,795	1,837,615	4,673,418
1999	1,707,277	461,061	1,697	68,394	83,399	186	372,965	639,878	2,170,427	5,639,616
2000	1,839,093	488,323	3,125	81,196	86,707	134	568,121	934,000	2,138,811	6,324,284
2001	1,790,346	494,131	2,580	82,487	92,439	92	633,769	861,853	1,855,789	6,065,138
2002	2,046,902	574,455	3,504	157,633	87,709	150	627,881	845,181	1,882,660	6,477,659
2003	1,770,355	561,482	2,943	207,158	119,773	298	692,863	680,214	1,811,892	6,127,485
2004	1,727,065	547,008	3,373	185,621	98,131	2,417	860,424	652,509	2,035,345	6,521,248
2005	1,832,534	547,191	5,377	184,716	93,736	412	730,500	693,149	1,967,985	6,564,844
2006	2,347,532	532,022	5,469	148,014	81,008	567	697,061	947,824	1,963,922	7,380,077
2007	2,300,913	466,458	5,650	108,576	92,600	1,746	676,594	889,474	1,912,744	7,220,792
2008	2,190,013	502,971	5,783	110,737	59,638	28,198	612,300	928,273	1,609,005	6525,836

NA = Not available. (1) Excludes cars assembled in U.S. foreign trade zones. (2) Figures prior to 1991 are for West Germany. (3) Includes units imported from countries not shown in table.

Passenger Car Production in U.S. Plants, 2007-08

Source: Ward's AutoInfoBank, Ward's Automotive Group, Penton Media Inc.

(in number of units)

	2008	2007		2008	2007
AUTOALLIANCE TOTAL[1]	**167,490**	**198,780**	G5	58,013	54,138
Ford Mustang	92,345	144,459	G6	157,154	150,397
Mazda6	75,145	54,321	Solstice	6,843	24,049
BMW TOTAL	**9,771**	**25,559**	**Pontiac total**	**222,010**	**228,584**
BMW Z4	9,771	25,559	Aura	64,510	60,853
CHRYSLER TOTAL	**290,547**	**401,310**	Sky	8,902	14,735
Sebring Convertible	25,592	32,646	**Saturn total**	**73,412**	**103,090**
Sebring Sedan	53,664	79,593	**HONDA TOTAL**	**553,045**	**589,556**
Chrysler total	**79,256**	**112,239**	Opel GT	3,128	4,109
Avenger	82,247	125,292	Acura TL	57,207	66,654
Caliber	127,499	163,447	Honda Accord	381,533	366,870
Viper	1,545	332	Honda Civic	114,305	156,032
Dodge total	**211,291**	**289,071**	**HYUNDAI TOTAL**	**152,588**	**133,534**
FORD TOTAL	**318,614**	**302,080**	Hyundai Sonata	152,588	133,534
Focus	236,612	191,115	**MITSUBISHI TOTAL**	**54,480**	**62,810**
Taurus	46,546	54,218	Mitsubishi Eclipse	15,944	30,365
Ford total	**283,158**	**258,682**	Mitsubishi Galant	38,536	32,445
MKS	23,388	—	**NISSAN TOTAL**	**373,882**	**384,651**
Lincoln total	**23,388**	**21,478**	Nissan Altima	320,628	338,609
Sable	12,068	17,879	Nissan Maxima	53,254	46,042
Mercury total	**12,068**	**21,920**	**NUMMI[2] TOTAL**	**220,192**	**249,556**
Lucerne	53,301	81,217	Pontiac Vibe	70,843	49,367
Buick total	**53,301**	**81,217**	Toyota Corolla	149,349	200,189
GM TOTAL	**1,019,184**	**938,848**	**SUBARU TOTAL**	**165,160**	**122,932**
CTS	86,333	55,934	Subaru Legacy	73,489	84,960
DTS	32,558	52,226	Toyota Camry	91,671	37,972
STS	14,796	18,836	**TOYOTA TOTAL**	**451,688**	**514,652**
XLR	1,451	1,343	Toyota Avalon	51,563	76,219
Cadillac total	**135,138**	**128,339**	Toyota Camry	382,433	409,946
Cobalt	250,002	226,314	Toyota Solara	17,692	28,487
Corvette	30,897	36,597	**TOTAL CARS**	**3,776,641**	**3,924,268**
Malibu	251,296	130,598			
Chevrolet total	**532,195**	**393,509**			

— = No production. (1) Joint venture between Ford and Mazda. (2) NUMMI (New United Motor Manufacturing, Inc.) is a joint venture between GM and Toyota.

Domestic and Imported Retail Car Sales in the U.S., 1980-2008

Source: Ward's AutoInfoBank, Ward's Automotive Group, Penton Media Inc.

(in number of units)

		Imports				Total	Imports (% total U.S. sales)		
Year	Domestic[1]	Japan	Germany	Other countries[2]	Total	U.S. sales	Japan	Germany	Total
1980	6,581,307	1,905,968	305,219	186,700	2,397,887	8,979,194	21.2%	3.3%	26.7%
1981	6,208,760	1,858,896	282,881	185,502	2,327,279	8,536,039	21.8	3.3	27.3
1982	5,758,586	1,801,969	247,080	174,508	2,223,557	7,982,143	22.6	3.0	27.9
1983	6,795,295	1,915,621	279,748	191,403	2,386,772	9,182,067	20.9	3.0	26.0
1984	7,951,523	1,906,206	344,416	188,220	2,438,842	10,390,365	18.3	3.8	23.5
1985	8,204,670	2,170,898	407,684	195,935	2,774,517	10,979,187	19.8	3.7	25.3
1986	8,215,017	2,339,503	431,453	418,286	3,189,222	11,404,239	20.5	3.8	28.0
1987	7,085,279	2,114,224	337,232	655,142	3,106,598	10,191,877	20.7	3.3	30.5
1988	7,543,116	2,022,602	280,097	700,993	3,003,692	10,546,808	19.2	2.7	28.5
1989	7,098,098	1,897,957	246,206	536,256	2,680,419	9,778,517	19.4	2.5	27.4
1990	6,918,869	1,719,384	263,263	401,699	2,384,346	9,303,215	18.5	2.8	25.6
1991	6,161,573	1,500,239	192,713	330,454	2,023,406	8,184,979	18.3	2.4	24.7
1992	6,285,916	1,451,766	200,851	274,580	1,927,197	8,213,113	17.7	2.4	23.5
1993	6,741,667	1,328,445	186,177	261,570	1,776,192	8,517,859	15.6	2.2	20.9
1994	7,255,303	1,239,450	192,275	303,489	1,735,214	8,990,517	13.8	2.1	19.3
1995	7,128,707	981,506	207,482	317,269	1,506,257	8,634,964	11.4	2.4	17.4
1996	7,254,557	726,940	237,009	308,247	1,272,196	8,526,753	8.5	2.8	14.9
1997	6,916,769	726,104	297,028	332,173	1,355,305	8,272,074	8.8	3.6	16.4
1998	6,761,940	691,162	366,724	321,895	1,379,781	8,141,721	8.5	4.5	16.9
1999	6,979,357	757,568	466,870	494,489	1,718,927	8,698,284	8.7	5.4	19.8
2000	6,830,505	862,780	516,614	636,726	2,016,120	8,846,625	9.8	5.8	22.8
2001	6,324,996	836,685	522,659	738,285	2,097,629	8,422,625	9.9	6.2	24.9
2002	5,877,645	930,253	546,654	748,677	2,225,584	8,103,229	11.5	6.7	27.5
2003	5,527,430	830,355	543,823	708,873	2,083,051	7,610,481	10.9	7.1	27.4
2004	5,396,090	810,004	541,940	797,115	2,149,059	7,545,149	10.7	7.2	28.5
2005	5,533,020	922,934	534,286	729,313	2,186,533	7,719,553	12.0	6.9	28.3
2006	5,476,090	1,154,455	560,726	629,583	2,344,764	7,820,854	14.8	7.2	30.0
2007	5,253,350	1,183,144	567,287	614,632	2,365,063	7,618,413	15.5	7.4	31.0
2008	4,535,098	1,141,768	506,736	629,767	2,278,271	6,813,369	16.8	7.4	33.4

(1) Includes cars manufactured in Canada and Mexico. (2) Australia, Belgium, Brazil, Hungary, Portugal, South Korea, Sweden, UK.

U.S. Retail Car Sales by Vehicle Size and Type, 1985-2008
Source: Ward's AutoInfoBank, Ward's Automotive Group, Penton Media Inc.
(percent of total U.S. sales)

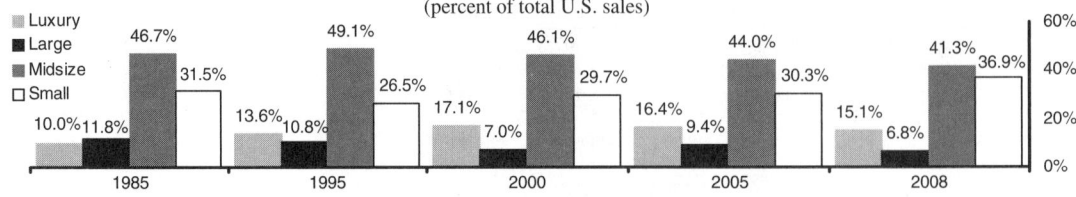

Top-Selling Passenger Cars in the U.S. by Calendar Year, 2005-08
Source: Ward's Automotive Group, Penton Media Inc.
(ranked by number of vehicles sold)

2008
1. Toyota Camry	436,617
2. Honda Accord	372,789
3. Toyota Corolla/Matrix	351,007
4. Honda Civic	339,289
5. Nissan Altima	269,668
6. Chevrolet Impala	265,840
7. Ford Focus	195,823
8. Chevrolet Cobalt	188,045
9. Chevrolet Malibu	178,253
10. Toyota Prius	158,884
11. Ford Fusion	147,569
12. Pontiac G6	140,240
13. Hyundai Sonata	117,357
14. BMW 3 Series	112,464
15. Mazda3	109,957
16. Toyota Yaris	102,328
17. Nissan Sentra	99,797
18. Volkswagen Jetta	97,461
19. Dodge Charger	97,367
20. Hyundai Elantra	94,720

2007
1. Toyota Camry	473,108
2. Honda Accord	392,231
3. Toyota Corolla/Matrix	371,390
4. Honda Civic	331,095
5. Chevrolet Impala	311,128
6. Nissan Altima	284,762
7. Chevrolet Cobalt	200,620
8. Toyota Prius	181,221
9. Ford Focus	173,213
10. Pontiac G6	150,001

2006
1. Toyota Camry	448,445
2. Toyota Corolla/Matrix	387,388
3. Honda Accord	354,441
4. Honda Civic	316,638
5. Chevrolet Impala	289,868
6. Nissan Altima	232,457
7. Chevrolet Cobalt	211,449
8. Ford Focus	177,006
9. Ford Taurus	174,803
10. Ford Mustang	166,530

2005
1. Toyota Camry	431,703
2. Honda Accord	369,293
3. Toyota Corolla/Matrix	341,290
4. Honda Civic	308,415
5. Nissan Altima	255,371
6. Chevrolet Impala	246,481
7. Chevrolet Cobalt	212,667
8. Chevrolet Malibu	203,503
9. Ford Taurus	196,919
10. Ford Focus	184,825

Top-Selling Light Trucks in the U.S. by Calendar Year, 2006-08

2008
1. Ford F-Series	476,469
2. Chevrolet Silverado	465,065
3. Dodge Ram Pickup	240,454
4. Honda CR-V	197,279
5. GMC Sierra	168,544
6. Ford Escape	156,544
7. Toyota Tacoma	144,655
8. Toyota Tundra	137,249
9. Toyota RAV4	137,020
10. Honda Odyssey	135,493

2007
1. Ford F-Series	633,949
2. Chevrolet Silverado	618,257
3. Dodge Ram Pickup	357,707
4. Honda CR-V	219,160
5. GMC Sierra	208,243
6. Toyota Tundra	196,555
7. Dodge Caravan	176,150
8. Toyota Tacoma	173,238
9. Honda Odyssey	173,046
10. Toyota RAV4	172,752

2006
1. Ford F-Series	744,996
2. Chevrolet Silverado	636,069
3. Dodge Ram Pickup	364,177
4. Dodge Caravan	211,140
5. GMC Sierra	210,736
6. Ford Econoline	180,457
7. Ford Explorer	179,229
8. Toyota Tacoma	178,351
9. Honda Odyssey	177,919
10. Chevrolet TrailBlazer	174,797

Number of Sport Utility Vehicles Sold in the U.S., 1988-2008
Source: Ward's AutoInfoBank, Ward's Automotive Group, Penton Media Inc.

In 1988, 960,852 sport utility vehicles (**SUVs**)—a term that comprises **cross utility vehicles**, or crossovers, which are generally smaller and get better gas mileage—were sold in the U.S. That number accounted for slightly more than 6% of all light vehicles (i.e., cars, SUVs, minivans, vans, pickup trucks, and trucks under 14,000 lbs) sold that year.

Excluding cross utility vehicles, SUV sales continued to slow, with a 58.1% decrease between 2004 (2,781,457 sold) and 2008 (1,164,209 sold). Over that same period of time, crossover vehicle sales increased, up 26.6% from 1,906,953 sales in 2004 to 2,413,685 sales in 2008.

U.S. Sport Utility and Cross Utility Vehicle Sales

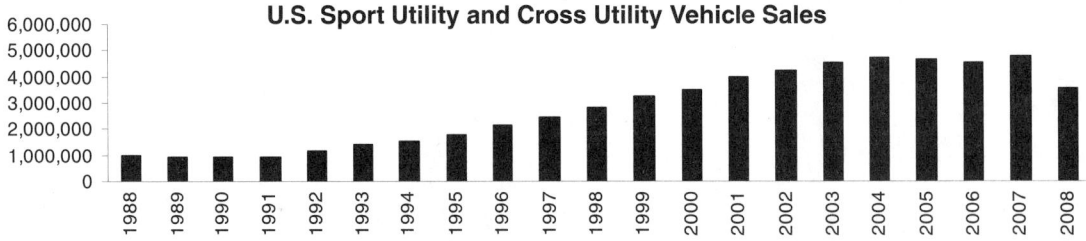

Most Popular Colors, by Vehicle Type, 2008 Model Year
Source: Ward's Automotive Group, Penton Media Inc.; Du Pont Automotive Products

Luxury cars		Full size/intermediate cars		Compact/sports cars		Light trucks	
Color	Percent	Color	Percent	Color	Percent	Color	Percent
Black/black effect	26%	Silver	20%	Silver	20%	White/white pearl	30%
White/white pearl	23	Blue	18	Black/black effect	18	Black/black effect	17
Silver	12	White/white pearl	16	Gray	17	Red	14
Red	10	Black/black effect	13	Blue	15	Silver	12
Gray	9	Gray	12	Red	12	Gray	11
Blue	8	Red	8	White/white pearl	10	Blue	8
Beige/brown	6	Beige/brown	8	Beige/brown	2	Beige/brown	3
Yellow/gold	5	Green	5	Yellow/gold	4	Green	3
Green	1	Yellow/gold	1	Green	2	Yellow/gold	3
Other	1	Other	1	Other	1	Other	1

U.S. Light-Duty Vehicle Fuel Efficiency, 1975-2008

Source: Natl. Vehicle and Fuel Emissions Laboratory, Office of Transportation and Air Quality, U.S. Environmental Protection Agency

Cars and light-duty trucks (SUVs, minivans, passenger vans, and pickup trucks) showed significant fuel-efficiency improvements from 1975 through 1987, when the fuel economy for both reached a high of 22 miles per gallon (mpg). After 1987, the fuel economy value entered a long-term decline, reaching 19.3 mpg in 2004 before the trend reversed itself. Since 2005, fuel economy has increased. Most of this increase has been due to higher truck fuel economy.

In Dec. 2006, the EPA changed its method of calculating adjusted real-world fuel economy values due to changed driving habits, including more aggressive driving and increased air conditioning use, among other factors. Data from 1986 on were revised under this method. Comparing laboratory 55/45 fuel economy values, however, shows an all-time high was reached in 2008.

Sales of light-duty trucks, which in recent years have had an average fuel efficiency 5-7 mpg less than cars, accounted for only 19% of the market in 1975 but have been at about 50% since 2002. This increase has been a major factor in the leveling off in the fuel efficiency of the average light-duty vehicle. But technological innovations have helped to boost fuel efficiency in recent years.

Year[1]	Cars (mpg[2])	Light-duty trucks (mpg[2])	All light-duty vehicles (mpg[2])	Year[1]	Cars (mpg[2])	Light-duty trucks (mpg[2])	All light-duty vehicles (mpg[2])
1975.........	13.5	11.6	13.1	2000	22.9	16.9	19.8
1980.........	20.0	15.8	19.2	2001	23.0	16.7	19.6
1985.........	23.0	17.5	21.3	2002	23.1	16.7	19.4
1990.........	23.3	17.4	21.2	2003	23.2	16.9	19.6
1995.........	23.4	17.0	20.5	2004	23.1	16.7	19.3
1996.........	23.3	17.2	20.4	2005	23.5	17.2	19.9
1997.........	23.4	17.0	20.1	2006	23.3	17.6	20.2
1998.........	23.4	17.1	20.1	2007	23.4	17.7	20.2
1999.........	23.0	16.7	19.7	2008	24.1	18.1	20.8

(1) Because of changes in methodology, mpg figures before 1986 are not entirely comparable with later values. (2) Adjusted composite (city and highway fuel efficiency combined in a 55%/45% ratio) values reflecting real-world use.

Registered Cars in the U.S., 1900-2007[1]

Source: Office of Highway Policy Information, Federal Highway Administration, U.S. Dept. of Transportation

(includes automobiles for public and private use)

Year	Reg. cars	Year	Reg. cars	Year	Reg. cars	Year	Reg. cars	Year	Reg. cars
1900....	8,000	1940.....	27,465,826	1975	106,705,934	1994	127,883,469	2001.....	137,633,467
1905....	77,400	1945.....	25,796,985	1980	121,600,843	1995	128,386,775	2002.....	135,920,677
1910....	458,377	1950.....	40,339,077	1985	127,885,193	1996	129,728,311	2003.....	135,669,897
1915....	2,332,426	1955.....	52,144,739	1990	133,700,497	1997	129,748,704	2004.....	136,430,651
1920....	8,131,522	1960.....	61,671,390	1991	128,299,601	1998	131,838,538	2005.....	136,568,083
1925....	17,481,001	1965.....	75,257,588	1992	126,581,148	1999	132,432,044	2006.....	135,399,945
1930....	23,034,753	1970.....	89,243,557	1993	127,327,189	2000	133,621,420	2007.....	135,932,930
1935....	22,567,827								

(1) There were no publicly owned vehicles before 1925; statistics also exclude military vehicles for all years. Alaska and Hawaii data included since 1960.

Licensed Drivers, by Age and Sex, 1980-2007

Source: Office of Highway Policy Information, Federal Highway Administration, U.S. Dept. of Transportation

(numbers in thousands)

	1980			1990			2007			
Age	Male	Female	Total[1]	Male	Female	Total[1]	Male	Female	Total[1]	% total drivers[2]
Under 16	52	41	93	23	20	43	127	124	252	0.1%
16.........	1,001	822	1,823	769	674	1,443	682	670	1,352	0.7
17.........	1,530	1,260	2,790	1,136	996	2,132	1,150	1,108	2,258	1.1
18.........	1,763	1,484	3,247	1,378	1,217	2,595	1,480	1,394	2,874	1.4
19.........	1,900	1,643	3,542	1,608	1,429	3,037	1,638	1,547	3,185	1.5
19 and under...	**6,246**	**5,249**	**11,496**	**4,913**	**4,336**	**9,249**	**5,077**	**4,843**	**9,920**	**4.8**
20..........	1,930	1,706	3,636	1,691	1,538	3,229	1,682	1,624	3,306	1.6
21..........	1,961	1,772	3,733	1,694	1,555	3,249	1,712	1,677	3,389	1.6
22..........	1,998	1,813	3,811	1,701	1,561	3,262	1,740	1,715	3,455	1.7
23..........	2,062	1,876	3,938	1,767	1,631	3,398	1,743	1,726	3,469	1.7
24..........	2,047	1,868	3,915	1,951	1,807	3,758	1,792	1,778	3,570	1.7
20-24	9,998	9,034	19,032	8,804	8,093	16,897	8,669	8,520	17,190	8.4
25-29	9,865	9,060	18,925	10.239	9,656	19,895	9,073	9,077	18,150	8.8
30-34	9,010	8,359	17,369	10,507	10,071	20,578	8,852	8,767	17,619	8.6
35-39	7,113	6,583	13,696	9,684	9,371	19,055	9,763	9,635	19,398	9.4
40-44	5,828	5,306	11,134	8,610	8,295	16,905	10,117	10,042	20,159	9.8
45-49	5,311	4,765	10,076	6,642	6,378	13,020	10,583	10,642	21,225	10.3
50-54	5,351	4,739	10,090	5,376	5,108	10,484	9,870	9,994	19,864	9.7
55-59	5,198	4,572	9,770	4,855	4,583	9,438	8,581	8,724	17,305	8.4
60-64	4,439	3,793	8,232	4,738	4,497	9,235	6,891	6,976	13,867	6.7
65-69	3,631	2,949	6,580	4,266	4,109	8,375	4,982	5,095	10,077	4.9
70-74	NA	NA	NA	NA	NA	NA	3,734	3,877	7,611	3.7
75-79	NA	NA	NA	NA	NA	NA	2,933	3,188	6,121	3.0
80-84	NA	NA	NA	NA	NA	NA	2,000	2,306	4,306	2.1
85 and over	**NA**	**NA**	**NA**	**NA**	**NA**	**NA**	**1,340**	**1,590**	**2,930**	**1.4**
Total.........	**77,187**	**68,108**	**145,295**	**85,792**	**81,223**	**167,015**	**102,465**	**103,277**	**205,742**	**100.0**

NA = Not available. (1) Figures may not add to totals due to rounding. (2) Percentages are calculated using Census Bureau population estimates.

Selected Motor Vehicle Statistics

Source: Federal Highway Admin., U.S. Dept. of Transportation; Insurance Inst. for Highway Safety; American Petroleum Inst.

Driver's license age requirements, state gas tax, and safety belt use laws (incl. laws passed, but not in effect) as of 2009. Other figures are for 2007.

STATE	Driver's license age requirements		State gas tax (cents/ gal.)	Safety belt use law[7]	Licensed drivers		Reg. motor vehicles per 1,000 pop.	Fuel use per reg. vehicle (gallons)	Annual miles driven		
	Learner's permit	Regular[1]			Per 1,000 total resident pop.	Per reg. motor vehicle			Per gal. used	Per reg. vehicle	Per lic. driver
Alabama	15	17	16.0	P	798	0.80	1,011	756	17.37	13,128	16,634
Alaska	14	16y, 6m	0.0	P	725	0.74	995	798	9.50	7,576	10,405
Arizona	15y, 6m	16y, 6m	18.0	S(a)	655	0.96	690	864	16.68	14,401	15,158
Arkansas	14	18	21.5	S	722	1.03	709	1,062	15.53	16,501	16,212
California	15y, 6m	17	18.0	P	642	0.70	928	556	17.40	9,675	13,990
Colorado	15	17	22.0	S(a)	720	2.10	351	1,629	17.52	28,535	13,907
Connecticut	16	18[2]	25.0	P	813	0.95	870	614	17.12	10,518	11,252
Delaware	16	17[2]	23.0	P	722	0.74	984	631	17.65	11,140	15,186
Dist. of Columbia	16	18[3]	20.0	P	673	1.93	370	725	22.89	16,592	9,109
Florida	15	18	4.0	S(a)	775	0.88	903	625	20.02	12,512	14,578
Georgia	15	18[2]	7.5	P	643	0.73	892	765	17.29	13,221	18,346
Hawaii	15y, 6m	17[2]	17.0	P	672	0.89	774	578	18.02	10,417	11,989
Idaho	14y, 6m	16[2]	25.0	S	685	0.82	855	744	16.54	12,311	15,360
Illinois	15	18[2]	19.0	P	637	0.85	759	684	16.09	11,016	13,124
Indiana	15y, 6m	18[2]	18.0	P	679	0.89	781	920	15.68	14,424	16,589
Iowa	14	17[2]	21.0	P	701	0.63	1,125	688	13.51	9,301	14,928
Kansas	14	16y, 6m	24.0	S(a)	727	0.84	875	750	16.50	12,370	14,888
Kentucky	16	17[2]	21.1[6]	P	692	0.84	836	876	15.47	13,552	16,385
Louisiana	15	17[2]	20.0	P	707	0.79	915	792	14.60	11,556	14,956
Maine	15	16y, 6m[2]	29.5	P	767	0.96	820	835	16.67	13,923	14,889
Maryland	15y, 9m	18	23.5	P	665	0.84	803	757	16.55	12,527	15,116
Massachusetts	16	18[2]	21.0	S	729	0.89	832	618	16.60	10,262	11,719
Michigan	14y, 9m	17[2]	19.0	P	701	0.88	813	695	18.38	12,771	14,820
Minnesota	15	17[2]	27.1	S	606	0.67	915	709	16.98	12,034	18,174
Mississippi	15	16y, 6m	18.0	P	660	0.97	688	1,154	18.70	21,584	22,490
Missouri	15	17y, 11m	17.0	S(a)	708	0.85	836	882	15.94	14,064	16,615
Montana	14y, 6m	16[2]	27.0	S	768	0.80	990	808	14.75	11,921	15,368
Nebraska	15	17	26.4[6]	S(a)	750	0.78	980	736	15.20	11,178	14,608
Nevada	15y, 6m	18[2]	23.0	S	648	1.19	555	1,099	14.15	15,548	13,328
New Hampshire	15y, 6m	17y, 1m	18.0	None	780	0.88	900	704	16.13	11,359	13,111
New Jersey	16	18	10.5	P	666	0.95	719	859	14.20	12,190	13,170
New Mexico	15	16y, 6m[2]	17.0	P	693	0.88	812	931	18.04	16,788	19,667
New York	16	18[2,4]	8.0	P	589	1.01	596	624	19.07	11,896	12,027
North Carolina	15	16y, 6m[2]	29.9[6]	P(b)	705	1.03	697	888	18.47	16,399	16,229
North Dakota	14	16	23.0	S(a)	736	0.68	1,111	766	14.42	11,040	16,663
Ohio	15y, 6m	18[2]	28.0	S	696	0.75	946	626	16.30	10,198	13,871
Oklahoma	15y, 6m	17[4]	16.0	P	631	0.73	891	841	17.54	14,753	20,836
Oregon	15	17[2]	24.0	P	754	0.94	824	690	16.30	11,252	12,291
Pennsylvania	16	18[4]	12.0	S	692	0.88	799	677	16.15	10,938	12,638
Rhode Island	16	17y, 6m[2]	32.0	S(a)	703	0.95	753	589	18.40	10,840	11,611
South Carolina	15	16y, 6m	16.0	P	709	0.90	799	927	15.67	14,515	16,345
South Dakota	14	16	22.0	S(a)	739	0.70	1,086	740	14.07	10,412	15,300
Tennessee	15	17	20.0	P	719	0.84	867	792	16.82	13,330	16,082
Texas	15	17[2,4]	20.0	P	635	0.86	756	902	14.94	13,471	16,033
Utah	15	17[5]	24.5	S(a)	624	0.72	877	686	16.86	11,565	16,244
Vermont	15	16y, 6m[2]	19.0	S	860	0.96	909	726	18.76	13,618	14,395
Virginia	15y, 6m	18[2]	17.5	S	682	0.81	858	790	15.70	12,410	15,605
Washington	15	17[2]	37.5	P	754	0.86	890	599	16.52	9,889	11,669
West Virginia	15	17	20.5	P	750	0.99	780	799	18.22	14,549	15,137
Wisconsin	15y, 6m	16y, 9m[2]	30.9	S	726	0.82	896	669	17.73	11,856	14,631
Wyoming	15	16y, 6m[2]	13.0	S	762	0.63	1,247	1,162	12.36	14,363	23,516
U.S. AVERAGE			18.5		682	0.85	820	733	16.71	12,253	14,726

Note: Most states have graduated licensing systems that phase in full driving privileges. During the learner's stage, driving generally is not permitted without adult supervision. In an intermediate stage, young licensees may be allowed to drive unsupervised only under certain conditions. (1) Min. age at which all restrictions may be lifted on private passenger car operation. (2) Applicants under a specified age (typically between 17 and 19) must complete driver education. Some states allow applicants to substitute home training, state-sponsored traffic school, or a number of hrs. of supervised driving for driver ed. (3) Learner's stage mandatory for all license applicants regardless of age. (4) Minimum age for an unrestricted driver's license may be lower if the applicant has completed driver education. Unsupervised driving in New York City prohibited for all drivers under 18. (5) Driver ed. required regardless of age. (6) Variable tax. Price as of July 2009. (7) P = officer may stop vehicle for violation (primary); S = officer may issue seat belt citation only when vehicle is stopped for another moving violation (secondary). (a) Primary enforcement for children under a specified age. (b) Secondary enforcement for rear seat occupants. (8) The number of registered vehicles does not include some farm trucks registered at a nominal fee and restricted to use in the vicinity of the owner's farm.

Highway Speed Limits by State

Source: Insurance Institute for Highway Safety (IIHS)

Under the National Highway System Designation Act of 1995, states are allowed to set their own highway speed limits. Under federal legislation enacted in 1974 during the energy crisis, states had been, in effect, restricted to a National Maximum Speed Limit of 55 miles per hour (raised in 1987 to 65 mph on rural interstates).

Maximum posted speed limits, in miles per hour, are given by state in the table below. (Speeds shown in parentheses are for commercial use trucks.) Data is current as of Sept. 2009. For more information, visit the IIHS website at www.iihs.org.

State	Rural interstates[1]	Urban interstates[1]	Limited access roads[2]	Other roads	State	Rural interstates[1]	Urban interstates[1]	Limited access roads[2]	Other roads
AL	70	65	65	65	MO	70	60	70	65
AK	65	55	65	55	MT	75 (65)	65	70[5]	70[5]
AZ	75	65	55	55	NE	75	65	65	60
AR	70 (65)	55	60[3]	55	NV	75	65	70	70
CA	70 (55)	65 (55)	70	65	NH	65	65	55	55
CO	75	65	65	65	NJ	65	55	65	55
CT	65	55	65	55	NM	75	75	65	55
DC	NA	55	NA	25	NY	65	65	65	55
DE	65	55	65	55	NC	70	70	70	55
FL	70	65	70	65	ND	75	75	70	65
GA	70	65	65	65	OH	65 (55)[6]	65	55	55
HI	60	50	45	45	OK	75	70	70	70
ID	75 (65)	75	65	65	OR	65 (55)	55	55	55
IL	65 (55)	55	65	55	PA	65	55	65	55
IN	70 (65)	55	60	55	RI	65	55	55	55
IA	70	55	70	55	SC	70	70	60	55
KS	70	70	70	65	SD	75	75	70	70
KY	65[4]	65	65	55	TN	70	70	70	65
LA	70	70	70	65	TX	75 (70)[5,7]	70[5]	75[5]	60[8]
ME	65	65	65	60	UT	75[9]	65	75	65
MD	65	65	65	55	VT	65	55	50	50
MA	65	65	65	55	VA	65[10]	65[10]	65	55
MI	70 (60); <70 (55)	65	70	55	WA	70 (60)	60	60	60
					WV	70	55	65	55
MN	70	65	65	55	WI	65	65	65	55
MS	70	70	70	65	WY	75	60	65	65

NA = Not applicable. (1) The distinction between urban and rural interstates is based on U.S. Census Bureau population data, which is adjusted by state and local governments to reflect planning and other issues. (2) Multiple-lane roads with restricted access via exit and entrance ramps rather than intersections. (3) Might be raised to 65 mph on 2- or 4-lane highways based upon the results of a study that was to be completed by mid-Sept. 2008. (4) 70 mph on specified road segments. (5) 65 mph at night (½ hour after sunset to ½ hour before sunrise). (6) For trucks on OH Turnpike, speed limit is 65 mph. (7) 80 mph (70 mph for comm. use trucks) on certain sections of I-10, I-20 in rural western TX. (8) 55 mph at night (½ hour after sunset to ½ hour before sunrise). (9) Portions of I-15 have a posted speed limit of 80 mph. (10) Posted speed limit may be as high as 70 mph on I-85.

Tourism Trends

World tourist arrivals increased by 6.0% between 2005 and 2006 and 6.1% between 2006 and 2007, according to the World Tourism Organization's (UNWTO) *Barometer* publication. The number of international tourist arrivals in 2008 was an estimated 922 mil, an increase of 2.0% over the previous year. Worldwide tourism receipts, as measured in constant U.S. dollars, rose 10.2% in 2007-08 to reach a record estimated value of $944 bil. Europe as a region again commanded the largest share of international tourist arrivals (53%) and receipts (50%) in 2008. Asia and the Pacific posted the second-largest share in each category, with 20% of international tourist arrivals and 22% of receipts worldwide. With 147 mil arrivals, the Americas held a 16% share of the world total, with the greatest increase in Central America (6.4%). Compared to 2006-07, the growth in international tourist arrivals in 2007-08 was somewhat lower in Africa (4.2%) but higher in the Middle East (18.2%).

Preliminary data for the first four months of 2009 indicated a decline of about 8% in international tourist arrivals, continuing the downward trend that began in late 2008. Because of the global economic uncertainty and continued concerns about the influenza A (H1N1) virus, the UNWTO predicted a decline overall in 2009, but with the pace of decline slowing from the start of the year.

The International Air Transport Association (IATA) reported a 1.8% increase in actual international passenger traffic (as measured in revenue passenger kilometers) in 2007-08 but an 8% decline for the first five months of 2009. The IATA forecasted a continued decline in the volume of passenger traffic in 2009 but an upturn for 2010. It expected a decline in the global airline industry's net profits in those years, although with some improvement in 2010. The price of fuel remains a challenge, having risen from 14% of airline operating costs in 2003 to 32% in 2008. Because of decreasing oil prices, among other reasons, IATA forecasted that fuel will have accounted for 25% of operating costs in 2009.

World Tourism Receipts, 1990-2008[1]

Source: World Tourism Organization (UNWTO)
(in billions of U.S. dollars)

Year	Receipts	Year	Receipts	Year	Receipts	Year	Receipts	Year	Receipts	Year	Receipts
1990	$264	1994	$356	1997	$443	2000	$475	2003	$529	2006	$742
1991	278	1995	405	1998	445	2001	464	2004	633	2007	856
1992	317	1996	439	1999	455	2002	482	2005	680	2008	944*
1993	323										

*Preliminary. (1) Total of all transactions made by or on behalf of visitors for the duration of their visit. Does not include receipts from international passenger transport contracted from companies outside a traveler's country of residence.

Top 10 Countries in Tourism Earnings, 2008

Source: World Tourism Organization (UNWTO)
(in billions of dollars; ranked by receipts from most recent year)

Rank	Country	Receipts[1] 2008*	2007	% change	Rank	Country	Receipts[1] 2008*	2007	% change
1.	United States	$110.1	$96.7	13.9%	6.	Germany	$40.0	$36.0	11.1%
2.	Spain	61.6	57.6	6.9	7.	United Kingdom	36.0	38.6	-0.7
3.	France	55.6	54.3	2.4	8.	Australia	24.7	18.5	18.9
4.	Italy	45.7	42.7	7.0	9.	Turkey	21.8	18.9	115.3
5.	China[2]	40.8	37.2	9.7	10.	Austria	18.5	16.9	9.7

*Preliminary. (1) Excluding receipts from international passenger transport contracted from companies outside a traveler's country of residence. (2) Not including Hong Kong, Macao, and Taiwan.

World's Top 10 Tourist Destinations, 2008

Source: World Tourism Organization (UNWTO)

(numbers in millions; preliminary)

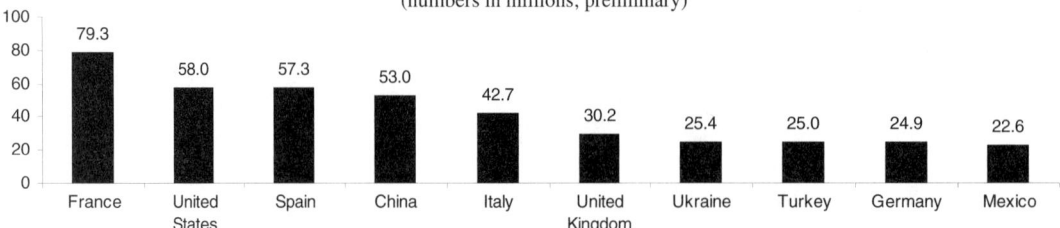

International Travel to the U.S., 1986-2008

Source: Office of Travel and Tourism Industries, Intl. Trade Admin., U.S. Dept. of Commerce; World Tourism Organization

(Visitors each year are in millions; some figures are revised and may differ from other sources.)

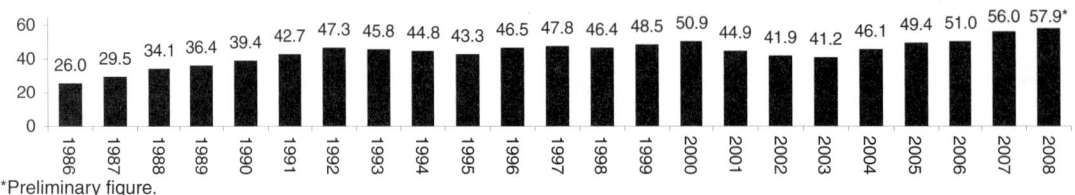

*Preliminary figure.

International Visitors to the U.S., 2008[1]

Source: Office of Travel and Tourism Industries, Intl. Trade Admin., U.S. Dept. of Commerce

(ranked by number of visitors)

Country of origin	Visitors (thousands)	Expenditures (millions)[2]	Expenditures per visitor	Country of origin	Visitors (thousands)	Expenditures (millions)[2]	Expenditures per visitor
1. Canada	18,910,000	$18,664	$1,013.18	12. Netherlands	607,802	$2,217	$274.16
2. Mexico	13,686,000	9,742	1,404.85	13. India	598,971	4,289	139.65
3. UK	4,564,895	16,716	273.09	14. Ireland	531,198	NA	NA
4. Japan	3,249,578	14,554	223.28	15. Venezuela	507,153	2,702	187.70
5. Germany	1,782,299	6,683	266.69	16. China	492,958	3,614	136.40
6. France	1,243,942	4,782	260.13	17. Colombia	419,268	NA	NA
7. Italy	779,463	3,703	210.50	18. Sweden	397,017	NA	NA
8. Brazil	769,232	4,162	184.82	19. Switzerland	341,955	NA	NA
9. South Korea	759,394	NA	NA	20. Israel	332,257	NA	NA
10. Australia	689,927	3,733	184.82	**All countries . . . .**	**57,937,451**	**141,713**	**408.84**
11. Spain	658,333	NA	NA				

NA = Not available. (1) Excludes cruise travel. (2) Does not include fares received by U.S. air carriers from international visitors for travel between the U.S. and foreign countries and between two foreign points. (3) Not including Hong Kong, Macao, and Taiwan.

Traveler Spending in the U.S., 1987-2008

Source: Office of Travel and Tourism Industries, Intl. Trade Admin., U.S. Dept. of Commerce

(in billions of dollars; NA = not available)

Year	Travelers Domestic	Travelers International	Year	Travelers Domestic	Travelers International	Year	Travelers Domestic	Travelers International
1987	$235	$31	1995	$360	$63	2002	$478	$67
1988	258	38	1996	385	70	2003	496	65
1989	273	47	1997	406	73	2004	532	75
1990	291	43	1998	425	71	2005	572	82
1991	296	48	1999	458	75	2006	NA	86
1992	306	55	2000	503	82	2007	NA	97
1993	323	58	2001	484	72	2008	NA	110
1994	340	58						

U.S. Domestic Leisure Travel Volume, 1995-2007[1]

Source: Travel Industry Association of America, TravelScope

(in millions of person-trips of 50 mi or more, one-way)

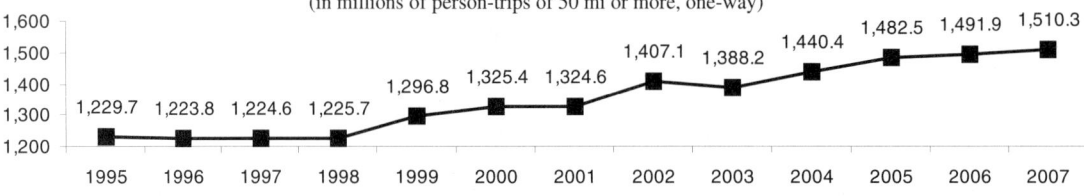

(1) Method of collecting travel data has been revised; data for earlier years have been adjusted to maintain comparability.

Top 10 U.S. States by Domestic Traveler Spending, 2007

Source: Travel Industry Association of America

(in billions of dollars)

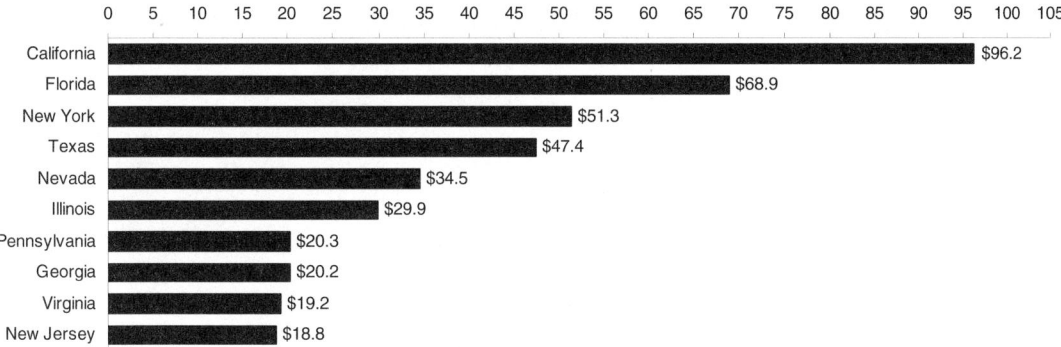

State	Spending
California	$96.2
Florida	$68.9
New York	$51.3
Texas	$47.4
Nevada	$34.5
Illinois	$29.9
Pennsylvania	$20.3
Georgia	$20.2
Virginia	$19.2
New Jersey	$18.8

U.S. Resident Travelers Visiting Overseas Destinations, 2008

Source: Survey of Intl. Air Travelers, Office of Travel and Tourism Industries, Intl. Trade Admin., U.S. Dept. of Commerce

Total U.S. resident travelers	**30,789,000**
Males (adults).	53%
Females (adults).	47%
Avg. age of males (yrs.)	45.7
Avg. age of females (yrs.).	43.4
Median annual household income	$107,200
Avg. total trip expend. per visitor (incl. airfare) . .	$3,315
Avg. expend. outside the U.S. per visitor per day	$85
Median number of nights	10.0

Place of residence	% of travelers
Middle Atlantic	40%
Pacific (incl. California, Washington)	16
South Atlantic (incl. Florida, DC metro area)	17
New England	8
East North Central (incl. Illinois, Ohio)	7
West South Central (incl. Texas)	5
Mountain	3
West North Central.	2
East South Central	1

Main purpose of trip	
Leisure/recreation/holidays	40%
Visit friends/relatives	34
Business.	18
Study/teaching	3
Convention/conference	2
Religion/pilgrimages.	1
Health treatment.	1

Occupation	% of travelers
Professional/technical	38%
Manager/executive	25
Retired.	11
Student	9
Homemaker.	6
Clerical/sales.	4
Craftsman/factory worker	3
Government/military	2

Leisure/recreational activities[1]	
Dining in restaurants	83%
Shopping.	71
Visit historical places.	51
Visit small towns/villages.	42
Sightseeing in cities.	40
Cultural heritage sights	32
Touring the countryside	32
Art gallery, museum.	25
Water sports/sunbathing	24
Nightclub/dancing	21
Guided tours	17
Ethnic heritage sites	13
Concert, play, musical	12
Amusement/theme parks	11
Visit national parks	11

(1) Percentages based on multiple responses.

U.S. Resident Travel Abroad, 1997-2008[1]

Source: Office of Travel and Tourism Industries, Intl. Trade Admin., U.S. Dept. of Commerce

(numbers in thousands; regions ranked by most recent numbers)

Region/country[2]	2008	2000	1997	Region/country[2]	2008	2000	1997
Total outbound[3]	**63,549**	**61,326**	**52,735**	Asia	6,404	4,914	NA
				Japan.	1,601	1,262	1,082
Mexico	20,271	19,285	17,909	China[5]	1,201	644	476
Canada.	12,489	15,188	13,401	India.	1,016	457	NA
Overseas subtotal[4].	**30,789**	**26,853**	**21,634**	Caribbean	5,973	3,867	NA
Europe	11,238	13,373	NA	Jamaica.	1,447	886	1,341
Western Europe	10,468	12,916	NA	South America.	3,017	2,095	NA
United Kingdom	2,894	4,189	3,570	Central America.	2,001	886	NA
Italy.	1,940	2,148	1,471	Middle East	1,724	1,370	NA
France	2,124	2,927	2,098	Eastern Europe	1,201	806	NA
Germany	1,601	2,309	1,796	Oceania.	801	1,047	NA
Spain	1,139	1,262	714	Africa.	801	483	NA

NA = Not available. **Note:** Visitation estimates for Canada and Mexico include all modes of transportation used. Estimates for all other countries are available only for air travel to that country and are based upon data from the airlines who voluntarily provide it. (1) Visits of one or more nights. (2) Only individual countries that received more than 1 mil visitors in 2008 are shown. Region figures include U.S. resident travelers to all countries in region. (3) Travelers to Canada, Mexico, and overseas. (4) Travelers to all countries except Canada and Mexico. (5) Not including Hong Kong, Macao, and Taiwan.

U.S. Airline Safety, Scheduled Commercial Carriers, 1985-2008

Source: National Transportation Safety Board; Federal Aviation Administration, U.S. Dept. of Transportation

Year	Departures (millions)	Fatal accidents	Fatalities[1]	Rate of fatal accidents[2]	Year	Departures (millions)	Fatal accidents	Fatalities[1]	Rate of fatal accidents[2]
1985....	6.1	4	197	0.066	2000	11.1	2	89	0.018
1990....	7.8	6	39	0.077	2001[3]....	10.6	6	531	0.019
1992....	7.5	4	33	0.053	2002	10.3	0	0	0.000
1993....	7.7	1	1	0.013	2003	10.2	2	22	0.020
1994[3]....	7.8	4	239	0.051	2004	10.8	1	13	0.009
1995....	8.1	1	160	0.012	2005	10.9	3	22	0.027
1996....	7.9	3	342	0.038	2006	10.6	2	50	0.019
1997....	9.9	3	3	0.030	2007	10.7	0	0	—
1998....	10.5	1	1	0.009	2008*....	10.6	0	0	—
1999....	10.9	2	12	0.018					

*Preliminary. (1) Except for fatalities resulting from the Sept. 11, 2001, terrorist attacks, any deaths that may have occurred on the ground as a result of an accident are included in the fatality counts. (2) Per 100,000 departures. (3) An illegal act, such as suicide or sabotage, is counted among fatal accidents and fatalities for this year but was not used in the calculation of accident rates.

U.S. Scheduled Airline Traffic, 2000-08

Source: Courtesy of Air Transport Association of America, Inc. Reprinted with permission.
Copyright © 2009 by Air Transport Association of America, Inc. All rights reserved.
(in millions, except where otherwise noted)

	2000	2001	2002	2003	2004	2005	2006	2007	2008
Passengers enplaned	666.2	622.1	614.1	646.5	702.9	738.3	744.2	769.2	741.4
Revenue passenger miles[1]	692,757	651,700	642,242	656,938	733,680	778,563	796,795	829,033	811,440
Available seat miles[2]	956,950	930,511	894,217	893,941	971,466	1,002,735	1,005,534	1,037,116	1,020,147
Cargo revenue (ton miles)[1]	23,888	24,784	25,983	26,735	27,978	28,036	29,339	29,524	28,383
% of seating utilized...........	72.4	70.0	71.8	73.5	75.5	77.6	79.2	79.9	79.5
Passenger operating revenue ...	$93,622	$80,947	$73,577	$77,379	$85,646	$93,500	$101,419	$107,011	$111,535
Net profit[3]...................	$2,486	–$8,275	–$11,008	–$2,371	–$7,643	–$5,782	$3,123	$4,998	–$9,464
Total employment[4]...........	679,967	671,949	601,355	569,778	569,498	562,467	545,695	560,997	556,920

(1) One fare-paying passenger or one ton of revenue cargo transported one mile. (2) One seat transported one mile. (3) Excludes bankruptcy-related charges (reorganization expenses and fresh-start accounting gains). (4) Not in millions. Figures are of avg. full-time equivalents (FTE), i.e., the number of full-time employees that could have been employed if the reported number of hours worked by part-time employees had been worked by full-time employees. In this table, part-time employees are treated as 0.5 FTEs.

Top 25 U.S. Passenger Airlines, 2008

Source: Courtesy of Air Transport Association of America, Inc. Reprinted with permission.
Copyright © 2009 by Air Transport Association of America, Inc. All rights reserved.
(in thousands; ranked by number of passengers)

Airline	Passengers[2]	Airline	Passengers[2]	Airline	Passengers[2]	Airline	Passengers[2]
1. Delta	120,387	8. JetBlue	21,824	14. Mesa	11,182	20. Republic	7,100
2. Southwest	101,921	9. SkyWest	20,668	15. Frontier	10,577	21. Spirit	6,800
3. American.....	92,772	10. Alaska	16,789	16. Pinnacle......	10,332	22. Chautauqua...	6,300
4. United	63,071	11. American Eagle	16,558	17. Comair.......	8,098	23. Air Wisconsin...	5,594
5. US Airways ...	54,776	12. ExpressJet....	14,753	18. Hawaiian	7,849	24. Mesaba	5,294
6. Continental ...	46,919	13. Atlantic		19. Horizon	7,390	25. PSA..........	4,744
7. AirTran.......	24,574	Southeast ..	12,457				

(1) Domestic and international. Does not include passengers on flights with both origin and destination in a foreign country. (2) US Airways and America West merged in Sept. 2005. In Oct. 2007, US Airways started reporting a combined number for both.

Top North American Airports by Passenger Traffic, 2008

Source: Airports Council International-North America

City/airport name (airport code)	Total passengers[2]
1. Hartsfield-Jackson Atlanta Intl. (ATL)	90,039,280
2. Chicago O'Hare Intl. (ORD).................	69,353,876
3. Los Angeles Intl. (LAX)...................	59,497,539
4. Dallas/Fort Worth Intl. (DFW)...............	57,093,187
5. Denver Intl. (DEN)......................	51,245,334
6. New York Kennedy Intl. (JFK)...............	47,807,816
7. Las Vegas McCarran Intl. (LAS)..............	43,208,724
8. Houston George Bush Intercontinental (IAH)	41,709,389
9. Phoenix Sky Harbor Intl. (PHX)..............	39,891,193
10. San Francisco Intl. (SFO)	37,234,592
11. Orlando Intl. (MCO)	35,660,742
12. Newark Liberty Intl. (EWR)	35,360,848
13. Detroit Metro. Wayne Co. (DTW).............	35,135,828
14. Charlotte Douglas Intl. (CLT)...............	34,739,020
15. Miami Intl. (MIA)	34,063,531
16. Minneapolis-St. Paul Intl. (MSP)..............	34,056,443
17. Toronto Pearson Intl. (YYZ)................	32,334,831
18. Seattle-Tacoma Intl. (SEA)	32,196,528
19. Philadelphia Intl. (PHL)	31,834,725
20. Boston Logan Intl. (BOS)	26,102,651
21. Washington Dulles Intl. (IAD)..............	23,703,729
22. New York LaGuardia (LGA)................	23,073,056
23. Fort Lauderdale-Hollywood Intl. (FLL)..........	22,621,698
24. Baltimore/Washington Thurgood Marshall Intl. (BWI)	20,889,416
25. Salt Lake City Intl. (SLC).................	20,790,400

(1) Excludes U.S. airports and airports that do not participate in ACI's Airport Traffic Statistics collection. (2) Arriving and departing passengers and direct transit passengers counted once.

Top World Airports by Passenger Traffic, 2008[1]

Source: Airports Council International

City/airport name (airport code)	Total passengers[2]
1. London Heathrow (UK; LHR)	67,056,379
2. Tokyo Haneda (Japan; HND)	66,754,829
3. Paris Charles de Gaulle (France; CDG)	60,874,681
4. Beijing Capital (China; PEK)	55,937,289
5. Frankfurt (Germany; FRA)	53,467,450
6. Madrid Barajas (Spain; MAD)	50,824,435
7. Hong Kong (China; HKG)	47,857,746
8. Amsterdam Schiphol (Netherlands; AMS)	47,430,019
9. Bangkok Suvarnabhumi (Thailand; BKK)	38,603,490
10. Singapore Changi (Singapore; SIN)	37,694,824
11. Dubai (United Arab Emirates; DXB)	37,441,440
12. Rome Fiumicino Leonardo da Vinci (Italy; FCO)	35,132,224
13. Munich (Germany; MUC)	34,530,593
14. London Gatwick (UK; LGW)	34,214,740
15. Tokyo Narita (Japan; NRT)	33,466,347
16. Guangzhou Baiyun (China; CAN)............	33,435,472
17. Sydney (Australia; SYD)	33,308,977
18. Toronto Pearson (Canada; YYZ)............	32,334,831
19. Jakarta Soekarno-Hatta (Indonesia; CGK).....	32,233,493
20. Barcelona (Spain; BCN)	30,195,886
21. Incheon (South Korea; ICN)	30,166,816
22. Istanbul (Turkey; IST)	28,625,269
23. Shanghai Pudong (China; PVG).............	28,235,691
24. Kuala Lumpur (Malaysia; KUL)	27,529,355
25. Mexico City Benito Juárez (Mexico; MEX)	26,210,217

Top Travel Websites, Aug. 2009

Source: comScore Media Metrix
(ranked by number of visitors)

Website	Visitors (1,000)[1]	% of all travel websites	Website	Visitors (1,000)[1]	% of all travel websites
1. Expedia Inc	24,562	30.9%	12. American Airlines	4,621	5.8%
2. TravelAdNetwork	13,849	17.4	13. Hilton Hotels	4,532	5.7
3. Priceline.com Incorporated	11,069	13.9	14. LOWFARES.COM	4,319	5.4
4. Orbitz Worldwide	10,747	13.5	15. InterContinental Hotels Group	4,120	5.2
5. Yahoo! Travel	9,945	12.5	16. About.com Travel	3,914	4.9
6. Southwest Airlines Co.	9,029	11.3	17. JetBlue Airways	3,895	4.9
7. Travelocity	9,023	11.3	18. Disney Travel	3,299	4.1
8. Delta Airlines	5,802	7.3	19. Wyndham Worldwide	3,252	4.1
9. AOL Travel	5,140	6.5	20. Enterprise Rent-A-Car Company	2,965	3.7
10. Kayak.com Network	4,988	6.3	**Total travel audience[2]**	**79,608**	**100.0**
11. Marriott	4,820	6.1	**Total Internet audience[2]**	**197,311**	**—**

(1) Number of unique users who visited at least once. (2) Audience comprises all persons at U.S. home/work/college-university locations.

Number of Paid Days Off Per Year in Selected Countries

Source: *No-Vacation Nation* (2007) by Rebecca Ray and John Schmitt, Center for Economic and Policy Research

The figures below represent the amount of paid time off that workers in selected countries are entitled to each year by law. Individual employers may offer additional paid time off beyond the legal guaranteed minimum. Countries may refer to workdays, calendar days, or weeks in their legal mandates. For sake of comparison, table assumes a five-day workweek.

Country	Paid vacation days	Paid holidays	Total paid days off	Country	Paid vacation days	Paid holidays	Total paid days off
France	30	1	31	Ireland	20	9	29
Denmark	25	9	34	Australia	20	7	27
Finland[1]	25	9	34	New Zealand	20	7	27
Norway	25	2	27	Greece	20	6	26
Sweden	25	0	25	Netherlands	20	0	20
Germany[1]	24	10	34	Switzerland	20	0	20
Portugal	22	13	35	United Kingdom	20	0	20
Spain	22	12	34	Canada[1]	10	8	18
Italy	20	13	33	Japan	10	0	10
Belgium	20	10	30	U.S.	0	0	0

(1) Number of paid vacation days and/or paid holidays varies by regional jurisdiction. Figures represent national average.

Record-Breaking Roller Coasters

Source: UltimateRollercoaster.com; speeds measured in mph, lengths and heights in ft

Steel-Tracked Roller Coasters

Fastest

	Roller coaster	Theme park, location
128	Kingda Ka	Six Flags Great Adventure, Jackson, NJ
120	Top Thrill Dragster	Cedar Point, Sandusky, OH
106.8	Dodonpa	Fuji-Q High Land, Fujiyoshida-shi, Japan
100	Tower of Terror	Dreamworld, Gold Coast, Australia
100	Superman the Escape	Six Flags Magic Mountain, Valencia, CA

Tallest

	Roller coaster	Theme park, location
456	Kingda Ka	Six Flags Great Adventure, Jackson, NJ
420	Top Thrill Dragster	Cedar Point, Sandusky, OH
415	Superman the Escape	Six Flags Magic Mountain, Valencia, CA
377	Tower of Terror	Dreamworld, Gold Coast, Australia
318	Steel Dragon 2000	Nagashima Spa Land, Mie, Japan

Largest drop

	Roller coaster	Theme park, location
418	Kingda Ka	Six Flags Great Adventure, Jackson, NJ
400	Top Thrill Dragster	Cedar Point, Sandusky, OH
306	Steel Dragon 2000	Nagashima Spa Land, Mie, Japan
300	Millennium Force	Cedar Point, Sandusky, OH
255	Goliath	Six Flags Magic Mountain, Valencia, CA

Longest

	Roller coaster	Theme park, location
8,133	Steel Dragon 2000	Nagashima Spa Land, Mie, Japan
7,450	The Ultimate	Lightwater Valley, UK
6,709	Fujiyama	Fuji-Q High Land, Fujiyoshida-shi, Japan
6,595	Millennium Force	Cedar Point, Sandusky, OH
6,072	California Screamin'	Disney's California Adventure, Anaheim, CA

Most inversions

	Roller coaster	Theme park, location
10	Colossus	Thorpe Park, Surrey, UK
10	10 Inversion Roller Coaster	Chimelong Paradise, Guangzhou, China

Wood-Tracked Roller Coasters

Fastest

	Roller coaster	Theme park, location
78.3	Son of Beast	Kings Island, Cincinnati, OH
74.6	Colossos	Heide Park, Soltau, Germany
70	El Toro	Six Flags Great Adventure, Jackson, NJ
67.4	The Voyage	Holiday World & Splashin' Safari, Santa Claus, IN
66.3	The Boss	Six Flags St. Louis, Eureka, MO

Tallest

	Roller coaster	Theme park, location
218	Son of Beast	Kings Island, Cincinnati, OH
183	T Express	Everland, Yongin, S. Korea
181	El Toro	Six Flags Great Adventure, Jackson, NJ
179	The Rattler	Six Flags Fiesta Texas, San Antonio, TX
173	The Voyage	Holiday World & Splashin' Safari, Santa Claus, IN

Largest drop

	Roller coaster	Theme park, location
214	Son of Beast	Kings Island, Cincinnati, OH
176	El Toro	Six Flags Great Adventure, Jackson, NJ
159	Colossos	Heide Park, Soltau, Germany
155	Mean Streak	Cedar Point, Sandusky, OH
154	The Voyage	Holiday World & Splashin' Safari, Santa Claus, IN

Longest

	Roller coaster	Theme park, location
7,400	The Beast	Kings Island, Cincinnati, OH
7,032	Son of Beast	Kings Island, Cincinnati, OH
6,442	The Voyage	Holiday World & Splashin' Safari, Santa Claus, IN
5,427	Mean Streak	Cedar Point, Sandusky, OH
5,384	Shivering Timbers	Michigan's Adventure, Muskegon, MI

Passports, Health Regulations, and Travel Warnings for Foreign Travel

Source: Bureau of Consular Affairs, U.S. Dept. of State; Centers for Disease Control and Prevention (CDC), U.S. Dept. of Health and Human Services; World Health Organization (WHO); Transportation Security Administration, U.S. Dept. of Homeland Security

Passports, Visas

Passports are issued by the Dept. of State to U.S. citizens and nationals to provide documentation for foreign travel. As of Sept. 2008, the fees for a new passport for persons ages 16 and over total $100; provided certain criteria are met, passports can be renewed for $75.

In July 2008, the U.S. government began issuing passport cards. Travelers arriving by land or sea from Canada, Mexico, the Caribbean (17 nations), and Bermuda may present a passport card to enter the U.S. Passport cards may not be used for air travel, however. The fees for a new passport card for persons ages 16 and over total $45.

A U.S. passport is often sufficient for U.S. citizens to gain admission for a limited stay in another country. Some countries also require a visa before entering. Each country has its own specific guidelines concerning length and purpose of visit, among other considerations. Visitors may need to provide proof of sufficient funds for their intended stay, onward/return tickets, and/or at least 6-months remaining validity on their U.S. passports.

All persons traveling by air outside of the U.S. (excl. direct travel to and from a U.S. territory) are required to present a passport or other valid document upon reentering the U.S.

For up-to-date passport and international travel information, visit the Consular Affairs website (travel.state. gov) or call the National Passport Information Center at 1-877-4USA-PPT (1-877-487-2778).

Health Regulations

Under WHO regulations, first instituted in 1969, member countries agree to abide by resolutions meant to contain the spread of disease. For example, some countries require travelers to provide proof of vaccination against yellow fever before entering.

Detailed information can be found in *Health Information for International Travel*, or the "Yellow Book," published every two years by the CDC. The book is written primarily for health care providers but may be of use to other travelers. The CDC also issues travel notices of outbreaks, health precautions, and health warnings. For current notices and more on travelers' health, visit www.cdc.gov/travel.

WHO publishes a more technical guide, *International Travel and Health*, which can be found online at www. who.int/ith.

Travel Warnings and Alerts

The State Dept. issues travel warnings as recommendations that Americans avoid travel to certain countries. Long-term conditions in such countries may be dangerous or unstable; because of an embassy closure or limited personnel, the U.S. government's ability to assist U.S. citizens is also reduced. As of Sept. 21, 2009, travel warnings were in effect for the following countries: Afghanistan, Algeria, Bolivia, Burundi, Central African Republic, Chad, Colombia, Côte d'Ivoire, Dem. Rep. of the Congo, Eritrea, Georgia, Haiti, Iran, Iraq, Israel (incl. West Bank and Gaza), Kenya, Lebanon, Mali, Nepal, Nigeria, Pakistan, Philippines, Saudi Arabia, Somalia, Sri Lanka, Sudan, Syria, Uzbekistan, and Yemen.

The department issues travel alerts when it has concerns about short-term conditions—natural disasters, terrorist attacks, anniversaries of attacks, election-related demonstrations, and regional sporting events, among others—within a country or area. For the latest travel warnings and alerts, see travel.state.gov.

Summary of TSA Regulations

Airplane carry-ons. TSA promotes the "3-1-1" rule regarding carry-on items. Containers with liquids or gels may hold only **3** oz or less; these containers should be packed inside a single **1**-quart, clear plastic, zip-top bag; and this **1** bag must be placed in a bin when going through security. Exceptions to the 3-1-1 rule include medication, baby formula and food, and breast milk. Travelers must declare any exceptions at security.

Security checkpoint identification. Adult travelers (18 years of age and over) must present a U.S. federal or state-issued photo ID. The ID must have name, date of birth, sex, expiration date, and a tamper-resistant feature. Acceptable documents: U.S. passport or passport card; foreign government-issued passport; state-issued drivers license; permanent resident card; or U.S. military ID, among others.

Screening process. Travelers may wear loose fitting or religious garments (incl. head coverings) through security. They may be subject to additional screening if clothing could potentially conceal prohibited items. Travelers may request a private area if selected for personal screening. In most cases, travelers will be screened by someone of the same gender.

Disability-related permitted carry-on items:

- Wheelchairs
- Crutches, canes, and walkers
- Personal supplemental oxygen
- Slate and stylus
- Medications and associated supplies
- Service animals

Permitted carry-on items:

- Safety razors (incl. disposable razors)
- Eye drops (amounts greater than 3 oz must be declared)
- Nail clippers, tweezers
- Blunt-tipped plastic or metal scissors
- Mobile phones
- Umbrellas (must be inspected at security)
- Common lighters
- Beverages (any size) purchased after security screening
- Musical instruments (one per traveler going through security, though some airlines prohibit musical instruments as carry-ons)

Prohibited carry-on items:

- Knives (except for plastic or round bladed butter knives), incl. knives that are religious objects
- Baseball bats, golf clubs
- Flares
- Realistic firearm replicas
- Hammers, screwdrivers, wrenches, pliers, and other tools more than 7 in. in length
- Brass knuckles
- Lighter fluid
- Liquid bleach
- Spray paint
- Snow globes

For complete travel information, visit www.tsa.gov/travelers.

Road Mileage Between Selected U.S. Cities

	Atlanta	Boston	Chicago	Cincinnati	Cleveland	Dallas	Denver	Des Moines	Detroit	Houston
Atlanta, GA........	...	1,037	674	440	672	795	1,398	870	699	789
Boston, MA........	1,037	...	963	840	628	1,748	1,949	1,280	695	1,804
Chicago, IL........	674	963	...	287	335	917	996	327	266	1,067
Cincinnati, OH	440	840	287	...	244	920	1,164	571	259	1,029
Cleveland, OH	672	628	335	244	...	1,159	1,321	652	170	1,273
Dallas, TX........	795	1,748	917	920	1,159	...	781	684	1,143	243
Denver, CO	1,398	1,949	996	1,164	1,321	781	...	669	1,253	1,019
Detroit, MI........	699	695	266	259	170	1,143	1,253	584	...	1,265
Houston, TX.......	789	1,804	1,067	1,029	1,273	243	1,019	905	1,265	...
Indianapolis, IN	493	906	181	106	294	865	1,058	465	278	987
Kansas City, MO ...	798	1,391	499	591	779	489	600	195	743	710
Los Angeles, CA...	2,182	2,979	2,054	2,179	2,367	1,387	1,059	1,727	2,311	1,538
Memphis, TN	371	1,296	530	468	712	452	1,040	599	713	561
Milwaukee, WI	761	1,050	87	374	422	991	1,029	361	353	1,142
Minneapolis, MN....	1,068	1,368	405	692	740	936	841	252	671	1,157
New Orleans, LA ...	479	1,507	912	786	1,030	496	1,273	978	1,045	356
New York, NY......	841	206	802	647	473	1,552	1,771	1,119	637	1,608
Omaha, NE	986	1,412	459	693	784	644	537	132	716	865
Philadelphia, PA....	741	296	738	567	413	1,452	1,691	1,051	573	1,508
Pittsburgh, PA	687	561	452	287	129	1,204	1,411	763	287	1,313
Portland, OR	2,601	3,046	2,083	2,333	2,418	2,009	1,238	1,786	2,349	2,205
St. Louis, MO	541	1,141	289	340	529	630	857	333	513	779
San Francisco, CA..	2,496	3,095	2,142	2,362	2,467	1,753	1,235	1,815	2,399	1,912
Seattle, WA	2,618	2,976	2,013	2,300	2,348	2,078	1,307	1,749	2,279	2,274
Tulsa, OK.........	772	1,537	683	736	925	257	681	443	909	478
Washington, DC....	608	429	671	481	346	1,319	1,616	984	506	1,375

	Indianapolis	Kansas City	Los Angeles	Louisville	Memphis	Milwaukee	Minneapolis	New Orleans	New York	Omaha
Atlanta, GA........	493	798	2,182	382	371	761	1,068	479	841	986
Boston, MA........	906	1,391	2,979	941	1,296	1,050	1,368	1,507	206	1,412
Chicago, IL........	181	499	2,054	292	530	87	405	912	802	459
Cincinnati, OH	106	591	2,179	101	468	374	692	786	647	693
Cleveland, OH	294	779	2,367	345	712	422	740	1,030	473	784
Dallas, TX........	865	489	1,387	819	452	991	936	496	1,552	644
Denver, CO	1,058	600	1,059	1,120	1,040	1,029	841	1,273	1,771	537
Detroit, MI........	278	743	2,311	360	713	353	671	1,045	637	716
Houston, TX.......	987	710	1,538	928	561	1,142	1,157	356	1,608	865
Indianapolis, IN	...	485	2,073	111	435	268	586	796	713	587
Kansas City, MO ...	485	...	1,589	520	451	537	447	806	1,198	201
Los Angeles, CA....	2,073	1,589	...	2,108	1,817	2,087	1,889	1,883	2,786	1,595
Memphis, TN	435	451	1,817	367	...	612	826	390	1,100	652
Milwaukee, WI	268	537	2,087	379	612	...	332	994	889	493
Minneapolis, MN....	586	447	1,889	697	826	332	...	1,214	1,207	357
New Orleans, LA ...	796	806	1,883	685	390	994	1,214	...	1,311	1,007
New York, NY......	713	1,198	2,786	748	1,100	889	1,207	1,311	...	1,251
Omaha, NE	587	201	1,595	687	652	493	357	1,007	1,251	...
Philadelphia, PA....	633	1,118	2,706	668	1,000	825	1,143	1,211	100	1,183
Pittsburgh, PA	353	838	2,426	388	752	539	857	1,070	368	895
Portland, OR	2,272	1,809	959	2,320	2,259	2,010	1,678	2,505	2,885	1,654
St. Louis, MO	235	257	1,845	263	285	363	552	673	948	449
San Francisco, CA..	2,293	1,835	379	2,349	2,125	2,175	1,940	2,249	2,934	1,683
Seattle, WA	2,194	1,839	1,131	2,305	2,290	1,940	1,608	2,574	2,815	1,638
Tulsa, OK.........	631	248	1,452	659	401	757	695	647	1,344	387
Washington, DC....	558	1,043	2,631	582	867	758	1,076	1,078	233	1,116

	Philadelphia	Pittsburgh	Portland	St. Louis	Salt Lake City	San Francisco	Seattle	Toledo	Tulsa	Wash., DC
Atlanta, GA........	741	687	2,601	541	1,878	2,496	2,618	640	772	608
Boston, MA........	296	561	3,046	1,141	2,343	3,095	2,976	739	1,537	429
Chicago, IL........	738	452	2,083	289	1,390	2,142	2,013	232	683	671
Cincinnati, OH	567	287	2,333	340	1,610	2,362	2,300	200	736	481
Cleveland, OH	413	129	2,418	529	1,715	2,467	2,348	111	925	346
Dallas, TX........	1,452	1,204	2,009	630	1,242	1,753	2,078	1,084	257	1,319
Denver, CO	1,691	1,411	1,238	857	504	1,235	1,307	1,218	681	1,616
Detroit, MI........	576	287	2,349	513	1,647	2,399	2,279	59	909	506
Houston, TX.......	1,508	1,313	2,205	779	1,438	1,912	2,274	1,206	478	1,375
Indianapolis, IN	633	353	2,272	235	1,504	2,293	2,194	219	631	558
Kansas City, MO ...	1,118	838	1,809	257	1,086	1,835	1,839	687	248	1,043
Los Angeles, CA....	2,706	2,426	959	1,845	715	379	1,131	2,276	1,452	2,631
Memphis, TN	1,000	752	2,259	285	1,535	2,125	2,290	654	401	867
Milwaukee, WI	825	539	2,010	363	1,423	2,175	1,940	319	757	758
Minneapolis, MN....	1,143	857	1,678	552	1,186	1,940	1,608	637	695	1,076
New Orleans, LA ...	1,211	1,070	2,505	673	1,738	2,249	2,574	986	647	1,078
New York, NY......	100	368	2,885	948	2,182	2,934	2,815	578	1,344	233
Omaha, NE	1,183	895	1,654	449	931	1,683	1,638	681	387	1,116
Philadelphia, PA....	...	288	2,821	868	2,114	2,866	2,751	514	1,264	133
Pittsburgh, PA	288	...	2,535	588	1,826	2,578	2,465	228	984	221
Portland, OR	2,821	2,535	...	2,060	767	636	172	2,315	1,913	2,754
St. Louis, MO	868	588	2,060	...	1,337	2,089	2,081	454	396	793
San Francisco, CA..	2,866	2,578	636	2,089	752	...	808	2,364	1,760	2,799
Seattle, WA	2,751	2,465	172	2,081	836	808	...	2,245	1,982	2,684
Tulsa, OK.........	1,264	984	1,913	396	1,172	1,760	1,982	850	...	1,189
Washington, DC....	133	221	2,754	793	2,047	2,799	2,684	447	1,189	...

Air Distances Between Selected World Cities in Statute Miles

Point-to-point measurements are usually from City Hall.

	Bangkok	Beijing	Berlin	Cairo	Cape Town	Caracas	Chicago	Hong Kong	Honolulu	Lima
Bangkok..........	...	2,046	5,352	4,523	6,300	10,555	8,570	1,077	6,609	12,244
Beijing	2,046	...	4,584	4,698	8,044	8,950	6,604	1,217	5,077	10,349
Berlin	5,352	4,584	...	1,797	5,961	5,238	4,414	5,443	7,320	6,896
Cairo............	4,523	4,698	1,797	...	4,480	6,342	6,141	5,066	8,848	7,726
Cape Town.......	6,300	8,044	5,961	4,480	...	6,366	8,491	7,376	11,535	6,072
Caracas	10,555	8,950	5,238	6,342	6,366	...	2,495	10,165	6,021	1,707
Chicago	8,570	6,604	4,414	6,141	8,491	2,495	...	7,797	4,256	3,775
Hong Kong.......	1,077	1,217	5,443	5,066	7,376	10,165	7,797	...	5,556	11,418
Honolulu.........	6,609	5,077	7,320	8,848	11,535	6,021	4,256	5,556	...	5,947
London..........	5,944	5,074	583	2,185	5,989	4,655	3,958	5,990	7,240	6,316
Los Angeles	7,637	6,250	5,782	7,520	9,969	3,632	1,745	7,240	2,557	4,171
Madrid	6,337	5,745	1,165	2,087	5,308	4,346	4,189	6,558	7,872	5,907
Melbourne	4,568	5,643	9,918	8,675	6,425	9,717	9,673	4,595	5,505	8,059
Mexico City.......	9,793	7,753	6,056	7,700	8,519	2,234	1,690	8,788	3,789	2,639
Montreal.........	8,338	6,519	3,740	5,427	7,922	2,438	745	7,736	4,918	3,970
Moscow	4,389	3,607	1,006	1,803	6,279	6,177	4,987	4,437	7,047	7,862
New York	8,669	6,844	3,979	5,619	7,803	2,120	714	8,060	4,969	3,639
Paris............	5,877	5,120	548	1,998	5,786	4,732	4,143	5,990	7,449	6,370
Rio de Janeiro	9,994	10,768	6,209	6,143	3,781	2,804	5,282	11,009	8,288	2,342
Rome	5,494	5,063	737	1,326	5,231	5,195	4,824	5,774	8,040	6,750
San Francisco	7,931	5,918	5,672	7,466	10,248	3,902	1,859	6,905	2,398	4,518
Singapore........	883	2,771	6,164	5,137	6,008	11,402	9,372	1,605	6,726	11,689
Stockholm	5,089	4,133	528	2,096	6,423	5,471	4,331	5,063	6,875	7,166
Tokyo	2,865	1,307	5,557	5,958	9,154	8,808	6,314	1,791	3,859	9,631
Warsaw	5,033	4,325	322	1,619	5,935	5,559	4,679	5,147	7,366	7,215
Washington, DC....	8,807	6,942	4,181	5,822	7,895	2,047	596	8,155	4,838	3,509

	London	Los Angeles	Madrid	Melbourne	Mexico City	Montreal	Moscow	New Delhi	New York	Paris
Bangkok..........	5,944	7,637	6,337	4,568	9,793	8,338	4,389	1,813	8,669	5,877
Beijing	5,074	6,250	5,745	5,643	7,753	6,519	3,607	2,353	6,844	5,120
Berlin	583	5,782	1,165	9,918	6,056	3,740	1,006	3,598	3,979	548
Cairo............	2,185	7,520	2,087	8,675	7,700	5,427	1,803	2,758	5,619	1,998
Cape Town.......	5,989	9,969	5,308	6,425	8,519	7,922	6,279	5,769	7,803	5,786
Caracas	4,655	3,632	4,346	9,717	2,234	2,438	6,177	8,833	2,120	4,732
Chicago	3,958	1,745	4,189	9,673	1,690	745	4,987	7,486	714	4,143
Hong Kong........	5,990	7,240	6,558	4,595	8,788	7,736	4,437	2,339	8,060	5,990
Honolulu.........	7,240	2,557	7,872	5,505	3,789	4,918	7,047	7,412	4,969	7,449
London...........	...	5,439	785	10,500	5,558	3,254	1,564	4,181	3,469	214
Los Angeles	5,439	...	5,848	7,931	1,542	2,427	6,068	7,011	2,451	5,601
Madrid	785	5,848	...	10,758	5,643	3,448	2,147	4,530	3,593	655
Melbourne	10,500	7,931	10,758	...	8,426	10,395	8,950	6,329	10,359	10,430
Mexico City.......	5,558	1,542	5,643	8,426	...	2,317	6,676	9,120	2,090	5,725
Montreal.........	3,254	2,427	3,448	10,395	2,317	...	4,401	7,012	331	3,432
Moscow	1,564	6,068	2,147	8,950	6,676	4,401	...	2,698	4,683	1,554
New York	3,469	2,451	3,593	10,359	2,090	331	4,683	7,318	...	3,636
Paris............	214	5,601	655	10,430	5,725	3,432	1,554	4,102	3,636	...
Rio de Janeiro	5,750	6,330	5,045	8,226	4,764	5,078	7,170	8,753	4,801	5,684
Rome	895	6,326	851	9,929	6,377	4,104	1,483	3,684	4,293	690
San Francisco	5,367	347	5,803	7,856	1,887	2,543	5,885	7,691	2,572	5,577
Singapore........	6,747	8,767	7,080	3,759	10,327	9,203	5,228	2,571	9,534	6,673
Stockholm	942	5,454	1,653	9,630	6,012	3,714	716	3,414	3,986	1,003
Tokyo	5,959	5,470	6,706	5,062	7,035	6,471	4,660	3,638	6,757	6,053
Warsaw	905	5,922	1,427	9,598	6,337	4,022	721	3,277	4,270	852
Washington, DC....	3,674	2,300	3,792	10,180	1,885	489	4,876	7,500	205	3,840

	Rio de Janeiro	Rome	San Francisco	Singapore	Stockholm	Tehran	Tokyo	Vienna	Warsaw	Wash., DC
Bangkok..........	9,994	5,494	7,931	883	5,089	3,391	2,865	5,252	5,033	8,807
Beijing	10,768	5,063	5,918	2,771	4,133	3,490	1,307	4,648	4,325	6,942
Berlin	6,209	737	5,672	6,164	528	2,185	5,557	326	322	4,181
Cairo............	6,143	1,326	7,466	5,137	2,096	1,234	5,958	1,481	1,619	5,822
Cape Town.......	3,781	5,231	10,248	6,008	6,423	5,241	9,154	5,656	5,935	7,895
Caracas	2,804	5,195	3,902	11,402	5,471	7,320	8,808	5,372	5,559	2,047
Chicago	5,282	4,824	1,859	9,372	4,331	6,502	6,314	4,698	4,679	596
Hong Kong........	11,009	5,774	6,905	1,605	5,063	3,843	1,791	5,431	5,147	8,155
Honolulu.........	8,288	8,040	2,398	6,726	6,875	8,070	3,859	7,632	7,366	4,838
London...........	5,750	895	5,367	6,747	942	2,743	5,959	771	905	3,674
Los Angeles	6,330	6,326	347	8,767	5,454	7,682	5,470	6,108	5,922	2,300
Madrid	5,045	851	5,803	7,080	1,653	2,978	6,706	1,128	1,427	3,792
Melbourne	8,226	9,929	7,856	3,759	9,630	7,826	5,062	9,790	9,598	10,180
Mexico City.......	4,764	6,377	1,887	10,327	6,012	8,184	7,035	6,320	6,337	1,885
Montreal.........	5,078	4,104	2,543	9,203	3,714	5,880	6,471	4,009	4,022	489
Moscow	7,170	1,483	5,885	5,228	716	1,532	4,660	1,043	721	4,876
New York	4,801	4,293	2,572	9,534	3,986	6,141	6,757	4,234	4,270	205
Paris............	5,684	690	5,577	6,673	1,003	2,625	6,053	645	852	3,840
Rio de Janeiro	...	5,707	6,613	9,785	6,683	7,374	11,532	6,127	6,455	4,779
Rome	5,707	...	6,259	6,229	1,245	2,127	6,142	477	820	4,497
San Francisco	6,613	6,259	...	8,448	5,399	7,362	5,150	5,994	5,854	2,441
Singapore........	9,785	6,229	8,448	...	5,936	4,103	3,300	6,035	5,843	9,662
Stockholm	6,683	1,245	5,399	5,936	...	2,173	5,053	780	494	4,183
Tokyo	11,532	6,142	5,150	3,300	5,053	4,775	...	5,689	5,347	6,791
Warsaw	6,455	820	5,854	5,843	494	1,879	5,689	347	...	4,472
Washington, DC....	4,779	4,497	2,441	9,662	4,183	6,341	6,791	4,438	4,472	...

AGRICULTURE

Number and Acreage of Farms by State, 2000, 2008

Source: National Agricultural Statistics Service, U.S. Dept. of Agriculture

State	No. of farms (1,000) 2008	No. of farms (1,000) 2000[1]	Acreage in farms (mil.) 2008	Acreage in farms (mil.) 2000	Acreage per farm 2008	Acreage per farm 2000	State	No. of farms (1,000) 2008	No. of farms (1,000) 2000[1]	Acreage in farms (mil.) 2008	Acreage in farms (mil.) 2000	Acreage per farm 2008	Acreage per farm 2000
AL....	48.5	47.0	9.0	9.0	185	191	NE....	47.4	46.1	45.6	46.1	962	887
AK....	0.7	0.6	0.9	0.9	1,309	1,569	NV....	3.1	3.1	5.9	6.4	1,903	2,065
AZ....	15.6	10.7	26.1	26.9	1,673	2,518	NH....	4.2	3.3	0.5	0.4	113	133
AR....	49.3	48.0	13.7	14.6	278	304	NJ....	10.3	9.7	0.7	0.8	71	86
CA....	81.5	83.1	25.4	28.0	312	337	NM....	20.6	18.0	43.0	44.9	2,087	2,494
CO....	36.5	30.0	31.3	31.6	858	1,060	NY....	36.6	37.5	7.1	7.7	194	205
CT....	4.9	4.2	0.4	0.4	82	86	NC....	52.5	55.5	8.6	9.2	164	166
DE....	2.5	2.6	0.5	0.6	200	215	ND....	32.0	30.8	39.6	39.4	1,238	1,279
FL....	47.5	44.0	9.3	10.4	195	238	OH....	75.0	79.0	13.9	14.8	185	187
GA....	47.8	49.1	10.4	10.9	218	223	OK....	86.6	84.5	35.1	33.8	405	401
HI....	7.5	5.5	1.1	1.4	148	251	OR....	38.6	40.0	16.4	17.3	425	433
ID....	25.2	24.5	11.4	11.9	452	486	PA....	63.2	59.0	7.8	7.7	123	130
IL....	75.9	77.0	26.7	27.5	352	357	PR[2]....	11.2	NA	0.5	NA	42	NA
IN....	61.0	63.4	14.8	15.2	243	240	RI....	1.2	0.8	0.1	0.1	57	75
IA....	92.6	94.0	30.8	32.5	333	346	SC....	26.9	24.2	4.9	4.9	182	203
KS....	65.5	64.5	46.2	47.5	705	736	SD....	31.3	32.4	43.7	44.0	1,396	1,358
KY....	85.3	90.0	14.0	13.7	164	152	TN....	79.0	88.0	10.9	11.8	138	134
LA....	30.0	29.0	8.1	8.0	268	277	TX....	247.5	228.3	130.4	130.9	527	573
ME....	8.0	7.1	1.4	1.4	169	190	UT....	16.5	15.5	11.1	11.6	673	747
MD....	12.9	12.4	2.1	2.1	160	172	VT....	7.0	6.6	1.2	1.3	174	192
MA....	7.7	6.1	0.5	0.5	66	89	VA....	47.0	48.5	8.0	8.7	170	180
MI....	55.0	53.0	10.0	10.2	182	192	WA....	39.5	37.0	14.8	15.6	375	420
MN....	81.0	81.0	26.9	27.9	332	344	WV....	23.2	20.8	3.7	3.6	159	173
MS....	42.0	42.0	11.0	11.2	262	266	WI....	78.0	77.5	15.2	16.0	195	206
MO....	108.0	109.0	29.1	30.2	269	277	WY....	11.0	9.2	30.1	34.5	2,736	3,750
MT....	29.5	27.8	60.8	59.3	2,061	2,133	U.S.[3]...	2,200.0	2,166.8	919.9	945.1	418	436

NA = Not available. (1) Some figures for 2000 are revised. (2) Puerto Rico not incl. in U.S. total. (3) Totals may be different due to rounding.

U.S. Farms, Number and Average Size, 1940-2008

Source: National Agricultural Statistics Service, U.S. Dept. of Agriculture

The number of farms in the United States in 2008 was estimated at 2.2 million, about 5,000 fewer than in 2007. Total land in farms decreased 1.56 million acres from 2007, to 919.9 million acres. The average farm size in 2008 was 418 acres, unchanged from the previous year. The continuing decline in the number of farms and land being farmed reflected consolidation in farming operations and the use of agricultural land for other purposes.

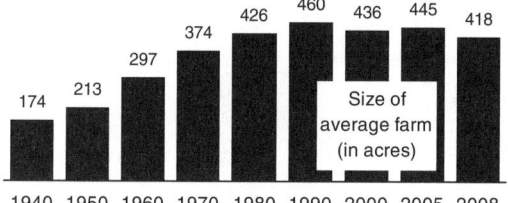

Size of average farm (in acres)

1940	1950	1960	1970	1980	1990	2000	2005	2008
174	213	297	374	426	460	436	445	418

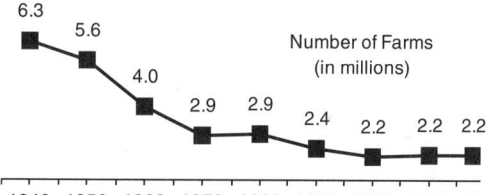

Number of Farms (in millions)

1940	1950	1960	1970	1980	1990	2000	2005	2008
6.3	5.6	4.0	2.9	2.9	2.4	2.2	2.2	2.2

U.S. Federal Food Assistance Programs, 1990-2008[1]

Source: Food and Nutrition Service, U.S. Dept. of Agriculture

(in millions of dollars)

	1990	1995	2000	2003	2004	2005	2006	2007	2008
Supplemental Nutrition Assistance Program (SNAP)[2]...............	$15,491	$24,620	$17,054	$23,816	$27,098	$31,073	$32,912	$33,206	$37,658
Puerto Rico nutrition asst.[3]..........	937	1,131	1,268	1,395	1,413	1,495	1,518	1,551	1,623
Natl. school lunch[4]................	3,834	5,160	6,149	7,189	7,626	8,030	8,191	8,741	9,318
School breakfast[4,5].................	596	1,048	1,393	1,652	1,776	1,927	2,043	2,164	2,366
WIC (Women, Infants, and Children)[6] ..	2,122	3,440	3,982	4,524	4,887	4,994	5,076,	5,414	6,205
Summer food service[7]	164	237	267	257	263	267	276	290	326
Child/adult care[8].................	813	1,464	1,683	1,926	2,020	2,111	2,153	2,234	2,403
Special milk[9].....................	19	17	15	14	14	17	15	14	15
Nutrition for the elderly (NSIP)[10]	142	148	137	3	4	4	3	3	2
Food distrib. to Indian reserv.[11]	66	65	76	75	78	76	76	81	96
Commodity supp. food prog.[11]	85	99	98	122	145	156	131	142	161
Food dist. to charitable inst.[12]	104	64	2	6	10	4	3	0	0
Emergency food assistance[13]	334	135	225	456	420	373	300	255	283
Total[14]	**$24,707**	**$37,628**	**$32,317**	**$41,565**	**$45,891**	**$50,673**	**$52,868**	**$54,254**	**$60,625**

(1) Data are for fiscal years ending Sept. 30. All 2008 data are preliminary; all data subject to revision by the FNS. (2) Formerly known as the Food Stamp Program. Includes benefits and admin. expenses. (3) Provides benefits analogous to SNAP. (4) Data are 9-month averages (summer months excluded). (5) Costs are cash payments (federal reimbursements to states). (6) Includes food benefits, nutrition services and admin. funds, Farmers' Market Nutrition Program, infrastructure, breastfeeding promotion and peer counseling, program evaluation, and technical assistance. (7) Includes cash payments, commodity costs, and admin. expenses. Similar services provided by Natl. School Lunch and Breakfast programs. (8) Includes cash payments, entitlement and bonus commodities, cash-in-lieu of commodities, sponsor admin. costs, start-up costs, and audits. (9) Costs are cash payments. (10) For years 2003 and on, program was administered by the Agency on Aging; Food and Nutrition Service costs limited to value of commodities distributed. (11) Includes commodity distribution costs and admin. expenses. (12) Includes summer camps. (13) Food made available to hunger relief orgs. such as food banks and soup kitchens. (14) Totals may not add because of rounding and administrative costs not shown.

Average Retail Food Prices, 1980-2009

Source: Average Price Data, Bureau of Labor Statistics, U.S. Dept. of Labor

Prices in U.S. dollars per pound, with the exception of orange juice (dollars per 12 oz. can), ice cream (dollars per half-gallon), and eggs (dollars per dozen Grade A). Prices are not seasonally adjusted for inflation and reflect the U.S. city average in June of each given year.

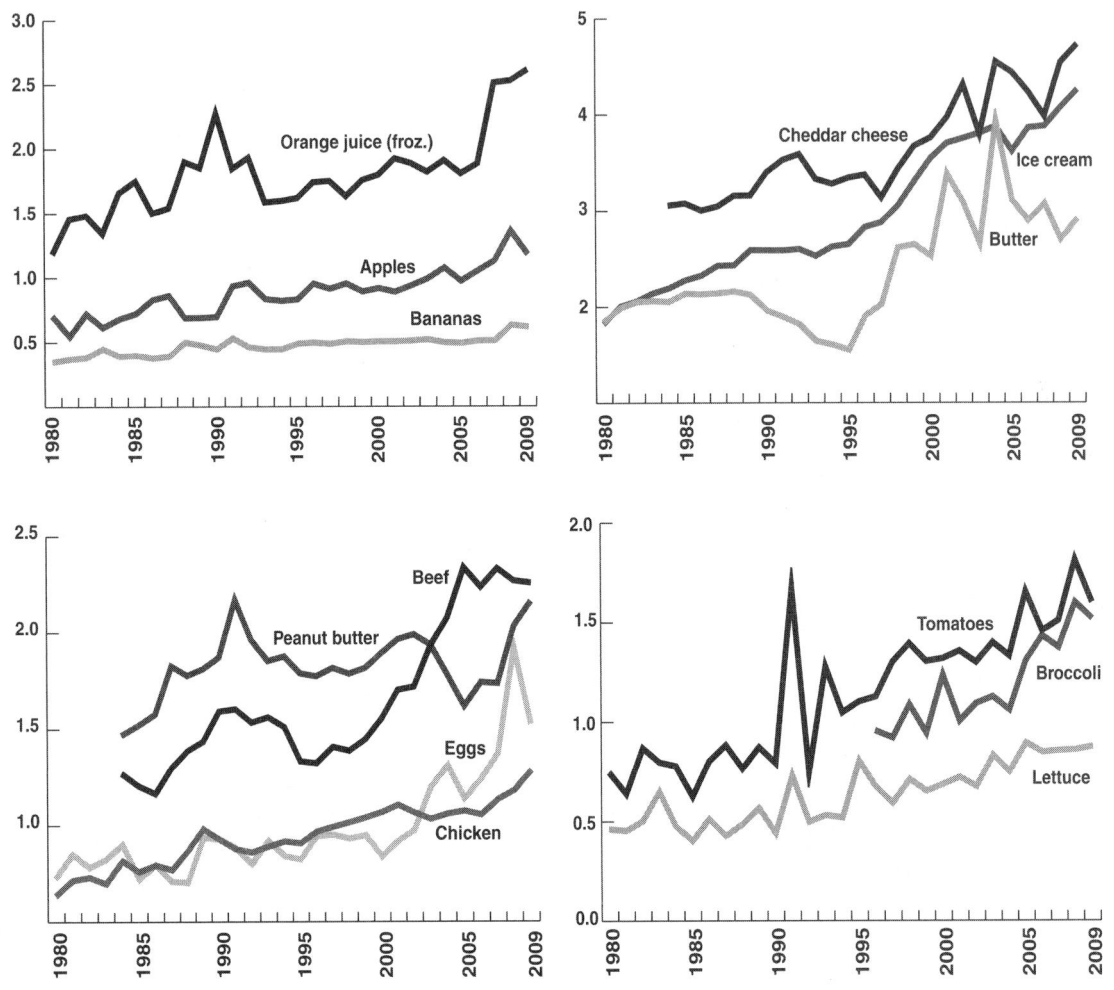

U.S. Annual Per Capita Consumption of Selected Foods, 1970-2007

Source: Economic Research Service, U.S. Dept. of Agriculture

(fruits and vegetables in pounds; beverages in gallons)

	1970	1990	2007	% change, 1970-2007		1970	1990	2007	% change, 1970-2007
Fresh fruit	96.2	111.0	119.7	24.4%	**Fresh vegetables**	154.3	170.5	202.2	31.0%
Apples	16.3	18.8	15.8	−3.1	Broccoli	0.5	3.1	5.5	1,000.0
Avocados	0.4	1.3	3.2	700.0	Carrots	5.8	8.0	8.7	50.0
Bananas	17.4	24.3	26.0	49.4	Celery	6.8	6.7	5.9	−13.2
Cherries	0.5	0.4	1.2	140.0	Corn	7.2	6.2	8.4	16.7
Grapes	2.6	7.1	7.3	180.8	Onions	9.5	14.2	20.4	114.7
Melons	19.6	22.3	25.6	30.6	Potatoes	59.3	44.9	37.7	−36.4
Grapefruit	8.0	4.3	2.8	−65.0	Tomatoes	10.3	13.2	17.3	68.0
Oranges	15.7	12.0	7.2	−54.1					
Peaches/nectarines	5.5	5.3	4.3	−21.8	**Beverages**				
Pears	1.8	3.1	2.9	61.1	Coffee	33.4	26.8	24.6	−26.3
Strawberries	1.6	3.0	5.9	268.8	Bottled water	NA	8.8	29.1	NA
					Carbonated soft drinks	NA	47.1	48.8	NA
Vegetables	336.8	385.7	417.0	23.8	Fruit juice	5.5	7.0	8.2	49.1
Canned vegetables	100.6	110.3	97.2	−3.4	Beer	18.5	23.9	21.8	17.8
Frozen vegetables	43.8	66.8	76.0	73.5	Wine	1.3	2.0	2.5	92.3
					Distilled spirits	1.8	1.5	1.4	−22.2

U.S. Meat Production and Consumption, 1940-2009

Source: Economic Research Service, U.S. Dept. of Agriculture
(in millions of pounds)

Year	Beef Prod.	Beef Cons.	Veal Prod.	Veal Cons.	Lamb and mutton Prod.	Lamb and mutton Cons.	Pork Prod.	Pork Cons.	All red meats[1] Prod.	All red meats[1] Cons.	All poultry Prod.	All poultry Cons.
1940	7,175	7,257	981	981	876	873	10,044	9,701	19,076	18,812	NA	NA
1950	9,534	9,529	1,230	1,206	597	596	10,714	10,390	22,075	21,721	3,174	3,097
1960	14,728	15,465	1,109	1,118	769	857	13,905	14,057	30,511	31,497	6,310	6,168
1970	21,684	23,451	588	613	551	669	14,699	14,957	37,522	39,689	10,193	9,981
1980	21,643	23,560	400	420	318	351	16,617	16,838	38,978	41,170	14,173	13,525
1990	22,743	24,030	327	325	363	397	15,354	16,025	38,787	40,778	23,468	22,152
1995	25,222	25,534	319	319	285	346	17,849	17,768	43,675	43,967	30,393	25,944
2000	26,888	27,338	225	225	234	354	18,952	18,643	46,299	46,560	36,073	30,508
2005	26,787	27,754	165	164	191	355	20,705	19,112	45,848	47,385	40,935	34,947
2006	26,256	28,137	156	155	190	356	21,074	19,048	47,675	47,696	41,231	35,544
2007	26,523	28,144	145	144	188	384	21,962	19,763	48,817	48,435	42,117	35,667
2008	26,663	27,302	152	150	180	343	23,367	19,415	50,361	47,210	43,235	35,379
2009*	25,922	27,059	142	146	173	339	22,959	19,550	49,196	47,094	41,407	34,380

* Preliminary. NA = Not available. (1) Meats may not add to total because of rounding. (2) Consumption (also called total disappearance) is estimated as production plus beginning stocks, plus imports, minus exports, minus ending stocks.

U.S. Annual Per Capita Consumption of Meat and Dairy, 1910-2007

Source: Economic Research Service, U.S. Dept. of Agriculture
(in pounds per capita, unless otherwise noted)

Meat	1910	1930	1950	1970	1990	2007	% change, 1910-2007
Beef	48.5	33.7	44.6	79.6	63.9	62.2	28.2%
Fish/shellfish	11.2	10.2	11.9	11.7	14.9	16.3	45.5
Pork	38.2	41.1	43.0	48.1	46.4	47.3	23.8
Chicken	11.0	11.1	14.3	27.4	42.4	59.9	444.5
Red meat	96.0	83.6	95.8	131.9	112.2	110.6	15.2
Dairy							
Butter	18.4	17.6	10.9	5.4	4.0	4.7	−74.5
American cheese	2.5	3.2	5.5	7.0	11.1	12.8	412.0
Other cheese	1.4	1.5	2.2	4.4	13.5	19.9	1,321.4
Skim/lower fat milk (gallons)	7.1	5.0	3.0	5.8	15.2	14.3	101.4
Whole milk (gallons)	25.2	28.2	34.3	25.5	10.5	6.4	−74.6
Ice cream	1.9	9.7	17.4	17.8	15.8	14.0	636.8

U.S. Organic Farmland and Animals, 1995-2005

Source: Economic Research Service, U.S. Dept. of Agriculture

Organic acreage[1]	1995	2000	2001	2002	2003	2004	2005	% change, 2000-05	Total U.S. farmland[2]
Grains									
Corn	32,650	77,912	93,551	96,270	105,574	99,111	130,672	67.7%	81,759,000
Wheat	96,100	181,262	194,640	217,611	234,221	214,244	277,487	53.1	57,229,000
Oats	13,250	29,771	33,254	53,459	46,074	42,616	46,465	56.1	4,246,000
Barley	17,150	41,904	31,478	34,031	30,265	26,629	39,271	−6.3	3,875,000
Rice	8,400	26,870	29,022	22,381	20,152	22,173	26,428	−1.6	3,384,000
Beans									
Soybeans	47,200	136,071	174,467	126,540	122,403	114,239	122,217	−10.2	72,142,000
Dry beans	NA	14,010	15,080	2,430	9,836	7,642	10,561	−24.6	1,659,300
Dry peas & lentils	5,900	10,144	9,362	7,476	16,188	15,893	17,757	75.1	571,000
Hay and silage	84,100	231,207	253,641	267,827	327,538	356,590	411,342	77.9	61,649,000
All vegetables	NA	62,342	71,667	69,887	78,905	86,822	98,525	58.0	2,114,110
All fruits	NA	43,481	55,675	60,693	77,989	80,707	97,277	123.7	3,911,200
Other cropland									
Cotton	32,850	15,027	11,456	10,551	9,875	9,213	9,537	−36.5	14,195,400
Peanuts	NA	2,085	4,653	5,134	5,698	9,514	11,940	472.8	1,657,000
Potatoes	NA	5,433	7,533	6,593	6,569	7,300	6,581	21.1	1,107,200
Trees for maple syrup	10,200	11,965	12,030	1,121	1,514	13,357	12,247	2.3	NA
Fallow land	NA	57,688	72,595	64,668	83,003	116,582	165,040	186.1	16,559,229
Total cropland	**638,500**	**1,218,905**	**1,302,392**	**1,299,632**	**1,451,601**	**1,452,353**	**1,723,271**	**41.4**	**340,650,083**
Total pasture and rangeland	**276,300**	**557,167**	**789,505**	**625,902**	**745,273**	**1,592,756**	**2,331,158**	**318.4**	**455,786,634**
Total farmland	**914,800**	**1,776,073**	**2,094,272**	**1,925,534**	**2,196,874**	**3,045,109**	**4,054,429**	**128.3**	**796,436,717**

Organic animals[1]	1995	2000	2001	2002	2003	2004	2005	% change, 2000-05	Total U.S. animals
Total livestock	NA	56,028	72,209	108,362	124,346	157,253	196,506	250.7%	162,917,000
Beef cows	NA	13,829	15,197	23,384	27,285	36,662	36,113	161.1	32,915,000
Milk cows	NA	38,196	48,677	67,207	74,435	74,840	87,082	128.0	9,058,000
Other cows[3]	NA	NA	993	10,103	11,501	36,598	58,822	NA	53,517,000
Hogs and pigs	NA	1,724	3,135	2,753	6,564	4,883	10,018	481.1	61,197,000
Sheep and lambs	NA	2,279	4,207	4,915	4,561	4,270	4,471	96.2	6,230,000
Total poultry	NA	3,159,050	5,014,015	6,270,181	8,780,152	7,304,566	13,757,270	335.5	NA
Layer hens	NA	1,113,746	1,611,662	1,052,272	1,591,181	1,787,901	2,415,056	116.8	347,917,000
Broilers	NA	1,924,807	3,286,456	3,032,189	6,301,014	4,769,104	10,405,879	440.6	8,740,650,000
Turkeys	NA	9,138	98,653	305,605	217,353	164,292	144,086	1,476.8	NA
Other/unclassified	NA	111,359	17,244	1,880,115	670,604	583,269	792,249	611.4	NA

NA = Not available. (1) Certified by USDA's National Organic Program. (2) Total organic and nonorganic land used for agricultural purposes. (3) Includes unclassified cows and some young stock.

Production of Principal U.S. Crops, 1990-2008

Source: National Agricultural Statistics Service, U.S. Dept. of Agriculture

Year	Corn for grain (1,000 bu)	Oats (1,000 bu)	Barley (1,000 bu)	Sorghum for grain (1,000 bu)	All wheat (1,000 bu)	Rye (1,000 bu)	Flaxseed (1,000 bu)	Upland Cotton (1,000 b)	Cottonseed (1,000 t)
1990	7,934,028	357,654	422,196	573,303	2,729,778	10,176	3,812	15,505.4	5,968.5
1995	7,373,876	162,027	359,562	460,373	2,182,591	10,064	2,211	17,532.2	6,848.7
1996	9,293,435	155,273	395,751	802,974	2,285,133	9,016	1,602	18,413.5	7,143.5
1997	9,206,832	167,246	359,878	633,545	2,481,466	8,132	2,420	18,245.0	6,934.6
1998	9,758,685	165,981	352,125	519,933	2,547,321	12,161	6,708	13,475.9	5,365.4
1999	9,430,612	146,193	280,292	595,166	2,299,010	11,038	7,864	16,293.7	6,354.0
2000	9,915,051	149,545	318,728	470,526	2,232,460	8,386	10,730	16,799.2	6,435.6
2001	9,506,840	117,024	249,420	514,524	1,957,043	6,971	11,455	19,602.4	7,452.2
2002	8,966,787	116,002	226,906	360,713	1,605,878	6,488	11,863	16,530.3	6,183.9
2003	10,089,222	144,383	278,283	411,237	2,344,760	8,634	10,516	17,822.9	6,664.6
2004	11,807,086	115,695	279,743	453,654	2,158,245	8,255	10,368	22,505.1	8,242.1
2005	11,114,082	114,878	211,896	392,933	2,104,690	7,537	19,695	23,259.7	8,172.1
2006[1]	10,534,868	93,638	180,165	277,538	1,812,036	7,193	11,019	20,822.4	7,347.9
2007[1]	13,037,875	90,430	210,110	497,445	2,051,088	6,311	5,896	18,355.1	6,588.7
2008	12,101,238	88,635	239,498	472,342	2,499,524	7,979	5,716	12,589.0	4,429.0

Year	Tobacco (1,000 lb)	All hay (1,000 t)	Beans, dry edible (1,000 cwt)	Peas, dry edible (1,000 cwt)	Peanuts[2] (1,000 lb)	Soybeans[3] (1,000 bu)	Potatoes (1,000 cwt)	Sweet potatoes (1,000 cwt)
1990	1,626,380	146,212	32,379	2,372	3,602,770	1,925,947	402,110	12,594
1995	1,268,538	154,166	30,812	4,765	4,247,455	2,176,814	443,606	12,906
1996	1,517,334	149,457	27,960	2,671	3,661,205	2,382,364	498,633	13,456
1997	1,787,399	152,536	29,370	5,752	3,539,380	2,688,750	467,091	13,327
1998	1,479,867	151,780	30,418	5,934	3,963,440	2,741,014	475,771	12,382
1999	1,292,692	159,707	33,085	4,773	3,829,490	2,653,758	478,216	12,234
2000	1,052,999	151,921	26,409	3,474	3,265,505	2,757,810	513,621	13,794
2001	991,223	156,764	19,583	3,763	4,276,704	2,890,682	437,888	14,637
2002	871,122	149,467	30,312	4,727	3,321,040	2,756,147	458,171	12,799
2003	802,560	157,585	22,492	5,202	4,144,150	2,453,665	457,814	15,891
2004	881,973	158,247	17,788	11,419	4,288,200	3,123,686	456,041	16,112
2005	645,015	151,017	26,772	14,003	4,869,860	3,063,237	423,926	15,730
2006[1]	727,347	142,336	24,247	13,203	3,464,250	3,188,247	441,348	16,248
2007[1]	787,653	146,901	25,586	16,287	3,672,250	2,667,117	444,875	18,070
2008	800,527	145,672	25,558	12,270	5,147,900	2,959,174	412,580	18,345

Year	Rice (1,000 cwt)	Sugarcane (1,000 t)	Sugar beets (1,000 t)	Pecans[4] (1,000 lb)	Apples (1,000 t)	Grapes (1,000 t)	Peaches (1,000 t)	Oranges[5] (1,000 bx)	Grapefruit[5] (1,000 bx)
1990	156,088	28,136	27,513	205,000	4,828	5,660	1,121	184,415	49,300
1995	173,871	30,944	27,954	268,000	5,293	5,922	1,150	263,605	71,050
1996	171,321	29,462	26,680	209,500	5,196	5,554	1,058	263,890	66,200
1997	182,992	31,709	29,886	335,000	5,162	7,291	1,312	292,620	70,200
1998	184,443	32,743	32,499	146,400	5,823	5,820	1,190	315,525	63,150
1999	206,027	35,299	33,420	406,100	5,316	6,236	1,252	224,580	61,200
2000	190,872	36,114	32,541	209,850	5,291	7,688	1,276	299,760	66,980
2001	215,270	34,587	25,764	338,500	4,712	6,569	1,204	280,935	59,750
2002	210,960	35,553	27,707	172,900	4,262	7,339	1,268	283,760	58,660
2003	199,897	33,858	30,710	282,100	4,397	6,664	1,260	267,040	50,080
2004	232,362	29,013	30,021	185,800	5,220	6,240	1,307	294,620	52,540
2005	223,235	26,606	27,433	280,250	4,853	7,814	1,185	216,500	25,640
2006[1]	193,736	29,564	34,064	207,300	4,912	6,378	1,010	210,750	30,600
2007[1]	198,388	29,969	31,834	387,305	4,545	7,057	1,127	177,280	39,900
2008	203,733	30,690	26,820	193,890	4,885	7,303	1,133	236,814	38,500

Note: Some 2008 figures are preliminary estimates. (1) Some totals revised. (2) Harvested for nuts. (3) Harvested for beans. (4) Utilized production only. (5) Crop year ending in year cited.

Livestock on Farms in the U.S., 1900-2009

Source: National Agricultural Statistics Service, U.S. Dept. of Agriculture
(in thousands)

Year (on Jan. 1)	All cattle[1]	Milk cows	Sheep and lambs	Hogs and pigs[2]	Year (on Jan. 1)	All cattle[1]	Milk cows	Sheep and lambs	Hogs and pigs[2]
1900	59,739	16,544	48,105	51,055	1990	95,816	10,015	11,358	53,788
1910	58,993	19,450	50,239	48,072	1995	102,755	9,487	8,886	57,150
1920	70,400	21,455	40,743	60,159	2000	98,199	9,183	7,036	59,335
1930	61,003	23,032	51,565	55,705	2001	97,298	9,172	6,908	59,110
1940	68,309	24,940	52,107	61,165	2002	96,723	9,106	6,623	59,722
1950	77,963	23,853	29,826	58,937	2003	96,100	9,142	6,321	59,554
1955	96,592	23,462	31,582	50,474	2004	94,888	8,990	6,105	60,444
1960	96,236	19,527	33,170	59,026	2005	95,838	9,005	6,135	60,975
1965	109,000	16,981	25,127	56,106	2006	96,702	9,063	6,230	61,449
1970	112,369	12,091	20,423	57,046	2007	97,003	9,132	6,165	62,490
1975	132,028	11,220	14,515	54,693	2008	96,035	9,257	5,950	66,963
1980	111,242	10,758	12,699	67,318	2009	94,491	9,333	5,747	66,768
1985	109,582	10,777	10,716	54,073					

(1) From 1970, includes milk cows and heifers that have calved. (2) As of Dec. 1 of preceding year.

Animal Products: Average Prices Received by U.S. Farmers, 1940-2008

Source: National Agricultural Statistics Service, U.S. Dept. of Agriculture

Figures below represent dollars per 100 lb for hogs, beef cattle, veal calves, sheep, lamb, and milk (wholesale); dollars per head for milk cows; cents per lb for chickens, broilers, turkeys, and wool; cents per dozen for eggs; weighted calendar year prices for livestock and livestock products other than wool. For 1943-63, wool prices were weighted on marketing year basis. The marketing year was changed in 1964 from a calendar year to a Dec.-Nov. basis for hogs, chickens, broilers, and eggs.

Year	Broilers	Calves (veal)	Cattle (beef)	Chickens (excl. broilers)	Eggs	Hogs	Lambs	Milk cows	Milk	Sheep	Turkeys	Wool
1940	17.3	8.83	7.56	13.0	18.0	5.39	8.10	61	1.82	3.95	15.2	28.4
1950	27.4	26.30	23.30	22.2	36.3	18.00	25.10	198	3.89	11.60	32.8	62.1
1960	16.9	22.90	20.40	12.2	36.1	15.30	17.90	223	4.21	5.61	25.4	42.0
1970	13.6	34.50	27.10	9.1	39.1	22.70	26.40	332	5.71	7.51	22.6	35.4
1975	26.3	27.20	32.20	9.9	54.5	46.10	42.10	412	8.75	11.30	34.8	44.8
1980	27.7	76.80	62.40	11.0	56.3	38.00	63.60	1,190	13.05	21.30	41.3	88.1
1985	30.1	62.10	53.70	14.8	57.1	44.00	67.70	860	12.76	23.90	49.1	63.3
1990	32.6	95.60	74.60	9.3	70.9	53.70	55.50	1,160	13.74	23.20	39.4	80.0
1995	34.4	73.10	61.80	6.5	62.4	40.50	78.20	1,130	12.78	28.00	41.6	104.0
2000	33.6	104.00	68.60	5.7	61.8	42.30	79.80	1,340	12.40	34.30	40.7	33.0
2001	39.3	106.00	71.30	4.5	62.2	44.30	66.90	1,500	15.04	34.60	39.0	36.0
2002	30.5	96.40	66.50	4.8	58.9	33.40	73.80	1,600	12.18	27.90	36.5	53.0
2003	34.6	102.00	79.70	4.9	73.2	37.20	94.40	1,340	12.55	34.90	36.1	73.0
2004	44.6	119.00	85.80	5.8	71.4	49.30	101.00	1,580	16.13	38.80	42.0	80.0
2005	43.6	135.00	89.70	6.5	54.0	50.20	110.00	1,770	15.19	45.10	44.9	71.0
2006	36.3	133.00	87.20	5.8	58.2	46.00	95.50	1,730	12.96	35.20	47.9	68.0
2007[1]	43.6	119.00	89.90	5.6	88.5	46.60	98.50	1,830	19.21	31.00	52.3	87.0
2008	45.8	110.00	89.10	6.6	109.0	47.00	99.60	1,950	18.40	27.20	56.5	99.0

(1) Some prices revised.

Crops: Average Prices Received by U.S. Farmers, 1940-2008

Source: National Agricultural Statistics Service, U.S. Dept. of Agriculture

Figures below represent cents per lb for cotton, apples, and peanuts; dollars per bushel for oats, wheat, corn, barley, and soybeans; dollars per 100 lb for rice, sorghum, and potatoes; dollars per ton for cottonseed and baled hay; weighted crop year prices. The marketing year is described as follows: apples, June-May; wheat, oats, barley, hay, and potatoes, July-June; cotton, rice, peanuts, and cottonseed, Aug.-July; soybeans, Sept.-Aug.; and corn and sorghum grain, Oct.-Sept.

Year	Apples	Barley	Corn	Cottonseed	Cotton (upland)*	Hay	Oats	Peanuts	Potatoes	Rice	Sorghum	Soybeans	Wheat
1940	NA	0.39	0.62	21.70	9.8	9.78	0.30	3.7	0.85	1.80	0.87	0.89	0.67
1950	NA	1.19	1.52	86.60	39.9	21.10	0.79	10.9	1.50	5.09	1.88	2.47	2.00
1960	2.7	0.84	1.00	42.50	30.1	21.70	0.60	10.0	2.00	4.55	1.49	2.13	1.74
1970	6.5	0.97	1.33	56.40	21.9	26.10	0.62	12.8	2.21	5.17	2.04	2.85	1.33
1975	8.8	2.42	2.54	97.00	51.1	52.10	1.45	19.0	4.48	8.35	4.21	4.92	3.55
1980	12.1	2.86	3.11	129.00	74.4	71.00	1.79	25.1	6.55	12.80	5.25	7.57	3.91
1985	17.3	1.98	2.23	66.00	56.8	67.60	1.23	24.4	3.92	6.53	3.45	5.05	3.08
1990	20.9	2.14	2.28	121.00	67.1	80.60	1.14	34.7	6.08	6.68	3.79	5.74	2.61
1995	24.0	2.89	3.24	106.00	75.4	82.20	1.67	29.3	6.77	9.15	5.69	6.72	4.55
2000	17.8	2.11	1.85	105.00	49.8	84.60	1.10	27.4	5.08	5.61	3.37	4.54	2.62
2001	22.9	2.22	1.97	90.50	29.8	96.50	1.59	23.4	6.99	4.25	4.25	4.38	2.78
2002	25.6	2.72	2.32	101.00	44.5	92.40	1.81	18.2	6.69	4.49	4.14	5.53	3.56
2003	29.4	2.83	2.42	117.00	61.8	85.50	1.48	19.3	5.89	8.08	4.26	7.34	3.40
2004	21.8	2.48	2.06	107.00	41.6	92.00	1.48	18.9	5.67	7.33	3.19	5.74	3.40
2005	24.4	2.53	2.00	96.00	47.7	98.20	1.63	17.3	7.06	7.65	3.33	5.66	3.42
2006	31.7	2.85	3.04	111.00	46.5	110.00	1.87	17.7	7.33	9.96	5.88	6.43	4.26
2007[1]	38.3	4.02	4.20	162.00	59.3	128.00	2.63	20.5	7.51	12.80	7.80	10.10	6.48
2008[2]	29.6	5.37	3.90	223.00	55.2	157.00	3.15	20.5	9.46	16.50	5.70	9.25	6.78

*Beginning in 1964, 480-lb net weight bales. NA = Not available. (1) Some prices revised. (2) Preliminary.

Value of U.S. Agricultural Exports and Imports, 1978-2008

Source: Economic Research Service, U.S. Dept. of Agriculture

(in billions of dollars)

Year[1]	Agric. trade surplus	Agric. exports	% of all exports	Agric. imports	% of all imports	Year[1]	Agric. trade surplus	Agric. exports	% of all exports	Agric. imports	% of all imports
1978	$13.4	$27.3	21%	$13.9	8%	1994	$19.2	$46.2	10%	$27.0	4%
1979	15.8	32.0	19	16.2	8	1995	26.0	56.3	10	30.3	4
1980	23.2	40.5	19	17.3	7	1996	26.8	60.3	10	33.5	4
1981	26.4	43.8	19	17.3	7	1997	21.0	57.2	9	36.1	4
1982	23.6	39.1	18	15.5	6	1998	14.9	51.8	8	36.9	4
1983	18.5	34.8	18	16.3	7	1999	10.7	48.4	8	37.7	4
1984	19.1	38.0	18	18.9	6	2000	12.2	51.2	7	39.0	3
1985	11.5	31.2	15	19.7	6	2001	14.3	53.7	8	39.4	4
1986	5.4	26.3	13	20.9	6	2002	11.2	53.1	8	41.9	4
1987	7.2	27.9	12	20.7	5	2003	10.3	56.0	9	45.7	4
1988	14.3	35.3	12	21.0	5	2004	9.7	62.4	9	52.7	4
1989	18.1	39.7	12	21.6	5	2005	4.8	62.5	8	57.7	4
1990	16.6	39.5	11	22.9	5	2006	4.7	68.7	8	64.0	3
1991	16.4	39.3	10	22.9	5	2007	12.1	82.2	8	70.1	4
1992	18.3	43.1	10	24.8	5	2008	36.0	115.3	10	79.3	4
1993	17.7	42.9	10	25.1	4						

(1) Fiscal year (Oct.-Sept.).

World Meat Production, 2000, 2007

Source: UN Food and Agriculture Organization; in thousands of metric tons; ranked by top producers in 2007

Rank	Top beef producers Country	2000	2007	Rank	Top poultry producers Country	2000	2007	Rank	Top pork producers Country	2000	2007
1.	U.S.	12,298	12,044	1.	U.S.	16,416	19,481	1.	China	41,406	61,150
2.	Brazil	6,579	7,900	2.	China	12,873	16,034	2.	U.S.	8,597	9,953
3.	China	5,352	7,633	3.	Brazil	6,125	8,907	3.	Germany	3,982	4,670
4.	Argentina	2,718	2,830	4.	Mexico	1,858	2,543	4.	Spain	2,905	3,222
5.	India	2,858	2,782	5.	India	1,136	2,273	5.	Brazil	2,600	3,130
6.	Australia	1,988	2,261	6.	Russia	775	1,769	6.	Vietnam	1,409	2,500
7.	Russia	1,894	1,828	7.	UK	1,513	1,523	7.	Poland	1,923	2,100
8.	Mexico	1,409	1,650	8.	France	2,220	1,473	8.	France	2,312	1,982
9.	France	1,528	1,450	9.	Iran	826	1,444	9.	Canada	1,640	1,894
10.	Canada	1,263	1,279	10.	Indonesia	818	1,356	10.	Russia	1,569	1,788
11.	Germany	1,304	1,190	11.	Japan	1,195	1,290	11.	Denmark	1,625	1,750
12.	Pakistan	886	1,113	12.	Canada	1,065	1,207	12.	Italy	1,479	1,600
13.	Italy	1,153	1,101	13.	Argentina	1,000	1,204	13.	Philippines	1,008	1,501
14.	UK	705	850	14.	Thailand	1,194	1,136	14.	Netherlands	1,623	1,296
15.	South Africa	625	805	15.	Spain	987	1,087	15.	Mexico	1,030	1,200
16.	Colombia	745	790	16.	Malaysia	714	1,042	16.	Japan	1,256	1,165
17.	Spain	651	705	17.	Germany	801	1,026	17.	Belgium	1,042	1,000
18.	New Zealand	572	632	18.	South Africa	821	982	18.	South Korea	916	915
19.	Egypt	544	590	19.	Italy	1,092	947	19.	Thailand	475	700
20.	Uzbekistan	390	586	20.	Turkey	661	915	20.	UK	899	700
21.	Uruguay	453	570	21.	Poland	589	878	21.	Ukraine	676	650
22.	Ukraine	754	563	22.	Australia	643	850	22.	Indonesia	413	597
23.	Ireland	577	560	23.	Peru	542	800	23.	Serbia	0	560
24.	Japan	530	491	24.	Colombia	504	760	24.	Romania	502	526
25.	Indonesia	386	464	25.	Venezuela	693	740	25.	Austria	620	515
	Africa	4,280	4,899		Africa	2,998	3,610		Africa	657	821
	Asia	13,874	16,945		Asia	23,358	30,852		Asia	48,248	70,410
	Europe	11,777	11,213		Europe	11,898	13,297		Europe	25,377	25,694
	North America	13,561	13,323		North America	17,480	20,688		North America	10,237	11,847
	Oceania	2,581	2,913		Oceania	767	1,023		Oceania	488	518
	South America	11,857	13,529		South America	9,743	13,484		South America	3,725	4,600
	World total	**59,920**	**65,083**		**World total**	**69,096**	**86,772**		**World total**	**90,075**	**115,454**

World Wheat, Rice, and Corn Production, 2000, 2007

Source: UN Food and Agriculture Organization; in millions of metric tons; ranked by top producers in 2007

Rank	Top corn producers Country	2000	2007	Rank	Top rice producers Country	2000	2007	Rank	Top wheat producers Country	2000	2007
1.	U.S.	251.9	332.1	1.	China	189.8	187.0	1.	China	99.6	109.9
2.	China	106.2	152.0	2.	India	127.4	141.1	2.	India	76.4	74.9
3.	Brazil	31.9	51.6	3.	Indonesia	51.9	57.0	3.	U.S.	60.8	53.6
4.	Mexico	17.6	22.5	4.	Bangladesh	37.6	43.5	4.	Russia	34.5	49.4
5.	Argentina	16.8	21.8	5.	Vietnam	32.5	35.6	5.	France	37.4	33.2
6.	India	12.0	16.8	6.	Myanmar (Burma)	21.3	32.6	6.	Pakistan	21.1	23.5
7.	France	16.0	13.1	7.	Thailand	25.8	27.9	7.	Germany	21.6	21.4
8.	Indonesia	9.7	12.4	8.	Philippines	12.4	16.0	8.	Canada	26.5	20.6
9.	Canada	7.0	10.6	9.	Brazil	11.1	11.1	9.	Turkey	21.0	17.7
10.	Italy	10.1	9.9	10.	Japan	11.9	11.0	10.	Kazakhstan	9.1	16.5
11.	Hungary	5.0	8.4	11.	U.S.	8.7	9.0	11.	Iran	8.1	15.0
12.	Nigeria	4.1	7.8	12.	Pakistan	7.2	8.3	12.	Argentina	16.1	14.0
13.	South Africa	11.4	7.3	13.	Egypt	6.0	6.7	13.	Ukraine	10.2	13.8
14.	Egypt	6.5	7.0	14.	Cambodia	4.0	6.0	14.	UK	16.7	13.4
15.	Philippines	4.5	6.7	15.	South Korea	7.2	6.0	15.	Australia	22.1	13.0
16.	Ukraine	3.8	6.7	16.	Nigeria	3.3	4.7	16.	Poland	8.5	8.4
17.	Vietnam	2.0	4.3	17.	Nepal	4.2	3.7	17.	Egypt	6.6	7.4
18.	Ethiopia	2.7	4.0	18.	Madagascar	2.5	3.6	18.	Italy	7.5	7.3
19.	Russia	1.5	4.0	19.	Iran	2.0	3.5	19.	Spain	7.3	6.4
20.	Serbia	3.0	3.9	20.	Sri Lanka	2.9	3.1	20.	Uzbekistan	3.5	5.9
21.	Turkey	2.3	3.9	21.	Laos	2.2	2.9	21.	Denmark	4.7	4.5
22.	Romania	4.9	3.7	22.	Peru	1.9	2.5	22.	Syria	3.1	4.5
23.	Spain	4.0	3.6	23.	Colombia	2.3	2.3	23.	Brazil	1.7	4.0
24.	Thailand	4.5	3.6	24.	Malaysia	2.1	2.2	24.	Hungary	3.7	4.0
25.	Germany	3.3	3.5	25.	North Korea	1.7	2.2	25.	Czech Republic	4.1	4.0
	Africa	44.3	51.1		Africa	17.5	23.5		Africa	14.4	19.3
	Asia	149.1	213.0		Asia	545.5	591.7		Asia	254.5	285.8
	Europe	63.5	68.6		Europe	3.2	3.5		Europe	183.7	190.4
	North America	258.8	342.6		North America	8.7	9.0		North America	87.3	74.2
	Oceania	0.6	0.6		Oceania	1.1	0.2		Oceania	22.4	13.3
	South America	55.4	82.6		South America	20.5	21.4		South America	20.2	21.0
	World total	**592.5**	**784.8**		**World total**	**598.9**	**651.7**		**World total**	**586.1**	**607.0**

Note: North America comprises Canada and the U.S.

Crop Consumption Per Capita, Selected Nations, 1980-2003

Source: UN Food and Agriculture Organization

(in kg per capita per year)

Countries	Corn				Rice				Wheat			
	1980	1990	2003	% change, 1980-2003	1980	1990	2003	% change, 1980-2003	1980	1990	2003	% change, 1980-2003
Australia	1	4	5	400.0%	5	10	14	180.0%	81	71	68	−16.0%
Bangladesh	0	0	2	NA	209	234	240	14.8	27	20	21	−22.2
Brazil	22	21	26	18.2	58	61	54	−6.9	49	43	53	8.2
Cambodia.	11	8	12	9.1	203	231	223	9.9	4	0	2	−50.0
Canada.	3	3	20	566.7	5	7	8	60.0	76	77	86	13.2
Chad.	4	5	9	125.0	9	16	14	55.6	2	4	7	250.0
China	25	24	15	−40.0	126	140	117	−7.1	60	80	61	1.7
Congo Republic	4	2	6	50.0	2	5	20	900.0	33	36	52	57.6
Cuba.	0	0	28	NA	77	70	112	45.5	78	73	57	−26.9
Egypt	49	57	60	22.4	43	47	62	44.2	125	147	130	4.0
France	1	13	12	1,100.0	5	5	8	60.0	95	91	98	3.2
Germany	3	6	9	200.0	2	3	5	150.0	69	67	82	18.8
India	7	7	5	−28.6	89	116	106	19.1	44	49	63	43.2
Indonesia	22	28	37	68.2	182	221	211	15.9	9	9	17	88.9
Iran.	0	0	2	NA	43	44	53	23.3	152	163	171	12.5
Israel	11	23	18	63.6	8	11	13	62.5	136	123	120	−11.8
Italy.	4	3	3	−25.0	6	7	8	33.3	173	149	151	−12.7
Japan	6	9	12	100.0	109	96	85	−22.0	43	43	44	2.3
Kenya	113	83	88	−22.1	3	2	10	233.3	20	18	26	30.0
Korea, North.	43	56	42	−2.3	107	135	109	1.9	31	24	28	−9.7
Korea, South	1	13	15	1,400.0	202	155	116	−42.6	48	47	48	0.0
Mexico	122	128	125	2.5	7	6	7	0.0	43	43	36	−16.3
New Zealand	1	3	2	100.0	3	6	14	366.7			60	NA
Nigeria	6	36	20	233.3	25	34	42	68.0	17	3	17	0.0
Pakistan	6	6	8	33.3	33	21	25	−24.2	112	128	109	−2.7
Philippines	21	21	5	−76.2	142	148	165	16.2	16	20	29	81.3
Rwanda	14	15	9	−35.7	2	2	5	150.0	2	3	3	50.0
Saudi Arabia.	11	12	16	45.5	51	25	42	−17.6	89	101	86	−3.4
South Africa	111	107	115	3.6	44	45	99	125.0	55	61	45	−18.2
Spain	0	1	1	NA	8	9	10	25.0	98	92	88	−10.2
Thailand	4	5	6	50.0	215	164	156	−27.4	4	5	11	175.0
Turkey	8	19	21	162.5	0	1	2	NA	199	208	184	−7.5
United Arab Emirates	0	0	0	NA	51	48	71	39.2	62	78	93	50.0
United Kingdom	3	3	3	0.0	2	3	7	250.0	83	82	102	22.9
United States	7	13	13	85.7	5	10	13	160.0	69	80	83	20.3
Uruguay	22	28	34	54.5	11	15	15	36.4	104	95	118	13.5
Venezuela	75	54	46	−38.7	44	43	90	104.5	50	51	47	−6.0
Vietnam	6	6	8	33.3	31	19	23	−25.8	17	3	10	−41.2
Developed countries.	7	9	12	71.4	17	16	17	0.0	98	99	98	0.0
Developing countries	21	22	20	−4.8	98	108	98	0.0	52	60	58	11.5
Africa	37	41	41	10.8	22	24	29	31.8	43	45	47	9.3
Asia	15	16	11	−26.7	119	133	119	0.0	54	64	63	16.7
Europe	5	6	7	40.0	5	5	7	40.0	108	103	111	2.8
North & Central America	32	39	41	28.1	10	13	17	70.0	61	67	67	9.8
Oceania	1	3	3	200.0	13	19	26	100.0	70	60	60	−14.3
South America	23	21	26	13.0	43	47	45	4.7	58	53	59	1.7
World per capita consumption.	**17**	**19**	**18**	**5.9%**	**76**	**86**	**81**	**6.6%**	**64**	**69**	**67**	**4.7%**

Meat Consumption Per Capita, Selected Nations, 1980-2003

Source: UN Food and Agriculture Organization

(in kg per capita per year)

Countries	Beef				Pork				Poultry			
	1980	1990	2003	% change, 1980-2003	1980	1990	2003	% change, 1980-2003	1980	1990	2003	% change, 1980-2003
Australia	53	47	46	−13.2%	14	18	21	50.0%	20	24	35	75.0%
Bangladesh	1	1	1	0.0	0	0	0	NA	0	0	0	NA
Brazil	22	27	33	50.0	7	6	13	85.7	10	14	33	230.0
Cambodia.	2	3	4	100.0	0	6	8	NA	0	1	1	NA
Canada.	40	35	34	−15.0	34	27	27	−20.6	22	27	36	63.6
Chad.	7	12	9	28.6	0	0	0	NA	0	0	0	NA
China	0	1	4	NA	11	20	35	218.2	1	3	10	900.0
Congo Republic	3	1	1	−66.7	0	1	1	NA	1	4	11	1,000.0
Cuba.	15	12	5	−66.7	4	9	9	125.0	9	12	16	77.8
Egypt	7	8	8	14.3	0	0	0	NA	3	4	9	200.0
France	32	33	26	−18.8	37	33	38	2.7	16	20	24	50.0
Germany	23	22	11	−52.2	60	60	54	−10.0	9	11	13	44.4
India.	2	2	2	0.0	0	0	0	NA	0	0	1	NA
Indonesia	1	1	1	0.0	1	3	2	100.0	1	2	5	400.0
Iran.	6	6	5	−16.7	0	0	0	NA	5	6	11	120.0
Israel	13	14	23	76.9	2	2	2	0.0	35	38	69	97.1
Italy.	26	27	24	−7.7	24	31	43	79.2	18	19	15	−16.7
Japan	4	8	8	100.0	13	15	18	38.5	10	13	15	50.0
Kenya	11	9	9	−18.2	0	0	0	NA	1	2	1	0.0
Korea, North.	1	1	0	−100.0	9	11	6	−33.3	2	2	1	−50.0
Korea, South	2	5	12	500.0	7	12	27	285.7	2	6	10	400.0
Mexico	11	14	17	54.5	18	9	12	−33.3	6	10	25	316.7
New Zealand	58	39	26	−55.2	7	13	20	185.7	9	16	35	288.9

Countries	Beef 1980	Beef 1990	Beef 2003	Beef % change, 1980-2003	Pork 1980	Pork 1990	Pork 2003	Pork % change, 1980-2003	Poultry 1980	Poultry 1990	Poultry 2003	Poultry % change, 1980-2003
Nigeria	6	2	2	−66.7%	0	1	1	NA	2	2	1	−50.0%
Pakistan	4	6	6	50.0	0	0	0	NA	0	1	2	NA
Philippines	2	2	3	50.0	8	11	17	112.5%	4	3	8	100.0
Rwanda	2	2	2	0.0	0	0	0	NA	0	0	0	NA
Saudi Arabia.	6	4	3	−50.0	—	—	—	—	24	28	35	45.8
South Africa	19	17	14	−26.3	2	3	3	50.0	7	15	22	214.3
Spain	11	12	15	36.4	31	47	66	112.9	20	23	30	50.0
Thailand	5	5	3	−40.0	5	6	9	80.0	7	9	11	57.1
Turkey	3	6	4	33.3	0	0	0	NA	5	7	12	140.0
United Arab Emirates. . . .	14	11	7	−50.0	—	—	—	—	43	34	64	48.8
United Kingdom	23	20	20	−13.0	26	25	25	−3.8	13	18	29	123.1
United States	47	43	41	−12.8	32	28	30	−6.3	26	39	50	92.3
Uruguay	75	47	40	−46.7	8	7	8	0.0	4	7	15	275.0
Venezuela	22	18	16	−27.3	6	5	4	−33.3	17	12	26	52.9
Vietnam	1	2	2	100.0	5	10	22	340.0	1	2	5	400.0
Developed countries.	26	27	22	−15.4	29	30	29	0.0	14	20	25	78.6
Developing countries	4	5	6	50.0	5	7	11	120.0	2	3	8	300.0
Africa	6	5	5	−16.7	0	0	0	NA	2	3	4	100.0
Asia	1	2	4	300.0	6	9	14	133.3	2	3	7	250.0
Europe	21	21	16	−23.8	38	41	35	−7.9	13	15	18	38.5
North & Central America .	35	32	31	−11.4	26	21	22	−15.4	20	28	39	95.0
Oceania	44	37	33	−25.0	12	15	18	50.0	15	18	28	86.7
South America	28	27	28	0.0	7	6	9	28.6	9	11	25	177.8
World per capita consumption.	10	10	9	−10.0%	11	13	15	36.4%	5	7	11	120.0%

Trade in Wheat, Rice, Corn, and Meat, 1997, 2007

Source: UN Food and Agriculture Organization; in thousands of dollars

Wheat exports

Rank	Country	1997	Country	2007
1.	U.S.	$4,181,746	U.S.	$8,344,749
2.	Australia. . . .	3,279,041	Canada	4,359,492
3.	Canada	3,156,955	Australia.	3,887,832
4.	France	2,369,088	Russia	3,608,763
5.	Argentina	1,346,762	France	3,540,589
6.	Germany	661,947	Argentina. . . .	2,015,981
7.	UK	574,907	Kazakhstan . .	1,170,509
8.	Kazakhstan . .	430,414	Germany	1,168,131
9.	Syria	190,824	China	480,895
10.	Denmark	163,612	UK	463,602

Wheat imports

Rank	Country	1997	Country	2007
1.	Japan	$1,363,393	Italy	$1,822,396
2.	Italy	1,336,575	Japan	1,632,245
3.	Iran	1,107,780	Egypt.	1,566,617
4.	Brazil.	974,490	Brazil.	1,391,955
5.	Egypt.	821,048	Algeria.	1,385,843
6.	Indonesia	776,521	Indonesia. . . .	1,181,313
7.	Algeria.	730,842	Netherlands. .	1,133,135
8.	S. Korea	593,850	Morocco	1,125,687
9.	China.	571,428	Spain	940,432
10.	Spain	509,846	Belgium	938,025

Rice exports

Rank	Country	1997	Country	2007
1.	U.S.	$143,500	U.S.	$409,582
2.	Argentina	26,515	China	28,328
3.	Uruguay	24,401	Paraguay	9,892
4.	Greece.	21,827	India.	8,908
5.	France	14,794	France	7,290
6.	Italy	7,207	Italy	7,061
7.	Guinea	5,519	Saudi Arabia	4,277
8.	Guyana	3,239	Spain	2,695
9.	Kazakhstan . .	2,000	Bangladesh . .	2,378
10.	China	1,926	Thailand.	2,157

Rice imports

Rank	Country	1997	Country	2007
1.	Mexico.	$108,685	Mexico.	$213,530
2.	Brazil.	48,953	Costa Rica . . .	60,442
3.	Costa Rica . . .	25,494	Nicaragua . . .	46,469
4.	Italy	21,553	Uzbekistan . .	32,000
5.	Colombia.	12,832	Saudi Arabia	26,701
6.	Portugal.	12,001	Guatemala. . .	26,626
7.	Turkey	10,307	El Salvador . .	21,303
8.	Spain.	9,890	Panama	21,276
9.	Bangladesh . . .	8,929	Honduras. . . .	20,540
10.	El Salvador . . .	8,504	Bangladesh . .	11,553

Corn exports

Rank	Country	1997	Country	2007
1.	U.S.	$5,418,929	U.S.	$10,099,898
2.	France	1,391,675	Argentina	2,253,083
3.	Argentina	1,348,385	Brazil.	1,918,840
4.	China	858,946	France	1,522,375
5.	South Africa. .	250,274	Hungary	1,091,173
6.	Hungary	157,270	China	874,301
7.	Germany	76,628	India.	592,045
8.	Brazil.	52,008	Paraguay	282,742
9.	Zimbabwe . . .	50,522	Chile	232,335
10.	Chile	50,244	Germany	211,985

Corn imports

Rank	Country	1997	Country	2007
1.	Japan	$2,448,789	Japan	$3,842,474
2.	S. Korea	1,251,256	S. Korea	1,825,690
3.	China.	843,164	Spain.	1,571,184
4.	Malaysia	414,973	Mexico.	1,554,320
5.	Spain.	400,088	Egypt.	940,096
6.	Egypt.	385,391	China.	928,949
7.	Mexico.	379,525	Netherlands. .	874,117
8.	Netherlands . .	319,006	Colombia. . . .	679,823
9.	UK.	294,787	Germany	667,476
10.	Colombia.	272,557	Italy	641,582

Meat exports

Rank	Country	1997	Country	2007
1.	U.S.	$6,337,965	Brazil	$10,957,298
2.	Netherlands. .	4,179,018	U.S.	8,677,125
3.	France	4,084,058	Netherlands. .	7,812,996
4.	Denmark	4,003,672	Germany	7,505,327
5.	Belgium-Luxembourg	2,795,510	Australia.	5,155,497
6.	Australia.	2,435,787	Denmark	5,130,285
7.	Germany	1,939,132	France	4,392,806
8.	New Zealand .	1,875,730	Belgium	4,002,110
9.	Canada	1,713,546	Canada	3,467,246
10.	China	1,559,715	New Zealand	3,151,710

Meat imports

Rank	Country	1997	Country	2007
1.	Japan	$7,112,986	Japan	$8,366,287
2.	Germany	4,485,297	UK	8,030,083
3.	Italy	3,410,714	Germany	6,948,224
4.	UK.	3,348,888	Italy	5,693,121
5.	France	3,000,407	U.S.	5,221,534
6.	U.S.	2,737,860	France	5,073,577
7.	Russian	2,612,321	Russia	4,690,570
8.	China.	1,351,230	Netherlands. .	3,779,813
9.	Netherlands . .	1,215,460	Mexico.	2,552,748
10.	Belgium-Luxembourg	1,033,831	S. Korea	2,004,829

World Capture of Fish, Crustaceans, and Mollusks, 2000-06

Source: UN Food and Agriculture Organization
(in thousands of metric tons; ranked by 2006 captures)

Country	2000	2003	2004	2005	2006	Country	2000	2003	2004	2005	2006
China	16,987	16,756	16,893	17,053	17,092	Myanmar (Burma)	1,093	1,344	1,587	1,743	2,007
Peru	10,657	6,086	9,605	9,389	7,017	Vietnam	1,623	1,856	1,879	1,930	1,960
U.S.	4,718	4,939	4,960	4,889	4,860	South Korea	1,825	1,643	1,575	1,639	1,750
Indonesia	4,083	4,627	4,642	4,381	4,759	Bangladesh	1,004	1,141	1,187	1,334	1,436
Japan	4,986	4,670	4,312	4,073	4,187	Iceland	1,983	1,981	1,728	1,661	1,327
Chile	4,300	3,613	4,919	4,330	4,168	Mexico	1,316	1,357	1,259	1,305	1,300
India	3,666	3,712	3,391	3,481	3,855	Malaysia	1,289	1,287	1,336	1,214	1,296
Russia	3,974	3,281	2,942	3,191	3,284	Argentina	922	916	946	931	1,182
Thailand	2,997	2,850	2,840	2,599	2,776	Canada	998	1,111	1,176	1,081	1,063
Philippines	1,897	2,166	2,216	2,246	2,319	**World total**	**95,610**	**90,354**	**94,364**	**93,253**	**91,994**
Norway	2,699	2,549	2,524	2,393	2,256						

World Aquaculture Production, 2000-06

Source: UN Food and Agriculture Organization

Country	Metric tons[1] 2000	2003	2004	2005	2006	Value ($)[2] 2000	2003	2004	2005	2006
China	24,581	28,886	30,615	32,416	34,429	$24,317	$29,876	$30,870	$34,552	$38,423
India	1,942	2,313	2,795	2,962	3,123	2,511	2,588	3,784	3,758	3,431
Vietnam	499	938	1,199	1,437	1,658	991	1,968	2,444	2,931	3,316
Thailand	738	1,064	1,260	1,304	1,386	2,514	1,463	1,705	1,740	2,220
Indonesia	789	997	1,045	1,197	1,293	2,246	1,699	1,993	1,999	2,255
Bangladesh	657	857	915	882	892	1,039	1,243	1,363	1,246	1,359
Chile	392	563	665	698	802	1,250	2,138	2,745	3,108	4,428
Japan	763	824	776	746	734	3,317	3,368	3,205	3,178	3,099
Norway	491	584	637	662	709	1,385	1,352	1,681	2,136	2,716
Philippines	394	460	512	557	623	681	601	701	794	982
Egypt	340	445	472	540	595	815	615	613	792	951
Myanmar (Burma)	99	252	400	485	575	781	775	1,231	1,504	1,785
South Korea	293	388	406	437	514	573	889	980	1,195	1,419
U.S.	456	544	607	492	465	843	805	907	900	898
Taiwan	244	352	318	305	310	836	906	943	969	880
Spain	309	269	294	220	293	334	312	330	315	362
Brazil	172	273	270	258	272	264	478	470	444	469
France	267	240	261	259	239	425	581	701	696	661
Italy	214	192	118	181	173	446	524	375	598	602
UK	152	182	207	173	172	461	517	593	619	769
World total[3]	**35,475**	**42,674**	**45,922**	**48,490**	**51,653**	**$50,627**	**$58,395**	**$63,900**	**$70,371**	**$78,758**

Note: Does not include aquatic plants or marine mammals. (1) In thousands. (2) In millions of dollars. (3) Includes nations not shown.

U.S. Commercial Landings of Fish and Shellfish, 1990-2008[1]

Source: U.S. Dept. of Commerce, Natl. Oceanic and Atmospheric Admin., Natl. Marine Fisheries Service

Year	Landings for human food Weight (mil lbs)	Value (mil $)	Landings for industrial purposes[2] Weight (mil lbs)	Value (mil $)	Total Weight (mil lbs)	Value (mil $)
1990	7,041	$3,366	2,363	$156	9,404	$3,522
1991	7,031	3,169	2,453	139	9,484	3,308
1992	7,618	3,531	2,019	147	9,637	3,678
1993	8,214	3,317	2,253	154	10,467	3,471
1994	7,936	3,751	2,525	95	10,461	3,846
1995	7,667	3,625	2,121	145	9,788	3,770
1996	7,474	3,355	2,091	132	9,565	3,487
1997	7,244	3,285	2,598	163	9,842	3,448
1998	7,173	3,009	2,021	119	9,194	3,128
1999	6,832	3,265	2,507	202	9,339	3,467
2000	6,912	3,398	2,157	152	9,069	3,550
2001	7,314	3,074	2,178	154	9,492	3,228
2002	7,205	2,940	2,192	152	9,397	3,092
2003	7,521	3,185	1,986	157	9,507	3,347
2004	7,794	3,611	1,889	145	9,683	3,756
2005	7,997	3,825	1,710	117	9,707	3,942
2006	7,842	3,911	1,641	113	9,483	4,024
2007	7,490	4,015	1,819	177	9,309	4,192
2008[3]	6,633	4,231	1,692	152	8,325	4,383

Note: Does not include products of aquaculture, except oysters and clams. (1) Statistics on landings are shown in round (live) weight for all items except univalve and bivalve mollusks such as clams, oysters, and scallops, which are shown in weight of meats (excluding the shell). (2) Processed into meal, oil, solubles, and shell products or used as bait or animal food. (3) Preliminary data.

U.S. Domestic Landings, by Region, 2005, 2008[1]

Source: U.S. Dept. of Commerce, Natl. Oceanic and Atmospheric Admin., Natl. Marine Fisheries Service

Region	2005[2] Weight (1,000 lbs)	Value ($1,000)	2008[3] Weight (1,000 lbs)	Value ($1,000)
New England	684,090	$971,663	590,273	$791,651
Middle Atlantic	199,937	221,505	200,926	232,555
Chesapeake	508,953	218,933	477,091	219,058
South Atlantic	122,422	125,117	116,021	167,087
Gulf	1,196,355	620,987	1,273,424	697,591
Pacific Coast incl. Alaska	6,950,647	1,700,927	5,619,149	2,174,233
Great Lakes	16,732	12,434	18,279	16,767
Hawaii	28,139	70,811	30,651	84,878
Total	**9,707,275**	**$3,942,376**	**8,325,814**	**$4,383,820**

(1) Landings reported in round (live) weight items except for univalve and bivalve mollusks (e.g., clams, oysters, scallops, which are reported in weight of meats (excluding shell). (2) Revised. (3) Preliminary.

EMPLOYMENT

Employment and Unemployment in the U.S., 1900-2008

Source: Bureau of Labor Statistics, U.S. Dept. of Labor
(civilian labor force, persons 16 years of age and older; annual averages; in thousands)

Year[1]	Employed	Unemployed Number	Rate	Year[1]	Employed	Unemployed Number	Rate	Year[1]	Employed	Unemployed Number	Rate
1900[2] ...	26,956	1,420	5.0%	1985....	107,150	8,312	7.2%	1997[5]...	129,558	6,739	4.9%
1910[2] ...	34,599	2,150	5.9	1986....	109,597	8,237	7.0	1998[5]...	131,463	6,210	4.5
1920[2] ...	39,208	2,132	5.2	1987....	112,440	7,425	6.2	1999[6]...	133,488	5,880	4.2
1930[2] ...	44,183	4,340	8.9	1988....	114,968	6,701	5.5	2000[7]...	136,891	5,692	4.0
1940[2] ...	47,520	8,120	14.6	1989....	117,342	6,528	5.3	2001 ...	136,933	6,801	4.7
1950....	58,918	3,288	5.0	1990[3]....	118,793	7,047	5.6	2002 ...	136,485	8,378	5.8
1955....	62,170	2,852	4.4	1991....	117,718	8,628	6.8	2003 ...	137,736	8,774	6.0
1960....	65,778	3,852	5.5	1992....	118,492	9,613	7.5	2004 ...	139,252	8,149	5.5
1965....	71,088	3,366	4.5	1993....	120,259	8,940	6.9	2005 ...	141,730	7,591	5.1
1970....	78,678	4,093	4.9	1994[4]...	123,060	7,996	6.1	2006 ...	144,427	7,001	4.6
1975....	85,846	7,929	8.5	1995....	124,900	7,404	5.6	2007 ...	146,047	7,078	4.6
1980....	99,303	7,637	7.1	1996....	126,708	7,236	5.4	2008 ...	145,362	8,924	5.8

(1) **Other unemployment rates (1905-45): 1905**, 4.3; **1915**, 8.5; **1925**, 3.2; **1935**, 20.3; **1936**, 16.9; **1937**, 14.3; **1938**, 19.0; **1939**, 17.2; **1945**, 1.9; all for 14 years of age and older. (2) Persons 14 years of age and older. (3) Beginning in 1990, data incorporate 1990 census-based population controls, adjusted for estimated undercount. (4) Beginning in 1994, not strictly comparable with prior years because of major redesign of the survey used. (5) From 1997, not strictly comparable with 1994-96 because of revisions in population controls used in household survey. (6) From 1999, not strictly comparable with 1998 and earlier years because of further revisions in population controls used in household survey. (7) From 2000, not strictly comparable with earlier years because of revisions to the controls used in the survey.

Unemployment Insurance Data, by State, 2008

Source: Employment and Training Admin., U.S. Dept. of Labor; state programs only

STATE	Monetarily eligible claimants	Number of first payments	Number of final payments	Initial claims	Benefits paid	Average weekly benefit	Employers subject to state law
AL	191,733	147,870	35,443	346,895	$299,235,072	$196	90,639
AK	44,121	37,665	15,736	81,551	101,205,628	202	17,289
AZ	212,575	136,526	50,630	295,888	432,137,669	218	135,009
AR	113,282	104,782	32,714	258,973	318,702,746	265	68,361
CA	1,816,849	1,389,228	573,674	2,999,765	6,654,997,105	307	1,193,485
CO	137,800	95,711	36,446	163,141	416,045,120	341	157,608
CT	159,644	153,263	46,181	260,145	693,266,319	322	99,466
DE	39,923	29,520	9,680	65,474	125,001,121	257	26,821
FL	670,704	510,018	225,600	938,721	1,708,790,165	238	506,697
GA	409,928	310,660	109,407	742,488	917,418,410	273	218,372
HI	50,292	39,333	9,069	92,924	212,675,370	413	31,373
ID	87,691	71,476	18,963	146,550	211,272,513	272	51,219
IL	502,597	445,417	148,766	872,368	2,209,467,511	312	300,337
IN	343,535	261,334	93,086	613,106	952,344,107	298	131,397
IA	150,081	126,309	26,425	264,683	408,661,289	302	72,152
KS	94,086	72,762	23,211	175,595	259,544,854	316	71,311
KY	213,660	138,934	29,491	433,698	539,389,829	300	86,410
LA	160,813	75,494	24,262	214,687	211,949,054	209	103,093
ME	55,090	39,358	12,331	82,579	135,880,772	265	42,360
MD	182,658	139,541	44,399	295,832	609,656,770	305	142,874
MA	306,982	256,698	94,366	460,371	1,498,915,273	391	187,950
MI	640,355	513,255	177,270	1,102,497	2,149,286,913	300	220,398
MN	228,015	163,871	58,585	311,726	835,865,783	347	136,525
MS	114,906	76,960	19,831	189,372	180,367,992	183	56,740
MO	257,234	176,288	51,774	478,999	569,001,812	244	139,330
MT	43,567	30,260	8,875	67,128	97,727,968	255	37,773
NE	56,002	38,268	13,976	82,236	101,325,871	241	48,233
NV	148,431	128,702	45,601	254,060	568,995,205	292	60,479
NH	43,843	33,874	6,501	72,192	118,453,444	272	41,074
NJ	420,539	368,176	162,112	623,106	2,215,054,849	377	245,594
NM	59,122	37,710	15,084	68,952	169,963,606	278	45,839
NY	815,456	578,770	192,473	1,214,987	2,528,050,419	307	491,598
NC	482,650	353,511	132,019	924,716	1,022,205,401	287	202,817
ND	20,450	15,397	4,561	29,298	47,326,208	286	20,380
OH	400,198	357,192	97,460	868,810	1,440,643,756	303	228,606
OK	74,803	52,858	16,698	129,566	182,300,886	272	82,328
OR	248,718	198,479	55,343	498,553	784,323,786	302	111,748
PA	634,083	562,343	166,335	1,367,977	2,607,423,849	335	288,686
RI	55,289	46,446	20,492	90,827	279,122,771	370	33,860
SC	230,271	157,489	56,488	411,657	474,039,788	240	99,996
SD	13,847	9,219	913	20,997	25,041,374	239	25,225
TN	214,918	193,988	60,847	419,522	548,089,998	221	115,859
TX	645,271	404,589	135,761	894,733	1,487,453,695	303	446,958
UT	79,580	46,737	14,053	101,885	188,009,216	312	70,893
VT	32,908	27,605	5,254	49,284	105,114,831	294	22,063
VA	226,328	149,759	47,232	356,220	501,279,390	282	189,003
WA	328,782	232,831	47,498	555,199	1,008,305,566	355	200,521
WV	61,559	48,800	10,709	80,068	159,731,787	242	36,385
WI	371,287	321,164	77,371	738,041	997,815,135	273	132,568
WY	29,267	12,595	3,397	23,542	49,944,949	309	21,815
DC	23,040	21,182	10,360	20,700	105,198,804	291	28,057
PR	56,810	109,613	48,438	188,769	221,622,289	112	70,717
VI	3,120	2,454	1,180	3,525	12,387,590	328	3,477
U.S.	**13,004,693**	**10,049,915**	**3,423,977**	**22,040,113**	**40,698,031,628**	**297**	**7,690,062**

Unemployed Persons[1] by Industry and Duration of Unemployment, Sept. 2009

Source: Bureau of Labor Statistics, U.S. Dept. of Labor

OCCUPATION	Total	Less than 5 weeks	5 to 14 weeks	15 weeks and over Total	15 to 26 weeks	27 weeks and over	Weeks of Unemployment Average (mean) duration	Median duration
Management, professional, and related occupations	2,859	526	696	1,637	533	1,103	27.6	18.6
Management, business, and financial operations occupations	1,188	198	258	732	231	500	28.5	20.6
Professional and related occupations	1,671	328	438	905	302	603	26.9	17.0
Service occupations	2,556	628	654	1,274	433	841	24.7	14.4
Sales and office occupations.	3,367	528	812	2,028	635	1,392	29.6	20.3
Sales and related occupations	1,521	265	351	905	277	628	27.7	20.5
Office and administrative support occupations	1,846	264	460	1,122	358	764	31.1	20.1
Natural resources, construction, and maintenance occupations	2,210	544	456	1,210	377	833	26.0	17.7
Farming, fishing, and forestry occupations	156	53	56	47	17	31	17.1	9.7
Construction and extraction occupations.	1,605	408	324	874	255	618	25.3	17.9
Installation, maintenance, and repair occupations	449	83	77	289	105	184	31.7	21.1
Production, transportation, and material moving occupations	2,388	408	519	1,461	465	996	28.9	20.9
Production occupations.	1,264	184	247	833	269	564	30.1	22.9
Transportation and material moving occupations	1,125	224	272	628	196	432	27.7	18.2
INDUSTRY[2]								
Agriculture and related industries	158	47	57	54	14	41	21.2	10.1
Mining, quarrying, and oil and gas extraction	81	12	24	45	10	35	26.4	19.5
Construction	1,610	372	303	935	271	663	26.8	19.9
Manufacturing.	1,890	296	411	1,183	402	781	29.1	21.0
Durable goods.	1,286	177	317	792	266	525	28.6	20.4
Nondurable goods.	604	119	94	392	135	256	30.0	22.4
Wholesale and retail trade.	1,835	284	445	1,107	350	756	29.0	20.7
Transportation and utilities.	560	106	126	327	130	197	27.7	17.9
Information.	379	64	90	225	50	175	31.2	22.7
Financial activities	669	94	141	433	143	291	30.8	21.4
Professional and business services.	1,628	326	385	917	280	637	27.5	18.6
Education and health services.	1,669	333	478	858	281	577	26.1	15.4
Leisure and hospitality.	1,535	379	378	778	278	500	23.4	14.9
Other services	468	96	98	273	92	182	29.7	19.3
Public administration	263	52	68	142	55	87	29.3	17.1
No previous work experience	1,127	210	421	495	219	277	23.7	13.4

(1) Numbers are in thousands. (2) Includes wage and salary workers only.

Persons Not in the Labor Force, 2008

Source: Bureau of Labor Statistics, U.S. Dept. of Labor

The Labor Dept.'s unemployment rate, based on its household survey, shows the number of people out of work as a percentage of U.S. adults in the labor force. That rate excludes, however, the millions of adults considered not to be in the labor force.

(in thousands)

	Total	Age 16 to 24 years	Age 25 to 54 years	Age 55 years and over	Sex Men	Sex Women
Total not in the labor force	79,501	15,452	21,255	42,794	30,593	48,908
Do not want a job now[1]	74,519	13,719	19,087	41,712	28,365	46,154
Want a job[1]	4,983	1,733	2,168	1,082	2,228	2,755
Did not search for work in previous year	2,826	913	1,145	768	1,187	1,639
Searched for work in previous year[2] . . .	2,157	819	1,023	314	1,041	1,115
Not available to work now	543	252	244	48	214	329
Available to work now	1,614	568	780	266	827	787
Reason not currently looking						
Discouragement over job prospects[3].	462	145	226	90	282	180
Reasons other than discouragement.	1,152	422	554	176	545	607
Family responsibilities	171	35	111	25	45	126
In school or training.	218	173	42	3	108	109
Ill health or disability	124	16	68	40	55	69
Other[4]	640	199	332	108	337	303

(1) Includes some persons who are not asked if they want a job. (2) Persons who had a job in the prior 12 months must have searched since the end of that job; those available to work now are also referred to as being "marginally attached" to the labor force. (3) Includes believes no work available, could not find work, lacks necessary schooling or training, employer thinks too young or old, and other types of discrimination. (4) Includes those who did not actively look for work in the prior 4 weeks for such reasons as child care and transportation problems, as well as a small number for which reason for nonparticipation was not ascertained.

Displaced Workers, Jan. 2008

Source: Bureau of Labor Statistics, U.S. Dept. of Labor

	Total (thousands)	Percent distribution by reason of job loss Plant or company closed down or moved	Insufficient work	Position or shift abolished
Total, 20 years and over	3,641	45.3%	23.9%	30.8%
20 to 24 years	127	42.4	39.8	17.7
25 to 54 years	2,602	44.8	25.2	30.0
55 to 64 years	708	45.7	17.6	36.7
65 years and over	204	52.2	19.2	28.5
Men	2,024	43.6	27.9	28.5
Women	1,617	47.4	19.0	33.6
White	3,032	45.4	23.5	31.1
Black or African American	408	46.6	26.9	26.4
Asian	172	44.7	15.7	39.5
Hispanic or Latino	423	43.5	39.5	17.0

Note: Displaced workers are persons 20 years or older who lost or left jobs they had held for at least 3 years. Workers in this table were displaced between Jan. 2005 and Dec. 2007. Hispanic/Latino persons may be of any race.

U.S. Unemployment Rates by Selected Characteristics, 1995-2009[1]

Source: Bureau of Labor Statistics, U.S. Dept. of Labor

	1995	2000	2003	2004	2005	2006	2007	2008 Jan.	2008 June	2008 Yr.	2009 Jan.	2009 June
Total (all civilian workers)	5.6%	4.0%	6.0%	5.5%	5.1%	4.6%	4.6%	5.4%	5.7%	5.8%	7.6%	9.5%
Men, 20 years and older	4.8	3.3	5.6	5.0	4.4	4.0	4.1	5.2	4.8	5.4	11.0	9.5
Women, 20 years and older	4.9	3.6	5.1	4.9	4.6	4.1	4.0	4.4	4.9	4.9	9.6	7.9
Both sexes, 16 to 19 years	17.3	13.1	17.5	17.0	16.6	15.4	15.7	18.2	21.9	18.7	24.3	27.8
White	4.9	3.5	5.2	4.8	4.4	4.0	4.1	4.9	5.1	5.2	6.9	8.7
Black	10.4	7.6	10.8	10.4	10.0	8.9	8.3	9.4	9.8	10.1	12.6	14.7
Hispanic (of any race)	9.3	5.7	7.7	7.0	6.0	5.2	5.6	7.2	7.6	7.6	9.7	12.2
Asian	—	3.6	6.0	4.4	4.0	3.0	3.2	3.2	4.5	4.0	6.2	8.2
Married men, spouse present	3.3	—	—	—	—	—	—	2.7	3.0	3.4	5.0	6.9
Married women, spouse present	3.9	—	—	—	—	—	—	3.1	3.3	3.6	4.7	5.6
Women who maintain families	8.0	5.9	8.5	8.0	7.8	7.1	6.5	7.0	7.9	8.0	10.3	11.7
OCCUPATION												
Management, professional, and related	2.4	1.8	3.1	2.7	2.3	2.1	2.1	2.2	2.7	2.7	4.1	5.0
Service	7.5	5.2	7.1	6.6	6.4	5.9	5.9	7.0	6.5	6.7	9.1	10.2
Sales and office	5.0	3.8	5.5	5.2	4.8	4.4	4.3	4.8	5.2	5.3	7.5	8.6
Nat. resources, constr., and maintenance	—	5.3	8.1	7.3	6.5	6.0	6.3	8.9	7.3	8.8	15.5	14.2
Prod., trans., material moving	—	5.1	7.9	7.2	6.5	5.8	5.8	7.3	7.3	7.6	12.9	13.9
INDUSTRY												
Nonagricultural, private wage, and salary workers	5.8	4.1	6.3	5.7	5.2	4.7	4.7	5.6	5.6	5.9	9.0	10.0
Mining	5.2	4.4	6.7	3.9	3.1	3.2	3.4	4.0	3.3	3.1	7.0	13.6
Construction	11.5	6.2	9.3	8.4	7.4	6.7	7.4	11.0	8.2	10.6	18.2	17.4
Manufacturing	4.9	3.5	6.6	5.7	4.9	4.2	4.3	5.1	5.2	5.8	10.9	12.6
Durable goods	4.4	3.2	6.9	5.5	4.6	3.9	4.2	4.4	5.1	5.6	11.2	13.9
Non durable goods	5.7	4.0	6.1	5.9	5.3	4.8	4.5	6.4	5.5	6.0	10.3	10.5
Wholesale and retail trade	6.5	4.3	6.0	5.8	5.4	4.9	4.7	5.4	5.7	5.9	8.7	9.1
Transportation and utilities	4.5	3.4	5.3	4.4	4.1	4.0	3.9	4.4	5.1	5.1	8.4	8.4
Information	—	3.2	6.8	5.7	5.0	3.7	3.6	5.1	4.7	5.0	7.4	11.1
Financial activities	3.3	2.4	3.5	3.6	2.9	2.7	3.0	3.0	3.4	3.9	6.0	5.5
Professional and business services	—	4.8	8.2	6.8	6.2	5.6	5.3	6.4	6.2	6.5	10.4	11.3
Education and health services	—	2.5	3.6	3.4	3.4	3.0	3.0	2.9	3.4	3.5	3.8	6.1
Leisure and hospitality	—	6.6	8.7	8.3	7.8	7.3	7.4	9.4	8.9	8.6	11.5	12.1
Other services	8.4	3.9	5.7	5.3	4.8	4.7	3.9	4.4	5.0	5.3	7.1	8.4
Agriculture and related	11.1	9.0	10.2	9.9	8.3	7.2	6.3	9.5	6.1	9.2	18.7	12.3
Government	2.9	2.1	2.8	2.7	2.6	2.3	2.3	2.2	3.0	2.4	3.0	4.4
Self-employed and unpaid family workers	—	2.1	2.7	2.8	2.7	2.7	2.8	3.3	3.3	3.6	6.5	4.4

— = Not available. (1) All monthly rates unadjusted, except for married men and women, which are seasonally adjusted.

Employed Persons in the U.S. by Occupation and Sex, 2007 and 2008

Source: Bureau of Labor Statistics, U.S. Dept. of Labor

(in thousands)

	Total 16 years and older 2007	Total 16 years and older 2008	Men 16 years and older 2007	Men 16 years and older 2008	Women 16 years and older 2007	Women 16 years and older 2008
Total	146,047	145,362	78,254	77,486	67,792	67,876
Management, professional, and related	51,788	52,761	25,593	25,948	26,195	26,813
Management, business, and financial operations	21,577	22,059	12,375	12,647	9,203	9,412
Management	15,486	15,852	9,686	9,925	5,800	5,926
Business and financial operations	6,091	6,207	2,688	2,721	3,403	3,486
Professional and related	30,210	30,702	13,218	13,301	16,992	17,401
Computer and mathematical	3,441	3,676	2,560	2,765	881	911
Architecture and engineering	2,932	2,931	2,511	2,536	421	395
Life, physical, and social science	1,382	1,307	792	704	591	603
Community and social services	2,265	2,293	890	909	1,375	1,383
Legal	1,668	1,671	809	803	858	867
Education, training, and library	8,485	8,605	2,267	2,234	6,218	6,371
Arts, design, entertainment, sports, and media	2,789	2,820	1,476	1,471	1,313	1,349
Healthcare practitioner and technical	7,248	7,399	1,913	1,878	5,335	5,521
Service	24,137	24,451	10,337	10,471	13,800	13,980
Healthcare support	3,138	3,212	338	359	2,800	2,853
Protective service	3,071	3,047	2,380	2,352	691	695
Food preparation and serving related	7,699	7,824	3,354	3,443	4,345	4,381
Building and grounds cleaning and maintenance	5,469	5,445	3,280	3,254	2,189	2,192
Personal care and service	4,760	4,923	986	1,064	3,774	3,859
Sales and office	36,212	35,544	13,264	13,067	22,948	22,477
Sales and related	16,698	16,295	8,424	8,221	8,275	8,073
Office and administrative support	19,513	19,249	4,840	4,845	14,673	14,404
Natural resources, construction, and maintenance	15,740	14,806	15,078	14,181	662	626
Farming, fishing, and forestry	960	988	759	780	201	208
Construction and extraction	9,535	8,667	9,276	8,448	258	219
Installation, maintenance, and repair	5,245	5,152	5,043	4,953	202	199
Production, transportation, and material moving	18,171	17,800	13,983	13,820	4,188	3,980
Production	9,395	8,973	6,563	6,313	2,832	2,661
Transportation and material moving	8,776	8,827	7,420	7,507	1,355	1,319

Note: Updated population controls are introduced annually with the release of January data. Totals may not add because of independent rounding.

Projected Openings for Selected High-Paying Occupations, 2006-16

Source: Bureau of Labor Statistics, U.S. Dept. of Labor

Job openings shown below represent the average number expected each year for workers in the U.S. who are entering these occupations for the first time.

Occupation	Annual avg. job openings[1]	Median annual earnings[2]	Occupation	Annual avg. job openings[1]	Median annual earnings[2]
Registered nurses	100,000	$57,280	First-line retail superv. or mgrs	42,000	$33,960
Postsecondary teachers	66,000	56,120	Secondary school teachers[3]	37,000	47,740
Elementary school teachers[3]	55,000	45,570	First-line office superv. or mgrs	37,000	43,510
Truck drivers, heavy & tractor trailer . .	52,000	35,040	Carpenters	35,000	36,550
Exec. secretaries, admin. assists.	50,000	37,240	Lic. practical and voc. nurses	31,000	36,550
Sales representatives[4]	48,000	49,610	Computer software eng., applications	30,000	79,780
Accountants and auditors	45,000	54,630	Auto mechanics/technicians	27,000	33,780
Gen. and operations mgrs.	44,000	85,230			

(1) As a result of growth and net replacement needs. (2) Median earnings are for 2006. (3) Except special and vocational education. (4) Wholesale and manufacturing, except technical and scientific products.

Top-Paying U.S. Counties by Average Weekly Wage, 4th Quarter 2008

Source: Bureau of Labor Statistics, U.S. Dept. of Labor

County	Avg. weekly wage	% change 4th qtr. 2007-08	County	Avg. weekly wage	% change 4th qtr. 2007-08
New York, NY	$1,856	−0.6%	San Francisco, CA.	$1,491	−2.4%
Fairfield, CT.	1,596	1.1	San Mateo, CA	1,439	−5.4
Washington, DC	1,570	5.1	Fairfax, VA.	1,407	3.5
Suffolk, MA	1,568	1.3	Morris, NJ	1,351	2.5
Santa Clara, CA.	1,566	−7.8	Alexandria City, VA	1,311	5.6
Arlington, VA	1,509	3.1	Middlesex, MA.	1,296	−1.1
St. Louis City, MO	1,508	56.8	Mercer, NJ	1,249	7.7
Somerset, NJ.	1,498	2.9	**United States**	**918**	**2.2**

Note: Hidalgo County, TX, recorded the lowest average weekly earnings among the 335 largest counties, with an average weekly wage of $574 in the fourth quarter of 2008. It was followed by: Horry County, SC ($581); Cameron County, TX ($584); Webb County, TX ($600); San Juan, PR ($621); and Yakima, WA ($624). The top 15 were derived from a list of the 335 largest U.S. counties, which comprise 71.5% of total covered workers. Data includes all workers covered by state and federal unemployment insurance programs.

Federal Minimum Hourly Wage Rates Since 1950

Source: Bureau of Labor Statistics, U.S. Dept. of Labor

Effective date	NONFARM WORKERS Under laws prior to 1966[1]	Percent of avg. earnings[2]	NONFARM WORKERS Under 1966 and later provis.[3]	FARM WORKERS[4]	Effective date	NONFARM WORKERS Under laws prior to 1966[1]	Percent of avg. earnings[2]	NONFARM WORKERS Under 1966 and later provis.[3]	FARM WORKERS[4]
Jan. 25, 1950. . .	$0.75	54%	NA	NA	Jan. 1, 1977. . . .	(5)	(5)	$2.30	$2.20
Mar. 1, 1956. . .	1.00	52	NA	NA	Jan. 1, 1978. . . .	$2.65	44%	2.65	2.65
Sept. 3, 1961. . .	1.15	50	NA	NA	Jan. 1, 1979. . . .	2.90	45	2.90	2.90
Sept. 3, 1963. . .	1.25	51	NA	NA	Jan. 1, 1980. . . .	3.10	43	3.10	3.10
Feb. 1, 1967. . . .	1.40	50	$1.00	$1.00	Jan. 1, 1981. . . .	3.35	42	3.35	3.35
Feb. 1, 1968. . . .	1.60	54	1.15	1.15	Apr. 1, 1990. . . .	3.80[6]	35	3.80	3.80[6]
Feb. 1, 1969. . . .	(5)	(5)	1.30	1.30	Apr. 1, 1991. . . .	4.25[6]	38	4.25	4.25[6]
Feb. 1, 1970. . . .	(5)	(5)	1.45	(5)	Oct. 1, 1996. . . .	4.75[7]	37	4.75	4.75[7]
Feb. 1, 1971. . . .	(5)	(5)	1.60	(5)	Sept. 1, 1997. . . .	5.15[7]	39	5.15	5.15[7]
May 1, 1974. . . .	2.00	46	1.90	1.60	July 24, 2007 . . .	5.85[7]	NA	5.85	5.85[7]
Jan. 1, 1975. . . .	2.10	45	2.00	1.80	July 24, 2008 . . .	6.55[7]	NA	6.55	6.55[7]
Jan. 1, 1976. . . .	2.30	46	2.20	2.00	July 24, 2009 . . .	7.25[7]	NA	7.25	7.25[7]

NA = Not applicable. (1) Applies to workers covered prior to 1961 Amendments and, after Sept. 1965, to workers covered by 1961 Amendments. Rates set by 1961 Amendments were: Sept. 1961, $1.00; Sept. 1964, $1.15; and Sept. 1965, $1.25. (2) Percent of gross average hourly earnings of production workers in manufacturing. (3) Applies to workers newly covered by Amendments of 1966, 1974, and 1977, and Title IX of Education Amendments of 1972. (4) Included in coverage as of 1966, 1974, and 1977 Amendments. (5) No change in rate. (6) Training wage for workers age 16-19 in first 6 months of first job: Apr. 1, 1990, $3.35; Apr. 1, 1991, $3.62. The training wage expired Mar. 31, 1993. (7) Under 1996 legislation, a subminimum training wage of $4.25 an hour was established for employees under 20 years of age during their first 90 consecutive calendar days of employment with an employer. For workers receiving gratuities, the minimum wage remained $2.13 per hour.

Fatal Occupational Injuries, 2008

Source: Bureau of Labor Statistics, U.S. Dept. of Labor, in cooperation with other agencies, Census of Fatal Occupational Injuries

	FATALITIES Number	%		FATALITIES Number	%
Total	**5,071**	**100%**	**Contact with objects and equipment**	**923**	**18%**
			Struck by object or equipment	508	10
Transportation incidents	**2,053**	**40**	Struck by falling object or equipment	349	7
Highway	1,149	23	Struck by flying object or equipment	50	1
Collision bet. vehicles, mobile equipment	562	11	Caught in or compressed by equipment or objects	299	6
Vehicle struck object on side of road	303	6	Caught in running equipment or machinery. . . .	109	2
Noncollision	264	5	Caught in or crushed in collapsing materials.	101	2
Jack-knifed or overturned	230	5			
Nonhighway (farm, industrial premises)	283	6	**Falls**	**680**	**13**
Overturned	151	3	**Exposure to harmful substances or environments**	**432**	**9**
Worker struck by vehicle	322	6	Contact with electric current	192	4
Railway accident.	34	1	Contact with overhead power lines	102	2
Water vehicle accident.	75	1	Contact with temperature extremes.	35	1
Aircraft accident.	189	4	Exposure to caustic, noxious, or allergenic		
			substances	127	3
Assaults and violent acts	**794**	**16**	Inhalation of substance	56	1
Homicides	517	10	Oxygen deficiency	77	2
Shooting	413	8	Drowning, submersion.	59	1
Stabbing	32	1	**Fires and explosions**	**173**	**3**
Self-inflicted injuries.	251	5			

Note: Totals for categories may include subcategories not shown separately. Percentages based on incidence rate per total fatalities.

U.S. Occupational Injuries or Illnesses, by Industry, 2007

Source: Bureau of Labor Statistics, U.S. Dept. of Labor

(percent distribution)

	Private industry [1,2,3]	Goods producing			Service providing					
		Natural resources & mining [1,2]	Con-struc-tion	Manu-facturing	Trade, trans. & utilities [3]	Info.	Financial	Prof. & business	Educ. & health	Leisure and hospitality
Total (1,158,870 cases) ..	100.0%	100.0%	100.0%	100.0%	100.0%	100.0%	100.0%	100.0%	100.0%	100.0%
Nature of injury or illness										
Sprains, strains, tears.....	38.7	32.2	32.8	33.6	41.8	39.5	35.3	37.4	49.9	31.1
Bruises, contusions	8.7	10.3	6.2	8.2	9.6	8.7	5.7	8.8	9.0	10.4
Cuts, lacerations	7.9	8.0	11.5	10.0	7.0	4.4	6.3	6.2	2.8	13.7
Punctures..............	1.4	1.4	3.6	1.9	0.9	0.5	0.4	1.7	0.6	0.6
Fractures	8.2	14.3	12.8	9.0	7.6	8.3	7.6	7.1	5.4	7.2
Heat burns	1.5	1.0	0.9	1.8	0.8	0.4	0.5	0.7	0.9	6.9
Carpal tunnel syndrome...	1.0	0.2	0.2	2.2	0.9	1.6	2.3	1.6	0.7	0.3
Tendonitis.............	0.4	0.2	0.2	0.7	0.3	0.4	0.3	0.5	0.4	0.4
Chemical burns	0.5	0.9	0.4	0.8	0.3	—	1.3	0.4	0.4	1.2
Amputations...........	0.6	1.3	0.6	1.7	0.4	0.1	0.3	0.3	0.1	0.7
Multiple traumatic injuries	4.0	3.6	5.0	3.9	3.8	5.2	3.8	4.6	4.1	2.9
Part of body affected by the injury or illness										
Head.................	6.8	8.9	7.8	7.4	6.5	5.9	7.4	6.8	4.7	7.7
Eye.................	2.8	4.5	3.8	4.4	2.3	1.4	3.4	2.2	1.2	2.9
Neck.................	1.5	1.1	1.4	1.0	1.6	0.9	2.1	1.7	1.9	0.8
Trunk	33.2	29.6	30.4	31.0	35.7	29.8	29.9	30.5	40.9	25.4
Shoulder.............	6.5	5.2	6.1	7.3	7.5	5.5	4.1	5.5	6.8	4.5
Back................	20.4	16.1	16.7	16.6	21.7	18.2	19.8	19.2	29.0	15.5
Upper extremities........	23.2	20.8	23.5	33.1	20.1	18.4	21.7	23.0	16.0	29.9
Arm	4.7	4.3	5.1	5.2	4.6	3.8	4.8	4.0	3.7	4.7
Wrist..............	4.5	2.0	2.8	5.7	4.1	5.3	6.3	6.2	4.3	4.7
Hand, except finger	4.1	3.7	5.5	5.4	3.4	3.0	3.1	3.9	2.3	6.6
Finger..............	8.8	9.7	9.3	15.3	7.0	5.1	6.3	7.4	4.5	12.5
Lower extremities........	22.5	27.9	25.4	18.6	23.7	23.6	22.7	22.4	20.2	24.2
Knee	8.2	9.4	8.8	6.5	8.2	8.6	8.2	7.6	8.5	9.3
Ankle..............	5.4	5.7	6.3	3.6	5.7	5.8	4.9	6.5	5.0	6.5
Foot, except toe.......	3.8	5.7	4.3	3.8	4.2	3.6	4.6	3.3	2.7	3.7
Toe	1.0	0.8	1.2	1.0	1.4	1.3	0.5	0.5	0.6	0.6
Body systems..........	1.5	1.0	1.2	1.2	1.4	3.8	2.0	2.4	1.6	1.3
Multiple parts	10.4	9.8	9.5	7.0	10.0	16.9	12.5	12.4	14.0	9.8
Source of injury or illness										
Chemicals and chemical products	1.5	3.1	1.0	2.1	1.0	1.9	2.1	1.6	1.4	2.4
Containers	11.8	7.3	4.3	11.1	19.6	8.9	7.8	8.1	5.3	16.0
Furniture and fixtures.....	4.0	0.6	2.2	2.8	4.3	2.0	6.3	4.0	5.1	5.8
Machinery	6.0	8.8	6.2	12.4	5.0	4.5	6.3	5.2	2.0	4.7
Parts and materials	10.1	11.4	22.1	18.4	9.2	5.5	3.2	6.0	1.2	1.9
Floors, walkways, ground surfaces	19.9	18.1	21.7	12.9	18.3	26.1	26.9	22.0	23.5	24.8
Tools, instruments, and equipment.........	6.8	6.6	11.4	7.2	5.0	9.1	7.7	7.0	5.0	8.8
Vehicles	8.4	10.1	5.4	5.2	13	8.7	7.6	10.4	5.4	4.7
Person, injured or ill worker	14.7	11.2	12.2	17.6	14.1	21.2	18.7	16.8	12.7	14.6
Worker motion or position	14.2	10.9	11.8	17.3	13.7	20.7	17.8	16.3	12.4	14.3
Person, other than injured or ill worker	5.5	0.3	0.1	0.2	0.8	0.6	1.9	1.8	30.6	2.4
Health-care patient.......	4.4	—	—	—	0.1	—	0.1	0.8	27.3	<0.1
Event or exposure leading to injury or illness										
Contact with objects and equipment.........	27.4	39.4	35.4	37.5	26.5	19.3	21.9	22.8	13.7	29.4
Struck by object	14.1	20.1	19.9	16.6	13.7	8.1	13.1	11.9	7.1	17.2
Struck against object ...	6.5	7.5	7.9	7.2	6.6	6.2	5.6	5.8	4.3	7.8
Caught in equipment or object	4.6	8.6	4.1	10.7	4.2	3.3	2.0	3.4	1.4	2.4
Fall to lower level	6.7	8.4	14.7	3.9	6.5	9.1	9.3	7.4	3.5	4.4
Fall on same level.......	14.4	10.0	9.3	1.00	13.2	17.2	19.5	15.1	20.3	21.3
Slip, trip, loss of balance—without fall........	3.3	3.7	2.8	2.6	3.1	4.4	2.4	4.0	3.8	4.5
Overexertion...........	22.9	14.3	17.4	21.0	26.2	16.7	16.1	18.2	33.6	13.7
Overexertion in lifting ...	12.1	5.8	9.7	10.7	14.8	8.4	8.8	11.0	15.1	8.5

Note: Dashes (—) indicate data are not available. Because of rounding and classifications not shown, percentages may not add to 100. All injuries and illnesses reported involved days away from work. (1) Excludes farms with fewer than 11 employees. (2) Data conforming to OSHA definitions for mining operators in coal, metal, and nonmetal mining are provided by the Mine Safety and Health Administration, U.S. Dept. of Labor. Independent mining contractors are excluded from the coal, metal, and nonmetal industries. Data for mining include establishments not governed by Mine Safety and Health Administration rules, such as those in oil and gas extraction. (3) Data for employers in railroad transportation are provided by the Federal Railroad Administration, U.S. Department of Transportation.

Civilian Employment of the Federal Government, Nov. 2008

Source: Statistical Analysis and Services Division, U.S. Office of Personnel Management

(monthly payroll in thousands of dollars)

	ALL AREAS		UNITED STATES		WASH., DC, MSA[1]		OVERSEAS	
	Employ-ment	Payroll	Employ-ment	Payroll	Employ-ment	Payroll	Employ-ment	Payroll
TOTAL, all agencies[2,3]	2,716,978	$13,516,103	2,628,888	$13,124,522	333,499	$2,287,898	88,090	$391,581
Legislative Branch[2,3]	**29,871**	**181,263**	**29,865**	**181,199**	**28,761**	**172,182**	**6**	**64**
Congress[3]	17,531	97,263	17,531	97,263	17,531	97,263	—	—
U.S. Senate[3]	6,820	38,200	6,820	38,200	6,820	38,200	—	—
House of Representatives[3]	10,711	59,063	10,711	59,063	10,711	59,063	—	—
Architect of the Capitol[3]	2,212	11,404	2,212	11,404	2,212	11,404	—	—
Congressional Budget Ofc.[3]	233	2,119	233	2,119	233	2,119	—	—
Govt. Accountability Ofc.	3,129	28,194	3,129	28,194	2,257	20,337	—	—
Govt. Printing Ofc.[3]	2,378	13,882	2,378	13,882	2,188	12,936	—	—
Library of Congress[3]	3,871	24,700	3,865	24,636	3,831	24,465	6	64
U.S. Tax Court[3]	234	1,633	234	1,633	234	1,633	—	—
Judicial Branch[3]	**33,754**	**187,679**	**33,385**	**185,884**	**2,815**	**18,911**	**369**	**1,795**
Supreme Court[3]	483	2,484	483	2,484	483	2,484	—	—
U.S. courts[3]	33,271	185,195	32,902	183,400	2,332	16,427	369	1,795
Executive Branch	**2,653,353**	**13,147,161**	**2,565,638**	**12,757,439**	**301,923**	**2,096,805**	**87,715**	**389,722**
Exec. Ofc. of the President	1,707	12,815	1,694	12,710	1,694	12,710	13	105
White House Office	401	2,266	401	2,266	401	2,266	—	—
Ofc. of Vice President	17	159	17	159	17	159	—	—
Ofc. of Mgmt. and Budget	485	3,947	485	3,947	485	3,947	—	—
Ofc. of Administration.	234	1,646	234	1,646	234	1,646	—	—
Council Economic Advisors	23	157	23	157	23	157	—	—
Council Environmental Quality . . .	21	147	21	147	21	147	—	—
Ofc. of Policy Development	22	137	22	137	22	137	—	—
National Security Council.	58	411	58	411	58	411	—	—
Ofc. of Natl. Drug Control Policy .	98	829	98	829	98	829	—	—
Ofc. of U.S. Trade Rep.	228	2,160	215	2,055	215	2,055	13	105
Executive Departments	1,746,063	8,877,343	1,664,491	8,520,106	238,474	1,646,155	81,572	357,237
State.	36,472	241,904	14,788	92,305	11,981	73,813	21,684	149,599
Treasury	88,245	581,951	87,648	578,965	11,631	115,101	597	2,986
Defense, total.	699,103	2,530,457	652,087	2,396,970	68,179	271,195	47,016	133,487
Defense, mil. function.	676,696	2,469,943	629,732	2,336,537	67,461	269,372	46,964	133,406
Defense, civ. function	22,407	60,514	22,355	60,433	718	1,823	52	81
Dept. of the Army	264,241	729,339	244,324	672,556	20,285	43,469	19,917	56,783
Army, mil. function	241,835	668,826	221,970	612,124	19,568	41,647	19,865	56,702
Army, civil function	22,406	60,513	22,354	60,432	717	1,822	52	81
Corps of Engineers	22,334	60,330	22,282	60,249	645	1,639	52	81
Dept. of the Navy	182,329	737,852	175,238	709,100	24,780	100,351	7,091	28,752
Dept. of the Air Force	154,778	626,003	148,919	602,323	5,844	23,652	5,859	23,680
Defense Logist. Agency	22,624	93,931	22,044	89,381	2,029	11,452	580	4,550
Other defense activities	75,131	343,332	61,562	323,610	15,241	92,271	13,569	19,722
Justice	110,032	705,909	108,041	691,952	23,853	178,928	1,991	13,957
Interior	67,528	335,163	67,186	333,930	7,407	47,514	342	1,233
Agriculture	82,437	476,177	81,659	471,483	7,877	77,408	778	4,694
Commerce	39,220	316,683	38,940	313,929	19,809	207,651	280	2,754
Labor	16,238	114,854	16,201	114,629	5,798	45,674	37	225
Health and Human Services	64,072	412,237	63,778	410,023	29,893	216,489	294	2,214
Housing and Urban Dev.	8,868	68,767	8,800	68,302	3,102	25,811	68	465
Transportation	55,810	431,948	55,487	429,924	9,233	76,464	323	2,024
Energy	15,215	122,302	15,198	122,121	5,134	46,774	17	181
Education.	4,160	31,006	4,150	30,947	3,030	23,272	10	59
Veterans Affairs	283,491	1,518,326	279,536	1,500,728	8,209	63,345	3,955	17,598
Homeland Security.	175,172	989,659	170,992	963,898	23,338	176,716	4,180	25,761
Independent agencies[2,3]	**905,583**	**4,257,003**	**899,453**	**4,224,623**	**61,755**	**437,940**	**6,130**	**32,380**
Bd. of Govt., Fed. Rsrv. Sys.[3]	1,873	13,535	1,873	13,535	1,873	13,535	—	—
Environmtl. Protect. Agcy.	18,249	130,000	18,189	129,656	5,308	36,393	60	344
Equal Employ. Opp. Comm.	2,198	13,843	2,189	13,798	484	3,701	9	45
Federal Communic. Comm.	1,776	15,355	1,774	15,336	1,508	13,202	2	19
Federal Deposit Ins. Corp.	5,100	41,847	5,085	41,763	1,556	14,676	15	84
Federal Trade Comm.[3]	1,131	8,533	1,131	8,533	976	7,287	—	—
General Svcs. Admin.	12,021	79,600	11,968	79,303	4,134	31,180	53	297
Natl. Aero. and Space Admin.	18,445	146,783	18,432	146,660	4,020	34,022	13	123
Natl. Fdn. Arts & Humanities[3]	400	3,324	400	3,324	399	3,319	—	—
Natl. Science Foundation	1,395	11,321	1,389	11,268	1,386	11,252	6	53
Nuclear Regulatory Comm.	4,088	33,311	4,087	33,296	2,960	24,868	1	15
Ofc. Personnel Management	5,433	31,130	5,414	31,095	1,670	13,298	19	35
Peace Corps	979	5,863	622	3,744	511	3,234	357	2,119
Securities and Exch. Comm.	3,664	37,420	3,664	37,420	2,181	21,876	—	—
Small Business Adm.	5,018	30,346	4,917	29,836	957	7,306	101	510
Smithsonian Inst.[3]	4,512	29,008	4,490	28,827	4,152	26,588	22	181
Social Security Admin.	63,975	336,191	63,563	334,407	1,666	10,031	412	1,784
Tennessee Valley Authority	11,515	86,898	11,515	86,898	5	42	—	—
U.S. Postal Service	723,171	3,057,562	719,737	3,041,051	13,959	69,936	3,434	16,511

— = Not applicable. (1) Metropolitan Statistical Area. (2) Totals include agencies not listed. (3) Denotes figures that are preliminary or are based in whole or part on figures for the previous month.

U.S. Median Weekly Earnings, 2nd Quarter 2009*

Source: Bureau of Labor Statistics, U.S. Dept. of Labor

AGE, RACE, HISPANIC OR LATINO ETHNICITY	Total Number of workers (thousands)	Total Median weekly earnings	Men Number of workers (thousands)	Men Median weekly earnings	Women Number of workers (thousands)	Women Median weekly earnings
All workers, by age						
16 years and over.	100,130	$734	55,419	$815	44,711	$652
16 to 24 years	9,039	432	5,128	450	3,911	413
16 to 19 years	1,211	327	695	340	515	317
20 to 24 years	7,828	455	4,433	471	3,395	435
25 years and over.	91,091	770	50,290	872	40,801	679
25 to 54 years	73,878	762	41,032	854	32,846	674
25 to 34 years	24,027	672	13,500	710	10,527	632
35 to 44 years	24,624	823	13,942	915	10,682	699
45 to 54 years	25,227	824	13,591	961	11,636	703
55 years and over.	17,213	823	9,258	945	7,955	703
55 to 64 years	14,618	840	7,797	964	6,821	721
65 years and over.	2,594	705	1,461	826	1,134	635
White[1]						
16 years and over.	81,012	754	45,921	842	35,091	666
16 to 24 years	7,432	443	4,251	462	3,181	422
25 years and over.	73,580	797	41,670	896	31,910	698
25 to 54 years	59,158	785	33,744	879	25,413	694
55 years and over.	14,422	852	7,926	963	6,497	717
Black or African American[1]						
16 years and over.	11,785	592	5,436	620	6,349	567
16 to 24 years	1,031	395	509	412	522	374
25 years and over.	10,754	613	4,926	660	5,827	583
25 to 54 years	9,060	610	4,163	649	4,897	583
55 years and over.	1,694	643	763	730	930	583
Asian[1]						
16 years and over.	4,976	909	2,739	969	2,237	781
16 to 24 years	272	451	180	475	93	430
25 years and over.	4,704	938	2,560	1,009	2,145	813
25 to 54 years	3,908	950	2,127	1,060	1,782	810
55 years and over.	796	841	433	856	363	829
Hispanic and Latino[2]						
16 years and over.	14,900	547	9,265	575	5,635	511
16 to 24 years	1,802	416	1,105	424	697	401
25 years and over.	13,099	582	8,161	605	4,938	535
25 to 54 years	11,601	580	7,277	603	4,324	531
55 years and over.	1,497	599	84	628	613	564
OCCUPATION						
Managerial, professional, and related	38,820	1,046	18,979	1,250	19,841	900
Management, business, and financial	15,634	1,145	8,630	1,342	7,004	968
Professional and related	23,186	994	10,348	1,188	12,838	862
Service.	14,530	468	7,225	520	7,305	419
Sales and office	23,747	622	9,078	726	14,669	589
Sales and related.	9,575	665	5,349	782	4,226	541
Office and administrative support.	14,172	607	3,729	638	10,442	599
Natural resources, construction, and maintenance	10,469	707	10,021	716	448	548
Farming, fishing, and forestry.	736	440	589	455	147	394
Construction and extraction.	5,325	702	5,192	704	133	629
Installation, maintenance, and repair.	4,407	763	4,240	772	167	563
Production, transportation, and material moving	12,564	611	10,115	656	2,448	478
Production.	6,453	622	4,774	696	1,679	479
Transportation and material moving.	6,111	595	5,341	616	769	476

*Not seasonally adjusted; figures are for median usual weekly earnings of full-time wage and salary workers. (1) Persons who selected this race group only; persons who selected more than one race group are not included. (2) May be of any race.

Average Hours and Earnings of U.S. Production Workers, 1969-2008[1]

Source: Bureau of Labor Statistics, U.S. Dept. of Labor
(annual averages)

	Weekly hours	Hourly earnings	Weekly earnings		Weekly hours	Hourly earnings	Weekly earnings		Weekly hours	Hourly earnings	Weekly earnings
1969 . . .	37.5	$3.22	$120.75	1983	34.9	$8.20	$286.18	1996 . . .	34.3	$12.04	$413.28
1970 . . .	37.0	3.40	125.80	1984	35.1	8.49	298.00	1997 . . .	34.5	12.51	431.86
1971 . . .	36.8	3.63	133.58	1985	34.9	8.74	305.03	1998 . . .	34.5	13.01	448.56
1972 . . .	36.9	3.90	143.91	1986	34.7	8.93	309.87	1999 . . .	34.3	13.49	463.15
1973 . . .	36.9	4.14	152.77	1987	34.7	9.14	317.16	2000 . . .	34.3	14.02	481.01
1974 . . .	36.4	4.43	161.25	1988	34.6	9.44	326.62	2001 . . .	34.0	14.54	493.79
1975 . . .	36.0	4.73	170.28	1989	34.5	9.80	338.10	2002 . . .	33.9	14.97	506.72
1976 . . .	36.1	5.06	182.67	1990	34.3	10.20	349.75	2003 . . .	33.7	15.37	518.06
1977 . . .	35.9	5.44	195.30	1991	34.1	10.52	358.51	2004 . . .	33.7	15.69	529.09
1978 . . .	35.8	5.88	210.50	1992	34.2	10.77	368.25	2005 . . .	33.8	16.13	544.33
1979 . . .	35.6	6.34	225.70	1993	34.3	11.05	378.89	2006 . . .	33.9	16.76	567.87
1980 . . .	35.2	6.85	241.12	1994	34.5	11.34	391.22	2007 . . .	33.9	17.43	589.04
1981 . . .	35.2	7.44	261.89	1995	34.3	11.65	400.07	2008 . . .	33.6	18.08	607.99
1982 . . .	34.7	7.87	273.09								

(1) Data refer to production workers in natural resources, mining and manufacturing, construction workers, and non-supervisory workers in the service industries. Figures may be revised.

Elderly in U.S. Labor Force, 1890-2008

Source: Bureau of the Census, U.S. Dept. of Commerce

(labor force participation rate; 1910 figures not available)

□ Men
■ Women

	1890	1900	1920	1930	1940	1950	1960	1970	1980	1990	2000	2008
Men	68.3	63.1	55.6	54.0	41.8	45.8	33.1	26.8	19.0	16.3	17.7	21.5
Women	7.6	8.3	7.3	7.3	6.1	9.7	10.8	9.7	8.1	8.6	9.4	13.3

Union Affiliation and Median Weekly Earnings of Wage and Salary Workers in the U.S., 1996, 2008

Source: Bureau of Labor Statistics, U.S. Dept. of Labor

	1996				2008			
Sex and age	Total	Members of unions[1]	Represented by unions[2]	Non-union	Total	Members of unions[1]	Represented by unions[2]	Non-union
Total, 16 years and older	$490	$615	$610	$462	$722	$886	$880	$691
16 to 24 years	298	371	362	294	443	560	549	434
25 years and older	520	625	621	498	761	903	898	736
25 to 34 years	463	554	548	447	666	801	793	645
35 to 44 years	559	636	632	530	804	933	926	775
45 to 54 years	594	687	686	552	822	944	941	785
55 to 64 years	535	620	616	505	825	927	922	790
65 years and older	384	510	510	367	644	771	773	627
Men, 16 years and older	557	653	651	520	798	939	937	766
16 to 24 years	307	375	369	303	461	571	565	451
25 years and older	599	669	668	580	857	957	956	828
25 to 34 years	499	591	587	485	704	845	839	682
35 to 44 years	632	683	683	617	915	994	991	896
45 to 54 years	698	718	721	682	944	1,003	1,005	922
55 to 64 years	643	667	664	633	943	967	965	935
65 years and older	477	589	593	424	753	864	886	736
Women, 16 years and older	418	549	543	398	638	809	800	615
16 to 24 years	284	358	339	280	420	546	530	416
25 years and older	444	560	555	420	670	825	818	645
25 to 34 years	415	497	495	405	623	748	740	609
35 to 44 years	463	561	556	439	682	842	838	657
45 to 54 years	481	620	616	445	707	853	847	674
55 to 64 years	420	524	523	395	711	875	866	675
65 years and older	334	417	413	321	563	693	672	542

Note: Data refer to the sole or principal job of full-time workers. Excluded are self-employed workers regardless of whether or not their businesses are incorporated. (1) Including members of an employee association similar to a union. (2) Including members of a labor union or employee association similar to a union, and others whose jobs are covered by a union or an employee-association contract.

Work Stoppages (Strikes and Lockouts) in the U.S., 1950-2008[1]

Source: Bureau of Labor Statistics, U.S. Dept. of Labor; involving 1,000 workers or more

Year	Number[1]	Workers (thous.)	Days idle (thous.)	Year	Number[1]	Workers (thous.)	Days idle (thous.)	Year	Number[1]	Workers (thous.)	Days idle (thous.)
1950....	424	1,698	30,390	1983.....	81	909	17,461	1996	37	273	4,889
1955....	363	2,055	21,180	1984.....	62	376	8,499	1997	29	339	4,497
1960....	222	896	13,260	1985.....	54	324	7,079	1998	34	387	5,116
1965....	268	999	15,140	1986.....	69	533	11,861	1999	17	73	1,996
1970....	381	2,468	52,761	1987.....	46	174	4,481	2000	39	394	20,419
1975....	235	965	17,563	1988.....	40	118	4,381	2001	29	99	1,151
1976....	231	1,519	23,962	1989.....	51	452	16,996	2002	19	46	660
1977....	298	1,212	21,258	1990.....	44	185	5,926	2003	14	129	4,091
1978....	219	1,006	23,774	1991.....	40	392	4,584	2004	17	171	3,344
1979....	235	1,021	20,409	1992.....	35	364	3,989	2005	22	100	1,736
1980....	187	795	20,844	1993.....	35	182	3,981	2006	20	70	2,688
1981....	145	729	16,908	1994.....	45	322	5,020	2007	21	189	1,265
1982....	96	656	9,061	1995.....	31	192	5,771	2008	15	72	1,954

(1) Numbers cover stoppages that began in the year indicated. Workers are counted more than once if they are involved in more than 1 stoppage during the year. For work stoppages ongoing at the end of a calendar year, days idle include only the days for the calendar year.

U.S. Union Membership, 1930-2008[1]

Source: Bureau of Labor Statistics, U.S. Dept. of Labor

(figures in thousands)

Year	Total employed[1]	% in unions	Union members[2]	Year	Total employed[1]	% in unions	Union members[2]	Year	Total employed[1]	% in unions	Union members[2]
1930....	29,424	11.6%	3,401	1965....	60,815	28.4%	17,299	1995 ...	110,038	14.9%	16,360
1935....	27,053	13.2	3,584	1970....	70,920	27.3	19,381	2000 ...	120,786	13.5	16,258
1940....	32,376	26.9	8,717	1975....	76,945	25.5	19,611	2005[4]...	125,889	12.5	15,685
1945....	40,394	35.5	14,322	1980....	90,564	21.9	19,843	2006[4]...	128,237	12.0	15,359
1950....	45,222	31.5	14,267	1985....	94,521	18.0	16,996	2007[4]...	129,767	12.1	15,670
1955....	50,675	33.2	16,802	1990....	103,905	16.1	16,740	2008 ...	129,377	12.4	16,098
1960....	54,234	31.4	17,049								

(1) Does not include agricultural employment; from 1985, does not include self-employed or unemployed persons. (2) From 1930 to 1980, includes dues-paying members of traditional trade unions, regardless of employment status; after that includes employed only. From 1985, includes members of employee associations that engage in collective bargaining with employers. (3) Revised to incorporate changes to the class of worker status associated with the introduction of the 2002 Census industry and occupational classification systems into the Current Population Survey. (4) Data reflect revised population controls used in the household survey.

ENERGY

U.S. Energy Overview, 1960-2008

Source: Energy Information Administration, U.S. Dept. of Energy, *Annual Energy Review 2008*; in quadrillion Btu

	1960	1965	1970	1975	1980	1985	1990	1995	2000	2005	2008P
Production	42.80	50.68	63.50	61.36	67.23	67.80	70.87	71.32	71.49	69.63	73.71
Fossil fuels	39.87	47.23	59.19	54.73	59.01	57.54	58.56	57.54	57.37	55.06	57.94
Coal[1]	10.82	13.06	14.61	14.99	18.60	19.33	22.49	22.13	22.74	23.19	23.86
Natural gas (dry)	12.66	15.78	21.67	19.64	19.91	16.98	18.33	19.08	19.66	18.57	21.15
Crude oil[2]	14.93	16.52	20.40	17.73	18.25	18.99	15.57	13.89	12.36	10.96	10.52
Natural gas plant liquids (NGPL)	1.46	1.88	2.51	2.37	2.25	2.24	2.17	2.44	2.61	2.33	2.41
Nuclear electric power	0.01	0.04	0.24	1.90	2.74	4.08	6.10	7.08	7.86	8.16	8.46
Renewable energy	2.93	3.40	4.08	4.72	5.49	6.18	6.21	6.70	6.26	6.41	7.32
Conventional hydroelectric power[3]	1.61	2.06	2.63	3.15	2.90	2.97	3.05	3.21	2.81	2.70	2.45
Biomass[4]	1.32	1.33	1.43	1.50	2.48	3.02	2.74	3.10	3.01	3.12	3.90
Geothermal energy	(*)	(*)	0.01	0.07	0.11	0.20	0.34	0.29	0.32	0.34	0.36
Solar	NA	NA	NA	NA	NA	(*)	0.06	0.07	0.07	0.07	0.09
Wind	NA	NA	NA	NA	NA	(*)	0.03	0.03	0.06	0.18	0.51
Imports	4.19	5.89	8.34	14.03	15.80	11.78	18.82	22.26	28.97	34.71	32.84
Coal	0.01	(*)	(*)	0.02	0.03	0.05	0.07	0.24	0.31	0.76	0.86
Natural gas	0.16	0.47	0.85	0.98	1.01	0.95	1.55	2.90	3.87	4.45	4.06
All crude oil and petroleum prods.[5]	4.00	5.40	7.47	12.95	14.66	10.61	17.12	18.88	24.53	29.25	27.56
Electricity[6]	0.02	0.01	0.02	0.04	0.09	0.16	0.06	0.15	0.17	0.15	0.19
Fuel ethanol	NA	NA	NA	NA	NA	NA	NA	(*)	(*)	0.01	0.84
Exports	1.48	1.83	2.63	2.32	3.69	4.20	4.75	4.51	4.01	4.56	7.06
Coal	1.02	1.38	1.94	1.76	2.42	2.44	2.77	2.32	1.53	1.27	2.07
Natural gas	0.01	0.03	0.07	0.07	0.05	0.06	0.09	0.16	0.25	0.74	1.01
All crude oil and petroleum prods.[5]	0.43	0.39	0.55	0.44	1.16	1.66	1.82	1.99	2.15	2.44	3.77
Electricity[6]	(*)	0.01	0.01	0.02	0.01	0.02	0.06	0.01	0.05	0.07	0.08
Consumption	45.09	54.02	67.84	72.00	78.12	76.49	84.65	91.17	98.98	100.51	99.30
Fossil fuels	42.14	50.58	63.52	65.35	69.83	66.09	72.33	77.26	84.73	85.82	83.44
Coal	9.84	11.58	12.26	12.66	15.42	17.48	19.17	20.09	22.58	22.80	22.42
Coal coke net imports	−0.01	−0.02	−0.06	0.01	−0.04	−0.01	0.00	0.06	0.07	0.04	0.04
Natural gas[7]	12.39	15.77	21.80	19.95	20.24	17.70	19.60	22.67	23.82	22.58	23.84
Petroleum[8]	19.92	23.25	29.52	32.73	34.20	30.92	33.55	34.44	38.26	40.39	37.14
Nuclear electric power	0.01	0.04	0.24	1.90	2.74	4.08	6.10	7.08	7.86	8.16	8.46
Renewable energy	2.93	3.40	4.08	4.72	5.49	6.18	6.21	6.71	6.26	6.42	7.30
Conventional hydroelectric power[3]	1.61	2.06	2.63	3.15	2.90	2.97	3.05	3.21	2.81	2.70	2.45
Biomass[4]	1.32	1.33	1.43	1.50	2.48	3.02	2.74	3.10	3.01	3.13	3.88
Geothermal energy	(*)	(*)	0.01	0.07	0.11	0.20	0.34	0.29	0.32	0.34	0.36
Solar	NA	NA	NA	NA	NA	(*)	0.06	0.07	0.07	0.07	0.09
Wind	NA	NA	NA	NA	NA	(*)	0.03	0.03	0.06	0.18	0.51

NA = Not available. P = preliminary. (*) = Less than 0.005 quadrillion Btu. **Note:** Some figures have been revised. Some totals may not add because of rounding. (1) Incl. waste coal supplied beginning in 1989 and refuse recovery beginning in 2001. (2) Incl. lease condensate. (3) Starting in 1990, pumped storage is removed and expanded coverage of industrial use of hydroelectric power is included. (4) Substituted in 2000 for former "wood, waste, and alcohol" category. Includes wood, waste, and alcohol fuels (ethanol blended into motor gasoline). Ethanol is included in both "Petroleum" and "Biomass" categories, but is only counted once in totals. (5) Incl. imports of crude oil for the Strategic Petroleum Reserve, which began in 1977. (6) Small amts. of electricity transmitted across borders with Canada and Mexico. (7) Incl. supplemental gaseous fuels. (8) Petroleum products supplied, incl. natural gas plant liquids and crude oil burned as fuel.

U.S. Energy Flow, 2008[1]

Source: Energy Information Administration, U.S. Dept. of Energy, *Annual Energy Review 2008*; in quadrillion Btu

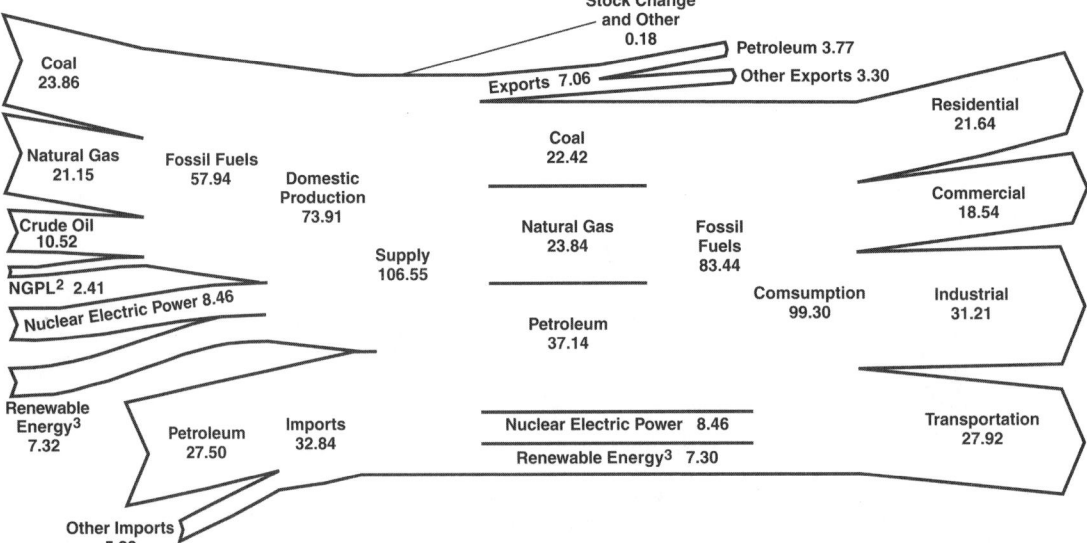

Note: Some totals may not add because of rounding. (1) Preliminary figures. (2) Natural Gas Plant Liquids. (3) Conventional hydro-electric power; wood, waste, and ethanol blended into gasoline; geothermal; solar; and wind power.

U.S. Energy Consumption by Source, 1949-2008

Source: Energy Information Administration, U.S. Dept. of Energy, *Annual Energy Review 2008*

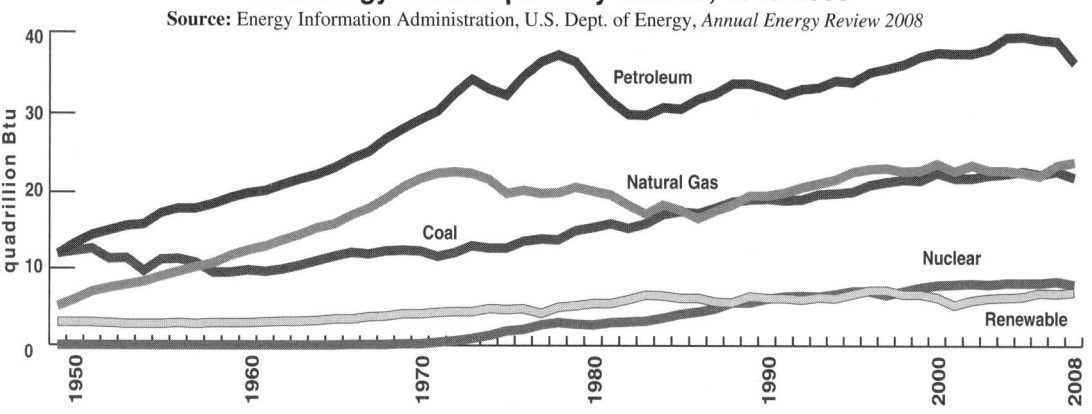

World's Largest Energy Producers and Consumers, 1980-2006

Source: Energy Information Administration, U.S. Dept. of Energy, *International Energy Annual 2008*

(primary energy in quadrillion Btu, ranked by top producers/consumers in 2006)

Production	1980	1985	1990	1995	2000	2005	2006	% change, 1980-2006
1. United States	67.233	67.798	70.871	71.319	71.490	69.640	71.025	5.6%
2. China	18.122	24.303	29.385	35.140	35.343	63.229	67.738	273.8
3. Russia	NA	NA	NA	41.776	43.603	52.717	53.341	NA
4. Saudi Arabia.	22.434	8.642	15.920	20.659	21.593	25.508	24.681	10.0
5. Canada.	10.276	12.020	13.403	16.830	18.124	19.087	19.250	87.3
6. Iran	3.944	5.587	7.670	9.347	10.400	13.012	13.119	232.6
7. India	3.101	5.266	6.821	9.484	9.831	11.731	12.388	299.5
8. Australia.	3.263	4.888	6.169	7.436	9.677	11.226	11.402	249.4
9. Mexico	5.734	7.867	7.709	8.033	9.340	10.261	10.349	80.5
10. Norway.	2.929	3.771	5.804	8.347	10.270	10.658	10.232	249.3

Consumption	1980	1985	1990	1995	2000	2005	2006	% change, 1980-2006
1. United States	78.121	76.491	84.652	91.173	98.975	100.691	99.856	27.8%
2. China	17.503	22.006	26.999	34.850	37.488	67.093	73.808	321.7
3. Russia	NA	NA	NA	28.299	27.709	30.293	30.386	NA
4. Japan	15.210	15.698	18.488	20.643	22.278	22.572	22.786	49.8
5. India	4.041	5.914	7.879	11.442	13.461	16.205	17.677	337.4
6. Germany[1].	14.872	14.874	14.832	14.326	14.261	14.506	14.629	−1.6
7. Canada.	9.695	10.152	10.997	12.202	12.932	14.308	13.950	43.9
8. France	8.389	8.350	9.126	10.051	10.854	11.433	11.445	36.4
9. United Kingdom	8.841	8.735	9.277	9.460	9.706	10.015	9.802	10.9
10. Brazil	4.017	4.584	5.748	7.019	8.573	9.332	9.635	139.9
Total world production	**287.594**	**307.259**	**349.833**	**363.933**	**396.263**	**460.139**	**469.412**	**63.2%**
Total world consumption	**283.481**	**308.494**	**347.424**	**365.046**	**398.134**	**462.798**	**472.274**	**66.6%**

NA = Not available. (1) Data for Germany 1980-90 represents sum of figures for East and West Germany and may not be directly comparable.

Gasoline Retail Prices in Selected Countries, 1990-2008

Source: Energy Information Administration, U.S. Dept. of Energy, *Annual Energy Review 2008*

(average price in dollars per gallon, including taxes)

Year	Regular unleaded									Premium unleaded						
	Australia	Canada	China	Germany	Japan	Mexico	S. Korea	Taiwan	U.S.	France	Italy	S. Africa	Spain	Thailand	UK	U.S.
1990	NA	$1.87	NA	$2.65	$3.16	$1.00	$2.05	$2.49	$1.16	$3.63	$4.59	NA	NA	NA	$2.82	$1.35
1991	$1.96	1.92	NA	2.90	3.46	1.30	2.49	2.39	1.14	3.45	4.50	NA	NA	NA	3.01	1.32
1992	1.89	1.73	NA	3.27	3.58	1.50	2.65	2.42	1.13	3.56	4.53	NA	$3.50	$1.35	3.06	1.32
1993	1.73	1.57	NA	3.07	4.16	1.56	2.88	2.27	1.11	3.41	3.68	NA	3.01	1.26	2.84	1.30
1994	1.84	1.45	NA	3.52	4.36	1.48	2.87	2.14	1.11	3.59	3.70	NA	2.99	1.21	2.99	1.31
1995	1.95	1.53	NA	3.96	4.43	1.11	2.94	2.23	1.15	4.26	4.00	NA	3.24	1.25	3.21	1.34
1996	2.12	1.61	NA	3.94	3.64	1.25	3.18	2.15	1.23	4.41	4.39	NA	3.32	1.49	3.34	1.41
1997	2.05	1.62	NA	3.53	3.26	1.47	3.34	2.23	1.23	4.00	4.07	$1.72	3.01	1.27	3.83	1.42
1998	1.63	1.38	NA	3.34	2.82	1.49	3.04	1.86	1.06	3.87	3.84	1.51	2.80	1.09	4.06	1.25
1999	1.72	1.52	NA	3.42	3.27	1.79	3.80	1.86	1.17	3.85	3.87	1.55	2.82	1.22	4.29	1.36
2000	1.94	1.86	NA	3.45	3.65	2.01	4.18	2.15	1.51	3.80	3.77	1.78	2.86	1.38	4.58	1.69
2001	1.71	1.72	$1.22	3.40	3.27	2.20	3.76	2.02	1.46	3.51	3.57	1.59	2.73	1.33	4.13	1.66
2002	1.76	1.69	1.21	3.67	3.15	2.24	3.84	1.93	1.36	3.62	3.74	1.41	2.90	1.35	4.16	1.56
2003	2.19	1.99	1.33	4.59	3.47	2.04	4.11	2.16	1.59	4.35	4.53	1.91	3.49	1.52	4.70	1.78
2004	2.72	2.37	1.48	5.24	3.93	2.03	4.51	2.46	1.88	4.99	5.29	2.58	4.09	1.76	5.56	2.07
2005	3.23	2.89	1.70	5.66	4.28	2.22	5.28	2.76	2.30	5.46	5.74	3.05	4.49	2.25	5.97	2.49
2006	3.54	3.26	2.11	6.03	4.47	2.31	5.92	3.05	2.59	5.88	6.10	3.42	4.84	2.76	6.36	2.81
2007	3.85	3.59	2.29	6.88	4.49	2.40	6.21	3.20	2.80	6.60	6.73	3.64	5.36	3.20	7.13	3.03
2008	4.45	4.08	3.11	7.75	5.74	2.45	5.83	3.53	3.27	7.51	7.63	4.13	6.13	4.01	7.42	3.52

NA = Not available. **Note:** Some countries report only premium averages and some do not sell unleaded regular gasoline.

Gasoline Retail Prices, U.S. City Average, 1974-2009

Source: Energy Information Administration, U.S. Dept. of Energy, *Monthly Energy Review*, Sept. 2009

(in cents per gallon, including taxes)

Average	Leaded regular	Unleaded regular	Unleaded premium	All types[1]	Average	Leaded regular	Unleaded regular	Unleaded premium	All types[1]
1974..........	53.2	NA	NA	NA	1992	NA	112.7	131.6	119.0
1975..........	56.7	NA	NA	NA	1993	NA	110.8	130.2	117.3
1976..........	59.0	61.4	NA	NA	1994	NA	111.2	130.5	117.4
1977..........	62.2	65.6	NA	NA	1995	NA	114.7	133.6	120.5
1978..........	62.6	67.0	NA	65.2	1996	NA	123.1	141.3	128.8
1979..........	85.7	90.3	NA	88.2	1997	NA	123.4	141.6	129.1
1980..........	119.1	124.5	NA	122.1	1998	NA	105.9	125.0	111.5
1981[2]	131.1	137.8	147.0	135.3	1999	NA	116.5	135.7	122.1
1982..........	122.2	129.6	141.5	128.1	2000	NA	151.0	169.3	156.3
1983..........	115.7	124.1	138.3	122.5	2001	NA	146.1	165.7	153.1
1984..........	112.9	121.2	136.6	119.8	2002	NA	135.8	157.8	144.1
1985..........	111.5	120.2	134.0	119.6	2003	NA	159.1	177.7	163.8
1986..........	85.7	92.7	108.5	93.1	2004	NA	188.0	206.8	192.3
1987..........	89.7	94.8	109.3	95.7	2005	NA	229.5	249.1	233.8
1988..........	89.9	94.6	110.7	96.3	2006	NA	258.9	280.5	263.5
1989..........	99.8	102.1	119.7	106.0	2007	NA	280.1	303.3	284.9
1990..........	114.9	116.4	134.9	121.7	2008	NA	326.6	351.9	331.7
1991..........	NA	114.0	132.1	119.6	2009 (Aug.)	NA	262.7	288.7	267.7

Note: Until unleaded gas became available in 1976, leaded was the only type used in automobiles. Average retail prices (in cents per gallon) for selected years preceding those in the table above were as follows: 1950: 27; 1955: 29; 1960: 31; 1965: 31; 1970: 36. Covers 56 urban areas (1974-77), 85 urban areas for 1978 and after. NA = Not applicable. (1) Also includes types of motor gasoline not shown separately. (2) In Sept. 1981, the Bureau of Labor Statistics changed the weights in the calculation of average motor gasoline prices. Starting in Sept. 1981, gasohol is included in average for all types, and unleaded premium is weighted more heavily.

Energy Consumption, Total and Per Capita, by State, 2007

Source: Energy Information Administration, U.S. Dept. of Energy, *State Energy Data Report 2007*

	Total Consumption					Consumption Per Capita		
Rank/State	Trillion Btu	Rank/State	Trillion Btu	Rank/State	Million Btu	Rank/State	Million Btu
1. Texas........	11,834.5	27. Colorado.....	1,479.3	1. Alaska.......	1,062.3	27. Missouri	334.1
2. California.....	8,491.5	28. Mississippi....	1,239.5	2. Wyoming.....	948.6	28. Wisconsin....	329.8
3. Florida.......	4,601.9	29. Iowa	1,235.2	3. Louisiana.....	861.2	29. Georgia......	329.0
4. New York.....	4,064.3	30. Arkansas.....	1,149.3	4. North Dakota .	671.1	30. Pennsylvania .	322.6
5. Ohio.........	4,048.9	31. Kansas	1,136.2	5. Texas	496.3	31. Washington ..	320.5
6. Illinois	4,043.2	32. Oregon	1,108.2	6. Montana	483.1	32. Wash., DC ...	318.5
7. Pennsylvania .	4,006.2	33. Connecticut...	870.7	7. Kentucky.....	477.5	33. New Jersey ..	317.1
8. Louisiana.....	3,766.2	34. West Virginia..	850.5	8. West Virginia .	469.9	34. Illinois.......	315.2
9. Georgia......	3,133.0	35. Utah	805.5	9. Alabama.....	460.8	35. Colorado.....	305.5
10. Michigan	3,026.9	36. Nevada	777.4	10. Indiana	458.4	36. Nevada......	304.3
11. Indiana.......	2,904.0	37. Alaska.......	723.6	11. Oklahoma....	445.8	37. Utah	301.8
12. New Jersey ..	2,743.7	38. New Mexico ..	710.7	12. Mississippi ...	424.3	38. Michigan.....	301.2
13. North Carolina .	2,700.0	39. Nebraska.....	692.9	13. Iowa	414.0	39. North Carolina	298.6
14. Virginia	2,610.9	40. Idaho........	529.6	14. Kansas	409.1	40. Oregon......	296.7
15. Tennessee....	2,330.5	41. Wyoming.....	496.4	15. Arkansas.....	406.1	41. Hawaii	269.1
16. Alabama	2,132.0	42. Montana	462.1	16. Nebraska....	391.6	42. Maryland	265.0
17. Washington ..	2,067.2	43. Maine	455.6	17. South Carolina	384.2	43. Vermont	261.2
18. Kentucky	2,023.0	44. North Dakota..	428.1	18. Tennessee ...	379.0	44. Florida	252.9
19. Missouri......	1,964.1	45. Hawaii.......	343.7	19. South Dakota .	367.2	45. Connecticut ..	249.5
20. Minnesota	1,874.6	46. New Hampshire	314.2	20. New Mexico ..	361.8	46. Arizona......	248.3
21. Wisconsin	1,846.3	47. Delaware.....	302.0	21. Minnesota....	361.7	47. New Hampshire	239.5
22. South Carolina .	1,692.3	48. South Dakota .	292.2	22. Idaho........	354.0	48. Massachusetts	234.2
23. Oklahoma	1,608.5	49. Rhode Island..	217.6	23. Ohio........	352.8	49. California	233.4
24. Arizona	1,577.8	50. Wash., DC....	187.2	24. Delaware	350.4	50. New York	209.2
25. Massachusetts	1,514.6	51. Vermont	162.1	25. Maine	346.3	51. Rhode Island ..	206.6
26. Maryland	1,488.7	**U.S. ....**	**101,468.0[1]**	26. Virginia	339.1	**U.S. ....**	**336.8**

(1) Includes 25.2 tril Btu in coal coke imports and 378.0 tril Btu of energy losses and co-products from the production of fuel ethanol not allocated to states.

U.S. Production of Crude Oil by State, 2008

Source: Energy Information Administration, *Petroleum Supply Monthly*, Oct. 2009

(in thousand barrels)

State	Total	State	Total	State	Total	State	Total
1. Texas........	398,014	9. Kansas	39,582	17. Arkansas......	6,079	25. West Virginia ..	1,593
2. Alaska.......	249,874	10. Montana	31,545	18. Ohio	5,715	26. Nevada.......	436
3. California.....	214,544	11. Colorado.....	24,054	19. Pennsylvania ..	3,611	27. New York	386
4. Louisiana.....	73,011	12. Mississippi....	22,102	20. Kentucky......	2,645	28. Tennessee	344
5. Oklahoma....	64,065	13. Utah	21,998	21. Nebraska	2,394	29. Missouri	99
6. North Dakota..	62,776	14. Illinois	9,423	22. Florida.......	1,956	30. Arizona......	52
7. New Mexico...	59,403	15. Alabama	7,546	23. Indiana	1,858	31. Virginia.......	7
8. Wyoming	52,943	16. Michigan	6,223	24. South Dakota ..	1,697	**U.S. total[1] ......**	**1,811,817**

(1) Includes 445,844 thousand barrels of federal offshore production and 102,538 offshore production by individual states (Alaska, 83,206 thousand; California, 12,500 thousand; Louisiana, 6,222 thousand; and Texas, 610 thousand).

U.S. Petroleum Trade, 1976-2009

Source: Energy Information Administration, U.S. Dept. of Energy, *Monthly Energy Review*, Aug. 2009
(in thousands of barrels per day; average for the year)

Year	Imports from Persian Gulf[1]	Total imports	Total exports	Net imports[2]	Petroleum products supplied[3]	Year	Imports from Persian Gulf[1]	Total imports	Total exports	Net imports[2]	Petroleum products supplied[3]
1976...	1,840	7,313	223	7,090	17,461	1993...	1,782	8,620	1,003	7,618	17,237
1977...	2,448	8,807	243	8,565	18,431	1994...	1,728	8,996	942	8,054	17,718
1978...	2,219	8,363	362	8,002	18,847	1995...	1,573	8,835	949	7,886	17,725
1979...	2,069	8,456	471	7,985	18,513	1996...	1,604	9,478	981	8,498	18,309
1980...	1,519	6,909	544	6,365	17,056	1997...	1,755	10,162	1,003	9,158	18,620
1981...	1,219	5,996	595	5,401	16,058	1998...	2,136	10,708	945	9,764	18,917
1982...	696	5,113	815	4,298	15,296	1999...	2,464	10,852	940	9,912	19,519
1983...	442	5,051	739	4,312	15,231	2000...	2,488	11,459	1,040	10,419	19,701
1984...	506	5,437	722	4,715	15,726	2001...	2,761	11,871	971	10,900	19,649
1985...	311	5,067	781	4,286	15,726	2002...	2,269	11,530	984	10,546	19,761
1986...	912	6,224	785	5,439	16,281	2003...	2,501	12,264	1,027	11,238	20,034
1987...	1,077	6,678	764	5,914	16,665	2004...	2,493	13,145	1,048	12,097	20,731
1988...	1,541	7,402	815	6,587	17,283	2005...	2,334	13,714	1,165	12,549	20,802
1989...	1,861	8,061	859	7,202	17,325	2006...	2,211	13,707	1,317	12,390	20,687
1990...	1,966	8,018	857	7,161	16,988	2007...	2,163	13,468	1,433	12,036	20,680
1991...	1,845	7,627	1,001	6,626	16,714	2008...	2,370	12,915	1,802	11,114	19,498
1992...	1,778	7,888	950	6,938	17,033	2009[4]..	NA	12,102	1,902	10,199	18,772

Note: Beginning in Oct. 1977, imports for the Strategic Petroleum Reserves are included. U.S. exports include shipments to U.S. territories; imports include receipts from U.S. territories. Totals may not add because of rounding. Some figures are revised. NA = Not available. (1) Bahrain, Iran, Iraq, Kuwait, Qatar, Saudi Arabia, and United Arab Emirates. (2) Net imports are total imports minus total exports. (3) Includes domestic production and imports minus change in stocks, refinery imports, and exports. (4) Annualized 8-month average, for Jan.-Aug. 2009.

World Crude Oil and Natural Gas Reserves, 2007

Source: Energy Information Administration, U.S. Dept. of Energy, *International Energy Annual 2006*; *Oil and Gas Journal (OGJ)*, Dec. 2006; *World Oil (WO)*, Sept. 2007

Region/country	Crude oil (billion barrels) OGJ	WO	Natural gas (trillion cubic feet) OGJ	WO	Region/country	Crude oil (billion barrels) OGJ	WO	Natural gas (trillion cubic feet) OGJ	WO
North America	**212.5**	**58.2**	**283.6**	**286.8**	**Eurasia**	**98.9**	**123.4**	**2,014.8**	**2,136.7**
Canada...........	179.2	25.6	57.9	56.8	Azerbaijan	7.0	NA	30.0	NA
Mexico	12.4	11.7	14.6	19.0	Kazakhstan	30.0	NA	100.0	NA
United States	21.0	21.0	211.1	211.1	Russia	60.0	74.4	1,680.0	1,688.8
Central and South					Turkmenistan	0.6	NA	100.0	NA
America..........	**102.8**	**77.1**	**240.7**	**242.2**	Ukraine...........	0.4	NA	39.0	NA
Argentina	2.5	2.6	16.1	15.8	Uzbekistan.........	0.6	NA	65.0	NA
Bolivia	0.4	0.0	24.0	25.7	Other	NA	48.9	NA	447.9
Brazil	11.8	12.3	10.8	12.3	**Africa**.............	**114.1**	**111.7**	**484.4**	**500.7**
Chile.............	0.2	0.0	3.5	1.0	Algeria	12.3	11.9	161.7	161.2
Colombia	1.5	1.4	4.0	6.7	Angola	8.0	9.3	2.0	4.1
Cuba.............	0.1	0.6	2.5	0.6	Cameroon	0.4	NA	3.9	NA
Ecuador	4.5	4.9	0.0	0.3	Congo Republic	1.6	1.9	3.2	4.2
Peru	0.9	1.1	8.7	12.0	Egypt	3.7	3.6	58.5	67.4
Trinidad and Tobago..	0.7	0.6	18.8	16.7	Equatorial Guinea ...	1.1	1.8	1.3	3.4
Venezuela	80.0	52.9	152.4	151.1	Gabon	2.0	2.0	1.0	1.5
Europe.............	**15.8**	**14.5**	**180.3**	**175.7**	Libya	41.5	35.0	52.7	51.7
Austria	0.1	0.1	0.6	0.8	Mozambique	0.0	0.0	4.5	0.0
Croatia	0.1	0.1	1.1	1.0	Nigeria	36.2	37.2	181.9	184.5
Denmark..........	1.3	1.2	2.5	2.9	Sudan............	5.0	6.6	3.0	4.0
Germany	0.4	0.2	9.0	5.8	Tunisia	0.4	0.6	2.3	3.4
Hungary	0.0	0.1	0.3	2.0	Other	NA	1.7	NA	15.3
Italy.............	0.6	0.4	5.8	3.7	**Asia and Oceania**.....	**33.4**	**36.0**	**419.5**	**497.9**
Netherlands	0.0	0.0	50.0	50.8	Afghanistan	0.0	NA	1.8	NA
Norway...........	7.8	7.1	82.3	81.3	Australia...........	1.6	4.3	30.4	153.0
Poland	0.1	0.3	5.8	4.9	Bangladesh	0.0	NA	5.0	NA
Romania..........	0.6	0.5	2.2	4.5	Brunei.............	1.1	1.2	13.8	11.5
Serbia............	0.1	NA	1.7	NA	China	16.0	16.3	80.0	60.9
United Kingdom	3.9	3.8	17.0	15.7	India	5.6	3.8	38.0	27.2
Middle East	**739.2**	**722.5**	**2,566.0**	**2,555.1**	Indonesia	4.3	4.8	97.8	93.0
Bahrain...........	0.1	NA	3.3	NA	Japan	0.1	NA	1.4	NA
Iran..............	136.3	133.0	974.0	974.0	Malaysia	3.0	2.8	75.0	60.0
Iraq..............	115.0	125.1	112.0	90.0	Myanmar (Burma) ...	0.1	0.2	10.0	16.0
Kuwait............	101.5	100.1	55.0	56.2	New Zealand	0.1	0.1	0.9	1.8
Oman	5.5	4.7	30.0	28.0	Pakistan	0.3	0.3	28.0	30.5
Qatar	15.2	20.4	910.5	905.5	Papua New Guinea ..	0.2	0.2	12.2	13.7
Saudi Arabia........	262.3	262.3	240.0	252.5	Philippines	0.1	0.1	3.5	1.8
Syria.............	2.5	2.9	8.5	12.8	Thailand	0.3	0.5	14.8	11.7
United Arab Emirates	97.8	70.6	214.4	205.6	Vietnam	0.6	1.3	6.8	8.3
Yemen	3.0	2.8	16.9	17.0	Other	NA	0.1	NA	8.6
Other	NA	0.7	NA	13.6	**World**...............	**1,316.7**	**1,143.4**	**6,189.4**	**6,395.0**

NA = Not reported separately, amounts included in totals. **Note:** Totals may not add because of rounding. Some countries omitted for lack of appreciable reserves. Data for Kuwait and Saudi Arabia include one-half of the reserves in the Neutral Zone between Kuwait and Saudi Arabia. All reserve figures except those for the former USSR and natural gas reserves in Canada are *proved reserves*. Former USSR and Canadian natural gas figures include amounts understood as *proved*, and some *probable reserves*. Totals may include small amounts not listed. (1) Figure includes 5.2 bil barrels of conventional crude oil and 174 bil barrels contained in Alberta's oil sands, according to *Oil & Gas Journal*.

U.S. Crude Oil Imports by Selected Country, 1990-2008

Source: Energy Information Administration, *Petroleum Supply Monthly*; ranked by 2008 figures

(in thousands of barrels per day)

The United States has become increasingly dependent on foreign oil. From 1990 to 2008, total U.S. oil imports rose by 65%. Over the same period, oil imports from OPEC countries increased 54%. The proportion of U.S. oil imports from OPEC nations in 2008 was 55%, up from 53% in 2007 and 47% in 2006. Although OPEC countries, especially in the Persian Gulf region, have a significant production advantage because of the relatively low cost of developing their oil resources, non-OPEC countries have also increased their oil production. Canada dominated this growth in the early 1970s, the North Sea and Mexico became major producers in the 1980s, and more recent production increases have come from oil supplies in West Africa and the former Soviet Union. Sanctions do not permit the U.S. to import oil from Iran.

Country	2008	2007	2006	2005	2004	2003	2002	2000	1995	1990
Canada................	1,956	1,888	1,802	1,633	1,616	1,549	1,445	1,348	1,040	643
Saudi Arabia#..........	1,503	1,447	1,423	1,445	1,495	1,726	1,519	1,523	1,260	1,195
Mexico	1,187	1,409	1,577	1,556	1,598	1,569	1,500	1,313	1,027	689
Venezuela#	1,039	1,148	1,142	1,241	1,297	1,183	1,201	1,223	1,151	666
Nigeria#	922	1,084	1,037	1,077	1,078	832	589	875	621	784
Iraq#.................	627	484	553	527	655	481	459	620	0	514
Angola#[1]	504	498	513	456	306	363	315	295	360	236
Algeria#	312	443	362	228	215	112	30	1	27	63
Brazil	231	165	133	94	51	50	58	5	0	0
Ecuador[2]	214	198	272	276	232	139	100	125	96	38
Kuwait#	206	175	179	227	241	208	212	261	213	79
Colombia	178	137	141	156	142	166	233	308	207	140
Russia[3]...............	116	112	108	199	158	151	85	7	14	1
Chad.................	102	77	95	74	57	3	NA	NA	NA	NA
United Kingdom	78	101	130	224	238	359	405	291	341	155
Equatorial Guinea	74	55	57	68	66	59	39	61	NA	NA
Azerbaijan	73	57	27	0	NA	0	0	NA	NA	NA
Libya#................	68	84	66	44	18	NA	NA	0	0	0
Congo Republic	67	63	27	25	8	27	23	42	20	NA
Gabon[4]...............	58	63	60	127	142	131	143	143	229	64
Australia..............	33	2	5	10	21	27	51	49	16	47
Norway...............	30	56	98	119	143	181	348	302	258	96
Argentina	29	33	29	56	59	54	70	53	44	NA
Vietnam	29	31	42	31	25	25	20	9	1	NA
Non-OPEC imports......	**4,369**	**4,643**	**5,335**	**5,310**	**5,046**	**5,087**	**5,058**	**4,526**	**3,660**	**NA**
OPEC imports..........	**5,415**	**5,388**	**4,783**	**4,816**	**5,042**	**4,578**	**4,083**	**4,544**	**3,570**	**3,514**
TOTAL................	**9,783**	**10,031**	**10,118**	**10,126**	**10,088**	**9,665**	**9,140**	**9,071**	**7,230**	**5,894**

OPEC member. NA = Not available. (1) Angola became a member of OPEC as of Jan. 1, 2007, and is not included in OPEC totals from before that year. (2) Ecuador suspended its OPEC membership from Dec. 1992-Nov. 2007. Ecuador's imports between 1993 and 2007, inclusive, appear in non-OPEC totals. (3) May include oil from USSR states before 1992. (4) Gabon withdrew from OPEC Dec. 31, 1994. Imports after Jan. 1, 1995, appear in non-OPEC totals.

U.S. Coal Production and Consumption, 1950-2008

Source: Energy Information Administration, U.S. Dept. of Energy, *Annual Energy Review 2008*

(in short tons)

	Coal production[1]			Coal consumption				
Year	Surface mining	Underground mining	Total production	Residential	Commercial	Industrial	Electric power[2]	Total consumption
1950...	139,388,000	421,000,000	560,388,000	51,562,350	63,020,650	224,637,000	91,870,770	494,101,770
1960...	141,745,000	292,584,000	434,329,000	24,159,320	16,788,680	177,402,000	176,685,359	398,081,359
1970...	272,131,000	340,530,000	612,661,000	9,023,840	7,090,160	186,637,000	320,181,708	523,230,708
1975...	361,174,000	293,467,000	654,641,000	2,823,000	6,587,000	147,244,000	405,962,432	562,640,432
1980...	492,192,000	337,508,000	829,700,000	1,354,920	5,097,080	127,004,000	569,273,735	702,729,735
1985...	532,838,000	350,800,000	883,638,117	1,711,426	6,067,781	116,428,686	693,840,766	818,048,659
1990...	604,529,000	424,546,000	1,029,075,527	1,344,774	5,379,096	115,207,053	782,566,645	904,497,568
1995...	636,724,750	396,249,022	1,032,973,772	754,871	5,051,832	106,066,596	850,230,475	962,103,774
2000...	699,952,835	373,658,726	1,073,611,561	453,949	3,672,864	94,147,215	985,820,847	1,084,094,875
2001...	747,061,973	380,626,833	1,127,688,806	480,600	3,888,487	91,343,512	964,432,933	1,060,145,532
2002...	736,898,094	357,384,967	1,094,283,061	533,410	3,911,676	84,402,776	977,506,711	1,066,354,573
2003...	718,967,887	352,784,686	1,071,752,573	550,638	3,685,042	85,509,001	1,005,116,162	1,094,860,843
2004...	744,541,615	367,557,255	1,112,098,870	512,176	4,609,588	85,864,763	1,016,268,012	1,107,254,539
2005...	762,886,599	368,611,500	1,131,498,099	377,528	4,341,573	83,773,950	1,037,484,561	1,125,977,612
2006...	803,727,844	359,021,815	1,162,749,659	290,389	2,936,157	82,429,188	1,026,636,031	1,112,291,765
2007...	794,854,411	351,780,934	1,146,635,345	352,607	3,173,460	79,330,575	1,045,141,487	1,127,998,129
2008[E]..	813,923,721	357,559,146	1,171,482,867	350,582	3,155,236	76,605,719	1,041,602,860	1,121,714,397

E = Estimated or based on preliminary figures. (1) A small amount of refuse recovery has been included in coal production figures since 2001. (2) Electricity-only and combined-heat-and-power (CHP) plants whose primary business is to sell electricity, or electricity and heat, to the public. Through 1988, data are for electric utilities only; beginning in 1989, data are for electric utilities and independent power producers.

World Nuclear Power Summary, 2009

Source: International Atomic Energy Agency, *Nuclear Technology Review 2009*, as of Dec. 31, 2008

Country	Reactors in operation No. of units	Reactors in operation Total MW(e)	Reactors under construction No. of units	Reactors under construction Total MW(e)	Nuclear electricity supplied in 2008 TW(e).h[1]	Nuclear electricity supplied in 2008 % of nation's total	Total operating experience[2] Years	Total operating experience[2] Months
Argentina	2	935	1	692	6.9	6.2%	60	7
Armenia	1	376	—	—	2.2	39.4	34	8
Belgium	7	5,824	—	—	43.4	53.8	226	7
Brazil	2	1,766	—	—	13.2	3.1	35	3
Bulgaria	2	1,906	2	1,906	14.7	32.9	145	3
Canada	18	12,577	—	—	88.3	14.8	564	2
China	11	8,438	11	10,220	65.3	2.2	88	3
Czech Republic	6	3,634	—	—	25.0	32.5	104	10
Finland	4	2,696	1	1,600	22.1	29.7	119	4
France	59	63,260	1	1,600	419.8	76.2	1,641	2
Germany	17	20,470	—	—	140.9	28.8	734	5
Hungary	4	1,859	—	—	13.9	37.2	94	2
India	17	3,782	6	2,910	13.2	2.0	301	4
Iran	—	—	1	915	—	—	—	—
Japan	55	47,278	2	2,191	241.3	24.9	1,386	8
Korea, South	20	17,647	5	5,180	144.3	35.6	319	8
Lithuania	1	1,185	—	—	9.1	72.9	42	6
Mexico	2	1,300	—	—	9.4	4.0	33	11
Netherlands	1	482	—	—	3.9	3.8	64	0
Pakistan	2	425	1	300	1.7	1.9	45	10
Romania	2	1,300	—	—	10.3	17.5	13	11
Russia	31	21,743	8	5,809	152.1	16.9	963	4
Slovakia	4	1,711	—	—	15.5	56.4	128	7
Slovenia	1	666	—	—	6.0	41.7	27	3
South Africa	2	1,800	—	—	12.8	5.3	48	3
Spain	8	7,450	—	—	56.5	18.3	261	6
Sweden	10	8,996	—	—	61.3	42.0	362	6
Switzerland	5	3,220	—	—	26.3	39.2	168	10
Taiwan	6	4,949	2	2,600	39.3	17.5	164	1
Ukraine	15	13,107	2	1,900	84.5	47.4	353	6
United Kingdom	19	10,097	—	—	48.2	13.5	1,438	8
United States	104	100,683	1	1,165	806.7	19.7	3,395	9
TOTAL	**438**	**371,562**	**44**	**38,988**	**2,597.8**	**14.0**	**13,475**	**7**

MW(e) = Megawatt electricity. (1) 1 terawatt-hour [TW(e).h] = 10^6 megawatt-hour [MW(e).h]. For an average power plant, 1 TW(e).h = 0.39 megatons of coal equivalent (input) and 0.23 megatons of oil equivalent (input). (2) Through Dec. 31, 2008. Also includes shutdown plants for countries not listed here: Italy (81 years) and Kazakhstan (25 years, 10 months).

Nations Most Reliant on Nuclear Energy, 2008

Source: International Atomic Energy Agency
(nuclear electricity generation as % of total electricity generated)

Country	%	Country	%	Country	%	Country	%
1. France	76.2	9. Switzerland	39.2	17. **United States**	19.7	24. South Africa	5.3
2. Lithuania	72.9	10. Hungary	37.2	18. Spain	18.3	25. Mexico	4.0
3. Slovakia	56.4	11. South Korea	35.6	19. Romania	17.5	26. Netherlands	3.8
4. Belgium	53.8	12. Bulgaria	32.9	20. Russia	16.9	27. Brazil	3.1
5. Ukraine	47.4	13. Czech Republic	32.5	21. Canada	14.8	28. China	2.2
6. Sweden	42.0	14. Finland	29.7	22. United Kingdom	13.5	29. India	2.0
7. Slovenia	41.7	15. Germany	28.3	23. Argentina	6.2	30. Pakistan	1.9
8. Armenia	39.4	16. Japan	24.9				

U.S. Nuclear Reactors and Power Plant Operations, 1955-2008

Source: Energy Information Administration, U.S. Dept. of Energy, *Annual Energy Review 2008*

Years	Ordered[1]	Cancelled	Number of reactor units Construction permits[2]	Number of reactor units Low-power licensed[3]	Number of reactor units Full-power licensed[4]	Number of reactor units Shutdown[5]	Operable units[6]	Capacity factor[6,7] (percent)	Nuclear electricity generation (million net KW-hrs)[6]	Nuclear share of domestic electricity generation (percent)[6]
1955-59	14	0	8	2	2	0	2	NA	188.1	NA
1960-64	7	0	12	13	12	1	13	NA	3,342.7	0.3%
1965-69	81	0	50	8	9	5	17	NA	13,927.8	1.0
1970-74	143	16	59	41	41	3	55	47.8%	113,975.7	6.1
1975-79	13	43	48	17	17	3	69	58.4	255,154.6	11.3
1980-84	0	54	0	24	19	1	87	56.3	327,633.5	13.5
1985-89	0	7	0	24	28	4	111	62.2	529,354.7	17.8
1990-94	0	15	0	49	58	9	109	73.8	640,439.8	19.7
1995-99	0	2	0	1	1	6	104	85.3	728,254.1	19.7
2000-04	0	0	0	0	0	0	104	90.1	788,528.4	19.9
2005-08	0	0	0	0	0	0	104	91.9	806,200.0	19.6
Total	**259**	**124**	**177**	**132**	**132**	**28**				

Note: Revised permit/license procedures eliminate the historical categories shown. According to Senate testimony, the Nuclear Regulatory Commission anticipates 16 or more new "combined license applications" over the next few years—the first of which was submitted Sept. 25, 2007—which may amount to 25 or more new reactor units. (1) Order placed by a utility or government agency for a nuclear steam supply system. (2) Numbers show permits issued in a given period, not extant permits. (3) Licenses granted to conduct testing. (4) Licenses granted for full power operation. (5) Permanently ceased operation. (6) As of the last year of designated period. (7) The ratio of electric energy produced to the amount that could be produced at continuous full power operation.

Renewable Energy Sources

Source: U.S. Department of Energy

Concern over the environmental impact of burning fossil fuels has helped spur interest in alternative fuels that are less polluting. And since the supply of fossil fuels is finite and diminishing, there is interest in "renewable" sources that do not deplete existing supplies. However, renewable energy sources still make up only a small share of U.S. domestic energy production (about 10% in 2008). The major reason for this is their relatively higher cost (in some cases 2 to 4 times that of power obtained from traditional fuels). The following are the major renewable energy sources available.

Biomass is plant-derived material usable as a renewable energy source, including wood energy crops such as hybrid poplars and willow trees, agricultural crops including soybeans and corn, and animal and other wastes. Biomass is one of the two most common energy sources in the U.S. today along with hydropower. Forms of biomass such as wood can be burned to produce heat and generate electricity. Agricultural crops can be chemically converted into fuels such as ethanol and biodiesel; these are the only known renewable liquid energy sources, and may one day replace petroleum and fossil-fuel produced diesel. But bringing ethanol and biodiesel into wide use would require more energy-efficient methods of production and transportation. Overall, biomass fuels are much cleaner-burning than fossil fuels, though biomass fuels do produce carbon dioxide and other pollutants.

Geothermal energy is generated from heat from inside Earth. This form of energy is both clean and renewable. The technology has caught on in countries with substantial geothermal activity such as Iceland, where it accounted for 54% of primary energy use. In the U.S. the best sources for geothermal power are in the West, where there are many underground lakes of heated water; however, large-scale access would require drilling. A major goal in this field is to find a way to harness energy directly from magma (molten rock material), which has great potential because of its high temperature.

Hydrogen is the 3rd most abundant element on Earth. It does not naturally occur on Earth as a pure gas or liquid, but is always combined with other elements (such as with oxygen to form water or carbon to form methane). For energy use it is produced from hydrocarbons using heat, bacteria or algae through photosynthesis, or by using sunlight or electricity to split water into hydrogen and oxygen. Hydrogen batteries, or fuel cells, are already used by NASA on the space shuttle. In a fuel cell, electrons are released from the hydrogen atoms in a chemical reaction and flow through an external circuit as electricity. The protons then combine with oxygen (and some of the electrons in the electric current) to make heat and water suitable for drinking. Fuel cells do not run down, but work as long as hydrogen is supplied. Some experts think hydrogen will be the power source of the future. However, an infrastructure would need to be created for safe and cost-effective transportation and storage of hydrogen.

Hydropower, or hydroelectric power, is generated by water flowing through turbines. With biomass fuels, it is one of the two most common renewable energy sources in the U.S. today. A dam on a river is a common hydropower producer. No harmful greenhouse gases are produced, but the dams needed to generate the power can harm river ecosystems. Researchers are working on turbine technologies that may maximize use of hydropower and reduce adverse environmental effects.

Ocean energy is generated in two ways. Thermal ocean energy uses the heat that the ocean absorbs from the sun to power generators, and sometimes drinkable desalinated water is a by-product. Mechanical ocean energy is generated by the movement of tides and waves through a turbine. In both cases, power generation is not very efficient with current technology. Much more research is needed to make thermal ocean energy generation a reality. Mechanical ocean energy requires large dams or breakwater-type structures called tidal barrages to be built, which could cause harm to coastal ecosystems.

Solar energy is generated using heat and light from the sun. Solar energy is an increasingly common source of electricity. Photovoltaic (PV) solar cells are made of semiconducting materials that can directly convert sunlight to electricity without any harmful waste product. Solar collectors are made more efficient by using arrays of mirrors to concentrate the sun's rays onto PV panels. Another way of using sunlight is to heat water directly. According to the DOE, homes incorporating solar heating designs can save as much as 50% on heating bills. The downside to solar energy is that it depends heavily on a range of factors including location, time of year, and weather.

Wind energy uses wind turbines to produce energy. They are perched on high towers, usually 100 feet or higher, and often placed in large groups ("farms") to generate electricity for towns and cities. On a much smaller scale, stand-alone turbines are sometimes used by farmers and homeowners to generate supplemental electricity. In the past 20 years, government incentives in the form of tax credits to producers and incentives for homeowners have helped lower the price of wind power by 85%, making it a more feasible option. Some people object to wind farms because of their appearance or the noise the turbines make. Wind power raises few other environmental problems, but the turbines can pose a danger to birds. In addition, because weather is involved, consistent generation is a challenge.

Alternative-Fueled Vehicles in Use in the U.S., by Fuel, 1995-2007

Source: Energy Information Administration, U.S. Dept. of Energy

Fuel	1995	2000	2004	2005	2006	2007[P]	% change, 2000-07
Liquefied petroleum gases (LPG) ..	172,806	181,994	182,864	173,795	164,846	158,254	−13.0%
Compressed natural gas (CNG).....	50,218	100,750	118,532	117,699	116,131	114,391	13.5
Liquefied natural gas (LNG)........	603	2,090	2,717	2,748	2,798	2,781	33.1
Methanol, 85 percent (M85)[1]......	18,319	10,426	0	0	0	0	NA
Ethanol, 85 percent (E85)[1,2]......	1,527	87,570	211,800	246,363	297,099	364,384	316.1
Ethanol, 95 percent (E95)[1]........	136	4	0	0	0	0	NA
Electricity[3]....................	2,860	11,830	49,536	51,398	53,526	55,730	371.1
Hydrogen.....................	386	0	43	119	159	223	NA
Total[4].......................	**246,855**	**394,664**	**565,492**	**592,125**	**634,562**	**695,766**	**76.3**

P = Preliminary. (1) The remaining portion of 85-percent methanol and both ethanol fuels is gasoline. (2) In 1997, some vehicle manufacturers began including E85-fueling capability in certain model lines of vehicles. For 2006, the EIA estimated that the number of E-85 vehicles that are capable of operating on E85, gasoline, or both, is about 6 mil. Many are sold and used as traditional gasoline-powered vehicles. In this table, AFVs in use include only those E85 vehicles believed to be intended for use as AFVs (primarily fleet-operated vehicles). (3) Excludes gasoline-electric and diesel-electric hybrids. (4) Includes other fuels.

CRIME

Measuring Crime

The U.S. Dept. of Justice administers two statistical programs to measure trends in crime in the U.S. Because of differences in focus and methodology, their results are not strictly comparable.

The Federal Bureau of Investigation (FBI) conducts the **Uniform Crime Report (UCR)** program, which aims to provide statistics for law enforcement administration, operation, and management. It collects actual counts on the crimes of homicide, forcible rape, robbery, aggravated assault, burglary, larceny-theft, motor vehicle theft, and arson as they are reported to law enforcement authorities. Each year, the program releases a preliminary report in the spring, followed by a more detailed, final report in the fall.

The **National Crime Victimization Survey (NCVS)** is conducted annually by the Bureau of Justice Statistics through interviews with members of a nationally representative sample of households about their experiences with crime. The survey complements the UCR by providing alternative and previously unavailable information, including information about the victims of crime and their offenders (e.g., age, sex, ethnicity, victim-offender relationship) and information on crimes not reported to law enforcement. In contrast to the UCR, the NCVS does not cover homicide, arson, commercial crimes, or crimes against children under age 12.

Further explanation of the UCR and NCVS is available at www.ojp.usdoj.gov/bjs/abstract/ntmc.htm.

Uniform Crime Report for 2008

Source: *Crime in the United States, 2008*, Federal Bureau of Investigation, U.S. Dept. of Justice

In 2008, nearly 17,800 city, county, college and university, state, tribal, and federal agencies—representing about 95% of the U.S. population—voluntarily participated in the UCR program.

Between 2007 and 2008, there was a 1.9% dip in the number of violent crimes reported, marking the second straight year violent crime declined. The number of property crimes reported was also down, by 0.8% from 2007, making it the sixth year in a row property crime reports declined.

Victims of all property crimes, excluding arson, lost an estimated $17.2 bil in 2008. Although arson is considered a property crime, it is not included in estimates of totals because of variations in the level of participation by reporting agencies. The FBI estimates that on average, each arson offense did about $16,015 worth of damages.

Additional highlights from the 2008 report:
- Males accounted for 78.2% of all murder victims whose gender was known. Of all murder offenders whose gender was known, 90.0% were male.
- Firearms were used in 67% of all murders.
- Of the 7,912 murder victims whose relation to the offender was known, 23.2% were killed by a family member, and about the same percentage were killed by a stranger. Some 38.8% were killed by an acquaintance (e.g., friend, neighbor, employee, same-sex partner).
- Most robberies (43.1%) took place on a street or highway.
- The majority of property crimes reported were larceny-thefts (67.5%). Excluding motor vehicle thefts, 26% of all larceny-thefts involved items taken from motor vehicles (except for accessories), 16.2% were shoplifting, 11.4% were from buildings, and 3.4% were of bikes.

National Crime Victimization Survey for 2008

Source: *Criminal Victimization, 2008*, Bureau of Justice Statistics, U.S. Dept. of Justice

Victimizations of U.S. residents age 12 and over were at or near their lowest rates in over three decades, according to the NCVS estimates for 2008. The violent crime rate—19.3 victimizations per 1,000 persons—was down slightly from the 2007 estimate of 20.7, while the property crime rate (135 victimizations per 1,000 households) dropped significantly from the 147 per 1,000 households recorded in 2007. The

biggest declines came in the numbers of rapes or sexual assaults (down 18.5%) and motor vehicle theft (down 19.9%). Over the 10-year period between 1999 and 2008, violent crime fell 41% while property crime declined 32%. Note that the NCVS does not include figures for murders because published data are based on victim interviews.

Criminal Victimization, 2007-08

Source: *Criminal Victimization, 2008*, Bureau of Justice Statistics, U.S. Dept. of Justice

A crime committed against an individual or single household counts as one **victimization**. Because a personal crime may involve more than one victim, the number of victimizations may be greater than the number of personal crime incidents. In property crimes, the affected household is considered one victim.

Victimization rates measure the frequency with which victimizations occur. Personal crime victimization rates are based on the number of victimizations per 1,000 persons in the total population age 12 and over. Property crime victimization rates are calculated per 1,000 of total households.

Type of crime	Number of victimizations		Victimization rate		Percent Change
	2007	2008	2007	2008	
All crimes	22,879,720	21,312,400	NA	NA	NA
Crimes of violence[1]	5,177,130	4,856,510	20.7%	19.3%	−6.9%
Rape/sexual assault[2]	248,280	203,830	1.0	0.8	−18.5
Robbery	597,320	551,830	2.4	2.2	−8.3
Assault	4,331,530	4,100,850	17.3	16.3	−6.0
Aggravated	858,940	839,940	3.4	3.3	−2.9
Simple	3,472,590	3,260,920	13.9	12.9	−6.8
Personal theft[3]	194,060	136,710	0.8	0.5	−30.1
Property crimes	17,508,530	16,319,180	146.5	134.7	−8.1
Household burglary	3,215,090	3,188,620	26.9	26.3	−2.2
Motor vehicle theft	979,640	795,160	8.2	6.6	−19.9
Theft	13,313,800	12,335,400	111.4	101.8	−8.6
Total population age 12 and over	250,344,870	252,242,520			
Total households	119,503,530	121,141,060			

NA = Not applicable. **Note:** Details may not add up to totals due to rounding. (1) Excludes murder because the NCVS is based on interviews with victims. (2) Includes male as well as female victims and both heterosexual and homosexual rape. (3) Includes pocket picking, completed purse snatching, and attempted purse snatching.

Crime in the U.S., 1989-2008

Source: *Crime in the United States, 2008*, Federal Bureau of Investigation, U.S. Dept. of Justice

In the FBI's Uniform Crime Reporting (UCR) Program, offenses are classified as **violent crimes** if they involve force or the threat of force: murder and nonnegligent manslaughter, forcible rape, robbery, and aggravated assault. The following offenses are considered **property crimes**: burglary, larceny-theft, motor vehicle theft, and arson. Arson data is excluded from this table because of variations in the level of participation by reporting agencies. That data is presented separately online at www.fbi.gov/ucr/ucr.htm, under Crime in the United States.

Year(s)	Population[1]	VIOLENT CRIME					PROPERTY CRIME			
		All violent crimes	Murder & nonnegligent manslaughter	Forcible rape[2]	Robbery	Aggravated assault[3]	All property crimes	Burglary	Larceny-theft[4]	Motor vehicle theft
NUMBER OF OFFENSES										
1989	246,819,230	1,646,037	21,500	94,504	578,326	951,707	12,605,412	3,168,170	7,705,872	7,872,442
1990	249,464,396	1,820,127	23,438	102,555	639,271	1,054,863	12,655,486	3,073,909	7,945,670	1,635,907
1994	260,327,021	1,857,670	23,326	102,216	618,949	1,113,179	12,131,873	2,712,774	7,879,812	1,539,287
1995	262,803,276	1,798,792	21,606	97,470	580,509	1,099,207	12,063,935	2,593,784	7,997,710	1,472,441
1996	265,228,572	1,688,540	19,645	96,252	535,594	1,037,049	11,805,323	2,506,400	7,904,685	1,394,238
1997	267,783,607	1,636,096	18,208	96,153	498,534	1,023,201	11,558,475	2,460,526	7,743,760	1,354,189
1998	270,248,003	1,533,887	16,974	93,144	447,186	976,583	10,951,827	2,332,735	7,376,311	1,242,781
1999	272,690,813	1,426,044	15,522	89,411	409,371	911,740	10,208,334	2,100,739	6,955,520	1,152,075
2000	281,421,906	1,425,486	15,586	90,178	408,016	911,706	10,182,584	2,050,992	6,971,590	1,160,002
2001[5]	285,317,559	1,439,480	16,037	90,863	423,557	909,023	10,437,189	2,116,531	7,092,267	1,228,391
2002	287,973,924	1,423,677	16,229	95,235	420,806	891,407	10,455,277	2,151,252	7,057,379	1,246,646
2003	290,788,976	1,383,676	16,528	93,883	414,235	859,030	10,442,862	2,154,834	7,026,802	1,261,226
2004	293,656,842	1,360,088	16,148	95,089	401,470	847,381	10,319,386	2,144,446	6,937,089	1,237,851
2005	296,507,061	1,390,745	16,740	94,347	417,438	862,220	10,174,754	2,155,448	6,783,447	1,235,859
2006	299,398,484	1,418,043	17,030	92,757	447,403	860,853	9,983,568	2,183,746	6,607,013	1,192,809
2007	301,621,157	1,408,337	16,929	90,427	445,125	855,856	9,843,481	2,179,140	6,568,572	1,095,769
2008	304,059,724	1,382,012	16,272	89,000	441,855	834,885	9,767,915	2,222,196	6,588,873	956,846
PERCENT CHANGE: NUMBER OF OFFENSES										
2008/2007		−1.9	−3.9	−1.6	−0.7	−2.5	−0.8	2.0	0.3	−12.7
2008/2004		1.6	0.8	−6.4	10.1	−1.5	−5.3	3.6	−5.0	−22.7
2008/1999		−3.1	4.8	−0.5	7.9	−8.4	−4.3	5.8	−5.3	−16.9
RATE PER 100,000 RESIDENTS										
1989		666.9	8.7	38.3	234.3	385.6	5,107.1	1,283.6	3,189.6	634.0
1990		729.6	9.4	41.1	256.3	422.9	5,073.1	1,232.2	3,185.1	655.8
1994		713.6	9.0	39.3	237.8	427.6	4,660.2	1,042.1	3,026.9	591.3
1995		684.5	8.2	37.1	220.9	418.3	4,590.5	987.0	3,043.2	560.3
1996		636.6	7.4	36.3	201.9	391.0	4,451.0	945.0	2,980.3	525.7
1997		611.0	6.8	35.9	186.2	382.1	4,316.3	918.8	2,891.8	505.7
1998		567.6	6.3	34.5	165.5	361.4	4,052.5	863.2	2,729.5	459.9
1999		523.0	5.7	32.8	150.1	334.3	3,743.6	770.4	2,550.7	422.5
2000		506.5	5.5	32.0	145.0	324.0	3,618.3	728.8	2,477.3	412.2
2001		504.5	5.6[5]	31.8	148.5	318.6	3,658.1	741.8	2,485.7	430.5
2002		494.4	5.6	33.1	146.1	309.5	3,630.6	747.0	2,450.7	432.9
2003		475.8	5.7	32.3	142.5	295.4	3,591.2	741.0	2,416.5	433.7
2004		463.2	5.5	32.4	136.7	288.6	3,514.1	730.3	2,362.3	421.5
2005		469.0	5.6	31.8	140.8	290.8	3,431.5	726.9	2,287.8	416.8
2006		473.6	5.7	31.0	149.4	287.5	3,334.5	729.4	2,206.8	398.4
2007		466.9	5.6	30.0	147.6	283.8	3,263.5	722.5	2,177.8	363.3
2008		454.5	5.4	29.3	145.3	274.6	3,212.5	730.8	2,167.0	314.7
PERCENT CHANGE: RATE PER 100,000 RESIDENTS										
2008/2007		−2.7	−4.7	−2.4	−1.5	−3.2	−1.6	1.2	−0.5	−13.4
2008/2004		−1.9	−2.7	−9.6	6.3	−4.8	−8.6	0.1	−8.3	−25.3
2008/1999		−13.1	−6.0	−10.7	−3.2	−17.9	−14.2	−5.1	−15.0	−25.5

(1) U.S. Census Bureau estimates for July 1 of each year except for 1990 and 2000, which show Apr. 1 decennial census counts. (2) Does not include statutory rape (i.e., rape not involving force) and other offenses of a sexual nature. Also does not include sexual attacks on males, which are considered aggravated assaults or sex offenses, depending on circumstances and extent of injuries. (3) Attack upon another with the intent of doing serious bodily harm; usually accompanied by the use of a weapon or other means likely to produce death or great bodily harm. (4) The unlawful taking of another's property not involving force or fraud (e.g., theft of motor vehicle parts, shoplifting). Excludes crimes such as embezzlement and check fraud. (5) The murder and nonnegligent homicides that occurred as a result of the Sept. 11, 2001, terrorist attacks are not included.

Law Enforcement Civilian Employees and Officers, 2008

Source: *Crime in the United States, 2008*; *Law Enforcement Officers Killed and Assaulted, 2008*; Federal Bureau of Investigation, U.S. Dept. of Justice

As of Oct. 31, 2008, 14,169 city, county, state, college and university, and tribal agencies around the country collectively employed 1,024,228 full-time law enforcement workers. About 69.2% of employees were sworn officers. The FBI's UCR program defines a sworn **law enforcement officer** as a person who ordinarily carries a firearm and badge, has full arrest powers, and is paid from government funds specifically dedicated to law enforcement. Civilians (e.g., clerks, radio dispatchers, correctional officers) made up the remaining 30.8% of law enforcement employees.

Altogether, they provided service to an estimated 286.2 mil people around the country, meaning there were 3.6 full-time law enforcement employees (civilian and sworn officers) and 2.5 sworn officers per 1,000 residents.

California employed the greatest number of full-time law enforcement workers (123,506) of any state. DC, however, had the highest rate, with 8.8 full-time law enforcement employees (and 7.5 sworn officers) for every 1,000 residents in its population.

Females made up 61.6% of all full-time civilian law enforcement employees in the U.S. while males made up 88.1% of the nation's sworn officers.

Nationwide, 41 law enforcement officers were killed in the line of duty in 2008. Of that number, 10 were involved in arrest situations, 8 were performing traffic stops, 7 were killed during tactical situations, and 6 died while investigating suspicious persons or circumstances. Thirty-five of the 41 officers were killed with firearms. The majority of these firearms (25) were handguns. Another 67 officers died accidentally while performing official duties.

U.S. Crime Rates by Region, Geographic Division, and State, 2008

Source: *Crime in the United States, 2008*, Federal Bureau of Investigation, U.S. Dept. of Justice
(per 100,000 population, as estimated by U.S. Census Bureau for July 1 of year)

	VIOLENT CRIME					PROPERTY CRIME[1]			
	All violent crimes	Murder & nonnegligent manslaughter	Forcible rape[2]	Robbery	Aggra-vated assault[3]	All property crimes	Burglary	Larceny-theft[4]	Motor vehicle theft
TOTAL U.S.[5,6,7]	454.5	5.4	29.3	145.3	274.6	3,212.5	730.8	2,167.0	314.7
NORTHEAST.........	370.8	4.2	20.0	138.5	208.2	2,248.8	429.5	1,644.9	174.4
New England.......	326.4	2.7	25.0	88.8	209.9	2,429.3	497.3	1,736.0	196.1
Connecticut	297.8	3.5	19.3	111.6	163.5	2,458.7	428.7	1,774.0	256.0
Maine	117.5	2.4	28.5	25.3	61.4	2,452.4	495.4	1,867.7	89.3
Massachusetts.....	449.0	2.6	26.7	108.8	310.9	2,400.1	555.5	1,648.6	196.0
New Hampshire	157.2	1.0	29.7	31.8	94.7	2,091.9	325.7	1,660.8	105.4
Rhode Island	249.4	2.8	26.4	83.7	136.7	2,840.6	547.2	1,988.9	304.5
Vermont	135.9	2.7	20.4	14.3	98.3	2,538.5	557.2	1,887.1	94.2
Middle Atlantic	386.4	4.7	18.2	156.0	207.5	2,185.3	405.6	1,612.9	166.8
New Jersey	326.5	4.3	12.9	146.3	163.0	2,293.4	465.3	1,595.7	232.4
New York	398.1	4.3	14.4	163.0	216.4	1,993.5	337.3	1,527.3	128.9
Pennsylvania	410.0	5.6	27.9	151.6	224.8	2,410.2	470.9	1,758.8	180.5
MIDWEST[5,6]	400.1	4.8	34.0	126.8	234.5	3,066.5	681.1	2,122.8	262.6
East North Central[5,6]	419.5	5.1	34.2	147.4	232.8	3,085.7	715.2	2,098.3	272.3
Illinois[5,6]	525.4	6.1	31.9	186.4	300.9	2,932.6	612.1	2,068.1	252.5
Indiana	333.8	5.1	27.0	118.1	183.5	3,335.8	762.8	2,299.2	273.7
Michigan...........	501.5	5.4	45.0	129.6	321.5	2,934.8	741.5	1,831.1	362.3
Ohio	348.2	4.7	38.5	163.0	142.1	3,411.7	892.8	2,270.5	248.4
Wisconsin..........	274.0	2.6	19.9	91.1	160.4	2,756.4	488.3	2,063.4	204.7
West North Central[6]	355.4	4.2	33.4	79.3	238.4	3,022.2	602.9	2,179.1	240.2
Iowa	283.8	2.5	29.6	41.6	210.1	2,420.9	547.9	1,728.8	144.3
Kansas............	410.6	4.0	42.5	60.1	304.0	3,377.2	699.9	2,413.4	263.9
Minnesota[6]........	262.8	2.1	34.6	80.0	146.1	2,850.6	505.9	2,151.6	193.1
Missouri	504.4	7.7	27.3	125.0	344.4	3,663.7	774.5	2,537.9	351.3
Nebraska	303.7	3.8	32.7	72.8	194.3	2,878.6	492.0	2,151.8	234.8
North Dakota	166.5	0.5	36.2	11.2	118.6	1,894.4	328.3	1,428.6	137.5
South Dakota	201.4	3.2	53.7	14.9	129.6	1,645.6	302.2	1,244.0	99.5
SOUTH[7]	533.9	6.6	30.4	159.1	337.8	3,780.8	941.3	2,515.9	323.6
South Atlantic[7]	553.7	6.6	27.2	175.3	344.5	3,788.5	923.2	2,525.7	339.6
Delaware	703.4	6.5	41.9	210.5	444.4	3,585.3	774.3	2,520.0	291.0
District of Columbia[7]	1,437.7	31.4	31.4	748.5	626.4	5,104.6	640.0	3,372.2	1,092.4
Florida	688.9	6.4	32.6	197.9	452.0	4,140.8	1,028.3	2,766.0	346.5
Georgia	478.9	6.6	22.7	179.2	270.5	4,015.5	1,038.9	2,567.5	409.1
Maryland	628.2	8.8	20.0	234.4	365.1	3,517.6	689.6	2,378.3	449.7
North Carolina	467.3	6.5	24.8	155.4	280.6	4,044.1	1,210.1	2,544.0	290.0
South Carolina	729.7	6.8	36.6	147.3	539.1	4,234.2	1,026.1	2,814.1	394.0
Virginia	255.9	4.7	22.6	95.7	132.8	2,518.1	411.8	1,935.6	170.7
West Virginia	273.8	3.3	20.0	49.0	201.5	2,568.6	609.9	1,782.2	176.6
East South Central..	481.2	6.6	33.1	139.2	302.4	3,529.6	941.6	2,329.8	258.2
Alabama...........	452.8	7.6	34.7	157.6	253.0	4,082.9	1,081.3	2,713.0	288.7
Kentucky	296.2	4.6	33.0	93.8	164.8	2,583.9	675.5	1,728.8	179.6
Mississippi	284.9	8.1	30.3	102.6	143.9	2,940.4	885.6	1,838.7	216.2
Tennessee	722.4	6.6	33.2	173.8	508.9	4,042.6	1,046.0	2,687.3	309.3
West South Central	528.1	6.5	34.4	142.4	344.9	3,896.9	971.2	2,595.1	330.6
Arkansas	503.4	5.7	48.9	95.8	353.1	3,835.1	1,180.0	2,427.1	228.0
Louisiana	656.2	11.9	27.9	135.9	480.4	3,823.1	982.1	2,529.4	311.6
Oklahoma..........	526.7	5.8	40.2	101.1	379.5	3,442.4	963.1	2,180.5	298.7
Texas	507.9	5.6	32.9	155.2	314.1	3,985.6	946.0	2,688.8	350.8
WEST..............	445.4	4.8	30.2	146.4	264.0	3,200.7	679.3	2,063.0	458.3
Mountain	417.8	4.4	36.4	108.5	268.6	3,444.7	723.0	2,327.8	393.8
Arizona............	447.0	6.3	25.7	149.2	265.9	4,291.0	868.9	2,849.5	572.6
Colorado...........	343.1	3.2	42.5	68.1	229.3	2,849.0	572.0	2,003.3	273.7
Idaho	228.6	1.5	36.2	15.8	175.1	2,101.2	439.8	1,552.0	109.5
Montana	258.1	2.4	30.4	17.8	207.6	2,603.0	344.4	2,095.9	162.6
Nevada	724.5	6.3	42.4	248.9	426.9	3,447.5	929.0	1,906.8	611.6
New Mexico	649.9	7.2	57.4	109.5	475.9	3,909.2	1,094.2	2,411.6	403.4
Utah	221.8	1.4	32.6	51.9	135.8	3,357.4	536.5	2,557.9	262.9
Wyoming	232.0	1.9	33.8	16.1	180.2	2,717.3	410.0	2,173.4	133.9
Pacific	457.7	5.0	27.5	163.2	261.9	3,092.3	659.9	1,945.5	487.0
Alaska	651.9	4.1	64.3	94.0	489.6	2,932.3	472.1	2,221.5	238.7
California	503.8	5.8	24.2	188.8	285.0	2,940.3	647.1	1,769.4	523.8
Hawaii	272.6	1.9	28.3	84.3	158.1	3,571.2	728.1	2,444.7	398.5
Oregon............	257.2	2.2	30.5	69.7	154.8	3,282.2	550.9	2,432.3	299.0
Washington	331.2	2.9	40.1	96.9	191.2	3,758.4	801.3	2,524.6	432.6
Puerto Rico........	239.9	20.4	2.4	138.3	78.8	1,498.6	484.0	837.4	177.1

Note: Offense totals are based on all reporting agencies and estimates for unreported areas. Figures may not add up to totals due to rounding. (1) Data for arson, considered a property crime, are not included in this table. (2) Does not include statutory rape (i.e., rape not involving force) and other offenses of a sexual nature. Also does not include sexual attacks on males, which are considered aggravated assaults or sex offenses, depending on circumstances and extent of injuries. (3) Attack upon another with the intent of doing serious bodily harm; usually accompanied by the use of a weapon or other means likely to produce death or great bodily harm. (4) The unlawful taking of another's property not involving force or fraud (e.g., theft of motor vehicle parts, shoplifting). Excludes crimes such as embezzlement and check fraud. (5) Limited data available for Illinois. (6) Illinois and Minnesota—with the exception of Rockford, IL, and Minneapolis and St. Paul, MN—collect data on forcible rape offenses using methodology not consistent with national UCR guidelines. Forcible rape offenses in the two states, with the exception of the previously mentioned cities, have been estimated for inclusion in this table. (7) Includes offenses reported by National Zoological Park Police and Washington Metro Transit Police.

State and Federal Prison Population; Death Penalty, 2007-08

Source: *Prison Inmates at Midyear 2008, Capital Punishment, 2006*; Bureau of Justice Statistics, U.S. Dept. of Justice

As of June 30, 2008, 1,610,584 prisoners—about two-thirds of the nation's incarcerated population—were under the jurisdiction, or legal authority, of federal (12.5%) or state (87.5%) correctional authorities. The prison population increased by 1.0% over the preceding 12 months, which is slower than the 2.0% annual average growth recorded between 2000 and 2007. **Jails**, which are locally operated and typically hold persons awaiting trial or sentencing as well as those sentenced to one year or less, held most of the remaining inmate population (785,556).

As of mid-2008, the incarceration rate in state and federal prisons for those with sentences of more than one year was 509 per 100,000 U.S. residents, the same as the year before, but up significantly from 478 at year-end 2000. Among inmates held in custody in prisons or jails, black males were incarcerated at 6.6 times the rate of white males. One in 21 black males was incarcerated in June 2008, compared to one in 138 white males. Black males (846,000) outnumbered white males (712,500) and Hispanic males (427,000) among inmates in prisons and jails. An estimated 94,724 non-U.S. citizens were held in state or federal prisons as of June 2008.

In 2007, 42 persons were executed, while another 44 were removed from death row. Of the 3,220 persons under sentence of death at year-end 2007, 98.3% were male; 56.0% were white, and 41.8% were black. The median age of this population was 42 years.

Region/jurisdiction	SENTENCED PRISONERS[1]			DEATH PENALTY[2]				
	Mid-2007	Mid-2008	% change, mid-2007 to mid-2008	Death penalty	Under sentence of death, year-end 2007	Executed, 2007	Executed, as of 2007[3] Since 1930	Since 1977
U.S. TOTAL[4]	1,594,611	1,610,584	1.0	—	3,220	42	4,958[5]	1,099[5]
Federal[6]	199,118	201,142	1.0	Y	48	0	36	3
State[4]	1,395,493	1,409,442	1.0	37	3,172	42	4,882	1,096
Northeast	**180,096**	**179,120**	**-0.5**	—	**230**	**0**	**612**	**4**
Connecticut[7]......	20,780	21,099	1.5	Y	9	0	22	1
Maine	2,185	2,246	2.8	N	—	—	—	—
Massachusetts....	11,440	11,662	1.9	N	—	—	27	—
New Hampshire ...	2,814	2,827	0.5	Y	0	0	1	0
New Jersey.......	27,494	26,490	-3.7	N	—	—	74	0
New York	63,536	62,211	-2.1	Y	0	0	329	0
Pennsylvania	45,563	46,313	1.6	Y	221	0	155	3
Rhode Island[7]	4,119	4,190	1.7	N	—	—	—	—
Vermont[7]	2,165	2,082	-3.8	N	—	—	4	—
Midwest	**264,524**	**265,342**	**0.3**	—	**273**	**5**	**530**	**127**
Illinois	45,565	45,675	0.2	Y	13	0	102	12
Indiana	26,833	27,380	2.0	Y	14	2	60	19
Iowa[8]	8,837	8,778	-0.7	N	—	—	18	—
Kansas..........	8,850	8,633	-2.5	Y	7	0	15	0
Michigan	50,648	50,482	-0.3	N	—	—	—	—
Minnesota.......	9,891	9,964	0.7	N	—	—	—	—
Missouri	30,423	30,466	0.1	Y	45	0	128	66
Nebraska	4,435	4,419	-0.4	Y	9	0	7	3
North Dakota	1,435	1,450	1.0	N	—	—	—	—
Ohio	50,418	51,160	1.5	Y	—	2	198	26
South Dakota	3,446	3,358	-2.6	Y	182	1	2	1
Wisconsin........	23,743	23,577	-0.7	N	3	—	—	—
South	**633,236**	**648,126**	**2.4**	—	**1,739**	**36**	**3,164**	**898**
Alabama.........	29,244	29,871	2.1	Y	199	3	173	38
Arkansas	13,914	14,552	4.6	Y	38	0	145	27
Delaware[7]........	7,521	7,362	-2.1	Y	19	0	26	14
Florida	95,078	100,494	5.7	Y	389	0	234	64
Georgia[8]........	53,226	54,016	1.5	Y	105	1	406	40
Kentucky.........	21,644	21,610	-0.2	Y	39	0	105	2
Louisiana	36,981	38,137	3.1	Y	86	0	160	27
Maryland	23,123	23,293	0.7	Y	5	0	73	5
Mississippi	21,758	22,764	4.6	Y	65	0	162	8
North Carolina	38,179	39,042	2.3	Y	167	0	306	43
Oklahoma........	25,686	26,155	1.8	Y	80	3	146	86
South Carolina	24,093	25,275	4.9	Y	59	1	199	37
Tennessee	26,453	26,998	2.1	Y	96	2	97	4
Texas	172,626	173,232	0.4	Y	372	26	702	405
Virginia	37,824	39,224	3.7	Y	20	0	190	98
West Virginia	5,886	6,101	3.7	N	—	—	40	—
West	**317,637**	**316,854**	**-0.2**	—	**930**	**1**	**576**	**67**
Alaska[7].........	5,312	5,223	-1.7	N	—	—	—	—
Arizona[8]	37,088	38,988	5.1	Y	116	1	61	23
California	176,059	173,320	-1.6	Y	655	0	305	13
Colorado.........	22,662	23,130	2.1	Y	1	0	48	1
Hawaii[7].........	6,039	6,003	-0.6	N	—	—	—	—
Idaho	7,357	7,338	-0.3	Y	17	0	4	1
Montana	3,469	3,592	3.5	Y	2	0	9	3
Nevada..........	13,034	12,915	-0.9	Y	83	0	41	12
New Mexico	6,526	6,330	-3.0	Y	2	0	9	1
Oregon..........	14,012	14,079	0.5	Y	35	0	21	2
Utah	6,527	6,459	-1.0	Y	9	0	19	6
Washington	17,438	17,404	-0.2	Y	8	0	51	4
Wyoming	2,114	2,073	-1.9	Y	2	0	8	1

(—) = Not available or applicable. (1) Inmates sentenced to more than one year. (2) Figures do not include persons held under Armed Forces jurisdiction with a military death sentence for murder. (3) Military authorities carried out an additional 160 executions between 1930 and 1961. (4) Includes estimates for Illinois for June 30, 2008, and Nevada for Dec. 31, 2007. (5) Total executed includes 40 executions performed under the District of Columbia's jurisdiction. (6) Prisoners sentenced under DC's criminal code are housed in federal facilities. (7) Prisons and jails form one integrated system. Data includes total jail and prison population. (8) Sentenced prisoner population based on custody count.

Prison Situation Under State or Federal Correctional Authorities' Jurisdiction

Source: *Prison Inmates at Midyear 2008*, Bureau of Justice Statistics, U.S. Dept. of Justice

Largest prison populations, 2008		Imprisonment rates of sentenced prisoners, 2008		Largest percent increases in prison populations			
Jurisdiction	Number	Jurisdiction	Rate[1]	Jurisdiction	% change, 2007-08	Jurisdiction	% change, 2000-08
U.S. TOTAL[2]	1,610,584	U.S. TOTAL[2]...	509	U.S. TOTAL[2]	0.8	U.S. TOTAL[2]	15.7
Federal.....	201,142	Federal......	59	Federal.....	0.8	Federal.....	38.3
State[2]......	1,409,442	State[2].......	450	State[2].....	0.8	State[2]......	13.1
1. California....	173,320	1. Louisiana.....	858	1. Minnesota...	5.2	1. Minnesota...	59.7
2. Texas......	173,232	2. Mississippi.....	749	2. Maine	4.6	2. West Virginia	58.2
3. Florida.....	100,494	3. Oklahoma	668	3. Rhode Island[4]	4.3	3. Arizona[3]	47.1
4. New York....	62,211	Texas	668	South Carolina	4.3	4. Kentucky....	44.8
5. Georgia[3]	54,016	5. Alabama	619	5. Montana	3.8	5. Florida......	40.9
6. Ohio........	51,160	6. Arizona[3]......	565	6. Arizona[3]	3.3	6. Colorado....	37.4
7. Michigan	50,482	7. Florida........	548	7. Virginia	3.0	7. Indiana	36.0
8. Pennsylvania	46,313	8. Georgia[3]	542	8. North Carolina	2.8	8. North Dakota	34.7
9. Illinois[2]......	45,675	9. South Carolina	537	Tennessee ...	2.8	9. Maine	33.7
10. Virginia	39,224	10. Missouri.......	515	10. North Dakota	2.4	10. Oregon	33.1

(1) Prisoners sentenced to more than one year. Rates are per 100,000 population, based upon census population estimates for July 1, 2008. (2) Data for Illinois are estimated. (3) Population based on custody count (number of prisoners held in its facilities) as opposed to jurisdiction count (number of prisoners under its legal authority). Some states are unable to provide both counts. (4) Prisons and jails form one integrated system. Data includes total jail and prison population.

Arrests by Race, 2008

Source: *Crime in the United States, 2008*, Federal Bureau of Investigation, U.S. Dept. of Justice

Each instance in which a person is arrested, cited, or summoned for an offense is counted as one arrest. The figures below therefore do not represent the number of individuals arrested but the number of times persons were arrested, assuming an individual may be arrested multiple times in one year. Arrest estimates are based on statistics from law enforcement agencies that reported 12 months of arrest data.

Offense charged	Total	Number of arrests where arrestee was—				% distrib. for offense charged[1]			
		White	Black	Amer. Indian/ Alaska Native	Asian/ Pacific Islander	White	Black	Amer. Indian/ Alaska Native	Asian/ Pacific Islander
PART I OFFENSES[2]									
Violent crime..............	455,967	265,754	179,636	5,431	5,146	58.3	39.4	1.2	1.1
Murder and nonnegligent manslaughter	9,859	4,721	4,935	99	104	47.9	50.1	1.0	1.1
Forcible rape	16,847	10,990	5,428	198	231	65.2	32.2	1.2	1.4
Robbery	100,525	41,962	56,948	681	934	41.7	56.7	0.7	0.9
Aggravated assault	328,736	208,081	112,325	4,453	3,877	63.3	34.2	1.4	1.2
Property crime	1,300,167	876,425	391,645	15,688	16,409	67.4	30.1	1.2	1.3
Burglary	235,407	157,252	73,960	2,077	2,118	66.8	31.4	0.9	0.9
Larceny-theft	979,145	666,360	286,844	12,684	13,257	68.1	29.3	1.3	1.4
Motor vehicle theft	74,881	44,674	28,510	795	902	59.7	38.1	1.1	1.2
Arson	10,734	8,139	2,331	132	132	75.8	21.7	1.2	1.2
PART II OFFENSES[3]									
Other assaults[4]	991,225	645,870	319,498	14,237	11,620	65.2	32.2	1.4	1.2
Forgery and counterfeiting....	68,586	46,425	21,073	334	754	67.7	30.7	0.5	1.1
Fraud	173,567	117,217	53,508	1,424	1,418	67.5	30.8	0.8	0.8
Embezzlement.............	16,314	10,517	5,455	95	247	64.5	33.4	0.6	1.5
Stolen property: buying, receiving, possessing......	85,351	52,719	31,258	663	711	61.8	36.6	0.8	0.8
Vandalism	218,188	164,334	47,974	3,359	2,521	75.3	22.0	1.5	1.2
Weapons: carrying, possessing, etc...........	137,869	78,114	57,454	1,010	1,291	56.7	41.7	0.7	0.9
Prostitution and commercialized vice.......	58,678	32,682	23,987	491	1,518	55.7	40.9	0.8	2.6
Sex offenses (except forcible rape and prostitution)	60,582	44,553	14,546	646	837	73.5	24.0	1.1	1.4
Drug abuse violations........	1,299,708	829,432	452,590	8,408	9,278	63.8	34.8	0.6	0.7
Gambling	7,611	1,720	5,712	21	158	22.6	75.0	0.3	2.1
Offenses against the family and children.................	86,051	57,292	26,527	1,646	586	66.6	30.8	1.9	0.7
Driving under the influence ...	1,104,342	964,583	110,682	14,706	14,371	87.3	10.0	1.3	1.3
Liquor laws...............	475,198	400,995	54,878	13,997	5,328	84.4	11.5	2.9	1.1
Drunkenness	472,562	390,057	70,969	8,901	2,635	82.5	15.0	1.9	0.6
Disorderly conduct	527,626	334,697	180,073	8,641	4,215	63.4	34.1	1.6	0.8
Vagrancy	26,283	15,705	9,945	500	133	59.8	37.8	1.9	0.5
All other offenses (except traffic violations)...............	2,907,265	1,931,327	898,881	40,237	36,820	66.4	30.9	1.4	1.3
Suspicion[5]	1,247	584	642	14	7	46.8	51.5	1.1	0.6
Curfew and loitering law violations	103,992	65,661	36,223	828	1,280	63.1	34.8	0.8	1.2
Runaways	83,827	55,400	22,749	1,631	4,047	66.1	27.1	1.9	4.8
TOTAL ARRESTS.........	**10,662,206**	**7,382,063**	**3,015,905**	**142,908**	**121,330**	**69.2**	**28.3**	**1.3**	**1.1**

(1) Percentages may not add up to 100 due to rounding. (2) In the UCR program, serious crimes that occur in all areas of the country and are likely to be reported to police are classified as part I offenses. Refer to "Crime in the U.S." table footnotes for offense definitions. (3) Arrest data only is collected for UCR program-designated part II offenses. (4) Simple assaults, where no weapons were used and where the victim did not sustain serious injury (e.g., stalking). (5) Arrested for no specific offense and released without formal charges being placed against a person.

Inmate Population by Gender, Race, Hispanic Origin, and Age, Mid-2008

Source: *Prison Inmates at Midyear 2008*, Bureau of Justice Statistics, U.S. Dept. of Justice

(number of inmates per 100,000 of each group in the U.S. resident population)

Age	Male All races[1]	Male White[2]	Male Black[2]	Male Hispanic	Age	Female All races[1]	Female White[2]	Female Black[2]	Female Hispanic
18-19	1,934	976	5,543	2,376	18-19	129	86	236	185
20-24	3,256	1,564	9,776	4,281	20-24	302	221	608	367
25-29	3,241	1,550	10,408	3,792	25-29	308	225	691	326
30-34	3,328	1,793	11,137	3,446	30-34	367	281	892	328
35-39	2,919	1,643	10,120	2,868	35-39	373	279	961	313
40-44	2,580	1,529	8,622	2,510	40-44	303	208	827	262
45-49	1,641	912	5,854	2,011	45-49	157	101	451	166
50-54	920	520	3,330	1,320	50-54	73	52	178	93
55-59	556	356	1,790	976	55-59	34	25	61	74
60-64	299	213	899	607	60-64	16	11	50	22
65 or older	106	75	383	191	65 or older	4	3	7	4
Total[3]	**1,403**	**727**	**4,777**	**1,760**	**Total[3]**	**135**	**93**	**349**	**147**

Note: Rates are based on census population estimates for July 1, 2008. Detailed categories exclude persons who reported two or more races. (1) Includes American Indians, Alaska natives, Asians, Native Hawaiians, other Pacific Islanders, and persons identifying two or more races. (2) Not including persons of Hispanic or Latino origin. (3) Includes persons under age 18.

Hate Crimes by Offense Type, Bias Motivation, 2007

Source: *Hate Crime Statistics, 2007*, Federal Bureau of Investigation, U.S. Dept. of Justice

Hate crimes are defined as crimes in which victims are chosen because of one or more personal characteristics, such as race, ethnicity, or religion. Congress enacted the Hate Crime Statistics Act of 1990, which led to the collection of hate crime data as part of the FBI's UCR program beginning in 1992. Not all agencies that participate in the UCR program submit hate crime data, so the data presented is not representative of the nation as a whole.

Bias motivation	Total offenses	Crimes against persons[1] Aggravated assault	Crimes against persons[1] Simple assault	Crimes against persons[1] Intimidation	Crimes against persons[1] Other[1]	Crimes against persons[1] Total crimes against persons	Crimes against property[2] Robbery	Crimes against property[2] Burglary	Crimes against property[2] Larceny-theft	Crimes against property[2] Destruction/damage/vandalism	Crimes against property[2] Other[2]	Crimes against property[2] Total crimes against property	Total crimes against society[3]
Single-bias incidents	8,999	1,116	1,683	2,561	43	5,403	178	159	221	2,913	106	3,577	19
Race	4,724	623	845	1,546	17	3,031	67	75	120	1,361	63	1,686	7
Anti-White	871	107	246	190	9	552	39	25	76	155	22	317	2
Anti-Black	3,275	450	518	1,186	7	2,161	21	41	26	992	30	1,110	4
Anti-American Indian/ Alaskan native	75	9	18	22	0	49	0	1	10	9	6	26	0
Anti-Asian/Pacific Islander	219	19	33	79	0	131	6	5	5	71	1	88	0
Anti-multiple races, group	284	38	30	69	1	138	1	3	3	134	4	145	1
Religion	1,477	44	82	290	5	421	3	36	33	972	10	1,054	2
Anti-Jewish	1,010	16	42	201	4	263	1	17	6	718	5	747	0
Anti-Catholic	65	0	7	4	0	11	0	4	10	38	2	54	0
Anti-Protestant	59	4	5	3	0	12	0	2	4	41	0	47	0
Anti-Islamic	133	12	21	51	0	84	1	4	3	41	0	49	0
Anti-other religion	140	10	5	24	0	39	0	6	3	88	2	99	2
Anti-multiple religions, group	64	1	2	7	1	11	0	3	7	42	1	53	0
Anti-atheism/agnosticism/ etc.	6	1	0	0	0	1	1	0	0	4	0	5	0
Sexual orientation	1,460	242	448	335	14	1,039	53	16	23	314	12	418	3
Anti-male homosexual...	864	142	280	203	10	635	37	4	9	173	4	227	2
Anti-female homosexual	184	37	48	47	0	132	2	4	3	41	2	52	0
Anti-homosexual	362	61	104	74	2	241	14	3	6	93	4	120	1
Anti-heterosexual	27	1	7	8	2	18	0	4	1	3	1	9	0
Anti-bisexual	23	1	9	3	0	13	0	1	4	4	1	10	0
Ethnicity/national origin ..	1,256	203	292	375	4	874	53	28	24	257	15	377	874
Anti-Hispanic	775	147	172	247	4	570	43	19	11	123	5	201	570
Anti-other ethnicity/ national origin	481	56	120	128	0	304	10	9	13	134	10	176	304
Disability	82	4	16	15	3	38	2	4	21	9	6	42	2
Anti-physical	20	2	7	7	0	16	0	0	2	1	1	4	0
Anti-mental	62	2	9	8	3	22	2	4	19	8	5	38	2
Multiple-bias incidents[4] ..	7	0	1	4	0	5	0	0	0	2	0	2	0
Total offenses	**9,006**	**1,116**	**1,684**	**2,565**	**43**	**5,408**	**178**	**159**	**221**	**2,915**	**106**	**3,579**	**19**

(1) Includes murder, non-negligent manslaughter, forcible rape, and additional offenses not shown here in details. (2) Includes arson, motor vehicle theft, and additional offenses not shown here in detail. (3) Includes drug or narcotic offenses, gambling and prostitution offenses, and weapon law violations where society as a whole is considered the victim. (4) More than one offense type must occur and at least two offense types must be motivated by different biases to count as a multiple-bias incident.

Notable Assassinations Since 1865

1865—Apr. 14: U.S. Pres. Abraham Lincoln shot by John Wilkes Booth, well-known actor with Confederate sympathies, at Ford's Theater in Washington, DC; died Apr. 15.

1881—Mar. 13: Alexander II of Russia. **July 2:** U.S. Pres. James A. Garfield shot by Charles J. Guiteau, disappointed office seeker, in Washington, DC; died Sept. 19.

1894—June 24: French Pres. Sadi Carnot, by Sante Caserio, Italian anarchist, in Lyon.

1898—Sept. 10: Empress Elizabeth of Austria stabbed by Luigi Lucheni, Italian anarchist.

1900—July 29: Umberto I, king of Italy.

1901—Sept. 6: U.S. Pres. William McKinley shot by Leon Czolgosz, anarchist, in Buffalo, NY; died Sept. 14.

1908—Feb. 1: King Carlos I of Portugal and his son Luis Felipe in Lisbon.

1913—Feb. 23: Mexican Pres. Francisco I. Madero and Vice Pres. José María Pino Suárez. **Mar. 18:** King George of Greece.

1914—June 28: Archduke Francis Ferdinand of Austria-Hungary and his wife shot by Gavrilo Princip, Serb nationalist, in Sarajevo, Bosnia.

1916—Dec. 30: Grigory Rasputin, mystic and court figure, by group of aristocrats.

1918—July 12: Grand Duke Michael of Russia, at Perm. **July 16:** Nicholas II, former (abdicated) czar of Russia; his wife, Czarina Alexandra; their son, Czarevitch Alexis; their daughters, Grand Duchesses Olga, Tatiana, Marie, Anastasia; and 4 members of household executed by Bolsheviks at Ekaterinburg.

1920—May 20: Mexican Pres. Gen. Venustiano Carranza in Tlaxcalantongo.

1922—Aug. 22: Michael Collins, Irish revolutionary, in ambush in West Cork. **Dec. 16:** Polish Pres. Gabriel Narutowicz in Warsaw.

1923—July 20: Gen. Francisco "Pancho" Villa, ex-rebel leader, in Parral, Mexico.

1928—July 17: Gen. Alvaro Obregon, president-elect of Mexico, in San Angel.

1932—May 6: French Pres. Paul Doumer shot by Russian émigré, Pavel Gorgulov, in Paris.

1934—July 25: Austrian Chancellor Engelbert Dollfuss by Nazis, in Vienna.

1935—Sept. 8: Sen. Huey P. Long, former Louisiana governor, shot by Dr. Carl Austin Weiss, son-in-law of political opponent, in Baton Rouge; died Sept. 10.

1940—Aug. 20: Leon Trotsky (Lev Bronstein), exiled Soviet commissar of war, fatally wounded with ice ax by Soviet agent near Mexico City.

1948—Jan. 30: Mohandas K. Gandhi (Mahatma) shot by Nathuram Godse, Hindu fanatic, in New Delhi. **Sept. 17:** Count Folke Bernadotte, UN mediator for Palestine, by Jewish extremists in Jerusalem.

1951—July 20: Jordanian King Abdullah ibn Hussein. **Oct. 16:** Prime Min. Liaquat Ali Khan of Pakistan shot, in Rawalpindi.

1956—Sept. 21: Pres. Anastasio Somoza of Nicaragua shot in Leon; died Sept. 29.

1957—July 26: Guatemalan Pres. Carlos Castillo Armas, in Guatemala City by one of own guards.

1958—July 14: King Faisal of Iraq, Crown Prince Abdullah, and **July 15,** Prem. Nuri as-Said, by rebels in Baghdad.

1959—Sept. 25: Prime Min. Solomon Bandaranaike of Ceylon, by Buddhist monk in Colombo.

1961—Jan. 17: Ex-Prem. Patrice Lumumba of the Congo, in Katanga Province. **May 30:** Dominican dictator Rafael Leonidas Trujillo Molina, nr. Ciudad Trujillo.

1963—June 12: Medgar Evers, NAACP's Mississippi field secretary, shot by Byron De La Beckwith in Jackson, MS. **Nov. 2:** Pres. Ngo Dinh Diem of South Vietnam and his brother, Ngo Dinh Nhu, in military coup. **Nov. 22:** U.S. Pres. John F. Kennedy shot while riding in motorcade through downtown Dallas, TX; accused gunman Lee Harvey Oswald murdered by nightclub owner Jack Ruby while awaiting trial.

1965—Jan. 21: Iranian Prem. Hassan Ali Mansour in Tehran; 4 executed. **Feb. 21:** Malcolm X, black nationalist leader, shot by three men linked to Nation of Islam at New York City rally.

1966—Sept. 6: Prime Min. Hendrik F. Verwoerd of South Africa stabbed to death in parliament at Cape Town.

1968—Apr. 4: Rev. Martin Luther King Jr. fatally shot in Memphis, TN; James Earl Ray convicted of crime. **June 5:** Sen. Robert F. Kennedy (D, NY) shot in Los Angeles; died June 6. Sirhan Sirhan convicted of crime.

1971—Nov. 28: Jordanian Prime Min. Wasfi Tal by Palestinian guerrillas, in Cairo.

1973—Mar. 2: U.S. Amb. Cleo A. Noel Jr., U.S. Charge d'Affaires George C. Moore, and Belgian Charge d'Affaires Guy Eid, by Palestinian guerrillas in Khartoum, Sudan. **Dec. 20:** Spanish Prem. Luis Carrero Blanco in car bombing by Basque separatist group ETA, in Madrid.

1974—Aug. 19: U.S. Amb. to Cyprus, Rodger P. Davies, by sniper's bullet in Nicosia.

1975—Feb. 11: Pres. Richard Ratsimandrava of Madagascar shot in Tananarive. **Mar. 25:** Saudi Arabian King Faisal shot by nephew Prince Musad Abdel Aziz, in Riyadh. **Aug. 15:** Bangladesh Pres. Sheik Mujibur Rahman killed in coup.

1976—Feb. 13: Nigerian head of state, Gen. Murtala Ramat Mohammed, by self-styled "young revolutionaries."

1977—Mar. 16: Kamal Jumblat, Lebanese Druse chieftain, shot near Beirut. **Mar. 18:** Congo Pres. Marien Ngouabi shot in Brazzaville.

1978—May 9: Former Italian Prem. Aldo Moro killed by Red Brigades terrorists who abducted him Mar. 16 in Rome, held him hostage for several weeks. **July 9:** Former Iraqi Prem. Abdul Razak Al-Naif shot in London.

1979—Feb. 14: U.S. Amb. Adolph Dubs shot by Afghan Muslim extremists in Kabul. **Aug. 27:** Lord Mountbatten, WWII hero, and 2 others killed when a bomb exploded on his fishing boat off coast of Co. Sligo, Ireland. IRA claimed responsibility. **Oct. 26:** S. Korean Pres. Park Chung Hee and 6 bodyguards fatally shot by Kim Jae Kyu, head of S. Korean CIA.

1980—Apr. 12: Liberian Pres. William R. Tolbert slain in military coup. **Sept. 17:** Former Nicaraguan Pres. Anastasio Somoza Debayle shot in Paraguay.

1981—Oct. 6: Egyptian Pres. Anwar al-Sadat shot by commandos while reviewing military parade in Cairo; 7 others killed, 28 wounded. 4 convicted as assassins and executed.

1982—Sept. 14: Lebanese Pres.-elect Bashir Gemayel killed by bomb in east Beirut.

1983—Aug. 21: Philippine opposition leader Benigno Aquino Jr. shot by gunman at Manila Intl. Airport.

1984—Oct. 31: Indian Prime Min. Indira Gandhi shot and killed by 2 Sikh bodyguards, in New Delhi.

1986—Feb. 28: Swedish Prem. Olof Palme shot by gunman on Stockholm street.

1987—June 1: Lebanese Prem. Rashid Karami killed when bomb exploded aboard helicopter.

1988—Apr. 16: PLO military chief Khalil Wazir (Abu Jihad) gunned down by Israeli commandos in Tunisia.

1989—Aug. 18: Colombian pres. candidate Luis Carlos Galan killed by Medellín cartel drug traffickers at campaign rally in Bogotá. **Nov. 22:** Lebanese Pres. Rene Moawad killed when bomb exploded next to his motorcade.

1990—Mar. 22: Colombian pres. candidate Bernardo Jaramillo Ossa shot by gunman at airport in Bogotá.

1991—May 21: Former Indian Prime Min. Rajiv Gandhi killed by bomb during election rally in Madras.

1992—June 29: Algerian Pres. Mohammed Boudiaf shot by gunman in Annaba.

1993—May 1: Sri Lankan Pres. Ranasinghe Premadasa killed by bomb in Colombo.

1994—Mar. 23: Mexican pres. candidate Luis Donaldo Colosio Murrieta shot by gunman Mario Aburto Martinez. **Apr. 6:** Burundian Pres. Cyprien Ntaryamira and Rwandan Pres. Juvenal Habyarimana killed with 8 others when their plane was apparently shot down.

1995—Nov. 4: Israeli Prime Min. Yitzhak Rabin shot by Yigal Amir, Jewish extremist, at peace rally in Tel Aviv.

1996—Oct. 2: Andrei Lukanov, former Bulgarian prime min., shot outside home by unidentified gunman.

1998—Feb. 6: Prefect of Corsica, Claude Erigmac, shot in the back by 2 unidentified gunmen while walking to concert. **Apr. 26:** Guatemalan Roman Catholic Bishop Juan Gerardi Conedera, human rights champion, found beaten to death in Guatemala City.

1999—Mar. 23: Paraguayan Vice-Pres. Luis Maria Argaña, ambushed and shot to death along with his driver, by 4 unidentified assailants, in Asunción. **Apr. 9:** Niger Pres. Ibrahim Bare Mainassara ambushed and killed by dissident soldiers. **Oct. 27:** Armenian Prime Min. Vazgen Sarkissian, along with 7 others, shot to death during session of parliament.

2000—Jan. 15: Serbian paramilitary leader Zeljko Raznjatovic (Arkan), with 2 others, shot and killed by unidentified gunman in Belgrade. **June 8:** Brig. Gen. Stephen Saunders, Britain's senior military representative in Greece, fatally shot by 2 men on motorcycle, while driving car in Athens suburb.

2001—Jan. 16: Dem. Rep. of the Congo Pres. Laurent Kabila shot to death by bodyguard at pres. palace in Kinshasa. **June 1:** Nepal's King Birendra, Queen Aiswarya, and 7 other royals fatally shot by Crown Prince Dipendra, who also fatally wounded himself. **Sept. 9:** Afghan Northern Alliance (anti-Taliban) guerrilla leader Ahmed Shah Massoud injured in suicide-attack bombing by 2 people posing as journalists, in N. Afghanistan; died Sept. 15. **Oct. 14:** Abdel Rahman Hamad, a leader of Palestinian militant group Hamas, shot by Israeli military snipers. **Oct. 17:** Israeli tourism min. Rehavam Zeevifatally shot; Popular Front for the Liberation of Palestine claimed responsibility.

2002—Mar. 16: Colombian cleric Isaias Duarte Cancino, critic of Colombian guerrillas and drug traffickers, shot by unidentified gunmen outside of church in Cali. **May 6:** Dutch right-wing politician Pim Fortuyn shot outside radio station in Hilversum. **July 6:** Afghan Vice-Pres. Haji Abdul Qadir shot outside his office in Kabul. **July 23:** Salah Sherhada, a founder of armed wing of Hamas, killed with 14 others in air strike on Gaza City by Israeli fighter jet.

2003—Mar. 12: Serbian Prime Min. Zoran Djindjic shot by snipers (paramilitary) outside govt. headquarters in Belgrade. **Apr. 10:** Shiite Muslim cleric Abdul Majid al-Khoei attacked by crowd, hacked to death at Imam Ali mosque, Najaf, Iraq. **Apr. 17:** Sergei Yushenkov, former Russian legislator and Liberal Party head, shot outside apartment in Moscow. **Aug. 29:** Shiite Muslim cleric Bakir al-Hakim killed in car bombing at Imam Ali mosque in Najaf, Iraq. **Sept. 10:** Swedish Foreign Min. Anna Lindh stabbed in Stockholm dept. store; died Sept. 11.

2004—Feb. 13: Former Chechen Pres. Zelimkhan Yandarbiyev killed after car exploded in Qatar. **Mar. 22:** Sheik Ahmed Yassin, spiritual leader of Hamas, by Israeli missile attack in Gaza City. **Apr. 17:** Hamas leader Abdel Aziz Rantisi, by Israeli missile strike in Gaza City. **May 9:** Chechen Pres. Akhmad Kadyrov, by bomb explosion at WWII memorial service in Grozny. **May 17:** Iraqi Gov. Council Pres. Ezzedine Salim, by car bomb explosion at Green Zone checkpoint in Baghdad. **Nov. 2:** Filmmaker Theo van Gogh, critic of Islam and great-grandnephew of painter Vincent van Gogh, shot and stabbed by Muslim militant in Amsterdam.

2005—Jan. 4: Baghdad Gov. Ali al-Haidari gunned down by insurgents in Baghdad, Iraq. **Feb. 14:** Former Lebanese Prime Min. Rafik al-Hariri killed when motorcade bombed in Beirut. **Mar. 8:** Former Chechen pres. Aslan Maskhadov killed in raid by Russian special forces, in village outside Grozny. **July 1:** Sheik Kamaledding al-Ghuraifi, senior aide to Grand Ayatollah Ali Sistani, shot and killed on way to Friday prayers, in Baghdad.

2006—Feb. 11: Leading Kazakhstan opposition politician Altynbek Sarsenbayev (also known as Sarsenbaiuly) kidnapped, found murdered outside Almaty. **July 10:** Shamil Basayev, leader of Chechen separatist movement who claimed responsibility for many of Russia's worst terrorist attacks, killed in massive explosion nr. village of Ekazhevo. Chechen rebel website said explosion was accidental, but Russian security director said killing was result of special forces operation. **July 14:** Prominent Shiite Muslim cleric Allama Hassan Turabi killed in suicide bombing at his home in Karachi, Pakistan. **Sept. 14:** Andrei Kozlov, Russian central banker active in reforming industry, shot by unidentified gunmen in Moscow. **Oct. 7:** Anna Politkovskaya, reporter critical of Kremlin's Chechnya policies, fatally shot by unidentified gunman in apartment building in Moscow. **Nov. 21:** Pierre Gemayel, Lebanese cabinet minister opposed to Syria, shot by unknown gunmen while driving through Beirut. **Nov. 23:** Aleksandr Litvinenko, former Russian intelligence agent and critic of Russia's government and security service, died after apparent poisoning by radioactive isotope; another former KGB agent suspected.

2007—June 13: Walid Eido, Lebanese parliament member who was part of anti-Syria coalition, killed by car bomb in Beirut. **Aug. 2:** *Oakland Post* editor Chauncey Bailey, who was investigating financial status of black Muslim organization, shot dead in downtown Oakland, CA. **Sept. 19:** Antoine Ghanem, member of ruling anti-Syria coalition in Lebanese parliament, killed by bomb in parked car nr. Beirut. **Dec. 27:** Benazir Bhutto, former Pakistani prime min. and first female elected leader of a Muslim state, by gunfire and/or bomb as she was leaving political rally for Pakistan People's Party.

2008—Feb. 12: Imad Mughniyeh, top Hezbollah commander, by car bomb in Syria. Mughniyeh had been on FBI's Most Wanted Terrorist list and was believed to have orchestrated the 1983 bombing of U.S. embassy in Beirut, among other terrorist acts.

May 8: Edgar Eusebio Millán Gómez, Mexico's acting national police chief and opponent of drug cartels, by gunmen outside his home in Mexico City. **Aug. 1:** Brig. gen. and top presidential aide Mohammed Suleiman reportedly shot by sniper nr. Tartus, Syria; Suleiman had been Syria's primary contact with investigators from Intl. Atomic Energy Agency. **Oct. 23:** Ivo Pukanic, owner and editor-in-chief of the Croatian weekly political newspaper *Nacional* was killed in Zagreb when a bomb exploded near his car. The bombing was widely attributed to organized crime groups. **Oct.-Nov.:** A total of 12 police officers, including the state police commanders in two districts of Mexico, are assassinated over a five-day stretch of drug-related violence.

2009—Jan.: Six candidates for elected office are killed in several regions of Iraq shortly before scheduled provincial elections. **Mar. 2:** Heavily armed men launch rocket grenades into the home of Guinea-Bissau's longtime President João Bernardo Vieira and Gen. Batista Tagme Na Waie, killing both men. **Mar. 31:** Sulim Yamadeyev, a former Chechen general and enemy of the Kremlin-installed president, is killed by gunmen in Dubai. **May 31:** Dr. George Tiller, one of the few doctors in Kansas to provide abortions and one of the few in U.S. to perform abortions late in pregnancy, is shot to death in his Wichita church by an anti-abortion protester. **June 12:** Harith al-Obaidi, a Sunni member of Iraq's Parliament, is shot at point-blank range. His aide and three bodyguards are also killed in the attack. **June 13:** Gunmen kill Bashir Aushev, a former vice premier of the Ingushetia region of Russia. **Sept. 2:** A suicide bomber in Mehtar Lam, Afghanistan, kills at least 16 people, including Abdullah Lahgmani, deputy director of the country's National Directorate for Security.

Notable Assassination Attempts Since 1912

1912—Oct. 14: Former U.S. Pres. Theodore Roosevelt shot and wounded by demented man in Milwaukee, WI.

1933—Feb. 15: In Miami, FL, Joseph Zangara, anarchist, shot at Pres.-elect Franklin D. Roosevelt, but a woman seized his arm; bullet fatally wounded Chicago Mayor Anton J. Cermak, who died Mar. 6.

1944—July 20: Adolf Hitler injured when bomb, planted by a German officer, exploded in his headquarters; 1 aide killed,12 injured.

1950—Nov. 1: In attempt to assassinate Pres. Harry Truman, 2 members of a Puerto Rican nationalist movement—Griselio Torresola and Oscar Collazo—tried to shoot their way into Blair House, across the street from White House. Torresola killed. Pvt. Leslie Coffelt, White House policeman, fatally shot.

1970—Nov. 27: Pope Paul VI unharmed by knife-wielding assailant who attempted to attack him in airport in Manila, Philippines.

1972—May 15: Alabama Gov. George Wallace seriously wounded when shot in Laurel, MD, by Arthur Bremer.

1975—Sept. 5: Pres. Gerald R. Ford unharmed when Secret Service agent grabbed pistol aimed at him by Lynette (Squeaky) Fromme, a follower of cult leader Charles Manson, in Sacramento, CA. **Sept. 22:** Pres. Ford again unharmed when bystander grabbed arm of Sara Jane Moore as she fired upon Ford in San Francisco.

1980—May 29: Civil rights leader Vernon E. Jordan Jr. shot and wounded in Ft. Wayne, IN.

1981—Jan. 16: Irish political activist Bernadette Devlin McAliskey and her husband shot and seriously wounded by 3 members of a Protestant paramilitary group in Co. Tyrone, Ireland. **Mar. 30:** Pres. Ronald Reagan, along with Press Sec. James Brady, Secret Service agent Timothy J. McCarthy, and Washington, DC, policeman Thomas Delahanty shot and seriously wounded by John W. Hinckley Jr. in Washington, DC. **May 13:** Pope John Paul II and 2 bystanders shot and wounded by Mehmet Ali Agca, an escaped Turkish prisoner, in St. Peter's Square, Rome.

1982—May 12: Pope John Paul II wounded by ultra-conservative priest wielding bayonet, in Fatima, Portugal.

1984—Oct. 12: British Prime Min. Margaret Thatcher unharmed when a bomb, said to have been planted by the IRA, exploded at the Grand Hotel in Brighton, England, during a Party conference; 4 died, incl. a member of Parliament.

1986—Sept. 7: Chilean Pres. Gen. Augusto Pinochet Ugarte unharmed after motorcade was attacked by rebels.

1995—June 26: Egyptian Pres. Hosni Mubarak unharmed when gunmen fired on his motorcade in Addis Ababa, Ethiopia; 4 died, incl. 2 Ethiopian police officers.

1997—Feb. 12: Colombian Pres. Ernesto Samper Pizano unharmed when bomb exploded on a runway in Barranquilla as his plane was preparing to land. **Apr. 30:** Tajik Pres. Imamali Rakhmanov injured when a grenade was thrown at him.

1998—Feb. 9: Georgian Pres. Eduard A. Shevardnadze unharmed when gunmen fired on his motorcade in Tbilisi.

2000—Sept. 18: Armed men attempted to assassinate Côte d'Ivoire military leader Gen. Robert Guei in predawn raid.

2002—Apr. 14: Leading Colombian pres. candidate Alvaro Uribe Velez unharmed after bomb exploded under parked bus as his motorcade passed in Barranquilla; 3 bystanders killed. **July 14:** French Pres. Jacques Chirac unharmed after Maxime Brunerie, gunman with ties to neo-Nazi groups, fired at his open-top jeep during a Bastille Day parade in Paris. **Sept. 5:** Afghan Pres. Hamid Karzai unharmed after militant shot at car in Kandahar. **Nov. 25:** Turkmenistan Pres. Saparmurat Niyazov unharmed after gunmen opened fire on his motorcade in Ashgabat.

2003—Dec. 1: Pakistani Pres. Pervez Musharraf unharmed after bomb detonated on bridge in Rawalpindi seconds after his motorcade crossed over.

2004—Mar. 19: Taiwanese Pres. Chen Shui-bian shot while campaigning in motorcade; minor injuries. **July 13:** Separatists bombed motorcade of Sergei Abramov, Chechnya's acting pres. **Sept. 5:** Ukrainian opposition presidential candidate Viktor Yushchenko, who later won office, fell ill after meeting; diagnosed with dioxin poisoning. **Sept. 16:** Rocket fired at helicopter carrying Afghan Pres. Hamid Karzai, near Gardez.

2005—Mar. 15: Kosovo Pres. Ibrahim Rugova survived after bomb damaged the vehicle he was in as his motorcade traveled through Pristina. **July 12:** Lebanon's pro-Syrian defense min. Elias Murr wounded by car explosion in Beirut suburb.

2006—Apr. 12: Pro-democracy activist Edil Baisalov was beaten as he left his office in Bishkek, Kyrgyzstan. He had sought to block the parliamentary candidacy of a reputed crime boss. **Sept. 5:** Lt. Col. Samir Shehade, involved in investigation of 2005 assassination of former Lebanese Prime Min. Rafik al-Hariri, wounded by bomb as he drove in village near Sidon.

2007—June 29: Rockets hit a plane carrying former rebel chief and current Côte d'Ivoire Prime Min. Guillaume Soro, shortly after plane landed in Bouake; Soro unhurt.

2008—Feb. 11: Pres. José Ramos-Horta shot in attack led by fugitive former army official, in Dili, Timor-Leste. Ambush on Prime Min. Xanana Gusmão's motorcade a short time later unsuccessful. **Apr. 27:** Afghan President Hamid Karzai is unharmed after Taliban gunmen fire on a military parade in Kabul where Karzai and other members of Afghanistan's government were in attendance.

2009—Jan. 21: Ziad al-Ani, a leader of one of Iraq's main Sunni Arab parties participating in forthcoming provincial elections, survives a car bombing that leaves four dead. **June 22:** Yunus-Bek Yevkurov, president of the Ingushetia region of Russia, is seriously wounded when a suicide bomber in a car packed with explosives crashes into his motorcade. **Sept. 2:** Hamid Saeed Kami, Pakistan's Minister of Religious Affairs, is wounded by two men firing at his car from a motorcycle.

Notable U.S. Kidnappings Since 1924

Bobby Franks, 14, in Chicago, **May 21, 1924**, by 2 youths from wealthy families—Richard Loeb, 18, and Nathan Leopold, 19—who killed boy. Demand for $10,000 ignored. Loeb killed in prison; Leopold paroled 1958.

Charles A. Lindbergh Jr., 20 mos. old, nr. Hopewell, NJ, **Mar. 1, 1932**; found dead **May 12**. Ransom of $50,000 paid to man identified as Bruno Richard Hauptmann, 35, paroled German convict who entered U.S. illegally. Hauptmann convicted, electrocuted in Trenton, NJ, prison, Apr. 3, 1936.

William A. Hamm Jr., 39, brewing company pres. in St. Paul, **June 15, 1933**, by Karpis-Barker gang. $100,000 paid. Alvin Karpis given life, paroled in 1969.

Charles F. Urschel, in Oklahoma City, **July 22, 1933**. Released **July 31** after $200,000 paid. George "Machine Gun" Kelly and 5 others sentenced to life.

Brooke L. Hart, 22, in San Jose, CA. Thomas Thurmond and John Holmes arrested after demanding $40,000. When Hart's body was found in San Francisco Bay, **Nov. 26, 1933**, a mob forced its way into county jail and lynched the 2 kidnappers.

June Robles, 6, abducted in Tucson, AZ, **Apr. 25, 1934**. Missing for 19 days after ransom note sent to parents. Found alive in iron cage buried in desert. No arrests ever made.

George Weyerhaeuser, 9, of Weyerhaeuser lumber company, in Tacoma, WA, **May 24, 1935**. Returned home **June 1** after $200,000 paid. Kidnappers given 20 to 60 years.

Charles Mattson, 10, in Tacoma, WA, **Dec. 27, 1936**. Kidnapper initially asked for $28,000 but subsequent communication with parents was confusing. Charles found dead **Jan. 11, 1937**.

Robert C. Greenlease, 6, son of wealthy car dealer, taken from Kansas City, MO, school **Sept. 28, 1953**, held for $600,000. Body was found **Oct. 7**. Bonnie Brown Heady and Carl A. Hall pleaded guilty, were executed.

Peter Weinberger, 32 days old, Westbury, NY, **July 4, 1956**, for $2,000 ransom, not paid. Child found dead, abandoned by kidnapper Angelo John LaMarca, 31, who was convicted, executed.

Lee Crary, 8, in Everett, WA, **Sept. 22, 1957**; $10,000 ransom, not paid. Escaped after 3 days, led police to George E. Collins, who was convicted.

Frank Sinatra Jr., 19, from hotel room in Lake Tahoe, CA, **Dec. 8, 1963**. Released **Dec. 11** after his father paid $240,000 ransom. Three men sentenced to prison.

Barbara Jane Mackle, 20, abducted **Dec. 17, 1968**, from Atlanta, GA, motel; found unharmed 3 days later, buried in a coffin-like box 18 in. underground, after her father paid $500,000 ransom. Gary Steven Krist sentenced to life, Ruth Eisenmann-Schier to 7 years.

Virginia Piper, 49, abducted **July 27, 1972**, from her home in suburban Minneapolis; found unharmed near Duluth 2 days later after husband, retired banker, paid $1 mil ransom, then largest ransom ever reported in U.S.

J. Paul Getty III, 17, grandson of the oil billionaire, disappeared **July 10, 1973**, in Italy. Reported payment of $2.8 mil ransom not made until after Getty's ear was sent to a newspaper with a warning that other parts of his body would be mutilated unless ransom was paid. Getty freed **Dec. 15**; 2 men sentenced to prison.

Patricia "Patty" Hearst, 19, taken from her Berkeley, CA, apartment **Feb. 4, 1974**; "Symbionese Liberation Army" captors demanded her father, publisher Randolph Hearst, give millions to area poor. Patricia implicated in a San Francisco bank holdup, **Apr. 15**. The FBI, **Sept. 18, 1975**, captured her and others; they were indicted on various charges. Patricia convicted of bank robbery, Mar. 20, 1976; released from prison under executive clemency, Feb. 1, 1979. In 1978, William and Emily Harris were sentenced to 10 years to life for the kidnapping; both were paroled in 1983.

J. Reginald Murphy, 40, an editor of *Atlanta Constitution* (GA), kidnapped **Feb. 20, 1974**; freed **Feb. 22** after newspaper paid $700,000 ransom. William A. H. Williams arrested; most of the money recovered.

Jack Teich, Kings Point, NY, steel executive, seized **Nov. 12, 1974**; released **Nov. 19** after payment of $750,000.

Adam Walsh, 6, abducted from a Hollywood, FL, dept. store, **July 27, 1981**. Severed head found 2 weeks later. John Walsh, Adam's father, became active in raising awareness about missing children.

Terry Anderson, 37, Middle East bureau chief for Associated Press, in Beirut, Lebanon, by members of Islamic fundamentalist group Hezbollah on **Mar. 16, 1985**. Freed **Dec. 4, 1991**. Anderson had been held hostage along with **William Buckley**, 55, CIA sta-

tion chief in Beirut who was kidnapped **Mar. 16, 1984**, and died in captivity.

Jaycee Dugard, 11, kidnapped near her home in South Lake Tahoe, CA, **June 10, 1991**; held for 18 years by Nancy and Philip Garrido, who fathered two girls with Dugard during her captivity. Dugard, along with her 11- and 15-year-old daughters, was reunited with her family **Aug. 27, 2009**, after police arrested the Garridos.

Sidney J. Reso, oil company executive, seized **Apr. 29, 1992**; died **May 3**. Arthur D. Seale—former security official at oil company—and his wife, Irene, arrested June 19. Arthur pleaded guilty, sentenced to life in prison; Irene sentenced to 20-year prison term.

Polly Klaas, 12, Petaluma, CA, abducted at knife point, **Oct. 1, 1993**, during a slumber party at her home. Police arrested Richard Allen Davis on **Nov. 30**; he led them to her body, found **Dec. 4** in wooded area of Cloverdale, CA. Davis found guilty June 18, 1996, and sentenced to death Sept. 26.

Marshall I. Wais, 79, owner of 2 San Francisco steel companies, kidnapped **Nov. 19, 1996**, from his San Francisco home. Released unharmed the same day after $500,000 ransom paid; Thomas William Taylor and Michael K. Robinson arrested same day.

Tionda Z. Bradley, 10, and sister **Diamond Yvette Bradley**, 3, went missing **July 6, 2001**, in Chicago, IL. Note left by Tionda at home stated the 2 girls were going to the store and the playground. Believed kidnapped, case still unsolved.

Daniel Pearl, 38, reporter for *Wall Street Journal*, disappeared **Jan. 23, 2002**, while researching story in Karachi, Pakistan. British-born militant Ahmad Omar Saeed Sheikh **Feb. 14** admitted to organizing the kidnapping and said Pearl was dead. Sheikh and 3 others convicted July 15 of kidnapping and murder by a judge in Hyderabad.

Elizabeth Smart, 14, abducted from her home in Salt Lake City, UT, **June 5, 2002**, allegedly by Brian D. Mitchell, and forced to live with Mitchell and wife Wanda for 9 months in various U.S. cities; found walking down street with captors in Sandy, UT, 15 miles from Smart family home, **Mar. 12, 2003**.

Natalee Holloway, 18, of Birmingham, AL, vanished **May 30, 2005**, on high school graduation trip to Aruba, Netherlands dependency in West Indies. Officials believed she was kidnapped and murdered. Several suspects were detained but later released.

Jill Carroll, 28, freelance journalist, in Baghdad by group called the Revenge Brigade, **Jan. 7, 2006**. She was on assignment for the *Christian Science Monitor* when she was seized. She was released **Mar. 30**; 4 Iraqis arrested in connection with her kidnapping in Aug.

Steve Centanni, 60, a Fox News reporter released **Aug. 26, 2006** (along with a colleague), after being kidnapped and held hostage for 13 days by Palestinian militant group Holy Jihad Brigades. The group had demanded that the U.S. release all Muslims held in its prisons.

Reigh Storrow Mills, 7, abducted **July 27, 2008**, by her father Christian Gerhartsreiter (who used the alias Clark Rockefeller); reunited with her mother **Aug. 2, 2008**, by FBI agents who took Gerhartsreiter into custody.

Felix Batista, 55, who negotiated the release of numerous kidnapping victims in Latin America was abducted in Mexico in early **Dec. 2008**.

Melissa Roxas, 31, a volunteer health worker released **May 24, 2009**, five days after being kidnapped in the Philippines **May 19, 2009**.

David Rohde, 41, a *New York Times* reporter captured by the Taliban in Afghanistan **Nov. 10, 2008**, escaped **June 19, 2009**.

Notable Terrorist Incidents Worldwide Since 1971

Source: U.S. Dept. of State; *Facts On File World News Digest @ Facts.com*; World Almanac research

Selected noteworthy incidents, excluding most assassinations, kidnappings, and military targets. Does not include all incidents in Iraq or Afghanistan, 2001-present; *see* Chronology of the Year's Events.

1971—Mar. 1: Senate wing of U.S. Capitol Building in Wash., DC, bombed by Weather Underground; no deaths.

1972—July 21: "Bloody Friday." Provisional IRA exploded 20+ bombs across Belfast, N. Ireland; 9 killed, hundreds injured. **Sept. 5:** Members of Palestinian group Black September killed 2 Israeli athletes and seized 9 others at Olympic Village in Munich, W. Germany, during Summer Olympics. 9 hostages, 5 militants, 1 Ger. officer died in botched rescue.

1973—Dec. 17: Palestinian gunmen attacked Rome airport and bombed plane on tarmac; hijacked Lufthansa plane with 5 Italian hostages to Athens, Greece, then to Kuwait; 31 killed in all.

1974—June 17: Houses of Parliament in London, England, bombed by Provisional IRA; 11 injured.

1975—Jan. 27: Puerto Rican FALN nationalists bombed Fraunces Tavern in New York City; 4 killed, 53 injured. **Jan. 29:** U.S. State Dept. building in Wash., DC, bombed by Weather Underground; no deaths.

1976—June 27: Palestinian and Baader-Meinhof militants forced Air France jet to land at Entebbe, Uganda. Israeli army rescued 103 hostages from airport terminal in battle with terrorists and Ugandan troops, July 3-4; 32 killed in all.

1978—Mar. 11: Palestinian militants landed on beach near Haifa, Israel. Shot civilians and hijacked bus with hostages to Tel Aviv. Exploded at roadblock; 43 killed.

1979—Nov. 4: Iranian radicals seized U.S. embassy in Tehran, taking 66 Americans hostage. 52 were held until Jan. 20, 1981. **Nov. 20:** 200 Islamic terrorists seized Grand Mosque in Mecca, Saudi Arabia, and held hundreds of pilgrims hostage. Saudi forces retook mosque Dec. 4; about 250 died.

1980—Feb. 27: Members of leftist guerrilla group April 19 Movement (M-19) seized Dominican Republic embassy in Bogota, Colombia; 80 hostages taken. 18 held until Apr. 27.

1983—April 18: Hezbollah suicide truck bomb at U.S. embassy in Beirut, Lebanon, killed 63. **Oct. 9:** N. Korean agents ambushed a S. Korean govt. delegation in Rangoon, Burma, killing 21. **Oct. 23:** Hezbollah suicide truck bombings of U.S. and French military bases, Beirut, Lebanon; 242 Americans, 58 French killed.

1984—Sept. 20: U.S. embassy annex nr. Beirut, Lebanon, bombed, killing approx. 20.

1985—June 14: Hezbollah members hijacked TWA Flight 847 with 153 passengers and crew to Beirut, Lebanon; 39 held for 17 days; 1 U.S. Navy sailor killed. **June 23:** Air India Flight 182 destroyed by bomb off coast of Ireland; 329 killed. Blamed on Sikh terrorists. **Apr. 12:** Bomb blast at restaurant nr. Air Force base in Torrejon, Spain; 18 killed. **Oct. 7:** Four Palestinians hijacked Italian cruise ship *Achille Lauro*; 1 passenger killed. **Nov. 23:** EgyptAir Flight 648 from Athens to Cairo hijacked to Malta by Palestinian group Abu Nidal; 60 killed in rescue. **Dec. 27:** Palestinian militants opened fire at El-Al airline counters at Rome and Vienna airports; 19 killed.

1986—Apr. 5: Nightclub in Berlin, W. Germany, bombed; 3 killed, incl. 2 U.S. servicemen, 200+ hurt. 3 Libyan embassy workers in Germany convicted in bombing.

1987—Apr. 17: Bomb in Sri Lankan capital killed 100+; blamed on Tamil rebels who, 4 days later, attacked Sinhalese travelers on highway, killing 127. **June 19:** Basque group ETA bombed supermarket garage in Barcelona, Spain; 21 killed, 45 injured. **Nov. 29:** Bomb planted by N. Korean agents exploded on Korean Air Lines Flight 858 over Indian Ocean; 115 killed.

1988—Dec. 21: Pan Am Flight 103 exploded over Lockerbie, Scotland, killing all 259 aboard and 11 on ground; Libya took responsibility for bombing in Aug. 2003.

1989—Sept. 19: French UTA Flight 722 from Congo to Paris destroyed by bomb in midair over Niger; 171 killed. Several Libyan officials convicted in absentia; no official admission.

1992—Mar. 17: Israeli embassy in Buenos Aires, Argentina, bombed; 28 killed, 200+ injured. Hezbollah suspected.

1993—Feb. 26: Truck bomb exploded in World Trade Center garage in New York City; 6 killed. Blast later linked to al- Qaeda.
Mar. 12-19: At least 11 bombs ripped through Bombay and Calcutta, India; 300+ killed.

1994—Feb. 25: U.S.-born Israeli settler Baruch Goldstein opened fire in mosque in Hebron, West Bank; about 30 Muslim worshippers killed. **July 18:** Buenos Aires Jewish center bombed; 87 killed. Blamed on Hezbollah.

1995—Mar. 20: Twelve killed and over 5,000 injured when Japanese Aum Shinri-kyu cult members released Sarin nerve gas in several Tokyo subway cars. **Apr. 19:** Murrah Federal Building in Oklahoma City bombed, killing 168 and injuring 500+. Timothy McVeigh and Terry Nichols convicted in bombing. McVeigh executed in 2001; Nichols sentenced to life in prison, 1998 on state charges, 2004 on federal charges. **Nov. 13:** U.S. miltary compound in Riyadh, Saudi Arabia, bombed by Islamic Movement of Change; 7 killed.

1996—Jan. 31: Tamil Tigers drove explosives-laden truck into Central Bank in Colombo, Sri Lanka; 90 killed. **June 25:** Bomb-laden fuel truck exploded outside Khobar Towers, a U.S. military complex in Dhahran, Saudi Arabia; killed 19. **June 27:** Bomb exploded at Centennial Olympic Park in Atlanta, GA, during Summer Games; killed 2, injured 100+. Suspect Eric Robert Rudolph arrested in 2003, pleaded guilty; sentenced to life in prison, 2005. **Dec. 3:** Bomb exploded on subway train in Paris; 4 killed, 86 injured. Blamed on Algerian extremists.

1997—Nov. 17: Gamaa al-Islamiya gunmen killed 58 tourists and 4 Egyptians in Valley of the Kings near Luxor, Egypt.

1998—Aug. 7: U.S. embassies in Nairobi, Kenya, and Dar-es-Salaam, Tanzania, bombed; 257 people killed. Al-Qaeda blamed. **Aug. 15:** IRA car bomb exploded outside courthouse in Omagh, N. Ireland; killed 29, injured 300+. **Oct. 18:** National Liberation Army of Colombia blew up Ocensa oil pipeline; about 71 killed, 100+ injured.

1999—Sept. 9-16: Three apt. buildings bombed in Moscow and Volgodonsk, Russia; about 300 killed. Chechen rebels blamed.

2000—Oct. 12: Small boat assisting in docking of U.S.S. *Cole* exploded while alongside it in Aden, Yemen; 17 U.S. sailors killed, 39 injured. Blamed on al-Qaeda.

2001—Sept. 11: 19 al-Qaeda terrorists hijacked 4 U.S. domestic flights, including 2 planes that crashed into World Trade Center towers and 1 into Pentagon. Total dead minus hijackers: 2,973; deadliest attack of terrorism yet on U.S. soil. **Sept.-Nov. 7:** Letters tainted with deadly anthrax bacteria mailed through U.S. postal system killed 5.

2002—Mar. 27: Suicide bombing at hotel in Netanya, Israel, during Passover celebration; 27 killed. **Oct 12:** Resort in Bali, Indonesia, bombed; 202 dead. Jemaah Islamiah blamed. **Oct. 23:** Chechen guerrillas seized theater in Moscow, held 700+ hostages. Russian authorities gassed theater; most guerrillas and about 128 hostages killed. **Nov. 28:** Suicide bombers destroyed Israeli-owned hotel near Mombasa, Kenya; 13 killed. At same time, 2 missiles narrowly missed Israeli plane taking off from Mombasa airport; blamed on al-Qaeda. **Dec. 27:** Chechen rebels plowed truck bomb into pro-Russian gov. headquarters in Grozny, Chechnya; 80 killed, 152 injured.

2003—May 12-13: Al-Qaeda militants detonated car bombs at 3 residential complexes used by Westerners in Riyadh, Saudi Arabia; 34 killed. **May 16:** Five explosions in Casablanca, Morocco; 44 killed, 100+ wounded. Blamed on al-Qaeda. **May 17-19:** Five

suicide bombings in Israel; 17 killed. Hamas and al-Aqsa Martyrs brigade blamed. **Aug. 5:** Car bomb hit Marriott hotel in Jakarta, Indonesia; 12 killed, 150 injured. Blamed on Jemaah Islamiah. **Aug. 19:** UN headquarters in Baghdad bombed by truck; 22 killed, incl. UN envoy to Iraq. **Aug. 25:** 2 bombs exploded in taxis in Mumbai (Bombay), India; 46 killed, 100+ injured. Islamic militants suspected. **Oct. 27:** Suicide bombings at Intl. Red Cross and police stations; 40 killed. **Nov. 15:** Two synagogues in Istanbul, Turkey, bombed; 25 killed. **Nov. 20:** British consulate and offices of British bank HSBC bombed in Istanbul, Turkey; 27 killed incl. Br. cons. gen. Blamed on al-Qaeda. **Dec. 5:** Suicide bombing on commuter train in Yessentuki, Russia; 44 killed, 150 injured. Blamed on Chechen rebels.

2004—Feb. 6: Bomb exploded on Moscow subway; 39 killed, 130 injured. Chechen rebels blamed. **Mar. 11:** Al-Qaeda cell bombed 4 commuter trains during morning rush hour in Madrid, Spain; 191 killed, about 1,200 injured. **Apr. 21:** Car bomb destroyed Saudi govt. security building in Riyadh; 4 killed, 148 injured. **May 29:** Al-Qaeda militants stormed foreigner compound in Khobar, Saudi Arabia, taking hostages; 22 killed. **Aug. 24:** Two Russian passenger planes crashed nearly simultaneously in diff. parts of Russia; 90 killed. Blamed on Chechen rebels. **Sept. 1:** Militants seized school in Beslan, in northern Ossetia, Russia; held 1,000+ hostage for 3 days before Russian troops stormed school. About 330 killed, incl. 27 hostage-takers. Blamed on Chechen militants.

2005—July 7: Four bombs exploded on 3 separate subways and a bus in central London, UK; 52 killed, incl. bombers, about 700 injured. **July 21:** Four bombs placed on 3 subways and a bus in London malfunction. **July 23:** Three car bombs explode nr. resorts at Sharm el Sheik, Egypt; about 90 killed. **Aug. 17:** More than 400 small bombs exploded in cities and towns across Bangladesh, killing 2 and injuring at least 125. Jamaat ul-Mujahedeen Bangladesh claimed responsibility. **Aug. 19:** Three rockets fired from Jordan hit cities of Eilat, Israel, and Aqaba, Jordan. One missile flies over a docked U.S. naval ship; 1 death. **Nov. 9:** 3 suicide bombings targeting hotels in Amman, Jordan; killed 56+, injured about 100. Al-Qaeda in Iraq took responsibility.

2006—Apr. 24: Three deadly bombs within 5 minutes struck Egyptian Red Sea resort town of Dahab; 18 killed, 85 injured. Nasser Khamis el-Mallah, supposed "mastermind and leader" of Tawhid wal Jihad (Unity and Holy War), the terrorist cell that launched the attack, reported killed during gun battle in May. **July 11:** 8 explosions struck 7 different trains and 1 station of public commuter rail system in Mumbai, India; 207 killed, 700+ wounded. Lashkar-e-Qahhar (Army of Terror) claimed responsibility.

2007—Feb. 19: Train traveling between New Delhi and border with Pakistan caught fire, 68 killed; Indian ministers blamed Muslim militants for trying to disrupt peace talks between India and Pakistan. **June 30:** In apparent attempt at suicide attack, two men crashed their SUV into the main terminal of Scotland's Glasgow Airport; both also allegedly planted bombs on two cars parked in central London before attacking airport; driver later died of burns sustained in attack. **Dec. 11:** 2 coordinated car bombs went off outside govt. building and UN office building in Algiers, Algeria; 41 killed, incl. 17 UN employees, 170 wounded.

2008—Sept. 20: Suicide bomber in truck set off explosion outside of Marriott Hotel in Islamabad, Pakistan. Hotel was popular among foreigners and wealthy residents and was located nr. prime min.'s house and parliament building; 53 killed, 271 wounded. **Nov. 26-29:** A series of attacks and bombings on luxury hotels and high profile targets in Mumbai, India; 171 killed, 300 injured. Gunmen take dozens of hostages before Mumbai police and Indian National Security Guards secure the buildings. Pakistan officials later arrest 20 suspected militant Islamic extremists in connection with the attack. **Dec. 5:** A car bomb explodes in the central bazaar in Peshawar, Pakistan; 29 killed, about 90 injured.

2009—Feb. 9: Female suicide bomber at a checkpoint in northern Sri Lanka where government soldiers are fighting rebel troops; 28 killed. **Feb. 20:** Suicide bomber targets Shiite funeral in Dera Ismail Khan, Pakistan; 30 killed, 50+ wounded.

Homeland Security Advisories Timeline

Source: U.S. Dept of Homeland Security

Date	Event
Mar. 12, 2002	Homeland Security Advisory System established, with national threat level at Elevated, New York City at High.
Sept. 10-24, 2002	National threat level raised to High around the anniversary of Sept. 11.
Feb. 7-27, 2003	National threat level raised to High based on threats of attacks during the Hajj pilgrimage in Mecca.
Mar. 17-Apr. 16, 2003	National threat level raised to High during beginning of the Iraq War.
May 20-30, 2003	National threat level raised to High following terrorist bombings in Saudi Arabia and Morocco and as a precaution for Memorial Day.
Dec. 21, 2003-Jan. 9, 2004	National threat level raised to High based on threats specific to the holiday season.
Aug. 1-Nov. 10, 2004	Threat level raised to High for financial services sectors in New York City, northern New Jersey, and Washington, DC, based on gathered intelligence.
July 7-Aug. 12, 2005	Threat level raised to High for mass transit following London railway bombings.
Aug. 10-13, 2006	Threat level raised from Elevated to Severe for flights originating in UK bound for U.S. following arrest by British authorities of 21 individuals allegedly involved in plot to detonate liquid explosives on board U.S.-bound commercial aircraft. Threat level raised to High for all other commercial flights destined for or operating within U.S.
Aug. 13, 2006-present (as of Oct. 2009)	National threat level remains at Elevated; New York City threat level remains at High; threat level for all domestic and international flights at High.

MILITARY AFFAIRS

Chief Commanding Officers of the U.S. Military

Chairman, Joint Chiefs of Staff: Adm. Michael G. Mullen (USN)
Vice Chairman: Gen. James E. "Hoss" Cartwright (USMC)

The **Joint Chiefs of Staff** consists of the Chairman and Vice Chairman of the Joint Chiefs of Staff; the Chief of Staff, U.S. Army; the Chief of Naval Operations; the Chief of Staff, U.S. Air Force; and the Commandant of the Marine Corps. Date of rank is date when the individual achieved his or her current rank. While serving in any of these positions, or as Commander of a unified or specified combatant command, basic pay is $19,326.60 per month. Officers hold positions listed as of Sept. 2009.

Army

Chief of Staff	Date of rank
Casey Jr., George W.	Apr. 10, 2007

Other Generals

Campbell, Charles C.	Jan. 9, 2007
Chiarelli, Peter	June 4, 2008
Dempsey, Martin	July 23, 2008
Dunwoody, Ann	Nov. 14, 2008
Ham, Carter	July 23, 2008
McChrystal, Stanley A.	June 10, 2009
Odierno, Raymond T.	July 10, 2008
Petraeus, David H.	Feb. 10, 2007
Sharp, Walter	Apr. 29, 2008
Ward, William E.	May 3, 2006

Air Force

Chief of Staff	Date of rank
Schwartz, Norton A.	Aug. 12, 2008

Other Generals

Brady, Roger A.	Jan. 9, 2008
Carlson, Bruce	Sept. 1, 2005
Chandler, Carrol H. "Howie"	Nov. 30, 2007
Chilton, Kevin P.	June 26, 2006
Fraser, Douglas M.	June 25, 2009
Fraser III, William M.	Oct. 8, 2008
Hoffman, Donald	Nov. 21, 2008
Johns Jr., Raymond E.	July 31, 2009
Kehler, C. Robert	Oct. 12, 2007
Lorenz, Stephen R.	July 2, 2008
McKinley, Craig R.	Nov. 17, 2008

McNabb, Duncan J.	Dec. 1, 2005
North, Gary L.	Aug. 19, 2009
Renuart Jr., Victor E. "Gene"	Mar. 23, 2007

Navy

Chief of Naval Operations	Date of rank
Roughead, Gary (surface warfare)	Sept. 29, 2007

Other Admirals

Donald, Kirkland H. (submariner)	Jan. 1, 2005
Fitzgerald, Mark P. (aviator)	Nov. 30, 2007
Greenert, Jonathan W. (submariner)	Sept. 29, 2007
Harvey Jr., John C. (nuclear propulsion)	July 24, 2009
Keating, Timothy J. (aviator)	Jan. 1, 2005
Olson, Eric T. (special operations)	July 9, 2007
Stavridis, James, G. (surface warfare)	Oct. 19, 2006
Walsh, Patrick M. (aviator)	April, 2007
Willard, Robert F. (aviator)	Mar. 18, 2005

Marine Corps

Commandant of the Marine Corps (CMC)	Date of rank
Conway, James T.	Nov. 13, 2006

Other Generals

Amos, James F.	July 2, 2008
Cartwright, James E.	July 9, 2004
Mattis, James N.	Nov. 9, 2007

Coast Guard

Commandant, with rank of Admiral	Date of rank
Allen, Thad W.	May 25, 2006

Vice Commandant, with rank of Vice Admiral	
Pekoske, David P.	Aug. 7, 2009

Unified Combatant Commands Commanders-in-Chief

U.S. European Command, Stuttgart-Vaihingen, Germany—Adm. James Stavridis (USAF)
U.S. Pacific Command, Honolulu, Hawaii—Adm. Timothy J. Keating (USN)
U.S. Joint Forces Command, Norfolk, Virginia—Gen. James N. Mattis (USMC)
U.S. Special Operations Command, MacDill AFB, Florida—Adm. Eric T. Olson (USN)
U.S. Transportation Command, Scott AFB, Illinois—Gen. Duncan J, McNabb (USAF)
U.S. Central Command, MacDill AFB, Florida—Gen. David Petraeus (U.S. Army)
U.S. Southern Command, Miami, Florida—Gen. Douglas Fraser (USAF)
U.S. Northern Command, Peterson AFB, Colorado—Gen. Victor E. "Gene" Renuart Jr. (USAF)
U.S. Strategic Command, Offutt AFB, Nebraska—Gen. Kevin P. Chilton (USAF)
U.S. Africa Command, Kelley Barracks, Stuttgart, Germany—Gen. William "Kip" Ward (U.S. Army)

North Atlantic Treaty Organization (NATO) International Commands

NATO Headquarters: Chairman, NATO Military Committee—Adm. Giampaolo Di Paola (Italian Navy)
Strategic Commands:
    Allied Command Operations (ACO)—Adm. James G. Stavridis (USN), Supreme Allied Commander, Europe
    Allied Command Transformation (ACT)—Gen. Stéphane Abrial (French Air Force), Supreme Allied Commander Transformation
ACO Subordinate Commands:
    Joint Force Command Brunssum (JFC Brunssum)—Gen. Egon Ramms (German Army), Commander
    Joint Force Command Naples (JFC Naples)—Adm. Mark Fitzgerald (USN), Commander
    Joint Headquarters Lisbon (JHQ Lisbon)—Lt. Gen. Philippe Stoltz (French Army), Commander

Chairmen of the Joint Chiefs of Staff, 1949-2009

Gen. of the Army Omar N. Bradley, USA	8/16/49-8/15/53	Gen. John W. Vessey Jr., USA	6/18/82-9/30/85
Adm. Arthur W. Radford, USN	8/15/53-8/15/57	Adm. William J. Crowe Jr., USN	10/1/85-9/30/89
Gen. Nathan F. Twining, USAF	8/15/57-9/30/60	Gen. Colin L. Powell, USA	10/1/89-9/30/93
Gen. Lyman L. Lemnitzer, USA	10/1/60-9/30/62	Gen. John M. Shalikashvili, USA	10/25/93-9/30/97
Gen. Maxwell D. Taylor, USA	10/1/62-7/1/64	Gen. Henry H. Shelton, USA	9/30/97-9/30/01
Gen. Earle G. Wheeler, USA	7/3/64-7/2/70	Gen. Richard B. Myers, USAF	10/1/01-9/30/05
Adm. Thomas H. Moorer, USN	7/2/70-7/1/74	Gen. Peter Pace, USMC	9/30/05-9/30/07
Gen. George S. Brown, USAF	7/1/74-6/20/78	Adm. Michael G. Mullen, USN	10/1/07-
Gen. David C. Jones, USAF	6/21/78-6/18/82		

Directors of the Central Intelligence Agency

In 1942, Pres. Franklin D. Roosevelt established the Office of Strategic Services (OSS); it was disbanded in 1945. In 1946, Pres. Harry Truman established the Central Intelligence Group (CIG) to operate under the National Intelligence Authority (NIA). A 1947 law replaced the NIA with the National Security Council and the CIG with the Central Intelligence Agency.

Director	Served	Appointed by President	Director	Served	Appointed by President
Adm. Sidney W. Souers	1946	Truman	Adm. Stansfield Turner	1977-1981	Carter
Gen. Hoyt S. Vandenberg	1946-1947	Truman	William J. Casey	1981-1987	Reagan
Adm. Roscoe H. Hillenkoetter	1947-1950	Truman	William H. Webster	1987-1991	Reagan
Gen. Walter Bedell Smith	1950-1953	Truman	Robert M. Gates	1991-1993	Bush
Allen W. Dulles	1953-1961	Eisenhower	R. James Woolsey	1993-1995	Clinton
John A. McCone	1961-1965	Kennedy	John M. Deutch	1995-1997	Clinton
Adm. William F. Raborn Jr.	1965-1966	Johnson	George J. Tenet	1997-2004	Clinton
Richard Helms	1966-1973	Johnson	Porter Goss	2004-2006	Bush
James R. Schlesinger	1973	Nixon	Gen. Michael V. Hayden	2006-2009	Bush
William E. Colby	1973-1976	Nixon	Leon E. Panetta	2009-	Obama
George H. W. Bush	1976-1977	Ford			

Military Units, U.S. Army and Air Force

ARMY UNITS. Squad: In infantry usually 8-16 enlisted personnel under a staff sergeant. **Platoon:** In infantry 2-4 squads under a lieutenant. **Company:** Headquarters section and 3-5 platoons under a captain. (Company-size unit in the artillery is a battery; in the cavalry, a troop.) **Battalion:** Hdqts. and 4-6 companies under a lieutenant colonel. (Battalion-size unit in the cavalry is a squadron.) **Brigade:** Hdqts. and 2-5 battalions under a colonel. (Brigade-size unit in the cavalry and rangers is a regiment; in the special forces, a group.) **Division:** Hdqts. and 3 brigades with artillery, combat support, and combat service support units under a major general. **Corps:** Two or more divisions with corps troops under a lieutenant general. **Army:** Hdqts. and 2 or more corps with operational and support responsibilities under a general.

AIR FORCE UNITS. Flight: Numerically designated flights are the lowest level unit in the Air Force. They are used primarily where there is a need for small mission elements to be incorporated into an organized unit. **Squadron:** The basic unit. Designates specific operational or support capability like mission units in operational commands. **Group:** A flexible unit composed of 2 or more squadrons whose functions may be operational, support, or administrative in nature. **Wing:** A primary group with supporting groups on a distinct mission with significant scope such as combat, flying training, or airlift. **Numbered Air Forces:** Normally an operationally oriented agency, the numbered air force is designed for the control of subordinate units with the same mission and/or geographical location. **Major Command:** A major subdivision of the Air Force with full staff that manages a major segment of the USAF mission. Major Command is composed of 3 or more numbered air forces.

Active Duty U.S. Military Personnel Strengths Worldwide, 2009

Source: U.S. Dept. of Defense

(as of Mar. 31, 2009)

TOTAL WORLDWIDE[1] **1,385,122**	**EUROPE**	**EAST ASIA & PACIFIC**
U.S. TERRITORIES & SPEC. LOCATIONS	Belgium 1,266	Australia 138
	Germany 54,043	Japan 34,554
U.S., 48 contiguous states 917,284	Greece 371	Korea, South . . . . NA
Alaska 20,807	Greenland 139	Philippines 190
Hawaii 38,757	Italy 9,219	Singapore 124
Guam 3,145	Netherlands 534	Thailand 122
Puerto Rico 181	Portugal 745	Afloat 9,064
Transients 51,928	Serbia (incl. Kosovo) 1	**Regional total[2]** **44,382**
Afloat 86,717	Spain 1,234	**NORTH AFRICA, NEAR EAST, &**
Regional total[2] **1,118,828**	Turkey 1,557	**SOUTH ASIA***
	United Kingdom 9,398	Afghanistan[3] 41,300
OTHER WESTERN HEMISPHERE	Afloat 661	Bahrain 1,456
Canada 127	**Regional total[2]** **79,636**	Diego Garcia 268
Colombia 88		Egypt 279
Cuba (Guantánamo) 971	**SUB-SAHARAN AFRICA**	Iraq[3] 174,200
Honduras 418	Djibouti 1,294	Qatar 444
Afloat 9	**Regional Total[2]** **1,601**	Saudi Arabia 264
Regional total[2] **2,060**		United Arab Emirates 103
	FORMER SOVIET UNION	Afloat 2,878
	Total **150**	**Regional total[2,4]** **5,994**

NA = Not available. *Special Forces personnel involved in Operation Enduring Freedom in Afghanistan not reported by Dept. of Defense. (1) Total worldwide also includes undistributed personnel. (2) Most countries and areas with fewer than 100 assigned U.S. military members not listed; regional totals include personnel stationed in those countries and areas not shown. (3) Rounded strengths for Operation Enduring Freedom (OEF) and Operation Iraqi Freedom (OIF) deployment; includes troops in surrounding areas and deployed Reserve/National Guard. (4) Excludes troops deployed for OEF/OIF.

U.S. Army Personnel on Active Duty[1]

Source: Dept. of the Army, U.S. Dept. of Defense

(as of mid-year, except where noted)

Date	Total strength[2]	Commissioned officers Total	Male	Female[3]	Warrant officers Male[4]	Female	Enlisted personnel Total	Male	Female
1940	267,767	17,563	16,624	939	763	—	249,441	249,441	—
1942	3,074,184	203,137	190,662	12,475	3,285	—	2,867,762	2,867,762	—
1943	6,993,102	557,657	521,435	36,222	21,919	—	6,413,526	6,358,200	55,325
1944	7,992,868	740,077	692,351	47,726	36,893	10	7,215,888	7,144,601	71,287
1945	8,266,373	835,403	772,511	62,892	56,216	44	7,374,710	7,283,930	90,780
1946	1,889,690	257,300	240,658	16,642	9,826	18	1,622,546	1,605,847	16,699
1950	591,487	67,784	63,375	4,409	4,760	22	518,921	512,370	6,551
1955	1,107,606	111,347	106,196	5,151	10,552	48	985,659	977,943	7,716
1960	871,348	91,056	86,832	4,224	10,141	39	770,112	761,833	8,279
1965	967,049	101,812	98,029	3,783	10,285	23	854,929	846,409	8,520
1970	1,319,735	143,704	138,469	5,235	23,005	13	1,153,013	1,141,537	11,476
1975	781,316	89,756	85,184	4,572	13,214	22	678,324	640,621	37,703
1980 (Sept. 30) . . .	772,661	85,339	77,843	7,496	13,265	113	673,944	612,593	61,351
1985 (Sept. 30) . . .	776,244	94,103	83,563	10,540	15,296	288	666,557	598,639	67,918
1990 (Mar. 31) . . .	746,220	91,330	79,520	11,810	15,177	470	639,713	567,015	72,698
1995	521,036	72,646	62,250	10,396	12,053	599	435,807	377,832	57,975
2000	471,633	66,344	56,391	9,953	10,608	781	393,900	333,947	59,953
2002	485,536	66,446	55,715	10,731	10,900	812	404,363	341,794	62,569
2003 (Sept. 30) . . .	499,301	68,198	56,980	11,218	11,273	854	414,769	351,921	62,848
2004 (Sept. 30) . . .	499,543	68,640	57,245	11,395	11,414	914	414,438	354,043	60,395
2005 (Sept. 30) . . .	492,728	69,174	57,675	11,499	11,506	976	406,923	346,194	57,354
2006 (Sept. 30) . . .	505,402	68,742	57,318	11,424	11,931	1,035	419,353	361,528	57,825
2007 (Sept. 30) . . .	522,017	70,657	58,854	11,803	13,844	1,160	433,109	374,989	58,120
2008 (Sept. 30) . . .	539,170	72,650	60,357	12,293	13,428	1,246	451,846	392,163	59,683
2009	550,722	75,724	NA	NA	15,137	NA	455,275	NA	NA

NA = Not available. (1) Represents strength of the active Army, including Philippine Scouts (1940-46), retired Regular Army personnel on extended active duty, and National Guard and Reserve personnel on extended active duty; excludes U.S. Military Academy cadets, contract surgeons, and National Guard and Reserve personnel not on extended active duty. (2) Includes categories not listed, e.g. West Point Cadets. Data for 1940 to 1946 include personnel in the Army Air Forces and its predecessors (Air Service and Air Corps). (3) Includes Army Nurse Corps for all years, Women's Army Corps (1942-78), Medical Specialists Corps (1949 and subsequent years). (4) Act of Congress approved Apr. 27, 1926, directed the appointment as warrant officers of field clerks still in active service. Includes flight officers as follows: 1943, 5,700; 1944, 13,615; 1945, 31,117; 1946, 2,580.

U.S. Navy Personnel on Active Duty
Source: U.S. Dept. of Defense
(as of mid-year, except where noted)

Date	Officers	Nurses	Enlisted	Officer candi-dates	Total[1]	Date	Officers	Nurses	Enlisted	Officer candi-dates	Total[1]
1940	13,162	442	144,824	2,569	160,997	1999	55,726	—	322,372	—	378,098
1945	320,293	11,086	2,988,207	61,231	3,380,817	2000 (Oct.).	53,698	—	320,212	—	373,910
1950	42,687	1,964	331,860	5,037	381,538	2001 (Aug.)	54,177	—	317,100	—	375,618
1960	67,456	2,103	544,040	4,385	617,984	2002	55,506	—	324,712	—	384,576
1970	78,488	2,273	605,899	6,000	692,660	2003	55,852	—	324,927	—	380,779
1980[2]	63,100	—	464,100	—	527,200	2004	55,592	—	319,929	—	375,521
1990 (Sept.)	74,429	—	530,133	—	604,562	2005	54,039	—	305,368	—	363,858
1995 (May)	61,075	—	402,626	—	463,701	2006	53,209	—	295,773	—	353,496
1996	60,013	—	376,595	—	436,608	2007 (Sept.)	51,385	—	281,772	—	337,547
1997	57,341	—	340,616	—	397,957	2008	52,184	—	276,346	—	331,785
1998 (Sept.)	55,007	—	326,196	—	381,203	2009	52,233	—	274,858	—	331,637

(1) May include categories not shown, e.g., midshipmen. (2) Starting in 1980, "Nurses" are included with "Officers," and "Officer candidates" are included with "Enlisted."

U.S. Air Force Personnel on Active Duty
Source: U.S. Dept. of Defense
(as of mid-year)

Year[1]	Strength	Year[1]	Strength	Year[1]	Strength	Year[1]	Strength	Year[1]	Strength	Year[1]	Strength
1918 . . .	195,023	1943 . .	2,197,114	1980 . .	557,969	1994 . . .	426,327	2000 . . .	357,777	2005 . .	358,705
1920 . . .	9,050	1944 . .	2,372,292	1986 . .	608,200	1995 . . .	400,051	2001 . . .	351,935	2006 . .	352,620
1930 . . .	13,531	1945 . .	2,282,259	1990 . .	535,233	1996 . . .	389,400	2002 . . .	369,721	2007 . .	340,596
1940 . . .	51,165	1950 . .	411,277	1991 . .	510,432	1997 . . .	378,681	2003 . . .	373,116	2008 . .	328,771
1941 . . .	152,125	1960 . .	814,213	1992 . .	470,315	1998 . . .	363,479	2004 . . .	379,887	2009 . .	334,009
1942 . . .	764,415	1970 . .	791,078	1993 . .	444,351	1999 . . .	357,929				

(1) Prior to 1947, data are for U.S. Army Air Corps and Air Service of the Signal Corps.

U.S. Marine Corps Personnel on Active Duty
Source: U.S. Dept. of Defense
(as of mid-year)

Year	Officers	Enlisted	Total	Year	Officers	Enlisted	Total	Year	Officers	Enlisted	Total
1940	1,800	26,545	28,345	1994	18,430	159,949	178,379	2002	18,472	154,913	173,385
1945	37,067	437,613	474,680	1995	18,017	153,929	171,946	2003	18,908	160,814	179,722
1950	7,254	67,025	74,279	1996	18,146	154,141	172,287	2004	19,052	157,150	176,202
1960	16,203	154,418	170,621	1997	18,089	154,240	172,329	2005	19,118	159,113	178,231
1970	24,941	234,796	259,737	1998	17,984	154,648	172,632	2006	19,218	159,705	178,923
1980	18,198	170,271	188,469	1999	17,892	155,250	173,142	2007	19,456	162,085	181,541
1990	19,958	176,694	196,652	2000	17,897	154,744	172,641	2008	20,137	172,903	193,040
1993	18,878	161,205	180,083	2001	18,072	152,559	170,631	2009	21,031	183,243	204,274

U.S. Coast Guard Personnel on Active Duty
Source: U.S. Dept. of Defense
(as of mid-year)

Year	Total	Officers	Cadets	Enlisted	Year	Total	Officers	Cadets	Enlisted	Year	Total	Officers	Cadets	Enlisted
1970 . . .	37,689	5,512	653	31,524	1996 . . .	35,229	7,270	830	27,129	2003 . . .	39,000	7,532	983	30,859
1980 . . .	39,381	6,463	877	32,041	1997 . . .	34,717	7,079	868	26,770	2004 . . .	40,151	7,835	1,030	31,286
1985 . . .	38,595	6,775	733	31,087	1998 . . .	34,890	7,140	805	26,945	2005 . . .	40,814	7,908	1,006	31,900
1990 . . .	37,308	6,475	820	29,860	1999 . . .	35,266	7,135	880	27,251	2006 . . .	40,639	8,032	1,004	32,001
1993 . . .	38,832	7,724	691	30,417	2000 . . .	35,712	7,154	863	27,695	2007 . . .	41,265	8,231	720	32,314
1994 . . .	37,284	7,401	881	29,002	2001 . . .	35,328	7,112	631	27,585	2008 . . .	42,424	8,282	1,005	33,137
1995 . . .	36,731	7,489	841	28,401	2002 . . .	37,166	7,267	694	29,205	2009 . . .	43,514	8,497	993	34,024

Women in the U.S. Armed Forces
Source: U.S. Dept. of Defense; U.S. Census Bureau; Women In Military Service For America Memorial Foundation

Women in the Army, Navy, Air Force, Marines, and Coast Guard are fully integrated with male personnel. All enlisted jobs were open to women when the draft ended June 30, 1973. Admission to service academies began in 1976. Under rules instituted in 1993, women were allowed to fly combat aircraft and serve aboard warships. By the mid-1990s, 80% of all jobs and more than 90% of all career fields had been opened to women. In 2009, the first woman achieved the rank of four-star general. Women remained restricted from service in ground combat units. Women on active duty as of Sept. 30; Coast Guard as of Oct. 15.

Women Active Duty Troops, 2008

Service	% women
Army	13.6
Navy	15.0
Marines	6.1
Air Force	19.6
Coast Guard	12.2

Women on Active Duty, All Services, 1973-2008

Year	% women	Year	% women
1973	2.5	1993	11.6
1975	4.6	1997	13.6
1981	8.9	2000	14.4
1987	10.2	2005	14.6
		2008	14.2

African American Service in U.S. Wars
Source: U.S. Dept. of Defense; U.S. Census Bureau

American Revolution. About 5,000 served in the Continental Army, mostly in integrated units, some in all-black combat units.

Civil War. Some 180,000 served in 163 units of the Union Army's U.S. Colored Troops, 200,000 worked in service units—10% of the Union Army in all; about 37,000 died, 31,000 wounded.

World War I. 350,000-400,000 served in the armed forces, 100,000 in France. Some 40,000 fought.

World War II. Some 1 mil served in the armed forces—8% of all troops—mostly in Army service units; all-black fighter and bomber AAF units and infantry divisions gave distinguished service.

Korean War. More than 600,000 served in the military; 3,075 lost their lives in combat. By 1954, armed forces were completely desegregated.

Vietnam War. 274,937 served in the armed forces (1965-74)—9.8% of all troops; 7,241 were killed in combat.

Persian Gulf War. About 104,000 served in the Kuwait theater—20% of all U.S. troops. 66 died in combat.

Operation Enduring Freedom. 73 military deaths and 223 wounded in Afghanistan and other locations (as of Oct. 3, 2009).

Iraq War. 416 military deaths and 2,636 wounded (as of Oct. 3, 2009).

Monthly Military Pay Scale[1]

Source: U.S. Dept. of Defense

(effective Jan. 1, 2009; Salaries rounded to nearest dollar.)

	<2	2	3	4	6	8	Cumulative Years of Service 10	12	14	16	18	20	22	24	26
Commissioned officers															
O-10	NA	NA	NA	NA	NA	NA	NA	NA	NA	NA	NA	14,689	14,760	15,067	15,602
O-9	NA	NA	NA	NA	NA	NA	NA	NA	NA	NA	NA	12,847	13,032	13,299	13,766
O-8	9,090	9,388	9,585	9,641	9,887	10,299	10,395	10,786	10,898	11,235	11,723	12,172	12,473	12,473	12,473
O-7	7,553	7,904	8,066	8,195	8,429	8,660	8,927	9,193	9,460	10,299	11,007	11,007	11,007	11,007	11,063
O-6	5,598	6,150	6,554	6,554	6,579	6,861	6,898	6,898	7,290	7,983	8,390	8,797	9,028	9,262	9,717
O-5	4,667	5,257	5,621	5,690	5,917	6,053	6,352	6,571	6,854	7,287	7,493	7,697	7,929	7,929	7,929
O-4	4,027	4,661	4,972	5,042	5,330	5,640	6,025	6,326	6,534	6,654	6,723	6,723	6,723	6,723	6,723
O-3	3,540	4,013	4,332	4,723	4,949	5,197	5,358	5,622	5,760	5,760	5,760	5,760	5,760	5,760	5,760
O-2	3,059	3,484	4,013	4,148	4,233	4,233	4,233	4,233	4,233	4,233	4,233	4,233	4,233	4,233	4,233
O-1	2,655	2,764	3,341	3,341	3,341	3,341	3,341	3,341	3,341	3,341	3,341	3,341	3,341	3,341	3,341
Commissioned officers with over 4 years' active duty service as enlisted member or warrant officer															
O-3E	NA	NA	NA	4,723	4,949	5,197	5,358	5,622	5,845	5,973	6,147	6,147	6,147	6,147	6,147
O-2E	NA	NA	NA	4,148	4,233	4,368	4,596	4,772	4,902	4,902	4,902	4,902	4,902	4,902	4,902
O-1E	NA	NA	NA	3,341	3,568	3,699	3,834	3,967	4,148	4,148	4,148	4,148	4,148	4,148	4,148
Warrant officers															
W-5	NA	NA	NA	NA	NA	NA	NA	NA	NA	NA	NA	6,506	6,836	7,081	7,354
W-4	3,659	3,936	4,049	4,160	4,351	4,541	4,732	5,021	5,274	5,515	5,711	5,903	6,186	6,417	6,682
W-3	3,341	3,480	3,623	3,670	3,820	4,114	4,421	4,565	4,732	4,904	5,213	5,422	5,547	5,680	5,861
W-2	2,957	3,236	3,322	3,382	3,573	3,871	4,019	4,164	4,342	4,481	4,607	4,757	4,856	4,935	4,935
W-1	2,595	2,874	2,950	3,108	3,296	3,573	3,702	3,882	4,060	4,199	4,328	4,484	4,484	4,484	4,484
Enlisted members															
E-9[2]	NA	NA	NA	NA	NA	NA	4,421	4,521	4,647	4,796	4,945	5,185	5,388	5,602	5,928
E-8	NA	NA	NA	NA	NA	3,619	3,779	3,878	3,997	4,125	4,357	4,475	4,675	4,786	5,060
E-7	2,516	2,746	2,851	2,990	3,099	3,285	3,390	3,578	3,733	3,839	3,951	3,995	4,142	4,221	4,521
E-6	2,176	2,394	2,500	2,602	2,709	2,951	3,045	3,226	3,282	3,323	3,370	3,370	3,370	3,370	3,370
E-5	1,994	2,127	2,230	2,335	2,499	2,671	2,811	2,828	2,828	2,828	2,828	2,828	2,828	2,828	2,828
E-4	1,828	1,921	2,025	2,128	2,219	2,219	2,219	2,219	2,219	2,219	2,219	2,219	2,219	2,219	2,219
E-3	1,650	1,754	1,860	1,860	1,860	1,860	1,860	1,860	1,860	1,860	1,860	1,860	1,860	1,860	1,860
E-2	1,569	1,569	1,569	1,569	1,569	1,569	1,569	1,569	1,569	1,569	1,569	1,569	1,569	1,569	1,569
E-1[3]	1,400	1,400	1,400	1,400	1,400	1,400	1,400	1,400	1,400	1,400	1,400	1,400	1,400	1,400	1,400

NA = Not applicable. **Notes:** In 2007, the military pay scale was expanded to 40 years. **Over 30 years**—O-10: $16,382; O-9: $14,455; O-8: $12,785; O-7: $11,285; O-6: $9,911; W-5: $7,721; W-4: $6,815; E-9: $6,225; E-8: $5,161. **Over 34 years**—O-10: $17,201; O-9: $15,177; O-8: $13,104; W-5: $8,108; E-9: $6,536. **Over 38 years**—O-10: $18,061; O-9: $15,936; W-5: $8,513; E-9: $6,863. (1) Basic pay is limited for O-7 to O-10 to $14,750. Basic pay for O-6 and below is limited to $11,958. (2) Basic pay for the Master Chief Petty Officer of the Navy, Chief Master Sergeant of the Air Force, Sergeant Major of the Army or Marine Corps, or Senior Enlisted Advisor of the Joint Chiefs of Staff is $7,143. (3) E-1 with 4 months or more of active duty. Basic pay for an E-1 with less than 4 months of active duty is $1,295.

Outlays for Individual Payments to Veterans

Source: White House Office of Management and Budget

(in millions of dollars)

Year	Total	Compen- sation	Pen- sions	Hospital, medical	Edu- cation	Insurance & burial	Year	Total	Compen- sation	Pen- sions	Hospital, medical	Edu- cation	Insurance & burial
1940..	$578	$244	$185	$69	—	$80	2002...	$50,969	$22,418	$3,166	$22,384	$1,681	$1,320
1950..	8,827	1,533	476	764	$2,739	3,315	2003...	55,792	24,696	3,229	24,487	2,049	1,331
1960..	5,355	2,049	1,263	931	392	720	2004...	55,021	26,297	3,334	21,590	2,408	1,392
1970..	8,808	2,980	2,255	1,723	1,002	848	2005...	62,206	30,877	3,663	23,073	3,224	1,369
1980..	20,927	7,446	3,585	6,290	2,418	1,188	2006...	63,658	30,991	3,547	24,445	3,325	1,350
1990..	28,545	10,735	3,594	12,021	795	1,400	2007...	69,740	31,055	3,376	30,537	3,427	1,345
1995..	36,822	14,842	3,024	16,196	1,386	1,374	2008...	76,113	36,256	3,790	31,096	3,607	1,364
2000..	46,086	20,775	2,969	19,343	1,636	1,363	2009*..	85,573	40,990	4,029	34,009	5,132	1,413
2001..	45,435	18,579	2,760	20,966	1,783	1,347	2010*..	95,644	42,855	4,027	38,202	9,141	1,419

* Estimate. **Note:** Compensation is service-connected; pension is not.

U.S. Veteran Population, 2009

Source: U.S. Dept. of Veterans Affairs

(projection of population, in thousands, as of Sept. 30, 2009)

TOTAL VETERANS IN CIVILIAN LIFE[1]	**23,067.0**	Total Korean conflict[3]	2,621.2
Total wartime veterans[2]	**17,175.1**	Korean conflict with no prior wartime service	2,175.5
Total Gulf War[3]	5,506.5	Korean conflict with service in WWII	172.0
Gulf War with no prior wartime service	5,149.9	Total World War II[3]	2,272.4
Gulf War with service in Vietnam era	351.0	WWII only	2,024.3
Gulf War, with service in Vietnam and Korea	5.0		
Gulf War with service in Vietnam, Korea, and WWII	0.7	**Total peacetime veterans**[4]	**5,891.8**
Total Vietnam era[3]	7,653.3	Service between Vietnam era and Gulf War only	3,423.0
Vietnam era with no prior wartime service	7,028.7	Service between Korean conflict and Vietnam era only	2,343.0
Vietnam era with service in Korean conflict	192.6		
Vietnam era with service in Korea and WWII	75.4	Pre-Korean conflict without service in WWII	125.9

Note: Figures are for U.S. veterans worldwide. (1) Includes those who served on active duty in Army, Navy, Air Force, Marines, Coast Guard, uniformed Public Health Service and NOAA, and reservists called to federal active duty. Excludes those dishonorably discharged, those whose only active duty was training, and those currently on active duty. (2) Veterans serving in more than one period are counted only once in total. (3) Total includes veterans who also served in previous periods. (4) Veterans with both wartime and peacetime service are counted only as "wartime veterans."

Nations with Largest Armed Forces, by Active-Duty Troop Strength[1]

Source: *The Military Balance 2009* (International Institute for Strategic Studies, published by Routledge Journals, Taylor & Francis, UK)

	Troop strength Active troops (thousands)	Reserve troops (thousands)	Defense expend. ($ bil)	Tanks (MBT) (army only)	Navy Cruisers/ Frigates/ Destroyers	Sub-marines	Combat aircraft FGA (air force only)	Fighters (air force only)
China	2,185	800	46.174	7,660+	50F/28D	62	283	1,136+
United States	1,540	979	552.568	7,620+	22/22F/52D*	71	2,622 tactical	
India	1,281	1,155	26.513	4,065	14F/8D*	16	507	96
North Korea	1,106	4,700	—	3,500+	3F	63	152	388
Russia	1,027	20,000	32.215	23,000	5C/15D/17F*	67	807	725
South Korea	687	4,500	26.588	2,330	9F/10D	12	468 FTR/FGA	
Pakistan	617	—	4.53	2,461	6F	8	104	233
Iraq	577	—	NA	149+	—	—	—	—
Iran	523	350	7.451	1,613+	4F	9	168	118
Turkey	510	379	13.643	4,205	23F	14	348	87
Egypt	469	479	4.64	3,505	10F/1D	4	235	165
Vietnam	455	5,000	3.709	1,315	5F	2	64	140
Myanmar	406	—	7.009	150	—	—	22	58
France	353	70	60.662	637	20F/12D*	9	50	10
Brazil	326	1,340	20.559	224	10F*	5	204	71
Thailand	307	200	3.333	333	10F*	—	87 FTR/FGA	
Indonesia	302	400	4.329	—	8F	2	48	24
Italy	293	42	37.77	320	12F/2D*	7	138	56
Syria	293	314	1.465	4,950	2F	—	289	150+
Taiwan	290	1,657	9.585	926+	22F/4D	4	150	292
Colombia	267	62	6.806	—	—	4	22	—
Mexico	256	40	3.982	—	6F/1D	—	—	10
Germany	244	162	42.108	2,035	15F	12	156	109
Japan	230	42	41.039	880	8F/44D	16	—	260
Spain	222	319	17.495	404	11F*	4	91	83
Saudi Arabia	222	—	35.446	910	7F	—	155	121
Eritrea	202	120	—	150	—	—	—	16
Morocco	196	150	2.409	580	3F	—	—	66
Israel	177	565	11.61	3,501	—	3	267	168
United Kingdom	160	199	63.2	386	17F/8D*	13	176	128

— = Not available. MBT = Main battle tank. FGA = Fighter, ground attack. FTR = Fighter. *Denotes navies with aircraft carriers, as follows: United States 11, United Kingdom 2, France 2, Italy 2, India 1, Russia 1, Spain 1, Brazil 1, Thailand 1. (1) All figures are for Aug. 2009, except defense expenditure, which is for 2007.

Budget for Global War on Terror Operations: Fiscal Years 2001-09

Source: Congressional Research Service
(Estimates in billions of dollars)

	2001/02[1]	2003	2004	2005	2006	2007	2008	2009	Total
Total: All missions	$33.8	$81.2	$94.1	$107.6	$121.4	$171.0	$183.3	$149.1	$941.3
Dept. of Defense	33.0	77.4	72.4	102.6	116.8	165.0	179.1	141.6	888.0
Foreign aid and diplomacy[2]	0.8	3.7	21.7	4.8	4.3	5.0	3.1	5.9	49.1
Veterans Affairs medical.	0.0	0.0	0.0	0.2	0.4	1.0	1.0	1.6	4.2
Op. Iraqi Freedom[3]	0.0	53.0	75.9	85.5	101.7	133.6	140.9	93.5	684.0
Dept. of Defense	0.0	50.0	56.4	83.4	98.1	129.6	138.3	89.7	645.5
Foreign aid and diplomacy[2]	0.0	3.0	19.5	2.0	3.2	3.2	1.7	2.6	35.1
Veterans Affairs medical.	0.0	0.0	0.0	0.2	0.4	0.9	0.8	1.2	3.5
Op. Enduring Freedom[4].	20.8	14.7	14.5	20.0	19.0	36.9	42.1	55.2	223.2
Dept. of Defense	20.0	14.0	12.4	17.2	17.9	34.9	40.6	51.7	208.6
Foreign aid and diplomacy[2]	0.8	0.7	2.2	2.8	1.1	1.9	1.3	3.1	13.9
Veterans Affairs medical.	0.0	0.0	0.0	0.0	0.0	0.1	0.2	0.4	0.7
Op. Noble Eagle[5]	13.0	8.0	3.7	2.1	0.8	0.5	0.1	0.1	28.4
Dept. of Defense unallocated.	0.0	5.5	0.0	0.0	0.0	0.0	0.0	0.0	5.5

(1) FY01 & FY02 funds combined because most were obligated in FY02 after the 9/11 attacks at the end of FY01. (2) Foreign aid and diplomacy figures include monies for reconstruction, development and humanitarian aid, embassy operations, counternarcotics, initial training of the Afghan and Iraqi army, foreign military sales credits, and Economic Support Funds. (3) Began in the fall of 2002 with the buildup of troops for the March 2003 invasion of Iraq and continues with counterinsurgency and stability operations. (4) Covering Afghanistan and other ongoing Global War on Terror (GWOT) operations, ranging from the Philippines to Djibouti, that began immediately after the 9/11 attacks. (5) Dept. of Defense funds that rebuilt the Pentagon, provide higher security at U.S. military bases, and other homeland security, including combat air patrol.

Leading Purchasers of U.S. Defense Articles and Services

Source: Congressional Research Service
(in current U.S. dollars)

Worldwide Deliveries[1]

2000-03				2004-07			
1. Saudi Arabia	$6.0 billion	6. South Korea	$2.5 billion	1. Israel	$5.7 billion	6. Japan	$2.3 billion
2. Egypt	5.1 billion	7. Japan	1.8 billion	2. Egypt	5.5 billion	7. Poland	2.3 billion
3. Taiwan	4.0 billion	8. UK	1.6 billion	3. Saudi Arabia	4.4 billion	8. Australia	1.7 billion
4. Israel	3.0 billion	9. Netherlands	1.4 billion	4. Taiwan	4.3 billion	9. Greece	1.7 billion
5. Greece	3.0 billion	10. Turkey	1.2 billion	5. South Korea	2.8 billion	10. UK	1.5 billion

(1) Total dollar value of all U.S. defense articles and services actually delivered to top 10 purchasers worldwide. Figures include government-to-government sales through the Foreign Military Sales (FMS) system (which accounts for the overwhelming majority of U.S. conventional arms deliveries) concluded in calendar years listed, as well as commercially licensed exports concluded in pertinent fiscal years.

U.S. Foreign Military Financing Worldwide, Select Countries

Source: Defense Security Cooperation Agency, U.S. Dept. of Defense

(in thousands of U.S. dollars)

	2008	2002-07		2008	2002-07
Africa.	**$6,757**	**$140,275**	**Europe**	**$93,429**	**$1,224,822**
Djibouti.	1,983	33,606	Bosnia & Herzegovina	3,292	48,990
Near East & S. Asia	**4,298,120**	**26,385,995**	Bulgaria	6,584	62,419
Afghanistan	—	1,051,877	Czech Republic	2,845	56,923
Bahrain.	3,968	192,620	Georgia	9,000	107,884
Egypt	1,289,470	7,760,480	Poland	26,980	207,548
Israel	2,380,560	14,073,046	Romania	11,097	83,549
Jordan	298,380	1,628,937	Turkey	6,817	163,160
Lebanon.	6,943	34,463	Ukraine	6,036	37,866
Morocco.	3,625	58,143	**Americas**.	**64,143**	**487,750**
Oman	4,712	178,044	Colombia	52,570	389,350
Pakistan	297,570	1,266,060	El Salvador	5,631	27,593
Tunisia	8,345	46,332	**World total**	**4,505,945**	**28,495,703**
Yemen	3,952	65,370			
E. Asia & Pacific.	**43,495**	**256,861**			
Philippines	27,757	213,220			

Note: Grants extended to foreign governments in a fiscal year to pay for military equipment and services. May be from DOD or, for specific countries, negotiated directly with U.S. commercial suppliers with DOD approval.

Defense Contracts, 2009

Source: U.S. Dept. of Defense

Listed are the 50 companies or organizations receiving the largest dollar volume of prime contract awards from the U.S. Dept. of Defense during fiscal year 2009.

Rank	Company	Contracts awarded[1]	Rank	Company	Contracts awarded[1]
1.	Lockheed Martin Corporation	$21,031,414,248	27.	Alliant Techsystems Inc.	$988,853,840
2.	The Boeing Company	15,944,563,479	28.	Hensel Phelps Construction Co.	971,465,644
3.	General Dynamics Corporation.	9,903,425,049	29.	Textron Inc.	946,123,804
4.	Northrop Grumman Corporation	9,887,967,366	30.	BP PLC	906,666,718
5.	Raytheon Company	8,506,837,538	31.	Rockwell Collins, Inc.	902,032,360
6.	United Technologies Corporation	4,927,603,480	32.	Dyncorp International Inc.	856,817,121
7.	L-3 Communications Holdings, Inc.	4,152,960,451	33.	Honeywell International Inc.	842,883,762
8.	BAE Systems PLC	3,705,706,722	34.	Navistar Defense LLC	830,719,973
9.	Humana Inc.	2,887,522,910	35.	CACI International Inc.	813,847,765
10.	KBR, Inc.	2,798,378,992	36.	Valero Energy Corporation.	774,830,930
11.	Saic, Inc.	2,550,974,639	37.	Anthem Health of Indiana Inc.	750,304,989
12.	Oshkosh Corporation	2,549,227,677	38.	Clark Enterprises, Inc.	737,656,556
13.	Health Net, Inc.	2,532,929,140	39.	General Atomic Technologies Corp.	730,295,130
14.	Bell Boeing Joint Project Office.	2,519,107,055	40.	Amerisourcebergen Corporation	705,395,545
15.	General Electric Company	2,426,963,263	41.	The Mitre Corporation	694,272,117
16.	TriWest Healthcare Alliance Corp.	2,322,983,927	42.	The Aerospace Corporation	672,850,250
17.	Bechtel Group, Inc.	2,030,501,070	43.	Harris Corporation	667,576,716
18.	Royal Dutch Shell PLC	2,015,752,163	44.	Rolls-Royce Grp. PLC	636,013,934
19.	Computer Sciences Corporation.	1,776,068,422	45.	SK Energy Co., Ltd.	633,779,878
20.	ITT Corporation.	1,748,171,844	46.	Government of the United States.	628,201,324
21.	Bahrain Petroleum Co.	1,738,252,617	47.	Jacobs Engineering Group Inc.	591,280,691
22.	MIT	1,538,195,428	48.	McKesson Corporation.	581,545,668
23.	URS Corporation.	1,429,671,241	49.	Hawker Beechcraft, Inc.	563,971,451
24.	MacAndrews & Forbes Holdings Inc. . .	1,345,740,315	50.	Petromax Refining Company LLC	538,622,439
25.	Booz Allen Hamilton Inc.	1,083,184,025	Other	. . . .	70,752,494,837
26.	Finmeccanica SpA	1,028,227,637	**Total**	. . . .	**203,100,834,141**

(1) Totals include subsidiaries of each company.

Arms Transfer Agreements with the World, by Supplier, 2001-08

Source: Congressional Research Service

(in millions of current U.S. dollars)

Supplier	2001	2002	2003	2004	2005	2006	2007	2008	2001-08
United States	$11,340	$12,990	$14,477	$12,681	$12,803	$16,026	$24,719	$37,796	$142,832
Russia	5,600	5,700	4,600	7,400	6,000	14,700	10,500	3,500	58,000
France	4,400	600	2,800	2,900	7,300	5,600	2,000	2,600	28,200
United Kingdom	600	700	2,500	4,200	2,800	4,100	9,800	200	24,900
China	1,100	400	600	1,000	2,600	1,400	1,300	800	9,200
Germany	2,000	1,000	1,500	4,000	2,100	1,400	1,500	1,000	14,500
Italy.	1,100	400	600	600	1,500	1,200	1,200	3,700	10,300
All other European	2,700	4,600	2,200	5,400	7,500	5,800	5,100	3,200	36,500
All others	2,600	2,200	1,700	3,300	2,300	4,000	2,100	2,400	20,600
TOTAL	**31,440**	**28,590**	**30,977**	**41,481**	**44,903**	**54,226**	**58,219**	**55,196**	**345,032**

Note: All data are for the calendar year given except for U.S. MAP (Military Assistance Program), IMET (International Military Education, and Training), and Excess Defense Article data, which are included for the particular fiscal year. All amounts given include the values of all categories of weapons, spare parts, construction, all associated services, military assistance, excess defense articles, and training programs. Statistics for foreign countries are based upon estimated selling prices. All foreign data are rounded to the nearest $100 million.

Personal Salutes and Honors

The U.S. **national salute**, 21 guns, is also the salute to a national flag. U.S. independence is commemorated by the salute to the Union—one gun for each state—fired at noon July 4, at all military posts provided with suitable artillery.

A 21-gun salute on arrival and departure, with 4 ruffles and flourishes, is rendered to the **president** of the United States, to a former president, and to a president-elect. The national anthem or "Hail to the Chief," as appropriate, is played for the president, and the national anthem for the others. A 21-gun salute on arrival and departure, with 4 ruffles and flourishes, also is rendered to the **sovereign or chief of state of a foreign country** or a member of a reigning royal family, and the national anthem of his or her country is played. The music is considered an inseparable part of the salute and immediately follows the ruffles and flourishes without pause. For the Honors March, generals receive the "General's March," admirals receive the "Flag Officer's March," and all others receive the 32-bar medley of "The Stars and Stripes Forever."

GRADE, TITLE, OR OFFICE	SALUTE (IN GUNS) Arriving	Leaving	Ruffles and flourishes	Music
Vice President of U.S.	19	—	4	Hail, Columbia
Speaker of the House	19	—	4	Honors March
U.S. or foreign ambassador in country to which accredited	19	—	4	Nat. anthem of official
Premier or prime minister	19	—	4	Nat. anthem of official
Secretary of Defense, Army, Navy, or Air Force	19	19	4	Honors March
Other cabinet members, Senate president pro tempore, governor, or chief justice of U.S.	19	—	4	Honors March
Chairman, Joint Chiefs of Staff	19	19	4	Honors March
Army chief of staff, chief of naval operations, Air Force chief of staff, Marine commandant	19	19	4	Honors March
General of the Army, general of the Air Force, fleet admiral	19	19	4	Honors March
Generals, admirals	17	17	4	Honors March
Assistant secretaries of Defense, Army, Navy, or Air Force	17	17	4	Honors March
Chair of a committee of Congress	17	—	4	Honors March

OTHER SALUTES (on arrival only, with Honors March) include 17 guns, with 3 ruffles and flourishes, for U.S. ambassadors returning to the U.S. on official business; 15 guns, with 3 ruffles and flourishes, for U.S. envoys or ministers, foreign envoys or ministers accredited to the U.S., and lieutenant generals or vice admirals; 13 guns, with 2 ruffles and flourishes, for a major general or rear admiral (upper half) and for U.S. ministers resident and ministers resident accredited to the U.S.; 11 guns, with 1 ruffle and flourish, for a brigadier general or rear admiral (lower half) and for U.S. chargés d'affaires and like officials accredited to the U.S.; 11 guns, no ruffles and flourishes, for consuls general accredited to the U.S.

U.S. Military Awards
The Medal of Honor

Source: Congressional Medal of Honor Society; Army, U.S. Dept. of Defense

The Medal of Honor is the highest military award for bravery that can be given to any individual in the United States. The first Army Medals were awarded on Mar. 25, 1863; the first Navy Medals went to sailors and Marines on Apr. 3, 1863.

On Dec. 21, 1861, Pres. Abraham Lincoln signed a bill to create the Navy Medal of Honor. Lincoln, on July 14, 1862, approved a resolution providing for the presentation of Medals of Honor to enlisted men of the Army and Voluntary Forces, making it a law. The law was amended on March 3, 1863, to extend its provisions to include officers as well as enlisted men.

The Medal of Honor is awarded in the name of Congress to a person who, while a member of the armed forces, distinguishes himself or herself conspicuously by gallantry and intrepidity at the risk of life above and beyond the call of duty while engaged in an action against any enemy of the United States; while engaged in military operations involving conflict with an opposing foreign force; or while serving with friendly foreign forces engaged in an armed conflict against an opposing armed force in which the United States is not a belligerent party.

The deed performed must have been one of personal bravery or self-sacrifice so conspicuous as to clearly distinguish the individual above his or her comrades and must have involved risk of life. Incontestable proof of the performance of service is required, and each recommendation for award of this decoration is considered on the standard of extraordinary merit.

Prior to World War I, the 2,625 Army Medal of Honor awards up to that time were reviewed to determine which past awards met new stringent criteria. The Army removed 911 names from the list, most of them former members of a volunteer infantry group during the Civil War who had been induced to extend their enlistments when they were promised the medal. However, in 1977 a medal was restored to Dr. Mary Walker, and in 1989 medals were restored to Buffalo Bill Cody and 7 other Indian scouts.

Seven African American soldiers were awarded Medals of Honor for service in World War II (6 of them posthumously) in Jan. 1997. Previously, no black soldier had received the medal for World War II service; an Army inquiry begun in 1993 concluded that the prevailing political climate and Army practices of the time had prevented proper recognition of heroism on the part of black soldiers in that war. In June 2002, 22 Asian Americans received the award for World War II service.

As of Oct. 1, 2009, four Medals of Honor had been awarded for actions in Operation Iraqi Freedom. On Apr. 4, 2003, Army Sgt. First Class Paul R. Smith was mortally wounded while holding an exposed position, near Baghdad International Airport, against enemy attack. On Apr. 14, 2004, Marine Cpl. Jason L. Dunham was mortally wounded at Karbala when he covered a live grenade with his helmet and body to protect his fellow Marines. On Sept. 29, 2006, Navy Petty Officer Second Class (SEAL) Michael A. Monsoor was mortally wounded at Ar Ramadi when he threw himself onto a grenade, saving the lives of two teammates. The most recent recipient was Army Private First Class Ross A. McGinnis, whose posthumous award was presented June 5, 2008. While manning a machine gun in northern Baghdad on Dec. 4, 2006, an insurgent threw a grenade into his vehicle. He covered the grenade with his body and was mortally wounded while saving his four crew members from serious injury.

Two Medals of Honor had been awarded for actions in Afghanistan. On June 28, 2005, Navy Lt. Michael P. Murphy's SEAL team came under attack by Taliban fighters. Heavily outnumbered and with all four team members wounded, Lt. Murphy left cover to radio for help and was shot in the back. One of his men survived the attack. On June 21, 2006, Army Sgt. First Class Jared C. Monti and his patrol were ambushed. Monti repeatedly tried to rescue a wounded soldier despite overwhelming gunfire and his men being outnumbered by more than 3 to 1. Monti was killed by a grenade on his third attempt. His heroism inspired his comrades to fend off the enemy.

Other Selected Awards

Source: U.S. Army Institute of Heraldry; Navy Department Awards Web Service; Air Force Personnel Center

Distinguished Service Cross

Established in Congress July 9, 1918, on recommendation of Gen. John J. "Black Jack" Pershing, and awarded for extraordinary heroism not justifying the award of a Medal of Honor. The act or acts of heroism must have been so notable and have involved risk of life so extraordinary as to set the individual apart from his or her comrades.

Silver Star

An earlier version of this award, the Citation Star, was established by Congress on July 19, 1918, and retroactively awarded to soldiers for "gallantry in action," back to the Spanish-American War. The Silver Star medal replaced the Citation Star in 1932 and is awarded for gallantry in action which, while of a lesser degree than that required for award of the Distinguished Service Cross, must nevertheless have been performed with marked distinction.

Legion of Merit

Established by Congress on July 20, 1942, and awarded to individuals who have distinguished themselves by exceptionally meritorious conduct in the performance of outstanding services. There are different designs depending on the level of command of the award recipient.

Distinguished Flying Cross

Established by Congress July 2, 1926, and awarded for heroism or extraordinary achievement while participating in aerial flight. Awards are made only to recognize single acts of heroism or extraordinary achievement, not sustained operational activities against an armed enemy. Initial awards were given to persons who made record breaking long-distance and endurance flights or who set altitude records. The first DFC was awarded to Cpt. Charles A. Lindbergh on May 31, 1927, and DFCs were awarded retroactively to Orville and Wilbur Wright.

Soldier's Medal

Established by Congress July 2, 1926, to recognize acts of heroism not involving actual conflict with an enemy. The same degree of heroism is required as for the award of the Distinguished Flying Cross. The performance must have involved personal hazard or danger and the voluntary risk of life under conditions not involving conflict with an armed enemy. Awards are not made solely on the basis of having saved a life.

Bronze Star

Established by Executive Order Feb. 4, 1944, largely to raise the morale of ground troops in WWII, on the recommendation of Gen. George C. Marshall. It is awarded to any person who, while serving in any capacity in or with the U.S. military, distinguishes himself or herself by heroic or meritorious achievement or service, not involving participation in aerial flight.

Purple Heart

The original Purple Heart, designated as the Badge of Military Merit, was established by Gen. George Washington on Aug. 7, 1782. Following the American Revolution, the badge fell into disuse until 1932, the 200th anniversary of Washington's birth. During WWII, the Order of the Purple Heart was awarded for both wounds received in action and for meritorious service; following the introduction of the Legion of Merit, it was awarded only for combat wounds. Today, the Purple Heart is awarded to any member of an armed force who, while serving with the U.S. Armed Services, has been wounded or killed, or who has died or may hereafter die after being wounded in action against an enemy of the U.S. or in an armed conflict in which the U.S. or friendly foreign forces are engaged; as the result of an act of any hostile foreign force; as a result of an international terrorist attack against the U.S. or a friendly foreign nation; as a result of military operations outside the U.S. as part of a peacekeeping force. Wounds must be inflicted by weapon fire while directly engaged in armed conflict, regardless of the fire causing the wound; or while held as a prisoner of war or while being taken captive.

Air Medal

Authorized by Pres. Roosevelt on May 11, 1942, and awarded for heroism or meritorious achievement while participating in aerial flight. Awards may be made to recognize single acts of merit or heroism, or for meritorious service. Awards are not made to individuals who use air transportation solely for the purpose of moving from point to point in a combat zone.

Army Commendation

Established Dec. 18, 1945, and awarded for heroism, meritorious achievement, or meritorious service. It may also be awarded to a member of the Armed Forces of a friendly foreign nation who distinguishes him or herself by an act of heroism, extraordinary achievement, or meritorious service which has been of mutual benefit to a friendly nation and the United States.

U.S. Military Awards in Selected Wars and Conflicts

Source: U.S. Army Human Resources Command, U.S. Dept. of Defense

AWARD	Civil War	WWI	WWII	Korea	Vietnam	Gulf War	OEF[1]	OIF[2]
Medal of Honor.	1,522	124	464	133	246	0	2	4
Distinguished Service Cross . . .	NA	6,430	4,434	724	848	0	4	15
Silver Star.	NA	(3)	73,654	10,061	21,634	75	156	398
Legion of Merit	NA	NA	20,273	(3)	10,356	158	15	75
Distinguished Flying Cross.	NA	NA	126,318	(3)	21,697	108	97	102
Soldier's Medal.	NA	NA	12,485	581	5,402	43	28	111
Bronze Star (Total)[4]	NA	NA	395,380	30,359	719,968	27,967	24,424	82,258
Purple Heart.	NA	NA	(3)	(3)	220,516	504	2,723	20,831
Air Medal (Total)[4]	NA	NA	1,166,471	0	1,039,124	6,399	6,765	16,284
Army Commendation (Total)[4]. . .	NA	NA	0	0	837,037	81,979	43,087	276,688

(1) Operation Enduring Freedom (primarily Afghanistan). (2) Operation Iraqi Freedom. (3) Numbers for the individual decorations shown on these charts represent only those awards that were properly processed and reported to Headquarters, Department of the Army. The actual number of individual decorations awarded under combat conditions, when award approval authority is delegated to field commanders, cannot be stated with absolute certainty. These charts reflect the current statistics recorded by the Military Awards Branch, as of July 21, 2009. (4) Includes awards for valor/heroism and for meritorious service or achievement.

The Federal Service Academies

U.S. Military Academy, West Point, NY. Founded 1802. Awards BS degree and Army commission for a 5-year service obligation. For admissions information, write USMA Admissions, Bldg. 606, USMA, West Point, NY 10996. www.usma.edu

U.S. Naval Academy, Annapolis, MD. Founded 1845. Awards BS degree and Navy or Marine Corps commission for a 5-year service obligation. For admissions information, write Candidate Guidance Office, United States Naval Academy, 117 Decatur Rd., Annapolis, MD 21402-5018. www.usna.edu

U.S. Air Force Academy, Colorado Springs, CO. Founded 1954. Awards BS degree and Air Force commission for a 6-year service obligation. For admissions information, write HQ USAFA/RRS, 2304 Cadet Dr., Ste. 200, USAF Academy, CO 80840-5025. www.usafa.edu

U.S. Coast Guard Academy, New London, CT. Founded 1876. Awards BS degree and Coast Guard commission for a 5-year service obligation. For admissions information, write Director of Admissions, U.S. Coast Guard Academy, 31 Mohegan Ave., New London, CT 06320-8103. www.cga.edu

U.S. Merchant Marine Academy, Kings Point, NY. Founded 1943. Awards BS degree, a license as a deck, engineer, or dual officer, and a U.S. Naval Reserve commission. Service obligations vary according to options taken by the graduate. For admissions information, write Admissions Office, U.S. Merchant Marine Academy, 300 Steamboat Rd., Kings Point, NY 11024-1699. www.usmma.edu

Casualties in Principal Wars of the U.S.

Source: U.S. Dept. of Defense, U.S. Coast Guard

Data prior to World War I are based on incomplete records in many cases. Casualty data are confined to dead and wounded personnel and, therefore, exclude personnel captured or missing in action who were subsequently returned to military control. Dash (—) indicates information is not available. off. = officers.

	Branch of service	Number serving	CASUALTIES Battle deaths	Other deaths	Wounds not mortal[7]	Total[13]
Revolutionary War	**Total**	—	**4,435**	—	**6,188**	**10,623**
1775-83	Army	184,000	4,044	—	6,004	10,048
	Navy	to	342	—	114	456
	Marines	250,000[11]	49	—	70	119
War of 1812	**Total**	**286,730[8]**	**2,260**	—	**4,505**	**6,765**
1812-15	Army	—	1,950	—	4,000	5,950
	Navy	—	265	—	439	704
	Marines	—	45	—	66	111
Mexican War	**Total**	**78,718[8]**	**1,733**	**11,550**	**4,152**	**17,435**
1846-48	Army	—	1,721	11,550	4,102	17,373
	Navy	—	1	—	3	4
	Marines	—	11	—	47	58
	Coast Guard[12]	71 off.	—	—	—	—
Civil War						
Union forces	**Total**	**2,213,363**	**140,414**	**224,097**	**281,881**	**646,392**
1861-65	Army	2,128,948[8]	138,154	221,374	280,040	639,568
	Navy	—	2,112	2,411	1,710	6,233
	Marines	(in Navy total)	148	312	131	591
	Coast Guard[12]	219 off.	1	—	—	1
Confederate forces	**Total**	—	**74,524**	**59,297**	—	**133,821**
(estimate)[1]	Army	600,000	—	—	—	—
	Navy	to	—	—	—	—
	Marines	1,500,000	—	—	—	—
Spanish-American War	**Total**	**306,760**	**385**	**2,061**	**1,662**	**4,108**
1898	Army[3]	280,564	369	2,061	1,594	4,024
	Navy	22,875	10	—	47	57
	Marines	3,321	6	—	21	27
	Coast Guard[12]	660	0	—	—	—
World War I	**Total**	**4,734,991**	**53,402**	**63,114**	**204,002**	**320,518**
April 6, 1917-Nov. 11, 1918	Army[4]	4,057,101	50,510	55,868	193,663	300,041
	Navy	599,051	431	6,856	819	8,106
	Marines	78,839	2,461	390	9,520	12,371
	Coast Guard	8,835	111	81	—	192
World War II	**Total**	**16,112,566**	**291,557**	**113,842**	**671,846**	**1,077,245**
Dec. 7, 1941-Dec. 31, 1946[2]	Army[5]	11,260,000	234,874	83,400	565,861	884,135
	Navy[6]	4,183,466	36,950	25,664	37,778	100,392
	Marines	669,100	19,733	4,778	68,207	92,718
	Coast Guard	241,093	574	1,343	—	1,917
Korean War[9]	**Total**	**5,720,000**	**33,574**	**2,833**	**103,284**	**139,691**
June 25, 1950-July 27, 1953	Army	2,834,000	27,731	2,125	77,596	107,452
	Navy	1,177,000	506	152	1,576	2,234
	Marines	424,000	4,266	242	23,744	28,252
	Air Force	1,285,000	1,238	314	368	1,920
	Coast Guard	44,143	—	—	—	—
Vietnam War[10]	**Total**	**8,744,000**	**47,424**	**10,785**	**153,303**	**211,512**
Aug. 4, 1964-Jan. 27, 1973	Army	4,368,000	30,957	7,261	96,802	135,020
	Navy	1,842,000	1,631	934	4,178	6,743
	Marines	794,000	13,091	1,749	51,392	66,232
	Air Force	1,740,000	1,745	841	931	3,517
	Coast Guard	8,000	7	2	60	69
Persian Gulf War	**Total**	**2,225,000**	**147**	**235**	**467**	**849**
1991	Army	782,000	98	126	—	578
	Navy	669,000	5	50	—	67
	Marines	213,000	24	44	92	160
	Air Force	561,000	20	15	9	44
	Coast Guard	400	—	—	—	—
Iraq War[14]	**Total**	**269,363[15]**	**3,465**	**873**	**31,527**	**35,865**
Mar. 19, 2003-Oct. 3, 2009	Army	99,664[15]	2,520	646	21,843	25,009
	Navy	61,018[15]	64	36	632	732
	Marines	66,166[15]	851	169	8,623	9,643
	Air Force	42,515[15]	29	22	429	480
	Coast Guard	1,250[15]	1	—	—	1

(1) From the final report of the Provost Marshal General, 1863-66. Authoritative statistics for the Confederate forces are not available. In addition, an estimated 26,000-31,000 Confederate personnel died in Union prisons. (2) Data are for Dec. 1, 1941, through Dec. 31, 1946, when hostilities were officially terminated by presidential proclamation; few battle deaths or wounds not mortal were incurred after Japanese acceptance of Allied peace terms on Aug. 14, 1945. Numbers serving Dec. 1, 1941-Aug. 31, 1945, were: Total—14,903,213; Army—10,420,000; Navy—3,883,520; Marine Corps—599,693. (3) Number serving covers the period Apr. 21-Aug. 13, 1898, while dead and wounded data are for the period May 1-Aug. 31, 1898. Active hostilities ceased on Aug. 13, 1898, but ratifications of the treaty of peace were not exchanged between the U.S. and Spain until Apr. 11, 1899. (4) Includes Army Air Forces battle deaths and wounds not mortal, as well as casualties suffered by American forces in northern Russia to Aug. 25, 1919, and in Siberia to Apr. 1, 1920. Other deaths covered the period Apr. 1, 1917-Dec. 31, 1918. (5) Includes Army Air Forces. (6) Battle deaths and wounds not mortal include casualties incurred in Oct. 1941 due to hostile action. (7) Marine Corps data for Iraq War, World War II, the Spanish-American War, and prior wars represent the number of individuals wounded, whereas all other data in this column represent the total number (incidence) of wounds. (8) As reported by Commissioner of Pensions in his Annual Report for Fiscal Year 1903. (9) As a result of an ongoing Dept. of Defense review of available Korean War casualty record information, updates to previously reported figures for battle deaths and other deaths are reflected in this table. (10) Number serving covers the period Aug. 4, 1964-Jan. 27, 1973 (date of cease-fire). Includes casualties incurred in Mayaguez incident. Wounds not mortal exclude 150,332 persons not requiring hospital care. (11) Estimated. (12) Actually the U.S. Revenue Cutter Services, predecessor to the U.S. Coast Guard. (13) Totals do not include categories for which no data are listed. (14) Military deaths during the invasion phase, which ended Apr. 30, 2003, totaled 115 combat-related and 23 other. (15) These serving figures for the Iraq War are current as of Mar. 31, 2003, and do not include numbers of troops deployed since then. **Note:** As of Oct. 3, 2009, there have been 616 battle deaths, 247 non-hostile deaths, and 4,198 wounded in Op. Enduring Freedom, mostly in Afghanistan and the Persian Gulf area.

U.S. Army, Navy, Air Force, Marine Corps, and Coast Guard Insignia

Source: Dept. of the Army, Dept. of the Navy, Dept. of the Air Force, U.S. Dept. of Defense, U.S. Coast Guard, U.S. Dept. of Homeland Security

Army

General of the Armies—Gen. John J. Pershing (1860-1948), the only person to have held this rank while living, was authorized to prescribe his own insignia but never wore in excess of four stars. The rank originally was established posthumously by Congress for George Washington in 1799, and he was promoted to the rank by joint resolution of Congress, approved by Pres. Gerald Ford, Oct. 19, 1976.

General of the Army—Five silver stars fastened together in a circle and the coat of arms of the United States in gold color metal with shield and crest enameled. Reserved for wartime use only.

Rank	Insignia
General of the Army*	Five silver stars
General	Four silver stars
Lieutenant General	Three silver stars
Major General	Two silver stars
Brigadier General	One silver star
Colonel	Silver eagle
Lieutenant Colonel	Silver oak leaf
Major	Gold oak leaf
Captain	Two silver bars
First Lieutenant	One silver bar
Second Lieutenant	One gold bar

Warrant Officers

Grade Five—Silver bar with enamel black line.
Grade Four—Silver bar with 4 enamel black squares.
Grade Three—Silver bar with 3 enamel black squares.
Grade Two—Silver bar with 2 enamel black squares.
Grade One—Silver bar with 1 enamel black square.

Noncommissioned Officers

Sergeant Major of the Army (E-9)—Three chevrons above 3 arcs, with a U.S. Coat of Arms centered on the chevrons, flanked by 2 stars—one star on each side of the eagle. Also wears distinctive red and white shield collar insignia.

Command Sergeant Major (E-9)—Three chevrons above 3 arcs with a 5-pointed star with a wreath around the star between the chevrons and arcs.

Sergeant Major (E-9)—Three chevrons above 3 arcs with a 5-pointed star between the chevrons and arcs.

First Sergeant (E-8)—Three chevrons above 3 arcs with a lozenge between the chevrons and arcs.

Master Sergeant (E-8)—Three chevrons above 3 arcs.

Sergeant First Class (E-7)—Three chevrons above 2 arcs.

Staff Sergeant (E-6)—Three chevrons above 1 arc.

Sergeant (E-5)—Three chevrons.

Corporal (E-4)—Two chevrons.

Specialists

Specialist (E-4)—Eagle device only.

Other Enlisted

Private First Class (E-3)—One chevron above 1 arc.
Private (E-2)—One chevron.
Private (E-1)—None.

*Rank reserved for wartime use only.

Air Force

Insignia for Air Force officers are identical to those of the Army. Insignia for enlisted personnel are worn on both sleeves and consist of a star and an appropriate number of rockers. Chevrons appear above 5 rockers for the top 3 noncommissioned officer ranks, as follows (in ascending order): Master Sergeant, 1 chevron; Senior Master Sergeant, 2 chevrons; and Chief Master Sergeant, 3 chevrons. The insignia of the Chief Master Sergeant of the Air Force has 3 chevrons and a wreath around the star design. General of the Air Force is reserved for wartime use only.

Navy

The following stripes are worn on the lower sleeves of the Service Dress Blue uniform. They are of gold embroidery.

Rank	Insignia
Fleet Admiral*	1 two inch with 4 one-half inch
Admiral	1 two inch with 3 one-half inch
Vice Admiral	1 two inch with 2 one-half inch
Rear Admiral (upper half)	1 two inch with 1 one-half inch
Rear Admiral (lower half)	1 two inch
Captain	4 one-half inch
Commander	3 one-half inch
Lieutenant Commander	2 one-half inch with 1 one-quarter inch between
Lieutenant	2 one-half inch
Lieutenant (j.g.)	1 one-half inch with one-quarter inch above
Ensign	1 one-half inch
Warrant Officer W-4	½" stripe with 1 break
Warrant Officer W-3	½" stripe with 2 breaks, 2" apart
Warrant Officer W-2	½" stripe with 3 breaks, 2" apart

Enlisted personnel (noncommissioned petty officers)—A rating badge worn on the upper left sleeve, consisting of a spread eagle, appropriate number of chevrons, and centered specialty mark.

*Rank reserved for wartime use only.

Marine Corps

Marine Corps' distinctive cap and collar ornament is the Marine Corps Emblem—a combination of the American eagle, a globe, and an anchor. Marine Corps and Army officer insignia are similar. Marine Corps enlisted insignia, although basically similar to the Army's, feature crossed rifles beneath the chevrons. Marine Corps enlisted rank insignia are as follows:

Sergeant Major of the Marine Corps (E-9)—Same as Sergeant Major (below) but with Marine Corps emblem in the center with a 5-pointed star on both sides of the emblem.

Sergeant Major (E-9)—Three chevrons above 4 rockers with a 5-pointed star in the center.

Master Gunnery Sergeant (E-9)—Three chevrons above 4 rockers with a bursting bomb insignia in the center.

First Sergeant (E-8)—Three chevrons above 3 rockers with a diamond in the middle.

Master Sergeant (E-8)—Three chevrons above 3 rockers with crossed rifles in the middle.

Gunnery Sergeant (E-7)—Three chevrons above 2 rockers with crossed rifles in the middle.

Staff Sergeant (E-6)—Three chevrons above 1 rocker with crossed rifles in the middle.

Sergeant (E-5)—Three chevrons above crossed rifles.

Corporal (E-4)—Two chevrons above crossed rifles.

Lance Corporal (E-3)—One chevron above crossed rifles.

Private First Class (E-2)—One chevron.

Private (E-1)—None.

Coast Guard

Coast Guard insignia follow Navy custom, with certain minor changes such as the officer cap insignia. The Coast Guard shield is worn on both sleeves of officers and on the right sleeve of all enlisted personnel.

For Further Information on the U.S. Armed Forces

Additional information on all the U.S. Armed Forces branches, as well as many other related organizations, can be accessed through **DefenseLINK**, the official Internet site of the Dept. of Defense: www.defenselink.mil

Army—Office of the Chief of Public Affairs, Attn: Media Relations Division—MRD, 1500 Army Pentagon, Washington, DC 20310-1500. **Website:** www.army.mil

Navy—Chief of Information, 1200 Navy Pentagon, Washington, DC 20350-1200. **Website:** www.navy.mil

Air Force—Office of Public Affairs, 1690 Air Force Pentagon, Washington, DC 20330-1690. **Website:** www.af.mil

Marine Corps—Marine Corps Headquarters, Division of Public Affairs, U.S. Marine Corps, Washington, DC 20380-1775. **Website:** www.usmc.mil

Coast Guard—Commandant (G-IPA-2), U.S. Coast Guard Headquarters, 2100 Second St. SW, Washington, DC 20593. **Website:** www.uscg.mil

Timeline of Major Wars Since 1066

Norman Conquest 1066-71	William I, duke of Normandy, landed on the English coast near Hastings on Sept. 28, 1066, and defeated Harold II, Saxon king of England, at Battle of Hastings Oct. 14. William crowned king Dec. 25 in Westminster Abbey. Most revolts were suppressed by 1071. **Conquest linked England's interests with those of the continent and led to its rise as a powerful monarchy.**
Crusades 1095-1270/1291	Military expeditions undertaken by **Western European Christians** usually at the behest of the **papacy**, to recover **Jerusalem** and other Biblical places of pilgrimage from **Muslim** control; in the long term, stimulated trade and flow of ideas between East and West. Pope Urban II called Nov. 27, 1095, for the **First Crusade**; Crusaders took Jerusalem on July 15, 1099, massacred inhabitants, and founded four temporary states: Antioch, Edessa, Jerusalem, and Tripoli. The failed **Second Crusade** was prompted by Muslims' capture of Edessa in 1144. Jerusalem was captured by Ayyubid sultan Saladin on Oct. 2, 1187, launching the **Third Crusade**, which involved the Holy Roman emperor, Frederick I (Barbarossa); the French king, Philip II (Augustus); and the English king, Richard I (Lion-Heart), but did not lead to a Crusader victory. The **Fourth Crusade** sacked Constantinople on Apr. 13, 1204. The **Fifth Crusade** began with capture of Damietta in Egypt (1219) but failed at Cairo. A **Sixth Crusade** led to the Treaty of Jaffa in 1229, giving Jerusalem to the Crusaders until 1244, when it was taken by the Khwarizmians, launching a **Seventh Crusade**. The last crusade abruptly ended when its leader, French King Louis IX, died in 1270. The last major Crusader stronghold, Acre (now Akko, Israel), was lost on May 18, 1291.
Hundred Years War 1337-1453	Series of armed conflicts over rival claims to the French throne, broken by a number of truces and peace treaties. Edward III declared self king of France in 1338 and invaded, with victories at Crécy in 1346 and Poitiers in 1356. **Treaty of Brétigny** signed May 8, 1360, but French king Charles V renewed fighting in 1369. Truce from 1396 until **Henry V** of England invaded in 1415 and **defeated French army at Agincourt**, capturing land north of Loire River including Paris. **Treaty of Troyes** in 1420 made Henry VI heir of both thrones. The siege of French stronghold Orléans, lifted in 1429 with help from **Joan of Arc**, turned the tide in favor of the French. **War ended English claims to France, paved the way for French absolute monarchy.**
Wars of the Roses 1455-85	Series of dynastic civil wars in England fought by the **rival houses of Lancaster and York for the throne**. Richard, third duke of York, in conflict with the Lancastrian King **Henry VI**, won victories at St. Albans (1455) and Northampton (1460); Richard died at battle of Wakefield on Dec. 30, 1460, before coronation, leaving his son to become King Edward IV. Henry VI imprisoned in tower of London, 1465. Edward died in 1483; his brother became **Richard III** after usurping throne from Edward V. Henry Tudor defeated Richard III at the Battle of Bosworth Field (1485). As Henry VII, he married Edward's daughter Elizabeth, 1486, **finally uniting the houses**.
Thirty Years War 1618-48	A series of religious and political conflicts involving **most countries of western Europe**; most fighting in Germany, devastating it. Protestants stormed Hapsburg palace in the "Defenestration of Prague" (May 23, 1618). Major conflicts included defeat of King Christian IV of Denmark and Norway by Catholic League (1626); victories by Lutheran King Gustav II Adolph of Sweden at Breitenfeld (1631) and Lützen (1632). France, under cardinal and statesman **Richelieu**, chief minister of King Louis XIII, declared war on the Hapsburgs in May 1635; defeated Austro-Bavarian army (Aug. 3, 1645), leading to Truce of Ulm. **Peace of Westphalia** signed at Münster on Oct. 24, 1648, bringing peace by recognizing the rulers' sovereignty within their lands and their right to determine the religious beliefs of their subjects.
English Civil Wars 1638-60	Series of conflicts between followers of King Charles (Cavaliers) and Parliament (Roundheads), over divine right of king versus Parliament's right to control national finances. Presbyterian Scots, allied with Parliament, rioted and in 1640 occupied the northern counties of England. **Oliver Cromwell**, second in command of Parliament's New Model Army, destroyed the king's army at the Battle of Naseby (June 14, 1645); first civil war ended May 1646 when Charles surrendered to the Scots. Charles later allied with Scots, but was defeated by Cromwell at Preston Aug. 17-19, 1648, and executed Jan. 30, 1649. Parliament abolished monarchy and House of Lords. Cromwell suppressed Irish and Scottish rebellions, was briefly succeeded by son Richard after death (1658); **Charles II restored to the throne** by "The Long Parliament," May 1660.
War of the Spanish Succession 1701-14	War fought by the Grand Alliance (originally England, Netherlands, Denmark, and Austria; later also Portugal), against coalition of France, Spain, and a number of small Italian and German principalities to preserve balance of power after death of Spanish king Charles II. Opened with invasion of Italy, via Venice, by an Austrian army under Prince Eugène of Savoy in May 1701. French forced to withdraw from Netherlands and Italy in 1706 and finally defeated 1709 in bloodiest battle of the war at the French village of Malplaquet. Treaty of Rastatt and Baden signed in 1714; gave **Austria control of Spanish Netherlands and settled peace between Austria and France.**
War of the Austrian Succession 1740-48	Conflict over rival claims for the **hereditary dominions of the Habsburg family**, following death (1740) of Charles VI, Holy Roman emperor and archduke of Austria. An alliance of Bavaria, France, Spain, Sardinia, Prussia, and Saxony fought against Austria, allied with Holland and Great Britain. King Frederick the Great of Prussia captured Silesia from Austria in the First (1740-42) and Second Silesian Wars (1744-45). British king George II defeated French army at Battle of Dettingen am Main (June 27, 1743). French conquered Austrian Netherlands (1745-46). Treaty of Aix-la-Chapelle Oct. 18, 1748, **restored most original borders, and Prussia became a significant force.**
Seven Years War 1756-63	Worldwide conflicts fought for the **control of Germany** and for **supremacy in colonial N America and India**. French defeated British Gen. Edward Braddock on the Monongahela in 1754, leading to formal declaration of **French-Indian War**, May 1756. Frederick II of Prussia invaded Saxony on Aug. 29, 1756; defeated French at Rossbach (1757), Austrians at Leuthen (1757), Russians at Zorndorf (1758). By 1760, British conquered French Canada. Peter III signed armistice with Prussia, 1762. Treaty of Paris signed Feb. 10, 1763; Peace of Hubertusburg Feb. 15, 1763, between Prussia and Austria. **England emerged as leading world naval power.**
American Revolution 1775-83	Conflict between Great Britain and 13 British colonies on the eastern seaboard of North America. George Washington took command of the Continental Army, July 2, 1775, and King George III declared colonies traitors on Aug. 23. **Independence of colonies declared July 4, 1776.** France recognized the colonies' independence Feb. 6, 1778, followed by Spain on June 21, 1779; both pledged support. French fleet drove British fleet under Adm. Thomas Graves from the Chesapeake Bay on Sept. 5, 1781. French and Americans laid siege to Yorktown Sept. 28-Oct. 19, forcing British Gen. Cornwallis to surrender. **Treaty of Paris** (Sept. 3, 1783) recognized U.S. independence.
Wars of French Revolution & Napoleonic Wars 1792-1815	Large-scale wars fought between France and two multinational coalitions. France declared war on the Austrian part of the Holy Roman Empire for aiding King Louis XVI, Apr. 20, 1792. Newly created French Republic declared war on monarchs of Britain and Holland, Feb. 1, 1793, and Spain, Mar. 7. **Napoleon Bonaparte** defeated Austria in N Italy (1796-97), captured Egypt from Britain (1798-99; Battle of the Pyramids, July 21, 1798), and became First Consul after coup d'état of Nov. 9-10, 1799. French Grande Armée later swept through Europe using innovative and aggressive tactics. French navy defeated by British under Adm. Horatio Nelson at **Trafalgar** (Oct. 21, 1805), but Napoleon defeated Austro-Russian forces at Austerlitz (Dec. 2) and controlled most of Europe except Russia and Great Britain by 1808. France suffered its first major defeat by Austria at Aspern-Essling, May 21-22, 1809. **Napoleon invaded Russia**, captured Moscow Sept. 14, 1812, but was forced to flee the bitter Russian winter and abandoned Germany after defeat at Leipzig, Oct. 16-19, 1813. Paris captured by Allied armies Mar. 30-31, 1814. Napoleon exiled to Elba May 4 but returned for "Hundred Days" reign, Mar. 20-June 28, 1815; **final defeat at Waterloo** by British and Prussian troops (June 18). **The Bourbon monarchy was restored under Louis XVIII**, and Britain, Prussia, Russia, and Austria maintained European peace.

Crimean War 1853-56	Conflict between **Russia** and a coalition of **Great Britain, France, Sardinia, and Turkey for influence over Balkans** and the straits between the Black Sea and the Mediterranean. Russia destroyed Turkish fleet at Sinope on Nov. 30, 1853. Britain and France declared war in Mar. 1854 and with Turkish troops defeated Russians at Battle of Alma River on Sept. 20. Lord Lucan of Britain prevented Russia from capturing Balaklava on Oct. 25 ("Charge of the Light Brigade"). Siege of Sevastopol ended when Russia evacuated Sept. 8, 1855. Treaty of Paris signed Mar. 30, 1856; **curbed Russian expansion and loosened European power alignments**.
American Civil War 1861-65	Conflict between the United States (the Union) and 11 secessionist Southern states, organized as the Confederate States of America. Union garrison at Fort Sumter off Charleston, SC, surrendered to Brig. Gen. Pierre Beauregard (Apr. 12-13, 1861). 22,000 Confederates under Beauregard repelled 35,000 Union troops under Gen. Irvin McDowell along Bull Run stream near Manassas, VA (July 21). The *Merrimack* (renamed the *Virginia*) battled the *Monitor* Mar. 9, 1862. In **Battle of Antietam** (Sept. 17), some 12,000 Northerners and 12,700 Southerners were killed or wounded. Pres. Abraham Lincoln announced **Emancipation Proclamation** on Sept. 22. Confederate Gen. Robert E. Lee's forces numbering 75,000 battled 88,000 Union troops under Gen. George Meade at **Gettysburg** July 1-3, 1863, forcing Lee's army back across the Potomac River. Lee surrendered to Ulysses S. Grant at **Appomattox Court House** (Apr. 9, 1865). **The Union was preserved and slavery abolished.**
Franco-Prussian War 1870-71	German states led by Prussia defeated France, seizing Alsace and part of Lorraine. French defeated in several major battles, culminating at **Sedan** Sept. 1, 1870, when Prussian forces decisively defeated the French army and captured emperor Napoleon III. Prussian king crowned William I, emperor of a unified Germany, Jan 18, 1871. **France surrendered** Jan. 28. Final treaty signed May 10; set the stage for later **German imperialistic expansion**.
Spanish-American War 1898	War waged by the U.S. to **liberate Cuba from Spanish rule**. A mysterious explosion, blamed on Spain by American newspapers, sank the U.S. battleship *Maine* in Havana's harbor (Feb. 15, 1898), killing 260. The U.S. called for Spain's withdrawal from Cuba, and Spain declared war (Apr. 24). Rufus Shafter led 17,000 U.S. troops from Daiquirí to Santiago de Cuba, taking **San Juan Hill** with help of the Rough Riders under Teddy Roosevelt. Santiago de Cuba surrendered July 17. The Treaty of Paris (Dec. 10, 1898) provided for the **independence of Cuba**; the cession by Spain to the U.S. of **Puerto Rico, Guam, and for a $20 mil payment, the Philippine Islands**.
World War I 1914-18	Local European war that grew into a global war involving 32 nations: the Allies and the Associated Powers—28 nations including Great Britain, France, Russia, Italy, and the U.S.—versus the Central Powers of Germany, Austria-Hungary, Turkey, and Bulgaria. Archduke Francis Ferdinand assassinated at Sarajevo, Bosnia (June 28, 1914). Germany invaded France through Belgium and the Netherlands; advance on Paris halted by the French under Gen. Joseph Jacques Césaire Joffre at the **First Battle of the Marne**, Sept. 5-12. Germany checked the Russian army at the Battle of Tannenberg, Aug. 26-30. The British suffered 57,470 casualties (19,240 dead) in the opening day of the **First Battle of the Somme** (July 1-Nov. 18, 1916), first of 12 battles that forced Germany back to the Hindenburg Line. **U.S. declared war on Germany Apr. 6, 1917.** Russian involvement ended when Bolshevik party seized power on Nov. 7; signed armistice Dec. 15. German offensive halted by U.S. and French troops at **Second Battle of the Marne** (July 15-Aug. 5, 1918), the turning point of the war. Allied counteroffensive broke the Hindenburg Line, and an armistice was signed Nov. 11.
World War II 1939-45	Global military conflict stemming from European unrest after World War I and Japan's aggressive expansion into Asia and the Pacific. **The War in Europe:** The Nazi-Soviet nonaggression pact (Aug. 23, 1939) freed Germany and the Soviet Union to attack Poland in Sept. **Britain and France declared war on Germany** Sept. 3. German forces raced through Europe (Apr.-June 1940), capturing Paris June 14. **Italy declared war on France and Britain** June 10; German-Italian campaigns won the Balkans and N Africa by June 1941. U.S. entered war Dec. 1941. Three million Axis troops invaded Russia June 22, 1941, but Russian counterthrusts stopped the German advance (**Stalingrad**, Aug. 20, 1942-Feb. 2, 1943), and Allies took N Africa (Nov. 8, 1942-May 13, 1943), Italy (July 10, 1943-May 2, 1945). Normandy invaded on **D-Day**, June 6, 1944; Paris liberated Aug. 25. Yalta Conference (Feb. 4-11, 1945) to defeat and split Germany into quarters. Adolf Hitler committed suicide Apr. 30. **Germany surrendered unconditionally** May 7. **The War in the Pacific:** Japan invaded China (July 7, 1937), joined alliance with Germany and Italy (Sept. 27, 1940) and signed nonaggression pact with Russia (Apr. 13, 1941); attacked Hawaii's Pearl Harbor, Dec. 7, 1941; U.S. declared war on Japan Dec. 8. **Battle of Midway** (June 4-7, 1942) repulsed the Japanese advance. Marines landed on Guadalcanal Aug. 7. Navy defeated Japanese fleet at **Leyte Gulf**, Oct. 23-26, 1944. B-29 bombing raids on Japan began in Nov. Marines invaded Iwo Jima (Feb. 19-Mar. 16, 1945) with heavy casualties, then Okinawa (Apr. 1-June 21). **U.S. atom bombs dropped** on Hiroshima (Aug. 6) and Nagasaki (Aug. 9) and the Soviet invasion of Manchuria (Aug. 8) **forced Japan to agree, on Aug. 14, to surrender**; formal surrender on Sept. 2.
Korean War 1950-53	Military struggle fought on the Korean Peninsula between the Democratic Peoples' Republic of Korea (N Korea) and the Republic of Korea (S Korea) that developed into an international war involving China allied with N Korea against the U.S. and other nations under the UN flag. DPRK army crossed the 38th parallel and invaded S Korea (June 25, 1950), entering Seoul (June 26). Amphibious assault launched at **Inchon** by Gen. Douglas MacArthur (Sept. 15) helped U.S. forces rout DPRK close to the Yalu River by Nov. 24. Chinese counterattack retook Seoul (Jan. 4, 1951), but forced back to the 38th parallel by Apr. 22. Armistice was signed (July 27, 1953) by the UN, DPRK, and China, but not ROK, **leaving the peninsula partitioned at 38th parallel**.
Vietnam War 1959-75	Struggle primarily in S Vietnam that widened into a war between S Vietnam supported mainly by the U.S. and N Vietnam supported by the USSR and China. Viet Minh, led by Communist leader Ho Chi Minh, formed the Democratic Republic of Vietnam (Sept. 2, 1945). Colonial power France withdrew after fortress at Dien Bien Phu fell (May 8, 1954). Pres. John F. Kennedy pledged U.S. commitment to S Vietnamese independence Dec. 14, 1961. USS *Maddox* destroyer damaged in **Gulf of Tonkin** (Aug. 2, 1964) prompted Congress to increase involvement. Regular bombing of N Vietnam began (Feb. 24, 1965) and the first U.S. combat ground-forces arrived (Mar. 6). North Vietnamese Army siege of **Khe Sanh** (Jan. 21-Apr. 7, 1968) and the **"Tet" offensive** (Jan. 30) aimed to cause insurrection in the south. **My Lai Massacre** by U.S. soldiers against civilians (Mar. 16, 1968) created scandal, fueled U.S. disaffection with war. U.S. forces peaked at 543,400 in Apr. 1969. NVA **"Easter Offensive"** (Mar. 30, 1972) rebuffed, and U.S. responded with aerial bombings in May and Dec. U.S. withdrew after ceasefire, Jan. 1973. **NVA offensive captured Saigon, Apr. 30, 1975, and unified Vietnam under Communist rule.**
Persian Gulf Wars 1991, 2003	Conflicts fought principally between Iraq and the U.S. concerning Iraq's influence in the Middle East and its development of weapons of mass destruction. **First Gulf War:** Iraq under dictator Saddam Hussein invaded Kuwait Aug 2, 1990, and annexed it; UN Security Council ordered Iraqi forces to withdraw by Jan. 15, 1991. Beginning Jan. 17, a multinational force (**Operation Desert Storm**) led by the U.S. bombed military targets in Iraq and Kuwait. A coordinated air-land offensive (**Operation Desert Sabre**, begun Feb. 24) retook Kuwait City Feb. 26, and permanent ceasefire was signed on Apr. 6. Iraq was ordered to pay reparations to Kuwait, reveal locations of biological and chemical weapons, and eliminate weapons of mass destruction. **Second Gulf War:** The U.S. and UK mistakenly asserted that Iraq was still producing WMD and posed an imminent threat. The UN passed Resolution 1441, Nov. 8, 2002, warning Iraq of "serious consequences" if it failed to cooperate fully and unconditionally with UN weapons inspectors. Iraq rejected a Mar. 17, 2003, U.S. ultimatum demanding Hussein and his sons leave Iraq; U.S. launched **Operation Iraqi Freedom** Mar. 19, 2003, with support from UK and other allies, but without full UN Security Council support. Baghdad fell Apr. 9, and major combat operations declared over May 1. Saddam Hussein was captured Dec. 13, but guerrilla opposition to U.S. troops and violence between Iraqi Shiites and Sunnis continued.

HEALTH

U.S. Health Expenditures, 1960-2006

Source: *Health, United States, 2008*, National Center for Health Statistics, U.S. Dept. of Health and Human Services

	1960	1970	1980	1990	1995	2000	2003	2004	2005	2006
					Amount in billions					
National health expenditures	$27.5	$74.9	$253.4	$714.0	$1,016.5	$1,353.6	$1,732.4	$1,852.3	$1,973.3	$2,105.5
					Percent distribution					
Health services and supplies	90.6	89.6	92.1	93.4	93.7	93.4	93.5	93.4	93.4	93.4
Personal health care	84.7	84.0	84.8	85.1	85.0	84.2	83.5	83.6	83.8	83.7
Hospital care	33.3	36.8	39.9	35.2	33.5	30.8	30.3	30.5	30.7	30.8
Professional services..............	30.2	27.6	26.5	30.4	31.1	31.5	31.3	31.4	31.5	31.4
Physician and clinical services......	19.4	18.7	18.6	22.1	21.7	21.3	21.2	21.3	21.4	21.3
Other professional services	1.4	1.0	1.4	2.5	2.8	2.9	2.8	2.8	2.8	2.8
Dental services	7.1	6.2	5.3	4.4	4.4	4.6	4.4	4.4	4.4	4.3
Other personal health care.........	2.2	1.7	1.3	1.3	2.3	2.7	2.9	2.9	2.9	3.0
Nursing home and home health.......	3.2	5.7	8.2	9.1	10.3	9.3	8.6	8.5	8.5	8.4
Home health care[1]	0.2	0.3	0.9	1.8	3.0	2.3	2.2	2.3	2.4	2.5
Nursing home care[1]	2.9	5.4	7.3	7.4	7.3	7.0	6.4	6.2	6.1	5.9
Retail outlet sales of medical products..	18.0	14.0	10.1	10.4	10.0	12.6	13.2	13.2	13.0	13.1
Prescription drugs	9.7	7.3	4.8	5.6	6.0	8.9	10.1	10.2	10.1	10.3
Other medical products	8.2	6.6	5.4	4.7	4.0	3.7	3.2	3.0	2.9	2.8
Government administration and net cost of private health insurance ...	4.4	3.7	4.8	5.5	5.7	6.0	7.0	7.0	6.8	6.9
Government public health activities[2] ...	1.5	1.9	2.5	2.8	3.0	3.2	3.1	2.9	2.9	2.8
Investment	**9.4**	**10.4**	**7.9**	**6.6**	**6.3**	**6.6**	**6.5**	**6.6**	**6.6**	**6.6**
Research[3]	2.5	2.6	2.1	1.8	1.8	1.9	2.1	2.1	2.1	2.0
Structures and equipment	6.9	7.8	5.7	4.9	4.5	4.7	4.4	4.5	4.5	4.6
				Average annual percent change from previous year shown						
National health expenditures	—	10.5	13.0	10.9	7.3	5.9	8.0	6.9	6.5	6.7
Health services and supplies	—	10.4	13.3	11.1	7.4	5.8	8.1	6.8	6.5	6.6
Personal health care	—	10.4	13.1	11.0	7.3	5.7	7.8	7.0	6.8	6.6
Hospital care	—	11.6	13.9	9.6	6.3	4.1	7.5	7.4	7.3	7.0
Professional services..............	—	9.5	12.5	12.4	7.9	6.2	7.9	7.0	7.1	6.1
Physician and clinical services......	—	10.1	12.9	12.8	7.0	5.5	8.5	7.3	7.4	5.9
Other professional services	—	6.6	17.1	17.5	9.5	6.5	7.5	7.0	7.1	4.9
Dental services	—	9.1	11.1	9.0	7.1	6.9	4.8	6.0	6.3	5.7
Other personal health care.........	—	7.3	10.1	11.4	19.2	10.0	8.7	5.7	6.8	9.5
Nursing home and home health.......	—	17.2	17.2	12.1	9.9	3.8	6.1	6.3	6.9	5.3
Home health care[1]	—	14.5	26.9	18.1	19.4	0.0	11.1	12.3	12.3	9.9
Nursing home care[1]	—	17.4	16.4	11.0	7.1	5.2	4.5	4.2	4.9	3.5
Retail outlet sales of medical products..	—	7.8	9.4	11.2	6.6	10.8	9.5	6.8	5.2	7.3
Prescription drugs	—	7.5	8.2	12.8	8.6	14.6	10.5	8.4	5.8	8.5
Other medical products	—	8.1	10.6	9.5	4.0	3.9	6.5	1.8	3.1	3.0
Government administration and net cost of private health insurance	—	8.6	16.0	12.4	8.2	7.1	13.6	6.6	3.6	8.8
Government public health activities[2] ...	—	12.8	16.5	12.0	9.2	7.0	3.2	0.2	4.4	4.3
Investment	—	**11.7**	**9.9**	**9.0**	**6.1**	**6.9**	**7.5**	**8.9**	**6.6**	**7.4**
Research[3]	—	10.9	10.8	8.9	7.7	6.9	9.2	9.1	4.8	2.9
Structures and equipment	—	11.9	9.5	9.1	5.5	6.8	6.7	8.8	7.4	9.5

Note: Numbers may not add to totals because of rounding. (1) Freestanding facilities only. (2) Includes personal care services delivered by government public health agencies. (3) Excludes R&D expenditures of drug companies and other manufacturers and suppliers of medical equip. and supplies.

Health Coverage for Persons Under 65, by Characteristics, 1984-2007

Source: *Health, United States, 2008*, National Center for Health Statistics, U.S. Dept. of Health and Human Services

	PRIVATE INSURANCE				MEDICAID[1]				NOT COVERED[2]			
	1984[3]	2000	2004	2007	1984[3]	2000	2004	2007	1984[3]	2000	2004	2007
					Percent of each population group							
Total......................	76.8%	71.5%	68.8%	66.8%	6.8%	9.5%	12.5%	13.9%	14.5%	17.0%	16.4%	16.6%
Age												
Under 18 years	72.6	66.6	63.2	59.8	11.9	19.6	26.4	29.8	13.9	12.6	9.2	9.0
18-44 years	76.5	70.5	67.3	65.5	5.1	5.6	7.7	8.7	17.1	22.4	23.5	23.9
45-64 years	83.3	78.7	77.1	75.5	3.4	4.5	5.5	5.9	9.6	12.6	12.8	13.5
Race and Hispanic origin[4,5]												
White, non-Hispanic	79.9	75.7	71.4	69.7	4.6	7.1	10.4	11.4	13.6	15.4	16.1	16.3
Black, non-Hispanic..........	58.1	55.9	53.9	51.8	20.5	21.2	24.9	27.7	19.9	19.5	17.6	17.0
All Hispanic	55.7	47.8	41.7	41.7	13.3	15.5	22.5	24.7	29.5	35.6	34.4	31.8
Percent of poverty level[4]												
Below 100%	32.2	25.2	21.8	21.4	33.0	38.4	45.0	47.6	33.9	34.2	31.0	28.4
100-149%	62.2	41.7	39.0	32.7	7.7	20.7	27.1	31.8	27.2	34.9	30.8	31.5
150-199%	77.2	58.5	52.5	47.5	3.2	11.5	16.9	20.3	17.3	27.0	27.2	28.5
200% or more	91.5	85.7	84.2	83.1	0.6	2.3	3.5	3.8	6.0	10.1	10.2	10.6
Geographic region[4]												
Northeast..................	80.5	76.3	74.0	72.2	8.6	10.6	13.0	15.4	10.2	12.2	11.8	11.0
Midwest....................	80.6	78.8	76.3	72.0	7.4	8.0	10.4	13.7	11.3	12.3	12.4	13.0
South.....................	74.3	66.8	64.1	62.6	5.1	9.4	12.4	12.9	17.7	20.5	19.9	20.1
West	71.9	66.5	64.1	64.0	7.0	10.4	14.4	14.5	18.2	20.7	18.9	18.9

Note: Data based on household interviews of a sample of the civilian noninstitutionalized population. Percents do not add to 100 because other types of health insurance (e.g., Medicare, military) are not shown and persons with both private insurance and Medicaid appear in both sections. (1) Includes Medicaid and other public assistance. In 2007, the age-adjusted percent of the population under 65 covered by Medicaid was 11.3%; 1.2% were covered by state-sponsored health plans and 1.5% were covered by State Children's Health Insurance Program (SCHIP). (2) Includes persons not covered by private insurance, Medicaid or other public assistance, Medicare, or military plans. (3) A change in the questionnaire in 1997 prevents direct comparison with later years. (4) Age adjusted. (5) Changed reporting methods make percentages for race before 1999 not strictly comparable with those from 1999 on.

Spending on Health in the 50 Most Populous Countries, 2006

Source: *World Health Statistics 2009*, The World Health Organization

Country	As % of GDP	Per capita[1]	Country	As % of GDP	Per capita[1]	Country	As % of GDP	Per capita[1]	Country	As % of GDP	Per capita[1]
Afghanistan ..	9.2%	$27	Germany.....	10.6%	$3,718	Nepal	5.1%	$17	Sudan	3.8%	$37
Algeria	4.2	148	Ghana.......	5.1	33	Nigeria	3.8	33	Tanzania	6.4	23
Argentina	10.1	551	India	3.6	29	North Korea .	3.5	<1	Thailand	3.5	113
Bangladesh ..	3.2	12	Indonesia	2.5	39	Pakistan	2.0	16	Turkey	5.1	352
Brazil	7.5	427	Iran	6.8	215	Peru	4.4	149	Uganda	7.0	24
Canada......	10.0	3,917	Iraq	3.5	62	Philippines ..	3.8	52	Ukraine	6.9	160
China	4.6	94	Italy	9.0	2,813	Poland......	6.2	555	United		
Colombia	7.3	217	Japan	8.1	2,759	Romania	4.5	256	Kingdom...	8.2	3,332
Congo, Dem.			Kenya	4.6	29	Russia......	5.3	367	**United States**	**15.3**	**6,719**
Rep. of the	6.8	10	Malaysia	4.3	259	Saudi Arabia	3.3	492	Uzbekistan ..	4.7	30
Egypt	6.3	92	Mexico	6.6	527	South Africa	8.0	425	Venezuela ...	4.9	332
Ethiopia	3.9	7	Morocco	5.3	113	South Korea	6.4	1,168	Vietnam.....	6.6	46
France	11.0	3,937	Myanmar.....	2.2	5	Spain.......	8.4	2,328	Yemen......	4.5	40

(1) At average exchange rates.

Health Insurance Coverage,[1] by State, 1990-2008

Source: Bureau of the Census, U.S. Dept. of Commerce

	2006-08[2] Not covered[3]	2006-08[2] % not covered	2000 Not covered[3]	2000 % not covered	1990 Not covered[3]	1990 % not covered		2006-08[2] Not covered[3]	2006-08[2] % not covered	2000 Not covered[3]	2000 % not covered	1990 Not covered[3]	1990 % not covered
AL	600	13.0%	582	13.3%	710	17.4%	MT	155	16.3%	150	16.8%	115	14.0%
AK	122	18.2	117	18.7	77	15.4	NE	220	12.5	154	9.1	138	8.5
AZ	1,249	19.6	869	16.7	547	15.5	NV	475	18.5	344	16.8	201	16.5
AR	492	17.6	379	14.3	421	17.4	NH	140	10.7	103	8.4	107	9.9
CA	6,742	18.5	6,299	18.5	5,683	19.1	NJ	1,297	15.1	1,021	12.2	773	10.0
CO	802	16.5	620	14.3	495	14.7	NM	450	23.0	435	24.2	339	22.2
CT	331	9.6	330	9.8	226	6.9	NY	2,634	13.8	3,056	16.3	2,176	12.1
DE	98	11.4	72	9.3	96	13.9	NC	1,505	16.6	1,084	13.6	883	13.8
DC	60	10.4	78	14.0	109	19.2	ND	70	11.4	71	11.3	40	6.3
FL	3,698	20.5	2,829	17.7	2,376	18.0	OH	1,256	11.1	1,248	11.2	1,123	10.3
GA	1,675	17.7	1,166	14.3	971	15.3	OK	597	16.9	641	18.9	574	18.6
HI	101	8.1	113	9.4	81	7.3	OR	639	17.0	433	12.7	360	12.4
ID	224	15.0	199	15.4	159	15.2	PA	1,208	9.8	1,047	8.7	1,218	10.1
IL	1,705	13.4	1,704	13.9	1,272	10.9	RI	109	10.4	77	7.4	105	11.1
IN	746	11.8	674	11.2	587	10.7	SC	700	16.1	480	12.1	550	16.2
IA	288	9.8	253	8.8	225	8.1	SD	90	11.5	81	11.0	81	11.6
KS	337	12.4	289	10.9	272	10.8	TN	874	14.4	615	10.9	673	13.7
KY	630	15.0	545	13.6	480	13.2	TX	5,917	24.9	4,748	22.9	3,569	21.1
LA	855	20.1	789	18.1	797	19.7	UT	382	14.5	281	12.5	156	9.0
ME	125	9.5	138	10.9	139	11.2	VT	63	10.2	52	8.6	54	9.5
MD	736	13.2	547	10.4	601	12.7	VA	1,034	13.5	814	11.6	996	15.7
MA	450	7.1	549	8.7	530	9.1	WA	764	11.8	792	13.5	557	11.4
MI	1,115	11.3	901	9.2	865	9.4	WV	256	14.2	250	14.1	249	13.8
MN	450	8.7	399	8.1	389	8.9	WI	489	8.9	406	7.6	321	6.7
MS	555	19.1	380	13.6	531	19.9	WY	72	13.9	76	15.7	58	12.5
MO	747	12.8	524	9.5	665	12.7	**U.S.**	**46,330**	**15.5**	**39,804**	**14.2**	**34,719**	**13.9**

(1) For population, all ages, including those 65 or over, an age group largely covered by Medicare. (2) 3-year average. (3) In thousands.

Persons Not Covered by Health Insurance, by Selected Characteristics, 2008

Source: Bureau of the Census, U.S. Dept. of Commerce

Race and Ethnicity	Number[1]	% of specified population
White.....................	34,890	14.5%
Non-Hispanic	21,322	10.8
Black.......................	7,284	19.1
Asian and Pacific Islander.......	2,344	17.6
Hispanic[2]...................	14,558	30.7
Nativity		
Native	34,036	12.9
Foreign born	12,304	33.5
Naturalized citizen	2,792	18.0
Not a citizen	9,511	44.7
Age		
Under 18 years	7,348	9.9
18 to 24 years	8,200	28.6
25 to 34 years	10,754	26.5
35 to 44 years	8,035	19.4
45 to 64 years	11,355	14.4
65 years and over	646	1.7

Region	Number[1]	% of specified population
Northeast	6,277	11.6%
Midwest	7,588	11.6
South	20,154	18.2
West......................	12,321	17.4
Household Income		
Less than $25,000	13,673	24.5
$25,000 to $49,999............	14,908	21.1
$50,000 to $74,999............	8,034	14.0
$75,000 or more.............	9,725	8.2
Work Experience		
Worked during year	27,772	18.7
Worked full-time	20,908	17.2
Worked part-time.............	6,864	25.4
Did not work	10,573	26.0
Total	**46,340**	**15.4**

(1) In thousands. (2) Persons of Hispanic origin may be of any race.

Enrollment in Health Maintenance Organizations (HMOs), 1976-2004

Source: *Health, United States, 2004*, National Center for Health Statistics, U.S. Dept. of Health and Human Services

	1976	1980	1990	1995	1997	1998	1999	2000	2001	2002	2003	2004
						Number of enrolled in millions						
TOTAL	6.0	9.1	33.0	50.9	66.8	76.6	81.3	80.9	79.5	76.1	71.6	68.8
Model type[1]												
Individual practice												
assoc.[2]	0.4	1.7	13.7	20.1	26.7	32.6	32.8	33.4	33.1	31.6	27.9	24.6
Group[3]	5.6	7.4	19.3	13.3	11.0	13.8	15.9	15.2	15.6	15.0	16.1	15.3
Mixed	—	—	—	17.6	29.0	30.1	32.6	32.3	30.9	29.6	27.8	28.9
Federal program[4]												
Medicaid[5]	—	0.3	1.2	3.5	5.6	7.8	10.4	10.8	11.4	12.8	14.5	14.3
Medicare	—	0.4	1.8	2.9	4.8	5.7	6.5	6.6	6.1	5.4	4.9	4.9
						Percent of population enrolled in HMOs						
TOTAL	2.8%	4.0%	13.4%	19.4%	25.2%	28.6%	30.1%	30.0%	28.3%	26.4%	24.6%	23.4%
Geographic region												
Northeast	2.0	3.1	14.6	24.4	32.4	37.8	36.7	36.5	35.1	33.4	31.8	30.1
Midwest	1.5	2.8	12.6	16.4	19.5	22.7	23.3	23.2	21.7	20.6	19.7	18.7
South	0.4	0.8	7.1	12.4	17.9	21.0	23.9	22.6	21.0	19.8	17.1	16.0
West	9.7	12.2	23.2	28.6	36.4	39.1	41.4	41.7	40.7	38.2	35.8	34.4

— = Not available. **Note:** Data as of June 30 in 1976-80, Jan. 1 from 1990 onwards. HMOs in Guam included starting in 1994; Puerto Rico, 1998; Guam HMO enrollment was 32,000 in 2003 and Puerto Rico enrollment was 1,726,000 in 2003. Open-ended enrollment in HMO plans, amounting to 7.6 mil on Jan. 1, 2003, included from 1994 onwards. (1) Enrollment may not equal total because some plans did not report these characteristics. (2) This type of HMO contracts with an association of physicians from various settings (a mixture of solo and group practices) to provide health services. (3) Group includes staff, group, and network model types. (4) Enrollment by Medicaid or Medicare beneficiaries, where the Medicaid or Medicare program contracts directly with the HMO to pay the premium. (5) Data for 1990 and later include enrollment in managed-care health insuring organizations.

Health Care Visits, by Selected Characteristics, 1997-2007

Source: Centers for Disease Control and Prevention, National Center for Health Statistics. National Health Interview Survey, family core and sample adult questionnaires.

	No visits			1-3 visits			4-9 visits			10 or more visits		
	1997	2000	2007	1997	2000	2007	1997	2000	2007	1997	2000	2007
						Percent distribution						
All persons	16.5%	16.7%	20.1%	46.2%	45.4%	43.5%	23.6%	24.6%	23.1%	13.7%	13.3%	13.4%
Age												
Under 6 years	5.0	6.3	NA	44.9	44.5	NA	37.0	38.1	NA	13.0	11.1	NA
6-17 years	15.3	15.2	NA	58.7	58.2	NA	19.3	20.6	NA	6.8	6.0	NA
18-44 years	NA	NA	26.4	NA	NA	45.5	NA	NA	17.8	NA	NA	10.4
45-64 years	NA	NA	15.7	NA	NA	45.6	NA	NA	24.0	NA	NA	14.7
65-74 years	9.8	9.0	9.3	36.9	34.5	35.4	31.6	34.5	36.7	21.6	22.1	18.6
75 years and over	7.7	5.8	6.4	31.8	29.3	32.0	33.8	39.3	39.3	26.6	25.6	22.3
Sex												
Male	21.3	21.7	26.7	47.1	45.9	43.9	20.6	22.3	19.2	11.0	10.1	10.3
Female	11.7	11.9	13.6	45.4	44.8	43.2	26.5	27.0	26.8	16.3	16.3	16.4
Race and Hispanic origin												
White, non-Hispanic	14.7	14.5	19.7	46.6	45.4	43.4	24.4	25.9	23.3	14.3	14.1	13.6
Black, non-Hispanic	16.9	17.1	20.1	46.1	46.8	43.3	23.1	23.5	23.6	13.8	12.6	12.9
Hispanic[1]	24.9	26.8	30.5	42.3	41.8	40.1	20.3	19.8	18.8	12.5	11.6	10.6
Health insurance status[2]												
Insured continuously	14.1	14.0	NA	49.2	48.8	NA	23.6	24.6	NA	13.0	12.6	NA
Uninsured for any period . . .	18.9	20.6	NA	46.0	44.5	NA	20.8	20.8	NA	14.4	14.1	NA
Uninsured	39.0	43.2	NA	41.4	39.6	NA	13.2	12.1	NA	6.4	5.1	NA

Note: Covers visits to doctor's offices, emergency departments, and home visits in a 12-month period prior to interview. Estimates are age-adjusted to the year 2000 standard population. Includes all races not shown separately and unknown health insurance status. 2007 data are for persons 18 years and older. (1) Persons of Hispanic origin may be of any race. (2) In 12 months prior to interview, for under-65 population only; persons with both Medicaid and private coverage are classified as having private coverage.

Top 20 Reasons Given by Patients for Physicians' Office Visits, 2006

Source: National Center for Health Statistics, U.S. Dept. of Health and Human Services

Rank	Number of visits (1,000)	% distrib. Total	Rank	Number of visits (1,000)	% distrib. Total
1. General medical examination	66,389	7.4%	11. Back symptoms	13,346	1.5%
2. Progress visit, not otherwise			12. Symptoms referable to throat	13,309	1.5
specified	51,296	5.7	13. For other and unspecified test		
3. Cough	26,738	3.0	results	13,077	1.4
4. Postoperative visit	23,355	2.6	14. Vision	12,184	1.4
5. Prenatal examination, routine	21,718	2.4	15. Fever	12,167	1.3
6. Gynecological examination	19,379	2.1	16. Hypertension	11,604	1.3
7. Medication, other and unspecified			17. Earache or ear infection	11,366	1.3
kinds	19,034	2.1	18. Headache, pain in head	10,243	1.1
8. Stomach and abdominal pain,			19. Skin rash	10,088	1.1
cramps, and spasms	16,007	1.8	20. Nasal congestion	9,448	1.0
9. Knee symptoms	14,957	1.7	**All other reasons**	512,714	56.8
10. Well-baby examination	13,555	1.5	**All visits**	901,954	100.0

(1) Based on 533,292,000 visits by women and 368,662,000 by men.

Top 20 Reasons Given by Patients for Emergency Room Visits, 2006

Source: National Center for Health Statistics, U.S. Dept. of Health and Human Services

Rank	Principal reason for visit	Number (1,000)	%	Rank	Principal reason for visit	Number (1,000)	%
1.	Stomach and abdominal pain, cramps, and spasms	8,057	6.8%	12.	Nausea	1,804	1.5%
2.	Chest pain and related symptoms	6,392	5.4	13.	Accident, not otherwise specified	1,737	1.5
3.	Fever	4,485	3.8	14.	Motor vehicle accident	1,714	1.4
4.	Headache, pain in head	3,354	2.8	15.	Earache	1,677	1.4
5.	Back symptoms	3,304	2.8	16.	Vertigo—dizziness	1,657	1.4
6.	Shortness of breath	3,007	2.5	17.	Leg symptoms	1,645	1.4
7.	Cough	2,956	2.5	18.	Skin rash	1,613	1.4
8.	Vomiting	2,635	2.2	19.	Injury, other and unspecified type—head, neck, and face	1,586	1.3
9.	Pain, site not referable to a specific body system	2,512	2.1	20.	Low back symptoms	1,511	1.3
10.	Symptoms referable to throat	2,278	1.9		**All other reasons**	**63,399**	**53.2**
11.	Lacerations and cuts—upper extremity	1,870	1.6		**All visits**	**119,191**	**100.0**

Drugs Most Frequently Prescribed in Ambulatory Care Settings, 2006

Source: National Center for Health Statistics, *National Health Statistics Report*

Rank	Therapeutic Classification[1]	Times prescribed (1,000)	% distrib.[2]	Rank	Therapeutic Classification[1]	Times prescribed (1,000)	% distrib.[2]
1.	Analgesics	319,598	13.6%	11.	Dermatological agents	63,972	2.7%
2.	Antihyperlipidemic agents	112,430	4.8	12.	Diuretics	63,658	2.7
3.	Antidepressants	97,812	4.2	13.	Anticonvulsants	62,664	2.7
4.	Anxiolytics, sedatives, and hypnotics	84,627	3.6	14.	ACE[3] inhibitors	56,147	2.4
5.	Antidiabetic agents	81,926	3.5	15.	Adrenal cortical steroids	46,553	2.0
6.	Bronchodilators	74,696	3.2	16.	Ophthalmic preparations	44,234	1.9
7.	Antiplatelet agents	72,834	3.1	17.	Antiemetic/antivertigo agents	44,187	1.9
8.	Beta-adrenergic blocking agents	72,786	3.1	18.	Penicillins	43,611	1.9
9.	Proton pump inhibitors	68,591	2.9	19.	Calcium channel blockers	42,051	1.8
10.	Antihistamines	64,985	2.8	20.	Minerals and electrolytes	41,957	1.8

(1) Based on the Multum Lexicon second-level therapeutic drug category. (2) Based on an estimated 2,356,882,000 drug mentions at ambulatory care visits in 2006. A drug mention is defined as any medication that is provided, prescribed, or continued at the visit, including over-the-counter preparations, immunizations, desensitizing agents, and anesthetics. (3) Angiotensin-converting enzyme.

Transplant Waiting List, Oct. 2009*

Transplants Performed, 2008

Source: United Network for Organ Sharing

Type of transplant	Patients waiting
Kidney	86,833
Liver	16,586
Heart	2,898
Kidney-pancreas	2,255
Lung	1,899
Pancreas	1,515
Intestine	232
Heart-lung	82
Total[1]	**112,300**

Type of transplant	Number
Kidney	16,518
Liver	6,319
Heart	2,163
Lung	1,478
Kidney-pancreas	837
Pancreas	436
Intestine	185
Heart-lung	27
Total	**27,963**

* As of Oct. 2, 2009. (1) Some patients are waiting for more than one organ; therefore total number of patients waiting is less than the sum of patients waiting for each organ.

Physicians by Sex and Specialty, 2005

Source: American Medical Assn., as of Dec. 31, 2005

	Male	Female		Male	Female		Male	Female
All Specialties[1]	649,347	235,627	General Preventive Med.	1,297	751	Pediatrics	33,515	36,636
Aerospace Medicine	442	33	General Surgery	32,329	5,173	Physical Med./Rehab.	4,812	2,478
Allergy & Immunology	3,056	1,050	Internal Medicine	104,688	46,245	Plastic Surgery	6,075	777
Anaesthesiology	30,452	8,370	Medical Genetics	250	226	Psychiatry	27,213	13,079
Cardiovascular Disease	20,060	2,054	Neurological Surgery	4,976	312	Public Health	1,091	464
Child Psychiatry	3,829	3,019	Neurology	10,396	3,266	Pulmonary Diseases	8,385	1,422
Colon/Rectal Surgery	1,116	149	Nuclear Medicine	1,164	283	Radiation Oncology	3,271	1,017
Dermatology	6,535	3,906	Obstetrics/Gynecology	24,801	17,258	Radiology	7,465	1,270
Diagnostic Radiology	18,527	5,126	Occupational Medicine	2,172	502	Thoracic Surgery	4,750	166
Emergency Medicine	21,877	5,987	Ophthalmology	15,529	3,177	Transplantation Surgery	94	10
Family Practice	54,022	26,305	Orthopedic Surgery	22,775	1,021	Urology	10,060	508
Forensic Pathology	413	207	Otolaryngology	8,777	1,084	Vascular	17	5
Gastroenterology	10,473	1,255	Pathology-Anat./Clin.	12,523	6,037	Other Speciality	4,427	908
General Practice	9,544	2,120	Pediatric Cardiology	1,276	480	Unspecified	3,813	1,720

(1) Includes "Inactive," "Address Unknown," and certain specialties with very few practitioners.

Drug Use in the General U.S. Population, 2008

Source: Substance Abuse and Mental Health Services Administration (SAMHSA), U.S. Dept. of Health and Human Services

According to the Substance Abuse and Mental Health Service Administration's *2008 National Survey on Drug Use and Health*, an estimated 117,325,000 Americans 12 years of age and older (47.0%) had used an illicit drug at least once during their lifetimes, 14.2% had used one in the previous year, and 8.0% had used one in the most recent month. The rate of current illicit drug use (in the past month) in 2008 was 9.9% for men and 6.3% for women. An estimated 30.3% of Americans 12 or older (75.6 mil) had used an il-

licit drug other than marijuana at least once in their lives. The overall rate of illicit drug use between 2007 and 2008 increased slightly. The Substance Abuse and Mental Health Services Administration's Drug Abuse Warning Network (DAWN) reported 1.74 mil drug abuse or misuse-related episodes in hospital emergency departments in 2006. Cocaine was a factor in 31% of these. Alcohol in combination with illegal drug use was a factor in 13%.

Illicit Drug Use Among Persons 12 or Older, 2003-08

Source: *2008 National Survey on Drug Use & Health*, Substance Abuse and Mental Health Services Admin. (SAMHSA), U.S. Dept. of Health and Human Services.

(numbers in thousands)

	2003 No.	2003 %	2004 No.	2004 %	2005 No.	2005 %	2006 No.	2006 %	2007 No.	2007 %	2008 No.	2008 %
Used in lifetime												
Illicit drugs	110,205	46.4	110,057	45.8	112,085	46.1	111,774	45.4	114,275	46.1	117,325	47.0
Illicit drugs other than marijuana	71,128	29.9	70,657	29.4	71,822	29.5	72,906	29.6	73,494	29.7	75,573	30.3
Used in past month												
Illicit drugs	19,470	8.2	19,071	7.9	19,720	8.1	20,357	8.3	19,857	8.0	20,077	8.0
Illicit drugs other than marijuana	8,849	3.7	8,247	3.4	8,963	3.7	9,615	3.9	9,270	3.7	8,565	3.4
Used in past year												
Illicit drugs	34,993	14.7	34,807	14.5	35,041	14.4	35,775	14.5	35,692	14.4	35,525	14.2
Marijuana and hashish	25,231	10.6	25,451	10.6	25,375	10.4	25,378	10.3	25,085	10.1	25,768	10.3
Illicit drugs other than marijuana	20,305	8.5	19,658	8.2	20,109	8.3	21,254	8.6	21,144	8.5	19,990	8.0
Cocaine	5,908	2.5	5,658	2.4	5,523	2.3	6,069	2.5	5,738	2.3	5,255	2.1
Crack	1,406	0.6	1,304	0.5	1,381	0.6	1,479	0.6	1,451	0.6	1,109	0.4
Heroin	314	0.1	398	0.2	379	0.2	560	0.2	366	0.1	453	0.2
Hallucinogens	3,936	1.7	3,878	1.6	3,809	1.6	3,956	1.6	3,762	1.5	3,678	1.5
LSD	558	0.2	592	0.2	563	0.2	666	0.3	620	0.3	802	0.3
PCP	219	0.1	210	0.1	164	0.1	187	0.1	137	0.1	99	0.0
Ecstasy	2,119	0.9	1,915	0.8	1,960	0.8	2,130	0.9	2,132	0.9	2,139	0.9
Inhalants	2,075	0.9	2,255	0.9	2,187	0.9	2,218	0.9	2,080	0.8	2,047	0.8
Nonmedical use of psychotherapeutics	15,163	6.4	14,849	6.2	15,346	6.3	16,482	6.7	16,280	6.6	15,166	6.1
Pain relievers	11,671	4.9	11,256	4.7	11,815	4.9	12,649	5.1	12,466	5.0	11,885	4.8
OxyContin®	—	—	1,213	0.5	1,226	0.5	1,323	0.5	1,422	0.6	1,459	0.6
Tranquilizers	5,051	2.1	5,068	2.1	5,249	2.2	5,058	2.1	5,282	2.1	5,103	2.0
Stimulants	3,031	1.3	3,254	1.4	3,088	1.3	3,791	1.5	2,998	1.2	2,639	1.1
Sedatives	831	0.3	737	0.3	750	0.3	926	0.4	864	0.3	621	0.2

NA = Not available/applicable.

Drug Use: America's High School Seniors, 1975-2008

Source: *Monitoring the Future*, Univ. of Michigan Inst. for Social Research and National Inst. on Drug Abuse

Class of:	1975	1980	1985	1990	1995	2000	2003	2004	2005	2006	2007	2008	2007-08 change[7]
Marijuana/hashish	47.3%	60.3%	54.2%	40.7%	41.7%	48.8%	46.1%	45.7%	44.8%	42.3%	41.8%	42.6%	0.8%
Inhalants[1]	—	17.3	18.1	18.5	17.8	14.6	12.2	11.4	11.9	11.5	11.0	10.1	−0.6
Amyl & butyl nitrites	—	11.1	7.9	2.1	1.5	0.8	1.6	1.3	1.1	1.2	1.2	0.6	−0.9
Hallucinogens[2]	—	15.6	12.1	9.7	13.1	13.6	10.9	9.9	9.3	8.8	8.9	9.0	−0.7
LSD	11.3	9.3	7.5	8.7	11.7	11.1	5.9	4.6	3.5	3.3	3.4	4.0	0.1
PCP	—	9.6	4.9	2.8	2.7	3.4	2.5	1.6	2.4	2.2	2.1	1.8	−0.3
Ecstasy	—	—	—	—	—	11.0	8.3	7.5	5.4	6.5	6.5	6.2	−0.3
Cocaine	9.0	15.7	17.3	9.4	6.0	8.6	7.7	8.1	8.0	8.5	7.8	7.2	−0.6
Crack	—	—	—	3.5	3.0	3.9	3.6	3.9	3.5	3.5	3.2	2.8	−0.5
Heroin[3]	2.2	1.1	1.2	1.3	1.6	2.4	1.5	1.5	1.5	1.4	1.5	1.3	−0.5
Other narcotics[4]	9.0	9.8	10.2	8.3	7.2	10.6	13.2	13.5	12.8	13.4	13.1	13.2	−0.3
Amphetamines[4,5]	22.3	26.4	26.2	17.5	15.3	15.6	14.4	15.0	13.1	12.4	11.4	10.5	+0.1
Methamphetamine	—	—	—	—	—	7.9	6.2	6.2	4.5	4.4	3.0	2.8	−0.9
Crystal Meth.	—	—	—	2.7	3.9	4.0	3.9	4.0	4.0	3.4	3.4	2.8	−0.3
Barbiturates[4]	16.9	11.0	9.2	6.8	7.4	9.5	8.8	9.9	10.5	10.2	9.3	8.5	−0.6
Methaqualone[4]	8.1	9.5	6.7	2.3	1.2	0.8	1.0	1.3	1.3	1.2	1.0	0.8	−0.2
Tranquilizers[4]	17.0	15.2	11.9	7.2	7.1	8.9	10.2	10.6	9.9	10.3	9.5	8.9	−0.2
Alcohol[6]	90.4	93.2	92.2	89.5	80.7	80.3	76.6	76.8	75.1	72.7	72.2	71.9	−0.6
Cigarettes	73.6	71.0	68.8	64.4	64.2	62.5	53.7	52.8	50.0	47.1	46.2	44.7	−0.2
Steroids	—	—	—	2.9	2.3	2.5	3.5	3.4	2.6	2.7	2.2	2.2	0.0

— Data not available. (1) Adjusted for underreporting of amyl and butyl nitrites. (2) Adjusted for underreporting of PCP. (3) Reflects use with or without injection. (4) Includes only drug use that was not under a doctor's orders. (5) Data for 1990-2007 are not directly comparable to prior years. (6) Data for 1995-2007 are not directly comparable to prior years. (7) In percentage points.

Cigarette Use in the U.S., 1985-2007

Source: Substance Abuse and Mental Health Services Administration (SAMHSA), U.S. Dept. of Health and Human Services
(percentage reporting use in the month prior to the survey; figures exclude persons under age 12)

	1985	2000	2004	2005	2006	2007		1985	2000	2004	2005	2006	2007
TOTAL	38.7	24.9	24.9	24.9	25.0	24.2	**Race/Ethnicity**						
							White	38.9	25.9	26.4	26.0	26.1	25.6
Sex							Black	38.0	23.3	23.5	24.5	24.4	23.2
Male	43.4	26.9	27.7	27.4	27.8	27.1	Hispanic	40.0	20.7	21.3	22.1	22.4	20.5
Female	34.5	23.1	22.3	22.5	22.4	21.5	**Education[2]**						
Age group							Non-high school graduate	37.3	32.4	34.8	34.8	35.6	32.9
12-17	29.4	13.4	11.9	10.8	10.4	9.8	High school graduate	37.0	31.1	30.4	31.8	31.9	31.9
18 and older	47.4	38.3	39.5	39.0	38.4	36.2	Some college	32.6	27.7	29.0	28.1	27.7	26.8
26 and older	45.7[1]	24.2	24.1	24.3	24.7	24.1	College graduate	23.0	13.9	13.6	13.8	14.3	14.0

(1) Figures are for all persons aged 26 to 34 only. (2) Estimates for education are for persons aged 18 and older.

Daily Use of Cigarettes by U.S. 8th, 10th, and 12th Graders[1]

Source: *Monitoring the Future*, Univ. of Michigan Inst. for Social Research and National Inst. on Drug Abuse
(percent who smoked daily in last 30 days; change 2007-08 in percentage points)

	8th grade					2007-08 change	10th grade					2007-08 change	12th grade					2007-08 change
	1995	2000	2005	2007	2008		1995	2000	2005	2007	2008		1995	2000	2005	2007	2008	
TOTAL	9.3	7.4	4.0	3.0	3.1	0.0%	16.3	14.0	7.5	7.2	5.9	−1.3%	21.6	20.6	13.6	12.3	11.4	0.9%
Sex																		
Male	9.2	7.0	3.9	3.4	3.2	−0.2	16.3	13.7	7.2	7.7	6.2	−1.5	21.7	20.9	14.6	13.0	12.0	−1.0
Female	9.2	7.5	4.0	2.6	2.9	0.3	16.1	14.1	7.7	6.6	5.5	−1.1	20.8	19.7	11.9	11.2	10.6	−0.6
College plans																		
None or under 4 yrs.	22.5	21.7	14.4	12.3	10.8	−1.5	32.7	28.8	19.2	18.9	17.9	−1.0	33.7	31.7	24.9	22.5	21.1	−1.4
Complete 4 yrs.	7.5	5.6	2.9	2.2	2.3	0.2	13.3	11.6	5.9	5.6	4.3	−1.4	17.4	16.6	10.5	9.9	9.0	−0.9
Region																		
Northeast	9.2	6.9	3.2	1.7	2.4	0.7	15.8	14.1	7.6	6.8	5.3	−1.5	22.5	22.8	13.3	14.3	11.3	−2.9
North central	11.0	9.0	4.8	3.8	3.9	0.1	17.6	16.3	8.6	10.0	7.6	−2.4	25.7	23.6	16.3	14.5	12.9	−1.6
South	9.4	7.8	5.0	3.8	3.7	0.0	19.3	15.7	8.8	7.2	6.9	−0.3	21.7	19.4	15.4	12.9	13.1	0.3
West	7.0	4.9	2.4	1.9	2.0	0.0	9.4	7.8	4.0	4.7	3.4	−1.3	14.5	16.9	7.6	7.4	7.0	−0.4
Race/Ethnicity[2]																		
White	10.5	9.0	4.6	3.9	3.3	−0.5	23.9	25.7	17.1	14.5	14.3	−0.2	23.9	25.7	17.1	14.5	14.3	−0.2
Black	2.8	3.2	2.1	2.1	1.9	−0.2	6.1	8.0	5.6	5.8	5.8	0.0	6.1	8.0	5.6	5.8	5.8	−0.1
Hispanic	9.2	7.1	3.1	2.8	2.5	−0.3	11.6	15.7	7.6	6.6	6.7	−1.3	11.6	15.7	7.7	6.6	6.7	0.0

(1) Totals and percentage changes may not add up due to rounding. (2) For each of these groups, data for the specified year and previous year have been combined to increase sample size and thus provide a more reliable estimate.

Alcohol Use by 8th and 12th Graders, 1980-2008

Source: *Monitoring the Future*, Univ. of Michigan Inst. for Social Research and National Inst. on Drug Abuse

	1980	1990	1995	2000	2003	2005	2006	2007	2008	2007-08 change
ALCOHOL[1]			Percent using alcohol in the month before the survey							
All 12th graders	72.0%	57.1%	51.3%	50.0%	47.5%	47.0%	45.3%	44.4%	43.1%	−1.3%
Male	77.4	61.3	55.7	54.0	51.7	50.7	47.3	47.1	45.8	−1.3
Female	66.8	52.3	47.0	46.1	43.8	43.3	43.0	41.4	40.9	−0.6
White	75.4	63.8	54.5	55.1	52.3	52.3	50.7	49.3	48.6	−0.6
Black	47.6	35.8	35.2	30.0	29.9	29.0	29.2	28.7	28.6	−0.1
Hispanic	63.6	49.1	48.7	51.2	46.4	43.3	43.4	41.4	38.9	−2.5
All 8th graders	—	—	24.6	22.4	19.7	17.1	17.2	15.9	15.9	0.1
Male	—	—	25.0	22.5	19.4	16.2	16.3	15.6	15.4	−0.2
Female	—	—	24.0	22.0	19.8	17.9	17.6	16.0	16.4	0.4
White	—	—	25.4	24.7	20.1	17.9	16.9	15.6	15.2	−0.4
Black	—	—	18.7	16.0	15.5	14.9	13.1	12.3	12.9	0.6
Hispanic	—	—	32.4	26.7	25.3	20.6	21.2	23.0	21.5	−1.5
HEAVY ALCOHOL[2]			Percent heavily using the 2 weeks before the survey							
All 12th graders	41.2%	32.2%	29.8%	30.0%	27.9%	27.1%	25.4%	25.9%	24.6%	−1.3%
Male	52.1	39.1	36.9	36.7	34.2	32.6	28.9	30.7	28.4	−2.2
Female	30.5	24.4	23.0	23.5	22.1	21.6	21.5	21.5	21.3	−0.2
White	44.3	36.6	32.3	34.6	32.4	32.5	30.4	29.7	29.9	0.2
Black	17.7	14.4	14.9	11.5	10.8	11.3	11.4	11.5	10.9	−0.5
Hispanic	33.1	25.6	26.6	31.0	25.9	23.9	23.3	22.5	21.5	−1.1
All 8th graders	—	—	12.3	11.7	9.8	8.4	8.7	8.3	8.1	−0.2
Male	—	—	12.5	11.7	10.2	8.2	8.6	8.2	8.1	−0.1
Female	—	—	12.1	11.3	9.4	8.6	8.5	8.2	8.0	−0.2
White	—	—	12.1	13.0	10.0	9.0	8.4	8.0	7.8	−0.2
Black	—	—	8.3	7.3	7.5	6.1	5.7	5.6	5.7	0.1
Hispanic	—	—	18.4	16.0	13.8	12.1	11.6	12.5	12.3	−0.2

— Data not available. **Note:** *Monitoring the Future* study excludes high school dropouts (about 3-6% of the class group, according to a 1996 report) and absentees (about 16-17% of 12th graders and 9-10% of 8th graders). High school dropouts and absentees have higher alcohol usage than those included in the survey. (1) Since 1993 the alcohol question has indicated that a "drink" is defined as "more than a few sips." (2) Five or more drinks in a row at least once in the prior 2-week period.

Acquired Immune Deficiency Syndrome (AIDS)

Source: Centers for Disease Control and Prevention; www.cdc.gov

AIDS (Acquired Immune Deficiency Syndrome) is caused by the human immunodeficiency virus (**HIV**). HIV kills or disables crucial cells of the immune system, progressively destroying the body's ability to fight disease.

HIV is commonly spread through unprotected sexual contact with an infected partner. It is also spread through contact with infected blood. Where modern screening techniques are used it is rare to contract HIV from transfusion, but it can be contracted when intravenous drug users share syringes with others. Though HIV can be spread through semen, vaginal fluids, and breast milk, there is no evidence it can be spread through saliva. The rate of transmission from a pregnant woman to her infant is about 25% without treatment, but can be reduced to less than 2% with treatment. Studies have indicated no evidence of HIV transmission through casual contact such as the sharing of food utensils, towels and bedding, telephones, or toilet seats.

Some people experience flu-like symptoms a short time after infection with HIV, and scientists estimate that about half of those infected with HIV develop more serious, often chronic symptoms within ten years. Even when symptoms are not present, HIV is active in the body, multiplying, infecting, and killing CD4+ T cells, or "T-helper cells," the crucial immune cells that signal other cells in the immune system to perform its functions.

The term **AIDS** applies to the most advanced stages of HIV infection. According to the official definition set by the Centers for Disease Control and Prevention (CDC), an HIV–infected person with fewer than 200 CD4+ T cells can be said to have AIDS. (Healthy adults usually have 1,000 or more). An HIV-infected person, regardless of T cell count, is diagnosed with AIDS if he or she develops one of 26 conditions that typically affect people with advanced HIV. Most of these conditions are "opportunistic infections" that occur when the immune system is so ravaged by HIV that the body cannot fight off certain bacteria, viruses and microbes.

Months or years prior to the onset of AIDS, many people experience such symptoms as swollen glands, lack of energy, fevers and sweats, and skin rashes. People with full-blown AIDS may develop infections of the intestinal tract, lungs, brain, eyes, and other organs, with a variety of symptoms, and may become severely debilitated. They also are prone to developing certain cancers, especially those caused by viruses, such as Kaposi's sarcoma, cervical cancer, and lymphoma. Children with AIDS may have delayed development or failure to thrive.

HIV is primarily **detected** by testing a person's blood for the presence of antibodies (disease-fighting proteins) to HIV. In about 5% of infected individuals, HIV antibodies may take more than 6 months after exposure to reach detectable levels, but in most cases the antibodies are detectable in about 6 weeks. HIV testing may also be performed on oral fluid and urine samples. New rapid HIV tests can provide preliminary results in about 20 minutes.

Patients are typically given a combination of different drugs, because HIV can much more easily become resistant to a single drug. While these drugs extend the period between HIV infection and serious illness, they do not prevent the spread of the disease to others, and can have severe side effects.

The **U.S. Food and Drug Administration** has approved a number of **drugs** that may slow down the growth of HIV in the body and treat the infections and cancers associated with AIDS. The first group of drugs used to treat HIV, called nucleoside analog reverse transcriptase inhibitors (NRTIs), include the drug zidovudine (commonly known as AZT). Non-nucleoside reverse transcriptase inhibitors (NNRTIs) have also been approved to treat HIV. A third class of drugs, called protease inhibitors, are also approved for HIV. In 2003 the FDA granted accelerated approval of Fuzeon for use with other anti-HIV drugs to treat advanced cases of infection. Fuzeon was the first among a new class of medications called fusion inhibitors; drugs in this class interfered with HIV's entry into cells by hindering the fusion of viral and cellular membranes. The FDA in July 2006 approved the first once-a-day, single-pill drug combination treatment for AIDS. The development was regarded as a significant milestone in treatment of the disease, which often required the daily administration of several drugs. Two drug companies, Bristol-Myers Squibb Co. and Gilead Sciences Inc., had cooperated to develop the drug, called Atripla. The pill combined three drugs—Sustiva, Viread and Emtriva—and would cost roughly $1,100 per month in the U.S. FDA officials said complicated AIDS drug regimens had often dissuaded patients from taking their pills as directed. They said the new drug would simplify drug regimens and help prevent HIV, the virus that caused AIDS, from gaining resistance to drugs. Health experts expect the drug to dramatically improve AIDS treatment in the developing world.

Since there is no vaccine or cure for AIDS, the only **protection** is to avoid activities that carry a risk. When it cannot be known with certainty whether a sexual partner has HIV, the CDC recommends abstinence (the only certain protection), mutual monogamy with an uninfected partner, or correct and consistent use of male latex condoms.

New AIDS Cases in the U.S., 1985-2007, by Transmission Category

Source: *HIV/AIDS Surveillance Report, 2007*, CDC, National Center for HIV, STD, and TB Prevention, Div. of HIV/AIDS Prevention

TRANSMISSION CATEGORY	All years[1]	1985	1990	2000	2003	2004	2005	2006	2007
All males 13 years and older	810,676	7,504	36,193	30,251	28,370	27,545	26,525	26,185	26,355
Men who have sex with men	487,695	5,348	23,658	13,648	16,782	16,627	16,172	16,235	16,749
Injection drug use	175,704	1,103	6,923	5,554	5,098	4,527	4,243	3,940	3,750
Men who have sex with men and injecting drug use	71,242	661	2,943	1,587	2,129	1,964	1,972	1,748	1,664
Heterosexual contact[2]	63,927	32	715	2,537	4,140	4,204	3,909	4,054	4,011
Other[3]	12,108	—	—	—	220	222	230	209	181
All females 13 years and older	198,544	524	4,547	9,979	10,450	10,033	9,548	9,471	9,579
Injection drug use	80,155	287	2,347	2,545	3,002	2,884	2,604	2,331	2,260
Heterosexual contact[2]	112,230	119	1,538	4,025	7,247	6,956	6,768	6,955	7,100
Other[3]	6,158	—	—	—	202	193	176	186	220
Child under 12	9,209	—	—	—	73	55	54	38	28
Perinatal	8,434	—	—	—	66	53	48	33	24
Other[3]	775	—	—	—	7	2	5	6	4

Note: The definition of AIDS cases for reporting purposes was expanded in 1985, 1987, and 1993, as more was learned about the spectrum of human immunodeficiency virus-associated diseases. Data exclude residents of U.S. territories. (1) Includes cases prior to 1985 and for years not shown. (2) Includes persons who have had heterosexual contact with a person with human immunodeficiency virus (HIV) infection or at risk of HIV infection. (3) For 2003-07, includes hemophilia, blood transfusion, perinatal exposure, and risk factors not reported or identified.

AIDS Deaths and New AIDS Cases in the U.S., 1985-2006

Source: *Health, United States, 2008;* National Center for Health Statistics, U.S. Dept. of Health and Human Services

	Percent Distribu-tion	All Years[1]	1985	1990	1995	2000	2002	2003	2004	2005	2006
TOTAL DEATHS	—	583,298	6,981	31,988	52,254	17,741	18,017	17,679	17,154	15,564	14,561
					NEW AIDS CASES						
All	—	982,498	8,131	41,449	70,373	40,165	38,132	38,538	37,726	36,552	36,828
All males, 13 years and over	100.0	783,786	7,484	36,180	56,650	30,047	28,067	28,079	27,532	26,787	26,989
Race White[2]	45.2	353,945	4,743	20,818	25,972	11,224	9,523	9,363	9,347	9,120	9,267
Black[2]	36.6	286,741	1,695	10,244	20,812	13,041	12,552	12,470	12,141	11,625	11,540
Hispanic[3]	16.5	129,540	989	4,746	9,128	5,295	5,269	5,511	5,330	5,305	5,388
American Indian or Alaska Native[2]	0.9	6,780	9	81	196	135	349	366	358	360	423
Asian or Pacific Islander[2]	0.3	2,626	47	254	463	275	130	132	122	132	118
Age 13-14 years	0.1	603	NA	NA	NA	NA	30	31	40	32	24
15-24 years	3.7	28,682	NA	NA	NA	NA	1,045	1,219	1,316	1,436	1,472
25-34 years	32.0	250,746	NA	NA	NA	NA	6,198	5,915	5,840	5,519	5,498
35-44 years	40.0	313,667	NA	NA	NA	NA	11,868	11,615	10,975	10,330	10,304
45-54 years	17.6	137,779	NA	NA	NA	NA	6,538	6,798	6,671	6,886	6,820
55-64 years	5.2	40,645	NA	NA	NA	NA	1,888	1,940	2,087	2,046	2,256
65 years and over	1.5	11,656	NA	NA	NA	NA	501	561	603	539	616
All females, 13 years and over	100.0	189,566	519	4,544	12,978	9,932	9,959	10,389	10,141	9,713	9,801
Race White[2]	20.3	38,478	143	1,230	3,031	1,841	1,696	1,573	1,711	1,552	1,659
Black[2]	62.0	117,586	275	2,557	7,581	6,455	6,624	6,996	6,735	6,418	6,391
Hispanic[3]	15.9	30,218	98	724	2,244	1,476	1,424	1,581	1,432	1,509	1,516
American Indian or Alaska Native[2]	0.6	1,117	2	9	38	68	74	84	85	89	95
Asian or Pacific Islander[2]	0.4	688	1	20	69	71	47	44	59	39	37
Age 13-14 years	0.2	475	5	67	157	168	33	43	30	33	49
15-24 years	7.0	13,167	175	1,117	2,676	1,749	670	651	643	649	598
25-34 years	34.1	63,882	230	2,088	5,937	3,965	2,640	2,665	2,501	2,259	2,273
35-44 years	37.3	70,436	45	780	3,055	2,851	3,753	4,028	3,800	3,527	3,395
45-54 years	15.0	29,336	26	273	818	859	2,091	2,183	2,318	2,369	2,495
55-64 years	4.5	8,848	38	219	335	340	591	616	662	687	771
65 years and over	1.8	3,419	NA	NA	NA	NA	181	202	188	188	219
All children, under 13 years	100.0	9,144	128	725	745	186	106	70	53	53	38
Race White[2]	17.5	1,599	26	156	117	30	14	12	7	4	4
Black[2]	61.8	5,654	84	390	483	121	70	46	33	38	30
Hispanic[3]	19.1	1,748	18	169	135	30	18	10	9	8	3
American Indian or Alaska Native[2]	0.6	54	—	5	2	1	1	0	1	0	0
Asian or Pacific Islander[2]	0.3	31	—	4	5	3	1	0	1	1	1
Age Under 5 years	74.8	6,812	108	586	553	116	14	12	7	4	4
5-12 years	23.4	2,127	20	139	192	70	68	—	—	—	—

Note: The definition of AIDS cases for reporting purposes was expanded in 1985, 1987, and 1993, as more was learned about the spectrum of human immunodeficiency virus-associated diseases. Data exclude residents of U.S. territories. Figures may differ from previous reports of *Health, United States.* (1) Revised figures; includes cases and deaths prior to 1985 and for years not shown. Through June 30, 2007. (2) Excludes persons of Hispanic origin. (3) Persons of Hispanic origin may be of any race.

Allergies and Asthma

Source: Asthma and Allergy Foundation of America, 8201 Corporate Drive, Suite 1000, Landover, MD 20785; phone: (800) 7-ASTHMA; www.aafa.org

One out of five Americans suffers from **allergies** of some kind. People with allergies have extra-sensitive immune systems that react to normally harmless substances. Common allergens that may produce this reaction include plant pollens, dust mites, or animal dander; plants such as poison ivy; certain drugs, such as penicillin; and certain foods such as eggs, milk, nuts, or seafood.

The **tendency to develop allergies** is usually inherited, and allergies usually begin to appear in childhood, but they can show up at any age. **Common allergies** for infants include food allergies and eczema (patches of dry skin). Older children and adults may often develop allergic rhinitis (hay fever), a reaction to an inhaled allergen; common symptoms include nasal congestion, runny nose, and sneezing.

It is best to avoid contact with the allergen, if feasible. In some cases, **medications** such as antihistamines and nasal steroids are used to decrease the reaction. Other effective allergy treatments include decongestants, eye drops, and ointments. There also are treatments aimed at gradually desensitizing the patient to the allergen.

Some people with allergies also have **asthma**, and allergens are a common asthma trigger. Asthma is a disease of chronic inflammation affecting the passages that carry air into and out of the lungs. It can develop at any age.

People with asthma have inflamed, supersensitive airways that tighten and become filled with mucus during an asthma episode. Wheezing, difficulty in breathing, tightening of the chest, and coughing are common symptoms. Asthma can progress through stages to become life-threatening if not controlled. **Emergency symptoms** include: no improvement minutes after initial treatment; struggling to breathe, with patient hunched over and/or chest and neck pulled in; trouble walking or talking; stopping activity and not starting activity again; gray or blue lips or fingernails.

Besides common allergens, tobacco smoke, cold air, and pollution can trigger an asthma attack, as can viral infections or physical exercise. An accurate diagnosis by a physician is important. Although there is no cure for asthma or allergies, they can be controlled with medications and lifestyle changes.

Alzheimer's Disease

Source: Alzheimer's Association, 225 N Michigan Ave., 17th Fl., Chicago, IL 60601-7633; phone: (800) 272-3900; www.alz.org

Alzheimer's disease, the most common form of dementia, is a progressive, degenerative disease of the brain in which nerve cells deteriorate and die for unknown reasons. Its first symptoms usually involve impaired memory and confusion about recent events. As the disease advances, it results in greater impairment of memory, thinking, judgement, language, behavior, and physical health.

The **rate of progression** of Alzheimer's varies, ranging from 3 to 20 years; the average length of time from onset of symptoms until death is 5 years. Eventually, affected individuals lose their ability to care for themselves and become susceptible to infections of the lungs, urinary tract, or other organs as they grow progressively debilitated.

Alzheimer's disease affects an estimated 5.2 mil Americans, striking men and women of all ethnic groups. Although most people diagnosed with Alzheimer's are older than age 60, some cases occur in people in their 40s and 50s. An estimated 13% of the population over age 65 have Alzheimer's, In the United States, annual costs of diagnosis, treatment, and long-term care are estimated at $100 billion.

Diagnosis involves a comprehensive evaluation that may include a complete health history, a physical examination, neurological and mental status assessments, and other testing as needed. Skilled health care professionals can generally diagnose Alzheimer's with about 90% accuracy. Other conditions that can cause similar symptoms include depression, drug interactions, nutritional imbalances, infections such as AIDS, meningitis, and syphilis, and other forms of dementia, such as those associated with stroke, Huntington's disease, Parkinson's disease, frontotemporal dementia, and vascular disease. Absolute confirmation of diagnosis requires a brain biopsy or autopsy.

Treatments for cognitive and behavioral symptoms are available, but no intervention has yet been developed that prevents Alzheimer's or reverses its course. Some research suggests that risk factors for heart disease, such as high blood pressure, elevated cholesterol, diabetes and excess body weight may also increase risk of developing Alzheimer's. Studies also suggest that staying physically and mentally active and socially connected may be associated with a lower risk for the disease.

Providing care for people with Alzheimer's is physically and psychologically demanding. Nearly 70% of affected individuals live at home, where family or friends care for them. In advanced stages of the disease, many individuals require long-term residential care. Nearly half of all nursing home residents in the U.S. have Alzheimer's.

People with Alzheimer's need a safe, stable environment and a regular daily schedule offering appropriate stimulation. Physical exercise and social interaction are important, as are proper nutritionand adequate pain management. Security is also a consideration, because many people with Alzheimer's tend to wander. An identification bracelet listing the person's name, address, and condition may help ensure the safe return of an individual who wanders.

Warning Signs of Alzheimer's Disease

- Forgetting recently learned information or inability to learn new information
- Difficulty with everyday tasks such as cooking or dressing
- Inability to remember simple words
- Use of inappropriate words when communicating
- Disorientation to time and place
- Poor or decreased judgment
- Problems with abstract thinking
- Putting objects in inappropriate places
- Rapid changes in mood or behavior
- Increased irritability, anxiety, depression, confusion, and restlessness
- Prolonged loss of initiative

Arthritis

Source: Arthritis Foundation, P.O. Box 7669, Atlanta, GA 30357-0669; phone: (800) 283-7800; www.arthritis.org

The term "arthritis" refers to more than 100 different diseases that cause pain, stiffness, swelling, and restricted movement in joints. The condition is usually chronic. The Centers for Disease Control and Prevention (CDC) estimates that nearly 70 million adults suffer from arthritis and/or chronic joint symptoms. Arthritis annually results in 36 mil doctor visits, 744,000 hospitalizations. The cause for most types of arthritis is unknown; scientists are studying the roles played by genetics, lifestyle, and the environment.

Symptoms of arthritis may develop either slowly or suddenly. A visit to the doctor is indicated when pain, stiffness, or swelling in a joint or difficulty in moving a joint persists for more than two weeks. To make a diagnosis of arthritis, the doctor records the patient's symptoms and examines joints, looking for any swelling or limited movement. In addition, the doctor checks for other signs often seen with arthritis, such as rashes, mouth sores, or eye involvement. Finally, the doctor may test the blood, urine, or joint fluid, or take X-rays of the joints.

Of the 3 most prevalent forms of arthritis, **osteoarthritis** is the most common, affecting more than 27 mil Americans; it usually occurs after age 45. In this type, which is also called degenerative arthritis, the protective cartilage of joints is lost and changes occur in the bone, leading to pain and stiffness. It usually occurs in the fingers, knees, feet, hips, and back.

Fibromyalgia, another common arthritis condition, affects more than 5 million Americans and affects more women than men. In this form, widespread pain and tenderness occur in muscles and their attachments to the bone. Common symptoms include fatigue, disturbed sleep, stiffness, and psychological distress.

Rheumatoid arthritis, which affects an estimated 1.3 mil people in the U.S., is one of the most serious and disabling forms of the disease. In this type, which is also more common and more degenerative in women, inflammation of the joints leads to damage of the cartilage and bone. The areas of the body that can be affected are the hands, wrists, feet, knees, ankles, shoulders, neck, jaw, and elbows.

Other forms of arthritis and related conditions include lupus, gout, ankylosing spondylitis, and scleroderma; also related are bursitis and tendinitis, which may result from injuring or overusing a joint.

Medications to treat arthritis include drugs that relieve pain and swelling such as analgesics, anti-inflammatory drugs, biologic response modifiers, glucocorticoids and antirheumatic drugs that also tend to slow the disease process. Most treatment programs call for exercise, use of heat or cold, and joint-protection techniques, such as avoiding excess stress on joints, using assistive devices, and controlling weight. In some cases, surgery can help.

Cancer Prevention

Source: American Cancer Society, 1599 Clifton Road NE, Atlanta, GA 30329-4251; phone: (800) 227-2345

PRIMARY PREVENTION: Modifiable determinants of cancer risk.

Smoking	Lung cancer mortality rates are about 23 times higher for current male smokers, and 13 times higher for current female smokers, than for those who have never smoked. Smoking accounts for about 30% of all cancer deaths in the U.S. Tobacco use is responsible for nearly 1 in 5 deaths in the U.S. Smoking is associated with cancer of the lung, mouth, nasal cavities, pharynx, larynx, esophagus, stomach, pancreas, uterine cervix, kidney, bladder, and myeloid leukemia.
Nutrition and Diet	Risk for colon, breast (among postmenopausal women), kidney, prostate, and endometrial cancers increases in obese people. While a diet high in fat may be a factor in the development of certain cancers, the link between obesity and cancer is more the result of an imbalance between caloric intake and energy expenditure than fat per se. Eating 5 or more servings of fruits and vegetables each day, and eating other foods from plant sources (especially grains and beans), may reduce risk for many cancers. Physical activity can help protect against some cancers.
Sunlight	Many of the 1 million skin cancers that are diagnosed annually in the U.S. could have been prevented by protection from the sun's rays. Epidemiological evidence shows that sun exposure is a major factor in the development of melanoma and that the incidence rates are increasing around the world.
Alcohol	Heavy drinking, especially when accompanied by cigarette smoking or smokeless tobacco use, increases risk of cancers of the mouth, larynx, pharynx, esophagus, and liver. Studies have also noted an association between regular alcohol consumption and an increased risk of breast cancer.
Smokeless Tobacco	Use of chewing tobacco or snuff increases risk of cancers of the mouth and pharynx. The excess risk of cancer of the cheek and gum may reach nearly 50-fold among long-term snuff users.
Estrogen	Estrogen replacement therapy (ERT) to control menopausal symptoms can increase the risk of endometrial cancer. However, adding progesterone to estrogen (hormone replacement therapy, or HRT) helps to minimize this risk. Most studies suggest that long-term use (5 years or more) of HRT after menopause increases the risk of breast cancer, and recent studies suggest that risks from taking HRT exceed benefits. The benefits and risks of the use of HRT or ERT by menopausal women should be discussed carefully by the woman and her doctor.
Radiation	Excessive exposure to ionizing radiation can increase cancer risk. Medical and dental X rays are adjusted to deliver the lowest dose possible without sacrificing image quality. Excessive radon exposure in the home may increase lung cancer risk, especially in cigarette smokers.
Environmental Hazards	Exposure to various chemicals (including benzene, asbestos, vinyl chloride, arsenic, and aflatoxin) increases risk of various cancers. Risk of lung cancer from asbestos is greatly increased when combined with smoking.

Cancer-Detection Guidelines

SECONDARY PREVENTION: Steps to diagnose a cancer or precursor as early as possible after it has developed.

In addition to indicated screening for cancers of the breast, colon, and rectum, prostate, and uterine cervix, a cancer-related checkup should include health counseling and, depending on a person's age, might include examinations for cancers of the thyroid, oral cavity, skin, lymph nodes, testes, and ovaries, as well as for some nonmalignant diseases. Special tests for certain cancer sites for individuals at average risk are recommended as outlined below:

Breast Cancer	Women should start getting annual mammograms beginning at age 40. Women who are at increased risk because of family history, genetic predisposition, or past breast cancer should discuss the benefits and limitations of initiating screening at an earlier age. Clinical breast exam should be part of a periodic health exam, about every 3 years for women in their 20's and 30's, and every year for women 40 and older. Women should be aware of any changes in their breasts and report these promptly to their health care provider.
Cervical Cancer	Women should begin cervical cancer screening about 3 years after they begin having vaginal intercourse, but no later than when they are 21 years old. Screening should be done every year with the regular Pap test or every 2 years using the newer liquid-based Pap test.
	Beginning at age 30, women who have had 3 normal Pap test results in a row may get screened every 2 to 3 years. Women who have certain risk factors such as diethylstilbestrol (DES) exposure before birth, HIV infection, or a weakened immune system due to organ transplant, chemotherapy, or chronic steroid use should continue to be screened annually.
	Another reasonable option for women over 30 is to get screened every 3 years (but no more frequently) with either the conventional or liquid-based Pap test, *plus* the HPV DNA test.
	Women 70 years of age or older who have had 3 or more normal Pap tests in a row and no abnormal Pap test results in the last 10 years may choose to stop having cervical cancer screening. Women with a history of cervical cancer, DES exposure before birth, HIV infection or a weakened immune system should continue to have screening as long as they are in good health. Women who have had a total hysterectomy (removal of the uterus and cervix) may also choose to stop having cervical cancer screening, unless the surgery was done as a treatment for cervical cancer or precancer. Women who have had a hysterectomy without removal of the cervix should continue to follow the guidelines above.
Colorectal Cancer	Beginning at age 50, both men and women should follow one of these testing schedules: • Yearly fecal occult blood test; or flexible sigmoidoscopy every 5 years; or • yearly fecal occult blood test plus flexible sigmoidoscopy every 5 years; or • colonoscopy every 10 years; or • double-contrast barium enema every 5-10 years. **Note:** Persons known to be at increased risk for colorectal cancer (due to inflammatory bowel disease, personal or family history, etc.) need to begin screening at an early age and may need more frequent screening.
Endometrial Cancer	For women with or at high risk of hereditary nonpolyposis colon cancer (HNPCC), annual screening including endometrial biopsy should be obtained beginning at age 35.
Prostate Cancer	The prostate specific antigen (PSA) test and the digital rectal examination should offered annually, beginning at age 50, by men who have a 10-year life expectancy. Men at high risk such as African-American men and men with a strong family history of one or more first-degree relatives (father, brother, or son) diagnosed with prostate cancer at an early age, should start getting tested at age 45. For both men at average risk and high risk, information should be provided about what is known and what is uncertain about the benefits and limitations of early detection and treatment of prostate cancer so that they can make an informed decision about testing.
Skin Cancer	Adults should practice skin self-exam regularly. Suspicious lesions and moles should be evaluated promptly by a physician.

Expected New Cancer Cases and Deaths, by Sex, for Leading Sites, 2009

Source: American Cancer Society

The estimates of expected new cases are offered as a rough guide only. They exclude basal and squamous cell skin cancers and in situ carcinomas, except urinary bladder. Carcinoma in situ of the breast accounts for about 62,280 new cases annually, melanoma carcinoma in situ for about 53,120. More than 1 mil cases of basal cell and squamous cell cancer, which are highly curable forms of skin cancer, occur annually.

EXPECTED NEW CASES

Both sexes		Women		Men	
Lung & bronchus	219,440	Breast	192,370	Prostate	192,280
Breast	194,280	Lung & bronchus	103,350	Lung & bronchus	116,090
Prostate	192,280	Colon and rectum	54,090	Urinary bladder	52,810
Colon and rectum	106,100	Uterine corpus	42,160	Colon and rectum	52,010
Urinary bladder	70,980	Non-Hodgkin lymphoma	29,990	Melanoma	39,080
Melanoma	68,720	Melanoma	29,640	Non-Hodgkin lymphoma	35,990
Non-Hodgkin lymphoma	65,980	Thyroid	27,200	Kidney & renal pelvis	35,430
Kidney	57,760	Kidney	22,330	Rectum	23,580
Pancreas	42,470	Ovary	21,550	Pancreas	21,050
Uterine corpus	42,160	Pancreas	21,420	Liver	16,410
ALL SITES	**1,479,350**	**ALL SITES**	**713,220**	**ALL SITES**	**766,130**

EXPECTED DEATHS

Both sexes		Women		Men	
Lung & bronchus	159,390	Lung & bronchus	70,490	Lung & bronchus	88,900
Colon and rectum	49,920	Breast	40,170	Prostate	27,360
Breast	40,610	Colon	24,680	Colon and rectum	25,240
Pancreas	35,240	Pancreas	17,210	Pancreas	18,030
Prostate	27,360	Ovary	14,600	Liver & intrahepatic bile duct	12,090
Non-Hodgkin lymphoma	19,500	Non-Hodgkin lymphoma	9,670	Esophagus	11,490
Liver & intrahepatic bile duct	18,160	Uterine corpus	7,780	Urinary bladder	10,180
Ovary	14,600	Liver & intrahepatic bile duct	6,070	Non-Hodgkin lymphoma	9,830
Esophagus	14,530	Brain & other nervous system	5,590	Kidney	8,160
Urinary bladder	14,300	Myeloma	4,940	Stomach	6,320
ALL SITES	**562,340**	**ALL SITES**	**269,800**	**ALL SITES**	**292,540**

Cancer Survival Rates[1] by Year of Diagnosis, 1960-2005

Source: Surveillance, Epidemiology, and End Results (SEER) Program, National Cancer Institute

	Total	Males	Females	White All	White Male	White Female	Black All	Black Male	Black Female
1960-1963	—	—	—	39.0%	—	—	27.0%	—	—
1970-1973	—	—	—	43.0	—	—	31.0	—	—
1975-1977	50.1%	42.3%	57.1%	51.0	43.3%	57.8%	39.7	32.7%	47.1%
1978-1980	50.4	44.0	56.4	51.4	45.3	57.1	39.6	33.3	46.6
1981-1983	51.6	46.1	56.7	52.8	47.6	57.6	39.6	34.3	45.6
1984-1986	53.5	47.7	58.9	54.7	49.1	59.9	40.8	35.5	46.4
1987-1989	56.4	51.6	61.1	57.8	53.3	62.1	43.7	38.8	48.9
1990-1992	60.9	59.6	62.4	62.4	61.3	63.5	48.2	47.3	49.3
1993-1995	62.2	61.2	63.4	63.4	62.4	64.5	53.0	53.7	52.0
1996-1998	64.4	63.6	65.3	65.6	64.7	66.4	55.5	57.2	53.5
1999-2005	67.8	68.0	67.7	69.1	69.3	68.9	59.4	62.2	56.2

Note: Area and scope of surveillance varies. (1) 5-year relative survival rate, for all invasive cancer sites.

Cancer Survival Rates[1] by Age at Diagnosis, 1999-2005

Source: Surveillance, Epidemiology, and End Results (SEER) Program, National Cancer Institute

Age	Total	Males	Females	White All	White Male	White Female	Black All	Black Male	Black Female
Under age 45	78.6%	73.4%	82.0%	80.4%	75.8%	83.5%	65.1%	56.8%	70.2%
Ages 45-54	71.2	64.9	76.3	72.9	66.5	78.0	59.0	56.3	61.6
Ages 55-64	68.4	68.3	68.5	69.4	69.1	69.8	60.7	64.6	54.7
Ages 65-74	64.2	67.9	59.3	64.9	68.2	60.4	58.1	65.1	47.9
Under age 65	71.7	68.3	74.9	73.1	69.7	76.3	61.1	60.6	61.6
Ages 65+	59.7	64.2	54.5	60.3	64.5	55.6	53.1	60.8	43.9
Ages 75+	53.8	58.5	49.5	54.4	58.7	50.6	44.8	51.7	38.7

Note: Area and scope of surveillance varies. (1) 5-year relative survival rate, for all invasive cancer sites.

Breast Cancer

Source: American Cancer Society, Inc., 1599 Clifton Road NE, Atlanta, GA 30329-4251; phone: (800) 227-2345

In 2009, an estimated 192,370 women and 1,910 men in the U.S. will have been diagnosed with breast cancer, and about 40,610 women and 440 men will have died from it. Currently, an estimated 2.4 mil women are living with a history of breast cancer, the 2nd biggest cause of cancer death for women in the U.S. (lung cancer ranks first). But mortality rates have been declining, especially among younger women, probably because of earlier detection and improved treatment.

The **risk** for breast cancer increases with age. It is higher for women with a personal or family history of cancer, a long menstrual history (menstrual periods that started early and ended late in life), recent use of birth control pills, long-term use of postmenopausal hormone replacement therapy, and no children or no live birth until age 30 or older. Other risk factors include alcohol consumption and obesity. Inherited mutations such as in the BRCA1 and BRCA2 genes greatly increase risk, but these probably account for 5% to

10% of all breast cancers. By far the majority of women who develop breast cancer have no family history of it.

Breast cancer is often **manifested** first as an abnormality on a mammogram, a type of X-ray. Physical symptoms that show up later, which may be detectable by a woman or her doctor, include a breast lump and, less commonly, breast thickening, swelling, distortion, or tenderness; skin irritation or dimpling; or pain, scaliness, or retraction of the nipple. Breast pain is more commonly associated with benign (non-cancerous) conditions.

Studies show that **early detection** increases survival and treatment options (*See* "Cancer Prevention" p. 154). Although most breast lumps that are detected are noncancerous, any suspicious lump needs to be biopsied.

Treatment for breast cancer may involve lumpectomy (local removal of a tumor), mastectomy (surgical removal of the breast), radiation therapy, chemotherapy, hormone therapy, immunotherapy, or some combination. For early-stage breast cancer, long-term survival rates following lumpectomy plus radiation therapy are similar to survival rates after mastectomy.

Prostate Cancer
Source: Prostate Cancer Foundation, 1250 Fourth Street Santa Monica, CA 90401

The **prostate** is a male gland located between the bladder and scrotum that secretes seminal fluid. Prostate cancer is the most common non-skin cancer in America, and the most common cause of cancer death among American men after lung cancer. In 2009, more than 192,280 men will be diagnosed with prostate cancer, and more than 27,630 men will die from the disease. One new case occurs every 2.5 minutes, and a man dies from prostate cancer every 19 minutes. It is estimated that more than 2 million men are currently living with prostate cancer.

The exact **cause** of prostate cancer is unknown. The most identifiable risk factors are age, family history, and race. About 63% of all prostate cancers are diagnosed in men over the age of 65, and the chances of developing the disease rise dramatically with age. Men with a single relative with a history of prostate cancer are twice as likely to develop the disease, and those with two or more relatives are more than four times as likely to get it. African-American men are much more likely to get the disease than white men and are twice as likely to die from it. The cause for this disparity remains unknown; it is likely that both socioeconomic and biologic differences are involved.

Usually, the disease has no **symptoms** in its early stages. If symptoms arise, they may include: a need to urinate frequently; difficulty starting urination; weak or interrupted flow; pain during urination; difficulty having an erection; painful ejaculation; blood in urine or semen; frequent pain or stiffness in lower back, hips or upper thighs.

White men over 50 with no family history of prostate cancer are typically encouraged to be screened annually for the disease with both a prostate specific antigen (**PSA) blood test** and a **digital rectal exam** (DRE). African-American men or those with a family history of the disease may be encouraged to undergo screening beginning at age 40 or 45. Men under 40 seldom get prostate cancer.

Treatment may include surgery, radiation, hormone deprivation therapy, chemotherapy, or a combination. If caught early, while tumor cells are localized within the prostate, the cure rate is over 90%.

Skin Cancer
Source: American Cancer Society

Skin cancer is generally divided into two main classes, nonmelanomas and melanomas, both types affecting different types of skin cells. Melanoma develops in skin cells called melanocytes, which are cells that produce melanin, a pigment that gives skin a tan or brown color and helps to protect the deeper layers of skin from the harmful effects of the sun. Melanoma is the most dangerous type of skin cancer because it can easily spread to other parts of the body.

Although skin cancer is the most common type of cancer diagnosed, Melanoma only accounts for about 4% of skin cancers. According to the American Cancer Society, in 2009 there will be 68,720 new cases of melanoma diagnosed in the U.S., and about 11,590 people will die from the disease.

The exact causes of melanoma are not clear, but there are several risk factors that have been associated with the disease, which include:

- Over-exposure to UV light (sunlight)
- Presence of moles; moles themselves are not harmful but they are associated with an increased risk for skin cancer
- Family history
- Taking immune suppression drugs
- Age; melanoma is more likely to happen in older people
- Gender; men get melanoma more often than women
- Past history with melanoma
- Xeroderma pigmentosum (XP), a rare, genetic condition in which people are less able to repair damage caused by sunlight.
- Melanomas generally look like abnormal moles on the surface of the skin. Normal moles are most often an evenly colored brown, tan, or black spot on the skin that can either be flat or raised. They normally have a distinct border that separates them from normal skin cells. Moles can be present at birth, form over time, or even

disappear. Abnormal moles differ from regular skin cells and may be a sign of skin cancer. If you suspect you have an irregular mole, it is important to have it examined as soon as possible. Irregular moles generally have the following characteristics:

- Asymmetry—one half of the mole does not match the other half.
- Irregular border—the edge of the mole is jagged and doesn't have as distinct divide between it and regular skin.
- Color—it is not the same all over the mole; there may be shades of tan, brown, black, and sometimes patches of red, blue, or white.
- Diameter—moles wider than ¼ inch are abnormal (however, melanomas can be smaller)
- After examination, if a melanoma is suspected, the doctor will perform a biopsy using either cells extracted from the suspected cancer or by removing the whole mass and examining it. If a melanoma is found, doctors will often check to see if the cancer has spread to other parts of the body. This is called staging and it is represented by Roman numerals I-IV (1-4). The lower the number, the less the cancer has spread. This will determine what course of treatment is necessary.

If caught early melanoma is highly curable. The 5-year survival rates for the various stages are as follows:
- All stages   91.2%
- Local   98.7%
- Regional   65.1%
- Distant   15.5%

Treatment may include: simple removal of the melanoma; amputation if the cancer is found on the finger or toe; or treatment of cancer in other parts of the body if the melanoma spread, which may involve chemotherapy, immunotherapy, or radiation.

Depression

Source: National Institute of Mental Health (NIMH)

Depression is a serious illness that affects thoughts, feelings, and the ability to function in everyday life. It strikes across all age groups, and often goes unrecognized or inadequately treated. The National Institutes of Health estimates that about 20.9 million Americans suffer from depression in any given year and that more than 16% of all Americans will have had depression at some point in life. Young people are among those at risk; in a one-year period, 3 times as many persons with depression were 18 to 29 years old as were 60 or older.

Nearly twice as many women as men suffer from a depressive illness in a given year. Although conventional wisdom holds that depression is most closely associated with menopause, in fact, the childbearing years are marked by the highest rates of depression, followed by the years prior to menopause. The influence of hormones on depression in women has been an active area of NIMH research.

In a given year, 1-2% of people over age 65 living in the community (outside of institutions) suffer from major depression. Depression frequently occurs with other physical illnesses, including heart disease, stroke, cancer, and diabetes. It is not a normal part of aging.

The **treatments** that are now available can alleviate symptoms, and with awareness growing, more people with depression are seeking the help they need. But many depressed people—and those around them—still fail to realize that they have an illness or could benefit from medical help. According to the NIH, more than half of those seeking help do not get adequate treatment, often because they consult family practitioners who do not deal aggressively enough with the problem.

Symptoms and Types of Depression

- Persistent sad mood
- Loss of interest or pleasure in activities once enjoyed, including sex
- Significant change in appetite or body weight
- Difficulty sleeping or oversleeping
- Lethargy or agitation
- Loss of energy
- Feelings of worthlessness or inappropriate guilt
- Difficulty thinking or concentrating
- Recurrent thoughts of death or suicide

A diagnosis of **major depressive disorder** (or **unipolar major depression**) is made if an individual has 5 or more of these symptoms during the same two-week period. Unipolar major depression typically comes to the fore in episodes that recur during a person's lifetime.

Bipolar disorder (or **manic-depressive illness**) is characterized by episodes of major depression as well as episodes of mania—abnormally and persistently elevated mood or irritability, accompanied by such symptoms as inflated self-esteem, less need for sleep, increased talkativeness, racing thoughts, distractibility, agitation, and excessive involvement in pleasurable activities that have a high potential for painful consequences. While sharing some of the features of major depression, bipolar disorder is a distinct illness.

Dysthymic disorder (or **dysthymia**), a less severe yet typically more chronic form of depression, is diagnosed when a depressed mood persists for at least two years in adults (one year in children or adolescents) and is accompanied by at least 2 other depressive symptoms. Many people with dysthymic disorder also experience major depressive episodes.

In contrast to the normal experiences of sadness, or passing moods, depression is extreme and persistent and can interfere significantly with an individual's ability to function. A recent study sponsored by the World Health Organization and the World Bank found unipolar major depression to be the leading cause of disability in the U.S. and worldwide.

Treatments for Depression

A variety of **medicines** are used to treat depression. These drugs influence the functioning of certain neurotransmitters in the brain, primarily serotonin and norepinephrine, known as monoamines. Older drugs—so-called tricyclic antidepressants (TCAs) and monoamine oxidase inhibitors (MAOIs)—affect the functioning of both of these neurotransmitters. But they can have strong side effects or, in the case of MAOIs, require dietary restrictions. Newer medications, such as the selective serotonin reuptake inhibitors (SSRIs), have fewer side effects. All of these medications can be effective, but some people respond to one type and not another.

NIMH research has shown that certain types of **psychotherapy**, particularly cognitive-behavioral therapy (CBT) and interpersonal therapy (IPT), can help relieve depression. CBT helps patients change the negative styles of thinking and behaving often associated with depression. IPT focuses on working through disturbed personal relationships that may contribute to depression. Studies of adults have shown that a combination of psychotherapy and antidepressant medication is most effective in treating moderate-to-severe depression.

Electroconvulsive therapy (ECT) has been found effective in treating some of cases of severe depression, particularly those that have not responded to other forms of treatment. ECT involves producing a seizure in the brain of a patient under general anesthesia by applying electrical stimulation through electrodes placed on the scalp. Memory loss and other cognitive problems are common, but typically short-lived, side effects.

Diabetes

Source: American Diabetes Association, 1701 N Beauregard St., Alexandria, VA 22311; phone: (800) 342-2383; www.diabetes.org

Diabetes is a chronic disease in which the body does not produce or properly use **insulin**, a hormone needed to convert sugar, starches, and other foods into energy necessary for daily life. Both genetics and environment appear to play roles in the onset of diabetes. This disease, which has no cure, is the 6th leading cause of death by disease in the U.S. According to death certificate data, 72,449 people in the U.S. died as a result of diabetes in 2006.

It is estimated that there are 23.6 mil Americans with diabetes, 5.7 mil of whom are undiagnosed.

The American Diabetes Association recommends the following **guidelines for diagnosing diabetes**: lowering the acceptable level of blood sugar in a fasting glucose test from 140 mg of glucose/deciliter of blood to 126 mg/deciliter; testing all adults 45 years and older, and then every 3 years if normal; and testing at a younger age, or more frequently, in high-risk individuals. The American Diabetes Association supports studies that have proven that detection at an earlier stage and modest lifestyle changes, such as eating better and exercising more, will help prevent or delay complications.

There are 2 major types of diabetes:

Type 1 (formerly known as insulin dependent, or juvenile diabetes). The body produces very little or no insulin; disease most often begins in childhood or early adulthood. People with type 1 diabetes must take daily insulin injections to stay alive.

Type 2 (formerly known as non-insulin dependent, or adult-onset diabetes). The body does not produce enough or cannot properly use insulin. It is the most common form of the disease (90-95% of cases in people over age 20) and often begins later in life.

Pre-Diabetes

Among U.S. adults 40-74 years of age, 57 mil (40.1% of the population) have **pre-diabetes**, the state that occurs when a person's blood glucose levels are higher than normal but not high enough for a diagnosis of diabetes.

About 11% of people with pre-diabetes developed type 2 diabetes during each year of the study. Other studies show that most people with pre-diabetes develop type 2 diabetes in 10 years.

Complications of Diabetes

People often have diabetes many years before it is diagnosed. During that time, serious complications have a chance to develop. Potential complications include:

Blindness. Diabetes is the leading cause of blindness in people ages 20-74. Each year, from 12,000 to 24,000 people lose their sight because of diabetes.

Kidney disease. 10% to 21% of all people with diabetes develop kidney disease. In 2005, a total of 46,739 people initiated treatment for end-stage renal disease (kidney failure) because of diabetes.

Amputations. Diabetes is the most frequent cause of non-traumatic lower limb amputations. The risk of a leg amputation is 15 to 40 times greater for a person with diabetes than for the average American. In 2004, there were approximately 71,000 lower-limb amputations as a result of complications brought on by diabetes.

Heart disease and stroke. People with diabetes are 2 to 4 times more likely to have heart disease. And they are 2 to 4 times more likely to suffer a stroke. About 68% of deaths among people with diabetes are due to heart disease and stroke.

Warning Signs of Diabetes

Type 1 Diabetes (usually occurs suddenly):

frequent urination	unusual weight loss
unusual thirst	extreme fatigue
extreme hunger	irritability

Type 2 Diabetes (occurs less suddenly):

any type 1 symptoms	cuts/bruises slow to heal
frequent infections	tingling/numbness in hands or feet
blurred vision	recurring skin, gum, or bladder infections

Eating Disorders

Source: National Institute of Mental Health

Eating disorders involve serious disturbances in eating behavior, usually in the form of extreme and unhealthy reduction of food intake or severe overeating. They are not due to a failure of will; rather, they are real and treatable medical illnesses in which certain patterns of behavior get out of control. The **main types** are anorexia nervosa, bulimia nervosa, and binge-eating disorder. These disorders usually develop in adolescence or early adulthood and often occur with other illnesses such as depression, substance abuse, and anxiety disorders. They are much more common among females; only about 5% to 15% of anorexia or bulimia patients and 35% of binge eaters are male.

If not treated, eating disorders can lead serious complications, including heart conditions and kidney failure, which may lead to death.

Anorexia nervosa affects an estimated 0.5% to 3.7% of females during their lifetime. Symptoms include resistance to maintaining weight at even minimally normal levels, intense fear of gaining weight, exaggerated importance of body weight or shape in one's self image, and infrequent or absent menstrual periods. Anorexics see themselves as overweight even though they are dangerously thin. In response, they avoid food, and often take other extreme measures to lose weight, such as compulsive exercise or purging by means of vomiting or laxatives and enemas. While some anorexics fully recover after a single episode, others may relapse frequently or experience chronic deterioration.

Bulimia nervosa affects an estimated 1.1% to 4.2% of females. It is characterized by recurrent uncontrolled binge-eating episodes followed by a compensatory behavior to prevent weight gain, such as self-induced vomiting, excessive exercise, or fasting. Persons with bulimia usually end up weighing within a normal range for their age and height, but they may fear gaining weight and feel intensely dissatisfied with their bodies. They often perform their behaviors in secret, feeling ashamed when they binge and relieved when they purge.

Binge-eating disorder (not officially approved as a psychiatric diagnosis) affects an estimated 2% to 5% of Americans in any given 6-month period. Like bulimia, a binge-eating disorder involves episodes of excessive eating during which the sufferer may lose all control, but individuals with this disorder do not compensate by purging, exercising, or fasting. Many are thus overweight, and the shame associated with the illness can lead to further bingeing.

Eating disorder sufferers may not admit they are ill and may resist treatment. Early diagnosis and a comprehensive treatment program are essential to recovery. Some patients may need immediate hospitalization. For anorexia, treatment usually follows 3 established steps: weight restoration (usually in an inpatient hospital setting), treatment of any accompanying psychological disturbances, and achieving long-term remission or recovery. Medications may be helpful in treating underlying depression or anxiety. Families are sometimes involved in the therapeutic process.

Heart and Blood Vessel Disease

Sources: American Heart Association, 7272 Greenville Ave., Dallas, TX 75231; phone: (800) 242-8721; Centers for Disease Control and Prevention; National Center for Health Statistics; National Institutes of Health; National Heart, Blood, and Lung Institute

Warning Signs of Heart Attack

- Chest discomfort. Most heart attacks involve discomfort in the center of the chest that lasts more than a few minutes, or that goes away and comes back. It can feel like uncomfortable pressure, squeezing, fullness, or pain.
- Discomfort in other areas of the upper body. Symptoms can include pain or discomfort in one or both arms, the back, neck, jaw, or stomach.
- Shortness of breath. This feeling may occur with or without chest discomfort.
- Other signs: These may include breaking out in a cold sweat, nausea, or lightheadedness.
- The American Heart Assoc. advises immediate action at onset of symptoms, as more than half of heart attack victims die within an hour of symptoms. Call 9-1-1. Get to a hospital right away.

Warning Signs of Stroke

- Sudden numbness or weakness of face, arm or leg, especially on one side of the body
- Sudden confusion, trouble speaking or understanding
- Sudden trouble seeing in one or both eyes
- Sudden trouble walking, dizziness, loss of balance or coordination
- Sudden severe headache with no known cause
- Prompt treatment of stroke can be a major factor in controlling the effects. If you have one or more stroke symptoms that last more than a few minutes, don't delay! Immediately call 9-1-1 or the emergency medical service (EMS) number so an ambulance (ideally with advanced life support) can quickly be sent for you.

Some Major Modifiable Risk Factors

High Blood pressure: High blood pressure, or hypertension, increases the risk of stroke, heart attack, kidney failure, and heart failure. It affects people of all races, sexes, ethnic origins, and ages. Obesity, physical inactivity, and an unhealthy diet can contribute to this **often symptomless** disease, and it is recommended that individuals have a blood pressure reading at least once every 2 years (more often if advised by a physician).

A blood pressure reading is really two measurements in one, with one written over the other, such as 122/78 mmHg. The **upper number (systolic pressure)** represents the amount of pressure in the blood vessels when the heart contracts (beats) and pushes blood through the circulatory system. The **lower number (diastolic pressure)** represents the pressure in the blood vessels between beats, when the heart is resting. According to recent National Institutes of Health guidelines, a blood pressure reading below 120/80 is considered normal, while readings from 120/80 to 139/89 are considered "prehypertension."

High blood pressure is divided into 2 stages:

Stage 1 is 140-159 (systolic) over 90-99 (diastolic);

Stage 2 is 160+ (systolic) over 100+ (diastolic).

The diagnosis can be based on either the systolic or the diastolic reading.

High blood pressure usually cannot be cured, but it can be controlled in a variety of ways, including lifestyle modifications and medication. Treatment always should be at the direction and under the supervision of a physician. The treatment goal for patients with hypertension is below 140/90. For individuals with hypertension and diabetes or chronic kidney disease, your doctors will want your blood pressure to be lower than 130/80.

High Blood Cholesterol: Cholesterol is a waxy fat-like substance found in all cells of the body. It is produced by the body and also comes in some foods. The body needs some cholesterol, but excess levels increase the risk of heart disease. High cholesterol itself **usually does not cause symptoms**, so many people are unaware that they have a problem.

There are 2 major kinds of cholesterol: **LDL (low-density lipoprotein)**, often called "bad" cholesterol, leads to narrowing of the arteries; **HDL (high-density lipoprotein)**, known as "good" cholesterol, helps reduce this risk.

National Institutes of Health guidelines classify total cholesterol levels (determined by a blood test) of less than 200 mg/dl as desirable, 200-239 as borderline high, and 240 and above as high. About 37 mil Americans have a cholesterol level of 240 mg/dl or higher. LDL levels of less than 100 are considered optimal, 130-159 as borderline high, 160-189 as high, and 190 and over as very high. For HDL, levels of 60 mg/dl and above are considered protective against heart disease, while levels under 40 mg/dl are considered a risk factor for heart disease.

Like high-blood pressure, high blood cholesterol can be controlled by life-style modification and medication, and should be treated under supervision of a physician.

Triglycerides, another form of fat in the blood, can also raise the risk of heart disease. Levels that are borderline high (150-199) or high (200 or more) may need treatment.

Diabetes: Diabetes is a major risk factor for heart disease; at least 65% of people with diabetes mellitus die of some form of heart or blood vessel disease. *See also* "Diabetes" on page 157.

Smoking: Cigarette smokers are 2-4 times more likely to develop CHD. Smoking is also associated with the risk of sudden cardiac death.

Obesity: Using a body mass index (BMI) of 25 and higher for overweight and 30 and higher for obesity, an estimated 142 mil Americans age 20 and over are overweight and obese. Of these, more than 67 mil are obese. *See also* "Weight Guidelines for Adults" on page 165.

Physical Inactivity: An inactive lifestyle is a risk factor for coronary heart disease (CHD). This increase in risk is comparable to that observed for high blood cholesterol, high blood pressure, or cigarette smoking.

Women and Cardiovascular Disease

The American Heart Association reports that diseases of the heart and stroke, respectively, are the no. 1 and no. 3 killers of women over the age of 25 (cancer is the 2nd); one in 2.6 women died of some form of cardiovascular disease in 2004. Because heart disease was long viewed as a "man's" disease, many of the major cardiovascular studies were conducted only on men. Much recent attention has been directed toward understanding the influence of gender on cardiovascular disease risk and prevention, but important gaps in knowledge remain.

Women often present some of the same "classic" symptoms of heart attack that men feel, such as chest pain that spreads to the shoulders and arms, but they may more often report atypical chest pain or complain of abdominal pain, difficulty breathing (dyspnea), and nausea. Another problem in diagnosis is that women tend to have heart attacks later in life than men, so symptoms may more often be masked by other age-related diseases such as arthritis or osteoporosis. Even certain diagnostic tests and procedures such as the exercise stress test may not be as accurate in women, with the result that the disease process that leads to heart attack or stroke may not be detected early on, with potentially serious consequences.

Irritable Bowel Syndrome

Source: National Institutes of Health, 9000 Rockville Pike, Bethesda, MD 20892

Irritable Bowel Syndrome (IBS) is a functional disorder, not a disease, that occurs in the large intestine and is one of the most common disorders diagnosed by physicians. Nearly 1 in 5 Americans has symptoms of IBS, and it accounts for more than one out of every 10 doctor visits in the U.S. IBS occurs more frequently in women than in men and it usually begins before the age of 35 for about 50% those affected. Though IBS causes discomfort and may even be painful, it does not damage the bowel.

Most people are not comfortable discussing IBS because of its embarrassing symptoms. They include:

- bloating
- gas
- diarrhea
- constipation
- abdominal pain or cramping
- mucus in the stool
- feeling like you have not finished with a bowel movement

For most people, IBS is a chronic condition and there will likely be times where the symptoms are worse than during other times, or they may disappear altogether only to reappear again in the future. Most complications are derived from the symptoms such as hemorrhoids, which may form as a result of the diarrhea and constipation. Often people with chronic IBS may feel discouraged and go through periods of depression partly because of the constant discomfort, but also because the symptoms can interfere with work and personal relationships.

The specific causes for IBS are unknown. The walls of the intestines are lined with layers of muscle that contract and relax in a coordinated manner as they move food through the digestive system. When a person has IBS, the contractions cause food to either speed up or slow down as it moves though the bowel, subsequently causing the gas, bloating, diarrhea, and/or constipation. Some researchers believe that people who suffer from IBS have a colon that is particularly sensitive to certain foods. In particular, milk products, alcohol, caffeine, carbonated drinks, chocolate, and fatty foods can trigger IBS symptoms. Another common factor is a low tolerance for stretching of the large intestine. Women tend to get IBS more often than men and they usually have more severe symptoms during menstrual periods, leading researchers to believe that IBS may have a hormonal trigger. Recent research has shown that serotonin, a neurotransmitter hormone, may be linked with gastrointestinal functioning.

IBS can sometimes be the result of infection or other problems in the body. Researchers have found that people who have had gastroenteritis have later developed IBS. But because symptoms of IBS can match those many serious diseases, it is important for chronic sufferers to consult their doctors. If symptoms began early in life and have been stable, a patient may require a colonoscopy to rule out any inflammatory bowel diseases, such as Crohn's, or even colon cancer.

Patients over 50 should be regularly screened for colon cancer.

Despite the uncertainty over the cause of IBS, there are known precautionary measures that people with sensitive digestive systems can take. Having a well-balanced diet is the best possible prevention. High fiber foods such as bread and cereal reduce IBS symptoms, particularly constipation. In addition, vegetables, beans and bran can reduce symptoms if part of a daily diet. Eating large meals has been shown to worsen the condition, so eating smaller meals can also help reduce symptoms.

There is no particular cure for IBS, and treatment usually involves lessening the symptoms so that the sufferer may lead a more normal life.

Common Infectious Diseases

Sources: National Institutes of Health; Centers for Disease Control; World Health Organization

The following is a list of major infectious diseases. It is meant to be used for reference purposes only and not as a tool for diagnosis. If you think you may have a serious disease, you should see your doctor immediately. Statistics may appear uneven because of different methods of reporting by the various agencies, and because not all diseases are surveyed in the same year.

Chicken Pox

(Varicella simplex.) Usually non-threatening viral disease commonly associated with children. In adults, the disease can be serious. **Transmission:** highly contagious; transmitted by direct contact with rash, coughing, or sneezing of infected persons. **Symptoms:** blister-like rash, discomfort, high fever. Infected people may develop shingles later in life. **Vaccine:** became available 1995. **Treatment:** none; antibiotics in some severe cases. **Annual U.S. cases:** before 1995, about 4 mil, mostly children; in 2004, 32,931 reported cases.

Chlamydia

(Chlamydia trachomatis.) One of the most widely spread sexually transmitted diseases. **Transmission:** sexually transmitted. **Symptoms:** 70% of those infected have no symptoms. In women, vaginal discharge, infection of the cervix and urinary tract, can cause pelvic inflammatory disease; in men, infection of urinary tract and epididymitis (inflammation of testicular duct); can also infect the throat, rectum, and eye. **Treatment:** curable with antibiotics. **Annual U.S. cases:** 1,030,911 in 2006.

Common Cold

(More than 200 different viruses.) An upper respiratory viral infection. **Transmission:** touching your nose, eyes, or mouth after touching something contaminated by the virus; inhalation of airborne virus. **Symptoms:** irritated nose or scratchy throat, sneezing and watery nasal discharge; green or yellow nasal discharge, cough, muscle aches, headache, postnasal drip, decreased appetite. **Treatment:** no cure, over-the-counter remedies can relieve symptoms; effectiveness of antiviral drugs is debated. **Annual U.S. cases:** about 1 billion.

Gonorrhea

(Neisseria Gonorrhoeae.) Common bacterial STD. **Transmission:** sexually transmitted. **Symptoms:** in men, discomfort in urethra, yellow or green discharge, burning during urination; in women, pelvic pain, bleeding associated with intercourse, burning during urination, yellow or bloody discharge. **Treatment:** highly curable with antibiotics. **Annual U.S. cases:** 358,366 (2006).

Hepatitis

A viral disease that causes inflammation of the liver. In the U.S., five forms are endemic: A, B, C, D, and E; A, B, and C are the most common. **Symptoms:** all forms have generally similar symptoms including jaundice, fatigue, abdominal pain, loss of appetite, nausea, mild flu like symptoms; many cases cause no symptoms; in extreme cases, liver transplants may be necessary.

Hepatitis A *(Hepatovirus Picornaviridae).* **Transmission:** food or water contaminated with feces from infected persons. **Vaccine:** effective; travelers are advised to not drink tap water in countries where disease is common. **Treatment:** disease usually resolves itself on its own; alcohol consumption should be avoided. **Est. annual U.S. cases:** 25,000; 3,579 acute lab-confirmed cases in 2006.

Hepatitis B *(Orthohepadnavirus Hepadnaviridae).* **Transmission:** unsterilized needle sharing; contaminated blood transfusions; sexual contact. **Vaccine:** highly effective. **Treatment:** for chronic cases, drug treatment is necessary; for acute cases, disease usually resolves itself, severe cases treated with lamivudine. **Est. annual U.S. cases:** 43,000; 4,713 acute lab-confirmed cases in 2006.

Hepatitis C *(Hepacivirus Flavinviridae).* **Transmission:** unsterilized needle sharing, contaminated blood transfusions; sexual contact. **Vaccine:** none. **Treatment:** chronic cases treated with drugs, eliminating virus in about 50% of patients; for acute cases, treatment recommended if disease present after 2-3 months. **Est. annual U.S. cases:** 17,000 new hepatitis C infections in 2006.

HPV Infection

(More than 100 strains of human papillomavirus.) Common viral infection; leading cause of cervical cancer. **Transmission:** sexually transmitted. **Symptoms:** most of those infected have no symptoms but can still transmit virus; in some cases, genital warts; pre-cancerous bumps on anus, cervix or vulva (women), or penis (men). **Vaccine:** Gardasil vaccine was approved by the FDA in 2006. **Treatment:** while there is no cure, a healthy immune system can usually fight off HPV naturally. Women with HPV should have pap smear and pelvic exam every 6 months. **Annual U.S. cases:** 5.5 mil new cases of HPV; approximately 20 million Americans currently infected with HPV.

Influenza

(Various influenza viruses.) Highly contagious viral respiratory infection. **Transmission:** airborne transmission; contact with face after touching infected surface. **Symptoms:** chills, fatigue, fever, headache, sore throat, sinus congestion, coughing. "Stomach flu" is not influenza. **Vaccine:** yearly vaccinations recommended. **Treatment:** antiviral drugs; disease normally runs its course in a matter of days. **Annual U.S. Cases:** 5-20% of U.S. population; 200,000 hospitalized and 36,000 killed annually.

Lyme Disease

(Borrelia burgdorferi.) Bacterial inflammatory disease, first identified 1975 in Old Lyme, CT. Found across the U.S., usually in areas with large deer populations. **Transmission:** bite of infected deer ticks. Mice and deer are most common hosts. **Symptoms:** mimic those of other diseases: flu-like symptoms; fatigue; stiff neck, joint inflammation; skin rash may appear at site of tick bite. **Treatment:** antibiotics in early stages; anti-inflammation drugs to relieve symptoms; without treatment, long-term complications (some fatal) involving joints, heart, and nervous system. **Annual U.S. cases:** during the 15-year study period, the number of cases reported increased 101%, from 9,908 cases in 1992 to 19,931 cases in 2006.

Malaria

(Plasmodium parasite.) Infectious disease known from as early as 2700 BCE. Virtually eradicated in developed countries; still a major killer in tropical regions. **Transmission:** bite from an infected mosquito. **Symptoms:** high fever, shaking chills, heavy sweating, headache, fatigue, enlarged spleen; if left untreated, organ damage and death. **Treatment:** the FDA approved the use of Coartem tablets for the treatment of acute, uncomplicated malaria in 2009. Antimalarial drugs, including chloroquine, for treatment and prevention. **Annual U.S. Cases:** 1,505 new cases in the U.S. (2007); worldwide, as many as 2.7 million people killed each year, 75% of them African children.

Measles

(Rubeola virus.) Once-common viral infection; today almost nonexistent in U.S. and Canada. **Transmission:** airborne transmission by infected people. **Symptoms:** itchy and raised rash, sore throat, cough, pink-eye, high fever; in rare cases, encephalitis, seizures, permanent deafness, death. **Vaccine:** highly effective. **Treatment:** no specific treatment; symptoms relieved with bed rest, acetaminophen, humidified air. **Annual U.S. cases:** 55 new U.S. cases in 2006.

Mumps

(Mumps virus.) Acute and contagious viral infection. **Transmission:** direct contact with mucus or saliva of infected persons. **Symptoms:** painful, visible swelling of the salivary or parotid glands in the face; chills, headache, fever, painful swallowing; in some cases, inflammation of testes, pancreas, ovaries; in severe cases, brain swelling and symptoms ranging from nausea and drowsiness to seizures and permanent deafness. **Vaccine**: MMR vaccine is effective. **Treatment:** no specific treatment; symptoms may be relieved by applying ice or heat to swollen glands. **Annual U.S. cases:** 6,584 new U.S. cases in 2006.

Peptic Ulcer

(Most from *Helicobacter pylori* [*H. pylori*] bacteria; also overuse of aspirin or other anti-inflammatory drugs.) Weakening of the stomach's protective mucous coating, allowing stomach acid and bacteria to irritate stomach lining. **Transmission:** *H. Pylori* may be transmitted through food and water. **Symptoms:** indigestion; bloating; dull, transient abdominal pain or discomfort; nausea; vomiting. **Treatment:** antibiotics, acid-suppressing drugs. **Annual U.S. cases:** about 20% of Americans under 40 and half of those over 60 years may be infected with *H. pylori*. An estimated 500,000 to 850,000 develop peptic ulcers each year.

Pertussis or Whooping cough

(Bordetella pertussis or *B. parepertussis.)* Upper respiratory bacterial infection. **Transmission:** highly contagious; airborne transmission by infected people. **Symptoms:** initially, mild cold-like symptoms, fever, diarrhea, difficulty breathing; later, violent coughing with characteristic "whooping" heard when patient tries to breathe between coughs, vomiting; in severe cases, apnea, pneumonia, seizures, encephalopathy. **Vaccine:** TDaP vaccine or pertussis only vaccine. **Treatment:** antibiotics in early cases, otherwise disease must run its course. **Annual U.S. Cases:** 15,632 new U.S. cases (2006). After 25 years of increasing rates of infection, the number of annual infections dropped between 2005 and 2006.

Salmonella or Salmonellosis

(Salmonella enteritidis.) Bacterial infection. **Transmission:** eating foods contaminated by feces carrying the bacteria; undercooked meats or raw eggs contaminated by bacteria; contact with feces of infected animal/pet. **Symptoms:** fever, diarrhea, abdominal cramps 12 to 72 hours after infection. **Treatment:** no standard treatment; runs its course in 4 to 7 days; antibiotics in severe cases. **Annual U.S. cases:** 45,808 new U.S. lab-confirmed cases in 2006.

Shigellosis

(Four species of *Shigella: boydii, dysenteriae, flexneri,* and *sonnei*.) Bacterial infection and a form of dysentery (an intestinal disease). **Transmission:** food contaminated by infected feces; vegetables grown in fields containing contaminated sewage; swimming in contaminated water. **Symptoms:** watery or bloody diarrhea 1 to 4 days after infection, high fever, vomiting, painful bowel movements, severe diarrhea; in extreme cases, seizures in children, intestinal perforation. **Treatment:** mild infection allowed to run its course; replacement of fluids and salts lost through excessive diarrhea; antibiotics in severe cases. Although severe diarrhea is symptomatic, antidiarrheal medicines may make illness worse. **Annual U.S. Cases:** 15,503 cases reported in 2006.

Syphilis

(Treponema pallidum.) Bacterial infection known since ancient times, and spread rampantly throughout Europe in the Middle Ages. **Transmission:** sexually transmitted. **Symptoms:** primary stage: painless ulcer where bacteria enters the body; usually heals in 3 to 12 weeks with or without treatment. Without treatment, disease enters secondary stage: skin rash 2-10 weeks after chancre. Without treatment, enters tertiary stage: mouth sores, fever, fatigue, loss of appetite, weight loss, hair loss, jaundice, syphilitic meningitis, aortal aneurysms, lesions, damage to nervous system, heart, and eyes. Most infected do not progress beyond primary or secondary stage. **Treatment:** curable with antibiotics (mostly penicillin). **Annual U.S. Cases:** 36,953 total U.S. cases in 2006; 9,756 primary and secondary.

Tetanus or Lockjaw

(Clostridium tetani.) Bacterial infection. **Transmission**: Bacteria, found in soil, enters body through broken skin. **Symptoms**: muscle stiffness and spasm or "locking" of muscles of the jaw, neck, and limbs. **Vaccine:** 4 forms of tetanus immunization. **Treatment:** tetanus immune globulin can fight infection; with treatment, less than 10% of cases are fatal. **Annual U.S. Cases:** approx. 100 cases per year, most due to lack of immunization.

Tuberculosis

(Mycobacterium tuberculosis.) Bacterial infection that primarily affects the lungs. **Transmission:** airborne transmission by people with active TB infection. **Symptoms:** weight loss, fever, cough with discharge (sometimes with bloody sputum), night sweats, growing shortness of breath over time, chest pains. **Vaccine**: BCG (Bacille Calmette Guerin) vaccine only effective in protecting young children and used where TB is common; not recommended by health experts in U.S. **Treatment**: BCG (Bacille Calmette Guerin) vaccine is generally effective in protecting young children and is used where TB is prevalent; not recommended for use in the U.S. because of the low risk of infection and its variable effectiveness. **Annual U.S. Cases**: 13,299 U.S. cases in 2007.

Yellow Fever

(Yellow fever virus, in *flavivirus* group.) Viral infection that has caused large epidemics in S. America, the Caribbean and Africa. **Transmission:** bite from mosquitoes carrying the virus. **Symptoms:** headaches, muscle aches, fever, jaundice (yellowing skin), nausea and vomiting, kidney failure, severe generalized pain; in severe cases, shock, coma, and death. **Vaccine:** available, safe and effective. **Treatment:** symptoms are treated until disease runs its course. **Annual U.S. cases:** 0; 200,000 estimated new cases worldwide per year, with 30,000 deaths.

Food Guide Pyramid

MyPyramid.gov
STEPS TO A HEALTHIER YOU

In 2005 the U.S. Dept. of Agriculture issued a revised food guide pyramid called MyPyramid, along with new dietary guidelines for Americans. The new pyramid represents the latest findings in health and nutrition, with a focus on reducing calorie consumption and increasing physical activity. More specifically, the new system factors in weight, age, gender, and physical activity in putting together a nutrition plan, and distinguishes between necessary and unnecessary types of fats and sugars. In addition, the new pyramid allows for variation and personalization according to an individual's caloric needs. The guidelines below are general guidelines for better health and nutrition. To get a personalized nutrition and exercise assessment and for dietary recommendations visit MyPyramid.gov

Dietary Guidelines for Americans—Some Key Recommendations:

- Choose nutrient-dense foods and beverages among the basic food groups, while limiting the intake of foods with saturated and trans fats, cholesterol, added sugars, salt, and alcohol.
- To maintain a healthy body weight, balance calories consumed with calories expended.
- To prevent gradual weight gain over time, make small decreases in calories and increase physical activity.
- Engage in regular physical activity and cut down on sedentary activities.
- Keep fit through cardiovascular conditioning, stretching exercises for flexibility, and resistance exercises or calisthenics for muscle strength and endurance.
- Eat a sufficient amount of fruits and vegetables each day.
- Choose from all 5 vegetable subgroups, dark greens, orange, legumes, starchy vegetables, and other vegetables.

- Consume 3 cups per day of fat-free or low-fat milk or equivalent milk products.
- Consume less than 10% of calories from saturated fatty acids and less than 300 mg/day of cholesterol, and keep trans fatty acid consumption as low as possible.
- Keep total fat intake between 20%-35% of calories, with most fats coming from sources of polyunsaturated and monounsaturated fatty acids, such as fish, nuts, and vegetable oils.
- Choose lean, low-fat, or fat-free meat, poultry, dry beans, and milk or milk products.
- Eat fiber-rich fruits, vegetables, and whole grains often.
- Consume less than 2,300 mg (approx. 1 teaspoon of salt) of sodium per day. Eat potassium-rich foods, such as fruits and vegetables.
- If you drink alcoholic beverages, do so in moderation: up to 1 drink per day for women and up to 2 drinks per day for men.

Food Ingredients

Protein

Proteins, composed of amino acids, are essential to good nutrition. They build, maintain, and repair the body. Best sources: eggs, milk, fish, meat, poultry, soybeans, nuts. High-quality proteins such as eggs, meat, or fish supply all 8 amino acids needed in the diet. Plant foods can be combined to meet protein needs as well: whole grain breads and cereals, rice, oats, soybeans, other beans, split peas, and nuts.

Fats

Fats provide energy by furnishing calories to the body, and they also carry vitamins A, D, E, and K. They are the most concentrated source of energy in the diet. Best sources of polyunsaturated and monounsaturated fats: margarine, vegetable/plant oils, nuts. Meats, cheeses, butter, cream, egg yolks, lard are concentrated sources of saturated fats.

Carbohydrates

Carbohydrates provide energy for body function and activity by supplying immediate calories. The carbohydrate group includes sugars, starches, fiber, and starchy vegetables. Best sources: grains, legumes, potatoes, vegetables, fruits.

Fiber

The portion of plant foods that our bodies cannot digest is known as fiber. There are 2 basic types: *insoluble* ("roughage") and *soluble*. Insoluble fibers help move food materials through the digestive tract; soluble fibers tend to slow them down. Both types absorb water, thus prevent and treat constipation by softening and increasing the bulk of the undigested food components passing through the digestive tract. Soluble fibers have also been reported to be helpful in reducing blood cholesterol levels. Best sources: beans, bran, fruits, whole grains, vegetables.

Water

Water dissolves and transports other nutrients throughout the body, aiding the processes of digestion, absorption, circulation, and excretion. It helps regulate body temperature.

Vitamins

Vitamin A—promotes good eyesight and helps keep the skin and mucous membranes resistant to infection. Best sources: liver, sweet potatoes, carrots, kale, cantaloupe, turnip greens, collard greens, broccoli, fortified milk.

Vitamin B_1 (thiamine)—prevents beriberi. Essential to carbohydrate metabolism and health of nervous system. Best sources: pork, enriched cereals, grains, soybeans, nuts.

Vitamin B_2 (riboflavin)—protects the skin, mouth, eyes, eyelids, and mucous membranes. Essential to protein and energy metabolism. Best sources: milk, meat, poultry, cheese, broccoli, spinach.

Vitamin B_6 (pyridoxine)—important in the regulation of the central nervous system and in protein metabolism. Best sources: whole grains, meats, fish, poultry, nuts, brewers' yeast.

Vitamin B_{12} (cobalamin)—needed to form red blood cells. Best sources: meat, fish, poultry, eggs, dairy products.

Niacin—maintains health of skin, tongue, digestive system. Best sources: poultry, peanuts, fish, enriched flour and bread.

Folic acid (folacin)—required for normal blood cell formation, growth, and reproduction and for important chemical reactions in body cells. Best sources: yeast, orange juice, green leafy vegetables, wheat germ, asparagus, broccoli, nuts.

Other B vitamins—biotin, pantothenic acid.

Vitamin C (ascorbic acid)—maintains collagen, a protein necessary for the formation of skin, ligaments, and bones. It helps heal wounds and mend fractures and aids in resisting some types of viral and bacterial infections. Best sources: citrus fruits and juices, cantaloupe, broccoli, brussels sprouts, potatoes and sweet potatoes, tomatoes, cabbage.

Vitamin D—important for bone development. Best sources: sunlight, fortified milk and milk products, fish-liver oils, egg yolks.

Vitamin E (tocopherol)—helps protect red blood cells. Best sources: vegetable oils, wheat germ, whole grains, eggs, peanuts, margarine, green leafy vegetables.

Vitamin K—necessary for formation of prothrombin, which helps blood to clot. Also made by intestinal bacteria. Best dietary sources: green leafy vegetables, tomatoes.

Minerals

Calcium—works with phosphorus in building and maintaining bones and teeth. Best sources: milk and milk products, cheese, blackstrap molasses, some types of tofu.

Phosphorus—performs more functions than any other mineral, and plays a part in nearly every chemical reaction in the body. Best sources: cheese, milk, meats, poultry, fish, tofu.

Iron—Necessary for the formation of myoglobin, which is a reservoir of oxygen for muscle tissue, and hemoglobin, which transports oxygen in the blood. Best sources: lean meats, beans, green leafy vegetables, shellfish, enriched breads and cereals, whole grains.

Other minerals—chromium, cobalt, copper, fluorine, iodine, magnesium, manganese, molybdenum, potassium, selenium, sodium, sulfur, and zinc.

Understanding Food Label Claims

Source: U.S. Food and Drug Admin., Center for Food Safety and Applied Nutrition

The federal Nutrition Labeling and Education Act of 1990 provides that manufacturers can make certain claims on processed food labels only if they meet the definitions specified here:

Sugar

Sugar free: less than 0.5g per serving
No added sugar; Without added sugar; No sugar added:
No sugars added during processing or packing, including ingredients that contain sugars (for example, fruit juices, applesauce, or dried fruit).
Processing does not increase sugar content above the amount naturally in the ingredients. (A functionally insignificant increase in sugars is acceptable from processes used for purposes other than increasing sugar content.)
Food for which it substitutes normally contains added sugars.
Reduced sugar: at least 25% less sugar than reference food

Fat

Fat free: less than 0.5g of fat per serving
Saturated fat free: less than 0.5g of saturated fat per serving, and the level of trans fatty acids does not exceed 1% of total fat
Low fat: 3g or less per serving and, if the serving is 30g or less or 2 tbs or less, per 50g of the food
Low saturated fat: 1g or less per serving and not more than 15% of calories from saturated fatty acids
Reduced or Less fat: at least 25% less per serving than reference food

Fiber

High fiber: 5g or more per serving. (Also, must meet low-fat definition, or must state level of total fat.)
Good source of fiber: 2.5g to 4.9g per serving
More or Added fiber: at least 2.5g more per serving than reference food

Sodium

Sodium free: less than 5mg per serving
Low sodium: 140 mg or less per serving and, if the serving is 30g or less or 2 tbs or less, per 50g of the food
Very low sodium: 35 mg or less per serving and, if the serving is 30g or less or 2 tbs or less, per 50g of the food
Reduced or Less sodium: at least 25% less per serving than reference food

Calories

Low calorie: 40 calories or less per serving; if the serving is 30g or less or 2 tablespoons or less, 40 calories or less per 50g of food
Calorie free: under 5 calories per serving
Reduced or Fewer calories: at least 25% fewer calories than reference food

Cholesterol

Cholesterol free: less than 2mg of cholesterol and 2g or less of saturated fat per serving
Low cholesterol: 20mg or less and 2g or less of saturated fat per serving and, if the serving is 30g or less or 2 tbs or less, per 50g of the food
Reduced or Less cholesterol: at least 25% less than reference food

Other Food Label Claims

Source: Food Safety and Inspection Service, U.S. Department of Agriculture

The FDA allows food producers and marketers to use language on their packaging that advertises the health benefits and production methods of their products. Products marked as "certified" have been formally evaluated for class, grade, or other quality characteristics by the USDA's Food Safety and Inspection Service. Below are some common packaging terms and their meanings.

Organic: Produced by farmers who use environmentally friendly methods to raise their crops or animals. Before a product can be labeled "organic," the farm where the food is grown must pass a special inspection by a USDA official. Organic foods must be produced without conventional pesticides; fertilizers made with synthetic ingredients, sewage or sludge; bioengineering; or ionizing radiation.

The official *USDA Organic* label may appear on vegetables, fruit, packages of meat, cartons of milk, eggs, cheese, and other single-ingredient foods. Foods with more than one ingredient can place the official seal on their packaging if at least 95% of the ingredients are organic. Products with at least 70% organic ingredients may advertise prominently on the front of the package that the item contains organic ingredients. Products with some organic ingredients, but less than 70%, may not make any organic claims on the front of the package, but may list organic ingredients on the side panel. Foods that contain 100% organic ingredients may advertise that fact on the front of the packaging along with the organic seal.

Natural: A product that does not contain any artificial ingredient or added color, and which has been minimally processed. The label must explain the specific use of the term natural with regard to the product, such as: no added colorings, no artificial ingredients, minimally processed.

Free-range: Generally means that the product comes from an animal that was given access to the outdoors to roam for an unspecified amount of time each day. Animals raised in slaughterhouses are not considered free range. Free range products do not necessarily mean healthier or more disease-free.

Halal and **Zabiah Halal:** Produced in federally inspected meat packing plants and handled in accordance with Islamic law and under Islamic authority.

Kosher: Only used on meat and poultry products prepared under Rabbinical supervision.

Minimal Processing: Produced using only traditional physical processes which do not fundamentally alter the raw products, in order to make food edible, to preserve it, or to make it safe for human consumption. Includes smoking, roasting, freezing, drying, and fermenting; applies mostly to meat and poultry.

No Hormones: Hormones are not allowed in raising hogs or poultry, so those products may not make this claim. If sufficient documentation is provided to the USDA to prove that hormones were not used, this term may be used on packages of beef.

No Antibiotics: This claim may be made on a package if sufficient documentation is provided to the USDA that shows the animals were raised without being administered antibiotics.

Recommended Levels for Elements (Minerals)

Source: Food and Nutrition Board, National Academy of Sciences—Institute of Medicine, 2005

in milligrams per day (mg/d) or in micrograms per day (µg/d); asterisks denote levels defined as "adequate intake" (AI).

		Calcium (mg/d)	Chromium (µg/d)	Copper (µg/d)	Fluoride (mg/d)	Iodine (µg/d)	Iron (mg/d)	Magnesium (mg/d)	Manganese (mg/d)	Molybdenum (µg/d)	Phosphorus (mg/d)	Selenium (µg/d)	Zinc (mg/d)
Infants	0-6 mos	210*	0.2*	200*	0.01*	110*	0.27*	30*	0.003*	2*	100*	15*	2*
	7-12 mos	270*	5.5*	220*	0.5*	130*	11	75*	0.6*	3*	275*	20*	3
	1-3 yrs	500*	11*	340	0.7*	90	7	80	1.2*	17	460	20	3
	4-8 yrs	800*	15*	440	1*	90	10	130	1.5*	22	500	30	5
Males	9-13 yrs	1,300*	25*	700	2*	120	8	240	1.9*	34	1,250	40	8
	14-18 yrs	1,300*	35*	890	3*	150	11	410	2.2*	43	1,250	55	11
	19-30 yrs	1,000*	35*	900	4*	150	8	400	2.3*	45	700	55	11
	31-50 yrs	1,000*	35*	900	4*	150	8	420	2.3*	45	700	55	11
	51-70 yrs	1,200*	30*	900	4*	150	8	420	2.3*	45	700	55	11
	over 70 yrs	1,200*	30*	900	4*	150	8	420	2.3*	45	700	55	11
Females	9-13 yrs	1,300*	21*	700	2*	120	8	240	1.6*	34	1,250	40	8
	14-18 yrs	1,300*	24*	890	3*	150	15	360	1.6*	43	1,250	55	9
	19-30 yrs	1,000*	25*	900	3*	150	18	310	1.8*	45	700	55	8
	31-50 yrs	1,000*	25*	900	3*	150	18	320	1.8*	45	700	55	8
	51-70 yrs	1,200*	20*	900	3*	150	8	320	1.8*	45	700	55	8
	over 70 yrs	1,200*	20*	900	3*	150	8	320	1.8*	45	700	55	8
Pregnancy	18 yrs. or less	1,300*	29*	1,000	3*	220	27	400	2.0*	50	1,250	60	12
	19-30 yrs.	1,000*	30*	1,000	3*	220	27	350	2.0*	50	700	60	11
	31-50 yrs.	1,000*	30*	1,000	3*	220	27	360	2.0*	50	700	60	11
Lactation	18 yrs. or less	1,300*	44*	1,300	3*	290	10	360	2.6*	50	1,250	70	13
	19-30 yrs.	1,000*	45*	1,300	3*	290	9	310	2.6*	50	700	70	12
	31-50 yrs.	1,000*	45*	1,300	3*	290	9	320	2.6*	50	700	70	12

Recommended Levels for Vitamins

Source: Food and Nutrition Board, National Academy of Sciences—Institute of Medicine, 2005

in milligrams per day (mg/d) or in micrograms per day (µg/d); asterisks denote levels defined as "adequate intake" (AI).

		Vitamin A (µg/d)[1]	Vitamin C (mg/d)	Vitamin D (µg/d)[2]	Vitamin E (mg/d)	Vitamin K (µg/d)	Thiamin (mg/d)	Riboflavin (mg/d)	Niacin (mg/d)[3]	Vitamin B6 (mg/d)	Folate (µg/d)[4]	Vitamin B12 (µg/d)	Pantothenic Acid (mg/d)	Biotin (µg/d)	Choline (mg/d)[5]
Infants	0-6 mos	400*	40*	5*	4*	2.0*	0.2*	0.3*	2*	0.1*	65*	0.4*	1.7*	5*	125*
	7-12 mos	500*	50*	5*	5*	2.5*	0.3*	0.4*	4*	0.3*	80*	0.5*	1.8*	6*	150*
Children	1-3 yrs	300	15	5*	6	30*	0.5	0.5	6	0.5	150	0.9	2*	8*	200*
	4-8 yrs	400	25	5*	7	55*	0.6	0.6	8	0.6	200	1.2	3*	12*	250*
Males	9-13 yrs	600	45	5*	11	60*	0.9	0.9	12	1.0	300	1.8	4*	20*	375*
	14-18 yrs	900	75	5*	15	75*	1.2	1.3	16	1.3	400	2.4	5*	25*	550*
	19-30 yrs	900	90	5*	15	120*	1.2	1.3	16	1.3	400	2.4	5*	30*	550*
	31-50 yrs	900	90	5*	15	120*	1.2	1.3	16	1.3	400	2.4	5*	30*	550*
	51-70 yrs	900	90	10*	15	120*	1.2	1.3	16	1.7	400	2.46	5*	30*	550*
	over 70 yrs	900	90	15*	15	120*	1.2	1.3	16	1.7	400	2.46	5*	30*	550*
Females	9-13 yrs	600	45	5*	11	60*	0.9	0.9	12	1.0	300	1.8	4*	20*	375*
	14-18 yrs	700	65	5*	15	75*	1.0	1.0	14	1.2	400[7]	2.4	5*	25*	400*
	19-30 yrs	700	75	5*	15	90*	1.1	1.1	14	1.3	400[7]	2.4	5*	30*	425*
	31-50 yrs	700	75	5*	15	90*	1.1	1.1	14	1.3	400[7]	2.4	5*	30*	425*
	51-70 yrs	700	75	10*	15	90*	1.1	1.1	14	1.5	400	2.46	5*	30*	425*
	over 70 yrs	700	75	15*	15	90*	1.1	1.1	14	1.5	400	2.46	5*	30*	425*
Pregnancy	18 yrs. or less	750	80	5*	15	75*	1.4	1.4	18	1.9	600[8]	2.6	6*	30*	450*
	19-30 yrs.	770	85	5*	15	90*	1.4	1.4	18	1.9	600[8]	2.6	6*	30*	450*
	31-50 yrs.	770	85	5*	15	90*	1.4	1.4	18	1.9	600[8]	2.6	6*	30*	450*
Lactation	18 yrs. or less	1,200	115	5*	19	75*	1.4	1.6	17	2.0	500	2.8	7*	35*	550*
	19-30 yrs.	1,300	120	5*	19	90*	1.4	1.6	17	2.0	500	2.8	7*	35*	550*
	31-50 yrs.	1,300	120	5*	19	90*	1.4	1.6	17	2.0	500	2.8	7*	35*	550*

NOTE: For healthy breastfed infants, the AI is the mean intake. The AI for other life stage and gender groups is believed to cover needs of all individuals in the group, but lack of data or uncertainty in the data prevent being able to specify with confidence the percentage of individuals covered by this intake. (1) As retinol activity equivalents. (2) In the absence of adequate exposure to sunlight. (3) As niacin equivalents (NE). 1 mg of niacin = 60 mg of tryptophan; 0-6 months = preformed niacin (not NE). (4) As dietary folate equivalents (DFE). 1 DFE = 1 µg food folate = 0.6 µg of folic acid from fortified food or as a supplement consumed with food = 0.5 µg of a supplement taken on an empty stomach. (5) Although AIs have been set for choline, there are few data to assess whether a dietary supply of choline is needed at all stages of the life cycle, and it may be that the choline requirement can be met by endogenous synthesis at some of these stages. (6) Because 10-30% of older people may malabsorb food-bound B_{12}, it is advisable for those older than 50 years to meet their RDA mainly by consuming foods fortified with B_{12} or a supplement containing B_{12}. (7) In view of evidence linking folate intake with neural tube defects in the fetus, it is recommended that all women capable of becoming pregnant consume 400 µg from supplements or fortified foods in addition to intake of food folate from a varied diet. (8) It is assumed that women will continue consuming 400 µg from supplements or fortified food until their pregnancy is confirmed and they enter prenatal care, which ordinarily occurs after the end of the periconceptional period—the critical time for formation of the neural tube.

Dietary Requirements

The Food and Nutrition Board of the National Academy of Sciences' Institute of Medicine, in reports published from 1997 to 2005, set **Dietary Reference Intakes (DRIs)** for vitamins and elements (often called minerals). The DRIs, based on recent scientific research, establish daily consumption values that aim to optimize health at all stages of life, not just to guard against nutritional deficiencies.

The DRIs include 4 categories of values. The **Recommended Dietary Allowance (RDA)** gives an intake that meets the nutrient requirements of almost all (97-98%) healthy individuals in a specified group. The **Estimated Average Requirement (EAR)** is the intake that meets the estimated nutrient need of half the individuals in a specified group, while the **Adequate Intake (AI)** is the value given when adequate scientific evidence is not available to calculate an EAR. For healthy breastfed infants, the AI is the mean intake; for other life stage groups the AI is thought to cover the needs of all individuals in the group, but lack of data or uncertainty in the data prevents the percentage of individuals covered from being specified with confidence. The **Tolerable Upper Intake Level (UL)** designates the maximum intake that is unlikely to pose risks of adverse health effects in almost all healthy individuals in a specified group; taking the nutrient above that level could be bad for one's health. RDAs and AIs may both be used as goals for individual intake.

Weight Guidelines for Adults

Source: Dietary Guidelines for Americans, 2005, U.S. Dept. of Agriculture.

Guidelines on identification, evaluation, and treatment of overweight and obesity in adults were released in June 1998 by the National Heart, Lung, and Blood Institute (NHLBI), in cooperation with the National Institute of Diabetes and Digestive and Kidney Diseases. The guidelines, based on research into risk factors in heart disease, stroke, and other conditions, define degrees of overweight and obesity in terms of **body mass index (BMI)**, which is based on weight and height and is strongly correlated with total body fat content. A BMI of 25-29 is said to indicate **overweight**; a BMI of 30 or above is said to indicate **obesity**. Weight reduction is advised for persons with a BMI of 25 or higher. (Previous guidelines have been less stringent.) Factors such as large waist circumference, high blood pressure or cholesterol, and a family history of obesity-related disease may increase risk.

Despite growing awareness of the health problems associated, more than $1/3$ of Americans adults are obese (have a BMI of 30 or greater), according to the National Center for Health Statistics. A high prevalence of overweight and obesity is a huge public health concern because excess body fat has been associated with type 2 diabetes, hypertension, dyslipidemia, cardiovascular disease, stroke, gall bladder disease, respiratory dysfunction, gout, osteoarthritis, and certain kinds of cancers. Over the last 2 decades, the prevalence of overweight children has doubled, and among adolescents it has tripled. It is estimated that, in 2005, as many as 16% of children and adolescents were overweight.

The table below shows the BMI for certain heights and weights. For weight reduction tips, contact the Weight-control Information Network, 1 WIN Way, Bethesda, MD 20892-3665. Phone: 1-877-946-4627. Website: win.niddk.nih.gov

Weight (lbs)

Height	HEALTHY						OVERWEIGHT					OBESE								
4'10"	91	96	100	105	110	115	119	124	129	134	138	143	148	153	158	162	167	172	177	181
4'11"	94	99	104	109	114	119	124	128	133	138	143	148	153	158	163	168	173	178	183	188
5'0"	97	102	107	112	118	123	128	133	138	143	148	153	158	163	168	174	179	184	189	194
5'1"	100	106	111	116	122	127	132	137	143	148	153	158	164	169	174	180	185	190	195	201
5'2"	104	109	115	120	126	131	136	142	147	153	158	164	169	175	180	186	191	196	202	207
5'3"	107	113	118	124	130	135	141	146	152	158	163	169	175	180	186	191	197	203	208	214
5'4"	110	116	122	128	134	140	145	151	157	163	169	174	180	186	192	197	204	209	215	221
5'5"	114	120	126	132	138	144	150	156	162	168	174	180	186	192	198	204	210	216	222	228
5'6"	118	124	130	136	142	148	155	161	167	173	179	186	192	198	204	210	216	223	229	235
5'7"	121	127	134	140	146	153	159	166	172	178	185	191	198	204	211	217	223	230	236	242
5'8"	125	131	138	144	151	158	164	171	177	184	190	197	203	210	216	223	230	236	243	249
5'9"	128	135	142	149	155	162	169	176	182	189	195	203	209	216	223	230	236	243	250	257
5'10"	132	139	146	153	160	167	174	181	188	195	202	209	216	222	229	236	243	250	257	264
5'11"	136	143	150	157	165	172	179	186	193	200	208	215	222	229	236	243	250	257	265	272
6'0"	140	147	154	162	169	177	184	191	199	206	213	221	228	235	242	250	258	265	272	279
6'1"	144	151	159	166	174	182	189	197	204	212	219	227	235	242	250	257	265	272	280	288
6'2"	148	155	163	171	179	186	194	202	210	218	225	233	241	249	256	264	272	280	287	295
6'3"	152	160	168	176	184	192	200	208	216	224	232	240	248	256	264	272	279	287	295	303
6'4"	156	164	172	180	189	197	205	213	221	230	238	246	254	263	271	279	287	295	304	312
BMI[1]	19	20	21	22	23	24	25	26	27	28	29	30	31	32	33	34	35	36	37	38

(1) The BMI numbers apply to both men and women. Some very muscular people may have a high BMI without health risks.

Estimated Calorie Requirements[1]

Estimated amounts of calories, rounded to the nearest 200, needed to maintain energy balance for various gender, age groups, and levels of physical activity.

	Age (years)	Sedentary[2]	Moderately[3] Active	Active[4]		Age (years)	Sedentary[2]	Moderately[3] Active	Active[4]
Child	2–3	1,000	1,000–1,400	1,000–1,400	Male	4–8	1,400	1,400–1,600	1,600–2,000
Female	4–8	1,200	1,400–1,600	1,400–1,800		9–13	1,800	1,800–2,200	2,000–2,600
	9–13	1,600	1,600–2,000	1,800–2,200		14–18	2,200	2,400–2,800	2,800–3,200
	14–18	1,800	2,000	2,400		19–30	2,400	2,600–2,800	3,000
	19–30	2,000	2,000–2,200	2,400		31–50	2,200	2,400–2,600	2,800–3,000
	31–50	1,800	2,000	2,200		51+	2,000	2,200–2,400	2,400–2,800
	51+	1,600	1,800	2,000–2,200					

(1) Based on median height and weight for ages up to age 18 years and Body Mass Index (BMI) of 21.5 for adult females and 22.5 for adult males. (2) Engaging only in minimal activities associated with ordinary day-to-day life. (3) Includes physical activity equivalent to walking 1.5 to 3 miles per day at 3-4 mph. (4) Includes physical activity equivalent to walking more than 3 miles per day at 3-4 mph.

Calories Used During Physical Activity

Source: U.S. Dept. of Agriculture

Amounts of calories burned during physical activities are estimates for a 154-pound person. The more an individual weighs the more calories he or she will burn up with the same degree of exercise.

Moderate physical activities	In 1 hour	In 30 min.	Vigorous physical activities	In 1 hour	In 30 min.
Hiking	370	185	Running/jogging (5 miles per hour) . . .	590	295
Light gardening/yard work	330	165	Bicycling (more than 10 miles per hour)	590	295
Dancing	330	165	Swimming (slow freestyle laps)	510	255
Golf (walking and carrying clubs)	330	165	Aerobics	480	240
Bicycling (less than 10 miles per hour)	290	145	Walking (4 ½ miles per hour)	460	230
Walking (3 ½ miles per hour)	280	140	Heavy yard work (e.g., chopping wood)	440	220
Weight training (general light workout).	220	110	Weight lifting (vigorous effort)	440	220
Stretching	180	90	Basketball (vigorous)	440	220

Finding Your Target Heart Rate

Source: Carole Casten, EdD, *Aerobics Today;* Peg Jordan, RN, Aerobics and Fitness Assoc. of America

The target heart rate is the heartbeat rate a person should have during aerobic exercise (such as running, fast walking, cycling, or cross-country skiing) to get the full benefit of the exercise for cardiovascular conditioning.

First, determine the intensity level at which one would like to exercise. A sedentary person may want to begin an exercise regimen at the 60% level and work up gradually to the 70% level. Athletes and highly fit individuals must work at an 85% or higher level to receive benefits. *Second,* calculate the target heart rate. One common way is by using the American College of Sports Medicine Method.

To obtain cardiovascular fitness benefits from aerobic exercise, it is recommended that an individual participate in an aerobic activity at least 3-5 times a week for 20-30 minutes per session, although cardiac patients and very sedentary individuals can obtain benefits with shorter periods (15-20 minutes). Generally, training changes occur in 4-6 weeks, but they can occur in as little as 2 weeks.

Using the American College of Sports Medicine Method to calculate one's target heart rate, an individual should subtract his or her age from 220, then multiply by the desired intensity level of the workout. Then divide the answer by 6 for a 10-second pulse count. (The 10-second pulse count is useful for checking whether the target heart rate is being achieved during the workout. One can easily check one's pulse—at the wrist or side of the neck—counting the number of beats in 10 seconds.)

For example, a 20-year-old wishing to exercise at 70% intensity would employ the following steps:

Maximum Heart Rate	220 – 20 = 200
Target Heart Rate	200× .70 = 140
10-second Pulse Count	140/6 = 23

To work at the desired level of intensity, this 20-year-old would strive for a target heart rate of 140 beats per minute, or a 10-second pulse count of 23.

Overweight, Obesity, and Healthy Weight in the U.S.[1], 1960-2006

Source: National Center for Health Statistics, National Health and Nutrition Examination Survey

	1960-62	1971-74	1976-80	1988-94	1999-2002	2001-04	2003-06
				Percent of population			
Overweight[2]							
Both sexes[3,4]	44.8%	47.7%	47.4%	56.0%	65.2%	66.0%	66.9%
Male	49.5	54.7	52.9	61.0	68.8	70.7	72.6
Female[3]	40.2	41.1	42.0	51.2	61.7	61.4	61.2
Obese[5]							
Both sexes[3,4]	13.3	14.6	15.1	23.3	31.1	32.1	34.1
Male.	10.7	12.2	12.8	20.6	28.1	30.2	33.1
Female[3]	15.7	16.8	17.1	26.0	34.0	34.0	35.2
Healthy weight[6]							
Both sexes[3,4]	51.2	48.8	49.6	41.7	32.9	32.2	31.4
Male	48.3	43.0	45.4	37.9	30.2	28.1	26.1
Female[3]	54.1	54.3	53.7	45.3	35.6	36.2	36.6

NOTE: Percents do not sum to 100 because the percent of persons with BMI less than 18.5 is not shown and the percent of persons with obesity is a subset of the percent with overweight. Height was measured without shoes; two pounds were deducted from data for 1960-62 to allow for weight of clothing. (1) In persons age 20-74, age-adjusted to 2000 standard population group; Data based on measured height and weight of a sample of the civilian noninstitutionalized population. (2) Body mass index (BMI) greater than or equal to 25. (3) Excludes pregnant women. (4) Includes persons of all races and Hispanic origins. (5) Body mass index (BMI) greater than or equal to 30. (6) BMI of 18.5 to less than 25. See pg. 153 for tables to calculate BMI.

Basic First Aid

Source: Courtesy of the American National Red Cross. All rights reserved in all countries.

NOTE: This information is not intended to be a substitute for formal training. It is recommended that you contact your local American Red Cross chapter (www.redcross.org) to sign up for a First Aid/CPR/AED course.

It is important to get medical assistance as soon as possible, but knowing what to do until a doctor or other trained person gets to the scene can save a life, especially in cases of severe bleeding, choking, poisoning, and shock.

People with special medical problems, such as diabetes, cardiovascular disease, epilepsy, or allergies, are urged to wear some sort of emblem identifying the problem, as a safeguard against receiving medication that might be harmful or even fatal. Emblems may be obtained from Medic Alert Foundation, 2323 Colorado Ave., Turlock, CA 95382; 888-633-4298.

Animal bite: Call 9-1-1 or the local emergency number if the wound is bleeding seriously or if you suspect the animal might have rabies. Control any bleeding. Wash minor wounds with soap under running water and apply triple antibiotic ointment and a dressing. When possible, proper authorities should test the animal for rabies.

Asphyxiation: Call 9-1-1, or the local emergency number. Give care for any life-threatening conditions.

Bleeding: Use a barrier between your hand and the wound to help prevent infection. Cover wound with a sterile compress. Apply direct pressure until bleeding stops. Cover compress with a bandage. Call 9-1-1, or the local emergency number if bleeding is severe.

Burn: Check for life-threatening conditions. If the burn is mild, with skin unbroken and no blisters, flush with cold running water until pain subsides. Apply a loose, sterile, dry dressing to prevent infection. If severe, call 9-1-1 or the local emergency number. Care for shock (see below). Keep the person from getting chilled or overheated until advanced medical assistance arrives. Do not try to clean a severe burn or break blisters.

Chemical in eye: Call 9-1-1 or the local emergency number. With the victim's head turned to the side with the affected eye lower than the unaffected eye, continuously flush the injured eye with water.

Choking: *See* **First Aid for Choking**, below.

Convulsions (seizures): Remove nearby objects that might cause injury. Protect the person's head by placing a thin folded towel or clothing under it. If there is fluid in the person's mouth, roll him or her on one side so that the fluid may drain from the mouth. Do not place anything between the person's teeth. Stay with the person until he or she is fully conscious. If convulsions do not stop, get medical attention immediately.

Cut (minor): Use a clean barrier between your hand and the wound to prevent infection. Apply direct pressure for a few minutes to control any bleeding. Wash the wound thoroughly with soap and water and apply triple-antibiotic ointment or cream. Cover the wound with a sterile compress and a bandage (or an adhesive bandage).

Fainting: If the victim feels faint, lower him or her to the ground. Lay the victim down on his or her back. If possible, elevate the victim's legs 8 to 12 inches. Care for any life-threatening conditions. Loosen any restrictive clothing and check for any other signs of injury. Call 9-1-1 or the local emergency number.

Foreign object in eye: If an object is embedded in someone's eye do not remove it. If not embedded, try to remove the object by having the victim blink several times. If the object doesn't come out, try gently flushing the eye with water. Do not rub the eye. If the object still doesn't come out, the victim should receive professional medical attention.

Frostbite: Handle frostbitten area gently. Do not rub., Soak affected area in warm water (not warmer than 105°F), if there is no danger of area refreezing. Do not allow frostbitten area to touch the container. Keep the frostbitten part in the water until normal color returns and it feels warm. Loosely bandage the area with dry, sterile dressings. If fingers or toes are frostbitten, put sterile gauze between them. Call 9-1-1 or seek emergency help as soon as possible.

Heat Stroke and Heat Exhaustion: Remove the victim from the heat. Loosen any tight clothing. Fan the person and apply cool, wet cloths to the skin. If the victim is conscious, give him or her cool water to drink slowly. Call 9-1-1 if the victim's condition does not improve or if you suspect heat stroke.

Heart Attack and Stroke: *See* page 158.

Hypothermia: Call 9-1-1 or the local emergency number. Move victim to a warm place. Remove wet clothing and dry victim, if necessary. Warm victim gradually by wrapping the person in warm blankets or clothing. Apply heat pads or other heat sources if available, but not directly to the body. If the person is alert, give the victim warm, non-alcoholic and decaffeinated liquids to drink.

Loss of Limb: Call 9-1-1 or the local emergency number and care for any life-threatening conditions. If a limb is severed, it is important to properly protect the limb so that it can possibly be reattached. After the victim is cared for, the limb should be wrapped in a sterile gauze or clean material and placed in a clean plastic bag, garbage can, or other suitable container. Pack ice around the limb on the OUTSIDE of the bag to keep the limb cold. Be sure the limb is taken to the hospital with the person.

Poisoning: Care for any life-threatening conditions. Call the National Poison Control Center (800-222-1222) , 9-1-1 or the local emergency number and follow their directions. Do not give the victim any food or drink or induce vomiting, unless specified by medical professionals.

Shock (injury-related): Monitor breathing and consciousness. Have the victim lie down and keep him or her as comfortable as possible. Elevate legs 8 to 12 in. if you do not suspect a head, neck or back injury or broken bones in the hips or legs. Maintain normal body temperature; if the weather is cold or damp, place blankets or extra clothing over and under the victim; if weather is hot, provide shade. Do not attempt to move victim if spinal injury is suspected.

Snakebite: Call 9-1-1 or the local emergency number. Wash the injury. Keep the area still and at a lower level than the heart. Keep the victim calm. If the victim cannot get professional medical help within 30 minutes, consider using a snakebite kit if available. Care for a bite from an elapid snake, such as a coral snake, the same except that after washing the wound you should apply an elastic roller bandage.

Sprains and fractures: Apply ice to reduce swelling and pain. Do not try to straighten or move broken limbs. Apply a splint to immobilize the injured area only if you have to move or transport the victim to seek medical attention and if it does not cause more pain. If you suspect a serious injury, call 9-1-1 or the local emergency number.

Sting from insect: If possible, remove stinger by scraping it away with your finger, a plastic card (like a credit card) or using tweezers. If you use tweezers, grasp the stinger, not the venom sac. Wash the area with soap and water; cover it to keep it clean. Apply a cold pack to reduce pain and swelling. Call 9-1-1 or the local emergency number immediately if body swells, patient collapses, or you know that the victim is allergic to the sting.

Unconsciousness: Call 9-1-1 or the local emergency number immediately. Care for any life-threatening conditions. If the person shows signs of life (movement and breathing), place him or her in the recovery position (i.e., lying on a side, with head supported, so that the airway is open). Do not move the person if a spinal injury is suspected.

First Aid for Choking

The recommended first aid for a conscious choking victim who is unable to speak, cough or breathe, is to deliver a series of 5 back blows and 5 abdominal thrusts. Have someone call 9-1-1 or the local emergency number. Obtain consent. Lean the victim forward and give 5 back blows with the heel of your hand. Stand or kneel behind the victim and wrap your arms around his or her waist. Make a fist with one hand and place the thumb side against the middle of the person's abdomen, just above the navel and well below the lower tip of the breastbone. Grasp the fist with the other hand and give 5 quick, upward thrusts into the abdomen. Continue back blows and abdominal thrusts until the object is dislodged and the person can breathe or cough forcefully, or becomes unconscious.

VITAL STATISTICS

Recent Trends in Vital Statistics

Source: National Center for Health Statistics, U.S. Dept. of Health and Human Services; latest years available

Births

An estimated 4,247,000 babies were born in the U.S. in 2008, a decrease from 4,315,000 in 2007. The birth rate decreased to 13.9 per 1,000 total population, to match the record low in 2002.

The fertility rate (number of live births per 1,000 women aged 15-44 years) decreased slightly to an estimated 68.4 for 2008, down from the 2007 rate of 69.2.

Deaths

The number of deaths during 2008 was estimated at 2,453,000 according to provisional data, up from 2,415,000 in 2007. The death rate in 2008 increased to 8.1 deaths per 1,000 population, up from 8.0 in 2007. The infant death rate was 6.5 deaths under 1 year per 1,000 live births in 2008, down from 6.6 in 2007.

Natural Increase

As a result of natural increase (the excess of births over deaths), an estimated 1,794,000 persons were added to the population in 2008. The rate fell to 5.8 per 1,000 population, down from 6.3 in 2007.

Marriages

An estimated 2,162,000 marriages were performed in 2008, compared to 2,197,000 in 2007. The provisional marriage rate for 2008 (7.1 per 1,000 population) was down from the 2007 rate of 7.3.

Divorces

The divorce rate went down slightly from 3.6 per 1,000 population in 2007 to 3.5 per 1,000 population in 2008, according to provisional data. Data are incomplete however. The NCHS does not include divorce data for California, Georgia, Hawaii, Indiana, Louisiana, and Minnesota.

Births and Deaths in the U.S., 1960-2008

Source: National Center for Health Statistics, U.S. Dept. of Health and Human Services

Year	BIRTHS Total number	BIRTHS Rate	DEATHS Total number	DEATHS Rate	Year	BIRTHS Total number	BIRTHS Rate	DEATHS Total number	DEATHS Rate
1960	4,257,850	23.7	1,711,982	9.5	1999	3,959,417	14.2	2,391,399	8.6
1970	3,731,386	18.4	1,921,031	9.5	2000	4,058,814	14.4	2,403,351	8.5
1980	3,612,258	15.9	1,989,841	8.8	2001	4,025,933	14.1	2,416,425	8.5
1990	4,092,994	16.7	2,148,463	8.6	2002	4,021,726	13.9	2,443,387	8.5
1992	4,049,024	15.8	2,175,613	8.5	2003	4,089,950	14.1	2,448,288	8.4
1993	4,000,240	15.4	2,268,553	8.7	2004	4,112,052	14.0	2,397,615	8.2
1994	3,952,767	15.0	2,278,994	8.7	2005	4,138,349	14.0	2,448,017	8.3
1995	3,899,589	14.6	2,312,132	8.7	2006	4,265,555	14.2	2,426,264	8.1
1996	3,891,494	14.4	2,314,690	8.6	2007P	4,315,000	14.3	2,415,000	8.0
1997	3,880,894	14.2	2,314,245	8.5	2008P	4,247,000	13.9	2,453,000	8.1
1998	3,941,553	14.3	2,337,256	8.5					

P = Provisional data. **Note:** Statistics cover only events occurring within the U.S. and exclude fetal deaths. Rates per 1,000 population; enumerated as of Apr. 1 for census years; estimated as of July 1 for all other years. Beginning 1970 statistics exclude births and deaths occurring among nonresidents of the U.S. Data include revisions. Birth and death rates for years in the 1990s revised on basis of the 2000 Census.

Marriage and Divorce Rates, 1920-2008

Source: National Center for Health Statistics, U.S. Dept. of Health and Human Services

The U.S. marriage rate dipped during the Depression and peaked sharply just after World War II; the trend after that has been more gradual. The divorce rate generally rose from the 1920s through 1981, when it peaked at 5.3 per 1,000 population, before declining somewhat. The graph below shows marriage and divorce rates since 1920. (2006-08 divorce rates were calculated excluding data and populations from the non-reporting states California, Georgia, Hawaii, Indiana, Louisiana, and Minnesota. Some data are provisional.)

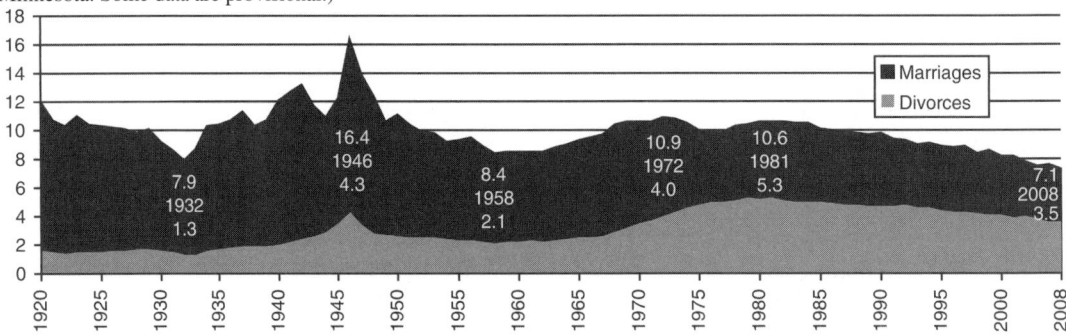

U.S. Median Age at First Marriage, 1890-2008

Source: Bureau of the Census, U.S. Dept. of Commerce

Year[1]	Men	Women	Year[1]	Men	Women	Year[1]	Men	Women	Year[1]	Men	Women	Year[1]	Men	Women
1890	26.1	22.0	1960	22.8	20.3	1991	26.3	24.1	1997	26.8	25.0	2003	27.1	25.3
1900	25.9	21.9	1965	22.8	20.6	1992	26.5	24.4	1998	26.7	25.0	2004	27.4	25.3
1910	25.1	21.6	1970	23.2	20.8	1993	26.5	24.5	1999	26.9	25.1	2005	27.1	25.3
1920	24.6	21.2	1975	23.5	21.1	1994	26.7	24.5	2000	26.8	25.1	2006	27.5	25.5
1930	24.3	21.3	1980	24.7	22.0	1995	26.9	24.5	2001	26.9	25.1	2007	27.5	25.6
1940	24.3	21.5	1985	25.5	23.3	1996	27.1	24.8	2002	26.9	25.3	2008	27.6	25.9
1950	22.8	20.3	1990	26.1	23.9									

(1) Figures after 1947 based on pop. 15 to 54 years in Current Population Survey data; earlier figures based on decennial censuses.

Birth Rates; Fertility Rates by Age of Mother, 1950-2007
Source: National Center for Health Statistics, U.S. Dept. of Health and Human Services

				AGE OF MOTHER							
Year	Birth rate[1]	Fertility rate[2]	10-14 years	15-19 years Total	15-17	18-19	20-24 years	25-29 years	30-34 years	35-39 years	40-44 years	45-49 years
				Live births per 1,000 women by age group							
1950	24.1	106.2	1.0	81.6	40.7	132.7	196.6	166.1	103.7	52.9	15.1	1.2
1960	23.7	118.0	0.8	89.1	43.9	166.7	258.1	197.4	112.7	56.2	15.5	0.9
1970	18.4	87.9	1.2	68.3	38.8	114.7	167.8	145.1	73.3	31.7	8.1	0.5
1980	15.9	68.4	1.1	53.0	32.5	82.1	115.1	112.9	61.9	19.8	3.9	0.2
1990	16.7	70.9	1.4	59.9	37.5	88.6	116.5	120.2	80.8	31.7	5.5	0.2
1992	15.8	68.4	1.4	60.3	37.6	93.6	113.7	115.7	79.6	32.3	5.9	0.3
1993	15.4	67.0	1.4	59.0	37.5	91.1	111.3	113.2	79.9	32.7	6.1	0.3
1994	15.0	65.9	1.4	58.2	37.2	90.2	109.2	111.0	80.4	33.4	6.4	0.3
1995	14.6	64.6	1.3	56.0	35.5	87.7	107.5	108.8	81.1	34.0	6.6	0.3
1996	14.4	64.1	1.2	53.5	33.3	84.7	107.8	108.6	82.1	34.9	6.8	0.3
1997	14.2	63.6	1.1	51.3	31.4	82.1	107.3	108.3	83.0	35.7	7.1	0.4
1998	14.3	64.3	1.0	50.3	29.9	80.9	108.4	110.2	85.2	36.9	7.4	0.4
1999	14.2	64.4	0.9	48.8	28.2	79.1	107.9	111.2	87.1	37.8	7.4	0.4
2000	14.4	65.9	0.9	47.7	26.9	78.1	109.7	113.5	91.2	39.7	8.0	0.5
2001	14.1	65.3	0.8	45.3	24.7	76.1	106.2	113.4	91.9	40.6	8.1	0.5
2002	13.9	64.8	0.7	43.0	23.2	72.8	103.6	113.6	91.5	41.4	8.3	0.5
2003	14.1	66.1	0.6	41.6	22.4	70.7	102.6	115.6	95.1	43.8	8.7	0.5
2004	14.0	66.3	0.7	41.1	22.1	70.0	101.7	115.5	95.3	45.4	8.9	0.5
2005	14.0	66.7	0.7	40.5	21.4	69.9	102.2	115.5	95.8	46.3	9.1	0.6
2006	14.2	68.5	0.6	41.9	22.0	73.0	105.9	116.7	97.7	47.3	9.4	0.6
2007[3]	14.3	69.5	0.6	42.5	22.2	73.9	106.4	117.5	99.9	47.5	9.5	0.6

(1) Live births per 1,000 population. (2) Live births per 1,000 women 15-44 years of age. (3) Preliminary.

Numbers of Multiple Births in the U.S., 1990-2006
Source: National Center for Health Statistics, U.S. Dept. of Health and Human Services
The general upward trend in multiple births reflects greater numbers of births to older women and increased use of fertility drugs.

Year	Twins	Triplets	Quadruplets	Quintuplets[1]	Year	Twins	Triplets	Quadruplets	Quintuplets[1]
1990	93,865	2,830	185	13	2000	118,916	6,742	506	77
1993	96,445	3,834	277	57	2001	121,246	6,885	501	85
1994	97,064	4,233	315	46	2002	125,134	6,898	434	69
1995	96,736	4,551	365	57	2003	128,665	7,110	468	85
1996	100,750	5,298	560	81	2004	132,219	6,750	439	86
1997	104,137	6,148	510	79	2005	133,122	6,208	418	68
1998	110,670	6,919	627	79	2006	137,085	6,118	355	67
1999	114,307	6,742	512	67					

(1) Quintuplets and other multiple births of 5 or more.

Top 15 Countries for U.S. Foreign Adoptions, 1999-2008[1]
Source: Dept. of Homeland Security, Office of Immigration Statistics

Country	2008	2007	2006	2005	2004	2003	2002	2001	2000	1999
Guatemala	4,082	4,728	4,135	3,783	3,264	2,328	2,419	1,609	1,518	1,504
China	3,852	5,453	6,493	7,906	7,044	6,859	6,119	4,681	5,053	4,101
Russia	1,859	2,310	3,706	4,639	5,865	5,209	4,939	4,279	4,269	4,348
Ethiopia	1,666	1,255	732	441	289	135	105	158	95	100
South Korea	1,038	939	1,376	1,630	1,716	1,790	1,779	1,870	1,794	2,008
Vietnam	737	828	163	NA	25	382	766	737	724	709
Ukraine	487	606	460	821	723	702	1,106	1,246	659	323
Kazakhstan	380	540	587	755	826	825	819	672	398	108
Colombia	308	310	344	291	287	272	334	407	246	231
India	306	416	320	323	406	472	464	543	503	499
Haiti	300	190	309	234	356	250	187	192	131	93
Philippines	279	265	245	271	196	214	221	219	173	195
Taiwan	262	184	187	141	89	107	41	44	24	26
Liberia	243	314	353	183	86	22	23	51	20	20
Nigeria	114	35	53	62	59	46	41	33	5	7
Mexico	108	89	70	88	89	67	61	73	106	145
Total[2]	**17,229**	19,741	20,705	22,710	22,911	21,320	20,100	19,087	18,120	16,363

NA = Not available. (1) Ranked by fiscal year 2008 totals. (2) Total includes countries not shown.

10 Leading Causes of Infant Death in the U.S., 2006
Source: National Center for Health Statistics, U.S. Dept. of Health and Human Services

Cause	Number	Percent of total deaths	Mortality rate[1]
Congenital malformations, deformations, and chromosomal abnormalities	5,819	20.4%	136.4
Disorders related to short gestation and low birth weight, not elsewhere classified	4,841	17.0	113.5
Sudden infant death syndrome	2,323	8.1	54.5
Newborn affected by maternal complications of pregnancy	1,683	5.9	39.5
Accidents (unintentional injuries)	1,147	4.0	26.9
Newborn affected by complications of placenta, cord, and membranes	1,140	4.0	26.7
Respiratory distress of newborn	825	2.9	19.3
Bacterial sepsis[2] of newborn	807	2.8	18.9
Neonatal hemorrhage	618	2.2	14.5
Diseases of the circulatory system	543	1.9	12.7
All other causes	8,781	30.8	205.9
All causes	**28,527**	**100.0**	**668.8**

(1) Infant deaths per 100,000 live births. (2) Toxic condition resulting from the spread of bacteria.

Nonmarital Childbearing in the U.S., 1970-2006

Source: National Center for Health Statistics, U.S. Dept. of Health and Human Services

	1970	1975	1980	1985	1990	1995	2000	2001	2002	2003	2004	2005	2006
Births to unmarried mothers (1,000s) . .	399	448	666	828	1,165	1,254	1,347	1,349	1,366	1,416	1,470	1,527	1,642
Race of mother						Percent of live births to unmarried mothers							
All races	10.7	14.3	18.4	22.0	28.0	32.2	33.2	33.5	34.0	34.6	35.8	36.9	38.5
White	5.5	7.1	11.2	14.7	20.4	25.3	27.1	27.7	28.5	29.4	30.5	31.7	—
Black	37.5	49.5	56.1	61.2	66.5	69.9	68.5	68.4	68.2	68.2	68.8	69.3	—
American Indian or Alaska Native	22.4	32.7	39.2	46.8	53.6	57.2	58.4	59.7	59.7	61.3	62.3	63.5	64.6
Asian or Pacific Islander	—	—	7.3	9.5	13.2	16.3	14.8	14.9	14.9	15.0	15.5	16.2	16.3
Hispanic origin (selected states)[1],[2]. . . .	—	—	23.6	29.5	36.7	40.8	42.7	42.5	43.5	45.0	46.4	48.0	49.9
White, non-Hispanic (selected states)[1]	—	—	9.5	12.4	16.9	21.2	22.1	22.5	23.0	23.6	24.5	25.3	26.6
Black, non-Hispanic (selected states)[1]	—	—	57.2	62.0	66.7	70.0	68.7	68.6	68.4	68.5	69.3	69.9	70.7
Maternal age						Percent distribution of live births to unmarried mothers							
Under 20 years	50.1	52.1	40.8	33.8	30.9	30.9	28.0	26.6	25.4	24.3	23.7	23.1	22.7
20-24 years	31.8	29.9	35.6	36.3	34.7	34.5	37.4	38.2	38.6	38.8	38.5	38.3	38.1
25 years and over	18.1	18.0	23.5	29.9	34.4	34.7	34.6	35.2	36.9	36.9	37.8	38.6	39.2
Race of mother						Live births per 1,000 unmarried women 15-44 years of age[3]							
All races and origins	26.4	24.5	29.4	32.8	43.8	44.3	44.0	43.8	43.7	44.9	46.1	47.5	—
White[4]	13.9	12.4	18.1	22.5	32.9	37.0	38.2	38.5	38.9	40.4	41.6	43.0	—
Black[4]	95.5	84.2	81.1	77.0	90.5	74.5	70.5	68.2	66.2	66.3	67.2	67.8	—
Hispanic origin (selected states)[1],[2]. . . .	—	—	—	—	89.6	88.7	87.2	87.8	87.9	92.2	95.7	100.3	—
White, non-Hispanic	—	—	—	—	—	28.1	28.0	27.8	27.8	28.6	29.4	30.1	—

— = Not available. (1) Data for Hispanics and non-Hispanics are affected by expansion of the reporting area for an Hispanic-origin item on the birth certificate and by immigration. The states in the reporting area increased from 22 in 1980, to 23 and the District of Columbia in 1983, 48 and DC by 1990, and 50 and DC by 1993. (2) Includes mothers of all races. (3) Rates computed by relating births to unmarried mothers, regardless of mother's age, to unmarried women 15-44 years of age. (4) For 1970 and 1975, birth rates are by race of child.

Number, Ratio, and Rate of Legal Abortions in U.S., 1970-2005

Source: Centers for Disease Control, *Abortion Surveillance, U.S., 2005*

Year	Legal Abortions	Ratio[1]	Rate[2]	Year	Legal Abortions	Ratio[1]	Rate[2]	Year	Legal Abortions	Ratio[1]	Rate[2]
1970	193,491	52	5	1982	1,303,980	354	24	1994	1,267,415	321	21
1971	485,816	137	11	1983	1,268,987	349	23	1995	1,210,883	311	20
1972	586,760	180	13	1984	1,333,521	364	24	1996	1,225,937	315	21
1973	615,831	196	14	1985	1,328,570	354	24	1997	1,186,039	306	20
1974	763,476	242	17	1986	1,328,112	354	23	1998[3]	884,273	264	17
1975	854,853	272	18	1987	1,353,671	356	24	1999[3]	861,789	256	17
1976	988,267	312	21	1988	1,371,285	352	24	2000[4]	857,475	245	16
1977	1,079,430	325	22	1989	1,396,658	346	24	2001[4]	853,485	246	16
1978	1,157,776	347	23	1990	1,429,247	344	24	2002[4]	854,122	246	16
1979	1,251,921	358	24	1991	1,388,937	338	24	2003[5]	848,163	241	16
1980	1,297,606	359	25	1992	1,359,146	334	23	2004[5]	839,226	238	16
1981	1,300,760	358	24	1993	1,330,414	333	23	2005[6]	820,151	233	15

(1) Number of abortions per 1,000 live births. (2) Number of abortions per 1,000 women aged 15-44 years. (3) Without estimates for AK, CA, NH, and OK. (4) Without estimates for AK, CA, and NH. (5) Without estimates for CA, NH, and WV. (6) Without estimates for CA, NH, and LA.

Sexual Behavior in the U.S.

Data released by the National Center for Health Statistics in 2005 show that about 90% of U.S. men and women 18-44 years of age think of themselves as heterosexual; 2.3% of men and 1.3% of women as homosexual; and 1.8% of men and 2.8% of women as bisexual. However, 6.2% of men 18-44 years of age reported ever having had sex with another male as of 2002 (up from 2.3% in 1991), and 11.5% of women reported ever having had a sexual experience with another woman (up from 4.1% in 1992).

Ten percent of males age 15-44 had never had sex with a female, but this percentage varied greatly with age: more than half (52%) of males age 15-17 had never had sex with a female, but only 1.8% of males age 40-44 had not done so.

Percentages were slightly lower for women, with only 8.4% of females age 15-44 having never had sex with a male, with specific percentages ranging from 50.2% for females age 15-17 to only 1.3% for females age 40-44.

Among men age 15-44 who had sex with at least one partner in the previous year, 39% reported using a condom in their most recent sexual encounter (24% of married men and 65% of never-married men). Among women, only 22% reported using a condom (13% of married and 42% of never-married women). Condom use was also more frequent among younger men and women: in the 15-19 age group, 66% of males and 44% of females used a condom in their most recent sexual encounter.

Median Number of Opposite-Sex Partners in Past Year

Source: National Center for Health Statistics,
Sexual Behavior and Selected Health Measures, 2002
Note: U.S. males and females 15-44 years of age.

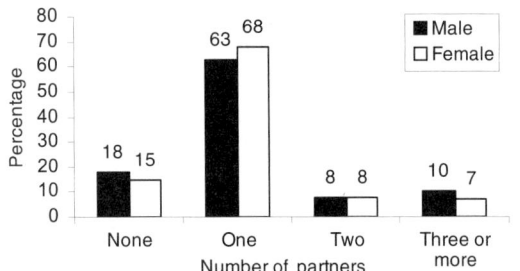

Median Number of Opposite-Sex Partners in Lifetime

Source: National Center for Health Statistics,
Sexual Behavior and Selected Health Measures, 2002

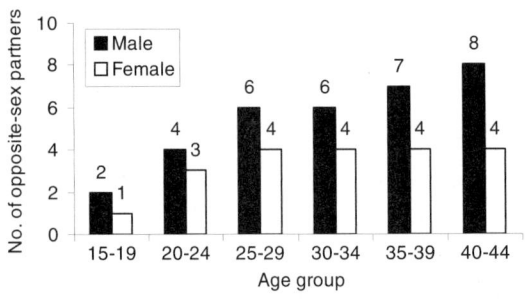

Lifetime and Median Number of Sexual Partners, by Age and Race, 2002

Source: National Center for Health Statistics, Sexual Behavior and Selected Health Measures, 2002

	Number of opposite-sex partners in lifetime, % distrib.						Median no.[1]		Number of opposite-sex partners in lifetime, % distrib.						Median no.[1]
	0	1	2	3-6	7-14	15+			0	1	2	3-6	7-14	15+	
Males 15-44 years[2]	9.6	12.5	8.0	27.2	19.5	23.2	5.6	**Females 15-44 years[2]**	8.6	22.5	10.8	32.6	16.3	9.2	3.3
Age								**Age**							
15-19	43.5	23.4	9.0	17.0	4.9	2.3	1.6	15-19	37.8	27.2	9.0	19.1	5.0	1.9	1.4
20-24	9.9	15.7	11.6	33.1	13.9	15.8	3.8	20-24	8.9	24.6	13.0	32.2	14.4	6.9	2.8
25-44	2.9	9.5	6.9	27.7	23.7	29.2	6.7	25-44	1.7	20.9	10.7	36.0	19.4	11.4	3.8
Race								**Race**							
White, non-Hispanic . .	9.8	13.4	8.3	27.0	19.2	22.3	5.3	White, non-Hispanic . .	7.8	21.0	10.6	32.1	18.2	10.2	3.6
Black, non-Hispanic . .	8.6	5.8	5.9	24.0	22.1	33.7	8.3	Black, non-Hispanic . .	7.7	12.4	8.4	44.8	18.0	8.8	4.1
Hispanic or Latino. . . .	9.1	13.5	8.5	32.5	18.4	17.9	4.5	Hispanic or Latina . . .	10.5	34.6	14.9	27.2	8.2	4.6	1.7

(1) Excludes people who have never had intercourse with an opposite-sex partner. (2) Includes people of other or multiple race and origin groups, not shown separately.

Sexual Activity of High School Students, 2007

Source: CDC, *Youth Risk Behavior Surveillance—United States, 2007*

	Ever had sexual intercourse			First sexual intercourse before age 13			Currently sexually active[1]			Condom use[2]		
	Female	Male	Total	Female	Male	Total	Female	Male	Total	Female	Male	Total
Race/Ethnicity												
White[3]	43.7%	43.6%	43.7%	3.1%	5.7%	4.4%	35.1%	30.6%	32.9%	53.9%	66.4%	59.7%
Black[3]	60.9	72.6	66.5	6.9	26.2	16.3	43.5	48.7	46.0	60.1	74.0	67.3
Hispanic	45.8	58.2	52.0	4.5	11.9	8.2	35.3	39.6	37.4	52.1	69.9	61.4
Grade												
9	27.4	38.1	32.8	4.9	13.5	9.2	18.0	22.2	20.1	61.0	75.8	69.3
10	41.9	45.6	43.8	4.7	9.1	6.9	31.8	29.4	30.6	59.5	73.2	66.1
11	53.6	57.3	55.5	3.4	9.9	6.6	41.5	42.0	41.8	55.1	69.3	62.0
12	66.2	62.8	64.6	2.4	6.7	4.5	56.7	48.3	52.6	49.9	59.6	54.2
Total	45.9	49.8	47.8	4.0	10.1	7.1	35.6	34.3	35.0	54.9	68.5	61.5

(1) Sexual intercourse during the 3 months preceding the survey. (2) Among the 35.0% who were sexually active. (3) Non-Hispanic.

Sexual Activity of Older Adults

Source: National Social Life, Health, and Aging Project at the Univ. of Chicago

		% sexually active with a partner		% reporting sexual behavior			% reporting sexual problem[1]				
Sex	Age	In prev. 12 mo.	2-3+ times per mo.[1]	Inter-course[1]	Oral sex[1]	Mastur-bation[2]	Lack of interest	Stimulation problems	No Pleasure	Anxiety	Pain
Men	57-64	83.7%	67.5%	91.1%	62.1%	63.4%	28.2%	30.7%	3.8%	25.1%	3.0%
	65-74	67.0	65.4	78.5	47.9	53.0	28.5	44.6	7.0	28.9	3.2
	75-85	38.5	54.2	83.5	28.3	27.9	24.2	43.5	5.1	29.3	1.0
Women	57-64	61.6	62.6	86.8	52.7	31.6	44.2	35.9	24.0	10.4	17.8
	65-74	39.5	65.4	85.4	46.5	21.9	38.4	43.2	22.0	12.5	18.6
	75-85	16.7	54.1	74.4	35.0	16.4	49.3	43.6	24.9	9.9	11.8

Note: Based on in-home interviews of 3,005 U.S. adults (1,550 women and 1,455 men) between July 2005 and Mar. 2006. (1) If reported having sex in prev. 12 months. (2) In prev. 12 months asked of all respondents by questionnaire.

U.S. Fires, 2008

Source: National Fire Protection Assn.

Fires

- Public fire departments responded to 1,451,500 fires in 2008, a 6.8% decrease from 2007. Every 22 seconds, a fire department responds to a fire somewhere in the United States.
- There were 515,000 structure fires in 2008, a decrease of 2.9% from 2007. 78% of them (403,000 fires) occurred in homes.
- Fires in vehicles dropped 8.5% from the previous year, totaling 236,000 in 2008.
- There were 700,500 fires in outside properties, a decrease of 8.9% from 2007.

Civilian deaths

- There were an estimated 3,320 civilian fire deaths in 2008. This was a 3.2% increase from the year before.
- The number of civilian fire deaths that occurred in home structure fires decreased 3.8% to 2,755, and fires in the home caused 83% of all fire deaths.
- Fires caused an average of one civilian death every 158 minutes.

Civilian injuries

- There were an estimated 16,705 civilian fire injuries reported in 2008, a 5.5% drop from 2007. Nationwide, a civilian was injured in a fire every 31 minutes.

- Home structure fires were the site of 13,560 civilian fire injuries in 2008, and non-home structure fires accounted for 1,400 civilian injuries.

Property damage

- Direct property damage from fires amounted to an estimated $15.5 bil in 2008, an increase of 5.7% from 2007. Structure fires accounted for $12.3 billion of property damage.
- Property loss associated with home fires came to $8.6 bil for 2008.

Intentionally set fires

- There were an estimated 30,500 intentionally set structure fires in 2008, a decrease of 6.2% from 2007.
- Intentionally set structure fires are believed to have resulted in 315 civilian deaths in 2008, an increase of 6.8% from the year before. Property damage from intentionally set structure fires totaled $866 mil, an increase of 18.2% from the 2007 figure.
- The number of intentionally set vehicle fires in 2008 was 17,500, about the same amount as the previous year. Intentionally set vehicle fires caused an estimated $139 mil in property damage, a decrease of 4.1% from 2007.

U.S. Motor Vehicle Accidents, 2006

Sources: National Safety Council; Natl. Highway Traffic Safety Admin.

A total of 42,642 people in the U.S. were killed in motor vehicle accidents in 2006, according to figures from the National Safety Council, down 2% from the total for 2005. As the number of drivers (202.8 million) and vehicle miles driven (3 trillion) increased in 2006, the death rate per 100 million vehicle miles decreased 5.6% to 1.41.

Motor vehicle deaths per 10,000 registered vehicles dropped from 1.8 in 2005 to 1.7 in 2006, and are down from 2.1 in 1996, a decrease of 11% over 10 years. This rate has declined in most years since the introduction of the automobile. The rate of fatalities per 100,000 population declined 11% from 1996 to 2006, and 3% from 2005 to 2006.

The split between male and female licensed drivers was basically 50-50. Male drivers were involved in about 6.1 mil accidents, whereas female drivers were in 4.4 mil. Male drivers were also involved in 73% of fatal accidents, about 42,000, compared with 15,000 female drivers.

In 2006, 13,470 traffic fatalities, or 32%, involved an intoxicated (blood alcohol concentration of 0.08 or greater) driver or motorcycle operator, a decline of 0.5% from 2005. In cases where a driver or nonoccupant drank at all, traffic fatalities totaled 17,602 people, or 41%. Alcohol factored in about 9% of all traffic accidents.

Seat belt use was 82% in 2007. In 2006, safety belts and child restraints saved an estimated 15,808 lives. Another 2,796 lives were saved by air bags. Women used safety belts more often, 86%, than men, 79%. The least likely safety belt users were rural drivers, 78%, and drivers of pickup trucks, 72%.

	Deaths	Injuries
All motor vehicle accidents	42,642	2,575,000
Collision between motor vehicles	14,718	1,189,000
Rear end collision.	2,102	503,000
Collision with fixed object	12,607	316,000
Pedestrian accidents	4,424	54,000
Noncollision accidents (e.g., rollovers) . . .	4,861	93,000
Collision with pedal cycle	756	43,000
Collision with parked motor vehicle	412	29,000
Collision with railroad train	210	1,000
Collision with animal	204	15,000

Note: NSC numbers are rounded. NHTSA intoxication data is final.

Improper Driving Reported in Accidents, 2000, 2002, 2006

Source: National Safety Council

	Percentage of fatal accidents			Percentage of injury accidents			Percentage of all accidents		
Type	2006	2002	2000	2006	2002	2000	2006	2002	2000
Improper driving	65.1%	59.5%	61.6%	65.8%	54.7%	60.3%	62.6%	50.3%	57.8%
Speed too fast or unsafe.	19.6	21.9	18.6	15.1	12.6	16.3	12.9	10.1	13.6
Right of way	11.4	17.4	10.1	17.3	18.9	19.9	14.4	16.4	20.1
Failed to yield	7.5	10.1	4.6	12.4	14.3	15.0	10.9	11.4	12.7
Disregarded signal	1.9	4.0	8.2	3.0	3.3	1.3	2.1	3.4	2.2
Passed stop sign	2.0	3.3	3.8	1.9	1.3	3.6	1.4	1.6	5.3
Drove left of center	7.8	5.7	0.7	1.9	0.9	1.1	1.6	0.7	1.0
Improper overtaking	1.5	1.0	0.9	0.7	0.5	2.0	0.8	0.8	2.4
Made improper turn.	3.8	0.5	0.7	4.3	1.2	0.6	4.6	1.7	0.9
Followed too closely	0.9	0.4	0.9	7.3	2.8	4.3	9.0	3.8	5.7
Other improper driving	20.1	12.5	9.0	19.2	17.9	16.1	19.3	16.8	14.1
No improper driving stated	34.9	40.5	38.4	34.2	45.3	39.7	37.4	49.7	42.2

Note: Based on reports from state traffic authorities. When a driver was under the influence of alcohol or drugs, the accident was considered a result of the driver's physical condition—not a driving error. For this reason, accidents in which the driver was reported to be under the influence are included under "no improper driving stated."

Risk Behaviors in High School Students, 2007

Source: CDC, *Youth Risk Behavior Surveillance—United States, 2007*

		Percent rarely or never wear seat belts[1]			Percent rarely or never wear bicycle helmets[2]			Percent who rode with a driver who had been drinking alcohol[3]		
		Female	Male	Total	Female	Male	Total	Female	Male	Total
Race	Non-Hispanic white	7.3%	13.0%	10.1%	79.5%	85.6%	82.9%	28.0%	27.8%	27.9%
	Non-Hispanic black	10.0	14.7	12.4	93.0	95.0	94.2	26.9	28.1	27.4
	Hispanic.	11.4	14.3	12.9	86.6	90.3	88.7	35.1	36.0	35.5
Grade	9	9.2	15.1	12.3	80.1	86.4	83.7	27.6	27.6	27.6
	10	8.3	13.2	10.8	83.0	88.1	85.9	30.4	27.1	28.7
	11	8.9	12.2	10.6	83.0	88.1	85.9	26.8	31.4	29.2
	12	7.3	13.8	10.5	83.8	86.9	85.5	30.5	32.5	31.5
Total		8.5	13.6	11.1	82.2	87.4	85.1	28.8	29.5	29.1

(1) When riding in a car or truck driven by someone else. (2) Among the 62.3% of students who rode bicycles during the 12 months preceding the survey. (3) In a car or truck one or more times during the 30 days preceding the survey.

Death Rates[1] for Suicide at Selected Ages, 1960, 1980, 2000, 2005

Source: *Health, United States, 2007*, National Center for Health Statistics, U.S. Dept. of Health and Human Services

	2005			2000			1980			1960		
Age	Both sexes	Male	Female	Both sexes	Male	Female	Both sexes	Male	Female	Both sexes	Male	Female
15-24.	10.0	16.2	3.5	10.2	17.1	3.0	12.3	20.2	4.3	5.2	8.2	2.2
25-44.	13.7	21.6	5.8	13.4	21.3	5.4	15.6	24.0	7.7	12.2	17.9	6.6
45-64.	15.4	24.0	7.2	13.5	21.3	6.2	15.9	23.7	8.9	22.0	34.4	10.2
65 and older	14.7	29.5	4.0	15.2	31.1	4.0	17.6	35.0	6.1	24.5	44.0	8.4
All ages	10.9	18.0	4.4	10.4	17.7	4.0	12.2	19.9	5.7	12.5	20.0	5.6

(1) Per 100,000 population.

Leading Causes of Death in the U.S., 2006

Source: National Center for Health Statistics, U.S. Dept. of Health and Human Services

	Number	% of total deaths	Death rate[1]		Number	% of total deaths	Death rate[1]
All causes	2,426,264	100.0%	810.4	9. Kidney disease.	45,344	1.9%	15.1
1. Diseases of heart.	631,636	26.0	211.0	10. Septicemia	34,234	1.4	11.4
2. Cancer.	559,888	23.1	187.0	11. Intentional self-harm (suicide) . . .	33,300	1.4	11.1
3. Stroke.	137,119	5.7	45.8	12. Chronic liver disease and cirrhosis	27,555	1.1	9.2
4. Chronic lower respiratory diseases	124,583	5.1	41.6	13. Hypertension and hypertensive			
5. Accidents (unintentional injuries) .	121,599	5.0	40.6	renal disease	23,855	1.0	8.0
6. Diabetes.	72,449	3.0	24.2	14. Parkinson's disease	19,566	0.8	6.5
7. Alzheimer's disease.	72,432	3.0	24.2	15. Assault (homicide)	18,573	0.8	6.2
8. Influenza and pneumonia.	56,326	2.3	18.8	All other causes (residual).	447,805	18.5	149.6

(1) Per 100,000 population.

Principal Types of Accidental Deaths in the U.S., 1970-2006

Source: National Safety Council

Year	Total	Motor vehicle	Falls	Poisoning	Drowning	Fires, flames, smoke	Suffocation: ingestion of food, object	Firearms	Mechanical suffocation
1970	NA	54,633	16,926	5,299	7,860	6,718	2,753	2,406	NA
1980	105,718	53,172	13,294	4,331	7,257	5,822	3,249	1,955	NA
1985	93,457	45,901	12,001	5,170	5,316	4,938	3,551	1,649	NA
1990	91,983	46,814	12,313	5,803	4,685	4,175	3,303	1,416	NA
1992	86,777	40,982	12,646	7,082	3,542	3,958	3,182	1,409	NA
1993	90,437	41,893	13,141	8,537	3,807	3,900	3,160	1,521	NA
1994	91,437	42,524	13,450	8,994	3,942	3,986	3,065	1,356	NA
1995	93,320	43,363	13,986	9,072	4,350	3,761	3,185	1,225	NA
1996	94,948	43,649	14,986	9,510	3,959	3,741	3,206	1,134	NA
1997	95,644	43,458	15,447	10,163	4,051	3,490	3,275	981	NA
1998	97,835	43,501	16,274	10,801	4,406	3,255	3,515	866	NA
1999[1]	97,860	42,401	13,162	12,186	3,529	3,348	3,885	824	1,618
2000	97,900	43,354	13,322	12,757	3,482	3,377	4,313	776	1,335
2001	101,537	43,788	15,019	14,078	3,281	3,309	4,185	802	1,370
2002	106,742	45,380	16,257	18,550	3,447	3,159	4,128	762	1,389
2003	109,277	44,757	17,229	19,457	3,306	3,369	4,272	730	1,309
2004[2]	112,012	44,933	18,807	20,950	3,308	3,229	4,470	649	1,421
2005[2]	118,000	45,500	20,800	23,200	3,600	2,700	4,900	630	1,300
2006[3]	120,000	44,700	21,200	25,300	3,800	2,800	4,100	680	1,100
Death rates per 100,000 population									
1970	NA	26.8	8.3	2.6	3.9	3.3	1.4	1.2	NA
1980	47.8	23.4	5.9	1.9	3.2	2.6	1.4	0.9	NA
1985	39.3	19.3	5.0	2.2	2.2	2.1	1.5	0.7	NA
1990	36.9	18.8	4.9	2.3	1.9	1.7	1.3	0.6	NA
1992	34.0	16.1	5.0	2.7	1.4	1.6	1.2	0.6	NA
1993	35.1	16.3	5.1	3.4	1.5	1.5	1.2	0.6	NA
1994	35.1	16.3	5.2	3.5	1.5	1.5	1.2	0.5	NA
1995	35.5	16.5	5.3	3.4	1.7	1.4	1.2	0.5	NA
1996	35.8	16.5	5.6	3.5	1.5	1.4	1.2	0.4	NA
1997	35.7	16.2	5.8	3.8	1.5	1.3	1.2	0.4	NA
1998	36.2	16.1	6.0	4.0	1.6	1.2	1.3	0.3	NA
1999[1]	35.9	15.5	4.8	4.5	1.3	1.2	1.4	0.3	0.6
2000	35.6	15.7	4.8	4.6	1.3	1.2	1.6	0.3	0.5
2001	35.6	15.4	5.3	4.9	1.2	1.2	1.5	0.3	0.5
2002	37.1	15.8	5.6	6.4	1.2	1.1	1.4	0.3	0.5
2003	37.6	15.4	5.9	6.7	1.1	1.2	1.5	0.3	0.4
2004[2]	38.1	15.3	6.4	7.1	1.1	1.1	1.5	0.2	0.5
2005[2]	39.8	15.3	7.0	7.8	1.2	0.9	1.7	0.2	0.4
2006[3]	40.1	14.9	7.1	8.5	1.3	0.9	1.4	0.2	0.4

NA = Not available. **Note:** There were 16,320 other accidental deaths in 2006. All figures include on-the-job deaths. (1) Data for 1999 and later not comparable with earlier data because of classification changes. (2) Revised data.

Worldwide Airline Fatalities, 1987-2007[1]

Source: National Safety Council

Year	Aircraft accidents[2]	Passenger deaths	Death rate[3]	Year	Aircraft accidents[2]	Passenger deaths	Death rate[3]
1987	25	900	0.06	1998	20	904	0.03
1988	29	742	0.04	1999	21	499	0.02
1989	29	879	0.05	2000	18	757	0.03
1990	27	544	0.03	2001	13	577	0.02
1991	29	638	0.03	2002	13	791	0.03
1992	28	1,070	0.06	2003	7	466	0.02
1993	33	864	0.04	2004	9	203	0.01
1994	27	1,170	0.05	2005	17	712	0.02
1995	25	711	0.03	2006	23	755	0.02
1996	24	1,146	0.05	2007	11	587	0.01
1997	25	921	0.04				

(1) Excluding accidents due to acts of unlawful interference. (2) Involving 1 or more passenger fatalities and an aircraft with a maximum takeoff mass greater than 2,250 kg. (3) Passenger deaths per 100 mil passenger kilometers.

Deaths in the U.S. Involving Firearms, by Age and Sex, 2004

Source: National Safety Council

	All ages	Under 5	5-14	15-19	20-24	25-44	45-64	65-74	75 & over
Total firearms deaths	**29,625**	**58**	**300**	**2,499**	**4,053**	**11,044**	**7,450**	**1,887**	**2,334**
Male	25,546	31	231	2,206	3,700	9,463	6,127	1,665	2,123
Female	4,079	27	69	293	353	1,581	1,323	222	211
Unintentional	651	15	48	81	92	198	141	40	36
Male	575	11	40	75	86	180	119	33	31
Female	76	4	8	6	6	18	22	7	5
Suicide	16,756	—	59	787	1,318	5,155	5,677	1,631	2,129
Male	14,529	—	50	688	1,202	4,358	4,755	1,475	2,001
Female	2,227	—	9	99	116	797	922	156	128
Homicide	11,672	42	184	1,582	2,555	5,430	1,533	195	151
Male	9,961	20	134	1,399	2,328	4,693	1,171	140	76
Female	1,711	22	50	183	227	737	362	55	75
Legal Intervention	311	0	0	27	52	172	50	5	5
Male	302	0	0	26	52	169	46	4	5
Female	9	0	0	1	0	3	4	1	0
Undetermined[1]	235	1	9	22	36	89	49	16	13
Male	179	0	7	18	32	63	36	13	10
Female	56	1	2	4	4	26	13	3	3

Note: There were 29,625 firearms deaths in 2004. (1) "Undetermined" means that the intention involved (whether accident, suicide, or homicide) could not be determined.

U.S. Infant Mortality Rates, by Race and Sex, 1960-2006[1]

Source: National Center for Health Statistics, U.S. Dept. of Health and Human Services

Year	ALL RACES Total	Male	Female	WHITE Total	Male	Female	BLACK Total	Male	Female
1960	26.0	29.3	22.6	22.9	26.0	19.6	44.3	49.1	39.4
1970	20.0	22.4	17.5	17.8	20.0	15.4	32.6	36.2	29.0
1980	12.6	13.9	11.2	11.0	12.3	9.6	21.4	23.3	19.4
1985	10.6	11.9	9.3	9.3	10.6	8.0	18.2	19.9	16.5
1989	9.8	10.8	8.8	8.1	9.0	7.1	18.6	20.0	17.2
1990	9.2	10.3	8.1	7.6	8.5	6.6	18.0	19.6	16.2
1991	8.9	10.0	7.8	7.3	8.3	6.3	17.6	19.4	15.7
1992	8.5	9.4	7.6	6.9	7.7	6.1	16.8	18.4	15.3
1993	8.4	9.3	7.4	6.8	7.6	6.0	16.5	18.3	14.7
1994	8.0	8.8	7.2	6.6	7.2	5.9	15.8	17.5	14.1
1995	7.6	8.3	6.8	6.3	7.0	5.6	15.1	16.3	13.9
1996	7.3	8.0	6.6	6.1	6.7	5.4	14.7	16.0	13.3
1997	7.2	8.0	6.5	6.0	6.7	5.4	14.2	15.5	12.8
1998	7.2	7.8	6.5	6.0	6.5	5.4	14.3	15.7	12.8
1999	7.1	7.7	6.4	5.8	6.4	5.2	14.6	15.9	13.2
2000	6.9	7.6	6.2	5.7	6.2	5.1	14.1	15.5	12.6
2001	6.8	7.5	6.1	5.7	6.2	5.1	14.0	15.5	12.5
2002	7.0	7.6	6.3	5.8	6.4	5.1	14.4	15.4	13.3
2003	6.9	7.6	6.1	5.7	6.3	5.0	14.0	15.5	12.4
2004	6.8	7.5	6.1	5.7	6.2	5.1	13.8	15.2	12.3
2005	6.9	7.6	6.2	5.7	6.3	5.1	13.7	15.2	12.3
2006	6.7	7.3	6.0	5.6	6.1	5.0	13.3	14.4	12.2

(1) Rates per 1,000 live births in specified group.

Years of Life Expected at Birth in U.S., 1900-2006

Source: National Center for Health Statistics, U.S. Dept. of Health and Human Services

Year[1]	ALL RACES Total	Male	Female	WHITE Total	Male	Female	BLACK Total	Male	Female
1900	47.3	46.3	48.3	47.6	46.6	48.7	NA	NA	NA
1910	50.0	48.4	51.8	50.3	48.6	52.0	NA	NA	NA
1920	54.1	53.6	54.6	54.9	54.4	55.6	NA	NA	NA
1930	59.7	58.1	61.6	61.4	59.7	63.5	NA	NA	NA
1940	62.9	60.8	65.2	64.2	62.1	66.6	NA	NA	NA
1950	68.2	65.6	71.1	69.1	66.5	72.2	NA	NA	NA
1960	69.7	66.6	73.1	70.6	67.4	74.1	NA	NA	NA
1970	70.8	67.1	74.7	71.7	68.0	75.6	64.1	60.0	68.3
1975	72.6	68.8	76.6	73.4	69.5	77.3	68.8	62.4	71.3
1980	73.7	70.0	77.5	74.4	70.7	78.1	68.1	63.8	72.5
1985	74.7	71.2	78.2	75.3	71.9	78.7	69.3	65.0	73.4
1990	75.4	71.8	78.8	76.1	72.7	79.4	69.1	64.5	73.6
1992	75.5	72.1	78.9	76.4	73.0	79.5	69.6	65.0	73.9
1993	75.5	72.1	78.9	76.3	73.0	79.5	69.2	64.6	73.7
1994	75.7	72.4	79.0	76.5	73.3	79.6	69.5	64.9	73.9
1995	75.8	72.5	78.9	76.5	73.4	79.6	69.6	65.2	73.9
1996	76.1	73.1	79.1	76.8	73.9	79.7	70.2	66.1	74.2
1997	76.5	73.6	79.4	77.1	74.3	79.9	71.1	67.2	74.7
1998	76.7	73.8	79.5	77.3	74.5	80.0	71.3	67.6	74.8
1999	76.7	73.9	79.4	77.3	74.6	79.9	71.4	67.8	74.7
2000	76.8	74.1	79.3	77.3	74.7	79.9	71.8	68.2	75.1
2001	76.9	74.2	79.4	77.4	74.8	79.9	72.0	68.4	75.2
2002	76.9	74.3	79.5	77.4	74.9	79.9	72.1	68.6	75.4
2003	77.1	74.5	79.6	77.6	75.0	80.0	72.3	68.8	75.6
2004	77.5	74.9	79.9	77.9	75.4	80.4	72.8	69.3	76.0
2005	77.4	74.9	79.9	77.9	75.4	80.4	72.8	69.3	76.1
2006	77.7	75.1	80.2	78.2	75.7	80.6	73.2	69.7	76.5

NA = Not available. (1) Data prior to 1940 for death-registration states only.

U.S. Life Expectancy at Selected Ages, 2006

Source: National Center for Health Statistics, U.S. Dept. of Health and Human Services

Exact age in years	ALL RACES[1] Both sexes	Male	Female	WHITE Both sexes	Male	Female	BLACK Both sexes	Male	Female
0	77.7	75.1	80.2	78.2	75.7	80.6	73.2	69.7	76.5
1	77.2	74.7	79.7	77.6	75.1	80.0	73.2	69.7	76.5
5	73.3	70.8	75.8	73.7	71.2	76.1	69.4	65.8	72.6
10	68.4	65.8	70.8	68.7	66.3	71.1	64.4	60.9	67.7
15	63.4	60.9	65.9	63.8	61.3	66.1	59.5	56.0	62.7
20	58.6	56.1	61.0	59.0	56.6	61.3	54.7	51.3	57.8
25	53.9	51.5	56.1	54.2	51.9	56.4	50.1	46.8	53.0
30	49.2	46.9	51.3	49.5	47.3	51.5	45.5	42.4	48.2
35	44.4	42.2	46.4	44.7	42.6	46.7	40.9	37.9	43.5
40	39.7	37.6	41.7	40.0	37.9	41.9	36.4	33.5	38.9
45	35.2	33.1	37.0	35.4	33.4	37.2	32.0	29.2	34.5
50	30.7	28.8	32.5	30.9	29.0	32.6	27.9	25.2	30.2
55	26.5	24.7	28.0	26.6	24.9	28.2	24.1	21.6	26.1
60	22.4	20.7	23.8	22.5	20.9	23.8	20.4	18.2	22.2
65	18.5	17.0	19.7	18.6	17.1	19.8	17.1	15.1	18.6
70	14.9	13.6	15.9	14.9	13.6	15.9	13.9	12.3	15.1
75	11.6	10.5	12.3	11.5	10.5	12.3	11.1	9.8	12.0
80	8.7	7.8	9.3	8.7	7.8	9.3	8.7	7.7	9.3
85	6.4	5.7	6.8	6.3	5.7	6.7	6.7	5.9	7.1
90	4.6	4.1	4.8	4.5	4.0	4.7	5.1	4.5	5.3
95	3.2	2.9	3.3	3.2	2.8	3.3	3.8	3.5	3.9
100	2.3	2.0	2.3	2.2	2.0	2.2	2.8	2.6	2.8

(1) Includes races other than white and black.

NOTED PERSONALITIES

Widely Known Americans of the Present

Political leaders, journalists, other prominent living persons. As of Oct. 2009. Excludes most who fall in categories listed elsewhere in Noted Personalities, such as Writers of the Present and Entertainment Personalities of the Present, or in Sports Personalities. Includes some figures active in American life but not U.S. citizens.

Jack Abramoff, b 2/28/58 (Atlantic City, NJ), former lobbyist; convicted in 2006 of crimes including bribing public officials.

Roger Ailes, b 5/15/40 (Warren, OH), TV exec.

Madeleine K. Albright, b 5/15/37 (Prague, Czech.), former sec. of state.

Edwin "Buzz" Aldrin, b 1/20/30 (Montclair, NJ), former astronaut; 2nd person to walk on the Moon.

Samuel A. Alito Jr., b 4/1/50 (Trenton, NJ), Supreme Court justice.

Paul Allen, b 1/21/53 (Mercer Is., WA), co-founder of Microsoft.

Christiane Amanpour, b 1/12/58 (London, Eng.), TV journalist.

Richard K. Armey, b 7/7/40 (Cando, ND), former U.S. rep. (TX), House majority leader.

Neil Armstrong, b 8/5/30 (Wapakoneta, OH), former astronaut, 1st person to walk on the Moon.

John Ashcroft, b 5/9/42 (Chicago, IL), former MO gov., attorney gen.

David Axelrod, b 1955 (NYC), sr. advisor to Pres. Obama, political strategist.

F. Lee Bailey, b 6/10/33 (Waltham, MA), attorney.

Russell Baker, b 8/14/25 (Loudoun Co., VA), columnist.

Haley Barbour, b 10/22/47 (Yazoo City, MS), MS governor.

Bob Barr, b 11/5/48 (Iowa City, IA), former U.S. rep. (GA), 2008 Libertarian presid. nominee.

Dave Barry, b 7/3/47 (Armonk, NY), humorist.

Marion Barry, b 3/6/36 (Itta Bena, MS), former Wash., DC, mayor; DC city council member.

Max Baucus, b 12/11/41 (Helena, MT), senator (MT), Finance commitee chair.

Gary Bauer, b 5/4/46 (Covington, KY), domestic policy advisor to Pres. Reagan; founder, Campaign for Working Families.

William Bennett, b 7/31/43 (Brooklyn, NY), author, former education secretary.

Chris Berman, b 5/10/55 (Greenwich, CT), sportscaster.

Ben Bernanke, b 12/13/53 (Augusta, GA), Federal Reserve Chairman.

Carl Bernstein, b 2/14/44 (Washington, DC), journalist; with Woodward cracked Watergate scandal.

Jeff Bezos, b 1/12/64 (Albuquerque, NM), founder and CEO of Amazon.com.

Jill Biden, b 6/5/51 (Hammonton, NJ), English college professor, wife of vice pres. Joe Biden.

Joseph R. Biden Jr., b 11/20/42 (Scranton, PA), senator (DE), U.S. vice-president.

James H. Billington, b 6/1/29 (Bryn Mawr, PA), librarian of U.S. Congress.

Rod Blagojevich, b 12/10/56 (Chicago, IL), impeached IL governor.

Dennis Blair, b 2/4/47 (Kittery, ME), director of national intelligence.

Wolf Blitzer, b 3/22/48 (Buffalo, NY), TV journalist.

Harold Bloom, b 7/11/30 (New York City), literary critic.

Michael R. Bloomberg, b 2/14/42 (Medford, MA), NYC mayor; financial information/media entrepreneur.

Roy Blunt, b 1/10/50 (Niangua, MO), House minority whip.

John Boehner, b 11/17/49 (Cincinnati, OH), U.S. rep. (R, OH), House minority leader.

Julian Bond, b 1/14/40 (Nashville), civil rights leader; NAACP chairman.

Barbara Boxer, b 11/11/40 (Brooklyn, NY), senator (CA).

Bill Bradley, b 7/28/43 (Crystal City, MO), former senator (NJ), basketball player, presid. candidate.

James Brady, b 8/29/40 (Centralia, IL), former presid. press sec.; gun control advocate.

L. Paul Bremer III, b 9/30/41 (Hartford, CT), diplomat, former top U.S. civilian administrator in Iraq.

Jimmy Breslin, b 10/17/30 (Queens, NY), columnist, author.

Stephen Breyer, b 8/15/38 (San Francisco), Supreme Court justice.

Sergey Brin, b 3/26/73 (Moscow, Russia), co-founder of Google.

David Broder, b 9/11/29 (Chicago Heights, IL), journalist.

Tom Brokaw, b 2/6/40 (Webster, SD), TV journalist, retired NBC anchor.

David Brooks, b 8/11/61 (NYC), columnist, political commentator.

Joyce Brothers, b 10/20/28 (NYC), psychologist.

Aaron Brown, b 11/10/48 (Hopkins, MN), broadcast journalist.

Jerry (Edmund G.) Brown Jr., b 4/7/38 (San Francisco), atty. gen. (CA); former CA gov., pres. candidate.

Michael Brown, b 11/11/54 (Guymon, OK), former FEMA head, resigned under fire after Hurricane Katrina.

Pat Buchanan, b 11/2/38 (Washington, DC), journalist, former presid. candidate.

Warren Buffett, b 8/30/30 (Omaha, NE), investor, leading philanthropist.

Roland Burris, b 8/3/37 (Centralia, IL), senator (IL), first African American IL atty. gen.

Barbara Bush, b 6/8/25 (NYC), former first lady.

Barbara Bush, b 11/25/81 (Dallas, TX), daughter of former Pres. George W. Bush.

George H. W. Bush, b 6/12/24 (Milton, MA), former U.S.president.

George W. Bush, b 7/6/46 (New Haven, CT), former U.S. president.

Jeb Bush, b 2/11/53 (Midland, TX), former FL governor.

Jenna Bush Hager, b 11/25/81(Dallas, TX), daughter of former Pres. George W. Bush.

Laura Bush, b 11/4/46 (Midland, TX), former first lady.

Robert Byrd, b 11/20/17 (N. Wilkesboro, NC), senator (WV), former majority leader, President pro tempore.

Eric Cantor, b 6/6/63 (Richmond, VA), U.S. rep. (VA), House minority whip.

Andrew Card, b 5/10/47 (Brockton, MA), former White House chief of staff.

Tucker Carlson, b 5/16/69 (San Francisco), journalist, TV commentator.

Jimmy Carter, b 10/1/24 (Plains, GA), former U.S. president; won 2002 Nobel Peace Prize.

Rosalynn Carter, b 8/18/27 (GA), former first lady.

James Carville Jr., b 10/25/44 (Fort Benning, GA), TV political commentator.

Steve Case, b 8/21/58 (Honolulu, HI), former AOL Time Warner chairman.

Elaine Chao, b 3/26/53 (Taipei, Taiwan), former sec. of labor.

Julie Chen, b 1/6/70 (New York, NY), co-host of *The Early Show* and *Big Brother*.

Dick Cheney, b 1/30/41 (Lincoln, NE), former U.S. vice president.

Lynne Cheney, b 8/14/41 (Casper, WY), political commentator, wife of Dick Cheney.

Michael Chertoff, b 11/28/53 (Elizabeth, NJ), former sec. of homeland security.

Noam Chomsky, b 12/7/28 (Philadelphia), linguist; activist.

Steven Chu, b 2/28/48, (St. Louis, MO), energy secretary, atomic physicist.

Connie Chung, b 8/20/46 (Washington, DC), TV journalist.

Bill Clinton, b 8/19/46 (Hope, AR), former U.S. president.

Chelsea Clinton, b 2/27/80 (Little Rock, AR), daughter of former pres. Clinton and Sec. Hillary Rodham Clinton.

Hillary Rodham Clinton, b 10/26/47 (Chicago), sec. of state, former senator (NY), former first lady, 2008 presid. contender.

James Clyburn, b 7/21/40 (Sumter, SC), U.S. rep. (SC) House majority whip.

Anderson Cooper, b 6/3/67 (NYC), CNN anchor.

Jon Corzine, b 1/1/47 (Willey's Station, IL), NJ governor.

Bob Costas, b 3/22/52 (Queens, NY), TV sports journalist.

Ann Coulter, b 12/8/61 (New Canaan, CT), political commentator, author.

Katie Couric, b 1/7/57 (Arlington, VA), TV journalist; former NBC morning anchor; anchor of *CBS Evening News.*

Mark Cuban, b 7/31/58 (Pittsburgh, PA), entrepreneur, Dallas Mavericks owner.

Mario Cuomo, b 6/15/32 (Queens, NY), former NY governor.

Ann Curry, b 11/19/56 (Guam), news anchor on *Today* show.

Richard M. Daley, b 4/24/42 (Chicago), Chicago mayor.

John Danforth, b 9/5/36 (St, Louis, MO), former senator (MO); former ambassador to the UN.

Thomas Daschle, b 12/9/47 (Aberdeen, SD), former senator (SD) and Senate minority leader.

Howard Dean, b 11/17/48 (NYC), former VT gov., presid. contender; former Dem. Natl. Committee chair.

Oscar de la Renta, b 7/22/36 (Santo Domingo, Dominican Rep.), fashion designer.

Tom DeLay, b 4/8/47 (Laredo, TX), former U.S. rep. (TX), House Majority leader.

Michael Dell, b 2/23/65 (Houston, TX), founder, chairman, and CEO of Dell computers.

Alan Dershowitz, b 9/1/38 (Brooklyn, NY), attorney.

Barry Diller, b 2/2/42 (San Francisco), media exec.

Lou Dobbs, b 9/24/45 (Childress, TX), TV journalist.

Christopher Dodd, b 5/27/44 (Willimantic, CT), senator (CT), 2008 presid. contender.

James Dobson, b 4/21/36 (Shreveport, LA), evangelical Christian leader, chairman of Focus on the Family.

Elizabeth Hanford Dole, b 7/29/36 (Salisbury, NC), former senator (NC); former Red Cross pres., cabinet member.

Robert Dole, b 7/22/23 (Russell, KS), former Senate majority leader (KS), 1996 presid. nominee.

Sam Donaldson, b 3/11/34 (El Paso, TX), TV journalist.

Elizabeth Drew, b 11/16/35 (Cincinnati), journalist.

Matt Drudge, b 10/27/66 (Tacoma Park, MD), internet journalist.

Michael S. Dukakis, b 11/3/33 (Brookline, MA), former MA gov., presid. nominee.

Arne Duncan, b 11/6/64 (Chicago, IL), education secretary.

Dick Durbin, b 11/21/44 (East. St. Louis, IL), Senate majority whip (IL).

Bernard Ebbers, b 8/27/41 (Edmonton, Alberta, Can.), former WorldCom CEO, jailed for fraud.

Roger Ebert, b 6/18/42 (Urbana, IL), film critic.

Marian Wright Edelman, b 6/6/39 (Bennettsville, SC), pres. and founder of the Children's Defense Fund.

Elizabeth Edwards, b 7/3/49 (Jacksonville, FL), attorney, wife of John Edwards.

John Edwards, b 6/10/53 (Seneca, SC), former senator (NC); 2004 vice-presid. candidate; 2008 presid. contender.

Edward Egan, b 4/2/32 (Oak Park, IL), Rom. Cath. cardinal, archbishop emeritus of New York.

Michael Eisner, b 3/7/42 (Mt. Kisco, NY), former Disney Co. CEO.

Lawrence J. Ellison, b 8/17/44 (NYC), Oracle Corp. founder, CEO.

Rahm Emanuel, b 11/29/59 (Chicago, IL), White House Chief of Staff, former U.S. rep. (IL).

Louis Farrakhan, b 5/11/33 (Roxbury, MA), Nation of Islam leader.

Russell Feingold, b 3/2/53 (Janesville, WI), senator (WI).

Dianne Feinstein, b 6/22/33 (San Francisco), senator (CA).

Geraldine Ferraro, b 8/26/35 (Newburgh, NY), former U.S. rep. (NY), vice-presid. nominee.

Carleton S. (Carly) Fiorina, b 9/6/54 (Austin, TX), former CEO of Hewlett-Packard.

Larry Flynt, b 11/1/42 (Salyersville, KY), publisher.

Steve (Malcolm) Forbes Jr., b 7/18/47 (Morristown, NJ), publisher, former presid. contender.

Betty Ford, b 4/8/18 (Chicago), former first lady.

Al Franken, b 5/21/51 (NYC), senator (MN); humorist, political writer, radio host.

Barney Frank, b 3/31/40 (Bayonne, NJ), attorney, U.S. rep. (MA), chairman of House Financial Services Committee.

Thomas Friedman, b 7/20/53 (Minneapolis), columnist, author.

Bill Frist, b 8/19/42 (Nashville, TN), former Senate majority leader (TN); physician.

Bill Gates, b 10/28/55 (Seattle), software pioneer; Microsoft exec.

Henry Louis Gates Jr., b 9/16/50 (Keyser, WV), African American studies scholar.

Robert M. Gates, b 9/25/43 (Wichita, KS), sec. of defense.

David Geffen, b 2/21/43 (Brooklyn, NY), entertainment exec.

Timothy Geithner, b 8/18/61 (NYC), treasury secretary, former CEO Federal Reserve Bank of NY.

Louis Gerstner, b 3/1/42 (Mineola, NY), retired IBM exec.

Robert Gibbs, b 3/29/71 (Auburn, AL), White House press secretary.

Charles Gibson, b 3/4/43 (Evanston, IL), TV journalist; host of ABC's *World News*.

Kirsten Gillibrand, b 12/9/66 (Albany, NY), senator (NY); attorney.

Newt Gingrich, b 6/17/43 (Harrisburg, PA), former House Speaker (GA).

Ruth Bader Ginsburg, b 3/15/33 (Brooklyn, NY), Sup. Ct. justice.

Rudolph Giuliani, b 5/28/44 (Brooklyn, NY), 2008 presid. contender; former NYC mayor.

John Glenn, b 7/18/21 (Cambridge, OH), former senator (OH); astronaut.

Alberto Gonzales, b 8/4/55 (San Antonio, TX), former Attorney General.

Roger Goodell, b 2/19/59 (Jamestown, NY), NFL commissioner.

Ellen Goodman, b 4/11/41 (Newton, MA), columnist.

Doris Kearns Goodwin, b 1/4/43 (Rockville Centre, NY), historian, TV commentator.

Berry Gordy, b 11/28/29 (Detroit), Motown record label founder.

Al Gore Jr., b 3/31/48 (Washington, DC), former senator, U.S. vice president, 2000 presid. candidate; Nobel Peace Prize winner.

Tipper Gore, b 8/19/48 (Washington, DC), wife of Al Gore.

Porter Goss, b 11/26/38 (Waterbury, CT), former CIA director; former U.S. rep. (FL).

Rev. Billy Graham, b 11/7/18 (Charlotte, NC), evangelist.

(William) Franklin Graham III, b 7/14/52 (Asheville, NC), evangelist, son of Billy Graham.

Andrew Greeley, b 2/5/28 (Oak Park, IL), Rom. Cath. priest, sociologist, writer.

Jeff Greenfield, b 6/10/43 (NYC), TV journalist.

Alan Greenspan, b 3/6/26 (NYC), former Fed chairman.

Michael Griffin, b 11/1/49 (Aberdeen, MD), NASA head.

Bryant Gumbel, b 9/29/48 (New Orleans), TV journalist.

Greg Gumbel, b 5/3/46 (New Orleans), sportscaster.

Chuck Hagel, b 10/4/46 (North Platte, NE), U.S. senator (NE).

Pete Hamill, b 6/24/35 (Brooklyn, NY), journalist, author.

Lee Hamilton, b 4/20/31 (Daytona Beach, FL), 9/11 commission vice-chair; former U.S. rep. (IN).

Sean Hannity, b 12/30/61 (New York, NY), radio and TV host, author, political commentator.

J. Dennis Hastert, b 1/2/42 (Aurora, IL), former Speaker of the House (IL).

Orrin Hatch, b 3/22/34 (Homestead Park, PA), senator (UT).

Hugh Hefner, b 4/9/26 (Chicago), publisher.

Tommy Hilfiger, b 3/24/51 (Elmira, NY), fashion designer.

Anita Hill, b 7/30/56 (Morris, OK), legal scholar, complainant against Clarence Thomas.

Paris Hilton, b 2/17/81 (New York, NY), heiress, actress.

Christopher Hitchens, b 4/13/49 (Portsmouth, England), journalist, author.

James P. Hoffa, b 5/19/41, (Detroit), Teamsters Union head.

Richard Holbrooke, b 4/24/41 (Scarsdale, NY), spec. envoy to Afghanistan and Pakistan, former U.S. amb. to UN.

Eric Holder Jr., b 1/21/51 (NYC), first African American attorney general.

David Horowitz, b 1/10/39 (NYC), consumer advocate, columnist, author.

Steny H. Hoyer, b 6/14/39 (NYC), U.S. House majority leader (MD).

Mike Huckabee, b 8/24/55 (Hope, AR), former gov (AR), minister, 2008 presid. contender, TV host.

Arianna Huffington, b 7/15/50 (Athens, Greece), political commentator.

H. Wayne Huizenga, b 12/29/39 (Evergreen Park, IL), entrepreneur, sports exec.

Brit Hume, b 6/22/43 (Washington DC), TV journalist (FOX).

Kay Bailey Hutchison, b 7/22/43 (Galveston, TX), senator (TX).

Lee Iacocca, b 10/15/24 (Allentown, PA), former auto exec.

Carl Icahn, b 1936 (Queens, NY), financier.

Gwen Ifill, b 9/29/55 (Queens, NY), TV journalist, moderator (PBS).

Jeffrey Immelt, b 2/19/56 (Cincinnati, OH), General Electric CEO.

Don Imus, b 7/23/40 (Riverside, CA), talk-show host.

Patricia Ireland, b 10/19/45 (Oak Park, IL), feminist leader.

Rev. Jesse Jackson, b 10/8/41 (Greenville, SC), civil rights leader, former presid. contender.

Valerie Jarrett, b 11/14/56 (Shiraz, Iran), sr. advisor to Pres. Obama.

Bobby Jindal, b 6/10/71 (Baton Rouge, LA), LA governor, first elected Indian American governor.

Steve Jobs, b 2/24/55 (San Francisco), Apple Computer exec.; Pixar exec.

Jasper Johns, b 5/15/30 (Augusta, GA), artist.

Vernon E. Jordan Jr., b 8/15/35 (Atlanta, GA), attorney, former presid. adviser, civil rights leader.

Tim Kaine, b 2/26/58 (St. Paul, MN), chair of Democratic National Committee, VA governor.

Donna Karan, b 10/2/48 (Queens, NY), fashion designer.

Jeffrey Katzenberg, b 12/21/50 (NYC), entertainment exec.

Thomas Kean, b 4/21/35 (NYC), 9/11 commission chair, former Drew Univ. presid., former NJ gov.

Garrison Keillor, b 8/7/42 (Anoka, MN), author, broadcaster.

Anthony M. Kennedy, b 7/23/36 (Sacramento, CA), Supreme Court. justice.

Robert ("Bob") Kerrey, b 8/27/43 (Lincoln, NE), former senator (NE), president of the New School (NYC).

John Kerry, b 12/11/43 (Aurora, CO), senator (MA), foreign relations chair, 2004 presid. candidate.

Jack Kevorkian, b 5/26/28 (Pontiac, MI), physican, assisted-suicide activist.

Larry King, b 11/19/33 (Brooklyn, NY), TV talk show host.

Michael Kinsley, b 3/9/51 (Detroit), editor, pol. commentator.

Paul Kirk Jr., b 1/18/38 (Newton, MA), senator (D, MA), former Dem. Natl. Committee chair.

Henry Kissinger, b 5/27/23 (Fuerth, Germany), former sec. of state, nat. security adviser; won 1973 Nobel Peace Prize.

Calvin Klein, b 11/19/42 (Bronx, NY), fashion designer.

Philip H. Knight, b 2/24/38 (Portland, OR), founder and chairman of the board of Nike.

Edward I. Koch, b 12/12/24 (NYC), former NYC mayor.

Ted Koppel, b 2/8/40 (Lancashire, England), former ABC network TV journalist; former anchor of *Nightline*.

Larry Kramer, b 6/25/35 (Bridgeport, CT), AIDS activist, writer.

William Kristol, b 12/23/52 (NYC), editor, columnist.

Steve Kroft, b 8/22/45 (Kokomo, IN), TV journalist.

Dennis Kucinich, b 10/8/46 (Cleveland, OH), U.S. rep. (OH), presid. contender.

Brian Lamb, b 10/9/41 (Lafayette, IN), cable TV exec., journalist.

Matt Lauer, b 12/30/57 (NYC), TV journalist; NBC morning show.

Ralph Lauren, b 10/14/39 (Bronx, NY), fashion designer.

Bernard F. Law, b 11/4/31 (Torreon, Mexico), cardinal archbishop emeritus of Boston.

Patrick Leahy, b 3/31/40 (Montpelier, VT), senator (VT), Judiciary Committee chair.

Norman Lear, b 7/27/22 (New Haven, CT), TV producer, political activist.

Jim Lehrer, b 5/19/34 (Wichita, KS), TV journalist, author.

Carl Levin, b 6/28/34 (Detroit), senator (MI), Armed Services Committee chair.

Monica Lewinsky, b 7/23/73 (San Francisco), former White House intern.

Joseph Lieberman, b 2/24/42 (Stamford, CT), senator (CT), former vice presid. candidate; 2004 presid. contender.

Rush Limbaugh, b 1/12/51 (Cape Girardeau, MO), radio talk-show host.

Gary Locke, b 1/21/50 (Seattle, WA), commerce secretary, former WA gov.

Trent Lott, b 10/9/41 (Grenada, MS), senator (MS), former Senate minority whip.

Shannon Lucid, b 1/14/43 (Shanghai, China), NASA scientist, astronaut.

Richard Lugar, b 4/4/32 (Indianapolis), senator (IN).

Rachel Maddow, b 4/1/73 (Castro Valley, CA), TV and radio host, political commentator.

Bernie Madoff, b 4/29/38 (NYC), financier who swindled investors; sentenced to 150 years in prison.

Roger Mahony, b 2/27/36 (Hollywood, CA), Rom. Cath. cardinal, archbishop of Los Angeles.

Mary Matalin, b 8/19/53 (Chicago), political commentator.

Chris Matthews, b 12/18/45 (Philadelphia), TV journalist.

John McCain, b 8/29/36 (Panama Canal Zone), senator (AZ); 2008 Republican presidential candidate.

Mitch McConnell, b 2/20/42 (Tuscumbia, AL), senator (KY), Senate minority leader.

David McCullough, b 7/7/33 (Pittsburgh, PA), historian, biographer.

George McGovern, b 7/19/22 (Avon, SD), former senator (SD), 1972 presid. nominee.

Dr. Phil McGraw, b 9/1/50 (Vinita, OK), talk-show host, motivational speaker, author.

James McGreevey, b 8/6/57 (Jersey City, NY), former NJ governor; resigned amid allegations of sexual harassment and admitted he was gay.

John McLaughlin, b 3/29/27 (Providence, RI), TV journalist.

Russell Means, b 11/10/39 (Pine Ridge Indian Reserv., SD), Native American activist.

Kate Michelman, b 8/4/42 (NJ), abortion-rights activist.

Ken Mehlman, b 1967 (Baltimore, MD), former Republican National Comm. chair.

Kate Millett, b 9/14/34 (St. Paul, MN), author, feminist.

George Mitchell, b 8/20/33, (Waterville, ME), spec. envoy for Middle East peace, former Senate majority leader (ME); diplomat, Disney Co. chairman.

Walter Mondale, b 1/5/28 (Ceylon, MN), former vice pres., senator (MN), 1984 presid. nominee.

Michael Moore, b 4/23/54 (Davison, MI), activist, documentary filmmaker; author.

Bill Moyers, b 6/5/34 (Hugo, OK), TV journalist, author.

Robert S. Mueller III, b 8/7/44 (NYC), FBI director.

Michael Mullen, b 10/4/46 (Los Angeles, CA), chairman of Joint Chiefs of Staff.

Rupert Murdoch, b 3/11/31 (Melbourne, Aust.), media exec.

John Murtha, b 6/17/32 (New Martinsville, WV), U.S. rep. (PA); Vietnam War hero; outspoken critic of Iraq War.

Ralph Nader, b 2/27/34 (Winsted, CT), consumer advocate, independent presid. cand. in 1996, 2000, 2004, and 2008.

(Clarence) Ray Nagin, b 6/11/56 (New Orleans, LA), New Orleans mayor.

Janet Napolitano, b 11/29/57 (NYC), homeland security sec.; former AZ governor.

John Negroponte, b 7/21/39 (London, Eng.), former director of National Intelligence; former U.S. rep. to UN.

Craig Newmark, b 12/6/52 (Morristown, NY), founder of Craigslist.com.

Peggy Noonan, b 9/7/50 (Brooklyn, NY), columnist, speechwriter.

Oliver North, b 10/7/43 (San Antonio, TX), talk-show host, former Nat. Sec. Council aide, fig. in Iran-contra scandal.

Eleanor Holmes Norton, b 6/13/37 (Washington, DC), U.S. House delegate for Washington, DC.

Sam Nunn, b 9/8/38 (Perry, GA), former senator (GA).

Barack Obama, b 8/4/61 (Hawaii), U.S. President, former senator (IL).

Michelle Obama, b 1/17/64 (Chicago, IL), first lady, lawyer.

Soledad O'Brien, b 9/19/66 (Smithtown, NY), TV journalist.

Sandra Day O'Connor, b 3/26/30 (El Paso, TX), former Supreme Court justice.

Keith Olbermann, b 1/27/59 (New York, NY), TV news anchor and commentator, former ESPN host.

Paul O'Neill, b 12/4/35 (St. Louis, MO), former treasury sec.

Bill O'Reilly, b 9/10/49 (NYC), TV commentator, host.

Peter Orszag, b 12/16/68 (Boston, MA), dir., office of management and budget.

Joel Osteen, b 3/5/63 (Houston, TX), televangelist, author.

Michael Ovitz, b 12/14/46 (Encino, CA), entertainment exec.

Clarence Page, b 6/2/47 (Dayton, OH), journalist, TV commentator.

Lawrence Page, b 9/26/73 (East Lansing, MI), co-founder of Google.

Camille Paglia, b 4/2/47 (Endicott, NY), scholar, author.

Sarah Palin, b 2/11/64 (Sandpoint, ID), former AK governor, 2008 Republican vice presidential nominee.

Leon E. Panetta, b 6/28/38 (Monterey, CA), CIA director, former White House chief of staff, U.S. rep. (CA).

Richard Parsons, b 4/4/48 (NYC), chairman Citigroup, former Time Warner CEO.

George Pataki, b 6/24/45 (Peekskill, NY), former NY gov.

David Paterson, b 5/20/54 (Brooklyn, NY), attorney, first African American NY governor.

Ron Paul, b 8/20/35 (Pittsburgh, PA), physician, U.S. rep. (R, TX), 2008 presid. contender.

Jane Pauley, b 10/31/50 (Indianapolis), TV journalist.

Henry Paulson, b 3/28/46 (Palm Beach, FL), former sec. of treasury, former CEO/chairman of Goldman Sachs.

Nancy Pelosi, b 3/26/40 (Baltimore, MD), U.S. rep. (CA); Speaker of the House.

Ross Perot, b 6/27/30 (Texarkana, TX), entrepreneur, former presid. nominee.

David Petraeus, b 11/7/52 (Cornwall on Hudson, NY), U.S. Central Command cmdr.

Colin Powell, b 4/5/37 (NYC), former sec. of state, nat. security adviser, Joint Chiefs of Staff chairman.

Dan Quayle, b 2/4/47 (Indianapolis), former U.S. vice pres., senator (IN), presid. contender.

Anna Quindlen, b 7/8/53 (Philadelphia), author, columnist.

Dan Rather, b 10/31/31 (Wharton, TX), TV journalist, retired CBS anchor.

Nancy Reagan, b 7/6/21 (NYC), former first lady.

Sumner Redstone, b 5/27/23 (Boston), Viacom/CBS chairman.

Ralph Reed Jr., b 6/24/61 (Portsmouth, VA), political adviser.

Robert B. Reich, b 6/24/46 (Scranton, PA), economist, author, former labor sec.

Harry Reid, b 12/2/39 (Searchlight, NV), Senate majority leader (NV).

Janet Reno, b 7/21/38 (Miami, FL), former attorney gen.

Condoleezza Rice, b 11/14/54 (Birmingham, AL) former sec. of state, former nat. security advisor.

Susan Rice, b 11/17/64 (Washington, DC), U.S. Amb. to UN.

Bill Richardson, b 11/15/47 (Pasadena, CA), NM gov.; former energy sec., UN ambassador, U.S. Rep; 2008 presid. contender.

Sally K. Ride, b 5/26/51 (Encino, CA), former astronaut, 1st U.S. woman in space.

Tom (Thomas Joseph) Ridge, b 8/26/45 (Munhall, PA), former sec. of homeland security; former PA gov.

Geraldo Rivera, b 7/4/43 (NYC), TV journalist.

Cokie Roberts, b 12/27/43 (New Orleans), TV journalist.

John G. Roberts, b 1/27/55 (Buffalo, NY), Sup. Ct. chief justice.

Rev. Oral Roberts, b 1/24/18 (nr. Ada, OK), TV evangelist, educator.

Robin Roberts, b 11/23/60 (Tuskeegee, AL), co-anchor *Good Morning America*

Rev. Pat Robertson, b 3/22/30 (Lexington, VA), religious broadcasting exec, former presid. contender.

V. Gene Robinson, b 5/29/47 (Lexington, KY), first openly gay Episcopal bishop.

David Rockefeller, b 6/12/15 (NYC), banker.

John D. "Jay" Rockefeller 4th, b 6/18/37 (NYC), senator (WV), former WV gov.

Al Roker, b 8/20/54 (Queens, NY), TV weather person.

Mitt Romney, b 3/12/47 (Detroit), former MA gov, former Olympics organizer; 2008 pres. contender.

Andy Rooney, b 1/14/19 (Albany, NY), TV commentator.

Charlie Rose, b 1/5/42 (Henderson, NC), TV journalist.

Karl Rove, b 12/25/50 (Denver, CO), former White House senior domestic policy advisor.

Donald Rumsfeld, b 7/9/32 (Chicago), former Sec of Defense.

Morley Safer, b 11/8/31 (Toronto, Can.), TV journalist.

Ken Salazar, b 3/2/55 (Alamosa, CO), interior sec., former sen. (D, CO), rancher.

Diane Sawyer, b 12/22/45 (Glasgow, KY), TV journalist; ABC morning anchor.

Antonin Scalia, b 3/11/36 (Trenton, NJ), Sup. Ct. justice.

Bob Schieffer, b 2/25/37 (Austin, TX), CBS TV news anchor.

Phyllis Schlafly, b 8/15/24 (St. Louis, MO), political activist.

Caroline Kennedy Schlossberg, b 11/27/57 (NYC), author, daughter of Pres. Kennedy.

Patricia Schroeder, b 7/30/40 (Portland, OR), former U.S. rep (CO).

Rev. Robert Schuller, b 9/16/26 (Alton, IA), TV evangelist.

Charles Schumer, b 11/23/50 (Brooklyn, NY), senator (NY).

Arnold Schwarzenegger, b 7/30/47 (Thal, Styria, Austria), CA governor; former actor.

H. Norman Schwarzkopf, b 8/22/34 (Trenton, NJ), former military leader.

Willard Scott, b 3/7/34 (Alexandria, VA), former TV weather person.

Kathleen Sebelius, b 5/15/58 (Cincinnati, OH), health and human services secretary, former KS governor.

Allan H. ("Bud") Selig, b 7/30/34 (Milwaukee), MLB comm.

Richard Serra, b 11/2/39 (San Francisco), sculptor.

Eric Shinseki, b 11/28/42 (Lihue, HI), veterans affairs secretary, former Army chief of staff.

Rev. Al Sharpton, b 10/3/54 (Brooklyn, NYC), activist, civil rights leader; 2004 presid. contender.

Maria Shriver, b 11/6/55 (Chicago), TV journalist; CA first lady.

George P. Shultz, b 12/13/20 (NYC), former sec. of state; other cabinet posts.

Russell Simmons, b 10/4/57 (Queens, NY), music producer.

O. J. Simpson, b 7/9/47 (San Francisco), former football star, murder defendant.

Harry Smith, b 8/21/51 (Lansing, IL), TV journalist; CBS morning anchor.

Liz Smith, b 2/2/23 (Ft. Worth, TX), gossip columnist.

John Snow, b 8/2/39 (Toledo, OH), former treasury sec, former CSX CEO.

Hilda Solis, b 10/20/57 (Los Angeles, CA), labor sec., former U.S. rep. (CA).

George Soros, b 8/12/30 (Budapest, Hungary), financier, philanthropist.

Sonia Sotomayor, b 6/25/54 (Bronx, NY), Supreme Court justice.

David H. Souter, b 9/17/39 (Melrose, MA), former Supreme Court justice.

Arlen Specter, b 2/12/30 (Wichita, KS), senator (PA).

Margaret Spellings, b 11/30/57 (Michigan), former sec of education.

Steven Spielberg, b 12/18/46 (Cincinnati, OH), movie director, producer.

Ellot Spitzer, b 6/10/59 (Bronx, NY), former NY gov.; resigned after involvement with prostitutes.

Lesley Stahl, b 12/16/41 (Swampscott, MA), TV journalist.

Kenneth Starr, b 7/21/46 (Vernon, TX), former Whitewater indep. counsel.

Michael Steele, b 10/19/58 (Prince George's, MD), Republican Natl. Committee chair, former MD lt. governor.

Shelby Steele, b 1/1/46 (Chicago), scholar, critic.

Ben Stein, b 11/25/44 (Washington, DC), attorney, columnist, former speechwriter, actor and TV personality.

George Steinbrenner, b 7/4/30 (Rocky River, OH), NY Yankees owner.

Gloria Steinem, b 3/25/34 (Toledo, OH), author, feminist.

Frank Stella, b 5/12/36 (Malden, MA), painter.

George Stephanopoulos, b 2/10/61 (Fall River, MA), TV journalist, former presid. adviser.

David J. Stern, b 9/22/42 (NYC), NBA comm.

Howard Stern, b 1/12/54 (Roosevelt, NY), radio talk show host.

John Paul Stevens, b 4/20/20 (Chicago), Supreme Court justice.

Ted Stevens, b 11/18/23 (Indianapolis, IN), former senator (AK).

Martha Stewart, b 8/3/41 (Nutley, NJ), homemaking adviser, entrepreneur; TV personality.

Chesley (Sully) Sullenberger III, b 1/23/51 (Denison, TX), US Airways pilot who safely landed a jet in the Hudson River.

Arthur Ochs Sulzberger Jr., b 9/22/51 (Mt. Kisco, NY), newspaper publisher.

Lawrence H. Summers, b 11/30/54 (New Haven, CT), dir., Council of Economic Advisers, former Harvard Univ. pres.

George Tenet, b 1/5/53 (Queens, NY), former CIA director.

Clarence Thomas, b 6/23/48 (Savannah, GA), Supreme Court justice.

Helen Thomas, b 8/4/20 (Winchester, KY), journalist.

Fred Thompson, b 8/19/42 (Sheffield, AL), former senator (TN); actor; 2008 presid. contender.

Tommy G. Thompson, b 11/19/41 (Elroy, WI), former sec. of health and human services; former WI gov.

Richard Trumka, b 7/24/49 (Waynesburg, PA), pres. of AFL-CIO.

Donald Trump, b 6/14/46 (NYC), real estate exec.; TV personality.

Ted Turner, b 11/19/38 (Cincinnati), TV exec., philanthropist.

Neil deGrasse Tyson, b 10/5/58 (New York, NY), astrophysicist, director of NYC's Hayden Planetarium, author, television host.

Abigail Van Buren, b 7/4/18 (Sioux City, IA), retired advice columnist.

Gloria Vanderbilt, 2/20/24 (NYC), fashion designer, heiress.

Greta Van Susteren, b 6/11/54 (Appleton, WI), TV journalist, former attorney.

Jesse Ventura, b 7/15/51 (Minneapolis), former wrestler, former MN governor; radio talk show host.

Meredith Vieira, b 12/30/53 (Providence, RI), co-host *Today* show.

Antonio Villaraigosa, b 1/23/53 (East LA), 1st Hispanic mayor of LA since 1870s.

Paul Volcker, b 9/5/27 (Cape May, NJ), economist, former Fed chairman.

Mike Wallace, b 5/9/18 (Brookline, MA), TV journalist.

Barbara Walters, b 9/25/31 (Boston), TV journalist.

Rick Warren, b 1/28/54 (San Jose, CA), evangelical Christian pastor, founder of Saddleback Church, author.

James Watson, b 4/6/28 (Chicago), biochemist, DNA pioneer, co-winner 1962 Nobel Prize.

Dr. Andrew Weil, b 6/8/42 (Philadelphia), health adviser.

Harvey Weinstein, b 3/19/52 (NYC), movie exec.

Jack Welch, b 11/19/35 (Peabody, MA), former General Electric CEO.

Jann Wenner, b 1/7/46 (NYC), publisher, founder *Rolling Stone*.

Cornel West, b 6/23/53 (Tulsa, OK), African American scholar, critic.

Ruth Westheimer, b 6/4/28 (Frankfurt am Main, Germany), human sexuality expert.

Christine Todd Whitman, b 9/26/46 (NYC), former EPA head, NJ gov.

Meg Whitman, b 8/4/56 (Cold Spring Harbor, NY), former eBay pres. and CEO.

Elie Wiesel, b 9/30/28 (Sighet, Romania), scholar, author, 1986 Nobel Peace Prize winner.

George Will, b 5/4/41 (Champaign, IL), journalist, author.

Brian Williams, b 5/5/59 (Elmira, NY), NBC TV news anchor.

Oprah Winfrey, b 1/29/54 (Kosciusko, MS), TV and media personality, businesswoman, actress.

Bob Woodward, b 3/26/43 (Geneva, IL), journalist; with Bernstein cracked Watergate scandal.

Steve Wynn, b 1/27/42 (New Haven, CT), casino developer.

Paula Zahn, b 2/24/56 (Omaha, NE), TV journalist.

Mortimer Zuckerman, b 6/4/37 (Montreal, Quebec, Can.), publisher, columnist.

Widely Known World Personalities of the Present

Living non-Americans only. Generally excludes current heads of state or government (see Nations chapter) and excludes most others covered elsewhere, such as in Widely Known Americans, Entertainers and Writers lists or Sports Personalities.

Mahmoud Abbas (Abu Mazen), b 3/26/35 (Safed, Palestine [now Israel]), president of the Palestinian National Authority.

Gerry Adams, b 10/6/48 (Belfast, N. Ireland), Sinn Fein leader.

Theo Albrecht, b 3/28/22 (Schonebeck, Ger.), billionaire, former CEO of Aldi.

Prince Andrew, b 2/19/60 (London, Eng.), Duke of York (2nd son of Queen Elizabeth II).

Kofi Annan, b 4/8/38 (Kumasi, Ghana), former UN sec.-gen.; 2001 Nobel laureate.

Princess Anne, b 8/15/50 (London, Eng.), Princess Royal (daughter of Queen Elizabeth II).

Oscar Arias Sánchez, b 9/13/41 (Heredia, Costa Rica), former Costa Rican pres., peace negotiator, 1987 Nobel laureate.

Giorgio Armani, b 7/30/34 (Piacenza, Italy), fashion designer.

Ban Ki-Moon, b 6/13/44 (Umsong, [now] South Korea), UN sec-gen.

Ehud Barak, b 2/12/42 (Mishmar Ha-Sharon Kibbutz, Israel), Israel minister of defense, former Israeli prime min.

Ahmed Ben Bella, b 12/25/18 (Marnia, Algeria), 1st Algerian prime min.; revolutionary leader.

Benedict XVI (Joseph Ratzinger), b 4/16/27 (Marktl am Inn, Germany), pope of Rom. Cath. Church, elected 2005.

Boris Berezovsky, b 1/23/46 (Moscow, USSR), businessman, politician.

Tim Berners-Lee, b 6/8/55 (London, Eng.), World Wide Web inventor.

Osama bin Laden, b 3/10/57 (Riyadh, Saudi Ar.), leader of al-Qaeda terrorist organization.

Tony Blair, b 5/6/53 (Edinburgh, Scot.), former British Prime minister.

Hans Blix, b 6/28/28 (Uppsala, Sweden), former UN weapons inspector.

Bono (Paul David Hewson), b 5/20/60 (Glasnevin, Dublin, Ire.), musician, social activist, and philanthropist.

Fernando Botero, b 4/19/32 (Medellín, Col.), Colombian artist.

Boutros Boutros-Ghali, b 11/14/22 (Cairo, Egypt), former UN sec.-gen.

Richard Branson, b 7/18/50 (S. London, Eng.), British Virgin Records and Airways founder.

Tina Brown, b 11/21/53 (Maidenhead, Eng.), journalist, TV talk show host, author.

Carla Bruni, b 12/23/67 (Turin, Italy), first lady of France, musician, actress, model.

Mark Burnett, b 7/17/60 (Myland, England), reality TV producer.

Rhonda Byrne, b 3/12/51 (Australia), author, TV writer and producer.

David Cameron, 10/9/66 (London, Eng.), leader of UK Conservative Party.

Kim Campbell, b 3/10/47 (Port Alberni, British Columbia, Can.), former Canadian prime min.

Pierre Cardin, b 7/7/22 (Venice, Italy), fashion designer.

Princess Caroline, b 1/23/57 (Monte Carlo, Monaco), Monaco royal (eldest daughter of Prince Rainier and Princess Grace).

Fidel Castro, b 8/13/26 (Birán, Cuba), former prime minister of Cuba.

Prince Charles, b 11/14/48 (London, Eng.), Prince of Wales (eldest son of Queen Elizabeth II); heir to British throne.

Jean Chrétien, b 1/11/34 (Shawinigan, Que., Can.), former Canadian prime min.

Christo (Javacheff), b 6/13/35 (Gabrovo, Bulg.), artist.

Joe (Charles Joseph) Clark, b 6/5/39 (High River, Alberta, Can.), former Canadian prime min.

King Constantine II, b 6/2/40 (Psychiko, Greece), former king of Greece.

Simon Cowell, b 10/7/59 (Brighton, East Sussex, Eng.), music executive, TV producer, *American Idol* host.

Dalai Lama (Tenzin Gyatso), b 7/6/35 (Taktser, Amdo, Tibet), Buddhist leader; 1989 Nobel laureate.

Richard Dawkins, b 3/26/41 (Nairobi, Kenya), ethologist, evolutionary biologist, author.

Shirin Ebadi, b 6/21/47 (Hamadan, Iran), human rights activist, 2003 Nobel laureate.

Prince Edward, b 3/10/64 (London, Eng.), Earl of Essex (3rd son of Queen Elizabeth II).

Mohammed ElBaradei, b 6/17/42 (Cairo, Egypt), Director general of the International Atomic Energy Agency (IAEA).

Prince Felipe, b 1/30/68 (Madrid, Spain), heir to Spanish throne.

Sarah Ferguson, b 10/15/58 (London, Eng.), Duchess of York; ex-wife of Prince Andrew.

John Galliano, b 11/28/60 (Gibraltar), fashion designer.

Valery Giscard d'Estaing, b 2/2/26 (Koblenz, Ger.), former French pres.

Jane Goodall, b 4/3/34 (London, Eng.), British anthropologist and primatologist.

Mikhail Gorbachev, b 3/2/31 (Privolnoye, USSR), former Soviet pres.; 1990 Nobel laureate.

Jürgen Habermas, b 6/18/29 (Dusseldorf, Ger.), philosopher.

Prince Henry ("Harry") of Wales, b 9/15/84 (London, Eng.), son of Prince Charles; 3rd in line to British throne.

Vaclav Havel, b 10/5/36 (Prague, Czech.), former Czech pres.; playwright.

Stephen Hawking, b 1/8/42 (Oxford, Eng.), physicist; author.

Damien Hirst, b 6/7/65 (Bristol, England), artist.

David Hockney, b 7/9/37 (Bradford, Eng.), artist.

Jiang Zemin, b 8/17/26 (Yangzhou, Jiangsu Prov., China), former pres. of China.

Garry Kasparov, b 4/13/63 (Baku, Azerbaijan, USSR), former world chess champion; Russian pro-democracy leader.

Ayatullah Ali Khamenei, b 7/17/39 (Mashhad, Iran), Supreme Leader and former president of Iran, cleric, author.

F.W. (Frederik Willem) de Klerk, b 3/18/36 (Johannesburg, S. Africa), former S. African pres.; 1993 Nobel laureate.

Helmut Kohl, b 4/3/30 (Ludwigshafen, Ger.), former German chancellor.

Vladimir Kramnik, b 7/25/75 (Tuapse, Russia, USSR), world chess champion.

Hans Kung, b 3/19/28 (Sursee, Switz.), Rom. Cath. theologian.

Karl Lagerfeld, b 9/10/38 (Hamburg, Germany), fashion designer.

Richard Leakey, b 12/19/44 (Nairobi, Kenya), anthropologist, paleontologist, conservationist.

Claude Lévi-Strauss, b 11/28/08 (Brussels, Belg.), French anthropologist, developed structuralism.

Tzipi Livni, b 7/5/58 (Tel Aviv, Israel), attorney, head of Israeli Kadima party, foreign affairs minister of Israel.

Wangari Maathai, b 4/1/40 (Nyeri, Kenya), Nobel Peace Prize-winning Kenyan environmental and political activist.

John Major, b 3/29/43 (Wimbledon, Eng.), former British prime min.

Nelson Mandela, b 7/18/18 (Transkei, S. Africa), former pres. of S. Africa; 1993 Nobel laureate.

Imelda Marcos, b 7/2/29 (Manila, Philip.), former first lady of Philippines.

Paul Martin, b 8/28/38 (Ontario, Can.), former prime minister Canada.

Peter Max, b 10/19/37 (Berlin, Ger.), artist, designer.

Thabo Mbeki, b 1942 (Idutywa, S. Africa), former S. African prime min.

Angela Merkel, b 7/17/54 (Hamburg, Ger.), chancellor of Germany; 1st woman to hold the office.

Jean-Marie Messier, b 12/13/56 (Grenoble, Fr.), former CEO of Vivendi Universal.

Empress Michiko, b 10/20/34 (Tokyo, Jap.), empress of Japan.

Heather Mills, b 1/12/68 (Aldershot, Hampshire, Eng.), former model, animal rights activist, ex-wife of Paul McCartney.

Rev. Sun Myung Moon, b 1/6/20 (Kwangju Sangsa Ri, N. Korea), Unification Church founder.

Kate Moss, b 1/16/74 (Addiscombe, Surrey, Eng.), model.

Mir Hussein Moussavi, b 9/29/41 (Khameneh, Iran), challenger in Iran's 2009 presidential election.

Brian Mulroney, b 3/20/39 (Baie-Corneau, Quebec, Can.), former Canadian prime min.

Prince Naruhito, b 2/23/60 (Tokyo, Jap.), crown prince of Japan.

Hassan Nasrallah, b 1960 (Beirut, Lebanon), leader of the Hezbollah in Lebanon.

Benjamin Netanyahu, b 10/21/49 (Tel Aviv, Israel), Israeli prime min. 2009, 1996-1999.

Queen Noor (Lisa Halaby), b 8/23/51 (Washington, DC), American-born widow of Jordan's King Hussein.

Ehud Olmert, b 9/30/45 (Binyamina, Palestine), former prime minister of Israel.

Daniel Ortega Saavedra, b 11/11/45 (La Libertad, Nicar.), Nicaraguan pres., Sandinista leader.

Camilla Parker-Bowles, Duchess of Cornwall, b 7/17/47 (London, Eng.), wife of Prince Charles.

Jean-Marie le Pen, b 6/20/28 (La Trinite-sur-Mer, Fr.), French right-wing politician

Javier Perez de Cuellar, b 1/19/20 (Lima, Peru), former UN sec. gen.

Prince Philip, b 6/10/21 (Corfu, Greece), Duke of Edinburgh (husband of Queen Elizabeth II).

Gerhard Richter, b 2/9/32 (Dresden, Ger.), artist.

Mary Robinson, b 5/21/44 (Ballina, Co. Mayo, Ireland), former Irish pres., former UN High Commissioner for Human Rights.

Ségolène Royal, b 9/22/53 (Dakar, Senegal), French socialist politician, 2007 candidate for president of France.

Moqtada al-Sadr, b 1974 (Iraq), extremist Shiite cleric.

Carlos Salinas de Gortari, b 4/3/48 (Mexico City, Mex.), former Mexican pres.

Ariel Sharon, b 2/26/28 (Kfar Malal, Palestine), former Israeli prime min. 2000-2006.

Eduard Shevardnadze, b 1/25/28 (Mamati, Georgia, USSR), former Georgian pres.

Ayatollah Ali al-Sistani, b 8/4/30 (Mashhad, Iran), major Iraqi Shiite religious leader.

Princess Stephanie, b 2/1/65 (Monte Carlo, Monaco), youngest daughter and child of Prince Rainier and Princess Grace.

Aung San Suu Kyi, b 6/19/45 (Rangoon, Myanmar), political activist, 1991 Nobel laureate, under effective house arrest.

Valentina Tereshkova, b 3/6/37 (Maslennikovo, Russia, USSR), 1st woman in space.

Margaret Thatcher, b 10/13/25 (Grantham, Eng.), former British prime min.

Morgan Tsvangirai, b 3/10/52 (Gutu, Southern Rhodesia), prime minister of Zimbabwe, trade unionist.

John Napier Turner, b 6/7/29 (Richmond, Surrey, Eng.), former Canadian prime min.

Desmond Tutu, b 10/7/31 (Klerksdorp, Transvaal, S. Africa), former S. African archbishop; 1984 Nobel laureate.

Lech Walesa, b 9/29/43 (Popowo, Pol.), Solidarity leader; 1983 Nobel laureate; former president of Poland.

Prince William (of Wales), b 6/21/82 (London, Eng.), son of Prince Charles; 2nd in line to British throne.

Rowan Williams, b 6/14/50 (Ystradgynlais, Wales), Archbishop of Canterbury.

Muhammad Yunus, b 6/28/40 (Chittagong, India), Nobel Peace prize winner, economics professor.

Ayman al-Zawahiri, b 6/19/51 (Cairo, Egypt), reputed high-ranking al-Qaeda leader.

Architects

Max Abramovitz, 1908-2004, Avery Fisher Hall, NYC; U.S. Steel Bldg. (now USX Towers), Pittsburgh, PA.

Tadao Ando, b 1941, Modern Art Museum, Ft. Worth, TX, Stone Hill Center, MA.

Henry Bacon, 1866-1924, Lincoln Memorial, Washington, DC.

Benjamin Banneker, 1731-1806, African American inventor, astronomer, mathematician; helped design and lay out Washington, D.C.

Pietro Belluschi, 1899-1994, Juilliard School; Lincoln Center; Pan Am, now MetLife, Bldg. (with Walter Gropius), NYC.

Marcel Breuer, 1902-81, Whitney Museum of American Art (with Hamilton Smith), NYC.

Charles Bulfinch, 1763-1844, State House, Boston; Capitol (part), Washington, DC.

Gordon Bunshaft, 1909-90, Lever House, Park Ave, NYC; Hirshhorn Museum, Washington, DC.

Daniel H. Burnham, 1846-1912, Union Station, Washington DC; Flatiron Bldg., NYC.

Irwin Chanin, 1892-1988, theaters, skyscrapers, NYC.

David Childs, b 1941, Washington Mall Master Plan/Constitution Gardens, Washington, DC; WTC Freedom Tower, NYC.

Lucio Costa, 1902-98, master plan for city of Brasilia, with Oscar Niemeyer.

Ralph Adams Cram, 1863-1942, Cath. of St. John the Divine, NYC; U.S. Military Acad. (part), West Point, NY.

Norman Foster, b 1935, Commerzbank Headquarters, Frankfurt-am-Main, Ger.; London Millennium Bridge, London.

James Ingo Freed, 1930-2005, Holocaust Memorial Museum, Washington, DC; Jacob K. Javits Center, NYC.

R. Buckminster Fuller, 1895-1983, U.S. Pavilion (geodesic domes), Expo 67, Montreal.

Frank O. Gehry, b 1929, Guggenheim Museum, Bilbao, Spain; Experience Music Project, Seattle, WA.

Cass Gilbert, 1859-1934, Custom House, Woolworth Bldg., NYC; Supreme Court Bldg., Washington, DC.

Bertram G. Goodhue, 1869-1924, Capitol, Lincoln, NE; St. Thomas's Church, St. Bartholomew's Church, NYC.

Michael Graves, b 1934, Portland Bldg., Portland, OR; Humana Bldg., Louisville, KY.

Walter Gropius, 1883-1969, Pan Am Bldg. (now MetLife Bldg.) (with Pietro Belluschi), NYC.

Lawrence Halprin, 1916-2009, Ghirardelli Sq., San Francisco; Nicollet Mall, Minneapolis; FDR Memorial, Washington, DC.

Peter Harrison, 1716-75, Touro Synagogue, Redwood Library, Newport, RI.

Wallace K. Harrison, 1895-1981, Metropolitan Opera House, Lincoln Center, NYC.

Thomas Hastings, 1860-1929, NY Public Library (with John Carrère), Frick Mansion, NYC.

James Hoban, 1762-1831, White House, Washington, DC.

Raymond Hood, 1881-1934, Rockefeller Center (part), Daily News, NYC; Tribune, Chicago, IL.

Richard M. Hunt, 1827-95, Metropolitan Museum (part), NYC; National Observatory, Washington, DC.

Helmut Jahn, b 1940, United Airlines Terminal, O'Hare Airport, Chicago.

William Le Baron Jenney, 1832-1907, Home Insurance (demolished 1931), Chicago, IL.

Philip C. Johnson, 1906-2005, AT&T headquarters (now 550 Madison Ave.), NYC; Transco Tower, Houston, TX.

Albert Kahn, 1869-1942, General Motors Bldg., Detroit, MI.

Louis Kahn, 1901-74, Salk Laboratory, La Jolla, CA; Yale Art Gallery, New Haven, CT.

Christopher Grant LaFarge, 1862-1938, Roman Catholic Chapel, West Point, NY.

Benjamin H. Latrobe, 1764-1820, Capitol (part), Washington, DC; State Capitol Bldg., Richmond, VA.

Le Corbusier (Charles-Edouard Jeanneret), 1887-1965, Salvation Army Hostel and Swiss Dormitory, both Paris; master plan for cities of Algiers and Buenos Aires.

William Lescaze, 1896-1969, Philadelphia Savings Fund Society; Borg-Warner Bldg., Chicago.

Maya Lin, b 1959, Vietnam Veterans Mem., Washington, DC.

Charles Rennie Mackintosh, 1868-1928, Glasgow School of Art; Hill House, Helensburgh.

Bernard R. Maybeck, 1862-1957, Hearst Hall, Univ. of CA, Berkeley; First Church of Christ Scientist, Berkeley, CA.

Charles F. McKim, 1847-1909, Public Library, Boston; Columbia Univ. (part), NYC.

Charles M. McKim, b 1920, KUHT-TV Transmitter Bldg., Lutheran Church of the Redeemer, Houston, TX.

Richard Meier, b 1934, Getty Center Museum, Los Angeles, CA; High Museum of Art, Atlanta, GA.

Ludwig Mies van der Rohe, 1886-1969, Seagram Bldg. (with Philip C. Johnson), NYC; National Gallery, Berlin.

Robert Mills, 1781-1855, Washington Monument, Wash., DC.

Charles Moore, 1925-93, Sea Ranch, near San Francisco; Piazza d'Italia, New Orleans, LA.

Richard J. Neutra, 1892-1970, Mathematics Park, Princeton, NJ; Orange Co. Courthouse, Santa Ana, CA.

Oscar Niemeyer, b 1907, government buildings, Brasilia Palace Hotel, all Brasilia.

Gyo Obata, b 1923, Natl. Air & Space Museum, Smithsonian Inst., Washington, DC; Dallas-Ft. Worth Airport.

Frederick L. Olmsted, 1822-1903, Central Park, NYC; Fairmount Park, Philadelphia, PA.

I(eoh) M(ing) Pei, b 1917, East Wing, Natl. Gallery of Art, Washington, DC; Pyramid, The Louvre, Paris; Rock & Roll Hall of Fame and Museum, Cleveland, OH.

Cesar Pelli, b 1926, World Financial Center, Carnegie Hall Tower, NYC; Petronas Twin Towers, Malaysia.

William Pereira, 1909-85, Cape Canaveral; Transamerica Bldg., San Francisco, CA.

Renzo Piano, b 1937, Pompidou Centre, Paris; New York Times Building, NYC,

John Russell Pope, 1874-1937, National Gallery, Wash., DC.

John Portman, b 1924, Peachtree Center, Atlanta, GA.

George Browne Post, 1837-1913, NY Stock Exchange; Capitol, Madison, WI.

James Renwick Jr., 1818-95, Grace Church, St. Patrick's Cath., NYC.; Corcoran (Renwick) Gallery, Wash., DC.

Henry H. Richardson, 1838-86, Trinity Church, Boston, MA.

Kevin Roche, b 1922, Oakland Museum, Oakland, CA; Fine Arts Center, University of Massachusetts, Amherst.

James Gamble Rogers, 1867-1947, Columbia-Presbyterian Medical Center, NYC; Northwestern Univ., Evanston, IL.

John Wellborn Root, 1887-1963, Palmolive Bldg., Chicago; Hotel Statler, Washington, DC.

Paul Rudolph, 1918-97, Jewitt Art Center, Wellesley Colllege, MA; Art & Architecture Bldg., Yale Univ., New Haven, CT.

Eero Saarinen, 1910-61, Gateway to the West Arch, St. Louis, MO; Trans World Airlines Flight Center, NYC.

Louis Skidmore, 1897-1962, Atomic Energy Commission town site, Oak Ridge, TN; Terrace Plaza Hotel, Cincinnati, OH.

Clarence S. Stein, 1882-1975, Temple Emanu-El, NYC.

Edward Durell Stone, 1902-78, U.S. Embassy, New Delhi, India; (H. Hartford) Gallery of Modern Art, NYC.

Louis H. Sullivan, 1856-1924, Auditorium Bldg., Chicago, IL.

Kenzo Tange, 1913-2005, Hiroshima Peace Park, 1964 Tokyo Olympics twin stadiums.

Richard Upjohn, 1802-78, Trinity Church, NYC.

Max O. Urbahn, 1912-95, Vehicle Assembly Bldg., Cape Canaveral, FL.

Robert Venturi, b 1925, Gordon Wu Hall, Princeton, NJ; Mielparque Nikko Kirifuri Resort, Japan.

Ralph T. Walker, 1889-1973, NY Telephone Bldg. (now NYNEX); IBM Research Lab, Poughkeepsie, NY.

Roland A. Wank, 1898-1970, Cincinnati Union Terminal, OH; head architect (1933-44), Tennessee Valley Authority.

Stanford White, 1853-1906, Washington Arch in Washington Square Park, first Madison Square Garden, NYC.

Christopher Wren, 1632-1723, St. Paul's Cathedral, London.

Frank Lloyd Wright, 1867-1959, Imperial Hotel, Tokyo; Guggenheim Museum, NYC; Kaufmann "Fallingwater" house, Bear Run, PA.; Taliesin West, Scottsdale, AZ.

William Wurster, 1895-1973, Ghirardelli Sq., San Francisco.

Minoru Yamasaki, 1912-86, World Trade Center, NYC.

Artists, Photographers, and Sculptors of the Past

Artists are painters unless otherwise indicated.

Berenice Abbott, 1898-1991, (U.S.) photographer. Documentary of New York City, *Changing New York* (1939).

Ansel Easton Adams, 1902-84, (U.S.) photographer. Landscapes of the American Southwest.

Washington Allston, 1779-1843, (U.S.) landscapist. *Belshazzar's Feast.*

Albrecht Altdorfer, 1480-1538, (Ger.) landscapist.

Andrea del Sarto, 1486-1530, (It.) frescoes. *Madonna of the Harpies.*

Fra Angelico, c.1400-55, (It.) Renaissance muralist. *Madonna of the Linen Drapers' Guild.*

Diane Arbus, 1923-71, (U.S.) photographer. Disturbing images.

Alexsandr Archipenko, 1887-1964, (U.S.) sculptor. *Boxing Match, Medranos.*

Jean Arp, 1887-1966, (Fr.) sculptor and painter, founder of Dada movement.

Eugène Atget, 1856-1927, (Fr.) photographer. Paris life.

John James Audubon, 1785-1851, (U.S.) *Birds of America.*

Hans Baldung-Grien, 1484-1545, (Ger.) *Todentanz.*

Ernst Barlach, 1870-1938, (Ger.) Expressionist sculptor. *Man Drawing a Sword.*

Frederic-Auguste Bartholdi, 1834-1904, (Fr.) *Liberty Enlightening the World, Lion of Belfort.*

Fra Bartolommeo, 1472-1517, (It.) *Vision of St. Bernard.*

Romare Bearden, 1911-88, (U.S.) collage and other media. *The Visitation.*

Aubrey Beardsley, 1872-98, (Br.) illustrator. *Salome, Lysistrata, Morte d'Arthur, Volpone.*

Max Beckmann, 1884-1950, (Ger.) Expressionist. *The Descent From the Cross.*

Gentile Bellini, 1426-1507, (It.) Renaissance. *Procession in St. Mark's Square.*

Giovanni Bellini, 1428-1516, (It.) *St. Francis in Ecstasy.*

Jacopo Bellini, 1400-70, (It.) *Crucifixion.*

George Wesley Bellows, 1882-1925, (U.S.) sports artist, portraitist, landscapist. *Stag at Sharkey's, Edith Clavell.*

Thomas Hart Benton, 1889-1975, (U.S.) American regionalist. *Threshing Wheat, Arts of the West.*

Gianlorenzo Bernini, 1598-1680, (It.) Baroque sculpture. *The Assumption.*

Ruth Bernhard, 1905-2006, (Ger.-U.S.) photographer, black and white studies of female nudes.

Albert Bierstadt, 1830-1902, (U.S.) landscapist. *The Rocky Mountains, Mount Corcoran.*

George Caleb Bingham, 1811-79, (U.S.) *Fur Traders Descending the Missouri.*

William Blake, 1752-1827, (Br.) engraver. *Book of Job, Songs of Innocence, Songs of Experience.*

Rosa Bonheur, 1822-99, (Fr.) *The Horse Fair.*

Pierre Bonnard, 1867-1947, (Fr.) Intimist. *The Breakfast Room, Girl in a Straw Hat.*

Gutzon Borglum, 1871-1941, (U.S.) sculptor. Mt. Rushmore Memorial.

Hieronymus Bosch, 1450-1516, (Flem.) religious allegories. *The Crowning With Thorns.*

Sandro Botticelli, 1444-1510, (It.) Renaissance. *Birth of Venus, Adoration of the Magi, Guiliano de'Medici.*

Margaret Bourke-White, 1906-71, (U.S.) photographer, photojournalist. WW2, USSR, rural South during the Depression.

Mathew Brady, c.1823-96, (U.S.) Official photographer of the Civil War.

Constantin Brancusi, 1876-1957, (Romanian-Fr.) Nonobjective sculptor. *Flying Turtle, The Kiss.*

Georges Braque, 1882-1963, (Fr.) Cubist. *Violin and Palette.*

Pieter Bruegel the Elder, c.1525-69, (Flem.) *The Peasant Dance, Hunters in the Snow, Magpie on the Gallows.*

Pieter Bruegel the Younger, 1564-1638, (Flem.) *Village Fair, The Crucifixion.*

Edward Burne-Jones, 1833-98, (Br.) Pre-Raphaelite artist-craftsman. *The Mirror of Venus.*

Alexander Calder, 1898-1976, (U.S.) sculptor. *Lobster Trap and Fish Tail.*

Julia Cameron, 1815-79, (Br.) photographer. Prominent portraitist of the 19th cent.

Robert Capa (Andrei Friedmann), 1913-54, (Hung.-U.S.) photographer. War photojournalist; invasion of Normandy.

Michelangelo Merisi da Caravaggio, 1573-1610, (It.) Baroque. *The Supper at Emmaus.*

Emily Carr, 1871-1945, (Can.) landscapist. *Blunden Harbour, Big Raven, Rushing Sea of Undergrowth.*

Carlo Carrà, 1881-1966, (It.) Metaphysical school. *Lot's Daughters, The Enchanted Room.*

Henri Cartier-Bresson, 1908-2004, (Fr.) photographer. *Imagenes à la sauvette.*

Mary Cassatt, 1844-1926, (U.S.) Impressionist. *The Cup of Tea, Woman Bathing, The Boating Party.*

Oleg Cassini, 1913-2006, (Fr.-U.S.) fashion designer.

George Catlin, 1796-1872, (U.S.) American Indian life. *Gallery of Indians, Buffalo Dance.*

Benvenuto Cellini, 1500-71, (It.) Mannerist sculptor, goldsmith. *Perseus and Medusa.*

Paul Cézanne, 1839-1906, (Fr.) *Card Players, Mont-Sainte-Victoire With Large Pine Trees.*

Marc Chagall, 1887-1985, (Russ.) Jewish life and folklore. *I and the Village, The Praying Jew.*

Jean Simeon Chardin, 1699-1779, (Fr.) still lifes. *The Kiss, The Grace.*

Giorgio de Chirico, 1888-1978, (It.) painter, founded the metaphysical school. *Enigma of an Autumn Night.*

Frederick Church, 1826-1900, (U.S.) Hudson River school. *Niagara, Andes of Ecuador.*

Giovanni Cimabue, 1240-1302, (It.) Byzantine mosaicist. *Madonna Enthroned With St. Francis.*

Claude Lorrain (Claude Gellée), 1600-82, (Fr.) Ideal-landscapist. *The Enchanted Castle.*

Thomas Cole, 1801-48, (U.S.) Hudson River school. *The Ox-Bow, In the Catskills.*

John Constable, 1776-1837, (Br.) landscapist. *Salisbury Cathedral From the Bishop's Grounds.*

John Singleton Copley, 1738-1815, (U.S.) portraitist. *Samuel Adams, Watson and the Shark.*

Lovis Corinth, 1858-1925, (Ger.) Expressionist. *Apocalypse.*

Jean-Baptiste-Camille Corot, 1796-1875, (Fr.) landscapist. *Souvenir de Mortefontaine, Pastorale.*

Correggio, 1494-1534, (It.) Renaissance muralist. *Mystic Marriages of St. Catherine.*

Gustave Courbet, 1819-77, (Fr.) Realist. *The Artist's Studio.*

Lucas Cranach the Elder, 1472-1553, (Ger.) Protestant Reformation portraitist. *Luther.*

Imogen Cunningham, 1883-1976, (U.S.) photographer, portraitist. Plant photography.

Nathaniel Currier, 1813-88, and **James M. Ives**, 1824-95, (both U.S.) lithographers. *A Midnight Race on the Mississippi, American Forest Scene—Maple Sugaring.*

John Steuart Curry, 1897-1946, (U.S.) Americana, murals. *Baptism in Kansas.*

Salvador Dalí, 1904-89, (Sp.) Surrealist. *Persistence of Memory, The Crucifixion.*

Honoré Daumier, 1808-79, (Fr.) caricaturist. *The Third-Class Carriage.*

Jacques-Louis David, 1748-1825, (Fr.) Neoclassicist. *The Oath of the Horatii.*

Arthur Davies, 1862-1928, (U.S.) Romantic landscapist. *Unicorns, Leda and the Dioscuri.*

Aaron Douglas, 1900-79, Harlem Renaissance artist.

Willem de Kooning, 1904-97, (Dutch-U.S.) abstract expressionist. *Excavation, Woman I, Door to the River.*

Edgar Degas, 1834-1917, (Fr.) *The Ballet Class.*

Eugène Delacroix, 1798-1863, (Fr.) Romantic. *Massacre at Chios, Liberty Leading the People.*

Paul Delaroche, 1797-1856, (Fr.) historical themes. *Children of Edward IV.*

Luca Della Robbia, 1400-82, (It.) Renaissance terracotta artist. *Cantoria* (singing gallery), Florence cathedral.

Donatello, 1386-1466, (It.) Renaissance sculptor. *David, Gattamelata.*

Jean Dubuffet, 1902-85, (Fr.) painter, sculptor, printmaker. *Group of Four Trees.*

Marcel Duchamp, 1887-1968, (Fr.) Dada artist. *Nude Descending a Staircase, No. 2.*

Raoul Dufy, 1877-1953, (Fr.) Fauvist. *Chateau and Horses.*

Asher Brown Durand, 1796-1886, (U.S.) Hudson River school. *Kindred Spirits.*

Albrecht Dürer, 1471-1528, (Ger.) Renaissance painter, engraver, woodcuts. *St. Jerome in His Study, Melencolia I.*

Anthony van Dyck, 1599-1641, (Flem.) Baroque portraitist. *Portrait of Charles I Hunting.*

Thomas Eakins, 1844-1916, (U.S.) Realist. *The Gross Clinic.*

Alfred Eisenstaedt, 1898-1995, (Ger.-U.S.) photographer, photojournalist. Famous photo, V-J Day, Aug. 14, 1945.

Peter Henry Emerson, 1856-1936, (Br.) photographer. Promoted photography as an independent art form.

Jacob Epstein, 1880-1959, (Br.) religious and allegorical sculptor. *Genesis, Ecce Homo.*

Erté, 1892-1990, (Fr.) b Romain de Tiertoff; painter, fashion and stage designer.

Jan van Eyck, c.1390-1441, (Flem.) naturalistic panels. *Adoration of the Lamb.*

Roger Fenton, 1819-68, (Br.) photographer. Crimean War.

Anselm Feuerbach, 1829-80, (Ger.) Romantic Classicist. *Judgment of Paris, Iphigenia.*

John Bernard Flannagan, 1895-1942, (U.S.) animal sculptor. *Triumph of the Egg.*

Jean-Honoré Fragonard, 1732-1806, (Fr.) Rococo. *The Swing.*

Daniel Chester French, 1850-1931, (U.S.) *The Minute Man of Concord;* seated *Lincoln,* Lincoln Memorial, Washington, DC.

Caspar David Friedrich, 1774-1840, (Ger.) Romantic landscapes. *Man and Woman Gazing at the Moon.*

Thomas Gainsborough, 1727-88, (Br.) portraitist. *The Blue Boy, The Watering Place, Orpin the Parish Clerk.*

Alexander Gardner, 1821-82, (U.S.) photographer. Civil War; railroad construction; Great Plains Indians.

Paul Gauguin, 1848-1903, (Fr.) Post-impressionist. *The Tahitians, Spirit of the Dead Watching.*

Lorenzo Ghiberti, 1378-1455, (It.) Renaissance sculptor. Gates of Paradise baptistery doors, Florence.

Alberto Giacometti, 1901-66, (Swiss) attenuated sculptures of solitary figures. *Man Pointing.*

Giorgione, c.1477-1510, (It.) Renaissance. *The Tempest.*

Giotto di Bondone, 1267-1337, (It.) Renaissance. *Presentation of Christ in the Temple.*

François Girardon, 1628-1715, (Fr.) Baroque sculptor of classical themes. *Apollo Tended by the Nymphs.*

Vincent van Gogh, 1853-90, (Dutch) *The Starry Night, L'Arlesienne, Bedroom at Arles, Self-Portrait.*

Edward Gorey, 1925-2000, (U.S.) artist, illustrator. *The Doubtful Guest.*

Arshile Gorky, 1905-48, (U.S.) Surrealist. *The Liver Is the Cock's Comb.*

Francisco de Goya y Lucientes, 1746-1828, (Sp.) *The Naked Maja, The Disasters of War* (etchings).

El Greco, 1541-1614, (Sp.) *View of Toledo, Assumption of the Virgin.*

Horatio Greenough, 1805-52, (U.S.) Neoclassical sculptor.

Matthias Grünewald, 1480-1528, (Ger.) mystical religious themes. *The Resurrection.*

Frans Hals, c.1580-1666, (Dutch) portraitist. *Laughing Cavalier, Gypsy Girl.*

Austin Hansen, 1910-96, (U.S.) photographer. Harlem, NY, life.

Childe Hassam, 1859-1935, (U.S.) Impressionist. *Southwest Wind, July 14 Rue Daunon.*

Edward Hicks, 1780-1849, (U.S.) folk painter. *The Peaceable Kingdom.*

Lewis Wickes Hine, 1874-1940, (U.S.) photographer. Studies of immigrants, children in industry.

Hans Hofmann, 1880-1966, (U.S.) early abstract Expressionist. *Spring, The Gate.*

William Hogarth, 1697-1764, (Br.) caricaturist. *The Rake's Progress.*

Katsushika Hokusai, 1760-1849, (Jpn.) printmaker. *Crabs.*

Hans Holbein the Elder, 1460-1524, (Ger.) late Gothic. *Presentation of Christ in the Temple.*

Hans Holbein the Younger, 1497-1543, (Ger.) portraitist. *Henry VIII, The French Ambassadors.*

Winslow Homer, 1836-1910, (U.S.) naturalist painter, marine themes. *Marine Coast, High Cliff.*

Edward Hopper, 1882-1967, (U.S.) realistic urban scenes. *Nighthawks, House by the Railroad.*

Horst P. Horst, 1906-99, (Ger.) fashion, celebrity photographer.

Jean-Auguste-Dominique Ingres, 1780-1867, (Fr.) Classicist. *Valpincon Bather.*

George Inness, 1825-94, (U.S.) luminous landscapist. *Delaware Water Gap.*

William Henry Jackson, 1843-1942, (U.S.) photographer. American West, building of Union Pacific Railroad.

Donald Judd, 1928-94, (U.S.) sculptor, major Minimalist.

Frida Kahlo, 1907-54, (Mex.) painter; *Self-Portrait With Monkey.*

Vasily Kandinsky, 1866-1944, (Russ.) Abstractionist. *Capricious Forms, Improvisation 38* (second version).

Paul Klee, 1879-1940, (Swiss) Abstractionist. *Twittering Machine, Pastoral, Death and Fire.*

Gustav Klimt, 1862-1918, (Austrian) cofounder of Vienna Secession Movement, *The Kiss.*

Oscar Kokoschka, 1886-1980, (Austrian) Expressionist. *View of Prague, Harbor of Marseilles.*

Kathe Kollwitz, 1867-1945, (Ger.) printmaker, social justice themes. *The Peasant War.*

Gaston Lachaise, 1882-1935, (U.S.) figurative sculptor. *Standing Woman.*

John La Farge, 1835-1910, (U.S.) muralist. *Red and White Peonies, The Ascension.*

Sir Edwin (Henry) Landseer, 1802-73, (Br.) painter, sculptor. *Shoeing, Rout of Comus.*

Dorothea Lange, 1895-1965, (U.S.) photographer. Depression photographs, migrant farm workers.

Fernand Léger, 1881-1955, (Fr.) Machine art. *The Cyclists.*

Leonardo da Vinci, 1452-1519, (It.) *Mona Lisa, Last Supper, The Annunciation.*

Emanuel Leutze, 1816-68, (U.S.) historical themes. *Washington Crossing the Delaware.*

Roy Lichtenstein, 1923-97, (U.S.) pop artist.

Jacques Lipchitz, 1891-1973, (Fr.) Cubist sculptor. *Harpist.*

Filippino Lippi, 1457-1504, (It.) Renaissance.

Fra Filippo Lippi, 1406-69, (It.) Renaissance. *Coronation of the Virgin, Madonna and Child With Angels.*

Morris Louis, 1912-62, (U.S.) abstract Expressionist. *Signa, Stripes, Alpha-Phi.*

René Magritte, 1898-1967, (Belgian) Surrealist. *The Descent of Man, The Betrayal of Images.*

Aristide Maillol, 1861-1944, (Fr.) sculptor. *L'Harmonie.*

Édouard Manet, 1832-83, (Fr.) forerunner of Impressionism. *Luncheon on the Grass, Olympia.*

Andrea Mantegna, 1431-1506, (It.) Renaissance frescoes. *Triumph of Caesar.*

Franz Marc, 1880-1916, (Ger.) Expressionist. *Blue Horses.*

John Marin, 1870-1953, (U.S.) Expressionist seascapes. *Maine Island.*

Reginald Marsh, 1898-1954, (U.S.) satirical artist. *Tattoo and Haircut.*

Agnes Martin, 1912-2004, (U.S.) abstract artist. *Night Sea.*

Masaccio, 1401-28, (It.) Renaissance. *The Tribute Money.*

Henri Matisse, 1869-1954, (Fr.) Fauvist. *Woman With the Hat.*

Michelangelo Buonarroti, 1475-1564, (It.) *Pietà, David, Moses, The Last Judgment*, Sistine Chapel ceiling.

Jean-Francois Millet, 1814-75, (Fr.) painter of peasant subjects. *The Gleaners, The Man With a Hoe.*

Joan Miró, 1893-1983, (Sp.) Exuberant colors, playful images. Catalan landscape, *Dutch Interior.*

Amedeo Modigliani, 1884-1920, (It.) *Reclining Nude.*

Piet Mondrian, 1872-1944, (Dutch) Abstractionist. *Composition With Red, Yellow and Blue.*

Claude Monet, 1840-1926, (Fr.) Impressionist. *The Bridge at Argenteuil, Haystacks.*

Henry Moore, 1898-1986, (Br.) sculptor of large-scale, abstract works. *Reclining Figure* (several).

Gustave Moreau, 1826-98, (Fr.) Symbolist. *The Apparition, Dance of Salome.*

James Wilson Morrice, 1865-1924, (Can.) landscapist. *The Ferry, Quebec, Venice, Looking Over the Lagoon.*

William Morris, 1834-96, (Br.) decorative artist, leader of the Arts and Crafts movement.

Grandma Moses, 1860-1961, (U.S.) folk painter. *Out for the Christmas Trees, Thanksgiving Turkey.*

Edvard Munch, 1863-1944, (Nor.) Expressionist. *The Cry.*

Bartolome Murillo, 1618-82, (Sp.) Baroque religious artist. *Vision of St. Anthony, The Two Trinities.*

Elizabeth Murray, 1940-2007, (U.S.) abstract color painter.

Eadweard Muybridge, 1830-1904, (Br.-U.S.) photographer. Studies of motion, *Animal Locomotion.*

Nadar (Gaspar-Félix Tournachon), 1820-1910, (Fr.) photographer, caricaturist, portraitist. Invented photo-essay.

Arnold Newman, 1918-2006, (U.S.) portrait photographer.

Barnett Newman, 1905-70, (U.S.) Abstract Expressionist. *Stations of the Cross.*

Isamu Noguchi, 1904-88, (U.S.) abstract sculptor, designer. *Kouros, BirdC(MU)*, sculptural gardens.

Georgia O'Keeffe, 1887-1986, (U.S.) Southwest motifs. *Cow's Skull: Red, White, and Blue, The Shelton With Sunspots.*

José Clemente Orozco, 1883-1949, (Mex.) frescoes. *House of Tears, Pre-Columbian Golden Age.*

Timothy H. O'Sullivan, 1840-82, (U.S.) Civil War photographer.

Gordon Parks, 1912-2006, (U.S.) African American photographer and film maker. *Life* photographer 1948-68.

Charles Willson Peale, 1741-1827, (U.S.) Amer. Revolutionary portraitist. *The Staircase Group*, U.S. presidents.

Rembrandt Peale, 1778-1860, (U.S.) portraitist. *Thomas Jefferson.*

Irving Penn, 1917-2009, (U.S.) portraitist, fashion photographer.

Pietro Perugino, 1446-1523, (It.) Renaissance. *Delivery of the Keys to St. Peter.*

Pablo Picasso, 1881-1973, (Sp.) painter, sculptor. *Guernica; Dove; Head of a Woman; Head of a Bull, Metamorphosis.*

Piero della Francesca, c.1415-92, (It.) Renaissance. *Duke of Urbino, Flagellation of Christ.*

Camille Pissarro, 1830-1903, (Fr.) Impressionist. *Boulevard des Italiens, Morning, Sunlight; Bather in the Woods.*

Jackson Pollock, 1912-56, (U.S.) Abstract Expressionist. *Autumn Rhythm.*

Nicolas Poussin, 1594-1665, (Fr.) Baroque pictorial classicism. *St. John on Patmos.*

Maurice B. Prendergast, c.1860-1924, (U.S.) Post-impressionist water colorist. *Umbrellas in the Rain.*

Pierre-Paul Prud'hon, 1758-1823, (Fr.) Romanticist. *Crime Pursued by Vengeance and Justice..*

Pierre Cecile Puvis de Chavannes, 1824-98, (Fr.) muralist. *The Poor Fisherman.*

Niki de Saint Phalle,1930-2002, (Fr.) creator of paintings, sculptures, prints and large public installations.

Raphael Sanzio, 1483-1520, (It.) Renaissance. *Disputa, School of Athens, Sistine Madonna.*

Robert Rauschenberg, 1925-2008, (U.S.) printmaker. *Combine, Bed, Revolvers, Outpost.*

Man Ray, 1890-1976, (U.S.) Dada and Surrealist artist. *Observing Time, The Lovers, Marquis de Sade.*

Odilon Redon, 1840-1916, (Fr.) Symbolist painter, lithographer. *In the Dream, Vase of Flowers.*

Rembrandt van Rijn, 1606-69, (Dutch) *The Bridal Couple, The Night Watch.*

Frederic Remington, 1861-1909, (U.S.) painter, sculptor. Portrayer of the American West, *Bronco Buster.*

Pierre-Auguste Renoir, 1841-1919, (Fr.) Impressionist. *The Luncheon of the Boating Party, Dance in the Country.*

Joshua Reynolds, 1723-92, (Br.) portraitist. *Mrs. Siddons as the Tragic Muse.*

Herb Ritts, 1952-2002, (U.S.) photographer. Nudes, celebrities.

Diego Rivera, 1886-1957, (Mex.) frescoes. *The Fecund Earth.*

Larry Rivers, 1923-2002, (U.S.) painter, sculptor, often realistic; *Dutch Masters* series.

Henry Peach Robinson, 1830-1901 (Br.) photographer. A leader of "high art" photography.

Norman Rockwell, 1894-1978, (U.S.) painter, illustrator. *Saturday Evening Post* covers.

Auguste Rodin, 1840-1917, (Fr.) sculptor. *The Thinker.*

Willy Ronis, 1910-2009 (Fr.) photographer of post-war Paris.

Mark Rothko, 1903-70, (U.S.) abstract Expressionist. *Light, Earth and Blue.*

Georges Rouault, 1871-1958, (Fr.) Expressionist. *Three Judges.*

Henri Rousseau, 1844-1910, (Fr.) primitive exotic themes. *The Snake Charmer.*

Theodore Rousseau, 1812-67, (Swiss-Fr.) landscapist. *Under the Birches, Evening.*

Peter Paul Rubens, 1577-1640, (Flem.) Baroque. *Mystic Marriage of St. Catherine.*

Jacob van Ruisdael, c.1628-82, (Dutch) landscapist. *Jewish Cemetery.*

Charles M. Russell, 1866-1926, (U.S.) Western life.

Salomon van Ruysdael, c.1600-70, (Dutch) landscapist. *River With Ferry-Boat.*

Albert Pinkham Ryder, 1847-1917, (U.S.) seascapes and allegories. *Toilers of the Sea.*

Augustus Saint-Gaudens, 1848-1907, (U.S.) memorial statues. *Farragut, Mrs. Henry Adams (Grief).*

Andrea Sansovino, 1460-1529, (It.) Renaissance sculptor. *Baptism of Christ.*

Jacopo Sansovino, 1486-1570, (It.) Renaissance sculptor. *St. John the Baptist.*

John Singer Sargent, 1856-1925, (U.S.) Edwardian society portraitist. *The Wyndham Sisters, Madam X.*

George Segal, 1924-2000, (U.S.) sculptor of life-sized figures realistically depicting daily life.

Georges Seurat, 1859-91, (Fr.) Pointillist. *Sunday Afternoon on the Island of La Grande Jatte.*

Gino Severini, 1883-1966, (It.) Futurist and Cubist. *Dynamic Hieroglyph of the Bal Tabarin.*

Ben Shahn, 1898-1969, (U.S.) social and political themes. Sacco and Vanzetti series, *Seurat's Lunch, Handball.*

Charles Sheeler, 1883-1965, (U.S.) abstractionist.

David Alfaro Siqueiros, 1896-1974, (Mex.) political muralist. *March of Humanity.*

David Smith, 1906-65, (U.S.) welded metal sculpture. *Hudson River Landscape, Zig, Cubi* series.

Edward Steichen, 1879-1973, (U.S.) photographer. Credited with transforming photography into an art form.

Alfred Stieglitz, 1864-1946, (U.S.) photographer, editor; helped create acceptance of photography as art.

Paul Strand, 1890-1976, (U.S.) photographer. People, nature, landscapes.

Gilbert Stuart, 1755-1828, (U.S.) portraitist. *George Washington, Thomas Jefferson, James Madison.*

Thomas Sully, 1783-1872, (U.S.) portraitist. *Col. Thomas Handasyd Perkins, The Passage of the Delaware.*

William Henry Fox Talbot, 1800-77, (Br.) photographer. *Pencil of Nature*, early photographically illustrated book.

George Tames, 1919-94, (U.S.) photographer. Chronicled presidents, political leaders.

Yves Tanguy, 1900-55, (Fr.) Surrealist. *Rose of the Four Winds, Mama, Papa Is Wounded!*

Giovanni Battista Tiepolo, 1696-1770, (It.) Rococo frescoes. *The Crucifixion.*

Jacopo Tintoretto, 1518-94, (It.) Mannerist. *The Last Supper.*

Titian, c.1485-1576, (It.) Renaissance. *Venus and the Lute Player, The Bacchanal.*

Jose Rey Toledo, 1916-94, (U.S.) Native American artist. Captured the essence of tribal dances on canvas.

Henri de Toulouse-Lautrec, 1864-1901, (Fr.) *At the Moulin Rouge.*

John Trumbull, 1756-1843, (U.S.) historical themes. *The Declaration of Independence.*

J(oseph) M(allord) W(illiam) Turner, 1775-1851, (Br.) Romantic landscapist. *Snow Storm.*

Paolo Uccello, 1397-1475, (It.) Gothic-Renaissance. *The Rout of San Romano.*

Maurice Utrillo, 1883-1955, (Fr.) Impressionist. *Sacre-Coeur de Montmartre.*

John Vanderlyn, 1775-1852, (U.S.) Neoclassicist. *Ariadne Asleep on the Island of Naxos.*

Diego Velázquez, 1599-1660, (Sp.) Baroque. *Las Meninas, Portrait of Juan de Pareja.*

Jan Vermeer, 1632-75, (Dutch) interior genre subjects. *Young Woman With a Water Jug.*

Paolo Veronese, 1528-88, (It.) devotional themes, vastly peopled canvases. *The Temptation of St. Anthony.*

Andrea del Verrocchio, 1435-88, (It.) Floren. sculptor. *Colleoni.*

Maurice de Vlaminck, 1876-1958, (Fr.) Fauvist landscapist. *Red Trees.*

Andy Warhol, 1928-87, (U.S.) Pop Art. *Campbell's Soup Cans, Marilyn Diptych.*

Antoine Watteau, 1684-1721, (Fr.) Rococo painter of "scenes of gallantry." *The Embarkation for Cythera.*

George Frederic Watts, 1817-1904, (Br.) painter and sculptor of grandiose allegorical themes. *Hope.*

Benjamin West, 1738-1820, (U.S.) realistic historical themes. *Death of General Wolfe.*

Edward Weston, 1886-1958, (U.S.) photographer. Landscapes of American West.

James Abbott McNeill Whistler, 1834-1903, (U.S.) *Arrangement in Grey and Black, No. 1: The Artist's Mother.*

Archibald M. Willard, 1836-1918, (U.S.) *The Spirit of '76.*

Grant Wood, 1891-1942, (U.S.) Midwestern regionalist. *American Gothic, Daughters of Revolution.*

Andrew Wyeth, 1917-2009, (U.S.), painter, regionalist style. *Christina's World.*

Ossip Zadkine, 1890-1967, (Russ.) School of Paris sculptor. *The Destroyed City, Musicians, Christ.*

Business Leaders and Philanthropists of the Past

Giovanni Agnelli, 1921-2003, (It.) industrialist, principal shareholder of Fiat.

Walter Annenberg, 1908-2002, (U.S.) publisher, founder *TV Guide*, philanthropist.

Elizabeth Arden (F. N. Graham), 1884-1966, (U.S.) Canadian-born founder of cosmetics empire.

Philip D. Armour, 1832-1901, (U.S.) industrialist; streamlined meatpacking.

Brooke Astor, 1902-2007, philanthropist; president of Vincent Astor Foundation.

John Jacob Astor, 1763-1848, (U.S.) German-born fur trader, banker, real estate magnate; at death, richest in U.S.

Francis W. Ayer, 1848-1923, (U.S.) ad industry pioneer.

August Belmont, 1816-90, (U.S.) German-born financier.

James B. (Diamond Jim) Brady, 1856-1917, (U.S.) financier, philanthropist, legendary bon vivant.

Adolphus Busch, 1839-1913, (U.S.) German-born businessman; established brewery empire.

Asa Candler, 1851-1929, (U.S.) founded Coca-Cola Co.

Andrew Carnegie, 1835-1919, (U.S.) Scottish-born industrialist; philanthropist; founded Carnegie Steel Co.

Tom Carvel, 1908-89, (Gr.-U.S.) founded ice cream chain.

William Colgate, 1783-1857, (Br.-U.S.) Br.-born businessman, philanthropist; founded soap-making empire.

Jay Cooke, 1821-1905, (U.S.) financier; sold $1 billion in Union bonds during Civil War.

Peter Cooper, 1791-1883, (U.S.) industrialist, inventor, philanthropist; founded Cooper Union (1859).

Ezra Cornell, 1807-74, (U.S.) businessman, philanthropist; headed Western Union, established university.

Erastus Corning, 1794-1872, (U.S.) financier; headed N.Y. Central.

Charles Crocker, 1822-88, (U.S.) railroad builder, financier.

Samuel Cunard, 1787-1865, (Can.) pioneered trans-Atlantic steam navigation.

Marcus Daly, 1841-1900, (U.S.) Irish-born copper magnate.

W. Edwards Deming, 1900-93, (U.S.) quality-control expert who revolutionized Japanese manufacturing.

Walt Disney, 1901-66, (U.S.) pioneer in cinema animation; built entertainment empire.

Herbert H. Dow, 1866-1930, (U.S.) founder of chemical co.

James Duke, 1856-1925, (U.S.) founded American Tobacco, Duke Univ.

Eleuthere I. du Pont, 1771-1834, (Fr.-U.S.) gunpowder manufacturer; founded one of the largest business empires.

Thomas C. Durant, 1820-85, (U.S.) railroad official, financier.

William C. Durant, 1861-1947, (U.S.) industrialist; formed General Motors.

George Eastman, 1854-1932, (U.S.) inventor; manufacturer of photographic equipment.

Marshall Field, 1834-1906, (U.S.) merchant; founded Chicago's largest department store.

Harvey Firestone, 1868-1938, (U.S.) founded tire company.

Avery Fisher, 1906-94, (U.S.) industrialist, philanthropist, founded Fisher electronics.

Henry M. Flagler, 1830-1913, (U.S.) financier; helped form Standard Oil; developed Florida as resort state.

Malcolm Forbes, 1919-90, (U.S.) magazine publisher.

Henry Ford, 1863-1947, (U.S.) auto maker; developed first popular low-priced car.

Henry Ford 2nd, 1917-87, (U.S.) headed auto company founded by grandfather.

Henry C. Frick, 1849-1919, (U.S.) steel and coke magnate; had prominent role in development of U.S. Steel.

Jakob Fugger (Jakob the Rich), 1459-1525, (Ger.) headed leading banking, trading house, in 16th-cent. Europe.

Alfred C. Fuller, 1885-1973, (U.S.) Canadian-born businessman; founded brush company.

Elbert H. Gary, 1846-1927, (U.S.) one of the organizers of U.S. Steel; chaired board of directors, 1903-27.

Jean Paul Getty, 1892-1976, (U.S.) founded oil empire.

Amadeo Giannini, 1870-1949, (U.S.) founded Bank of America.

Stephen Girard, 1750-1831, (U.S.) French-born financier, philanthropist; richest man in U.S. at his death.

Leonard H. Goldenson, 1905-99, (U.S.) turned ABC into major TV network.

Jay Gould, 1836-92, (U.S.) railroad magnate, financier.

Hetty Green, 1834-1916, (U.S.) financier, the "witch of Wall St."; richest woman in U.S. in her day.

William Gregg, 1800-67, (U.S.) launched textile industry in S.

Meyer Guggenheim, 1828-1905, (U.S.) Swiss-born merchant, philanthropist; built merchandising, mining empires.

Armand Hammer, 1898-1990, (U.S.) headed Occidental Petroleum; promoted U.S.-Soviet ties.

Edward H. Harriman, 1848-1909, (U.S.) railroad financier, administrator; headed Union Pacific.

Henry J. Heinz, 1844-1919, (U.S.) founded food empire.

Leona Helmsley, 1920-2007, real estate, philanthropist.

Milton Snavely Hershey, 1857-1945, (U.S.) chocolate co. founder, philanthropist.

James J. Hill, 1838-1916, (U.S.) Canadian-born railroad magnate, financier; founded Great Northern Railway.

Conrad N. Hilton, 1888-1979, (U.S.) hotel chain founder.

Howard Hughes, 1905-76, (U.S.) industrialist, aviator, movie maker.

H. L. Hunt, 1889-1974, (U.S.) oil magnate.

Collis P. Huntington, 1821-1900, (U.S.) railroad magnate.

Henry E. Huntington, 1850-1927, (U.S.) railroad builder, philanthropist.

Walter L. Jacobs, 1898-1985, (U.S.) founder of the first rental car agency, which later became Hertz.

Howard Johnson, 1896-1972, (U.S.) founded restaurants.

John H. Johnson, 1918-2005; built publishing empire based on *Ebony* and *Jet*.

Samuel Curtis Johnson, 1928-2004, (U.S.) headed S.C. Johnson & Sons.

Henry J. Kaiser, 1882-1967, (U.S.) industrialist; built empire in steel, aluminum.

Minor C. Keith, 1848-1929, (U.S.) railroad magnate; founded United Fruit Co.

Will K. Kellogg, 1860-1951, (U.S.) businessman, philanthropist; founded breakfast food co.

Richard King, 1825-85, (U.S.) cattleman; founded half-million-acre King Ranch in Texas.

William S. Knudsen, 1879-1948, (U.S.) Danish-born auto industry executive.

Samuel H. Kress, 1863-1955, (U.S.) businessman, art collector, philanthropist; founded "dime store" chain.

Ray A. Kroc, 1902-84, (U.S.) original CEO of McDonald's Corp.; oversaw company's vast expansion.

Alfred Krupp, 1812-87, (Ger.) armaments magnate.

Kenneth L. Lay, 1942-2006, (U.S.), former CEO of Enron, indicted on fraud charges.

William Levitt, 1907-94, (U.S.) industrialist, "suburb maker."

Thomas Lipton, 1850-1931, (Scot.) merchant, tea empire.

James McGill, 1744-1813, (Scot.-Can.) founded university.

Andrew W. Mellon, 1855-1937, (U.S.) financier, industrialist; benefactor of National Gallery of Art.

Charles E. Merrill, 1885-1956, (U.S.) financier; developed firm of Merrill Lynch.

John Pierpont Morgan, 1837-1913, (U.S.) most powerful figure in finance and industry at the turn of the cent.

Akio Morita, 1921-99, (Japan) co-founded Sony Corp.

Malcolm Muir, 1885-1979, (U.S.) created *Business Week* magazine; headed *Newsweek*, 1937-61.

Samuel Newhouse, 1895-1979, (U.S.) publishing and broadcasting magnate; built communications empire.

Aristotle Onassis, 1906-75, (Gr.) shipping magnate.

William S. Paley, 1901-90, (U.S.) built CBS communic. empire.

Frederick D. Patterson, 1901-88, founder of United Negro College Fund, 1944.

George Peabody, 1795-1869, (U.S.) merchant, financier, philanthropist.

James C. Penney, 1875-1971, (U.S.) businessman; developed department store chain.

William C. Procter, 1862-1934, (U.S.) headed soap co.

Frank Perdue, 1920-2005, (U.S.) founder of Perdue Farms, chicken-processing company.

John D. Rockefeller, 1839-1937, (U.S.) industrialist; established Standard Oil.

John D. Rockefeller Jr., 1874-1960, (U.S.) philanthropist; established foundation; provided land for UN.

Laurance S. Rockefeller, 1910-2004, (U.S.) philanthropist, conservationist.

Meyer A. Rothschild, 1743-1812, (Ger.) founded international banking house.

Thomas Fortune Ryan, 1851-1928, (U.S.) financier; a founder of American Tobacco.

Edmond J. Safra, 1932-99, (U.S.) banker.

David Sarnoff, 1891-1971, (U.S.) broadcasting pioneer; established first radio network, NBC.

Richard Sears, 1863-1914, (U.S.) founded mail-order co.

Werner von Siemens, 1816-92, (Ger.) industrialist; inventor.

Alfred P. Sloan, 1875-1966, (U.S.) industrialist, philanthropist; headed General Motors.

A. Leland Stanford, 1824-93, (U.S.) railroad official, philanthropist; founded university.

Frank Stanton, 1908-2006, (U.S.) president of CBS network, 1946-71.

Larry Stewart, 1948-2007, "Kansas City's Secret Santa."

Nathan Straus, 1848-1931, (U.S.) German-born merchant, philanthropist; headed Macy's.

Levi Strauss, c.1829-1902, (U.S.) pants manufacturer.

Clement Studebaker, 1831-1901, (U.S.) wagon, carriage maker.

Gustavus Swift, 1839-1903, (U.S.) pioneer meatpacker.

Gerard Swope, 1872-1957, (U.S.) industrialist, economist; headed General Electric.

Dave Thomas, 1932-2002, (U.S.) Wendy's founder.

James Walter Thompson, 1847-1928, (U.S.) ad executive.

Alice Tully, 1902-93, (U.S.) philanthropist, arts patron.

Theodore N. Vail, 1845-1920, (U.S.) organized Bell Telephone system; headed AT&T.

Cornelius Vanderbilt, 1794-1877, (U.S.) financier; established steamship, railroad empires.

Henry Villard, 1835-1900, (U.S.) German-born railroad executive, financier.

George Westinghouse, 1846-1914, (U.S) inventor, manufacturer; organized Westinghouse Electric Co., 1886.

Charles R. Walgreen, 1873-1939, (U.S.) founded drugstore chain.

DeWitt Wallace, 1889-1981, (U.S.) and Lila Wallace, 1889-1984, (U.S.) cofounders of Reader's Digest magazine.

Sam Walton, 1918-92, (U.S.) founder of Wal-Mart stores.

John Wanamaker, 1838-1922, (U.S.) department-store merchandising pioneer.

Aaron Montgomery Ward, 1843-1913, (U.S.) established first mail-order firm.

Thomas J. Watson, 1874-1956, (U.S.) IBM head, 1914-56.

John Hay Whitney, 1905-82, (U.S.) publisher, sportsman, philanthropist.

Charles E. Wilson, 1890-1961, (U.S.) auto exec., public official.

Frank W. Woolworth, 1852-1919, (U.S.) created 5 & 10 chain.

William Wrigley Jr., 1861-1932, (U.S.) founded Wrigley chewing gum company.

American Cartoonists

Reviewed by Lucy Shelton Caswell, Professor and Curator, Cartoon Research Library, Ohio State University.

Scott Adams, b 1957, Dilbert.

Charles Addams, 1912-88, macabre cartoons.

Brad Anderson, b 1924, Marmaduke.

Sergio Aragones, b 1937, MAD Magazine.

Peter Arno, 1904-68, The New Yorker.

Tex Avery, 1908-80, animator, Bugs Bunny, Porky Pig.

George Baker, 1915-75, The Sad Sack.

Carl Barks, 1901-2000, Donald Duck comic books.

C. C. Beck, 1910-89, Captain Marvel.

Dave Berg, 1920-2002, Mad Magazine.

Jim Berry, b 1932, Berry's World.

Herb Block (Herblock), 1909-2001, political cartoonist.

George Booth, b 1926, The New Yorker.

Berkeley Breathed, b 1957, Bloom County.

Dik Browne, 1917-89, Hi & Lois, Hagar the Horrible.

Marjorie Buell, 1904-93, Little Lulu.

Ernie Bushmiller, 1905-82, Nancy.

Milton Caniff, 1907-88, Terry & the Pirates, Steve Canyon.

Al Capp, 1909-79, Li'l Abner.

Roz Chast, b 1954, The New Yorker.

Paul Conrad, b 1924, political cartoonist.

Roy Crane, 1901-77, Captain Easy, Buz Sawyer.

Robert Crumb, b 1943, underground cartoonist.

Shamus Culhane, 1908-96, animator.

Jay N. Darling (Ding), 1876-1962, political cartoonist.

Jack Davis, b 1926, MAD Magazine.

Jim Davis, b 1945, Garfield.

Billy DeBeck, 1890-1942, Barney Google.

Rudolph Dirks, 1877-1968, The Katzenjammer Kids.

Walt Disney, 1901-66, produced animated cartoons, created Mickey Mouse, Donald Duck.

Steve Ditko, b 1927, Spider-Man.

Mort Drucker, b 1929, MAD Magazine.

Will Eisner, 1917-2005, The Spirit.

Jules Feiffer, b 1929, political cartoonist.

Bud Fisher, 1884-1954, Mutt & Jeff.

Ham Fisher, 1900-55, Joe Palooka.

Max Fleischer, 1883-1972, Betty Boop.

Hal Foster, 1892-1982, Tarzan, Prince Valiant.

Fontaine Fox, 1884-1964, Toonerville Folks.

Isadore "Friz" Freleng, 1905-95, animator, Yosemite Sam, Porky Pig, Sylvester and Tweety Bird.

Rube Goldberg, 1883-1970, Boob McNutt.

Chester Gould, 1900-85, Dick Tracy.

Harold Gray, 1894-1968, Little Orphan Annie.

Matt Groening, b 1954, Life in Hell, The Simpsons.

Cathy Guisewite, b 1950, Cathy.

Bill Hanna, 1910-2001, & Joe Barbera, 1911-2006, animators, Tom & Jerry, Yogi Bear, Flintstones.

Oliver Harrington, 1912-95, Bootsie.

Johnny Hart, 1931-2007, BC, Wizard of Id.

Alfred Harvey, 1913-94, created Casper the Friendly Ghost.

Jimmy Hatlo, 1898-1963, Little Iodine.

John Held Jr., 1889-1958, Jazz Age.

George Herriman, 1881-1944, Krazy Kat.

Harry Hershfield, 1885-1974, Abie the Agent.

Al Hirschfeld, 1903-2003, N.Y. Times theater caricaturist.

Burne Hogarth, 1911-96, Tarzan.

Helen Hokinson, 1900-49, The New Yorker.

Nicole Hollander, b 1939, Sylvia.

Oliver Johnston, 1912-2008, Disney animator.

Chuck Jones, 1912-2002, animator, Bugs Bunny, Porky Pig.

Mike Judge, b 1962, Beavis and Butthead, King of the Hill.

Bob Kane, b 1916-98, Batman.

Bil Keane, b 1922, The Family Circus.

Walt Kelly, 1913-73, Pogo.

Hank Ketcham, 1920-2001, Dennis the Menace.

Ted Key, 1912-2008, Hazel.

Frank King, 1883-1969, Gasoline Alley.

Jack Kirby, 1917-94, Fantastic Four, The Incredible Hulk.

Rollin Kirby, 1875-1952, political cartoonist.

B(ernard) Kliban, 1935-91, cat books.

Edward Koren, b 1935, The New Yorker.

Harvey Kurtzman, 1921-93, MAD Magazine.

Walter Lantz, 1900-94, Woody Woodpecker.

Gary Larson, b 1950, The Far Side.

Mell Lazarus, b 1929, Momma, Miss Peach.

Stan Lee, b 1922, Marvel Comics.

David Levine, b 1926, N.Y. Review of Books caricatures.

Doug Marlette, 1949-2007, political cartoonist, Kudzu.

Don Martin, 1931-2000, MAD Magazine.

Bill Mauldin, 1921-2003, political cartoonist.

Jeff MacNelly, 1947-2000, political cartoonist, Shoe.

Winsor McCay, 1872-1934, Little Nemo.

John T. McCutcheon, 1870-1949, political cartoonist.

Aaron McGruder, b 1974, The Boondocks.

George McManus, 1884-1954, Bringing Up Father.

Dale Messick, 1906-2005, Brenda Starr.

Norman Mingo, 1896-1980, Alfred E. Neuman.

Bob Montana, 1920-75, Archie.

Dick Moores, 1909-86, Gasoline Alley.

Willard Mullin, 1902-78, sports cartoonist; Dodgers "Bum," Mets "Kid."

Russell Myers, b 1938, Broom Hilda.

Thomas Nast, 1840-1902, political cartoonist; Republican elephant and Democratic donkey.

Pat Oliphant, b 1935, political cartoonist.

Frederick Burr Opper, 1857-1937, Happy Hooligan.

Richard Outcault, 1863-1928, Yellow Kid, Buster Brown.

Brant Parker, 1920-2007, Wizard of Id.

Trey Parker, b 1969, animator, co-creator of South Park.

Mike Peters, b 1943, cartoonist, Mother Goose & Grimm.

George Price, 1901-95, The New Yorker.

Antonio Prohias, 1921-98, Spy vs. Spy.

Alex Raymond, 1909-56, Flash Gordon, Jungle Jim.

Forrest (Bud) Sagendorf, 1915-94, Popeye.

Art Sansom, 1920-91, The Born Loser.

Charles Schulz, 1922-2000, Peanuts.

Elzie C. Segar, 1894-1938, Popeye.

Joe Shuster, 1914-92, & Jerry Siegel, 1914-96, Superman.

Sidney Smith, 1887-1935, The Gumps.

Otto Soglow, 1900-75, Little King.

Art Spiegelman, b 1948, Raw, Maus.

William Steig, b 1907-2003, The New Yorker.

Matt Stone, b 1971, animator, co-creator of South Park.

Paul Szep, b 1941, political cartoonist.

James Swinnerton, 1875-1974, Little Jimmy, Canyon Kiddies.

Paul Terry, 1887-1971, animator of Mighty Mouse.

Bob Thaves, 1924-2006, Frank and Ernest.

James Thurber, 1894-61, The New Yorker.

Garry Trudeau, b 1948, Doonesbury.

Mort Walker, b 1923, Beetle Bailey.

Bill Watterson, b 1958, Calvin and Hobbes.

Russ Westover, 1887-1966, Tillie the Toiler.

Signe Wilkinson, b 1950, political cartoonist.

Frank Willard, 1893-1958, Moon Mullins.

J. R. Williams, 1888-1957, The Willets Family, Out Our Way.

Gahan Wilson, b 1930, The New Yorker.

Tom Wilson, b 1931, Ziggy.

Art Young, 1866-1943, political cartoonist.

Chic Young, 1901-73, Blondie.

Economists, Educators, Historians, and Social Scientists of the Past

For Psychologists see Scientists of the Past.

Brooks Adams, 1848-1927, (U.S.) historian, political theoretician; *The Law of Civilization and Decay.*

Henry Adams, 1838-1918, (U.S.) historian, autobiographer; *The Education of Henry Adams.*

Francis Bacon, 1561-1626, (Eng.) philosopher, essayist, and statesman; championed observation and induction.

George Bancroft, 1800-91, (U.S.) historian; wrote 10-volume *History of the United States.*

Jack Barbash, 1911-94, (U.S.) labor economist who helped create the AFL-CIO.

Henry Barnard, 1811-1900, (U.S.) public school reformer.

Charles A. Beard, 1874-1948, (U.S.) historian; *The Economic Basis of Politics.*

(St.) Bede (the Venerable), c.673-735, (Br.) scholar, historian; *Ecclesiastical History of the English People.*

Ruth Benedict, 1887-1948, (U.S.) anthropologist; studied Indian tribes of the Southwest.

Sir Isaiah Berlin, 1909-97, (Br.) philosopher, historian; *The Age of Enlightenment.*

Leonard Bloomfield, 1887-1949, (U.S.) linguist; *Language.*

Franz Boas, 1858-1942, (U.S.) German-born anthropologist; studied American Indians.

Van Wyck Brooks, 1886-1963, (U.S.) historian; critic of New England culture, especially literature.

William Edward Burghardt (W.E.B.) Du Bois, 1868-1963, (U.S.) historian, sociologist; and NAACP founder, 1909.

Edmund Burke, 1729-97, (Ir.) British parliamentarian and political philosopher; *Reflections on the Revolution in France.*

Nicholas Murray Butler, 1862-1947, (U.S.) educator; headed Columbia Univ., 1902-45; Nobel Peace Prize, 1931.

Joseph Campbell, 1904-87, (U.S.) author, editor, teacher; wrote books on mythology, folklore.

Thomas Carlyle, 1795-1881, (Sc.) historian, critic; *Sartor Resartus, Past and Present, The French Revolution.*

Edward Channing, 1856-1931, (U.S.) historian; wrote 6-volume *History of the United States.*

Henry Steele Commager, 1902-98, (U.S.) historian, educator; wrote *The Growth of the American Republic.*

John R. Commons, 1862-1945, (U.S.) economist, labor his- torian; *Legal Foundations of Capitalism.*

James B. Conant, 1893-1978, (U.S.) educator, diplomat; *The American High School Today.*

Benedetto Croce, 1866-1952, (It.) philosopher, statesman, and historian; *Philosophy of the Spirit.*

Bernard A. De Voto, 1897-1955, (U.S.) historian; wrote trilogy on American West; edited Mark Twain manuscripts.

Melvil Dewey, 1851-1931, (U.S.) devised decimal system of library-book classification.

Donald Herbert Donald, 1920-2009, (U.S.) Pulitzer Prize-winning Civil War and Lincoln historian.

St. Clair Drake, 1911-90, (U.S.) Sociologist, black studies pioneer, *Black Metropolis* (1945), with Horace R. Cayton.

Emile Durkheim, 1858-1917, (Fr.) a founder of modern sociology; *The Rules of Sociological Method.*

Jean Baptiste Point du Sable, c.1750-1818, (U.S.) pioneer trader and first settler of Chicago, 1779.

Charles Eliot, 1834-1926, (U.S.) educator, Harvard president.

Friedrich Engels, 1820-95, (Ger.) political writer; with Marx wrote the *Communist Manifesto.*

Irving Fisher, 1867-1947, (U.S.) economist; contributed to the development of modern monetary theory.

John Fiske, 1842-1901, (U.S.) historian and lecturer; popularized Darwinian theory of evolution.

Charles Fourier, 1772-1837, (Fr.) utopian socialist.

John Hope Franklin, 1915-2009, (U.S.), historian, *From Slavery to Freedom: A History of African Americans.*

Milton Friedman, 1912-2006, (U.S.) economist.

John Kenneth Galbraith, 1908-2006, (Can.-U.S.) economist, author, professor, former amb. to India.

Giovanni Gentile, 1875-1944, (It.) philosopher, educator; reformed Italian educational system.

Sir James George Frazer, 1854-1941, (Br.) anthropologist; studied myth in religion; *The Golden Bough.*

Henry George, 1839-97, (U.S.) economist, reformer; led single-tax movement.

Edward Gibbon, 1737-94, (Br.) historian; *The History of the Decline and Fall of the Roman Empire.*

Francesco Guicciardini, 1483-1540, (It.) historian; *Storia d'Italia,* principal historical work of the 16th cent.

Thomas Hobbes, 1588-1679, (Eng.) philosopher, political theorist; *Leviathan.*

Richard Hofstadter, 1916-70, (U.S.) historian; *The Age of Reform.*

Charles Hamilton Houston, 1895-1950, (U.S.) African American lawyer, Howard University instructor, champion of minority rights.

Samuel Huntington, 1927-2008, (U.S.), political scientist, Harvard University professor, *The Clash of Civilizations.*

George F. Kennan, 1904-2005, (U.S.) diplomat; main architect of the U.S. Cold War "containment" strategy.

John Maynard Keynes, 1883-1946, (Br.) economist; principal advocate of deficit spending.

Alfred Kinsey, 1894-1956, (U.S.) zoologist; pioneering human sex researcher.

Russell Kirk, 1918-94, (U.S.), social philosopher; *The Conservative Mind.*

Alfred L. Kroeber, 1876-1960, (U.S.) cultural anthropologist; studied Indians of North and South America.

Elisabeth Kubler-Ross, 1926-2004, (Swiss) psychiatrist, author. *On Death and Dying.*

Christopher Lasch, 1932-94, (U.S.) social critic, historian; *The Culture of Narcissism.*

James L. Laughlin, 1850-1933, (U.S.) economist; helped establish Federal Reserve System.

Lucien Lévy-Bruhl, 1857-1939, (Fr.) philosopher; studied the psychology of primitive societies; *Primitive Mentality.*

John Locke, 1632-1704, (Eng.) philosopher and political theorist; *Two Treatises of Government.*

Thomas B. Macaulay, 1800-59, (Br.) historian, statesman.

Niccolò Machiavelli, 1469-1527, (It.) writer, statesman. *The Prince.*

Bronislaw Malinowski, 1884-1942, (Pol.) considered the father of social anthropology.

Thomas R. Malthus, 1766-1834, (Br.) economist; famed for *Essay on the Principle of Population.*

Horace Mann, 1796-1859, (U.S.) pioneered modern public school system.

Karl Mannheim, 1893-1947, (Hung.) sociologist, historian; *Ideology and Utopia.*

Harriet Martineau, 1802-76, (Eng.) writer, feminist; *Society in America*

Karl Marx, 1818-83, (Ger.) political theorist, proponent of Communism; *Communist Manifesto, Das Kapital.*

Benjamin Mays, 1895-1984, (U.S.) minister, educator, civil rights leader; headed Morehouse College, 1940-67.

Giuseppe Mazzini, 1805-72, (It.) political philosopher.

William H. McGuffey, 1800-73, (U.S.) whose *Reader* was a mainstay of 19th-cent. U.S. public education.

George H. Mead, 1863-1931, (U.S.) philosopher, social psychologist.

Margaret Mead, 1901-78, (U.S.) cultural anthropologist; popularized field; *Coming of Age in Samoa.*

Alexander Meiklejohn, 1872-1964, (U.S.) Br.-born educator; championed academic freedom and experimental curricula.

James Mill, 1773-1836, (Sc.) philosopher, historian, economist; a proponent of utilitarianism.

John Stuart Mill, 1806-73, (Eng.) philosopher, economist, *Utilitarianism*; eldest son of James Mill.

Perry G. Miller, 1905-63, (U.S.) historian; interpreted 17th-cent. New England.

Theodor Mommsen, 1817-1903, (Ger.) historian; *The History of Rome.*

Ashley Montagu, 1905-99, (Eng.) anthropologist; *The Natural Superiority of Women.*

Charles-Louis Montesquieu, 1689-1755, (Fr.) social philosopher; *The Spirit of Laws.*

Maria Montessori, 1870-1952, (It.) educator, physician; started Montessori method of student self-motivation.

Samuel Eliot Morison, 1887-1976, (U.S.) historian; chronicled voyages of early explorers.

Lewis Mumford, 1895-1990, (U.S.) sociologist, critic; *The Culture of Cities.*

Gunnar Myrdal, 1898-1987, (Swed.) economist, social scientist; *Asian Drama: An Inquiry Into the Poverty of Nations.*

Allan Nevins, 1890-1971, (U.S.) historian, biographer; *The Ordeal of the Union.*

José Ortega y Gasset, 1883-1955, (Sp.) philosopher; advocated control by elite, *The Revolt of the Masses.*

Robert Owen, 1771-1858, (Br.) political philosopher, reformer; pioneer in cooperative movement.

Thomas (Tom) Paine, 1737-1809, (U.S.) political theorist, writer. *Common Sense.*

Vilfredo Pareto, 1848-1923, (It.) economist, sociologist.

Francis Parkman, 1823-93, (U.S.) historian; *France and England in North America.*

Elizabeth P. Peabody, 1804-94, (U.S.) education pioneer; founded 1st kindergarten in U.S., 1860.

William Prescott, 1796-1859, (U.S.) early American historian; *The Conquest of Peru.*

Pierre Joseph Proudhon, 1809-65, (Fr.) social theorist; father of anarchism; *The Philosophy of Property.*

François Quesnay, 1694-1774, (Fr.) economic theorist.

David Ricardo, 1772-1823, (Br.) economic theorist; advocated free international trade.

David Riesman, 1909-2002, (U.S.) sociologist, coauthor *The Lonely Crowd.*

Jean-Jacques Rousseau, 1712-78, (Fr.) social philosopher; the father of romantic sensibility; *Confessions.*

Edward Sapir, 1884-1939, (Ger.-U.S.) anthropologist; studied ethnology and linguistics of U.S. Indian groups.

Ferdinand de Saussure, 1857-1913, (Swiss) a founder of modern linguistics.

Arthur Schlesinger Jr., 1917-2007, (U.S.) historian, author; *The Imperial Presidency.*

Joseph Schumpeter, 1883-1950, (Czech.-U.S.) economist, sociologist.

Elizabeth Seton, 1774-1821, (U.S.) nun; est. parochial school education in U.S.; first native-born American saint.

Georg Simmel, 1858-1918, (Ger.) sociologist, philosopher; helped establish German sociology.

Adam Smith, 1723-90, (Br.) economist; advocated laissez-faire economy, free trade; *The Wealth of Nations*.

Jared Sparks, 1789-1866, (U.S.) historian, educator, editor; *The Library of American Biography*.

Oswald Spengler, 1880-1936, (Ger.) philosopher and historian; *The Decline of the West*.

William G. Sumner, 1840-1910, (U.S.) social scientist, economist; laissez-faire economy, Social Darwinism.

Hippolyte Taine, 1828-93, (Fr.) historian; basis of naturalistic school; *The Origins of Contemporary France*.

A(lan) J(ohn) P(ercivale) Taylor, 1906-89, (Br.) historian; *The Origins of the Second World War*.

Nikolaas Tinbergen, 1907-88, (Dutch-Br.) ethologist; pioneer in study of animal behavior.

Alexis de Tocqueville, 1805-59, (Fr.) political scientist, historian; *Democracy in America*.

Francis E. Townsend, 1867-1960, (U.S.) led old-age pension movement, 1933.

Arnold Toynbee, 1889-1975, (Br.) historian; *A Study of History*, sweeping analysis of hist. of civilizations.

George Trevelyan, 1838-1928, (Br.) historian, statesman; favored "literary" over "scientific" history; *History of England*.

Henri Troyat, 1911-2007 (Rus.-Fr.), biographies of major figures in Russian history.

Frederick J. Turner, 1861-1932, (U.S.) historian, educator; *The Frontier in American History*.

Thorstein B. Veblen, 1857-1929, (U.S.) economist, social philosopher; *The Theory of the Leisure Class*.

Giovanni Vico, 1668-1744, (It.) historian, philosopher; regarded by many as first modern historian; *New Science*.

Izaak Walton, 1593-1683, (Eng.) wrote biographies; political-philosophical study of fishing, *The Compleat Angler*.

Booker T. Washington, 1856-1915, (U.S.) founder, 1881, and first pres. of Tuskegee Institute; *Up From Slavery*.

Sidney J., 1859-1947, and **Beatrice**, 1858-1943, **Webb**, (Br.) leading figures in Fabian Society and Labor Party.

Max Weber, 1864-1920, (Ger.) sociologist; *The Protestant Ethic and the Spirit of Capitalism*.

Walter White, 1893-1955, (U.S.) exec. sec., NAACP, 1931-55.

Roy Wilkins, 1901-81, (U.S.) exec. director, NAACP, 1955-77.

Emma Hart Willard, 1787-1870, (U.S.) pioneered higher education for women.

Carter G. Woodson, 1875-1950, (U.S.) historian; founded Assn. for the Study of Negro Life and History.

C. Vann Woodward, 1908-99, (U.S.) historian; *The Strange Career of Jim Crow*.

American Journalists of the Past

Reviewed by Dean Mills, Dean, Missouri School of Journalism.

See also Business Leaders, Cartoonists, Writers of the Past.

Franklin P. Adams (F.P.A.), 1881-1960, humorist; wrote column "The Conning Tower."

Joseph W. Alsop, 1910-89, and **Stewart Alsop**, 1914-74, Washington-based political analysts, columnists.

Jack Anderson, 1922-2006, muckraking Washington, DC, syndicated columnist.

Brooks Atkinson, 1894-1984, theater critic.

Robert L. Bartley, 1937-2003, editorial-page editor for *Wall Street Journal*.

James Gordon Bennett, 1795-1872, editor and publisher; founded *NY Herald*.

James Gordon Bennett, 1841-1918, succeeded father, financed expeditions, founded afternoon paper.

Elias Boudinot, d 1839, founding editor of first Native American newspaper in U.S., *Cherokee Phoenix* (1828-34).

Margaret Bourke-White, 1904-71, photojournalist.

Ed Bradley, 1941-2006, TV journalist (*60 Minutes*); one of the first African American journalists to report on the Vietnam War.

David Brinkley, 1920-2003, co-anchor of NBC's *Huntley-Brinkley Report*, host of ABC's *This Week With David Brinkley*.

Arthur Brisbane, 1864-1936, editor; helped introduce "yellow journalism" with sensational, simply written articles.

Heywood Broun, 1888-1939, author, columnist; founded American Newspaper Guild.

Art Buchwald, 1925-2007, journalist, humorist, syndicated columnist.

William F. Buckley Jr., 1925-2008, columnist and commentator; founder of *National Review*.

Herb Caen, 1916-97, longtime columnist for *San Francisco Chronicle* and *Examiner*.

John Campbell, 1653-1728, published *Boston News-Letter*, first continuing newspaper in the American colonies.

Jimmy Cannon, 1909-73, syndicated sports columnist.

John Chancellor, 1927-96, NBC TV reporter, anchor.

Harry Chandler, 1864-1944, *Los Angeles Times* publisher, 1917-41; made it a dominant force.

Otis Chandler, 1928-2006, *Los Angeles Times* publisher, 1960-80.

Marquis Childs, 1903-90, reporter and columnist for *St. Louis Post-Dispatch* and United Feature syndicate.

Craig Claiborne, 1920-2000, *NY Times* food editor and critic; key in internationalizing American taste.

Elizabeth Cochrane (Nellie Bly), 1867-1922, pioneer woman journalist, investig. reporter, noted for series on trip around the world.

Charles Collingwood, 1917-85, CBS news correspondent.

Alistair Cooke, 1908-2004, journalist, TV narrator, naturalized American citizen, "Letter from America" series.

Howard Cosell, 1920-95, TV and radio sportscaster.

Gardner Cowles, 1861-1946, founded newspaper chain.

Walter Cronkite, 1916-2009, evening news anchor, TV journalist.

Cyrus Curtis, 1850-1933, publisher of *Saturday Evening Post*, *Ladies' Home Journal*, *Country Gentleman*.

John Charles Daly, 1914-91, war correspondent; TV journalist; Voice of America head.

Charles Anderson Dana, 1819-97, editor, publisher; made *NY Sun* famous for its news reporting.

Elmer (Holmes) Davis, 1890-1958, *NY Times* editorial writer; radio commentator.

Richard Harding Davis, 1864-1916, war correspondent, travel writer, fiction writer.

Benjamin Day, 1810-89, published *NY Sun* beginning in 1833, introducing penny press to the U.S.

Finley Peter Dunne, 1867-1936, humorist, social critic, wrote "Mr. Dooley" columns.

Mary Baker Eddy, 1821-1910, founded Christian Science movement and *Christian Science Monitor*.

Rowland Evans Jr., 1921-2001, Washington columnist.

Fanny Fern (Sarah Willis Parton), 1811-72, newspaper columnist, author.

Marshall Field III, 1893-1956, retail magnate, *Chicago Sun* founder.

Doris Fleeson, 1901-70, war correspondent, columnist.

James Franklin, 1697-1735, printer, pioneer journalist, publisher of *New England Courant* and *Rhode Island Gazette*.

Fred W. Friendly, 1915-98, radio, TV reporter, producer, executive, collaborator with Edward R. Murrow.

Margaret Fuller, 1810-50, social reformer, transcendentalist, critic and foreign correspondent for *NY Tribune*.

Frank E. Gannett, 1876-1957, founded newspaper chain.

William Lloyd Garrison, 1805-79, abolitionist; publisher of *The Liberator*.

Elizabeth Meriwether Gilmer (Dorothy Dix), 1861-1951, reporter, pioneer of the advice column genre.

Edwin Lawrence Godkin, 1831-1902, founder of *The Nation*, editor of *N.Y. Evening Post*.

Katharine Graham, 1917-2001, *Washington Post* publisher.

Sheilah Graham, 1904-89, Hollywood gossip columnist.

Horace Greeley, 1811-72, editor and politician; founded *NY Tribune*.

Meg Greenfield, 1930-99, *Newsweek* columnist, editorial page editor *Washington Post*.

Gilbert Hovey Grosvenor, 1875-1966, longtime editor of *National Geographic* magazine.

John Gunther, 1901-70, *Chicago Daily News* foreign correspondent, author.

David Halberstam, 1934-2007, journalist, sports reporter, author; *The Best and the Brightest*, *Summer of '49*.

Sarah Josepha Buell Hale, 1788-1879, first female magazine editor, (Ladies' Magazine, later Godey's Lady's Book)

William Randolph Hearst, 1863-1951, founder of Hearst newspaper chain and one of the pioneer yellow journalists.

Gabriel Heatter, 1890-1972, radio commentator.

John Hersey, 1914-98, foreign correspondent for *Time*, *Life*, and *The New Yorker*, author.

Marguerite Higgins, 1920-66, reporter, war correspondent.

Hedda Hopper, 1885-1966, Hollywood gossip columnist.

Roy Howard, 1883-1964, editor, executive, Scripps-Howard papers and United Press (later United Press International).

Chet (Chester Robert) Huntley, 1911-74, co-anchor of NBC's *Huntley-Brinkley Report*.

Ralph Ingersoll, 1900-85, editor, *Fortune*, *Time*, *Life* exec.

Molly Ivins, 1944-2007, author, syndicated political columnist.

Peter Jennings, 1938-2005, ABC TV correspondent, anchor.

H. V. (Hans von) Kaltenborn, 1878-1965, radio commentator, reporter.

Murray Kempton, 1917-97, reporter, columnist for magazines and newspapers, including *NY Post*.

Dorothy Kilgallen, 1913-65, crime reporter; columnist.

John S. Knight, 1894-1981, editor, publisher; founded Knight newspaper group, which merged into Knight-Ridder.

Joseph Kraft, 1942-86, foreign policy columnist.

Irving Kristol, 1920-2009, columnist and commentator.

Arthur Krock, 1886-1974, *NY Times* political writer, Washington bureau chief.

Charles Kuralt, 1934-97, TV anchor and host of CBS "On the Road" featuring stories about life in the U.S.

Ann Landers (Eppie Lederer), 1918-2002, advice columnist.

David Lawrence, 1888-1973, reporter, columnist, publisher; founded *U.S. News & World Report*.

Frank Leslie, 1821-80, engraver and publisher of newspapers and magazines, notably *Leslie's Illustrated Newspaper*.

Alexander Liberman, 1912-99, editorial director for Conde Nast magazines.

A(bbott) J(oseph) Liebling, 1904-63, foreign correspondent, critic, principally with *The New Yorker*.

Walter Lippmann, 1889-1974, political analyst, social critic, columnist, author.

Peter Lisagor, 1915-76, Washington bureau chief, *Chicago Daily News*; broadcast commentator.

David Ross Locke, 1833-88, humorist, satirist under pseudonym P.V. Nasby; owned *Toledo (Ohio) Blade*.

Elijah Parish Lovejoy, 1802-37, abolitionist editor in St. Louis and in Alton, IL; killed by proslavery mob.

Clare Booth Luce, 1903-87, war correspondent for *Life*; diplomat, playwright.

Henry R. Luce, 1898-1967, founded *Time, Fortune, Life, Sports Illustrated*.

Dwight Macdonald, 1906-82, reporter, social critic.

C(harles) K(enny) McClatchy, 1858-1936, founder of McClatchy newspaper chain.

Sarah McClendon, 1910-2003, veteran White House correspondent.

Samuel McClure, 1857-1949, founder (1893) of *McClure's Magazine*, famous for its investigative reporting.

Anne O'Hare McCormick, 1889-1954, foreign correspondent, first woman on *NY Times* editorial board.

Robert R. McCormick, 1880-1955, editor, publisher, executive of *Chicago Tribune* and *NY Daily News*.

Ralph McGill, 1893-1969, crusading editor and publisher of *Atlanta Constitution*.

Mary McGrory, 1918-2004, Washington, DC, columnist.

O(scar) O(dd) McIntyre, 1884-1938, feature writer, syndicated columnist on everyday life in New York City.

Don Marquis, 1878-1937, humor columnist for *NY Sun* and *N.Y. Tribune*; wrote "archy and mehitabel" stories.

Robert Maynard, 1937-97, first African American editor and then owner of major U.S. paper, the *Oakland Tribune*.

Joseph Medill, 1823-99, longtime *editor of Chicago Tribune*.

H(enry) L(ouis) Mencken, 1880-1956, reporter, editor, columnist with *Baltimore Sun* papers; anti-establishment viewpoint.

Edwin Meredith, 1876-1928, founder of magazine company.

Frank A. Munsey, 1854-1925, owner, editor, and publisher of newspapers and magazines, including *Munsey's Magazine*.

Edward R. Murrow, 1908-65, broadcast reporter, executive; reported from Britain in WW2; hosted *See It Now, Person to Person*.

Louella Parsons, 1881-1972, Hollywood gossip columnist.

Daniel Pearl, 1963-2002, American journalist, kidnapped and murdered in Pakistan.

Drew (Andrew Russell) Pearson, 1897-1969, investigative reporter and columnist.

(James) Westbrook Pegler, 1894-1969, reporter, columnist.

Shirley Povich, 1905-98, sports columnist.

Joseph Pulitzer, 1847-1911, *NY World* publisher; founded Columbia Journalism School, Pulitzer Prizes.

Joseph Pulitzer II, 1885-1955, longtime *St. Louis Post-Dispatch* editor, publisher; built it into major paper.

Ernie (Ernest Taylor) Pyle, 1900-45, reporter, war correspondent; killed in WW2.

Henry Raymond, 1820-69, cofounder, editor, *NY Times*.

Harry Reasoner, 1923-91, ABC and CBS news reporter, anchor.

John Reed, 1887-1920, reporter, foreign correspondent famous for coverage of Bolshevik Revolution; buried at the Kremlin.

Whitelaw Reid, 1837-1912, longtime editor, *NY Tribune*.

James Reston, 1909-95 *NY Times* political reporter, columnist.

Frank Reynolds, 1923-83, ABC reporter, anchor.

(Henry) Grantland Rice, 1880-1954, sportswriter.

Jacob Riis, 1849-1914, reporter, photographer; exposed slum conditions in *How the Other Half Lives*.

Max Robinson, 1939-88, first African American to anchor network news (ABC), 1978.

Harold Ross, 1892-1951, founder, editor, *The New Yorker*.

Carl T. Rowan, 1925-2000, reporter, columnist, author.

Mike Royko, 1932-97, Chicago newspaper columnist; wrote *Boss*, biography of Mayor Richard Daley.

Adela Rogers St. Johns, 1894-1988, reporter, sportswriter for Hearst newspapers.

A. M. Rosenthal, 1922-2006, reporter and editor for the *New York Times* (1943-99).

Joe Rosenthal, 1911-2006, (U.S.) photojournalist; photographed six marines raising the U.S. flag over Iwo Jima in WWII.

Louis Rukeyser, 1933-2006, TV journalist, financial analyst, hosted "Wall Street Week" on public television.

(Alfred) Damon Runyon, 1884-1946, sportswriter, columnist; stories collected in *Guys and Dolls*.

Tim Russert, 1950-2008, TV journalist, moderator of *Meet the Press* (NBC).

John B. Russwurm, 1799-1851, cofounded (1827) nation's first black newspaper, *Freedom's Journal*, in NYC.

William Safire, 1929-2009, Pulitzer Prize-winning columnist, *New York Times*.

Pierre Salinger, 1925-2004, press secretary under Pres. Kennedy and Johnson; foreign correspondent.

Harrison Salisbury, 1908-93, reporter, foreign correspondent; a Soviet specialist.

E(dward) W(lyllis) Scripps, 1854-1926, founded first large U.S. newspaper chain, pioneered syndication.

Eric Sevareid, 1912-92, war correspondent, radio newscaster, CBS commentator.

William L. Shirer, 1904-93, broadcaster, foreign correspondent; wrote *The Rise and Fall of the Third Reich*.

Howard K. Smith, 1914-2002, ABC TV reporter, anchor.

Red (Walter) Smith, 1905-82, sportswriter.

Edgar P. Snow, 1905-71, correspondent, expert on Chinese Communist movement.

Tony Snow, 1955-2008, columnist, radio/TV journalist, White House press sec.

Tom Snyder, 1936-2007, television journalist.

Lawrence Spivak, 1900-94, co-creator, moderator, producer of *Meet the Press*.

(Joseph) Lincoln Steffens, 1866-1936, muckraking journalist.

I(sidor) F(einstein) Stone, 1907-89, one-man editor of *I.F. Stone's Weekly*.

Arthur Hays Sulzberger, 1891-1968, longtime publisher of *NY Times*.

C(yrus) L(eo) Sulzberger, 1912-93, *N.Y. Times* foreign correspondent and columnist.

David Susskind, 1920-87, TV producer, public affairs talk-show host (*Open End*).

John Cameron Swayze, 1906-95, early TV newscaster (NBC).

Herbert Bayard Swope, 1882-1958, war correspondent and editor of *N.Y. World*.

Ida Tarbell, 1857-1944, muckraking journalist.

Isaiah Thomas, 1750-1831, printer, publisher, cofounder of revolutionary journal, *Massachusetts Spy*.

Lowell Thomas, 1892-1981, radio newscaster, world traveler.

Dorothy Thompson, 1894-1961, foreign correspondent, columnist, radio commentator.

Hunter S. Thompson, 1937-2005, political journalist, author *Fear and Loathing on the Campaign Trail* (1972).

Kenneth Thompson, 1923-2006, Canadian media magnate; owned Toronto *Globe and Mail* newspaper.

Ida Bell Wells-Barnett, 1862-1931, African American reporter, editor, anti-lynching crusader.

William Allen White, 1868-1944, newspaper editor, publisher.

Walter Winchell, 1897-1972, reporter, columnist, broadcaster of celebrity news.

John Peter Zenger, 1697-1746, printer and journalist; acquitted in precedent-setting libel suit (1735).

Military and Naval Leaders of the Past

Reviewed by Alan C. Aimone, USMA Library.

Alexander the Great, 356-323 BCE, (Maced.) conquered Persia and much of the world known to Europeans.

Harold Alexander, 1891-1969, (Br.) led Allied invasion of Italy, 1943, WW2.

Ethan Allen, 1738-89, (U.S.) headed Green Mountain Boys; captured Ft. Ticonderoga, 1775, Amer. Rev.

Edmund Allenby, 1861-1936, (Br.) in Boer War, WW1; led Egyptian expeditionary force, 1917-18.

Benedict Arnold, 1741-1801, (U.S.) victorious at Saratoga; tried to betray West Point to British, Amer. Rev.

Henry "Hap" Arnold, 1886-1950, (U.S.) commanded Army Air Force in WW2.

Ashurnasirpal II, 884-859 BCE, (Assyria) king, began Assyrian conquest of Middle East.

John Barry, 1745-1803, (U.S.) won numerous sea battles during Amer. Rev.

Belisarius, c.505-565, (Byzant.) won remarkable victories for Byzantine Emperor Justinian I.

Pierre Beauregard, 1818-93, (U.S.) Confed. general, ordered bombardment of Ft. Sumter that began Civil War.

Gebhard von Blücher, 1742-1819, (Ger.) helped defeat Napoleon at Waterloo.

Simón Bolívar, 1783-1830, (Venez.) S. Amer. Revolutionary who liberated much of the continent from Spanish rule.

Napoleon Bonaparte, 1769-1821, (Fr.) defeated Russia and Austria at Austerlitz, 1805; invaded Russia, 1812; defeated at Waterloo, 1815.

Edward Braddock, 1695-1755, (Br.) commanded forces in French and Indian War.

Omar N. Bradley, 1893-1981, (U.S.) headed U.S. ground troops in Normandy invasion, 1944, WW2.

John Burgoyne, 1722-92, (Br.) general, defeated at Saratoga, Amer. Rev.

Julius Caesar, 100-44 BCE, (Rom.) general and politician; conquered northern Gaul; overthrew Roman Republic.

Charlemagne, 742-814, (Fr.) king of the Franks, Holy Roman Emperor, conqured most of Western Europe.

El Cid (Rodrigo Diaz de Vivar), 1040-99, (Sp.) renowned knight, captured Valencia (1094); hero of "Song of Cid" epic.

Claire Lee Chennault, 1893-1958, (U.S.) headed Flying Tigers in WW2.

Mark W. Clark, 1896-1984, (U.S.) helped plan N. African invasion in WW2; commander of UN forces, Korean War.

Karl von Clausewitz, 1780-1831, (Pruss.) military theorist.

Lucius D. Clay, 1897-1978, (U.S.) led Berlin airlift, 1948-49.

Henry Clinton, 1738-95, (Br.) commander of forces in Amer. Rev., 1778-81.

Cochise, c.1815-74, (Nat. Am.) chief of Chiricahua band of Apache Indians in Southwest.

Charles Cornwallis, 1738-1805, (Br.) victorious at Brandywine, 1777; surrendered at Yorktown, Amer. Rev.

Hernán Cortés, 1485-1547, (Sp.) led Spanish conquistadors in the defeat of the Aztec empire, 1519-28.

Crazy Horse, 1849-77, (Nat. Am.) Sioux war chief victorious at battle of Little Bighorn.

George Armstrong Custer, 1839-76, (U.S.) U.S. army officer defeated and killed at battle of Little Bighorn.

Moshe Dayan, 1915-81, (Isr.) directed campaigns in the 1967, 1973 Arab-Israeli wars.

Benjamin O. Davis Jr., 1912-2002, leader of World War II black aviators, first African American general in U.S. Air Force.

Benjamin O. Davis Sr., 1877-1970, first African American general, 1940, in U.S. Army.

Stephen Decatur, 1779-1820, (U.S.) naval hero of Barbary wars, War of 1812.

Anton Denikin, 1872-1947, (Russ.) led White forces in Russian civil war.

George Dewey, 1837-1917, (U.S.) destroyed Spanish fleet at Manila, 1898, Span.-Amer. War.

Karl Doenitz, 1891-1980, (Ger.) submarine com. in chief and naval commander, WW2.

Jimmy Doolittle, 1896-1993, (U.S.) led 1942 air raid on Tokyo and other Japanese cities in WW2.

Hugh C. Dowding, 1883-1970, (Br.) headed RAF, 1936-40, WW2.

Jubal Early, 1816-94, (U.S.) Confed. general, led raid on Washington, 1864, Civil War.

Dwight D. Eisenhower, 1890-1969, (U.S.) commanded Allied forces in Europe, WW2.

Erich von Falkenhayn, 1861-1922, (Ger.) minister of war, general, commander at Verdun in WW1.

David Farragut, 1801-70, (U.S.) Union admiral, captured New Orleans, Mobile Bay, Civil War.

John Arbuthnot Fisher, 1841-1920, (Br.) WW1 admiral, naval reformer.

Ferdinand Foch, 1851-1929, (Fr.) headed victorious Allied armies, 1918, WW1.

Nathan Bedford Forrest, 1821-77, (U.S.) Confed. general, led raids against Union supply lines, Civil War.

Frederick the Great, 1712-86, (Pruss.) led Prussia in Seven Years War.

Horatio Gates, 1728-1806, (U.S.) commanded army at Saratoga, Amer. Rev.

Daniel James Jr., 1920-78, first black 4-star general, 1975; commander, North American Air Defense Command.

Genghis Khan, 1162-1227, (Mongol) unified Mongol tribes and subjugated much of Asia, 1206-21.

Geronimo, 1829-1909, (Nat. Am.) leader of Chiricahua band of Apache Indians.

Charles G. Gordon, 1833-85, (Br.) led forces in China, Crimean War; killed at Khartoum.

Ulysses S. Grant, 1822-85, (U.S.) headed Union army, Civil War, 1864-65; forced Lee's surrender, 1865.

Nathanael Greene, 1742-86, (U.S.) defeated British in Southern campaign, 1780-81, Amer. Rev.

Heinz Guderian, 1888-1953, (Ger.) tank theorist, led panzer forces in Poland, France, Russia, WW2.

Gustavus Adolphus, 1594-1632, (Swed.) King; military tactician; reformer; led forces in Thirty Years' War.

Douglas Haig, 1861-1928, (Br.) led British armies in France, 1915-18, WW1.

William F. Halsey, 1882-1959, (U.S.) defeated Japanese fleet at Leyte Gulf, 1944, WW2.

Hannibal, 247-183 BCE, (Carthage) invaded Rome, crossing Alps, in Second Punic War, 218-201 BCE.

Sir Arthur Travers Harris, 1895-1984, (Br.) led Britain's WW2 bomber command.

Paul von Hindenburg, 1847-1934, (Ger.) chief of general staff, WW1; 2nd pres. of Weimar Republic.

Richard Howe, 1726-99, (Br.) commanded navy in Amer. Rev., 1776-78; June 1 victory against French, 1794.

William Howe, 1729-1814, (Br.) commanded forces in Amer. Rev., 1776-78.

Isaac Hull, 1773-1843, (U.S.) sunk British frigate *Guerriere*, War of 1812.

Thomas (Stonewall) Jackson, 1824-63, (U.S.) Confed. general, led Shenandoah Valley campaign, Civil War.

Joseph Joffre, 1852-1931, (Fr.) headed Allied armies, won Battle of the Marne, 1914, WW1.

Chief Joseph, c.1840-1904, (Nat. Am.) chief of the Nez Percé, forced by army to retreat and surrender.

John Paul Jones, 1747-92, (U.S.) commanded *Bonhomme Richard* in victory over *Serapis*, Amer. Rev., 1779.

Stephen Kearny, 1794-1848, (U.S.) headed Army of the West in Mexican War.

Albert Kesselring, 1885-1960 (Ger.) field marshal who led the defense of Italy in WW2.

Ernest J. King, 1878-1956, (U.S.) key WW2 naval strategist.

Horatio H. Kitchener, 1850-1916, (Br.) led forces in Boer War; victorious at Khartoum; organized army in WW1.

Henry Knox, 1750-1806, (U.S.) general in Amer. Rev.; first sec. of war under U.S. Constitution.

Lavrenti Kornilov, 1870-1918, (Russ.) commander-in-chief, 1917; led counter-revolutionary march on Petrograd.

Thaddeus Kosciusko, 1746-1817, (Pol.) aided Amer. Rev.

Walter Krueger, 1881-1967, (U.S.) led Sixth Army in WW2 in Southwest Pacific.

Mikhail Kutuzov, 1745-1813, (Russ.) fought at Borodino, Napol. Wars, 1812; abandoned Moscow; forced French retreat.

Marquis de Lafayette, 1757-1834, (Fr.) fought in, secured French aid for Amer. Rev.

T(homas) E. Lawrence (of Arabia), 1888-1935, (Br.) organized revolt of Arabs against Turks in WW1.

William Daniel Leahy, 1875-1959, (U.S.) chief of staff to Pres. Roosevelt in WWII, Fleet Admiral.

Henry (Light-Horse Harry) Lee, 1756-1818, (U.S.) cavalry officer in Amer. Rev.

Robert E. Lee, 1807-70, (U.S.) Confed. general defeated at Gettysburg, Civil War; surrendered to Grant, 1865.

Curtis LeMay, 1906-90, (U.S.) Air Force commander in WW2, Korean War, and Vietnam War.

Lyman Lemnitzer, 1899-1988, (U.S.) WW2 hero, later general, chairman of Joint Chiefs of Staff.

James Longstreet, 1821-1904, (U.S.) aided Lee at Gettysburg, Civil War.

Erich Ludendorff, 1865-1937, (Ger.) general, victor at Tannenberg, WW1.

Maurice, Count of Nassau, 1567-1625, (Dutch) military innovator; led forces in Thirty Years' War.

Douglas MacArthur, 1880-1964, (U.S.) commanded forces in SW Pacific in WW2; headed occupation forces in Japan, 1945-51; UN commander in Korean War.

Erich von Manstein, 1887-1973, (Ger.) served WW1–2, planned inv. of France (1940), convicted of war crimes.

Carl Gustaf Mannerheim, 1867-1951, (Finn.) army officer and pres. of Finland 1944-46.

Francis Marion, 1733-95, (U.S.) led guerrilla actions in South Carolina during Amer. Rev.

Duke of Marlborough, 1650-1722, (Br.) led forces against Louis XIV in War of the Spanish Succession.

George C. Marshall, 1880-1959, (U.S.) chief of staff in WW2; authored Marshall Plan.

George B. McClellan, 1826-85, (U.S.) Union general, commanded Army of the Potomac, 1861-62, Civil War.

George Meade, 1815-72, (U.S.) commanded Union forces at Gettysburg, Civil War.

Dorie Miller, 1919-43, Navy hero of Pearl Harbor attack.

Billy Mitchell, 1879-1936, (U.S.) WW1 air-power advocate; court-martialed for insubordination, later vindicated.

Helmuth von Moltke, 1800-91, (Ger.) victorious in Austro-Prussian, Franco-Prussian wars.

Louis de Montcalm, 1712-59, (Fr.) headed troops in Canada, French and Indian War; defeated at Quebec, 1759.

Bernard Law Montgomery, 1887-1976, (Br.) stopped German offensive at Alamein, 1942, WW2; helped plan Normandy.

Daniel Morgan, 1736-1802, (U.S.) victorious at Cowpens, 1781, Amer. Rev.

Louis Mountbatten, 1900-79, (Br.) Supreme Allied Commander of SE Asia, 1943-46, WW2.

Joachim Murat, 1767-1815, (Fr.) led cavalry at Marengo, Austerlitz, and Jena, Napoleonic Wars.

Horatio Nelson, 1758-1805, (Br.) naval commander, destroyed French fleet at Trafalgar.

Michel Ney, 1769-1815, (Fr.) commanded forces in Switz., Aust., Russ., Napoleonic Wars; defeated at Waterloo.

Chester Nimitz, 1885-1966, (U.S.) commander of naval forces in Pacific in WW2.

George S. Patton, 1885-1945, (U.S.) led assault on Sicily, 1943, Third Army invasion of Europe, WWII.

Oliver Perry, 1785-1819, (U.S.) won Battle of Lake Erie in War of 1812.

John Pershing, 1860-1948, (U.S.) commanded Mexican border campaign, 1916, Amer. Expeditionary Force, WW1.

Henri Philippe Pétain, 1856-1951, (Fr.) defended Verdun, 1916; headed Vichy government in WW2.

George E. Pickett, 1825-75, (U.S.) Confed. general famed for "charge" at Gettysburg, Civil War.

Charles Portal, 1893-1971, (Br.) chief of staff, Royal Air Force, 1940-45, led in Battle of Britain.

Manfred Frieherr von Richthofen (Red Baron), 1892-1918, (Ger.) WW1 flying ace, led elite fighter squadron.

Hyman Rickover, 1900-86, (U.S.) father of nuclear navy.

Matthew Bunker Ridgway, 1895-1993, (U.S.) commanded Allied ground forces in Korean War.

Erwin Rommel, 1891-1944, (Ger.) headed Afrika Korps, WW2.

Gerd von Rundstedt, 1875-1953, (Ger.) supreme commander in West, 1942-45, WW2.

Saladin, 1138-93, (Kurdish Muslim) recaptured Jerusalem from Crusaders.

Aleksandr Samsonov, 1859-1914, (Russ.) led invasion of E Prussia, WW1, defeated at Tannenberg, 1914.

Antonio Lopez de Santa Anna, 1794-1876, (Mex.) defeated Texans at the Alamo; defeated in Mexican War.

Maurice, Count of Saxe, 1696-1750, (Fr.) general, War of Aust. Succession, War of Pol. Succession; noted tactician.

Scipio Africanus the Elder, 234?-183 BCE, (Rom.) hero of 2nd Punic War, defeated Hannibal, invaded N. Africa.

Winfield Scott, 1786-1866, (U.S.) hero of War of 1812; headed forces in Mexican War, took Mexico City.

Philip Sheridan, 1831-88, (U.S.) Union cavalry officer, headed Army of the Shenandoah, 1864-65, Civil War.

William T. Sherman, 1820-91, (U.S.) Union general, sacked Atlanta during "march to the sea," 1864, Civil War.

Carl Spaatz, 1891-1974, (U.S.) directed strategic bombing against Germany, later Japan, in WW2.

Raymond Spruance, 1886-1969, (U.S.) victorious at Midway Island, 1942, WW2.

Joseph W. Stilwell, 1883-1946, (U.S.) headed forces in the China, Burma, India theater in WW2.

J.E.B. Stuart, 1833-64, (U.S.) Confed. cavalry commander, Civil War.

Sun Tzu, 6th? cent. BCE, (Chin.) general, author of *The Art of War.*

Aleksandr Suvorov, 1729-1800, (Rus.) commanded Allied Russian and Austrian armies, Russo-Turkish War.

Tamerlane, 1336-1405, (Turkoman Mongol) conqueror, established empire from India to Mediterranean Sea.

George H. Thomas, 1816-70, (U.S.) saved Union army at Chattanooga, 1863; won at Nashville, 1864, Civil War.

Semyon Timoshenko, 1895-1970, (USSR) defended Moscow, Stalingrad, WW2; led winter offensive, 1942-43.

Alfred von Tirpitz, 1849-1930, (Ger.) responsible for submarine blockade in WW1.

Henri de la Tour d'Auvergne, Viscount of Turenne, 1611-75, (Fr.) marshal, Thirty Years' War, Fronde, War of Devolution.

Sebastien Le Prestre de Vauban, 1633-1707, (Fr.) innovative military engineer and theorist.

Jonathan M. Wainwright, 1883-1953, (U.S.) forced to surrender on Corregidor, 1942, WW2.

George Washington, 1732-99, (U.S.) led Continental army, 1775-83, Amer. Rev.

Archibald Wavell, 1883-1950, (Br.) commanded forces in N and E Africa, and SE Asia in WW2.

Anthony Wayne, 1745-96, (U.S.) captured Stony Point, 1779, Amer. Rev.

Duke of Wellington, 1769-1852, (Br.) defeated Napoleon at Waterloo, 1815.

William Westmoreland, 1914-2005, (U.S.) commanded forces in Vietnam 1964-68.

William I (The Conqueror), 1027-87, (Br.) victor Battle of Hastings 1066, became first Norman king of England.

James Wolfe, 1727-59, (Br.) captured Quebec from French, 1759, French and Indian War.

Isoroku Yamamoto, 1884-1943, (Jpn.) com. in chief of Japanese fleet and naval planner before and during WW2.

Georgi Zhukov, 1895-1974, (Russ.) defended Moscow, 1941, led assault on Berlin, 1945, WW2.

Philosophers and Religious Figures of the Past

Excludes most biblical figures and popes (see Religion). For Greeks and Romans, see also Historical Figures chapter.

Lyman Abbott, 1835-1922, (U.S.) clergyman, reformer; advocate of Christian Socialism.

Pierre Abelard, 1079-1142, (Fr.) philosopher, theologian, teacher; used dialectic method to support Christian beliefs.

Mortimer Adler, 1902-2001, (U.S.) philosopher, helped create "Great Books" program.

Felix Adler, 1851-1933, (U.S.) German-born founder of the Ethical Culture Soc.

(St.) Anselm, c.1033-1109, (It.) philosopher-theologian, church leader; "ontological argument" for God's existence.

(St.) Thomas Aquinas, 1225-74, (It.) preeminent medieval philosopher-theologian; *Summa Theologica.*

Aristotle, 384-322 BCE, (Gr.) pioneering wide-ranging philosopher, logician, ethician, naturalist.

(St.) Augustine, 354-430, (N Africa) philosopher, theologian, bishop; *Confessions, City of God, On the Trinity.*

J. L. Austin, 1911-60, (Br.) ordinary-language philosopher.

Averroes (Ibn Rushd), 1126-98, (Sp.) Islamic philosopher, physician.

Avicenna (Ibn Sina), 980-1037, (Iran.) Islamic philosopher, scientist.

A(lfred) J(ules) Ayer, 1910-89, (Br.) philosopher; logical positivist; *Language, Truth, and Logic.*

Roger Bacon, c.1214-94, (Eng.) philosopher and scientist.

Bahaullah (Mirza Husayn Ali), 1817-92, (Pers.) founder of Bahá'í faith.

Karl Barth, 1886-1968, (Swiss) theologian; a leading force in 20th-cent. Protestantism.

Thomas à Becket, 1118-70, (Eng.) archbishop of Canterbury; opposed Henry II; murdered by King's men.

(St.) Benedict, c.480-547, (It.) founded the Benedictines.

Jeremy Bentham, 1748-1832, (Br.) philosopher, reformer; enunciated utilitarianism.

Henri Bergson, 1859-1941, (Fr.) philosopher of evolution.

George Berkeley, 1685-1753, (Ir.) idealist philosopher, bishop.

John Biddle, 1615-62, (Eng.) founder of English Unitarianism.

Jakob Boehme, 1575-1624, (Ger.) theosophist and mystic.

Dietrich Bonhoeffer, 1906-45, (Ger.) Lutheran theologian, pastor; executed as opponent of Nazis.

William Brewster, 1567-1644, (Eng.) headed Pilgrims.

Emil Brunner, 1889-1966, (Swiss) Protestant theologian.

Giordano Bruno, 1548-1600, (It.) philosopher, pantheist.

Martin Buber, 1878-1965, (Ger.) Jewish philosopher, theologian; *I and Thou.*

Buddha (Siddhartha Gautama), c.563-c.483 BCE, (Indian) phil-osopher; founded Buddhism.

John Calvin, 1509-64, (Fr.) theologian; a key figure in the Protestant Reformation.

Rudolph Carnap, 1891-1970, (U.S.) German-born analytic philosopher; a founder of logical positivism.

William Ellery Channing, 1780-1842, (U.S.) clergyman; early spokesman for Unitarianism.

Auguste Comte, 1798-1857, (Fr.) philosopher; originated positivism.

Confucius, 551-479 BCE, (Chin.) founder of Confucianism.

John Cotton, 1584-1652, (Eng.) Puritan theologian.

Thomas Cranmer, 1489-1556, (Eng.) Anglican churchman; wrote much of *Book of Common Prayer.*

Jacques Derrida, 1930-2004 (Fr.), deconstructionist philosopher.

René Descartes, 1596-1650, (Fr.) philosopher, mathematician; "father of modern philosophy." *Discourse on Method, Meditations on First Philosophy.*

John Dewey, 1859-1952, (U.S.) philosopher, educator; instrumentalist theory of knowledge; progressive education.

Denis Diderot, 1713-84, (Fr.) philosopher, encyclopedist.

John Duns Scotus, c.1266-1308, (Sc.) Franciscan philosopher and theologian.

Mary Baker Eddy, 1821-1910, (U.S.) founder of Christian Science; *Science and Health.*

Jonathan Edwards, 1703-58, (U.S.) preacher, theologian; "Sinners in the Hands of an Angry God."

(Desiderius) Erasmus, c.1466-1536, (Dutch) Renaissance humanist; *On the Freedom of the Will.*

Rev. Jerry Falwell, 1933-2007, (U.S.) TV evangelist, religious commentator.

Johann Fichte, 1762-1814, (Ger.) idealist philosopher.

Michel Foucault, 1926-84, (Fr.) structuralist philosopher, historian.

George Fox, 1624-91, (Br.) founder of Society of Friends.

(St.) Francis of Assisi, 1182-1226, (It.) espoused voluntary poverty; founded Franciscans.

al-Ghazali, 1058-1111, Islamic philosopher.

Billy James Hargis, 1925-2004, (U.S.) anti-Communist televangelist; founder of the Church of the Christian Crusade.

Georg W. F. Hegel, 1770-1831, (Ger.) idealist philosopher; *Phenomenology of Mind.*

Martin Heidegger, 1889-1976, (Ger.) existentialist philosopher; affected many fields; *Being and Time.*

Johann G. Herder, 1744-1803, (Ger.) philosopher, cultural historian; a founder of German Romanticism.

Thomas Hobbes, 1588-1679, (Eng.) philosopher, political theorist; *Leviathan.*

David Hume, 1711-76, (Sc.) empiricist philosopher; *Enquiry Concerning Human Understanding.*

Jan Hus, 1369-1415, (Czech.) religious reformer.

Edmund Husserl, 1859-1938, (Ger.) philosopher; founded the phenomenological movement.

Thomas Huxley, 1825-95, (Br.) philosopher, educator.

William Inge, 1860-1954, (Br.) theologian; explored mystic aspects of Christianity.

William James, 1842-1910, (U.S.) philosopher, psychologist; pragmatist; studied religious experience.

Karl Jaspers, 1883-1969, (Ger.) existentialist philosopher.

Joan of Arc, 1412-31, (Fr.) national heroine and a patron saint of France; key figure in the Hundred Years' War.

Immanuel Kant, 1724-1804, (Ger.) philosopher; founder of modern critical philosophy; *Critique of Pure Reason.*

Thomas à Kempis, c.1380-1471, (Ger.) monk, devotional writer; *Imitation of Christ* attributed to him.

Soren Kierkegaard, 1813-55, (Dan.) religious philosopher; pre-existentialist; *Either/Or, The Sickness Unto Death.*

John Knox, 1505-72, (Sc.) leader of the Protestant Reformation in Scotland.

Lao-Tzu, 604-531 BCE, (Chin.) philosopher; considered the founder of the Taoist religion.

Gottfried von Leibniz, 1646-1716, (Ger.) rationalistic philosopher, logician, mathematician.

John Locke, 1632-1704, (Eng.) political theorist, empiricist philosopher; *Essay Concerning Human Understanding.*

(St.) Ignatius Loyola, 1491-1556, (Sp.) founder of the Jesuits; *Spiritual Exercises.*

Martin Luther, 1483-1546, (Ger.) leader of the Protestant Reformation, founded Lutheran church.

Jean-Francois Lyotard, 1924-98, (Fr.) postmodern philosopher, lecturer; *The Post-Modern Condition.*

Maimonides, 1135-1204, (Sp.) major Jewish philosopher.

Gabriel Marcel, 1889-1973, (Fr.) Rom. Cath. existentialist philosopher, dramatist,

Jacques Maritain, 1882-1973, (Fr.) neo-Thomist philosopher.

Cotton Mather, 1663-1728, (U.S.) defender of orthodox Puritanism; founded Yale, 1701.

Philipp Melanchthon, 1497-1560, (Ger.) theologian, humanist; an important voice in the Reformation.

Maurice Merleau-Ponty, 1908-61, (Fr.) existentialist philosopher; *Phenomenology of Perception.*

Thomas Merton, 1915-68, (U.S.) Trappist monk, spiritual writer; *The Seven Storey Mountain.*

Dwight Moody, 1837-99, (U.S.) evangelist.

G(eorge) E(dward) Moore, 1873-1958, (Br.) philosopher; *Principia Ethica*, "A Defense of Common Sense."

Muhammad, c.570-632, (Arab) the prophet of Islam.

Elijah Muhammad, 1897-1975, (U.S.) Black Muslim sect leader.

Heinrich Muhlenberg, 1711-87, (Ger.) organized the Lutheran Church in America.

John H. Newman, 1801-90, (Br.) Rom. Cath. convert, cardinal; led Oxford Movement; *Apologia pro Vita Sua.*

Reinhold Niebuhr, 1892-1971, (U.S.) Protestant theologian.

Richard Niebuhr, 1894-1962 (U.S.) Protestant theologian.

Friedrich Nietzsche, 1844-1900, (Ger.) philosopher; *The Birth of Tragedy, Beyond Good and Evil, Thus Spake Zarathustra.*

Robert Nozick, 1938-2002, (U.S.) political philosopher; *Anarchy, State, and Utopia.*

Blaise Pascal, 1623-62, (Fr.) philosopher, mathematician; *Pensées.*

(St.) Patrick, c.389-c.461, (Br.) brought Christianity to Ireland.

Norman Vincent Peale, 1898-1993, (U.S.) minister, author; *The Power of Positive Thinking.*

C(harles) S. Peirce, 1839-1914, (U.S.) philosopher, logician; originated concept of pragmatism, 1878.

Plato, c.428-347 BCE, (Gr.) philosopher; wrote Socratic dialogues; argued for immortality of soul, indep. reality of ideas or forms; *Republic, Meno, Phaedo, Apology.*

Plotinus, 205-70, (Rom.) a founder of neo-Platonism; *Enneads.*

W(illard) V(an) O(rman) Quine, 1908-2001, (U.S.) philosopher, logician; "On What There Is."

John Rawls, 1922-2002, (U.S.) political philosopher; *A Theory of Justice* (1971).

Josiah Royce, 1855-1916, (U.S.) idealist philosopher

Bertrand Russell, 1872-1970, (Br.) philosopher, logician; one of the founders of modern logic; a prolific popular writer.

Charles T. Russell, 1852-1916, (U.S.) founder of Jehovah's Witnesses.

Gilbert Ryle, 1900-76, (Br.) analytic philosopher; *The Concept of Mind.*

George Santayana, 1863-1952, (U.S.) philosopher, writer, critic; *The Sense of Beauty, The Realms of Being.*

Jean-Paul Sartre, 1905-80, (Fr.) philosopher, novelist, playwright. *Nausea, No Exit, Being and Nothingness.*

Friedrich von Schelling, 1775-1854, (Ger.) philosopher of romantic movement.

Friedrich Schleiermacher, 1768-1834, (Ger.) theologian; a founder of modern Protestant theology.

Arthur Schopenhauer, 1788-1860, (Ger.) philosopher; *The World as Will and Idea.*

Albert Schweitzer, 1875-1965, (Ger.) theologian, social philosopher, medical missionary.

Joseph Smith, 1805-44, (U.S.) founded Latter-Day Saints (Mormon) movement, 1830.

Socrates, 469-399 BCE, (Gr.) philosopher immortalized by Plato.

Herbert Spencer, 1820-1903, (Br.) philosopher of evolution.

Baruch de Spinoza, 1632-77, (Dutch) rationalist philosopher; *Ethics.*

Billy Sunday, 1862-1935, (U.S.) evangelist.

Emanuel Swedenborg, 1688-1772, (Swed.) philosopher, mystic; *Principia.*

Pierre Teilhard de Chardin, 1881-1955, (Fr.) Jesuit priest, paleontologist, philosopher-theologian; *The Divine Milieu.*

Daisetz Teitaro Suzuki, 1870-1966, (Jpn.) Buddhist scholar.

(St.) Therese of Lisieux, 1873-97, (Fr.) Carmelite nun ("Little Flower"), revered for everyday sanctity; *The Story of a Soul.*

Paul Tillich, 1886-1965, (U.S.) German-born philosopher and theologian; brought depth psychology to Protestantism.

John Wesley, 1703-91, (Br.) theologian, evangelist; founded Methodism.

Alfred North Whitehead, 1861-1947, (Br.) philosopher, mathematician; *Process and Reality.*

William of Occam, c.1285-c.1349 (Eng.) medieval scholastic philosopher; nominalist.

Roger Williams, c.1603-83, (U.S.) clergyman; championed religious freedom and separation of church and state.

Ludwig Wittgenstein, 1889-1951, (Austrian) philosopher; major influence on contemporary language philosophy; *Tractatus Logico-Philosophicus, Philosophical Investigations.*

John Woolman, 1720-72, (U.S.) Quaker social reformer, abolitionist, writer; *The Journal.*

John Wycliffe, 1320-84, (Eng.) theologian, reformer.

(St.) Francis Xavier, 1506-52, (Sp.) Jesuit missionary, "Apostle of the Indies."

Brigham Young, 1801-77, (U.S.) Mormon leader after Smith's assassination; colonized Utah.

Huldrych Zwingli, 1484-1531, (Swiss) theologian; led Swiss Protestant Reformation.

Political Leaders of the Past

(U.S. presidents, vice presidents, Supreme Ct. justices, signers of Declaration of Independence listed elsewhere.)

Abu Bakr, 573-634, Muslim leader, first caliph, chosen successor to Muhammad.

Dean Acheson, 1893-1971, (U.S.) sec. of state; architect of cold war foreign policy.

Samuel Adams, 1722-1803, (U.S.) patriot, Boston Tea Party firebrand.

Konrad Adenauer, 1876-1967, (Ger.) first West German chancellor.

Emilio Aguinaldo, 1869-1964, (Philip.) revolutionary; fought against Spain and the U.S.

Corazon Aquino, 1933-2009 (Philip.), president of Philippines 1986-92.

Akbar, 1542-1605, greatest Mogul emperor of India.

Carl Albert, 1908-2000 (U.S.) House rep. from OK, Speaker, 1971-76.

Salvador Allende Gossens, 1908-73, (Chilean) Marxist pres. 1970-73; ousted and died in coup.

Idi Amin, 1925-2003 (Uganda), Ugandan ruler from 1971 to 1979, blamed for hundreds of thousands of deaths.

Hafez al Assad, 1930-2000 (Syr.), Syrian ruler from 1970.

Herbert H. Asquith, 1852-1928, (Br.) liberal prime min.; instituted major social reform.

Atahualpa, ?-1533, Inca (ruling chief) of Peru.

Kemal Ataturk, 1881-1938, (Turk.) founded modern Turkey.

Clement Attlee, 1883-1967, (Br.) Labour party leader, prime min.; enacted natl. health, nationalized many industries.

Stephen F. Austin, 1793-1836, (U.S.) led Texas colonization.

Mikhail Bakunin, 1814-76, (Rus.) revolutionary; leading exponent of anarchism.

Arthur J. Balfour, 1848-1930, (Br.) foreign sec. under Lloyd George; issued Balfour Declaration backing Zionism.

Bernard M. Baruch, 1870-1965, (U.S.) financier, govt. adviser.

Fulgencio Batista y Zaldívar, 1901-73, (Cub.) Cuban pres. (1940-44, 1952-59), overthrown by Castro.

Lord Beaverbrook, 1879-1964, (Br.) financier, statesman, newspaper owner.

Menachem Begin, 1913-92, (Isr.) Israeli prime min., shared 1978 Nobel Peace Prize.

Eduard Benes, 1884-1948, (Czech.) pres. during interwar and post-WW2 eras.

David Ben-Gurion, 1886-1973, (Isr.) first prime min. of Israel, 1948-53, 1955-63.

Thomas Hart Benton, 1782-1858, (U.S.) Missouri senator; championed agrarian interests and westward expansion.

Lloyd Bentsen, 1921-2006 (U.S.), former senator, treasury sec., vice-pres. nominee.

Aneurin Bevan, 1897-1960, (Br.) Labour party leader.

Benazir Bhutto, 1953-2007, (Pak.) former prime minister of Pakistan.

Ernest Bevin, 1881-1951, (Br.) Labour party leader, foreign minister; helped lay foundation for NATO.

Otto von Bismarck, 1815-98, (Ger.) statesman known as the Iron Chancellor; uniter of Germany, 1870.

James G. Blaine, 1830-93, (U.S.) Republican politician, diplomat; influential in Pan-American movement.

Léon Blum, 1872-1950, (Fr.) socialist leader, writer; headed first Popular Front government.

William E. Borah, 1865-1940, (U.S.) isolationist senator; helped block U.S. membership in League of Nations.

Cesare Borgia, 1476-1507, (It.) soldier, politician; an outstanding figure of the Italian Renaissance.

P. W. Botha, 1916-2006, (So. Africa) So. African president, prime minister

Tom Bradley, 1917-98, (U.S.) first African American LA mayor.

Willy Brandt, 1913-92, (Ger.) statesman, chancellor of West Germany, 1969-74; promoted East/West peace, *Ostpolitik.*

Leonid Brezhnev, 1906-82, (USSR) Soviet leader, 1964-82.

Aristide Briand, 1862-1932, (Fr.) foreign min.; chief architect of Locarno Pact and anti-war Kellogg-Briand Pact.

William Jennings Bryan, 1860-1925, (U.S.) Democratic, populist leader, orator; 3 times lost race for presidency.

Ralph Bunche, 1904-71, (U.S.) first black person to win the Nobel Peace Prize, 1950; undersecretary of the UN, 1950.

John C. Calhoun, 1782-1850, (U.S.) political leader; champion of states' rights and a symbol of the Old South.

James Callaghan (Baron Callaghan), 1912-2005 (Br.) Labour Party politican, prime min. 1976-79.

Robert Castlereagh, 1769-1822, (Br.) foreign sec.; guided Grand Alliance against Napoleon.

Camillo Benso Cavour, 1810-61, (It.) statesman; largely responsible for uniting Italy under the House of Savoy.

Nicolae Ceausescu, 1918-89, (Roman.) Communist leader, head of state 1967-89; executed.

Austen Chamberlain, 1863-1937, (Br.) statesman; helped finalize Locarno Treaties, both 1925.

Neville Chamberlain, 1869-1940, (Br.) Conservative prime min. whose appeasement of Hitler led to Munich Pact.

Chiang Kai-shek, 1887-1975, (Chin.) Nationalist Chinese pres. whose government was driven from mainland to Taiwan.

Chiang Kai-shek, Madame, 1898-2003, (Chin.) highly influential wife of Nationalist Chinese leader Chiang Kai-shek.

Shirley Chisholm, 1924-2005, first black woman elected to U.S. House (1968); pres. contender, 1972.

Winston Churchill, 1874-1965, (Br.) prime min., soldier, author; guided Britain through WW2.

Galeazzo Ciano, 1903-44, (It.) fascist foreign minister; helped create Rome-Berlin Axis, executed by Mussolini.

Henry Clay, 1777-1852, (U.S.) "The Great Compromiser," one of the most influential pre-Civil War political leaders.

Georges Clemenceau, 1841-1929, (Fr.) twice prem., Wilson's antagonist at Paris Peace Conference after WW1.

DeWitt Clinton, 1769-1828, (U.S.) political leader; responsible for promoting the Erie Canal.

Robert Clive, 1725-74, (Br.) first administrator of Bengal; laid foundation for British Empire in India.

Jean Baptiste Colbert, 1619-83, (Fr.) statesman; influential under Louis XIV, created the French navy.

Bettino Craxi, 1934-2000, (It.) Italy's first post-WWII Socialist premier.

David Crockett, 1786-1836, (U.S.) frontiersman, congressman, died defending the Alamo.

Oliver Cromwell, 1599-1658, (Br.) Lord Protector of England, led parliamentary forces during Civil War.

Curzon of Kedleston, 1859-1925, (Br.) viceroy of India, foreign sec.; major force in post-WW1 world.

Édouard Daladier, 1884-1970, (Fr.) Radical Socialist politician, arrested by Vichy, interned by Germans until 1945.

Richard J. Daley, 1902-76, (U.S.) Chicago mayor.

Georges Danton, 1759-94, (Fr.) leading French Rev. figure.

Jefferson Davis, 1808-89, (U.S.) pres. of the Confederacy.

Charles G. Dawes, 1865-1951, (U.S.) statesman, banker; advanced plan to stabilize post-WW1 German finances.

William L. Dawson, 1886-1970, Illinois congressman, first black chairman of a major U.S. House committee.

Alcide De Gasperi, 1881-1954, (It.) prime min.; founder of Christian Democratic party.

Charles De Gaulle, 1890-1970, (Fr.) general, statesman; first pres. of the Fifth Republic.

Deng Xiaoping, 1904-97, (Chin.) "paramount leader" of China; backed economic modernization.

Eamon De Valera, 1882-1975, (Ir.-U.S.) statesman; led fight for Irish independence.

Thomas E. Dewey, 1902-71, (U.S.) NY governor; twice loser in try for presidency.

Ngo Dinh Diem, 1901-63, (Viet.) South Vietnamese pres.; assassinated in government takeover.

Everett M. Dirksen, 1896-1969, (U.S.) Senate Republican minority leader, orator.

Benjamin Disraeli, 1804-81, (Br.) prime min.; considered founder of modern Conservative party.

Engelbert Dollfuss, 1892-1934, (Austrian) chancellor; assassinated by Austrian Nazis.

Andrea Doria, 1466-1560, (It.) Genoese admiral, statesman; called "Father of Peace" and "Liberator of Genoa."

Stephen A. Douglas, 1813-61, (U.S.) Democratic leader, orator; opposed Lincoln for the presidency.

Alexander Dubcek, 1921-92, (Czech.) statesman whose attempted liberalization was crushed, 1968.

John Foster Dulles, 1888-1959, (U.S.) sec. of state under Eisenhower, cold war policy-maker.

Abba Eban, 1915-2002, (Isr.) diplomat, foreign min. 1966-74.

Friedrich Ebert, 1871-1925, (Ger.) Social Democratic movement leader; 1st pres., Weimar Republic, 1919-25.

Sir Anthony Eden, 1897-1977, (Br.) foreign sec., prime min. during Suez invasion of 1956.

Ludwig Erhard, 1897-1977, (Ger.) economist, West German chancellor; led nation's economic rise after WW2.

King Fahid, 1921-2005, (Saudi Arab.) monarch since 1982, but inactive since 1995 stroke; encouraged U.S. relations.

Joao Baptista de Figueiredo, 1918-99, (Braz.) president of Brazil, restored the nation's democracy.

Hamilton Fish, 1808-93, (U.S.) sec. of state, successfully mediated disputes with Great Britain, Latin America.

James V. Forrestal, 1892-1949, (U.S.) sec. of navy, first sec. of defense.

Francisco Franco, 1892-1975, (Sp.) leader of rebel forces during Spanish Civil War and longtime ruler of Spain.

Benjamin Franklin, 1706-90, (U.S.) printer, publisher, author, inventor, scientist, diplomat.

Louis de Frontenac, 1620-98, (Fr.) governor of New France (Canada); encouraged explorations, fought Iroquois.

J. William Fulbright, 1905-95, (U.S.) U.S. senator; leading figure in U.S. foreign policy during cold war years.

Hugh Gaitskell, 1906-63, (Br.) Labour party leader; major force in reversing its stand for unilateral disarmament.

Albert Gallatin, 1761-1849, (U.S.) sec. of treasury; instrumental in negotiating end of War of 1812.

Léon Gambetta, 1838-82, (Fr.) statesman, politician; one of the founders of the Third Republic.

Indira Gandhi, 1917-84, (In.) daughter of Jawaharlal Nehru, prime min. of India, 1966-77, 1980-84; assassinated.

Mohandas K. Gandhi, 1869-1948, (In.) political leader, ascetic; led movement against British rule; assassinated.

Giuseppe Garibaldi, 1807-82, (It.) patriot, soldier; a leader in the Risorgimento, Italian unification movement.

William E. Gladstone, 1809-98, (Br.) prime min. 4 times; dominant force in Liberal party from 1868 to 1894.

Paul Joseph Goebbels, 1897-1945, (Ger.) Nazi propagandist, master of mass psychology.

Barry Goldwater, 1909-98 (U.S.) conservative U.S. senator and 1964 Republican presid. nominee.

Klement Gottwald, 1896-1953, (Czech.) Communist leader; ushered Communism into his country.

Alexander Hamilton, 1755-1804, (U.S.) first treasury sec.; champion of strong central government.

Dag Hammarskjold, 1905-61, (Swed.) statesman; UN sec.-general.

Hassan II, King, 1929-99, (Moroc.), ruler of Morocco,1962-99.

John Hay, 1838-1905, (U.S.) sec. of state; primarily associated with Open Door Policy toward China.

Sir Edward Heath, 1916-2005, (Br.) conserative prime min., 1970-74; promoted European unity.

Jesse Helms, 1921-2008, (U.S.) former senator (NC).

Patrick Henry, 1736-99, (U.S.) major Revolutionary War figure, remarkable orator.

Édouard Herriot, 1872-1957, (Fr.) Radical Socialist leader; twice prem., pres. of National Assembly.

Theodor Herzl, 1860-1904, (Hung.) founded modern Zionism.

Heinrich Himmler, 1900-45, (Ger.) head of Nazi SS and Gestapo.

Paul von Hindenburg, 1847-1934, (Ger.) field marshal, WW1; 2nd pres. of Weimar Republic, 1925-34.

Adolf Hitler, 1889-1945, (Ger.) dictator; built Nazism, launched WW2, presided over the Holocaust.

Ho Chi Minh, 1890-1969, (Viet.) N Vietnamese pres., Vietnamese Communist leader.

Harry L. Hopkins, 1890-1946, (U.S.) New Deal administrator; closest adviser to FDR during WW2.

Edward M. House, 1858-1938, (U.S.) diplomat; confidential adviser to Woodrow Wilson.

Samuel Houston, 1793-1863, (U.S.) leader of struggle for Texas independence.

Cordell Hull, 1871-1955, (U.S.) sec. of state, 1933-44; initiated reciprocal trade to lower tariffs, helped organize UN.

Hubert H. Humphrey, 1911-78, (U.S.) MN Democrat; senator; vice presid., presid. candidate.

Hussein, King, 1935-99 (Jordan), peacemaker; ruler of Jordan, 1952-99.

Saddam Hussein, 1937-2006, (Iraq) Iraqi ruler, put to death for crimes against humanity.

Jinnah, Muhammad Ali, 1876-1948, (Pak.) founder, first governor-general of Pakistan.

Barbara Jordan, 1936-96, (U.S.) congresswoman, orator, educator; first black woman to win a seat in the Texas senate, 1966.

Benito Juarez, 1806-72, (Mex.) rallied his country against foreign threats, sought to create democratic, federal republic.

Kim Dae Jung, 1925-2009 (near Mokpo, S. Korea), former S. Korean dissident, opposition leader, pres.; 2000 Nobelist.

Constantine Karamanlis, 1907-98, (Gr.) Greek prime min., restored democracy; later president.

Frank B. Kellogg, 1856-1937, (U.S.) sec. of state; negotiated Kellogg-Briand Pact to outlaw war.

Jack Kemp, 1935-2009, (U.S.) sec. of HUD, U.S. Rep. (NY), football player.

Edward M. Kennedy, 1932-2009 (U.S.) senator (MA), championed progressive causes.

Robert F. Kennedy, 1925-68, (U.S.) attorney general, senator; assassinated while seeking presidency.

Aleksandr Kerensky, 1881-1970, (Russ.) headed provisional government after Feb. 1917 revolution.

Ayatollah Ruhollah Khomeini, 1900-89, (Iranian), religious-political leader, spearheaded overthrow of shah, 1979.

Nikita Khrushchev, 1894-1971, (USSR) prem., first sec. of Communist party; initiated de-Stalinization.

Kim Il Sung, 1912-94, (Korean) N Korean dictator, 1948-94.

Lajos Kossuth, 1802-94, (Hung.) principal figure in 1848 Hungarian revolution.

Pyotr Kropotkin, 1842-1921, (Russ.) anarchist; championed the peasants but opposed Bolshevism.

Kublai Khan, c.1215-94, (Mongol) emperor; founder of Yüan dynasty in China.

Béla Kun, 1886-c.1939, (Hung.) member of 3rd Communist Internat.; tried to foment worldwide revolution.

Robert M. LaFollette, 1855-1925, (U.S.) Wisconsin public official; leader of progressive movement.

Fiorello La Guardia, 1882-1947, (U.S.) colorful NYC reform mayor.

Pierre Laval, 1883-1945, (Fr.) politician, Vichy foreign min.; executed for treason.

Andrew Bonar Law, 1858-1923, (Br.) Conservative party politician; led opposition to Irish home rule.

Vladimir Ilyich Lenin (Ulyanov), 1870-1924, (Russ.) revolutionary; founded Bolshevism; Soviet leader 1917-24.

Ferdinand de Lesseps, 1805-94, (Fr.) diplomat, engineer; conceived idea of Suez Canal.

Rene Levesque, 1922-87, (Can.) prem. of Quebec, 1976-85; led unsuccessful separartist campaign.

Maxim Litvinov, 1876-1951, (Pol.-Russ.) revolutionary, commissar of foreign affairs; favored cooperation with West.

Liu Shaoqi, c.1898-1974, (Chin.) Communist leader; fell from grace during Cultural Revolution.

David Lloyd George, 1863-1945, (Br.) Liberal party prime min.; laid foundations for modern welfare state.

Henry Cabot Lodge, 1850-1924, (U.S.) Republican senator; led opposition to participation in League of Nations.

Huey P. Long, 1893-1935, (U.S.) Louisiana political demagogue, governor, U.S. senator; assassinated.

Rosa Luxemburg, 1871-1919, (Ger.) revolutionary; leader of the German Social Democratic party and Spartacus party.

J. Ramsay MacDonald, 1866-1937, (Br.) first Labour party prime min. of Great Britain.

Harold Macmillan, 1895-1986, (Br.) prime min. of Great Britain, 1957-63.

Eugene McCarthy, 1916-2005, (U.S.) political leader and author; 1968 presidential contender.

Joseph R. McCarthy, 1908-57, (U.S.) senator, extremist in searching out alleged Communists and pro-Communists.

Makarios III, 1913-77, (Cypriot) Greek Orthodox archbishop; first pres. of Cyprus.

Mao Zedong, 1893-1976, (Chin.) chief Chinese Marxist theorist, revolutionary, political leader; led Chinese revolution establishing his nation as Communist state.

Jean Paul Marat, 1743-93, (Fr.) revolutionary, politician; identified with radical Jacobins; assassinated.

Thurgood Marshall, 1908-93, (U.S.) first black U.S. solicitor general, 1965; first black justice of U.S. Sup. Ct., 1967-91.

José Martí, 1853-95, (Cub.) patriot, poet; leader of Cuban struggle for independence.

Jan Masaryk, 1886-1948, (Czech.) foreign min.; died by mysterious alleged suicide following Communist coup.

Thomas G. Masaryk, 1850-1937, (Czech.) statesman, philosopher; first pres. of Czechoslovak Republic.

Jules Mazarin, 1602-61, (Fr.) cardinal, statesman; prime min. under Louis XIII and queen regent Anne of Austria.

Giusseppe Mazzini, 1805-72, (It.), reformer dedicated to Risorgimento movement for renewal of Italy.

Tom Mboya, 1930-69, (Kenyan) political leader; instrumental in securing independence for Kenya.

Cosimo I de' Medici, 1519-74, (It.) Duke of Florence, grand duke of Tuscany.

Lorenzo de' Medici, the Magnificent, 1449-92, (It.) merchant prince; a towering figure in Italian Renaissance.

Catherine de Médicis, 1519-89, (Fr.) queen consort of Henry II, regent of France; influential in Catholic-Huguenot wars.

Golda Meir, 1898-1978, (Isr.) a founder of the state of Israel and prime min., 1969-74.

Klemens W. N. L. Metternich, 1773-1859, (Austrian) statesman; arbiter of post-Napoleonic Europe.

Slobodan Milosevic, 1941-2006, (Serbian/Yugoslavian), former Yugoslav pres.; tried for war crimes.

François Mitterrand, 1916-96, (Fr.) pres. of France, 1981-95.

Mobutu Sese Seko, 1930-97, (Zaire) long-time ruler of Zaire (now Congo) (1965-97); exiled after rebellion.

Guy Mollet, 1905-75, (Fr.) socialist politician, resistance leader.

Henry Morgenthau Jr., 1891-1967, (U.S.) sec. of treasury; fund-raiser for New Deal and U.S. WW2 activities.

Gouverneur Morris, 1752-1816, (U.S.) statesman, diplomat. financial expert, helped plan decimal coinage.

Daniel Patrick Moynihan, 1927-2003, (U.S.) senator, diplomat, social scientist, and author.

Benito Mussolini, 1883-1945, (It.) leader of the Italian fascist state; assassinated.

Imre Nagy, c.1896-1958, (Hung.) Communist prem.; assassinated after Soviets crushed 1956 uprising.

Gamal Abdel Nasser, 1918-70, (Egypt.) leader of Arab unification, 2nd Egyptian pres.

Jawaharlal Nehru, 1889-1964, (In.) prime min.; guided India through its early years of independence.

Kwame Nkrumah, 1909-72, (Ghan.) 1st prime min., 1957-60, and pres., 1960-66, of Ghana.

Frederick North, 1732-92, (Br.) prime min.; his inept policies led to loss of American colonies.

Julius K. Nyerere, 1923?-99, (Tanz.) founding father, 1st pres., 1962-85, of Tanzania.

Daniel O'Connell, 1775-1847, (Ir.) nationalist political leader; known as The Liberator.

Omar, c.581-644, Muslim leader; 2nd caliph, led Islam to become an imperial power.

Thomas P. (Tip) O'Neill Jr., 1912-94, (U.S.) U.S. congressman, Speaker of the House, 1977-86.

Ignace Paderewski, 1860-1941, (Pol.) statesman, pianist; composer, briefly prime min., an ardent patriot.

Viscount Palmerston, 1784-1865, (Br.) Whig-Liberal prime min., foreign min.; embodied British nationalism.

Andreas George Papandreou, 1919-96, (Gk.) leftist politician, served 2 times as prem. (1981-89, 1993-96).

Georgios Papandreou, 1888-1968, (Gk.) Republican politician; served 3 times as prime min.

Franz von Papen, 1879-1969, (Ger.) politician; major role in overthrow of Weimar Republic and rise of Hitler.

Charles Stewart Parnell, 1846-1891, (Ir.) nationalist leader; "uncrowned king of Ireland."

Lester Pearson, 1897-1972, (Can.) diplomat, Liberal party leader, prime min.

Robert Peel, 1788-1850, (Br.) reformist prime min., founder of Conservative party.

Eva (Evita) Perón, 1919-52 (Arg.) highly influential 2nd wife of Juan Perón.

Juan Perón, 1895-1974, (Arg.) dynamic pres. of Argentina (1946-55, 1973-74).

Joseph Pilsudski, 1867-1935, (Pol.) statesman; instrumental in reestablishing Polish state in the 20th cent.

Charles Pinckney, 1757-1824, (U.S.) founding father; his Pinckney plan largely incorporated into Constitution.

Christian Pineau, 1905-95, (Fr.) leader of French Resistance during WW2; French foreign min., 1956-58.

Augusto Pinochet (Ugarte), 1915-2006, (Chile) former Chilean ruler; indicted for human rights abuses while in office.

William Pitt the Elder, 1708-78, (Br.) statesman; the "Great Commoner," transformed Britain into imperial power.

William Pitt the Younger, 1759-1806, (Br.) prime min. during French Revolutionary wars.

Georgi Plekhanov, 1857-1918, (Russ.) revolutionary, social philosopher; called "father of Russian Marxism."

Raymond Poincaré, 1860-1934, (Fr.) 9th pres. of the Republic; advocated harsh punishment of Germany after WW1.

Pol Pot, 1925-98, (Camb.) leader of Khmer Rouge; ruled Cambodia, 1975-79; responsible for mass deaths.

Georges Pompidou, 1911-74, (Fr.) Gaullist political leader; pres. 1969-74.

Grigori Potemkin, 1739-91, (Russ.) field marshal; favorite of Catherine II.

Adam Clayton Powell Jr., 1908-72, (U.S.) civil rights leader, congressman, 1945-69.

Yitzhak Rabin, 1922-95, (Isr.) military, political leader; prime min. of Israel, 1974-77, 1992-95; assassinated.

Joseph H. Rainey, 1832-87, (U.S.) first black person elected to U.S. House, 1869, from South Carolina.

Edmund Randolph, 1753-1813, (U.S.) attorney; prominent in drafting, ratification of constitution.

John Randolph, 1773-1833, (U.S.) southern planter; strong advocate of states' rights.

Jeannette Rankin, 1880-1973, (U.S.) pacifist; first woman member of U.S. Congress.

Walter Rathenau, 1867-1922, (Ger.) industrialist, statesman.

Sam Rayburn, 1882-1961, (U.S.) Democratic leader; representative for 47 years, House Speaker for 17.

Hiram R. Revels, 1822-1901, (U.S.) first African American U.S. senator, elected in Mississippi, served 1870-71.

Paul Reynaud, 1878-1966, (Fr.) statesman; prem. in 1940 at the time of France's defeat by Germany.

Syngman Rhee, 1875-1965, (Korean) first pres. of S Korea.

Cecil Rhodes, 1853-1902, (Br.) imperialist, industrial magnate; established Rhodes scholarships in his will.

Ann Richards, 1933-2006, (U.S.) former TX gov.

Cardinal de Richelieu, 1585-1642, (Fr.) statesman, known as "red eminence"; chief minister to Louis XIII.

Maximilien Robespierre, 1758-94, (Fr.) leading figure in French Revolution and Reign of Terror.

Year in Pictures

History in the Making ▲

Barack Obama was inaugurated as the 44th president of the United States Jan. 20, 2009; First Lady Michelle Obama and daughters Malia and Sasha were nearby to witness the swearing in of the first African American president.

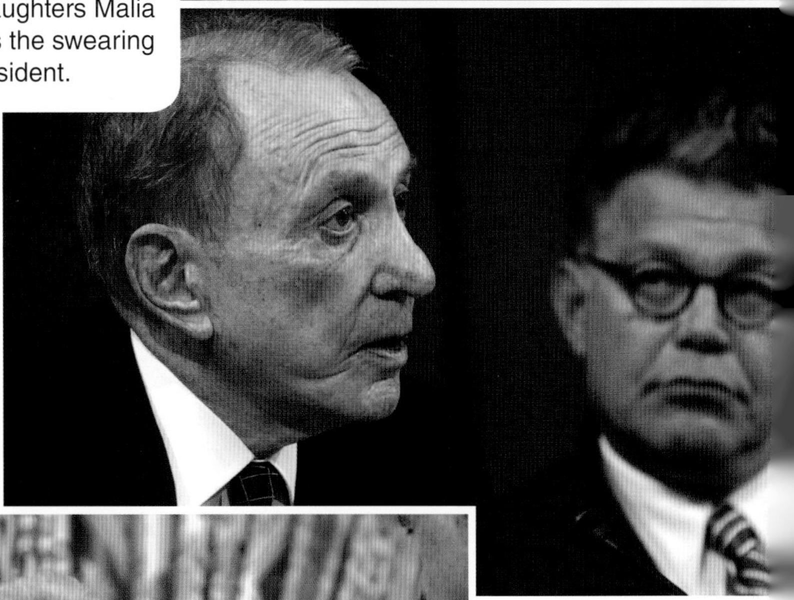

Senate Shifts ▶

Comedian Al Franken (right) became the junior Democratic senator from Minnesota July 7, 2009, following a controversial election recount battle against incumbent Sen. Norm Coleman (R). Sen. Arlen Specter (left) (R, PA since 1981) defected to the Democratic party Apr. 28, 2009.

◀ New Allies

Hillary Rodham Clinton was sworn in as Pres. Barack Obama's secretary of state Feb. 2, 2009; Clinton joined Obama's administration after a heated 2008 Democratic primary in which she was his chief opponent.

Economic Recovery ▶

Pres. Barack Obama signed the $787 billion American Recovery and Reinvestment Act into law Feb. 17, 2009; the multifaceted bill allocated funds for everything from "green-collar" jobs to increased unemployment benefits and tax cuts.

PUTTING AMERICA TO WORK

PROJECT FUNDED BY THE American Recovery and Reinvestment Act

USDOT TIGER

Banks Under Pressure ▼

The nation's banking giants found themselves under new oversight as a condition of the Troubled Assets Relief Program (TARP), which gave banks desperately needed infusions of cash in Oct. 2008 and Jan. 2009.

$4500 FOR this CLUNKE

IF YOUR CAR QUALIFIES THIS CAR QUALIFIES CARS

Cash for Clunkers ▲

Despite turbulence and restructuring in the U.S. auto industry, the so-called "cash for clunkers" program was a resounding success in July-Aug. 2009, as many Americans exchanged older, less fuel efficient cars for new models.

Out of Work

Unemployment reached its highest levels in more than 25 years during 2009 as the manufacturing and service sectors contracted with the economic downturn.

195

◀ Marriage Equality
Iowa became the third state in the union to legalize gay marriage Apr. 3, 2009, joining Connecticut and Massachusetts; Vermont, Maine, and New Hampshire also legalized same-sex marriage in 2009.

◀ Doctor Murdered
Dr. George Tiller, a doctor who performed late-term abortions at his Kansas clinic, was shot to death by a militant pro-life activist May 31, 2009, eliciting furor on both sides of the abortion debate.

▲ California Wildfires
Wildfires raged north of Los Angeles, CA, in late-summer 2009, threatening thousands of homes; two firefighters died fighting the blaze Aug. 30, 2009.

Polarizing Question
The debate over health care reform raged across the country in 2009; thousands nationwide went to town halls to express their support for or opposition to proposed reform plans.

The Supremes

Supreme Court Justice David H. Souter announced his retirement May 1, 2009. Pres. Barack Obama chose Sonia Sotomayor, a federal appeals court judge, to fill the vacancy; she was sworn in Aug. 8, 2009.

Crime and Punishment

Disgraced financier Bernie Madoff was sentenced June 29, 2009, to 150 years in federal prison; Madoff's Ponzi scheme had cost hundreds of people their life savings for a total fraud estimated at $65 billion.

◀ Lion in Winter

Sen. Ted Kennedy (D, MA) died Aug. 25, 2009, from brain cancer diagnosed in May 2008; Kennedy had served in the Senate for more than 45 years as a champion of liberal causes.

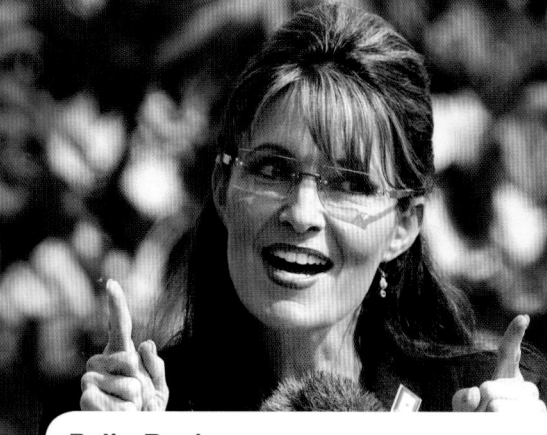

Palin Resigns

Alaska Gov. Sarah Palin, the Republican nominee for vice president and a polarizing figure on the American political scene, resigned and left her office midterm, July 26, 2009.

◀ Tainted Power

Illinois Gov. Rod Blagojevich (left) was removed from office Jan. 29, 2009, following a Dec. arrest on federal corruption charges. Blagojevich was accused of trying to profit from his ability to appoint a successor to Barack Obama in the Senate; he appointed Roland Burris (right), a former Illinois attorney general, Dec. 30, 2008.

Heroic Flight

U.S. Airways pilot Chesley B. "Sully" Sullenberger III safely landed a distressed plane on the Hudson River Jan. 15, 2009, ensuring that all 155 people on board were evacuated safely.

Beauty Pageant Controversy

Miss California USA beauty queen Carrie Prejean made headlines when she claimed that revealing her opposition to same-sex marriage at the Miss USA pageant Apr. 19, 2009, cost her the crown.

That's the Way It Is ▶

Respected anchorman Walter Cronkite died July 17, 2009; Cronkite had retired from CBS News in 1981 after a long and distinguished career as a journalist.

◀ Beer Summit

Vice Pres. Joe Biden, Harvard Prof. Henry Louis Gates Jr., Cambridge police Sgt. James Crowley, and Pres. Barack Obama sat down for a beer outside the White House July 30, 2009. Crowley had arrested Gates at his home July 16, 2009, in an incident that sparked racial debate.

Separating Reality

Jon and Kate Gosselin, who appeared on reality series *Jon & Kate Plus 8*, about raising sextuplets and twins, announced June 22, 2009, that they planned to divorce.

Octomom

Nadya Suleman gave birth to octuplets Jan. 26, 2009, in Bellflower, CA; she became a controversial tabloid subject after subsequent reports revealed that Suleman, who had conceived using in vitro fertilization, was mother of six other children.

Distressed Governor

South Carolina Gov. Mark Sanford was censured by the SC Republican Party July 6, 2009, after admitting to an extramarital affair.

King of Pop Passes

Controversial pop star Michael Jackson died unexpectedly from a prescription drug overdose June 25, 2009; Jackson was remembered perhaps as much for his scandalous personal life as for selling 750 million records.

▲ Baton Passed

Conan O'Brien took over NBC's long-running *Tonight Show* June 1, 2009; former host Jay Leno moved on to *The Jay Leno Show*, his own nightly NBC show.

Three Billies ▶

The Broadway musical *Billy Elliot* and the three boys who shared the title role were honored with Tony Award wins May 3, 2009.

Overnight Sensation ▲

Scottish amateur singer Susan Boyle became an international sensation after her April 11, 2009, performance on *Britain's Got Talent* got more than 100 million hits after being posted on YouTube.

◀ Critical Succes

Sleeper hit *Slumdo Millionaire* won eigh Academy Awards F 22, 2009, including Best Picture and B Director.

◀ New Judge

Long-time *American Idol* judge Paula Abdul announced Apr. 4, 2009, that she would be leaving the show; comedienne and talk-show host Ellen DeGeneres was named the show's new judge Sept. 9, 2009.

Nelson Rockefeller, 1908-79, (U.S.) Republican governor of NY, 1959-73; U.S. vice pres., 1974-77.

George W. Romney, 1907-95, (U.S.) auto exec.; 3-term Republican governor of Michigan.

Eleanor Roosevelt, 1884-1962, (U.S.) influential First Lady, humanitarian, UN diplomat.

Elihu Root, 1845-1937, (U.S.) lawyer, statesman, diplomat; leading Republican supporter of the League of Nations.

Dean Rusk, 1909-95, (U.S.) statesman; sec. of state, 1961-69.

John Russell, 1792-1878, (Br.) Liberal prime min. during the Irish potato famine.

Anwar al-Sadat, 1918-81, (Egypt.) pres., 1970-1981, promoted peace with Israel; Nobel laureate; assassinated.

António de Oliveira Salazar, 1889-1970, (Port.) longtime dictator.

José de San Martin, 1778-1850, S Amer. revolutionary; protector of Peru.

Eisaku Sato, 1901-75, (Jpn.) prime min.; presided over Japan's post-WW2 emergence as major world power.

Abdul Aziz Ibn Saud, c.1880-1953, (Saudi Arabia) king of Saudi Arabia, 1932-53.

Robert Schuman, 1886-1963, (Fr.) statesman; founded European Coal and Steel Community.

Carl Schurz, 1829-1906, (U.S.) German-American political leader, journalist, orator, dedicated reformer.

Kurt Schuschnigg, 1897-1977, (Austrian) chancellor; unsuccessful in stopping Austria's annexation by Germany.

William H. Seward, 1801-72, (U.S.) anti-slavery activist; as U.S. sec. of state purchased Alaska.

Carlo Sforza, 1872-1952, (It.) foreign min., anti-fascist.

Sitting Bull, c.1831-90, (Nat. Am.) Sioux leader in Battle of Little Bighorn over George A. Custer, 1876.

Alfred E. Smith, 1873-1944, (U.S.) NY Democratic governor; first Roman Catholic to run for presidency.

Margaret Chase Smith, 1897-1995, (U.S.) congresswoman, senator; 1st woman elected to both houses of Congress.

Jan C. Smuts, 1870-1950, (S. African) statesman, philosopher, soldier, prime min.

Paul Henri Spaak, 1899-1972, (Belg.) statesman, socialist leader.

Joseph Stalin, 1879-1953, (USSR) Soviet dictator, 1924-53; instituted forced collectivization, massive purges, and labor camps, causing millions of deaths.

Edwin M. Stanton, 1814-69, (U.S.) sec. of war, 1862-68.

Edward R. Stettinius Jr., 1900-49, (U.S.) industrialist, sec. of state who coordinated aid to WW2 allies.

Adlai E. Stevenson, 1900-65, (U.S.) Democratic leader, diplomat, Illinois governor, presidential candidate.

Henry L. Stimson, 1867-1950, (U.S.) statesman; served in 5 administrations, foreign policy adviser in 30s and 40s.

Carl Stokes, 1927-96, (U.S.) first black mayor of a major American city (Cleveland), 1967-72.

Suharto, 1921-2008, (Indon.) former long-time Indonesian ruler.

Sukarno, 1901-70, (Indon.) dictatorial first pres. of the Indonesian republic.

Sun Yat-sen, 1866-1925, (Chin.) revolutionary; leader of Kuomintang, regarded as the father of modern China.

Robert A. Taft, 1889-1953, (U.S.) conservative Senate leader, called "Mr. Republican."

Charles de Talleyrand, 1754-1838, (Fr.) statesman, diplomat; the major force of the Congress of Vienna of 1814-15.

U Thant, 1909-74 (Bur.) statesman, UN sec.-general.

Norman M. Thomas, 1884-1968, (U.S.) social reformer; 6 times Socialist party presidential candidate.

Josip Broz Tito, 1892-1980, (Yug.) pres. of Yugoslavia from 1953, WW2 guerrilla chief, postwar rival of Stalin.

Palmiro Togliatti, 1893-1964, (It.) major Italian Communist leader.

Hideki Tojo, 1885-1948, (Jpn.) statesman, soldier; prime min. during most of WW2.

François Toussaint L'Ouverture, c.1744-1803, (Haitian) patriot, martyr; thwarted French colonial aims.

Leon Trotsky, 1879-1940, (Russ.) revolutionary, founded Red Army, expelled from party in conflict with Stalin; assassinated.

Pierre Elliott Trudeau, 1919-2000, (Can.) longtime liberal prime minister of Canada, 1968-79, 1980-84; achieved native Canadian constitution.

Rafael L. Trujillo Molina, 1891-1961, (Dom.) dictator of Dominican Republic, 1930-61; assassinated.

Moise K. Tshombe, 1919-69, (Cong.) pres. of secessionist Katanga, prem. of Congo.

William M. Tweed, 1823-78, (U.S.) political boss of Tammany Hall, NYC's Democratic political machine.

Walter Ulbricht, 1893-1973, (Ger.) Communist leader of German Democratic Republic.

Arthur H. Vandenberg, 1884-1951, (U.S.) senator; proponent of bipartisan anti-Communist foreign policy.

Eleutherios Venizelos, 1864-1936, (Gk.) most prominent Greek statesman of early 20th cent.

Hendrik F. Verwoerd, 1901-66, (S. African) prime min.; rigorously applied apartheid policy despite protest.

Kurt Waldheim, 1918-2007, (Austria) UN sec.-gen, and Austrian pres.

George Wallace, 1919-98, (U.S.) former segregationist governor of Alabama and presid. candidate.

Robert Walpole, 1676-1745, (Br.) statesman; generally considered Britain's first prime min.

Harold Washington, 1922-87, (U.S.) first black mayor of Chicago.

Robert C. Weaver, 1907-97, (U.S.) first African American appointed to cabinet; secretary of HUD.

Daniel Webster, 1782-1852, (U.S.) orator, politician; advocate of business interests during Jacksonian agrarianism.

Caspar Weinberger, 1917-2006 (U.S.), business exec, former defense sec., other cabinet posts.

Chaim Weizmann, 1874-1952, (Russ.-Isr.) Zionist leader, scientist; first Israeli pres.

Wendell L. Willkie, 1892-1944, (U.S.) Republican who tried to unseat FDR when he ran for his 3rd term.

Harold Wilson, 1916-95, (Br.) Labour party leader; prime min., 1964-70, 1974-76.

Boris Yeltsin, 1931-2007, (USSR-Russia) first freely elected president of post-Soviet Russia.

Coleman A. Young, 1918-97, (U.S.) first Afr.-Amer. mayor of Detroit, 1974-93.

Emiliano Zapata, c.1879-1919, (Mex.) revolutionary; major influence on modern Mexico.

Todor Zhivkov, 1911-98, (Bulg.) Communist ruler of Bulgaria from 1954 until ousted in a 1989 coup.

Zhou Enlai, 1898-1976, (Chin.) diplomat, prime min.; a leading figure of the Chinese Communist party.

Scientists of the Past

Revised by Peter Barker, Prof. & Chair, Dept. of the History of Science, Univ. of Oklahoma.

For pre-modern scientists see also Philosophers and Religious Figures of the Past and Historical Figures chapter.

Albertus Magnus, c.1200-1280, (Ger.) theologian, philosopher; helped found medieval study of natural science.

Alhazen (Ibn al-Haytham), c.965-c.1040, mathematician, astronomer; optical theorist.

Andre-Marie Ampère, 1775-1836, (Fr.) mathematician, chemist; founder of electrodynamics.

John V. Atanasoff, 1903-95, (U.S.) physicist; co-invented Atanasoff-Berry Computer (1939-41).

Amedeo Avogadro, 1776-1856, (It.) chemist, physicist; proposed that equal volumes of gas contain equal numbers of molecules, permitting determination of molecular weights.

John Bardeen, 1908-91, (U.S.) double Nobel laureate in physics (transistor, 1956; superconductivity, 1972).

A. H. Becquerel, 1852-1908, (Fr.) physicist; discovered radioactivity in uranium (1896).

Alexander Graham Bell, 1847-1922, (U.S.) inventor; first to patent and commercially exploit the telephone (1876).

Daniel Bernoulli, 1700-82, (Swiss) mathematician; developed fluid dynamics and kinetic theory of gases.

Clifford Berry, 1918-1963, (U.S.) collaborated with Atanasoff on the ABC computer (1939-41).

Jöns Jakob Berzelius, 1779-1848, (Swed.) chemist; developed modern chemical symbols and formulas.

Henry Bessemer, 1813-98, (Br.) engineer; invented Bessemer steel-making process.

Hans Bethe, 1906-2005, (Ger.-U.S.) physicist; won Nobel Prize in 1967 for describing how stars generate energy.

Bruno Bettelheim, 1903-90, (Austrian-U.S.) psychoanalyst; studied disturbed children; *Uses of Enchantment* (1976).

Louis Blériot, 1872-1936, (Fr.) engineer; monoplane pioneer, first Channel flight (1909).

Franz Boas, 1858-1942, (Ger.-U.S.) founded modern anthropology; studied Pacific Coast tribes.

Niels Bohr, 1885-1962, (Dan.) atomic and nuclear physicist; founded quantum mechanics.

Norman Borlaug, 1914-2009, (U.S.) plant pathologist and geneticist, father of "green" (agricultural) revolution.

Max Born, 1882-1970, (Ger.) atomic and nuclear physicist; helped develop quantum mechanics.

Satyendranath Bose, 1894-1974, (Indian) physicist; forerunner of modern quantum theory for integral-spin particles.

Louis de Broglie, 1892-1987, (Fr.) physicist; proposed quantum wave-particle duality.

Robert Bunsen, 1811-99, (Ger.) chemist; pioneered spectroscopic analysis; discovered rubidium, caesium.

Luther Burbank, 1849-1926, (U.S.) naturalist; developed plant breeding into a modern science.

Vannevar Bush, 1890-1974, (U.S.) electrical engineer; developed differential analyzer, an early analogue computer; headed WWII Office of Scientific Res. and Dev.

Marvin Camras, 1916-95, (U.S.) inventor, electrical engineer; invented magnetic tape recording.

Alexis Carrel, 1873-1944, (Fr.) surgeon, biologist; developed methods of suturing blood vessels and transplanting organs.

Rachel Carson, 1907-64, (U.S.) marine biologist, environmentalist; *Silent Spring* (1962).

James Chadwick, 1891-1974, (Br.) physicist; discovered the neutron (1932); led Brit. Manhattan Project group in U.S..

Albert Claude, 1898-1983, (Belg.-U.S.) a founder of modern cell biology; determined role of mitochondria.

Nicolaus Copernicus, 1473-1543, (Pol.) first modern astronomer to propose sun as center of the planets' motions.

Jacques Yves Cousteau, 1910-1997, (Fr.) oceanographer; co-inventor, with E. Gagnan, of the Aqualung (1943).

Seymour Cray, 1925-96, (U.S.) computer industry pioneer; developed supercomputers.

Francis Crick, 1916-2004, (Br.) biophysicist; co-discoverer of genetic code; shared 1962 Nobel Prize.

Marie, 1867-1934 (Pol.-Fr.) and **Pierre Curie**, 1859-1906, (Fr.) physical chemists; pioneer investigators of radioactivity, discovered radium and polonium (1898).

Gottlieb Daimler, 1834-1900, (Ger.) engineer, inventor; pioneer automobile manufacturer.

John Dalton, 1766-1844, (Br.) chemist, physicist; formulated atomic theory, made first table of atomic weights.

Charles Darwin, 1809-82, (Br.) naturalist; established theory of organic evolution; *Origin of Species* (1859).

Lee De Forest, 1873-1961, (U.S.) inventor of triode, pioneer in wireless telegraphy, sound pictures, television.

Pierre-Gilles de Gennes, 1932-2007, (Fr.) physicist whose research furthered the development of liquid-crystal-display (LCD) technology; awarded Nobel Prize for Physics in 1991.

Max Delbruck, 1906-81, (Ger.-U.S.) founded molecular biology.

Rudolf Diesel, 1858-1913, (Ger.) mechanical engineer; patented Diesel engine (1892).

Theodosius Dobzhansky, 1900-75, (Russ.-U.S.) biologist; reconciled genetics and natural selection.

Christian Doppler, 1803-53, (Austrian) physicist; showed change in wave frequency caused by motion of source, now known as Doppler effect.

J. Presper Eckert Jr., 1919-95, (U.S.) co-inventor, with Mauchly, of the ENIAC computer (1943-45).

Thomas A. Edison, 1847-1931, (U.S.) inventor; held more than 1,000 patents, including incandescent electric lamp.

Paul Ehrlich, 1854-1915, (Ger.) medical researcher in immunology and bacteriology; pioneered antitoxin production.

Albert Einstein, 1879-1955, (Ger.-U.S.) theoretical physicist; founded relativity theory.

John F. Enders, 1897-1985, (U.S.) virologist; helped discover vaccines against polio, measles, mumps and chicken pox.

Erik Erikson, 1902-94, (U.S.) psychoanalyst, author; theory of developmental stages of life, *Childhood and Society* (1950).

Leonhard Euler, 1707-83, (Swiss) mathematician, physicist; pioneer of calculus, revived ideas of Fermat.

Gabriel Fahrenheit, 1686-1736, (Ger.) physicist; improved thermometers and introduced Fahrenheit temperature scale.

Michael Faraday, 1791-1867, (Br.) chemist, physicist; discovered electrical induction and invented dynamo (1831).

Philo T. Farnsworth, 1906-71, (U.S.) inventor; built first television system (San Francisco, 1928).

Pierre de Fermat, 1601-65, (Fr.) mathematician; founded modern theory of numbers.

Enrico Fermi, 1901-54, (It.-U.S.) nuclear physicist; demonstrated first controlled chain reaction (Chicago, 1942).

Richard Feynman, 1918-88, (U.S.) theoretical physicist, author; founder of Quantum Electrodynamics (QED).

Alexander Fleming, 1881-1955, (Br.) bacteriologist; discovered penicillin (1928).

Jean B. J. Fourier, 1768-1830, (Fr.) introduced method of analysis in math and physics known as Fourier Series.

Sigmund Freud, 1856-1939, (Austrian) psychiatrist; founder of psychoanalysis. *Interpretation of Dreams* (1901).

Erich Fromm, 1900-80, (U.S.) psychoanalyst. *Man for Himself* (1947).

Galileo Galilei, 1564-1642, (It.) physicist; used telescope to vindicate Copernicus, founded modern science of motion.

Carl Friedrich Gauss, 1777-1855, (Ger.) math. physicist; completed work of Fermat and Euler in number theory.

Josiah W. Gibbs, 1839-1903, (U.S.) theoretical physicist, chemist; founded chemical thermodynamics.

Robert H. Goddard, 1882-1945, (U.S.) physicist; invented liquid fuel rocket (1926).

George W. Goethals, 1858-1928, (U.S.) chief engineer who completed Panama Canal (1907-14).

William C. Gorgas, 1854-1920, (U.S.) physician; pioneer in prevention of yellow fever and malaria.

Stephen Jay Gould, 1941-2002, (U.S.) paleontologist, evolutionary biologist, writer.

Ernest Haeckel, 1834-1919, (Ger.) zoologist, evolutionist; early Darwinist, introduced concept of "ecology."

Otto Hahn, 1879-1968, (Ger.) chemist; with Meitner discovered nuclear fission (1938).

Edmund Halley, 1656-1742, (Br.) astronomer; predicted return of 1682 comet ("Halley's Comet") in 1759.

William Harvey, 1578-1657, (Br.) physician, anatomist; discovered circulation of the blood (1628).

Werner Heisenberg, 1901-76, (Ger.) physicist; developed matrix mechanics and uncertainty principle (1927).

Hermann von Helmholtz, 1821-94, (Ger.) physicist, physiologist; formulated principle of conservation of energy.

William Herschel, 1738-1822, (Ger.-Br.) astronomer; discovered Uranus (1781).

Heinrich Hertz, 1857-94, (Ger.) physicist; discovered radio waves and photo-electric effect (1886-7).

David Hilbert, 1862-1943, (Ger.) mathematician; contributed to algebra, calculus and foundational studies (formalism).

Albert Hofmann, 1906-2008, (U.S.) father of LSD.

Edwin P. Hubble, 1889-1953, (U.S.) astronomer; discovered observational evidence of expanding universe.

Alexander von Humboldt, 1769-1859, (Ger.) naturalist, author; explored S America, created ecology.

Edward Jenner, 1749-1823, (Br.) physician; pioneered vaccination, introduced term "virus."

James Joule, 1818-89, (Br.) physicist; found relation between heat and mechanical energy (conservation of energy).

Carl Jung, 1875-1961, (Swiss) psychiatrist; founder of analytical psychology.

Ernest Everett Just, 1883-1941, (U.S.) marine biologist; studied egg development; author, *Biology of Cell Surfaces*, 1941.

Johannes Kepler, 1571-1630, (Ger.) astronomer; discovered laws of planetary motion.

Al-Khawarizmi, early 9th cent., (Arab.), mathematician; regarded as founder of algebra.

Robert Koch, 1843-1910 (Ger.) bacteriologist; isolated bacterial causes of tuberculosis and other diseases.

Georges Köhler, 1946-95, (Ger.) immunologist; with Cesar Milstein he developed monoclonal antibody technique.

Willem Kolff, 1911-2009, (Dutch-U.S.) physician, biomedical engineer, developed the first practical kidney dialysis machine, considered the "father of artificial" organs.

Jacques Lacan, 1901-81, (Fr.) influential psychoanalyst.

Joseph Lagrange, 1736-1813, (Fr.) geometer, astronomer; showed that gravity of earth and moon cancels creating stable points in space around them.

Jean B. Lamarck, 1744-1829, (Fr.) naturalist; forerunner of Darwin in evolutionary theory.

Pierre Simon de Laplace, 1749-1827, (Fr.) astronomer, physicist; proposed nebular origin for solar system.

Lewis H. Latimer, 1848-1928, (U.S.) African American scientist; associate of Edison; supervised installation of first electric street lighting in NYC.

Antoine Lavoisier, 1743-94, (Fr.) a founder of mod. chemistry.

Ernest O. Lawrence, 1901-58, (U.S.) physicist; invented the cyclotron.

Jerome Lejeune, 1927-94, (Fr.) geneticist; discovered chromosomal cause of Down syndrome (1959).

Louis 1903-72, and **Mary Leakey**, 1913-96, (Br.) early hominid paleoanthropologists; discovered remains in Africa.

Anton van Leeuwenhoek, 1632-1723, (Dutch) founder of microscopy.

Kurt Lewin, 1890-1947, (Ger.-U.S.) social psychologist; studied human motivation and group dynamics.

Justus von Liebig, 1803-73, (Ger.) founded quantitative organic chemistry.

Joseph Lister, 1827-1912, (Br.) physician; pioneered antiseptic surgery.

Hendrik Lorentz, 1853-1928 (Neth.), physicist, developed electron theory of matter, contrib. to relativity theory.

Konrad Lorenz, 1903-89, (Austrian) ethologist; pioneer in study of animal behavior.

Percival Lowell, 1855-1916, (U.S.) astronomer; predicted the existence of Pluto.

Louis, 1864-1948, and **Auguste Lumière**, 1862-1954, (Fr.) invented cinematograph and made first motion picture (1895).

Theodore H. Maiman, 1927-2007, (U.S.) physicist who invented the first workable laser, which he displayed in 1960.

Guglielmo Marconi, 1874-1937, (It.) physicist; developed wireless telegraphy.

John W. Mauchly, 1907-80, (U.S.) co-inventor, with Eckert, of computer ENIAC (1943-45).

James Clerk Maxwell, 1831-79, (Br.) physicist; unified electricity and magnetism; electromagnetic theory of light.

Maria Goeppert Mayer, 1906-72, (Ger.-U.S.) physicist; developed shell model of atomic nuclei.

Barbara McClintock, 1902-92, (U.S.) geneticist; showed that some genetic elements are mobile.

Lise Meitner, 1878-1968, (Austrian) co-discoverer, with Hahn, of nuclear fission (1938).

Gregor J. Mendel, 1822-84, (Austrian) botanist, monk; his experiments became the foundation of modern genetics.

Dmitri Mendeleyev, 1834-1907, (Russ.) chemist; established Periodic Table of the Elements.

Bruce R. Merrifield, 1921-2006, (U.S.) chemist; discovered how to synthesize proteins quickly and efficiently.

Franz Mesmer, 1734-1815, (Ger.) physician; introduced hypnotherapy.

Albert A. Michelson, 1852-1931, (U.S.) physicist; invented interferometer.

Robert A. Millikan, 1868-1953, (U.S.) physicist; measured electronic charge.

Thomas Hunt Morgan, 1866-1945, (U.S.) geneticist, embryologist; established role of chromosomes in heredity.

Isaac Newton, 1642-1727, (Br.) natural philosopher; discovered laws of gravitation, motion; with Leibniz, founded calculus.

Robert N. Noyce, 1927-90, (U.S.) invented microchip.

J. Robert Oppenheimer, 1904-67, (U.S.) physicist; scientific director of Manhattan project.

Wilhelm Ostwald, 1853-1932, (Ger.) chemist, philosopher; main founder of modern physical chemistry.

Louis Pasteur, 1822-95, (Fr.) chemist; showed that germs cause disease and fermentation, originated pasteurization.

Linus C. Pauling, 1901-94, (U.S.) chemist; studied chemical bonds; campaigned for nuclear disarmament.

Jean Piaget, 1896-1980, (Swiss) psychologist; four-stage theory of intellectual development in children.

Max Planck, 1858-1947, (Ger.) physicist; introduced quantum hypothesis (1900).

Jules Henri Poincaré, 1854-1912, (Fr.) mathematician, founded algebraic topology, many other discoveries.

Walter S. Reed, 1851-1902, (U.S.) army physician; proved mosquitoes transmit yellow fever.

Theodor Reik, 1888-1969, (Austrian-U.S.) psychoanalyst, major Freudian disciple.

Bernhard Riemann, 1826-66, (Ger.) mathematician; developed non-Euclidean geometry used by Einstein.

Norbert Rillieux, 1806-94, (U.S.) African American inventor of a vacuum pan evaporator, 1846, revolutionized sugar-refining industry.

Wilhelm Roentgen, 1845-1923, (Ger.) physicist; discovered X-rays (1895).

Carl Rogers, 1902-87, (U.S.) psychotherapist, author; originated nondirective therapy.

Ernest Rutherford, 1871-1937, (Br.) physicist; pioneer investigator of radioactivity, identified the atomic nucleus.

Albert B. Sabin, 1906-93, (Russ.-U.S.), developed oral polio live-virus vaccine.

Carl Sagan, 1934-96, (U.S.) astronomer, author.

Jonas Salk, 1914-95, (U.S.) developed first successful polio vaccine, widely used in U.S. after 1955.

Giovanni Schiaparelli, 1835-1910, (It.) astronomer; reported canals on Mars.

Erwin Schrödinger, 1887-1961, (Austrian) physicist; developed wave equation for quantum systems.

Glenn T. Seaborg, 1912-99, (U.S.) chemist, Nobel Prize winner (1951); codiscoverer of plutonium.

Harlow Shapley, 1885-1972, (U.S.) astronomer; mapped galactic clusters and position of Sun in our own galaxy.

Norman E. Shumway, 1923-2006, (U.S.) surgeon; performed the world's first successful heart-lung transplant.

B(urrhus) F(rederick) Skinner, 1904-89, (U.S.) psychologist; leading advocate of behaviorism.

Richard E. Smalley, 1943-2006, (U.S.) chemist; along with three other scientists, discovered "buckminsterfullerenes," a previously unknown class of carbon molecules.

Roger W. Sperry, 1913-94, (U.S.) neurobiologist; established different functions of right and left sides of brain.

Benjamin Spock, 1903-98, (U.S.) pediatrician, child care expert; *Common Sense Book of Baby and Child Care*.

Charles P. Steinmetz, 1865-1923, (Ger.-U.S.) electrical engineer; developed basic ideas on alternating current.

Ernst Stuhlinger, 1913-2008, (Ger.) rocket scientist; electric propulsion for NASA in early space age.

Leo Szilard, 1898-1964, (Hung.-U.S.) physicist; helped on Manhattan project, later opposed nuclear weapons.

Edward Teller, 1908-2003, (Hung.-U.S.) physicist, aided on Manhattan project, had key role in development of H-bomb.

Nikola Tesla, 1856-1943, (Serb.-U.S.) invented electrical devices including a.c. dynamos, transformers and motors.

William Thomson (Lord Kelvin), 1824-1907, (Br.) physicist; aided in success of transatlantic telegraph cable (1865); proposed Kelvin absolute temperature scale.

Alan Turing, 1912-54, (Br.) mathematician; helped develop basis for computers.

Rudolf Virchow, 1821-1902, (Ger.) pathologist; pioneered the modern theory that diseases affect the body through cells.

James Van Allen, 1914-2006, (U.S.) physicist; discovered the presence of radiation belts around Earth (Van Allen belts).

Alessandro Volta, 1745-1827, (It.) physicist; electricity pioneer.

Werner von Braun, 1912-77, (Ger.-U.S.) developed rockets for warfare and space exploration.

John Von Neumann, 1903-57, (Hung.-U.S.) mathematician; originated game theory; basic design for modern computers.

Alfred Russell Wallace, 1823-1913, (Br.) naturalist; proposed concept of evolution independently of Darwin.

John B. Watson, 1878-1958, (U.S.) psychologist; a founder of behaviorism.

James E. Watt, 1736-1819, (Br.) mechanical engineer, inventor; invented modern steam engine (1765).

Alfred L. Wegener, 1880-1930, (Ger.) meteorologist, geophysicist; postulated continental drift.

Norbert Wiener, 1894-1964, (U.S.) mathematician; founder of cybernetics.

Daniel Hale Williams, 1858-1931, (U.S.) African American surgeon; performed one of first two open-heart operations, 1893.

Sewall Wright, 1889-1988, (U.S.) evolutionary theorist; helped found population genetics.

Wilhelm Wundt, 1832-1920, (Ger.) founder of experimental psychology.

Ferdinand von Zeppelin, 1838-1917, (Ger.) soldier, aeronaut, airship designer.

Social Reformers, Activists, and Humanitarians of the Past

Ralph David Abernathy, 1926-90, (U.S.) black civil rights activist; pres., 1968, Southern Christian Leadership Conf.

Jane Addams, 1860-1935, (U.S.) cofounder of Hull House; won Nobel Peace Prize, 1931.

Susan B. Anthony, 1820-1906, (U.S.) a leader in temperance, anti-slavery, and woman suffrage movements.

Thomas Barnardo, 1845-1905, (Br.) social reformer; pioneered in care of destitute children.

Clara Barton, 1821-1912, (U.S.) organized American Red Cross.

Daisy Bates, 1914-99, (U.S.) black civil rights leader who fought for school integration; leading advocate for the "Little Rock 9" during the Arkansas desegregation crisis in 1957.

Henry Ward Beecher, 1813-87, (U.S.) clergyman, abolitionist.

Peter Benenson, 1921-2005, (Br.) activist; founded Amnesty International in 1961.

Mary McLeod Bethune, 1875-1955, (U.S.) black educator and civil rights activist; adviser to FDR and Truman; founder, pres., Bethune-Cookman College.

Amelia Bloomer, 1818-94, (U.S.) suffragette, social reformer.

William Booth, 1829-1912, (Br.) founded Salvation Army.

John Brown, 1800-59, (U.S.) abolitionist who led murder of 5 pro-slavery men, was hanged.

Stokely Carmichael (Kwame Toure), 1941-98, (U.S.) black power activist, major proponent of Pan-Africanism. Prime Min. Black Panthers.

Frances Xavier (Mother) Cabrini, 1850-1917, (It.-U.S.) Italian-born nun; founded charitable institutions; first American canonized as a saint, 1946.

Carrie Chapman Catt, 1859-1947, (U.S.) suffragette.

Eldridge Cleaver, 1935-98, (U.S.) revolutionary social critic; former "minister of information" for Black Panthers; *Soul on Ice*.

Cesar Chavez, 1927-93, (U.S.) labor leader; helped establish United Farm Workers of America.

Clarence Darrow, 1857-1938, (U.S.) lawyer; defender of "underdog," opponent of capital punishment.

Ossie Davis, 1917-2005, (U.S.) black civil rights activist, actor, director.

Dorothy Day, 1897-1980, (U.S.) founder of Catholic Worker movement.

Eugene V. Debs, 1855-1926, (U.S.) labor leader; led Pullman strike, 1894; 4-time Socialist presidential candidate.

Vine Deloria Jr., 1933-2005, (U.S) Native American activist and author; wrote *Custer Died for Your Sins*.

Dorothea Dix, 1802-87, (U.S.) crusader for mentally ill.

Thomas Dooley, 1927-61, (U.S.) "jungle doctor," noted for efforts to supply medical aid to developing countries.

Frederick Douglass, 1817-95, (U.S.) slave, author, editor, orator, diplomat; edited abolitionist weekly *The North Star*.

Marjory Stoneman Douglas, 1890-1998, (U.S.) writer and environmentalist; campaigned to save Florida Everglades.

Andrea Dworkin, 1946-2005, (U.S.) radical feminist and antipornography crusader.

Betty Friedan, 1921-2006, (U.S.) author, feminist; wrote *The Feminine Mystique*.

Medgar Evers, 1925-63, (U.S.) black civil rights leader; campaigned to register black voters; assassinated.

James Farmer, 1920-99, (U.S.) black civil rights leader; founded Congress of Racial Equality (CORE).

William Lloyd Garrison, 1805-79, (U.S.) abolitionist.

Emma Goldman, 1869-1940, (Russ.-U.S.) published anarchist *Mother Earth*, birth-control advocate.

Samuel Gompers, 1850-1924, (U.S.) labor leader. First president of the American Federation of Labor (AFL).

Prince Hall, 1735-1807, (U.S.) activist; founded black Freemasonry; served in American Revolutionary war.

Michael Harrington, 1928-89, (U.S.) exposed poverty in affluent U.S. in *The Other America*, 1963.

Sidney Hillman, 1887-1946, (U.S.) labor leader; helped organize CIO.

Samuel G. Howe, 1801-76, (U.S.) social reformer; changed public attitudes toward the handicapped.

Helen Keller, 1880-1968, (U.S.) crusader for better treatment for the handicapped; deaf and blind herself.

Coretta Scott King, 1927-2006, (U.S.) black civil rights leader; wife of Rev. Martin Luther King Jr.

Rev. Martin Luther King Jr., 1929-68, (U.S.) civil rights leader; led 1955-56 Montgomery, AL, boycott; founder, pres., Southern Christian Leadership Conference, 1957; Nobel laureate (1964); assassinated.

Malcolm X (Little), 1925-65, (U.S.) Black Muslim, black nationalist leader; promoted black pride; assassinated.

Maggie Kuhn, 1905-95, (U.S.) founded Gray Panthers, 1970.

William Kunstler, 1919-95, (U.S.) civil liberties attorney.

John L. Lewis, 1880-1969, (U.S.) labor leader; headed United Mine Workers, 1920-60.

Karl Menninger, 1893-1990, (U.S.) with brother William founded Menninger Clinic and Menninger Foundation.

Lucretia Mott, 1793-1880, (U.S.) reformer, pioneer feminist.

Philip Murray, 1886-1952, (U.S.) Scottish-born labor leader.

Huey P. Newton, 1942-89, (U.S.) co-founded Black Panther Party, 1966.

Florence Nightingale, 1820-1910, (Br.) founder of modern nursing.

Rosa Parks,1913-2005, (U.S.), black civil rights activist; her actions sparked 1955-56 Montgomery bus boycott.

Emmeline Pankhurst, 1858-1928, (Br.) woman suffragist.

A. Philip Randolph, 1889-1979, (U.S.) organized Brotherhood of Sleeping Car Porters, 1925; an organizer of 1941 and 1963 March on Washington movements.

Walter Reuther, 1907-70, (U.S.) labor leader; headed UAW.

Jacob Riis, 1849-1914, (U.S.) crusader for urban reforms.

Paul Robeson, 1898-1976, (U.S.) actor, singer, black civil rights activist.

Bayard Rustin, 1910-87, (U.S.) an organizer of the 1963 March on Washington; exec. director, A. Philip Randolph Institute.

Margaret Sanger, 1883-1966, (U.S.) social reformer; pioneered the birth-control movement.

Earl of Shaftesbury (A. A. Cooper), 1801-85, (Br.) social reformer.

Eunice Kennedy Shriver, 1921-2009, (U.S.), co-founder of the Special Olympics for mentally challenged athletes.

Elizabeth Cady Stanton, 1815-1902, (U.S.) woman suffrage pioneer.

Lucy Stone, 1818-93, (U.S.) feminist, abolitionist.

Mother Teresa of Calcutta, 1910-97, (Alban.) nun; founded order to care for sick, dying poor; 1979 Nobel Peace Prize.

Willard Townsend, 1895-1957, (U.S.) organized the United Transport Service Employees (Red Caps), 1935.

Sojourner Truth (Isabella Baumfree), 1797-1883, (U.S.) preacher, abolitionist; worked for black educ. opportunity.

Harriet Tubman, 1823-1913, (U.S.) prominent figure in the Underground Railroad, which helped runaway slaves in the south reach safety in the north; nurse and spy for Union Army in the Civil War.

Nat Turner, 1800-31, (U.S.) slave who led the most significant of more than 200 slave revolts in U.S., in Southampton, VA; hanged.

Philip Vera Cruz, 1905-94, (Filipino-U.S.) helped to found the United Farm Workers Union.

William Wilberforce, 1759-1833, (Br.) social reformer; prominent in struggle to abolish the slave trade.

Frances E. Willard, 1839-98, (U.S.) temperance, women's rights leader.

Mary Wollstonecraft, 1759-97, (Br.) wrote *Vindication of the Rights of Women*.

Sports Personalities of the Past and Present

Henry (Hank) Aaron, b 1934, Milwaukee-Atlanta outfielder; hit record 755 home runs, led NL 4 times; record 2,297 RBI.

Kareem Abdul-Jabbar, b 1947, Milwaukee, L.A. Lakers center; MVP 6 times; all-time leading NBA scorer, 38,387 points.

Freddy Adu, b 1989, AS Monaco midfielder; youngest player ever to play in the MLS at 14 years, 308 days, in 2004.

Andre Agassi, b 1970, won: Wimbledon, '92; U.S. Open, '94, '99, '99; Aust. Open, '95, 2000-01, 2003; French Open, '99.

Troy Aikman, b 1966, quarterback; led Dallas Cowboys to Super Bowl wins in 1993-94, 1996; Super Bowl MVP, 1993.

Amy Alcott, b 1956, golfer; 29 career wins (5 majors), inducted into World Golf Hall of Fame in 1999.

Shaun Alexander, b 1977, Washington Redskins running back; 2005 NFL MVP.

Grover Cleveland "Pete" Alexander,1887-1950, pitcher; won 373 NL games; pitched 16 shutouts, 1916.

Muhammad Ali, b 1942, 3-time heavyweight champion.

Fernando Alonso, b 1981, Spanish Formula 1 racer; youngest ever to win a World Grand Prix championship, 2005.

Morten Andersen, b 1960, kicker; NFL's career points leader, with 2,544 through the end of the 2007 season.

Gary Anderson, b 1959, kicker; NFL's 2nd in career points, with 2,434 through the end of the 2003 season.

Sparky Anderson, b 1934, only manager to win World Series in the NL (Cincinnati, 1975-76) and the AL (Detroit, 1984).

Mario Andretti, b 1940, race-car driver; won Daytona 500 (1967), Indy 500 (1969); Formula 1 world title (1978).

Earl Anthony, 1938-2001, bowler; won record 6 PBA Championships (1973-75, 1981-83), 41 career PBA tournaments.

Eddie Arcaro, 1916-97, only jockey to win racing's Triple Crown twice, 1941,1948; rode to 4,779 wins in his career.

Lance Armstrong, b 1971, cyclist; record 7-time winner of the Tour de France (1999-2005).

Arthur Ashe, 1943-93, tennis player; won U.S. Open (1968); Wimbledon (1975); died of AIDS.

Evelyn Ashford, b 1957, sprinter; won 100m gold (1984) and silver (1988); member of 5 U.S. Olympic teams (1976-1992).

Red Auerbach, 1917-2006, coached Boston to 9 NBA titles.

Tracy Austin, b 1962: youngest player to win U.S. Open tennis title (age 16 in 1979), 2-time AP Female Athlete of the Year.

Ernie Banks, b 1931, Chicago Cubs slugger; hit 512 NL homers; twice MVP; never played in World Series.

Roger Bannister, b 1929, British physician; ran first sub 4-minute mile, May 6, 1954 (3 min. 59.4 sec.).

Charles Barkley, b 1963, NBA MVP, 1993; 4th player ever to surpass 20,000 pts, 10,000 rebounds, and 4,000 assists.

Rick Barry, b 1944: NBA scoring leader, 1967; ABA, 1969.

Sammy Baugh, 1914-2008: Washington Redskins quarterback; held numerous records upon retirement after 16 seasons.

Elgin Baylor, b 1934, L.A. Lakers forward; 11-time all-star.

Bob Beamon, b 1946, Olympic long jump gold medalist in 1968; world record jump of 29' 2½" stood until 1991.

Boris Becker, b 1967, German tennis star; won U.S. Open 1989; Wimbledon champ 3 times.

David Beckham, b 1975, English soccer star; captain of 2002 World Cup team; joined Los Angeles Galaxy, 2007, with record-breaking $250 million contract.

Bill Belichick, b 1952, NFL coach; led New England Patriots to 3 Super Bowl wins (2001, 2003, 2004); best all-time post-season coaching record; fined $500,000 in 2007 for violating rules about videotaping the opposing sideline.

Jean Beliveau, b 1931, Montreal Canadiens center; scored 507 goals; twice MVP.

Johnny Bench, b 1947, Cincinnati Reds catcher; MVP twice; led league in home runs twice, RBIs 3 times.

Patty Berg, 1918-2006, won more than 80 golf tournaments; AP Woman Athlete of the Year 3 times.

Chris Berman, b 1955, sportscaster and anchor for ESPN.

Yogi Berra, b 1925, Yankee catcher (1946-63); 3-time MVP.

Abebe Bikila, 1932-73, Ethiopian runner; won consecutive Olympic marathon gold medals in 1960 (barefoot), 1964.

Matt Biondi, b 1965, swimmer; won 5 golds, 1988 Olympics.

Larry Bird, b 1956, Boston Celtics forward (1979-92); NBA MVP, 1984-86; 1998 coach of the year with Indiana Pacers.

Bonnie Blair, b 1964, speed skater; won 5 individual gold medals in 3 Olympics (1988, '92, '94).

George Blanda, b 1927, quarterback, kicker; 26 years as active player, scored 2,002 career points.

Fanny Blankers-Koen, 1918-2004, track; won 4 golds in 1948 Olympics.

Wade Boggs, b 1958, AL batting champ, 1983, 1985-88; reached 3,000 career hits, 1999 (3,010).

Usain Bolt, b 1986, Jamaican sprinter; won 3 golds in 2008 Olympics, world record for men's 100 & 200 meter runs.

Barry Bonds, b 1964, outfielder; hit record 73 homers in 2001; NL MVP 1990, 1992-93, 2001-04; 1st all-time in HRs (762).

Björn Borg, b 1956, led Sweden to first Davis Cup, 1975; Wimbledon champion 5 times.

Ray Bourque, b 1960, Boston defenseman,1979-2000; 5-time Norris Trophy winner; won Stanley Cup with Colorado, 2001.

Bill Bradley, b 1943, All-America at Princeton; led NY Knicks to 2 NBA titles (1970, '73); U.S. senator, 1979-97.

Donald Bradman, 1908-2001, Australian widely regarded as the greatest cricketer ever; set several batting records.

Terry Bradshaw, b 1948, quarterback; led Pittsburgh to 4 Super Bowl wins (1975-76, 1979-80); NFL MVP, 1978.

Tom Brady, b 1977, quarterback; led New England Patriots to 3 Super Bowl titles, 2002, 2004, 2005; Super Bowl MVP, 2002, 2004; NFL MVP, 2007; most single-season TD passes (50), 2007.

Christine Brennan, b 1958, sports journalist for *USA Today*, radio and television commentator, specializing in figure skating.

George Brett, b 1953, Kansas City Royals infielder; led AL in batting, 1976, 1980, 1990; MVP, 1980.

Lou Brock, b 1939, St. Louis Cardinals outfielder; stole NL single-season record 118 bases, 1974; led NL 8 times.

Jim Brown, b 1936, Clev. fullback; 12,312 career yds.; 2-time Associated Press MVP.

Paul Brown, 1908-91, football owner, coach; led eponymous Cleveland Browns to 3 NFL championships.

Kobe Bryant, b 1978, guard; won 3 straight titles with Lakers (2000-02); leading NBA scorer, 2005-06 and 2006-07; 2007-08 NBA MVP; member of 2008 U.S. Olympic gold-medal basketball team, NBA Final MVP 2009.

Paul "Bear" Bryant, 1913-83, college football coach with 323 wins; led Alabama to 5 national titles (1961, '64, '65, '78, '79).

Sergei Bubka, b 1963, Ukrainian pole vaulter; first to clear 20 feet; gold medal, 1988 Olympics.

Don Budge, 1915-2000, won numerous amateur and pro tennis titles; Grand Slam, 1938.

Reggie Bush, b 1985, New Orleans Saints running back drafted 2nd overall in 2006; helped USC to 2 National Titles (2003-04); Heisman Trophy winner (2005).

Dick Butkus, b 1942, Chicago Bears linebacker; twice chosen NFL defensive player of the year.

Dick Button, b 1929, figure skater; won 1948, 1952 Olympic gold medals; world titlist, 1948-52.

Walter Camp, 1859-1925, Yale football player, coach, athletic director; established many rules for modern football.

Roy Campanella, 1921-93, Hall of Fame catcher for the Brooklyn Dodgers (1948-57); 3-time NL MVP.

Earl Campbell, b 1955, NFL running back; MVP 1978-79.

Jose Canseco, b 1964, outfielder; led Oakland A's to the World Series, 1988; wrote book about steroids in baseball, 2005.

Eric Cantona, b 1966, French soccer star; Manchester United 1992-97; named Premier League Overseas Player of the Decade (to mark the 1st 10 years of the Premiere League, 1993-2003) in 2003.

Jennifer Capriati, b 1976, won Aust. (2001-02) and French Opens (2001), at 14 in 1990 was youngest top-10 player.

Rod Carew, b 1945, AL infielder; 7 batting titles, 1977 MVP.

Steve Carlton, b 1944, NL pitcher; won 20 games 6 times, Cy Young award 4 times; 4,136 career strikeouts.

Pete Carroll, b 1951, college football coach; coached the USC Trojans to 2 championships (2003-04).

Billy Casper, b 1931, PGA Player of the Year 3 times; U.S. Open champ twice.

Wilt Chamberlain, 1936-99, center; was NBA leading scorer 7 times, MVP 4 times; scored 100 pts. in a game, 1962.

Fred Chapman, 1872-1957, pitcher, Philadelphia A's; became the youngest ever U.S. pro athlete on July 22, 1887 when he pitched against the Cleveland Spiders; he was 14 years, 7 months, 29 days old.

Stewart Cink, b 1973, golfer; winner of British Open 2009.

Bobby Clarke, b 1949, Philadelphia Flyers center; led team to 2 Stanley Cup championships; MVP 3 times.

Roger Clemens, b 1962, pitcher; 1986 AL MVP; only 7-time Cy Young winner (1986-87, '91, '97-98, 2001, '04); twice recorded record 20 Ks in a game; 354 wins, 4,672 Ks (2nd all-time).

Roberto Clemente, 1934-72, Pittsburgh Pirates outfielder; won 4 batting titles; MVP, 1966; killed in plane crash.

Ty Cobb, 1886-1961, Detroit Tigers outfielder; had record .367 lifetime batting average, 12 batting titles.

Sebastian Coe, b 1956, British runner; won Olympic 1,500m gold medal and 800m silver medal in 1980 and 1984.

Nadia Comaneci, b 1961, Romanian gymnast; won 3 gold medals, achieved 7 perfect scores, 1976 Olympics.

Maureen Connolly, 1934-69, won tennis Grand Slam, 1953; AP Woman-Athlete-of-the-Year 3 times.

Jimmy Connors, b 1952, tennis; 5 U.S. titles, 2 Wimbledon.

Alberto Contador, b 1982, Spanish cyclist, won Tour de France 2007, 2009.

Cynthia Cooper, b 1963, basketball; 4-time MVP of the WNBA finals and 2-time league MVP for the Houston Comets.

James J. Corbett, 1866-1933, heavyweight champion, 1892-97; credited with being the first "scientific" boxer.

Angel Cordero Jr., b 1942, jockey; leading money winner, 1976, 1982-83; rode 3 Kentucky Derby winners.

Margaret Smith Court, b 1942, Australian tennis great; won 24 Grand Slam events.

Bob Cousy, b 1928, Boston guard; 6 NBA titles; 1957 MVP.

Mark Cuban, b 1958, Dallas Mavericks owner; known for criticism of NBA.

Al Davis, b 1929, Oakland Raiders owner and former coach.

Bjoern Daehlie, b 1967, Norwegian cross-country skier; won record 8 Winter Olympic gold medals.

Lindsay Davenport, b 1976, tennis; won Olympic gold (1996), U.S. Open (1998), Wimbledon (1999), Aust. Open (2000).

Dizzy Dean, 1910-74, pitcher; St. Louis Cardinals' "Gashouse Gang" in the 30s.

Mary Decker Slaney, b 1958, runner; has held 6 separate American records from the 800m to 10,000m.

Frank Deford, b 1938, senior contributing writer for *Sports Illustrated,* author and commentator.

Oscar De La Hoya, b 1972, won IBF lightweight (1995); WBC super lightweight (1996) and welterweight (1997, 2000) titles.

Jose Martin Del Potro, b 1988, Argentinian tennis player, won U.S. Open (2009).

Donna de Varona, b 1947, 2 Olympic swimming golds,1964; 1st female sportscaster at a major network (ABC), 1965.

Jack Dempsey, 1895-1983, heavyweight champ, 1919-26.

Gail Devers, b 1966, Olympic 100m gold medalist, 1992, '96.

Eric Dickerson, b 1960, NFL record 2,105 rushing yds.,1984.

Joe DiMaggio, 1914-99, N.Y. Yankees outfielder; hit safely in record 56 consecutive games, 1941; AL MVP 3 times.

Tony Dorsett, b 1954, Heisman winner who led the Dallas Cowboys to an NFL title in his rookie year (1977).

Tim Duncan, b 1976, San Antonio center; 3-time NBA Finals MVP (1999, 2003, 2005); NBA MVP, 2002-03.

Roberto Duran, b 1951, Panamanian boxer, held titles at 3 weights; lost 1980 "no mas" fight to Sugar Ray Leonard.

Leo Durocher, 1905-91, manager; won 3 NL pennants (Brooklyn-1941, N.Y. Giants-1951, '54) and 1954 World Series.

Dale Earnhardt, 1951-2001, 7-time NASCAR Winston Cup champ; died in a last-lap crash at 2001 Daytona 500.

Stefan Edberg, b 1966, Swedish tennis player; U.S. Open champ, 1991, 1992; Wimbledon champ, 1988, 1990.

Gertrude Ederle, 1906-2003, first woman to swim English Channel, broke existing men's record, 1926.

Teresa Edwards, b 1964, basketball; 5-time Olympian; gold medalist in 1984, '88, '96, 2000 and bronze medal in 1992.

Hicham El Guerrouj, b 1974, Moroccan runner; holds world records in mile (3:43.13) and 1,500m (3:26); won gold medals in 1,500m and 5,000m in 2004 Olympics.

John Elway, b 1960, quarterback; led Denver Broncos to 2 Super Bowl wins, 1998, 1999; regular-season MVP, 1987.

Julius "Dr. J" Erving, b 1950, 3-time ABA MVP, 1981 NBA MVP.

Phil Esposito, b 1942, NHL scoring leader 5 times.

Janet Evans, b 1971, 4 Olympic swimming golds, 1988-92.

Lee Evans, b 1947, Olympic 400m gold medalist in 1968 with a 43.86 sec. world record not broken until 1988.

Chris Evert, b 1954, U.S. Open tennis champ 6 times, Wimbledon champ 3 times.

Ray Ewry, 1873-1937, track-and-field star; won 8 gold medals, 1900, 1904, and 1908 Olympics.

Nick Faldo, b 1957, British golfer; won Masters, British Open 3 times each.

Juan Manuel Fangio, 1911-95, Argentinian; 5-time World Grand Prix driving champ (1951, 1954-57).

Marshall Faulk, b 1973, 2000 NFL MVP; scored then-record 26 TDs in 2001; 3-time Off. Player of the Year (1999-2001).

Brett Favre, b 1969, quarterback; led Green Bay to Super Bowl win, 1997; NFL MVP, 1995, 1996; co-MVP, 1997; left retirement in 2008 to play for NY Jets, joined Minnesota Vikings in 2009 .

Roger Federer, b 1981, Swiss tennis star; won Aust. Open (2004, 2006-07), Wimbledon (2003-07, 2009), U.S. Open (2004-08), French Open (2009).

Bob Feller, b 1918, Cleveland Indians pitcher; won 266 games; pitched 3 no-hitters, 12 one-hitters.

Rollie Fingers, b 1946, pitcher; 341 career saves; AL MVP, Cy Young Award, 1981; World Series MVP, 1974.

Peggy Fleming, b 1948, world figure skating champion, 1966-68; gold medalist, 1968 Olympics.

Whitey Ford, b 1928, NY Yankees pitcher; won record 10 World Series games.

George Foreman, b 1949, heavyweight champion, 1973-74, 1994-95; at 45, the oldest to win a heavyweight title.

Dick Fosbury, b 1947, high jumper; won 1968 Olympic gold medal; developed the "Fosbury Flop."

Jimmie Foxx, 1907-67, Red Sox, Athletics slugger; MVP 3 times; triple crown, 1933.

A. J. Foyt, b 1935, won Indy 500 4 times; U.S. Auto Club champ 7 times.

Joe Frazier, b 1944, heavyweight champion, 1970-73.

Walt Frazier, b 1945, Hall of Fame guard for N.Y. Knicks' NBA championship teams (1970, '73).

Peter Gammons, b 1945, sportswriter for ESPN, named to Major League Baseball Hall of Fame.

Lou Gehrig, 1903-41, N.Y. Yankees 1st baseman; MVP, 1927, 1936; triple crown, 1934; AL record 184 RBIs, 1931; played in 2,130 straight games (1925-39), a record that stood until 1995.

Althea Gibson, 1927-2003, 2-time U.S. and Wimbledon champ.

Bob Gibson, b 1935, St. Louis Cardinals pitcher; won Cy Young award twice; struck out 3,117 batters.

Josh Gibson, 1911-47, Hall of Fame catcher; known as "Babe Ruth of the Negro Leagues"; credited with as many as 84 homers in 1 season and about 800 in his career.

Marc Girardelli, b 1963, skier (Lux.); won 5 World Cup titles.

Raul Gonzalez, b 1977, Spanish soccer player; led Real Madrid to 3 Champions League titles 1998, 2000, 2002; all-time top UEFA goal scorer (63).

Jeff Gordon, b 1971, race car driver; youngest to win NASCAR title 4 times (1995, 1997-98, 2001).

Steffi Graf, b 1969, German; won tennis Grand Slam, 1988; U.S. champ 5 times; Wimbledon champ 7 times.

Otto Graham, 1921-2003, Cleveland quarterback; 4-time all-pro.

Red Grange, 1903-91, All-American at Univ. of Illinois, 1923-25; played for Chicago Bears, 1925-35.

"Mean" Joe Greene, b 1946, Pittsburgh Steelers lineman; twice NFL outstanding defensive player.

Wayne Gretzky, b 1961, top scorer in NHL history with record 894 goals, 1,963 assists, 2,857 points; MVP, 1980-87, 1989.

Bob Griese, b 1945, All-Pro quarterback; led Miami Dolphins to 17-0 season (1972) and 2 Super Bowl titles (1973-74).

Ken Griffey Jr., b 1969, outfielder; led AL in homers 1994, 1997-1999; 1997 AL MVP; 10 gold gloves.

Archie Griffin, b 1954, Ohio State running back; only 2-time winner of the Heisman Trophy (1974-75).

Florence Griffith Joyner, 1959-98, sprinter; won 3 gold medals at 1988 Olympics; world and Olympic record for 100m.

Lefty Grove, 1900-75, pitcher; won 300 AL games.

Vladimir Guerrero, b 1976, Dominican right fielder for Los Angeles Angels; 2004 American League MVP award.

Janet Guthrie, b 1938, 1st woman driver in Indy 500 (1977).

Tony Gwynn, b 1960, 8-time NL batting champ, 1984, 1987-89, 1994-97; 3,141 career hits.

Walter Hagen, 1892-1969, golfer; 5 PGA, 4 British Open titles.

Mika Hakkinen, b 1968, Finnish Formula One racing driver; Formula One champion 1998, 1999.

George Halas, 1895-1983, founder/player/coach of Chicago Bears; won 6 NFL championships as a coach.

Dorothy Hamill, b 1956, figure skater; gold medalist at the Olympics and World championships in 1976.

Scott Hamilton, b 1958, U.S. and world figure skating champion, 1981-84; Olympic gold medalist, 1984.

Mia Hamm, b 1972, led U.S. to World Cup (1991, '99) and Olympic ('96, 2004) titles; most career internat. goals (144).

Franco Harris, b 1950, running back; 4 Super Bowls with Steelers (1975-76, 1979-80); 1,000+ yds. in a season 8 times.

Marvin Harrison, b 1972, Indianapolis Colts wide receiver; NFL record for single-season receptions (143), 2002.

Bill Hartack, 1932-2007, jockey; rode 5 Kentucky Derby winners.

Dominik Hasek, b 1965, NHL goaltender; won Vezina Trophy, 1994-95, 1997-99, 2001; NHL MVP, 1997-98.

John Havlicek, b 1940, Boston Celtics forward; scored 26,395 career pts.

Eric Heiden, b 1958, speed skater; won 5 Olympic golds, 1980.

Rickey Henderson, b 1958, outfielder; 1990 AL MVP; record 130 stolen bases, 1982; all-time leader in steals, runs.

Sonja Henie, 1912-69, Norwegian world champion figure skater, 1927-36; Olympic gold medalist, 1928, 1932, 1936.

Martina Hingis, b 1980, Swiss; won Aust. and U.S. Opens, Wimbledon; youngest No. 1 player (16 yrs., 6 m.), 1997.

Trevor Hoffman, b 1967; relief pitcher; holds all-time career saves record (591).

Ben Hogan, 1912-97, golfer; won 4 U.S. Open titles, 2 PGA Championships, 2 Masters.

Evander Holyfield, b 1962, 4-time heavyweight champion.

Santonio Holmes, b 1984, wide receiver, Pittsburgh Steelers, Super Bowl MVP 2009.

Rogers Hornsby, 1896-1963, NL 2nd baseman; batted record .424 in 1924; twice won triple crown.

Paul Hornung, b 1935, Green Bay Packers running back, placekicker; scored record 176 points, 1960.

Ryan Howard, b 1979, first baseman for Philadelphia Phillies, known for his hitting; 2006 NL MVP award.

Gordie Howe, b 1928, hockey forward; NHL MVP 6 times; scored 801 goals in 26 NHL seasons.

Carl Hubbell, 1903-88, N.Y. Giants pitcher; 20-game winner 5 consecutive years, 1933-37.

Bobby Hull, b 1939, NHL all-star 10 times; MVP, 1965-66.

Brett Hull, b 1964: St. Louis Blues forward; led NHL in goals, 1990-92; MVP, 1991.

Catfish Hunter, 1946-99, pitched perfect game, 1968; 20-game winner 5 times.

Don Hutson, 1913-97, Packers receiver; caught 99 TD passes; 2-time NFL MVP.

Juli Inkster, b 1960, Hall of Fame golfer; 2nd to win all 4 of LPGA's modern majors; won 7 career major titles.

Phil Jackson, b 1945, won 9 NBA titles as coach of Bulls and Lakers; 1973 title as a player with N.Y. Knicks.

Reggie Jackson, b 1946, slugger; led AL in home runs 4 times; MVP, 1973; hit 5 World Series home runs, 1977.

"Shoeless" Joe Jackson, 1889-1951, outfielder; 3rd highest career batting average (.356); one of the "Black Sox" banned for allegedly throwing 1919 World Series.

Jaromir Jagr, b 1972, Czech hockey player; NHL MVP in 1999; Art Ross Trophy (leading scorer) 1995, 1998-2001.

LeBron James, b 1984, Cleveland Cavaliers forward; won Rookie of the Year, 2004; 2008 scoring leader; member of 2008 U.S. Olympic gold medal basketball team, NBA Most Valuable Player 2008-09.

Ron Jaworski, b 1951, former NFL quarterback (1974-89), NFL analyst on ESPN.

Sally Jenkins, b 1960, sports journalist and writer for *The Washington Post.*

Bruce Jenner, b 1949, Olympic decathlon gold medalist, 1976.

Lynn Jennings, b 1960, runner; 3-time World and 9-time U.S. cross country champ; bronze at 1992 Olympics (10,000m).

Derek Jeter, b 1974, shortstop; 10-time All-Star; led NY Yankees to 4 World Series titles; World Series MVP, 2000; record for most hits by a shortstop, and most hits by a Yankee.

Earvin "Magic" Johnson, b 1959, NBA MVP, 1987, 1989, 1990; Playoff MVP, 1980, 1982, 1987; 2nd in career assists.

Jack Johnson, 1878-1946, heavyweight champion, 1908-15.

Michael Johnson, b 1967, 5-time Olympic gold medalist (1996, 2000); world and Olympic record, 200m and 400m.

Randy Johnson, b 1963, 5-time Cy Young winner; strikeout leader: 1992-95, 1999-2004; 4,789 strikeouts (2nd all-time); pitched perfect game, 2004.

Walter Johnson, 1887-1946, Washington Senators pitcher; won 416 games; record 110 shutouts.

Bobby Jones, 1902-71, won golf's Grand Slam, 1930; U.S. Amateur champ 5 times, U.S. Open champ 4 times.

Cobi Jones, b 1970, soccer; most U.S. national team appearances with 164.

David "Deacon" Jones, b 1938, 5-time All-Pro with L.A. Rams (1965-69); "sack" specialist credited with inventing the term.

Marion Jones, b 1975, 2000 Olympic 100m, 200m, 1,600m relay gold medalist, bronze in long jump and 400m relay. Stripped of medals in 2007 after admitting use of performance-enhancing drugs.

Roy Jones Jr., b 1969, light heavyweight champ, 1999-2004.

Michael Jordan, b 1963, guard; leading NBA scorer, 1987-93, 1996-98; MVP, 1988, 1991-92, '96, '98; playoff MVP, 1991-93, 1996-98; ESPN Athlete of the Century.

Dorothy Kamenshek, b 1925, led Rockford (IL) Peaches to 4 All-American Girls Baseball League titles in the 1940s.

Kasey Keller, b 1969, U.S. goalkeeper; U.S. record for most career international victories, 39.

Jackie Joyner-Kersee, b 1962, Olympic gold medalist in heptathlon (1988,'92) and long jump (1988).

Harmon Killebrew, b 1936, Minnesota Twins slugger; led AL in home runs 6 times; 573 lifetime.

Jean Claude Killy, b 1943, French skier; 3 Olympic golds, 1968.

Ralph Kiner, b 1922, Pittsburgh Pirates slugger; led NL in home runs 7 consecutive years, 1946-52.

Billie Jean King, b 1943, U.S. singles champ 4 times; Wimbledon champ 6 times; beat Bobby Riggs, 1973.

Peter King, b 1957, senior writer for *Sports Illustrated.*

Bob Knight, b 1940, ESPN studio analyst, ret. basketball coach; led Indiana U. to NCAA title in 1976, '81, '87, winningest men's college basketball coach (900).

Olga Korbut, b 1955, Soviet gymnast; 3 1972 Olympic golds.

Sandy Koufax, b 1935, 3-time Cy Young winner; lowest ERA in NL, 1962-66; pitched 4 no-hitters, one a perfect game.

Jack Kramer, 1921-2009, world's number one tennis player 1946-53, first Wimbledon competitor to wear shorts.

Ingrid Kristiansen, b 1956, Norwegian; only runner to have held world records in 5,000m, 10,000m, and marathon.

Julie Krone, b 1963, winningest female jockey; only woman to ride a winner in a Triple Crown race (Belmont, 1993).

Michelle Kwan, b 1980, figure skater; 9 U.S. and 5 World titles; silver medalist at 1998 Olympics, bronze in 2002.

Guy Lafleur, b 1951, 3-time NHL scoring leader; 1977-78 MVP.

Alexi Lalas, b 1970, soccer player; first American to play in Italian League Serie A.

Kenesaw Mountain Landis, 1866-1944, 1st commissioner of baseball (1920-44); banned the 8 "Black Sox" involved in fixing 1919 World Series.

Tom Landry, 1924-2000, Dallas Cowboys head coach, 1960-88; won 2 Super Bowls (1972, '78); 3rd in career wins (270).

Dick "Night Train" Lane, 1928-2002, Hall of Fame defensive back, intercepted an NFL season record 14 passes (1952).

Don Larsen, b 1929, As N.Y. Yankee, pitched only World Series perfect game, Oct. 8, 1956—a 2-0 win over Brooklyn.

Rod Laver, b 1938, Australian; won tennis Grand Slam twice, 1962, 1969; Wimbledon champ 4 times.

Mario Lemieux, b 1965, 6-time NHL leading scorer; MVP, 1988, 1993, 1996; playoff MVP, 1991-92.

Greg Lemond, b 1961, cyclist; 3-time Tour de France winner (1986, '89-90); first American to win the event.

Ivan Lendl, b 1960, Czech; U.S. Open tennis champ, 1985-87.

Sugar Ray Leonard, b 1956: boxer; held titles in 5 different weight classes.

Carl Lewis, b 1961, track-and-field star; won 9 Olympic gold medals in sprinting and the long jump.

Lennox Lewis, b 1965, Brit.; heavyweight champ, 1997-2004.

Ray Lewis, b 1975, linebacker for the Baltimore Ravens; Super Bowl XXXV MVP.

Tara Lipinski, b 1982, youngest figure skater to win U.S. and world championships, 1997, and Winter Olympic gold, 1998.

Vince Lombardi, 1913-70, Green Bay Packers coach; led team to 5 NFL championships and 2 Super Bowl victories.

Nancy Lopez, b 1957, Hall of Fame golfer; 4-time LPGA Player of the Year, 3-time winner of the LPGA Championship.

Greg Louganis, b 1960, won Olympic gold medals in both springboard and platform diving, 1984, 1988.

Joe Louis, 1914-81, heavyweight champion, 1937-49.

Sid Luckman, 1916-98, Chicago Bears quarterback; led team to 4 NFL championships; MVP, 1943.

Connie Mack, 1862-1956, Philadelphia Athletics manager, 1901-50; won 9 pennants, 5 championships.

John Madden, b 1936, won Super Bowl as coach of the Oakland Raiders (1977); former NFL TV analyst.

Greg Maddux, b 1966, NL pitcher, won 4 consecutive Cy Young awards, 1992-95; 355 career wins.

Karl Malone, b 1963, Utah Jazz, L.A. Laker forward; MVP, 1997, 1999; 14-time All-Star; 36,928 career points (2nd all-time).

Moses Malone, b 1955, NBA center; MVP, 1979, 1982-83.

Eli Manning, b 1981, NY Giants quarterback; Super Bowl XLII MVP.

Peyton Manning, b 1976, Indianapolis Colts quarterback; NFL MVP, 2003, 2004, 2008; Super Bowl XLI MVP; highest single-season passer rating (121.1), 2004.

Mickey Mantle, 1931-95, N.Y. Yankees outfielder; triple crown, 1956; 18 World Series home runs; MVP 3 times.

Diego Maradona, b 1960, soccer player; led Argentina to World Cup in 1986.

"Pistol" Pete Maravich, 1947-88, guard; scored NCAA record 44.2 ppg during collegiate career; led NBA in scoring, 1977.

Rocky Marciano, 1923-69, heavyweight champion, 1952-56; retired undefeated.

Dan Marino, b 1961, Miami quarterback; NFL record single-season yards passing (5,084), 1984.

Roger Maris, 1934-85, N.Y. Yankees outfielder; hit AL record 61 home runs, 1961; MVP, 1960 and 1961.

Curtis Martin, b 1973: Jets running back; 5-time Pro-Bowler; 4th all-time in rushing yards with 14,101.

Eddie Mathews, 1931-2001, Milwaukee-Atlanta Braves 3rd baseman; hit 512 career home runs.

Christy Mathewson, 1880-1925, pitcher; won 373 games.

Bob Mathias, 1930-2006, decathlon gold, 1948, 1952 Olympics.

Willie Mays, b 1931, N.Y.-S.F. Giants center fielder; hit 660 home runs, led NL 4 times; had 3,283 hits; twice MVP.

Willie McCovey, b 1938, S.F. Giants slugger; hit 521 home runs; led NL 3 times; MVP, 1969.

John McEnroe, b 1959, U.S. Open tennis champ, 1979-81, 1984; Wimbledon champ, 1981, 1983-84.

John McGraw, 1873-1934, N.Y. Giants manager; led team to 10 pennants, 3 championships.

Mark McGwire, b 1963, hit then-record 70 home runs in 1998; 583 career home runs (8th).

Tamara McKinney, b 1962, 1st U.S. skier to win overall Alpine World Cup championship (1983).

Andrea Mead Lawrence, 1932-2009, skier; only woman to win 2 gold medals in alpine skiing at one Olympics (1952).

Mark Messier, b 1961, center; NHL MVP, 1990, 1992; Conn Smythe Trophy, 1984.

Debbie Meyer, b 1952, 1st swimmer to win 3 individual Olympic golds (1968).

Al Michaels, b 1944, *NBC Sunday Night Football* announcer, 5 time Outstanding Sports Personality Emmy winner.

George Mikan, 1924-2005, Minn. Lakers center; considered the best basketball player of the first half of the 20th century.

Stan Mikita, b 1940, Chicago Blackhawks center; led NHL in scoring 4 times; MVP twice.

Billy Mills, b 1938, runner; upset winner of the 1964 Olympic 10,000m; only American man ever to win the event.

Yao Ming, b 1980, Chinese center for the Houston Rockets, one of the tallest in NBA at 7'6".

Joe Montana, b 1956, S.F. 49ers quarterback; Super Bowl MVP, 1982, 1985, 1990.

Archie Moore, 1913-98, light-heavyweight champ, 1952-62.

Howie Morenz, 1902-37, Montreal Canadiens forward; considered best hockey player of first half of the 20th century.

Edwin Moses, b 1955, undefeated in 122 consecutive 400m hurdles races, 1977-87; Olympic gold medalist, 1976, '84.

Shirley Muldowney, b 1940, 1st woman to race National Hot Rod Assoc. Top Fuel dragsters; 3-time NHRA points champ.

Eddie Murray, b 1956, 3rd player with both 3,000+ hits with 500+ home runs.

Stan Musial, b 1920, St. Louis Cardinals star; won 7 NL batting titles; MVP 3 times.

Rafael Nadal, b 1986, Spanish tennis player; won French Open (2005-08), Wimbledon (2008), Australian Open (2009); Olympic gold medal in men's singles (2008).

Bronko Nagurski, 1908-90, Chicago Bears fullback and tackle; gained more than 4,000 yds. rushing.

Joe Namath, b 1943, Jets quarterback; 1969 Super Bowl MVP.

Steve Nash, b 1974, Phoenix Suns point guard; NBA MVP, in 2005, 2006.

Martina Navratilova, b 1956, Wimbledon champ 9 times, U.S. Open champ 1983-84, 1986-87.

Byron Nelson, b 1912-2006, won 11 consecutive golf tournaments in 1945; twice Masters and PGA titlist.

Ernie Nevers, 1903-76, Stanford football star; selected as best college fullback to play between 1919-69.

Paula Newby-Fraser, b 1972, 8-time Ironman Triathlon World Champ; holds women's course record.

John Newcombe, b 1943, Australian; twice U.S. Open tennis champ; Wimbledon titlist 3 times.

Jack Nicklaus, b 1940, PGA Player of the Year, 1967, 1972; leading money winner 8 times; won 18 majors (6 Masters).

Chuck Noll, b 1932, Pittsburgh coach; won 4 Super Bowls.

Paavo Nurmi, 1897-1973, Finnish distance runner; won 6 Olympic gold medals, 1920, 1924, 1928.

Al Oerter, 1936-2007, discus thrower; won gold medal at 4 consecutive Olympics, 1956-68.

Hakeem Olajuwon, b 1963, Houston center; NBA MVP, 1994, playoffs MVP, 1994-95; career blocked shots leader.

Barney Oldfield, 1878-1946, pioneer auto racer; was first to drive a car 60 mph (1903).

Shaquille O'Neal, b 1972, center; led L.A. Lakers to NBA titles, 2000-2002; and Miami Heat to NBA title, 2006; Finals MVP 2000, 2002; NBA MVP 2000.

Magglio Ordonez, b 1974, Venezuelan right fielder for the Detroit Tigers.

Bobby Orr, b 1948, Boston Bruins defenseman; 8-time Norris Trophy winner; led NHL in scoring twice, assists 5 times.

Mel Ott, 1909-58, N.Y. Giants rightfielder; hit 511 home runs; led NL 6 times.

Jesse Owens, 1913-80, track and field; 4 1936 Olympic golds.

Terrell Owens, b 1973: wide receiver; NFL record for single-game receptions with 20 in 2000.

Satchel Paige, 1906-82, pitcher; starred in Negro leagues, 1924-48; entered major leagues at age 42.

Arnold Palmer, b 1929, golf's first $1 million winner; won 4 Masters, 2 British Opens.

Jim Palmer, b 1945, Baltimore Orioles pitcher; won Cy Young award 3 times; 20-game winner 8 times.

Joe Paterno, b 1926, football coach; most wins in NCAA Div. I-A (380); led Penn St. to titles, 1982, 1986.

Danica Patrick, b 1982, race car driver; 4th woman to race at Indy 500, and 1st to lead (2005).

Floyd Patterson, 1935-2006, 2-time heavyweight champion; first to ever regain the title after losing it.

Walter Payton, 1954-99, Chicago Bears running back; most rushing yards in NFL history; top NFC rusher, 1976-80.

Pelé (Edson Arantes do Nascimento), b 1940, Brazilian soccer player; led Brazil to 3 World Cups (1958, '62, '70); scored 1,281 goals.

Bob Pettit, b 1932, first NBA player to score 20,000 points; twice NBA scoring leader.

Richard Petty, b 1937, NASCAR national champ 7 times; 7-time Daytona 500 winner.

Michael Phelps, b 1985, swimmer; holds record for most Olympic gold medals won by a single athlete (14); won 8 medals (6 gold, 2 bronze) at 2004 Olympics and 8 gold in 2008; holds 6 world records in swimming events.

Picabo Street, b 1971, skier; 2-time World Cup downhill champion (1995-96); Olympic super G gold medalist, 1998.

Laffit Pincay Jr., b 1946, jockey; leading money-winner, 1970-74, 1979, 1985.

Jacques Plante, 1929-86, NHL goaltender; 7 Vezina trophies; first goalie to wear a mask in a game.

Gary Player, b 1935, South African golfer; won 3 Masters, 3 British Opens, 2 PGA Championships, and the U.S. Open.

Mike Powell, b 1963, U.S. track and field athlete; holds world record for long jump (29 ft., 4.5 in.).

Steve Prefontaine, 1951-75, runner; 1st to win 4 NCAA titles in same event (5,000m, 1970-73); died in auto accident.

Kirby Puckett, 1960-2006, Minnesota Twins center fielder (1984-95); led team to World Series titles in 1987 and 1991.

Albert Pujols, b 1980, St. Louis first baseman; NL MVP, 2005, 2008.

Paula Radcliffe, b 1973, British runner; set marathon world record of 2:15:25 in London, 2003.

Kimi Räikkönen, b 1979, Finnish Formula One race car driver, currently driving for Scuderia Ferrari; 2007 Formula One World Drivers' Champion.

Manny Ramirez, b 1972, LA Dodgers slugger; 2004 World Series MVP; suspended for 50 games in 2009 for violating MLB performance enhancing drug policy.

Willis Reed, b 1942, N.Y. Knicks center; MVP, 1970; playoff MVP, 1970, 1973.

Mary Lou Retton, b 1968, gymnast; won all-around gold medal at 1984 Olympics; also won 2 silvers and 2 bronzes.

José Reyes, b 1983, shortstop for the New York Mets; 2006-07 All-Star; NY Mets career leader in stolen bases, triples.

Claudio Reyna, b 1973, former midfielder; U.S. National Team; named to the FIFA World Cup All-Star team in 2002.

Jerry Rice, b 1962, receiver; 1989 Super Bowl MVP; NFL record for career touchdowns (208) and receptions (1,549).

Maurice Richard, 1921-2000, Montreal Canadiens forward; scored 544 regular season goals, 82 playoff goals.

Branch Rickey, 1881-1965, MLB executive; helped break baseball's color barrier, 1947; initiated farm system, 1919.

Cal Ripken Jr., b 1960, Baltimore shortstop; AL MVP 1983, 1991; most consecutive games played (2,632).

Mariano Rivera, b 1969: relief pitcher; helped NY Yankees to 4 World Series titles; World Series MVP, 1999; all-time MLB leader in post-season saves with 34.

Oscar Robertson, b 1938, NBA guard; averaged career 25.7 points per game; 4th in career assists (9,887); MVP, 1964.

Brooks Robinson, b 1937, Baltimore Orioles 3rd baseman; played in 4 World Series; MVP, 1964; 16 gold gloves.

Frank Robinson, b 1935, MVP in both NL and AL; triple crown, 1966; 586 career home runs; first black manager in majors.

Jackie Robinson, 1919-72, broke baseball's color barrier with Brooklyn Dodgers, 1947; MVP, 1949.

Sugar Ray Robinson, 1920-89, boxer; middleweight champion 5 times, welterweight champion.

Knute Rockne, 1888-1931, Notre Dame football coach, 1918-31; revolutionized game by stressing forward pass.

Bill Rodgers, b 1947, runner; won Boston and New York City marathons 4 times each, 1975-80.

Alex Rodriguez, b 1975, New York Yankees third baseman; AL MVP in 2003, 2005, 2007; 12-time All Star; youngest player to ever hit 500 HRs.

Juan "Chi Chi" Rodriguez, b 1935, champion golfer; 8 PGA tour wins and 22 Champions tour wins.

Ben Roethlisberger, b 1982, quarterback, Pittsburgh Steelers; youngest Super Bowl winning quarterback (2005).

Ronaldinho, b 1980, soccer midfielder; led Brazil to World Cup Finals in 2006; FIFA World Player of the Year, 2004, 2005.

Ronaldo (Ronaldo Luiz Nazario de Lima), b 1976, soccer forward; led Brazil to 2002 World Cup title; 3-time FIFA world player of the year (1996-97, 2002); most World Cup goals, 15.

Art Rooney, 1901-88, famous NFL owner; bought Pittsburgh Pirates in 1933, renamed Steelers, in 1940.

Pete Rose, b 1941, won 3 NL batting titles; hit in 44 consecutive games, 1978; most career hits, 4,256; banned for gambling, 1989; admitted betting on his team, 2004.

Ken Rosewall, b 1934, Australian tennis player; 2-time U.S. champ, 8 Grand Slam singles titles.

Patrick Roy, b 1965, Montreal-Colorado goalie; only 3-time NHL Playoffs MVP (Conn Smythe Trophy), 1986, '93, 2001.

Wilma Rudolph, 1940-94, sprinter; won 3 1960 Olympic golds.

Adolph Rupp, 1901-77, NCAA basketball coach; led Kentucky to 4 national titles, 1948-49, 1951, 1958.

Bill Russell, b 1934, Boston Celtics center; led team to 11 NBA titles; MVP 5 times; first black coach of major pro sports team.

Babe Ruth, 1895-1948, N.Y. Yankees outfielder; hit 60 home runs, 1927; 714 lifetime (2nd all-time); led AL 12 times.

Johnny Rutherford, b 1938, auto racer; won 3 Indy 500s.

Nolan Ryan, b 1947, pitcher; holds season (383), career (5,714) strikeout records; won 324 games (7 no-hitters).

Pete Sampras, b 1971, tennis star; 1st man in Open era to win 7 Wimbledons; 2nd-most career Grand Slam wins (14).

Joan Benoit Samuelson, b 1968, won 1st Olympic women's marathon (1984), Boston Marathon (1979, '83).

Barry Sanders, b 1968, rushed for 2,053 yards in 1997; led NFL in rushing, 1990, 1994, 1996, 1997.

Gale Sayers, b 1943, Chicago back; twice led NFL in rushing.

Mike Schmidt, b 1949, Phillies 3rd baseman; led NL in home runs 8 times; 548 lifetime; NL MVP, 1980, 1981, 1986.

Michael Schumacher, b 1969, German race-car driver; 7-time Formula 1 world champ (1994-95, 2000-2004).

Tom Seaver, b 1944, pitcher; won NL Cy Young award 3 times; won 311 major league games.

Monica Seles, b 1973, tennis; won U.S. ('91-92), Aust. ('91-93, '96), French ('90-92) Opens; stabbed on court by fan, 1993.

Maria Sharapova, b 1987, Russian tennis star; won Wimbledon 2004, U.S. Open 2006; Australian Open 2008.

Patty Sheehan, b 1956, Hall of Fame golfer; 3 LPGA Championships (1983-84, '93).

Willie Shoemaker, 1931-2003, jockey; rode 4 Kentucky Derby and 5 Belmont Stakes winners; leading career money winner.

Frank Shorter, b 1947, runner, only American to win men's Olympic marathon (1972) since 1908; silver medalist (1976).

Don Shula, b 1930, all-time winningest NFL coach (347 games).

Al Simmons, 1902-56, AL outfielder; lifetime .334 batting avg.

Bill Simmons, b 1969, columnist for *Page 2* on ESPN.com known as "The Sports Guy."

O. J. Simpson, b 1947, running back; rushed for 2,003 yds., 1973; AFC leading rusher 4 times; acquitted of murder, 1995; found guilty of robbery and kidnapping, 2008.

George Sisler, 1893-1973, St. Louis Browns 1st baseman; had then-record 257 hits, 1920; batted .340 lifetime.

Dean Smith, b 1931, retired basketball coach; most career Division I wins (879); led North Carolina to 2 NCAA titles (1982, '93).

Emmitt Smith, b 1969, running back; NFL and Super Bowl MVP, 1993; third-season winner on TV's "Dancing With the Stars."

Conn Smythe, 1895-1980, won 7 Stanley Cups as Toronto GM (1929-1961); playoff MVP award named in his honor.

Sam Snead, 1912-2002, PGA and Masters champ 3 times each, record 82 PGA tournament victories.

Annika Sorenstam, b 1970, Swedish golfer; set LPGA 18-hole record of 59 (–13) and 72-hole record of 27-under-par, 2001; won 10 LPGA majors, including career Grand Slam.

Sammy Sosa, b 1968, right fielder; 66 homers, NL MVP, 1998; 1st to hit 60+ homers 3 times (1998, 1999, 2001).

Warren Spahn, 1921-2003, pitcher; won 363 NL games; 20-game winner 13 times; Cy Young award, 1957.

Tris Speaker, 1888-1958, AL outfielder; batted .345 over 22 seasons; hit record 793 career doubles.

Mark Spitz, b 1950, swimmer; won 7 golds at 1972 Olympics.

Amos Alonzo Stagg, 1862-1965, football innovator; Univ. of Chicago football coach for 41 years, 5 undefeated seasons.

Bart Starr, b 1934, Green Bay Packers quarterback; led team to 5 NFL titles and 2 Super Bowl victories.

Roger Staubach, b 1942, Dallas Cowboys quarterback; leading NFC passer 5 times.

Casey Stengel, 1890-1975, managed Yankees to 10 pennants, 7 championships, 1949-60.

Jackie Stewart, b 1939, Scot auto racer; 27 Grand Prix wins.

John Stockton, b 1962, Utah Jazz guard; NBA career leader in assists, steals; NBA assists leader, 1988-96.

Louise Suggs, b 1923, golfer; U.S. Women's Open champ., 1949, '52; 11 major victories, ranks 3rd all-time.

John L. Sullivan, 1858-1918, last bareknuckle heavyweight champion, 1882-1892.

Pat Summit, b 1952, women's basketball coach; led Tennessee Lady Vols to 8 NCAA titles (1987, '89, '91, '96-98, 2007-08); all-time winningest NCAA coach.

Ichiro Suzuki, b 1973, Japanese center fielder for the Seattle Mariners; Pacific League MVP, 1994, 1995, 1996; American League MVP, 2001; single-season hits record (262), 2004.

Fran Tarkenton, b 1940, Minnesota, N.Y. Giants quarterback; 3rd in career TD passes (342); 1975 Player of the Year.

Diana Taurasi, b 1982, WNBA shooting guard; Phoenix Mercury; gold medalist 2008 Olympics, WNBA MVP 2009.

Lawrence Taylor, b 1959, linebacker; led N.Y. Giants to 2 Super Bowl titles; played in 10 Pro Bowls.

Jenny Thompson, b 1973, swimmer; most decorated U.S. female Olympian; 12 medals (8 gold) in 1992, '96, 2000, '04.

Daley Thompson, b 1958, British decathlete; Olympic gold medalist in 1980, '84.

Jim Thorpe, 1888-1953, football All-America, 1911, 1912; won pentathlon and decathlon, 1912 Olympics.

Bill Tilden, 1893-1953, won 7 U.S. tennis titles, 3 Wimbledon.

Y. A. Tittle, b 1926, N.Y. Giants quarterback; MVP, 1961, 1963.

Alberto Tomba "La Bomba", b 1966, Italian skier; 5 Olympic alpine medals (3 golds, 2 silver) in 1988, 1992.

LaDainian "L.T." Tomlinson, b 1979, running back for the San Diego Chargers; NFL records for single season touchdowns (31), rushing touchdowns (28) & most points scored in a single season (186).

Joe Torre, b 1940 (Brooklyn, NY) manager of the Los Angeles Dodgers; former MLB player, former manager of the NY Yankees, St. Louis Cardinals, Atlanta Braves and NY Mets.

Lee Trevino, b 1939, golfer; won U.S., British Open twice.

Bryan Trottier, b 1956, Islanders, Penguins center for 6 Stanley Cup champs.

Gene Tunney, 1897-1978, heavyweight champion, 1926-28.

Mike Tyson, b 1966, undisputed heavyweight champ, 1987-1990; at 20, youngest to win a heavyweight title (WBC) (1986).

Wyomia Tyus, b 1945, Olympic 100m gold medalist, 1964, '68.

Johnny Unitas, 1933-2002, Baltimore Colts quarterback; passed for more than 40,000 yds; MVP, 1957, 1967.

Al Unser, b 1939, Indy 500 winner 5 times.

Bobby Unser, b 1934, Indy 500 winner 3 times.

Brian Urlacher, b 1978, Chicago Bears linebacker; Defensive Rookie of the Year, 2000; 6-time Pro Bowler.

Norm Van Brocklin, 1926-83, quarterback; passed for game record 554 yds., 1951; MVP, 1960.

Amy Van Dyken, b 1973, swimmer, first American woman to win 4 gold medals in one Olympics (1996).

Michael Vick, b 1980, quarterback for the Philadelphia Eagles; suspended and convicted (2007) of illegal dog fighting and gambling activities.

Lasse Viren, b 1949, Finnish runner; Olympic 5,000m and 10,000m gold medalist in 1972 and 1976.

Dwyane Wade, b 1982, guard; led Miami Heat to NBA title in 2006; finals MVP 2006; member of 2008 U.S. Olympic gold medal basketball team; NBA scoring title 2009.

Honus Wagner, 1874-1955, Pirates shortstop; 8 NL batting titles.

Grete Waitz, b 1953, Norwegian; 9-time winner of the New York City Marathon (1978-80, 1982-86, '88).

"Jersey" Joe Walcott, 1914-94, boxer; became heavyweight champion at age 37, 1951-52.

Bill Walton, b 1952, center; led Portland Trail Blazers to 1977 NBA title; MVP, 1978; NBA TV commentator.

Kurt Warner, b 1971, Rams, Giants, Cardinals quarterback; NFL MVP 1999, 2001; Super Bowl MVP, 2000.

Tom Watson, b 1949, golfer; 6-time PGA Player of the Year, won 5 British Opens, 2 Masters, U.S. Open.

Karrie Webb, b 1974, Australian golfer; youngest woman (26 yrs. 6 mos.) to win career Grand Slam, 1999-2001.

Johnny Weissmuller, 1903-84, swimmer; won 52 national championships, 5 Olympic gold medals; set 67 world records.

Jerry West, b 1938, L.A. Lakers guard; had career average 27 points per game; first team all-star 10 times.

Byron "Whizzer" White, 1917-2002, running back; led NCAA in scoring and rushing at Colorado (1937); led NFL in rushing twice (1938, '40); Supreme Court justice, 1962-93.

Kathy Whitworth, b 1939, 7-time LPGA Player of the Year (1966-69, 1971-73); 88 tour wins most on LPGA or PGA tour.

Michelle Wie, b 1989, golfer; in 2002 became youngest-ever qualifier for an LPGA event; turned pro at age 15.

Michael Wilbon, b 1958, sportswriter and columnist for *The Washington Post* and ESPN.

Lenny Wilkens, b 1937, winningest coach in NBA history; in Hall of Fame as player and coach.

Serena Williams, b 1981, tennis; champ at Wimbledon (2002, 2009), U.S. Open (1999, 2002, 2008); Australian Open (2003, 2005, 2007, 2009); French Open (2002); two-time Olympic gold medal winner in doubles (2000, 2008, 2009) with sister Venus.

Ted Williams, 1918-2002, Boston Red Sox outfielder; won 6 batting titles, 2 triple crowns; hit .406 in 1941.

Venus Williams, b 1980, singles champ at Wimbledon (2000, 2001, 2005, 2007, 2008), Olympic gold medal in singles (2000) and doubles, with sister Serena (2000, 2008, 2009).

Helen Wills Moody, 1905-98, tennis star; won U.S. Open 7 times, Wimbledon 8 times.

Katarina Witt, b 1965, German figure skater; won Olympic gold medal, 1984, 1988; world champ, 1984-84, 1987-88.

John Wooden, b 1910, UCLA basketball coach; 10 NCAA titles.

Tiger Woods, b 1975, golfer; youngest to win career Grand Slam, at age 24 (1997-2000); 14 career major titles.

Mickey Wright, b 1935, golfer; won LPGA and U.S. Open championship 4 times; 82 career wins, including 13 majors.

Eric Wynalda, b 1969, soccer; all-time leading U.S. international goal scorer with 34.

Kristi Yamaguchi, b 1971, figure skater; won national, world, and Olympic titles in 1992.

Carl Yastrzemski, b 1939, Boston Red Sox slugger; won 3 batting titles; triple crown, 1967.

Cy Young, 1867-1955, pitcher; won record 511 games.

Steve Young, b 1961, 49ers quarterback; led NFL in passing, 1991-94, 1996, 1997; NFL MVP, 1992, 1994; Super Bowl MVP, 1995.

Vince Young, b 1983, quarterback for the Tennessee Titans.

Babe Didrikson Zaharias, 1911-56, all-around athlete; 3 track & field medals (2 golds), 1932 Olympics; won 10 golf majors; also played baseball; 6-time AP Female Athlete of the Year.

Emil Zátopek, 1922-2000, Czech runner; won 3 gold medals at 1952 Olympics (5,000m, 10,000m, and marathon).

Zinedine Zidane, b 1972, soccer midfielder; led France to 1998 World Cup title; named top player in 2006; 3-time FIFA world player of the year (1998, 2000, 2003).

Writers of the Present

Name (Birthplace)	Birthdate
Chinua Achebe (Ogidi, Nigeria)	11/16/30
Richard Adams (Newbury, Eng.)	5/9/20
Edward Albee (Wash., DC)	3/12/28
Mitch Albom (Passaic, NJ)	5/23/58
Isabel Allende (Lima, Peru)	8/2/42
Elizabeth Alexander (NYC)	5/30/62
Dorothy Allison (Greenville, SC)	4/11/49
Martin Amis (Oxford, Eng.)	8/25/49
Maya Angelou (St. Louis, MO)	4/4/28
Piers Anthony (Oxford, Eng.)	8/6/34
Jeffrey Archer (Somerset, Eng.)	4/15/40
Oscar Arias Sanchez (Heredia, Costa Rica)	9/13/41
John Ashbery (Rochester, NY)	7/28/27
Margaret Atwood (Ottawa, Ont.)	11/18/39
David Auburn (Chicago)	1969
Louis Auchincloss (Lawrence, NY)	9/27/17
Jean Auel (Chicago)	2/18/36
Paul Auster (Newark, NJ)	2/3/47
Alan Ayckbourn (Hampstead, Eng.)	4/12/39
Nicholson Baker (Rochester, NY)	1/7/57
David Baldacci (Richmond, VA)	1960
Russell Banks (Newton, MA)	3/28/40
John Barth (Cambridge, MD)	5/27/30
Ann Beattie (Wash., DC)	9/8/47
John Berendt (Syracuse, NY)	12/5/39
Thomas Berger (Cincinnati, OH)	7/20/24
Maeve Binchy (Dalkey, Ireland)	3/28/40
Judy Blume (Elizabeth, NJ)	2/12/38
T. Coraghessan Boyle (Peekskill, NY)	12/2/48
Ray Bradbury (Waukegan, IL)	8/22/20
Barbara Taylor Bradford (Leeds, Eng.)	5/10/33
Christopher Bram (Buffalo, NY)	2/22/52
Geraldine Brooks (Sydney, Australia)	1955
Dan Brown (Exeter, NH),	6/22/64
Rita Mae Brown (Hanover, PA)	11/28/44
Christopher Buckley (NYC)	9/28/52
James Lee Burke (Houston, TX)	12/5/36
Augusten Burroughs (Pittsburgh, PA)	10/23/65
Robert Olen Butler (Granite City, IL)	1/20/45
A. S. Byatt (Sheffield, England)	8/24/36
Ethan Canin (Ann Arbor, MI)	7/19/60
Peter Carey (Bacchus-Marsh, Victoria, Australia)	5/7/43
Caleb Carr (NYC)	5/19/63
Michael Chabon (Wash., DC)	5/19/63
Tracy Chevalier (Wash., DC)	10/62
Sandra Cisneros (Chicago)	12/20/54
Tom Clancy (Baltimore, MD)	4/12/47
Mary Higgins Clark (NYC)	12/24/29
Beverly Cleary (McMinnville, OR)	4/12/16
Paulo Coelho (Rio de Janeiro, Brazil)	8/24/47
J(ohn) M(axwell) Coetzee (Capetown, S. Africa)	2/9/40
Billy Collins (NYC)	3/22/41
Jackie Collins (London, Eng.)	10/4/41
Evan S. Connell (Kansas City, MO)	8/17/24
Pat Conroy (Atlanta, GA)	10/26/45
Robin Cook (NYC)	5/4/40
Patricia Cornwell (Miami, FL)	6/9/56
Harry Crews (Alma, GA)	6/6/35
Michael Cunningham (Cincinnati, Ohio)	11/6/52
Don DeLillo (NYC)	11/20/36
Nelson DeMille (NYC)	8/23/43
Junot Díaz (Santo Domingo, Dominican Republic)	12/31/68
Joan Didion (Sacramento, CA)	12/5/34
Annie Dillard (Pittsburgh, PA)	4/30/45
E. L. Doctorow (NYC)	1/6/31
Rita Dove (Akron, OH)	8/28/52
Roddy Doyle (Dublin, Ireland)	5/5/58
Umberto Eco (Alessandria, Italy)	1/5/32
Bret Easton Ellis (Los Angeles)	3/7/64
Dave Eggers (Chicago)	3/12/70
James Ellroy (Los Angeles)	3/4/48
Louise Erdrich (Little Falls, MN)	7/6/54
Laura Esquivel (Mexico City, Mexico)	9/30/51
Jeffrey Eugenides (Detroit, MI)	3/8/60
Lawrence Ferlinghetti (Yonkers, NY)	3/24/19

Name (Birthplace)	Birthdate
Helen Fielding (Morley, Yorkshire, Eng.)	2/19/58
Ken Follett (Cardiff, Wales)	6/5/49
Dario Fo (San Giano, Italy)	3/26/26
Richard Ford (Jackson, MS)	2/16/44
Frederick Forsyth (Ashford, Eng.)	8/25/38
Paula Fox (NYC)	4/22/23
Dick Francis (Tenby, Pembrokeshire, Wales)	10/31/20
Jonathan Franzen (Western Springs, IL)	8/17/59
Michael Frayn (London, Eng.)	9/8/33
Charles Frazier (Asheville, NC)	11/4/50
Marilyn French (NYC)	11/21/29
Brian Friel (Omagh, County Tyrone, N. Ireland)	1/9/29
Carlos Fuentes (Panama City, Panama)	11/11/28
Ernest J. Gaines (Oscar, LA)	1/15/33
Gabriel Garcia Marquez (Aracataca, Colombia)	3/6/28
Frank Gilroy (Bronx, NY)	10/13/25
Malcolm Gladwell (Gosport, Hampshire, England)	9/3/63
Robert Goddard (Fareham, Hampshire, England)	11/13/54
Gail Godwin (Birmingham, AL)	6/18/37
William Goldman (Highland Park, IL)	8/12/31
Nadine Gordimer (Springs, S. Africa)	11/20/23
Mary Gordon (Far Rockaway, Long Island, NY)	12/8/49
Sue Grafton (Louisville, KY)	4/24/40
Günter Grass (Danzig, now Gdansk, Poland)	10/16/27
Shirley Ann Grau (New Orleans, LA)	7/8/29
John Grisham (Jonesboro, AR)	2/8/55
John Guare (NYC)	2/5/38
David Handler (Los Angeles)	9/14/52
David Hare (St. Leonards, Sussex, Eng.)	6/5/47
Jim Harrison (Grayling, MI)	12/11/37
Robert Hass (San Francisco, CA)	3/1/41
Vaclav Havel (Prague, Czech.)	10/5/36
Seamus Heaney (Mossbaum, Cty. Derry, N. Ire.)	4/13/39
Mark Helprin (NYC)	6/28/47
Carl Hiaasen (S. Florida)	3/12/53
Oscar Hijuelos (NYC)	8/24/51
S. E. Hinton (Tulsa, OK)	7/22/50
Alice Hoffman (NYC)	3/16/52
Khaled Hosseini (Afghanistan)	1965
John Irving (Exeter, NH)	3/2/42
Kazuo Ishiguro (Nagasaki, Japan)	11/8/54
John Jakes (Chicago)	3/31/32
P. D. James (Oxford, Eng.)	8/3/20
Ha Jin (Liaoning, China)	2/21/56
Edward P. Jones (Wash., DC)	10/5/50
Erica Jong (NYC)	3/26/42
Garrison Keillor (Anoka, MN)	8/7/42
Thomas Keneally (Sydney, Austral.)	10/7/35
William Kennedy (Albany, NY)	1/16/28
Sue Monk Kidd (Sylvester, GA)	8/12/48
Jamaica Kincaid (St. Johns, Antigua)	5/25/49
Stephen King (Portland, ME)	9/21/47
Barbara Kingsolver (Annapolis, MD)	4/8/55
Maxine Hong Kingston (Stockton, CA)	10/27/40
Galway Kinnell (Providence, RI)	2/1/27
Dean Koontz (Everett, PA)	7/9/45
Ted Kooser (Ames, IA)	4/25/39
Jon Krakauer (Brookline, MA)	4/12/54
Judith Krantz (NYC)	1/9/28
Maxine Kumin (Philadelphia, PA)	6/6/25
Milan Kundera (Brno, Czechoslovakia)	4/1/29
Tony Kushner (NYC)	7/16/56
Jhumpa Lahiri (London, England)	1967
David Leavitt (Pittsburgh, PA)	6/23/61
John Le Carré (Poole, Eng.)	10/19/31
Harper Lee (Monroeville, AL)	4/28/26
Jean Marie Gustave Le Clézio (Nice, France)	4/13/40
Ursula K. Le Guin (Berkeley, CA)	10/21/29
Elmore Leonard (New Orleans, LA)	10/11/25
Doris Lessing (Kermanshah, Persia)	10/22/19
Jonathan Lethem (Brooklyn, NY)	2/19/64
David Lodge (South London, Eng.)	1/28/35
Alison Lurie (Chicago)	9/3/26
Gregory Maguire (Albany, NY)	6/9/54
David Malouf (Brisbane, Queensland, Australia)	3/20/34

Name (Birthplace)	Birthdate	Name (Birthplace)	Birthdate
Thomas Mallon (Glen Cove, Long Island, NY)	11/2/51	Anne Rice (New Orleans, LA)	10/4/41
David Mamet (Chicago)	11/30/47	Adrienne Rich (Baltimore, MD)	5/16/29
Yann Martel (Salamanca, Spain)	6/25/63	Nora Roberts (Wash., DC)	10/10/50
Bobbie Ann Mason (nr. Mayfield, KY)	5/1/40	Marilynne Robinson (Sandpoint, IL)	11/26/43
Peter Matthiessen (NYC)	5/22/27	Philip Roth (Newark, NJ)	3/19/33
Armistead Maupin (Wash., DC)	4/13/44	J.K. Rowling (Chipping Sodbury, Eng.)	7/31/65
Cormac McCarthy (Providence, RI)	7/20/33	Norman Rush (Oakland, CA)	10/24/33
Colleen McCullough (Wellington, N.S.W., Austral.)	6/1/37	Salman Rushdie (Bombay, India)	6/19/47
Alice McDermott (Brooklyn, NY)	6/27/53	Richard Russo (Johnstown, NY)	7/15/49
Ian McEwan (Aldershot, England)	6/21/48	J. D. Salinger (NYC)	1/1/19
Thomas McGuane (Wyandotte, MI)	12/11/39	Jose Saramago (Azinhaga, Portugal)	11/16/22
Terry McMillan (Port Huron, MI)	10/18/51	Alice Sebold (Madison, WI)	1963
Larry McMurtry (Wichita Falls, TX)	6/3/36	David Sedaris (Johnson City, NY)	12/26/56
Terrence McNally (St. Petersburg, FL)	11/3/39	Vikram Seth (Calcutta, India)	6/20/52
John McPhee (Princeton, NJ)	3/8/31	John Patrick Shanley (NYC)	10/13/50
W(illiam) S(tanley) Merwin (NYC)	9/30/27	Sam Shepard (Ft. Sheridan, IL)	11/5/43
Stephenie Meyer (Hartford, CT)	12/24/73	Neil Simon (Bronx, NY)	7/4/27
Steven Millhauser (NYC)	8/3/43	Jane Smiley (Los Angeles, CA)	9/26/49
Toni Morrison (Lorain, OH)	2/18/31	Wole Soyinka (Abeokuta, Nigeria)	7/13/34
Walter Mosley (Los Angeles, CA)	1/12/52	Nicholas Sparks (Omaha, NE)	12/31/65
Andrew Motion (London)	10/26/52	Danielle Steel (NYC)	8/14/47
Bharati Mukherjee (Calcutta, India)	7/27/40	Richard Stern (NYC)	2/25/28
Herta Müller (Nitzkydorf, Banat, Romania)	8/17/53	Mary Stewart (Sunderland, Eng.)	9/17/16
Alice Munro (Wingham, Ont., Canada)	7/10/31	R(obert) L(awrence) Stine (Columbus, OH)	10/8/43
Haruki Murakami (Kyoto, Japan)	1/12/49	Tom Stoppard (Zlin, Czech.)	7/3/37
V. S. Naipaul (Chaguanas, Trinidad)	8/17/32	Mark Strand (P.E.I., Can.)	4/11/34
Joyce Carol Oates (Lockport, NY)	6/16/38	Elizabeth Strout (Portland, ME)	1/6/56
Edna O'Brien (Tuamgraney, Ir.)	12/15/32	Wislawa Szymborska (Kornik, Pol.)	7/2/23
Tim O'Brien (Austin, MN)	10/1/46	Amy Tan (Oakland, CA)	2/19/52
Kenzaburo Oe (Uchiko, Japan)	1/31/35	Donna Tartt (Greenwood, MS)	12/23/63
Michael Ondaatje (Colombo, Sri Lanka)	9/12/43	Paul Theroux (Medford, MA)	4/10/41
Cynthia Ozick (NYC)	4/17/28	Calvin Trillin (Kansas City, MO)	12/5/35
Orhan Pamuk (Istanbul, Turk.)	6/7/52	Scott F. Turow (Chicago)	4/12/49
Robert B. Parker (Springfield, MA)	9/17/32	Anne Tyler (Minneapolis, MN)	10/25/41
Suzan-Lori Parks (Fort Knox, KY)	5/10/63	Mario Vargas Llosa (Arequipa, Peru)	3/28/36
James Patterson (Newburgh, NY)	3/22/47	Gore Vidal (West Point, NY)	10/3/25
Jodi Picoult (New York)	5/19/66	Paula Vogel (Wash., DC)	11/16/51
Marge Piercy (Detroit, MI)	3/31/36	Derek Walcott (Castries, Saint Lucia)	1/23/30
Robert Pinsky (Long Branch, NJ)	10/20/40	Alice Walker (Eatonton, GA)	2/9/44
Michael Pollan (NYC)	2/6/55	Robert James Waller (Rockford, IA)	8/1/39
Richard Powers (Evanston, IL)	6/18/57	Joseph Wambaugh (East Pittsburgh, PA)	1/22/37
Reynolds Price (Macon, NC)	2/1/33	Elie Wiesel (Sighet, Romania)	9/30/28
Richard Price (Bronx, NY)	10/12/49	Edmund White (Cincinnati, OH)	1/19/40
E. Annie Proulx (Norwich, CT)	8/22/35	Lanford Wilson (Lebanon, MO)	4/13/37
Philip Pullman (Norwich, Eng.)	10/19/46	Tom Wolfe (Richmond, VA)	3/2/31
Thomas Pynchon (Glen Cove, Long Island, NY)	5/8/37	Tobias Wolff (Birmingham, AL)	6/19/45
David Rabe (Dubuque, IA)	3/10/40	Herman Wouk (NYC)	5/27/15
Ishmael Reed (Chattanooga, TN)	2/22/38	Yevgeny Yevtushenko (Irkutsk, Russia)	7/18/33
Ruth Rendell (London, England)	2/17/30		

Writers of the Past

See also Journalists of the Past, and Greeks and Romans in Historical Figures chapter.

Alice Adams, 1926-99, (U.S.) novelist, short-story writer. *Superior Woman.*

James Agee, 1909-55, (U.S.) novelist. *A Death in the Family.*

S(hmuel) Y(osef)Agnon, 1888-1970, (Is.) Hebrew novelist. *Only Yesterday.*

Conrad Aiken, 1889-1973, (U.S.) poet, critic. *Ushant.*

Anna Akhmatova, 1889-1966, (Russ.) poet. *Requiem.*

Louisa May Alcott, 1832-88, (U.S.) novelist. *Little Women.*

Sholom Aleichem, 1859-1916, (Russ.) Yiddish writer. *Tevye's Daughters, The Old Country.*

Vicente Aleixandre, 1898-1984, (Sp.) poet. *La destrucción o el amor, Dialogolos del conocimiento.*

Horatio Alger, 1832-99, (U.S.) "rags-to-riches" books.

Jorge Amado, 1912-2001, (Brazil) novelist. *Dona Flor and Her Two Husbands, The Violent Land.*

Eric Ambler, 1909-98, (Br.) suspense novelist. *A Coffin for Dimitrios.*

Kingsley Amis, 1922-95, (Br.) novelist, critic. *Lucky Jim.*

Hans Christian Andersen, 1805-75, (Dan.) author of fairy tales. *The Ugly Duckling.*

Maxwell Anderson, 1888-1959, (U.S.) playwright. *What Price Glory?, High Tor, Winterset, Key Largo.*

Sherwood Anderson, 1876-1941, (U.S.) short-story writer. "Death in the Woods;" *Winesburg, Ohio.*

Reinaldo Arenas, 1943-90, (Cuba) short-story writer, novelist. *Before Night Falls.*

Ludovico Ariosto, 1474-1533, (It.) poet. *Orlando Furioso.*

Matthew Arnold, 1822-88, (Br.) poet, critic. "Thrysis," "Dover Beach," "Culture and Anarchy."

Isaac Asimov, 1920-92, (U.S.) versatile writer, espec. of science-fiction. *I Robot.*

Miguel Angel Asturias, 1899-1974, (Guatemala) novelist. *El Señor Presidente.*

W(ystan) H(ugh) Auden, 1907-73, (Br.) poet, playwright, literary critic. "The Age of Anxiety."

Jane Austen, 1775-1817, (Br.) novelist. *Pride and Prejudice, Sense and Sensibility, Emma, Mansfield Park.*

Isaac Babel, 1894-1941, (Russ.) short-story writer, playwright. *Odessa Tales, Red Cavalry.*

James Baldwin, 1924-87, (U.S.) author, playwright. *The Fire Next Time, Blues for Mister Charlie.*

Honoré de Balzac, 1799-1850, (Fr.) novelist. *Le Père Goriot, Cousine Bette, Eugénie Grandet.*

James M. Barrie, 1860-1937, (Br.) playwright, novelist. *Peter Pan, Dear Brutus, What Every Woman Knows.*

Charles Baudelaire, 1821-67, (Fr.) poet. *Les Fleurs du Mal.*

L(yman) Frank Baum, 1856-1919, (U.S.) *Wizard of Oz* series.

Simone de Beauvoir, 1908-86, (Fr.) novelist, essayist. *The Second Sex, Memoirs of a Dutiful Daughter.*

Samuel Beckett, 1906-89, (Ir.) novelist, playwright. *Waiting for Godot, Endgame* (plays); *Murphy, Watt, Molloy* (novels).

Brendan Behan, 1923-64, (Ir.) playwright. *The Quare Fellow, The Hostage, Borstal Boy.*

Saul Bellow, 1915-2005, (U.S.) novelist. *The Adventures of Augie March, Humboldt's Gift.*

Robert Benchley, 1889-1945, (U.S.) humorist.

Stephen Vincent Benét, 1898-1943, (U.S.) poet, novelist. *John Brown's Body.*

Stan Berenstain, 1923-2005, (U.S.) co-writer and illustrator of *Berenstain Bears* series of children's books.

John Berryman, 1914-72, (U.S.) poet. *Homage to Mistress Bradstreet.*

Ambrose Bierce, 1842-1914, (U.S.) short-story writer, journalist. *In the Midst of Life, The Devil's Dictionary.*

Elizabeth Bishop, 1911-79, (U.S.) poet. *North and South—A Cold Spring.*

William Blake, 1757-1827, (Br.) poet, artist. *Songs of Innocence, Songs of Experience.*

Aleksandr Blok, 1880-1921, (Russ.) poet. "The Twelve", "The Scythians."

Giovanni Boccaccio, 1313-75, (It.) poet. *Decameron.*

Heinrich Böll, 1917-85, (Ger.) novelist, short-story writer. *Group Portrait With Lady.*

Jorge Luis Borges, 1900-86, (Arg.) short-story writer, poet, essayist. *Labyrinths.*

James Boswell, 1740-95, (Sc.) biographer. *The Life of Samuel Johnson.*

Pierre Boulle, 1913-94, (Fr.) novelist. *The Bridge Over the River Kwai, Planet of the Apes.*

Paul Bowles, 1910-99, (U.S.) novelist, short-story writer. *The Sheltering Sky.*

Anne Bradstreet, c.1612-72, (U.S.) poet. *The Tenth Muse Lately Sprung Up in America.*

Bertolt Brecht, 1898-1956, (Ger.) dramatist, poet. *The Three-penny Opera, Mother Courage and Her Children.*

Charlotte Brontë, 1816-55, (Br.) novelist. *Jane Eyre.*

Emily Brontë, 1818-48, (Br.) novelist. *Wuthering Heights.*

Elizabeth Barrett Browning, 1806-61, (Br.) poet. *Sonnets From the Portuguese, Aurora Leigh.*

Joseph Brodsky, 1940-96, (Russ.-U.S.) poet. *A Part of Speech, Less Than One, To Urania.*

Sterling A. Brown, 1901-89, (U.S.) poet, literature professor. *Southern Road.*

William Wells Brown, 1815-84, (U.S.) writer, memoirist, first African American to publish a novel, *Clotel*, 1853.

Robert Browning, 1812-89, (Br.) poet. "My Last Duchess," "Fra Lippo Lippi," *The Ring and The Book.*

Pearl S. Buck, 1892-1973, (U.S.) novelist. *The Good Earth.*

Charles Bukowski, 1920-94, (U.S.) novelist, poet. *Ham on Rye, Women.*

Mikhail Bulgakov, 1891-1940, (Russ.) novelist, playwright. *The Heart of a Dog, The Master and Margarita.*

John Bunyan, 1628-88, (Br.) writer. *Pilgrim's Progress.*

Anthony Burgess, 1917-93, (Br.) author. *A Clockwork Orange.*

Frances Hodgson Burnett, 1849-1924, (Br.-U.S.) novelist. *The Secret Garden.*

Robert Burns, 1759-96, (Sc.) poet. "Flow Gently, Sweet Afton," "My Heart's in the Highlands," "Auld Lang Syne."

Edgar Rice Burroughs, 1875-1950, (U.S.) "Tarzan" books.

William S. Burroughs, 1914-97, (U.S.) novelist. *Naked Lunch.*

George Gordon, Lord Byron, 1788-1824, (Br.) poet. *Don Juan, Childe Harold, Manfred, Cain.*

Pedro Calderon de la Barca, 1600-81, (Sp.) playwright. *Life Is a Dream.*

Hortense Calisher, 1911-2009, (U.S.) novelist, short story writer. *False Entry.*

Italo Calvino, 1923-85, (It.) novelist, short-story writer. *If on a Winter's Night a Traveler.*

Luis Vaz de Camoes, 1524?-80 (Port.) poet. *The Lusiads.*

Albert Camus, 1913-60, (Fr.) writer. *The Stranger, The Fall.*

Elias Canetti, 1905-94, (Bulg.) novelist, essayist. *Auto-Da-Fe.*

Karel Capek, 1890-1938, (Czech.) playwright, novelist, essayist. *R.U.R. (Rossum's Universal Robots).*

Truman Capote, 1924-84, (U.S.) author. *Other Voices, Other Rooms, Breakfast at Tiffany's, In Cold Blood.*

Lewis Carroll (Charles Dodgson), 1832-98, (Br.) writer, mathematician. *Alice's Adventures in Wonderland.*

Giacomo Casanova, 1725-98, (It.) adventurer, memoirist.

Willa Cather, 1873-1947, (U.S.) novelist. *O Pioneers!, My Ántonia, Death Comes for the Archbishop.*

Constantine Cavafy, 1863-1933, (Gr.) poet. "Ithaka," "Sensual Pleasures."

Camilo Jose Cela, 1916-2001, (Sp.) novelist. *The Family of Pascual Duarte, The Hive.*

Miguel de Cervantes Saavedra, 1547-1616, (Sp.) novelist, dramatist, poet. *Don Quixote.*

Raymond Chandler, 1888-1959, (U.S.) writer of detective fiction. Philip Marlowe series.

Geoffrey Chaucer, c.1340-1400, (Br.) poet. *The Canterbury Tales, Troilus and Criseyde.*

John Cheever, 1912-82, (U.S.) novelist, short-story writer. *The Wapshot Scandal,* "The Country Husband."

Anton Chekhov, 1860-1904, (Russ.) short-story writer, dramatist. *Uncle Vanya, The Cherry Orchard, The Three Sisters.*

Charles Waddell Chesnutt, 1858-1932, (U.S.) author known for his short stories, such as in *The Conjure Woman (1899).*

G(ilbert) K(eith) Chesterton, 1874-1936, (Br.) critic, novelist, relig. apologist. Father Brown series of mysteries.

Kate Chopin, 1851-1904, (U.S.) writer. *The Awakening.*

Agatha Christie, 1890-1976, (Br.) mystery writer; created Miss Marple, Hercule Poirot; *And Then There Were None, Murder on the Orient Express, Murder of Roger Ackroyd.*

James Clavell, 1924-94, (Br.-U.S.) novelist. *Shogun, King Rat.*

Arthur C. Clarke, 1917-2008, (Br.) science fiction writer. *2001: A Space Odyssey.*

Jean Cocteau, 1889-1963, (Fr.) writer, visual artist, filmmaker. *The Beauty and the Beast, Les Enfants Terribles.*

Samuel Taylor Coleridge, 1772-1834, (Br.) poet, critic. "Kubla Khan," "The Rime of the Ancient Mariner."

(Sidonie) Colette, 1873-1954, (Fr.) novelist. *Claudine, Gigi.*

Wilkie Collins, 1824-89, (Br.) novelist. *The Moonstone.*

Joseph Conrad, 1857-1924, (Br.) novelist. *Lord Jim, Heart of Darkness, The Secret Agent.*

James Fenimore Cooper, 1789-1851, (U.S.) novelist. *Leatherstocking Tales, The Last of the Mohicans.*

Pierre Corneille, 1606-84, (Fr.) dramatist. *Medeé, Le Cid.*

Hart Crane, 1899-1932, (U.S.) poet. "The Bridge."

Stephen Crane, 1871-1900, (U.S.) novelist, short-story writer. *The Red Badge of Courage,* "The Open Boat."

Michael Crichton, 1942-2008, (U.S.) writer. *The Andromeda Strain, Jurassic Park.*

Countee Cullen, 1903-46, (U.S.) poet, prominent in the Harlem Renaissance of the 1920s; *The Black Christ.*

E. E. Cummings, 1894-1962, (U.S.) poet. *Tulips and Chimneys.*

Roald Dahl, 1916-90, (Br.-U.S.) writer. *Charlie and the Chocolate Factory, James and the Giant Peach.*

Gabriele D'Annunzio, 1863-1938, (It.) poet, novelist, dramatist. *The Child of Pleasure, The Intruder, The Victim.*

Dante Alighieri, 1265-1321, (It.) poet. *The Divine Comedy.*

Robertson Davies, 1913-95, (Can.) novelist, playwright, essayist. Salterton, Deptford, and Cornish trilogies.

Daniel Defoe, 1660-1731, (Br.) writer. *Robinson Crusoe, Moll Flanders, Journal of the Plague Year.*

Charles Dickens, 1812-70, (Br.) novelist. *David Copperfield, Oliver Twist, Great Expectations, A Tale of Two Cities.*

Philip K. Dick, 1928-82, (U.S.) science fiction writer. *Do Androids Dream of Electric Sheep?*

James Dickey, 1923-97, (U.S.) poet, novelist. *Deliverance.*

Emily Dickinson, 1830-86, (U.S.) lyric poet. "Because I could not stop for Death . . .," "Success is counted sweetest . . ."

Isak Dinesen (Karen Blixen), 1885-1962, (Dan.) author. *Out of Africa, Seven Gothic Tales, Winter's Tales.*

John Donne, 1573-1631, (Br.) poet. *Songs and Sonnets.*

José Donoso, 1924-96, (Chil.) surreal novelist and short-story writer. *The Obscene Bird of Night.*

John Dos Passos, 1896-1970, (U.S.) novelist. *U.S.A.*

Fyodor Dostoyevsky, 1821-81, (Russ.) novelist. *Crime and Punishment, The Brothers Karamazov, The Possessed.*

Arthur Conan Doyle, 1859-1930, (Br.) novelist. Sherlock Holmes mystery stories.

Theodore Dreiser, 1871-1945, (U.S.) novelist. *An American Tragedy, Sister Carrie.*

John Dryden, 1631-1700, (Br.) poet, dramatist, critic. *All for Love, Mac Flecknoe, Absalom and Achitophel.*

Alexandre Dumas (père), 1802-70, (Fr.) novelist, dramatist. *The Three Musketeers, The Count of Monte Cristo.*

Alexandre Dumas (fils), 1824-95, (Fr.) dramatist, novelist. *La Dame aux Camélias, Le Demi-Monde.*

Paul Laurence Dunbar, 1872-1906, (U.S.) poet, novelist; won fame with *Lyrics of Lowly Life,* 1896.

Lawrence Durrell, 1912-90, (Br.) novelist, poet. *Alexandria Quartet.*

Ilya G. Ehrenburg, 1891-1967, (Russ.) writer. *The Thaw.*

George Eliot (Mary Ann Evans or Marian Evans), 1819-80, (Br.) novelist. *Silas Marner, Middlemarch.*

T(homas) S(tearns) Eliot, 1888-1965, (Br.) poet, critic. *The Waste Land,* "The Love Song of J. Alfred Prufrock."

Stanley Elkin, 1930-95, (U.S.) novelist, short story writer. *George Mills.*

Ralph Ellison, 1914-94, (U.S.) writer. *Invisible Man.*

Ralph Waldo Emerson, 1803-82, (U.S.) poet, essayist. "Brahma," "Nature," "The Over-Soul," "Self-Reliance."

James T. Farrell, 1904-79, (U.S.) novelist. *Studs Lonigan.*

William Faulkner, 1897-1962, (U.S.) novelist. *Sanctuary, Light in August, The Sound and the Fury, Absalom, Absalom!*

Edna Ferber, 1887-1968, (U.S.) novelist, short-story writer, playwright. *So Big, Cimarron, Show Boat.*

Henry Fielding, 1707-54, (Br.) novelist. *Tom Jones.*

F(rancis) Scott Fitzgerald, 1896-1940, (U.S.) short-story writer, novelist. *The Great Gatsby, Tender Is the Night.*

Gustave Flaubert, 1821-80, (Fr.) novelist. *Madame Bovary.*

Ian Fleming, 1908-64, (Br.) novelist; James Bond spy thrillers. *Dr. No, Goldfinger.*

Horton Foote, 1916-2009, (U.S.) playwright, screenwriter. *The Trip to Bountiful.*

Ford Madox Ford, 1873-1939, (Br.) novelist, critic, poet. *The Good Soldier.*

C(ecil) S(cott) Forester, 1899-1966, (Br.) writer. Horatio Hornblower books.

E(dward) M(organ) Forster, 1879-1970, (Br.) novelist. *A Passage to India, Howards End.*

Anatole France, 1844-1924, (Fr.) writer. *Penguin Island, My Friend's Book, The Crime of Sylvestre Bonnard.*

Robert Frost, 1874-1963, (U.S.) poet. "Birches," "Fire and Ice," "Stopping by Woods on a Snowy Evening."

William Gaddis, 1922-98, (U.S.) novelist. *The Recognitions.*

John Galsworthy, 1867-1933, (Br.) novelist, dramatist. *The Forsyte Saga.*

Federico Garcia Lorca, 1898-1936, (Sp.) poet, dramatist. *Blood Wedding.*

Erle Stanley Gardner, 1889-1970, (U.S.) mystery writer; created Perry Mason.

Jean Genet, 1911-86, (Fr.) playwright, novelist. *The Maids.*

Kahlil Gibran, 1883-1931, (Lebanese-U.S.) mystical novelist, essayist, poet. *The Prophet.*

André Gide, 1869-1951, (Fr.) writer. *The Immoralist, The Pastoral Symphony, Strait Is the Gate.*

Allen Ginsberg, 1926-97, (U.S.) Beat poet. "Howl."

Jean Giraudoux, 1882-1944, (Fr.) novelist, dramatist. *Electra, The Madwoman of Chaillot, Ondine, Tiger at the Gate.*

Johann Wolfgang von Goethe, 1749-1832, (Ger.) poet, dramatist, novelist. *Faust, Sorrows of Young Werther.*

Nikolai Gogol, 1809-52, (Russ.) short-story writer, dramatist, novelist. *Dead Souls, The Inspector General.*

William Golding, 1911-93, (Br.) novelist. *Lord of the Flies.*

Oliver Goldsmith, 1728-74, (Br.-Ir.) dramatist, novelist. *The Vicar of Wakefield, She Stoops to Conquer.*

Maxim Gorky, 1868-1936, (Russ.) dramatist, novelist. *The Lower Depths.*

Robert Graves, 1895-1985, (Br.) poet, classical scholar, novelist. *I, Claudius; The White Goddess.*

Thomas Gray, 1716-71, (Br.) poet. "Elegy Written in a Country Churchyard," "The Progress of Poesy."

Julien Green, 1900-98, (U.S.-Fr.) expatriate American, French novelist. *Moira, Each Man in His Darkness.*

Graham Greene, 1904-91, (Br.) novelist. *The Power and the Glory, The Heart of the Matter, The Ministry of Fear.*

Zane Grey, 1872-1939, (U.S.) writer of Western stories.

Jakob Grimm, 1785-1863, (Ger.) philologist, folklorist; with brother **Wilhelm**, 1786-1859, collected *Grimm's Fairy Tales.*

Alex Haley, 1921-92, (U.S.) author. *Roots.*

Dashiell Hammett, 1894-1961, (U.S.) detective-story writer; created Sam Spade. *The Maltese Falcon.*

Jupiter Hammon, c.1720-1800, (U.S.) poet; first African American to have his works published, 1761.

Knut Hamsun, 1859-1952, (Nor.) novelist. *Hunger.*

Lorraine Hansberry, 1930-65, (U.S.) playwright; won New York Drama Critics Circle Award, 1959; *A Raisin in the Sun.*

Thomas Hardy, 1840-1928, (Br.) novelist, poet. *The Return of the Native, Tess of the D'Urbervilles, Jude the Obscure.*

E. Lynn Harris, 1955-2009, (U.S.) novelist. *Invisible Life, Basketball Jones.*

Joel Chandler Harris, 1848-1908, (U.S.) Uncle Remus stories.

Moss Hart, 1904-61, (U.S.) playwright. *Once in a Lifetime, You Can't Take It With You, The Man Who Came to Dinner.*

Bret Harte, 1836-1902, (U.S.) short-story writer, poet. *The Luck of Roaring Camp.*

Jaroslav Hasek, 1883-1923, (Czech.) writer, playwright. *The Good Soldier Schweik.*

John Hawkes, 1925-98, (U.S.) experimental fiction writer. *The Goose on the Grave, Blood Oranges.*

Nathaniel Hawthorne, 1804-64, (U.S.) novelist, short-story writer. *The Scarlet Letter,* "Young Goodman Brown."

Heinrich Heine, 1797-1856, (Ger.) poet. *Book of Songs.*

Robert Heinlein, 1907-88, (U.S.) science fiction writer. *Stranger in a Strange Land.*

Joseph Heller, 1923-99, (U.S.) novelist. *Catch-22.*

Lillian Hellman, 1905-84, (U.S.) playwright, author of memoirs. *The Little Foxes, An Unfinished Woman, Pentimento.*

Ernest Hemingway, 1899-1961, (U.S.) novelist, short-story writer. *A Farewell to Arms, For Whom the Bell Tolls.*

O. Henry (W. S. Porter), 1862-1910, (U.S.) short-story writer. "The Gift of the Magi."

George Herbert, 1593-1633, (Br.) poet. "The Altar," "Easter Wings."

Zbigniew Herbert, 1924-98, (Pol.) poet. "Apollo and Marsyas."

Robert Herrick, 1591-1674, (Br.) poet. "To the Virgins to Make Much of Time."

John Hersey, 1914-93, (U.S.) novelist, journalist. *Hiroshima, A Bell for Adano.*

Hermann Hesse, 1877-1962, (Ger.) novelist, poet. *Death and the Lover, Steppenwolf, Siddhartha.*

Tony Hillerman, 1925-2008, (U.S.) novelist. *Dance Hall of the Dead.*

James Hilton, 1900-54, (Br.) novelist. *Lost Horizon.*

Chester Himes, 1909-84, (U.S.) novelist; *Cotton Comes to Harlem.*

Oliver Wendell Holmes, 1809-94, (U.S.) poet, novelist. *The Autocrat of the Breakfast-Table.*

Gerard Manley Hopkins, 1844-89, (Br.) poet. "Pied Beauty," "God's Grandeur."

A(lfred) E. Housman, 1859-1936, (Br.) poet. *A Shropshire Lad.*

William Dean Howells, 1837-1920, (U.S.) novelist, critic. *The Rise of Silas Lapham.*

Langston Hughes, 1902-67, (U.S.) poet, lyric writer, author; a major influence in 1920s Harlem Renaissance.

Ted Hughes, 1930-98, (Br.) British poet laureate, 1984-98. *Crow, The Hawk in the Rain.*

Victor Hugo, 1802-85, (Fr.) poet, dramatist, novelist. *Notre Dame de Paris, Les Misérables.*

Zora Neale Hurston, 1903-60, (U.S.) novelist, folklorist. *Their Eyes Were Watching God, Mules and Men.*

Aldous Huxley, 1894-1963, (Br.) writer. *Brave New World.*

Henrik Ibsen, 1828-1906, (Nor.) dramatist, poet. *A Doll's House, Ghosts, The Wild Duck, Hedda Gabler.*

William Inge, 1913-73, (U.S.) playwright. *Picnic; Come Back, Little Sheba; Bus Stop.*

Eugene Ionesco, 1910-94, (Fr.) surrealist dramatist. *The Bald Soprano, The Chairs.*

Washington Irving, 1783-1859, (U.S.) writer. "Rip Van Winkle," "The Legend of Sleepy Hollow."

Christopher Isherwood, 1904-86, (Br.) novelist, playwright. *The Berlin Stories.*

Shirley Jackson, 1919-65, (U.S.) short-story writer. "The Lottery."

Henry James, 1843-1916, (U.S.) novelist, short-story writer, critic. *The Portrait of a Lady, The Ambassadors, Daisy Miller.*

Robinson Jeffers, 1887-1962, (U.S.) poet, dramatist. *Tamar and Other Poems, Medea.*

Samuel Johnson, 1709-84, (Br.) author, scholar, critic. *Dictionary of the English Language, Vanity of Human Wishes.*

Ben Jonson, 1572-1637, (Br.) dramatist, poet. *Volpone.*

James Weldon Johnson, 1871-1938, (U.S.) poet, novelist, diplomat; lyricist for *Lift Every Voice and Sing.*

James Joyce, 1882-1941, (Ir.) writer. *Ulysses, Dubliners, A Portrait of the Artist as a Young Man, Finnegans Wake.*

Ernst Junger, 1895-1998, (Ger.) novelist, essayist. *The Peace, On the Marble Cliff.*

Franz Kafka, 1883-1924, (Austro-Hung./Czech) novelist, short-story writer. *The Trial, The Castle,* "The Metamorphosis."

George S. Kaufman, 1889-1961, (U.S.) playwright. *The Man Who Came to Dinner, You Can't Take It With You.*

Yasunari Kawabata, 1899-1972, (Japan) novelist. *The Sound of the Mountains.*

Nikos Kazantzakis, 1883-1957, (Gk.) novelist. *Zorba the Greek, A Greek Passion.*

Alfred Kazin, 1915-98 (U.S.) author, critic, teacher. *On Native Grounds.*

John Keats, 1795-1821, (Br.) poet. "Ode on a Grecian Urn," "Ode to a Nightingale," "La Belle Dame Sans Merci."

Jack Kerouac, 1922-1969, (U.S.), author, Beat poet. *On the Road, The Dharma Bums,* "Mexico City Blues."

Joyce Kilmer, 1886-1918, (U.S.) poet. "Trees."

Rudyard Kipling, 1865-1936, (Br.) author, poet. "The White Man's Burden," "Gunga Din," *The Jungle Book.*

Jean de la Fontaine, 1621-95, (Fr.) poet. *Fables choisies.*

Pär Lagerkvist, 1891-1974, (Swed.) poet, dramatist, novelist. *Barabbas, The Sybil.*

Selma Lagerlöf, 1858-1940, (Swed.) novelist. *Jerusalem, The Ring of the Lowenskolds.*

Alphonse de Lamartine, 1790-1869, (Fr.) poet, novelist, statesman. *Méditations poétiques.*

Charles Lamb, 1775-1834, (Br.) essayist. *Specimens of English Dramatic Poets, Essays of Elia.*

Giuseppe di Lampedusa, 1896-1957, (It.) novelist. *The Leopard.*

William Langland, c.1332-1400, (Eng.) poet. *Piers Plowman.*

Ring Lardner, 1885-1933, (U.S.) short-story writer, humorist.

Louis L'Amour, 1908-88, (U.S.) western author, screenwriter. *Hondo, The Cherokee Trail.*

D(avid) H(erbert) Lawrence, 1885-1930, (Br.) novelist. *Sons and Lovers, Women in Love, Lady Chatterley's Lover.*

Halldor Laxness, 1902-98, (Icelandic) novelist. *Iceland's Bell.*

Madeleine L'Engle, 1918-2007, (U.S.) novelist of young adult fiction. *A Wrinkle in Time.*

Mikhail Lermontov, 1814-41, (Russ.) novelist, poet. "Demon," *Hero of Our Time.*

Alain-René Lesage, 1668-1747, (Fr.) novelist. *Gil Blas de Santillane.*

Gotthold Lessing, 1729-81, (Ger.) dramatist, philosopher, critic. *Miss Sara Sampson, Minna von Barnhelm.*

Ira Levin, 1929-2007, (U.S.) novelist, playwright. *Deathtrap.*

C(live) S(taples) Lewis, 1898-1963, (Br.) critic, novelist, religious writer. *Allegory of Love; The Lion, the Witch and the Wardrobe; Out of the Silent Planet.*

Sinclair Lewis, 1885-1951, (U.S.) novelist. *Babbitt, Main Street, Arrowsmith, Dodsworth.*

Li Po, 701-762, (China) poet. "Song Before Drinking," "She Spins Silk."

Vachel Lindsay, 1879-1931, (U.S.) poet. *General William Booth Enters Into Heaven, The Congo.*

Hugh Lofting, 1886-1947, (Br.) writer. Dr. Doolittle series.

Jack London, 1876-1916, (U.S.) novelist, journalist. *Call of the Wild, The Sea-Wolf, White Fang.*

Henry Wadsworth Longfellow, 1807-82, (U.S.) poet. *Evangeline, The Song of Hiawatha.*

Lope de Vega, 1562-1635, (Sp.) playwright. *Noche de San Juan, Maestro de Danzar.*

H(oward) P(hillips) Lovecraft, 1890-1937, (U.S.) novelist, short-story writer. "At the Mountains of Madness."

Amy Lowell, 1874-1925, (U.S.) poet, critic. "Lilacs."

James Russell Lowell, 1819-91, (U.S.) poet, editor. *Poems, The Biglow Papers.*

Robert Lowell, 1917-77, (U.S.) poet. "Lord Weary's Castle."

Joaquim Maria Machado de Assis, 1839-1908, (Brazil) novelist, poet. *The Posthumous Memoirs of Bras Cubas.*

Archibald MacLeish, 1892-1982, (U.S.) poet. *Conquistador.*

Naguib Mahfouz, 1911-2006, (Egypt) novelist; first Arabic-language writer to win the Nobel Prize for Literature. *Cairo Trilogy.*

Norman Mailer, 1923-2007, (U.S.) novelist, essayist, journalist. *The Naked and the Dead.*
Bernard Malamud, 1914-86, (U.S.) short-story writer, novelist. "The Magic Barrel," *The Assistant, The Fixer.*
Stéphane Mallarmé, 1842-98, (Fr.) poet. *Poésies.*
Sir Thomas Malory, ?-1471, (Br.) writer. *Morte d'Arthur.*
Andre Malraux, 1901-76, (Fr.) novelist. *Man's Fate.*
Osip Mandelstam, 1891-1938, (Russ.) poet. *Stone, Tristia.*
Thomas Mann, 1875-1955, (Ger.) novelist, essayist. *Buddenbrooks, The Magic Mountain,* "Death in Venice."
Katherine Mansfield, 1888-1923, (Br.) short-story writer. "Bliss."
Christopher Marlowe, 1564-93, (Br.) dramatist, poet. *Tamburlaine the Great, Dr. Faustus, The Jew of Malta.*
Andrew Marvell, 1621-78, (Br.) poet. "To His Coy Mistress."
John Masefield, 1878-1967, (Br.) poet. "Sea Fever," "Cargoes," *Salt Water Ballads.*
Edgar Lee Masters, 1869-1950, (U.S.) poet, biographer. *Spoon River Anthology.*
W(illiam) Somerset Maugham, 1874-1965, (Br.) author. *Of Human Bondage, The Moon and Sixpence.*
Guy de Maupassant, 1850-93, (Fr.) novelist, short-story writer. "A Life," "Bel-Ami," "The Necklace."
François Mauriac, 1885-1970, (Fr.) novelist, dramatist. *Viper's Tangle, The Kiss to the Leper.*
Vladimir Mayakovsky, 1893-1930, (Russ.) poet, dramatist. *The Cloud in Trousers.*
Mary McCarthy, 1912-89, (U.S.) critic, novelist, memoirist. *Memories of a Catholic Girlhood.*
Frank McCourt, 1930-2009, (U.S.) memoirist. *Angela's Ashes, 'Tis, Teacher Man.*
Carson McCullers, 1917-67, (U.S.) novelist. *The Heart Is a Lonely Hunter, Member of the Wedding.*
Herman Melville, 1819-91, (U.S.) novelist, poet. *Moby-Dick, Typee, Billy Budd, Omoo.*
George Meredith, 1828-1909, (Br.) novelist, poet. *The Ordeal of Richard Feverel, The Egoist.*
Prosper Mérimée, 1803-70, (Fr.) author. *Carmen.*
James Merrill, 1926-95, (U.S.) poet. *Divine Comedies.*
James Michener, 1907-97, (U.S.) novelist. *Tales of the South Pacific.*
Edna St. Vincent Millay, 1892-1950, (U.S.) poet. *The Harp Weaver and Other Poems.*
Arthur Miller, 1915-2005, (U.S.) playwright. *The Crucible, After the Fall, Death of a Salesman.*
Henry Miller, 1891-1980, (U.S.) erotic novelist. *Tropic of Cancer.*
A(lan) A(lexander) Milne, 1882-1956, (Br.) author. *Winnie-the-Pooh.*
Czeslaw Milosz, 1911-2004, (Pol.) essayist, poet. "Esse," "Encounter."
John Milton, 1608-74, (Br.) poet, writer. *Paradise Lost, Comus, Lycidas, Areopagitica.*
Mishima Yukio (Hiraoka Kimitake) 1925-70, (Jpn.) writer. *Confessions of a Mask.*
Gabriela Mistral, 1889-1957, (Chil.) poet. *Sonnets of Death.*
Margaret Mitchell, 1900-49, (U.S.) novelist. *Gone With the Wind.*
Jean Baptiste Molière, 1622-73, (Fr.) dramatist. *Tartuffe, Le Misanthrope, Le Bourgeois Gentilhomme.*
Ferenc Molnár, 1878-1952, (Hung.) dramatist, novelist. *Liliom, The Guardsman, The Swan.*
Michel de Montaigne, 1533-92, (Fr.) essayist. *Essais.*

Eugenio Montale, 1896-1981, (It.) poet.
Brian Moore, 1921-99, (Ir.-U.S.) novelist. *The Lonely Passion of Judith Hearne.*
Clement C. Moore, 1779-1863, (U.S.) poet, educator. "A Visit From Saint Nicholas."
Marianne Moore, 1887-1972, (U.S.) poet.
Alberto Moravia, 1907-90, (It.) novelist, short-story writer. *The Time of Indifference.*
Sir Thomas More, 1478-1535, (Br.) writer, statesman, saint. *Utopia.*
Wright Morris, 1910-98 (U.S.) novelist. *My Uncle Dudley.*
Murasaki Shikibu, c.978-1026, (Jpn.) novelist. *The Tale of Genji.*
Iris Murdoch, 1919-99 (Br.), novelist, philosopher. *The Sea, The Sea.*
Alfred de Musset, 1810-57, (Fr.) poet, dramatist. *La Confession d'un Enfant du Siècle.*
Vladimir Nabokov, 1899-1977, (Russ.-U.S.) novelist. *Lolita, Pale Fire.*
R. K. Narayan, 1906-2001, (India), novelist, *The Guide.*
Ogden Nash, 1902-71, (U.S.) poet of light verse.
Irène Némirovsky, 1903-42, (Ukraine) novelist. *David Golder, Suite Française.*
Pablo Neruda, 1904-73, (Chil.) poet. *Twenty Love Poems and One Song of Despair, Toward the Splendid City.*
Patrick O'Brian, 1914-2000, (Br.) historical novelist. *Master and Commander, Blue at the Mizzen.*
Sean O'Casey, 1884-1964, (Ir.) dramatist. *Juno and the Paycock, The Plough and the Stars.*
Frank O'Connor (Michael Donovan), 1903-66, (Ir.) short-story writer. "Guests of a Nation."
Flannery O'Connor, 1925-64, (U.S.) novelist, short-story writer. *Wise Blood,* "A Good Man Is Hard to Find."
Clifford Odets, 1906-63, (U.S.) playwright. *Waiting for Lefty, Awake and Sing, Golden Boy, The Country Girl.*
John O'Hara, 1905-70, (U.S.) novelist, short-story writer. *From the Terrace, Appointment in Samarra, Pal Joey.*
Omar Khayyam, c.1028-1122, (Per.) poet. *Rubaiyat.*
Eugene O'Neill, 1888-1953, (U.S.) playwright. *Emperor Jones, Anna Christie, Long Day's Journey Into Night.*
George Orwell (Eric Arthur Blair), 1903-50, (Br.) novelist, essayist. *Animal Farm, Nineteen Eighty-Four.*
John Osborne, 1929-95, (Br.) dramatist, novelist. *Look Back in Anger, The Entertainer.*
Wilfred Owen, 1893-1918 (Br.) poet. "Dulce et Decorum Est."
Grace Paley, 1922-2007, (U.S.) short-story writer, poet. *The Little Disturbances of Man.*
Dorothy Parker, 1893-1967, (U.S.) poet, short-story writer. *Enough Rope, Laments for the Living.*
Boris Pasternak, 1890-1960, (Russ.) poet, novelist. *Doctor Zhivago.*
Alan Paton, 1903-88, (S. Africa) novelist. *Cry, the Beloved Country.*
Octavio Paz, 1914-98, (Mex.) poet, essayist. *The Labyrinth of Solitude, They Shall Not Pass!, The Sun Stone.*
Samuel Pepys, 1633-1703, (Br.) public official, diarist.
S(idney) J(oseph) Perelman, 1904-79, (U.S.) humorist. *The Road to Miltown, Under the Spreading Atrophy.*
Charles Perrault, 1628-1703, (Fr.) writer. *Tales From Mother Goose (Sleeping Beauty, Cinderella).*
Petrarch (Francesco Petrarca), 1304-74, (It.) poet. *Africa, Trionfi, Canzoniere.*
Harold Pinter, 1930-2008, (Br.) playwright. *The Birthday Party, The Caretaker, The Homecoming.*

Luigi Pirandello, 1867-1936, (It.) novelist, dramatist. *Six Characters in Search of an Author.*
Sylvia Plath, 1932-63, (U.S.) author, poet. *The Bell Jar.*
Edgar Allan Poe, 1809-49, (U.S.) poet, short-story writer, critic. "Annabel Lee," "The Raven," "The Purloined Letter."
Alexander Pope, 1688-1744, (Br.) poet. *The Rape of the Lock, The Dunciad, An Essay on Man.*
Katherine Anne Porter, 1890-1980, (U.S.) novelist, short-story writer. *Ship of Fools.*
Chaim Potok, 1929-2002, (U.S.) novelist. *The Chosen.*
Ezra Pound, 1885-1972, (U.S.) poet. *Cantos.*
Anthony Powell, 1905-2000, (Br.) novelist. *A Dance to the Music of Time* series.
J(ohn) B(oynton) Priestley, 1894-1984, (Br.) novelist, dramatist. *The Good Companions.*
Marcel Proust, 1871-1922, (Fr.) novelist. *Remembrance of Things Past.*
Aleksandr Pushkin, 1799-1837, (Russ.) poet, novelist. *Boris Godunov, Eugene Onegin.*
Mario Puzo, 1920-99, (U.S.) novelist. *The Godfather.*
François Rabelais, 1495-1553, (Fr.) writer. *Gargantua.*
Jean Racine, 1639-99, (Fr.) dramatist. *Andromaque, Phèdre, Bérénice, Britannicus.*
Ayn Rand, 1905-82, (Russ.-U.S.) novelist, moral theorist. *The Fountainhead, Atlas Shrugged.*
Terence Rattigan, 1911-77, (Br.) playwright. *Separate Tables, The Browning Version.*
Erich Maria Remarque, 1898-1970, (Ger.-U.S.) novelist. *All Quiet on the Western Front.*
Samuel Richardson, 1689-1761, (Br.) novelist. *Pamela; or Virtue Rewarded.*
Rainer Maria Rilke, 1875-1926, (Ger.) poet. *Life and Songs, Duino Elegies, Poems From the Book of Hours.*
Arthur Rimbaud, 1854-91, (Fr.) poet. *A Season in Hell.*
Edwin Arlington Robinson, 1869-1935, (U.S.) poet. "Richard Cory," "Miniver Cheevy," *Merlin.*
Theodore Roethke, 1908-63, (U.S.) poet. *Open House, The Waking, The Far Field.*
Romain Rolland, 1866-1944, (Fr.) novelist, biographer. *Jean-Christophe.*
Pierre de Ronsard, 1524-85, (Fr.) poet. *Sonnets pour Hélène, La Franciade.*
Christina Rossetti, 1830-94, (Br.) poet. "When I Am Dead, My Dearest."
Dante Gabriel Rossetti, 1828-82, (Br.) poet, painter. "The Blessed Damozel."
Edmond Rostand, 1868-1918, (Fr.) poet, dramatist. *Cyrano de Bergerac.*
Damon Runyon, 1880-1946, (U.S.) short-story writer, journalist. *Guys and Dolls, Blue Plate Special.*
John Ruskin, 1819-1900, (Br.) critic, social theorist. *Modern Painters, The Seven Lamps of Architecture.*
François Sagan (Françoise quoirez), 1935-2004, (Fr.) novelist *Bonjour Tristesse.*
Antoine de Saint-Exupéry, 1900-44, (Fr.) writer. *Wind, Sand and Stars, The Little Prince.*
Saki or H(ector) H(ugh) Munro, 1870-1916, (Br.) writer. *The Chronicles of Clovis.*
George Sand (Amandine Lucie Aurore Dupin), 1804-76, (Fr.) novelist. *Indiana, Consuelo.*
Carl Sandburg, 1878-1967, (U.S.) poet. *The People, Yes; Chicago Poems, Smoke and Steel, Harvest Poems.*
William Saroyan, 1908-81, (U.S.) playwright, novelist. *The Time of Your Life, The Human Comedy.*
Nathalie Sarraute, 1900-99, (Fr.) Nouveau Roman novelist. *Tropismes.*

May Sarton, 1914-95, (Belg.-U.S.) poet, novelist. *Encounter in April, Anger.*

Dorothy L. Sayers, 1893-1957, (Br.) mystery writer; created Lord Peter Wimsey.

Richard Scarry, 1920-94, (U.S.) author of children's books. *Richard Scarry's Best Story Book Ever.*

Friedrich von Schiller, 1759-1805, (Ger.) dramatist, poet, historian. *Don Carlos, Maria Stuart, Wilhelm Tell.*

Sir Walter Scott, 1771-1832, (Sc.) novelist, poet. *Ivanhoe.*

Jaroslav Seifert, 1902-86, (Czech.) poet.

Dr. Seuss (Theodor Seuss Geisel), 1904-91, (U.S.) children's book author and illustrator. *The Cat in the Hat.*

William Shakespeare, 1564-1616, (Br.) dramatist, poet. *Romeo and Juliet, Hamlet, King Lear, Julius Caesar,* sonnets.

Karl Shapiro, 1913-2000, (U.S.) poet. "Elegy for a Dead Soldier."

George Bernard Shaw, 1856-1950, (Ir.-Br.) playwright, critic. *St. Joan, Pygmalion, Major Barbara, Man and Superman.*

Sidney Sheldon, 1917-2007, (U.S.) screenwriter; novelist. *Rage of Angels, Memories of Midnight.*

Mary Wollstonecraft Shelley, 1797-1851, (Br.) novelist, feminist. *Frankenstein. The Last Man.*

Percy Bysshe Shelley, 1792-1822, (Br.) poet. *Prometheus Unbound, Adonais,* "Ode to the West Wind," "To a Skylark."

Richard B. Sheridan, 1751-1816, (Br.) dramatist. *The Rivals, School for Scandal.*

Robert Sherwood, 1896-1955, (U.S.) playwright, biographer. *The Petrified Forest, Abe Lincoln in Illinois.*

Mikhail Sholokhov, 1906-84, (Russ.) writer. *The Silent Don.*

Shel Silverstein, 1932-99, (U.S.) poet, writer. *The Giving Tree, Where the Sidewalk Ends.*

Georges Simenon (Georges Sims), 1903-89, (Belg.-Fr.) mystery writer; created Inspector Maigret.

Upton Sinclair, 1878-1968, (U.S.) novelist. *The Jungle.*

Isaac Bashevis Singer, 1904-91, (Pol.-U.S.) novelist, short-story writer, in Yiddish. *The Magician of Lublin.*

C(harles) P(ercy) Snow, 1905-80, (Br.) novelist, scientist. *Strangers and Brothers, Corridors of Power.*

Aleksandr Solzhenitsyn, 1918-2008, (Russ.) novelist, dramatist. *One Day in the Life of Ivan Denisovich.*

Susan Sontag, 1933-2004, (U.S.) critic, essayist, novelist. *Notes on Camp, The Volcano Lover, In America.*

Stephen Spender, 1909-95, (Br.) poet, critic, novelist. *Twenty Poems,* "Elegy for Margaret."

Edmund Spenser, 1552-99, (Br.) poet. *The Faerie Queen.*

Mickey Spillane, 1918-2006, (U.S.) novelist; series of novels with the character detective Mike Hammer. *The Killing Man.*

Johanna Spyri, 1827-1901, (Swiss) children's author. *Heidi.*

Christina Stead, 1903-83, (Austral.) novelist, short-story writer. *The Man Who Loved Children.*

Richard Steele, 1672-1729, (Br.) essayist, playwright, began the *Tatler* and *Spectator. The Conscious Lovers.*

Gertrude Stein, 1874-1946, (U.S.) writer. *Three Lives.*

John Steinbeck, 1902-68, (U.S.) novelist. *The Grapes of Wrath, Of Mice and Men, The Winter of Our Discontent.*

Stendhal (Marie Henri Beyle), 1783-1842, (Fr.) novelist. *The Red and the Black, The Charterhouse of Parma.*

Laurence Sterne, 1713-68, (Br.) novelist. *Tristram Shandy.*

Wallace Stevens, 1879-1955, (U.S.) poet. *Harmonium, The Man With the Blue Guitar, Notes Toward a Supreme Fiction.*

Robert Louis Stevenson, 1850-94, (Br.) novelist, poet, essayist. *Treasure Island, A Child's Garden of Verses.*

Bram Stoker, 1845-1910, (Br.) writer. *Dracula.*

Rex Stout, 1886-1975, (U.S.) mystery writer; created Nero Wolfe.

Harriet Beecher Stowe, 1811-96, (U.S.) novelist. *Uncle Tom's Cabin.*

Lytton Strachey, 1880-1932, (Br.) biographer, critic. *Eminent Victorians. Queen Victoria, Elizabeth and Essex.*

August Strindberg, 1849-1912, (Swed.) dramatist, novelist. *The Father, Miss Julie, The Creditors.*

William Styron, 1925-2006, (U.S.) novelist, essayist. *The Confessions of Nat Turner, Sophie's Choice, Darkness Visible: A Memoir of Madness.*

Jonathan Swift, 1667-1745, (Br.) satirist, poet. *Gulliver's Travels,* "A Modest Proposal."

Algernon C. Swinburne, 1837-1909, (Br.) poet, dramatist. *Atalanta in Calydon.*

John M. Synge, 1871-1909, (Ir.) poet, dramatist. *Riders to the Sea, The Playboy of the Western World.*

Rabindranath Tagore, 1861-1941, (In.) author, poet. *Sadhana, The Realization of Life, Gitanjali.*

Booth Tarkington, 1869-1946, (U.S.) novelist. *Seventeen.*

Peter Taylor, 1917-94, (U.S.) novelist. *A Summons to Memphis.*

Sara Teasdale, 1884-1933, (U.S.) poet. *Helen of Troy and Other Poems, Rivers to the Sea.*

Alfred, Lord Tennyson, 1809-92, (Br.) poet. *Idylls of the King, In Memoriam,* "The Charge of the Light Brigade."

William Makepeace Thackeray, 1811-63, (Br.) novelist. *Vanity Fair, Henry Esmond, Pendennis.*

Dylan Thomas, 1914-53, (Welsh) poet. *Under Milk Wood, A Child's Christmas in Wales.*

Hunter S. Thompson, 1937-2005, (U.S.) author, journalist. *Hell's Angels, Fear and Loathing in Las Vegas.*

Henry David Thoreau, 1817-62, (U.S.) writer, philosopher, naturalist. *Walden,* "Civil Disobedience."

James Thurber, 1894-1961, (U.S.) humorist; "The Secret Life of Walter Mitty," *My Life and Hard Times.*

J(ohn) R(onald) R(euel) Tolkien, 1892-1973, (Br.) writer. *The Hobbit, Lord of the Rings* trilogy.

Leo Tolstoy, 1828-1910, (Russ.) novelist, short-story writer. *War and Peace, Anna Karenina,* "The Death of Ivan Ilyich."

Lionel Trilling, 1905-75 (U.S.) critic, author, teacher. *The Liberal Imagination.*

Anthony Trollope, 1815-82, (Br.) novelist. *The Warden, Barchester Towers,* the Palliser novels.

Ivan Turgenev, 1818-83, (Russ.) novelist, short-story writer. *Fathers and Sons, First Love, A Month in the Country.*

Amos Tutuola, 1920-97, (Nigerian) novelist. *The Palm-Wine Drunkard, My Life in the Bush of Ghosts.*

Mark Twain (Samuel Clemens), 1835-1910, (U.S.) novelist, humorist. *The Adventures of Huckleberry Finn.*

Sigrid Undset, 1881-1949, (Nor.) novelist, *Kristin Lavransdatter.*

John Updike, 1932-2009, (U.S.), novelist, literary critic. *Rabbit is Rich, The Witches of Eastwick.*

Paul Valéry, 1871-1945, (Fr.) poet, critic. *La Jeune Parque, The Graveyard by the Sea.*

Paul Verlaine, 1844-96, (Fr.) Symbolist poet. *Songs Without Words.*

Jules Verne, 1828-1905, (Fr.) novelist. *Twenty Thousand Leagues Under the Sea.*

François Villon, 1431-63?, (Fr.) poet. *The Lays, The Grand Testament.*

Voltaire (F. M. Arouet), 1694-1778, (Fr.) writer of "philosophical romances"; philosopher, historian; *Candide.*

Kurt Vonnegut Jr., 1922-2007, (U.S.) novelist, essayist; *Cat's Cradle, Slaughterhouse-Five,* and *Breakfast of Champions.*

David Foster Wallace, 1962-2008, (U.S.) novelist, essayist. *Infinite Jest, A Supposedly Fun Thing I'll Never Do Again.*

Robert Penn Warren, 1905-89, (U.S.) novelist, poet, critic. *All the King's Men.*

Wendy Wasserstein, 1950-2006, (U.S.) playwright; *The Heidi Chronicles.*

Evelyn Waugh, 1903-66, (Br.) novelist. *The Loved One, Brideshead Revisited, A Handful of Dust.*

H(erbert) G(eorge) Wells, 1866-1946, (Br.) novelist. *The Time Machine, The Invisible Man, The War of the Worlds.*

Eudora Welty, 1909-2001, (U.S.) southern short story writer, novelist. "Why I Live at the P.O.," "The Ponder Heart."

Rebecca West, 1893-1983, (Br.) novelist, critic, journalist. *Black Lamb and Grey Falcon.*

Edith Wharton, 1862-1937, (U.S.) novelist. *The Age of Innocence, The House of Mirth, Ethan Frome.*

Phillis Wheatley, c.1753-84, (U.S.) poet; 2nd American woman and first black woman to be published, 1770.

E(lwyn) B(rooks) White, 1899-1985, (U.S.) essayist, novelist. *Charlotte's Web, Stuart Little.*

Patrick White, 1912-90, (Austral.) novelist. *The Tree of Man.*

T(erence) H(anbury) White, 1906-64, (Br.) author. *The Once and Future King, A Book of Beasts.*

Walt Whitman, 1819-92, (U.S.) poet. *Leaves of Grass.*

John Greenleaf Whittier, 1807-92, (U.S.) poet, journalist. *Snow-Bound.*

Oscar Wilde, 1854-1900, (Ir.) novelist, playwright. *The Picture of Dorian Gray, The Importance of Being Earnest.*

Laura Ingalls Wilder, 1867-1957, (U.S.) novelist. *Little House on the Prairie* series of children's books.

Thornton Wilder, 1897-1975, (U.S.) playwright. *Our Town, The Skin of Our Teeth, The Matchmaker.*

Tennessee Williams, 1911-83, (U.S.) playwright. *A Streetcar Named Desire, Cat on a Hot Tin Roof, The Glass Menagerie.*

William Carlos Williams, 1883-1963, (U.S.) poet, physician. *Tempers, Al Que Quiere! Paterson,* "This Is Just to Say."

Edmund Wilson, 1895-1972, (U.S.) critic, novelist. *Axel's Castle, To the Finland Station.*

P(elham) G(renville) Wodehouse, 1881-1975, (Br.-U.S.) humorist. The "Jeeves" novels, *Anything Goes.*

Thomas Wolfe, 1900-38, (U.S.) novelist. *Look Homeward, Angel; You Can't Go Home Again.*

Virginia Woolf, 1882-1941, (Br.) novelist, essayist. *Mrs. Dalloway, To the Lighthouse, A Room of One's Own.*

William Wordsworth, 1770-1850, (Br.) poet. "Tintern Abbey," "Ode: Intimations of Immortality," *The Prelude.*

Richard Wright, 1908-60, (U.S.) novelist, short-story writer. *Native Son, Black Boy, Uncle Tom's Children.*

Elinor Wylie, 1885-1928, (U.S.) poet. *Nets to Catch the Wind.*

William Butler Yeats, 1865-1939, (Ir.) poet, playwright. "The Second Coming," *The Wild Swans at Coole.*

Frank Yerby, 1916-91, (U.S.) first bestselling African American novelist; *The Foxes of Harrow.*

Émile Zola, 1840-1902, (Fr.) novelist. *Nana, Thérèse Raquin.*

Poets Laureate

There is no record of the origin of the office of Poet Laureate of England. Henry III (1216-72) reportedly had a Versificator Regis, or King's Poet, paid 100 shillings per year. Other poets said to have filled the role include Geoffrey Chaucer (d 1400), Edmund Spenser (d 1599), Ben Jonson (d 1637), and Sir William d'Avenant (d 1668). The first official English poet laureate was John Dryden, appointed 1668, for life (as was customary). Then came Thomas Shadwell, in 1689; Nahum Tate, 1692; Nicholas Rowe, 1715; Rev. Laurence Eusden, 1718; Colley Cibber, 1730; William Whitehead, 1757; Rev. Thomas Warton, 1785; Henry James Pye, 1790; Robert Southey, 1813; William Wordsworth, 1843; Alfred, Lord Tennyson, 1850; Alfred Austin, 1896; Robert Bridges, 1913; John Masefield, 1930; C. Day Lewis, 1968; Sir John Betjeman, 1972; Ted Hughes, 1984; Andrew Motion, 1999; Carol Ann Duffy, 2009.

In U.S., appointment is by Librarian of Congress and is not for life: Robert Penn Warren, appointed 1986; Richard Wilbur, 1987; Howard Nemerov, 1988; Mark Strand, 1990; Joseph Brodsky, 1991; Mona Van Duyn, 1992; Rita Dove, 1993; Robert Hass, 1995; Robert Pinsky, 1997; Stanley Kunitz, 2000; Billy Collins, 2001; Louise Gluck, 2003; Ted Kooser, 2004; Donald Hall, 2006; Charles Simic, 2007; Kay Ryan, 2008.

Composers of Classical and Avant Garde Music

John Adams, b 1947, (U.S.) *Nixon in China, The Death of Klinghoffer.*

Carl Philipp Emanuel Bach, 1714-88, (Ger.) Cantatas, passions, numerous keyboard and instrumental works.

Johann Christian Bach, 1735-82, (Ger.) Concertos, operas, sonatas. Known as the "English" Bach.

Johann Sebastian Bach, 1685-1750, (Ger.) *St. Matthew Passion, The Well-Tempered Clavier.*

Samuel Barber, 1910-81, (U.S.) *Adagio for Strings, Vanessa.*

Béla Bartók, 1881-1945, (Hung.) *Concerto for Orchestra, The Miraculous Mandarin.*

Amy Beach (Mrs. H. H. A. Beach), 1867-1944, (U.S.) *The Year's at the Spring, Fireflies, The Chambered Nautilus.*

Ludwig van Beethoven, 1770-1827, (Ger.) Concertos (*Emperor*), sonatas (*Moonlight, Pathetique*), 9 symphonies.

Vincenzo Bellini, 1801-35, (It.) *I Puritani, La Sonnambula, Norma.*

Alban Berg, 1885-1935, (Austrian) *Wozzeck, Lulu.*

Hector Berlioz, 1803-69, (Fr.) *Damnation of Faust, Symphonie Fantastique, Requiem.*

Leonard Bernstein, 1918-90, (U.S.) *Chichester Psalms, Jeremiah Symphony, Mass.*

Georges Bizet, 1838-75, (Fr.) *Carmen, Pearl Fishers.*

Ernest Bloch, 1880-1959, (Swiss-U.S.) *Macbeth* (opera), *Schelomo, Voice in the Wilderness.*

Luigi Boccherini, 1743-1805, (It.) Chamber music and guitar pieces.

Alexander Borodin, 1833-87, (Russ.) *Prince Igor, In the Steppes of Central Asia, Polovtzian Dances.*

Pierre Boulez, b 1925, (Fr.) *Le Visage nuptial, Edats/Multiple, Domaines.*

Johannes Brahms, 1833-97, (Ger.) Lie-beslieder Waltzes, *Acad. Festival Overture,* chamber music, 4 symphonies.

Henry Brant, 1913-2008, (Can.) spatial music.

Benjamin Britten, 1913-76, (Br.) *Peter Grimes, Turn of the Screw, A Ceremony of Carols, War Requiem.*

Anton Bruckner, 1824-96, (Austrian) 9 symphonies.

Dietrich Buxtehude, 1637-1707, (Dan.) Organ works, vocal music.

William Byrd, 1543-1623, (Br.) Masses, motets.

John Cage, 1912-92, (U.S.) *Winter Music, Fontana Mix.*

Elliott Carter, b 1908, (U.S.) *Second String Quartet, Third String Quartet.*

Emmanuel Chabrier, 1841-94, (Fr.) *Le Roi Malgré Lui, España.*

Gustave Charpentier, 1860-1956, (Fr.) *Louise.*

Frédéric Chopin, 1810-49, (Pol.) Mazurkas, waltzes, etudes, nocturnes, polonaises, sonatas.

Aaron Copland, 1900-90, (U.S.) *Appalachian Spring, Fanfare for the Common Man, Lincoln Portrait.*

Claude Debussy, 1862-1918, (Fr.) *Pelleas et Melisande, La Mer, Prelude to the Afternoon of a Faun.*

David Del Tredici, b 1937, (U.S.) *Child Ace, In Memory of a Summer Day.*

Gaetano Donizetti, 1797-1848, (It.) *Elixir of Love, Lucia di Lammermoor, Daughter of the Regiment.*

Paul Dukas, 1865-1935, (Fr.) *Sorcerer's Apprentice.*

Antonin Dvorak, 1841-1904, (Czech.) *Songs My Mother Taught Me, Symphony in E Minor (From the New World).*

Edward Elgar, 1857-1934, (Br.) *Enigma Variations, Pomp and Circumstance.*

Manuel de Falla, 1876-1946, (Sp.) *El Amor Brujo, La Vida Breve, The Three-Cornered Hat.*

Gabriel Faurè, 1845-1924, (Fr.) *Requiem, Elègie for Cello and Piano.*

Cesar Franck, 1822-90, (Belg.) Symphony in D minor, Violin Sonata.

George Gershwin, 1898-1937, (U.S.) *Rhapsody in Blue, An American in Paris, Porgy and Bess.*

Philip Glass, b 1937, (U.S.) *Einstein on the Beach, The Voyage.*

Mikhail Glinka, 1804-57, (Russ.) *A Life for the Tsar, Ruslan and Ludmilla.*

Christoph W. Gluck, 1714-87, (Ger.) *Alceste, Iphigènie en Tauride.*

Charles Gounod, 1818-93, (Fr.) *Faust, Romeo and Juliet.*

Edvard Grieg, 1843-1907, (Nor.) *Peer Gynt Suite,* Concerto in A minor for piano.

George Frideric Handel, 1685-1759, (Ger.-Br.) *Messiah, Water Music.*

Howard Hanson, 1896-1981, (U.S.) Symphonies No. 1 (Nordic) and No. 2 (Romantic).

Roy Harris, 1898-1979, (U.S.) Symphonies.

(Franz) Joseph Haydn, 1732-1809, (Austrian) Symphonies (*Clock, London, Toy*), chamber music, oratorios.

Paul Hindemith, 1895-1963, (U.S.) *Mathis der Maler.*

Gustav Holst, 1874-1934, (Br.) *The Planets.*

Arthur Honegger, 1892-1955, (Fr.) *Judith, Le Roi David, Pacific 231.*

Alan Hovhaness, 1911-2000, (U.S.) Symphonies, *Magnificat.*

Engelbert Humperdinck, 1854-1921, (Ger.) *Hansel and Gretel.*

Charles Ives, 1874-1954, (U.S.) *Concord Sonata,* symphonies.

Aram Khachaturian, 1903-78, (Russ.) Ballets, piano pieces, *Sabre Dance.*

Zoltán Kodaly, 1882-1967, (Hung.) *Háry János, Psalmus Hungaricus.*

Fritz Kreisler, 1875-1962, (Austrian) *Caprice Viennois, Tambourin Chinois.*

Edouard Lalo, 1823-92, (Fr.) *Symphonie Espagnole.*

David Lang, b 1957, (U.S.) *The Little Match Girl Passion.*

Ruggero Leoncavallo, 1857-1919, (It.) *Pagliacci.*

Franz Liszt, 1811-86, (Hung.) 20 Hungarian rhapsodies, symphonic poems.

Edward MacDowell, 1861-1908, (U.S.) *To a Wild Rose.*

Gustav Mahler, 1860-1911, (Austrian) *Das Lied von der Erde;* 9 complete symphonies.

Pietro Mascagni, 1863-1945, (It.) *Cavalleria Rusticana.*

Jules Massenet, 1842-1912, (Fr.) *Manon, Le Cid, Thaïs.*

Felix Mendelssohn, 1809-47, (Ger.) *A Midsummer Night's Dream, Songs Without Words,* violin concerto.

Gian Carlo Menotti, 1911-2007, (It.-U.S.) *The Medium, The Consul, Amahl and the Night Visitors.*

Claudio Monteverdi, 1567-1643, (It.) Opera, masses, madrigals.

Modest Mussorgsky, 1839-81, (Russ.) *Boris Godunov, Pictures at an Exhibition.*

Wolfgang Amadeus Mozart, 1756-91, (Austrian) Chamber music, concertos, operas (*Magic Flute, Marriage of Figaro*), 41 symphonies.

Jacques Offenbach, 1819-80, (Fr.) *Tales of Hoffmann.*

Carl Orff, 1895-1982, (Ger.) *Carmina Burana.*

Johann Pachelbel, 1653-1706, (Ger.) Canon and Fugue in D major.

Ignacy Paderewski, 1860-1941, (Pol.) Minuet in G.

Niccolò Paganini, 1782-1840, (It.) Caprices for violin solo.

Giovanni Palestrina, c.1525-94, (It.) Masses, madrigals.

Krzysztof Penderecki, b 1933, (Pol.) *Psalmus, Polymorphia, De natura sonoris.*

Francis Poulenc, 1899-1963, (Fr.) *Dialogues des Carmèlites.*

Mel Powell, 1923-98, (U.S.) *Duplicates: A Concerto for Two Pianos and Orchestra, Cantilena Concertante.*

Sergei Prokofiev, 1891-1953, (Russ.) *Classical Symphony, Love for Three Oranges, Peter and the Wolf.*

Giacomo Puccini, 1858-1924, (It.) *La Boheme, Manon Lescaut, Tosca, Madama Butterfly.*

Henry Purcell, 1659-95, (Eng.) *Dido and Aeneas.*

Sergei Rachmaninoff, 1873-1943, (Russ.) Concertos, preludes (Prelude in C sharp minor), symphonies.

Maurice Ravel, 1875-1937, (Fr.) *Bolèro, Daphnis et Chloè,* Piano Concerto in D for Left Hand Alone.

Steve Reich, b 1936, (U.S.) *Double Sextet, Three Tales.*

Nikolai Rimsky-Korsakov, 1844-1908, (Russ.) *Golden Cockerel, Scheherazade, Flight of the Bumblebee.*

Gioacchino Rossini, 1792-1868, (It.) *Barber of Seville, Otello, William Tell.*

John Rutter, b 1945, (Br.) *Magnificat, Requiem.*

Camille Saint-Saëns, 1835-1921, (Fr.) *Carnival of Animals (The Swan), Samson and Delilah, Danse Macabre.*

Alessandro Scarlatti, 1660-1725, (It.) Cantatas, oratorios, operas.

Domenico Scarlatti, 1685-1757, (It.) Harpsichord works.

Alfred Schnittke, 1934-98 (Sov.-Ger.) *Life With an Idiot.*

Arnold Schoenberg, 1874-1951, (Austrian) *Pelleas and Melisande, Pierrot Lunaire, Verklärte Nacht.*

Franz Schubert, 1797-1828, (Austrian) Chamber music (*Trout Quintet*), lieder, symphonies (Unfinished).

Robert Schumann, 1810-56, (Ger.) *Die Frauenliebe und Leben, Träumerei.*

Dmitri Shostakovich, 1906-75, (Russ.) Symphonies, *Lady Macbeth of the District Mzensk.*

Jean Sibelius, 1865-1957, (Finn.) *Finlandia.*

Bedrich Smetana, 1824-84, (Czech.) *The Bartered Bride.*

Karlheinz Stockhausen, 1928-2008, (Ger.) *Kontra-Punkte, Kontakte* for Electronic Instruments.

Richard Strauss, 1864-1949, (Ger.) *Salome, Elektra, Der Rosenkavalier, Thus Spake Zarathustra.*

Igor Stravinsky, 1882-1971, (Russ.) *Noah and the Flood, The Rake's Progress, The Rite of Spring.*

Toru Takemitsu, 1930-96, (Jpn.) *Requiem for Strings, Dorian Horizon.*

Peter I. Tchaikovsky, 1840-93, (Russ.) *Nutcracker, Swan Lake, The Sleeping Beauty.*

Georg Philipp Telemann, 1681-1767, (Ger.) church music, orchestral suites, chamber music.

Virgil Thomson, 1896-1989, (U.S.) Opera, film music, *Four Saints in Three Acts.*

Dmitri Tiomkin, 1894-1979, (Russ.-U.S.) film scores, including *High Noon.*

Sir Michael Tippett, 1905-98, (Br.) *A Child of Our Time, The Midsummer Marriage, The Knot Garden.*

Ralph Vaughan Williams, 1872-1958, (Eng.) *Fantasia on a Theme by Thomas Tallis*, symphonies, vocal music.

Giuseppe Verdi, 1813-1901, (It.) *Aida, Rigoletto, Don Carlo, Il Trovatore, La Traviata, Falstaff, Macbeth.*

Heitor Villa-Lobos, 1887-1959, (Brazil) *Bachianas Brasileiras.*

Antonio Vivaldi, 1678-1741, (It.) Concerto grossos (*The Four Seasons*).

Richard Wagner, 1813-83, (Ger.) *Rienzi, Tannhäuser, Lohengrin, Tristan und Isolde.*

Carl Maria von Weber, 1786-1826, (Ger.) *Der Freischutz.*

Composers of Operettas, Musicals, and Popular Music

Richard Adler, b 1921, (U.S.) *Pajama Game; Damn Yankees.*

Milton Ager, 1893-1979, (U.S.) I Wonder What's Become of Sally; Hard-Hearted Hannah; Ain't She Sweet?

Arthur Altman, 1910-94, (U.S.) *All or Nothing at All.*

Leroy Anderson, 1908-75, (U.S.) Sleigh Ride, Blue Tango, Syncopated Clock.

Paul Anka, b 1941, (Can.) My Way; *Tonight Show* theme.

Harold Arlen, 1905-86, (U.S.) Stormy Weather; Over the Rainbow; Blues in the Night; That Old Black Magic.

Burt Bacharach, b 1928, (U.S.) Raindrops Keep Fallin' on My Head; Walk on By; What the World Needs Now Is Love.

Ernest Ball, 1878-1927, (U.S.) Mother Machree; When Irish Eyes Are Smiling.

Irving Berlin, 1888-1989, (U.S.) *Annie Get Your Gun; Call Me Madam;* God Bless America; White Christmas.

Leonard Bernstein, 1918-90, (U.S.) *On the Town; Wonderful Town; Candide; West Side Story.*

Eubie Blake, 1883-1983, (U.S.) *Shuffle Along;* I'm Just Wild About Harry.

Jerry Bock, b 1928, (U.S.) *Mr. Wonderful; Fiorello; Fiddler on the Roof; The Rothschilds.*

Carrie Jacobs Bond, 1862-1946, (U.S.) I Love You Truly.

Nacio Herb Brown, 1896-1964, (U.S.) Singing in the Rain; You Were Meant for Me; All I Do Is Dream of You.

Hoagy Carmichael, 1899-1981, (U.S.) Stardust; Georgia on My Mind; Old Buttermilk Sky.

James Cleveland, 1931-91, (U.S.) composer, musician, singer; first black gospel artist to appear at Carnegie Hall.

George M. Cohan, 1878-1942, (U.S.) Give My Regards to Broadway; You're a Grand Old Flag; Over There.

Cy Coleman, 1929-2004, (U.S.) *Sweet Charity;* Witchcraft.

John Frederick Coots, 1895-1985, (U.S.) Santa Claus Is Coming to Town; You Go to My Head; For All We Know.

Noel Coward, 1899-1973, (Br.) *Bitter Sweet;* Mad Dogs and Englishmen; Mad About the Boy.

Neil Diamond, b 1941, (U.S.) I'm a Believer; Sweet Caroline.

Walter Donaldson, 1893-1947, (U.S.) My Buddy; Carolina in the Morning; Makin' Whoopee.

Vernon Duke, 1903-69, (U.S.) April in Paris.

Bob Dylan, b 1941, (U.S.) Blowin' in the Wind.

Gus Edwards, 1879-1945, (U.S.) School Days; By the Light of the Silvery Moon; In My Merry Oldsmobile.

Sherman Edwards, 1919-81, (U.S.) See You in September; Wonderful! Wonderful!

Duke Ellington, 1899-1974, (U.S.) Sophisticated Lady; Satin Doll; It Don't Mean a Thing; Solitude.

Sammy Fain, 1902-89, (U.S.) I'll Be Seeing You; Love Is a Many-Splendored Thing.

Fred Fisher, 1875-1942, (U.S.) Peg O' My Heart; Chicago.

Stephen Collins Foster, 1826-64, (U.S.) My Old Kentucky Home; Old Folks at Home; Beautiful Dreamer.

Rudolf Friml, 1879-1972, (Czech-U.S.) *The Firefly; Rose Marie; Vagabond King; Bird of Paradise.*

John Gay, 1685-1732, (Br.) *The Beggar's Opera.*

George Gershwin, 1898-1937, (U.S.) Someone to Watch Over Me; I've Got a Crush on You; Embraceable You.

Morton Gould, 1913-96, (U.S.) Fall River Suite, Holocaust Suite, Spirituals for Orchestra, Stringmusic.

Ferde Grofe, 1892-1972, (U.S.) Grand Canyon Suite.

Marvin Hamlisch, b 1944, (U.S.) The Way We Were; Nobody Does It Better; *A Chorus Line.*

Ray Henderson, 1896-1970, (U.S.) *George White's Scandals;* That Old Gang of Mine; Five Foot Two, Eyes of Blue.

Victor Herbert, 1859-1924, (Ir.-U.S.) *Mlle. Modiste; Babes in Toyland; The Red Mill; Naughty Marietta; Sweethearts.*

Jerry Herman, b 1931, (U.S.) *Hello Dolly; Mame.*

Brian Holland, b 1941, **Lamont Dozier**, b 1941, **Eddie Holland**, b 1939, (all U.S.) Heat Wave; Stop! In the Name of Love; Baby, I Need Your Loving.

Rupert Holmes, b 1947, (Eng.-U.S.) *The Mystery of Edwin Drood, Curtains.*

Antonio Carlos Jobim, 1927-94, (Brazil) *The Girl From Ipanema; Desafinado; One Note Samba.*

Billy (William Martin) Joel, b 1949, (U.S.) *Just the Way You Are; Honesty;* Piano Man.

Elton John, b 1947 (Br.) *The Lion King;* Candle in the Wind; Your Song.

Scott Joplin, 1868-1917, (U.S.) Maple Leaf Rag; *Treemonisha.*

John Kander, b 1927, (U.S.) *Cabaret; Chicago; Funny Lady.*

Jerome Kern, 1885-1945, (U.S.) *Sally; Sunny; Show Boat.*

Carole King, b 1942, (U.S.) Will You Love Me Tomorrow?; Natural Woman; One Fine Day; Up on the Roof.

Burton Lane, 1912-97, (U.S.) *Finian's Rainbow.*

Jonathan Larson, 1960-96, (U.S.), *tick, tick... BOOM!; Rent.*

Franz Lehar, 1870-1948, (Hung.) *Merry Widow.*

Jerry Leiber & **Mike Stoller**, both b 1933, (both U.S.) Hound Dog; Searchin'; Yakety Yak; Love Me Tender.

Mitch Leigh, b 1928, (U.S.) *Man of La Mancha.*

John Lennon, 1940-80, & **Paul McCartney**, b 1942, (both Br.) I Want to Hold Your Hand; She Loves You.

Jay Livingston, 1915-2001 (U.S.) Mona Lisa; Que Sera, Sera.

Andrew Lloyd Webber, b 1948, (Br.) *Jesus Christ Superstar; Evita; Cats; The Phantom of the Opera.*

Frank Loesser, 1910-69, (U.S.) *Guys and Dolls; Where's Charley?; The Most Happy Fella; How to Succeed....*

Frederick Loewe, 1901-88, (Austrian-U.S.) *Brigadoon; Paint Your Wagon; My Fair Lady; Camelot.*

Henry Mancini, 1924-94, (U.S.) Moon River; Days of Wine and Roses; Pink Panther Theme.

Barry Mann, b 1939, & **Cynthia Weil**, b 1937, (both U.S.) You've Lost That Loving Feeling.

Jimmy McHugh, 1894-1969, (U.S.) Don't Blame Me; I'm in the Mood for Love; I Feel a Song Coming On.

Alan Menken, b 1949, (U.S.) *Little Shop of Horrors, Beauty and the Beast.*

Joseph Meyer, 1894-1987, (U.S.) If You Knew Susie; California, Here I Come; Crazy Rhythm.

Chauncey Olcott, 1858-1932, (U.S.) Mother Machree.

Jerome "Doc" Pomus, 1925-91, (U.S.) Save the Last Dance for Me; A Teenager in Love.

Cole Porter, 1893-1964, (U.S.) *Anything Goes; Kiss Me Kate; Can Can; Silk Stockings.*

Smokey Robinson, b 1940, (U.S.) Shop Around; My Guy; My Girl; Get Ready.

Richard Rodgers, 1902-79, (U.S.) *Oklahoma!; Carousel; South Pacific; The King and I; The Sound of Music.*

Sigmund Romberg, 1887-1951, (Hung.) *Maytime; The Student Prince; Desert Song; Blossom Time.*

Harold Rome, 1908-93, (U.S.) *Pins and Needles; Call Me Mister; Wish You Were Here; Fanny; Destry Rides Again.*

Vincent Rose, b 1880-1944, (U.S.) Avalon; Whispering; Blueberry Hill.

Harry Ruby, 1895-1974, (U.S.) Three Little Words; Who's Sorry Now?

Arthur Schwartz, 1900-84, (U.S.) *The Band Wagon;* Dancing in the Dark; By Myself; That's Entertainment.

Steven Schwartz, b 1948, (U.S.) *Godspell, Pippin, Wicked.*

Neil Sedaka, b 1939, (U.S.) Breaking Up Is Hard to Do.

Paul Simon, b 1942, (U.S.) Sounds of Silence; I Am a Rock; Mrs. Robinson; Bridge Over Troubled Waters.

Stephen Sondheim, b 1930, (U.S.) *A Little Night Music; Company; Sweeney Todd; Sunday in the Park With George.*

John Philip Sousa, 1854-1932, (U.S.) *El Capitan;* Stars and Stripes Forever.

Oskar Straus, 1870-1954, (Austrian) *Chocolate Soldier.*

Johann Strauss, 1825-99, (Austrian) *Gypsy Baron; Die Fledermaus;* waltzes: Blue Danube; Artist's Life.

Charles Strouse, b 1928, (U.S.) *Bye Bye, Birdie; Annie.*

Jule Styne, 1905-94, (Br.-U.S.) *Gentlemen Prefer Blondes; Bells Are Ringing; Gypsy; Funny Girl.*

Arthur S. Sullivan, 1842-1900, (Br.) *H.M.S. Pinafore; Pirates of Penzance; The Mikado.*

Deems Taylor, 1885-1966, (U.S.) *Peter Ibbetson.*

Harry Tobias, 1905-94, (U.S.) *I'll Keep the Lovelight Burning.*

Egbert van Alstyne, 1882-1951, (U.S.) In the Shade of the Old Apple Tree; Memories; Pretty Baby.

Jimmy Van Heusen, 1913-90, (U.S.) Moonlight Becomes You; Swinging on a Star; All the Way; Love and Marriage.

Albert von Tilzer, 1878-1956, (U.S.) I'll Be With You in Apple Blossom Time; Take Me Out to the Ball Game.

Harry von Tilzer, 1872-1946, (U.S.) Only a Bird in a Gilded Cage; On a Sunday Afternoon.

Fats Waller, 1904-43, (U.S.) Honeysuckle Rose; Ain't Misbehavin'.

Harry Warren, 1893-1981, (U.S.) You're My Everything; We're in the Money; I Only Have Eyes for You.

Jimmy Webb, b 1946, (U.S.) Up, Up and Away; By the Time I Get to Phoenix; Didn't We?; Wichita Lineman.

Kurt Weill, 1900-50, (Ger.-U.S.) Threepenny Opera; Lady in the Dark; Knickerbocker Holiday; One Touch of Venus.

Percy Wenrich, 1887-1952, (U.S.) When You Wore a Tulip; Moonlight Bay; Put On Your Old Gray Bonnet.

Richard A. Whiting, 1891-1938, (U.S.) Till We Meet Again; Sleepytime Gal; Beyond the Blue Horizon; My Ideal.

Fred Wildhorn, b 1959, (U.S.) Jekyll and Hyde; Victor/Victoria; The Civil War.

John Williams, b 1932, (U.S.) Jaws; E.T.; Star Wars series; Raiders of the Lost Ark series.

Meredith Willson, 1902-84, (U.S.) The Music Man.

Stevie Wonder, b 1950, (U.S.) You Are the Sunshine of My Life; Signed, Sealed, Delivered, I'm Yours.

Vincent Youmans, 1898-1946, (U.S.) Two Little Girls in Blue; Wildflower; No, No, Nanette; Hit the Deck; Rainbow; Smiles.

Lyricists

Howard Ashman, 1950-91, (U.S.) Little Shop of Horrors; The Little Mermaid.

Johnny Burke, 1908-84, (U.S.) Misty; Imagination.

Irving Caesar, 1895-1996, (U.S.) Swanee; Tea for Two; Just a Gigolo.

Sammy Cahn, 1913-93, (U.S.) High Hopes; Love and Marriage; The Second Time Around; It's Magic.

Leonard Cohen, b 1934, (Can.) Suzanne; Stranger Song.

Betty Comden, 1917-2006, (U.S.) and **Adolph Green**, 1915-2002, (U.S.) The Party's Over; New York, New York.

Hal David, b 1921, (U.S.) What the World Needs Now Is Love.

Buddy De Sylva, 1895-1950, (U.S.) When Day Is Done; Look for the Silver Lining; April Showers.

Howard Dietz, 1896-1983, (U.S.) Dancing in the Dark; That's Entertainment.

Al Dubin, 1891-1945, (U.S.) Tiptoe Through the Tulips; Lullaby of Broadway.

Fred Ebb, b 1936-2004, (U.S.) Cabaret; Zorba; Woman of the Year; Chicago.

Ray Evans, 1915-2007, (U.S.) Mona Lisa; Que Sera, Sera.

Dorothy Fields, 1905-74, (U.S.) On the Sunny Side of the Street; Don't Blame Me; The Way You Look Tonight.

Ira Gershwin, 1896-1983, (U.S.) The Man I Love; S'Wonderful; Embraceable You.

William S. Gilbert, 1836-1911, (Br.) H.M.S. Pinafore; Pirates of Penzance.

Gerry Goffin, b 1939, (U.S.) Will You Love Me Tomorrow; Take Good Care of My Baby; Up on the Roof.

Mack Gordon, 1905-59, (Pol.-U.S.) You'll Never Know; The More I See You; Chattanooga Choo-Choo.

Oscar Hammerstein II, 1895-1960, (U.S.) Ol' Man River; Oklahoma!; Carousel.

E. Y. (Yip) Harburg, 1898-1981, (U.S.) Brother, Can You Spare a Dime; April in Paris; Over the Rainbow.

Sheldon Harnick, b 1924, (U.S.) Fiddler on the Roof; She Loves Me.

Lorenz Hart, 1895-1943, (U.S.) Isn't It Romantic; Blue Moon; Lover; Manhattan; My Funny Valentine.

DuBose Heyward, 1885-1940, (U.S.) Summertime.

Gus Kahn, 1886-1941, (U.S.) Memories; Ain't We Got Fun.

Alan J. Lerner, 1918-86, (U.S.) Brigadoon; My Fair Lady; Camelot; Gigi; On a Clear Day You Can See Forever.

Johnny Mercer, 1909-76, (U.S.) Blues in the Night; Come Rain or Come Shine; Laura; That Old Black Magic.

Bob Merrill, 1921-98, (U.S.) People; (How Much Is That) Doggie in the Window.

Jack Norworth, 1879-1959, (U.S.) Take Me Out to the Ball Game; Shine On Harvest Moon.

Mitchell Parish, 1901-93, (U.S.) Stardust; Stairway to the Stars.

Andy Razaf, 1895-1973, (U.S.) Honeysuckle Rose; Ain't Misbehavin'.

Leo Robin, 1900-84, (U.S.) Thanks for the Memory; Hooray for Love; Diamonds Are a Girl's Best Friend.

Bernie Taupin, b 1947 (Br.) Rocket Man; Your Song.

Paul Francis Webster, 1907-84, (U.S.) Secret Love; The Shadow of Your Smile; Love Is a Many-Splendored Thing.

Jack Yellen, 1892-1991, (U.S.) Down by the O-Hi-O; Ain't She Sweet; Happy Days Are Here Again.

Blues and Jazz Artists of the Past

Julian "Cannonball" Adderley, 1928-75, alto sax

Nat Adderley, 1931-2000, cornet

Henry "Red" Allen, 1908-67, trumpet

Louis "Satchmo" Armstrong, 1901-71, trumpet, singer, bandleader

Albert Ayler, 1936-70, tenor sax, alto sax

Mildred Bailey, 1907-51, singer

Chet Baker, 1929-88, trumpet, singer

Ray Barretto, 1930-2006, conga drummer

Count Basie, 1904-84, bandleader, piano, composer

Sidney Bechet, 1897-1959, soprano sax, clarinet

Bix Beiderbecke, 1903-31, cornet, composer, piano

Bunny Berigan, 1908-42, trumpet

Barney Bigard, 1906-80, clarinet

Eubie Blake, 1883-1983, composer, piano

Art Blakey, 1919-90, drums, bandleader

Jimmy Blanton, 1921-42, bass

Charles "Buddy" Bolden, 1877-1931, cornet, pioneer bandleader

Lester Bowie, 1941-99, trumpet, composer, bandleader

Michael Brecker, 1949-2007, saxophone

Big Bill Broonzy, 1893-1958, blues singer, guitar

Clarence "Gatemouth" Brown, 1924-2006, guitar, singer

Clifford Brown, 1930-56, trumpet

Ray Brown, 1926-2002, bass

Don Byas, 1912-72, tenor sax

Charlie Byrd, 1925-99, guitarist; popularized bossanova

Cab Calloway, 1907-94, bandleader, singer

Harry Carney, 1910-74, baritone sax, clarinet

Benny Carter, 1907-2003, alto saxophone

Betty Carter, 1930-98, jazz singer

Sidney "Big Sid" Catlett, 1910-51, drums

Adolphus Anthony "Doc" Cheatham, 1905-97, trumpet

Don Cherry, 1936-95, trumpet

Charlie Christian, 1916-42, guitar

Kenny "Klook" Clarke, 1914-85, drums

Buck Clayton, 1911-91, trumpet

Al Cohn, 1925-88, tenor sax

Cozy Cole, 1909-81, drums

Alice Coltrane, 1937-2007, pianist, composer

John Coltrane, 1926-67, tenor sax, soprano sax, composer

Eddie Condon, 1905-73, guitar, bandleader

Tadd Dameron, 1917-65, piano, composer

Eddie "Lockjaw" Davis, 1921-86, tenor sax

Miles Davis, 1926-91, trumpet, composer

Wild Bill Davison, 1906-89, cornet

Blossom Dearie, 1924-2009, singer

Paul Desmond, 1924-77, alto sax

Vic Dickenson, 1906-84, trombone

Willie Dixon, 1915-92, composer, bass

Johnny Dodds, 1892-1940, clarinet

Warren "Baby" Dodds, 1898-1959, drums

Eric Dolphy, 1928-64, alto sax, bass clarinet, flute

Jimmy Dorsey, 1904-57, alto sax, bandleader

Tommy Dorsey, 1905-56, trombone, bandleader

Billy Eckstine, 1914-93, singer, bandleader

Harry "Sweets" Edison, 1915-99, trumpet

Roy Eldridge, 1911-89, trumpet, singer

Duke Ellington, 1899-1974, piano, bandleader, composer

Bill Evans, 1929-80, piano

Gil Evans, 1912-88, composer, arranger, piano

Art Farmer, 1928-99, trumpet, flugelhorn

Maynard Ferguson, 1926-2006, trumpeter, bandleader

Ella Fitzgerald, 1917-96, singer

Tommy Flanagan, 1930-2001, piano

Erroll Garner, 1921-77, piano, composer

Stan Getz, 1927-91, tenor sax

Dizzy Gillespie, 1917-93, trumpet, composer, singer

Benny Goodman, 1909-86, clarinet, bandleader

Dexter Gordon, 1923-90, tenor sax

Stéphane Grappelli, 1908-97, violin

Bobby Hackett, 1915-76, trumpet, cornet

Lionel Hampton, 1908-2002, vibraphone, bandleader

W. C. Handy, 1873-1958, composer

Jimmy Harrison, 1900-31, trombone

Coleman Hawkins, 1904-69, tenor sax

Percy Heath, 1923-2005, bass

Fletcher Henderson, 1898-1952, bandleader, arranger

Woody Herman, 1913-87, clarinet, alto sax, bandleader

Jay C. Higginbotham, 1906-73, trombone

Ruiz Hilton, 1952-2006, piano, composer

Earl "Fatha" Hines, 1903-83, piano

Milt Hinton, 1910-2000, bass

Al Hirt, 1922-99, trumpet

Johnny Hodges, 1906-70, alto sax

Billie Holiday, 1915-59, singer

John Lee Hooker, 1917-2001, blues guitar, singer

Sam "Lightnin'" Hopkins, 1912-82, blues singer, guitar

Shirley Horn, 1934-2005, piano, singer

Howlin' Wolf, 1910-1976, blues singer, harmonica, guitar

Alberta Hunter, 1895-1984, singer

Mahalia Jackson, 1911-72, gospel singer

Milt Jackson, 1923-99, vibraphone

Elmore James, 1918-63, blues singer, guitar

Blind Lemon Jefferson, 1897-1930, blues singer, guitar

Bunk Johnson, 1879-1949, trumpet

J. J. Johnson, 1924-2001, trombone

James P. Johnson, 1891-1955, piano, composer

Robert Johnson, 1912-38, blues singer, guitar
Elvin Jones, 1927-2004, drums
Jo Jones, 1911-85, drums
Philly Joe Jones, 1923-85, drums
Thad Jones, 1923-86, cornet, bandleader, composer
Scott Joplin, 1868-1917, ragtime composer
Louis Jordan, 1908-75, singer, alto sax
Stan Kenton, 1911-79, bandleader, composer, piano
Barney Kessel, 1923-2004, guitar
Albert King, 1923-92, blues guitar
John Kirby, 1908-52, bandleader, bass
Rahsaan Roland Kirk, 1936-77, saxophones, composer
Gene Krupa, 1909-73, drums, bandleader
Scott LaFaro, 1936-61, bass
Huddie Ledbetter (Lead Belly), 1888-1949, folk and blues singer, guitar
Peggy Lee, 1920-2002, singer
John Lewis, 1920-2001, piano, Modern Jazz Quartet founder
Mel Lewis, 1929-90, drums, bandleader
Jimmie Lunceford, 1902-47, bandleader
Machito (Frank Grillo), 1912-84, Latin percussion, singer, bandleader
Shelly Manne, 1920-84, drums, bandleader
Jackie McLean, 1931-2006, saxophone, composer
Jimmy McPartland, 1907-91, trumpet
Carmen McRae, 1920-94, singer
Glenn Miller, 1904-44, trombone, bandleader
Charles Mingus, 1922-79, bass, composer, bandleader
Thelonious Monk, 1917-82, piano, composer
Wes Montgomery, 1925-68, guitar
"Jelly Roll" Morton, 1885-1941, composer, piano
Bennie Moten, 1894-1935, piano, bandleader
Gerry Mulligan, 1927-96, baritone sax, composer
"Fats" Navarro, 1923-50, trumpet
Red Nichols, 1905-65, cornet, bandleader

Red Norvo, 1908-99, vibraphone, xylophone, bandleader
Anita O'Day, 1919-2006, singer
Arturo "Chico" O'Farrill, 1921-2001, Latin composer, arranger
King Oliver, 1885-1938, cornet, band leader
Sy Oliver, 1910-88, arranger, composer
Kid Ory, 1886-1973, trombone, bandleader
Oran "Hot Lips" Page, 1908-54, trumpet, singer
Charlie "Bird" Parker, 1920-55, alto sax, composer
Joe Pass, 1929-94, guitar
Art Pepper, 1925-82, alto sax
Oscar Peterson, 1925-2007, pianist
Oscar Pettiford, 1922-60, bass
Bud Powell, 1924-66, piano
Chano Pozo, 1915-48, Cuban percussion, singer
Louis Prima, 1911-78, singer, bandleader
Tito Puente, 1923-2000, Latin percussion, bandleader
Gertrude "Ma" Rainey, 1886-1939, blues singer
Lou Rawls, 1933- 2006, singer
Dewey Redman, 1931-2006, tenor saxophone
Don Redman, 1900-64, composer, arranger
Django Reinhardt, 1910-53, guitar
Buddy Rich, 1917-87, drums
Max Roach, 1924-2007, drummer, composer
Red Rodney, 1928-94, trumpet
Jimmy Rowles, 1918-96, piano
Jimmy Rushing, 1903-72, blues and jazz singer
Pee Wee Russell, 1906-69, clarinet
Artie Shaw, 1910-2004, swing-era bandleader, clarinet
Zoot Sims, 1925-85, tenor sax
Zutty Singleton, 1898-1975, drums
Bessie Smith, 1894-1937, blues singer
Clarence "Pinetop" Smith, 1904-29, piano, singer; boogie woogie pioneer
Willie "The Lion" Smith, 1897-1973, piano, composer

Muggsy Spanier, 1906-67, cornet
Sonny Stitt, 1924-82, tenor sax, alto sax
Billy Strayhorn, 1915-67, composer, piano; Duke Ellington collaborator
Sun Ra, 1915?-93, bandleader, piano, composer
Art Tatum, 1910-56, piano
Art Taylor, 1929-95, drums
Jack Teagarden, 1905-64, trombone, singer
Mel Tormé, 1925-99, singer ("the Velvet Fog")
Dave Tough, 1908-48, drums
Lennie Tristano, 1919-78, piano, composer
Joe Turner, 1911-85, blues singer
Sarah Vaughan, 1924-90, singer
Joe Venuti, 1904-78, violin
T-Bone Walker, 1910-75, blues guitar
Thomas "Fats" Waller, 1904-43, piano, singer, composer
Dinah Washington, 1924-63, singer
Grover Washington Jr., 1943-99, pop-jazz sax, composer
Ethel Waters, 1896-1977, jazz and blues singer
Muddy Waters, 1915-83, blues singer, songwriter
Julius Watkins, 1921-77, French horn
Chick Webb, 1902-39, bandleader, drums
Ben Webster, 1909-73, tenor sax
Junior Wells, 1934-98, blues singer, harmonica
Paul Whiteman, 1890-1967, bandleader
Charles "Cootie" Williams, 1910-85, trumpet, bandleader
Joe Williams, 1918-99, singer
Mary Lou Williams, 1910-81, piano, composer
Tony Williams, 1945-97, drums
John Lee "Sonny Boy" Williamson, 1914-48, blues singer, harmonica
Sonny Boy Williamson (Aleck "Rice" Miller), 1900?-65, blues singer, harmonica
Teddy Wilson, 1912-86, piano
Kai Winding, 1922-83, trombone
Jimmy Yancey, 1894-1951, piano
Lester "Pres" Young, 1909-59, tenor sax

Noted Country Music Artists of the Past and Present

Roy Acuff, 1903-92, fiddler, singer, songwriter; "Wabash Cannon Ball"
Alabama (Randy Owen, b 1949; Jeff Cook, b 1949; Teddy Gentry, b 1952; Mark Herndon, b 1955); "Feels So Right"
Eddy Arnold, 1918-2008, singer, guitarist, the "Tennessee Plowboy"
Chet Atkins, 1924-2001, guitarist, composer, producer, helped create the "Nashville sound"
Gene Autry, 1907-98, first great singing movie cowboy; "Back in the Saddle Again"
Garth Brooks, b 1962, singer, songwriter; "Friends in Low Places"
Brooks & Dunn (Kix Brooks, b 1955; Ronnie Dunn, b 1953); "Hard Workin' Man"
Boudleaux and Felice Bryant (Boudleaux, 1920-87; Felice, 1925-2003), songwriting team; "Hey Joe"
Mary Chapin Carpenter, b 1958, singer, songwriter; "I Feel Lucky"
Carter Family (original members, **"Mother" Maybelle**, 1909-78; **A. P.**, 1891-1960; **Sara**, 1898-1979); "Wildwood Flower"
Johnny Cash, 1932-2003, singer, songwriter; "I Walk the Line," "Ring of Fire," "Folsom Prison Blues"
Kenny Chesney, b 1968, guitar, singer, songwriter; "You Had Me from Hello"
Patsy Cline, 1932-63, singer; "Walkin' After Midnight," "Crazy," "Sweet Dreams"
John Denver, 1943-97, singer, songwriter; "Rocky Mountain High"
Dixie Chicks (Natalie Maines, b 1974; Martie Seidel, b 1969; Emily Erwin Robison, b 1972); "Wide Open Spaces"
Dale Evans (Lucille Wood Smith), 1912-2001, singer, actress, married Roy Rogers

Flatt & Scruggs (Lester Flatt, 1914-79; Earl Scruggs, b 1924), guitar-banjo duo and soloists; "Foggy Mountain Breakdown"
Red Foley, 1910-68, singer; "Chattanoogie Shoe Shine Boy"
Tennessee Ernie Ford, 1919-91, singer, TV host; "Sixteen Tons"
Lefty Frizzell, 1928-75, singer, guitarist; "Long Black Veil"
Vince Gill, b 1957, singer, songwriter; "When I Call Your Name"
Merle Haggard, b 1937, singer, songwriter; "Okie from Muskogee"
Emmylou Harris, b 1947, singer, songwriter, folk-country crossover artist; "If I Could Only Win Your Love"
Faith Hill, b 1967, singer, songwriter, married Tim McGraw; "Breathe"
Alan Jackson, b 1958, singer, songwriter, "Where Were You (When the World Stopped Turning)"
Waylon Jennings, 1937-2002, singer, songwriter; "outlaw country" pioneer; "Luckenbach, Texas"
George Jones, b 1931, singer; "He Stopped Loving Her Today"
The Judds (Naomi, 1946- ; Wynonna, 1964-), mother-daughter duo; Wynonna also a solo act
Toby Keith, b 1961, singer, songwriter, guitarist; "Should've Been a Cowboy"
Alison Krauss, b 1971, bluegrass fiddler, singer, bandleader; "When You Say Nothing at All"
Kris Kristofferson, b 1936, singer, songwriter, actor; "Me and Bobby McGee"
Patty Loveless, b 1957, singer, songwriter; "How Can I Help You Say Goodbye"
Lyle Lovett, b 1957, singer, songwriter, bandleader, actor; "Cowboy Man"

Loretta Lynn, b 1935, singer, songwriter; "Coal Miner's Daughter"
Kathy Mattea, b 1959, singer, songwriter; "Eighteen Wheels and a Dozen Roses"
Martina McBride, b 1966, singer, songwriter; "Independence Day"
Reba McEntire, b 1955, singer, songwriter, actress; "Whoever's in New England"
Tim McGraw, b 1967, singer; "It's Your Love," with wife, Faith Hill
Roger Miller, 1936-92, singer, songwriter; "King of the Road"
Ronnie Milsap, b 1944, singer, songwriter; "There's No Gettin' Over Me"
Bill Monroe, 1911-96, singer, songwriter, mandolin player, "father of bluegrass music"; "Mule Skinner Blues"
Willie Nelson, b 1933, singer, songwriter, actor; "On the Road Again"
Mark O'Connor, b 1961, fiddler, country-classical crossover composer
Brad Paisley, b 1972, singer, songwriter; "Whiskey Lullaby," "When I Get Where I'm Going"
Dolly Parton, b 1946, singer, songwriter, actress; "Dollywood" theme park; "Here You Come Again," "9 to 5"
Minnie Pearl, 1912-96, comedienne, Grand Ole Opry star
Charley Pride, b 1938, singer, 1st African American country star; "Kiss an Angel Good Mornin'"
Rascal Flatts (Jay DeMarcus, b 1971; Gary LeVox, b 1970; Joe Don Rooney, b 1975); "Life Is A Highway"
Jim Reeves, 1923-64, singer, songwriter; "Four Walls"
Charlie Rich, 1932-95, singer, songwriter called the "Silver Fox"; "The Most Beautiful Girl"

LeAnn Rimes, b 1982, singer; "Blue"
Tex Ritter, 1905-74, singer, songwriter; "Jingle, Jangle, Jingle"
Marty Robbins, 1925-82, singer, songwriter; "A White Sport Coat and a Pink Carnation"
Jimmie Rodgers, 1897-1933, singer, songwriter; "T for Texas"
Kenny Rogers, b 1938, singer, songwriter; "The Gambler"
Roy Rogers (Leonard Slye), 1911-98, singer, actor, "King of the Cowboys," sang with Sons of the Pioneers.
Fred Rose, 1898-1954, songwriter, singer, producer; "Blue Eyes Cryin' in the Rain"
Ricky Skaggs, b 1954, singer, songwriter, bandleader; "Don't Cheat in Our Hometown"
Ralph Stanley, b 1927, singer, banjo player; "Man of Constant Sorrow"

George Strait, b 1952, singer, bandleader; "Ace in the Hole"
Sugarland (Kristian Bush, b 1970; Jennifer Nettles, b 1974); "Stay"
Taylor Swift, b 1989, singer; "You Belong With Me"
Merle Travis, 1917-83, singer, guitarist, songwriter; "Divorce Me C.O.D."
Randy Travis, b 1959, singer, songwriter; "Forever and Ever, Amen"
Ernest Tubb, 1914-84, singer, songwriter, guitarist; "Walking the Floor Over You"
Shania Twain, b 1965, singer, songwriter; "You're Still the One"
Conway Twitty, 1933-93, singer, songwriter; "Hello Darlin'"
Carrie Underwood, b 1983, singer, American Idol winner
Keith Urban, b 1967, guitar, singer, songwriter; "It's a Love Thing"

Dottie West, 1932-91, singer, songwriter; "Here Comes My Baby"
Hank Williams Jr., b 1949, singer, songwriter; "Bocephus"; "All My Rowdy Friends (Have Settled Down)"
Hank Williams Sr., 1923-53, singer, songwriter; "Your Cheatin' Heart"
Bob Wills, 1905-75, Western Swing fiddler, singer, bandleader, songwriter; "New San Antonio Rose"
Lee Ann Womack, b 1966, singer, songwriter; "I Hope You Dance"
Tammy Wynette, 1942-98, singer; "Stand By Your Man"
Trisha Yearwood, b 1964, singer, songwriter; "How Do I Live"
Dwight Yoakam, b 1957, singer, songwriter, actor; "Ain't That Lonely Yet"

Dance Figures of the Past

Alvin Ailey, 1931-89, (U.S.) modern dancer, choreographer; melded modern dance and Afro-Caribbean techniques.
Frederick Ashton, 1904-88, (Br.) ballet choreographer; director of Great Britain's Royal Ballet, 1963-70.
Fred Astaire, 1899-1987, (U.S.) dancer, actor; teamed with dancer/actress **Ginger Rogers**, 1911-95, (U.S.) in movie musicals.
George Balanchine, 1904-83, (Russ.-U.S.) ballet choreographer, teacher; most influential exponent of neoclassical style; founded, with Lincoln Kirstein, School of American Ballet and New York City Ballet.
Carlo Blasis, 1803-78, (It.) ballet dancer, choreographer, writer; his teaching methods are standards of classical dance.
August Bournonville, 1805-79, (Dan.) ballet dancer, choreographer, teacher; exuberant, light style.
Fernando Bujones, 1955-2005, (Cuba-U.S.) ballet dancer.
Gisella Caccialanza, 1914-97, (U.S.) ballerina, charter member of Balanchine's American Ballet.
Irene and **Vernon Castle** (Irene, 1893-1969; Vernon, 1887-1918), husband-and-wife ballroom dancers.
Enrico Cecchetti, 1850-1928, (It.) ballet dancer, leading dancer of Russia's Imperial Ballet; his technique was basis for Britain's Imperial Soc. of Teachers of Dancing.
Gower Champion, 1921-80, (U.S.) dancer, choreographer, director; with his wife **Marge**, b 1923, (U.S.) choreographed, danced in Broadway musicals and films.
John Cranko, 1927-73, (S. African) choreographer; created narrative ballets based on literary works.
Merce Cunningham, 1919-2009, (U.S.) dancer, choreographer of avant-garde dance.
Agnes de Mille, 1909-93, (U.S.) ballerina, choreographer; known for using American themes, she choreographed the ballet *Rodeo* and the musical *Oklahoma!*
Alexandra Danilova, 1903-97, (Russ.) ballerina; noted teacher at the School of American Ballet.
Dame Ninette DeValois, 1898-2001, (Br.) choreographer, founding director London's Royal Ballet; *The Rake's Progress*.
Sergei Diaghilev, 1872-1929, (Russ.) impresario; founded Les Ballet Russes; saw ballet as an art unifying dance, drama, music, and decor.
Isadora Duncan, 1877-1927, (U.S.) expressive dancer who united free movement with serious music; one of the founders of modern dance.
Katherine Dunham, 1910-2006, (U.S.) dancer, choreographer; internationally known for African, Caribbean, and Afri can American dance forms.

Fanny Elssler, 1810-84, (Austrian) ballerina of the Romantic era; known for dramatic skill, sensual style.
Michel Fokine, 1880-1942, (Russ.) ballet dancer, choreographer, teacher; rejected strict classicism in favor of dramatically expressive style.
Margot Fonteyn, 1919-91, (Br.) prima ballerina, Royal Ballet of Great Britain; famed performance partner of Rudolf Nureyev.
Bob Fosse, 1927-87, (U.S.) jazz dancer, choreographer, director; Broadway musicals and film.
Serge Golovine, 1924-98, (Fr.) ballet dancer with Grand Ballet du Marquis de Cuevas; choreographer.
Martha Graham, 1893-1991, (U.S.) modern dancer, choreographer; created and codified her own dramatic technique.
Melissa Hayden, 1923-2006, (Canada) ballet dancer.
Martha Hill, 1901-95, (U.S.) educator; leading figure in modern dance; founded American Dance Festival.
Gregory Hines, 1946-2003, (U.S.) tap-dance innovator and master of improvisation.
Doris Humphrey, 1895-1958, (U.S.) modern dancer, choreographer, writer, teacher.
Michael Jackson, 1958-2009, (U.S.) singer and dancer who perfected the "moonwalk."
Robert Joffrey, 1930-88, (U.S.) ballet dancer, choreographer; cofounded with **Gerald Arpino**, b 1928, (U.S.), the Joffrey Ballet.
Kurt Jooss, 1901-79, (Ger.) choreographer, teacher; created expressionist works using modern and classical techniques.
Tamara Karsavina, 1885-1978, (Russ.) prima ballerina of Russia's Imperial Ballet and Diaghilev's Ballets Russes; partner of Nijinsky.
Nora Kaye, 1920-87, (U.S.) ballerina with Metropolitan Opera Ballet and Ballet Theater (now American Ballet Theatre).
Lincoln Kirstein, 1907-96 (U.S.) brought ballet as an art form to U.S.; founded, with George Balanchine, School of American Ballet and New York City Ballet.
Serge Lifar, 1905-86, (Russ.-Fr.) prem. danseur, choreographer; director of dance at Paris Opera, 1930-45, 1947-58.
José Limón, 1908-72, (Mex.-U.S.) modern dancer, choreographer, teacher; developed technique based on Humphrey.
Catherine Littlefield, 1908-51, (U.S.) ballerina, choreographer, teacher; pioneer of American ballet.
Alicia Markova, 1910-2004, (Br.), ballet dancer.
Léonide Massine, 1896-1979, (Russ.-U.S.) ballet dancer, choreographer; known for his "symphonic ballet."
Kenneth MacMillan, 1929-92, (Br.) dancer, choreographer; directed Royal Ballet of Great Britain 1970-77.

Dame Alicia Markova, 1910-2004, (Br.) ballerina; helped popularize ballet in U.S. and Britain; known for title role in *Giselle*.
Fayard Nicholas, 1914-2006, (U.S.) tap dancer, choreographer, actor; together with brother **Harold Nicholas**, 1921-2000, (U.S.) formed the "Nicholas Brothers."
Vaslav Nijinsky, 1890-50, (Russ.) prem. danseur, choreographer; leading member of Diaghilev's Ballets Russes; his ballets were revolutionary for their time.
Alwin Nikolais, 1910-93, (U.S.) modern choreographer; created dance theater utilizing mixed media effects.
Jean-George Noverre, 1727-1810, (Fr.) ballet choreographer, teacher, writer; "Shakespeare of the Dance."
Rudolf Nureyev, 1938-93, (Russ.) prem. danseur, choreographer; leading male dancer of his generation; director of dance at Paris Opera, 1983-89.
Ruth Page, 1903-91, (U.S.) ballerina, choreographer; danced and directed ballet at Chicago Lyric Opera.
Anna Pavlova, 1881-1931, (Russ.) prima ballerina; toured with her own company to world acclaim.
Marius Petipa, 1818-1910, (Fr.) ballet dancer, choreographer; ballet master of the Imperial Ballet; established Russian classicism as leading style of late 19th cent.
Pearl Primus, 1919-95, (Trinidad-U.S.) modern dancer, choreographer, scholar; combined African, Caribbean, and African American styles.
Jerome Robbins, 1918-98, (U.S.) choreographer, director, dancer; *The King and I, West Side Story, Fiddler on the Roof*.
Bill (Bojangles) Robinson, 1878-1949, (U.S.) famed tap dancer; called King of Tapology on stage and screen.
Ruth St. Denis, 1877-1968, (U.S.) influential interpretive dancer, choreographer, teacher.
Ted Shawn, 1891-1972, (U.S.) modern dancer, choreographer; formed dance company and school with Ruth St. Denis; established Jacob's Pillow Dance Festival.
Marie Taglioni, 1804-84, (It.) ballerina, teacher; in title role of *La Sylphide* established image of the ethereal ballerina.
Glen Tetley, 1926-2007, (U.S.) dancer, choreographer, ballet director; fused elements of modern dance with ballet.
Antony Tudor, 1908-87, (Br.) choreographer, teacher; exponent of the "psychological ballet."
Galina Ulanova, 1910-98, (Russ.) revered ballerina with Bolshoi Ballet.
Agrippina Vaganova, 1879-1951, (Russ.) ballet teacher, director; codified Soviet ballet technique that developed virtuosity; called "queen of variations."
Mary Wigman, 1886-1973, (Ger.) modern dancer, choreographer, teacher; influenced European expressionist dance.

Opera Singers of the Past

Frances Alda, 1883-1952, (N.Z.) soprano
Pasquale Amato, 1878-1942, (It.) baritone
Marian Anderson, 1897-1993, (U.S.) contralto
Jussi Björling, 1911-60, (Swed.) tenor
Lucrezia Bori, 1887-1960, (It.) soprano
Maria Callas, 1923-77, (U.S.) soprano
Emma Calvé, 1858-1942, (Fr.) soprano
Enrico Caruso, 1873-1921, (It.) tenor
Feodor Chaliapin, 1873-1938, (Russ.) bass
Boris Christoff, 1914-93, (Bulg.) bass
Franco Corelli, 1921-2003, (It.) tenor
Victoria De Los Angeles, 1923-2005, (Sp.) soprano
Giuseppe De Luca, 1876-1950, (It.) baritone
Fernando De Lucia, 1860-1925, (It.) tenor
Edouard De Reszke, 1853-1917, (Pol.) bass
Jean De Reszke, 1850-1925, (Pol.) tenor
Emmy Destinn, 1878-1930, (Czech.) soprano
Emma Eames, 1865-1952, (U.S.) soprano
(Carlo Broschi) Farinelli, 1705-82, (It.) castrato
Geraldine Farrar, 1882-1967, (U.S.) soprano
Eileen Farrell, 1920-2002, (U.S.) soprano
Kathleen Ferrier, 1912-53, (Eng.) contralto
Kirsten Flagstad, 1895-1962, (Nor.) soprano
Olive Fremstad, 1871-1951, (Swed.-U.S.) soprano
Amelita Galli-Curci, 1882-1963, (It.) soprano
Mary Garden, 1874-1967, (Br.) soprano

Nicolai Ghiaurov, 1929-2004, (Bulg.) bass
Beniamino Gigli, 1890-1957, (It.) tenor
Tito Gobbi, 1913-84, (It.) baritone
Giulia Grisi, 1811-69, (It.) soprano
Frieda Hempel, 1885-1955, (Ger.) soprano
Jerome Hines, 1921-2003, (U.S.) bass
Hans Hotter, 1909-2003, (Ger.) bass-baritone
Maria Jeritza, 1887-1982, (Czech.) soprano
Alexander Kipnis, 1891-1978, (Russ.-U.S.) bass
Dorothy Kirsten, 1910-92, (U.S.) soprano
Alfredo Kraus, 1927-99, (Sp.) tenor
Luigi Lablache, 1794-1858, (It.) bass
Lilli Lehmann, 1848-1929, (Ger.) soprano
Lotte Lehmann, 1888-1976, (Ger.-U.S.) soprano
Jenny Lind, 1820-87, (Swed.) soprano
Maria Malibran, 1808-36, (Sp.) mezzo-soprano
Giovanni Martinelli, 1885-1969, (It.) tenor
John McCormack, 1884-1945, (Ir.) tenor
Nellie Melba, 1861-1931, (Austral.) soprano.
Lauritz Melchior, 1890-1973, (Dan.) tenor
Robert Merrill, 1919-2004, (U.S.) baritone
Zinka Milanov, 1906-89, (Yugo.) soprano
Birgit Nilsson, 1918-2005, (Swed.) soprano
Lillian Nordica, 1857-1914, (U.S.) soprano
Giuditta Pasta, 1797-1865, (It.) soprano
Adelina Patti, 1843-1919, (It.) soprano
Luciano Pavarotti, 1934-2007, (It.) tenor
Peter Pears, 1910-86, (Eng.) tenor
Jan Peerce, 1904-84, (U.S.) tenor

Ezio Pinza, 1892-1957, (It.) bass
Lily Pons, 1898-1976, (Fr.) soprano
Rosa Ponselle, 1897-1981, (U.S.) soprano
Hermann Prey, 1929-98, (Ger.) baritone.
Elisabeth Rethberg, 1894-1976, (Ger.) soprano
Giovanni Battista Rubini, 1794-1854, (It.) tenor
Leonie Rysanek, 1926-98, (Austrian) soprano
Bidú Sayão, 1902-99, (Braz.) soprano
Friedrich Schorr, 1888-1953, (Hung.) bass-baritone
Elisabeth Schwarzkopf, 1915-2006, (Ger.) soprano
Marcella Sembrich, 1858-1935, (Pol.) soprano
Beverly Sills, 1929-2007, (U.S.) soprano
Eleanor Steber, 1916-90, (U.S.) soprano
Ferrucio Tagliavini, 1913-95, (It.) tenor
Renata Tebaldi, 1922-2004 (It.) soprano
Luisa Tetrazzini, 1871-1940, (It.) soprano
Lawrence Tibbett, 1896-1960, (U.S.) baritone
Tatiana Troyanos, 1938-93, (U.S.) mezzo-soprano
Richard Tucker, 1913-75, (U.S.) tenor
Pauline Viardot, 1821-1910, (Fr.) mezzo-soprano
William Warfield, 1920-2002, (U.S.) bass-baritone
Leonard Warren, 1911-60, (U.S.) baritone
Ljuba Welitsch, 1913-96, (Bulg.) soprano
Wolfgang Windgassen, 1914-74, (Ger.) tenor

Selected Rock and Roll, Rhythm and Blues, Rap Artists

Titles in quotation marks are singles; others are albums. *Inducted into Rock and Roll Hall of Fame as performer between 1986 and 2009; year is in parentheses.

Aaliyah: "More than a Woman"
Paula Abdul: "Straight Up"
*****AC/DC (2003):** "Back in Black"
Bryan Adams: "Cuts Like a Knife"
*****Aerosmith (2001):** "Sweet Emotion"
Christina Aguilera: "What a Girl Wants"
Alice In Chains: "Heaven Beside You"
*****The Allman Brothers Band (1995):** "Ramblin' Man"
*****The Animals (1994):** "House of the Rising Sun"
Paul Anka: "Lonely Boy"
Fiona Apple: "Criminal"
Ashanti: "Foolish"
Frankie Avalon: "Venus"
The B-52s: "Love Shack"
Bachman Turner Overdrive: "Takin' Care of Business"
Backstreet Boys: "I Want it That Way"
Bad Company: "Can't Get Enough"
Erykah Badu: "On and On"
*****La Vern Baker (1991):** "I Cried a Tear"
*****Hank Ballard[1] and the Midnighters (1990):** "Work With Me, Annie"
*****The Band (1994):** "The Weight"
Barenaked Ladies: "One Week"
*****The Beach Boys (1988):** "Good Vibrations"
Beastie Boys: "(You Gotta) Fight for Your Right (to Party)"
*****The Beatles (1988):** *Sgt. Pepper's Lonely Hearts Club Band*
Beck: "Loser"
*****Jeff Beck (2009):** "Escape"
*****The Bee Gees (1997):** "Stayin' Alive"
Pat Benatar: "Hit Me With Your Best Shot"
Beyoncé: "Crazy in Love"
Ben Folds Five: "Brick"
*****Chuck Berry (1986):** "Johnny B. Goode"
The Big Bopper: "Chantilly Lace"
Björk: "Human Behavior"
The Black Crowes: "Hard to Handle"
Black Eyed Peas: *Elephunk*
*****Black Sabbath (2006):** "Paranoid"
*****Bobby "Blue" Bland (1992):** "Turn On Your Love Light"
Mary J. Blige: *My Life*
Blind Faith: "Can't Find My Way Home"

Blink-182: "All the Small Things"
*****Blondie (2006):** "Heart of Glass"
Blood, Sweat, and Tears: "Spinning Wheel"
Blues Traveler: "Run-Around"
Gary "U.S." Bonds: "Quarter to Three"
Bon Jovi: "Livin' on a Prayer"
*****Booker T. and the M.G.'s (1992):** "Green Onions"
Earl Bostic: "Flamingo"
Boston: "More Than A Feeling"
*****David Bowie (1996):** "Space Oddity"
Boyz II Men: "I'll Make Love to You"
Toni Braxton: "Un-Break My Heart"
*****James Brown (1986):** "Papa's Got a Brand New Bag"
*****Ruth Brown (1993):** "Lucky Lips"
*****Jackson Browne (2004):** "Doctor My Eyes"
*****Buffalo Springfield (1997):** "For What It's Worth"
Jimmy Buffett: "Margaritaville"
*****Solomon Burke (2001):** "Over and Over (Huggin' and Lovin')"
Bush: "Glycerine"
*****The Byrds (1991):** "Turn! Turn! Turn!"
Mariah Carey: "Vision of Love"
The Carpenters: "(They Long to Be) Close to You"
The Cars: "Shake It Up"
*****Johnny Cash (1992):** "I Walk the Line"
*****Ray Charles (1986):** "Georgia on My Mind"
Cheap Trick: "Surrender"
Chicago: "Saturday in the Park"
Chubby Checker: "The Twist"
*****Eric Clapton (2000):** "Layla"
Kelly Clarkson: "Since U Been Gone"
*****The Clash (2003):** "Rock the Casbah"
*****The Coasters (1987):** "Yakety Yak"
*****Eddie Cochran (1987):** "Summertime Blues"
Joe Cocker: "With a Little Help From My Friends"
Coldplay: "Clocks"
*****Leonard Cohen (2008):** "Suzanne"
Collective Soul: "The World I Know"
Phil Collins: "Against All Odds"
*****Sam Cooke (1986):** "You Send Me"

Coolio: "Gangsta's Paradise"
Alice Cooper: "School's Out"
*****Elvis Costello and the Attractions (2003):** "Alison"
Counting Crows: "Mr. Jones"
*****Cream (1993):** "Sunshine of Your Love"
Creed: "Arms Wide Open"
*****Creedence Clearwater Revival (1993):** "Proud Mary"
*****Crosby, Stills, and Nash (1997):** "Suite: Judy Blue Eyes"
Sheryl Crow: "All I Want to Do"
The Crystals: "Da Doo Ron Ron"
The Cure: "Boys Don't Cry"
Cypress Hill: "Insane in the Brain"
Danny and the Juniors: "At the Hop"
*****Bobby Darin (1990):** "Splish Splash"
*****The Dave Clark Five (2008):** "Glad All Over"
*****Miles Davis (2006):** *Bitches Brew*
Spencer Davis Group: "Gimme Some Lovin' "
Daughtry: "It's Not Over"
Deep Purple: "Smoke on the Water"
Def Leppard: "Photograph"
*****The Dells (2004):** "Oh, What a Night"
Depeche Mode: "Strange Love"
Destiny's Child: "Survivor"
*****Bo Diddley (1987):** "Who Do You Love?"
*****Dion[1] and the Belmonts (1989):** "A Teenager in Love"
Celine Dion: "Because You Loved Me"
Dire Straits: "Money for Nothing"
DMX: "What's My Name"
*****Fats Domino (1986):** "Blueberry Hill"
Donovan: "Mellow Yellow"
The Doobie Brothers: "What a Fool Believes"
*****The Doors (1993):** "Light My Fire"
Dr. Dre: "Nothin' But a 'G' Thang"
*****The Drifters (1988):** "Save the Last Dance for Me"
Duran Duran: "Hungry Like the Wolf"
*****Bob Dylan (1988):** "Like a Rolling Stone"
*****The Eagles (1998):** "Hotel California"
*****Earth, Wind, and Fire (2000):** "Shining Star"
*****Duane Eddy (1994):** "Rebel-Rouser"

Missy Elliott: "Sock It 2 Me"
Eminem: "The Real Slim Shady"
En Vogue: "Hold On"
The Eurythmics: "Sweet Dreams (Are Made of This)"
Everclear: "Father Of Mine"
***The Everly Brothers (1986):** "Wake Up, Little Susie"
50 Cent (Curtis Jackson): *Get Rich Or Die Tryin'*
The Five Satins: "In the Still of the Night"
***The Flamingos (2001):** "I Only Have Eyes for You"
***Fleetwood Mac (1998):** *Rumours*
The Foo Fighters: "I'll Stick Around"
Foreigner: "Double Vision"
***The Four Seasons (1990):** "Sherry"
***The Four Tops (1990):** "I Can't Help Myself (Sugar Pie, Honey Bunch)"
***Aretha Franklin (1987):** "Respect"
Nelly Furtado: "I'm Like a Bird"
Peter Gabriel: "Shock the Monkey"
***Gamble (Kenny) and Huff (Leon) (2008):** "If You Don't Know Me By Now"
***Marvin Gaye (1987):** "I Heard It Through the Grapevine"
Genesis: "No Reply at All"
Goo Goo Dolls: "Iris"
Grand Funk Railroad: "We're an American Band"
***Grandmaster Flash and the Furious Five (2007):** "The Message"
***The Grateful Dead (1994):** "Uncle John's Band"
***Al Green (1995):** "Let's Stay Together"
Green Day: "Boulevard of Broken Dreams"
The Guess Who: "American Woman"
Guns N' Roses: "Sweet Child o' Mine"
***Buddy Guy (2005):** *A Man and His Blues*
***Bill Haley[1] and His Comets (1987):** "Rock Around the Clock"
Hall and Oates: "Kiss on My List"
Hanson: "MMMBop"
***Isaac Hayes (2002):** "Theme from 'Shaft'"
Heart: "Barracuda"
***Jimi Hendrix (1992):** "Purple Haze"
Lauryn Hill: "Doo-Wop (That Thing)"
Hole: "Doll Parts"
The Hollies: "Long Cool Woman (In a Black Dress)"
***Buddy Holly (1986):** "Peggy Sue"
***John Lee Hooker (1991):** "Boogie Chillen"
Hootie and the Blowfish: *Cracked Rear View*
Whitney Houston: "I Will Always Love You"
***The Impressions (1991):** "For Your Precious Love"
Indigo Girls: "Closer to Fine"
INXS: "Need You Tonight"
***The Isley Brothers (1992):** "It's Your Thing"
***The Jackson Five (1997):** "ABC"
Janet Jackson: *Rhythm Nation*
***Michael Jackson (2001):** *Thriller*
***Etta James (1993):** "At Last"
Tommy James & The Shondells: "Crimson and Clover"
Jane's Addiction: "Jane Says"
Ja Rule: *Venni, Vetti, Vecci*
Jay and the Americans: "This Magic Moment"
Jay-Z: "Can I Live"
***Jefferson Airplane (1996):** "White Rabbit"
Jethro Tull: *Aqualung*
Joan Jett: "I Love Rock 'n' Roll"
Jewel: "You Were Meant for Me"
***Billy Joel (1999):** "Piano Man"
***Elton John (1994):** "Candle in the Wind"
***Little Willie John (1996):** "Sleep"
Norah Jones: *Come Away With Me*
***Janis Joplin (1995):** "Me and Bobby McGee"
Journey: "Don't Stop Believin'"
K.C. and the Sunshine Band: "Get Down Tonight"
R. Kelly: "I Can't Sleep Baby (If I)"
Alicia Keys: "Fallin'"
Kid Rock: "Cowboy"
***B.B. King (1987):** "The Thrill Is Gone"
Carole King: *Tapestry*

***The Kinks (1990):** "You Really Got Me"
Kiss: "Rock 'n' Roll All Night"
***Gladys Knight and the Pips (1996):** "Midnight Train to Georgia"
Korn: "Blind"
Lenny Kravitz: "Are You Gonna Go My Way?"
***Led Zeppelin (1995):** "Stairway to Heaven"
***Brenda Lee (2002):** "I'm Sorry"
John Legend: "Ordinary People"
***John Lennon (1994):** "Imagine"
***Jerry Lee Lewis (1986):** "Whole Lotta Shakin' Going On"
Lil' Kim: "No Matter What They Say"
Limp Bizkit: "Break Stuff"
Linkin Park: "One Step Closer"
***Little Anthony and the Imperials (2009):** "Tears on My Pillow"
***Little Richard (1986):** "Tutti Frutti"
***Little Walter (2008):** "Juke"
Live: "Lightning Crashes"
L. L. Cool J: "Mama Said Knock You Out"
Jennifer Lopez: "Love Don't Cost a Thing"
***The Lovin' Spoonful (2000):** "Summer in the City"
Ludacris: "Money Maker"
***Frankie Lymon and the Teenagers (1993):** "Why Do Fools Fall in Love?"
***Lynyrd Skynyrd (2006):** "Free Bird"
***Madonna (2008):** "Material Girl"
Taj Mahal: "Going up to the Country, Paint My Mailbox Blue"
***The Mamas and the Papas (1998):** "Monday, Monday"
Aimee Mann: "Save Me"
Marilyn Manson: "Beautiful People"
***Bob Marley (1994):** *Exodus*
Maroon 5: *Songs About Jane*
***Martha and the Vandellas (1995):** "Dancin' in the Streets"
The Marvelettes: "Please, Mr. Postman"
Matchbox 20: "Push"
Dave Matthews Band: "Don't Drink the Water"
John Mayer: "Daughters"
***Curtis Mayfield (1999):** "Superfly"
***Paul McCartney (1999):** "Band on the Run"
Don McLean: "American Pie"
***Clyde McPhatter (1987):** "A Lover's Question"
Meat Loaf: "Paradise by the Dashboard Light"
***John (Cougar) Mellencamp (2008):** "Jack and Diane"
Men at Work: "Who Can It Be Now?"
***Metallica (2009):** "Enter Sandman"
George Michael: "Faith"
***Joni Mitchell (1997):** "Both Sides Now"
Moby: "Bodyrock"
The Monkees: "I'm a Believer"
Moody Blues: "Nights in White Satin"
***The Moonglows (2000):** "Blue Velvet"
Alanis Morissette: "Ironic"
***Van Morrison (1993):** "Brown-Eyed Girl"
Jason Mraz: "I'm Yours"
Nelly: *Country Grammar*
***Ricky Nelson (1987):** "Hello, Mary Lou"
Nine Inch Nails: "Closer"
Nirvana: *Nevermind*
No Doubt: *Rock Steady*
The Notorious B.I.G.: "Mo Money Mo Problems"
'N Sync: "Bye, Bye, Bye"
Oasis: "Wonderwall"
The Offspring: "Pretty Fly (for a White Guy)"
***The O'Jays (2005):** "Back Stabbers"
***Roy Orbison (1987):** "Oh, Pretty Woman"
OutKast: *Speakerboxxx/The Love Below*
Ozzy Osbourne: "Crazy Train"
***Parliament/Funkadelic (1997):** "One Nation Under a Groove"
Pearl Jam: "Jeremy"
***Carl Perkins (1987):** "Blue Suede Shoes"
Katy Perry: "I Kissed A Girl"
Peter, Paul, and Mary: "Leaving on a Jet Plane"
***Tom Petty and the Heartbreakers (2002):** "Refugee"
Liz Phair: *Exile in Guyville*
Phish: "Sample in a Jar"

***Wilson Pickett (1991):** "Land of 1,000 Dances"
Pink: *Missundaztood!*
***Pink Floyd (1996):** *The Wall*
***Gene Pitney (2002):** "Only Love Can Break a Heart"
***The Platters (1990):** "The Great Pretender"
***The Police (2003):** "Every Breath You Take"
Iggy Pop: "Lust for Life"
***Elvis Presley (1986):** "Love Me Tender"
***The Pretenders (2005):** "Back on the Chain Gang"
***Lloyd Price (1998):** "Stagger Lee"
***Prince (The Artist) (2004):** "Purple Rain"
Public Enemy: "Fight the Power"
Puff Daddy and the Family: *No Way Out*
***Queen (2001):** "Bohemian Rhapsody"
Radiohead: *OK Computer*
Rage Against the Machine: "Bulls on Parade"
***Bonnie Raitt (2000):** "Something to Talk About"
***The Ramones (2002):** "I Wanna Be Sedated"
***Otis Redding (1989):** "(Sittin' on) the Dock of the Bay"
Red Hot Chili Peppers: "Under the Bridge"
***Jimmy Reed (1991):** "Ain't That Loving You, Baby?"
Lou Reed: "Walk on the Wild Side"
***R.E.M. (2007):** "Losing My Religion"
REO Speedwagon: "Can't Fight This Feeling"
Busta Rhymes: "What's It Gonna Be?"
***The Righteous Brothers (2003):** "You've Lost That Lovin' Feelin'"
Johnny Rivers: "Poor Side of Town"
***Smokey Robinson[1] and the Miracles (1987):** "Shop Around"
***The Rolling Stones (1989):** "Satisfaction"
***The Ronettes (2007):** "Be My Baby"
Linda Ronstadt: "You're No Good"
***Run-D.M.C. (2009):** "Raisin' Hell"
Rush: "Tom Sawyer"
Sade: "Smooth Operator"
Salt-N-Pepa: "Shoop"
***Sam and Dave (1992):** "Soul Man"
***Santana (1998):** "Black Magic Woman"
Seal: "Kiss From a Rose"
Neil Sedaka: "Breaking Up Is Hard to Do"
***Bob Seger (2004):** "Old Time Rock & Roll"
***Sex Pistols (2006):** "Anarchy in the U.K."
Shaggy: "It Wasn't Me"
Shakira: "Whenever, Wherever"
Tupac Shakur: "How Do U Want It"
***Del Shannon (1999):** "Runaway"
***The Shirelles (1996):** "Soldier Boy"
Carly Simon: "You're So Vain"
***Paul Simon (2001):** "50 Ways to Leave Your Lover"
***Simon and Garfunkel (1990):** "Bridge Over Troubled Water"
***Percy Sledge (2005):** "When a Man Loves a Woman"
***Sly and the Family Stone (1993):** "Everyday People"
Smashing Pumpkins: "Today"
***Patti Smith (2007):** "Because the Night"
Will Smith: "Gettin' Jiggy With It"
The Smiths: "This Charming Man"
Snoop Dogg: "Gin and Juice"
Sonic Youth: "Bull in the Heather"
Soundgarden: "Black Hole Sun"
Britney Spears: "Hit Me Baby One More Time"
Spice Girls: "Wannabe"
***Dusty Springfield (1999):** "I Only Want to Be With You"
***Bruce Springsteen (1999):** "Born to Run"
Squeeze: "Tempted"
***Staple Singers (1999):** "I'll Take You There"
***Steely Dan (2001):** "Rikki Don't Lose That Number"
Gwen Stefani: "Hollaback Girl"
Steppenwolf: "Born to Be Wild"
***Rod Stewart (1994):** "Maggie Mae"

Sting: "If You Love Somebody, Set Them Free"
Stone Temple Pilots: "Plush"
Styx: "Come Sail Away"
Sublime: "What I Got"
The Sugar Hill Gang: "Rapper's Delight"
Donna Summer: "Bad Girls"
***The Supremes (1988):** "Stop! In the Name of Love"
***Talking Heads (2002):** "Once in a Life-time"
***James Taylor (2001):** "You've Got a Friend"
***The Temptations (1989):** "My Girl"
Three Dog Night: "Joy to the World"
Justin Timberlake: "SexyBack"
TLC: "Waterfalls"
T. Rex: "Bang a Gong (Get It On)"
***Traffic (2004):** *Traffic*
***Big Joe Turner (1987):** "Shake, Rattle & Roll"

***Ike and Tina Turner (1991):** "Proud Mary"
***Tina Turner:** "What's Love Got to Do With It?"
The Turtles: "Happy Together"
***U2 (2005):** "With or Without You"
Usher: "You Make Me Wanna"
***Ritchie Valens (2001):** "La Bamba"
***Van Halen (2007):** "Running With the Devil"
Stevie Ray Vaughan: "Crossfire"
***The Velvet Underground (1996):** "Sweet Jane"
***The Ventures (2008):** "Walk, Don't Run"
***Gene Vincent (1998):** "Be-Bop-A-Lula"
Tom Waits: "Downtown Train"
The Wallflowers: "One Headlight"
Dionne Warwick: "I Say a Little Prayer"
***Muddy Waters (1987):** "I Can't Be Satisfied"
Mary Wells: "My Guy"
Kanye West: "Gold Digger"
The White Stripes: "Seven Nation Army"

***The Who (1990):** *Tommy*
Lucinda Williams: *Car Wheels on a Gravel Road*
***Jackie Wilson (1987):** "That's Why"
***Bobby Womack (2009):** "Lookin for a Love"
***Stevie Wonder (1989):** "You Are the Sun-shine of My Life"
Wu-Tang Clan: "Protect Ya Neck"
Weird Al Yankovic: *Dare to Be Stupid*
***The Yardbirds (1992):** "For Your Love"
Yes: "Roundabout"
***Neil Young (1995):** "Down by the River"
***The Young Rascals/The Rascals (1997):** "Good Lovin' "
***Frank Zappa[1]/Mothers of Invention (1995):** *Hot Rats*
John Zorn: *News for Lulu*
***ZZ Top (2004):** "Legs"

(1) Only individual performer is in Rock and Roll Hall of Fame.

Entertainment Personalities of the Present

Living actors, musicians, dancers, singers, producers, directors, radio-TV performers.

Name	Birthplace	Birthdate
Abbado, Claudio	Milan, Italy	6/26/33
Abdul, Paula	San Fernando, CA	6/19/62
Abraham, F. Murray	Pittsburgh, PA	10/24/39
Abrams, J(effrey) J(acob)	New York, NY	6/27/66
Adams, Bryan	Kingston, Ontario	11/5/59
Adele	London, England	5/5/88
Adjani, Isabelle	Paris, France	6/27/55
Ad-Rock	South Orange, NJ	10/31/66
Affleck, Ben	Berkeley, CA	8/15/72
Affleck, Casey	Falmouth, MA	8/12/75
Aghdashloo, Shohreh	Tehran, Iran	1952
Aguilera, Christina	Staten Is., New York, NY	12/18/80
Agutter, Jenny	Taunton, Somerset, Eng.	12/20/52
Aiello, Danny	New York, NY	6/20/33
Aiken, Clay	Raleigh, NC	11/30/78
Aimee, Anouk	Paris, France	4/27/32
Alba, Jessica	Pomona, CA	4/28/81
Albanese, Licia	Bari, Italy	7/22/13
Alberghetti, Anna Maria	Pesaro, Italy	5/15/36
Albert, Marv	Brooklyn, New York, NY	6/12/41
Alda, Alan	New York, NY	1/28/36
Alexander, Jane	Boston, MA	10/28/39
Alexander, Jason	Newark, NJ	9/23/59
Allen, Debbie	Houston, TX	1/16/50
Allen, Joan	Rochelle, IL	8/20/56
Allen, Karen	Carrollton, IL	10/5/51
Allen, Kris	Jacksonville, AR	06/21/85
Allen, Krista	Ventura, CA	04/5/71
Allen, Ted	Carmel, IN	5/20/65
Allen, Tim	Denver, CO	6/13/53
Allen, Woody	Brooklyn, NY	12/1/35
Alley, Kirstie	Wichita, KS	1/12/51
Allman, Gregg	Nashville, TN	12/8/47
Alonso, Maria Conchita	Cienfuegos, Cuba	6/29/57
Alpert, Herb	Los Angeles, CA	3/31/35
Almodóvar, Pedro	Calzada de Calatrava, Spain	9/25/51
Ambrose, Lauren	New Haven, CT	2/20/78
Ames, Ed	Malden, Boston, MA	7/9/27
Amos, John	Newark, NJ	12/27/41
Amos, Tori	Newton, NC	8/22/63
André 3000	Atlanta, GA	5/27/75
Anderson, Gillian	Chicago, IL	8/9/68
Anderson, Harry	Newport, RI	10/14/52
Anderson, Ian	Dunfermline, Scotland	8/10/47
Anderson, Kevin	Gurnee, IL	1/13/60
Anderson, Loni	St. Paul, MN	8/5/46
Anderson, Lynn	Grand Forks, ND	9/26/47
Anderson, Melissa Sue	Berkeley, CA	9/26/62
Anderson, Pamela	Comox, Vancouver Isl., BC	7/1/67
Anderson, Richard	Long Branch, NJ	8/8/26
Anderson, Richard Dean	Minneapolis, MN	1/23/50
Anderson, Wes	Houston, TX	5/1/69
Andersson, Bibi	Stockholm, Sweden	11/11/35
Andress, Ursula	Bern, Switzerland	3/19/36
Andrews, Julie	Walton-on-Thames, Surrey, England	10/1/35
Andrews, Naveen	London, England	1/17/69
Andrews, Patty	Minneapolis, MN	2/16/18
Angel, Criss	Long Island, NY	12/19/67
Aniston, Jennifer	Sherman Oaks, CA	2/11/69
Anka, Paul	Ottawa, Ontario	7/30/41
Ann-Margret	Stockholm, Sweden	4/28/41
Anthony, Marc	New York, NY	9/16/68
Apatow, Judd	Syosset, NY	12/6/67
Apple, Fiona	New York, NY	9/13/77
Applegate, Christina	Los Angeles, CA	11/25/71
Archer, Anne	Los Angeles, CA	8/25/47
Archuleta, David	Miami, FL	12/28/90
Arkin, Adam	Brooklyn, NY	8/19/56
Arkin, Alan	New York, NY	3/26/34
Armisen, Fred	Valley Stream, NY	12/4/66
Arnaz, Desi, Jr.	Hollywood, CA	1/19/53
Arnaz, Lucie	Hollywood, CA	7/17/51
Arness, James	Minneapolis, MN	5/26/23
Arnett, Will	Toronto, ON	5/4/70
Arnold, Tom	Ottumwa, IA	3/6/59
Arquette, David	Winchester, VA	9/8/71
Arquette, Patricia	Chicago, IL	4/8/68
Arquette, Rosanna	New York, NY	8/10/59
Arroyo, Martina	Harlem, New York, NY	2/2/37
Ashanti (Douglas)	Glen Cove, NY	10/13/80
Ashley, Elizabeth	Ocala, FL	8/30/39
Asner, Ed	Kansas City, KS	11/15/29
Assante, Armand	New York, NY	10/4/49
Astin, John	Baltimore, MD	3/30/30
Astin, Sean	Santa Monica, CA	2/25/71
Atkins, Eileen	London, England	6/16/34
Atkins, Sharif	Pittsburgh, PA	1/29/75
Atkinson, Rowan	Newcastle-Upon-Tyne, Eng.	1/6/55
Attenborough, Richard	Cambridge, England	8/29/23
Auberjonois, Rene	New York, NY	6/1/40
Austin, Patti	New York, NY	8/10/48
Autry, Alan	Shreveport, LA	7/31/52
Avalon, Frankie	Philadelphia, PA	9/18/39
Aykroyd, Dan	Ottawa, Ontario	7/1/52
Azaria, Hank	Forest Hills, Queens, NY	4/25/64
Aznavour, Charles	Paris, France	5/22/24
Babyface (Kenneth Edmonds)	Indianapolis, IN	4/10/59
Bacall, Lauren	Bronx, New York, NY	9/16/24
Bacon, Kevin	Philadelphia, PA	7/8/58
Badalucco, Michael	Brooklyn, NY	12/20/54
Bader, Diedrich	Alexandria, VA	12/24/66
Badu, Erykah	Dallas, TX	2/26/71
Baez, Joan	Staten Island, NY	1/9/41
Bain, Conrad	Lethbridge, Alberta	2/4/23
Baio, Scott	Brooklyn, NY	9/22/61
Baker, Anita	Toledo, OH	1/26/58
Baker, Carroll	Johnstown, PA	5/28/31
Baker, Diane	Hollywood, CA	2/25/38
Baker, Joe Don	Groesbeck, TX	2/12/36
Baker, Kathy	Midland, TX	6/8/50
Baker, Simon	Launceston, Tasmania, Australia	7/30/69
Bakula, Scott	St. Louis, MO	10/9/54
Baldwin, Alec	Massapequa, NY	4/3/58
Baldwin, Daniel	Massapequa, NY	10/5/60
Baldwin, Stephen	Massapequa, NY	5/12/66
Baldwin, William	Massapequa, NY	2/21/63
Bale, Christian	Pembrokeshire, Wales	1/30/74
Ballard, Kaye	Cleveland, OH	11/20/26
Bana, Eric	Melbourne, Australia	8/9/68
Banderas, Antonio	Málaga, Spain	8/10/60
Banks, Elizabeth	Pittsfield, MA	2/10/75
Banks, Tyra	Los Angeles, CA	12/4/73
Bannon, Jack	Los Angeles, CA	6/14/40
Baranski, Christine	Buffalo, NY	5/2/52
Barbeau, Adrienne	Sacramento, CA	6/11/45

Name	Birthplace	Birthdate	Name	Birthplace	Birthdate
Bardem, Javier	Las Palmas, Canary Isl.	3/1/69	Blige, Mary J.	Bronx, NY.	1/11/71
Bardot, Brigitte	Paris, France	9/28/34	Bloom, Claire	London, England	2/15/31
Barker, Bob	Darrington, WA	12/12/23	Bloom, Orlando	Canterbury, England	1/13/77
Barkin, Ellen	Bronx, New York, NY	4/16/55	Blyth, Ann	Mt. Kisco, NY	8/16/28
Barrie, Barbara	Chicago, IL	5/23/31	Bochco, Steven	New York, NY	12/16/43
Barrino, Fantasia	High Point, NC	6/30/84	Bocelli, Andrea	Lajatico, Italy	9/22/58
Barry, Gene	New York, NY	6/14/19	Bogdanovich, Peter	Kingston, NY	7/30/39
Barrymore, Drew	Los Angeles, CA	2/22/75	Bogosian, Eric	Woburn, MA.	4/24/53
Bartoli, Cecilia	Rome, Italy	6/4/66	Bologna, Joseph	Brooklyn, NY	12/30/38
Barton, Misha	London, Eng.	1/24/86	Bolton, Michael	New Haven, CT	2/26/53
Baryshnikov, Mikhail	Riga, Latvia	1/28/48	Bonet, Lisa.	San Francisco, CA.	11/16/67
Basinger, Kim	Athens, GA	12/8/53	Bonham Carter, Helena	London, England	5/26/66
Bass, Lance	Laurel, MS.	5/4/79	Bon Jovi, Jon	Sayreville, NJ.	3/2/62
Bassett, Angela	Harlem, New York, NY	8/16/58	Bono (Vox)	Dublin, Ireland	5/10/60
Bassey, Shirley	Cardiff, Wales	1/8/37	Boone, Debby	Hackensack, NJ.	9/22/56
Bateman, Jason	Rye, NY.	1/14/69	Boone, Pat.	Jacksonville, FL	6/1/34
Bateman, Justine	Rye, NY.	2/19/66	Boreanaz, David	Buffalo, NY.	5/16/71
Bates, Kathy	Memphis, TN.	6/28/48	Borgnine, Ernest	Hamden, CT.	1/24/17
Batt, Bryan	New Orleans, LA.	3/1/63	Bosco, Philip	Jersey City, NJ.	9/26/30
Battle, Kathleen	Portsmouth, OH	8/13/48	Bosley, Tom.	Chicago, IL.	10/1/27
Baxter, Meredith	Los Angeles, CA	6/21/47	Bosson, Barbara	Charleroi, PA	11/1/39
Bean, Orson	Burlington, VT	7/22/28	Bostwick, Barry	San Mateo, CA.	2/24/45
Bean, Sean	Sheffield, England.	4/17/59	Bosworth, Kate	Los Angeles, CA	1/2/83
Beatty, Ned	Louisville, KY.	7/6/37	Bottoms, Timothy	Santa Barbara, CA.	8/30/51
Beatty, Warren	Richmond, VA.	3/30/37	Bow Wow	Columbus, OH	3/9/87
Beauvais, Garcelle	St. Marc, Haiti	11/26/66	Bowen, Julie	Baltimore, MD	3/3/70
Beck (Hansen)	Los Angeles, CA	7/8/70	Bowie, David	London, England	1/8/47
Beck, Jeff	Wallington, Surrey, Eng.	6/24/44	Bowles, Peter.	London, England	10/16/36
Beckham, Victoria	Hertfordshire, England	4/17/74	Boxleitner, Bruce	Elgin, IL	5/12/50
Beckinsale, Kate	London, England	7/26/73	Boy George	Bexleyheath, England	6/14/61
Bedelia, Bonnie	New York, NY	3/25/48	Boyle, Lara Flynn.	Davenport, IA.	3/24/70
Begley, Ed, Jr.	Los Angeles, CA	9/16/49	Bracco, Lorraine	Brooklyn, NY	10/2/55
Behar, Joy	Brooklyn, NY.	10/7/43	Brady, Wayne	Orlando, FL	6/2/72
Belafonte, Harry	Harlem, New York, NY	3/1/27	Braff, Zach	S. Orange, NJ	4/6/75
Bell, Art	Camp Lejeune, NC	6/17/45	Branagh, Kenneth	Belfast, N. Ireland	12/10/60
Bell, Catherine	London, England	8/14/68	Brandauer, Klaus Maria	Steiermark, Austria	6/22/44
Bell, Kristen	Huntington Woods, MI.	7/18/80	Brandy (Norwood)	McComb, MS.	2/11/79
Bello, Maria	Norristown, PA	4/18/67	Braschi, Nicoletta	Cesena, Italy	8/10/60
Belmondo, Jean-Paul	Neuilly-sur-Seine, France	4/9/33	Bratt, Benjamin	San Francisco, CA.	12/16/63
Belushi, Jim	Chicago, IL	6/15/54	Braugher, Andre	Chicago, IL.	7/1/62
Belzer, Richard	Bridgeport, CT.	8/4/44	Braxton, Toni	Severn, MD	10/7/66
Benatar, Pat	Brooklyn, NY	1/10/53	Bremner, Ewen	Edinburgh, Scotland.	1971
Benedict, Dirk	Helena, MT.	3/1/45	Brendon, Nicholas	Los Angeles, CA	4/12/71
Benigni, Roberto	Misericordia, Italy	10/27/52	Brennan, Eileen	Los Angeles, CA	9/3/35
Bening, Annette	Topeka, KS	5/29/58	Brenneman, Amy	Glastonbury, CT.	6/22/64
Benjamin, Richard	New York, NY	5/22/38	Brenner, David.	Philadelphia, PA.	2/4/45
Bennett, Alan	Leeds, England	5/9/34	Bridges, Beau	Hollywood, CA.	12/9/41
Bennett, Tony	Astoria, Queens, NY	8/3/26	Bridges, Jeff.	Los Angeles, CA	12/4/49
Benson, George	Pittsburgh, PA.	3/22/43	Brightman, Sarah.	Berkhamstead, England.	8/14/60
Benson, Robby	Dallas, TX	1/21/56	Brimley, Wilford	Salt Lake City, UT	9/27/34
Berenger, Tom	Chicago, IL.	5/31/50	Brinkley, Christie	Malibu, CA.	2/2/54
Berfield, Justin	Ventura County, CA	2/25/86	Broadbent, Jim.	Lincolnshire, England.	5/24/49
Bergen, Candice	Beverly Hills, CA	5/9/46	Brochtrup, Bill	Inglewood, CA.	3/7/63
Bergen, Polly.	Knoxville, TN.	7/14/30	Broderick, Matthew	New York, NY	3/21/62
Bergeron, Tom	Haverhill, MA.	5/6/55	Brody, Adam	San Diego, CA.	12/15/79
Berlinger, Warren	Brooklyn, NY.	8/31/37	Brody, Adrien.	New York, NY	4/14/73
Berman, Shelley	Chicago, IL.	2/3/26	Brolin, James.	Los Angeles, CA	7/18/40
Bernard, Crystal	Dallas, TX	9/30/64	Brolin, Josh	Los Angeles, CA	2/12/68
Bernhard, Sandra	Flint, MI	6/6/55	Brooks, Albert	Beverly Hills, CA	7/22/47
Bernsen, Corbin	N. Hollywood, CA	9/7/54	Brooks, Garth	Tulsa, OK.	2/7/62
Berry, Chuck	St. Louis, MO	10/18/26	Brooks, James L.	North Bergen, NJ.	5/9/40
Berry, Halle	Cleveland, OH.	8/14/66	Brooks, Mel	Brooklyn, NY	6/28/26
Berry, Ken	Moline, IL.	11/3/33	Brosnan, Pierce	Navan, Co. Meath, Ireland.	5/16/53
Bertinelli, Valerie	Wilmington, DE	4/23/60	Brown, Blair	Washington, DC.	4/23/46
Bertolucci, Bernardo	Parma, Italy	3/16/40	Brown, Bobby	Roxbury, Boston, MA.	2/5/69
Bettany, Paul.	London, England	5/27/71	Brown, Bryan	Panania, Australia	6/23/47
Biafra, Jello	Boulder, CO	6/17/58	Brown, Chris	Tappahannock, VA	5/5/89
Bialik, Mayim	San Diego, CA	12/12/75	Brown, Foxy.	Brooklyn, NY	9/6/79
Biel, Jessica	Ely, MN	3/3/82	Browne, Jackson	Heidelberg, Germany.	10/9/48
Big Boi.	Savannah, GA.	2/1/75	Brubeck, Dave	Concord, CA	12/6/20
Biggs, Jason	Pompton Plains, NJ.	5/12/78	Bryant, Paul (Cubby)	Virginia Beach, VA.	6/1/71
Bikel, Theodore	Vienna, Austria	5/2/24	Bryson, Peabo	Greenville, SC	4/13/51
Billingsley, Barbara	Los Angeles, CA	12/22/22	Buckley, Betty	Ft. Worth, TX	7/3/47
Bilson, Rachel.	Los Angeles, CA.	8/25/81	Buffett, Jimmy	Pascagoula, MS.	12/25/46
Binoche, Juliette	Paris, France.	3/9/64	Bujold, Geneviève	Montreal, Quebec	7/1/42
Birch, Thora	Beverly Hills, CA	3/11/82	Bullock, Sandra	Arlington, VA	7/26/64
Birney, David.	Washington, DC	4/23/39	Bumbry, Grace.	St. Louis, MO.	1/4/37
Bisset, Jacqueline	Weybridge, England.	9/13/44	Bunchen, Gisele	Horizontina, Brazil	7/20/80
Bissett, Josie	Seattle, WA.	10/5/70	Burghoff, Gary	Bristol, CT	5/24/43
Björk (Gudmundsdottir).	Reykjavik, Iceland	11/21/65	Burke, Delta	Orlando, FL	7/30/56
Black, Clint	Long Branch, NJ	2/4/62	Burnett, Carol.	San Antonio, TX.	4/26/33
Black, Jack	Los Angeles, CA	4/7/69	Burns, Edward	Woodside, Queens, NY	1/29/68
Black, Karen	Park Ridge, IL	7/1/42	Burrows, Darren E.	Winfield, KS	9/12/66
Blades, Ruben	Panama City, Panama	7/16/48	Burstyn, Ellen.	Detroit, MI	12/7/32
Blair, Linda	St. Louis, MO	1/22/59	Burton, LeVar	Landstuhl, W Germany	2/16/57
Blair, Selma.	Southfield, MI	6/23/72	Burton, Tim	Burbank, CA.	8/25/58
Blake, Robert	Nutley, NJ.	9/18/33	Buscemi, Steve	Brooklyn, NY	12/13/57
Blanchett, Cate	Melbourne, Australia.	5/14/69	Busey, Gary.	Goose Creek, TX.	6/29/44
Bledsoe, Tempestt	Chicago, IL	8/1/73	Busfield, Timothy	Lansing, MI	6/12/57
Bleeth, Yasmine	New York, NY	6/14/68	Butler, Brett	Montgomery, AL.	1/30/58
Blethyn, Brenda	Ramsgate, Kent, England	2/20/46	Buzzi, Ruth	Westerly, RI	7/24/36

Name	Birthplace	Birthdate
Bynes, Amanda	Thousand Oaks, CA	4/3/86
Byrne, David	Dumbarton, Scotland	5/14/52
Byrne, Gabriel	Dublin, Ireland	5/12/50
Byrne, Rose	Sydney, NSW, Australia	7/24/79
Caan, James	Bronx, NY	3/26/40
Caballe, Montserrat	Barcelona, Spain	4/12/33
Caesar, Sid	Yonkers, NY	9/8/22
Cage, Nicolas	Long Beach, CA	1/7/64
Cain, Dean	Mt. Clemens, MI	7/31/66
Caine, Michael	London, England	3/14/33
Caldwell, Zoe	Hawthorne, Australia	9/14/33
Callow, Simon	London, England	6/13/49
Cameron, James	Kapuskasing, Ontario	8/16/54
Cameron, Kirk	Panorama City, CA	10/12/70
Campanella, Joseph	New York, NY	11/21/27
Campbell, Bruce	Royal Oak, MI	6/22/58
Campbell, Glen	Delight, AR	4/22/36
Campbell, Naomi	South London, England	5/22/70
Campbell, Neve	Guelph, Ontario	10/3/73
Campion, Jane	Waikanae, New Zealand	4/30/54
Cannell, Stephen J.	Pasadena, CA	5/2/41
Cannon, Dyan	Tacoma, WA	1/4/37
Capshaw, Kate	Ft. Worth, TX	11/3/53
Cara, Irene	New York, NY	3/18/64
Carell, Steve	Concord, MA	8/16/62
Cardellini, Linda	Redwood City, CA	6/25/75
Cardinale, Claudia	Tunis, Tunisia	4/15/39
Carey, Drew	Cleveland, OH	5/23/58
Carey Jr., Harry	Saugus, CA	5/16/21
Carey, Mariah	Huntington, NY	3/27/70
Cariou, Len	Winnipeg, Manitoba	9/30/39
Carlton, Vanessa	Milford, PA	8/16/80
Carlyle, Robert	Glasgow, Scotland	4/14/61
Carmen, Eric	Cleveland, OH	8/11/49
Caron, Leslie	Boulogne, France	7/1/31
Carpenter, John	Carthage, NY	1/16/48
Carpenter, Mary Chapin	Princeton, NJ	2/21/58
Carr, Vikki	El Paso, TX	7/19/41
Carradine, David	Hollywood, CA	12/8/36
Carreras, Jose	Barcelona, Spain	12/5/46
Carrere, Tia	Honolulu, HI	1/2/67
Carrey, Jim	Newmarket, Ontario	1/17/62
Carroll, Diahann	Bronx, NY	7/17/35
Carroll, Pat	Shreveport, LA	5/5/27
Carter, Dixie	McLemoresville, TN	5/25/39
Carter, Jack	Brooklyn, New York, NY	6/24/23
Carter, Lynda	Phoenix, AZ	7/24/51
Carter, Nick	Jamestown, NY	1/28/80
Carter, Ron	Ferndale, MI	5/4/37
Cartwright, Nancy	Kettering, OH	10/25/59
Caruso, David	Forest Hills, Queens, NY	1/17/56
Carvey, Dana	Missoula, MT	6/2/55
Case, Sharon	Detroit, MI	2/9/71
Cash, Rosanne	Memphis, TN	5/24/55
Cassidy, David	New York, NY	4/12/50
Castellaneta, Dan	Chicago, IL	9/10/58
Castle-Hughes, Keisha	Donnybrook, W. Australia, Australia	3/24/90
Cates, Phoebe	New York, NY	7/16/63
Cattrall, Kim	Liverpool, England	8/21/56
Cavanagh, Tom	Ottawa, Ontario	10/26/68
Cavett, Dick	Gibbon, NE	11/19/36
Cavill, Henry	Jersey, Channel Islands, UK	5/5/83
Cedric the Entertainer	Jefferson City, MO	4/24/64
Cera, Michael	Brampton, Ont, Can.	6/7/88
Chabert, Lacey	Purvis, MS	9/30/82
Chalke, Sarah	Ottawa, Ontario	8/27/76
Carson, Lisa Nicole	Brooklyn, NY	7/12/69
Chamberlain, Richard	Beverly Hills, CA	3/31/34
Chambers, Justin	Springfield, OH	7/11/70
Chan, Jackie	Hong Kong	4/7/54
Channing, Carol	Seattle, WA	1/31/21
Channing, Stockard	New York, NY	2/13/44
Chaplin, Geraldine	Santa Monica, CA	7/31/44
Chapman, Tracy	Cleveland, OH	3/30/64
Chappelle, Dave	Washington, DC	8/24/73
Charisse, Cyd	Amarillo, TX	3/8/21
Charo	Murcia, Spain	1/15/41
Chase, Chevy	New York, NY	10/8/43
Chasez, Joshua (J.C.)	Washington, DC	8/8/76
Cheadle, Don	Kansas City, MO	11/29/64
Checker, Chubby	Spring Gulley, SC	10/3/41
Chenoweth, Kristin	Broken Arrow, OK	7/24/68
Cher	El Centro, CA	5/20/46
Chesney, Kenny	Knoxville, TN	3/26/68
Chianese, Dominic	Bronx, NY	2/24/31
Chiba, Sonny	Fukuoka, Kyushu, Japan	1/23/39
Chiklis, Michael	Lowell, MA	8/30/63
Cho, Margaret	San Francisco	12/5/68
Chong, Rae Dawn	Vancouver, BC	2/28/61
Chong, Thomas	Edmonton, Alberta	5/24/38

Name	Birthplace	Birthdate
Chow Yun-Fat	Hong Kong	5/18/55
Christensen, Hayden	Vancouver, BC	4/19/81
Christensen, Helena	Copenhagen, Denmark	12/25/68
Christie, Julie	Chukua, Assam, India	4/14/40
Christopher, William	Evanston, IL	10/20/32
Chuck D	New York, NY	8/1/60
Church, Charlotte	Llandaff, Cardiff, Wales	2/21/86
Church, Thomas Haden	El Paso, TX	6/17/61
Clapp, Gordon	North Conway, NH	9/24/48
Clapton, Eric	Surrey, England	3/30/45
Clark, Anthony	Lynchburg, VA	4/4/64
Clark, Dick	Mt. Vernon, NY	11/30/29
Clark, Petula	Ewell, Surrey, England	11/15/32
Clark, Roy	Meherrin, VA	4/15/33
Clarkson, Kelly	Burleson, TX	4/24/82
Clarkson, Patricia	New Orleans, LA	12/29/59
Clay, Andrew Dice	Brooklyn, NY	9/29/58
Clayburgh, Jill	New York, NY	4/30/44
Cleese, John	Weston-super-Mare, Eng.	10/27/39
Cliburn, Van	Shreveport, LA	7/12/34
Clooney, George	Lexington, KY	5/6/61
Close, Glenn	Greenwich, CT	3/19/47
Coen, Ethan	St. Louis Park, MN	9/21/57
Coen, Joel	St. Louis Park, MN	11/29/54
Cohen, Leonard	Montreal, Canada	9/21/34
Cohen, Sacha Baron	London, England	10/13/71
Colbert, Stephen	Charleston, SC	5/13/64
Cole, Gary	Park Ridge, IL	9/20/57
Cole, Natalie	Los Angeles, CA	2/6/50
Cole, Olivia	Memphis, TN	11/26/42
Cole, Paula	Manchester, CT	4/5/68
Coleman, Dabney	Austin, TX	1/3/32
Coleman, Gary	Zion, IL	2/8/68
Coleman, Ornette	Fort Worth, TX	3/19/30
Collette, Toni	Blacktown, Australia	11/1/72
Collins, Joan	London, England	5/23/33
Collins, Judy	Seattle, WA	5/1/39
Collins, Pauline	Exmouth, England	9/3/40
Collins, Phil	London, England	1/30/51
Collins, Stephen	Des Moines, IA	10/1/47
Colvin, Shawn	Vermillion, SD	1/10/56
Combs, Sean "Diddy"	Harlem, NY	11/4/69
Connelly, Jennifer	Catskill Mountains, NY	12/12/70
Connery, Sean	Edinburgh, Scotland	8/25/30
Connick, Harry, Jr.	New Orleans, LA	9/11/67
Connolly, Kevin	New York, NY	3/5/74
Connors, Mike	Fresno, CA	8/15/25
Conrad, Robert	Chicago, IL	3/1/35
Conroy, Frances	Monroe, GA	11/13/53
Constantine, Michael	Reading, PA	5/22/27
Conti, Tom	Paisley, Scotland	11/22/41
Conway, Tim	Willoughby, OH	12/15/33
Cook, Barbara	Atlanta, GA	10/25/27
Cook, David	Houston, TX	12/20/82
Coolidge, Rita	Nashville, TN	5/1/45
Coolio	Los Angeles, CA	8/1/63
Cooper, Alice	Detroit, MI	2/4/48
Cooper, Bradley	Philadelphia, PA	1/5/75
Cooper, Chris	Kansas City, MO	7/9/51
Cooper, Jackie	Los Angeles, CA	9/15/21
Copperfield, David	Metuchen, NJ	9/16/56
Coppola, Francis Ford	Detroit, MI	4/7/39
Coppola, Sofia	New York, NY	5/12/71
Corbett, John	Wheeling, WV	5/9/61
Corbin, Barry	Lamesa, TX	10/16/40
Cord, Alex	Floral Park, NY.	5/3/33
Corea, Chick	Chelsea, MA	6/12/41
Corgan, Billy	Elk Grove, IL	3/17/67
Corley, Pat	Dallas, TX	6/1/30
Cornell, Chris	Seattle, WA	7/20/64
Corwin, Jeff	Halifax, Nova Scotia	7/11/67
Cosby, Bill	Philadelphia, PA	7/12/37
Costas, Bob	Queens, New York, NY	3/22/52
Costello, Elvis	London, England	8/25/54
Costner, Kevin	Compton, CA	1/18/55
Cotillard, Marion	Paris, France	9/30/75
Courtenay, Tom	Hull, England	2/25/37
Cowell, Simon	London, England	10/7/59
Cox, Brian	Dundee, Scotland	6/1/46
Cox, Nikki	Los Angeles, CA	6/2/78
Cox, Ronny	Cloudcroft, NM	7/23/38
Cox Arquette, Courteney	Birmingham, AL	6/15/64
Coyote, Peter	New York, NY	10/10/42
Craig, Daniel	Chester, England	3/2/68
Cranston, Bryan	San Fernando Valley, CA	3/7/56
Crawford, Cindy	DeKalb, IL	2/20/66
Crawford, Michael	Salisbury, England	1/19/42
Cromwell, James	Los Angeles, CA	1/27/40
Crosby, David	Los Angeles, CA	8/14/41
Cross, Ben	London, England	12/16/47
Cross, Marcia	Marlborough, MA	3/25/62

Name	Birthplace	Birthdate
Crouse, Lindsay	New York, NY	5/12/48
Crow, Sheryl	Kennett, MO	2/11/62
Crowe, Cameron	Palm Springs, CA	7/13/57
Crowe, Russell	Wellington, New Zealand	4/7/64
Crowell, Rodney	Houston, TX	8/17/50
Crudup, Billy	Manhasset, NY	7/8/68
Cruise, Tom	Syracuse, NY	7/3/62
Cruz, Penelope	Madrid, Spain	4/28/74
Cryer, Jon	New York, NY	4/16/65
Crystal, Billy	Long Beach, NY	3/14/47
Culkin, Kieran	New York, NY	9/30/82
Culkin, Macaulay	New York, NY	8/26/80
Culkin, Rory	New York, NY	7/21/89
Cullum, John	Knoxville, TN	3/2/30
Culp, Robert	Oakland, CA	8/16/30
Cumming, Alan	Perthshire, Scotland	1/27/65
Curry, Tim	Cheshire, England	4/19/46
Curtin, Jane	Cambridge, MA	9/6/47
Curtis, Jamie Lee	Los Angeles, CA	11/22/58
Curtis, Tony	New York, NY	6/3/25
Cusack, Joan	New York, NY	10/11/62
Cusack, John	Evanston, IL	6/28/66
Cyrus, Billy Ray	Flatwoods, KY	8/25/61
Cyrus, Miley	Nashville, TN	11/23/92
Dafoe, Willem	Appleton, WI	7/22/55
Dahl, Arlene	Minneapolis, MN	8/11/28
Dale, Jim	Rothwell, England	8/15/35
Dalton, Abby	Las Vegas, NV	8/15/32
Dalton, Timothy	Colwyn Bay, Wales	3/21/46
Daltrey, Roger	London, England	3/1/44
Daly, Carson	Santa Monica, CA	6/22/73
Daly, Timothy	New York, NY	3/1/56
Daly, Tyne	Madison, WI	2/21/46
Damon, Matt	Cambridge, MA	10/8/70
Damone, Vic	Brooklyn, NY	6/12/28
Dane, Eric	San Francisco, CA	11/9/72
Danes, Claire	New York, NY	4/12/79
D'Angelo	Richmond, VA	2/11/74
D'Angelo, Beverly	Columbus, OH	11/15/54
Daniels, Anthony	Salisbury, England	2/21/46
Daniels, Charlie	Wilmington, NC	10/28/36
Daniels, Jeff	Athens, GA	2/19/55
Daniels, William	Brooklyn, NY	3/31/27
Danner, Blythe	Rosemont, PA	2/3/43
Danson, Ted	San Diego, CA	12/29/47
Danza, Tony	Brooklyn, New York, NY	4/21/51
Darby, Kim	Hollywood, CA	7/8/48
David, Larry	Brooklyn, NY	7/2/47
Davidson, John	Pittsburgh, PA	12/13/41
Davis, Ann B.	Schenectady, NY	5/5/26
Davis, Clifton	Chicago, IL	10/4/45
Davis, Geena	Wareham, MA	1/21/56
Davis, Hope	Englewood, NJ	3/23/64
Davis, Judy	Perth, Australia	4/23/55
Davis, Kristin	Boulder, CO	2/24/65
Davis, Mac	Lubbock, TX	1/21/42
Dawber, Pam	Farmington Hills, MI	10/18/51
Dawson, Richard	Gosport, Hampshire, Eng.	11/20/32
Dawson, Rosario	Bronx, New York, NY	5/9/79
Day, Doris	Cincinnati, OH	4/3/24
Day-Lewis, Daniel	London, England	4/29/57
Dean, Jimmy	Plainview, TX	8/10/28
Dee, Ruby	Cleveland, OH	10/27/24
DeFranco, Buddy	Camden, NJ	2/17/23
DeGeneres, Ellen	Metairie, LA	1/26/58
DeHaven, Gloria	Los Angeles, CA	7/23/25
De Havilland, Olivia	Tokyo, Japan	7/1/16
Delaney, Kim	Philadelphia, PA	11/29/61
Delany, Dana	New York, NY	3/13/56
De la Rocha, Zack	Long Beach, CA	1/12/70
De Laurentiis, Dino	Torre Annunziata, Italy	8/8/19
Delon, Alain	Sceaux, France	11/8/35
Del Toro, Benicio	Santurce, Puerto Rico	2/19/67
Demme, Jonathan	Baldwin, NY	2/22/44
De Mornay, Rebecca	Santa Rosa, CA	8/29/62
Dempsey, Patrick	Lewiston, ME	1/13/66
Dench, Judi	York, England	12/9/34
Deneuve, Catherine	Paris, France	10/22/43
De Niro, Robert	New York, NY	8/17/43
Dennehy, Brian	Bridgeport, CT	7/9/38
DePalma, Brian	Newark, NJ	9/11/40
Depardieu, Gerard	Chateauroux, France	12/27/48
Depp, Johnny	Owensboro, KY	6/9/63
Derek, Bo	Long Beach, CA	11/20/56
De Rossi, Portia	Melbourne, Victoria, Aust.	1/31/73
Dern, Bruce	Winnetka, IL	6/4/36
Dern, Laura	Santa Monica, CA	2/10/67
DeVito, Danny	Neptune, NJ	11/17/44
DeWitt, Joyce	Wheeling, WV	4/23/49
Dey, Susan	Pekin, IL	12/10/52
Diamond, Neil	Brooklyn, NY	1/24/41
Diaz, Cameron	San Diego, CA	8/30/72
DiCaprio, Leonardo	Hollywood, CA	11/11/74
Dick, Andy	Charleston, SC	12/21/65
Dickinson, Angie	Kulm, ND	9/30/31
Diesel, Vin	New York, NY	7/18/67
Diggs, Taye	Essex Co., NJ	1/2/72
Diller, Phyllis	Lima, OH	7/17/17
Dillman, Bradford	San Francisco, CA	4/14/30
Dillon, Kevin	Mamaroneck, NY	8/16/65
Dillon, Matt	New Rochelle, NY	2/18/64
Dinklage, Peter	Mendham, NJ.	6/11/69
Dion, Celine	Charlemagne, Quebec	3/30/68
Djalili, Omid	London, England	9/30/65
Dobson, Kevin	Queens, New York, NY	3/18/43
Dogg, Snoop	Long Beach, CA.	10/20/71
Doherty, Shannen	Memphis, TN	4/12/71
Dolenz, Mickey	Los Angeles, CA	3/8/45
Domingo, Placido	Madrid, Spain	1/21/41
Domino, Fats	New Orleans, LA	2/26/28
Donahue, Phil	Cleveland, OH	12/21/35
D'Onofrio, Vincent	Brooklyn, NY	6/30/59
Donovan (Leitch)	Glasgow, Scotland	5/10/46
Donovan, Tate	Tenafly, NJ.	9/25/63
Dorn, Michael	Luling, TX.	12/9/52
Dorough, Howie	Orlando, FL	8/22/73
Dotrice, Roy	Guernsey, England	5/26/23
Douglas, Kirk	Amsterdam, NY	12/9/16
Douglas, Michael	New Brunswick, NJ	9/25/44
Dourdan, Gary	Philadelphia, PA.	12/11/66
Dow, Tony	Hollywood, CA.	4/13/45
Down, Lesley-Anne	London, England	3/17/54
Downey, Robert, Jr.	New York, NY	4/4/65
Downey, Roma	Derry, Northern Ireland	5/6/60
Downs, Hugh	Akron, OH	2/14/21
Drescher, Fran	Flushing, Queens, NY	9/30/57
Dreyfuss, Richard	Brooklyn, NY	10/29/47
Driver, Minnie	London, England	1/31/70
Dryer, Fred	Hawthorne, CA.	7/6/46
Duchovny, David	New York, NY	8/7/60
Duff, Haylie	Houston, TX.	2/19/85
Duff, Hilary	Houston, TX.	9/28/87
Duffy, (Aimee Anne)	Bangor, Gwynedd, Wales	6/23/84
Duffy, Julia	Minneapolis, MN	6/27/51
Duffy, Patrick	Townsend, MT	3/17/49
Duhamel, Josh	Minot, ND	11/14/72
Dukakis, Olympia	Lowell, MA	6/20/31
Duke, Patty	Elmhurst, NY	12/14/46
Dullea, Keir	Cleveland, OH	5/30/36
Dunaway, Faye	Bascom, FL	1/14/41
Duncan, Lindsay	Edinburgh, Scotland	11/7/50
Duncan, Sandy	Henderson, TX	2/20/46
Dunne, Griffin	New York, NY	6/8/55
Dunst, Kirsten	Point Pleasant, NJ	4/30/82
Durbin, Deanna	Winnipeg, Manitoba	12/4/21
Durning, Charles	Highland Falls, NY	2/28/23
Dussault, Nancy	Pensacola, FL	6/30/36
Dutton, Charles S.	Baltimore, MD	1/30/51
Duvall, Robert	San Diego, CA	1/5/31
Duvall, Shelley	Houston, TX.	7/7/49
Dylan, Bob	Duluth, MN.	5/24/41
Dylan, Jakob	New York, NY	12/9/69
Dysart, Richard	Brighton, MA	3/30/29
Dzundza, George	Rosenheim, Germany	7/19/45
Eads, George	Fort Worth, TX.	3/1/67
Easton, Sheena	Bellshill, Scotland	4/27/59
Eastwood, Clint	San Francisco, CA.	5/31/30
Ebert, Roger	Urbana, IL	6/18/42
Eckhart, Aaron	Cupertino, CA	3/12/68
Eden, Barbara	Tucson, AZ	8/23/34
Edwards, Anthony	Santa Barbara, CA.	7/19/62
Edwards, Blake	Tulsa, OK.	7/26/22
Efron, Zac	San Luis Obispo, CA	10/18/87
Ehle, Jennifer	Winston-Salem, NC	12/29/69
Eichhorn, Lisa	Reading, PA	2/4/52
Eikenberry, Jill	New Haven, CT	1/21/47
Ekberg, Anita	Malmo, Sweden	9/29/31
Ekland, Britt	Stockholm, Sweden	10/6/42
Electra, Carmen	Cincinnati, OH	4/20/72
Elfman, Jenna	Los Angeles, CA	9/30/71
Elizabeth, Shannon	Houston, TX.	9/7/73
Elizondo, Hector	New York, NY	12/22/36
Elliott, Bob	Boston, MA	3/26/23
Elliott, Chris	New York, NY	5/31/60
Elliott, Sam	Sacramento, CA	8/9/44
Elvira	Manhattan, KS	9/17/51
Emerson, Michael	Cedar Rapids, IA	9/7/1954
Eminem	St. Joseph, MO	10/17/72
Enberg, Dick	Mt. Clemens, MI.	1/9/35
Englund, Robert	Glendale, CA.	6/6/49
Enya	Gweedore, Ireland	5/17/61
Ephron, Nora	New York, NY	5/19/41

Name	Birthplace	Birthdate
Ermey, R. Lee	Emporia, KS	3/24/44
Estefan, Gloria	Havana, Cuba	9/1/57
Estevez, Emilio	New York, NY	5/12/62
Estrada, Erik	New York, NY	3/16/49
Etheridge, Melissa	Leavenworth, KS	5/29/61
Evans, Linda	Hartford, CT	11/18/42
Evans, Robert	New York, NY	6/29/30
Everett, Chad	South Bend, IN	6/11/36
Everett, Rupert	Norfolk, England	5/29/59
Everly, Don	Brownie, KY	2/1/37
Everly, Phil	Chicago, IL	1/19/39
Evigan, Greg	South Amboy, NJ	10/14/53
Fabares, Shelley	Santa Monica, CA	1/19/44
Fabian (Forte)	Philadelphia, PA	2/6/43
Fabio	Milan, Italy	3/15/61
Fabolous	Brooklyn, NY	11/18/77
Fairchild, Morgan	Dallas, TX	2/3/50
Faison, Donald	New York, NY	6/22/74
Falana, Lola	Philadelphia, PA	9/11/43
Falco, Edie	Brooklyn, NY	7/5/63
Falk, Peter	New York, NY	9/16/27
Fallon, Jimmy	Brooklyn, NY	9/19/74
Farentino, James	Brooklyn, NY	2/24/38
Fargo, Donna	Mt. Airy, NC	11/10/49
Farina, Dennis	Chicago, IL	2/29/44
Farr, Jamie	Toledo, OH	7/1/34
Farrell, Colin	Dublin, Ireland	5/31/76
Farrell, Mike	St. Paul, MN	2/6/39
Farrell, Perry	Queens, NY	3/29/59
Farrelly, Bob	Cumberland, RI	6/17/58
Farrelly, Peter	Phoenixville, PA	12/17/56
Farrow, Mia	Los Angeles, CA	2/9/45
Fatone, Joey	Brooklyn, New York, NY	1/28/77
Feinstein, Michael	Columbus, OH	9/7/56
Feldon, Barbara	Pittsburgh, PA	3/12/41
Feldshuh, Tovah	New York, NY	12/27/52
Feliciano, Jose	Lares, Puerto Rico	9/10/45
Fenn, Sherilyn	Detroit, MI	2/1/65
Fergie	Hacienda Heights, CA	3/27/75
Ferrara, Jerry	Brooklyn, NY	11/29/79
Ferrell, Conchata	Charleston, WV	3/28/43
Ferrell, Will	Irvine, CA	7/16/67
Ferrera, America	Los Angeles, CA	4/18/84
Feuerstein, Mark	New York, NY	6/8/71
Fey, Tina	Upper Darby, PA	5/18/70
Field, Sally	Pasadena, CA	11/6/46
Fiennes, Joseph	Salisbury, England	5/27/70
Fiennes, Ralph	Suffolk, England	12/22/62
Fierstein, Harvey	Brooklyn, NY	6/6/54
50 Cent	Queens, NY	7/6/76
Filicia, Thom	Syracuse, NY	5/17/69
Fincher, David	Denver, CO	5/10/62
Finney, Albert	Salford, England	5/9/36
Fiorentino, Linda	Philadelphia, PA	3/9/60
Firth, Colin	Grayshott, England	9/10/60
Firth, Peter	Bradford, Yorkshire, Eng.	10/27/53
Fischer-Dieskau, Dietrich	Berlin, Germany	5/28/25
Fischer, Jenna	Ft. Wayne, IN	3/7/74
Fishburne, Laurence	Augusta, GA	7/30/61
Fisher, Carrie	Beverly Hills, CA	10/21/56
Fisher, Eddie	Philadelphia, PA	8/10/28
Flack, Roberta	Black Mountain, NC	2/10/39
Flanagan, Fionnula	Dublin, Ireland	12/10/41
Flavor Flav	New York, NY	3/16/59
Fleetwood, Mick	Redruth, Cornwall, Eng.	6/24/42
Fleming, Rhonda	Hollywood, CA	8/10/23
Fletcher, Louise	Birmingham, AL	7/22/34
Flockhart, Calista	Freeport, IL	11/11/64
Florek, Dann	Flat Rock, MI	5/1/50
Fogerty, John	Berkeley, CA	5/28/45
Foley, Dave	Etobicoke, Ontario	1/4/63
Fonda, Bridget	Los Angeles, CA	1/27/64
Fonda, Jane	New York, NY	12/21/37
Fonda, Peter	New York, NY	2/23/40
Fontaine, Joan	Tokyo, Japan	10/22/17
Ford, Faith	Alexandria, LA	9/14/64
Ford, Harrison	Des Plaines, IL	7/13/42
Forman, Milos	Caslav, Czechoslovakia	2/18/32
Forsythe, John	Penns Grove, NJ	1/29/18
Forte, Will	Alameda Co., CA	6/17/70
Foster, Jodie	Los Angeles, CA	11/19/62
Foster, Sutton	Statesboro, Georgia	3/18/75
Fox, James	London, England	5/19/39
Fox, Jorja	New York, NY	7/7/68
Fox, Matthew	Crowheart, WY	7/14/66
Fox, Megan	Rockwood, TN	5/16/86
Fox, Michael J.	Edmonton, Alberta	6/9/61
Fox, Vivica A.	Indianapolis, IN	7/30/64
Foxworth, Robert	Houston, TX	11/1/41
Foxworthy, Jeff	Atlanta, GA	9/6/58
Foxx, Jamie	Terrell, TX	12/13/67

Name	Birthplace	Birthdate
Frampton, Peter	Kent, England	4/22/50
Francis, Anne	Ossining, NY	9/16/30
Francis, Connie	Newark, NJ	12/12/38
Franco, James	Palo Alto, CA	4/19/78
Franken, Al	New York, NY	5/21/51
Franklin, Aretha	Memphis, TN	3/25/42
Franklin, Bonnie	Santa Monica, CA	1/6/44
Franz, Dennis	Maywood, IL	10/28/44
Fraser, Brendan	Indianapolis, IN	12/3/68
Freeman, Al, Jr.	San Antonio, TX	3/21/34
Freeman, Mona	Baltimore, MD	6/9/26
Freeman, Morgan	Memphis, TN	6/1/37
French, Dawn	Holyhead, Wales	10/11/57
Fricker, Brenda	Dublin, Ireland	2/17/45
Friedkin, William	Chicago, IL	8/29/39
Frost, David	Tenterden, England	4/7/39
Fry, Stephen	London, England	8/24/57
Fuentes, Daisy	Havana, Cuba	11/17/66
Fuller, Robert	Troy, NY	7/29/34
Funicello, Annette	Utica, NY	10/22/42
Furlong, Edward	Pasadena, CA	8/2/77
Furtado, Nelly	Victoria, British Columbia	12/2/78
Gabor, Zsa Zsa	Budapest, Hungary	2/6/17
Gabriel, John	Niagara Falls, NY	5/25/31
Gabriel, Peter	Surrey, England	2/13/50
Gaines, Boyd	Atlanta, GA	5/11/53
Gallagher, Peter	Armonk, NY	8/19/55
Gallo, Vincent	Buffalo, NY	4/11/62
Galway, James	Belfast, N. Ireland	12/8/39
Gandolfini, James	Westwood, NJ	9/18/61
Garagiola, Joe	St. Louis, MO	2/12/26
Garber, Victor	London, Ontario	3/16/49
Garcia, Andy	Havana, Cuba	4/12/56
Garfunkel, Art	Queens, New York, NY	11/5/41
Garlin, Jeff	Chicago, IL	6/5/62
Garner, James	Norman, OK	4/7/28
Garner, Jennifer	Houston, TX	4/17/72
Garofalo, Janeane	Newton, NJ	9/28/64
Garr, Teri	Lakewood, OH	12/11/49
Garrett, Betty	St. Joseph, MO	5/23/19
Garrett, Brad	Woodland Hills, CA	4/14/60
Garth, Jennie	Urbana, IL	4/3/72
Gatlin, Larry	Seminole, TX	5/2/48
Gavin, John	Los Angeles, CA	4/8/31
Gayle, Crystal	Paintsville, KY	1/9/51
Gaynor, Mitzi	Chicago, IL	9/4/31
Gazzara, Ben	New York, NY	8/28/30
Geary, Anthony	Coalville, UT.	5/29/47
Geary, Cynthia	Jackson, MS	3/21/65
Gedda, Nicolai	Stockholm, Sweden	7/11/25
Gellar, Sarah Michelle	New York, NY	4/14/77
Gere, Richard	Philadelphia, PA.	8/31/49
Gervais, Ricky	Reading, England	6/25/61
Giannini, Giancarlo	La Spezia, Italy	8/1/42
Gibb, Barry	Isle of Man, England	9/1/46
Gibb, Robin	Isle of Man, England	12/22/49
Gibbons, Leeza	Irmo, SC.	3/26/57
Gibbs, Marla	Chicago, IL	6/14/31
Gibson, Deborah	Brooklyn, New York, NY	8/31/70
Gibson, Mel	Peekskill, NY	1/3/56
Gibson, Thomas	Charleston, SC.	7/3/62
Gifford, Frank	Santa Monica, CA	8/16/30
Gifford, Kathie Lee	Neuilly-sur-Seine, France	8/16/53
Gilbert, Sara	Santa Monica, CA	1/29/75
Gilbert, Melissa	Los Angeles, CA	5/8/64
Gilberto, Astrud	Salvador, Brazil	3/30/40
Gill, Vince	Norman, OK.	4/12/57
Gillette, Anita	Baltimore, MD	8/16/36
Gilley, Mickey	Natchez, MS	3/9/36
Gilliam, Terry	Minneapolis, MN	11/22/40
Gilmour, David	Cambridge, England	3/6/44
Gilpin, Peri	Waco, TX	5/27/61
Ginty, Robert	New York, NY	11/14/48
Givens, Robin	New York, NY	11/27/64
Glaser, Paul Michael	Cambridge, MA	3/25/43
Gleeson, Brendan	Belfast, N. Ireland	11/9/55
Glenn, Scott	Pittsburgh, PA	1/26/42
Gless, Sharon	Los Angeles, CA	5/31/43
Glover, Crispin	New York, NY	9/20/64
Glover, Danny	San Francisco, CA.	7/22/47
Glover, John	Kingston, NY	8/7/44
Glover, Julian	London, England	3/27/35
Glover, Savion	Newark, NJ	11/19/73
Godard, Jean Luc	Paris, France	12/3/30
Goldberg, Whoopi	New York, NY	11/13/55
Goldblum, Jeff	Pittsburgh, PA	10/22/52
Goldthwait, Bobcat	Syracuse, NY	5/26/62
Goldwyn, Tony	Los Angeles, CA	5/20/60
Gooding, Cuba, Jr.	Bronx, NY.	1/2/68
Goodman, John	Affton, MO	6/20/52
Gordon-Levitt, Joseph	Los Angeles, CA	2/17/81

Name	Birthplace	Birthdate
Gorme, Eydie	Bronx, NY	8/16/32
Gosling, Ryan	London, Ontario	11/12/80
Gosselaar, Mark-Paul	Panorama City, CA	3/1/74
Gossett, Louis, Jr.	Brooklyn, NY	5/27/36
Gould, Elliott	Brooklyn, NY	8/29/38
Gould, Harold	Schenectady, NY	12/10/23
Grace, Topher	New York, NY	7/19/78
Graham, Heather	Milwaukee, WI	1/29/70
Grammer, Kelsey	St. Thomas, Virgin Isl.	2/21/55
Granger, Farley	San Jose, CA	7/1/25
Grant, Amy	Augusta, GA	11/25/60
Grant, Hugh	London, England	9/9/60
Grant, Lee	New York, NY	10/31/27
Graves, Peter	Minneapolis, MN	3/18/26
Gray, Linda	Santa Monica, CA	9/12/40
Gray, Macy	Canton, OH	9/9/70
Grayson, Kathryn	Winston-Salem, NC	2/9/22
Green, Al	Forrest City, AR	4/13/46
Green, Seth	Overbrook Park, PA	2/8/74
Green, Tom	Pembroke, Ontario	7/30/71
Greene, Shecky	Chicago, IL	4/8/26
Greenwood, Bruce	Noranda, Quebec	8/12/56
Gregory, Cynthia	Los Angeles, CA	7/8/46
Gregory, Dick	St. Louis, MO	10/12/32
Grenier, Adrian	Brooklyn, NY	7/10/76
Grey, Jennifer	New York, NY	3/26/60
Grey, Joel	Cleveland, OH	4/11/32
Grier, David Alan	Detroit, MI	6/30/55
Grier, Pam	Winston-Salem, NC	5/26/49
Gries, Jon	Glendale, CA	6/17/57
Griffith, Andy	Mount Airy, NC	6/1/26
Griffith, Melanie	New York, NY	8/9/57
Griffiths, Rachel	New Castle, Australia	2/20/68
Griffiths, Richard	Stockton-on-Tees, Cleveland, United Kingdom	7/31/47
Grimes, Tammy	Lynn, MA	1/30/34
Grint, Rupert	Hertfordshire, England	8/24/88
Groban, Josh	Los Angeles, CA	2/27/81
Grodin, Charles	Pittsburgh, PA	4/21/35
Grohl, David	Warren, OH	1/14/69
Grosbard, Ulu	Antwerp, Belgium	1/9/29
Gross, Michael	Chicago, IL	6/21/47
Guest, Christopher	New York, NY	2/5/48
Guillaume, Robert	St. Louis, MO	11/30/37
Gumbel, Greg	New Orleans, LA	5/3/46
Guthrie, Arlo	Brooklyn, New York, NY	7/10/47
Guttenberg, Steve	Brooklyn, New York, NY	8/24/58
Guy, Buddy	Lettsworth, LA	7/30/36
Guy, Jasmine	Boston, MA	3/10/64
Gyllenhaal, Jake	Los Angeles, CA	12/19/80
Gyllenhaal, Maggie	New York, NY	11/16/77
Hackman, Gene	San Bernardino, CA	1/30/30
Hader, Bill	Tulsa, OK	6/7/78
Hagerty, Julie	Cincinnati, OH	6/15/55
Haggard, Merle	Bakersfield, CA	4/6/37
Hagman, Larry	Fort Worth, TX	9/21/31
Haid, Charles	San Francisco, CA	6/2/43
Hale, Barbara	DeKalb, IL	4/18/22
Hale, Tony	West Point, NY	9/30/70
Hall, Anthony Michael	West Roxbury, MA	4/14/68
Hall, Arsenio	Cleveland, OH	2/12/55
Hall, Daryl	Pottstown, PA	10/11/49
Hall, Deidre	Milwaukee, WI	10/31/47
Hall, Michael C.	Raleigh, NC	2/1/71
Hall, Monty	Winnipeg, Manitoba	8/25/21
Hall, Tom T.	Olive Hill, KY	5/25/36
Halliwell, Geri	Watford, England	8/6/72
Hamill, Mark	Oakland, CA	9/25/51
Hamilton, George	Memphis, TN	8/12/39
Hamilton, Linda	Salisbury, MD	9/26/56
Hamlin, Harry	Pasadena, CA	10/30/51
Hamm, Jon	St. Louis, MO	3/10/71
Hammer (M.C.)	Oakland, CA	3/29/63
Hammond, Darrell	Melbourne, FL	10/8/60
Hampshire, Susan	London, England	5/12/37
Hancock, Herbie	Chicago, IL	4/12/40
Hanks, Tom	Concord, CA	7/9/56
Hannah, Daryl	Chicago, IL	12/3/60
Hannigan, Alyson	Washington, DC	3/24/74
Hanson, Curtis	Reno, NV	3/24/45
Hanson, Isaac	Tulsa, OK	11/17/80
Hanson, Taylor	Tulsa, OK	3/14/83
Hanson, Zac	Tulsa, OK	10/22/85
Harden, Marcia Gay	La Jolla, CA	8/14/59
Hardison, Kadeem	New York, NY	7/24/66
Harewood, Dorian	Dayton, OH	8/6/50
Hargitay, Mariska	Los Angeles, CA	1/23/64
Harmon, Angie	Highland Park, TX	8/10/72
Harmon, Mark	Burbank, CA	9/2/51
Harper, Ben	Claremont, CA	10/28/69
Harper, Jessica	Chicago, IL	10/10/49
Harper, Tess	Mammoth Springs, AR	8/15/50
Harper, Valerie	Suffern, NY	8/22/40
Harrelson, Woody	Midland, TX	7/23/61
Harrington, Pat.	New York, NY	8/13/29
Harris, Barbara	Evanston, IL	7/25/35
Harris, Ed	Tenafly, NJ	11/28/50
Harris, Emmylou	Birmingham, AL	4/2/47
Harris, Julie	Grosse Pte. Park, MI	12/2/25
Harris, Neil Patrick	Albuquerque, NM	6/15/73
Harris, Rosemary	Ashby, England	9/19/30
Harris, Steve	Chicago, IL	12/3/65
Harrison, Gregory	Avalon, CA	5/31/50
Harry, Deborah	Miami, FL	7/1/45
Hart, Mary	Madison, SD	11/8/50
Hart, Melissa Joan	Sayville, NY	4/18/76
Hartley, Hal	Lindenhurst, NY	11/3/59
Hartley, Mariette	New York, NY	6/21/40
Hartman, David	Pawtucket, RI	5/19/35
Hartman Black, Lisa	Houston, TX	6/1/56
Hartnett, Josh	San Francisco, CA	7/21/78
Harvey, P. J.	Yeovil, Somerset, England	10/9/69
Harvey, Steve	Welch, WV	11/23/56
Hasselbeck, Elisabeth	Cranston, RI	5/28/77
Hasselhoff, David	Baltimore, MD	7/17/52
Hatcher, Teri	Sunnyvale, CA	12/8/64
Hatfield, Juliana	Wiscasset, ME	7/27/67
Hathaway, Anne	Brooklyn, NY	11/12/82
Hauer, Rutger	Breukelen, Netherlands	1/23/44
Havoc, June	Seattle, WA	11/8/16
Hawke, Ethan	Austin, TX	11/6/70
Hawn, Goldie	Washington, DC	11/21/45
Hayek, Salma	Coatzacoalcos, Mexico	9/2/66
Hayes, Sean	Glen Ellyn, IL	6/26/70
Haynes, Roy	Roxbury, Boston, MA	3/13/26
Hays, Robert	Bethesda, MD	7/24/47
Head, Anthony Stewart	North London, England	2/20/54
Heard, John	Washington, DC	3/7/46
Hearn, George	St. Louis, MO	6/18/34
Heaton, Patricia	Bay Village, OH	3/4/58
Heche, Anne	Aurora, OH	5/25/69
Heder, Jon	Fort Collins, CO	10/26/77
Hedren, Tippi	Lafayette, MN	1/19/31
Heigl, Katherine	Washington, DC	11/24/78
Helfgott, David	Melbourne, Australia	5/19/47
Helgenberger, Marg.	Fremont, NE	11/16/58
Helmond, Katherine	Galveston, TX	7/5/34
Hemingway, Mariel	Mill Valley, CA	11/22/61
Hemsley, Sherman	Philadelphia, PA	2/1/38
Henderson, Florence	Dale, IN	2/14/34
Henley, Don	Gilmer, TX	7/22/47
Henner, Marilu	Chicago, IL	4/6/52
Hennessy, Jill	Edmonton, Alberta	11/25/68
Henry, Buck	New York, NY	12/9/30
Herman, Pee-Wee	Peekskill, NY	8/27/52
Herrmann, Edward	Washington, DC	7/21/43
Hershey, Barbara	Hollywood, CA	2/5/48
Hesseman, Howard	Lebanon, OR	2/27/40
Hetfield, James	Downey, CA	8/3/63
Hewitt, Jennifer Love	Waco, TX	2/21/79
Hicks, Catherine	Scottsdale, AZ	8/6/51
Higgins, John Michael	Boston, MA	2/12/63
Hill, Dulé	Orange, NJ	5/3/74
Hill, Faith	Jackson, MS	9/21/67
Hill, Lauryn	South Orange, NJ	5/25/75
Hill, Steven	Seattle, WA	2/24/22
Hillerman, John	Denison, TX	12/20/32
Hilton, Paris	New York, NY	2/17/81
Hines, Cheryl	Miami Beach, FL	9/21/65
Hirsch, Emile	Palms, CA	3/13/85
Hirsch, Judd	New York, NY	3/15/35
Hodgman, John	Cambridge, MA	6/3/71
Hoffman, Dustin	Los Angeles, CA	8/8/37
Hoffman, Philip Seymour	Fairport, NY	7/23/67
Hogan, Hulk	Augusta, GA	8/11/53
Hogan, Paul	Lightning Ridge, New South Wales, Australia	10/8/39
Holbrook, Hal	Cleveland, OH	2/17/25
Holder, Geoffrey	Port of Spain, Trinidad	8/1/30
Holliday, Polly	Jasper, AL	7/2/37
Holliman, Earl	Delhi, LA	9/11/28
Holloway, Josh	San Jose, CA	7/20/69
Holly, Lauren	Bristol, PA	10/28/63
Holm, Celeste	New York, NY	4/29/19
Holm, Ian	Ilford, England	9/12/31
Holmes, Katie	Toledo, OH	12/18/78
Hooks, Jan	Decatur, GA	4/23/57
Hopkins, Anthony	Port Talbot, South Wales	12/31/37
Hopkins, Bo	Greenville, SC	2/2/42
Hopkins, Telma	Louisville, KY	10/28/48
Hopper, Dennis	Dodge City, KS	5/17/36
Horne, Lena	Brooklyn, NY	6/30/17

Name	Birthplace	Birthdate
Horne, Marilyn	Bradford, PA	1/16/34
Hornsby, Bruce	Williamsburg, VA	11/23/54
Horsley, Lee	Muleshoe, TX	5/15/55
Horton, Robert	Los Angeles, CA	7/29/24
Hoskins, Bob	Suffolk, England	10/26/42
Hounsou, Djimon	Benin	4/24/64
Houston, Whitney	Newark, NJ	8/9/63
Howard, Ken	El Centro, CA	3/28/44
Howard, Ron	Duncan, OK	3/1/54
Howard, Terence	Chicago, IL	3/11/69
Howell, C. Thomas	Van Nuys, CA	12/7/66
Howes, Sally Ann	London, England	7/20/30
Hudgens, Vanessa	Salinas, CA	12/14/88
Hudson, Kate	Los Angeles, CA	4/19/79
Hudson, Jennifer	Chicago, IL	9/12/81
Huffman, Felicity	Bedford, NY	12/6/62
Hughley, D.L.	Los Angeles, CA	3/6/63
Hulce, Tom	Whitewater, WI	12/6/53
Humperdinck, Engelbert	Madras, India	5/2/36
Humphries, Barry	Melbourne, Australia	2/17/34
Hunt, Bonnie	Chicago, IL	9/22/64
Hunt, Helen	Culver City, CA	6/15/63
Hunt, Linda	Morristown, NJ	4/2/45
Hunter, Holly	Conyers, GA	3/20/58
Hunter, Tab	New York, NY	7/11/31
Hurley, Elizabeth	Hampshire, England	6/10/65
Hurt, John	Chesterfield, England	1/22/40
Hurt, Mary Beth	Marshalltown, IA	9/26/48
Hurt, William	Washington, DC	3/20/50
Huston, Anjelica	Santa Monica, CA	7/8/51
Hutton, Lauren	Charleston, SC	11/17/43
Hutton, Timothy	Malibu, CA	8/16/60
Hyman, Earle	Rocky Mount, NC	10/11/26
Ian, Janis	New York, NY	4/7/51
Ice Cube	Los Angeles, CA	6/15/69
Ice-T	Newark, NJ	2/16/58
Idle, Eric	S. Shields, England	3/29/43
Idol, Billy	Middlesex, England	11/30/55
Iglesias, Enrique	Madrid, Spain	5/8/75
Iglesias, Julio	Madrid, Spain	9/23/43
Iler, Robert	New York, NY	3/2/85
Iman	Mogadishu, Somalia	7/25/55
Imbruglia, Natalie	Sydney, Australia	2/4/75
Imperioli, Michael	Mount Vernon, NY	1/1/66
Imus, Don	Riverside, CA	7/23/40
Ingram, James	Akron, OH	2/16/56
Innes, Laura	Pontiac, MI	8/16/59
Ireland, Kathy	Glendale, CA	3/20/63
Irons, Jeremy	Isle of Wight, England	9/19/48
Irving, Amy	Palo Alto, CA	9/10/53
Irving, George S.	Springfield, MA	11/1/22
Irwin, Bill	Santa Monica, CA	4/11/50
Ivanek, Željko	Ljubljana, Yugoslavia	8/15/57
Ivey, Judith	El Paso, TX	9/4/51
Ivory, James	Berkeley, CA	6/7/28
Izzard, Eddie	Aden, Yemen	2/7/62
Jackée (Harry)	Winston-Salem, NC	8/14/56
Jackman, Hugh	Sydney, Australia	10/12/68
Jackson, Anne	Allegheny, PA	9/3/26
Jackson, Cheyenne	Newport, WA	7/12/75
Jackson, Glenda	Birkenhead, England	5/9/36
Jackson, Janet	Gary, IN	5/16/66
Jackson, Jermaine	Gary, IN	12/11/54
Jackson, Jonathan	Orlando, FL	5/11/82
Jackson, Joshua	Vancouver, Brit. Columbia	6/11/78
Jackson, Kate	Birmingham, AL	10/29/48
Jackson, La Toya	Gary, IN	5/29/56
Jackson, Peter	Wellington, New Zealand	10/31/61
Jackson, Samuel L.	Chattanooga, TN	12/21/48
Jacobi, Derek	London, England	10/22/38
Jagger, Mick	Dartford, England	7/26/43
James, Etta	Los Angeles, CA	1/25/38
James, Kevin	Mineola, NY	4/26/65
Janis, Conrad	New York, NY	2/11/28
Janney, Allison	Boston, MA	11/19/60
Janssen, Famke	Amsterdam, Netherlands	11/5/65
Jardine, Al	Lima, OH	9/3/42
Jarmusch, Jim	Akron, OH	1/22/53
Jarreau, Al	Milwaukee, WI	3/12/40
Jarrette, Keith	Allentown, PA	5/8/45
Ja Rule	Queens, NY	2/29/76
Jay Z	Brooklyn, NY	12/4/69
Jeffreys, Anne	Goldsboro, NC	1/26/23
Jett, Joan	Philadelphia, PA	9/22/60
Jewel (Kilcher)	Payson, UT	5/23/74
Jewison, Norman	Toronto, Ontario	7/21/26
Jillian, Ann	Cambridge, MA	1/29/50
Jillette, Penn	Greenfield, MA	3/5/55
Joel, Billy	Bronx, NY	5/9/49
Johansson, Scarlett	New York, NY	11/22/84
John, Elton	Pinner, Middlesex, Eng.	3/25/47

Name	Birthplace	Birthdate
Johns, Glynis	Durban, S Africa	10/5/23
Johnson, Arte	Benton Harbor, MI	1/20/34
Johnson, Beverly	Buffalo, NY	10/13/52
Johnson, Don	Flatt Creek, MO	12/15/49
Johnston, Bruce	Chicago, IL	6/24/44
Johnston, Kristen	Washington, DC	9/20/67
Jolie, Angelina	Los Angeles, CA	6/4/75
Jonas, Joe	Casa Grande, AZ	8/15/89
Jonas, Kevin	Teaneck, NJ	11/5/87
Jonas, Nick	Dallas, TX	9/16/92
Jones, Cherry	Paris, TN	11/21/56
Jones, Davy	Manchester, England	12/30/45
Jones, Dean	Morgan City, AL	1/25/31
Jones, Gemma	London, England	12/4/42
Jones, George	Saratoga, TX	9/12/31
Jones, Grace	Spanishtown, Jamaica	5/19/52
Jones, Jack	Hollywood, CA	1/14/38
Jones, James Earl	Arkabutla, MS	1/17/31
Jones, Jennifer	Tulsa, OK	3/2/19
Jones, Mick	London, England	6/26/55
Jones, Norah	New York, NY	3/30/79
Jones, Quincy	Chicago, IL	3/14/33
Jones, Shirley	Smithton, PA	3/31/34
Jones, Star	Badin, NC	3/24/62
Jones, Tom	Pontypridd, Wales	6/7/40
Jones, Tommy Lee	San Saba, TX	9/15/46
Jonze, Spike	Rockville, MD	10/22/69
Jourdan, Louis	Marseilles, France	6/19/19
Jovovich, Milla	Kiev, Ukraine	12/17/75
Judd, Ashley	Granada Hills, CA	4/19/68
Judd, Naomi	Ashland, KY	1/11/46
Judd, Wynonna	Ashland, KY	5/30/64
Kaczmarek, Jane	Milwaukee, WI	12/21/55
Kanaly, Steve	Burbank, CA	3/14/46
Kane, Carol	Cleveland, OH	6/18/52
Kaplan, Gabe	Brooklyn, NY	3/31/45
Karlen, John	Brooklyn, NY	5/28/33
Karn, Richard	Seattle, WA	2/17/56
Karras, Alex	Gary, IN	7/15/35
Kasem, Casey	Detroit, MI	4/27/32
Kattan, Chris	Sherman Oaks, CA	10/19/70
Kavner, Julie	Burbank, CA	9/7/51
Kazan, Lainie	New York, NY	5/15/42
Keach, Stacy	Savannah, GA	6/2/41
Keaton, Diane	Santa Ana, CA	1/5/46
Keaton, Michael	Pittsburgh, PA	9/9/51
Keener, Catherine	Miami FL	3/23/59
Keillor, Garrison	Anoka, MN	8/7/42
Keitel, Harvey	Brooklyn, NY	5/13/39
Keith, David	Knoxville, TN	5/8/54
Keith, Penelope	Sutton, Surrey, England	4/2/40
Kellerman, Sally	Long Beach, CA	6/2/37
Kelly, Jean Louisa	Worcester, MA	3/9/72
Kelly, Minka	Los Angeles, CA	6/24/80
Kelly, R(obert)	Chicago, IL	1/8/67
Kennedy, George	New York, NY	2/18/25
Kennedy, Jamie	Upper Darby, PA	5/25/70
Kennedy, Jayne	Washington, DC	10/27/51
Kenny G	Seattle, WA	6/5/56
Kent, Allegra	Santa Monica, CA	8/11/37
Keoghan, Phil	Christchurch, New Zealand	5/31/67
Kercheval, Ken	Wolcottville, IN	7/15/35
Kerns, Joanna	San Francisco, CA	2/12/53
Keys, Alicia	New York, NY	1/25/81
Khan, Chaka	Great Lakes, IL	3/23/53
Kidder, Margot	Yellowknife, N.W.T.	10/17/48
Kidman, Nicole	Honolulu, HI	6/20/67
Kiel, Richard	Detroit, MI	9/13/39
Kilborn, Craig	Kansas City, KS	8/24/62
Kilmer, Val	Los Angeles, CA	12/31/59
Kim, Daniel Dae	Pusan, Korea	8/4/68
Kimmel, Jimmy	Brooklyn, NY	11/13/67
King, B. B.	Itta Bena, MS	9/16/25
King, Carole	Brooklyn, NY	2/9/42
King, Larry	Brooklyn, NY	11/19/33
King, Perry	Alliance, OH	4/30/48
Kingsley, Ben	Scarborough, England	12/31/43
Kingston, Alex	London, England	3/11/63
Kinnear, Greg	Logansport, IN	6/17/63
Kinney, Kathy	Stevens Point, WI	11/3/53
Kinski, Nastassja	Berlin, W. Germany	1/24/60
Kirkland, Gelsey	Bethlehem, PA	12/29/52
Kirkpatrick, Chris	Clarion, PA	10/17/71
Kirshner, Mia	Toronto, Ontario	1/25/75
Klein, Robert	Bronx, New York, NY	2/8/42
Kline, Kevin	St. Louis, MO	10/24/47
Klugman, Jack	Philadelphia, PA	4/27/22
Klum, Heidi	Bergish-Gladbach, Germany	6/1/73
Knight, Gladys	Atlanta, GA	5/28/44
Knight, Shirley	Goessel, KS	7/5/36
Knight, T. R.	Minneapolis, MN	3/26/73

Name	Birthplace	Birthdate
Knight, Wayne	New York, NY	8/7/55
Knightley, Keira	Teddington, England	3/26/85
Knopfler, Mark	Glasgow, Scotland	8/12/49
Knowles, Beyoncé	Houston, TX	9/4/81
Knoxville, Johnny	Knoxville, TN	3/11/71
Konitz, Lee	Chicago, IL	10/13/27
Kopell, Bernie	New York, NY	6/21/33
Kotto, Yaphet	New York, NY	11/15/37
Krakowski, Jane	Parsippany, NJ	10/11/68
Krasinski, John	Newton, MA	10/20/79
Krause, Peter	Alexandria, MN	8/12/65
Kressley, Carson	Allentown, PA	11/11/69
Kretschmann, Thomas	Dessau, E. Germany	9/8/62
Kristofferson, Kris	Brownsville, TX	6/22/36
Kudrow, Lisa	Encino, CA	7/30/63
Kunis, Mila	Kiev, Ukraine, Soviet Union	8/14/83
Kuriyama, Chiaki	Tsuchiura, Ibaraki, Japan	10/10/84
Kurtz, Swoosie	Omaha, NE	9/6/44
Kutcher, Ashton	Cedar Rapids, IA	2/7/78
Kwan, Nancy	Hong Kong	5/19/39
LaBelle, Patti	Philadelphia, PA	5/24/44
LaBeouf, Shia	Los Angeles, CA	6/11/86
Lachey, Nick	Harlan, KY	11/9/73
Ladd, Cheryl	Huron, SD	7/12/51
Ladd, Diane	Meridian, MS	11/29/32
Lady Gaga	Yonkers, NY	3/28/86
Lagasse, Emeril	Fall River, MA	10/15/59
Lahti, Christine	Royal Oak, MI	4/4/50
Laine, Cleo	Southall, England	10/28/27
Lake, Ricki	Hastings-on-Hudson, NY	9/21/68
Lamas, Lorenzo	Santa Monica, CA	1/20/58
Lambert, Adam	Indianapolis, IN	1/29/82
Lambert, Christopher	Great Neck, NY	3/29/57
Landau, Martin	Brooklyn, NY	6/20/28
Landis, John	Chicago, IL	8/3/50
Lane, Diane	New York, NY	1/22/65
Lane, Nathan	Jersey City, NJ	2/3/56
lang, k.d.	Consort, Alberta	11/2/61
Lang, Stephen	Queens, New York, NY	7/11/52
Lange, Jessica	Cloquet, MN	4/20/49
Langella, Frank	Bayonne, NJ	1/1/40
Lansbury, Angela	London, England	10/16/25
LaPaglia, Anthony	Adelaide, Australia	1/31/59
Larroquette, John	New Orleans, LA	11/25/47
LaSalle, Eriq	Hartford, CT	6/23/62
Lauper, Cyndi	Brooklyn, NY	6/20/53
Laurie, Hugh	Oxford, England	6/11/59
Laurie, Piper	Detroit, MI	1/22/32
Lavigne, Avril	Napanee, Ontario	9/27/84
Lavin, Linda	Portland, ME	10/15/37
Law, Jude	London, England	12/29/72
Lawless, Lucy	Mount Albert, New Zealand	3/29/68
Lawrence, Carol	Melrose Park, IL	9/5/34
Lawrence, Joey	Montgomery, PA	4/20/76
Lawrence, Martin	Frankfurt, Germany	4/16/65
Lawrence, Steve	Brooklyn, NY	7/8/35
Lawrence, Vicki	Inglewood, CA	3/26/49
Leach, Robin	London, England	8/29/41
Leachman, Cloris	Des Moines, IA	4/30/26
Lear, Norman	New Haven, CT	7/27/22
Learned, Michael	Washington, DC	4/9/39
Leary, Denis	Worcester, MA	8/18/57
LeBlanc, Matt	Newton, MA	7/25/67
LeBon, Simon	Bushey, England	10/27/58
Lee, Ang	Pingtung, Taiwan	10/23/54
Lee, Brenda	Lithonia, GA	12/11/44
Lee, Christopher	London, England	5/27/22
Lee, Jason	Huntington Beach, CA	4/25/70
Lee, Michele	Los Angeles, CA	6/24/42
Lee, Spike	Atlanta, GA	3/20/57
Leeves, Jane	London, England	4/18/61
Legrand, Michel	Paris, France	2/24/32
Leguizamo, John	Bogotá, Colombia	7/22/64
Leibman, Ron	New York, NY	10/11/37
Leigh, Jennifer Jason	Hollywood, CA	2/5/62
Leighton, Laura	Iowa City, IA	7/24/68
Lennox, Annie	Aberdeen, Scotland	12/25/54
Leno, Jay	New Rochelle, NY	4/28/50
Leonard, Robert Sean	Westwood, NJ	2/25/69
Leoni, Tea	New York, NY	2/25/66
Leslie, Joan	Detroit, MI	1/26/25
Leto, Jared	Bossier City, LA	12/26/71
Letterman, David	Indianapolis, IN	4/12/47
Levine, Adam	Los Angeles, CA	3/18/79
Levine, James	Cincinnati, OH	6/23/43
Levine, Ted	Parma, OH	5/29/58
Levinson, Barry	Baltimore, MD	4/6/42
Levy, Eugene	Hamilton, Ontario	12/17/46
Lewis, Huey	New York, NY	7/5/50
Lewis, Jason	Newport Beach, CA	6/25/71
Lewis, Jerry	Newark, NJ	3/16/26
Lewis, Jerry Lee	Ferriday, LA	9/29/35
Lewis, Juliette	San Fernando Valley, CA	6/21/73
Lewis, Leona	London, England	4/3/85
Lewis, Richard	Brooklyn, NY	6/29/47
Li, Jet	Beijing, China	4/26/63
Light, Judith	Trenton, NJ	2/9/49
Lightfoot, Gordon	Orillia, Ontario	11/17/38
Lil' Kim	Brooklyn, NY	7/11/75
Lil' Romeo	New Orleans, LA	8/19/89
Lilly, Evangeline	Fort Saskatchewan, Alberta	8/3/79
Linden, Hal	Bronx, New York, NY	3/20/31
Ling, Lisa	Sacramento, CA	8/30/73
Linkletter, Art	Moose Jaw, Saskatchewan	7/17/12
Linn-Baker, Mark	St. Louis, MO	6/17/54
Linney, Laura	New York, NY	2/5/64
Liotta, Ray	Newark, NJ	12/18/55
Lithgow, John	Rochester, NY	10/19/45
Little, Rich	Ottawa, Ontario	11/26/38
Little Richard	Macon, GA	12/5/32
Littrell, Brian	Lexington, KY	2/20/75
Liu, Lucy	Queens, NY	12/2/68
L. L. Cool J	St. Albans, Queens, NY	1/14/68
Lloyd, Christopher	Stamford, CT	10/22/38
Lloyd, Emily	North London, England	9/29/70
Lloyd Webber, Andrew	London, England	3/22/48
Locke, Sondra	Shelbyville, TN	5/28/47
Lockhart, June	New York, NY	6/25/25
Locklear, Heather	Westwood, CA	9/25/61
Loggia, Robert	Staten Island, NY	1/3/30
Loggins, Kenny	Everett, WA	1/7/48
Logue, Donal	Ottawa, Ontario	2/27/66
Lohan, Lindsay	New York, NY	7/2/86
Lollobrigida, Gina	Subiaco, Italy	7/4/27
Lom, Herbert	Prague, Czechoslovakia	1/9/17
Lonergan, Kenneth	New York, NY	10/16/62
Long, Nia	Brooklyn, NY	10/30/70
Long, Shelley	Ft. Wayne, IN	8/23/49
Longoria, Eva	Corpus Christi, TX	3/15/75
Lopez, George	Mission Hills, CA	4/23/61
Lopez, Jennifer	Bronx, NY	7/24/70
Lopez, Mario	San Diego, CA	10/10/73
Loren, Sophia	Rome, Italy	9/20/34
Loring, Gloria	New York, NY	12/10/46
Louis-Dreyfus, Julia	New York, NY	1/13/61
Love, Courtney	San Francisco, CA	7/9/64
Love, Mike	Baldwin Hills, CA	3/15/41
Loveless, Patty	Pikeville, KY	1/4/57
Lovett, Lyle	Klein, TX	11/1/57
Lovitz, Jon	Tarzana, CA	7/21/57
Lowe, Rob	Charlottesville, VA	3/17/64
Lowell, Carey	Huntington, NY	2/11/61
Lucas, George	Modesto, CA	5/14/44
Lucci, Susan	Scarsdale, NY	12/23/46
Luckinbill, Laurence	Ft. Smith, AR	11/21/34
Ludacris	Champaign, IL	9/11/77
Ludwig, Christa	Berlin, Germany	3/16/24
Luhrmann, Baz	Sydney, Australia	9/17/62
Lumet, Sidney	Philadelphia, PA	6/25/24
LuPone, Patti	Northport, NY	4/21/49
Lynch, David	Missoula, MT	1/20/46
Lynch, Susan	Corrinshego, N. Ireland, UK	6/5/71
Lynley, Carol	New York, NY	2/13/42
Lynn, Loretta	Butcher Hollow, KY	4/14/35
Lynn, Vera	London, England	3/20/17
Lynne, Shelby	Quantico, VA	10/22/68
Lyonne, Natasha	Great Neck, NY	4/4/79
Ma, Yo-Yo	Paris, France	10/7/55
Maazel, Lorin	Neuilly-sur-Seine, France	3/6/30
MacArthur, James	Los Angeles, CA	12/8/37
Macchio, Ralph	Huntington, NY	11/4/62
MacCorkindale, Simon	Ely, England	2/12/52
MacDonald, Kelly	Glasgow, Scotland	2/23/76
MacDowell, Andie	Gaffney, SC	4/21/58
MacFarlane, Seth	Kent, CT	11/26/73
MacGowan, Shane	Tunbridge, Kent, England	12/25/57
MacGraw, Ali	Pound Ridge, NY	4/1/38
MacLachlan, Kyle	Yakima, WA	2/22/59
MacLaine, Shirley	Richmond, VA	4/24/34
MacLeod, Gavin	Mt. Kisco, NY	2/28/31
MacNee, Patrick	London, England	2/6/22
MacNeil, Cornell	Minneapolis, MN	9/24/22
MacNicol, Peter	Dallas, TX	4/10/54
MacPherson, Elle	Sydney, Australia	3/29/64
Macy, Bill	Revere, MA	5/18/22
Macy, William H.	Miami, FL	3/13/50
Madden, John	Austin, MN	4/10/36
Madigan, Amy	Chicago, IL	9/11/50
Madonna (Ciccone)	Bay City, MI	8/16/58
Madsen, Michael	Chicago, IL	9/25/58
Maguire, Tobey	Santa Monica, CA	6/27/75
Maher, Bill	New York, NY	1/20/56

Name	Birthplace	Birthdate
Mahoney, John	Manchester, England	6/20/40
Majors, Lee	Wyandotte, MI	4/23/39
Malick, Terrence	Ottawa, IL	11/30/43
Malick, Wendie	Buffalo, NY	12/13/50
Malina, Joshua	New York, NY	1/17/66
Malkovich, John	Christopher, IL.	12/9/53
Malone, Dorothy	Chicago, IL	1/30/25
Mamet, David	Chicago, IL	11/30/47
Manchester, Melissa	Bronx, NY	2/15/51
Mandel, Howie	Toronto, Ontario	11/29/55
Mandrell, Barbara	Houston, TX	12/25/48
Mangione, Chuck	Rochester, NY	11/29/40
Manheim, Camryn	Caldwell, NJ	3/8/61
Manilow, Barry	Brooklyn, NY	6/17/46
Mann, Aimee	Richmond, VA	8/9/60
Manoff, Dinah	New York, NY	1/25/58
Manson, Marilyn	Canton, OH	1/5/69
Mantegna, Joe	Chicago, IL	11/13/47
Marcil, Vanessa	Indio, CA	10/15/69
Margulies, Julianna	Spring Valley, NY	6/8/66
Marie, Constance	Hollywood, CA.	9/9/69
Marin, Cheech	Los Angeles, CA	7/13/46
Marinaro, Ed	New York, NY	3/31/50
Marriner, Neville	Lincoln, England	4/15/24
Marsalis, Branford	New Orleans, LA	8/26/60
Marsalis, Wynton	New Orleans, LA	10/18/61
Marsh, Jean	London, England	7/1/34
Marshall, Garry	Bronx, NY	11/13/34
Marshall, Penny	Bronx, NY	10/15/42
Marshall, Peter	Huntington, WV.	3/30/27
Martin, Chris	Devon, England.	3/22/77
Martin, Jesse L.	Rocky Mount, VA	1/18/69
Martin, Kellie	Riverside, CA	10/16/75
Martin, Ricky	San Juan, Puerto Rico	12/24/71
Martin, Steve	Waco, TX	8/14/45
Martin, Tony	Oakland, CA	12/25/13
Martins, Peter	Copenhagen, Denmark	10/27/46
Mason, Jackie	Sheboygan, WI	6/9/34
Mason, Marsha	St. Louis, MO	4/3/42
Masterson, Christopher	Long Island, NY	1/22/80
Masterson, Mary Stuart	New York, NY	6/28/66
Mastrantonio, Mary Elizabeth	Lombard, IL.	11/17/58
Masur, Kurt	Brieg, Germany	7/18/27
Masur, Richard	New York, NY	11/20/48
Mathers, Jerry	Sioux City, IA.	6/2/48
Matheson, Tim	Glendale, CA.	12/31/47
Mathis, Johnny	Gilmer, TX.	9/30/35
Matlin, Marlee	Morton Grove, IL	8/24/65
Matthews, Dave	Johannesburg, S. Africa	1/9/67
May, Elaine	Philadelphia, PA	4/21/32
Mayer, John	Bridgeport, CT.	10/16/77
Mazar, Debi.	Queens, NY.	8/15/64
Mazursky, Paul	Brooklyn, NY	4/25/30
MCA	Brooklyn, NY	11/20/65
McAdams, Rachel	London, Ontario	10/7/86
McArdle, Andrea	Abington, PA	11/5/63
McAvoy, James	Glasgow, Scotland	1/1/79
McBride, Patricia	Teaneck, NJ	8/23/42
McCallum, David	Glasgow, Scotland	9/19/33
McCarthy, Andrew	Westfield, NJ.	11/29/62
McCarthy, Jenny	Chicago, IL	11/1/72
McCarthy, Kevin	Seattle, WA	2/15/14
McCartney, Paul	Liverpool, England	6/18/42
McCarver, Tim	Memphis, TN.	10/16/41
McClanahan, Rue	Healdton, OK.	2/21/34
McConaughey, Matthew	Uvalde, Texas	11/4/69
McCoo, Marilyn	Jersey City, NJ	9/30/43
McCormack, Eric	Toronto, Ontario	4/18/63
McCormack, Mary	Plainsfield, NJ	2/8/69
McCrane, Paul	Philadelphia, PA	1/19/61
McDaniel, James	Washington, DC	3/25/58
McDermott, Dylan	Waterbury, CT.	10/26/61
McDiarmid, Ian	Carnoustie, Tayside, Scotland	4/17/47
McDonald, Audra	Berlin, Germany	7/3/70
McDonnell, Mary	Wilkes-Barre, PA.	4/28/52
McDormand, Frances	Chicago, Illinois	6/23/57
McDowell, Malcolm	Leeds, England	6/13/43
McEntire, Reba	McAlester, OK.	3/28/55
McFerrin, Bobby	New York, NY	3/11/50
McGillis, Kelly	Newport Beach, CA	7/9/57
McGovern, Elizabeth	Evanston, IL	7/18/61
McGovern, Maureen	Youngstown, OH	7/27/49
McGraw, Tim	Delhi, LA	5/1/67
McGregor, Ewan	Crieff, Scotland	3/31/71
McKean, Michael	New York, NY	10/17/47
McKechnie, Donna	Pontiac, MI	11/16/42
McKellen, Ian	Burnley, England.	5/25/39
McKenzie, Benjamin	Austin, TX	9/12/78
McLachlan, Sarah	Halifax, Nova Scotia	1/28/68
McLean, A. J.	West Palm Beach, FL	1/9/78
McNichol, Kristy	Los Angeles, CA	9/11/62
McPartland, Marian	Stough, England	3/20/20
McRaney, Gerald	Collins, MS.	8/19/47
McShane, Ian	Blackburn, England	9/29/42
Meadows, Jayne	Wu Chang, China.	9/27/20
Meara, Anne	Brooklyn, NY	9/20/29
Meat Loaf	Dallas, TX	9/27/51
Meester, Leighton	Marco Island, FL	4/9/86
Mehta, Zubin	Bombay, India	4/29/36
Mellencamp, John	Seymour, IN.	10/7/51
Meloni, Christopher	Washington, DC.	4/2/61
Mendes, Sam	Redding, England	8/1/65
Mendes, Sergio	Niteroi, Brazil	2/11/41
Menzel, Idina	Syosset, NY	5/30/71
Mercer, Marian	Akron, OH	11/26/35
Merchant, Natalie	Jamestown, NY	10/26/63
Merkerson, S. Epatha	Saginaw, MI	11/28/52
Merrill, Dina	New York, NY	12/9/25
Messing, Debra	Brooklyn, NY	8/15/68
Metcalf, Laurie	Carbondale, IL	6/16/55
Meyers, Seth	Bedford, NH	12/28/73
Michael, George	London, England	6/25/63
Michaels, Al	Brooklyn, NY	11/12/44
Michaels, Lorne	Toronto, Ontario	11/17/44
Midler, Bette	Honolulu, HI	12/1/45
Midori	Osaka, Japan.	10/25/71
Mike D	Brooklyn, NY	11/20/65
Milano, Alyssa	Brooklyn, NY	12/19/72
Miles, Sarah	Ingatestone, England.	12/31/41
Miles, Vera	near Boise City, OK	8/23/29
Miller, Dennis	Pittsburgh, PA	11/3/53
Miller, Mitch	Rochester, NY	7/4/11
Miller, Penelope Ann	Santa Monica, CA	1/13/64
Mills, Donna	Chicago, IL.	12/11/43
Mills, Hayley	London, England	4/18/46
Milner, Martin	Detroit, MI	12/28/27
Milnes, Sherrill	Downers Grove, IL.	1/10/35
Milsap, Ronnie	Robinsville, NC	1/16/44
Mimieux, Yvette	Hollywood, CA.	1/8/42
Ming-Na	Macao	11/20/63
Minnelli, Liza	Los Angeles, CA	3/12/46
Minogue, Kylie	Melbourne, Australia	5/28/68
Mirren, Helen	London, England	7/26/45
Mitchell, Brian Stokes	Seattle, WA	10/31/57
Mitchell, Elizabeth	Los Angeles, CA	3/27/70
Mitchell, Joni	Fort McLeod, Alberta	11/7/43
Moby	Harlem, New York, NY.	9/11/65
Modine, Matthew	Loma Linda, CA	3/22/59
Moffat, Donald	Plymouth, England.	12/26/30
Molina, Alfred	London, England	5/24/53
Molinaro, Al	Kenosha, WI	6/24/19
Moll, Richard	Pasadena, CA	1/13/43
Moloney, Janel	Woodland Hills, CA	10/3/69
Monaghan, Dominic	Berlin, Germany	12/8/76
Monica (Arnold)	College Park, GA	10/24/80
Mo'Nique	Woodlawn, MD.	12/11/67
Moody, Ron	London, England	1/8/24
Moore, Demi	Roswell, NM.	11/11/62
Moore, Julianne	Fort Bragg, NC	12/3/60
Moore, Mandy	Nashua, NH	4/10/84
Moore, Mary Tyler	Brooklyn, NY	12/29/36
Moore, Melba	New York, NY	10/29/45
Moore, Michael	Flint, MI	4/23/54
Moore, Roger	London, England	10/14/27
Moore, Terry	Los Angeles, CA	1/7/29
Morales, Esai	Brooklyn, NY	10/1/62
Moranis, Rick	Toronto, Ontario	4/18/54
Moreau, Jeanne	Paris, France	1/23/28
Moreno, Rita	Humacao, PR.	12/11/31
Morgan, Harry	Detroit, MI	4/10/15
Morgan, Tracy	Bronx, NY.	11/10/68
Moriarty, Michael	Detroit, MI	4/5/41
Morissette, Alanis	Ottawa, Ontario	6/1/74
Morris, Garrett	New Orleans, LA	2/1/37
Morrison, Van	Belfast, N. Ireland	8/31/45
Morrissey	Manchester, England.	5/22/59
Morrow, Rob	New Rochelle, NY	9/21/62
Morse, David	Beverly, MA	10/11/53
Morse, Robert	Newton, MA	5/18/31
Mortensen, Viggo	New York, NY	10/20/58
Mortimer, Emily	London, England	12/1/71
Morton, Joe	Brooklyn, NY	10/18/47
Morton, Samantha	Nottingham, England.	5/13/77
Moses, William	Los Angeles, CA	11/17/59
Moss, Carrie-Anne	Vancouver, BC.	8/21/67
Moss, Elisabeth	Los Angeles, CA	7/24/82
Moss, Kate	Croydon, Surrey, England	1/16/74
Mueller-Stahl, Armin	Tilsit, E. Prussia	12/17/30
Muldaur, Diana	Brooklyn, NY	8/19/38
Mulgrew, Kate	Dubuque, IA	4/29/55
Mull, Martin	Chicago, IL.	8/18/43

Name	Birthplace	Birthdate
Mullally, Megan	Los Angeles, CA	11/12/58
Mullan, Peter	Peterhead, Scotland	1960
Mulroney, Dermot	Alexandria, VA	10/31/63
Muniz, Frankie	Ridgewood, NJ	12/5/85
Munsel, Patrice	Spokane, WA	5/14/25
Murphy, Ben	Jonesboro, AR	3/6/42
Murphy, Brittany	Atlanta, GA	11/10/77
Murphy, Donna	Queens, NY	3/7/58
Murphy, Eddie	Brooklyn, NY	4/3/61
Murphy, Michael	Los Angeles, CA	5/5/38
Murray, Anne	Springhill, Nova Scotia	6/20/45
Murray, Bill	Wilmette, IL	9/21/50
Murray, Don	Hollywood, CA	7/31/29
Musburger, Brent	Portland, OR	5/26/39
Muti, Riccardo	Naples, Italy	7/28/41
Myers, Mike	Scarborough, Ontario	5/25/63
Nabors, Jim	Sylacauga, AL	6/12/30
Nagra, Parminder	Leicester, England	10/5/75
Nash, Graham	Blackpool, England	2/2/42
Naughton, James	Middletown, CT	12/6/45
Navarro, Dave	Santa Monica, CA	6/7/67
Neal, Patricia	Packard, KY	1/20/26
Nealon, Kevin	Bridgeport, CT	11/18/53
Neeson, Liam	Ballymena, N. Ireland	6/7/52
Neill, Sam	Ulster, N. Ireland	9/14/47
Nelligan, Kate	London, Ontario	3/16/51
Nelly	Austin, TX	11/2/74
Nelson, Craig T.	Spokane, WA	4/4/46
Nelson, Ed	New Orleans, LA	12/21/28
Nelson, Judd	Portland, ME	11/28/59
Nelson, Tracy	Santa Monica, CA	10/25/63
Nelson, Willie	Abbott, TX	4/30/33
Nero, Peter	Brooklyn, NY	5/22/34
Nesmith, Mike	Houston, TX	12/30/42
Neuwirth, Bebe	Newark, NJ	12/31/58
Neville, Aaron	New Orleans, LA	1/24/41
Newhart, Bob	Oak Park, IL	9/5/29
Newman, Randy	New Orleans, LA	11/28/43
Newton, Wayne	Norfolk, VA	4/3/42
Newton-John, Olivia	Cambridge, England	9/26/48
Nicholas, Denise	Detroit, MI	7/12/44
Nichols, Mike	Berlin, Germany	11/6/31
Nicholson, Jack	Neptune, NJ	4/22/37
Nicks, Stevie	Phoenix, AZ	5/26/48
Nielsen, Connie	Copenhagen, Denmark	7/3/65
Nielsen, Leslie	Regina, Sask.	2/11/26
Nighy, Bill	Caterham, Surrey, Eng.	12/12/49
Nimoy, Leonard	Boston, MA	3/26/31
Nixon, Cynthia	New York, NY	4/9/66
Nolte, Nick	Omaha, NE	2/8/41
Noone, Peter	Manchester, England	11/5/47
Norman, Jessye	Augusta, GA	9/15/45
Norris, Chuck	Ryan, OK	3/10/40
Northam, Jeremy	Cambridge, England	12/1/61
Norton, Edward	Columbia, MD	8/18/69
Noth, Christopher	Madison, WI	11/13/54
Novak, Kim	Chicago, IL	2/13/33
Nuyen, France	Marseilles, France	7/31/39
Oates, John	New York, NY	4/7/49
Obradors, Jacqueline	San Fernando Valley, CA	10/6/66
O'Brian, Hugh	Rochester, NY	4/19/25
O'Brien, Conan	Brookline, MA	4/18/63
O'Brien, Margaret	Los Angeles, CA	1/15/37
Ocean, Billy	Fyzabad, Trinidad	1/21/50
O'Connor, Frances	Oxford, England	6/12/69
O'Connor, Sinead	Glenageary, Ireland	12/8/66
O'Donnell, Chris	Winnetka, IL	6/26/70
O'Donnell, Rosie	Commack, NY	3/21/62
O'Grady, Gail	Detroit, MI	1/23/63
Oh, Sandra	Nepean, Ontario	7/20/71
O'Hara, Catherine	Toronto, Canada	3/4/54
O'Hara, Maureen	Dublin, Ireland	8/17/20
Oka, Masi	Tokyo, Japan	12/27/74
Oldman, Gary	South London, England	3/21/58
Olin, Ken	Chicago, IL	7/30/54
Olin, Lena	Stockholm, Sweden	3/22/55
Olmos, Edward James	E. Los Angeles, CA	2/24/47
Olsen, Ashley	Sherman Oaks, CA	6/13/86
Olsen, Mary-Kate	Sherman Oaks, CA	6/13/86
Olsen, Merlin	Logan, UT	9/15/40
Olson, Nancy	Milwaukee, WI	7/14/28
O'Malley, Mike	Boston, MA	10/31/69
O'Neal, Ryan	Los Angeles, CA	4/20/41
O'Neal, Tatum	Los Angeles, CA	11/5/63
O'Neill, Ed	Youngstown, OH	4/12/46
Ontkean, Michael	Vancouver, B.C.	1/24/46
O'Quinn, Terry	Newbury, MI	7/15/52
Orlando, Tony	New York, NY	4/3/44
Ormond, Julia	Epsom, England	1/4/65
Osbourne, Jack	London, England	11/8/85
Osbourne, Kelly	London, England	10/27/84

Name	Birthplace	Birthdate
Osbourne, Ozzy	Birmingham, England	12/3/48
Osbourne, Sharon	London, England	10/10/52
O'Shea, Milo	Dublin, Ireland	6/2/26
Oslin, K.T.	Crossett, AR	5/15/42
Osment, Haley Joel	Los Angeles, CA	4/10/88
Osmond, Donny	Ogden, UT	12/9/57
Osmond, Marie	Ogden, UT	10/13/59
O'Toole, Annette	Houston, TX	4/1/53
O'Toole, Peter	Connemara, Ireland	8/2/32
Otto, Miranda	Brisbane, Australia	12/16/67
Owen, Clive	Keresley, England	10/3/64
Oz, Frank	Herford, England	5/25/44
Ozawa, Seiji	Shenyang, China	9/1/35
Pacino, Al	East Harlem, NY	4/25/40
Packer, Billy	Wellsville, NY	2/25/40
Page, Ellen	Halifax, Nova Scotia	2/21/87
Page, Jimmy	Heston, England	1/9/44
Page, Patti	Claremore, OK	11/8/27
Paget, Debra	Denver, CO	8/19/33
Paige, Janis	Tacoma, WA	9/16/22
Paisley, Brad	Glen Dale, WV	10/28/72
Palin, Michael	Sheffield, England	5/5/43
Palmer, Betsy	East Chicago, IN	11/1/29
Palmer, Geoffrey	London, England	6/4/27
Palminteri, Chazz	Bronx, NY	5/15/51
Paltrow, Gwyneth	Los Angeles, CA	9/28/72
Panettiere, Hayden	Palisades, NY	8/21/89
Pantoliano, Joe	Hoboken, NJ	9/12/51
Papas, Irene	Chiliomodion, Greece	9/3/26
Paquin, Anna	Wellington, New Zealand	7/24/82
Parker, Alan	London, England	2/14/44
Parker, Eleanor	Cedarville, OH	6/26/22
Parker, Fess	Ft. Worth, TX	8/16/25
Parker, Jameson	Baltimore, MD	11/18/47
Parker, Mary-Louise	Fort Jackson, SC	8/2/64
Parker, Sarah Jessica	Nelsonville, OH	3/25/65
Parsons, Estelle	Marblehead, MA.	11/20/27
Parton, Dolly	Sevierville, TN	1/19/46
Pasdar, Adrian	Pittsfield, MA	4/30/65
Patinkin, Mandy	Chicago, IL	11/30/52
Patric, Jason	Queens, NY	6/17/66
Pattinson, Robert	London, England	5/13/86
Patton, Will	Charleston, SC.	6/14/54
Paul, Adrian	London, England	5/29/59
Paulson, Sarah	Tampa, FL	12/17/75
Paxton, Bill	Fort Worth, TX	5/17/55
Pearce, Guy	Ely, England	10/5/67
Peet, Amanda	New York, NY	1/11/72
Pendergrass, Teddy	Philadelphia, PA.	3/26/50
Penn, Arthur	Philadelphia, PA.	9/27/22
Penn, Kal	Montclair, NJ	4/23/77
Penn, Sean	Burbank, CA.	8/17/60
Perez, Rosie	Brooklyn, NY	9/6/64
Perkins, Elizabeth	Queens, NY	11/18/60
Perlman, Itzhak	Tel Aviv, Israel	8/31/45
Perlman, Rhea	Brooklyn, NY	3/31/48
Perlman, Ron	New York, NY	4/13/50
Perrine, Valerie	Galveston, TX	9/3/43
Perry, Luke	Fredericktown, OH	10/11/66
Perry, Matthew	Williamstown, MA.	8/19/69
Persoff, Nehemiah	Jerusalem, Israel	8/2/20
Pesci, Joe	Newark, NJ	2/9/43
Peters, Bernadette	Queens, NY	2/28/48
Peters, Roberta	Bronx, NY	5/4/30
Petersen, Wolfgang	Emden, Germany	3/14/41
Petty, Lori	Chattanooga, TN	3/23/63
Petty, Tom	Gainesville, FL	10/20/50
Pfeiffer, Michelle	Santa Ana, CA.	4/29/58
Phair, Liz	New Haven, CT	4/17/67
Philbin, Regis	New York, NY	8/25/31
Phillippe, Ryan	New Castle, DE	9/10/74
Phillips, Lou Diamond	Subic Bay, Philippines	2/17/62
Phillips, Mackenzie	Alexandria, VA	11/10/59
Phillips, Michelle	Long Beach, CA.	6/4/44
Phillips, Sian	Bettws, Wales, UK	5/14/34
Phoenix, Joaquin	San Juan, Puerto Rico	10/28/74
Pierce, David Hyde	Albany, NY.	4/3/59
Pinchot, Bronson	New York, NY	5/20/59
Pink (Alecia Moore)	Doylestown, PA	9/8/79
Pinkett Smith, Jada	Baltimore, MD	9/18/71
Pirner, David	Green Bay, WI	4/16/64
Piscopo, Joe	Passaic, NJ	6/17/51
Pitt, Brad	Shawnee, OK.	12/18/63
Piven, Jeremy	New York, NY	7/26/65
Plant, Robert	W. Bromwich, England.	8/20/48
Plowright, Joan	Brigg, England	10/28/29
Plummer, Amanda	New York, NY	3/23/57
Plummer, Christopher	Toronto, Ontario	12/13/27
Poelher, Amy	Burlington, MA	9/16/71
Poitier, Sidney	Miami, FL	2/20/27
Polanski, Roman	Paris, France	8/18/33

Name	Birthplace	Birthdate
Pompeo, Ellen	Everett, MA	11/10/69
Pop, Iggy	Muskegon, MI	4/21/47
Portman, Natalie	Jerusalem, Israel	6/9/81
Posey, Parker	Baltimore, MD	11/8/68
Post, Markie	Palo Alto, CA	11/4/50
Potente, Franka	Dulmen, Germany	7/22/74
Potts, Annie	Nashville, TN	10/28/52
Povich, Maury	Bethesda, MD	1/17/39
Powell, Jane	Portland, OR	4/1/28
Powers, Stefanie	Hollywood, CA	11/2/42
Prentiss, Paula	San Antonio, TX	3/4/39
Prepon, Laura	Watchung, NJ	3/7/80
Presley, Priscilla	Brooklyn, NY	5/24/45
Pressly, Jaime	Kinston, NC	7/30/77
Previn, Andre	Berlin, Germany	4/6/29
Price, Leontyne	Laurel, MS	2/10/27
Price, Molly	North Plainfield, NJ	12/15/66
Price, Ray	Perryville, TX	1/12/26
Pride, Charley	Sledge, MS	3/18/38
Priestley, Jason	Vancouver, Brit. Columbia	8/28/69
Prince (The Artist)	Minneapolis, MN	6/7/58
Prince, Faith	Augusta, GA	8/5/57
Principal, Victoria	Fukuoka, Japan	1/3/50
Prinze, Freddie, Jr.	Albuquerque, NM	3/8/76
Probst, Jeff	Wichita, KS	11/1/61
Proctor, Emily	Raleigh, NC	10/18/68
Provine, Dorothy	Deadwood, SD	1/20/37
Pryce, Jonathan	Holywell, N. Wales	6/1/47
Puck, Wolfgang	St. Veit, Austria	1/8/49
Pulliam, Keshia Knight	Newark, NJ	4/9/79
Pullman, Bill	Hornell, NY	12/17/53
Purcell, Sarah	Richmond, IN	10/8/48
Quaid, Dennis	Houston, TX	4/9/54
Quaid, Randy	Houston, TX	10/1/50
Queen Latifah	Newark, NJ	3/18/70
Quinn, Aidan	Chicago, IL	3/8/59
Quinn, Colin	Brooklyn, NY	8/15/59
Quinn, Martha	Albany, NY	5/11/59
Quinto, Zachary	Pittsburgh, PA	1/1/77
Rachins, Alan	Cambridge, MA	10/3/42
Radcliffe, Daniel	London, England	7/23/89
Rae, Charlotte	Milwaukee, WI	4/22/26
Raffi	Cairo, Egypt	7/8/48
Rainer, Luise	Vienna, Austria	1/12/10
Raitt, Bonnie	Burbank, CA	11/8/49
Ramey, Samuel	Colby, KS	3/28/42
Ramirez, Efren	Los Angeles, CA	10/2/83
Ramirez, Sara	Mazatlan, Mexico	09/31/76
Ramone, Tommy	Budapest, Hungary	1/29/52
Randolph, Joyce	Detroit, MI	10/21/25
Raphael, Sally Jessy	Easton, PA	2/25/35
Rashad, Phylicia	Houston, TX	6/19/48
Ratzenberger, John	Bridgeport, CT	4/6/47
Raver, Kim	New York, NY	3/15/69
Ray, Rachael	Cape Cod, MA	8/25/68
Reddy, Helen	Melbourne, Australia	10/25/41
Redford, Robert	Santa Monica, CA	8/18/37
Redgrave, Lynn	London, England	3/8/43
Redgrave, Vanessa	London, England	1/30/37
Reed, Lou	Brooklyn, NY	3/2/42
Reed, Rex	Ft. Worth, TX	10/2/38
Reese, Della	Detroit, MI	7/6/31
Reeves, Keanu	Beirut, Lebanon	9/2/64
Reeves, Martha	Eufaula, AL	7/18/41
Regalbuto, Joe	Brooklyn, NY	8/24/49
Reid, Tara	Wyckoff, NJ	11/8/75
Reid, Tim	Norfolk, VA	12/19/44
Reid, Vernon	London, England	8/22/58
Reilly, John C.	Chicago, IL	5/24/65
Reiner, Carl	Bronx, NY	3/20/22
Reiner, Rob	Bronx, NY	3/6/47
Reinhold, Judge	Wilmington, DE	5/21/57
Reinking, Ann	Seattle, WA	11/10/49
Reiser, Paul	New York, NY	3/30/57
Reitman, Ivan	Komarno, Czechoslovakia	10/26/46
Remini, Leah	Brooklyn, NY	6/15/70
Resnik, Regina	New York, NY	8/30/22
Reynolds, Burt	Waycross, GA	2/11/36
Reynolds, Debbie	El Paso, TX	4/1/32
Reynolds, Ryan	Vancouver, BC	10/23/76
Reznor, Trent	Mercer, PA	5/17/65
Rhames, Ving	Harlem, New York, NY	5/12/59
Rhys Meyers, Jonathan	Dublin, Ireland	7/27/77
Rhymes, Busta	Brooklyn, NY	5/20/72
Ribisi, Giovanni	Los Angeles, CA	12/17/74
Ricci, Christina	Santa Monica, CA	2/12/80
Richards, Denise	Downers Grove, IL	2/17/71
Richards, Keith	Dartford, Kent, England	12/18/43
Richards, Michael	Culver City, CA	7/24/49
Richardson, Kevin	Lexington, KY	10/3/71
Richardson, Miranda	Lancashire, England	3/3/58

Name	Birthplace	Birthdate
Richardson, Patricia	Bethesda, MD	2/23/51
Richie, Lionel	Tuskegee, AL	6/20/49
Richie, Nicole	Berkeley, CA	9/21/81
Richter, Andy	Grand Rapids, MI	8/28/66
Rickles, Don	Queens, NY	5/8/26
Rickman, Alan	Hammersmith, England	2/21/46
Riegert, Peter	New York, NY	4/11/47
Rigg, Diana	Doncaster, England	7/20/38
Rihanna	St. Michael, Barbados	2/20/88
Rimes, LeAnn	Flowood, MS	8/28/82
Ringwald, Molly	Roseville, CA	2/18/68
Ripa, Kelly	Stratford, NJ	10/2/70
Rivera, Chita	Washington, DC	1/23/33
Rivera, Geraldo	New York, NY	7/4/43
Rivers, Joan	Brooklyn, NY	6/8/33
Robbins, Tim	W. Covina, CA	10/16/58
Roberts, Doris	St. Louis, MO	11/4/29
Roberts, Eric	Biloxi, MS	4/18/56
Roberts, Julia	Smyrna, GA	10/28/67
Roberts, Pernell	Waycross, GA	5/18/28
Roberts, Tony	New York, NY	10/22/39
Robertson, Cliff	La Jolla, CA	9/9/25
Robertson, Dale	Harrah, OK	7/14/23
Robinson, Smokey	Detroit, MI	2/19/40
Rochon, Lela	Torrance, CA	4/17/64
Rock, Chris	South Carolina	2/7/66
Rock, The	Hayward, CA	5/2/72
Rodgers, Jimmy	Camas, WA	9/18/33
Rodriguez, Jai	Brentwood, NY	6/22/77
Rodriguez, Johnny	Sabinal, TX	12/10/51
Rogan, Joe	Newark, NJ	8/11/67
Rogen, Seth	Vancouver, BC	4/15/82
Rogers, Kenny	Houston, TX	8/21/38
Rogers, Mimi	Coral Gables, FL	1/27/56
Rogers, Wayne	Birmingham, AL	4/7/33
Rohm, Elisabeth	Dusseldorf, Germany	4/28/73
Rollins, Henry	Washington, DC	2/13/61
Rollins, Sonny	Harlem, NY	9/7/30
Romano, Ray	Queens, NY	12/21/57
Romijn, Rebecca	Berkeley, CA	11/6/72
Ronstadt, Linda	Tucson, AZ	7/15/46
Rooney, Mickey	Brooklyn, NY	9/23/20
Root, Stephen	Sarasota, FL	11/17/51
Rose, Axl	Lafayette, IN	2/6/62
Rose Marie	New York, NY	8/15/23
Roseanne	Salt Lake City, UT	11/3/52
Ross, Charlotte	Winnetka, IL	1/21/68
Ross, Diana	Detroit, MI	3/26/44
Ross, Katharine	Hollywood, CA	1/29/40
Ross, Marion	Albert Lea, MN	10/25/28
Rossdale, Gavin	London, England	10/30/67
Rossellini, Isabella	Rome, Italy	6/18/52
Rossum, Emmy	New York, NY	9/12/86
Roth, David Lee	Bloomington, IN	10/10/55
Roth, Tim	London, England	5/14/61
Rotten, Johnny	London, England	1/31/56
Rourke, Mickey	Schenectady, NY	9/16/56
Routh, Brandon	Des Moines, IA	10/9/79
Routledge, Patricia	Birkenhead, England	2/17/29
Rowan, Kelly	Ottawa, Ontario	1967
Rowlands, Gena	Cambria, WI	6/19/36
Rubinstein, John	Beverly Hills, CA	12/8/46
Rudd, Paul	Passaic, NJ	4/6/1969
Rudner, Rita	Miami, FL	9/17/56
Rudolph, Maya	Gainesville, FL	7/27/72
Ruehl, Mercedes	Queens, NY	2/28/48
Ruffalo, Mark	Kenosha, WI	11/22/67
Rupp, Debra Jo	Glendale, CA	2/24/51
Rush, Barbara	Denver, CO	1/4/27
Rush, Geoffrey	Toowoomba, Australia	7/6/51
Russell, Jane	Bemidji, MN	6/21/21
Russell, Ken	Southampton, England	7/3/27
Russell, Keri	Fountain Valley, CA	3/23/76
Russell, Kurt	Springfield, MA	3/17/51
Russell, Leon	Lawton, OK	4/2/41
Russell, Mark	Buffalo, NY	8/23/32
Russell, Theresa	San Diego, CA	3/20/57
Russo, Rene	Burbank, CA	2/17/54
Rutherford, Ann	Toronto, Ontario	11/2/20
Ruttan, Susan	Oregon City, OR	9/16/50
Ryan, Meg	Fairfield, CT	11/19/61
Ryan, Roz	Detroit, MI	7/7/51
Rydell, Bobby	Philadelphia, PA	4/26/42
Ryder, Winona	Winona, MN	10/29/71
Sabato, Antonio, Jr.	Rome, Italy	2/29/72
Sade	Ibadan, Nigeria	1/16/59
Sagal, Katey	Hollywood, CA	1/19/53
Saget, Bob	Philadelphia, PA	5/17/56
Sagnier, Ludivine	La Celle-St.-Cloud, France	7/3/79
Sahl, Mort	Montreal, Quebec	5/11/27
Saint, Eva Marie	Newark, NJ	7/4/24

Name	Birthplace	Birthdate
St. James, Susan	Hollywood, CA	8/14/46
St. John, Jill	Los Angeles, CA	8/19/40
St. Patrick, Mathew	Philadelphia, PA	3/17/69
Sajak, Pat	Chicago, IL	10/26/46
Saks, Gene	New York, NY	11/8/21
Salonga, Lea	Manila, Philippines	2/22/71
Samberg, Andy	Berkeley, CA	8/18/78
Samms, Emma	London, England	8/28/60
Sandler, Adam	Brooklyn, NY	9/9/66
Sands, Julian	West Yorkshire, England	1/15/58
San Giacomo, Laura	West Orange, NJ	11/14/61
Santana, Carlos	Autlan, Mexico	7/20/47
Sara, Mia	Brooklyn, NY	6/19/67
Sarandon, Susan	New York, NY	10/4/46
Sarnoff, Dorothy	New York, NY	5/25/17
Sartain, Gailard	Tulsa, OK	9/18/46
Savage, Ben	Highland Park, IL	9/13/80
Savage, Fred	Highland Park, IL	7/9/76
Sawa, Devon	Vancouver, BC	9/7/78
Saxon, John	Brooklyn, NY	8/5/35
Sayles, John	Schenectady, NY	9/28/50
Scacchi, Greta	Milan, Italy	2/18/60
Scaggs, Boz	Canton, OH	6/8/44
Scales, Prunella	Sutton Abinger, England	6/22/32
Scalia, Jack	Brooklyn, NY	11/10/51
Schallert, William	Los Angeles, CA	7/6/22
Schell, Maximilian	Vienna, Austria	12/8/30
Schiff, Richard	Bethesda, MD	5/27/55
Schiffer, Claudia	Rheinbach, Germany	8/25/70
Schneider, John	Mt. Kisco, NY	4/8/54
Schneider, Rob	San Francisco, CA	10/31/63
Schram, Bitty	New York, NY	7/17/68
Schreiber, Liev	San Francisco, CA	10/4/67
Schroder, Rick	Staten Island, NY	4/13/70
Schwarzenegger, Arnold	Thal, Austria	7/30/47
Schwimmer, David	Astoria, Queens, NY	11/2/66
Sciorra, Annabella	New York, NY	3/24/64
Scolari, Peter	New Rochelle, NY	9/12/54
Scorsese, Martin	Flushing, Queens, NY	11/17/42
Scott, Lizabeth	Scranton, PA	9/29/22
Scott, Ridley	South Shields, England	11/30/37
Scott, Seann William	Cottage Grove, MN	10/3/76
Scott-Heron, Gil	Chicago, IL	4/1/49
Scott Thomas, Kristin	Redruth, England	5/24/60
Scotto, Renata	Savona, Italy	2/24/35
Scully, Vin	Bronx, NY	11/29/27
Seacrest, Ryan	Atlanta, GA	12/24/74
Seagal, Steven	Lansing, MI	4/10/51
Secor, Kyle	Tacoma, WA	5/31/58
Sedaka, Neil	Brooklyn, NY	3/13/39
Sedgwick, Kyra	New York, NY	8/19/65
Seeger, Pete	New York, NY	5/3/19
Segal, George	Great Neck, NY	2/13/34
Seidelman, Susan	Abington, PA	12/11/52
Seinfeld, Jerry	Brooklyn, NY	4/29/54
Sellecca, Connie	Bronx, NY	5/25/55
Selleck, Tom	Detroit, MI	1/29/45
Severinsen, Doc	Arlington, OR	7/7/27
Sevigny, Chloë	Springfield, MA	11/18/74
Sewell, Rufus	London, England	10/29/67
Seymour, Jane	Hillingdon, England	2/15/51
Shackelford, Ted	Oklahoma City, OK	6/23/46
Shaffer, Paul	Thunder Bay, Ontario	11/28/49
Shakira	Barranquilla, Colombia	2/2/77
Shalhoub, Tony	Green Bay, WI	10/9/53
Shandling, Garry	Chicago, IL	11/29/49
Shankar, Ravi	Benares, India	4/7/20
Shannon, Molly	Shaker Heights, OH	9/16/64
Sharif, Omar	Alexandria, Egypt	4/10/32
Shatner, William	Montreal, Quebec	3/22/31
Shaughnessy, Charles	London, England	2/9/55
Shaver, Helen	St. Thomas, Ontario	2/24/51
Shawkat, Alia	Riverside, CA	4/18/89
Shea, John	N. Conway, NH	4/14/49
Shearer, Harry	Los Angeles, CA	12/23/43
Shearing, George	London, England	8/13/19
Sheedy, Ally	New York, NY	6/13/62
Sheen, Charlie	Los Angeles, CA	9/3/65
Sheen, Martin	Dayton, OH	8/3/40
Sheindlin, Judy	Brooklyn, NY	10/21/42
Shelley, Carole	London, England	8/16/39
Shepard, Sam	Ft. Sheridan, IL	11/5/43
Shepherd, Cybill	Memphis, TN	2/18/50
Shepherd, Sherri	Chicago, IL	4/22/67
Sheridan, Nicollette	Worthing, England	11/21/63
Shields, Brooke	New York, NY	5/31/65
Shire, Talia	Lake Success, NY	4/25/46
Short, Martin	Hamilton, Ontario	3/26/50
Shortz, Will	Crawfordsville, IN	8/26/52
Show, Grant	Detroit, MI	2/27/62
Shue, Andrew	S. Orange, NJ	2/20/67

Name	Birthplace	Birthdate
Shue, Elisabeth	Wilmington, DE	10/6/63
Shyamalan, M. Night	Pondicherry, India	8/6/70
Siepi, Cesare	Milan, Italy	2/14/23
Sigler, Jamie-Lynn	Jericho, NY	5/15/81
Sikking, James B.	Los Angeles, CA	3/5/34
Silverman, Jonathan	Beverly Hills, CA	8/5/66
Silverman, Sarah	Bedford, NH	12/1/70
Silverstone, Alicia	Hillsborough, CA	10/4/76
Simmons, Gene	Haifa, Israel	8/25/49
Simmons, Henry	Stamford, CT	7/1/70
Simmons, Jean	London, England	1/31/29
Simmons, Richard	New Orleans, LA	7/12/48
Simon, Carly	Riverdale, NY	6/25/45
Simon, Paul	Newark, NJ	10/13/41
Simpson, Ashlee	Waco, TX	10/3/84
Simpson, Jessica	Abilene, TX	7/10/80
Sinatra, Nancy	Jersey City, NJ	6/8/40
Sinbad	Benton Harbor, MI	11/10/56
Singleton, John	Los Angeles, CA	1/6/68
Sinise, Gary	Blue Island, IL	3/17/55
Sirico, Tony	Brooklyn, NY	7/29/42
Sisto, Jeremy	Grass Valley, CA	10/6/74
Sizemore, Tom	Detroit, MI	9/29/64
Skerritt, Tom	Detroit, MI	8/25/33
Skye, Ione	Hertfordshire, England	9/4/70
Slater, Christian	New York, NY	8/18/69
Slater, Helen	Massapequa, NY	12/15/63
Slattery, John	Boston, MA	8/13/63
Slezak, Erika	Hollywood, CA	8/5/46
Slick, Grace	Evanston, IL	10/30/39
Smirnoff, Yakov	Odessa, Ukraine	1/24/51
Smith, Allison	Bronx, NY	12/9/69
Smith, Jaclyn	Houston, TX	10/26/47
Smith, Keely	Norfolk, VA	3/9/32
Smith, Kevin	Red Bank, NJ	8/2/70
Smith, Maggie	Ilford, England	12/28/34
Smith, Patti	Chicago, IL	12/30/46
Smith, Robert	Blackpool, England	4/21/59
Smith, Will	West Philadelphia, PA	9/25/68
Smits, Jimmy	New York, NY	7/9/55
Smothers, Dick	Governor's Island, NY	11/20/38
Smothers, Tom	Governor's Island, NY	2/2/37
Snipes, Wesley	Orlando, FL	7/31/62
Snoop Dogg	Long Beach, CA	10/20/72
Soderbergh, Steven	Atlanta, GA	1/14/63
Somers, Suzanne	San Bruno, CA	10/16/46
Sommer, Elke	Berlin, Germany	11/5/40
Sorbo, Kevin	Mound, MN	9/24/58
Sorvino, Mira	Tenafly, NJ	9/28/67
Sorvino, Paul	Brooklyn, NY	4/13/39
Soul, David	Chicago, IL	8/28/43
Spacek, Sissy	Quitman, TX	12/25/49
Spacey, Kevin	S. Orange, NJ	7/26/59
Spade, David	Birmingham, MI	7/22/64
Spader, James	Boston, MA	2/7/60
Spano, Joe	San Francisco, CA	7/7/46
Sparks, Jordin	Phoenix, AZ	12/22/89
Spears, Britney	Kentwood, LA	12/2/81
Spears, Jamie-Lynn	McComb, MS	4/4/91
Spector, Phil	Bronx, NY	12/26/40
Spelling, Tori	Los Angeles, CA	5/16/73
Spielberg, Steven	Cincinnati, OH	12/18/46
Spiner, Brent	Houston, TX	2/2/49
Springer, Jerry	London, England	2/13/44
Springfield, Rick	Sydney, Australia	8/23/49
Springsteen, Bruce	Freehold, NJ	9/23/49
Spurlock, Morgan	Parksburg, WV	11/7/70
Stahl, Nick	Harlingen, TX	12/5/79
Stallone, Sylvester	New York, NY	7/6/46
Stamos, John	Cypress, CA	8/19/63
Stamp, Terence	Stepney, England	7/22/39
Stang, Arnold	Chelsea, MA	9/28/25
Stanton, Harry Dean	West Irvine, KY	7/14/26
Stapleton, Jean	New York, NY	1/19/23
Starr, Ringo	Liverpool, England	7/7/40
Steenburgen, Mary	Newport, AR	2/8/53
Stefani, Gwen	Anaheim, CA	10/3/69
Stein, Ben	Washington, DC	11/25/44
Stephens, James	Mt. Kisco, NY	5/18/51
Stern, Daniel	Bethesda, MD	8/28/57
Stern, Howard	Roosevelt, NY	1/12/54
Sternhagen, Frances	Washington, DC	1/13/30
Stevens, Andrew	Memphis, TN	6/10/55
Stevens, Cat	London, England	7/21/48
Stevens, Connie	Brooklyn, NY	8/8/38
Stevens, Rise	Bronx, NY	6/11/13
Stevens, Stella	Hot Coffee, MS	10/1/36
Stevenson, Parker	Philadelphia, PA	6/4/52
Stewart, French	Albuquerque, NM	2/20/64
Stewart, Jon	Trenton, NY	11/28/62
Stewart, Kristen	Los Angeles, CA	4/9/90

Name	Birthplace	Birthdate
Stewart, Patrick	Mirfield, England	7/13/40
Stewart, Rod	London, England	1/10/45
Stiers, David Ogden	Peoria, IL	10/31/42
Stiles, Julia	New York, NY	3/28/81
Stiller, Ben	New York, NY	11/30/65
Stiller, Jerry	Brooklyn, NY	6/8/27
Stills, Stephen	Dallas, TX	1/3/45
Sting	Newcastle, England	10/2/51
Stipe, Michael	Decatur, GA	1/4/60
Stockwell, Dean	North Hollywood, CA	3/5/36
Stoltz, Eric	Whittier, CA	9/30/61
Stone, Dee Wallace	Kansas City, KS	12/14/48
Stone, Oliver	New York, NY	9/15/46
Stone, Sharon	Meadville, PA	3/10/58
Stookey, Paul	Baltimore, MD	12/30/37
Storch, Larry	New York, NY	1/8/23
Stowe, Madeleine	Eagle Rock, CA	8/18/58
Strait, George	Pearsall, TX	5/18/52
Strasser, Robin	New York, NY	5/7/45
Stratas, Teresa	Toronto, Ontario	5/26/38
Strathairn, David	San Francisco, CA	1/26/49
Strauss, Peter	Croton-on-Hudson, NY	2/20/47
Streep, Meryl	Summit, NJ	6/22/49
Streisand, Barbra	Brooklyn, NY	4/24/42
Stringfield, Sherry	Colorado Springs, CO	6/24/67
Stritch, Elaine	Detroit, MI	2/2/26
Stroman, Susan	Wilmington, DE	10/17/54
Struthers, Sally	Portland, OR	7/28/48
Stuart, Gloria	Santa Monica, CA	7/4/10
Studdard, Ruben	Birmingham, AL	9/12/78
Suchet, David	London, England	5/2/46
Sullivan, Erik Per	Worcester, MA	7/12/91
Sullivan, Susan	New York, NY	11/18/42
Sumac, Yma	Ichocan, Peru	9/10/27
Summer, Donna	Dorchester, MA	12/31/48
Sutherland, Donald	St. John, New Brunswick	7/17/34
Sutherland, Joan	Sydney, Australia	11/7/26
Sutherland, Kiefer	London, England	12/21/66
Suvari, Mena	Newport, RI	2/9/79
Swank, Hilary	Bellingham, WA	7/30/74
Swinton, Tilda	London, England	11/5/60
Swit, Loretta	Passaic, NJ	11/4/37
Swift, Taylor	Wyomissing, PA	12/13/89
Sykes, Wanda	Portsmouth, VA	3/7/64
Szmanda, Eric	Milwaukee, WI	7/24/75
T, Mr.	Chicago, IL	5/21/52
Takei, George	Los Angeles, CA	4/20/37
Tallchief, Maria	Fairfax, OK	1/24/25
Tamblyn, Amber	Santa Monica, CA	5/14/83
Tamblyn, Russ	Los Angeles, CA	12/30/34
Tambor, Jeffrey	San Francisco, CA	7/8/44
Tarantino, Quentin	Knoxville, TN	3/27/63
Tautou, Audrey	Beaumont, France	8/9/78
Taylor, Billy	Greenville, NC	7/21/21
Taylor, Buck	Hollywood, CA	5/13/38
Taylor, Elizabeth	London, England	2/27/32
Taylor, James	Boston, MA	3/12/48
Taylor, Rip	Washington, DC	1/13/34
Taylor, Rod	Sydney, Australia	1/11/30
Taymor, Julie	Newton, MA	12/15/52
Te Kanawa, Kiri	Gisborne, New Zealand	3/6/44
Teller	Philadelphia, PA	2/14/48
Temple Black, Shirley	Santa Monica, CA	4/23/28
Tennant, Victoria	London, England	9/30/50
Tennille, Toni	Montgomery, AL	5/8/43
Tesh, John	Garden City, NY	7/9/52
Tharp, Twyla	Portland, IN	7/1/41
Thaxter, Phyllis	Portland, ME	11/20/21
Theron, Charlize	South Africa	8/7/75
Thicke, Alan	Kirkland Lake, Ontario	3/1/47
Thiessen, Tiffani	Long Beach, CA	1/23/74
Thomas, Jay	Kermit, TX	7/12/48
Thomas, Jonathan Taylor	Bethlehem, PA	9/8/81
Thomas, Marlo	Deerfield, MI	11/21/38
Thomas, Michael Tilson	Hollywood, CA	12/21/44
Thomas, Philip Michael	Columbus, OH	5/26/49
Thomas, Richard	New York, NY	6/13/51
Thomas, Sean Patrick	Wilmington, DE	12/17/70
Thompson, Emma	London, England	4/15/59
Thompson, Jack	Sydney, Australia	8/31/40
Thompson, Lea	Rochester, MN	5/31/61
Thompson, Sada	Des Moines, IA	9/27/29
Thorne-Smith, Courtney	San Francisco, CA	11/8/67
Thornton, Billy Bob	Hot Springs, AR	8/4/55
Thurman, Uma	Boston, MA	4/29/70
Tiegs, Cheryl	Breckenridge, MN	9/25/47
Tierney, Maura	Boston, MA	2/3/65
Tillis, Mel	Tampa, FL	8/8/32
Tilly, Jennifer	Harbor City, CA	9/16/58
Tilly, Meg	Long Beach, CA	2/14/60
Timberlake, Justin	Memphis, TN	1/31/81

Name	Birthplace	Birthdate
Tisdale, Ashley	West Deal, NJ	7/2/85
Todd, Richard	Dublin, Ireland	6/11/19
Tomei, Marisa	Brooklyn, NY	12/4/64
Tomlin, Lily	Detroit, MI	9/1/39
Tork, Peter	Washington, DC	2/13/42
Torn, Rip	Temple, TX	2/6/31
Townsend, Robert	Chicago, IL	2/6/57
Townshend, Peter	Chiswick, England	5/19/45
Travanti, Daniel J.	Kenosha, WI	3/7/40
Travis, Nancy	Astoria, Queens, NY	9/21/61
Travis, Randy	Marshville, NC	5/4/59
Travolta, John	Englewood, NJ	2/18/54
Trebek, Alex	Sudbury, Ontario	7/22/40
Tripplehorn, Jean	Tulsa, OK	6/10/63
Tritt, Travis	Marietta, GA	2/9/63
Tucci, Stanley	Katonah, NY	1/11/60
Tucker, Chris	Decatur, GA	8/31/72
Tucker, Michael	Baltimore, MD	2/6/44
Tucker, Tanya	Seminole, TX	10/10/58
Tune, Tommy	Wichita Falls, TX	2/28/39
Turlington, Christy	Walnut Creek, CA	1/2/69
Turner, Janine	Lincoln, NE	12/6/62
Turner, Kathleen	Springfield, MO	6/19/54
Turner, Tina	Brownsville, TN	11/26/39
Turturro, John	Brooklyn, NY	2/28/57
Twain, Shania	Windsor, Ontario	8/28/65
Twiggy (Lawson)	London, England	9/19/49
Tyler, Liv	New York, NY	7/1/77
Tyler, Steven	Yonkers, NY	3/26/48
Tyson, Cicely	Harlem, NY	12/19/33
Uecker, Bob	Milwaukee, WI	1/26/35
Uggams, Leslie	New York, NY	5/25/43
Ullman, Tracey	Slough, England	12/30/59
Ullmann, Liv	Tokyo, Japan	12/16/39
Ulrich, Skeet	New York, NY	1/20/69
Underwood, Carrie	Checotah, OK	3/10/83
Underwood, Blair	Tacoma, WA	8/25/64
Urban, Keith	Whangarei, North Island, New Zealand	10/26/67
Urie, Michael	Dallas, TX	8/8/80
Usher (Raymond IV)	Chattanooga, TN	10/14/78
Vaccaro, Brenda	Brooklyn, NY	11/18/39
Vale, Jerry	Bronx, NY	7/8/32
Valente, Caterina	Paris, France	1/14/31
Valley, Mark	Ogdensburg, NY	12/24/64
Valli, Frankie	Newark, NJ	5/3/37
Van Ark, Joan	New York, NY	6/16/43
Vance, Courtney B.	Birmingham, MI	3/12/60
Van Damme, Jean-Claude	Brussels, Belgium	10/18/60
Van Der Beek, James	Cheshire, CT	3/8/77
Van Doren, Mamie	Rowena, SD	2/6/31
Van Dyke, Dick	West Plains, MO	12/13/25
Van Dyke, Jerry	Danville, IL	7/27/31
Van Halen, Eddie	Nijmegen, Netherlands	1/26/55
Van Patten, Dick	Queens, NY	12/9/28
Van Peebles, Mario	Mexico City, Mexico	1/15/57
Van Sant, Gus	Louisville, KY	7/24/52
Van Zandt, Steven	Boston, MA	11/22/50
Vardalos, Nia	Winnipeg, Manitoba	9/24/62
Vaughn, Robert	New York, NY	11/22/32
Vaughn, Vince	Minneapolis, MN	3/28/70
Vedder, Eddie	Evanston, IL	12/23/64
Vega, Alexa	Miami, FL	8/27/88
Ventimiglia, Milo	Anaheim, CA	7/8/77
Vereen, Ben	Miami, FL	10/10/46
Verrett, Shirley	New Orleans, LA	5/31/31
Vickers, Jon	Prince Albert, Sask.	10/29/26
Vieira, Meredith	Providence, RI	12/30/53
Vigoda, Abe	New York, NY	2/24/21
Vincent, Jan-Michael	Denver, CO	7/15/44
Vinton, Bobby	Canonsburg, PA	4/16/35
Visnjic, Goran	Sibenik, Yugo. (Croatia)	9/9/72
Vitale, Dick	East Rutherford, NJ	6/9/39
Voight, Jon	Yonkers, NY	12/29/38
Von Stade, Frederica	Somerville, NJ	6/1/45
Von Sydow, Max	Lund, Sweden	4/10/29
Von Trier, Lars	Copenhagen, Denmark	4/30/56
Wagner, Jack	Washington, MO	10/3/59
Wagner, Lindsay	Los Angeles, CA	6/22/49
Wagner, Robert	Detroit, MI	2/10/30
Wahl, Ken	Chicago, IL	2/14/56
Wahlberg, Mark	Dorchester, MA	6/5/71
Wain, Bea	Bronx, NY	4/30/17
Waite, Ralph	White Plains, NY	6/22/28
Waits, Tom	Pomona, CA	12/7/49
Walden, Robert	New York, NY	9/25/43
Walken, Christopher	Astoria, Queens, NY	3/31/43
Walker, Clint	Hartford, IL	5/30/27
Wallace, Marcia	Creston, IA	11/1/42
Wallach, Eli	Brooklyn, NY	12/7/15

Name	Birthplace	Birthdate
Walsh, Kate	San Jose, CA	10/13/67
Walter, Jessica	Brooklyn, NY	1/31/40
Ward, Fred	San Diego, CA	12/30/42
Ward, Sela	Meridian, MS	7/11/56
Ward, Simon	Kent, London, England	10/19/41
Warfield, Marsha	Chicago, IL	3/5/54
Warner, Malcolm-Jamal	Jersey City, NJ	8/18/70
Warren, Lesley Ann	New York, NY	8/16/46
Warwick, Dionne	East Orange, NJ	12/12/40
Washington, Denzel	Mt. Vernon, NY	12/28/54
Washington, Isaiah	Houston, TX	8/3/63
Watanabe, Ken	Koide, Niigata, Japan	10/21/59
Waters, John	Baltimore, MD	4/22/46
Waters, Roger	Great Bookham, England	9/6/44
Waterston, Sam	Cambridge, MA	11/15/40
Watson, Emily	London, England	1/14/67
Watson, Emma	Oxford, England	4/15/90
Watts, Andre	Nuremberg, Germany	6/20/46
Watts, Naomi	Shoreham, England	9/28/68
Wayans, Damon	New York, NY	9/4/60
Wayans, Keenen Ivory	Brooklyn, NY	6/8/58
Wayans, Marlon	New York, NY	723/72
Wayans, Shawn	New York, NY	1/19/71
Weathers, Carl	New Orleans, LA	1/14/48
Weaver, Fritz	Pittsburgh, PA	1/19/26
Weaver, Sigourney	New York, NY	10/8/49
Weiland, Scott	Santa Cruz, CA	10/27/67
Weir, Peter	Sydney, Australia	8/8/44
Weisz, Rachel	London, England	3/7/71
Weitz, Bruce	Norwalk, CT	5/27/43
Welch, Raquel	Chicago, IL	9/5/40
Weld, Tuesday	New York, NY	8/27/43
Weller, Peter	Stevens Point, WI	6/24/47
Welling, Tom	Putnam Valley, NY	4/26/77
Wells, Kitty	Nashville, TN	8/30/19
Wendt, George	Chicago, IL	10/17/48
Wentz, Pete	Wilmette, IL	6/5/79
West, Adam	Walla Walla, WA	9/19/28
West, Kayne	Atlanta, GA	6/8/77
West, Shane	Baton Rouge, LA	6/10/78
Wettig, Patricia	Cincinnati, OH	12/4/51
Whalley, Joanne	Manchester, England	8/25/64
Wheaton, Wil	Burbank, CA	7/29/72
Whitaker, Forest	Longview, TX	7/15/61
White, Betty	Oak Park, IL	1/17/22
White, Jack	Detroit, MI	7/9/75
White, Jaleel	Pasadena, CA	11/27/76
White, Vanna	N. Myrtle Beach, SC	2/18/57
Whitford, Bradley	Madison, WI	10/10/59
Whiting, Margaret	Detroit, MI	7/22/24
Whitman, Stuart	San Francisco, CA	2/1/26
Wiest, Dianne	Kansas City, MO	3/28/48
Wiig, Kristen	Canandaigua, NY	8/22/73
Wilder, Gene	Milwaukee, WI	6/11/33
Wilkinson, Tom	Leeds, England	12/12/48
Williams, Andy	Wall Lake, IA	12/3/27
Williams, Armstrong	Marion, SC	2/5/59
Williams, Barry	Santa Monica, CA	9/30/54
Williams, Billy Dee	Harlem, NY	4/6/37
Williams, Cindy	Van Nuys, CA	8/22/47
Williams, Esther	Los Angeles, CA	8/8/23
Williams, Hal	Columbus, OH	12/14/38
Williams, Hank, Jr.	Shreveport, LA	5/26/49
Williams, JoBeth	Houston, TX	12/6/48
Williams, Kimberly	Rye, NY	9/14/71
Williams, Lucinda	Lake Charles, LA	1/26/53
Williams, Michelle	Kalispell, MT	9/9/80
Williams, Montel	Baltimore, MD	7/3/56
Williams, Paul	Omaha, NE	9/19/40
Williams, Robin	Chicago, IL	7/21/51
Williams, Treat	Rowayton, CT	12/1/51
Williams, Vanessa	Tarrytown, NY	3/18/63
Williamson, Kevin	New Bern, NC	3/14/65
Williamson, Nicol	Hamilton, Scotland	9/14/38
Willis, Bruce	Idar-Oberstein, W. Germ.	3/19/55
Wilson, Brian	Hawthorne, CA	6/20/42
Wilson, Cassandra	Jackson, MS	12/4/55
Wilson, Chandra	Houston, TX	8/27/69
Wilson, Demond	Valdosta, GA	10/13/46
Wilson, Elizabeth	Grand Rapids, MI	4/4/21
Wilson, Luke	Dallas, TX	9/21/71
Wilson, Nancy	Chillicothe, OH	2/20/37
Wilson, Owen	Dallas, TX	11/18/68
Wilson, Rainn	Seattle, WA	1/20/66
Windom, William	New York, NY	9/28/23
Winehouse, Amy	Enfield, London, England	9/14/83
Winfrey, Oprah	Kosciusko, MS	1/29/54
Winger, Debra	Cleveland, OH	5/16/55
Winkler, Henry	New York, NY	10/30/45
Winningham, Mare	Phoenix, AZ	5/16/59
Winokur, Marissa Jaret	New York, NY	2/2/73
Winslet, Kate	Reading, England	10/5/75
Winter, Johnny	Beaumont,TX	2/23/44
Winters, Jonathan	Dayton, OH	11/11/25
Winwood, Steve	Birmingham, England	5/12/48
Wiseman, Joseph	Montreal, Quebec	5/15/18
Withers, Jane	Atlanta, GA	4/12/26
Witherspoon, Reese	New Orleans, LA	3/22/76
Witt, Alicia	Worcester, MA	8/21/75
Wolf, Scott	Boston, MA	6/4/68
Wonder, Stevie	Saginaw, MI	5/13/50
Wong, Faye	Beijing, China	8/8/69
Woo, John	Guangzhou, China	5/1/46
Wood, Elijah	Cedar Rapids, IA	1/28/81
Woodard, Alfre	Tulsa, OK	11/8/53
Woods, James	Vernal, UT	4/18/47
Woodward, Edward	Croyden, England	6/1/30
Woodward, Joanne	Thomasville, GA	2/27/30
Wopat, Tom	Lodi, WI	9/9/51
Wright, Jeffrey	Washington, DC	12/7/65
Wright, Max	Detroit, MI	8/2/43
Wright, Steven	New York, NY	12/6/55
Wright Penn, Robin	Dallas, TX	4/8/66
Wyle, Noah	Hollywood, CA	6/4/71
Wyman, Bill	London, England	10/24/36
Yankovic, Weird Al	Lynwood, CA	10/23/59
Yanni	Kalamata, Greece	11/14/54
Yarrow, Peter	New York, NY	5/31/38
Yearwood, Trisha	Monticello, GA	9/19/64
Yoakam, Dwight	Pikesville, KY	10/23/56
York, Michael	Fulmer, England	3/27/42
York, Susannah	London, England	1/9/41
Young, Alan	North Shields, England	11/19/19
Young, Burt	New York, NY	4/30/40
Young, Neil	Toronto, Ontario	11/12/45
Young, Sean	Louisville, KY	11/20/59
Zane, Billy	Chicago, IL	2/24/66
Zeffirelli, Franco	Florence, Italy	2/12/23
Zellweger, Renée	Katy, TX	4/25/69
Zemeckis, Robert	Chicago, IL	5/14/52
Zerbe, Anthony	Long Beach, CA	5/20/36
Zeta-Jones, Catherine	Swansea, Wales	9/25/69
Zimbalist, Efrem, Jr.	New York, NY	11/30/18
Zimbalist, Stephanie	New York, NY	10/8/56
Zimmer, Kim	Grand Rapids, MI	2/2/55
Zhang, Ziyi	Beijing, China	2/9/79
Zukerman, Pinchas	Tel Aviv, Israel	7/16/48
Zuniga, Daphne	San Francisco, CA	10/28/62

Entertainment Personalities of the Past

See also other lists for some deceased entertainers not included here.

Name	Born	Died	Name	Born	Died	Name	Born	Died
Aaliyah	1979	2001	Albertson, Jack	1907	1981	Andre the Giant	1946	1993
Abbott, Bud	1895	1974	Alda, Robert	1914	1986	Andrews, Dana	1909	1992
Abbott, George	1887	1995	Allen, Fred	1894	1956	Andrews, Laverne	1913	1967
Acuff, Roy	1903	1992	Allen, Gracie	1906	1964	Andrews, Maxine	1918	1995
Adams, Don	1923	2005	Allen, Mel	1913	1996	Angeli, Pier	1933	1971
Adams, Joey	1911	1999	Allen, Peter	1944	1992	Anita Louise	1915	1970
Adams, Maude	1872	1953	Allen, Steve	1921	2000	Antonioni, Michelangelo	1912	2007
Adams, Mason	1919	2005	Allgood, Sara	1883	1950	Arbuckle, Fatty (Roscoe)	1887	1933
Adler, Jacob P	1855	1926	Allyson, June	1917	2006	Archerd, Army	1922	2009
Adoree, Renee	1898	1933	Altman, Robert	1926	2006	Arden, Eve	1908	1990
Agar, John	1921	2002	Ameche, Don	1908	1993	Arlen, Richard	1900	1976
Aherne, Brian	1902	1986	Ames, Leon	1903	1993	Arliss, George	1868	1946
Ailey, Alvin	1931	1989	Amsterdam, Morey	1908	1996	Armstrong, Louis	1901	1971
Akins, Claude	1918	1994	Anderson, G. M. "Bronco Billy"	1882	1971	Arnaz, Desi	1917	1986
Albert, Eddie	1908	2005	Anderson, Judith	1897	1992	Arnold, Eddy	1918	2008
Albertson, Frank	1909	1964	Anderson, Marian	1897	1993	Arnold, Edward	1890	1956

Name	Born	Died	Name	Born	Died	Name	Born	Died
Arquette, Cliff	1905	1974	Blore, Eric	1888	1959	Carson, Jack	1910	1963
Arthur, Beatrice	1923	2009	Blue, Ben	1901	1975	Carson, Jean	1923	2005
Arthur, Jean	1900	1991	Blyden, Larry	1925	1975	Carson, Johnny	1925	2005
Ashcroft, Peggy	1907	1991	Bogarde, Dirk	1920	1999	Carter, Benny	1907	2003
Astaire, Fred	1899	1987	Bogart, Humphrey	1899	1957	Carter, Nell	1948	2003
Astor, Mary	1906	1987	Boland, Mary	1880	1965	Caruso, Enrico	1873	1921
Atkins, Chet	1924	2001	Boles, John	1895	1969	Casals, Pablo	1876	1973
Atwill, Lionel	1885	1946	Bolger, Ray	1904	1987	Cash, Johnny	1932	2003
Auer, Mischa	1905	1967	Bond, Ward	1903	1960	Cash, June Carter	1929	2003
Aumont, Jean-Pierre	1911	2001	Bondi, Beulah	1892	1981	Cass, Peggy	1924	1999
Austin, Gene	1900	1972	Bono, Sonny	1935	1998	Cassidy, Jack	1927	1976
Autry, Gene	1907	1998	Boone, Richard	1917	1981	Cassavetes, John	1929	1989
Axton, Hoyt	1938	1999	Booth, Edwin	1833	1893	Castle, Irene	1893	1969
Ayres, Lew	1908	1996	Booth, Junius Brutus	1796	1852	Castle, Vernon	1887	1918
Backus, Jim	1913	1989	Booth, Shirley	1898	1992	Caulfield, Joan	1922	1991
Bailey, Pearl	1918	1990	Borge, Victor	1909	2000	Chaliapin, Feodor	1873	1938
Bainter, Fay	1892	1968	Bow, Clara	1905	1965	Champion, Gower	1919	1980
Baker, Josephine	1906	1975	Bowes, Maj. Edward	1874	1946	Chandler, Jeff	1918	1961
Balanchine, George	1904	1983	Bowman, Lee	1914	1979	Chaney, Lon	1883	1930
Ball, Lucille	1911	1989	Boxcar Willie	1931	1999	Chaney, Lon, Jr.	1905	1973
Balsam, Martin	1919	1996	Boyd, Stephen	1928	1977	Chapin, Harry	1942	1981
Bancroft, Anne	1931	2005	Boyd, William	1898	1972	Chaplin, Charles	1889	1977
Bancroft, George	1882	1956	Boyer, Charles	1899	1978	Chapman, Graham	1941	1989
Bankhead, Tallulah	1903	1968	Boyle, Peter	1933	2006	Charisse, Cyd	1921	2008
Bara, Theda	1890	1955	Bracken, Eddie	1915	2002	Charles, Ray	1930	2004
Barnett, Etta Moten	1902	2004	Brady, Alice	1893	1939	Chase, Ilka	1905	1978
Barnum, Phineas T.	1810	1891	Brand, Neville	1921	1992	Chatterton, Ruth	1893	1961
Barrett, Syd	1946	2006	Brando, Marlon	1924	2004	Cherrill, Virginia	1908	1996
Barrymore, Ethel	1879	1959	Branigan, Laura	1957	2004	Chevalier, Maurice	1888	1972
Barrymore, John	1882	1942	Brazzi, Rossano	1916	1994	Child, Julia	1912	2004
Barrymore, Lionel	1878	1954	Brennan, Walter	1894	1974	Clair, René	1898	1981
Barrymore, Maurice	1848	1905	Brent, George	1904	1979	Clayton, Jan	1917	1983
Bartel, Paul	1938	2000	Brett, Jeremy	1935	1995	Clift, Montgomery	1920	1966
Barthelmess, Richard	1897	1963	Brewer, Teresa	1931	2007	Cline, Patsy	1932	1963
Bartholomew, Freddie	1924	1992	Brice, Fanny	1891	1951	Clooney, Rosemary	1928	2002
Bartok, Eva	1926	1998	Bridges, Lloyd	1913	1998	Clyde, Andy	1892	1967
Barty, Billy	1924	2000	Broderick, Helen	1891	1959	Cobain, Kurt	1967	1994
Basehart, Richard	1914	1984	Bronson, Charles	1921	2003	Cobb, Lee J.	1911	1976
Basie, Count	1904	1984	Brooks, Foster	1912	2001	Coburn, Charles	1877	1961
Bates, Alan	1934	2003	Brooks, Louise	1906	1985	Coburn, James	1928	2002
Bates, Clayton (Peg Leg)	1907	1998	Brown, James	1933	2006	Coca, Imogene	1908	2001
Bavier, Francis	1902	1989	Brown, Joe E.	1892	1973	Cochran, Steve	1917?	1965
Baxter, Anne	1923	1985	Brown, Les	1912	2001	Coco, James	1930	1987
Baxter, Warner	1889	1951	Browne, Roscoe Lee	1925	2007	Cody, Buffalo Bill	1846	1917
Beaumont, Hugh	1909	1982	Bruce, Lenny	1925	1966	Cody, Iron Eyes	1907	1999
Beavers, Louise	1902	1962	Bruce, Nigel	1895	1953	Cohan, George M.	1878	1942
Beery, Noah, Sr.	1884	1946	Bruce, Virginia	1910	1982	Cohen, Myron	1902	1986
Beery, Noah, Jr.	1913	1994	Brynner, Yul	1915	1985	Colbert, Claudette	1903	1996
Beery, Wallace	1889	1949	Buchanan, Edgar	1903	1979	Cole, Nat "King"	1919	1965
Begley, Ed	1901	1970	Buchholz, Horst	1933	2003	Collins, Ray	1890	1965
Bel Geddes, Barbara	1922	2005	Buñuel, Luis	1900	1983	Colman, Ronald	1891	1958
Bellamy, Ralph	1904	1991	Buono, Victor	1938	1982	Columbo, Russ	1908	1934
Belushi, John	1949	1982	Burke, Billie	1885	1970	Comden, Betty	1917	2006
Benaderet, Bea	1906	1968	Burnette, Smiley	1911	1967	Como, Perry	1912	2001
Bendix, William	1906	1964	Burns, George	1896	1996	Conniff, Ray	1916	2002
Bennett, Constance	1904	1965	Burr, Raymond	1917	1993	Connors, Chuck	1921	1992
Bennett, Joan	1910	1990	Burton, Richard	1925	1984	Conrad, William	1920	1994
Bennett, Michael	1943	1987	Busch, Mae	1897	1946	Conried, Hans	1917	1982
Benny, Jack	1894	1974	Bushman, Francis X.	1883	1966	Conte, Richard	1911	1975
Berg, Gertrude	1899	1966	Buttons, Red	1919	2006	Convy, Bert	1933	1991
Bergen, Edgar	1903	1978	Byington, Spring	1893	1971	Conway, Tom	1904	1967
Bergman, Ingmar	1918	2007	Cabot, Bruce	1904	1972	Coogan, Jackie	1914	1984
Bergman, Ingrid	1915	1982	Cabot, Sebastian	1918	1977	Cook, Elisha, Jr.	1904	1995
Berkeley, Busby	1895	1976	Cagney, James	1899	1986	Cooke, Alistair	1908	2004
Berle, Milton	1908	2002	Caldwell, Sarah	1924	2006	Cooke, Sam	1935	1964
Berlin, Irving	1888	1989	Calhern, Louis	1895	1956	Cooper, Gary	1901	1961
Bernardi, Herschel	1923	1986	Calhoun, Rory	1923	1999	Cooper, Gladys	1888	1971
Berman, Lazar	1930	2005	Callas, Maria	1923	1977	Cooper, Melville	1896	1973
Bernhardt, Sarah	1844	1923	Calloway, Cab	1907	1994	Copland, Aaron	1900	1990
Bernstein, Leonard	1918	1990	Cambridge, Godfrey	1933	1976	Corby, Ellen	1913	1999
Berry, Jan	1941	2004	Camp, Hamilton	1934	2005	Corelli, Franco	1923	2003
Bessell, Ted	1939	1996	Campbell, Mrs. Patrick	1865	1940	Corey, Jeff	1914	2002
Bickford, Charles	1889	1967	Candy, John	1950	1994	Corio, Ann	1914	1999
Big Bopper, The	1930	1959	Cantinflas	1911	1993	Corley, Pat	1930	2006
Bing, Rudolf	1902	1997	Cantor, Eddie	1892	1964	Cornell, Katharine	1893	1974
Bishop, Joey	1918	2007	Capra, Frank	1897	1991	Correll, Charles ("Andy")	1890	1972
Bissell, Whit	1909	1996	Carey, Harry	1878	1947	Costello, Dolores	1905	1979
Bixby, Bill	1934	1993	Carey, Macdonald	1913	1994	Costello, Lou	1906	1959
Bjoerling, Jussi	1911	1960	Carle, Frankie	1903	2001	Cotten, Joseph	1905	1994
Blackmer, Sidney	1895	1973	Carlin, George	1937	2008	Coward, Noel	1899	1973
Blackstone, Harry	1885	1965	Carlisle Hart, Kitty	1910	2007	Cox, Wally	1924	1973
Blaine, Vivian	1921	1995	Carney, Art	1918	2003	Crabbe, Buster	1908	1983
Blake, Amanda	1931	1989	Carpenter, Karen	1950	1983	Crain, Jeanne	1925	2003
Blake, Eubie	1883	1983	Carradine, David	1936	2009	Crane, Bob	1928	1978
Blanc, Mel	1908	1989	Carradine, John	1906	1988	Crawford, Broderick	1911	1986
Blocker, Dan	1928	1972	Carrillo, Leo	1880	1961	Crawford, Joan	1904	1977
Blondell, Joan	1909	1979	Carroll, Leo G.	1892	1972	Crenna, Richard	1926	2003
Blondin, Charles	1824	1897	Carroll, Madeleine	1906	1987	Crews, Laura Hope	1880	1942

Name	Born	Died	Name	Born	Died	Name	Born	Died
Crisp, Donald	1880	1974	Dunne, Irene	1898	1990	Franchi, Sergio	1933?	1990
Croce, Jim	1942	1973	Dunnock, Mildred	1904	1991	Franciosa, Anthony	1929	2006
Cronyn, Hume	1911	2003	Durante, Jimmy	1893	1980	Francis, Arlene	1908	2001
Crosby, Bing	1903	1977	Duryea, Dan	1907	1968	Francis, Kay	1903	1968
Crothers, Scatman	1910	1986	Duse, Eleanora	1858	1924	Franciscus, James	1934	1991
Cruz, Celia	1925	2003	Dvorak, Ann	1912	1979	Frankenheimer, John	1930	2002
Cugat, Xavier	1900	1990	Eagels, Jeanne	1894	1929	Frann, Mary	1943	1998
Cukor, George	1899	1983	Ebsen, Buddy	1908	2003	Frawley, William	1887	1966
Cullen, Bill	1920	1990	Eckstine, Billy	1914	1993	Frederick, Pauline	1885	1938
Cummings, Constance	1910	2005	Eddington, Paul	1927	1995	Freed, Alan	1921	1965
Cummings, Robert	1908	1990	Eddy, Nelson	1901	1967	French, Victor	1934	1989
Currie, Finlay	1878	1968	Edelman, Herb	1933	1996	Friganza, Trixie	1870	1955
Curtis, Keene	1923	2002	Edwards, Cliff	1897	1971	Frisco, Joe	1890	1958
Curtis, Ken	1916	1991	Edwards, Ralph	1913	2005	Froman, Jane	1907	1980
Cushing, Peter	1913	1994	Edwards, Vince	1928	1996	Fuller, Samuel	1912	1997
Dailey, Dan	1914	1978	Egan, Richard	1923	1987	Funt, Allen	1914	1999
Dandridge, Dorothy	1923	1965	Eisenstein, Sergei	1898	1948	Furness, Betty	1916	1994
Dangerfield, Rodney	1921	2004	Elam, Jack	1916	2003	Gabin, Jean	1904	1976
Daniell, Henry	1894	1963	Ellington, Duke	1899	1974	Gable, Clark	1901	1960
Daniels, Bebe	1901	1971	Elliot, Cass	1941	1974	Gabor, Eva	1920	1995
Darin, Bobby	1936	1973	Elliott, Denholm	1922	1992	Garbo, Greta	1905	1990
Darnell, Linda	1921	1965	Ellis, Mary	1897	2003	Garcia, Jerry	1942	1995
Darwell, Jane	1879	1967	Elman, Mischa	1891	1967	Gardenia, Vincent	1922	1992
Da Silva, Howard	1909	1986	Errol, Leon	1881	1951	Gardner, Ava	1922	1990
Davenport, Harry	1866	1949	Evans, Dale	1912	2001	Garfield, John	1913	1952
Davies, Marion	1897	1961	Evans, Edith	1888	1976	Garland, Beverly	1926	2008
Davis, Bette	1908	1989	Evans, Maurice	1901	1989	Garland, Judy	1922	1969
Davis, Joan	1907	1961	Ewell, Tom	1909	1994	Garson, Greer	1904	1996
Davis, Sammy, Jr.	1925	1990	Fadiman, Clifton	1904	1999	Gassman, Vittorio	1922	2000
Davis, Ossie	1917	2005	Fairbanks, Douglas	1883	1939	Gaye, Marvin	1939	1984
Day, Dennis	1917	1988	Fairbanks, Douglas, Jr.	1909	2000	Gaynor, Janet	1906	1984
Day, Laraine	1917	2007	Falkenburg, Jinx	1919	2003	Gebel-Williams, Gunther	1934	2001
Dean, James	1931	1955	Farley, Chris	1964	1997	Geer, Will	1902	1978
Dearie, Blossom	1924	2009	Farmer, Frances	1914	1970	George, Gladys	1900	1954
De Carlo, Yvonne	1922	2007	Farnsworth, Richard	1920	2000	Gershwin, George	1898	1937
Dee, Frances	1907	2004	Farnum, Dustin	1870	1929	Getty, Estelle	1923	2008
Dee, Sandra	1942	2005	Farnum, William	1876	1953	Ghostley, Alice	1926	2007
Defore, Don	1917	1993	Farrar, Geraldine	1882	1967	Gibb, Andy	1958	1988
Dekker, Albert	1905	1968	Farrell, Charles	1901	1990	Gibb, Maurice	1949	2003
Del Rio, Dolores	1908	1983	Farrell, Eileen	1920	2002	Gibson, Henry	1935	2009
DeLuise, Dom	1933	2009	Fassbinder, Rainer Werner	1946	1982	Gibson, Hoot	1892	1962
Demarest, William	1892	1983	Fawcett, Farrah	1947	2009	Gielgud, John	1904	2000
DeMille, Agnes	1905	1993	Fay, Frank	1897	1961	Gilbert, Billy	1894	1971
DeMille, Cecil B.	1881	1959	Faye, Alice	1912	1998	Gilbert, John	1895	1936
Denison, Michael	1915	1998	Fazenda, Louise	1895	1962	Gilford, Jack	1907	1990
Denning, Richard	1914	1998	Feld, Fritz	1900	1993	Gillespie, Dizzy	1917	1993
Dennis, Sandy	1937	1992	Feldman, Marty	1933	1982	Gillette, William	1855	1937
Denny, Reginald	1891	1967	Fell, Norman	1924	1998	Gingold, Hermione	1897	1987
Denver, Bob	1935	2005	Fellini, Federico	1920	1993	Gish, Dorothy	1898	1968
Denver, John	1943	1997	Fenneman, George	1919	1997	Gish, Lillian	1893	1993
Derek, John	1926	1998	Ferrer, Jose	1912	1992	Giulini, Carlo Maria	1914	2005
DeSica, Vittorio	1901	1974	Ferrer, Mel	1917	2008	Gleason, Jackie	1916	1987
Devine, Andy	1905	1977	Fetchit, Stepin	1898	1985	Gleason, James	1886	1959
Dewhurst, Colleen	1924	1991	Fiedler, Arthur	1894	1979	Gluck, Alma	1884	1938
De Wilde, Brandon	1942	1972	Fiedler, John	1925	2005	Gobel, George	1919	1991
De Wolfe, Billy	1907	1974	Field, Betty	1918	1973	Goddard, Paulette	1905	1990
Diamond, Selma	1920	1985	Fields, Gracie	1898	1979	Godfrey, Arthur	1903	1983
Diddley, Bo	1928	2008	Fields, W.C.	1879	1946	Godunov, Alexander	1949	1995
Dietrich, Marlene	1901	1992	Fields, Totie	1931	1978	Goldwyn, Samuel	1882	1974
Digges, Dudley	1879	1947	Finch, Peter	1916	1977	Goodman, Benny	1909	1986
Disney, Walt	1901	1966	Fine, Larry	1902	1975	Gorcey, Leo	1915	1969
Dix, Richard	1894	1949	Firkusny, Rudolf	1912	1994	Gordon, Gale	1906	1995
Dmytryk, Edward	1908	1999	Fiske, Minnie Maddern	1865	1932	Gordon, Ruth	1896	1985
Donahue, Troy	1936	2001	Fitzgerald, Barry	1888	1961	Gorshin, Frank	1934	2005
Donat, Robert	1905	1958	Fitzgerald, Ella	1917	1996	Gosden, Freeman ("Amos")	1899	1982
Donlevy, Brian	1901?	1972	Fitzgerald, Geraldine	1913	2005	Gottschalk, Ferdinand	1869	1944
Dors, Diana	1931	1984	Flagstad, Kirsten	1895	1962	Gottschalk, Louis	1829	1869
Dorsey, Tommy	1905	1956	Fleischer, Richard	1916	2006	Gould, Glenn	1932	1982
Douglas, Melvyn	1901	1981	Fleming, Art	1924	1995	Gould, Morton	1913	1996
Douglas, Paul	1907	1959	Flynn, Errol	1909	1959	Goulet, Robert	1933	2007
Dove, Billie	1900	1998	Flynn, Joe	1925	1974	Grable, Betty	1916	1973
Downey, Morton, Jr.	1933	2001	Foch, Nina	1924	2008	Graham, Martha	1894	1991
Doyle, David	1929	1997	Fogelberg, Dan	1951	2008	Graham, Virginia	1912	1998
Drake, Alfred	1914	1992	Foley, Red	1910	1968	Grahame, Gloria	1925	1981
Draper, Ruth	1889	1956	Fonda, Henry	1905	1982	Granger, Stewart	1913	1993
Dresser, Louise	1881	1965	Fontaine, Frank	1920	1978	Grant, Cary	1904	1986
Dressler, Marie	1869	1934	Fontanne, Lynn	1887	1983	Granville, Bonita	1923	1988
Drew, Ellen	1915	2003	Fonteyn, Margot	1919	1991	Gray, Dolores	1924	2002
Drew, Mrs. John	1820	1897	Ford, Glenn	1916	2006	Gray, Spalding	1941	2004
Dru, Joanne	1923	1996	Ford, John	1895	1973	Greco, Jose	1918	2001
Duchin, Eddy	1909	1951	Ford, Paul	1901	1976	Green, Adolph	1915	2002
Duff, Howard	1917	1990	Ford, Tennessee Ernie	1919	1991	Greene, Lorne	1915	1987
Duggan, Andrew	1923	1988	Forrest, Helen	1918	1999	Greenstreet, Sydney	1879	1954
Dumbrille, Douglass	1890	1974	Fosse, Bob	1927	1987	Greenwood, Charlotte	1890	1978
Dumont, Margaret	1889	1965	Foster, Phil	1914	1985	Gregory, James	1911	2002
Duncan, Isadora	1878	1927	Foster, Preston	1901	1970	Griffin, Merv	1925	2007
Dunham, Katherine	1910	2006	Foxx, Redd	1922	1991	Griffith, David Wark	1874	1948
Dunn, James	1905	1967	Foy, Eddie	1857	1928	Griffith, Hugh	1912	1980

Name	Born	Died	Name	Born	Died	Name	Born	Died
Grizzard, George	1928	2007	Hopkins, Miriam	1902	1972	Kaye, Stubby	1918	1997
Guardino, Harry	1925	1995	Hopper, DeWolf	1858	1935	Kazan, Elia	1909	2003
Guinness, Sir Alec	1914	2000	Hopper, Hedda	1885	1966	Kean, Charles	1811	1868
Guthrie, Woody	1912	1967	Hopper, William	1915	1970	Kean, Mrs. Charles	1806	1880
Gwenn, Edmund	1875	1959	Horowitz, Vladimir	1904	1989	Kean, Edmund	1787	1833
Gwynne, Fred	1926	1993	Horton, Edward Everett	1886	1970	Keaton, Buster	1895	1966
Hackett, Buddy	1924	2003	Houdini, Harry	1874	1926	Keel, Howard	1919	2005
Hackett, Joan	1934	1983	Houseman, John	1902	1988	Keeler, Ruby	1910	1993
Hagen, Uta	1919	2004	Hovis, Larry	1936	2003	Keeshan, Bob (Captain		
Hale, Alan	1892	1950	Howard (Horwitz), Curly	1903	1952	Kangaroo)	1927	2004
Hale, Alan, Jr.	1918	1990	Howard, Leslie	1890	1943	Keith, Brian	1921	1997
Haley, Bill	1925	1981	Howard (Horwitz), Moe	1897	1975	Kellaway, Cecil	1894	1973
Haley, Jack	1899	1979	Howard (Horwitz), Shemp	1895	1955	Kelley, DeForest	1920	1999
Hall, Huntz	1919	1999	Howard, Trevor	1916	1988	Kelly, Emmett	1898	1979
Hall, Jon	1915	1979	Hudson, Rock	1925	1985	Kelly, Gene	1912	1996
Hamilton, Margaret	1902	1985	Hughes, Bernard	1915	2006	Kelly, Grace	1929	1982
Hammerstein, Oscar	1847	1919	Hughes, John	1950	2009	Kelly, Jack	1927	1992
Hammerstein II, Oscar	1895	1960	Hull, Henry	1890	1977	Kelly, Nancy	1921	1985
Hampton, Lionel	1908	2002	Hull, Josephine	1886	1957	Kelly, Patsy	1910	1981
Hardwicke, Cedric	1893	1964	Humphrey, Doris	1895	1958	Kelton, Pert	1907	1968
Hardy, Oliver	1892	1957	Hunter, Jeffrey	1925	1969	Kendall, Kay	1926	1959
Harlow, Jean	1911	1937	Hunter, Kim	1922	2002	Kennedy, Arthur	1914	1990
Harris, Phil	1904	1995	Hunter, Ross	1921	1996	Kennedy, Edgar	1890	1948
Harris, Richard	1930	2002	Husing, Ted	1901	1962	Kerr, Deborah	1921	2007
Harrison, George	1943	2001	Hussey, Ruth	1911	2005	Kibbee, Guy	1886	1956
Harrison, Rex	1908	1990	Huston, John	1906	1987	Kilbride, Percy	1888	1964
Hart, William S.	1870	1946	Huston, Walter	1884	1950	Kiley, Richard	1922	1999
Hartman, Phil	1948	1998	Hutchence, Michael	1960	1997	King, Alan	1927	2004
Harvey, Laurence	1928	1973	Hutton, Betty	1921	2007	Kinski, Klaus	1926	1991
Harvey, Paul	1918	2009	Hutton, Jim	1934	1979	Kirby, Bruno	1949	2006
Hatfield, Bobby	1940	2003	Hutton, Robert	1920	1994	Kirby, George	1923	1995
Haver, June	1926	2005	Hyde-White, Wilfrid	1903	1991	Kirby, Durward	1912	2000
Hawkins, Jack	1910	1973	Ingram, Rex	1895	1969	Kirsten, Dorothy	1910	1992
Hawkins, Screamin' Jay	1929	2000	Ireland, Jill	1936	1990	Kitt, Eartha	1927	2008
Hawthorne, Nigel	1929	2001	Ireland, John	1915	1992	Klemperer, Werner	1919	2000
Hayakawa, Sessue	1890	1973	Irving, Henry	1838	1905	Knight, Ted	1923	1986
Hayden, Sterling	1916	1986	Ives, Burl	1909	1995	Knotts, Don	1924	2006
Hayes, Gabby	1885	1969	Irwin, Steve	1962	2006	Korman, Harvey	1927	2008
Hayes, Helen	1900	1993	Iturbi, Jose	1895	1980	Kostelanetz, Andre	1901	1980
Hayes, Isaac	1942	2008	Jack, Wolfman	1938	1995	Kovacs, Ernie	1919	1962
Hayward, Leland	1902	1971	Jackson, Joe	1875	1942	Kramer, Stanley	1913	2001
Hayward, Louis	1909	1985	Jackson, Mahalia	1911	1972	Kruger, Otto	1885	1974
Hayward, Susan	1917	1975	Jackson, Michael	1958	2009	Kubrick, Stanley	1928	1999
Hayworth, Rita	1918	1987	Jackson, Milt	1922	1999	Kulp, Nancy	1921	1991
Head, Edith	1907	1981	Jaeckel, Richard	1926	1997	Kurosawa, Akira	1910	1998
Healy, Ted	1896	1937	Jaffe, Sam	1891	1984	Kyser, Kay	1906	1985
Heckart, Eileen	1919	2001	Jagger, Dean	1903	1991	Ladd, Alan	1913	1964
Heflin, Van	1910	1971	Jam Master Jay	1965	2003	Lahr, Bert	1895	1967
Heifetz, Jascha	1901	1987	James, Dennis	1917	1997	Laine, Frankie	1913	2007
Held, Anna	1873	1918	James, Harry	1916	1983	Lake, Arthur	1905	1987
Hemingway, Margaux	1955	1996	James, Rick	1948	2004	Lake, Veronica	1919	1973
Hemmings, David	1941	2003	Janis, Elsie	1889	1956	Lamarr, Hedy	1913	2000
Henderson, Skitch	1918	2005	Jannings, Emil	1886	1950	Lamas, Fernando	1915	1982
Hendrix, Jimi	1942	1970	Janssen, David	1930	1980	Lamour, Dorothy	1914	1996
Henie, Sonja	1912	1969	Jenkins, Allen	1900	1974	Lancaster, Burt	1913	1994
Henreid, Paul	1908	1992	Jennings, Waylon	1937	2002	Lanchester, Elsa	1902	1986
Henson, Jim	1936	1990	Jessel, George	1898	1981	Lane, Priscilla	1917	1995
Hepburn, Audrey	1929	1993	Jeter, Michael	1952	2003	Landis, Carole	1919	1948
Hepburn, Katharine	1907	2003	Johnson, Ben	1918	1996	Landis, Jessie Royce	1904	1972
Hersholt, Jean	1886	1956	Johnson, Celia	1908	1982	Landon, Michael	1936	1991
Heston, Charlton	1923	2008	Johnson, Chic	1892	1962	Lang, Fritz	1890	1976
Hewett, Christopher	1922	2001	Johnson, J.J.	1924	2001	Langdon, Harry	1884	1944
Hickey, William	1928	1997	Johnson, Robert	1911	1938	Lange, Hope	1931	2003
Hickson, Joan	1906	1998	Johnson, Van	1916	2008	Langford, Frances	1914	2005
Hildegarde	1906	2005	Jolson, Al	1886	1950	Langtry, Lillie	1853	1929
Hill, Arthur	1922	2006	Jones, Brian	1942	1969	Lanza, Mario	1921	1959
Hill, Benny	1925	1992	Jones, Buck	1889	1942	LaRue, Lash (Alfred)	1917	1996
Hill, George Roy	1921	2002	Jones, Carolyn	1933	1983	Lauder, Harry	1870	1950
Hiller, Wendy	1912	2003	Jones, Charlie	1930	2008	Laughton, Charles	1899	1962
Hines, Gregory	1946	2003	Jones, Elvin	1927	2004	Laurel, Stan	1890	1965
Hines, Jerome	1921	2003	Jones, Henry	1912	1999	Lawford, Peter	1923	1984
Hingle, Pat	1924	2009	Jones, Spike	1911	1965	Lawrence, Florence	1886	1938
Hirt, Al	1922	1999	Joplin, Janis	1943	1970	Lawrence, Gertrude	1898	1952
Hitchcock, Alfred	1899	1980	Joplin, Scott	1868	1917	Lean, David	1908	1991
Ho, Don	1930	2007	Jordan, Richard	1938	1993	Ledger, Heath	1979	2008
Hobson, Valerie	1917	1998	Jory, Victor	1902	1982	Lee, Anna	1913	2004
Hodiak, John	1914	1955	Joslyn, Allyn	1905	1981	Lee, Bernard	1908	1981
Holden, William	1918	1981	Julia, Raul	1940	1994	Lee, Bruce	1940	1973
Holiday, Billie	1915	1959	Jump, Gordon	1932	2003	Lee, Canada	1907	1952
Holliday, Judy	1922	1965	Jurado, Katy	1924	2002	Lee, Gypsy Rose	1914	1970
Holloway, Sterling	1905	1992	Jurgens, Curt	1915	1982	Lee, Peggy	1920	2002
Holly, Buddy	1936	1959	Kahn, Madeline	1942	1999	LeGallienne, Eva	1899	1991
Holt, Jack	1888	1951	Kane, Helen	1910	1966	Lehmann, Lotte	1888	1976
Holt, Tim	1918	1973	Kanin, Garson	1912	1999	Leigh, Janet	1927	2004
Homolka, Oscar	1898	1978	Karloff, Boris	1887	1969	Leigh, Vivien	1913	1967
Hooker, John Lee	1917	2001	Karns, Roscoe	1893	1970	Leighton, Margaret	1922	1976
Hoon, Shannon	1967	1995	Kaufman, Andy	1949	1984	Lemmon, Jack	1925	2001
Hope, Bob	1903	2003	Kaye, Danny	1913	1987	Lennon, John	1940	1980

Name	Born	Died	Name	Born	Died	Name	Born	Died
Lenya, Lotte	1898	1981	Mayfield, Curtis	1942	1999	Morrow, Vic	1932	1982
Leonard, Eddie	1870	1941	Maynard, Ken	1895	1973	Morton, Jelly Roll	1885	1941
Leonard, Sheldon	1907	1997	Mayo, Virginia	1920	2005	Mostel, Zero	1915	1977
LeRoy, Mervyn	1900	1987	Mazurki, Mike	1909	1990	Mowbray, Alan	1897	1969
Levant, Oscar	1906	1972	McCambridge, Mercedes	1916	2004	Mulhare, Edward	1923	1997
Levene, Sam	1905	1980	McCartney, Linda	1941	1998	Mulligan, Gerry	1927	1996
Levenson, Sam	1911	1980	McClure, Doug	1935	1995	Mulligan, Richard	1932	2000
Lewis, Al	1923	2006	McCormack, John	1884	1945	Muni, Paul	1895	1967
Lewis, Joe E.	1902	1971	McCrary, Tex	1910	2003	Munshin, Jules	1915	1970
Lewis, Shari	1934	1998	McCrea, Joel	1905	1990	Murphy, Audie	1924	1971
Lewis, Ted	1892	1971	McDaniel, Hattie	1895	1952	Murphy, George	1902	1992
Liberace	1919	1987	McDowall, Roddy	1928	1998	Murray, Arthur	1895	1991
Lillie, Beatrice	1894	1989	McFarland, George "Spanky"	1928	1993	Murray, Kathryn	1906	1999
Lind, Jenny	1820	1887	McGoohan, Patrick	1928	2009	Murray, Mae	1885	1965
Lindfors, Viveca	1920	1995	McGuire, Al	1931	2001	Nagel, Conrad	1896	1970
Lindley, Audra	1918	1997	McGuire, Dorothy	1916	2001	Naish, J. Carroll	1900	1973
Linville, Larry	1939	2000	McHugh, Frank	1899	1981	Naldi, Nita	1898	1961
Little, Cleavon	1939	1992	McIntire, John	1907	1991	Nance, Jack	1943	1997
Llewelyn, Desmond	1914	1999	McKay, Gardner	1932	2001	Natwick, Mildred	1908	1994
Lloyd, Harold	1893	1971	McKern, Leo	1920	2002	Nazimova, Alla	1879	1945
Lloyd, Marie	1870	1922	McLaglen, Victor	1883	1959	Negri, Pola	1897	1987
Lockhart, Gene	1891	1957	McMahon, Ed	1923	2009	Nelson, Harriet (Hilliard)	1909	1994
Logan, Ella	1913	1969	McNally, Stephen	1913	1994	Nelson, Ozzie	1906	1975
Lombard, Carole	1909	1942	McNeill, Don	1907	1996	Nelson, Rick	1940	1985
Lombardo, Guy	1902	1977	McQueen, Butterfly	1911	1995	Nesbit, Evelyn	1885	1967
Long, Richard	1927	1974	McQueen, Steve	1930	1980	Nettleton, Lois	1929	2008
Lopes, Lisa	1971	2002	Meader, Vaughn	1936	2004	Newley, Anthony	1931	1999
Lopez, Vincent	1895	1975	Meadows, Audrey	1924	1996	Newman, Paul	1925	2008
Lord, Jack	1920?	1998	Medford, Kay	1920	1980	Newton, Robert	1905	1956
Lorne, Marion	1888	1968	Meek, Donald	1880	1946	Nicholas, Harold	1924	2000
Lorre, Peter	1904	1964	Meeker, Ralph	1920	1988	Nijinsky, Vaslav	1890	1950
Loudon, Dorothy	1933	2003	Melba, Nellie	1861	1931	Nilsson, Anna Q.	1893	1974
Lovejoy, Frank	1912	1962	Melchior, Lauritz	1890	1973	Niven, David	1910	1983
Lowe, Edmund	1890	1971	Menjou, Adolphe	1890	1963	Nolan, Lloyd	1902	1985
Loy, Myrna	1905	1993	Menken, Helen	1902	1966	Normand, Mabel	1894	1930
Lubitsch, Ernst	1892	1947	Menuhin, Yehudi	1916	1999	North, Sheree	1933	2005
Ludden, Allen	1918	1981	Mercouri, Melina	1925	1994	Notorious B.I.G.	1972	1997
Lugosi, Bela	1882	1956	Mercury, Freddie	1946	1991	Novarro, Ramon	1899	1968
Lukas, Paul	1894	1971	Meredith, Burgess	1909	1997	Nureyev, Rudolf	1938	1993
Lunt, Alfred	1892	1977	Merman, Ethel	1908	1984	Oakie, Jack	1903	1978
Lupino, Ida	1918	1995	Merrick, David	1911	2000	Oakley, Annie	1860	1926
Lymon, Frankie	1942	1968	Merrill, Gary	1915	1990	Oates, Warren	1928	1982
Lynde, Paul	1926	1982	Mifune, Toshiro	1920	1997	Oberon, Merle	1911	1979
Lynn, Diana	1926	1971	Milland, Ray	1905	1986	O'Brien, Edmond	1915	1985
Mac, Bernie	1958	2008	Miller, Ann	1923	2004	O'Brien, Pat	1899	1983
MacDonald, Jeanette	1903	1965	Miller, Glenn	1904	1944	O'Connell, Arthur	1908	1981
Mack, Ted	1904	1976	Miller, Marilyn	1898	1936	O'Connell, Helen	1921	1993
MacKenzie, Gisele	1927	2003	Miller, Roger	1936	1992	O'Connor, Carroll	1924	2001
MacLane, Barton	1902	1969	Mills, Harry	1913	1982	O'Connor, Donald	1925	2003
MacMurray, Fred	1908	1991	Mills, Sir John	1908	2005	O'Connor, Una	1880	1959
MacRae, Gordon	1921	1986	Mineo, Sal	1939	1976	Odetta	1930	2008
Macready, George	1909	1973	Miner, Jan	1917	2004	O'Keefe, Dennis	1908	1968
Madison, Guy	1922	1996	Minghella, Anthony	1954	2008	O'Herlihy, Daniel	1919	2005
Magnani, Anna	1908	1973	Mingus, Charles	1922	1979	Oland, Warner	1880	1938
Mancini, Henry	1924	1994	Miranda, Carmen	1913	1955	Olcott, Chauncey	1860	1932
Main, Marjorie	1890	1975	Mitchell, Cameron	1918	1994	Oliver, Edna May	1883	1942
Malden, Karl	1912	2009	Mitchell, Thomas	1892	1962	Olivier, Laurence	1907	1989
Malle, Louis	1932	1995	Mitchum, Robert	1917	1997	Olsen, Ole	1892	1963
Mann, Herbie	1930	2003	Mix, Tom	1880	1940	O'Neal, Ron	1937	2004
Mansfield, Jayne	1932	1967	Monica, Corbett	1930	1998	O'Neill, James	1849	1920
Mantovani, Annunzio	1905	1980	Moffo, Anna	1934	2006	Orbach, Jerry	1935	2004
Marais, Jean	1913	1998	Monroe, Marilyn	1926	1962	Orbison, Roy	1936	1988
March, Fredric	1897	1975	Monroe, Vaughn	1911	1973	Ormandy, Eugene	1899	1985
March, Hal	1920	1970	Montalban, Ricardo	1920	2009	O'Sullivan, Maureen	1911	1998
Marchand, Nancy	1928	2000	Montand, Yves	1921	1991	Ouspenskaya, Maria	1876	1949
Markova, Alicia	1910	2004	Montez, Maria	1917	1951	Owen, Reginald	1887	1972
Marley, Bob	1945	1981	Montgomery, Elizabeth	1933	1995	Owens, Buck	1929	2006
Marshall, E.G.	1910	1998	Montgomery, George	1916	2000	Paar, Jack	1918	2004
Marshall, Herbert	1890	1966	Montgomery, Robert	1904	1981	Paderewski, Ignace	1860	1941
Martin, Barney	1923	2005	Moore, Clayton	1914	1999	Page, Bettie	1923	2008
Martin, Dean	1917	1995	Moore, Colleen	1900	1988	Page, Geraldine	1924	1987
Martin, Dick	1922	2008	Moore, Dudley	1935	2002	Pakula, Alan	1928	1998
Martin, Mary	1913	1990	Moore, Grace	1901	1947	Palance, Jack	1919	2006
Martin, Ross	1920	1981	Moore, Garry	1914	1993	Pallette, Eugene	1889	1954
Marvin, Lee	1924	1987	Moore, Victor	1876	1962	Palmer, Lilli	1914	1986
Marx, Arthur (Harpo)	1888	1964	Moorehead, Agnes	1906	1974	Palmer, Robert	1949	2003
Marx, Herbert (Zeppo)	1901	1979	Moreland, Mantan	1902	1973	Pangborn, Franklin	1894	1958
Marx, Julius (Groucho)	1890	1977	Morgan, Dennis	1910	1994	Parker, Jean	1915	2005
Marx, Leonard (Chico)	1886	1961	Morgan, Frank	1890	1949	Parks, Bert	1914	1992
Marx, Milton (Gummo)	1893	1977	Morgan, Helen	1900	1941	Parks, Larry	1914	1975
Mason, James	1909	1984	Morgan, Henry	1915	1994	Pasternack, Josef A.	1881	1940
Massey, Daniel	1933	1998	Morita, Pat	1932	2005	Pastor, Tony (vaudevillian)	1837	1908
Massey, Raymond	1896	1983	Morley, Robert	1908	1992	Pastor, Tony (bandleader)	1907	1969
Mastroianni, Marcello	1924	1996	Morris, Chester	1901	1970	Patrick, Gail	1911	1980
Matthau, Walter	1920	2000	Morris, Greg	1934	1996	Patti, Adelina	1843	1919
Mature, Victor	1916	1999	Morris, Howard	1919	2005	Patti, Carlotta	1840	1889
Maxwell, Marilyn	1921	1972	Morris, Wayne	1914	1959	Paul, Les	1915	2009
Mayer, Louis B.	1885	1957	Morrison, Jim	1943	1971	Pavarotti, Luciano	1935	2007

Name	Born	Died	Name	Born	Died	Name	Born	Died
Pavlova, Anna	1885	1931	Reeves, George	1914	1959	Scott-Siddons, Mrs.	1843	1896
Paycheck, Johnny	1938	2003	Reeves, Steve	1926	2000	Scofield, Paul	1922	2008
Payne, John	1912	1989	Reid, Wallace	1891	1923	Seberg, Jean	1938	1979
Pearl, Minnie	1912	1996	Reilly, Charles Nelson	1931	2007	Seeley, Blossom	1892	1974
Peck, Gregory	1916	2003	Reinhardt, Max	1873	1943	Segovia, Andres	1893	1987
Peckinpah, Sam	1925	1984	Remick, Lee	1935	1991	Selena	1971	1995
Peerce, Jan	1904	1984	Renaldo, Duncan	1904	1980	Sellers, Peter	1925	1980
Penn, Chris	1965	2006	Rennie, Michael	1909	1971	Selznick, David O.	1902	1965
Penner, Joe	1905	1941	Renoir, Jean	1894	1979	Sennett, Mack	1884	1960
Peppard, George	1928	1994	Rettig, Tommy	1941	1996	Señor Wences	1896	1999
Perkins, Anthony	1932	1992	Reynolds, Marjorie	1923	1997	Serling, Rod	1924	1975
Perkins, Carl	1932	1998	Rich, Charlie	1932	1995	Shakur, Tupac.	1971	1996
Perkins, Marlin	1905	1986	Richardson, Ian	1934	2007	Shaw, Robert (actor)	1927	1978
Peters, Brock	1927	2005	Richardson, Natasha	1963	2009	Shaw, Robert (conductor)	1916	1999
Peters, Jean	1926	2000	Richardson, Ralph	1902	1983	Shawn, Ted.	1891	1972
Peters, Susan	1921	1952	Riddle, Nelson	1921	1985	Shean, Al	1868	1949
Peterson, Oscar	1925	2007	Riefenstahl, Leni	1902	2003	Shearer, Moira	1926	2006
Phillips, John	1935	2001	Ripperton, Minnie	1947	1979	Shearer, Norma	1902	1983
Phoenix, River	1970	1993	Ritchard, Cyril	1898	1977	Sheridan, Ann	1915	1967
Piaf, Edith	1915	1963	Ritter, John	1948	2003	Shore, Dinah	1917	1994
Pickens, Slim	1919	1983	Ritter, Tex	1907	1974	Short, Bobby	1924	2005
Pickett, Wilson	1941	2006	Ritter, Thelma	1905	1969	Shubert, Lee	1875	1953
Pickford, Mary	1893	1979	Ritz, Al	1901	1965	Shull, Richard B.	1929	1999
Picon, Molly	1898	1992	Ritz, Harry	1906	1986	Siddons, Mrs. Sarah	1755	1831
Pidgeon, Walter	1897	1984	Ritz, Jimmy	1903	1985	Sidney, Sylvia	1910	1999
Pinza, Ezio	1892	1957	Roach, Max	1924	2007	Signoret, Simone	1921	1985
Pitney, Gene	1941	2006	Robards, Jason	1922	2000	Sills, Beverly	1929	2007
Pitts, Zasu	1898	1963	Robbins, Jerome	1918	1998	Silver, Ron	1946	2009
Plato, Dana	1964	1999	Robbins, Marty	1925	1982	Silverheels, Jay.	1912	1980
Pleasence, Donald	1919	1995	Roberts, Rachel	1927	1980	Silvers, Phil	1912	1985
Pleshette, Suzanne	1937	2008	Robeson, Paul	1898	1976	Sim, Alastair	1900	1976
Pollack, Sydney	1934	2008	Robinson, Bill	1878	1949	Simmons, Richard.	1913	2003
Pons, Lily	1904	1976	Robinson, Edward G.	1893	1973	Simone, Nina	1933	2003
Ponselle, Rosa	1897	1981	Robson, Flora	1902	1984	Sims, Irene	1930	2001
Ponti, Carlo	1922	2007	Roche, Eugene	1928	2004	Sinatra, Frank	1915	1998
Porter, Eric.	1928	1995	Rochester (E. Anderson)	1905	1977	Sinclair, Madge	1938	1995
Porter, Edwin S.	1870	1941	Roddenberry, Gene	1921	1991	Singleton, Penny	1908	2003
Porter, Nyree Dawn	1940	2001	Rodgers, Jimmie	1897	1933	Siskel, Gene	1946	1999
Poston, Tom	1921	2007	Rogers, Buddy.	1904	1999	Sitka, Emil	1914	1998
Powell, Dick	1904	1963	Rogers, Fred	1928	2003	Sjostrom, Victor	1879	1960
Powell, Eleanor	1912	1982	Rogers, Ginger	1911	1995	Skelton, Red	1913	1997
Powell, William	1892	1984	Rogers, Roy	1911	1998	Skinner, Otis	1858	1942
Power, Tyrone	1913	1958	Rogers, Will	1879	1935	Smith, Alexis	1921	1993
Preminger, Otto	1905	1986	Roland, Gilbert	1905	1994	Smith, Bessie	1894?	1937
Presley, Elvis	1935	1977	Rolle, Esther	1920?	1998	Smith, Buffalo Bob	1917	1998
Preston, Billy	1946	2006	Rollins, Howard	1950	1996	Smith, C. Aubrey	1863	1948
Preston, Robert	1918	1987	Roman, Ruth	1924	1999	Smith, Elliott	1969	2003
Price, Vincent	1911	1993	Romero, Cesar	1907	1994	Smith, Jeff	1939	2004
Prima, Louis	1911	1978	Rooney, Pat.	1880	1962	Smith, Kate	1907	1986
Prinze, Freddie	1954	1977	Rose, Billy	1899	1966	Smith, Kent	1907	1985
Prosky, Robert	1930	2008	Rossellini, Roberto	1906	1977	Snodgress, Carrie	1946	2004
Prowse, Juliet	1936	1996	Rostropovich, Mstislav	1927	2007	Snow, Hank.	1914	1999
Pryor, Richard	1940	2005	Rowan, Dan.	1922	1987	Snyder, Tom	1936	2007
Puente, Tito	1923	2000	Rubinstein, Artur	1887	1982	Solti, George	1912	1997
Pyle, Denver	1920	1997	Ruggles, Charles	1886	1970	Sondergaard, Gale	1899	1985
Quayle, Anthony	1913	1989	Russell, Harold	1914	2002	Sothern, Ann	1909	2001
Questel, Mae	1908	1998	Russell, Lillian	1861	1922	Sousa, John Philip	1854	1932
Quinn, Anthony	1915	2001	Russell, Nipsey	1923	2005	Sparks, Ned	1884	1957
Quintero, José	1924	1999	Russell, Rosalind	1911	1976	Spelling, Aaron	1928	2006
Rabb, Ellis	1930	1998	Rutherford, Margaret.	1892	1972	Spencer, John	1946	2005
Rabbit, Eddie	1941	1998	Ryan, Irene	1903	1973	Sperber, Wendy Jo	1958	2005
Radner, Gilda	1946	1989	Ryan, Robert	1909	1973	Springfield, Dusty	1939	1999
Raft, George	1895	1980	Sabu	1924	1963	Stack, Robert	1919	2003
Rains, Claude	1890	1967	St. Cyr, Lili	1917	1999	Stafford, Jo	1917	2008
Raitt, John	1917	2005	St. Denis, Ruth	1877	1968	Stander, Lionel	1908	1994
Ralston, Esther	1902	1994	Sakall, S.Z.	1884	1955	Stanley, Kim	1925	2001
Ramone, Dee Dee	1952	2002	Sale (Chic), Charles	1885	1936	Stanwyck, Barbara	1907	1990
Ramone, Joey	1951	2001	Sales, Soupy	1926	2009	Stapleton, Maureen.	1925	2006
Ramone, Johnny	1951	2004	Sanders, George	1906	1972	Steiger, Rod	1925	2002
Rampal, Jean-Pierre	1922	2000	Sanford, Isabel	1917	2004	Sterling, Jan	1921	2004
Randall, Tony	1920	2004	Sargent, Dick	1933	1994	Stern, Isaac	1920	2001
Randolph, John	1915	2004	Savalas, Telly	1924	1994	Stevens, Craig	1918	2000
Rathbone, Basil	1892	1967	Scheider, Roy	1935	2008	Stevens, Inger	1934	1970
Ratoff, Gregory	1897	1960	Schell, Maria	1926	2005	Stevens, Mark	1916	1994
Rawls, Lou	1933	2006	Schenkel, Chris	1923	2005	Stevenson, McLean	1929	1996
Ray, Aldo	1926	1991	Schiavelli, Vincent	1948	2005	Stewart, James	1908	1997
Ray, Johnnie	1927	1990	Schildkraut, Joseph	1895	1964	Stickney, Dorothy	1896	1998
Rayburn, Gene	1917	1999	Schipa, Tito	1889	1965	Stokowski, Leopold	1882	1977
Raye, Martha	1916	1994	Schlesinger, John	1926	2003	Stone, Lewis	1879	1953
Raymond, Gene	1908	1998	Schnabel, Artur	1882	1951	Stone, Milburn	1904	1980
Reagan, Ronald	1911	2004	Schneider, Romy	1938	1982	Storm, Gale	1922	2009
Redding, Otis	1941	1967	Schwartzkopf, Elizabeth	1915	2006	Straight, Beatrice	1918	2001
Redgrave, Michael.	1908	1985	Scott, George C.	1927	1999	Strasberg, Lee	1901	1982
Reed, Donna	1921	1986	Scott, Gordon	1926	2007	Strasberg, Susan	1938	1999
Reed, Jerry	1937	2008	Scott, Hazel	1920	1981	Strode, Woody	1914	1994
Reed, Oliver	1938	1999	Scott, Martha	1914	2003	Strummer, Joe	1952	2002
Reed, Robert	1932	1992	Scott, Randolph.	1898	1987	Stuarti, Enzo	1919	2005
Reeve, Christopher	1952	2004	Scott, Zachary	1914	1965	Sturges, Preston	1898	1959

Name	Born	Died	Name	Born	Died	Name	Born	Died
Sullavan, Margaret	1911	1960	Urich, Robert	1947	2002	White, Barry	1944	2003
Sullivan, Barry	1912	1994	Ustinov, Peter	1921	2004	White, Jesse	1919	1997
Sullivan, Ed	1902	1974	Valens, Ritchie	1941	1959	White, Pearl	1889	1938
Sullivan, Francis L.	1903	1956	Valentino, Rudolph	1895	1926	Whiteman, Paul	1891	1967
Summerville, Slim	1892	1946	Vallee, Rudy	1901	1986	Whitmore, James	1921	2009
Swanson, Gloria	1899	1983	Van, Bobby	1928	1980	Whitty, May	1865	1948
Swarthout, Gladys	1904	1969	Vance, Vivian	1912	1979	Wickes, Mary	1910	1995
Swayze, Patrick	1952	2009	Van Cleef, Lee	1925	1989	Widmark, Richard	1914	2008
Sweet, Blanche	1896	1986	Vandross, Luther	1951	2005	Wilde, Cornel	1918	1989
Switzer, Carl "Alfalfa"	1926	1959	Van Fleet, Jo	1922	1996	Wilder, Billy	1906	2002
Talbot, Lyle	1904	1996	Varney, Jim	1949	2000	Wilding, Michael	1912	1979
Talmadge, Norma	1893	1957	Vaughan, Sarah	1924	1990	Williams, Bert	1877	1922
Tamiroff, Akim	1899	1972	Veidt, Conrad	1893	1943	Williams, Guy	1924	1989
Tandy, Jessica	1909	1994	Velez, Lupe	1908	1944	Williams, Hank Sr.	1923	1953
Tanguay, Eva	1878	1947	Vera-Ellen	1926	1981	Wills, Bob	1905	1975
Tati, Jacques	1908	1982	Verdon, Gwen	1925	2000	Wills, Chill	1903	1978
Taylor, Deems	1885	1966	Vernon, Jackie	1925	1987	Wilson, Carl	1946	1998
Taylor, Dub	1907	1994	Vernon, John	1932	2005	Wilson, Dennis	1944	1983
Taylor, Estelle	1899	1958	Villechaize, Herve	1943	1993	Wilson, Dooley	1894	1953
Taylor, Laurette	1887	1946	Vincent, Gene	1935	1971	Wilson, Flip	1933	1998
Taylor, Robert	1911	1969	Vicious, Sid	1957	1979	Wilson, Jackie	1934	1984
Tebaldi, Renata	1922	2004	Vinson, Helen	1907	1999	Wilson, Marie	1917	1972
Terry, Ellen	1847	1928	Von Stroheim, Erich	1885	1957	Windsor, Marie	1919	2000
Thalberg, Irving	1899	1936	Von Zell, Harry	1906	1981	Winfield, Paul	1941	2004
Thaw, John	1942	2002	Walker, Junior	1942	1995	Winninger, Charles	1884	1969
Thigpen, Lynne	1948	2003	Walker, Nancy	1922	1992	Winters, Shelley	1920	2006
Thomas, Danny	1912	1991	Walker, Robert	1918	1951	Wise, Robert	1914	2005
Thomas, John Charles	1892	1960	Wallenda, Karl	1905	1978	Withers, Grant	1904	1959
Thorndike, Sybil	1882	1976	Walsh, J. T.	1943	1998	Wong, Anna May	1907	1961
Thulin, Ingrid	1926	2004	Walsh, Raoul	1887	1980	Wood, Natalie	1938	1981
Tibbett, Lawrence	1896	1960	Walston, Ray	1914	2001	Wood, Peggy	1892	1978
Tierney, Gene	1920	1991	Walter, Bruno	1876	1962	Wooley, Sheb	1921	2003
Tiny Tim	1923	1996	Ward, Helen	1916	1998	Woolley, Monty	1888	1963
Tippett, Sir Michael	1905	1998	Warden, Jack	1914	2006	Worth, Irene	1916	2002
Todd, Michael	1909	1958	Waring, Fred	1900	1984	Wray, Fay	1907	2004
Tomlinson, David	1917	2000	Warner, H. B.	1876	1958	Wright, Teresa	1918	2005
Tone, Franchot	1903	1968	Warrick, Ruth	1915	2005	Wyatt, Jane	1910?	2006
Torme, Mel	1925	1999	Washington, Dinah	1924	1963	Wyler, William	1902	1981
Toscanini, Arturo	1867	1957	Waters, Ethel	1896	1977	Wyman, Jane	1914?	2007
Tracy, Lee	1898	1968	Waters, Muddy	1915	1983	Wynette, Tammy	1942	1998
Tracy, Spencer	1900	1967	Waxman, Al	1935	2001	Wynn, Ed	1886	1966
Traubel, Helen	1903	1972	Wayne, David	1914	1995	Wynn, Keenan	1916	1986
Travers, Henry	1874	1965	Wayne, John	1907	1979	Yankovic, Frank	1915	1998
Travers, Mary	1937	2009	Weaver, Dennis	1924	2006	York, Dick	1929	1992
Treacher, Arthur	1894	1975	Webb, Clifton	1891	1966	Young, Clara Kimball	1890	1960
Tree, Herbert Beerbohm	1853	1917	Webb, Jack	1920	1982	Young, Gig	1913	1978
Trevor, Claire	1909	2000	Weems, Ted	1901	1963	Young, Loretta	1913	2000
Truex, Ernest	1890	1973	Weissmuller, Johnny	1904	1984	Young, Robert	1907	1998
Truffaut, Francois	1932	1984	Welk, Lawrence	1903	1992	Young, Roland	1887	1953
Tucker, Forrest	1919	1986	Welles, Orson	1915	1985	Youngman, Henny	1906	1998
Tucker, Richard	1913	1975	Wellman, William	1896	1975	Zanuck, Darryl F.	1902	1979
Tucker, Sophie	1884	1966	Werner, Oskar	1922	1984	Zappa, Frank	1940	1993
Turner, Ike	1931	2008	West, Mae	1893	1980	Zevon, Warren	1947	2003
Turner, Lana	1920	1995	Weston, Jack	1924	1996	Zinneman, Fred	1907	1997
Turpin, Ben	1874	1940	Whale, James	1889	1957	Ziegfeld, Florenz	1869	1932
Twelvetrees, Helen	1908	1958	Wheeler, Bert	1895	1968	Zukor, Adolph	1873	1976
Twitty, Conway	1933	1993						

Original Names of Selected Entertainers

CLAY AIKEN: Clayton Grissom
ALI G: Sacha Baron Cohen
EDDIE ALBERT: Edward Albert Heimberger
ALAN ALDA: Alphonso D'Abruzzo
JASON ALEXANDER: Jay Greenspan
FRED ALLEN: John Sullivan
WOODY ALLEN: Allen Konigsberg
JUNE ALLYSON: Ella Geisman
ANDRÉ 3000: Andre Benjamin
JULIE ANDREWS: Julia Wells
CRISS ANGEL: Christopher Sarantakos
EVE ARDEN: Eunice Quedens
BEATRICE ARTHUR: Bernice Frankel
JEAN ARTHUR: Gladys Greene
ASHANTI: Ashanti Douglas
FRED ASTAIRE: Frederick Austerlitz
BABYFACE: Kenneth Edmonds
LAUREN BACALL: Betty Joan Perske
ERYKAH BADU: Erica Wright
ERIC BANA: Eric Banadinovich
ANNE BANCROFT: Anna Maria Italiano
THEDA BARA: Theodosia Goodman
PAT BENATAR: Patricia Andrejewski
TONY BENNETT: Anthony Benedetto
IRVING BERLIN: Israel Baline
JACK BENNY: Benjamin Kubelsky

SARAH BERNHARDT: Henriette-Rosine Bernard
MILTON BERLE: Mendel Berlinger
JELLO BIAFRA: Eric Reed Boucher
ROBERT BLAKE: Michael James Vijencio Gubitosi
BIG BOI: Antwan Patton
JON BON JOVI: John Francis Bongiovi
JOEY BISHOP: Joseph Gottlieb
THE BIG BOPPER: Jiles Perry "J.P." Richardson
BONO (VOX): Paul Hewson
BOW WOW: Shad Gregory Moss
DAVID BOWIE: David Robert Jones
BOY GEORGE: George Alan O'Dowd
FANNY BRICE: Fanny Borach
CHARLES BRONSON: Charles Buchinski
ALBERT BROOKS: Albert Einstein
MEL BROOKS: Melvin Kaminsky
FOXY BROWN: Inga Marchand
GEORGE BURNS: Nathan Birnbaum
ELLEN BURSTYN: Edna Gilhooley
RICHARD BURTON: Richard Jenkins
RED BUTTONS: Aaron Chwatt
NICOLAS CAGE: Nicholas Coppola
MICHAEL CAINE: Maurice Micklewhite
MARIA CALLAS: Maria Kalogeropoulos

CEDRIC THE ENTERTAINER: Cedric Kyles
JACKIE CHAN: Chan Kwong-Sung
CYD CHARISSE: Tula Finklea
RAY CHARLES: Ray Charles Robinson
CHARO: Maria Rosario Pilar Martinez Molina Baeza
CHUBBY CHECKER: Ernest Evans
CHUCK D: Carlton Ridenhour
CHER: Cherilyn Sarkisian
PATSY CLINE: Virginia Patterson Hensley
CLAUDETTE COLBERT: Lily Chauchoin
COOLIO: Artis Leon Ivey Jr.
ALICE COOPER: Vincent Furnier
DAVID COPPERFIELD: David Kotkin
HOWARD COSELL: Howard Cohen
ELVIS COSTELLO: Declan McManus
LOU COSTELLO: Louis Cristillo
PETER COYOTE: Peter Cohon
TOM CRUISE: Thomas Mapother IV
TONY CURTIS: Bernard Schwartz
VIC DAMONE: Vito Farinola
RODNEY DANGERFIELD: Jacob Cohen
BOBBY DARIN: Walden Robert Cassotto
DORIS DAY: Doris von Kappelhoff
YVONNE DE CARLO: Peggy Middleton
SANDRA DEE: Alexandra Zuck

JOHN DENVER: Henry John Deutschendorf Jr.
BO DEREK: Mary Cathleen Collins
DIVINE: Harris Glenn Milstead
DANNY DEVITO: Daniel Michaeli
ANGIE DICKINSON: Angeline Brown
BO DIDDLEY: Elias Bates
PHYLLIS DILLER: Phyllis Driver
DMX: Earl Simmons
EARL TROY DONAHUE: Merle Johnson Jr.
KIRK DOUGLAS: Issur Danielovitch
MELVYN DOUGLAS: Melvyn Hesselberg
DUFFY: Aimee Anne Duffy
BOB DYLAN: Robert Zimmerman
BARBARA EDEN: Barbara Huffman
CARMEN ELECTRA: Tara Leigh Patrick
ELVIRA: Cassandra Peterson
EMINEM: Marshall Mathers
ENYA: Eithne Ni Bhraonian
DALE EVANS: Frances Smith
CHAD EVERETT: Raymond Cramton
FABOLOUS: Skylar Jackson
DOUGLAS FAIRBANKS: Douglas Ullman
MORGAN FAIRCHILD: Patsy McClenny
JAMIE FARR: Jameel Farah
ALICE FAYE: Alice Jeanne Leppert
STEPIN FETCHIT: Lincoln Perry
W. C. FIELDS: William Claude Dukenfield
50 CENT: Curtis Jackson
BARRY FITZGERALD: William Shields
FLAVOR FLAV: William Drayton
JOAN FONTAINE: Joan de Havilland
JODIE FOSTER: Alicia Christian Foster
REDD FOXX: John Sanford
ARLENE FRANCIS: Arlene Kazanjian
CONNIE FRANCIS: Concetta Franconero
KENNY G: Kenneth Gorelick
GRETA GARBO: Greta Gustafsson
VINCENT GARDENIA: Vincent Scognamiglio
JOHN GARFIELD: Julius Garfinkle
JUDY GARLAND: Frances Gumm
JAMES GARNER: James Bumgarner
CRYSTAL GAYLE: Brenda Gayle Webb
GEORGE GERSHWIN: Jacob Gershowitz
KATHIE LEE GIFFORD: Kathie Epstein
WHOOPI GOLDBERG: Caryn Johnson
EYDIE GORME: Edith Gormezano
STEWART GRANGER: James Stewart
CARY GRANT: Archibald Leach
LEE GRANT: Lyova Rosenthal
ROBERT GUILLAUME: Robert Williams
BUDDY HACKETT: Leonard Hacker
HAMMER: Stanley Kirk Burrell
JEAN HARLOW: Harlean Carpentier
REX HARRISON: Reginald Carey
LAURENCE HARVEY: Larushka Skikne
HELEN HAYES: Helen Brown
SUSAN HAYWARD: Edythe Marriner
RITA HAYWORTH: Margarita Cansino
PEE-WEE HERMAN: Paul Reubenfeld
CHARLTON HESTON: John Charlton Carter
HULK HOGAN: Terry Gene Bollea
WILLIAM HOLDEN: William Beedle
BILLIE HOLIDAY: Eleanora Fagan
BUDDY HOLLY: Charles Hardin Holley
JUDY HOLLIDAY: Judith Tuvim
BOB HOPE: Leslie Townes Hope
HARRY HOUDINI: Ehrich Weiss
LESLIE HOWARD: Leslie Stainer
HOWLIN' WOLF: Chester Burnett
ROCK HUDSON: Roy Scherer Jr. (later Fitzgerald)
ENGELBERT HUMPERDINCK: Arnold Dorsey
KIM HUNTER: Janet Cole
ICE CUBE: O'Shea Jackson
ICE-T: Tracy Morrow
BILLY IDOL: William Broad
JA RULE: Jeffrey Atkins
ETTA JAMES: Jamesetta Hawkins
JAY-Z: Shawn Carter
JEWEL: Jewel Kilcher
ELTON JOHN: Reginald Dwight

DON JOHNSON: Donald Wayne
ANGELINA JOLIE: Angelina Jolie Voight
AL JOLSON: Asa Yoelson
JENNIFER JONES: Phylis Isley
TOM JONES: Thomas Woodward
SPIKE JONZE: Adam Spiegel
LOUIS JOURDAN: Louis Gendre
WYNONNA JUDD: Christina Ciminella
BORIS KARLOFF: William Henry Pratt
DANNY KAYE: David Kaminsky
DIANE KEATON: Diane Hall
MICHAEL KEATON: Michael Douglas
ALICIA KEYS: Alicia Augello Cook
CHAKA KHAN: Yvette Stevens
CAROLE KING: Carole Klein
LARRY KING: Larry Zeiger
BEN KINGSLEY: Krishna Banji
TED KNIGHT: Tadeus Wladyslaw Konopka
CHERYL LADD: Cheryl Stoppelmoor
LADY GAGA: Stefani Germanotta
VERONICA LAKE: Constance Ockleman
HEDY LAMARR: Hedwig Kiesler
DOROTHY LAMOUR: Mary Leta Dorothy Slaton
MICHAEL LANDON: Eugene Orowitz
MARIO LANZA: Alfredo Cocozza
QUEEN LATIFAH: Dana Owens
STAN LAUREL: Arthur Jefferson
STEVE LAWRENCE: Sidney Leibowitz
BRENDA LEE: Brenda Mae Tarpley
GYPSY ROSE LEE: Rose Louise Hovick
MICHELLE LEE: Michelle Dusiak
PEGGY LEE: Norma Egstrom
JANET LEIGH: Jeanette Morrison
VIVIEN LEIGH: Vivian Hartley
HUEY LEWIS: Hugh Cregg
JERRY LEWIS: Joseph Levitch
LIL' KIM: Kimberly Denise Jones
LIL' ROMEO: Percy Romeo Miller Jr.
CAROLE LOMBARD: Jane Peters
SOPHIA LOREN: Sophia Scicolone
PETER LORRE: Laszio Lowenstein
MYRNA LOY: Myrna Williams
BELA LUGOSI: Bela Ferenc Blasko
MOMS MABLEY: Loretta Mary Aitken
SHIRLEY MACLAINE: Shirley Beaty
ELLE MACPHERSON: Eleanor Gow
MADONNA: Madonna Louise Veronica Ciccone
LEE MAJORS: Harvey Lee Yeary
KARL MALDEN: Mladen Sekulovich
BARRY MANILOW: Barry Alan Pincus
JAYNE MANSFIELD: Vera Jane Palmer
MARILYN MANSON: Brian Warner
FREDRIC MARCH: Frederick Bickel
RICKY MARTIN: Enrique Jose Martin Morales
GROUCHO MARX: Julius Henry Marx
WALTER MATTHAU: Walter Matuschanskayasky
DEAN MARTIN: Dino Crocetti
MEAT LOAF: Marvin Lee Aday
FREDDIE MERCURY: Frederick Bulsara
ETHEL MERMAN: Ethel Zimmerman
GEORGE MICHAEL: Georgios Panayiotou
RAY MILLAND: Reginald Truscott-Jones
ANN MILLER: Lucille Collier
HELEN MIRREN: Ilynea Lydia Mironoff
JONI MITCHELL: Roberta Joan Anderson
MOBY: Richard Melville Hall
MARILYN MONROE: Norma Jean Mortenson (later Baker)
YVES MONTAND: Ivo Livi
DEMI MOORE: Demetria Guynes
RITA MORENO: Rosita Alverio
HARRY MORGAN: Harry Bratsburg
MR. T: Lawrence Tero
PAUL MUNI: Muni Weisenfreund
MIKE NICHOLS: Michael Igor Peschowsky
CHUCK NORRIS: Carlos Ray
NOTORIOUS B.I.G.: Christopher Wallace
HUGH O'BRIAN: Hugh Krampke
MAUREEN O'HARA: Maureen FitzSimons
OZZY OSBOURNE: John Michael Osbourne
JACK PALANCE: Walter Palanuik

MINNIE PEARL: Sarah Ophelia Cannon
BERNADETTE PETERS: Bernadette Lazzara
EDITH PIAF: Edith Gassion
SLIM PICKENS: Louis Lindley
MARY PICKFORD: Gladys Smith
PINK: Alecia Moore
ROBERT PRESTON: Robert Preston Meservey
PRINCE: Prince Rogers Nelson
DEE DEE RAMONE: Douglas Colvin
JOEY RAMONE: Jeffrey Hyman
JOHNNY RAMONE: John Cummings
TOMMY RAMONE: Tom Erdelyi
TONY RANDALL: Leonard Rosenberg
MARTHA RAYE: Margaret O'Reed
DELLA REESE: Delloreese Patricia Early
BUSTA RHYMES: Trevor Smith Jr.
JOAN RIVERS: Joan Sandra Molinsky
EDWARD G. ROBINSON: Emmanuel Goldenberg
THE ROCK: Dwayne Johnson
GINGER ROGERS: Virginia McMath
ROY ROGERS: Leonard Franklin Slye
MICKEY ROONEY: Joe Yule Jr.
JOHNNY ROTTEN: John Lydon
LILLIAN RUSSELL: Helen Leonard
MEG RYAN: Margaret Hyra
WINONA RYDER: Winona Horowitz
SADE: Helen Folsad Abu
SOUPY SALES: Milton Hines
SUSAN SARANDON: Susan Tomaling
SEAL: Seal Henry Olusegun Olumide Adeola Samuel
RANDOLPH SCOTT: George Randolph Crane
JANE SEYMOUR: Joyce Frankenberg
SHAKIRA: Shakira Isabel Mebarak Ripoll
OMAR SHARIF: Michael Shalhoub
CHARLIE SHEEN: Carlos Irwin Estevez
MARTIN SHEEN: Ramon Estevez
TALIA SHIRE: Talia Coppola
BEVERLY SILLS: Belle Silverman
GENE SIMMONS: Haim Witz
PHIL SILVERS: Philip Silversmith
SINBAD: David Atkins
SNOOP DOGGY DOG: Calvin Broadus
ANNA NICOLE SMITH: Vickie Lynn Hogan
ANN SOTHERN: Harriette Lake
ROBERT STACK: Robert Modini
BARBARA STANWYCK: Ruby Stevens
JEAN STAPLETON: Jeanne Murray
RINGO STARR: Richard Starkey
CAT STEVENS: Stephen Demetre Georgiou
CONNIE STEVENS: Concetta Ingolia
STING: Gordon Sumner
JOE STRUMMER: John Graham Mellor
DONNA SUMMER: La Donna Gaines
RIP TAYLOR: Charles Elmer Jr.
ROBERT TAYLOR: Spangler Brugh
DANNY THOMAS: Muzyad Yakhoob, later Amos Jacobs
TINY TIM: Herbert Khaury
RIP TORN: Elmore Rual Torn Jr.
RANDY TRAVIS: Randy Traywick
SOPHIE TUCKER: Sophia Kalish
TINA TURNER: Annie Mae Bullock
SHANIA TWAIN: Eilleen Regina Edwards
TWIGGY: Leslie Hornby
CONWAY TWITTY: Harold Lloyd Jenkins
USHER: Usher Raymond IV
RUDOLPH VALENTINO: Rudolpho D'Antonguolla
FRANKIE VALLI: Frank Castelluccio
EDDIE VEDDER: Edward Louis Seversen III
SID VICIOUS: John Simon Ritchie
JOHN WAYNE: Marion Morrison
RAQUEL WELCH: Raquel Tejada
GENE WILDER: Jerome Silberman
SHELLEY WINTERS: Shirley Schrift
STEVIE WONDER: Stevland Morris
JANE WYMAN: Sarah Jane Fulks
LORETTA YOUNG: Gretchen Michaels
BUCKWHEAT ZYDECO: Stanley Dural Jr.

ARTS AND MEDIA

Some Notable Movies, Sept. 2008-Aug. 2009

Film	Stars	Director
Adventureland (R)	Jesse Eisenberg, Martin Starr, Kristen Stewart	Greg Mottola
Angels & Demons (PG-13)	Tom Hanks, Ewan McGregor	Ron Howard
Away We Go (R)	John Krasinski, Catherine O'Hara, Maya Rudolph	Sam Mendes
Beverly Hills Chihuahua (PG)	Drew Barrymore, Andy Garcia, George Lopez, Piper Perabo	Raja Gosnell
Body of Lies (R)	Russell Crowe, Leonardo DiCaprio	Ridley Scott
Bolt (PG)	Susie Essman, John Travolta	Byron Howard, Chris Williams
Brüno (R)	Sacha Baron Cohen	Larry Charles
Changeling (R)	Jeffrey Donovan, Angelina Jolie, John Malkovich, Amy Ryan	Clint Eastwood
Che (NR)	Demián Bichir, Benicio Del Toro	Steven Soderbergh
Confessions of a Shopaholic (PG)	Joan Cusack, Hugh Dancy, Isla Fisher	P. J. Hogan
Coraline (PG)	Dakota Fanning, Dawn French, Teri Hatcher, Jennifer Saunders	Henry Selick
The Curious Case of Benjamin Button (PG-13)	Cate Blanchett, Brad Pitt	David Fincher
The Day the Earth Stood Still (PG-13)	Kathy Bates, Jennifer Connelly, Jon Hamm, Keanu Reeves	Scott Derrickson
District 9 (R)	Nathalie Boltt, Jason Cope, Sharlto Copley	Neill Blomkamp
Doubt (PG-13)	Amy Adams, Philip Seymour Hoffman, Meryl Streep	John Patrick Shanley
Duplicity (PG-13)	Clive Owen, Julia Roberts	Tony Gilroy
Food, Inc. (PG)	Documentary	Robert Kenner
Frost/Nixon (R)	Toby Jones, Frank Langella, Sam Rockwell, Michael Sheen	Ron Howard
Funny People (R)	Leslie Mann, Seth Rogen, Adam Sandler	Judd Apatow
G.I. Joe: The Rise of Cobra (PG-13)	Adewale Akinnuoye-Agbaje, Joseph Gordon-Leavitt, Sienna Miller	Stephen Sommers
G-Force (PG)	Will Arnett, Zack Galifianakis, Bill Nighy	Hoyt Yeatman
Gran Torino (R)	Clint Eastwood	Clint Eastwood
The Hangover (R)	Bradley Cooper, Zack Galifianakis, Ed Helms	Todd Phillips
Hannah Montana: The Movie (G)	Miley Cyrus	Peter Chelsom
Happy-Go-Lucky (R)	Sally Hawkins, Eddie Marsan, Alexis Zegerman	Mike Leigh
Harry Potter & the Half-Blood Prince (PG)	Rupert Grint, Daniel Radcliffe, Emma Watson	David Yates
He's Just Not That Into You (PG-13)	Jennifer Aniston, Jennifer Connelly, Kevin Connolly, Scarlett Johansson	Ken Kwapis
High School Musical 3: Senior Year (G)	Zac Efron, Vanessa Hudgens, Ashley Tisdale	Kenny Ortega
I Love You, Man (R)	Paul Rudd, Jason Segel	John Hamburg
Ice Age: Dawn of the Dinosaurs (PG)	Queen Latifah, Dennis Leary, Ray Romano	Carlos Saldanha, Mike Thurmeier
Inglourious Basterds (R)	Brad Pitt	Quentin Tarantino
I've Loved You So Long (PG-13)	Kristin Scott Thomas	Philippe Claudel
Julie & Julia (PG-13)	Amy Adams, Meryl Streep	Nora Ephron
Madagascar: Escape 2 Africa (PG)	Andy Richter, Chris Rock, Jada Pinkett Smith, Ben Stiller	Eric Darnell, Tom McGrath
Marley and Me (PG)	Jennifer Aniston, Alan Arkin, Eric Dane, Owen Wilson	David Frankel
Milk (R)	Josh Brolin, Victor Garber, Sean Penn	Gus Van Sant
Miracle at St. Anna (R)	Laz Alonzo, Michael Ealy, Derek Luke, John Turturro, Kerry Washington	Spike Lee
Monsters vs. Aliens (PG)	Will Arnett, Hugh Laurie, Seth Rogen, Reese Witherspoon	Rob Letterman, Conrad Vernon
Night at the Museum: Battle of the Smithsonian (PG)	Amy Adams, Hank Azaria, Ben Stiller, Owen Wilson	Shawn Levy
Notorious (R)	Angela Bassett, Derek Luke, Jamal Woolard	George Tillman Jr.
Observe and Report (R)	Anna Faris, Ray Liotta, Seth Rogen	Jody Hill
Paul Blart: Mall Cop (PG)	Kevin James	Steve Carr
Pride and Glory (R)	Jennifer Ehle, Colin Farrell, Edward Norton	Gavin O'Connor
Public Enemies (R)	Christian Bale, Marion Cotillard, Johnny Depp	Michael Mann
Quantum of Solace (PG-13)	Daniel Craig, Judi Dench	Marc Forster
Rachel Getting Married (R)	Rosemarie DeWitt, Anne Hathaway, Bill Irwin, Debra Winger	Jonathan Demme
The Reader (R)	Ralph Fiennes, Kate Winslet	Stephen Daldry
Religulous (R)	Bill Maher (Documentary)	Larry Charles
Revolutionary Road (R)	Kathy Bates, Leonardo DiCaprio, David Harbour, Kate Winslet	Sam Mendes
The Secret Life of Bees (PG-13)	Dakota Fanning, Jennifer Hudson, Queen Latifah, Sophie Okonedo	Gina Prince-Bythewood
The September Issue (PG-13)	Documentary	R. J. Cutler
Seven Pounds (PG-13)	Will Smith	Gabriele Muccino
Slumdog Millionaire (R)	Dev Patel, Freida Pinto	Danny Boyle
The Spirit (PG-13)	Samuel L. Jackson	Frank Miller
Star Trek (PG-13)	Chris Pine, Zachary Quinto	J. J. Abrams
State of Play (PG-13)	Ben Affleck, Russell Crowe, Rachel McAdams, Helen Mirren	Kevin Macdonald
Synecdoche, New York (R)	Philip Seymour Hoffman, Catherine Keener, Michelle Williams	Charlie Kaufman
Taking Woodstock (R)	Dan Fogler, Demetri Martin	Ang Lee
The Tale of Despereaux (G)	Matthew Broderick, Dustin Hoffman, Kevin Kline, William H. Macy	Sam Fell, Robert Stevenhagen
The Class (Entre les murs) (PG-13)	François Bégaudeau	Laurent Cantet
The Time Traveler's Wife (PG-13)	Eric Bana, Rachel McAdams	Robert Schwentke
Transformers: Revenge of the Fallen (PG-13)	Megan Fox, Shia LaBeouf	Michael Bay
Twilight (PG-13)	Robert Pattinson, Kristen Stewart	Catherine Hardwicke
Up (PG)	Ed Asner, Christopher Plummer, John Ratzenberger	Pete Docter, Bob Peterson
Valkyrie (PG-13)	Tom Cruise, Bill Nighy, Tom Wilkinson	Bryan Singer
W. (PG-13)	Josh Brolin, Richard Dreyfuss	Oliver Stone
Waltz With Bashir (R)	Animated documentary	Ari Folman
Watchmen (R)	Malin Akerman, Billy Crudup, Matthew Goode, Jackie Earle Haley	Zack Snyder
Whatever Works (PG-13)	Larry David, Evan Rachel Wood	Woody Allen
The Women (PG-13)	Annette Bening, Debra Messing, Meg Ryan, Jada Pinkett Smith	Diane English
The Wrestler (R)	Mickey Rourke, Marisa Tomei, Evan Rachel Wood	Darren Aronofsky
X-Men Origins: Wolverine (PG-13)	Hugh Jackman	Gavin Hood

50 Top-Grossing Movies, 2008

Source: *Variety* magazine, box-office grosses in the U.S. and Canada during calendar year 2008

Rank	Title	Gross (mil)	Rank	Title	Gross (mil)
1.	The Dark Knight	$530.9	27.	Beverly Hills Chihuahua	$93.5
2.	Iron Man	318.3	28.	The Bucket List	92.6
3.	Indiana Jones and the Kingdom of the Crystal Skull	317.0	29.	High School Musical 3: Senior Year	90.0
4.	Hancock	227.9	30.	Pineapple Express	87.3
5.	WALL-E	223.8	31.	Marley and Me	82.4
6.	Kung Fu Panda	215.4	32.	21	81.2
7.	Madagascar: Escape 2 Africa	176.1	33.	What Happens in Vegas	80.2
8.	Twilight	172.3	34.	Jumper	80.2
9.	Quantum of Solace	165.7	35.	Cloverfield	80.0
10.	Horton Hears a Who	154.5	36.	National Treasure: Book of Secrets	77.0
11.	Sex and the City	152.6	37.	27 Dresses	76.8
12.	Mamma Mia!	144.1	38.	Hellboy II: The Golden Army	76.0
13.	The Chronicles of Narnia: Prince Caspian	141.6	39.	Vantage Point	72.3
14.	The Incredible Hulk	134.8	40.	The Spiderwick Chronicles	71.2
15.	Wanted	134.5	41.	Fool's Gold	70.2
16.	Get Smart	130.3	42.	The Day the Earth Stood Still	69.4
17.	Four Christmases	115.4	43.	Role Models	66.5
18.	Juno	112.0	44.	Yes Man	65.6
19.	Tropic Thunder	110.5	45.	Hannah Montana/Miley Cyrus: Best of Both Worlds Concert Tour	65.3
20.	Bolt	106.6	46.	Bedtime Stories	65.0
21.	The Mummy: Tomb of the Dragon Emperor	102.5	47.	The Happening	64.5
22.	Journey to the Center of the Earth	101.7	48.	Alvin and the Chipmunks	63.7
23.	Eagle Eye	101.3	49.	Forgetting Sarah Marshall	63.2
24.	Step Brothers	100.5	50.	The Curious Case of Benjamin Button	60.6
25.	You Don't Mess With the Zohan	100.0			
26.	10,000 B.C.	94.8			

All-Time Top-Grossing American Movies[1]

Source: *Variety* magazine

Rank	Title (original release)	Gross[2]	Rank	Title (original release)	Gross[2]
1.	Titanic (1997)	$600.8	26.	Pirates of the Caribbean: At World's End (2007)	$309.4
2.	The Dark Knight (2008)	530.9	27.	Star Wars: Episode VI—Return of the Jedi (1983)	309.2
3.	Star Wars: Episode IV—A New Hope (1977)	461.0	28.	Independence Day (1996)	306.2
4.	Shrek 2 (2004)	436.7	29.	Pirates of the Caribbean: The Curse of the Black Pearl (2003)	305.4
5.	E.T.: The Extra-Terrestrial (1982)	435.0	30.	The Sixth Sense (1999)	293.5
6.	Star Wars: Episode I—The Phantom Menace (1999)	431.1	31.	Harry Potter and the Order of the Phoenix (2007)	292.0
7.	Pirates of the Caribbean: Dead Man's Chest (2006)	423.3	32.	The Chronicles of Narnia: The Lion, the Witch and the Wardrobe (2005)	291.7
8.	Spider-Man (2002)	403.7	33.	Star Wars: Episode V—The Empire Strikes Back (1980)	290.3
9.	Star Wars: Episode III—Revenge of the Sith (2005)	380.3	34.	Harry Potter and the Goblet of Fire (2005)	290.0
10.	The Lord of the Rings: The Return of the King (2003)	377.0	35.	Home Alone (1990)	285.8
11.	Spider-Man 2 (2004)	373.4	36.	The Matrix: Reloaded (2003)	281.5
12.	The Passion of the Christ (2004)	370.3	37.	Meet the Fockers (2004)	279.2
13.	Jurassic Park (1993)	357.1	38.	Shrek (2001)	267.7
14.	The Lord of the Rings: The Two Towers (2002)	341.8	39.	Harry Potter and the Chamber of Secrets (2002)	262.0
15.	Finding Nemo (2003)	339.7	40.	The Incredibles (2004)	261.4
16.	Spider-Man 3 (2007)	336.5	41.	Dr. Seuss' How the Grinch Stole Christmas (2000)	260.0
17.	Forrest Gump (1994)	329.7	42.	Jaws (1975)	260.0
18.	The Lion King (1994)	328.5	43.	Monsters, Inc. (2001)	255.9
19.	Shrek the Third (2007)	321.0	44.	Batman (1989)	251.2
20.	Transformers (2007)	319.2	45.	Night at the Museum (2006)	250.9
21.	Iron Man (2008)	318.3	46.	Men in Black (1997)	250.7
22.	Harry Potter and the Sorcerer's Stone (2001)	317.6	47.	Harry Potter and the Prisoner of Azkaban (2004)	249.5
23.	Indiana Jones and the Kingdom of the Crystal Skull (2008)	317.0	48.	Toy Story 2 (1999)	245.9
24.	The Lord of the Rings: The Fellowship of the Ring (2001)	314.8	49.	Raiders of the Lost Ark (1981)	245.0
25.	Star Wars: Episode II—Attack of the Clones (2002)	310.7	50.	Cars (2006)	244.1

(1) Through 2008. (2) Gross is in millions of absolute dollars based on box office sales in the U.S. and Canada. Rising ticket prices favor newer films. Revenues from re-releases are included.

100 Best American Movies of All Time

Source: American Film Institute

First unveiled in 1998 based on ballots sent to 1,500 individuals, mostly from the film world, in 1997. Updated in 2007 (the version shown here) to include newly eligible films and reflect shifting cultural perspectives. Criteria for judging included historical significance, cultural impact, critical recognition and awards, and popularity. The year each film was first released is in parentheses.

1. Citizen Kane (1941)
2. The Godfather (1972)
3. Casablanca (1942)
4. Raging Bull (1980)
5. Singin' in the Rain (1952)
6. Gone With the Wind (1939)
7. Lawrence of Arabia (1962)
8. Schindler's List (1993)
9. Vertigo (1958)
10. The Wizard of Oz (1939)
11. City Lights (1931)
12. The Searchers (1956)
13. Star Wars (1977)
14. Psycho (1960)
15. 2001: A Space Odyssey (1968)
16. Sunset Boulevard (1950)
17. The Graduate (1967)
18. The General (1927)
19. On the Waterfront (1954)
20. It's a Wonderful Life (1946)
21. Chinatown (1974)
22. Some Like It Hot (1959)
23. The Grapes of Wrath (1940)
24. E.T.: The Extra-Terrestrial (1982)
25. To Kill a Mockingbird (1962)
26. Mr. Smith Goes to Washington (1939)
27. High Noon (1952)
28. All About Eve (1950)
29. Double Indemnity (1944)
30. Apocalypse Now (1979)
31. The Maltese Falcon (1941)
32. The Godfather Part II (1974)
33. One Flew Over the Cuckoo's Nest (1975)
34. Snow White and the Seven Dwarfs (1937)
35. Annie Hall (1977)
36. The Bridge on the River Kwai (1957)
37. The Best Years of Our Lives (1946)
38. The Treasure of the Sierra Madre (1948)
39. Dr. Strangelove (1964)

40. The Sound of Music (1965)
41. King Kong (1933)
42. Bonnie and Clyde (1967)
43. Midnight Cowboy (1969)
44. The Philadelphia Story (1940)
45. Shane (1953)
46. It Happened One Night (1934)
47. A Streetcar Named Desire (1951)
48. Rear Window (1954)
49. Intolerance (1916)
50. The Lord of the Rings: The
    Fellowship of the Ring (2001)
51. West Side Story (1961)
52. Taxi Driver (1976)
53. The Deer Hunter (1978)
54. M*A*S*H (1970)
55. North By Northwest (1959)
56. Jaws (1975)
57. Rocky (1976)
58. The Gold Rush (1925)
59. Nashville (1975)

60. Duck Soup (1933)
61. Sullivan's Travels (1941)
62. American Graffiti (1973)
63. Cabaret (1972)
64. Network (1976)
65. The African Queen (1951)
66. Raiders of the Lost Ark (1981)
67. Who's Afraid of Virginia Woolf? (1966)
68. Unforgiven (1992)
69. Tootsie (1982)
70. A Clockwork Orange (1971)
71. Saving Private Ryan (1998)
72. The Shawshank Redemption (1994)
73. Butch Cassidy and the Sundance Kid
    (1969)
74. The Silence of the Lambs (1991)
75. In the Heat of the Night (1967)
76. Forrest Gump (1994)
77. All the President's Men (1976)
78. Modern Times (1936)
79. The Wild Bunch (1969)

80. The Apartment (1960)
81. Spartacus (1960)
82. Sunrise (1927)
83. Titanic (1997)
84. Easy Rider (1969)
85. A Night at the Opera (1935)
86. Platoon (1986)
87. 12 Angry Men (1957)
88. Bringing Up Baby (1938)
89. The Sixth Sense (1999)
90. Swing Time (1936)
91. Sophie's Choice (1982)
92. Goodfellas (1990)
93. The French Connection (1971)
94. Pulp Fiction (1994)
95. The Last Picture Show (1971)
96. Do the Right Thing (1989)
97. Blade Runner (1982)
98. Yankee Doodle Dandy (1942)
99. Toy Story (1995)
100. Ben-Hur (1959)

Film and Television Production by State, 2007-08

Source: Motion Picture Association of America

State	Movies and TV filming in 2007	in 2008	Recent examples
Alabama*	14	21	Final Destination: Death Trip 3D
Alaska*	2	4	Star Trek, Deadliest Catch (TV), Into the Wild
Arizona*	147	106	Away We Go, Middle Men (TV), The Kingdom, Kids in America (TV)
Arkansas*	2	5	Chasing the Dragon, 17 Kids & Counting (TV)
California*	529	480	American Idol (TV), Angels & Demons, G.I. Joe: The Rise of the Cobra, 24 (TV), Frost/Nixon
Colorado*	14	16	Imagine That, E-Vet Interns, The Bucket List, The Prestige
Connecticut*	45	31	Indiana Jones and the Kingdom of the Crystal Skull, Revolutionary Road, College Road Trip
Delaware	1	1	Detox, National Treasure: Book of Secrets
District of Columbia*	36	21	Night at the Museum: Battle of the Smithsonian, Bones (TV), Get Smart, The Bourne Ultimatum
Florida*	41	35	New in Town, Burn Notice (TV), Ace Ventura 3
Georgia*	82	92	Road Trip II, House of Payne (TV), Stomp the Yard
Hawaii*	22	18	Lost (TV), The Informant, Forgetting Sarah Marshall, Pirates of the Caribbean: At World's End
Idaho	4	3	Norman Waiting, Vagabond Lane, Baby Borrowers (TV)
Illinois*	72	38	Judge Mathis (TV), Eagle Eye, The Dark Knight, ER (TV)
Indiana*	4	9	American Teen, Made (TV)
Iowa*	3	7	Ticket Out, South Dakota
Kansas	3	9	My Own Love Song, Bunker Hill
Kentucky	5	6	Jefferson Davis: An American President (TV)
Louisiana*	54	56	The Open Road, Cirque du Freak, Imagination Movers (TV), The Curious Case of Benjamin Button
Maine*	9	2	Shutter Island
Maryland*	10	7	My One and Only, Step Up 2: The Streets, The Wire (TV)
Massachusetts*	15	27	Paul Blart: Mall Cop, Surrogates, The Game Plan
Michigan*	11	43	Gran Torino, Prayers for Bobby (TV), Semi-Pro
Minnesota*	4	14	A Serious Man, Transylvania Television (TV)
Mississippi*	3	9	Austin's Attic, M for Mississippi
Missouri*	10	14	The Apology Dance, Works in Progress, Farmer Wants a Wife (TV)
Montana*	47	51	My Sister's Keeper, Modern Marvels (TV), Taking Chance (TV)
Nebraska	9	1	For The Benefit of Mr. Buffett, Yes Man
Nevada	234	264	Race to Witch Mountain, The Bachelor (TV), What Happens in Vegas
New Hampshire	15	29	Mystery Team, The American Experience: We Shall Remain (TV)
New Jersey*	26	38	The Wrestler, The Sopranos (TV)
New Mexico*	36	47	Terminator Salvation, Breaking Bad (TV), Wild Hogs, No Country for Old Men
New York*	371	351	Confessions of a Shopaholic, Saturday Night Live (TV), Enchanted, Duplicity, I Am Legend
North Carolina*	43	26	Nights in Rodanthe, One Tree Hill (TV), The Guardian
North Dakota	4	4	Kristen Dunst/Jacob Soboroff documentary, Dangers From Within
Ohio	8	6	The Soloist, Spider-Man 3
Oklahoma*	2	6	Barking Water, Four Sheets to the Wind, Saving Grace (TV)
Oregon*	6	9	Twilight, Without a Paddle: Nature's Calling, Mr. Brooks
Pennsylvania*	57	52	Marley & Me, She's Out of My League, Baby Mama
Rhode Island*	23	21	Brotherhood (TV), Underdog, Dan in Real Life, 27 Dresses
South Carolina*	6	9	Nailed, Army Wives (TV), Leatherheads
South Dakota	18	39	Rez Bomb, Dinosaur Dig (TV)
Tennessee*	30	26	Can You Duet (TV), Gone Country (TV), Hannah Montana: The Movie
Texas*	134	115	Open Season 2, Friday Night Lights (TV), There Will Be Blood, Prison Break (TV)
Utah*	28	47	High School Musical 3: Senior Year, Dogtown (TV), Unaccompanied Minors, High School Musical 2
Vermont*	10	2	Dumping Lisa, Moonlight and Mistletoe (TV)
Virginia*	29	31	Body of Lies, Code Breakers (TV), John Adams (TV)
Washington*	11	13	Traveling, The Last Mimzy
West Virginia*	32	25	The Road to Emmaus, PA; We Are Marshall
Wisconsin*	4	25	Nephilim, The Watch (TV)
Wyoming*	1	11	The Real Cowboys (TV), This American Life (TV), Flicka

* Denotes state that has enacted incentives to increase production.

National Film Registry, 2009

Source: National Film Registry, Library of Congress

The National Film Registry adds 25 "culturally, historically, or aesthetically significant" American films annually.

The Asphalt Jungle (1950)
Deliverance (1972)
Disneyland Dream (1956)
A Face in the Crowd (1957)
Flower Drum Song (1961)
Foolish Wives (1922)
Free Radicals (1979)

Hallelujah (1929)
In Cold Blood (1967)
The Invisible Man (1933)
Johnny Guitar (1954)
The Killers (1946)
The March (1964)
No Lies (1973)

On the Bowery (1957)
One Week (1920)
The Pawnbroker (1965)
The Perils of Pauline (1914)
Sergeant York (1941)
The 7th Voyage of Sinbad (1958)

So's Your Old Man (1926)
George Stevens World War II Footage (1943-46)
The Terminator (1984)
Water and Power (1989)
White Fawn's Devotion (1910)

U.S. Movie Theaters, 1946-2008

Source: Motion Picture Association of America

Year	Box office (millions)	Admissions (mil)	Admissions per week (mil)	Screens	Avg. ticket price	Films produced	Films released
1946	$1,692.0	4,067.3	78.2	NA	$0.42	NA	400
1950	1,379.0	3,017.5	58.0	NA	0.46	NA	483
1955	1,204.0	2,072.3	39.9	NA	0.58	NA	319
1960	984.4	1,304.5	25.1	NA	0.76	NA	248
1965	1,041.8	1,031.5	19.8	NA	1.01	NA	279
1970	1,429.2	920.6	17.7	NA	1.55	279	306
1975	2,114.8	1,032.8	19.9	15,030	2.05	258	233
1980	2,748.5	1,021.5	19.6	17,590	2.69	214	233
1985	3,749.4	1,056.1	20.3	21,147	3.55	264	470
1990	5,021.8	1,188.6	22.9	23,689	4.23	346	410
1995	5,269.0	1,211.0	23.3	27,805	4.35	631	411
2000	7,468.0	1,383.0	26.6	37,396	5.39	683	475
2001	8,125.0	1,438.0	27.7	36,764	5.66	611	482
2002	9,272.0	1,599.0	30.8	35,280	5.81	546	466
2003	9,165.0	1,521.0	29.3	35,786	6.03	593	473
2004	9,215.0	1,484.0	28.5	36,594	6.21	611	528
2005	8,832.0	1,376.0	26.5	38,852	6.41	699	549
2006	9,138.0	1,395.0	26.8	39,668	6.55	485	607
2007	9,629.0	1,400.0	26.9	40,077	6.88	453	603
2008	9,791.0	1,364.0	26.2	40,194	7.18	520	610

NA = Not applicable.

Top Film Websites, Aug. 2009

Source: comScore Media Metrix, Inc.

Rank		Visitors[1]	% change[2]	Rank		Visitors[1]	% change[2]
1.	IMDb.com	21,875	−1.2%	11.	RottenTomatoes.com	2,381	35.8%
2.	Yahoo! Movies	15,594	8.5	12.	Disney Movies	2,228	−44.6
3.	Moviefone	12,729	−26.8	13.	WarnerBros.com	2,225	−9.8
4.	MSN Movies	10,068	−27.5	14.	AMC Entertainment Inc.	1,859	13.3
5.	Fandango Movies Network	8,918	NA	15.	Paramount Online	1,679	628.9
6.	Hollywood.com Network	6,305	0.8	16.	Summit Entertainment, L.L.C.	1,448	NA
7.	UGO Film-TV	3,505	14.8	17.	Regal Entertainment	1,395	29.8
8.	FILM.com	3,141	26.4	18.	ComingSoon.net	1,197	NA
9.	Flixster.com	2,900	NA	19.	Lions Gate Entertainment	992	−40.3
10.	TotalFilm	2,529	NA	20.	ZML.COM	948	1,413.4

NA = Not applicable. (1) Number of unique visitors, in thousands, who visited website at least once in Aug. 2009. (2) Percent change over Aug. 2008.

Most Popular DVDs, 2008

Source: Rentrak Home Video Essentials

Top Rentals, 2008

Rank	Title
1.	I Am Legend
2.	The Bucket List
3.	3:10 to Yuma
4.	No Country for Old Men
5.	Juno
6.	National Treasure 2: Book of Secrets
7.	American Gangster
8.	Good Luck Chuck
9.	Fool's Gold
10.	27 Dresses
11.	The Game Plan
12.	21
13.	Iron Man
14.	Jumper
15.	Michael Clayton

Top Selling DVDs, 2008

Rank	Title
1.	The Dark Knight
2.	Iron Man
3.	Alvin and the Chipmunks
4.	I Am Legend
5.	Kung Fu Panda
6.	WALL-E
7.	National Treasure 2: Book of Secrets
8.	Indiana Jones and the Kingdom of the Crystal Skull
9.	Enchanted
10.	Bee Movie
11.	Mamma Mia!
12.	Juno
13.	American Gangster
14.	Hancock
15.	Sex and the City: The Movie

Top-Selling Video Games, 2008

Source: The NPD Group / NPD Funworld; ranked by units sold, in millions.

The video game industry (which includes hardware, software, and accessories) generated record retail sales in 2008 totaling $21.3 billion—a 19% increase over $18.0 bil in 2007.

Rank	Title (console)[1]	Units sold	Rank	Title (console)[1]	Units sold
1. Wii Play w/ remote (Wii)		5.28	6. Call of Duty: World at War* (360)		2.75
2. Wii Mario Kart w/ wheel (Wii)		5.00	7. Gears of War 2* (360)		2.31
3. Wii Fit w/ balance board (Wii)		4.53	8. Grand Theft Auto IV* (PS3)		1.89
4. Wii Super Smash Brothers: Brawl (Wii)		4.17	9. Madden NFL 09* (360)		1.87
5. Grand Theft Auto IV* (360)		3.29	10. Mario Kart (NDS)		1.65

*Includes collector's, limited, legendary, and bundled editions. (1) Primary console listed; software may be available for other systems. 360 = Microsoft Xbox 360; NDS = Nintendo DS; PS3 = PlayStation 3; Wii = Nintendo Wii.

Film and TV Content Ratings

The Motion Picture Association of America (MPAA) began rating movies in 1968. The system was heavily revised in 1984 and again in 1990. The MPAA, National Cable Television Association, and National Association of Broadcasters developed and revised the TV ratings system in 1997, in accordance with the Telecommunications Act of 1996; it was implemented in Oct. 1997.

Film Ratings

G: General Audience. All ages admitted. Does not contain themes, language, nudity, sex, or violence that the MPAA ratings board believes would offend parents whose younger children see the film. Does not necessarily denote a "certificate of approval" nor "children's" movie. No nudity, sex scenes, or drug use depicted.

PG: Parental Guidance Suggested. Some material may not be suited for children. The MPAA ratings board recommends that parents determine whether the content of the film is appropriate for their children. The film may contain more mature themes, some profanity, violence, or brief nudity. No drug use depicted.

PG-13: Parents Strongly Cautioned. Some material may be inappropriate for children under 13. The MPAA urges more strongly that parents vet the movie to see if its content is appropriate for their children. Any movie depicting drug use or more than brief nudity is automatically rated at least PG-13. Violence is permitted, though it is generally not both realistic or extreme and persistent violence. The single use of one sexually-derived expletive rates a PG-13; more than one use requires at least an R rating.

R: Restricted. Under 17 requires accompanying parent or adult guardian. Movies given R ratings contain some adult material, defined as adult themes or activity, hard language, intense or persistent violence, sexually-oriented nudity, or drug abuse.

NC-17: No One 17 and Under Admitted. The ratings board considers NC-17 films those that most parents would consider too adult for children under 17. An NC-17 rating does not mean the film is obscene or pornographic. The rating can be based on violence, sex, aberrational behavior, drug abuse, or any other element that most parents would consider too adult for children.

TV Ratings

Y: All Children. Program designed to be acceptable for children of all ages. Its themes and elements are designed for a very young audience.

Y7: Directed to Older Children. Program designed for children ages 7 and older, and more appropriate for those who have the skills to distinguish between make-believe and reality. May include mild fantasy/comedic violence. Programs with more than mild fantasy violence are denoted with FV.

G: General Audience. Program not necessarily designed for children, but most parents would find it suitable for all ages. Little or no violence, no strong language, and little or no sexual dialogue or situations.

PG: Parental Guidance Suggested. Program might contain material that parents would consider inappropriate for children, such as an adult theme or one or more of the following: suggestive dialogue (D), infrequent coarse language (L), some sexual situations (S), or moderate violence (V).

TV-14: Parents Strongly Cautioned. Program contains material that many parents would consider inappropriate for children under 14, such as one or more of the following: intensely suggestive dialogue (D), strong coarse language (L), intense sexual situations (S), or intense violence.

TV-MA: Mature Audience Only. Program specifically designed for adults and may be unsuitable for children under 17. Contains one or more of the following: crude indecent language (L), explicit sexual activity (S), or graphic violence (V).

Longest-Running Broadway Plays[1]

Source: The Broadway League, New York, NY

Title (run)	Performances[2]	Title (run)	Performances[2]	Title (run)	Performances[2]
1. *The Phantom of the Opera (1988-)	9,003	17. Hello, Dolly! (1964-70)	2,844	34. Gemini (1977-81)	1,819
2. Cats (1982-2000)	7,485	18. My Fair Lady (1956-62)	2,717	35. Deathtrap (1978-82)	1,793
3. Les Misérables (1987-2003)	6,680	19. Hairspray (2002-09)	2,642	36. Harvey (1944-49)	1,775
4. A Chorus Line (1975-90)	6,137	20. Threepenny Opera (revival, 1955-61)	2,611	37. Dancin' (1978-82)	1,774
5. Oh! Calcutta! (revival, 1976-89)	5,959	21. Avenue Q (2003-09)	2,534	38. La Cage aux Folles (1983-87)	1,761
6. Beauty and the Beast (1994-2007)	5,461	22. The Producers (2001-07)	2,502	39. Hair (1968-72)	1,750
7. *Chicago (revival, 1996-)	5,332	23. *Wicked (2003-)	2,438	40. The Wiz (1975-79)	1,672
8. Rent (1996-2008)	5,123	24. Annie (1977-83)	2,377	41. Born Yesterday (1946-49)	1,642
9. *The Lion King (1997-)	4,917	Cabaret (revival, 1998-2004)	2,377	42. Crazy For You (1992-96)	1,622
10. Miss Saigon (1991-2001)	4,092	26. Man of La Mancha (1965-71)	2,328	43. Ain't Misbehavin' (1978-82)	1,604
11. 42nd Street (1980-89)	3,486	27. Abie's Irish Rose (1922-27)	2,327	44. Jersey Boys (2005-)	1,595
12. Grease (1972-80)	3,388	28. Oklahoma! (1943-48)	2,212	45. The Best Little Whorehouse in Texas (1978-82)	1,584
13. *Mamma Mia! (2001-)	3,280	29. Smokey Joe's Cafe (1995-2000)	2,036	46. Spamalot (2005-09)	1,575
14. Fiddler on the Roof (1964-72)	3,242	30. Pippin (1972-77)	1,944	47. Mary, Mary (1961-64)	1,572
15. Life With Father (1939-47)	3,224	31. South Pacific (1949-54)	1,925	48. Evita (1979-83)	1,567
16. Tobacco Road (1933-41)	3,182	32. The Magic Show (1974-78)	1,920	49. The Voice of the Turtle (1943-48)	1,557
		33. Aida (2000-04)	1,852	50. Jekyll & Hyde (1997-2001)	1,543

*Still running Sept. 28, 2009. (1) Unless noted, listings reflect a play's first run on Broadway. (2) Number of performances through Sept. 28, 2009.

Broadway Season Statistics, 1959-2009

Source: The Broadway League, New York, NY

Season	Gross (mil $)	Attendance (mil)	Playing weeks	New productions	Season	Gross (mil $)	Attendance (mil)	Playing weeks	New productions
1959-1960	$46	7.9	1,156	58	1994-1995	$406	9.0	1,120	33
1964-1965	50	8.2	1,250	67	1999-2000	603	11.4	1,464	37
1969-1970	53	7.1	1,047	62	2004-2005	769	11.5	1,494	39
1974-1975	57	6.6	1,101	54	2005-2006	862	12.0	1,501	39
1979-1980	146	9.6	1,540	61	2006-2007	939	12.3	1,509	35
1984-1985	209	7.3	1,078	33	2007-2008	938	12.3	1,560	36
1989-1990	282	8.0	1,070	40	2008-2009	943	12.2	1,548	43

Notable U.S. Museums

This unofficial list of some of the largest (by budget) museums in the U.S. was compiled with the assistance of the American Association of Museums, a national association representing the concerns of the museum community. Association members also include zoos, aquariums, arboretums, botanical gardens, and planetariums, but these are not included in *The World Almanac* listing.

Museum	City	State	Museum	City	State
American Museum of Natural History	New York	NY	Museum of African American History	Detroit	MI
Amon Carter Museum of Western Art	Ft. Worth	TX	Museum of the American West	Los Angeles	CA
The Art Institute of Chicago	Chicago	IL	Museum of Contemporary Art	Los Angeles	CA
Brooklyn Museum of Art	Brooklyn	NY	Museum of Fine Arts	Boston	MA
Busch-Reisinger Museum	Cambridge	MA	Museum of Fine Arts	Houston	TX
California Academy of Sciences	San Francisco	CA	Museum of Modern Art	New York	NY
California Science Center	Los Angeles	CA	Museum of New Mexico	Santa Fe	NM
Carnegie Museums of Pittsburgh	Pittsburgh	PA	Museum of Science	Boston	MA
Chicago Historical Society	Chicago	IL	Mystic Seaport Museum	Mystic	CT
Children's Museum of Indianapolis	Indianapolis	IN	National Air and Space Museum	Washington	DC
Cincinnati Art Museum	Cincinnati	OH	National Baseball Hall of Fame and		
Cincinnati Museum Center	Cincinnati	OH	Museum, Inc.	Cooperstown	NY
Cleveland Museum of Art	Cleveland	OH	National Gallery of Art	Washington	DC
Colonial Williamsburg	Williamsburg	VA	National Museum of American History	Washington	DC
Corning Museum of Glass	Corning	NY	National Museum of the American Indian	Washington	DC
Dallas Museum of Art	Dallas	TX	National Museum of Natural History	Washington	DC
Denver Art Museum	Denver	CO	Nelson-Atkins Museum of Art	Kansas City	MO
Denver Museum of Nature and Science	Denver	CO	New York Historical Society	New York	NY
Detroit Institute of Arts	Detroit	MI	New York State Museum	Albany	NY
Exploratorium	San Francisco	CA	Peabody Essex Museum	Salem	MA
The Field Museum	Chicago	IL	Pennsylvania Historical and Museum		
Fine Arts Museums of San Francisco	San Francisco	CA	Commission	Harrisburg	PA
Franklin Institute	Philadelphia	PA	Philadelphia Museum of Art	Philadelphia	PA
The Frick Collection	New York	NY	Public Museum of Grand Rapids	Grand Rapids	MI
J. Paul Getty Museum	Los Angeles	CA	Rock and Roll Hall of Fame and Museum,		
Harvard University Art Museums	Cambridge	MA	Inc.	Cleveland	OH
Henry F. Dupont Winterthur Museum	Winterthur	DE	San Diego Museum of Art	San Diego	CA
Henry Ford Museum/Greenfield Village	Dearborn	MI	San Francisco Museum of Modern Art	San Francisco	CA
High Museum of Art	Atlanta	GA	Science Museum of Minnesota	Saint Paul	MN
Houston Museum of Natural Science	Houston	TX	Scottsdale Museum of Contemp. Art	Scottsdale	AZ
Jamestown-Yorktown Foundation	Williamsburg	VA	Sports Museum of America	New York	NY
Jewish Museum	New York	NY	St. Louis Science Center	St. Louis	MO
L.A. County Museum of Art	Los Angeles	CA	Toledo Museum of Art	Toledo	OH
Liberty Science Center, Liberty State Park	Jersey City	NJ	U.S. Holocaust Memorial Museum	Washington	DC
Maryland Science Center	Baltimore	MD	Univ. of Pennsylvania Museum of		
Mashantucket Pequot Museum and			Archaeology and Anthropology	Philadelphia	PA
Research Center	Mashantucket	CT	Virginia Museum of Fine Arts	Richmond	VA
Metropolitan Museum of Art	New York	NY	Wadsworth Atheneum	Hartford	CT
Milwaukee Public Museum	Milwaukee	WI	Walker Art Center	Minneapolis	MN
Minneapolis Institute of Art	Minneapolis	MN	Whitney Museum of American Art	New York	NY

Symphony Orchestras: Most Performed Composers, 2007-08

Source: League of American Orchestras

Composer	Performances	Composer	Performances	Composer	Performances
Ludwig Van Beethoven	1,044	Igor Stravinsky	330	Gustav Mahler	253
Wolfgang Amadeus Mozart	900	Felix Mendelssohn	319	Franz Schubert	246
Piotr Ilyich Tchaikovsky	628	Sergei Rachmaninoff	296	Sergei Prokofiev	236
Johannes Brahms	555	Richard Strauss	285	Hector Berlioz	213
Antonin Dvorak	418	Jean Sibelius	284	Claude Debussy	210
Maurice Ravel	367	Franz Joseph Haydn	277	Aaron Copland	206
Johann Sebastian Bach	359	Dmitri Shostakovich	275		

Note: Number of performances of a given composer's work(s) scheduled during the 2007-08 season (generally Oct.-Sept.) by members of the League of American Orchestras.

Opera: Most Produced Works, 2007-08

Source: Opera America

Work, composer	Productions	Work, composer	Productions	Work, composer	Productions
La bohème, Giacomo Puccini	20	*Carmen*, Georges Bizet	9	*Aida*, Giuseppe Verdi	8
Tosca, Giacomo Puccini	15	*Don Giovanni*, Wolfgang Amadeus Mozart	9	*Madama Butterfly*, Giacomo Puccini	8
La traviata, Giuseppe Verdi	13	*The Elixir of Love*, Gaetano Donizetti	9	*Turandot*, Giacomo Puccini	8
The Marriage of Figaro, Wolfgang Amadeus Mozart	10	*The Magic Flute*, Wolfgang Amadeus Mozart	9		

Note: Number of productions (not individual performances) of a given opera by professional member companies of OPERA America and Opera.ca during the 2007-08 opera season (roughly Oct.-Sept.).

Best-Selling U.S. Magazines, 2008

Source: Audit Bureau of Circulations, Schaumburg, IL

General magazines, exclusive of comics; also excluding magazines that failed to file reports to ABC by press time. Based on total average paid and verified circulation during the 6 months ending Dec. 31, 2008, ranked by paid circ. size.

Publication	Paid circ.	Publication	Paid circ.	Publication	Paid circ.
1. AARP Bulletin	24,500,078	6. Good Housekeeping	4,684,811	12. Game Informer	3,517,598
2. AARP The Magazine	24,349,637	7. Woman's Day	3,920,867	13. Time	3,360,135
3. Reader's Digest	8,168,667	8. Family Circle	3,914,927	14. Prevention	3,339,616
4. Better Homes and Gardens	7,659,823	9. AAA Westways	3,842,577	15. TV Guide	3,256,962
5. National Geographic	5,060,377	10. Ladies' Home Journal	3,840,645	16. Sports Illustrated	3,218,133
		11. People	3,691,819	17. Taste of Home	3,202,493

Publication	Paid circ.	Publication	Paid circ.	Publication	Paid circ.
18. Cosmopolitan	2,926,683	46. Every Day with Rachael Ray	1,783,542	73. Home and Away	1,241,944
19. Southern Living	2,834,589	47. In Style	1,757,429	74. Popular Mechanics	1,231,830
20. AAA	2,807,830	48. Shape	1,701,023	75. Star	1,225,521
21. Newsweek	2,701,893	49. Golf Digest	1,657,821	76. Sunset	1,202,831
22. Playboy	2,617,116	50. Country Living	1,626,722	77. Women's Health	1,196,898
23. AAA Going Places	2,561,201	51. U.S. News and World Report	1,583,914	78. Vanity Fair	1,190,997
24. Maxim	2,521,709	52. Fitness	1,557,370	79. Country	1,176,940
25. American Legion Magazine	2,430,285	53. VFW Magazine	1,548,271	80. Boys' Life	1,169,295
26. O, The Oprah Magazine	2,365,333	54. Field and Stream	1,529,413	81. Family Handyman	1,162,231
27. Glamour	2,290,452	55. Birds & Blooms	1,514,986	82. Lucky	1,160,603
28. Redbook	2,209,059	56. Self	1,482,664	83. Reminisce	1,127,278
29. Guideposts	2,195,872	57. Rolling Stone	1,469,213	84. Elle	1,124,674
30. AAA World	2,130,386	58. American Rifleman	1,435,323	85. Motor Trend	1,117,016
31. Parenting	2,128,913	59. Bon Appetit	1,426,992	86. Essence	1,101,289
32. Parents	2,061,406	60. Golf Magazine	1,414,751	87. Allure	1,095,034
33. ESPN The Magazine	2,059,571	61. Cosmo Girl!	1,410,797	88. Major Market Magazine Network	1,064,093
34. Seventeen	2,034,494	62. Health	1,371,279	89. The New Yorker	1,051,152
35. Martha Stewart Living	2,030,150	63. Woman's World	1,332,904	90. Domino	1,047,916
36. Smithsonian	2,029,532	64. Scholastic Parent and Child	1,327,703	91. Scouting	1,041,369
37. Real Simple	1,980,061	65. Popular Science	1,319,602	92. Teen Vogue	1,025,016
38. Remedy/Remedy MD	1,959,801	66. Car and Driver	1,316,358	93. National Geographic International	1,024,627
39. Money	1,913,459	67. First	1,315,269	94. Cottage Living	1,022,092
40. US Weekly	1,902,964	68. More	1,303,566	95. Marie Claire	1,007,814
41. FamilyFun	1,882,287	69. Country Home	1,299,939	96. Everyday Food	991,056
42. Men's Health	1,859,701	70. Ebony	1,294,177	97. Traditional Home	987,191
43. Entertainment Weekly	1,796,560	71. Vogue	1,293,078	98. Gourmet	977,267
44. Endless Vacation	1,794,458	72. Weight Watchers	1,278,094	99. Midwest Living	972,279
45. Cooking Light	1,793,191			100. Travel + Leisure	960,147

Most Challenged Books, 2008

Source: Office of Intellectual Freedom, American Library Association

A challenge is a formal, written complaint filed with a library or school requesting that materials be removed because of content or appropriateness. From 2001-08, 3,736 challenges were reported: 1,225 challenges due to "sexually explicit" material; 1,008 for "offensive language"; 720 for material deemed "unsuited to age group"; 458 for "violence"; 269 challenges for "homosexuality"; 233 for "religious viewpoints"; and 103 for being "anti-family." Approximately 31% of challenges were to material in classrooms; 37% in school libraries; 24% in public libraries. ALA estimates that for every challenge received, 4-5 were not reported.

Rank	Title, author	Common reasons given for challenge
1.	*And Tango Makes Three*, Justin Richardson and Peter Parnell	Anti-ethnic, anti-family, homosexuality, religious viewpoint, and unsuited to age group
2.	*His Dark Materials* trilogy, Philip Pullman	Political viewpoint, religious viewpoint, and violence
3.	*TTYL; TTFN; L8R, G8R* (series), Lauren Myracle	Offensive language, sexually explicit, and unsuited to age group
4.	*Scary Stories* (series), Alvin Schwartz	Occult/satanism, religious viewpoint, and violence
5.	*Bless Me, Ultima*, Rudolfo Anaya	Occult/satanism, offensive language, religious viewpoint, sexually explicit, and violence
6.	*The Perks of Being a Wallflower*, Stephen Chbosky	Drugs, homosexuality, nudity, offensive language, sexually explicit, suicide, and unsuited to age group
7.	*Gossip Girl* (series), Cecily von Ziegesar	Offensive language, sexually explicit, and unsuited to age group
8.	*Uncle Bobby's Wedding*, Sarah S. Brannen	Homosexuality and unsuited to age group
9.	*The Kite Runner*, Khaled Hosseini	Offensive language, sexually explicit, and unsuited to age group
10.	*Flashcards of My Life*, Charise Mericle Harper	Sexually explicit and unsuited to age group

Some Notable New Books, 2008

Source: Reference and User Services Assn. and Young Adult Library Services Assn., divisions of the American Library Association.

Fiction

The Hawakati, Rabih Alameddine
The Wasted Vigil, Nadeem Aslam
Peace, Richard Bausch
City of Thieves: A Novel, David Benioff
The Plague of Doves, Louise Erdrich
Atmospheric Disturbances, Rivka Galchen
Unaccustomed Earth, Jhumpa Lahiri
Dangerous Laughter: Thirteen Stories, Steven Millhauser
Resistance, Owen Sheers
Olive Kitteridge, Elizabeth Strout
The Ginseng Hunter, Jeff Talarigo

Nonfiction

The Bin Ladens: An Arabian Family in the American Century, Steve Coll
This Republic of Suffering: Death and the American Civil War, Drew Gilpin Faust
The Forever War, Dexter Filkins

Defying Dixie: The Radical Roots of Civil Rights, 1919-1950, Glenda Elizabeth Gilmore
The Hemingses of Monticello: An American Family, Annette Gordon-Reed
Pictures at a Revolution: Five Movies and the Birth of the New Hollywood, Mark Harris
A Voyage Long and Strange: Rediscovering the New World, Tony Horwitz
The Dark Side: The Inside Story of How the War on Terror Turned into a War on American Ideals, Jane Mayer
In Defense of Food: An Eater's Manifesto, Michael Pollan
American-Made: The Enduring Legacy of the WPA: When FDR Put the Nation to Work, Nick Taylor
Traffic: Why We Drive the Way We Do (and What It Says About Us, Tom Vanderbilt
The Suicide Index: Putting My Father's Death in Order, Joan Wickersham

Poetry

Special Orders: Poems, Edward Hirsch
Ghost Soldiers: Poems, James Tate

Some Notable New Books for Children, 2008

Source: Association for Library Service to Children, a division of the American Library Association, for books published in 2008.

Younger Readers

A Visitor for Bear, Bonny Becker
Beware of the Frog, William Bee
Wolfsnail: A Backyard Predator, Sarah C. Campbell
Stinky, Eleanor Davis
Papá and Me, Arthur Dorros
Buster Goes to Cowboy Camp, Denise Fleming
A Couple of Boys Have the Best Week Ever, Marla Frazee
Goose and Duck, Jean Craighead George
How to Heal a Broken Wing, Bob Graham
Chicken Said, "Cluck!", Judyann Ackerman Grant
Maybe a Bear Ate It!, Robie H. Harris
Old Bear, Kevin Henkes
What's Up, Duck? A Book of Opposites, Tad Hills
Garmann's Summer, Stian Hole
Ghosts in the House!, Kazuno Kohara
The Hinky Pink, Megan McDonald
Just in Case: A Trickster Tale and Spanish Alphabet Book, Yuyi Morales
One Boy, Laura Vaccaro Seeger
The House in the Night, Susan Marie Swanson
What Can You Do with a Rebozo?, Carmen Tafolla
Before John Was a Jazz Giant: A Song of John Coltrane, Carole Boston Weatherford
Are You Ready to Play Outside?, Mo Willems

Middle Readers

The Underneath, Kathi Appelt
Frogs, Nic Bishop
Masterpiece, Elise Broach
All Stations! Distress!: April 15, 1912, the Day the Titanic Sank, Don Brown
A River of Words: The Story of William Carlos Williams, Jen Bryant
The London Eye Mystery, Siobhan Dowd
Bird, Zetta Elliott
The Porcupine Year, Louise Erdrich
Buffalo Music, Tracey E. Fern
The Graveyard Book, Neil Gaiman
The Storyteller's Candle/La velita de los cuentos, Lucía González
Christo and Jeanne-Claude: Through the Gates and Beyond, Jan Greenberg and Sandra Jordan
Rapunzel's Revenge, Shannon and Dean Hale
Abe Lincoln Crosses a Creek: A Tall, Thin Tale (Introducing His Forgotten Frontier Friend), Deborah Hopkinson
What to Do About Alice? How Alice Roosevelt Broke the Rules, Charmed the World, and Drove Her Father Teddy Crazy!, Barbara Kerley
Savvy, Ingrid Law

Horse Song: The Naadam of Mongolia, Ted and Betsy Lewin
Way Up and Over Everything, Alice McGill
Ways to Live Forever, Sally Nicholls
Planting the Trees of Kenya: The Story of Wangari Maathai, Claire A. Nivola
Boys of Steel: The Creators of Superman, Marc Tyler Nobleman
Piano Starts Here: The Young Art Tatum, Robert Andrew Parker
When the Wolves Returned: Restoring Nature's Balance in Yellowstone, Dorothy Hinshaw Patent
Six Innings: A Game in the Life, James Preller
Wanda Gág: The Girl Who Lived to Draw, Deborah Kogan Ray
Silent Music: A Story of Baghdad, James Rumford
Knucklehead: Tall Tales & Mostly True Stories About Growing Up Scieszka, Jon Scieszka
Pale Male: Citizen Hawk of New York City, Janet Schulman
How I Learned Geography, Uri Shulevitz
Elizabeth Leads the Way: Elizabeth Cady Stanton and the Right to Vote, Tanya Lee Stone
The Blacker the Berry, Joyce Carol Thomas
Moribito: Guardian of the Spirit, Nahoko Uehashi

Older Readers

Chains, Lauri Halse Anderson
The Hunger Games, Suzanne Collins
Waiting for Normal, Leslie Connor
Bodies from the Ice: Melting Glaciers and the Recovery of the Past, James M. Deem
The Surrender Tree: Poems of Cuba's Struggle for Freedom, Margarita Engle
The Trouble Begins at 8: A Life of Mark Twain in the Wild, Wild West, Sid Fleischman
The Lincolns: A Scrapbook Look at Abraham and Mary, Candace Fleming
Washington at Valley Forge, Russell Freedman
Reaching Out, Francisco Jiménez
The Way We Work: Getting to Know the Amazing Human Body, David Macaulay with Richard Walker
Tiger Moon, Antonia Michaelis
We Are the Ship: The Story of Negro League Baseball, Kadir Nelson
Ain't Nothing But a Man: My Quest to Find the Real John Henry, Scott Reynolds Nelson with Marc Aronson
Afghan Dreams: Young Voices of Afghanistan, Tony O'Brien and Mike Sullivan
Nation, Terry Pratchett
Here Lies Arthur, Philip Reeve
Keeping the Night Watch, Hope Anita Smith
After Tupac and D Foster, Jacqueline Woodson

Best-Selling Books, 2008

Source: Publishers Weekly

Hardcover Fiction

1. *The Appeal*, John Grisham
2. *The Story of Edgar Sawtelle*, David Wroblewski
3. *The Host*, Stephenie Meyer
4. *Cross Country*, James Patterson
5. *The Lucky One*, Nicholas Sparks
6. *Fearless Fourteen*, Janet Evanovich
7. *Christmas Sweater*, Glenn Beck
8. *Scarpetta*, Patricia Cornwell
9. *Your Heart Belongs to Me*, Dean Koontz
10. *Plum Lucky*, Janet Evanovich
11. *7th Heaven*, James Patterson
12. *Sail*, James Patterson
13. *A Good Woman*, Danielle Steel
14. *Divine Justice*, David Baldacci
15. *The Gate House*, Nelson DeMille

Hardcover Nonfiction

1. *The Last Lecture*, Randy Pausch
2. *The Purpose of Christmas*, Rick Warren
3. *You: Being Beautiful*, Michael F. Roizen and Mehmet C. Oz
4. *Outliers*, Malcolm Gladwell
5. *A Bold Fresh Piece of Humanity*, Bill O'Reilly

6. *Dewey: The Small-Town Library Cat Who Touched the World*, Vicki Myron with Brett Witter
7. *Audition*, Barbara Walters
8. *Barefoot Contessa Back to Basics*, Ina Garten
9. *The Snowball: Warren Buffett and the Business of Life*, Alice Schroeder
10. *Hot, Flat, and Crowded*, Thomas L. Friedman
11. *When You Are Engulfed in Flames*, David Sedaris
12. *Multiple Blessings*, Jon and Kate Gosselin and Beth Carson
13. *American Lion*, Jon Meacham
14. *Are You There, Vodka? It's Me, Chelsea*, Chelsea Handler
15. *Just Who Will You Be?*, Maria Shriver

Trade Paperback

1. *A New Earth*, Eckhart Tolle
2. *The Shack*, William P. Young
3. *Three Cups of Tea*, Greg Mortenson
4. *The Audacity of Hope*, Barack Obama
5. *Dreams from My Father*, Barack Obama
6. *Eat This, Not That!*, David Zinczenko and Matt Goulding
7. *Eat, Pray, Love*, Elizabeth Gilbert
8. *The Secret Life of Bees*, Sue Monk Kidd
9. *The Friday Night Knitting Club*, Kate Jacobs
10. *The Power of Now*, Eckhart Tolle

Mass Market

1. *The Appeal*, John Grisham
2. *The Hollow*, Nora Roberts
3. *The Pagan Stone*, Nora Roberts
4. *Double Cross*, James Patterson
5. *Playing for Pizza*, John Grisham
6. *The 5th Horseman*, James Patterson
7. *High Noon*, Nora Roberts
8. *Simple Genius*, David Baldacci
9. *Step on a Crack*, James Patterson
10. *You've Been Warned*, James Patterson

Children's Hardcover

1. *Breaking Dawn*, Stephenie Meyer
2. *The Tales of Beedle the Bard*, J. K. Rowling
3. *Brisingr (The Inheritance Cycle)*, Christopher Paolini

4. *Diary of a Wimpy Kid #2: Rodrick Rules*, Jeff Kinney
5. *Burning Up: On Tour with the Jonas Brothers*, Kevin, Joe, and Nick Jonas
6. *Percy Jackson and the Olympians, Book Four: The Battle of the Labyrinth*, Rick Riordan
7. *Diary of a Wimpy Kid: Do-It-Yourself Book*, Jeff Kinney
8. *If You Give a Cat a Cupcake*, Laura Numeroff
9. *Fancy Nancy's Favorite Fancy Words*, Jane O'Connor
10. *Swing!*, Rufus Butler Seder

Almanacs, Atlases, & Annuals

1. *The World Almanac and Book of Facts 2009*
2. *The Old Farmer's Almanac 2008*
3. *Europe TravelBook, 9th Edition*, Des Hannigan
4. *What Color Is Your Parachute? 2009*, Richard Nelson Bolles
5. *2008 AAA Road Atlas*

Note: Bestseller calculations are based on shipped-and-billed figures supplied by publishers and reflect 2008 sales only.

Leading U.S. Daily Newspapers, 2008

Source: 2008 *Editor & Publisher International Yearbook*

As of Feb. 1, 2009, the number of U.S. daily newspapers had fallen to 1,408, for a net loss of 14 since Feb. 1, 2008. Average daily circulation fell by 2.1 mil, from 50.7 mil in 2008 to 48.6 mil in 2009. The overall number of Sunday papers fell by 5, to 902. Average Sunday circulation as of Feb. 1, 2009, fell 2.1 mil, from 51.2 mil to 49.1 mil.

(circulation as of Sept. 30, 2008; m = morning, e = evening, d = all day)

Newspaper	Circulation	Newspaper	Circulation
1. Arlington (VA) *USA Today* (m)	2,293,310	52. Oklahoma City (OK) *Oklahoman* (m)	179,703
2. New York (NY) *Wall Street Journal* (m)	2,011,999	53. Detroit (MI) *News* (m)	178,280
3. New York (NY) *Times* (m)	1,000,665	54. Little Rock (AR) *Democrat-Gazette* (m)	176,275
4. Los Angeles (CA) *Times* (m)	739,147	55. Buffalo (NY) *News* (d)	175,984
5. New York (NY) *Daily News* (m)	632,595	56. New Orleans (LA) *Times-Picayune* (m)	175,530
6. New York (NY) *Post* (m)	625,421	57. Norfolk (VA) *Virginian-Pilot* (m)	174,573
7. Washington (DC) *Post* (m)	622,714	58. Omaha (NE) *World-Herald* (d)	169,722
8. Chicago (IL) *Tribune* (m)	516,032	59. Boston (MA) *Herald* (m)	167,506
9. Houston (TX) *Chronicle* (m)	448,271	60. Las Vegas (NV) *Review-Journal* (m)	165,010
10. Long Island (NY) *Newsday* (m)	377,517	61. Hartford (CT) *Courant* (m)	164,338
11. Phoenix (AZ) *Republic* (m)	361,333	62. Richmond (VA) *Times-Dispatch* (m)	160,886
12. San Francisco (CA) *Chronicle* (d)	339,440	63. Raleigh (NC) *News & Observer* (m)	158,573
13. Dallas (TX) *Morning News* (m)	338,933	64. Los Angeles (CA) *Investor's Business Daily* (m)	156,882
14. Boston (MA) *Globe* (m)	323,983	65. Bergen Co. (NJ) *Record* (m)	156,817
15. Minneapolis (MN) *Star Tribune* (m)	322,360	66. Austin (TX) *American-Statesman* (m)	151,520
16. Newark (NJ) *Star-Ledger* (m)	316,280	67. Nashville (TN) *Tennessean* (m)	149,686
17. Chicago (IL) *Sun-Times* (m)	313,176	68. Riverside (CA) *Press-Enterprise* (m)	149,608
18. Cleveland (OH) *Plain Dealer* (m)	305,529	69. West Palm Beach (FL) *Post* (m)	149,412
19. Philadelphia (PA) *Inquirer* (m)	300,674	70. Memphis (TN) *Commercial Appeal* (m)	147,598
20. Detroit (MI) *Free Press* (m)	298,243	71. Greensburg (PA) *Tribune-Review* (m)	146,520
21. St. Petersburg (FL) *Times* (m)	292,471	72. Rochester (NY) *Democrat and Chronicle* (m)	141,812
22. Portland (OR) *Oregonian* (d)	283,321	73. Fresno (CA) *Bee* (m)	139,649
23. Atlanta (GA) *Journal-Constitution* (m)	274,999	74. Chicago (IL) *Daily Herald* (m)	138,186
24. San Diego (CA) *Union-Tribune* (m)	269,819	75. Jacksonville (FL) *Times-Union* (m)	136,026
25. New York (NY) *am New York* (m)	266,852	76. Des Moines (IA) *Register* (m)	135,056
26. Washington (DC) *Examiner* (m)	259,906	77. Neptune (NJ) *Asbury Park Press* (m)	133,241
27. Sacramento (CA) *Bee* (m)	253,249	78. Honolulu (HI) *Advertiser* (d)	132,894
28. Indianapolis (IN) *Star* (m)	244,796	79. Providence (RI) *Journal* (m)	131,620
29. St. Louis (MO) *Post-Dispatch* (m)	240,796	80. Birmingham (AL) *News* (m)	131,133
30. Kansas City (MO) *Star* (m)	239,358	81. Los Angeles (CA) *Daily News* (m)	129,647
31. Orange County (CA) *Register* (m)	236,270	82. Grand Rapids (MI) *Press* (e)	123,893
32. Miami (FL) *Herald* (m)	225,554	83. Salt Lake City (UT) *Tribune* (m)	119,976
33. San Jose (CA) *Mercury News* (m)	224,199	84. Seattle (WA) *Post-Intelligencer* (m)	117,572
34. Baltimore (MD) *Sun* (m)	218,923	85. Toledo (OH) *Blade* (m)	115,058
35. Orlando (FL) *Sentinel* (d)	216,978	86. Knoxville (TN) *News Sentinel* (m)	112,132
36. Milwaukee (WI) *Journal Sentinel* (m)	212,156	87. Dayton (OH) *Daily News* (m)	111,855
37. Denver (CO) *Post* (m)	210,585	88. Akron (OH) *Beacon Journal* (m)	110,999
38. Denver (CO) *Rocky Mountain News* (m)	210,281	89. Tulsa (OK) *World* (m)	110,467
39. San Antonio (TX) *Express-News* (m)	206,933	90. Syracuse (NY) *Post-Standard* (m)	107,272
40. Tampa (FL) *Tribune* (m)	204,106	91. Tacoma (WA) *News Tribune* (m)	106,335
41. Pittsburgh (PA) *Post-Gazette* (m)	203,588	92. Albuquerque (NM) *Journal* (m)	102,266
42. Ft. Lauderdale (FL) *South Florida Sun-Sentinel* (m)	200,924	93. Wilmington (DE) *News Journal* (d)	102,171
43. Seattle (WA) *Times* (m)	198,741	94. Allentown (PA) *Morning Call* (m)	101,432
44. Columbus (OH) *Dispatch* (m)	195,317	95. Los Angeles (CA) *La Opinion* (m)	100,462
45. Fort Worth (TX) *Star-Telegram* (m)	194,257	96. Lexington (KY) *Herald-Leader* (m)	100,185
46. Charlotte (NC) *Observer* (m)	193,577	97. Westchester Co. (NY) *Journal News* (m)	99,971
47. Cincinnati (OH) *Enquirer* (m)	193,326	98. Sarasota (FL) *Herald-Tribune* (m)	99,598
48. Louisville (KY) *Courier-Journal* (m)	192,896	99. Stuart (FL) *Treasure Coast News/Press-Tribune* (m)	99,116
49. San Francisco (CA) *Examiner* (m)	186,335	100. Philadelphia (PA) *Daily News* (m)	97,694
50. St. Paul (MN) *Pioneer Press* (m)	184,973		
51. Walnut Creek (CA) *Contra Costa Times* (m)	180,605		

Leading Canadian Daily Newspapers, 2008

Source: 2008 *Editor & Publisher International Yearbook*

(circulation as of Sept. 30, 2008; all morning papers)

Newspaper	Circulation	Newspaper	Circulation
1. Toronto (ON) *Star*	430,931	6. Toronto (ON) *National Post*	190,187
2. Toronto (ON) *Globe and Mail*	329,504	7. Vancouver (BC) *Sun*	165,740
3. Montreal (QC) *Le Journal de Montreal*	265,764	8. Vancouver (BC) *Province*	160,055
4. Montreal (QC) *La Presse*	200,049	9. Montreal (QC) *Gazette*	143,783
5. Toronto (ON) *Sun*	195,211	10. Ottawa (ON) *Citizen*	124,656

Paid U.S. Newspaper Circulation, 1940-2008

Source: Newspaper Association of America

(circulation figures in thousands)

Year	Number of daily newspapers			Circulation of daily newspapers			Sunday newspapers	
	Morning	Evening	Total	Morning	Evening	Total	Number	Circulation
1940	380	1,498	1,878	16,114	25,018	41,132	525	32,371
1945	330	1,419	1,749	19,240	29,144	48,384	485	39,860
1950	322	1,450	1,772	21,266	32,563	53,829	549	46,582
1955	316	1,454	1,760	22,183	33,964	56,147	541	46,448
1960	312	1,459	1,763	24,029	34,853	58,882	563	47,699
1965	320	1,444	1,751	24,107	36,251	60,358	562	48,600
1970	334	1,429	1,748	25,934	36,174	62,108	586	49,217
1975	339	1,436	1,756	25,490	35,165	60,655	639	51,096
1980	387	1,388	1,745	29,414	32,787	62,202	736	54,676
1985	482	1,220	1,676	36,362	26,405	62,766	798	58,826
1990	559	1,084	1,611	41,311	21,017	62,328	863	62,635
1995	656	891	1,533	44,310	13,883	58,193	888	61,229
2000	766	727	1,480	46,772	9,000	55,773	917	59,421
2005	817	645	1,452	46,122	7,222	53,345	914	55,270
2006	833	614	1,437	45,441	6,888	52,329	907	53,179
2007	867	565	1,422	44,548	6,194	50,742	907	51,246
2008	872	546	1,408	42,757	5,840	48,597	902	49,115

Newspaper Advertising Revenues, 1950-2008

Source: Newspaper Association of America

(in millions of dollars)

Year	National ad revenue (mil $)	Retail ad revenue (mil $)	Classified ad revenue (mil $)	Print advertising total revenue (mil $)	% change[1]	Online advertising total revenue (mil $)	% change	Total advertising revenue (mil $)	% change
1950	$518	$1,175	$377	$2,070	—	—	—	—	—
1955	712	1,755	610	3,077	48.7%	—	—	—	—
1960	778	2,100	803	3,681	19.6	—	—	—	—
1965	783	2,429	1,214	4,426	20.2	—	—	—	—
1970	891	3,292	1,521	5,704	28.9	—	—	—	—
1975	1,109	4,966	2,159	8,234	44.4	—	—	—	—
1980	1,963	8,609	4,222	14,794	79.7	—	—	—	—
1985	3,352	13,443	8,375	25,170	70.1	—	—	—	—
1990	4,122	16,652	11,506	32,280	28.3	—	—	—	—
1995	4,251	18,099	13,742	36,092	11.8	—	—	—	—
2000	7,653	21,409	19,608	48,670	5.1	—	—	—	—
2005	7,910	22,187	17,312	47,408	1.5	$2,027	31.5%	$49,435	2.5%
2006	7,505	22,121	16,986	46,611	−1.7	2,664	31.5	49,275	−0.3
2007	7,005	21,018	14,186	42,209	−9.4	3,166	18.8	45,375	−7.9
2008	5,996	18,769	9,975	34,740	−17.7	3,109	−1.8	37,848	−16.6

(1) Percent change for 1950-2000 refers to the rate of change over the preceding 5-year period; 2005-08 figures represent the rate of change over the past year.

Top Newspaper Websites, Aug. 2009

Source: comScore Media Metrix, Inc.

Rank	Website	Visitors[1]	% change[2]	Rank	Website	Visitors[1]	% change[2]
1.	Tribune Newspapers	11,889	−4.7%	11.	MediaNews Group	5,971	14.8%
2.	The New York Times Brand	11,312	−2.7	12.	Lee Enterprises, Incorporated	4,611	−9.1
3.	Advance Internet	8,708	14.0	13.	Mail Online	3,993	49.9
4.	McClatchy Corporation	8,147	12.3	14.	Cox Newspapers	3,812	−11.1
5.	WashingtonPost.com	7,917	7.1	15.	Boston.com	3,607	11.6
6.	Hearst Newspapers	6,777	10.4	16.	DallasNews.com Sites	3,132	NA
7.	Wall Street Journal Online	6,558	44.3	17.	Telegraph Media Group	3,045	NA
8.	NYDailyNews.com	6,461	95.9	18.	NYPost.com	2,981	26.7
9.	USAToday Sites	6,341	−12.2	19.	PostChronicle.com	2,882	170.6
10.	Topix.com	6,117	−3.3	20.	Guardian.co.uk	2,880	24.6

(1) Number of unique visitors, in thousands, who visited website at least once in Aug 2009. (2) Percent change over Aug. 2008.

Top News/Information Websites, Aug. 2009
Source: comScore Media Metrix, Inc.

Rank	Website	Visitors[1]	% change[2]	Rank	Website	Visitors[1]	% change[2]
1.	Yahoo! News	47,260	6.8%	11.	Tribune Newspapers	11,889	−4.7%
2.	New York Times Digital	45,754	5.5	12.	ABCNews Digital	9,965	30.7
3.	The Weather Channel	41,684	13.9	13.	Belo	9,960	NA
4.	CNN	33,410	3.7	14.	Wunderground.com	9,744	NA
5.	MSNBC	31,738	−28.7	15.	FoxNews.com	8,737	−9.2
6.	AOL News	27,220	−4.0	16.	AccuWeather Sites	8,711	NA
7.	Weatherbug Property	23,182	11.6	17.	Advance Internet	8,708	14.0
8.	Gannett Sites	21,196	−1.3	18.	McClatchy Corporation	8,147	12.3
9.	WorldNow Sites	17,061	−5.8	19.	Legacy.com	7,134	−6.1
10.	The Washington Post Company	16,063	14.8	20.	CBS News Digital	6,902	5.5

(1) Number of unique visitors, in thousands, who visited website at least once in Aug. 2009. (2) Percent change over Aug. 2008.

Multi-Platinum and Platinum Awards for Recorded Music and Music Videos, 2008-09
Source: Recording Industry Assn. of America, Washington, DC

To achieve platinum status, an **album** must reach a minimum sale of 1 mil units in LPs, tapes, and CDs, with a manufacturer's dollar volume of at least $2 mil based on one-third of the suggested retail list price for each record, tape, or CD sold. To achieve multi-platinum status, an album must reach a minimum sale of at least 2 mil units in LPs, tapes, and CDs, with a manufacturer's dollar volume of at least $4 mil based on one-third of the list price.

Singles must sell 1 mil units to achieve a platinum award (created in 1976) and 2 mil to achieve a multi-platinum award (created in 1984). **Digital singles** are certified at the same levels; the digital sales award was first created in 2004. In 1999, the Diamond Award, honoring sales of 10 mil or more copies of an album or single, was introduced. EP singles count as 2 units. Double-CD sets count as 2 units. **Music videos** (long form) must sell 100,000 units to qualify for a platinum award, more than 200,000 units for a multi-platinum award. As of July 2006, master **ringtones**—the original recording and not synthesized versions of songs—could be awarded gold (500,000 downloads), platinum (1 mil), and multi-platinum (2 mil+) status.

Awards listed here are for albums and digital singles (released Sept. 2007-Sept. 2009) and for music videos (released at any time) that were certified Sept. 2008-Aug. 2009. Number in parentheses = millions sold. V = Various artists. Alphabetized by artist name.

Albums, Multi-Platinum
Black Ice (2), AC/DC
Sold Out at Madison Square Garden (2), Aventura
The Last (2), Aventura
I Am Sasha Fierce (2), Beyoncé
It's Time (3), Michael Bublé
Viva La Vida (2), Coldplay
Talento de Barrio (2), Daddy Yankee
Los Mejores Corridos (2), El Potro de Sinaloa
Noel (5), Josh Groban
Rock 'N' Roll Jesus (3), Kid Rock
Tha Carter, Vol. 3 (3), Lil Wayne
Si Tu Te Vas (2), Los Temerarios
Dark Horse (2), Nickelback
Una Noche en Madrid (2), Marco Antonio Solis
No Molestar, Marco Antonio Solis
Paper Trail (2), T.I.
Twilight soundtrack (V) (2)

Albums, Platinum
Alvin and the Chipmunks soundtrack (V)
Across the Universe soundtrack (V)
Quinto Piso, Ricardo Arjona
Te Presumo, Banda el Recodo
The Foundation, Zac Brown Band
Camp Rock soundtrack (V)
David Cook, David Cook
Breakout, Miley Cyrus
Hannah Montana: The Movie soundtrack, Miley Cyrus as Hannah Montana
Con Banda, Los Dareyes de la Sierra
Indestructible, Disturbed
Palabras del Silencio, Luis Fonsi
Intuition, Jamie Foxx
Nosotros Somos, Grupo Montéz de Durango
Chinese Democracy, Guns N' Roses
High School Musical 3 soundtrack (V)
A Little Bit Longer, Jonas Brothers
Juno soundtrack (V)
Only by the Night, Kings of Leon
The Fame, Lady Gaga
Vámanos Pa'l Río, Los Pikadientes de Caborca
Death Magnetic, Metallica
We Sing, We Dance, We Steal Things, Jason Mraz
Year of the Gentleman, Ne-Yo
One of the Boys, Katy Perry
Funhouse, Pink
Unstoppable, Rascal Flatts
Learn to Live, Darius Rucker
Jordin Sparks, Jordin Sparks
Circus, Britney Spears
Troubadour, George Strait

Love on the Inside, Sugarland
Here I Stand, Usher
Now That's What I Call Music!, Vol. 27 (V)
Now That's What I Call Music!, Vol. 29 (V)
808s & Heartbreak, Kanye West
Wisin Y Yandel Present: La Mente Maestra, DJ Nesty and Wisin y Yandel

Videos, Multi-Platinum
The Red Piano, Elton John (2)
The McCartney Years, Paul McCartney (2)
No Bull, AC/DC (5)
Live Unplugged, Jeremy Camp (2)
Live in Las Vegas: A New Day, Celine Dion (7)
Morning Constitutions, Larry the Cable Guy (4)
Elvis: '68 Comeback Special Deluxe Edition, Elvis Presley (4)
Elvis: Aloha From Hawaii Deluxe Edition, Elvis Presley (3)
Get Ready: Definitive Performances 1965-1972, The Temptations (2)
Radio City Christmas Spectacular Featuring the Rockettes (V) (3)
Billy Graham Homecoming, Vol. 1, (V) (2)

Digital Singles, Platinum and Multi-Platinum
"It's Not My Time," "Kryptonite," 3 Doors Down
"Don't Trust Me" (2), 3OH!3,
"Honky Tonk Badonkadonk," Trace Adkins
"Right Now (Na Na Na)," Akon
"Potential Break Up Song," Aly & AJ
"Cyclone" (2), Baby Bash
"Pocketful of Sunshine" (2), Natasha Bedingfield
"Halo," "If I Were a Boy," "Single Ladies (Put a Ring on It)" (2), Beyoncé
"Beautiful Liar," Beyoncé & Shakira
"Chicken Fried," Zac Brown Band
"Everything," "Home," Michael Bublé
"Sorry," Buckcherry
"Realize," Colbie Caillat
"Touch My Body," Mariah Carey
"Viva La Vida" (3), Coldplay
"Time of My Life," David Cook
"The Climb" (2), Miley Cyrus
"Damaged," Danity Kane
"Down with the Sickness," Disturbed
"Mercy," Duffy
"Hotel California," Eagles
"American Boy," Estelle
"Call Me When You're Sober," Evanescence

"Sugar, We're Goin' Down" (2), Fall Out Boy
"Superstar," Lupe Fiasco
"In the Ayer," "Low" (5), "Right Round" (3), "Sugar," Flo Rida
"Handlebars," Flobots
"You Found Me" (2), The Fray
"I Don't Wanna Be in Love," Good Charlotte
"Upside Down," Jack Johnson
"Day 'N' Nite," Kid Cudi
"Mr. Brightside" (2), "When You Were Young," The Killers
"Sex on Fire," "Use Somebody," Kings of Leon
"Fire Burning," Sean Kingston
"Just Dance" (3), Lady Gaga
"Got Money," "A Milli," Lil Wayne
"Bleed It Out," "New Divide," "What I've Done" (2), Linkin Park
"Paper Planes" (2), M.I.A.
"Say," John Mayer
"Shake It" (2), Metro Station
"This Is Why I'm Hot," Mims
"I'm Yours" (4), Jason Mraz
"Come on Get Higher," Matt Nathanson
"Closer," "Miss Independent," Ne-Yo
"Over and Over," Nelly
"Shattered," O.A.R.
"Misery Business," Paramore
"Hot 'N' Cold" (3), "I Kissed a Girl" (3), Katy Perry
"My Wish," Rascal Flatts
"Under the Bridge," Red Hot Chili Peppers
"Disturbia" (3), "Don't Stop the Music" (2), "Shut Up and Drive," "Take a Bow," "Umbrella" (3), Rihanna
"I Love College," Asher Roth
"Let It Rock" (3), Kevin Rudolf
"Swing," Savage
"Addicted," Saving Abel
"Fall for You," Secondhand Serenade
"Fake It," Seether
"Second Chance," Shinedown
"Stay," Sugarland
"Live Your Life" (3), "Whatever You Like" (3), T.I.
"Dead and Gone" (2), T.I. feat. Justin Timberlake
"Lolli Lolli," Three 6 Mafia
"That's Not My Name," The Ting Tings
"All-American Girl," Carrie Underwood
"Untouched," The Veronicas
"Heartless" (2), "Love Lockdown" (2), "Stronger" (3), Kanye West
"Wait for You," Elliott Yamin
"Soul Survivor," Young Jeezy

Top-Selling Albums of All-Time[1]

Source: Recording Industry Assn. of America, Washington, DC

Rank	Title, artist	Unit sales (mil)	Rank	Title, artist	Unit sales (mil)
1.	*Eagles/Their Greatest Hits 1971-1975*, Eagles	29.0		*The Bodyguard* (soundtrack), Whitney Houston	17.0
2.	*Thriller*, Michael Jackson	28.0	15.	*The Beatles 1967-1970*, The Beatles	16.0
3.	*Led Zeppelin IV*, Led Zeppelin	23.0		*Hotel California*, Eagles	16.0
	The Wall, Pink Floyd	23.0		*Cracked Rear View*, Hootie & the Blowfish	16.0
5.	*Back in Black*, AC/DC	22.0		*Greatest Hits*, Elton John	16.0
6.	*Greatest Hits Volume I & Volume II*, Billy Joel	21.0		*Physical Graffiti*, Led Zeppelin	16.0
	Double Live, Garth Brooks	21.0		*Jagged Little Pill*, Alanis Morissette	16.0
8.	*Come on Over*, Shania Twain	20.0	21.	*The Beatles 1962-1966*, The Beatles	15.0
9.	*The Beatles*, The Beatles	19.0		*Saturday Night Fever* (soundtrack), Bee Gees	15.0
	Rumours, Fleetwood Mac	19.0		*Greatest Hits*, Journey	15.0
11.	*Appetite for Destruction*, Guns N' Roses	18.0		*Dark Side of the Moon*, Pink Floyd	15.0
12.	*Boston*, Boston	17.0		*Supernatural*, Santana	15.0
	No Fences, Garth Brooks	17.0		*Born in the U.S.A.*, Bruce Springsteen	15.0

(1) As of Sept. 2009; sales figures represent RIAA multi-platinum certifications, albums ranked by latest sales certification.

U.S. Commercial Radio Stations, by Format, 1998-2009[1]

Source: The M Street Radio Directory, M Street Corporation, Littleton, NH © 2009; counts are for June of each year

Primary format	2009	2008	2007	2006	2005	2004	2003	2002	2001	1998
1. Country	1,997	2,028	2,034	2,035	2,019	2,047	2,088	2,131	2,190	2,368
2. News/Talk	1,401	1,363	1,370	1,336	1,324	1,282	1,224	1,179	1,139	1,131
3. Spanish	800	799	777	705	703	665	628	603	574	493
4. Oldies	669	711	711	727	773	816	807	813	786	799
5. Sports	635	587	557	530	497	469	429	388	338	251
6. Adult Contemporary (AC)	626	665	661	660	684	703	692	713	709	844
7. Top 40	483	467	473	485	502	497	491	474	468	379
8. Classic Rock	479	468	456	454	461	450	425	384	338	282
9. Hot AC	407	370	377	375	380	416	399	395	369	281
10. Classic Hits	367	311	296	276	262	229	237	258	265	192
11. Adult Standards	330	362	370	366	405	460	497	547	569	561
12. Religion (Teaching, Variety)	328	296	290	312	318	336	347	332	356	356
13. Rock	294	290	282	278	270	280	273	278	282	266
14. Black Gospel	241	246	255	266	286	273	253	254	264	238
15. Southern Gospel	212	207	206	208	207	208	207	240	255	273
16. Soft AC	207	228	243	302	324	322	336	340	375	368
Adult Hits	207	200	171	149	54	0	0	0	0	0
18. Urban AC	161	157	162	166	153	136	128	121	118	127
19. Contemporary Christian	153	143	151	150	174	159	167	164	164	164
20. R&B	129	135	134	138	150	159	189	193	183	171
Off air	202	138	88	93	70	79	123	110	113	102
Total operating stations[2]	**10,956**	**10,843**	**10,755**	**10,696**	**10,729**	**10,727**	**10,728**	**10,679**	**10,629**	**10,292**

(1) Data for 2000 unavailable. (2) Totals include stations that are changing or did not report format.

Top-Grossing North American Concert Tours, 1985-2008

Source: Pollstar, Fresno, CA; ranked by total gross

Artist (year)	Total gross[1]	Cities/ shows	Artist (year)	Total gross[1]	Cities/ shows
1. The Rolling Stones (2005)	$162.0	38/42	13. Barbra Streisand (2006)	$92.5	16/20
2. U2 (2005)	138.9	43/78	14. The Rolling Stones (1997)	89.3	26/33
3. The Rolling Stones (2006)	138.5	35/39	15. Tim McGraw/Faith Hill (2006)	88.8	55/73
4. The Police (2007)	133.2	41/54	16. The Rolling Stones (2002)	87.9	33/34
5. The Rolling Stones (1994)	121.2	43/60	17. Prince (2004)	87.4	69/96
6. Bruce Springsteen & The E Street Band (2003)	115.9	30/47	18. 'N Sync (2001)	86.8	36/43
7. U2 (2001)	109.7	56/80	19. Madonna (2006)	85.9	14/34
8. Madonna (2008)	105.3	19/30	20. Backstreet Boys (2001)	82.1	73/98
9. Pink Floyd (1994)	103.5	39/59	Cirque du Soleil: Delirium (2006)	82.1	61/156
10. Paul McCartney (2002)	103.3	43/53	22. Celine Dion (2005)	81.3	1/155
11. The Rolling Stones (1989)	98.0	33/60	23. Celine Dion (2003)	80.5	1/145
12. Celine Dion (2008)	94.0	31/47	24. Celine Dion (2004)	80.4	1/154
			25. Tina Turner (2000)	80.2	88/95

(1) In millions. Not adjusted for inflation.

Sales of Recorded Music and Music Videos, by Units Shipped and Value, 2000-08

Source: Recording Industry Assn. of America, Washington, DC

(in millions, net after returns)

	2000	2001	2002	2003	2004	2005	2006	2007	2008	% change 2007-08
Physical units shipped	1,079.2	968.5	859.7	798.4	814.1	748.7	648.2	543.9	401.8	−26.1%
Dollar value	14,323.7	13,740.9	12,614.2	11,854.4	12,154.7	11,195.0	9,868.6	7,985.8	5,758.5	−27.9
Compact discs (CD)	942.5	881.9	803.3	746.0	767.0	705.4	619.7	511.1	384.7	−24.7
Dollar value	13,214.5	12,909.4	12,044.1	11,232.9	11,446.5	10,520.2	9,372.6	7,452.3	5,471.3	−26.6
Cassettes	76.0	45.0	31.1	17.2	5.2	2.5	0.7	0.4	0.1	−62.8
Dollar value	626.0	363.4	209.8	108.1	23.7	13.1	3.7	3.0	0.9	−70.7
LP/EP	2.2	2.3	1.7	1.5	1.4	1.0	0.9	1.3	2.9	124.1
Dollar value	27.7	27.4	20.5	21.7	19.3	14.2	15.7	22.9	56.7	147.7
CD singles	34.2	17.3	4.5	8.3	3.1	2.8	1.7	2.6	0.7	−71.7
Dollar value	142.7	79.4	19.6	36.0	15.0	10.9	7.7	12.2	3.5	−71.3
Vinyl singles	4.8	5.5	4.4	3.8	3.5	2.3	1.5	0.6	0.4	−30.9
Dollar value	26.3	31.4	24.9	21.5	19.9	13.2	9.9	4.0	2.9	−27.4

	2000	2001	2002	2003	2004	2005	2006	2007	2008	% change 2007-08
Physical Units Shipped										
Music videos[1]........	18.2	17.7	14.7	19.9	32.8	33.8	23.2	27.5	12.8	−53.6%
Dollar value........	281.9	329.2	288.4	399.9	607.2	602.2	451.1	484.9	218.9	−54.9
Digital formats[2]........	—	—	—	—	143.9	383.1	625.3	868.4	1,112.3	28.1
Dollar value..........	—	—	—	—	183.4	503.6	878.0	1,257.5	1,635.4	30.1
Download albums......	—	—	—	—	4.6	13.6	27.6	42.5	56.9	33.9
Dollar value........	—	—	—	—	45.5	135.7	275.9	424.9	568.9	33.9
Download singles......	—	—	—	—	139.4	366.9	586.4	809.9	1,033.0	27.5
Dollar value........	—	—	—	—	138.0	363.3	580.6	801.6	1,022.7	27.6
Music videos........	—	—	—	—	—	1.9	9.9	14.2	20.8	46.7
Dollar value........	—	—	—	—	—	3.7	19.7	28.2	41.3	46.7
Mobile formats[3]........	—	—	—	—	—	170.0	315.0	362.0	338.4	−6.5
Dollar value........	—	—	—	—	—	421.6	773.8	880.8	816.3	−7.3
Subscription formats[4].....	—	—	—	—	—	1.3	1.3	1.8	1.6	−15.0
Dollar value...........	—	—	—	—	—	149.2	206.2	201.3	188.2	−6.5
Digital performances[5].....	—	—	—	—	6.9	27.4	31.5	47.0	81.8	74.1
TOTAL UNITS[6]........	1,079.2	968.5	859.7	798.4	958.0	1,301.8	1,588.5	1,774.3	1,852.5	4.4
TOTAL VALUE........	14,323.7	13,740.9	12,614.2	11,854.4	12,345.0	12,296.9	11,758.2	10,372.1	8,480.2	−18.2

(1) Includes DVD videos. (2) Includes kiosk singles and albums. (3) Includes master ringtones, ringbacks, music videos, full-length downloads, and other mobile music. (4) Weighted annual average. (5) Estimated royalty payments, to artists/record companies distributed by SoundExchange, based on prior year's collections and airplay. (6) Includes albums and singles, excludes subscriptions and royalties.

Sales of Recorded Music and Music Videos, by Genre and Format, 2000-08
Source: Recording Industry Assn. of America, Washington, DC
Percentage of sales revenue for all recorded music sold, ranked for 2008.

Genre	2008	2007	2006	2005	2000	Genre	2008	2007	2006	2005	2000
Rock............	31.8%	32.4%	34.0%	31.5%	24.8%	New Age............	0.6%	0.3%	0.3%	0.4%	0.5%
Country..............	11.9	11.5	13.0	12.5	10.7	Other[3].............	9.1	7.1	7.3	8.5	8.3
Rap/Hip-Hop.........	10.7	10.8	11.4	13.3	12.9						
R&B/Urban[1]........	10.2	11.8	11.0	10.2	9.7	**Format**	**2008**	**2007**	**2006**	**2005**	**2000**
Pop............	9.1	10.7	7.1	8.1	11.0	Compact disc (CD).....	77.8%	82.6%	85.6%	87.0%	89.3%
Religious[2]...........	6.5	3.9	5.5	5.3	4.8	Digital download[4].......	12.8	11.2	6.7	5.7	NA
Children's...........	3.0	2.9	2.9	2.3	0.6	Singles (all types)......	3.8	2.4	3.4	2.7	2.5
Classical............	1.9	2.3	1.9	2.4	2.7	DVD audio...........	1.0	1.2	1.3	0.8	NA
Jazz................	1.1	2.6	2.0	1.8	2.9	Vinyl LPs............	1.0	0.7	0.6	0.7	0.5
Soundtracks..........	0.8	0.8	0.8	0.9	0.7	Music videos/DVDs[4]....	0.8	0.4	1.1	0.7	0.8
Oldies..............	0.7	0.4	1.1	1.1	0.9	Cassette............	0.4	0.3	0.8	1.1	4.9

(1) Includes R&B, blues, dance, disco, funk, fusion, Motown, reggae, soul. (2) Includes Christian, gospel, inspirational, religious, and spiritual. (3) "Other" includes big band, Broadway, comedy, contemporary, electronic, emo, ethnic, exercise, folk, gothic, grunge, holiday music, house music, humor, instrumental, language, Latin, love songs, mix, mellow, modern, ska, spoken-word, standards, swing, top-40, trip-hop. (4) 2001 is the first year that data were collected on digital download purchases and that music video/DVD data was recorded separately from audio DVD.

Top Cable TV Networks, 2009
Source: Natl. Cable Television Assn., Mar. 2009; ranked by number of subscribers in millions

Network[1]	Subscribers	Network	Subscribers
1. Discovery (1985)...........................	98.0	11. ABC Family (2001).........................	97.0
TNT (1988).................................	98.0	ESPN2 (1993).............................	97.0
3. ESPN (1979).............................	97.8	13. C-Span (1979)...........................	96.5
4. CNN (1980)...............................	97.5	HGTV (1994).............................	96.5
USA Network (1980)......................	97.5	15. Food Network (1993).....................	96.3
6. Lifetime Television (1984)...............	97.3	MTV (1981).............................	96.3
Nickelodeon (1979)......................	97.3	17. Comedy Central (1991)...................	96.0
TBS (1976)................................	97.3	Fox News (1996).........................	96.0
The Weather Channel (1982)...................	97.3	VH1 (1985).............................	96.0
TLC–The Learning Channel (1980)............	97.3		

Note: Data include noncable affiliates. (1) Date in parentheses is year service began.

U.S. Households With Cable Television, 1977-2009
Source: Nielsen Media Research

Year[1]	Subscribers[2] (mil)	As % of households with TVs	Year[1]	Subscribers[2] (mil)	As % of households with TVs	Year[1]	Subscribers[2] (mil)	As % of households with TVs
1977	12.2	16.6%	1988	46.3	52.0%	1999	76.4	76.9%
1978	13.4	17.9	1989	50.2	55.6	2000	78.6	77.9
1979	14.9	19.4	1990	53.9	58.6	2001	81.5	79.8
1980	17.7	22.6	1991	56.1	60.3	2002	87.8	83.8
1981	23.2	28.3	1992	56.2	61.1	2003	88.4	82.9
1982	27.4	33.4	1993	57.6	61.9	2004	92.4	85.3
1983	31.8	37.9	1994	59.7	63.4	2005	94.0	85.7
1984	35.8	42.5	1995	62.1	65.1	2006	95.0	86.2
1985	38.7	45.3	1996	63.6	66.3	2007	94.5	83.8
1986	40.9	47.4	1997	65.1	67.2	2008	99.7	88.2
1987	43.3	49.2	1998	65.9	67.2	2009	103.0	89.7

(1) After 1998, figures include wired-cable households as well as households that receive TV programming via alternate delivery systems (including satellite receivers, SMATV, MMDS). (2) Households that subscribe to basic cable service.

U.S. Television Set Owners, 2009
Source: Nielsen Media Research, Oct. 2009

Of the 114.9 million U.S. households that owned at least one TV set in 2009:

83% had 2 or more TV sets	67% had a VCR	88% received basic cable
54% had 3 or more TV sets	89% had a DVD player	35% received premium cable

TV Viewing Shares, Broadcast Years 1990-2008[1]

Source: *Cable TV Facts*, Cable Advertising Bureau, New York, NY

	All television households[2]						All cable households[2]						Pay cable households[2]					
	'90	'95	'00	'05	'07	'08	'90	'95	'00	'05	'07	'08	'90	'95	'00	'05	'07	'08
Network affiliates[3]	55	48	44	30	38	26	46	41	40	27	25	23	43	38	37	24	23	21
Ind. TV stations[4]	20	22	12	9	6	4	16	17	9	7	4	3	16	17	9	6	4	3
Public TV stations	3	3	3	2	2	1	3	3	2	2	1	1	2	2	2	1	1	1
Basic cable[5]	21	30	46	48	51	50	32	42	55	54	57	54	30	41	55	52	55	52
Pay cable	6	6	6	5	4	4	10	8	7	5	5	5	18	15	11	10	9	8

(1) Broadcast years represent the 12-month period of the preceding October through September of the year listed. (2) Share figures refer to percentage of the viewing audience for all television viewing, 24 hours/day. As a result of multiset use and rounding, share figures add to more than 100. (3) Includes CBS, NBC, ABC, and FOX after 1998. (4) Varies year-to-year; 2008 includes ION, MNT, and CW. (5) Includes ad-supported cable and all other cable (non-pay and non-ad-supported channels).

Average U.S. Television Viewing Time

Source: Nielsen Media Research (hours: minutes per week), Sept. 1, 2008-Aug. 30, 2009

Group	Age	Total per week	M-F 7-10 AM	M-F 10 AM-4:00 PM	M-Sun. 8-11 PM	Sat. 7 AM-1 PM	M-F 11:30 PM-1 AM	Sunday 1-7:00 PM
Men	18+	34:23	1:56	4:21	8:31	0:59	2:59	1:52
	18-24	24:22	1:05	3:23	5:14	0:36	2:34	1:14
	25-54	32:38	1:45	3:45	8:09	0:59	3:04	1:48
	55+	42:12	2:39	5:55	10:42	1:09	3:02	2:16
Women	18+	38:39	2:31	5:48	9:19	1:05	3:12	1:45
	18-24	27:43	1:22	4:33	6:05	0:42	2:42	1:13
	25-54	35:56	2:22	4:57	8:46	1:04	3:12	1:38
	55+	47:02	3:11	7:37	11:24	1:17	3:24	2:07
Children	2-11	24:32	1:49	4:06	5:05	1:12	1:16	1:15
Teens	12-17	24:04	1:02	2:52	5:41	0:48	2:03	1:13
ALL VIEWERS		33:50	2:04	4:46	8:07	1:02	2:45	1:40

Selected Reality TV Show Winners, 2000-09

Numbers in parentheses represent the season, edition, or cycle of the show. As of Sept. 30, 2009.

The Amazing Race. Debuted Aug. 2001 on CBS. Rob Frisbee & Brennan Swain (1); Chris Luca & Alex Boylan (2); Flo Pesenti & Zach Behr (3); Reichen Lehmkuhl & Chip Arndt (4); Chip & Kim McAllister (5); Freddy Holliday & Kendra Bentley (6); Uchenna & Joyce Agu (7); The Linz Family (8); B. J. Averell & Tyler MacNiven (9); Tyler Denk & James Branaman (10); All-Stars: Eric Sanchez & Danielle Turner (11); TK Erwin & Rachel Morales (12); Nick & Starr Spangler (13); Tammy & Victor Jih (14).

American Idol. Debuted July 2002 on Fox. Kelly Clarkson (1); Ruben Studdard (2); Fantasia Barrino (3); Carrie Underwood (4); Taylor Hicks (5); Jordin Sparks (6); David Cook (7); Kris Allen (8).

America's Got Talent. Debuted June 2006 on NBC. Bianca Ryan (1); Terry Fator (2); Neil E. Boyd (3); Kevin Skinner (4).

America's Next Top Model. Debuted May 2003. Adrianne Curry (1); Yoanna House (2); Eva Pigford (3); Naima Mora (4); Nicole Linkletter (5); Danielle Evans (6); CariDee English (7); Jaslene Gonzalez (8); Saleisha Stowers (9); Whitney Thompson (10); McKey Sullivan (11); Teyona Anderson (12).

The Apprentice. Debuted Jan. 2004 on NBC. Bill Rancic (1); Kelly Perdew (2); Kendra Todd (3); Randal Pinkett (4); Sean Yazbeck (5); Stefani Schaeffer (6). Celebrity Apprentice: Piers Morgan (1); Joan Rivers (8).

The Bachelor. Debuted Mar. 2002 on ABC. Alex Michel chose Amanda Marsh (1); Aaron Buerge chose Helene Eksterowicz (2); Andrew Firestone chose Jen Schefft (3); Bob Guiney chose Estella Gardinier (4); Jesse Palmer chose Jessica Bowlin (5); Byron Velvick chose Mary Delgado (6); Charlie O'Connell chose Sarah Brice (7); Travis Stork chose Sarah Stone (8); Lorenzo Borghese chose Jennifer Wilson (9); Andy Baldwin chose Tessa Horst (10); Brad Womack chose no one (11); Matt Grant chose Shayne Lamas (12); Jason Mesnick chose Melissa Rycroft (13).

The Bachelorette. Debuted Jan. 2003 on ABC. Trista Rehn chose Ryan Sutter (1); Meredith Phillips chose Ian McKee (2); Jen Schefft chose Jerry Ferris (3); DeAnna Pappas chose Jesse Csincsak (4); Jillian Harris chose Ed Swiderski (5).

The Biggest Loser. Debuted Oct. 2004 on NBC. Ryan Benson (1); Matt Hoover (2); Erik Chopin (3); Bill Germanakos (4); Ali Vincent (5); Michelle Aguilar (6); Helen Phillips (7).

Big Brother. Debuted July 2000 on CBS. Eddie McGee (1); Will Kirby (2); Lisa Donahue (3); Jun Song (4); Drew Daniel (5); Maggie Ausburn (6); Mike Malinto (7); Dick Donato (8); Adam Jasinski (9); Dan Gheesling (10); Jordan Lloyd (11).

The Contender. Debuted Mar. 2005 on NBC; 2nd and 3rd seasons on ESPN; 4th season on Versus. Sergio Mora (1); Grady Brewer (2); Sakio Bika (3); Troy Ross (4).

Dancing With the Stars. Debuted June 2005 on ABC. Kelly Monaco & Alex Mazo (1); Drew Lachey & Cheryl Burke (2); Emmitt Smith & Cheryl Burke (3); Apolo Anton Ohno & Julianne Hough (4); Helio Castroneves & Julianne Hough (5); Kristi Yamaguchi & Mark Ballas (6); Brooke Burke & Derek Hough (7); Shawn Johnson & Mark Ballas (8).

Hell's Kitchen. Debuted Mar. 2005 on FOX. Michael Wray (1); Heather West (2); Rock Harper (3); Christina Machamer (4); Danny Veltri (5).

Last Comic Standing. Debuted June 2003 on NBC. Dat Phan (1); John Heffron (2); Alonzo Bodden (3); Josh Blue (4); Jon Reep (5); Iliza Shlesinger (6).

Make Me a Supermodel. Debuted Jan. 2008 on Bravo. Holly Kiser (1); Branden Rickman (2).

Nashville Star. Debuted Mar. 2003 on USA Network; 6th season aired on NBC. Buddy Jewell (1); Brad Cotter (2); Erika Jo Heriges (3); Chris Young (4); Angela Hacker (5); Melissa Lawson (6).

The Next Food Network Star. Debuted June 2005 on Food Network. Steve McDonagh & Dan Smith (1); Guy Fieri (2); Amy Finley (3); Aaron McCargo Jr. (4); Melissa d'Arabian (5).

Project Runway. Debuted Dec. 2004 on Bravo. Jay McCarroll (1); Chloe Dao (2); Jeffrey Sebelia (3); Christian Siriano (4); Leanne Marshall (5).

So You Think You Can Dance. Debuted July 2005 on FOX. Nick Lazzarini (1); Benji Schwimmer (2); Sabra Johnson (3); Joshua Allen (4); Jeanine Mason (5).

Survivor. Debuted May 2000 on CBS. Borneo: Richard Hatch (1); Outback: Tina Wesson (2); Africa: Ethan Zohn (3); Marquesas: Vecepia Towery (4); Thailand: Brian Heidik (5); The Amazon: Jenna Morasca (6); Pearl Islands: Sandra Diaz-Twine (7); All-Stars, Panama: Amber Brkich (8); Vanuatu: Chris Daugherty (9); Palau: Tom Westman (10); Guatemala: Danni Boatwright (11); Panama: Aras Baskauskas (12); Cook Islands: Yul Kwon (13); Fiji: Earl Cole (14); China: Todd Herzog (15); Micronesia: Parvati Shallow (16); Gabon: Robert Crowley (17); Tocantins: James "JT" Thomas (18).

Top Chef. Debuted Mar. 2006 on Bravo. Harold Dieterle (1); Ilan Hall (2); Hung Huynh (3); Stephanie Izard (4); Hosea Rosenberg (5); Masters: Rick Bayless.

Favorite Prime-Time Television Programs, 2008-09

Source: Nielsen Media Research

Data are for regularly scheduled network programs in 2008-09; ranked by average audience percentage. Average audience percentages, or ratings, are estimates of the percentage of all TV-owning households that are watching a particular program. Audience share percentages are estimates of the percentage of those watching TV that are tuned into a particular program.

Rank Program	Avg. audience	Audience share	Rank Program	Avg. audience	Audience share
1. American Idol-Wednesday	15.1%	23%	27. E.R.	6.7%	11%
2. American Idol-Tuesday	14.6	22	Sunday Night NFL Pre-Kick	6.7	11
3. Dancing With the Stars	12.9	19	Amazing Race 13	6.7	10
4. Dancing With the Stars: Results	10.7	16	30. Lie to Me	6.6	11
5. NBC Sunday Night Football	10.0	16	Lost	6.6	10
6. NCIS	9.8	16	32. Law & Order: SVU	6.5	11
7. CSI	9.5	15	33. Brothers & Sisters	6.4	10
8. The Mentalist	9.4	15	Cold Case	6.4	10
9. Desperate Housewives	8.8	13	35. Amazing Race 14	6.3	10
10. Two and a Half Men	8.3	12	Biggest Loser 7	6.3	9
11. Criminal Minds	8.1	13	37. Boston Legal	6.2	10
CSI: Miami	8.1	13	38. Fox Nascar Sprint Cup	6.1	10
Survivor: Gabon	8.1	13	Worst Week	6.1	9
14. 60 Minutes	8.0	14	40. Harper's Island	6.0	10
15. Eleventh Hour	7.8	13	The Unit	6.0	10
Grey's Anatomy	7.8	12	Fringe	6.0	9
17. America's Got Talent-Tuesday	7.7	13	43. The Big Bang Theory	5.9	9
18. Without a Trace	7.6	13	44. Ghost Whisperer	5.7	11
19. CSI: NY	7.5	13	So You Think You Can Dance-Thursday	5.7	10
Survivor: Tocantins	7.5	12	46. Numb3rs	5.6	10
The Bachelor	7.5	11	Rules of Engagement	5.6	9
America's Got Talent-Wednesday	7.5	11	Bones	5.6	9
23. 24	7.3	11	Apprentice 8	5.6	9
24. The OT	7.1	12	50. The Bachelorette	5.5	9
25. The Mentalist-Tuesday	6.9	11			
26. House	6.8	11			

Favorite Syndicated Programs, 2008-09

Source: Nielsen Media Research, Sept. 22, 2008-Sept. 20, 2009

Average audience percentages, or ratings, are estimates of the percentage of TV-owning households watching a program.

Rank Program	Avg. audience	Rank Program	Avg. audience
1. ESPN NFL Regular Season	7.8%	14. Everybody Loves Raymond	3.0%
2. Wheel of Fortune	6.8	Law & Order: SVU	3.0
3. Jeopardy	5.6	16. George Lopez	2.9
4. Oprah Winfrey Show	4.8	Inside Edition	2.9
Two and a Half Men	4.8	Seinfeld (weekend)	2.9
6. Judge Judy	4.3	Wheel of Fortune (weekend)	2.9
7. 2008 NFL Regular Season Saturday	4.2	20. 2008 NFL Regular Season Games	2.8
Entertainment Tonight	4.2	Buena Vista VI (package)	2.8
9. Family Guy	3.9	22. Century 19 (package)	2.7
10. ESPN NFL Preseason Thursday	3.5	23. 2008 NFL Regular Season Postgame	2.6
11. CSI: New York	3.4	Live with Regis and Kelly	2.6
Seinfeld	3.4	25. 2008 NFL Regular Season Pre-Kick Saturday	2.5
13. Dr. Phil	3.2		

All-Time Most Watched Television Programs

Source: Nielsen Media Research, Jan. 1961-May 2009

Estimates exclude unsponsored or joint network telecasts (e.g., presidential addresses) or programs under 30 minutes long. Ranked by number of TV-owning households tuned in to the program.

Rank	Program	Telecast date	Network	Rating (%)	Avg. households (in thousands)
1.	M*A*S*H (last episode)	2/28/83	CBS	60.2%	50,150
2.	Super Bowl XLII	2/3/08	FOX	43.2	48,721
3.	Super Bowl XLIII	2/1/09	NBC	42.1	48,239
4.	Super Bowl XLI	2/4/07	CBS	42.7	47,535
5.	Super Bowl XL	2/5/06	ABC	41.6	45,869
6.	XVII Winter Olympics (Women's figure skating)	2/23/94	CBS	48.5	45,690
7.	Super Bowl XXXIX	2/6/05	FOX	41.1	45,080
8.	Super Bowl XXXVIII	2/1/04	CBS	41.4	44,910
9.	Super Bowl XXX	1/28/96	NBC	46.0	44,150
10.	Super Bowl XXXII	1/25/98	NBC	44.5	43,630
11.	Super Bowl XXXIV	1/30/00	ABC	43.3	43,620
12.	Super Bowl XXXVII	1/26/03	ABC	40.7	43,430
13.	Super Bowl XXVIII	1/30/94	NBC	45.5	42,860
14.	Super Bowl XXXVI	2/3/02	FOX	40.4	42,660
15.	Cheers	5/20/93	NBC	45.5	42,360
16.	Super Bowl XXXI	1/26/97	FOX	43.3	42,000
17.	Super Bowl XXVII	1/31/93	NBC	45.1	41,990
18.	XVII Winter Olympics (Women's figure skating)	2/25/94	CBS	44.1	41,540
19.	Super Bowl XX	1/26/86	NBC	48.3	41,490
20.	Dallas	11/21/80	CBS	53.3	41,470

Highest-Rated TV Programs of Each Season, 1950-51 to 2008-09

Source: Nielsen Media Research; regular series programs, Sept.-May season

Season	Program	Rating[1]	TV-owning households (in thousands)	Season	Program	Rating[1]	TV-owning households (in thousands)
1950-51	Texaco Star Theatre	61.6%	10,320	1980-81	Dallas	31.2%	79,900
1951-52	Godfrey's Talent Scouts	53.8	15,300	1981-82	Dallas	28.4	81,500
1952-53	I Love Lucy	67.3	20,400	1982-83	60 Minutes	25.5	83,300
1953-54	I Love Lucy	58.8	26,000	1983-84	Dallas	25.7	83,800
1954-55	I Love Lucy	49.3	30,700	1984-85	Dynasty	25.0	84,900
1955-56	$64,000 Question	47.5	34,900	1985-86	Cosby Show	33.8	85,900
1956-57	I Love Lucy	43.7	38,900	1986-87	Cosby Show	34.9	87,400
1957-58	Gunsmoke	43.1	41,920	1987-88	Cosby Show	27.8	88,600
1958-59	Gunsmoke	39.6	43,950	1988-89	Roseanne	25.5	90,400
1959-60	Gunsmoke	40.3	45,750	1989-90	Roseanne	23.4	92,100
1960-61	Gunsmoke	37.3	47,200	1990-91	Cheers	21.6	93,100
1961-62	Wagon Train	32.1	48,555	1991-92	60 Minutes	21.7	92,100
1962-63	Beverly Hillbillies	36.0	50,300	1992-93	60 Minutes	21.6	93,100
1963-64	Beverly Hillbillies	39.1	51,600	1993-94	Home Improvement	21.9	94,200
1964-65	Bonanza	36.3	52,700	1994-95	Seinfeld	20.5	95,400
1965-66	Bonanza	31.8	53,850	1995-96	E.R.	22.0	95,900
1966-67	Bonanza	29.1	55,130	1996-97	E.R.	21.2	97,000
1967-68	Andy Griffith	27.6	56,670	1997-98	Seinfeld	22.0	98,000
1968-69	Rowan & Martin's Laugh-In	31.8	58,250	1998-99	E.R.	17.8	99,400
1969-70	Rowan & Martin's Laugh-In	26.3	58,500	1999-2000	Who Wants to Be a Millionaire	18.6	100,800
1970-71	Marcus Welby, M.D.	29.6	60,100	2000-01	Survivor II	17.4	102,200
1971-72	All in the Family	34.0	62,100	2001-02	Friends	15.3	105,500
1972-73	All in the Family	33.3	64,800	2002-03	CSI	16.1	106,700
1973-74	All in the Family	31.2	66,200	2003-04	CSI	15.9	108,400
1974-75	All in the Family	30.2	68,500	2004-05	CSI	16.3	106,900
1975-76	All in the Family	30.1	69,600	2005-06	American Idol-Tuesday	17.6	110,200
1976-77	Happy Days	31.5	71,200	2006-07	American Idol-Wednesday	17.3	112,800
1977-78	Laverne & Shirley	31.6	72,900	2007-08	American Idol-Tuesday	16.1	113,050
1978-79	Laverne & Shirley	30.5	74,500	2008-09	American Idol-Wednesday	15.1	114,900
1979-80	60 Minutes	28.2	76,300				

(1) Rating is percent of TV-owning households tuned in to the program. Data prior to 1988-89 exclude Alaska and Hawaii.

All-Time Highest-Rated Television Programs

Source: Nielsen Media Research, Jan. 1961-May 2009

Estimates exclude unsponsored or joint network telecasts (e.g., presidential addresses) or programs under 30 minutes long. Ranked by rating (percentage of TV-owning households tuned in to the program).

Rank	Program	Telecast date	Network	Rating (%)	Avg. households (in thousands)
1.	M*A*S*H (last episode)	2/28/83	CBS	60.2%	50,150
2.	Dallas (Who Shot J.R.?)	11/21/80	CBS	53.3	41,470
3.	Roots-Pt. 8	1/30/77	ABC	51.1	36,380
4.	Super Bowl XVI	1/24/82	CBS	49.1	40,020
5.	Super Bowl XVII	1/30/83	NBC	48.6	40,480
6.	XVII Winter Olympics (Women's figure skating)	2/23/94	CBS	48.5	45,690
7.	Super Bowl XX	1/26/86	NBC	48.3	41,490
8.	Gone With the Wind-Pt. 1	11/7/76	NBC	47.7	33,960
9.	Gone With the Wind-Pt. 2	11/8/76	NBC	47.4	33,750
10.	Super Bowl XII	1/15/78	CBS	47.2	34,410
11.	Super Bowl XIII	1/21/79	NBC	47.1	35,090
12.	Bob Hope Christmas Show	1/15/70	NBC	46.6	27,260
13.	Super Bowl XIX	1/20/85	ABC	46.4	39,390
	Super Bowl XVIII	1/22/84	CBS	46.4	38,800
15.	Super Bowl XIV	1/20/80	CBS	46.3	35,330
16.	Super Bowl XXX	1/28/96	NBC	46.0	44,150
	ABC Theater (The Day After)	11/20/83	ABC	46.0	38,550
18.	Roots-Pt. 6	1/28/77	ABC	45.9	32,680
	The Fugitive	8/29/67	ABC	45.9	25,700
20.	Super Bowl XXI	1/25/87	CBS	45.8	40,030
21.	Roots-Pt. 5	1/27/77	ABC	45.7	32,540
22.	Super Bowl XXVIII	1/30/94	NBC	45.5	42,860
	Cheers (last episode)	5/20/93	NBC	45.5	42,360
24.	Ed Sullivan	2/9/64	CBS	45.3	23,240
25.	Super Bowl XXVII	1/31/93	NBC	45.1	41,990

AWARDS — MEDALS — PRIZES

The Alfred B. Nobel Prize Winners, 1901-2009

Alfred B. Nobel (1833-96) bequeathed $9 mil, the interest on which was to be distributed yearly to those judged to have most benefited humankind in physics, chemistry, medicine-physiology, literature, and promotion of peace. Prizes were first awarded in 1901. The 1st prize in economics was awarded in 1969, funded by Sweden's central bank. Each prize is now worth 10 mil Swedish krona (about $1.4 mil). If year is omitted, no award was given. The 2009 Nobel Prizes were announced Oct. 5-12.

2009 Nobel Prizes

Chemistry: Venkatraman Ramakrishnan, UK; Thomas A. Steitz, U.S.; and Ada E. Yonath, Israel, shared the prize for their independent research on the structure and function of ribosomes. Yonath was only the fourth woman to receive the chemistry prize and the first since 1964.

Economics: Americans Elinor Ostrom and Oliver E. Williamson were honored for their separate analyses of "economic governance." Their work demonstrated the likelihood that in business, problems that arise from free market competition are resolved through implicit supplementary relationships between parties, including competitors.

Literature: Romanian-born German author Herta Müller, "who, with the concentration of poetry and the frankness of prose, depicts the landscaped of the dispossessed," according to the Nobel committee, won the prize for her novels and essays. Like the 2008 prize winner, Jean-Marie Gustave Le Clézio, Müller was considered a relative unknown outside of her home country.

Peace: In an unanticipated move, Pres. Barack Obama was awarded the prize "for his extraordinary efforts to strengthen international diplomacy and cooperation between peoples." Obama was the fourth U.S. president to be honored with the peace prize and the first sitting president to receive it since Woodrow Wilson (1919).

Physics: Half of the physics prize was given to Charles K. Kao (U.S.-UK), for his work that led to developments in fiber optic cables. The other half of the prize was shared by Willard S. Boyle, U.S.-Can., and George E. Smith, U.S., for their invention of the CCD sensor, an imaging semiconductor circuit used in digital cameras.

Physiology or Medicine: Americans Elizabeth H. Blackburn, Carol W. Greider, and Jack W. Szostak were awarded the prize "for the discovery of how chromosomes are protected by telomeres and the enzyme telomerase." Their work, done in the 1970-80s, has been the basis for experimental cancer treatments and may offer insight on aging.

Physics

1901	Wilhelm C. Röntgen, Ger.
1902	Hendrik A. Lorentz, Pieter Zeeman, Neth.
1903	Antoine Henri Becquerel, Pierre Curie, Fr.; Marie Curie, Pol.-Fr.
1904	Lord Rayleigh (John W. Strutt), UK
1905	Philipp E. A. von Lenard, Ger.
1906	Sir Joseph J. Thomson, UK
1907	Albert A. Michelson, U.S.
1908	Gabriel Lippmann, Fr.
1909	Carl F. Braun, Ger.; Guglielmo Marconi, It.
1910	Johannes D. van der Waals, Neth.
1911	Wilhelm Wien, Ger.
1912	Nils G. Dalén, Swed.
1913	Heike Kamerlingh Onnes, Neth.
1914	Max von Laue, Ger.
1915	Sir William H. Bragg, Sir William L. Bragg, UK
1917	Charles G. Barkla, UK
1918	Max K. E. L. Planck, Ger.
1919	Johannes Stark, Ger.
1920	Charles E. Guillaume, Fr.-Switz.
1921	Albert Einstein, Ger.-U.S.
1922	Niels Bohr, Den.
1923	Robert A. Millikan, U.S.
1924	Karl M. G. Siegbahn, Swed.
1925	James Franck, Gustav Hertz, Ger.
1926	Jean B. Perrin, Fr.
1927	Arthur H. Compton, U.S.; Charles T. R. Wilson, UK
1928	Owen W. Richardson, UK
1929	Prince Louis-Victor de Broglie, Fr.
1930	Sir Chandrasekhara V. Raman, India
1932	Werner Heisenberg, Ger.
1933	Paul A. M. Dirac, UK; Erwin Schrödinger, Austria
1935	Sir James Chadwick, UK
1936	Carl D. Anderson, U.S.; Victor F. Hess, Austria
1937	Clinton J. Davisson, U.S.; Sir George P. Thomson, UK
1938	Enrico Fermi, It.-U.S.
1939	Ernest O. Lawrence, U.S.
1943	Otto Stern, U.S.
1944	Isidor Isaac Rabi, U.S.
1945	Wolfgang Pauli, U.S.-Austria
1946	Percy W. Bridgman, U.S.
1947	Sir Edward V. Appleton, UK
1948	Patrick M. S. Blackett, UK
1949	Hideki Yukawa, Jpn.
1950	Cecil F. Powell, UK
1951	Sir John D. Cockcroft, UK; Ernest T. S. Walton, Ire.
1952	Felix Bloch, Edward M. Purcell, U.S.
1953	Frits Zernike, Neth.
1954	Max Born, UK; Walter Bothe, Ger.
1955	Polykarp Kusch, Willis E. Lamb, U.S.
1956	John Bardeen, Walter H. Brattain, William Shockley, U.S.
1957	Tsung-Dao Lee, Chen Ning Yang, U.S.-China
1958	Pavel Cherenkov, Il'ja Frank, Igor Y. Tamm, USSR
1959	Owen Chamberlain, Emilio G. Segre, U.S.
1960	Donald A. Glaser, U.S.
1961	Robert Hofstadter, U.S.; Rudolf L. Mossbauer, Ger.
1962	Lev D. Landau, USSR
1963	Maria Goeppert-Mayer, Eugene P. Wigner, U.S.; J. Hans D. Jensen, Ger.
1964	Nicolay G. Basov, Aleksandr M. Prokhorov, USSR; Charles H. Townes, U.S.
1965	Richard P. Feynman, Julian S. Schwinger, U.S.; Sin-Itiro Tomonaga, Jpn.
1966	Alfred Kastler, Fr.
1967	Hans A. Bethe, U.S.
1968	Luis W. Alvarez, U.S.
1969	Murray Gell-Mann, U.S.
1970	Louis Néel, Fr.; Hannes Alfvén, Swed.
1971	Dennis Gabor, UK
1972	John Bardeen, Leon N. Cooper, John R. Schrieffer, U.S.
1973	Ivar Giaever, U.S.; Leo Esaki, Jpn.; Brian D. Josephson, UK
1974	Sir Martin Ryle, Antony Hewish, UK
1975	Leo James Rainwater, U.S.; Ben Mottelson, U.S.-Den.; Aage Bohr, Den.
1976	Burton Richter, Samuel C. C. Ting, U.S.
1977	John H. van Vleck, Philip W. Anderson, U.S.; Sir Nevill F. Mott, UK
1978	Pyotr Kapitsa, USSR; Arno Penzias, Robert Wilson, U.S.
1979	Steven Weinberg, Sheldon L. Glashow, U.S.; Abdus Salam, Pakistan
1980	James W. Cronin, Val L. Fitch, U.S.
1981	Nicolaas Bloembergen, Arthur Schawlow, U.S.; Kai M. Siegbahn, Swed.
1982	Kenneth G. Wilson, U.S.
1983	Subramanyan Chandrasekhar, William A. Fowler, U.S.
1984	Carlo Rubbia, It.; Simon van der Meer, Neth.
1985	Klaus von Klitzing, Ger.
1986	Ernst Ruska, Gerd Binnig, Ger.; Heinrich Rohrer, Switz.
1987	K. Alex Müller, Switz.; J. Georg Bednorz, Ger.
1988	Leon M. Lederman, Melvin Schwartz, Jack Steinberger, U.S.
1989	Norman F. Ramsey, U.S.; Hans G. Dehmelt, Ger.-U.S.; Wolfgang Paul, Ger.
1990	Richard E. Taylor, Can.; Jerome I. Friedman, Henry W. Kendall, U.S.
1991	Pierre-Gilles de Gennes, Fr.
1992	Georges Charpak, Pol.-Fr.
1993	Joseph H. Taylor, Russell A. Hulse, U.S.
1994	Bertram N. Brockhouse, Can.; Clifford G. Shull, U.S.
1995	Martin Perl, Frederick Reines, U.S.
1996	David M. Lee, Douglas D. Osheroff, Robert C. Richardson, U.S.
1997	Steven Chu, William D. Phillips, U.S.; Claude Cohen-Tannoudji, Fr.
1998	Robert B. Laughlin, U.S.; Horst L. Störmer, Ger.-U.S; Daniel C. Tsui, China-U.S.
1999	Gerardus`t Hooft, Martinus J. G. Veltman, Netherlands
2000	Jack S. Kilby, U.S.; Herbert Kroemer, Ger.-U.S.; Zhores I. Alferov, Russ.
2001	Eric A. Cornell, Carl E. Wieman, U.S.; Wolfgang Ketterle, Ger.
2002	Raymond Davis Jr., Riccardo Giacconi, U.S.; Masatoshi Koshiba, Jpn.
2003	Vitaly L. Ginzburg, Alexei A. Abrikosov, Russ.; Anthony J. Leggett, UK
2004	David J. Gross, H. David Politzer, Frank Wilczek, U.S.
2005	Roy J. Glauber, John L. Hall, U.S.; Theodor W. Hänsch, Ger.
2006	John C. Mather, George F. Smoot, U.S.
2007	Albert Fert, Fr.; Peter Grünberg, Ger.
2008	Yoichiro Nambu, U.S.; Makoto Kobayashi, Toshihide Maskawa, Jpn.

Chemistry

1901 Jacobus H. van 't Hoff, Neth.	1950 Kurt Alder, Otto P. H. Diels, Ger.	1985 Herbert A. Hauptman,
1902 Emil Fischer, Ger.	1951 Edwin M. McMillan,	Jerome Karle, U.S.
1903 Svante A. Arrhenius, Swed.	Glenn T. Seaborg, U.S.	1986 Dudley Herschbach, Yuan T. Lee,
1904 Sir William Ramsay, UK	1952 Archer J. P. Martin,	U.S.; John C. Polanyi, Can.
1905 Adolf von Baeyer, Ger.	Richard L. M. Synge, UK	1987 Donald J. Cram,
1906 Henri Moissan, Fr.	1953 Hermann Staudinger, Ger.	Charles J. Pedersen, U.S.;
1907 Eduard Buchner, Ger.	1954 Linus C. Pauling, U.S.	Jean-Marie Lehn, Fr.
1908 Ernest Rutherford, UK	1955 Vincent du Vigneaud, U.S.	1988 Johann Deisenhofer, Robert Huber,
1909 Wilhelm Ostwald, Ger.	1956 Sir Cyril N. Hinshelwood, UK;	Hartmut Michel, Ger.
1910 Otto Wallach, Ger.	Nikolay N. Semenov, USSR	1989 Thomas R. Cech,
1911 Marie Curie, Pol.-Fr.	1957 Lord (Alexander R.) Todd, UK	Sidney Altman, U.S.
1912 Victor Grignard, Paul Sabatier, Fr.	1958 Frederick Sanger, UK	1990 Elias James Corey, U.S.
1913 Alfred Werner, Switz.	1959 Jaroslav Heyrovsky, Czech.	1991 Richard R. Ernst, Switz.
1914 Theodore W. Richards, U.S.	1960 Willard F. Libby, U.S.	1992 Rudolph A. Marcus, Can.-U.S.
1915 Richard M. Willstätter, Ger.	1961 Melvin Calvin, U.S.	1993 Kary B. Mullis, U.S.;
1918 Fritz Haber, Ger.	1962 John C. Kendrew, Max F. Perutz, UK	Michael Smith, UK-Can.
1920 Walther H. Nernst, Ger.	1963 Giulio Natta, It.; Karl Ziegler, Ger.	1994 George A. Olah, U.S.
1921 Frederick Soddy, UK	1964 Dorothy C. Hodgkin, UK	1995 Paul Crutzen, Neth.; Mario Molina,
1922 Francis W. Aston, UK	1965 Robert B. Woodward, U.S.	Mex.-U.S.; Sherwood Rowland, U.S.
1923 Fritz Pregl, Austria	1966 Robert S. Mulliken, U.S.	1996 Sir Harold W. Kroto, UK;
1925 Richard A. Zsigmondy, Ger.	1967 Manfred Eigen, Ger.; Ronald G. W.	Robert F. Curl Jr.,
1926 Theodor Svedberg, Swed.	Norrish, George Porter, UK	Richard E. Smalley, U.S.
1927 Heinrich O. Wieland, Ger.	1968 Lars Onsager, U.S.	1997 Paul D. Boyer, U.S., & John E.
1928 Adolf O. R. Windaus, Ger.	1969 Derek H. R. Barton, UK;	Walker, UK; Jens C. Skou, Den.
1929 Sir Arthur Harden, UK;	Odd Hassel, Nor.	1998 Walter Kohn, U.S.;
Hans von Euler-Chelpin, Swed.	1970 Luis F. Leloir, Arg.	John A. Pople, UK
1930 Hans Fischer, Ger.	1971 Gerhard Herzberg, Can.	1999 Ahmed H. Zewail, U.S.
1931 Friedrich Bergius, Carl Bosch, Ger.	1972 Christian B. Anfinsen, Stanford	2000 Alan J. Heeger, U.S.;
1932 Irving Langmuir, U.S.	Moore, William H. Stein, U.S.	Alan G. MacDiarmid, N. Zea.-U.S.;
1934 Harold C. Urey, U.S.	1973 Ernst Otto Fischer, Ger.;	Hideki Shirakawa, Jpn.
1935 Frédéric and Irene Joliot-Curie, Fr.	Geoffrey Wilkinson, UK	2001 K. Barry Sharpless,
1936 Peter J. W. Debye, Neth.	1974 Paul J. Flory, U.S.	William S. Knowles, U.S.;
1937 Walter N. Haworth, UK;	1975 John Cornforth, Austral.-UK;	Ryoji Noyori, Jpn.
Paul Karrer, Switz.	Vladimir Prelog, Bosnia-Switz.	2002 John B. Fenn, U.S.;
1938 Richard Kuhn, Ger.	1976 William N. Lipscomb, U.S.	Koichi Tanaka, Jpn.;
1939 Adolf F. J. Butenandt, Ger.;	1977 Ilya Prigogine, Belg.	Kurt Wüthrich, Switz.
Leopold Ruzicka, Switz.	1978 Peter Mitchell, UK	2003 Peter Agre,
1943 George de Hevesy, Hung.	1979 Herbert C. Brown, U.S.;	Roderick MacKinnon, U.S.
1944 Otto Hahn, Ger.	Georg Wittig, Ger.	2004 Aaron Ciechanover, Avram Hershko,
1945 Artturi I. Virtanen, Fin.	1980 Paul Berg, Walter Gilbert, U.S.;	Isr.; Irwin Rose, U.S.
1946 James B. Sumner, John H.	Frederick Sanger, UK	2005 Yves Chauvin, Fr.; Robert H.
Northrop, Wendell M. Stanley, U.S.	1981 Kenichi Fukui, Jpn.;	Grubbs, Richard R. Schrock, U.S.
1947 Sir Robert Robinson, UK	Roald Hoffmann, U.S.	2006 Roger D. Kornberg, U.S.
1948 Arne W. K. Tiselius, Swed.	1982 Aaron Klug, UK-Lith.	2007 Gerhard Ertl, Ger.
1949 William F. Giauque, U.S.	1983 Henry Taube, Can.	2008 Martin Chalfie, Roger Y. Tsien,
	1984 Robert Bruce Merrifield, U.S.	Osamu Shimomura, U.S.

Physiology or Medicine

1901 Emil A. von Behring, Ger.	1931 Otto H. Warburg, Ger.	1954 John F. Enders, Frederick C.
1902 Sir Ronald Ross, UK	1932 Edgar D. Adrian,	Robbins, Thomas H. Weller, U.S.
1903 Niels R. Finsen, Den.	Sir Charles S. Sherrington, UK	1955 Alex H. T. Theorell, Swed.
1904 Ivan P. Pavlov, Russ.	1933 Thomas H. Morgan, U.S.	1956 André F. Cournand,
1905 Robert Koch, Ger.	1934 George R. Minot, William P. Murphy,	Dickinson W. Richards, U.S.;
1906 Camillo Golgi, It.;	G. H. Whipple, U.S.	Werner Forssmann, Ger.
Santiago Ramon y Cajal, Spain	1935 Hans Spemann, Ger.	1957 Daniel Bovet, It.
1907 Charles L. A. Laveran, Fr.	1936 Sir Henry H. Dale, UK;	1958 George W. Beadle, Edward L.
1908 Paul Ehrlich, Ger.;	Otto Loewi, U.S.	Tatum, Joshua Lederberg, U.S.
Ilya Mechnikov, Fr.	1937 Albert Szent-Gyorgyi, Hung.-U.S.	1959 Arthur Kornberg,
1909 Emil T. Kocher, Switz.	1938 Corneille J. F. Heymans, Belg.	Severo Ochoa, U.S.
1910 Albrecht Kossel, Ger.	1939 Gerhard Domagk, Ger.	1960 Sir F. MacFarlane Burnet, Austral.;
1911 Allvar Gullstrand, Swed.	1943 Henrik C. P. Dam, Den.;	Peter B. Medawar, UK
1912 Alexis Carrel, Fr.	Edward A. Doisy, U.S.	1961 Georg von Békésy, U.S.
1913 Charles R. Richet, Fr.	1944 Joseph Erlanger,	1962 Francis H. C. Crick,
1914 Robert Bárány, Austria	Herbert S. Gasser, U.S.	Maurice H. F. Wilkins, UK;
1919 Jules Bordet, Belg.	1945 Ernst B. Chain, Sir Alexander	James D. Watson, U.S.
1920 Schack A. S. Krogh, Den.	Fleming, Sir Howard W. Florey, UK	1963 Sir John C. Eccles, Austral.;
1922 Archibald V. Hill, UK;	1946 Hermann J. Muller, U.S.	Alan L. Hodgkin,
Otto F. Meyerhof, Ger.	1947 Carl F. Cori, Gerty T. Cori, U.S.;	Andrew F. Huxley, UK
1923 Frederick G. Banting, Can.;	Bernardo A. Houssay, Arg.	1964 Konrad E. Bloch, U.S.;
John J. R. Macleod, Scot.	1948 Paul H. Müller, Switz.	Feodor Lynen, Ger.
1924 Willem Einthoven, Neth.	1949 Walter R. Hess, Switz.;	1965 François Jacob, André Lwoff,
1926 Johannes A. G. Fibiger, Den.	Antonio Moniz, Port.	Jacques Monod, Fr.
1927 Julius Wagner-Jauregg, Austrian	1950 Philip S. Hench, Edward C. Kendall,	1966 Charles B. Huggins,
1928 Charles J. H. Nicolle, Fr.	U.S.; Tadeus Reichstein, Switz.	Peyton Rous, U.S.
1929 Christiaan Eijkman, Neth.;	1951 Max Theiler, U.S.	1967 Ragnar Granit, Swed.;
Sir Frederick G. Hopkins, UK	1952 Selman A. Waksman, U.S.	Haldan Keffer Hartline,
1930 Karl Landsteiner, U.S.	1953 Hans A. Krebs, UK;	George Wald, U.S.
	Fritz A. Lipmann, U.S.	

1968 Robert W. Holley,
H. Gobind Khorana,
Marshall W. Nirenberg, U.S.
1969 Max Delbrück, Alfred D. Hershey,
Salvador Luria, U.S.
1970 Julius Axelrod, U.S.;
Sir Bernard Katz, UK;
Ulf von Euler, Swed.
1971 Earl W. Sutherland Jr., U.S.
1972 Gerald M. Edelman, U.S.;
Rodney R. Porter, UK
1973 Karl von Frisch, Ger.;
Konrad Lorenz, Austria;
Nikolaas Tinbergen, UK
1974 Albert Claude, Lux.-U.S.;
George Emil Palade, Rom.-U.S.;
Christian de Duve, Belg.
1975 David Baltimore,
Howard Temin, U.S.;
Renato Dulbecco, It.-U.S.
1976 Baruch S. Blumberg,
Daniel Carleton Gajdusek, U.S.
1977 Rosalyn S. Yalow,
Roger C.L. Guillemin,
Andrew V. Schally, U.S.
1978 Daniel Nathans,
Hamilton O. Smith, U.S.;
Werner Arber, Switz.
1979 Allan M. Cormack, U.S.;
Godfrey N. Hounsfield, UK

1980 Baruj Benacerraf, George Snell,
U.S.; Jean Dausset, Fr.
1981 Roger W. Sperry, David H. Hubel,
Torsten N. Wiesel, U.S.
1982 Sune K. Bergström,
Bengt I. Samuelsson, Swed.;
John R. Vane, UK
1983 Barbara McClintock, U.S.
1984 César Milstein, UK-Arg.;
Georges J. F. Köhler, Ger.;
Niels K. Jerne, UK-Den.
1985 Michael S. Brown,
Joseph L. Goldstein, U.S.
1986 Rita Levi-Montalcini, It.-U.S.;
Stanley Cohen, U.S.
1987 Susumu Tonegawa, Jpn.
1988 Gertrude B. Elion,
George H. Hitchings, U.S;
Sir James Black, UK
1989 J. Michael Bishop,
Harold E. Varmus, U.S.
1990 Joseph E. Murray,
E. Donnall Thomas, U.S.
1991 Edwin Neher, Bert Sakmann, Ger.
1992 Edmond H. Fisher,
Edwin G. Krebs, U.S.
1993 Phillip A. Sharp, U.S.;
Richard J. Roberts, UK
1994 Alfred G. Gilman,
Martin Rodbell, U.S.

1995 Edward B. Lewis,
Eric F. Wieschaus, U.S.;
Christiane Nüsslein-Volhard, Ger.
1996 Peter C. Doherty, Austral.;
Rolf M. Zinkernagel, Switz.
1997 Stanley B. Prusiner, U.S.
1998 Robert F. Furchgott,
Louis J. Ignarro, Ferid Murad, U.S.
1999 Günter Blobel, U.S.
2000 Arvid Carlsson, Swed.;
Paul Greengard, U.S.;
Eric R. Kandel, Austria-U.S.
2001 Leland H. Hartwell, U.S.;
R. Timothy (Tim) Hunt,
Sir Paul M. Nurse, UK
2002 Sydney Brenner, John E. Sulston,
UK; H. Robert Horvitz, U.S.
2003 Paul C. Lauterbur, U.S.;
Sir Peter Mansfield, UK
2004 Richard Axel, Linda B. Buck, U.S.
2005 Barry J. Marshall,
J. Robin Warren, Australia
2006 Andrew Z. Fire, Craig C. Mello, U.S.
2007 Mario R. Capecchi,
Oliver Smithies, U.S.;
Sir Martin J. Evans, UK
2008 Harald zur Hausen, Ger.;
Françoise Barré-Sinoussi,
Luc Montagnier, Fr.

Literature

1901 Rene F. A. Sully Prudhomme, Fr.
1902 Theodor Mommsen, Ger.
1903 Bjørnstjerne Bjørnson, Nor.
1904 Fréderic Mistral, Fr.;
José Echegaray y Eizaguirre, Spain
1905 Henryk Sienkiewicz, Pol.
1906 Giosuè Carducci, It.
1907 Rudyard Kipling, UK
1908 Rudolf C. Eucken, Ger.
1909 Selma Lagerlöf, Swed.
1910 Paul J. L. Heyse, Ger.
1911 Maurice Maeterlinck, Belg.
1912 Gerhart Hauptmann, Ger.
1913 Rabindranath Tagore, India
1915 Romain Rolland, Fr.
1916 Verner von Heidenstam, Swed.
1917 Karl A. Gjellerup,
Henrik Pontoppidan, Den.
1919 Carl F. G. Spitteler, Switz.
1920 Knut Hamsun, Nor.
1921 Anatole France, Fr.
1922 Jacinto Benavente, Spain
1923 William Butler Yeats, Ire.
1924 Wladyslaw S. Reymont, Pol.
1925 George Bernard Shaw, Ire.-UK
1926 Grazia Deledda, It.
1927 Henri Bergson, Fr.
1928 Sigrid Undset, Nor.
1929 Thomas Mann, Ger.
1930 Sinclair Lewis, U.S.
1931 Erik A. Karlfeldt, Swed.
1932 John Galsworthy, UK
1933 Ivan A. Bunin, USSR
1934 Luigi Pirandello, It.
1936 Eugene O'Neill, U.S.
1937 Roger Martin du Gard, Fr.

1938 Pearl S. Buck, U.S.
1939 Frans E. Sillanpää, Fin.
1944 Johannes V. Jensen, Den.
1945 Gabriela Mistral, Chile
1946 Hermann Hesse, Ger.-Switz.
1947 André Gide, Fr.
1948 T. S. Eliot, UK
1949 William Faulkner, U.S.
1950 Bertrand Russell, UK
1951 Pär F. Lagerkvist, Swed.
1952 François Mauriac, Fr.
1953 Sir Winston Churchill, UK
1954 Ernest Hemingway, U.S.
1955 Halldór K. Laxness, Ice.
1956 Juan Ramón Jiménez, Spain
1957 Albert Camus, Fr.
1958 Boris L. Pasternak, USSR
(declined)
1959 Salvatore Quasimodo, It.
1960 Saint-John Perse, Fr.
1961 Ivo Andric, Yugo.
1962 John Steinbeck, U.S.
1963 Giorgos Seferis, Greece
1964 Jean-Paul Sartre, Fr. (declined)
1965 Mikhail Sholokhov, USSR
1966 Shmuel Yosef Agnon, Isr.;
Nelly Sachs, Swed.
1967 Miguel Angel Asturias, Guat.
1968 Yasunari Kawabata, Jpn.
1969 Samuel Beckett, Ire.
1970 Aleksandr I. Solzhenitsyn, USSR
1971 Pablo Neruda, Chile
1972 Heinrich Böll, Ger.
1973 Patrick White, Austral.
1974 Eyvind Johnson,
Harry Edmund Martinson, Swed.

1975 Eugenio Montale, It.
1976 Saul Bellow, U.S.
1977 Vicente Aleixandre, Spain
1978 Isaac Bashevis Singer, U.S.
1979 Odysseus Elytis, Greece
1980 Czeslaw Milosz, Pol.-U.S.
1981 Elias Canetti, Bulg.-UK
1982 Gabriel García Márquez, Colombia
1983 William Golding, UK
1984 Jaroslav Siefert, Czech.
1985 Claude Simon, Fr.
1986 Wole Soyinka, Nigeria
1987 Joseph Brodsky, USSR-U.S.
1988 Naguib Mahfouz, Egypt
1989 Camilo José Cela, Spain
1990 Octavio Paz, Mex.
1991 Nadine Gordimer, S. Afr.
1992 Derek Walcott, St. Lucia
1993 Toni Morrison, U.S.
1994 Kenzaburo Oe, Jpn.
1995 Seamus Heaney, Ire.
1996 Wislawa Szymborska, Pol.
1997 Dario Fo, It.
1998 Jose Saramago, Por.
1999 Günter Grass, Ger.
2000 Gao Xingjian, China-Fr.
2001 Sir V.S. Naipaul, UK
2002 Imre Kertész, Hung.
2003 J. M. Coetzee, S. Afr.
2004 Elfriede Jelinek, Austria
2005 Harold Pinter, UK
2006 Orhan Pamuk, Turk.
2007 Doris Lessing, UK
2008 Jean-Marie Gustave Le Clézio, Fr.

Peace

1901 Jean H. Dunant, Switz.;
Frédéric Passy, Fr.
1902 Élie Ducommun,
Charles A. Gobat, Switz.
1903 Sir William R. Cremer, UK
1904 Institute of International Law
1905 Baroness Bertha von Suttner,
Austria
1906 Theodore Roosevelt, U.S.

1907 Ernesto T. Moneta, It.;
Louis Renault, Fr.
1908 Klas P. Arnoldson, Swed.;
Fredrik Bajer, Den.
1909 Auguste M. F. Beernaert, Belg.;
Paul H. B. B. d'Estournelles
de Constant, Fr.
1910 Permanent Intl. Peace Bureau
1911 Tobias M. C. Asser, Neth.;
Alfred H. Fried, Austria

1912 Elihu Root, U.S.
1913 Henri La Fontaine, Belg.
1917 International Red Cross
1919 Woodrow Wilson, U.S.
1920 Léon V. A. Bourgeois, Fr.
1921 Karl H. Branting, Swed.;
Christian L. Lange, Nor.
1922 Fridtjof Nansen, Nor.

1925 Sir J. Austen Chamberlain, UK; Charles G. Dawes, U.S.	1961 Dag Hammarskjöld, Swed.	1988 UN Peacekeeping Forces
1926 Aristide Briand, Fr.; Gustav Stresemann, Ger.	1962 Linus C. Pauling, U.S.	1989 Dalai Lama (Tenzin Gyatso), Tibet
1927 Ferdinand E. Buisson, Fr.; Ludwig Quidde, Ger.	1963 International Red Cross, League of Red Cross Societies	1990 Mikhail S. Gorbachev, USSR
1929 Frank B. Kellogg, U.S.	1964 Martin Luther King Jr., U.S.	1991 Aung San Suu Kyi, Burm.
1930 Nathan Söderblom, Swed.	1965 UN Children's Fund (UNICEF)	1992 Rigoberta Menchú Tum, Guat.
1931 Jane Addams, Nicholas Murray Butler, U.S.	1968 René Cassin, Fr.	1993 Frederik W. de Klerk, Nelson Mandela, S. Afr.
1933 Sir Norman Angell, UK	1969 Intl. Labor Organization	1994 Yasser Arafat, Pal.; Shimon Peres, Yitzhak Rabin, Isr.
1934 Arthur Henderson, UK	1970 Norman E. Borlaug, U.S.	1995 Joseph Rotblat, Pol.-UK; Pugwash Conference
1935 Carl von Ossietzky, Ger.	1971 Willy Brandt, Ger.	
1936 Carlos Saavedra Lamas, Arg.	1973 Henry Kissinger, U.S.; Le Duc Tho, N. Viet. (Tho declined)	1996 Bishop Carlos Ximenes Belo, José Ramos-Horta, Timor-Leste
1937 Viscount Cecil of Chelwood, UK	1974 Eisaku Sato, Jpn.; Seán MacBride, Ire.	1997 Jody Williams, U.S.; International Campaign to Ban Landmines
1938 Nansen International Office for Refugees	1975 Andrei Sakharov, USSR	1998 John Hume, David Trimble, N. Ire.
1944 International Red Cross	1976 Mairead Corrigan, Betty Williams, N. Ire.	1999 Doctors Without Borders (Médecins Sans Frontières), Fr.
1945 Cordell Hull, U.S.	1977 Amnesty International	2000 Kim Dae-Jung, S. Kor.
1946 Emily G. Balch, John R. Mott, U.S.	1978 Anwar al-Sadat, Egypt; Menachem Begin, Isr.	2001 UN; Kofi Annan, Ghana
1947 Friends Service Council, UK; Amer. Friends Service Committee, U.S.	1979 Mother Teresa of Calcutta, Alb.-Ind.	2002 Jimmy Carter, U.S.
1949 Lord John Boyd Orr of Brechin, UK	1980 Adolfo Pérez Esquivel, Arg.	2003 Shirin Ebadi, Iran
1950 Ralph J. Bunche, U.S.	1981 Office of UN High Com. for Refugees	2004 Wangari Maathai, Kenya
1951 Léon Jouhaux, Fr.		2005 Mohamed ElBaradei, Egypt; International Atomic Energy Agency, Austria
1952 Albert Schweitzer, Fr.	1982 Alva Myrdal, Swed.; Alfonso García Robles, Mex.	
1953 George C. Marshall, U.S.	1983 Lech Walesa, Pol.	2006 Muhammad Yunus, Grameen Bank, Bang.
1954 Office of UN High Com. for Refugees	1984 Bishop Desmond Tutu, S. Afr.	2007 Intergovernmental Panel on Climate Change, Switz.; Albert Arnold Gore Jr., U.S.
1957 Lester B. Pearson, Can.	1985 Intl. Physicians for the Prevention of Nuclear War, U.S.	
1958 Georges Pire, Belg.	1986 Elie Wiesel, Rom.-U.S.	
1959 Philip J. Noel-Baker, UK	1987 Oscar Arias Sánchez, Costa Rica	2008 Martti Ahtisaari, Finland
1960 Albert J. Lutuli, S. Afr.		

Nobel Memorial Prize in Economic Science

1969 Ragnar Frisch, Nor.; Jan Tinbergen, Neth.	1983 Gerard Debreu, Fr.-U.S.	1997 Robert C. Merton, U.S.; Myron S. Scholes, Can.-U.S.
1970 Paul A. Samuelson, U.S.	1984 Richard Stone, UK	1998 Amartya Sen, India
1971 Simon Kuznets, U.S.	1985 Franco Modigliani, It.-U.S.	1999 Robert A. Mundell, Can.
1972 Kenneth J. Arrow, U.S.; John R. Hicks, UK	1986 James M. Buchanan, U.S.	2000 James J. Heckman, Daniel L. McFadden, U.S.
1973 Wassily Leontief, U.S.	1987 Robert M. Solow, U.S.	
1974 Gunnar Myrdal, Swed.; Friedrich A. von Hayek, Austria	1988 Maurice Allais, Fr.	2001 George A. Akerlof, A. Michael Spence, Joseph E. Stiglitz, U.S.
	1989 Trygve Haavelmo, Nor.	
1975 Tjalling Koopmans, Neth.-U.S.; Leonid Kantorovich, USSR	1990 Harry M. Markowitz, William F. Sharpe, Merton H. Miller, U.S.	2002 Daniel Kahneman, U.S.-Isr.; Vernon L. Smith, U.S.
1976 Milton Friedman, U.S.		2003 Robert F. Engle, U.S.; Clive W. J. Granger, UK
1977 Bertil Ohlin, Swed.; James E. Meade, UK	1991 Ronald H. Coase, UK-U.S.	
	1992 Gary S. Becker, U.S.	2004 Finn E. Kydland, Nor.; Edward C. Prescott, U.S.
1978 Herbert A. Simon, U.S.	1993 Robert W. Fogel, Douglass C. North, U.S.	
1979 Theodore W. Schultz, U.S.; Sir Arthur Lewis, UK	1994 John C. Harsanyi, John F. Nash, U.S.; Reinhard Selten, Ger.	2005 Robert J. Aumann, Israel-U.S.; Thomas C. Schelling, U.S.
1980 Lawrence R. Klein, U.S.	1995 Robert E. Lucas Jr., U.S.	2006 Edmund S. Phelps, U.S.
1981 James Tobin, U.S.	1996 James A. Mirrlees, UK; William Vickrey, Can.-U.S.	2007 Leonid Hurwicz, Eric S. Maskin, Roger B. Myerson, U.S.
1982 George J. Stigler, U.S.		2008 Paul Krugman, U.S.

Pulitzer Prizes in Journalism, Letters, and Music

Endowed by Joseph Pulitzer (1847-1911), publisher of the *New York World*, in a bequest to Columbia Univ. and awarded annually, in years shown, for work the previous year. Prizes are now $10,000 in each category, except Public Service (in Journalism), for which a medal is given. For letters and music, prizes in past years are listed; if a year is omitted, no award was given that year.

Journalism, 2009

Public Service: *Las Vegas Sun*, notably reporting by Alexandra Berzon, for exposing the high death rate of construction workers on the Las Vegas strip amid lax regulation enforcement.

Breaking News Reporting: *NY Times* staff for coverage of the sex scandal that resulted in the resignation of Gov. Eliot Spitzer, breaking and developing the story on its website.

Investigative Reporting: David Barstow, *NY Times*, for reporting on retired generals working as radio and TV analysts, and their ties with the Pentagon and/or companies that profited from military policies they defended.

Explanatory Reporting: Bettina Boxall and Julie Cart, *LA Times*, for exploration of the cost/effectiveness of fighting wildfires in the western U.S.

Local Reporting: *Detroit Free Press* staff, notably Jim Schaefer and M. L. Elrick, for uncovering a pattern of lies by Mayor Kwame Kilpatrick; and Ryan Gabrielson and Paul Giblin, *East Valley Tribune* (Mesa, AZ) for revealing how a sheriff's focus on illegal immigration endangered public safety and violent crime investigation.

National Reporting: *St. Petersburg Times* (FL), for "PolitiFact," its fact-checking initiative of the 2008 presidential campaign that separated rhetoric from truth to enlighten voters.

International Reporting: *NY Times* staff, for coverage of escalating military and political challenges in Afghanistan and Pakistan, reporting under perilous conditions.

Feature Writing: Lane DeGregory, *St. Petersburg Times* (FL), for her story of a neglected girl—unable to talk or feed herself—adopted by a new family committed to her nurturing.

Commentary: Eugene Robinson, *Washington Post*, for eloquent columns on the 2008 presidential campaign that focus on the election of the first African American president.

Criticism: Holland Cotter, *NY Times*, for his art reviews marked by acute observation, luminous writing, and dramatic storytelling.

Editorial Writing: Mark Mahoney, *The Post-Star* (Glens Falls, NY), for editorials on the perils of local government secrecy.

Editorial Cartooning: Steve Breen, *San Diego Union Tribune*.

Breaking News Photog.: Patrick Farrell, *Miami Herald*, for images of the humanitarian disaster in Haiti after Hurricane Ike.

Feature Photog.: Damon Winter, *NY Times*, for his pictures capturing multiple facets of Barack Obama's campaign.

Pulitzer Prizes—Letters

Fiction

1918 Ernest Poole, *His Family*
1919 Booth Tarkington, *The Magnificent Ambersons*
1921 Edith Wharton, *The Age of Innocence*
1922 Booth Tarkington, *Alice Adams*
1923 Willa Cather, *One of Ours*
1924 Margaret Wilson, *The Able McLaughlins*
1925 Edna Ferber, *So Big*
1926 Sinclair Lewis, *Arrowsmith* (refused prize)
1927 Louis Bromfield, *Early Autumn*
1928 Thornton Wilder, *Bridge of San Luis Rey*
1929 Julia M. Peterkin, *Scarlet Sister Mary*
1930 Oliver LaFarge, *Laughing Boy*
1931 Margaret Ayer Barnes, *Years of Grace*
1932 Pearl S. Buck, *The Good Earth*
1933 T. S. Stribling, *The Store*
1934 Caroline Miller, *Lamb in His Bosom*
1935 Josephine W. Johnson, *Now in November*
1936 Harold L. Davis, *Honey in the Horn*
1937 Margaret Mitchell, *Gone With the Wind*
1938 John P. Marquand, *The Late George Apley*
1939 Marjorie Kinnan Rawlings, *The Yearling*
1940 John Steinbeck, *The Grapes of Wrath*
1942 Ellen Glasgow, *In This Our Life*
1943 Upton Sinclair, *Dragon's Teeth*
1944 Martin Flavin, *Journey in the Dark*
1945 John Hersey, *A Bell for Adano*
1947 Robert Penn Warren, *All the King's Men*
1948 James A. Michener, *Tales of the South Pacific*
1949 James Gould Cozzens, *Guard of Honor*
1950 A. B. Guthrie Jr., *The Way West*
1951 Conrad Richter, *The Town*
1952 Herman Wouk, *The Caine Mutiny*
1953 Ernest Hemingway, *The Old Man and the Sea*
1955 William Faulkner, *A Fable*
1956 MacKinlay Kantor, *Andersonville*
1958 James Agee, *A Death in the Family*
1959 Robert Lewis Taylor, *The Travels of Jaimie McPheeters*
1960 Allen Drury, *Advise and Consent*
1961 Harper Lee, *To Kill a Mockingbird*
1962 Edwin O'Connor, *The Edge of Sadness*
1963 William Faulkner, *The Reivers*
1965 Shirley Ann Grau, *The Keepers of the House*
1966 Katherine Anne Porter, *Collected Stories*
1967 Bernard Malamud, *The Fixer*
1968 William Styron, *The Confessions of Nat Turner*
1969 N. Scott Momaday, *House Made of Dawn*
1970 Jean Stafford, *Collected Stories*
1972 Wallace Stegner, *Angle of Repose*
1973 Eudora Welty, *The Optimist's Daughter*
1975 Michael Shaara, *The Killer Angels*
1976 Saul Bellow, *Humboldt's Gift*
1978 James Alan McPherson, *Elbow Room*
1979 John Cheever, *The Stories of John Cheever*
1980 Norman Mailer, *The Executioner's Song*
1981 John Kennedy Toole, *A Confederacy of Dunces*
1982 John Updike, *Rabbit Is Rich*
1983 Alice Walker, *The Color Purple*
1984 William Kennedy, *Ironweed*
1985 Alison Lurie, *Foreign Affairs*
1986 Larry McMurtry, *Lonesome Dove*
1987 Peter Taylor, *A Summons to Memphis*
1988 Toni Morrison, *Beloved*
1989 Anne Tyler, *Breathing Lessons*
1990 Oscar Hijuelos, *The Mambo Kings Play Songs of Love*
1991 John Updike, *Rabbit at Rest*
1992 Jane Smiley, *A Thousand Acres*
1993 Robert Olen Butler, *A Good Scent From a Strange Mountain*
1994 E. Annie Proulx, *The Shipping News*
1995 Carol Shields, *The Stone Diaries*
1996 Richard Ford, *Independence Day*
1997 Steven Millhauser, *Martin Dressler: The Tale of an American Dreamer*
1998 Philip Roth, *American Pastoral*
1999 Michael Cunningham, *The Hours*
2000 Jhumpa Lahiri, *Interpreter of Maladies*
2001 Michael Chabon, *The Amazing Adventures of Kavalier & Clay*
2002 Richard Russo, *Empire Falls*
2003 Jeffrey Eugenides, *Middlesex*
2004 Edward P. Jones, *The Known World*
2005 Marilynne Robinson, *Gilead*
2006 Geraldine Brooks, *March*
2007 Cormac McCarthy, *The Road*
2008 Junot Díaz, *The Brief Wondrous Life of Oscar Wao*
2009 Elizabeth Strout, *Olive Kitteridge*

Drama

1918 Jesse Lynch Williams, *Why Marry?*
1920 Eugene O'Neill, *Beyond the Horizon*
1921 Zona Gale, *Miss Lulu Bett*
1922 Eugene O'Neill, *Anna Christie*
1923 Owen Davis, *Icebound*
1924 Hatcher Hughes, *Hell-Bent for Heaven*
1925 Sidney Howard, *They Knew What They Wanted*
1926 George Kelly, *Craig's Wife*
1927 Paul Green, *In Abraham's Bosom*
1928 Eugene O'Neill, *Strange Interlude*
1929 Elmer Rice, *Street Scene*
1930 Marc Connelly, *The Green Pastures*
1931 Susan Glaspell, *Alison's House*
1932 George S. Kaufman, Morrie Ryskind, and Ira Gershwin, *Of Thee I Sing*
1933 Maxwell Anderson, *Both Your Houses*
1934 Sidney Kingsley, *Men in White*
1935 Zoe Akins, *The Old Maid*
1936 Robert E. Sherwood, *Idiot's Delight*
1937 George S. Kaufman and Moss Hart, *You Can't Take It With You*
1938 Thornton Wilder, *Our Town*
1939 Robert E. Sherwood, *Abe Lincoln in Illinois*
1940 William Saroyan, *The Time of Your Life*
1941 Robert E. Sherwood, *There Shall Be No Night*
1943 Thornton Wilder, *The Skin of Our Teeth*
1945 Mary Chase, *Harvey*
1946 Russel Crouse and Howard Lindsay, *State of the Union*
1948 Tennessee Williams, *A Streetcar Named Desire*
1949 Arthur Miller, *Death of a Salesman*
1950 Richard Rodgers, Oscar Hammerstein II, and Joshua Logan, *South Pacific*
1952 Joseph Kramm, *The Shrike*
1953 William Inge, *Picnic*
1954 John Patrick, *Teahouse of the August Moon*
1955 Tennessee Williams, *Cat on a Hot Tin Roof*
1956 Frances Goodrich and Albert Hackett, *The Diary of Anne Frank*
1957 Eugene O'Neill, *Long Day's Journey Into Night*
1958 Ketti Frings, *Look Homeward, Angel*
1959 Archibald MacLeish, *J. B.*
1960 George Abbott, Jerome Weidman, Sheldon Harnick, and Jerry Bock, *Fiorello!*
1961 Tad Mosel, *All the Way Home*
1962 Frank Loesser and Abe Burrows, *How to Succeed in Business Without Really Trying*
1965 Frank D. Gilroy, *The Subject Was Roses*
1967 Edward Albee, *A Delicate Balance*
1969 Howard Sackler, *The Great White Hope*
1970 Charles Gordone, *No Place to Be Somebody*
1971 Paul Zindel, *The Effect of Gamma Rays on Man-in-the-Moon Marigolds*
1973 Jason Miller, *That Championship Season*
1975 Edward Albee, *Seascape*
1976 Michael Bennett, James Kirkwood, Nicholas Dante, Marvin Hamlisch, and Edward Kleban, *A Chorus Line*
1977 Michael Cristofer, *The Shadow Box*
1978 Donald L. Coburn, *The Gin Game*
1979 Sam Shepard, *Buried Child*
1980 Lanford Wilson, *Talley's Folly*
1981 Beth Henley, *Crimes of the Heart*
1982 Charles Fuller, *A Soldier's Play*
1983 Marsha Norman, *'night, Mother*
1984 David Mamet, *Glengarry Glen Ross*
1985 Stephen Sondheim and James Lapine, *Sunday in the Park With George*
1987 August Wilson, *Fences*
1988 Alfred Uhry, *Driving Miss Daisy*
1989 Wendy Wasserstein, *The Heidi Chronicles*
1990 August Wilson, *The Piano Lesson*
1991 Neil Simon, *Lost in Yonkers*
1992 Robert Schenkkan, *The Kentucky Cycle*
1993 Tony Kushner, *Angels in America: Millennium Approaches*
1994 Edward Albee, *Three Tall Women*
1995 Horton Foote, *The Young Man From Atlanta*
1996 Jonathan Larson, *Rent*
1998 Paula Vogel, *How I Learned to Drive*
1999 Margaret Edson, *Wit*
2000 Donald Margulies, *Dinner With Friends*
2001 David Auburn, *Proof*
2002 Suzan-Lori Parks, *Topdog/Underdog*
2003 Nilo Cruz, *Anna in the Tropics*
2004 Doug Wright, *I Am My Own Wife*
2005 John Patrick Shanley, *Doubt, a parable*
2007 David Lindsay-Abaire, *Rabbit Hole*
2008 Tracy Letts, *August: Osage County*
2009 Lynn Nottage, *Ruined*

History (U.S.)

1917 J. J. Jusserand, *With Americans of Past and Present Days*
1918 James Ford Rhodes, *History of the Civil War*
1920 Justin H. Smith, *The War With Mexico*
1921 William Sowden Sims, *The Victory at Sea*
1922 James Truslow Adams, *The Founding of New England*
1923 Charles Warren, *The Supreme Court in United States History*
1924 Charles Howard McIlwain, *The American Revolution: A Constitutional Interpretation*
1925 Frederick L. Paxton, *A History of the American Frontier*
1926 Edward Channing, *A History of the U.S.*
1927 Samuel Flagg Bemis, *Pinckney's Treaty*
1928 V. L. Parrington, *Main Currents in American Thought*
1929 Fred A. Shannon, *The Organization and Administration of the Union Army, 1861-65*
1930 Claude H. Van Tyne, *The War of Independence*
1931 Bernadotte E. Schmitt, *The Coming of the War, 1914*
1932 Gen. John J. Pershing, *My Experiences in the World War*
1933 Frederick J. Turner, *The Significance of Sections in American History*
1934 Herbert Agar, *The People's Choice*
1935 Charles McLean Andrews, *The Colonial Period of American History*
1936 Andrew C. McLaughlin, *The Constitutional History of the United States*
1937 Van Wyck Brooks, *The Flowering of New England*
1938 Paul Herman Buck, *The Road to Reunion, 1865-1900*
1939 Frank Luther Mott, *A History of American Magazines*
1940 Carl Sandburg, *Abraham Lincoln: The War Years*
1941 Marcus Lee Hansen, *The Atlantic Migration, 1607-1860*
1942 Margaret Leech, *Reveille in Washington*
1943 Esther Forbes, *Paul Revere and the World He Lived In*
1944 Merle Curti, *The Growth of American Thought*
1945 Stephen Bonsal, *Unfinished Business*
1946 Arthur M. Schlesinger Jr., *The Age of Jackson*
1947 James Phinney Baxter III, *Scientists Against Time*
1948 Bernard De Voto, *Across the Wide Missouri*
1949 Roy F. Nichols, *The Disruption of American Democracy*
1950 O. W. Larkin, *Art and Life in America*
1951 R. Carlyle Buley, *The Old Northwest: Pioneer Period 1815-1840*
1952 Oscar Handlin, *The Uprooted*
1953 George Dangerfield, *The Era of Good Feelings*
1954 Bruce Catton, *A Stillness at Appomattox*
1955 Paul Horgan, *Great River: The Rio Grande in North American History*
1956 Richard Hofstadter, *The Age of Reform*
1957 George F. Kennan, *Russia Leaves the War*
1958 Bray Hammond, *Banks and Politics in America—From the Revolution to the Civil War*
1959 Leonard D. White and Jean Schneider, *The Republican Era; 1869-1901*
1960 Margaret Leech, *In the Days of McKinley*
1961 Herbert Feis, *Between War and Peace: The Potsdam Conference*
1962 Lawrence H. Gibson, *The Triumphant Empire: Thunderclouds Gather in the West*
1963 Constance McLaughlin Green, *Washington: Village and Capital, 1800-1878*
1964 Sumner Chilton Powell, *Puritan Village: The Formation of a New England Town*
1965 Irwin Unger, *The Greenback Era*
1966 Perry Miller, *Life of the Mind in America*
1967 William H. Goetzmann, *Exploration and Empire: The Explorer and Scientist in the Winning of the American West*
1968 Bernard Bailyn, *The Ideological Origins of the American Revolution*
1969 Leonard W. Levy, *Origin of the Fifth Amendment*
1970 Dean Acheson, *Present at the Creation: My Years in the State Department*
1971 James McGregor Burns, *Roosevelt: The Soldier of Freedom*
1972 Carl N. Degler, *Neither Black nor White*
1973 Michael Kammen, *People of Paradox: An Inquiry Concerning the Origins of American Civilization*
1974 Daniel J. Boorstin, *The Americans: The Democratic Experience*
1975 Dumas Malone, *Jefferson and His Time*
1976 Paul Horgan, *Lamy of Santa Fe*
1977 David M. Potter, *The Impending Crisis*
1978 Alfred D. Chandler Jr., *The Visible Hand: The Managerial Revolution in American Business*
1979 Don E. Fehrenbacher, *The Dred Scott Case: Its Significance in American Law and Politics*
1980 Leon F. Litwack, *Been in the Storm So Long*

1981 Lawrence A. Cremin, *American Education: The National Experience, 1783-1876*
1982 C. Vann Woodward, ed., *Mary Chesnut's Civil War*
1983 Rhys L. Issac, *The Transformation of Virginia, 1740-1790*
1985 Thomas K. McCraw, *Prophets of Regulation*
1986 Walter A. McDougall, *The Heavens and the Earth*
1987 Bernard Bailyn, *Voyagers to the West*
1988 Robert V. Bruce, *The Launching of Modern American Science, 1846-1876*
1989 Taylor Branch, *Parting the Waters: America in the King Years, 1954-63*; and James M. McPherson, *Battle Cry of Freedom: The Civil War Era*
1990 Stanley Karnow, *In Our Image: America's Empire in the Philippines*
1991 Laurel Thatcher Ulrich, *A Midwife's Tale: The Life of Martha Ballard,* based on her diary, 1785-1812
1992 Mark E. Neely Jr., *The Fate of Liberty: Abraham Lincoln and Civil Liberties*
1993 Gordon S. Wood, *The Radicalism of the American Revolution*
1995 Doris Kearns Goodwin, *No Ordinary Time: Franklin and Eleanor Roosevelt: The Home Front in World War II*
1996 Alan Taylor, *William Cooper's Town: Power and Persuasion on the Frontier of the Early American Republic*
1997 Jack N. Rakove, *Original Meanings: Politics and Ideas in the Making of the Constitution*
1998 Edward J. Larson, *Summer for the Gods: The Scopes Trial and America's Continuing Debate Over Science and Religion*
1999 Edwin G. Burrows and Mike Wallace, *Gotham: A History of New York City to 1898*
2000 David M. Kennedy, *Freedom From Fear: The American People in Depression and War, 1929-1945*
2001 Joseph J. Ellis, *Founding Brothers: The Revolutionary Generation*
2002 Louis Menand, *The Metaphysical Club: A Story of Ideas in America*
2003 Rick Atkinson, *An Army at Dawn: The War in North Africa, 1942-1943*
2004 Steven Hahn, *A Nation Under Our Feet: Black Political Struggles in the Rural South from Slavery to the Great Migration*
2005 David Hackett Fischer, *Washington's Crossing*
2006 David M. Oshinsky, *Polio: An American Story*
2007 Gene Roberts and Hank Klibanoff, *The Race Beat: The Press, the Civil Rights Struggle, and the Awakening of a Nation*
2008 Daniel Walker Howe, *What Hath God Wrought: The Transformation of America, 1815-1848*
2009 Annette Gordon-Reed, *The Hemingses of Monticello: An American Family*

Biography or Autobiography

1917 Laura E. Richards and Maude Howe Elliott, assisted by Florence Howe Hall, *Julia Ward Howe*
1918 William Cabell Bruce, *Benjamin Franklin, Self-Revealed*
1919 Henry Adams, *The Education of Henry Adams*
1920 Albert J. Beveridge, *The Life of John Marshall*
1921 Edward Bok, *The Americanization of Edward Bok*
1922 Hamlin Garland, *A Daughter of the Middle Border*
1923 Burton J. Hendrick, *The Life and Letters of Walter H. Page*
1924 Michael Pupin, *From Immigrant to Inventor*
1925 M. A. DeWolfe Howe, *Barrett Wendell and His Letters*
1926 Harvey Cushing, *Life of Sir William Osler*
1927 Emory Holloway, *Whitman: An Interpretation in Narrative*
1928 Charles Edward Russell, *The American Orchestra and Theodore Thomas*
1929 Burton J. Hendrick, *The Training of an American: The Earlier Life and Letters of Walter H. Page*
1930 Marquis James, *The Raven* (Sam Houston)
1931 Henry James, *Charles W. Eliot*
1932 Henry F. Pringle, *Theodore Roosevelt*
1933 Allan Nevins, *Grover Cleveland*
1934 Tyler Dennett, *John Hay*
1935 Douglas Southall Freeman, *R. E. Lee*
1936 Ralph Barton Perry, *The Thought and Character of William James*
1937 Allan Nevins, *Hamilton Fish: The Inner History of the Grant Administration*
1938 Odell Shepard, *Pedlar's Progress* (Bronson Alcott); and Marquis James, *Andrew Jackson, 2 vols.*
1939 Carl Van Doren, *Benjamin Franklin*
1940 Ray Stannard Baker, *Woodrow Wilson, Life and Letters*
1941 Ola Elizabeth Winslow, *Jonathan Edwards*
1942 Forrest Wilson, *Crusader in Crinoline* (Harriet Beecher Stowe)

1943 Samuel Eliot Morison, *Admiral of the Ocean Sea* (Christopher Columbus)
1944 Carleton Mabee, *The American Leonardo: The Life of Samuel F. B. Morse*
1945 Russell Blaine Nye, *George Bancroft: Brahmin Rebel*
1946 Linny Marsh Wolfe, *Son of the Wilderness* (John Muir)
1947 William Allen White, *Autobiography of William Allen White*
1948 Margaret Clapp, *Forgotten First Citizen: John Bigelow*
1949 Robert E. Sherwood, *Roosevelt and Hopkins*
1950 Samuel Flagg Bemis, *John Quincy Adams and the Foundations of American Foreign Policy*
1951 Margaret Louise Coit, *John C. Calhoun: American Portrait*
1952 Merlo J. Pusey, *Charles Evans Hughes*
1953 David J. Mays, *Edmund Pendleton, 1721-1803*
1954 Charles A. Lindbergh, *The Spirit of St. Louis*
1955 William S. White, *The Taft Story*
1956 Talbot F. Hamlin, *Benjamin Henry Latrobe*
1957 John F. Kennedy, *Profiles in Courage*
1958 Douglas Southall Freeman (I-VI), John Alexander Carroll and Mary Wells Ashworth (VII), *George Washington*
1959 Arthur Walworth, *Woodrow Wilson: American Prophet*
1960 Samuel Eliot Morison, *John Paul Jones*
1961 David Donald, *Charles Sumner and the Coming of the Civil War*
1963 Leon Edel, *Henry James: Vols. 2-3*
1964 Walter Jackson Bate, *John Keats*
1965 Ernest Samuels, *Henry Adams*
1966 Arthur M. Schlesinger Jr., *A Thousand Days*
1967 Justin Kaplan, *Mr. Clemens and Mark Twain*
1968 George F. Kennan, *Memoirs (1925-1950)*
1969 B. L. Reid, *The Man From New York: John Quinn and His Friends*
1970 T. Harry Williams, *Huey Long*
1971 Lawrence Thompson, *Robert Frost: The Years of Triumph, 1915-1938*
1972 Joseph P. Lash, *Eleanor and Franklin*
1973 W. A. Swanberg, *Luce and His Empire*
1974 Louis Sheaffer, *O'Neill, Son and Artist*
1975 Robert A. Caro, *The Power Broker: Robert Moses and the Fall of New York*
1976 R. W. B. Lewis, *Edith Wharton: A Biography*
1977 John E. Mack, *A Prince of Our Disorder: The Life of T. E. Lawrence*
1978 Walter Jackson Bate, *Samuel Johnson*
1979 Leonard Baker, *Days of Sorrow and Pain: Leo Baeck and the Berlin Jews*
1980 Edmund Morris, *The Rise of Theodore Roosevelt*
1981 Robert K. Massie, *Peter the Great: His Life and World*
1982 William S. McFeely, *Grant: A Biography*
1983 Russell Baker, *Growing Up*
1984 Louis R. Harlan, *Booker T. Washington*
1985 Kenneth Silverman, *The Life and Times of Cotton Mather*
1986 Elizabeth Frank, *Louise Bogan: A Portrait*
1987 David J. Garrow, *Bearing the Cross: Martin Luther King Jr. and the Southern Christian Leadership Conference*
1988 David Herbert Donald, *Look Homeward: A Life of Thomas Wolfe*
1989 Richard Ellmann, *Oscar Wilde*
1990 Sebastian de Grazia, *Machiavelli in Hell*
1991 Steven Naifeh and Gregory White Smith, *Jackson Pollock: An American Saga*
1992 Lewis B. Puller Jr., *Fortunate Son: The Healing of a Vietnam Vet*
1993 David McCullough, *Truman*
1994 David Levering Lewis, *W.E.B. DuBois: Biography of a Race, 1868-1919*
1995 Joan D. Hedrick, *Harriet Beecher Stowe: A Life*
1996 Jack Miles, *God: A Biography*
1997 Frank McCourt, *Angela's Ashes: A Memoir*
1998 Katharine Graham, *Personal History*
1999 A. Scott Berg, *Lindbergh*
2000 Stacy Schiff, *Véra (Mrs. Vladimir Nabokov)*
2001 David Levering Lewis, *W.E.B. Du Bois: The Fight for Equality and the American Century, 1919-1963*
2002 David McCullough, *John Adams*
2003 Robert Caro, *The Years of Lyndon Johnson: Master of the Senate*
2004 William Taubman, *Khrushchev: The Man and His Era*
2005 Mark Stevens and Annalyn Swan, *de Kooning: An American Master*
2006 Kai Bird and Martin J. Sherwin, *American Prometheus: The Triumph and Tragedy of J. Robert Oppenheimer*
2007 Debby Applegate, *The Most Famous Man in America: The Biography of Henry Ward Beecher*
2008 John Matteson, *Eden's Outcasts: The Story of Louisa May Alcott and Her Father*
2009 Jon Meacham, *American Lion: Andrew Jackson in the White House*

American Poetry

Before 1922, awards were funded by the Poetry Society.

1918 Sara Teasdale, *Love Songs*
1919 Margaret Widdemer, *Old Road to Paradise*; Carl Sandburg, *Corn Huskers*
1922 Edwin Arlington Robinson, *Collected Poems*
1923 Edna St. Vincent Millay, *The Ballad of the Harp-Weaver; A Few Figs From Thistles*; other works
1924 Robert Frost, *New Hampshire: A Poem With Notes and Grace Notes*
1925 Edwin Arlington Robinson, *The Man Who Died Twice*
1926 Amy Lowell, *What's O'Clock*
1927 Leonora Speyer, *Fiddler's Farewell*
1928 Edwin Arlington Robinson, *Tristram*
1929 Stephen Vincent Benet, *John Brown's Body*
1930 Conrad Aiken, *Selected Poems*
1931 Robert Frost, *Collected Poems*
1932 George Dillon, *The Flowering Stone*
1933 Archibald MacLeish, *Conquistador*
1934 Robert Hillyer, *Collected Verse*
1935 Audrey Wurdemann, *Bright Ambush*
1936 Robert P. Tristram Coffin, *Strange Holiness*
1937 Robert Frost, *A Further Range*
1938 Marya Zaturenska, *Cold Morning Sky*
1939 John Gould Fletcher, *Selected Poems*
1940 Mark Van Doren, *Collected Poems*
1941 Leonard Bacon, *Sunderland Capture*
1942 William Rose Benet, *The Dust Which Is God*
1943 Robert Frost, *A Witness Tree*
1944 Stephen Vincent Benet, *Western Star*
1945 Karl Shapiro, *V-Letter and Other Poems*
1947 Robert Lowell, *Lord Weary's Castle*
1948 W. H. Auden, *The Age of Anxiety*
1949 Peter Viereck, *Terror and Decorum*
1950 Gwendolyn Brooks, *Annie Allen*
1951 Carl Sandburg, *Complete Poems*
1952 Marianne Moore, *Collected Poems*
1953 Archibald MacLeish, *Collected Poems*
1954 Theodore Roethke, *The Waking*
1955 Wallace Stevens, *Collected Poems*
1956 Elizabeth Bishop, *Poems, North and South*
1957 Richard Wilbur, *Things of This World*
1958 Robert Penn Warren, *Promises: Poems 1954-1956*
1959 Stanley Kunitz, *Selected Poems 1928-1958*
1960 W. D. Snodgrass, *Heart's Needle*
1961 Phyllis McGinley, *Times Three: Selected Verse From Three Decades*
1962 Alan Dugan, *Poems*
1963 William Carlos Williams, *Pictures From Breughel*
1964 Louis Simpson, *At the End of the Open Road*
1965 John Berryman, *77 Dream Songs*
1966 Richard Eberhart, *Selected Poems*
1967 Anne Sexton, *Live or Die*
1968 Anthony Hecht, *The Hard Hours*
1969 George Oppen, *Of Being Numerous*
1970 Richard Howard, *Untitled Subjects*
1971 William S. Merwin, *The Carrier of Ladders*
1972 James Wright, *Collected Poems*
1973 Maxine Winokur Kumin, *Up Country*
1974 Robert Lowell, *The Dolphin*
1975 Gary Snyder, *Turtle Island*
1976 John Ashbery, *Self-Portrait in a Convex Mirror*
1977 James Merrill, *Divine Comedies*
1978 Howard Nemerov, *Collected Poems*
1979 Robert Penn Warren, *Now and Then: Poems 1976-1978*
1980 Donald Justice, *Selected Poems*
1981 James Schuyler, *The Morning of the Poem*
1982 Sylvia Plath, *The Collected Poems*
1983 Galway Kinnell, *Selected Poems*
1984 Mary Oliver, *American Primitive*
1985 Carolyn Kizer, *Yin*
1986 Henry Taylor, *The Flying Change*
1987 Rita Dove, *Thomas and Beulah*
1988 William Meredith, *Partial Accounts*
1989 Richard Wilbur, *New and Collected Poems*
1990 Charles Simic, *The World Doesn't End*
1991 Mona Van Duyn, *Near Changes*
1992 James Tate, *Selected Poems*
1993 Louise Glück, *The Wild Iris*
1994 Yusef Komunyakaa, *Neon Vernacular*
1995 Philip Levine, *The Simple Truth*
1996 Jorie Graham, *The Dream of the Unified Field*
1997 Lisel Mueller, *Alive Together: New and Selected Poems*
1998 Charles Wright, *Black Zodiac*
1999 Mark Strand, *Blizzard of One*
2000 C. K. Williams, *Repair*
2001 Stephen Dunn, *Different Hours*

2002 Carl Dennis, *Practical Gods*
2003 Paul Muldoon, *Moy Sand and Gravel*
2004 Franz Wright, *Walking to Martha's Vineyard*
2005 Ted Kooser, *Delights & Shadows*
2006 Claudia Emerson, *Late Wife*
2007 Natasha Trethewey, *Native Guard*
2008 Robert Hass, *Time and Materials*; Philip Schultz, *Failure*
2009 W. S. Merwin, *The Shadow of Sirius*

General Nonfiction

1962 Theodore H. White, *The Making of the President 1960*
1963 Barbara W. Tuchman, *The Guns of August*
1964 Richard Hofstadter, *Anti-Intellectualism in American Life*
1965 Howard Mumford Jones, *O Strange New World*
1966 Edwin Way Teale, *Wandering Through Winter*
1967 David Brion Davis, *The Problem of Slavery in Western Culture*
1968 Will and Ariel Durant, *Rousseau and Revolution*
1969 Norman Mailer, *The Armies of the Night*; Rene Jules Dubos, *So Human an Animal: How We Are Shaped by Surroundings and Events*
1970 Eric H. Erikson, *Gandhi's Truth*
1971 John Toland, *The Rising Sun*
1972 Barbara W. Tuchman, *Stilwell and the American Experience in China, 1911-1945*
1973 Frances FitzGerald, *Fire in the Lake: The Vietnamese and the Americans in Vietnam*; Robert Coles, *Children of Crisis*, Volumes II & III
1974 Ernest Becker, *The Denial of Death*
1975 Annie Dillard, *Pilgrim at Tinker Creek*
1976 Robert N. Butler, *Why Survive? Being Old in America*
1977 William W. Warner, *Beautiful Swimmers*
1978 Carl Sagan, *The Dragons of Eden*
1979 Edward O. Wilson, *On Human Nature*
1980 Douglas R. Hofstadter, *Gödel, Escher, Bach: An Eternal Golden Braid*
1981 Carl E. Schorske, *Fin-de-Siecle Vienna: Politics and Culture*
1982 Tracy Kidder, *The Soul of a New Machine*
1983 Susan Sheehan, *Is There No Place on Earth for Me?*
1984 Paul Starr, *Social Transformation of American Medicine*
1985 Studs Terkel, *The Good War*
1986 Joseph Lelyveld, *Move Your Shadow*; J. Anthony Lukas, *Common Ground*
1987 David K. Shipler, *Arab and Jew*
1988 Richard Rhodes, *The Making of the Atomic Bomb*
1989 Neil Sheehan, *A Bright Shining Lie: John Paul Vann and America in Vietnam*

1990 Dale Maharidge and Michael Williamson, *And Their Children After Them*
1991 Bert Holldobler and Edward O. Wilson, *The Ants*
1992 Daniel Yergin, *The Prize: The Epic Quest for Oil*
1993 Garry Wills, *Lincoln at Gettysburg*
1994 David Remnick, *Lenin's Tomb: The Last Days of the Soviet Empire*
1995 Jonathan Weiner, *The Beak of the Finch: A Story of Evolution in Our Time*
1996 Tina Rosenberg, *The Haunted Land: Facing Europe's Ghosts After Communism*
1997 Richard Kluger, *Ashes to Ashes: America's Hundred-Year Cigarette War, the Public Health, and the Unabashed Triumph of Philip Morris*
1998 Jared Diamond, *Guns, Germs, and Steel: The Fates of Human Societies*
1999 John McPhee, *Annals of the Former World*
2000 John W. Dower, *Embracing Defeat: Japan in the Wake of World War II*
2001 Herbert P. Bix, *Hirohito and the Making of Modern Japan*
2002 Diane McWhorter, *Carry Me Home: Birmingham, Alabama, the Climactic Battle of the Civil Rights Revolution*
2003 Samantha Power, *A Problem From Hell: America and the Age of Genocide*
2004 Anne Applebaum, *Gulag: A History*
2005 Steve Coll, *Ghost Wars*
2006 Caroline Elkins, *Imperial Reckoning: The Untold Story of Britain's Gulag in Kenya*
2007 Lawrence Wright, *The Looming Tower: Al-Qaeda and the Road to 9/11*
2008 Saul Friedländer, *The Years of Extermination: Nazi Germany and the Jews, 1939-1945*
2009 Douglas A. Blackmon, *Slavery by Another Name: The Re-Enslavement of Black Americans from the Civil War to World War II*

Special Citation in Letters

1944 Richard Rodgers and Oscar Hammerstein II, for *Oklahoma!*
1957 Kenneth Roberts, for his historical novels
1960 *The Armada*, by Garrett Mattingly
1961 *American Heritage Picture History of the Civil War*
1973 *George Washington, Vols. I-IV*, by James Thomas Flexner
1977 Alex Haley, for *Roots*
1978 E. B. White
1984 Theodore Seuss Geisel (Dr. Seuss)
1992 Art Spiegelman, for *Maus*
2006 Edmund S. Morgan
2007 Ray Bradbury

Pulitzer Prizes—Music

1943 William Schuman, *Secular Cantata No. 2, A Free Song*
1944 Howard Hanson, *Symphony No. 4, Op. 34*
1945 Aaron Copland, *Appalachian Spring*
1946 Leo Sowerby, *The Canticle of the Sun*
1947 Charles E. Ives, *Symphony No. 3*
1948 Walter Piston, *Symphony No. 3*
1949 Virgil Thomson, *Louisiana Story*
1950 Gian-Carlo Menotti, *The Consul*
1951 Douglas Moore, *Giants in the Earth*
1952 Gail Kubik, *Symphony Concertante*
1954 Quincy Porter, *Concerto for Two Pianos and Orchestra*
1955 Gian-Carlo Menotti, *The Saint of Bleecker Street*
1956 Ernest Toch, *Symphony No. 3*
1957 Norman Dello Joio, *Meditations on Ecclesiastes*
1958 Samuel Barber, *Vanessa*
1959 John La Montaine, *Concerto for Piano and Orchestra*
1960 Elliott Carter, *Second String Quartet*
1961 Walter Piston, *Symphony No. 7*
1962 Robert Ward, *The Crucible*
1963 Samuel Barber, *Piano Concerto No. 1*
1966 Leslie Bassett, *Variations for Orchestra*
1967 Leon Kirchner, *Quartet No. 3*
1968 George Crumb, *Echoes of Time and The River*
1969 Karel Husa, *String Quartet No. 3*
1970 Charles W. Wuorinen, *Time's Encomium*
1971 Mario Davidovsky, *Synchronisms No. 6*
1972 Jacob Druckman, *Windows*
1973 Elliott Carter, *String Quartet No. 3*
1974 Donald Martino, *Notturno*
1975 Dominick Argento, *From the Diary of Virginia Woolf*
1976 Ned Rorem, *Air Music*
1977 Richard Wernick, *Visions of Terror and Wonder*
1978 Michael Colgrass, *Deja Vu for Percussion and Orchestra*
1979 Joseph Schwantner, *Aftertones of Infinity*
1980 David Del Tredici, *In Memory of a Summer Day*
1982 Roger Sessions, *Concerto for Orchestra*
1983 Ellen T. Zwilich, *Three Movements for Orchestra*
1984 Bernard Rands, *Canti del Sole*
1985 Stephen Albert, *Symphony, RiverRun*

1986 George Perle, *Wind Quintet IV*
1987 John Harbison, *The Flight Into Egypt*
1988 William Bolcom, *12 New Etudes for Piano*
1989 Roger Reynolds, *Whispers Out of Time*
1990 Mel Powell, *Duplicates: A Concerto for Two Pianos and Orchestra*
1991 Shulamit Ran, *Symphony*
1992 Wayne Peterson, *The Face of the Night, The Heart of the Dark*
1993 Christopher Rouse, *Trombone Concerto*
1994 Gunther Schuller, *Of Reminiscences and Reflections*
1995 Morton Gould, *Stringmusic*
1996 George Walker, *Lilacs*
1997 Wynton Marsalis, *Blood on the Fields*
1998 Aaron Jay Kernis, *String Quartet No. 2*
1999 Melinda Wagner, *Concerto for Flute, Strings and Percussion*
2000 Lewis Spratlan, *Life is a Dream, Opera in Three Acts: Act II, Concert Version*
2001 John Corigliano, *Symphony No. 2 for String Orchestra*
2002 Henry Brant, *Ice Field*
2003 John Adams, *On the Transmigration of Souls*
2004 Paul Moravec, *Tempest Fantasy*
2005 Steven Stucky, *Second Concerto for Orchestra*
2006 Yehudi Wyner, *Piano Concerto: 'Chiavi in Mano'*
2007 Ornette Coleman, *Sound Grammar*
2008 David Lang, *The Little Match Girl Passion*
2009 Steve Reich, *Double Sextet*

Special Citation in Music

1974 Roger Sessions
1976 Scott Joplin
1982 Milton Babbitt
1985 William Schuman
1998 George Gershwin
1999 Edward Kennedy "Duke" Ellington
2006 Thelonious Monk
2007 John Coltrane
2008 Bob Dylan

The Man Booker Prize for Fiction, 1969-2009

The Booker Prize for fiction, established in 1968, is awarded annually in October for what is judged the best full-length novel written in English by a citizen of the UK, the Commonwealth, or the Irish Republic. In 2002 sponsorship of the award was taken over by Man Group PLC, the name was changed to the Man Booker Prize, and the amount was increased from £20,000 to £50,000.

Year	Author, Book
1969	P. H. Newby, *Something to Answer For*
1970	Bernice Rubens, *The Elected Member*
1971	V. S. Naipaul, *In a Free State*
1972	John Berger, *G*
1973	J. G. Farrell, *The Siege of Krishnapur*
1974	Nadine Gordimer, *The Conservationist*; Stanley Middleton, *Holiday*
1975	Ruth Prawer Jhabvala, *Heat & Dust*
1976	David Storey, *Saville*
1977	Paul Scott, *Staying On*
1978	Iris Murdoch, *The Sea, The Sea*
1979	Penelope Fitzgerald, *Offshore*
1980	William Golding, *Rites of Passage*
1981	Salman Rushdie, *Midnight's Children*[1]
1982	Thomas Keneally, *Schindler's Ark*
1983	J. M. Coetzee, *Life and Times of Michael K*
1984	Anita Brookner, *Hotel du Lac*
1985	Keri Hulme, *The Bone People*
1986	Kingsley Amis, *The Old Devils*
1987	Penelope Lively, *Moon Tiger*
1988	Peter Carey, *Oscar and Lucinda*
1989	Kazuo Ishiguro, *The Remains of the Day*
1990	A. S. Byatt, *Possession*
1991	Ben Okri, *The Famished Road*
1992	Michael Ondaatje, *The English Patient*; Barry Unsworth, *Sacred Hunger*
1993	Roddy Doyle, *Paddy Clarke Ha Ha Ha*
1994	James Kelman, *How Late It Was, How Late*
1995	Pat Barker, *The Ghost Road*
1996	Graham Swift, *Last Orders*
1997	Arundhati Roy, *The God of Small Things*
1998	Ian McEwan, *Amsterdam*
1999	J. M. Coetzee, *Disgrace*
2000	Margaret Atwood, *The Blind Assassin*
2001	Peter Carey, *True History of the Kelly Gang*
2002	Yann Martel, *Life of Pi*
2003	DBC Pierre, *Vernon God Little*
2004	Alan Hollinghurst, *The Line of Beauty*
2005	John Banville, *The Sea*
2006	Kiran Desai, *The Inheritance of Loss*
2007	Anne Enright, *The Gathering*
2008	Aravind Adiga, *The White Tiger*
2009	Hilary Mantel, *Wolf Hall*

(1) Salman Rushdie's *Midnight's Children* also won the "Booker of Booker" prize in 1993 and the "Best of the Booker" prize in 2008.

Newbery Medal Books, 1922-2009

The Newbery Medal was awarded annually in the years shown, by the Association for Library Service to Children, a division of the American Library Association, to the author of the most distinguished contribution to American literature for children.

Year	Book, Author
1922	*The Story of Mankind*, Hendrik Willem van Loon
1923	*The Voyages of Dr. Dolittle*, Hugh Lofting
1924	*The Dark Frigate*, Charles Boardman Hawes
1925	*Tales From Silver Lands*, Charles Joseph Finger
1926	*Shen of the Sea*, Arthur Bowie Chrisman
1927	*Smoky, the Cowhorse*, Will James
1928	*Gay-Neck*, Dhan Gopal Mukerji
1929	*The Trumpeter of Krakow*, Eric P. Kelly
1930	*Hitty, Her First Hundred Years*, Rachel Field
1931	*The Cat Who Went to Heaven*, Elizabeth Coatsworth
1932	*Waterless Mountain*, Laura Adams Armer
1933	*Young Fu of the Upper Yangtze*, Elizabeth Foreman Lewis
1934	*Invincible Louisa*, Cornelia Lynde Meigs
1935	*Dobry*, Monica Shannon
1936	*Caddie Woodlawn*, Carol Ryrie Brink
1937	*Roller Skates*, Ruth Sawyer
1938	*The White Stag*, Kate Seredy
1939	*Thimble Summer*, Elizabeth Enright
1940	*Daniel Boone*, James Daugherty
1941	*Call It Courage*, Armstrong Sperry
1942	*The Matchlock Gun*, Walter D. Edmonds
1943	*Adam of the Road*, Elizabeth Janet Gray
1944	*Johnny Tremain*, Esther Forbes
1945	*Rabbit Hill*, Robert Lawson
1946	*Strawberry Girl*, Lois Lenski
1947	*Miss Hickory*, Carolyn S. Bailey
1948	*Twenty-One Balloons*, William Pène Du Bois
1949	*King of the Wind*, Marguerite Henry
1950	*The Door in the Wall*, Marguerite de Angeli
1951	*Amos Fortune, Free Man*, Elizabeth Yates
1952	*Ginger Pye*, Eleanor Estes
1953	*Secret of the Andes*, Ann Nolan Clark
1954	*. . . And Now Miguel*, Joseph Krumgold
1955	*The Wheel on the School*, Meindert DeJong
1956	*Carry On, Mr. Bowditch*, Jean Lee Latham
1957	*Miracles on Maple Hill*, Virginia Sorensen
1958	*Rifles for Watie*, Harold Keith
1959	*The Witch of Blackbird Pond*, Elizabeth George Speare
1960	*Onion John*, Joseph Krumgold
1961	*Island of the Blue Dolphins*, Scott O'Dell
1962	*The Bronze Bow*, Elizabeth George Speare
1963	*A Wrinkle in Time*, Madeleine L'Engle
1964	*It's Like This, Cat*, Emily Cheney Neville
1965	*Shadow of a Bull*, Maja Wojciechowska
1966	*I, Juan de Pareja*, Elizabeth Borton de Trevino
1967	*Up a Road Slowly*, Irene Hunt
1968	*From the Mixed-Up Files of Mrs. Basil E. Frankweiler*, E. L. Konigsburg
1969	*The High King*, Lloyd Alexander
1970	*Sounder*, William H. Armstrong
1971	*The Summer of the Swans*, Betsy Byars
1972	*Mrs. Frisby and the Rats of NIMH*, Robert C. O'Brien
1973	*Julie of the Wolves*, Jean George
1974	*The Slave Dancer*, Paula Fox
1975	*M. C. Higgins the Great*, Virginia Hamilton
1976	*Grey King*, Susan Cooper
1977	*Roll of Thunder, Hear My Cry*, Mildred D. Taylor
1978	*Bridge to Terabithia*, Katherine Paterson
1979	*The Westing Game*, Ellen Raskin
1980	*A Gathering of Days*, Joan Blos
1981	*Jacob Have I Loved*, Katherine Paterson
1982	*A Visit to William Blake's Inn: Poems for Innocent and Experienced Travelers*, Nancy Willard
1983	*Dicey's Song*, Cynthia Voigt
1984	*Dear Mr. Henshaw*, Beverly Cleary
1985	*The Hero and the Crown*, Robin McKinley
1986	*Sarah, Plain and Tall*, Patricia MacLachlan
1987	*The Whipping Boy*, Sid Fleischman
1988	*Lincoln: A Photobiography*, Russell Freedman
1989	*Joyful Noise: Poems for Two Voices*, Paul Fleischman
1990	*Number the Stars*, Lois Lowry
1991	*Maniac Magee*, Jerry Spinelli
1992	*Shiloh*, Phyllis Reynolds Naylor
1993	*Missing May*, Cynthia Rylant
1994	*The Giver*, Lois Lowry
1995	*Walk Two Moons*, Sharon Creech
1996	*The Midwife's Apprentice*, Karen Cushman
1997	*The View From Saturday*, E. L. Konigsburg
1998	*Out of the Dust*, Karen Hesse
1999	*Holes*, Louis Sachar
2000	*Bud, Not Buddy*, Christopher Paul Curtis
2001	*A Year Down Yonder*, Richard Peck
2002	*A Single Shard*, Linda Sue Park
2003	*Crispin: The Cross of Lead*, Avi
2004	*The Tale of Despereaux*, Kate DiCamillo
2005	*Kira-Kira*, Cynthia Kadohata
2006	*Criss Cross*, Lynne Rae Perkins
2007	*The Higher Power of Lucky*, Susan Patron
2008	*Good Masters! Sweet Ladies! Voices From a Medieval Village*, Laura Amy Schlitz
2009	*The Graveyard Book*, Neil Gaiman

Caldecott Medal Books, 1938-2009

The Caldecott Medal was awarded annually in the years shown, by the Association for Library Service to Children, a division of the American Library Association, to the illustrator of the most distinguished American picture book for children.

Year	Book, Illustrator
1938	*Animals of the Bible*, Dorothy P. Lathrop
1939	*Mei Li*, Thomas Handforth
1940	*Abraham Lincoln*, Ingri & Edgar Parin d'Aulaire
1941	*They Were Strong and Good*, Robert Lawson
1942	*Make Way for Ducklings*, Robert McCloskey
1943	*The Little House*, Virginia Lee Burton
1944	*Many Moons*, Louis Slobodkin
1945	*Prayer for a Child*, Elizabeth Orton Jones
1946	*The Rooster Crows*, Maude and Miska Petersham
1947	*The Little Island*, Leonard Weisgard
1948	*White Snow, Bright Snow*, Roger Duvoisin
1949	*The Big Snow*, Berta and Elmer Hader
1950	*Song of the Swallows*, Leo Politi
1951	*The Egg Tree*, Karherine Milhous
1952	*Finders Keepers*, Nicolas, pseud. (Nicholas Mordvinoff)
1953	*The Biggest Bear*, Lynd Ward
1954	*Madeline's Rescue*, Ludwig Bemelmans
1955	*Cinderella, or the Little Glass Slipper*, Marcia Brown
1956	*Frog Went A-Courtin'*, Feodor Rojankovsky
1957	*A Tree Is Nice*, Marc Simont
1958	*Time of Wonder*, Robert McCloskey
1959	*Chanticleer and the Fox*, Barbara Cooney
1960	*Nine Days to Christmas*, Marie Hall Ets
1961	*Baboushka and the Three Kings*, Nicolas Sidjakov
1962	*Once a Mouse*, Marcia Brown
1963	*The Snowy Day*, Ezra Jack Keats
1964	*Where the Wild Things Are*, Maurice Sendak
1965	*May I Bring a Friend?*, Beni Montressor
1966	*Always Room for One More*, Nonny Hogrogian
1967	*Sam, Bang, and Moonshine*, Evaline Ness
1968	*Drummer Hoff*, Ed Emberley
1969	*The Fool of the World and the Flying Ship*, Uri Shulevitz
1970	*Sylvester and the Magic Pebble*, William Steig
1971	*A Story A Story*, Gail E. Haley
1972	*One Fine Day*, Nonny Hogrogian
1973	*The Funny Little Woman*, Blair Lent
1974	*Duffy and the Devil*, Margot Zemach
1975	*Arrow to the Sun*, Gerald McDermott
1976	*Why Mosquitoes Buzz in People's Ears*, Leo & Diane Dillon
1977	*Ashanti to Zulu: African Traditions*, Leo & Diane Dillon
1978	*Noah's Ark*, Peter Spier
1979	*The Girl Who Loved Wild Horses*, Paul Goble
1980	*Ox-Cart Man*, Barbara Cooney
1981	*Fables*, Arnold Lobel
1982	*Jumanji*, Chris Van Allsburg
1983	*Shadow*, Marcia Brown
1984	*The Glorious Flight: Across the Channel with Louis Bleriot*, Alice and Martin Provensen
1985	*Saint George and the Dragon*, Trina Schart Hyman
1986	*The Polar Express*, Chris Van Allsburg
1987	*Hey, Al*, Richard Egielski
1988	*Owl Moon*, John Schoenherr
1989	*Song and Dance Man*, Stephen Grammell
1990	*Lon Po Po: A Red-Riding Hood Story From China*, Ed Young
1991	*Black and White*, David Macaulay
1992	*Tuesday*, David Wiesner
1993	*Mirette on the High Wire*, Emily Arnold McCully
1994	*Grandfather's Journey*, Allen Say
1995	*Smoky Night*, David Diaz
1996	*Officer Buckle and Gloria*, Peggy Rathmann
1997	*Golem*, David Wisniewski
1998	*Rapunzel*, Paul O. Zelinsky
1999	*Snowflake Bentley*, Mary Azarian
2000	*Joseph Had a Little Overcoat*, Simms Taback
2001	*So You Want to be President?*, David Small
2002	*The Three Pigs*, David Wiesner
2003	*My Friend Rabbit*, Eric Rohmann
2004	*The Man Who Walked Between the Towers*, Mordicai Gerstein
2005	*Kitten's First Full Moon*, Kevin Henkes
2006	*The Hello, Goodbye Window*, Chris Raschka
2007	*Flotsam*, David Wiesner
2008	*The Invention of Hugo Cabret*, Brian Selznick
2009	*The House in the Night*, Beth Krommes

National Book Awards, 1950-2008

The National Book Awards (known as American Book Awards 1980-86) are administered by the National Book Foundation and have been given annually in the years shown, since 1950. The prizes, each valued at $10,000, are awarded to U.S. citizens for works published in the U.S. In some years, multiple awards were given for nonfiction in various categories; in such cases, the history and biography (if any) or biography winner is listed. Selected additional awards in nonfiction are listed in footnotes.

Other National Book Awards, 2008: Poetry: Mark Doty, *Fire to Fire: New and Collected Poems*; Young People's Literature: Judy Blundell, *What I Saw and How I Lied*. Medal for Distinguished Contribution to American Letters: Maxine Hong Kingston. Literarian Award for Outstanding Service to the American Literary Community: Barney Rosset.

Fiction

Year	Author, Book
1950	Nelson Algren, *The Man With the Golden Arm*
1951	William Faulkner, *The Collected Stories*
1952	James Jones, *From Here to Eternity*
1953	Ralph Ellison, *Invisible Man*
1954	Saul Bellow, *The Adventures of Augie March*
1955	William Faulkner, *A Fable*
1956	John O'Hara, *Ten North Frederick*
1957	Wright Morris, *The Field of Vision*
1958	John Cheever, *The Wapshot Chronicle*
1959	Bernard Malamud, *The Magic Barrel*
1960	Philip Roth, *Goodbye, Columbus*
1961	Conrad Richter, *The Waters of Kronos*
1962	Walker Percy, *The Moviegoer*
1963	J. F. Powers, *Morte d'Urban*
1964	John Updike, *The Centaur*
1965	Saul Bellow, *Herzog*
1966	Katherine Anne Porter, *The Collected Stories*
1967	Bernard Malamud, *The Fixer*
1968	Thornton Wilder, *The Eighth Day*
1969	Jerzy Kosinski, *Steps*
1970	Joyce Carol Oates, *Them*
1971	Saul Bellow, *Mr. Sammler's Planet*
1972	Flannery O'Connor, *The Complete Stories*
1973	John Barth, *Chimera*
1974	Thomas Pynchon, *Gravity's Rainbow*
1974	Isaac Bashevis Singer, *A Crown of Feathers*
1975	Robert Stone, *Dog Soldiers*
1976	William Gaddis, *JR*
1977	Wallace Stegner, *The Spectator Bird*
1978	Mary Lee Settle, *Blood Ties*
1979	Tim O'Brien, *Going After Cacciato*
1980	William Styron, *Sophie's Choice*
1981	Wright Morris, *Plains Song*
1982	John Updike, *Rabbit Is Rich*
1983	Alice Walker, *The Color Purple*
1984	Ellen Gilchrist, *Victory Over Japan*
1985	Don DeLillo, *White Noise*
1986	E. L. Doctorow, *World's Fair*
1987	Larry Heinemann, *Paco's Story*
1988	Pete Dexter, *Paris Trout*
1989	John Casey, *Spartina*
1990	Charles Johnson, *Middle Passage*
1991	Norman Rush, *Mating*
1992	Cormac McCarthy, *All the Pretty Horses*
1993	E. Annie Proulx, *The Shipping News*
1994	William Gaddis, *A Frolic of His Own*
1995	Philip Roth, *Sabbath's Theater*
1996	Andrea Barrett, *Ship Fever and Other Stories*
1997	Charles Frazier, *Cold Mounatin*
1998	Alice McDermott, *Charming Billy*
1999	Ha Jin, *Waiting*
2000	Susan Sontag, *In America*
2001	Jonathan Franzen, *The Corrections*
2002	Julia Glass, *Three Junes*
2003	Shirley Hazzard, *The Great Fire*
2004	Lily Tuck, *The News from Paraguay*
2005	William T. Vollmann, *Europe Central*
2006	Richard Powers, *The Echo Maker*
2007	Denis Johnson, *Tree of Smoke*
2008	Peter Matthiessen, *Shadow Country*

Nonfiction

Year	Author, Title
1950	Ralph L. Rusk, *Ralph Waldo Emerson*
1951	Newton Arvin, *Herman Melville*
1952	Rachel Carson, *The Sea Around Us*
1953	Bernard A. De Voto, *The Course of an Empire*
1954	Bruce Catton, *A Stillness at Appomattox*
1955	Joseph Wood Krutch, *The Measure of Man*
1956	Herbert Kubly, *An American in Italy*
1957	George F. Kennan, *Russia Leaves the War*
1958	Catherine Drinker Bowen, *The Lion and the Throne*
1959	J. Christopher Herold, *Mistress to an Age: A Life of Madame De Stael*
1960	Richard Ellman, *James Joyce*
1961	William L. Shirer, *The Rise and Fall of the Third Reich*
1962	Lewis Mumford, *The City in History: Its Origins, Its Transformations, and Its Prospects*
1963	Leon Edel, *Henry James: Vol. II: The Conquest of London; Vol. III: The Middle Years*
1964	WIlliam H. McNeill, *The Rise of the West: A History of the Human Community*
1965	Louis Fisher, *The Life of Lenin*
1966	Arthur M. Schlesinger Jr., *A Thousand Days: John F. Kennedy in the White House*
1967	Peter Gay, *The Enlightenment, An Interpretation, Vol I: The Rise of Modern Paganism*
1968	George F. Kennan, *Memoirs: 1925-1950*[1]
1969	Winthrop D. Jordan, *White Over Black: American Attitudes Toward the Negro, 1550-1812*[2]
1970	T. Harry Williams, *Huey Long*[3]
1971	James MacGregor Burns, *Roosevelt: The Soldier of Freedom*
1972	Joseph P. Lash, *Eleanor and Franklin: The Story of Their Relationship, Based on Eleanor Roosevelt's Private Papers*
1973	James Thomas Flexner, *George Washington, Vol. IV: Anguish and Farewell, 1793-1799*[4]
1974	John Clive, *Macaulay, The Shaping of the Historian;* Douglas Day, *Malcolm Lowry: A Biography*[5]
1975	Richard B. Sewall, *The Life of Emily Dickinson*[6]
1976	David Brion Davis, *The Problem of Slavery in the Age of Revolution, 1770-1823*
1977	W. A. Swanberg, *Norman Thomas: The Last Idealist*[7]
1978	W. Jackson Bate, *Samuel Johnson*
1979	Arthur M. Schlesinger Jr., *Robert Kennedy and His Times*
1980	Tom Wolfe, *The Right Stuff*

Year	Author, Title
1981	Maxine Hong Kingston, *China Men*
1982	Tracy Kidder, *The Soul of a New Machine*
1983	Fox Butterfield, *China: Alive in the Bitter Sea*
1984	Robert V. Remini, *Andrew Jackson and the Course of American Democracy, 1833-1845*
1985	J. Anthony Lukas, *Common Ground: A Turbulent Decade in the Lives of Three American Families*
1986	Barry Lopez, *Arctic Dreams*
1987	Richard Rhodes, *The Making of the Atom Bomb*
1988	Neil Sheehan, *A Bright Shining Lie: John Paul Vann and America in Vietnam*
1989	Thomas L. Friedman, *From Beirut to Jerusalem*
1990	Ron Chernow, *The House of Morgan: An American Banking Dynasty and the Rise of Modern Finance*
1991	Orlando Patterson, *Freedom*
1992	Paul Monette, *Becoming a Man: Half a Life Story*
1993	Gore Vidal, *United States: Essays 1952-1992*
1994	Sherwin B. Nuland, *How We Die: Reflections on Life's Final Chapter*
1995	Tina Rosenberg, *The Haunted Land: Facing Europe's Ghosts After Communism*
1996	James Carroll, *An American Requiem: God, My Father, and the War That Came Between Us*
1997	Joseph J. Ellis, *American Sphinx: The Character of Thomas Jefferson*
1998	Edward Ball, *Slaves in the Family*
1999	John W. Dower, *Embracing Defeat: Japan in the Wake of World War II*
2000	Nathaniel Philbrick, *In the Heart of the Sea: The Tragedy of the Whaleship Essex*
2001	Andrew Solomon, *The Noonday Demon: An Atlas of Depression*
2002	Robert A. Caro, *Master of the Senate: The Years of Lyndon Johnson*
2003	Carlos Eire, *Waiting for Snow in Havana: Confessions of a Cuban Boy*
2004	Kevin Boyle, *Arc of Justice: A Saga of Race, Civil Rights, and Murder in the Jazz Age*
2005	Joan Didion, *The Year of Magical Thinking*
2006	Timothy Egan, *The Worst Hard Time: The Untold Story of Those Who Survived the Great American Dust Bowl*
2007	Tim Weiner, *Legacy of Ashes: The History of the CIA*
2008	Annette Gordon-Reed, *The Hemingses of Monticello: An American Family*

(1) Science, Philosophy, and Religion: Jonathan Kozol, *Death at an Early Age*. (2) Arts & Letters: Norman Mailer, *The Armies of the Night: History as a Novel, The Novel as History*. (3) Arts & Letters: Lillian Hellman, *An Unfinished Woman: A Memoir*. (4) Contemp. Affairs: Frances FitzGerald, *Fire in the Lake: The Vietnamese and the Americans in Vietnam*. (5) Arts & Letters: Pauline Kael, *Deeper Into the Movies*. (6) Arts & Letters: Roger Shattuck, *Marcel Proust*; Lewis Thomas, *The Lives of a Cell: Notes of a Biology Watcher*. (7) Contemp. Thought: Bruno Bettelheim, *The Uses of Enchantment: The Meaning and Importance of Fairy Tales*.

Journalism Awards, 2009

National Journalism Awards, by Scripps Howard Foundation. Investigative Reporting: Rob Barry, Jack Dolan, and Matthew Haggman, *Miami Herald*. Public Service Reporting: *Las Vegas Sun*. Editorial Writing: David Barham, *Arkansas Democrat-Gazette* (Little Rock). Commentary: Paul Krugman, *NY Times*. Human Interest Writing: Sean Kirst, *Post-Standard* (Syracuse, NY). Web Reporting: *LA Times*. Environmental Reporting: *Milwaukee Journal Sentinel* (WI). Washington Reporting: David Willman, *LA Times*. Editorial Cartooning: Mike Luckovich, *Atlanta Journal-Constitution*. First Amendment: Josh Margolin and Ted Sherman, *Star-Ledger* (Newark, NJ). Photojournalism: Michael Robinson Chavez, *LA Times*. Business/Economics Reporting: Farah Stockman, *Boston Globe*. Excellence in Electronic Media: National Public Radio; Downtown Community Television Center (NY). College Cartooning: Grant Snider, *University News*, Univ. of Missouri–Kansas City. Journalism Teacher of the Year: Charles Davis, University of Missouri–Columbia. Journalism Administrator of the Year: Marilyn Weaver, Ball State University, Muncie, IN.

National Magazine Awards, by American Society of Magazine Editors and Columbia Univ. Graduate School of Journalism. General Excellence, circ. over 2 mil: *Reader's Digest*; 1 mil-2 mil: *Field & Stream*; 500,000 to 1 mil: *Wired*; 250,000-500,000: *Texas Monthly*; 100,000-250,000: *Foreign Policy*; under 100,000: *Print*. Single-Topic Issue: *Saveur*. Magazine Section: *Wired*. Reporting: *NY Times Magazine*. Public Interest: *Bicycling*. Feature Writing: *Esquire*. Profile Writing: *Rolling Stone*. Essays: *Backpacker*. Columns and Commentary: *Automobile*. Reviews and Criticism: *The New Yorker*. Fiction: *The New Yorker*. Personal Service: *Esquire*. Leisure Interests: *Esquire*. Design: *Wired*. Photography: *GQ*. Photojournalism: *National Geographic*. Photo Portfolio: *The*

New Yorker. General Excellence Online, less than 1 mil avg. monthly unique visitors: Backpacker.com; 1 mil+ avg. monthly unique visitors: NYmag.com. Personal Service Online: Backpacker.com. Interactive Feature: *AARP The Magazine* Online.

George Foster Peabody Awards, by Univ. of Georgia. *Lost*, ABC. *Breaking Bad*, AMC. *John Adams*, HBO. *Entourage*, HBO. *The Metropolitan Opera: Live in HD* series, PBS. *Beijing Olympics Opening Ceremony* dir. Zhang Yimou, NBC. *Jungle Fish*, Korean Broadcasting System. *Avatar: The Last Airbender*, Nickelodeon. YouTube.com, Google. NYTimes.com, *New York Times*. Onion News Network, *The Onion*. *The Red Race*, Shanghai Media Group. *Hopkins*, ABC. *Black Magic*, ESPN. *P.O.V.: Campaign*, PBS. *Depression: Out of the Shadows*, PBS. *Ape Genius*, PBS. *Independent Lens: Mapping Stem Cell Research–Terra Incognita*, PBS. *Independent Lens: King Corn*, PBS. *Hear and Now*, HBO. *The Gates*, HBO. *Nanking*, HBO. *Crossfire: Water, Power and Politics*, KLAS-TV, Las Vegas. "NOAH Housing Program Investigation," WWL-TV, New Orleans. "Sichuan Earthquake Coverage," Sichuan Television. "Coverage of 2008 Presidential Primary Campaigns and Debates," CNN. "Failing the Children: Deadly Mistakes," KMGH-TV, Denver. "Lifeline," *60 Minutes*, CBS. *Richard Engel Reports: Tip of the Spear*, NBC. "The Giant Pool of Money," *This American Life*, Chicago Public Radio, NPR. "China: The Earthquake of Chungdu," NPR. "36 Years of Solitary: Murder, Death, and Justice on Angola," NPR/*All Things Considered*. "Commitment 2008," Hearst-Argyle TV. Turner Classic Movies (TCM). *Washington Week with Gwen Ifill* and *National Journal*, PBS. "Political Satire, 2008," *Saturday Night Live*, NBC.

Reuben Award, by National Cartoonists Society. For Outstanding Cartoonist of the Year: Dave Coverly.

Miscellaneous Book Awards, 2009

(Awarded in 2009 unless otherwise noted.)

Academy of American Poets Awards. Wallace Stevens Award, for poetry mastery, $100,000 (2008): Louise Glück. Academy Fellowship, $25,000 (2008): Brigit Pegeen Kelly. Lenore Marshall Poetry Prize, $25,000 (2008): Henri Cole, *Blackbird and Wolf*. James Laughlin Award, $5,000 (2008): Rusty Morrison, *the true keeps calm biding its story*. Walt Whitman Award, $5,000: J. Michael Martinez, *Heredities*. Harold Morton Landon Translation Award, $1,000: Avi Sharon, *C. P. Cavafy: Selected Poems*. Raiziss/de Palchi Translation Prize, $5,000 (2008): Patrick Barron, *The Selected Poetry and Prose of Andrea Zanzotto*.

American Academy of Arts and Letters. Gold Medal for Poetry: Mark Strand. Award of Merit Medal for the Novel, $10,000: Denis Johnson. Academy Awards in Literature ($7,500 each): Rilla Askew, Michael Collier, Tracy Letts, D. Nurkse, Marie Ponsot, George Saunders, Susan Stewart. E. M. Forster Award, $20,000: Paul Farley. Sue Kaufman Prize for First Fiction, $5,000: Charles Bock, *Beautiful Children*. Addison M. Metcalf Award, $10,000: Ron Currie Jr. Rome Fellowships in Literature: Peter Campion, Eliza Griswold. Rosenthal Family Foundation Award, $5,000: Chris Adrian, *A Better Angel*. Harold D. Vursell Memorial Award, $10,000: Sharon Cameron. Thornton Wilder Prize for Translation, $20,000: Gregory Rabassa.

Bollingen Prize in Poetry, $100,000, by the Yale Univ. Library: Allen Grossman.

Coretta Scott King Awards, by American Library Assn., for African American authors and illustrators of outstanding books for children and young adults. Author: Kadir Nelson, *We Are the Ship: The Story of Negro League Baseball*. Illustrator: Floyd Cooper, *The Blacker the Berry*. John Steptoe New Talent Award (illustrator): Shadra Strickland, *Bird*.

Costa Book of the Year (formerly Whitbread Award): £25,000: *The Secret Scripture*, Sebastian Barry.

Edgar Awards, by the Mystery Writers of America. Best Novel: *Blue Heaven*, C. J. Box. Best First Novel by an American Author: *The Foreigner*, Francie Lin. Best Paperback Original: *China Lake*, Meg Gardiner. Best Fact Crime: *American Lightning: Terror, Mystery and the Birth of Hollywood, and the Crime of the Century*, Howard Blum. Best Critical/Biographical: *Edgar Allan Poe: An Illustrated Companion to His Tell-Tale Stories*, Dr. Harry Lee Poe. Best Short Story: "Skinhead Central," T. Jefferson Parker. Best Juvenile: *The Postcard*, Tony Abbott. Best Young Adult: *Paper Towns*, John Green. Best Play: *The Ballad of Emmett Till*, Ifa Bayeza. Best Teleplay: "Prayer of the Bone," *Wire in the Blood*, Patrick Harbinson. Best Screenplay: *In Bruges*, Martin McDonagh.

Golden Kite Awards, $2,500, by Society of Children's Book Writers and Illustrators. Fiction: *Down Sand Mountain*, Steve Watkins. Nonfiction: *A Life in the Wild*, Pamela S. Turner. Picture Book Text: *A Visitor for Bear*, Bonnie Becker. Picture Book Illustration: *Last Night*, Hyewon Yum.

Hugo Awards, by the World Science Fiction Convention. Novel: *The Graveyard Book*, Neil Gaiman. Novella: *The Erdman Nexus*, Nancy Kress. Novelette: *Shoggoths in Bloom*, Elizabeth Bear. Short story: "Exhalation," Ted Chiang. Related Book: *Your Hate Mail Will Be Graded*, John Scalzi. Graphic Story: *Girl Genius, Vol. 8: Agatha Heterodyne and the Chapel of Bones*, Kaja and Phil Foglio. Dramatic, long form: *WALL-E*, dir. Andrew Stanton. Dramatic, short form: *Doctor Horrible's Sing-Along Blog*, dir. Joss Whedon. Best New Writer (not a Hugo): David Anthony Durham.

Lincoln Prize, by Lincoln and Soldiers Institute at Gettysburg College, for contribution to Civil War studies ($50,000 and a bust of Lincoln): James L. McPherson, *Tried by War: Abraham Lincoln as Commander in Chief* and Craig L. Symonds, *Lincoln and His Admirals: Abraham Lincoln, the U.S. Navy, and the Civil War*.

National Book Critics Circle Awards. Fiction: Roberto Bolaño, *2666*. General Nonfiction: Dexter Filkins, *The Forever War*. Biography: Patrick French, *The World Is What It Is: The Authorized Biography of V. S. Naipaul*. Autobiography: Ariel Sabar, *My Father's Paradise: A Son's Search for His Jewish Past in Kurdish Iraq*. Criticism: Seth Lerer, *Children's Literature: A Reader's History from Aesop to Harry Potter*. Poetry: August Kleinzahler, *Sleeping It Off in Rapid City* and Juan Felipe Herrera, *Half the World in Light*. Ivan Sandrof Lifetime Achievement Award: PEN American Center. Nona Balakian Citation for Excellence in Reviewing: Ron Charles, *Washington Post Book World*.

Nebula Awards, by the Science Fiction and Fantasy Writers of America. Novel: *Powers*, Ursula K. LeGuin. Novella: *The Spacetime Pool*, Catherine Asaro. Novelette: *Pride and Prometheus*, John Kessel. Short Story: "Trophy Wives," Nina Kiriki Hoffman. Script: *WALL-E*, Andrew Stanton, Jim Reardon. Andre Norton Award: *Flora's Dare: How a Girl of Spirit Gambles All to Expand Her Vocabulary, Confront a Bouncing Boy Terror, and Try to Save Califa from a Shaky Doom (Despite Being Confined to Her Room)*, Ysabeau S. Wilce.

PEN/Faulkner Award, for fiction, $15,000: Joseph O'Neill, *Netherland*.

Prix Goncourt, by Académie Goncourt (2008): Atiq Rahimi, *Syngué sabour* (*Patience Stone*).

The Spingarn Medal, 1915-2009

The Spingarn Medal has been awarded annually since 1915 (except in 1938) by the National Assoc. for the Advancement of Colored People for outstanding achievement by an African American.

1915 Ernest E. Just	**1940** Louis T. Wright	**1963** Medgar W. Evers	**1987** Percy E. Sutton
1916 Charles Young	**1941** Richard Wright	**1964** Roy Wilkins	**1988** Frederick D. Patterson
1917 Harry T. Burleigh	**1942** A. Philip Randolph	**1965** Leontyne Price	**1989** Jesse Jackson
1918 William S. Braithwaite	**1943** William H. Hastie	**1966** John H. Johnson	**1990** L. Douglas Wilder
1919 Archibald H. Grimké	**1944** Charles Drew	**1967** Edward W. Brooke	**1991** Gen. Colin L. Powell
1920 W. E. B. Du Bois	**1945** Paul Robeson	**1968** Sammy Davis Jr.	**1992** Barbara Jordan
1921 Charles S. Gilpin	**1946** Thurgood Marshall	**1969** Clarence M. Mitchell Jr.	**1993** Dorothy I. Height
1922 Mary B. Talbert	**1947** Dr. Percy L. Julian	**1970** Jacob Lawrence	**1994** Maya Angelou
1923 George W.Carver	**1948** Channing H. Tobias	**1971** Leon H. Sullivan	**1995** John Hope Franklin
1924 Roland Hayes	**1949** Ralph J. Bunche	**1972** Gordon Parks	**1996** A. Leon Higginbotham
1925 James W. Johnson	**1950** Charles H. Houston	**1973** Wilson C. Riles	**1997** Carl T. Rowan
1926 Carter G. Woodson	**1951** Mabel K. Staupers	**1974** Damon Keith	**1998** Myrlie Evers-Williams
1927 Anthony Overton	**1952** Harry T. Moore	**1975** Henry (Hank) Aaron	**1999** Earl G. Graves Sr.
1928 Charles W. Chesnutt	**1953** Paul R. Williams	**1976** Alvin Ailey	**2000** Oprah Winfrey
1929 Mordecai W. Johnson	**1954** Theodore K. Lawless	**1977** Alex Haley	**2001** Vernon E. Jordan Jr.
1930 Henry A. Hunt	**1955** Carl Murphy	**1978** Andrew Young	**2002** John Lewis
1931 Richard B. Harrison	**1956** Jack R. Robinson	**1979** Rosa L. Parks	**2003** Constance Baker Motley
1932 Robert R. Moton	**1957** Martin Luther King Jr.	**1980** Dr. Rayford W. Logan	**2004** Robert L. Carter
1933 Max Yergan	**1958** Daisy Bates and the	**1981** Coleman Young	**2005** Oliver W. Hill
1934 William T. B. Williams	Little Rock Nine	**1982** Dr. Benjamin E. Mays	**2006** Dr. Benjamin S. Carson
1935 Mary McLeod Bethune	**1959** Duke Ellington	**1983** Lena Horne	**2007** John Conyers Jr.
1936 John Hope	**1960** Langston Hughes	**1984** Thomas Bradley	**2008** Ruby Dee
1937 Walter White	**1961** Kenneth B. Clark	**1985** Bill Cosby	**2009** Julian Bond
1939 Marian Anderson	**1962** Robert C. Weaver	**1986** Dr. Benjamin L. Hooks	

Miscellaneous Awards, 2009

(Awarded in 2009, unless otherwise noted.)

American Academy of Arts and Letters Architecture Awards. Arthur W. Brunner Memorial Prize, $5,000: Juhani Pallasmaa. Academy Awards, $7,500 each: Stan Allen, Wendell Burnette, Jeffrey Kipnis.

American Academy of Arts and Letters Art Awards. Academy Awards, $7,500 each: Stephen Antonakos, Gregory Crewdson, John Dubrow, Duncan Johnson, Susan Jane Walp. Jimmy Ernst Award, $5,000: Charles Cajori. John Koch Award, $10,000: Elisa Jensen. Rosenthal Family Foundation Award in Painting, $5,000: Hilary Harkness.

American Academy of Arts and Letters Music Awards. Academy Awards, $7,500 each: David Gompper, David Lang, Andrew Waggoner, Barbara White. Benjamin H. Danks Award, $20,000: Sean Shepherd. Goddard Lieberson Fellowships, $15,000 each: Laura Elise Schwendinger, Kurt Stallmann. Walter Hinrichsen Award: Victoria Bond. Charles Ives Fellowships, $15,000 each: Yu-Hui Chang, Ray Lustig. Charles Ives Scholarships, $5,000 each: Matthew Barnson, Ryan Gallagher, Michael Gilbertson, David M. Gordon, Andrew Norman, Carolyn O'Brien. Charles Ives Living, $75,000 annually for 3 years (2007): George Tsontakis. Richard Rodgers Awards for Musical Theater: *Cheer Wars*, Karlan Judd and Gordon Leary; *Rosa Parks*, Scott Ethier and Jeff Hughes.

Congressional Gold Medal, by Congress: Dr. Michael Ellis DeBakey (Oct. 10, 2007); Daw Aung San Suu Kyi (May 6, 2008); Constantino Brumidi, Edward William Brooke III (July 1, 2008)' Women Airforce Service Pilots of WWII (July 1, 2009).

Intel Science Talent Search (formerly given by Westinghouse). First place ($100,000 scholarship): Eric Larson, Eugene, OR; second place ($75,000 scholarship): William Sun, Chesterfield, MO; third place ($50,000 scholarship): Philip Streich, Platteville, WI.

John F. Kennedy Center Honors (Dec. 2008): Morgan Freeman, George Jones, Barbra Streisand, Twyla Tharp, Pete Townshend and Roger Daltry.

John W. Kluge Prize, by Library of Congress, $500,000 each (2008): Peter Robert Lamont Brown, Romila Thapar.

Library of the Year Award, by Gale and *Library Journal*, $10,000: Queens Library, New York, NY.

National Humanities Medal, by National Endowment for the Humanities. $5,000 each (2008): Gabor S. Boritt, Richard Brookhiser, Harold Holzer, Myron Magnet, Albert Marrin, Milton J. Rosenberg, Thomas A. Saunders III and Jordan Horner Saunders, Robert H. Smith, John Templeton Foundation, Norman Rockwell Museum.

National Inventor of the Year Awards, by Intellectual Property Owners Education Foundation: James Baughman, David Cook, Keith Kowalsky, and Daniel Marantz.

National Medal of the Arts, by the National Endowment for the Arts and the White House (2008): Olivia de Havilland, Fisk Jubilee Singers, Ford's Theatre Society, Hank Jones, Stan Lee, José Limón Dance Foundation, Jesús Moroles, the Presser Foundation, the Sherman Brothers.

Presidential Medal of Freedom, by the White House. By Pres. G. W. Bush, Jan. 13, 2009: Tony Blair, John Howard, Alvaro Uribe. By Pres. Obama, Aug. 12, 2009: Nancy Goodman Brinker, Pedro José Greer Jr., Stephen Hawking, Jack Kemp (posthumous), Sen. Edward Kennedy, Billie Jean King, Rev. Joseph Lowery, Joe Medicine Crow, Harvey Milk (posthumous), Sandra Day O'Connor, Sidney Poitier, Chita Rivera, Mary Robinson, Janet Davison Rowley, Desmond Tutu, Muhammad Yunus.

Pritzker Architecture Prize, by the Hyatt Foundation, $100,000: Peter Zumthor, Switzerland.

Teacher of the Year, by Council of Chief State School Officers and ING: Anthony J. Mullen, Special Education, ARCH School, Greenwich, CT.

Templeton Prize for Progress Toward Research or Discoveries about Spiritual Realities, by Templeton Foundation, £1,000,000 (about $1.6 million): Bernard d'Espagnat.

Miss America Winners, 1921-2009

Year	Winner	Year	Winner
1921	Margaret Gorman, Washington, DC	1970	Pamela Anne Eldred, Birmingham, Michigan
1922-23	Mary Campbell, Columbus, Ohio	1971	Phyllis Ann George, Denton, Texas
1924	Ruth Malcolmson, Philadelphia, Pennsylvania	1972	Laurie Lea Schaefer, Columbus, Ohio
1925	Fay Lamphier, Oakland, California	1973	Terry Anne Meeuwsen, DePere, Wisconsin
1926	Norma Smallwood, Tulsa, Oklahoma	1974	Rebecca Ann King, Denver, Colorado
1927	Lois Delander, Joliet, Illinois	1975	Shirley Cothran, Fort Worth, Texas
1933	Marion Bergeron, West Haven, Connecticut	1976	Tawney Elaine Godin, Yonkers, New York
1935	Henrietta Leaver, Pittsburgh, Pennsylvania	1977	Dorothy Kathleen Benham, Edina, Minnesota
1936	Rose Coyle, Philadelphia, Pennsylvania	1978	Susan Perkins, Columbus, Ohio
1937	Bette Cooper, Bertrand Island, New Jersey	1979	Kylene Barker, Galax, Virginia
1938	Marilyn Meseke, Marion, Ohio	1980	Cheryl Prewitt, Ackerman, Mississippi
1939	Patricia Donnelly, Detroit, Michigan	1981	Susan Powell, Elk City, Oklahoma
1940	Frances Marie Burke, Philadelphia, Pennsylvania	1982	Elizabeth Ward, Russellville, Arkansas
1941	Rosemary LaPlanche, Los Angeles, California	1983	Debra Maffett, Anaheim, California
1942	Jo-Caroll Dennison, Tyler, Texas	1984[1]	Suzette Charles, Mays Landing, New Jersey
1943	Jean Bartel, Los Angeles, California	1985	Sharlene Wells, Salt Lake City, Utah
1944	Venus Ramey, Washington, DC	1986	Susan Akin, Meridian, Mississippi
1945	Bess Myerson, New York City, New York	1987	Kellye Cash, Memphis, Tennessee
1946	Marilyn Buferd, Los Angeles, California	1988	Kaye Lani Rae Rafko, Monroe, Michigan
1947	Barbara Walker, Memphis, Tennessee	1989	Gretchen Carlson, Anoka, Minnesota
1948	BeBe Shopp, Hopkins, Minnesota	1990	Debbye Turner, Columbia, Missouri
1949	Jacque Mercer, Litchfield, Arizona	1991	Marjorie Vincent, Oak Park, Illinois
1951	Yolande Betbeze, Mobile, Alabama	1992	Carolyn Suzanne Sapp, Honolulu, Hawaii
1952	Coleen Kay Hutchins, Salt Lake City, Utah	1993	Leanza Cornett, Jacksonville, Florida
1953	Neva Jane Langley, Macon, Georgia	1994	Kimberly Aiken, Columbia, South Carolina
1954	Evelyn Margaret Ay, Ephrata, Pennsylvania	1995	Heather Whitestone, Birmingham, Alabama
1955	Lee Meriwether, San Francisco, California	1996	Shawntel Smith, Muldrow, Oklahoma
1956	Sharon Ritchie, Denver, Colorado	1997	Tara Dawn Holland, Overland Park, Kansas
1957	Marian McKnight, Manning, South Carolina	1998	Kate Shindle, Evanston, Illinois
1958	Marilyn Van Derbur, Denver, Colorado	1999	Nicole Johnson, Roanoke, Virginia
1959	Mary Ann Mobley, Brandon, Mississippi	2000	Heather Renee French, Maysville, Kentucky
1960	Lynda Lee Mead, Natchez, Mississippi	2001	Angela Perez Baraquio, Honolulu, Hawaii
1961	Nancy Fleming, Montague, Michigan	2002	Katie Harman, Gresham, Oregon
1962	Maria Fletcher, Asheville, North Carolina	2003	Erika Harold, Urbana, Illinois
1963	Jacquelyn Mayer, Sandusky, Ohio	2004	Ericka Dunlap, Orlando, Florida
1964	Donna Axum, El Dorado, Arkansas	2005[2]	Deidre Downs, Birmingham, Alabama
1965	Vonda Kay Van Dyke, Phoenix, Arizona	2006	Jennifer Berry, Tulsa, Oklahoma
1966	Deborah Irene Bryant, Overland Park, Kansas	2007	Lauren Nelson, Lawton, Oklahoma
1967	Jane Anne Jayroe, Laverne, Oklahoma	2008	Kirsten Haglund, Farmington Hills, Michigan
1968	Debra Dene Barnes, Moran, Kansas	2009	Katie Stam, Seymour, Indiana
1969	Judith Anne Ford, Belvidere, Illinois		

(1) Miss New York, Vanessa Williams, resigned July 23, 1984. (2) The Sept. 2005 Miss America Pageant and award were postponed until Jan. 2006, when the pageant was broadcast from Las Vegas, NV, by Country Music Television (CMT).

Entertainment Awards
Tony (Antoinette Perry) Awards, 2009

Play: *God of Carnage*, Yasmina Reza
Musical: *Billy Elliot, The Musical*
Book of a Musical: Lee Hall, *Billy Elliot, The Musical*
Original Score: Tom Kitt and Brian Yorkey, *Next to Normal*
Play Revival: *The Norman Conquests*
Musical Revival: *Hair*
Special Theatrical Event: *Liza's at the Palace*
Actor, Play: Geoffrey Rush, *Exit the King*
Actress, Play: Marcia Gay Harden, *God of Carnage*
Actor, Musical: David Alvarez, Trent Kowalik, and Kiril Kulish, *Billy Elliot, The Musical*
Actress, Musical: Alice Ripley, *Next to Normal*
Featured Actor, Play: Roger Robinson, *Joe Turner's Come and Gone*
Featured Actress, Play: Angela Lansbury, *Blithe Spirit*

Featured Actor, Musical: Gregory Jbara, *Billy Elliot, The Musical*
Featured Actress, Musical: Karen Olivo, *West Side Story*
Director, Play: Matthew Warchus, *God of Carnage*
Director, Musical: Stephen Daldry, *Billy Elliot, The Musical*
Choreography: Peter Darling, *Billy Elliot, The Musical*
Orchestrations: Martin Koch, *Billy Elliot, The Musical*, and Matthew Starobin and Tom Kitt, *Next to Normal*
Scenic Design, Play: Derek McLane, *33 Variations*
Scenic Design, Musical: Ian MacNeil, *Billy Elliot, The Musical*
Costume Design, Play: Anthony Ward, *Mary Stuart*
Costume Design, Musical: Tim Hatley, *Shrek The Musical*
Regional Theater: Signature Theatre, Arlington, VA
Special Tony Award, Lifetime Achievement: Jerry Herman
Isabelle Stevenson Award: Phyllis Newman
Tony Honors for Excellence in the Theatre: Shirley Herz

Tony Awards, 1948-2009

Year	Play	Musical	Year	Play	Musical
1948	Mister Roberts	No Award	1978	Da	Ain't Misbehavin'
1949	Death of a Salesman	Kiss Me Kate	1979	The Elephant Man	Sweeney Todd
1950	The Cocktail Party	South Pacific	1980	Children of a Lesser God	Evita
1951	The Rose Tattoo	Guys and Dolls	1981	Amadeus	42nd Street
1952	The Fourposter	The King and I	1982	The Life and Adventures of Nicholas Nickelby	Nine
1953	The Crucible	Wonderful Town			
1954	The Teahouse of the August Moon	Kismet	1983	Torch Song Trilogy	Cats
			1984	The Real Thing	La Cage aux Folles
1955	The Desperate Hours	The Pajama Game	1985	Biloxi Blues	Big River
1956	The Diary of Anne Frank	Damn Yankees	1986	I'm Not Rappaport	The Mystery of Edwin Drood
1957	Long Day's Journey Into Night	My Fair Lady	1987	Fences	Les Miserables
1958	Sunrise at Campobello	The Music Man	1988	M. Butterfly	Phantom of the Opera
1959	J.B.	Redhead	1989	The Heidi Chronicles	Jerome Robbins' Broadway
1960	The Miracle Worker	(tie) Fiorello!, The Sound of Music	1990	The Grapes of Wrath	City of Angels
			1991	Lost in Yonkers	The Will Rogers Follies
1961	Becket	Bye, Bye Birdie	1992	Dancing at Lughnasa	Crazy for You
1962	A Man for All Seasons	How to Succeed in Business Without Really Trying	1993	Angels in America: Millennium Approaches	Kiss of the Spider Woman
1963	Who's Afraid of Virginia Woolf?	A Funny Thing Happened on the Way to the Forum	1994	Angels in America: Perestroika	Passion
			1995	Love! Valour! Compassion!	Sunset Boulevard
1964	Luther	Hello, Dolly!	1996	Master Class	Rent
1965	The Subject Was Roses	Fiddler on the Roof	1997	The Last Night of Ballyhoo	Titanic
1966	Marat/Sade	Man of La Mancha	1998	Art	The Lion King
1967	The Homecoming	Cabaret	1999	Side Man	Fosse
1968	Rosencrantz and Guildenstern Are Dead	Hallelujah, Baby!	2000	Copenhagen	Contact
1969	The Great White Hope	1776	2001	Proof	The Producers
1970	Borstal Boy	Applause	2002	Edward Albee's The Goat or Who Is Sylvia?	Thoroughly Modern Millie
1971	Sleuth	Company			
1972	Sticks and Bones	Two Gentleman of Verona	2003	Take Me Out	Hairspray
1973	That Championship Season	A Little Night Music	2004	I Am My Own Wife	Avenue Q
1974	The River Niger	Raisin	2005	Doubt	Monty Python's Spamalot
1975	Equus	The Wiz	2006	The History Boys	Jersey Boys
1976	Travesties	A Chorus Line	2007	The Coast of Utopia	Spring Awakening
1977	The Shadow Box	Annie	2008	August: Osage County	In the Heights
			2009	God of Carnage	Billy Elliot, The Musical

Selected 2009 Daytime Emmy Awards

Drama series: *The Bold and the Beautiful*, CBS
Actress: Susan Haskell, *One Life to Live*, ABC
Actor: Christian LeBlanc, *The Young and the Restless*, CBS
Sup. actress: Tamara Braun, *Days of Our Lives*, NBC
Sup. actor: Jeff Branson, *Guiding Light*, CBS; Vincent Irizarry, *All My Children*, ABC
Younger actress: Julie Berman, *General Hospital*, ABC
Younger actor: Darin Brooks, *Days of Our Lives*, NBC
Drama series directing team: *One Life to Live*, ABC
Drama series writing team: *General Hospital*, ABC

Game show host: Meredith Vieira, *Who Wants to Be a Millionaire*, synd.
Talk show host: Barbara Walters, Sherri Shepherd, Elisabeth Hasselbeck, Joy Behar, Whoopi Goldberg, *The View*, ABC
Talk show, entertainment: *Rachael Ray*, synd.
Talk show, informative: *The Tyra Banks Show*, synd.
Legal/courtroom show: *Cristina's Court*, synd.
Morning show: *Good Morning America*, ABC
Game show: *Cash Cab*, Discovery Channel
Performer, children's series: Kevin Clash, *Sesame Street*, PBS

Selected 2009 Prime-Time Emmy Awards (for 2008-09 TV season)

Drama series: *Mad Men*, AMC
Comedy series: *30 Rock*, NBC
Miniseries: *Little Dorrit*, PBS
Variety, music, or comedy series: *The Daily Show with Jon Stewart*, Comedy Central
Made-for-television movie: *Grey Gardens*, HBO
Lead actor, drama: Bryan Cranston, *Breaking Bad*, AMC
Lead actress, drama: Glenn Close, *Damages*, FX
Lead actor, comedy: Alec Baldwin, *30 Rock*, NBC
Lead actress, comedy: Toni Collette, *United States of Tara*, Showtime
Lead actor, miniseries/movie: Brendan Gleeson, *Into the Storm*, HBO
Lead actress, miniseries/movie: Jessica Lange, *Grey Gardens*, HBO

Sup. actor, drama: Michael Emerson, *Lost*, ABC
Sup. actress, drama: Cherry Jones, *24*, FOX
Sup. actor, comedy: Jon Cryer, *Two and a Half Men*, CBS
Sup. actress, comedy: Kristin Chenoweth, *Pushing Daisies*, ABC
Sup. actor, miniseries/movie: Ken Howard, *Grey Gardens*, HBO
Sup. actress, miniseries/movie: Shohreh Aghdashloo, *House of Saddam*, HBO
Host, reality/competition program: Jeff Probst, *Survivor*, CBS
Reality/competition program: *The Amazing Race*, CBS
Director, drama: Rod Holcomb, *ER*, NBC
Director, comedy: Jeffrey Blitz, *The Office*, NBC
Writing, drama: Katie Gordon, Matthew Weiner, *Mad Men*, AMC
Writing, comedy: Matt Hubbard, *30 Rock*, NBC
Writing, variety, music, or comedy: *The Daily Show with Jon Stewart*, Comedy Central

Prime-Time Emmy Awards, 1952-2009

The Academy of Television Arts and Sciences presented the first Emmy Awards in 1949. Through the years, award categories have changed, but since 1952, the Academy has given out an outstanding comedy and drama award each year.

Year	Comedy	Drama	Year	Comedy	Drama
1952	*Red Skelton Show*, NBC	*Studio One*, CBS	1978	*All in the Family*, CBS	*The Rockford Files*, NBC
1953	*I Love Lucy*, CBS	*Robert Montgomery Presents*, NBC	1979	*Taxi*, ABC	*Lou Grant*, CBS
			1980	*Taxi*, ABC	*Lou Grant*, CBS
1954	*I Love Lucy*, CBS	*The U.S. Steel Hour*, ABC	1981	*Taxi*, ABC	*Hill Street Blues*, NBC
1955	*Make Room for Daddy*, ABC	*The U.S. Steel Hour*, ABC	1982	*Barney Miller*, ABC	*Hill Street Blues*, NBC
1956	*Phil Silvers Show*, CBS	*Producer's Showcase*, NBC	1983	*Cheers*, NBC	*Hill Street Blues*, NBC
1957	*Phil Silvers Show*, CBS	*Requiem for a Heavyweight*, CBS[1]	1984	*Cheers*, NBC	*Hill Street Blues*, NBC
			1985	*The Cosby Show*, NBC	*Cagney & Lacey*, CBS
1958	*Phil Silvers Show*, CBS	*Gunsmoke*, CBS	1986	*Golden Girls*, NBC	*Cagney & Lacey*, CBS
1959[2]	*Jack Benny Show*, CBS	*	1987	*Golden Girls*, NBC	*L.A. Law*, NBC
1960	*Art Carney Special*, NBC	*Playhouse 90*, CBS	1988	*The Wonder Years*, ABC	*thirtysomething*, ABC
1961	*Jack Benny Show*, CBS	*Hallmark Hall of Fame: Macbeth*, NBC	1989	*Cheers*, NBC	*L.A. Law*, NBC
			1990	*Murphy Brown*, CBS	*L.A. Law*, NBC
1962	*Bob Newhart Show*, CBS	*The Defenders*, CBS	1991	*Cheers*, NBC	*L.A. Law*, NBC
1963	*Dick Van Dyke Show*, CBS	*The Defenders*, CBS	1992	*Murphy Brown*, CBS	*Northern Exposure*, CBS
1964	*Dick Van Dyke Show*, CBS	*The Defenders*, CBS	1993	*Seinfeld*, NBC	*Picket Fences*, CBS
1965	*Dick Van Dyke Show*, CBS	*Hallmark Hall of Fame: The Magnificent Yankee*, NBC	1994	*Frasier*, NBC	*Picket Fences*, CBS
			1995	*Frasier*, NBC	*NYPD Blue*, ABC
1966	*Dick Van Dyke Show*, CBS	*The Fugitive*, ABC	1996	*Frasier*, NBC	*ER*, NBC
1967	*The Monkees*, NBC	*Mission: Impossible*, CBS	1997	*Frasier*, NBC	*Law & Order*, NBC
1968	*Get Smart*, NBC	*Mission: Impossible*, CBS	1998	*Frasier*, NBC	*The Practice*, ABC
1969	*Get Smart*, NBC	*NET Playhouse*, NET	1999	*Ally McBeal*, Fox	*The Practice*, ABC
1970	*My World and Welcome to It*, NBC	*Marcus Welby, M.D.*, ABC	2000	*Will & Grace*, NBC	*The West Wing*, NBC
1971	*All in the Family*, CBS	*The Bold Ones: "The Senator,"* NBC	2001	*Sex and the City*, HBO	*The West Wing*, NBC
			2002	*Friends*, NBC	*The West Wing*, NBC
1972	*All in the Family*, CBS	*Masterpiece Theatre: Elizabeth R*, PBS	2003	*Everybody Loves Raymond*, CBS	*The West Wing*, NBC
1973	*All in the Family*, CBS	*The Waltons*, CBS	2004	*Arrested Development*, Fox	*The Sopranos*, HBO
1974	*M*A*S*H*, CBS	*Masterpiece Theatre: Upstairs, Downstairs*, PBS	2005	*Everybody Loves Raymond*, CBS	*Lost*, ABC
1975	*Mary Tyler Moore Show*, CBS	*Masterpiece Theatre: Upstairs, Downstairs*, PBS	2006	*The Office*, NBC	*24*, Fox
1976	*Mary Tyler Moore Show*, CBS	*Police Story*, NBC	2007	*30 Rock*, NBC	*The Sopranos*, HBO
1977	*Mary Tyler Moore Show*, CBS	*Masterpiece Theatre: Upstairs, Downstairs*, PBS	2008	*30 Rock*, NBC	*Mad Men*, AMC
			2009	*30 Rock*, NBC	*Mad Men*, AMC

(1) "Best Single Program of the Year," shown on *Playhouse 90*, which was named "Best New Series." (2) Beginning in 1959, Emmys awarded for work in the season encompassing the previous and current year. (*) *Playhouse 90* (CBS) was best drama of 1 hour or longer; *Alcoa-Goodyear Theatre* (NBC) was best drama of less than 1 hour.

2009 Golden Globe Awards

The Hollywood Foreign Press Association (then the Hollywood Foreign Correspondents Assn.) presented its first awards for achievement in film in 1944; television was considered for the first time in 1955.

Film

Drama: *Slumdog Millionaire*
Comedy/Musical: *Vicky Cristina Barcelona*
Actress, Drama: Kate Winslet, *Revolutionary Road*
Actor, Drama: Mickey Rourke, *The Wrestler*
Actress, Comedy/Musical: Sally Hawkins, *Happy-Go-Lucky*
Actor, Comedy/Musical: Colin Farrell, *In Bruges*
Sup. Actress: Kate Winslet, *The Reader*
Sup. Actor: Heath Ledger, *The Dark Knight*
Director: Danny Boyle, *Slumdog Millionaire*
Screenplay: Simon Beaufoy, *Slumdog Millionaire*
Animated Film: *WALL-E*
Foreign-Language Film: *Waltz With Bashir*
Original Score: A. R. Rahman, *Slumdog Millionaire*
Original Song: "The Wrestler" (*The Wrestler*), w/m by Bruce Springsteen
Cecil B. DeMille Award: Steven Spielberg

Television

Series, Drama: *Mad Men*, AMC
Series, Comedy/Musical: *30 Rock*, NBC
Actress, Drama: Anna Paquin, *True Blood*, HBO
Actor, Drama: Gabriel Byrne, *In Treatment*, HBO
Actress, Comedy/Musical: Tina Fey, *30 Rock*, NBC
Actor, Comedy/Musical: Alec Baldwin, *30 Rock*, NBC
Miniseries or Movie Made for TV: *John Adams*, HBO
Actress, Miniseries/Movie: Laura Linney, *John Adams*, HBO
Actor, Miniseries/Movie: Paul Giamatti, *John Adams*, HBO
Sup. Actress: Laura Dern, *Recount*, HBO
Sup. Actor: Tom Wilkinson, *John Adams*, HBO

2009 People's Choice Awards

The first People's Choice Awards were presented in 1975. Sponsored by Procter & Gamble, the nominees and awards were initially selected by a Gallup Poll. Since 2005, winners have been selected by Internet voting.

Film

Picture: *The Dark Knight*
Drama: *The Secret Life of Bees*
Comedy: *27 Dresses*
Family Movie: *WALL-E*
Movie Stars: Reese Witherspoon, Will Smith
Leading Lady/Man: Kate Hudson, Brad Pitt
Action Movie Stars: Angelina Jolie, Will Smith
On-Screen Matchup: Christian Bale and Heath Ledger in *The Dark Knight*

Music

Singers: Carrie Underwood, Chris Brown
Group or Band: Rascal Flatts
R&B Song: "No One," Alicia Keys
Hip-Hop Song: "Low," Flo Rida feat. T-Pain

Pop Song: "I Kissed a Girl," Katy Perry
Country Song: "Last Name," Carrie Underwood
Rock Song: "All Summer Long," Kid Rock

Television

Drama: *House*
Comedy: *Two and a Half Men*
Animated Show: *The Simpsons*
Competition/Reality Program: *Dancing With the Stars*
Game Show: *Deal or No Deal*
TV Stars: Christina Applegate, Hugh Laurie
New Comedy: *Gary Unmarried*
New Drama: *The Mentalist*
Talk Show Host: Ellen DeGeneres

Academy Awards (Oscars), 1927-2008

Year	Picture	Actor	Actress	Sup. Actor[1]	Sup. Actress[1]	Director
1927 -28	*Wings*	Emil Jannings *The Way of All Flesh*	Janet Gaynor *Seventh Heaven*			Frank Borzage *Seventh Heaven*; Lewis Milestone *Two Arabian Knights*
1928 -29	*Broadway Melody*	Warner Baxter *In Old Arizona*	Mary Pickford *Coquette*			Frank Lloyd *The Divine Lady*
1929 -30	*All Quiet on the Western Front*	George Arliss *Disraeli*	Norma Shearer *The Divorcee*			Lewis Milestone *All Quiet on the Western Front*
1930 -31	*Cimarron*	Lionel Barrymore *Free Soul*	Marie Dressler *Min and Bill*			Norman Taurog *Skippy*
1931 -32	*Grand Hotel*	Fredric March *Dr. Jekyll and Mr. Hyde*; Wallace Beery *The Champ* (tie)	Helen Hayes *The Sin of Madelon Claudet*			Frank Borzage *Bad Girl*
1932 -33	*Cavalcade*	Charles Laughton *The Private Life of Henry VIII*	Katharine Hepburn *Morning Glory*			Frank Lloyd *Cavalcade*
1934	*It Happened One Night*	Clark Gable *It Happened One Night*	Claudette Colbert *It Happened One Night*			Frank Capra *It Happened One Night*
1935	*Mutiny on the Bounty*	Victor McLaglen *The Informer*	Bette Davis *Dangerous*			John Ford *The Informer*
1936	*The Great Ziegfeld*	Paul Muni *Story of Louis Pasteur*	Luise Rainer *The Great Ziegfeld*	Walter Brennan *Come and Get It*	Gale Sondergaard *Anthony Adverse*	Frank Capra *Mr. Deeds Goes to Town*
1937	*Life of Emile Zola*	Spencer Tracy *Captains Courageous*	Luise Rainer *The Good Earth*	Joseph Schildkraut *Life of Emile Zola*	Alice Brady *In Old Chicago*	Leo McCarey *The Awful Truth*
1938	*You Can't Take It With You*	Spencer Tracy *Boys Town*	Bette Davis *Jezebel*	Walter Brennan *Kentucky*	Fay Bainter *Jezebel*	Frank Capra *You Can't Take It With You*
1939	*Gone With the Wind*	Robert Donat *Goodbye Mr. Chips*	Vivien Leigh *Gone With the Wind*	Thomas Mitchell *Stage Coach*	Hattie McDaniel *Gone With the Wind*	Victor Fleming *Gone With the Wind*
1940	*Rebecca*	James Stewart *The Philadelphia Story*	Ginger Rogers *Kitty Foyle*	Walter Brennan *The Westerner*	Jane Darwell *The Grapes of Wrath*	John Ford *The Grapes of Wrath*
1941	*How Green Was My Valley*	Gary Cooper *Sergeant York*	Joan Fontaine *Suspicion*	Donald Crisp *How Green Was My Valley*	Mary Astor *The Great Lie*	John Ford *How Green Was My Valley*
1942	*Mrs. Miniver*	James Cagney *Yankee Doodle Dandy*	Greer Garson *Mrs. Miniver*	Van Heflin *Johnny Eager*	Teresa Wright *Mrs. Miniver*	William Wyler *Mrs. Miniver*
1943	*Casablanca*	Paul Lukas *Watch on the Rhine*	Jennifer Jones *The Song of Bernadette*	Charles Coburn *The More the Merrier*	Katina Paxinou *For Whom the Bell Tolls*	Michael Curtiz *Casablanca*
1944	*Going My Way*	Bing Crosby *Going My Way*	Ingrid Bergman *Gaslight*	Barry Fitzgerald *Going My Way*	Ethel Barrymore *None But the Lonely Heart*	Leo McCarey *Going My Way*
1945	*The Lost Weekend*	Ray Milland *The Lost Weekend*	Joan Crawford *Mildred Pierce*	James Dunn *A Tree Grows in Brooklyn*	Anne Revere *National Velvet*	Billy Wilder *The Lost Weekend*
1946	*The Best Years of Our Lives*	Fredric March *The Best Years of Our Lives*	Olivia de Havilland *To Each His Own*	Harold Russell *The Best Years of Our Lives*	Anne Baxter *The Razor's Edge*	William Wyler *The Best Years of Our Lives*
1947	*Gentleman's Agreement*	Ronald Colman *A Double Life*	Loretta Young *The Farmer's Daughter*	Edmund Gwenn *Miracle on 34th Street*	Celeste Holm *Gentleman's Agreement*	Elia Kazan *Gentleman's Agreement*
1948	*Hamlet*	Laurence Olivier *Hamlet*	Jane Wyman *Johnny Belinda*	Walter Huston *Treasure of Sierra Madre*	Claire Trevor *Key Largo*	John Huston *Treasure of Sierra Madre*
1949	*All the King's Men*	Broderick Crawford *All the King's Men*	Olivia de Havilland *The Heiress*	Dean Jagger *Twelve O'Clock High*	Mercedes McCambridge *All the King's Men*	Joseph L. Mankiewicz *Letter to Three Wives*
1950	*All About Eve*	Jose Ferrer *Cyrano de Bergerac*	Judy Holliday *Born Yesterday*	George Sanders *All About Eve*	Josephine Hull *Harvey*	Joseph L. Mankiewicz *All About Eve*
1951	*An American in Paris*	Humphrey Bogart *The African Queen*	Vivien Leigh *A Streetcar Named Desire*	Karl Malden *A Streetcar Named Desire*	Kim Hunter *A Streetcar Named Desire*	George Stevens *A Place in the Sun*
1952	*The Greatest Show on Earth*	Gary Cooper *High Noon*	Shirley Booth *Come Back Little Sheba*	Anthony Quinn *Viva Zapata!*	Gloria Grahame *The Bad and the Beautiful*	John Ford *The Quiet Man*
1953	*From Here to Eternity*	William Holden *Stalag 17*	Audrey Hepburn *Roman Holiday*	Frank Sinatra *From Here to Eternity*	Donna Reed *From Here to Eternity*	Fred Zinnemann *From Here to Eternity*

Year	Picture	Actor	Actress	Sup. Actor[1]	Sup. Actress[1]	Director
1954	On the Waterfront	Marlon Brando *On the Waterfront*	Grace Kelly *The Country Girl*	Edmond O'Brien *The Barefoot Contessa*	Eva Marie Saint *On the Waterfront*	Elia Kazan *On the Waterfront*
1955	Marty	Ernest Borgnine *Marty*	Anna Magnani *The Rose Tattoo*	Jack Lemmon *Mister Roberts*	Jo Van Fleet *East of Eden*	Delbert Mann *Marty*
1956	Around the World in 80 Days	Yul Brynner *The King and I*	Ingrid Bergman *Anastasia*	Anthony Quinn *Lust for Life*	Dorothy Malone *Written on the Wind*	George Stevens *Giant*
1957	The Bridge on the River Kwai	Alec Guinness *The Bridge on the River Kwai*	Joanne Woodward *The Three Faces of Eve*	Red Buttons *Sayonara*	Miyoshi Umeki *Sayonara*	David Lean *The Bridge on the River Kwai*
1958	Gigi	David Niven *Separate Tables*	Susan Hayward *I Want to Live*	Burl Ives *The Big Country*	Wendy Hiller *Separate Tables*	Vincente Minnelli *Gigi*
1959	Ben-Hur	Charlton Heston *Ben-Hur*	Simone Signoret *Room at the Top*	Hugh Griffith *Ben-Hur*	Shelley Winters *Diary of Anne Frank*	William Wyler *Ben-Hur*
1960	The Apartment	Burt Lancaster *Elmer Gantry*	Elizabeth Taylor *Butterfield 8*	Peter Ustinov *Spartacus*	Shirley Jones *Elmer Gantry*	Billy Wilder *The Apartment*
1961	West Side Story	Maximilian Schell *Judgment at Nuremberg*	Sophia Loren *Two Women*	George Chakiris *West Side Story*	Rita Moreno *West Side Story*	Jerome Robbins, Robert Wise *West Side Story*
1962	Lawrence of Arabia	Gregory Peck *To Kill a Mockingbird*	Anne Bancroft *The Miracle Worker*	Ed Begley *Sweet Bird of Youth*	Patty Duke *The Miracle Worker*	David Lean *Lawrence of Arabia*
1963	Tom Jones	Sidney Poitier *Lilies of the Field*	Patricia Neal *Hud*	Melvyn Douglas *Hud*	Margaret Rutherford *The V.I.P.s*	Tony Richardson *Tom Jones*
1964	My Fair Lady	Rex Harrison *My Fair Lady*	Julie Andrews *Mary Poppins*	Peter Ustinov *Topkapi*	Lila Kedrova *Zorba the Greek*	George Cukor *My Fair Lady*
1965	The Sound of Music	Lee Marvin *Cat Ballou*	Julie Christie *Darling*	Martin Balsam *A Thousand Clowns*	Shelley Winters *A Patch of Blue*	Robert Wise *The Sound of Music*
1966	A Man for All Seasons	Paul Scofield *A Man for All Seasons*	Elizabeth Taylor *Who's Afraid of Virginia Woolf?*	Walter Matthau *The Fortune Cookie*	Sandy Dennis *Who's Afraid of Virginia Woolf?*	Fred Zinnemann *A Man for All Seasons*
1967	In the Heat of the Night	Rod Steiger *In the Heat of the Night*	Katharine Hepburn *Guess Who's Coming to Dinner*	George Kennedy *Cool Hand Luke*	Estelle Parsons *Bonnie and Clyde*	Mike Nichols *The Graduate*
1968	Oliver!	Cliff Robertson *Charly*	Katharine Hepburn *The Lion in Winter;* Barbra Streisand *Funny Girl* (tie)	Jack Albertson *The Subject Was Roses*	Ruth Gordon *Rosemary's Baby*	Sir Carol Reed *Oliver!*
1969	Midnight Cowboy	John Wayne *True Grit*	Maggie Smith *The Prime of Miss Jean Brodie*	Gig Young *They Shoot Horses, Don't They?*	Goldie Hawn *Cactus Flower*	John Schlesinger *Midnight Cowboy*
1970	Patton	George C. Scott *Patton* (refused)	Glenda Jackson *Women in Love*	John Mills *Ryan's Daughter*	Helen Hayes *Airport*	Franklin Schaffner *Patton*
1971	The French Connection	Gene Hackman *The French Connection*	Jane Fonda *Klute*	Ben Johnson *The Last Picture Show*	Cloris Leachman *The Last Picture Show*	William Friedkin *The French Connection*
1972	The Godfather	Marlon Brando *The Godfather* (refused)	Liza Minnelli *Cabaret*	Joel Grey *Cabaret*	Eileen Heckart *Butterflies Are Free*	Bob Fosse *Cabaret*
1973	The Sting	Jack Lemmon *Save the Tiger*	Glenda Jackson *A Touch of Class*	John Houseman *The Paper Chase*	Tatum O'Neal *Paper Moon*	George Roy Hill *The Sting*
1974	The Godfather Part II	Art Carney *Harry and Tonto*	Ellen Burstyn *Alice Doesn't Live Here Anymore*	Robert DeNiro *The Godfather Part II*	Ingrid Bergman *Murder on the Orient Express*	Francis Ford Coppola *The Godfather Part II*
1975	One Flew Over the Cuckoo's Nest	Jack Nicholson *One Flew Over the Cuckoo's Nest*	Louise Fletcher *One Flew Over the Cuckoo's Nest*	George Burns *The Sunshine Boys*	Lee Grant *Shampoo*	Milos Forman *One Flew Over the Cuckoo's Nest*
1976	Rocky	Peter Finch *Network*	Faye Dunaway *Network*	Jason Robards *All the President's Men*	Beatrice Straight *Network*	John G. Avildsen *Rocky*
1977	Annie Hall	Richard Dreyfuss *The Goodbye Girl*	Diane Keaton *Annie Hall*	Jason Robards *Julia*	Vanessa Redgrave *Julia*	Woody Allen *Annie Hall*
1978	The Deer Hunter	Jon Voight *Coming Home*	Jane Fonda *Coming Home*	Christopher Walken *The Deer Hunter*	Maggie Smith *California Suite*	Michael Cimino *The Deer Hunter*
1979	Kramer vs. Kramer	Dustin Hoffman *Kramer vs. Kramer*	Sally Field *Norma Rae*	Melvyn Douglas *Being There*	Meryl Streep *Kramer vs. Kramer*	Robert Benton *Kramer vs. Kramer*
1980	Ordinary People	Robert DeNiro *Raging Bull*	Sissy Spacek *Coal Miner's Daughter*	Timothy Hutton *Ordinary People*	Mary Steenburgen *Melvin & Howard*	Robert Redford *Ordinary People*
1981	Chariots of Fire	Henry Fonda *On Golden Pond*	Katharine Hepburn *On Golden Pond*	John Gielgud *Arthur*	Maureen Stapleton *Reds*	Warren Beatty *Reds*
1982	Gandhi	Ben Kingsley *Gandhi*	Meryl Streep *Sophie's Choice*	Louis Gossett Jr. *An Officer and a Gentleman*	Jessica Lange *Tootsie*	Richard Attenborough *Gandhi*
1983	Terms of Endearment	Robert Duvall *Tender Mercies*	Shirley MacLaine *Terms of Endearment*	Jack Nicholson *Terms of Endearment*	Linda Hunt *The Year of Living Dangerously*	James L. Brooks *Terms of Endearment*

Year Picture	Actor	Actress	Sup. Actor[1]	Sup. Actress[1]	Director
1984 *Amadeus*	F. Murray Abraham *Amadeus*	Sally Field *Places in the Heart*	Haing S. Ngor *The Killing Fields*	Peggy Ashcroft *A Passage to India*	Milos Forman *Amadeus*
1985 *Out of Africa*	William Hurt *Kiss of the Spider Woman*	Geraldine Page *The Trip to Bountiful*	Don Ameche *Cocoon*	Anjelica Huston *Prizzi's Honor*	Sydney Pollack *Out of Africa*
1986 *Platoon*	Paul Newman *The Color of Money*	Marlee Matlin *Children of a Lesser God*	Michael Caine *Hannah and Her Sisters*	Dianne Wiest *Hannah and Her Sisters*	Oliver Stone *Platoon*
1987 *The Last Emperor*	Michael Douglas *Wall Street*	Cher *Moonstruck*	Sean Connery *The Untouchables*	Olympia Dukakis *Moonstruck*	Bernardo Bertolucci *The Last Emperor*
1988 *Rain Man*	Dustin Hoffman *Rain Man*	Jodie Foster *The Accused*	Kevin Kline *A Fish Called Wanda*	Geena Davis *The Accidental Tourist*	Barry Levinson *Rain Man*
1989 *Driving Miss Daisy*	Daniel Day-Lewis *My Left Foot*	Jessica Tandy *Driving Miss Daisy*	Denzel Washington *Glory*	Brenda Fricker *My Left Foot*	Oliver Stone *Born on the Fourth of July*
1990 *Dances With Wolves*	Jeremy Irons *Reversal of Fortune*	Kathy Bates *Misery*	Joe Pesci *Goodfellas*	Whoopi Goldberg *Ghost*	Kevin Costner *Dances With Wolves*
1991 *The Silence of the Lambs*	Anthony Hopkins *The Silence of the Lambs*	Jodie Foster *The Silence of the Lambs*	Jack Palance *City Slickers*	Mercedes Ruehl *The Fisher King*	Jonathan Demme *The Silence of the Lambs*
1992 *Unforgiven*	Al Pacino *Scent of a Woman*	Emma Thompson *Howards End*	Gene Hackman *Unforgiven*	Marisa Tomei *My Cousin Vinny*	Clint Eastwood *Unforgiven*
1993 *Schindler's List*	Tom Hanks *Philadelphia*	Holly Hunter *The Piano*	Tommy Lee Jones *The Fugitive*	Anna Paquin *The Piano*	Steven Spielberg *Schindler's List*
1994 *Forrest Gump*	Tom Hanks *Forrest Gump*	Jessica Lange *Blue Sky*	Martin Landau *Ed Wood*	Dianne Wiest *Bullets Over Broadway*	Robert Zemeckis *Forrest Gump*
1995 *Braveheart*	Nicolas Cage *Leaving Las Vegas*	Susan Sarandon *Dead Man Walking*	Kevin Spacey *The Usual Suspects*	Mira Sorvino *Mighty Aphrodite*	Mel Gibson *Braveheart*
1996 *The English Patient*	Geoffrey Rush *Shine*	Frances McDormand *Fargo*	Cuba Gooding Jr. *Jerry Maguire*	Juliette Binoche *The English Patient*	Anthony Minghella *The English Patient*
1997 *Titanic*	Jack Nicholson *As Good As It Gets*	Helen Hunt *As Good As It Gets*	Robin Williams *Good Will Hunting*	Kim Basinger *L.A. Confidential*	James Cameron *Titanic*
1998 *Shakespeare in Love*	Roberto Benigni *Life Is Beautiful*	Gwyneth Paltrow *Shakespeare in Love*	James Coburn *Affliction*	Judi Dench *Shakespeare in Love*	Steven Spielberg *Saving Private Ryan*
1999 *American Beauty*	Kevin Spacey *American Beauty*	Hilary Swank *Boys Don't Cry*	Michael Caine *The Cider House Rules*	Angelina Jolie *Girl, Interrupted*	Sam Mendes *American Beauty*
2000 *Gladiator*	Russell Crowe *Gladiator*	Julia Roberts *Erin Brockovich*	Benicio Del Toro *Traffic*	Marcia Gay Harden *Pollock*	Steven Soderbergh *Traffic*
2001 *A Beautiful Mind*	Denzel Washington *Training Day*	Halle Berry *Monster's Ball*	Jim Broadbent *Iris*	Jennifer Connelly *A Beautiful Mind*	Ron Howard *A Beautiful Mind*
2002 *Chicago*	Adrien Brody *The Pianist*	Nicole Kidman *The Hours*	Chris Cooper *Adaptation*	Catherine Zeta-Jones *Chicago*	Roman Polanski *The Pianist*
2003 *The Lord of the Rings: The Return of the King*	Sean Penn *Mystic River*	Charlize Theron *Monster*	Tim Robbins *Mystic River*	Renée Zellweger *Cold Mountain*	Peter Jackson *The Lord of the Rings: The Return of the King*
2004 *Million Dollar Baby*	Jamie Foxx *Ray*	Hilary Swank *Million Dollar Baby*	Morgan Freeman *Million Dollar Baby*	Cate Blanchett *The Aviator*	Clint Eastwood *Million Dollar Baby*
2005 *Crash*	Philip Seymour Hoffman, *Capote*	Reese Witherspoon *Walk the Line*	George Clooney *Syriana*	Rachel Weisz *The Constant Gardener*	Ang Lee *Brokeback Mountain*
2006 *The Departed*	Forest Whitaker *The Last King of Scotland*	Helen Mirren *The Queen*	Alan Arkin *Little Miss Sunshine*	Jennifer Hudson *Dreamgirls*	Martin Scorsese *The Departed*
2007 *No Country for Old Men*	Daniel Day-Lewis *There Will Be Blood*	Marion Cotillard *La Vie en Rose*	Javier Bardem *No Country for Old Men*	Tilda Swinton *Michael Clayton*	Joel Coen and Ethan Coen, *No Country for Old Men*
2008 *Slumdog Millionaire*	Sean Penn *Milk*	Kate Winslet *The Reader*	Heath Ledger *The Dark Knight*	Penelope Cruz *Vicky Cristina Barcelona*	Danny Boyle *Slumdog Millionaire*

(1) These awards not given until 1936.

Other Oscar Winners, 2008

Original Screenplay: Dustin Lance Black, *Milk*
Adapted Screenplay: Simon Beaufoy, *Slumdog Millionaire*
Foreign Language Film: *Departures*, Japan
Animated Feature: *WALL-E*
Documentary Feature: *Man on Wire*
Short Films: *La Maison en Petits Cubes* (animated), *Spielzeugland* [*Toyland*] (live action), *Smile Pinki* (documentary)
Art Direction: *The Curious Case of Benjamin Button*

Cinematography: *Slumdog Millionaire*
Visual Effects: *The Curious Case of Benjamin Button*
Costume Design: *The Duchess*
Film Editing: *Slumdog Millionaire*
Sound Mixing: *Slumdog Millionaire*
Sound Editing: *The Dark Knight*
Original Score: A. R. Rahman, *Slumdog Millionaire*
Original Song: "Jai Ho," *Slumdog Millionaire*
Makeup: *The Curious Case of Benjamin Button*

Other Film Awards, 2009
(Awarded in 2009, unless otherwise noted.)

Berlin International Film Festival

Best Film (Golden Bear): *La teta asustada* [*The Milk of Sorrow*], Claudia Llosa, Peru

Jury Grand Prix (Silver Bear): *Alle Anderen* [*Everyone Else*], Maren Ade, Germany; *Gigante*, Adrián Biniez, Uruguay

Director: Asghar Farhadi, *Darbareye Elly* [*About Elly*], Iran

Actress: Birgit Minichmayr, *Alle Anderen* [*Everyone Else*], Germany

Actor: Sotigui Kouyate, *London River*, UK

Artistic Contribution: György Kovács, Gábor Erdély, and Tamás Székely for sound design of *Katalin Varga*, Romania

Script: Oren Moverman and Alessandro Camon, *The Messenger*, U.S.

Alfred Bauer Prize: *Gigante*, Adrián Biniez, Uruguay; *Tatarak* [*Sweet Rush*], Andrzej Wajda, Poland

British Academy of Film and Television Awards (BAFTAs, 2008)

Best Film: *Slumdog Millionaire*

British Film: *Man on Wire*

Director: Danny Boyle, *Slumdog Millionaire*

Original Screenplay: *In Bruges*, Martin McDonagh

Adapted Screenplay: *Slumdog Millionaire*, Simon Beaufoy

Foreign Language Film: *I've Loved You So Long* (France)

Animated Film: *WALL-E*

Actor: Mickey Rourke, *The Wrestler*

Actress: Kate Winslet, *The Reader*

Supporting Actor: Heath Ledger, *The Dark Knight*

Supporting Actress: Penélope Cruz, *Vicky Cristina Barcelona*

Cannes International Film Festival Awards

Cannes: Feature Films

Palme d'Or (Golden Palm): *Das Weisse Band* [*The White Ribbon*], Michael Haneke, Austria

Grand Prix: *Un Prophète* [*A Prophet*], Jacques Audiard, France

Director: Brillante Mendoza, *Kinatay*, France/Philippines

Jury Prize: *Fish Tank*, Andrea Arnold, UK; *Bak-Jwi* [*Thirst*], Park Chan-Wook

Actor: Christoph Waltz, *Inglourious Basterds*, Germany/U.S.

Actress: Charlotte Gainsbourg, *Antichrist*, Denmark/Germany/France/Sweden/Italy

Screenplay: Lou Ye, *Chun Feng Chen Zui De Ye Wan* [*Spring Fever*], Hong Kong/France

Vulcain Prize: *Map of the Sounds of Tokyo*, Isabel Coixet, Spain

Cannes: Short Films

Palme d'Or: *Arena*, João Salaviza, Portugal

Special Distinction: *The Six Dollar Fifty Man*, Louis Sutherland, Mark Albiston, New Zealand

Director's Guild of America Awards (2008)

Feature Film: Danny Boyle, *Slumdog Millionaire*

Documentary: Ari Folman, *Waltz with Bashir*

Genie Awards (Canada)

Best Motion Picture: *Passchendaele*

Best Actor: Natar Ungalaaq, *C'est qu'il faut pour vivre* [*The Necessities of Life*]

Best Actress: Ellen Burstyn, *The Stone Angel*

Best Supporting Actor: Callum Keith Rennie, *Normal*

Best Supporting Actress: Kristin Booth, *Young People Fucking*

Best Documentary: *Up the Yangtze*

Director: Benoit Pilon, *C'est qu'il faut pour vivre* [*The Necessities of Life*]

Sundance Film Festival Awards

Grand Jury Prize: *Push: Based on the Novel by Sapphire*, Lee Daniels (drama); *We Live in Public*, Ondi Timoner (doc.)

World Cinema Grand Jury Prize: *La Nana* [*The Maid*], Sebastián Silva, Chile (drama); *Rough Aunties*, Kim Longinotto, UK (doc.)

Audience Award: *Push: Based on the Novel by Sapphire*, Lee Daniels (drama); *The Cove*, Louie Psilhoyos (doc.)

World Cinema Audience Award: *An Education*, Lone Scherfig, UK (drama); *Afghan Star*, Havana Marking, Afghanistan/UK (doc.)

Directing: Cary Joji Fukunaga, *Sin Nombre* (drama); Natalia Almada, *El General* (doc.)

World Cinema Directing Award: Oliver Hirschbiegel, *Five Minutes of Heaven*, UK/Ireland (drama); Havana Marking, *Afghan Star*, Afghanistan/UK (doc.)

Waldo Salt Screenwriting Award: Nicholas Jasenovec and Charlene Yi, *Paper Heart*

World Cinema Screenwriting Award: Guy Hibbert, *Five Minutes of Heaven*, UK/Ireland

Documentary Editing: Karen Schmeer, *Sergio*

World Cinema Doc. Editing: Janus Billeskov Jansen and Thomas Papapetros, *Burma VJ*, Denmark

Cinematography: Adriano Goldman, *Sin Nombre* (drama); Bob Richman, *The September Issue* (doc.)

World Cinema Cinematography: John De Borman, *An Education*, UK (drama); John Maringouin, *Big River Man*, U.S./UK (doc.)

Special Jury Prize: Jeff Stilson, *Good Hair* (doc.); Lynn Shelton, *Humpday* (spirit of independence); Mo'Nique, *Push: Based on the Novel by Sapphire* (acting)

World Cinema Special Jury Prize: Benoît Delépine and Gustave de Kervern, *Louise-Michel*, France (originality); Ngawang Choephel, *Tibet in Song*, Tibet (doc.); Catalina Saavedra, *La Nana* [*The Maid*], Chile (acting)

Toronto International Film Festival

Prize of the International Critics (FIPRESCI Prize) for Discovery: Laxmikant Shetgoankar's *The Man Beyond the Bridge*

FIPRESCI Prize for Special Presentation: Bruno Dumont's *Hadewijch*

Cadillac People's Choice Award: Lee Daniels's *Precious*

Best Canadian Short Film: Pedro Pires's *Danse Macabre*

Best Canadian First Feature Film: Alexandre Franchi's *The Wild Hunt*

Best Canadian Feature Film: Ruba Nadda's *Cairo Time*

2009 MTV Video Music Awards

Video of the Year: "Single Ladies (Put a Ring on It)," Beyoncé

Best Female Video: "You Belong With Me," Taylor Swift

Best Male Video: "Live Your Life," T.I. feat. Rihanna

Breakthrough Video: "Lessons Learned," Matt & Kim

Best Hip-Hop Video: "We Made You," Eminem

Best Rock Video: "21 Guns," Green Day

Best Pop Video: "Womanizer," Britney Spears

Best New Artist: "Poker Face," Lady Gaga

Best Art Direction: "Paparazzi," Lady Gaga

Best Choreography: "Single Ladies (Put a Ring on It)," Beyoncé

Best Cinematography: "21 Guns," Green Day

Best Direction: "21 Guns," Green Day

Best Editing: "Single Ladies (Put a Ring on It)," Beyoncé

Best Special Effects: "Paparazzi," Lady Gaga

2009 Academy of Country Music Awards

Entertainer of the Year: Carrie Underwood

Album of the Year: *Fearless*, Taylor Swift

Record of the Year (single): "You're Gonna Miss This," Trace Adkins

Song of the Year: "In Color," Jamey Johnson

Vocal Event of the Year: "Start a Band," Brad Paisley, Keith Urban

Female Vocalist: Carrie Underwood

Male Vocalist: Brad Paisley

Vocal Duo: Sugarland

Vocal Group: Rascal Flatts

New Artist: Julianne Hough

New Female Vocalist: Julianne Hough

New Male Vocalist: Jake Owen

New Duo/Group: Zac Brown Band

Video of the Year: "Waitin' on a Woman," Brad Paisley

Crystal Milestone Award: Taylor Swift, Jennifer Nettles

Humanitarian Award: Leann Rimes

Grammy Awards

Source: National Academy of Recording Arts & Sciences
2008 Grammy Awards are for albums released Oct. 1, 2007-Sept. 30, 2008, and were presented in Feb. 2009.

Selected Grammy Awards for 2008

Record of the Year (single): "Please Read the Letter," Robert Plant & Alison Krauss
Album of the Year: *Raising Sand*, Robert Plant & Alison Krauss
Song of the Year: "Viva La Vida," Coldplay
New Artist: Adele
Pop Vocal Perf., Female: "Chasing Pavements," Adele
Pop Vocal Perf., Male: "Say," John Mayer
Pop Vocal Perf., Duo/Group: "Viva La Vida," Coldplay
Pop Vocal Perf., Collaboration: "Rich Woman," Robert Plant & Alison Krauss
Pop Vocal Album: *Rockferry*, Duffy
Dance Recording: "Harder Better Faster Stronger," Daft Punk
Rock Vocal Perf., Solo: "Gravity," John Mayer
Rock Vocal Perf., Duo/Group: "Sex On Fire," Kings of Leon
Hard Rock Perf.: "Wax Simulacra," The Mars Volta
Rock Song: "Girls in Their Summer Clothes," Bruce Springsteen
Rock Album: *Viva La Vida or Death and All His Friends*, Coldplay
Alternative Album: *In Rainbows*, Radiohead
R&B Vocal Perf., Female: "Superwoman," Alicia Keys
R&B Vocal Perf., Male: "Miss Independent," Ne-Yo
R&B Vocal Perf., Duo/Group: "Stay With Me (By the Sea)," Al Green feat. John Legend

R&B Song: "Miss Independent," Ne-Yo
R&B Album: *Jennifer Hudson*, Jennifer Hudson
R&B Album, Contemporary: *Growing Pains*, Mary J. Blige
Rap Perf., Solo: "A Milli," Lil Wayne
Rap Perf., Duo/Group: "Swagga Like Us," Jay-Z & T.I. feat. Kanye West & Lil Wayne
Rap Song: "Lollipop," Lil Wayne feat. Static Major
Rap Album: *Tha Carter III*, Lil Wayne
Country Vocal Perf., Female: "Last Name," Carrie Underwood
Country Vocal Perf., Male: "Letter to Me," Brad Paisley
Country Vocal Perf., Duo/Group: "Stay," Sugarland
Country Song: "Stay," Sugarland (w/m by Jennifer Nettles)
Country Album: *Troubadour*, George Strait
Comedy Album: *It's Bad For Ya*, George Carlin
Soundtrack Album, Compilation: *Juno*, various artists
Soundtrack Album, Score: *The Dark Knight*, James Newton Howard & Hans Zimmer
Song, Motion Picture/TV: "Down to Earth," Peter Gabriel & Thomas Newman, *WALL-E*
Music Video, Short Form: "Pork and Beans," Weezer
Music Video, Long Form: *Runnin' Down a Dream*, Tom Petty and the Heartbreakers

Grammy Awards for 1958-2008

Record of the Year (single)	Year	Album of the Year
Domenico Modugno, "Nel Blu Dipinto Di Blu (Volare)"	1958	Henry Mancini, *The Music From Peter Gunn*
Bobby Darin, "Mack the Knife"	1959	Frank Sinatra, *Come Dance With Me*
Percy Faith, "Theme From a Summer Place"	1960	Bob Newhart, *Button Down Mind*
Henry Mancini, "Moon River"	1961	Judy Garland, *Judy at Carnegie Hall*
Tony Bennett, "I Left My Heart in San Francisco"	1962	Vaughn Meader, *The First Family*
Henry Mancini, "The Days of Wine and Roses"	1963	Barbra Streisand, *The Barbra Streisand Album*
Stan Getz, Astrud Gilberto, "The Girl From Ipanema"	1964	Stan Getz, João Gilberto, *Getz/Gilberto*
Herb Alpert, "A Taste of Honey"	1965	Frank Sinatra, *September of My Years*
Frank Sinatra, "Strangers in the Night"	1966	Frank Sinatra, *A Man and His Music*
5th Dimension, "Up, Up and Away"	1967	The Beatles, *Sgt. Pepper's Lonely Hearts Club Band*
Simon and Garfunkel, "Mrs. Robinson"	1968	Glen Campbell, *By the Time I Get to Phoenix*
5th Dimension, "Aquarius/Let the Sunshine In"	1969	Blood, Sweat & Tears, *Blood, Sweat & Tears*
Simon and Garfunkel, "Bridge Over Troubled Water"	1970	Simon and Garfunkel, *Bridge Over Troubled Water*
Carole King, "It's Too Late"	1971	Carole King, *Tapestry*
Roberta Flack, "The First Time Ever I Saw Your Face"	1972	George Harrison and friends, *The Concert for Bangla Desh*
Roberta Flack, "Killing Me Softly With His Song"	1973	Stevie Wonder, *Innervisions*
Olivia Newton-John, "I Honestly Love You"	1974	Stevie Wonder, *Fulfillingness' First Finale*
Captain & Tennille, "Love Will Keep Us Together"	1975	Paul Simon, *Still Crazy After All These Years*
George Benson, "This Masquerade"	1976	Stevie Wonder, *Songs in the Key of Life*
Eagles, "Hotel California"	1977	Fleetwood Mac, *Rumours*
Billy Joel, "Just the Way You Are"	1978	Bee Gees, *Saturday Night Fever*
The Doobie Brothers, "What a Fool Believes"	1979	Billy Joel, *52nd Street*
Christopher Cross, "Sailing"	1980	Christopher Cross, *Christopher Cross*
Kim Carnes, "Bette Davis Eyes"	1981	John Lennon, Yoko Ono, *Double Fantasy*
Toto, "Rosanna"	1982	Toto, *Toto IV*
Michael Jackson, "Beat It"	1983	Michael Jackson, *Thriller*
Tina Turner, "What's Love Got to Do With It"	1984	Lionel Richie, *Can't Slow Down*
USA for Africa, "We Are the World"	1985	Phil Collins, *No Jacket Required*
Steve Winwood, "Higher Love"	1986	Paul Simon, *Graceland*
Paul Simon, "Graceland"	1987	U2, *The Joshua Tree*
Bobby McFerrin, "Don't Worry, Be Happy"	1988	George Michael, *Faith*
Bette Midler, "Wind Beneath My Wings"	1989	Bonnie Raitt, *Nick of Time*
Phil Collins, "Another Day in Paradise"	1990	Quincy Jones, *Back on the Block*
Natalie Cole, with Nat "King" Cole, "Unforgettable"	1991	Natalie Cole, with Nat "King" Cole, *Unforgettable*
Eric Clapton, "Tears in Heaven"	1992	Eric Clapton, *Unplugged*
Whitney Houston, "I Will Always Love You"	1993	Whitney Houston, *The Bodyguard*
Sheryl Crow, "All I Wanna Do"	1994	Tony Bennett, *MTV Unplugged*
Seal, "Kiss From a Rose"	1995	Alanis Morissette, *Jagged Little Pill*
Eric Clapton, "Change the World"	1996	Celine Dion, *Falling Into You*
Shawn Colvin, "Sunny Came Home"	1997	Bob Dylan, *Time Out of Mind*
Celine Dion, "My Heart Will Go On"	1998	Lauryn Hill, *The Miseducation of Lauryn Hill*
Santana featuring Rob Thomas, "Smooth"	1999	Santana, *Supernatural*
U2, "Beautiful Day"	2000	Steely Dan, *Two Against Nature*
U2, "Walk On"	2001	Various Artists, *O Brother, Where Art Thou?*
Norah Jones, "Don't Know Why"	2002	Norah Jones, *Come Away With Me*
Coldplay, "Clocks"	2003	OutKast, *Speakerboxxx/The Love Below*
Ray Charles & Norah Jones, "Here We Go Again"	2004	Ray Charles & Various Artists, *Genius Loves Company*
Green Day, "Boulevard of Broken Dreams"	2005	U2, *How to Dismantle an Atomic Bomb*
Dixie Chicks, "Not Ready to Make Nice"	2006	Dixie Chicks, *Taking the Long Way*
Amy Winehouse, "Rehab"	2007	Herbie Hancock, *River: The Joni Letters*
Robert Plant & Alison Krauss, "Please Read the Letter"	2008	Robert Plant & Alison Krauss, *Raising Sand*

SCIENCE AND TECHNOLOGY

Science and Technology News 2009

The following were some of the more newsworthy developments in science and technology in the past year. (See also Astronomy, Computers and Telecommunications, and the Chronology of the Year's Events.)

Minerals Evolved With Life

Life and minerals on Earth may have "co-evolved"—the presence of one affecting how the other diversified and flourished—according to a study by Robert Hazen and colleagues in the Nov. 2008 issue of *American Mineralogist*. Hazen's team found that two out of every three minerals, or nonliving solids with specific chemical compositions occurring in nature, on Earth would not exist if not for living things.

Earth's mineral evolution began billions of years ago. Before the solar system was formed, there existed a giant cloud of gas and dust comprised of the ashes of dying stars. The cloud contained all of the 94 naturally occurring elements found in the periodic table but only about a dozen minerals. More minerals were formed once the sun grew massive and hot enough to achieve thermonuclear fusion, bringing the total to about 60. Gravitational forces and high temperatures led to the creation of more minerals as the planets formed. Hazen estimates that about 10 mil years after Earth formed, some 250 minerals were present. Earthquakes and volcanoes, both powerful forces of mineral creation resulting from plate tectonics, ensured an increase. By the time Earth was about 2.5 billion years old, it contained about 1,500 minerals.

But the biggest boost to mineral evolution didn't occur until life (in the form of photosynthesizing cyanobacteria) arrived. The bacteria created an oxygen-rich atmosphere that contributed to the creation of new mineral species. Hazen estimates that two-thirds of the approximately 4,300 minerals found on Earth today stem from biological processes, either directly or indirectly. The new findings could aid astronomers searching for life beyond our solar system.

Scientists Figure Out How Bleach Kills Bacteria

More than 140 years after discovering bleach's use as a disinfectant, scientists have finally figured out exactly how it kills germs. A research team, led by Ursula Jakob, showed in the Nov. 2008 issue of *Cell* that bleach kills bacteria in much the same way a fever or boiling does—it "cooks" cell proteins by destroying their shape and causing them to unfold and clump together, thus killing the cells.

The team focused their research on Hsp33, a protein found in some bacteria. Bleach causes Hsp33, which protects the bacteria's other proteins, to unfold. Unlike other proteins, Hsp33 is not damaged permanently, and returns to normal once conditions change. (Hsp33 serves the same function in high temperatures, enabling bacteria with it to survive.) In bacteria without Hsp33, the acid in bleach warps the unprotected proteins, killing the cell.

Early Whales Gave Birth on Land

A team of paleontologists led by Philip Gingerich concluded that a previously undiscovered species of protocetid (an early ancestor of modern-day whales) gave birth on land, according to fossil evidence-based findings published in Feb. in the online journal *PLoS ONE*. The approximately 47.5 mil-year-old fossils were discovered at a rock formation in central Pakistan in 2000 and 2004. (Much of the Indian subcontinent was underwater during the Eocene epoch nearly 50 million years ago.) After the team uncovered what appeared to be the fossil of a small protocetid, further excavation revealed that it was surrounded by the fossil of a much larger protocetid, indicating that the remains were those of a fetus inside its mother. The fetus was positioned for a headfirst birth, as are most land mammals, so that the offspring are able to breathe during delivery. Contemporary cetaceans, the group of mammals to which whales and dolphins belong, deliver their offspring tail first underwater to lessen the chances of the offspring drowning before it is free of its mother's body. The fossils, along with other evidence, led the team to conclude that while these early whales hunted in the sea, they gave birth on land.

(Piezoelectric) Energy Is All Around

Cell phones, calculators, iPods, flashlights, insulin pumps, and other medical devices: one thing these items have in common is that they require lots of energy to power. That may change someday, thanks in part to the work of a research team led by Zhong Lin Wang whose work was published in the Feb. issue of *Nano Letters*. Wang's group looked into ways to build devices that "scavenge" small amounts of mechanical energy from the environment—including sound waves, ground vibrations, body motions, even blood moving through the body—and turn it into electricity.

Piezoelectricity, first described in 1880, is a phenomenon associated with compressing or stretching. When one compresses or stretches a piezoelectric material, that action creates an electric potential. Much of Wang's work focused on the use of zinc oxide (ZnO), a commonly found material. In addition to being piezoelectric, zinc oxide is biosafe and can be made into different shapes, including tiny nanowires that can be grown on a wide variety of substrates. Wang's team tested ZnO nanowires one at a time, manipulating each with an atomic force microscope equipped with a probe. As the wire was pushed to one side by the microscope's tip, one part of the wire would stretch and develop a positive electrical charge while the other side would compress and develop a negative charge. The contact between the tip and the ZnO wire forms what is called a Schottky barrier, preventing the flow of electrons from the microscope's tip into the nanowire. Charge built up in the wire, and the Schottky contact acted like a gate for separating and slowly accumulating the charges. As the tip slid to the compressed side, there was a sudden spike in the flow of electrons from the nanowire into the tip of the microscope, as if electrons were pumped into the tip of the nanowire, then released into the electrode—and into a circuit that could be used to potentially power a device. Wang's nanogenerator, in photomicrographs, looks like a tiny brush with thousands of ZnO nanowire bristles. When the tip of the microscope was replaced with a zigzag electrode capable of bending many wires at the same time, the nanowires could produce electricity in parallel, increasing the current from the nanogenerator.

Possible short-term uses for the nanogenerators include powering censors in biomedical devices or for military or industrial purposes. But someday—perhaps a decade from now—it may be possible to apply the technology to create products for the consumer market.

Stem Cell Restrictions Lifted

Pres. Barack Obama issued an executive order Mar. 9 removing the tight restrictions on federal funding for embryonic stem-cell research that were put in place by former Pres. George W. Bush early in his first term. Many scientists and patient advocates believe stem cells could be a particularly fruitful line of research into the treatment of a number of diseases. But Obama's order was opposed by those who, on religious or other grounds, see such research as crossing an ethical line.

Climate Models May Underestimate Global Warming

According to Richard E. Zeebe and colleagues in the Aug. issue of *Nature Geoscience*, it's getting hotter than we think. Zeebe's findings suggest that the current climate models may vastly underestimate global warming and might be failing to account for important warming mechanisms.

The scientists examined rock dating back 55 mil years, to a time when the climate warmed dramatically. This extreme shift, called the Paleocene-Eocene Thermal Maximum (PETM), caused massive species extinctions. Using a popular climate model that emphasizes the role of carbon dioxide in warming, they estimated that temperatures during the PETM would have risen by 2 to 6 degrees Fahrenheit. But by examining the composition of rock from the PETM, scientists were able to determine actual carbon levels and average temperatures. They found that temperatures actually rose by 9 to 16 degrees Fahrenheit, indicating that the model they had used may fail to account for undetermined factors, such as an overlooked feedback mechanism or other greenhouse gases. The position of the continents was different 55 mil years ago, permitting greater interaction between the Atlantic and Pacific Oceans, so the PETM is not a perfect analogue to modern times.

Is Primate Fossil the "Missing Link"?

The exquisitely preserved fossil of a 47 mil-year-old lemur-like creature could shed new light on the evolution of the ancestral lines from which humans arose, according to researchers led by Jens L. Franzen in the May 19 issue of *PLoS One*. The authors theorized that the primate could have been an early cousin of one of the common ancestors of today's monkeys, apes, and humans. Nicknamed "Ida," the fossil was that of a juvenile female and was so complete that the outline of the creature's fur was discernible and the contents of its last meal could be determined. Ida, whose official name is *Darwinius masillae*, lived during the Eocene period, when rainforest covered much of the planet, and many different species of primates thrived and underwent rapid evolution. The near-perfect remains were originally found in 1983 by a team of amateur fossil hunters.

While Ida has features similar to those of humans—such as nails instead of claws, a human-shaped ankle bone, a grasping hand, and an opposable thumb—she is probably not a direct ancestor, according to Franzen: "We're not dealing with our grand, grand, grandmother, but perhaps with our grand, grand, grand aunt."

Although the fossil was considered a great specimen in and of itself, many in the scientific community were skeptical of the paper's claims that Ida was a close relative of humans. In addition, many also protested the hype and fanfare that accompanied the research as unnecessary and premature.

See-Through Aluminum

Spray a sheet of aluminum with an ultra-intense beam of photons, and you'll see through to the other side, according to Bob Nagler and colleagues in the July 26 issue of *Nature Physics*. The team discovered the surprising new phenomenon while working at FLASH, a photon science facility in Hamburg, Germany. The FLASH laser, known as a free-electron laser, produces brief pulses of intense light on various wavelengths. The team exposed aluminum wafers 53 nanometers thick to beams of laser light. When bombarded by FLASH's laser—which, in terms of intensity (energy per time per area) is about 1,019 times stronger than the noonday sun—the solid aluminum changed into a special high-energy state called warm dense matter (WDM). For as long as the aluminum remained in that state (only 15 quadrillionths of a second), additional light rays traveled through the metal as if it were transparent. The researchers believe this new approach is an ideal way to create and study exotic states of matter and will lead to further work relevant to areas as diverse as planetary science, astrophysics, and nuclear fusion power.

Forensics Solves Mystery of Missing Russian Royalty

The Bolsheviks' clandestine murder of the Romanovs, the last imperial family of Russia, took place in 1918 in the cellar of a mansion in Yekaterinburg, Russia. For decades, the actual events were shrouded in secrecy and remained a mystery to historians. The 1991 unearthing of the Romanovs' burial site, which was discovered in 1979, fueled more questions into the circumstances of their deaths. The bodies of two of the Romanov children were not found at the site. This fed speculation that some members of the family had survived.

New, unidentified remains were found near the burial site in 2007. DNA tests conducted by scientists at the Armed Forces DNA Identification Laboratory in Rockville, MD, and the Institute for Legal Medicine in Innsbruck, Austria, confirmed that the new remains belonged to the two Romanov children. The findings, presented by Michael D. Coble and colleagues Mar. 11 in *PLoS ONE*, showed mitochondrial DNA, autosomal STR, and Y-STR evidence eliminating the possibility that any member of the Romanov family survived the killings.

As for why the two children were not buried alongside the rest of their family, Coble said historical record indicates that the Bolsheviks tried to cremate the bodies in an effort to destroy evidence. He hypothesized that they first tried with the two children's bodies but gave up the effort after failing to generate high enough temperatures to fully dispose of the remains.

Markov Models: Decryption by Probability

The Indus Valley civilization, which flourished between 2600 and 1900 BCE, has long puzzled scientists because its written record is indecipherable. Archaeologists have found nearly 4,000 artifacts with what appear to be short inscriptions. Without a key, modern-day investigators could not decipher the language. Translations have been proposed, but there has been no widespread agreement on their accuracy. A team of researchers led by Rajesh Rao decided to tackle the problem by using probability, and their findings were published in *Proceedings of the National Academy of Sciences* in Aug. Though they did not produce translations, the researchers claim that their approach may facilitate that goal. The aim was to construct a Markov model—a matrix of probabilities of one sign following another. If they could build a model that determined the likelihood of sequences of marks, it might in turn shed light on word usage and grammar.

The analysis of the samples of Indus Valley script revealed that certain signs were significantly more likely to start a text than others, and similarly, certain symbols were more likely to occur at the end. The researchers said that an inspection of the transition matrix (i.e., the Markov matrix of probabilities) showed that for a given sign in the language, there is a specific subset of signs that have a high probability of following it. In terms of the order of signs, the texts occupy a middle ground between a rigid order and flexibility or randomness. Most natural languages exhibit this flexibility, which the researchers note is a sign that grammar-like rules are playing a role in determining the sequence of the signs. Further analysis along these lines may one day produce a key by which archaeologists can translate this civilization's texts.

Science Glossary

This glossary covers some concepts that come up frequently in the news, in biology, chemistry, geology, and physics. *See also* Astronomy, Computers and Telecommunications, Environment, Health, Meteorology, Weights and Measures.

Biology

Note: For classification terms such as *kingdom*, *phylum*, etc., *see* p. 292.

Amino acid: one of about 20 similar small molecules that are the building blocks of proteins.

Antibiotic: a substance produced by or derived from a bacterium, fungus, or other organism that battles bacterial infections and diseases, by killing bacteria or halting their growth.

Autoimmunity: a condition in which an individual's immune system reacts against his or her own tissues; leads to diseases such as lupus, diabetes, inflammatory bowel disease, and rheumatoid arthritis.

Bacteriophage: a virus that infects, or lyses, bacteria. Also called "phage."

Bacterium (plural, bacteria): one of a large, varied class of microscopic and simple, single-celled organisms; bacteria live almost everywhere—some forms cause disease, while others are useful in digestion and other natural processes.

Biodiversity: richness of variety of life-forms—both plant and animal—in a given environment.

Cell: the smallest unit of life capable of living independently, or with other cells; usually bounded by a membrane. May include a nucleus and other specialized parts.

Cholesterol: a fatty substance in animal tissues; it is produced by the liver in humans, is found in foods such as butter, eggs, and meat, and is an essential body constituent.

Chromosome: one of the rod-like structures in cell nuclei that carry genetic material (DNA).

Cloning: the process of copying a particular piece of DNA to allow it to be sequenced, studied, or used in some other way; can also refer to producing a genetic copy of an organism.

DNA (deoxyribonucleic acid): the chemical substance that carries genetic information, which determines the form and functioning of all living things.

Ecosystem: an interdependent community of living organisms and their climatic and geographical habitat.

Enzyme: a protein that promotes a particular chemical reaction in the body.

Estrogen: one of a group of hormones that promote development of female secondary sex characteristics and the growth and health of the female reproductive system; males also produce small amounts of estrogen.

Eukaryote: single- or multi-celled organisms whose cells have distinct nuclei.

Evolution: the process of gradual change that may occur as a species adapts to its environment; natural selection is the process by which evolution occurs.

Gene: a portion of a DNA molecule that provides the blueprint for the assembly of a protein.

Gene pool: the collection and total diversity of genes in an interbreeding population.

Gene therapy: a treatment in which scientists try to implant functioning genes into a person's cells so the genes can produce proteins that the person lacks or that help the person fight disease.

Genetic sequencing: the process of determining the order of subunits within a gene or even the order of all genes for an organism.

Genome: the complete set of an organism's genetic material.

Hormone: a substance secreted in one part of an organism that regulates the functioning of other tissues or organs.

Meiosis: the process of cell division that results in gametes (sperm or egg cells), all of which contain half the number of chromosomes as their precursor.

Metabolism: the sum total of the body's chemical processes providing energy for vital functions and enabling new material to be synthesized.

Mitosis: the process by which a cell divides its nucleus and other cell materials into two duplicate daughter cells with the same DNA.

Neuron: a nerve cell, of the type found in the brain or spinal cord, that sends electrical and chemical messages to other cells.

Nucleus (plural, nuclei): the center of an atom; or the portion of a cell that contains genetic material and regulates growth and metabolism.

Organism: a living entity, capable of growth, metabolism, and usually reproduction.

Phenotype: the observable properties and characteristics of an organism arising at least in part from its genetic makeup.

Pheromone: a chemical secreted by an animal to influence the behavior of other members of its species.

Placebo effect: a phenomenon in which patients show improvements even though they have taken a medically inactive substance, called a placebo.

Prokaryote: a single-celled organism that does not have a distinct nucleus, such as bacteria and blue-green algae.

Protein: a complex molecule made up of one or more chains of amino acids; essential to the structure and function of all cells.

RNA (ribonucleic acid): a complex molecule similar to the genetic material DNA but usually single-stranded; several forms of RNA translate the genetic code of DNA and use that code to assemble proteins for structural and biological functions in the body.

Species: a population of organisms that breed with each other in nature and produce fertile offspring; other definitions of species exist to accommodate the diversity of life on Earth.

Stem cell: a cell that can give rise to other types of cells; for instance, bone marrow stem cells divide and produce different types of blood cells.

Steroid: type of hormone that freely enters cells (other hormones bind to cell surfaces). Different varieties can suppress immune response or influence stress reaction, blood pressure, or sexual development; includes testosterone- and estrogen-related compounds.

Testosterone: a hormone that stimulates the development and maintenance of male sexual characteristics and the production of sperm; women also produce small amounts of testosterone.

Virus: a microscopic, often disease-causing, organism made of genetic material surrounded by a protein shell; can only reproduce inside a living cell.

Chemistry

Acid: a class of compound that contrasts with bases. Acids taste sour, turn litmus red/pink, and often produce hydrogen gas in contact with some metals. Acids donate protons (hydrogen atoms minus the electron) in chemical reactions.

Base: a substance that yields hydroxyl ions (OH-) when dissolved in water; any of a class of compounds whose aqueous solutions taste bitter, feel slippery, turn litmus blue, and react with acids to form salts; also known as **alkaline**.

Carbon fiber: an extremely strong, thin fiber made by pyrolyzing (decomposing by heat) synthetic fibers, such as rayon, until charred; used to make high-strength composites.

Chlorofluorocarbon (CFC): one of a group of industrial chemicals that contain chlorine, fluorine, and carbon and have been found to damage Earth's ozone layer.

Element: a substance that cannot be chemically decomposed into simpler substances; the atoms of an element all have the same number of protons and electrons.

Isotope: an atom of a chemical element with the same number of protons in its nucleus as other atoms of that element, but with a different number of neutrons.

Molecule: the basic unit of a chemical compound, composed of two or more atoms bound together.

Noble gases: a group of gases including helium, neon, argon, krypton, xenon, and radon that are not reactive except in rare and limited instances. Also called **inert gases**.

Osmosis: the transfer of a fluid from an area of higher concentration to an area of lower concentration, usually through a membrane.

Phase: any of the possible states of matter—solid, liquid, gas, or plasma—that change according to temperature and pressure.

Polymer: a huge molecule containing hundreds or thousands of smaller molecules arranged in repeating units.

Salt: a neutral compound produced by the reaction of an acid and a base.

Geology

Fault, tectonic: a crack or break in Earth's crust, often due to the slippage of tectonic plates past or over one another; usually geologically unstable.

Igneous: a type of rock formed by solidification from a molten state, especially from molten magma.

Magma: hot liquid rock material under Earth's crust, from which igneous rock is formed by cooling.

Metamorphic: in geology, the name given to sedimentary rocks or minerals that have recrystallized under the influence of heat and pressure since their original deposition.

Pangaea: a single supercontinent that scientists believe broke apart about 170 mil years ago to form the current continents.

Plate tectonics: theory that Earth's crust is made up of many separate rigid plates of rock that float on top of hot semi-liquid rock.

Sedimentary rock: rock formed by the buildup of material at the bottoms of bodies of water.

Physics

Absolute zero: the theoretical temperature at which all motion within a molecule stops, corresponding to $-273.15°$ C ($-459.67°$ F).

Antimatter: matter that consists of antiparticles, such as antiprotons, that have an opposite charge from normal particles; when matter meets antimatter, both are destroyed, and their combined mass is converted to energy. Antimatter is created in certain radioactive decay processes but appears to be present in only small amounts in the universe.

Atom: the basic unit of a chemical element.

Atomic mass: the total mass of an atom of a given element; atoms of the same element with different atomic masses (different numbers of neutrons, not protons) are called **isotopes**.

Atomic number: the number of protons in an atom of a given element of the periodic table; the characteristic that sets atoms of different elements apart.

Axion: a hypothetical subatomic particle with low mass and energy that is thought to exist because of the properties of the strong nuclear force.

Bose-Einstein condensate (BEC): a "super-atom" comprised of thousands of atoms super-cooled to within a few billionths of a degree of absolute zero and thus condensed into the lowest energy state; atoms bound in the BEC behave synchronously, giving the BEC wavelike properties.

Boson: force-carrying particles including photons, gluons, and the W and Z particles; one of the two primary categories of particles in the Standard Model, the other being fermions.

Dark energy: a mysterious, undefined energy leading to a repulsive force pervading all of space-time; proposed by cosmologists as counteracting gravity and accelerating the expansion of the universe; predicted to make up 65% of the universe's composition.

Dark matter: hypothetical, invisible matter that some scientists believe makes up 90% of the matter in the universe; its existence was proposed to account for otherwise inexplicable gravitational forces observed in space.

Doppler effect: a change in the frequency of sound, light, or radio waves caused by the motion of the source emitting the waves or the motion of the person or instrument perceiving the waves.

Electron: negatively charged particle that is the least massive electrically charged fundamental particle; the most common charged lepton in the Standard Model.

Energy: capacity to perform work. Energy can take various forms, such as potential energy, kinetic energy, and chemical energy.

Entropy: a measure of disorder in a system.

Fermion: any one of a number of matter particles including electrons, protons, neutrons, and quarks; one of the two primary categories of particles in the Standard Model, the other being bosons.

Field: the effects of forces (gravitational, electric, etc.) are visualized and described mathematically by physicists in terms of fields, which show the strength and direction of a force at a given position.

Fission: a nuclear reaction that occurs when the nuclei of large, unstable atoms break apart, releasing large amounts of energy.

Fluorescence: luminescence that is caused by the absorption of radiation at one wavelength followed by an immediate re-radiation, usually at a different wavelength, that stops almost immediately when the radiation stops.

Force: In classical physics, a force is something that causes acceleration in a body and can be thought of as a push or pull.

Fusion: a nuclear reaction occurring when atomic nuclei collide at high temperatures and combine to form one heavier atomic nucleus, releasing enormous energy in the process.

Gravity: an attractive force between any 2 objects or particles, proportional to the mass (or energy) of the objects; strength of the force decreases with greater distance; the only fundamental force still unaccounted for by the Standard Model.

Half-life: the time it takes for half of a given amount of a radioactive element to decay.

Hertz (Hz): a measure of frequency, or how many times a given event occurs per second; applied to sound waves, electrical current, microchip clock speeds.

Laser: light consisting of a cascade of photons all having the same wavelength; stands for Light Amplification by Stimulated Emission of Radiation.

Light-emitting diode (LED): a semiconductor that emits light when an electrical current is passed through it. The color of the light depends on the material used in making the diode.

Neutrino: a tiny fundamental particle with no electrical charge and very small mass that moves very quickly through the universe; comes in three varieties, or flavors, called electron, muon, and tau.

Neutron: a neutral particle found in the nuclei of atoms.

Particle accelerator: a large machine with a long tunnel in which atoms smash into each other at high speeds; physicists use these machines to study subatomic particles.

Phosphorescence: luminescence that is caused by the absorption of radiation at one wavelength followed by a delayed re-radiation, usually at a different wavelength, that continues for a noticeable time after the radiation stops.

Photon: the elementary unit, or quantum, of light or electromagnetic radiation having no mass or electrical charge; one of the fundamental force-carrying particles, or bosons, described by the Standard Model.

Plasma: a high-energy state of matter different from solid, liquid, or gas in which atomic nuclei and the electrons orbiting them separate from each other.

Proton: a positively charged subatomic particle found in the nuclei of atoms.

Quantum: a natural unit of some physically measurable property, such as energy or electrical charge.

Quark: a fermion and a fundamental matter particle that makes up neutrons and protons, forming atomic nuclei; there are 6 different "flavors" of quarks grouped in pairs; up and down, charm and strange, top and bottom.

Radiation: energy emitted as rays or particles; radiation includes heat, light, ultraviolet rays, gamma rays, X-rays, cosmic rays, alpha particles, beta particles, and the protons, neutrons, and electrons of radioactive atoms.

Relativity, general theory of: a theory of space-time proposed by Albert Einstein in 1915; gravitational and other forces are transmitted through the effects of the curvature of space-time.

Relativity, special theory of: Einstein's theory of space and time: all laws of physics are valid in all uniformly moving frames of reference, and the speed of light in a vacuum is always the same, so long as the source and the observer are moving uniformly (not accelerating).

Standard Model: prevailing theory of the interaction of subatomic particles; matter particles are fermions: either leptons or quarks; force-carrying particles are bosons: either gluons, W or Z bosons, or photons; successfully explains three of the four elementary forces acting on particles (strong, weak, electromagnetic) but thus far has not incorporated gravity.

String theory: a theory that seeks to unify quantum mechanics and general relativity, positing that the basic constituents of matter can best be understood not as point objects but as tiny closed loops ("strings").

Subatomic particle: one of the small particles, such as electrons, neutrons, and protons, which make up an atom.

Superconductivity: the property of certain materials, usually metals and chemically complex ceramics, to conduct electricity without resistance, generally at very cold temperatures.

Thermodynamics: the branch of physics that describes how energy, heat, and temperature flow in physical systems.

Ultraviolet radiation: a form of light, invisible to the human eye, that has a shorter wavelength and greater energy than visible light but a longer wavelength and less energy than X rays.

Virtual particle: subatomic particles that rapidly pop into and out of existence and can exert real forces; usually occur in particle-antiparticle pairs and are rapidly annihilated.

Mohs Scale of Hardness

Hardness is the ability of a solid substance to resist abrasion or deformation on the surface. Soft minerals scratch easier than hard ones. For example, a diamond will scratch graphite because the graphite is softer. In 1812, German mineralogist Frederich Mohs (1773-1839) created the arbitrary scale shown below to measure relative hardness using ten minerals that were readily available at that time. The numbers in the Mohs scale are arranged in order of increasing hardness. A mineral's hardness is obtained by determining which mineral in the Mohs scale will scratch the specimen.

Mohs Scale		Selected items and their relative hardness	
1. Talc	6. Orthoclase feldspar	2.5 ..... Fingernails	5.5 ...... Knife blade
2. Gypsum	7. Quartz	2.5-3 .... Gold, silver	6-7 ...... Glass
3. Calcite	8. Topaz	3 .... Copper penny	6.5 ...... Iron pyrite
4. Fluorite	9. Corundum	4-4.5 .... Platinum	7+ .... Hardened steel file
5. Apatite	10. Diamond	4-5 ..... Iron	

Chemical Elements, Atomic Numbers, Year Discovered

Reviewed by Darleane C. Hoffman, Ph.D., Lawrence Berkeley National Laboratory and Dept. of Chemistry, Univ. of California, Berkeley. See Periodic Table of the Elements on page 284 for atomic weights.

Element	Atomic symbol	number	Year discov.	Element	Atomic symbol	number	Year discov.	Element	Atomic symbol	number	Year discov.
Actinium	Ac	89	1899	Hafnium	Hf	72	1923	Radon	Rn	86	1900
Aluminum	Al	13	1825	Hassium	Hs	108	1984	Rhenium	Re	75	1925
Americium	Am	95	1944	Helium	He	2	1868	Rhodium	Rh	45	1803
Antimony	Sb	51	1450	Holmium	Ho	67	1878	Roentgenium	Rg	111	1995
Argon	Ar	18	1894	Hydrogen	H	1	1766	Rubidium	Rb	37	1861
Arsenic	As	33	13th cent.	Indium	In	49	1863	Ruthenium	Ru	44	1845
Astatine	At	85	1940	Iodine	I	53	1811	Rutherfordium	Rf	104	1969
Barium	Ba	56	1808	Iridium	Ir	77	1804	Samarium	Sm	62	1879
Berkelium	Bk	97	1949	Iron	Fe	26	BCE	Scandium	Sc	21	1879
Beryllium	Be	4	1798	Krypton	Kr	36	1898	Seaborgium	Sg	106	1974
Bismuth	Bi	83	15th cent.	Lanthanum	La	57	1839	Selenium	Se	34	1817
Bohrium	Bh	107	1981	Lawrencium	Lr	103	1961	Silicon	Si	14	1823
Boron	B	5	1808	Lead	Pb	82	BCE	Silver	Ag	47	BCE
Bromine	Br	35	1826	Lithium	Li	3	1817	Sodium	Na	11	1807
Cadmium	Cd	48	1817	Lutetium	Lu	71	1907	Strontium	Sr	38	1790
Calcium	Ca	20	1808	Magnesium	Mg	12	1829	Sulfur	S	16	BCE
Californium	Cf	98	1950	Manganese	Mn	25	1774	Tantalum	Ta	73	1802
Carbon	C	6	BCE	Meitnerium	Mt	109	1982	Technetium	Tc	43	1937
Cerium	Ce	58	1803	Mendelevium	Md	101	1955	Tellurium	Te	52	1782
Cesium	Cs	55	1860	Mercury	Hg	80	BCE	Terbium	Tb	65	1843
Chlorine	Cl	17	1774	Molybdenum	Mo	42	1782	Thallium	Tl	81	1861
Chromium	Cr	24	1797	Neodymium	Nd	60	1885	Thorium	Th	90	1828
Cobalt	Co	27	1735	Neon	Ne	10	1898	Thulium	Tm	69	1879
Copernicium	Cn	112	1996	Neptunium	Np	93	1940	Tin	Sn	50	BCE
Copper	Cu	29	BCE	Nickel	Ni	28	1751	Titanium	Ti	22	1791
Curium	Cm	96	1944	Niobium[2]	Nb	41	1801	Tungsten (Wolfram)	W	74	1783
Darmstadtium	Ds	110	1995	Nitrogen	N	7	1772	*Ununhexium	Uuh	116	2000
Dubnium (Hahnium)[1]	Db (Ha)	105	1970	Nobelium	No	102	1958	*Ununoctium	Uuo	118	2006
Dysprosium	Dy	66	1886	Osmium	Os	76	1804	*Ununpentium	Uup	115	2004
Einsteinium	Es	99	1952	Oxygen	O	8	1774	*Ununquadium	Uuq	114	1999
Erbium	Er	68	1843	Palladium	Pd	46	1803	*Ununseptium	Uus	117	—
Europium	Eu	63	1901	Phosphorus	P	15	1669	*Ununtrium	Uut	113	2004
Fermium	Fm	100	1953	Platinum	Pt	78	1735	Uranium	U	92	1789
Fluorine	F	9	1771	Plutonium	Pu	94	1941	Vanadium	V	23	1830
Francium	Fr	87	1939	Polonium	Po	84	1898	Xenon	Xe	54	1898
Gadolinium	Gd	64	1886	Potassium	K	19	1807	Ytterbium	Yb	70	1878
Gallium	Ga	31	1875	Praseodymium	Pr	59	1885	Yttrium	Y	39	1794
Germanium	Ge	32	1886	Promethium	Pm	61	1945	Zinc	Zn	30	BCE
Gold	Au	79	BCE	Protactinium	Pa	91	1917	Zirconium	Zr	40	1789
				Radium	Ra	88	1898				

Note: 118 elements are listed here; only 112 have been independently confirmed. The most recent of these, element 112 (with a mass number of 270), was reported by S. Hoffman et al. in 1996 and was approved by the International Union of Pure and Applied Chemistry (IUPAC) in June 2009. The discoverers proposed the name Copernicium with a symbol of Cn, in honor of the astronomer Nicolaus Copernicus, but as of Sept. 2009, full approval of the name was still pending. (*) Indicates element whose existence has been reported or hypothesized, but not yet confirmed. Between 1999 and 2006, observation of many isotopes of elements 113-116 and 118 have been reported in refereed journals. These reports all await confirmation and are shown in italics in the periodic table. Evidence for element 117 has not been published in refereed journals and is shown in parentheses. (1) The name Dubnium (Db) has been approved by IUPAC for element 105, but the name Hahnium (Ha) is used in most of the scientific literature before 1998 and is still sometimes used in the U.S. (2) Formerly Columbium.

Periodic Table of the Elements

Source: © 1996 Lawrence Berkeley National Laboratory

Parentheses indicate undiscovered elements.

Legend:

14	28.09
Si	← symbol
Silicon	

14 — atomic number
28.09 — atomic weight
Si — symbol
Silicon — name

Categories: alkali metals · alkaline earth metals · transitional metals · nonmetals · noble gases · other metals

1	2	3	4	5	6	7	8	9	10	11	12	13	14	15	16	17	18
1 1.01 **H** Hydrogen																	2 4.003 **He** Helium
3 6.94 **Li** Lithium	4 9.01 **Be** Beryllium											5 10.81 **B** Boron	6 12.01 **C** Carbon	7 14.01 **N** Nitrogen	8 15.999 **O** Oxygen	9 18.998 **F** Fluorine	10 20.18 **Ne** Neon
11 22.99 **Na** Sodium	12 24.31 **Mg** Magnesium											13 26.98 **Al** Aluminum	14 28.09 **Si** Silicon	15 30.97 **P** Phosphorus	16 32.06 **S** Sulfur	17 35.45 **Cl** Chlorine	18 39.95 **Ar** Argon
19 39.10 **K** Potassium	20 40.08 **Ca** Calcium	21 44.96 **Sc** Scandium	22 47.90 **Ti** Titanium	23 50.94 **V** Vanadium	24 51.996 **Cr** Chromium	25 54.94 **Mn** Manganese	26 55.85 **Fe** Iron	27 58.93 **Co** Cobalt	28 58.70 **Ni** Nickel	29 63.55 **Cu** Copper	30 65.37 **Zn** Zinc	31 69.72 **Ga** Gallium	32 72.59 **Ge** Germanium	33 74.92 **As** Arsenic	34 78.96 **Se** Selenium	35 79.90 **Br** Bromine	36 83.80 **Kr** Krypton
37 85.47 **Rb** Rubidium	38 87.62 **Sr** Strontium	39 88.91 **Y** Yttrium	40 91.22 **Zr** Zirconium	41 92.91 **Nb** Niobium	42 95.94 **Mo** Molybdenum	43 98 **Tc** Technetium	44 101.07 **Ru** Ruthenium	45 102.91 **Rh** Rhodium	46 106.40 **Pd** Palladium	47 107.87 **Ag** Silver	48 112.41 **Cd** Cadmium	49 114.82 **In** Indium	50 118.69 **Sn** Tin	51 121.75 **Sb** Antimony	52 127.60 **Te** Tellurium	53 126.90 **I** Iodine	54 131.30 **Xe** Xenon
55 132.91 **Cs** Cesium	56 137.33 **Ba** Barium	57 138.91 **La** Lanthanum	72 178.49 **Hf** Hafnium	73 180.95 **Ta** Tantalum	74 183.85 **W** Tungsten	75 186.21 **Re** Rhenium	76 190.20 **Os** Osmium	77 192.22 **Ir** Iridium	78 195.09 **Pt** Platinum	79 196.97 **Au** Gold	80 200.59 **Hg** Mercury	81 204.37 **Tl** Thallium	82 207.19 **Pb** Lead	83 208.98 **Bi** Bismuth	84 209 **Po** Polonium	85 210 **At** Astatine	86 222 **Rn** Radon
87 223 **Fr** Francium	88 226.03 **Ra** Radium	89 227.03 **Ac** Actinium	104 261 **Rf** Rutherfordium	105 262 **Db (Ha)** Dubnium (Hahnium)	106 266 **Sg** Seaborgium	107 267 **Bh** Bohrium	108 269 **Hs** Hassium	109 268 **Mt** Meitnerium	110 271 **Ds** Darmstadtium	111 272 **Rg** Roentgenium	112 **112**	113 **113**	114 **114**	115 **115**	116 **116**	85 (117) **(117)**	118 **118**

Lanthanide series

58	59	60	61	62	63	64	65	66	67	68	69	70	71
140.12 **Ce** Cerium	140.91 **Pr** Praseodymium	144.24 **Nd** Neodymium	145 **Pm** Promethium	150.35 **Sm** Samarium	151.96 **Eu** Europium	157.25 **Gd** Gadolinium	158.93 **Tb** Terbium	162.50 **Dy** Dysprosium	164.93 **Ho** Holmium	167.26 **Er** Erbium	168.93 **Tm** Thulium	173.04 **Yb** Ytterbium	174.97 **Lu** Lutetium

Actinide series

90	91	92	93	94	95	96	97	98	99	100	101	102	103
232.04 **Th** Thorium	231.04 **Pa** Protactinium	238.03 **U** Uranium	237.05 **Np** Neptunium	244 **Pu** Plutonium	243 **Am** Americium	247 **Cm** Curium	247 **Bk** Berkelium	251 **Cf** Californium	252 **Es** Einsteinium	257 **Fm** Fermium	258 **Md** Mendelevium	259 **No** Nobelium	262 **Lr** Lawrencium

Basic Laws of Physics

Isaac Newton's Laws of Motion

1. An object in motion moves at a constant velocity in a straight line unless acted upon by a force. Likewise, an object at rest will stay at rest. This is known as inertia.

2. The acceleration of an object is proportional to the force acting on it and inversely proportional to the mass of an object.

Force (F) equals mass (m) times acceleration (a)

$$F = ma$$

3. For every action, there is an equal and opposite reaction.

Law of Gravity

In common usage, gravity only refers to the gravitational force between the Earth and objects on or near it. More specifically, gravitation is one of four basic forces controlling the interactions of matter, the others being strong and weak nuclear forces and electromagnetic force. The gravitational force (F) between objects is proportional to the product of their masses (m_1 and m_2) and inversely proportional to the square of the distance (d) between them. G represents the "gravitational constant" in Newton's law of gravity, a fixed ratio measured in metric terms as, $G = 6.67390 \times 10^{-11}$ newton m^2/kg^2.

The basic law of gravity is:

$$F = G \frac{m_1 \, m_2}{d_2}$$

Excluding factors such as high winds and wind resistance, objects close to the Earth's surface will fall at a constant acceleration of 32.174 ft/sec^2 (9.8 m/sec^2), which is usually written as g. Using g will yield the velocity (v) and the distance travelled by a falling object (d) after any amount of time, (t) in seconds. (Positive numbers represent up, negative numbers down.)

$$v = -g\,t$$
$$d = -\tfrac{1}{2}\,g(t^2)$$

If an object has an initial velocity of v_0 and an initial height above ground called a, the equations become:

$$v = v_0 - g\,t$$
$$d = -\tfrac{1}{2}\,g(t^2) + v_0 t + a$$

Assuming that height is measured in feet and speeds in feet per second, the maximum height (H) reached by an object with a positive initial velocity (v_0) and a known initial height (a) is expressed as:

$$H = a + \frac{v_0{}^2}{64}$$

The force of gravity on Earth is lessened by the centrifugal force caused by the Earth's rotation. This counteracts the gravitational effect to a small degree. At the poles, where technically there is no centrifugal force, acceleration due to gravity is greater.

The force of gravity decreases slightly with an increase in distance from the Earth's center; gravity is weaker on a mountaintop than it is at sea level.

Conservation Laws

In physics, laws of conservation state that in a closed system certain measurable quantities remain constant. Anything added from outside the system could affect the quantity of the entity being conserved.

Conservation of Mass: Mass is neither created nor destroyed within a closed system except when converted to energy.

Conservation of Momentum: All moving objects have momentum, and in a closed system, momentum is always conserved. Linear momentum is the product of the mass of an object and its velocity. In the following equation, M and V represent the initial total mass and velocity of objects within a closed system. After a collision between those objects, the mass and velocity of individual objects may change (for example, one object could break into smaller pieces, each traveling at a different velocity) but the product of the total mass and velocity in the system after the collision (mv) will remain the same.

$$MV = mv$$

Any object moving in a circle has angular momentum. Motion in a circle requires acceleration which is directed towards the center of the circle and which depends on the speed of the object and the square of the radius of the circle. (Angular momentum is the product of this speed, the mass of the object and the square of the radius.)

Conservation of Energy: The amount of energy of a closed system will not change except when converted to mass.

Conservation of Mass-Energy: According to Einstein, as part of his special theory of relativity, mass and energy are related. Because they can be converted into one another, mass and energy alone cannot be conserved. However, the total amount of mass and energy together must be conserved. This is reflected in the following equation where m is mass, E is energy, and c is the speed of light in a vacuum (which is constant):

$$E = mc^2$$

Einstein also discovered that mass increases with velocity. The following equation—where m is the mass of a moving object, m_0 is the object's mass when not moving, v is its velocity in relation to a stationary observer, and c is the speed of light—shows how mass is related to velocity in this context.

$$m = \frac{m_0}{\sqrt{1 - \dfrac{v^2}{c^2}}}$$

This equation accounts for the theory that no object can travel faster than the speed of light. As an object approaches c, so much energy is converted to mass that it no longer accelerates.

Laws of Thermodynamics

1. Heat is a form of energy. Within a closed system energy must be conserved except in nuclear reactions or other extreme conditions. It is neither created nor destroyed.

2. Within a self-sustaining system, heat can never go from an area of low temperature to an area of high temperature. Disorder, or entropy, can only increase in closed system.

3. Absolute zero cannot be attained by any procedure in a finite number of steps. Absolute zero can be approached arbitrarily closely, but it can never be reached.

Laws of Current Electricity

Electricity is the result of electrons flowing through a conductor. When electrons flow through a conductor, the amount of current generated, measured in amperes, is defined in terms of the coulomb (an amount of electric charge equal to about 6.25 quintillion or 6.25×10^{18} electrons) and the time it takes for electrons to pass through the conductor. One ampere is equal to 1 coulomb of charge moving past a point in 1 second. As an electric current moves through a conductor, energy can vary depending on varying charges within the conductor. This variation is known as the potential difference and is measured in volts.

Certain substances are more prone to conductivity. The resistance to conductivity is measured in ohms.

Ohm's Law: Electric current is directly proportional to the potential difference and inversely proportional to the total resistance of the circuit. I is electric current (measured in amperes), and V is the potential difference (measured in volts), and R is resistance (measured in ohms):

$$I = \frac{V}{R}$$

Law of Electric Power: The rate at which electricity is used is electric power. If electric power (P) is measured in watts, then P is the product of current and potential difference.

$$P = IV$$

Two Basic Laws of Quantum Physics

1. Heisenberg's uncertainty principle: Certain pairs of observable quantities like energy and time or position and momentum cannot be measured with complete accuracy simultaneously. Also known as the indeterminacy principle.

2. Pauli's exclusion principle: Two electrons in an atom cannot simultaneously occupy the same quantum or energy state. This has since been shown to be true for many subatomic particles.

Breaking the Sound Barrier; Speed of Sound

The prefix **Mach** is used to describe supersonic speed. It was named for Ernst Mach (1838-1916), a Czech-born Austrian physicist. When a plane moves at the speed of sound, it is Mach 1. When the plane is moving at twice the speed of sound, it is Mach 2. Mach may be defined as the ratio of the velocity of a rocket or a jet to the velocity of sound in the medium being considered.

When a plane passes the sound barrier—flying faster than sound travels—listeners in the area hear thunderclaps, but the pilot of the plane does not hear them.

Sound is produced by vibrations of an object and is transmitted by alternate increase and decrease in pressures that radiate outward through a material media of molecules, somewhat like waves spreading out on a pond after a rock has been tossed into it.

The **frequency of sound** is determined by the number of times the vibrating waves undulate per second and is measured in cycles per second. The slower the cycle of waves, the lower the frequency. As frequencies increase, the sound is higher in pitch. The human ear is usually not sensitive to frequencies of fewer than 20 vibrations per second or greater than about 20,000 vibrations per second, although this range varies among individuals.

Intensity, or loudness, is the strength of the pressure of these radiating waves and is measured in decibels. (*See* Weights and Measures.)

The **speed of sound** is generally defined as 1,088 feet per second at sea level at 32° F. It varies in other temperatures and in different media. Sound travels faster in water than in air and even faster in iron and steel.

Light; Colors of the Spectrum

Light, a form of electromagnetic radiation similar to radiant heat, radio waves, and X-rays, is emitted from a source in straight lines and spreads out over larger areas as it travels; light per unit area diminishes as the square of the distance.

The English mathematician and physicist Sir Isaac Newton (1642-1727) described light as an **emission of particles**; the Dutch astronomer, mathematician, and physicist Christiaan Huygens (1629-95) developed the theory that light travels by a **wave motion**. It is now believed that these 2 theories are essentially complementary, and the development of quantum theory has led to results where light acts like a series of particles in some experiments and like a wave in others.

The **speed of light** was first measured in a laboratory experiment by the French physicist Armand Hippolyte Louis Fizeau (1819-96). Today the speed of light is known very precisely as 299,792.458 km per sec (or 186,282.396 mi per sec) in a vacuum; in water the speed of light is about 25% less, and in glass, 33% less.

Color sensations are produced through the excitation of the retina of the eye by light vibrating at different frequencies. The different colors of the spectrum may be produced by viewing a light beam that is refracted by passage through a prism, which breaks the light into its wavelengths.

Customarily, the **primary colors** are taken to be the 6 monochromatic colors that occupy relatively large areas of the spectrum: red, orange, yellow, green, blue, and violet. Scientists have differed, however, in how many and which primary colors they recognized. The color sensation of **black** is due to complete lack of stimulation of the retina, that of **white** to complete stimulation.

Infrared and **ultraviolet rays**, below the red (long) end of the spectrum and above the violet (short) end of the spectrum, respectively, are invisible to the naked eye. Heat is the principal effect of infrared rays, and chemical action that of ultraviolet rays.

Discoveries and Innovations: Chemistry, Physics, Biology, Medicine

Discovery	Date	Discoverer(s)	Nationality
Acetylene gas	1862	Berthelot	French
ACTH	1927	Evans, Long	U.S.
Adrenaline	1901	Takamine	Japan
Aluminum, electrolytic process	1886	Hall	U.S.
Aluminum, isolated	1825	Oersted	Danish
Anesthesia, ether	1842	Long	U.S.
Anesthesia, local	1885	Koller	Austrian
Anesthesia, spinal	1898	Bier	German
Aniline dye	1856	Perkin	English
Anti-rabies	1885	Pasteur	French
Antiseptic surgery	1867	Lister	English
Antitoxin, diphtheria	1891	Von Behring	German
Argyrol	1897	Bayer	German
Arsphenamine	1910	Ehrlich	German
Aspirin	1853	Gerhardt	French
Atabrine	1932	Mietzsch, et al.	German
Atomic numbers	1913	Moseley	English
Atomic theory	1803	Dalton	English
Atomic time clock	1948	Lyons	U.S.
Atomic time clock, cesium beam	1948	Essen	English
Atom-smashing theory	1919	Rutherford	English
Bacitracin	1943	Johnson, Meleneyl	U.S.
Bacteria, description	1676	Leeuwenhoek	Dutch
Bleaching powder	1798	Tennant	English
Blood, circulation	1628	Harvey	English
Blood plasma storage (blood banks)	1940	Drew	U.S.
Bordeaux mixture	1885	Millardet	French
Bromine from the sea	1826	Balard	French
Calcium carbide	1888	Wilson	U.S.
Calculus	1670	Newton	English
Camphor synthetic	1896	Haller	French
Canning (food)	1804	Appert	French
Carbon oxides	1925	Fisher	German
Chemotherapy	1909	Ehrlich	German
Chloamphenicol	1947	Burkholder	U.S.
Chlorine	1774	Scheele	Swedish
Chloroform	1831	Guthrie, S.	U.S.
Chlortetracycline	1948	Duggen	U.S.
Classification of plants and animals	1735	Linnaeus	Swedish

Discovery	Date	Discoverer(s)	Nationality
Cloning, DNA	1973	Boyer, Cohen	U.S.
Cloning, mammal	1996	Wilmut, et al.	Scottish
Cocaine	1860	Niermann	German
Combustion explained	1777	Lavoisier	French
Conditioned reflex	1914	Pavlov	Russian
Cortisone	1936	Kendall	U.S.
Cortisone, synthesis	1946	Sarett	U.S.
Cosmic rays	1910	Gockel	Swiss
Cyanamide	1905	Frank, Caro	German
Cyclotron	1930	Lawrence	U.S.
DDT (not applied as insecticide until 1939)	1874	Zeidler	German
Deuterium	1932	Urey, Brickwedde, Murphy	U.S.
DNA (structure)	1953	Crick	English
		Watson	U.S.
		Wilkins	English
Electric resistance, law of	1827	Ohm	German
Electric waves	1888	Hertz	German
Electrolysis	1852	Faraday	English
Electromagnetism	1819	Oersted	Danish
Electron	1897	Thomson, J.	English
Electron diffraction	1936	Thomson	English
		Davisson, G.	U.S.
Electroshock treatment	1938	Cerletti, Bini	Italian
Erythromycin	1952	McGuire	U.S.
Evolution, natural selection	1858	Darwin	English
Falling bodies, law of	1590	Galileo	Italian
Gases, law of combining volumes	1808	Gay-Lussac	French
Geometry, analytic	1619	Descartes	French
Gold, cyanide process for extraction	1887	MacArthur, Forest	British
Gravitation, law	1687	Newton	English
HIV (human immuno-deficiency virus)	1984	Montagnier	French
		Gallo	U.S.
Holograph	1948	Gabor	British
Human heart transplant	1967	Barnard	S. African
Indigo, synthesis of	1880	Baeyer	German
Induction, electric	1830	Henry	U.S.
Insulin	1922	Banting, Best	Canadian
		Macleod	Scottish
Intelligence testing	1905	Binet, Simon	French

Discovery	Date	Discoverer(s)	Nationality
In vitro fertilization	1978	Steptoe, Edwards	English
Isotopes, theory	1912	Soddy	English
Laser	1957	Gould	U.S.
Light, velocity	1675	Roemer	Danish
Light, wave theory	1690	Huygens	Dutch
Lithography	1796	Senefelder	Bohemian
Logarithms	1614	Napier	Scottish
LSD-25	1943	Hoffman	Swiss
Mendelian laws	1866	Mendel	Austrian
Mercator projection (map)	1568	Mercator (Kremer)	Flemish
Methanol	1661	Boyle	Irish
Milk condensation	1853	Borden	U.S.
Molecular hypothesis	1811	Avogadro	Italian
Motion, laws of	1687	Newton	English
Neomycin	1949	Waksman, Lechevalier	U.S.
Neutron	1932	Chadwick	English
Nitric acid	1648	Glauber	German
Nitric oxide	1772	Priestley	English
Nitroglycerin	1846	Sobrero	Italian
Oil cracking process	1891	Dewar	U.S.
Oxygen	1774	Priestley	English
Oxytetracycline	1950	Finlay, et al.	U.S.
Ozone	1840	Schonbein	German
Paper, sulfite process	1867	Tilghman	U.S.
Paper, wood pulp, sulfate process	1884	Dahl	German
Penicillin	1928	Fleming	Scottish
practical use	1941	Florey, Chain	English
Periodic law and table of elements	1869	Mendeleyev	Russian
Physostigmine synthesis	1935	Julian	U.S.
Pill, birth-control	1954	Pincus, Rock	U.S.
Planetary motion, laws	1609	Kepler	German
Plutonium fission	1940	Kennedy, Wahl, Seaborg, Segre	U.S.
Polymyxin	1947	Ainsworth	English
Positron	1932	Anderson	U.S.
Proton	1919	Rutherford	N. Zealand
Psychoanalysis	1900	Freud	Austrian
Quantum theory	1900	Planck	German
Quasars	1963	Matthews, Sandage	U.S.
Quinine synthetic	1946	Woodward, Doering	U.S.
Radioactivity	1896	Becquerel	French
Radiocarbon dating	1947	Libby	U.S.

Discovery	Date	Discoverer(s)	Nationality
Radium	1898	Curie, Pierre	French
		Curie, Marie	Pol.-Fr.
Relativity theory	1905	Einstein	German
Reserpine	1949	Jal Vaikl	Indian
Schick test	1913	Schick	U.S.
Silicon	1823	Berzelius	Swedish
Smallpox eradication	1979	World Health Org.	UN
Streptomycin	1944	Waksman, et al	U.S.
Sulfanilamide	1935	Bovet, Trefouel	French
Sulfanilamide theory	1908	Gelmo	German
Sulfapyridine	1938	Ewins, Phelps	English
Sulfathiazole	1939	Fosbinder, Walter	U.S.
Sulfuric acid	1831	Phillips	English
Sulfuric acid, lead	1746	Roebuck	English
Syphilis test	1906	Wassermann	German
Tuberculin	1890	Koch	German
Uranium fission theory	1939	Hahn, Meitner, Strassmann	German
		Bohr	Danish
		Fermi	Italian
		Einstein, Pegram, Wheeler	U.S.
Uranium fission, atomic reactor	1942	Fermi, Szilard	U.S.
Vaccine, measles	1963	Enders	U.S.
Vaccine, meningitis (first conjugate)	1987	Gordon, et al., Connaught Lab.	U.S.
Vaccine, polio	1954	Salk	U.S.
Vaccine, polio, oral	1960	Sabin	U.S.
Vaccine, rabies	1885	Pasteur	French
Vaccine, smallpox	1796	Jenner	English
Vaccine, typhus	1909	Nicolle	French
Vaccine, varicella	1974	Takahashi	Japan
Van Allen belts, radiation	1958	Van Allen	U.S.
Vitamin A	1913	McCollum, Davis	U.S.
Vitamin B	1916	McCollum	U.S.
Vitamin C	1928	Szent-Gyorgyi	Hungarian
		King	U.S.
Vitamin D	1922	McCollum	U.S.
Vitamin K	1935	Dam, Doisy	U.S.
Xerography	1938	Carlson	U.S.
X-ray	1895	Roentgen	German

Inventions

Invention	Date	Inventor(s)	Nationality
Adding machine	1642	Pascal	French
Adding machine	1885	Burroughs	U.S.
Aerosol spray	1926	Rotheim	Norwegian
Airbag	1952	Hetrick	U.S.
Air brake	1868	Westinghouse	U.S.
Air conditioning	1902	Carrier	U.S.
Air pump	1654	Guericke	German
Airplane, automatic pilot	1912	Sperry	U.S.
Airplane, experimental	1896	Langley	U.S.
Airplane, hydro	1911	Curtiss	U.S.
Airplane jet engine	1939	Ohain	German
Airplane with motor	1903	Wright Bros.	U.S.
Airship	1852	Giffard	French
Arc welder	1919	Thomson	U.S.
Aspartame	1965	Schlatter	U.S.
Autogyro	1920	de la Cierva	Spanish
Automobile, differential gear	1885	Benz	German
Automobile, electric	1892	Morrison	U.S.
Automobile, exp'mtl	1864	Marcus	Austrian
Automobile, gasoline	1889	Daimler	German
Automobile, gasoline	1892	Duryea	U.S.
Automobile magneto	1897	Bosch	German
Automobile muffler	1904	Pope	U.S.
Automobile self-starter	1911	Kettering	U.S.
Bakelite	1907	Baekeland	Belg., U.S.
Balloon	1783	Montgolfier	French
Barometer	1643	Torricelli	Italian
Bicycle, modern	1885	Starley	English
Bifocal lens	1780	Franklin	U.S.
Bottle machine	1895	Owens	U.S.
Braille printing	1829	Braille	French
Bubble gum	1928	Diemer	U.S.
Burner, gas	1855	Bunsen	German
Calculating machine	1833	Babbage	English
Calculator, electronic pocket	1972	Merryman, Van Tassel	U.S.
Camera, Kodak	1888	Eastman, Walker	U.S
Camera, Polaroid Land	1948	Land	U.S.

Invention	Date	Inventor(s)	Nationality
Car coupler	1873	Janney	U.S.
Carburetor, gasoline	1893	Maybach	German
Carding machine	1797	Whittemore	U.S.
Carpet sweeper	1876	Bissell	U.S.
Cash register	1879	Ritty	U.S.
Cassette, audio	1963	Philips Co.	Dutch
Cassette, videotape	1969	Sony	Japanese
Cathode-ray tube	1897	Braun	German
CAT, or CT, scan	1973	Hounsfield	English
Cellophane	1908	Brandenberger	Swiss
Celluloid	1870	Hyatt	U.S.
Cement, Portland	1824	Aspdin	English
Chronometer	1735	Harrison	English
Circuit breaker	1925	Hilliard	U.S.
Circuit, integrated	1959	Kilby, Noyce, Texas Instr.	U.S.
Clock, pendulum	1657	Huygens	Dutch
Coaxial cable system	1929	Affel, Espensched	U.S.
Coffeemaker, automatic drip	1963	Bunn Corp.	U.S.
Compressed air rock drill	1871	Ingersoll	U.S.
Comptometer	1887	Felt	U.S.
Computer, automatic sequence	1944	Aiken, et al.	U.S.
Computer, electronic	1942	Atanasoff, Berry	U.S.
Computer, laptop	1987	Sinclair	English
Computer, mini	1960	Digital Corp	U.S.
Condenser microphone (telephone)	1916	Wente	U.S.
Contact lens, corneal	1948	Tuohy	U.S.
Contraceptive, oral	1954	Pincus, Rock	U.S.
Corn, hybrid	1917	Jones	U.S.
Cotton gin	1793	Whitney	U.S.
Cream separator	1878	DeLaval	Swedish
Cultivator, disc	1878	Mallon	U.S.
Cystoscope	1878	Nitze	German
Diapers, disposable	1950	Donovan	U.S.
Diesel engine	1895	Diesel	German
Disc, compact	1972	RCA	U.S.

Invention	Date	Inventor(s)	Nationality
Disc player, compact	1979	Sony, Philips Co.	Japan-Dutch
Dishwasher	1893	Cochrane	U.S.
Disk, floppy	1970	IBM	U.S.
Disk, video	1972	Philips Co.	Dutch
Dynamite	1866	Nobel	Swedish
Dynamo, contin. current	1871	Gramme	Belgian
Electric battery	1800	Volta	Italian
Electric fan	1882	Wheeler	U.S.
Electrocardiograph	1903	Einthoven	Dutch
Electroencephalograph	1929	Berger	German
Electromagnet	1824	Sturgeon	English
Electron spectrometer	1944	Deutsch, Elliott, Evans	U.S.
Electron tube multigrid	1913	Langmuir	U.S.
Electroplating	1805	Brugnatelli	Italian
Electrostatic generator	1929	Van de Graaff	U.S.
Elevator brake	1852	Otis	U.S.
Elevator, push button	1922	Larson	U.S.
Engine, automatic transmission	1910	Fottinger	German
Engine, coal-gas 4-cycle	1876	Otto	German
Engine, compression ignition	1883	Daimler	German
Engine, electric ignition	1883	Benz	German
Engine, gas, compound	1926	Eickemeyer	U.S.
Engine, gasoline	1872	Brayton, Geo.	U.S.
Engine, gasoline	1889	Daimler	German
Engine, jet	1930	Whittle	English
Engine, steam, piston	1705	Newcomen	English
Engine, steam, piston	1769	Watt	Scottish
Engraving, half-tone	1852	Talbot	U.S.
Fiberglass	1938	Owens-Corning	U.S.
Fiber optics	1955	Kapany	English
Fiber optic wire	1970	Keck, Maurer Schulz	U.S.
Filament, tungsten	1913	Coolidge	U.S.
Flanged rail	1831	Stevens	U.S.
Flatiron, electric	1882	Seely	U.S.
Food, frozen	1923	Birdseye	U.S.
Freon	1930	Midgley, et al.	U.S.
Furnace (for steel)	1858	Siemens	German
Galvanometer	1820	Sweigger	German
Garbage bag, polyethylene	1950	Wasylyk	Canadian
Gas discharge tube	1922	Hull	U.S.
Gas lighting	1792	Murdoch	Scottish
Gas mantle	1885	Welsbach	Austrian
Gasoline (lead ethyl)	1922	Midgley	U.S.
Gasoline, cracked	1913	Burton	U.S.
Gasoline, high octane	1930	Ipatieff	Russian
Geiger counter	1913	Geiger	German
Glass, laminated safety	1909	Benedictus	French
Glider	1853	Cayley	English
Gun, breechloader	1811	Thornton	U.S.
Gun, Browning	1897	Browning	U.S.
Gun, magazine	1875	Hotchkiss	U.S.
Gun, silencer	1908	Maxim, H. P.	U.S.
Guncotton	1847	Schoenbein	German
Gyrocompass	1911	Sperry	U.S.
Gyroscope	1852	Foucault	French
Harvester-thresher	1818	Lane	U.S.
Heart, artificial	1982	Jarvik	U.S.
Helicopter	1939	Sikorsky	U.S.
Hydrometer	1768	Baume	French
Iron lung	1928	Drinker, Slaw	U.S.
Kaleidoscope	1817	Brewster	Scottish
Kevlar	1965	Kwolek, Blades	U.S.
Kinetoscope	1889	Edison	U.S.
Lamp, arc	1847	Staite	English
Lamp, fluorescent	1938	General Electric, Westinghouse	U.S.
Lamp, incandescent	1879	Edison	U.S.
Lamp, incand., gas	1913	Langmuir	U.S.
Lamp, klieg	1911	Kliegl, A. & J.	U.S.
Lamp, mercury vapor	1912	Hewitt	U.S.
Lamp, miner's safety	1816	Davy	English
Lamp, neon	1909	Claude	French
Lathe, turret	1845	Fitch	U.S.
Launderette	1934	Cantrell	U.S.
Lens, achromatic	1758	Dollond	English
Lens, fused bifocal	1908	Borsch	U.S.
Leyden jar (condenser)	1745	von Kleist	German
Lightning rod	1752	Franklin	U.S.
Linoleum	1860	Walton	English
Linotype	1884	Mergenthaler	U.S.
Liquid Paper	c.1951	Graham	U.S.
Lock, cylinder	1851	Yale	U.S.
Locomotive, electric	1851	Vail	U.S.
Locomotive, exp'mtl.	1802	Trevithick	English
Locomotive, exp'mtl.	1812	Fenton, et al.	English
Locomotive, exp'mtl.	1814	Stephenson	English
Locomotive, practical	1829	Stephenson	English
Locomotive, 1st U.S.	1830	Cooper, P.	U.S.
Loom, power	1785	Cartwright	English
Loudspeaker, dynamic	1924	Rice, Kellogg	U.S.
Machine gun	1862	Gatling	U.S.
Machine gun, improved	1872	Hotchkiss	U.S.
Machine gun (Maxim)	1883	Maxim, H.S.	U.S., Eng.
Magnet, electro	1828	Henry	U.S.
Magnetic Resonance Imaging (MRI)	1971	Damadian	U.S.
Mason jar	1858	Mason, J.	U.S.
Match, friction	1827	Walker, J.	English
Mercerized textiles	1843	Mercer, J.	English
Meter, induction	1888	Shallenberger	U.S.
Metronome	1816	Malezel	German
Microcomputer	1973	Truong, et al.	French
Micrometer	1636	Gascoigne	English
Microphone	1877	Berliner	U.S.
Microprocessor	1971	Intel Corp.	U.S.
Microscope, compound	1590	Janssen	Dutch
Microscope, electronic	1931	Knoll, Ruska	German
Microscope, field ion	1951	Mueller	German
Microwave oven	1947	Spencer	U.S.
Monitor, warship	1861	Ericsson	U.S.
Monotype	1887	Lanston	U.S.
Motor, AC	1892	Tesla	U.S.
Motor, DC	1837	Davenport	U.S.
Motor, induction	1887	Tesla	U.S.
Motorcycle	1885	Daimler	German
Movie machine	1894	Jenkins	U.S.
Movie, panoramic	1952	Waller	U.S.
Movie, talking	1927	Warner Bros.	U.S.
Mower, lawn	1831	Budding, Ferrabee	English
Mowing machine	1822	Bailey	U.S.
Neoprene	1930	Carothers	U.S.
Nylon	1937	Du Pont lab	U.S.
Nylon synthetic	1930	Carothers	U.S.
Oil cracking furnace	1891	Gavrilov	Russian
Oil filled power cable	1921	Emanueli	Italian
Oleomargarine	1869	Mege-Mouries	French
Ophthalmoscope	1851	Helmholtz	German
Pacemaker	1952	Zoll	U.S.
Paper	105	Ts'ai	Chinese
Paper clip	1900	Waaler	Norwegian
Paper machine	1809	Dickinson	U.S.
Parachute	1785	Blanchard	French
Pen, ballpoint	1888	Loud	U.S.
Pen, fountain	1884	Waterman	U.S.
Pen, steel	1780	Harrison	English
Pendulum	1583	Galileo	Italian
Percussion cap	1807	Forsythe	Scottish
Phonograph	1877	Edison	U.S.
Photo, color	1892	Ives	U.S.
Photo film, celluloid	1893	Reichenbach	U.S.
Photo film, transparent	1884	Eastman, Goodwin	U.S.
Photoelectric cell	1895	Elster	German
Photocopier	1938	Carlson	U.S.
Photographic paper	1835	Talbot	English
Photography	1816	Niepce	French
Photography	1835	Talbot	English
Photography	1835	Daguerre	French
Photophone	1880	Bell	U.S.-Scot.
Phototelegraphy	1925	Bell Labs	U.S.
Piano	1709	Cristofori	Italian
Piano, player	1863	Fourneaux	French
Pin, safety	1849	Hunt	U.S.
Pistol (revolver)	1836	Colt	U.S.
Plow, cast iron	1785	Ransome	English
Plow, disc	1896	Hardy	U.S.
Pneumatic hammer	1890	King	U.S.
Post-it note	1980	Fry, Silver	U.S.
Powder, smokeless	1884	Vieille	French
Printing press, rotary	1845	Hoe	U.S.
Printing press, web	1865	Bullock	U.S.
Propeller, screw	1804	Stevens	U.S.
Propeller, screw	1837	Ericsson	Swedish

Invention	Date	Inventor(s)	Nationality
Pulsars	1967	Bell	English
Punch card accounting	1889	Hollerith	U.S.
Radar	1940	Watson-Watt	Scottish
Radio, magnetic detector	1902	Marconi	Italian
Radio, signals	1895	Marconi	Italian
Radio amplifier	1906	De Forest	U.S.
Radio beacon	1928	Donovan	U.S.
Radio crystal oscillator	1918	Nicolson	U.S.
Radio receiver, cascade tuning	1913	Alexanderson	U.S.
Radio receiver, heterodyne	1913	Fessenden	Canadian
Radio transmitter triode modulation	1914	Alexanderson	U.S.
Radio tube diode	1904	Fleming	English
Radio tube oscillator	1915	De Forest	U.S.
Radio tube triode	1906	De Forest	U.S.
Radio FM, 2-path	1933	Armstrong	U.S.
Rayon (acetate)	1895	Cross	English
Rayon (cuprammonium)	1890	Despeissis	French
Rayon (nitrocellulose)	1884	Chardonnet	French
Razor, electric	1917	Schick	U.S.
Razor, safety	1895	Gillette	U.S.
Reaper	1834	McCormick	U.S.
Record, cylinder	1887	Bell, Tainter	U.S.
Record, disc	1887	Berliner	U.S.
Record, long playing	1947	Goldmark	U.S.
Record, wax cylinder	1888	Edison	U.S.
Refrigerator car	1868	David	U.S.
Remote control	1898	Tesla	U.S.
Resin, synthetic	1931	Hill	English
Richter scale	1935	Richter	U.S.
Rifle, repeating	1860	Henry	U.S.
Rocket, liquid fuel	1926	Goddard	U.S.
Rollerblades	1980	Olson	U.S.
Rubber, vulcanized	1839	Goodyear	U.S.
Saccharin	1879	Remsen, Fahlberg	U.S.
Saw, circular	1777	Miller	English
Scotch tape	1930	Drew	U.S.
Seat belt	1959	Volvo	Swedish
Sewing machine	1846	Howe	U.S.
Shoe-lasting machine	1883	Matzeliger	U.S.
Shoe-sewing machine	1860	McKay	U.S.
Shrapnel shell	1784	Shrapnel	English
Shuttle, flying	1733	Kay	English
Sleeping-car	1865	Pullman	U.S.
Slide rule	1620	Oughtred	English
Smoke detector	1969	Smith, House	U.S.
Soap, hardwater	1928	Bertsch	German
Spectroscope	1859	Kirchoff, Bunsen	German
Spectroscope (mass)	1918	Dempster	U.S.
Spinning jenny	c.1764	Hargreaves	English
Spinning mule	1779	Crompton	English
Steamboat, exp'mtl	1778	Jouffroy	French
Steamboat, exp'mtl	1785	Fitch	U.S.
Steamboat, exp'mtl	1787	Rumsey	U.S.
Steamboat, exp'mtl	1803	Fulton	U.S.
Steamboat, exp'mtl	1804	Stevens	U.S.
Steamboat, practical	1802	Symington	Scottish
Steamboat, practical	1807	Fulton	U.S.
Steam car	1770	Cugnot	French
Steam turbine	1884	Parsons	English
Steel (converter)	1856	Bessemer	English
Steel alloy	1891	Harvey	U.S.
Steel alloy, high-speed	1901	Taylor, White	U.S.
Steel, manganese	1884	Hadfield	English
Steel, stainless	1916	Brearley	English
Stereoscope	1838	Wheatstone	English
Stethoscope	1819	Laennec	French
Stethoscope, binaural	1840	Cammann	U.S.
Stock ticker	1870	Edison	U.S.
Storage battery, rechargeable	1859	Plante	French
Stove, electric	1896	Hadaway	U.S.
Submarine	1891	Holland	U.S.
Submarine, even keel	1894	Lake	U.S.
Submarine, torpedo	1776	Bushnell	U.S.
Superconductivity	1957	Bardeen, Cooper, Schreiffer	U.S.

Invention	Date	Inventor(s)	Nationality
Superconductivity in ceramics at high temp	1986	Bednorz	German
		Muller	Swiss
Synthesizer	1964	Moog	U.S.
Tank, military	1914	Swinton	English
Tape recorder, magnetic	1899	Poulsen	Danish
Teflon	1938	Du Pont	U.S.
Telegraph, magnetic	1837	Morse	U.S.
Telegraph, quadruplex	1864	Edison	U.S.
Telegraph, railroad	1887	Woods	U.S.
Telegraph, wireless high frequency	1895	Marconi	Italian
Telephone[1]	1871	Meucci	U.S.-Italian
Telephone[1]	1876	Bell	U.S.-Scot.
Telephone answering machine (1st practical)	1954	Hashimoto	Japanese
Telephone, automatic	1891	Strowger	U.S.
Telephone, cellular	1947	Bell Labs	U.S.
Telephone, cordless[2]	1950	Gross	U.S.
Telephone, radio	1900	Poulsen	Danish
		Fessenden	Canadian
Telephone, radio	1906	De Forest	U.S.
Telephone, radio, long dist.	1915	AT&T	U.S.
Telephone, recording	1898	Poulsen	Danish
Telephone amplifier	1912	De Forest	U.S.
Telescope	1608	Lippershey	Neth.
Telescope	1609	Galileo	Italian
Telescope, astronomical	1611	Kepler	German
Teletype	1928	Morkrum, Kleinschmidt	U.S.
Television, color	1928	Baird	Scottish
Television, electronic	1927	Farnsworth	U.S.
Television, iconoscope	1923	Zworykin	U.S.
Television, mech. scanner	1923	Baird	Scottish
Tesla Coil	1891	Tesla	U.S.
Thermometer	1593	Galileo	Italian
Thermometer	1730	Reaumur	French
Thermometer, mercury	1714	Fahrenheit	German
Time recorder	1890	Bundy	U.S.
Tire, double-tube	1845	Thomson	Scottish
Tire, pneumatic	1888	Dunlop	Scottish
Toaster, automatic	1918	Strite	U.S.
Toilet, flush	1589	Harington	English
Tool, pneumatic	1865	Law	English
Torpedo, marine	1804	Fulton	U.S.
Tractor, crawler	1904	Holt	U.S.
Transformer, AC	1885	Stanley	U.S.
Transistor	1947	Shockley, Brattain, Bardeen	U.S.
Trolley car, electric	1884-87	Van DePoele, Sprague	U.S.
Tungsten, ductile	1912	Coolidge	U.S.
Tupperware®	1945	Tupper	U.S.
Turbine, gas	1849	Bourdin	French
Turbine, hydraulic	1849	Francis	U.S.
Turbine, steam	1884	Parsons	English
Type, movable	1447	Gutenberg	German
Typewriter	1867	Sholes, Soule, Glidden	U.S.
Vacuum cleaner, electric	1907	Spangler	U.S.
Vacuum evaporating pan	1846	Rillieux	U.S.
Velcro	1948	de Mestral	Swiss
Video game ("Pong")	1972	Bushnell	U.S.
Video home system (VHS)	1975	Matsushita, JVC	Japanese
Washer, electric	1901	Fisher	U.S.
Welding, atomic hydrogen	1924	Langmuir, Palmer	U.S.
Welding, electric	1877	Thomson	U.S.
Windshield wiper	1903	Anderson	U.S.
Wind tunnel	1912	Eiffel	French
Wire, barbed	1874	Glidden	U.S.
Wrench, double-acting	1913	Owen	U.S.
X-ray tube	1913	Coolidge	U.S.
Zeppelin	1900	Zeppelin	German
Zipper, early model	1893	Judson	U.S.
Zipper, improved	1913	Sundback	Canadian

(1) While Alexander Graham Bell has traditionally been credited with invention of the telephone, which he patented, Antonio Meucci developed a working model before Bell. (2) Al Gross held a number of important early patents in the field of wireless communication; other people were also involved in the development of practical cordless telephones.

Top 20 Corporations Receiving U.S. Patents in 2008

Source: U.S. Patent and Trademark Office, U.S. Department of Commerce

Rank Company	No. of patents	Rank Company	No. of patents
1. International Business Machines Corporation	4,169	11. Hitachi, Ltd	1,301
2. Samsung Electronics Co., Ltd.	3,502	12. Micron Technology, Inc.	1,250
3. Canon Kabushiki Kaisha	2,107	13. Seiko Epson Corporation	1,219
4. Microsoft Corporation	2,026	14. General Electric Company	911
5. Intel Corporation	1,772	15. Fujifilm Corporation	863
6. Toshiba Corporation	1,575	16. Ricoh Company, Ltd.	851
7. Fujitsu Limited	1,475	17. Infineon Technologies AG	809
8. Matsushita Electric Industrial Co., Ltd.	1,469	18. LG Electronics, Inc.	805
9. Sony Corporation	1,461	19. Texas Instruments, Inc.	755
10. Hewlett-Packard Development Company, L.P.	1,422	20. Siemens Aktiengesellschaft	721

Note: Reflects patent ownership at time of patent grant. Changes may occur after patent grant. Where more than one assignee exists, patents are attributed to first-named assignee.

Foreign Countries Receiving Most U.S. Patents, 2008

Source: U.S. Patent and Trademark Office

2008 rank	Country (2007 rank)	2008 patents	Share of total issued	Change, 2007-08	2008 rank	Country (2007 rank)	2008 patents	Share of total issued	Change, 2007-08
1.	Japan (1)	33,682	21.3%	1.0%	7.	United Kingdom (6)	3,094	2.0%	−6.0%
2.	Germany (2)	8,915	5.7	−1.5	8.	Italy (8)	1,357	0.9	4.2
3.	South Korea (3)	7,549	4.8	19.9	9.	Netherlands (10)	1,329	0.8	6.3
4.	Taiwan (4)	6,339	4.0	3.4	10.	Australia (9)	1,292	0.8	2.1
5.	Canada (5)	3,393	2.2	2.3		United States	77,501	49.1	−2.5
6.	France (7)	3,163	2.0	1.1		All countries	157,772	100.0	0.3

Note: Country of origin is determined by residence of first-named inventor.

Top 20 U.S. Patent Categories, 1988-2008

Source: U.S. Patent and Trademark Office

(ranked by number of patents issued in 2008)

Rank	Category	Pre-1988	1988	1998	2008	Change, 1988-2008
1.	Multiplex Communications	2,199	350	1,232	4,527	1,193.4%
2.	Semiconductor Device Manufacturing: Process	3,711	533	2,298	4,526	749.2
3.	Active Solid-State Devices (e.g., Transistors, Solid-State Diodes)	3,377	485	2,417	4,119	749.3
4.	Recording, Communication, or Information Retrieval Equipment	3,298	478	1,243	3,325	595.6
5.	Telecommunications	2,093	209	1,199	3,130	1,397.6
6.	Drug, Bio-Affecting and Body Treating Compositions	17,160	1,857	3,940	2,983	60.6
7.	Chemistry: Molecular Biology and Microbiology	4,763	701	4,006	2,681	282.5
8.	Electrical Computers and Digital Processing Systems: Multicomputer Data Transferring	166	40	941	2,676	6,590.0
9.	Image Analysis	1,122	237	1,320	2,427	924.1
10.	Computer Graphics Processing and Selective Visual Display Systems	1,915	334	1,665	2,352	604.2
11.	Static Information Storage and Retrieval	2,639	383	1,513	2,338	510.4
12.	Pulse or Digital Communications	1,885	284	1,242	2,289	706.0
13.	Radiant Energy	6,667	1,009	1,153	2,210	119.0
14.	Electrical Connectors	5,221	771	1,313	2,177	182.4
15.	Optical: Systems and Elements	4,896	663	1,604	2,065	211.5
16.	Electricity: Electrical Systems and Devices	4,709	626	1,388	2,003	220.0
17.	Data Processing: Database and File Management or Data Structures	162	23	967	1,965	8,443.5
18.	Error Detection/Correction and Fault Detection/Recovery	1,782	268	1,069	1,947	626.5
19.	Measuring and Testing	11,190	1,016	1,653	1,917	88.7
20.	Furnishings	5,747	628	1,472	1,914	204.8

Bottom 20 U.S. Patent Categories, 1988-2008

Source: U.S. Patent and Trademark Office

(ranked by number of patents issued in 2008)

Rank	Category	Pre-1988	1988	1998	2008	Change, 1988-2008
1.	Button Making	1	1	0	0	−100%
2.	Wood Turning	27	1	1	0	−100
3.	Coopering	2	0	1	0	NA
4.	Needle and Pin Making	9	2	0	0	−100
5.	Motors: Spring, Weight, or Animal Powered	52	4	3	0	−100
6.	Type Casting	0	0	0	0	NA
7.	Railway Mail Delivery	2	0	0	0	NA
8.	Typesetting	0	0	0	0	NA
9.	Land Vehicles: Animal Draft Appliances	1	0	0	0	NA
10.	Electric Lamp and Discharge Devices: Consumable Electrodes	4	1	0	0	−100
11.	Leather Manufactures	85	5	1	1	−80
12.	Unearthing Plants or Buried Objects	119	5	6	1	−80
13.	Wire Fabrics and Structure	14	1	1	1	0
14.	Track Sanders	10	4	0	1	−75
15.	Railway Wheels and Axles	33	2	0	1	−50
16.	Telegraphy	372	37	36	2	−95
17.	Electricity: Transmission to Vehicles	167	11	18	2	−82
18.	Mineral Oils: Apparatus	68	5	5	2	−60
19.	Wooden Receptacles	39	4	5	2	−50
20.	Tuners	90	1	4	2	100

Note: Excludes patents for which design classification could not be determined.

Geologic Time Scale

Our understanding of Earth's ancient history is largely a result of geoscientists' study of climate, rock strata, ice samples, mineral deposits, and fossils from around the world; clues to the planet's origin have also been found through the study of extraterrestrial bodies. Geologists divide Earth's history into the following units (MYA = million years ago):

PRECAMBRIAN TIME (4,600-542 MYA)

HADEAN EON (4,600-3,800 MYA) Earth has no continents, oceans, or life; surface conditions are defined by intense volcanic activity and widespread meteorite impact. Oldest known minerals and rocks, many of meteoric origin, date to this era.

ARCHEAN EON (3,800-2,500 MYA) Earth's surface cools and water vapor in atmosphere condenses to form early oceans, which define small protocontinents; the first single-celled organisms, primarily bacteria, appear in these oceans.

PROTEROZOIC EON (2,500-542 MYA) Protocontinents merge into larger landmasses as Earth's crust continues to shift. Atmospheric oxygen levels increase, and first known multicellular life (a form of algae) appears. Later, soft-bodied marine animals emerge.

PHANEROZOIC EON

Paleozoic Era (542-251 MYA)

Cambrian Period (542-488 MYA) Collisions between Earth's plates create a supercontinent of the southern hemisphere known as Gondwanaland. Seas experience an explosion of invertebrate animal life, including thousands of species of trilobites; there is no life on land.

Ordovician Period (488-443 MYA) Gondwanaland extends from South Pole to tropic regions; northern hemisphere is mostly open ocean. Average global temperatures are warmer than present era. First primitive land plants, early ancestors of starfish and mollusks, and first known vertebrates (armored, jawless fishes) appear. The period ends in extinction of a majority of species, possibly a result of a global drop in sea level due to glaciation.

Silurian Period (443-416 MYA) South Pole remains covered by supercontinent, but precursors of present-day N America, Europe, and Asia coalesce around the equator and middle latitudes. Appearance of first known vascular land plants, first freshwater fish, first jawed fish, first coral reefs, and first air-breathing animals (*eurypterids*, a scorpion-like creature).

Devonian Period (416-359 MYA) Collisions between Gondwanaland and ancestral landmasses of N America and Eurasia produce mountains visible today as northern Appalachians. Newly-formed ozone layer offers protection from sun's rays, allowing first air-breathing spiders and mites to appear on dry land; emergence of first jawed fish, fish with fins and scales, and first amphibians.

Carboniferous Period (359-299 MYA) Precursors of modern N America and Northern Europe lie in tropical latitudes north of the Equator; warm and humid conditions there facilitate spread of lush forests and peat swamps that later form most of the world's coal and limestone. Later period sees emergence of first true conifers, *lepidodendrales* ("scale trees") as tall as 100 ft, and first true reptiles.

Permian Period (299-251 MYA) All major landmasses collide to form the supercontinent Pangaea, surrounded by the world ocean Panthalassa. Gradual warming throughout the Permian allows for initial flourishing of species—including dinosaur precursors (up to 10 ft in length) and marine species in shallow inland seas—but later precipitates mass extinction of as much as 95% of all species.

Mesozoic Era (251-65.5 MYA)

Triassic Period (251-199 MYA) Pangea separates into supercontinents of Laurasia and Gondwana; subtropical conditions extend as far north as present-day Wyoming and New England. Emergence of *icthyosaurs* and *plesiosaurs* (large marine reptiles), several species of dinosaurs (up to 15 ft long), first true mammals, and first insects to undergo metamorphosis from larva to pupa to adult.

Jurassic Period (199-145 MYA) North American continent drifts westward, opening Gulf of Mexico; rift forms between South America and Africa. Warm, moist climate contributes to flourishing of coral reefs and temperate and subtropical forests. Appearance of first angiosperms (flowering plants), *pterosaurs* (winged reptiles), earliest known bird (*Archaeopteryx*), and huge dinosaurs such as the carnivorous *Allosaurus* and herbivorous *Apatosaurus*.

Cretaceous Period (145-65.5 MYA) African continental plate drifts north, creating roots of European Alps; gap between S America and Africa broadens; western movement of N America drives formation of Sierra Nevada and Rocky Mountains, turning the western interior of continent into a vast swamp. Later, sea levels rise and cover about one-third of Earth's present land area; global climate is warm and mild. The period ends in a mass extinction of plant and animal species (including dinosaurs), possibly caused by volcanic activity or impact of one or more asteroids or comet fragments.

Cenozoic Era (65.5 MYA-present)

Paleogene Period (65.5-23 MYA)
- Paleocene Epoch (65.5-55.8 MYA) Australia separates from Antarctica; N America and Greenland spread apart. Mammalian life predominates, including early marsupials, insectivores, creodonts (carnivorous ancestors to both cats and dogs), and primitive hoofed mammals.
- Eocene Epoch (55.8-33.9 MYA) Australia drifts farther from Antarctica; the Indian subcontinent becomes welded to Asia, and tectonic forces drive the upheaval of the Alpine-Himalayan system. Climate in N America and Europe is subtropical and moist, with temperate forests as far north as Greenland and Siberia. Ancestors of modern horses, rhinoceroses, camels, bats, primates, and squirrel-like rodents emerge; earliest known marine mammals appear in later Eocene.
- Oligocene Epoch (33.9-23 MYA) San Andreas fault develops between N American and Pacific plates. Mammalian species continue to diversify, producing the first elephants, modern horses, and multiple rodent, camel, and rhinoceros-like species, as well as first known species of great ape. Long-term cooling trend begins that would later cause Pleistocene ice ages.

Neogene Period (23 MYA-present)
- Miocene Epoch (23-5.3 MYA) Crustal plate collisions continue to drive uplift of Alps, Himalayas, and Cordilleran Ranges in Americas; eroded sediment is deposited in shallow marine basins, forming reservoirs for oil fields of California, Romania, and Caspian Sea. Ocean currents prevent Antarctica from receiving warmer waters, fostering growth of Antarctic ice sheet; northern forests become grassy prairies. Elephants give rise to first mastodons, and large apes related to the orangutan live in Asia and southern Europe; oldest hominid fossils from Africa date to this epoch.
- Pliocene Epoch (5.3-1.8 MYA) Alps continue to rise in Europe, and subduction of the Pacific tectonic plate elevates the Sierra Nevada and volcanic Cascade Range. Climate becomes cooler and drier, driving formation of permanent Arctic ice cap. Rapid primate evolution produces *Australopithecus*, earliest direct ancestor of *Homo sapiens*.
- Pleistocene Epoch (1.8 MYA-11,800 years ago) Glacier ice covers as much as 25% or more of Earth's land surface, carving numerous present-day features including the Great Lakes; increased rainfall in lower latitudes allows plant and animal life to flourish in northern and eastern Africa. Late Pleistocene brings worldwide extinction of many large mammals, including the mastodon, saber-toothed tiger, and ground sloth.
- Holocene Epoch (11,800 years ago to the present) Melting ice caused sea levels to rise 100 ft or more in early Holocene, covering large areas of land and extending continental shelf of North America. Humans proliferate, and civilization begins.

Classification

Source: *Funk & Wagnalls New Encyclopedia*

In biology, classification is the identification, naming, and grouping of organisms into a formal system. The 2 fields that are most directly concerned with classification are taxonomy and systematics. Although the 2 disciplines overlap considerably, taxonomy is more concerned with nomenclature (naming) and with constructing hierarchical systems, and systematics with uncovering evolutionary relationships. Two kingdoms of living forms, Plantae and Animalia, have been recognized since Aristotle established the first taxonomy in the 4th century BCE. In addition, there are the following 3 kingdoms: Protista (one-celled organisms), Monera (bacteria and blue-green algae; also known as kingdom Procaryotae), and Fungi. The 7 basic categories of classification (from most general to most specific) are kingdom, phylum (or division), class, order, family, genus, and species. Below are 2 examples:

ZOOLOGICAL HIERARCHY

Kingdom	Phylum	Class	Order	Family	Genus	Species name	Common name
Animalia	Chordata	Mammalia	Primates	Hominidae	Homo	Homo sapiens	Human

BOTANICAL HIERARCHY

Kingdom	Division*	Class	Order	Family	Genus	Species name	Common name
Plantae	Magnoliophyta	Magnoliopsida	Magnoliales	Magnoliaceae	Magnolia	M. virginiana	Sweet Bay

* In botany, the division is generally used in place of the phylum.

Gestation, Longevity, and Incubation of Selected Animals

Information reviewed by Ronald M. Nowak, author of *Walker's Mammals of the World* (6th ed., Johns Hopkins University Press, 1999). Average longevity figures supplied by Ronald T. Reuther. These apply to animals in captivity; the potential life span of animals is rarely attained in nature. Figures on gestation and incubation are averages based on estimates.

Animal	Gestation (days)	Average longevity (years)	Maximum longevity (yrs.-mos.)	Animal	Gestation (days)	Average longevity (years)	Maximum longevity (yrs.-mos.)
Ass	365	12	47	Leopard	98	12	23
Baboon	187	20	45	Lion	100	15	30
Bear (black)	219	18	36-10	Monkey (rhesus)	166	15	37
Bear (grizzly)	225	25	50	Moose	240	12	27
Bear (polar)	240	20	45	Mouse (meadow)	21	3	4
Beaver	105	5	50	Mouse (dom. white)	19	3	6
Bison	285	15	40	Opossum (American)	13	1	5
Camel	406	12	50	Pig (domestic)	112	10	27
Cat (domestic)	63	12	37	Puma	90	12	20
Chimpanzee	230	20	60	Rabbit (domestic)	31	5	13
Chipmunk	31	6	10	Rhinoceros (black)	450	15	45-10
Cow	284	15	30	Rhinoceros (white)	480	20	50
Deer (white-tailed)	201	8	20	Sea lion (California)	350	12	34
Dog (domestic)	61	12	20	Sheep (domestic)	154	12	20
Elephant (African)	660	35	70	Squirrel (gray)	44	10	23-6
Elephant (Asian)	645	40	77	Tiger	105	16	26-3
Elk	250	15	26-8	Wolf (maned)	63	5	15-8
Fox (red)	52	7	14	Zebra (Grant's)	365	15	50
Giraffe	457	10	36-2				
Goat (domestic)	151	8	18			**Incubation time (days)**	
Gorilla	258	20	54	Chicken			21
Guinea pig	68	4	8	Duck			30
Hippopotamus	238	41	61	Goose			30
Horse	330	20	50	Pigeon			18
Kangaroo (gray)	36	7	24	Turkey			26

Major Venomous Animals

Snakes

Asian pit viper—from 2 ft to 5 ft long; throughout Asia; reactions and mortality vary, but most bites cause tissue damage, and mortality is generally low.

Australian brown snake—4 ft to 7 ft long; very slow onset of cardiac or respiratory distress; moderate mortality, but because death can be sudden and unexpected, it is the most dangerous of the Australian snakes; antivenom.

Barba Amarilla or fer-de-lance—up to 7 ft long; from tropical Mexico to Brazil; severe tissue damage common; moderate mortality; antivenom.

Black mamba—up to 14 ft long, fast-moving; S and C Africa; rapid onset of dizziness, difficulty breathing, erratic heartbeat; mortality high, nears 100% without antivenom.

Boomslang—less than 6 ft long; in African savannahs; rapid onset of nausea and dizziness, often followed by slight recovery and then sudden death from internal hemorrhaging; bites rare, mortality high; antivenom.

Bushmaster—up to 12 ft long; wet tropical forests of C and S America; few bites occur, but mortality rate is high.

Common, or Asian, cobra—4 ft to 8 ft long; throughout southern Asia; considerable tissue damage, sometimes paralysis; mortality probably not more than 10%; antivenom.

Copperhead—less than 4 ft long; from New England to Texas; pain and swelling; very seldom fatal; antivenom seldom needed.

Coral snake—2 ft to 5 ft long; in Americas south of Canada; bite may be painless; slow onset of paralysis, impaired breathing; mortalities rare, but high without antivenom and mechanical respiration.

Cottonmouth water moccasin—up to 5 ft long; wetlands of southern U.S. from Virginia to Texas. Rapid onset of severe pain, swelling; mortality low, but tissue destruction can be extensive; antivenom.

Death adder—less than 3 ft long; Australia; rapid onset of faintness, cardiac and respiratory distress; at least 50% mortality without antivenom.

Desert horned viper—in dry areas of Africa and western Asia; swelling and tissue damage; low mortality; antivenom.

European viper—1 ft to 3 ft long; bleeding and tissue damage; mortality low; antivenom.

Gaboon viper—more than 6 ft long; fat; 2-in. fangs; south of the Sahara; massive tissue damage, internal bleeding; few recorded bites.

King cobra—up to 16 ft long; throughout southern Asia; rapid swelling, dizziness, loss of consciousness, difficulty breathing, erratic heartbeat; mortality varies sharply with amount of venom involved, but most bites involve nonfatal amounts; antivenom.

Krait—up to 5 ft long; in SE Asia; rapid onset of sleepiness, numbness; up to 50% mortality even with use of antivenom.

Puff adder—up to 5 ft long; fat; south of the Sahara and throughout the Middle East; rapid large swelling, great pain, dizziness; moderate mortality, often from internal bleeding; antivenom.

Rattlesnake—2 ft to 6 ft long; throughout W Hemisphere; rapid onset of severe pain, swelling; mortality low, but amputation of affected digits is sometimes necessary; antivenom. Mojave rattler may produce temporary paralysis.

Ringhals, or spitting, cobra—5 ft to 7 ft long; southern Africa; squirts venom through holes in front of fangs as a defense; venom is severely irritating, can cause blindness.

Russell's viper or tic-polonga—more than 5 ft long; throughout Asia; internal bleeding; bite reports common; moderate mortality rate; antivenom.

Saw-scaled, or carpet, viper—as much as 2 ft long; in dry areas from India to Africa; severe bleeding, fever; high mortality, causes more human fatalities than any other snake; antivenom.

Sea snakes—throughout Pacific, Indian oceans except NE Pacific; almost painless bite; variety of muscle pain, paralysis; mortality rate low, many bites not envenomed; some antivenoms.

Sharp-nosed pit viper or one hundred pace snake—up to 5 ft long; in S Vietnam, Taiwan, and China; the most toxic of Asian pit vipers; very rapid onset of swelling and tissue damage, internal bleeding; moderate mortality; antivenom.

Taipan—up to 11 ft long; in Australia and New Guinea; rapid paralysis with severe breathing difficulty; mortality nears 100% without antivenom.

Tiger snake—2 ft to 6 ft long; S Australia; pain, numbness, mental disturbances with rapid paralysis; may be deadliest of all land snakes, but antivenom is quite effective.

Yellow, or cape, cobra—7 ft long; in S Africa; most toxic venom of any cobra; rapid onset of swelling, breathing and cardiac difficulties; mortality is high without treatment; antivenom.

Note: Not all bites by venomous snakes are actually envenomed. Any animal bite, however, carries the danger of tetanus, and anyone suffering a venomous snake bite should seek medical attention. Antivenoms do not cure; they are only an aid in the treatment of bites. Mortality rates above are for envenomed bites; low mortality, c. 2% or less; moderate, 2-5%; high, 5-15%.

Lizards

Gila monster—as much as 24 in. long, with heavy body and tail; in high desert in SW U.S. and N Mexico; immediate severe pain and transient low blood pressure; no recent mortality.

Mexican beaded lizard—similar to Gila monster; Mexican west coast; reaction and mortality rate similar to Gila monster.

Insects

Ants, bees, wasps, hornets, etc. Global distribution. Usual reaction is piercing pain in area of sting. Not directly fatal, except in cases of massive multiple stings. However, many people suffer allergic reactions—swelling and rashes—and a few may die within minutes from severe sensitivity to the venom (anaphylactic shock).

Spiders, scorpions

Atrax spider—also known as funnel web spider; several varieties, often large; in Australia; slow onset of breathing, circulation difficulties; low mortality; antivenom.

Black widow—small, round-bodied with red hourglass marking; the widow and its relatives are found in tropical and temperate zones; severe musculoskeletal pain, weakness, breathing difficulty, convulsions; may be more serious in small children; low mortality; antivenom. The **redback** spider of Australia has the hourglass marking on its back, rather than on its front, but is otherwise identical to the black widow.

Brown recluse, or fiddleback, spider—small, oblong body; throughout U.S.; pain with later ulceration at place of bite; in severe cases fever, nausea, and stomach cramps; ulceration may last months; very low mortality.

Scorpion—crablike body with stinger in tail, various sizes; many varieties throughout tropical and subtropical areas; various symptoms may include severe pain spreading from the wound, numbness, severe agitation, cramps; severe reaction may include respiratory failure; low mortality, usually in children; antivenoms.

Tarantula—large, hairy spider found around the world; the American tarantula, and probably all other tarantulas, are harmless to humans, though their bite may cause some pain and swelling.

Sea life

Cone-shell—mollusk in small, beautiful shell; in the S Pacific and Indian oceans; shoots barbs into victims; paralysis; low mortality.

Octopus—global distribution, usually in warm waters; all varieties produce venom, but only a few can cause death; rapid onset of paralysis with breathing difficulty.

Portuguese man-of-war—jellyfish-like, with tentacles up to 100 ft long; in most warm water areas; immediate severe pain; not directly fatal, though shock may cause death in rare cases.

Sea wasp—jellyfish, with tentacles up to 30 ft long, in the S Pacific; very rapid onset of circulatory problems; high mortality because of speed of toxic reaction; antivenom.

Stingray—several varieties of differing sizes; found in tropical and temperate seas and some fresh water; severe pain, rapid onset of nausea, vomiting, breathing difficulties; wound area may ulcerate, gangrene may appear; seldom fatal.

Stonefish—brownish fish that lies motionless on bottom in shallow water; throughout S Pacific and Indian oceans; extraordinary pain, rapid paralysis; low mortality; antivenom available, amount determined by number of puncture wounds; warm water relieves pain.

Speeds of Selected Animals

Source: Natural History magazine. © American Museum of Natural History

Animal	mph	Animal	mph	Animal	mph
Cheetah	70	Mongolian wild ass	40	Human	27.89
Pronghorn antelope	61	Greyhound	39.35	Elephant	25
Wildebeest	50	Whippet	35.50	Black mamba snake	20
Lion	50	Rabbit (domestic)	35	Six-lined race runner (lizard)	18
Thomson's gazelle	50	Mule deer	35	Wild turkey	15
Quarterhorse	47.5	Jackal	35	Squirrel	12
Elk	45	Reindeer	32	Pig (domestic)	11
Cape hunting dog	45	Giraffe	32	Chicken	9
Coyote	43	White-tailed deer	30	Spider (Tegenaria atrica)	1.17
Gray fox	42	Wart hog	30	Giant tortoise	0.17
Hyena	40	Grizzly bear	30	Three-toed sloth	0.15
Zebra	40	Cat (domestic)	30	Garden snail	0.03

Note: Most of these measurements are for maximum speeds over approximate quarter-mile distances. Exceptions are the lion and elephant, whose speeds were clocked in the act of charging; the whippet, which was timed over a 200-yd course; the cheetah, timed over a 100-yd distance; humans, timed over a 15-yd segment of a 100-yd run; and the black mamba, six-lined race runner, spider, giant tortoise, three-toed sloth, and garden snail, which were measured over various small distances.

Top 50 American Kennel Club Registrations

Source: American Kennel Club, New York, NY; covers newly registered dogs during calendar year shown

Breed	2008 Rank	2008 Number registered	2007 Rank	2007 Number registered	Breed	2008 Rank	2008 Number registered	2007 Rank	2007 Number registered
Labrador Retriever	1.	100,736	1.	114,113	French Bulldog	26.	6,963	34.	6,399
Yorkshire Terrier	2.	41,914	2.	47,850	English Springer Spaniel	27.	6,690	27.	7,915
German Shepherd	3.	40,909	3.	43,376	Mastiff	28.	6,657	28.	7,160
Golden Retriever	4.	34,485	4.	39,659	Australian Shepherd	29.	6,471	33.	6,471
Beagle	5.	33,722	5.	37,021	Brittany	30.	6,270	29.	7,015
Boxer	6.	29,705	6.	33,548	Weimaraner	31.	5,732	30.	6,932
Dachshund	7.	26,075	7.	32,598	Miniature Pinscher	32.	5,648	26.	7,952
Bulldog	8.	23,413	10.	22,160	Basset Hound	33.	5,277	31.	6,790
Poodle	9.	21,545	8.	26,369	West Highland White Terrier	34.	4,755	35.	5,666
Shih Tzu	10.	20,219	9.	24,951	Bichons Frise	35.	4,675	32.	6,494
Miniature Schnauzer	11.	17,040	11.	20,747	Havanese	36.	4,435	37.	4,460
Chihuahua	12.	15,985	12.	19,801	Papillon	37.	4,396	36.	5,393
Pomeranian	13.	13,215	13.	16,605	Collie	38.	4,016	38.	4,268
Rottweiler	14.	13,059	15.	14,211	Bullmastiff	39.	3,447	40.	3,735
Pug	15.	12,202	14.	16,525	Bernese Mountain Dog	40.	3,338	41.	3,522
German Shorthaired Pointer	16.	11,110	18.	12,173	Dogue de Bordeaux	41.	3,223	—	—
Boston Terrier	17.	10,930	16.	13,201	Black and Tan Coonhound	42.	3,222	136.	132
Doberman Pinscher	18.	10,547	21.	11,381	Bloodhound	43.	3,203	43.	3,324
Shetland Sheepdog	19.	10,188	20.	11,755	Vizsla	44.	3,010	42.	3,431
Maltese	20.	10,056	19.	11,964	St. Bernard	45.	3,007	39.	3,767
Cocker Spaniel	21.	9,481	17.	12,483	Newfoundland	46.	2,938	44.	3,159
Great Dane	22.	8,994	23.	9,303	Chinese Shar-Pei	47.	2,583	46.	2,940
Siberian Husky	23.	8,465	24.	9,048	Chesapeake Bay Retriever	48.	2,463	47.	2,840
Pembroke Welsh Corgi	24.	8,102	22.	9,437	Scottish Terrier	49.	2,429	45.	3,084
Cavalier King Charles Spaniel	25.	7,626	25.	8,268	Rhodesian Ridgeback	50.	2,199	53.	2,165

Breed Registration for Top 10 Pedigreed Cats, 1979-2005[1]

Source: The Cat Fanciers' Association, Manasquan, NJ; ranked by new registrations, 2005

Breed	2005	2004	2000	1995	1990	1979	Breed	2005	2004	2000	1995	1990	1979
Persian	16,657	18,176	25,524	44,735	60,661	25,819	Birman	991	945	998	990	969	258
Maine Coon	3,932	4,162	4,539	4,332	2,727	401	American Shorthair	802	846	885	1,050	1,176	738
Exotic	3,006	2,838	2,094	1,610	1,311	289	Oriental	764	854	1,085	1,237	1,288	260
Siamese	1,445	1,621	2,131	3,025	3,860	3,607	Tonkinese	704	717	803	780	618	—
Abyssinian	1,344	1,462	1,683	2,469	2,702	1,524	Total	NA	41,606	49,551	70,288	84,729	37,630
Ragdoll	1,215	981	—	—	—	—							

(1) Latest figures available. 2006 rankings were identical to 2005, except the 10th most popular breed was the Sphynx.

Trees of the U.S.

Source: American Forests, Washington, DC

Approximately 826 native and naturalized species of trees are grown in the U.S. The oldest living tree in the U.S. is believed to be a bristlecone pine tree in California named Methuselah, estimated to be 4,700 years old. The world's largest known living tree*, the General Sherman giant sequoia in California, weighs more than 6,167 tons—as much as 41 blue whales or 740 elephants. Listed here are the 10 largest National Champion trees as listed by American Forests, as of Oct. 8, 2008.

10 Largest National Champion Trees

Tree type	Girth at 4.5 ft (in.)	Height (ft)	Crown spread (ft)	Total points*	Location
Giant sequoia (Gen. Sherman tree)	1,020	274	107	1,321	Sequoia National Park, CA
Coast redwood	950	321	75	1,290	Jedediah Smith Redwoods State Park, CA
Coast redwood	895	307	83	1,223	Jedediah Smith Redwoods State Park, CA
Coast redwood	867	311	101	1,203	Prairie Creek Redwoods State Park, CA
Western red cedar	761	159	45	931	Olympic National Park, WA
Sitka spruce	668	191	96	883	Olympic National Park, WA
Douglas-fir	512	301	65	829	Jedediah Smith Redwoods State Park, CA
Douglas-fir	505	281	71	804	Olympic National Forest, WA
Port-Orford Cedar	522	242	35	773	Siskiyou National Forest, OR
Common Baldcypress	647	96	74	762	Cat Island, LA

* American Forests uses a point system to determine the largest trees. The following calculation to determine a tree's total points: trunk circumference (in inches) + height (in feet) + ¼ average crown spread (in feet) = total points.

ENVIRONMENT

U.S. Greenhouse Gas Emissions from Human Activities, 1990-2007

Source: U.S. Environmental Protection Agency

GAS AND MAJOR SOURCE(S)	1990	1995	2000	2004	2005	2006	2007	% change, 2000-07
Carbon dioxide (CO_2)	5,076.7	5,407.9	5,955.2	6,048.1	6,090.8	6,014.9	6,103.4	2.5%
Fossil fuel combustion	4,708.9	5,013.9	5,561.5	5,669.3	5,723.5	5,635.4	5,735.8	3.1
Methane (CH_4)	616.6	615.8	591.1	562.7	561.7	582.0	585.3	−1.0
Landfills	149.2	144.3	122.3	126.2	127.8	130.4	132.9	8.7
Enteric fermentation[1]	133.2	143.6	134.4	133.8	136.0	138.2	139.0	3.4
Natural gas systems	129.6	132.6	130.8	118.0	106.3	104.8	104.7	−20.0
Coal mining	84.1	67.1	60.5	58.2	57.1	58.4	57.6	−4.8
Nitrous oxide (N_2O)	315.0	334.1	329.2	317.8	315.9	312.1	311.9	−5.3
Agricultural soil management	200.3	202.3	204.5	211.2	210.6	208.4	207.9	1.7
Hydrofluorocarbons (HFCs), perfluorocarbons (PFCs), and sulfur hexafluoride (SF_6)	181.9	211.9	266.5	273.6	281.3	285.3	300.0	12.6
Total U.S. emissions	**6,098.7**	**6,463.3**	**7,008.2**	**7,064.9**	**7,108.6**	**7,051.1**	**7,150.1**	**2.0**
Net U.S. emissions[2]	**5,257.3**	**5,612.3**	**6,290.7**	**5,770.4**	**5,985.9**	**6,000.6**	**6,087.5**	**−3.2**

Note: Emissions given in terms of equivalent emissions of carbon dioxide (CO_2), using units of teragrams of carbon dioxide equivalents (Tg CO_2 Eq.). (1) Digestive process of ruminant animals, such as cattle and sheep, producing methane as a by-product. (2) Total emissions minus carbon dioxide absorbed by forests or other means.

U.S. Carbon Dioxide Emissions from Fossil Fuel Combustion, 1990-2007

Source: U.S. Environmental Protection Agency

The concept of Global Warming Potential (GWP) was developed by the Intergovernmental Panel on Climate Change (IPCC) to compare the ability of each greenhouse gas to trap heat in the atmosphere relative to another gas. Carbon dioxide (CO_2) from fossil fuel combustion is the largest source of U.S. greenhouse gas emissions, accounting for approximately 79% of global warming potential (GWP) weighted emissions since 1990.

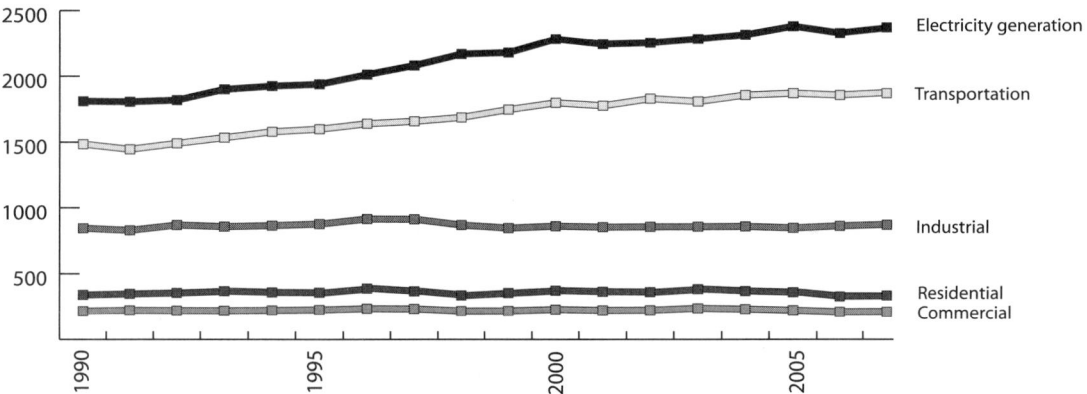

Top 15 Nations Producing Carbon Dioxide Emissions, 1980-2007

Source: U.S. Department of Energy

(million metric tons of carbon dioxide emitted from the consumption of energy; ranked by 2007 totals)

Region/country	1980	1985	1990	1995	2000	2007	% change, 1980-2007	% change, 1990-2007
China	1,460.20	1,873.52	2,288.95	2,885.42	2,871.53	6,283.56	330%	175%
United States	4,794.68	4,623.99	5,035.50	5,331.85	5,869.04	6,006.71	25	19
Russia[1]	3,092.69	3,547.09	3,833.32	1,607.08	1,560.42	1,672.62	NA	NA
India	293.17	450.47	582.50	876.39	1,009.76	1,400.71	378	140
Japan	948.93	928.55	1,051.00	1,121.00	1,206.46	1,262.39	33	20
Germany[2]	762.03	690.84	700.81	887.36	857.97	835.13	NA	NA
Canada	458.35	444.80	474.57	509.94	563.96	589.90	29	24
United Kingdom	616.34	591.73	604.36	561.79	560.59	564.02	−8	−7
Korea, South	132.27	173.24	243.06	382.48	440.29	515.98	290	112
Iran	116.85	159.97	202.14	262.24	320.67	490.29	320	143
Italy	372.20	366.32	415.96	431.89	448.21	460.80	24	11
Australia	201.45	228.85	270.28	291.21	359.87	456.36	127	69
Mexico	240.43	280.83	302.31	321.57	383.33	452.96	88	50
South Africa	236.95	304.60	300.44	350.32	390.16	452.28	91	21
Saudi Arabia	176.92	179.22	208.02	235.29	290.54	433.93	145	109
World total[3]	**18,512.25**	**19,628.62**	**21,691.22**	**22,227.62**	**23,876.45**	**29,914.24**	**62**	**38**

NA = Not applicable. (1) Numbers for 1980-90 are for the former Soviet Union. (2) Numbers for 1980-90 are for the former West Germany. (3) Includes nations not listed.

Air Pollution in Selected World Cities

Source: World Bank, *World Development Indicators 2007*

Particulate matter in the following table refers to smoke, soot, dust, and liquid droplets from combustion that are in the air—specifically, to particulates less than 10 microns in diameter capable of reaching deep into the respiratory tract. The level of particulates, an important indicator of air quality, is significantly affected by the state of technology and pollution controls. Particulate pollution causes an estimated 500,000 premature deaths each year. **Sulfur dioxide** is a pollutant formed when fossil fuels containing sulfur are burned. **Nitrogen dioxide** is a poisonous, pungent gas formed when nitric oxide combines with hydrocarbons and sunlight, producing a photochemical reaction. Nitrogen oxides are emitted by bacteria, nitrogenous fertilizers, aerobic decomposition of organic matter, biomass combustion, and, especially, burning fuel for vehicles and industrial activities. Emissions of sulfur dioxide and nitrogen oxides lead to **acid rain**.

Data in the following table are average concentrations based on reports from urban monitoring sites, measured in micrograms per cubic meter (mpcm); the figures give a general indication of air quality, but results should be interpreted with caution. World Health Organization standards for acceptable air quality are annual mean concentrations of 20 mpcm for particulate matter less than 10 microns in diameter and 40 mpcm for nitrogen dioxide; and daily mean concentrations of 20 mpcm for sulfur dioxide.

City, country	Particulate matter[1]	Sulfur dioxide[2]	Nitrogen dioxide[2]	City, country	Particulate matter[1]	Sulfur dioxide[2]	Nitrogen dioxide[2]
Accra, Ghana	33	NA	NA	Montréal, Canada	19	10	42
Amsterdam, Netherlands	34	10	58	Moscow, Russia	21	109	NA
Athens, Greece	43	34	64	Mumbai, India	63	33	39
Bangkok, Thailand	79	11	23	Nairobi, Kenya	43	NA	NA
Barcelona, Spain	35	11	43	New York, NY-Newark, NJ, U.S.	21	26	79
Beijing, China	89	90	122	Oslo, Norway	14	8	43
Berlin, Germany	22	18	26	Paris, France	11	14	57
Cairo, Egypt	169	69	NA	Prague, Czech Republic	23	14	33
Calcutta, India	128	49	34	Quito, Ecuador	30	22	NA
Capetown, South Africa	16	21	72	Rio de Janeiro, Brazil	35	129	NA
Caracas, Venezuela	10	33	57	Rome, Italy	29	NA	NA
Chicago, U.S.	25	14	57	São Paulo, Brazil	40	43	83
Delhi, India	150	24	41	Seoul, South Korea	41	44	60
Jakarta, Indonesia	104	NA	NA	Shanghai, China	73	53	73
London, United Kingdom	21	25	77	Sofia, Bulgaria	61	39	122
Los Angeles, U.S.	34	9	74	Tokyo, Japan	40	18	68
Manila, Philippines	39	33	NA	Toronto, Canada	22	17	43
Mexico City, Mexico	51	74	130	Warsaw, Poland	43	16	32
Milan, Italy	30	31	248				

NA = Not available. (1) Data collected in 2004. (2) Average of data collected between 1995 and 2001.

Air Quality of Selected U.S. Metropolitan Areas, 2000-08

Source: U.S. Environmental Protection Agency, Office of Air Quality Planning and Standards

Data indicate the number of days metropolitan statistical areas failed to meet acceptable air-quality standards.

Metropolitan Statistical Area	2000	2005	2006	2007	2008
Atlanta, GA	26	5	14	15	4
Bakersfield, CA	62	33	41	28	26
Baltimore, MD	7	6	4	5	4
Baton Rouge, LA	13	6	4	4	0
Boston, MA-NH	1	3	0	2	0
Chicago, IL	0	4	0	2	0
Cincinnati, OH-KY-IN	3	5	1	2	0
Cleveland-Lorain-Elyria, OH	3	6	3	3	0
Dallas, TX	15	9	9	3	0
Denver, CO	0	0	2	2	0
Detroit, MI	1	7	1	4	1
Fresno, CA	69	19	16	19	15
Greensboro-Winston Salem-High Point, NC	5	0	1	3	1
Houston, TX	29	19	16	3	2
Indianapolis, IN	3	1	0	0	0
Las Vegas, NV-AZ	1	3	3	3	0
Los Angeles-Long Beach, CA	35	29	26	17	28
Memphis, TN-AR-MS	6	4	4	2	1
Miami, FL	0	1	1	0	0
Minneapolis-St. Paul, MN-WI	1	2	0	0	0
Nashville, TN	5	1	2	2	0
Nassau-Suffolk, NY	2	5	5	1	1
New Orleans, LA	5	0	0	1	0
New York, NY	4	8	4	4	1
Newark, NJ	4	0	2	2	0
Orange County, CA	7	0	2	3	1
Philadelphia, PA-NJ	8	6	5	7	4
Phoenix-Mesa, AZ	2	1	134	94	84
Pittsburgh, PA	7	13	4	8	1
Riverside-San Bernardino, CA	65	50	46	52	53
Sacramento, CA	22	22	22	4	20
San Francisco, CA	0	0	1	0	0
Seattle-Bellevue-Everett, WA	0	0	5	1	0
Washington, DC-MD-VA-WV	5	4	8	3	3

U.S. Greenhouse Gas Emissions, 2007

Source: U.S. Environmental Protection Agency

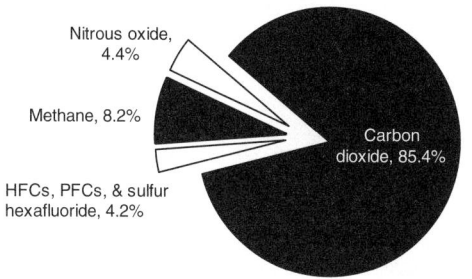

Nitrous oxide, 4.4%

Methane, 8.2%

HFCs, PFCs, & sulfur hexafluoride, 4.2%

Carbon dioxide, 85.4%

World Carbon Dioxide Emissions from the Use of Fossil Fuels, 2006

Source: U.S. Energy Information Administration

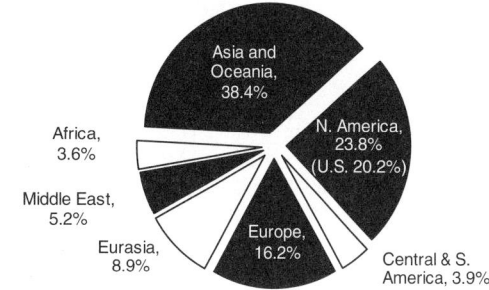

Asia and Oceania, 38.4%

Africa, 3.6%

Middle East, 5.2%

Eurasia, 8.9%

N. America, 23.8% (U.S. 20.2%)

Europe, 16.2%

Central & S. America, 3.9%

Note: Emissions sources are independently rounded; percentages may not add up to 100.

Atmospheric Concentration of Carbon Dioxide, 1744-2008

Sources: Carbon Dioxide Information Analysis Center, U.S. Dept. of Energy

Year[1]	CO$_2$ in ppm[2]	Year[1]	CO$_2$ in ppm[2]	Year[1]	CO$_2$ in ppm[2]	Year[1]	CO$_2$ in ppm[2]	Year[1]	CO$_2$ in ppm[2]
1744	277	1869	289	1927	306	1980	339	2005	377
1791	280	1878	290	1943	308	1990	354	2006	379
1816	284	1903	295	1960	317	2000	367	2007	381
1843	287	1915	301	1970	326	2004	375	2008	383

(1) Measurements for the years 1744-1943 were derived from a 200m ice core sample drilled near Siple Station in Antarctica between 1983-84. Measurements from 1960-2004 were taken directly from the atmosphere at Mauna Loa Observatory in Hawaii. Measurements for 2005-08 were taken directly from the atmosphere at Jubany Station, Antarctica. (2) Parts per million.

Emissions of Principal Air Pollutants in the U.S., 1970-2008

Source: U.S. Environmental Protection Agency, Office of Air Quality Planning and Standards; in est. million tons

Pollutant	1970	1975	1980	1985	1990	1995	2000	2005	2008
Carbon monoxide	204.0	188.4	185.4	176.8	154.2	126.8	114.5	93.0	77.7
Nitrogen oxides[1]	26.9	26.4	27.1	25.8	25.5	25.0	22.6	19.1	16.3
Particulate matter[2]									
PM$_{10}$	13.0	7.6	7.0	41.3	27.8	25.8	23.0	18.3	11.9
PM$_{2.5}$	NA	NA	NA	NA	7.6	6.9	6.5	3.0	2.4
Sulfur dioxide	31.2	28.0	25.9	23.3	23.1	18.6	16.3	14.8	11.4
Volatile org. compounds[1]	3.5	30.8	31.1	27.4	24.1	22.06	17.5	18.4	15.9
Lead	0.221	0.160	0.074	0.022	0.005	0.004	0.003	0.001	0.001
Total[3]	**278.8**	**281.4**	**276.5**	**294.6**	**254.7**	**91.5**	**193.9**	**163.6**	**133.2**

NA = Not available (1) Ozone, a major air pollutant and the primary constituent of smog, is not emitted directly to the air but is formed by sunlight acting on emissions of nitrogen oxides and volatile organic compounds. (2) PM$_{10}$, particulates 10 microns or smaller diameter. PM$_{2.5}$, particulates 2.5 microns or smaller diameter. (3) Totals are rounded, as are components of totals.

Carbon Monoxide Emission Estimates, 1970-2008

(in thousand tons)

Source	1970	1975	1980	1985	1990	1995	2000	2006	2007	2008
Fuel combustion, elec. util.	237	276	322	291	363	372	484	661	680	699
Industrial processes[1]	10,610	8,304	7,700	5,894	5,572	5,631	3,628	3,143	3,213	3,283
Transportation[2]	174,602	167,884	160,512	153,216	131,702	107,755	92,239	65,111	61,007	56,902
Total[3]	**204,042**	**188,398**	**185,408**	**176,845**	**154,188**	**126,778**	**114,465**	**87,915**	**82,801**	**77,685**

(1) Industrial fuel combustion, chemical and allied manufacturing, metals processing, and petroleum and other industrial sectors. (2) Highway and off-highway vehicles. (3) Totals may not add because not all categories are listed.

Nitrogen Oxides Emission Estimates, 1970-2008

(in thousand tons)

Source	1970	1975	1980	1985	1990	1995	2000	2006	2007	2008
Fuel combustion, elec. util.	4,900	5,694	7,024	6,127	6,663	6,384	5,330	3,446	3,320	3,006
Industrial processes[1]	5,100	4,546	4,110	4,009	3,831	3,909	3,518	2,769	2,755	2,741
Transportation[2]	15,276	15,029	14,846	14,508	13,373	12,989	12,561	10,740	10,101	9,461
Total[3]	**26,882**	**26,378**	**27,080**	**25,757**	**25,527**	**24,955**	**22,599**	**18,110**	**17,321**	**16,339**

(1) Industrial fuel combustion, chemical and allied manufacturing, metals processing, and petroleum and other industrial sectors. (2) Highway and off-highway vehicles. (3) Totals may not add because not all categories are listed.

Sulfur Dioxide Emissions Estimates, 1970-2008

(in thousand tons)

Source	1970	1975	1980	1985	1990	1995	2000	2006	2007	2008
Fuel combustion, elec. util.	17,398	18,268	17,469	16,272	15,909	12,080	11,396	9,404	8,941	7,552
Industrial processes[1]	11,661	7,993	6,725	5,597	5,402	4,945	3,516	2,701	2,683	2,663
Transportation[2]	551	635	717	809	874	741	697	827	673	520
Total[3]	**31,218**	**28,044**	**25,926**	**23,307**	**23,077**	**18,619**	**16,348**	**13,655**	**13,006**	**11,429**

(1) Industrial fuel combustion, chemical and allied manufacturing, metals processing, and petroleum and other industrial sectors. (2) Highway and off-highway vehicles. (3) Totals may not add because not all categories are listed.

Average Global Temperatures, 1900-2008

Source: National Oceanic and Atmospheric Administration; in degrees Fahrenheit

1900-09	56.58	1940-49	57.13	1980-89	57.35	2002	58.02	2006	57.99
1910-19	56.56	1950-59	56.98	1990-99	57.64	2003	58.02	2007	58.01
1920-29	56.76	1960-69	57.04	2000	57.67	2004	57.98	2008	57.88
1930-39	57.01	1970-79	57.06	2001	57.90	2005	58.11		

Note: The warmest year on record was 2005, when the average global temperature reached 58.11°F. The second warmest year on record was 1998.

Toxics Release Inventory, U.S., 2004-05

Source: U.S. Environmental Protection Agency

Releases of toxic chemicals into the environment, by manner of release and industry sector; pollutant transfers by destination of transfer. Totals below may not add because of rounding.

	2004 mil lbs	2005 mil lbs		2004 %	2005 %
Pollutant releases			**Top industries, total releases**		
Air releases	1,540	1,512	Metal mining	25%	27%
Surface water discharges	235	240	Electric utilities	25	25
Underground injection	238	231	Chemicals	13	11
On-site land releases	1,701	1,824	Primary metals	12	12
Off-site releases	508	533	Hazardous waste/solvent recovery	5	5
Total on- and off-site releases	**4,223**	**4,339**	All others	15	20
Pollutant transfers			**Top carcinogens, air/water/land releases**	mil lbs	mil lbs
To recycling	2,036	2,014	Lead compounds	451	426
To energy recovery	650	608	Arsenic compounds	184	119
To treatment	326	337	Chromium compounds	52	56
To publicly owned treatment works	260	265	Styrene	55	55
Other transfers	71	<1	Nickel compounds	32	33
Off-site to disposal	606	637	Formaldehyde	22	25
Total	**3,950**	**3,862**			

Note: This information does not indicate whether (or to what degree) the public has been exposed to toxic chemicals.

Top 10 States, Total Toxics Releases, 2006

Source: U.S. Environmental Protection Agency

State	Total lbs	State	Total lbs	State	Total lbs	State	Total lbs
Alaska	667,686,056	Indiana	237,002,637	Pennsylvania	154,108,216	Tennessee	131,262,217
Ohio	291,070,520	Nevada	217,093,821	North Carolina	134,222,456		
Texas	238,775,263	Utah	193,525,829	Louisiana	132,062,553	**U.S. total***	**4,294,568,027**

*Total includes District of Columbia, Puerto Rico, American Samoa, Guam, Northern Marianas, and the Virgin Islands.

Hazardous Waste Sites in the U.S., 2008

Source: U.S. Environmental Protection Agency, *National Priorities List,* Sept. 2008

State/territory	Proposed Gen.	Proposed Fed.	Final Gen.	Final Fed.	Total	State/territory	Proposed Gen.	Proposed Fed.	Final Gen.	Final Fed.	Total
Alabama	2	0	10	3	15	Nevada	0	0	1	0	1
Alaska	0	0	0	5	5	New Hampshire	1	0	19	1	21
Arizona	0	0	7	2	9	New Jersey	2	0	106	8	116
Arkansas	0	0	9	0	9	New Mexico	1	0	12	1	14
California	3	0	70	24	97	New York	1	0	81	4	86
Colorado	2	0	15	3	20	North Carolina	0	0	30	2	32
Connecticut	1	0	13	1	15	North Dakota	0	0	0	0	0
Delaware	0	0	13	1	14	Ohio	7	2	28	3	40
District of Columbia	0	0	0	1	1	Oklahoma	1	0	7	1	9
Florida	3	0	43	6	52	Oregon	0	0	10	2	12
Georgia	1	0	13	2	16	Pennsylvania	3	0	88	6	97
Hawaii	0	0	1	2	3	Rhode Island	0	0	10	2	12
Idaho	3	0	4	2	9	South Carolina	1	0	23	2	26
Illinois	5	1	39	4	49	South Dakota	0	0	1	1	2
Indiana	1	0	31	0	32	Tennessee	0	1	10	3	14
Iowa	1	0	10	1	12	Texas	3	0	42	4	49
Kansas	1	0	10	1	12	Utah	4	0	11	4	19
Kentucky	0	0	13	1	14	Vermont	0	0	11	0	11
Louisiana	3	0	9	1	13	Virginia	0	0	19	11	30
Maine	0	0	9	3	12	Washington	0	0	35	13	48
Maryland	1	1	8	9	19	West Virginia	0	0	7	2	9
Massachusetts	1	0	25	6	32	Wisconsin	1	0	37	0	38
Michigan	1	1	65	0	67	Wyoming	0	0	1	1	2
Minnesota	0	0	23	2	25	Guam	0	0	1	1	2
Mississippi	2	0	4	0	6	Puerto Rico	0	0	12	1	13
Missouri	0	0	26	3	29	Virgin Islands	0	0	2	0	2
Montana	1	0	14	0	15	**Total**	**57**	**6**	**1,100**	**157**	**1,318**
Nebraska	0	0	12	1	13						

Note: Fed. = Hazardous waste produced by federal agency; Gen. = Non-Fed. sites. Proposed = Proposed for federal Superfund financing; Final = Qualified for Superfund financing.

Renewable Water Resources

Source: Food and Agriculture Organization, United Nations, 2007

Globally, water supplies are abundant, but they are unevenly distributed among and within countries. In some areas, water withdrawals are so high, relative to supply, that surface water supplies are shrinking, and groundwater reserves are being depleted faster than they can be replenished by precipitation. The U.S. (including Alaska and Hawaii) has a total of 2,818 cubic kilometers of internal renewable water resources, an actual total (which takes into account incoming water flow from outside the country) of 3,069 cubic kilometers, and 10,333 cubic meters per capita. Totals for all countries are 43,219 cubic kilometers of internal resources, 55,273 cubic kilometers of actual resources, and 8,549 cubic meters per capita.

These numbers, and those in the tables below, were published by the Food and Agriculture Organization in 2007; the tables draw upon studies done over a number of years and use 2005 population data.

Countries With Greatest Water Resources*
(ranked by per capita resources)

Country	Cubic meters per capita	Total cubic km
Greenland............	10,578,947.4	603.0
French Guiana	683,673.5	134.0
Iceland	566,666.7	170.0
Guyana.............	320,478.7	241.0
Suriname	268,131.9	88.0
Congo, Republic of....	196,319.0	222.0
Papua New Guinea....	131,010.8	801.0
Gabon..............	114,765.6	164.0
Solomon Islands......	89,043.8	44.7
Canada.............	88,335.6	2,850.0

*Data not available from all nations.

Countries With Lowest Water Resources*
(ranked by per capita resources)

Country/territory	Cubic meters per capita	Total cubic km
Andorra.............	0.0	0.0
Kuwait..............	7.0	0.0
United Arab Emirates ..	31.4	0.2
Bahamas............	60.2	0.0
Qatar...............	61.8	0.1
Maldives	86.7	0.0
Saudi Arabia	93.0	2.4
Libya	98.6	0.6
Malta	123.5	0.1
Singapore	135.3	0.6

Top 50 Countries by Forest Area, 1990-2005

Source: World Resources Institute; United Nations
(in thousand hectares; ranked by 2005 hectares)

Country	Total forest area 2005	Total forest area 2000	Total forest area 1990	Percent change in forest area 1990-2005	Country	Total forest area 2005	Total forest area 2000	Total forest area 1990	Percent change in forest area 1990-2005
Russian Federation	808,790	809,268	808,950	0%	Congo	22,471	22,556	22,726	−1%
Brazil	477,698	493,213	520,027	−8	Gabon	21,775	21,826	21,927	−1
Canada.........	310,134	310,134	310,134	0	Cameroon	21,245	22,345	24,545	−13
United States	303,089	302,294	298,648	1	Malaysia	20,890	21,591	22,376	−7
China	197,290	177,001	157,141	26	Mozambique	19,262	19,512	20,012	−4
Australia	163,678	164,645	167,904	−3	Paraguay........	18,475	19,368	21,157	−13
Congo, Dem. Rep.	133,610	135,207	140,531	−5	Spain	17,915	16,436	13,479	33
Indonesia	88,495	97,852	116,567	−24	Zimbabwe	17,540	19,105	22,234	−21
Peru	68,742	69,213	70,156	−2	Laos............	16,142	16,532	17,314	−7
India	67,701	67,554	63,939	6	Chile	16,121	15,834	15,263	6
Sudan..........	67,546	70,491	76,381	−12	France..........	15,554	15,351	14,538	7
Mexico	64,238	65,540	69,016	−7	Guyana	15,104	15,104	15,104	0
Colombia	60,728	60,963	61,439	−1	Suriname........	14,776	14,776	14,776	0
Angola	59,104	59,728	60,976	−3	Thailand........	14,520	14,814	15,965	−9
Bolivia..........	58,740	60,091	62,795	−6	Ethiopia	13,000	13,705	15,114	−14
Venezuela	47,713	49,151	52,026	−8	Vietnam.........	12,931	11,725	9,363	38
Zambia	42,452	44,676	49,124	−14	Madagascar......	12,838	13,023	13,692	−6
Tanzania	35,257	37,318	41,441	−15	Mali	12,572	13,072	14,072	−11
Argentina	33,021	33,770	35,262	−6	Botswana........	11,943	12,535	13,718	−13
Myanmar	32,222	34,554	39,219	−18	Chad	11,921	12,317	13,110	−9
Papua New Guinea	29,437	30,132	31,523	−7	Nigeria..........	11,089	13,137	17,234	−36
Sweden	27,528	27,474	27,367	−1	Germany	11,076	11,076	10,741	3
Japan	24,868	24,876	24,950	0	Iran	11,075	11,075	11,075	0
Central African Rep.	22,755	22,903	23,203	−2	Ecuador........	10,853	11,841	13,817	−21
Finland	22,500	22,475	22,194	1	Cambodia	10,447	11,541	12,946	−19
					World	**3,952,025**	**3,988,610**	**4,077,291**	**−3**

Selected Endangered Animal Species

Source: Fish and Wildlife Service, U.S. Dept. of the Interior

Common name	Scientific name	Range
Albatross, Amsterdam	Diomedia amsterdamensis	Amsterdam Island, Indian Ocean
Antelope, giant sable	Hippotragus niger variani................	Angola
Armadillo, giant	Pridontes maximus	Venezuela, Guyana to Argentina
Babirusa.......................	Babyrousa babyrussa	Indonesia
Bandicoot, desert...................	Perameles eremiana	Australia
Bat, gray.......................	Myotis grisescens	Central, southeastern U.S.
Bear, Mexican grizzly.................	Ursus aretos	Mexico
Bison, wood	Bison bison athabascae	Canada, northwestern U.S.
Bobcat, Mexican...................	Felis rufus escuinapae................	Central Mexico
Caiman, black	Melanosuchus niger	Amazon basin
Camel, Bactrian	Camelus bactrianus..................	Mongolia, China
Caribou, woodland.................	Rangifer tarandus caribou	Canada, Northwestern U.S.

Common name	Scientific name	Range
Cheetah	Acinonyx jubatus	Africa to India
Chimpanzee, pygmy	Pan paniscus	Dem. Rep. of the Congo
Condor, California	Gymnogyps californianus	U.S. (AZ, CA, OR), Mexico (Baja California)
Crane, whooping	Grus americana	Canada, Mexico, U.S. (Rocky Mts. to Carolinas)
Crocodile, American	Crocodylus acutus	U.S. (FL), Mexico, Caribbean Sea, Central and S America
Deer, Columbian white-tailed	Odocoileus virginianus leucurus	U.S. (OR, WA)
Dolphin, Chinese river	Lipotes vexillifer	China
Dugong	Dugong dugon	East Africa to southern Japan
Elephant, Asian	Elephas maximus	S central and southeastern Asia
Fox, northern swift	Vulpes velox hebes	Canada
Frog, mountain yellow-legged	Rano capito sevosa	Western U.S. (CA, NV)
Gorilla	Gorilla gorilla	Central and W Africa
Hartebeest, Tora	Alcelaphus buselaphus tora	Egypt, Ethiopia, Sudan
Hawk, Hawaiian	Buteo solitarius	U.S. (HI)
Hyena, brown	Hyaena brunnea	Southern Africa
Impala, black-faced	Aepyceros melampus petersi	Angola, Namibia
Kangaroo, Tasmanian forester	Macropus giganteus tasmaniensis	Australia (Tasmania)
Leopard	Panthera pardus	Africa and Asia
Lion, Asiatic	Panthera leo persica	Turkey to India
Manatee, West Indian	Trichechus manatus	Southeastern U.S., Caribbean Sea, Mexico
Monkey, spider	Ateles geoffroyi frontatus	Costa Rica, Nicaragua
Ocelot	Felis pardalis	U.S. (AZ, TX) to Central and S America
Orangutan	Pongo pygmaeus	Borneo, Sumatra
Ostrich, West African	Struthio camelus spatzi	W Sahara
Otter, marine	Lutra felina	Peru south to Straits of Magellan
Panda, giant	Ailuropoda melanoleuca	China
Panther, Florida	Felis concolor coryi	U.S. (FL)
Parakeet, golden	Aratinga guarouba	Brazil
Parrot, imperial	Amazona imperialis	West Indies (Dominica)
Penguin, Galapagos	Spheniscus mendiculus	Ecuador (Galapagos Islands)
Puma, eastern	Felis concolor couguar	Eastern N America (presumed extinct in wild)
Python, Indian	Python molurus molurus	Sri Lanka, India
Rat-kangaroo, brush-tailed	Bettongia penicillata	Australia
Rhinoceros, black	Diceros bicornis	Sub-Saharan Africa
Rhinoceros, northern white	Ceratotherium simum cottoni	Dem. Rep. of the Congo, Sudan, Uganda, Central African Rep.
Salamander, Chinese giant	Andrias davidianus	Western China
Sea lion, Steller	Eumetopias jubatus	Alaska, Russia
Sheep, bighorn	Ovis canadensis	California
Squirrel, Carolina northern flying	Glaucomys sabrinus coloratus	U.S. (NC, TN)
Tiger	Panthera tigris	Asia
Tortoise, Galapagos	Geochelone elephantopus	Ecuador (Galapagos Islands)
Turtle, Plymouth red-bellied	Pseudemys rubriventris bangsi	U.S. (MA)
Whale, gray	Eschrichtius robustus	N Pacific Ocean
Whale, humpback	Megaptera novaeangliae	Oceania
Wolf, red	Canis rufus	U.S. (FL, NC, SC)
Woodpecker, ivory-billed	Campephilus principalis	Cuba
Yak, wild	Bos grunniens mutus	China (Tibet), India
Zebra, mountain	Equus zebra zebra	South Africa

List of Endangered and Threatened Species, 2009

Source: Fish and Wildlife Service, U.S. Dept. of Interior; as of Oct. 2009

Group	Endangered U.S.	Endangered Foreign	Threatened U.S.	Threatened Foreign	Total species[1]	U.S. species with recovery plans
Mammals	70	255	15	20	360	59
Birds	75	182	15	6	278	85
Reptiles	13	66	24	16	119	38
Amphibians	14	8	11	1	34	17
Fishes	74	11	65	1	151	102
Clams	62	2	8	0	72	70
Snails	24	1	11	0	36	30
Insects	47	4	10	0	61	40
Arachnids	12	0	0	0	12	12
Crustaceans	19	0	3	0	22	18
Corals	0	0	2	0	2	0
Animal subtotal	**410**	**529**	**164**	**44**	**1,147**	**471**
Flowering plants	573	1	143	0	717	633
Conifers and cycads	2	0	1	2	5	3
Ferns and allies	24	0	2	0	26	26
Lichens	2	0	0	0	2	2
Plant subtotal	**601**	**1**	**146**	**2**	**750**	**664**
GRAND TOTAL	**1,011**	**530**	**310**	**46**	**1,897**	**1,135**

(1) Some species are classified as both endangered and threatened. The table tallies these "dual status" species only once, as endangered, except for the olive ridley sea turtle, which is dual status but tallied as a U.S. threatened species. The other dual status species, all tallied as endangered, are (U.S.) California tiger salamander, chinook salmon, gray wolf, green sea turtle, piping plover, roseate tern, sockeye salmon, steelhead, Steller sea lion; (non-U.S.) argali, chimpanzee, leopard, saltwater crocodile.

METEOROLOGY

National Weather Service Watches and Warnings

Source: National Weather Service, National Oceanic and Atmospheric Admin. (NOAA),
U.S. Dept. of Commerce; *Glossary of Meteorology*, American Meteorological Society

The **National Weather Service** issues watches, warnings, and advisories for specific geographic areas to alert people to the possibility or imminent arrival of severe weather. A severe thunderstorm or tornado watch is issued when a severe convective storm, covering a relatively small geographic area or moving in a narrow path, is sufficiently intense to threaten life and property. Excessive localized convective rains are not classified as severe storms but are often the product of severe local storms. Such rainfall may result in phenomena, such as flash floods, that threaten life and property. Lightning occurs with all thunderstorms and, along with flash floods, is a leading cause of storm deaths and injuries.

Cyclone: atmospheric circulation of winds rotating counterclockwise in the Northern Hemisphere and clockwise in the Southern Hemisphere. Tornadoes, hurricanes, and the lows shown on weather maps are all examples of cyclones. Cyclones are usually accompanied by precipitation or stormy weather.

Severe thunderstorm: thunderstorm (any local atmospheric disturbance) that produces a tornado, winds more than 50 knots (58 mph), and/or hail at least ¾ inch in diameter. A **severe thunderstorm watch** indicates a severe thunderstorm is likely to develop within a 3- to 6-hr period. A **severe thunderstorm warning** indicates a severe thunderstorm has been sighted by radar or reported by a spotter.

Tornado: violent rotating column of air that extends from the base of a thunderstorm to the ground. On a local scale, it is the most destructive of all atmospheric phenomena. Tornado paths range from a few feet to more than 100 mi long (avg. 5 mi) and from a few feet to more than 1 mi in diameter (avg. 220 yds). The average forward speed is 30 mph.

Subtropical storm: cyclone that develops over subtropical waters (N of 20° lat.) with 1-min. sustained surface winds of 34 knots (39 mph) or more. It may form over warm or cold water and can develop into a tropical storm or hurricane.

Tropical storm: cyclone that develops over tropical waters (23.5° N-23.5° S lat.) with 1-min. sustained surface winds between 34 and 63 knots (39-72 mph). A **tropical storm watch** is issued when tropical storm conditions pose a threat to specified coastal areas within 36 hours. A **tropical storm warning** is issued when such conditions are expected in a specified coastal area within 24 hours.

Hurricane: severe cyclone originating over tropical ocean waters and having 1-min. sustained surface winds of 64 knots (74 mph) or more. (West of the international date line, north of the equator, such storms are known as **typhoons**.) The hurricane-force winds form a circle or oval, sometimes as wide as 300 mi in diameter. In the lower latitudes, hurricanes usually move W or NW at 10-15 mph. When the center approaches 25° to 30° N lat., the direction of motion often changes to the NE, with increased forward speed. In the Atlantic, hurricane season is June 1-Nov. 30. Hurricane season is May 15-Nov. 30 in the eastern Pacific. A **hurricane warning** is issued when a hurricane is forecast for an area within 24 hours.

Winter storm and blizzard: A **winter storm watch** is issued when conditions are favorable for hazardous winter weather, such as heavy snow, sleet, or freezing rain. A **winter storm warning** is issued when hazardous conditions are imminent. A **blizzard warning** is issued for winter storm conditions where winds are 35 mph or more and there is sufficient falling and/or blowing snow to frequently reduce visibility to less than ¼ mi for at least 3 hours.

Floods take many forms. **River flooding:** occurs when rains, sometimes coupled with melting snow, quickly fill river basins with an excess of water. Torrential rains from decaying hurricanes or tropical systems are also a major cause. **Coastal flooding:** tropical storm and hurricane winds or intense offshore low pressure systems can drive ocean water inland. Coastal floods can also be produced by sea waves called **tsunamis**, sometimes referred to as tidal waves, produced by earthquakes or volcanic activity. **Flash flooding:** usually due to copious amounts of rain falling in a short time, flash flooding typically occurs within 6 hours of a rain event. Ice can also cause flash flooding. When ice accumulates at natural or artificial obstructions, it can stop the flow of water. The resulting buildup of water can lead to flooding upstream. If the jam suddenly gives way, a flash flood can occur downstream.

Flash floods account for the majority of flood deaths in the U.S. and are the leading cause of deaths associated with thunderstorms. Urbanization significantly increases runoff because less rain is absorbed by the terrain, making flash flooding in urban areas extremely dangerous. Streets can become swift-moving rivers, and basements can fill with water.

A **(flash) flood watch** indicates flooding or flash flooding is possible within a designated area. A **(flash) flood warning** indicates flooding is imminent or has been reported.

National Weather Service Marine Warnings and Advisories

Primary sources of dissemination are commercial radio, TV, U.S. Coast Guard radio stations, and NOAA VHF-FM broadcasts. NOAA broadcasts on a group of frequencies, the most common being 162.40 to 162.55 MHz. These broadcasts can usually be received within 50 mi of the transmission site.

Small craft advisory: alerts mariners to sustained (more than 2 hours) weather and/or sea conditions, present or forecast, potentially hazardous to small boats, including winds 18-33 knots (21-38 mph) and/or dangerous wave conditions. The advisory is also issued for lower wind speeds that may affect small craft. Criteria vary depending on region and type of marine environment.

Special marine warning: indicates potentially hazardous weather conditions, usually of short duration (2 hours or less) and producing wind speeds of 34 knots (39 mph) or more, not adequately covered by existing marine warnings.

Gale warning: indicates winds of 34-47 knots (39-54 mph) not directly associated with a tropical storm are forecast for the area.

Tropical storm warning: indicates that winds 34-63 knots (39-72 mph) associated with a tropical storm are forecast to occur within 24 hours.

Storm warning: indicates winds 48 knots (55 mph) or more not directly associated with a tropical storm are forecast for the area.

Hurricane warning: indicates that winds 64 knots (74 mph) or greater associated with a hurricane are forecast for the area within 24 hours.

Monthly Normal Mean Temperatures, Normal Precipitation, U.S. Cities

Source: National Climatic Data Center, NESDIS, NOAA, U.S. Dept. of Commerce

Normals are averages covering a 30-year period. The temperature and precipitation normals given here are based on records for 1971-2000. Temperatures listed below represent means of the normal daily maximum and normal daily minimum temperatures for each month. For stations that did not have continuous records from the same site for the entire 30 years, the means have been adjusted to the record at the present site. (*) = city station. Other figures are for airport stations. T = Temperature in Fahrenheit; P = Precipitation in inches.

	Jan.		Feb.		Mar.		Apr.		May		June		July		Aug.		Sept.		Oct.		Nov.		Dec.	
Station	T	P	T	P	T	P	T	P	T	P	T	P	T	P	T	P	T	P	T	P	T	P	T	P
Albany, NY	22	2.7	25	2.3	35	3.2	47	3.3	58	3.7	66	3.7	71	3.5	69	3.7	61	3.3	49	3.2	39	3.3	28	2.8
Albuquerque, NM	36	0.5	41	0.4	48	0.6	56	0.5	65	0.6	75	0.7	79	1.3	76	1.7	69	1.1	57	1.0	44	0.6	36	0.5
Anchorage, AK	16	0.7	19	0.7	26	0.7	36	0.5	47	0.7	55	1.1	58	1.7	56	2.9	48	2.9	34	2.1	22	1.1	18	1.1
Asheville, NC	36	3.1	39	3.2	46	3.9	54	3.2	62	3.5	69	3.2	73	3.0	72	3.3	66	3.0	55	2.4	46	2.9	39	2.6
Atlanta, GA	43	5.0	47	4.7	54	5.4	62	3.6	70	4.0	77	3.6	80	5.1	79	3.7	73	4.1	63	3.1	53	4.1	45	3.8
Atlantic City, NJ	32	3.6	34	2.9	42	4.1	51	3.5	61	3.4	70	2.7	75	3.9	74	4.3	66	3.1	55	2.9	46	3.3	37	3.2
Baltimore, MD	32	3.5	36	3.0	44	3.9	53	3.0	63	3.9	72	3.4	77	3.9	75	3.7	67	4.0	55	3.2	46	3.1	37	3.4
Barrow, AK	–14	0.1	–16	0.1	–14	0.1	–1	0.1	20	0.1	35	0.3	40	0.9	39	1.0	31	0.7	15	0.4	–1	0.2	–11	0.1
Birmingham, AL	43	5.5	47	4.2	55	6.1	61	4.7	69	4.8	76	3.8	80	5.1	80	3.5	74	4.1	63	3.2	53	4.6	46	4.5
Bismarck, ND	10	0.5	18	0.5	30	0.9	43	1.5	56	2.2	65	2.6	70	2.6	69	2.2	58	1.6	45	1.3	28	0.7	15	0.4
Boise, ID	30	1.4	37	1.1	44	1.4	51	1.3	59	1.3	67	0.7	75	0.4	74	0.3	64	0.8	53	0.8	40	1.4	31	1.4
Boston, MA	29	3.9	32	3.3	39	3.9	48	3.6	59	3.2	68	3.2	74	3.1	72	3.4	65	3.5	54	3.8	45	4.0	35	3.7
Buffalo, NY	25	3.2	26	2.4	34	3.0	45	3.0	57	3.4	66	3.8	71	3.1	69	3.9	62	3.8	51	3.2	40	3.9	30	3.8
Burlington, VT	18	2.2	20	1.7	31	2.3	44	2.9	57	3.3	66	3.4	71	4.0	68	4.0	59	3.8	48	3.1	37	3.1	25	2.2
Caribou, ME	10	3.0	13	2.1	25	2.6	38	2.6	52	3.3	61	3.3	66	3.9	63	4.2	54	3.3	43	3.0	31	3.1	16	3.2
Charleston, SC	48	4.1	51	3.1	58	4.0	64	2.8	72	3.7	78	5.9	82	6.1	81	6.9	76	6.0	66	3.1	58	2.7	51	3.2
Charleston, WV	33	3.3	37	3.2	45	3.9	54	3.3	62	4.3	70	4.1	74	4.9	73	4.1	66	3.5	55	2.7	46	3.7	38	3.3
Chicago, IL	22	1.8	27	1.6	37	2.7	48	3.7	59	3.4	68	3.6	73	3.5	72	4.6	64	3.3	52	2.7	39	3.0	27	2.4
Cleveland, OH	26	2.5	28	2.3	38	2.9	48	3.4	59	3.5	68	3.9	72	3.5	70	3.7	63	3.8	52	2.7	42	3.4	31	3.1
Columbus, OH	28	2.5	32	2.2	42	2.9	52	3.3	63	3.9	71	4.1	75	4.6	74	3.7	67	2.9	55	2.3	44	3.2	34	2.9
Dallas-Ft. Worth, TX	44	1.9	49	2.4	57	3.1	65	3.2	73	5.2	81	3.2	85	2.1	84	2.0	78	2.4	67	4.1	55	2.6	47	2.6
Denver, CO	29	0.5	33	0.5	40	1.3	48	1.9	57	2.3	68	1.6	73	2.2	72	1.8	62	1.1	51	1.0	38	1.0	30	0.6
Des Moines, IA	20	1.0	27	1.2	38	2.2	51	3.6	62	4.3	71	4.6	76	4.2	74	4.5	65	3.2	53	2.6	38	2.1	25	1.3
Detroit, MI	25	1.9	27	1.9	37	2.5	48	3.1	60	3.1	69	3.6	74	3.2	72	3.1	64	3.3	52	2.2	41	2.7	30	2.5
Dodge City, KS	30	0.6	36	0.7	44	1.8	54	2.3	64	3.0	74	3.2	80	3.2	78	2.7	69	1.7	57	1.5	42	1.0	33	0.8
Duluth, MN	8	1.1	15	0.8	25	1.7	39	2.1	52	3.0	60	4.3	66	4.2	64	4.2	55	4.1	44	2.5	28	2.1	14	0.9
Fairbanks, AK	–10	0.6	–4	0.4	11	0.3	32	0.2	49	0.6	60	1.4	62	1.7	56	1.7	45	1.1	24	1.0	2	0.7	–6	0.7
Fresno, CA	46	2.2	51	2.1	56	2.2	61	0.8	69	0.4	76	0.2	81	0.0	80	0.0	75	0.3	65	0.7	53	1.1	45	1.3
Galveston, TX*	56	4.1	58	2.6	64	2.8	70	2.6	77	3.7	82	4.0	84	3.5	84	4.2	81	5.8	74	3.5	65	3.6	58	3.5
Grand Rapids, MI	22	2.0	25	1.5	35	2.6	46	3.5	58	3.4	67	3.7	71	3.6	69	3.8	61	4.3	50	2.8	38	3.4	28	2.7
Hartford, CT	26	3.8	29	3.0	38	3.9	49	3.9	60	4.4	69	3.9	74	3.7	72	4.0	63	4.1	52	3.9	42	4.1	31	3.6
Helena, MT	20	0.5	26	0.4	35	0.6	44	0.9	53	1.8	61	1.8	68	1.3	67	1.3	56	1.1	45	0.7	31	0.5	21	0.5
Honolulu, HI	73	2.7	73	2.4	74	1.9	76	1.1	77	0.8	80	0.4	81	0.5	82	0.5	82	0.7	80	2.2	78	2.3	75	2.9
Houston, TX	52	3.7	55	3.0	62	3.4	69	3.6	76	5.2	81	5.4	84	3.2	83	3.8	79	4.3	70	4.5	61	4.2	54	3.7
Huron, SD	14	0.5	21	0.6	33	1.7	46	2.3	58	3.0	68	3.3	73	2.9	72	2.1	61	1.8	48	1.6	31	0.9	19	0.4
Indianapolis, IN	27	2.5	31	2.4	42	3.4	52	3.6	63	4.4	72	4.1	75	4.4	74	3.8	66	2.9	55	2.8	43	3.6	32	3.0
Jackson, MS	45	5.7	49	4.5	57	5.7	63	6.0	72	4.9	79	3.8	81	4.7	81	3.7	76	3.2	64	3.4	55	5.0	48	5.3
Jacksonville, FL	53	3.7	56	3.2	62	3.9	67	3.1	73	3.5	79	5.4	82	6.0	81	6.9	78	7.9	69	3.9	62	2.3	55	2.6
Juneau, AK	26	4.8	29	4.0	34	3.5	41	3.0	48	3.5	54	3.4	57	4.1	56	5.4	50	7.6	42	8.3	33	5.4	29	5.4
Kansas City, MO	27	1.2	33	1.3	44	2.4	54	3.4	64	5.4	74	4.4	79	4.4	77	3.5	68	4.6	57	3.3	43	2.3	31	1.6
Knoxville, TN	38	4.6	42	4.0	50	5.2	58	4.0	66	4.7	74	4.0	78	4.7	77	2.9	71	3.0	59	2.7	49	4.0	41	4.5
Lander, WY	20	0.5	26	0.5	36	1.2	44	2.1	53	2.4	64	1.2	71	0.8	69	0.6	59	1.1	46	1.4	30	1.0	21	0.6
Lexington, KY	32	3.3	36	3.3	46	4.4	55	3.7	64	4.8	72	4.6	76	4.8	75	3.8	68	3.1	57	2.7	46	3.4	36	4.0
Little Rock, AR	40	3.6	45	3.3	53	4.9	61	5.5	70	5.1	78	4.0	82	3.3	81	2.9	74	3.7	63	4.3	52	5.7	43	4.7
Los Angeles, CA*	57	3.0	58	3.1	58	2.4	61	0.6	63	0.2	66	0.1	69	0.0	71	0.1	70	0.3	67	0.4	62	1.1	58	1.8
Louisville, KY	33	3.3	38	3.3	47	4.4	56	3.9	66	4.9	74	3.8	78	4.3	77	3.4	70	3.1	59	2.8	48	3.8	38	3.7
Marquette, MI*	12	2.6	15	1.9	24	3.1	36	2.8	50	3.1	59	3.2	64	3.0	62	3.6	54	3.7	43	3.7	29	3.3	17	2.4
Memphis, TN	40	4.2	45	4.3	54	5.6	62	5.8	71	5.2	79	4.3	83	4.2	81	3.0	75	3.3	64	3.3	52	5.8	43	5.7
Miami, FL	68	1.9	69	2.1	72	2.6	76	3.4	80	5.5	82	8.5	84	5.8	84	8.6	82	8.4	79	6.2	74	3.4	70	2.2
Milwaukee, WI	21	1.9	25	1.7	35	2.6	45	3.8	56	3.1	66	3.6	72	3.6	71	4.0	63	3.3	51	2.5	38	2.7	26	2.2
Minneapolis, MN	13	1.0	20	0.8	32	1.9	47	2.3	59	3.2	68	4.3	73	4.0	71	4.1	61	2.7	49	2.1	33	1.9	19	1.0
Mobile, AL	61	5.8	65	5.1	71	7.2	77	5.1	84	6.1	89	5.0	91	6.5	91	6.2	87	6.0	79	3.3	70	5.4	63	4.7
Moline, IL	21	1.6	27	1.5	39	2.9	51	3.8	62	4.3	71	4.6	75	4.0	73	4.4	65	3.2	53	2.8	39	2.7	26	2.2
Nashua, NH	23	3.9	26	3.1	35	4.1	46	3.9	57	3.7	66	3.9	71	3.7	69	3.8	61	3.6	49	3.9	39	4.2	28	3.7
Nashville, TN	37	4.0	41	3.7	50	4.9	59	3.9	67	5.1	75	4.1	79	3.8	78	3.3	71	3.6	60	2.9	49	4.5	41	4.5
Newark, NJ	31	4.0	34	3.0	42	4.2	52	3.9	63	4.5	72	3.4	77	4.7	76	4.0	68	4.0	56	3.2	46	3.9	36	3.6
New Orleans, LA	53	5.9	56	5.5	62	5.2	68	5.0	76	4.6	81	6.8	83	6.2	83	6.2	79	5.6	70	3.1	61	5.1	55	5.1
New York, NY*	33	3.6	35	2.8	42	3.9	52	3.7	62	4.2	72	3.6	77	4.4	76	4.1	69	3.8	58	3.3	48	3.7	38	3.5
Norfolk, VA	40	3.9	42	3.3	49	4.1	57	3.4	66	3.7	75	3.8	79	5.2	77	4.8	72	4.1	61	3.5	52	3.0	44	3.0
Oklahoma City, OK	37	1.3	42	1.6	51	2.9	60	3.0	68	5.4	77	4.6	82	2.9	81	2.5	73	4.0	62	3.6	49	2.1	40	1.9
Omaha, NE	22	0.8	28	0.8	39	2.1	51	2.9	62	4.4	72	4.0	77	3.9	75	3.2	65	3.2	53	2.2	38	1.8	26	0.9
Philadelphia, PA	32	3.5	35	2.7	43	3.8	53	3.5	64	3.9	72	3.3	78	4.4	76	3.8	69	3.9	57	2.8	47	3.2	37	3.3
Phoenix, AZ	54	0.8	58	0.8	63	1.1	70	0.3	79	0.2	89	0.1	93	1.0	91	0.9	86	0.8	75	0.8	62	0.7	54	0.9
Pittsburgh, PA	28	2.7	31	2.4	40	3.2	50	3.0	60	3.8	68	4.1	73	4.0	71	3.4	64	3.2	53	2.3	42	3.0	33	2.9
Portland, ME	22	4.1	25	3.1	34	4.1	44	4.3	54	3.8	63	3.3	69	3.3	67	3.1	59	3.4	48	4.4	38	4.7	28	4.2
Portland, OR	40	5.1	43	4.2	47	3.7	51	2.6	57	2.4	63	1.6	68	0.7	69	0.9	64	1.7	54	2.9	46	5.6	40	5.7
Providence, RI	29	4.4	31	3.5	39	4.4	49	4.2	59	3.7	68	3.4	73	3.2	72	3.9	64	3.7	53	3.7	44	4.4	34	4.1
Raleigh, NC	40	4.0	43	3.5	51	4.0	59	2.8	67	3.8	75	3.4	79	4.3	77	3.8	71	4.3	60	3.2	51	3.0	43	3.0
Rapid City, SD	22	0.4	27	0.5	35	1.0	45	1.9	55	3.0	65	2.8	72	2.0	71	1.6	61	1.1	48	1.4	33	0.6	25	0.4
Reno, NV	34	1.1	39	1.1	43	0.9	49	0.4	56	0.6	65	0.5	71	0.2	70	0.3	62	0.5	52	0.4	41	0.8	34	0.9
Richmond, VA	36	3.6	40	3.0	48	4.1	57	3.2	65	4.0	74	3.5	78	4.7	76	4.2	70	4.0	58	3.6	49	3.1	40	3.1
St. Louis, MO	30	2.1	35	2.3	46	3.6	57	3.7	67	4.1	77	3.8	80	3.9	78	3.0	70	3.0	58	2.8	45	3.7	34	2.9
Salt Lake City, UT	29	1.4	35	1.3	43	1.9	50	2.0	59	2.1	69	0.8	77	0.7	76	0.8	65	1.3	53	1.6	40	1.4	30	1.2
San Antonio, TX	51	1.7	55	1.8	63	1.9	69	2.6	76	4.7	81	4.3	84	2.0	84	2.6	79	3.0	71	3.9	60	2.6	53	2.0
San Diego, CA	58	2.3	59	2.0	60	2.3	63	0.8	65	0.2	67	0.1	71	0.0	73	0.1	72	0.2	68	0.4	62	1.1	58	1.3
San Francisco, CA	49	4.5	52	4.0	54	3.3	56	1.2	59	0.4	61	0.1	63	0.0	64	0.1	64	0.2	61	1.0	55	2.5	50	2.9
San Juan, PR	77	3.0	77	2.3	78	2.1	79	3.7	81	5.3	82	3.5	82	4.2	82	5.2	82	5.6	82	5.1	80	6.2	78	4.6
Santa Fe, NM	29	0.6	35	0.5	41	0.8	48	0.7	57	1.3	66	1.2	70	2.3	68	2.1	62	1.7	51	1.3	38	1.1	30	0.7
Savannah, GA	49	4.0	53	2.9	59	3.6	65	3.3	73	3.6	79	5.5	82	6.0	81	7.2	77	5.1	67	3.1	59	2.4	51	2.8
Seattle, WA	41	5.1	43	4.2	46	3.8	50	2.6	56	1.8	61	1.5	65	0.8	66	1.0	61	1.6	53	3.2	45	5.9	41	5.6
Spokane, WA	27	1.8	33	1.5	40	1.5	47	1.3	54	1.6	62	1.2	69	0.8	69	0.7	59	0.8	47	1.1	35	2.2	27	2.3
Springfield, MO	32	2.1	37	2.3	46	3.8	56	4.3	65	4.6	73	5.0	79	3.6	78	3.4	69	4.8	58	3.5	46	4.5	36	3.2
Tampa, FL	61	2.3	63	2.7	67	2.9	72	1.8	78	2.9	82	5.5	83	6.5	83	7.6	82	6.5	76	2.3	69	1.6	63	2.3
Washington, DC	34	3.6	36	2.8	44	3.9	54	3.3	64	4.3	73	3.6	78	4.2	76	3.9	69	4.1	57	3.4	47	3.3	38	3.2
Wilmington, DE	32	3.4	34	2.8	43	4.0	52	3.4	63	4.1	72	4.0	77	4.3	75	3.5	68	4.0	56	3.0	46	3.2	36	3.4

Normal High and Low Temperatures, Precipitation, U.S. Cities

Source: National Climatic Data Center, NESDIS, NOAA, U.S. Dept. of Commerce

The normal temperatures and precipitation data given here are based on records for the period 1971-2000. The extreme temperatures are based on records from the time of each station's installation. (*) = city station. Other figures are for airport stations.

State	Station	NORMAL TEMPERATURE (°F) January Max.	January Min.	July Max.	July Min.	EXTREME TEMPERATURE (°F) Highest	Lowest	AVG. ANNUAL PRECIPITATION (in.)
Alabama	Mobile	61	40	91	72	105	3	66.29
Alaska	Anchorage	22	9	65	52	85	−34	16.08
Alaska	Barrow	−8	−20	47	34	79	−56	4.16
Alaska	Juneau	31	21	64	49	90	−22	58.33
Arizona	Phoenix	65	43	104	81	122	17	8.29
Arkansas	North Little Rock	49	31	94	73	111	−6	49.19
California	Los Angeles*	66	49	75	63	110	23	13.15
California	San Francisco	56	43	71	55	106	20	20.11
Colorado	Denver	43	15	88	59	101	−19	15.81
Connecticut	Hartford	34	17	85	62	102	−26	46.16
Delaware	Wilmington	39	24	86	67	102	−14	42.81
District of Columbia	Washington–National	43	27	89	67	105	−5	39.35
Florida	Jacksonville	64	42	91	72	105	7	52.34
Florida	Miami	77	60	91	77	98	30	58.53
Georgia	Atlanta	52	34	89	71	105	−8	50.20
Georgia	Savannah	60	38	92	72	105	3	49.58
Hawaii	Honolulu	80	66	88	74	95	53	18.29
Idaho	Boise	37	24	89	60	111	−25	12.19
Illinois	Chicago	30	14	84	63	104	−27	36.27
Indiana	Indianapolis	35	19	86	65	104	−27	40.95
Iowa	Des Moines	29	12	86	66	108	−26	34.72
Kansas	Dodge City	41	19	93	67	110	−21	22.35
Kentucky	Lexington	40	24	86	66	103	−21	45.91
Kentucky	Louisville	41	25	87	70	106	−22	44.54
Louisiana	New Orleans	62	43	91	74	102	11	64.16
Maine	Caribou	19	0	76	55	96	−41	37.44
Maine	Portland	31	13	79	59	103	−39	45.83
Maryland	Baltimore	41	24	87	66	105	−7	41.94
Massachusetts	Boston	37	22	82	66	102	−12	42.53
Michigan	Detroit	31	18	83	64	104	−21	32.89
Michigan	Grand Rapids	29	16	82	61	100	−22	37.13
Michigan	Sault Ste. Marie*	22	5	76	52	98	−36	34.67
Minnesota	Duluth	18	−1	76	55	97	−39	31.00
Minnesota	Minneapolis-St. Paul	22	4	83	63	105	−34	29.41
Mississippi	Jackson	55	35	91	71	107	2	55.95
Missouri	Kansas City	36	18	89	68	109	−23	37.98
Missouri	St. Louis	38	21	90	71	107	−18	38.75
Montana	Helena	31	10	83	52	105	−42	11.32
Nebraska	Omaha	32	12	87	66	114	−23	30.22
Nevada	Reno	46	22	91	51	108	−16	7.48
New Hampshire	Concord	31	10	83	57	102	−37	37.60
New Jersey	Atlantic City	41	23	85	65	106	−11	40.59
New Mexico	Albuquerque	48	24	92	65	107	−17	9.47
New York	Albany	31	13	82	60	100	−28	38.60
New York	Buffalo	31	18	80	62	99	−20	40.54
New York	New York–Central Park*	38	26	84	69	106	−15	49.69
North Carolina	Raleigh	50	30	89	69	105	−9	43.05
North Dakota	Bismarck	21	−1	85	56	111	−44	16.84
Ohio	Cleveland	33	19	81	62	104	−20	38.71
Ohio	Columbus	36	20	85	65	102	−22	38.52
Oklahoma	Oklahoma City	47	26	93	71	110	−8	35.85
Oregon	Portland	46	34	79	57	107	−3	37.07
Pennsylvania	Philadelphia	39	26	86	70	104	−7	42.05
Pennsylvania	Pittsburgh	35	20	83	62	103	−22	37.85
Puerto Rico	San Juan	82	71	87	77	98	46	50.76
Rhode Island	Providence	37	20	83	64	104	−13	46.45
South Carolina	Charleston	59	37	91	73	105	6	51.53
South Dakota	Huron	25	4	86	61	112	−41	20.90
South Dakota	Rapid City	34	11	86	58	110	−31	16.64
Tennessee	Memphis	49	31	92	73	108	−13	54.65
Tennessee	Nashville	46	28	89	70	107	−17	48.11
Texas	Dallas-Fort Worth	54	34	95	75	109	17	34.73
Texas	Houston	62	41	94	74	109	17	47.84
Utah	Salt Lake City	37	21	91	63	107	−30	16.50
Vermont	Burlington	27	9	81	60	101	−30	36.05
Virginia	Norfolk	48	32	87	71	104	−3	45.74
Virginia	Richmond	45	28	88	68	105	−12	43.91
Washington	Seattle-Tacoma	46	36	75	55	100	0	37.07
Washington	Spokane	33	22	83	55	108	−25	16.67
West Virginia	Charleston	43	24	85	63	104	−16	44.05
Wisconsin	Milwaukee	28	13	81	63	103	−26	34.81
Wyoming	Lander	32	9	86	55	101	−37	13.42

Mean annual snowfall (in.): Based on climate normals 1971-2000: Boston, MA, 41.8; Sault Ste. Marie, MI, 132.6; Albany, NY, 62.7; Burlington, VT, 83.1; Lander, WY, 102.9; Anchorage, AK, 69.5.

Wettest spot: Mount Waialeale, HI, on the island of Kauai, is the rainiest place in the world. It has an average annual rainfall of 460 in.

Temperature extremes: A temperature of 136°F observed at El Azizia (Al Aziziyah), near Tripoli, Libya, on Sept. 13, 1922, is generally accepted as the world's highest temperature recorded under standard conditions. The record high in the U.S. was 134°F in Death Valley, CA, July 10, 1913. The world record low of −129°F was recorded at the Soviet station of Vostok in Antarctica on July 21, 1983. The record low in the U.S. was −80°F at Prospect Creek, AK, Jan. 23, 1971.

Annual Climatological Data for U.S. Cities, 2008

Source: National Climatic Data Center, NESDIS, NOAA, U.S. Dept. of Commerce

Station	Elev. (ft)	TEMPERATURE (°F) Highest	Date	Lowest	Date	PRECIPITATION[1] Total (in.)	Greatest in 24 hrs. (in.)	Date	Snowfall[2] Total snowfall (in.)	Greatest in 24 hrs. (in.)	Date	FASTEST WIND MPH	Date	NO. OF DAYS Prec. 0.01 in. or more	Snow, sleet 1 in. or more
Albany, NY	281	96	6/10	−5	1/3	47.79	3.14	7/23-24	57.5	7.8	12/19	41	1/09	146	13
Albuquerque, NM	5,308	97	8/1	10	1/19	8.35	1.25	10/4-5	7.0	2.2	12/15	47	6/28	54	2
Anchorage, AK	222	71	7/4+	−15	12/31	17.03	1.32	4/25	130.0	15.5	4/25	32	2/20	119	39
Asheville, NC	2,174	93	8/6+	9	1/21	35.63	4.23	8/26-27	3.7	1.5	1/17+	44	5/12	116	2
Atlanta, GA	974	98	6/9	15	1/3	41.43	2.35	12/10-11	1.4	1.0	1/19	48	8/2	101	1
Atlantic City, NJ	117	98	6/9	10	1/4+	46.55	4.36	12/11-12	5.9	2.5	1/24	43	5/12	116	3
Baltimore, MD	196	96	6/10	8	1/21	44.97	3.78	9/26-27	4.3	2.4	1/17	44	6/4	119	1
Barrow, AK	38	61	6/29	−47	1/14	4.82	0.43	7/19-20	65.5	3.8	4/5	40	12/15	116	17
Birmingham, AL	630	99	7/21	53	1/3	55.09	3.66	8/25-26	0.1	0.1	3/8	53	7/29	104	0
Bismarck, ND	1,654	100	8/30	−25	12/31	18.71	1.57	6/10-11	59.5	9.2	11/6-7	45	7/30	111	15
Boise, ID	2,861	105	6/29	5	1/24	9.25	0.90	9/20	44.8	4.7	12/22	46	6/21	79	19
Boston, MA	180	95	7/19	7	1/3	54.46	3.32	12/11-12	49.6	8.9	2/22	40	11/15	133	6
Buffalo, NY	717	89	6/9	2	2/10+	47.31	1.61	9/13-14	124.6	13.1	3/8	53	12/28	194	34
Burlington, VT	348	93	6/10	−12	2/29	40.59	1.63	7/18-19	115.3	11.3	2/6	35	12/15	157	28
Caribou, ME	626	87	7/8	−29	1/25	52.67	2.12	10/26	176.8	10.6	3/20	43	1/10	173	44
Charleston, SC	48	100	8/6	19	1/4	47.32	6.57	10/24	T	T	4/19	40	3/15	118	0
Chicago, IL	658	94	9/2	−6	12/21	50.86	6.83	9/12-13	64.9	4.8	12/16	38	6/28	138	21
Cleveland, OH	805	93	6/9+	1	12/21	44.49	2.53	2/5-6	85.3	10.8	3/8	51	1/30	175	24
Columbus, OH	812	93	9/3	3	12/22+	45.44	3.64	6/25-26	40.4	15.5	3/8	54	9/14	139	9
Dallas-Ft. Worth, TX	562	107	8/3	23	1/2	27.10	3.89	11/10-11	2.1	1.1	3/6	61	4/10	61	2
Denver, CO	5,382	104	8/1	−19	12/15	10.18	1.31	8/6-7	29.8	3.6	12/4	46	5/2	63	11
Des Moines, IA	971	95	8/3	−12	1/24	49.45	4.29	6/5-6	55.3	5.7	2/17	53	5/25	128	20
Detroit, MI	631	93	9/3	0	12/21	33.98	2.97	9/13	82.6	7.9	12/19	46	12/28	141	23
Duluth, MN	1,429	86	7/6	−22	12/16	31.00	2.49	6/5-6	79.1	8.8	12/14	43	4/11	140	21
Fairbanks, AK	464	85	7/4	−48	2/10	14.02	1.64	7/28-29	68.6	4.0	1/17	31	2/29	123	19
Fresno, CA	375	112	7/10	31	12/18	8.46	1.23	1/4	T	T	12/15	33	12/25	43	0
Grand Rapids, MI	788	92	9/2	−5	2/21	48.80	3.76	9/4-5	143.7	10.2	12/19	48	12/28	168	44
Hartford, CT	165	98	6/10	−3	1/4+	65.35	5.24	9/6-7	48.4	8.4	12/19	43	5/31	140	5
Helena, MT	3,867	99	8/18	−18	1/21	9.24	1.05	5/22-23	44.8	4.1	1/19	43	2/7	91	19
Honolulu, HI	18	90	9/5	62	1/18	14.76	3.35	12/11	—	—	—	37	12/11	92	—
Houston, TX	107	101	8/2	27	1/3	53.00	7.73	9/13	1.4	1.4	12/10	47	9/12	92	1
Huron, SD	1,284	96	7/11	−20	2/20	25.44	2.45	9/1-9/2	55.1	9.0	4/25	48	10/26	111	18
Indianapolis, IN	797	93	9/2	0	1/20	49.02	2.70	6/6-7	15.1	1.3	2/20	49	9/14	136	5
Jackson, MS	296	101	7/27+	19	1/3	59.60	5.11	12/10-11	—	—	—	37	2/12	116	—
Jacksonville, FL	34	96	8/7+	25	1/3	57.18	9.14	8/21-22	—	—	—	47	6/25	103	—
Kansas City, MO	1,008	97	8/4+	−4	1/19	44.66	4.37	9/12-13	21.4	4.4	2/17	51	5/2	116	8
Knoxville, TN	982	95	7/21	12	12/22	47.75	2.30	7/13	T	T	11/21+	44	7/28	112	0
Lander, WY	5,560	98	8/1	−22	1/22	14.14	1.99	5/25-26	93.0	14.5	10/11	59	3/29	75	22
Lexington, KY	984	94	7/21	12	12/22	47.46	4.65	4/3-4	13.6	4.0	3/8	47	2/6	131	4
Los Angeles, CA	326	96	10/22	40	12/27	11.02	1.89	12/15	—	—	—	40	3/15	32	—
Louisville, KY	484	97	9/1	5	12/22	46.79	4.03	4/3-4	19.8	6.1	3/8	53	9/14	128	3
Marquette, MI	1,415	90	9/2	−21	3/8	33.79	2.22	4/11	244.3	16.8	11/19-20	—	—	169	50
Memphis, TN	286	101	7/29	14	12/22	64.21	3.50	12/9-10	5.4	4.0	3/7	48	2/5	111	2
Miami, FL	29	96	5/11	39	1/3	60.27	3.83	8/18-19	—	—	—	40	7/2	138	—
Milwaukee, WI	680	89	9/2	−6	1/20	44.44	5.89	6/7-8	106.6	11.6	2/6	38	1/29	130	25
Minn.-St. Paul, MN	874	94	7/29	−15	1/20	22.38	2.16	8/27-28	48.1	5.5	3/31	49	6/14	122	17
Mobile, AL	212	97	7/21	21	1/3	69.10	8.32	4/4-5	T	T	1/19	41	7/12	103	0
Moline, IL	607	92	8/4	−15	1/25+	48.59	6.32	9/12-13	57.1	5.3	2/6	60	7/21	129	43
Nashville, TN	574	97	8/5	9	12/22	48.17	3.36	12/9-10	3.0	1.0	12/11	40	1/31	106	1
Newark, NJ	28	99	6/10+	10	2/11	48.83	3.75	9/5-6	18.6	6.8	2/22	53	3/8	140	4
New Orleans, LA	7	97	7/28+	28	1/3	54.04	3.29	9/2	—	—	—	45	9/1	109	—
New York, NY	161	96	7/19	10	2/11	53.61	3.54	9/5-6	15.0	6.0	2/22	32	3/8	141	4
Norfolk, VA	69	101	6/7	20	1/4	44.80	3.24	9/10-11	0.2	0.2	2/14	44	3/8	115	0
North Little Rock, AR	565	104	8/3	12	12/22	51.93	4.96	9/2-3	4.0	2.5	3/7	—	—	115	2
Oklahoma City, OK	1,284	106	8/4+	11	12/21	35.82	4.62	8/11	0.8	0.6	1/31	51	5/1	66	0
Philadelphia, PA	62	98	6/10	11	2/11	40.33	3.52	2/21-22	6.1	3.2	2/22	49	3/8	117	3
Phoenix, AZ	1,106	115	6/21	34	12/28+	9.58	1.30	7/13	—	—	—	54	8/28	39	—
Pittsburgh, PA	1,175	91	6/9	2	12/22	39.69	2.23	6/26	43.9	5.0	2/26	47	1/9	173	14
Portland, ME	72	88	9/4	−5	1/4	61.24	5.52	9/6-7	91.4	14.5	12/21	39	11/25	137	20
Portland, OR	223	102	8/14	20	12/21+	27.12	1.17	5/24-25	—	—	—	36	12/20	165	—
Providence, RI	53	97	6/9	7	1/4	57.12	4.06	9/6-7	30.7	8.0	12/19	43	12/12	127	9
Raleigh, NC	430	101	6/10+	15	1/21	50.47	5.19	9/5-6	0.9	0.5	1/19	41	3/8	116	0
Rapid City, SD	3,153	99	8/31+	−19	12/22	20.55	2.21	5/22-23	54.6	11.0	5/2	62	11/6	101	19
Reno, NV	4,407	102	8/15	3	12/18	6.09	1.94	1/4-5	26.9	6.5	2/23	52	4/14	46	8
Richmond, VA	167	101	6/10	12	1/21	49.55	5.22	8/28-29	0.8	0.8	1/19	48	3/8	117	0
St. Louis, MO	710	99	7/20	4	12/22	57.96	4.58	9/14	26.3	10.0	3/4	43	1/29	121	5
Salt Lake City, UT	4,224	103	8/1	−2	1/22	11.74	1.08	10/4-5	67.1	8.4	12/25-26	48	7/27	83	25
San Antonio, TX	821	102	6/19	26	1/20	13.76	1.89	8/18-19	T	T	12/10+	37	8/22	60	0
San Diego, CA	81	94	10/8	41	12/16-17	11.11	1.63	12/16-17	—	—	—	31	1/27	36	—
San Francisco, CA	89	96	6/20	34	12/17	14.42	2.55	1/25-26	—	—	—	54	1/4	52	—
San Juan, PR	10	95	8/30	68	1/27	54.70	4.08	9/21-22	0	0	—	30	12/24	196	—
Sault Ste. Marie, MI	727	87	9/2	−12	2/27	34.88	1.35	4/8-9	174.2	8.5	1/11	39	1/30	188	53
Savannah, GA	143	102	8/6	23	1/4	47.29	3.61	10/24	T	T	7/30	33	6/25	104	0
Scottsbluff, NE	3,949	101	8/2	−14	12/15	14.27	1.66	8/14-15	26.7	4.1	3/22	56	9/1	88	11
Seattle, WA	434	92	6/29	14	12/20	30.73	2.74	11/6-7	—	—	—	39	2/7	161	—
Spokane, WA	2,384	103	8/17	−18	12/20	16.28	1.22	12/17-18	132.6	12.5	12/17	43	8/18	132	36
Springfield, MO	1,280	98	8/4	3	12/22	60.12	4.59	3/17-18	12.1	6.7	3/4	48	1/8	113	2
Tampa, FL	40	98	6/6	29	1/3	43.77	3.53	6/21-22	0	0	—	30	6/26	108	0
Washington, DC	3	98	7/7	16	12/22	46.49	3.90	9/5-6	2.3	1.3	1/17	46	3/8	112	2
Wilmington, DE	77	96	7/19+	12	2/11	40.44	3.32	9/5-6	6.3	2.6	1/17	47	3/8	118	4

(+): Indicates value for extreme also occurred on an earlier date(s). (T): Trace amount. (—): Data not available or unreported. (1) Where one date is shown, it is the starting date of the storm. (2) Comprises all forms of frozen precipitation, including hail and sleet. (3) Sustained for at least 2 mins., not peak gust.

Record Temperatures by State

Source: National Climatic Data Center, NESDIS, NOAA, U.S. Dept. of Commerce
(through Aug. 2006)

State	°F	Latest date	Station	Approx. elevation (ft)	°F	Latest date	Station	Approx. elevation (ft)
		LOWEST TEMPERATURE				**HIGHEST TEMPERATURE**		
Alabama	−27	Jan. 30, 1966	New Market	760	112	Sept. 5, 1925	Centerville	345
Alaska	−80	Jan. 23, 1971	Prospect Creek Camp	1,100	100	June 27, 1915	Fort Yukon	c. 420
Arizona	−40	Jan. 7, 1971	Hawley Lake	8,180	128	June 29, 1994	Lake Havasu City	505
Arkansas	−29	Feb. 13, 1905	Pond	1,250	120	Aug. 10, 1936	Ozark	396
California	−45	Jan. 20, 1937	Boca	5,532	134	July 10, 1913	Furnace Creek Ranch	−178
Colorado	−61	Feb. 1, 1985	Maybell	5,920	118	July 11, 1888	Bennett	5,484
Connecticut	−32	Jan. 22, 1961[1]	Coventry	480	106	July 15, 1995	Danbury	450
Delaware	−17	Jan. 17, 1893	Millsboro	20	110	July 21, 1930	Millsboro	20
Florida	−2	Feb. 13, 1899	Tallahassee	193	109	June 29, 1931	Monticello	207
Georgia	−17	Jan. 27, 1940	CCC Camp F-16	1,000	112	Aug. 20, 1983[1]	Greenville	860
Hawaii	12	May 17, 1979	Mauna Kea Obs.	13,770	100	Apr. 27, 1931	Pahala	850
Idaho	−60	Jan. 18, 1943	Island Park Dam	6,285	118	July 28, 1934	Orofino	1,027
Illinois	−36	Jan. 5, 1999	Congerville	635	117	July 14, 1954	East St. Louis	410
Indiana	−36	Jan. 19, 1994	New Whiteland	785	116	July 14, 1936	Collegeville	672
Iowa	−47	Feb. 3, 1996[1]	Elkader	770	118	July 20, 1934	Keokuk	614
Kansas	−40	Feb. 13, 1905	Lebanon	1,812	121	July 24, 1936[1]	Alton (near)	1,651
Kentucky	−37	Jan. 19, 1994	Shelbyville	730	114	July 28, 1930	Greensburg	581
Louisiana	−16	Feb. 13, 1899	Minden	194	114	Aug. 10, 1936	Plain Dealing	268
Maine	−48	Jan. 19, 1925	Van Buren	510	105	July 10, 1911[1]	North Bridgton	450
Maryland	−40	Jan. 13, 1912	Oakland	2,461	109	July 10, 1936[1]	Cumberland Frederick	623 325
Massachusetts	−35	Jan. 12, 1981	Chester	640	107	Aug. 2, 1975	Chester New Bedford	640 120
Michigan	−51	Feb. 9, 1934	Vanderbilt	785	112	July 13, 1936	Mio	963
Minnesota	−60	Feb. 2, 1996	Tower	1,460	114	July 6, 1936[1]	Moorhead	904
Mississippi	−19	Jan. 30, 1966	Corinth	420	115	July 29, 1930	Holly Springs	600
Missouri	−40	Feb. 13, 1905	Warsaw	700	118	July 14, 1954[1]	Warsaw Union	705 560
Montana	−70	Jan. 20, 1954	Rogers Pass	5,470	117	July 5, 1937	Medicine Lake	1,950
Nebraska	−47	Dec. 22, 1989[1]	Oshkosh	3,379	118	July 24, 1936[1]	Minden	2,169
Nevada	−50	Jan. 8, 1937	San Jacinto	5,200	125	June 29, 1994[1]	Laughlin	605
New Hampshire	−47	Jan. 29, 1934	Mt. Washington	6,262	106	July 4, 1911	Nashua	125
New Jersey	−34	Jan. 5, 1904	River Vale	70	110	July 10, 1936	Runyon	18
New Mexico	−50	Feb. 1, 1951	Gavilan	7,350	122	June 27, 1994	Waste Isolat. Pilot Plt.	3,418
New York	−52	Feb. 18, 1979	Old Forge	1,720	108	July 22, 1926	Troy	35
North Carolina	−34	Jan. 21, 1985	Mt. Mitchell	6,525	110	Aug. 21, 1983	Fayetteville	213
North Dakota	−60	Feb. 15, 1936	Parshall	1,929	121	July 6, 1936	Steele	1,857
Ohio	−39	Feb. 10, 1899	Milligan	800	113	July 21, 1934[1]	Gallipolis (near)	673
Oklahoma	−27	Jan. 18, 1930[1]	Watts	958	120	June 27, 1994[1]	Tipton	1,350
Oregon	−54	Feb. 10, 1933[1]	Seneca	4,700	119	Aug. 10, 1898[1]	Pendleton	1,074
Pennsylvania	−42	Jan. 5, 1904	Smethport	1,500	111	July 10, 1936[1]	Phoenixville	100
Rhode Island	−25	Feb. 5, 1996	Greene	425	104	Aug. 2, 1975	Providence	51
South Carolina	−19	Jan. 21, 1985	Caesars Head	3,115	111	June 28, 1954[1]	Camden	170
South Dakota	−58	Feb. 17, 1936	McIntosh	2,277	120	July 15, 2006[1]	Kelly Ranch/Usta	2,339
Tennessee	−32	Dec. 30, 1917	Mountain City	2,471	113	Aug. 9, 1930[1]	Perryville	377
Texas	−23	Feb. 8, 1933[1]	Seminole	3,275	120	June 28, 1994[1]	Monahans	2,660
Utah	−69	Feb. 1, 1985	Peter's Sink	8,092	117	July 5, 1985	Saint George	2,880
Vermont	−50	Dec. 30, 1933	Bloomfield	915	105	July 4, 1911	Vernon	310
Virginia	−30	Jan. 22, 1985	Mountain Lake Bio. Station	3,870	110	July 15, 1954	Balcony Falls	725
Washington	−48	Dec. 30, 1968	Mazama Winthrop	2,120 1,755	118	Aug. 5, 1961[1]	Ice Harbor Dam	475
West Virginia	−37	Dec. 30, 1917	Lewisburg	2,200	112	July 10, 1936[1]	Martinsburg	435
Wisconsin	−55	Feb. 4, 1996	Couderay	1,300	114	July 13, 1936	Wisconsin Dells	900
Wyoming	−66	Feb. 9, 1933	Riverside R.S.	6,500	115	Aug. 8, 1983	Basin	3,500

(1) Also on earlier dates at the same or other places.

Hurricane and Tornado Classifications

Source: National Weather Service, NOAA, U.S. Dept. of Commerce

The Saffir-Simpson Hurricane Scale rates a hurricane's intensity from 1 to 5. The scale is used to give an estimate of the potential property damage and flooding expected along the coast from a hurricane landfall. Wind speed is the determining factor in the scale. The Fujita (or F) Scale, created by T. Theodore Fujita, is used to classify tornadoes. The F Scale uses a 0-5 rating system, based on the amount and type of wind damage. The Enhanced Fujita Scale, an update to the original, was implemented in the U.S. in Feb. 2007.

	Saffir-Simpson Scale (Hurricanes)				**Enhanced Fujita Scale (Tornadoes)**			
Category	Wind speed	Severity	Storm surge[1]	Rank	3-sec. gust	Damage	Strength	
1	74-95 mph	Weak	4-5 ft	EF-0	65-85 mph	Light	Weak	
2	96-110 mph	Moderate	6-8 ft	EF-1	86-110 mph	Moderate	Weak	
3	111-130 mph	Strong	9-12 ft	EF-2	111-135 mph	Considerable	Strong	
4	131-155 mph	Very Strong	13-18 ft	EF-3	136-165 mph	Severe	Strong	
5	Over 155 mph	Devastating	Above 18 ft	EF-4	166-200 mph	Devastating	Violent	
				EF-5	Over 200 mph	Incredible	Violent	

(1) Above normal tides.

Tropical Cyclone Names in 2010
Source: National Weather Service, NOAA, U.S. Dept. of Commerce

Atlantic: Alex, Bonnie, Colin, Danielle, Earl, Fiona, Gaston, Hermine, Igor, Julia, Karl, Lisa, Matthew, Nicole, Otto, Paula, Richard, Shary, Tomas, Virginie, and Walter. If there are more than 21 named Atlantic storms in one season, remaining storms take names from the Greek alphabet, starting with Alpha.

Eastern North Pacific: Agatha, Blas, Celia, Darby, Estelle, Frank, Georgette, Howard, Isis, Javier, Kay, Lester, Madeline, Newton, Orlene, Paine, Roslyn, Seymour, Tina, Virgil, Winifred, Xavier, Yolanda, Zeke.

World Temperature and Precipitation
Source: World Meteorological Organization

Average daily maximum and minimum temperatures and annual precipitation based on records for the period 1961-90. Records of extreme temperatures include all available years of data for a given location and are usually for a longer period. Surface elevations are supplied by the WMO and may differ from figures in other sections of *The World Almanac*. NA = Not available.

Station	Surface elevation (ft)	Temperature (°F) AVERAGE DAILY January Max.	January Min.	July Max.	July Min.	EXTREME Max.	EXTREME Min.	Avg. annual precipitation (in.)
Algiers, Algeria	82	61.7	42.6	87.1	65.3	NA	NA	27.0
Athens, Greece	49	56.1	44.6	88.9	73.0	NA	NA	14.6
Auckland, New Zealand	20	74.8	61.2	58.5	46.4	NA	NA	49.4
Bangkok, Thailand	66	89.6	69.8	90.9	77.0	104	51	59.0
Berlin, Germany	190	35.2	26.8	73.6	55.2	107	-4	23.3
Bogotá, Colombia	8,357	67.3	41.7	64.6	45.5	75	21	32.4
Bombay (Mumbai), India	36	85.3	66.7	86.2	77.5	110	46	85.4
Bucharest, Romania	298	34.7	22.1	83.8	60.1	105	-18	23.4
Budapest, Hungary	456	34.2	24.8	79.7	59.7	103	-10	20.3
Buenos Aires, Argentina	82	85.8	67.3	59.7	45.7	104	22	45.2
Cairo, Egypt	243	65.8	48.2	93.9	71.1	118	34	1.0
Cape Town, South Africa	138	79.0	60.3	63.3	44.6	105	28	20.5
Caracas, Venezuela	2,739	79.9	60.8	81.3	66.0	96	45	36.1
Casablanca, Morocco	203	62.8	47.1	77.7	66.7	NA	NA	16.8
Copenhagen, Denmark	16	35.6	28.4	68.9	55.0	NA	NA	NA
Damascus, Syria	2,004	54.3	32.9	97.2	61.9	NA	NA	5.6
Dublin, Ireland	279	45.7	36.5	66.0	52.5	86	8	28.8
Geneva, Switzerland	1,364	38.3	27.9	76.3	53.2	101	-3	35.6
Havana, Cuba	164	78.4	65.5	88.3	74.8	NA	NA	46.9
Hong Kong, China	203	65.5	56.5	88.7	79.9	97	32	87.2
Istanbul, Turkey	108	47.8	37.2	82.8	65.3	105	7	27.4
Jerusalem, Israel	2,483	53.4	39.4	83.8	63.0	107	26	23.2
Lagos, Nigeria	125	90.0	72.3	82.8	72.1	NA	NA	59.3
Lima, Peru	43	79.0	66.9	66.4	59.4	NA	NA	0.2
London, England	203	44.1	32.7	71.1	52.3	99	2	29.7
Manila, Philippines	79	85.8	74.8	89.1	76.8	NA	NA	49.6
Mexico City, Mexico	7,570	70.3	43.7	73.8	53.2	NA	NA	33.4
Montreal, Canada	118	21.6	5.2	79.2	59.7	100	-36	37.0
Nairobi, Kenya	5,897	77.9	50.9	71.6	48.6	NA	NA	41.9
Paris, France	213	42.8	33.6	75.2	55.2	105	-1	25.6
Prague, Czech Republic	1,197	32.7	22.5	73.9	53.2	98	-16	20.7
Reykjavik, Iceland	200	35.4	26.6	55.9	46.9	76	-3	31.5
Rome, Italy	79	53.8	35.4	88.2	62.1	NA	NA	33.0
San Salvador, El Salvador	2,037	86.5	61.3	86.2	66.4	105	45	68.3
São Paulo, Brazil	2,598	81.1	65.7	71.2	53.1	NA	NA	57.4
Shanghai, China	23	45.9	32.9	88.9	76.6	104	10	43.8
Singapore	52	85.8	73.6	87.4	75.6	NA	NA	84.6
Stockholm, Sweden	171	30.7	23.0	71.4	56.1	97	-26	21.2
Sydney, Australia	10	79.5	65.5	62.4	43.9	114	32	46.4
Tehran, Iran	3,906	45.0	30.0	98.2	75.2	109	-5	9.1
Tokyo, Japan	118	49.1	34.2	83.8	72.1	NA	NA	55.4
Toronto, Canada	567	27.5	12.0	80.2	57.6	105	-26	30.8

Speed of Winds in the U.S.
Source: National Climatic Data Center, NESDIS, NOAA, U.S. Dept. of Commerce

In miles per hour. Based on available records through 2008. Average and maximum speeds are annual. Max. speeds are highest 1-min. average values recorded by observers, except where noted.

Station	Avg.	Max.	Station	Avg.	Max.	Station	Avg.	Max.
Albuquerque, NM	8.9	52	Helena, MT[2]	7.7	73	New York (Central Park), NY	9.1	40
Anchorage, AK[1,2]	7.1	64	Honolulu, HI	11.2	46	Oklahoma City, OK	12.2	67
Atlanta, GA	9.1	52	Houston, TX	7.6	46	Omaha (Eppley Airfield), NE	10.5	58
Baltimore, MD[2]	8.7	80	Indianapolis, IN	9.6	47	Philadelphia, PA[2]	9.5	67
Bismarck, ND	10.2	64	Jackson, MS	6.9	50	Phoenix, AZ	6.2	51
Boise, ID[2]	8.7	61	Jacksonville, FL	7.8	57	Pittsburgh, PA	9.0	58
Boston, MA	12.3	54	Las Vegas, NV	9.1	51	Portland, ME	8.7	57
Buffalo, NY[2]	11.8	91	Little Rock, AR[2]	7.7	65	Portland, OR	7.9	70
Burlington, VT	9.0	39	Los Angeles (Co.), CA[2]	5.2	49	Providence, RI	10.4	60
Cape Hatteras, NC	10.8	66	Louisville, KY	8.3	56	Richmond, VA	7.7	46
Charleston (Intl. Airport), SC	8.6	46	Miami, FL	9.2	80	St. Louis, MO	9.6	52
Charleston, WV	5.8	55	Milwaukee, WI	11.5	54	Salt Lake City, UT[2]	8.8	71
Cheyenne, WY	12.9	71	Minn.-St. Paul, MN	10.5	51	San Francisco (Co.), CA[2]	8.7	47
Chicago, IL	10.3	58	Mobile, AL	8.8	63	Seattle (Intl. Airport), WA[2]	8.8	66
Cleveland, OH	10.5	53	Mt. Washington, NH[1,2]	35.1	230	Sioux Falls, SD	11.0	70
Denver, CO	8.7	54	Nashville, TN	8.0	58	Washington (Natl. Airport), DC	9.4	49
Des Moines, IA[2]	10.7	76	Newark, NJ	10.2	58	Wichita, KS	12.2	70
Detroit, MI	10.2	61	New Orleans, LA	8.2	49	Wilmington, DE	9.0	58
Hartford, CT	8.4	46						

(1) Max. speed based on short gusts. (2) Max. speed calculated from minimum time during which one mile of wind passed the station.

Tides and Their Causes

Source: National Ocean Service, NOAA, U.S. Dept. of Commerce

The tides are natural phenomena involving the movement of waves in the Earth's large fluid bodies as a result of the gravitational attraction of the sun and moon. These two variable influences combined produce the complex recurrent cycle of the tides. Tides may occur in both oceans and seas; to a limited extent in large lakes and in the atmosphere; and, to a very minute degree, in the Earth itself. The length of time between succeeding tides can vary.

The tide-generating force represents the difference between (1) the centrifugal force produced by Earth's revolution around the common center-of-gravity of the Earth-moon system and (2) the gravitational attraction of the moon acting upon the Earth's overlying waters. The moon is about 400 times closer to Earth than is the sun. So despite its smaller mass, the moon's tide-raising force is 2.5 times greater.

The tide-generating forces of the moon and sun acting tangentially to the Earth's surface tend to cause a maximum accumulation of waters at two diametrically opposite points on the Earth's surface and to withdraw compensating amounts of water from all points 90° removed from these tidal bulges. As the Earth rotates beneath the maxima and minima of these tide-generating forces, a sequence of two high tides, separated by two low tides, is produced each day in what is called a **semidiurnal tide**. Each ocean basin reacts differently to tidal forces.

Twice each month, when the sun, moon, and Earth are directly aligned—the moon between the Earth and sun (at new moon) or on the opposite side of Earth from the sun (at full moon)—the sun and moon exert gravitational forces in a mutual or additive fashion. The highest high tides and lowest low tides, called **spring tides**, are produced at these times. At two positions 90° in between—at right angles—counteract

each other to the greatest extent, and the range between high and low tides is reduced, resulting in **neap tides**.

The inclination of the moon's monthly orbit and of the sun to the equator during Earth's yearly rotation through its orbit produce a difference in the height of succeeding high and low tides, known as the diurnal inequality. In most cases, this produces a so-called **mixed tide**. In extreme cases, these phenomena may result in a **diurnal tide**, with only one high tide and one low tide each day. There are other monthly and yearly variations in the tides because of the elliptical shape of the orbits.

U.S. convention distinguishes between mean higher high water (MHHW), mean high water (MHW), mean tide level (MTL), mean sea level (MSL), mean low water (MLW), and mean lower low water (MLLW). Diurnal range of tide is the difference in height between MHHW and MLLW. Mean range of tide is the difference between MHW and MLW.

The range of tides in the open ocean is generally less than in the coastal regions, where the incoming tide can be augmented by the continental shelves, as well as by bays and estuaries. In some shallow inlets and bays, though, the range may be diminished. The range of tide, or difference between high and low waters, may reach 43½ ft or more under spring tide conditions in Nova Scotia's Bay of Fundy.

In New Orleans, the periodic rise and fall of the diurnal tide is affected by the seasonal stages of the Mississippi River, being about 10 in. at low stage and 0 at high. The Canadian Tide Tables for 1972 gave a maximum range of nearly 50 ft at Leaf Basin, Ungava Bay, Quebec.

In every case, actual high or low tide can vary considerably from the average, as a result of weather conditions such as strong winds, abrupt barometric pressure changes, or prolonged periods of extreme high or low pressure.

Average Rise and Fall of Tides[1]

Place	Ft	In.	Place	Ft	In.	Place	Ft	In.
Baltimore, MD	1	8	Hampton Roads, VA	2	10	St. John's, NL, Canada	2	7
Boston, MA.	10	4	Key West, FL	1	10	St. Petersburg, FL	2	3[2]
Charleston, SC.	5	10	Mobile, AL	1	6[2]	San Diego, CA	5	9
Cristobal, Panama	1	1	New London, CT	3	1	Sandy Hook, NJ	5	2
Eastport, ME	19	4	Newport, RI	3	11	San Francisco, CA.	5	10
Ft. Pulaski, GA.	7	6	New York, NY.	5	1	Seattle, WA	11	4
Galveston, TX	1	5[2]	Philadelphia, PA.	6	9	Vancouver, BC, Canada	10	6
Halifax, NS, Canada.	4	5[2]	Portland, ME	9	11	Washington, DC.	3	2

(1) Mean ranges, except where noted. (2) Diurnal range.

El Niño and La Niña

Source: National Weather Service, NOAA, U.S. Dept. of Commerce

El Niño is a climatically significant disruption of the ocean-atmosphere system characterized by large-scale weakening of trade winds and warming of the surface layers in the central and eastern equatorial Pacific. The term *El Niño*, Spanish for "the little boy" or "The Christ Child," was originally used by fishermen to refer to a warm ocean current that appeared around Christmas off the west coasts of Ecuador and Peru that lasted several months. The term has come to be reserved for exceptionally strong, warm currents that bring heavy rains.

El Niño events generally occur at irregular intervals of 2 to 7 years, at an average of once every 3 to 4 years. They typically last 12 to 18 months. The intensity of El Niño events varies depending on the area encompassed by the abnormally warm ocean temperatures. Some are strong, such as in 1982-83 and 1997-98. Others are considerably weaker, such as the 2004-05 event. The eastward extent of warmer than normal water varies from episode to episode.

El Niño influences weather around the globe, and its impacts are most clearly seen in the winter. During El Niño years, winter temperatures in the continental U.S. tend to be warmer than normal in the North and West Coast states and

cooler than normal in the Southeast. Conditions tend to be wetter than normal over central and southern California, the Southwest states and across much of the South, and drier than normal over the northern portions of the Rocky Mountains and in the Ohio valley. Globally, El Niño brings wetter than normal conditions to Peru and Chile and dry conditions to Australia and Indonesia. It should be noted that El Niño is only one of a number of factors influencing seasonal variations of climate.

La Niña ("the little girl") is characterized by colder than normal sea surface temperatures in the equatorial Pacific. La Niña typically brings wetter, cooler conditions to the Pacific Northwest and drier, warmer conditions to much of the southern U.S. El Niño and La Niña are opposite phases of the El Niño-Southern Oscillation (ENSO) cycle, a shift in tropical sea-level pressure between the Eastern and Western hemispheres.

The National Weather Service's Climate Prediction Center, using satellites and buoys in the Pacific Ocean, monitors these events. Highly sophisticated numerical computer models of the ocean and atmosphere use these data to predict the onset and evolution of El Niño and La Niña.

Wind Chill Table

Source: National Weather Service, NOAA, U.S. Dept. of Commerce

Temperature and wind combine to cause heat loss from body surfaces. For example, a temperature of 5°F, plus a 10-mph wind, causes body heat loss equal to that which would occur in –10°F with no wind. In other words, a 10-mph wind makes 5°F feel like –10°F. Wind speeds greater than 45 mph have little additional chilling effect. Direct sunlight can increase the wind chill temperature 10° to 15°F. When the wind chill temperature falls within the shaded area, frostbite can occur in 30 mins. or less.

Calm	Air temperature (°F)																	
	40	35	30	25	20	15	10	5	0	–5	–10	–15	–20	–25	–30	–35	–40	–45
Wind speed (mph)	Wind chill temperature (°F)																	
5	36	31	25	19	13	7	1	–5	–11	–16	–22	–28	–34	–40	–46	–52	–57	–63
10	34	27	21	15	9	3	–4	–10	–16	–22	–28	–35	–41	–47	–53	–59	–66	–72
15	32	25	19	13	6	0	–7	–13	–19	–26	–32	–39	–45	–51	–58	–64	–71	–77
20	30	24	17	11	4	–2	–9	–15	–22	–29	–35	–42	–48	–55	–61	–68	–74	–81
25	29	23	16	9	3	–4	–11	–17	–24	–31	–37	–44	–51	–58	–64	–71	–78	–84
30	28	22	15	8	1	–5	–12	–19	–26	–33	–39	–46	–53	–60	–67	–73	–80	–87
35	28	21	14	7	0	–7	–14	–21	–27	–34	–41	–48	–55	–62	–69	–76	–82	–89
40	27	20	13	6	–1	–8	–15	–22	–29	–36	–43	–50	–57	–64	–71	–78	–84	–91
45	26	29	12	5	–2	–9	–16	–23	–30	–37	–44	–51	–58	–65	–72	–79	–86	–93

Heat Index

Source: National Weather Service, NOAA, U.S. Dept. of Commerce

The heat index is a measure of the impact humidity, in combination with abnormally high temperatures, has on the body's ability to cool itself. In other words, it measures what hot weather feels like to the average person. For example, when the air temperature is 100°F, and the relative humidity is 50%, it will feel as if it's 120°F (with no humidity). Full sunlight can make one feel even hotter. Sunstroke and heat exhaustion are likely when the heat index reaches 105°F, within the shaded area.

	Air temperature (°F)										
	70	75	80	85	90	95	100	105	110	115	120
Relative humidity	Apparent temperature (°F)										
0%	64	69	73	78	83	87	91	95	99	103	107
10	65	70	75	80	85	90	95	100	105	111	116
20	66	72	77	82	87	93	99	105	112	120	130
30	67	73	78	84	90	96	104	113	123	135	148
40	68	74	79	86	93	101	110	123	137	151	
50	69	75	81	88	96	107	120	135	150		
60	70	76	82	90	100	114	132	149			
70	70	77	85	93	106	124	144				
80	71	78	86	97	113	136					
90	71	79	88	102	122						
100	72	80	91	108							

Ultraviolet (UV) Index Forecast

Source: National Weather Service, NOAA, U.S. Dept. of Commerce; U.S. Environmental Protection Agency

The National Weather Service (NWS), Environmental Protection Agency (EPA), and Centers for Disease Control and Prevention (CDC) developed and began offering a UV index on June 28, 1994, in response to increasing incidences of skin cancer, cataracts, and other effects from exposure to the sun's harmful rays. In 2004, the Global Solar UV Index was released. The UV index is now a regular element of NWS atmospheric forecasts.

The UV index, ranging from 0 to 11+, is an indication of the expected intensity of UV radiation reaching the Earth's surface during the solar noon hour (11:30 AM-2:30 PM standard time). The lower the UV index value, the less the radiation. The UV index forecast is produced daily for 58 cities by the NWS Climate Prediction Center and uses the following scale.

UV index	Exposure	Minimum precautions
0-2	Low	Sunscreen with an SPF of at least 15
3-5	Moderate	Sunscreen, covering up
6-7	High	Sunscreen, hat, UV-blocking sunglasses, avoid sun 10 AM-4 PM
8-10	Very high	Same as above
11+	Extreme	Same as above

The index value is valid for a radius of about 30 miles around a listed city and is based on several factors:

Ozone. Ozone, a form of oxygen, the molecules of which consist of three atoms rather than two, blocks UV radiation. The more ozone, the lower the UV radiation at the surface.

Cloudiness. Clear skies allow 100% UV transmission to the surface, broken clouds allow about 73%, and overcast conditions allow 32%.

Reflectivity. Reflective surfaces intensify UV exposure. Grass reflects 2.5% to 3% of UV radiation reaching the surface; sand, 20% to 30%; snow and ice, 80% to 90%; water, up to 100% depending on reflection angle.

Elevation. At higher elevations, UV radiation travels a shorter distance to reach Earth's surface so there is less atmosphere to absorb the rays. For every 4,000 ft one travels above sea level, the UV index value increases by one unit. Snow and lack of pollutants intensify UV exposure at higher altitudes.

Latitude. The closer a location is to the equator, the higher the UV radiation level.

SPF number. The UV index is not linked in any way to the SPF number on suntan lotions and sunscreens. For an explanation of the SPF factor, contact the product's manufacturer or refer to the Food and Drug Administration website www.fda.gov/ForConsumers/ConsumerUpdates

Further information. For precautions to take after learning the UV index value, call the EPA's stratospheric ozone protection hotline (800-296-1996). For questions on scientific aspects, visit the NWS Climate Prediction Center online at www.cpc.noaa.gov.

Lightning

Source: National Weather Service, NOAA, U.S. Dept. of Commerce

Lightning occurs as a result of ice in storm clouds. As ice particles rise and sink in a cloud, collisions between them cause a separation of electrical charge. Positively charged crystals rise to the top, while negatively charged crystals drop. As the storm travels, a pool of positive charges gathers in the ground below and follows along, traveling up objects like trees and telephone poles. In a common form of lightning, the negatively charged area in a storm sends charges downward, attracted to positively charged objects. A channel develops and the electrical transfer seen is lightning. Lightning can travel miles away from the area of a storm.

The transfer of charges in lightning generates a huge amount of heat, sending the temperature in the channel to 50,000°F and causing the air within it to expand rapidly. The sound of that expansion is thunder. Sound travels more slowly than light, so lightning is usually observed before thunder is heard.

To (very roughly) gauge one's danger, use the 30-30 rule. In good visibility, count the time between a lightning flash and the crack of thunder. If it's less than 30 secs., the storm is within 6 miles. Find shelter immediately. The threat of more lightning does not stop right away; one needs to wait about 30 mins. after the last flash of the storm to be sure.

An estimated 25 mil cloud-to-ground lightning bolts happen in the U.S. each year, killing an annual average of 62 people in 1978-2007. This is a small number compared to U.S. deaths from fire (about 3,000 a year) and motor vehicle accidents (40,000-50,000), but it is still significant. In comparison, tornadoes caused an average of 54 deaths a year and hurricanes an average of 49 over the same 30-year time period. The NWS reported that in 2008, 28 people were struck and killed by lightning; 215 more were injured.

Most lightning deaths and injuries occur in the summer months when people are outdoors. Even while indoors, one is advised to stay away from windows and avoid contact with anything conducting electricity.

More information about lightning can be found online at www.lightningsafety.noaa.gov.

Global Measured Extremes of Temperature and Precipitation Records

Source: World Weather/Climate Extremes Archive, World Meteorological Organization Commission for Climatology

(records in each category ranked from most to least extreme)

Highest Temperature Extremes

Continent	Highest temp. (°F)	Place	Elevation (ft)	Date
Africa	136	El Azizia, Libya	367	Sept. 13, 1922
North America	134	Death Valley, CA, U.S. (Furnace Creek Ranch)	−179	July 10, 1913
Asia	129	Tirat Tsvi, Israel	−722	June 21, 1942
Australia	123	Oodnadatta, South Australia	367	Jan. 2, 1960
South America	120	Rivadavia, Argentina	2,192	Dec. 11, 1905
Europe	118.4	Athens, Greece (and Elefsina, Greece)	774	July 10, 1977
Oceania	108	Tuguegarao, Philippines	676	Apr. 29, 1912
Antarctica	59	Vanda Station (New Zealand), Wright Valley	49	May 1, 1974

Lowest Temperature Extremes

Continent	Lowest temp. (°F)	Place	Elevation (ft)	Date
Antarctica	−129	Vostok Station (Russia)	11,220	July 21, 1983
Asia	−90	Verkhoyansk, Russia	350	Feb. 5 & 7, 1892
	−90	Oimekon, Russia	2,625	Feb. 6, 1933
North America	−81.4	Snag, Yukon Territory, Canada	2,120	Mar. 2, 1947
Europe	−72.6	Ust'Shchugor, Russia	279	Dec. 31, 1978
South America	−27	Sarmiento, Argentina	879	June 1, 1907
Africa	−11	Ifrane, Morocco	5,364	Feb. 11, 1935
Australia	−9.4	Charlotte Pass, New South Wales	5,758	June 29, 1994

Highest Measured Average Annual Precipitation Extremes

Continent	Highest avg. (in.)[1]	Place	Elevation (ft)	Years in averaging period
Asia	467.4	Mawsynram, India	4,695	38
Oceania	460	Mt. Waialeale, Kauai, HI, U.S.	5,148	30
Africa	405	Debundscha, Cameroon	30	32
South America	354	Quibdo, Colombia	230	29
Australia	316.3	Bellenden Ker, Queensland	5,102	34
North America	276	Henderson Lake, British Columbia, Canada	115	15
Europe	183	Crkvica, Bosnia-Herzegovina	4,298	22
Antarctica	31.5[2]	Along coast of E and W and over the Antarctic Peninsula		3[3]

(1) Official greatest average annual precipitation. The average annual precipitation record of 523.6 in., set in Lloro, Colombia (14 mi SE and at a higher elevation than Quibdo), is an estimated amount. (2) 460 in. water equivalent. (3) July 1996-June 1999.

Lowest Measured Average Annual Precipitation Extremes

Continent	Lowest avg. (in.)	Place	Elevation (ft)	Years in averaging period
South America	0.03	Arica, Chile	213	59
Africa	<0.1	Wadi Halfa, Sudan	590	39
Antarctica	0.8	Amundsen-Scott South Pole Station (U.S.)	9,301	10
North America	1.2	Batagues, Mexico	69	14
Asia	1.8	Aden, Yemen	63	50
Australia	4.05	Troudaninna, South Australia	46	42
Europe	6.4	Astrakhan, Russia	66	25
Oceania	7.41	Mauna Kea Observatory, HI, U.S.	13,780	11[1]

(1) 1972-1982

DISASTERS

Some Notable Aircraft Disasters Since 1937

Source: National Transportation Safety Board; World Almanac research. As of Sept. 2009.

Particularly notable disasters are in bold. Asterisk (*) indicates number of deaths includes those on ground.

Date	Aircraft	Site of accident	Deaths
1937, May 6	**German zeppelin Hindenburg**	**Burned at mooring, Lakehurst, NJ**	**36***
1944, Aug. 23	U.S. Air Force B-24 Liberator bomber	Hit school, Freckleton, England	61*
1945, July 28	U.S. Army B-25	Hit Empire State Building after getting lost in fog, New York, NY	14*
1952, Dec. 20	U.S. Air Force C-124	Crashed at Moses Lake, WA	87
1953, Mar. 3	**Canadian Pacific DH-106 Comet**	**Crashed on takeoff from Karachi, Pakistan; world's first fatal commercial passenger jet crash**	**11**
1953, June 18	U.S. Air Force C-124	Crashed, burned near Tokyo, Japan	129
1955, Oct. 6	United Airlines DC-4	Crashed in Medicine Bow Peak, WY	66
1955, Nov. 1	United Airlines DC-6	Bomb on board exploded near Longmont, CO	44[1]
1956, June 20	Venezuelan Super Constellation	Crashed into Atlantic off Asbury Park, NJ	74
1956, June 30	TWA Super Const., United DC-7	Collided over Grand Canyon, AZ	128
1960, Dec. 16	United DC-8, TWA Super Const.	Collided over New York, NY, killing all 128 on planes, 6 on ground	134*
1962, Mar. 16	Flying Tiger Super Constellation	Vanished in W Pacific en route to Philippines from Guam	107
1962, June 3	Air France Boeing 707	Crashed on takeoff from Paris	130
1962, June 22	Air France Boeing 707	Crashed in storm, Guadeloupe, French West Indies	113
1963, Feb. 1	Lebanese Middle East Airlines Vickers Viscount 754, Turkish Mil. Douglas C-47	Collided over Ankara, Turkey, killing all 17 on planes, 87 on ground	104*
1963, June 3	Northwest Airlines DC-7	Crashed into Pacific off British Columbia, Canada	101
1963, Nov. 29	Trans-Canada Air Lines DC-8	Crashed after takeoff from Montreal, Quebec, Canada	118
1965, May 20	Pakistani Boeing 720	Crashed at airport in Cairo, Egypt	121
1966, Jan. 24	Air India Boeing 707	Crashed on Mont Blanc, France-Italy	117
1966, Feb. 4	All-Nippon Boeing 727	Plunged into Tokyo Bay, Japan	133
1966, Mar. 5	BOAC Boeing 707	Crashed into Mt. Fuji, Japan, after encountering severe turbulence.	124
1966, Dec. 24	U.S. military-chartered CL-44	Crashed into village in S Vietnam	129*
1967, Apr. 20	Globe Air Bristol Britannia	Crashed on approach to airport, Nicosia, Cyprus	126
1967, July 19	Piedmont Boeing 727, Cessna 310	Collided over Hendersonville, NC	82
1968, Apr. 20	S. African Airways Boeing 707	Crashed on takeoff from Windhoek, South-West Africa	122
1968, May 3	Braniff International Electra	Crashed in storm near Dawson, TX	85
1969, Mar. 16	Venezuelan DC-9	Crashed after takeoff from Maracaibo, Venezuela	155[2]
1969, Dec. 8	Olympic Airways DC-6B	Crashed in storm near Athens, Greece	93
1970, Feb. 15	Dominicana DC-9	Crashed into sea on takeoff from Santo Domingo, Dominican Rep.	102
1970, July 3	British-chartered DH-106 Comet	Crashed near Barcelona, Spain	112
1970, July 5	Air Canada DC-8	Crashed near Toronto International Airport.	108
1970, Aug. 9	LANSA Lockheed L-188A Electra	Crashed on takeoff from Cuzco, Peru	101*
1970, Nov. 14	Southern Airways DC-9	Crashed into mountains near Huntington, WV	75[3]
1971, July 30	All-Nippon Boeing 727, Japan Air Force F-86 fighter	Collided over Morioka, Japan	162[4]
1971, Sept. 4	Alaska Airlines Boeing 727	Crashed into mountain near Juneau, AK	111
1972, Aug. 14	East German IL-62	Crashed on takeoff from East Berlin	156
1972, Oct. 13	Aeroflot IL-62	Crashed near Moscow, U.S.S.R.	176
1972, Dec. 3	Spanish-chartered Convair CV-990	Crashed on takeoff from Canary Islands, Spain	155
1972, Dec. 29	Eastern Airlines Lockheed Tristar	Crashed on approach to Miami Intl. Airport, FL	101
1973, Jan. 22	Nigerian-chartered Boeing 707	Burst into flames upon landing at Kano Airport, Nigeria	176
1973, Feb. 21	**Libyan Arab Boeing 727**	**Flew off course, shot down by Israeli fighter planes over Sinai Desert**	**108**
1973, Apr. 10	British Vickers Vanguard	Crashed during snowstorm on approach to Basel, Switzerland	104
1973, June 3	Soviet Supersonic Tu-144	Crashed near Goussainville, France.	14[5]
1973, July 11	Brazilian Boeing 707	Crashed on approach to Orly Airport, Paris, France	122
1973, July 31	Delta Airlines DC-9	Crashed while attempting landing in fog, Logan Airport, Boston, MA.	89
1974, Mar. 3	Turkish DC-10	Crashed in Ermenonville, near Paris, France	346
1974, Apr. 22	Pan American Boeing 707	Crashed in Bali, Indonesia	107
1974, Dec. 1	TWA Boeing 727	Crashed on approach in storm, Upperville, VA	92
1974, Dec. 4	Dutch-chartered DC-8	Crashed in storm near Colombo, Sri Lanka	191
1975, Apr. 4	Air Force Galaxy C-5A	Crashed on takeoff near Saigon, S Viet.; carried orphans	172
1975, June 24	Eastern Airlines 727	Crashed in storm, JFK Airport, New York, NY	113
1975, Aug. 3	Alia Royal Jordanian Boeing 707	Hit mountainside in heavy fog near Agadir, Morocco	188
1976, Sept. 10	Brit. Airways Trident, Yug. DC-9	Collided near Zagreb, Yugoslavia	176
1976, Sept. 19	Turkish 727	Hit mountain in S Turkey	155
1976, Oct. 13	LAB Boeing 707	Crashed after takeoff from Santa Cruz, Bolivia	100[6]
1977, Mar. 27	**KLM 747, Pan American 747**	**Collided on runway, Tenerife, Canary Islands, Spain; world's worst airline disaster**	**583**
1977, Nov. 19	TAP Portugal Boeing 727	Crashed in Madeira, Portugal	130
1977, Dec. 4	Malaysian Airlines Boeing 737	Hijacked and forced to fly to Singapore, crashed near Johor Strait	100
1977, Dec. 13	National Jet Service DC-3	Crashed after takeoff from Evansville, IN; passengers incl. Univ. of Evansville men's basketball team	29
1978, Jan. 1	Air India 747	Crashed into sea after takeoff from Bombay	213
1978, Sept. 25	Boeing 727, Cessna 172	Collided over San Diego, CA	150
1978, Nov. 15	Indonesian-chartered DC-8	Crashed on approach to airport, Colombo, Sri Lanka	183
1979, May 25	**American Airlines DC-10**	**Crashed after takeoff from O'Hare Airport, Chicago, IL; highest death toll in U.S. aviation history**	**275***
1979, Aug. 11	Aeroflot/Moldova Tu-134, Aeroflot Tu-134	Collided over Ukraine	178
1979, Nov. 26	Pakistani Boeing 707	Crashed near Jidda, Saudi Arabia	156
1979, Nov. 28	Air New Zealand DC-10	Crashed into mountain after takeoff from Antarctica	257
1980, Mar. 14	PLL LOT IL-62	Crashed making emergency landing, Warsaw, Poland	87[7]
1980, Aug. 19	Saudi Arabian Tristar	Burned after emergency landing in Riyadh	301
1981, Dec. 1	Inex Adria DC-9	Crashed into mountain on island of Corsica, France	180
1982, Jan. 13	Air Florida Boeing 737	Crashed into Potomac R. after takeoff from Washington, DC	78
1982, July 9	Pan Am Boeing 727	Crashed after takeoff from Kenner, LA, near New Orleans	153*
1983, Sept. 1	**S. Korean Boeing 747**	**Shot down after violating Soviet airspace near Sakhalin; plane apparently misidentified**	**269**
1983, Nov. 27	Avianca Boeing 747	Crashed near Barajas Airport, Madrid, Spain	183

Date	Aircraft	Site of accident	Deaths
1984, Oct. 11	Aeroflot/East Siberia Tu-154	Crashed into vehicles on runway while landing in poor weather, Omsk, Russia	178*
1985, Feb. 19	Spanish Boeing 727	Crashed into Mt. Oiz, Spain	148
1985, June 23	Air India Boeing 747	Crashed into Atlantic off Ireland after bomb detonated on board	329
1985, Aug. 2	Delta Air Lines L-1011	Crashed at Dallas-Ft. Worth Airport, TX	137
1985, Aug. 12	**Japan Air Lines Boeing 747**	**Crashed into Mt. Ogura, Japan; world's worst single-plane disaster**	**520**
1985, Dec. 12	Arrow Air DC-8	Crashed after takeoff from Gander, Newfoundland, Canada	256[8]
1986, Mar. 31	Mexican Boeing 727	Crashed NW of Mexico City	166
1986, Aug. 31	Aeromexico DC-9, Piper PA-28	Collided over Cerritos, CA.	82*
1987, May 9	Polish IL-62M	Crashed after takeoff from Warsaw, Poland	183
1987, Aug. 16	Northwest Airlines MD-82	Crashed after takeoff from Romulus, MI	156
1987, Nov. 28	S. African Boeing 747	Crashed into Indian Ocean near Mauritius	159
1987, Nov. 29	S. Korean Boeing 707	Bomb planted by 2 N. Korean agents exploded while plane over Thai-Burmese border	155
1988, Mar. 17	Colombian Boeing 707	Crashed into mountainside near Venezuela border	137
1988, July 3	**Iran Air Airbus A300**	**Misidentified as hostile aircraft, shot down by U.S. Navy warship _Vincennes_ over Pers. Gulf**	**290**
1988, Dec. 21	**Pan Am Boeing 747**	**Libyan agent planted bomb on board; exploded over Lockerbie, Scotland**	**270[9]**
1989, Feb. 8	U.S.-chartered Boeing 707	Crashed into mountain on Azores Isls., off Portugal	144
1989, June 7	Suriname DC-8	Crashed near Paramaribo Airport, Suriname	168
1989, July 19	United Airlines DC-10	Crashed on landing in Sioux City, IA.	111
1989, Sept. 19	**UTA DC-10**	**Bomb exploded on board flight from Chad to France while over desert in Niger**	**171**
1989, Nov. 27	Avianca Boeing 727	Bomb exploded on flight from Bogotá, Colombia	107
1990, Jan. 25	Avianca Air Boeing 707	Crashed on landing at JFK Airport, New York, NY	73
1990, Feb. 14	Indian Airlines Airbus 320	Crashed and burned on landing in Bangalore, India	91
1990, Oct. 2	Xiamen Airlines Boeing 737	Hijacked after takeoff from Xiamen; struck empty 707, then 757, on runway, Guangzhou, China	132
1991, May 26	Lauda-Air Boeing 767-300	Exploded over rural Thailand	223
1991, July 11	Nigerian DC-8	Crashed on landing at Jidda, Saudi Arabia	261
1991, Oct. 5	Air Force Lockheed C-130 Hercules	Crashed after takeoff from Jakarta, Indonesia	137*
1992, July 31	Thai Airbus A300-310	Crashed into mountain N of Kathmandu, Nepal	113
1992, Oct. 4	**El Al Boeing 747-200F**	**Crashed into 2 apartment bldgs., Amsterdam, Netherlands.**	**120***
1993, Feb. 8	Iran Air Tu-154, Iranian Air Force jet	Collided after military jet took off from Tehran, Iran	133
1993, Mar. 5	Macedonian Pal Air Fokker 100	Crashed after takeoff in snowstorm from Skopje, Macedonia	83
1994, Jan. 3	Aeroflot Tu-154	Crashed and exploded after takeoff from Irkhutsk, Russia	125*
1994, Apr. 26	China Airlines Airbus A300	Crashed on approach to Nagoya Airport, Japan	264
1994, June 6	China Northwest Airlines Tu-154	Crashed near Xian, China	160
1994, Sept. 8	USAir Boeing 737-300	Crashed near Pittsburgh Intl. Airport, Aliquippa, PA	132
1994, Oct. 31	American Eagle ATR-72-210	Crashed in field near Roselawn, IN.	68
1995, Aug. 11	Aviateca Boeing 737	Crashed into Chichontepec volcano, El Salvador	65
1995, Dec. 20	American Airlines Boeing 757	Crashed into mountain N of Cali, Colombia	160
1996, Jan. 8	Antonov-32 cargo plane	Crashed into central market in Kinshasa, Zaire	350+*
1996, Feb. 6	Turkish Boeing 757	Crashed into Atlantic off Dominican Republic	189
1996, Apr. 3	U.S. Air Force Boeing T-43A	Crashed into mountain near Dubrovnik, Croatia	35[10]
1996, May 11	ValuJet DC-9	Crashed into Florida Everglades after takeoff	110
1996, July 17	Trans World Airlines Boeing 747	Exploded and crashed into Atlantic off Long Isl., NY	230
1996, Aug. 29	Vnukovo Tu-154	Crashed into mountain on Arctic island of Spitsbergen	141
1996, Oct. 2	Aeroperu Boeing 757	Crashed into Pacific after takeoff from Lima, Peru	70
1996, Oct. 31	Brazilian TAM Fokker-100	Crashed shortly after takeoff from São Paulo, Brazil	97*
1996, Nov. 7	ADG Boeing 727	Crashed into lagoon SE of Lagos, Nigeria	143
1996, Nov. 12	**Saudi Arabian Boeing 747, Kazakh IL-76 cargo plane**	**Collided near New Delhi, India; world's worst midair collision**	**349**
1996, Nov. 23	Ethiopian Airlines Boeing 767	Hijacked, then crashed into Indian Ocean off the Comoros	127
1997, Aug. 6	Korean Air Boeing 747-300	Crashed into jungle on Guam on approach to airport	228
1997, Sept. 3	Vietnamese Airlines Tu-134	Crashed on approach to Phnom Penh airport.	64
1997, Sept. 26	Indonesian Airbus A300	Crashed near airport, Medan, Indonesia.	234
1997, Oct. 10	Austral Airlines DC-9-32	Crashed and exploded near Neuvo Berlin, Uruguay	74
1997, Dec. 6	Russian AN-124 transport cargo plane	Crashed into apartment complex near Irkutsk, Siberia	67*
1997, Dec. 15	Tajik Air Tu-154	Crashed in desert near airport, Sharja, UAE.	85
1997, Dec. 17	AeroSvit Airlines Yakovlev-42	Crashed into mountains near Katerini, Greece.	70
1997, Dec. 19	SilkAir Boeing 737-300	Crashed into Musi River, Sumatra, Indonesia	104
1998, Feb. 2	Cebu Pacific Air DC-9-32	Crashed into mountain near Cagayan de Oro, Philippines	104
1998, Feb. 16	China Airlines Airbus A300	Crashed on approach to airport in Taipei, Taiwan	203*
1998, Apr. 20	Air France Boeing 727-200	Crashed into mountain after takeoff from Bogotá, Colombia	53
1998, Sept. 2	Swissair MD-11	Crashed into Atlantic off Nova Scotia, Canada	229
1998, Oct. 11	Congo Air Lines Boeing 727	Shot down by rebels in Kindu, Congo	40
1998, Dec. 11	Thai Airways Airbus A310	Crashed on third landing attempt at Surat Thani airport, Thailand	101
1999, Feb. 24	China Southwest Airlines Tu-154	Crashed on approach to airport in Wenzhou, China	61
1999, Sept. 1	LAPA Boeing 737-200	Crashed on takeoff from airport, Buenos Aires, Argentina	74*
1999, Oct. 31	EgyptAir Boeing 767	Crashed off Nantucket, MA; result of deliberate actions by copilot, motives unknown	217
2000, Jan. 30	Kenya Airways Airbus A310	Crashed into Atlantic after takeoff from Abidjan, Ivory Coast	169
2000, Jan. 31	Alaska Airlines MD-83	Crashed into Pacific off coast of Southern CA	88
2000, Apr. 19	Air Philippines Boeing 737-200	Crashed on approach to airport, Davao, Philippines	131
2000, July 25	**Air France Concorde**	**Crashed into hotel after takeoff from Paris; world's first Concorde crash.**	**113***
2000, Aug. 23	Gulf Air Airbus A320	Crashed into Persian Gulf on approach to airport in Bahrain	143
2000, Oct. 31	Singapore Airlines Boeing 747	Crashed immediately after takeoff from Taipei, Taiwan	81
2001, Apr. 7	M-17 helicopter	Crashed into mountain S of Hanoi, Vietnam	16[11]
2001, July 3	Vladivostokavia Tu-154	Crashed on approach to airport, Irkutsk, Russia	145
2001, Sept. 11	**2 Boeing 767s, 2 Boeing 757s**	**September 11 terrorist attacks.**	**265[12]**
2001, Oct. 4	Sibir Boeing 757	Crashed into Black Sea after strike by errant Ukrainian missile	78
2001, Oct. 8	Cessna 525A Citation, Scandinavian Airlines System (SAS) MD-87	Collided in heavy fog on takeoff from Milan, Italy	118*

Date	Aircraft	Site of accident	Deaths
2001, Nov. 12	**American Airlines Airbus A300**	**Crashed after takeoff from JFK Airport, New York, NY**	**265***
2002, Jan. 28	TAME Ecuador Boeing 727	Crashed into Andes mountains, S Colombia	92
2002, Feb. 12	Iran Air Tours Tu-154	Crashed in Khorramabad, Iran	119
2002, Apr. 15	Air China Boeing 767	Crashed into mountainside in rain and fog on approach to airport, Pusan, S. Korea	129
2002, May 4	EAS Airlines BAC 1-11	Crashed shortly after takeoff from Kano, Nigeria	149
2002, May 7	China Northern Airlines MD-82	Plunged into sea, apparently after a passenger started fire in cabin, NE China	112
2002, May 25	China Airlines Boeing 747	Broke apart in midair, plunged into Taiwan Strait en route to Hong Kong airport	225
2002, July 1	Bashkirian Airlines Tu-154, DHL Boeing 757 cargo	Collided over S Germany	71
2002, July 27	**Ukraine Air Force Sukhoi Su-27**	**Crashed while performing, Lviv, Ukraine; world's worst air-show crash**	**77[13]**
2002, Aug. 19	Russian Mi-26 transport helicopter	Hit by Chechen missile near Grozny, Chechnya	127
2003, Jan. 8	Turkish Airlines British Aerospace RJ-100	Crashed on approach to airport in Diyarbakir, Turkey	75
2003, Feb. 19	Iranian Revolutionary Guard Il-76	Crashed into mountain near Kerman, Iran; passengers were Revolutionary Guard members	275
2003, Mar. 6	Air Algérie Boeing 737-200	Crashed on takeoff from Tamanrasset, Algeria	102
2003, May 8	Congolese Air Force Il-76	On flight from Kinshasa, Dem. Rep. of Congo, cargo door opened, passengers sucked out	7+[14]
2003, May 26	Ukrain.-Medit. Airlines Yak-42	Crashed into mountain in fog approaching Trabzon, Turkey; passengers incl. Spanish peacekeepers returning from Afghan.	75
2003, July 8	Sudan Airways Boeing 737-200	Mechanical problems reported shortly after takeoff; crashed upon return to Port Sudan Airport	115
2003, Dec. 25	Union Transp. Africains Boeing 727	Overloading caused crash on takeoff from Cotonou, Benin	138
2004, Jan. 3	Flash Airlines Boeing 737-300	Crashed into Red Sea after takeoff from Sharm el-Sheik, Egypt	148
2004, Jan. 13	Uzbekistan Airways Yakovlev YAK-40	Crashed on landing attempt in fog at Tashkent, Uzbekistan	37
2004, Feb. 10	Iranian Kish Airline Fokker-50	Crashed on approach to Sharjah, UAE	43
2004, May 15	Rico Linhas Aereas Embraer 120ER Brasilia	Crashed in Amazon jungle near Manaus, Brazil	33
2004, Aug. 24	Volga-Aviaexpress Tu-134, Sibir Airlines Tu-154	2 planes that took off from Moscow crashed within minutes of each other; brought down by Chechen suicide bombers	90
2005, Feb. 3	Kam Air Boeing 737-200	Crashed on approach to airport in Kabul, Afghan.	104
2005, Aug. 14	Helios Airways Boeing 737-300	Crashed after air pressure failure on board, near Athens, Greece	121
2005, Aug. 16	West Caribbean Airways MD-82	Crashed after engine failure, near Machiques, Venezuela	160
2005, Sept. 5	Mandala Airlines Boeing 737-200	Crashed shortly after takeoff from Medan, Sumatra, Indonesia	145[15]
2005, Oct. 22	Bellview Airlines Boeing 737-200	Crashed during heavy electrical storm near Lagos, Nigeria	117
2005, Dec. 6	Islamic Rep. of Iran Air Force Lockheed C-130	Crashed into apartment building after reportedly attempting emergency landing back at airport, Tehran, Iran	116+[16]
2005, Dec. 10	Sosoliso Airlines DC-9-30	Crashed during storm on approach to Port Harcourt, Nigeria	107
2006, May 3	Armavia Airbus A320	Crashed into Black Sea on approach to airport, Sochi, Russia	113
2006, July 9	S7 Airlines Airbus A310	Skidded off runway, crashed into concrete barrier after landing, Irkutsk, Russia	125
2006, Aug. 22	Pulkovo Aviation Tu-154	Crashed after encountering storm, near Donetsk, Ukraine	170
2006, Aug. 27	Comair Bombardier CRJ-100	Crashed after takeoff from Lexington, KY	49
2006, Sept. 29	Gol Airlines Boeing 737	Crashed into Amazon jungle after midair collision with Embraer Legacy jet, Brazil	154
2006, Oct. 29	ADC Airlines Boeing 737-200	Crashed in stormy weather shortly after takeoff from Abuja, Nigeria	96
2007, Jan. 1	Adam Air Boeing 737-400	Crashed into sea off coast, Makassar, Indonesia	102
2007, May 5	Kenya Airways Boeing 737-800	Crashed shortly after takeoff from Douala, Cameroon	114
2007, July 17	TAM Airlines Airbus 320	Crashed into cargo depot, gas station after skidding off airport runway, São Paulo, Brazil	199*
2007, Sept. 16	One-Two-Go Airlines Boeing-MD-82	Skidded off runway, caught fire after landing, Phuket, Thailand	89
2007, Nov. 30	Atlasjet MD-83	Crashed on approach to airport, Isparta, Turkey	57
2008, Aug. 20	Spanair Boeing-MD-82	Swerved off runway, caught fire on takeoff attempt, Madrid, Spain	154
2008, Aug. 24	Itek Air Boeing 737	Crashed after takeoff from Bishkek, Kyrgyzstan	65
2008, Sept. 14	Aeroflot-Nord Boeing 737-500	Crashed on approach to airport, Perm, Russia	88
2009, Feb. 12	Colgan Air Bombardier Dash 8 Q400	Crashed into house near airport, Buffalo, NY	50*
2009, May 20	Indonesian military C-130 Hercules	Crashed into houses and a rice field, Java, Indonesia	98
2009, June 1	Air France Airbus A330	Plunged into Atlantic Ocean en route from Rio de Janeiro, Brazil, to Paris, France	228
2009, June 29	Yemenia Airbus A310-300	Fell into Indian Ocean on approach to Moroni, Comoros	152
2009, July 15	Caspian Airlines Tupolev 154	Crashed after takeoff from Tehran, Iran	168

(1) Bomb was planted by Jack G. Graham in insurance plot to kill his mother, Daisie E. King, a passenger. (2) 84 on plane, 71 on ground killed. (3) Incl. 43 Marshall Univ. football players and coaches. (4) Fighter pilot parachuted to safety. (5) First supersonic plane crash; killed 8 on ground. (6) Crew of 3, 97 on ground killed. (7) Incl. 22 members of U.S. amateur boxing team. (8) Incl. 248 members of U.S. 101st Airborne Division. (9) Incl. 11 on ground. (10) Incl. U.S. Sec. of Commerce Ron Brown. (11) Carried U.S. mil. personnel searching for MIAs from Vietnam War. (12) 4 planes were hijacked and crashed, with all on board killed (265, incl. 19 hijackers). American Airlines Flight 11, a Boeing 767-200, with 81 passengers, 11 crew, crashed into Tower 1 of World Trade Center; United Airlines Flight 175, a Boeing 767-200, with 56 passengers, 9 crew, crashed into Tower 2 of World Trade Center; American Airlines Flight 77, a Boeing 757-200, with 58 passengers, 6 crew, crashed into Pentagon outside Washington, DC; United Air Lines Flight 93, a Boeing 757-200, with 37 passengers, 7 crew, crashed near Shanksville, PA. About 125 died on ground in the Pentagon. In May 2007, for first time, medical examiner linked a death to exposure to dust from collapsed towers on Sept. 11. Additional deaths from such exposure brought number of World Trade Center victims to 2,752 as of Sept. 2009. (13) Pilots ejected to safety. All spectator deaths. (14) 7 confirmed dead. Actual number might be 60-100+. (15) Incl. 44 on ground. (16) 94 on plane plus 22+ on ground.

Disaster Averted

Date: Jan. 15, 2009. **Location:** Hudson River, NY-NJ. **Fatalities:** 0.

Chesley B. "Sully" Sullenberger III, the captain of U.S. Airways Flight 1549, made a spectacular emergency landing on the surface of a chilly Hudson River after apparent bird strikes took out both of the plane's engines shortly after takeoff from New York's LaGuardia Airport. Ferry boats and other nearby watercrafts safely evacuated the five crew members and all 150 passengers to shore soon after the emergency water landing.

Some Notable Shipwrecks Since 1854

Figures are estimated deaths. Does not include most wartime disasters.

1854, Mar. 1—City of Glasgow; Brit. steamer left Liverpool for Philadelphia, never heard from again; 480.

1854, Sept. 27—Arctic and Vesta; U.S. Collins Line steamer sunk in collision with French steamer nr. Cape Race, Canada; 285-351.

1856, Jan. 23—Pacific; U.S. Collins Line steamer went missing in N Atlantic; 186-286.

1858, Sept. 23—Austria; German steamer destroyed by fire in N Atlantic; 471.

1863, Apr. 27—Anglo-Saxon; Brit. steamer wrecked at Cape Race, Canada; 238.

1865, Apr. 27—Sultana; Mississippi R. steamer blew up nr. Memphis, TN; 1,450.

1869, Oct. 27—Stonewall; steamer burned, Mississippi R. below Cairo, IL; 200.

1870, Jan. 25—City of Boston; Brit. Inman Line steamer vanished between New York and Liverpool; 177.

1870, Oct. 19—Cambria; Brit. steamer off N Ireland; 196.

1872, Nov. 7—Mary Celeste; U.S. half-brig sailing from New York to Genoa, Italy, found abandoned; loss of life unknown.

1873, Jan. 22—Northfleet; Brit. steamer foundered off Dungeness, England; 300.

1873, Apr. 1—Atlantic; Brit. White Star steamer off Nova Scotia, Can.; 585.

1873, Nov. 23—Ville du Havre and Loch Earn; French steamer sank after collision with Brit. sailing ship; 226.

1875, May 7—Schiller; German steamer off Scilly Isles, UK; 312.

1875, Nov. 4—Pacific; U.S. steamer sank after collision off Cape Flattery, WA; 236.

1878, Sept. 3—Princess Alice; Brit. steamer sank after collision with *Bywell Castle* in Thames R.; 700.

1878, Dec. 18—Byzantin; French steamer sank after collision in Dardanelles, off Turkey; 210.

1881, May 24—Victoria; steamer capsized in Thames R., ON, Canada; 200.

1883, Jan. 19—Cimbria and Sultan; German steamer sank in collision with Brit. steamer in North Sea; 389.

1890, Feb. 17—Duburg; Brit. steamer wrecked, China Sea; 400.

1890, Sept. 19—Ertogrul; Turkish frigate off Japan; 540.

1891, Mar. 17—Utopia and Anson; Brit. steamer sank in collision with Brit. ironclad off Gibraltar; 562.

1895, Jan. 30—Elbe and Craithie; German steamer sank in collision with Brit. steamer in North Sea; 332.

1895, Mar. 11—Reina Regenta; Spanish cruiser foundered nr. Gibraltar; 400.

1898, Feb. 15—USS Maine; explosion caused battleship to sink in Havana Harbor, Cuba; 260.

1898, July 4—La Bourgogne and Cromartyshire; French steamer sank in collision with Brit. sailing ship off Nova Scotia, Can.; 549.

1898, Nov. 26—Portland; U.S. steamer, off Cape Cod, MA; 157.

1904, June 15—General Slocum; excursion steamer burned in East R., New York, NY; 1,021.

1904, June 28—Norge; Danish steamer wrecked on Rockall Isl., Scotland; 620.

1906, Aug. 4—Sirio; Italian steamer wrecked off Cape Palos, Spain; 350.

1908, Mar. 23—Mutsu Maru; Japanese steamer sank in collision with another steamer nr. Hakodate, Japan; 300.

1909, Aug. 1—Waratah; Brit. steamer vanished en route from Sydney to London; 300.

1910, Feb. 9—General Chanzy; French steamer wrecked off Minorca, Spain; 200.

1911, Sept. 25—Liberté; French battleship exploded at Toulon; 285.

1912, Mar. 5—Principe de Asturias; Spanish steamer wrecked off Spanish coast; 500.

1912, Apr. 14-15—Titanic; Brit. White Star steamer hit iceberg in N Atlantic; 1,503.

1912, Sept. 28—Kichemaru; Japanese steamer sank off Japan coast; 1,000.

1914, May 29—Empress of Ireland; Canadian Pacific steamer collided with Norwegian coal transporter *Storstad* in St. Lawrence R., Can.; 1,014.

1915, May 7—Lusitania; Brit. Cunard Line steamer torpedoed and sunk by German submarine off Ireland; 1,198.

1915, July 24—Eastland; steamer capsized, Chicago R., IL; 844.

1916, Feb. 26—Provence; French cruiser sank in Medit.; 3,100.

1916, Mar. 3—Principe de Asturias; Spanish steamer wrecked nr. Santos, Brazil; 558.

1917, Dec. 6—Mont Blanc and Imo; French ammunition ship and Belgian steamer collided in Halifax Harbor, Can.; 1,600.

1918, Apr. 25—Kiang-Kwan; Chinese steamer sank in collision off Hankow; 500.

1918, July 12—Kawachi; Japanese battleship blew up in Tokayama Bay; 500.

1918, Oct. 25—Princess Sophia; Canadian steamer sank off Alaskan coast; 398.

1919, Jan. 17—Chaonia; French steamer lost in Straits of Messina, Italy; 460.

1919, Sept. 9—Valbanera; Spanish steamer lost off FL coast; 500.

1921, Mar. 18—Hong Kong; steamer wrecked, S China Sea; 1,000.

1922, Aug. 26—Niitaka; Japanese cruiser sank in storm off Kamchatka, USSR; 300.

1924, June 12—USS Mississippi; explosions in battleship's gun turret, off San Pedro, CA; 48.

1927, Oct. 25—Principessa Mafalda; Italian steamer blew up, sank off Porto Seguro, Brazil; 314.

1928, Nov. 12—Vestris; Brit. steamer sank off VA coast; 113.

1934, Sept. 8—Morro Castle; U.S. steamer en route from Havana to New York, burned off Asbury Park, NJ; 134.

1939, May 23—Squalus; U.S. submarine sank off Portsmouth, NH; 26.

1939, June 1—Thetis; Brit. submarine sank, Liverpool Bay; 99.

1942, Feb. 18—USS Truxtun and USS Pollux; destroyer and cargo ship ran aground, sank off Newfoundland, Can.; 204.

1942, Oct. 2—Curacao and Queen Mary; Brit. cruiser sank after collision with liner; 338.

1944, Dec. 17-18—3 U.S. Third Fleet destroyers sank during typhoon, Philippine Sea; 790.

1945, Jan. 30—Wilhelm Gustloff; liner with German refugees, soldiers sunk by Soviet submarine in Baltic; 5,000-9,000.

1945, Apr. 16—Goya; cargo ship carrying German refugees, soldiers sunk by Soviet submarine in Baltic; 6,000-7,000.

1945, May 3—Cap Arcona and Thielbek; German liners carrying concentration camp inmates sunk by British warplanes in Lubeck Bay, Ger.; 7,000-8,000.

1947, Jan. 19—Himera; Greek steamer hit mine off Athens, Greece; 392.

1947, Apr. 16—Grandcamp; French freighter exploded, Texas City, TX, harbor, started fires; 576+.

1948, Dec. 3—Kiangya; Chinese refugee ship wrecked in explosion S of Shanghai; 1,100+.

1949, Sept. 17—Noronic; Canadian Great Lakes Cruiser burned in dock, Toronto, Can.; 130.

1952, Apr. 26—USS Hobson and USS Wasp; destroyer and aircraft carrier collided in Atlantic; 176.

1954, Sept. 26—Toya Maru; Japanese ferry sank, Tsugaru Strait, Japan; 1,172.

1956, July 26—Andrea Doria and Stockholm; Italian liner and Swedish liner collided off Nantucket Isl., MA; 51.

1957, July 14—Eshghabad; Soviet ship ran aground in Caspian Sea; 270.

1961, Apr. 8—Dara; Brit. liner exploded in Persian Gulf; 236.

1961, July 8—Save; Portuguese ship ran aground off Mozambique; 259.

1963, Apr. 10—Thresher; U.S. Navy atomic submarine sank in N Atlantic; 129.

1964, Feb. 10—Voyager; Australian destroyer sank after collision with aircraft carrier *Melbourne* off New South Wales; 82.

1965, Nov. 13—Yarmouth Castle; Panamanian-registered cruise ship burned, sank off Nassau, Bahamas; 89.

1968, Jan. 25—Dakar; Israeli submarine vanished in Medit.; 69.

1968, May 27—Scorpion; U.S. nuclear submarine went missing, later found to have sunk in Atlantic nr. Azores; 99.

1969, June 2—Evans and Melbourne; U.S. destroyer cut in half by Australian carrier, S China Sea; 74.

1970, Mar. 4—Eurydice; French submarine sank in Medit. nr. Toulon; 57.

1970, Dec. 15—Namyong-Ho; S. Korean ferry sank in Korea Strait; 308.

1974, Sept. 26—Soviet destroyer sank in Black Sea; 200+.

1975, Nov. 10—Edmund Fitzgerald; U.S. cargo ship sank during storm on Lake Superior; 29.

1976, Oct. 20—George Prince and Frosta; U.S. ferryboat and Norwegian tanker collided, Mississippi R., at Luling, LA; 77.

1976, Dec. 25—Patria; Egyptian liner caught fire, sank in Red Sea; 100.

Sinking of the *General Slocum*

Date: June 15, 1904. **Location:** New York, NY. **Fatalities:** 1,021.

The highest death toll of any incident in New York City prior to the Sept. 11, 2001, terrorist attacks. The *General Slocum* caught fire while on the East River. Most of its 1,300-1,500 passengers were women and children, German immigrants on a daylong church outing. Shortly after the ship launched, a fire erupted on board. The inexperienced crew didn't know how to respond, and the ship, which was in poor condition, lacked adequate safety measures. Those who didn't know how to swim died in the fire or drowned when they jumped into the water.

1979, Aug. 14—23 yachts competing in Fastnet yacht race sank or abandoned during storm in S Irish Sea; 18.
1980, Apr. 22—**Don Juan;** sank off Mindoro Isl., Philippines, after colliding with barge; 1,000+.
1981, Jan. 27—**Tamponas II;** Indonesian passenger ship caught fire and sank in Java Sea; 580.
1983, Feb. 12—**Marine Electric;** coal freighter sank during storm off Chincoteague, VA; 33.
1983, May 25—**10th of Ramadan;** Nile steamer caught fire and sank in Lake Nasser, Egypt; 357.
1986, Apr. 20—**Atlas Star;** ferry sank in storm, Dhaleswari R. nr. Dhaka, Bangladesh; 300+.
1986, May 25—**Shamia;** ferry capsized in storm, Meghna R., Bangladesh; 500+.
1986, Sept. 1—**Admiral Nakhimov** and **Pyotr Vasev;** Soviet cruise ship collided with Soviet freighter in Black Sea; 425.
1987, Mar. 6—**Herald of Free Enterprise;** Brit. ferry capsized off Zeebrugge, Belgium; 189.
1987, Dec. 20—**Doña Paz** and **Victor;** Philippine ferry and oil tanker collided in Tablas Strait; 4,341.
1988, Aug. 6—Indian ferry capsized on Ganges R.; 400+.
1989, Apr. 7—**Komsolets;** Soviet submarine sank after fire off Norwegian coast; 42.
1989, Aug. 20—**Bowbelle** and **Marchioness;** Brit. barge struck Brit. pleasure cruiser on Thames R. in central London; 56.
1991, Apr. 10—**Moby Prince** and **Agip Abruzzo;** auto ferry and oil tanker collided outside Livorno Harbor, Italy; 140.
1991, Dec. 14—**Salem Express;** ferry rammed coral reef nr. Safaga, Egypt; 462.
1993, Feb. 17—**Neptune;** ferry capsized off Port-au-Prince, Haiti; 500+.
1993, Oct. 10—**Seohae;** capsized in Yellow Sea nr. W S. Korea during storm; 285.
1994, Sept. 28—**Estonia;** ferry sank in Baltic Sea; 852.
1996, May 21—**Bukoba;** overcrowded Tanzanian ferry sank in Lake Victoria; 500+.
1997, Feb. 20—Tamil refugee boat sank off Sri Lanka; 165.
1997, Mar. 28—Albanian refugee boat sank in Adriatic after being rammed by Italian navy warship *Sibilla;* 83.
1997, Sept. 8—**Pride of la Gonâve;** Haitian ferry sank off Montrouis, Haiti; 200+.
1998, Apr. 4—Passenger boat capsized off coast nr. Ibaka beach, Nigeria; 280.
1998, Sept. 2—2 passenger boats capsized on Lake Kivu, nr. Bukavu, Congo; 200+.
1999, Feb. 6—**Harta Rimba;** cargo ship sank off Indonesia; 280+.
1999, May 1—**Miss Majestic;** "duck" boat on tour sank, Lake Hamilton, AR; 13.
1999, Nov. 24—**Dashun;** passenger ferry capsized nr. Yantai, China; 280.

2000, June 29—**Cahaya Bahari;** overloaded ferry carrying refugees from religious strife capsized in storm off Sulawesi Isl., Indonesia; 500+.
2000, Aug. 12—**Kursk;** faulty torpedo exploded on board Russian submarine, causing it to sink in Barents Sea; 118.
2000, Sept. 26—**Express Samina;** Greek ferry sank off Paros, Greece; 81+.
2001, Feb. 9—**Ehime Maru;** Japanese trawler sunk by surfacing U.S. submarine *Greeneville,* nr. Hawaii; 9.
2001, Oct. 19—Fishing boat overloaded with refugees, mainly from Middle East, sank off Indonesia; 350+.
2001, Dec. 22—Suspected N. Korean spy ship sank after exchanging fire with Japanese coast guard; 15.
2002, May 4—**Salahuddin-2;** overloaded Bangladesh ferry sank in Meghna R.; 300+.
2002, Sept. 26—**Joola;** overloaded Senegalese ferry capsized in ocean off The Gambia; 1,863.
2003, Mar. 23—**Kashowgwe;** overloaded ferry capsized in Lake Tanganyika, off Burundi; 111+.
2003, July 8—**MV-Nasrin 1;** overcrowded ferry sank nr. Chandpur in Bangladesh R.; 400.
2003, Oct. 15—**Andrew J. Barberi;** NYC ferry crashed into dock on approach to Staten Isl.; 11.
2003, Nov. 25—**Dieu Merci;** overloaded ferry sank on Lake Mayi Ndombe, Dem. Rep. of Congo; 130-200.
2004, Jan. 26—**Convoi Lengi;** ferry caught fire on Congo R., Dem. Rep. of Congo; 200.
2004, Mar 6—**Lady D;** water taxi capsized in storm, Inner Harbor, Baltimore, MD; 5.
2004, Mar. 11—**Samson;** ferry sank off Madagascar during cyclone; 113.
2005, July 7—**KMP Digul;** ferry capsized in rough waters nr. Merauke, Indonesia; 150+.
2005, Aug. 12—Fishing boat overloaded with Ecuadorans attempting to migrate to U.S. sank off Colombia; 94.
2005, Oct. 2—**Ethan Allen;** glass boat carrying senior citizens capsized on tour, Lake George, NY; 20.
2006, Feb. 3—**Al-Salam Boccaccio 98;** ferry caught fire, sank in Red Sea off Egypt; 1,000+.
2006, Dec. 30—**Senopati Nusantara;** high waves capsized ferry en route to Java, Indonesia; 400+.
2007, May 4—Boat overloaded with illegal Haitian immigrants capsized in storm nr. Turks and Caicos Isls.; 61+.
2007, Nov. 23—**Explorer;** Canadian cruise ship sank off Antarctica, first comm. passenger ship to sink in region; none.
2008, June 23—**Princess of the Stars;** Philippine ferry capsized during Typhoon *Fengshen* nr. Manila; 800.
2009, Mar. 30—Passenger boat carrying African immigrants to Italy capsized off coast of Libya; 200+.

Some Notable Railroad Disasters Since 1925

Date	Location	Deaths	Date	Location	Deaths
1925, June 16	Hackettstown, NJ	50	1957, Sept. 1	Kendal, Jamaica	178
1925, Oct. 27	Victoria, MS	21	1957, Sept. 29	Montgomery, W Pakistan	250
1926, Sept. 5	Waco, CO	30	1957, Dec. 4	London, England	90
1937, July 16	Bhita, India	107	1958, May 8	Rio de Janeiro, Brazil	128
1938, June 19	Saugus, MT	47	1958, Sept. 15	Elizabethport, NJ	48
1939, Aug. 12	Harney, NV	24	1960, Nov. 14	Pardubice, Czechoslovakia	110
1939, Dec. 22	Near Magdeburg, Germany	132	1962, Jan. 8	Woerden, Netherlands	91
1939, Dec. 22	Near Friedrichshafen, Germany	99	1962, May 3	Tokyo, Japan	163
1940, Apr. 19	Little Falls, NY	31	1963, Nov. 9	Yokohama, Japan	120+
1940, July 31	Cuyahoga Falls, OH	43	1964, July 26	Porto, Portugal	94
1943, Aug. 29	Wayland, NY	27	1967, July 6	Madgeburg, Germany	94
1943, Sept. 6	Frankford Junction, Philad., PA	79	1970, Feb. 1	Buenos Aires, Argentina	236
1943, Dec. 16	Between Rennert and Buie, NC	72	1972, June 16	Vierzy, France	107
1944, Jan. 16	León Province, Spain	500	1972, July 21	Seville, Spain	76
1944, Mar. 2	Salerno, Italy	521	1972, Oct. 6	Saltillo, Mexico	208
1944, July 6	High Bluff, TN	35	1972, Oct. 30	Chicago, IL	45
1944, Aug. 4	Near Stockton, GA	47	1974, Aug. 30	Zagreb, Yugoslavia	153
1944, Sept. 14	Dewey, IN	29	1975, Feb. 28	Subway train, London, England	41
1944, Dec. 31	Bagley, UT	50	1977, Jan. 18	Granville, Australia	83
1945, Aug. 9	Michigan, ND	34	1981, June 6	Bihar, India	800+
1946, Mar. 20	Aracaju, Mexico	185	1982, Jan. 27	El Asnam, Algeria	130
1946, Apr. 25	Naperville, IL	45	1982, July 11	Tepic, Mexico	120
1947, Feb. 18	Gallitzin, PA	24	1983, Feb. 19	Empalme, Mexico	100
1949, Oct. 22	Near Dwor, Poland	200+	1985, Feb. 23	Madhya Pradesh state, India	50
1950, Feb. 17	Rockville Centre, NY	31	1987, July 2	Kasumbalesha Shaba, Zaire	125
1950, Sept. 11	Coshocton, OH	33	1988, June 27	Gare de Lyon train station, Paris	57
1950, Nov. 22	Richmond Hill, NY	79	1988, Dec. 12	London, England	35
1951, Feb. 6	Woodbridge, NJ	84	1989, Jan. 15	Maizdi Khan, Bangladesh	110+
1952, Mar. 4	Near Rio de Janeiro, Brazil	119	1989, June 9	Train collided with bus, S Russia	31
1952, July 9	Rzepin, Poland	160	1990, Jan. 4	Sindh Province, Pakistan	210+
1952, Oct. 8	Harrow, England	112	1993, Sept. 22	Big Bayou Conot, AL	47
1953, Mar. 27	Conneaut, OH	21	1994, Mar. 8	Near Durban, South Africa	63
1953, Dec. 24	Tangiwai, New Zealand	151	1994, Sept. 22	Tolunda, Angola	300
1955, Apr. 3	Guadalajara, Mexico	300	1995, Aug. 20	Firozabad, India	358
1956, Jan. 22	Los Angeles, CA	30	1997, Mar. 3	Punjab Province, Pakistan	125

Date	Location	Deaths	Date	Location	Deaths
1997, Apr. 29	Rongjiawan, China	58	2003, Feb. 1	NW Zimbabwe	46
1997, May 4	Rwandan refugees on overcrowded trains, Kisangani, Zaire	100+	2003, May 8	Near Lake Balaton, Hungary	33
			2003, May 15	Ludhiana, India	36
1997, Sept. 14	Madhya Pradesh state, India	77	2003, June 3	Albacete Province, Spain	19
1998, Feb. 19	Yaounde, Cameroon	100+	2003, June 22	Rajapur, India	33
1998, June 3	Eschede, Germany	102	2003, July 2	Andhra Pradesh state, India	22
1998, Nov. 26	Khanna, India	200+	2004, Feb. 18	Neyshabur, NE Iran	300+
1998, Mar. 15	Bourbonnais, IL	11	2004, Apr. 22	Ryongchon, North Korea	161
1999, Mar. 24	Nairobi, Kenya	32+	2004, July 22	Mekece, NW Turkey	36
1999, Aug. 2	Gauhati, India	285+	2005, Jan. 26	Glendale, CA	11
1999, Oct. 5	London, England	31	2005, Apr. 25	Near Amagasaki, Japan	107+
2000, Jan. 4	Rena, Norway	35	2005, July 13	3 commuter trains, Ghotki, Pakistan	133
2000, Nov. 11	Kaprun, Austria	155	2005, Oct. 29	Near Veligonda, India	114+
2001, Feb. 28	Great Heck, England	13	2006, Jan. 23	Podgorica, Montenegro	46
2001, June 22	Cochin, India	64	2007, Aug. 2	Nr. Benaleka, Dem. Rep. of Congo	70+
2002, Feb. 20	S of Cairo, Egypt	373	2008, July 16	Near Marsa Matruh, Egypt	37+
2002, May 25	Muamba, Mozambique	196+	2008, Sept. 12	Commuter train collided head-on with freight train, Los Angeles, CA	25
2002, June 24	Igandu, Tanzania	281+			
2002, Sept. 10	Bihar, India	118	2009, June 22	Moving DC Metro train collided with stationary train nr. Takoma Park, MD	9
2002, Nov. 6	Nancy, France	12			
2003, Jan. 3	Maharashtra, India	18			

Some Notable U.S. Tornadoes Since 1925

Date	Location	Deaths	Date	Location	Deaths
1925, Mar. 18	MO, IL, IN	689	1971, Feb. 21	Mississippi Delta: MS, LA, AR, TN	110
1927, Apr. 12	Rocksprings, TX	74	1973, May 26-27	South, Midwest	47
1927, May 9	AR; Poplar Bluff, MO	92	1974, Apr. 3-4	AL; GA; KY; Xenia, OH; other states	315
1927, Sept. 29	St. Louis, MO	90	1977, Apr. 4	AL, MS, GA	22
1930, May 6	Hill, Navarro, Ellis Cos., TX	41	1979, Apr. 10	TX, OK	60
1932, Mar. 21	Alabama	268	1984, Mar. 28	NC, SC	57
1936, Apr. 5-6	Tupelo, MS; Gainesville, GA	454	1985, May 31	NY; PA; OH; Ontario, Can	75
1938, Sept. 29	Charleston, SC	32	1987, May 22	Saragosa, TX	30
1942, Mar. 16	Central to NE Mississippi	75	1989, Nov. 15	Huntsville, AL	18
1942, Apr. 27	Rogers and Mayes Cos., OK	52	1990, Aug. 28	Northern IL	25
1944, June 23	OH, PA, WV, MD	150	1991, Apr. 26	KS, OK	23
1945, Apr. 12	OK, AR	102	1992, Nov. 21-23	South, Midwest	26
1947, Apr. 9	TX; Woodward, OK; KS	181	1994, Mar. 27-28	AL, TN, GA, NC, SC	52
1948, Mar. 19	Bunker Hill and Gillespie, IL	33	1995, May 6-7	S Oklahoma, N Texas	23
1949, Jan. 3	LA, AR	58	1997, Mar. 1	Central AR	26
1952, Mar. 21-22	AR, MO, TN	208	1997, May 27	Jarrell, TX	27
1953, May 11	Waco, TX	114	1998, Feb. 22-23	Central FL	42
1953, June 8	Flint-Beecher, MI; OH	142	1998, Apr. 8	AL, GA, MS	39
1953, June 9	Worcester and vicinity, MA	90	1999, May 3	OK, KS	54
1953, Dec. 5	Vicksburg, MS	38	2000, Feb. 14	SW Georgia	22+
1955, May 25	Udall, KS; MO; Blackwell, OK; TX	115	2000, Dec. 16	Alabama	12
1957, May 20	KS, MO	48	2001, Nov. 23-24	AL, AR, MS	13
1958, June, 4	NW Wisconsin	30	2002, Nov. 10-11	AL, MS, TN, IN, OH, PA	36
1959, Feb. 10	St. Louis, MO	21	2003, May 4-11	TN, MO, KS, IL, OK, WV, AL	48
1960, May 5-6	Southeastern OK, AR	30	2005, Nov. 6	KY, IN	22
1962, Mar. 31	Milton, FL	17	2006, Apr. 7-8	Central U.S., TX to WV	12
1965, Apr. 11	IA, IN, IL, OH, MI, WI	271	2007, Mar. 1	AL, GA, MO, Midwest	20
1966, Mar. 3	Jackson, MS	57	2007, May 4	Greensburg, KS	11
1966, Mar. 3	MS, AL	61	2008, Feb. 25	"Super Tuesday" outbreak, TN, AR, KY, AL, MO	57
1967, Apr. 21	IL, MO, IA, MI	33			
1968, May 15	Midwest	71	2008, May 10	MS, OK, GA	23
1969, Jan. 23	Mississippi	32	2009, Feb. 10	Lone Grove and Ardmore, OK	9
1970, May 11	Lubbock, TX	23			

Principal U.S. Mine Disasters Since 1900

Source: Bureau of Mines, U.S. Dept. of the Interior; Mine Safety and Health Admin., U.S. Dept. of Labor; World Almanac research
All are bituminous-coal mines unless otherwise noted.

Date	Location	Deaths	Date	Location	Deaths	Date	Location	Deaths
1900, May 1	Scofield, UT	200	1913, Oct. 22	Dawson, NM	263	1940, Jan. 10	Bartley, WV	91
1902, May 19	Coal Creek, TN	184	1914, Apr. 28	Eccles, WV	181	1940, Mar. 16	St. Clairesville, OH	72
1902, July 10	Johnstown, PA	112	1915, Mar. 2	Layland, WV	115	1942, Mar. 26	Allentown, PA[3]	31
1903, June 30	Hanna, WY	169	1917, Apr. 27	Hastings, CO	121	1943, Feb. 27	Washoe, MT	74
1904, Jan. 25	Cheswick, PA	179	1917, June 8	Butte, MT[1]	163	1947, Mar. 25	Centralia, IL	111
1905, Feb. 20	Virginia City, AL	112	1919, June 5	Wilkes-Barre, PA[2]	92	1951, Dec. 21	West Frankfort, IL	119
1907, Jan. 29	Stuart, WV	84	1922, Nov. 6	Spangler, PA	77	1968, Mar. 6	Belle Isle, LA[4]	21
1907, Dec. 6	Monongah, WV	362	1922, Nov. 22	Dolomite, AL	90	1968, Nov. 20	Farmington, WV	78
1907, Dec. 19	Jacobs Creek, PA	239	1923, Feb. 8	Dawson, NM	120	1972, May 2	Kellogg, ID[1]	91
1908, Nov. 28	Marianna, PA	154	1923, Aug. 14	Kemmerer, WY	99	1976, Mar. 9	Oven Fork, KY	15
1909, Nov. 13	Cherry, IL	259	1924, Mar. 8	Castle Gate, UT	172	1981, Apr. 15	Redstone, CO	15
1910, Jan. 31	Primero, CO	75	1924, Apr. 28	Benwood, WV	119	1981, Dec. 8	Whitwell, TN	13
1910, May 5	Palos, AL	84	1926, Jan. 13	Wilburton, OK	91	1984, Dec. 19	Orangeville, UT	27
1910, Nov. 8	Delagua, CO	79	1926, Nov. 3	Ishpeming, MI[1]	51	1989, Sept. 13	Wheatcroft, KY	10
1911, Apr. 8	Littleton, AL	128	1927, Apr. 30	Everettville, WV	97	2001, Sept. 23	Brookwood, AL	13
1911, Dec. 9	Briceville, TN	84	1928, May 19	Mather, PA	195	2006, Jan. 2	Sago, WV	12
1912, Mar. 26	Jed, WV	83	1930, Nov. 5	Millfield, OH	82	2007, Aug. 6	Huntington, UT	6[5]
1913, Apr. 23	Finleyville, PA	98						

Note: World's worst mine disaster killed 1,549 workers in Manchuria, Apr. 25, 1942. (1) Metal mine. (2) Anthracite mine. (3) Limestone mine. (4) Salt mine. (5) Trapped after mine collapse; presumed dead. Does not incl. deaths of 3 rescue workers in tunnel collapse.

Some Notable Hurricanes, Typhoons, Blizzards, Other Storms

C.—cyclone; H.—hurricane; TS.—tropical storm; T.—typhoon[1]

Date	Location	Deaths	Date	Location	Deaths
1881, Aug. 24-29	H., GA, SC	700	1987, Nov. 25	T. *Nina*, Philippines	650
1888, Mar. 11-14	Blizzard, eastern U.S.	400	1988, Sept. 10-17	H. *Gilbert*, Carib., Gulf of Mex.	260
1893, Aug. 15-Sept. 2	H., GA, SC	1,000+	1989, Sept. 16-22	H. *Hugo*, Caribbean, SE U.S.	86
1893, Oct. 1	H., LA	1,100+	1990, May 6-11	C. (mult.), SE India	450
1900, Sept. 8	H., Galveston, TX	8,000+	1991, Apr. 30	C., Bangladesh	139,000
1906, Sept. 19-24	H., LA, MS	350	1991, Nov. 5	TS. *Thelma*, flash floods, central	
1906, Sept. 18	T., Hong Kong	10,000+		Philippines	7,000+
1909, Sept. 20	H., LA	350+	1992, Aug. 24-26	H. *Andrew*, southern FL, LA	65
1915, Aug. 16	H., Galveston, TX	275	1993, Mar. 12-14	Blizzard, eastern U.S.	270+
1915, Sept. 29	H., LA	275	1993, June	Monsoon, Bangladesh.	2,000
1919, Sept. 6-14	H., Carib., Florida Keys, Gulf, TX	600+[2]	1994, Nov. 8-18	TS. *Gordon*, Caribbean, FL.	830
1926, Sept. 11-22	H., FL, AL, MS	370+	1995, Oct. 2-4	H. *Opal*, S Mexico, FL, AL.	59
1926, Oct. 20	H., Cuba	600	1995, Nov. 2-3	T. *Angela*, Philippines	600+
1928, Sept. 6-20	H., southern FL.	2,500+	1996, Jan. 7-8	Blizzard, northeast U.S.	100
1930, Sept. 3	H., Dominican Republic	2,000	1996, Aug. 22	Blizzard, Himalayas, N India	239
1935, Aug. 29-Sept. 10	H., Carib., SE U.S.	400+	1996, Aug. 29-Sept. 6	H. *Fran*, Carib., NC, VA, WV.	30
1937, Sept. 2	T., "The Great Typhoon," Hong		1996, Sept. 9	T. *Sally*, S China	114
	Kong	10,000+	1996, Nov. 6	C., Andhra Pradesh, India.	1,000+
1938, Sept. 21	H., "Long Isl. Express," NY; New		1996, Nov. 24-25	Ice storms, TX to MO	26
	England	682	1996, Dec. 25	TS. *Greg*, E Malaysia	100+
1940, Nov. 11-12	Blizzard, NE, Midwest U.S.	144	1997, May 19	C., Bangladesh	108
1942, Oct. 15-16	H., Bengal, India	40,000	1997, Aug. 18-21	T. *Winnie*, Taiwan, E China.	140+
1947, Dec. 26	Blizzard, NYC, N Atl. states	55	1997, Oct. 8-10	H. *Pauline*, SW Mexico	230
1952, Oct. 22	T., Philippines	440	1998, June 9	C., Gujarat, India	1,320
1954, Aug. 30	H. *Carol*, northeastern U.S.	68	1998, Aug.	Monsoon, Bangladesh.	326
1954, Oct. 5-18	H. *Hazel*, E Canada, U.S., Haiti	347	1998, Sept. 21-23	H. *Georges*, Carib., FL, U.S. Gulf	600+
1955, Aug. 7-21	H. *Diane*, eastern U.S.	400	1998, Oct. 27-29	H. *Mitch*, Honduras, Nicaragua,	
1955, Sept. 19	H. *Hilda*, Mexico	200		Guatemala, El Salvador	10,866+
1956, Feb. 1-29	Blizzard, W Europe	1,000	1999, Sept. 4-17	H. *Floyd*, Baha., E seaboard U.S	56
1957, June 25-30	H. *Audrey*, TX to AL	390	1999, Oct. 29	C., E India	9,392
1958, Feb. 15-16	Blizzard, northeastern U.S.	171	1999, Dec. 26-29	Gales, France, Switz., Germany	120
1959, Sept. 17-19	T. *Sarah*, Japan, S. Korea	2,000	2000, Dec. 27	Winter storm, TX, OK, AR	40+
1959, Sept. 26-27	T. *Vera*, Honshu, Japan	4,466	2001, July 30	T. *Toraji*, Taiwan	200
1960, Sept. 4-12	H. *Donna*, Caribbean, E U.S.	148	2001, Nov. 2-5	H. *Michelle*, Cuba, Jamaica.	17
1961, Oct. 31	H. *Hattie*, Brit. Honduras.	400	2001, Nov. 6-12	T. *Lingling*, S Philip., Vietnam	220+
1962, Sept. 1	T. *Wanda*, Hong Kong	130-200	2002, July 1-11	T. *Chata'an*, Micron., Philip., Jap.	70+
1963, May 28-29	Windstorm, Bangladesh	22,000	2002, Aug.-Sept.	T. *Rusa*, N. and S. Korea	115+
1963, Oct. 4-8	H. *Flora*, Caribbean	6,000	2003, Feb. 16-17	Blizzard, E seaboard U.S.	59
1964, June 30	T. *Winnie*, N Philippines	107	2003, Sept. 12	T. *Maemi*, S. Korea	130
1964, Sept. 5	T. *Ruby*, Hong Kong, China	735	2003, Sept. 7-19	H. *Isabel*, NC, VA, E seaboard	40+
1965, May 11-12	Windstorm, Bangladesh	17,000	2003, Dec. 17	C., S India	50
1965, June 1-2	Windstorm, Bangladesh	30,000	2004, Jan. 26-Feb. 4	C. *Elita*, Madagascar.	29
1965, Sept. 7-12	H. *Betsy*, FL, MS, LA	74	2004, Mar. 7-19	C. *Gafilo*, Madagascar.	198
1965, Dec. 15	Windstorm, Bangladesh	10,000	2004, May 19	C., Myanmar	220
1966, June 4-10	H. *Alma*, Honduras, SE U.S.	51	2004, Aug. 12-15	T. *Rananim*, E China	164
1966, Sept. 24-30	H. *Inez*, Carib., FL, Mexico.	293	2004, Aug. 13-14	H. *Charley*, SC	36
1967, July 9	T. *Billie*, SW Japan	347	2004, Aug. 24-Sept. 10	T. *Aere*, China, Taiwan, Philip.	67
1967, Sept. 5-23	H. *Beulah*, Carib., Mex., TX	54	2004, Sept. 5-6	H. *Frances*, Bahamas, Florida.	35
1967, Dec. 12-20	Blizzard, southwest U.S.	51	2004, Sept. 7-16	H. *Ivan*, Barbados, Grenada,	
1968, Nov. 18-23	T. *Nina*, Philippines	63		U.S. Gulf Coast	115
1969, Aug. 17-18	H. *Camille*, MS, LA	256	2004, Sept. 16-26	H. *Jeanne*, Dom. Rep., Haiti, FL	1,500+
1970, Sept. 15	T. *Georgia*, Philippines	300	2005, July 7-11	H. *Dennis*, Jamaica, Haiti, Cuba,	
1970, Oct. 14	T. *Sening*, Philippines.	583		FL	50
1970, Oct. 15	T. *Titang*, Philippines	526	2005, Aug. 25-29	H. *Katrina*, LA, MS, FL, AL, GA.	1,833+[3]
1970, Nov. 13	C., Bay of Bengal, Bangladesh.	300,000	2005, Aug. 31-Sept. 1	T. *Talim*, Taiwan, E China.	129+
1971, Aug. 1	T. *Rose*, Hong Kong	130	2005, Sept. 21-24	H. *Rita*, TX, LA	62[4]
1972, June 19-29	H. *Agnes*, FL to NY.	118	2005, Sept. 21-28	T. *Damrey*, SE Asia; Philippines;	
1972, Dec. 3	T. *Theresa*, Philippines	169		Hainan, China	145
1973, June-Aug.	Monsoon rains, India	1,217	2005, Oct. 4	H. *Stan*, Central Amer., Mex.	1,000+[5]
1974, June 11	TS. *Dinah*, Luzon Isl., Philippines	71	2006, Jul. 14	TS. *Bilis*, SE China	612
1974, July 11	T. *Gilda*, Japan, S. Korea	108	2006, Aug. 10	T. *Saomai*, SE China.	295
1974, Sept. 19-20	H. *Fifi*, Honduras.	2,000	2006, Nov. 30	T. *Durian*, Philippines	450-1,000+
1974, Dec. 25	C. *Tracy*, Darwin, Australia.	65	2007, June 6-7	C. *Gonu*, Oman, Iran.	54[6]
1975, Sept. 13-27	H. *Eloise*, Caribbean, NE U.S.	71	2007, Nov. 15	C. *Sidr*, S Bangladesh.	3,363
1976, May 20	T. *Olga*, floods, Philippines.	215	2008, May 2-3	C. *Nargis*, S Myanmar.	84,500-125,000
1976, Sept. 25-Oct. 2	H. *Liza*, W Mexico.	630	2008, June 20-25	T. *Fengshen*, Philippines, China	233
1978, Oct. 27	T. *Rita*, Philippines	400	2008, Aug. 26-Sept. 1	H. *Gustav*, Haiti, Dom. Rep., U.S.	138
1979, Aug. 30-Sept. 7	H. *David*, Caribbean, E U.S.	1,100	2008, Sept. 1-4	TS. *Hanna*, Haiti	529
1980, Aug. 4-11	H. *Allen*, Caribbean, TX	272	2008, Sept. 7-13	H. *Ike*, Haiti; Cuba; Galveston, TX	164
1981, Nov. 25	T. *Irma*, Luzon Isl., Philippines	176	2009, May 23-26	C. *Alia*, India, Bangladesh	260
1983, June	Monsoon, India.	900	2009, Aug. 7-9	T. *Morakot*, mudslides, Taiwan	700+
1984, Sept. 2	T. *Ike*, S Philippines	1,363	2009, Sept. 23-30	T. *Ketsana*, Philippines, Vietnam,	
1985, May 25	C., Bangladesh.	10,000		Cambodia, Laos	600+
1985, Oct. 26-Nov. 6	T. *Juan*, SE U.S.	97			

(1) What hurricanes are called W of intl. date line and N of equator. (2) Incl. about 500 lost on ships at sea. (3) Official toll as of Aug. 2006 was 1,577 in LA, 238 in MS, 14 in FL, and 2 each in AL and GA. (4) Incl. 55 indirect deaths, among them 20 people, mostly elderly evacuees from a nursing home, whose bus exploded and caught fire outside Dallas. (5) Incl. deaths from floods and landslides generated by heavy rainstorms. (6) First documented super cyclone in Arabian Sea.

"Storm of the Century"

Dates: Mar. 12-14, 1993. **Location:** East Coast, U.S. **Fatalities:** 270+. **Damages:** $5-6 bil.

One of the worst winter storms to strike the eastern U.S. About 90 mil people were subjected to high wind gusts (max. 71-144 mph) and record low temperatures, from 31° in FL to –12°F in VT and ME. Snowfall totals ranged from 4 in. to 56 in. A reported 15 tornadoes struck FL, causing deadly storm surges. For the first time, every major airport on the East Coast experienced closings because of the storm. The National Weather Service estimated that 44 mil acre-ft of water fell as snow during the storm—comparable to the volume of water in the Mississippi R. that flows past New Orleans in 40 days.

Some Notable Floods, Tidal Waves

Date	Location	Deaths	Date	Location	Deaths
1703	Awa, Japan	100,000+	1996, June-July	S China	950+
1889, May 31	Johnstown, PA	2,200+	1996, Aug. 7	Pyrenees Mts., Spain	71
1903, June 15	Heppner, OR	325	1997, Mar.	Ohio R. Valley	35
1911	Chang Jiang R., China	100,000	1997, July	Poland, Czech Republic	98
1913, Mar. 25-27	OH, IN	732	1997, Nov.	Spanish-Portuguese border	31+
1915, Aug. 17	Galveston, TX	275	1997, Nov.	Bardera, Somalia	1,300+
1927, Jan.-July	Mississippi Valley	246+	1998, Jan.	Kenya	86
1928, Mar. 13	Dam collapse, Saugus, CA	450	1998, Feb.	CA to Tijuana, Mexico	30+
1928, Sept. 16	Lake Okeechobee, FL	1,770+	1998, Mar.	SW Pakistan	300+
1931, Aug.	Huang He R., China	3,700,000	1998, July-Aug.	China	4,150
1937, Jan. 22	OH, MS valleys	250	1998, July-Sept.	Bangladesh	1,441
1939	N China	200,000	1998, July 17	Papua New Guinea	3,000
1946, Apr. 1	HI, AK	159	1999, Aug. 1-4	Philippines, SE Asia	188+
1947, Sept. 20	Honshu Isl., Japan	1,900	1999, Sept.-Oct.	NE Mexico	350+
1951, Aug.	Manchuria	1,800	1999, Oct.-Dec.	Central Vietnam	700+
1953, Jan. 31	W Europe	2,000	1999, Feb. 6-11	Botswana	70+
1954, Aug. 17	Farahzad, Iran	2,000	1999, Dec. 15-17	NW Venezuela	9,000+
1955, Oct. 7-12	India, Pakistan	1,700	2000, Feb.-Mar.	Madagascar	150+
1959, Nov. 1	W Mexico	2,000	2000, Feb.-Mar.	Mozambique	700
1959, Dec. 2	Frejus, France	412	2000, Aug. 2	Himachal Pradesh, India	120+
1960, Oct. 10	Bangladesh	6,000	2000, Aug. 2	Bhutan	200+
1960, Oct. 31	Bangladesh	4,000	2000, Sept. 19-30	India, Bangladesh	1,000+
1962, Feb. 17	North Sea coast, Germany	343	2000, Oct. 12-17	France, Brit., Italy, Switz.	35
1962, Sept. 27	Barcelona, Spain	445	2001, Jan.-Feb.	Mozambique	84+
1963, Oct. 9	Dam collapse, Vaiont, Italy	1,800	2001, Aug.-Nov.	S Vietnam, Cambodia	360+
1966, Nov. 3-4	Florence, Venice, Italy	113	2001, Aug. 1-6	Taiwan	100+
1967, Jan. 18-24	E Brazil	894	2001, Aug. 10-12	NE Iran	247
1967, Mar. 19	Rio de Janeiro, Brazil	436	2001, Aug.	N Thailand	170
1967, Nov. 26	Lisbon, Portugal	464	2001, Nov. 9-10	N Algeria	711+
1968, Aug. 7-14	Gujarat state, India	1,000	2001, Dec. 23-31	Rio de Janeiro, Brazil	66
1968, Oct. 7	NE India	780	2002, Jan. 30-Feb. 15	Java Isl., Indonesia	147
1969, Jan. 18-26	Southern CA	100	2002, Feb. 19	La Paz, Bolivia	65
1969, Mar. 17	Mundau Valley, Alagoas, Brazil	218	2002, Apr.-May	E Africa	150+
1969, Aug. 20-22	Western VA	189	2002, Apr.-Aug.	China	800+
1969, Sept. 15	South Korea	250	2002, July-Aug.	India, Nepal, Bangladesh	1,100+
1969, Oct. 1-8	Tunisia	500	2002, Aug.	Russia	110
1970, May 20	Central Romania	160	2002, Aug.	Germany, Hungary, Austria,	
1970, July 22	Himalayas, India	500		Czech Rep.	100+
1971, Feb. 26	Rio de Janeiro, Brazil	130	2003, May 17-27	Sri Lanka	250
1972, Feb. 26	Buffalo Creek, WV	118	2003, Aug.-mid-Sept.	E India	200+
1972, June 9	Rapid City, SD	238	2003, early Nov.	Sumatra, Indonesia	65+
1972, Aug. 7	Luzon Isl., Philippines	454	2003, Dec. 10-		
1972, Aug. 19-31	Pakistan	1,500	Jan. 23, 2004	Sumatra, Indonesia	148
1974, Mar. 29	Tubaro, Brazil	1,000	2003, Dec. 19-		
1974, Aug. 12	Monty-Long, Bangladesh	2,500	Jan. 7, 2004	Central Philippines	200
1976, June 5	Teton Dam collapse, ID	11	2004, Jan. 10-Mar. 8	E Brazil	161
1976, July 31	Big Thompson Canyon, CO	140	2004, Apr. 9-May 11	W Kenya	50
1976, Nov. 17	East Java, Indonesia	136	2004, Apr. 12-16	Djibouti City, Djibouti	53
1977, July 19-20	Johnstown, PA	68	2004, May 23-25	Dom. Republic, Haiti	2,000
1977, Nov. 6	Toccoa, GA	39	2004, June-Sept.	Banglad., India, Myan., Nepal	2,000+
1978, June-Sept.	N India	1,200	2004, June-Sept.	China	500
1979, Jan.-Feb.	Brazil	204	2004, Aug. 8-12	NE Nigeria	65
1979, July 17	Lomblem Isl., Indonesia	539	2004, Nov.-Dec.	Philippines	1,060+
1979, Aug. 11	Morvi, India	15,000	2004, Dec. 26	12 Indian Ocean nations,	226,328[1]
1981, Apr.	N China	550	2005, July 26-Aug. 2	W Maharashtra state, India	1,000+
1981, July	Sichuan, Hubei Prov., China	1,300	2005, Aug. 21-23	Central Eur., espec. Romania	67
1982, Jan. 23	Near Lima, Peru	600	2006, Feb. 17	Leyte Isl., Philippines	1,000
1982, May 12	Guangdong, China	430	2006, July 17	S of Java, Indonesia	530+
1982, Sept. 17-21	El Salvador, Guatemala	1,300+	2007, Aug. 19-27	MN, WI, OH	25
1984, Aug.-Sept.	South Korea	200+	2008, June	IL, IN, WI, MN, MO.	24
1985, July 19	Dam collapse, N Italy	361	2008, Sept.	Eastern Orissa, India	173
1987, Aug.-Sept.	N Bangladesh	1,000+	2008, Oct.	Ghardaia, Algeria	65
1988, Sept.	N India	1,000+	2008, Oct. 14-16	Central America	40
1990, June 14	Shadyside, OH	26	2008, Oct. 24-25	Hadramaut, Mahaura, Yemen	100
1993, July-Aug.	Midwest, U.S.	47	2008, Oct.-Nov.	Central, N Vietnam	80
1995, Jan. 30-Feb. 9	NW Europe	40	2008, Nov. 22-Dec. 3	Santa Catarina, S Brazil	116
1995, July	NE China	1,200	2009, Mar. 27	Jakarta, Indonesia	77+
1995, Aug. 19	SW Morocco	136	2009, Mar.-Apr.	Zambia, Namibia	92
1995, Dec. 25	KwaZulu Natal, South Africa	166	2009, June-July	S China	66
1996, Feb. 17	Biak Isl., Indonesia	105	2009, Sept. 29	Amer. Samoa, Samoa, Tonga	170+
1996, April	Afghanistan	100+			

(1) Based on official estimates assembled by the Intl. Fed. of Red Cross and Red Crescent Societies, including 50,773 missing; as reported Dec. 15, 2005. The nearly 176,300 listed as dead include 128,645 from Indonesia; 31,147 from Sri Lanka; 10,749 from India; and 5,395 from Thailand.

Hurricane Katrina

Dates: Aug. 25-29, 2005. **Location:** FL, LA, MS, AL, other inland states. **Fatalities:** 1,833+. **Damages:** $125 bil.

The costliest storm to date in U.S. history first made landfall in SE Florida, Aug. 25, as a Category 1 hurricane. Katrina brought heavy rains that led to flooding in the FL peninsula. Katrina then weakened slightly, strengthened over the Gulf of Mexico, but was downgraded again to Category 3 status before hitting land south of Buras, LA, on Aug. 29. Despite weakening, Katrina caused massive storm surges measuring up to 25-28 ft. throughout SE Louisiana, S Mississippi, and SW Alabama. These storm surges, combined with strong winds and heavy rainfall, contributed to the failure of New Orleans's levee system Aug. 30. About 80% of the city eventually flooded. Approximately 1 mil were displaced from their homes.

Some Major Earthquakes

Source: Global Volcanism Network, Smithsonian Institution; U.S. Geological Survey, U.S. Dept. of the Interior; World Almanac research

Magnitude of earthquakes (mag.) is measured on the Richter scale; an increase of one whole point represents a release of about 30 times more energy. Adopted in 1935, the scale is applied to earthquakes as far back as reliable seismograms are available, but earlier figures should be considered estimates.

Date	Location	Deaths	Mag.	Date	Location	Deaths	Mag.
526, May 20	Antioch, Syria	250,000	NA	1977, Aug. 19	Indonesia	200	8.0
856	Corinth, Greece	45,000	NA	1978, Sept. 16	NE Iran	15,000	7.8
856, Dec. 22	Damghan, Iran	200,000	NA	1979, Sept. 12	Indonesia	100	8.1
893, Mar. 23	Ardabil, Iran	150,000	NA	1979, Dec. 12	Colombia, Ecuador	800	7.9
1057	Chihli, China	25,000	NA	1980, Oct. 10	NW Algeria	3,500	7.7
1138, Aug. 9	Aleppo, Syria	230,000	NA	1980, Nov. 23	S Italy	3,000	7.2
1169, Feb. 11	Nr. Mt. Etna, Sicily	15,000	NA[1]	1981, June 11	S Iran	3,000	6.9
1268	Silicia, Asia Minor	60,000	NA	1981, July 28	S Iran	1,500	7.3
1290, Sept. 27	Chihli, China	100,000	NA	1982, Dec. 13	W Arabian Peninsula	2,800	6.0
1293, May 20	Kamakura, Japan	30,000	NA	1983, Oct. 30	E Turkey	1,342	6.9
1531, Jan. 26	Lisbon, Portugal	30,000	NA	1985, Mar. 3	Valparaiso, Chile	146	7.8
1556, Jan. 24	Shaanxi, China	830,000	NA	1985, Sept. 19	Michoacan, Mexico	9,500	8.1
1667, Nov.	Shemakha, Caucasia	80,000	NA	1986, Oct. 10	El Salvador	1,000+	5.5
1693, Jan. 11	Catania, Italy	60,000	NA	1987, Mar. 6	Colombia-Ecuador	4,000+	7.0
1737, Oct. 11	India, Calcutta	300,000	NA	1988, Aug. 20	India-Nepal border	1,450	6.6
1755, June 7	N Persia (current-day Iran)	40,000	NA	1988, Nov. 6	China-Burma border	1,000	7.3
1755, Nov. 1	Lisbon, Portugal	60,000	8.75[2]	1988, Dec. 7	Soviet Armenia	55,000	7.0
1783, Feb. 4	Calabria, Italy	30,000	NA	1989, Oct. 17	San Fran. Bay, CA, area	63	6.9
1797, Feb. 4	Quito, Ecuador	41,000	NA	1990, May 30	N Peru	115	6.3
1822, Sept. 5	Asia Minor, Aleppo	22,000	NA	1990, June 20	W Iran	40,000+	7.7
1828, Dec. 28	Echigo, Japan	30,000	NA	1990, July 16	Luzon, Philippines	1,621	7.8
1868, Aug. 13-15	Peru, Ecuador	40,000	NA	1991, Feb. 1	Pakistan-Afgh. border	1,200	6.8
1875, May 16	Venezuela, Colombia	16,000	NA	1991, Oct. 19	N India	2,000	7.0
1886, Aug. 31	Charleston, SC	60	6.6	1992, Mar. 13/15	E Turkey	4,000	6.8/6.0
1896, June 15	Sanriku, Japan (tsunami)	27,120	8.5	1992, June 28	Landers, CA/Big Bear, CA	3	7.3/6.5
1905, Apr. 4	Kangra, India	19,000	8.6	1992, Oct. 12	Cairo, Egypt	450	5.9
1906, Apr. 18-19	San Francisco, CA	3,000+	7.7[3]	1992, Dec. 12	Flores Isl., Indonesia	2,500	7.5
1906, Aug. 17	Valparaiso, Chile	20,000	8.6	1993, July 12	Nr. Hokkaido, Japan	200+	7.7
1907, Oct. 21	Central Asia	12,000	8.1	1993, Sept. 30	Maharashtra, S India	9,748	6.3+
1908, Dec. 28	Messina, Italy	83,000	7.5	1994, Jan. 17	Northridge, CA	61	6.8
1915, Jan. 13	Avezzano, Italy	29,980	7.5	1994, Feb. 15	S Sumatra, Indonesia	215	7.0
1918, Oct. 11	Mona Passage, PR	116	7.5	1994, June 6	Cauca, SW Colombia	1,000	6.8
1920, Dec. 16	Gansu, China	200,000	8.6	1994, Aug. 19	N Algeria	164	6.0
1923, Sept. 1	Yokohama, Japan	143,000	8.3	1995, Jan. 16	Kobe, Japan	5,502	6.9
1925, Mar. 16	Yunnan, China	5,000	7.1	1995, May 27	Sakhalin Isl., Russia	1,989	7.5
1927, May 22	Tsinghai, China	200,000	8.3	1996, Feb. 3	SW China	200+	7.0
1932, Dec. 25	Gansu, China	70,000	7.6	1997, Feb. 27	W Pakistan	100+	7.3
1933, Mar. 2	Sanriku, Japan (tsunami)	2,990	8.4	1997, Feb. 28	NW Iran	1,000+	6.1
1933, Mar. 10	Long Beach, CA	115	6.2	1997, May 10	N Iran	1,560	7.5
1934, Jan. 15	India, Bihar-Nepal	10,700	8.4	1998, Feb. 4, 8	Takhar Prov., NE Afghan.	2,323	6.1
1935, Apr. 21	Hsinchu-Taichung, Taiwan	3,276	7.4	1998, May 30	NE Afghanistan	4,700+	6.9
1935, May 30	Quetta, Pakistan	50,000	7.5	1999, Jan. 25	Armenia, Colombia	1,185+	6.0
1939, Jan. 25	Chillan, Chile	28,000	7.8	1999, Aug. 17	Izmit, W Turkey	17,200+	7.4
1939, Dec. 26	Erzincan, Turkey	30,000	8.0	1999, Sept. 21	Taichung, Taiwan	2,474	7.6
1946, Dec. 20	Honshu, Japan	1,330	8.4	1999, Nov. 12	Duzce, Turkey	675+	7.2
1948, June 28	Fukui, Japan	5,390	7.3	2000, June 4	Sumatra, Indonesia	103	7.9
1948, Oct. 5	Ashgabat, Turkmenistan	110,000	7.3	2001, Jan. 13	San Vicente, El Salvador	800+	7.6
1949, Aug. 5	Pelileo, Ecuador	6,000	6.8	2001, Jan. 26	Gujarat, India	20,000+	7.9
1950, Aug. 15	Assam, India	1,530	8.7	2001, Feb. 13	San Vicente, El Salvador	255	6.6
1953, Mar. 18	NW Turkey	1,200	7.2	2001, June 23	Arequipa, Peru	102	8.1
1956, June 10-17	N Afghanistan	2,000	7.7	2002, Mar. 3	N Afghanistan	166	7.4
1957, July 2	N Iran	1,200	7.4	2002, Mar. 25-26	Nahrin, N Afghanistan	1,000+	6.1
1957, Dec. 13	W Iran	1,130	7.3	2002, Apr. 12	Hindu Kush, Afghanistan	50+	5.9
1960, Feb. 29	Agadir, Morocco	12,000	5.8	2002, June 22	W Iran	261+	6.5
1960, May 21-30	S Chile	5,000	9.5[4]	2003, Feb. 24	S Xinjiang Prov., China	261	6.4
1962, Sept. 1	NW Iran	12,230	7.3	2003, May 1	E Turkey	177	6.4
1963, July 26	Skopje, Yugoslavia	1,100	6.0	2003, May 21	N Algeria	2,200+	6.8
1964, Mar. 27	Prince Wm. Sound, Alaska	131	9.2[5]	2003, Dec. 26	Bam, SE Iran	26,271	6.6
1966, Aug. 19	E Turkey	2,520	7.1	2004, Feb. 24	Al Hoceima, NE Morocco	629	6.4
1968, Aug. 31	NE Iran	12,000	7.3	2004, Dec. 26	Nr. Sumatra, Indonesia	226,328	9.16
1970, Jan. 5	Yunnan Prov., China	15,621	7.7	2005, Feb. 22	Central Iran	549	6.4
1970, Mar. 28	W Turkey	1,100	7.3	2005, Mar. 28	Isls. off Sumatra, Indon.	1,000+	8.7
1970, May 31	N Peru	66,000	7.8	2005, Oct. 8	Kashmir, Pakistan, India	80,000+	7.6
1971, Feb. 9	San Fernando Val., CA	65	6.6	2006, Mar. 31	W Iran	70+	6.1
1972, Apr. 10	S Iran	5,054	7.1	2006, May 27	Java, Indonesia	6,200+	6.3
1972, Dec. 23	Managua, Nicaragua	5,000	6.2	2006, July 17	S of Java, Indonesia	530+	7.7
1974, Dec. 28	N Pakistan	5,200	6.3	2007, Mar. 6	S Sumatra, Indonesia	70	6.4
1975, Sept. 6	E Turkey	2,300	6.7	2007, Aug. 15	Nr. coast of central Peru	519	8.0
1976, Feb. 4	Guatemala	23,000	7.5	2008, May 12	E Sichuan Prov., China	87,857	7.9
1976, May 6	NE Italy	1,000	6.5	2008, Oct. 5	Kyrgyzstan	74	6.7
1976, June 25	Irian Jaya, New Guinea	422	7.1	2008, Oct. 28	Pakistan	166	6.4
1976, July 28	Tangshan, China	255,000	7.5	2009, Jan. 8	Costa Rica	40	6.1
1976, Aug. 16	Mindanao, Philippines	8,000	7.8	2009, Apr. 6	Central Italy	295	6.3
1976, Nov. 24	NW Iran-USSR border	5,000	7.3	2009, Sept. 2	Java, Indonesia	47	7.0
1977, Mar. 4	Romania	1,500	7.2	2009, Sept. 30	Sumatra, Indonesia	777	7.6

NA = Not available. (1) Once thought to have been a volcanic eruption; evidence indicates a destructive earthquake and tsunami occurred on this date. (2) This earthquake caused the most deadly tsunami to date in the Atlantic Ocean. (3) Incl. deaths from resulting fires; revised estimates of magnitude range from 7.7 to 7.9. (4) The largest recorded earthquake; caused a deadly tsunami that spread across the Pacific Ocean as far as Japan. (5) The "Good Friday" earthquake sent a tsunami that hit British Columbia, Canada, and the U.S. Pacific coast. (6) This undersea earthquake triggered devastating tsunamis that hit 12 Indian Ocean nations. See listing above under Floods; see also Nations of the World.

Some Notable Fires Since 1930

See also Some Notable Explosions Since 1920.

Date	Location	Deaths	Date	Location	Deaths
1930, Apr. 21	Penitentiary, Columbus, OH	320	1981, Feb. 14	Discotheque, Dublin, Ireland	44
1931, July 24	Home for aged, Pittsburgh, PA	48	1982, Nov. 8	County jail, Biloxi, MS	29
1934, Dec. 11	Hotel Kerns, Lansing, MI.	34	1983, Feb. 13	Movie theater, Turin, Italy	64
1938, May 16	Terminal Hotel, Atlanta, GA	35	1983, Dec. 17	Discotheque, Madrid, Spain.	83
1940, Apr. 23	Nightclub, Natchez, MS.	198	1984, May 11	Great Adventure Amusement Pk., NJ	8
1942, Nov. 28	Cocoanut Grove Nightclub, Boston, MA	492	1985, Apr. 21	Movie theaters, Tabaco, Philippines	44
1942, Dec. 12	Hostel, St. John's, NL, Canada.	100	1985, Apr. 26	Hospital, Buenos Aires, Argentina	79
1943, Sept. 7	Gulf Hotel, Houston, TX	55	1985, May 11	Soccer stadium, Bradford, England	53
1944, July 6	Ringling Circus, Hartford, CT	168	1985, May 13	MOVE headquarters, row houses, Philadelphia, PA	11
1946, June 5	LaSalle Hotel, Chicago, IL.	61			
1946, Dec. 7	Winecoff Hotel, Atlanta, GA	119	1986, Dec. 31	Dupont Plaza Hotel, Puerto Rico	96
1946, Dec. 12	Ice plant, tenement, New York, NY	37	1987, May 6–		
1949, Apr. 5	Hospital, Effingham, IL	77	June 2	Forest fire, N China	193
1950, Jan. 7	Mercy Hospital, Davenport, IA	41	1987, Nov. 17	Subway, London, England.	30
1953, Mar. 29	Nursing home, Largo, FL	35	1988, Mar. 20	2000 buildings, Lashio, Burma	134
1953, Apr. 16	Metalworking plant, Chicago, IL	35	1990, Mar. 25	Social club, Bronx, NY	87
1957, Feb. 17	Home for aged, Warrenton, MO	72	1991, Mar. 3	Munitions dump, Addis Ababa, Ethiopia	260+
1958, Mar. 19	Loft building, New York, NY	24	1991, Sept. 3	Processing plant, Hamlet, NC	25
1958, Dec. 1	Parochial school, Chicago, IL	95	1991, Oct. 20-21	Wildfire, Oakland, Berkeley, CA	24
1958, Dec. 16	Store, Bogotá, Colombia.	83	1993, Apr. 19	Cult compound, Waco, TX.	72
1959, June 23	Resort hotel, Stalheim, Norway.	34	1994, May 10	Toy factory, Bangkok, Thailand	213
1960, Mar. 12	Chemical plant, Pusan, Korea.	68	1994, July 4-10	(Firefighters) Glenwood Springs, CO.	14
1960, July 14	Mental hospital, Guatemala City	225	1994, Nov. 2	Burning fuel flood, Durunka, Egypt	500
1960, Nov. 13	Movie theater, Amude, Syria.	152	1994, Dec. 10	Theater, Karamay, China.	300
1960, Dec. 19	USS *Constellation*, Brooklyn, NY	49	1995, Oct. 28	Subway train, Baku, Azerbaijan.	300
1961, Jan. 6	Thomas Hotel, San Francisco, CA	20	1995, Dec. 23	School, Mandi Dabwali, India	500+
1961, Dec. 17	Circus, Niteroi, Brazil.	323	1996, Mar. 19	Nightclub, Quezon City, Philippines	150+
1963, May 4	Theater, Diourbel, Senegal.	64	1996, Mar. 28	Shopping mall, Bogor, Indonesia.	78
1963, Nov. 18	Surfside Hotel, Atlantic City, NJ	25	1996, Nov. 20	Building, Hong Kong	39
1963, Nov. 23	Rest home, Fitchville, OH.	63	1997, Feb. 23	Worship site, Baripada, India.	164
1963, Dec. 29	Roosevelt Hotel, Jacksonville, FL.	22	1997, Apr. 15	Encampment, Mina, Saudi Arabia	343
1964, May 8	Apt. bldg., Manila, Philippines.	30	1997, June 7	Temple, Thanjavur, India.	60+
1964, Dec. 18	Nursing home, Fountaintown, IN.	20	1997, June 13	Movie theater, New Delhi, India.	60
1965, Mar. 1	Apartment, LaSalle, Quebec. Can.	28	1997, July 11	Hotel, Pattaya, Thailand	90
1965, Aug. 11-16	Watts riot fires, Los Angeles, CA	30+	1997, Sept. 29	Children's home, nr. Colina, Chile	30
1966, Mar. 11	2 ski resorts, Numata, Japan	31	1998, Dec. 3	Orphanage, Manila, Philippines.	28
1966, Oct. 17	Bldg. (firefighters), New York, NY	12	1999, Mar. 24	Mt. Blanc Tunnel, France and Italy	40
1966, Dec. 7	Barracks, Erzurum, Turkey	68	1999, Oct. 30	Karaoke salon, Inchon, S. Korea	55+
1967, Feb. 7	Restaurant, Montgomery, AL	25	2000, Mar. 17	Church, Kanungu, Uganda	530
1967, May 22	Store, Brussels, Belgium.	322	2000, Oct. 20	Nightclub, Mexico City, Mexico	20
1967, July 16	State prison, Jay, FL.	37	2000, Nov. 11	Cable car, Kaprun, Austria.	155
1967, July 29	USS *Forrestal*, off N Vietnam	134	2000, Dec. 25	Shopping center, Luoyang, China	309
1968, May 11	Wedding hall, Vijayawada, India	58	2001, Mar. 6	School, Central China	41
1969, Dec. 2	Nursing home, Notre Dame, Can.	54	2001, Mar. 26	School, Machakos, Kenya	64
1970, Jan. 9	Nursing home, Marietta, OH	27	2001, Aug. 18	Hotel, Quezon City, Philippines	73
1970, Nov. 1	Dance hall, Grenoble, France	145	2001, Sept. 1	Nightclub, Tokyo, Japan	44
1970, Dec. 20	Hotel, Tucson, AZ	28	2001, Dec. 29	Fireworks accident, Lima, Peru	291
1971, Dec., 25	Hotel, Seoul, South Korea.	162	2002, Mar. 11	Girls' school, Mecca, Saudi Arabia	15
1972, May 13	Nightclub, Osaka, Japan.	116	2002, June 16	Internet cafe, Beijing, China.	24
1972, July 5	Hospital, Sherborne, England	30	2002, July 7	Coal mine, Donetsk region, Ukraine	34+
1973, June 24	Bar, New Orleans, LA	32	2002, July 20	Disco, Lima, Peru	25+
1973, Aug. 3	Amusement park, Isle of Man, Eng.	51	2002, July 31	Coal mine, Donetsk region, Ukraine	20
1973, Sept. 1	Hotel, Copenhagen, Denmark.	35	2003, Feb. 18	Subway train, Taegu, S. Korea	198
1973, Nov. 29	Dept. store, Kumamoto, Japan.	107	2003, Feb. 20	Pyrotechnics in nightclub, Warwick, RI	100
1973, Dec. 2	Theater, Seoul, South Korea.	50	2003, Sept. 15	Prison, Riyadh, Saudi Arabia.	94
1974, Feb. 1	Bank building, São Paulo, Brazil.	189	2003, Nov. 24	Students' hostel, Moscow, Russia	36
1974, June 30	Discotheque, Port Chester, NY	24	2004, May 17	Prison, San Pedro Sula, Honduras	104
1974, Nov. 3	Hotel, disco, Seoul, S. Korea	88	2004, July 16	Pvt. school, Kumbakonam, India	80+
1975, Dec. 12	Tent city, Mina, Saudi Arabia	138	2004, Aug. 1	Market, Asunción, Paraguay	400+
1976, Oct. 24	Social club, Bronx, NY	25	2004, Dec. 30	Club, Buenos Aires, Argentina.	194
1977, Feb. 25	Rossiya hotel, Moscow, Russia	45	2005, Feb. 14	Mosque, Tehran, Iran	59
1977, May 28	Nightclub, Southgate, KY	164	2005, Mar. 7	Prison, Higuey, Dom. Republic	159
1977, June 9	Nightclub, Abidjan, Ivory Coast.	41	2005, Apr. 15	Hotel, Paris, France	22
1977, June 26	Jail, Columbia, TN.	42	2005, Sept. 5	Theater, Beni Suef, Egypt	32
1977, Nov. 14	Hotel, Manila, Philippines	47	2006, Dec. 9	Drug treatment center, Moscow, Russia	45
1978, Jan. 28	Coates House Hotel, Kansas City, MO.	16	2007, Mar. 20	Nursing home for elderly and disabled, Kamyshevatskaya, Russia.	62
1978, Aug. 19	Movie theater, Abadan, Iran	425+			
1979, July 14	Hotel, Saragossa, Spain	80	2007, Aug. 24–		
1979, Dec. 31	Social club, Chapais, Quebec, Can.	42	Sept. 2	Wildfires (arson), Greece.	65
1980, May 20	Nursing home, Kingston, Jamaica	157	2008, Apr. 26	Factory fire, Casablanca, Morocco	55
1980, Nov. 21	MGM Grand Hotel, Las Vegas, NV.	84	2008, Sept.	Wildfires, Mozambique, S Africa, Swaziland	89
1980, Dec. 4	Stouffer Inn, Harrison, NY.	26	2009, Jan.-Feb.	Wildfires (arson), Victoria, Australia.	210
1981, Jan. 9	Boarding home, Keansburg, NJ	30			
1981, Feb. 10	Las Vegas Hilton, Las Vegas, NV	8			

Cocoanut Grove Nightclub Fire

Date: Nov. 28, 1942. **Location:** Boston, MA. **Fatalities:** 492.

More than 1,000 people were packed into the popular Cocoanut Grove nightclub one Saturday night when a lit match accidentally set an artificial palm tree ablaze. The fire quickly spread from a downstairs lounge through the rest of the nightclub, which was furnished with highly flammable material. The crowds—larger than should have been allowed in the club—panicked and mobbed the exits that weren't locked. Hundreds were trampled or were consumed by the conflagration. The survivors suffered burns, smoke inhalation, and other injuries.

Some Notable Explosions Since 1920

See also Principal U.S. Mine Disasters Since 1900. Some bombings related to political conflicts and terrorism are not included.

Date	Location	Deaths	Date	Location	Deaths
1920, Sept. 16	Wall Street, New York, NY	30	1996, Nov. 21	Propane gas leak in bldg., San Juan, Puerto Rico	33
1921, Sept. 21	Chem. storage facility, Oppau, Ger.	561	1996, Nov. 27	Coal mine, Shanxi Prov., China	91+
1924, Jan. 3	Food plant, Pekin, IL	42	1996, Dec. 30	Train, Assam, India	59+
1927, May 18	Bath school, Lansing, MI	38	1997, Jan. 18	Nr. courthouse, Lahore, Pakistan	25
1928, April 13	Dance hall, West Plains, MO	40	1997, July 8	Train, Punjab, India	36
1937, Mar. 18	School, New London, TX	311	1997, Nov. 19	Car, Hyderabad, India	23
1940, Sept. 12	Hercules Powder factory, Kenvil, NJ	55	1997, Dec. 2	Coal mine, Novokuznetsk, Siberia	68
1942, June 5	Ordnance plant, Elwood, IL	49	1998, Jan. 17	Coal mine, Sokobanja, Serbia	29
1944, Apr. 14	Harbor, Bombay, India	700	1998, Feb. 14	2 oil tankers, Yaounde, Cameroon	120
1944, July 17	Munitions ships, depot, Port Chicago, CA	322	1998, Feb. 14	17 bombs, Coimbatore, India	50
1944, Oct. 21	Liquid gas plant, Cleveland, OH	135	1998, Mar. 5	Bus, Colombo, Sri Lanka	32
1947, Apr. 16	Freighter, chemical co. plant, Texas City, TX	576	1998, Apr. 4	Coal mine, Donetsk, Ukraine	63
1948, July 28	Farben works, Ludwigshafen, Ger.	184	1998, Aug. 7	Bomb, U.S. emb., Nairobi, Kenya	213
1950, May 19	Munitions barges, S. Amboy, NJ	30		Bomb, U.S. emb., Dar-es-Salaam, Tanz.	11
1954, May 26	USS Bennington, off RI	103	1998, Aug. 15	Car bomb, Omagh, Ireland	29
1956, Aug. 7	Dynamite trucks, Cali, Colombia	1,100	1998, Sept. 8	Two buses, São Paulo, Brazil	59
1958, Apr. 18	Sunken munitions plant, Okinawa, Japan	40	1998, Oct. 17	Oil pipeline, Jesse, Nigeria	700+
1958, May 22	Nike missiles, Leonardo, NJ	10	1999, May 16	Fuel truck, Punjab Prov., Pakistan	75
1959, Apr. 10	WWII bomb, Philippines	38	1999, Sept. 10	Apartment building, Moscow, Russia	94
1959, June 28	Rail tank cars, Meldrim, GA	25	1999, Sept. 13	Apartment building, Moscow, Russia	118
1959, Aug. 7	Dynamite truck, Roseburg, OR	13	1999, Sept. 16	Apartment building, Moscow, Russia	18
1959, Nov. 2	Explosives, Jamuri Bazar, India	46	1999, Sept. 26	Fireworks factory, Celaya, Mexico	56
1959, Dec. 13	2 apt. bldgs., Dortmund, Ger.	26	2000, Feb. 25	Bombs on 2 buses, Ozamis, Philippines	41
1960, Mar. 4	Belgian munitions ship, Havana, Cuba	100	2000, Mar. 11	Coal mine, Krasnodon, Ukraine	80
1962, Oct. 3	Telephone Co. office, New York, NY	23	2000, Apr. 16	Airport hangar, Dem. Rep. of Congo	100+
1963, Jan. 2	Packing plant, Terre Haute, IN	17	2000, July 16	Oil pipeline, Warri, Nigeria	30
1963, Mar. 9	Dynamite plant, S. Africa	45	2000, Sept. 9	Truck explosion, Urumqi, China	60
1963, Aug. 13	Explosives dump, Gauhaiti, India	32	2000, Oct. 12	U.S. destroyer, Yemen	17
1963, Oct. 31	State Fair Coliseum, Indianapolis, IN	73	2001, Mar. 6	School, Wanzai Co., China	41
1964, July 23	Harbor munitions, Bone, Algeria	100	2001, Apr. 21	Coal mine, Shaanxi, China	51
1965, Aug. 9	Missile silo, Searcy, AR	53	2001, June 1	Dance club, Tel Aviv, Israel	21
1965, Oct. 21	Bridge, Tila Bund, Pakistan	80	2001, July 17	Coal mine, Guanxi, China	76+
1965, Nov. 24	Armory, Keokuk, IA	20	2001, Aug. 19	Coal mine, Donetsk region, Ukraine	52
1967, Dec. 25	Apartment bldg., Moscow, USSR	20	2001, Sept. 21	Chem. plant, Toulouse, France	29
1968, Apr. 6	Sports store, Richmond, IN	43	2002, Jan. 21	Volcanic lava caused gas station blast, Goma, Dem. Rep. of Congo	50+
1969, Mar. 31	Coal mine, nr. Barroteran, Mexico	180	2002, Jan. 27	Munitions dump, Lagos, Nigeria	1,000+
1970, Apr. 8	Subway construction, Osaka, Japan	73	2002, Apr. 11	Truck nr. synagogue, Djerba, Tunisia	17
1971, June 24	Tunnel, Sylmar, CA	17	2002, Apr. 21	Bomb, dept. store, Mindanao, Philip.	14
1973, Feb., 10	Liquid gas tank, Staten Island, NY	40	2002, May 8	Bomb on bus outside hotel, Karachi, Pak.	14
1975, Dec. 27	Coal mine, Chasnala, India	431	2002, May 9	Land mine at parade, Kaspiisk, Russia	34+
1976, Apr. 13	Munitions works, Lapua, Finland	40	2002, June 14	Car bomb outside U.S. consulate, Karachi, Pakistan	12
1977, Nov. 11	Freight train, Iri, S. Korea	57	2002, June 18	Bomb on bus, Jerusalem, Israel	20
1977, Dec. 22	Grain elevator, Westwego, LA	35	2002, July 5	Bomb in market, Larba, Algeria	35+
1978, Feb. 24	Derailed tank car, Waverly, TN	12	2002, Aug. 9	Explosion, Jalalabad, Afghanistan	25+
1978, July 11	Propylene tank truck, Tarragona, Spain	150	2002, Sept. 5	Car bomb, Kabul, Afghanistan	30
1980, Oct. 23	School, Ortuella, Spain	64	2002, Oct. 12	Nightclub bombings, Bali, Indonesia	202
1982, Apr. 25	Antiques exhibition, Todi, Italy	33	2003, Aug. 25	Bombs in 2 taxis, Mumbai, India	52
1982, Nov. 2	Salang Tunnel, Afghanistan	1,000+	2003, Dec. 5	Bomb on train, Yessentuki, Russia	45
1984, Feb. 25	Oil pipeline, Cubatao, Brazil	508	2003, Dec. 23	Gas well explosion, Chongqing, China	233
1984, June 21	Naval supply depot, Severomorsk, USSR	200+	2004, Jan. 19	Natural gas facility, Skikda, Algeria	27
1984, Nov. 19	Gas storage area, NE Mexico City	334	2004, Feb. 6	Bomb on subway car, Moscow, Russia	39
1984, Dec. 3	Chemical plant, Bhopal, India	3,849	2004, Mar. 11	Bombs on commuter trains, Madrid, Spain	191
1984, Dec. 5	Coal mine, Taipei, Taiwan	94	2004, July 19	Coal mine, Ukraine	31
1985, June 25	Fireworks factory, Hallett, OK	21	2005, Feb. 14	Coal mine, NE China	214
1988, Apr. 10	Army ammunitions dump nr. Rawalpindi and Islamabad, Pakistan	100	2005, Mar. 23	Oil refinery, Texas City, TX	15
1988, July 6	Oil rig, North Sea off NE Scotland	167	2005, May 2	Arms cache, Baghlan Prov., Afghan.	34+
1989, June 3	Gas pipeline, between Ufa, Asha, USSR	650+	2005, July 7	Bombs in mass transit, London, Eng.	56
1992, Mar. 3	Coal mine, Kozlu, Turkey	270+	2005, Oct. 1	Bombings of restaurants, Bali, Indonesia	26
1992, Apr. 22	Gas leak in sewers, Guadalajara, Mexico	200+	2005, Nov. 27	Coal mine, NE China	161+
1992, May 9	Coal mine, Plymouth, Nova Scotia	26	2006, May 12	Oil pipeline, nr. Lagos, Nigeria	200
1993, Feb. 26	World Trade Center, New York, NY	6	2006, July 1	Bombings of trains, station, Mumbai, India	207
1994, July 18	Jewish com. center, Buenos Aires, Arg.	100	2007, Mar. 19	Coal mine, Siberia, Russia	108
1995, Apr. 19	Fed. office building, Oklahoma City, OK	168	2007, Mar. 22	Natl. weapons depot, Maputo, Mozambique	117
1995, Apr. 29	Subway construction, S. Korea	110	2007, June 9	Oil pipeline, Pyongan Prov., N. Korea	110
1995, Nov. 13	Military facility, Riyadh, Saudi Arabia	7	2007, Nov. 18	Methane gas buildup in coal mine, E Ukraine	90
1996, Jan. 31	Bank, Colombo, Sri Lanka	53	2008, May 15	Pipeline explosion in Lagos, Nigeria	100+
1996, Mar. 3-4	Jerusalem and Tel Aviv, Israel	33	2008, Sept. 20	Truck bomb outside hotel, Islamabad, Pakistan	40+
1996, June 25	U.S. military housing complex, nr. Dhahran, Saudi Arabia	19	2009, Feb. 22	Coal mine explosion, N China	74
1996, July 24	Train, Colombo, Sri Lanka	86			
1996, Nov. 16	Military apt., Dagestan region, Russia	68			

Bhopal Industrial Disaster

Date: Dec. 3, 1984. **Location:** Bhopal, India. **Fatalities:** 16,000 (est.). **Damages:** $470 mil+.

Tons of toxic methyl isocyanate gas leaked from a defective storage tank at a Union Carbide pesticide plant in Bhopal, central India. Between 2,000 and 3,000—many of them residents of slums adjacent to the plant—died shortly thereafter. About 50,000 were treated for severe injuries to their eyes, lungs, and kidneys. An estimated 15,000-20,000 may have subsequently died from exposure to the lethal gas. In 1989, Union Carbide settled a lawsuit by agreeing to provide $470 mil in compensation. Bhopal residents still contend with the effects of the disaster, including health problems and contaminated groundwater.

Notable Nuclear Accidents

Oct. 7, 1957—Fire in the Windscale plutonium production reactor N of Liverpool, England, released radioactive material; later blamed for 39 cancer deaths.

Jan. 3, 1961—Reactor explosion at a federal installation near Idaho Falls, ID, killed 3 workers. Radiation contained.

Oct. 5, 1966—Sodium cooling system malfunction caused a partial core meltdown at the Enrico Fermi demonstration breeder reactor, near Detroit, MI. Radiation contained.

Jan. 21, 1969—Coolant malfunction from an experimental underground reactor at Lucens Vad, Switzerland, released radiation into a cavern, which was then sealed.

Mar. 22, 1975—Fire at the Brown's Ferry reactor in Decatur, AL, caused dangerous lowering of cooling water levels.

Mar. 28, 1979—Worst commercial nuclear accident in the U.S. occurred as equipment failures and human mistakes led to a loss of coolant and a partial core meltdown at the Three Mile Island reactor in Middletown, PA.

Feb. 11, 1981—8 workers were contaminated when 100,000 gallons of radioactive coolant fluid leaked into containment building of TVA's Sequoyah 1 plant near Chattanooga, TN.

Apr. 25, 1981—Some 100 workers were exposed to radiation during repairs of a nuclear plant at Tsuruga, Japan.

Jan. 6, 1986—Cylinder of nuclear material burst after being improperly heated at a Kerr-McGee plant at Gore, OK. One worker died; 100 were hospitalized.

Apr. 26, 1986—In the worst nuclear accident in the history of nuclear power, fires and explosions resulting from an unauthorized experiment at the Chernobyl nuclear power plant near Kiev, USSR (now in Ukraine), left at least 31 dead in the immediate aftermath and spread radioactive material over much of Europe. An estimated 135,000 people were evacuated from the region, some of which was uninhabitable for years. As a result of the radiation released, tens of thousands of excess cancer deaths (as well as increased birth defects) were expected.

Sept. 30, 1999—Japan's worst nuclear accident ever occurred at a uranium-reprocessing facility in Tokaimura, NE of Tokyo, when workers accidentally overloaded a container with uranium, thereby exposing workers and area residents to extremely high radiation levels.

Record Oil Spills

The number of tons can be multiplied by 7 to estimate roughly the number of barrels spilled; the exact number of barrels in a ton varies with the type of oil. Each barrel contains 42 gallons.

Name, location	Date	Cause	Tons
Ixtoc I oil well, S Gulf of Mexico	June 3, 1979	Blowout	600,000
Nowruz oil field, Persian Gulf	Feb. 1983	Blowout	600,000 (est.)
Atlantic Empress and *Aegean Captain*, off Trinidad and Tobago	July 19, 1979	Collision	300,000
ABT Summer, off Angola	May 28, 1991	Explosion	260,000
Castillo de Bellver, off Cape Town, South Africa	Aug. 6, 1983	Fire	250,000
Amoco Cadiz, near Portsall, France	Mar. 16, 1978	Grounding	223,000
Torrey Canyon, off Land's End, England	Mar. 18, 1967	Grounding	119,000
Sea Star, Gulf of Oman	Dec. 19, 1972	Collision	115,000
Urquiola, La Coruna, Spain	May 12, 1976	Grounding	100,000

Other Notable Oil Spills

Name, location	Date	Cause	Gallons
Persian Gulf	Began Jan. 23, 1991	Spillage by Iraq	130,000,000[1]
Braer, off Shetland Islands, UK	Jan. 5, 1993	Grounding	26,000,000
Prestige, off N Spain	Nov. 13-19, 2002	Ship broke in half	22,600,000
Aegean Sea, off N Spain	Dec. 3, 1992	Unknown	21,500,000
Sea Empress, off SW Wales	Feb. 15, 1996	Grounding	18,000,000
World Glory, off South Africa	June 13, 1968	Hull failure	13,524,000
Newtown Creek, Greenpoint, Brooklyn, NY	Oct. 5, 1950-present	Industrial explosion, preceded by leaks in 1940s-50s	17,000,000
Exxon Valdez, Prince William Sound, AK	Mar. 24, 1989	Grounding	10,080,000
Ashland Oil facility, Floreffe, PA; Monongahela R.	Jan. 2, 1988	Storage tank collapse	3,850,000

(1) Est. by Saudi Arabia. Some estimates as low as 25 mil gal.

Some Notable Miscellaneous Disasters Since 1950

Date	Event	Location	Details	Est. deaths
1952, Dec.	Pollution	London, England	Heavy smog blanketed city; caused breathing difficulties	4,000
1973-74	Drought and famine	Ethiopia	Caused by 6-year drought	200,000
1974	Famine	Bangladesh	Caused by flooding	26,000+
1974-75	Famine	Sub-Saharan Africa	Drought in some regions, torrential rains in others, compounded by government mismanagement	40,000+
1980, summer	Heat wave	United States	June through Sept.	1,265
1984, Dec. 3	Industrial accident	Bhopal, India	Toxic gas leaked from a Union Carbide factory	16,000
1984	Famine	Africa, espec. Ethiopia	Several years of drought compounded by government mismanagement	800,000-1 mil
1986, Aug. 21	Gas	Nr. Lake Nyos, Cameroon	Volcanic lake released cloud of carbon dioxide gas	1,700
1990, July 2	Stampede	Mecca, Saudi Arabia	Pilgrims panicked in tunnel leading to the holy city	1,426
2003, summer	Heat wave	Europe	Abnormally high temperatures from Russia to Britain; France suffered most, with 14,800 dead	35,000
2005, Aug. 31	Stampede	Baghdad, Iraq	Fear of suicide bomber caused bridge stampede	1,000

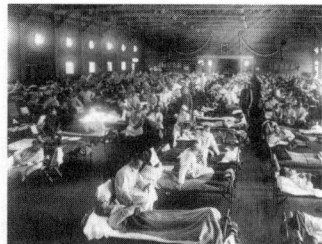

The 1918 Flu Pandemic

Dates: 1918-19. **Location:** Worldwide. **Fatalities:** 50-100 mil.

One of the most devastating epidemics in history, also known as the Spanish flu, in which approximately one-third of the world's population, or 500 mil, were infected by the flu virus. In spring of 1918, a deadly new strain of influenza appeared within the army training grounds of Camp Funston, KS. American soldiers are believed to have carried the virus to W Europe, where they had been shipped to fight in World War I. The pandemic peaked in fall 1918: many of those infected with the flu also developed complications from pneumonia and died within days of the first appearance of their symptoms.

AEROSPACE

Memorable Moments in Human Spaceflight

Sources: National Aeronautics and Space Administration; Congressional Research Service; World Almanac research

The spaceflights listed are a selection of notable U.S. missions by the National Aeronautics and Space Administration (NASA), unless otherwise noted, plus non-U.S. missions (shown with an asterisk). The non-U.S missions were sponsored by the USSR (later, the Commonwealth of Independent States and, from 1997, Russia) or by China. Dates are Eastern standard time. EVA = extravehicular activity. ASTP = Apollo-Soyuz Test Project. STS = Space Transportation System, NASA's name for the overall Shuttle program. Number of total flights by each crew member is given in parentheses when flight listed is not the first.

Launch date	Mission[1]	Crew (no. of flights)	Duration (hr:min)	Remarks
4/12/61	*Vostok 1	Yuri A. Gagarin	1:48	**1st human orbital flight**
5/5/61	Mercury-Redstone 3	Alan B. Shepard Jr.	0:15	**1st American in space**
7/21/61	Mercury-Redstone 4	Virgil I. Grissom	0:15	Spacecraft sank, Grissom rescued
8/6/61	*Vostok 2	Gherman S. Titov	25:18	1st spaceflight of more than 24 hrs
2/20/62	Mercury-Atlas 6	John H. Glenn Jr.	4:55	**1st American in orbit**; 3 orbits
5/24/62	Mercury-Atlas 7	M. Scott Carpenter	4:56	Manual retrofire error caused 250-mi landing overshoot
8/11/62	*Vostok 3	Andrian G. Nikolayev	94:22	*Vostok 3* and *4* made 1st group flight
8/12/62	*Vostok 4	Pavel R. Popovich	70:57	On 1st orbit, it came within 3 mi of *Vostok 3*
10/3/62	Mercury-Atlas 8	Walter M. Schirra Jr.	9:13	Landed 5 mi from target
5/15/63	Mercury-Atlas 9	L. Gordon Cooper	34:19	1st U.S. evaluation of effects of one day in space on a person; 22 orbits
6/14/63	*Vostok 5	Valery F. Bykovsky	119:06	*Vostok 5* and *6* made 2nd group flight
6/16/63	*Vostok 6	Valentina V. Tereshkova	70:50	**1st woman in space**; passed within 3 mi of *Vostok 5*
10/12/64	*Voskhod 1	Vladimir M. Komarov, Konstantin P. Feoktistov, Boris B. Yegorov	24:17	1st 3-person orbital flight; 1st without space suits
3/18/65	*Voskhod 2	Pavel I. Belyayev, Aleksei A. Leonov	26:02	Leonov made **1st "space walk"** (10 min)
3/23/65	Gemini-Titan 3	Grissom (2), John W. Young	4:53	1st piloted spacecraft to change its orbital path
6/3/65	Gemini-Titan 4	James A. McDivitt, Edward H. White 2nd	97:56	White was 1st American to "walk in space" (36 min)
8/21/65	Gemini-Titan 5	Cooper (2), Charles Conrad Jr.	190:55	Longest-duration human flight to date
12/15/65	Gemini-Titan 6A	Schirra (2), Thomas P. Stafford	25:51	Completed 1st U.S. space rendezvous, with *Gemini 7*
12/4/65	Gemini-Titan 7	Frank Borman, James A. Lovell	330:35	Longest-duration *Gemini* flight
3/16/66	Gemini-Titan 8	Neil A. Armstrong, David R. Scott	10:41	**1st docking of one space vehicle with another**; mission aborted, control malfunction; 1st Pacific landing
6/3/66	Gemini-Titan 9A	Stafford (2), Eugene A. Cernan	72:21	Performed simulation of lunar module rendezvous
7/18/66	Gemini-Titan 10	Young (2), Michael Collins	70:47	1st use of Agena target vehicle's propulsion systems; 1st orbital docking
9/12/66	Gemini-Titan 11	Conrad (2), Richard F. Gordon Jr.	71:17	1st tethered flight; highest Earth-orbit altitude (850 mi)
11/11/66	Gemini-Titan 12	Lovell (2), Edwin E. "Buzz" Aldrin Jr.	94:34	Final *Gemini* mission; 5-hr EVA
4/23/67	*Soyuz 1	Komarov (2)	26:40	Crashed on reentry, killing Komarov
10/11/68	Apollo-Saturn 7	Schirra (3), Donn F. Eisele, R. Walter Cunningham	260:09	1st piloted flight of *Apollo* spacecraft command-service module only; live TV footage of crew
12/21/68	Apollo-Saturn 8	Borman (2), Lovell (3), William A. Anders	147:00	**1st lunar orbit** and piloted lunar return reentry (command-service module only); views of lunar surface televised to Earth
1/14/69	*Soyuz 4	Vladimir A. Shatalov	71:21	Docked with *Soyuz 5*
1/15/69	*Soyuz 5	Boris V. Volyanov, Aleksei S. Yeliseyev, Yevgeny V. Khrunov	72:54	Docked with *Soyuz 4*; Yeliseyev and Khrunov transferred to *Soyuz 4* via a spacewalk
3/3/69	Apollo-Saturn 9	McDivitt (2), Scott (2), Russell L. Schweickart	241:00	1st piloted flight of lunar module
5/18/69	Apollo-Saturn 10	Stafford (3), Young (3), Cernan (2)	192:03	1st lunar module orbit of Moon, 50,000 ft from Moon surface
7/16/69	Apollo-Saturn 11	Armstrong (2), Collins (2), Aldrin (2)	195:18	**1st lunar landing** made by Armstrong and Aldrin (7/20); collected 48.5 lbs of soil, rock samples; lunar stay time 21:36:21
10/11/69	*Soyuz 6	Georgi S. Shonin, Valery N. Kubasov	118:43	1st welding of metals in space
10/12/69	*Soyuz 7	Anatoly V. Flipchenko, Vladislav N. Volkov, Viktor V. Gorbatko	118:40	Space lab construction test made; *Soyuz 6, 7,* and *8*: 1st time 3 spacecraft, 7 crew members orbited the Earth at once
10/13/69	*Soyuz 8	Shatalov (2), Yeliseyev (2)	118:51	Part of space lab construction team
11/14/69	Apollo-Saturn 12	Conrad (3), Gordon (2), Alan L. Bean	244:36	Conrad and Bean made **2nd Moon landing** (11/18); collected 74.7 lbs of samples; lunar stay time 31:31
4/11/70	Apollo-Saturn 13	Lovell (4), Fred W. Haise Jr., John L. Swigert Jr.	142:54	Aborted after service module oxygen tank ruptured; crew returned in lunar module
6/1/70	*Soyuz 9	Nikolayev (2), Vitaliy I. Sevastyanov	424:59	Longest human spaceflight to date
1/31/71	Apollo-Saturn 14	A. Shepard (2), Stuart A. Roosa, Edgar D. Mitchell	216:01	Shepard and Mitchell made **3rd Moon landing** (2/3); collected 96 lbs of lunar samples; lunar stay 33:31
4/19/71	*Salyut 12	(Occupied by *Soyuz 11* crew)	—	**1st space station**
4/22/71	*Soyuz 10	Shatalov (3), Yeliseyev (3), Nikolay N. Rukavishnikov	47:46	**1st successful docking with a space station**; failed to enter space station
6/6/71	*Soyuz 11	Georgi T. Dobrovolskiy, V. Volkov, Viktor I. Patsayev	570:22	Docked and entered *Salyut 1* space station; **crew died** during reentry from loss of pressurization
7/26/71	Apollo-Saturn 15	Scott (3), James B. Irwin, Alfred M. Worden	295:12	Scott and Irwin made **4th Moon landing** (7/30); 1st lunar rover use; 1st deep space walk; 170 lbs of samples; 66:55 stay
4/16/72	Apollo-Saturn 16	Young (4), Charles M. Duke Jr., Thomas K. Mattingly 2nd	265:51	Young and Duke made **5th Moon landing** (4/20); collected 213 lbs of lunar samples; lunar stay 71:2
12/7/72	Apollo-Saturn 17	Cernan (3), Ronald E. Evans, Harrison H. Schmitt	301:51	Cernan and Schmitt made 6th and **last lunar landing** (12/11); collected 243 lbs of samples; record lunar stay over 75 hrs

Launch date	Mission[1]	Crew (no. of flights)	Duration (hr:min) Remarks
5/14/73[2]	Skylab 1	(Occupied by Skylab 2, 3, and 4 crews)	— **1st U.S. space station**; fell out of orbit 7/11/79
5/25/73	Skylab 2	Conrad (4), Joseph P. Kerwin, Paul J. Weitz	672:49 1st Amer. piloted orbiting space station; crew repaired damage caused in boost
7/28/73	Skylab 3	Bean (2), Owen K. Garriott, Jack R. Lousma	1,427:09 Crew systems and operational tests; scientific activities; 3 EVAs, 13:44
11/16/73	Skylab 4	Gerald P. Carr, Edward G. Gibson, William Pogue	2,017:15 Final Skylab mission
7/15/75	*Soyuz 19 (ASTP)	Leonov (2), Kubasov (2)	143:31 U.S.-USSR joint flight; crews linked up in space (7/17), conducted experiments, shared meals, held a joint news conf.
7/15/75	Apollo (ASTP)	Vance Brand, Stafford (4), Donald K. Slayton	217:28 Joint flight with *Soyuz 19*
12/10/77	*Soyuz 26	Yuri V. Romanenko, Georgiy M. Grechko (2)	2,314:00 1st multiple docking at a space station (*Soyuz 26* and *27* docked at *Salyut 6*)
1/10/78	*Soyuz 27	Vladimir A. Dzhanibekov	142:59 See *Soyuz 26*
3/2/78	*Soyuz 28	Aleksei A. Gubarev (2), Vladimir Remek	190:16 1st international crew launch; Remek was 1st Czech in space
4/12/81	Columbia (STS-1)	Young (5), Robert L. Crippen	54:21 **1st space shuttle** to fly into Earth's orbit
11/12/81	Columbia (STS-2)	Joe H. Engle, Richard H. Truly	54:13 1st scientific payload; 1st reuse of space shuttle
11/11/82	Columbia (STS-5)	Brand (2), Robert Overmyer, William Lenoir, Joseph Allen	122:14 1st 4-person crew
6/18/83	Challenger (STS-7)	Crippen (2), Frederick Hauck, Sally K. Ride, John M. Fabian, Norman Thagard	146:24 Ride was **1st U.S. woman in space**; 1st 5-person crew
6/27/83	*Soyuz T-9	Vladimir A. Lyakhov (2), Aleksandr Pavlovich	3,585:46 Docked at *Salyut 7*; 1st construction in space
8/30/83	Challenger (STS-8)	Truly (2), Daniel Brandenstein, William Thornton, Guion Bluford, Dale Gardner	145:09 Bluford was **1st African-American in space**
11/28/83	Columbia (STS-9)	Young (6), Brewster Shaw Jr., Robert Parker, Garriott (2), Byron Lichtenberg, Ulf Merbold	247:47 1st 6-person crew; 1st Spacelab mission
2/3/84	Challenger (41-B)	Brand (3), Robert Gibson, Ronald McNair, Bruce McCandless, Robert Stewart	191:16 1st untethered EVA
2/8/84	*Soyuz T-10B	Leonid Kizim, Vladimir Solovyov, Oleg Atkov	1,510:43 Docked with *Salyut 7*; crew set space duration record of 237 days
4/3/84	*Soyuz T-11	Yury Malyshev (2), Gennady Strekalov (3), Rakesh Sharma	4,365:48 Docked with *Salyut 7*; Sharma 1st Indian in space
4/6/84	Challenger (41-C)	Crippen (3), Francis R. Scobee, George D. Nelson, Terry J. Hart, James D. van Hoften	167:40 1st in-orbit satellite repair
7/17/84	*Soyuz T-12	Dzhanibekov (4), Svetlana Y. Savitskaya (2), Igor P. Volk	283:14 Docked at *Salyut 7*; Savitskaya was 1st woman to perform EVA
8/30/84	Discovery (41-D)	Henry W. Hartsfield (2), Michael L. Coats, Richard M. Mullane, Steven A. Hawley, Judith A. Resnik, Charles D. Walker	144:56 1st flight of U.S. nonastronaut (Walker)
10/5/84	Challenger (41-G)	Crippen (4), Jon A. McBride, Kathryn D. Sullivan, Ride (2), Marc Garneau, David C. Leestma, Paul D. Scully-Power	197:24 1st 7-person crew
11/8/84	Discovery (51-A)	Hauck (2), David M. Walker, Dr. Anna L. Fisher, J. Allen (2), Gardner (2)	191:45 1st satellite retrieval/repair
4/12/85	Discovery (51-D)	Karol J. Bobko, Donald E. Williams, Jake Garn, C. Walker (2), Jeffrey A. Hoffman, S. David Griggs, M. Rhea Seddon	167:55 Garn (R, UT) was **1st U.S. senator in space**
6/17/85	Discovery (51-G)	Brandenstein (2), John O. Creighton, Shannon W. Lucid, Steven R. Nagel, Fabian (2), Prince Sultan Salman al-Saud, Patrick Baudry	169:39 Launched 3 satellites; Salman al-Saud was 1st Arab in space; Baudry was 1st French person on U.S. mission
10/3/85	Atlantis (51-J)	Bobko (3), Ronald J. Grabe, David C. Hilmers, Stewart (2), William A. Pailes	97:47 1st *Atlantis* flight
10/30/85	Challenger (61-A)	Hartsfield (2), Nagel (2), Buchli (2), Bluford (2), Bonnie J. Dunbar, Wubbo J. Ockels, Richard Furrer, Ernst Messerschmid	168:45 1st 8-person crew; 1st German Spacelab mission
1/12/86	Columbia (61-C)	R. Gibson (2), Charles F. Bolden Jr., Hawley (2), G. Nelson (2), Franklin R. Chang-Diaz, Robert J. Cenker, Bill Nelson	146:04 B. Nelson (D, FL) was **1st U.S. representative in space**; material and astronomy experiments conducted
1/28/86	Challenger (51-L)	Scobee (2), Michael J. Smith, Resnik (2), Ellison S. Onizuka (2), Ronald E. McNair, Gregory B. Jarvis, Christa McAuliffe	— **Exploded 73 sec after liftoff**; all aboard were killed
2/20/86	*Mir[2]	—	— *Mir* **space station** with 6 docking ports **launched**
3/13/86	*Soyuz T-15	Kizim (3), Solovyov (2)	3,000:01 Ferry between stations; docked at *Mir*
2/5/87	*Soyuz TM-2	Romanenko (3), Aleksandr I. Laveikin	7,835:38 Romanenko set endurance record, since broken
7/22/87	*Soyuz TM-3	Aleksandr Viktorenko, Aleksandr Pavlovich Aleksandrov (2), Mohammed Faris	3,847:16 Docked with *Mir*; Faris 1st Syrian in space
9/29/88	Discovery (STS-26)	Hauck (3), Richard O. Covey (2), Hilmers (2), G. Nelson (2), John M. Lounge (2)	97:00 **1st shuttle flight since *Challenger* explosion** 1/28/86
5/4/89	Atlantis (STS-30)	D. Walker (2), Grabe (2), Thagard (2), Mary L. Cleave (2), Mark C. Lee	96:56 Launched Venus orbiter *Magellan*
10/18/89	Atlantis (STS-34)	Donald E. Williams (2), Michael J. McCulley, Lucid (2), Chang-Diaz (2), Ellen S. Baker	119:39 Launched Jupiter probe and orbiter *Galileo*
4/24/90	Discovery (STS-31)	McCandless (2), Sullivan (2), Loren J. Shriver (2), Bolden (2), Hawley (3)	121:16 **Launched Hubble Space Telescope**
10/6/90	Discovery (STS-41)	Richard N. Richards (2), Robert D. Cabana, Bruce E. Melnick, William M. Shepherd (2), Thomas D. Akers	98:10 Launched *Ulysses* spacecraft to investigate interstellar space and the Sun
5/18/91	*Soyuz TM-12	Anatoly Artsebarskiy, Sergei Krikalev (2) (to *Mir*), Helen Sharman	3,471:22 Docked with *Mir*; Sharman 1st from United Kingdom in space
3/17/92	*Soyuz TM-14	Viktorenko (3) (to *Mir*), Alexandr Kaleri (to *Mir*), Klaus-Dietrich Flade, Aleksandr Volkov (3) (from *Mir*), Krikalev (2) (from *Mir*)	3,495:11 First human CIS space mission; docked with *Mir* 3/19; Viktorenko and Kaleri to *Mir*; Volkov and Krikalev from *Mir*; Krikalev was in space 313 days

Launch date	Mission[1]	Crew (no. of flights)	Duration (hr:min)	Remarks
5/7/92	Endeavour (STS-49)	Brandenstein (4), Kevin C. Chilton, Melnick (2), Pierre J. Thuot (2), Richard J. Hieb (2), Kathryn Thornton (2), Akers (2)	213:30	1st 3-person EVA; satellite recovery and redeployment
9/12/92	Endeavour (STS-47)	R. Gibson (4), Curtis L. Brown Jr., Lee (2), Jay Apt (2), N. Jan Davis, Mae Carol Jemison, Mamoru Mohri	190:30	Jemison was **1st black woman in space**; Lee and Davis **1st married couple to travel together in space**; 1st Japanese Spacelab
6/21/93	Endeavour (STS-57)	Grabe (4), Brian J. Duffy (2), G. David Low (3), Nancy J. Sherlock, Peter J. K. Wisoff, Janice E. Voss	239:46	Carried Spacelab commercial payload module
12/2/93	Endeavour (STS-61)	Covey (3), Kenneth D. Bowersox (2), Claude Nicollier (2), Story Musgrave (5), Akers (3), K. Thornton (3), Hoffman (4)	259:58	Hubble Space Telescope repaired; Akers set new U.S. EVA duration record (29 hrs, 40 mins)
2/3/94	Discovery (STS-60)	Bolden (3), Kenneth S. Reightier Jr. (2), Davis (2), Chang-Diaz (3), Ronald M. Sega, Krikalev (3)	199:10	Krikalev was 1st Russian on U.S. shuttle
7/1/94	*Soyuz TM-19	Yuri I. Malenchenko, Talgat A. Musabayev, Merbold (2) (from *Mir*)	3,022:53	Docked with *Mir;* Merbold from *Mir*
9/9/94	Discovery (STS-64)	Richards (4), L. Blaine Hammond Jr. (2), Jerry M. Linenger, Susan J. Helms (2), Carl J. Meade (3), Lee (3)	262:50	Performed atmospheric research; 1st untethered EVA in more than 10 years
2/3/95	Discovery (STS-63)	James D. Wetherbee (3), Eileen M. Collins, Bernard A. Harris (2), C. Michael Foale (3), Janice E. Voss (2), Vladimir Titov (4)	198:29	*Discovery* and Russian space station rendezvous
3/2/95	Endeavour (STS-67)	Stephen S. Oswald (3), William G. Gregory, Samuel T. Durrance (2), Ronald Parise (2), Wendy B. Lawrence, Tamara E. Jernigan (3), John M. Grunsfeld	399:09	Shuttle data made available on the Internet; astronomy research conducted
3/14/95	*Soyuz TM-21	Thagard (2), Vladimir Dezhurov, Strekalov (5)	2,688[3]	Docked with *Mir* 3/16/95; Thagard was 1st Amer. onboard; Valery Polyakov returned to Earth, 3/22/95, after record stay in space (439 days)
6/27/95	Atlantis (STS-71)	R. Gibson (5), Charles J. Precourt (2), E. Baker (3), Gregory J. Harbaugh (3), Dunbar (4), Anatoly Solovyev (4) (to *Mir*), Nikolai M. Budarin (to *Mir*), Thagard (5) (from *Mir*), Strekalov (from *Mir*), Dezhurov (from *Mir*)	269:47	**1st shuttle-*Mir* docking**; exchanged crew members with *Mir;* Thagard, with his stay on *Mir*, had spent 115 days in space
11/12/95	Atlantis (STS-74)	Kenneth D. Cameron (3), James D. Halsell Jr. (2), Chris Hadfield (2), Jerry L. Ross (5), William S. McArthur (2)	196:30	2nd shuttle-*Mir* docking (11/15-11/18); erected a 15-ft permanent docking tunnel to *Mir* for future use by U.S. orbiters
2/22/96	Columbia (STS-75)	Andrew M. Allen (3), Scott J. Horowitz, Chang-Diaz (5), Umberto Guidoni, Hoffman (5), Maurizio Cheli, Nicollier (3)	377:40	Lost an Italian satellite when its tether was severed; microgravity experiments performed; singe marks found on 2 O-rings
3/22/96	Atlantis (STS-76)	Chilton (3), Richard A. Searfoss (2), Sega (2), Michael R. Clifford (3), Linda Godwin (3), Lucid (5) (to *Mir*)	221:15	3rd shuttle-*Mir* docking (5 days); Lucid to *Mir*, 2-person EVA
9/16/96	Atlantis (STS-79)	Apt (4), Terry Wilcutt (2), William Readdy (3), Akers (4), Carl E. Walz (3), Lucid (5) (from *Mir*), John E. Blaha (5) (to *Mir*)	243:19	Docked with *Mir* 9/18; exchanged crew members; Lucid set **U.S. and women's duration in space record** (188 days)
11/19/96	Columbia (STS-80)	Kenneth D. Cockrell (3), Kent V. Rominger (2), Jernigan (4), Thomas D. Jones (3), Musgrave (6)	423:53	Longest-duration shuttle flight; Musgrave, 61, oldest thus far to fly in space; 2 science satellites deployed, retrieved
1/12/97	Atlantis (STS-81)	Michael A. Baker (4), Brent W. Jett (2), Wisoff (3), Grunsfeld (2), Marsha Ivins (4), Linenger (2) (to *Mir*), Blaha (5) (from *Mir*)	243:30	Docked with *Mir* 1/14-1/19; Linenger to *Mir;* Blaha from *Mir*, spent 128 days in space
2/11/97	Discovery (STS-82)	Bowersox (3), Horowitz (2), Joe Tanner (2), Hawley (4), Harbaugh (4), Lee (4), Steve Smith (2)	238:47	Increased capabilities of Hubble Space Telescope; 5 EVAs used to service it
5/15/97	Atlantis (STS-84)	Precourt (3), E. Collins (2), Jean-François Clervoy (2), Carlos Noriega, Ed Lu, Elena Kondakova, Foale (4) (to *Mir*), Linenger (2) (from *Mir*)	221:20	Docked with *Mir* 5/16-5/21; Foale to *Mir;* Linenger from *Mir*, 132 days in space, 2nd-longest time for an American; stay on *Mir* marked by troubles incl. fire 2/23
8/5/97	*Soyuz TM-26	Solovyev (5), Pavel Vinogradov	4,743:35	Docked with *Mir* 8/7; repaired damaged space station
8/7/97	Discovery (STS-85)	Brown (4), Rominger (3), Davis (3), Robert L. Curbeam Jr., Stephen K. Robinson, Bjarni V. Tryggvason	284:27	Deployed and retrieved satellite designed to study Earth's middle atmosphere; demonstrated robotic arm
9/25/97	Atlantis (STS-86)	Wetherbee (4), Michael J. Bloomfield, V. Titov (5), Scott Parazynski (2), Jean-Loup Chrétien (3), Lawrence (2), David A. Wolf (2) (to *Mir*), Foale (4) (from *Mir*)	236:24	Docked with *Mir* 9/27-10/3; delivered new computer to *Mir;* Wolf to *Mir*, Foale from *Mir*, stay on *Mir* marked by major collision with cargo ship 6/25
4/17/98	Columbia (STS-90)	Searfoss (2), Scott D. Altman, Richard M. Linnehan (2), Dafydd Rhys Williams, Kathryn P. Hire (2), Jay C. Buckey, James A. Pawelczyk	381:50	Studied effects of microgravity on the nervous systems of the crew and more than 2,000 live animals; 1st surgery in space on animals meant to survive
6/2/98	Discovery (STS-91)	Precourt (4), Dominic L. Gorie, Lawrence (3), Chang-Diaz (6), Janet L. Kavandi, Valery Ryumin (4), A. Thomas (2) (from *Mir*)	235:53	Final docking mission with *Mir;* Thomas from *Mir*, 141 days in space
10/29/98	Discovery (STS-95)	Brown (5), Steven W. Lindsey (2), Parazynski (3), Robinson (2), Pedro Duque, Chiaki Mukai (2), Glenn (2)	213:44	Sen. John Glenn (D, OH), 77, was **oldest person to fly in space**; Duque was 1st Spaniard in space; experiments to study aging performed on Glenn
12/4/98	Endeavour (STS-88)	Cabana (4), Frederick W. Sturckow, Nancy J. Currie (3), Ross (6), James H. Newman (3), Krikalev (4)	283:18	**1st assembly of International Space Station (ISS)**; attached U.S.-built *Unity* connecting module to Russian-built *Zarya* control module; 1st crew to enter ISS
7/23/99	Columbia (STS-93)	E. Collins (3), Jeffrey S. Ashby, Hawley (5), Catherine G. Coleman (2), Michel Tognini (2)	118:50	Collins was **1st woman space shuttle commander**; deployed Chandra X-ray Observatory telescope

Launch date	Mission[1]	Crew (no. of flights)	Duration (hr:min)	Remarks
2/11/00	Endeavour (STS-99)	Kevin Kregel (4), Gorie (2), Kavandi (2), Janice E. Voss (5), Mohri (2), Gerhard P.J. Thiele	269:38	Used radar to make most complete topographic map of Earth's surface ever produced
9/8/00	Atlantis (STS-106)	Wilcutt (4), Altman (2), Lu (2), Richard A. Mastracchio, Daniel C. Burbank, Malenchenko (2), Boris V. Morukov	283:10	Prepared ISS for 1st permanent crew; 1 EVA by all 7 crew members
10/31/00	*Soyuz TM-204	Shepherd (4), Yuri Gidzenko (2), Krikalev (5)	—	Established **1st permanent manning of ISS** with 3-person crew for a 4-month stay
3/8/01	Discovery (STS-102)	Wetherbee (5), James M. Kelly, Helms (4) (to ISS), James S. Voss (5) (to ISS), Paul Richards, Andrew S.W. Thomas (2), Usachev (4) (to ISS), Shepherd (4) (from ISS), Gidzenko (2) (from ISS), Krikalev (5) (from ISS)	307:49	Transported 2nd permanent crew (Voss, Helms, Usachev) to ISS and returned 1st crew to Earth; 2 EVAs
7/12/01	Atlantis (STS-104)	Lindsey (3), Charles O. Hobaugh, Michael L. Gernhardt (4), Kavandi (3), James F. Reilly II (2)	259:58	Installed a Joint Airlock, with nitrogen and oxygen tanks to permit future spacewalks from the ISS; 3 EVAs
3/1/02	Columbia (STS-109)	Altman (3), Duane G. Carey, Grunsfeld (4), Currie (4), Linnehan (3), Newman (4), Michael J. Massimino	262:10	Installed powerful new camera and upgraded other equipment on Hubble Space Telescope; 5 EVAs
4/8/02	Atlantis (STS-110)	Bloomfield (3), Stephen N. Frick, Rex J. Walheim, Ellen Ochoa (4), Lee M.E. Morin, Ross (7), S. Smith (4)	259:42	Installed S0 Truss, backbone for expansion of ISS; Ross set records with 7th spaceflight, 9th spacewalk; 4 EVAs
10/30/02	*Soyuz TMA-1	Sergei Zalyotin (2), Frank De Winne, Yuri Lonchakov (2)	—	1st launch of *Soyuz* TMA (Crew returned 11/10/02 on *Soyuz* TM-34 already docked at ISS)
1/16/03	Columbia (STS 107)	Rick Husband (2), William McCool, Michael Anderson (2), David Brown, Kalbana Chawla (2), Laurel Clark, Ilan Ramon	382:20	**Entire crew lost when *Columbia* burned up** during reentry, 2/1; Ramon first Israeli astronaut
10/15/03	*Shenzhou 5	Yang Liwei	21:00	**1st Chinese manned spacecraft**
6/21/04	SpaceShipOne	Mike Melvill	0:90	**1st privately funded manned spaceflight[4]**
7/26/05	Discovery (STS-114)	Charles Camarda, E. Collins (4), J. Kelly (2), Lawrence (4), Soichi Noguchi, Robinson (3), A. Thomas (3)	333:33	**1st space shuttle flight since *Columbia* disaster**; tested new safety modifications to craft; delivered supplies to ISS
7/4/06	Discovery (STS-121)	Lindsey (4), J. Kelly (3), Michael E. Fossum, Sellers (4), Lisa M. Nowak, Thomas Reiter (to ISS), Stephanie D. Wilson	306:36	**1st shuttle to launch on Independence Day**; conducted more safety tests to craft; brought supplies to and performed maintenance on ISS.
4/7/07	*Soyuz TMA-10[5]	Oleg Kotov (to ISS), Sheikh Muszaphar Shukor (from ISS), Charles Simonyi (US), Fyodor Yurchikhin (to ISS)	—	Kotov and Yurchikhin joined ISS expedition 15; Simonyi became **fifth space tourist** (returned on TMA-9); Shukor was **first Malaysian in space** (arrived on TMA-11)
6/8/07	Atlantis (STS-117)	Clayton Anderson (to ISS), Lee Archambault, Patrick Forrester (2), John "Danny" Olivas, Jim Reilly (3), Frederick Sturckow (3), Steven Swanson, S.L. Williams (from ISS)	332:11	Delivered truss segments and solar arrays to ISS; Williams set record for **longest spaceflight by a woman**
8/8/07	Endeavour (STS-118)	Alvin Drew, Barbara R. Morgan, Scott Kelly (2), Charlie Hobaugh (2), Tracy Caldwell, Rick Mastracchio (2), Dave Williams (2)	305:55	Brought **Teacher in Space Project** participant Morgan to ISS; attached new truss segment, repaired faulty gyroscope
10/10/07	*Soyuz TMA-11[5]	Malenchenko (3), Shukor (to ISS), Whitson (2) (from ISS), Yi So-Yeon (from ISS)	—	Delivered and installed components of ISS; malfunctioned on return to Earth, landing short of its touchdown area but causing no fatalities
10/23/07	Discovery (STS-120)	C. Anderson (from ISS), Melroy (3), Paolo Nespoli, Parazynski (5), Tani (2) (to ISS), Douglas Wheelock, Stephanie Wilson, George Zamka	362:24	Continued construction of ISS, installing living space (Harmony Node 2) and repositioning truss
2/7/08	Atlantis (STS-122)	Léopold Eyharts (to ISS), S. Frick (2), Stanley Love, Leland Melvin, Alan Poindexter, Hans Schlegel (2), Tani (from ISS), Walheim (2)	306:22	Installed European Space Agency's Columbus laboratory on the ISS; minor damage to a thermal plate caused concern about the shuttle's safety during re-entry, but *Atlantis* landed safely
3/11/08	Endeavor (STS-123)	Robert L. Behnken, Takao Doi (2), Eyharts (from ISS), Michael J. Foreman, Gorie (4), Gregory H. Johnson, Linnehan (4), Garrett Reisman (to ISS)	378:00	Delivered and installed components of the Japanese Kibo science laboratory
4/8/08	*Soyuz TMA-12[5]	Oleg Kononenko, Sergei Volkov, Yi (to ISS); Richard Garriott (from ISS)	—	Yi became **1st S. Korean in space**
5/31/08	Discovery (STS-124)	Gregory E. Chamitoff (to ISS), Fossum (2), Ronald J. Garan Jr., Kenneth T. Ham, Akihiko Hoshide, Mark Kelly (3), Karen Nyberg, Reisman (from ISS)	330:13	Delivered and installed pressurized and experimental modules of Kibo
9/25/08	*Shenzhou 7	Jing Haipeng, Liu Boming, Zhai Zhigang	68:00	Zhai completed **1st Chinese spacewalk**
10/12/08	*Soyuz TMA-13[5]	Richard Garriott (to ISS), Lonchakov, Michael Fincke		Garriott became 6th space tourist
3/15/09	Discovery (STS-119)	Archambault (2), Dominic A. Antonelli, Joseph M. Acaba, Swanson (2), Richard R. Arnold, John L. Phillips, Koichi Wakata (to ISS), Sandra H. Magnus (from ISS)	307:29	Delivered final solar panels and last U.S.-made truss segment.
5/11/09	Atlantis (STS-125)	Altman (4), Gregory C. Johnson, Michael T. Good, K. Megan McArthur, Grunsfeld (5), Massimino (2), Andrew J. Feustel	309:37	Final Hubble Space Telescope servicing mission

Note: As of Oct. 2009, there have been 128 space shuttle flights, 102 since the 1986 *Challenger* explosion, 15 since the 2003 loss of *Columbia*. Totals include the final (28th) *Columbia* flight. There are 3 remaining shuttles: *Discovery* (37 flights), *Atlantis* (30), and *Endeavour* (23); the *Challenger* completed 9 missions in all. Four Soviets have died during spaceflight: Vladimir Komarov was killed on *Soyuz 1* (1967) when parachute lines tangled during descent; the 3-person *Soyuz 11* crew (1971) was asphyxiated. Six Americans and an Israeli astronaut died aboard the *Columbia*; 7 Americans died in the *Challenger* explosion; and 3 astronauts—Virgil I. Grissom, Edward H. White, and Roger B. Chaffee—died in the Jan. 27, 1967, *Apollo 1* fire on the ground at Cape Canaveral, FL.

(1) For shuttle flights, mission name is in parentheses following name of orbiter. (2) Space stations, such as the *Salyuts* and *Mir*, were used to house crews starting in 1971. (3) Approx. crew duration for Thagard's stay. Crew did not return together. (4) Date of first successful flight; later, SpaceShipOne flew at least 100 km (62 mi) into space, 9/29/04, piloted by Mike Melvill, and 10/4/04, piloted by Brian Binnie, winning the $10 mil Ansari Prize for 1st private venture to accomplish this feat twice within 2 weeks. (5) Soyuz crew often return from ISS on spacecraft that launched and were docked at the station before their arrival.

U.S. Manned Space Program

Following the Feb. 1, 2003, *Columbia* disaster, when the craft broke up on re-entry, all space shuttle flights were grounded. Improvements to future spacecrafts were made, including a redesigned external tank, new sensors to register impact, and a boom with a camera to allow astronauts to inspect the shuttle in flight for potential damage. On July 26, 2005, a modified *Discovery* made it into orbit, but onboard cameras showed that foam insulation broke off from the external fuel tank during launch—the same problem that caused the *Columbia* disaster. Despite a successful return, the shuttle program was grounded again until July 4, 2006, when *Discovery* lifted off with new safety features in place. The crew visited the International Space Station and returned to Earth without incident.

Even before the *Columbia* disaster it was clear that a new vehicle was needed to replace the space shuttle, which is due to be retired in 2010. President George W. Bush in 2004 outlined his vision for future space exploration: Following the retirement of the space shuttle fleet, NASA will employ a new space vessel to aid not only in finishing the ISS, but also in sending astronauts to the moon and eventually to Mars. In Aug. 2006, NASA unveiled plans for the new spacecraft, a multipurpose orbital capsule called *Orion*. Its developer, Lockheed Martin, plans to deliver the first craft in 2014. *Orion* will carry astronauts into orbit, ferry personnel and equipment to the ISS, serve as the orbital vehicle for missions to the Moon, and eventually deliver astronauts to a Mars-bound spacecraft that will be built in Earth's orbit.

The reusable *Orion* craft abandons the 30-year-old space shuttle design for an *Apollo*-style capsule. A novel expendable rocket, the *Ares* (currently under development), will propel the craft into space. *Orion*, expected to cost $8.1 bil through 2020, will incorporate the latest technology in electronics, life support, computers, propulsion, and heat protection systems. At 16.5 ft in diameter, *Orion* will have 2.5 times the interior volume of the original *Apollo* capsules, and like the Russian *Soyuz* capsules, *Orion* will use parachutes to touch down on land (the *Apollo* capsules landed in water). Like the *Apollo* craft, *Orion* will launch on top of its booster rocket, which will prevent ice or insulating foam from the booster rocket from hitting the capsule. In addition, the capsule will be able to jettison from its booster in the event of launch failure—a safety mechanism unavailable to space shuttle crews.

The earliest *Orion* flight is scheduled for 2014, with a manned Moon mission expected by 2020.

International Space Station

The International Space Station (ISS) is considered the largest cooperative scientific project in history.

16 cooperating nations: U.S., Russia, Canada, Belgium, Denmark, France, Germany, Italy, Netherlands, Norway, Spain, Sweden, Switzerland, United Kingdom, Japan, and Brazil.

Impact of *Columbia* disaster: The grounding of U.S. space shuttles after the *Columbia* disaster and then after complications with *Discovery* in 2005 interrupted further assembly of the station. Since lower-capacity Russian *Soyuz* and *Progress* craft were the usual means of ferrying provisions and crew to and from Earth, the size of the crew aboard the ISS was reduced to 2.

In 2006, the flights resumed, allowing operations on the station to move forward and bringing the ISS crew back up to 3. Over the course of the year, the crew tested new equipment and safety procedures and performed maintenance on the station, notably the station's mobile transporter (a device that moves along exterior rails and facilitates repair, maintenance, and module additions). New and updated research equipment was installed inside the Leonardo Multi-Purpose Logistics Module. In Sept. the space shuttle *Atlantis* arrived with a new truss segment, two solar arrays, and a rotary joint that is used to position the solar panels so that they face the sun as the ISS moves through its orbit. In 2007 and 2008, the ISS crew added the Japanese Kibo laboratory and a maintenance robot, Dextre.

Operations to assemble and supply the station continued throughout 2008 and 2009. Space shuttle *Endeavour* delivered additional crew quarters, exercise eqiupment, and supplies in Nov. 2008, and returned in July 2009 with a new module for the Kibo laboratory. Discovery brought the final U.S.-made truss segment and the final pair of power-generating solar wings in Mar. 2009, and made a second delivery of ISS science components in September. The European Space Agency's unmanned Automated Transfer Vehicle made its first delivery of supplies in 2008; the second ATV is scheduled to launch in mid-2010.

The station when completed:
- mass of 1,040,000 lbs
- 356' x 290', with almost an acre of solar panels
- internal volume roughly equivalent to passenger cabin of a 747 jumbo jet
- 6 laboratories; living space for up to 7 people

Examples of research conducted or planned:
- growing living cells in a gravity-free environment
- studying the effects on humans of long-term exposure to reduced gravity
- studying large-scale long-term changes in Earth's environment by observing Earth from orbit

Summary of Worldwide Successful Launches, 1957-2009

Source: National Aeronautics and Space Administration

Year	Total[1]	Russia[2]	U.S.	ESA[3]	China	Japan	France	India	UK	Germany	Canada	Israel	Iran	S. Korea
1957-59	24	6	18	—	—	—	—	—	—	—	—	—	—	—
1960-69	1,035	399	614	2	—	—	4	—	1	—	—	—	—	—
1970-79	1,366	1,028	247	5	8	18	14	1	6	3	4	—	—	—
1980-89	1,431	1,132	191	14	16	26	5	9	4	7	5	—	—	—
1990-99	1,045	542	300	55	33	23	16	11	7	6	4	—	—	—
2000-09[4]	583	237	201	61	49	17	0	13	0	0	0	3	1	1
Total	5,357	3,334	1,571	137	106	84	39	34	18	16	13	3	1	1

(1) Includes launches sponsored by countries not shown. (2) Data for 1957-91 apply to the Soviet Union, for 1992-96 to the Commonwealth of Independent States, after 1996 to Russia. (3) European Space Agency. Member states are Austria, Belgium, Denmark, Finland, France, Germany, Greece, Ireland, Italy, Luxembourg, the Netherlands, Norway, Portugal, Spain, Sweden, Switzerland, and the United Kingdom. Canada, Hungary, and the Czech Republic also participate in some projects under cooperation agreements. (4) As of Oct. 11, 2009.

Notable Proposed U.S. Space Missions in 2010

Source: National Aeronautics and Space Administration

Planned Launch	Mission	Purpose
Feb. 3	Solar Dynamics Observatory (SDO)	Study the Sun's influence on Earth and near-Earth space.
Sept.	Space Shuttle Discovery (STS-133)	Final U.S. space shuttle flight.
Oct. 1	Glory	Study human and solar effects on climate.

Notable Lunar and Planetary Science Missions

Source: National Aeronautics and Space Administration

Spacecraft	Launch date[1]	Mission	Remarks
Mariner 2	Aug. 27, 1962	Venus	Passed within 22,000 mi of Venus 12/14/62; confirmed high surface temperature on planet; contact lost 1/3/63 at 54 mil mi
Ranger 7	July 28, 1964	Moon	Yielded over 4,000 photos of lunar surface
Mariner 4	Nov. 28, 1964	Mars	1st probe to fly by Mars; passed behind planet 7/14/65; took 22 photos from 6,000 mi above surface
Ranger 8	Feb. 17, 1965	Moon	Yielded over 7,000 photos of lunar surface
Surveyor 3	Apr. 17, 1967	Moon	Scooped and tested lunar soil
Venera 3	Nov. 16, 1965	Venus	Soviet probe; first artificial probe to impact on the surface of another planet 3/1/66; probe failed to send back data
Mariner 5	June 14, 1967	Venus	In solar orbit; closest Venus flyby 10/19/67; allowed scientists to obtain accurate readings on the composition of the Venusian atmosphere
Mariner 6	Feb. 24, 1969	Mars	Came within 2,000 mi of Mars 7/31/69; collected data, photos
Mariner 7	Mar. 27, 1969	Mars	Came within 2,000 mi of Mars 8/5/69
Venera 7	Aug. 17, 1970	Venus	Soviet probe; first probe to land safely on the surface of another planet; because of high atmospheric temperatures, probe is thought to have melted
Mariner 9	May 30, 1971	Mars	First craft to orbit Mars 11/13/71; sent back over 7,000 photos
Pioneer 10	Mar. 2, 1972	Jupiter	Passed Jupiter 12/4/73; took readings on Jupiter's composition, found that the planet is composed mostly of hydrogen; exited the planetary system 6/13/83; transmission ended 3/31/97 at 6.39 bil mi
Pioneer 11	Apr. 5, 1973	Jupiter, Saturn	Passed Jupiter 12/3/74, Saturn 9/1/79; discovered an additional ring and 2 moons around Saturn; operating in outer solar system; transmission ended 9/30/95
Mariner 10	Nov. 3, 1973	Venus, Mercury	Passed Venus 2/5/74; arrived Mercury 3/29/74. 1st time gravity of 1 planet (Venus) used to whip spacecraft toward another (Mercury); 1st probe to visit 2 planets; took readings of cloud and wind patterns in Venusian atmosphere
Viking 1	Aug. 20, 1975	Mars	Landed on Mars 7/20/76; 1st probe to land safely on Mars; performed chemical analysis of soil; functioned 6 years
Viking 2	Sept. 9, 1975	Mars	Sister probe of *Viking 1*; landed on Mars 9/3/76; functioned 3 years
Voyager 2	Aug. 20, 1977	Jupiter, Saturn, Uranus, Neptune	Encountered Jupiter 7/9/79; Saturn 8/25/81; Uranus 1/24/86; Neptune 8/25/89; confirmed existence of rings around Uranus; observed Neptune's "great dark spot," which has since dissipated. Entered boundary of solar system Oct. 2007
Voyager 1	Sept. 5, 1977	Jupiter, Saturn	Encountered Jupiter 3/5/79, provided evidence of rings around Jupiter; passed near Saturn 11/12/80; passed *Pioneer 10* to become most distant human-made object 2/17/98; 8/15/06 reached a distance of 100 AUs from sun
Pioneer Venus 1	May 20, 1978	Venus	Entered Venus orbit 12/4/78; studied atmosphere, magnetic field, weather, and surface; fuel ran out and probe was destroyed in atomospheric entry, Aug. 1992
Pioneer Venus 2 (multiprobe)	Aug. 8, 1978	Venus	Consisted of a "bus" which carried 1 large and 3 small atmospheric probes. All 4 probes entered the Venus atmosphere 12/9/78, followed by the bus; took readings of Venusian atmosphere; probes impacted on surface
Magellan	May 4, 1989	Venus	Landed on Venus 8/10/90; monitored geological activity; mapped more than 99% of planet surface, observed more than 1,600 volcanoes and volcanic features, enabling creation of a 3-dimensional map; showed that about 85% of the surface is covered by volcanic flows; ceased operating 10/11/94
Galileo	Oct. 18, 1989	Jupiter	Used Earth's gravity to propel it toward Jupiter; encountered Venus Feb. 1990; encountered Jupiter 12/7/95; encountered moons; released probe into Jovian atmosphere; intentionally flown into Jupiter 9/21/03 to prevent accidental contamination of Jupiter's moon Europa
Mars Global Surveyor	Nov. 7, 1996	Mars	Began orbiting Mars 9/11/97; began mapping survey of entire surface 3/9/99; discovered a weak magnetic field on planet; observed Martian moon Phobos; found evidence of liquid water in past 6/22/00
Mars Pathfinder	Dec. 4, 1996	Mars	Landed on Mars 7/4/97; rover *Sojourner* made measurements of climate and soil composition, sending thousands of surface images; ceased operating 9/27/97
Cassini-Huygens	Oct. 15, 1997	Saturn	Began orbiting Saturn 6/30/04; 4-year mission to study planet's atmosphere, rings, and moons; spotted evidence of a subterranean ocean and 300-mi-wide hot spot region on Titan; detected an atmosphere on Saturn's moon Enceladus; *Huygens* probe landed on Titan 1/14/05; found a muddy surface, possible deposits of water ice, channels carved by liquid methane springs
Lunar Prospector	Jan. 6, 1998	Moon	Began orbiting Moon 1/11/98; mapped abundance of 11 elements on Moon's surface; discovered evidence of water ice at both lunar poles; crashed into crater near Moon's south pole 7/31/99 to end mission
Deep Space 1	Oct. 24, 1998	Comet Borrelly	Flew within 1,500 mi of comet; sent back photos showing a 6 mi long nucleus
Stardust	Feb. 7, 1999	Comet Wild-2	Reached comet 1/2/04; gathered dust samples, returned to Earth 1/15/06
2001 Mars Odyssey	Apr. 7, 2001	Mars	Reached Mars 10/24/01; detected evidence of water ice near south pole; primary mission to study climate and geologic history completed Aug. 2004; began extended mission, aiming to identify minerals on Mars
Genesis	Aug. 8, 2001	Sun	Orbited Sun, collected particles from solar wind; capsule containing specimens crashed to Earth 9/8/04; some samples survived
Mars Express/ Beagle 2 lander	June 3, 2003	Mars	First European Space Agency probe to another planet; arrived at Mars Dec. 2003; performing remote sensing including photography in search for subsurface water; *Beagle 2* lander was deployed 12/19/03 but contact was lost soon after
Mars Exploration Rovers	June 7 & July 10, 2003	Mars	Rovers *Spirit* and *Opportunity* landed on Mars Jan. 2004, found further evidence that water existed on surface; *Spirit* took first photo of a Martian meteor; survived severe dust storms in 2007; *Opportunity* explored massive Victoria Crater Sept. 2007-Aug. 2008 and sighted larger Endeavor Crater Mar. 2009
MESSENGER	Mar. 2, 2004	Mercury	Flew by Mercury 10/6/08, expected to enter orbit in 2011; provided images of 20% of Mercury's surface; reached 2-bil-mi mark in Sept. 2007
Deep Impact	Jan. 12, 2005	Comet Tempel 1	Reached Tempel 1; deployed an impact probe which slammed into the comet on 7/4/05, impacting with a force equivalent to roughly 5 tons of TNT; orbiter probe passed Earth 12/31/07; en route to Comet Hartley 2 in Oct. 2010
Mars Reconnaissance Orbiter	Aug. 12, 2005	Mars	Reached Mars 3/10/06 and began taking detailed images of the Martian surface; in Mar. 2008, found salt deposits suggesting ancient water supplies; June 2008 found largest known crater in solar system

Spacecraft	Launch date[1]	Mission	Remarks
New Horizons (Pluto)	Jan. 19, 2006	Pluto & Charon	Flew by Jupiter July 2007. Due to reach Pluto and Charon in July 2015; may examine other Kuiper Belt Objects
Phoenix Mars Lander	Aug. 4, 2007	Mars	Landed 5/25/08; examining northern polar region, monitoring weather and analyzing minerals; evidence of water ice verified 7/31; lost contact 11/2/08
Dawn	Sept. 27, 2007	Asteroid Belt (bet. Jupiter and Mars)	Will compare the evolution of Ceres, a dwarf planet, with Vesta, an asteroid, in an effort to shed light on the formation of the solar system
Lunar CRater Observation and Sensing Satellite (LCROSS)	June 18, 2009	Moon	Launch vehicle's upper stage and LCROSS impacted Cabeus crater on 10/9/09; impacts were intended to create plumes of lunar debris that could be analyzed for water content

(1) Coordinated Universal Time

General Aviation and Air Taxi Active Aircraft, 2007

Source: Federal Aviation Administration; aircraft not associated with major airlines or the military.

	Total active	Personal	Busi- ness	Cor- porate	Instruc- tional	Aerial apps	External load	Other work	Sight- seeing	Air medical	Other	On demand operations
Fixed wing.....	186,806	120,616	23,796	10,128	12,301	7,544	6	572	588	59	3,817	7,378
Piston	166,907	118,180	21,094	2,433	12,129	5,856	0	413	560	25	2,982	3,234
Turboprop	9,514	1,687	1,822	2,224	117	1,649	6	85	4	26	428	1,463
Turbojet	10,385	749	880	5,472	54	37	0	73	24	7	407	2,681
Rotorcraft	9,567	1,492	567	537	1,083	2,850	175	69	97	159	585	1,954
Piston	2,769	910	235	21	866	501	6	12	63	0	86	68
Turbine.......	6,798	582	332	516	217	2,349	169	56	34	159	499	1,885
Other aircraft ..	5,940	4,726	4	23	330	5	2	132	558	0	118	41
Gliders.......	1,947	1,635	2	10	211	0	2	8	44	0	34	0
Lighter-than-air	3,993	3,091	2	13	119	5	0	123	513	0	85	41
Experimental...	23,228	20,404	594	168	422	277	4	147	18	4	1,084	107
Amateur......	19,538	17,895	428	5	353	105	2	70	11	0	670	0
Exhibition.....	2,101	1,807	42	7	29	18	0	23	0	0	175	0
Other........	1,589	702	123	156	40	153	2	54	7	4	240	107
Light sport	6,066	5,277	32	7	514	34	0	17	14	0	171	0
Total all aircraft	231,607	152,514	24,993	10,864	14,650	10,710	188	936	1,275	222	5,776	9,479

Note: Columns may not add to totals due to rounding. Personal—Flying for personal reasons; Business—Individual or group use for business transportation without a paid, professional crew; Corporate—Individual or group business transportation with a paid, professional crew (includes fractional ownership); Instructional—Flying under the supervision of a flight instructor; Aerial applications—Includes observation (Aerial mapping/photography, patrol, search and rescue, hunting, traffic advisory, ranching, surveillance, oil and mineral exploration, etc.), agriculture, forestry, public health, fire fighting, and other applications; External load—Operations such as helicopter hoists, hauling logs, etc.; Other work use—Construction work, parachuting, aerial advertising, towing gliders, etc.; Sight-seeing—Commercial sight-seeing; Air medical services—Air ambulance services, rescue, human organ transportation, emergency medical services; Other—Positioning flights, proficiency flights, training, ferrying, sales demos; On demand operations—On demand air taxi, air tours, commuter, and air medical services.

Estimated Active Airmen Certificates Held, 2008

Source: U.S. Dept. of Transportation, Federal Aviation Administration

Category	Certificates	Category	Certificates	Category	Certificates
Pilot total.................613,746		Sport 2,623		Parachute Rigger......... 8,248	
Airplane[1]		Rotorcraft only (helicopters) 14,647		Ground Instructor......... 74,983	
Private 222,596		Glider 21,055		Dispatcher 19,590	
Commercial 124,746		Nonpilot total 678,181		Flight Navigator........... 222	
Airline Transport........146,838		Mechanic 326,276		Flight Attendant 154,671	
Student................. 80,989		Repairmen 41,056		Flight Engineer........... 53,135	
Recreational............. 252					

Note: The term airmen includes men and women certified as pilots, mechanics, or other aviation technicians. (1) Includes pilots with an airplane-only certificate as well as those with an airplane and a helicopter and/or glider certificate.

Aircraft Operating Statistics

Source: Courtesy of Air Transport Association of America, Inc. Reprinted with permission. © 2003 by Air Transport Association of America, Inc. All rights reserved. Figures are averages for most commonly used models.

	No. of seats	Speed airborne (mph)	Flight length (mi)	Fuel (gal per hr)	Operating cost per hr		No. of seats	Speed airborne (mph)	Flight length (mi)	Fuel (gal per hr)	Operating cost per hr
B747-200/300*..	370	520	3,148	3,625	$9,153	B727-200*.....	148	430	644	1,289	$4,075
B747-400	367	534	3,960	3,411	8,443	B727-100*.....	—	417	468	989	13,667
B747-100*	—	503	2,022	1,762	3,852	A320	146	454	1,065	767	2,359
B747-F*.......	—	506	2,512	3,593	7,138	B737-400......	141	409	646	703	2,595
L-1011	325	494	2,023	1,981	8,042	MD-80	134	432	791	953	2,718
DC-10*........	286	497	1,637	2,405	7,374	B737-700LR ...	132	441	879	740	1,692
B767-400	265	495	1,682	1,711	3,124	B737-300/700 ..	132	403	542	723	2,388
B-777	263	525	3,515	2,165	5,105	A319	122	442	904	666	1,913
A330..........	261	509	3,559	1,407	3,076	A310-200*.....	—	455	847	1,561	8,066
MD-11*........	261	515	2,485	2,473	7,695	B737-100/200 ..	119	396	465	824	2,377
A300-600*	235	460	947	1,638	6,518	B717-200......	112	339	175	573	3,355
B757-300	235	472	1,309	985	2,345	B737-500......	110	407	576	756	2,347
B767-300ER*...	207	497	2,122	1,579	4,217	DC-9	101	387	496	826	2,071
DC-8*.........	—	437	686	1,712	8,065	F-100.........	87	398	587	662	2,303
B757-200*	181	464	1,175	1,045	3,312	B737-200C	55	387	313	924	3,421
B767-200ER....	175	487	1,987	1,404	3,873	ERJ-145	50	360	343	280	1,142
A321.........	169	454	1,094	673	1,347	CRJ-145	49	397	486	369	1,433
B737-800/900...	151	454	1,035	770	2,248	ERJ-135	37	357	382	267	969
MD-90	150	446	886	825	2,716	SD 340B	33	230	202	84	644

* Data include cargo operations.

Notable Aviation Firsts[1]

1903: On Dec. 17, near Kitty Hawk, NC, brothers Wilbur and Orville Wright made the 1st human-carrying, powered flight. Each made 2 flights; the longest, about 852 ft, lasted 59 sec.

1907: U.S. airplane manufacturing company formed by Glenn H. Curtiss.

1908: 1st airplane passenger, Lt. Frank P. Lahm, rode with Wilbur Wright in a brief (6 min, 24 sec) flight.

1911: 1st transportation of mail by airplane officially approved by the U.S. Postal Service began on Sept. 23. It lasted one week. In 1918, limited scheduled airmail service began. By 1921, scheduled transcontinental airmail service began between New York City and San Francisco.

1914: 1st scheduled passenger airline service began. It operated between St. Petersburg and Tampa, FL.

1919: 1st airline food, a basket lunch, was served as part of a commercial airline service.

1930: Ellen Church became 1st flight attendant.

1939: On Aug. 27, the German Heinkel He 178 made the 1st successful flight powered by a jet engine.

1947: Amer. Chuck Yeager broke the sound barrier, reaching Mach 1 speed in a Bell X-1 rocket-powered aircraft.

1947: Largest airplane ever flown, Howard Hughes's "Spruce Goose," flew 1 mi at an altitude of 80 ft.

1953: Jacqueline Cochran became 1st woman to fly faster than the speed of sound.

1960: Convair B-58, 1st supersonic bomber, was introduced.

1969: Tupolev Tu-144 became first passengr airliner to reach Mach 2. The plane had an approximate maximum speed of 1,200 mph.

1970: The Tupolev Tu-144, during commercial transport, reached about 1,335 mph at 53,475 ft.

1976: The Concorde began 1st scheduled supersonic commercial service.

1977: The Gossamer Condor successfully demonstrated human-powered flight through pedalling, completing figure-8 course of 1.15 mi.

1979: The human-powered Gossamer Albatross crossed the English Channel in 2 hrs, 49 mins.

1981: Solar Challenger became the 1st solar-powered airplane to cross the English Channel.

2001: Solar powered, propeller-driven plane Helios (NASA) reached 96,863 ft, breaking altitude record for non-rocket-powered aircraft.

2005: The Airbus 380, the biggest-ever commercial jet, was unveiled. It was 240 ft long, had a wingspan of 262 ft, and could seat a maximum of 840 passengers. Began commercial flights Oct. 25, 2007.

(1) Excludes notable around-the-world and international trips.

Notable Around-the-World and Intercontinental Trips

Aviator or craft	From/to	Miles	Time	Date
J. Alcock-A.W. Brown[1]	Newfoundland/Ireland	1,960	16h 12m	June 14-15, 1919
2 U.S. Army airplanes	Seattle/Seattle	26,103	35d 01h 11m	1924
Richard E. Byrd, Floyd Bennett[2]	Spitsbergen (Nor.)/N. Pole	1,545	15h 30m	May 9, 1926
Amundsen-Ellsworth-Nobile Polar Expedition (in a dirigible)	Spitsbergen (Nor.)/over N. Pole to Teller, Alaska	—	80h	May 11-14,1926
E. S. Evans and L. Wells (*New York World*)	New York/ New York	18,410[3]	28d 14h 36m 05s	June 16-July 14, 1926
Charles Lindbergh[4]	New York/Paris	3,610	33h 29m 30s	May 20-21, 1927
Amelia Earhart, W. Stultz, L. Gordon	Newfoundland/Wales	—	20h 40m	June 17-18, 1928
Graf Zeppelin	Friedrichshafen, Ger./Lakehurst, NJ	6,630	4d 15h 46m	Oct. 11-15, 1928
Graf Zeppelin	Lakehurst, NJ/Lakehurst, NJ	20,373	21d 05h 31m	Aug. 8-29, 1929
Wiley Post and Harold Gatty (Monoplane Winnie Mae)	New York/New York	15,474	8d 15h 51m	July 1, 1931
C. Pangborn-H. Herndon Jr.[5]	Misawa, Japan/Wenatchee, WA	4,458	41h 34m	Oct. 3-5, 1931
Amelia Earhart[6]	Newfoundland/Ireland	2,026	14h 56m	May 20-21, 1932
Wiley Post (Monoplane Winnie Mae)[7]	New York/New York	15,596	115h 36m 30s	July 15-22, 1933
Hindenburg Zeppelin	Lakehurst, NJ/Frankfort, Ger.	—	42h 53m	Aug. 9-11, 1936
Howard Hughes and 4 assistants	New York/New York	14,824	3d 19h 08m 10s	July 10-13, 1938
America, Pan American 4-engine Lockheed Constellation[8]	New York/New York	22,219	101h 32m	June 17-30, 1947
Col. Edward Eagan	New York/New York	20,559	147h 15m	Dec. 13, 1948
USAF B-50 Lucky Lady II (Capt. James Gallagher)[9]	Ft. Worth, TX/Ft. Worth, TX	23,452	94h 01m	Mar. 2, 1949
Col. D. Schilling, USAF [10]	England/Limestone, ME.	3,300	10h 01m	Sept. 22, 1950
C. F. Blair Jr.	Norway/Alaska	3,300	10h 29m	May 29, 1951
Canberra Bomber[11]	N. Ireland/Newfoundland	2,073	04h 34m	Aug. 26, 1952
	Newfoundland/N. Ireland	2,073	03h 25m	Aug. 26, 1952
3 USAF B-52 Strato-fortresses[12]	Merced, CA/CA	24,325	45h 19m	Jan. 15-18, 1957
USSR TU-114[13]	Moscow/New York	5,092	11h 06m	June 28, 1959
Peter Gluckmann (solo)	San Francisco/San Francisco	22,800	29d	Aug. 22-Sept. 20, 1959
Robert & Joan Wallick	Manila/Manila	23,129	5d 06h 17m 10s	June 2-7, 1966
Trevor K. Brougham	Darwin, Australia/Darwin, Australia	24,800	5d 05h 57m	Aug. 5-10, 1972
Arnold Palmer	Denver/Denver	22,985	57h 7m 12s	May 17-19, 1976
Boeing 747[14]	San Francisco/San Francisco	26,382	57h 25m 42s	Oct. 28-31, 1977
Richard Rutan, Jeana Yeager[15]	Edwards AFB/Edwards AFB (CA)	24,986	09d 03m 44s	Dec. 14-23, 1986
Concorde	New York/New York (A-T-W record)	(1,114 mph)	31h 27m 49s	Aug. 15-16, 1995
Col. Douglas L. Raaberg and crew, B1 bomber[16]	Dyess AFB, Abilene, TX/Dyess AFB	6,250	36h 13m 36s	June 3, 1995
Linda Finch[17]	Oakland, CA/Oakland, CA	26,000	73d	Mar. 17-May 28, 1997
Bertrand Piccard, Brian Jones[18]	Switzerland/Egypt	29,054.6	19d 21h 55m	Mar. 1-21, 1999
Steve Fossett[19]	Australia/Australia	21,109.6	14d 20h 01m	June 19-July 4, 2002
Steve Fossett[20]	Salina, KS/Salina, KS	26,366	67h 2m 38s	Mar. 1-3, 2005
Steve Fossett[21]	Cape Canaveral, FL/Bournemouth, UK	26,389.3	76h 45m	Feb. 8-11, 2006

(1) Nonstop transatlantic flight. (2) Claim of reaching N. Pole in dispute; if claim is untrue, then Amundsen-Ellsworth-Nobile were the first to fly over N. Pole. (3) Includes mileage by train and auto, 4,110; by plane, 6,300; by steamship, 8,000. (4) Solo transatlantic flight in the Ryan monoplane Spirit of St. Louis. (5) Nonstop transpacific flight. (6) First woman to complete a transoceanic solo flight. Earhart disappeared in the Pacific in 1937 while attempting an around-the-world flight. (7) First to fly solo around N circumference of the world, and first to fly twice around the world. (8) Inception of regular commercial global air service. (9) First nonstop round-the-world flight, refueled 4 times in flight. (10) Nonstop jet transatlantic flight. (11) Transatlantic round-trip on same day. (12) First nonstop global flight by jet planes; refueled in flight by KC-97 aerial tankers; average speed approx. 525 mph. (13) Nonstop between Moscow and New York. (14) Speed record around the world over both Earth's poles. (15) Circled Earth nonstop without refueling. (16) Refueled in flight 6 times. Tested B-1B bomber by bombing 3 pre-arranged target sites on 3 continents. (17) Followed the intended around-the-world route (1937) of Amelia Earhart. (18) First to circumnavigate the globe nonstop in a balloon. (19) First solo circumnavigation of globe nonstop in a balloon; time, dates, and distance are for complete flight, which exceeded circumnavigation because winds prevented landing. (20) First nonstop solo circumnavigation in an airplane without refueling. (21) Longest nonstop, non-refueled solo flight.

Edited by Michael J. Kaufman, Dept. of Physics and Astronomy, San Jose State University

Celestial Events Summary, 2010

There are 4 eclipses in 2010: one annular solar eclipse, one partial lunar eclipse, one total solar eclipse, and one total lunar eclipse. Neither solar eclipse will be visible in N America, but both lunar eclipses will be visible over wide portions of the continent. *See* page 338.

The Perseids meteor shower will be visible in Aug.; the Geminids in Dec. *See* page 333.

At the start of the year Saturn is up most of the night. Jupiter is low in the West at sunset, Mars is visible all night, and Mercury is low in the East before sunrise. Venus becomes a bright evening object by Mar., and remains present in the evening sky through Oct. By Nov., it is visible in the early morning sky. Jupiter is visible in the morning sky beginning in Mar., is up most of the night from Aug. through Nov., and is visible low in the West at sunset by the end of the year. Mars begins the year spending most of the night in

the sky; by mid-year, it can be seen following the sunset in the SW. Saturn is up all night long in Jan. and Feb., then begins its move into the evening sky; by Sept. it is lost in the glare of the Sun, reappearing in the morning sky in late Oct. The best opportunities for seeing Mercury occur in late Jan., late May, and late Sept. in the morning sky and in mid-Apr., early Aug., and early Dec. in the evening sky.

The crescent Moon, with its subdued light, regularly makes pretty pairings with the 2 brightest planets, Venus and Jupiter. Waxing crescent pairings are visible in the early evening soon after sunset, while waning crescent pairings are visible in the early morning before sunrise. The waxing crescent Moon pairs with Venus in each of the months from Apr. through Sept. The waxing crescent Moon pairs with Jupiter in the evening in Jan., and the waning crescent pairs with Jupiter in Apr., May, and June.

Astronomical Positions and Constants

Two celestial bodies are in **conjunction** when they are due North and South of each other, either in **right ascension** (with respect to the North celestial pole) or in **celestial longitude** (with respect to the North ecliptic pole). Celestial bodies in conjunction will rise and set at nearly the same time. For the inner planets—Mercury and Venus—**inferior conjunction** occurs when either planet passes between Earth and the Sun, while **superior conjunction** occurs when either Mercury or Venus is on the far side of the Sun. Celestial bodies are in **opposition** when their right ascensions differ by exactly 12 hours, or when their celestial longitudes differ by 180°. In this case one of the 2 objects in opposition will rise while the other is setting. **Quadrature** refers to the arrangement where the coordinates of 2 bodies differ by exactly 90°. These terms may refer to the relative positions of any 2 bodies as seen from Earth, but one of the bodies is so frequently the Sun that mention of the Sun is omitted in that case.

When objects are in conjunction, the alignment is not perfect, and one is usually passing above or below the other.

The geocentric angular separation between the Sun and an object is termed **elongation**. Elongation is limited only for Mercury and Venus; the greatest elongation for each of these bodies is approximately the time for longest observation. **Perihelion** is the point in an orbit that is nearest to the Sun, and **aphelion** is the point farthest from the Sun. **Perigee** is the point in an orbit that is nearest Earth, **apogee** the point that is farthest from Earth. An **occultation** of a planet or a star is an eclipse of it by some other body, usually the Moon. A **transit** of the Sun occurs when Mercury or Venus passes directly between Earth and the Sun, appearing to cross the disk of the Sun.

The following were adopted as part of the International Astronomical Union System of Astronomical Constants (1976): **Speed of light**, 299,792.458 km per sec., or about 186,282 statute mi per sec.; **solar parallax**, 8".794143; **Astronomical Unit** (the mean distance between the Earth and the Sun), 149,597,870 km, or 92,955,807 mi; **constant of nutation**, 9".2052; and **constant of aberration**, 20".49551.

Celestial Events Highlights, 2010

(Coordinated Universal Time, or UTC—the standard time of the prime meridian)

January

Mercury is visible low in the SE before sunrise the second half of the month.

Venus is too close to the Sun to be seen all month.

Mars rises after sunset all month.

Jupiter, **Uranus**, and **Neptune** are low in the SW after sunset all month.

Saturn rises in the middle of the night and is visible high in the W at sunrise.

Jan. 1: Sun in Sagittarius, Mercury in Sagittarius, Venus in Sagittarius, Mars in Leo, Jupiter in Capricorn, Saturn in Virgo all year, Uranus in Aquarius, Neptune in Capricorn; Moon passes 7.1° S of Pollux

Jan. 3: Moon passes 6.8° S of Mars

Jan. 4: Moon passes 4.2° S of Regulus, Mercury in inferior conjunction 2.7° N

Jan. 5: Mercury passes 3.4° N of Venus

Jan. 6: Moon passes 8.1° S of Saturn, Jupiter enters Aquarius

Jan. 7: Last Quarter Moon

Jan. 8: Moon passes 3.5° S of Spica

Jan. 10: Mars enters Cancer

Jan. 11: Venus in superior conjunction 0.8° S, Moon passes 1.1° N of Antares, occults Antares (like all occultations, this one is only visible from some locations on Earth)

Jan. 13: Moon passes 4.6° S of Mercury

Jan. 15: New Moon, Annular Solar eclipse (*see* details under Eclipses), Moon passes 1.4° N of Venus, occults Venus

Jan. 16: Uranus enters Pisces, where it remains for the rest of the year

Jan. 17: Moon passes 3.7° N of Neptune

Jan. 18: Moon passes 4.7° N of Jupiter, Venus enters Capricorn

Jan. 20: Moon passes 6° N of Uranus, Sun enters Capricorn

Jan. 23: First Quarter Moon

Jan. 26: Moon passes 9° N of Aldebaran

Jan. 27: Mercury at greatest elongation 24.8° W

Jan. 29: Moon passes 7.1° S of Pollux, Mars at opposition

Jan. 30: Full Moon, Moon passes 6.6° S of Mars

Jan. 31: Moon passes 4.2° S of Regulus

February

Mercury is visible low in the SE before sunrise all month.

Venus, **Jupiter**, and **Neptune** are too close to the Sun to be seen most of the month.

Mars rises before sunset and is visible most of the night.

Saturn rises late in the evening and is visible most of the night.

Uranus is low in the SW after sunset all month.

Feb. 3: Moon passes 8.2° S of Saturn

Feb. 4: Moon passes 3.4° S of Spica

Feb. 6: Last Quarter Moon

Feb. 7: Moon passes 1.1° N of Antares, occults Antares, Venus passes 1.1° S of Neptune

Feb. 9: Venus enters Aquarius

Feb. 10: Mercury enters Capricorn

Feb. 12: Moon passes 2.3° N of Mercury

Feb. 14: New Moon, Moon passes 3.8° N of Neptune, Neptune in conjunction with the Sun

Feb. 15: Moon passes 5.9° N of Venus, Moon passes 5.1° N of Jupiter

Feb. 16: Moon passes 5.9° N of Uranus, Venus passes 0.6° S of Jupiter, Sun enters Aquarius

Feb. 22: First Quarter Moon, Moon passes 8.8° N of Aldebaran

Feb. 25: Moon passes 7.2° S of Pollux

Feb. 26: Moon passes 5.3° S of Mars

Feb. 27: Mercury passes 1.8° S of Neptune

Feb. 28: Full Moon, Moon passes 4.1° S of Regulus, Mercury enters Aquarius, Jupiter in conjunction with the Sun

March

Mercury is too close to the Sun to be seen all month.
Venus is visible low in the SW after sunset all month.
Mars is high in the E at sunset and up much of the night.
Jupiter and **Neptune** low in the SE before sunrise.
Saturn rises around sunset and is visible all night.
Uranus is too close to the Sun to be seen.

Mar. 2: Moon passes 8.2° S of Saturn

Mar. 3: Moon passes 3.3° S of Spica, Venus passes 0.7° S of Uranus, Venus enters Pisces

Mar. 7: Last Quarter Moon; Moon passes 1.3° N of Antares, occults Antares, Mercury passes 1.2° S of Jupiter

Mar. 13: Moon passes 3.9° N of Neptune, Sun enters Pisces, Venus enters Cetus

Mar. 14: Mercury in superior conjunction 1.5° S

Mar. 15: New Moon, Moon passes 5.6° N of Jupiter, Mercury passes 0.7° S of Uranus, Venus enters Pisces

Mar. 16: Moon passes 5.9° N of Uranus, Moon passes 6.7° N of Mercury, Mercury enters Pisces

Mar. 17: Moon passes 6.6° N of Venus, Uranus in conjunction with the Sun

Mar. 20: Vernal Equinox 17:32 UTC (13:32 EDT)

Mar. 21: Moon passes 8.7° N of Aldebaran

Mar. 22: Saturn at opposition

Mar. 23: First Quarter Moon, Neptune enters Aquarius

Mar. 25: Moon passes 7.4° S of Pollux, Moon passes 4.5° S of Mars

Mar. 27: Moon passes 4.2° S of Regulus

Mar. 29: Moon passes 8.1° S of Saturn

Mar. 30: Full Moon

Mar. 31: Moon passes 3.1° S of Spica, Venus enters Aries

April

Mercury and Venus are low in the SW after sunset, with Mercury too close to the Sun by the end of the month.
Mars is high overhead at sunset and sets before sunrise.
Jupiter, **Uranus**, and **Neptune** are low in the SE before sunrise.
Saturn is low in the SE at sunset and is visible most of the night.
Watch for the waxing crescent **Moon** paired with Mercury and Venus after sunset on the 16th.

Apr. 3: Moon passes 1.6° N of Antares, occults Antares, Mercury enters Aries

Apr. 6: Last Quarter Moon

Apr. 8: Mercury at greatest elongation 19° E

Apr. 10: Moon passes 4.1° N of Neptune

Apr. 11: Moon passes 6.1° N of Jupiter

Apr. 12: Moon passes 6.0° N of Uranus

Apr. 14: New Moon

Apr. 15: Moon passes 1.5° N of Mercury, occults Mercury

Apr. 16: Moon passes 4.1° N of Venus

Apr. 18: Moon passes 8.4° N of Aldebaran

Apr. 19: Sun enters Aries

Apr. 20: Venus enters Taurus

Apr. 21: First Quarter Moon, Moon passes 7.7° S of Pollux

Apr. 22: Moon passes 4.6° S of Mars

Apr. 23: Moon passes 4.4° S of Regulus

Apr. 26: Moon passes 8.1° S of Saturn

Apr. 27: Moon passes 3.1° S of Spica

Apr. 28: Full Moon, Mercury in inferior conjunction 0.9° N

Apr. 30: Moon passes 1.7° N of Antares, occults Antares

May

Mercury is low in the SE before sunrise all month, though very close to the Sun for the first week of May.
Venus is visible low in the SW after sunset all month.
Mars is high overhead at sunset and sets after midnight.
Jupiter, **Uranus**, and **Neptune** are low in the SE for several hours before sunrise.
Saturn is nearly overhead at sunset and visible until just before sunrise.

May 3: Jupiter enters Pisces

May 4: Venus passes 6.5° N of Aldebaran

May 6: Last Quarter Moon

May 7: Moon passes 4.4° N of Neptune

May 9: Moon passes 6.5° N of Jupiter

May 10: Moon passes 6.2° N of Uranus, Mercury enters Pisces

May 12: Moon passes 7.8° N of Mercury

May 13: Mars enters Leo

May 14: New Moon, Sun enters Taurus

May 15: Moon passes 8.3° N of Aldebaran, Mercury enters Cetus

May 16: Moon passes 0.1° N of Venus, occults Venus

May 18: Moon passes 7.9° S of Pollux

May 20: Moon passes 5.2° S of Mars, Venus enters Gemini

May 21: First Quarter Moon, Moon passes 4.7° S of Regulus

May 23: Moon passes 8.2° S of Saturn, Mercury enters Aries

May 24: Moon passes 3.2° S of Spica

May 26: Mercury at greatest elongation 25° W

May 27: Full Moon

May 28: Moon passes 1.8° N of Antares, occults Antares

June

Mercury is low in the SE before sunrise the first half of the month, becoming difficult to spot as it nears the Sun later in the month.
Venus is visible low in the SW after sunset all month.
Mars and **Saturn** are high in the W at sunset and visible the first half of the night.
Jupiter, **Uranus**, and **Neptune** rise around midnight and are high overhead at sunrise.
Watch for the waxing crescent **Moon** near Mars and between Venus and Saturn at sunset on the 17th.

June 3: Moon passes 4.6° N of Neptune

June 4: Last Quarter Moon

June 6: Moon passes 6.9° N of Jupiter, Moon passes 6.4° N of Uranus, Mars passes 0.9° N of Regulus, Jupiter passes 0.5° S of Uranus, Mercury enters Taurus

June 9: Venus passes 4.8° S of Pollux

June 11: Moon passes 5.2° N of Mercury, Moon passes 8.3° N of Aldebaran

June 12: New Moon, Venus enters Cancer

June 14: Moon passes 8° S of Pollux

June 15: Moon passes 3.9° S of Venus

June 16: Mercury passes 4.6° N of Aldebaran

June 17: Moon passes 4.8° S of Regulus, Moon passes 5.9° S of Mars

June 19: First Quarter Moon, Moon passes 8.2° S of Saturn

June 21: Moon passes 3.3° S of Spica, Northern Solstice 11:28 UTC (07:28 EDT), Sun enters Gemini

June 24: Moon passes 1.8° N of Antares, occults Antares

June 26: Full Moon, Partial lunar eclipse (*see* details under Eclipses), Mercury enters Gemini

June 28: Mercury in superior conjunction 1.2° N

June 30: Venus enters Leo

July

Mercury is low in the SW after sunset the second half of the month.

Venus is visible in the SW after sunset all month.

Mars and **Saturn** are high in the SW at sunset and set before midnight.

Jupiter, **Uranus**, and **Neptune** rise before midnight and are high overhead at sunrise.

Watch for the waxing crescent **Moon** below Mars, Venus, and Saturn at sunset on the 15th. Mars, Venus, and Saturn are separated by less than 10° at the end of the month.

July 1: Moon passes 4.7° N of Neptune

July 3: Moon passes 6.5° N of Uranus

July 4: Last Quarter Moon, Moon passes 7.1° N of Jupiter

July 6: Mercury passes 4.9° S of Pollux

July 9: Moon passes 8.3° N of Aldebaran, Mercury enters Cancer

July 10: Venus passes 1.1° N of Regulus, occults Regulus

July 11: New Moon, Total solar eclipse (*see* details under Eclipses)

July 12: Moon passes 8° S of Pollux

July 13: Moon passes 4.2° S of Mercury

July 14: Moon passes 4.8° S of Regulus

July 15: Moon passes 6.0° S of Venus

July 16: Moon passes 6.2° S of Mars, Moon passes 8.2° S of Saturn

July 18: First Quarter Moon, Moon passes 3.3° S of Spica

July 20: Mercury enters Leo, Mars enters Virgo

July 21: Moon passes 1.8° N of Antares, occults Antares, Sun enters Cancer

July 26: Full Moon

July 27: Mercury passes 0.3° S of Regulus

July 28: Moon passes 4.6° N of Neptune

July 31: Moon passes 6.5° N of Uranus, Moon passes 7.2° N of Jupiter

August

Mercury is low in the SW after sunset, becoming difficult to spot as it nears the Sun the last week of the month.

Venus, **Mars**, and **Saturn** are visible in the SW after sunset all month.

Jupiter, **Uranus**, and **Neptune** rise around sunset and are visible all night.

Watch for the waxing crescent **Moon** just W and below Mars, Venus, and Saturn at sunset on the 13th. Mars, Venus, and Saturn make a tight grouping after sunset the first half of the month.

Aug. 1: Mars passes 1.9° S of Saturn, Venus enters Virgo

Aug. 3: Last Quarter Moon

Aug. 5: Moon passes 8.2° N of Aldebaran

Aug. 6: Mercury enters Sextans

Aug. 7: Mercury at greatest elongation 27° E

Aug. 8: Moon passes 8° S of Pollux, Mercury enters Leo

Aug. 10: New Moon, Venus passes 3.1° S of Saturn

Aug. 11: Moon passes 4.8° S of Regulus, Sun enters Leo

Aug. 12: Moon passes 2.4° S of Mercury

Aug. 13: Moon passes 8.0° S of Saturn, Moon passes 4.5° S of Venus, Moon passes 5.9° S of Mars

Aug. 14: Moon passes 3.2° S of Spica

Aug. 15: Neptune enters Capricorn

Aug. 16: First Quarter Moon

Aug. 17: Moon passes 1.9° N of Antares, occults Antares

Aug. 20: Venus at greatest elongation 46° E, Neptune at opposition

Aug. 23: Venus passes 2.5° S of Mars

Aug. 24: Full Moon, Moon passes 4.6° N of Neptune

Aug. 27: Moon passes 6.3° N of Uranus, Moon passes 7.2° N of Jupiter

September

Mercury is visible low in the SE before sunrise the second half of the month.

Venus and **Mars** are visible in the SW after sunset all month.

Jupiter, **Uranus**, and **Neptune** are low in the E at sunset and visible all night.

Saturn is low in the SW after sunset all month, becoming difficult to spot as it nears the Sun late in the month.

Watch for the waxing crescent **Moon** paired with Mars and Venus on the 11th.

Sept. 1: Last Quarter Moon, Moon passes 8.0° N of Aldebaran, Venus passes 1.2° S of Spica, Mercury enters Sextans

Sept. 3: Mercury in inferior conjunction 3.9° S

Sept. 4: Mars passes 2.2° N of Spica

Sept. 5: Moon passes 8.1° S of Pollux

Sept. 7: Moon passes 4.8° S of Regulus, Moon passes 1.7° S of Mercury, occults Mercury

Sept. 8: New Moon, Mercury enters Leo

Sept. 9: Moon passes 7.9° S of Saturn

Sept. 11: Moon passes 3.0° S of Spica, Moon passes 5.0° S of Mars, Moon passes 0.3° S of Venus, occults Venus

Sept. 14: Moon passes 2.1° N of Antares

Sept. 15: First Quarter Moon

Sept. 17: Sun enters Virgo

Sept. 19: Mercury at greatest elongation 18° W

Sept. 20: Moon passes 4.6° N of Neptune

Sept. 21: Jupiter at opposition, Uranus at opposition

Sept. 22: Jupiter passes 0.9° S of Uranus

Sept. 23: Full Moon, Moon passes 7.1° N of Jupiter, Moon passes 6.3° N of Uranus, Autumnal Equinox 03:09 UTC (23:09 EDT Sept. 22)

Sept. 25: Venus enters Libra

Sept. 26: Mars enters Libra

Sept. 29: Moon passes 7.8° N of Aldebaran, Venus passes 6.5° S of Mars

Sept. 30: Mercury enters Virgo

October

Mercury is visible low in the SE before sunset the first few days of the month.

Venus is low in the SW after sunset, becoming difficult to spot as it nears the Sun the last week of the month.

Mars is low in the SW after sunset all month.

Jupiter, **Uranus**, and **Neptune** are in the E at sunset and set soon before sunrise.

Saturn is visible low in the SE at sunrise the second half of the month.

Oct. 1: Last Quarter Moon, Saturn in conjunction with the Sun

Oct. 2: Moon passes 8.4° S of Pollux

Oct. 4: Moon passes 4.9° S of Regulus

Oct. 7: New Moon, Moon passes 7.3° S of Mercury, Moon passes 7.8° S of Saturn

Oct. 8: Moon passes 2.9° S of Spica, Mercury passes 0.6° S of Saturn

Oct. 9: Moon passes 3.3° N of Venus

Oct. 10: Moon passes 3.5° S of Mars

Oct. 11: Moon passes 2.4° N of Antares

Oct. 14: First Quarter Moon, Jupiter enters Aquarius

Oct. 16: Mercury passes 3.2° N of Spica

Oct. 17: Moon passes 4.7° N of Neptune, Mercury in superior conjunction 0.9° N

Oct. 20: Moon passes 7.1° N of Jupiter, Moon passes 6.3° N of Uranus, Venus enters Virgo

Oct. 23: Full Moon

Oct. 24: Mercury passes 7.2° N of Venus

Oct. 26: Moon passes 7.6° N of Aldebaran, Mercury enters Libra

Oct. 27: Mars enters Scorpius

Oct. 29: Moon passes 8.6° S of Pollux, Venus in inferior conjunction 6.0° S

Oct. 30: Last Quarter Moon

Oct. 31: Sun enters Libra

November

Mercury is visible low in the SW after sunset the second half of the month.

Venus and **Saturn** are visible low in the SE before sunrise all month.

Mars is visible low in the SW after sunset all month.

Jupiter, **Uranus**, and **Neptune** are high overhead at sunset and set several hours before sunrise.

Nov. 1: Moon passes 5.1° S of Regulus

Nov. 4: Moon passes 7.8° S of Saturn, Moon passes 2.9° S of Spica

Nov. 5: Moon passes 0.2° S of Venus, occults Venus

Nov. 6: New Moon

Nov. 7: Moon passes 1.7° S of Mercury, occults Mercury, Moon passes 1.6° S of Mars, occults Mars

Nov. 8: Moon passes 2.5° N of Antares, Mars enters Ophiucus

Nov. 9: Mercury enters Scorpius

Nov. 10: Mars passes 4.0° N of Antares

Nov. 13: First Quarter Moon

Nov. 14: Moon passes 5.0° N of Neptune

Nov. 15: Mercury passes 2.5° N of Antares, Mercury enters Ophiucus

Nov. 16: Moon passes 7.2° N of Jupiter, Moon passes 6.5° N of Uranus

Nov. 21: Full Moon, Mercury passes 1.7° S of Mars

Nov. 22: Moon passes 7.5° N of Aldebaran

Nov. 24: Sun enters Scorpius

Nov. 25: Moon passes 8.8° S of Pollux

Nov. 28: Last Quarter Moon, Moon passes 5.3° S of Regulus, Mercury enters Sagittarius

Nov. 30: Sun enters Ophiucus

December

Mercury is visble low in the SW at sunset the first half of the month.

Venus and **Saturn** are visible low in the SE before sunrise all month.

Mars is visible low in the SW after sunset the first half of the month.

Jupiter, **Uranus**, and **Neptune** are high overhead at sunset and set several hours before sunrise.

Watch for the waxing crescent **Moon** near Mars and Mercury after sunset on the 6th and 7th.

Dec. 1: Moon passes 8.0° S of Saturn, Mercury at greatest elongation 21.5° E

Dec. 2: Moon passes 3.0° S of Spica, Moon passes 6.4° S of Venus

Dec. 3: Mars enters Sagittarius

Dec. 5: New Moon, Moon passes 2.5° N of Antares

Dec. 6: Moon passes 0.5° N of Mars, occults Mars

Dec. 7: Moon passes 1.8° N of Mercury

Dec. 11: Moon passes 5.1° N of Neptune

Dec. 13: First Quarter Moon, Venus enters Libra

Dec. 14: Moon passes 7.2° N of Jupiter, Mercury passes 1.0° N of Mars, Moon passes 6.6° N of Uranus

Dec. 18: Sun enters Sagittarius, Jupiter enters Pisces

Dec. 20: Moon passes 7.5° N of Aldebaran, Mercury in inferior conjunction 2.0° N

Dec. 21: Full Moon, Total lunar eclipse (*see* details under Eclipses), Southern Solstice 23:38 UTC (18:38 EST)

Dec. 22: Mercury enters Ophiucus

Dec. 23: Moon passes 8.8° S of Pollux

Dec. 25: Moon passes 5.4° S of Regulus

Dec. 28: Last Quarter Moon

Dec. 29: Moon passes 8.1° S of Saturn, Moon passes 3.1° S of Spica

Dec. 31: Moon passes 7.0° S of Venus

Meteorites and Meteor Showers

When a chunk of material, ice or rock, plunges into Earth's atmosphere and burns up in a fiery display, the event is a **meteor**. While the chunk of material is still in space, it is a **meteoroid**. If a portion of the material survives passage through the atmosphere and reaches the ground, the remnant on the ground is a **meteorite**.

Meteorites found on Earth are classified into types, depending on their composition: **irons**, those composed chiefly of iron, a small percentage of nickel, and traces of other metals such as cobalt; **stones**, stony meteors consisting of silicates; and **stony irons**, containing varying proportions of both iron and stone.

Serious study of meteorites as non-earth objects began in the 20th century. Scientists use sophisticated chemical analysis, X-rays, and mass spectrography in determining their origin and composition. Although most meteorites are now believed to be fragments of asteroids or comets, geochemical studies have shown that a few Antarctic stones came from the Moon or from Mars, presumably ejected by the explosive impact of asteroids.

The **largest known meteorite**, estimated to weigh about 55 metric tons, is situated at Hoba West near Grootfontein, Namibia. The Manicouagan impact crater in Quebec, Canada, with an estimated diameter of 60 mi, is one of the largest crater structures still visible on the surface of the Earth. Although not visible to the eye, other still larger impact craters identified include the Vredefort crater in South Africa at 185 mi across and the Sudbury crater in Ontario, Canada, es-

timated at 125 mi across. The Bedout impact site off the NW coast of Australia gained attention in 2004, when scientists identified further evidence in support of the idea that it may be linked to the Permian extinction event 250 million years ago.

Meteor showers vary in strength, but usually the 3 most visible meteor showers of the year are the **Perseids**, around Aug. 13, the **Orionids**, around Oct. 21, and the **Geminids**, around Dec. 14. These showers feature meteors at the rate of about 60 per hour. Best observing conditions occur with the absence of moonlight, usually when the Moon's phase is between waning crescent Moon and waxing quarter Moon.

For most meteor showers the cometary debris is relatively uniformly scattered along the comet's orbit. However, in the case of the **Leonid** meteor shower, which occurs every year around Nov. 17-18, the cometary debris, from Comet Temple-Tuttle, seems to be bunched up in one stretch. Hence, most years when Earth crosses the orbit of this comet, the meteor shower produced is relatively weak. However, about every 33 years, Earth encounters the bunched-up debris. Sometimes the storm is a disappointment, as it was in 1899 and 1933; at other times it is a roaring success, as in 1833 and 1866. The Leonids stormed again more recently, producing rates of 1,000-3,000 meteors per hour in 2001. Best showers in 2010 are the Perseids in mid-Aug., with a several day old Moon, and the Geminids in mid-Dec., with a first quarter Moon. The Orionids in late Oct. will be more difficult to see as the Moon will be full.

Rising and Setting of Planets, 2010

(In Coordinated Universal Time. 0 in the *h* col. designates 12 AM.)

Venus, 2010

Date	20° N Latitude Rise h m	20° N Latitude Set h m	30° N Latitude Rise h m	30° N Latitude Set h m	40° N Latitude Rise h m	40° N Latitude Set h m	50° N Latitude Rise h m	50° N Latitude Set h m	60° N Latitude Rise h m	60° N Latitude Set h m
Jan. 1	6 27	17 19	6 48	16 58	7 15	16 31	7 54	15 52	9 02	14 44
11	6 40	17 36	7 01	17 16	7 26	16 50	8 03	16 14	9 06	15 11
21	6 50	17 54	7 09	17 36	7 31	17 13	8 03	16 41	8 56	15 48
31	6 57	18 11	7 12	17 56	7 31	17 37	7 57	17 12	8 39	16 30
Feb. 10	7 01	18 27	7 12	18 16	7 26	18 02	7 45	17 43	8 15	17 13
20	7 02	18 42	7 09	18 35	7 18	18 26	7 30	18 14	7 49	17 56
Mar. 2	7 02	18 56	7 05	18 53	7 08	18 50	7 13	18 45	7 20	18 38
12	7 00	19 09	6 59	19 11	6 57	19 13	6 55	19 16	6 51	19 20
22	6 59	19 23	6 53	19 29	6 46	19 36	6 36	19 46	6 21	20 02
Apr. 1	6 58	19 37	6 48	19 47	6 35	20 00	6 18	20 17	5 52	20 45
11	6 59	19 51	6 45	20 06	6 27	20 24	6 03	20 48	5 23	21 29
21	7 02	20 07	6 44	20 25	6 22	20 48	5 51	21 20	4 58	22 14
May 1	7 08	20 23	6 47	20 44	6 21	21 11	5 44	21 49	4 37	22 57
11	7 18	20 39	6 55	21 02	6 26	21 31	5 43	22 14	4 25	23 34
21	7 30	20 54	7 06	21 18	6 36	21 48	5 51	22 32	4 27	23 57
31	7 43	21 06	7 20	21 29	6 50	21 59	6 07	22 42	4 46	00 03
June 10	7 58	21 15	7 36	21 36	7 09	22 03	6 30	22 42	5 19	23 52
20	8 12	21 20	7 53	21 38	7 30	22 02	6 56	22 35	5 58	23 32
30	8 25	21 21	8 09	21 36	7 50	21 55	7 23	22 21	6 39	23 05
July 10	8 36	21 19	8 24	21 30	8 10	21 44	7 50	22 03	7 19	22 34
20	8 45	21 13	8 37	21 21	8 28	21 30	8 15	21 42	7 56	22 01
30	8 51	21 06	8 48	21 09	8 44	21 13	8 39	21 18	8 30	21 26
Aug. 9	8 56	20 56	8 57	20 55	8 58	20 54	9 00	20 52	9 02	20 49
19	8 59	20 45	9 04	20 39	9 10	20 33	9 19	20 24	9 32	20 11
29	8 59	20 31	9 08	20 22	9 20	20 10	9 35	19 55	9 59	19 31
Sept. 8	8 56	20 15	9 09	20 02	9 25	19 46	9 47	19 23	10 22	18 48
18	8 47	19 55	9 04	19 38	9 24	19 18	9 52	18 49	10 39	18 03
28	8 30	19 28	8 49	19 09	9 12	18 45	9 46	18 12	10 43	17 15
Oct. 8	7 59	18 52	8 19	18 32	8 45	18 06	9 21	17 30	10 24	16 27
18	7 10	18 05	7 30	17 45	7 55	17 21	8 30	16 46	9 30	15 46
28	6 07	17 11	6 24	16 54	6 45	16 33	7 14	16 04	8 03	15 16
Nov. 7	5 03	16 20	5 16	16 07	5 32	15 51	5 54	15 29	6 29	14 54
17	4 12	15 39	4 22	15 29	4 34	15 17	4 51	15 00	5 17	14 34
27	3 38	15 11	3 47	15 02	3 58	14 51	4 12	14 36	4 35	14 14
Dec. 7	3 18	14 51	3 27	14 42	3 39	14 31	3 54	14 15	4 17	13 52
17	3 09	14 37	3 19	14 27	3 32	14 14	3 49	13 57	4 16	13 30
27	3 07	14 29	3 19	14 17	3 34	14 02	3 54	13 41	4 27	13 08

Mars, 2010

Date	20° N Latitude Rise h m	20° N Latitude Set h m	30° N Latitude Rise h m	30° N Latitude Set h m	40° N Latitude Rise h m	40° N Latitude Set h m	50° N Latitude Rise h m	50° N Latitude Set h m	60° N Latitude Rise h m	60° N Latitude Set h m
Jan. 1	20 13	09 17	19 56	09 34	19 34	09 55	19 04	10 26	18 14	11 16
11	19 23	08 31	19 05	08 49	18 42	09 12	18 10	09 44	17 15	10 39
21	18 28	07 40	18 09	08 00	17 44	08 24	17 09	08 59	16 09	10 00
31	17 31	06 47	17 10	07 08	16 44	07 34	16 06	08 11	15 00	09 18
Feb. 10	16 34	05 54	16 12	06 15	15 45	06 43	15 05	07 22	13 53	08 34
20	15 41	05 03	15 19	05 25	14 51	05 53	14 10	06 34	12 55	07 49
Mar. 2	14 55	04 16	14 32	04 38	14 04	05 06	13 23	05 47	12 07	07 03
12	14 14	03 34	13 52	03 56	13 24	04 24	12 43	05 04	11 29	06 18
22	13 38	02 56	13 17	03 18	12 50	03 45	12 10	04 24	11 00	05 35
Apr. 1	13 08	02 23	12 47	02 44	12 21	03 10	11 43	03 47	10 37	04 54
11	12 41	01 53	12 21	02 12	11 56	02 37	11 20	03 13	10 19	04 15
21	12 16	01 25	11 58	01 43	11 34	02 07	11 01	02 40	10 05	03 37
May 1	11 55	00 58	11 37	01 16	11 16	01 37	10 45	02 08	09 54	02 59
11	11 35	00 33	11 19	00 49	10 59	01 09	10 31	01 37	09 45	02 23
21	11 16	00 09	11 02	00 24	10 44	00 42	10 19	01 06	09 39	01 47
31	10 58	23 44	10 46	23 56	10 30	00 14	10 09	00 36	09 34	01 11
June 10	10 42	23 21	10 31	23 31	10 18	23 45	09 59	00 06	09 30	00 35
20	10 26	22 58	10 17	23 07	10 06	23 18	09 51	23 33	09 27	23 56
30	10 10	22 36	10 03	22 43	09 55	22 51	09 43	23 03	09 25	23 20
July 10	09 55	22 14	09 51	22 19	09 45	22 25	09 36	22 33	09 24	22 45
20	09 41	21 53	09 38	21 56	09 35	21 59	09 30	22 03	09 23	22 10
30	09 27	21 32	09 27	21 32	09 26	21 33	09 25	21 34	09 23	21 35
Aug. 9	09 14	21 11	09 16	21 09	09 18	21 07	09 20	21 05	09 24	21 00
19	09 01	20 51	09 05	20 47	09 10	20 42	09 16	20 36	09 26	20 26
29	08 49	20 32	08 55	20 25	09 03	20 18	09 13	20 08	09 28	19 52
Sept. 8	08 38	20 13	08 46	20 04	08 57	19 54	09 10	19 40	09 32	19 19
18	08 27	19 55	08 38	19 44	08 51	19 31	09 09	19 13	09 36	18 46
28	08 18	19 38	08 31	19 25	08 46	19 09	09 08	18 48	09 42	18 14
Oct. 8	08 09	19 22	08 24	19 08	08 42	18 49	09 07	18 24	09 48	17 43
18	08 01	19 08	08 18	18 51	08 38	18 30	09 07	18 01	09 55	17 14
28	07 54	18 55	08 12	18 37	08 35	18 13	09 07	17 41	10 02	16 47
Nov. 7	07 47	18 44	08 07	18 24	08 32	17 59	09 07	17 23	10 08	16 22
17	07 41	18 34	08 02	18 13	08 29	17 46	09 06	17 08	10 13	16 02
27	07 35	18 25	07 57	18 03	08 25	17 36	09 04	16 56	10 14	15 46
Dec. 7	07 29	18 18	07 51	17 56	08 19	17 28	08 59	16 48	10 12	15 36
17	07 23	18 13	07 45	17 50	08 13	17 23	08 52	16 43	10 04	15 31
27	07 16	18 08	07 37	17 46	08 04	17 19	08 43	16 41	09 51	15 33

Jupiter, 2010

Date	20° N Latitude Rise	Set	30° N Latitude Rise	Set	40° N Latitude Rise	Set	50° N Latitude Rise	Set	60° N Latitude Rise	Set
	h m	h m	h m	h m	h m	h m	h m	h m	h m	h m
Jan. 1	09 30	20 53	09 42	20 42	09 56	20 27	10 15	20 08	10 46	19 37
11	08 58	20 23	09 09	20 12	09 22	19 59	09 40	19 40	10 09	19 12
21	08 25	19 53	08 36	19 43	08 48	19 31	09 05	19 14	09 32	18 47
31	07 54	19 24	08 03	19 14	08 15	19 03	08 31	18 47	08 55	18 23
Feb. 10	07 22	18 55	07 31	18 46	07 41	18 35	07 56	18 21	08 18	17 59
20	06 50	18 26	06 58	18 18	07 08	18 08	07 21	17 55	07 41	17 35
Mar. 2	06 19	17 57	06 26	17 50	06 35	17 41	06 46	17 29	07 04	17 11
12	05 47	17 28	05 53	17 21	06 01	17 14	06 12	17 03	06 28	16 48
22	05 15	16 59	05 21	16 53	05 28	16 46	05 37	16 37	05 51	16 23
Apr. 1	04 43	16 29	04 48	16 25	04 54	16 19	05 02	16 11	05 14	15 59
11	04 11	16 00	04 15	15 56	04 20	15 51	04 27	15 44	04 37	15 34
21	03 39	15 30	03 42	15 26	03 46	15 22	03 51	15 17	03 59	15 09
May 1	03 06	14 59	03 08	14 56	03 12	14 53	03 16	14 49	03 22	14 43
11	02 32	14 28	02 35	14 26	02 37	14 23	02 40	14 20	02 45	14 16
21	01 59	13 56	02 00	13 55	02 02	13 53	02 04	13 51	02 07	13 48
31	01 24	13 24	01 25	13 23	01 27	13 21	01 28	13 20	01 30	13 18
June 10	00 49	12 50	00 50	12 50	00 51	12 49	00 51	12 48	00 52	12 47
20	00 14	12 16	00 14	12 15	00 14	12 15	00 14	12 15	00 14	12 15
30	23 34	11 40	23 34	11 40	23 33	11 40	23 33	11 40	23 32	11 41
July 10	22 56	11 03	22 56	11 03	22 56	11 04	22 55	11 04	22 54	11 05
20	22 18	10 25	22 17	10 25	22 17	10 25	22 16	10 26	22 15	10 27
30	21 38	09 45	21 38	09 45	21 38	09 46	21 37	09 46	21 36	09 47
Aug. 9	20 58	09 04	20 58	09 04	20 58	09 04	20 57	09 05	20 57	09 05
19	20 17	08 22	20 17	08 22	20 17	08 22	20 17	08 21	20 17	08 21
29	19 34	07 39	19 35	07 38	19 36	07 37	19 36	07 37	19 37	07 36
Sept. 8	18 51	06 54	18 52	06 53	18 54	06 52	18 55	06 51	18 57	06 49
18	18 08	06 10	18 10	06 08	18 11	06 06	18 13	06 04	18 17	06 01
28	17 25	05 25	17 27	05 23	17 29	05 21	17 32	05 18	17 36	05 13
Oct. 8	16 42	04 40	16 44	04 38	16 47	04 35	16 50	04 31	16 56	04 26
18	15 59	03 56	16 01	03 53	16 05	03 50	16 09	03 46	16 15	03 40
28	15 17	03 13	15 20	03 10	15 23	03 07	15 28	03 02	15 35	02 55
Nov. 7	14 36	02 31	14 39	02 28	14 43	02 25	14 47	02 20	14 55	02 12
17	13 56	01 51	13 59	01 48	14 03	01 44	14 07	01 39	14 15	01 32
27	13 17	01 12	13 20	01 09	13 23	01 05	13 28	01 01	13 35	00 53
Dec. 7	12 39	00 35	12 41	00 32	12 45	00 29	12 49	00 24	12 56	00 17
17	12 02	23 55	12 04	23 53	12 07	23 50	12 11	23 46	12 17	23 40
27	11 25	23 21	11 28	23 18	11 30	23 16	11 34	23 13	11 39	23 08

Saturn, 2010

Date	20° N Latitude Rise	Set	30° N Latitude Rise	Set	40° N Latitude Rise	Set	50° N Latitude Rise	Set	60° N Latitude Rise	Set
	h m	h m	h m	h m	h m	h m	h m	h m	h m	h m
Jan. 1	23 31	11 39	23 31	11 39	23 30	11 40	23 29	11 41	23 28	11 43
11	22 53	11 00	22 52	11 01	22 51	11 01	22 50	11 02	22 49	11 04
21	22 13	10 21	22 12	10 21	22 12	10 22	22 11	10 23	22 09	10 25
31	21 33	09 41	21 32	09 42	21 31	09 43	21 30	09 44	21 28	09 46
Feb. 10	20 52	09 01	20 51	09 01	20 50	09 02	20 48	09 04	20 46	09 06
20	20 10	08 20	20 09	08 21	20 08	08 22	20 06	08 24	20 03	08 27
Mar. 2	19 28	07 38	19 27	07 40	19 25	07 41	19 23	07 44	19 19	07 47
12	18 46	06 57	18 44	06 58	18 42	07 00	18 39	07 03	18 35	07 07
22	18 03	06 15	18 01	06 17	17 59	06 19	17 56	06 22	17 51	06 28
Apr. 1	17 20	05 34	17 18	05 36	17 16	05 38	17 12	05 42	17 06	05 48
11	16 38	04 52	16 36	04 54	16 33	04 57	16 29	05 01	16 22	05 07
21	15 56	04 11	15 53	04 13	15 50	04 16	15 46	04 21	15 39	04 27
May 1	15 14	03 30	15 12	03 32	15 08	03 36	15 04	03 40	14 56	03 48
11	14 33	02 49	14 30	02 52	14 27	02 55	14 22	03 00	14 14	03 08
21	13 53	02 09	13 50	02 12	13 46	02 15	13 42	02 20	13 34	02 28
31	13 13	01 29	13 10	01 32	13 07	01 35	13 02	01 40	12 54	01 48
June 10	12 34	00 50	12 32	00 53	12 28	00 56	12 23	01 01	12 16	01 09
20	11 56	00 11	11 53	00 14	11 50	00 17	11 46	00 22	11 38	00 29
30	11 19	23 29	11 16	23 32	11 13	23 35	11 09	23 39	11 02	23 46
July 10	10 42	22 52	10 39	22 54	10 37	22 57	10 33	23 01	10 26	23 07
20	10 05	22 15	10 03	22 17	10 01	22 19	09 57	22 23	09 52	22 28
30	09 30	21 38	09 28	21 39	09 26	21 42	09 23	21 45	09 18	21 49
Aug. 9	08 54	21 01	08 53	21 03	08 51	21 04	08 49	21 07	08 45	21 11
19	08 19	20 25	08 18	20 26	08 17	20 27	08 15	20 29	08 12	20 32
29	07 45	19 49	07 44	19 50	07 43	19 51	07 42	19 52	07 40	19 54
Sept. 8	07 10	19 13	07 10	19 14	07 10	19 14	07 09	19 14	07 08	19 15
18	06 36	18 38	06 36	18 38	06 36	18 37	06 36	18 37	06 36	18 37
28	06 02	18 02	06 03	18 02	06 03	18 01	06 04	18 00	06 05	17 59
Oct. 8	05 28	17 27	05 29	17 26	05 30	17 25	05 31	17 23	05 33	17 21
18	04 54	16 51	04 55	16 50	04 57	16 48	04 59	16 46	05 02	16 43
28	04 19	16 16	04 21	16 14	04 23	16 12	04 26	16 09	04 30	16 05
Nov. 7	03 45	15 40	03 47	15 38	03 50	15 35	03 53	15 32	03 58	15 27
17	03 10	15 04	03 13	15 01	03 16	14 58	03 19	14 55	03 25	14 49
27	02 35	14 28	02 38	14 25	02 41	14 22	02 45	14 17	02 52	14 11
Dec. 7	01 59	13 51	02 02	13 48	02 06	13 44	02 11	13 40	02 18	13 32
17	01 23	13 14	01 26	13 11	01 30	13 07	01 35	13 02	01 43	12 54
27	00 46	12 37	00 50	12 34	00 54	12 29	00 59	12 24	01 07	12 16

Morning and Evening "Stars," 2010

(Coordinated Universal Time)

	Morning	Evening		Morning	Evening
Jan.	Mercury from Jan. 5 Venus to Jan. 11 Mars to Jan. 29	Mercury to Jan. 4 Venus from Jan. 12 Mars from Jan. 30 Jupiter Saturn Uranus Neptune	July	Jupiter Saturn Uranus Neptune	Mercury Venus Mars
			Aug.	Jupiter Saturn Uranus Neptune to Aug. 20	Mercury Venus Mars Neptune from Aug. 21
Feb.	Mercury Neptune from Feb. 15	Venus Mars Jupiter to Feb. 28 Saturn Neptune to Feb. 14	Sept.	Mercury from Sept. 3 Jupiter to Sept. 21 Saturn Uranus to Sept. 21	Mercury to Sept. 3 Venus Mars Jupiter from Sept. 22 Uranus from Sept. 22 Neptune
Mar.	Mercury to Mar. 14 Jupiter Saturn from Mar. 23 Uranus from Mar. 18 Neptune	Mercury from Mar. 15 Venus Mars Saturn to Mar. 22 Uranus to Mar. 17	Oct.	Mercury to Oct. 17 Venus from Oct. 30 Saturn to Oct. 1	Mercury from Oct. 18 Venus to Oct. 29 Mars Jupiter Saturn from Oct. 2 Uranus Neptune
Apr.	Mercury from Apr. 29 Jupiter Saturn Uranus Neptune	Mercury to Apr. 28 Venus Mars	Nov.	Venus	Mercury Mars Jupiter Saturn Uranus Neptune
May	Mercury Jupiter Saturn Uranus Neptune	Venus Mars	Dec.	Mercury from Dec. 21 Venus	Mercury to Dec. 20 Mars Jupiter Saturn Uranus Neptune
June	Mercury to June 28 Jupiter Saturn Uranus Neptune	Mercury from June 29 Venus Mars			

Greenwich Sidereal Time for 0h UTC*, 2010

(Add 12 hours to obtain Right Ascension of Mean Sun)

Date	d	h	m	Date	d	h	m	Date	d	h	m	Date	d	h	m
Jan.	1	6	42.2	Apr.	1	12	37.0	July	10	19	11.2	Oct.	8	1	6.1
	11	7	21.6		11	13	16.4		20	19	50.7		18	1	45.5
	21	8	1.0		21	13	55.8		30	20	30.1		28	2	24.9
	31	8	40.4	May	1	14	35.3	Aug.	9	21	9.5	Nov.	7	3	4.4
Feb.	10	9	19.9		11	15	14.7		19	21	48.9		17	3	43.8
	20	9	59.3		21	15	54.1		29	22	28.4		27	4	23.2
Mar.	2	10	38.7		31	16	33.5	Sept.	8	23	7.8	Dec.	7	5	2.6
	12	11	18.1	June	10	17	13.0		18	23	47.2		17	5	42.1
	22	11	57.6		20	17	52.4		28	0	26.6		27	6	21.5
					30	18	31.8								

* Coordinated Universal Time.

Largest Telescopes

Astronomers indicate the size of telescopes not by length or magnification, but by the diameter of the primary light-gathering component of the system—such as the lens or mirror. This measurement is a direct indication of the telescope's light-gathering power. The bigger the diameter, the fainter the objects you are able to detect. The Earth's atmosphere limits the resolution of what you see. That is why the Hubble Space Telescope, which is outside the atmosphere, can have better resolution than larger telescopes on the Earth.

Refracting (lens) telescopes are currently not made with lens diameters of more than 40 in. Mirror telescopes can be made less expensively than lens telescopes, so all modern large optical telescopes are made with mirrors. **Radio telescopes**, also reflecting telescopes, view at wavelengths not visible to optical telescopes or to the human eye. Radio telescopes are made larger than optical telescopes because larger diameters are required at longer wavelengths to obtain equivalent resolution. Arrays of telescopes are used to achieve even better resolution through a technique called interferometry. Originally developed for radio telescopes, the technique is now also used with optical and infrared telescopes.

Largest Refracting (lens) Optical Telescope: Yerkes Observatory—1 m (40 in.), at Williams Bay, WI

Largest Reflecting (mirror) Optical/Infrared Telescope: Keck—9.8 m (32 ft), on Mauna Kea, HI (segmented mirror; 2 equal-size telescopes)

Largest Infrared Interferometer: Four 8.2 m (27 ft) telescopes of the Very Large Telescope Interferometer (VLTI) with a 200 m (656 ft) baseline on Cerro Paranal in Chile

Largest Fully Steerable Radio Dish: 100 m x 110 m (328 ft x 360 ft) Robert Byrd Green Bank Telescope (GBT) in Green Bank, WV

Largest Single Radio Dish: Arecibo Observatory—305 m (1,000 ft), in Puerto Rico

Largest Radio Interferometer: Ten 25 m (82 ft) diameter telescopes of the Very Long Baseline Array (VLBA), dispersed from Hawaii to the Virgin Islands with a resolution equal to a radio dish of 8,600 km (5,000 mi), making it the highest resolution telescope in the solar system

Constellations

Culturally, constellations are imagined patterns among the stars that, in some cases, have been recognized through millennia. Knowledge of constellations was once necessary in order to function as an astronomer. For today's astronomers, constellations are simply areas on the entire sky in which interesting objects await observation and interpretation.

Because Western culture has prevailed in establishing modern science, equally viable and interesting constellations and celestial traditions of other cultures are not well known outside their regions of origin. Even the patterns with which we are most familiar today have undergone considerable change over the centuries.

Today, **88 constellations** are officially recognized. Although many have ancient origins, some are "modern," devised out of unclaimed stars by astronomers a few centuries ago. Unclaimed stars were those too faint or inconveniently placed to be included in the more prominent constellations. Stars in a constellation are not necessarily near each other; they are just located in the same direction on the celestial sphere.

When astronomers began to travel to South Africa in the 16th and 17th centuries, they found an unfamiliar sky that showed numerous brilliant stars. Thus, we find constellations in the southern hemisphere that depict technological marvels of the time, as well as some arguably traditional forms, such as the "fly."

Many of the commonly recognized constellations had their **origins** in ancient Asia Minor. These were adopted by the Greeks and Romans, who translated their names and stories into their own languages, modifying some details in the process. After the declines of these cultures, most such knowledge entered oral tradition or remained hidden in monastic libraries. From the 8th century Muslim civilization spread through the Mediterranean world. Wherever possible, everything was translated into Arabic to be taught in the universities the Muslims established all over their new-found world.

In the 13th century, Alfonso X of Castile, an avid student of astronomy, had Ptolemy's *Almagest* translated into Latin. It thus became widely available to European scholars. In the process, the constellation names were translated, but the star names were retained in their Arabic forms. Thus the names of many stars—e.g., Altair, Alnitak, Mirfak—have Arabic roots, although linguistic adaptation and the inaccuracies of transliteration have wrought changes.

Until the 1920s, astronomers used curved boundaries for the constellation areas. As these were rather arbitrary at best, the International Astronomical Union adopted new constellation boundaries that ran due north-south and east-west, filling the sky much as the contiguous states fill up the area of the "lower 48" United States.

Common names of stars often referred to parts of the traditional figures they represented, e.g., Deneb, the tail of the swan, or Betelgeuse, the armpit of the giant. Avoiding traditional names, astronomers may label stars by using Greek letters, generally to denote order of brightness. Thus, the "alpha star" would generally be the brightest star of that constellation. The "of" implies possession, so the genitive (possessive) form of the constellation name is used, as in Alpha Orionis, the first star of Orion (Betelgeuse). Astronomers usually use a 3-letter abbreviation for the constellation name, as indicated here.

Within these boundaries, and occasionally crossing them, popular "asterisms" are recognized: the so-called Big Dipper is a small part of the constellation Ursa Major, the big bear; the Sickle is the traditional head and mane of Leo, the lion; the three stars of the Summer Triangle are each in a different constellation, with Vega in Lyra the lyre, Deneb in Cygnus the swan, and Altair in Aquila the eagle; the northeast star of the Great Square of Pegasus is Alpha Andromedae.

Name	Genitive case	Abbr.	Meaning
Andromeda	Andromedae	And	Chained Maiden
Antlia	Antliae	Ant	Air Pump
Apus	Apodis	Aps	Bird of Paradise
Aquarius	Aquarii	Aqr	Water Bearer
Aquila	Aquilae	Aql	Eagle
Ara	Arae	Ara	Altar
Aries	Arietis	Ari	Ram
Auriga	Aurigae	Aur	Charioteer
Boötes	Boötis	Boo	Herdsmen
Caelum	Caeli	Cae	Chisel
Camelopardalis	Camelopardalis	Cam	Giraffe
Cancer	Cancri	Cnc	Crab
Canes Venatici	Canum Venaticorum	CVn	Hunting Dogs
Canis Major	Canis Majoris	CMa	Greater Dog
Canis Minor	Canis Minoris	CMi	Littler Dog
Capricornus	Capricorni	Cap	Sea-goat
Carina	Carinae	Car	Keel
Cassiopeia	Cassiopeiae	Cas	Queen
Centaurus	Centauri	Cen	Centaur
Cepheus	Cephei	Cep	King
Cetus	Ceti	Cet	Whale
Chamaeleon	Chamaeleontis	Cha	Chameleon
Circinus	Circini	Cir	Compasses (art)
Columba	Columbae	Col	Dove
Coma Berenices	Comae Berenices	Com	Berenice's Hair
Corona Australis	Coronae Australis	CrA	Southern Crown
Corona Borealis	Coronae Borealis	CrB	Northern Crown
Corvus	Corvi	Crv	Crow
Crater	Crateris	Crt	Cup
Crux	Crucis	Cru	Cross (southern)
Cygnus	Cygni	Cyg	Swan
Delphinus	Delphini	Del	Dolphin
Dorado	Doradus	Dor	Goldfish
Draco	Draconis	Dra	Dragon
Equuleus	Equulei	Equ	Little Horse
Eridanus	Eridani	Eri	River
Fornax	Fornacis	For	Furnace
Gemini	Geminorum	Gem	Twins
Grus	Gruis	Gru	Crane (bird)
Hercules	Herculis	Her	Hercules
Horologium	Horologii	Hor	Clock
Hydra	Hydrae	Hya	Water Snake (female)
Hydrus	Hydri	Hyi	Water Snake (male)
Indus	Indi	Ind	Indian

Name	Genitive case	Abbr.	Meaning
Lacerta	Lacertae	Lac	Lizard
Leo	Leonis	Leo	Lion
Leo Minor	Leonis Minoris	LMi	Littler Lion
Lepus	Leporis	Lep	Hare
Libra	Librae	Lib	Balance
Lupus	Lupi	Lup	Wolf
Lynx	Lyncis	Lyn	Lynx
Lyra	Lyrae	Lyr	Lyre
Mensa	Mensae	Men	Table Mountain
Microscopium	Microscopii	Mic	Microscope
Monoceros	Monocerotis	Mon	Unicorn
Musca	Muscae	Mus	Fly
Norma	Normae	Nor	Square (rule)
Octans	Octantis	Oct	Octant
Ophiuchus	Ophiuchi	Oph	Serpent Bearer
Orion	Orionis	Ori	Hunter
Pavo	Pavonis	Pav	Peacock
Pegasus	Pegasi	Peg	Flying Horse
Perseus	Persei	Per	Hero
Phoenix	Phoenicis	Phe	Phoenix
Pictor	Pictoris	Pic	Painter
Pisces	Piscium	Psc	Fishes
Piscis Austrinus	Piscis Austrini	PsA	Southern Fish
Puppis	Puppis	Pup	Stern (deck)
Pyxis	Pyxidis	Pyx	Compass (sea)
Reticulum	Reticuli	Ret	Reticle
Sagitta	Sagittae	Sge	Arrow
Sagittarius	Sagittarii	Sgr	Archer
Scorpius	Scorpii	Sco	Scorpion
Sculptor	Sculptoris	Scl	Sculptor
Scutum	Scuti	Sct	Shield
Serpens	Serpentis	Ser	Serpent
Sextans	Sextantis	Sex	Sextant
Taurus	Tauri	Tau	Bull
Telescopium	Telescopii	Tel	Telescope
Triangulum	Trianguli	Tri	Triangle
Triangulum Australe	Trianguli Australis	TrA	Southern Triangle
Tucana	Tucanae	Tuc	Toucan
Ursa Major	Ursae Majoris	UMa	Greater Bear
Ursa Minor	Ursae Minoris	UMi	Littler Bear
Vela	Velorum	Vel	Sail
Virgo	Virginis	Vir	Maiden
Volans	Volantis	Vol	Flying Fish
Vulpecula	Vulpeculae	Vul	Fox

Eclipses, 2010

(In Coordinated Universal Time (UTC), standard time of the prime meridian)

There are 4 eclipses in 2010: an annular eclipse of the Sun, a partial eclipse of the Moon, a total eclipse of the Sun, and a total eclipse of the Moon. During an annular eclipse of the Sun, the Moon's angular diameter is not large enough to block the entire disk of the Sun, and the Sun appears as a bright ring about the dark disk of the Moon. The tables below give the times, in UTC, when the Moon or Sun reaches certain phases of eclipse. In the case of the lunar eclipses, the times are relevant for any observer who can see the Moon. In the case of solar eclipses, the tabulated times refer to when the given event may begin or end from specific points along the eclipse path. The Moon's shadow sweeps quickly across the Earth; observed duration of totality depends precisely on an observer's location.

I. Annular Eclipse of the Sun, Jan. 15

The path of the annular eclipse will begin over equatorial Africa and will proceed across the Indian Ocean, grazing Southern India and Sri Lanka, finally ending after crossing parts of southern and eastern China. A partial eclipse will be visible over a much wider area extending from Eastern Europe, much of Africa, and across nearly all of Asia. The maximum duration of the annular eclipse is slightly more than 11 minutes.

Event	Date		h	m
Penumbral eclipse begins	Jan.	15	4	5.5
Annular eclipse begins		15	5	21.2
Greatest eclipse		15	7	7.6
Annular eclipse ends		15	8	51.6
Penumbral eclipse ends		15	10	7.6

III. Total Eclipse of the Sun, July 11

The path of totality lies nearly entirely over the South Pacific, with landfall in the Cook Islands and Easter Island, finally ending in southern Chile and Argentina. A partial eclipse will be visible across much of the South Pacific and south eastern South America. The maximum duration of totality is just over 5 minutes.

Event	Date		h	m
Penumbral eclipse begins	July	11	17	9.6
Total eclipse begins		11	18	18.5
Greatest eclipse		11	19	34.6
Total eclipse ends		11	20	48.3
Penumbral eclipse ends		11	21	57.2

II. Partial Eclipse of the Moon, June 26

Portions of the eclipse will be visible over a wide area of the Americas, excluding the NE U.S. and much of Brazil. The entire eclipse will be visible from Hawaii, much of Australia, and other locations in the Pacific.

Event	Date		h	m
Penumbral eclipse begins	June	26	8	57.3
Partial eclipse begins		26	10	16.9
Greatest eclipse		26	11	39.5
Partial eclipse ends		26	12	59.8
Penumbral eclipse ends		26	14	19.6

IV. Total Eclipse of the Moon, Dec. 21

This eclipse is visible from the entire United States and Canada.

Event	Date		h	m
Penumbral eclipse begins	Dec.	21	5	29.3
Total eclipse begins		21	7	40.8
Greatest eclipse		21	8	18.1
Total eclipse ends		21	8	53.1
Penumbral eclipse ends		21	11	4.5

Total Solar Eclipses, 2010-20

Total solar eclipses actually take place nearly as often as total lunar eclipses. Total lunar eclipses are visible over at least half of the Earth, while total solar eclipses can be seen only along a very narrow path up to a few hundred miles wide and a few thousand miles long. Observing a total solar eclipse is thus a rarity for most people.

Solar eclipses can be dangerous to observe. This is not because the Sun emits more potent rays during an eclipse, but because the Sun is always dangerous to observe directly and people are particularly likely to stare at it during a solar eclipse.

Date	Duration[1] m	s	Width (mi)	Path of Totality
2010, July 11	5	20	164	Pacific Ocean, southern S America
2012, Nov. 13	4	2	112	N Australia, Pacific Ocean
2013, Nov. 3[h]	1	40	36	Atlantic Ocean, Africa
2015, Mar. 20	2	47	304	N Atlantic Ocean, Arctic Ocean
2016, Mar. 9	4	10	96	Indonesia, Pacific Ocean
2017, Aug. 21	2	40	71	Pacific Ocean, U.S., Atlantic Ocean
2019, July 2	4	33	125	S Pacific Ocean, S America
2020, Dec. 14	2	10	56	S Pacific Ocean, S America, S Atlantic Ocean

h = indicates annular-total hybrid eclipse. (1) Duration refers to length of time at optimal viewing area.

Total Solar Eclipses in the U.S. in the 21st Century

During the 21st century there will be 8 total solar eclipses visible somewhere in the continental U.S. The first comes after a long gap; the last total solar eclipse visible in the U.S. was on Feb. 26, 1979, in the northwestern U.S.

Date	Path of Totality	Date	Path of Totality
Aug. 21, 2017	Oregon to South Carolina	Mar. 30, 2052	Florida to Georgia
Apr. 8, 2024	Mexico to Texas and up through Maine	May 11, 2078	Louisiana to North Carolina
Aug. 23, 2044	Montana to North Dakota	May 1, 2079	New Jersey to the lower edge of New England
Aug. 12, 2045	N California to Florida	Sept. 14, 2099	North Dakota to Virginia

Beginnings of the Universe

One of the dominating astronomical discoveries of the 20th century was that the galaxies of the universe all seem to be moving away from us. Doppler redshifts were observed for the spiral nebulae around 1920, even though they were not yet known to be galaxies. By the early 1930s, Edwin Hubble and M. L. Humason had established that the more distant a galaxy, the faster it was receding. It turned out that they are moving away not just from us but from one another—that is, the **universe is expanding**. Scientists conclude that the universe must once, very long ago, have been extremely compact and dense, until an explosion or a similar event caused the matter to spread out. The explosion that gave birth to the universe is called the **Big Bang**.

On the subatomic level, according to this theory, there were vast changes of energy and matter and the way physical laws operated during the first few minutes. After those early minutes the percentages of the basic matter of the universe—hydrogen, helium, and lithium—were set. Everything was so compact and so hot that **radiation dominated the early universe** and there were no stable, un-ionized atoms. At first, the universe was opaque, in the sense that any energy emitted was quickly absorbed and then re-emitted by free electrons. As the universe expanded, **density and temperature continued to drop.** A few hundred thousand years after the Big Bang, the temperature dropped far enough that electrons and nuclei could combine to form stable atoms as the universe became transparent. Once that occurred, the radiation that had been trapped was free to escape.

In the 1940s, George Gamov and others predicted that astronomers should be able to see remnants of this escaped radiation. They were starting to search for this background radiation when physicists Arno Penzias and Robert Wilson, using a radio telescope, inadvertently beat them to the punch (Penzias and Wilson were later awarded a Nobel Prize).

In 2003, NASA's Wilkinson Microwave Anisotropy Probe made measurements of the temperature of this **cosmic microwave background** radiation to within millionths of a degree. From these measurements, scientists were able to deduce that our universe is **13.7 bil years old** and that first-generation stars began to form a mere 200 mil years after the Big Bang.

A related mystery is that evidence suggests there is hidden matter and hidden energy that cannot be directly observed. This **dark matter** may be composed of gas, large numbers of cool, small objects, or even sub-atomic particles. The presence of dark matter is indicated by the rotation curves of galaxies and the dynamics of clusters of galaxies. Evidence for **dark energy** is derived from studies of distant Type Ia supernovae in far galaxies indicating that the expansion of the universe is accelerating, rather than slowing. The visible matter we see seems to constitute only about 4% of the total mass of the universe, while the rest of the mass of the universe is in the form of dark matter (23%) and dark energy (73%). Dark energy is a mysterious force that seems to work on the very fabric of the universe, spreading it apart.

Galaxies

The 20th century might be called the century of the galaxy. By the start of the century, more than 10,000 **nebulae**—cloud-like luminous objects in the sky—had been discovered. Some were correctly identified as star clusters and others as clouds of gas and dust. Those nebulae which were spiral or elliptical in shape were found in regions of the sky far from the glowing band that is our own Milky Way Galaxy. Immanuel Kant had written in 1775 that some of these fuzzy objects might be "**island universes**" apart from our own. But the idea remained speculative until 1923-24, when Edwin Hubble discovered the existence of variable stars in some of these nebulae. This provided conclusive evidence that these systems were outside our own "island universe," the Milky Way Galaxy.

Galaxies range in size from small dwarf elliptical ones, with perhaps 1 mil stars, to spiral galaxies containing 300 bil stars, to giant elliptical galaxies that may be home to more than 10 tril stars. The diameters of galaxies range from 3,000 light-years in dwarf elliptical galaxies to over 500,000 light-years in giant elliptical galaxies. It is estimated that the Milky Way galaxy is about 100,000 light-years in diameter with about 400 bil stars.

Galaxies also congregate into **clusters**. The smallest are poor clusters of only a few dozen galaxies, while the largest rich clusters may contain thousands of galaxies. The Milky Way is part of a poor cluster of about 3 dozen galaxies called the **Local Group**. The largest member of the Local Group is the Andromeda Galaxy, a spiral galaxy visible to the unaided eye in the constellation of Andromeda on a very dark night away from lights. The Milky Way is the second largest galaxy in this group; most other galaxies in our Local Group are small.

The Solar System

The major planets of the solar system, in order of mean distance from the Sun, are **Mercury, Venus, Earth, Mars, Jupiter, Saturn, Uranus**, and **Neptune**. The dwarf planets in order of average distance from the Sun are **Ceres** (located between Mars and Jupiter), **Pluto, Haumea, Makemake,** and **Eris**. All planets orbit counterclockwise around the Sun as viewed from above the Earth's North Pole.

Because **Mercury and Venus** are nearer to the Sun than is Earth, their motions about the Sun appear from Earth as wide swings first to one side of the Sun then to the other, though both planets move around the Sun in almost circular orbits. When their passage takes them between Earth and the Sun or beyond the Sun from Earth's perspective, they cannot be seen. The **planets that lie farther from the Sun** than does Earth may be seen for longer periods and are invisible only when so located in our sky so that they rise and set at about the same time as the Sun—and thus become overwhelmed by the Sun's light.

The giant planets emit their own energy. On occasion, radio emissions from Jupiter exceed even those emitted by the Sun in intensity.

Mercury and Venus, because they are between Earth and the Sun, show phases much as the Moon does. The planets farther from the Sun are always seen as full, although Mars does occasionally present a slightly gibbous phase—like the Moon when not quite full.

The **planets appear to move rapidly among the stars** because they are relatively closer to Earth than the stars. The stars are also in motion, some at tremendous speeds, but they are so far away that their motion does not change their apparent positions in the heavens enough to be perceived. The nearest star is about 9,000 times farther away than Neptune. The count for identified **moons** in the solar system orbiting planets and dwarf planets stood at 173 in fall 2009.

Planet Superlatives			
Largest, most massive planet	Jupiter	Smallest, least massive planet	Mercury
Fastest orbiting planet	Mercury	Slowest orbiting planet	Neptune
Fastest sidereal rotation	Jupiter	Slowest sidereal rotation	Venus
Longest (synodic) day	Mercury	Shortest (synodic) day	Jupiter
Rotational pole closest to ecliptic	Uranus	Hottest planet	Venus
Most moons	Jupiter	No moons	Mercury, Venus
Planet with largest moon	Jupiter	Planet with moon with most eccentric orbit	Neptune
Greatest average density	Earth	Lowest average density	Saturn
Tallest mountain	Mars	Deepest oceans	Jupiter
Strongest magnetic fields	Jupiter	Greatest amount of liquid, surface water	Earth
Most circular orbit	Venus		

Planets and the Sun, by Selected Characteristics

Sun and planets	Radius— at unit distance[1] "	at mean least distance[2] "	in mi mean radius	Volume[3]	Mass[3]	Density[3]	Sidereal period d	h	m	s	Gravity at surface[3]	Reflecting power Pct°	Daytime surface temp. °F
Sun	959.5	976.0	432,500	1,304,000	333,000	0.26	25	9	7		28.00		+9,941
Mercury	3.36	6.5	1,516	0.0562	0.0553	0.98	58	15	36		0.38	0.11	845
Venus	8.34	33.0	3,760	0.857	0.815	0.95	243		30R		0.91	0.65	867
Earth	8.78	—	3,959	1.000	1.000	1.00		23	56	4.2	1.00	0.37	59
Moon	2.40	986.2	1,079	0.0203	0.0123	0.61	27	7	43	40	0.16	0.12	260
Mars	4.67	12.8	2,106	0.151	0.107	0.71		24	37	22	0.38	0.15	−24
Jupiter	96.40	24.5	43,441	1,321	317.8	0.24		9	55	30	2.53	0.52	−162
Saturn	80.29	10.05	36,184	764	95.16	0.12		10	39	20	1.06	0.47	−218
Uranus	34.97	2.05	15,759	63.1	14.54	0.23		17	14	20R	0.90	0.51	−323
Neptune	33.95	1.2	15,301	57.7	17.15	0.30		16	6	40	1.14	0.41	−330

(1) Angular radius, in seconds of arc, if object were seen at a distance of 1 astronomical unit. (2) Angular radius, in seconds of arc, when object is closest to Earth. (3) Earth = 1. R = Retrograde rotation.

The Planets: Motion, Distance, and Brightness

Planet	Mean daily motion[1]	Orbital velocity mi per sec.[2]	Sidereal revolution days[3]	Synodic revolution days[4]	Distance from Sun in millions of mi Max.	Min.	Distance from Earth in millions of mi Max.	Min.	Light at[5] perihelion	aphelion
Mercury	14,732	29.75	87.97	115.9	43.4	28.6	137.9	48.0	10.56	4.59
Venus	5,768	21.76	224.7	583.9	67.7	66.8	162.2	23.7	1.94	1.89
Earth	3,548	18.50	365.256	—	94.5	91.4	—	—	1.03	0.97
Mars	1,887	15.00	686.98	779.9	154.9	128.4	249.4	33.9	0.52	0.36
Jupiter	299	8.12	4,332.6	398.9	507.4	460.1	602	366.0	0.041	0.034
Saturn	120	6.02	10,759.2	378.1	941.1	840.4	1,031	743.0	0.012	0.0098
Uranus	42	4.23	30,685.4	369.7	1,866.4	1,703.4	1,962	1,605.0	0.0030	0.0025
Neptune	22	3.37	60,189.0	367.5	2,824.5	2,761.7	2,913	2,676.0	0.0011	0.0011

(1) Average angular motion measured in seconds of arc per day. (2) Speed of revolution around Sun. (3) Number of Earth days to orbit Sun with respect to background stars. (4) Number of Earth days to get back to the same position in its orbit around Sun, relative to Earth. (5) Light at perihelion and aphelion is solar illumination measured in units of mean illumination at Earth.

Planets of the Solar System

Note: AU = astronomical unit (92.96 mil mi, mean distance of Earth from the Sun); **d** = 1 Earth synodic (solar) day (24 hrs); **synodic day** = rotation period of a planet measured with respect to the Sun (the "true" day, i.e. the time from midday to midday, or from sunrise to sunrise); **sidereal day** = the rotation period of a planet with respect to the stars.

The International Astronomical Union (IAU) on Aug. 24, 2006, at their General Assembly in Prague, agreed on a new definition for "planet," and in the process effectively removed Pluto's planet status. The ruling came after years of debate as to whether Pluto, discovered in 1930, should still be considered the ninth planet in our solar system because of its size, orbit, and other characteristics. New discoveries of other Pluto-like objects in the solar system, such as the 2003 discovery of Eris, a **Kuiper Belt object** (KBO) bigger than Pluto, also contributed to the debate.

Under the IAU's new definition, Mercury, Venus, Earth, Mars, Jupiter, Saturn, Uranus, and Neptune are regarded as "classical" planets. A **planet** is now defined as a celestial body that (a) is in orbit around the Sun, (b) has sufficient mass for its self-gravity to overcome rigid body forces so that it assumes a hydrostatic equilibrium (nearly round) shape, and (c) has cleared the neighborhood around its orbit.

Pluto, Eris, Ceres, MakeMake, and Haumea are now regarded as "dwarf planets," with the status of Pluto's largest moon, Charon, to be determined at a later date. A **dwarf planet** is a celestial body that (a) is in orbit around the Sun, (b) has sufficient mass for its self-gravity to overcome rigid body forces so that is assumed a hydrostatic equilibrium (nearly round) shape, (c) has not cleared the neighborhood around its orbit, and (d) is not a satellite.

The IAU also created a new category, **small solar system bodies**, for all other objects, except satellites, orbiting the Sun, including comets, asteroids, KBOs, and other small objects, although it has not yet established a process by which other solar system objects will be classified.

Mercury

```
Distance from the Sun
  Perihelion . . . . . . . . . . . . . . . . . . . . . . . . . .28.6 mil mi
  Aphelion . . . . . . . . . . . . . . . . . . . . . . . . . . .43.4 mil mi
  Semi-major axis (mean distance)   36.0 mil mi (0.387 AU)
Period of revolution around Sun . . . . . . . . . . . . . . 87.97 d
Orbital eccentricity. . . . . . . . . . . . . . . . . . . . . . 0.2056
Orbital inclination. . . . . . . . . . . . . . . . . . . . . . . . 7.00°
Synodic day (midday to midday) . . . . . . . . . . . . 175.94 d
Sidereal day. . . . . . . . . . . . . . . . . . . . . . . . . . . 58.65 d
Rotational inclination . . . . . . . . . . . . . . . . . . . . . . 0.01°
Mass (Earth = 1) . . . . . . . . . . . . . . . . . . . . . . . 0.0553
Mean radius. . . . . . . . . . . . . . . . . . . . . . . . . . 1,516 mi
Mean density (Earth = 1). . . . . . . . . . . . . . . . . . 0.984
Natural satellites . . . . . . . . . . . . . . . . . . . . . . . . . . 0
Average surface temperature . . . . . . . . . . . . . . . 333°F
```

Mercury, named for the Roman gods' messenger, is the closest planet to the Sun and the smallest in the solar system. Mercury is too much in line with the Sun to be observed against a dark sky; therefore it is always seen during morning or evening twilight. In 2008, the MESSENGER spacecraft made the first flybys of Mercury since the 1970s. Messenger is scheduled to go into orbit about Mercury in 2011 for a year-long reconnaisance mission.

Orbit and Rotation. Mercury moves with great speed around the Sun, averaging about 30 mi per second to complete its orbit, which takes about 88 Earth days. Mercury takes nearly 59 days to rotate on its axis. Because its orbital period is only about 50% longer than its sidereal rotation, the time from one sunrise to the next on Mercury is about 176 days—twice as long as a Mercurial year. Oddly, Mercury has a magnetic field, albeit very weak. It has been held that both a fluid core and rapid rotation—neither of which Mercury is believed to have—are necessary for the generation of a planetary magnetic field. Mercury may demonstrate the contrary.

Atmosphere. Mercury's atmosphere is almost non-existent. What very little it has is composed of 42% oxygen, 29% sodium, 22% hydrogen, 6% helium, 0.5% potassium, and 0.5% other particles. Because of Mercury's lack of atmosphere to regulate temperatures between day and night, the surface during the day may reach a temperature of about 845°F, while the temperature at night may fall as low as −300°F. Earth-based observation has provided evidence of water ice near the poles.

Surface and Composition. Mercury's surface is rocky and cratered similar to that of Earth's Moon. The most imposing feature on Mercury, the Caloris Basin, is a huge impact crater more than 800 mi in diameter. Mercury has a huge iron core that takes up about 75% of the planet's radius; it has higher percentage of iron than any other planet.

Venus

Distance from the Sun	
Perihelion	66.8 mil mi
Semi-major axis (mean distance)	67.2 mil mi (0.723 AU)
Aphelion	67.7 mil mi
Period of revolution around Sun	224.7 d
Orbital eccentricity	0.0067
Orbital inclination	3.39°
Synodic day (midday to midday)	116.75 d (retrograde)
Sidereal day	243.02 d (retrograde)
Rotational inclination	177.4°
Mass (Earth = 1)	0.815
Mean radius	3,760 mi
Mean density (Earth = 1)	0.951
Natural satellites	0
Average surface temperature	867°F

Venus, named for the Roman goddess of love, is the second planet out from the Sun. Almost the same size as Earth, it is believed that the two planets were formed at the same time by the same general process and from the same mixture of chemical elements. Venus can easily be seen from Earth with the naked eye; it is the 3rd-brightest object in the sky, exceeded only by the Sun and the Moon.

Orbit and Rotation. It takes Venus 225 Earth days to complete its orbit around the sun. Its synodic revolution—its return to the same relationship with Earth and the Sun, which is a result of the combination of its own motion with that of Earth—is 584 days. Because of this, every 19 months Venus is closer to Earth than any other planet. The rotation period of Venus appears to be 243 days clockwise—in other words, contrary to the spin of the other planets and contrary to its own motion around the Sun. This rate and sense of rotation makes for a solar day (sunrise to sunrise) on Venus of 116.8 Earth days; night lasts 58 days and day lasts 58 days. Venus has no detectible magnetic field.

Atmosphere. The Venusian atmosphere is very thick and toxic. It is composed of 96.5% carbon dioxide, 3.5% nitrogen, trace concentrations of sulfur dioxide, argon, water, carbon monoxide, helium, and neon. In addition, it exerts an atmospheric pressure at the surface more than 90 times Earth's normal sea-level pressure. The planet is covered with a dense, white, cloudy atmosphere that conceals whatever is below it. These clouds are believed to contain sulfuric acid, meaning that when it rains on Venus, it may rain sulfuric acid. Due to the thickness of the atmosphere and resulting extreme greenhouse effect, the temperature is essentially the same day and night; the planet has an average surface temperature of about 867°F making it the hottest planet in the solar system. Winds of about 200 mph in the clouds may account for the transfer of heat into the night side despite the low rotation speed of the planet. However, at the surface, the winds are very slow.

Surface and Composition. Radar-produced maps of the entire planet show large craters, continent-sized highlands, and extensive dry lowlands. No tectonic activity has been found similar to Earth's moving tectonic plates, but a system of global rift zones and numerous broad, low, dome-like structures, called coronae, may have been produced by the upwelling and subsidence of magma from the mantle. Volcanic surface features, such as vast lava plains, fields of small lava domes, and large shield volcanoes, are common. About 1,600 volcanoes and volcanic features appear on the Venusian surface; more than 85% of the surface is covered by volcanic flows. Theia Mons, a huge shield volcano, has a diameter of over 600 mi and a height of over 3.5 mi. (The largest Hawaiian volcano is only about 125 mi in diameter, but rises nearly 5.5 mi from the ocean floor.) Aside from volcanoes, there are highly deformed mountain belts across Venus along with a few meteor-impact craters more than 20 mi wide. Erosion is a very slow process on Venus due to the lack of water. There are indications of some wind movement of dust and sand. The few impact craters on Venus suggest that the surface is generally geologically young—less than 800 million years old. Despite the fact that probes have landed on Venus, there are very few pictures because the probes themselves couldn't survive the high temperature and atmospheric pressure.

Mars

Distance from the Sun	
Perihelion	128.4 mil mi
Semi-major axis (mean distance)	141.6 mil mi (1.524 AU)
Aphelion	154.9 mil mi
Period of revolution around Sun	686.98 d (1.88 y)
Orbital eccentricity	0.0935
Orbital inclination	1.85°
Synodic day (midday to midday)	24h 39m 35s
Sidereal day	24h 37m 22s
Rotational inclination	25.19°
Mass (Earth = 1)	0.107
Mean radius	2,106 mi
Mean density (Earth = 1)	0.713
Natural satellites	2
Average surface temperature	−81°F

Named for the Roman god of war, the "Red Planet" has some features much like Earth. Mars has climate, seasons, volcanoes, and possibly once had liquid water flowing across its surface. Mars can easily be seen with the naked eye on most clear nights, which is why it was one of the first planets to be studied by ancient astronomers. Later, when telescopes came into use, many observers claimed that canals made by Martians existed on the planet's surface, which led to speculation as to whether there was intelligent life there. Unmanned probes have since put all those theories to rest; the canals turned out to be topographic patterns and dust storms.

Orbit and Rotation. Although Mars's orbital path is nearly circular, it is somewhat more eccentric than that of most other planets; Mars is more than 26 mil mi farther from the Sun at its most distant point compared to its closest approach. Its orbit and speed in relation to Earth's bring it fairly close to Earth about every 2 years. Every 15-17 years the close approaches are especially favorable for observation.

Mars rotates in 24 hours and 37 minutes, almost the same period of time as Earth. Mars's mean distance from the Sun is 142 mil mi. Because Mars's axis of rotation is inclined by about 25° from the vertical to the plane of its solar orbit about the Sun, the planet has seasons.

Unlike Earth's global magnetic field, the Martian magnetic field is small, weak, and localized and may be the remnant of a stronger field from the planet's past.

Atmosphere. The Martian atmosphere is composed of 95.32% carbon dioxide, 2.7% nitrogen, 1.6% argon, 0.13% oxygen, 0.08% carbon monoxide, and in very minor quantities, water, hydrogen oxide, and neon. The atmosphere on Mars is very thin; it has an atmospheric pressure between 1% and 2% of Earth's (if Earth's atmosphere were that thin, we would not have enough oxygen to breathe). Because the Martian atmosphere is so thin and because of the planet's weak magnetic field, its surface is bombarded by cosmic radiation about 100 times as intense as on Earth.

Martian weather systems consist mainly of huge dust storms. On the poles, white caps (believed to be both water ice and carbon dioxide ice) grow in winter and shrink in summer. It is mainly the carbon dioxide that comes and goes with the seasons. The water ice is apparently in many layers with dust between them, indicating climatic cycles.

Surface and Composition. Mars is an alien world with rust-red sand and pink skies. In the planet's beginning stages when it was much hotter, Mars's surface melted to a sufficient extent to separate into dense and lighter layers. At some point later, Mars cooled enough to allow liquid water to possibly flow across its surface. Today, Mars is very dry.

Natural Satellites. Mars has 2 satellites called Phobos and Deimos, each discovered in 1877 by Asaph Hall. (Phobos measures about 11 by 17 mi and Deimos about 7 by 9 mi.) Deimos, the outer satellite, revolves around the planet in about 31 hours. Phobos, the inner satellite, whips around Mars in a little more than 7 hours, making 3 trips each Martian day. Since it orbits Mars faster than the planet rotates, Phobos rises in the west and sets in the east, opposite to what other bodies appear to do in the Martian sky. Both moons are irregularly shaped and pitted with numerous craters. Their origins are not known; however, some astronomers consider them to be asteroid-like objects that were captured by Mars very early in its existence.

Jupiter

Distance from the Sun	
Perihelion	460.1 mil mi
Semi-major axis (mean distance)	483.8 mil mi (5.204 AU)
Aphelion	507.4 mil mi
Period of revolution around Sun	11.862 y
Orbital eccentricity	0.0489
Orbital inclination	1.304°
Synodic day (midday to midday)	9h 55m 33s
Sidereal day	9h 55m 30s
Rotational inclination	3.13°
Mass (Earth = 1)	317.8
Mean radius	43,441 mi
Mean density (Earth = 1)	0.24
Natural satellites	63
Average temperature*	−162°F

*i.e., temperature where atmosphere pressure equals 1 Earth atmosphere.

Jupiter, named for the Roman ruler of the gods, is the largest planet in the solar system (11 times the diameter of Earth). Its mass is more than twice the mass of all the other planets, moons, and asteroids put together. Visible to the naked eye and known to the ancients, it was a focus of the Italian scientist Galileo Galilei who viewed the planet and its 4 largest moons through a homemade telescope.

Orbit and Rotation. Jupiter is at an average distance of 484 mil mi from the Sun and takes almost 12 Earth years to make a complete revolution. The largest of the planets, Jupiter has an equatorial diameter of 88,846 mi; however, its polar diameter is more than 5,700 mi shorter. This noticeable oblateness is a result of the liquidity of the planet and its extremely rapid rotation rate—a Jupiter day is less than 10 Earth hours long. For a planet this size, this rotational speed is amazing. A point on Jupiter's equator moves at a speed of 22,000 mph, as compared with 1,000 mph for a point on Earth's equator. Jupiter's magnetic field is by far the strongest of any planet. Electrical activity caused by this field is so strong that it discharges billions of watts into Earth's magnetic field daily.

Atmosphere. Jupiter's atmosphere is composed of 90% molecular hydrogen and 10% helium. Minor constituents include methane, ammonia, hydrogen deuteride, ethane, and water. Jupiter has a turbulent atmosphere characterized by thick clouds, high winds, and huge lightning storms many times larger than those on Earth. The atmospheric temperature varies but the temperature at the tops of clouds may be about −280°F. The Great Red Spot seen prominently on Jupiter is a huge hurricane-like storm that is three times the diameter of Earth. In 2006, the Hubble Space Telescope detected the appearance of a second, smaller red spot.

Surface and Composition. Gas giant planets like Jupiter, Saturn, and Neptune do not have a surface like Earth or any of the other rocky planets. The gases become denser with depth, until they may turn into a slush or slurry. Jupiter has a liquid hydrogen ocean more than 35,000 mi deep. It likely has a rocky core about the size of Earth, but 13 times more massive. There is no sharp interface between the gaseous atmosphere and the hydrogen ocean that accounts for most of Jupiter's volume. At lower depths, under enormous pressure, the liquid hydrogen takes on the properties of a metal. It is likely that this liquid metallic hydrogen is the source for both Jupiter's persistent radio noise and for its improbably strong magnetic field.

Natural Satellites. Jupiter has 63 known satellites, 23 of which were found as recently as 2003. Four of the moons (in order of distance from Jupiter), Io, Europa, Ganymede, and Callisto—all discovered by Galileo in 1610—are large and bright and are close in diameter to Earth's Moon and Mercury. Because they move so rapidly around Jupiter, their change in position from night to night can be seen from Earth using binoculars.

Io is one of the most intriguing moons because it is the most volcanically active body in the solar system. A gaseous, doughnut-shaped ring, or torus, enveloping Io's orbit around Jupiter may have been formed by material ejected from Io's active volcanoes. (This is not to be confused with Jupiter's rings.) These volcanoes, hotter than Earth's volcanoes, erupt mainly molten sulfur.

Europa may have a 30-mi-deep salty, liquid ocean beneath its icy crust, perhaps a small metallic core, and a very tenuous atmosphere. Ganymede is the biggest moon in the solar system. With a diameter of 3,120 mi, it is bigger than both Mercury and Pluto. Ganymede also has ita own magnetic field produced by a molten core perhaps of iron sulfide. Callisto has the oldest, most heavily cratered surface in the solar system, a very thin atmosphere of carbon dioxide, and possibly a subsurface liquid ocean.

The other satellites are much smaller, with 4 closer to Jupiter than Io, 5 between Ganymede and Callisto, and the rest farther out. Most of Jupiter's moons revolve around Jupiter clockwise as seen from the north, contrary to the motions of most satellites in the solar system and to the direction of revolution of planets around the Sun. These moons may be captured asteroids.

Jupiter has a set of rings that cannot be seen from Earth without powerful telescopes. They are composed of small dust grains possibly blasted off the 4 innermost moons by meteoroid impacts.

Saturn

Distance from the Sun	
Perihelion	840.44 mil mi
Semi-major axis (mean distance)	890.8 mil mi (9.582 AU)
Aphelion	941.07 mil mi
Period of revolution around Sun	29.458 y
Orbital eccentricity	0.0565
Orbital inclination	2.485°
Synodic day (midday to midday)	10h 39m 23s
Sidereal day	10h 39m 22s
Rotational inclination	26.73°
Mass (Earth = 1)	95.159
Mean radius	36,184 mi
Mean density (Earth = 1)	0.125
Natural satellites	60
Average temperature*	−218°F

*i.e., temperature where atmosphere pressure equals 1 Earth atmosphere.

Saturn, named for the Roman ruler of the Titans, is the 6th planet from the sun and most distant of the planets visible to the unaided eye. Saturn is 2nd in size to Jupiter, but its mass is much smaller. Saturn is the only planet less dense than water, meaning that Saturn would float if there were a pool of water gigantic enough to hold it.

Orbit and Rotation. Saturn's diameter is almost 74,900 mi at the equator, while its polar diameter is more than 7,300 mi shorter. Like Jupiter, its noticeable oblateness is a result of the liquidity of the planet and its extremely rapid rate of rotation; a day is little more than 10 Earth hours long.

Atmosphere. Saturn's atmosphere is composed of 96.3% hydrogen, 3.3% helium, and traces of methane, ammonia, hydrogen deuteride, ethane, and water. Saturn's atmosphere is much like that of Jupiter, except that the temperature at the top of its cloud layer is at least 50°F colder.

Surface and Composition. Saturn's atmosphere resembles Jupiter's; it likely has a small dense center surrounded by a deep ocean of hydrogen.

Natural Satellites. Saturn has 61 known natural satellites, most of which were not discovered until space probes reached the planet. Saturn's moon Mimas has an impact crater 81 mi across (the moon itself is only 249 miles across). Enceladus has an atmosphere and shows evidence of geysers that spit water ice and vapor. Two tiny moons orbit within the rings, plowing through and making gaps in the rings along their orbits. Pan, the innermost satellite, creates the Encke Gap of Saturn's A-ring. 2005 S1 creates the Keeler Gap. The most intriguing Saturnian moon is Titan. The second biggest moon in the solar system, Titan is bigger than Mercury. Its atmosphere is similar to Earth's atmosphere of long ago; it is made up of approximately 95% nitrogen with traces of methane. Titan's atmosphere extends about 360 mi into space whereas Earth's atmosphere extends about 37 mi. Photographs from the surface show a muddy terrain, with possible deposits of water ice, channels carved by liquid methane springs, and an interesting boundary between light and dark material on the surface. In addition, in 2006, scientists found sand dunes on Titan's surface. The "sand" is believed to be tiny water ice crystals or organic compounds. Surface phenomenon such as sand dunes are signs of erosion and wind. However, unlike on Earth or Mars, Titan's winds are not the result of uneven solar heating on the moon's surface, but rather the strong gravitational pull from Saturn that creates atmospheric "tides" almost in the same way Earth's moon does to the oceans.

Rings. Saturn's ring system is the planet's most recognizable feature. It begins about 4,000 mi above the visible disk of Saturn lying above its equator and extends about 260,000 mi into space. The diameter of the ring system visible from Earth is about 170,000 mi; the rings are estimated to be about 700 feet thick. The rings are composed of rock and ice and range in size from tiny particles to large chunks of material the size of a bus. There are several divisions in the rings. The 2,920 mi Cassini division, the gap between the A and B rings, is the largest division.

Uranus

Distance from the Sun	
Perihelion	1,703.4 mil mi
Semi-major axis (mean distance)	1,784.8 mil mi (19.201 AU)
Aphelion	1,866.4 mil mi
Period of revolution around Sun	84.01 y
Orbital eccentricity	0.0457
Orbital inclination	0.772°
Synodic day (midday to midday)	17h 14m 23s (retrograde)
Sidereal day	17h 14m 24s (retrograde)
Rotational inclination	97.77°
Mass (Earth = 1)	14.536
Mean radius	15,759mi
Mean density (Earth = 1)	0.23
Natural satellites	27
Average temperature*	–323°F

*i.e., temperature where atmosphere pressure equals 1 Earth atmosphere.

Uranus, discovered by Sir William Herschel in 1781, was the first planet discovered using a telescope. It was named for the father of the Titans in Roman mythology.

Rotation and Orbit. Uranus has a diameter of over 31,000 mi and spins once in approximately 17.23 hours, according to flyby magnetic data. One of the most fascinating features of Uranus is how far over it is tipped. Its north pole lies 98° from being directly up and down to its orbit plane. Thus, its seasons are extreme. Over its 84 year orbit, when the Sun rises at the north pole, it shines there for about 42 Earth years; then it sets, and the north pole is in darkness for 42 Earth years. In addition to its rotational tilt, Uranus's magnetic field axis is tipped an incredible 58.6° from its rotational axis and is displaced about 30% of its radius away from the planet's center.

Atmosphere. The atmosphere is composed of 82.5% hydrogen, 15.2% helium, 2.3% methane, with small amounts of hydrogen deuteride, ammonia ice, water ice, ammonia hydrosulfide, and methane ice.

Surface and Composition. Uranus has no solid surface, and likely no rocky core but rather a mixture of rocks and assorted ices with about 15% hydrogen and some helium.

Natural Satellites. Uranus has 27 known moons, which have orbits lying in the plane of the planet's equator. Five moons are relatively large, while 22 are very small and were only discovered with the Voyager 2 mission or in later observations. Miranda has grooved markings, reminiscent of Jupiter's Ganymede, but often arranged in a chevron pattern. Rifts and channels on Ariel provide evidence of liquid flowing over its surface in the past. Umbriel is extremely dark, prompting some observers to regard its surface as among the oldest in the system. Titania has rifts and fractures, but not the evidence of flow found on Ariel. Oberon's main feature is its surface saturated with craters, unrelieved by other formations.

In the equatorial plane there is also a complex of 11 rings, 9 of which were discovered in 1978 by observers watching Uranus pass before a star.

Neptune

Distance from the Sun	
Perihelion	2,761.7 mil mi
Semi-major axis (mean distance)	2,793.1 (30.047 AU)
Aphelion	2,824.5 mil mi
Period of revolution around Sun	164.79 y
Orbital eccentricity	0.0113
Orbital inclination	1.769°
Synodic day (midday to midday)	16h 6m 37s
Sidereal day	16h 6m 36s
Rotational inclination	28.32°
Mass (Earth = 1)	17.147
Mean radius	15,301 mi
Mean density (Earth = 1)	0.297
Natural satellites	13
Average temperature*	–330°F

*i.e., temperature where atmosphere pressure equals 1 Earth atmosphere.

Named for the Roman god of the sea, Neptune was the first planet discovered through mathematical calculations and not observation. Its approximate orbit and position was first calculated independently by John Couch Adams and Urbain Le Verrier in 1845. In 1846, Johann Galle first observed Neptune through a telescope.

Orbit and Rotation. Neptune orbits the Sun in 164.8 years in a nearly circular orbit. Its magnetic field is considerably asymmetric to the planet's structure, similar to, but not so extreme as, Uranus's. Neptune's magnetic field axis is tipped 46.9° from its rotational axis and is displaced more than 55% of its radius away from the planet's center.

Atmosphere. The Neptunian atmosphere is composed of 80% hydrogen, 19% helium, 1.5% methane, and small amounts of hydrogen deuteride, ethane, ammonia ice, water ice, ammonia hydrosulfide, and methane ice. Neptune's atmosphere is quite blue, with quickly changing white clouds often suspended high above an apparent surface. A Great Dark Spot was discovered in 1989 when Voyager 2 visited the planet, reminiscent of the Great Red Spot of Jupiter. Observations with the Hubble Space Telescope have shown that the Great Dark Spot originally seen by Voyager has apparently dissipated, but a new dark spot has since appeared. Lightning and auroras have been found on other giant planets, but only the aurora phenomenon has been seen on Neptune. As with the other giant planets, Neptune is emitting more energy than it receives from the Sun. The excess has been found to be 2.7 times the solar contribution.

Surface and Composition. As with other giant planets, Neptune may have no solid surface or exact diameter. However, a mean value of 30,600 mi may be assigned to a diameter between atmosphere levels where the pressure is about the same as sea level on Earth.

Natural Satellites. Largest of Neptune's 13 satellites is Triton. It is the only large moon in a retrograde orbit, which suggests that it was captured rather than having been there from Neptune's creation. Triton's large size, sufficient to raise significant tides on the planet, may one day, billions of years from now, cause Triton to come close enough to Neptune for it to be torn apart. Triton has a tenuous atmosphere of nitrogen with a trace of hydrocarbons and evidence of active geysers injecting material into it. Triton is the coldest object yet measured in the solar system with a surface temperature of –391°F. Only about half of Triton has been observed, but its terrain shows cratering and a strange regional feature described as resembling the skin of a cantaloupe. Nereid has the highest orbital eccentricity (0.75) of any moon. Its long looping orbit suggests that it was also captured. In 2003, 2 more moons, which orbit farther from their parent planet than any other moon, were discovered. The *Voyager* 2 probe in 1989 confirmed the existence of 6 rings around Neptune composed of very fine particles. There may be some clumpiness in the rings' structure. It is not known whether Neptune's satellites influence the formation or maintenance of the rings.

Dwarf Planets

Note: See page 340 for the definition of a dwarf planet.

Ceres

Distance from the Sun	
Perihelion	237 mil mi (2.55 AU)
Semi-major axis (mean distance)	257 mil mi (2.77 AU)
Period of revolution around Sun	4.6 y
Orbital eccentricity	0.0789
Orbital inclination	10.58°
Sidereal day	9.075 hours
Mass (Earth = 1)	0.00016
Mean radius	300 mi

Ceres was the first asteroid ever discovered, on Jan. 1, 1801, by Guiseppe Piazzi. In the 1800s, it was considered a planet, but as more asteroids were discovered, it lost that designation. In Aug. of 2006, it was designated a "dwarf planet" by the International Astronomical Union.

No probe has ever visited Ceres. NASA's DAWN space probe, launched in Sept. 2007, may become the first. The Dawn probe's mission is to Vesta and Ceres, the solar system's two largest asteroids. When Dawn arrives at Ceres in Feb. 2015, months before the New Horizons probe arrives at Pluto, it will be the first mission to study a dwarf planet.

Orbit and Rotation. Ceres orbits the sun in the asteroid belt region between Mars and Jupiter.

Surface and Composition. Ceres is in a class of stony meteorites known as carbonaceous chondrites. These are considered to be the oldest materials in the solar system, with a composition reflecting that of the primitive solar nebula. Extremely dark in color, probably because of their hydrocarbon content, they show evidence of having absorbed water of hydration. Thus, unlike the Earth and the Moon, they have never either melted or been reheated since they first formed.

Pluto

Distance from the Sun	
Perihelion	2,756.9 mil mi
Semi-major axis (mean distance)	3,647.2 mil mi (39.482 AU)
Aphelion	4,583.2 mil mi
Period of revolution around Sun	247.68 y
Orbital eccentricity	0.2488
Orbital inclination	17.16°
Synodic day (midday to midday)	6d 9h 17m (retrograde)
Sidereal day	6d 9h 18m (retrograde)
Rotational inclination	122.53°
Mass (Earth = 1)	0.0021
Mean radius	742.5 mi
Mean density (Earth = 1)	0.317
Natural satellites	3
Average surface temperature	–369°

Pluto, named for the Roman god of the underworld, is the second largest known KBO (Kuiper Belt object) in the solar system. It was first discovered in 1930 by Clyde Tombaugh and was classified as a planet until 2006 when the International Astronomical Union changed its designation to dwarf planet. The New Horizons spacecraft was launched on a voyage to Pluto and beyond in 2006; the spacecraft will make its closest approach to Pluto in July of 2015. In 2008, Pluto was designated by the IAU as the prototype for a class of objects called **plutoids**, bodies (a) whose average distance from the Sun is greater than Neptune's; (b) are large enough that gravity determines their shape; and (c) have not cleared their orbit of other objects. Haumea, Makemake and Eris are also plutoids, and at least 10 other plutoid candidates have been identified as of fall 2009.

Orbit and Rotation. Highly irregular. Although Pluto on the average stays about 3.6 bil mi from the Sun, it may get as close as 2.76 bil mi, and for about 20 years of its orbit, it is closer to the Sun than Neptune. Currently, it is beyond Neptune's orbit.

Atmosphere and Surface. Because no probes have visited Pluto, it is difficult for astronomers to accurately take readings of the planet's atmospheric composition. It is believed that an atmosphere of methane, nitrogen, and carbon monoxide exists when the planet is closer to the Sun. When Pluto is farther away from the sun during its orbit, the atmosphere freezes and becomes part of the surface. Large regions on Pluto are dark, others light; Pluto has spots and perhaps polar caps. There is also evidence of temperature fluctuations on the planet that may indicate primitive weather. Its core may be rocky with a mantle of water ice surrounding it.

Natural Satellites. Pluto has 3 natural satellites. Charon, the biggest, has a diameter of 737 mi—about half of Pluto's diameter of 1,485 mi. No other planet of any kind has a moon so close to its size. Discovered in 1978, Charon orbits Pluto at a distance of 12,200 mi and takes 6.39 days to move around the planet. In this same length of time, Pluto and Charon both rotate once around their axes, meaning that a person standing on Pluto would always see the same face of Charon in the same part of the sky, every day and night. The Pluto-Charon system thus appears to rotate as virtually a rigid body. Both worlds are roughly spherical and have comparable densities. Because of these similarities and their peculiar relationship, there is a debate as to whether Charon should one day be designated a dwarf planet.

The 2 other moons, discovered in 2005 and 2006, were officially named Nix and Hydra.

Haumea

Distance from the Sun	
Semi-major axis (mean distance)	43.335 AU
Period of revolution around Sun	285 y
Mean radius	420 mi
Orbital eccentricity	0.189
Orbital inclination	28.19°
Mass (Earth = 1)	0.0007

Haumea was discovered in 2004 and was accepted as a dwarf planet by the IAU in 2008.

Orbit and Rotation. Haumea has a moderately eccentric orbit and takes about 285 years to go around the Sun.

Surface and Composition. Spectra of Haumea indicate the presence of almost pure crystalline water ice. The surface reflects about 60% of sunlight shining on it. Haumea has a very oblong shape, twice as long as it is wide.

Natural Satellites. Haumea has two natural satellites.

Makemake

Distance from the Sun	
Semi-major axis (mean distance)	45.791 AU
Period of revolution around Sun	310 y
Mean radius	450 mi
Orbital eccentricity	0.159
Orbital inclination	28.96°
Mass (Earth = 1)	0.0007

Makemake was discovered in 2005 and was accepted as a dwarf planet by the IAU in 2008.

Orbit and Rotation. Makemake has a moderately eccentric orbit and takes about 310 years to go around the Sun.

Surface and Composition. Spectra of Makemake indicate the presence of frozen methane, as well as several organic compounds. The surface is highly reflective and appears similar to that of Pluto.

Eris

Distance from the Sun	
Semi-major axis (mean distance)	67.6681 AU
Period of revolution around Sun	560 y
Mean radius	925 mi
Orbital eccentricity	0.44177
Orbital inclination	44.177°
Natural satellites	1
Mass (Earth = 1)	0.0027

Eris is the largest dwarf planet. Discovered in 2003 by astronomers at the California Institute of Technology, it is the most distant object ever seen in orbit around the Sun.

Orbit and Rotation. Eris has a highly elliptical orbit and takes about 560 years to go around the Sun—more than twice the time it takes Pluto. Its inclination is steep, tilted at 44° to the planetary plane. It also has an extremely eccentric orbit. It will be at its closest to the Sun, actually coming inside part of Pluto's orbit, in about 280 years.

Surface and Composition. Eris, with a surface covered in frozen methane, may be similar to Pluto and the Neptunian moon Triton. Observations made by the Hubble Space Telescope show that Eris's surface is almost white and uniform, reflecting 86% of the light that hits it. This makes it the most reflective body in the solar system. The dwarf planet's interior is likely a mixture of rock and ice.

Natural Satellites. Eris has one moon, Dysnomia.

Small Solar System Bodies: Asteroids, Comets, Kuiper Belt, and the Oort Cloud

Asteroids

Besides planets and moons, there are many smaller objects that orbit the sun. In 2006, the IAU officially designated these objects "small solar system bodies." **Asteroids** or minor planets are found mainly in a belt between the orbits of Mars and Jupiter, but some may be found outside this region. Within this belt there may be millions of asteroids of varying sizes. Most asteroids are very small. Ceres, which can be classified both as an asteroid and a dwarf planet, is 588 mi in diameter, about one-quarter the diameter of our Moon.

Some of these objects, or asteroids, are gravitationally locked with Jupiter and the Sun so that they have roughly the same orbit as Jupiter but are either 60° ahead or behind the planet. These are the **Trojan asteroids**. Many of the smaller moons of the solar system, especially those in retrograde orbits, may be captured asteroids. Asteroids whose orbits either cross or come close to the Earth's orbit are labeled **near Earth asteroids** or NEAs. A handful of asteroids have actually been imaged by the Arecibo and Goldstone radio telescopes, and by the NEAR Shoemaker space probe, while the *Galileo* spacecraft imaged the asteroids Gaspra and Ida (including its moon Dactyl) on its way to Jupiter.

Comets

Comets are small icy bodies that orbit the Sun. When they approach the Sun, the energy from the Sun boils off material from the comet's nucleus, producing an enlarged head (or **coma**), and in many cases an extended tail. Because of the proximity to the Sun and the expanded head and tail, comets are brighter when near the Sun. For large comets, the head may be a 100,000 mi across and the tail more than a million mi long, though both are mainly empty space.

Comets have been known since ancient times; ultimately, British astronomer Edmund Halley (1656-1742) realized that a group of historical reports were just repeated visits of the same object. Comets are the only astronomical objects named after their discoverers. In 1986, the European spacecraft *Giotto* took the first close-up images of a comet's nucleus, specifically of Comet Halley, showing it had a peanut-shaped nucleus whose longest dimension was about 10 mi.

In 1995, Alan Hale and Thomas Bopp independently discovered a comet that was then beyond the orbit of Jupiter. It was the farthest comet ever discovered by amateurs and one of the brightest of all time. It also holds the record for length of naked-eye visibility—19 months—and is the most photographed comet in history. In July 2009, an amateur astronomer discovered a large impact scar in the upper atmosphere of Jupiter, likely the result of another cometary impact.

Kuiper Belt

The **Kuiper Belt** is a donut-shaped region that extends to about 50 AU from the Sun and is thought to be the source of short-period comets such as Comet Halley or Comet Swift-Tuttle. It is filled with icy bodies that are in solar orbit. The more than 1,000 objects found in this region in recent years are called Kuiper Belt objects (KBOs). It is estimated that there are more than 70,000 objects 60 mi in diameter or larger within the Kuiper Belt. Dwarf planets Pluto and Eris are considered KBOs. There are at least 6 KBOs larger than 300 mi in diameter.

Oort Cloud

The Oort Cloud is a vast spherical shell hypothesized to exist around the Sun. Astronomer Jan Oort proposed its existence as the origin for long-period comets that enter the inner part of the solar system where the planets orbit. As of yet, our technology is not sufficient to detect any members of the Oort Cloud, other than those comets that have been observed that indicate the most distant parts of their orbits may reach out to 50,000 AU. Recent examples of such long-period comets are Comet Hale-Bopp and Comet Hyakutake.

The Sun

Distance from Earth, mean	92.96 mil mi (1 AU)
Sidereal day	25.38 d
Mass (Earth=1)	332,900
Mean Radius	432,200 mi
Mean Density (Earth=1)	0.255
Average surface temperature	9,941°F

The Sun is the Earth's primary source of light and heat and its closest star. The biggest object in the solar system, the Sun is 332,900 times more massive than Earth and contains 99.86% of the mass of the entire solar system. On the whole, the Sun is made up of about 92.1% hydrogen and 7.8% helium, with trace amounts of other elements. It has a mass and luminosity greater than that of 90% of the stars in the Milky Way galaxy. Although most of the stars that can be easily seen on a clear night are bigger and brighter than the Sun, its proximity to Earth makes it appear tremendously large and bright. The Sun is 400,000 times as bright as the full moon and it gives Earth 6 mil times as much light as do all other stars put together. Because of the great distance between the Sun and Earth, it takes about 499 seconds, or slightly more than 8 minutes, for light from the Sun to reach Earth.

Composition. The Sun has six regions. The first three from the inside out are the core, the radiative zone, and the convective zone. Together they form the interior. The others, which comprise the visible surface, are the photosphere, the chromosphere, and the outermost region, the corona.

The Sun's core is where its heat and energy are produced. Through a series of nuclear fusion reactions, hydrogen nuclei are converted to helium nuclei. Temperatures in the core are theorized to be 28 mil°F. From the core, photons transport the energy outward through the radiative zone. It can take photons several millions of years to pass through this area. In the convective zone, gases move energy outward at a faster rate. Like a boiling pot, bubbles of gas bring energy to the surface.

The photosphere is the visible surface of the sun, that is, the light from here is what we see as sunlight. When sunlight is analyzed with a spectroscope, it is found to consist of a continuous spectrum composed of all the colors of the rainbow in order, crossed by many dark lines. The dark "absorption lines" are produced by gaseous materials in the outer layers of the Sun. More than 60 of the natural terrestrial elements have been identified in the Sun, all in gaseous form because of the Sun's intense heat.

Just above the photosphere is the chromosphere, which is visible to the naked eye only at total solar eclipses, appearing then to be a pinkish-violet layer with occasional great prominences projecting above its general level. With proper instruments, the chromosphere can be seen or photographed whenever the Sun is visible. Above the chromosphere is the corona, also visible to the naked eye only at times of total eclipse or with instruments that permit the brighter portions of the corona to be seen. The light of the corona surges millions of miles from the Sun, where atoms of which it is composed are all in a state of extreme attenuation and high ionization that indicates temperatures nearly 2 mil°F.

Sunspots. These dark, irregularly shaped regions may reach diameters of thousands of miles. There is an intimate connection between sunspots and the corona. At times of low sunspot activity, the fine streamers of the corona are longer above the Sun's equator than over the polar regions of the Sun; during periods of high sunspot activity, the corona extends fairly evenly outward from all regions of the Sun, but to a much greater distance in space. The average life of a sunspot group is 2 months, but some have lasted for more than a year.

Sunspots reach a low point, on average, every 11.3 years, with a peak of activity occurring irregularly between 2 successive periods of minimal activity. Currently, the number of sunspots is declining. Solar minimum occurred late in 2006.

Solar Wind and Magnetic Field. Magnetic arches, called prominences, may extend tens of thousands of miles into the corona, and may release enormous amounts of energy heating the corona. Coronal mass ejections are enormous releases of solar energy. Coronal holes are regions where the corona appears dark in X-rays and are associated with open magnetic field lines, where the magnetic field lines project out into space instead of back towards the Sun. It is in these regions where the high-speed solar wind originates.

The solar wind carries the Sun's magnetic field, which extends beyond the planets. This is called the interplanetary magnetic field (IMF). Far past Pluto and the Kuiper Belt, the solar wind and the IMF lose their influence, and the boundary between them and interstellar space is called the heliopause.

Searching for Extrasolar Planets

During the last 10 years of the 20th century, astronomers began to detect the presence of planets orbiting stars other than the Sun. Except for a few possible instances, they have not seen those objects, but merely inferred their existence by their effect on their parent star. The Sun is a typical star in many respects. With over 200 billion stars in the Milky Way, it seems plausible that many other stars might have planets.

As of fall 2009, astronomers had found a total of 374 planets orbiting 316 stars. Of those, 237 were at least as massive as Jupiter, which is about 318 times more massive than the Earth. About 137 star systems may have planets less massive than Jupiter. In June 2005, astronomers reported detecting a planet that is only about 6 times the mass of the Earth. The planet orbits much closer to its parent star; Gliese 876 takes less than 2 days to complete one orbit.

Using the Doppler effect to detect radial velocity changes in the motions of individual stars, astronomers are more likely to find high-mass planets in close and eccentric orbits around stars, because that situation produces larger and more noticeable changes.

In addition to the radial velocity method, astronomers are now using an optical gravitational lensing means of detecting extrasolar planets. Using this technique, Southern Hemisphere astronomers found the most distant planet yet detected, about halfway to the center of our own Milky Way galaxy. Astronomers have also found planets by looking for the periodic dimming of starlight as orbiting planets pass in front of their host stars. About 25 planets have been discovered this way.

In 2005, astronomers obtained the first direct photograph of an extra-solar planet. The unnamed planet orbits a star called GQ Lupi, which is a star like our Sun but younger. The planet is about 100 AUs away from its star, and it is estimated to be about twice as massive as Jupiter.

In 2006, astronomers discovered what they call a "super Earth" orbiting a red dwarf star 9,000 light-years away. The planet appears to have about 13 times the mass of Earth and may be composed of rock and ice. Although the planet is similar in structure to the Earth, it is believed to orbit too far from its star for there to be any liquid on the surface. In 2007, astronomers for the first time detected water in the atmosphere of an extra-solar planet.

In Apr. 2009, NASA launched Kepler, the first telescope sensitive enough to detect Earth-sized planets around other stars. The mission is planned to last four years and should help determine how common Earth-like planets are.

Earth: Size, Computation of Time, Seasons

Distance from the Sun	
Perihelion	91.4 mil mi
Semi-major axis	93 mil mi (1.0000 AU)
Aphelion	94.5 mil mi
Period of revolution	365.256 d
Orbital eccentricity	0.0167
Orbital inclination	0°
Sidereal day (rotation period)	23h 56m 4.2s
Synodic day (midday to midday)	24h 0m 0s
Rotational inclination	23.45°
Mass (Earth = 1)	1
Mean radius	3,958.8 mi
Mean density (Earth = 1)	1
Natural satellites	1
Average surface temperature	59°F

Earth is the 5th-largest planet and the 3rd from the Sun. Its mass is 5.9736 x 10^{24} kg. Earth's equatorial diameter is 7,926 mi while its polar diameter is only 7,900 mi.

Size and Dimensions. Earth is considered a solid mass, yet it has a large, liquid iron, **magnetic core** with a radius of about 2,160 mi. Surprisingly, it has a solid **inner core** that may be a large iron crystal, with a radius of 760 mi. Around the core is a thick shell, or **mantle**, of dense rock. This mantle is composed of materials rich in iron and magnesium. It is somewhat plastic-like, and under slow steady pressure, it can flow like a liquid. The mantle, in turn, is covered by a thin **crust** forming the solid granite and basalt base of the continents and ocean basins. Over broad areas of Earth's surface, the crust has a thin cover of sedimentary rock such as sandstone, shale, and limestone formed by weathering and by deposits of sands, clays, and plant and animal remains.

The temperature inside the Earth increases about 1° F with every 100 to 200 feet in depth, in the upper 100 km of Earth, and reaches nearly 8,000-9,000° F at the center. The heat is believed to come from radioactivity in rocks, pressures within Earth, and the original heat of Earth's formation.

Atmosphere of Earth. Earth's atmosphere is a blanket composed of 78% nitrogen, 21% oxygen, and 1% argon. Present in minute quantities are carbon dioxide, hydrogen, neon, helium, krypton, and xenon. Water vapor displaces other gases and varies from nearly zero to about 4% by volume. The atmosphere rests on Earth's surface with a weight equivalent to a layer of water 34 ft deep. For about 300,000 ft upward, the gases remain in the proportions stated. Gravity holds the gases

to Earth. The weight of the air compresses it at the bottom so that the greatest density is at Earth's surface. Pressure and density decrease as height increases.

The lowest layer of the atmosphere extending up about 7.5 mi is the **troposphere**, which contains 90% of the air and the tallest mountains. This is also where most weather phenomena occur. The temperature drops with increasing height throughout this layer. The atmosphere for about 23 mi above the troposphere is the **stratosphere**, where the temperature generally increases with height. The stratosphere contains **ozone**, which prevents ultraviolet rays from reaching Earth's surface. Since there is very little convection in the stratosphere, jets regularly cruise in the lower parts to provide a smoother ride for passengers.

Above the stratosphere is the **mesosphere**, where the temperature again decreases with height for another 19 mi. Extending above the mesosphere to the outer fringes of the atmosphere is the **thermosphere**, a region where temperature once more increases with height to a value measured in thousands of degrees Fahrenheit. The lower portion of this region, extending from 50 to about 400 mi in altitude, is characterized by a high ion density and is thus called the **ionosphere**. Most meteors are in the lower thermosphere or the mesosphere at the time they are observed.

Longitude, Latitude. Position on the globe is measured by meridians and parallels. Meridians, which are imaginary lines drawn around Earth through the poles, determine **longitude**. The meridian running through Greenwich, England, is the **prime meridian** of longitude, and all others are either E or W. Parallels, which are imaginary circles parallel with the equator, determine **latitude**. The length of a degree of longitude varies as the cosine of the latitude. At the equator a degree of longitude is 69.171 statute mi; this is gradually reduced toward the poles. Value of a longitude degree at the poles is zero.

Latitude is reckoned by the number of degrees N or S of the **equator**, an imaginary circle on Earth's surface everywhere equidistant between the two poles. According to the International Astronomical Union, the length of a degree of latitude is 68.708 statute mi at the equator and varies slightly N and S because of the oblate form of the globe; at the poles it is 69.403 statute mi.

Definitions of Time. Earth rotates on its axis and follows an elliptical orbit around the Sun. The rotation makes the Sun appear to move across the sky from E to W. This rotation determines day and night, and the complete rotation, in relation to the Sun, is called the **apparent or true solar day**. A sundial thus measures **apparent solar time**. This length of time varies, but an average determines the mean solar day of 24 hours.

The mean solar day and **mean solar time** are in universal use for civil purposes. Mean solar time may be obtained from apparent solar time by correcting observations of the Sun for the **equation of time**. Mean solar time may be up to 16 minutes different from apparent solar time.

Sidereal time is the measure of time defined by the diurnal motion of the vernal equinox and is determined from observation of the meridian transits of stars. One complete rotation of Earth relative to the equinox is called the **sidereal day**. The **mean sidereal day** is 23 hours, 56 minutes, 4.091 seconds of mean solar time.

The interval required for Earth to make one absolute revolution around the Sun is a **sidereal** year; it consisted of 365 days, 6 hours, 9 minutes, and 9.5 seconds of mean solar time (approximately 24 hours per day) in 1900 and has been increasing at the rate of 0.0001 second annually.

The **tropical year**, upon which our calendar is based, is the interval between 2 consecutive returns of the Sun to the vernal equinox. The tropical year consisted of 365 days, 5 hours, 48 minutes, and 46 seconds in 1900. It has been decreasing at the rate of 0.53 second per century. The **calendar year** begins at 12 o'clock midnight precisely, local clock time, on the night of Dec. 31-Jan. 1. The day and the calendar month also begin at midnight by the clock.

On Jan. 1, 1972, the Bureau International des Poids et Mesures in Paris introduced **International Atomic Time** (TAI) as the most precisely determined time scale for astronomical usage. The fundamental unit of TAI in the international system of units is the second, defined as the duration of 9,192,631,770 periods of the radiation corresponding to the transition between 2 hyperfine levels of the ground state of the cesium-133 atom. **Coordinated Universal Time** (UTC), which serves as the basis for civil timekeeping and is the standard time of the prime meridian, is officially defined by a formula which relates UTC to mean sidereal time in Greenwich, England. (UTC has replaced GMT as the basis for standard time for the world.)

The Zones and Seasons. The 5 zones of Earth's surface are the Torrid, lying between the Tropics of Cancer and Capricorn; the N Temperate, between Cancer and the Arctic Circle; the S Temperate, between Capricorn and the Antarctic Circle; and the 2 Frigid Zones, between the Polar Circles and the Poles.

The inclination, or tilt, of Earth's axis, 23° 27′ away from a perpendicular to Earth's orbit of the Sun, determines the seasons. These are commonly marked in the N Temperate Zone, where spring begins at the vernal equinox, summer at the summer solstice, autumn at the autumnal equinox, and winter at the winter solstice. In the S Temperate Zone, the seasons are reversed. Spring begins at the autumnal equinox, summer at the winter solstice, etc.

The points at which the Sun crosses the equator are the **equinoxes**, when day and night are most nearly equal. The points at which the Sun is at a maximum distance from the equator are the **solstices**. Days and nights are then most unequal. However, at the equator, day and night are equal throughout the year.

In June, the North Pole is tilted 23°27′ toward the Sun, and the days in the Northern Hemisphere are longer than the nights, while the days in the Southern Hemisphere are shorter than the nights. In Dec., the North Pole is tilted 23°27′ away from the Sun, and the situation is reversed.

The Seasons in 2010. In 2010, the 4 seasons begin in the Northern Hemisphere as shown. (Add 1 hour to Eastern Standard Time for Atlantic Time; subtract 1 hour for Central, 2 for Mountain, 3 for Pacific, 4 for Alaska, 5 for Hawaii-Aleutian. Also shown is Coordinated Universal Time.)

Seasons	Date	UTC	EST/EDT
Vernal Equinox (spring)	Mar. 20	17:32	13:32 EDT
Northern Solstice (summer)	June 21	11:28	07:28 EDT
Autumnal Equinox (fall)	Sept. 23	03:09	23:09 EDT Sept. 22
Southern Solstice (winter)	Dec. 21	23:38	18:38 EST

Poles of Earth. The geographic (rotation) poles, or points where Earth's axis of rotation cuts the surface, are not absolutely fixed in the body of Earth. The pole of rotation describes an irregular curve about its mean position.

Two periods have been detected in this motion: (1) an annual period due to seasonal changes in barometric pressure, to load of ice and snow on the surface, and to other seasonal phenomena; (2) a period of about 14 months due to the shape and constitution of Earth. In addition, there are small but as yet unpredictable irregularities. The whole motion is so small that the actual pole at any time remains within a circle of 30 or 40 feet in radius centered at the mean position of the pole.

The pole of rotation for the time being is of course the pole having a latitude of 90° and an indeterminate longitude.

Magnetic Poles. Although Earth's magnetic field resembles that of an ordinary bar magnet, this magnetic field is probably produced by electric currents in the liquid currents of the Earth's outer core. The **north magnetic pole** of Earth is that region where the magnetic force is vertically downward, and the **south magnetic pole** is that region where the magnetic force is vertically upward. A compass placed at the magnetic poles experiences no directive force in azimuth (i.e., direction).

There are slow changes in the distribution of Earth's magnetic field. This slow temporal change is referred to as the secular change of the main magnetic field, and the magnetic poles shift due to this. The location of the N magnetic pole was first measured in 1831 at Cape Adelaide on the west coast of Boothia Peninsula in Canada's Northwest Territories (about latitude 70° N and longitude 96° W). Since then it has moved over 500 mi. It is now estimated to be at 82.7° N and 114.4° W, northwest of Ellef Ringnes Island in northern Canada. Measurement for several decades by Canadian scientists indicates the motion of the pole has accelerated, now averaging about 25 mi per year.

The direction of the horizontal components of the magnetic field at any point is known as magnetic N at that point, and the angle by which it deviates E or W of true N is known as the magnetic declination.

A compass without error points in the direction of magnetic north. (In general, this is not the direction of the true rotational north pole.) If you follow the direction indicated by the N end of the compass, you will go along an irregular curve that eventually reaches the north magnetic pole (though not usually by a great-circle route). However, the action of the compass should not be thought of as due to any influence of the distant pole, but simply as an indication of the distribution of Earth's magnetism at the place of observation.

Rotation of Earth. The speed of rotation of Earth about its axis is slightly variable. The variations may be classified as:

(A) **Secular.** Tidal friction acts as a brake on the rotation and causes a slow secular increase in the length of the day, about 1 millisecond per century.

(B) **Irregular.** The speed of rotation may increase for a number of years, about 5 to 10, and then start decreasing. The maximum difference from the mean in the length of the day during a century is about 5 milliseconds. The accumulated difference in time has amounted to approximately 44 seconds since 1900. The cause is probably motion in the interior of Earth.

(C) **Periodic.** Seasonal variations exist with periods of 1 year and 6 months. The cumulative effect is such that each year, Earth is late about 30 milliseconds near June 1 and is ahead about 30 milliseconds near Oct. 1. The maximum seasonal variation in the length of the day is about 0.5 millisecond. It is believed that the principal cause of the annual variation is the seasonal change in the wind patterns of the northern and southern hemispheres. The semiannual variation is due chiefly to tidal action of the Sun, which distorts the shape of Earth slightly.

The Moon

Distance from Earth	
Perigee	225,744 mi
Semi-major axis	238,855 mi
Apogee	251,966 mi
Period of revolution	27.322 d
Synodic orbital period (period of phases)	29.53 d
Orbital eccentricity	0.0549
Orbital inclination	5.145°
Sidereal day (rotation period)	27.322 d
Rotational inclination	6.68°
Mass (Earth = 1)	0.0123
Mean radius	1,079 mi
Mean density (Earth = 1)	0.607
Average surface temperature	−100°F

The Moon is the second brightest object in the sky (the sun is the first). Earth's only natural satellite, the Moon is the force behind the rising and falling of tides, and it helps to regulate the Earth's orbit around the sun. Many probes have been sent to the moon and between 1969 and 1972, 12 U.S. astronauts walked on its surface. The Moon is the subject of renewed international interest. In 2007, Japan and China orbited satellites around the Moon. India orbited a spacecraft in fall 2008, while the U.S. sent an orbiter and impactor in 2009. It is expected that several nations, including the U.S. and China, will send humans back to the Moon in the next 15 years. In Sept. 2009, American scientists announced the discovery of a thin layer of water ice near the lunar poles. The LCROSS mission, which was scheduled to impact the Moon, is designed to search for water buried beneath the surface near the lunar south pole.

Orbit and Rotation. The Moon completes a circuit around Earth in a period that averages 27 days, 7 hours, 43.2 minutes. This is the Moon's sidereal period. Because of the motion of the Moon in common with Earth around the Sun, the mean duration of the lunar month—the period from one New Moon to the next New Moon—is 29 days, 12 hours, 44.05 minutes. This is the Moon's synodic period.

The mean distance of the Moon from Earth is 238,855 mi, but its orbit about Earth is elliptical, and thus the actual distance varies considerably. The maximum distance from Earth that the Moon may reach is 251,966 mi and the least distance is 225,744 mi.

The Moon rotates on its axis in a period of time that is exactly equal to its sidereal revolution about Earth—27.322 days. Thus the backside, or farside, of the Moon always faces away from Earth. But this does not mean that the backside is always dark. The farside of the Moon gets just as much direct sunlight as the nearside; at New Moon phase, the farside of the Moon is fully lit but not visible from Earth.

The Moon's revolution about Earth is irregular because of its elliptical orbit. The Moon's rotation, however, is regular, and this, together with the irregular revolution, produces what is called "libration in longitude," which permits an observer on Earth to see first farther around the eastern side and then farther around the western side of the Moon. The Moon's variation north or south of the ecliptic permits one to see farther over first one pole of the Moon and then the other; this is called "libration in latitude." These two libration effects permit observers on Earth to see a total of about 60% of the Moon's surface over a period of time.

Atmosphere and Surface. The Moon, like the planet Mercury, has no real atmosphere to speak of. What little exists is variable and tenuous. With its long day and night, the daytime temperature can reach 260°F, while the coldest nighttime temperature may reach −280°F. This day-to-night contrast is exceeded only by that on Mercury.

The lunar surface has not changed much since humans have been observing it. The side visible from Earth has large craters and vast dark areas called maria (Latin word for "seas") that were once lava. The farside has almost no maria but is pockmarked with craters.

Recent findings show that up to 300 mil metric tons of water ice may exist in craters at the lunar poles. The Moon may have a small core in its interior, which supports the idea that most of the mass of the Moon was ripped away from the early Earth when a Mars-size object collided with Earth. The hidden side of the Moon was first photographed in 1959 by the Soviet space probe Lunik III.

Harvest Moon and Hunter's Moon. The Harvest Moon, the full Moon nearest the autumnal equinox, ushers in a period of several successive days when the Moon rises soon after sunset. This phenomenon gives farmers in temperate latitudes extra hours of light in which to harvest their crops before frost and winter. The 2010 Harvest Moon falls on Sept. 23. Harvest Moon in the Southern Hemisphere temperate latitudes falls on Mar. 30.

The next full Moon after Harvest Moon is called the Hunter's Moon; it is accompanied by a similar but less marked phenomenon. In 2010, the Hunter's Moon occurs on Oct. 23 in the Northern Hemisphere and on Apr. 28 in the Southern Hemisphere.

Moon's Perigee and Apogee, 2010

Perigee is the point in the moon's orbit where it is closest to the Earth. Apogee is the point where it is farthest.

(Coordinated Universal Time, standard time of the prime meridian)

Perigee			Perigee			Apogee			Apogee		
Date	Hour		Date	Hour		Date	Hour		Date	Hour	
Jan. 1	21		July 13	11		Jan. 17	2		July 1	10	
30	9		Aug. 10	18		Feb. 13	2		29	0	
Feb. 27	22		Sept. 8	4		Mar. 12	10		Aug. 25	6	
Mar. 28	5		Oct. 6	13		Apr. 9	3		Sept. 21	8	
Apr. 24	21		Nov. 3	17		May 6	22		Oct. 18	18	
May 20	9		30	19		June 3	17		Nov. 15	12	
June 15	15		Dec. 25	12					Dec. 13	4	

Moon Phases, 2010

(Coordinated Universal Time, standard time of the prime meridian)

New Moon				Waxing Quarter				Full Moon				Waning Quarter			
Month	d	h	m	Month	d	h	m	Month	d	h	m	Month	d	h	m
Jan.	15	7	11	Jan.	23	10	53	Jan.	30	6	18	Jan.	5	23	48
Feb.	14	2	51	Feb.	22	0	42	Feb.	28	16	38	Feb.	7	15	42
Mar.	15	21	1	Mar.	23	11	0	Mar.	30	2	25	Mar.	6	9	37
Apr.	14	12	29	Apr.	21	18	20	Apr.	28	12	18	Apr.	6	4	15
May	14	1	4	May	20	23	43	May	27	23	7	May	4	22	13
June	12	11	15	June	19	4	29	June	26	11	30	June	4	14	35
July	11	19	40	July	18	10	11	July	26	1	37	July	3	4	59
Aug.	10	3	8	Aug.	16	18	14	Aug.	24	17	5	Aug.	1	17	22
Sept.	8	10	30	Sept.	15	5	50	Sept.	23	9	17	Sept.	1	3	52
Oct.	7	18	44	Oct.	14	21	27	Oct.	23	1	36	Oct.	30	12	46
Nov.	6	4	52	Nov.	13	16	39	Nov.	21	17	27	Nov.	28	20	36
Dec.	5	17	36	Dec.	13	13	59	Dec.	21	8	13	Dec.	28	4	18

CALENDAR

Julian and Gregorian Calendars; Leap Year; Century

The **Julian calendar**, under which all Western nations measured time until 1582 CE, was authorized by Julius Caesar in 46 BCE. It called for a year of 365¼ days, starting in January, with every 4th year being a **leap year** of 366 days. St. Bede, an Anglo-Saxon monk also known as the Venerable Bede, announced in 730 CE that the Julian year was 11 min, 14 sec too long, a cumulative error of about a day every 128 years, but nothing was done about this for centuries.

By 1582 the accumulated error was estimated at 10 days. In that year Pope Gregory XIII decreed that the day following Oct. 4, 1582, should be called Oct. 15, thus dropping 10 days and initiating the **Gregorian calendar**.

The Gregorian calendar continued a system devised by the monk Dionysius Exiguus (6th century), starting from the first year following the birth of Jesus Christ, which was inaccurately taken to be year 753 in the Roman calendar. Leap years were continued but, to prevent further displacements, centesimal years (years ending in 00) were made common years, not leap years, unless divisible by 400. Under this plan, **1600** and **2000** were leap years (as was **2004**); 1700, 1800, and 1900 were not.

The Gregorian calendar was adopted at once by France, Italy, Spain, Portugal, and Luxembourg. Within 2 years most German Catholic states, Belgium, and parts of Switzerland and the Netherlands were brought under the new calendar, and Hungary followed in 1587. The rest of the Netherlands, along with Denmark and the German Protestant states, made the change in 1699-1700.

The British government adopted the Gregorian calendar and imposed it on all its possessions, including the American colonies, in 1752, decreeing that the day following Sept. 2, 1752, should be called Sept. 14, a loss of 11 days. All dates preceding were marked OS, for Old Style. In addition, New Year's Day was moved to Jan. 1 from Mar. 25 (under the old reckoning, for example, Mar. 24, 1700, had been followed by Mar. 25, 1701). Thus George Washington's birthdate, which was Feb. 11, 1731, OS, became Feb. 22, 1732, NS (New Style). In 1753 Sweden also went Gregorian.

In 1793 the French revolutionary government adopted a calendar of 12 months of 30 days with 5 extra days in September of each common year and 6 extra days every 4th year. Napoleon reinstated the Gregorian calendar in 1806.

The Gregorian system later spread to non-European regions, replacing traditional calendars at least for official purposes. Japan in 1873, Egypt in 1875, China in 1912, and Turkey in 1925 made the change, usually in conjunction with political upheaval. In China, the republican government began reckoning years from its 1911 founding. After 1949, the People's Republic adopted the Common, or Christian Era, year count, even for the traditional lunar calendar, which it also retained. In 1918 the Soviet Union decreed that the day after Jan. 31, 1918, OS, would be Feb. 14, 1918, NS. Greece changed over in 1923. For the first time in history, all major nations had one calendar. The Russian Orthodox church and some other Christian sects retained the Julian calendar.

To convert from the Julian to the Gregorian calendar, add 10 days to dates Oct. 5, 1582, through Feb. 28, 1700; after that date add 11 days through Feb. 28, 1800; 12 days through Feb. 28, 1900; and 13 days through Feb. 28, 2100.

A **century** consists of 100 consecutive years. The 1st century CE may be said to have run from the years 1 through 100. The 20th century by this reckoning consisted of the years 1901 through 2000 and ended Dec. 31, 2000, as did the 2nd millennium CE. The 21st century thus technically began Jan. 1, 2001.

For a **Perpetual Calendar**, *see* pages 354-55.

Gregorian Calendar

Choose the desired year from the table below or from the Perpetual Calendar (for years 1803 to 2080). The number after each year designates which calendar to use for that year, as shown in the Perpetual Calendar. (The Gregorian calendar was inaugurated Oct. 15, 1582. From that date to Dec. 31, 1582, use calendar 6.)

1583-1802

1583	7	1603	4	1623	1	1643	5	1663	2	1683	6	1703	2	1723	6	1743	3	1763	7	1783	4
1584	8	1604	12	1624	9	1644	13	1664	10	1684	14	1704	10	1724	14	1744	11	1764	8	1784	12
1585	3	1605	7	1625	4	1645	1	1665	5	1685	2	1705	5	1725	2	1745	6	1765	3	1785	7
1586	4	1606	1	1626	5	1646	2	1666	6	1686	3	1706	6	1726	3	1746	7	1766	4	1786	1
1587	5	1607	2	1627	6	1647	3	1667	7	1687	4	1707	7	1727	4	1747	1	1767	5	1787	2
1588	13	1608	10	1628	14	1648	11	1668	8	1688	12	1708	8	1728	12	1748	9	1768	13	1788	10
1589	1	1609	5	1629	2	1649	6	1669	3	1689	7	1709	3	1729	7	1749	4	1769	1	1789	5
1590	2	1610	6	1630	3	1650	7	1670	4	1690	1	1710	4	1730	1	1750	5	1770	2	1790	6
1591	3	1611	7	1631	4	1651	1	1671	5	1691	2	1711	5	1731	2	1751	6	1771	3	1791	7
1592	11	1612	8	1632	12	1652	9	1672	13	1692	10	1712	13	1732	10	1752	14	1772	11	1792	8
1593	6	1613	3	1633	7	1653	4	1673	1	1693	5	1713	1	1733	5	1753	2	1773	6	1793	3
1594	7	1614	4	1634	1	1654	5	1674	2	1694	6	1714	2	1734	6	1754	3	1774	7	1794	4
1595	1	1615	5	1635	2	1655	6	1675	3	1695	7	1715	3	1735	7	1755	4	1775	1	1795	5
1596	9	1616	13	1636	10	1656	14	1676	11	1696	8	1716	11	1736	8	1756	12	1776	9	1796	13
1597	4	1617	1	1637	5	1657	2	1677	6	1697	3	1717	6	1737	3	1757	7	1777	4	1797	1
1598	5	1618	2	1638	6	1658	3	1678	7	1698	4	1718	7	1738	4	1758	1	1778	5	1798	2
1599	6	1619	3	1639	7	1659	4	1679	5	1699	5	1719	1	1739	5	1759	2	1779	6	1799	3
1600	14	1620	11	1640	8	1660	12	1680	9	1700	6	1720	9	1740	13	1760	10	1780	14	1800	4
1601	2	1621	6	1641	3	1661	7	1681	4	1701	7	1721	4	1741	1	1761	5	1781	2	1801	5
1602	3	1622	7	1642	4	1662	1	1682	5	1702	1	1722	5	1742	2	1762	6	1782	3	1802	6

The Julian Period

How many days have you lived? To determine this, multiply your age by 365, add the number of days since your last birthday, and account for all leap years. Chances are your calculations will go wrong somewhere. Astronomers, however, find it convenient to express dates and time intervals in days rather than in years, months, and days. This is done by placing events within the Julian period.

The Julian period was devised in 1582 by the French classical scholar Joseph Scaliger (1540-1609), and it was named after his father, Julius Caesar Scaliger, not after the Julian calendar as might be supposed.

Scaliger began with a zero hour, or starting time, of noon on Jan. 1, 4713 BCE (on the Julian calendar). This was the most recent time that 3 major chronological cycles began on the same day: (1) the 28-year solar cycle, after which dates in the Julian calendar (e.g., Feb. 11) return to the same days of the week (e.g., Monday); (2) the 19-year lunar cycle, after which the phases of the moon return to the same dates of the year; and (3) the 15-year indiction cycle, used in ancient Rome to regulate taxes.

It will take 7,980 years to complete the period, the product of 28, 19, and 15.

Noon (Universal Time) of Dec. 31, 2009, will be Julian Date (JD) 2,455,197; that many days will have passed since the start of the Julian period. The JD at noon of any date in 2010 may be found by adding to this figure the day of the year for that date, which can be obtained from the left half of the "How Far Apart Are Two Dates?" chart on the next page.

Julian Calendar

To find which of the 14 calendars of the Perpetual Calendar (pages 354-55) applies to any year under the Julian system, find the century for the desired year in the 3 leftmost columns below. Read across and find the year in the 4 top rows. Then read down. The number in the intersection is the calendar designation for that year. For some years and countries the Julian new year did not start Jan. 1; to find the correct Perpetual Calendar for Britain and its possessions, you can generally add one year for dates from Jan. 1-Mar. 24. For example, to look up Feb. 2, 1705, Old Style, use the year 1706.

Year (last 2 figures of desired year)

Century			01	02	03	04	05	06	07	08	09	10	11	12	13	14	15	16	17	18	19	20	21	22	23	24	25	26	27	28
			29	30	31	32	33	34	35	36	37	38	39	40	41	42	43	44	45	46	47	48	49	50	51	52	53	54	55	56
			57	58	59	60	61	62	63	64	65	66	67	68	69	70	71	72	73	74	75	76	77	78	79	80	81	82	83	84
		00	85	86	87	88	89	90	91	92	93	94	95	96	97	98	99													
0	700	1400	12	7	1	2	10	5	6	7	8	3	4	5	13	1	2	3	11	6	7	1	9	4	5	6	14	2	3	4	12
100	800	1500	11	6	7	1	9	4	5	6	14	2	3	4	12	7	1	2	10	5	6	7	8	3	4	5	13	1	2	3	11
200	900	1600	10	5	6	7	8	3	4	5	13	1	2	3	11	6	7	1	9	4	5	6	14	2	3	4	12	7	1	2	10
300	1000	1700	9	4	5	6	14	2	3	4	12	7	1	2	10	5	6	7	8	3	4	5	13	1	2	3	11	6	7	1	9
400	1100	1800	8	3	4	5	13	1	2	3	11	6	7	1	9	4	5	6	14	2	3	4	12	7	1	2	10	5	6	7	8
500	1200	1900	14	2	3	4	12	7	1	2	10	5	6	7	8	3	4	5	13	1	2	3	11	6	7	1	9	4	5	6	14
600	1300	2000	13	1	2	3	11	6	7	1	9	4	5	6	14	2	3	4	12	7	1	2	10	5	6	7	8	3	4	5	13

How Far Apart Are Two Dates?

This table covers a range of 2 years. To use, **find the numbers in the tables for each date and subtract** the smaller from the larger. For example, to find the number of days from Mar. 15, 2009, to Sept. 22, 2010 subtract 74 from 630; the result is 556. For leap years, such as 2008, where Feb. 29 intervenes, one day must be then added; thus Feb. 4, 2008, and Mar. 13, 2009, were 403 days apart.

First Year

Date	Jan.	Feb.	Mar.	April	May	June	July	Aug.	Sept.	Oct.	Nov.	Dec.
1	1	32	60	91	121	152	182	213	244	274	305	335
2	2	33	61	92	122	153	183	214	245	275	306	336
3	3	34	62	93	123	154	184	215	246	276	307	337
4	4	35	63	94	124	155	185	216	247	277	308	338
5	5	36	64	95	125	156	186	217	248	278	309	339
6	6	37	65	96	126	157	187	218	249	279	310	340
7	7	38	66	97	127	158	188	219	250	280	311	341
8	8	39	67	98	128	159	189	220	251	281	312	342
9	9	40	68	99	129	160	190	221	252	282	313	343
10	10	41	69	100	130	161	191	222	253	283	314	344
11	11	42	70	101	131	162	192	223	254	284	315	345
12	12	43	71	102	132	163	193	224	255	285	316	346
13	13	44	72	103	133	164	194	225	256	286	317	347
14	14	45	73	104	134	165	195	226	257	287	318	348
15	15	46	74	105	135	166	196	227	258	288	319	349
16	16	47	75	106	136	167	197	228	259	289	320	350
17	17	48	76	107	137	168	198	229	260	290	321	351
18	18	49	77	108	138	169	199	230	261	291	322	352
19	19	50	78	109	139	170	200	231	262	292	323	353
20	20	51	79	110	140	171	201	232	263	293	324	354
21	21	52	80	111	141	172	202	233	264	294	325	355
22	22	53	81	112	142	173	203	234	265	295	326	356
23	23	54	82	113	143	174	204	235	266	296	327	357
24	24	55	83	114	144	175	205	236	267	297	328	358
25	25	56	84	115	145	176	206	237	268	298	329	359
26	26	57	85	116	146	177	207	238	269	299	330	360
27	27	58	86	117	147	178	208	239	270	300	331	361
28	28	59	87	118	148	179	209	240	271	301	332	362
29	29	—	88	119	149	180	210	241	272	302	333	363
30	30	—	89	120	150	181	211	242	273	303	334	364
31	31	—	90	—	151	—	212	243	—	304	—	365

Second Year

Date	Jan.	Feb.	Mar.	April	May	June	July	Aug.	Sept.	Oct.	Nov.	Dec.
1	366	397	425	456	486	517	547	578	609	639	670	700
2	367	398	426	457	487	518	548	579	610	640	671	701
3	368	399	427	458	488	519	549	580	611	641	672	702
4	369	400	428	459	489	520	550	581	612	642	673	703
5	370	401	429	460	490	521	551	582	613	643	674	704
6	371	402	430	461	491	522	552	583	614	644	675	705
7	372	403	431	462	492	523	553	584	615	645	676	706
8	373	404	432	463	493	524	554	585	616	646	677	707
9	374	405	433	464	494	525	555	586	617	647	678	708
10	375	406	434	465	495	526	556	587	618	648	679	709
11	376	407	435	466	496	527	557	588	619	649	680	710
12	377	408	436	467	497	528	558	589	620	650	681	711
13	378	409	437	468	498	529	559	590	621	651	682	712
14	379	410	438	469	499	530	560	591	622	652	683	713
15	380	411	439	470	500	531	561	592	623	653	684	714
16	381	412	440	471	501	532	562	593	624	654	685	715
17	382	413	441	472	502	533	563	594	625	655	686	716
18	383	414	442	473	503	534	564	595	626	656	687	717
19	384	415	443	474	504	535	565	596	627	657	688	718
20	385	416	444	475	505	536	566	597	628	658	689	719
21	386	417	445	476	506	537	567	598	629	659	690	720
22	387	418	446	477	507	538	568	599	630	660	691	721
23	388	419	447	478	508	539	569	600	631	661	692	722
24	389	420	448	479	509	540	570	601	632	662	693	723
25	390	421	449	480	510	541	571	602	633	663	694	724
26	391	422	450	481	511	542	572	603	634	664	695	725
27	392	423	451	482	512	543	573	604	635	665	696	726
28	393	424	452	483	513	544	574	605	636	666	697	727
29	394	—	453	484	514	545	575	606	637	667	698	728
30	395	—	454	485	515	546	576	607	638	668	699	729
31	396	—	455	—	516	—	577	608	—	669	—	730

Signs of the Zodiac

The **zodiac** is the apparent yearly path of the sun among the stars as viewed from earth, and was divided by the ancients into 12 equal sections or signs, each named for the constellation situated within its limits in ancient times. Astrologers claim that the temperament and destiny of each individual depend on the zodiac sign under which the person was born and the relationships between the planets at that time and throughout life.

Below are the 12 traditional signs and the traditional range of dates pertaining to each:

♈ **Aries** (Ram), March 2–April 19

♉ **Taurus** (Bull), April 20–May 20

♊ **Gemini** (Twins), May 21–June 21

♋ **Cancer** (Crab), June 22–July 22

♌ **Leo** (Lion), July 23–August 22

♍ **Virgo** (Virgin), August 23–September 22

♎ **Libra** (Scales), September 23–October 23

♏ **Scorpio** (Scorpion), October 24–November 21

♐ **Sagittarius** (Archer), November 22–December 21

♑ **Capricorn** (Goat), December 22–January 19

♒ **Aquarius** (Water Bearer), January 20–February 18

♓ **Pisces** (Fishes), February 19–March 20

Calendar for the Year 2010

JANUARY						
S	M	T	W	T	F	S
					1	2
3	4	5	6	7	8	9
10	11	12	13	14	15	16
17	18	19	20	21	22	23
24	25	26	27	28	29	30
31						

FEBRUARY						
S	M	T	W	T	F	S
	1	2	3	4	5	6
7	8	9	10	11	12	13
14	15	16	17	18	19	20
21	22	23	24	25	26	27
28						

MARCH						
S	M	T	W	T	F	S
	1	2	3	4	5	6
7	8	9	10	11	12	13
14	15	16	17	18	19	20
21	22	23	24	25	26	27
28	29	30	31			

APRIL						
S	M	T	W	T	F	S
				1	2	3
4	5	6	7	8	9	10
11	12	13	14	15	16	17
18	19	20	21	22	23	24
25	26	27	28	29	30	

MAY						
S	M	T	W	T	F	S
						1
2	3	4	5	6	7	8
9	10	11	12	13	14	15
16	17	18	19	20	21	22
23	24	25	26	27	28	29
30	31					

JUNE						
S	M	T	W	T	F	S
		1	2	3	4	5
6	7	8	9	10	11	12
13	14	15	16	17	18	19
20	21	22	23	24	25	26
27	28	29	30			

JULY						
S	M	T	W	T	F	S
				1	2	3
4	5	6	7	8	9	10
11	12	13	14	15	16	17
18	19	20	21	22	23	24
25	26	27	28	29	30	31

AUGUST						
S	M	T	W	T	F	S
1	2	3	4	5	6	7
8	9	10	11	12	13	14
15	16	17	18	19	20	21
22	23	24	25	26	27	28
29	30	31				

SEPTEMBER						
S	M	T	W	T	F	S
			1	2	3	4
5	6	7	8	9	10	11
12	13	14	15	16	17	18
19	20	21	22	23	24	25
26	27	28	29	30		

OCTOBER						
S	M	T	W	T	F	S
					1	2
3	4	5	6	7	8	9
10	11	12	13	14	15	16
17	18	19	20	21	22	23
24	25	26	27	28	29	30
31						

NOVEMBER						
S	M	T	W	T	F	S
	1	2	3	4	5	6
7	8	9	10	11	12	13
14	15	16	17	18	19	20
21	22	23	24	25	26	27
28	29	30				

DECEMBER						
S	M	T	W	T	F	S
			1	2	3	4
5	6	7	8	9	10	11
12	13	14	15	16	17	18
19	20	21	22	23	24	25
26	27	28	29	30	31	

Federal Holidays and Other Notable Dates, 2010

Some dates may be subject to change.

The days marked on the calendar above and shown below *in italics* are U.S. federal holidays, designated by the president or Congress and applicable to federal employees and the District of Columbia. Most U.S. states also observe these holidays, and many states observe others; practices vary from state to state. In most states the secretary of state's office can provide details.

January
1 *New Year's Day*; Rose Bowl; Sugar Bowl
4 Fiesta Bowl
5 Orange Bowl
7 BCS Football Championship Game (Pasadena, CA)
18 *Martin Luther King Jr. Day* (3rd Mon. in Jan.)
18-31 Australian Open tennis tournament
26 Australia Day, Australia
31 NFL Pro Bowl (Miami, FL)

February
2 Groundhog Day
7 Super Bowl XLIV (Miami, FL)
12 Lincoln's Birthday
13-16 Carnival, Brazil
14 Valentine's Day
 Daytona 500
 NBA All-Star Game (Arlington, TX)
15 *Washington's Birthday* (observed), Presidents' Day, or *Washington-Lincoln Day* (3rd Mon. in Feb.)
15-16 Westminster Dog Show
16 Mardi Gras
17 Ash Wednesday
28 Purim (Feast of Lots), starts previous night

March
6 Iditarod Trail Sled Dog Race begins
7 Academy Awards
14 Daylight Saving Time begins in U.S.
17 St. Patrick's Day
20 First day of spring (Northern Hemisphere)
21 Benito Juárez's Birthday, Mexico
30 First full day of Passover

April
1 April Fool's Day
2 Good Friday
3-5 NCAA men's basketball Final Four
4 Easter
4-6 NCAA women's basketball Final Four
5-11 Masters golf tournament
19 Patriots' Day
 Boston Marathon (Third Mon. in Apr.)
22 Earth Day
 Take Our Daughters and Sons to Work Day
30 Arbor Day, U.S.

May
1 May Day
 Kentucky Derby
4 National Teacher Day, U.S.
5 Cinco de Mayo (Battle of Puebla Day), Mexico
9 Mother's Day
15 Armed Forces Day
 Preakness Stakes
21 Buddha's Birthday, Korea, Hong Kong
24 Victoria Day, Canada
24-June 6 French Open tennis tournament
31 *Memorial Day*, or *Decoration Day* (last Mon. in May)

June
5 Belmont Stakes
14 Flag Day
16 Dragon Boat Festival, China
17-20 U.S. Open golf tournament (Pebble Beach, CA)
20 Father's Day
21 First day of summer (Northern Hemisphere)
21-July 4 Wimbledon tennis tournament

July
1 Canada Day
4 *Independence Day*
7-14 Running of the Bulls (Pamplona, Spain)
14 Bastille Day, France
15-18 British Open golf tournament

August
9-15 PGA Championship
11 Ramadan (Islamic month of fasting), 1st full day

September
6 *Labor Day*, U.S. (1st Monday in Sept.); *Labor Day*, Canada
9 Rosh Hashanah (New Year), 1st full day
12 Grandparents' Day, U.S.
16 Independence Day, Mexico
17 Constitution Day and Citizenship Day, U.S.
18 Yom Kippur (Day of Atonement), starts previous night
22 First day of autumn (Northern Hemisphere)

October
3 German Unity Day, Germany
4 U.S. Supreme Court session begins
11 *Columbus Day* (2nd Mon. in Oct.)
 Thanksgiving Day, Canada
12 Día de la Raza, Spain, Mexico
24 United Nations Day
31 Halloween

November
1 All Saints' Day
1-2 Día de los Muertos, Mexico
2 Election Day (1st Tues. after 1st Mon. in Nov.)
5 Guy Fawkes Day, UK
7 New York City Marathon
 Daylight Saving Time ends in U.S.
11 *Veterans Day*; Remembrance Day, Canada
14 Remembrance Sunday, UK
25 *Thanksgiving Day* (4th Thurs. in Nov.)

December
2-9 Hanukkah (Festival of Lights), starts previous night
7 Islamic New Year (Muharram 1), starts previous night
10 Nobel Prizes awarded (winners announced in Oct.)
12 Día de la Virgen de Guadalupe, Mexico
21 First day of winter (Northern Hemisphere)
25 *Christmas Day*
26 Boxing Day, Australia, Canada, New Zealand, UK
26-Jan. 1 Kwanzaa

Chinese Calendar, Asian Festivals

Source: Chinese Information and Culture Center, New York, NY

The Chinese calendar, like the Jewish and Islamic calendars (see the Religion chapter), is a lunar calendar. It is divided into 12 months of 29 or 30 days (compensating for the lunar month's mean duration of 29 days, 12 hr, 44.05 min). This calendar is synchronized with the solar year by the addition of extra months at fixed intervals.

The Chinese calendar runs on a 60-year cycle. The cycles 1876-1935 and 1936-95, with the years grouped under their 12 animal designations, are printed below, along with the first 24 years of the current cycle. This cycle began in 1996 and will last until 2055. Feb. 14, 2010, marks the beginning of the year 4708 in the Chinese calendar, and is designated the Year of the Tiger. Readers can find the animal name for the year of their birth in the chart below. (Note: The first 3-7 weeks of each Western year belong to the previous Chinese year and animal designation.)

Both the Western (Gregorian) and traditional lunar calendars are used publicly in China and in North and South Korea, and 2 New Year's celebrations are held. In Taiwan, in overseas Chinese communities, and in Vietnam, the lunar calendar is used only to set the dates for traditional festivals, with the Gregorian system in general use.

The 4-day Chinese New Year, Hsin Nien, the 3-day Vietnamese New Year festival, Tet, and the 3-to-4-day Korean festival, Suhl, begin at the 2nd new moon after the winter solstice. The new moon in the Far East, which is west of the International Date Line, may be a day later than the new moon in the U.S. The festivals may start, therefore, anywhere between Jan. 21 and Feb. 19 of the Gregorian calendar.

Rat	Ox	Tiger	Hare (Rabbit)	Dragon	Snake	Horse	Sheep (Goat)	Monkey	Rooster	Dog	Pig (Boar)
1876	1877	1878	1879	1880	1881	1882	1883	1884	1885	1886	1887
1888	1889	1890	1891	1892	1893	1894	1895	1896	1897	1898	1899
1900	1901	1902	1903	1904	1905	1906	1907	1908	1909	1910	1911
1912	1913	1914	1915	1916	1917	1918	1919	1920	1921	1922	1923
1924	1925	1926	1927	1928	1929	1930	1931	1932	1933	1934	1935
1936	1937	1938	1939	1940	1941	1942	1943	1944	1945	1946	1947
1948	1949	1950	1951	1952	1953	1954	1955	1956	1957	1958	1959
1960	1961	1962	1963	1964	1965	1966	1967	1968	1969	1970	1971
1972	1973	1974	1975	1976	1977	1978	1979	1980	1981	1982	1983
1984	1985	1986	1987	1988	1989	1990	1991	1992	1993	1994	1995
1996	1997	1998	1999	2000	2001	2002	2003	2004	2005	2006	2007
2008	2009	2010	2011	2012	2013	2014	2015	2016	2017	2018	2019

Other Calendars: Year and New Year's in 2010

Era	Year	Begins in 2010	Era	Year	Begins in 2010
Byzantine	7519	Sept. 14	Grecian (Seleucidae)	2322	Sept. 14 or Oct. 14
Jewish	5771	Sept. 9[1]	Diocletian	1727	Sept. 11
Roman (Ab Urbe Condita)	2763	Jan. 14	Indian (Saka)	1932	Mar. 22
Nabonassar (Babylonian)	2759	Apr. 23	Islamic/Muslim (Hijra)	1431	Dec. 18 (2009)[2]
Japanese (starts at 0 with new emperor)	22	Jan. 1	Chinese (Year of the Tiger)	4708	Feb. 14

(1) Year begins at sunset of the previous day. (2) Year begins previous evening at moon crescent.

Chronological Cycles, 2010

Dominical Letter	C	Roman Indiction	3	Solar Cycle	3
Golden Number (Lunar Cycle)	16	Epact	14	Julian Period (year of)	6723

Special Months

There are many thousands of special months, days, and weeks because of anniversaries, official proclamations, and promotional events, both trivial and serious. Here are a few of the special months:

January: Jump Out of Bed Month, National Mentoring Month, National Poverty in America Awareness Month

February: Black History Month, American Heart Month, Library Lovers Month, Youth Leadership Month, Return Shopping Carts to the Supermarket Month

March: Irish-American Heritage Month, Women's History Month, American Red Cross Month, National Frozen Foods Month, National Talk With Your Teen About Sex Month

April: National Child Abuse Prevention Month, National Humor Month, Stress Awareness Month, Grange Month

May: Clean Air Month, Get Caught Reading Month, National Barbecue Month, Asian Pacific American Heritage Month, National Mental Health Month

June: National Candy Month, Gay and Lesbian Pride Month, Potty Training Awareness Month, National Safety Month

July: Cell Phone Courtesy Month, National Hot Dog Month, Women's Motorcycle Month

August: Black Business Month, National Inventors' Month, Happiness Happens Month, National Toddler Month

September: Library Card Sign-Up Month, National Hispanic Heritage Month (Sept. 15-Oct. 15), National Biscuit Month

October: National Domestic Violence Awareness Month, National Breast Cancer Awareness Month, Diversity Awareness Month, National Popcorn Poppin' Month

November: National AIDS Awareness Month, National American Indian Heritage Month, National Adoption Month, American Diabetes Month, Peanut Butter Lovers' Month

December: Universal Human Rights Month, National Drunk and Drugged Driving Prevention Month, National Tie Month, Colorectal Cancer Education and Awareness Month

Wedding Anniversaries

The traditional names for wedding anniversaries go back many years in social usage and have been used to suggest types of appropriate anniversary gifts. Traditional products for gifts are listed here in CAPITAL LETTERS, with a few allowable revisions in parentheses, followed by common modern gifts in each category.

1st	PAPER, clocks	**9th**	POTTERY (CHINA), leather goods	**25th**	SILVER, sterling silver
2nd	COTTON, china	**10th**	TIN, ALUMINUM, diamond	**30th**	PEARL, diamond
3rd	LEATHER, crystal, glass	**11th**	STEEL, fashion jewelry	**35th**	CORAL (JADE), jade
4th	LINEN (SILK), appliances	**12th**	SILK, pearls, colored gems	**40th**	RUBY, ruby
5th	WOOD, silverware	**13th**	LACE, textiles, furs	**45th**	SAPPHIRE, sapphire
6th	IRON, wood objects	**14th**	IVORY, gold jewelry	**50th**	GOLD, gold
7th	WOOL (COPPER), desk sets	**15th**	CRYSTAL, watches	**55th**	EMERALD, emerald
8th	BRONZE, linens, lace	**20th**	CHINA, platinum	**60th**	DIAMOND, diamond

Birthstones

Source: Jewelry Industry Council

MONTH	Ancient	Modern	MONTH	Ancient	Modern
January	Garnet	Garnet	July	Onyx	Ruby
February	Amethyst	Amethyst	August	Carnelian	Sardonyx or Peridot
March	Jasper	Bloodstone or Aquamarine	September	Chrysolite	Sapphire
April	Sapphire	Diamond	October	Aquamarine	Opal or Tourmaline
May	Agate	Emerald	November	Topaz	Topaz
June	Emerald	Pearl, Moonstone, or Alexandrite	December	Ruby	Turquoise or Zircon

Standard Time, Daylight Saving Time, and Others

Source: National Geospatial-Intelligence Agency, Dept. of Defense

See also Time Zone map, page 460.

Standard Time

Standard Time is reckoned from the Prime Meridian of Longitude in Greenwich, England. The world is divided into 24 zones, each 15 deg of arc, or one hour in time apart. The Greenwich meridian (0 deg) extends through the center of the initial zone, and the zones to the east are numbered from 1 to 12, with the prefix "minus" indicating the number of hours to be subtracted to obtain Greenwich Time. Each zone extends 7.5 deg on either side of its central meridian.

Westward zones are similarly numbered, but prefixed "plus," showing the number of hours that must be added to get Greenwich Time. Although these zones apply generally to sea areas, the Standard Time maintained in many countries does not coincide with zone time.

The U.S. and possessions are divided into 10 Standard Time zones. Each zone is approximately 15 deg of longitude in width. All places in each zone use, instead of their own local time, the time counted from the transit of the "mean sun" across the Standard Time meridian that passes near the middle of that zone. These time zones are designated as Atlantic, Eastern, Central, Mountain, Pacific, Alaska, Hawaii-Aleutian, Samoa, Wake Island, and Guam; the time in these zones is reckoned from the 60th, 75th, 90th, 105th, 120th, 135th, 150th, and 165th meridians west of Greenwich and the 165th and 150th meridians east of Greenwich. The time zone line wanders to conform to local geographical regions. The time in the various zones in the U.S. and U.S. territories west of Greenwich is earlier than Greenwich Time by 4, 5, 6, 7, 8, 9, 10, and 11 hours, respectively. However, Wake Island and Guam cross the International Date Line and are 12 and 10 hours later than Greenwich Time, respectively.

24-Hour Time

Twenty-four-hour time is widely used in scientific work throughout the world. In the U.S. it is also used in operations of the armed forces. In Europe it is frequently used by the transportation networks in preference to the 12-hour AM and PM system. With the 24-hour system the day begins at midnight, and times are designated 00:00 through 23:59.

International Date Line

The Date Line, approximately coinciding with the 180th meridian, separates the calendar dates. The date must be advanced one day when crossing in a westerly direction and set back one day when crossing in an easterly direction. The Date Line frequently deviates from the 180th meridian because of decisions made by individual nations affected. The line is deflected eastward through the Bering Strait and westward of the Aleutians to prevent separating these areas by date. The line is deflected eastward of the Tonga and New Zealand Islands in the South Pacific for the same reason. In 1995, Kiribati announced that all of its islands east of the Date Line would observe the same date as islands to the west, though most maps and atlases do not depict this as a deviation in the Date Line. The line is established by international custom; there is no international authority prescribing its exact course.

Daylight Saving Time

Daylight Saving Time is achieved by advancing the clock one hour. As of 2007, Daylight Saving Time begins at 2 AM on the 2nd Sunday in Mar. and ends at 2 AM on the first Sunday in Nov. **In 2010, Daylight Saving Time begins at 2 AM on Mar. 14 and ends at 2 AM on Nov. 7.** Prior to 2007, Daylight Saving Time traditionally ran from the first Sunday in Apr. to the last Sunday in Oct.

Daylight Saving Time was first observed in the U.S. during World War I, and then again during World War II. In the intervening years, some states and communities observed Daylight Saving Time, using whatever beginning and ending dates they chose. In 1966, Congress passed the Uniform Time Act, which provided that any state or territory that chooses to observe Daylight Saving Time must begin and end on the federal dates. Any state could, by law, exempt itself; a 1972 amendment to the act authorized states split by time zones to observe Daylight Saving Time in one time zone and standard time in the other time zone. Currently, Arizona, Hawaii, Puerto Rico, the U.S. Virgin Islands, Guam, and American Samoa do not observe Daylight Saving Time. On Apr. 2, 2006, all of Indiana observed Daylight Saving Time for the first time. The state remains divided between two time zones.

Congress and the secretary of transportation both have authority to change time zone boundaries. Since 1966 there have been a number of changes to U.S. time zone boundaries. In addition, efforts to conserve energy have prompted various changes in the times that Daylight Saving Time is observed.

Daylight Saving Time: International Usage

Adjusting clock time so as to gain the added daylight on summer evenings is common throughout the world.

Canada, which extends over 6 time zones, generally observes Daylight Saving Time during the same period as the U.S. Most provincial governments—with the exceptions of Newfoundland, Nunavut, and Yukon—pledged to observe the 4 week extension to Daylight Saving Time that went into effect in 2007. Most of Saskatchewan remains on standard time all year. Communities elsewhere in Canada also may exempt themselves from Daylight Saving Time. Except for the state of Sonora, which shares a border with Arizona, most of Mexico observes Daylight Saving Time.

Member nations of the European Union (EU) observe a "summer-time period," a version of Daylight Saving Time, from the last Sunday of Mar. until the last Sunday in Oct.

Russia, which extends over 11 time zones, maintains its Standard Time 1 hour fast for its zone designation. Additionally, it proclaims Daylight Saving Time from the last Sunday in Mar. until the 4th Sunday in Oct.

China, which extends across 5 time zones, has decreed that the entire country be placed on Greenwich Time plus 8 hours. Daylight Saving Time is not observed. Japan, which lies within one time zone, also does not modify its legal time during the summer months.

Many countries in the Southern Hemisphere maintain Daylight Saving Time, generally from Oct. to Mar.; however, most countries near the equator do not deviate from Standard Time.

Perpetual Calendar

The number shown for each year indicates which Gregorian calendar to use. For 1583-1802, see "Gregorian Calendar" on page 349. For 1803-20, use numbers for 1983-2000, respectively. For Julian Calendar, see "Julian Calendar" on page 350.

The main table consists of six numbered perpetual-calendar panels and a set of year-index columns.

Calendar panels (numbered, with representative years):

No.	Year(s)	Months shown
1	2006	January, February, March, April, May, June, July, August, September, October, November, December
2	2007	January–December
3	2013	January–December
4	2014	January–December
5	2009/2015	January–December
6	2010	January–December

Each panel lists the weekdays S M T W T F S across the top of every month.

Year-index columns (year ... calendar number):

1821 ... 2	1925 ... 5	2029 ... 2	2055 ... 6
1822 ... 3	1926 ... 6	2030 ... 3	2056 ... 14
1823 ... 4	1927 ... 7	2031 ... 5	2057 ... 3
1824 ... 12	1928 ... 8	2032 ... 13	2058 ... 4
1825 ... 7	1929 ... 3	2033 ... 7	2059 ... 5
1826 ... 1	1930 ... 4	2034 ... 1	2060 ... 13
1827 ... 2	1931 ... 5	2035 ... 2	2061 ... 7
1828 ... 10	1932 ... 13	2036 ... 10	2062 ... 1
1829 ... 5	1933 ... 1	2037 ... 5	2063 ... 2
1830 ... 6	1934 ... 2	2038 ... 6	2064 ... 10
1831 ... 7	1935 ... 3	2039 ... 7	2065 ... 5
1832 ... 8	1936 ... 11	2040 ... 8	2066 ... 6
1833 ... 3	1937 ... 6	2041 ... 3	2067 ... 7
1834 ... 4	1938 ... 7	2042 ... 4	2068 ... 8
1835 ... 5	1939 ... 1	2043 ... 5	2069 ... 3
1836 ... 13	1940 ... 9	2044 ... 13	2070 ... 4
1837 ... 1	1941 ... 4	2045 ... 1	2071 ... 5
1838 ... 2	1942 ... 5	2046 ... 2	2072 ... 13
1839 ... 3	1943 ... 6	2047 ... 3	2073 ... 1
1840 ... 11	1944 ... 14	2048 ... 11	2074 ... 2
1841 ... 6	1945 ... 2	2049 ... 6	2075 ... 3
1842 ... 7	1946 ... 3	2050 ... 7	2076 ... 11
1843 ... 1	1947 ... 4	2051 ... 1	2077 ... 6
1844 ... 9	1948 ... 12	2052 ... 9	2078 ... 7
1845 ... 4	1949 ... 7	2053 ... 4	2079 ... 1
1846 ... 5	1950 ... 1	2054 ... 5	2080 ... 9

1847 ... 6	1951 ... 2	1977 ... 7
1848 ... 14	1952 ... 10	1978 ... 1
1849 ... 2	1953 ... 5	1979 ... 2
1850 ... 3	1954 ... 6	1980 ... 10
1851 ... 4	1955 ... 7	1981 ... 5
1852 ... 12	1956 ... 8	1982 ... 6
1853 ... 7	1957 ... 3	1983 ... 7
1854 ... 1	1958 ... 4	1984 ... 8
1855 ... 2	1959 ... 5	1985 ... 3
1856 ... 10	1960 ... 13	1986 ... 4
1857 ... 5	1961 ... 1	1987 ... 5
1858 ... 6	1962 ... 2	1988 ... 13
1859 ... 7	1963 ... 3	1989 ... 1
1860 ... 8	1964 ... 11	1990 ... 2
1861 ... 3	1965 ... 6	1991 ... 3
1862 ... 4	1966 ... 7	1992 ... 11
1863 ... 5	1967 ... 1	1993 ... 6
1864 ... 13	1968 ... 9	1994 ... 7
1865 ... 1	1969 ... 4	1995 ... 1
1866 ... 2	1970 ... 5	1996 ... 9
1867 ... 3	1971 ... 6	1997 ... 4
1868 ... 11	1972 ... 14	1998 ... 5
1869 ... 6	1973 ... 2	1999 ... 6
1870 ... 7	1974 ... 3	2000 ... 14
1871 ... 1	1975 ... 4	2001 ... 2
1872 ... 9	1976 ... 12	2002 ... 3

1873 ... 6	1899 ... 1
1874 ... 14	1900 ... 2
1875 ... 2	1901 ... 3
1876 ... 10	1902 ... 4
1877 ... 7	1903 ... 5
1878 ... 1	1904 ... 13
1879 ... 2	1905 ... 1
1880 ... 10	1906 ... 2
1881 ... 5	1907 ... 3
1882 ... 6	1908 ... 11
1883 ... 7	1909 ... 6
1884 ... 8	1910 ... 7
1885 ... 3	1911 ... 1
1886 ... 4	1912 ... 9
1887 ... 5	1913 ... 4
1888 ... 13	1914 ... 5
1889 ... 1	1915 ... 6
1890 ... 2	1916 ... 14
1891 ... 3	1917 ... 2
1892 ... 11	1918 ... 3
1893 ... 6	1919 ... 4
1894 ... 7	1920 ... 12
1895 ... 1	1921 ... 7
1896 ... 9	1922 ... 1
1897 ... 4	1923 ... 2
1898 ... 5	1924 ... 10

Perpetual Calendar — Dominical Letter / Year Reference Grid

The page consists of twelve calendar blocks arranged in a grid. Each block is identified by a large index number (left margin) and a sample year (top-right), with the twelve months (January–December) laid out in S M T W T F S columns.

Index	Year
7	2011
8	2012
9	—
10	2008
11	—
12	—
13	—
14	2000

Months shown in each block: JANUARY, FEBRUARY, MARCH, APRIL, MAY, JUNE, JULY, AUGUST, SEPTEMBER, OCTOBER, NOVEMBER, DECEMBER

Standard Time Differences—World Cities

The time indicated in the table is fixed by law and is called the legal time or, more generally, Standard Time. Use of Daylight Saving Time varies widely. *Indicates morning of the following day. At 12:00 noon, Eastern Standard Time, the Standard Time (in 24-hour time) in selected cities is as follows:

Addis Ababa	20	00	Helsinki	19	00	Paris	18	00
Amsterdam	18	00	Ho Chi Minh City	0	00*	Prague	18	00
Ankara	19	00	Hong Kong	1	00*	Quito	12	00
Athens	19	00	Islamabad	22	00	Rio de Janeiro	14	00
Auckland	5	00*	Istanbul	19	00	Riyadh	20	00
Baghdad	20	00	Jakarta	0	00*	Rome	18	00
Bangkok	0	00*	Jerusalem	19	00	St. Petersburg	20	00
Beijing	1	00*	Johannesburg	19	00	Santiago	13	00
Belfast	17	00	Kabul	21	50	Sarajevo	18	00
Belgrade	18	00	Karachi	22	00	Seoul	2	00*
Berlin	18	00	Kathmandu	22	45	Shanghai	1	00*
Bogotá	12	00	Kiev	19	00	Singapore	1	00*
Bombay (Mumbai)	22	30	Lagos	18	00	Stockholm	18	00
Brussels	18	00	Lima	12	00	Sydney	3	00*
Bucharest	19	00	Lisbon	17	00	Taipei	1	00*
Budapest	18	00	London	17	00	Tashkent	22	00
Buenos Aires	14	00	Madrid	18	00	Tehran	20	30
Cairo	19	00	Manila	1	00*	Tel Aviv	19	00
Calcutta (Kolkata)	22	30	Mecca	20	00	Tokyo	2	00*
Cape Town	19	00	Melbourne	3	00*	Vladivostok	3	00*
Caracas	13	00	Montevideo	14	00	Vienna	18	00
Casablanca	17	00	Moscow	20	00	Warsaw	18	00
Copenhagen	18	00	Munich	18	00	Wellington	5	00*
Dhaka	23	00	Nagasaki	2	00*	Yangon (Rangoon)	23	30
Dublin	17	00	Nairobi	20	00	Yokohama	2	00*
Edinburgh	17	00	New Delhi	22	30	Zurich	18	00
Geneva	18	00	Oslo	18	00			

Standard Time Differences—North American Cities

At 12:00 noon, Eastern Standard Time, the Standard Time in selected North American cities is as follows:

Akron, OH	12	00	Noon	Fort Wayne, IN[1]	12	00	Noon	Ottawa, ON	12	00	Noon
Albuquerque, NM	10	00	AM	Frankfort, KY	12	00	Noon	*Panama City, Panama	12	00	Noon
Anchorage, AK	8	00	AM	Havana, Cuba	12	00	Noon	Peoria, IL	11	00	AM
Atlanta, GA	12	00	Noon	Helena, MT	10	00	AM	*Phoenix, AZ	10	00	AM
Austin, TX	11	00	AM	*Honolulu, HI	7	00	AM	Pierre, SD	11	00	AM
Baltimore, MD	12	00	Noon	Houston, TX	11	00	AM	Pittsburgh, PA	12	00	Noon
Birmingham, AL	11	00	AM	Indianapolis, IN[1]	12	00	Noon	*Regina, SK	11	00	AM
Bismarck, ND	11	00	AM	Jackson, MS	11	00	am	Reno, NV	9	00	AM
Boise, ID	10	00	AM	Jacksonville, FL	12	00	Noon	Richmond, VA	12	00	Noon
Boston, MA	12	00	Noon	Juneau, AK	8	00	AM	Rochester, NY	12	00	Noon
Buffalo, NY	12	00	Noon	Kansas City, MO	11	00	AM	Sacramento, CA	9	00	AM
Butte, MT	10	00	AM	*Kingston, Jamaica	12	00	Noon	St. John's, NL	1	30	PM
Calgary, AB	10	00	AM	Knoxville, TN	12	00	Noon	St. Louis, MO	11	00	AM
Charleston, SC	12	00	Noon	Las Vegas, NV	9	00	AM	St. Paul, MN	11	00	AM
Charleston, WV	12	00	Noon	Lexington, KY	12	00	Noon	Salt Lake City, UT	10	00	AM
Charlotte, NC	12	00	Noon	Lincoln, NE	11	00	AM	San Antonio, TX	11	00	AM
Charlottetown, PE	1	00	PM	Little Rock, AR	11	00	AM	San Diego, CA	9	00	AM
Chattanooga, TN	12	00	Noon	Los Angeles, CA	9	00	AM	San Francisco, CA	9	00	AM
Cheyenne, WY	10	00	AM	Louisville, KY	12	00	Noon	San Jose, CA	9	00	AM
Chicago, IL	11	00	AM	Madison, WI	11	00	am	*San Juan, PR	1	00	PM
Cincinnati, OH	12	00	Noon	Mexico City, Mexico	11	00	AM	Santa Fe, NM	10	00	AM
Cleveland, OH	12	00	Noon	Memphis, TN	11	00	AM	Savannah, GA	12	00	Noon
Colorado Spr., CO	10	00	AM	Miami, FL	12	00	Noon	Seattle, WA	9	00	AM
Columbus, OH	12	00	Noon	Milwaukee, WI	11	00	AM	Shreveport, LA	11	00	AM
Dallas, TX	11	00	AM	Minneapolis, MN	11	00	AM	Sioux Falls, SD	11	00	AM
*Dawson, YT	9	00	AM	Mobile, AL	11	00	AM	Spokane, WA	9	00	AM
Dayton, OH	12	00	Noon	Montreal, QC	12	00	Noon	Tampa, FL	12	00	Noon
Denver, CO	10	00	AM	Nashville, TN	11	00	AM	Toledo, OH	12	00	Noon
Des Moines, IA	11	00	AM	Nassau, Bahamas	12	00	Noon	Topeka, KS	11	00	AM
Detroit, MI	12	00	Noon	New Haven, CT	12	00	Noon	Toronto, ON	12	00	Noon
Duluth, MN	11	00	AM	New Orleans, LA	11	00	AM	*Tucson, AZ	10	00	AM
Edmonton, AB	10	00	AM	New York, NY	12	00	Noon	Tulsa, OK	11	00	AM
El Paso, TX	10	00	AM	Nome, AK	8	00	AM	Vancouver, BC	9	00	AM
Erie, PA	12	00	Noon	Norfolk, VA	12	00	Noon	Washington, DC	12	00	Noon
Evansville, IN[1]	11	00	AM	Oklahoma City, OK	11	00	AM	Wichita, KS	11	00	AM
Fairbanks, AK	8	00	AM	Omaha, NE	11	00	AM	Wilmington, DE	12	00	Noon
Flint, MI	12	00	Noon	Orlando, FL	12	00	Noon	Winnipeg, MB	11	00	AM

(1) While most of Indiana is in the Eastern Time Zone, 18 counties in the southwestern and northwestern parts of the state observe Central Time. **Note:** This same table can be used for Daylight Saving Time when it is in effect, but allowance must be made for cities that do not observe it; they are marked with an asterisk (*). Daylight Saving Time is one hour later than Standard Time.

WEIGHTS AND MEASURES

Source: National Institute of Standards and Technology, U.S. Dept. of Commerce

The International System of Units (SI)

Two systems of weights and measures coexist in the U.S. today: the **U.S. Customary System** and the **International System of Units** (SI, after the initials of Système International). SI, commonly identified with the **metric system**, is actually a more complete, coherent version of it. Throughout U.S. history, the Customary System (inherited from, but now different from, the British Imperial System) has been generally used; federal and state legislation has given it, through implication, standing as the primary weights and measures system. The metric system, however, is the only system that Congress has ever specifically sanctioned. An 1866 law reads:

"It shall be lawful throughout the United States of America to employ the weights and measures of the metric system; and no contract or dealing, or pleading in any court, shall be deemed invalid or liable to objection because the weights or measures expressed or referred to therein are weights or measures of the metric system."

Since that time, use of the metric system in the U.S. has slowly and steadily increased, particularly in the scientific community, the pharmaceutical industry, and the manufacturing sector—the last motivated by the practice in international commerce, in which the metric system is now predominantly used.

On Feb. 10, 1964, the National Bureau of Standards (now known as the National Institute of Standards and Technology) issued the following statement:

"Henceforth it shall be the policy of the National Bureau of Standards to use the units of the International System (SI), as adopted by the 11th General Conference on Weights and Measures (October 1960), except when the use of these units would obviously impair communication or reduce the usefulness of a report."

On Dec. 23, 1975, Pres. Gerald R. Ford signed the Metric Conversion Act of 1975. It defines the metric system as being the International System of Units as interpreted in the U.S. by the secretary of commerce. The Trade Act of 1988 and other legislation declare the metric system the preferred system of weights and measures for U.S. trade and commerce, call for the federal government to adopt metric specifications, and mandate the Commerce Dept. to oversee the program. However, the metric system has still not become the system of choice for most Americans' daily use.

The following 7 units serve as the base units for the system: **length**—meter; **mass**—kilogram; **time**—second; **electric current**—ampere; **thermodynamic temperature**—kelvin; **amount of substance**—mole; and **luminous intensity**—candela.

Frequently Used Conversions

Boldface indicates exact values. For greater accuracy, use the "multiply by" number in parentheses. For weights, *avdp* is an abbreviation for avoirdupois weight, the system of weights applied to all goods except medicines, precious metals, and precious stones (see p. 360). For more detailed tables, see pp. 359-362.

U.S. Customary to Metric

	If you have:	Multiply by:		To get:
Length	inches	**25.4**		millimeters
	inches	**2.54**		centimeters
	inches	**0.0254**		meters
	feet	0.3	(**0.3048**)	meters
	yards	0.9	(**0.9144**)	meters
	miles[1]	1.6	(**1.609344**)	kilometers
Area	sq. inches	6.5	(**6.4516**)	sq. cm.
	sq. feet	0.09	(0.09290341)	sq. meters
	sq. yards	0.84	(0.83612736)	sq. meters
	acres	0.4	(0.4046873)	hectares
	sq. miles	2.6	(2.58998811)	sq. kilometers
Weight	ounces (avdp)	28	(**28.349523125**)	grams
	pounds (avdp)	454	(**453.59237**)	grams
	pounds (avdp)	0.45	(**0.45359237**)	kilograms
	short tons[2]	0.91	(**0.90718474**)	metric tons
	long tons[3]	1	(**1.0160469088**)	metric tons
Liquid meas.	ounces	0.03	(0.02957353)	liters
	cups	0.24	(0.23658824)	liters
	pints	0.47	(0.473176473)	liters
	quarts	0.95	(0.946352946)	liters
	gallons	3.79	(3.785411784)	liters

Metric to U.S. Customary

	If you have:	Multiply by:		To get:
Length	millimeters	0.04	(0.03937)	inches
	centimeters	0.4	(0.3937)	inches
	meters	39	(39.37)	inches
	meters	3.3	(3.280840)	feet
	meters	1.1	(1.093613)	yards
	kilometers	0.6	(0.621371)	miles
Area	sq. cm.	0.16	(0.15500)	sq. inches
	sq. meters	10.8	(0.3937)	sq. feet
	sq. meters	1.2	(39.37)	sq. yards
	hectares	2.5	(3.280840)	acres
	sq. kilometers	0.39	(1.093613)	sq. miles
Weight	grams	0.035	(0.03527396)	ounces (avdp)
	grams	0.002	(0.00220462)	pounds (avdp)
	kilograms	2.2	(0.3937)	pounds (avdp)
	metric tons	1.1	(39.37)	short tons
	metric tons	0.98	(3.280840)	long tons
Liquid meas.	liters	33.8	(33.81402)	ounces
	liters	4.2	(0.3937)	cups
	liters	2.1	(39.37)	pints
	liters	1.1	(3.280840)	quarts
	liters	0.26	(1.093613)	gallons

(1) Statute mile. (2) A short ton is 2,000 pounds. (3) A long ton is 2,240 pounds.

Temperature Conversions

The left-hand column below gives a temperature according to the **Celsius** scale, and the right-hand gives the same temperature according to the **Fahrenheit** scale. The lowest number on each scale is equivalent to absolute zero, the temperature at which all motion within a molecule would stop.

For temperatures not shown: To convert Fahrenheit to Celsius by formula, subtract 32 degrees and divide by 1.8; to convert Celsius to Fahrenheit, multiply by 1.8 and add 32 degrees.

Note: Although the term *centigrade* is still frequently used, the International Committee on Weights and Measures and the National Institute of Standards and Technology have recommended since 1948 that this scale be called *Celsius*.

Celsius	Fahrenheit	Celsius	Fahrenheit	Celsius	Fahrenheit	Celsius	Fahrenheit	Celsius	Fahrenheit
−273.15	−459.67	−45.6	−50	−1.1	30	30	86	66	150
−250	−418	**−40**	**−40**	**0**	**32**	32.2	90	70	158
−200	−328	−34.4	−30	4.4	40	35	95	80	176
−184	−300	−30	−22	10	50	**37**	**98.6**	90	194
−157	−250	−28.9	−20	15.6	60	37.8	100	93	200
−150	−238	−23.3	−10	**20**	**68**	40	104	**100**	**212**
−129	−200	−20	−4	21.1	70	43	110	121	250
−101	−150	−17.8	0	23.9	75	49	120	149	300
−100	−148	−12.2	10	25	77	50	122	150	302
−73.3	−100	−10	14	26.7	80	54	130	200	392
−50	−58	−6.7	20	29.4	85	60	140	300	572

Boiling and Freezing Points

Water boils at 212°F (100°C) at sea level. For every 550 feet above sea level, boiling point of water is lower by about 1°F. Methyl alcohol boils at 148°F. Average human oral temperature, 98.6°F. **Water freezes** at 32°F (0°C).

Mathematical Formulas

Note: The value of π (the Greek letter pi) is approximately 3.14159265 (equal to the ratio of the circumference of a circle to the diameter). The equivalence is typically rounded further to 3.1416 or 3.14.

To find the Circumference of a:
Circle: Multiply the diameter by π.

To find the Area of a:
Circle: Multiply the square of the radius (equal to ½ the diameter) by π.
Rectangle: Multiply the length of the base by the height.
Sphere (surface): Multiply the square of the radius by π and multiply by 4.
Square: Square the length of one side.
Trapezoid: Add the 2 parallel sides, multiply by the height, and divide by 2.
Triangle: Multiply the base by the height, divide by 2.

To find the Volume of a:
Cone: Multiply the square of the radius of the base by π, multiply by the height, and divide by 3.
Cube: Cube the length of one edge.
Cylinder: Multiply the square of the radius of the base by π and multiply by the height.
Pyramid: Multiply the area of the base by the height and divide by 3.
Rectangular Prism: Multiply the length by the width by the height.
Sphere: Multiply the cube of the radius by π, multiply by 4, and divide by 3.

Playing Cards and Dice Chances

5-Card Poker Hands

Hand	Number possible	Odds against
Royal flush	4	649,739 to 1
Other straight flush	36	72,192 to 1
Four of a kind	624	4,164 to 1
Full house	3,744	693 to 1
Flush	5,108	508 to 1
Straight	10,200	254 to 1
Three of a kind	54,912	46 to 1
Two pairs	123,552	20 to 1
One pair	1,098,240	4 to 3 (1.37 to 1)
Nothing	1,302,540	1 to 1
TOTAL	**2,598,960**	

Bridge

The odds—against suit distribution in a hand of 4-4-3-2 are about 4 to 1; against 5-4-2-2 about 8 to 1; against 6-4-2-1 about 20 to 1; against 7-4-1-1 about 254 to 1; against 8-4-1-0 about 2,211 to 1; and against 13-0-0-0 about 158,753,389,899 to 1.

Dice
(probabilities on 2 dice)

Total	Odds against (single toss)	Total	Odds against (single toss)
2	35 to 1	8	31 to 5
3	17 to 1	9	8 to 1
4	11 to 1	10	11 to 1
5	8 to 1	11	17 to 1
6	31 to 5	12	35 to 1
7	5 to 1		

Large Numbers

No. of zeros	U.S.	British[1], French, German	No. of zeros	U.S.	British[1], French, German
6	million	million	42	tredecillion	septillion
9	billion	milliard	45	quattuordecillion	1,000 septillion
12	trillion	billion	48	quindecillion	octillion
15	quadrillion	1,000 billion	51	sexdecillion	1,000 octillion
18	quintillion	trillion	54	septendecillion	nonillion
21	sextillion	1,000 trillion	57	octodecillion	1,000 nonillion
24	septillion	quadrillion	60	novemdecillion	decillion
27	octillion	1,000 quadrillion	63	vigintillion	1,000 decillion
30	nonillion	quintillion	100	googol	googol
33	decillion	1,000 quintillion	303	centillion	—
36	undecillion	sextillion	600	—	centillion
39	duodecillion	1,000 sextillion	googol	googolplex	googolplex

(1) In recent years, it has become more common in Britain to use U.S. terminology for large numbers.

Prime Numbers

A prime number is any positive integer greater than 1 that is divisible only by two positive integers, 1 and itself.

Prime Numbers to 1,009

	2	3	5	7	11	13	17	19	23
29	31	37	41	43	47	53	59	61	67
71	73	79	83	89	97	101	103	107	109
113	127	131	137	139	149	151	157	163	167
173	179	181	191	193	197	199	211	223	227
229	233	239	241	251	257	263	269	271	277
281	283	293	307	311	313	317	331	337	347
349	353	359	367	373	379	383	389	397	401
409	419	421	431	433	439	443	449	457	461
463	467	479	487	491	499	503	509	521	523
541	547	557	563	569	571	577	587	593	599
601	607	613	617	619	631	641	643	647	653
659	661	673	677	683	691	701	709	719	727
733	739	743	751	757	761	769	773	787	797
809	811	821	823	827	829	839	853	857	859
863	877	881	883	887	907	911	919	929	937
941	947	953	967	971	977	983	991	997	1,009

Common Fractions Converted to Decimals

8ths	16ths	32nds	64ths	Decimal
			1	= 0.015625
		1	2	= 0.03125
			3	= 0.046875
	1	2	4	= 0.0625
			5	= 0.078125
		3	6	= 0.09375
			7	= 0.109375
1	2	4	8	= 0.125
			9	= 0.140625
		5	10	= 0.15625
			11	= 0.171875
	3	6	12	= 0.1875
			13	= 0.203125
		7	14	= 0.21875
			15	= 0.234375
2	4	8	16	= 0.25

8ths	16ths	32nds	64ths	Decimal
			17	= 0.265625
		9	18	= 0.28125
			19	= 0.296875
	5	10	20	= 0.3125
			21	= 0.328125
		11	22	= 0.34375
			23	= 0.359375
3	6	12	24	= 0.375
			25	= 0.390625
		13	26	= 0.40625
			27	= 0.421875
	7	14	28	= 0.4375
			29	= 0.453125
		15	30	= 0.46875
			31	= 0.484375
4	8	16	32	= 0.5

8ths	16ths	32nds	64ths	Decimal
			33	= 0.515625
		17	34	= 0.53125
			35	= 0.546875
		18	36	= 0.5625
			37	= 0.578125
		19	38	= 0.59375
			39	= 0.609375
5	10	20	40	= 0.625
			41	= 0.640625
		21	42	= 0.65625
			43	= 0.671875
	11	22	44	= 0.6875
			45	= 0.703125
		23	46	= 0.71875
			47	= 0.734375
6	12	24	48	= 0.75

8ths	16ths	32nds	64ths	Decimal
			49	= 0.765625
		25	50	= 0.78125
			51	= 0.796875
	13	26	52	= 0.8125
			53	= 0.828125
		27	54	= 0.84375
			55	= 0.859375
7	14	28	56	= 0.875
			57	= 0.890625
		29	58	= 0.90625
			59	= 0.921875
	15	30	60	= 0.9375
			61	= 0.953125
		31	62	= 0.96875
			63	= 0.984375
8	16	32	64	= 1.0

Roman Numerals

I — 1	IV — 4	VII — 7	X — 10	XX — 20	L — 50	C — 100	D — 500
II — 2	V — 5	VIII — 8	XI — 11	XXX — 30	LX — 60	CC — 200	CM — 900
III — 3	VI — 6	IX — 9	XIX — 19	XL — 40	XC — 90	CD — 400	M — 1,000

Note: The numerals V, X, L, C, D, or M shown with a horizontal line on top denote 1,000 times the original value.

Ancient Measures

Biblical
Cubit. . . . . = 21.8 inches
Omer . . . . = 0.45 peck
= 3.964 liters
Ephah. . . . . = 10 omers
Shekel . . . . = 0.497 ounce
= 14.1 grams

Greek
Cubit . . . . = 18.3 inches
Stadion . . . . . . = 607.2 or 622 feet
Obolos. . . . . . . = 715.38 milligrams
Drachma . . . . . = 4.2923 grams
Mina. . . . . = 0.9463 pound
Talent. . . . . = 60 mina

Roman
Cubit . . . . = 17.5 inches
Stadium. . . . . . . = 202 yards
As, libra,
pondus . . . . . . = 325.971 grams
= 0.71864 pound

Metric System Prefixes

The following prefixes, in combination with the basic unit names, provide the multiples and submultiples in the metric system. For example, the unit name *meter*, with the prefix *kilo* added, produces *kilometer*, meaning "1,000 meters."

Prefix	Symbol	Multiples	Equivalent
yotta	Y	10^{24}	septillionfold
zetta	Z	10^{21}	sextillionfold
exa	E	10^{18}	quintillionfold
peta	P	10^{15}	quadrillionfold
tera	T	10^{12}	trillionfold
giga	G	10^{9}	billionfold
mega	M	10^{6}	millionfold
kilo	k	10^{3}	thousandfold
hecto	h	10^{2}	hundredfold
deka	da	10	tenfold

Prefix	Symbol	Multiples	Equivalent
deci	d	10^{-1}	tenth part
centi	c	10^{-2}	hundredth part
milli	m	10^{-3}	thousandth part
micro	μ	10^{-6}	millionth part
nano	n	10^{-9}	billionth part
pico	p	10^{-12}	trillionth part
femto	f	10^{-15}	quadrillionth part
atto	a	10^{-18}	quintillionth part
zepto	z	10^{-21}	sextillionth part
yocto	y	10^{-24}	septillionth part

Metric Weights and Measures

The metric system generally uses the term *mass* instead of *weight*. Mass is a measure of an object's inertial property, or the amount of matter it contains. Weight is a measure of the force exerted on an object by gravity or the force needed to support it. Also, the metric system does not make a distinction between "dry volume" and "liquid volume."

Length

10 millimeters (mm) . . . . = 1 centimeter (cm)
10 centimeters . . . . = 1 decimeter (dm)
= 100 millimeters
10 decimeters. . . . . = 1 meter (m)
= 1,000 millimeters
10 meters . . . . = 1 dekameter (dam)
10 dekameters . . . . = 1 hectometer (hm)
= 100 meters
10 hectometers . . . . = 1 kilometer (km)
= 1,000 meters

Area

100 square millimeters (mm²) = 1 square centimeter (cm²)
10,000 square centimeters. . . . = 1 square meter (m²)
= 1,000,000 square millimeters
100 square meters . . . . = 1 are (a)
100 ares . . . . = 1 hectare (ha)
= 10,000 square meters
100 hectares . . . . = 1 square kilometer (km²)
= 1,000,000 square meters

Volume

10 milliliters (mL) . . . . = 1 centiliter (cL)
10 centiliters. . . . . = 1 deciliter (dL)
= 100 milliliters
10 deciliters . . . . = 1 liter (L)
= 1,000 milliliters

10 liters . . . . = 1 dekaliter (daL)
10 dekaliters . . . . = 1 hectoliter (hL)
= 100 liters
10 hectoliters. . . . . = 1 kiloliter (kL)
= 1,000 liters

Volume (Cubic Measure)

1,000 cubic millimeters (mm³) = 1 cubic centimeter (cm³)
1,000 cubic centimeters . . . . . = 1 cubic decimeter (dm³)
= 1,000,000 cubic millimeters
1,000 cubic decimeters . . . . . . = 1 cubic meter (m³)
= 1 stere (s)
= 1,000,000 cubic centimeters
= 1,000,000,000 cubic millimeters

Weight (Mass)

10 milligrams (mg). . . . . = 1 centigram (cg)
10 centigrams . . . . = 1 decigram (dg)
= 100 milligrams
10 decigrams. . . . . = 1 gram (g)
= 1,000 milligrams
10 grams . . . . = 1 dekagram (dag)
10 dekagrams . . . . = 1 hectogram (hg)
= 100 grams
10 hectograms. . . . . = 1 kilogram (kg)
= 1,000 grams
1,000 kilograms . . . . = 1 metric ton (t)

U.S. Customary Weights and Measures

Length

12 inches (in.).	= 1 foot (ft)
3 feet	= 1 yard (yd)
5½ yards	= 1 rod (rd), pole, or perch (16½ feet)
40 rods.	= 1 furlong (fur)
	= 220 yards
	= 660 feet
8 furlongs	= 1 statute mile (mi)
	= 1,760 yards
	= 5,280 feet
3 miles	= 1 league (on land)
	= 5,280 yards
	= 15,840 feet
6,076.11549 feet	= 1 international nautical mile (nm)

Volume (Liquid Measure)

When necessary to distinguish the liquid pint or quart from the dry pint or quart, the word *liquid* or the abbreviation *liq* is used in combination with the name or abbreviation of the liquid unit.

4 gills (gi)	= 1 pint (pt)
	= 28.875 cubic inches
2 pints.	= 1 quart (qt)
	= 57.75 cubic inches
4 quarts	= 1 gallon (gal)
	= 231 cubic inches
	= 8 pints
	= 32 gills

Volume (Dry Measure)

When necessary to distinguish the dry pint or quart from the liquid pint or quart, the word *dry* is used in combination with the name or abbreviation of the dry unit.

2 pints (pt)	= 1 quart (qt)
	= 67.2006 cubic inches
8 quarts	= 1 peck (pk)
	= 537.605 cubic inches
	= 16 pints
4 pecks.	= 1 bushel (bu)
	= 2,150.42 cubic inches
	= 32 quarts

Area

Squares and cubes of units are sometimes abbreviated by using superscripts. For example, ft² means square foot, and ft³ means cubic foot.

144 square inches	= 1 square foot (ft²)
9 square feet	= 1 square yard (yd²)
	= 1,296 square inches
30¼ square yards	= 1 square rod (rd²)
	= 272¼ square feet
160 square rods	= 1 acre (A)
	= 4,840 square yards
	= 43,560 square feet

640 acres.	= 1 square mile (mi²)
1 mile square.	= 1 section (of land)
6 miles square	= 1 township
	= 36 sections
	= 36 square miles

Cubic Measure

1 cubic foot (ft³)	= 1,728 cubic inches (in³)
27 cubic feet	= 1 cubic yard (yd³)

Gunter's, or Surveyor's, Chain Measure

7.92 inches (in)	= 1 link (li)
100 links	= 1 chain (ch)
	= 4 rods
	= 66 feet
80 chains.	= 1 statute mile (mi)
	= 320 rods
	= 5,280 feet

Avoirdupois Weight

When necessary to distinguish the avoirdupois ounce or pound from the troy ounce or pound, the word *avoirdupois* or the abbreviation *avdp* is used in combination with the name or abbreviation of the avoirdupois unit. The *grain* is the same in avoirdupois and troy weight.

27¹¹/₃₂ grains (gr)	= 1 dram (dr)
16 drams	= 1 ounce (oz)
	= 437½ grains
16 ounces	= 1 pound (lb)
	= 256 drams
	= 7,000 grains
100 pounds	= 1 hundredweight (cwt)*
20 hundredweights	= 1 ton (t)
	= 2,000 pounds*

In *gross* or *long* measure, the following values are recognized.

112 pounds	= 1 gross or long hundredweight*
20 gross or long hundredweights.	= 1 gross or long ton
	= 2,240 pounds*

*When the terms *hundredweight* and *ton* are used unmodified, they are commonly understood to mean the 100-pound hundredweight and the 2,000-pound ton, respectively; these units may be designated *net* or *short* when necessary to distinguish them from the corresponding units in gross or long measure.

Troy Weight

24 grains	= 1 pennyweight (dwt)
20 pennyweights	= 1 ounce troy (oz t)
	= 480 grains
12 ounces troy.	= 1 pound troy (lb t)
	= 240 pennyweights
	= 5,760 grains

Weight and Measurement Equivalents

In this table it is necessary to distinguish between the *international* and the *survey* foot. The international foot, defined in 1959 as exactly equal to 0.3048 meter, is shorter than the old survey foot by exactly 2 parts in 1 million. The survey foot is still used in data expressed in feet in geodetic surveys within the U.S. In this table the survey foot is indicated with capital letters.

When the name of a unit is enclosed in brackets, e.g., [1 hand], either (1) the unit is not in general current use in the U.S. or (2) the unit is believed to be based on custom and usage rather than on formal definition.

Equivalents involving decimals are, in most instances, rounded to the 3rd decimal place; exact equivalents are so designated.

Lengths

1 angstrom (Å)	= 0.1 nanometer (exactly)
	= 0.000 1 micrometer (exactly)
	= 0.000 000 1 millimeter (exactly)
	= 0.000 000 004 inch
1 cable's length	= 120 fathoms (exactly)
	= 720 FEET (exactly)
	= 219 meters
1 centimeter (cm)	= 0.3937 inch
1 chain (ch) (Gunter's or surveyor's)	= 66 FEET (exactly)
	= 20.1168 meters
1 chain (engineer's)	= 30.48 meters (exactly)
	= 100 feet
1 decimeter (dm)	= 3.937 inches
1 degree (geographical)	= 364,566.929 feet
	= 69.047 miles (avg.)
	= 111.123 kilometers (avg.)
of latitude	= 68.708 miles at equator
	= 69.403 miles at poles
of longitude.	= 69.171 miles at equator

1 dekameter (dam)	= 32.808 feet
1 fathom (fath)	= 6 FEET (exactly)
	= 1.8288 meters
1 foot (ft)	= 0.3048 meters (exactly)
	= 0.015 chains (surveyor's)
1 furlong (fur)	= 660 FEET (exactly)
	= ⅛ statute mile (exactly)
	= 201.168 meters
[1 hand] (height measure for horses from ground to top of shoulders)	= 4 inches
1 inch (in)	= 2.54 centimeters (exactly)
1 kilometer (km).	= 0.621371 mile
	= 3,280.8 feet
1 league (land)	= 3 statute miles (exactly)
	= 4.828 kilometers
1 link (Gunter's or surveyor's)	= 7.92 inches (exactly)
	= 0.201 meter
1 link (engineer's)	= 1 foot
	= 0.305 meter

1 meter (m). . . . . = 39.37 inches
                          = 1.09361 yards
1 micrometer (μm) . . . . = 0.001 millimeter (exactly)
                          = 0.00003937 inch
1 mil . . . . = 0.001 inch (exactly)
                          = 0.0254 millimeter (exactly)
1 mile (mi) (statute or land) . . . = 5,280 FEET (exactly)
                          = 1.609344 kilometers (exactly)
1 international nautical mile
   (nmi). . . . . = 1.852 kilometers (exactly)
                          = 1.150779 statute miles
                          = 6,076.11549 feet
1 millimeter (mm) . . . . = 0.03937 inch
1 nanometer (nm). . . . . = 0.001 micrometer (exactly)
                          = 0.00000003937 inch
1 pica (typography) . . . . = 12 points
1 point (pt) (typography). . . . . . = 0.013837 inch (exactly)
                          = 0.351 millimeter
1 rod (rd), pole, or perch . . . . . = 16½ FEET (exactly)
                          = 5.029 meters
1 yard (yd) . . . . = 0.9144 meter (exactly)

Areas or Surfaces

1 acre. . . . . = 43,560 square FEET (exactly)
                          = 4,840 square yards
                          = 0.405 hectare
1 are (a) . . . . = 119.599 square yards
                          = 0.025 acre
1 bolt (cloth measure):
   length . . . . = 100 yards (on modern looms)
   width . . . . = 45 or 60 inches
1 hectare (ha). . . . . = 2.471 acres
[1 square (building)] . . . . = 100 square feet
1 square centimeter (cm²) . . . . = 0.155 square inch
1 square decimeter (dm²). . . . . = 15.500 square inches
1 square foot (ft²) . . . . = 929.030 square centimeters
1 square inch (in²) . . . . = 6.4516 square centimeters
                          (exactly)
1 square kilometer (km²) . . . . . = 247.104 acres
                          = 0.386102 square mile
1 square meter (m²) . . . . = 1.196 square yards
                          = 10.764 square feet
1 square mile (mi²) . . . . = 258.999 hectares
1 square millimeter (mm²) . . . . = 0.002 square inch
1 square rod (rd²), sq. pole,
   or sq. perch . . . . = 25.293 square meters
1 square yard (yd²). . . . . = 0.836127 square meter

Capacities or Volumes

1 barrel (bbl), liquid. . . . . = 31 to 42 gallons*

*There are a variety of "barrels" established by law or usage. For example: federal taxes on fermented liquors are based on a barrel of 31 gallons; many state laws fix the "barrel for liquids" as 31½ gallons; one state fixes a 36-gallon barrel for cistern measurement; federal law recognizes a 40-gallon barrel for "proof spirits"; by custom, 42 gallons constitute a barrel of crude oil or petroleum products for statistical purposes, and this equivalent is recognized "for liquids" by 4 states.

1 barrel (bbl), standard for
   fruits, vegetables, and other
   dry commodities except dry
   cranberries . . . . = 7,056 cubic inches
                          = 105 dry quarts
                          = 3.281 bushels, struck measure
1 barrel (bbl), standard,
   cranberry . . . . = 86 $\frac{45}{64}$ dry quarts
                          = 2.709 bushels, struck measure
                          = 5,826 cubic inches
1 board foot (lumber measure) = a foot-square board 1 inch
                          thick
1 bushel (bu) (U.S.) (struck
   measure) . . . . = 2,150.42 cu in (exactly)
                          = 35.239 liters
[1 bushel, heaped (U.S.)] . . . . . = 2,747.715 cubic inches
                          = 1.278 bushels, struck
                          measure*
*Frequently recognized as 1¼ bushels, struck measure.
[1 bushel (bu) (British Imperial)
   (struck measure)] . . . . = 1.032 U.S. bushels, struck
                          measure
                          = 2,219.36 cubic inches
1 cord (cd) firewood . . . . = 128 cubic feet (exactly)
1 cubic centimeter (cm³). . . . . . = 0.061 cubic inch

1 cubic decimeter (dm³). . . . . . = 61.024 cubic inches
1 cubic inch (in³) . . . . = 0.554 fluid ounce
                          = 4.433 fluid drams
                          = 16.387 cubic centimeters
1 cubic foot (ft³) . . . . = 7.481 gallons
                          = 28.317 cubic decimeters
1 cubic meter (m³) . . . . = 1.308 cubic yards
1 cubic yard (yd³). . . . . = 0.765 cubic meter
1 cup, measuring. . . . . = 8 fluid ounces (exactly)
                          = ½ liquid pint (exactly)
[1 dram, fluid (fl dr) (British)] . . = 0.961 U.S. fluid dram
                          = 0.217 cubic inch
                          = 3.552 milliliters
1 dekaliter (daL) . . . . = 2.642 gallons
                          = 1.135 pecks
1 gallon (gal) (U.S.) . . . . = 231 cubic inches (exactly)
                          = 3.785 liters
                          = 0.833 British gallon
                          = 128 U.S. fluid ounces (exactly)
[1 gallon (gal) British Imperial] = 277.42 cubic inches
                          = 1.201 U.S. gallons
                          = 4.546 liters
                          = 160 British fluid ounces
                          (exactly)
1 gill (gi) . . . . = 7.219 cubic inches
                          = 4 fluid ounces (exactly)
                          = 0.118 liter
1 hectoliter (hL) . . . . = 26.418 gallons
                          = 2.838 bushels
1 liter (L) (1 cubic decimeter
   exactly) . . . . = 1.057 liquid quarts
                          = 0.908 dry quart
                          = 61.024 cubic inches
1 milliliter (mL) (1 cu cm
   exactly) . . . . = 0.271 fluid dram
                          = 16.231 minims
                          = 0.061 cubic inch
1 ounce, liquid (U.S.). . . . . = 1.805 cubic inches
                          = 29.574 milliliters
                          = 1.041 British fluid ounces
[1 ounce, fluid (fl oz) (British)] = 0.961 U.S. fluid ounce
                          = 1.734 cubic inches
                          = 28.412 milliliters
1 peck (pk). . . . . = 8.810 liters
1 pint (pt), dry . . . . = 33.600 cubic inches
                          = 0.551 liter
1 pint (pt), liquid. . . . . = 28.875 cubic inches (exactly)
                          = 0.473 liter
1 quart (qt), dry (U.S.) . . . . = 67.201 cubic inches
                          = 1.101 liters
                          = 0.969 British quart
1 quart (qt), liquid (U.S.) . . . . . = 57.75 cubic in (exactly)
                          = 0.946 liter
                          = 0.833 British quart
[1 quart (qt) (British)] . . . . = 69.354 cubic inches
                          = 1.032 U.S. dry quarts
                          = 1.201 U.S. liquid quarts
1 tablespoon . . . . = 3 teaspoons*(exactly)
                          = 4 fluid drams
                          = ½ fluid ounce (exactly)
1 teaspoon. . . . . = ⅓ tablespoon*(exactly)
                          = 1⅓ fluid drams*

*The equivalent "1 teaspoon = 1⅓ fluid drams" has been found to correspond more closely with the actual capacities of teaspoons in use than the equivalent "1 teaspoon = 1 fluid dram" which is given by many dictionaries.

Weights or Masses

1 assay ton" (AT) . . . . = 29.167 grams

**Used in assaying. The assay ton bears the same relation to the milligram that a ton of 2,000 pounds avoirdupois bears to the ounce troy; hence, the weight in milligrams of precious metal obtained from one assay ton of ore gives directly the number of troy ounces to the net ton.

1 bale (cotton measure) . . . . . = 500 pounds in U.S.
                          = 750 pounds in Egypt
1 carat (c) . . . . = 200 milligrams (exactly)
                          = 3.086 grains
1 dram avoirdupois (dr avdp) = 27 $\frac{11}{32}$ (= 27.344) grains
                          = 1.772 grams
1 gamma (g) . . . . = 1 microgram (exactly),
                          see below
1 grain (gr). . . . . = 64.7989 milligrams

1 gram (g)	= 15.432 grains
	= 0.035 ounce, avoirdupois
1 hundredweight, gross or long*** (gross cwt)	= 112 pounds (exactly)
	= 50.802 kilograms
1 hundredweight, net or short (cwt or net cwt)	= 100 pounds (exactly)
	= 45.359 kilograms
1 kilogram (kg)	= 2.20462 pounds
1 microgram (μg)	= 0.000001 gram (exactly)
1 milligram (mg)	= 0.015 grain
1 ounce, avoirdupois (oz avdp)	= 437.5 grains (exactly)
	= 0.911 troy ounce
	= 28.3495 grams
1 ounce, troy (oz t)	= 480 grains (exactly)
	= 1.097 avoirdupois ounces
	= 31.103 grams
1 pennyweight (dwt)	= 1.555 grams
1 pound, avoirdupois (lb avdp)	= 7,000 grains (exactly)
	= 1.215 troy pounds
	= 453.59237 grams (exactly)

1 pound, troy (lb t)	= 5,760 grains (exactly)
	= 0.823 pound, avoirdupois
	= 373.242 grams
1 stone (st)	= 14 pounds avdp (exactly)
	= 6.350 kilograms
1 ton, gross or long	= 2,240 pounds (exactly)
	= 1.12 net tons (exactly)
	= 1.016 metric tons

***The gross, or long, ton and hundredweight are used commercially in the U.S. to only a limited extent, usually in restricted industrial fields. These units are the same as the British ton and hundredweight.

1 ton, metric (t)	= 2,204.623 pounds
	= 0.984 gross ton
	= 1.102 net tons
1 ton, net or short (sh ton)	= 2,000 pounds (exactly)
	= 0.893 gross ton
	= 0.907 metric ton

Electrical Units

The **watt** (W) is the unit of power (electrical, mechanical, thermal, etc.). Electrical power is given by the product of the voltage and the current.

Energy is sold by the **joule** (J), but in common practice the billing of electrical energy is expressed in terms of the **kilowatt-hour** (kWh), which is 3,600,000 joules or 3.6 megajoules.

The **horsepower** (hp) is a nonmetric unit sometimes used in mechanics. It is equal to 746 watts.

The **ohm** is the unit of electrical resistance and represents the physical property of a conductor that offers a resistance to the flow of electricity, permitting just 1 ampere to flow at 1 volt of pressure.

Measures of Force and Pressure

Dyne (dyn) = force necessary to accelerate a 1-gram mass 1 centimeter per second squared = 0.000072 poundal

Poundal (pdl) = force necessary to accelerate a 1-pound mass 1 foot per second squared = 13,825.5 dynes = 0.138255 newtons

Newton (N) = force needed to accelerate a 1-kilogram mass 1 meter per second squared

Pascal (pressure) (Pa) = 1 newton per square meter = 0.020885 pound per square foot

Atmosphere (air pressure at sea level) (atm) = 2,116.102 pounds per square foot = 14.6952 pounds per square inch = 1.0332 kilograms per square centimeter = 101,323 newtons per square meter

Spirits Measures

Pony	= 0.5 jigger	Quart (qt)	= 32 shots	For champagne only:	
Shot	= 0.667 jigger		= 1.25 fifths	Rehoboam	= 3 magnums
	= 1.0 ounce	Magnum	= 2 quarts	Methuselah	= 4 magnums
Jigger	= 1.5 shots		= 2.49797 bottles (wine)	Salmanazar	= 6 magnums
Pint (pt)	= 16 shots			Balthazar	= 8 magnums
	= 0.625 fifth			Nebuchadnezzar	= 10 magnums
Fifth	= 25.6 shots	For champagne and brandy only:		Wine bottle (standard)	= 0.800633 quart
	= 1.6 pints	Jeroboam	= 6.4 pints		= 0.7576778 liter
	= 0.8 quart		= 1.6 magnums		
	= 0.75706 liter		= 0.8 gallon		

Miscellaneous Modern Measures

Caliber (cal)—the diameter of a gun bore. In the U.S., caliber is traditionally expressed in hundredths of inches, e.g., .22. In Britain, caliber is often expressed in thousandths of inches, e.g., .270. Now it is commonly expressed in millimeters, e.g., the 5.56 mm M16 rifle. Heavier weapons' caliber has long been expressed in millimeters, e.g., the 155 mm howitzer. Naval guns' caliber refers to the barrel length as a multiple of the bore diameter. A 5-inch, 50-caliber naval gun has a 5-inch bore and a barrel length of 250 inches.

Decibel (dB)—a measure of the relative loudness or intensity of sound. A 20-decibel sound is 10 times louder than a 10-decibel sound; 30 decibels is 100 times louder; 40 decibels is 1,000 times louder, etc.

One decibel is the smallest difference between sounds detectable by the human ear. A 120-decibel sound is painful.

10 decibels	light whisper
20	quiet conversation
30	normal conversation
40	light traffic
50	typewriter, loud conversation
60	noisy office
70	normal traffic, quiet train
80	rock music, subway
90	heavy traffic, thunder
100	jet plane at takeoff

Em—a printer's measure designating the square width of any given type size. Thus, an em of 10-point type is 10 points. An en is half an em.

Gauge (ga)—a measure of shotgun bore diameter. Gauge numbers originally referred to the number of lead balls just fitting the gun barrel diameter required to make a pound. Thus, a 16-gauge shotgun's bore was smaller than a 12-gauge shotgun's. Today, an international agreement assigns millimeter measures to each gauge.

Gauge	Bore diameter (in mm)	Gauge	Bore diameter (in mm)
6	23.34	14	17.60
10	19.67	16	16.81
12	18.52	20	15.90

Horsepower (hp)—the power needed to lift 550 pounds 1 foot in 1 second or to lift 33,000 pounds 1 foot in 1 minute. Equivalent to 746 watts or 2,546.0756 Btu/h.

Karat or carat (k or c)—a measure of fineness for gold equal to $1/24$ part of pure gold in an alloy. Thus 24-karat gold is pure; 18-karat gold is ¼ alloy. The carat is also used as a unit of weight for precious stones; it is equal to 200 milligrams or 3.086 grains.

Knot (kn or kt)—a measure of the speed of ships. A knot equals 1 nautical mile per hour.

Quire (qr)—25 sheets of paper.

Ream (rm)—500 sheets of paper.

Computer Milestones

1623: German mathematician Wilhelm Schickard developed the 1st mechanical calculator, capable of adding, subtracting, multiplying, and dividing.

1642: French mathematician Blaise Pascal built the 1st of more than 4 dozen copies of an adding and subtracting machine that he invented.

1801: French inventor Joseph Marie Jacquard demonstrated a new control system for looms. He "programmed" the loom, communicating desired weaving operations to the machine via patterns of holes in paper cards.

1833-71: British mathematician and scientist Charles Babbage used the Jacquard punch-card system in his design for a sophisticated, programmable "Analytical Engine" that foreshadowed basic features of today's computers. Babbage's conception was beyond the capabilities of the technology of his time, and the machine remained unfinished at his death in 1871.

1889: American engineer Herman Hollerith patented an electromechanical punch-card tabulating system that facilitated the handling of large amounts of statistical data and quickly found use in censuses in the U.S. and other countries.

1911: Hollerith's Tabulating Machine Company merged with 2 other enterprises to form the Computing-Tabulating-Recording Company, which was renamed the International Business Machines Corporation (IBM) in 1924.

1941: German engineer Konrad Züse completed the Z3, the 1st fully functional digital computer to be controlled by a program; the Z3 was not electronic—it was based on electrical switches called relays.

1942: Iowa State Coll. physicist John Vincent Atanasoff and his assistant Clifford Berry completed a working model of the 1st fully electronic computer, using vacuum tubes, which could operate much more quickly than relays; the rudimentary machine was not programmable.

1943: IBM and Harvard professor Howard Aiken completed the 1st large-scale automatic digital computer, the Mark I, a relay-based machine 55 ft long and 8 ft high.

1943: British scientists built the Colossus, an electronic computer designed specifically for breaking German codes.

1946: ENIAC (Electronic Numerical Integrator and Computer), a 30-ton room-sized electronic computer with more than 18,000 vacuum tubes, was completed by physicist John Mauchly and engineer J. Presper Eckert at the Univ. of Pennsylvania for the U.S. Army. ENIAC could be programmed to do different tasks, but cables had to be plugged in and switches set by hand.

1951: Eckert and Mauchly's UNIVAC (Universal Automatic Computer) became the 1st computer commercially available in the U.S. The 1st customer: the Census Bureau. CBS-TV used a UNIVAC in 1952 to predict election results.

1969-71: The powerful Unix operating system was developed at Bell Laboratories; later versions became widely used on large computers and formed the basis for Linux and Macintosh OS X operating systems for personal computers.

1971: Intel released the 4004, the 1st commercial microprocessor (an entire computer processing unit on a chip).

1973: The Alto computer, developed at Xerox's Palo Alto Research Center, became operational, implementing many features used years later in commercial personal computers, including a graphical user interface (GUI) featuring windows, icons, a mouse, and pointers.

1975: The 1st widely marketed personal computer, the MITS Altair 8800, was introduced in kit form, with no keyboard, video display, or printer, for under $400.

1975: Microsoft was founded by college dropouts Bill Gates and Paul Allen.

1976: The 1st word-processing program for personal computers, Electric Pencil, was written.

1976: Apple Computer Company was founded by Steven Jobs and Stephen Wozniak.

1977: Apple introduced the Apple II; capable of displaying text and graphics in color, the machine enjoyed phenomenal success.

1981: IBM unveiled its "Personal Computer," which used Microsoft's DOS (disk operating system).

1984: Apple introduced the 1st Macintosh. The easy-to-use Macintosh came with a proprietary operating system and was the 1st popular computer to have a GUI and a mouse.

1990: Microsoft released Windows 3.0, the 1st workable version of its own GUI.

1991: The Linux operating system was invented for the personal computer by Helsinki University student Linus Torvalds and made available for free.

1996: The Palm Pilot, the 1st widely successful handheld computer and personal information manager, arrived.

1997: The IBM computer Deep Blue beat world chess champion Garry Kasparov in a 6-game match, 2-1, with 3 draws.

2000: Microsoft was found guilty of antitrust violations by a federal district judge. Microsoft settled in 2001 by accepting certain restrictions on its competitive practices and creating an antitrust compliance committee.

2001: Apple introduced the Unix-based operating system OS X for the Macintosh.

2002: The total number of personal computers (PCs), including desktop and laptop machines of all types, shipped by manufacturers since 1975 reached 1 bil, according to computer industry research firm Gartner Dataquest.

2004: The European Union (EU) found Microsoft guilty of anticompetitive practices and fined the company $613 mil. In mid-2006 the EU levied an additional penalty of $357 mil for noncompliance.

2006: Apple began using Intel microprocessors in its Macintosh computers instead of the IBM PowerPC.

2007: Microsoft released Windows Vista, the successor to its 6-year-old Windows XP operating system.

Nations with the Most Personal Computers in Use, 2008

Source: Computer Industry Almanac at www.c-i-a.com for year end 2008

Rank	PCs in use[1]	% of worldwide total	Rank	PCs in use[1]	% of worldwide total
1. U.S.	264.10	22.19%	10. Brazil	33.30	2.80%
2. China	98.67	8.29	11. India	32.03	2.69
3. Japan	86.22	7.24	12. Canada	27.63	2.32
4. Germany	61.96	5.21	13. Mexico	19.13	1.61
5. UK	47.04	3.95	14. Australia	17.01	1.43
6. France	43.11	3.62	15. Spain	16.71	1.40
7. Russia	36.42	3.06			
8. Italy	35.69	3.00	**Top 15 countries**	**853.90**	**71.70**
9. South Korea	34.87	2.93	**World total**	**1,190.10**	**100.00**

(1) In millions.

Status of Electronics Sold, 1980-2007

Source: U.S. Environmental Protection Agency
(millions of units)

	Disposed or recycled		In storage		Still in use		Total
	units	%	units	%	units	%	units
Desktop PCs	277.6	50.6	65.7	12.0	205.8	37.5	549.0
PC monitors.	339.0	57.6	42.4	7.2	207.2	35.2	588.7
Portable PCs	67.1	39.3	2.1	1.2	101.7	59.5	170.8
Hard copy peripherals[1]	209.3	51.3	25.2	6.2	173.7	42.6	408.2
Televisions.	306.6	43.5	99.1	14.1	299.1	42.4	704.9
Total	**1,199.6**	**49.5**	**234.6**	**9.7**	**987.6**	**40.8**	**2,421.7**

Note: Estimates as of 2008. (1) Printers, scanners, fax machines.

Computer Products Disposal, 1999-2007

Source: U.S. Environmental Protection Agency
(millions of units and thousands of tons)

Year	Desktops Units	Tons	Portables Units	Tons	Peripherals* Units	Tons	CRT monitors Units	Tons	Flat-panel monitors Units	Tons	Total Units	Tons	Total recycled Units	Tons
1999	12.6	138.3	3.2	13.5	90.4	141.7	15.7	238.3	1.8	21.7	123.7	553.5	19.2	82.4
2000	15.4	174.3	3.9	16.0	77.6	162.7	18.9	314.8	1.8	22.7	117.7	690.4	18.5	102.5
2001	18.4	204.4	4.8	19.0	89.8	190.9	21.1	386.6	1.8	22.6	135.9	823.5	21.2	119.7
2002	21.9	244.8	5.8	22.0	96.7	217.8	23.9	480.7	1.8	21.7	150.1	987.0	25.5	151.4
2003	24.7	275.0	6.9	25.4	112.4	263.7	27.7	597.8	2.8	34.3	174.5	1,196.2	29.3	178.8
2004	26.6	293.6	7.8	28.2	124.5	278.0	27.8	627.8	3.7	45.3	190.4	1,272.9	34.7	199.9
2005	28.4	322.6	9.0	31.8	130.8	278.9	28.5	673.1	5.0	61.5	201.6	1,368.0	38.1	217.9
2006	28.3	311.6	10.2	35.2	120.8	267.9	23.8	550.3	6.3	77.1	189.4	1,242.1	42.8	223.0
2007	29.9	341.3	12.0	40.3	131.8	295.4	22.8	533.6	9.1	111.4	205.5	1,321.9	48.2	244.0

Note: Estimated figures. * Includes printers, scanners, fax machines, mice, and keyboards.

Top-Selling Software, 2008-09

Source: The NPD Group/Retail Tracking Service
(based on unit U.S. sales, July 2008-June 2009; does not include software bundled with computers at point of sale)
Software is Windows-only unless otherwise noted; M = Macintosh, W/M = Windows/Mac,
SBE = small business edition, Upgr = Upgrade, Pers. = personal, Ed. = edition, Fed = federal.

All Software
1. MS Office 2007 Home & Student . . . . .Microsoft
2. TurboTax 2008 Deluxe Fed + State + e-File (W/M). . . . . . . Intuit
3. MS Office 2008 Home & Student (M) . . . . .Microsoft
4. QuickBooks 2009 Pro. . . . . Intuit
5. World of Warcraft: Wrath of the Lich King
   Expansion Pack (W/M) . . . . Vivendi
6. Norton 360 2.0 . . . . Symantec
7. TurboTax 2008 Home & Business
   Federal + State + e-File (W/M) . . . . Intuit
8. Norton Internet Security 2009. . . . . Symantec
9. Kaspersky Internet Security 2009. . . . . Kaspersky Lab
10. PC Spore (W/M). . . . . Electronic Arts

Business
1. MS Office 2007 Home & Student . . . . .Microsoft
2. MS Office 2008 Home & Student (M) . . . . .Microsoft
3. MS Office 2007 Govt. Promo . . . . .Microsoft
4. MobileMe (W/M) . . . . Apple
5. iWork 2009 (M). . . . . Apple
6. MS Office 2009 SBE Upgr . . . . .Microsoft
7. iWork 2008 (M) . . . . Apple
8. MS Office 2007 Pro . . . . .Microsoft
9. MS Office 2007 Upgr . . . . .Microsoft
10. MS Office 2007 SBE . . . . .Microsoft

Education
1. Spanish Pers. Ed. Level 1-2-3 (W/M) . . . . .Rosetta Stone Ltd
2. Spanish Pers. Ed. Level 1 (W/M) . . . . .Rosetta Stone Ltd
3. French Pers. Ed. Level 1-2-3 (W/M). . . . . . .Rosetta Stone Ltd
4. Spanish Pers. Ed. Level 1 & 2 (W/M) . . . . .Rosetta Stone Ltd
5. I SPY Fun House (W/M) . . . . .Scholastic
6. Italian Pers. Ed. Level 1-2-3 (W/M) . . . . . .Rosetta Stone Ltd
7. Mavis Beacon Teaches Typing 20.0 Deluxe (W/M) . . . . . Encore
8. Learning QuickBooks 2009 . . . . Intuit
9. German Pers. Ed. Level 1-2-3 (W/M) . . . .Rosetta Stone Ltd
10. Japanese Pers. Ed. Level 1-2-3 (W/M) . . . .Rosetta Stone Ltd

Finance
1. TurboTax 2008 Deluxe Fed + State + e-File (W/M) . . . . . Intuit
2. QuickBooks 2009 Pro. . . . . Intuit
3. TurboTax 2008 Home & Business Fed + State + e-File
   (W/M). . . . . Intuit
4. TurboTax 2008 Premier Fed + State + e-File (W/M) . . . . Intuit
5. Taxcut 2008 Premium Fed + State + e-File (W/M) . . . H&R Block
6. TurboTax 2008 Deluxe Fed + e-File (W/M) . . . . Intuit
7. Quicken 2009 Deluxe. . . . . Intuit
8. QuickBooks 2008 Pro. . . . . Intuit
9. TurboTax 2008 Basic Fed + e-File (W/M) . . . . Intuit
10. QuickBooks 2009 Premier . . . . Intuit

Imaging/Graphics
1. iLife 2009 (M) . . . . .Apple
2. Adobe Photoshop Elements 7.0 . . . . Adobe
3. Final Cut Studio 2.0 (M). . . . . Apple
4. Adobe Photoshop Elements 7.0/
   Premiere Elements 7.0 Bundle . . . . Adobe

5. iLife 2008 Family Pack (M). . . . . .Apple
6. Autocad Lt 2009 . . . . .Autodesk
7. Acrobat 9.0. . . . . Adobe
8. Final Cut Express 4.0 HD (M) . . . . .Apple
9. Adobe Photoshop Elements 6.0 (M) . . . . Adobe
10. MS Publisher 2007. . . . . .Microsoft

Operating Systems
1. Mac OS X 10.5 Leopard (M) . . . . .Apple
2. MS Windows Vista Home Premium . . . . Microsoft
3. MS Windows Vista Ultimate Upgr . . . . Microsoft
4. MS Windows XP Home Ed. . . . . Microsoft
5. MS Windows XP Pro . . . . Microsoft
6. MS Windows Vista Ultimate. . . . . Microsoft
7. MS Windows Vista Home Premium Upgr . . . . Microsoft
8. MS Windows Vista Home Basic. . . . . Microsoft
9. Mac OS X 10.5 Leopard Family Pack (M) . . . . .Apple
10. MS Windows XP Pro Upgr. . . . . Microsoft

PC Games
1. World of Warcraft: Wrath of the Lich King
   Expansion Pack (W/M) . . . . Vivendi
2. PC Spore (W/M). . . . . .Electronic Arts
3. The Sims 3 (W/M) .Electronic Arts
4. Warhammer Online: Age of Reckoning . . . . . . .Electronic Arts
5. World of Warcraft: Battle Chest (W/M). . . . . Vivendi
6. Fallout 3 . . . . Bethesda SoftWorks
7. The Sims 2 Double Deluxe . . . . .Electronic Arts
8. Call of Duty: World at War . . . . .Activision
9. World of Warcraft: Wrath of the Lich King
   Expansion Pack Collector's Edition (W/M) . . . . Vivendi
10. Left 4 Dead . . . . .Electronic Arts

Personal Productivity
1. City Navigator 2009 Update (W/M) . . . . Garmin
2. Nero 9.0 . . . . Nero Inc
3. Roxio Creator 2009 . . . . .Roxio
4. Logic 8.0 Studio (M). . . . . .Apple
5. MS Streets & Trips 2009 . . . . Microsoft
6. Easy CD & DVD Burning . . . . .Roxio
7. MS Streets & Trips 2009 with GPS locator . . . . Microsoft
8. MS Works 9.0. . . . . Microsoft
9. Nero 8.0 Ultra Ed . . . . Nero Inc
10. Acid Music Studio 7.0 . . . . Sony

System Utilities
1. Norton 360 2.0 . . . . Symantec
2. Norton Internet Security 2009 . . . . Symantec
3. Kaspersky Internet Security 2009 . . . . Kaspersky Lab
4. Norton Antivirus 2009. Symantec
5. Trend Micro AntiVirus 2008 Plus Anti-Spyware . . . . . Trend Micro
6. Kaspersky Antivirus 2009. . . . . Kaspersky Lab
7. Spy Sweeper with Antivirus . . . . Webroot
8. Norton 360 3.0 . . . . Symantec
9. Trend Micro Internet Security 2009 . . . . .Trend Micro
10. Norton Internet Security 2008 . . . . Symantec

U.S. Sales of Selected Hardware, 1997-2009

Source: Consumer Electronics Association

(factory sales to dealers in millions of dollars and millions of units)

	1997	2000	2003		2007		2008		2009 (est.)	
	$	$	$	units	$	units	$	units	$	units
Computers	$15,950[1]	$16,400[1]	$15,584	18.1	$21,156	24.5	$20,931	27.6	$16,481	27.9
Desktop	—	—	7,212	10.9	8,500	10.5	6,744	10.2	4,806	9.2
Notebook	—	—	8,372	7.2	12,656	14.0	14,187	17.4	11,675	18.7
Smartphones	—	—	925	2.3	7,960	24.2	11,393	28.6	11,729	30.7
Electronic Gaming Hardware . . .	1,650	2,700	3,188	—	6,710	—	7,780	—	7,037	—
Digital Video Recorders	—	46	57	0.2	975	5.0	3,237	20.2	2,764	19.2
Digital Cameras	483	1,823	3,921	14.8	6,517	32.2	6,813	33.2	5,969	30.5
Digital Camcorder	—	2,838	2,002	5.3	2,112	5.6	1,885	5.6	1,897	5.7
Portable Media/MP3 Players . . .	—	107	424	3.0	5,968	48.0	5,844	43.7	5,207	40.7

(1) Desktop and notebook computers were not separated.

About the Internet

The Internet is a vast and rapidly growing computer network. In 1994, a total of 3 mil people (most of them in the U.S.) made use of it; by the end of 2008 the number of users worldwide exceeded 1.6 bil (Computer Industry Almanac Inc.).

The Internet is not owned or funded by any one institution, organization, or government. It has no CEO and is not a commercial service. Its development is guided by the Internet Society (ISOC), which is composed of volunteers. The ISOC appoints the Internet Architecture Board (IAB), which oversees issues of standards, network resources, etc.

Major Historical Highlights

1969: ARPANET, an experimental 4-computer network, was established by the Advanced Research Projects Agency (ARPA) of the U.S. Defense Dept. Two years later, ARPANET linked about 23 computers ("hosts") at 15 sites, including MIT and Harvard.

1978: The 1st spam, or junk e-mail, message was sent over ARPANET.

1983: The set of communications rules (protocol) known as TCP/IP became the main networking protocol of ARPANET. TCP/IP facilitates connection between networks. Its adoption was tantamount to the birth of the Internet.

1983: The military portion of ARPANET was moved onto the MILNET.

1986: The U.S. National Science Foundation (NSF) launched NSFNET, the 1st large-scale network using Internet technology.

1988: Internet Relay Chat (IRC) was developed by Finnish student Jarkko Oikarinen, enabling people to communicate via the Internet in "real time."

1988: A "worm" crafted by Cornell Univ. graduate student Robert Morris Jr. infected thousands of computers, shutting many down and causing millions of dollars of damage—the 1st known case of large-scale damage caused by a computer virus spread via the Internet.

1989: The World—the 1st commercial Internet service provider supplying dial-up access—debuted.

1989-90: Tim Berners-Lee invented the World Wide Web. Created as an environment in which scientists at the European Center for Nuclear Research in Switzerland could share information, it gradually evolved into a medium with text, graphics, audio, animation, and video.

1990: ARPANET was disbanded.

1991: The NSFNET was opened to commercial traffic.

1991: Berners-Lee introduced the 1st browser, or software for accessing the Web.

1993: The U.S. National Center for Supercomputing Applications released versions of Mosaic, the 1st Web browser able to present both text and images in a single page, for Microsoft Windows, Unix systems running the X Window GUI, and Apple Macintosh.

1994: Netscape Communications released the Netscape Navigator browser.

1995: Microsoft released its Internet Explorer browser. It initially failed to make a dent in Netscape's dominance of the browser market but surpassed it by 1999.

1996: A group of universities launched Internet2, an advanced, high-performance network for the research community and a test bed for development of new capabilities that might find use in the commercial Internet.

1998: Under a contract with the U.S. Dept. of Commerce, the nonprofit Internet Corporation for Assigned Numbers and Names (ICANN) took over the management of such basic Internet functions as assignment of domain names and Internet (IP) addresses.

1999: Release of the free Napster file-sharing service enabled users to easily exchange files containing music or other content without regard to copyright restrictions.

2003: Niue, a self-governing Pacific island associated with New Zealand, became the 1st "country" to offer free nationwide wireless access to the Internet (using Wi-Fi technology).

2004: The Mozilla Foundation released the first official version of the open-source browser Mozilla Firefox.

2006: Websites with rich user interfaces that encourage collective participation and personalization through online applications and scripts, known as Web 2.0, became prevalent.

2007: Apple Inc. releases the iPhone, a touchscreen-equipped smartphone; the company sold 1 mil units within 3 days of its launch.

Safety and Security on the Internet

Common sense dictates some basic security rules:

• Pick passwords that are difficult to guess, preferably consisting of both letters and numbers, and other symbols, if permitted. Using the same password at multiple websites is not recommended.

• Do not give out your phone number, address, credit card number, or other personal information unless needed for a transaction at a site you trust.

• If you feel someone is being threatening or dangerous, inform your Internet service provider.

• Use protective "firewall," antivirus, and antispyware software to guard your system against attacks by hackers.

• Be careful about opening e-mail and file attachments from unknown correspondents.

• If you have programs that can make use of macros—bits of auxiliary coding that are meant to play a helpful role but can be taken advantage of by some viruses—make sure the programs' macro virus protection (if any) is turned on. Disable macros if you do not know how to use them.

• Users of so-called **peer-to-peer** (P2P) file-sharing networks or protocols should open up only part of their computer system to sharing, not the entire hard drive.

• When manufacturers provide **patches** to solve security flaws or other problems with operating systems, software, or web browsers, it is usually advisable to install these fixes. If a fix is not available for a serious security problem, you may want to consider switching to an alternative program.

Malware. Software designed to harm a computer system—such as a virus (malicious code carried within a program) or a worm (a self-contained malicious program)—may be transmitted via the Internet, received on a disk, or communicated via e-mail.

Malicious software may install a "back door" on an infected system, giving hackers access; attempt to turn off any antivirus program on the system; or try to log the user's keystrokes.

A **Trojan horse** is computer code concealed within harmless code or data that is capable of taking control and causing damage. It can be used to mount a massive "**denial-of-service**" attack, which overwhelms targeted computers by inundating them with messages. The infected computers, acting under hacker control without their owners' knowledge, are called **zombies**, and the network of zombie computers that carry out the attack is called a **botnet**.

Spyware. Software that observes your computer activity without your knowledge is often regarded as a type of malware. Spyware programs, which can gain entry to your machine via a Trojan horse, may record your keystrokes and report passwords or other personal information to a hacker. Some can flood your screen with ads.

Phishing. A popular scam is **phishing**—the use of a forged e-mail message purportedly from a respectable organization, such as a bank, to elicit personal data. The e-mail typically contains a hyperlink that leads to a fabricated website resembling the site of the ostensible sender. To avoid falling victim to a phishing scam, do not click on any links in e-mails sent by companies with whom you do business. If you want to visit such a company's website, open your browser and manually enter the site's normal address.

Spam. Junk e-mail, or **spam**, can be a time-wasting annoyance or worse—spam may offer pornography or products dangerous to health; seek to defraud the recipient; carry a destructive virus; or turn the recipient's machine into a zombie that stores illicit material, takes part in a denial-of-service attack, or distributes spam. Net administrators worry that the flood of spam could cause a breakdown in the flow of Internet traffic.

In 2003 Congress enacted a law that attempted to restrict spam, but it had little effect on the volume of spam received by e-mail accounts.

While filtering software can help reduce the deluge of spam—some e-mail programs include filters—it is not completely accurate. Experts recommend that you be wary of revealing your e-mail address as you surf the Web. If possible, do not list your e-mail address on a public website.

Internet Addresses

The fundamental part of an address on the Internet is called the domain. The final part of a domain name, known as the **top-level domain (TLD)**, is its most basic part. For example, in *The World Almanac*'s web address (www.worldalmanac.com), .com is the top-level domain.

So-called generic top-level domains (gTLDs), consisting of 3 or more letters, include:

Domain	What it is (usually)
.aero	an organization in the air-transport industry
.asia	legal entities within the Pan-Asia and Asia-Pacific region
.biz	a business
.cat	a site associated with Catalan language and culture
.com	generally a commercial organization, business, or company
.coop	a nonprofit business cooperative, such as a rural electric co-op
.edu	an educational institution
.gov	a nonmilitary U.S. governmental entity, usually federal
.info	an informational site for an individual or organization, without restriction
.int	an international organization
.jobs	information about employment, such as job openings
.mil	a U.S. military organization
.mobi	a site providing content for mobile devices
.museum	a museum
.name	an individual
.net	suggested for a network administration, but actually used by a wide variety of sites
.org	suggested for a nonprofit organization, but actually used by a wide variety of sites
.pro	a professional, such as an accountant, lawyer, or physician
.tel	Internet communications identifier for an individual or organization
.travel	information about travel

Domain names with 2 letters are generally for countries or regions. The **top-level domain** .us, for instance, is available to persons, organizations, and entities in the U.S. More examples: .eu (European Union), .jp (Japan), .ru (Russia), .uk (United Kingdom).

Internet Lingo

The following abbreviations are sometimes used on the Internet and in e-mail.

BTW	By the way	GOK	God only knows	LOL	Laughing out loud
CBLO	See below	GTG	Got to go	PLS	Please
F2F	Face to face; a personal meeting	HHOK	Ha, ha—only kidding	ROFL	Rolling on the floor laughing
FCOL	For crying out loud	IMHO	In my humble opinion	TAFN	That's all for now
FWIW	For what it's worth	IMO	In my opinion	TTFN	Ta-ta for now

Emoticons, or **smileys**, are a series of typed characters that, when turned sideways, resemble a face and express an emotion. Here are some smileys often encountered on the Internet.

:-)	Smile	:-D	Laugh	:-(	Unhappy	:-b..	Drooling
;-)	Wink	:-*	Kiss	:-o	Surprised	{*}	A hug and a kiss

Nations with the Most Internet Users, 2008

Source: Computer Industry Almanac at www.c-i-a.com for year-end 2008

Rank Country	Internet users[1]	% of worldwide users	Rank Country	Internet users[1]	% of worldwide users	Rank Country	Internet users[1]	% of worldwide users
1. China	235,100	14.76%	7. Brazil	41,170	2.59%	13. Canada. . . .	26,060	1.64%
2. U.S.	234,240	14.71	8. France	39,460	2.48	14. Mexico	25,450	1.60
3. India	108,410	6.81	9. Italy	37,370	2.35	15. Spain	22,910	1.44
4. Japan	99,010	6.22	10. S.Korea . . .	36,940	2.32	Top 15 total	1,077,230	67.65
5. Germany . . .	57,030	3.58	11. Russia	35,890	2.25			
6. UK	44,890	2.82	12. Indonesia . .	33,300	2.09	World total.	1,592,404	100.00

(1) In thousands.

U.S. Broadband Internet Access, 2008-09

Source: Horrigan, John B., Home Broadband Adoption 2009, Pew Internet & American Life Project, June 17, 2009

	% with broadband at home		Percentage increase,		% with broadband at home		Percentage increase,
	2008	2009	2008-09		2008	2009	2008-09
Total.	55%	63%	15%	**Race/ethnicity**			
Gender				White (not Hispanic)	57%	65%	14%
Male.	58	64	10	Black (not Hispanic)	43	46	7
Female	53	63	19	Hispanic (English-speaking)	56	68	21
Age				**Annual household income**			
18-29.	70	77	10	Under $20K	25	35	40
30-49.	69	72	4	$20K-$30K	42	53	26
50-64.	50	61	22	$30K-$40K	49	54	10
65+	19	30	58	$40K-$50K	60	71	18
Educational attainment				$50K-$75K	67	80	19
Less than high school	28	30	7	$75K-$100K	82	82	0
High school grad	40	52	30	Over $100K	85	88	4
Some college.	66	71	8	**Community type**			
College+	79	83	5	Nonrural	59	67	13
				Rural.	38	46	21

NA = Not applicable. **Note:** 2008 data comes from the Pew Internet Project's Apr.-May survey of 2,251 adults; 1,153 were home broadband users. 2009 data comes from the Pew Internet Project's Apr. survey of 2,253 adults; 1,332 were home broadband users.

Most-Visited Websites, Aug. 2009

Source: comScore Media Metrix, Inc.

Some websites represent an aggregation of commonly owned domain names; popular domains within a group added in parenthesis by World Almanac editors.

Overall Visitors

Rank	Website	Visitors[1]	Rank	Website	Visitors[1]
1.	Google Sites (YouTube; Blogger)	161,148	11.	Apple Inc. (iTunes)	56,608
2.	Yahoo! Sites (Flickr; Delicious)	158,043	12.	CBS Corporation	52,781
3.	Microsoft Sites (Bing)	129,992	13.	Glam Media	51,250
4.	America Online LLC (Mapquest; TMZ)	101,719	14.	Viacom Digital (MTV; BET; Paramount)	50,123
5.	Facebook.com	92,208	15.	Turner Network	48,562
6.	Fox Interactive Media (MySpace; Photobucket). . .	77,450	16.	craigslist, inc.	47,130
7.	Ask Network (Evite; Dictionary.com)	76,595	17.	New York Times Digital (About.com)	45,754
8.	eBay (PayPal; Skype; Stubhub).	71,788	18.	Answers.com Sites	45,082
9.	Amazon Sites (IMDb)	68,103	19.	Weather Channel, The	41,684
10.	Wikimedia Foundation Sites (Wikipedia)	63,929	20.	Adobe Sites	39,613

Social Networking

Rank	Website	Visitors[1]	Rank	Website	Visitors[1]
1.	Facebook.com	92,208	6.	Betawave Partners	12,146
2.	MySpace	64,242	7.	MyLife.com Sites	11,394
3.	Twitter.com	20,830	8.	Windows Live Profile	10,280
4.	Digg.com	17,410	9.	Buzz Media.	10,140
5.	Classmates.com Sites	13,939	10.	LinkedIn.com	8,744

Blog Networks

Rank	Website	Visitors[1]	Rank	Website	Visitors[1]
1.	Blogger	51,663	6.	BlogHer.	7,001
2.	WordPress.	26,443	7.	Gawker Media	6,990
3.	Federated Media Publishing	21,709	8.	Hubpages.com	6,230
4.	Technorati Media.	19,736	9.	Windows Live Spaces.	2,957
5.	Six Apart Sites.	13,954	10.	b5media	2,139

Search/Navigation

Rank	Website	Visitors[1]
1.	Google Search	140,038
2.	Yahoo! Search	89,668
3.	Ask Network	76,595
4.	Bing	63,761
5.	AOL Search Network	27,550

E-mail

Rank	Website	Visitors[1]
1.	Yahoo! Mail.	106,621
2.	Windows Live Hotmail	46,692
3.	MySpace Mail	40,417
4.	Google Gmail	38,831
5.	AOL Email.	34,906

(1) Number of visitors, in thousands, who visited website at least once in Aug. 2009.

Internet Access in the U.S., 2000-08

Source: 2009 Digital Future Report, USC Annenberg School Center for the Digital Future

Type of Internet access	% of Americans accessing internet[1]						Avg. hours per week spent online[1]					
	2000	2002	2005	2006	2007	2008	2000	2002	2005	2006	2007	2008
All access	67	71	79	78	79	80	9.4	11.1	13.3	14.0	15.3	17.3
at home	47	59	66	68	66	72	3.3	6.8	7.8	8.9	10.0	10.1
at school[2]	55	63	67	67	70	66	NA	NA	NA	NA	NA	NA
at work[3]	42	40	55	56	52	59	NA	5.5	5.6	7.8	7.4	8.3
by cell phone/mobile devices[4]	NA	5	9	11	13	16	NA	NA	2.0	1.8	1.4	1.7
by wireless computer[4]	NA	3	7	11	27	32	NA	NA	5.7	8.6	7.2	9.7

NA = Not available. (1) Internet users age 12 and older who connect from all locations. (2) Adult respondents with children in household. (3) Work outside the home. (4) Via wireless device.

Frequency of Internet Activities in the U.S., 2008

Source: 2009 Digital Future Report, USC Annenberg School Center for the Digital Future

(among Internet users age 12 and older who connect from any location)

Online activities	Daily[1]	Weekly	Monthly	Occas-ionally	Never	Online activities	Daily[1]	Weekly	Monthly	Occas-ionally	Never
Browse (surf)	51%	23%	9%	7%	9%	Find or check a fact	11%	23%	19%	25%	24%
Pay bills	3	17	28	7	44	Read blogs	9	10	8	16	56
Use E-mail	78	14	3	1	3	Watch/download videos	9	16	10	13	52
Read news	37	23	12	14	16	Make/receive phone calls	3	3	1	4	90
Social networking or video sharing	24	20	NA	20	37	Work on a blog	2	4	4	6	84
Play games	20	13	8	12	47	Buy products/services	2	11	32	38	17
Instant message	17	12	7	14	51	Gamble	2	2	2	8	87
Listen/download music	16	18	12	18	36						

(1) One or more times daily.

Informative and Useful Websites[1]

Name	URL	Description
Daily Data		
MetaFilter	www.metafilter.com	A community weblog where users share and discuss interesting links.
ResourceShelf	www.resourceshelf.com	Librarians and researchers share the websites they find.
Shorpy	www.shorpy.com	"The 100-year-old photography blog" provides a continuous supply of historical photos.
Today's Front Pages	www.newseum.org/todaysfrontpages	Today's front page from more than 500 newspapers worldwide.
Education and Exhibits		
American Memory	memory.loc.gov	More than 5 million items from the Library of Congress, including audio, maps, movies, photos, prints, and sheet music.
British Library	www.bl.uk/onlinegallery/	Scanned rarities from (among others) Gutenberg, Shakespeare, Leonardo as well as audio, maps, music, and photos.
Internet Archive	www.archive.org	Digital library of free cultural artifacts and Internet sites.
Library of Congress	www.loc.gov/exhibits	Online counterparts to LOC exhibits since 1992.
MIT OpenCourseWare	ocw.mit.edu	Free and open educational course material from Massachusetts Institute of Technology.
New York Public Library Digital Gallery	digitalgallery.nypl.org	More than 550,000 images digitized from primary sources and printed rarities in the library's collections.
Our Documents	www.ourdocuments.gov	Digitized images and text of 100 milestone documents from America's history.
World Digital Library	www.wdl.org	Collection of significant primary documents from countries around the world.
Statistics		
FedStats	www.fedstats.gov	Find statistics by topic or program from more than 100 federal agencies.
Swivel	www.swivel.com	Community for users to visually map out and share statistics.
United Nations Statistics Division	unstats.un.org	International data sets and country profiles with demographics and stats on society, industry, and the environment.
U.S. Economy at a Glance	stats.bls.gov/eag	Quick reference tables on employment and wages from the Bureau of Labor Statistics.
Online Tools		
Kayak	www.kayak.com	One stop search of multiple travel-booking sites for the lowest fares and price trends.
LibraryThing	www.librarything.com	Track the books you've read, receive suggestions for new books, and compare lists with similar readers.
Open Congress	www.opencongress.org	Easily follow Congress and find news about specific members, bills, committees, and issues. Receive updates by RSS feed.
Downloadable Tools		
Google Earth	earth.google.com	Free downloadable interactive world atlas and mapping software.
Stellarium	www.stellarium.org	Free downloadable planetarium that visualizes astronomical phenomena in real time from any point on Earth.

(1) Websites are subject to change. The World Almanac cannot take responsibility for contents.

TELECOMMUNICATIONS

Worldwide Telecommunications: Market Data (1990-2008)

Source: © International Telecommunication Union

	1990	1999	2000	2004	2005	2006	2007	2008
Total market revenue (bil $)[1]	$508	$1,123	$1,210	NA	NA	NA	NA	NA
Intl. phone traffic (bil minutes)[2]	33	103	114	166	179	183	NA	NA
Main telephone lines (mil)	520	904	975	1,204	1,262	1,263	1,278	1,267
Mobile cellular subscriptions (mil)	11	490	738	1,763	2,219	2,757	3,305	4,100

NA = Not available. (1) Revenue from installation, subscription, and local, trunk, and international call charges. (2) From 1994, including traffic between countries of the former Soviet Union.

Top 50 Nations for Use of Cellular Telephones, 2008

Source: © International Telecommunication Union, estimated; top countries or regions ranked by subscriptions at year-end.

Country/region	Subscriptions (thousands)	per 100 pop.	Country/region	Subscriptions (thousands)	per 100 pop.
China	634,000.0	47.41	Colombia	41,364.8	91.90
India	346,890.0	29.36	Egypt	41,272.5	50.62
United States	270,500.0	86.79	Saudi Arabia	36,000.0	142.85
Russia	187,500.0	132.61	Algeria	31,871.0	92.72
Brazil	150,641.4	78.47	Malaysia	27,125.0	100.41
Indonesia	140,578.2	61.83	Venezuela	27,083.8	96.31
Japan	110,395.0	86.73	Taiwan	25,412.5	110.31
Germany	107,245.0	130.37	Romania	24,467.0	114.54
Italy	88,580.0	148.61	Morocco	22,815.7	72.19
Pakistan	88,019.7	49.74	Australia	22,120.0	104.96
United Kingdom	75,565.4	123.41	Canada	21,455.2	64.51
Mexico	75,303.5	69.37	Peru	20,951.8	72.66
Vietnam	70,000.0	80.37	Netherlands	19,927.0	120.57
Philippines	68,101.8	75.38	Iraq	17,529.0	58.24
Turkey	65,824.1	89.05	Kenya	16,233.8	41.88
Nigeria	62,988.5	41.66	Guatemala	14,948.6	109.22
Thailand	62,000.0	92.01	Kazakhstan	14,910.6	96.06
France	57,972.0	93.45	Portugal	14,909.6	139.64
Ukraine	55,694.5	121.09	Chile	14,796.6	88.05
Spain	49,681.6	111.68	Greece	13,799.3	123.90
Argentina	46,508.8	116.61	Czech Republic	13,780.2	133.54
South Korea	45,607.0	94.71	Tanzania	13,006.8	30.62
South Africa	45,000.0	90.60	Uzbekistan	12,733.7	46.52
Bangladesh	44,640.0	27.90	Hungary	12,224.2	122.09
Poland	44,004.0	115.48			
Iran	43,000.0	58.65	**World**	**4,017,817.9**	**59.33**

U.S. Wireless Industry, 1985-2008[1]

Source: The CTIA Semi-Annual Industry Survey, used with permission of CTIA

Date	Est. total subscribers	Twelve-month total service revenues (in $000s)	Cell phone antennas	Avg. local monthly bill	Avg. local call length (min.)
1985	340,213	$482,428	913	NA	NA
1987	1,230,855	1,151,519	2,305	$96.83	2.33
1988	2,069,441	1,959,548	3,209	98.02	2.26
1989	3,508,944	3,340,595	4,169	89.30	2.48
1990	5,283,055	4,548,820	5,616	80.90	2.20
1991	7,557,148	5,708,522	7,847	72.74	2.38
1992	11,032,753	7,822,726	10,307	68.68	2.58
1993	16,009,461	10,892,175	12,824	61.49	2.41
1994	24,134,421	14,229,922	17,920	56.21	2.24
1995	33,785,661	19,081,239	22,663	51.00	2.15
1996	44,042,992	23,634,971	30,045	47.70	2.32
1997	55,312,293	27,485,633	51,600	42.78	2.31
1998	69,209,321	33,133,175	65,887	39.43	2.39
1999	86,047,003	40,018,489	81,698	41.24	2.38
2000	109,478,031	52,466,020	104,288	45.27	2.56
2001	128,374,512	65,316,235	127,540	47.37	2.74
2002	140,766,842	76,508,187	139,338	48.40	2.73
2003	158,721,981	87,624,093	162,986	49.91	3.07
2004	182,140,362	102,121,210	175,725	50.64	3.05
2005	207,896,198	113,538,221	183,689	49.98	3.00
2006	233,040,781	125,456,825	195,613	50.56	3.03
2007	255,395,599	138,869,304	213,299	49.79	NA
2008	270,333,881	148,084,170	242,130	50.07	2.27

NA = Not available. (1) In Dec. of each year.

U.S. Sales and Household Penetration, Selected Products[1], 1985-2009

Source: Consumer Electronics Association

	1985		1990		1995		2000		2008		2009 (est.)	
	Sales[2]	% of all house-holds	Sales[2]	% of all house-holds	Sales[2]	% of all house-holds	Sales[2]	% of all house-holds	Sales[2]	% of all house-holds	Sales[2]	% of all house-holds
Cordless telephones	$280	11	$842	28	$1,141	55	$1,307	80	$330	NA	$315	NA
Pagers	—	—	118	1	300	11	750	23	191	NA	64	NA
Modems/fax modems	10	0	191	2.7	770	16	1,564	55	1,090	NA	1,110	NA
Telephone answering devices	325	7	827	35	1,077	57	984	75	954	NA	747	NA
Cellular phones	116	0.1	1,098	5	2,574	29	8,995	60	22,814	NA	20,811	NA

NA = Not available. (1) Data may differ slightly from other sources. (2) In millions of dollars.

Telephone Area Codes, by Number

As of Oct. 2009.

Code	Location or Service	Code	Location or Service	Code	Location or Service	Code	Location or Service
201	New Jersey	404	Georgia	614	Ohio	808	Hawaii
202	District of Columbia	405	Oklahoma	615	Tennessee	809	Dominican Republic
203	Connecticut	406	Montana	616	Michigan	810	Michigan
204	Manitoba	407	Florida	617	Massachusetts	*811*	*Pipeline excavation*
205	Alabama	408	California	618	Illinois		*damage prevention*
206	Washington	409	Texas	619	California	812	Indiana
207	Maine	410	Maryland	620	Kansas	813	Florida
208	Idaho	*411*	*Directory Assistance*	623	Arizona	814	Pennsylvania
209	California	412	Pennsylvania	626	California	815	Illinois
210	Texas	413	Massachusetts	630	Illinois	816	Missouri
211	*Community Info.*	414	Wisconsin	631	New York	817	Texas
212	New York	415	California	636	Missouri	818	California
213	California	416	Ontario	641	Iowa	819	Quebec
214	Texas	417	Missouri	646	New York	828	North Carolina
215	Pennsylvania	418	Quebec	647	Ontario	829	Dominican Republic
216	Ohio	419	Ohio	649	Turks & Caicos Isl.	830	Texas
217	Illinois	423	Tennessee	650	California	831	California
218	Minnesota	424	California	651	Minnesota	832	Texas
219	Indiana	425	Washington	657	California	843	South Carolina
224	Illinois	430	Texas	660	Missouri	845	New York
225	Louisiana	432	Texas	661	California	847	Illinois
226	Ontario	434	Virginia	662	Mississippi	848	New Jersey
228	Mississippi	435	Utah	664	Montserrat	849	Dominican Republic
229	Georgia	438	Quebec	670	N. Mariana Islands	850	Florida
231	Michigan	440	Ohio	671	Guam	856	New Jersey
234	Ohio	441	Bermuda	678	Georgia	857	Massachusetts
239	Florida	443	Maryland	681	West Virginia	858	California
240	Maryland	450	Quebec	682	Texas	859	Kentucky
242	Bahamas	456	Inbound Intl.	684	American Samoa	860	Connecticut
246	Barbados	469	Texas	*700*	*IC Services*	862	New Jersey
248	Michigan	473	Grenada	701	North Dakota	863	Florida
250	British Columbia	478	Georgia	702	Nevada	864	South Carolina
251	Alabama	479	Arkansas	703	Virginia	865	Tennessee
252	North Carolina	480	Arizona	704	North Carolina	*866*	*Toll-Free Service*
253	Washington	484	Pennyslvania	705	Ontario	867	Yukon, NW Terr., Nunavut
254	Texas	*500*	*Personal Comm. Serv.*	706	Georgia	868	Trinidad & Tobago
256	Alabama	501	Arkansas	707	California	869	St. Kitts & Nevis
260	Indiana	502	Kentucky	708	Illinois	870	Arkansas
262	Wisconsin	503	Oregon	709	Newfoundland	876	Jamaica
264	Anguilla	504	Louisiana	710	U.S. Government	*877*	*Toll-Free Service*
267	Pennsylvania	505	New Mexico	*711*	*Telecommunications*	878	Pennsylvania
268	Antigua/Barbuda	506	New Brunswick		*Relay Service (TRS)*	*880*	*Paid Toll-Free Serv.*
269	Michigan	507	Minnesota	712	Iowa	*881*	*Paid Toll-Free Serv.*
270	Kentucky	508	Massachusetts	713	Texas	*882*	*Paid Toll-Free Serv.*
276	Virginia	509	Washington	714	California	*888*	*Toll-Free Service*
281	Texas	510	California	715	Wisconsin	*900*	*Premium Service*
284	British Virgin Islands	*511*	*Traffic Info.*	716	New York	901	Tennessee
289	Ontario	512	Texas	717	Pennsylvania	902	Nova Scotia, Prince Ed. Isl.
301	Maryland	513	Ohio	718	New York	903	Texas
302	Delaware	514	Quebec	719	Colorado	904	Florida
303	Colorado	515	Iowa	720	Colorado	905	Ontario
304	West Virginia	516	New York	724	Pennsylvania	906	Michigan
305	Florida	517	Michigan	727	Florida	907	Alaska
306	Saskatchewan	518	New York	731	Tennessee	908	New Jersey
307	Wyoming	519	Ontario	732	New Jersey	909	California
308	Nebraska	520	Arizona	734	Michigan	910	North Carolina
309	Illinois	530	California	740	Ohio	*911*	*Emergency*
310	California	540	Virginia	747	California	912	Georgia
311	*Non-Emergency Access*	541	Oregon	754	Florida	913	Kansas
312	Illinois	551	New Jersey	757	Virginia	914	New York
313	Michigan	559	California	758	St. Lucia	915	Texas
314	Missouri	561	Florida	760	California	916	California
315	New York	562	California	762	Georgia	917	New York
316	Kansas	563	Iowa	763	Minnesota	918	Oklahoma
317	Indiana	567	Ohio	765	Indiana	919	North Carolina
318	Louisiana	570	Pennsylvania	767	Dominica	920	Wisconsin
319	Iowa	571	Virginia	769	Mississippi	925	California
320	Minnesota	573	Missouri	770	Georgia	928	Arizona
321	Florida	574	Indiana	772	Florida	931	Tennessee
323	California	575	New Mexico	773	Illinois	936	Texas
325	Texas	580	Oklahoma	774	Massachusetts	937	Ohio
330	Ohio	581	Quebec	775	Nevada	939	Puerto Rico
331	Illinois	585	New York	778	British Columbia	940	Texas
334	Alabama	586	Michigan	779	Illinois	941	Florida
336	North Carolina	587	Alberta	780	Alberta	947	Michigan
337	Louisiana	*600*	*Canadian Services*	781	Massachusetts	949	California
339	Massachusetts	601	Mississippi	784	St. Vincent & Gren.	951	California
340	U.S. Virgin Islands	602	Arizona	785	Kansas	952	Minnesota
345	Cayman Islands	603	New Hampshire	786	Florida	954	Florida
347	New York	604	British Columbia	787	Puerto Rico	956	Texas
351	Massachusetts	605	South Dakota	*800*	*Toll-Free Service*	970	Colorado
352	Florida	606	Kentucky	801	Utah	971	Oregon
360	Washington	607	New York	802	Vermont	972	Texas
361	Texas	608	Wisconsin	803	South Carolina	973	New Jersey
385	Utah	609	New Jersey	804	Virginia	978	Massachusetts
386	Florida	610	Pennsylvania	805	California	979	Texas
401	Rhode Island	*611*	*Repair Service*	806	Texas	980	North Carolina
402	Nebraska	612	Minnesota	807	Ontario	985	Louisiana
403	Alberta	613	Ontario			989	Michigan

POSTAL INFORMATION

Basic U.S. Postal Service

The Postal Reorganization Act, creating a government-owned postal service under the executive branch and replacing the old Post Office Department, was signed into law by Pres. Richard Nixon, Aug. 12, 1970. The service officially came into being on July 1, 1971. The U.S. Postal Service is governed by an 11-person board of governors. Nine of the members are appointed by the president, with Senate approval. These 9 choose a postmaster general. The board and the postmaster general choose the 11th member, who serves as deputy postmaster general.

Congress passed the Postal Accountability and Enhancement Act, which overhauled postal service operations for the first time since 1971, on Dec. 8, 2006. New operating provisions included the ability to adjust rates annually, negotiate for contracts, and invest profits in internal improvements.

U.S. Domestic Rates

(Domestic rates apply to the U.S., to its territories and possessions, and to APOs and FPOs. Many changes in domestic postal rates, fees, and services took effect May 11, 2009.)

First-Class Mail

First-Class Mail includes written matter such as letters, postal cards, and postcards (private mailing cards), plus all other matter wholly or partly in writing, whether sealed or unsealed, except book manuscripts, periodical articles and music, manuscript copy accompanying proof sheets or corrected proof sheets of the same, and the writing authorized by law on matter of other classes. Also included: matter sealed or closed against inspection, bills, and statements of accounts.

Written letters and matter sealed against inspection cost **44¢** for first ounce, **17¢** for each additional ounce or fraction thereof. Postcard postage is **28¢**. Large envelopes, measuring up to 12 in. by 15 in., cost **88¢** for the first ounce and 17¢ for each additional ounce or fraction thereof. Presort- and automation-compatible mail can qualify for lower rates if certain piece minimums, mailing permits, and other requirements are met.

Express Mail

Express Mail provides guaranteed expedited service for any mailable article (up to 70 lbs and not over 108 in. in combined length and girth). Offers next day delivery by noon to most destinations; there is a $12.50 extra charge for Sunday or holiday delivery. Second-day service is available to locations not on the Next Day Delivery Network. Prices start at $13.05 for items weighing up to 8 oz., but are dependent on distance. All rates include insurance up to $100, shipment receipt, record of delivery at the destination post office, and free tracking.

Express Mail Flat Rate: $17.50, regardless of weight, if matter fits into a special Postal Service flat-rate envelope.

Pickup On Demand service is available for **$15.30** per stop, regardless of the number of pieces or service used.

Standard Mail

Standard Mail is limited to items less than 16 oz. such as solicitations, newsletters, advertising materials, books, cassettes, and other merchandise. It may not be used for personal correspondence. A minimum volume of 200 pieces or 50 lbs of such items is necessary, and specific bulk mail preparation and sortation requirements apply.

The minimum rate per piece for pieces 3.3 oz. or less is $0.330 for basic nonmachinable letters. Contact your post office for the discounts offered for automation, presorted, carrier route, destination entry, and other discounts. Separate rates are available for some nonprofit organizations.

Any mailer who uses standard mail is required to pay an annual fee of $185, good for 365 days. Additional standards apply to mailings of nonidentical-weight pieces.

Priority Mail

Due to expeditious handling and transportation, Priority Mail is delivered in 2 days, in most cases. Priority Mail may include any mailable article up to 70 lbs and not over 108 in. in length and girth combined, including written and other First-Class material.

Pickup On Demand service costs an additional $15.30, regardless of the number of pieces or service used (e.g., Express Mail, Priority Mail, or Parcel Post can be picked up together).

Priority Mail Flat Rate: $4.95, regardless of weight, if matter fits into a special Postal Service flat-rate envelope. **$10.35 or $13.95**, regardless of weight (under 70 lbs), if matter fits into special Postal Service flat-rate boxes.

Priority Mail Rates

Weight not over	ZONES						
	1-2	3	4	5	6	7	8
1 lb	$4.95	$4.95	$4.95	$4.95	$4.95	$4.95	$4.95
2	4.95	5.20	5.75	7.10	7.60	8.10	8.70
3	5.50	6.25	7.10	9.05	9.90	10.60	11.95
4	6.10	7.10	8.15	10.80	11.95	12.95	14.70
5	6.85	8.15	9.45	12.70	13.75	15.20	17.15
6	7.55	9.25	10.75	14.65	15.50	17.50	19.60
7	8.30	10.30	12.05	16.55	17.30	19.75	22.05
8	8.80	10.70	13.10	17.95	18.80	21.70	24.75
9	9.25	11.45	13.95	19.15	20.30	23.60	27.55
10	9.90	12.35	15.15	20.75	22.50	25.90	29.95
11	10.55	13.30	16.40	22.40	24.75	28.20	32.40
12	11.20	14.20	17.60	24.00	26.95	30.50	34.80
13	11.50	14.55	18.10	25.30	28.90	31.70	36.00
14	11.90	16.20	18.90	26.45	30.50	33.50	37.80
15[1]	12.40	15.85	19.85	27.25	31.15	33.85	38.60

(1) See postmaster for pieces over 15 lbs.

Periodicals

Periodicals include newspapers and magazines.

For the general public, the applicable Package Services or First-Class postage is paid for periodicals.

For publishers, rates vary according to the following:
(1) whether item is sent to same county,
(2) percentage of editorial and advertising matter,
(3) whether the publishing org. is nonprofit or produces educational material for use in classrooms,
(4) weight,
(5) distance,
(6) level of presort, and
(7) automation compatibility.

Historical Postage Rates

Postage cost for a prepaid, one-ounce letter (the first-class standard after July 1, 1885).

Effective date	Rate	2009 Dollars	Effective date	Rate	2009 Dollars	Effective date	Rate	2009 Dollars
July 1, 1851	$0.06[1]	$1.57	Jan. 7, 1968	$0.06	$0.37	Feb. 3, 1991	$0.29	$0.46
July 1, 1863	0.06	1.06	May 16, 1971	0.08	0.42	Jan. 1, 1995	0.32	0.45
Oct. 1, 1883	0.04	0.93	Mar. 2, 1974	0.10	0.43	Jan. 10, 1999	0.33	0.42
July 1, 1885	0.02	0.48	Dec. 31, 1975	0.13	0.52	Jan. 7, 2001	0.34	0.41
Nov. 2, 1917[2]	0.03	0.50	May 29, 1978	0.15	0.49	June 30, 2002	0.37	0.44
July 1, 1919	0.02	0.25	Mar. 22, 1981	0.18	0.42	Jan. 8, 2006	0.39	0.41
July 6, 1932	0.03	0.47	Nov. 1, 1981	0.20	0.47	May 14, 2007	0.41	0.42
Aug.1, 1958	0.04	0.30	Feb. 17, 1985	0.22	0.44	May 12, 2008	0.42	0.42
Jan. 7, 1963	0.05	0.35	Apr. 3, 1988	0.25	0.45	May 11, 2009	0.44	0.44

(1) For domestic letters traveling under 3,000 miles. (2) The price increased one cent during World War I; Congress restored the prewar rate in 1919.

Package Services

Package Services, formerly "Standard Mail (B)," is any mailable matter that is not included in First-Class or Periodicals (unless permitted or required by regulations). There are currently 5 subclasses of Package Services: Parcel Post, Parcel Select, Bound Printed Matter, Media Mail (formerly "Special Standard Mail"), and Library Mail.

The post office determines charges for Package Services according to the weight of the package in pounds and the zone distance shipped (Media Mail and Library Mail rates are determined by weight alone). There is no minimum weight; see separate headings for maximum weight. Presort- and automation-compatible mail for all Package Services can qualify for lower rates if certain piece minimums, mailing permits, and other requirements are met. Contact your local post office for further information. Package Services is not sealed against postal inspection.

Parcel Post

Parcel Post is any Package Services not mailed as Bound Printed Matter, Media Mail, or Library Mail. (Parcel Select, a separate service, is used for medium-to-large volumes of packages.) Any Package Services matter may be mailed at the Parcel Post rates, subject to these basic standards: not to exceed 70 lbs or 130 in. in combined length and girth (packages over 84 in., but not more than 108 in. in combined length and girth and under 20 lbs are subject to the 20 lb "balloon price"). All fractions of a pound are counted as a full pound. Parcel Post subclass consists of two basic retail rate categories and three drop-shipped categories, the latter collectively known as Parcel Select.

Parcel Post Basic Rates

(Inter BMC/ASF ZIP codes only, machinable[1] parcels, no discount, no surcharge)

Weight not over	ZONES						
	1-2	3	4	5	6	7	8
1 lb	$4.90	$4.90	$4.90	$4.90	$4.90	$4.90	$4.90
2	4.90	5.15	5.70	7.02	7.33	7.62	8.09
3	5.45	6.20	7.05	8.18	8.85	9.27	9.92
4	6.05	7.05	7.94	9.20	10.05	10.66	11.57
5	6.80	8.10	9.02	10.05	10.78	11.37	12.34
6	7.50	9.20	9.94	10.94	11.45	12.02	13.03
7	8.25	10.00	10.49	11.80	12.36	13.01	14.15
8	8.56	10.34	10.86	12.17	12.96	13.74	15.03
9	8.87	10.69	11.24	12.55	13.56	14.47	15.90
10	9.18	11.03	11.61	12.92	14.16	15.21	16.77
11	9.49	11.38	11.99	13.29	14.76	15.94	17.65
12	9.80	11.72	12.36	13.66	15.36	16.67	18.52
13	10.11	12.06	12.74	14.03	15.96	17.40	19.39
14	10.42	12.41	13.11	14.40	16.56	18.13	20.27
15	10.73	12.75	13.49	14.77	17.16	18.86	21.14
16	11.04	13.10	13.87	15.14	17.76	19.59	22.01
17	11.34	13.44	14.24	15.51	18.36	20.33	22.89
18	11.65	13.79	14.60	15.99	18.96	21.06	23.76
19	11.96	14.13	14.95	16.47	19.56	21.79	24.64
20[2]	12.27	14.48	15.30	16.94	20.16	22.52	25.51

(1) Machinable parcels must be not less than 6 in. long, 3 in. high, and 0.25 in. thick or more than 34 in. long, 17 in. high, and 17 in. thick; at least 6 oz. but not more than 35 lbs. (2) Consult postmaster for pieces greater than 20 lbs.

Library Mail

(minimum weight: none; maximum weight: 70 lbs)

Applies to books, printed music, bound academic theses, periodicals, sound recordings, museum materials, and other library materials mailed between schools, colleges, universities, public libraries, museums, veteran and fraternal organizations, and nonprofit religious, educational, scientific, and labor organizations or associations (or to or from these organizations). Advertising restrictions apply. All packages must be marked "Library Mail," and may not exceed 108 in. in combined length and girth. Contact your local post office for further information.

Rates are calculated by weight only. Single-piece rates: $2.26, up to 1 lb; 37¢ for each additional pound or fraction thereof.

Media Mail

(minimum weight: none; maximum weight: 70 lbs)

Applies to books of at least 8 printed pages; 16-mm or narrower-width films; printed music; printed test materials; sound recordings, playscripts, and manuscripts for books; printed educational charts; loose-leaf pages and binders consisting of medical information; computer-readable media. Advertising restrictions apply. Packages must be marked "Media Mail" and may not exceed 108 in. in combined length and girth. Contact your local post office for further information.

Rates are calculated by weight only. Single-piece rates: $2.38, up to 1 lb; additional pounds thereafter, 39¢ each.

Bound Printed Matter

(minimum weight: none; maximum weight: 15 lbs)

Applies to advertising, promotional, directory, or editorial material that is bound by permanent fastening and consists of sheets of which at least 90% are imprinted by any process other than handwriting or typewriting. Does not include stationery (or pads of blank forms) or personal correspondence. Packages may not exceed 108 in. in combined length and girth and must be marked "Bound Printed Matter" or "BPM."

Bound Printed Matter Rates

(zone rate for parcels)

Weight not over	ZONES						
	1-2	3	4	5	6	7	8
1.0 lb	$2.33	$2.37	$2.43	$2.52	$2.63	$2.69	$2.88
1.5	2.33	2.37	2.43	2.52	2.63	2.69	2.88
2.0	2.43	2.49	2.57	2.69	2.83	2.91	3.17
2.5	2.54	2.61	2.71	2.86	3.04	3.14	3.46
3.0	2.64	2.73	2.85	3.03	3.24	3.36	3.75
3.5	2.75	2.85	2.99	3.20	3.45	3.59	4.04
4.0	2.85	2.97	3.13	3.37	3.65	3.81	4.33
4.5	2.96	3.09	3.27	3.54	3.86	4.04	4.62
5.0	3.06	3.21	3.41	3.71	4.06	4.26	4.91
6.0	3.27	3.45	3.69	4.05	4.47	4.71	5.49
7.0	3.48	3.69	3.97	4.39	4.88	5.16	6.07
8.0	3.69	3.93	4.25	4.73	5.29	5.61	6.65
9.0	3.90	4.17	4.53	5.07	5.70	6.06	7.23
10.0	4.11	4.41	4.81	5.41	6.11	6.51	7.81
11.0	4.32	4.65	5.09	5.75	6.52	6.96	8.39
12.0	4.53	4.89	5.37	6.09	6.93	7.41	8.97
13.0	4.74	5.13	5.65	6.43	7.34	7.86	9.55
14.0	4.95	5.37	5.93	6.77	7.75	8.31	10.13
15.0	5.16	5.61	6.21	7.11	8.16	8.76	10.71

Domestic Mail Special Services

Delivery Confirmation

Applies to First-Class Mail parcels, Priority Mail, and Package Services. Available for purchase at the time of mailing only. Provides mailer with the date and time an article was delivered and, if delivery was attempted but not successful, the date and time of the attempt. Electronic confirmation is available for bar-coded matter.

Confirmation is accessible to retail purchasers on the Internet (www.usps.com) or toll-free by phone, (800) 222-1811).

Priority Mail fees: retail, 70¢; electronic, free. First-Class Mail parcels and Package Services fees: retail, 80¢; electronic, 19¢. Standard Mail fee: electronic, 19¢.

Change of Address

The USPS will forward mail to another address provided a Change of Address (COA) card has been filed, either in person (free), on www.usps.com ($1 fee), or by phone at (800) ASK-USPS ($1). The COA card, which can be picked up at any post office or printed off the Internet, can also be dropped in any mailbox for filing, free of charge.

Special Handling

Provides preferential handling, but not preferential delivery, to the extent practicable in dispatch and transportation. Available for First-Class Mail, Priority Mail, and Package Services for the following surcharge: up to 10 lb, $7.40; over 10 lb, $10.40. Pieces must be marked "Special Handling."

The USPS introduced the "Forever" stamp Apr. 12, 2007. The "Forever" stamp initially cost 41¢ and would always be valid as First-Class postage on standard envelopes weighing one ounce or less, even if rates change. The "Forever" stamp can be purchased at the current First-Class standard rate.

Registered Mail

Provides sender with mailing receipt, and a delivery record is maintained. Only matter prepaid with postage at First Class or Priority Mail rates may be registered. Stamps or meter stamps must be attached. The face of the article must be at least 5 in. long, 3½ in. high.

Declared value	Fee
$0.00	$10.60
$0.01 to $100.00	11.50
$100.01 to $500.00	13.10
$500.01 to $1,000.00	14.45
$1,000.01 to $2,000.00	15.80
$2,000.01 to $3,000.00	17.15
$3,000.01 to $4,000.00	18.50
$4,000.01 to $5,000.00	19.85
$5,000.01 to $6,000.00	21.20
$6,000.01 to $7,000.00	22.55
$7,000.01 to $8,000.00	23.90
$8,000.01 to $9,000.00	25.25
$9,000.01 to $10,000.00	26.60
$10,000.01 to $25,000.00	27.95 plus $1.35 for each $1,000 or fraction thereof over $10,000
$25,000.01 to $15 million	46.85 plus $1.35 for each $1,000 or fraction thereof over $25,000
Over $15 million	20,263.10 plus any additional amount determined by the Postal Service

Note: The mailer is required to declare the value of mail presented for registration. Fee for articles with declared value over $0.00 up to $25,000 includes insurance.

International Mail Special Services

Insurance: Available to many countries for loss of or damage to items paid at parcel post rate. Consult postmaster for indemnity limits for individual countries.

Priority Mail Intl. Insurance Rates

Limit of indemnity not over	Canada[1]	Other countries[1]
$50	$1.75	$2.50
$100	2.25	3.40
$200	2.75	4.40
$300	4.70	5.40
$400	5.70	6.40
$500	6.70	7.40
$600	7.70	8.40
$675	8.70	—
$700	—	9.40
Each additional $100 or fraction thereof	—	1.00

(1) Not all countries insure items up to the amounts listed in the table. Canada does not insure items for more than $675.

Collect on Delivery (C.O.D.): Fee: **$5.50** for up to $50; increases incrementally. Items must be sent as bona fide orders or be in conformity with agreements between senders and addressees. Maximum amount collectible is $1,000. For details, consult postmaster.

Certified mail: Available for any matter having no intrinsic value on which First Class or Priority Mail postage is paid. A receipt is furnished at the time of mailing, and evidence of delivery is obtained. Basic fee is **$2.80** in addition to regular postage. Return receipt and restricted delivery available upon payment of additional fees. No indemnity.

Insured Mail

Applicable to Standard Mail, Package Services, and First-Class or Priority Mail items eligible to be mailed as Package Services. Matter for sale addressed to prospective purchasers who have not ordered it or authorized its sending cannot be insured. **Note:** For Express Mail, insurance is included up to $100, and additional insurance can be purchased for slightly higher fees than those shown here.

Declared value	Insured mail fee[1]
$0.01 to $50.00	$1.75
$50.01 to $100.00	2.25
$100.01 to $200.00	2.75
$200.01 to $300.00	4.70
$300.01 to $400.00	5.70
$400.01 to $500.00	6.70
$500.01 to $600.00	7.70
$600.01 to $5,000.00	7.70 plus $1.00 per each $100 or fraction thereof over $600 in desired coverage

(1) In addition to postage. (Maximum liability is $5,000.) See postmaster for details on bulk discounts.

International postcards (single): 75¢ to Canada; 79¢ to Mexico; 98¢ to all other countries.

Registration: Available, for letter-post items only, to most countries. Fee: $11.50.

Return Receipt: Shows to whom and when delivered. Fee: $2.30 (must be purchased at time of mailing).

First-Class Mail International: Letter-post items weighing under 1 oz. can be sent airmail for 98¢ to most countries daily; 75¢ to Canada; 79¢ to Mexico.

International Reply Coupons (IRC): Provide foreign addressees with a prepaid means of responding to communications initiated by a U.S. sender. Each IRC is equivalent to the destination country's minimum postage rate for an unregistered airmail letter. Fee: $2.10 per coupon.

Restricted Delivery: Places restrictions on who receives an item. Available to many countries for registered mail; some limitations. Fee: $4.50.

Post Office-Authorized 2-Letter State Abbreviations

The abbreviations below are approved by the U.S. Postal Service for use in addresses.

Alabama	AL	Hawaii	HI	Missouri	MO	Pennsylvania	PA
Alaska	AK	Idaho	ID	Montana	MT	Puerto Rico	PR
American Samoa	AS	Illinois	IL	Nebraska	NE	Rhode Island	RI
Arizona	AZ	Indiana	IN	Nevada	NV	South Carolina	SC
Arkansas	AR	Iowa	IA	New Hampshire	NH	South Dakota	SD
California	CA	Kansas	KS	New Jersey	NJ	Tennessee	TN
Colorado	CO	Kentucky	KY	New Mexico	NM	Texas	TX
Connecticut	CT	Louisiana	LA	New York	NY	Utah	UT
Delaware	DE	Maine	ME	North Carolina	NC	Vermont	VT
District of Columbia	DC	Marshall Islands[1]	MH	North Dakota	ND	Virgin Islands	VI
Federated States of Micronesia[1]	FM	Maryland	MD	Northern Mariana Is.	MP	Virginia	VA
		Massachusetts	MA	Ohio	OH	Washington	WA
Florida	FL	Michigan	MI	Oklahoma	OK	West Virginia	WV
Georgia	GA	Minnesota	MN	Oregon	OR	Wisconsin	WI
Guam	GU	Mississippi	MS	Palau[1]	PW	Wyoming	WY

(1) Although an independent nation, this country is currently subject to domestic rates and fees.

Canadian Province and Territory Postal Abbreviations

Source: Canada Post

Alberta	AB	Newfoundland and Labrador	NL	Nunavut	NU	Quebec	QC
British Columbia	BC			Ontario	ON	Saskatchewan	SK
Manitoba	MB	Northwest Territories	NT	Prince Edward Island	PE	Yukon	YT
New Brunswick	NB	Nova Scotia	NS				

SOCIAL SECURITY AND WELFARE

Old-Age, Survivors, and Disability Insurance; Medicare; Supplemental Security Income; Temporary Assistance to Needy Families

Source: Social Security Administration; World Almanac research; provisions shown are as under current law, Sept. 2009

Social Security Benefits

Social Security benefits are based on a worker's **primary insurance amount (PIA)**, which is related by law to the average indexed monthly earnings (AIME) on which Social Security contributions have been paid. The full PIA is payable to a worker retiring at age 65 (plus a certain number of months after the 65th birthday, depending on birth year), and to an entitled disabled worker at any age. Spouses and children of retired or disabled workers and survivors of deceased workers receive set proportions of the PIA subject to a family maximum amount.

The PIA is calculated by applying varying percentages to succeeding parts of the AIME. The formula is adjusted annually to reflect changes in average annual wages.

Automatic increases in Social Security benefits are initiated for December of each year, assuming the Consumer Price Index (CPI) for the 3rd calendar quarter of the year increased relative to the base quarter, which is either the 3rd calendar quarter of the preceding year or the quarter in which an increase legislated by Congress became effective. The size of the benefit increase is determined by the percentage rise of the CPI between the quarters measured.

The **average monthly benefit** payable to all retired workers amounted to $1,153 in Dec. 2008. The average benefit for disabled workers in that month amounted to $1,063.

Minimum and maximum monthly retired-worker benefits payable for individuals who retired at age 65[1]

Year attaining age 65	Maximum benefit Payable at retirement	Payable effective Dec. 2008
1990	$975	$1,701
1995	1,199	1,762
1996	1,248	1,789
1997	1,326	1,847
1998	1,342	1,831
1999	1,373	1,848
2000	1,434	1,885
2001	1,538	1,952
2002	1,660	2,054
2003	1,721	2,100
2004	1,784	2,133
2005	1,874	2,181
2006	1,961	2,193
2007	1,998	2,163
2008	2,030	2,148
2009	2,172	2,172

(1) Assumes retirement at beginning of year.

Amount of Work Required

To qualify for benefits, the worker generally must have worked a certain length of time in covered employment. Just how long depends on when the worker reaches age 62 or, if earlier, when he or she dies or becomes disabled. A person born after 1929 who dies, becomes disabled, or reaches age 62 after 1991 must generally have had at least 10 years work credit to qualify for benefits.

Contribution and benefit base

Calendar year	OASDI[1]	Calendar year	OASDI[1]	Calendar year	OASDI[1]
1994	$60,600	2000	$76,200	2005	$90,000
1995	61,200	2001	80,400	2006	94,200
1996	62,700	2002	84,900	2007	97,500
1997	65,400	2003	87,000	2008	102,000
1998	68,400	2004	87,900	2009	106,800
1999	72,600				

(1) Old-Age, Survivors, and Disability Ins.

A person is **fully insured** who has 1 quarter of coverage for every year after 1950 (or year age 21 is reached, if later) up to but not including the year the worker reaches 62, dies, or becomes disabled. In 2009, a person earns 1 quarter of coverage for each $1,090 of annual earnings in covered employment, up to 4 quarters per year.

To receive **disability benefits**, the worker, in addition to being fully insured, must generally have credit for 20 quar-

ters of coverage out of the 40 calendar quarters before he or she became disabled. A disabled blind worker need meet only the fully insured requirement. Persons disabled before age 31 can qualify with a briefer period of coverage. Certain survivor benefits are payable if the deceased worker had 6 quarters of coverage in the 13 quarters preceding death.

Tax Rate Schedule
(percentage of covered earnings)

Year	Total (for employees and employers, each)	OASDI	HI
1979-80	6.13%	5.08%	1.05%
1981	6.65	5.35	1.30
1982-83	6.70	5.40	1.30
1984	7.00	5.70	1.30
1985	7.05	5.70	1.35
1986-87	7.15	5.70	1.45
1988-89	7.51	6.06	1.45
1990 and after	7.65	6.20	1.45
	(for self-employed)		
1979-80	8.10%	7.05%	1.05%
1981	9.30	8.00	1.30
1982-83	9.35	8.05	1.30
1984	14.00	11.40	2.60
1985	14.10	11.40	2.70
1986-87	14.30	11.40	2.90
1988-89	15.02	12.12	2.90
1990 and after	15.30	12.40	2.90

What Aged Workers Receive

A person may receive monthly old-age benefits when he or she has enough work in covered employment and has reached retirement age—age 62 for reduced benefits, the age below for full benefits.

Full-Benefit Retirement Age (FRA) by birth year

Year of birth	FRA	Year of birth	FRA
1937 or earlier	65	1955	66 and 2 months
1938	65 and 2 months	1956	66 and 4 months
1939	65 and 4 months	1957	66 and 6 months
1940	65 and 6 months	1958	66 and 8 months
1941	65 and 8 months	1959	66 and 10 months
1942	65 and 10 months	1960 or later	67
1943-54	66		

Note: If born on Jan. 1, refer to the previous birth year.

In 2000, the retirement **earnings test** was eliminated beginning with the month when the beneficiary reaches **full-benefit retirement age (FRA)**. A person at and above FRA no longer has benefits reduced because of earnings. However, in the calendar year a beneficiary reaches FRA, benefits are reduced $1 for every $3 of earnings above the limit allowed by law ($37,680 in 2009) for the months prior to FRA. For years before the beneficiary attains FRA, the reduction is $1 for every $2 of earnings over the exempt amount ($14,160 in 2009).

For workers who reached age 65 between 1982 and 1989, Social Security benefits are raised by 3% for each year for which the worker between FRA and 70 (72 before 1984) failed to receive benefits, whether because of earnings from work, because the worker had not applied for benefits, or because the worker declined benefits after entitlement. The **delayed retirement credit** is 1% per year for workers who reached age 65 before 1982. The delayed retirement credit rose to 8% per year for 2008 and years after. The rate for workers who reached age 65 in 1998-99 is 5.5%; 2000-01, 6.0%; 2002-03, 6.5%; 2004-05, 7.0%. For 2006-07 it is 7.5%.

For workers retiring early, before full retirement age, benefits are **permanently reduced** $5/9$ of 1% for each month before FRA, up to 36 months. If the number of months exceeds 36, then the benefit is further reduced $5/12$ of 1% per month.

For example, when FRA reaches 67, for workers who retire at exactly age 62, there are a total of 60 months of reduction. The reduction for the first 36 months is $5/9$ of 36%, or 20%. The reduction for the remaining 24 months is $5/12$ of 24%, or 10%. Thus, when the FRA reaches 67, the amount of reduction at age 62 will be 30%. The nearer to FRA the worker is when he or she begins collecting a benefit, the larger the monthly benefit will be.

Benefits for Worker's Spouse

The spouse of a worker who is getting Social Security retirement or disability payments may become entitled to an insurance benefit of **one-half of the worker's PIA** if he or she claims benefits at full retirement age. Reduced spouse's benefits are available at age 62 and are permanently reduced $^{25}/_{36}$ of 1% for each month before FRA, up to 36 months. If the number of months exceeds 36, then the benefit is further reduced $^5/_{12}$ of 1% per month. Benefits are also payable to the aged divorced spouse of an insured worker if he or she was married to the worker for at least 10 years. To qualify for divorced spouse benefits, the insured worker does not have to be receiving benefits if the divorce occurred at least 2 years earlier. Benefits received as a spouse are reduced by the amount of one's own PIA based on their own earnings.

Benefits for Children of Workers

If a retired or disabled worker has a child under age 18, the **child** will usually get a benefit equal to half of the worker's unreduced benefit. So will the worker's spouse, even if under age 62, if he or she is **caring for an entitled child** of the worker who is under 16 or became disabled before age 22. However, total benefits paid on a worker's earnings record are subject to a family maximum. Total monthly benefits paid to the family of a worker who retired in 2009 at age 66 and always had the maximum earnings creditable under Social Security cannot exceed $4,104.

When entitled children reach age 18, their benefits generally stop, but a child disabled before age 22 may get a benefit as long as the disability meets the definition in the law. Benefits will be paid until age 19 to a child attending elementary or secondary school full-time.

Benefits may also be paid to a grandchild or step-grandchild of a worker or of his or her spouse, in special circumstances.

OASDI beneficiaries

Beneficiaries	May 2006	May 2007	May 2008	May 2009
Total (in thousands)[1]	48,877	49,614	50,417	51,800
Aged 65 and over, total ...	34,232	34,752	35,478	36,182
Retired workers	27,897	28,448	29,152	29,920
Disabled workers	143	200	285	336
Survivors/dependents ..	6,192	6,105	6,041	5,926
Under age 65, total.......	14,645	14,862	14,939	15,618
Retired workers	2,883	2,874	2,749	3,002
Disabled workers	6,465	6,702	6,924	7,227
Survivors/dependents ..	5,297	5,286	5,266	5,389
Total monthly benefits (in millions)	$44,956	$47,592	$49,948	$54,797

(1) Totals may not add because of rounding or incomplete enumeration.

What Disabled Workers Receive

A worker who becomes unable to work may be eligible for a monthly **disability benefit**. Benefits continue until it is determined that the individual is no longer disabled. When a disabled-worker beneficiary reaches FRA (66 years for workers born in 1943), the disability benefit becomes a retired-worker benefit.

Benefits—generally like those for dependents of retired-worker beneficiaries—may be paid to dependents of disabled beneficiaries. However, the maximum family benefit in disability cases is generally lower than in retirement cases.

Survivor Benefits

If an insured worker should die, one or more types of benefits may be payable to survivors, again subject to a maximum family benefit as described above.

1. If claiming benefits at FRA, the **surviving spouse** will receive a benefit equal to 100% of the deceased worker's benefit. Benefits claimed before FRA are reduced for age with a maximum reduction of 28.5% at age 60. However, if the deceased worker claimed benefits before FRA, the surviving spouse's benefits are limited to the reduced amount the worker would be getting if alive, but not less than 82.5% of the worker's PIA. Remarriage after the worker's death ends the surviving spouse's benefit rights. However, if the widow(er) marries and the marriage is ended, he or she regains benefit rights. (A marriage after age 60, age 50 if disabled, is deemed not to have occurred for benefit purposes.) Survivor benefits may also be paid to a divorced spouse if the marriage lasted for at least 10 years.

Disabled widows and widowers may under certain circumstances qualify for benefits after attaining age 50 at the rate of 71.5% of the deceased worker's PIA. The widow or widower must have become totally disabled before or within 7 years after the spouse's death or the last month in which he or she received mother's or father's insurance benefits.

2. There is a benefit for each **child under age 18**. The monthly benefit for a child of a deceased worker is $^3/_4$ of the PIA, subject to the family maximum. A child with a disability that began before age 22 may also receive benefits. Also, a child may receive benefits until reaching age 19 if he or she is in full-time attendance at an elementary or secondary school.

3. There is a **mother's or father's benefit** for the widow(er) if children of the worker under age 16 are in his or her care. The benefit is 75% of the PIA (subject to the family maximum), and it continues until the youngest child reaches age 16, at which time payments stop even if the child's benefit continues. However, if the widow(er) has a disabled child beneficiary age 16 or over in care, benefits may continue.

4. **Dependent parents** may be eligible for benefits if they have been receiving at least half their support from the worker before his or her death, have reached age 62, and (except in certain circumstances) have not remarried since the worker's death. Each parent gets 75% of the worker's PIA; if only one parent survives, the benefit is 82%, but could be reduced for the family maximum.

5. A **lump sum** cash payment of **$255** is made when there is a spouse who was living with the worker or a spouse or child eligible for immediate monthly survivor benefits.

Self-Employed Workers

A self-employed person who has **net earnings of $400** or more in a year must report such earnings for Social Security tax and credit purposes. The person reports net returns from the business. Income from real estate, savings, dividends, loans, pensions, or insurance policies are not included unless it is part of the business.

A self-employed person receives 1 quarter of coverage for each $1,090 (for 2009), up to a maximum of 4 quarters per year.

The nonfarm self-employed have the option of reporting their earnings as $^2/_3$ of their gross income from self-employment. This option can be used only if actual net earnings from self-employment income are less than $1,600 and less than $^2/_3$ of their gross income. The option may be used only 5 times. Also, the self-employed person must have actual net earnings of $400 or more in 2 of the 3 taxable years immediately preceding the year in which he or she uses the option.

When a person has both taxable wages and earnings from self-employment, wages are credited for Social Security purposes first; only as much self-employment income as brings total earnings up to the current taxable maximum becomes subject to the self-employment tax.

Farm Owners and Workers

Self-employed farmers whose gross annual earnings from farming are from **$600-2,400** may report $^2/_3$ of their gross earnings instead of net earnings for Social Security purposes. (Farmers whose gross annual earnings are under $600 cannot use the optional method.) Farmers whose gross income is over $2,400 and whose net earnings are less than $1,600 can report $1,600. Cash or crop shares received from a tenant or share farmer count if the owner participated materially in production or management. The self-employed farmer pays contributions at the same rate as other self-employed persons.

Agricultural employees. A worker's earnings from farm work count toward benefits (1) if the employer pays the worker $150 or more in cash during the year; or (2) if the employer spends $2,500 or more in the year for agricultural labor. Under these rules, a person gets credit for 1 calendar quarter for each $1,090 in cash pay in 2009.

Foreign farm workers admitted to the U.S. on a temporary basis are not covered.

Household Workers

If an employer pays a household worker (e.g. maid, cook, laundry worker, nurse, babysitter, chauffeur, gardener, or other worker), who is age 18 or older, $1,700 or more in wages in 2009, the wages are covered under Social Security. This includes transportation costs paid for in cash. The job need not be regular or full-time. The employee should get a Social Security card at the Social Security office and show it to the employer. The employer deducts the amount of the employee's Social Security tax from the worker's pay, adds an identical amount as the employer's Social Security tax, and sends the total amount to the federal government.

Medicare Coverage

The Medicare health insurance program provides acute-care coverage for Social Security and Railroad Retirement beneficiaries age 65 and over, for persons entitled to receive Social Security or Railroad Retirement disability benefits, and for certain persons with end-stage kidney disease. What follows is a basic description and may not cover all circumstances.

The **basic Medicare plan**, available nationwide, is a fee-for-service arrangement, where the beneficiary may use any provider accepting Medicare; some services are not covered and there are some out-of-pocket costs.

Hospital insurance (Part A). The basic hospital insurance program pays covered services for hospital and post-hospital care including the following:
- All necessary inpatient hospital care for the first 60 days of each benefit period, except for a deductible ($1,068 in 2009). For days 61-90, Medicare pays for services over and above a coinsurance amount ($267 per day in 2009). After 90 days, the beneficiary has 60 lifetime reserve days for which Medicare helps pay. The coinsurance amount for reserve days was $534 in 2009.
- Up to 100 days of care in a skilled-nursing facility in each benefit period. Hospital insurance pays for all covered services for the first 20 days; for the 21-100th day, the beneficiary pays coinsurance ($134 per day in 2009).
- Part-time home health care provided by nurses or other health workers.
- Limited coverage of hospice care for individuals certified to be terminally ill.
- There is a premium for this insurance in certain cases.

Medical insurance (Part B). Elderly persons can receive benefits under this supplementary program only if they sign up for them and agree to a monthly premium. As of 2007, the monthly premium is tied to annual income. Individuals with income less than $85,000 and couples with income under $170,000 pay $96.40 per person if signing up upon becoming eligible in 2009. The federal government pays the covered costs of treatment. The Part B deductible was $135 in 2009; as of 2006, the deductible rose annually in proportion to the increase in average cost of Part B services to beneficiaries. After the deductible, the medical insurance program usually pays 80% of the approved amount for the following services:
- Covered services received from a doctor in his or her office, in a hospital, in a skilled-nursing facility, at home, or in other locations.
- Medical and surgical services, including anesthesia.
- Diagnostic tests and procedures that are part of the patient's treatment.
- Radiology and pathology services by doctors while the individual is a hospital inpatient or outpatient.
- Other services such as X-rays, services of a doctor's office nurse, drugs and biologicals that cannot be self-administered, transfusions of blood and blood components, medical supplies, physical/occupational therapy, and speech pathology services.

In addition to the above, certain other tests or preventive measures are now covered without an additional premium. These include a "Welcome to Medicare" physical exam and related services, mammograms, bone mass measurement, colorectal cancer screening, and flu shots. Routine physical exams, dental care, hearing aids, and routine eye care are generally not covered under the basic plan. There is limited coverage for nonhospital treatment of mental illness.

To get medical insurance (Part B), persons approaching age 65 may enroll in the **Initial Enrollment Period** that lasts from 3 months before to 3 months after the 65th birthday, and the month of their birthday. If new enrollers desire coverage to begin in the month they reach age 65, they must enroll in the 3 months before their birthday. Persons not enrolling within their first enrollment period may enroll later, but late-enrollment premiums may apply.

The monthly premium is deducted from the cash benefit for persons receiving Social Security, Railroad Retirement, or Civil Service retirement benefits. Income from the medical premiums and the federal matching payments are put in a Supplementary Medical Insurance Trust Fund, from which benefits and administrative expenses are paid.

Under **Medicare Advantage (Part C)** (formerly Medicare+ Choice), persons eligible for Medicare may have the option of getting services through a health maintenance organization (HMO) or other **managed care** plan. Any such plan must provide at least the same benefits, except for hospice services, and may provide added benefits—such as lower or no deductibles and coverage for some prescription drugs—but is usually subject to restrictions in choice of health care providers. In some plans services by outside providers are still covered for an extra out-of-pocket cost. Also available as options in some areas are Medicare-approved private fee-for-service plans and Medicare medical savings accounts.

Prescription Drug Coverage (Part D). Effective Jan. 1, 2006, a Medicare prescription drug plan provides insurance coverage for prescription drugs. Medicare recipients pay a monthly premium (averaging $28 in 2009, depending on the provider) and a portion of drug costs. **Enrollment is scheduled to take place Nov. 15-Dec. 31 each year**, and is optional. Coverage varies depending on the drug plan selected.

Part D Benefits
(parameters determined annually by the Centers for Medicare and Medicaid Services)

Standard benefit parameters	2008	2009
Deductible	$275	$295
Initial coverage limit	2,510	2,700
Out-of-pocket threshold	4,050	4,350
Minimum generic cost-sharing[1]	2.25	2.40
Minimum other drug cost-sharing	5.60	6.00
Retiree drug subsidy		
Cost threshold	$275	$295
Cost limit	5,600	6,000

(1) For generic/preferred multi-source drugs in the catastrophic phase.

Further details are available on the Internet at www.medicare.gov or by calling 1-800-MEDICARE (1-800-633-4227).

Medicare card. Persons qualifying for hospital insurance under Social Security receive a health insurance card similar to cards used by other health insurers. The card indicates whether the individual has taken out medical insurance protection. It is to be shown to the hospital, skilled-nursing facility, home health agency, doctor, or whoever provides the covered services.

Payments are generally made only in the 50 states, Puerto Rico, Virgin Islands, Guam, and American Samoa.

Social Security Financing

Social Security is paid for by a tax on certain earnings (for 2009, on earnings up to $106,800) for **Old Age, Survivors, and Disability Insurance** and on all earnings (no upper limit) for Hospital Insurance with the **Medicare** Program; the taxable earnings base for OASDI has been adjusted annually to reflect increases in average wages. The employed worker and his or her employer share Social Security taxes equally.

Employers remit amounts withheld from employee wages for Social Security and income taxes to the Internal Revenue Service; employer Social Security taxes are also payable at the same time. (Self-employed workers pay Social Security taxes when filing their regular income tax forms.) The Social Security taxes (along with revenues arising from partial taxation of the Social Security benefits of certain high-income people) are transferred to the Social Security Trust Funds; they can be used only to pay benefits, the cost of rehabilitation services, and administrative expenses. Money not immediately needed for these purposes is by law invested in obligations of the federal government, which must pay interest on the money borrowed and must repay the principal when the obligations are redeemed or mature.

Supplemental Security Income

On Jan. 1, 1974, the **Supplemental Security Income (SSI)** program established by the 1972 Social Security Act amendments replaced the former federal grants to states for aid to the needy aged, blind, and disabled in the 50 states and the District of Columbia. The program provides both for federal payments, based on uniform national standards and eligibility requirements, and for state supplementary payments varying from state to state. The Social Security Administration administers the federal payments financed from general funds of the Treasury—and the state supplements as well, if the state elects to have its supplementary program federally administered. States may supplement the federal payment for all recipients and must supplement it for persons otherwise adversely affected by the transition from the former public assistance programs. In May 2009, the number of persons receiving federally administered SSI payments was 7,596,745 and the payments totaled about $4.1 billion.

The **maximum** monthly federal SSI payment for individuals with no other countable income, living in their own household, was $674 in 2009. For couples the maximum payment was $1,011.

Social Security Statement

On Oct. 1, 1999, the Social Security Administration initiated regular mailings of an annual *Social Security Statement* to all workers age 25 and older not already receiving benefits. Workers will automatically receive statements about 3 months before their birth month. The statement provides estimates of potential monthly Social Security retirement, disability, and survivor benefits as well as a record of lifetime earnings. The statement also gives workers an easy way to determine whether their earnings are accurately posted in Social Security records.

For further information contact the Social Security Administration toll-free at 1-800-772-1213 or visit its website at www.socialsecurity.gov.

Examples of Monthly Benefits Available, 2009

Description of benefit or beneficiary	For low earnings ($18,756)[1]	For med. earnings ($41,680)[1]	For max. earnings ($95,047)[1,2]
Primary insurance amount (worker retiring at 66 years, 0 months) . . .	$900.50	$1,484.10	$2,323.80
Maximum family benefit (worker retiring at 66 years, 0 months)	1,350.80	2,708.10	4,066.80
Maximum family disability benefit (worker disabled at 55; in 2009) . . .	1,314.10	2,296.00	3,617.10
Disabled worker (worker disabled at 55)—			
Worker alone	926.00	1,530.00	2,411.00
Worker, spouse, and 1 child	1,314.00	2,296.00	3,617.00
Retired worker claiming benefits at age 62—			
Worker alone[3]	687.00	1,132.00	1,759.00
Worker with spouse claiming benefits at—			
NRA or over.	1,145.00	1,886.00	2,932.00
Age 62[3]	1,007.00	1,660.00	2,579.00
Widow or widower claiming benefits at—			
Age 66 or over[4]	900.00	1,484.00	2,323.00
Age 60[4]	643.00	1,061.00	1,661.00
Disabled widow or widower claiming benefits at age 50-59[5]	643.00	1,061.00	1,661.00
1 surviving child[4]	675.00	1,113.00	1,742.00
Widow or widower NRA or over and 1 child[4]	1,350.00	2,597.00	4,065.00
Widowed mother or father and 1 child[4].	1,350.00	2,226.00	3,484.00
Widowed mother or father and 2 children[4].	1,350.00	2,708.00	4,066.00

Effective Jan. 2009. (1) Career average earnings: an average of lifetime earnings indexed to the year prior to entitlement (2008 in this case). (2) Assumes work beginning at age 22. (3) Assumes maximum reduction. (4) Assumes worker lived and worked until NRA without receiving reduced benefits. (5) Effective Jan. 1984, disabled widow(er) claiming a benefit at ages 50-59 receive a benefit equal to 71.5% of the PIA.

Social Security Recipients[1] by Age, Sex, Race, and Hispanic Origin, 2008

Source: Social Security Administration

Social Security beneficiaries (thousands)	Total[2]	White	Black	American Indian, Alaska Native	Asian	Hispanic
Total	41,896	36,060	4,070	293	1,002	2,736
Sex						
Male	18,153	15,662	1,714	124	438	1,156
Female	23,743	20,398	2,356	169	564	1,580
Age						
15-54	4,731	3,584	906	62	81	475
55-64	5,609	4,647	690	64	119	424
65-74	16,102	13,978	1,387	98	455	1,077
75 or older	15,454	13,851	1,086	68	347	761
Supplemental Security Income recipients (thousands)						
Total	5,039	3,411	1,218	70	223	777
Sex						
Male	2,051	1,407	473	24	92	304
Female	2,989	2,004	745	47	130	473
Age						
15-54	2,933	2,004	768	30	51	406
55-64	969	697	206	19	29	144
65-74	572	331	150	6	72	116
75 or older	565	378	94	15	71	113
Average annual benefit in 2007						
Social Security	$11,759	$11,946	$10,419	$9,342	$11,717	$10,217
Supplemental Security Income.	6,550	6,706	6,267	5,160	6,677	6,153

Note: Race categories include people who reported themselves as that race alone or in combination with one or more other races. Persons of Hispanic origin may be of any race. (1) Persons 15 or older receiving Social Security benefits or Supplemental Security Income in Mar. 2008. (2) The sum of the individual categories may not equal the total because of independent rounding.

OASDI Recipients and Monthly Payments, 1940-2008

Source: Social Security Administration

Year	Total recipients	Total (thousands)	Avg.[1]	Avg. (2008 dollars[2])	Year	Total recipients	Total (thousands)	Avg.[1]	Avg. (2008 dollars[2])
		Monthly benefits					Monthly benefits		
1940	222,488	$4,070	$18.29	$262.88	1995	43,387,259	$28,148,078	$648.76	$877.93
1945	1,288,107	23,801	18.48	207.01	2000	45,414,794	34,848,920	767.35	920.77
1950	3,477,243	126,857	36.48	305.60	2001	45,877,506	36,504,206	795.69	929.33
1955	7,960,616	411,613	51.71	388.85	2002	46,444,317	37,854,453	815.05	939.18
1960	14,844,589	936,321	63.07	429.64	2003	47,038,486	39,541,528	840.62	947.45
1965	20,866,767	1,516,802	72.69	464.59	2004	47,687,722	41,574,363	871.80	957.70
1970	26,228,629	2,628,326	100.21	520.40	2005	48,434,445	44,351,772	915.71	971.74
1975	32,085,372	5,727,903	178.52	668.33	2006	49,122,831	46,938,176	955.53	982.29
1980	35,618,840	10,694,022	300.23	733.73	2007	49,864,982	49,218,232	987.03	1,024.93
1985	37,058,353	15,901,643	429.10	813.36	2008	50,898,396	53,666,202	1,054.38	1,054.38
1990	39,832,125	21,686,763	544.45	855.06					

Note: OASDI = Old Age, Survivors, and Disability Insurance. Disability insurance payments began in 1957. (1) Avg. monthly benefit does not necessarily reflect individual payments to OASDI recipients. (2) Monthly benefit adjusted for inflation.

Social Security Trust Funds
Old-Age and Survivors Insurance Trust Fund, 1940-2008
(in millions)

Fiscal year[1]	Total	Net contribs.[2]	Income from taxing benefits	Payments from the Treasury fund[3]	Net interest[4]	Total	Benefit payments[5]	Admin. expenses	Transfers to Railroad Retirement program	Net increase in fund[6]	Fund at end of period
			INCOME					DISBURSEMENTS			
1940	$592	$550	—	—	$42	$28	$16	$12	—	$564	$1,745
1950	2,367	2,106	—	$4	257	784	727	57	—	1,583	12,893
1960	10,360	9,843	—	—	517	11,073	10,270	202	$600	−713	20,829
1970	31,746	29,955	—	442	1,350	27,321	26,268	474	579	4,425	32,616
1980	100,051	97,608	—	557	1,886	103,228	100,626	1,160	1,442	−3,177	24,566
1990	278,607	261,506	$2,924	34	14,143	223,481	218,948	1,564	2,969	55,126	203,445
1995	326,067	289,529	5,114	7	31,417	294,456	288,607	1,797	4,052	31,611	447,946
2000	484,228	418,219	12,476	—	53,532	353,396	347,868	1,990	3,538	130,832	893,003
2001	513,834	440,819	11,771	—	61,243	372,996	367,654	2,069	3,273	140,837	1,033,840
2002	529,257	448,133	12,597	414	68,113	389,546	383,942	2,111	3,493	139,711	1,173,551
2003	542,343	456,014	12,340	—	73,990	402,814	396,710	2,522	3,580	139,530	1,313,080
2004	556,523	466,807	13,269	1	76,446	417,053	411,148	2,274	3,628	139,470	1,452,550
2005	599,992	502,998	15,332	—	81,662	436,919	430,439	2,900	3,579	163,073	1,615,623
2006	632,157	530,006	15,176	−350	87,324	455,560	449,191	2,911	3,458	176,597	1,792,220
2007	663,376	553,414	16,661	—	93,300	488,553	481,828	3,151	3,575	174,822	1,967,042
2008	692,873	573,750	16,396	—	102,727	509,864	502,973	3,259	3,632	183,009	2,150,052

(1) Fiscal years 1980 and later consist of the 12 months ending on Sept. 30 of each year. Fiscal years prior to 1977 consisted of the 12 months ending on June 30 of each year. (2) Beginning in 1983, includes transfers from general fund of Treasury representing contributions that would have been paid on deemed wage credits for military service in 1957 and later, if such credits were considered covered wages. (3) Includes payments (a) in 1947-52 and in 1967 and later, for costs of noncontributory wage credits for military service performed before 1957; (b) in 1972-83, for costs of deemed wage credits for military service performed after 1956; and (c) in 1969 and later, for costs of benefits to certain uninsured persons who attained age 72 before 1968. (4) Net interest includes net profits or losses on marketable investments. Beginning in 1967, administrative expenses were charged currently to the trust fund on an estimated basis, with a final adjustment, including interest, made in the next fiscal year. The amounts of these interest adjustments are included in net interest. For years prior to 1967, the method of accounting for administrative expenses is described in the 1970 Annual Report. Beginning in Oct. 1973, the figures shown include relatively small amounts of gifts to the fund. During 1983-91, interest paid from the trust fund to the general fund on advance tax transfers is reflected. (5) Beginning in 1967, includes payments for vocational rehabilitation services furnished to disabled persons receiving benefits because of their disabilities. Beginning in 1983, amounts are reduced by amount of reimbursement for unnegotiated benefit checks. (6) Net change in assets during fiscal year, including amounts borrowed or repaid by other funds.

Disability Insurance Trust Fund, 1960-2008
(in millions)

Fiscal year[1]	Total	Net contribs.[2]	Income from taxing benefits	Payments from the Treasury fund[3]	Net interest[4]	Total	Benefit pymts.[5]	Admin. expenses	Transfers to Railroad Retirement program	Net increase in fund[6]	Fund at end of period
			INCOME					DISBURSEMENTS			
1960	$1,034	$987	—	—	$47	$533	$528	$32	−$27	$501	$2,167
1970	4,380	4,141	—	$16	223	2,954	2,795	149	10	1,426	5,104
1980	17,376	16,805	—	118	453	15,320	14,998	334	−12	2,056	7,680
1990	28,215	27,291	$158	—	766	25,124	24,327	717	80	3,091	11,455
1995	70,209	67,987	335	—	1,888	41,374	40,234	1,072	68	28,835	35,206
2000	77,023	70,001	756	—	6,266	56,008	54,244	1,608	159	21,014	113,752
2001	82,079	74,611	732	−836	7,573	59,930	58,098	1,762	10	22,149	135,901
2002	85,720	76,067	936	—	8,717	66,364	64,138	2,005	154	19,356	155,258
2003	87,909	77,431	919	—	9,559	71,907	69,716	1,968	167	16,002	171,260
2004	90,105	79,269	1,047	—	9,789	78,471	76,139	2,070	215	11,634	182,893
2005	96,765	85,418	1,164	—	10,183	86,360	83,721	2,301	338	10,405	193,298
2006	101,571	90,001	1,174	—	10,396	92,932	90,064	2,480	388	8,640	201,938
2007	108,396	93,973	1,351	—	13,072	96,758	93,955	2,357	445	11,638	213,577
2008	109,816	97,432	1,373	8	11,003	107,153	104,222	2,513	418	2,663	216,239

(1) Fiscal years 1977 and later consist of the 12 months ending Sept. 30 of each year. Fiscal years prior to 1977 consisted of the 12 months ending June 30 of each year. (2) Beginning in 1983, includes transfers from general fund of Treasury representing contributions that would have been paid on deemed wage credits for military service in 1957 and later, if such credits were considered to be covered wages. (3) Includes payments (a) for costs of noncontributory wage credits for military service performed before 1957; and (b) in 1972-83, for costs of deemed wage credits for military service performed after 1956. (4) Net interest includes net profits or losses on marketable investments. Administrative expenses are charged currently to the trust fund on an estimated basis, with a final adjustment, including interest, made in the following fiscal year. Figures shown include relatively small amounts of gifts to the fund. During the years 1983-91, interest paid from the trust fund to the general fund on advance tax transfers is reflected. (5) Includes payments for vocational rehabilitation services. Beginning in 1983, amounts are reduced by amount of reimbursement for unnegotiated benefit checks. (6) Net change in assets during fiscal year, including amounts borrowed or repaid by other funds. **Note:** Totals may not add because of rounding.

Supplementary Medical Insurance Trust Fund (Medicare SMI), 1975-2008

(in millions)

Fiscal year[1]	Total	INCOME Premium from participants[2]	Government contribs.[3]	Transfers from states[4]	Interest and other income[5,6]	Total	DISBURSEMENTS Benefit payments[6,7,8]	Admin. expenses	Net change	Balance in fund at end of year[9]
1975	$4,322	$1,887	$2,330	—	$106	$4,170	$3,765	$404	$152	$1,424
1980	10,275	2,928	6,932	—	416	10,737	10,144	593	−462	4,532
1990	46,138[10]	11,494[10]	33,210	—	1,434[10]	43,022[10]	41,498	1,524[10]	3,115[10]	14,527[10]
1995	58,169	19,244	36,988	—	1,937	65,213	63,491	1,722	−7,044	13,874
1996	82,025	18,931	61,702	—	1,392	68,946	67,176	1,771	13,079	26,953
1997	80,806	19,141	59,471	—	2,193	72,553	71,133	1,420	8,252	35,206
1998	81,955	19,427	59,919	—	2,608	76,272	74,837	1,435	5,683	40,889
1999	85,278	20,160	62,185	—	2,933	80,518	79,008	1,510	4,760	45,649
2000	89,239	20,515	65,561	—	3,164	88,992	87,212[11]	1,780	247	45,896
2001	95,336	22,307	69,838	—	3,191	99,452	97,466[11]	1,986	−4,116	41,780
2002	105,705	24,427	78,318	—	2,960	108,825	106,995[11]	1,830	−3,120	38,659
2003	110,194	26,834	80,905	—	2,455	124,055	121,699[11]	2,356	−13,861	24,799
2004	126,805	30,341	94,734	—	1,730	134,490	131,673	2,817	−7,684	17,114
2005	152,505	35,939	115,200	—	1,366	152,735	149,820	2,914	−230	16,885
2006	211,951	44,241[12]	162,601	$3,630	1,478	195,557	192,083[12,13]	3,474	16,394	33,279
2007	237,869	49,649[12]	179,181	6,977	2,065	232,002	228,576[12,13]	3,426	5,867	39,146
2008	244,840	54,126[12]	180,434	7,042	3,238	224,837	221,414[13,14]	3,423	20,003	59,149

(1) Fiscal year 1975 consists of the 12 months ending on June 30, 1975; fiscal years 1980 and later consist of the 12 months ending on Sept. 30 of each year. (2) For Part D, premiums include both amounts withheld from Social Security benefit checks (and certain other federal benefit payments) and amounts paid directly to Part D plans (estimated). (3) For Part B, includes matching payments from the general fund, plus certain interest-adjustment items. For Part D, includes all federal govt. transfers. Includes amounts for the transitional assistance benefits in 2004-05. (4) As of 2006, Medicaid is no longer the primary payer for full-benefit dual eligibles. States must pay a portion of their estimated forgone drug costs for this population. As of 2006, states pay 90% of estimated costs, with the percentage phasing down, to 75% in 2015 and later. (5) "Other income" includes recoveries of amounts reimbursed from the trust fund that are not obligations of the trust fund and other small amounts of miscellaneous income. (6) In 2008, includes an adjustment of $812 million for interest inadvertently unearned as a result of HI hospice costs that were misallocated to, and paid from, the Part B account from May 2005 to September 2007. (7) Includes costs of Peer Review Organizations from 1983-2001 and costs of Quality Review Organizations beginning in 2002. (8) For Part D, includes payments to plans, subsidies to employer-sponsored retiree drug plans, payments to states for low-income eligibility determinations, and Part D drug premiums (the amount collected from beneficiaries and transferred to plans and an estimated amount for premiums paid directly by enrollees to plans). (9) Includes amounts for the transitional assistance benefits in 2004-06. The financial status of SMI depends on the assets and liabilities of the trust fund. (10) Includes the impact of the Medicare Catastrophic Coverage Act of 1988. (11) Benefit payments less monies transferred from the HI trust fund for home health agency costs. (12) Certain HI hospice costs were misallocated to, and paid from, the Part B account of the SMI trust fund. See also footnote (14). (13) Includes an estimated $1.804 billion (2006), $2.275 billion (2007), and $2.938 billion (2008) for premiums paid directly to Part D plans. (14) Benefit payments were $229,898 million. Amount shown includes −$8,484 million, which represents a transfer from the general fund of the Treasury to the Part B account of the SMI trust fund for HI hospice costs that were misallocated to, and paid from, the Part B account from May 2005 to September 2007. (The HI trust fund, in turn, transferred $8,484 million to the general fund.) **Note:** Totals may not add because of rounding.

Hospital Insurance Trust Fund (Medicare HI), 1975-2008

(in millions)

Fisc. year[1]	Total	Payroll taxes	Taxation of benefits	INCOME Transfers from Railroad Retire- ment acct.	Rmbrs. for uninsured persons	Premiums from voluntary enrollees	Pymts. for military wage credits	Interest and other income[2,3]	Total	DISBURSEMENTS Benefit pymts.[3,4]	Admin. expenses[5]	Net change	Balance
1975	$12,568	$11,291	—	$132	$481	$6	$48	$609	$10,612	$10,353	$259	$1,956	$9,870
1980	25,415	23,244	—	244	697	17	141	1,072	24,288	23,790	497	1,127	14,490
1990	79,563	70,655	—	367	413	113	107	7,908	66,687	65,912	774	12,876	95,631
1995	114,847	98,053	$3,913	396	462	998	61	10,963	114,883	113,583	1,300	−36	129,520
1996	121,135	106,934	4,069	401	419	1,107	−2,293[5]	10,496	125,317	124,088	1,229	−4,182	125,338
1997	128,548	112,725	3,558	419	481	1,279	70	10,017	137,836	136,175	1,661	−9,287	116,050
1998	138,203	121,913	5,067	419	34	1,320	67	9,382	137,140	135,487[6]	1,653	1,063	117,113
1999	153,015	134,385	6,552	430	652	1,401	71	9,523	131,441	129,463[6]	1,978	21,574	138,687
2000	159,681	137,738	8,787	465	470	1,392	2	10,827	130,284	127,934[6]	2,350	29,397	168,084
2001	171,014	151,931	4,903	470	453	1,440	−1,175[7]	12,993	141,723	139,356[6]	2,368	29,290	197,374
2002	179,762	151,575	10,946	425	442	1,525	0	14,850	148,031	145,566[6]	2,464	31,731	229,105
2003	175,813	149,839	8,318	426	393	1,598	0	15,239	153,792	151,250[6]	2,541	22,021	251,127
2004	180,815	153,448	8,577	419	365	1,799	173	16,034	166,998	164,079	2,920	13,816	264,943
2005	196,921	168,954	8,765	445	286	2,303	0	16,168	184,142	181,292[8]	2,850	12,779	277,723
2006	210,309	180,392	10,319	471	408	2,632	0	16,086	184,901	181,815[8]	3,086	25,408	303,130
2007	219,207	187,992	10,593	483	468	2,761	0	16,910	202,827	200,191[8]	2,636	16,380	319,510
2008	229,729	197,195	11,733	526	506	2,913	0	16,856	230,240	227,008[9]	3,231	−511	319,000

(1) Fiscal year 1975 consists of the 12 months ending on June 30, 1975; fiscal years 1980 and later consist of the 12 months ending Sept. 30 of each year. (2) Other income includes recoveries of amounts reimbursed from the trust fund that are not obligations of the trust fund, receipts from the fraud and abuse control program, and other small amounts of miscellaneous income. In 2008, includes an adjustment of −$853 million for interest inadvertently earned as a result of HI hospice costs that were misallocated to, and paid from, the Part B account of the SMI trust fund from May 2005 to September 2007. (3) Values after 2005 include additional premiums for Medicare Advantage (MA) plans that are deducted from beneficiaries' Social Security checks, transferred to the HI and SMI trust funds, and then transferred to the plans. (These additional premiums are incurred when an MA plan is chosen with a monthly payment exceeding the benchmark amount. Enrollees may pay plans directly or have the amounts deducted from their Social Security checks.) (4) Includes costs of Peer Review Organizations from 1983 through 2001 (beginning with the implementation of the Prospective Payment System on Oct. 1, 1983), and costs of Quality Improvement Organizations beginning in 2002. (5) Includes costs of experiments and demonstration projects. Beginning in 1997, includes fraud and abuse control expenses, as provided for by PL 104-191. (6) Includes monies transferred to the SMI trust fund for home health agency costs, as provided for by PL 105-33. (7) Includes the lump-sum general review adjustment of −$1,117 million, as provided for by sec. 151 of PL 98-21. (8) Certain HI hospice costs were misallocated to, and paid from, the Part B account of the SMI trust fund. See also footnote (9). (9) Benefit payments were $218,525 million. Amount shown includes a transfer of $8,484 million to the general fund of the Treasury for HI hospice costs that were misallocated to, and paid from, the Part B account of the SMI trust fund from May 2005 to September 2007. (The general fund, in turn, transferred $8,484 million to the Part B account.) **Note:** Totals may not add because of rounding.

Block Grants for Welfare (Temporary Assistance for Needy Families), 2007[1]

Source: Office of Family Assistance, Admin. for Children and Families, U.S. Dept. of Health and Human Services

State	Total federal and state TANF expenditures, 2007[2]	2007 average monthly expenditure per—		2007 average monthly number of—		
		Family	Recipient	Families	Recipients	Children
Alabama	$155,789	$703.35	$301.67	18,458	43,035	33,413
Alaska.	77,608	1,991.28	753.00	3,248	8,589	5,944
Arizona	325,107	747.44	346.84	36,247	78,111	59,313
Arkansas	107,323	1,040.25	459.60	8,598	19,460	14,550
California	6,586,129	1,162.92	473.63	471,955	1,158,811	928,969
Colorado	200,301	1,520.28	606.09	10,979	27,540	20,777
Connecticut	485,092	2,313.64	1,169.64	17,472	34,561	24,930
Delaware	64,207	1,300.03	620.43	4,116	8,624	6,945
Dist. of Columbia	149,381	2,014.66	851.89	6,179	14,613	11,893
Florida	834,107	1,452.85	908.94	47,843	76,672	65,680
Georgia.	499,788	1,677.20	923.37	24,832	45,106	41,662
Hawaii.	201,774	2,951.42	1,196.31	5,697	14,055	10,335
Idaho	37,336	1,922.14	1,239.32	1,619	2,511	2,312
Illinois	1,024,658	2,808.31	1,163.87	30,406	73,366	60,078
Indiana	284,535	571.52	197.30	41,488	120,177	91,865
Iowa	166,431	828.55	330.06	16,739	42,020	29,033
Kansas	168,935	954.70	371.31	14,746	37,914	25,994
Kentucky.	199,295	552.47	271.50	30,061	61,171	47,808
Louisiana	201,184	1,525.74	687.85	10,988	24,374	21,214
Maine	109,792	882.63	370.11	10,366	24,721	16,903
Maryland.	384,491	1,728.79	762.93	18,534	41,997	31,898
Massachusetts	868,582	1,606.06	792.86	45,068	91,292	63,132
Michigan.	1,133,698	1,290.30	496.12	73,219	190,426	139,797
Minnesota.	394,020	1,237.73	519.15	26,528	63,247	46,845
Mississippi	82,732	594.20	292.68	11,603	23,556	18,383
Missouri	341,432	751.34	311.31	37,869	91,396	63,516
Montana	40,488	1,057.05	419.50	3,192	8,043	5,732
Nebraska	108,417	1,355.14	593.69	6,667	15,218	11,923
Nevada.	68,501	851.25	346.97	6,706	16,452	12,568
New Hampshire	87,877	1,430.87	667.52	5,118	10,971	7,905
New Jersey.	830,573	1,973.99	833.47	35,063	83,044	59,023
New Mexico	95,686	566.56	223.66	14,074	35,652	26,610
New York	4,399,712	2,996.93	1,360.95	122,340	269,401	202,942
North Carolina	435,246	1,401.36	742.86	25,882	48,825	40,508
North Dakota	35,733	1,426.86	569.33	2,087	5,230	3,797
Ohio	1,339,117	1,423.88	668.15	78,373	167,017	128,343
Oklahoma.	153,072	1,361.62	628.70	9,368	20,289	16,901
Oregon	257,449	1,154.51	510.37	18,583	42,036	31,228
Pennsylvania	897,732	1,169.56	487.44	63,965	153,476	116,566
Puerto Rico.	83,992	511.56	199.54	13,682	35,077	24,588
Rhode Island	142,215	1,409.44	590.35	8,409	20,075	14,200
South Carolina	151,614	813.66	357.76	15,528	35,316	27,287
South Dakota	28,595	827.45	392.82	2,880	6,066	5,110
Tennessee	284,052	384.19	148.23	61,613	159,688	114,862
Texas	789,679	1,074.17	477.92	61,263	137,695	116,496
Utah	90,210	1,484.62	615.88	5,064	12,206	8,909
Vermont	70,092	1,309.88	532.24	4,459	10,974	7,154
Virginia	255,136	703.50	314.92	30,222	67,513	48,999
Washington	614,862	1,009.37	429.76	50,763	119,225	84,705
West Virginia	106,551	903.04	373.97	9,833	23,743	16,235
Wisconsin	445,765	2,163.15	1,018.74	17,173	36,464	30,834
Wyoming	25,882	8,005.51	4,400.92	269	490	432
2007 totals.	**26,921,973**	**1,321.70**	**566.92**	**1,697,432**	**3,957,330**	**3,047,043**
2006 totals.	**25,593,809**	**1,191.88**	**510.33**	**1,789,460**	**4,179,295**	**3,207,216**
2005 totals.	**25,580,110**	**1,120.87**	**474.21**	**1,901,810**	**4,495,175**	**3,428,885**
2004 totals.	**25,821,230**	**1,094.51**	**455.63**	**1,965,960**	**4,722,588**	**3,581,448**
2003 totals.	**26,339,994**	**1,092.22**	**447.88**	**2,009,666**	**4,900,889**	**3,693,056**
2002 totals.	**25,414,383**	**1,039.00**	**417.89**	**2,038,373**	**5,067,963**	**3,791,560**
2001 totals.	**25,667,381**	**1,024.57**	**400.86**	**2,087,646**	**5,335,891**	**3,968,499**
2000 totals.	**24,780,711**	**926.32**	**353.72**	**2,229,315**	**5,838,043**	**4,303,943**
1999 totals.	**23,114,572**	**267.99**	**267.99**	**2,673,610**	**7,187,658**	**NA**
1998 totals.	**22,036,420**	**208.91**	**208.91**	**3,199,700**	**8,790,149**	**NA**
1997 totals.	**19,010,190**	**144.87**	**144.87**	**3,936,610**	**10,935,125**	**NA**

Note: Under 1996 legislation, the Aid to Families with Dependent Children (AFDC) program was converted to this state block-grant program. (1) Fiscal year 2007; covers period from Oct. 2006 to Sept. 2007. (2) In thousands.

Adults Receiving TANF[1] (Welfare) Funds, by Employment Status, 2007[2]

Source: Office of Family Assistance, Admin. for Children and Families, U.S. Dept. of Health and Human Services

State	Adults	Employed	State	Adults	Employed	State	Adults	Employed	State	Adults	Employed
AL.	9,592	30.0%	IL	13,935	12.8%	NE	3,294	68.6%	SC	9,713	37.6%
AK.	2,640	32.7	IN	25,757	29.2	NV	3,897	36.4	SD	989	14.4
AZ.	19,180	20.0	IA	12,801	41.9	NH	3,105	26.9	TN	45,174	22.8
AR	4,969	24.7	KS	11,829	21.8	NJ	24,281	9.1	TX	20,733	34.5
CA	236,830	28.3	KY	13,317	20.6	NM.	9,586	23.3	UT	2,305	42.5
CO	6,592	31.9	LA.	3,265	36.4	NY	69,762	25.4	VT	3,808	22.0
CT.	9,548	34.7	ME	7,508	25.1	NC	8,913	22.0	Virgin Isls.	366	4.4
DE	1,751	0.0	MD	9,550	8.8	ND	1,429	32.4	VA	18,522	31.7
DC	2,811	25.0	MA	27,389	14.0	OH	38,600	20.5	WA	34,913	21.2
FL	31,307	27.1	MI	51,262	24.2	OK	3,167	8.9	WV	5,467	11.0
GA	3,611	18.0	MN	16,931	28.2	OR	10,660	9.6	WI	5,520	18.1
Guam	NA	NA	MS	5,086	24.2	PA	38,005	30.3	WY.	59	10.5
HI	3,669	34.3	MO	28,099	18.8	Puerto Rico	11,242	1.7			
ID	205	35.5	MT	2,245	28.1	RI.	5,823	23.3	**U.S.. . . . .**	**941,040**	**24.9**

NA = Not available. (1) TANF = The state block grant program known as Temporary Assistance for Needy Families. (2) Fiscal year 2007; covers period from Oct. 2006 to Sept. 2007.

TAXES

Federal Income Tax

Source: George W. Smith III, CPA, Managing Partner, George W. Smith & Company, P.C.

Highlights of Recent Legislation

American Recovery and Reinvestment Act of 2009

Pres. Barack H. Obama signed into law a massive stimulus package Feb. 17, 2009. The total cost was estimated at $787 billion, including nearly $300 billion in tax relief, and the following highlights:

First-Time Homebuyer Credit. Increases the credit for first-time homebuyers to a maximum $8,000 for purchases made after Dec. 31, 2008, and before Dec. 1, 2009. The repayment requirement is eliminated for purchases made during this period. There is a recapture rule if the home is disposed of within 36 months from the date of purchase.

American Opportunity Tax Credit. This addition to the Hope educational credit increases the credit to a maximum $2,500 per year for each eligible student and includes tuition, textbooks, and course materials. The credit can be claimed each year for up to four years. 40% of the eligible expenses are refundable for 2009 and 2010. There are phase-out rules for higher incomes.

Vehicle Sales Tax. Starting Feb. 17, 2009, through Jan. 1, 2010, purchasers of new automobiles, motorcycles, trucks and motor homes will be entitled to a deduction for state and local sales tax. The deduction will be limited to the sales tax imposed on the first $49,500 of the purchase price. There is an adjustment for higher amounts. There is also an income phase-out rule for taxpayers.

Making Work Pay Credit. This provision provides a limited earned income credit of $400 for single filers, $800 for joint filers, for the years 2009 and 2010. The credit will phase out depending upon the individual's gross income.

Fixed Income. The bill provides a one-time stimulus payment of $250 in 2009 primarily for Social Security recipients, disabled veterans, and retired railroad workers.

Alternative Powered Vehicles. A new 10% credit up to $4,000 will be available for the conversion of existing vehicles into plug-in electric drive motor vehicles before 2012.

Excludable Revenue. First $2,400 of unemployment compensation received in 2009 is excludable from gross income.

Equipment. The Sec. 179 expense election for machinery and equipment is extended one additional year for 2009.

Energy Credit. The new law increases the tax credit for residential energy property to a maximum $1,500 for 2009 and 2010. The credit includes insulation, exterior windows/doors, skylights, central air conditioners, furnaces, etc.

"Cash-for-Clunkers" Program. Consumers could have rebates of up to $4,500 for vehicles traded in with a combined city/highway mileage rating of 18 miles per gallon or lower for a more fuel-efficient automobile. The program ended Aug. 24, 2009.

Housing and Economic Recovery Act of 2008

Former Pres. George W. Bush signed into law this act, which included $15.1 billion in tax incentives, July 30, 2008.

New Homebuyers. Provides first-time homebuyers a refundable tax credit equal to 10% of the purchase price of a home with a maximum credit for singles up to $3,750; $7,500 for married couples. The credit is effective for homes purchased on or after Apr. 9, 2008. The taxpayer has 15 years to repay the credit. For homes purchased after 2008, the American Recovery Act of 2009 increased the credit to $8,000 for either singles or married couples filing jointly and modified the repayment requirement.

Military Tax Relief Bill of 2008

Congress unanimously passed this legislation in May 2008; it includes tax breaks for members of the military. Also requires civilian employers of service members to keep their jobs available if called to active duty.

Combat Pay. This provision allows military personnel to permanently treat combat pay as tax free. Military personnel can include tax-free combat pay to compute the Earned Income Credit.

Retirement Plan. For military reservists called to active duty, the law makes permanent the ability to make penalty-free withdrawals from IRAs.

Bonuses. Some states include as income veterans' bonuses to military personnel who returned from a combat zone. This provision requires that these bonuses be excluded from the recipient's state gross income.

Economic Stimulus Act of 2008

This bill was signed into law Feb. 13, 2008, and comes in two parts.

Stimulus Tax Rebates. Rebates were $600 for singles, $1,200 for married couples who file jointly, plus an additional $300 for each eligible child younger than 17 years of age. There were income phase-out rules.

Bonus Depreciation. The Stimulus Act of 2008 allows a business to depreciate 50% of the cost of new assets placed into service. Among the eligible items are machinery, business equipment, farm buildings, and computer software.

Small Business and Work Opportunity Tax Act of 2007

This business tax-incentives bill (which included an increase in the federal minimum wage) was signed into law by Pres. Bush on May 25, 2007.

"Kiddie Tax." Children under age 19 (previously 18) and students under age 24, who have unearned income over $1,800—non-wage income such as interest, dividends, and capital gains—will be subject to tax at the parents' higher rate, not the child's.

Negligence. The penalty for the understatement of tax caused by the preparer for "willful or reckless conduct," such as taking obviously improper deductions, was increased to the greater of $5,000 or 50% of the income derived by the tax return preparer. Lesser amounts apply to an "unreasonable position."

IRS Rulings and Other Tax Matters

Weight Loss. The IRS allows a medical deduction for costs of certain weight loss programs. Participation must be for treatment of a physician-diagnosed disease, including obesity. No deduction is allowed for diets that are used for purely cosmetic reasons or special diet foods.

Same-Sex Marriage. The IRS ruled that it is unlawful for same-sex couples to file federal tax returns under any married status, even if the jurisdiction in which the couple lives recognizes such marriages.

Property Taxes. Renters may not deduct a portion of rent that is included as property taxes, even when state or local law identifies a portion of the rent as being tied to tax increases.

Auto Damage. Damage to a person's car may be a deductible casualty loss unless it was caused by the person's willful conduct, such as drunken driving.

Smoking. Taxpayers can deduct the cost of two types of aids for quitting cigarette smoking as a medical expense: (1) participation in a smoking-cessation program; (2) prescription drugs to alleviate the effects of nicotine withdrawal. Over-the-counter products such as nicotine patches and chewing gum remain nondeductible.

Alimony. Payments to an individual under a written separation agreement constitute alimony for federal tax purposes even if the agreement is not enforceable under state law.

Working Abroad. Many Americans who live and work abroad are eligible to exclude a certain amount of their pay from U.S. income taxes. The amount of earned income that is excludable for 2009 increased to $91,400, up from $87,600 for 2008.

Penalties. Penalties and fines paid to a governmental agency or department are not deductible. This includes parking and speeding tickets as well as penalties for the late filing of a tax return.

Death Benefits. Qualified accelerated death benefits paid under a life insurance contract to terminally ill persons (certified as expected to die within 24 months) are excludable from gross income.

Sale of Residence. Married couples filing jointly who have lived in their principal residence for at least 2 years out of the last 5-year period can exclude from income up to $500,000 of the gain on the sale of their residence. Single taxpayers can exclude up to $250,000.

Domestic Workers. The annual threshold dollar amount for reporting and paying social security and federal unemployment taxes on domestic employees, including nannies and housekeepers, increased in 2009 to $1,700. Household workers under 18 are exempt unless household work is their principal occupation.

Student Loans. The income phase-out range for 2009 for the $2,500 student loan interest deduction increased to $60,000-$75,000 for single taxpayers and $120,000-$150,000 for married taxpayers filing jointly.

Personal Auto Mileage. The mileage allowance deduction for moving and medical expense decreased from 27 cents per mile for 2008 to 24 cents in 2009. The rate used for volunteer work for charitable activities remains at 14 cents per mile. Rates were set by Congress, not the IRS.

Business Auto Mileage. The standard mileage rate method starting in 2009 for calculating the business use of an individual's automobile is 55 cents. The business portion of parking fees and tolls may be deducted in addition to the standard mileage rate.

Investment Expenses. Investors may take a miscellaneous deduction on Schedule A for financial newspapers, reports, and other expenses incurred in managing their investment portfolio. However, investors cannot deduct expenses for attending a convention, seminar, or similar meeting.

Garage Sales. Revenues received from a garage sale usually do not result in taxable income. In most cases, the item that was sold cost more than the revenue received. Losses are considered personal and, therefore, not deductible.

"Hands Off." In a unanimous decision, the U.S. Supreme Court held that Individual Retirement Accounts (IRAs) are beyond the reach of creditors. This includes IRA assets of taxpayers who have filed for bankruptcy.

Full-Time Student. Starting in 2009, a taxpayer may not claim a dependency exemption for an individual who qualifies as a full-time student and is over age 23 at the end of the year, unless the student's gross income is less than $3,650.

First Job. Graduates may not deduct the expenses of seeking their first job.

Day Camps. The cost of computer camps, soccer camps and other specialty day camps (not overnight) for children may qualify for the child care credit. The child must be under 13 and the expenses must be incurred so the parent or parents can work.

Top Five List. Periodically, the IRS issues a list of the most commonly made income tax errors. The top five in 2007:

1. Incorrect or missing Social Security numbers.
2. Incorrect tax entered from tax tables.
3. Mathematical errors or wrong ID numbers listed for tax credits.
4. Entering withholding and estimated tax payments on the wrong line.
5. General math mistakes.

Income Tax Filing and Payment Due Dates

Filing Dates. The due date for filing a 2009 U.S. Individual Income Tax Return Form 1040, 1040A, 1040EZ including 2009 partnership tax returns, Form 1065, is Thursday, Apr. 15, 2010. Calendar-year-ending corporate returns are due Monday, Mar. 15, 2010.

Estimated Tax Payments. Due dates for filing individual quarterly federal estimated tax payments, Form 1040-ES: 1st quarter, Thurs., Apr. 15, 2010; 2nd quarter, Tues., June 15; 3rd quarter, Wed., Sept. 15; and 4th quarter, Mon., Jan. 17, 2011. Different filing dates may apply for state/local taxes.

Refunds. Individuals can call the IRS toll-free number at 1-800-829-4477 for a recorded message to check on the status of their expected refund. Or visit the IRS Website at www.irs.gov.

Filing Penalties. The IRS can levy two potential penalties after the filing due date when there is a balance owing. One penalty is for failing to file a timely tax return, the other is for failure to pay the tax when due. In addition, interest will be charged on any unpaid tax balance.

Installment Payments. Depending on the amount of tax owed, taxpayers may apply for monthly installment payments by attaching Form 9465 to their tax return. There is an IRS filing fee if the request is approved.

Need More Time to File? Individuals who cannot file their 2009 tax return by the due date, Apr. 15, 2010, may apply for an automatic 6-month extension of time to Friday, Oct. 15, 2010. To qualify for the extension, Form 4868 must be filed no later than Apr. 15, 2010.

Other Due Dates. The extension of time to file for calendar year partnerships and estates and trusts has been reduced to five months, to Sept. 15, 2010. The same due date applies to most year-ending Dec. 31, 2009, corporate returns. Approximately nine million extensions were filed last year.

Statute of Limitations. Taxpayers who have not yet filed their 2006 federal tax return have until Apr. 15, 2010, to file and claim their refund. After that date any refunds for income tax or withholding tax for 2006, including the refundable earned income tax credit, will be lost.

Electronic Filing. More than 90.6 million individual tax returns were e-filed in the 2009 tax filing season. More than 30 million returns were filed from home computers.

Tax Tip. For security purposes, taxpayers should request that tax refunds be deposited directly into their bank accounts. If you choose, you may be able to split the refund and have it deposited among two or three accounts.

IRS Services and Information

For Tax Questions: 1-800-829-1040
Website: www.irs.gov
Fax: 1-703-368-9694
For Forms/Publications: 1-800-829-3676
For English and Spanish: The IRS provides videotaped instructions both in English and Spanish at participating libraries. Many IRS publications and tax forms, including instructions, are also printed in Spanish. For more information, call 1-800-TAX-FORM and ask for the free IRS Publication 1SP, *Derechos del Contribuyente*.

For Hearing Impaired: The IRS telephone service for hearing impaired persons is available for taxpayers with access to TDD equipment. The toll-free number is 1-800-829-4059.

Meeting with Your Tax Preparer

More than 60% of all individual income tax returns are signed by paid tax professionals. Here are some ideas to keep in mind when visiting your tax preparer:

- **Review** last year's tax return. Make notes of any changes since then such as marriage, divorce, number of dependents, retirement, job changes, additional income, new deductions, etc.
- **Organize** your records with income items first, followed by itemized deductions in sequence: medical, taxes, interest, charitable, and other miscellaneous deductions, followed by gains, losses, rentals, or other items.
- **Time** spent with your preparer may affect your bill. If you bring in jumbled records and deductions, there may be an additional cost to have your tax preparer organize your records.

- **Prepare** a list of questions in advance. Bring with you any invoices or bills that you are not sure of.
- **Alert** your preparer if you're waiting to receive additional information. He or she can begin preparing your tax return and include the missing data later to finalize your return.
- **Don't hesitate** to call the preparer if you receive additional information at a later time. However, if you call after the return is completed, the changes may cost you additional fees.
- **Don't forget** to review your tax return before signing it. Ask questions about any item you don't understand. Remember, even though your preparer is required to sign the return, you are responsible for its contents.

Additional Help: For more information about choosing tax preparers, call the IRS Tele-Tax information at 1-800-829-4477. Follow the prompts and select Topic 254. This information is also available online at www.irs.gov/taxtopics/tc254.html.

Individual Income Tax Rates and Tax Brackets

Taxable Income and Rates for 2009

Tax rate	Single	Married filing separately	Married filing jointly or qualifying widow(er)	Head of household	Estates and trusts
10%	$1 to $8,350	$1 to $8,350	$1 to $16,700	$1 to $11,950	$0
15%	$8,351 to $33,950	$8,351 to $33,950	$16,701 to $67,900	$11,951 to $45,500	$1 to $2,300
25%	$33,951 to $82,250	$33,951 to $68,525	$67,901 to $137,050	$45,501 to $117,450	$2,301 to $5,350
28%	$82,251 to $171,550	$68,526 to $104,425	$137,051 to $208,850	$117,451 to $190,200	$5,351 to $8,250
33%	$171,551 to $372,950	$104,426 to $186,475	$208,851 to $372,950	$190,201 to $372,950	$8,201 to $11,150
35%	Over $372,950	Over $186,475	Over $372,950	Over $372,950	Over $11,150

Personal Exemptions

Dollar Amounts. The personal exemption amount for each taxpayer, spouse, and dependent for 2009 is $3,650, an increase of $150 from the prior year. The exemption amount is adjusted each year for cost-of-living increases. The personal exemption of an individual who is a dependent of another taxpayer is zero.

Exemption Phase-Out. The exemption deduction for higher-income taxpayers begins to be phased out when their income exceeds certain threshold dollar amounts, and is adjusted annually for cost-of-living. Each exemption is reduced by 2% for each $2,500 ($1,250 for married persons filing separately) or fraction thereof by which adjusted gross income for year 2009 exceeds the following:

Married filing jointly	$250,200
Qualifying widow(er)	$250,200
Head of household	$208,500
Single	$166,800
Married filing separately	$125,100

Standard Deduction

The standard deduction is a flat dollar amount that is subtracted from the adjusted gross income of taxpayers who do not itemize their deductions.

2009 Standard Deduction Amount

Single	$5,700
Married filing jointly or qualifying widow(er)	$11,400
Married filing separately	$5,700
Head of household	$8,350

These figures are not applicable if an individual can be claimed as a dependent on another person's tax return.

Dependents Tax Return. An individual reported as a dependent on another person's 2009 income tax return generally may claim on his or her own tax return only the greater of $950 or the sum of $300 plus earned income not to exceed the regular standard deduction.

Additional Standard Deduction

Taxpayers in 2009 who are 65 or older and/or blind may claim an additional standard deduction:

Single or head of household, 65 or older OR blind	$1,400
Single or head of household, 65 or older AND blind	$2,800
Married filing jointly or qualifying widow(er), 65 or older OR blind (per person)	$1,100
Married filing jointly or qualifying widow(er), 65 or older AND blind (per person)	$2,200
Married filing separately, 65 or older OR blind	$1,100
Married filing separately, 65 or older AND blind	$2,200

Savings Plans for Traditional and Roth IRAs

Traditional IRA. The maximum 2009 tax-deferred Individual Retirement Arrangement (IRA) deduction for a married couple filing jointly is $10,000 ($5,000 for singles). Each spouse can contribute up to $5,000 annually even if one spouse has little or no income. Individuals age 50 or older can fund an additional "catch-up" amount of $1,000. However, there are income limitations and phase-outs.

Withdrawals. There is a 10% penalty for IRA distributions before age 59½. Distributions paid to the beneficiary due to a disability or death of the owner are not subject to this penalty, nor are payments used for certain unreimbursed medical expenses, higher-education expenses or first-time homebuyer acquisition costs (up to $10,000).

Caution. Contributions to a traditional IRA or Roth IRA made after Apr. 15, 2010, will automatically be considered deposits for a 2010 IRA.

Roth IRA. Although contributions paid into a Roth IRA are not deductible, distributions of funds including investment earnings held in the account for 5 years or longer and distributed after age 59½ are both free of income tax and the 10% early withdrawal penalty at the time of distribution. Withdrawals in less than 5 years can be subject to income tax and the 10% withdrawal penalty regardless of age. There are income limitations on contributions.

401(k) Plan. The maximum amount that an individual under age 50 can contribute to a 401(k) plan for 2009 rose to $16,500 from $15,500. Those 50 or older can put away an additional $5,500 this year, for a total of $22,000, up from $20,500.

Distributions. The owner of a traditional IRA (or a SIMPLE, pension, or profit-sharing plan account) must begin receiving distributions by Apr. 1 of the calendar year following the year in which he or she reaches age 70½. Any employee who works beyond 70½ and is not a 5% or more owner of the business can continue to defer profit-sharing and pension plan distributions.

IRA Publication. For more information on IRAs call the IRS at 1-800-829-3676 for a free copy of Publication 590, *Individual Retirement Arrangements* (IRAs).

Itemized Deductions for 2009

If the total amount of itemized deductions is more than the standard deduction, taxpayers generally should itemize their deductions on Schedule A, Form 1040. The following examples are just a few of the many deductions that may be itemized. Some are subject to income limitations.

Medical expenses that exceed 7.5% of the taxpayer's adjusted gross income are deductible. Medicines, birth control pills, and insulin qualify if prescribed by a physician. Cosmetic surgery for congenital abnormality, for personal injury from an accident or trauma, or for a disfiguring disease is also allowed as a medical deduction.

Tax Tip. A mother-to-be may deduct the cost of classes taken in Lamaze breathing and relaxation techniques, stages of labor, and delivery procedures as a medical expense.

Medical Traveling. Taxpayers may deduct part of the expense of having to travel to seek health care.

Long-Term Care. Based on various annual limits, long-term care insurance premiums are deductible as medical expenses. For 2009 taxpayers age 71 and older can claim as much as $3,980 per person. There are lesser amounts for taxpayers between ages 41 and 70. People age 40 and younger can deduct $320.

Interest. Mortgage interest paid on a primary residence or a second home is deductible. However, there are limitations on mortgages in excess of $1 million. Interest on home equity loans also is deductible, but only covering the first $100,000 of equity debt. Credit card interest is not deductible.

Taxes. State and local income taxes including real estate taxes are deductible. Sales taxes may be deductible if taken in lieu of state taxes. You may not deduct an auto license fee based on weight, model, year, or horsepower. A tax based on the car's value qualifies as a personal property tax.

Charitable Contributions. You may not deduct the value of volunteer work you perform for charities.

Personal Losses. Casualty and theft losses are deductible subject to a $100 reduction and further reduced 10% for each occurrence. Separate rules apply for federally declared disasters. Unreimbursed automobile accident damage may be a deductible casualty loss.

Miscellaneous Deductions. Certain miscellaneous expenses are deductible, but only the amount that exceeds 2% of adjusted gross income. These include investment expenses, union and professional dues, tax preparation fees, safe deposit box rental fees, and most (but not all) expenses for a job search.

Employee Business Expenses. Deductible miscellaneous expenses include unreimbursed employee business expenses such as travel, automobile, telephone, and gifts. However, only 50% of the cost of customer meals and entertainment is deductible.

Moving Expenses. Taxpayers who change jobs or are transferred usually can deduct part of their moving expenses, including travel and the cost of moving household goods, but not meals.

Gambling. Lottery, slots, Texas Hold-Em poker, craps, bingo, or other gambling expenses are deductible if the taxpayer itemizes on Schedule A. However, expenses are limited to gambling winnings reported on page one, Form 1040. If there are no winnings, there are no deductions allowed.

Tax Credits

There Is a Difference. A tax deduction reduces a taxpaycr's taxable income. Tax credits reduce, dollar-for-dollar, the amount of tax owed.

Energy Credits. There are many energy-related credits—from the purchase of an alternative fuel vehicle, the installation of solar/fuel cell property in a residence, to the production of biodiesel or ethanol.

Earned Income Credit. Lower-income workers who maintain a household may be eligible for an Earned Income Credit (EIC). This credit is based on total earned income such as wages, commissions, and tips. Military personnel can include tax-free combat pay in income to compute the credit.

The phase-out range for 2009 of the earned income credit for joint filers with one qualifying child is $19,540 to $38,583, and $43,415 with 2 or more qualifying children.

American Opportunity Tax Credit. Modifying the Hope credit will provide a partially refundable $2,500 credit to cover each of four years of college.

Adoption Credit. The adoption credit for qualified expenses increased to $12,150 in 2009. The credit limit is per person, not per year, and is adjusted annually for inflation. The exclusion phases out for taxpayers whose income is between $182,180 and $222,180, when the credit is completely phased out.

Alternative Minimum Tax

The Alternative Minimum Tax (AMT) was established in 1969 to prevent people with very high incomes from using special tax breaks to pay little or no tax. It was never indexed or adjusted for inflation. Because of changes in the tax law, this tax now affects more and more middle-income taxpayers every year.

The instructions included with tax forms 1040 and 1040A provide help for individuals to determine whether they are subject to the AMT. Form 6251, Alternative Minimum Tax, is used to figure how much additional tax, if any, is owed.

Estate and Gift Taxes

Exclusion. The Tax Relief Reconciliation Act of 2001 increased the estate tax exclusion from $675,000 in 2001 to $1 million in 2002 and 2003, and $1.5 million in 2004 and 2005. For the years 2006 through 2008, the exclusion increased to $2 million. Starting in 2009 the amount tops out at $3.5 million. As the law stands now, the estate tax for 2010 is expected to be repealed.

Estate Tax Rates. The maximum tax rate in 2001 on the value of an estate was 55%. This was reduced to 50% in 2002, 47% in 2005 and 46% for 2006. The rate decreased for 2007-09 to a maximum of 45%.

Repeal. The estate tax laws (including many other recent tax changes, rules, and regulations) revert to the old lower exclusion of $1 million and the higher maximum tax rate of 55% in 2010.

Resident Aliens. The estate of a resident alien is subject to the same rules as that of an American citizen. All property owned worldwide is subject to the U.S. estate tax rules and regulations.

Gifting. U.S. citizens, residents, and non-resident aliens can make tax-free gifts of up to $13,000 in 2009 to as many individuals as he or she chooses. For married couples, the gift is twice that amount, $26,000, even if only one spouse does all the gifting.

Lifetime Gifting. A $1 million gift tax exclusion is the total limit an individual is allowed to give to other individuals (other than charities and the annual $13,000 gifting) during his or her lifetime before having to pay gift taxes.

Taxable Social Security Benefits

Earnings Limitations. Social Security recipients who have not reached full retirement age lose $1 of their benefits for every $2 of earned income over $14,160 in 2009, an increase of $600 over 2008. Recipients will have to pay back some benefits into the system if their income exceeds that amount.

Taxable Benefits. Up to 50% of Social Security benefits may be taxable if the person's total income is more than $25,000 but less than $34,000 for a single individual, head of household, qualifying widow(er), or a married person who is filing separately if spouses lived apart all year; or more than $32,000 but less than $44,000 for married individuals filing jointly. For higher incomes, 85% of Social Security benefits may become taxable.

Tax-Free. If the only income received during the year was Social Security, these benefits are not taxable and you probably do not have to file a tax return.

Retention of Income Tax Records

How long to keep your records is a combination of judgment and the statutes of limitations. Since federal tax returns generally can be audited for up to three years after filing, or six years if the IRS suspects underreported income, it's wise to keep income tax records at least seven years after a return is filed.

IRS Tax Audits

The IRS conducted more than 1.3 million audits in 2008 of individual taxpayers, less than 1% of all the tax returns filed. Most taxpayers have no reason to be concerned—unless they happen to be one of 1.3 million taxpayers.

The audit selection process is not random. It is based on a set of formulas that are designed to spot questionable returns. If the IRS concludes that you owe more and you disagree with the findings, you can meet with a supervisor. If you still do not agree, you can appeal to a separate Appeals Office, or you can take it to the U.S. Tax Court, Federal District Court, or the U.S. Court of Federal Claims.

The U.S. Tax Court is a federal court where taxpayers can dispute tax deficiencies as determined by the Commissioner of Internal Revenue before payment of the disputed amounts. The Tax Court is composed of presidentially appointed members. Many people choose the Tax Court because they are not required to pay the contested tax up front.

For more information about audits, call the IRS at 1-800-829-3676 for its free Publication 556, *Examination of Returns, Appeal Rights, and Claims for Refund*. Or visit www.irs.gov.

Your Rights as a Taxpayer

Congress has enacted "taxpayer bill of rights" legislation and created an Office of the Taxpayer Advocate within the IRS, with authority to order IRS personnel to issue refund checks and meet deadlines for resolving disputes. Taxpayer advocates can be contacted at 1-877-777-4778 (1-800-829-4059 for TTY/TDD). The IRS must pay legal fees if the taxpayer wins the case and the IRS cannot show it was "substantially justified" in pursuing it.

To confidentially report misconduct, waste, fraud or abuse by an IRS employee, call 1-800-366-4484.

For more information ask for free IRS Publication 1, *Your Rights as a Taxpayer*, by calling 1-800-TAX-FORM.

More Services

To find out what additional services are available, ask for Publication 910, *IRS Guide to Free Tax Services*. This guide contains a list of free tax publications and other information including tax education and assistance programs and a list of Tele-Tax topics.

State Government Personal Income Tax Rates, 2008

Source: Reproduced with permission from *CCH State Tax Guide*, published and copyrighted by CCH Inc., a Wolters Kluwer business

Alaska, Florida, Nevada, South Dakota, Texas, Washington, and Wyoming did not have state income taxes and are thus not listed. Tax rates apply in stages—for example, a single person in Arizona making $60,000 in taxable income would pay 2.59% on the first $10,000 of income, 2.88% on the next $15,000, etc. For further details, see notes at end of table.

Alabama

Single, Head of household, or Married filing separately
- $0 to $500 . . . . 2%
- $501 to $3,000 . . . . 4%
- $3,001 and over 5%

Married filing jointly
- $0 to $1,000 . . . . 2%
- $1,001 to $6,000 . . . . 4%
- $6,001 and over 5%

Arizona[1]

Single or Married filing separately
- $0 to $10,000 . . . . 2.59%
- $10,001 to $25,000 . . . . 2.88%
- $25,001 to $50,000 . . . . 3.36%
- $50,001 to $150,000 . . . . 4.24%
- $150,001 and over 4.54%

Married filing jointly, Head of household
- $0 to $20,000 . . . . 2.59%
- $20,001 to $50,000 . . . . 2.88%
- $50,001 to $100,000 . . . 3.36%
- $100,001 to $300,000 . . . 4.24%
- $300,001 and over 4.54%

Arkansas[2,3]

Single, Head of household, Married filing jointly, or Married filing separately
- $0 to $3,799 . . . . 1%
- $3,800 to $7,599 . . . . . . 2.5%
- $7,600 to $11,399 . . . . . . 3.5%
- $11,400 to $18,999 . . . . . . 4.5%
- $19,000 to $31,699 . . . . . . 6%
- $31,700 and over 7%

California[1,2]

Single or Married filing separately, or Registered domestic partners filing separately
- $0 to $7,060 . . . . 1.25%
- $7,061 to $16,739 . . . . 2.25%
- $16,740 to $26,419 . . . . 4.25%
- $26,420 to $36,675 . . . . 6.25%
- $36,676 to $46,349 . . . . 8.25%
- $46,350 and over 9.55%

Head of household
- $0 to $14,130 . . . . 1.25%
- $14,131 to $33,479 . . . . 2.25%
- $33,480 to $43,157 . . . . 4.25%
- $43,158 to $53,412 . . . . 6.25%
- $53,413 to $63,089 . . . . 8.25%
- $63,090 and over 9.55%

Married filing jointly, Registered domestic partners filing jointly, or Surviving spouse
- $0 to $14,120 . . . . 1.25%
- $14,121 to $33,478 . . . . 2.25%
- $33,479 to $52,838 . . . . 4.25%
- $52,839 to $73,350 . . . . 6.25%
- $73,351 to $92,698 . . . . 8.25%
- $92,699 and over 9.55%

Colorado

4.63% of federal taxable income

Connecticut

Single or Married filing separately
- $0 to $10,000 . . . . 3%
- $10,001 to $500,000 . . . . . . 5%
- $500,001 and over 6.5%

Head of household
- $0 to $16,000 . . . . 3%
- $16,001 to $800,000 . . . . . 5%
- $800,001 and over 6.5%

Married filing jointly or Surviving spouse
- $0 to $20,000 . . . . 3%
- $20,001 to $1,000,000 . . . . . 5%
- $1,000,001 and over 6.5%

Delaware

Single, Head of household, Married filing jointly, or Married filing separately
- $0 to $2,000 . . . . 0%
- $2,000 to $5,000 . . . . 2.2%
- $5,001 to $10,000 . . . . . . 3.9%
- $10,001 to $20,000 . . . . . 4.8%
- $20,001 to $25,000 . . . . . 5.2%
- $25,001 to $60,000 . . . . 5.55%
- $60,001 and over 5.95%

District of Columbia

- $0 to $10,000 . . . . 4%
- $10,001 to $40,000 . . . . . . 6%
- $40,001 and over 8.5%

Georgia

Single
- $0 to $750 . . . . 1%
- $751 to $2,250 . . . . 2%
- $2,251 to $3,750 . . . . 3%
- $3,751 to $5,250 . . . . 4%
- $5,251 to $7,000 . . . . 5%
- $7,001 and over 6%

Head of household, Married filing jointly, or Surviving spouse
- $0 to $1,000 . . . . 1%
- $1,001 to $3,000 . . . . 2%
- $3,001 to $5,000 . . . . 3%
- $5,001 to $7,000 . . . . 4%
- $7,001 to $10,000 . . . . 5%
- $10,001 and over 6%

Married filing separately
- $0 to $500 . . . . 1%
- $501 to $1,500 . . . . 2%
- $1,501 to $2,500 . . . . 3%
- $2,501 to $3,500 . . . . 4%
- $3,501 to $5,000 . . . . 5%
- $5,001 and over 6%

Hawaii

Single or Married filing separately
- $0 to $2,400 . . . . 1.4%
- $2,401 to $4,800 . . . . 3.2%
- $4,801 to $9,600 . . . . 5.5%
- $9,601 to $14,400 . . . . . . 6.4%
- $14,401 to $19,200 . . . . . 6.8%
- $19,201 to $24,000 . . . . . 7.2%
- $24,001 to $36,000 . . . . . 7.6%
- $36,001 to $48,000 . . . . . 7.9%
- $48,001 to $150,000 . . . 8.25%
- $150,001 to $175,000 . . . . 9%
- $175,001 to $200,000 . . . 10%
- $200,001 and over 11%

Head of household
- $0 to $3,600 . . . . 1.4%
- $3,601 to $7,200 . . . . 3.2%
- $7,201 to $14,400 . . . . . . 5.5%
- $14,401 to $21,600 . . . . . 6.4%
- $21,601 to $28,800 . . . . . 6.8%
- $28,801 to $36,000 . . . . . 7.2%
- $36,001 to $54,000 . . . . . 7.6%
- $54,001 to $72,000 . . . . . 7.9%
- $72,001 to $225,000 . . 8.25%
- $225,001 to $262,500 . . . . 9%
- $262,501 to $300,000 . . . 10%
- $300,001 and over 11%

Married filing jointly or Surviving spouse
- $0 to $4,800 . . . . 1.4%
- $4,801 to $9,600 . . . . 3.2%
- $9,601 to $19,200 . . . . . . 5.5%
- $19,201 to $28,800 . . . . . 6.4%
- $28,801 to $38,400 . . . . . 6.8%
- $38,401 to $48,000 . . . . . 7.2%
- $48,001 to $72,000 . . . . . 7.6%
- $72,001 to $96,000 . . . . . 7.9%
- $96,001 to $300,000 . . 8.25%
- $300,001 to $350,000 . . . . 9%
- $350,001 to $400,000 . . . 10%
- $400,000 and over 11%

Idaho[1,2]

Single or Married filing separately
- $0 to $1,320 . . . . 1.6%
- $1,321 to $2,641 . . . . 3.6%
- $2,642 to $3,962 . . . . 4.1%
- $3,963 to $5,283 . . . . 5.1%
- $5,284 to $6,603 . . . . 6.1%
- $6,604 to $9,906 . . . . 7.1%
- $9,907 to $26,417 . . . . . . 7.4%
- $26,418 and over 7.8%

Head of household, Married filing jointly, or Surviving spouse
- $0 to $2,641 . . . . 1.6%
- $2,642 to $5,283 . . . . 3.6%
- $5,284 to $7,925 . . . . 4.1%
- $7,926 to $10,567 . . . . . . 5.1%
- $10,568 to $13,207 . . . . . 6.1%
- $13,208 to $19,813 . . . . . 7.1%
- $19,814 to $52,835 . . . . . 7.4%
- $52,836 and over 7.8%

Illinois

3% of taxable net income

Indiana

3.4% of adjusted gross income

Iowa[2]

- $0 to $1,407 . . . . 0.36%
- $1,408 to $2,814 . . . . . . 0.72%
- $2,815 to $5,628 . . . . . . 2.43%
- $5,629 to $12,663 . . . . . 4.5%
- $12,664 to $21,105 . . . 6.12%
- $21,106 to $28,140 . . . 6.48%
- $28,141 to $42,210 . . . . 6.8%
- $42,211 to $63,315 . . . 7.92%
- $63,316 and over 8.98%

Kansas

Single, Head of household, or Married filing separately
- $0 to $15,000 . . . . 3.5%
- $15,001 to $30,000 . . . 6.25%
- $30,001 and over 6.45%

Married filing jointly
- $0 to $30,000 . . . . 3.5%
- $30,001 to $60,000 . . . 6.25%
- $60,001 and over 6.45%

Kentucky

Single, Head of household, Married filing jointly, or Married filing separately
- $0 to $3,000 . . . . 2%
- $3,001 to $4,000 . . . . 3%
- $4,001 to $5,000 . . . . 4%
- $5,001 to $8,000 . . . . 5%
- $8,001 to $75,000 . . . . . 5.8%
- 75,001 and over 6%

Louisiana[1]

Single, Head of household, or Married filing separately
- $0 to $12,500 . . . . 2%
- $12,501 to $50,000 . . . . . . 4%
- $50,001 and over 6%

Married filing jointly
- $0 to $25,000 . . . . 2%
- $25,001 to $100,000 . . . . . . 4%
- $100,001 and over 6%

Maine[2]

Single or Married filing separately
- $0 to $5,049 . . . . 2%
- $5,050 to $10,049 . . . . . 4.5%
- $10,050 to $20,149 . . . . . 7%
- $20,150 and over 8.5%

Head of household
- $0 to $7,599 . . . . 2%
- $7,600 to $15,099 . . . . . 4.5%
- $15,100 to $30,249 . . . . . 7%
- $30,250 and over 8.5%

Married filing jointly, Qualifying widow(er)
- $0 to $10,149 . . . . 2%
- $10,150 to $20,149 . . . . 4.5%
- $20,150 to $40,349 . . . . . 7%
- $40,350 and over 8.5%

Maryland

Single or Married filing separately
- $0 to $1,000 . . . . 2%
- $1,001 to $2,000 . . . . 3%
- $2,001 to $3,000 . . . . 4%
- $3,001 to $150,000 . . . . 4.75%
- $150,001 to $300,000 . . . . 5%
- $300,001 to $500,000 . . 5.25%
- $500,001 to $1,000,000 . . 5.5%
- $1,000,001 and over . . . 6.25%

Head of household, Married filing jointly, or Qualifying Widow(er)
- $0 to $1,000 . . . . 2%
- $1,001 to $2,000 . . . . 3%
- $2,001 to $3,000 . . . . 4%
- $3,001 to $200,000 . . . . 4.75%
- $200,001 to $350,000 . . . . 5%
- $350,001 to $500,000 . . 5.25%
- $500,001 to $1,000,000 . . 5.5%
- $1,000,001 and over . . . 6.25%

Massachusetts

Short-term capital gains 12%
All other income 5.3%

Michigan

4.35% of taxable income

Minnesota[2]

Single
- $0 to $22,730 . . . . 5.35%
- $22,731 to $74,650 . . . . 7.05%
- $74,651 and over 7.85%

Head of household
- $0 to $27,980 . . . . 5.35%
- $27,981 to $112,420 . . . 7.05%
- $112,421 and over 7.85%

Married filing jointly
- $0 to $33,220 . . . . 5.35%
- $33,221 to $131,970 . . . 7.05%
- $131,971 and over 7.85%

Married filing separately
- $0 to $16,610 . . . . 5.35%
- $16,611 to $65,990 . . . . 7.05%
- $65,991 and over 7.85%

Mississippi

- $0 to $5,000 . . . . 3%
- $5,001 to $10,000 . . . . 4%
- $10,001 and over 5%

Missouri

- $0 to $1,000 . . . . 1.5%
- $1,001 to $2,000 . . . . 2%
- $2,001 to $3,000 . . . . 2.5%
- $3,001 to $4,000 . . . . 3%
- $4,001 to $5,000 . . . . 3.5%
- $5,001 to $6,000 . . . . 4%
- $6,001 to $7,000 . . . . 4.5%
- $7,001 to $8,000 . . . . 5%
- $8,001 to $9,000 . . . . 5.5%
- $9,001 and over 6%

Montana[2]

- $0 to $2,600 . . . . 1%
- $2,601 to $4,500 . . . . 2%
- $4,501 to $6,900 . . . . 3%
- $6,901 to $9,300 . . . . 4%
- $9,301 to $12,000 . . . . 5%
- $12,001 to $15,400 . . . . . . 6%
- $15,401 and over 6.9%

Nebraska

Single
- $0 to $2,400 . . . . 2.56%
- $2,401 to $17,500 . . . . . 3.57%
- $17,501 to $27,000 . . . . 5.12%
- $27,001 and over 6.84%

Head of household
- $0 to $4,500 . . . . 2.56%
- $4,501 to $28,000 . . . . . 3.57%
- $28,001 to $40,000 . . . . 5.12%
- $40,001 and over 6.84%

Married filing jointly or Surviving spouse
- $0 to $4,800 . . . . 2.56%
- $4,801 to $35,000 . . . . . 3.57%
- $35,001 to $54,000 . . . . 5.12%
- $54,001 and over 6.84%

Married filing separately
- $0 to $2,400 . . . . 2.56%
- $2,401 to $17,500 . . . . . 3.57%
- $17,501 to $27,000 . . . . 5.12%
- $27,001 and over 6.84%

New Hampshire

5% on interest and dividends only

New Jersey

Single or Married filing separately
- $0 to $20,000 . . . . 1.4%
- $20,001 to $35,000 . . . . 1.75%
- $35,001 to $40,000 . . . . . 3.5%
- $40,001 to $75,000 . . . 5.525%
- $75,001 to $400,000 . . . 6.37%
- $400,001 to $500,000 . . . . 8%
- $500,001 to $1,000,000 10.25%
- $1,000,001 and over . . 10.75%

Head of household, Married filing jointly, or Surviving spouse
- $0 to $20,000 . . . . 1.4%
- $20,001 to $50,000 . . . . 1.75%
- $50,001 to $70,000 . . . . 2.45%
- $70,001 to $80,000 . . . . . 3.5%
- $80,001 to $150,000 . . 5.525%
- $150,001 to $400,000 . . 6.37%
- $400,001 to $500,000 . . . . 8%
- $500,001 to $1,000,000 10.25%
- $1,000,001 and over . . 10.75%

New Mexico[1]

Single
- $0 to $5,500 .... 1.7%
- $5,501 to $11,000 ...... 3.2%
- $11,001 to $16,000 ..... 4.7%
- $16,001 and over 4.9%

Head of household
- $0 to $8,000 .... 1.7%
- $8,001 to $16,000 ...... 3.2%
- $16,001 to $24,000 ..... 4.7%
- $24,001 and over 4.9%

Married filing jointly or Surviving spouse
- $0 to $8,000 .... 1.7%
- $8,001 to $16,000 ...... 3.2%
- $16,001 to $24,000 ..... 4.7%
- $24,001 and over 4.9%

Married filing separately
- $0 to $4,000 .... 1.7%
- $4,001 to $8,000 .... 3.2%
- $8,001 to $12,000 ...... 4.7%
- $12,001 and over 4.9%

New York

Single or Married filing separately
- $0 to $8,000 .... 4%
- $8,001 to $11,000 ...... 4.5%
- $11,001 to $13,000 .... 5.25%
- $13,001 to $20,000 ..... 5.9%
- $20,001 to $200,000 ... 6.85%
- $200,001 to $500,000 .. 7.85%
- $500,001 and over 8.97%

Head of household
- $0 to $11,000 .... 4%
- $11,001 to $15,000 ..... 4.5%
- $15,001 to $17,000 .... 5.25%
- $17,001 to $30,000 ..... 5.9%
- $30,001 to $250,000 ... 6.85%
- $250,001 to $500,000 .. 7.85%
- $500,001 and over 8.97%

Married filing jointly or Surviving spouse
- $0 to $16,000 .... 4%
- $16,001 to $22,000 ..... 4.5%
- $22,001 to $26,000 .... 5.25%
- $26,001 to $40,000 ..... 5.9%
- $40,001 to $300,000 ... 6.85%
- $300,001 to $500,000 .. 7.85%
- $500,001 and over 8.97%

North Carolina

Single
- $0 to $12,750 .... 6%
- $12,751 to $60,000 .... 7%
- $60,001 and over 7.75%

Head of household
- $0 to $17,000 .... 6%
- $17,001 to $80,000 .... 7%
- $80,001 and over 7.75%

Married filing jointly or Surviving spouse
- $0 to $21,250 .... 6%
- $21,251 to $100,000 ...... 7%
- $100,001 and over 7.75%

Married filing separately
- $0 to $10,625 .... 6%
- $10,626 to $50,000 ...... 7%
- $50,001 and over 7.75%

North Dakota[2]

Single
- $0 to $33,950 .... 1.84%
- $33,951 to $82,850 .... 3.44%
- $82,851 to $171,550 ... 3.81%
- $171,551 to $372,950 .. 4.42%
- $372,951 and over 4.86%

Head of household
- $0 to $45,500 .... 1.84%
- $45,501 to $117,450 ... 3.44%
- $117,451 to $190,200 .. 3.81%
- $190,201 to $372,950 .. 4.42%
- $372,951 and over 4.86%

Married filing jointly or Surviving spouse
- $0 to $56,750 .... 1.84%
- $56,751 to $137,050 ... 3.44%
- $137,051 to $208,850 .. 3.81%
- $208,851 to $372,950 .. 4.42%
- $372,951 and over 4.86%

Married filing separately
- $0 to $28,375 .... 1.84%
- $28,376 to $68,525 .... 3.44%
- $68,526 to $104,425 ... 3.81%
- $104,426 to $186,475 .. 4.42%
- $186,476 and over 4.86%

Ohio

- $0 to $5,000 .... 0.587%
- $5,001 to $10,000 .... 1.174%
- $10,001 to $15,000 ... 2.348%
- $15,001 to $20,000 ... 2.935%
- $20,001 to $40,000 ... 3.521%
- $40,001 to $80,000 ... 4.109%
- $80,001 to $100,000 .. 4.695%
- $100,001 to $200,000 . 5.451%
- $200,001 and over 5.925%

Oklahoma

Single or Married filing separately
- $0 to $1,000 .... 0.5%
- $1,001 to $2,500 .... 1%
- $2,501 to $3,750 .... 2%
- $3,751 to $4,900 .... 3%
- $4,901 to $7,200 .... 4%
- $7,201 to $8,700 .... 5%
- $8,701 and over 5.50%

Head of household, Married filing jointly, or Surviving spouse
- $0 to $2,000 .... 0.5%
- $2,001 to $5,000 .... 1%
- $5,001 to $7,500 .... 2%
- $7,501 to $9,800 .... 3%
- $9,801 to $12,200 .... 4%
- $12,201 to $15,000 ...... 5%
- $15,001 and over 5.5%

Oregon[2]

Single
- $0 to $2,000 .... 5%
- $2,001 to $5,000 .... 7%
- $5,001 to $125,000 ...... 9%
- $125,001 to $250,000 .. 10.8%
- $250,001 and over 11%

Married filing jointly, Head of household, or Surviving spouse
- $0 to $4,000 .... 5%
- $4,001 to $10,000 .... 7%
- $10,001 to $250,000 ...... 9%
- $250,001 to $500,000 ...10.8%
- $500,001 and over 11%

Pennsylvania

3.07% of taxable compensation, net profits, net gains from the sale of property, rent, royalties, patents or copyrights, income from estates or trusts, dividends, interest, and winnings

Rhode Island

Single
- $0 to $33,950 ....3.75%
- $33,951 to $82,250 .... 7%
- $82,251 to $171,550 ....7.75%
- $171,551 to $372,950 ..... 9%
- $372,951 and over 9.9%

Head of household
- $0 to $45,500 ....3.75%
- $45,501 to $117,450 ...... 7%
- $117,451 to $190,200 ...7.75%
- $190,201 to $372,950 ..... 9%
- $372,951 and over 9.9%

Married filing jointly or Surviving spouse
- $0 to $56,700 ....3.75%
- $56,701 to $137,050 ...... 7%
- $137,051 to $208,850 ...7.75%
- $208,851 to $372,950 ..... 9%
- $372,951 and over 9.9%

Married filing separately
- $0 to $28,350 ....3.75%
- $28,351 to $68,525 .... 7%
- $68,526 to $104,425 ....7.75%
- $104,426 to $186,475 ..... 9%
- $186,476 and over 9.9%

South Carolina[2]

- $0 to $2,740 .... 0%
- $2,741 to $5,480 .... 3%
- $5,481 to $8,220 .... 4%
- $8,221 to $10,960 .... 5%
- $10,961 to $13,700 .... 6%
- $13,701 and over 7%

Tennessee

6% of interest and dividends

Utah

5% on state taxable income

Vermont[2]

Single
- $0 to $33,950 ....3.55%
- $33,951 to $82,250 .... 7%
- $82,251 to $171,550 ....8.25%
- $171,551 to $372,950 ....8.9%
- $372,951 and over 9.4%

Head of household
- $0 to $45,500 .... 3.55%
- $45,501 to $117,450 ......7%
- $117,451 to $190,200 .. 8.25%
- $190,201 to $372,950 ... 8.9%
- $372,951 and over 9.4%

Married filing jointly, Surviving spouse, Civil Union filing jointly
- $0 to $56,700 .... 3.55%
- $56,701 to $137,050 ......7%
- $137,051 to $208,850 .. 8.25%
- $208,851 to $372,950 ... 8.9%
- $372,951 and over 9.4%

Married or Civil Union filing separately
- $0 to $28,350 .... 3.55%
- $28,351 to $68,525 ....7%
- $68,526 to $104,425 ... 8.25%
- $104,426 to $186,475 ... 8.9%
- $186,476 and over 9.4%

Virginia

Single, Head of household, Married filing jointly, or Married filing separately
- $0 to $3,000 ....2%
- $3,001 to $5,000 ....3%
- $5,001 to $17,000 ....5%
- $17,001 and over 5.75%

West Virginia

Single, Head of household, or Married filing jointly
- $0 to $10,000 ....3%
- $10,001 to $25,000 ....4%
- $25,001 to $40,000 ..... 4.5%
- $40,001 to $60,000 ....6%
- $60,001 and over 6.5%

Married filing separately
- $0 to $5,000 ....3%
- $5,001 to $12,500 ....4%
- $12,501 to $20,000 ..... 4.5%
- $20,001 to $30,000 ....6%
- $30,001 and over 6.5%

Wisconsin[1,2]

Single or Head of household
- $0 to $10,220 .... 4.6%
- $10,221 to $20,440 .... 6.15%
- $20,441 to $153,280 .... 6.5%
- $153,281 to $225,000 .. 6.75%
- $225,001 and over 7.75%

Married filing jointly
- $0 to $13,620 .... 4.6%
- $13,621 to $27,250 .... 6.15%
- $27,251 to $204,370 .... 6.5%
- $204,371 to $300,000 .. 6.75%
- $300,001 and over 7.75%

Married filing separately
- $0 to $6,810 .... 4.6%
- $6,811 to $13,620 ..... 6.15%
- $13,621 to $102,190 .... 6.5%
- $102,191 to $150,000 .. 6.75%
- $150,001 and over 7.75%

(1) Community property state in which, in general, one-half of the community income is taxable to each spouse. (2) Brackets indexed for inflation annually. (3) 2009 adjusted brackets were not available. Bracketed rates listed are for 2008. **Arkansas:** Married filing separately combined-status couples calculate taxes separately and add the results. **California:** An additional 1% tax is imposed on taxable income in excess of $1 million. **Colorado:** Alternative minimum tax imposed. Individual taxpayers are subject to an alternative minimum tax equal to the amount by which 3.47% of their Colorado alternative minimum taxable income exceeds their Colorado normal tax. **Connecticut:** Resident estates and trusts are subject to the 5% income tax rate on all of their income. Additional state minimum tax imposed on resident individuals, trusts, and estates that are subject to the federal alternative minimum tax, equal to the amount by which the Connecticut minimum tax exceeds the Connecticut basic income tax (the lesser of [a] 19% of adjusted federal tentative minimum tax or [b] 5.5% of adjusted federal alternative minimum taxable income). Separate provisions apply for non- and part-year resident individuals, trusts, and estates. **Illinois:** Additional personal property replacement tax of 1.5% of net income is imposed on partnerships, trusts, and S corporations. **Indiana:** Counties may impose an adjusted gross income tax on residents or on nonresidents, or a county option income tax. **Iowa:** An alternative minimum tax of 6.7% of alternative minimum income is imposed if the minimum tax exceeds the taxpayer's regular income tax liability. The minimum tax is 75% of the maximum regular tax rate. **Maine:** Additional state minimum tax is imposed equal to the amount by which the tentative minimum tax exceeds regular income tax liability. No state minimum tax on individuals beginning in 2010. **Massachusetts:** Part A income represents either interest and dividends or short-term capital gains. Part B income represents wages, salaries, tips, pensions, state bank interest, partnership income, business income, rents, alimony, winnings, and certain other items of income. Part C income represents gains from the sale of capital assets held for more than one year. **Michigan:** Business activity allocated or apportioned to Michigan is also subject to the Michigan business tax. **Minnesota:** A 6.4% alternative minimum tax is imposed. **Montana:** Minimum tax, $1. **Nebraska:** The tax rates in the schedules are determined by multiplying the primary rate set by the legislature by the following factors for the brackets, from lowest to highest bracket. For tax years beginning on or after January 1, 2003, the respective factors are: 0.6932, 0.9646, 1.3846, and 1.848. One rate schedule is to be established for each federal filing status (Sec. 77-2715.02). **New Mexico:** Qualified nonresident taxpayers may pay alternative tax of 0.75% of gross receipts from New Mexico sales. **New York:** A supplemental tax is imposed to recapture the tax table benefit. The supplemental tax is calculated in accordance with N.Y. Tax Law Sec. 601(d). **Rhode Island:** Taxpayers may elect to compute income tax liability based on a flat rate equal to 6.5% or a graduated rate schedule based on 25% of the federal income tax rates, including capital gains rates and any other special rates for other types of income, that were in effect prior to enactment of the Economic Growth and Tax Relief Reconciliation Act of 2001. **Vermont:** The tax amount in the schedules is increased by 24% of a taxpayer's federal tax liability for: additional taxes assessed due to early withdrawals from qualified retirement plans, individual retirement accounts, and medical savings accounts; recapture of the federal investment tax credit; or tax on qualified lump-sum distributions of pension income not included in federal taxable income. The amount of tax is decreased by 24% of the reduction in the taxpayer's federal liability due to farm income averaging. **West Virginia:** Minimum tax equal to the excess by which 25% of any federal minimum tax or alternative minimum tax for the taxable year exceeds the sum of the primary tax for West Virginia personal income tax purposes for the taxable year. The West Virginia minimum tax will expire for tax years on or after Jan. 1, 2010. **Wisconsin:** A permanent recycling surcharge is imposed on individuals, estates, trusts, and partnerships with at least $4 million in gross receipts at the rate of the greater of $25 or 0.2% of net business income as allocated or apportioned to Wisconsin with a maximum of $9,800. Farming is no longer treated preferentially.

EDUCATION

U.S. Public Schools: Students, Staff, Spending, 1899-2007

Source: National Center for Education Statistics, U.S. Dept. of Education

	1899-1900	1919-20	1939-40	1959-60	1969-70	1979-80	1989-90	1999-2000	2006-07
Population statistics (thous.)									
Total U.S. population[1]	75,995	104,514	131,028	177,830	201,385	225,055	246,819	279,040	298,363
Population 5-17 years of age	21,573	27,571	30,151	43,881	52,386	48,043	44,947	52,811	53,158
Percentage 5-17 years of age. . . .	28.4%	26.4%	23.0%	24.7%	26.0%	21.3%	18.2%	18.9%	17.8%
Enrollment (thousands)									
Elementary and secondary[2]	15,503	21,578	25,434	36,087	45,550	41,651	40,543	46,857	49,316
Pre-kindergarten to grades 1-8. . .	14,984	19,378	18,833	27,602	32,513	28,034	29,152	33,486	34,235
Grades 9-12	519	2,200	6,601	8,485	13,037	13,616	11,390	13,371	15,081
Percentage pop. 5-17 enrolled	71.9%	78.3%	84.4%	82.2%	87.0%	86.7%	90.2%	88.7%	92.8%
Percentage enrolled in high schools	3.3%	10.2%	26.0%	23.5%	28.6%	32.7%	28.1%	28.5%	30.6%
High school grads. (thousands)	62	231	1,143	1,627	2,589	2,748	2,320	2,554	2,892
Instructional staff									
Total instructional staff (thousands)	*	678	912	1,457	2,286	2,406	2,986	3,819	4,187
Teachers, librarians, and other non-supervisory instructional staff (thousands)	423	657	875	1,393	2,195	2,300	2,860	3681.858	4,033
Revenue and expenditures (mil)									
Total revenue.	$220	$970	$2,261	$14,747	$40,267	$96,881	$208,548	$372,944	$555,338
Total expenditures.	215	1,036	2,344	15,613	40,683	95,962	212,770	381,838	562,253
Current expenditures[3,4].	180	861	1,942	12,329	34,218	86,984	188,229	323,889	476,826
Capital outlay	35	154	258	2,662	4,659	6,506	17,781	43,357	62,910
Interest on school debt	*	18	131	490	1,171	1,874	3,776	9,135	14,713
Others.	*	3	13	133	636	598	2,983	5,457	7,804
Salaries and pupil cost									
Avg. annual salary of instruct. staff[5] .	$325	$871	$1,441	$4,995	$8,626	$15,970	$31,367	$41,807	$50,758
Expenditure per capita total pop. . . .	2.83	9.91	17.89	88	202	426	862	1,368	1,884
Current expenditure[4] per pupil ADA[6]	16.67	53.32	88.09	375	816	2,272	4,980	7,394	10,337

* = Data not collected. **Note:** Because of rounding, details may not add to totals. Prior to 1959-60, data do not include Alaska and Hawaii. (1) Population data for 1899-1900 are based on total population from the decennial census. From 1919-20 to 1959-60, population data are total population, including armed forces overseas, as of July 1 preceding the schoo-year. Data for later years are for resident population that excluding armed forces overseas. (2) Data for 1899 through 1960 are school year enrollment; data for later years are fall enrollment. (3) In 1899-1900, includes interest on school debt. (4) Because of changes in the definition of "current expenditures," data for 1959-60 and later years are not entirely comparable with prior years. (5) Data prior to 1959-60 include supervisors, principals, teachers, and nonsupervisory instructional staff. (6) ADA = average daily attendance.

U.S. Public High School Graduation Rates, 2005-06

Source: National Center for Education Statistics, U.S. Dept. of Education

State	Rate	Rank	State	Rate	Rank	State	Rate	Rank	State	Rate	Rank
Alabama	66.2%	44	Illinois	79.7%	17	Montana	81.9%	10	Rhode Island	77.8%	22
Alaska	66.5	43	Indiana	73.3	32	Nebraska	87.0	2	South Carolina	61.0	49
Arizona	70.5	39	Iowa	86.9	3	Nevada	55.8	51	South Dakota	84.5	6
Arkansas	80.4	15	Kansas	77.5	23	New Hampshire	81.1	11	Tennessee	70.7	38
California	69.2	40	Kentucky	77.2	24	New Jersey	84.8	5	Texas	72.5	35
Colorado	75.5	29	Louisiana	59.5	50	New Mexico	67.3	42	Utah	78.6	20
Connecticut	80.9	13	Maine	76.3	27	New York	67.4	41	Vermont	82.3	8
Delaware	76.3	26	Maryland	79.9	16	North Carolina	71.8	37	Virginia	74.5	31
Dist. of Columbia	65.4	45	Massachusetts	79.5	18	North Dakota	82.2	9	Washington	72.9	34
Florida	63.6	46	Michigan	72.2	36	Ohio	79.2	19	West Virginia	76.9	25
Georgia	62.4	48	Minnesota	86.2	4	Oklahoma	77.8	21	Wisconsin	87.5	1
Hawaii	75.5	30	Mississippi	63.5	47	Oregon	73.0	33	Wyoming	76.1	28
Idaho	80.5	14	Missouri	81.0	12	Pennsylvania	83.5	7	**TOTAL U.S.[1]**	73.4	

Note: The averaged freshman graduation rate provides an estimate of the percentage of high school students who graduate. The rate uses aggregate student enrollment data to estimate the size of an incoming freshman class and aggregate counts of the number of diplomas awarded 4 years later. (1) Includes estimates for nonreporting states.

Technology in U.S. Public Schools*

Source: Quality Education Data, Inc., Denver, CO

Number and percentage of schools in each category that have the technology indicated.

	Total		Elementary[1]		Middle/ jr. high[2]		Senior high[3]		K-12[4]		Special ed./ adult ed.	
TOTAL SCHOOLS	93,189	100%	56,232	100%	14,475	100%	20,161	100%	2,530	100%	2,310	100%
Schools with computers . .	83,057	89	51,418	91	12,911	89	17,100	85	2,026	80	1,625	70
by number of computers:												
1-10	3,170	3	1,990	4	194	1	597	3	59	2	389	17
11-20	4,590	5	3,123	6	345	2	829	4	129	5	293	13
21-50	16,741	18	11,934	21	1,728	12	2,628	13	493	19	449	19
51-100	23,753	25	16,940	30	3,372	23	3,178	16	607	24	262	11
100+	34,803	37	17,431	31	7,272	50	9,868	49	738	29	232	10
Schools with LANs[5]	61,104	66	36,791	66	10,652	74	14,030	72	1,614	65	707	30
by enrollment:												
100-299	13,607	15	8,610	15	1,212	8	3,309	17	774	31	476	20
300-499	18,256	20	13,802	25	2,098	15	2,294	12	403	16	62	3
500+	29,241	32	14,379	26	7,342	51	8,427	43	437	18	169	7
Schools with WANs[6]	45,933	50	27,549	49	8,011	56	9,932	51	996	40	441	19
by enrollment:												
100-299	8,816	10	5,701	10	769	5	2,032	10	434	18	314	13
300-499	14,574	16	11,100	20	1,735	12	1,707	9	289	12	32	1
500+	22,543	24	10,748	19	5,507	38	6,193	32	273	11	95	4

*Data for schools with computers as of 2005. All other data from 2004. (1) Includes preschools and schools with grade spans of preschool-3, K-6, K-8, and K-12. (2) Includes schools with grade spans of 4-8, 7-8, and 7-9. (3) Includes vocational, technical, and alternative high schools and schools with grade spans of 7-12, 9-12, and 10-12. (4) K-12 also included under elementary schools. (5) LAN = Local area computer network. (6) WAN = Wide area computer network.

Overview of U.S. Public Schools, Fall 2006-07*

Source: National Center for Education Statistics, U.S. Dept. of Education; National Education Association

State	Local school districts	Elementary schools[1]	Secondary schools[2]	Classroom teachers	Total enrollment	Pupils per teacher	Teacher's avg. pay[3]	Expend. per pupil[3]
Alabama	133	951	270	56,134	743,632	13.2	$43,389	$7,672
Alaska	53	201	50	7,903	132,608	16.8	54,658	10,392
Arizona	238	1,320	385	52,625	1,065,082	20.2	45,941	5,696
Arkansas	254	766	280	35,089	476,409	13.6	44,245	8,905
California	989	7,001	1,209	307,110	6,406,821	20.9	63,640	8,834
Colorado	179	1,298	280	46,973	794,026	16.9	45,833	8,895
Connecticut	169	858	154	39,115	575,100	14.7	60,822	13,005
Delaware	19	148	27	8,038	122,254	15.2	54,680	12,565
Dist. of Columbia	1	150	29	5,394	72,850	13.5	59,000	16,540
Florida	67	2,511	373	162,851	2,671,513	16.4	45,308	8,493
Georgia	182	1,721	337	113,597	1,629,157	14.3	49,905	8,799
Hawaii	1	218	41	11,271	180,728	16.0	51,922	10,431
Idaho	125	458	117	14,770	267,380	18.1	42,798	7,176
Illinois	873	3,283	655	140,988	2,118,276	15.0	58,246	10,404
Indiana	294	1,490	336	61,315	1,045,940	17.1	47,831	9,330
Iowa	365	1,060	326	35,653	483,122	13.6	43,130	8,141
Kansas	323	1,013	332	35,297	469,506	13.3	43,334	8,804
Kentucky	175	971	202	43,371	683,173	15.8	43,646	8,459
Louisiana	68	952	216	45,951	675,851	14.7	42,816	8,657
Maine	287	519	108	16,826	193,986	11.5	41,596	12,063
Maryland	24	1,110	187	58,443	851,640	14.6	56,927	10,298
Massachusetts	250	1,512	291	73,157	968,661	13.2	58,624	13,294
Michigan	552	2,683	603	98,037	1,714,709	17.5	54,895	10,209
Minnesota	340	1,171	415	51,880	840,565	16.2	49,634	10,143
Mississippi	152	637	193	32,351	495,026	15.3	40,182	6,866
Missouri	524	1,610	491	67,398	920,353	13.7	41,839	8,170
Montana	425	656	167	10,398	144,418	13.9	41,225	8,682
Nebraska	269	797	286	21,459	287,580	13.4	42,044	8,309
Nevada	17	439	84	22,908	424,240	18.5	45,342	6,963
New Hampshire	183	396	82	15,515	203,551	13.1	46,527	10,792
New Jersey	593	1,982	331	112,301	1,388,850	12.4	59,920	14,675
New Mexico	95	630	143	22,016	328,220	14.9	42,780	9,036
New York	697	3,354	791	218,879	2,809,649	12.8	58,537	14,206
North Carolina	125	1,824	398	104,412	1,444,481	13.8	46,410	8,000
North Dakota	198	323	169	8,007	96,670	12.1	38,822	8,228
Ohio	614	2,814	783	110,390	1,836,096	16.6	51,937	10,563
Oklahoma	540	1,300	462	42,206	639,391	15.1	42,379	7,084
Oregon	199	945	234	26,443	562,574	21.3	50,911	8,989
Pennsylvania	501	2,424	612	123,375	1,871,060	15.2	54,970	11,304
Rhode Island	32	256	44	11,381	151,612	13.3	55,956	11,503
South Carolina	101	895	194	49,733	703,119	14.1	44,133	9,274
South Dakota	171	508	165	9,070	121,158	13.4	35,378	8,237
Tennessee	136	1,297	275	62,176	978,368	15.7	43,816	7,255
Texas	1,033	5,731	1,116	311,649	4,599,509	14.8	44,897	8,048
Utah	40	662	117	23,640	523,586	22.1	40,566	5,551
Vermont	292	249	46	8,859	95,399	10.8	48,370	13,385
Virginia	134	1,527	301	105,039	1,220,440	11.6	44,727	9,785
Washington	296	1,472	306	53,743	1,026,774	19.1	47,882	8,730
West Virginia	57	439	107	19,414	281,939	14.5	40,531	10,071
Wisconsin	425	1,599	480	59,089	876,700	14.8	47,901	10,432
Wyoming	52	274	63	6,757	85,193	12.6	50,692	13,328
TOTAL U.S.	**13,862**	**68,405**	**15,663**	**3,180,396**	**49,298,945**	**15.5**	**50,816**	**9,557**

*Full-time elementary and secondary schools only. (1) Includes primary and middle schools (from kindergarten to no higher than grade 9). (2) Includes schools with no grade lower than 7. (3) 2006-07 estimates.

Programs for the Disabled, 1995-2007

Source: Office of Special Education and Rehabilitative Services, U.S. Dept. of Education

Number of children and young adults from 3-21 years old served annually in federally funded educational programs for the disabled; in thousands.

Type of disability	1995 -96	1996 -97	1997 -98	1998 -99	1999 -00	2000 -01	2001 -02	2002 -03	2003 -04	2004 -05	2005 -06	2006 -07
Learning disabilities	2,578	2,651	2,727	2,790	2,834	2,868	2,861	2,848	2,831	2,798	2,735	2,665
Speech impairments	1,022	1,045	1,060	1,068	1,080	1,409	1,391	1,412	1,441	1,463	1,468	1,475
Mental retardation	571	579	589	597	600	624	616	602	593	578	556	534
Emotional disturbance	437	446	454	462	469	481	483	485	489	489	477	464
Multiple disabilities	93	98	106	106	111	133	136	138	140	140	141	142
Hearing impairments	67	68	69	70	71	78	78	78	79	79	79	80
Orthopedic impairments	63	66	67	69	71	83	83	83	77	73	71	69
Other health impairments[1]	133	160	190	220	253	303	350	403	464	521	570	611
Visual impairments	25	25	26	26	26	29	28	29	28	29	29	29
Autism	28	34	42	53	65	94	114	137	163	191	223	258
Deaf-blindness	1	1	1	2	2	1	2	2	2	2	2	2
Traumatic brain injury	9	10	12	13	14	16	22	22	23	24	24	25
Developmental delay	—	—	2	12	19	178	242	283	305	332	339	333
All disabilities	**5,572**	**5,737**	**5,908**	**6,056**	**6,195**	**6,296**	**6,407**	**6,523**	**6,634**	**6,719**	**6,713**	**6,686**

— = Not available or not reliable data. **Note:** Counts based on reports from states and District of Columbia. Details may not add to totals because of rounding and/or incomplete enumeration. (1) Includes limited strength, vitality, or alertness due to chronic or acute health problems such as a heart condition, tuberculosis, rheumatic fever, nephritis, asthma, sickle cell anemia, hemophilia, epilepsy, lead poisoning, leukemia, or diabetes.

Trends in International Mathematics and Science Study (TIMSS), 1995-2007

Source: National Center for Education Statistics

The TIMSS is an international assessment test that was administered to 4th and 8th graders in 1995, 1999 (5th graders only), 2003, and 2007, to measure the degree to which students have learned concepts of mathematics and science. Listed below are the average scaled scores for each country. Scores are reported on a scale of 0 to 1,000, with the scale average set at 500. Student achievement is considered "high" with a score of at least 550; a score of at least 475 is considered "intermediate."

4th Grade

	Mathematics 2007	Mathematics Change 1995-2007	Science 2007	Science Change 1995-2007
Australia	516	22%	527	6%
Austria	505	−25	526	−12
Czech Republic	486	−54	515	−17
England	541	57	542	14
Hong Kong	607	50	554	46
Hungary	510	−12	536	28
Iran	402	15	436	55
Japan	568	1	548	−5
Latvia	537	38	542	56
Netherlands	535	−14	523	−7
New Zealand	492	23	504	−1
Norway	473	−3	477	−27
Scotland	494	1	500	−14
Singapore	599	9	587	63
Slovenia	502	40	518	54
United States	**529**	**11**	**539**	**−3**

8th Grade

	Mathematics 2007	Mathematics Change 1995-2007	Science 2007	Science Change 1995-2007
Australia	496	−13%	NA	NA
Bulgaria	464	−63	515	1%
Colombia	380	47	417	52
Cyprus	465	−2	452	0
Czech Republic	504	−42	539	−16
England	513	16	542	8
Hong Kong	572	4	530	20
Hungary	517	−10	539	2
Iran	403	−15	459	−4
Japan	570	−11	554	−1
South Korea	597	17	553	7
Lithuania	506	34	519	55
Norway	469	−29	487	−28
Romania	461	−12	462	−9
Russia	512	−12	530	7
Scotland	487	−6	496	−5
Singapore	593	−16	567	−13
Slovenia	501	7	538	24
Sweden	491	−48	511	−42
United States	**508**	**16**	**520**	**7**

Mathematics, Reading, and Science Achievement of U.S. Students, 1998-2007

Source: National Assessment of Educational Progress, National Center for Education Statistics, U.S. Dept. of Education

Percent of public school students who scored at or above basic levels in national tests.*

State	GRADE 4 Math 2000	2007	Reading 1998	2007	GRADE 8 Math 2000	2007	Reading 1998	2007	Science 2000	2005
AL	55	70	56	62	52	55	67	63	53	48
AK	NA	79	NA	62	NA	73	NA	70	NA	NA
AZ	57	74	51	56	62	66	72	65	55	49
AR	55	81	54	64	52	65	68	69	53	56
CA	50	70	48	53	52	59	63	60	38	44
CO	NA	82	69	70	NA	75	77	75	NA	66
CT	76	84	76	73	72	73	81	74	64	63
DE	NA	87	53	73	NA	74	64	80	NA	63
DC	24	49	27	39	23	34	44	45	NA	NA
FL	NA	86	53	70	NA	68	67	66	NA	51
GA	57	79	54	66	55	64	68	67	52	53
HI	55	77	45	59	52	59	59	58	40	44
ID	68	85	NA	70	71	75	NA	76	71	71
IL	63	79	NA	65	68	70	NA	75	59	58
IN	77	89	NA	68	76	76	NA	73	66	62
IA	75	87	67	74	NA	77	NA	79	NA	NA
KS	76	89	70	72	77	81	81	78	NA	NA
KY	59	79	62	68	63	69	74	75	60	63
LA	57	73	44	52	48	64	63	64	44	47
ME	73	85	72	73	76	78	83	81	72	72
MD	60	80	58	69	65	74	70	69	57	54
MA	77	93	70	81	76	85	79	83	70	72
MI	71	80	62	66	70	66	NA	73	68	66
MN	76	87	69	73	80	81	78	80	72	71
MS	45	70	47	51	41	54	62	60	41	40
MO	71	82	61	67	67	72	75	76	66	66

State	GRADE 4 Math 2000	2007	Reading 1998	2007	GRADE 8 Math 2000	2007	Reading 1998	2007	Science 2000	2005
MT	72	88	72	75	80	79	83	85	79	76
NE	65	80	NA	74	74	74	NA	79	52	48
NV	60	74	51	57	58	60	70	63	NA	NA
NH	NA	91	75	76	NA	78	NA	82	NA	76
NJ	NA	90	NA	77	NA	77	NA	81	NA	65
NM	50	70	51	58	50	50	71	62	48	46
NY	66	85	62	69	68	70	76	75	NA	NA
NC	73	85	58	64	70	73	74	71	54	53
ND	73	91	NA	75	77	86	NA	84	72	77
OH	73	87	NA	73	75	76	NA	79	72	67
OK	67	82	66	65	64	66	80	72	60	57
OR	65	79	58	62	71	73	78	77	68	66
PA	NA	85	NA	73	NA	77	NA	79	NA	NA
RI	65	80	64	65	64	65	76	69	58	58
SC	59	80	53	59	55	71	66	69	48	54
SD	NA	86	NA	71	NA	81	NA	83	NA	76
TN	59	76	57	61	53	64	71	71	55	55
TX	76	87	59	66	68	78	74	73	52	53
UT	69	83	62	69	68	72	77	75	67	65
VT	73	89	NA	74	75	81	NA	84	71	76
VA	71	87	62	74	67	77	78	79	61	66
WA	NA	84	64	70	NA	75	76	77	NA	66
WV	65	81	60	63	62	61	75	68	57	57
WI	NA	85	72	70	NA	76	78	76	NA	70
WY	71	88	64	73	70	80	76	80	69	74
U.S.	**64**	**81**	**58**	**66**	**65**	**70**	**71**	**73**	**57**	**57**

NA = Not administered. *"Basic level" denotes a partial mastery of prerequisite knowledge and skills fundamental for proficient work at each grade.

Enrollment in U.S. Public and Private Schools*, 1899-2016

Source: National Center for Education Statistics, U.S. Dept. of Education

School year[1]	Public school[2]	Private school[2]	% tot. private	School year[1]	Public school[2]	Private school[2]	% tot. private
1899-1900	15,503	1,352	8.7%	1979-80	41,651	5,000[3]	12.0%
1909-10	17,814	1,558	8.7	1989-90	40,543	5,599	13.8
1919-20	21,578	1,699	7.9	1999-2000	46,857	6,018	12.8
1929-30	25,678	2,651	10.3	2005-06	49,113	6,073	12.4
1939-40	25,434	2,611	10.3	2006-07	49,299	6,095[4]	12.4
1949-50	25,111	3,380	13.5	2007-08[4]	49,644	6,066	12.2
1959-60	35,182	5,675	16.1	2008-09[4]	49,825	6,054	12.2
1969-70	45,550	5,500[3]	12.1	2015-16[4]	52,910	6,217	11.8

*Private includes all nonpublic schools. (1) Fall enrollment. (2) In thousands. Data from fall 1980 onward covers an expanded universe of private schools; comparisons with earlier years should be avoided. (3) Estimated. (4) Projected.

Enrollment in U.S. Religious and Nonsectarian Private Schools, 2005-06

Source: U.S. Department of Education, National Center for Education Statistics, *Private School Universe Survey, 2005-06*

Number and percentage distribution of private school students, by school level and religious or nonsectarian orientation of school. Religious groups listed only if at least some data met reporting standards.

	Total		Elementary		Secondary		Combined	
	Students	Percent	Students	Percent	Students	Percent	Students	Percent
Total........................	5,057,520	100.0%	2,551,196	100.0%	859,453	100.0%	1,646,871	100.0%
Religious orientation..............	4,130,856	81.7	2,256,139	88.4	733,199	85.3	1,141,518	69.3
Nonsectarian	926,664	18.3	295,057	11.6	126,255	14.7	505,353	30.7
Roman Catholic....................	2,246,240	44.4	1,549,040	60.7	597,568	69.5	99,633	6.0
Amish...........................	25,589	0.5	23,489	0.9	(1)	(1)	2,089	0.1
Assembly of God	56,683	1.1	24,490	1.0	(1)	(1)	31,296	1.9
Baptist..........................	278,921	5.5	56,219	2.2	9,168	1.1	213,534	13.0
Brethren........................	11,512	0.2	3,983	0.2	(1)	(1)	6,126	0.4
Calvinist........................	32,642	0.6	14,687	0.6	6,726	0.8	11,229	0.7
Christian (unspecified).............	633,861	12.5	155,983	6.1	34,892	4.1	442,986	26.9
Church of Christ...................	37,549	0.7	7,318	0.3	(1)	(1)	30,189	1.8
Church of God	11,436	0.2	3,503	0.1	(1)	(1)	7,849	0.5
Church of God in Christ.............	3,698	0.1	2,798	0.1	(1)	(1)	(1)	(1)
Church of the Nazarene.............	9,440	0.2	4,652	0.2	0	0.0	4,788	0.3
Episcopal	100,961	2.0	41,895	1.6	10,626	1.2	48,440	2.9
Friends	20,222	0.4	5,485	0.2	1,036	0.1	13,701	0.8
Greek Orthodox	4,163	0.1	3,358	0.1	(1)	(1)	(1)	(1)
Islamic	26,209	0.5	10,688	0.4	(1)	(1)	15,230	0.9
Jewish	204,847	4.1	96,350	3.8	31,340	3.6	77,157	4.7
Lutheran Church—Missouri Synod	144,669	2.9	121,580	4.8	14,534	1.7	8,556	0.5
Evangelical Lutheran Church In America	17,672	0.3	14,888	0.6	(1)	(1)	(1)	(1)
Wisconsin Evangelical Lutheran Synod..	31,267	0.6	24,864	1.0	6,344	0.7	(1)	(1)
Other Lutheran....................	4,996	0.1	3,869	0.2	(1)	(1)	(1)	(1)
Mennonite	27,795	0.5	11,322	0.4	(1)	(1)	15,554	0.9
Methodist	19,394	0.4	10,172	0.4	(1)	(1)	8,248	0.5
Pentecostal......................	22,971	0.5	4,379	0.2	580	0.1	18,012	1.1
Presbyterian.....................	38,314	0.8	16,266	0.6	(1)	(1)	20,868	1.3
Seventh-Day Adventist..............	55,488	1.1	23,551	0.9	8,318	1.0	23,619	1.4
Other	61,473	1.2	19,022	0.7	4,912	0.6	37,539	2.3

Note: Details may not add up to totals because of rounding and/or missing data. (1) Reporting standards not met.

Homeschooled Students

A total of 1,508,000 U.S. students in grades K-12 were homeschooled in 2007, 84% of them full-time, according to the latest available statistics from the U.S. Dept. of Education.

In a 2007 U.S. Dept. of Education survey of parents who homeschool their children the reasons given as *most important* included concern over the school environment, including such factors as safety, drugs, or negative peer pressure (20.5%); desire to provide religious or moral instruction (35.8%); dissatisfaction with academic instruction in schools (17.1%); and a physical or mental health problem or other special need (5.7%). In all, 87.6% cited concern over school environment as one of their reasons, while 83.3% cited religious or moral instruction, and 72.7% cited dissatisfaction with academic instruction.

Below is a breakdown of homeschooled students by categories for 1999 and 2007.

	1999			2007		
Characteristic	No. of students	Percentage distribution	Home-schooling rate[1]	No. of students	Percentage distribution	Home-schooling rate[1]
Total.................................	850,000	100.0%	1.7%	1,508,000	100.0%	2.9%
Homeschooled entirely...................	697,000	82.0	—	1,266,000	84.0	—
Homeschooled and enrolled in school part-time	153,000	18.0	—	242,000	16.0	—
Race/ethnicity[2]						
White	640,000	75.3	2.0	1,159,000	76.8	3.9
Black	84,000	9.9	1.0	61,000	4.0	0.8
Hispanic................................	77,000	9.1	1.1	147,000	9.8	1.5
Other	49,000	5.8	1.9	141,000	9.3	3.4
Number of children in household						
One child	120,000	14.1	1.5	187,000	12.4	2.2
Two children...........................	207,000	24.4	1.0	412,000	27.3	2.0
Three or more children..................	523,000	61.6	2.4	909,000	60.3	4.1
Household income						
$25,000 or less........................	262,000	30.9	1.6	239,000	15.9	2.1
$25,001-50,000	278,000	32.7	1.8	364,000	24.1	3.4
$50,001-75,000	162,000	19.1	1.9	405,000	26.8	3.9
$75,001 or more........................	148,000	17.4	1.5	501,000	33.2	2.7
Parents' education						
High school diploma or less	160,000	18.9	0.9	206,000	13.7	1.4
Some college or vocational/technical.........	287,000	33.7	1.9	549,000	36.4	3.8
Bachelor's degree	213,000	25.1	2.6	444,000	29.4	3.9
Graduate/professional degree	190,000	22.3	2.3	309,000	20.5	2.7

(1) The homeschooling rate is the percentage of the total group or subgroup within the general population that is homeschooled. For example, in 2007, 1.1% of all Hispanic students K-12 in the U.S. were homeschooled. (2) Hispanic or Latino persons may be of any race. Race categories include non-Hispanic population only.

Revenues[1] for Public Elementary and Secondary Schools, by State, 2006-07

Source: National Education Association; in thousands

STATE	Total	Federal Amount	Federal % of tot. rev.	State Amount	State % of tot. rev.	Local and intermediate Amount	Local and intermediate % of tot. rev.
Alabama	$7,100,169	$720,476	10.1%	$4,070,907	57.3%	$2,001,570	28.2%
Alaska	1,896,849	284,203	15.0	1,146,630	60.4	446,188	23.5
Arizona	9,638,544	1,076,040	11.2	4,958,859	51.4	3,362,821	34.9
Arkansas	4,459,921	500,105	11.2	2,556,917	57.3	1,259,981	28.3
California	69,557,257	6,710,418	9.6	42,754,127	61.5	19,497,640	28.0
Colorado	7,717,989	541,519	7.0	3,323,182	43.1	3,543,206	45.9
Connecticut	9,050,539	419,906	4.6	3,509,495	38.8	5,001,042	55.3
Delaware	1,631,426	122,161	7.5	1,029,607	63.1	461,528	28.3
District of Columbia	1,282,317	155,019	12.1	NA	NA	1,119,711	87.3
Florida	27,372,359	2,533,503	9.3	11,133,826	40.7	12,766,986	46.6
Georgia	17,714,805	1,509,809	8.5	7,941,066	44.8	7,779,258	43.9
Hawaii	2,950,803	255,035	8.6	2,646,792	89.7	27,721	0.9
Idaho	2,039,338	209,685	10.3	1,371,187	67.2	420,405	20.6
Illinois	24,026,545	1,870,304	7.8	7,316,138	30.5	14,346,885	59.7
Indiana	10,062,766	805,079	8.0	5,354,404	53.2	3,602,508	35.8
Iowa	5,009,516	401,282	8.0	2,279,210	45.5	2,192,775	43.8
Kansas	5,259,228	445,010	8.5	2,980,534	56.7	1,716,551	32.6
Kentucky	6,141,245	687,706	11.2	3,483,546	56.7	1,856,212	30.2
Louisiana	7,142,552	1,233,167	17.3	3,043,752	42.6	2,801,766	39.2
Maine	2,537,228	231,870	9.1	1,147,116	45.2	1,114,825	43.9
Maryland	11,612,299	675,852	5.8	4,684,823	40.3	5,930,388	51.1
Massachusetts	14,179,328	763,031	5.4	6,641,467	46.8	6,574,725	46.4
Michigan	19,584,946	1,576,501	8.0	11,484,249	58.6	6,186,757	31.6
Minnesota	9,715,233	588,282	6.1	6,488,998	66.8	2,333,335	24.0
Mississippi	4,157,666	712,855	17.1	2,214,691	53.3	1,115,555	26.8
Missouri	9,345,716	787,309	8.4	3,111,235	33.3	5,099,403	54.6
Montana	1,474,331	192,940	13.1	709,781	48.1	515,189	34.9
Nebraska	3,123,329	293,223	9.4	990,277	31.7	1,696,805	54.3
Nevada	4,008,036	280,453	7.0	1,077,524	26.9	2,520,482	62.9
New Hampshire	2,502,258	137,549	5.5	937,660	37.5	1,376,859	55.0
New Jersey	24,190,490	1,055,816	4.4	10,194,361	42.1	12,427,778	51.4
New Mexico	3,352,094	468,393	14.0	2,399,420	71.6	434,203	13.0
New York	49,749,322	3,320,153	6.7	21,632,213	43.5	24,441,606	49.1
North Carolina	11,991,073	1,196,942	10.0	7,613,227	63.5	2,915,797	24.3
North Dakota	995,395	150,169	15.1	353,519	35.5	446,663	44.9
Ohio	22,242,577	1,589,201	7.1	9,888,710	44.5	10,074,699	45.3
Oklahoma	5,233,050	649,871	12.4	2,820,218	53.9	1,519,262	29.0
Oregon	5,661,558	547,425	9.7	2,908,103	51.4	2,061,087	36.4
Pennsylvania	23,988,602	1,762,026	7.3	8,675,316	36.2	13,132,108	54.7
Rhode Island	2,145,821	173,402	8.1	865,044	40.3	1,084,329	50.5
South Carolina	7,130,019	699,132	9.8	3,147,685	44.1	3,038,522	42.6
South Dakota	1,138,701	177,130	15.6	374,228	32.9	553,472	48.6
Tennessee	7,725,838	827,929	10.7	3,349,705	43.4	3,108,172	40.2
Texas	43,282,278	4,466,298	10.3	16,349,077	37.8	21,578,442	49.9
Utah	3,777,931	335,684	8.9	2,104,005	55.7	1,258,955	33.3
Vermont	1,441,199	97,252	6.7	1,238,582	85.9	85,173	5.9
Virginia	13,962,224	890,128	6.4	5,813,437	41.6	6,977,648	50.0
Washington	10,450,101	870,261	8.3	6,383,843	61.1	2,877,317	27.5
West Virginia	3,039,383	354,772	11.7	1,808,685	59.5	847,074	27.9
Wisconsin	10,069,345	577,878	5.7	5,197,595	51.6	4,054,513	40.3
Wyoming	1,476,046	111,264	7.5	721,925	48.9	625,680	42.4
50 states and DC	**$555,337,583**	**$47,041,419**	**8.5**	**$264,226,896**	**47.6**	**$232,211,575**	**41.8**

NA = Not applicable. (1) Included as revenue receipts are all appropriations from general funds of federal, state, county, and local governments; receipts from taxes levied for school purposes; income from permanent school funds and endowments; and income from leases of school lands and miscellaneous sources (interest on bank deposits, tuition, gifts, school lunch charges, etc.).

Percent of Population with Upper Secondary Education, Selected Countries, 2007

Source: Organization for Economic Cooperation and Development

Percentage of the population ages 25-64 that have received at least some upper secondary (senior high school) education; ranked by %

Country	%	Country	%	Country	%	Country	%	Country	%
Czech Republic	91	Switzerland	86	Hungary	79	Australia	68	Italy	52
Estonia	89	Sweden	85	Norway	79	Belgium	68	Spain	51
United States	88	Germany	84	Korea	78	Ireland	68	Chile[2]	50
Russian Federation[1]	88	Slovenia	82	Denmark	75	United Kingdom	68	Brazil	37
Canada	87	Finland	81	Netherlands	73	Luxembourg	66	Mexico	33
Slovak Republic	87	Austria	80	New Zealand	72	Iceland	65	Turkey	29
Poland	86	Israel	80	France	69	Greece	60	Portugal	27

(1) Year of reference 2002. (2) Year of reference 2004.

Teachers' Salaries in Upper Secondary Education, Selected Countries, 2007

Source: Organization for Economic Cooperation and Development

Annual statutory teachers' salaries in public institutions in upper secondary (senior high school) education, general programs, in equivalent U.S. dollars converted using PPPs[1]; ranked by starting salaries.

Country	Starting salary	Salary with 15 years' experience	Salary at top of scale	Country	Starting salary	Salary with 15 years' experience	Salary at top of scale
Luxembourg	$71,883	$89,864	$124,898	Scotland	$30,366	$48,436	$48,436
Switzerland	56,166	72,990	86,732	England	30,172	44,507	44,507
Germany	51,512	62,372	71,546	Austria	29,863	41,469	61,170
Spain	39,367	45,786	55,779	Sweden	29,554	35,005	39,813
Belgium (Fl.)[2]	36,850	53,233	64,007	Japan	27,284	48,742	63,296
Netherlands	35,858	63,169	71,738	Italy	26,877	33,778	42,179
Belgium (Fr.)[2]	35,260	51,195	61,674	Greece	26,326	32,107	38,619
Denmark	35,011	49,264	49,264	France	26,294	34,454	49,711
United States	**34,672**	**43,966**	**NA**	Iceland	25,389	32,251	33,828
Norway	34,336	38,684	42,325	Czech Republic	22,798	31,119	38,208
Australia	32,406	44,942	44,942	Portugal	21,304	34,876	54,698
Ireland	31,977	52,972	60,025	New Zealand	19,236	37,213	37,213
Finland	31,846	43,040	55,778	Turkey	14,063	15,693	17,515
Korea	31,590	54,671	87,617	Hungary	12,855	18,110	24,358

NA = Not available. (1) Purchasing power parities (PPPs) are the rates of currency conversion that equalize the purchasing power of different currencies by eliminating differences in price levels between countries. (2) Salaries in Belgium vary depending on whether French (Fr.) or Flemish (Fl.) Community.

Charges at U.S. Institutions of Higher Education, 1969-70 to 2007-08

Source: National Center for Education Statistics, U.S. Dept. of Education

Figures for 1969-70 are average charges for full-time resident degree-credit students; figures for later years are average charges per full-time equivalent student. Room and board are based on full-time students. These figures are enrollment-weighted, according to the number of full-time-equivalent undergraduates, and thus may vary from averages given elsewhere.

	TUITION AND FEES			BOARD RATES			DORMITORY CHARGES		
	All institutions	2-yr	4-yr	All institutions	2-yr	4-yr	All institutions	2-yr	4-yr
PUBLIC (in-state)									
1969-70	$323	$178	NA	$511	$465	NA	$369	$308	NA
1979-80	583	355	$738	867	893	$865	715	574	$725
1989-90	1,356	756	1,780	1,635	1,581	1,638	1,513	962	1,557
1990-91	1,454	824	1,888	1,691	1,594	1,698	1,612	1,050	1,657
1995-96	2,179	1,239	2,848	2,020	1,681	2,045	2,057	1,297	2,121
1996-97	2,271	1,276	2,987	2,111	1,789	2,133	2,148	1,339	2,214
1997-98	2,360	1,314	3,110	2,228	1,795	2,263	2,225	1,401	2,301
1998-99	2,430	1,327	3,229	2,347	1,828	2,389	2,330	1,450	2,409
1999-2000	2,506	1,338	3,349	2,364	1,834	2,406	2,440	1,549	2,519
2000-01	2,562	1,333	3,501	2,455	1,906	2,499	2,569	1,600	2,654
2001-02	2,700	1,380	3,735	2,598	2,036	2,645	2,723	1,722	2,816
2002-03	2,903	1,483	4,046	2,669	2,164	2,712	2,930	1,954	3,029
2003-04	3,319	1,702	4,587	2,823	2,233	2,875	3,107	2,086	3,212
2004-05	3,629	1,849	5,027	2,931	2,353	2,981	3,304	2,174	3,418
2005-06	3,874	1,935	5,351	3,035	2,306	3,093	3,545	2,251	3,664
2006-07	4,102	2,018	5,666	3,191	2,390	3,253	3,757	2,407	3,878
2007-08[1]	4,307	2,063	5,950	3,329	2,408	3,402	3,941	2,495	4,072
PRIVATE									
1969-70	1,533	1,034	NA	561	546	NA	436	413	NA
1979-80	3,130	2,062	3,225	955	923	957	827	766	831
1989-90	8,147	5,196	8,396	1,948	1,811	1,953	1,923	1,663	1,935
1990-91	8,772	5,570	9,083	2,074	1,989	2,077	2,063	1,744	2,077
1995-96	11,864	7,094	12,243	2,606	2,098	2,617	2,738	2,371	2,751
1996-97	12,498	7,236	12,881	2,663	2,181	2,672	2,878	2,537	2,889
1997-98	12,801	7,464	13,344	2,762	2,785	2,761	2,954	2,672	2,964
1998-99	13,428	7,854	13,973	2,865	2,884	2,865	3,075	2,581	3,091
1999-2000	14,081	8,235	14,588	2,882	2,922	2,881	3,224	2,808	3,237
2000-01	15,000	9,067	15,470	2,993	3,000	2,993	3,374	2,722	3,392
2001-02	15,742	10,076	16,211	3,104	2,633	3,109	3,567	3,116	3,576
2002-03	16,383	10,651	16,826	3,206	3,870	3,197	3,752	3,232	3,764
2003-04	17,327	11,546	17,777	3,364	4,432	3,354	3,945	3,581	3,952
2004-05	18,154	12,122	18,604	3,485	3,728	3,483	4,171	4,243	4,170
2005-06	18,862	12,450	19,292	3,647	4,726	3,639	4,380	3,994	4,386
2006-07	20,048	12,708	20,517	3,785	3,429	3,788	4,606	4,147	4,613
2007-08[1]	21,113	13,172	21,588	3,994	4,089	3,993	4,808	4,451	4,812

NA = Not available. (1) Preliminary data based on fall 2006 enrollment weights.

Top 20 Colleges and Universities in Endowment Assets, FY 2008[1]

Source: *2008 NACUBO Endowment Study*, National Association of College and University Business Officers (NACUBO)

College/university	Endowment assets[1]	% Change, 2007-08	College/university	Endowment assets[1]	% Change, 2007-08
1. Harvard University	$36,556,284	5.55%	11. University of Chicago	$6,632,311	6.90%
2. Yale University	22,869,700	1.51	12. University of Pennsylvania	6,233,281	−6.06
3. Stanford University	17,200,000	0.20	13. University of Notre Dame	6,225,688	4.16
4. Princeton University	16,349,329	3.56	14. University of California	6,217,340	−3.45
5. University of Texas System	16,111,184	3.19	15. Duke University	6,123,743	3.61
6. Massachusetts Institute of Technology	10,068,800	0.89	16. Emory University	5,472,528	−1.60
7. University of Michigan	7,571,904	6.80	17. Cornell University	5,385,482	−2.64
8. Northwestern University	7,243,948	11.39	18. Washington University	5,350,470	−3.90
9. Columbia University	7,146,806	−0.04	19. Rice University	4,610,164	−1.27
10. The Texas A&M University System and Foundations	6,659,352	1.05	20. University of Virginia	4,572,613	−4.63

Note: Market value of endowment assets, excluding pledges and working capital. (1) In thousands.

U.S. Higher Education Trends: Bachelor's Degrees Conferred

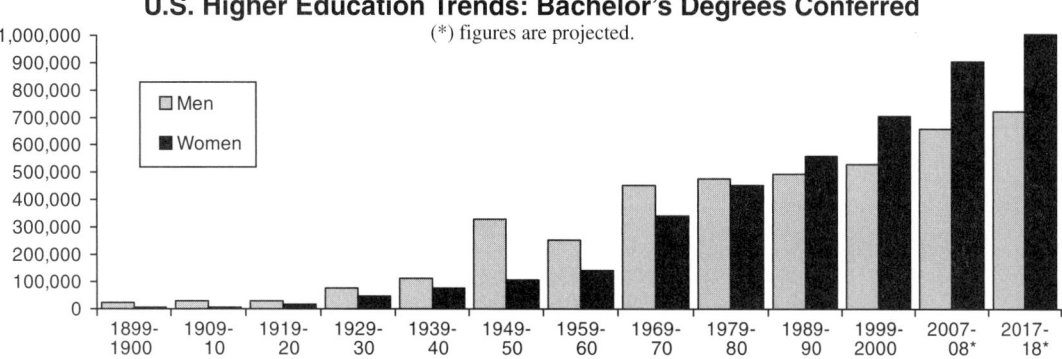

(*) figures are projected.

Financial Aid for College and Other Postsecondary Education

As of Sept. 2009. Reviewed by National Assoc. of Student Financial Aid Administrators.

The cost of postsecondary education in the U.S. has increased in recent years, but financial aid, which may be in the form of **grants** (no repayment needed), **loans**, and/or **work-study** programs, is widely available to help families meet these expenses. Most federal aid is limited to families that demonstrate financial need as determined by standard formulas. Student aid is designed to help students attend the college of their choice regardless of their ability to pay. Financial aid personnel at each school can provide information about all aid programs available to students, steps to apply for them, and deadlines, all of which may vary.

All applicants for federal aid must file a Free Application for Federal Student Aid (**FAFSA**), generally as soon as possible after Jan. 1 for the academic year starting the following September. Figures provided should agree with federal income tax forms filed for the previous year. Many other sources of aid—state governments, employers and unions, civic organizations, and the institutions themselves—also use the FAFSA to determine eligibility for aid. There are also special federal programs that pay for postsecondary education in return for service: AmeriCorps (phone: 1-800-942-2677), ROTC (phone: 1-800-USA-ROTC), and the GI Bill (phone: 1-888-442-4551). Additional forms and applications may be required if a student is to be considered for non-federal aid. Aid must be reapplied for annually.

A **federal formula**, based on information provided on the FAFSA, takes into account such factors as family income in the preceding calendar year, parental and student assets (excluding the parents' home or farm), length of time to parents' retirement, and unusual expenses (such as very high medical expenses). Outside scholarships (even non-need-based) are also taken into account in determining aid eligibility for federal, institutional, and state financial aid programs.

The formula determines a family's **Expected Family Contribution** (EFC), which is divided among the family members—excluding parents—in college. The EFC is subtracted from the total cost of attending college for each person (including tuition and fee charges, room and board or allowance for living costs, books and supplies, transportation to and from school, and other miscellaneous costs). The difference determines financial need and the maximum federal aid for which the family may be eligible. (Some institutions use a separate formula for need-based institutional aid.) Some schools guarantee to meet the full financial need of each admitted student; most do their best to cover a student's financial need using various forms of financial aid but may not be able to because of a lack of funds.

The **aid package** offered by each school may include one or more of the following resources: Federal Pell Grants, for those who demonstrate sufficient financial need; Federal Supplemental Educational Opportunity Grants, for those who still have need after receiving Pell Grants; grants from the school; Federal Work-Study or other work programs; low-interest Perkins loans; and subsidized and unsubsidized Stafford loans. Parents of undergraduates may also apply for a Federal PLUS loan. Unsubsidized Stafford loans and all PLUS loans to parents are available to all students regardless of their financial need but students and parents must still complete the FAFSA to get these loans.

Loans have varying interest rates and other requirements. Repayment of Perkins and Stafford loans does not begin until after graduation; deferments and loan forgiveness are available under certain circumstances. For PLUS loans, parents must pass a credit check and begin repayment of both principal and interest while the student is still in school.

Certain federal income **tax credits and refunds** are available to families who meet income and other requirements; see the chapter on Taxes.

Rules for financial aid are complex and changeable. *Funding Education Beyond High School: The Guide to Federal Student Aid*, a comprehensive resource on financial aid from the U.S. Dept. of Education, is available in English and Spanish on the Department's website: student aid.ed.gov/students/publications/student_guide/index.html

Further information and FAFSA forms are available from schools or from the Federal Student Aid Information Center, P.O. Box 84, Washington, DC 20044; phone: 1-800-4-FED-AID, Mon.-Fri., 8 AM-12 midnight EST. The Information Center also has a free booklet called *The EFC Formula Book*. FAFSA forms can be obtained online at www.fafsa.ed.gov

Average Salaries of U.S. College Professors, 2008-09

Source: American Association of University Professors. NA = Not available.

Teaching level		MEN Type of institution			WOMEN Type of institution		
		Public	Private/ Independent	Church-related	Public	Private/ independent	Church-related
Doctoral level .... Professor...........		$117,840	$153,860	$132,209	$106,977	$141,902	$121,366
Associate		82,181	98,740	89,645	76,448	91,145	83,547
Assistant...........		70,503	85,505	75,425	65,138	78,030	70,243
Master's level .... Professor...........		89,480	101,853	89,882	85,915	94,255	83,612
Associate		71,327	76,931	70,558	68,954	72,545	67,360
Assistant...........		60,482	63,385	58,531	58,366	60,662	56,850
Baccalaureate level ... Professor...........		86,240	100,523	76,214	81,108	95,311	72,699
Associate		69,440	73,215	64,275	66,525	72,090	60,025
Assistant...........		57,917	59,513	51,444	55,971	58,290	50,737
2-year.............. Professor...........		75,935	NA	NA	73,772	NA	NA
Associate		61,697	NA	NA	59,774	NA	NA
Assistant...........		54,021	NA	NA	52,920	NA	NA

ACT (formerly American College Testing) Mean Scores and Characteristics of College-Bound Students, 1990-2009

Source: ACT, Inc.

(for graduating class ending in year shown)

SCORES	Unit[1]	1990	1995	2000	2002	2003	2004	2005	2006	2007	2008	2009
Composite scores .. Points		20.6	20.8	21.0	20.8	20.8	20.9	20.9	21.1	21.2	21.1	21.1
Male........... Points		21.0	21.0	21.2	20.9	21.0	21.0	21.1	21.2	21.2	21.2	21.3
Female......... Points		20.3	20.7	20.9	20.7	20.8	20.9	20.9	21.0	21.0	21.0	20.9
English score ...... Points		20.5	20.2	20.5	20.2	20.3	20.4	20.4	20.6	20.7	20.6	20.6
Male........... Points		20.1	19.8	20.0	19.7	19.8	19.9	20.0	20.1	20.2	20.1	20.2
Female......... Points		20.9	20.6	20.9	20.6	20.7	20.8	20.8	21.0	21.0	21.0	20.9
Math score .... Points		19.9	20.2	20.7	20.6	20.6	20.7	20.7	20.8	21.0	21.0	21.0
Male........... Points		20.7	20.9	21.4	21.2	21.2	21.3	21.3	21.5	21.6	21.6	21.6
Female......... Points		19.3	19.7	20.2	20.1	20.1	20.2	20.2	20.3	20.4	20.4	20.4
PARTICIPANTS												
Total number....... (thous.)		817	945	1,065	1,116	1,175	1,171	1,186	1,206	1,301	1,422	1,480
Male........... Percent		46	44	43	44	44	43	44	44	42	44	45
White .... Percent		79	80	72	69	68	67	66	63	60	63	64
Black .... Percent		9	9	10	11	11	11	12	12	12	13	13
Hispanic[3] .... Percent		4	5	5	6	6	7	7	7	7	8	9
Composite scores												
27 or above ...... Percent		12	13	14	13	14	14	14	14	15	9[2]	12
18 or below....... Percent		35	34	32	35	35	34	34	34	33	33	34

(1) Minimum point score, 1; maximum score, 36. Test scores and characteristics of college-bound students are based on the performance of all ACT-tested students who graduated in the spring of a given school year and took the ACT assessment during junior or senior year of high school. (2) Composite scores of 28 or above. (3) Persons of Hispanic origin may be of any race.

ACT Average Composite Scores by State, 2008-09

Source: ACT, Inc.

State	Avg. comp. score	% grads taking ACT[1]	State	Avg. comp. score	% grads taking ACT[1]	State	Avg. comp. score	% grads taking ACT[1]
Alabama..........	20.3	76%	Kentucky	19.4	100%	Ohio	21.7	64%
Alaska	21.0	29	Louisiana	20.1	89	Oklahoma........	20.7	71
Arizona..........	21.9	15	Maine	23.1	9	Oregon...........	21.4	33
Arkansas	20.6	73	Maryland	22.1	17	Pennsylvania	22.1	14
California	22.2	19	Massachusetts.....	23.9	18	Rhode Island	22.8	10
Colorado.........	20.8	100	Michigan..........	19.6	100	South Carolina.....	19.8	50
Connecticut	23.5	21	Minnesota........	22.7	68	South Dakota	22.0	74
Delaware	22.6	11	Mississippi	18.9	93	Tennessee........	20.6	92
District of Columbia	19.4	30	Missouri	21.6	67	Texas............	20.8	30
			Montana..........	22.0	54	Utah	21.8	68
Florida	19.5	62	Nebraska.........	22.1	72	Vermont	23.1	24
Georgia	20.6	40	Nevada...........	21.5	30	Virginia..........	21.9	20
Hawaii	21.5	22	New Hampshire	23.5	15	Washington	22.8	18
Idaho	21.6	58	New Jersey	23.1	16	West Virginia	20.7	62
Illinois	20.8	97	New Mexico	20.0	65	Wisconsin.........	22.3	67
Indiana..........	22.2	24	New York	23.1	25	Wyoming	20.0	99
Iowa............	22.4	59	North Carolina	21.6	15			
Kansas..........	21.9	74	North Dakota	21.5	78	U.S. avg.	21.1	45

(1) Based on number of high school graduates in 2009, as projected by the Western Interstate Commission for Higher Education, and number of students in the class of 2009 who took the ACT.

The New SAT

The College Board administered a new version of the SAT in Mar. 2005 to the graduating high school class of 2006. The first revision to the test since 1995 adds a section in which test takers are asked to write an essay in 25 minutes, and changes other aspects of the traditional sections: the critical reading section (formerly the verbal section) places more emphasis on reading comprehension, and the math section includes more concepts learned in Algebra II and Geometry. Each section is still scored on an 800-point scale, making a perfect score 2,400. The new test has a time limit of 3 hours and 45 minutes, up from 3 hours for the old test.

Results for the graduating high school class of 2006 showed the sharpest drop in SAT scores in 31 years: composite reading and math scores fell by about 7 points. At the same time, the ACT, a competitor to the SAT, reported its largest composite score increase in 20 years. Some critics have charged that the drop in SAT scores may be attributed to the increased length, which leaves many test takers more tired. However, a College Board study of some 700,000 tests found no evidence to support this claim; College Board officials suggest that the drop may be due to a decrease in repeat test taking.

SAT Mean Verbal and Math Scores of College-Bound Seniors, 1975-2009

Source: The College Board

(recentered scale; for school year ending in year shown)

	1975	1980	1985	1990	1995	1999	2000	2001	2002	2003	2004	2005	2006	2007	2008	2009
Critical Reading scores	512	502	509	500	504	505	505	506	504	507	508	508	503	502	502	501
Male	515	506	514	505	505	509	507	509	507	512	512	513	505	504	504	503
Female	509	498	503	496	502	502	504	502	502	503	504	505	502	502	500	498
Math scores	498	492	500	501	506	511	514	514	516	519	518	520	518	515	515	515
Male	518	515	522	521	525	531	533	533	534	537	537	538	536	533	533	534
Female	479	473	480	483	490	495	498	498	500	503	501	504	502	499	500	499
Writing scores	NA	NA	NA	NA	NA	NA	NA	NA	NA	NA	NA	NA	497	494	494	493
Male	NA	NA	NA	NA	NA	NA	NA	NA	NA	NA	NA	NA	491	489	488	486
Female	NA	NA	NA	NA	NA	NA	NA	NA	NA	NA	NA	NA	502	500	501	499

Note: In 1995, the College Board recentered the scoring scale for the SAT by reestablishing the original mean score of 500 on the 200-800 scale. Earlier scores have been adjusted to account for this recentering. The Writing test was first given in Mar. 2005; however, only the scores of the first graduating class to take the revised test are given. NA = Not applicable.

SAT Mean Scores by State, 1990-2009

Source: The College Board

(recentered scale; for school year ending in year shown; V=Verbal, M=Math, CR=Critical Reading, W=Writing)

State	1990 V	1990 M	2000 V	2000 M	2005 V	2005 M	2008[1] CR	2008[1] M	2008[1] W	2009[1] CR	2009[1] M	2009[1] W	% grads taking SAT[2]
Alabama	545	534	559	555	567	559	565	557	554	557	552	549	7%
Alaska	514	501	519	515	523	519	520	520	493	520	516	492	46
Arizona	521	520	521	523	526	530	516	522	500	516	521	497	26
Arkansas	545	532	563	554	563	552	575	567	559	572	572	556	5
California	494	508	497	518	504	522	499	515	498	500	513	498	49
Colorado	533	534	534	537	560	560	564	570	553	568	575	555	20
Connecticut	506	496	508	509	517	517	509	513	513	509	513	512	83
Delaware	510	496	502	496	503	502	499	498	490	466	451	461	79
District of Columbia	483	467	494	486	490	478	470	455	465	495	498	484	71
Florida	495	493	498	500	498	498	496	497	481	497	498	480	59
Georgia	478	473	488	486	497	496	491	493	482	490	491	479	71
Hawaii	480	505	488	519	490	516	481	502	470	479	502	469	58
Idaho	542	524	540	541	544	542	540	540	517	541	540	520	18
Illinois	542	547	568	586	594	606	583	601	578	588	604	583	6
Indiana	486	486	498	501	504	508	496	508	481	496	507	480	63
Iowa	584	588	589	600	596	608	603	612	582	610	615	588	3
Kansas	566	563	574	580	585	588	580	589	564	581	589	564	7
Kentucky	548	541	548	550	561	559	568	570	554	573	573	561	7
Louisiana	551	537	562	558	565	562	566	564	558	563	558	555	7
Maine	501	490	504	500	509	505	469	466	461	468	467	455	90
Maryland	506	502	507	509	511	515	499	502	497	500	502	495	69
Massachusetts	503	498	511	513	520	527	514	525	513	514	526	510	84
Michigan	529	534	557	569	568	579	581	598	572	584	603	575	5
Minnesota	552	558	581	594	592	597	596	609	579	595	609	578	7
Mississippi	552	538	562	549	564	554	574	556	566	567	554	559	4
Missouri	548	541	572	577	588	588	594	597	584	595	600	584	5
Montana	540	542	543	546	540	540	541	548	523	541	542	519	22
Nebraska	559	562	560	571	574	579	581	585	567	587	594	572	4
Nevada	511	511	510	517	508	513	498	506	478	501	505	479	42
New Hampshire	518	510	520	519	525	525	521	523	511	523	523	510	75
New Jersey	495	498	498	513	503	517	495	513	496	496	513	496	76
New Mexico	554	546	549	543	558	547	557	548	540	553	546	534	11
New York	489	496	494	506	497	511	488	504	481	485	502	478	85
North Carolina	478	470	492	496	499	511	496	511	482	495	511	480	63
North Dakota	579	578	588	609	590	605	594	604	568	590	593	566	3
Ohio	526	522	533	539	539	543	534	544	521	537	546	523	22
Oklahoma	553	542	563	560	570	563	572	572	557	575	571	557	5
Oregon	515	509	527	527	526	528	523	527	502	523	525	499	52
Pennsylvania	497	490	498	497	501	503	494	501	483	493	501	483	71
Rhode Island	498	488	505	500	503	505	495	498	493	498	496	494	66
South Carolina	475	467	484	482	494	499	488	497	476	486	496	470	67
South Dakota	580	570	587	588	589	589	595	596	575	589	600	569	3
Tennessee	558	544	563	553	572	563	571	570	566	571	565	565	10
Texas	490	489	493	500	493	502	488	505	480	486	506	475	51
Utah	566	555	570	569	566	557	561	557	543	559	558	540	6
Vermont	507	493	513	508	521	517	519	523	507	518	518	506	64
Virginia	501	496	509	500	516	514	511	512	499	511	512	498	68
Washington	513	511	526	528	532	534	526	533	509	524	531	507	53

State	1990 V	1990 M	2000 V	2000 M	2005 V	2005 M	2008[1] CR	2008[1] M	2008[1] W	2009[1] CR	2009[1] M	2009[1] W	% grads taking SAT[2]
West Virginia	520	514	526	511	523	511	512	501	498	511	501	499	18%
Wisconsin	552	559	584	597	592	599	587	604	577	594	608	582	5
Wyoming	534	538	545	545	544	543	562	574	541	567	568	550	5
National avg.	**500**	**501**	**505**	**514**	**508**	**520**	**502**	**515**	**494**	**501**	**515**	**493**	**46**

Note: In 1995, the College Board recentered the scoring scale for the SAT by reestablishing the original mean score of 500 on the 200-800 scale. The College Board states that comparing states or ranking them on the basis of SAT scores alone is invalid, and the College Board discourages doing so. (1) In 2005, the SAT was changed. The Verbal portion became Critical Reading, and a new Writing test was added. The 2006 graduating class was the first to take the new test. (2) Based on number of high school graduates in 2009, as projected by the Western Interstate Commission for Higher Education, and number of students in the class of 2009 who took the SAT.

Top 100 Libraries in U.S. by Volumes Held, FY 2007

Source: American Library Association, *ALA Library Fact Sheet 22*

Institution	Volumes held*	Institution	Volumes held*
1. Library of Congress	32,332,832	51. North Carolina State University	3,857,365
2. Harvard University	15,965,675	52. University of Colorado	3,843,458
3. Boston Public Library	15,760,879	53. Houston Public Library	3,834,967
4. Yale University	12,283,594	54. King County Library System (WA)	3,767,233
5. University of California—Berkeley	10,725,334	55. Texas A&M University Libraries	3,739,081
6. University of Illinois—Urbana-Champaign	10,712,706	56. Johns Hopkins University	3,726,532
7. Columbia University	10,004,848	57. Brown University	3,720,244
8. University of Texas—Austin	9,323,252	58. University of Rochester	3,672,976
9. Public Library of Cincinnati & Hamilton County	9,154,039	59. State University of New York—Buffalo	3,655,089
10. Stanford University	8,500,000	60. University of Connecticut	3,637,190
11. University of Michigan	8,414,070	61. Hawaii State Public Library System	3,627,769
12. University of California—Los Angeles	8,272,112	62. University of Maryland	3,623,376
13. Cornell University	7,999,177	63. University of California—Davis	3,599,983
14. University of Chicago	7,926,905	64. University of South Carolina	3,579,504
15. University of Wisconsin—Madison	7,916,419	65. Louisiana State University	3,548,726
16. County of Los Angeles Public Library	7,838,277	66. Mid-Continent Public Library (MO)	3,537,916
17. Indiana University	7,553,823	67. University of Kentucky	3,537,710
18. Detroit Public Library	7,459,353	68. University of Massachusetts	3,529,419
19. University of Washington	7,304,234	69. Miami-Dade Public Library System	3,516,466
20. University of Minnesota	6,867,777	70. University of Hawaii	3,486,937
21. Princeton University	6,778,675	71. Wayne State University	3,458,773
22. Queens Borough Public Library (NY)	6,488,198	72. University of Missouri—Columbia	3,454,585
23. Free Library of Philadelphia	6,410,841	73. Florida State University Library	3,442,420
24. Los Angeles Public Library	6,285,760	74. San Diego Public Library	3,428,594
25. Ohio State University	6,244,095	75. University of Cincinnati Libraries	3,418,599
26. University of North Carolina—Chapel Hill	6,154,365	76. Montgomery Co. Dept. of Public Libraries (MD)	3,397,660
27. University of Pennsylvania	5,994,465	77. St. Louis Public Library	3,367,334
28. Chicago Public Library	5,891,306	78. University of California—San Diego	3,360,442
29. Duke University	5,872,136	79. University of Notre Dame	3,322,395
30. University of Arizona	5,632,559	80. University of Utah	3,320,167
31. University of Virginia	5,465,077	81. Vanderbilt University	3,311,665
32. Pennsylvania State University Libraries	5,220,080	82. Buffalo & Erie County Public Library	3,304,567
33. New York Public Library, The Branch Libraries	5,169,953	83. Emory University	3,298,971
34. Brooklyn Public Library (NY)	5,120,690	84. Broward County Libraries Division (FL)	3,289,920
35. University of Pittsburgh	5,116,305	85. University of Tennessee—Knoxville	3,251,893
36. University of Oklahoma	5,047,646	86. University of Miami	3,227,943
37. New York University	4,946,277	87. Cuyahoga County Public Library (OH)	3,182,260
38. Michigan State University	4,915,621	88. University of Nebraska—Lincoln	3,171,134
39. Northwestern University Library	4,768,588	89. Allen County Public Library (IN)	3,170,395
40. University of Iowa	4,765,690	90. Syracuse University	3,160,240
41. Dallas Public Library	4,609,883	91. Temple University	3,137,142
42. University of Georgia	4,559,220	92. Tulane University	3,106,645
43. Cleveland Public Library	4,552,843	93. Southern Illinois University—Carbondale	3,073,655
44. Rutgers University	4,462,249	94. Jacksonville Public Library	3,065,817
45. Arizona State University Libraries	4,342,425	95. Auburn University	3,016,986
46. University of Florida	4,229,717	96. Georgetown University	2,955,278
47. University of Kansas	4,210,639	97. University of California—Santa Barbara	2,914,539
48. Washington University—St. Louis	4,162,980	98. Ohio University	2,913,522
49. University of Southern California	4,039,228	99. University of Oregon	2,905,608
50. Brigham Young University	3,908,127	100. Massachusetts Institute of Technology	2,847,680

*Figures for public libraries include holdings by branches and include circulating books only.

Number of Public Libraries and Operating Income, by State, FY 2007

Source: Public Libraries Survey, National Center for Education Statistics, U.S. Dept. of Education

State	No.[1]	Income[2] (thous.)	State	No.[1]	Income[2] (thous.)	State	No.[1]	Income[2] (thous.)	State	No.[1]	Income[2] (thous.)
AL......	208	$92,585	IL......	623	$694,053	MT.....	80	$19,905	RI......	49	$45,739
AK.....	87	29,281	IN......	239	257,492	NE.....	271	48,359	SC......	42	110,378
AZ.....	83	184,243	IA......	539	94,692	NV.....	22	96,352	SD.....	123	21,098
AR.....	48	58,648	KS.....	326	105,298	NH.....	230	50,349	TN.....	187	100,723
CA.....	181	1,264,058	KY.....	116	140,736	NJ.....	303	470,863	TX.....	562	422,278
CO.....	115	243,153	LA......	67	169,353	NM.....	91	45,400	UT.....	70	79,167
CT.....	195	174,939	ME.....	272	38,535	NY.....	753	1,162,785	VT.....	183	18,887
DE.....	21	25,453	MD.....	24	266,960	NC.....	77	198,856	VA.....	90	259,121
DC.....	1	43,428	MA.....	370	251,013	ND.....	80	11,943	WA.....	66	326,363
FL......	79	658,866	MI.....	386	421,995	OH.....	251	736,068	WV.....	97	31,219
GA.....	58	201,189	MN.....	139	192,263	OK.....	113	$83,919	WI.....	382	204,245
HI......	1	31,220	MS.....	50	46,604	OR.....	128	155,298	WY.....	23	27,122
ID......	104	38,928	MO.....	152	206,038	PA.....	457	340,069	**U.S. total**	**9,214**	**10,997,532**

(1) Includes central libraries only. (2) Some totals may be underestimated because of nonresponse.

Four-Year Colleges and Universities

General Information for the 2008-09 Academic Year

Source: Peterson's College Database © 2009 Peterson's Nelnet, LLC. All rights reserved.

Note: These listings **include only accredited degree-granting institutions** in the U.S. and the U.S. territories with a total enrollment of 1,000 or more. Only **four-year** colleges and universities (which award a bachelor's degree as their highest undergraduate degree) are included. Data reported **only for institutions that provided updated information** on Peterson's Annual Survey of Undergraduate Institutions for the 2008-09 academic year.

All institutions are coeducational except those where the ZIP code is followed directly by a number in parentheses. (1) = men only, (2) = primarily men, (3) = women only, (4) = primarily women.

The **Tuition & Fees** column shows the annual tuition and required fees for full-time students, or, where indicated, the tuition and standard fees per unit for part-time students. Where tuition varies according to residence, the figure is given for the most local resident and is coded: (A) = area residents, (S) = state residents; all other figures apply to all students regardless of residence. Where annual expenses are expressed as a lump sum (including full-time tuition, mandatory fees, and room and board), the figure is entered under Tuition & Fees and coded: (C) = comprehensive fee. Rm. & Board is the average cost for one academic year. * indicates fee only.

Control: 1 = independent (nonprofit), 2 = independent-religious, 3 = proprietary (profit-making), 4 = federal, 5 = state, 6 = commonwealth (Puerto Rico), 7 = territory (U.S. territories), 8 = county, 9 = district, 10 = city, 11 = state and local, 12 = state-related, 13 = private (unspecified). **Degree** means the highest degree offered (B = bachelor's, M = master's, F = first professional, D = doctorate).

Enrollment is the total number of matriculated undergraduate and (if applicable) graduate students.

Faculty is the total number of faculty members teaching undergraduate courses and (if available) graduate courses.

NA or a dash indicates category is inapplicable or data not available from a consistent source.

Name, Address	Year Founded	Tuition & Fees	Room & Board	Control, Degree	Enroll- ment	Faculty
Abilene Christian Univ, Abilene, TX 79699-9100	1906	$18,930	$7,236	2-D	4,669	368
Acad of Art Univ, San Francisco, CA 94105-3410	1929	$18,050	$13,400	3-M	13,335	942
Adams State Coll, Alamosa, CO 81102	1921	$3,790(S)	$6,780	5-M	2,861	275
Adelphi Univ, Garden City, NY 11530-0701	1896	$23,925	$10,000	1-D	8,177	934
Adrian Coll, Adrian, MI 49221-2575	1859	$24,440	$7,460	2-B	1,469	177
Alabama Agr & Mech Univ, Huntsville, AL 35811	1875	$3,432(S)	$4,770	5-D	5,124	380
Alabama State Univ, Montgomery, AL 36101-0271	1867	$5,460(S)	$4,400	5-D	5,695	410
Albany Coll of Pharm & Health Sci, Albany, NY 12208-3425	1881	$22,640	$7,600	1-F	1,525	98
Albany State Univ, Albany, GA 31705-2717 (4)	1903	$3,710(S)	$4,018	5-M	4,176	250
Albertus Magnus Coll, New Haven, CT 06511-1189	1925	$22,624	$9,442	2-M	2,129	69
Albion Coll, Albion, MI 49224-1831	1835	$28,880	$8,190	2-B	1,860	171
Albright Coll, Reading, PA 19612-5234	1856	$30,570	$8,670	2-M	2,305	167
Alcorn State Univ, Alcorn State, MS 39096-7500	1871	$4,488(S)	$5,016	5-M	3,252	217
Alfred Univ, Alfred, NY 14802-1205	1836	$25,246	$16,174	1-D	2,416	197
Allegheny Coll, Meadville, PA 16335	1815	$32,000	$8,000	1-B	2,125	183
Alliant Intl Univ, San Diego, CA 92131-1799	1952	$15,220	NA	1-D	4,153	288
Alma Coll, Alma, MI 48801-1599	1886	$24,850	$8,120	2-B	1,384	138
Alvernia Univ, Reading, PA 19607-1799	1958	$24,350	$9,212	2-D	2,809	308
Alverno Coll, Milwaukee, WI 53234-3922	1887	$18,162	$6,336	2-M	2,480	226
Amberton Univ, Garland, TX 75041-5595	1971	$6,750	NA	2-M	1,562	40
Amer InterContinental Univ Online, Hoffman Estates, IL 60192	1970	NA	NA	3-M	22,424	396
Amer Intl Coll, Springfield, MA 01109-3189	1885	$24,100	$10,150	1-D	2,678	205
Amer Publ Univ System, Charles Town, WV 25414	1991	$6,000	NA	3-M	14,694	627
Amer Univ, Washington, DC 20016-8001	1893	$33,283	$12,418	2-D	11,684	1,078
Amer Univ of Puerto Rico, Bayamón, PR 00960-2037	1963	$4,175	NA	1-M	1,550	221
Amherst Coll, Amherst, MA 01002-5000	1821	$37,640	$9,790	1-B	1,697	223
Anderson Univ, Anderson, IN 46012-3495	1917	$22,910	$7,980	2-D	2,737	315
Anderson Univ, Anderson, SC 29621-4035	1911	$18,700	$7,050	2-M	2,064	168
Andrews Univ, Berrien Springs, MI 49104	1874	$19,930	$6,330	2-D	3,419	298
Angelo State Univ, San Angelo, TX 76909	1928	$4,596(S)	$6,612	5-D	6,155	348
Anna Maria Coll, Paxton, MA 01612	1946	$25,850	$9,350	2-M	1,333	179
Appalachian State Univ, Boone, NC 28608	1899	$4,275(S)	$6,200	5-D	16,610	1,132
Aquinas Coll, Grand Rapids, MI 49506-1799	1886	$22,314	$7,014	2-M	2,159	262
Arcadia Univ, Glenside, PA 19038-3295	1853	$29,700	$10,280	2-D	3,894	415
Argosy Univ, Sarasota, Sarasota, FL 34235	1974	NA	NA	3-D	NA	NA
Argosy Univ, Schaumburg, Schaumburg, IL 60173-5403	1979	NA	NA	3-D	NA	NA
Arizona State Univ, Tempe, AZ 85287	1885	$6,844(S)	$9,210	5-D	67,082	2,902
Arkansas State Univ, State University, AR 72467	1909	$6,370(S)	$5,056	5-D	11,490	630
Arkansas Tech Univ, Russellville, AR 72801	1909	$5,430(S)	$4,888	5-M	7,492	418
Armstrong Atlantic State Univ, Savannah, GA 31419-1997 (4)	1935	$3,876(S)	$5,472	5-M	7,042	491
Art Ctr Coll of Design, Pasadena, CA 91103-1999	1930	$29,594	NA	1-M	1,632	454
The Art Inst of Boston at Lesley Univ, Boston, MA 02215-2598	1912	$26,590	$12,400	1-D	6,686	225
Asbury Coll, Wilmore, KY 40390-1198	1890	$22,413	$5,414	2-M	1,550	141
Ashford Univ, Clinton, IA 52733-2967	1918	$16,106	$5,800	3-M	10,568	748
Ashland Univ, Ashland, OH 44805-3702	1878	$25,640	$7,358	2-D	6,475	581
Assumption Coll, Worcester, MA 01609-1296	1904	$28,851	$6,156	2-M	2,626	224
Athens State Univ, Athens, AL 35611	1822	$3,300(S)	NA	5-B	3,114	177
Atlantic Coll, Guaynabo, PR 00970	NA	$4,820	NA	1-M	1,080	NA
Auburn Univ, Auburn University, AL 36849	1856	$5,880(S)	$8,260	5-D	24,530	1,323
Auburn Univ Montgomery, Montgomery, AL 36124-4023	1967	$5,850(S)	$3,420	5-D	5,284	360
Augsburg Coll, Minneapolis, MN 55454-1351	1869	$27,513	NA	2-M	3,891	418
Augustana Coll, Rock Island, IL 61201-2296	1860	$30,150	$7,650	2-B	2,546	265
Augustana Coll, Sioux Falls, SD 57197	1860	$23,547	$6,188	2-M	1,754	174
Augusta State Univ, Augusta, GA 30904-2200	1925	$3,644(S)	NA	5-M	6,689	402
Aurora Univ, Aurora, IL 60506-4892	1893	$18,100	$7,850	1-D	4,291	393
Austin Coll, Sherman, TX 75090-4400	1849	$27,875	$9,090	2-M	1,298	126
Austin Peay State Univ, Clarksville, TN 37044	1927	$5,526(S)	$5,870	5-M	9,401	511
Avila Univ, Kansas City, MO 64145-1698	1916	$20,300	$6,200	2-M	1,939	193
Azusa Pacific Univ, Azusa, CA 91702-7000	1899	$26,640	$7,742	2-D	8,548	971
Babson Coll, Babson Park, MA 02457-0310	1919	$36,096	$12,020	1-M	3,439	247
Baker Coll of Allen Park, Allen Park, MI 48101 (4)	2003	$7,020	NA	1-B	2,551	88
Baker Coll of Auburn Hills, Auburn Hills, MI 48326-1586	1911	$7,020	NA	1-B	3,824	155
Baker Coll of Cadillac, Cadillac, MI 49601	1986	$7,020	NA	1-B	1,952	105
Baker Coll of Clinton Township, Clinton Township, MI 48035-4701	1990	$7,020	NA	1-B	5,637	208
Baker Coll of Flint, Flint, MI 48507-5508	1911	$7,020	$2,700	1-B	5,820	315
Baker Coll of Jackson, Jackson, MI 49202	1994	$7,020	NA	1-B	1,830	85
Baker Coll of Muskegon, Muskegon, MI 49442-3497	1888	$7,020	$2,700	1-B	5,232	177

Name, Address	Year Founded	Tuition & Fees	Room & Board	Control, Degree	Enroll-ment	Faculty
Baker Coll of Owosso, Owosso, MI 48867-4400	1984	$7,020	$2,700	1-B	2,926	144
Baker Coll of Port Huron, Port Huron, MI 48060-2597	1990	$7,020	NA	1-B	1,716	126
Baldwin-Wallace Coll, Berea, OH 44017-2088	1845	$23,524	$7,728	2-M	4,382	401
Ball State Univ, Muncie, IN 47306-1099	1918	$7,500(S)	$7,598	5-D	20,243	1,173
Bard Coll, Annandale-on-Hudson, NY 12504	1860	$38,374	$10,866	1-D	2,148	253
Barnard Coll, New York, NY 10027-6598 (3)	1889	$37,538	$11,926	1-B	2,359	340
Barry Univ, Miami Shores, FL 33161-6695	1940	$25,500	$8,600	2-D	8,581	636
Barton Coll, Wilson, NC 27893-7000	1902	$19,938	$6,782	2-B	1,155	104
Bates Coll, Lewiston, ME 04240-6028	1855	$49,350(C)	NA	1-B	1,776	193
Bayamón Central Univ, Bayamón, PR 00960-1725	1970	$3,880	NA	2-M	2,825	NA
Baylor Univ, Waco, TX 76798	1845	$27,910	$8,569	2-D	14,541	1,096
Bay Path Coll, Longmeadow, MA 01106-2292	1897	$23,840	$9,750	1-M	1,784	223
Becker Coll, Worcester, MA 01609	1784	$27,748	$9,760	1-B	1,752	184
Belhaven Coll, Jackson, MS 39202-1789	1883	$16,780	$6,120	2-M	2,619	120
Bellarmine Univ, Louisville, KY 40205-0671	1950	$28,900	$8,410	2-D	3,040	325
Bellevue Univ, Bellevue, NE 68005-3098	1965	$6,690	NA	1-M	6,808	370
Belmont Abbey Coll, Belmont, NC 28012-1802	1876	$20,094	$9,866	2-B	1,497	129
Belmont Univ, Nashville, TN 37212-3757	1951	$21,110	$10,000	2-D	4,991	592
Beloit Coll, Beloit, WI 53511-5596	1846	$31,540	$6,696	1-B	1,388	133
Bemidji State Univ, Bemidji, MN 56601-2699	1919	$7,360(S)	$6,325	5-M	5,009	254
Benedict Coll, Columbia, SC 29204	1870	$14,570	$6,702	2-B	2,641	NA
Benedictine Coll, Atchison, KS 66002-1499	1859	$18,800	$6,300	2-M	2,033	114
Benedictine Univ, Lisle, IL 60532-0900	1887	$22,310	$7,300	2-D	5,279	661
Bentley Univ, Waltham, MA 02452-4705	1917	$34,488	$11,320	1-D	5,664	484
Berea Coll, Berea, KY 40404	1855	$866	$5,768	1-B	1,549	183
Berklee Coll of Mus, Boston, MA 02215-3693	1945	$30,650	$15,080	1-B	4,054	529
Bernard M. Baruch Coll of the City Univ of New York, New York, NY 10010-5585	1919	$4,320(S)	NA	11-M	16,321	1,018
Berry Coll, Mount Berry, GA 30149-0159	1902	$22,370	$7,978	2-M	1,795	200
Bethel Coll, Mishawaka, IN 46545-5591	1947	$21,296	$5,936	2-M	2,075	220
Bethel Coll, McKenzie, TN 38201	1842	$12,242	$6,926	2-M	2,408	235
Bethel Univ, St. Paul, MN 55112-6999	1871	$25,860	$7,620	2-D	4,335	463
Bethune-Cookman Univ, Daytona Beach, FL 32114-3099	1904	$12,936	$7,672	2-F	3,633	225
Biola Univ, La Mirada, CA 90639-0001	1908	$26,579	$8,120	2-D	5,893	413
Birmingham-Southern Coll, Birmingham, AL 35254	1856	$25,586	$9,105	2-M	1,458	138
Black Hills State Univ, Spearfish, SD 57799	1883	$6,590(S)	$5,172	5-M	4,017	201
Bloomfield Coll, Bloomfield, NJ 07003-9981	1868	$20,080	$9,500	2-B	2,020	242
Bloomsburg Univ of Pennsylvania, Bloomsburg, PA 17815-1301	1839	$6,848(S)	$6,292	5-D	8,855	457
Bluefield State Coll, Bluefield, WV 24701-2198	1895	$4,272(S)	NA	5-B	1,868	150
Bluffton Univ, Bluffton, OH 45817	1899	$22,920	$7,596	2-M	1,149	113
Bob Jones Univ, Greenville, SC 29614	1927	$11,520	$5,100	2-D	4,141	367
Boise State Univ, Boise, ID 83725-0399	1932	$4,632(S)	$4,819	5-D	19,667	1,128
Boricua Coll, New York, NY 10032-1560	1974	$9,000	NA	1-M	1,058	133
Boston Arch Coll, Boston, MA 02115-2795	1889	$10,620	NA	1-M	1,176	229
Boston Coll, Chestnut Hill, MA 02467-3800	1863	$37,950	$12,395	2-D	13,903	1,224
Boston Univ, Boston, MA 02215	1839	$37,050	$11,418	1-D	32,053	2,499
Bowdoin Coll, Brunswick, ME 04011	1794	$38,190	$10,380	1-B	1,723	206
Bowie State Univ, Bowie, MD 20715-9465	1865	$6,005(S)	$6,460	5-D	5,291	359
Bowling Green State Univ, Bowling Green, OH 43403	1910	$9,060(S)	$7,220	5-D	17,874	1,022
Bradley Univ, Peoria, IL 61625-0002	1897	$22,814	$7,350	1-D	5,872	559
Brandeis Univ, Waltham, MA 02454-9110	1948	$37,294	$10,354	1-D	5,327	NA
Brewton-Parker Coll, Mt. Vernon, GA 30445	1904	$14,730	$5,620	2-B	1,017	199
Briarcliffe Coll, Bethpage, NY 11714	1966	NA	NA	3-B	2,343	247
Briar Cliff Univ, Sioux City, IA 51104-0100	1930	$21,510	$6,411	2-M	1,114	108
Bridgewater Coll, Bridgewater, VA 22812-1599	1880	$24,500	$9,900	2-B	1,514	131
Bridgewater State Coll, Bridgewater, MA 02325-0001	1840	$6,237(S)	$6,852	5-M	8,497	672
Brigham Young Univ, Provo, UT 84602-1001	1875	$440/cr. hr.	$6,840	2-D	34,244	1,781
Brigham Young Univ–Hawaii, Laie, HI 96762-1294	1955	$3,600	$5,568	2-B	2,473	184
Brooklyn Coll of the City Univ of New York, Brooklyn, NY 11210-2889	1930	$4,150(S)	NA	11-M	15,947	1,256
Brooks Inst, Santa Barbara, CA 93101	1945	$26,760	NA	3-M	1,743	120
Brown Univ, Providence, RI 02912	1764	$37,718	$10,022	1-D	6,095	828
Bryan Coll, Dayton, TN 37321-7000	1930	$17,860	$5,354	2-M	1,079	70
Bryant & Stratton Coll - Wauwatosa Cmps, Wauwatosa, WI 53226	NA	$13,080	NA	3-B	1,264	NA
Bryant Univ, Smithfield, RI 02917-1284	1863	$32,286	$11,757	1-M	3,800	260
Bryn Mawr Coll, Bryn Mawr, PA 19010-2899	1885	$38,034	$12,000	1-D	1,745	210
Bucknell Univ, Lewisburg, PA 17837	1846	$40,816	$9,504	1-M	3,719	358
Buena Vista Univ, Storm Lake, IA 50588	1891	$24,796	$7,014	2-M	1,070	111
Buffalo State Coll, State Univ of New York, Buffalo, NY 14222-1095	1867	$5,685(S)	$9,064	5-M	11,224	792
Butler Univ, Indianapolis, IN 46208-3485	1855	$28,266	$9,410	1-F	4,438	461
Cabrini Coll, Radnor, PA 19087-3698	1957	$30,010	$10,890	2-M	3,580	305
Caldwell Coll, Caldwell, NJ 07006-6195	1939	$23,600	$8,846	2-M	2,291	184
California Baptist Univ, Riverside, CA 92504-3206	1950	$22,330	$7,910	2-M	4,013	292
California Coll of the Arts, San Francisco, CA 94107	1907	$31,382	$6,600	1-M	1,354	485
California Inst of Integral Stds, San Francisco, CA 94103	1968	NA	NA	1-D	1,005	61
California Inst of Tech, Pasadena, CA 91125-0001	1891	$34,437	$10,146	1-D	2,126	360
California Inst of the Arts, Valencia, CA 91355-2340	1961	$35,406	$9,070	1-D	1,374	330
California Lutheran Univ, Thousand Oaks, CA 91360-2787	1959	$29,230	$10,090	2-D	3,499	287
California Polytechnic State Univ, San Luis Obispo, San Luis Obispo, CA 93407	1901	$5,043(S)	$9,256	5-D	19,471	1,293
California State Polytechnic Univ, Pomona, Pomona, CA 91768-2557	1938	$3,564(S)	$9,120	5-M	21,190	1,025
California State Univ, Bakersfield, Bakersfield, CA 93311-1022	1970	$4,383(S)	$7,137	5-M	7,684	416
California State Univ Channel Islands, Camarillo, CA 93012	2002	$3,482(S)	$10,200	5-F	3,599	294
California State Univ, Chico, Chico, CA 95929-0722	1887	$4,008(S)	$8,718	5-M	17,132	971
California State Univ, Dominguez Hills, Carson, CA 90747-0001	1960	$3,663(S)	$8,955	5-M	12,851	773
California State Univ, East Bay, Hayward, CA 94542-3000	1957	$3,810(S)	$9,228	5-M	14,167	813
California State Univ, Fresno, Fresno, CA 93740-8027	1911	$3,687(S)	$8,590	5-D	21,728	1,293
California State Univ, Fullerton, Fullerton, CA 92834-9480	1957	$3,658(S)	$8,722	5-M	36,996	1,852
California State Univ, Long Beach, Long Beach, CA 90840	1949	$3,698(S)	$10,832	5-M	37,891	2,289
California State Univ, Los Angeles, Los Angeles, CA 90032-8530	1947	$3,377(S)	$8,406	5-D	20,743	1,199
California State Univ, Monterey Bay, Seaside, CA 93955-8001	1994	$3,291(S)	$7,840	5-M	4,340	294
California State Univ, Northridge, Northridge, CA 91330	1958	$3,702(S)	$10,152	5-M	36,208	1,902
California State Univ, Sacramento, Sacramento, CA 95819-6048	1947	$3,048(S)	$9,428	5-D	29,011	1,583
California State Univ, San Bernardino, San Bernardino, CA 92407-2397	1965	$3,797(S)	$4,311	5-M	17,646	895
California State Univ, San Marcos, San Marcos, CA 92096-0001	1990	$3,650(S)	$9,000	5-M	8,676	527
California State Univ, Stanislaus, Turlock, CA 95382	1957	$3,819(S)	$7,832	5-D	8,601	506
California Univ of Pennsylvania, California, PA 15419-1394	1852	$7,679(S)	$8,804	5-M	7,720	402

Name, Address	Year Founded	Tuition & Fees	Room & Board	Control, Degree	Enroll-ment	Faculty
Calumet Coll of St Joseph, Whiting, IN 46394-2195	1951	$12,460	NA	2-M	1,213	116
Calvin Coll, Grand Rapids, MI 49546-4388	1876	$23,165	$7,970	2-M	4,171	418
Cambridge Coll, Cambridge, MA 02138-5304	1971	$10,959	NA	1-D	6,098	1,093
Cameron Univ, Lawton, OK 73505-6377	1908	$5,415(S)	$3,534	5-M	5,454	321
Campbellsville Univ, Campbellsville, KY 42718-2799	1906	$18,810	$6,540	2-M	2,830	278
Campbell Univ, Buies Creek, NC 27506	1887	$20,050	$6,830	2-D	4,743	305
Canisius Coll, Buffalo, NY 14208-1098	1870	$28,157	$10,150	2-M	4,916	494
Capella Univ, Minneapolis, MN 55402	1993	$11,160	NA	3-D	17,203	796
Capital Univ, Columbus, OH 43209-2394	1830	$27,680	$7,150	2-F	3,632	407
Cardinal Stritch Univ, Milwaukee, WI 53217-3985	1937	$20,510	$6,020	2-D	6,255	458
Caribbean Univ, Bayamón, PR 00960-0493	1969	$4,100	NA	1-M	1,670	NA
Carleton Coll, Northfield, MN 55057-4001	1866	$38,046	$9,993	1-B	2,000	232
Carlos Albizu Univ, Miami Cmps, Miami, FL 33172-2209 (4)	1980	$11,724	NA	1-D	1,139	61
Carlow Univ, Pittsburgh, PA 15213-3165 (4)	1929	$21,718	$8,554	2-D	2,128	236
Carnegie Mellon Univ, Pittsburgh, PA 15213-3891	1900	$40,920	$10,340	1-D	11,064	1,036
Carroll Coll, Helena, MT 59625-0002	1909	$22,592	$7,118	2-B	1,409	157
Carroll Univ, Waukesha, WI 53186-5593	1846	$21,926	$6,694	2-F	3,316	289
Carson-Newman Coll, Jefferson City, TN 37760	1851	$17,800	$5,790	2-M	2,032	213
Carthage Coll, Kenosha, WI 53140	1847	$26,500	$7,500	2-M	2,778	NA
Case Western Reserve Univ, Cleveland, OH 44106	1826	$35,202	$10,450	1-D	9,814	900
Castleton State Coll, Castleton, VT 05735	1787	$8,820(S)	$7,808	5-M	2,089	215
Catawba Coll, Salisbury, NC 28144-2488	1851	$23,740	$8,200	2-M	1,261	97
The Catholic Univ of America, Washington, DC 20064	1887	$31,520	$11,450	2-D	6,705	694
Cazenovia Coll, Cazenovia, NY 13035-1084	1824	$22,894	$9,502	1-B	1,062	188
Cedar Crest Coll, Allentown, PA 18104-6196 (3)	1867	$28,135	$9,321	2-M	1,872	173
Cedarville Univ, Cedarville, OH 45314-0601	1887	$22,304	$5,006	2-M	3,077	254
Centenary Coll, Hackettstown, NJ 07840-2100	1867	$24,930	$8,900	2-M	3,261	347
Central Coll, Pella, IA 50219-1999	1853	$23,944	$8,006	2-B	1,558	156
Central Connecticut State Univ, New Britain, CT 06050-4010	1849	$7,042(S)	$8,618	5-D	12,233	899
Central Methodist Univ, Fayette, MO 65248-1198	1854	$17,980	$6,000	2-M	1,031	88
Central Michigan Univ, Mount Pleasant, MI 48859	1892	$9,720(S)	$7,668	5-D	27,225	1,190
Central Pennsylvania Coll, Summerdale, PA 17093-0309	1881	$13,275	$6,015	3-B	1,091	113
Central State Univ, Wilberforce, OH 45384	1887	$5,294(S)	$7,402	5-M	2,171	196
Central Washington Univ, Ellensburg, WA 98926	1891	$5,723(S)	$8,052	5-M	10,662	601
Centre Coll, Danville, KY 40422-1394	1819	$37,000(C)	NA	2-B	1,197	122
Chadron State Coll, Chadron, NE 69337	1911	$4,557(S)	$4,654	5-M	2,636	110
Chamberlain Coll of Nurs, St. Louis, MO 63139-3215	1889	$12,730	$6,450	3-B	1,452	NA
Chaminade Univ of Honolulu, Honolulu, HI 96816-1578	1955	$16,140	$10,420	2-M	2,685	131
Champlain Coll, Burlington, VT 05402-0670	1878	$24,355	$11,210	1-M	2,857	313
Chapman Univ, Orange, CA 92866	1861	$36,764	$12,832	2-D	6,128	614
Charleston Southern Univ, Charleston, SC 29423-8087	1964	$18,678	$7,178	2-M	3,286	210
Charter Oak State Coll, New Britain, CT 06053-2142	1973	$186/cr. hr.(S)	NA	5-B	1,577	131
Chatham Univ, Pittsburgh, PA 15232-2826	1869	$27,495	$8,286	1-D	2,184	238
Chestnut Hill Coll, Philadelphia, PA 19118-2693	1924	$27,100	$8,800	2-D	2,085	299
Cheyney Univ of Pennsylvania, Cheyney, PA 19319-0200	1837	$7,089(S)	$7,156	5-M	1,488	100
Chicago State Univ, Chicago, IL 60628	1867	$8,878(S)	$7,250	5-D	6,810	433
Christian Brothers Univ, Memphis, TN 38104-5581	1871	$22,600	$5,880	2-M	1,869	164
Christopher Newport Univ, Newport News, VA 23606-2998	1960	$10,928(S)	$9,100	5-M	4,904	364
Cincinnati Christian Univ, Cincinnati, OH 45204-3200	1924	$11,900	$6,470	2-F	1,125	110
The Citadel, The Military Coll of South Carolina, Charleston, SC 29409	1842	$9,517(S)	$5,750	5-M	3,328	252
City Coll of the City Univ of New York, New York, NY 10031-9198	1847	$4,278(S)	$8,250	11-F	14,536	1,129
City Univ of Seattle, Bellevue, WA 98005	1973	$14,580	NA	1-M	3,592	1,172
Claflin Univ, Orangeburg, SC 29115	1869	$12,666	$6,806	2-M	1,773	146
Claremont McKenna Coll, Claremont, CA 91711	1946	$36,825	$11,930	1-M	1,212	157
Clarion Univ of Pennsylvania, Clarion, PA 16214	1867	$7,104(S)	$6,071	5-M	7,100	336
Clark Atlanta Univ, Atlanta, GA 30314	1865	$17,038	$7,120	2-D	4,068	325
Clarke Coll, Dubuque, IA 52001-3198	1843	$23,520	$6,840	2-D	1,156	130
Clarkson Univ, Potsdam, NY 13699	1896	$32,910	$11,118	1-D	3,045	217
Clark Univ, Worcester, MA 01610-1477	1887	$35,220	$6,750	1-D	3,330	299
Clayton State Univ, Morrow, GA 30260-0285	1969	$3,852(S)	$3,900	5-M	6,074	NA
Clemson Univ, Clemson, SC 29634	1889	$11,108(S)	$6,556	5-D	18,317	1,277
Cleveland State Univ, Cleveland, OH 44115	1964	$7,970(S)	$8,700	5-D	15,809	1,068
Coastal Carolina Univ, Conway, SC 29528-6054	1954	$8,650(S)	$7,080	5-M	8,154	561
Coe Coll, Cedar Rapids, IA 52402-5092	1851	$29,270	$7,150	2-M	1,326	NA
Colby Coll, Waterville, ME 04901-8840	1813	$48,520(C)	NA	1-B	1,846	225
Colgate Univ, Hamilton, NY 13346-1386	1819	$39,545	$9,625	1-M	2,844	315
The Coll at Brockport, State Univ of New York, Brockport, NY 14420-2997	1867	$5,444(S)	$8,615	5-M	8,275	590
Coll for Creative Stds, Detroit, MI 48202-4034	1926	$29,985	$8,500	1-M	1,369	248
Coll of Biblical Stds–Houston, Houston, TX 77036	1979	$5,490	NA	2-B	1,399	NA
Coll of Charleston, Charleston, SC 29424-0001	1770	$8,400(S)	$8,999	5-M	11,367	898
Coll of Mount St Joseph, Cincinnati, OH 45233-1670	1920	$22,000	$6,900	2-D	2,133	240
Coll of Mount St Vincent, Riverdale, NY 10471-1093	1911	$24,580	$9,370	1-M	1,797	185
The Coll of New Jersey, Ewing, NJ 08628	1855	$12,308(S)	$9,612	5-M	6,949	746
The Coll of New Rochelle, New Rochelle, NY 10805-2308 (4)	1904	$26,426	$9,600	1-M	1,890	232
Coll of Notre Dame of Maryland, Baltimore, MD 21210-2476	1873	$27,250	$9,100	2-D	2,935	243
Coll of St Benedict, Saint Joseph, MN 56374 (4)	1887	$28,668	$7,959	2-B	2,110	191
Coll of St Elizabeth, Morristown, NJ 07960-6989	1899	$24,042	$10,690	2-D	2,111	201
The Coll of St Rose, Albany, NY 12203-1419	1920	$21,972	$8,986	1-M	5,102	417
The Coll of St Scholastica, Duluth, MN 55811-4199	1912	$26,489	$6,972	2-D	3,593	281
Coll of Staten Island of the City Univ of New York, Staten Island, NY 10314-6600	1955	$4,378(S)	NA	11-D	13,092	944
Coll of the Holy Cross, Worcester, MA 01610-2395	1843	$38,722	$10,620	2-B	2,898	318
Coll of the Ozarks, Point Lookout, MO 65726	1906	$0	$5,000	2-B	1,331	119
The Coll of William & Mary, Williamsburg, VA 23187-8795	1693	$10,246(S)	$7,910	5-D	7,892	801
The Coll of Wooster, Wooster, OH 44691-2363	1866	$43,900(C)	NA	2-B	1,884	200
Collins Coll: A Sch of Design & Tech, Tempe, AZ 85281-5206	1978	$39,146	$4,860	3-B	1,287	102
Colorado Christian Univ, Lakewood, CO 80226	1914	$20,280	$8,050	2-M	2,221	46
The Colorado Coll, Colorado Springs, CO 80903-3294	1874	$36,044	$9,096	1-M	2,026	205
Colorado Sch of Mines, Golden, CO 80401-1887	1874	$11,238(S)	$7,626	5-D	4,488	345
Colorado State Univ, Fort Collins, CO 80523-0015	1870	$5,874(S)	$8,134	5-D	27,800	968
Colorado State Univ–Pueblo, Pueblo, CO 81001-4901	1933	$4,667(S)	$6,300	5-M	6,759	326
Colorado Tech Univ Colorado Springs, Colorado Springs, CO 80907-3896	1965	NA	NA	3-D	2,359	343
Colorado Tech Univ Online, Colorado Springs, CO 80907	NA	NA	NA	3-M	25,797	613
Columbia Coll, Columbia, MO 65216-0002	1851	$14,576	$5,898	2-M	1,353	99
Columbia Coll, Caguas, PR 00726	1966	$7,220	NA	3-M	1,076	85

Name, Address	Year Founded	Tuition & Fees	Room & Board	Control, Degree	Enroll-ment	Faculty
Columbia Coll, Columbia, SC 29203-5998	1854	$23,030	$6,450	2-F	1,444	163
Columbia Coll Chicago, Chicago, IL 60605-1996	1890	$17,634	$12,018	1-M	11,499	1,477
Columbia Southern Univ, Orange Beach, AL 36561 (2)	1993	$5,895	NA	3-D	14,057	127
Columbia Union Coll, Takoma Park, MD 20912-7796	1904	$19,430	$6,887	2-M	1,069	53
Columbia Univ, New York, NY 10027	1754	$38,552	$9,980	1-D	5,667	1,804
Columbia Univ, Sch of Genl Stds, New York, NY 10027-6939	1754	$37,958	$12,045	1-B	1,245	1,170
Columbus Coll of Art & Design, Columbus, OH 43215-1758	1879	$23,564	$6,750	1-B	1,599	183
Columbus State Univ, Columbus, GA 31907-5645	1958	$3,772(S)	$6,900	5-M	7,953	429
Concordia Coll, Moorhead, MN 56562	1891	$25,710	$6,825	2-M	2,823	266
Concordia Univ, Irvine, CA 92612-3299	1972	$24,950	$7,990	2-M	2,453	257
Concordia Univ, Ann Arbor, MI 48105-2797	1963	$19,700	$7,350	2-M	1,075	95
Concordia Univ, Portland, OR 97211-6099	1905	$23,400	$6,800	2-M	1,709	172
Concordia Univ Chicago, River Forest, IL 60305-1499	1864	$23,458	$7,700	2-D	4,185	287
Concordia Univ, Nebraska, Seward, NE 68434-1599	1894	$21,250	$5,520	2-M	1,344	161
Concordia Univ, St Paul, St. Paul, MN 55104-5494	1893	$26,400	$7,250	2-M	2,644	265
Concordia Univ Texas, Austin, TX 78726	1926	$20,490	$7,800	2-M	2,261	365
Concordia Univ Wisconsin, Mequon, WI 53097-2402	1881	$20,000	$7,700	2-D	6,549	245
Concord Univ, Athens, WV 24712-1000	1872	$4,578(S)	$6,530	5-M	2,837	199
Connecticut Coll, New London, CT 06320-4196	1911	$49,385(C)	NA	1-M	1,852	239
Converse Coll, Spartanburg, SC 29302-0006	1889	$24,500	$7,550	1-M	1,881	92
Coppin State Univ, Baltimore, MD 21216-3698	1900	$5,305(S)	$7,138	5-M	4,051	301
Corban Coll, Salem, OR 97301-9392	1935	$23,202	$8,068	2-M	1,031	101
Cornell Coll, Mount Vernon, IA 52314-1098	1853	$27,850	$7,220	2-B	1,083	97
Cornell Univ, Ithaca, NY 14853-0001	1865	$37,954	$12,110	1-D	20,273	1,896
Cornerstone Univ, Grand Rapids, MI 49525-5897	1941	$19,530	$6,500	2-F	2,440	127
Covenant Coll, Lookout Mountain, GA 30750	1955	$24,320	$6,900	2-M	1,073	83
Creighton Univ, Omaha, NE 68178-0001	1878	$28,542	$8,516	2-D	7,051	721
Crichton Coll, Memphis, TN 38111	1941	$12,114	$8,332	1-B	1,016	94
Crown Coll, St. Bonifacius, MN 55375-9001	1916	$19,774	$7,366	2-M	1,229	159
The Culinary Inst of America, Hyde Park, NY 12538-1499	1946	$22,270	$9,490	1-B	2,812	198
Cumberland Univ, Lebanon, TN 37087-3408	1842	$16,720	$6,070	1-M	1,335	90
Curry Coll, Milton, MA 02186-9984	1879	$27,720	$11,080	1-M	3,079	463
Daemen Coll, Amherst, NY 14226-3592	1947	$19,870	$9,050	1-D	2,716	269
Dakota State Univ, Madison, SD 57042-1799	1881	$6,498(S)	$4,612	5-D	2,675	121
Dallas Baptist Univ, Dallas, TX 75211-9299	1965	$16,440	$5,409	2-D	5,297	523
Dalton State Coll, Dalton, GA 30720-3797	1963	$1,994(S)	NA	5-B	4,349	199
Daniel Webster Coll, Nashua, NH 03063-1300	1965	$28,615	$9,698	1-M	1,007	62
Dartmouth Coll, Hanover, NH 03755	1769	$38,445	$10,779	1-D	5,848	647
Davenport Univ, Grand Rapids, MI 49503	1866	$10,640	$4,990	1-M	10,764	1,089
Davidson Coll, Davidson, NC 28035	1837	$33,479	$9,471	2-B	1,668	177
Defiance Coll, Defiance, OH 43512-1610	1850	$22,895	$7,750	2-M	1,001	101
Delaware State Univ, Dover, DE 19901-2277	1891	$7,261(S)	$8,752	5-D	3,534	339
Delaware Valley Coll, Doylestown, PA 18901-2697	1896	$27,292	$9,750	1-M	2,138	196
Delta State Univ, Cleveland, MS 38733-0001	1924	$4,450(S)	$5,476	5-D	4,065	258
Denison Univ, Granville, OH 43023	1831	$35,300	$8,610	1-B	2,200	218
DePaul Univ, Chicago, IL 60604-2287	1898	$26,067	$10,240	2-D	24,352	1,842
DePauw Univ, Greencastle, IN 46135-0037	1837	$31,825	$8,400	2-B	2,298	281
DeSales Univ, Center Valley, PA 18034-9568	1964	$25,800	$9,330	2-M	3,059	265
DeVry Coll of New York, Long Island City, NY 11101	1998	$14,720	NA	3-M	1,130	111
DeVry Univ, Phoenix, AZ 85021-2995	1967	$14,080	NA	3-M	1,277	102
DeVry Univ, Fremont, CA 94555	1998	$14,720	NA	3-M	1,447	254
DeVry Univ, Long Beach, CA 90806	1984	$14,080	NA	3-M	1,115	100
DeVry Univ, Pomona, CA 91768-2642	1983	$14,080	NA	3-M	1,934	156
DeVry Univ, Miramar, FL 33027-4150	2002	$14,080	NA	3-M	1,099	96
DeVry Univ, Orlando, FL 32839	2000	$14,080	NA	3-M	1,576	195
DeVry Univ, Decatur, GA 30030-2556	1969	$14,080	NA	3-M	2,719	197
DeVry Univ, Addison, IL 60101-6106	1982	$14,080	NA	3-B	1,403	121
DeVry Univ, Chicago, IL 60618-5994	1931	$14,080	NA	3-B	1,890	159
DeVry Univ, Naperville, IL 60563-2361	NA	$14,440	NA	3-M	8,828	2,248
DeVry Univ, Tinley Park, IL 60477	2000	$14,080	NA	3-M	1,401	75
DeVry Univ, Kansas City, MO 64131-3698	1931	$14,080	NA	3-M	1,116	88
DeVry Univ, North Brunswick, NJ 08902-3362	1969	$14,720	NA	3-B	1,290	169
DeVry Univ, Columbus, OH 43209-2705	1952	$14,080	NA	3-M	2,776	236
DeVry Univ, Fort Washington, PA 19034	2002	$14,720	NA	3-M	1,049	171
DeVry Univ, Houston, TX 77041	NA	$14,080	NA	3-M	1,283	174
DeVry Univ, Irving, TX 75063-2439	1969	$14,080	NA	3-M	1,806	142
DeVry Univ Online, Oakbrook Terrace, IL 60181	2000	$14,560	NA	3-M	12,276	3,111
Dickinson Coll, Carlisle, PA 17013-2896	1773	$38,234	$9,600	1-B	2,388	240
Dickinson State Univ, Dickinson, ND 58601-4896	1918	$5,083(S)	$4,280	5-B	2,572	217
Dixie State Coll of Utah, St. George, UT 84770-3876	1911	$2,893(S)	$3,498	5-B	6,086	332
Dominican Coll, Orangeburg, NY 10962-1210	1952	$20,300	$9,730	1-D	1,963	230
Dominican Univ, River Forest, IL 60305-1099	1901	$23,800	$7,350	2-M	3,413	407
Dominican Univ of California, San Rafael, CA 94901-2298	1890	$32,390	$11,200	2-M	2,071	332
Dordt Coll, Sioux Center, IA 51250-1697	1955	$22,080	$6,010	2-M	1,400	106
Dowling Coll, Oakdale, NY 11769-1999	1955	$20,310	$9,200	1-D	5,706	537
Drake Univ, Des Moines, IA 50311-4516	1881	$26,622	$7,800	1-D	5,668	407
Drew Univ, Madison, NJ 07940-1493	1867	$38,017	$10,368	2-D	2,605	233
Drexel Univ, Philadelphia, PA 19104-2875	1891	$30,440	$12,135	1-D	20,682	NA
Drury Univ, Springfield, MO 65802	1873	$19,013	$6,703	1-M	2,060	172
Duke Univ, Durham, NC 27708-0586	1838	$38,741	$11,154	2-D	14,060	1,155
Duquesne Univ, Pittsburgh, PA 15282-0001	1878	$25,480	$8,888	2-D	10,106	946
D'Youville Coll, Buffalo, NY 14201-1084	1908	$19,030	$9,300	1-D	2,943	316
Earlham Coll, Richmond, IN 47374-4095	1847	$34,030	$6,814	2-F	1,308	104
East Carolina Univ, Greenville, NC 27858-4353	1907	$4,290(S)	$7,773	5-D	27,677	1,329
East Central Univ, Ada, OK 74820-6899	1909	$3,436(S)	$4,080	5-M	4,463	253
Eastern Connecticut State Univ, Willimantic, CT 06226-2295	1889	$7,536(S)	$8,855	5-M	5,427	446
Eastern Illinois Univ, Charleston, IL 61920-3099	1895	$8,783(S)	$7,588	5-M	12,040	807
Eastern Kentucky Univ, Richmond, KY 40475-3102	1906	$6,080(S)	$6,360	5-M	15,839	1,039
Eastern Mennonite Univ, Harrisonburg, VA 22802-2462	1917	$23,180	$7,200	2-F	1,387	162
Eastern Michigan Univ, Ypsilanti, MI 48197	1849	$8,069(S)	$7,352	5-D	21,926	1,236
Eastern New Mexico Univ, Portales, NM 88130	1934	$3,342(S)	$5,222	5-M	4,300	291
Eastern Oregon Univ, La Grande, OR 97850-2899	1929	$6,225(S)	$8,800	5-M	3,666	124
Eastern Univ, St. Davids, PA 19087-3696	1952	$22,670	$8,610	2-F	3,918	343
Eastern Washington Univ, Cheney, WA 99004-2431	1882	$5,118(S)	$6,894	5-D	10,809	665

Name, Address	Year Founded	Tuition & Fees	Room & Board	Control, Degree	Enroll-ment	Faculty
East Stroudsburg Univ of Pennsylvania, East Stroudsburg, PA 18301-2999	1893	$7,090(S)	$6,148	5-M	7,234	359
East Tennessee State Univ, Johnson City, TN 37614	1911	$5,201(S)	$5,278	5-D	13,119	784
East Texas Baptist Univ, Marshall, TX 75670-1498	1912	$17,180	$5,164	2-B	1,210	95
East-West Univ, Chicago, IL 60605-2103	1978	$13,575	NA	1-B	1,170	77
Eckerd Coll, St. Petersburg, FL 33711	1958	$30,590	$8,754	2-B	1,819	160
Edgewood Coll, Madison, WI 53711-1997 (4)	1927	$20,040	$6,828	2-D	2,544	288
Edinboro Univ of Pennsylvania, Edinboro, PA 16444	1857	$7,042(S)	$6,650	5-M	7,671	418
Elizabeth City State Univ, Elizabeth City, NC 27909-7806	1891	$3,698(S)	$5,159	5-M	3,061	NA
Elizabethtown Coll, Elizabethtown, PA 17022-2298	1899	$30,650	$7,950	2-M	2,311	272
Elmhurst Coll, Elmhurst, IL 60126-3296	1871	$27,330	$7,874	2-M	3,316	351
Elmira Coll, Elmira, NY 14901	1855	$33,250	$10,100	1-M	1,551	204
Elms Coll, Chicopee, MA 01013-2839 (4)	1928	$25,152	$9,260	2-M	1,234	146
Elon Univ, Elon, NC 27244-2010	1889	$24,076	$7,770	2-D	5,628	457
Embry-Riddle Aeron Univ, Prescott, AZ 86301-3720	1978	$27,750	$8,008	1-M	1,719	130
Embry-Riddle Aeron Univ, Daytona Beach, FL 32114-3900	1926	$28,114	$9,964	1-M	5,062	322
Embry-Riddle Aeron Univ Worldwide, Daytona Beach, FL 32114-3900	1970	$5,304	NA	1-M	16,331	2,692
Emerson Coll, Boston, MA 02116-4624	1880	$28,884	$11,832	1-D	4,536	404
Emmanuel Coll, Boston, MA 02115	1919	$29,200	$11,950	2-M	1,902	235
Emory Univ, Atlanta, GA 30322-1100	1836	$36,336	$10,572	2-D	10,921	1,447
Emporia State Univ, Emporia, KS 66801-5087	1863	$4,136(S)	$5,858	5-D	6,404	293
Endicott Coll, Beverly, MA 01915-2096	1939	$24,530	$11,380	1-M	3,947	171
Eugene Lang Coll The New Sch for Lib Arts, New York, NY 10011-8601	1978	$33,060	$15,260	1-B	1,347	143
Evangel Univ, Springfield, MO 65802-2191	1955	$15,020	$5,410	2-M	1,911	161
Everest Univ, Pompano Beach, FL 33062	1940	$10,944	NA	3-M	1,377	61
Everest Univ, Tampa, FL 33614-5899	1890	NA	NA	3-M	1,320	61
Everest Univ, Tampa, FL 33619	1890	$17,040	NA	3-M	5,984	66
The Evergreen State Coll, Olympia, WA 98505	1967	$5,344(S)	$8,052	5-M	4,696	243
Excelsior Coll, Albany, NY 12203-5159	1970	$300/cr. hr.	NA	1-M	33,450	387
Fairfield Univ, Fairfield, CT 06824-5195	1942	$36,075	$10,850	2-M	5,128	510
Fairleigh Dickinson Univ, Coll at Florham, Madison, NJ 07940-1099	1942	$30,198	$10,548	1-M	3,465	NA
Fairleigh Dickinson Univ, Metropolitan Cmps, Teaneck, NJ 07666-1914	1942	$28,084	$10,914	1-D	8,693	NA
Fairmont State Univ, Fairmont, WV 26554	1865	$5,224(S)	$6,652	5-M	4,547	334
Farmingdale State Coll, Farmingdale, NY 11735	1912	$6,005(S)	$12,000	5-B	6,850	539
Fashion Inst of Tech, New York, NY 10001-5992 (4)	1944	$5,008(S)	$10,950	11-M	10,065	989
Faulkner Univ, Montgomery, AL 36109-3398	1942	$12,720	$6,350	2-F	2,873	117
Fayetteville State Univ, Fayetteville, NC 28301-4298	1867	$3,301(S)	$5,010	5-D	6,692	321
Felician Coll, Lodi, NJ 07644-2117	1942	$25,050	$9,700	2-M	2,042	191
Ferris State Univ, Big Rapids, MI 49307	1884	$9,162(S)	$7,944	5-F	13,537	857
Ferrum Coll, Ferrum, VA 24088-9001	1913	$22,500	$7,300	2-B	1,383	91
Fitchburg State Coll, Fitchburg, MA 01420-2697	1894	$6,400(S)	$7,148	5-M	6,761	270
Five Towns Coll, Dix Hills, NY 11746-6055	1972	$17,800	$11,850	1-D	1,163	129
Flagler Coll, St. Augustine, FL 32085-1027	1968	$12,520	$6,810	1-B	2,666	180
Florida Agr & Mech Univ, Tallahassee, FL 32307-3200	1887	$4,407(S)	$6,706	5-D	11,587	757
Florida Atlantic Univ, Boca Raton, FL 33431-0991	1961	$3,662(S)	$8,960	5-D	26,897	1,356
Florida Gulf Coast Univ, Fort Myers, FL 33965-6565	1991	$5,497(S)	$7,450	5-M	10,214	573
Florida Hosp Coll of Health Sci, Orlando, FL 32803	1913	$8,540	NA	1-B	2,207	84
Florida Inst of Tech, Melbourne, FL 32901-6975	1958	$30,440	$10,250	1-D	6,400	484
Florida Intl Univ, Miami, FL 33199	1965	$3,900(S)	$11,120	5-D	31,589	1,554
Florida Memorial Univ, Miami-Dade, FL 33054	1879	$12,254	$5,340	2-M	1,750	173
Florida Southern Coll, Lakeland, FL 33801-5698	1885	$23,245	$8,242	2-M	1,874	200
Florida State Univ, Tallahassee, FL 32306	1851	$4,196(S)	$8,178	5-D	38,682	1,666
Fontbonne Univ, St. Louis, MO 63105-3098 (4)	1917	$19,795	$7,411	2-M	2,967	347
Fordham Univ, New York, NY 10458	1841	$35,257	$12,980	2-D	14,448	1,210
Fort Hays State Univ, Hays, KS 67601-4099	1902	$3,051(S)	$5,450	5-M	7,403	291
Fort Lewis Coll, Durango, CO 81301-3999	1911	$6,956(S)	$7,170	5-B	3,746	269
Fort Valley State Univ, Fort Valley, GA 31030-4313	1895	$4,478(S)	$7,540	5-D	3,106	162
Framingham State Coll, Framingham, MA 01701-9101	1839	$6,141(S)	$7,509	5-M	6,097	266
Franciscan Univ of Steubenville, Steubenville, OH 43952-1763	1946	$19,650	$6,750	2-M	2,449	214
Francis Marion Univ, Florence, SC 29501-0547	1970	$7,960(S)	$6,024	5-M	4,019	256
Franklin & Marshall Coll, Lancaster, PA 17604-3003	1787	$38,630	$9,870	1-B	2,164	233
Franklin Coll, Franklin, IN 46131-2623	1834	$22,445	$6,640	2-B	1,153	105
Franklin Pierce Univ, Rindge, NH 03461-0060	1962	$28,700	$9,800	1-D	2,601	244
Franklin Univ, Columbus, OH 43215-5399	1902	$8,400	NA	1-M	7,559	NA
Freed-Hardeman Univ, Henderson, TN 38340-2399	1869	$13,860	$6,970	2-F	2,061	151
Fresno Pacific Univ, Fresno, CA 93702-4709	1944	$23,202	$6,800	2-M	2,353	355
Friends Univ, Wichita, KS 67213	1898	$9,175	$5,450	1-M	2,826	NA
Frostburg State Univ, Frostburg, MD 21532-1099	1898	$6,614(S)	$7,016	5-M	5,215	358
Full Sail Univ, Winter Park, FL 32792-7437 (2)	1979	NA	NA	3-M	5,916	702
Furman Univ, Greenville, SC 29613	1826	$34,588	$8,966	1-M	2,977	274
Gallaudet Univ, Washington, DC 20002-3625	1864	$10,950	$9,340	1-D	1,389	230
Gannon Univ, Erie, PA 16541-0001	1925	$22,662	$8,710	2-D	4,197	336
Gardner-Webb Univ, Boiling Springs, NC 28017	1905	$20,200	$6,500	2-D	3,892	322
Geneva Coll, Beaver Falls, PA 15010-3599	1848	$21,400	$7,770	2-M	1,624	184
George Fox Univ, Newberg, OR 97132-2697	1891	$25,190	$8,000	2-D	3,383	358
George Mason Univ, Fairfax, VA 22030	1957	$7,512(S)	$7,360	5-D	30,714	2,073
Georgetown Coll, Georgetown, KY 40324-1696	1829	$24,150	$6,700	2-M	1,856	149
Georgetown Univ, Washington, DC 20057	1789	$38,122	$12,153	2-D	15,318	1,589
The George Washington Univ, Washington, DC 20052	1821	$41,655	$10,120	1-D	25,116	2,080
Georgia Coll & State Univ, Milledgeville, GA 31061	1889	$5,476(S)	$7,698	5-M	6,506	412
Georgia Inst of Tech, Atlanta, GA 30332-0001 (2)	1885	$6,040(S)	$7,694	5-D	19,413	896
Georgian Court Univ, Lakewood, NJ 08701-2697	1908	$23,360	$9,112	2-M	3,189	309
Georgia Southern Univ, Statesboro, GA 30460	1906	$5,440(S)	$7,900	5-D	17,764	816
Georgia Southwestern State Univ, Americus, GA 31709-4693	1906	$3,816(S)	$5,694	5-M	2,405	155
Georgia State Univ, Atlanta, GA 30303-3083	1913	$6,056(S)	$9,330	5-D	28,238	1,573
Gettysburg Coll, Gettysburg, PA 17325-1483	1832	$37,600	$9,100	2-B	2,457	278
Glenville State Coll, Glenville, WV 26351-1200	1872	$4,486(S)	$6,150	5-B	1,443	93
Global Univ, Springfield, MO 65804	1948	$3,168	NA	2-F	7,096	633
Globe Inst of Tech, New York, NY 10018	NA	$12,150	NA	3-B	1,671	113
Golden Gate Univ, San Francisco, CA 94105-2968	1901	$12,960	NA	1-D	3,528	489
Goldey-Beacom Coll, Wilmington, DE 19808-1999	1886	$18,840	$4,982	1-M	1,208	52
Gonzaga Univ, Spokane, WA 99258	1887	$28,262	$7,860	2-D	7,272	713
Gordon Coll, Wenham, MA 01984-1899	1889	$27,294	$7,424	2-M	1,718	178
Goucher Coll, Baltimore, MD 21204-2794	1885	$33,786	$10,006	1-M	2,319	209
Governors State Univ, University Park, IL 60466-0975	1969	$4,896(S)	NA	5-M	5,405	212

Name, Address	Year Founded	Tuition & Fees	Room & Board	Control, Degree	Enroll-ment	Faculty
Grace Coll, Winona Lake, IN 46590-1294	1948	$20,376	$6,648	2-D	1,508	110
Graceland Univ, Lamoni, IA 50140	1895	$20,090	$6,780	2-M	2,444	97
Grambling State Univ, Grambling, LA 71245	1901	$3,804(S)	$5,202	5-D	5,253	291
Grand Canyon Univ, Phoenix, AZ 85017-1097	1949	$16,030	$7,896	2-D	13,415	514
Grand Valley State Univ, Allendale, MI 49401-9403	1960	$8,196(S)	$7,224	5-D	23,892	1,529
Grand View Univ, Des Moines, IA 50316-1599	1896	$18,614	$6,164	2-M	1,936	188
Granite State Coll, Concord, NH 03301 (4)	1972	$5,907(S)	NA	11-B	1,543	147
Grantham Univ, Kansas City, MO 64153	1951	$7,950	NA	3-M	6,423	163
Greensboro Coll, Greensboro, NC 27401-1875	1838	$22,248	$8,420	2-M	1,289	147
Greenville Coll, Greenville, IL 62246-0159	1892	$20,216	$6,796	2-M	1,618	153
Grinnell Coll, Grinnell, IA 50112-1690	1846	$35,428	$8,272	1-B	1,678	207
Grove City Coll, Grove City, PA 16127-2104	1876	$12,074	$6,440	2-B	2,499	209
Guilford Coll, Greensboro, NC 27410-4173	1837	$27,450	$7,560	2-B	2,641	219
Gustavus Adolphus Coll, St. Peter, MN 56082-1498	1862	$29,990	$7,460	2-B	2,578	251
Gwynedd-Mercy Coll, Gwynedd Valley, PA 19437-0901	1948	$22,790	$8,990	2-M	2,548	297
Hamilton Coll, Clinton, NY 13323-1296	1812	$38,600	$9,810	1-B	1,872	216
Hamline Univ, St. Paul, MN 55104-1284	1854	$28,152	$7,784	2-D	4,876	551
Hampden-Sydney Coll, Hampden-Sydney, VA 23943 (1)	1776	$29,511	$9,228	2-B	1,120	121
Hampshire Coll, Amherst, MA 01002	1965	$38,549	$10,080	1-B	1,428	164
Hampton Univ, Hampton, VA 23668	1868	$16,392	$7,440	1-D	5,427	447
Hannibal-LaGrange Coll, Hannibal, MO 63401-1999	1858	$14,506	$5,270	2-M	1,127	96
Harding Univ, Searcy, AR 72149-0001	1924	$13,130	$5,700	2-D	6,447	436
Hardin-Simmons Univ, Abilene, TX 79698-0001	1891	$19,790	$5,788	2-D	2,387	198
Harrington Coll of Design, Chicago, IL 60606 (4)	1931	$20,520	$2,600	3-B	1,563	142
Harris-Stowe State Univ, St. Louis, MO 63103-2136	1857	$5,320(S)	NA	5-B	1,852	162
Hartwick Coll, Oneonta, NY 13820-4020	1797	$31,900	$8,685	1-B	1,493	188
Harvard Univ, Cambridge, MA 02138	1636	$36,173	$11,042	1-D	19,230	2,265
Hastings Coll, Hastings, NE 68901-7696	1882	$20,782	$5,702	2-M	1,138	123
Haverford Coll, Haverford, PA 19041-1392	1833	$37,525	$11,450	1-B	1,169	132
Hawai`i Pacific Univ, Honolulu, HI 96813	1965	$14,960	$11,094	1-M	8,293	597
Heidelberg Univ, Tiffin, OH 44883-2462	1850	$21,330	$8,384	2-M	1,519	154
Henderson State Univ, Arkadelphia, AR 71999-0001	1890	$4,939(S)	$4,860	5-M	3,649	249
Hendrix Coll, Conway, AR 72032-3080	1876	$26,080	$7,950	2-M	1,350	131
Heritage Univ, Toppenish, WA 98948-9599	1982	$12,205	NA	1-M	1,311	187
High Point Univ, High Point, NC 27262-3598	1924	$34,200(C)	NA	2-M	3,384	277
Hilbert Coll, Hamburg, NY 14075-1597	1957	$17,350	$6,950	1-B	1,046	115
Hillsdale Coll, Hillsdale, MI 49242-1298	1844	$19,920	$7,750	1-B	1,378	154
Hiram Coll, Hiram, OH 44234-0067	1850	$25,160	$8,380	2-M	1,360	127
Hobart & William Smith Colls, Geneva, NY 14456-3397	1822	$38,860	$9,686	1-M	2,009	212
Hodges Univ, Naples, FL 34119	1990	$16,580	NA	1-M	1,906	116
Hofstra Univ, Hempstead, NY 11549	1935	$28,630	$10,825	1-D	12,333	1,185
Hollins Univ, Roanoke, VA 24020-1603	1842	$27,055	$9,650	1-M	1,058	108
Holy Family Univ, Philadelphia, PA 19114-2094 (4)	1954	$22,950	$9,900	2-M	3,524	384
Holy Names Univ, Oakland, CA 94619-1699 (4)	1868	$27,340	$9,320	2-M	1,105	138
Hood Coll, Frederick, MD 21701-8575	1893	$26,580	$8,980	1-M	2,533	260
Hope Coll, Holland, MI 49422-9000	1866	$24,920	$7,650	2-B	3,238	328
Hope Intl Univ, Fullerton, CA 92831-3138	1928	$22,761	$8,230	2-M	1,059	120
Houghton Coll, Houghton, NY 14744	1883	$22,990	$6,930	2-M	1,419	157
Houston Baptist Univ, Houston, TX 77074-3298	1960	$20,830	$6,975	2-M	2,564	260
Howard Payne Univ, Brownwood, TX 76801-2715	1889	$18,650	$5,160	2-M	1,388	146
Howard Univ, Washington, DC 20059-0002	1867	$15,270	$7,966	1-D	10,288	1,520
Humboldt State Univ, Arcata, CA 95521-8299	1913	$4,150(S)	$8,972	5-M	7,800	521
Hunter Coll of the City Univ of New York, New York, NY 10021-5085	1870	$4,349(S)	$5,311	11-M	21,258	1,642
Huntingdon Coll, Montgomery, AL 36106-2148	1854	$20,020	$6,950	2-B	1,082	116
Huntington Univ, Huntington, IN 46750-1299	1897	$20,300	$6,940	2-M	1,211	92
Husson Univ, Bangor, ME 04401-2999	1898	$12,990	$6,994	1-D	2,626	88
Idaho State Univ, Pocatello, ID 83209	1901	$4,664(S)	$5,270	5-D	12,653	767
Illinois Inst of Tech, Chicago, IL 60616-3793	1890	$27,513	$9,233	1-D	7,613	640
Illinois State Univ, Normal, IL 61790-2200	1857	$9,814(S)	$7,458	5-D	20,799	1,183
Illinois Wesleyan Univ, Bloomington, IL 61702-2900	1850	$32,434	$7,350	1-B	2,125	233
Immaculata Univ, Immaculata, PA 19345 (4)	1920	$24,575	$10,400	2-D	4,182	426
Indiana State Univ, Terre Haute, IN 47809-1401	1865	$7,148(S)	$6,672	5-D	10,457	627
Indiana Tech, Fort Wayne, IN 46803-1297	1930	$21,400	$8,040	1-M	3,512	295
Indiana Univ Bloomington, Bloomington, IN 47405-7000	1820	$8,231(S)	$7,138	5-D	40,354	2,361
Indiana Univ East, Richmond, IN 47374-1289	1971	$5,556(S)	NA	5-M	2,447	186
Indiana Univ Kokomo, Kokomo, IN 46904-9003	1945	$5,591(S)	NA	5-M	2,690	168
Indiana Univ Northwest, Gary, IN 46408-1197	1959	$5,669(S)	NA	5-M	4,794	362
Indiana Univ of Pennsylvania, Indiana, PA 15705-1087	1875	$6,959(S)	$8,224	5-D	14,310	712
Indiana Univ–Purdue Univ Fort Wayne, Fort Wayne, IN 46805-1499	1917	$5,936(S)	$5,400	5-M	12,338	778
Indiana Univ–Purdue Univ Indianapolis, Indianapolis, IN 46202-2896	1969	$7,191(S)	$3,140	5-D	30,300	3,252
Indiana Univ South Bend, South Bend, IN 46634-7111	1922	$5,763(S)	NA	5-M	7,712	525
Indiana Univ Southeast, New Albany, IN 47150-6405	1941	$5,644(S)	$3,276	5-M	6,482	453
Indiana Wesleyan Univ, Marion, IN 46953-4974	1920	$20,496	$6,770	2-D	3,201	312
Inter Amer Univ of Puerto Rico, Aguadilla Cmps, Aguadilla, PR 00605	1957	$5,308	NA	1-M	4,467	224
Inter Amer Univ of Puerto Rico, Arecibo Cmps, Arecibo, PR 00614-4050	1957	$4,212	NA	1-M	4,729	293
Inter Amer Univ of Puerto Rico, Barranquitas Cmps, Barranquitas, PR 00794	1957	$4,770	NA	1-M	2,329	135
Inter Amer Univ of Puerto Rico, Bayamón Cmps, Bayamón, PR 00957	1912	$4,110	NA	1-M	5,187	347
Inter Amer Univ of Puerto Rico, Fajardo Cmps, Fajardo, PR 00738-7003	1965	$4,854	NA	1-M	2,256	163
Inter Amer Univ of Puerto Rico, Guayama Cmps, Guayama, PR 00785	1958	$4,174	NA	1-M	2,157	182
Inter Amer Univ of Puerto Rico, Metropolitan Cmps, San Juan, PR 00919-1293	1960	$4,212	NA	1-D	10,610	NA
Inter Amer Univ of Puerto Rico, Ponce Cmps, Mercedita, PR 00715-1602	1962	$4,886	NA	1-M	5,367	257
Inter Amer Univ of Puerto Rico, San Germán Cmps, San Germán, PR 00683-5008	1912	$4,830	NA	1-D	5,706	308
Intl Acad of Design & Tech, Chicago, IL 60602-9736 (4)	1977	$23,640	NA	3-B	2,335	132
Iona Coll, New Rochelle, NY 10801-1890	1940	$27,500	$11,300	2-M	4,375	396
Iowa State Univ of Sci & Tech, Ames, IA 50011	1858	$6,651(S)	$7,277	5-D	26,856	1,641
Ithaca Coll, Ithaca, NY 14850-7020	1892	$30,606	$11,162	1-D	6,448	679
Jackson State Univ, Jackson, MS 39217	1877	$4,634(S)	$5,810	5-D	8,376	449
Jacksonville State Univ, Jacksonville, AL 36265-1602	1883	$5,700(S)	$4,215	5-M	9,481	321
Jacksonville Univ, Jacksonville, FL 32211-3394	1934	$23,900	$8,760	1-F	3,418	254
James Madison Univ, Harrisonburg, VA 22807	1908	$6,964(S)	$7,458	5-D	18,454	1,303
Jamestown Coll, Jamestown, ND 58405	1883	$15,585	$5,155	2-B	1,025	82
John Brown Univ, Siloam Springs, AR 72761-2121	1919	$18,066	$6,580	2-M	2,017	155
John Carroll Univ, University Heights, OH 44118-4581	1886	$28,840	$8,330	2-M	3,826	385
John F. Kennedy Univ, Pleasant Hill, CA 94523-4817 (4)	1964	$13,161	NA	1-D	1,580	237

Name, Address	Year Founded	Tuition & Fees	Room & Board	Control, Degree	Enroll- ment	Faculty
John Jay Coll of Criminal Justice of the City Univ of New York, New York, NY 10019-1093	1964	$4,330(S)	NA	11-M	14,844	1,014
The Johns Hopkins Univ, Baltimore, MD 21218-2699	1876	$37,700	$11,578	1-D	6,437	NA
Johnson & Wales Univ, Denver, CO 80220	1993	$22,585	$7,956	1-B	1,466	77
Johnson & Wales Univ, North Miami, FL 33181	1992	$22,585	$7,956	1-B	1,955	80
Johnson & Wales Univ, Providence, RI 02903-3703	1914	$22,585	$8,892	1-D	10,105	417
Johnson & Wales Univ - Charlotte Cmps, Charlotte, NC 28202	2004	$22,585	$8,892	1-B	2,569	101
Johnson C. Smith Univ, Charlotte, NC 28216-5398	1867	$15,754	$6,132	1-B	1,571	125
Johnson State Coll, Johnson, VT 05656-9405	1828	$9,039(S)	$7,810	5-M	1,898	146
Jones Intl Univ, Centennial, CO 80112	1995	$11,920	NA	3-D	1,882	116
Judson Univ, Elgin, IL 60123-1498	1963	$21,850	$7,500	2-M	1,230	133
Juniata Coll, Huntingdon, PA 16652-2119	1876	$30,280	$8,420	2-B	1,523	152
Kalamazoo Coll, Kalamazoo, MI 49006-3295	1833	$30,723	$7,443	2-B	1,387	111
Kansas State Univ, Manhattan, KS 66506	1863	$6,627(S)	$6,448	5-D	23,520	1,099
Kean Univ, Union, NJ 07083	1855	$9,179(S)	$9,677	5-D	14,203	1,280
Keene State Coll, Keene, NH 03435	1909	$8,778(S)	$7,796	5-M	5,271	422
Kendall Coll, Chicago, IL 60622	1934	NA	$13,980	2-B	1,913	80
Kennesaw State Univ, Kennesaw, GA 30144-5591	1963	$4,144(S)	$4,737	5-D	21,449	1,166
Kent State Univ, Kent, OH 44242-0001	1910	$8,430(S)	$7,200	5-D	22,923	1,569
Kent State Univ, Stark Cmps, Canton, OH 44720-7599	1967	$4,770(S)	NA	5-M	3,939	213
Kentucky State Univ, Frankfort, KY 40601	1886	$5,692(S)	$6,392	12-M	2,659	185
Kenyon Coll, Gambier, OH 43022-9623	1824	$40,980	$7,260	1-B	1,644	188
Kettering Univ, Flint, MI 48504-4898 (2)	1919	$26,936	$6,182	1-M	2,600	137
Keuka Coll, Keuka Park, NY 14478-0098	1890	$21,760	$8,850	2-M	1,613	105
Keystone Coll, La Plume, PA 18440	1868	$390/credit	NA	1-B	1,716	261
King Coll, Bristol, TN 37620-2699	1867	$20,582	$6,900	2-M	1,703	155
King's Coll, Wilkes-Barre, PA 18711-0801	1946	$24,680	$9,370	2-M	2,673	209
Knox Coll, Galesburg, IL 61401	1837	$31,911	$7,164	1-B	1,379	135
Kutztown Univ of Pennsylvania, Kutztown, PA 19530-0730	1866	$7,126(S)	$7,330	5-M	10,393	540
Laboratory Inst of Merchandising, New York, NY 10022-5268 (4)	1939	$18,625	$15,800	3-M	1,107	144
Lafayette Coll, Easton, PA 18042-1798	1826	$37,520	$11,799	2-B	2,382	234
Lake Erie Coll, Painesville, OH 44077-3389	1856	$25,296	$8,072	1-M	1,054	95
Lake Forest Coll, Lake Forest, IL 60045-2399	1857	$32,520	$7,724	1-M	1,400	159
Lakeland Coll, Sheboygan, WI 53082-0359	1862	$18,970	$6,778	2-M	3,941	70
Lake Superior State Univ, Sault Sainte Marie, MI 49783	1946	$7,894(S)	$7,567	5-M	2,583	184
Lamar Univ, Beaumont, TX 77710	1923	$6,014(S)	$6,290	5-D	13,465	520
Lander Univ, Greenwood, SC 29649-2099 (4)	1872	$8,930(S)	$6,642	5-M	2,614	222
Lane Coll, Jackson, TN 38301-4598	1882	$8,000	$5,520	2-B	1,982	83
Langston Univ, Langston, OK 73050-0907	1897	NA	NA	5-M	2,526	NA
La Roche Coll, Pittsburgh, PA 15237-5898	1963	$20,330	$8,338	2-M	1,425	182
La Salle Univ, Philadelphia, PA 19141-1199	1863	$31,200	$9,760	2-D	6,179	402
Lasell Coll, Newton, MA 02466-2709	1851	$25,300	$10,500	1-M	1,469	179
La Sierra Univ, Riverside, CA 92515	1922	$24,573	$6,990	2-D	1,899	187
Lawrence Tech Univ, Southfield, MI 48075-1058	1932	$21,979	$8,071	1-D	4,417	423
Lawrence Univ, Appleton, WI 54912-0599	1847	$33,264	$6,975	1-B	1,503	186
Lebanon Valley Coll, Annville, PA 17003-1400	1866	$29,350	$7,760	2-D	1,965	190
Lee Univ, Cleveland, TN 37320-3450	1918	$11,164	$5,470	2-M	4,147	327
Lehigh Univ, Bethlehem, PA 18015-3094	1865	$37,550	$9,770	1-D	6,994	648
Lehman Coll of the City Univ of New York, Bronx, NY 10468-1589	1931	$4,340(S)	NA	11-M	11,860	772
Le Moyne Coll, Syracuse, NY 13214	1946	$25,830	$9,990	2-M	3,479	325
Lenoir-Rhyne Univ, Hickory, NC 28601	1891	$23,070	$8,150	2-M	1,562	175
Lesley Univ, Cambridge, MA 02138-2790	1909	$28,460	$12,400	1-D	6,686	225
LeTourneau Univ, Longview, TX 75607-7001	1946	$19,140	$7,500	2-M	3,662	351
Lewis & Clark Coll, Portland, OR 97219-7899	1867	$33,726	$8,820	1-D	3,565	376
Lewis-Clark State Coll, Lewiston, ID 83501-2698	1893	$4,296(S)	$5,400	5-B	3,940	162
Lewis Univ, Romeoville, IL 60446	1932	$21,990	$8,750	2-D	5,536	563
Liberty Univ, Lynchburg, VA 24502	1971	$17,742	$5,996	2-D	33,604	582
Life Univ, Marietta, GA 30060-2903	1974	$7,830	$12,000	1-F	2,171	133
Lincoln Coll–Normal, Normal, IL 61761	1865	$20,000	$3,200	1-B	1,266	43
Lincoln Memorial Univ, Harrogate, TN 37752-1901	1897	$15,700	$5,680	1-F	3,365	247
Lincoln Univ, Jefferson City, MO 65102	1866	$5,995(S)	$4,590	5-M	3,109	242
Lincoln Univ, Lincoln University, PA 19352	1854	$7,980(S)	$7,532	12-M	2,524	194
Lindenwood Univ, St. Charles, MO 63301-1695	1827	$13,000	$6,500	2-D	10,085	617
Lindsey Wilson Coll, Columbia, KY 42728-1298	1903	$16,670	$6,925	2-M	2,003	158
Linfield Coll, McMinnville, OR 97128-6894	1849	$27,414	$7,860	2-B	1,720	191
Lipscomb Univ, Nashville, TN 37204-3951	1891	$18,580	$7,400	2-F	3,054	314
Lock Haven Univ of Pennsylvania, Lock Haven, PA 17745-2390	1870	$6,917(S)	$6,448	5-M	5,266	257
Logan Univ–Coll of Chiropractic, Chesterfield, MO 63006-1065	1935	$5,190	NA	1-F	1,143	100
Loma Linda Univ, Loma Linda, CA 92350	1905	$24,879	$2,490	2-D	4,270	840
Long Island Univ, Brentwood Cmps, Brentwood, NY 11717	1959	$27,230	NA	1-M	1,115	110
Long Island Univ, Brooklyn Cmps, Brooklyn, NY 11201-8423	1926	$27,358	$10,140	1-D	8,051	718
Long Island Univ, C.W. Post Cmps, Brookville, NY 11548-1300	1954	$27,400	$10,140	1-D	8,773	889
Longwood Univ, Farmville, VA 23909	1839	$8,499(S)	$6,856	5-M	4,024	287
Loras Coll, Dubuque, IA 52004-0178	1839	$25,348	$7,026	2-M	1,588	161
Louisiana Coll, Pineville, LA 71359-0001	1906	$12,030	$4,316	2-M	1,096	98
Louisiana State Univ & Agr & Mech Coll, Baton Rouge, LA 70803	1860	$5,086(S)	$7,238	5-D	28,628	1,503
Louisiana State Univ Health Sci Ctr, New Orleans, LA 70112-2223	1931	$4,577(S)	$4,470	5-D	2,233	1,044
Louisiana State Univ in Shreveport, Shreveport, LA 71115-2399	1965	$3,688(S)	NA	5-M	3,960	227
Louisiana Tech Univ, Ruston, LA 71272	1894	$4,911(S)	$4,740	5-D	10,917	504
Lourdes Coll, Sylvania, OH 43560-2898	1958	$14,730	NA	2-M	2,087	224
Loyola Marymount Univ, Los Angeles, CA 90045-2659	1911	$34,462	$11,810	2-D	9,011	942
Loyola Univ Chicago, Chicago, IL 60611-2196	1870	$30,656	$10,885	2-D	15,670	1,365
Loyola Univ Maryland, Baltimore, MD 21210-2699	1852	$36,240	$7,790	2-D	6,080	561
Loyola Univ New Orleans, New Orleans, LA 70118-6195	1912	$29,706	$9,826	2-F	4,474	399
Lubbock Christian Univ, Lubbock, TX 79407-2099	1957	$14,700	$5,884	2-M	1,868	167
Luther Coll, Decorah, IA 52101	1861	$32,290	$5,380	2-B	2,423	248
Luther Rice Univ, Lithonia, GA 30038-2454	1962	$199/sem. hr.	NA	2-D	1,047	NA
Lycoming Coll, Williamsport, PA 17701-5192	1812	$28,784	$7,672	2-B	1,431	126
Lynchburg Coll, Lynchburg, VA 24501-3199	1903	$28,105	$7,570	2-M	2,572	237
Lyndon State Coll, Lyndonville, VT 05851-0919	1911	$7,684(S)	$7,509	5-M	1,385	167
Lynn Univ, Boca Raton, FL 33431-5598	1962	$29,300	$10,900	1-D	2,410	157
Macalester Coll, St. Paul, MN 55105-1899	1874	$38,174	$8,768	2-B	1,900	225
Macon State Coll, Macon, GA 31206	1968	$2,044(S)	NA	5-B	6,244	293
Madonna Univ, Livonia, MI 48150-1173	1947	$12,430	$6,440	2-M	4,035	307
Malone Univ, Canton, OH 44709-3897	1892	$21,080	$7,100	2-M	2,442	208

Name, Address	Year Founded	Tuition & Fees	Room & Board	Control, Degree	Enrollment	Faculty
Manchester Coll, North Manchester, IN 46962-1225	1889	$22,720	$8,100	2-B	1,145	89
Manhattan Coll, Riverdale, NY 10471	1853	$23,385	$9,770	2-M	3,357	331
Manhattanville Coll, Purchase, NY 10577-2132	1841	$32,760	$13,580	1-M	1,802	268
Mansfield Univ of Pennsylvania, Mansfield, PA 16933	1857	$7,358(S)	$6,672	5-M	3,338	210
Marian Univ, Indianapolis, IN 46222-1997	1851	$22,400	$7,228	2-M	2,143	185
Marian Univ, Fond du Lac, WI 54935-4699	1936	$19,940	$5,380	2-D	2,891	304
Marietta Coll, Marietta, OH 45750-4000	1835	$26,080	$7,764	1-M	1,602	145
Marist Coll, Poughkeepsie, NY 12601-1387	1929	$25,596	$10,730	1-M	5,828	550
Marquette Univ, Milwaukee, WI 53201-1881	1881	$29,096	$6,330	2-D	11,633	1,096
Marshall Univ, Huntington, WV 25755	1837	$4,020(S)	$7,210	5-D	13,573	697
Mars Hill Coll, Mars Hill, NC 28754	1856	$19,894	$7,250	2-B	1,245	121
Martin Univ, Indianapolis, IN 46218-3867	1977	$13,520	NA	1-M	1,236	43
Mary Baldwin Coll, Staunton, VA 24401-3610	1842	$23,645	$6,730	1-M	1,738	143
Marygrove Coll, Detroit, MI 48221-2599 (4)	1905	$15,520	$6,800	2-M	2,953	64
Maryland Inst Coll of Art, Baltimore, MD 21217	1826	$32,680	$9,000	1-M	1,847	304
Marylhurst Univ, Marylhurst, OR 97036-0261 (4)	1893	$16,200	NA	2-M	1,802	265
Marymount Manhattan Coll, New York, NY 10021-4597	1936	$21,792	$12,660	1-B	1,988	285
Marymount Univ, Arlington, VA 22207-4299	1950	$21,528	$9,190	2-D	3,548	323
Maryville Coll, Maryville, TN 37804-5907	1819	$26,947	$8,240	2-B	1,114	121
Maryville Univ of St Louis, St. Louis, MO 63141-7299	1872	$21,145	$8,300	1-D	3,517	359
Marywood Univ, Scranton, PA 18509-1598	1915	$26,270	$11,498	2-D	3,378	323
Massachusetts Coll of Art & Design, Boston, MA 02115-5882	1873	$7,900(S)	$12,060	5-M	2,349	259
Massachusetts Coll of Lib Arts, North Adams, MA 01247-4100	1894	$6,425(S)	$7,754	5-M	1,942	171
Massachusetts Coll of Pharm & Health Sci, Boston, MA 02115-5896	1823	$23,620	$11,600	1-D	3,909	199
Massachusetts Inst of Tech, Cambridge, MA 02139-4307	1861	$37,782	$11,360	1-D	10,299	1,835
Massachusetts Maritime Acad, Buzzards Bay, MA 02532-1803 (2)	1891	$5,915(A)	$8,607	5-M	1,291	94
The Master's Coll & Sem, Santa Clarita, CA 91321-1200	1927	$24,650	$8,000	2-D	1,439	197
McDaniel Coll, Westminster, MD 21157-4390	1867	$30,780	$6,150	1-M	3,896	379
McKendree Univ, Lebanon, IL 62254-1299	1828	$21,270	$7,850	2-M	3,327	144
McMurry Univ, Abilene, TX 79697	1923	$17,985	$6,657	2-B	1,515	124
McNeese State Univ, Lake Charles, LA 70609	1939	$3,422(S)	$4,050	5-M	8,283	434
Medaille Coll, Buffalo, NY 14214-2695	1875	$18,230	$8,845	1-M	2,917	347
Medgar Evers Coll of the City Univ of New York, Brooklyn, NY 11225-2298	1969	$4,302(S)	NA	11-B	6,037	414
Med Coll of Georgia, Augusta, GA 30912	1828	$5,568(S)	$3,250	5-D	2,443	803
Med Univ of South Carolina, Charleston, SC 29425-0002	1824	NA	NA	5-D	2,531	224
Mercer Univ, Macon, GA 31207-0003	1833	$28,700	$8,450	2-D	5,464	606
Mercy Coll, Dobbs Ferry, NY 10522-1189	1951	$15,470	$10,588	1-D	9,043	809
Mercyhurst Coll, Erie, PA 16546	1926	$23,286	$8,196	2-M	4,253	302
Meredith Coll, Raleigh, NC 27607-5298	1891	$23,550	$6,740	1-M	2,250	256
Merrimack Coll, North Andover, MA 01845-5800	1947	$29,310	$10,190	2-M	2,147	217
Mesa State Coll, Grand Junction, CO 81501-3122	1925	$4,735(S)	$7,355	5-M	6,261	402
Messiah Coll, Grantham, PA 17027	1909	$25,670	$7,610	2-B	2,802	287
Methodist Univ, Fayetteville, NC 28311-1498	1956	$22,260	$8,400	2-M	2,190	213
Metropolitan State Coll of Denver, Denver, CO 80217-3362	1963	$3,241(S)	NA	5-B	21,729	1,248
Metropolitan State Univ, St. Paul, MN 55106-5000	1971	$5,473(S)	NA	5-D	8,237	711
Miami Univ, Oxford, OH 45056	1809	$11,887(S)	$8,998	12-D	17,191	1,261
Miami Univ Hamilton, Hamilton, OH 45011-3399	1968	$4,350(S)	NA	5-M	3,645	224
Michigan State Univ, East Lansing, MI 48824	1855	$10,214(S)	$7,026	5-D	46,648	2,997
Michigan Tech Univ, Houghton, MI 49931-1295	1885	$10,761(S)	$7,738	5-D	7,018	428
MidAmerica Nazarene Univ, Olathe, KS 66062-1899	1966	$18,216	$6,180	2-M	1,743	218
Mid-Continent Univ, Mayfield, KY 42066-9007	1949	$13,100	$6,300	2-B	1,541	98
Middlebury Coll, Middlebury, VT 05753-6002	1800	$49,210(C)	NA	1-D	2,455	311
Middle Tennessee State Univ, Murfreesboro, TN 37132	1911	$5,700(S)	$6,453	5-D	23,872	1,267
Midland Coll, Midland, TX 79705-6399	1969	$1,596(A)	$4,061	11-B	5,739	269
Midway Coll, Midway, KY 40347-1120 (4)	1847	$17,100	$6,600	2-M	1,323	114
Midwestern State Univ, Wichita Falls, TX 76308	1922	$5,571(S)	$5,350	5-M	6,027	309
Midwestern Univ, Glendale Cmps, Glendale, AZ 85308	1996	NA	NA	1-D	1,117	NA
Miles Coll, Birmingham, AL 35208	1905	$7,968	$5,516	2-B	1,738	147
Millersville Univ of Pennsylvania, Millersville, PA 17551-0302	1855	$6,866(S)	$7,308	5-M	8,319	452
Milligan Coll, Milligan College, TN 37682	1866	$20,560	$5,650	2-M	1,070	113
Millikin Univ, Decatur, IL 62522-2084	1901	$26,345	$7,866	2-M	2,344	291
Millsaps Coll, Jackson, MS 39210-0001	1890	$24,754	$8,800	2-M	1,118	114
Mills Coll, Oakland, CA 94613-1000	1852	$35,190	$10,550	1-D	1,476	199
Milwaukee Sch of Engr, Milwaukee, WI 53202-3109 (2)	1903	$28,665	$7,164	1-M	2,622	259
Minnesota State Univ Mankato, Mankato, MN 56001	1868	$6,263(S)	$5,732	5-D	14,515	763
Minnesota State Univ Moorhead, Moorhead, MN 56563-0002	1885	$6,144(S)	$5,936	5-D	7,520	484
Minot State Univ, Minot, ND 58707-0002	1913	$5,044(S)	$5,234	5-M	3,432	262
Misericordia Univ, Dallas, PA 18612-1098 (4)	1924	$23,150	$9,650	2-D	2,501	268
Mississippi Coll, Clinton, MS 39058	1826	$13,290	$5,800	2-D	4,741	404
Mississippi State Univ, Mississippi State, MS 39762	1878	$5,151(S)	$7,333	5-D	17,824	1,053
Mississippi Univ for Women, Columbus, MS 39701-9998 (4)	1884	$4,423(S)	$4,981	5-M	2,365	194
Mississippi Valley State Univ, Itta Bena, MS 38941-1400	1946	$9,423(S)	$4,748	5-M	2,929	166
Missouri Baptist Univ, St. Louis, MO 63141-8660	1964	$16,872	$7,070	2-M	4,614	236
Missouri Southern State Univ, Joplin, MO 64801-1595	1937	$4,535(S)	$5,440	5-M	5,264	304
Missouri State Univ, Springfield, MO 65804-0094	1905	$6,256(S)	NA	5-D	19,348	1,047
Missouri Univ of Sci & Tech, Rolla, MO 65409 (2)	1870	$8,498(S)	$7,035	5-D	6,371	446
Missouri Valley Coll, Marshall, MO 65340-3197	1889	$15,950	$6,050	2-B	1,639	90
Missouri Western State Univ, St. Joseph, MO 64507-2294	1915	$5,560(S)	$5,868	5-B	5,276	308
Molloy Coll, Rockville Centre, NY 11571-5002	1955	$19,450	NA	1-M	3,791	493
Monmouth Coll, Monmouth, IL 61462-1998	1853	$24,950	$7,300	2-B	1,328	126
Monmouth Univ, West Long Branch, NJ 07764-1898	1933	$24,098	$9,221	1-M	6,442	560
Monroe Coll, Bronx, NY 10468-5407	1933	$11,212	$7,240	3-M	4,737	251
Monroe Coll, New Rochelle, NY 10801-6410	1983	$11,272	$7,240	3-M	2,170	93
Montana State Univ, Bozeman, MT 59717	1893	$5,798(S)	$7,070	5-D	12,369	813
Montana State Univ–Billings, Billings, MT 59101-0298	1927	$5,172(S)	$5,134	5-M	4,912	268
Montana State Univ–Northern, Havre, MT 59501-7751	1929	$5,573(S)	$5,928	5-M	1,215	NA
Montana Tech of The Univ of Montana, Butte, MT 59701-8997	1895	$5,713(S)	$6,140	5-M	2,402	182
Montclair State Univ, Montclair, NJ 07043-1624	1908	$9,428(S)	$10,050	5-D	17,475	1,397
Montreat Coll, Montreat, NC 28757-1267	1916	$19,080	$6,000	2-M	1,039	86
Moravian Coll, Bethlehem, PA 18018-6650	1742	$30,062	$8,312	2-M	1,917	201
Morehead State Univ, Morehead, KY 40351	1922	$5,670(S)	$5,852	5-M	8,981	473
Morehouse Coll, Atlanta, GA 30314 (1)	1867	$21,376	$10,946	1-B	2,796	235
Morgan State Univ, Baltimore, MD 21251	1867	$6,438(S)	$8,030	5-D	7,005	558
Morningside Coll, Sioux City, IA 51106	1894	$22,246	$6,729	2-M	1,906	177

Name, Address	Year Founded	Tuition & Fees	Room & Board	Control, Degree	Enroll-ment	Faculty
Mountain State Univ, Beckley, WV 25802-9003	1933	$8,400	$6,116	1-M	5,108	452
Mount Aloysius Coll, Cresson, PA 16630-1999	1939	$17,280	$7,300	2-M	1,644	191
Mount Holyoke Coll, South Hadley, MA 01075 (3)	1837	$37,646	$11,020	1-M	2,241	240
Mount Ida Coll, Newton, MA 02459-3310	1899	$22,500	$11,100	1-B	1,460	174
Mount Marty Coll, Yankton, SD 57078-3724	1936	$18,250	$5,210	2-M	1,180	102
Mount Mary Coll, Milwaukee, WI 53222-4597	1913	$21,166	$7,280	2-M	1,862	212
Mount Mercy Coll, Cedar Rapids, IA 52402-4797	1928	$21,125	$6,650	2-M	1,555	150
Mount Olive Coll, Mount Olive, NC 28365	1951	$13,776	$5,540	2-B	3,390	319
Mount St Mary Coll, Newburgh, NY 12550-3494	1960	$20,745	$11,030	1-M	2,629	217
Mount St Mary's Coll, Los Angeles, CA 90049-1599	1925	$28,710	$9,830	2-D	2,343	351
Mount St Mary's Univ, Emmitsburg, MD 21727-7799	1808	$29,020	$9,878	2-F	2,079	185
Mount Union Coll, Alliance, OH 44601-3993	1846	$23,120	$7,050	2-B	2,204	232
Mount Vernon Nazarene Univ, Mount Vernon, OH 43050-9500	1964	$20,580	$5,890	2-M	2,558	271
Muhlenberg Coll, Allentown, PA 18104-5586	1848	$35,375	$8,060	2-B	2,492	275
Murray State Univ, Murray, KY 42071	1922	$5,748(S)	$6,004	5-M	10,014	562
Musicians Inst, Hollywood, CA 90028	1976	NA	NA	3-B	1,252	NA
Muskingum Coll, New Concord, OH 43762	1837	$18,910	$7,350	2-M	2,099	NA
Naropa Univ, Boulder, CO 80302-6697	1974	$22,074	$8,478	1-F	1,075	210
Natl-Louis Univ, Chicago, IL 60603	1886	$18,075	NA	1-D	7,056	726
Natl Univ, La Jolla, CA 92037-1011	1971	$10,284	NA	1-M	26,417	2,828
Nazareth Coll of Rochester, Rochester, NY 14618-3790	1924	$24,076	$9,916	1-D	3,250	364
Nebraska Wesleyan Univ, Lincoln, NE 68504-2796	1887	$21,392	$5,710	2-M	2,086	159
Neumann Univ, Aston, PA 19014-1298	1965	$20,402	$9,258	2-D	3,037	295
Nevada State Coll at Henderson, Henderson, NV 89015	2002	$2,340(S)	NA	5-B	1,959	141
Newbury Coll, Brookline, MA 02445	1962	$22,000	$10,700	1-B	1,202	107
New England Coll, Henniker, NH 03242-3293	1946	$27,450	$9,626	1-M	1,752	109
New Jersey City Univ, Jersey City, NJ 07305-1597	1927	$8,727(S)	$8,613	5-M	8,151	671
New Jersey Inst of Tech, Newark, NJ 07102	1881	$12,482(S)	$9,596	5-D	8,398	659
Newman Univ, Wichita, KS 67213-2097	1933	$19,650	$6,656	2-M	2,435	190
New Mexico Highlands Univ, Las Vegas, NM 87701	1893	$2,688(S)	$5,843	5-M	3,524	145
New Mexico Inst of Mining & Tech, Socorro, NM 87801	1889	$4,352(S)	$5,320	5-D	1,882	145
New Mexico State Univ, Las Cruces, NM 88003-8001	1888	$4,758(S)	$5,976	5-D	17,200	1,015
New Orleans Baptist Theol Sem, New Orleans, LA 70126-4858 (2)	1917	$2,100	$1,850	2-D	2,036	NA
The New Sch for Genl Stds, New York, NY 10011-8603	1919	$23,692	$15,260	1-M	1,820	421
New York City Coll of Tech of the City Univ of New York, Brooklyn, NY 11201-2983	1946	$4,339(S)	NA	11-B	14,268	1,010
New York Inst of Tech, Old Westbury, NY 11568-8000	1955	$22,780	$10,520	1-D	11,505	1,045
New York Univ, New York, NY 10012-1019	1831	$37,372	$12,910	1-D	42,189	4,662
Niagara Univ, Niagara University, NY 14109	1856	$24,700	$10,250	2-M	4,255	375
Nicholls State Univ, Thibodaux, LA 70310	1948	$3,710(S)	$5,098	5-M	6,920	301
Nichols Coll, Dudley, MA 01571-5000	1815	$26,970	$9,100	1-M	1,532	69
Norfolk State Univ, Norfolk, VA 23504	1935	$5,972(S)	$7,328	5-D	6,325	273
North Carolina Agr & Tech State Univ, Greensboro, NC 27411	1891	$3,583(S)	$5,459	5-D	11,098	NA
North Carolina Central Univ, Durham, NC 27707-3129	1910	$3,670(S)	$6,015	5-F	8,383	649
North Carolina State Univ, Raleigh, NC 27695	1887	$5,274(S)	$7,982	5-D	32,872	1,955
North Carolina Wesleyan Coll, Rocky Mount, NC 27804-8677	1956	$20,790	$7,380	2-B	1,510	169
North Central Coll, Naperville, IL 60566-7063	1861	$25,938	$8,217	2-M	2,726	228
Northcentral Univ, Prescott Valley, AZ 86314	NA	$8,340	NA	3-D	6,578	416
North Central Univ, Minneapolis, MN 55404-1322	1930	$15,701	$5,500	2-B	1,125	102
North Dakota State Univ, Fargo, ND 58105	1890	$5,264(S)	$6,220	5-D	13,229	740
Northeastern Illinois Univ, Chicago, IL 60625-4699	1961	$8,016(S)	NA	5-M	11,193	697
Northeastern State Univ, Tahlequah, OK 74464-2399	1846	$4,155(S)	$4,544	5-F	8,833	453
Northeastern Univ, Boston, MA 02115-5096	1898	$33,721	$11,940	1-D	21,324	1,378
Northern Arizona Univ, Flagstaff, AZ 86011	1899	$5,449(S)	$7,086	5-D	22,507	1,515
Northern Illinois Univ, De Kalb, IL 60115-2854	1895	$8,312(S)	$8,230	5-D	25,254	1,180
Northern Kentucky Univ, Highland Heights, KY 41099	1968	$6,528(S)	NA	5-D	15,082	1,072
Northern Michigan Univ, Marquette, MI 49855-5301	1899	$7,076(S)	$7,636	5-M	9,111	443
Northern State Univ, Aberdeen, SD 57401-7198	1901	$5,712(S)	$4,664	5-M	2,927	115
North Georgia Coll & State Univ, Dahlonega, GA 30597	1873	$4,070(S)	$5,244	5-M	5,500	350
North Greenville Univ, Tigerville, SC 29688-1892	1892	$11,680	$6,720	2-M	2,160	161
North Park Univ, Chicago, IL 60625-4895	1891	$17,600	$7,580	2-D	2,181	NA
Northwestern Coll, Orange City, IA 51041-1996	1882	$22,950	$6,580	2-B	1,315	135
Northwestern Coll, St. Paul, MN 55113-1598	1902	$23,180	$7,426	2-M	1,939	181
Northwestern Oklahoma State Univ, Alva, OK 73717-2799	1897	$4,111(S)	$3,430	5-M	2,030	133
Northwestern State Univ of Louisiana, Natchitoches, LA 71497	1884	$3,598(S)	$6,272	5-M	9,111	623
Northwestern Univ, Evanston, IL 60208	1851	$38,461	$11,703	1-D	18,431	1,153
Northwest Missouri State Univ, Maryville, MO 64468-6001	1905	$5,529(S)	$6,876	5-M	6,903	309
Northwest Nazarene Univ, Nampa, ID 83686-5897	1913	$22,250	$5,830	2-M	1,939	101
Northwest Univ, Kirkland, WA 98033	1934	$20,790	$6,578	2-M	1,290	110
Northwood Univ, Midland, MI 48640-2398	1959	$17,544	$7,548	1-M	2,269	129
Norwich Univ, Northfield, VT 05663 (2)	1819	$26,064	$9,032	1-M	3,104	311
Notre Dame Coll, South Euclid, OH 44121-4293	1922	$22,096	$7,372	2-M	1,393	118
Notre Dame de Namur Univ, Belmont, CA 94002-1908	1851	$27,200	$11,210	2-M	1,478	173
Nova Southeastern Univ, Fort Lauderdale, FL 33314-7796	1964	$20,350	$8,360	1-D	28,378	1,701
Nyack Coll, Nyack, NY 10960-3698	1882	$18,200	$3,900	2-F	3,250	290
Oakland City Univ, Oakland City, IN 47660-1099	1885	$15,360	$6,228	2-D	2,007	178
Oakland Univ, Rochester, MI 48309-4401	1957	$8,055(S)	$7,105	5-D	18,169	976
Oakwood Univ, Huntsville, AL 35896	1896	$13,174	$7,458	2-M	1,824	171
Oberlin Coll, Oberlin, OH 44074	1833	$38,280	$9,870	1-M	2,865	285
Occidental Coll, Los Angeles, CA 90041-3314	1887	$38,922	$10,780	1-M	1,868	251
Oglala Lakota Coll, Kyle, SD 57752-0490	1970	NA	NA	11-M	1,000	NA
Oglethorpe Univ, Atlanta, GA 30319-2797	1835	$25,580	$9,500	1-M	1,053	95
Ohio Dominican Univ, Columbus, OH 43219-2099	1911	$24,616	$8,100	2-M	3,117	205
Ohio Northern Univ, Ada, OH 45810-1599	1871	$31,866	$8,280	2-D	3,721	322
The Ohio State Univ, Columbus, OH 43210	1870	$8,676(S)	$7,755	5-D	53,715	4,402
The Ohio State Univ at Lima, Lima, OH 45804	1960	$5,664(S)	NA	5-M	1,409	82
The Ohio State Univ at Marion, Marion, OH 43302-5695	1958	$5,664(S)	NA	5-M	1,673	109
The Ohio State Univ–Mansfield Cmps, Mansfield, OH 44906-1599	1958	$5,664(S)	NA	5-M	1,545	103
The Ohio State Univ–Newark Cmps, Newark, OH 43055-1797	1957	$5,664(S)	NA	5-M	2,462	131
Ohio Univ, Athens, OH 45701-2979	1804	$8,907(S)	$8,946	5-D	20,960	1,178
Ohio Univ–Chillicothe, Chillicothe, OH 45601	1946	$4,581(S)	NA	5-M	1,836	NA
Ohio Univ–Lancaster, Lancaster, OH 43130-1097	1968	$4,581(S)	NA	5-M	1,728	NA
Ohio Univ–Southern Cmps, Ironton, OH 45638-2214	1956	$4,395(S)	NA	5-M	1,836	NA
Ohio Univ–Zanesville, Zanesville, OH 43701-2695	1946	$4,596(S)	NA	5-M	1,873	130
Ohio Wesleyan Univ, Delaware, OH 43015	1842	$33,700	$8,270	2-B	1,960	204

Name, Address	Year Founded	Tuition & Fees	Room & Board	Control, Degree	Enrollment	Faculty
Oklahoma Baptist Univ, Shawnee, OK 74804	1910	$16,790	$5,200	2-M	1,618	NA
Oklahoma Christian Univ, Oklahoma City, OK 73136-1100	1950	$16,266	$5,940	2-M	2,161	197
Oklahoma City Univ, Oklahoma City, OK 73106-1402	1904	$23,400	$9,200	2-F	3,897	329
Oklahoma Panhandle State Univ, Goodwell, OK 73939-0430	1909	$4,242(S)	$3,320	5-B	1,223	93
Oklahoma State Univ, Stillwater, OK 74078	1890	$6,202(S)	$7,402	5-D	22,768	1,263
Oklahoma Wesleyan Univ, Bartlesville, OK 74006-6299	1909	$16,585	$6,050	2-M	1,159	34
Old Dominion Univ, Norfolk, VA 23529	1930	$6,918(S)	$7,092	5-D	23,086	1,146
Olivet Coll, Olivet, MI 49076-9701	1844	$19,244	$6,772	2-M	1,049	NA
Olivet Nazarene Univ, Bourbonnais, IL 60914-2271	1907	$21,590	$6,400	2-D	4,636	NA
Oral Roberts Univ, Tulsa, OK 74171-0001	1963	$18,196	$7,610	2-D	3,067	291
Oregon Health & Sci Univ, Portland, OR 97239-3098	1974	$14,552(S)	NA	12-D	2,424	NA
Oregon Inst of Tech, Klamath Falls, OR 97601-8801	1947	$6,297(S)	$7,132	5-M	3,303	214
Oregon State Univ, Corvallis, OR 97331	1868	$6,187(S)	$8,208	5-D	20,320	1,112
Otis Coll of Art & Design, Los Angeles, CA 90045-9785	1918	$30,464	NA	1-M	1,206	266
Otterbein Coll, Westerville, OH 43081	1847	$26,319	$7,461	2-M	3,131	280
Ouachita Baptist Univ, Arkadelphia, AR 71998-0001	1886	$18,940	$5,660	2-B	1,493	146
Our Lady of Holy Cross Coll, New Orleans, LA 70131-7399	1916	$295/sem. hr.	NA	2-M	1,298	NA
Our Lady of the Lake Coll, Baton Rouge, LA 70808 (4)	1990	$6,920	NA	2-M	1,811	138
Our Lady of the Lake Univ of San Antonio, San Antonio, TX 78207-4689	1895	$20,232	$6,238	2-D	2,642	246
Pace Univ, New York, NY 10038	1906	$31,357	$11,180	1-D	12,704	1,064
Pacific Lutheran Univ, Tacoma, WA 98447	1890	$28,100	$8,600	2-M	3,672	268
Pacific Oaks Coll, Pasadena, CA 91103 (4)	1945	$21,540	NA	1-M	1,028	125
Pacific Union Coll, Angwin, CA 94508-9707	1882	$23,979	$6,750	2-M	1,278	107
Pacific Univ, Forest Grove, OR 97116-1797	1849	$28,137	$7,516	1-D	3,167	353
Palm Beach Atlantic Univ, West Palm Beach, FL 33416-4708	1968	$21,550	$8,220	2-F	3,211	301
Palmer Coll of Chiropractic, Davenport, IA 52803-5287	1897	$6,975	NA	1-F	1,284	NA
Park Univ, Parkville, MO 64152-3795	1875	$7,644	$5,805	1-M	12,457	1,019
Parsons The New Sch for Design, New York, NY 10011-8878	1896	$34,460	$15,260	1-M	4,241	1,066
Patten Univ, Oakland, CA 94601-2699	1944	$13,440	$7,090	2-M	1,056	125
Peirce Coll, Philadelphia, PA 19102-4699	1865	$14,350	NA	1-B	2,051	149
Penn State Abington, Abington, PA 19001	1950	$11,800(S)	NA	12-B	3,394	225
Penn State Altoona, Altoona, PA 16601-3760	1939	$12,182(S)	$7,670	12-B	4,013	315
Penn State Berks, Reading, PA 19610-6009	1924	$12,282(S)	$8,390	12-B	2,800	200
Penn State Erie, The Behrend Coll, Erie, PA 16563-0001	1948	$12,282(S)	$7,670	12-M	4,334	283
Penn State Harrisburg, Middletown, PA 17057-4898	1966	$12,282(S)	$8,780	12-D	3,936	292
Penn State Univ Park, University Park, PA 16802-1503	1855	$13,706(S)	$7,670	12-D	44,406	2,745
Pennsylvania Coll of Tech, Williamsport, PA 17701-5778	1965	$11,790(S)	$7,200	12-B	6,510	495
Pepperdine Univ, Malibu, CA 90263	1937	$36,770	$10,480	2-D	7,614	679
Peru State Coll, Peru, NE 68421	1867	$4,343(S)	$4,816	5-M	2,307	139
Pfeiffer Univ, Misenheimer, NC 28109-0960	1885	$18,570	$7,360	2-M	2,019	150
Philadelphia Biblical Univ, Langhorne, PA 19047-2990	1913	$18,872	$7,650	2-F	1,373	129
Philadelphia Univ, Philadelphia, PA 19144-5497	1884	$26,700	$8,692	1-D	3,360	433
Piedmont Coll, Demorest, GA 30535-0010	1897	$18,000	$6,000	2-M	2,640	222
Pikeville Coll, Pikeville, KY 41501	1889	$14,535	$6,000	2-F	1,077	72
Pittsburg State Univ, Pittsburg, KS 66762	1903	$4,322(S)	$5,394	5-M	7,127	312
Pitzer Coll, Claremont, CA 91711-6101	1963	$37,870	$10,930	1-B	1,025	104
Plymouth State Univ, Plymouth, NH 03264-1595	1871	$8,424(S)	$8,350	5-M	6,562	426
Point Loma Nazarene Univ, San Diego, CA 92106-2899	1902	$25,840	$8,170	2-M	3,490	345
Point Park Univ, Pittsburgh, PA 15222-1984	1960	$20,570	$8,940	1-M	3,846	436
Polytechnic Inst of NYU, Brooklyn, NY 11201-2990	1854	$32,644	$8,721	1-D	3,983	295
Polytechnic Univ of Puerto Rico, Hato Rey, PR 00919 (2)	1966	$6,330	NA	1-M	5,790	293
Pomona Coll, Claremont, CA 91711	1887	$35,625	$12,220	1-B	1,532	217
Pontifical Catholic Univ of Puerto Rico, Ponce, PR 00717-0777	1948	$5,018	$2,990	2-D	7,412	366
Portland State Univ, Portland, OR 97207-0751	1946	$6,147(S)	$9,486	5-D	26,382	1,465
Post Univ, Waterbury, CT 06723-2540	1890	$23,325	$9,000	1-B	1,101	122
Prairie View A&M Univ, Prairie View, TX 77446-0519	1878	$5,492(S)	$8,500	5-D	8,203	500
Pratt Inst, Brooklyn, NY 11205-3899	1887	$34,880	$9,756	1-M	4,763	1,000
Presbyterian Coll, Clinton, SC 29325	1880	$28,880	$8,345	2-B	1,174	115
Prescott Coll, Prescott, AZ 86301	1966	$21,792	$3,400	1-M	1,065	81
Princeton Univ, Princeton, NJ 08544-1019	1746	$34,290	$11,405	1-D	7,497	1,044
Providence Coll, Providence, RI 02918	1917	$31,394	$10,810	2-M	4,673	387
Purchase Coll, State Univ of New York, Purchase, NY 10577-1400	1967	$6,421(S)	$9,908	5-M	4,251	378
Purdue Univ, West Lafayette, IN 47907	1869	$7,750(S)	$7,930	5-D	40,090	2,427
Purdue Univ Calumet, Hammond, IN 46323-2094	1951	$5,757(S)	$6,155	5-M	9,325	399
Purdue Univ North Central, Westville, IN 46391-9542	1967	$6,080(S)	NA	5-M	4,245	289
Queens Coll of the City Univ of New York, Flushing, NY 11367-1597	1937	$4,447(S)	NA	11-M	19,572	1,425
Queens Univ of Charlotte, Charlotte, NC 28274-0002	1857	$22,068	$7,882	2-M	2,302	199
Quincy Univ, Quincy, IL 62301-2699	1860	$20,790	$7,900	2-M	1,424	137
Quinnipiac Univ, Hamden, CT 06518-1940	1929	$32,400	$12,380	1-D	7,434	845
Radford Univ, Radford, VA 24142	1910	$6,536(S)	$6,716	5-D	9,157	631
Ramapo Coll of New Jersey, Mahwah, NJ 07430-1680	1969	$10,765(S)	$10,830	5-M	5,847	394
Randolph-Macon Coll, Ashland, VA 23005-5505	1830	$28,355	$8,610	2-B	1,201	145
Reed Coll, Portland, OR 97202-8199	1908	$38,190	$9,920	1-M	1,471	137
Regent Univ, Virginia Beach, VA 23464-9800	1977	$14,000	$6,720	1-D	4,560	576
Regis Coll, Weston, MA 02493	1927	$27,800	$11,950	2-D	1,590	129
Regis Univ, Denver, CO 80221-1099	1877	$28,700	$8,982	2-D	11,038	967
Reinhardt Coll, Waleska, GA 30183-2981	1883	$16,070	$7,950	2-M	1,051	134
Rensselaer Polytechnic Inst, Troy, NY 12180-3590	1824	$37,990	$10,730	1-D	7,521	496
Rhode Island Coll, Providence, RI 02908-1991	1854	$5,771(S)	$8,250	5-D	9,085	705
Rhode Island Sch of Design, Providence, RI 02903-2784	1877	$34,925	$10,260	1-F	2,259	503
Rhodes Coll, Memphis, TN 38112-1690	1848	$32,446	$7,842	2-M	1,673	192
Rice Univ, Houston, TX 77251-1892	1912	$30,479	$10,750	1-D	5,243	NA
The Richard Stockton Coll of New Jersey, Pomona, NJ 08240-0195	1969	$10,469(S)	$10,204	5-D	7,307	499
Rider Univ, Lawrenceville, NJ 08648-3001	1865	$27,730	$10,280	1-M	6,011	591
Ringling Coll of Art & Design, Sarasota, FL 34234-5895	1931	$26,725	$10,350	1-B	1,229	144
Ripon Coll, Ripon, WI 54971	1851	$24,245	$6,770	1-B	1,057	92
Rivier Coll, Nashua, NH 03060	1933	$24,290	$9,154	2-M	2,231	178
Roanoke Coll, Salem, VA 24153-3794	1842	$27,935	$9,285	2-B	2,021	190
Robert Morris Coll, Chicago, IL 60605	1913	$19,200	NA	1-M	4,590	317
Robert Morris Univ, Moon Township, PA 15108-1189	1921	$19,740	$9,880	1-D	4,815	374
Roberts Wesleyan Coll, Rochester, NY 14624-1997	1866	$23,780	$8,520	2-M	1,902	235
Rochester Inst of Tech, Rochester, NY 14623-5603	1829	$28,035	$9,381	1-M	16,494	1,294
Rockford Coll, Rockford, IL 61108-2393	1847	$24,250	$6,750	1-M	1,391	144
Rockhurst Univ, Kansas City, MO 64110-2561	1910	$25,890	$7,080	2-D	3,086	223

Name, Address	Year Founded	Tuition & Fees	Room & Board	Control, Degree	Enrollment	Faculty
Rogers State Univ, Claremore, OK 74017-3252	1909	$4,277(S)	$6,615	5-B	3,858	222
Roger Williams Univ, Bristol, RI 02809	1956	$27,718	$11,880	1-F	5,159	584
Rollins Coll, Winter Park, FL 32789-4499	1885	$34,520	$10,780	1-M	2,511	230
Roosevelt Univ, Chicago, IL 60605-1394	1945	$21,300	$11,094	1-D	7,692	631
Rose-Hulman Inst of Tech, Terre Haute, IN 47803-3999 (2)	1874	$32,826	$8,868	1-M	1,923	172
Rowan Univ, Glassboro, NJ 08028-1701	1923	$10,908(S)	$9,616	5-D	10,271	937
Rush Univ, Chicago, IL 60612-3832	1969	$20,352	$9,960	1-D	1,566	796
Rutgers, The State Univ of New Jersey, Camden, Camden, NJ 08102-1401	1927	$11,358(S)	$9,378	5-D	5,398	421
Rutgers, The State Univ of New Jersey, Newark, Newark, NJ 07102	1892	$11,083(S)	$10,639	5-D	11,032	677
Rutgers, The State Univ of New Jersey, New Brunswick, Piscataway, NJ 08854-8097	1766	$11,540(S)	$10,232	5-D	36,041	2,395
Sacred Heart Univ, Fairfield, CT 06825-1000	1963	$28,990	$11,330	2-D	5,958	565
Saginaw Valley State Univ, University Center, MI 48710	1963	$6,492(S)	$6,830	5-M	9,837	594
St Ambrose Univ, Davenport, IA 52803-2898	1882	$22,590	$8,255	2-D	3,794	383
St Anselm Coll, Manchester, NH 03102-1310	1889	$29,205	$11,050	2-B	1,986	177
St Augustine Coll, Chicago, IL 60640-3501	1980	$7,680	NA	1-B	1,248	134
St Augustine's Coll, Raleigh, NC 27604-2298	1867	$14,124	$6,652	2-B	1,284	NA
St Bonaventure Univ, St. Bonaventure, NY 14778-2284	1858	$24,785	$8,980	2-M	2,614	207
St Catherine Univ, St. Paul, MN 55105-1789	1905	$27,414	$7,090	2-D	5,201	480
St Cloud State Univ, St. Cloud, MN 56301-4498	1869	$6,147(S)	$5,770	5-D	16,921	945
St Edward's Univ, Austin, TX 78704	1885	$24,440	$8,496	2-M	5,348	494
St Francis Coll, Brooklyn Heights, NY 11201-4398	1884	$15,720	NA	2-M	2,344	234
St Francis Univ, Loretto, PA 15940-0600	1847	$24,840	$8,422	2-D	2,210	200
St John Fisher Coll, Rochester, NY 14618-3597	1948	$23,390	$10,040	2-D	3,832	368
St John's Univ, Collegeville, MN 56321 (2)	1857	$28,628	$7,248	2-F	2,063	176
St John's Univ, Queens, NY 11439	1870	$28,790	$12,570	2-D	20,109	1,492
St Joseph Coll, West Hartford, CT 06117-2700	1932	$27,202	$12,437	2-M	1,926	246
St Joseph's Coll, Rensselaer, IN 47978	1889	$23,180	$7,170	2-M	1,076	107
St Joseph's Coll, Long Island Cmps, Patchogue, NY 11772-2399	1916	$15,963	NA	1-M	4,244	385
St Joseph's Coll, New York, Brooklyn, NY 11205-3688	1916	$15,963	NA	1-M	1,263	129
St Joseph's Coll of Maine, Standish, ME 04084-5263	1912	$25,060	$9,950	2-M	1,050	126
St Joseph's Univ, Philadelphia, PA 19131-1395	1851	$32,860	$11,180	2-D	7,900	622
St Lawrence Univ, Canton, NY 13617-1455	1856	$37,905	$9,645	1-M	2,325	194
St Leo Univ, Saint Leo, FL 33574-6665	1889	$17,150	$8,430	2-M	3,510	132
St Louis Coll of Pharm, St. Louis, MO 63110-1088	1864	$21,925	$8,154	1-F	1,191	106
St Louis Univ, St. Louis, MO 63103-2097	1818	$30,728	$8,760	2-D	12,733	1,076
St Martin's Univ, Lacey, WA 98503-1297	1895	$23,810	$8,040	2-M	1,659	198
St Mary-of-the-Woods Coll, Saint Mary-of-the-Woods, IN 47876 (4)	1840	$23,060	$8,450	2-M	1,572	133
St Mary's Coll, Notre Dame, IN 46556 (3)	1844	$28,212	$8,938	2-B	1,628	203
St Mary's Coll of California, Moraga, CA 94575	1863	$33,250	$11,680	2-D	3,840	478
St Mary's Coll of Maryland, St. Mary's City, MD 20686-3001	1840	$12,604(S)	$9,225	5-M	2,065	231
St Mary's Univ, San Antonio, TX 78228-8507	1852	$21,300	$7,188	2-D	3,889	351
St Mary's Univ of Minnesota, Winona, MN 55987-1399	1912	$25,570	$6,760	2-D	5,611	576
St Michael's Coll, Colchester, VT 05439	1904	$33,215	$8,280	2-M	2,460	209
St Norbert Coll, De Pere, WI 54115-2099	1898	$25,926	$6,781	2-M	2,137	180
St Olaf Coll, Northfield, MN 55057-1098	1874	$35,500	$8,200	2-B	3,073	323
St Peter's Coll, Jersey City, NJ 07306-5997	1872	$25,666	$10,336	2-M	3,081	NA
St Thomas Aquinas Coll, Sparkill, NY 10976	1952	$21,170	$9,980	1-M	2,100	157
St Thomas Univ, Miami Gardens, FL 33054-6459	1961	$20,664	$6,206	2-D	2,454	244
St Vincent Coll, Latrobe, PA 15650-2690	1846	$26,146	$8,184	2-M	2,021	196
St Xavier Univ, Chicago, IL 60655-3105	1847	$23,006	$8,007	2-M	5,337	419
Salem Intl Univ, Salem, WV 26426-0500	1888	$12,750	NA	1-M	NA	16
Salem State Coll, Salem, MA 01970-5353	1854	$6,460(S)	$6,038	5-M	10,157	771
Salisbury Univ, Salisbury, MD 21801-6837	1925	$6,492(S)	$7,798	5-M	7,868	655
Salve Regina Univ, Newport, RI 02840-4192	1934	$29,150	$10,700	2-D	2,691	255
Samford Univ, Birmingham, AL 35229	1841	$20,420	$6,624	2-D	4,469	437
Sam Houston State Univ, Huntsville, TX 77341	1879	$6,515(S)	$6,744	5-D	16,663	931
Samuel Merritt Univ, Oakland, CA 94609-3108 (4)	1909	$34,148	NA	1-D	1,311	227
San Diego State Univ, San Diego, CA 92182	1897	$3,754(S)	$11,266	5-D	35,832	1,792
San Francisco State Univ, San Francisco, CA 94132-1722	1899	$3,762(S)	$10,196	5-D	30,014	1,748
San Jose State Univ, San Jose, CA 95192-0001	1857	$3,992(S)	$8,663	5-M	32,746	1,888
Santa Clara Univ, Santa Clara, CA 95053	1851	$34,950	$11,070	2-D	8,758	772
Sarah Lawrence Coll, Bronxville, NY 10708-5999	1926	$40,350	$13,104	1-M	1,700	243
Savannah Coll of Art & Design, Savannah, GA 31402-3146	1978	$28,265	$11,710	1-M	9,332	568
Savannah State Univ, Savannah, GA 31404	1890	$3,726(S)	$5,644	5-M	3,188	167
Sch of the Art Inst of Chicago, Chicago, IL 60603-3103	1866	$31,020	$8,900	1-M	3,006	627
Sch of Visual Arts, New York, NY 10010-3994	1947	$23,520	$11,350	3-M	3,946	830
Seattle Pacific Univ, Seattle, WA 98119-1997	1891	$26,817	$8,454	2-D	3,891	347
Seattle Univ, Seattle, WA 98122-1090	1891	$28,260	$8,340	2-D	7,529	645
Seton Hall Univ, South Orange, NJ 07079-2697	1856	$29,630	$11,360	2-D	9,637	926
Seton Hill Univ, Greensburg, PA 15601	1883	$26,002	$8,170	2-M	2,093	197
Sewanee: The Univ of the South, Sewanee, TN 37383-1000	1857	$34,172	$9,760	2-D	1,562	169
Shawnee State Univ, Portsmouth, OH 45662-4344	1986	$5,832(S)	$7,670	5-M	3,976	304
Shaw Univ, Raleigh, NC 27601-2399	1865	$11,696	$7,200	2-F	2,866	272
Shenandoah Univ, Winchester, VA 22601-5195	1875	$23,340	$8,350	2-D	3,393	285
Shepherd Univ, Shepherdstown, WV 25443-3210	1871	$4,898(S)	$6,938	5-M	4,185	327
Shippensburg Univ of Pennsylvania, Shippensburg, PA 17257-2299	1871	$7,099(S)	$6,604	5-M	7,942	397
Shorter Coll, Rome, GA 30165	1873	$15,770	$7,400	2-M	1,136	126
Siena Coll, Loudonville, NY 12211-1462	1937	$23,950	$9,410	2-B	3,217	317
Siena Heights Univ, Adrian, MI 49221-1796	1919	$19,210	$7,070	2-M	2,307	216
Simmons Coll, Boston, MA 02115	1899	$30,000	$11,500	1-D	4,933	477
Simpson Coll, Indianola, IA 50125-1297	1860	$24,771	$6,988	2-M	2,054	203
Simpson Univ, Redding, CA 96003-8606	1921	$20,400	$6,900	2-M	1,147	108
Skidmore Coll, Saratoga Springs, NY 12866-1632	1903	$38,888	$10,378	1-M	2,777	366
Slippery Rock Univ of Pennsylvania, Slippery Rock, PA 16057-1383	1889	$6,934(S)	$8,066	5-D	8,458	387
Smith Coll, Northampton, MA 01063 (3)	1871	$36,058	$12,050	1-D	3,065	309
Sojourner-Douglass Coll, Baltimore, MD 21205-1814 (4)	1980	$7,478	NA	1-M	1,151	NA
Sonoma State Univ, Rohnert Park, CA 94928-3609	1960	$4,272(S)	$10,115	5-M	8,921	627
South Carolina State Univ, Orangeburg, SC 29117-0001	1896	$7,806(S)	$8,040	5-D	4,888	302
South Dakota Sch of Mines & Tech, Rapid City, SD 57701-3995	1885	$6,480(S)	$4,740	5-D	2,060	145
South Dakota State Univ, Brookings, SD 57007	1881	$5,808(S)	$5,423	5-D	11,995	674
Southeastern Louisiana Univ, Hammond, LA 70402	1925	$3,721(S)	$6,220	5-M	15,224	692
Southeastern Oklahoma State Univ, Durant, OK 74701-0609	1909	$4,316(S)	$4,290	5-M	3,889	252
Southeastern Univ, Lakeland, FL 33801-6099	1935	$15,000	$7,566	2-M	3,075	164
Southeast Missouri State Univ, Cape Girardeau, MO 63701-4799	1873	$6,255(S)	$5,935	5-M	10,814	604

Name, Address	Year Founded	Tuition & Fees	Room & Board	Control, Degree	Enroll- ment	Faculty
Southern Adventist Univ, Collegedale, TN 37315-0370	1892	$17,112	$5,080	2-M	2,640	263
Southern Arkansas Univ–Magnolia, Magnolia, AR 71753	1909	$5,646(S)	$4,250	5-M	3,117	245
Southern Baptist Theol Sem, Louisville, KY 40280-0004	1858	$5,736	$3,500	2-F	3,190	NA
Southern Connecticut State Univ, New Haven, CT 06515-1355	1893	$7,179(S)	$8,966	5-D	11,769	1,073
Southern Illinois Univ Carbondale, Carbondale, IL 62901-4701	1869	$9,813(S)	$7,137	5-D	20,673	1,073
Southern Illinois Univ Edwardsville, Edwardsville, IL 62026-0001	1957	$7,819(S)	$7,040	5-F	13,602	880
Southern Methodist Univ, Dallas, TX 75275	1911	$35,160	$12,445	2-D	10,965	1,034
Southern Nazarene Univ, Bethany, OK 73008	1899	$17,664	$6,490	2-M	2,069	198
Southern New Hampshire Univ, Manchester, NH 03106-1045	1932	$26,442	$10,176	1-D	4,211	388
Southern Oregon Univ, Ashland, OR 97520	1926	$5,718(S)	$8,250	5-M	4,437	290
Southern Polytechnic State Univ, Marietta, GA 30060-2896	1948	$4,232(S)	$5,870	5-M	4,818	265
Southern Univ & Agr & Mech Coll, Baton Rouge, LA 70813	1880	$3,906(S)	$5,558	5-D	7,699	546
Southern Univ at New Orleans, New Orleans, LA 70126-1009 (4)	1959	$2,970(S)	NA	5-M	3,104	101
Southern Utah Univ, Cedar City, UT 84720-2498	1897	$4,028(S)	$1,950	5-M	7,516	324
Southern Wesleyan Univ, Central, SC 29630-1020	1906	$18,700	$6,900	2-M	2,391	237
Southwest Baptist Univ, Bolivar, MO 65613-2597	1878	$16,530	$5,470	2-D	3,656	245
Southwestern Assemblies of God Univ, Waxahachie, TX 75165-5735	1927	$12,850	$4,994	2-M	1,834	NA
Southwestern Coll, Winfield, KS 67156-2499	1885	$19,630	$5,750	2-M	1,823	100
Southwestern Oklahoma State Univ, Weatherford, OK 73096-3098	1901	$4,110(S)	$3,900	5-F	4,869	230
Southwestern Univ, Georgetown, TX 78626	1840	$27,940	$8,870	2-B	1,270	170
Southwest Minnesota State Univ, Marshall, MN 56258	1963	$6,696(S)	$5,984	5-M	6,502	215
Spalding Univ, Louisville, KY 40203-2188	1814	$17,550	$4,560	2-D	1,712	162
Spelman Coll, Atlanta, GA 30314-4399 (3)	1881	$20,281	$9,734	1-B	2,270	249
Spring Arbor Univ, Spring Arbor, MI 49283-9799	1873	$19,240	$6,650	2-M	3,973	129
Springfield Coll, Springfield, MA 01109-3797	1885	$25,520	$9,160	1-D	3,155	342
Spring Hill Coll, Mobile, AL 36608-1791	1830	$24,240	$9,260	2-M	1,534	156
Stanford Univ, Stanford, CA 94305-9991	1891	$37,380	$11,463	1-D	17,833	1,002
State Univ of New York at Binghamton, Binghamton, NY 13902-6000	1946	$6,692(S)	$9,774	5-D	14,898	887
State Univ of New York at Fredonia, Fredonia, NY 14063-1136	1826	$6,208(S)	$9,140	5-M	5,573	437
State Univ of New York at New Paltz, New Paltz, NY 12561	1828	$6,039(S)	$8,690	5-M	8,205	722
State Univ of New York at Oswego, Oswego, NY 13126	1861	$6,651(S)	NA	5-M	8,909	516
State Univ of New York at Plattsburgh, Plattsburgh, NY 12901-2681	1889	$5,422(S)	$8,250	5-M	6,358	510
State Univ of New York Coll at Cortland, Cortland, NY 13045	1868	$6,145(S)	$9,790	5-M	7,234	575
State Univ of New York Coll at Geneseo, Geneseo, NY 14454-1401	1871	$6,278(S)	$9,070	5-M	5,585	352
State Univ of New York Coll at Old Westbury, Old Westbury, NY 11568-0210	1965	$4,350(S)	$9,032	5-M	3,505	273
State Univ of New York Coll at Oneonta, Oneonta, NY 13820-4015	1889	$6,230(S)	$8,680	5-M	5,757	489
State Univ of New York Coll at Potsdam, Potsdam, NY 13676	1816	$5,772(S)	$8,820	5-M	4,325	383
State Univ of New York Coll of Agr & Tech at Cobleskill, Cobleskill, NY 12043	1916	$6,311(S)	$9,460	5-B	2,619	175
State Univ of New York Coll of Agr & Tech at Morrisville, Morrisville, NY 13408-0901	1908	$223/credit(S)	NA	5-B	3,432	261
State Univ of New York Coll of Envir Sci & For, Syracuse, NY 13210-2779	1911	$4,970(S)	$11,920	5-D	2,201	173
State Univ of New York Coll of Tech at Canton, Canton, NY 13617	1906	$5,944(S)	$8,970	5-B	2,970	172
State Univ of New York Coll of Tech at Delhi, Delhi, NY 13753	1913	$6,225(S)	$9,024	5-B	2,971	187
State Univ of New York Downstate Med Ctr, Brooklyn, NY 11203-2098	1858	$7,453(S)	$11,898	5-D	1,608	981
State Univ of New York Empire State Coll, Saratoga Springs, NY 12866-4391	1971	$5,195(S)	NA	5-M	13,614	1,378
State Univ of New York Inst of Tech, Utica, NY 13504-3050	1966	$5,413(S)	$8,320	5-M	2,828	183
State Univ of New York Maritime Coll, Throggs Neck, NY 10465-4198 (2)	1874	$6,090(S)	$9,930	5-M	1,630	120
State Univ of New York Upstate Med Univ, Syracuse, NY 13210-2334	1950	$5,218(S)	$5,768	5-D	1,374	752
Stephen F. Austin State Univ, Nacogdoches, TX 75962	1923	$6,432(S)	$7,022	5-D	11,990	642
Stephens Coll, Columbia, MO 65215-0002	1833	$23,000	$8,730	1-M	1,147	110
Stetson Univ, DeLand, FL 32723	1883	$31,770	$8,934	1-F	3,696	361
Stevens Inst of Tech, Hoboken, NJ 07030	1870	$37,980	$12,150	1-D	5,563	438
Stevenson Univ, Stevenson, MD 21153	1952	$19,200	$9,856	1-M	3,409	352
Stillman Coll, Tuscaloosa, AL 35403-9990	1876	$12,712	$5,994	2-B	1,048	63
Stonehill Coll, Easton, MA 02357-5510	1948	$30,150	$11,830	2-B	2,426	242
Stony Brook Univ, State Univ of New York, Stony Brook, NY 11794	1957	$6,430(S)	$9,132	5-D	23,994	1,654
Suffolk Univ, Boston, MA 02108-2770	1906	$25,954	$13,970	1-D	9,435	1,037
Sullivan Univ, Louisville, KY 40205	1864	$14,940	$4,320	3-M	4,538	269
Sul Ross State Univ, Alpine, TX 79832	1920	$4,202(S)	$6,190	5-M	2,778	159
Susquehanna Univ, Selinsgrove, PA 17870	1858	$31,080	$8,400	2-B	2,137	249
Swarthmore Coll, Swarthmore, PA 19081-1397	1864	$36,490	$11,314	1-B	1,490	208
Syracuse Univ, Syracuse, NY 13244	1870	$33,440	$11,656	1-D	19,366	1,503
Tarleton State Univ, Stephenville, TX 76402	1899	$6,975(S)	$6,034	5-D	9,634	585
Taylor Univ, Upland, IN 46989-1001	1846	$24,546	$6,352	2-M	1,871	197
Temple Univ, Philadelphia, PA 19122-6096	1884	$11,448(S)	$8,884	12-D	35,489	2,890
Tennessee State Univ, Nashville, TN 37209-1561	1912	$5,132(S)	$5,462	5-D	8,254	603
Tennessee Tech Univ, Cookeville, TN 38505	1915	$5,244(S)	$7,290	5-D	10,793	648
Texas A&M Intl Univ, Laredo, TX 78041-1900	1969	$5,417(S)	$6,750	5-D	5,856	292
Texas A&M Univ, College Station, TX 77843	1876	$7,844(S)	$8,000	5-D	48,039	2,837
Texas A&M Univ at Galveston, Galveston, TX 77553-1675	1962	$6,454(S)	$5,508	5-M	1,612	170
Texas A&M Univ–Comm, Commerce, TX 75429-3011	1889	$5,130(S)	$6,650	5-D	8,882	811
Texas A&M Univ–Corpus Christi, Corpus Christi, TX 78412-5503	1947	$5,737(S)	$8,709	5-D	9,007	539
Texas A&M Univ–Kingsville, Kingsville, TX 78363	1925	$4,890(S)	$4,874	5-D	7,126	438
Texas A&M Univ–Texarkana, Texarkana, TX 75505-5518	1971	$3,392(S)	NA	5-M	1,670	108
Texas Christian Univ, Fort Worth, TX 76129-0002	1873	$28,298	$9,800	2-D	8,696	811
Texas Lutheran Univ, Seguin, TX 78155-5999	1891	$21,100	$6,140	2-B	1,432	142
Texas Southern Univ, Houston, TX 77004-4584	1947	$6,401(S)	$6,574	5-D	9,102	605
Texas State Univ–San Marcos, San Marcos, TX 78666	1899	$6,994(S)	$6,012	5-D	29,105	1,371
Texas Tech Univ, Lubbock, TX 79409	1923	$6,783(S)	$7,310	5-D	28,422	1,180
Texas Wesleyan Univ, Fort Worth, TX 76105-1536	1890	$16,730	$5,650	2-D	3,202	NA
Texas Woman's Univ, Denton, TX 76201 (4)	1901	$6,660(S)	$5,967	5-D	12,465	749
Thiel Coll, Greenville, PA 16125-2181	1866	$20,998	$8,790	2-B	1,137	119
Thomas Edison State Coll, Trenton, NJ 08608-1176	1972	$4,555(S)	NA	5-M	17,369	NA
Thomas Jefferson Univ, Philadelphia, PA 19107	1824	NA	NA	1-D	2,867	266
Thomas More Coll, Crestview Hills, KY 41017-3495	1921	$22,220	$5,870	2-M	1,894	138
Tiffin Univ, Tiffin, OH 44883-2161	1888	$17,730	$7,985	1-M	2,674	260
Touro Coll, New York, NY 10010	1971	$14,460	NA	1-F	17,129	NA
Towson Univ, Towson, MD 21252-0001	1866	$7,314(S)	$8,306	5-D	21,111	1,492
Transylvania Univ, Lexington, KY 40508-1797	1780	$23,810	$7,450	2-B	1,158	109
Trevecca Nazarene Univ, Nashville, TN 37210-2877	1901	$16,288	$7,134	2-D	2,366	201
Trine Univ, Angola, IN 46703-1764	1884	$24,200	$8,300	1-M	1,451	99
Trinity Christian Coll, Palos Heights, IL 60463-0929	1959	$20,046	$7,420	2-B	1,404	154
Trinity Coll, Hartford, CT 06106-3100	1823	$38,724	$9,900	1-M	2,566	255
Trinity Intl Univ, Deerfield, IL 60015-1284	1897	$21,980	$7,430	2-D	2,671	82
Trinity Univ, San Antonio, TX 78212-7200	1869	$27,699	$8,822	2-M	2,703	323

Name, Address	Year Founded	Tuition & Fees	Room & Board	Control, Degree	Enroll- ment	Faculty
Trinity (Washington) Univ, Washington, DC 20017-1094	1897	$19,357	$8,450	2-M	1,630	NA
Troy Univ, Troy, AL 36082	1887	$5,900(S)	$5,718	5-M	28,303	1,658
Truman State Univ, Kirksville, MO 63501-4221	1867	$6,692(S)	$6,290	5-M	5,842	384
Tufts Univ, Medford, MA 02155	1852	$38,840	$10,518	1-D	10,030	944
TUI Univ, Cypress, CA 90630	NA	$9,440	NA	1-D	8,004	213
Tulane Univ, New Orleans, LA 70118-5669	1834	$38,664	$9,296	1-D	11,157	1,557
Tusculum Coll, Greeneville, TN 37743-9997	1794	$18,870	$7,120	2-M	2,241	205
Tuskegee Univ, Tuskegee, AL 36088	1881	$16,160	$7,350	1-D	2,994	301
Union Coll, Barbourville, KY 40906-1499	1879	$17,894	$5,800	2-M	1,498	90
Union Coll, Schenectady, NY 12308-2311	1795	$48,552(C)	NA	1-B	2,240	227
Union Inst & Univ, Cincinnati, OH 45206-1925	1969	$10,528	NA	1-D	1,698	322
Union Univ, Jackson, TN 38305-3697	1823	$19,610	$6,500	2-D	3,700	185
United States Air Force Acad, USAF Academy, CO 80840-5025 (2)	1954	$0(C)	NA	4-B	4,537	530
United States Merchant Marine Acad, Kings Point, NY 11024-1699	1943	$0(C)	NA	4-M	1,003	NA
United States Military Acad, West Point, NY 10996	1802	$0(C)	NA	4-B	4,553	637
United States Naval Acad, Annapolis, MD 21402-5000 (2)	1845	$0(C)	NA	4-B	4,489	NA
United Talmudical Sem, Brooklyn, NY 11211-7900 (1)	1949	$6,000	$3,000	2-M	1,500	NA
Universidad del Este, Carolina, PR 00983	1949	$155/credit	NA	1-M	10,503	439
Universidad del Turabo, Gurabo, PR 00778-3030	1972	NA	NA	1-M	15,339	410
Universidad Metropolitana, San Juan, PR 00928-1150	1980	NA	NA	1-D	12,389	903
Univ at Albany, State Univ of New York, Albany, NY 12222-0001	1844	$6,388(S)	$9,778	5-D	18,202	1,273
Univ at Buffalo, the State Univ of New York, Buffalo, NY 14260	1846	$6,595(S)	$9,058	5-D	28,192	1,792
Univ of Advancing Tech, Tempe, AZ 85283-1042 (2)	1983	$17,800	$10,548	3-M	1,250	54
The Univ of Akron, Akron, OH 44325	1870	$8,612(S)	$8,311	5-D	24,119	1,616
The Univ of Alabama, Tuscaloosa, AL 35487	1831	$6,400(S)	$6,430	5-D	27,014	1,367
The Univ of Alabama at Birmingham, Birmingham, AL 35294	1969	$4,664(S)	$7,820	5-D	16,149	920
The Univ of Alabama in Huntsville, Huntsville, AL 35899	1950	$5,952(S)	$6,526	5-D	7,431	456
Univ of Alaska Anchorage, Anchorage, AK 99508-8060	1954	$4,580(S)	$7,962	5-M	17,361	1,258
Univ of Alaska Fairbanks, Fairbanks, AK 99775-7520	1917	$5,398(S)	$6,630	5-D	8,579	1,047
Univ of Alaska Southeast, Juneau, AK 99801	1972	$4,903(S)	$6,260	5-M	2,954	224
The Univ of Arizona, Tucson, AZ 85721	1885	$5,542(S)	$7,812	5-D	38,057	2,063
Univ of Arkansas, Fayetteville, AR 72701-1201	1871	$6,400(S)	$7,422	5-D	19,194	987
Univ of Arkansas at Fort Smith, Fort Smith, AR 72913-3649	1928	$4,410(S)	$4,282	11-B	6,784	389
Univ of Arkansas at Little Rock, Little Rock, AR 72204-1099	1927	$6,083(S)	$3,100	5-D	11,905	749
Univ of Arkansas at Monticello, Monticello, AR 71656	1909	$4,600(S)	$3,870	5-M	3,302	228
Univ of Arkansas at Pine Bluff, Pine Bluff, AR 71601-2799	1873	$4,676(S)	$6,198	5-M	3,200	240
Univ of Arkansas for Med Sci, Little Rock, AR 72205-7199	1879	$17,362(S)	NA	5-D	2,549	NA
Univ of Baltimore, Baltimore, MD 21201-5779	1925	$7,051(S)	NA	5-D	5,843	383
Univ of Bridgeport, Bridgeport, CT 06604	1927	$24,470	$10,600	1-D	5,323	552
Univ of California, Berkeley, Berkeley, CA 94720-1500	1868	$8,352(S)	$15,308	5-D	35,409	NA
Univ of California, Davis, Davis, CA 95616	1905	$9,364(S)	$12,361	5-D	30,568	1,903
Univ of California, Irvine, Irvine, CA 92697	1965	$8,775(S)	$10,527	5-D	26,984	1,969
Univ of California, Los Angeles, Los Angeles, CA 90095	1919	$8,310(S)	$12,891	5-D	39,650	2,654
Univ of California, Merced, Merced, CA 95343	NA	$4,476(S)	$10,550	5-D	2,718	202
Univ of California, Riverside, Riverside, CA 92521-0102	1954	$7,845(S)	$10,850	5-D	18,079	933
Univ of California, San Diego, La Jolla, CA 92093	1959	$8,062(S)	$10,820	5-D	27,520	1,166
Univ of California, Santa Barbara, Santa Barbara, CA 93106	1909	$8,573(S)	$12,485	5-D	21,410	1,067
Univ of California, Santa Cruz, Santa Cruz, CA 95064	1965	$10,131(S)	$13,641	5-D	16,625	803
Univ of Central Arkansas, Conway, AR 72035-0001	1907	$6,505(S)	$4,740	5-D	12,974	709
Univ of Central Florida, Orlando, FL 32816	1963	$3,947(S)	$8,492	5-D	50,254	1,659
Univ of Central Missouri, Warrensburg, MO 64093	1871	$7,311(S)	$6,320	5-M	11,063	562
Univ of Central Oklahoma, Edmond, OK 73034-5209	1890	$4,223(S)	$7,468	5-M	15,724	871
Univ of Charleston, Charleston, WV 25304-1099	1888	$23,150	$8,325	1-D	1,398	143
Univ of Chicago, Chicago, IL 60637-1513	1891	$37,632	$11,697	1-D	12,787	1,717
Univ of Cincinnati, Cincinnati, OH 45221	1819	$9,399(S)	$9,240	5-D	29,617	1,249
Univ of Colorado at Boulder, Boulder, CO 80309	1876	$7,287(S)	$9,860	5-D	32,191	1,932
Univ of Colorado at Colorado Springs, Colorado Springs, CO 80933-7150	1965	$5,878(S)	$8,750	5-D	8,912	615
Univ of Colorado Denver, Denver, CO 80217-3364	1912	$6,394(S)	$13,524	5-D	21,903	3,027
Univ of Connecticut, Storrs, CT 06269	1881	$9,338(S)	$9,300	5-D	24,273	1,360
Univ of Dallas, Irving, TX 75062-4736	1955	$26,294	$8,220	2-D	2,977	244
Univ of Dayton, Dayton, OH 45469-1300	1850	$27,330	$7,980	2-D	10,920	816
Univ of Delaware, Newark, DE 19716	1743	$8,646(S)	$8,478	12-D	19,832	1,424
Univ of Denver, Denver, CO 80208	1864	$35,481	$9,900	1-D	11,328	1,196
Univ of Detroit Mercy, Detroit, MI 48221	1877	$27,310	$8,250	2-D	5,521	708
Univ of Dubuque, Dubuque, IA 52001-5099	1852	$20,020	$6,790	2-D	1,441	158
Univ of Evansville, Evansville, IN 47722	1854	$25,845	$8,230	2-D	2,789	231
The Univ of Findlay, Findlay, OH 45840-3653	1882	$24,670	$8,306	2-F	5,761	363
Univ of Florida, Gainesville, FL 32611	1853	$3,778(S)	$7,150	5-D	51,474	1,989
Univ of Georgia, Athens, GA 30602	1785	$6,030(S)	$7,528	5-D	34,180	2,178
Univ of Guam, Mangilao, GU 96923	1952	$5,285(S)	$7,785	7-M	3,282	249
Univ of Hartford, West Hartford, CT 06117-1599	1877	$28,980	$11,328	1-D	7,366	928
Univ of Hawaii at Hilo, Hilo, HI 96720-4091	1970	$4,360(S)	$11,403	5-F	3,573	327
Univ of Hawaii at Manoa, Honolulu, HI 96822	1907	$7,168(S)	$7,564	5-D	20,169	1,306
Univ of Hawaii–West Oahu, Pearl City, HI 96782-3366	1976	$4,186(S)	NA	5-B	1,140	67
Univ of Houston, Houston, TX 77204	1927	$8,167(S)	$6,935	5-D	37,104	1,773
Univ of Houston–Clear Lake, Houston, TX 77058-1098	1971	$6,076(S)	$10,308	5-D	7,659	516
Univ of Houston–Downtown, Houston, TX 77002-1001	1974	$5,000(S)	NA	5-M	12,283	569
Univ of Houston–Victoria, Victoria, TX 77901-4450	1973	$5,220(S)	NA	5-M	3,174	176
Univ of Idaho, Moscow, ID 83844-2282	1889	$4,632(S)	$8,784	5-D	11,791	741
Univ of Illinois at Chicago, Chicago, IL 60607-7128	1946	$11,716(S)	$8,744	5-D	25,835	1,566
Univ of Illinois at Springfield, Springfield, IL 62703-5407	1969	$9,069(S)	$8,840	5-D	4,711	352
Univ of Illinois at Urbana–Champaign, Champaign, IL 61820	1867	$12,106(S)	$8,764	5-D	43,246	2,039
Univ of Indianapolis, Indianapolis, IN 46227-3697	1902	$20,510	$7,790	2-D	4,701	433
The Univ of Iowa, Iowa City, IA 52242-1316	1847	$6,824(S)	NA	5-D	29,747	1,673
The Univ of Kansas, Lawrence, KS 66045	1866	$7,725(S)	$6,474	5-D	29,365	1,301
Univ of Kentucky, Lexington, KY 40506-0032	1865	$8,123(S)	$9,125	5-D	26,054	1,661
Univ of La Verne, La Verne, CA 91750-4443	1891	$28,250	$11,110	1-D	3,923	389
Univ of Louisiana at Lafayette, Lafayette, LA 70504	1898	$3,574(S)	$4,200	5-D	16,345	743
Univ of Louisiana at Monroe, Monroe, LA 71209-0001	1931	$3,791(S)	$3,370	5-D	8,772	434
Univ of Louisville, Louisville, KY 40292-0001	1798	$7,564(S)	$6,058	5-D	20,834	1,354
Univ of Maine, Orono, ME 04469	1865	$9,100(S)	$8,008	5-D	11,818	829
The Univ of Maine at Augusta, Augusta, ME 04330-9410	1965	$6,495(S)	NA	5-B	5,202	253
Univ of Maine at Farmington, Farmington, ME 04938-1990	1863	$8,206(S)	$7,158	5-M	2,229	176
Univ of Maine at Fort Kent, Fort Kent, ME 04743-1292	1878	$6,413(S)	$6,940	5-B	1,102	72

Name, Address	Year Founded	Tuition & Fees	Room & Board	Control, Degree	Enroll- ment	Faculty
Univ of Maine at Machias, Machias, ME 04654-1321	1909	$6,871(S)	$6,574	5-B	1,023	76
Univ of Maine at Presque Isle, Presque Isle, ME 04769-2888	1903	$6,475(S)	$7,096	5-B	1,460	119
Univ of Mary, Bismarck, ND 58504-9652	1959	$12,584	$4,940	2-D	2,863	278
Univ of Mary Hardin-Baylor, Belton, TX 76513	1845	$20,650	$5,350	2-D	2,696	238
Univ of Maryland, Baltimore Cty, Baltimore, MD 21250	1963	$8,780(S)	$8,960	5-D	12,268	758
Univ of Maryland, Coll Park, College Park, MD 20742	1856	$8,005(S)	$9,109	5-D	36,956	2,273
Univ of Maryland Eastern Shore, Princess Anne, MD 21853-1299	1886	$6,042(S)	$6,880	5-D	3,762	283
Univ of Maryland Univ Coll, Adelphi, MD 20783	1947	$5,760(S)	NA	5-D	34,172	1,756
Univ of Mary Washington, Fredericksburg, VA 22401-5358	1908	$6,834(S)	$7,700	5-M	5,084	377
Univ of Massachusetts Amherst, Amherst, MA 01003	1863	$11,917(S)	$8,276	5-D	26,359	1,356
Univ of Massachusetts Boston, Boston, MA 02125-3393	1964	$9,111(S)	NA	5-D	14,117	913
Univ of Massachusetts Dartmouth, North Dartmouth, MA 02747-2300	1895	$8,858(S)	$8,716	5-D	9,155	611
Univ of Massachusetts Lowell, Lowell, MA 01854-2881	1894	$9,181(S)	$7,519	5-D	10,075	690
Univ of Memphis, Memphis, TN 38152	1912	$6,128(S)	$5,660	5-D	20,214	1,384
Univ of Miami, Coral Gables, FL 33124	1925	$34,834	$10,254	1-D	15,323	1,381
Univ of Michigan, Ann Arbor, MI 48109	1817	$11,927(S)	$8,590	5-D	41,028	3,005
Univ of Michigan–Dearborn, Dearborn, MI 48128-1491	1959	$8,529(S)	NA	5-M	8,311	487
Univ of Michigan–Flint, Flint, MI 48502-1950	1956	$7,775(S)	$6,800	5-D	7,260	469
Univ of Minnesota, Crookston, Crookston, MN 56716-5001	1966	$9,381(S)	$5,670	5-B	2,199	108
Univ of Minnesota, Duluth, Duluth, MN 55812-2496	1947	$10,260(S)	$6,078	5-D	11,365	599
Univ of Minnesota, Morris, Morris, MN 56267-2134	1959	$10,006(S)	$6,710	5-B	1,607	153
Univ of Minnesota, Twin Cities Cmps, Minneapolis, MN 55455-0213	1851	$10,273(S)	$7,280	5-D	51,140	2,892
Univ of Mississippi, University, MS 38677	1844	$5,106(S)	$7,778	5-D	15,289	867
Univ of Mississippi Med Ctr, Jackson, MS 39216-4505	1955	NA	NA	5-D	2,092	836
Univ of Missouri–Columbia, Columbia, MO 65211	1839	$8,467(S)	$8,100	5-D	30,200	1,337
Univ of Missouri–Kansas City, Kansas City, MO 64110-2499	1929	$8,273(S)	$7,881	5-D	14,499	1,165
Univ of Missouri–St Louis, St. Louis, MO 63121	1963	$8,595(S)	$7,782	5-D	15,617	900
Univ of Mobile, Mobile, AL 36613	1961	$13,970	$7,320	2-M	1,597	162
The Univ of Montana, Missoula, MT 59812-0002	1893	$5,180(S)	$6,258	5-D	14,207	800
The Univ of Montana Western, Dillon, MT 59725-3598	1893	$4,228(S)	$5,350	5-B	1,190	88
Univ of Montevallo, Montevallo, AL 35115	1896	$6,650(S)	$4,504	5-M	3,025	206
Univ of Nebraska at Kearney, Kearney, NE 68849-0001	1903	$5,426(S)	$6,330	5-M	6,543	400
Univ of Nebraska at Omaha, Omaha, NE 68182	1908	$5,880(S)	$6,980	5-D	14,213	880
Univ of Nebraska–Lincoln, Lincoln, NE 68588	1869	$6,857(S)	$7,260	5-D	23,537	1,081
Univ of Nebraska Med Ctr, Omaha, NE 68198	1869	$5,800(S)	NA	5-D	3,194	1,097
Univ of Nevada, Las Vegas, Las Vegas, NV 89154-9900	1957	$4,808(S)	$10,456	5-D	28,617	1,428
Univ of Nevada, Reno, Reno, NV 89557	1874	$4,616(S)	$10,595	5-D	16,867	635
Univ of New England, Biddeford, ME 04005-9526	1831	$27,920	$10,870	1-F	4,267	320
Univ of New Hampshire, Durham, NH 03824	1866	$11,738(S)	$8,596	5-D	14,964	976
Univ of New Haven, West Haven, CT 06516-1916	1920	$29,682	$12,204	1-M	5,233	503
Univ of New Mexico, Albuquerque, NM 87131-2039	1889	$4,834(S)	$7,336	5-D	NA	1,443
Univ of New Orleans, New Orleans, LA 70148	1958	$3,488(S)	$6,130	5-D	11,428	604
Univ of North Alabama, Florence, AL 35632-0001	1830	$5,598(S)	$4,658	5-M	7,203	418
The Univ of North Carolina at Asheville, Asheville, NC 28804-3299	1927	$4,255(S)	$6,620	5-M	3,629	331
The Univ of North Carolina at Chapel Hill, Chapel Hill, NC 27599	1789	$5,397(S)	$7,334	5-D	28,567	1,746
The Univ of North Carolina at Charlotte, Charlotte, NC 28223-0001	1946	$4,294(S)	$6,456	5-D	23,300	1,409
The Univ of North Carolina at Greensboro, Greensboro, NC 27412-5001	1891	$4,276(S)	$6,506	5-D	17,407	1,209
The Univ of North Carolina at Pembroke, Pembroke, NC 28372-1510	1887	$2,007(S)	$6,250	5-M	6,303	450
The Univ of North Carolina Wilmington, Wilmington, NC 28403-3297	1947	$4,528(S)	$7,370	5-D	12,195	933
Univ of North Dakota, Grand Forks, ND 58202	1883	$6,513(S)	$5,472	5-D	12,748	635
Univ of Northern Colorado, Greeley, CO 80639	1890	$4,680(S)	$7,784	5-D	11,925	620
Univ of Northern Iowa, Cedar Falls, IA 50614	1876	$6,636(S)	$7,082	5-D	12,998	856
Univ of North Florida, Jacksonville, FL 32224-2645	1965	$3,775(S)	$7,366	5-D	15,280	724
Univ of North Texas, Denton, TX 76203	1890	$6,767(S)	$6,026	5-D	34,698	1,435
Univ of Notre Dame, Notre Dame, IN 46556	1842	$36,847	$9,828	2-D	11,731	NA
Univ of Oklahoma, Norman, OK 73019-0390	1890	$5,245(S)	$7,376	5-D	26,185	1,387
Univ of Oklahoma Health Sci Ctr, Oklahoma City, OK 73190	1890	$5,557(S)	NA	5-D	3,913	463
Univ of Oregon, Eugene, OR 97403	1872	$6,435(S)	$8,211	5-D	21,452	1,209
Univ of Pennsylvania, Philadelphia, PA 19104	1740	$37,526	$10,621	1-D	19,018	2,789
Univ of Phoenix, Phoenix, AZ 85034-7209	1989	$12,090	NA	3-D	292,797	11,477
Univ of Phoenix–Atlanta Cmps, Sandy Springs, GA 30350-4153	NA	$12,000	NA	3-M	1,573	220
Univ of Phoenix–Bay Area Cmps, Pleasanton, CA 94588-3677	NA	$13,590	NA	3-M	2,240	318
Univ of Phoenix–Central Florida Cmps, Maitland, FL 32751-7057	1996	$11,040	NA	3-M	1,537	215
Univ of Phoenix–Central Valley Cmps, Fresno, CA 93720-1562	2004	$13,200	NA	3-M	2,235	272
Univ of Phoenix–Charlotte Cmps, Charlotte, NC 28273-3409	2003	$11,110	NA	3-M	1,149	141
Univ of Phoenix–Chicago Cmps, Schaumburg, IL 60173-4399	2002	$12,000	NA	3-M	1,178	191
Univ of Phoenix–Dallas Cmps, Dallas, TX 75251-2009	2001	$12,750	NA	3-M	1,371	181
Univ of Phoenix–Denver Cmps, Lone Tree, CO 80124-5453	NA	$10,590	NA	3-M	2,264	302
Univ of Phoenix–Houston Cmps, Houston, TX 77079-2004	2001	$12,000	NA	3-M	2,748	325
Univ of Phoenix–Las Vegas Cmps, Las Vegas, NV 89128	1994	$10,920	NA	3-M	3,162	279
Univ of Phoenix–Louisiana Cmps, Metairie, LA 70001-2082	1976	$10,350	NA	3-M	1,919	246
Univ of Phoenix–Metro Detroit Cmps, Troy, MI 48098-2623	NA	$12,690	NA	3-M	2,547	329
Univ of Phoenix–New Mexico Cmps, Albuquerque, NM 87109-4645	NA	$10,530	NA	3-M	4,170	427
Univ of Phoenix–North Florida Cmps, Jacksonville, FL 32216-0959	1976	$11,050	NA	3-M	1,276	210
Univ of Phoenix–Oregon Cmps, Tigard, OR 97223	1976	$11,700	NA	3-M	1,265	253
Univ of Phoenix–Phoenix Cmps, Phoenix, AZ 85040-1958	1976	$10,860	NA	3-M	5,379	985
Univ of Phoenix–Puerto Rico Cmps, Guaynabo, PR 00968	1995	$6,450	NA	3-M	2,815	228
Univ of Phoenix–Sacramento Valley Cmps, Sacramento, CA 95833-3632	1993	$13,200	NA	3-M	3,842	518
Univ of Phoenix–San Diego Cmps, San Diego, CA 92123	1988	$12,690	NA	3-M	3,212	399
Univ of Phoenix–Southern Arizona Cmps, Tucson, AZ 85711	1979	$10,860	NA	3-M	2,229	284
Univ of Phoenix–Southern California Cmps, Costa Mesa, CA 92626	1980	$15,000	NA	3-M	11,780	1,340
Univ of Phoenix–South Florida Cmps, Fort Lauderdale, FL 33309	NA	$11,340	NA	3-M	2,439	233
Univ of Phoenix–Utah Cmps, Salt Lake City, UT 84123-4617	1984	$10,950	NA	3-M	3,169	406
Univ of Pittsburgh, Pittsburgh, PA 15260	1787	$13,642(S)	$7,750	12-D	27,562	2,087
Univ of Pittsburgh at Bradford, Bradford, PA 16701-2812	1963	$11,722(S)	$7,050	12-B	1,504	150
Univ of Pittsburgh at Greensburg, Greensburg, PA 15601-5860	1963	$11,782(S)	$7,530	12-B	1,826	133
Univ of Pittsburgh at Johnstown, Johnstown, PA 15904-2990	1927	$11,674(S)	$6,860	12-B	3,032	159
Univ of Portland, Portland, OR 97203-5798	1901	$30,400	$8,756	2-D	3,661	307
Univ of Puerto Rico, Aguadilla Univ Coll, Aguadilla, PR 00604-6150	1972	$1,679(S)	NA	6-B	3,126	NA
Univ of Puerto Rico at Arecibo, Arecibo, PR 00613	1967	$1,872(S)	NA	6-B	3,923	NA
Univ of Puerto Rico at Bayamón, Bayamón, PR 00959	1971	$2,008(S)	NA	6-B	5,014	309
Univ of Puerto Rico at Humacao, Humacao, PR 00791	1962	$1,945(S)	NA	6-B	4,745	307
Univ of Puerto Rico at Ponce, Ponce, PR 00732-7186	1970	$1,747(S)	NA	6-B	3,232	197
Univ of Puerto Rico at Utuado, Utuado, PR 00641-2500	1979	$1,940(S)	NA	6-B	1,682	106

Name, Address	Year Founded	Tuition & Fees	Room & Board	Control, Degree	Enroll-ment	Faculty
Univ of Puerto Rico, Cayey Univ Coll, Cayey, PR 00736	1967	$1,504(S)	NA	6-B	3,659	174
Univ of Puerto Rico, Mayagüez Cmps, Mayagüez, PR 00681-9000	1911	$1,851(S)	NA	6-D	12,380	766
Univ of Puerto Rico, Med Sci Cmps, San Juan, PR 00936-5067 (4).	1950	NA	NA	6-D	2,420	693
Univ of Puerto Rico, Río Piedras, San Juan, PR 00931-3300	1903	$1,272(S)	$8,180	6-D	20,892	1,341
Univ of Puget Sound, Tacoma, WA 98416	1888	$35,635	$9,190	1-F	2,858	279
Univ of Redlands, Redlands, CA 92373-0999	1907	$32,294	$10,122	1-D	4,317	537
Univ of Rhode Island, Kingston, RI 02881	1892	$8,928(S)	$8,826	5-D	15,904	699
Univ of Richmond, University of Richmond, VA 23173	1830	$40,010	$8,480	1-F	3,445	367
Univ of Rio Grande, Rio Grande, OH 45674	1876	$18,260	$7,000	1-M	2,070	184
Univ of Rochester, Rochester, NY 14627-0250	1850	$37,250	$10,810	1-D	9,712	772
Univ of St Francis, Joliet, IL 60435-6169	1920	$21,860	$7,744	2-M	2,146	219
Univ of St Francis, Fort Wayne, IN 46808-3994	1890	$19,570	$6,006	2-M	2,112	222
Univ of St Thomas, St. Paul, MN 55105-1096	1885	$27,822	$7,614	2-D	10,984	840
Univ of St Thomas, Houston, TX 77006-4696	1947	$20,190	$7,700	2-D	3,246	273
Univ of San Diego, San Diego, CA 92110-2492	1949	$36,292	$12,602	2-D	7,882	801
Univ of San Francisco, San Francisco, CA 94117-1080	1855	$34,770	$11,540	2-D	8,750	891
Univ of Sci & Arts of Oklahoma, Chickasha, OK 73018	1908	$4,440(S)	$4,710	5-B	1,158	89
The Univ of Scranton, Scranton, PA 18510	1888	$33,124	$11,440	2-D	5,651	533
Univ of Sioux Falls, Sioux Falls, SD 57105-1699	1883	$20,270	$5,920	2-D	1,564	140
Univ of South Alabama, Mobile, AL 36688-0002	1963	$5,512(S)	$5,344	5-D	14,064	1,199
Univ of South Carolina, Columbia, SC 29208	1801	$8,838(S)	$7,318	5-D	27,488	1,709
Univ of South Carolina Aiken, Aiken, SC 29801-6309	1961	$7,582(S)	$6,620	5-M	3,232	223
Univ of South Carolina Beaufort, Beaufort, SC 29909	1959	$7,080(S)	$5,600	5-B	1,461	101
Univ of South Carolina Upstate, Spartanburg, SC 29303-4999	1967	$8,512(S)	$6,150	5-M	5,063	387
The Univ of South Dakota, Vermillion, SD 57069-2390	1862	$6,468(S)	$5,787	5-D	9,291	407
Univ of Southern California, Los Angeles, CA 90089	1880	$37,694	$11,298	1-D	33,747	2,747
Univ of Southern Indiana, Evansville, IN 47712-3590	1965	$5,219(S)	$6,648	5-D	10,126	624
Univ of Southern Maine, Portland, ME 04104-9300	1878	$7,467(S)	$8,344	5-D	7,879	710
Univ of Southern Mississippi, Hattiesburg, MS 39406-0001	1910	$5,096(S)	$6,032	5-D	14,793	929
Univ of South Florida, Tampa, FL 33620-9951	1956	$3,991(S)	$8,080	5-D	46,189	1,394
The Univ of Tampa, Tampa, FL 33606-1490	1931	$21,712	$7,978	1-M	5,800	484
The Univ of Tennessee, Knoxville, TN 37996	1794	$6,250(S)	$6,888	5-D	30,410	1,692
The Univ of Tennessee at Chattanooga, Chattanooga, TN 37403-2598	1886	$5,310(S)	$8,100	5-D	9,807	690
The Univ of Tennessee at Martin, Martin, TN 38238-1000	1900	$5,255(S)	$4,606	5-M	7,578	525
The Univ of Texas at Arlington, Arlington, TX 76019	1895	$7,780(S)	$6,412	5-D	25,084	1,176
The Univ of Texas at Austin, Austin, TX 78712-1111	1883	$8,532(S)	$9,246	5-D	49,984	2,983
The Univ of Texas at Brownsville, Brownsville, TX 78520-4991	1973	$4,355(S)	$2,920	5-D	17,189	701
The Univ of Texas at Dallas, Richardson, TX 75083-0688	1969	$9,850(S)	$6,828	5-D	14,944	772
The Univ of Texas at El Paso, El Paso, TX 79968-0001	1913	$5,925(S)	NA	5-D	20,458	1,121
The Univ of Texas at San Antonio, San Antonio, TX 78249-0617	1969	$4,800(S)	NA	5-D	28,413	1,224
The Univ of Texas at Tyler, Tyler, TX 75799-0001	1971	$5,742(S)	$7,510	5-M	6,117	399
The Univ of Texas Health Sci Ctr at Houston, Houston, TX 77225-0036	1972	$6,390(S)	NA	5-D	3,865	1,389
The Univ of Texas Health Sci Ctr at San Antonio, San Antonio, TX 78229-3900	1976	$5,050(S)	NA	5-D	2,754	1,372
The Univ of Texas Med Branch, Galveston, TX 77555	1891	$5,502(S)	NA	5-D	2,338	NA
The Univ of Texas of the Permian Basin, Odessa, TX 79762-0001	1969	$4,262(S)	$4,600	5-M	3,496	223
The Univ of Texas–Pan Amer, Edinburg, TX 78541-2999	1927	$3,898(S)	$4,994	5-D	17,534	812
The Univ of Texas Southwestern Med Ctr at Dallas, Dallas, TX 75390	1943	$4,628(S)	$11,353	5-D	2,461	1,964
The Univ of the Arts, Philadelphia, PA 19102-4944	1870	$30,600	$7,047	1-M	2,401	494
Univ of the Cumberlands, Williamsburg, KY 40769-1372	1889	$15,658	$6,826	2-M	2,553	143
Univ of the District of Columbia, Washington, DC 20008-1175	1976	$3,140(S)	NA	9-M	5,339	NA
Univ of the Incarnate Word, San Antonio, TX 78209-6397	1881	$21,290	$8,780	2-D	6,361	558
Univ of the Pacific, Stockton, CA 95211-0197	1851	$30,880	$10,118	1-D	6,251	724
Univ of the Sacred Heart, San Juan, PR 00914-0383	1935	$5,100	NA	2-M	5,666	367
Univ of the Sci in Philadelphia, Philadelphia, PA 19104-4495	1821	$28,506	$11,146	1-D	3,000	258
Univ of the Virgin Islands, Saint Thomas, VI 00802-9990	1962	$4,100(S)	$8,240	7-M	2,393	229
The Univ of Toledo, Toledo, OH 43606-3390	1872	$7,927(S)	$9,019	5-D	22,336	1,592
Univ of Tulsa, Tulsa, OK 74104-3189	1894	$23,940	$7,776	2-D	4,192	397
Univ of Utah, Salt Lake City, UT 84112-1107	1850	$5,285(S)	$5,972	5-D	28,211	1,932
Univ of Vermont, Burlington, VT 05405	1791	$12,844(S)	$8,534	5-D	12,800	765
Univ of Virginia, Charlottesville, VA 22903	1819	$9,300(S)	$7,820	5-D	24,541	1,344
The Univ of Virginia's Coll at Wise, Wise, VA 24293	1954	$6,748(S)	$7,933	5-B	1,964	166
Univ of Washington, Seattle, WA 98195	1861	$6,802(S)	$7,488	5-D	41,517	3,731
Univ of Washington, Bothell, Bothell, WA 98011-8246	1990	$7,409(S)	NA	5-M	2,261	178
Univ of Washington, Tacoma, Tacoma, WA 98402-3100	1990	$6,732(S)	NA	5-M	2,965	170
The Univ of West Alabama, Livingston, AL 35470	1835	$5,100(S)	$3,904	5-M	4,888	191
Univ of West Florida, Pensacola, FL 32514-5750	1963	$3,655(S)	$6,900	5-D	10,491	424
Univ of West Georgia, Carrollton, GA 30118	1933	$4,316(S)	$5,714	5-D	11,252	551
Univ of Wisconsin–Eau Claire, Eau Claire, WI 54702-4004	1916	$6,203(S)	$5,210	5-M	10,889	524
Univ of Wisconsin–Green Bay, Green Bay, WI 54311-7001	1968	$6,308(S)	$5,400	5-M	6,275	334
Univ of Wisconsin–La Crosse, La Crosse, WI 54601-3742	1909	$6,648(S)	$5,420	5-F	9,900	508
Univ of Wisconsin–Madison, Madison, WI 53706-1380	1848	$7,568(S)	$7,700	5-D	42,030	2,848
Univ of Wisconsin–Milwaukee, Milwaukee, WI 53201-0413	1956	$7,309(S)	$3,840	5-D	29,215	824
Univ of Wisconsin–Oshkosh, Oshkosh, WI 54901	1871	$6,038(S)	$5,898	5-M	12,669	599
Univ of Wisconsin–Parkside, Kenosha, WI 53141-2000	1968	$6,070(S)	$5,986	5-M	5,167	293
Univ of Wisconsin–Platteville, Platteville, WI 53818-3099	1866	$6,147(S)	$5,550	5-M	7,379	367
Univ of Wisconsin–River Falls, River Falls, WI 54022-5001	1874	$6,220(S)	$5,146	5-M	6,555	349
Univ of Wisconsin–Stevens Point, Stevens Point, WI 54481-3897	1894	$6,200(S)	$5,180	5-D	9,155	452
Univ of Wisconsin–Stout, Menomonie, WI 54751	1891	$7,584(S)	$5,170	5-M	8,811	420
Univ of Wisconsin–Superior, Superior, WI 54880-4500	1893	$6,359(S)	$5,154	5-M	2,688	187
Univ of Wisconsin–Whitewater, Whitewater, WI 53190-1790	1868	$7,062(S)	$4,740	5-M	10,962	501
Univ of Wyoming, Laramie, WY 82071	1886	$3,686(S)	$8,006	5-D	12,067	767
Urbana Univ, Urbana, OH 43078-2091	1850	$19,490	$7,860	1-M	1,551	120
Ursinus Coll, Collegeville, PA 19426-1000	1869	$36,910	$8,800	1-B	1,680	168
Ursuline Coll, Pepper Pike, OH 44124-4398	1871	$22,060	$7,350	2-M	1,426	216
Utah State Univ, Logan, UT 84322	1888	$4,445(S)	$4,650	5-D	15,099	945
Utah Valley Univ, Orem, UT 84058-5999	1941	$3,752(S)	NA	5-M	26,696	1,477
Utica Coll, Utica, NY 13502-4892	1946	$26,058	$10,430	1-F	3,101	322
Valdosta State Univ, Valdosta, GA 31698	1906	$4,158(S)	$6,230	5-D	11,490	622
Valley City State Univ, Valley City, ND 58072	1890	$5,781(S)	$4,071	5-M	1,019	89
Valparaiso Univ, Valparaiso, IN 46383	1859	$26,950	$7,620	2-D	3,976	376
Vanderbilt Univ, Nashville, TN 37240-1001	1873	$37,005	$12,028	1-D	12,093	NA
Vanguard Univ of Southern California, Costa Mesa, CA 92626-9601	1920	$25,452	$7,994	2-M	2,149	96
Vassar Coll, Poughkeepsie, NY 12604	1861	$40,210	$9,040	1-B	2,389	336
Vaughn Coll of Aeronautics & Tech, Flushing, NY 11369-1037 (2)	1932	$16,030	$10,130	1-M	1,082	121

Name, Address	Year Founded	Tuition & Fees	Room & Board	Control, Degree	Enroll- ment	Faculty
Vermont Tech Coll, Randolph Center, VT 05061-0500	1866	$9,984(A)	$7,510	5-B	1,651	229
Villanova Univ, Villanova, PA 19085-1699	1842	$37,655	$10,070	2-D	10,275	940
Virginia Coll at Birmingham, Birmingham, AL 35209	1989	$13,532	NA	3-M	3,826	NA
Virginia Commonwealth Univ, Richmond, VA 23284-9005	1838	$6,779(S)	$7,914	5-D	32,284	3,088
Virginia Military Inst, Lexington, VA 24450 (2)	1839	$10,556(S)	$6,444	5-B	1,428	172
Virginia Polytechnic Inst & State Univ, Blacksburg, VA 24061	1872	$8,198(S)	$5,476	5-D	30,739	1,598
Virginia State Univ, Petersburg, VA 23806-0001	1882	$5,644(S)	$7,710	5-D	5,042	359
Virginia Union Univ, Richmond, VA 23220-1170	1865	$13,662	$6,328	2-D	1,700	140
Virginia Wesleyan Coll, Norfolk, VA 23502-5599	1961	$27,476	$7,696	2-B	1,381	149
Viterbo Univ, La Crosse, WI 54601-4797 (4)	1890	$20,160	$7,510	2-M	2,093	232
Wagner Coll, Staten Island, NY 10301-4495	1883	$31,050	$9,250	1-M	2,294	256
Wake Forest Univ, Winston-Salem, NC 27109	1834	$38,622	$10,410	1-D	6,862	584
Walden Univ, Minneapolis, MN 55401	1970	$11,396	NA	3-D	29,456	883
Walla Walla Univ, College Place, WA 99324-1198	1892	$21,936	$4,320	2-M	1,800	205
Walsh Coll of Accountancy & Bus Admin, Troy, MI 48007-7006	1922	$10,959	NA	1-M	3,106	178
Walsh Univ, North Canton, OH 44720-3396	1958	$21,240	$8,110	2-D	2,738	289
Warren Wilson Coll, Asheville, NC 28815-9000	1894	$24,196	$7,770	2-M	1,002	84
Wartburg Coll, Waverly, IA 50677-0903	1852	$26,160	$7,255	2-B	1,799	176
Washburn Univ, Topeka, KS 66621	1865	$5,996(S)	$5,602	10-F	6,545	524
Washington & Jefferson Coll, Washington, PA 15301	1781	$31,496	$8,488	1-B	1,519	149
Washington & Lee Univ, Lexington, VA 24450-0303	1749	$37,412	$8,428	1-F	2,155	306
Washington Coll, Chestertown, MD 21620-1197	1782	$34,005	$7,180	1-M	1,402	149
Washington State Univ, Pullman, WA 99164	1890	$7,565(S)	$8,054	5-D	25,352	1,662
Washington Univ in St Louis, St. Louis, MO 63130-4899	1853	$38,864	$12,465	1-D	13,339	1,080
Wayland Baptist Univ, Plainview, TX 79072-6998	1908	$12,020	$3,691	2-M	1,234	120
Waynesburg Univ, Waynesburg, PA 15370 1222	1849	$17,080	$7,050	2-D	2,549	166
Wayne State Coll, Wayne, NE 68787	1910	$4,571(S)	$5,054	5-M	3,566	210
Wayne State Univ, Detroit, MI 48202	1868	$8,109(S)	$6,932	5-D	31,016	1,971
Weber State Univ, Ogden, UT 84408-1001	1889	$3,850(S)	NA	5-M	21,388	896
Webster Univ, St. Louis, MO 63119-3194	1915	$20,440	$9,000	1-D	8,010	863
Wellesley Coll, Wellesley, MA 02481 (3)	1870	$36,640	$11,336	1-B	2,344	326
Wentworth Inst of Tech, Boston, MA 02115-5998	1904	$21,800	$10,500	1-B	3,816	295
Wesleyan Univ, Middletown, CT 06459-0260	1831	$38,634	$10,636	1-D	3,149	356
Wesley Coll, Dover, DE 19901-3875	1873	$18,530	$8,400	2-M	1,871	157
West Chester Univ of Pennsylvania, West Chester, PA 19383	1871	$6,737(S)	$6,874	5-M	13,619	842
Western Carolina Univ, Cullowhee, NC 28723	1889	$4,325(S)	$5,462	5-D	9,050	705
Western Connecticut State Univ, Danbury, CT 06810-6885	1903	$7,088(S)	$9,158	5-D	6,462	537
Western Governors Univ, Salt Lake City, UT 84107	1998	$5,580	NA	1-M	9,022	NA
Western Illinois Univ, Macomb, IL 61455-1390	1899	$8,272(S)	$7,210	5-D	13,175	750
Western Intl Univ, Phoenix, AZ 85021-2718	1978	$8,760	NA	3-M	2,651	303
Western Kentucky Univ, Bowling Green, KY 42101	1906	$6,930(S)	$5,914	5-D	19,742	1,117
Western Michigan Univ, Kalamazoo, MI 49008-5202	1903	$7,928(S)	$7,377	5-D	24,818	1,436
Western New England Coll, Springfield, MA 01119	1919	$27,470	$10,554	1-D	3,722	305
Western New Mexico Univ, Silver City, NM 88062-0680	1893	$3,431(S)	$5,060	5-M	2,697	259
Western Oregon Univ, Monmouth, OR 97361-1394	1856	$5,868(S)	$7,600	5-M	5,371	334
Western State Coll of Colorado, Gunnison, CO 81231	1901	$3,778(S)	$7,516	5-B	1,990	161
Western Washington Univ, Bellingham, WA 98225-5996	1893	$5,535(S)	$7,712	5-M	14,620	735
Westfield State Coll, Westfield, MA 01086	1838	$6,515(S)	$7,204	5-M	5,548	421
West Liberty State Univ, West Liberty, WV 26074	1837	$4,464(S)	$6,282	5-M	2,511	169
Westminster Coll, Fulton, MO 65251-1299	1851	$17,990	$7,120	2-B	1,000	79
Westminster Coll, New Wilmington, PA 16172-0001	1852	$26,600	$8,110	2-M	1,593	149
Westminster Coll, Salt Lake City, UT 84105-3697	1875	$24,996	$7,006	1-M	2,863	298
Westmont Coll, Santa Barbara, CA 93108-1099	1937	$33,170	$10,080	2-B	1,336	136
West Texas A&M Univ, Canyon, TX 79016-0001	1909	$5,382(S)	$5,627	5-D	7,535	342
West Virginia State Univ, Institute, WV 25112-1000	1891	$4,346(S)	$6,020	5-M	3,502	198
West Virginia Univ, Morgantown, WV 26506	1867	$5,100(S)	$7,434	5-D	28,840	1,188
West Virginia Univ Inst of Tech, Montgomery, WV 25136	1895	$4,598(S)	$5,700	5-M	1,453	NA
West Virginia Wesleyan Coll, Buckhannon, WV 26201	1890	$22,880	$6,800	2-M	1,317	156
Wheaton Coll, Wheaton, IL 60187-5593	1860	$25,500	$7,618	2-D	2,915	300
Wheaton Coll, Norton, MA 02766	1834	$38,860	$9,150	1-B	1,655	181
Wheeling Jesuit Univ, Wheeling, WV 26003-6295	1954	$24,390	NA	2-M	1,303	125
Wheelock Coll, Boston, MA 02215-4176 (4)	1888	$28,160	$11,200	1-M	1,109	93
Whitman Coll, Walla Walla, WA 99362-2083	1859	$35,192	$8,812	1-B	1,489	183
Whittier Coll, Whittier, CA 90608-0634	1887	$32,470	$9,050	1-F	1,962	123
Whitworth Univ, Spokane, WA 99251-0001	1890	$27,420	$7,700	2-M	2,607	294
Wichita State Univ, Wichita, KS 67260	1895	$5,084(S)	$5,860	5-D	14,612	516
Widener Univ, Chester, PA 19013-5792	1821	$30,450	$10,840	1-D	6,601	668
Wilkes Univ, Wilkes-Barre, PA 18766-0002	1933	$25,170	$10,780	1-D	5,901	429
Willamette Univ, Salem, OR 97301-3931	1842	$33,960	$7,950	2-F	2,716	283
William Carey Univ, Hattiesburg, MS 39401-5499	1906	$9,015	$3,810	2-M	2,493	210
William Jewell Coll, Liberty, MO 64068-1843	1849	$24,600	$6,700	2-B	1,210	152
William Paterson Univ of New Jersey, Wayne, NJ 07470-8420	1855	$10,492(S)	$9,990	5-M	10,256	931
William Penn Univ, Oskaloosa, IA 52577-1799	1873	$18,034	$5,132	2-B	1,861	52
Williams Coll, Williamstown, MA 01267	1793	$37,640	$9,890	1-M	2,045	315
William Woods Univ, Fulton, MO 65251-1098	1870	$16,680	$6,750	2-M	2,185	249
Wilmington Coll, Wilmington, OH 45177	1870	$23,372	$8,010	2-M	1,501	122
Wilmington Univ, New Castle, DE 19720-6491	1967	$8,810	NA	1-D	8,496	894
Wingate Univ, Wingate, NC 28174-0159	1896	$20,140	$8,050	2-D	2,129	157
Winona State Univ, Winona, MN 55987-5838	1858	$7,627(S)	$6,430	5-M	8,220	501
Winston-Salem State Univ, Winston-Salem, NC 27110-0003	1892	$3,836(S)	$6,867	5-M	6,422	520
Winthrop Univ, Rock Hill, SC 29733	1886	$11,060(S)	$10,040	5-M	6,249	487
Wittenberg Univ, Springfield, OH 45501-0720	1845	$33,890	$8,772	2-M	1,976	196
Wofford Coll, Spartanburg, SC 29303-3663	1854	$29,465	$8,190	2-B	1,389	145
Woodbury Univ, Burbank, CA 91504-1099	1884	$26,978	$8,768	1-M	1,539	237
Worcester Polytechnic Inst, Worcester, MA 01609-2280	1865	$36,930	$10,880	1-D	4,561	314
Worcester State Coll, Worcester, MA 01602-2597	1874	$6,170(S)	$8,527	5-M	5,378	386
Wright State Univ, Dayton, OH 45435	1964	$7,278(S)	$7,180	5-D	16,672	863
Xavier Univ, Cincinnati, OH 45207	1831	$28,570	$9,530	2-D	6,584	630
Xavier Univ of Louisiana, New Orleans, LA 70125-1098	1925	$15,500	$6,800	2-F	3,236	240
Yale Univ, New Haven, CT 06520	1701	$35,300	$10,700	1-D	11,445	1,577
Yeshiva Univ, New York, NY 10033-3201	1886	NA	NA	1-D	5,998	NA
York Coll of Pennsylvania, York, PA 17405-7199	1787	$13,680	$7,800	1-M	5,627	526
York Coll of the City Univ of New York, Jamaica, NY 11451-0001	1967	$4,262(S)	NA	11-M	7,157	490
Youngstown State Univ, Youngstown, OH 44555-0001	1908	$6,721(S)	$7,090	5-D	13,704	964

DIRECTORY

Associations and Organizations
Source: World Almanac research

Selected list, generally by **category** and first distinctive **key word** in each title; e.g., Retired Persons, American Association of. Listed by acronym when that is the official name. Founding year in parentheses; religious entries include addresses and leadership information for 2009.

Academic and Educational

Academies, Natl. (1863): (202) 334-2000; www.nationalacademies.org

African-American Life and History, Assn. for the Study of (1915): (202) 865-0053; www.asalh.org

Alpha Delta Kappa (1947): (816) 363-5525; www.alphadeltakappa.org

AMIDEAST (formerly American Mideast Educational & Training Services) (1951): (202) 776-9600; www.amideast.org

Anthropological Assn., American (1902): (703) 528-1902; www.aaanet.org

Archaeological Institute of America (1879): (617) 353-9361; www.archaeological.org

Arts, Americans for the (1996): (202) 371-2830; www.artsusa.org

Arts and Sciences, American Academy of (1780): (617) 576-5000; www.amacad.org

Beta Gamma Sigma Honor Society (1913): (314) 432-5650; www.betagammasigma.org

Beta Sigma Phi (1931): (816) 444-6800; www.betasigmaphi.org

Biological Sciences, American Institute of (1947): (202) 628-1500; www.aibs.org

College Board, The (1900): (212) 713-8000; www.collegeboard.org

Colleges and Universities, Assn. of American (1915): (202) 387-3760; www.aacu.org

Community Colleges, American Assn. of (1920): (202) 728-0200; www.aacc.nche.edu

Consumer Interests, American Council on (ACCI) (1953): (414) 918-3189; www.consumerinterests.org

Delta Kappa Gamma Society Intl. (1929): (512) 478-5748; www.deltakappagamma.net

Education, American Council on (1918): (202) 939-9300; www.acenet.edu

Education, Council for Advancement and Support of (1974): (202) 328-2273; www.case.org

Education of Young Children, Natl. Assn. for the (1926): (202) 232-8777; www.naeyc.org

Educators for World Peace, Intl. Assn. of (1973): (256) 534-5501; www.iaewp.org

English-Speaking Union of the U.S. (1920): (212) 818-1200; www.esuus.org

Entomological Society of America (1889): (301) 731-4535; www.entsoc.org

Esperanto League for North America Inc. (1953): (510) 653-0998; www.esperanto-usa.org

Family Relations, Natl. Council on (1938): (888) 781-9331; www.ncfr.org

Foreign Study, The American Institute for (1964): (866) 906-2437; www.aifs.com

Freedom of Information Center (1958): (573) 882-5736; foi.missouri.edu

French Institute/Alliance Française (1971): (212) 355-6100; www.fiaf.org

Genealogical Society, Natl. (1903): (703) 525-0050; www.ngsgenealogy.org

Genetic Association, American (1903): (541) 867-0334; www.theaga.org

Geological Society of America (1888): (303) 357-1000; www.geosociety.org

Hemispheric Affairs, Council on (1975): (202) 223-4975; www.coha.org

Industrial and Applied Mathematics, Society for (1952): (215) 382-9800; www.siam.org

Intl. Education, Institute of (1919): (212) 883-8200; www.iie.org

Intl. Educational Exchange, Council on (1947): (207) 553-4000; www.ciee.org

Intl. Law, American Society of (1906): (202) 939-6000; www.asil.org

Irish American Cultural Inst. (1962): (973) 605-1991; www.irishaci.org

Law Libraries, American Assn. of (1906): (312) 939-4764; www.aallnet.org

Learned Societies, American Council of (1919): (212) 697-1505; www.acls.org

Libraries Assn., Special (1909): (703) 647-4900; www.sla.org

Linguistic Society of America (1924): (202) 835-1714; www.lsadc.org

Mathematical Society, American (1888): (401) 455-4000; www.ams.org

MENC: The Natl. Assn. for Music Education (formerly Music Educators Natl. Conference) (1907): (703) 860-4000; www.menc.org

Mensa, Ltd., American (1960): (817) 607-0060; www.us.mensa.org

Meteorological Society, American (1919): (617) 227-2425; www.ametsoc.org

Metric Assn., Inc., U.S. (1916): (818) 363-5606; www.metric.org

Microbiology, American Society for (1899): (202) 737-3600; www.asm.org

Modern Language Assn. of America (1883): (646) 576-5000; www.mla.org

Museums, American Assn. of (1906): (202) 289-9127; www.aam-us.org

Musicological Society, American (1934): (207) 798-4243; www.ams-net.org

Negro College Fund, United (1944): (800) 331-2244; www.uncf.org

Oriental Society, American (1842): (734) 647-4760; www. umich.edu/~aos

ORT Inc., American (Org. for Rehabilitation Through Training) (1922): (212) 505-7700; www.ortamerica.org

PEN American Center, Inc. (1922): (212) 334-1660; www.pen.org

Phi Beta Kappa Society (1776): (202) 265-3808; www.pbk.org

Phi Theta Kappa Intl. Honor Society (1918): (601) 984-3504; www.ptk.org

Philological Association, American (1869): (215) 898-4975; www.apaclassics.org

Philosophical Assn., American (1900): (302) 831-1112; www.apaonline.org

Physics, American Inst. of (1931): (301) 209-3100; www.aip.org

Physiological Society, American (1887): (301) 634-7164; www.the-aps.org

Poetry Society of America (1910): (212) 254-9628; www.poetrysociety.org

Poets, The Academy of American (1934): (212) 274-0343; www.poets.org

Political Science, Academy of (1880): (212) 870-2500; www.psqonline.org

Population Connection (1968): (202) 332-2200; www.populationconnection.org

Radio and Television Society Foundation, Intl. (1939): (212) 867-6650; www.irts.org

Reading Assn., Intl. (1956): (302) 731-1600; www.reading.org

Religion, American Academy of (1909): (404) 727-3049; www.aarweb.org

Science Fiction Society, World (1939): www.wsfs.org

Sciences, Natl. Academy of (1863): (202) 334-2000; www.nas.edu

Sigma Beta Delta (1994): (314) 516-4723; www.sigmabetadelta.org

Sociological Assn., American (1905): (202) 383-9005; www.asanet.org

Tall Buildings and Urban Habitat, Council on (1969): (312) 567-3307; www.ctbuh.org

Tau Beta Pi Association (1885): (865) 546-4578; www.tbp.org

Theological Schools in the U.S. and Canada, Assn. of (1918): (412) 788-6505; www.ats.edu

Theosophical Society in America (1875): (630) 668-1571, ext. 300; www.theosophical.org

Universities, Assn. of American (1900): (202) 408-7500; www.aau.edu

World Learning (1954): (802) 257-7751; www.worldlearning.org

Animal Welfare and Environment

Animals, American Society for Prevention of Cruelty to (ASPCA) (1866): (212) 876-7700; www.aspca.org

Animals, People for the Ethical Treatment of (PETA) (1980): (757) 622-7382; www.peta.org

Animal Welfare Institute (1951): (703) 836-4300; www.awionline.org

Appalachian Trail Conservancy (1925): (304) 535-6331; www.appalachiantrail.org

Audubon Soc., Natl. (1905): (212) 979-3000; www.audubon.org

Cat Fanciers' Assn., The (1906): (732) 528-9797; www.cfa.org

Defenders of Wildlife (1947): (800) 385-9712; www.defenders.org

Ducks Unlimited (1937): (901) 758-3825; www.ducks.org

Foresters, Society of American (1900): (301) 897-8720; www.safnet.org

Forest History Society (1946): (919) 682-9319; www.foresthistory.org

Friends of the Earth (1969): (202) 783-7400; www.foe.org

Garden Club of America (1913): (212) 753-8287; www.gcamerica.org

Garden Clubs, Inc., National Council of State (1929): (314) 776-7574; www.gardenclub.org

Geographic Society, Natl. (1888): (813) 979-6845; www.nationalgeographic.com

Green Mountain Club, The (1910): (802) 244-7037; www.greenmountainclub.org

Greenpeace, Inc. (1971): (202) 462-1177; www.greenpeaceusa.org

Hiking Society, American (1976): (301) 565-6714; www.americanhiking.org

Horse Council, American (1969): (202) 296-4031; www.horsecouncil.org

Humane Society of the U.S. (1954): (301) 258-8276; www.hsus.org

Lady Bird Johnson Wildflower Center (1982): (512) 232-0100; www.wildflower.org

Nature Conservancy, The (1951): (703) 841-5300; www.nature.org

Ocean Conservancy (1972): (202) 429-5609; www.oceanconservancy.org

Ornithologists' Union, American (1883): (505) 326-1579; www.aou.org

Recreation and Park Assn., Natl. (1965): (703) 858-0784; www.nrpa.org

Recycling Coalition, Natl. (1978): (202) 789-1430; www.nrc-recycle.org

Rose Society, American (1892): (318) 938-5402; www.ars.org

Save-the-Redwoods League (1918): (415) 362-2352; www.savetheredwoods.org

Sierra Club (1892): (415) 977-5500; www.sierraclub.org

Transportation Alternatives (1973): (212) 629-8080; www.transalt.org

Water Environment Federation (1928): (800) 666-0206; www.wef.org

Wildlife Federation, Natl. (1936): (800) 822-9919; www.nwf.org

World Wildlife Fund (1961): (202) 293-4800; www.worldwildlife.org

Children

Big Brothers/Big Sisters of America (1904): (215) 567-7000; www.bbbs.org

Boy Scouts of America (1910): (972) 580-2000; www.scouting.org

Boys & Girls Clubs of America (1906): (404) 487-5700; www.bgca.org

Camp Fire USA (formerly Camp Fire Boys & Girls) (1910): (816) 285-2010; www.campfireusa.org

Children's Aid Society (1912): (205) 251-7148; www.childrensaid.org

Children's Book Council, The (1945): (212) 966-1990; www.cbcbooks.org

Child Welfare League of America (1920): (703) 412-2400; www.cwla.org

4-H Clubs (1914): (301) 961-2800; www.4husa.org

Future Business Leaders of America/Phi Beta Lambda, Inc. (1942): (800) 325-2946; www.fbla-pbl.org

Future Farmers of America Org., Natl. (1928): (317) 802-6060; www.ffa.org

Gifted Children, Natl. Assn. for (1954): (202) 785-4268; www.nagc.org

Girl Scouts of the U.S.A. (1912): (212) 852-8000; www.girlscouts.org

Honor Society, Natl. (1921): (703) 860-0200; www.nhs.us

Junior Achievement, Inc. (1919): (719) 540-8000; www.ja.org

Junior Auxiliaries, Natl. Assn. of (1941): (662) 332-3000; www.najanet.org

Junior Chamber of Commerce, U.S. (1920): (800) 529-2337; www.usjaycees.org

Junior Honor Society, Natl. (1929): (703) 860-0200; www.njhs.us

Missing and Exploited Children, Natl. Center for (1984): 703-274-3900; www.missingkids.com

NA'AMAT USA (1921): (212) 563-5222; www.naamat.org

Pilot Intl. & Pilot Intl. Foundation (1921): (478) 477-1208; www.pilotinternational.org

Student Councils, Natl. Assn. of (1931): (703) 860-0200; www.nasc.us

Fraternal

Eagles, Fraternal Order of (1898): (614) 883-2200; www.foe.com

Eastern Star, General Grand Chapter, Order of the (1876): (202) 667-4737; www.eastern star.org

Elks of the U.S.A., Benevolent and Protective Order of (1868): (773) 755-4700; www.elks.org

Freemasonry, Supreme Council Ancient and Accepted Scottish Rite of, Northern Masonic Jurisdiction (1813): (781) 862-4410; www.supremecouncil.org

Freemasonry, Supreme Council Ancient and Accepted Scottish Rite of, Southern Jurisdiction (1802): (202) 232-3579; www.srmason-sj.org

Free Men, Natl. Coalition of (1977): (888) 223-1280; www.ncfm.org

Kiwanis International (1915): (317) 875-8755; www.kiwanis.org

Knights of Columbus (1882): (203) 752-4000; www.kofc.org

Knights of Pythias, Order of (1864): (617) 472-8800; www.pythias.org

Lions Clubs, Intl., Assn. of (1917): (630) 571-5466; www.lionsclubs.org

Moose Intl., Inc. (1888): (630) 859-2000; www.mooseintl.org

Odd Fellows, Independent Order of (1819): (336) 725-5955; www.ioof.org

Rotary Intl. (1905): (847) 866-3000; www.rotary.org

Shriners of North America, The (1872): (813) 281-0300; www.shrinershq.org

Sons of Italy in America, Order (1905): (202) 547-2900; www.osia.org

Sons of Norway (1895): (612) 827-3611; www.sofn.com

Woodmen of America, Modern (1883): (309) 558-3100; www.modern-woodmen.org

Historical

Colonial Dames XVII Century, Natl. Soc. (1915): (202) 293-1700; www.colonialdames17c.net

Daughters of the American Revolution Natl. Society (1890): (202) 628-1776; www.dar.org

Daughters of the Confederacy, United (1894): (804) 355-1636; www.hqudc.org

Historic Preservation, Natl. Trust for (1949): (202) 588-6000; www.preservationnation.org

Historical Assn., American (1884): (202) 544-2422; www.historians.org

Historical Society, United States (1971): (800) 788-4478; www.ushs.org

Lewis and Clark Trail Heritage Foundation (1969): (406) 454-1234; www.lewisand clark.org

Mayflower Descendants, General Society of (1897): (508) 746-3188; www.the mayflowersociety.com

Pilgrims Natl. Soc., Sons and Daughters of (1908): www.nssdp.com

Railway Historical Society, Natl. (1935): (215) 557-6606; www.nrhs.com

Sons of the American Revolution, Natl. Society of (1889): (502) 589-1776; www.sar.org

Sons of Confederate Veterans (1896): (800) 380-1896; www.scv.org

State & Local History, American Assn. for (1940): (615) 320-3203; www.aaslh.org

Supreme Court Historical Society (1974): (202) 543-0400; www.supremecourt history.org

Theodore Roosevelt Assn. (1920): (516) 921-6319; www.theodoreroosevelt.org

Thoreau Society (1941): (978) 369-5310; www.thoreausociety.org

Titanic Historical Society and Museum (1963): (413) 543-4770; www.titanichistorical society.org

Victorian Society in America (1966): (215) 636-9872; www.victoriansociety.org

Industrial and Trade

Aerospace Industries Assn. of America Inc. (1919): (703) 358-1000; www.aia-aerospace.org

Better Business Bureaus, Council of (1912): (703) 276-0100; www.bbb.org

Chamber of Commerce of the U.S.A. (1912): (202) 659-6000; www.uschamber.com

Chemistry Council, American (1872): (703) 741-5000; www.americanchemistry.com

Construction Specifications Institute (1948): (703) 684-0300; www.csinet.org

Croplife America (1933): (202) 296-1585; www.croplifeamerica.org

Cryogenic Soc. of America, Inc. (1964): (708) 383-6220; www.cryogenicsociety.org

Electrical Manufacturers Assn., Natl. (1926): (703) 841-3200; www.nema.org

Fire Protection Assn., Natl. (NFPA) (1896): (617) 770-3000; www.nfpa.org

Fisheries Soc., American (1870): (301) 897-8616; www.fisheries.org

Foreign Trade Council, Inc., Natl. (1914): (202) 887-0278; www.nftc.org

Funeral Consumers Alliance (1963): (800) 765-0107; www.funerals.org

Hotel & Lodging Assn., American (1910): (202) 289-3100; www.ahla.com

Insurance Assn., American (1866): (202) 828-7100; www.aiadc.org

Magazine Publishers of America (1919): (212) 872-3700; www.magazine.org

Manufacturers, Natl. Assn. of (1895): (202) 637-3000; www.nam.org

Newspaper Assn. of America (NAA) (1992): (571) 366-1000; www.naa.org

Nuclear Society, American (1954): (708) 352-6611; www.ans.org

Petroleum Institute, American (1919): (202) 682-8000; www.api.org

Printing Industries of America, Inc. (1887): (412) 741-6860; www.gain.net

Publishers, Assn. of American (1970): (202) 347-3375; www.publishers.org

Retail Federation, Natl. (1908): (800) 673-4692; www.nrf.com

Safety Council, Natl. (1913): (630) 285-1121; www.nsc.org

Shipbuilders Council of America (1920): (202) 347-5462; www.shipbuilders.org

Small Business Assn, Natl. (1937): (800) 345-6728; www.nsba.biz

Software and Information Industry Assn. (1999): (202) 289-7442; www.siia.net

Symphony Orchestra League, American (1942): (212) 262-5161; www.symphony.org

Toy Industry Assn., Inc. (1916): (212) 675-1141; www.toyassociation.org

Water Works Assn., American (1881): (303) 794-7711; www.awwa.org

Zoo and Aquarium Assn., American (1924): (301) 562-0777; www.aza.org

Lifestyle and Travel

AAA (American Automobile Assn.) (1902): (407) 444-7000; www.aaa.com

AARP. See Retired Persons, American Assn. of

AFS Intercultural Programs USA (1947): (212) 299-9000; www.afs.org/usa

Aircraft Owners and Pilots Assn. (1939): (800) 872-2672; www.aopa.org

Appalachian Mountain Club (1876): (617) 523-0655; www.outdoors.org

Boat Owners Assn. of the U.S. (1966): (703) 461-4666; www.boatus.com

Camping Assn., American (1910): (765) 342-8456; www.acacamps.org

Consumer Federation of America (1968): (202) 387-6121; www.consumerfed.org

Consumers Union of the U.S. (1914): (914) 378-2000; www.consumersunion.org

Green America (1982): (800) 584-7336; www.greenamericatoday.org.org

Helicopter Society, American (1944): (703) 684-6777; www.vtol.org

Hostelling Intl. USA (1934): (301) 495-1240; www.hiayh.org

Jewish Community Centers Assn. of North America (1917): (212) 532-4949; www.jcca.org

Motorcyclist Assn., American (1924): (800) 262-5646; www.amadirectlink.com

Nude Recreation, American Assn. for (1931): (407) 933-2064; www.aanr.com

Parents Without Partners, Inc. (1957): (561) 391-8833; www.parentswithoutpartners.org

Planetary Society (1980): (626) 793-5100; www.planetary.org

Retired Persons, American Assn. of (1958): (888) 687-2277; www.aarp.org

Scrabble® Assn., Natl. (1978): (631) 477-0033; www.scrabble-assoc.com

Sports Car Club of America (1944): (785) 357-7222; www.scca.org

Toastmasters Intl. (1924): (949) 858-8255; www.toastmasters.org

Travelers Protective Assn. of America (1890): (314) 371-0533; www.tpahq.org

YMCA (Young Men's Christian Assn.) of the USA (1851): (800) 872-9622; www.ymca.net

YWCA (Young Women's Christian Assn.) of the USA (1858): (202) 467-0801; www.ywca.org

Military and Veterans'

Air Force Assn. (1946): (703) 247-5800; www.afa.org

American Legion (1919): (317) 630-1200; www.legion.org

American Legion Auxiliary (1919): (317) 569-4500; www.legion-aux.org

AMVETS (American Veterans) (1944): (301) 459-9600; www.amvets.org

Army, Assn. of the United States (1950): (703) 841-4300; www.ausa.org

Blinded Veterans Assn. (1958): (202) 371-8880; www.bva.org

Civil Air Patrol (1941): (877) 227-9142; www.cap.gov

Coast Guard Combat Veterans Assn. (1985): (330) 887-5539; www.coastguard combatvets.com

Disabled American Veterans (1932): (859) 441-7300; www.dav.org

88th Infantry Division Assn. (1946): (508) 584-4169; www.88infdiv.org

82nd Airborne Division Assn., Inc. (1946): (910) 822-4534; www.82ndassociation.org

Ex-Prisoners of War, American (1942): (817) 649-2979; www.axpow.org

Fleet Reserve Association (1924): (703) 683-1400; www.fra.org

Jewish War Veterans of the U.S.A. (1896): (202) 265-6280; jwv.org

Legion of Valor Museum (1991): (559) 498-0510; www.legionofvalormuseum.org

Marine Corps League (1937): (703) 207-9588; www.mcleague.org

Military Officers Assn. (1929): (703) 549-2311; www.moaa.org

Military Order of the Purple Heart of the USA (1932): (703) 354-2140; www.purpleheart.org

Military Order of the World Wars (1919): (877) 320-3774; www.militaryorder.net

National Guard Assn. of the U.S. (1878): (202) 789-0031; www.ngaus.org

Naval Institute, U.S. (1873): (410) 268-6110; www.usni.org

Naval Reserve Assn. (1954): (866) 672-4968; www.navy-reserve.org

Navy League of the United States (1902): (703) 528-1775; www.navyleague.org

Ninety-Nines (Intl. Organization of Women Pilots) (1929): (405) 685-7969; www.ninety-nines.org

Non-Commissioned Officers Assn. (1960): (800) 662-2620; www.ncoausa.org

Paralyzed Veterans of America (1946): (800) 424-8200; www.pva.org

Reserve Officers Assn. of the U.S. (1922): (202) 479-2200; www.roa.org

Sons of the American Legion (1932): (317) 630-1200; www.sal.legion.org

Tin Can Sailors (1976): (508) 677-0515; www.destroyers.org

Uniformed Services, Natl. Assn. for (1968): (703) 750-1342; www.naus.org

USO World Headquarters (1941): (703) 908-6400; www.uso.org

USS Forrestal CVA/CV/AVT-59 Assn., Inc. (1990): (888) 434-5955; www.lancehatfield.com/cv59.htm

USS Missouri Memorial Assn., Inc. (1994): (808) 455-1600; www.ussmissouri.org

Veterans of Foreign Wars of the U.S. (1899): (816) 756-3390; www.vfw.org

Veterans of Foreign Wars of the U.S., Ladies Auxiliary to the (1914): (816) 756-3390; www.ladiesauxvfw.org

Veterans of the Vietnam War, Inc. (1978): (570) 603-9740; www.vvnw.org

War Mothers, American (1917): (202) 362-0090; www.americanwarmoms.org

Women's Army Corps Veterans Assn. (1946): www.armywomen.org

USS Idaho Assn. (1957), P.O. Box 711247, San Diego, CA 92171; 231

USS Los Angeles CA-135 Assn. (1977), c/o Jim Osborne, 1314 N. Alden Rd., Muncie, IN 47304; 365; www.uss-la-ca135.org

Political

Abortion Federation, National (1977): (202) 667-5881; www.prochoice.org

Advancement and Support of Education, Council for (1974): (202) 328-2273; www.case.org

American Indians, Natl. Congress of (1944): (202) 466-7767; www.ncai.org

American-Islamic Relations, Council on (1994): (202) 488-8787; www.cair.com

Cities, Natl. League of (1924): (202) 626-3000; www.nlc.org

Civil Liberties Union, American (ACLU) (1920): (888) 567-2258; www.aclu.org

Common Cause (1970): (202) 833-1200; www.commoncause.org

Concerned Women for America (1979): (202) 488-7000; www.cwfa.org

Congress of Racial Equality (CORE) (1942): (212) 598-4000; www.core-online.org

Conscientious Objectors, Central Committee for (1948): (510) 465-1617; www.objector.org

Crime and Delinquency, Natl. Council on (1907): (510) 208-0500; www.nccd-crc.org

Democratic Natl. Committee (1848): (202) 863-8000; www.democrats.org

Feminists for Life of America (1972): (703) 836-3354; www.feministsforlife.org

Gay & Lesbian Alliance Against Defamation (1985): (212) 629-3322; www.glaad.org

Gay and Lesbian Task Force, Natl. (1973): (202) 393-5177; www.thetaskforce.org

Governors' Assn., Natl. (1908): (202) 624-5300; www.nga.org

Grange Patrons of Husbandry, Natl. (1867): (202) 628-3507; www.nationalgrange.org

Gray Panthers (1970): (202) 737-6637; www.graypanthers.org

Green Party (1984): (866) 473-3672; www.greenparty.org

Homeless, Natl. Coalition for the (1984): (202) 462-4822; www.nationalhomeless.org

Japanese-American Citizens League (1929): (415) 921-5225; www.jacl.org

Jewish Committee, American (1906): (212) 751-4000; www.ajc.org

John Birch Society (1958): (920) 749-3780; www.jbs.org

Libertarian Party (1971): (202) 333-0008; www.lp.org

Mayors, U.S. Conference of (1932): (202) 293-7330; www.usmayors.org

Natl. Assn. for the Advancement of Colored People (NAACP) (1909): (410) 580-5777; www.naacp.org

Parliamentarians, Natl. Assn. of (1930): (816) 833-3892; www.parliamentarians.org

Reform Party of the U.S.A. (1995): (877) GO-REFORM; www.reformpartyusa.org

Republican National Committee (1856): (202) 863-8500; www.rnc.org

Rifle Assn., Natl. (1871): (800) 672-3888; www.nra.org

Science, American Assn. for the Advancement of (1848): (202) 326-6400; www.aaas.org

Southern Christian Leadership Conference (1957): (404) 522-1420; sclcnational.org

State Governments, Council of (1933): (859) 244-8000; www.csg.org

Tax Foundation (1937): (202) 464-6200; www.taxfoundation.org

Taxpayers Union, Natl. (1969): (703) 683-5700; www.ntu.org

Term Limits, U.S. (1992): (703) 383-0907; www.termlimits.org

Urban League, Natl. (1910): (212) 558-5300; www.nul.org

Women, Natl. Organization for (NOW) (1966): (202) 628-8669; www.now.org

Women and Families, Natl. Partnership for (1971): (202) 986-2600; www.nationalpartnership.org

Women's Christian Temperance Union, Natl. (1874): (847) 864-1397; www.wctu.org

Women Voters of the U.S., League of (1920): (202) 429-1965; www.lwv.org

Zionist Organization of America (1897): (212) 481-1500; www.zoa.org

Religious

African Methodist Episcopal Church (1787): 3801 Market St., Ste. 300, Philadelphia, PA 29204; (215) 662-0506; www.ame-church.com; Senior Bishop, Bishop Philip Robert Cousin

African Methodist Episcopal Zion Church (1796): 3225 West Sugar Creek Rd., Charlotte, NC 28269; (704) 688-2549; www.amez.org; Senior Bishop, George W. C. Walker Sr.

American Baptist Churches in the U.S.A. (1907): P.O. Box 851, Valley Forge, PA 19482; www.abc-usa.org; Pres., Arlee Griffin Jr.

Antiochian Orthodox Christian Archdiocese of North America (1895): 358 Mountain Rd., Englewood, NJ 07631; (201) 871-7954; www.antiochian.org; Primate, Archbishop Philip Saliba

Armenian Apostolic Church of America (1887): www.armprelacy.org; *Eastern Prelacy*: 138 E. 39th St., New York, NY 10016; (212) 689-7810; Prelate, Archbishop Oshagan Choloyan; *Western Prelacy*: 6252 Honolulu Ave., La Crescenta, CA 91214; (818) 248-7737; Prelate, Archbishop Moushegh Mardirossian

Assemblies of God (1914): 1445 N. Boonville Ave., Springfield, MO 65802; (417) 862-2781; www.ag.org/top; Gen. Supt., George O. Wood

Atheists, American (1963): P.O. Box 5733, Parsippany, NJ 07054; (908) 276-7300; www.atheists.org

Bahá'í Faith, National Spiritual Assembly of the Bahá'í's of the U.S. (1907): 1233 Central St., Evanston, IL 60201; (847) 733-3400; www.bahai.us; Sec. Gen., Dr. Robert C. Henderson

Baptist Bible Fellowship Intl. (1950): Baptist Bible Fellowship Missions Bldg., 720 E. Kearney St., Springfield, MO 65803; (417) 862-5001; www.bbfi.org; Pres., Rev. Bill Monroe

Baptist Convention, Southern (1845): 901 Commerce St., Nashville, TN 37203; (615) 244-2355; www.sbc.net; Pres. Frank Page

Baptist Convention, U.S.A., Inc., National (1895): 1700 Baptist World Center Dr., Nashville, TN 37207; (615) 228-6292; www.nationalbaptist.com; Pres., Dr. William J. Shaw

Baptist Convention of America, National (1880): 777 S.R.L. Thornton Freeway, Ste. 205, Dallas, TX 75203; (214) 946-8913; www.nbcamerica.net; Pres., Rev. Stephen J. Thurston

Baptist Convention of America, Natl. Missionary (1988): 4269 S. Figueroa St., Los Angeles, CA 90037; (323) 846-1950; www.nmbca.com; Pres., Dr. C. C. Robertson

Baptist General Conference (1852): 2002 S. Arlington Heights Rd., Arlington Heights, IL 60005; (847) 228-0200; www.bgcworld.org; Pres. and CEO, Dr. Gerald Sheveland

Bible Society, American (1816): 1865 Broadway, New York, NY 10023; (800) 322-4253; www.bibles.com

Biblical Literature, Society of (1880): 825 Houston Mill Rd., Atlanta, GA 30329; (404) 727-3100; www.sbl-site.org

B'nai B'rith Intl. (1843): 2020 K St. NW, 7th Fl., Washington, DC 20006; (202) 857-6600; www.bnaibrith.org

Brethren in Christ Church (1778): General Church Office, P.O. Box A, Grantham, PA 17027; (717) 697-2634; www.bic-church.org; Moderator, Dr. Warren L. Hoffman

Buddhist Churches of America (1899): 1710 Octavia St., San Francisco, CA 94109; (415) 776-5600; www.buddhistchurchesof america.com; Presiding Bishop, Socho Koshin Ogui

Christian Church (Disciples of Christ) (1832): Disciples Center, 130 E. Washington St., Indianapolis, IN 46206; (317) 635-3100; www.disciples.org; Pres., Rev. Dr. Sharon E. Watkins

Christian Churches and Churches of Christ, 4210 Bridgetown Rd., Box 11326, Cincinnati, OH 45211; (513) 598-6222; www.cctoday.org

Christian Methodist Episcopal Church (1870): First Memphis Plaza, 4466 Elvis Presley Blvd., Memphis, TN 38116; (216) 382-3559; www.c-m-e.org; Exec. Sec., Atty. Juanita Bryant

Church of the Brethren (1708): General Offices, 1451 Dundee Ave., Elgin, IL 60120; (847) 742-5100, ext. 206; www.brethren.org; Moderator, James M. Beckwith

Church of Christ (1830): Temple Lot, 200 S. River St., P.O. Box 472, Independence, MO 64051; (816) 833-3995; www.church-of-christ.com; Council of Apostles, Sec., Apostle Smith N. Brickhouse

Church of God (Anderson, IN) (1881): Box 2420, Anderson, IN 46018; (765) 642-0256; www.chog.org; Gen. Dir., Pres. Dr. Ronald V. Duncan

Church of God (Cleveland, TN) (1886): 2490 Keith St. NW, Cleveland, TN 37320; (423) 472-3361; www.churchofgod.org; Gen. Overseer, G. Dennis McGuire

Church of God in Christ (1897): Mason Temple, 938 Mason St., Memphis, TN 38126; (901) 947-9300; www.cogic.org; Presiding Bishop, Bishop C. E. Blake

Church of Jesus Christ (Bickertonites) (1862): 6th and Lincoln Sts., Monongahela, PA 15063; (412) 258-3066; Pres., Dominic Thomas

Church of Jesus Christ of Latter-day Saints, The (Mormons) (1830): 47 E. South Temple St., Salt Lake City, UT 84150; (801) 240-1000; www.lds.org; Pres., Gordon B. Hinckley

Church of the Nazarene (1907): 6401 The Paseo, Kansas City, MO 64131; (816) 333-7000; www.nazarene.org; Gen. Secy., David P. Wilson

Community of Christ (Reorganized Church of Jesus Christ of Latter-Day Saints) (1830): Intl. Headquarters, 1001 W. Walnut, Independence, MO 64050; www.CofChrist .org; Pres., Stephen M. Veazey

Community Churches, International Council of (1950): 21116 Washington Pkwy., Frankfort, IL 60423; (815) 464-5690; www.i cccusa.com; Exec. Dir., Michael Livingston

Conservative Judaism, United Synagogue of (1913): 820 Second Ave., New York, NY 10017; (212) 533-7800; www.uscj.org; Pres., Dr. Raymond B. Goldstein

Cumberland Presbyterian Church (1810): 1978 Union Ave., Memphis, TN 38104; (901) 276-4572; www.cumberland.org; Moderator, Rev. Frank Ward

Episcopal Church (1789): 815 Second Ave., New York, NY 10017; (212) 716-6240; www.ecusa.anglican.org; Presiding Bishop and Primate, Most Rev. Katharine Jefferts-Schori

Evangelical Lutheran Church in America (1987): 8765 W. Higgins Rd., Chicago, IL 60631; (773) 380-2700; www.elca.org; Presiding Bishop, Rev. Mark S. Hanson

First Church of Christ, Scientist, The (1879): 210 Massachusetts Ave., Boston, MA 02115; (617) 450-2000; www.tfccs.com; Pres., Barbara Vining

Free Methodist Church of North America (1860): World Ministries Center, 770 N. High School Rd., Indianapolis, IN 46214; (317) 244-1247; www.freemethodistchurch.org; The Board of Bishops

Freedom From Religion Foundation (1978): P.O. Box 750, Madison, WI 53701; (608) 256-8900; www.ffrf.org

Friends General Conference (1900): 1216 Arch St. 2B, Philadelphia, PA 19107; (215) 561-1700; www.fgcquaker.org; Gen. Sec., Bruce Birchard

Gideons Intl. (1899): P.O. Box 140800, Nashville, TN 37214; (615) 564-5000; www.gideons.org

Greek Orthodox Archdiocese of America (1922): 8-10 E. 79th St., New York, NY 10021; (212) 570-3500; www.goarch.org; Primate, Archbishop Demetrios

Hadassah, the Women's Zionist Organization of America (1912): 50 W. 58th St., New York, NY 10019; (888) 303-3640; www.hadassah.org

Interfaith Alliance, The (1994): 1212 New York Ave. NW, 7th Fl., Washington, DC 20005; (202) 238-3300; www.interfaithalliance.org

Islamic Society of North America: 6555 S. 750 East, Plainfield, IN 46168; (317) 839-8157; www.isna.net; Exec. Dir., Louay Safi

Jehovah's Witnesses (1884): 25 Columbia Heights, Brooklyn, NY 11201; (718) 560-5000; www.watchtower.org; Pres., Don Adams

Jewish Congress, American (1918): 825 Third Ave., New York, NY 10022; (212) 879-4500; www.ajcongress.org

Jewish Reconstructionist Federation (1955): Beit Devora, 101 Greenwood Ave., Ste. 340, Jenkintown, PA 19406; (215) 885-5601; www.jrf.org; Pres., Robert Barkin

Jewish Women, Natl. Council of (1893): 475 Riverside Dr., Ste. 520, New York, NY 10115; (212) 645-4048; www.ncjw.org

Lutheran Church—Missouri Synod (1847): 1333 S. Kirkwood Rd., St. Louis, MO 63122; (314) 996-1236; www.lcms.org; Pres., Dr. Gerald B. Kieschnick

Mennonite Brethren Churches, General Conference of (1860): 4812 E. Butler Ave., Fresno, CA, 93727; (209) 452-1713; Moderator, Ed Boschman

Mennonite Church USA (2001): 722 Main St., P.O. Box 347, Newton, KS 67114; (316) 283-5100; www.MennoniteChurchUSA.org; Moderator, Sharon Waltner

Moravian Church in North America (1735): www.moravian.org; *Northern Prov.*: 1021 Center St., P.O. Box 1245, Bethlehem, PA 18016; (610) 867-7566; Pres., David L. Wickmann; *Southern Prov.*: 459 S. Church St., Winston-Salem, NC 27101; (336) 725-5811; Pres., Rt. Rev. Wayne Burkette

North American Shi'a Muslim Communities Organization (NASIMCO) (1986) P.O. Box 29691, Minneapolis, MN 55429; (905) 763-7512; www.nasimco.org; Pres., Hussein Walji

Orthodox Jewish Congregations in America, Union of (1898): 11 Broadway, New York, NY 10004; (212) 563-4000; www.ou.org; Pres., Stephen J. Stavitsky

Pentecostal Assemblies of the World, Inc. (1925): 3939 Meadows Dr., Indianapolis, IN 46205; (317) 547-9541; www.pawinc.org; Presiding Bishop, Horace E. Smith

Presbyterian Church (U.S.A.) (1983): 100 Witherspoon St., Louisville, KY 40202; (888) 728-7228; www.pcusa.org; Exec. Dir., Linda Valentine

Progressive National Baptist Convention, Inc. (1961): 601 50th St. NE, Washington, DC 20019; (202) 396-0558; www.pnbc.org; Pres., Dr. T. DeWitt Smith Jr.

Rabbis, Central Conference of American (1889): 355 Lexington Ave., New York, NY 10017; (212) 972-3636; www.ccarnet.org

Reform Judaism, Union for (1873): 633 3rd Ave., New York, NY 10017; www.urj.org; (212) 650-4000; Pres., Rabbi Eric Yoffie

Roman Catholic Church (1634): U.S. Conference of Catholic Bishops, 3211 4th St. NE, Washington, DC 20017; (202) 541-3000; www.usccb.org; Gen. Sec., Msgr. David J. Malloy

Secular Humanism, Council for (1980): P.O. Box 664, Amherst, NY 14226; (716) 636-7571; www.secularhumanism.org

Separation of Church and State, Americans United for (1947): 518 C St. NE, Washington, DC 20002; (202) 466-3234; www.au.org

Seventh-day Adventist Church (1863): 12501 Old Columbia Pike, Silver Spring, MD 20904; (301) 680-6000; www.adventist.org; Pres., Jan Paulsen

Unitarian Universalist Association of Congregations (1961): 25 Beacon St., Boston, MA 02108; (617) 742-2100; www.uua.org; Pres., The Rev. William Sinkford

United Church of Christ (1957): 700 Prospect Ave., Cleveland, OH 44115; (216) 736-2100; www.ucc.org; Pres., Rev. John H. Thomas

United Methodist Church (1968): Council of Bishops, 100 Maryland Ave. NE, Washington, DC 20002; (615) 742-5406; www.umc.org; Pres. Bishop Peter D. Weaver

United Pentecostal Church Intl. (1945): 8855 Dunn Rd., Hazelwood, MO 63042; (314) 837-7300; www.upci.org; Gen. Supt. Rev. Kenneth F. Haney

Wesleyan Church (1968): P.O. Box 50434, Indianapolis, IN 46250; (317) 774-7900; www.wesleyan.org; Gen. Sec., Dr. Ronald D. Kelly

World Council of Churches, U.S. Office (1948): 475 Riverside Dr., Ste. 1370, New York, NY 10115; (212) 870-2533; www.wcc-usa.org

Businesses and Corporations

Listed below are major corporations offering products and services to U.S. consumers. Information as of Oct. 2009. Alphabetization is by first key word. Listings generally include examples of products offered.

Company Name (NYSE/NASDAQ symbol): Address; Telephone Number; Website; Top Executive; Business, Products, or Services.

A&P: see Great Atlantic & Pacific Tea Co.

Abbott Laboratories (ABT): 100 Abbott Park Rd., Abbott Park, IL 60064; (847) 937-6100; www.abbott.com; Miles D. White; develops and mfgr. pharmaceutical, nutritional, and hospital prods.

Advance Publications, Inc.: 950 Fingerboard Rd., Staten Island, NY, 10305; (718) 981-1234; www.advance.net; Samuel I. Newhouse Jr.; newspaper and magazine publisher (Parade; Condé Nast subsid.: New Yorker, Vanity Fair, Vogue).

Aetna, Inc. (AET): 151 Farmington Ave., Hartford, CT 06156; (860) 273-0123; www.aetna.com; Ronald A. Williams; health insurance, financial services.

Aflac, Inc. (AFL): 1932 Wynnton Rd., Columbus, GA 31999; (706) 323-3431; www.aflac.com; Daniel P. Amos; supplemental health and life insurance.

Alaska Air Group, Inc. (ALK): 19300 International Blvd., Seattle, WA 98188; (206) 392-5040; www.alaskaair.com; William S. Ayer; air travel (Alaska Airlines, Horizon Air).

Alberto Culver (ACV): 2525 Armitage Ave., Melrose Park, IL 60160; (708) 450-3000; www.alberto.com; Carol Lavin Bernick; personal care prods. (Alberto VO5, Nexxus, Noxzema), food prods. (Mrs. Dash).

Albertsons: see SUPERVALU.

Alcatel-Lucent (ALU): 54 rue La Boétie, Paris 75008, France; +33-1-40-76-10-10; www.alcatel-lucent.com; Philippe Camus; telecommunications equip.; wireless networks. France-based Alcatel merged with Lucent Technologies, 11/30/2006.

Alcoa Inc. (AA): 201 Isabella St., Pittsburgh, PA 15212; (412) 553-4545; www.alcoa.com; Alain J.P. Belda; aluminum products; aerospace & automotive components; industrial materials/tools.

Allegheny Technologies Inc. (ATI): 1000 Six PPG Place, Pittsburgh, PA 15222; (412) 394-2800; www.alleghenytechnologies.com; L. Patrick Hassey; metal mfgr. (steel, titanium, alloys).

Allstate Corp. (ALL): 2775 Sanders Rd., Northbrook, IL 60062; (847) 402-5000; www.allstate.com; Thomas J. Wilson; insurance (auto, homeowners, property/casualty, life); financial services.

Altria Group, Inc. (MO): 6601 West Broad St., Richmond, VA 23230; (807) 274-2200; www.altria.com. Michael E. Szymanczyk; largest U.S. tobacco company (Marlboro, Merit, Parliament, Virginia Slims). Spun off its Kraft Foods division, 3/16/2007; and its

Philip Morris International division, 3/28/2008. Acquired John Middleton, Inc. cigar co., 12/11/2007; acquired UST Inc. smokeless tobacco mfgr., 1/6/2009.

Amazon.com, Inc. (AMZN): 1200 12th Ave. S., Suite 1200, Seattle, WA 98144; (206) 266-1000; www.amazon.com; Jeffrey P. Bezos; online retailer of books, music, electronics, photo, and home and garden products.

American Electric Power Co., Inc. (AEP): 1 Riverside Plaza, Columbus, OH 43215; (614) 716-1000; www.aep.com; Michael G. Morris; utilities.

American Express Co. (AXP): World Financial Ctr., 200 Vesey St., NY, NY 10285; (212) 640-2000; www.american express.com; Kenneth I. Chenault; credit cards; travel and financial services.

American Greetings Corp. (AM): 1 American Rd., Cleveland, OH 44144; (216) 252-7300; www.americangreetings.com; Morry Weiss; greeting cards, stationery, party goods, gift items, photo services.

American Intl. Group, Inc. (AIG): 70 Pine St., NY, NY 10270; (212) 770-7000; www.aig corporate.com; Robert H. Benmosche; insurance, financial services; AIG received $85 bil govt. bailout, 9/16/2008; by July 2009, that amount had reached $182 billion.

American Standard Brands: 1 Centennial Ave., Piscataway, NJ 08855; (732) 980-6000; www.americanstandard-us.com; Donald C. Devine; kitchen and bath prods. Merger of American Standard America, Crane Plumbing, and Eljer, 3/6/2008.

AMR Corp. (AMR): 4333 Amon Carter Blvd., Ft. Worth, TX 76155; (817) 963-1234; www.aa.com; Gerard J. Arpey; one of the world's largest air carriers (American Airlines, American Eagle).

Anheuser-Busch Cos., Inc. (BUD): 1 Busch Pl., St. Louis, MO 63118; (314) 577-2000; www.anheuser-busch.com; Luiz F. Z. de Saint Edmond; world's largest brewer (Budweiser, Michelob, Busch, O'Doul's), aluminum can mfgr. and recycling; theme parks. U.S. subsidiary of Belgium-based Anheuser-Busch InBev. Takeover by InBev, 11/18/2008.

Apple Inc. (AAPL): 1 Infinite Loop, Cupertino, CA 95014; (408) 996-1010; www.apple.com; Steve Jobs; mfgr. computers (Mac), software, digital media devices (iPod, iPhone); distrib. digital media (iTunes store).

ARAMARK Corp.: 1101 Market St., Philadelphia, PA 19107; (215) 238-3000; www.aramark.com; Joseph Neubauer; food/support services, uniforms/career apparel, management svcs.

ArcelorMittal USA, Inc.: 3210 Watling St., East Chicago, IN 46312; (312) 899-3400; www.arcelormittal.com; Michael G. Rippey; U.S. subsidiary of Netherlands-based Arcelor Mittal, world's largest steel co.

Archer Daniels Midland Co. (ADM): 4666 Faries Pkwy., Decatur, IL 62525; (217) 424-5200; www.admworld.com; Patricia A. Woertz; agricultural commodities and prods.

Armstrong World Industries, Inc. (AWI): 2500 Columbia Ave., Lancaster, PA 17603; (717) 397-0611; www.armstrong.com; Michael D. Lockhart; carpeting, flooring, interior furnishings, building prods; emerged from Chap. 11, 10/2/2006.

ArvinMeritor, Inc. (ARM): 2135 W. Maple Rd., Troy, MI 48084; (248) 435-1000; www.arvinmeritor.com; Charles G. McClure Jr.; auto control systems; vehicle components.

Ashland Inc. (ASH): 50 E. RiverCenter Blvd., Covington, KY 41012; (859) 815-3333; www.ashland.com; James J. O'Brien Jr.; petroleum producer and refiner (Valvoline, plastics), chemicals, road construction. Acquired Hercules, 11/13/2008.

AT&T Inc. (T): 208 S. Akard St., Dallas, TX 75202; (210) 821-4105; www.att.com; Randall L. Stephenson.; telecommunications, global information management. Merger of SBC Communications and AT&T Corp. finalized, 11/18/2005; acquired BellSouth, 12/29/2006.

AutoNation, Inc. (AN): 110 SE 6th St., Ft. Lauderdale, FL 33301; (954) 769-6000; www.autonation.com; Michael J. Jackson; new and used auto vehicles; auto parts, maintenance, and repair; auto protection products.

Avon Products, Inc. (AVP): 1345 Ave. of the Americas, NY, NY 10105; (212) 282-5000; www.avon.com; Andrea Jung; cosmetics, fragrances, toiletries, jewelry, apparel.

Bank of America Corp. (BAC): Bank of America Corporate Center, 100 N. Tryon St., Charlotte, NC 28255; (704) 386-5681; www.bankofamerica.com; Kenneth D. Lewis. Acquired U.S. Trust, 7/2/2007; acquired LaSalle Bank, 10/1/2007; acquired Countrywide Financial, 7/1/2008; acquired Merrill Lynch, 1/1/2009.

Barnes & Noble, Inc. (BKS): 122 Fifth Ave., NY, NY 10011; (212) 633-3300; www.barnesandnobleinc.com; Leonard S. Riggio; leading U.S. bookstore chain (Barnes & Noble, B. Dalton stores), publishing (Sterling Pub. Co.).

Bausch & Lomb Inc.: One Bausch & Lomb Place, Rochester, NY 14604; (585) 338-6000; www.bausch.com; Gerald M. Ostrov; vision and health-care prods., surgical equip. Acquired by Warburg Pincus, 10/26/2007.

Baxter International Inc. (BAX): 1 Baxter Pkwy., Deerfield, IL 60015; (847) 948-2000; www.baxter.com; Robert Parkinson Jr.; health care prods. & services.

Bear Stearns Cos. Inc.: see JPMorgan Chase.

Becton, Dickinson & Co. (BDX): 1 Becton Dr., Franklin Lakes, NJ 07417; (201) 847-6800; www.bd.com; Edward J. Ludwig; medical, laboratory, diagnostic prods.

BellSouth Corp.: see AT&T Inc.

Berkshire Hathaway Inc. (BRK.A): 3555 Farnam St., Ste. 1440, Omaha, NE 68131; (402) 346-1400; www.berkshire hathaway.com; Warren E. Buffett; subsidiaries include GEICO, Johns Manville building materials, Fruit of the Loom apparel, Dairy Queen restaurants/desserts, Benjamin Moore & Co. paints, Shaw flooring.

Bertelsmann AG: Carl-Bertelsmann-Strasse 270, D-33311 Gütersloh, Germany; +49-5241-80-0; www.bertelsmann.de; Gunter Thielen; largest trade book publisher (Random House: Knopf, Ballantine, Bantam, Crown, Doubleday). Sold stake in Sony BMG to Sony Corp., 10/1/2008.

Best Buy Co., Inc. (BBY): 7601 Penn Ave. S., Richfield, MN 55423; (612) 291-1000; www.bestbuy.com; Richard M. Schulze; retailer of software, appliances, consumer electronics, cameras, music, DVDs.

Blackstone Group, LP (BX): 345 Park Ave., NY, NY 10154; (212) 583-5000; www.blackstone.com; Stephen Schwarzman; asset mgmt., financial services.

Black & Decker Corp. (BDK): 701 E. Joppa Rd., Towson, MD 21286; (410) 716-3900; www.bdk.com; Nolan D. Archibald; one of the top U.S. mfgrs. of power tools (DeWalt, Black & Decker), household prods. (Kwikset locks, Price Pfister faucets, Black & Decker small appliances).

H&R Block, Inc. (HRB): 1 H&R Block Way, Kansas City, MO 64105; (816) 854-3000; www.hrblock.com; Russ Smyth; tax return preparation, software; insurance.

Blockbuster Inc. (BBI): 1201 Elm St., Dallas, TX 75270; (214) 854-3000; www.blockbuster.com; James W. Keyes; DVD and video game rental; online rental, purchases.

Boeing Co. (BA): 100 N. Riverside Plaza, Chicago, IL 60606; (312) 544-2000; www.boeing.com; W. James McNerney Jr.; world's largest aerospace co.; world's 2nd-largest mfgr. of commercial jet aircraft; 2nd-largest U.S. defense contractor.

The Brink's Co. (BCO): 1801 Bayberry Ct., Richmond, VA 23226; (804) 289-9600; www.brinkscompany.com; Michael T. Dan; security (armored cars, alarm systems). Completed spin-off of Home Security into a publicly traded company, 10/31/2008.

Bristol-Myers Squibb Co. (BMY): 345 Park Ave., NY, NY 10154; (212) 546-4000; www.bms.com; James M. Cornelius; drugs (Plavix, Avapro, Abilify).

Brown-Forman Corp. (BFB): 850 Dixie Hwy., Louisville, KY 40210; (502) 585-1100; www.brown-forman.com; Paul C. Varga; distilled spirits (Jack Daniel's, Southern Comfort), wines (Bolla, Fetzer, Korbel).

Brown Shoe Co., Inc. (BWS): 8300 Maryland Ave., St. Louis, MO 63105; (314) 854-4000; www.brownshoe.com; Ronald A. Fromm; mfgr. and retailer of (Famous Footwear) of women's, men's, and children's shoes (Buster Brown, Naturalizer, Dr. Scholl's).

Brunswick Corp. (BC): 1 N. Field Ct., Lake Forest, IL 60045; (847) 735-4700; www.brunswick.com; Dustan McCoy; largest U.S. maker of leisure and recreation prods., incl. marine, billiards, and fitness equip.; bowling centers and equip.

Burger King Holdings, Inc. (BKC): 5505 Blue Lagoon Dr., Miami, FL 33126; (305) 378-3000; www.burgerking.com; John W. Chidsey; fast-food restaurants.

Burlington Northern Santa Fe Corp. (BNI): 2650 Lou Menk Dr., Ft. Worth, TX 76131; (817) 352-1000; www.bnsf.com; Matthew K. Rose; U.S. rail transportation co.

Cablevision Systems Corp. (CVC): 1111 Stewart Ave., Bethpage, NY 11714; (516) 803-2300; www.cablevision.com; James L. Dolan; cable & VoIP provider; cable channels (AMC, Fuse, IFC, WE); sports teams (NY Knicks, NY Rangers); arenas.

Cadbury plc (CBY): Cadbury House, Sanderson Rd., Uxbridge Business Pk., Uxbridge, London UB8 1DH, UK; +44-18-9561-5000; www.cadbury.com; Todd Stitzer; world's largest candy mfgr. by market share (Dentyne, Trident, Halls, Green & Black's). Created from separation of Cadbury Schweppes into Cadbury and Dr Pepper Snapple Group, 5/7/2008.

Campbell Soup Co. (CPB): One Campbell Pl., Camden, NJ 08103; (856) 342-4800; www.campbellsoup.com; Douglas R. Conant; world's largest soup mfgr., sauces (Pace, Prego), V8 juice, Pepperidge Farm baked goods.

Caterpillar Inc. (CAT): 100 NE Adams St., Peoria, IL 61629; (309) 675-1000; www.cat.com; James W. Owens; world's largest producer of earth-moving equip; mfgr. agricultural equip.

CBS Corp. (CBS): 51 W. 52nd St., NY, NY 10019; (212) 975-4321; www.cbs corporation.com; Sumner Redstone; TV stations, networks (CBS, Showtime); distrib. TV shows (Paramount, King World); radio stations; book publishing (Simon & Schuster). Split from parent co. Viacom, 12/31/2005.

Chevron Corp. (CVX): 6001 Bollinger Canyon Rd., San Ramon, CA 94583; (925) 842-1000; www.chevron.com; David J. O'Reilly; 2nd-largest integrated-energy co. in U.S.; acquired Unocal, 8/10/2005.

Chiquita Brands International, Inc. (CQB): 250 E. 5th St., Cincinnati, OH 45202; (513) 784-8000; www.chiquita.com; Fernando Aguirre; bananas; other fruits/vegetables.

Church & Dwight Co., Inc. (CHD): 469 N. Harrison St., Princeton, NJ 08543; (609) 683-5900; www.churchdwight.com; James R. Craigie; world's largest producer of sodium bicarbonate (ARM & HAMMER baking soda); household products (Brillo, SpinBrush); personal care products (Arrid antiperspirant, Trojan condoms, First Response pregnancy tests).

CIGNA Corp. (CI): 2 Liberty Pl., 1601 Chestnut St., Philadelphia, PA 19192; (215) 761-1000; www.cigna.com; H. Edward Hanway; accident, health, life insurance provider.

Cintas Corp. (CTAS): 6800 Cintas Blvd., Cincinnati, OH 45262; (513) 459-1200; www.cintas.com; Scott D. Farmer; largest U.S. uniform supplier; laundry services.

Circuit City Stores, Inc.: see Systemax Inc.

Cisco Systems, Inc. (CSCO): 170 West Tasman Dr., Bldg. 10, San Jose, CA 95134; (408) 526-4000; www.cisco.com; John T. Chambers; networking and communication products.

Citigroup, Inc. (C): 399 Park Ave., NY, NY 10043; (212) 559-1000; www.citigroup.com; Vikram Pandit; diversified financial services. Announced plans to realign into 2 businesses (Citicorp and Citi Holdings), 1/16/2009.

Clear Channel Communications, Inc. (CCMO): 200 E. Basse Rd., San Antonio, TX 78209; (210) 822-2828; www.clearchannel.com; Mark P. Mays; largest radio station owner in U.S. (850+ stations); outdoor advertising (billboards, mass transit ads). Acquired by CC Media Holdings, 7/30/2008.

Clorox Co. (CLX): 1221 Broadway, Oakland, CA 94612; (510) 271-7000; www.clorox.com; Donald R. Knauss; retail consumer prods. (Clorox, Formula 409, Pine-Sol, S.O.S., Tilex; ArmorAll, STP automotive prods.; Scoop Away, Fresh Step cat litters; Kingsford charcoal; Hidden Valley dressing; Glad plastic bags; Brita water systems; Burt's Bees personal care prods.).

Coca-Cola Co. (KO): 1 Coca-Cola Plaza, Atlanta, GA 30313; (404) 676-2121; www.coca-cola.com; Muhtar Kent; world's largest soft drink co. (Coca-Cola, Sprite, Dasani water, POWERade), world's largest dist. of juice prods. (Minute Maid).

Colgate-Palmolive Co. (CL): 300 Park Ave., NY, NY 10022; (212) 310-2000; www.colgate.com; Ian M. Cook; soap (Irish Spring), detergent (Palmolive), household cleansers (Ajax), toothpaste (Colgate, Tom's of Maine), pet food (Hill's Science Diet).

Collective Brands, Inc. (PSS): 3231 SE 6th Ave., Topeka, KS 66607; (785) 233-5171; www.collectivebrandsinc.com; Matthew E. Rubel; shoe mfgr./retailer. Formed by acquisition of StrideRite by Payless ShoeSource, 8/17/2007.

Comcast Corp. (CMCSA): 1 Comcast Ctr., Philadelphia, PA 19103; (215) 286-1700; www.comcast.com; Brian L. Roberts; largest U.S. cable company; broadband cable, internet, and voice services. Some programming (E!, Golf Channel).

Compaq Computer Corp.: see Hewlett-Packard Co.

CompUSA Inc.: see Systemax Inc.

Computer Sciences Corp. (CSC): 3170 Fairview Park Dr., Falls Church, VA 22042; (703) 876-1000; www.csc.com; Michael W. Laphen; technology services.

ConAgra Foods, Inc. (CAG): 1 ConAgra Dr., Omaha, NE 68102; (402) 595-4000; www.conagrafoods.com; Gary M. Rodkin; food processor (Chef Boyardee, Healthy Choice frozen dinners, Egg Beaters, Reddi-wip); food service supplier.

ConocoPhillips Co. (COP): 600 N. Dairy Ashford Rd., P.O. Box 2197, Houston, TX 77079; (281) 293-1000; www.conocophillips.com; James J. Mulva; 2nd-largest U.S. oil and gas company.

Consolidated Edison, Inc. (ED): 4 Irving Pl., New York, NY 10003; (212) 460-4600; www.conedison.com; Kevin Burke; electric, natural gas utilities.

Continental Airlines, Inc. (CAL): 1600 Smith St., Dept. HQSEO, Houston, TX 77002; (713) 324-2950; www.continental.com; Lawrence W. Kellner; air transportation.

Corning Inc. (GLW): 1 Riverfront Plaza, Corning, NY 14831; (607) 974-9000; www.corning.com; Wendell P. Weeks; mfgr. of telecommunications, specialty equipment, fiber optics.

Countrywide Financial: see Bank of America.

Costco Wholesale Corp. (COST): 999 Lake Dr., Issaquah, WA 98027; (425) 313-8100; www.costco.com; James D. Sinegal; wholesale warehouse stores.

Crane Co. (CR): 100 First Stamford Pl., Stamford, CT 06902; (203) 363-7300; www.craneco.com; Eric C. Fast; manuf. fluid control devices, vending machines, aircraft components.

A. T. Cross Co. (ATX): 1 Albion Rd., Lincoln, RI 02865; (401) 333-1200; www.cross.com; David G. Whalen; writing instruments, timepieces, personal accessories.

Crown Holdings, Inc. (CCK): 1 Crown Way, Philadelphia, PA 19154; (215) 698-5100; www.crowncork.com; John W. Conway; leading producer of packaging prods.

CSX Corp. (CSX): 500 Water St., 15th Fl., Jacksonville, FL 32202; (904) 359-3200; www.csx.com; Michael J. Ward; rail and road freight transport.

CVS Caremark Corp. (CVS): 1 CVS Dr., Woonsocket, RI 02895; (401) 765-1500; www.cvs.com; Thomas M. Ryan. Acquired Eckerd Corp. in Aug. 2004, to become nation's largest drugstore chain; announced acquisition of Long Drug Stores Corp., 8/12/2008.

Dana Holding Corp. (DAN): 4500 Dorr St., Toledo, OH 43615; (419) 535-4500; www.dana.com; John M. Devine; truck and auto parts, supplies; emerged from Chap. 11 reorganization, 2/1/2008.

Darden Restaurants, Inc. (DRI): 5900 Lake Ellenor Dr., Orlando, FL 32809; (407) 245-4000; www.dardenrestaurants.com; Clarence Otis Jr.; casual-dining restaurants (Red Lobster, Olive Garden).

Dean Foods Co. (DF): 2515 McKinney Ave., Ste. 1200, Dallas, TX 75201; (214) 303-3400; www.deanfoods.com; Gregg L. Engles; milk and specialty dairy products (Land O Lakes, Horizon Organic, Silk soy milk), yogurt (Mountain High).

Deere & Co. (DE): One John Deere Pl., Moline, IL 61265; (309) 765-8000; www.deere.com; Robert W. Lane; one of the world's largest mfgrs. of farm equip.; mfgr. industrial equip., lawn and garden tractors.

Dell Inc. (DELL): 1 Dell Way, Round Rock, TX 78682; (512) 338-4400; www.dell.com; Michael S. Dell; laptop and desktop computers, network accessories, peripherals.

Del Monte Foods Co. (DLM): One Market @ The Landmark, San Francisco, CA 94105; (415) 247-3000; www.delmonte.com; Richard G. Wolford; canned food (College Inn, Del Monte, Contadina); pet food (9Lives, Gravy Train, Milk-Bone, Meow Mix).

Delphi Corp. (DPHI): 5725 Delphi Dr., Troy, MI 48098; (248) 813-2000; www.delphi.com; Robert S. Miller Jr.; automotive systems, audio systems, mobile electronics; began Chap. 11 reorganization, 10/8/2005.

Delta Air Lines, Inc. (DAL): 1030 Delta Blvd., Atlanta, GA 30320; (404) 715-2600; www.delta.com; Edward H. Bastian; world's largest airline; emerged from Chap. 11, 4/30/2007; merged with Northwest Airlines, 10/29/2008.

Dial Corp.: 15501 N. Dial Blvd., Scottsdale, AZ 85260; (480) 754-3425; www.dialcorp.com; Bradley A. Casper; consumer prods. (Dial soap, Purex detergent, Right Guard antiperspirant, Renuzit air fresheners); U.S. subsidiary of Germany's Henkel company.

Diebold, Inc. (DBD): 5995 Mayfair Rd., North Canton, OH 44720; (330) 490-4000; www.diebold.com; Thomas W. Swidarski; mfgr. ATMs, security systems and prods.

Dillard's, Inc. (DDS): 1600 Cantrell Rd., Little Rock, AR 72201; (501) 376-5200; www.dillards.com; William Dillard II; dept. store chain.

Walt Disney Co. (DIS): 500 S. Buena Vista St., Burbank, CA 91521; (818) 560-1000; disney.go.com; Robert A. Iger; 2nd-largest media conglomerate; motion pictures (Touchstone, Pixar, Miramax); television (ESPN, ABC, Disney Channel); radio stations; theme parks (Walt Disney World, Disneyland); resorts; publishing; recordings. Agreed to acquire Marvel Entertainment, 8/31/2009.

Doctor's Associates Inc.: 325 Bic Dr., Milford, CT 06461; (203) 877-4281; www.subway.com; Frederick A. DeLuca; restaurants (Subway).

Dole Food Co., Inc.: One Dole Dr., Westlake Village, CA 91362; (818) 879-6600; www.dole.com; David H. Murdock; food prods., fresh fruits and vegetables. Announced plans to go public through an IPO, 8/14/2009.

R. R. Donnelley & Sons Co. (RRD): 111 S. Wacker Dr., Chicago, IL 60606; (312) 326-8000; www.rrdonnelley.com; Thomas J. Quinlan III; commercial printing; photos/graphics, translation; printer of *The World Almanac.*

Dow Chemical Co. (DOW): 2030 Dow Center, Midland, MI 48674; (989) 636-1000; www.dow.com; Andrew N. Liveris; chemicals, plastics (world's 2nd-largest chemical co.). Acquired Rohm and Haas, 4/1/2009.

Dow Jones & Co., Inc.: see News Corp.

Dr Pepper Snapple Group, Inc. (DPS): 5301 Legacy Dr., Plano, TX 75024; (972) 673-7000; www.drpeppersnapplegroup.com; Wayne R. Sanders; bottler and distributor of non-alcoholic beverages (Dr Pepper, Hawaiian Punch, 7UP, Snapple, Mott's). Created from separation of Cadbury Schweppes into Cadbury and Dr Pepper Snapple Group, 5/7/2008.

Duke Energy Corp. (DUK): 526 S. Church St., Charlotte, NC 28202; (704) 594-6200; www.duke-energy.com; James E. Rogers; utilities, fiber optics networks.

Dun & Bradstreet Corp. (DNB): 103 JFK Pkwy., Short Hills, NJ 07078; (973) 921-5500; www.dnb.com; Steven W. Alesio; business information, research.

E. I. du Pont de Nemours & Co. (Dupont) (DD): 1007 Market St., Wilmington, DE 19898; (302) 774-1000; www.dupont.com; Ellen J. Kullman; 3rd-largest U.S. chemical co.; petroleum, consumer prods.

Eastman Kodak Co. (EK): 343 State St., Rochester, NY 14650; (585) 724-4000; www.kodak.com; Antonio M. Perez; film; digital cameras; printers.

Eaton Corp. (ETN): Eaton Ctr., 1111 Superior Ave., Cleveland, OH 44114; (216) 523-5000; www.eaton.com; Alexander Cutler; mfgr. vehicle components, controls.

eBay Inc. (EBAY): 2145 Hamilton Ave., San Jose, CA 95125; (408) 376-7400; www.ebay.com; John Donahoe; online auctions. Acquired StubHub.com, 2/13/2007.

Edison Intl. (EIX): 2244 Walnut Grove Ave., Rosemead, CA 91770; (626) 302-2222; www.edison.com; Theodore F. Craver Jr.; electric utilities.

Electronic Arts Inc. (ERTS): 209 Redwood Shores Pkwy., Redwood City, CA 94065; (650) 628-1500; www.ea.com; Lawrence F. Probst III; leading U.S. video game publisher (Madden NFL, Battlefield, The Sims).

Electronic Data Systems: see Hewlett-Packard.

Eli Lilly and Co. (LLY): Lilly Corporate Center, 893 S. Delaware, Indianapolis, IN 46285; (317) 276-2000; www.lilly.com; John C. Lechleiter; pharmaceutical research, development, and manufacturing (Prozac, Strattera, Cialis).

El Paso Corp. (EP): 1001 Louisiana St., Houston, TX 77002; (713) 420-2600; www.elpaso.com; Ronald L. Kuehn Jr.; natural gas/oil transportation, storage, exploration, production.

EMC Corp. (EMC): 176 South St., Hopkinton, MA 01748; (508) 435-1000; www.emc.com; Joseph M. Tucci; data storage/protection.

Emerson Electric Co. (EMR): 8000 W. Florissant Ave., St. Louis, MO 63136; (314) 553-2000; www.gotoemerson.com; David Farr; electrical, electronics prods. & systems.

Energizer Holdings, Inc. (ENR): 533 Maryville Univ. Dr., St. Louis, MO 63141; (314) 985-2000; www.energizer.com; Ward M. Klein; batteries, flashlights.

Estée Lauder Cos. Inc. (EL): 767 5th Ave., NY, NY 10153; (212) 572-4200; www.elcompanies.com; William P. Lauder; cosmetics (Clinique, Bobbi Brown), fragrance, skin care prods.

Exelon Corp. (EXC): 10 S. Dearborn St., 37th Fl., Chicago, IL 60680; (312) 394-7398; www.exeloncorp.com; John W. Rowe; electricity generation/distribution; natural gas.

Exxon Mobil Corp. (XOM): 5959 Las Colinas Blvd., Irving, TX 75039; (972) 444-1000; www.exxon.mobil.com; Rex W. Tillerson; world's largest integrated oil co.

Federal Home Loan Mortgage Corp. (Freddie Mac) (FRE): 8200 Jones Branch Dr., McLean, VA 22102; (703) 903-2000; www.freddiemac.com; Charles E. Haldeman Jr.; residential mortgage provider. Taken over by U.S. government, 9/7/2008.

Federal National Mortgage Association (Fannie Mae) (FNM): 3900 Wisconsin Ave. NW, Washington, DC 20016; (202) 752-7000; www.fanniemae.com; Michael J. Williams; largest U.S. provider of residential mortgage funds. Taken over by U.S. government, 9/7/2008.

FedEx Corp. (FDX): 942 S. Shady Grove Rd., Memphis, TN 38120; (901) 818-7500; www.fedex.com; Frederick W. Smith; world's largest express delivery service.

First Data Corp.: 6200 S. Quebec St., Greenwood Village, CO, 80111; (303) 967-8000; www.firstdatacorp.com; Michael D. Capellas; financial transaction processing. Acquired by Kohlberg Kravis Roberts & Co., 9/24/2007.

FirstEnergy Corp. (FE): 76 S. Main St., Akron, OH 44308; (800) 633-4766; www.firstenergycorp.com; Anthony J. Alexander; public electricity supplier.

Fleetwood Enterprises, Inc. (FLE): 3125 Myers St., Riverside, CA 92503; (951) 351-3500; www.fleetwood.com; Elden L. Smith; manufactured homes. Filed for Chap. 11 reorganization, 3/10/2009.

Fluor Corp. (FLR): 6700 Las Colinas Blvd., Irving, TX 75039; (469) 398-7000; www.fluor.com; Alan L. Boeckmann; international engineering and construction co.

Foot Locker, Inc. (FL): 112 W. 34th St., NY, NY 10120; (212) 720-3700; www.footlocker-inc.com; Matthew D. Serra; retail athletic stores (Footaction, Foot Locker, Champs Sports).

Ford Motor Co. (F): 1 American Rd., Dearborn, MI 48126; (313) 322-3000; www.ford.com; William C. Ford Jr.; auto mfgr.; motor vehicle sales (Ford, Lincoln, Mercury, Volvo); largest U.S. auto. finance co. (Ford Motor Credit).

Fortune Brands, Inc. (FO): 520 Lake Cook Rd., Deerfield, IL 60015; (847) 484-4400; www.fortunebrands.com; Bruce A. Carbonari; spirits and wine (Jim Beam, Courvoisier, Sauza); home and hardware prods. (Moen, Master Lock); golf and leisure prods. (Titleist, Cobra, FootJoy).

Gannett Co., Inc. (GCI): 7950 Jones Branch Dr., McLean, VA 22107; (703) 854-6000; www.gannett.com; Craig A. Dubow; largest U.S. newspaper publisher (*USA Today*); network and cable TV.

Gap Inc. (GPS): 2 Folsom St., San Francisco, CA 94105; (650) 952-4400; www.gap.com; Glenn K. Murphy; casual apparel retailer (Gap, Banana Republic, Old Navy).

Gateway, Inc.: 7565 Irvine Ctr. Dr., Irvine, CA 92618; (949) 471-7000; www.gateway.com; personal computers, network servers, peripherals; acquired by Taiwan's Acer, Inc., 10/16/2007.

General Dynamics Corp. (GD): 2941 Fairview Park Dr., Ste. 100, Falls Church, VA 22042; (703) 876-3000; www.gendyn.com; Nicholas D. Chabraja; defense contractor: aerospace, combat systems, marine systems, computing devices.

General Electric Co. (GE): 3135 Easton Tpke., Fairfield, CT 06828; (203) 373-2211; www.ge.com; Jeffrey Immelt; electrical, electronic equip., financial services, radio and TV broadcasting (NBC, Bravo, USA, Telemundo), aircraft engines, power generation, appliances.

General Mills, Inc. (GIS): One General Mills Blvd., Minneapolis, MN 55426; (763) 764-7600; www.generalmills.com; Kendall J. Powell; food mfgr. (Betty Crocker, Bisquick, Cheerios, Chex, Colombo, Green Giant, Haagen-Dazs, Pillsbury, Progresso, Total, Wheaties).

General Motors Co. (GM): 300 Renaissance Ctr., Detroit, MI 48265; (313) 556-5000; www.gm.com; Frederick A. Henderson; world's largest auto mfgr. (Chevrolet, Cadillac, Buick, GMC); auto financing (GMAC). General Motors Corp. filed for Chap. 11 reorganization, 6/1/2009; sold its profitable components to a new, smaller company called General Motors Co., 7/10/2009.

Genuine Parts Co. (GPC): 2999 Circle 75 Pkwy., Atlanta, GA 30339; (770) 953-1700; www.genpt.com; Thomas C. Gallagher; auto replacement parts distributor (NAPA).

Goldman Sachs Group, Inc. (GS): 85 Broad St., NY, NY 10004; (212) 902-1000; www.goldmansachs.com; Lloyd C. Blankfein; investment banking, asset management, securities services.

Goodyear Tire & Rubber Co. (GT): 1144 E. Market St., Akron, OH 44316; (330) 796-2121; www.goodyear.com; Robert Keegan; tires and other auto prods.

Google, Inc. (GOOG): 1600 Amphitheatre Pkwy., Mountain View, CA 94043; (650) 253-0000; www.google.com; Eric E. Schmidt; leading internet search engine. Acquired YouTube, 10/9/2006, DoubleClick, 3/11/2008.

W. R. Grace & Co. (GRA): 7500 Grace Dr., Columbia, MD 21044; (410) 531-4000; www.grace.com; Alfred E. Festa; chemicals, construction prods.

Great Atlantic & Pacific Tea Co., Inc. (GAP): 2 Paragon Dr., Montvale, NJ 07645; (201) 573-9700; www.aptea.com; Christian Haub; supermarkets (A&P, The Food Emporium, Super Fresh, Waldbaum's, Pathmark). Acquired Pathmark, 12/3/2007.

Halliburton Co. (HAL): 5 Houston Center, 1401 McKinney St., Ste. 2400, Houston, TX 77010; (713) 759-2600; www.halliburton.com; David J. Lesar; oil field mgmt., energy services. Split off subsidiary KBR, Inc., 4/5/2007.

Hanesbrands Inc. (HBI): 1000 E. Hanes Mill Rd., Winston-Salem, NC 27105; (336) 519-4400; www.hanesbrands.com; Richard A. Knoll; apparel mfgr. (Hanes, L'eggs, Just My Size, Playtex, Wonderbra). Spun off from parent co. Sara Lee Corp., 9/5/2006.

Harley-Davidson, Inc. (HOG): 3700 W. Juneau Ave., Milwaukee, WI 53208; (414) 342-4680; www.harley-davidson.com; Keith E. Wandell; mfgr. motorcycles, parts, and accessories.

Harrah's Entertainment, Inc.: One Caesars Palace Dr., Las Vegas, NV 89109; (702) 407-6000; www.harrahs.com; Gary W. Loveman; casino-hotels (Bally's, Caesars), riverboats (Showboat). Acquired by Apollo Mgmt. and Texas Pacific Group, 1/28/2008.

Hartford Financial Services Group, Inc. (HIG): One Hartford Plaza, Hartford, CT 06155; (860) 547-5000; www.the hartford.com; Ramani Ayer; insurance, financial services.

Hartmarx Corp.: 101 N. Wacker Dr., Chicago, IL 60606; (312) 372-6300; www.hartmarx.com; apparel mfgr. (Hart Schaffner & Marx, Hickey-Freeman). Acquired by Emerisque Brands UK and SKNL North America, 8/7/2009.

Hasbro, Inc. (HAS): 1027 Newport Ave., Pawtucket, RI 02862; (401) 431-8697; www.hasbro.com; Alfred J. Verrecchia; toy and game mfgr. (Milton Bradley, Playskool, G.I. Joe, Parker Bros., Nerf, Play-Doh).

HCA Inc.: 1 Park Plaza, Nashville, TN 37203; (615) 344-9551; www.hcahealthcare.com; Jack O. Bovender Jr.; largest hospital mgmt. co. in the U.S.

H. J. Heinz Co. (HNZ): 1 PPG Place, Ste. 3100, Pittsburgh, PA 15222; (412) 456-5700; www.heinz.com; William R. Johnson; food mfgr. (Ore-Ida, 57 Varieties ketchup, Weight Watchers foods).

Hershey Co. (HSY): 100 Crystal A Dr., Hershey, PA 17033; (717) 534-4200; www.hersheys.com; David J. West; largest North American producer of chocolate prods. (Reese's, Kit Kat, Mounds, Almond Joy, Jolly Rancher, Twizzlers, Milk Duds, Good & Plenty).

Hertz Global Holdings, Inc. (HTZ): 225 Brae Blvd., Park Ridge, NJ 07656; (201) 307-2000; www.hertz.com; Mark P. Frissora; car rentals.

Hess Corp. (HES): 1185 Ave. of the Americas, NY, NY 10036; (212) 997-8500; www.hess.com; John B. Hess; integrated oil and gas co.

Hewlett-Packard Co. (HPQ): 3000 Hanover St., Palo Alto, CA 94304; (650) 857-1501; www.hp.com; Mark V. Hurd; computers, electronic prods. and systems. Merged with Compaq, 5/3/2002. Acquired Electronic Data Systems, 8/26/2008.

Hillenbrand, Inc. (HI): One Batesville Blvd., Batesville, IN 47006; (812) 934-7000; www.hillenbrandinc.com; Kenneth A. Camp; holder of Batesville Caskets, coffin mfgr. Spun off from Hill-Rom Holdings, 4/1/2008.

Hill-Rom Holdings, Inc. (HRC): 1069 State Rte. 46 E., Batesville, IN 47006; (812) 934-7777; www.hillenbrand.com; Rolf A. Classon; mfgr. hospital beds, other hospital equip. Hill-Rom separated its funeral casket mfgr., 4/1/2008.

Hilton Hotels Corp.: 7930 Jones Branch Dr., McLean, VA 22102; (310) 278-4321; www.hiltonworldwide.com; Christopher J. Nassetta; hotels, resorts. Merged with The Blackstone Group, 10/24/2007.

Home Depot, Inc. (HD): 2455 Paces Ferry Rd. NW, Atlanta, GA 30339; (770) 433-8211; www.homedepot.com; Francis S. Blake; world's largest home improvement retailer; 2nd-largest U.S. retailer; home improvement warehouse stores. Sold construction business, HD Supply, 8/30/2007.

Honeywell Intl. Inc. (HON): 101 Columbia Rd., Morristown, NJ 07962; (973) 455-2000; www.honeywell.com; David Cote; industrial and home control systems, aerospace guidance systems.

Hormel Foods Corp. (HRL): 1 Hormel Pl., Austin, MN 55912; (507) 437-5611; www.hormel.com; Jeffrey M. Ettinger; meat processor; pork, turkey, and beef prods. (SPAM, Dinty Moore, Jennie-O).

Houghton Mifflin Co.: 222 Berkeley St., Boston, MA 02116; (617) 351-5000; www.hmco.com; Anthony Lucki; publisher of textbooks, reference, general interest books.

Humana Inc. (HUM): 500 W. Main St., Louisville, KY 40202; (502) 580-1000; www.humana.com; Michael B. McCallister; managed health care service provider, related specialty products.

IAC/InterActive Corp (IACI): 555 W. 18th St., NY, NY 10011; (212) 314-7300; www.iac.com; Barry Diller; internet conglomerate (Ask.com, Match.com, Citysearch). Split off television, leisure, and financial holdings into 5 separate cos., 8/21/2008.

Illinois Tool Works Inc. (ITW): 3600 W. Lake Ave., Glenview, IL 60026; (847) 724-7500; www.itw.com; David B. Speer; consumer & industrial tools; food equip. (Hobart), packaging (Zip-Pak).

Ingersoll-Rand plc (IR): 170/175 Lakeview Dr., Airside Business Park, Swords, Dublin, Ireland; 353-1-870-7400; www.irco.com; Herbert L. Henkel; locks and security systems (Schlage, Kryptonite); refrigeration equip. (Thermo King, Hussmann); industrial equip.; air conditioning systems (Trane). Sold Bobcat, Utility Equip., & Attachments, 11/30/2007. Acquired Trane, 6/5/2008.

Intel Corp. (INTC): 2200 Mission College Blvd., Santa Clara, CA 95054; (408) 765-8080; www.intel.com; Paul S. Otellini; mfgr. semiconductors, microprocessors (Core, Centrino).

International Business Machines Corp. (IBM): One New Orchard Rd., Armonk, NY 10504; (914) 499-1900; www.ibm.com; Samuel Palmisano; world's largest supplier of advanced information processing technology equip., services.

International Paper Co. (IP): 6400 Poplar Ave., Memphis, TN 38197; (901) 419-7000; www.ipaper.com; John V. Faraci Jr.; world's largest paper/forest prods. co.

International Textile Group, Inc. (ITXN): 804 Green Valley Rd., Ste. 300, Greensboro, NC 29605; (336) 379-2865; www.itg-global.com; Joseph L. Gorga; apparel and home textiles/fabrics.

Interstate Bakeries Corp.: 6031 Connection Dr., Irving, TX 75039; (800) 483-7253; www.interstatebakeriescorp.com; Craig Jung; baked goods wholesaler, distributor (Wonder, Hostess, Dolly Madison, Drake's, Home Pride). Emerged from Chap. 11 reorganization, 2/3/2009.

J. Crew Group, Inc. (JCG): 770 Broadway, NY, NY 10003; (212) 209-2500; www.jcrew.com; Millard S. Drexler; retail and mail order apparel/accessories.

JetBlue Airways Corp. (JBLU): 118-29 Queens Blvd., Forest Hills, NY 11375; (718) 286-7900; www.jetblue.com; David Barger; air transportation.

Jo-Ann Stores, Inc. (JAS): 5555 Darrow Rd., Hudson, OH 44236; (330) 656-2600; www.joann.com; Darrell D. Webb; nation's largest specialty fabric and craft stores.

Johnson & Johnson (JNJ): 1 Johnson & Johnson Plaza, New Brunswick, NJ 08933; (732) 524-0400; www.jnj.com; William Weldon; health care prods. (Band-Aid), pharmaceuticals (Tylenol, Motrin, Risperdal), toiletries (Neutrogena, Aveeno); acquired Pfizer's consumer prods. division (Neosporin, Listerine, Sudafed), 12/20/2006.

S. C. Johnson & Son, Inc.: 1525 Howe St., Racine, WI 53403; (262) 260-2000; www.scjohnson.com; H. Fisk Johnson; cleaning and other household prods. (Johnson's Wax, Windex, Pledge, Fantastik, Raid, OFF!, Shout, Glade, Scrubbing Bubbles, Ziploc bags).

Johnson Controls, Inc. (JCI): 5757 N. Green Bay Ave., Milwaukee, WI 53209; (414) 524-1200; www.johnsoncontrols.com; Stephen A. Roell; fire protection services, auto interiors, batteries.

Jones Apparel Group, Inc. (JNY): 1411 Broadway, NY, NY 10018; (212) 642-3860; www.jny.com; Wesley R. Card; apparel (Jones New York, Gloria Vanderbilt), shoes (Nine West, Anne Klein); retail and outlet stores. Sold Barneys New York, 9/7/2007.

JPMorgan Chase & Co. (JPM): 270 Park Ave., NY, NY 10017; (212) 270-6000; www.jpmorganchase.com; James Dimon; financial services. Merged with Bank One Corp., 7/1/2004; acquired Bear Stearns, 6/2/2008; acquired Washington Mutual, 9/25/2008.

KBR, Inc. (KBR): 601 Jefferson St., Ste. 3400, Houston, TX 77002; (713) 753-3011; www.kbr.com; William P. Utt; engineering; construction mgmt. services. Separated from parent company Halliburton, 4/5/2007.

Kellogg Co. (K): One Kellogg Sq., Battle Creek, MI 49016; (269) 961-2000; www.kelloggcompany.com; James M. Jenness; world's largest mfgr. of ready-to-eat cereals, other food prods. (Frosted Flakes, Rice Krispies, Froot Loops, Pop-Tarts, Nutri-Grain, Keebler, Eggo).

Kelly Services, Inc. (KELYA): 999 W. Big Beaver Rd., Troy, MI 48084; (248) 362-4444; www.kellyservices.com; Carl T. Camden; temporary staffing services.

Kimberly-Clark Corp. (KMB): 351 Phelps Dr., Irving, TX 75038; (972) 281-1200; www.kimberly-clark.com; Thomas J. Falk; personal care prods. (Kleenex, Scott, Cottonelle, Huggies, Kotex).

Kmart Corp.: see Sears Holdings.

Koch Industries, Inc.: 4111 E. 37th St. N., Wichita, KS 67220; (316) 828-5500; www.kochind.com; Charles G. Koch; forest prod. mfgr.; oil refineries/pipeline; ranching. Acquired Georgia-Pacific, 12/23/2005.

Kraft Foods Inc. (KFT): 3 Lakes Dr., Northfield, IL 60093; (847) 646-2000; www.kraft.com; Irene B. Rosenfeld; world's largest cheese brand; Nabisco (world's largest cookie and cracker prod.); other food brands (Jell-O, Oscar Mayer, Tombstone Pizza). Spinoff from Altria completed, 3/16/2007; sold Post cereals to Ralcorp, 8/4/2008.

Kroger Co. (KR): 1014 Vine St., Cincinnati, OH 45202; (513) 762-4000; www.kroger.com; David B. Dillon; largest U.S. retail grocery chain, convenience stores, mall jewelry stores.

La-Z-Boy Inc. (LZB): 1284 N. Telegraph Rd., Monroe, MI 48162; (734) 242-1444; www.lazboy.com; Kurt L. Darrow; reclining chairs, other furniture.

Leggett & Platt, Inc. (LEG): No. 1 Leggett Rd., Carthage, MO 64836; (417) 358-8131; www.leggett.com; David S. Haffner; furniture and its components, industrial materials, automotive seating suspension, control and power train cable systems.

Lehman Bros. Holdings Inc.: 745 7th Ave., NY, NY 10019; (212) 526-7000; www.lehman.com; Bryan P. Marsal; investment bank. Filed for Chapter 11 bankruptcy, 9/15/2008.

Levi Strauss & Co.: 1155 Battery St., San Francisco, CA 94111; (415) 501-6000; www.levistrauss.com; R. John Anderson; blue jeans, casual sportswear (Dockers).

Lexmark Intl., Inc. (LXK): 740 W. New Circle Rd., Lexington, KY 40550; (859) 232-2000; www.lexmark.com; Paul J. Curlander; computer printers and peripherals.

Liberty Mutual Holding Co. Inc.: 175 Berkeley St., Boston, MA 02116; (617) 357-9500; www.libertymutual.com; Edmund F. Kelly; auto, home, and life insurance.

Limited Brands, Inc. (LTD): 3 Limited Pkwy., Columbus, OH 43216; (614) 415-7000; www.limitedbrands.com; Leslie H. Wexner; apparel stores (La Senza, Victoria's Secret, Henri Bendel), home decor (White Barn Candle Co.), personal care (Bath & Body Works).

Liz Claiborne, Inc. (LIZ): 1441 B'way., NY, NY 10018; (212) 354-4900; www.liz claiborne.com; William L. McComb; women's apparel (Kate Spade, Juicy Couture, Lucky Brand Jeans, Mexx).

L.L. Bean, Inc.: 3 Campus Dr., Freeport, ME 04033; (207) 552-3028; www.llbean.com; Chris McCormick; catalog and retail outdoor apparel, footwear, gear.

Lockheed Martin Corp. (LMT): 6801 Rockledge Dr., Bethesda, MD 20817; (301) 897-6000; www.lockheedmartin.com; Robert J. Stevens; leading U.S. defense contractor; commercial and military aircraft, electronics, missiles, information tech., and communications.

Loews Corp. (L): 667 Madison Ave., NY, NY 10065; (212) 521-2000; www.loews.com; Andrew H. Tisch; hotels, insurance (CNA Financial), offshore drilling (Diamond). Spun off Lorillard, Inc., tobacco prods. mfgr., 12/17/2007.

Longs Drug Stores: see CVS Caremark Corp.

Lorillard, Inc. (LO): 714 Green Valley Rd., Greensboro, NC 27408; (336) 335-7000; www.lorillard.com; Martin Orlowsky; 3rd-largest U.S. cigarette mfgr (Newport, Kent). Spun off from Loews Corp., 12/17/2007.

Lowe's Cos., Inc. (LOW): 1000 Lowe's Blvd. Mooresville, NC 28117; (704) 758-1000; www.lowes.com; Robert A. Niblock; building material and home improvement superstores.

Macy's, Inc. (M): 7 W. 7th St., Cincinnati, OH 45202; (513) 579-7000; www.federated-fds.com; Terry J. Lundgren; dept. stores (Macy's, Bloomingdale's). Acquired May Dept. Stores (Lord & Taylor, Marshall Field's), 2/28/2005. Federated Dept. Stores changed its name to Macy's, 6/1/2007.

Manpower Inc. (MAN): 100 Manpower Pl., Milwaukee, WI 53212; (414) 961-1000; www.manpower.com; Jeffrey A. Joerres; employment services.

Marathon Oil Corp. (MRO): 5555 San Felipe Rd., Houston, TX 77056; (713) 629-6600; www.marathon.com; Clarence P. Cazalot Jr.; integrated oil co.

Marriott International, Inc. (MAR): Marriott Dr., Washington DC 20058; (301) 380-3000; www.marriott.com; J. W. Marriott Jr.; hotels (Renaissance, Courtyard, Fairfield Inn, Ritz-Carlton).

Mars, Inc.: 6885 Elm St., McLean, VA 22101; (703) 821-4900; www.mars.com; John F. Mars; mfgr. chocolate (M&M's, Snickers, Milky Way); food (Uncle Ben's); pet food (Pedigree, Whiskas). Acquired Wm. Wrigley Jr., 10/6/2008.

Masco Corp. (MAS): 21001 Van Born Rd., Taylor, MI 48180; (313) 274-7400; www.masco.com; Richard A. Manoogian; mfgr. kitchen, bathroom prods. (Delta, Peerless faucets; Merillat cabinets); paints (Behr).

Massachusetts Mutual Life Insurance Co. (MassMutual Financial Group): 1295 State St., Springfield, MA 01111; (413) 744-1000; www.massmutual.com; Stuart H. Reese; financial planning and investment, life insurance.

Mattel, Inc. (MAT): 333 Continental Blvd., El Segundo, CA 90245; (310) 252-2000; www.mattel.com; Robert A. Eckert; largest U.S. toymaker (Barbie, Fisher-Price, Hot Wheels, Matchbox, American Girls).

McClatchy Co. (MNI): 2100 Q St., Sacramento, CA 95816; (916) 321-1846; www.mcclatchy.com; Gary B. Pruitt; 3rd-largest U.S. newspaper publisher. Acquired Knight Ridder papers, 6/27/2006.

McDonald's Corp. (MCD): 2111 McDonald's Dr., Oak Brook, IL 60523; (630) 623-3000; www.mcdonalds.com; James A. Skinner; world's largest fast food co.

McGraw-Hill Cos. (MHP): 1221 Ave. of the Americas, NY, NY 10020; (212) 512-2000; www.mcgraw-hill.com; Harold McGraw III; book, textbook, magazine publishing (*BusinessWeek*); information and financial services (Standard & Poor's); TV stations.

McKesson Corp. (MCK): 1 Post St., San Francisco, CA 94104; (415) 983-8300; www.mckesson.com; John H. Hammergren; distributor of drugs and toiletries; provides mgmt. software and services.

MeadWestvaco Corp. (MWV): 11013 W. Broad St., Glen Allen, VA 23060; (804) 327-5200; www.meadwestvaco.com; John A. Luke Jr.; packaging, shipping containers, chemicals, school supplies.

Medco Health Solutions, Inc. (MHS): 100 Parsons Pond Dr., Franklin Lakes, NJ 07417; (201) 269-3400; www.medco.com; David B. Snow Jr.; pharmacy benefits management.

Medtronic, Inc. (MDT): 710 Medtronic Pkwy., Minneapolis, MN 55432; (763) 514-4000; www.medtronic.com; William A. Hawkins III; mfgr. of implantable biomedical devices.

Merck & Co., Inc. (MRK): 1 Merck Dr., Whitehouse Station, NJ 08889; (908) 423-1000; www.merck.com; Richard T. Clark; pharmaceuticals (Gardasil, Propecia, Singulair, Vytorin, Zocor). Announced plans to merge with Schering-Plough Corp., 3/9/2009.

Meredith Corp. (MDP): 1716 Locust St., Des Moines, IA 50309; (515) 284-3000; www.meredith.com; Stephen M. Lacy; magazine publishing (*Better Homes and Gardens, Ladies' Home Journal, Parents, Family Circle*), book publishing, broadcasting.

Merrill Lynch & Co., Inc.: see Bank of America.

MetLife, Inc. (MET): 200 Park Ave., NY, NY 10166; (212) 578-2211; www.metlife.com; C. Robert Henrikson; insurance, financial services.

MGM MIRAGE (MGM): 3600 Las Vegas Blvd. S., Las Vegas, NV 89109; (702) 693-7120; www.mgmmirage.com; James J. Murren; hotel-casino operator (Mirage, New York-New York, Luxor, Circus Circus, Monte Carlo). Acquired Mandalay Resort Group, 4/25/2005.

Microsoft Corp. (MSFT): One Microsoft Way, Redmond, WA 98052; (425) 882-8080; www.microsoft.com; William H. Gates III; world's largest consumer software maker (Windows, Word, Excel); video game consoles (Xbox).

Miller Brewing Co.: see SABMiller.

Molson Coors Brewing Co. (TAP): 1225 17th St., Ste. 3200, Denver, CO 80202; (303) 279-6565; www.molsoncoors.com; Peter H. Coors; brewer (Coors, Killian's, Molson). Formed by merger of Adolph Coors and Molson, 2/9/2005. Announced creation of MillerCoors, joint venture with SABMiller, 7/1/2008.

Morgan Stanley (MS): 1585 Broadway, NY, NY 10036; (212) 761-4000; www.morganstanley.com; John J. Mack; diversified financial services.

Motorola, Inc. (MOT): 1303 E. Algonquin Rd., Schaumburg, IL 60196; (847) 576-5000; www.motorola.com; Greg Brown & Sanjay K. Jha; electronic equipment and components; communication devices.

National Semiconductor Corp. (NSM): 2900 Semiconductor Dr., Santa Clara, CA 95052; (408) 721-5000; www.national.com; Brian L. Halla; mfgr. semiconductors, integrated circuits.

Nationwide Mutual Insurance Co.: One Nationwide Plaza, Columbus, OH 43215; (614) 249-7111; www.nationwide.com; Stephen S. Rasmussen; property/casualty, life insurance; financial services.

Navistar Intl. Corp. (NAV): 4201 Winfield Rd., Warrenville, IL 60555; (630) 753-5000; www.navistar.com; Daniel Ustian; mfgr. heavy-duty trucks, parts, school buses.

NCR Corp. (NCR): 1700 S. Patterson Blvd., Dayton, OH 45479; (937) 445-5000; www.ncr.com; William R. Nuti; mfgr. ATMs, retail technology, hardware and software; computer services and supplies.

Nestlé USA, Inc.: 800 N. Brand Blvd., Glendale, CA 91203; (818) 549-6000; www.nestleusa.com; Brad Alford; candy (Baby Ruth, Raisinets), beverages (Nestea), frozen foods (Stouffer's), pet foods (Purina, Alpo, Friskies). Subsidiary of Nestlé SA in Switzerland; world's largest food co.

Netflix, Inc. (NFLX): 100 Winchester Cir., Los Gatos, CA 95032; (408) 540-3700; www.netflix.com; Reed Hastings; online DVD rentals.

New York Life Insurance Co.: 51 Madison Ave., Ste. 3200, NY, NY 10010; (212) 576-7000; www.newyorklife.com; Theodore A. Mathas; life insurance, annuities, mutual funds.

New York Times Co. (NYT): 620 8th Ave., NY, NY 10018; (212) 556-1234; www.nytco.com; Arthur O. Sulzberger Jr.; newspapers (New York Times, Boston Globe).

Newell Rubbermaid Inc. (NWL): 3 Glenlake Pkwy., Ste. 300, Atlanta, GA 30328; (770) 418-7000; www.newellrubbermaid.com; Mark D. Ketchum; housewares (Rubbermaid, Levolor); hair accessories (Goody); writing utensils (Parker, Sharpie); hardware and tools (Irwin, Amerock); juvenile prods. (Graco).

News Corp. (NWS): 1211 Ave. of the Americas, NY, NY 10036; (212) 852-7000; www.newscorp.com; K. Rupert Murdoch; newspaper, magazine, book publishing (HarperCollins); TV and CATV stations (FOX, Fox News Channel, FX); film (20th Century Fox, Fox Searchlight); websites (MySpace.com, RottenTomatoes.com). Acquired Dow Jones (*Wall Street Journal*), 12/13/2007.

NIKE, Inc. (NKE): 1 Bowerman Dr., Beaverton, OR 97005; (503) 671-6453; www.nike biz.com; Mark G. Parker; world's largest footwear mfgr. Acquired Umbro, 1/31/2008.

Nordstrom, Inc. (JWN): 1617 6th Ave., Seattle, WA 98101; (206) 628-2111; www.nordstrom.com; Enrique Hernandez Jr.; upscale dept. store chain.

Norfolk Southern Corp. (NSC): Three Commercial Pl., Norfolk, VA 23510; (757) 629-2600; www.nscorp.com; Charles W. Moorman IV; railway operator; freight carrier.

Northrop Grumman Corp. (NOC): 1840 Century Park East, Los Angeles, CA 90067; (310) 553-6262; www.northrop grumman.com; Ronald D. Sugar; world's largest shipbuilder; defense contractor: aircraft, electronics, data systems, information systems, missiles.

Northwest Airlines Corp.: 2700 Lone Oak Pkwy., Eagan, MN 55121; (612) 726-2111; www.nwa.com; Edward H. Bastian; air transportation; emerged from Chap. 11 reorganization, 5/31/2007; merged with Delta Air Lines, 10/29/2008.

Northwestern Mutual Life Insurance Co.: 720 E. Wisconsin Ave., Milwaukee, WI 53202; (414) 271-1444; www.nmfn.com; Edward J. Zore; life insurance, investment products and services, annuities.

Occidental Petroleum Corp. (OXY): 10889 Wilshire Blvd., Los Angeles, CA 90024; (310) 208-8800; www.oxy.com; Ray R. Irani; oil, natural gas, chemicals, plastics, fertilizers.

Office Depot, Inc. (ODP): 6600 N. Military Trail, Boca Raton, FL 33496; (561) 438-4800; www.officedepot.com; Steve Odland; office supply retail stores.

Omnicom Group Inc. (OMC): 437 Madison Ave., NY, NY 10022; (212) 415-3600; www.omnicomgroup.com; John D. Wren; advertising, marketing, interactive/digital media.

Oracle Corp. (ORCL): 500 Oracle Pkwy., Redwood City, CA 94065; (650) 506-7000; www.oracle.com; Lawrence J. Ellison; database and file management software. Acquired BEA Systems, 4/29/2008; announced plans to acquire Sun Microsystems, 4/20/2009.

Owens Corning (OC): 1 Owens Corning Pkwy., Toledo, OH 43659; (419) 248-8000; www.owenscorning.com; Michael H. Thaman; world leader in insulation, advanced glass, composite materials. Emerged from Chap. 11 reorganization, 10/31/2006.

Owens-Illinois, Inc. (OI): 1 Michael Owens Way, Perrysburg, OH 43551; (567) 336-5000; www.o-i.com; Albert P. L. Stroucken; mfgr. glass containers. Sold plastic packaging division, 8/1/2007.

J.C. Penney Co., Inc. (JCP): 6501 Legacy Dr., Plano, TX 75024; (972) 431-1000; www.jcpenney.com; Myron E. Ullman III; dept. stores, catalog sales.

Pepsi Bottling Group, Inc. (PBG): 1 Pepsi Way, Somers, NY 10589; (914) 767-6000; www.pbg.com; Eric J. Foss; world's #1 mfgr. & distrib. of PepsiCo prods. Announced plans to be acquired by PepsiCo, 8/4/2009.

PepsiCo, Inc. (PEP): 700 Anderson Hill Rd., Purchase, NY 10577; (914) 253-2000; www.pepsico.com; Indra K. Nooyi; soft drinks (Pepsi-Cola, Mountain Dew), fruit juice (Tropicana), sports drinks (Gatorade), FritoLay snacks (Ruffles, Lay's, Fritos, Doritos, Rold Gold), cereal (Quaker Oats, Life). Announced plans to acquire Pepsi Bottling Group, 8/4/2009.

Pfizer, Inc. (PFE): 235 E. 42nd St., NY, NY 10017; (212) 733-2323; www.pfizer.com; Jeffrey B. Kindler; pharmaceuticals (Celebrex, Lipitor, Viagra, Zoloft); hospital, veterinary prods. Announced plans to acquire Wyeth, 1/26/2009.

PG&E Corp. (PCG): One Market Spear Tower, Ste. 2400, San Francisco, CA 94105; (415) 267-7000; www.pgecorp.com; Peter A. Darbee; energy supplier.

Philip Morris Intl. Inc. (PM): 120 Park Ave., NY, NY 10017; (917) 663-2000; www.philip morrisinternational.com; Louis C. Camilleri; international tobacco mfgr. and distributor. Spun off from parent company Altria Group, 3/28/2008.

Phillips-Van Heusen Corp. (PVH): 200 Madison Ave., NY, NY 10016; (212) 381-3500; www.pvh.com; Emanuel Chirico; mfgr. of licensed apparel (Calvin Klein, IZOD, Geoffrey Beene, DKNY, Kenneth Cole, Sean John).

Pitney Bowes Inc. (PBI): 1 Elmcroft Rd., Stamford, CT 06926; (203) 356-5000; www.pb.com; Murray D. Martin; postage meters and mailing equip.

Plains All American Pipeline, L.P. (PAA): 333 Clay St., Ste. 1600, Houston, TX 77002; (713) 646-4100; www.plains allamerican.com; Greg L. Armstrong; oil transportation, storage.

Polo Ralph Lauren Corp. (RL): 650 Madison Ave., NY, NY 10022; (212) 318-7000; www.ralphlauren.com; Ralph Lauren; men's and women's apparel, home furnishings, fragrances.

PPG Industries, Inc. (PPG): 1 PPG Place, Pittsburgh, PA 15272; (412) 434-3131; www.ppg.com; Charles E. Bunch; glass prods., silicas, fiberglass, chemicals, sealants; world's leading supplier of automobile/industrial coatings. Acquired SigmaKalon, 1/2/2008.

Procter & Gamble Co. (PG): 1 Procter & Gamble Plaza, Cincinnati, OH 45202; (513) 983-1100; www.pg.com; Alan G. Lafley; soaps and detergents (Ivory, Cheer, Tide, Mr. Clean, Zest); toiletries (Crest, Scope, Head & Shoulders, Old Spice); pharmaceuticals (Pepto-Bismol, Vicks cough medicines); food (Pringles); paper prods. (Charmin toilet tissues, Bounty towels), Tampax tampons; Pampers & Luvs disposable diapers; CoverGirl and Max Factor cosmetics, Clairol hair care. Acquired Gillette (razors, batteries), 10/1/2005; sold Folgers to J. M. Smucker, 11/6/2008.

Prudential Financial, Inc. (PRU): 751 Broad St., Newark, NJ 07102; (973) 802-6000; www.prudential.com; John R. Strangfeld Jr.; insurance, financial services.

Publix Super Markets Inc.: 3300 Publix Corporate Pkwy., Lakeland, FL 33811; (863) 688-1188; www.publix.com; Charles H. Jenkins Jr.; supermarket chain.

Quest Diagnostics Inc. (DGX): 3 Giralda Farms, Madison, NJ 07940; (201) 393-5000; www.questdiagnostics.com; Surya N. Mohapatra; leading clinical laboratory.

Qwest Communications Intl. Inc. (Q): 1801 California St., Denver, CO 80202; (800) 899-7780; www.qwest.com; Edward A. Mueller; telecommunications; wireless and directory services.

RadioShack Corp. (RSH): 300 RadioShack Circle, Fort Worth, TX 76102; (817) 415-3011; www.radioshack.com; Julian C. Day; consumer electronics retailer.

Ralcorp Holdings, Inc. (RAH): 800 Market St., St. Louis, MO 63101; (314) 877-7000; www.ralcorp.com; William P. Stiritz; private-label breakfast cereals, snack foods. Acquired Post cereals, 8/4/2008

Raytheon Co. (RTN): 870 Winter St., Waltham, MA 02451; (781) 522-3000; www.raytheon.com; William Swanson; defense, communications systems.

Reader's Digest Assn., Inc.: Reader's Digest Road, Pleasantville, NY 10570; (914) 238-1000; www.rd.com; Mary G. Berner; world's best-selling gen. interest magazine; direct-mail marketer of magazines, books. Filed for Chap. 11 reorganization, 8/24/2009.

Reebok Intl. Ltd.: 1895 J.W. Foster Blvd., Canton, MA 02021; (781) 401-5000; www.reebok.com; Uli Becker; athletic and leisure footwear, apparel. Acquired by Germany's adidas AG, 1/31/2006.

Republic Services, Inc. (RSG): 18500 N. Allied Way, Phoenix, AZ 85054; (480) 627-2700; www.republicservices.com; James E. O'Connor; waste management co. Merged with Allied Waste Industries, 12/5/2008.

Revlon, Inc. (REV): 237 Park Ave., NY, NY 10017; (212) 527-4000; www.revlon.com; Ronald O. Perelman; cosmetics, skin care.

Reynolds American Inc. (RAI): 401 N. Main St., Winston-Salem, NC 27101; (336) 741-2000; www.reynoldsamerican.com; Susan M. Ivey; 2nd-largest U.S. producer of cigarettes (Winston, Camel, Pall Mall, Kool, Doral). Acquired Conwood smokeless tobacco co., 5/31/2006.

Rite Aid Corp. (RAD): 30 Hunter Ln., Camp Hill, PA 17011; (717) 761-2633; www.rite aid.com; Mary F. Sammons; 3rd-largest U.S. drugstore chain. Acquired Brooks and Eckerd drugstore chains, 6/4/2007.

Rockwell Automation, Inc. (ROK): 1201 S. 2nd St., Milwaukee, WI 53204; (414) 382-2000; www.rockwellautomation.com; Keith D. Nosbusch; industrial automation co.

Rohm and Haas Co.: 100 Independence Mall West, Philadelphia, PA 19106; (215) 592-3000; www.rohmhaas.com; Jerome A. Peribere; adhesives and sealants, performance chemicals, automotive coatings; salt (Morton). Acquired by Dow Chemical, 4/1/2009.

Ryder System, Inc. (R): 11690 NW 105th St., Miami, FL 33178; (305) 500-3726; www.ryder.com; Gregory T. Swienton; truck-leasing service.

SABMiller plc: 1 Stanhope Gate, London, W1K 1AF, United Kingdom; +44-20-7659-0100; www.sabmiller.com; Ernest A. Mackay; brewing company (Miller, Peroni, Grolsch). Announced creation of MillerCoors, joint venture with Molson Coors, 7/1/2008.

Safeway Inc. (SWY): 5918 Stoneridge Mall Rd., Pleasanton, CA 94588; (925) 467-3000; www.safeway.com; Steven A. Burd; supermarkets.

Sara Lee Corp. (SLE): 3500 Lacey Rd., Downers Grove, IL 60515; (630) 598-8100; www.saralee.com; Brenda Barnes; baked goods, fresh and processed meats (Ball Park, Jimmy Dean, Hillshire Farm, Kahn's). Spun off apparel business as Hanesbrands Inc., 9/5/2006.

SBC Communications, Inc.: see AT&T Inc.

Schering-Plough Corp. (SGP): 2000 Galloping Hill Rd., Kenilworth, NJ 07033; (908) 298-4000; www.sch-plough.com; Fred Hassan; pharmaceuticals (Clarinex, Levitra, Nasonex, Proventil), consumer prods. (Afrin, Claritin, Coppertone, Dr. Scholl's, MiraLAX), animal health prods. Announced plans to merge with Merck & Co., 3/9/2009.

Sears Holdings Corp. (SHLD): 3333 Beverly Rd., Hoffman Estates, IL 60179; (847) 286-2500; www.sears.com; Edward S. Lampert; 3rd-largest U.S. retailer; formed by merger of Kmart and Sears, 3/24/2005.

Shell Oil Co.: 910 Louisiana St., Houston, TX 77002; (713) 241-6161; www.shellus.com; Marvin Odum; integrated oil co; subsidiary of Royal Dutch Shell, world's 2nd-largest oil co.

Sherwin-Williams Co. (SHW): 101 Prospect Ave. NW, Cleveland, OH 44115; (216) 566-2000; www.sherwin-williams.com; Christopher M. Connor; largest North American paint and varnish producer (Dutch Boy, Krylon, Minwax).

Smithfield Foods, Inc. (SFD): 200 Commerce St., Smithfield, VA 23430; (757) 365-3000; www.smithfieldfoods.com; C. Larry Pope; world's largest producer of pork and processed meat products. Acquired Premium Standard Farms, 5/7/2007.

J. M. Smucker Co. (SJM): One Strawberry Ln., Orrville, OH 44667; (330) 682-3000; www.smucker.com; Timothy P. Smucker; largest U.S. producer of preserves, jams, jellies; toppings (Magic Shell), Jif peanut butter; Crisco oil. Merged with Folgers, 11/6/2008.

Smurfit-Stone Container Corp.: 222 N. LaSalle St., Chicago, IL 60601; (312) 346-6600; www.smurfit.com; Patrick J. Moore; industry leader for corrugated containers, paper bags, and sacks. Filed for Chap. 11 reorganization, 1/26/2009.

Sony Corp. of America: 550 Madison Ave., NY, NY 10022; (212) 833-6800; www.sony. com; Howard Stringer; U.S. subsidiary of Japan-based Sony Corp.; electronics, movies, music. Acquired Bertelsmann's stake in Sony BMG and renamed it Sony Music Entertainment, 10/1/2008.

Southwest Airlines Co. (LUV): 2702 Love Field Dr., Dallas, TX 75235; (214) 792-4000; www.southwest.com; Gary C. Kelly; air transportation.

Sprint Nextel Corp. (S): 6200 Sprint Pkwy., Overland Park, KS 66251; (703) 433-4000; www.sprint.com; Dan Hesse; wireless and long-distance telecommunications; merged with Nextel, 8/12/2005.

Staples, Inc. (SPLS): 500 Staples Dr., Framingham, MA 01702; (508) 253-5000; www.staples.com; Ronald L. Sargent; largest U.S. office-supply retailer.

Starbucks Corp. (SBUX): 2401 Utah Ave. S., Seattle, WA 98134; (206) 447-1575; www.starbucks.com; Howard D. Schultz; coffee producer; world's leading specialty coffee retailer.

Starwood Hotels & Resorts Worldwide, Inc. (HOT): 1111 Westchester Ave., White Plains, NY 10604; (914) 640-8100; www.starwood hotels.com; Bruce W. Duncan; hotel and resort co. (Westin, Sheraton, W Hotels).

State Farm Mutual Automobile Ins. Co.: 1 State Farm Plaza, Bloomington, IL 61710; (309) 766-2311; www.statefarm.com; Edward B. Rust Jr.; largest U.S. provider of auto/homeowners insurance.

Sun Microsystems, Inc. (JAVA): 4150 Network Cir., Santa Clara, CA 95054; (650) 960-1300; www.sun.com; Jonathan I. Schwartz; supplier of network computer systems. Announced plans to be acquired by Oracle, 4/20/2009.

Sunoco, Inc. (SUN): 1735 Market St., Ste. LL, Philadelphia, PA 19103; (215) 977-3000; www.sunocoinc.com; Lynn Elsenhans; energy resources co., gasoline retailer.

SUPERVALU Inc. (SVU): 11840 Valley View Rd., Eden Prairie, MN 55344; (952) 828-4000; www.supervalu.com; Jeffrey Noddle; food wholesaler, retailer. Acquired Albertsons, 6/2/2006.

SYSCO Corp. (SYY): 1390 Enclave Pkwy., Houston, TX 77077; (281) 584-1390; www.sysco.com; Manuel A. Fernandez; largest U.S. food-service distributor.

Systemax (SYX): 11 Harbor Park Dr., Port Washington, NY 11050; (516) 625-4300; www.systemax.com; Richard Leeds; computers, electronics, industrial prod. retailer. Acquired CompUSA, 1/6/2008; acquired Circuit City, 5/19/2009.

Target Corp. (TGT): 1000 Nicollet Mall, Minneapolis, MN 55403; (612) 304-6073; www.target.com; Gregg W. Steinhafel; 2nd-largest U.S. discount retailer.

Tenneco Inc. (TEN): 500 N. Field Dr., Lake Forest, IL 60045; (847) 482-5000; www.tenneco.com; Gregg M. Sherrill; automotive parts (Monroe, Walker).

Texas Instruments Inc. (TXN): 12500 TI Blvd., Dallas, TX 75266; (972) 995-2011; www.ti.com; Richard K. Templeton; processors, semiconductors, software, handheld calculators.

Textron Inc. (TXT): 40 Westminster St., Providence, RI 02903; (401) 421-2800; www.textron.com; Lewis B. Campbell; aircraft (Cessna, Bell), industrial, automotive prods.; financial services.

3M Co. (MMM): 3M Center, St. Paul, MN 55144; (651) 733-1110; www.mmm.com; George W. Buckley; abrasives, adhesives, electrical, health care, cleaning (Scotch-Brite, O-Cel-O sponges, Scotchgard), printing, consumer prods. (Scotch Tape, Post-it).

TIAA-CREF: 730 Third Ave., NY, NY 10017; (212) 490-9000; www.tiaa-cref.org; Roger W. Ferguson Jr.; financial services provider.

Timberland Co. (TBL): 200 Domain Dr., Stratham, NH 03885; (603) 772-9500; www.timberland.com; Jeffrey B. Swartz; footwear, apparel, accessories.

Time Warner Inc. (TWX): One Time Warner Ctr., NY, NY 10019; (212) 484-8000; www.timewarner.com; Jeffrey L. Bewkes; Internet service provider (AOL); magazine publishing (*Time, Sports Illustrated, Fortune, Money, People, DC Comics*), TV and CATV (Cartoon Network, HBO, CNN, TBS, TNT), motion pictures (Warner Bros., New Line Cinema), recordings. AOL and Time Warner completed the largest corporate merger in history in 2001; the largest U.S. media company. Sold book group to Hachette Livre UK, 3/31/2006.

TJX Cos., Inc. (TJX): 770 Cochituate Rd., Framingham, MA 01701; (508) 390-1000; www.tjx.com; Bernard Cammarata; world's largest off-price apparel retailer (T.J. Maxx, Marshalls); home furnishing retailer (Home Goods).

Toro Co. (TTC): 8111 Lyndale Ave. S, Bloomington, MN 55420; (952) 888-8801; www.thetorocompany.com; Michael J. Hoffman; lawn and turf maintenance prods. (Lawn-Boy); snow removal equip.; irrigation systems.

Toys "R" Us, Inc.: 1 Geoffrey Way, Wayne, NJ 07470; (973) 617-3500; www.toysrus.com; Gerald L. Storch; children's specialty retailer. Acquired FAO Schwarz, 5/28/2009.

Triarc: see Wendy's/Arby's Group.

Tribune Co.: 435 N. Michigan Ave., Chicago, IL 60611; (312) 222-9100; www.tribune.com; Sam Zell; newspapers (*Los Angeles Times*, *Chicago Tribune*), broadcasting (incl. WGN and 23 other television and radio stations), Chicago Cubs franchise. Filed for Chap. 11 reorganization, 12/8/2008.

Trinity Industries, Inc. (TRN): 2525 Stemmons Fwy., Dallas, TX 75207; (214) 631-4420; www.trin.net; Timothy R. Wallace; mfgr. metal prods., rail and freight equip.

Tyco Intl. Ltd. (TYC): 9 Roszel Rd., Princeton, NJ 08540; (609) 720-4200; www.tyco.com; Edward D. Breen Jr.; security and engineered prods. Spun off health care and electronics divisions, 6/29/2007.

Tyson Foods, Inc. (TSN): 2200 Don Tyson Pkwy., Springdale, AR 72762; (479) 290-4000 www.tysonfoodsinc.com; Leland E. Tollett; fresh and processed poultry; beef and pork prods.

UAL Corp. (UAUA): 77 W. Wacker Dr., Chicago IL 60601; (312) 997-8000; www.united.com; Glenn F. Tilton; air transportation (United Airlines).

UBS Financial Services Inc.: 1285 Ave. of the Americas, NY, NY 10019; (212) 713-2000; www.ubs.com; Marten Hoekstra; financial services; subsidiary of Switzerland's UBS AG.

Unilever US (UN/UL): 800 Sylvan Ave., Englewood Cliffs, NJ 07632; (201) 894-4000; www.unilever.com; Paul Polman; food (Hellmann's mayonnaise, Knorr soups, Ragu pasta sauce, Wish-Bone salad dressing, Lipton, Skippy peanut butter, Slim-Fast), hygiene prods. (Dove, Q-tips, Vaseline). Subsidiary of Unilever NV (Neth.) and Unilever plc (UK).

Union Pacific Corp. (UNP): 1400 Douglas St., Omaha, NE, 68179; (402) 544-5000; www.up.com; James R. Young; one of the largest railroad freight cos. in U.S.

Unisys Corp. (UIS): Unisys Way, Blue Bell, PA 19424; (215) 986-4011; www.unisys.com; J. Edward Coleman; designs, manuf. computer information systems; IT consulting.

UnitedHealth Group Inc. (UNH): UHG Center, 9900 Bren Rd. E., Minnetonka, MN 55343; (952) 936-1300; www.unitedhealthgroup.com; Stephen J. Hemsley; health insurer.

United Parcel Service, Inc. (UPS): 55 Glenlake Pkwy. NE, Atlanta, GA 30328; (404) 828-6000; www.ups.com; D. Scott Davis; world's largest package delivery co.

United States Steel Corp. (X): 600 Grant St., Pittsburgh, PA 15219; (412) 433-1121; www.ussteel.com; John P. Surma Jr.; steel, tin prods., resource mgmt.

United Technologies Corp. (UTX): One Financial Plaza, Hartford, CT 06103; (860) 728-7000; www.utc.com; George David; aerospace, industrial prods. and services (Carrier, Otis, Pratt & Whitney, Sikorsky).

US Airways Group, Inc. (LCC): 111 W. Rio Salado Pkwy., Tempe, AZ 85281; (480) 693-0800; www.usairways.com; William Douglas Parker; air transportation.

Verizon Communications Inc. (VZ): 140 West St., NY, NY 10007; (212) 395-1000; www.verizon.com; Ivan Seidenberg; broadband, wireless, wireline services provider. Acquired MCI, Inc., 1/6/2006.

V.F. Corp. (VFC): 105 Corporate Center Blvd., Greensboro, NC 27408; (336) 424-6000; www.vfc.com; Eric C. Wiseman; apparel (Lee, Wrangler, North Face).

Viacom Inc. (VIA): 1515 Broadway, NY, NY 10036; (212) 258-6000; www.viacom.com; Philippe P. Dauman; CATV (BET, Comedy Central, MTV, VH1, Nickelodeon); produces, distributes movies (Paramount); theme parks. Co. split into 2 separately traded entities, 12/31/2005. See CBS Corp.

Visteon Corp.: One Village Ctr. Dr., Van Buren Twp., MI 48111; (734) 710-2000; www.visteon.com; Donald J. Stebbins; automotive parts mfgr., architectural glass. Filed for Chap. 11 reorganization, 5/28/2009.

Wachovia Corp. (WB): 301 S. College St., Ste. 4000, Charlotte, NC 28288; (704) 590-0000; www.wachovia.com; financial services provider. Acquired by Wells Fargo, 12/31/2008.

Walgreen Co. (WAG): 200 Wilmot Rd., Deerfield, IL 60015; (847) 914-2500; www.walgreens.com; Alan G. McNally; drugstore chain.

Wal-Mart Stores, Inc. (WMT): 702 SW 8th St., Bentonville, AR 72716; (479) 273-4000; www.walmartstores.com; S. Robson Walton; world's largest retailer; discount stores, wholesale clubs (Sam's).

Washington Post Co. (WPO): 1150 15th St. NW, Washington, DC 20071; (202) 334-6000; www.washpostco.com; Donald E. Graham; newspapers, *Newsweek* magazine, Slate.com, TV and CATV stations, Kaplan educational services.

Waste Management, Inc. (WMI): 1001 Fannin St., Ste. 4000, Houston, TX 77002; (713) 512-6200; www.wm.com; David P. Steiner; N. America's largest solid waste collection and disposal co.

WellPoint, Inc. (WLP): 120 Monument Cir., Indianapolis, IN 46204; (317) 532-6000; www.wellpoint.com; Larry C. Glasscock; largest U.S. health insurer; HMOs and PPOs, incl. Blue Cross Blue Shield (licensed in some states), HealthLink, UniCare.

Wells Fargo & Co. (WFC): 420 Montgomery St., San Francisco, CA 94163; (866) 878-5865; www.wellsfargo.com; Richard Kovacevich; financial services. Acquired Wachovia, 12/31/2008.

Wendy's/Arby's Group, Inc. (WEN): 1155 Perimeter Ctr. W., Atlanta, GA 30338; (678) 514-4100; www.wendysarbys.com; Roland C. Smith; fast food restaurants (Pasta Pomodoro, Wendy's, Arby's). Merged with Triarc Inc., 9/29/2008.

Western Union Co. (WU): 12500 E. Belford Ave., Englewood, CO 80112; (720) 332-1000; www.westernunion.com; Christina A. Gold; money transfers, financial services.

Weyerhaeuser Co. (WY): 33663 Weyerhaeuser Way S., Federal Way, WA 98003; (253) 924-2345; www.weyerhaeuser.com; Daniel S. Fulton; produces and distributes paper and wood prods.

Whirlpool Corp. (WHR): 2000 N. M-63, Benton Harbor, MI 49022; (269) 923-5000; www.whirlpoolcorp.com; Jeff M. Fettig; mfgr. of major home appliances (KitchenAid, Amana). Acquired Maytag Corp. appliances, 3/31/2006.

Whole Foods Market, Inc. (WFMI): 550 Bowie St., Austin, TX 78703; (512) 477-4455; www.wholefoodsmarket.com; John P. Mackey; world's largest natural food market chain.

Winn-Dixie Stores, Inc. (WINN): 5050 Edgewood Ct., Jacksonville, FL 32254; (904) 783-5000; www.winn-dixie.com; Peter Lynch; supermarkets (Winn-Dixie, SaveRite); emerged from Chap. 11, 11/21/2006.

Winnebago Industries, Inc. (WGO): 605 W. Crystal Lake Rd., Forest City, IA 50436; (641) 585-3535; www.winnebagoind.com; Robert J. Olson; mfgr. of motor homes, recreational vehicles.

Wm. Wrigley Jr. Co.: 410 N. Michigan Ave., Chicago, IL 60611; (312) 644-2121; www.wrigley.com; William Wrigley Jr.; world's largest mfgr. of chewing gum. Acquired by Mars, Inc., 10/6/2008.

Wyeth (WYE): 5 Giralda Farms, Madison, NJ 07940; (973) 660-5000; www.wyeth.com; Bernard J. Poussot; mfgr. prescription (Alavert, Effexor) and over-the-counter drugs (Advil, Centrum, ChapStick, Robitussin). Announced plans to be acquired by Pfizer, 1/26/2009.

Xerox Corp. (XRX): 45 Glover Ave., Norwalk, CT 06856; (203) 968-3000; www.xerox.com; Anne Mulcahy; copiers, printers, scanners, document publishing equip.

Yahoo! Inc. (YHOO): 701 First Ave. Sunnyvale, CA 94089; (408) 349-3300; www.yahoo.com; Carol Bartz; internet media company.

YUM! Brands, Inc. (YUM): 1441 Gardiner Ln., Louisville, KY 40213; (502) 874-8300; www.yum.com; David C. Novak; fast food restaurants (Pizza Hut, KFC, Taco Bell).

Labor Unions and Professional Organizations

Source: Bureau of Labor Statistics, U.S. Dept. of Labor; AFL-CIO; *World Almanac* research.

(#) Member of Change to Win Coalition formed in 2005 by unions disaffiliated from AFL-CIO. (*) Independent union. All others are affiliated with AFL-CIO as of 2008. Year established in parenthesis.

Labor Unions

Air Line Pilots Association (1931): 55,000 members, 40 U.S. and Canadian airlines; (703) 689-2270; www.alpa.org

American Federation of Labor & Congress of Industrial Organizations (AFL-CIO) (1955): federation of 56 unions, 10.5 mil members, (202) 637-5000; www.aflcio.org

Automobile, Aerospace & Agricultural Implement Workers of America, International Union, United, (UAW) (1935): 640,000 active (500,000 ret.) members, 800 locals; (313) 926-5000; www.uaw.org

Bakery, Confectionery, Tobacco Workers, and Grain Millers International Union (BCTGM) (1881): 100,000+ members; (301) 933-8600; www.bctgm.org

Bricklayers and Allied Craftworkers, International Union of (BAC) (1865): 100,000 members, 50 locals; (202) 783-3788; www.bacweb.org

#Carpenters and Joiners of America, United Brotherhood of (1881): 520,000+ members, 1,035 locals; (732) 417-9229; www.carpenters.org

#Change to Win Coalition (2005): 7 unions, 6 ex-affiliates of AFL-CIO, 1 independent; (202) 721-0660; www.changetowin.org

Communications Workers of America (IUE-CWA) (1938): 700,000+ members, 1,200 locals; (202) 434-1100; www.cwa-union.org

*Education Association, National (1857): 3.2 mil members, 14,000+ affiliates; (202) 833-4000; www.nea.org

Electrical Workers, International Brotherhood of (IBEW) (1891): 750,000 members, 900 locals; (202) 833-7000; www.ibew.org

Engineers, International Union of Operating (IUOE) (1896): 400,000 members, 170 locals; (202) 429-9100; www.iuoe.org

#Farm Workers of America, United (UFW) (1962): 27,000+ members; (661) 823-6250; www.ufw.org

*Federal Employees, Federal District 1, National Federation of (NFFE FD1, IAMAW, AFL-CIO) (1917): 100,000 members, 200 locals; (202) 216-4420; www.nffe.org

Fire Fighters, International Association of (1918): 288,000 members, 3,100 locals; (202) 737-8484; www.iaff.org

Flight Attendants, Association of (1945): 55,000 members, 20 carriers; merged with Communications Workers of America in 2004; (202) 434-1300; www.afanet.org

#Food and Commercial Workers International Union, United (UFCW) (1979): 1.3 mil members, 500 locals; (202) 223-3111; www.ufcw.org

Glass, Molders, Pottery, Plastics & Allied Workers Intl. Union (GMP) (1842): 51,000 members, 290+ locals; (610) 565-5051; www.gmpiu.org

Government Employees, American Federation of (AFGE) (1932): 600,000 members, 1,100 locals; (202) 737-8700; www.afge.org

Graphic Communications Conference/ International Brotherhood of Teamsters (GCC/IBT) (1983): 150,000 members, 215 locals; merged with Teamsters in 2005; (202) 462-1400; www.gciu.org

Iron Workers, International Association of Bridge, Structural, Ornamental and Reinforcing (1896): 140,000 members, 213 locals; (202) 383-4800; www.ironworkers.org

#Laborers' International Union of North America (LIUNA) (1903): 500,000 members, 500+ locals; (202) 737-8320; www.liuna.org

Letter Carriers, National Association of (NALC) (1889): 300,058 members, 2,500 locals; (202) 393-4695; www.nalc.org

#Locomotive Engineers and Trainmen, Brotherhood of (BLET) (1863): 59,000+ members, 600+ divisions; (216) 241-2630; www.ble.org

Longshoremen's Association, International (ILA) (1892): 65,000+ members, approx. 200 locals; (212) 425-1200; www.ilaunion.org

Machinists and Aerospace Workers, International Association of (IAMAW) (1888): 730,000 members (current and retired), 1,174 locals; merged with TCU in 2006; (301) 967-4500; www.goiam.org

Maintenance of Way Employees, Brotherhood of (BMWE) (1887): 35,000 members, 770 locals; merged with Teamsters in 2005; (248) 948-1010; www.bmwe.org

Mine Workers of America, United (UMWA) (1890): 110,000 members, 600 locals; (703) 208-7200; www.umwa.org

Musicians of the United States and Canada, American Federation of (AFM) (1896): 90,000 members, 250 locals; (212) 869-1330; www.afm.org

Newspaper Guild-Communications Workers of America, The (CWA) (1933): 34,000+ members, 90 locals; (202) 434-7177; www.newsguild.org

*Nurses Association, American (ANA) (1897): 2.9 mil members, 54 constituent state & territorial assns.; (301) 628-5000; www.nursingworld.org

Office and Professional Employees International Union (OPEIU) (1945): 125,000 members, 200 locals; (800) 346-7348; www.opeiu.org

Painters and Allied Trades, International Union of (IUPAT) (1887): 140,000+ members, 425 locals; (202) 637-0700; www.ibpat.org

Plumbing and Pipe Fitting Industry of the U.S. and Canada, United Assn. of Journeymen and Apprentices of the (1889): 300,000 members, 317 locals; (202) 628-5823; www.ua.org

*Police, National Fraternal Order of (1915): 325,000 members, 2,100+ affiliates; (615) 399-0900; www.grandlodgefop.org

Police Associations, International Union of (1979): 80,000 members, 500 locals; (941) 487-2560; www.iupa.org

Postal Workers Union, American (APWU) (1971): 333,000+ U.S.P.S. employees, 2,000 private employees, 1,600+ locals; (202) 842-4200; www.apwu.org

Roofers, Waterproofers & Allied Workers, United Union of (1906): 22,000 members, 9 locals; (202) 463-7663; **www.unionroofers.com**

*Rural Letter Carriers' Association, National (1903): 100,000+ members; 50 state org; (703) 684-5545; **www.nrlca.org**

*Security, Police, and Fire Professionals of America (SPFPA) (1948): 30,000+ members, 300 locals; (800) 228-7492; www.spfpa.org

#Service Employees International Union (SEIU) (1921): 2 mil members, 325+ locals; (202) 730-7000; www.seiu.org

Sheet Metal Workers' International Association (SMWIA) (1888): 150,000 members, 200 locals; (202) 783-5880; www.smwia.org

State, County, and Municipal Employees, American Federation of (AFSCME), 1.4 mil members, 3,400+ locals; (202) 429-1000; www.afscme.org

Steelworkers of America, United (USWA) (1936): 850,000 active members, 2,700 locals; merged with PACE union in 2005; (412) 562-2400; www.usw.org

Teachers, American Federation of (AFT) (1916): 1.4+ mil members, 3,000 locals; (202) 879-4400; www.aft.org

#Teamsters, International Brotherhood of (IBT) (1903): 1.4 mil. members, 521 locals; (202) 624-6800; www.teamsters.org

Theatrical Stage Employees, Moving Picture Technicians, Artists and Allied Crafts of the United States, Its Territories, and Canada, International Alliance of (IATSE) (1893): 110,000+ members, 555+ locals; (212) 730-1770; www.iatse-intl.org

Transit Union, Amalgamated (ATU) (1892): 185,000+ members, 268 locals; (202) 537-1645; www.atu.org

Transportation-Communications International Union (TCU) (1899): merged with IAMAW in 2006; see Machinists and Aerospace Workers.

Transportation Union, United (UTU) (1969): 125,000 members, 600+ locals; (216) 228-9400; www.utu.org

Transport Workers Union of America (1934): 126,000 members, 92 locals; (212) 259-4900; www.twu.org

*Treasury Employees Union, National (NTEU) (1938): 150,000 represented, 270+ chapters; (202) 572-5500; www.nteu.org

#UNITE HERE (UNITE, 1900; HERE 1891) (unions merged, 2004): 440,000+ active members and 400,000+ retirees; (212) 265-7000; www.unitehere.org

Writers Guild of America, West (1933): 12,045 members; (323) 951-4000 www.wga.org

Professional Organizations and Societies

Accountants, American Institute of Certified Public (1887): 349,170 members; (888) 777-7077; www.aicpa.org

Actuaries, Society of (1949):18,000 members; (847) 706-3500; www.soa.org

Administrative Professionals, Intl. Assn. of (1942): 40,000 members; (816) 891-6600; www.iaap-hq.org

Aerospace Medical Assn. (1929): 3,200+ members; (703) 739-2240; www.asma.org

Agricultural and Biological Engineers, American Soc. of (ASABE) (1907): 9,000 members; (269) 429-0300; www.asabe.org

Air & Waste Management Assn. (1907): 8,000+ members; (412) 232-3444; www.awma.org

AMSUS (Society of the Federal Health Agencies) (1891): 9,000+ members; (301) 897-8800; www.amsus.org

APICS (Assn. for Operations Mgmt.) (1957): 43,000 members; (773) 867-1777; www.apics.org

Architects, American Institute of (1857): 83,000+; (202) 626-7300; www.aia.org

Astrologers, Inc., American Federation of (AFA, Inc.) (1938): 4,000; (480) 838-1751; www.astrologers.com

Astronautical Society, American (1954): 1,500 members; (703) 866-0020; www.astronautical.org

Astronomical Society, American (1899): 6,467 members; (202) 328-2010 www.aas.org

Authors Guild, The (1912): 9,000 members; (212) 563-5904; www.authorsguild.org

Authors Registry, The (1995): 40,000 members; (212) 563-6920; www.authorsregistry.org

Bankers of America, Independent Community (1930): 5,000 members; (202) 659-8111; www.icba.org

Bar Assn., American (1878): 400,000+; (312) 988-5000; www.abanet.org

Bar Assn., Federal (1920): 16,000 members; (571) 481-9100; www.fedbar.org

Biochemistry and Molecular Biology, American Society for (1906): 12,000+ members; (301) 634-7145; www.asbmb.org

Broadcasters, Natl. Assn. of (1923): 8,300 members; (202) 429-5300; www.nab.org

Business Women's Assn., American (1949): 40,000 members; (800) 228-0007; www.abwa.org

Cartoonists Society, Natl. (1948): 500+ members; (407) 647-8839; www.reuben.org

Ceramic Society, American (1899): 6,000+ members; (240) 646-7054; www.ceramics.org

Chamber Music Players, Inc., Amateur (1969): 5,400+ members; (212) 645-7424; www.acmp.net

Chemical Society, American (1876): 160,000+ members; (202) 872-4600; www.chemistry.org

Chiefs of Police, Intl. Assn. of (1893): 20,000+ members; (703) 836-6767; www.theiacp.org

Chiropractic Assn., American (1963): 15,000 members; (703) 276-8800; www.amerchiro.org

Civil Engineers, American Society of (1852): 141,000+ members; (800) 548-2723; www.asce.org

College Admission Counseling, Natl. Assn. for (1937): 10,000 members; (703) 836-2222; www.nacacnet.org

Commercial Law League of America (1895): 4,000 members; (312) 781-2000; www.clla.org

Communication Assn., Natl. (1914): 7,700 members; (202) 464-4622; www.natcom.org

Composers, Authors & Publishers, American Soc. of (ASCAP) (1914): 330,000+ members; (212) 621-6000; www.ascap.com

Computing Machinery, Assn. for (1947): 85,500 members; (212) 626-0500; www.acm.org

Computing Professionals, Institute for Certification of (1973): 50,000 members; (847) 299-4227; www.iccp.org

Construction Inspectors, Assn. of (1974): 1,000; (623) 580-4646; www.aci-assoc.org

Cosmetology Assn., Natl. (1921): 25,000 members; (866) 871-0656; www.ncacares.org

Counseling Assn., American (1952): 45,000 members; (800) 347-6647; www.counseling.org

Country Music Assn. (1958): 5,500 members; (615) 244-2840; www.CMAworld.com

Customs Brokers and Forwarders Assn. of America, Inc., Natl. (1897): 800 cos.; (202) 466-0222; www.ncbfaa.org

Dental Assn., American (1859): 155,000+ members; (312) 440-2500; www.ada.org

Directors Guild of America (1936): 13,400 members; (310) 289-2000; www.dga.org

Electrical and Electronics Engineers, Institute of (1963): 375,000+ members; (732) 981-0060; www.ieee.org

Electronics Technicians, Intl. Soc. of Certified (1980): 50,000 members; (800) 946-0201; www.iscet.org

Energy Engineers, Assn. of (1977): 8,500 members; (770) 447-5083; www.aeecenter.org

Engineers, Natl. Society of Professional (1934): 45,000 members; (703) 684-2800; www.nspe.org

Environmental Assessment Association (1972): 3,500 members; (623) 580-4646; www.eaa-assoc.org

Environmental Health Assn., Natl. (1937): 4,500 members; (303) 756-9090; www.neha.org

Family Physicians, American Academy of (1947): 93,000+; (913) 906-6000; www.aafp.org

Farm Bureau, American (1919): 6.2 mil members; (202) 406-3600; www.fb.org

Farmers Union, Natl. (1902): 250,000 families; (202) 554-1600; www.nfu.org

Financial Professionals, Assn. for (1979): 16,000+ members; (301) 907-2862; www.AFPonline.org

Financial Service Professionals, Soc. of (1928): 18,000 members; (610) 526-2600; www.financialpro.org

Financial Women Intl. (1921 as Natl. Assoc. of Bank Women): 1,000+ members; (651) 487-7632; www.fwi.org

Fire Chiefs, Intl. Assn. of (1873): 13,000 members; (703) 273-0911; www.iafc.org

Fire Protection Engineers, Soc. of (1950): 4,500 members; (301) 718-2910; www.sfpe.org

Food Technologists, Institute of (1939): 22,000 members; (312) 782-8424; www.ift.org

Forensic Sciences, American Academy of (1948): 6,000 members; (719) 636-1100; www.aafs.org

Funeral Directors Assn., Natl. (1882): 20,300 members; (262) 789-1880; www.nfda.org

General Contractors of America, Associated (1918): 32,000+ cos.; (703) 548-3118; www.agc.org

Geographers, Assn. of American (1904): 10,000 members; (202) 234-1450; www.aag.org

Graphic Arts, American Institute of (1914): 22,000 members; (212) 807-1990; www.aiga.org

Ground Water Assn., Natl. (1948): 14,000 members; (614) 898-7786; www.ngwa.org

Heating, Refrigerating & Air-Conditioning Engineers, Inc., American Soc. of (1894): 50,000 members; (404) 636-8400; www.ashrae.org

Home Builders, Natl. Assn. of (1942): 235,000 members; (202) 266-8200; www.nahb.org

Human Resource Management, Society for (SHRM) (1948): 225,000+ members; (703) 548-3440; www.shrm.org

Illustrators, Inc., Society of (1901): 1,000 members; (212) 838-2560; www.societyillustrators.org

Industrial Designers Society of America (1965): 3,300 members; (703) 707-6000; www.idsa.org

Industrial Security, American Soc. for (1955): 36,000+ members; (703) 519-6200; www.asisonline.org

Intelligence Officers, Assn. of Former (1975): 24 chap., 4,000 members; (703) 790-0320; www.afio.com

Interior Designers, American Society of (1975): 40,000 members; (202) 526-3240; www.asid.org

Investigative Pathology, American Soc. for (1900): 1,718 members; (301) 634-7130; www.asip.org

Jail Assn., American (1981): 5,000 members; (301) 790-3930; www.aja.org

Journalists, Society of Professional (1909): 10,000 members; (317) 927-8000; www.spj.org

Journalists and Authors, American Society of (1948): 1,100+ members; (212) 997-0947; www.asja.org

Judicature Society, American (1913): 6,000 members; (515) 271-2281; www.ajs.org

Landscape Architects, American Society of (1899): 18,000+ members; (202) 898-2444; www.asla.org

Legal Administrators, Assn. of (1971): 10,534 members; (847) 267-1252; www.alanet.org

Legal Secretaries, Natl. Assn. of (NALS) (1929): 6,000 members; (918) 582-5188; www.nals.org

Library Assn., American (1876): 66,000 members; (800) 545-2433; www.ala.org

Lifesaving Assn., U.S. (1964):11,000 members; (866) 367-8752; www.usla.org

Logistics, Intl. Society of (SOLE) (1966): 3,000+ members; (301) 459-8446; www.sole.org

Magicians, Intl. Brotherhood of (1922): 13,000 members; (314) 845-9200; www.magician.org

Management Accountants, Institute of (1919): 65,000 members; (201) 573-9000; www.imanet.org

Management Assn., American (1923): 4,100 cos., 38,000 ind.; (212) 903-7976; www.amanet.org

Marketing Assn., American (1915): 40,000 members; (312) 542-9000; www.marketingpower.com

Master Brewers Association of the Americas (1887): 3,500 members; (651) 454-7250; www.mbaa.com

Materials and Process Engineering, Soc. for the Advancement of (1944): 4,500 members; (626) 331-0616; www.sampe.org

Mechanical Engineers, American Soc. of (1880): 127,000 members; (973) 882-1170; www.asme.org

Medical Assn., American (1847): 250,000; (800) 621-8335; www.ama-assn.org

Medical Library Assn. (1898): 4,000 members; (312) 419-9094; www.mlanet.org

Motion Picture Arts & Sciences, Academy of (1927): 6,500+ members; (310) 247-3000; www.oscars.org

Motion Picture & Television Engineers, Soc. of (1916): 8,000 members; (914) 761-1100; www.smpte.org

Mystery Writers of America, Inc. (1945): 3,000+ members; (212) 888-8171; www.mysterywriters.org

Notaries, American Society of (1965): approx. 20,000 members; (850) 671-5164; www.notaries.org

Nursing, Natl. League for (1893): 20,000 members, 1,100 institutions; (212) 363-5555; www.nln.org

Optometric Assn., American (1898): 35,000+ members; (800) 365-2219; www.aoa.org

Organists, American Guild of (1896): 20,000 members; (212) 870-2310; www.agohq.org

Pen Women, Natl. League of American (1897): 3,000 members; (202) 785-1997; www.americanpenwomen.org

Pharmacists Assn., American (1852): 60,000+ members; (202) 628-4410; www.pharmacist.com

Physical Therapy Assn., American (1921): 72,000+ members; (703) 684-2782; www.apta.org

Plastics Engineers, Society of (1942): 20,000 members; (203) 775-0471; www.4spe.org

Police Assn., Intl. (1950 in UK, 1962 in U.S.): 300,000+ members; (248) 486-7137; www.ipa-usa.org

Population Assn. of America (1931): 3,000 members; (301) 565-6710; www.popassoc.org

Postmasters of the U.S., Natl. Assn. of (1898): 42,000 members, 95 clubs; (703) 683-9027; www.napus.org

Press Club, National (1908): 3,600; (202) 662-7500; www.press.org

Professional Ball Players of America, Assn. of (1924): 11,000 members; (714) 935-9993; www.apbpa.org

Psychiatric Assn., American (1844): 38,000 members; (703) 907-7300; www.psych.org

Psychological Assn., American (1892): 148,000 members; (202) 336-5500; www.apa.org

Public Administration, American Soc. for (1939): 9,000 members; (202) 393-7878; www.aspanet.org

Public Health Assn., American (1872): 50,000+ members; (202) 777-2042; www.apha.org

Public Relations Soc. of America (1947): 32,000 members; (212) 460-1400; www.prsa.org

Range Management, Society for (1948): 4,000 members; (303) 986-3309; www.rangelands.org

Real Estate Appraisers, Natl. Assn. of (1966): 5,500 members; (623) 580-4646; www.narea-assoc.org

Rehabilitation Assn., Natl. (1925): 6,000 members; (703) 836-0850; www.nationalrehab.org

Road & Transportation Builders Assn., American (1902): 5,000 members; (202) 289-4434; www.artba.org

Safety Engineers, American Soc. of (1911): 32,000+ members; (847) 699-2929; www.asse.org

School Administrators, American Assn. of (1865): 13,000+ members; (703) 528-0700; www.aasa.org

Science Teachers Assn., Natl. (1944): 55,000 members; (703) 243-7100; www.nsta.org

Science Writers, Natl. Assn. of (1955): 2,300 members; (304) 754-5077; www.nasw.org

Screen Actors Guild (1933): 120,000 members; (323) 954-1600; www.sag.com

Songwriters Guild of America (1931): 5,000+ members; (615) 742-9945; www.songwritersguild.com

Sportscasters Assn., The American (1980): 500+ members; (212) 227-8080; www.americansportscastersonline.com

Surgeons, American College of (1913): 70,000+ members; (312) 202-5000; www.facs.org

Tax Administrators, Federation of (1937): (202) 624-5890; www.taxadmin.org

Teachers of English, Natl. Council of (1911): 60,000+ members; (217) 328-3870; www.ncte.org

Teachers of English to Speakers of Other Languages (1966): 14,000 members; (703) 836-0774; www.tesol.org

Teachers of French, American Assn. of (1927): 10,000 members; (618) 453-5731; www.frenchteachers.org

Teachers of German, American Assn. of (1926): 5,500 members; (856) 795-5553; www.aatg.org

Teachers of Mathematics, Natl. Council of (1920): 100,000+ members; (703) 620-9840; www.nctm.org

Teachers of Spanish & Portuguese, American Assn. of (1917): 11,000 members; (248) 960-2180; www.aatsp.org

Television Academy, Natl. (1955): (212) 586-8424; www.emmyonline.org

Theological Library Assn., American (1946): 1,000+ members; (312) 454-5100; www.atla.com

Transportation Engineers, Inst. of (1930): 17,000 members; (202) 289-0222; www.ite.org

Travel Agents, American Soc. of (1931): 12,000 members; (703) 739-2782; www.astanet.com

Underwriters, Soc. of Chartered Property and Casualty (CPCU) (1944): 28,000+ members; (800) 932-2728; www.cpcusociety.org

University Women, American Assn. of (1881): 100,000 members; (202) 785-7700; www.aauw.org

Veterinary Medical Assn., American (1863): 76,000+ members; (847) 925-8070; www.avma.org

Women in Communications, the Association for (1909, as Theta Sigma Phi): 3,000+ members; (703) 370-7436; www.womcom.org

Women Engineers, Society of (1950): 17,000; (312) 596-5223; www.swe.org

Women in Radio and Television Inc., Amer. (1951): 1,500 members; (703) 506-3290; www.awrt.org

Sports Organizations

Major League Baseball

Office of the Commissioner, 245 Park Ave., 31st Fl., New York, NY 10167; www.mlb.com

American League

Baltimore Orioles (1953): 333 W. Camden St., Baltimore, MD 21201; (410) 685-9800; www.orioles.com

Boston Red Sox (1901): 4 Yawkey Way, Boston, MA 02215; (617) 267-9440; www.redsox.com

Chicago White Sox (1900, as Chicago White Stockings): 333 W. 35th St., Chicago, IL 60616; (312) 674-1000; www.whitesox.com

Cleveland Indians (1901): 2401 Ontario St., Cleveland, OH 44115; (216) 420-4200; www.indians.com

Detroit Tigers (1901): 2100 Woodward Ave., Detroit, MI 48201; (313) 471-2000; www.tigers.com

Kansas City Royals (1969): One Royal Way, Kansas City, MO 64129; (816) 921-8000; www.royals.com

Los Angeles Angels of Anaheim (1961): 2000 Gene Autry Way, Anaheim, CA 92806; (714) 940-2000; www.angelsbaseball.com

Minnesota Twins (1960): 34 Kirby Puckett Place, Minneapolis, MN 55415; (612) 375-1366; www.twinsbaseball.com

New York Yankees (1903): One East 61st St., Bronx, NY 10451; (718) 293-4300; www.yankees.com

Oakland Athletics (1901, as Philadelphia Athletics): 7000 Coliseum Way, Oakland, CA 94621; (510) 638-4900; www.oaklandathletics.com

Seattle Mariners (1977): P.O. Box 4100, Seattle, WA 98104; (206) 346-4000; www.mariners.com

Tampa Bay Rays (1995, as Tampa Bay Devil Rays): One Tropicana Dr., St. Petersburg, FL 33705; (727) 825-3137; www.raysbaseball.com

Texas Rangers (1960): 1000 Ballpark Way, Arlington, TX 76011; (817) 273-5222; www.texasrangers.com

Toronto Blue Jays (1976): One Blue Jays Way, Ste. 3200, Toronto, ON M5V1J1; (416) 341-1000; www.bluejays.com

National League

Arizona Diamondbacks (1998): 401 E. Jefferson St., Phoenix, AZ 85001; (602) 462-6500; www.dbacks.com

Atlanta Braves (1876, as Boston Red Stockings): 755 Hank Aaron Drive, Atlanta, GA 30315; (404) 522-7630; www.braves.com

Chicago Cubs (1876, as Chicago White Stockings): 1060 W. Addison St., Chicago, IL 60613; (773) 404-2827; www.cubs.com

Cincinnati Reds (1869, as Cincinnati Red Stockings): 100 Main St., Cincinnati, OH 45202; (513) 765-7000; www.reds.com

Colorado Rockies (1991): 2001 Blake St., Denver, CO 80205; (303) 292-0200; www.coloradorockies.com

Florida Marlins (1991): 2267 Dan Marino Blvd., Miami, FL 33056; (305) 626-7400; www.floridamarlins.com

Houston Astros (1962, as Houston Colt .45s): 501 Crawford St., Houston, TX 77002; (713) 259-8000; www.astros.com

Los Angeles Dodgers (1890): 1000 Elysian Park Ave., Los Angeles, CA 90012; (323) 224-1500; www.dodgers.com

Milwaukee Brewers (1970): One Brewers Way, Milwaukee, WI 53214; (414) 902-4400; www.brewers.com

New York Mets (1961): Roosevelt Ave., Flushing, NY 11368; (718) 507-6387; www.mets.com

Philadelphia Phillies (1883): One Citizens Bank Way, Philadelphia, PA 19148; (215) 463-6000; www.phillies.com

Pittsburgh Pirates (1887): 115 Federal St., Pittsburgh, PA 15212; (412) 323-5000; www.pirates.com

St. Louis Cardinals (1892): 700 Clark St., St. Louis, MO 63102; (314) 345-9600; www.stlcardinals.com

San Diego Padres (1968): 100 Park Blvd., San Diego, CA 92101; (619) 795-5000; www.padres.com

San Francisco Giants (1883, as New York Gothams): 24 Willie Mays Plaza, San Francisco, CA 94107; (415) 972-2000; www.sfgiants.com

Washington Nationals (1969, as Montreal Expos): 1500 South Capitol St., SE, Washington, DC 20003; (202) 349-0400; www.nationals.com

National Basketball Association

League Office, Olympic Tower, 645 5th Ave., New York, NY 10022; www.nba.com

Atlanta Hawks (1949, as Tri-City Blackhawks): 101 Marietta St. NW, Ste. 1900, Atlanta, GA 30303; (404) 878-3800; www.nba.com/hawks

Boston Celtics (1946): 226 Causeway St. Fourth Fl., Boston, MA 02114; (866) 423-5849; www.nba.com/celtics

Charlotte Bobcats (2004): 333 E. Trade St., Charlotte, NC 28202; (704) 688-8600; www.nba.com/bobcats

Chicago Bulls (1966): 1901 W. Madison St., Chicago, IL 60612; (312) 455-4500; www.nba.com/bulls

Cleveland Cavaliers (1970): One Center Court, Cleveland, OH 44115; (216) 420-2000; www.nba.com/cavaliers

Dallas Mavericks (1980): 2909 Taylor St., Dallas, TX 75226; (214) 747-6287; www.nba.com/mavericks

Denver Nuggets (1967, as Denver Rockets): 1000 Chopper Cir., Denver, CO 80204; (303) 405-1100; www.nba.com/nuggets

Detroit Pistons (1957): Five Championship Dr., Auburn Hills, MI 48326; (248) 377-0100; www.nba.com/pistons

Golden State Warriors (1946, as Philadelphia Warriors): 1011 Broadway, Oakland, CA 94607; (510) 986-2200; www.nba.com/warriors

Houston Rockets (1967, as San Diego Rockets): 1510 Polk St., Houston, TX 77002; (713) 627-3865; www.nba.com/rockets

Indiana Pacers (1967): 125 S. Pennsylvania St., Indianapolis, IN 46204; (317) 917-2500; www.nba.com/pacers

Los Angeles Clippers (1970, as Buffalo Braves): 1111 S. Figueroa St., Ste. 1100, Los Angeles, CA 90015; (888) 895-8662; www.nba.com/clippers

Los Angeles Lakers (1947, as Minneapolis Lakers): 555 N. Nash St., El Segundo, CA 90245; (310) 426-6000; www.nba.com/lakers

Memphis Grizzlies (1995, as Vancouver Grizzlies): 191 Beale St., Memphis, TN 38103; (901) 888-4667; www.nba.com/grizzlies

Miami Heat (1988): 601 Biscayne Blvd., Miami, FL 33132; (786) 777-4328; www.nba.com/heat

Milwaukee Bucks (1968): 1001 N. 4th St., Milwaukee, WI 53203; (414) 227-0599; www.nba.com/bucks

Minnesota Timberwolves (1989): 600 1st Ave. North, Minneapolis, MN 55403; (612) 673-1600; www.nba.com/timberwolves

New Jersey Nets (1967, as New Jersey Americans): 390 Murray Hill Pkwy., E. Rutherford, NJ 07073; (201) 935-8888; www.nba.com/nets

New Orleans Hornets (1988, as the Charlotte Hornets): 1250 Poydras St., 19th Fl., New Orleans, LA 70113; (504) 593-4700; www.nba.com/hornets

New York Knickerbockers (1946): Two Pennsylvania Plaza, New York, NY 10121; (212) 465-6471; www.nba.com/knicks

Oklahoma City Thunder (1967, as Seattle SuperSonics): 2 Leadership Square, 211 N. Robinson Ave., Ste. 300; Oklahoma City, OK 73102; (405) 208-4800; www.nba.com/thunder

Orlando Magic (1989): 8701 Maitland Summit Blvd., Orlando, FL 32810; (407) 916-2400; www.nba.com/magic

Philadelphia 76ers (1937, as Syracuse Nationals): 3601 S. Broad St., Philadelphia, PA 19148; (215) 336-3600; www.nba.com/sixers

Phoenix Suns (1968): 201 E. Jefferson St., Phoenix, AZ 85004; (602) 379-7900; www.nba.com/suns

Portland Trail Blazers (1970): One Center Ct., Ste. 200, Portland, OR 97227; (503) 234-9291; www.nba.com/blazers

Sacramento Kings (1945, as Rochester Royals): One Sports Pkwy., Sacramento, CA 95834; (916) 928-0000; www.nba.com/kings

San Antonio Spurs (1967, as Dallas Chaparrals): One AT&T Center, San Antonio, TX 78219; (210) 444-5000; www.nba.com/spurs

Toronto Raptors (1995): 40 Bay St., Toronto, ON M5J 2X2; (416) 366-3865; www.nba.com/raptors

Utah Jazz (1974, as New Orleans Jazz): 301 W. South Temple, Salt Lake City, UT 84101; (801) 325-2500; www.nba.com/jazz

Washington Wizards (1963, as Baltimore Bullets): 601 F St. NW, Washington, DC 20004; (202) 661-5000; www.nba.com/wizards

National Hockey League

NHL Headquarters, 1185 Ave. of the Americas, New York, NY 10036; www.nhl.com

Anaheim Ducks (1993): 2695 E. Katella Ave., Anaheim, CA 92806; (877) 945-3946; www.ducks.nhl.com

Atlanta Thrashers (1999): Centennial Tower, 101 Marietta St. NW, Ste. 1900, Atlanta, GA 30303; (404) 878-3000; www.thrashers.nhl.com

Boston Bruins (1924): 100 Legends Way, Boston, MA 02114; (617) 624-1900; www.bruins.nhl.com

Buffalo Sabres (1970): One Seymour H. Knox III Plaza, Buffalo, NY 14203; (716) 855-4100; www.sabres.nhl.com

Calgary Flames (1980): P.O. Box 1540, Station M, Calgary, AB T2P 3B9; (403) 777-2177; www.flames.nhl.com

Carolina Hurricanes (1972, as New England Whalers): 1400 Edwards Mill Rd., Raleigh, NC 27607; (919) 467-7825; www.hurricanes.nhl.com

Chicago Blackhawks (1926): 1901 W. Madison St., Chicago, IL 60612; (312) 455-7000; www.blackhawks.nhl.com

Colorado Avalanche (1972, as Quebec Nordiques): 1000 Chopper Cir., Denver, CO 80204; (303) 405-1100; www.avalanche.nhl.com

Columbus Blue Jackets (2000): 200 W. Nationwide Blvd., Columbus, OH 43215; (614) 246-4625; www.bluejackets.nhl.com

Dallas Stars (1967, as Minnesota North Stars): 2601 Avenue of the Stars, Frisco, TX 75034; (214) 387-5500; www.stars.nhl.com

Detroit Red Wings (1926, as Detroit Cougars): 600 Civic Center Dr., Detroit, MI 48226; (313) 983-6606; www.redwings.nhl.com

Edmonton Oilers (1972): 11230 110 St., Edmonton, AB T5G 3H7; (780) 414-4000; www.oilers.nhl.com

Florida Panthers (1993): One Panther Pkwy., Sunrise, FL 33323; (954) 835-7000; www.panthers.nhl.com

Los Angeles Kings (1967): 1111 S. Figueroa St., Ste. 3100, Los Angeles, CA 90015; (213) 742-7100; www.kings.nhl.com

Minnesota Wild (2000): 317 Washington St., St. Paul, MN 55102; (651) 602-6000; www.wild.nhl.com

Montreal Canadiens (1917): 1275 St. Antonie St. W, Montreal, QC H3C 5L2; (514) 932-2582; www.canadiens.nhl.com

Nashville Predators (1998): 501 Broadway, Nashville, TN 37203; (615) 770-2355; www.predators.nhl.com

New Jersey Devils (1974): Prudential Center, 165 Mulberry St., Newark, NJ 07102; (973) 757-6100; www.devils.nhl.com

New York Islanders (1972): 1255 Hempstead Tpke., Uniondale, NY 11553; (516) 501-6700; www.islanders.nhl.com

New York Rangers (1926): Two Pennsylvania Plaza, New York, NY 10121; (212) 465-6000; www.rangers.nhl.com

Ottawa Senators (1901): 1000 Palladium Dr., Ottawa, ON K2V 1A5; (613) 599-0250; www.senators.nhl.com

Philadelphia Flyers (1967): 3601 South Broad St., Philadelphia, PA 19148; (215) 336-3600; www.flyers.nhl.com

Phoenix Coyotes (1979, as Winnipeg Jets): 6751 N. Sunset Blvd. #200, Glendale, AZ 85305; (623) 772-3200; www.coyotes.nhl.com

Pittsburgh Penguins (1967): One Chatham Ctr., Ste. 400, Pittsburgh, PA 15219; (412) 642-1300; www.penguins.nhl.com

St. Louis Blues (1967): 1401 Clark Ave., St. Louis, MO 63103; (314) 622-2500; www.blues.nhl.com

San Jose Sharks (1991): 525 W. Santa Clara St., San Jose, CA 95113; (408) 287-7070; www.sharks.nhl.com

Tampa Bay Lightning (1992): 401 Channelside Dr., Tampa, FL 33602; (813) 301-6500; www.lightning.nhl.com

Toronto Maple Leafs (1919, as Toronto St. Pats): 40 Bay St., Ste. 400, Toronto, ON M5J 2X2; (416) 815-5700; www.mapleleafs.nhl.com

Vancouver Canucks (1946): 800 Griffiths Way, Vancouver, BC V6B 6G1; (604) 899-7400; www.canucks.nhl.com

Washington Capitals (1974): 627 N. Glebe Rd., Ste. 850, Arlington, VA 22203; (202) 266-2200; www.capitals.nhl.com

National Football League

League Office, 280 Park Ave., New York, NY 10017; www.nfl.com

Arizona Cardinals (1898): P.O. Box 888, Phoenix, AZ 85001; (602) 379-0101; www.azcardinals.com

Atlanta Falcons (1965): 4400 Falcon Pkwy., Flowery Branch, GA 30542; (770) 965-3115; www.atlantafalcons.com

Baltimore Ravens (1946, as Baltimore Colts): 1101 Russel St., Baltimore, MD 21230; (410) 261-7283; www.baltimoreravens.com

Buffalo Bills (1959): One Bills Dr., Orchard Park, NY 14127; (877) 228-4257; www.buffalobills.com

Carolina Panthers (1993): 800 S. Mint St., Charlotte, NC 28202; (704) 358-7000; www.panthers.com

Chicago Bears (1920, as Decatur Staleys): 1000 Football Dr., Lake Forest, IL 60045; (888) 792-3277; www.chicagobears.com

Cincinnati Bengals (1968): One Paul Brown Stadium, Cincinnati, OH 45202; (513) 621-3550; www.bengals.com

Cleveland Browns (1946): 100 Alfred Lerner Way, Cleveland, OH 44114; (440) 824-6284; www.clevelandbrowns.com

Dallas Cowboys (1960): 900 E. Randol Mill Rd., Arlington, TX 76011; (817) 892-5000; www.dallascowboys.com

Denver Broncos (1960): 13655 Broncos Pkwy., Englewood, CO 80112; (303) 649-9000; www.denverbroncos.com

Detroit Lions (1934): 222 Republic Dr., Allen Park, MI 48101; (313) 262-2002; www.detroitlions.com

Green Bay Packers (1919): 1265 Lombardi Ave., Green Bay, WI 54304; (920) 569-7500; www.packers.com

Houston Texans (2002): Two Reliant Park, Houston, TX 77054; (832) 667-2000; www.houstontexans.com

Indianapolis Colts (1946): 7001 W. 56th St., Indianapolis, IN 46254; (317) 297-2658; www.colts.com

Jacksonville Jaguars (1995): One Stadium Place, Jacksonville, FL 32202; (904) 633-2000; www.jaguars.com

Kansas City Chiefs (1960): One Arrowhead Dr., Kansas City, MO 64129; (816) 920-9300; www.kcchiefs.com

Miami Dolphins (1966): 7500 SW 30th St., Davie, FL 33314; (888) 346-7849; www.miamidolphins.com

Minnesota Vikings (1961): 9520 Viking Dr., Eden Prairie, MN 55344; (952) 858-6500; www.vikings.com

New England Patriots (1960): One Patriot Pl., Foxboro, MA 02035; (800) 543-1776; www.patriots.com

New Orleans Saints (1967): 5800 Airline Dr., Metairie, LA 70003; (504) 731-1700; www.neworleanssaints.com

New York Giants (1925): Giants Stadium, E. Rutherford, NJ 07073; (201) 935-8111; www.giants.com

New York Jets (1960): One Jets Dr., Florham Park, NJ 07932; (516) 560-8200; www.newyorkjets.com

Oakland Raiders (1960): 1220 Harbor Bay Pkwy., Alameda, CA 94502; (510) 864-5000; www.raiders.com

Philadelphia Eagles (1933): One NovaCare Way, Philadelphia, PA 19145; (215) 463-2500; www.philadelphiaeagles.com

Pittsburgh Steelers (1933): 100 Art Rooney Ave., Pittsburgh, PA 15212; (412) 432-7800; www.steelers.com

St. Louis Rams (1937): One Rams Way, St. Louis, MO 63045; (314) 982-7267; www.stlouisrams.com

San Diego Chargers (1960): 4020 Murphy Canyon Rd., San Diego, CA 92123; (858) 874-4500; www.chargers.com

San Francisco 49ers (1950): 4949 Centennial Blvd., Santa Clara, CA 95054; (408) 562-4949; www.sf49ers.com

Seattle Seahawks (1976): 12 Seahawks Way, Renton, WA 98056; (888) 635-4295; www.seahawks.com

Tampa Bay Buccaneers (1976): One Buccaneer Place, Tampa, FL 33607; (813) 870-2700; www.buccaneers.com

Tennessee Titans (1960): One Titans Way, Nashville, TN 37213; (615) 565-4000; www.titansonline.com

Washington Redskins (1937): 21300 Redskin Park Dr., Ashburn, VA 20147; (703) 726-7000; www.redskins.com

Other North American Sports Organizations

Athletic Union, Amateur (1888): P.O. Box 22409, Lake Buena Vista, FL 32830; (407) 934-7200; www.aausports.org

American Kennel Club (1884): 260 Madison Ave., New York, NY 10016; (919) 233-9767; www.akc.org

Auto Club, U.S. (1955): 4910 W. 16th St., Speedway, IN 46224; (317) 247-5151; www.usacracing.com

Badminton Assn., USA (1938): One Olympic Plaza, Colorado Springs, CO 80909; (719) 866-4808; www.usabadminton.org

Baseball Congress, American Amateur (1935): 100 W. Broadway, Farmington, NM 87401; (505) 327-3120; www.aabc.us

Baseball Congress, Natl. (1934): 300 S. Sycamore, Wichita, KS 67213; (316) 264-4625; www.nbcbaseball.com

Baseball Research, Inc., Society for American (1971): 812 Huron Rd., Ste. #719, Cleveland, OH 44115; (216) 575-0500; www.sabr.org

Bowling Congress, U.S. (2005): 621 Six Flags Dr., Arlington, TX 76011; (800) 514-2695; www.bowl.com

Canadian Football League (1958): 50 Wellington St. E., 3rd Fl., Toronto, ON M5E 1C8; (416) 322-9650; www.cfl.ca

Chess Federation, U.S. (1939): P.O. Box 3967, Crossville, TN 38557; (931) 787-1234; www.uschess.org

Contract Bridge League, American (1937): 2990 Airways Blvd., Memphis, TN 38116; (901) 332-5586; www.acbl.org

Disabled Sports USA (1967): 451 Hungerford Dr., Ste. 100, Rockville, MD 20850; (301) 217-0960; www.dsusa.org

Equestrian Federation, U.S. (1917): 4047 Iron Works Pkwy., Lexington, KY 40511; (859) 258-2472; www.usef.org

Figure Skating Assn., U.S. (1921): 20 First St., Colorado Springs, CO 80906; (719) 635-5200; www.usfigureskating.org

Game Fish Assn., Intl. (1939): 300 Gulf Stream Way, Dania Beach, FL 33004; (954) 927-2628; www.igfa.org

Golf Assn., U.S. (1894): P.O. Box 708, Far Hills, NJ 07931; (908) 234-2300; www.usga.org

LPGA (1950): 100 International Golf Dr., Daytona Beach, FL 32124; (386) 274-6200; www.lpga.com

Handball Assn., U.S. (1951): 2333 N. Tucson Blvd., Tucson, AZ 85716; (520) 795-0434; www.ushandball.org

Highpointers Club (1986): P.O. Box 6364, Sevierville, TN 37864; (303) 278-1915; www.highpointers.org

Hockey, U.S.A. (1936): 1775 Bob Johnson Dr., Colorado Springs, CO 80906; (719) 576-8724; www.usahockey.com

Hot Rod Assn., Natl. (1951): 2035 Financial Way, Glendora, CA 91741; (626) 914-4761; www.nhra.com

Indy Racing League (1994): 4565 W. 16th St., Indianapolis, IN 46222; (317) 492-6526; www.indycar.com

Intercollegiate Athletics, Natl. Assn. of (1937): 1200 Grand Blvd., Kansas City, MO 64106; (816) 595-8000; www.naia.org

Little League Baseball (1939): 539 US Rte. 15 Hwy, P.O. Box 3485, Williamsport, PA 17701; (570) 326-1921; www.littleleague.org

Muzzle Loading Rifle Assn., Natl. (1933): P.O. Box 67, Friendship, IN 47021; (812) 667-5131; www.nmlra.org

National Association for Stock Car Auto Racing (NASCAR, 1948): P.O. Box 2875, Daytona Beach, FL 32120; (386) 253-0611; www.nascar.com

National Collegiate Athletic Association (NCAA) (1906, as Intercollegiate Athletic Association of the United States): 700 W. Washington St., P.O. Box 6222, Indianapolis, IN 46206; (317) 917-6222; www.ncaa.org

National Rifle Assn. (1871): 11250 Waples Mill Rd., Fairfax, VA 22030; (800) 672-3888; www.nra.org

Olympic Committee, U.S. (1896, as American Olympic Association): One Olympic Plaza, Colorado Springs, CO 80909; (719) 632-5551; www.usoc.org

Polo Assn., U.S. (1890): 4037 Ironworks Pkwy., Ste. 110, Lexington, KY 40511; (859) 219-1000; www.us-polo.org

Power Boat Assn., American (1903): 17640 E. Nine Mile Rd., P.O. Box 377, Eastpointe, MI 48021; (586) 773-9700; www.apba-racing.com

Pro Bowlers Assn. (1958): 719 2nd Ave., Ste. 701, Seattle, WA 98104; (206) 332-9688; www.pbatour.org

Professional Golfers Association of America (PGA, 1916): 100 Avenue of the Champions, Palm Beach Gardens, FL 33418; (561) 624-8400; www.pga.com

Pro Rodeo Cowboys Assn. (1936): 101 Pro Rodeo Dr., Colorado Springs, CO 80919; (719) 593-8840; www.prorodeo.com

Roller Sports, U.S.A. (1937): 4730 South St., Lincoln, NE 68506; (402) 483-7551; www.usarollersports.org

Rugby, USA (1975): 2500 Arapahoe Ave., Ste. 200, Boulder, CO 80302; (303) 539-0300; www.usarugby.org

Running Assn., American (1968): 4405 East West Hwy., Ste. 405, Bethesda, MD 20814; (800) 776-2732; www.americanrunning.org

Ski and Snowboard Assn., U.S. (1964): 1 Victory Lane, P.O. Box 100, Park City, UT 84060; (435) 649-9090; www.ussa.org

Skeet Shooting Assn., Natl. (1928): 5931 Roft Rd., San Antonio, TX 78253; (210) 688-3371; www.mynssa.com

Soccer Federation, U.S. (1903): 1801 S. Prairie Ave., Chicago, IL 60616; (312) 808-1300; www.ussoccer.com

Major League Soccer (1993): 420 5th Ave., 7th Fl., New York, NY 10018; (212) 450-1200; www.mlsnet.com

Softball Assn., Amateur (1993): 2801 NE 50th St., Oklahoma City, OK 73111; (405) 424-5266; www.softball.org

Special Olympics (1968): 1133 19th St. NW, Washington, DC 20036; (202) 628-3630; www.specialolympics.org

Speedskating, U.S. (1966): 5662 S. 4800 W., Kearns, UT 84118; (801) 417-5360; www.usspeedskating.org

Speleological Society, Natl. (1941): 2813 Cave Ave., Huntsville, AL 35810; (256) 852-1300; www.caves.org

Swimming, USA (1979): One Olympic Plaza, Colorado Springs, CO 80909; (719) 866-4578; www.usa-swimming.org

Table Tennis Assn., U.S. (1933): One Olympic Plaza, Colorado Springs, CO 80909; (719) 866-4583; www.usatt.org

Tennis Assn., U.S. (1881): 70 W. Red Oak Lane, White Plains, NY 10604; (914) 696-7000; www.usta.com

Thoroughbred Racing Assn. (1942): 420 Fair Hill Dr. Ste. 1, Elkton, MD 21921; (410) 392-9200; www.tra-online.com

USA Track & Field (1878, as Amateur Athletic Union): 132 E. Washington St., Ste. 800, Indianapolis, IN 46204; (317) 261-0500; www.usatf.org

Trapshooting Assn. of America, Amateur (1900): 601 W. National Rd., Vandalia, OH 45377; (937) 898-4638; www.shootata.com

U.S. Trotting Assn. (1939): 750 Michigan Ave., Columbus, OH 43215; (614) 224-2291; www.ustrotting.com

Volleyball, USA (1928): 715 S. Circle Dr., Colorado Springs, CO 80910; (719) 228-6800; www.usavolleyball.org

Wheelchair Sports, USA (1956): 1236 Jungermann Rd., St. Peters, MO 63376; (636) 614-6784; www.wsusa.org

Women's National Basketball Association (WNBA, 1996): 645 5th Ave., New York, NY 10022; (212) 688-9622; www.wnba.com

Health Organizations

Source: World Almanac research

Entries are roughly alphabetized by the basic condition addressed, with general resources listed first. In addition to these selected sites, there is a vast array of medical information on the Internet; however, it is very important to be certain that the source of information is reliable and accurate. Always check with a physician before embarking on any new health-related undertaking.

Centers for Disease Control and Prevention (1946): (800) 311-3435; www.cdc.gov

Health Council, Natl. (1920): (202) 785-3910; www.nationalhealthcouncil.org

National Health Information Center (1979): (800) 336-4797; www.health.gov/NHIC

National Institutes of Health (1887): (301) 496-4000; www.nih.gov

Hospital Assn., American (1899): (312) 422-3000; www.aha.org

Al-Anon/Alateen (1951): (757) 563-1600; www.al-anon.alateen.org

Alcoholics Anonymous (1935): (212) 870-3400; www.alcoholics-anonymous.org

American Council on Alcoholism (1953): (800) 527-5344; www.aca-usa.org

Phoenix House (1967): (646) 505-2000; www.drughelp.org

National Clearinghouse for Alcohol and Drug Information: (800) 729-6686; www.ncadi.samhsa.gov

National Council on Alcoholism and Drug Dependence Hopeline (1944): (212) 269-7797; www.ncadd.org

Gamblers Anonymous (1957): (213) 386-8789; www.gamblersanonymous.org

Narcotics Anonymous (1953): (818) 773-9999; www.na.org

Wellplace (1976): (801) 569-4672; www.wellplace.com

Administration on Aging's Eldercare Locator Line (1991): (800) 677-1116; www.eldercare.gov

Geriatrics Society, American (1942): (212) 308-1414; www.americangeriatrics.org

National Institute on Aging (1974): (301) 496-1752; www.nia.nih.gov

AIDSinfo: (800) 448-0440; www.aidsinfo.nih.gov

Canadian AIDS Society (1988): (613) 230-3580; www.cdnaids.ca

Alzheimer's Association (1979): (312) 335-8700; www.alz.org

Alzheimer's Society of Canada (1978): (416) 488-8772; www.alzheimer.ca

ALS Association (1985): (818) 880-9007; www.alsa.org

Arthritis Foundation (1948): (800) 283-7800; www.arthritis.org

National Institute of Arthritis and Musculoskeletal and Skin Diseases (1986): (877) 226-4267; www.niams.nih.gov

Asthma and Allergy Foundation of America (1953): (800) 727-8462; www.aafa.org

American Academy of Allergy, Asthma, and Immunology (1943): (414) 272-6071; www.aaaai.org

Autism Society of America (1965): (800) 328-8476; www.autism-society.org

Blind, American Council of the (1961): (202) 467-5081; www.acb.org

Blind, Natl. Federation of the (1940): (410) 659-9314; www.nfb.org

Foundation Fighting Blindness (1971): (800) 683-5555, TDD (800) 683-5551; www.blindness.org

Blindness America, Prevent (1908): (800) 331-2020; www.preventblindness.org

Guide Dog Foundation for the Blind, Inc. (1946): (866) 282-8048; www.guidedog.org

Library of Congress National Library Service for the Blind and Physically Handicapped: (202) 707-5100; for the hearing impaired, TDD (202) 707-0744; www.loc.gov/nls

National Association for Parents of Children with Visual Impairments: (800) 562-6265; www.napvi.org

Cooley's Anemia Foundation (1954): (800) 522-7222; www.thalassemia.org

Sickle Cell Disease Association of America (1971): (800) 421-8453; www.sicklecelldisease.org

American Cancer Society (1913): (800) 227-2345; www.cancer.org

Canadian Cancer Society (1938): (416) 961-7223; www.cancer.ca

National Cancer Institute's Cancer Information Service (1975): (800) 422–6237; cis.nci.nih.gov

Breast Cancer Network of Strength (1978): (800) 221-2141 or (800) 986-9505 (Spanish); www.networkofstrength.org

Leukemia and Lymphoma Society (1949): (800) 955-4572; www.lls.org

Cerebral Palsy, Inc., United (1949): (202) 776-0406; www.ucp.org

American Academy of Pediatrics (1930): (847) 434-4000; www.aap.org

Children's Tumor Foundation (1978): (212) 344-6633; www.ctf.org

March of Dimes Birth Defects Foundation (1938): (914) 997-4488; www.marchofdimes.com

National Center for Missing and Exploited Children (1984): (703) 274-3900; www.missingkids.com

National Runaway Switchboard (1971): (773) 880-9860; www.nrscrisisline.org

CFIDS Association of America (1987): (704) 365-2343; www.cfids.org

Cystic Fibrosis Foundation (1955): (800) 344-4823 or (301) 951-4422; www.cff.org

American Diabetes Association (1940): (800) 342-2383; www.diabetes.org

Canadian Diabetes Association (1953): (416) 363-0177; www.diabetes.ca

Juvenile Diabetes Research Foundation Hotline (1973): (800) 533-2873; www.jdrf.org

Crohn's and Colitis Foundation of America (1967): (800) 932-2423; www.ccfa.org

Crohn's and Colitis Foundation of Canada: (416) 920-5035; www.ccfc.ca

Childhelp's USA National Child Abuse Hotline (1959): (800) 422-4453; www.childhelp.org

National Council on Child Abuse and Family Violence (1984): (202) 429-6695 (800) 422-4453, TTY (800) 787-3244; www.nccafv.org

National Domestic Violence Hotline (1996): (800) 799-7233; TTY (800) 787-3224; www.ndvh.org

National Down Syndrome Congress (1973): (800) 232-6372; www.ndsccenter.org

Arc of the United States, The (1950): (301) 565-3842; www.thearc.org

National Down Syndrome Society (1979): (800) 221-4602; www.ndss.org

Easter Seals (1919): (312) 726-6200, TTY (312) 726-4258; www.easterseals.com

International Dyslexia Association: (410) 296-0232; www.interdys.org

National Association of Anorexia Nervosa and Associated Disorders (1976): (847) 831-3438; www.anad.org

Overeaters Anonymous (1960): (505) 891-2664; www.oa.org

Endometriosis Association (1980): (414) 355-2200; www.endometriosisassn.org

Epilepsy Foundation's Answer Place (1967): (800) 332-1000; www.epilepsyfoundation.org/answerplace

Fat Acceptance, Natl. Assn. to Advance (NAAFA) (1969): (916) 558-6880; www.naafa.org

Meat and Poultry Hotline, U.S. Dept. of Agriculture's Food, Safety, and Inspection Service: (888) 674-6854, TTY (800) 256-7072; www.foodsafety.gov

FDA Center for Food Safety and Applied Nutrition Outreach & Information Center: (888) 723-3366; www.cfsan.fda.gov

National Headache Foundation (1970): (888) 643-5552; www.headaches.org

Deaf, Natl. Assn. of the (1880): (301) 587-1788, TTY (301) 587-1789; www.nad.org

Hearing Society, Intl. (1951): (734) 522-7200; www.ihsinfo.org

American Speech-Language-Hearing Association Action Center (1958): (800) 638-8255, TTY (301) 296-5650; www.asha.org

Canadian Hard of Hearing Association (1982): (613) 526-1584, TTY (613) 526-2692; www.chha.ca

Dial a Hearing Screening Test: (800) 222-EARS

Hearing Aid Helpline: (800) 521-5247, ext. 333; www.ihsinfo.org

American Heart Association: (800) 242-8721; www.americanheart.org

Mended Hearts, Inc. (1950): (214) 360-6149; www.mendedhearts.org

National Institute of Neurological Disorders and Stroke (1950): (800) 352-9424, TTY (301) 468-5981: www.ninds.nih.gov

National Stroke Association (1984): (800) 787-6537; www.stroke.org

Children's Hospice International (1983): (800) 242-4453; www.chionline.org

Hospice Education Institute Hospicelink (1985): (800) 331-1620; www.hospiceworld.org

Huntington's Disease Society of America (1967): (800) 345-4372; www.hdsa.org

Kidney Foundation of Canada (1964): (514) 369-4806; www.kidney.ca

National Kidney and Urologic Diseases Information Clearinghouse: (800) 891-5390; www.kidney.niddk.nih.gov

National Kidney Foundation (1950): (212) 889-2210; www.kidney.org

Kidney Fund, The American (1971): (800) 638-8299; www.kidneyfund.org

La Leche League Intl. (1957): (800) 525-3243, TTY (847) 592-7570; www.lalecheleague.org

American Liver Foundation (1976): (212) 668-1000; www.liverfoundation.org

American Lung Association (1904): (800) 586-4872; www.lungusa.org

Lung Line Information Service (1983): (800) 222-5864; www.nationaljewish.org/contact/lung/index.aspx

Lupus Foundation of America: (202) 349-1155; www.lupus.org

Lyme Disease Foundation (1988): (860) 870-0070; www.lyme.org

Depression and Bipolar Support Alliance (1985): (800) 826-3632; www.dbsalliance.org

Mental Health America (1909): (800) 969-6642; www.nmha.org

Mentally Ill, Natl. Alliance for the (1979): (703) 524-7600; www.nami.org

National Institute of Mental Health (1946): (301) 443-4513, TTY (301) 443-8431; www.nimh.nih.gov

Multiple Sclerosis Society of Canada (1948): (416) 922-6065; www.mssociety.ca

National Multiple Sclerosis Society (800) 344-4867; www.nationalmssociety.org

Muscular Dystrophy Association (1950): (800) 572-1717; www.mdausa.org

Organ Sharing, United Network for (1984): (804) 782-4800; www.unos.org

Living Bank (1968): (800) 528-2971; www.livingbank.org

National Osteoporosis Foundation (1984): (800) 231-4222; www.nof.org

National Chronic Pain Outreach Association: www.chronicpain.org

National Parkinson Foundation (1957): (800) 327-4545; www.parkinson.org

Parkinson's Disease Foundation, Inc. (1957): (212) 923-4700; www.pdf.org

Parkinson Society Canada (1965): (416) 227-9700; www.parkinson.ca

Physically Handicapped, Inc., Natl. Assn. of the (1958): www.naph.net

Planned Parenthood Federation of America, Inc. (1916): (212) 541-7800; www.plannedparenthood.org

Plastic Surgery Referral Service (1931): (847) 228-9900; www.plasticsurgery.org

Post-Polio Health International (1960): (314) 534-0475; www.post-polio.org

Psoriasis Foundation, Natl. (1968): (503) 244-7404; www.psoriasis.org

National Organization for Rare Disorders (1983): (203) 744-0100; www.rarediseases.org

National Rehabilitation Information Center: (800) 346-2742; TTY (301) 459-5984; www.naric.com

Reye's Syndrome Foundation, Natl. (1974): (419) 924-9000; www.reyessyndrome.org

United Scleroderma Foundation: (800) 722-4673; www.scleroderma.org

National STD Hotline (1914): (800) 227-8922; www.ashastd.org

Sjogren's Syndrome Foundation (1983): (800) 475-6473; www.sjogrens.org

National Center for Stuttering (1976): (800) 221-2483; www.stuttering.com

Stuttering Assn., Natl. (1977): (212) 944-4050; www.nsastutter.org

Stuttering Foundation of America (1947): (800) 992-9392; www.stutteringhelp.org

National Spinal Cord Injury Association (1948): (800) 962-9629; www.spinalcord.org

American Sudden Infant Death Syndrome Institute (1983): (800) 232-7437; www.sids.org

First Candle/SIDSAlliance (1987): (800) 221-7437; www.sidsalliance.org

Therapy Dogs Intl., Inc. (1976): (973) 252-9800; www.tdi-dog.org

Tourette Syndrome Association (1972): (718) 224-2999; tsa-usa.org

Tuberous Sclerosis Alliance (1974): (301) 562-9890; www.tsalliance.org

American Urological Association (1902): (866) 746-4282; www.auanet.org

National Association for Continence (1982): (843) 377-0900; www.nafc.org

Simon Foundation for Continence (1983): (800) 237-4666; www.simonfoundation.org

National Women's Health Network (1975): (202) 347-1140; www.nwhn.org

National Women's Health Resource Center (1988): (877) 986-9472; www.healthywomen.org

UNITED STATES GOVERNMENT

EXECUTIVE BRANCH	LEGISLATIVE BRANCH	JUDICIAL BRANCH
PRESIDENT **Vice President** **Executive Office of the President** White House Office* Office of the Vice President Council of Economic Advisers Council on Environmental Quality National Security Council Office of Administration Office of Management and Budget Office of National Drug Control Policy Office of Science and Technology Policy Office of the U.S. Trade Representative	**CONGRESS** **Senate/House** Architect of the Capitol U.S. Botanic Garden Government Accountability Office Government Printing Office Library of Congress Congressional Budget Office Medicare Payment Advisory Commission Stennis Center for Public Service	**Supreme Court of the United States** Courts of Appeals District Courts Territorial Courts Court of International Trade Bankruptcy Courts Court of Federal Claims Tax Court Court of Appeals for the Armed Forces Court of Appeals for Veterans Claims Administrative Office of the Courts Federal Judicial Center Sentencing Commission Judicial Panel on Multidistrict Litigation

*Includes Domestic Policy Council, Homeland Security Council, National Economic Council, Office of Faith-Based and Community Initiatives, Office of the First Lady, Office of National AIDS Policy, Privacy and Civil Liberties Oversight Board, USA Freedom Corps, White House Fellows Office, White House Military Office.

The Obama Administration

As of Oct. 15, 2009; mailing addresses are for Washington, DC, except for the Pentagon or where otherwise noted. Terms of office of the president and vice president: Jan. 20, 2009 to Jan. 20, 2013.

President: By law, Pres. Barack H. Obama received an annual salary of $400,000 (taxable) and an annual expense allowance of $50,000 (nontaxable) for costs resulting from official duties. In addition, up to $100,000 a year may be spent on travel expenses and $19,000 on official entertainment (both nontaxable). This does not include amounts available for expenditures within the Executive Office of the President, including $3,850,000 for necessary expenses for the White House and amounts for travel and entertainment.

Website: www.whitehouse.gov/administration/president_obama/; **E-mail:** comments@whitehouse.gov

Vice President: By law, Vice Pres. Joseph R. Biden received an annual salary of $227,300 (taxable) and an annual expense allowance of $20,000 for costs resulting from official duties, plus $90,000 for official entertainment expenses (nontaxable).

Website: www.whitehouse.gov/administration/vice_president_biden/; **E-mail:** vice_president@whitehouse.gov

The Cabinet Department Heads

(Salary: $196,700 per year)

Secretary of State: Hillary Rodham Clinton
Secretary of the Treasury: Timothy F. Geithner
Secretary of Defense: Robert M. Gates
Attorney General: Eric H. Holder Jr.
Secretary of the Interior: Kenneth L. Salazar
Secretary of Agriculture: Thomas J. Vilsack
Secretary of Commerce: Gary F. Locke
Secretary of Labor: Hilda L. Solis
Secretary of Health and Human Services: Kathleen Sebelius
Secretary of Housing and Urban Development: Shaun L.S. Donovan
Secretary of Transportation: Raymond L. LaHood
Secretary of Energy: Steven Chu
Secretary of Education: Arne Duncan
Secretary of Veterans Affairs: Eric K. Shinseki
Secretary of Homeland Security: Janet A. Napolitano

Executive Agencies

Council of Economic Advisers: Christina Romer, chair; www.whitehouse.gov/cea
Office of Administration: vacant; www.whitehouse.gov/oa
Office of Science & Technology Policy: John Holdren, dir.; www.ostp.gov
Office of Natl. Drug Control Policy: R. Gil Kerlikowske, dir.; www.whitehousedrugpolicy.gov
Office of Management and Budget: Peter R. Orszag, dir.; www.whitehouse.gov/omb
Office of the U.S. Trade Representative: Amb. Ronald Kirk; www.ustr.gov
Council on Environ. Quality: Nancy Sutley, chair; www.whitehouse.gov/ceq

The White House Staff

1600 Pennsylvania Ave. NW, 20500; www.whitehouse.gov

Counselor to the President and Director, Health Care Reform: Nancy-Ann E. DeParle
Physician to the President: Jeffrey C. Kuhlman
Director, National Intelligence: Dennis C. Blair
Assistants to the President:
 Chief of Staff: Rahm I. Emanuel
 Deputy Chief of Staff for Operations: James A. Messina
 Deputy Chief of Staff for Policy: Mona K. Sutphen
 Counsel to the President: Gregory B. Craig
 White House Press Secretary: Robert L. Gibbs
 Deputy National Security Advisor: Thomas E. Donilon
 Staff Secretary: Elizabeth M. Brown
 Communications: Anita B. Dunn
 Domestic Policy: Melody C. Barnes
 Economic Policy and Director of the National Economic Council: Lawrence H. Summers
 Homeland Security and Counterterrorism: John O. Brennan
 Legislative Affairs: Phillip M. Schiliro
 National Security Advisor: James L. Jones
 Presidential Personnel: Donald H. Gips
 Speechwriting: Jonathan E. Favreau
Chief of Staff to the Vice President: Ronald A. Klain
Special Assistant to the President & White House Social Secretary: Desiree G. Rogers
Assistant to the President and Chief of Staff to the First Lady: Susan S. Sher
Press Secretary, Office of the First Lady: Catherine M. Lelyveld

Cabinet-Level Departments

Department of State

2201 C St. NW, 20520; www.state.gov

Conducts U.S. foreign policy. The Foreign Service protects American citizens and interests through embassies in some 180 countries under eight geographic bureaus. Maintains contact with foreign governments, negotiates agreements and treaties, and supports U.S. foreign trade. Promotes democracy, international security, human rights—including issues related to AIDS, human trafficking, war crimes, and migration—and arms and narcotics control. Represents the nation in international organizations. Issues passports to U.S. citizens and visas to foreigners. **Budget:** $17.5 bil (2008); $22.4 bil (est. 2009); $28.6 bil (est. 2010).

- Intl. Boundary & Water Commission (4171 North Mesa, El Paso, TX 79902); www.ibwc.state.gov
- Intl. Information Programs (301 4th St. SW, 20547); www.america.gov
- Intl. Narcotics & Law Enforcement Affairs (2201 C St. NW, Rm. 7333, 20520); www.state.gov/p/inl/
- Intl. Organization Affairs (2201 C St. NW, Rm. 6323, 20520); www.state.gov/p/io/
- Population, Refugees, and Migration (2201 C St. NW, Rm. 5805, 20520); www.state.gov/g/prm/
- U.S. Global AIDS Coordinator (2201 C St. NW, SA-29, 20520); www.state.gov/s/gac/

Department of the Treasury

1500 Pennsylvania Ave. NW, 20220; www.ustreas.gov

Responsible for the fiscal affairs of the U.S. Serves as the government's financial agent; collects, borrows, and disburses funds for the federal government. Monitors the nation's financial infrastructure and economic development; recommends domestic and international financial, monetary, economic, trade, and tax policies. Manufactures currency and coins. Carries out monetary and tax law enforcement activities, sanctions, embargoes, and fights illicit finance—counterfeiting, money laundering, narcotics trafficking, terrorist financing. **Budget:** $548.8 bil (2008); $1.03 tril (est. 2009); $498.4 bil (est. 2010).

- Alcohol and Tobacco Tax and Trade Bureau (1310 G St. NW, Ste. 200 East, 20220); www.ttb.gov
- Bureau of Engraving and Printing (14th and C Sts. SW, 20228); www.moneyfactory.gov
- Bureau of the Public Debt (200 3rd St., Parkersburg, WV 26106); www.publicdebt.treas.gov
- Financial Crimes Enforcement Network (2070 Chain Bridge Rd., Vienna, VA 22182); www.fincen.gov
- Financial Management Service (401 14th St. SW, 20227); www.fms.treas.gov
- Internal Revenue Service (1111 Constitution Ave. NW, 20224); www.irs.gov
- U.S. Mint (801 9th St. NW, 20220); www.usmint.gov

Department of Defense

1400 Defense Pentagon, 20301; www.defenselink.mil

Directs and controls the armed forces and assists the president in protecting the nation's security. Military departments of the Army, Navy, and Air Force are each separately organized under its own secretary but functions under the command of the Secretary of Defense. They conduct military operations as unified commands. The Chairman of the Joint Chiefs of Staff is the principal military adviser to the President. Undersecretaries supervise acquisition, technology, and logistics; intelligence; personnel and readiness; and policy. **Budget:** $594.7 bil (2008); $665.0 bil (est. 2009); $685.1 bil (est. 2010).

- Def. Advanced Research Projects Agency (3701 North Fairfax Dr., Arlington, VA 22203); www.darpa.mil
- Def. Intelligence Agency (Bldg. 6000, 20340-5100); www.dia.mil
- Def. Security Cooperation Agency (2800 Defense Pentagon, 20301); www.dsca.osd.mil
- Missile Def. Agency (7100 Defense Pentagon, 20301); www.mda.mil
- Natl. Geospatial-Intelligence Agency (4600 Sangamore Rd., Bethesda, MD 20816); www.nga.mil
- Natl. Security Agency (9800 Savage Rd., Ft. Meade, MD 20755); www.nsa.gov

Department of Justice

950 Pennsylvania Ave. NW, 20530; www.usdoj.gov

Provides means for the enforcement of federal laws and investigating violations thereof; furnishes legal counsel in cases involving the federal government and interprets laws relating to the activities of other federal departments; supervises federal penal institutions. The Attorney General and Office of Legal Counsel render legal advice, upon request, to the president and department heads. The Solicitor General conducts all suits brought before the U.S. Supreme Court in which the federal government is concerned. The Civil Division represents the U.S. government in many civil or criminal matters. The 93 U.S. Attorneys are the principal litigators in the U.S. and its territories. Divisions for suits regarding antitrust laws, civil rights, civil and criminal statutes, natural resources and the environment, national security, and taxes. **Budget:** $26.5 bil (2008); $29.0 bil (est. 2009); $30.3 bil (est. 2010).

- Bureau of Alcohol, Tobacco, Firearms & Explosives (99 New York Ave. NE, Mail Stop 5S144, 20226); www.atf.gov
- Bureau of Prisons (320 First St. NW, 20534); www.bop.gov
- Drug Enforcement Admin. (AES, 8701 Morrissette Dr., Springfield, VA 22152); www.usdoj.gov/dea
- Executive Office for Immigration Review (5107 Leesburg Pike, Falls Church, VA 22041); www.usdoj.gov/eoir/
- Federal Bureau of Investigation (J. Edgar Hoover Building, 935 Pennsylvania Ave. NW, 20535); www.fbi.gov
- U.S. Marshals Service (Building CS-3, 20530-1000); www.usmarshals.gov
- Natl. Central Bureau of Interpol (20530); www.usdoj.gov/usncb
- U.S. Parole Commission (5550 Friendship Blvd., Ste. 420, Chevy Chase, MD 20815); www.justice.gov/uspc

Department of the Interior

1849 C St. NW, 20240; www.doi.gov

Custodian of natural resources; has the responsibility of protecting and conserving the country's land, water, minerals, fish, and wildlife; of promoting the wise use of all these natural resources; of maintaining national parks and recreation areas; and of preserving historic places. It also provides for the welfare of American Indian reservation communities and of inhabitants of island territories under U.S. administration. **Budget:** $9.9 bil (2008); $11.5 bil (est. 2009); $13.0 bil (est. 2010).

- Bureau of Indian Affairs (1849 C Street NW, 20240).
- Bureau of Land Management (1849 C St. NW, 20240); www.blm.gov
- Bureau of Reclamation (1849 C St. NW, 20240); www.usbr.gov
- Minerals Management Service (1849 C St. NW, 20240); www.mms.gov
- National Park Service (1849 C St. NW, 20240); www.nps.gov
- Fish & Wildlife Service (1849 C St. NW, 20240); www.fws.gov
- Office of Surface Mining (1951 Constitution Ave. NW, 20240); www.osmre.gov
- Office of Insular Affairs (1849 C St. NW, 20240); www.doi.gov/oia/
- U.S. Geological Survey (12201 Sunrise Valley Dr., Reston, VA 20192); www.usgs.gov

Department of Agriculture

1400 Independence Ave. SW, 20250; www.usda.gov

Provides leadership on food, agriculture, and natural resources; supports scientific research and education for agriculture, nutrition, and food safety. Develops nutrition assistance programs, promotes healthy eating, supplies food stamps, grades and inspects the commercial supply of food. Responsible for the health of the land through sustainable management and conservation, manages public lands in national forests and grasslands; safeguards against invasive pests and diseases; ensures the health and care of animals and plants. Oversees assistance and conservation programs for farmers and ranchers and programs to improve the rural economy and quality of life. Facilitates domestic and international marketing of U.S. agricultural products. **Budget:** $90.8 bil (2008); $116.2 bil (est. 2009); $132.9 bil (est. 2010).

- Agricultural Research Service (1400 Independence Ave. SW, 20250); www.ars.usda.gov
- Economic Research Service (1800 M St. NW, 20036); www.ers.usda.gov
- Food & Nutrition Service (3101 Park Center Dr., Alexandria, VA 22302); www.fns.usda.gov/fns
- Food Safety & Inspection Service (1400 Independence Ave. SW, 20250); www.fsis.usda.gov
- Foreign Agricultural Service (1400 Independence Ave. SW, 20250); www.fas.usda.gov
- Forest Service (1400 Independence Ave. SW, 20250); www.fs.fed.us
- Natl. Agricultural Statistics Service (1400 Independence Ave. SW, 20250); www.nass.usda.gov
- Natural Resources Conservation Service (P.O. Box 2890, 20013); www.nrcs.usda.gov

Department of Commerce

1401 Constitution Ave. NW, 20230; www.commerce.gov

Fosters, serves, and promotes the nation's economic development and technological advancement; supports the comprehension and use of the physical environment and its oceanic life; assists states, communities, and individuals with economic progress; promotes trade abroad and ensures an effective export control and treaty compliance system. Issues trademarks and patents, maintains measurement standards, and manages the federal telecommunications spectrum. Collects, analyzes, and distributes statistics regarding the nation and the economy through the Bureaus of the Census and Economic Analysis. The National Oceanic and Atmospheric Administration explores, monitors, and conserves oceans and coasts, tracks weather and other environmental data. **Budget:** $7.7 bil (2008); $11.8 bil (est. 2009); $15.8 bil (est. 2010).

- Bureau of the Census (4600 Silver Hill Rd., 20233); www.census.gov
- Bureau of Economic Analysis (1441 L St. NW, 20230); www.bea.gov
- Minority Business Development Agency (1401 Constitution Ave. NW, 20230); www.mbda.gov
- National Institute of Standards & Technology (100 Bureau Dr., Stop 1070, Gaithersburg, MD 20899); www.nist.gov
- National Oceanic and Atmospheric Admin. (1401 Constitution Ave. NW, 20230); www.noaa.gov
- National Technical Information Service (5285 Port Royal Rd., Springfield, VA 22161); www.ntis.gov
- National Telecommunications & Information Admin. (1401 Constitution Ave. NW, 20230); www.ntia.doc.gov

Department of Labor

200 Constitution Ave. NW, 20210; www.dol.gov

Administers federal labor laws to foster, promote, and develop the welfare of job seekers, wage earners, and retirees of the U.S., to improve working conditions, and to advance opportunities for profitable employment. Administers standards for wages and overtime pay, safety and health conditions, workers' compensation. Tracks changes in employment, prices, and other national economic measurements. Regulates pension and welfare benefit plans, the hiring and employment of migrant and seasonal workers, and requirements pertaining to the mining, construction, and transportation industries. Monitors labor unions and their funds. **Budget:** $58.8 bil (2008); $121.9 bil (est. 2009); $106.1 bil (est. 2010).

- Bureau of Labor Statistics (2 Massachusetts Ave. NE, 20212); www.bls.gov
- Employment Standards Admin. (200 Constitution Ave. NW, 20210); www.dol.gov/esa
- Job Corps (200 Constitution Ave. NW, 20210); www.jobcorps.dol.gov
- Mine Safety and Health Admin. (1100 Wilson Blvd., Arlington, VA 22209); www.msha.gov
- Occupational Safety & Health Admin. (200 Constitution Ave. NW, 20210); www.osha.gov

Department of Health and Human Services

200 Independence Ave. SW, 20201; www.hhs.gov

Administers a wide range of programs in the fields of health care and social services that affect nearly all Americans. Medicare and Medicaid provide health care insurance for one in four Americans. The HRSA improves health care services for people who are uninsured, isolated, or medically vulnerable; also oversees organ, tissue, and blood cell donations. The FDA assures the safety of food, drugs, cosmetics, biological products, and medical devices. The CDC monitors and safeguards against disease outbreaks. The NIH supports research projects nationwide and 27 health institutes and centers. The Surgeon General is the nation's chief health educator and leads the U.S. Public Health Service Commissioned Corps. **Budget:** $700.5 bil (2008); $817.8 bil (est. 2009); $880.8 bil (est. 2010).

- Agency for Healthcare Research & Quality (540 Gaither Rd., Rockville, MD 20850); www.ahrq.gov
- Centers for Disease Control & Prevention (1600 Clifton Rd., Atlanta, GA 30333); www.cdc.gov
- Centers for Medicare & Medicaid Services (7500 Security Blvd., Baltimore, MD 21244); www.cms.hhs.gov
- Food and Drug Admin. (5600 Fishers Ln., Rockville, MD 20857); www.fda.gov
- Health Resources and Services Admin. (5600 Fishers Ln., Rockville, MD 20857); www.hrsa.gov
- National Institutes of Health (9000 Rockville Pike, Bethesda, MD 20892); www.nih.gov
- Surgeon General (5600 Fishers Ln., Rm. 18-66, Rockville, MD 20857); www.surgeongeneral.gov

Department of Housing and Urban Development

451 7th St. SW, 20410; www.hud.gov

Responsible for housing needs and the improvement and development of urban areas. Supports affordable housing, provides grants for community development and redevelopment. Enforces fair and safe housing standards. Provides funds to assist homeless individuals and families with emergency and transitional shelters. The Federal Housing Administration provides mortgage insurance on loans made by approved lenders. **Budget:** $49.1 bil (2008); $65.1 bil (est. 2009); $54.8 bil (est. 2010).

- Fannie Mae (Federal National Mortgage Association) (3900 Wisconsin Ave. NW, 20016); www.fanniemae.com
- Federal Housing Administration (451 7th St. SW, 20410); www.fha.gov
- Freddie Mac (Federal Home Loan Mortgage Corporation) (8200 Jones Branch Dr., McLean, VA 22102); www.freddiemac.com
- Government National Mortgage Association (451 7th St. SW, Room B-133, 20410); www.ginniemae.gov

Note: Fannie Mae and Freddie Mac are government-sponsored enterprises (GSEs).

Department of Transportation

1200 New Jersey Ave. SE, 20590; www.dot.gov

Promotes and develops rapid, safe, efficient, and convenient transportation in the U.S.; monitors and administers assistance to transportation industries; negotiates and implements international transportation agreements. Manages airspace, commercial space transportation, and the movement of hazardous materials. Resolves railroad rate and service disputes and reviews proposed railroad mergers. Analyzes and shares research and statistics to develop and improve transportation through RITA. Develops and enforces regulations on the nation's pipeline transportation system. The Maritime Administration maintains a fleet of cargo ships in reserve for war or national emergencies and commissions officers of the merchant marines. Operates the U.S. portion of the St. Lawrence Seaway between Montreal and Lake Erie. **Budget:** $64.9 bil (2008); $79.7 bil (est. 2009); $90.5 bil (est. 2010).

- Federal Aviation Admin. (800 Independence Ave. SW, 20591); www.faa.gov
- Federal Highway Admin. (1200 New Jersey Ave. SE, 20590); www.fhwa.dot.gov
- Federal Transit Admin. (East Bldg., 1200 New Jersey Ave. SE, 20590); www.fta.dot.gov
- Federal Railroad Admin. (1200 New Jersey Ave. SE, 20590); www.fra.dot.gov
- Maritime Admin. (1200 New Jersey Ave. SE, 20590); www.marad.dot.gov
- National Highway Traffic Safety Admin. (West Bldg., 1200 New Jersey Ave. SE, 20590); www.nhtsa.dot.gov
- Research and Innovative Technology Admin. (RITA) (1200 New Jersey Ave. SE, 20590); www.rita.dot.gov

Department of Energy

1000 Independence Ave. SW, 20585; www.energy.gov

Secures the nation's energy and promotes scientific and technological innovation. Oversees the national energy supply and electric grid. Investigates and promotes clean and reliable energy. Manages and cleans up nuclear and other radioactive material, including nuclear weapons. The Office of Science supports much of America's scientific research through program offices, education initiatives, 10 national laboratories, and numerous user facilities. Four Power Marketing administrations sell hydroelectric power across the west and southeast. **Budget:** $21.4 bil (2008); $29.3 bil (est. 2009); $46.3 bil (est. 2010).

- Energy Information Admin. (1000 Independence Ave. SW, 20585); www.eia.doe.gov
- Federal Energy Regulatory Commission (888 1st St. NE, 20426); www.ferc.gov (independent regulatory agency)
- National Nuclear Security Admin. (1000 Independence Ave. SW, 20585); www.nnsa.energy.gov
- Office of Scientific and Technical Information (1 Science.gov Way, Oak Ridge, TN 37830); www.osti.gov

Department of Education

400 Maryland Ave. SW, 20202; www.ed.gov

Works with state agencies and local systems to ensure equal access to all levels of education and seeks to improve the quality of that education through federal support, research programs, and information sharing. Oversees a variety of financial aid distributed through competition, financial needs, or by a set formula. Sets policy goals and initiatives like No Child Left Behind. Conducts research and gathers educational information to disseminate to educators and the general public. **Budget:** $66.0 bil (2008); $49.7 bil (est. 2009); $100.5 bil (est. 2010).

Department of Veterans Affairs

810 Vermont Ave. NW, 20420; www.va.gov

Supports veterans and their families with nationwide programs for health care, financial assistance, and burial benefits. Compensates for disabilities incurred during wartime, provides pensions for veterans with low incomes, education assistance, loan guaranty, and life insurance. Manages America's largest medical education and health professions training program including hospitals, clinics, nursing homes, veterans centers, rehabilitation treatment, readjustment counseling, and home-care programs. Also funds medical research pertaining to veterans issues. Manages 120 National Cemeteries, provides headstones and markers. **Budget:** $84.8 bil (2008); $96.5 bil (est. 2009); $108.8 bil (est. 2010).

Department of Homeland Security

20528 (requires no street address); www.dhs.gov

Provides a unified core for the vast national network of organizations and institutions involved in efforts to secure the U.S., its borders, infrastructure, and major events. Provides funding, intelligence, and training for law enforcement and disaster relief. Leads and coordinates response teams to natural and man-made emergencies. Directs security for borders, customs, and transportation. Identifies threats, administers the color-coded Homeland Security Advisory System. **Budget:** $40.7 bil (2008); $49.2 bil (est. 2009); $49.3 bil (est. 2010).

- Federal Emergency Management Agency (500 C St. SW, 20472); www.fema.gov
- Immigration and Customs Enforcement (425 I St. NW, 20536); www.ice.gov
- Transportation Security Admin. (601 S 12th St., Arlington, VA 22202); www.tsa.gov
- U.S. Citizenship & Immigration Services (20 Massachusetts Ave. NW, 20529); www.uscis.gov

- U.S. Coast Guard (2100 2nd St., SW, 20593); www.uscg.mil
- U.S. Customs and Border Protection (1300 Pennsylvania Ave. NW, 20229); www.cbp.gov
- U.S. Fire Admin. (16825 S. Seton Ave., Emmitsburg, MD 21727); www.usfa.dhs.gov
- U.S. Secret Service (245 Murray Dr., Bldg. 410, 20223); www.secretservice.gov

Other Notable U.S. Government Agencies

Source: The U.S. Government Manual; National Archives and Records Administration; World Almanac research

All addresses are Washington, DC, unless otherwise noted; as of Oct. 2009.

African Development Foundation: Lloyd O. Pierson, pres. and CEO (1400 I St. NW, Ste. 1000, 20005); www.adf.gov

AMTRAK (National Railroad Passenger Corporation): Joseph H. Boardman, pres. and CEO (60 Mass. Ave. NE, 20002); www.amtrak.com

Broadcasting Board of Governors (330 Independence Ave. SW, 20237); www.bbg.gov

Central Intelligence Agency: Leon E. Panetta, dir. (20505); www.cia.gov

Commission on Civil Rights: Gerald A. Reynolds, chair (624 9th St. NW, 20425); www.usccr.gov

Commodity Futures Trading Commission: Gary Gensler, chair (3 Lafayette Ctr., 1155 21st St. NW, 20581); www.cftc.gov

Consumer Product Safety Commission: Inez Tenenbaum, chair (4330 East-West Hwy., Bethesda, MD 20814); www.cpsc.gov

Corporation for National and Community Service: Alan D. Solomont, chair (1201 New York Ave. NW, 20525); www.nationalservice.org

Court Services and Offender Supervision Agency for the District of Columbia: Adrienne Poteat, act. dir. (633 Indiana Ave. NW, 20004); www.csosa.gov

Defense Nuclear Facilities Safety Board: John E. Mansfield, vice chair (625 Indiana Ave. NW, Ste. 700, 20004); www.dnfsb.gov

Election Assistance Commission: Gineen Bresso Beach, chair (1225 New York Ave. NW, Ste. 1100, 20005); www.eac.gov

Environmental Protection Agency: Lisa P. Jackson, adm. (Cabinet rank) (Ariel Rios Bldg., 1200 Pennsylvania Ave. NW, 20460); www.epa.gov

Equal Employment Opportunity Commission: Stuart J. Ishimaru, act. chair (1801 L St. NW, 20507); www.eeoc.gov

Export-Import Bank of the United States: Fred P. Hochberg, pres. and chair (811 Vermont Ave. NW, 20571); www.exim.gov

Farm Credit Administration: Leland A. Strom, chair and CEO (1501 Farm Credit Dr., McLean, VA 22102); www.fca.gov

Federal Communications Commission: Julius Genachowski, chair (445 12th St. SW, 20554); www.fcc.gov

Federal Deposit Insurance Corporation: Sheila C. Bair, chair (550 17th St. NW, 20429); www.fdic.gov

Federal Election Commission: Steven T. Walther, chair (999 E St. NW, 20463); www.fec.gov

Federal Housing Finance Agency: James B. Lockhart III, dir. (1625 Eye St. NW, 20006); www.fhfa.gov

Federal Labor Relations Authority: Carol Waller Pope, chair (1400 K St. NW, 20005); www.flra.gov

Federal Maritime Commission: Joseph E. Brennan, act. chair (800 N Capitol St. NW, 20573); www.fmc.gov

Federal Mediation and Conciliation Service: Scot L. Beckenbaugh, act. dir. (2100 K St. NW, 20427); www.fmcs.gov

Federal Mine Safety & Health Review Commission: Mary Lucille Jordan, chair (601 New Jersey Ave. NW, Ste. 9500, 20001); www.fmshrc.gov

Federal Reserve System: Ben S. Bernanke, chair, Board of Governors (20th St. and Constitution Ave. NW, 20551); www.federalreserve.gov

Federal Retirement Thrift Investment Board: Andrew W. Saul, chair (1250 H St. NW, 20005); www.frtib.gov

Federal Trade Commission: Jon Leibowitz, chair (600 Pennsylvania Ave. NW, 20580); www.ftc.gov

General Services Administration: Paul F. Prouty, act. admin. (1800 F St. NW, 20405); www.gsa.gov

Institute of Museum and Library Services: Anne-Imelda M. Radice, Ph.D., dir. (1800 M St. NW, 9th Fl., 20036); www.imls.gov

Inter-American Foundation: Larry Palmer, pres. (901 N Stuart St., 10th Fl., Arlington, VA 22203); www.iaf.gov

Merit Systems Protection Board: Neil A. G. McPhie, chair (1615 M St. NW, 5th Fl., 20419); www.mspb.gov

National Aeronautics and Space Administration: Charles F. Bolden Jr., adm. (300 E St. SW, 20546); www.nasa.gov

National Archives & Records Administration: Adrienne Thomas, act. archivist (8601 Adelphi Rd., College Park, MD 20740-6001); www.archives.gov

National Capital Planning Commission: John V. Cogbill III, chair (401 9th St. NW, Ste. 500, 20004); www.ncpc.gov

National Council on Disability: John R. Vaughn, chair (1331 F St. NW, Ste. 850, 20004); www.ncd.gov

National Credit Union Administration: Debbie Matz, chair (1775 Duke St., Alexandria, VA 22314); www.ncua.gov

National Endowment for the Arts: Rocco Landesman, chair (1100 Pennsylvania Ave. NW, 20506); www.arts.gov

National Endowment for the Humanities: Jim Leach, chair (1100 Pennsylvania Ave. NW, 20506); www.neh.gov

National Indian Gaming Commission: Philip N. Hogen, chair (1441 L St. NW, Ste. 9100, 20005); www.nigc.gov

National Labor Relations Board: Wilma B. Liebman, chair (1099 14th St. NW, 20570); www.nlrb.gov

National Mediation Board: Elizabeth Dougherty, chair (1301 K St. NW, Ste. 250 East, 20005); www.nmb.gov

National Science Foundation: Dr. Arden L. Bement Jr., dir. (4201 Wilson Blvd., Arlington, VA 22230); www.nsf.gov

National Transportation Safety Board: Deborah A.P. Hersman, chair (490 L'Enfant Plaza SW, 20594); www.ntsb.gov

Nuclear Regulatory Commission: Gregory B. Jaczko, chair (U.S. Nuclear Regulatory Commission 20555); www.nrc.gov

Nuclear Waste Technical Review Board: B. John Garrick, Ph.D., chair (2300 Clarendon Blvd., Ste. 1300, Arlington, VA 22201); www.nwtrb.gov

Occupational Safety & Health Review Commission: Thomasina V. Rogers, chair (1120 20th St. NW, 9th Fl., 20036); www.oshrc.gov

Office of Government Ethics: Robert I. Cusick, dir. (1201 New York Ave. NW, Ste. 500, 20005); www.usoge.gov

Office of Personnel Management: John Berry, dir. (1900 E St. NW 20415); www.opm.gov

Office of Special Counsel: William E. Reukauf, assoc. spec. counsel (1730 M St. NW, Ste. 218, 20036); www.osc.gov

Overseas Private Investment Corporation: Lawrence Spinelli, Ph.D., act. pres. (1100 New York Ave. NW, 20527); www.opic.gov

Peace Corps: Aaron S. Williams, dir. (1111 20th St. NW, 20526); www.peacecorps.gov

Pension Benefit Guaranty Corporation: Hilda L. Solis, chair, Sec. of Labor (1200 K St. NW, 20005); www.pbgc.gov

Postal Regulatory Commission: Ruth Y. Goldway, chair (901 New York Ave. NW, Ste. 200, 20268); www.prc.gov

Railroad Retirement Board: Michael S. Schwartz, chair (844 N Rush St., Chicago, IL 60611); www.rrb.gov

Securities and Exchange Commission: Mary L. Schapiro, chair (100 F St. NE, 20549); www.sec.gov

Selective Service System: Ernest E. Garcia, act. dir. (1515 Wilson Blvd., Arlington, VA 22209); www.sss.gov

Small Business Administration: Karen G. Mills, adm. (409 Third St. SW, Ste. 7800, 20416); www.sba.gov

Social Security Administration: Michael J. Astrue, comm. (6401 Security Blvd., Baltimore, MD 21235); www.ssa.gov

Tennessee Valley Authority: Tom Kilgore, CEO and president (400 W. Summit Hill Dr., Knoxville, TN 37902); www.tva.com

U.S. Trade and Development Agency: Leocadia I. Zak, act. dir. (1000 Wilson Blvd., Ste. 1600, Arlington, VA 22209); www.ustda.gov

U.S. Agency for International Development: Alonzo Fulgham, act. adm. (1300 Pennsylvania Ave. NW, 20523); www.usaid.gov

United States International Trade Commission: Shara L. Aranoff, chair (Dept. of Commerce, 500 E St. SW, 20436); www.usitc.gov

United States Postal Service: John E. Potter, Postmaster General and CEO (475 L'Enfant Plaza SW, 20260); www.usps.com

CABINETS OF THE U.S.

The U.S. Cabinet and Its Role

The heads of major executive departments of government constitute the Cabinet. This institution, not provided for in the U.S. Constitution, developed as an advisory body out of the desire of presidents to consult on policy matters. Aside from its advisory role, the Cabinet as a body has no formal function and wields no executive authority. Individual members exercise authority as heads of their departments, reporting to the president.

In addition to the heads of federal departments as listed below, the Cabinet commonly includes other officials designated by the president as of Cabinet rank.

The officials so designated by Barack Obama include Vice Pres. Joseph R. Biden, Council of Economic Advisors Chair Christina Romer, Environmental Protection Agency Administrator Lisa P. Jackson, Office of Management and Budget Director Peter R. Orzag, United States Trade Representative Ronald Kirk, United States Ambassador to the United Nations Susan Rice, and Chief of Staff to the President Rahm I. Emanuel.

The Cabinet meets at times set by the president. Members of Pres. Obama's Cabinet listed in this chapter are as of Oct. 15, 2009.

Secretaries of State

The Department of Foreign Affairs was created by act of Congress on July 27, 1789, and the name changed to Department of State on Sept. 15, 1789.

President	Secretary	Home	Sworn in
Washington	Thomas Jefferson	VA	1789
	Edmund Randolph	VA	1794
	Timothy Pickering	PA	1795
Adams, J.	Timothy Pickering	PA	1797
	John Marshall	VA	1800
Jefferson	James Madison	VA	1801
Madison	Robert Smith	MD	1809
	James Monroe	VA	1811
Monroe	John Quincy Adams	MA	1817
Adams, J. Q.	Henry Clay	KY	1825
Jackson	Martin Van Buren	NY	1829
	Edward Livingston	LA	1831
	Louis McLane	DE	1833
	John Forsyth	GA	1834
Van Buren	John Forsyth	GA	1837
Harrison, W. H.	Daniel Webster	MA	1841
Tyler	Daniel Webster	MA	1841
	Abel P. Upshur	VA	1843
	John C. Calhoun	SC	1844
Polk	John C. Calhoun	SC	1845
	James Buchanan	PA	1845
Taylor	James Buchanan	PA	1849
	John M. Clayton	DE	1849
Fillmore	John M. Clayton	DE	1850
	Daniel Webster	MA	1850
	Edward Everett	MA	1852
Pierce	William L. Marcy	NY	1853
Buchanan	William L. Marcy	NY	1857
	Lewis Cass	MI	1857
	Jeremiah S. Black	PA	1860
Lincoln	Jeremiah S. Black	PA	1861
	William H. Seward	NY	1861
Johnson, A.	William H. Seward	NY	1865
Grant	Elihu B. Washburne	IL	1869
	Hamilton Fish	NY	1869
Hayes	Hamilton Fish	NY	1877
	William M. Evarts	NY	1877
Garfield	William M. Evarts	NY	1881
	James G. Blaine	ME	1881
Arthur	James G. Blaine	ME	1881
	F. T. Frelinghuysen	NJ	1881
Cleveland	F. T. Frelinghuysen	NJ	1885
	Thomas F. Bayard	DE	1885
Harrison, B.	Thomas F. Bayard	DE	1889
Harrison, B.	James G. Blaine	ME	1889
	John W. Foster	IN	1892
Cleveland	Walter Q. Gresham	IN	1893
	Richard Olney	MA	1895
McKinley	Richard Olney	MA	1897
	John Sherman	OH	1897
	William R. Day	OH	1898
	John Hay	DC	1898
Roosevelt, T.	John Hay	DC	1901
	Elihu Root	NY	1905
	Robert Bacon	NY	1909
Taft	Robert Bacon	NY	1909
	Philander C. Knox	PA	1909
Wilson	Philander C. Knox	PA	1913
	William J. Bryan	NE	1913
	Robert Lansing	NY	1915
	Bainbridge Colby	NY	1920

President	Secretary	Home	Sworn in
Harding	Charles E. Hughes	NY	1921
Coolidge	Charles E. Hughes	NY	1923
	Frank B. Kellogg	MN	1925
Hoover	Frank B. Kellogg	MN	1929
	Henry L. Stimson	NY	1929
Roosevelt, F. D.	Cordell Hull	TN	1933
	E.R. Stettinius Jr.	VA	1944
Truman	E.R. Stettinius Jr.	VA	1945
	James F. Byrnes	SC	1945
	George C. Marshall	PA	1947
	Dean G. Acheson	CT	1949
Eisenhower	John Foster Dulles	NY	1953
	Christian A. Herter	MA	1959
Kennedy	Dean Rusk	NY	1961
Johnson, L. B.	Dean Rusk	NY	1963
Nixon	William P. Rogers	NY	1969
	Henry A. Kissinger	DC	1973
Ford	Henry A. Kissinger	DC	1974
Carter	Cyrus R. Vance	NY	1977
	Edmund S. Muskie	ME	1980
Reagan	Alexander M. Haig Jr.	CT	1981
	George P. Shultz	CA	1982
Bush, G. H. W.	James A. Baker III	TX	1989
	Lawrence S. Eagleburger	MI	1992
Clinton	Warren M. Christopher	CA	1993
	Madeleine K. Albright	DC	1997
Bush, G. W.	Colin L. Powell	NY	2001
	Condoleezza Rice	AL	2005
Obama	Hillary Rodham Clinton	NY	2009

Secretaries of the Treasury

The Treasury Department was organized by act of Congress on Sept. 2, 1789.

President	Secretary	Home	Sworn in
Washington	Alexander Hamilton	NY	1789
	Oliver Wolcott	CT	1795
Adams, J.	Oliver Wolcott	CT	1797
	Samuel Dexter	MA	1801
Jefferson	Samuel Dexter	MA	1801
	Albert Gallatin	PA	1801
Madison	Albert Gallatin	PA	1809
	George W. Campbell	TN	1814
	Alexander J. Dallas	PA	1814
	William H. Crawford	GA	1816
Monroe	William H. Crawford	GA	1817
Adams, J. Q.	Richard Rush	PA	1825
Jackson	Samuel D. Ingham	PA	1829
	Louis McLane	DE	1831
	William J. Duane	PA	1833
	Roger B. Taney	MD	1833
	Levi Woodbury	NH	1834
Van Buren	Levi Woodbury	NH	1837
Harrison, W. H.	Thomas Ewing	OH	1841
Tyler	Thomas Ewing	OH	1841
	Walter Forward	PA	1841
	John C. Spencer	NY	1843
	George M. Bibb	KY	1844
Polk	Robert J. Walker	MS	1845
Taylor	William M. Meredith	PA	1849
Fillmore	Thomas Corwin	OH	1850
Pierce	James Guthrie	KY	1853
Buchanan	Howell Cobb	GA	1857
	Phillip F. Thomas	MD	1860
	John A. Dix	NY	1861

President	Secretary	Home	Sworn in
Lincoln	Salmon P. Chase	OH	1861
	William P. Fessenden	ME	1864
	Hugh McCulloch	IN	1865
Johnson, A.	Hugh McCulloch	IN	1865
Grant	George S. Boutwell	MA	1869
	William A. Richardson	MA	1873
	Benjamin H. Bristow	KY	1874
	Lot M. Morrill	ME	1876
Hayes	John Sherman	OH	1877
Garfield	William Windom	MN	1881
Arthur	Charles J. Folger	NY	1881
	Walter Q. Gresham	IN	1884
	Hugh McCulloch	IN	1884
Cleveland	Daniel Manning	NY	1885
	Charles S. Fairchild	NY	1887
Harrison, B.	William Windom	MN	1889
	Charles Foster	OH	1891
Cleveland	John G. Carlisle	KY	1893
McKinley	Lyman J. Gage	IL	1897
Roosevelt, T.	Lyman J. Gage	IL	1901
	Leslie M. Shaw	IA	1902
	George B. Cortelyou	NY	1907
Taft	Franklin MacVeagh	IL	1909
Wilson	William G. McAdoo	NY	1913
	Carter Glass	VA	1918
	David F. Houston	MO	1920
Harding	Andrew W. Mellon	PA	1921
Coolidge	Andrew W. Mellon	PA	1923
Hoover	Andrew W. Mellon	PA	1929
	Ogden L. Mills	NY	1932
Roosevelt, F. D.	William H. Woodin	NY	1933
	Henry Morgenthau, Jr.	NY	1934
Truman	Fred M. Vinson	KY	1945
	John W. Snyder	MO	1946
Eisenhower	George M. Humphrey	OH	1953
	Robert B. Anderson	CT	1957
Kennedy	C. Douglas Dillon	NJ	1961
Johnson, L. B.	C. Douglas Dillon	NJ	1963
	Henry H. Fowler	VA	1965
	Joseph W. Barr	IN	1968
Nixon	David M. Kennedy	IL	1969
	John B. Connally	TX	1971
	George P. Shultz	IL	1972
	William E. Simon	NJ	1974
Ford	William E. Simon	NJ	1974
Carter	W. Michael Blumenthal	MI	1977
	G. William Miller	RI	1979
Reagan	Donald T. Regan	NY	1981
	James A. Baker III	TX	1985
	Nicholas F. Brady	NJ	1988
Bush, G. H. W.	Nicholas F. Brady	NJ	1989
Clinton	Lloyd Bentsen	TX	1993
	Robert E. Rubin	NY	1995
	Lawrence H. Summers	CT	1999
Bush, G. W.	Paul H. O'Neill	MO	2001
	John W. Snow	OH	2003
	Henry M. Paulson, Jr.	FL	2006
Obama	Timothy F. Geithner	NY	2009

Secretaries of Defense

The Department of Defense, originally designated the National Military Establishment, was created on Sept. 18, 1947. It is headed by the secretary of defense, who is a member of the president's Cabinet. The departments of the Army, of the Navy, and of the Air Force function within the Defense Department, and since 1947 the secretaries of those departments have not been members of the president's Cabinet.

President	Secretary	Home	Sworn in
Truman	James V. Forrestal	NY	1947
	Louis A. Johnson	WV	1949
	George C. Marshall	PA	1950
	Robert A. Lovett	NY	1951
Eisenhower	Charles E. Wilson	MI	1953
	Neil H. McElroy	OH	1957
	Thomas S. Gates Jr.	PA	1959
Kennedy	Robert S. McNamara	MI	1961
Johnson, L. B.	Robert S. McNamara	MI	1963
	Clark M. Clifford	MD	1968
Nixon	Melvin R. Laird	WI	1969
	Elliot L. Richardson	MA	1973
	James R. Schlesinger	VA	1973

President	Secretary	Home	Sworn in
Ford	James R. Schlesinger	VA	1974
	Donald H. Rumsfeld	IL	1975
Carter	Harold Brown	CA	1977
Reagan	Caspar W. Weinberger	CA	1981
	Frank C. Carlucci	PA	1987
Bush, G. H. W.	Richard B. Cheney	WY	1989
Clinton	Les Aspin	WI	1993
	William J. Perry	CA	1994
	William S. Cohen	ME	1997
Bush, G. W.	Donald H. Rumsfeld	IL	2001
	Robert M. Gates	TX	2006
Obama	Robert M. Gates	TX	2009

Secretaries of War

The War Department (which included jurisdiction over the navy until 1798) was created by act of Congress on Aug. 7, 1789, and Gen. Henry Knox was commissioned secretary of war under that act on Sept. 12, 1789.

President	Secretary	Home	Sworn in
Washington	Henry Knox	MA	1789
	Timothy Pickering	PA	1795
	James McHenry	MD	1796
Adams, J.	James McHenry	MD	1797
	Samuel Dexter	MA	1800
Jefferson	Henry Dearborn	MA	1801
Madison	William Eustis	MA	1809
	John Armstrong	NY	1813
	James Monroe	VA	1814
	William H. Crawford	GA	1815
Monroe	John C. Calhoun	SC	1817
Adams, J. Q.	James Barbour	VA	1825
	Peter B. Porter	NY	1828
Jackson	John H. Eaton	TN	1829
	Lewis Cass	MI	1831
	Benjamin F. Butler	NY	1837
Van Buren	Joel R. Poinsett	SC	1837
Harrison, W. H.	John Bell	TN	1841
Tyler	John Bell	TN	1841
	John C. Spencer	NY	1841
	James M. Porter	PA	1843
	William Wilkins	PA	1844
Polk	William L. Marcy	NY	1845
Taylor	George W. Crawford	GA	1849
Fillmore	Charles M. Conrad	LA	1850
Pierce	Jefferson Davis	MS	1853
Buchanan	John B. Floyd	VA	1857
	Joseph Holt	KY	1861
Lincoln	Simon Cameron	PA	1861
	Edwin M. Stanton	PA	1862
Johnson, A.	Edwin M. Stanton	PA	1865
	John M. Schofield	IL	1868
Grant	John A. Rawlins	IL	1869
	William T. Sherman	OH	1869
	William W. Belknap	IA	1869
	Alphonso Taft	OH	1876
	James D. Cameron	PA	1876
Hayes	George W. McCrary	IA	1877
	Alexander Ramsey	MN	1879
Garfield	Robert T. Lincoln	IL	1881
Arthur	Robert T. Lincoln	IL	1881
Cleveland	William C. Endicott	MA	1885
Harrison, B.	Redfield Proctor	VT	1889
	Stephen B. Elkins	WV	1891
Cleveland	Daniel S. Lamont	NY	1893
McKinley	Russel A. Alger	MI	1897
	Elihu Root	NY	1899
Roosevelt, T.	Elihu Root	NY	1901
	William H. Taft	OH	1904
	Luke E. Wright	TN	1908
Taft	Jacob M. Dickinson	TN	1909
	Henry L. Stimson	NY	1911
Wilson	Lindley M. Garrison	NJ	1913
	Newton D. Baker	OH	1916
Harding	John W. Weeks	MA	1921
Coolidge	John W. Weeks	MA	1923
	Dwight F. Davis	MO	1925
Hoover	James W. Good	IL	1929
	Patrick J. Hurley	OK	1929
Roosevelt, F. D.	George H. Dern	UT	1933
	Harry H. Woodring	KS	1937
	Henry L. Stimson	NY	1940
Truman	Robert P. Patterson	NY	1945
	Kenneth C. Royall[1]	NC	1947

(1) Last member of the Cabinet with this title. The War Department became the Department of the Army, a branch of the Department of Defense, in 1947.

Secretaries of the Navy

The Navy Department was created by act of Congress on Apr. 30, 1798. The Marine Corps is part of this department.

President	Secretary	Home	Sworn in
Adams, J.	Benjamin Stoddert	MD	1798
Jefferson	Benjamin Stoddert	MD	1801
	Robert Smith	MD	1801
Madison	Paul Hamilton	SC	1809
	William Jones	PA	1813
	Benjamin W. Crowninshield	MA	1814
Monroe	Benjamin W. Crowninshield	MA	1817
	Smith Thompson	NY	1818
	Samuel L. Southard	NJ	1823
Adams, J. Q.	Samuel L. Southard	NJ	1825
Jackson	John Branch	NC	1829
	Levi Woodbury	NH	1831
	Mahlon Dickerson	NJ	1834
Van Buren	Mahlon Dickerson	NJ	1837
	James K. Paulding	NY	1838
Harrison, W. H.	George E. Badger	NC	1841
Tyler	George E. Badger	NC	1841
	Abel P. Upshur	VA	1841
	David Henshaw	MA	1843
	Thomas W. Gilmer	VA	1844
	John Y. Mason	VA	1844
Polk	George Bancroft	MA	1845
	John Y. Mason	VA	1846
Taylor	William B. Preston	VA	1849
Fillmore	William A. Graham	NC	1850
	John P. Kennedy	MD	1852
Pierce	James C. Dobbin	NC	1853
Buchanan	Isaac Toucey	CT	1857
Lincoln	Gideon Welles	CT	1861
Johnson, A.	Gideon Welles	CT	1865
Grant	Adolph E. Borie	PA	1869
	George M. Robeson	NJ	1869
Hayes	Richard W. Thompson	IN	1877
	Nathan Goff Jr.	WV	1881
Garfield	William H. Hunt	LA	1881
Arthur	William E. Chandler	NH	1882
Cleveland	William C. Whitney	NY	1885
Harrison, B.	Benjamin F. Tracy	NY	1889
Cleveland	Hilary A. Herbert	AL	1893
McKinley	John D. Long	MA	1897
Roosevelt, T.	John D. Long	MA	1901
	William H. Moody	MA	1902
	Paul Morton	IL	1904
	Charles J. Bonaparte	MD	1905
	Victor H. Metcalf	CA	1906
	Truman H. Newberry	MI	1908
Taft	George von L. Meyer	MA	1909
Wilson	Josephus Daniels	NC	1913
Harding	Edwin Denby	MI	1921
Coolidge	Edwin Denby	MI	1923
	Curtis D. Wilbur	CA	1924
Hoover	Charles Francis Adams	MA	1929
Roosevelt, F. D.	Claude A. Swanson	VA	1933
	Charles Edison	NJ	1940
	Frank Knox	IL	1940
	James V. Forrestal	NY	1944
Truman	James V. Forrestal[1]	NY	1945

(1) Last member of Cabinet with this title. The Navy Department became a branch of the Department of Defense when the latter was created on Sept. 18, 1947.

Attorneys General

The Office of Attorney General was established by act of Congress on Sept. 24, 1789. It officially reached Cabinet rank in Mar. 1792, when the first attorney general, Edmund Randolph, attended his initial Cabinet meeting. The Department of Justice, headed by the attorney general, was created June 22, 1870.

President	Attorney General	Home	Sworn in
Washington	Edmund Randolph	VA	1789
	William Bradford	PA	1794
	Charles Lee	VA	1795
Adams, J.	Charles Lee	VA	1797
Jefferson	Levi Lincoln	MA	1801
	John Breckenridge	KY	1805
	Caesar A. Rodney	DE	1807
Madison	Caesar A. Rodney	DE	1807
	William Pinkney	MD	1811
	Richard Rush	PA	1814
Monroe	Richard Rush	PA	1817
	William Wirt	VA	1817
Adams, J. Q.	William Wirt	VA	1825
Jackson	John M. Berrien	GA	1829
	Roger B. Taney	MD	1831
	Benjamin F. Butler	NY	1833
Van Buren	Benjamin F. Butler	NY	1837
	Felix Grundy	TN	1838
	Henry D. Gilpin	PA	1840
Harrison, W. H.	John J. Crittenden	KY	1841
Tyler	John J. Crittenden	KY	1841
	Hugh S. Legare	SC	1841
	John Nelson	MD	1843
Polk	John Y. Mason	VA	1845
	Nathan Clifford	ME	1846
	Isaac Toucey	CT	1848
Taylor	Reverdy Johnson	MD	1849
Fillmore	John J. Crittenden	KY	1850
Pierce	Caleb Cushing	MA	1853
Buchanan	Jeremiah S. Black	PA	1857
	Edwin M. Stanton	PA	1860
Lincoln	Edward Bates	MO	1861
	James Speed	KY	1864
Johnson, A.	James Speed	KY	1865
	Henry Stanbery	OH	1866
	William M. Evarts	NY	1868
Grant	Ebenezer R. Hoar	MA	1869
	Amos T. Akerman	GA	1870
	George H. Williams	OR	1871
	Edwards Pierrepont	NY	1875
	Alphonso Taft	OH	1876
Hayes	Charles Devens	MA	1877
Garfield	Wayne MacVeagh	PA	1881
Arthur	Benjamin H. Brewster	PA	1882
Cleveland	Augustus Garland	AR	1885
Harrison, B.	William H. H. Miller	IN	1889
Cleveland	Richard Olney	MA	1893
	Judson Harmon	OH	1895
McKinley	Joseph McKenna	CA	1897
	John W. Griggs	NJ	1898
	Philander C. Knox	PA	1901
Roosevelt, T.	Philander C. Knox	PA	1901
	William H. Moody	MA	1904
	Charles J. Bonaparte	MD	1906
Taft	George W. Wickersham	NY	1909
Wilson	J.C. McReynolds	TN	1913
	Thomas W. Gregory	TX	1914
	A. Mitchell Palmer	PA	1919
Harding	Harry M. Daugherty	OH	1921
Coolidge	Harry M. Daugherty	OH	1923
	Harlan F. Stone	NY	1924
	John G. Sargent	VT	1925
Hoover	William D. Mitchell	MN	1929
Roosevelt, F. D.	Homer S. Cummings	CT	1933
	Frank Murphy	MI	1939
	Robert H. Jackson	NY	1940
	Francis Biddle	PA	1941
Truman	Thomas C. Clark	TX	1945
	J. Howard McGrath	RI	1949
	J.P. McGranery	PA	1952
Eisenhower	Herbert Brownell Jr	NY	1953
	William P. Rogers	MD	1957
Kennedy	Robert F. Kennedy	MA	1961
Johnson, L. B.	Robert F. Kennedy	MA	1963
	N. de B. Katzenbach	IL	1964
	Ramsey Clark	TX	1967
Nixon	John N. Mitchell	NY	1969
	Richard G. Kleindienst	AZ	1972
	Elliot L. Richardson	MA	1973
	William B. Saxbe	OH	1974
Ford	William B. Saxbe	OH	1974
	Edward H. Levi	IL	1975

President	Attorney General	Home	Sworn in
Carter	Griffin B. Bell	GA	1977
	Benjamin R. Civiletti	MD	1979
Reagan	William French Smith	CA	1981
	Edwin Meese III	CA	1985
	Richard Thornburgh	PA	1988
Bush, G. H. W.	Richard Thornburgh	PA	1989
	William P. Barr	NY	1991
Clinton	Janet Reno	FL	1993
Bush, G. W.	John Ashcroft	MO	2001
	Alberto Gonzales	TX	2005
	Michael Mukasey	NY	2007
Obama	Eric H. Holder Jr.	DC	2009

Secretaries of the Interior

The Department of the Interior was created by act of Congress on Mar. 3, 1849.

President	Secretary	Home	Sworn in
Taylor	Thomas Ewing	OH	1849
Fillmore	Thomas M. T. McKennan	PA	1850
	Alex H. H. Stuart	VA	1850
Pierce	Robert McClelland	MI	1853
Buchanan	Jacob Thompson	MS	1857
Lincoln	Caleb B. Smith	IN	1861
	John P. Usher	IN	1863
Johnson, A.	John P. Usher	IN	1865
	James Harlan	IA	1865
	Orville H. Browning	IL	1866
Grant	Jacob D. Cox	OH	1869
	Columbus Delano	OH	1870
	Zachariah Chandler	MI	1875
Hayes	Carl Schurz	MO	1877
Garfield	Samuel J. Kirkwood	IA	1881
Arthur	Henry M. Teller	CO	1882
Cleveland	Lucius Q. C. Lamar	MS	1885
	William F. Vilas	WI	1888
Harrison, B.	John W. Noble	MO	1889
Cleveland	Hoke Smith	GA	1893
	David R. Francis	MO	1896
McKinley	Cornelius N. Bliss	NY	1897
	Ethan A. Hitchcock	MO	1898
Roosevelt, T.	Ethan A. Hitchcock	MO	1901
	James R. Garfield	OH	1907
Taft	Richard A. Ballinger	WA	1909
	Walter L. Fisher	IL	1911
Wilson	Franklin K. Lane	CA	1913
	John B. Payne	IL	1920
Harding	Albert B. Fall	NM	1921
	Hubert Work	CO	1923
Coolidge	Hubert Work	CO	1923
	Roy O. West	IL	1929
Hoover	Ray Lyman Wilbur	CA	1929
Roosevelt, F. D.	Harold L. Ickes	IL	1933
Truman	Harold L. Ickes	IL	1945
	Julius A. Krug	WI	1946
	Oscar L. Chapman	CO	1949
Eisenhower	Douglas McKay	OR	1953
	Fred A. Seaton	NE	1956
Kennedy	Stewart L. Udall	AZ	1961
Johnson, L. B.	Stewart L. Udall	AZ	1963
Nixon	Walter J. Hickel	AK	1969
	Rogers C.B. Morton	MD	1971
Ford	Rogers C.B. Morton	MD	1971
	Stanley K. Hathaway	WY	1975
	Thomas S. Kleppe	ND	1975
Carter	Cecil D. Andrus	ID	1977
Reagan	James G. Watt	CO	1981
	William P. Clark	CA	1983
	Donald P. Hodel	OR	1985
Bush, G. H. W.	Manuel Lujan	NM	1989
Clinton	Bruce Babbitt	AZ	1993
Bush, G. W.	Gale Norton	CO	2001
	Dirk Kempthorne	ID	2006
Obama	Kenneth L. Salazar	CO	2009

Secretaries of Agriculture

The Department of Agriculture was created by act of Congress on May 15, 1862. On Feb. 8, 1889, its commissioner was renamed secretary of agriculture and became a member of the Cabinet.

President	Secretary	Home	Sworn in
Cleveland	Norman J. Colman	MO	1889
Harrison, B.	Jeremiah M. Rusk	WI	1889
Cleveland	J. Sterling Morton	NE	1893
McKinley	James Wilson	IA	1897
Roosevelt, T.	James Wilson	IA	1901
Taft	James Wilson	IA	1909
Wilson	David F. Houston	MO	1913
	Edwin T. Meredith	IA	1920
Harding	Henry C. Wallace	IA	1921
Coolidge	Henry C. Wallace	IA	1923
	Howard M. Gore	WV	1924
	William M. Jardine	KS	1925
Hoover	Arthur M. Hyde	MO	1929
Roosevelt, F. D.	Henry A. Wallace	IA	1933
	Claude R. Wickard	IN	1940
Truman	Clinton P. Anderson	NM	1945
Truman	Charles F. Brannan	CO	1948
Eisenhower	Ezra Taft Benson	UT	1953
Kennedy	Orville L. Freeman	MN	1961
Johnson, L. B.	Orville L. Freeman	MN	1963
Nixon	Clifford M. Hardin	IN	1969
	Earl L. Butz	IN	1971
Ford	Earl L. Butz	IN	1974
	John A. Knebel	VA	1976
Carter	Bob Bergland	MN	1977
Reagan	John R. Block	IL	1981
	Richard E. Lyng	CA	1986
Bush, G. H. W.	Clayton K. Yeutter	NE	1989
	Edward Madigan	IL	1991
Clinton	Mike Espy	MS	1993
	Dan Glickman	KS	1995
Bush, G. W.	Ann M. Veneman	CA	2001
	Mike Johanns	NE	2005
	Ed Schafer	ND	2008
Obama	Thomas J. Vilsack	IA	2009

Secretaries of Commerce and Labor

The Department of Commerce and Labor, created by Congress on Feb. 14, 1903, was divided by Congress Mar. 4, 1913, into separate departments of Commerce and Labor. The secretary of each was made a Cabinet member.

President	Secretary	Home	Sworn in
Roosevelt, T.	George B. Cortelyou	NY	1903
	Victor H. Metcalf	CA	1904
	Oscar S. Straus	NY	1906
Taft	Charles Nagel	MO	1909

Secretaries of Labor

President	Secretary	Home	Sworn in
Wilson	William B. Wilson	PA	1913
Harding	James J. Davis	PA	1921
Coolidge	James J. Davis	PA	1923
Hoover	James J. Davis	PA	1929
	William N. Doak	VA	1930
Roosevelt, F. D.	Frances Perkins	NY	1933
Truman	L. B. Schwellenbach	WA	1945
	Maurice J. Tobin	MA	1949
Eisenhower	Martin P. Durkin	IL	1953
	James P. Mitchell	NJ	1953
Kennedy	Arthur J. Goldberg	IL	1961
	W. Willard Wirtz	IL	1962
Johnson, L. B.	W. Willard Wirtz	IL	1963
Nixon	George P. Shultz	IL	1969
	James D. Hodgson	CA	1970
	Peter J. Brennan	NY	1973
Ford	Peter J. Brennan	NY	1974
	John T. Dunlop	CA	1975
	W. J. Usery Jr.	GA	1976
Carter	F. Ray Marshall	TX	1977
Reagan	Raymond J. Donovan	NJ	1981
	William E. Brock	TN	1985
	Ann D. McLaughlin	DC	1987
Bush, G. H. W.	Elizabeth Hanford Dole	NC	1989
	Lynn Martin	IL	1991
Clinton	Robert B. Reich	MA	1993
	Alexis M. Herman	AL	1997
Bush, G. W.	Elaine L. Chao	KY	2001
Obama	Hilda L. Solis	CA	2009

Secretaries of Commerce

President	Secretary	Home	Sworn in
Wilson	William C. Redfield	NY	1913
	Joshua W. Alexander	MO	1919
Harding	Herbert C. Hoover	CA	1921
Coolidge	Herbert C. Hoover	CA	1923
	William F. Whiting	MA	1928
Hoover	Robert P. Lamont	IL	1929
	Roy D. Chapin	MI	1932
Roosevelt, F. D.	Daniel C. Roper	SC	1933
	Harry L. Hopkins	NY	1939
	Jesse Jones	TX	1940
	Henry A. Wallace	IA	1945
Truman	Henry A. Wallace	IA	1945
	W. Averell Harriman	NY	1947
	Charles Sawyer	OH	1948
Eisenhower	Sinclair Weeks	MA	1953
	Lewis L. Strauss	NY	1958
	Frederick H. Mueller	MI	1959
Kennedy	Luther H. Hodges	NC	1961
Johnson, L. B.	Luther H. Hodges	NC	1963
	John T. Connor	NJ	1965
	Alex B. Trowbridge	NJ	1967
	Cyrus R. Smith	NY	1968
Nixon	Maurice H. Stans	MN	1969
	Peter G. Peterson	IL	1972
	Frederick B. Dent	SC	1973
Ford	Frederick B. Dent	SC	1974
	Rogers C. B. Morton	MD	1975
	Elliot L. Richardson	MA	1975
Carter	Juanita M. Kreps	NC	1977
	Philip M. Klutznick	IL	1979
Reagan	Malcolm Baldrige	CT	1981
	C. William Verity Jr.	OH	1987
Bush, G. H. W.	Robert A. Mosbacher	TX	1989
	Barbara H. Franklin	PA	1992
Clinton	Ronald H. Brown	DC	1993
	Mickey Kantor	CA	1996
	William M. Daley	IL	1997
	Norman Y. Mineta	CA	2000
Bush, G. W.	Donald L. Evans	TX	2001
	Carlos Gutierrez	MI	2005
Obama	Gary F. Locke	WA	2009

Secretaries of Housing and Urban Development

The Department of Housing and Urban Development was created by act of Congress on Sept. 9, 1965.

President	Secretary	Home	Sworn in
Johnson, L. B.	Robert C. Weaver	WA	1966
	Robert C. Wood	MA	1969
Nixon	George W. Romney	MI	1969
	James T. Lynn	OH	1973
Ford	James T. Lynn	OH	1974
	Carla Anderson Hills	CA	1975
Carter	Patricia Roberts Harris	DC	1977
	Moon Landrieu	LA	1979
Reagan	Samuel R. Pierce Jr.	NY	1981
Bush, G. H. W.	Jack F. Kemp	NY	1989
Clinton	Henry G. Cisneros	TX	1993
	Andrew M. Cuomo	NY	1997
Bush, G. W.	Mel Martinez	FL	2001
	Alphonso Jackson	TX	2004
	Steve Preston	VA	2008
Obama	Shaun L. S. Donovan	IL	2009

Secretaries of Transportation

The Department of Transportation was created by act of Congress on Oct. 15, 1966.

President	Secretary	Home	Sworn in
Johnson, L. B.	Alan S. Boyd	FL	1966
Nixon	John A. Volpe	MA	1969
	Claude S. Brinegar	CA	1973
Ford	Claude S. Brinegar	CA	1974
	William T. Coleman Jr.	PA	1975
Carter	Brock Adams	WA	1977
	Neil E. Goldschmidt	OR	1979
Reagan	Andrew L. Lewis Jr.	PA	1981
	Elizabeth Hanford Dole	NC	1983
	James H. Burnley	NC	1987
Bush, G. H. W.	Samuel K. Skinner	IL	1989
	Andrew H. Card Jr.	MA	1992
Clinton	Federico F. Peña	CO	1993
	Rodney E. Slater	AR	1997
Bush, G. W.	Norman Y. Mineta	CA	2001
	Mary E. Peters	AZ	2006
Obama	Raymond L. LaHood	TX	2009

Secretaries of Energy

The Department of Energy was created by federal law on Aug. 4, 1977.

President	Secretary	Home	Sworn in
Carter	James R. Schlesinger	VA	1977
	Charles Duncan Jr.	WY	1979
Reagan	James B. Edwards	SC	1981
	Donald P. Hodel	OR	1982
	John S. Herrington	CA	1985
Bush, G. H. W.	James D. Watkins	CA	1989
Clinton	Hazel R. O'Leary	MN	1993
	Federico F. Peña	CO	1997
	Bill Richardson	NM	1998
Bush, G. W.	Spencer Abraham	MI	2001
	Samuel W. Bodman	MA	2005
Obama	Steven Chu	CA	2009

Secretaries of Health, Education, and Welfare

The Department of Health, Education, and Welfare was created by Congress on Apr. 11, 1953. On Sept. 27, 1979, it was divided by Congress into the departments of Education and of Health and Human Services, with the secretary of each becoming a Cabinet member.

President	Secretary	Home	Sworn in
Eisenhower	Oveta Culp Hobby	TX	1953
	Marion B. Folsom	NY	1955
	Arthur S. Flemming	OH	1958
Kennedy	Abraham A. Ribicoff	CT	1961
	Anthony J. Celebrezze	OH	1962
Johnson, L. B.	Anthony J. Celebrezze	OH	1963
	John W. Gardner	NY	1965
	Wilbur J. Cohen	MI	1968
Nixon	Robert H. Finch	CA	1969
	Elliot L. Richardson	MA	1970
	Caspar W. Weinberger	CA	1973
Ford	Caspar W. Weinberger	CA	1974
	Forrest D. Mathews	AL	1975
Carter	Joseph A. Califano Jr.	DC	1977
	Patricia Roberts Harris	DC	1979

Secretaries of Health and Human Services

President	Secretary	Home	Sworn in
Carter	Patricia Roberts Harris	DC	1979
Reagan	Richard S. Schweiker	PA	1981
	Margaret M. Heckler	MA	1983
Reagan	Otis R. Bowen	IN	1985
Bush, G. H. W.	Louis W. Sullivan	GA	1989
Clinton	Donna E. Shalala	WI	1993
Bush, G. W.	Tommy Thompson	WI	2001
	Michael O. Leavitt	UT	2005
Obama	Kathleen Sebelius	KS	2009

Secretaries of Education

President	Secretary	Home	Sworn in
Carter	Shirley Hufstedler	CA	1979
Reagan	Terrel Bell	UT	1981
	William J. Bennett	NY	1985
	Lauro F. Cavazos	TX	1988
Bush, G. H. W.	Lauro F. Cavazos	TX	1989
	Lamar Alexander	TN	1991
Clinton	Richard W. Riley	SC	1993
Bush, G. W.	Roderick R. Paige	TX	2001
	Margaret Spellings	TX	2005
Obama	Arne Duncan	IL	2009

Secretaries of Veterans Affairs

The Department of Veterans Affairs was created on Oct. 25, 1988, when Pres. Ronald Reagan signed a bill that made the Veterans Administration into a Cabinet department, effective Mar. 15, 1989.

President	Secretary	Home	Sworn in
Bush, G. H. W.	Edward J. Derwinski	IL	1989
Clinton	Jesse Brown	IL	1993
	Togo D. West Jr.	NC	1998
Bush, G. W.	Anthony Principi	CA	2001
	R. James Nicholson	CO	2005
	James B. Peake	MO	2007
Obama	Eric K. Shinseki	HI/VA	2009

Secretaries of Homeland Security

The Department of Homeland Security was created by act of Congress on Nov. 25, 2002.

President	Secretary	Home	Sworn in
Bush, G. W.	Thomas Ridge	PA	2003
	Michael Chertoff	DC	2005
Obama	Janet Napolitano	AZ	2009

U.S. SUPREME COURT

(as of Oct. 2009)

Justices of the U.S. Supreme Court

The Supreme Court comprises the chief justice of the U.S. and 8 associate justices, all appointed for life by the president with advice and consent of the Senate. Names of chief justices are in **boldface**. Terms of service begin with the year each justice took the judicial oath. Service years are the number of complete years served by a justice. Current salaries: chief justice, $217,400; associate justice, $208,100. The U.S. Supreme Court Bldg. is at 1 First St. NE, Washington, DC 20543. The Court website is www.supremecourtus.gov

Members at start of 2009-10 term (Oct. 5, 2009, but an unusual summer session was also convened Sept. 9, 2009): Chief justice: John G. Roberts Jr.; assoc. justices in seniority order: John Paul Stevens, Antonin Scalia, Anthony M. Kennedy, Clarence Thomas, Ruth Bader Ginsburg, Stephen G. Breyer, Samuel A. Alito Jr., Sonia Sotomayor.

Name, apptd. from	Service Term	Yrs.	Born	Died	Name, apptd. from	Service Term	Yrs.	Born	Died
John Jay, NY	1789-1795	5	1745	1829	Oliver W. Holmes, MA	1902-1932	29	1841	1935
John Rutledge, SC[1]	1790-1791	1	1739	1800	William R. Day, OH	1903-1922	19	1849	1923
William Cushing, MA	1790-1810*	20	1732	1810	William H. Moody, MA	1906-1910	3	1853	1917
James Wilson, PA.	1789-1798	8	1742	1798	Horace H. Lurton, TN	1910-1914	4	1844	1914
John Blair, VA.	1790-1795*	5	1732	1800	Charles E. Hughes, NY[1]	1910-1916	5	1862	1948
James Iredell, NC.	1790-1799	9	1751	1799	Willis Van Devanter, WY	1911-1937	26	1859	1941
Thomas Johnson, MD	1792-1793	<1	1732	1819	Joseph R. Lamar, GA	1911-1916	5	1857	1916
William Paterson, NJ	1793-1806	13	1745	1806	**Edward D. White,** LA[2]	1910-1921	10	1845	1921
John Rutledge, SC[2,3]	1795	<1	1739	1800	Mahlon Pitney, NJ	1912-1922	10	1858	1924
Samuel Chase, MD	1796-1811	15	1741	1811	James C. McReynolds, TN	1914-1941	26	1862	1946
Oliver Ellsworth, CT.	1796-1800	4	1745	1807	Louis D. Brandeis, MA	1916-1939	22	1856	1941
Bushrod Washington, VA	1799-1829*	30	1762	1829	John H. Clarke, OH	1916-1922	5	1857	1945
Alfred Moore, NC	1800-1804	3	1755	1810	**William H. Taft,** CT	1921-1930	8	1857	1930
John Marshall, VA.	1801-1835	34	1755	1835	George Sutherland, UT	1922-1938	15	1862	1942
William Johnson, SC	1804-1834	30	1771	1834	Pierce Butler, MN	1923-1939	16	1866	1939
Henry B. Livingston, NY	1807-1823	16	1757	1823	Edward T. Sanford, TN	1923-1930	7	1865	1930
Thomas Todd, KY.	1807-1826	18	1765	1826	Harlan F. Stone, NY[1]	1925-1941	16	1872	1946
Gabriel Duvall, MD	1811-1835	23	1752	1844	**Charles E. Hughes,** NY[2]	1930-1941	11	1862	1948
Joseph Story, MA.	1812-1845*	33	1779	1845	Owen J. Roberts, PA	1930-1945	15	1875	1955
Smith Thompson, NY	1823-1843	20	1768	1843	Benjamin N. Cardozo, NY	1932-1938	6	1870	1938
Robert Trimble, KY.	1826-1828	2	1777	1828	Hugo L. Black, AL	1937-1971	34	1886	1971
John McLean, OH	1830-1861*	31	1785	1861	Stanley F. Reed, KY	1938-1957	19	1884	1980
Henry Baldwin, PA	1830-1844	14	1780	1844	Felix Frankfurter, MA	1939-1962	23	1882	1965
James M. Wayne, GA.	1835-1867	32	1790	1867	William O. Douglas, CT	1939-1975	36[4]	1898	1980
Roger B. Taney, MD	1836-1864	28	1777	1864	Frank Murphy, MI.	1940-1949	9	1890	1949
Philip P. Barbour, VA.	1836-1841	4	1783	1841	**Harlan F. Stone,** NY[2]	1941-1946	4	1872	1946
John Catron, TN.	1837-1865	28	1786	1865	James F. Byrnes, SC	1941-1942	1	1879	1972
John McKinley, AL	1838-1852*	14	1780	1852	Robert H. Jackson, NY	1941-1954	13	1892	1954
Peter V. Daniel, VA.	1842-1860*	18	1784	1860	Wiley B. Rutledge, IA.	1943-1949	6	1894	1949
Samuel Nelson, NY	1845-1872	27	1792	1873	Harold H. Burton, OH	1945-1958	13	1888	1964
Levi Woodbury, NH.	1845-1851	5	1789	1851	**Fred M. Vinson,** KY	1946-1953	7	1890	1953
Robert C. Grier, PA.	1846-1870	23	1794	1870	Tom C. Clark, TX.	1949-1967	17	1899	1977
Benjamin R. Curtis, MA	1851-1857	5	1809	1874	Sherman Minton, IN	1949-1956	7	1890	1965
John A. Campbell, AL	1853-1861*	8	1811	1889	**Earl Warren,** CA	1953-1969	15	1891	1974
Nathan Clifford, ME	1858-1881	23	1803	1881	John Marshall Harlan, NY	1955-1971	16	1899	1971
Noah H. Swayne, OH.	1862-1881	18	1804	1884	William J. Brennan Jr., NJ	1956-1990	33	1906	1997
Samuel F. Miller, IA.	1862-1890	28	1816	1890	Charles E. Whittaker, MO	1957-1962	5	1901	1973
David Davis, IL	1862-1877	14	1815	1886	Potter Stewart, OH	1958-1981	22	1915	1985
Stephen J. Field, CA	1863-1897	33	1816	1899	Byron R. White, CO.	1962-1993	31	1917	2002
Salmon P. Chase, OH	1864-1873	8	1808	1873	Arthur J. Goldberg, IL	1962-1965	2	1908	1990
William Strong, PA	1870-1880	10	1808	1895	Abe Fortas, TN	1965-1969	3	1910	1982
Joseph P. Bradley, NJ.	1870-1892	21	1813	1892	Thurgood Marshall, NY	1967-1991	24	1908	1993
Ward Hunt, NY	1873-1882	9	1810	1886	**Warren E. Burger,** VA	1969-1986	17	1907	1995
Morrison R. Waite, OH	1874-1888	14	1816	1888	Harry A. Blackmun, MN.	1970-1994	24	1908	1999
John M. Harlan, KY	1877-1911	33	1833	1911	Lewis F. Powell Jr., VA.	1972-1987	15	1907	1998
William B. Woods, GA	1881-1887	6	1824	1887	William H. Rehnquist, AZ[1]	1972-1986	14	1924	2005
Stanley Matthews, OH	1881-1889	7	1824	1889	John Paul Stevens, IL	1975-		1920	
Horace Gray, MA	1882-1902	20	1828	1902	Sandra Day O'Connor, AZ.	1981-2006	24	1930	
Samuel Blatchford, NY.	1882-1893	11	1820	1893	**William H. Rehnquist,** VA[2]	1986-2005	18	1924	2005
Lucius Q.C. Lamar, MS	1888-1893	5	1825	1893	Antonin Scalia, VA.	1986-		1936	
Melville W. Fuller, IL	1888-1910	21	1833	1910	Anthony M. Kennedy, CA.	1988-		1936	
David J. Brewer, KS	1890-1910	20	1837	1910	David H. Souter, NH	1990-2009	18	1939	
Henry B. Brown, MI	1891-1906	15	1836	1913	Clarence Thomas, GA.	1991-		1948	
George Shiras Jr., PA.	1892-1903	10	1832	1924	Ruth Bader Ginsburg, NY	1993-		1933	
Howell E. Jackson, TN	1893-1895	2	1832	1895	Stephen G. Breyer, MA	1994-		1938	
Edward D. White, LA[1]	1894-1910	16	1845	1921	**John G. Roberts Jr.,** MD	2005-		1955	
Rufus W. Peckham, NY	1896-1909	13	1838	1909	Samuel A. Alito Jr., NJ.	2006-		1950	
Joseph McKenna, CA.	1898-1925	26	1843	1926	Sonia Sotomayor, NY	2009-		1954	

*Date of oath taken from questionable source. (1) Later, chief justice, as listed. (2) Formerly assoc. justice. (3) Named as acting chief justice; confirmation rejected by the Senate. (4) Longest term of service.

CONGRESS

As of Sept. 30, 2009. For complete 2008 Senate and House election results, see 111th Congress: 2008 Election Results.

Floor Leaders in the U.S. Senate, 1920-2009

Majority Leaders				Minority Leaders			
Name	Party	State	Tenure	Name	Party	State	Tenure
Charles Curtis[1]	Rep.	KS	1925-1929	Oscar W. Underwood[2]	Dem.	AL	1920-1923
James E. Watson	Rep.	IN	1929-1933	Joseph T. Robinson	Dem.	AR	1923-1933
Joseph T. Robinson	Dem.	AR	1933-1937	Charles L. McNary	Rep.	OR	1933-1944
Alben W. Barkley	Dem.	KY	1937-1947	Wallace H. White	Rep.	ME	1944-1947
Wallace H. White	Rep.	ME	1947-1949	Alben W. Barkley	Dem.	KY	1947-1949
Scott W. Lucas	Dem.	IL	1949-1951	Kenneth S. Wherry	Rep.	NE	1949-1951
Ernest W. McFarland	Dem.	AZ	1951-1953	Henry Styles Bridges	Rep.	NH	1952-1953
Robert A. Taft	Rep.	OH	1953	Lyndon B. Johnson	Dem.	TX	1953-1955
William F. Knowland	Rep.	CA	1953-1955	William F. Knowland	Rep.	CA	1955-1959
Lyndon B. Johnson	Dem.	TX	1955-1961	Everett M. Dirksen	Rep.	IL	1959-1969
Mike Mansfield	Dem.	MT	1961-1977	Hugh D. Scott	Rep.	PA	1969-1977
Robert C. Byrd	Dem.	WV	1977-1981	Howard H. Baker Jr.	Rep.	TN	1977-1981
Howard H. Baker Jr.	Rep.	TN	1981-1985	Robert C. Byrd	Dem.	WV	1981-1987
Robert J. Dole	Rep.	KS	1985-1987	Robert J. Dole	Rep.	KS	1987-1995
Robert C. Byrd	Dem.	WV	1987-1989	Thomas A. Daschle	Dem.	SD	1995-2001[3]
George J. Mitchell	Dem.	ME	1989-1995	Trent Lott	Rep.	MS	2001-2002[3,4]
Robert J. Dole	Rep.	KS	1995-1996	Thomas A. Daschle	Dem.	SD	2003-2005[5]
Trent Lott	Rep.	MS	1996-2001[3]	Harry M. Reid	Dem.	NV	2005-2007
Thomas A. Daschle	Dem.	SD	2001-2003[3]	Mitch McConnell	Rep.	KY	2007-
William Frist	Rep.	TN	2003-2007[4]				
Harry M. Reid	Dem.	NV	2007-				

Note: The offices of party (majority and minority) leaders in the Senate did not evolve until the 20th century. (1) First Republican to be designated floor leader. (2) First Democrat to be designated floor leader. (3) Democrats held the majority Jan. 3, 2001, until Dick Cheney (R) was installed as vice pres., Jan. 20. Republicans regained the majority Jan. 20 until Jim Jeffords (VT) switched from Republican to Independent, June 6, and gave Democrats the majority. (4) Trent Lott resigned from Republican leadership Dec. 20, 2002. William Frist was elected Republican leader Dec. 23, 2002, and began service Jan. 7, 2003, as majority leader. (5) Thomas Daschle was defeated in the 2004 election, and retired from the Senate Jan. 3, 2005; Democratic Whip Harry M. Reid was elected to the post for the 109th Congress.

Speakers of the House of Representatives, 1789-2009

Name	Party	State	Tenure	Name	Party	State	Tenure
Frederick Muhlenberg	Federalist	PA	1789-1791	James G. Blaine	Rep.	ME	1869-1875
Jonathan Trumbull	Federalist	CT	1791-1793	Michael C. Kerr	Dem.	IN	1875-1876
Frederick Muhlenberg	Federalist	PA	1793-1795	Samuel J. Randall	Dem.	PA	1876-1881
Jonathan Dayton	Federalist	NJ	1795-1799	J. Warren Keifer	Rep.	OH	1881-1883
Theodore Sedgwick	Federalist	MA	1799-1801	John G. Carlisle	Dem.	KY	1883-1889
Nathaniel Macon	Dem.-Rep.	NC	1801-1807	Thomas B. Reed	Rep.	ME	1889-1891
Joseph B. Varnum	Dem.-Rep.	MA	1807-1811	Charles F. Crisp	Dem.	GA	1891-1895
Henry Clay	Dem.-Rep.	KY	1811-1814	Thomas B. Reed	Rep.	ME	1895-1899
Langdon Cheves	Dem.-Rep.	SC	1814-1815	David B. Henderson	Rep.	IA	1899-1903
Henry Clay	Dem.-Rep.	KY	1815-1820	Joseph G. Cannon	Rep.	IL	1903-1911
John W. Taylor	Dem.-Rep.	NY	1820-1821	Champ Clark	Dem.	MO	1911-1919
Philip P. Barbour	Dem.-Rep.	VA	1821-1823	Frederick H. Gillett	Rep.	MA	1919-1925
Henry Clay	Dem.-Rep.	KY	1823-1825	Nicholas Longworth	Rep.	OH	1925-1931
John W. Taylor	Dem.	NY	1825-1827	John N. Garner	Dem.	TX	1931-1933
Andrew Stevenson	Dem.	VA	1827-1834	Henry T. Rainey	Dem.	IL	1933-1934
John Bell	Dem.	TN	1834-1835	Joseph W. Byrns	Dem.	TN	1935-1936
James K. Polk	Dem.	TN	1835-1839	William B. Bankhead	Dem.	AL	1936-1940
Robert M. T. Hunter	Dem.	VA	1839-1841	Sam Rayburn	Dem.	TX	1940-1947
John White	Whig	KY	1841-1843	Joseph W. Martin Jr.	Rep.	MA	1947-1949
John W. Jones	Dem.	VA	1843-1845	Sam Rayburn	Dem.	TX	1949-1953
John W. Davis	Dem.	IN	1845-1847	Joseph W. Martin Jr.	Rep.	MA	1953-1955
Robert C. Winthrop	Whig	MA	1847-1849	Sam Rayburn	Dem.	TX	1955-1961
Howell Cobb	Dem.	GA	1849-1851	John W. McCormack	Dem.	MA	1962-1971
Linn Boyd	Dem.	KY	1851-1855	Carl Albert	Dem.	OK	1971-1977
Nathaniel P. Banks	American	MA	1856-1857	Thomas P. O'Neill Jr.	Dem.	MA	1977-1987
James L. Orr	Dem.	SC	1857-1859	James Wright	Dem.	TX	1987-1989
William Pennington	Rep.	NJ	1860-1861	Thomas S. Foley	Dem.	WA	1989-1995
Galusha A. Grow	Rep.	PA	1861-1863	Newt Gingrich	Rep.	GA	1995-1999
Schuyler Colfax	Rep.	IN	1863-1869	J. Dennis Hastert	Rep.	IL	1999-2007
Theodore M. Pomeroy	Rep.	NY	1869	Nancy Pelosi	Dem.	CA	2007-

Political Divisions of the U.S. Senate and House of Representatives, 1901-2009

Source: Office of the Clerk; Congressional Research Service, Library of Congress

Note: All figures reflect immediate post-election party breakdown; **boldface** denotes party in majority immediately after election.

		SENATE					HOUSE OF REPRESENTATIVES				
Congress	Years	Total members	Dem.	Rep.	Other parties	Vacant	Total members	Dem.	Rep.	Other parties	Vacant
57th	1901-03	90	32	**56**	2		357	151	**200**	6	
58th	1903-05	90	33	**57**			386	176	**207**	3	
59th	1905-07	90	32	**58**			386	135	**251**		
60th	1907-09	92	31	**61**			391	167	**223**	1	
61st	1909-11	92	32	**60**			391	172	**219**		
62nd	1911-13	96	44	**52**			394	**230**	162	2	
63rd	1913-15	96	**51**	44	1		435	**291**	134	10	
64th	1915-17	96	**56**	40			435	**230**	196	9	
65th	1917-19	96	**54**	42			435	214[1]	**215**	6	
66th	1919-21	96	47	**49**			435	192	**240**	2	1
67th	1921-23	96	37	**59**			435	131	**302**	2	
68th	1923-25	96	42	**53**	1		435	207	**225**	3	
69th	1925-27	96	41	**54**	1		435	183	**247**	5	
70th	1927-29	96	46	**48**	1	1	435	194	**238**	3	
71st	1929-31	96	39	**56**	1		435	164	**270**	1	
72nd	1931-33	96	47	**48**	1		435	216[2]	**218**	1	

Congress	Years	SENATE Total members	Dem.	Rep.	Other parties	Vacant	HOUSE OF REPRESENTATIVES Total members	Dem.	Rep.	Other parties	Vacant
73rd	1933-35	96	59	36	1		435	313	117	5	
74th	1935-37	96	69	25	2		435	322	103	10	
75th	1937-39	96	76	16	4		435	334	88	13	
76th	1939-41	96	69	23	4		435	262	169	4	
77th	1941-43	96	66	28	2		435	267	162	6	
78th	1943-45	96	57	38	1		435	222	209	4	
79th	1945-47	96	57	38	1		435	242	191	2	
80th	1947-49	96	45	51			435	188	246	1	
81st	1949-51	96	54	42			435	263	171	1	
82nd	1951-53	96	49	47			435	235	199	1	
83rd	1953-55	96	47	48	1		435	213	221	1	
84th	1955-57	96	48	47	1		435	232	203		
85th	1957-59	96	49	47			435	234	201		
86th	1959-61	100	65	35			437[3]	283	153	1	
87th	1961-63	100	64	36			437[4]	263	174		
88th	1963-65	100	66	34			435	259	176		
89th	1965-67	100	68	32			435	295	140		
90th	1967-69	100	64	36			435	247	187		1
91st	1969-71	100	57	43			435	243	192		
92nd	1971-73	100	54	44	2		435	255	180		
93rd	1973-75	100	56	42	2		435	242	192	1	
94th	1975-77	100	60	38	2		435	291	144		
95th	1977-79	100	61	38	1		435	292	143		
96th	1979-81	100	58	41	1		435	277	158		
97th	1981-83	100	46	53	1		435	242	192	1	
98th	1983-85	100	46	54			435	269	166		
99th	1985-87	100	47	53			435	253	182		
100th	1987-89	100	55	45			435	258	177		
101st	1989-91	100	55	45			435	260	175		
102nd	1991-93	100	56	44			435	267	167	1	
103rd	1993-95	100	57	43			435	258	176	1	
104th	1995-97	100	48	52			435	204	230	1	
105th	1997-99	100	45	55			435	206	228	1	
106th	1999-2001	100	45	55			435	211	223	1	
107th	2001-03	100	50	50[5]			435	212	221	2	
108th	2003-05	100	48	51	1		435	204	229	1	1
109th	2005-07	100	44	55	1		435	202	232	1	
110th	2007-09	100	49	49	2[6]		435	233	202		
111th	2009-	100	58[7]	40	2[6]		435	256	178		1

(1) Democrats organized the House with help of other parties. (2) Democrats organized House because of Republican deaths. (3) Proclamation declaring Alaska a state issued Jan. 3, 1959. (4) Proclamation declaring Hawaii a state issued Aug. 21, 1959. (5) While the Senate was split 50-50, control was held by whichever party had an incumbent vice president. Republican Sen. James M. Jeffords (VT) changed his party designation to Independent on June 6, 2001, switching control of the Senate to Democrats. (6) Both Independent senators chose to caucus with the Democrats. (7) Sen. Arlen Spector (PA), reelected as a Republican in 2004, became a Democrat, Apr. 30, 2009; Sen. Al Franken (D, MN) was not seated until July 7, 2009.

Congressional Bills Vetoed, 1789-2009

Source: Senate Library

President	Regular vetoes	Pocket vetoes	Total vetoes	Vetoes overridden	President	Regular vetoes	Pocket vetoes	Total vetoes	Vetoes overridden
Washington	2	—	2	—	Benjamin Harrison	19	25	44	1
Adams, J.	—	—	—	—	Cleveland[2]	42	128	170	5
Jefferson	—	—	—	—	McKinley	6	36	42	—
Madison	5	2	7	—	Theodore Roosevelt	42	40	82	1
Monroe	1	—	1	—	Taft	30	9	39	1
Adams, J. Q.	—	—	—	—	Wilson	33	11	44	6
Jackson	5	7	12	—	Harding	5	1	6	—
Van Buren	—	1	1	—	Coolidge	20	30	50	4
William Harrison	—	—	—	—	Hoover	21	16	37	3
Tyler	6	4	10	1	Franklin Roosevelt	372	263	635	9
Polk	2	1	3	—	Truman	180	70	250	12
Taylor	—	—	—	—	Eisenhower	73	108	181	2
Fillmore	—	—	—	—	Kennedy	12	9	21	—
Pierce	9	—	9	5	Lyndon Johnson	16	14	30	—
Buchanan	4	3	7	—	Nixon	26	17	43	7
Lincoln	2	5	7	—	Ford	48	18	66	12
Andrew Johnson	21	8	29	15	Carter	13	18	31	2
Grant	45	48	93	4	Reagan	39	39	78	9
Hayes	12	1	13	1	George H. W. Bush[3]	29	15	44	1
Garfield	—	—	—	—	Clinton[4]	36	1	37	2
Arthur	4	8	12	1	George W. Bush	11	1[5]	12	4
Cleveland[1]	304	110	414	2	Total[3,4,6]	1,495	1,067	2,561	110

— = 0. (1) First term only. (2) Second term only. (3) Excluded from the figures are 2 additional bills that Pres. George H. W. Bush claimed to be vetoed but Congress considered enacted into law because the president failed to return them to Congress during a recess period. (4) Does not include line-item vetoes, which were ruled unconstitutional by the Supreme Court on June 25, 1998. (5) Pres. Bush characterized his Dec. 28, 2007, veto of H.R. 1585 as a pocket veto, although he did return the parchment to the House. (6) As of Oct. 15, 2009, Pres. Barack Obama had not vetoed any legislation.

Librarians of Congress

Librarian	Served	Appointed by	Librarian	Served	Appointed by
John J. Beckley	1802-1807	Jefferson	Herbert Putnam	1899-1939	McKinley
Patrick Magruder	1807-1815	Jefferson	Archibald MacLeish	1939-1944	F. D. Roosevelt
George Watterston	1815-1829	Madison	Luther H. Evans	1945-1953	Truman
John Silva Meehan	1829-1861	Jackson	L. Quincy Mumford	1954-1974	Eisenhower
John G. Stephenson	1861-1864	Lincoln	Daniel J. Boorstin	1975-1987	Ford
Ainsworth Rand Spofford	1864-1897	Lincoln	James H. Billington	1987-	Reagan
John Russell Young	1897-1899	McKinley			

111th Congress: 2008 Election Results

Official results as of Sept. 30, 2009.

Source: Federal Election Commission

The Senate

Dem., 58; Rep., 40; Ind., 1; Ind. Dem., 1. Total, 100. Boldface denotes the 2008 election winner. *Incumbent.

Terms are for 6 years and end Jan. 3 of the year preceding the senator's name in the following table. Annual salary, $174,000; President Pro Tempore, Majority Leader, and Minority Leader, $193,400. To be eligible for the Senate, one must be at least 30 years old, a U.S. citizen for at least 9 years, and a resident of the state from which chosen. The address is U.S. Senate, Washington DC 20510; telephone, (202) 224-3121; website, www.senate.gov

D-Democrat; **R**-Republican; **CFL**-Connecticut for Lieberman; **DFL**-Dem.-Farmer-Labor; **DNL**-Dem.-Nonpartisan League; **GR**-Green Party; **I**-Independent; **L**-Libertarian

Term ends	Senator (Party); Service from[1]	2008 election
Alabama		
2011	Richard Shelby (R); 1/6/87	
2015	**Jeff Sessions* (R); 1/7/97**	**1,305,383**
	Vivian Figures (D)	752,391
Alaska		
2011	Lisa Murkowski (R); 12/20/02	
2015	**Mark Begich (D); 1/6/09**	**151,767**
	Ted Stevens (R)*; 12/24/68	147,814
Arizona		
2011	John McCain (R); 1/6/87	
2013	Jon Kyl (R); 1/4/95	
Arkansas		
2011	Blanche L. Lincoln (D); 1/6/99	
2015	**Mark Pryor* (D); 1/7/03**	**804,678**
	Rebekah Kennedy (GR)	207,076
California		
2011	Barbara Boxer (D); 1993	
2013	Dianne Feinstein (D); 11/10/92	
Colorado		
2011	Michael F. Bennet (D); 1/22/09[2]	
2015	**Mark Udall (D); 1/6/09**	**1,231,049**
	Bob Schaffer (R)	990,784
Connecticut		
2011	Christopher J. Dodd (D); 1981	
2013	Joseph Lieberman (CFL); 1989	
Delaware		
2013	Thomas R. Carper (D); 2001	
2015	Edward E. Kaufman (D); 1/16/09[3]	
Florida		
2011	Mel Martinez (R); 2005	
2013	Bill Nelson (D); 2001	
Georgia		
2011	Johnny Isakson (R); 2005	
2015	**Saxby Chambliss* (R); 1/7/03**	**1,867,097**
	Jim Martin (D)	1,757,393
Hawaii		
2011	Daniel K. Inouye (D); 1963	
2013	Daniel K. Akaka (D); 4/28/90	
Idaho		
2011	Mike Crapo (R); 1/6/99	
2015	**Jim Risch (R); 1/6/09**	**371,744**
	Larry LaRocco (D)	219,903
Illinois		
2011	Roland W. Burris (D); 1/15/09[4]	
2015	**Richard J. Durbin* (D); 1/7/97**	**3,615,844**
	Steve Sauerberg (R)	1,520,621
Indiana		
2011	Evan Bayh (D); 1/6/99	
2013	Richard G. Lugar (R); 1977	

Term ends	Senator (Party); Service from[1]	2008 election
Iowa		
2011	Chuck Grassley (R); 1981	
2015	**Tom Harkin* (D); 1985**	**941,665**
	Christopher Reed (R)	560,006
Kansas		
2011	Sam Brownback (R); 11/27/96	
2015	**Pat Roberts* (R); 1/7/97**	**727,121**
	Jim Slattery (D)	441,399
Kentucky		
2011	Jim Bunning (R); 1/6/99	
2015	**Mitch McConnell* (R); 1985**	**953,816**
	Bruce Lunsford (D)	847,005
Louisiana		
2011	David Vitter (R); 2005	
2015	**Mary L. Landrieu* (D); 1/7/97**	**988,298**
	John Kennedy (R)	867,177
Maine		
2013	Olympia J. Snowe (R); 1/4/95	
2015	**Susan M. Collins* (R); 1/7/97**	**444,300**
	Tom Allen (D)	279,510
Maryland		
2011	Barbara Ann Mikulski (D); 1/6/87	
2013	Benjamin L. Cardin (D); 2007	
Massachusetts		
2013	Paul G. Kirk Jr.; 9/25/09[5]	
2015	**John F. Kerry* (D); 1/2/85**	**1,971,974**
	Jeff Beatty (R)	926,044
Michigan		
2013	Debbie Stabenow (D); 2001	
2015	**Carl Levin* (D); 1979**	**3,038,386**
	Jack Hoogendyk (R)	1,641,070
Minnesota		
2013	Amy Klobuchar (DFL); 2007	
2015	**Al Franken (DFL); 7/7/09**	**1,212,629**
	Norm Coleman* (R); 1/7/03	1,212,317
Mississippi		
2013	**Roger Wicker (R); 12/31/07[6]**	**683,409**
	Ronnie Musgrove (D)	560,064
2015	**Thad Cochran* (R); 12/27/78**	**766,111**
	Erik Fleming (D)	480,915
Missouri		
2011	Christopher (Kit) Bond (R); 1/6/87	
2013	Claire McCaskill (D); 2007	
Montana		
2013	Jon Tester (D); 2007	
2015	**Max Baucus* (D); 12/15/78**	**348,289**
	Bob Kelleher (R)	129,369
Nebraska		
2013	Ben Nelson (D); 2001	
2015	**Mike Johanns (R); 1/6/09**	**455,854**
	Scott Kleeb (D)	317,456

Term ends	Senator (Party); Service from[1]	2008 election
Nevada		
2011	Harry Reid (D); 1/6/87	
2013	**John Ensign (R); 2001**	
New Hampshire		
2011	Judd Gregg (R); 1993	
2015	**Jeanne Shaheen (D); 1/6/09**	358,438
	John Sununu* (R); 1/7/03	314,403
New Jersey		
2013	Robert Menendez (D); 1/18/06	
2015	**Frank Lautenberg* (D); 1/7/03**	1,951,218
	Dick Zimmer (R)	1,461,025
New Mexico		
2013	Jeff Bingaman (D); 1983	
2015	**Tom Udall (D); 1/6/09**	505,128
	Steve Pearce (R)	318,522
New York		
2011	Charles E. Schumer (D); 1/6/99	
2013	**Kirsten E. Gillibrand (D); 1/27/09[7]**	
North Carolina		
2011	Richard Burr (R); 2005	
2015	**Kay Hagan (D.); 1/6/09**	2,249,311
	Elizabeth H. Dole* (R); 1/7/03	1,887,510
North Dakota		
2011	Byron L. Dorgan (D); 12/14/92	
2013	Kent Conrad (DNL); 1/6/87	
Ohio		
2011	George V. Voinovich (R); 1/6/99	
2013	Sherrod Brown (D); 2007	
Oklahoma		
2011	Tom Coburn (R); 2005	
2015	**James M. Inhofe* (R); 11/21/94**	763,375
	Andrew Rice (D)	527,736
Oregon		
2011	Ron Wyden (D); 2/6/96	
2015	**Jeff Merkley (D); 1/6/09**	864,392
	Gordon Smith* (R); 1/7/97	805,159
Pennsylvania		
2011	Arlen Specter (R); 1981	
2013	Bob Casey Jr. (D); 2007	
Rhode Island		
2013	Sheldon Whitehouse (D); 2007	
2015	**John F. Reed* (D); 1/7/97**	320,644
	Bob Tingle (R)	116,174

Term ends	Senator (Party); Service from[1]	2008 election
South Carolina		
2011	Jim DeMint (R); 2005	
2015	**Lindsey Graham* (R); 1/7/03**	1,076,534
	Bob Conley (D)	790,621
South Dakota		
2011	John Thune (R); 2005	
2015	**Tim Johnson* (D); 1/7/97**	237,889
	Joel Dykstra (R)	142,784
Tennessee		
2013	Bob Corker (R); 2007	
2015	**Lamar Alexander* (R); 1/7/03**	1,579,477
	Robert Tuke (D)	767,236
Texas		
2013	Kay Bailey Hutchison (R); 6/5/93	
2015	**John Cornyn* (R); 12/2/02**	4,337,469
	Rick Noriega (D)	3,389,365
Utah		
2011	Robert F. Bennett (R); 1993	
2013	Orrin G. Hatch (R); 1977	
Vermont		
2011	Patrick Leahy (D); 1975	
2013	Bernard Sanders (I); 2007	
Virginia		
2013	James H. "Jim" Webb Jr. (D); 2007	
2015	**Mark Warner (D); 1/6/09**	2,369,327
	Jim Gilmore (R)	1,228,830
Washington		
2011	Patty Murray (D); 1993	
2013	Maria Cantwell (D); 2001	
West Virginia		
2013	Robert C. Byrd (D); 1959	
2015	**John D. "Jay" Rockefeller IV* (D); 1/15/85**	447,560
	Jay Wolf (R)	254,629
Wisconsin		
2011	Russ Feingold (D); 1993	
2013	Herb Kohl (D); 1989	
Wyoming		
2013	**John Barrasso* (R); 6/22/07[8]**	183,063
	Nick Carter (D)	66,202
2015	**Michael B. Enzi* (R); 1/7/97**	189,046
	Chris Rothfuss (D)	60,631

(1) Jan. 3, unless otherwise noted. (2) Appointed to fill seat vacated by Ken Salazar (D), who was appointed Sec. of the Interior, Jan. 20, 2009. (3) Appointed to fill seat vacated by Vice-Pres. Joseph Biden Jr. (D), Jan. 20, 2009; Biden had defeated Christine O'Donnell, 257,539-140,595, Nov. 4, 2008. (4) Appointed to fill seat vacated by Pres. Barack Obama (D), Jan. 20, 2009. (5) Appointed to fill seat vacated by death of Edward M. Kennedy, Aug. 25, 2009. (6) Appointed to fill seat vacated by Trent Lott (R), Dec. 31, 2007; he won a special election to keep the seat Nov. 4, 2008. (7) Appointed to fill seat vacated by Hillary Rodham Clinton (D), who was appointed Sec. of State, Jan. 21, 2009. (8) Appointed to fill seat vacated by death of Craig Thomas, June 4, 2007; he won a special election to keep the seat Nov. 4, 2008.

The House of Representatives
(as of Sept. 30, 2009)

Democrats, 256; Republicans, 177; 2 vacancies; Total 435. Boldface denotes the 2008 election winner. *Incumbent. Third-party or independent candidates receiving fewer than 10,000 votes are not listed.

The Democratic Party, which held a majority going into biannual elections Nov. 4, 2008, won 256 seats for a net gain of 21 seats. 218 seats were needed to hold a majority in the House.

Terms are for 2 years ending Jan. 3, 2011. Annual salary, $174,000; Speaker of the House, $223,500; Majority Leader and Minority Leader, $196,400. To be eligible for membership, a person must be at least 25 years of age, a U.S. citizen for at least 7 years, and a resident of the state from which he or she is chosen.

The address is U.S. House of Representatives, Washington, DC 20515; telephone, (202) 224-3121; website, www.house.gov

D-Democrat; **R**-Republican; **DFL**-Dem.-Farmer-Labor; **C**-Conservative; **CP**-Constitution Party; **GR**-Green; **Ind.**-Independent; **LB**-Libertarian

Dist.	Representative (Party)	2008 election
Alabama		
1	**Jo Bonner* (R)**	Unopposed
2	**Bobby Bright (D)**	144,368
	Jay Love (R)	142,578
3	**Mike Rogers* (R)**	142,708
	Joshua Segall (D)	121,080

Dist.	Representative (Party)	2008 election
4	**Robert B. Aderholt* (R)**	196,741
	Nicholas Sparks (D)	67,000
5	**Parker Griffith (D)**	158,324
	Wayne Parker (R)	147,314
6	**Spencer Bachus* (R)**	Unopposed
7	**Artur Davis (D)***	Unopposed

Dist.	Representative (Party)	2008 election
Alaska		
	Don E. Young* (R)	**158,939**
	Ethan Berkowitz (D).....................	142,560
Arizona		
1	**Ann Kirkpatrick (D)**	**155,791**
	Sydney Hay (R)	109,924
2	**Trent Franks* (R)**	**200,914**
	John Thrasher (D)	125,611
3	**John Shadegg* (R)**.	**148,800**
	Bob Lord (D)	115,759
4	**Ed Pastor* (D)**.	**89,721**
	Don Karg (R)	26,435
5	**Harry Mitchell* (D)**	**149,033**
	David Schweikert (R).	122,165
6	**Jeff Flake* (R)**.	**208,582**
	Rebecca Schneider (D)	115,457
7	**Raúl Grijalva* (D)**	**124,304**
	Joseph Sweeney (R).	64,425
8	**Gabrielle Giffords* (D)**	**179,629**
	Tim Bee (R)	140,553
Arkansas		
1	**Marion Berry* (D)**	**Unopposed**
2	**Vic Snyder* (D)**.	**212,303**
	Deb McFarland (GR)	64,398
3	**John Boozman* (R)**	**215,196**
	Abel Tomlinson (GR).	58,850
4	**Mike Ross* (D)**.	**203,178**
	Joshua Drake (GR)	32,603
California		
1	**Mike Thompson* (D)**	**197,812**
	Zane Starkewolf (R).	67,853
	Carol Wolman (GR)	24,793
2	**Wally Herger* (R)**	**163,459**
	Jeff Morris (D)	118,878
3	**Dan Lungren* (R)**.	**155,424**
	Bill Durston (D)	137,971
4	**Tom McClintock (R)**.	**185,790**
	Charlie Brown (D)	183,990
5	**Doris O. Matsui* (D)**.	**164,242**
	Paul Smith (R)	46,002
6	**Lynn Woolsey* (D)**.	**229,672**
	Mike Halliwell (R).	77,073
	Joel Smolen (LB)	13,617
7	**George Miller* (D)**.	**170,962**
	Roger Allen Petersen (R)	51,166
8	**Nancy Pelosi* (D)**.	**204,996**
	Cindy Sheehan (Ind.).	46,118
	Dana Walsh (R)	27,614
9	**Barbara Lee* (D)**.	**238,915**
	Charles Hargrave (R).	26,917
10	**Ellen O. Tauscher* (D)[1]**	**192,226**
	Nicholas Gerber (R).	91,877
11	**Jerry McNerney* (D)**	**164,500**
	Dean Andal (R)	133,104
12	**Jackie Speier* (D)**	**200,442**
	Greg Conlon (R)	49,258
13	**Fortney Pete Stark* (D)**	**166,829**
	Raymond Chui (R).	51,447
14	**Anna G. Eshoo* (D)**	**190,301**
	Ronny Santana (R)	60,610
15	**Mike Honda* (D)**.	**170,977**
	Joyce Stoer Cordi (R)	55,489
16	**Zoe Lofgren* (D)**.	**146,481**
	Charel Winston (R)	49,399
17	**Sam Farr* (D)**	**168,907**
	Jeff Taylor (R)	59,037
18	**Dennis A. Cardoza* (D)**	**Unopposed**
19	**George P. Radanovich* (R)**	**Unopposed**
20	**Jim Costa* (D)**	**93,023**
	Jim Lopez (R)	32,118
21	**Devin G. Nunes* (R)**.	**143,498**
	Larry Johnson (D)	66,317
22	**Kevin McCarthy* (R)**	**Unopposed**
23	**Lois Capps* (D)**	**171,403**
	Matt Kokkonen (R).	80,385
24	**Elton Gallegly* (R)**.	**174,492**
	Marta Ann Jorgensen (D)	125,560
25	**Howard P. "Buck" McKeon* (R)**	**144,660**
	Jackie Conaway (D).	105,929
26	**David Dreier* (R)**.	**140,615**
	Russ Warner (D)	108,039
	Ted Brown (LB)	18,476

Dist.	Representative (Party)	2008 election
27	**Brad Sherman* (D)**	**145,812**
	Navraj Singh (R)....................	52,852
	Tim Denton (LB)	14,171
28	**Howard L. Berman* (D).**	**Unopposed**
29	**Adam Schiff* (D)**.	**146,198**
	Charles Hahn (R)	56,727
30	**Henry A. Waxman* (D)**	**Unopposed**
31	**Xavier Becerra* (D)**	**Unopposed**
32	**Hilda L. Solis* (D)[2]**	**Unopposed**
33	**Diane E. Watson* (D)**	**186,924**
	David Crowley	26,536
34	**Lucille Roybal-Allard* (D).**	**98,503**
	Christopher Balding (R)	29,266
35	**Maxine Waters* (D)**	**150,778**
	Ted Hayes (R)	24,169
36	**Jane Harman* (D)**	**171,948**
	Brian Gibson (R).	78,543
37	**Laura Richardson* (D)**	**131,342**
	Nick Dibs (Ind.)	42,774
38	**Grace F. Napolitano* (D).**	**130,211**
	Christopher Agrella (LB).	29,113
39	**Linda T. Sanchez* (D)**	**125,289**
	Diane Lenning (R)	54,533
40	**Ed Royce* (R)**	**144,923**
	Christina Avalos (D)	86,772
41	**Jerry Lewis* (R)**	**159,486**
	Tim Prince (D)	99,214
42	**Gary G. Miller* (R).**	**158,404**
	Ed Chau (D)	104,909
43	**Joe Baca* (D)**	**108,259**
	John Roberts (R)	48,312
44	**Ken Calvert* (R)**	**129,937**
	Bill Hedrick (D)	123,890
45	**Mary Bono Mack* (R)**	**155,166**
	Julie Bornstein (D)	111,026
46	**Dana Rohrabacher* (R)**	**149,818**
	Debbie Cook (D).	122,891
47	**Loretta Sanchez* (D).**	**85,878**
	Rosie Avila (R)	31,432
48	**John Campbell* (R)**	**171,658**
	Steve Young (D)	125,537
49	**Darrell Issa* (R).**	**140,300**
	Robert Hamilton (D)	90,138
	Lars R. Grossmith (LB).	10,232
50	**Brian Bilbray* (R)**	**157,502**
	Nick Leibham (D)	141,635
	Wayne Dunlap (LB)	14,365
51	**Bob Filner* (D)**	**148,281**
	David Lee Joy (R).	49,345
52	**Duncan D. Hunter Jr. (R)**	**160,724**
	Mike Lumpkin (D)	111,051
	Michael Benoit (LB)	13,316
53	**Susan A. Davis* (D)**	**161,315**
	Michael Crimmins (R).	64,658
Colorado		
1	**Diana L. DeGette* (D)**	**203,756**
	George Lilly (R)	67,346
	Martin Buchanan (LB).	12,136
2	**Jared Polis (D)**.	**215,602**
	Scott Starin (R)	116,619
	J. A. Calhoun (G)	10,031
3	**John Salazar* (D)**	**203,457**
	Wayne Wolf (R)	126,762
4	**Betsy Markey (D).**	**187,348**
	Marilyn Musgrave* (R)	146,030
5	**Doug Lamborn* (R).**	**183,179**
	Hal Bidlack (D)	113,027
6	**Mike Coffman (R)**	**250,877**
	Hank Eng (D)	162,641
7	**Ed Perlmutter* (D).**	**173,937**
	John Lerew (R).	100,057
Connecticut		
1	**John B. Larson* (D)**	**211,493**
	Joe Visconti (R)	76,860
2	**Joe Courtney* (D).**	**212,148**
	Sean Sullivan (R)	104,574
3	**Rosa L. DeLauro* (D)**	**230,172**
	Bo Itshaky (R).	58,583
4	**Jim Himes (D)**	**158,475**
	Christopher Shays* (R).	146,854
5	**Chris Murphy* (D).**	**179,327**
	David Cappiello (R)	117,914

Dist.	Representative (Party)	2008 election
Delaware		
	Michael N. Castle* (R)	235,437
	Karen Hartley-Nagle (D)	146,434
Florida		
1	**Jeff Miller* (R)**	232,559
	Jim Bryan (D)	98,797
2	**Allen Boyd Jr.* (D)**	216,804
	Mark Mulligan (R)	133,404
3	**Corrine Brown* (D)**	Unopposed
4	**Ander Crenshaw* (R)**	224,112
	Jay McGovern (D)	119,330
5	**Virginia "Ginny" Brown-Waite* (R)**	265,186
	John T. Russell (D)	168,446
6	**Clifford "Cliff" Stearns* (R)**	228,302
	Tim Cunha (D)	146,655
7	**John L. Mica* (R)**	238,721
	Faye Armitage (D)	146,292
8	**Alan Grayson (D)**	172,854
	Ric Keller* (R)	159,490
9	**Gus Bilirakis* (R)**	216,591
	Bill Mitchell (D)	126,346
10	**C.W. Bill Young* (R)**	182,781
	Bob Hackworth (D)	118,430
11	**Kathy Castor* (D)**	184,106
	Eddie Adams (R)	72,825
12	**Adam H. Putnam* (R)**	185,698
	Doug Tudor (D)	137,465
13	**Vern Buchanan* (R)**	204,382
	Christine Jennings (D)	137,967
	Jan Schneider (Unaffiliated)	20,289
14	**Connie Mack* (R)**	224,602
	Robert Neeld (D)	93,590
	Burt Sanders (Unaffiliated)	54,750
15	**Bill Posey (R)**	192,151
	Stephen Blythe (D)	151,951
	Frank Zilaitis (Unaffiliated)	14,274
16	**Tom Rooney (R)**	209,874
	Tim Mahoney* (D)	139,373
17	**Kendrick B. Meek* (D)**	Unopposed
18	**Ileana Ros-Lehtinen* (R)**	140,617
	Annette Taddeo (D)	102,372
19	**Robert Wexler* (D)**	202,465
	Edward Lynch (R)	83,357
	Ben Graber (Unaffiliated)	20,214
20	**Debbie Wasserman Schultz* (D)**	202,832
	Margaret Hostetter (Unaffiliated)	58,958
21	**Lincoln Diaz-Balart* (R)**	137,226
	Raul L. Martinez (D)	99,776
22	**Ron Klein* (D)**	169,041
	Allen West (R)	140,104
23	**Alcee Hastings* (D)**	172,835
	Marion Thorpe (R)	37,431
24	**Suzanne Kosmas (D)**	211,284
	Tom Feeney* (R)	151,863
25	**Mario Diaz-Balart* (R)**	130,891
	Joe Garcia (D)	115,820
Georgia		
1	**Jack Kingston* (R)**	165,890
	Bill Gillespie (D)	83,444
2	**Sanford Bishop* (D)**	158,435
	Lee Ferrell (R)	71,351
3	**Lynn Westmoreland* (R)**	225,055
	Stephen Camp (D)	117,522
4	**Henry "Hank" Johnson* (D)**	Unopposed
5	**John Lewis* (D)**	Unopposed
6	**Tom Price* (R)**	231,520
	Bill Jones (D)	106,551
7	**John Linder* (R)**	209,354
	Doug Heckman (D)	128,159
8	**Jim Marshall* (D)**	157,241
	Rick Goddard (R)	117,446
9	**Nathan Deal* (R)**	217,493
	Jeff Scott (D)	70,537
10	**Paul Broun* (R)**	177,265
	Bobby Saxon (D)	114,638
11	**Phil Gingrey* (R)**	204,082
	Hugh "Bud" Gammon (D)	95,220
12	**John Barrow* (D)**	164,562
	John Stone (R)	84,773
13	**David Scott* (D)**	205,919
	Deborah Honeycutt (R)	92,320

Dist.	Representative (Party)	2008 election
Hawaii		
1	**Neil Abercrombie* (D)**	154,208
	Steve Tataii (R)	38,115
2	**Mazie Hirono* (D)**	165,748
	Roger Evans (R)	44,425
Idaho		
1	**Walt Minnick (D)**	175,898
	Bill Sali* (R)	171,687
2	**Mike Simpson* (R)**	205,777
	Deborah Holmes (D)	83,878
Illinois		
1	**Bobby L. Rush* (D)**	233,036
	Antoine Members (R)	38,361
2	**Jesse Jackson Jr.* (D)**	251,052
	Anthony Williams (R)	29,721
3	**Daniel Lipinski* (D)**	172,581
	Michael Hawkins (R)	50,336
	Jerome Pohlen (GR)	12,607
4	**Luis Gutierrez* (D)**	112,529
	Daniel Cunningham (R)	16,024
	Omar Lopez (GR)	11,053
5	**Rahm Emanuel* (D)[3]**	170,728
	Tom Hanson (R)	50,881
6	**Peter J. Roskam* (R)**	147,906
	Jill Morganthaler (D)	109,007
7	**Danny Davis* (D)**	235,343
	Steve Miller (R)	41,474
8	**Melissa Bean* (D)**	179,444
	Steve Greenberg (R)	116,081
9	**Janice D. Schakowsky* (D)**	181,948
	Michael Younan (R)	53,593
10	**Mark Kirk* (R)**	153,082
	Daniel Seals (D)	138,176
11	**Debbie Halvorson (D)**	185,652
	Marty Ozinga (R)	109,608
	Jason Wallace (GR)	22,635
12	**Jerry Costello* (D)**	212,891
	Timmy Richardson (R)	74,382
	Rodger Jennings (GR)	10,907
13	**Judy Biggert* (R)**	180,888
	Scott Harper (D)	147,430
14	**Bill Foster* (D)**	185,404
	Jim Oberweis (R)	135,653
15	**Timothy V. Johnson* (R)**	187,121
	Steve Cox (D)	104,393
16	**Donald Manzullo* (R)**	190,039
	Robert Abboud (D)	112,648
17	**Phil Hare* (D)**	Unopposed
18	**Aaron Schock (R)**	182,589
	Colleen Callahan (D)	117,642
19	**John M. Shimkus* (R)**	203,434
	Daniel Davis (D)	105,338
Indiana		
1	**Peter J. Visclosky* (D)**	199,954
	Mark Leyva (R)	76,647
2	**Joe Donnelly* (D)**	187,416
	Luke Puckett (R)	84,455
3	**Mark E. Souder* (R)**	155,693
	Michael Montagano (D)	112,309
	William Larsen (LB)	14,877
4	**Steve Buyer* (R)**	192,526
	Nels Ackerson (D)	129,038
5	**Dan Burton* (R)**	234,705
	Mary Ruley (D)	123,357
6	**Mike Pence* (R)**	180,608
	Barry Welsh (D)	94,265
7	**Andre Carson* (D)**	172,650
	Gabrielle Campo (R)	92,645
8	**Brad Ellsworth* (D)**	188,693
	Greg Goode (R)	102,769
9	**Baron Hill* (D)**	181,281
	Mike Sodrel (R)	120,529
	D. Eric Schansberg (LB)	11,994
Iowa		
1	**Bruce Braley* (D)**	186,991
	David Hartsuch (R)	102,439
2	**David Loebsack* (D)**	175,218
	Mariannette Miller-Meeks (R)	118,778
3	**Leonard Boswell* (D)**	176,904
	Kim Schmett (R)	132,136

Dist.	Representative (Party)	2008 election
4	**Tom Latham* (R)**	**185,458**
	Becky Greenwald (D)	120,746
5	**Steve King* (R)**	**159,430**
	Rob Hubler (D)	99,601

Kansas

Dist.	Representative (Party)	2008 election
1	**Jerry Moran* (R)**	**214,549**
	James Bordonaro (D)	34,771
2	**Lynn Jenkins (R)**	**155,532**
	Nancy Boyda* (D)	142,013
3	**Dennis Moore* (D)**	**202,541**
	Nick Jordan (R)	142,307
4	**Todd Tiahrt* (R)**	**177,617**
	Donald Betts (D)	90,706

Kentucky

Dist.	Representative (Party)	2008 election
1	**Ed Whitfield* (R)**	**178,107**
	Heather Ryan (D)	98,674
2	**Brett Guthrie (R)**	**158,936**
	David E. Boswell (D)	143,379
3	**John Yarmuth* (D)**	**203,843**
	Anne M. Northup (R)	139,527
4	**Geoff Davis* (R)**	**190,210**
	Michael Kelley (D)	111,549
5	**Harold "Hal" Rogers* (R)**	**177,024**
	Jim Holbert (Ind.)	33,444
6	**Ben Chandler* (D)**	**203,764**
	Jon Larson (R)	111,378

Louisiana

Dist.	Representative (Party)	2008 election
1	**Steve Scalise (R)**	**189,168**
	Jim Harlan (D)	98,839
2	**Joseph Cao (R)**	**33,132**
	William J. Jefferson* (D)	31,318
3	**Charlie Melancon* (D)**	**Unopposed**
4	**John Fleming (R)**	**44,501**
	Paul Carmouche (D)	44,151
5	**Rodney Alexander* (R)**	**Unopposed**
6	**Bill Cassidy (R)**	**150,332**
	Don Cazayoux (D)*	125,886
	Michael Jackson (Ind.)	36,198
7	**Charles Boustany* (R)**	**177,173**
	Don Cravins Jr. (D)	98,280
	Peter Vidrine (CP)	10,846

Maine

Dist.	Representative (Party)	2008 election
1	**Chellie Pingree (D)**	**205,629**
	Charlie Summers (R)	168,930
2	**Mike Michaud* (D)**	**226,274**
	John Frary (R)	109,268

Maryland

Dist.	Representative (Party)	2008 election
1	**Frank Kratovil (D)**	**177,065**
	Andy Harris (R)	174,213
2	**C. A. Dutch Ruppersberger* (D)**	**198,578**
	Richard Matthews (R)	68,561
3	**John P. Sarbanes* (D)**	**203,711**
	Thomas Harris (R)	87,971
4	**Donna Edwards* (D)**	**258,704**
	Peter James (R)	38,739
5	**Steny Hoyer* (D)**	**253,854**
	Collins Bailey (R)	82,631
6	**Roscoe Bartlett* (R)**	**190,926**
	Jennifer Dougherty (D)	128,207
	Gary Hoover (LB)	11,060
7	**Elijah Cummings* (D)**	**227,379**
	Michael Hargadon (R)	53,147
8	**Chris Van Hollen* (D)**	**229,740**
	Steve Hudson (R)	66,351

Massachusetts

Dist.	Representative (Party)	2008 election
1	**John W. Olver* (D)**	**215,696**
	Nate Bech (R)	80,067
2	**Richard E. Neal* (D)**	**Unopposed**
3	**James P. McGovern* (D)**	**Unopposed**
4	**Barney Frank* (D)**	**203,032**
	Earl Sholley (R)	75,571
	Susan Allen (Ind.)	19,848
5	**Niki Tsongas* (D)**	**Unopposed**
6	**John Tierney* (D)**	**226,216**
	Richard Baker (R)	94,845
7	**Edward Markey* (D)**	**212,304**
	John Cunningham (R)	67,978
8	**Michael Capuano* (D)**	**Unopposed**
9	**Stephen Lynch* (D)**	**Unopposed**
10	**William Delahunt* (D)**	**Unopposed**

Michigan

Dist.	Representative (Party)	2008 election
1	**Bart Stupak* (D)**	**213,216**
	Tom Casperson (R)	107,340
2	**Pete Hoekstra* (R)**	**214,100**
	Fred Johnson (D)	119,506
3	**Vernon J. Ehlers* (R)**	**203,799**
	Henry Sanchez (D)	117,961
	Erwin Haas (LB)	11,758
4	**Dave Camp* (R)**	**204,259**
	Andrew Concannon (D)	117,665
5	**Dale E. Kildee* (D)**	**221,841**
	Matt Sawicki (R)	85,017
6	**Fred Upton* (R)**	**188,157**
	Don Cooney (D)	123,257
7	**Mark Schauer (D)**	**157,213**
	Tim Walberg* (R)	149,781
8	**Mike Rogers* (R)**	**204,408**
	Robert Alexander (D)	145,491
9	**Gary Peters (D)**	**183,311**
	Joe Knollenberg* (R)	150,035
10	**Candice Miller* (R)**	**230,471**
	Robert Denison (D)	108,354
11	**Thaddeus McCotter* (R)**	**177,461**
	Joseph Larkin (D)	156,625
12	**Sander Levin* (D)**	**225,094**
	Bert Copple (R)	74,565
13	**Carolyn Cheeks Kilpatrick* (D)**	**167,481**
	Edward Gubics (R)	43,098
14	**John Conyers* (D)**	**227,841**
	Richard Secula (LB)	10,732
15	**John Dingell* (D)**	**231,784**
	John Lynch (R)	81,802

Minnesota

Dist.	Representative (Party)	2008 election
1	**Tim Walz* (DFL)**	**207,753**
	Brian Davis (R)	109,453
	Gregory Mikkelson (Ind.)	14,904
2	**John Kline* (R)**	**220,924**
	Steve Sarvi (DFL)	164,093
3	**Erik Paulsen (R)**	**178,932**
	Ashwin Madia (DFL)	150,787
	David Dillon (Ind.)	38,970
4	**Betty McCollum* (DFL)**	**216,267**
	Ed Matthews (R)	98,936
5	**Keith Ellison* (DFL)**	**228,776**
	Barb Davis White (R)	71,020
	Bill McGaughey (Ind.)	22,318
6	**Michele Bachmann* (R)**	**187,817**
	Elwyn Tinklenberg (DFL)	175,786
	Bob Anderson (Ind.)	40,643
7	**Collin C. Peterson* (DFL)**	**227,187**
	Glen Menze (R)	87,062
8	**James L. Oberstar* (DFL)**	**241,831**
	Michael Cummins (R)	114,871

Mississippi

Dist.	Representative (Party)	2008 election
1	**Travis Childers* (D)**	**185,959**
	Greg Davis (R)	149,818
2	**Bennie Thompson* (D)**	**201,606**
	Richard Cook (R)	90,364
3	**Gregg Harper (R)**	**213,171**
	Joel Gill (D)	127,698
4	**Gene Taylor* (D)**	**216,542**
	John McCay (R)	73,977

Missouri

Dist.	Representative (Party)	2008 election
1	**Wm. Lacy Clay* (D)**	**242,570**
	Robb Cunningham (LB)	36,700
2	**Todd Akin* (R)**	**232,276**
	Bill Haas (D)	132,068
3	**Russ Carnahan* (D)**	**202,470**
	Chris Sander (R)	92,759
4	**Ike Skelton* (D)**	**200,009**
	Jeff Parnell (R)	103,446
5	**Emanuel Cleaver* (D)**	**197,249**
	Jacob Turk (R)	109,166
6	**Sam Graves* (R)**	**196,526**
	Kay Barnes (D)	121,894
	Dave Browning (LB)	12,279
7	**Roy Blunt* (R)**	**219,016**
	Richard Monroe (D)	91,010
8	**Jo Ann Emerson* (R)**	**198,798**
	Joe Allen (D)	72,790
9	**Blaine Luetkemeyer (R)**	**161,031**
	Judy Baker (D)	152,956

Dist.	Representative (Party)	2008 election
Montana		
	Denny Rehberg* (R)	**308,470**
	John Driscoll (D)	155,930
	Mike Fellows (LB)	16,500
Nebraska		
1	**Jeff Fortenberry* (R)**	**184,923**
	Max Yashirin (D)	77,897
2	**Lee Terry* (R)**	**142,473**
	Jim Esch (D)	131,901
3	**Adrian Smith* (R)**	**183,117**
	Jay Stoddard (D)	55,087
Nevada		
1	**Shelley Berkley* (D)**	**154,860**
	Kenneth Wegner (R)	64,837
2	**Dean Heller* (R)**	**170,771**
	Jill Derby (D)	136,548
3	**Dina Titus (D)**	**165,912**
	Jon Porter* (R)	147,940
	Jeffrey C. Reeves (I)	14,922
	Joseph P. Silvestri (LB)	10,164
New Hampshire		
1	**Carol Shea-Porter* (D)**	**176,435**
	Jeb Bradley (R)	156,338
2	**Paul Hodes* (D)**	**188,332**
	Jennifer Horn (R)	138,222
New Jersey		
1	**Robert Andrews* (D)**	**206,453**
	Dale Glading (R)	74,001
2	**Frank A. LoBiondo* (R)**	**167,701**
	David Kurkowski (D)	110,990
3	**John Adler (D)**	**166,390**
	Chris Myers (R)	153,122
4	**Chris Smith* (R)**	**202,972**
	Joshua Zeitz (D)	100,036
5	**Scott Garrett* (R)**	**172,653**
	Dennis Shulman (D)	131,033
6	**Frank Pallone* (D)**	**164,077**
	Robert McLeod (R)	77,469
7	**Leonard Lance (R)**	**148,461**
	Linda Stender (D)	124,818
	Michael P. Hsing (Hsing for Congress)	16,419
8	**Bill Pascrell* (D)**	**159,279**
	Roland Straten (R)	63,107
9	**Steve Rothman* (D)**	**151,182**
	Vincent Micco (R)	69,503
10	**Donald M. Payne* (D)**	**169,945**
	Michael Taber (Ind.)	1,848
11	**Rodney Frelinghuysen* (R)**	**189,696**
	Tom Wyka (D)	113,510
12	**Rush Holt* (D)**	**193,732**
	Alan Bateman (R)	108,400
13	**Albio Sires* (D)**	**120,382**
	Joseph Turula (R)	34,735
New Mexico		
1	**Martin Heinrich (D)**	**166,271**
	Darren White (R)	132,485
2	**Harry Teague (D)**	**129,572**
	Edward R. Tinsley (R)	101,980
3	**Ben R. Lujan (D)**	**161,292**
	Daniel East (R)	86,618
	Carol Miller (Ind.)	36,348
New York		
1	**Timothy Bishop* (D)**	**162,083**
	Lee Zeldin (R)	115,545
2	**Steve Israel* (D)**	**161,279**
	Frank Stalzer (R)	79,641
3	**Peter King* (R)**	**172,774**
	Graham Long (D)	97,525
4	**Carolyn McCarthy* (D)**	**164,028**
	Jack Martins (R)	92,242
5	**Gary Ackerman* (D)**	**112,724**
	Elizabeth Berney (R)	43,039
6	**Gregory W. Meeks* (D)**	**Unopposed**
7	**Joseph Crowley* (D)**	**118,459**
	William Britt Jr. (R)	21,477
8	**Jerrold Nadler* (D)**	**160,775**
	Grace Lin (R)	39,062
9	**Anthony Weiner* (D)**	**112,205**
	Alfred Donohue (C)	8,378
10	**Edolphus Towns* (D)**	**155,090**
	Salvatore Grupico (R)	9,565
11	**Yvette D. Clarke* (D)**	**168,562**
	Hugh Carr (R)	11,644
12	**Nydia M. Velazquez* (D)**	**123,053**
	Allan E. Romaguera (R)	13,748
13	**Michael McMahon (D)**	**114,219**
	Robert Straniere (R)	62,441
14	**Carolyn Maloney* (D)**	**183,239**
	Robert Heim (R)	43,385
15	**Charles Rangel* (D)**	**177,151**
	Edward Daniels (R)	15,676
16	**Jose E. Serrano* (D)**	**127,179**
	Ali Mohamed (R)	4,488
17	**Eliot Engel* (D)**	**161,594**
	Robert Goodman (R)	40,707
18	**Nita Lowey* (D)**	**174,791**
	Jim Russell (R)	80,498
19	**John Hall* (D)**	**164,859**
	Kieran Lalor (R)	116,120
20	**Kirsten E. Gillibrand* (D)[4]**	**193,651**
	Sandy Treadwell (R)	118,031
21	**Paul Tonko (D)**	**171,286**
	James Buhrmaster (R)	96,599
22	**Maurice Hinchey* (D)**	**168,558**
	George Phillips (R)	85,126
23	**John McHugh* (R)[5]**	**143,029**
	Michael Oot (D)	75,871
24	**Michael Arcuri* (D)**	**130,799**
	Richard Hanna (R)	120,880
25	**Daniel Maffei (D)**	**157,375**
	Dale Sweetland (R)	120,217
26	**Christopher Lee (R)**	**148,607**
	Alice Kryzan (D)	109,615
27	**Brian Higgins* (D)**	**185,713**
	Daniel Humiston (R)	56,354
28	**Louise M. Slaughter* (D)**	**172,655**
	David Crimmen (R)	48,690
29	**Eric Massa (D)**	**140,529**
	Randy Kuhl Jr.* (R)	135,199
North Carolina		
1	**G. K. Butterfield* (D)**	**192,765**
	Dean Stephens (R)	81,506
2	**Bob Etheridge* (D)**	**199,730**
	Dan Mansell (R)	93,323
3	**Walter Jones* (R)**	**201,686**
	Craig Weber (D)	104,364
4	**David Price* (D)**	**265,751**
	William Lawson (R)	153,947
5	**Virginia Foxx* (R)**	**190,820**
	Roy Carter (D)	136,103
6	**Howard Coble* (R)**	**221,018**
	Teresa Sue Bratton (D)	108,873
7	**Mike McIntyre* (D)**	**215,383**
	Will Breazeale (R)	97,472
8	**Larry Kissell (D)**	**157,185**
	Robin Hayes* (R)	126,634
9	**Sue Myrick* (R)**	**241,053**
	Harry Taylor (D)	138,719
10	**Patrick McHenry* (R)**	**171,774**
	Daniel Johnson (D)	126,699
11	**Heath Shuler* (D)**	**211,112**
	Carl Mumpower (R)	122,087
12	**Mel Watt* (D)**	**215,908**
	Ty Cobb (R)	85,814
13	**Brad Miller* (D)**	**221,379**
	Hugh Webster (R)	114,383
North Dakota		
	Earl Pomeroy* (D)	**194,577**
	Duane Sand (R)	119,388
Ohio		
1	**Steve Driehaus (D)**	**155,455**
	Steve Chabot* (R)	140,683
2	**Jean Schmidt* (R)**	**148,671**
	Victoria Wulsin (D)	124,213
	David Krikorian (Ind.)	58,710
3	**Mike Turner* (R)**	**200,204**
	Jane Mitakides (D)	115,976
4	**Jim Jordan* (R)**	**186,154**
	Mike Carroll (D)	99,499
5	**Bob Latta* (R)**	**188,905**
	George Mays (D)	105,840
6	**Charlie Wilson Jr.* (D)**	**176,330**
	Richard Stobbs (R)	92,968
	Dennis Spisak (GR)	13,812

Dist.	Representative (Party)	2008 election
7	**Steve Austria (R)**	174,915
	Sharen Swartz Neuhardt (D)	125,547
8	**John Boehner* (R)**	202,063
	Nicholas von Stein (D)	95,510
9	**Marcy Kaptur* (D)**	222,054
	Bradley Leavitt (R)	76,512
10	**Dennis Kucinich* (D)**	157,268
	Jim Trakas (R)	107,918
	Paul Conroy (LB)	10,623
11	**Marcia Fudge (D)**	212,667
	Thomas Pekarek (R)	36,708
12	**Pat Tiberi* (R)**	197,447
	David Robinson (D)	152,234
	Steven Linnabary (LB)	10,707
13	**Betty Sutton* (D)**	192,593
	David Potter (R)	105,050
14	**Steven LaTourette* (R)**	188,488
	Bill O'Neill (D)	125,214
15	**Mary Jo Kilroy (D)**	139,584
	Steve Stivers (R)	137,272
	Mark Michael Noble (LB)	14,061
	Don Elijah Eckhart (Ind.)	12,915
16	**John Boccieri (D)**	169,044
	Kirk Schuring (R)	136,293
17	**Tim Ryan* (D)**	218,896
	Duane Grassell (R)	61,216
18	**Zack Space* (D)**	164,187
	Fred Dailey (R)	110,031

Oklahoma

Dist.	Representative (Party)	2008 election
1	**John Sullivan* (R)**	193,404
	Georgianna Oliver (D)	98,890
2	**Dan Boren* (D)**	173,757
	Raymond Wickson (R)	72,815
3	**Frank D. Lucas* (R)**	184,306
	Frankie Robbins (D)	62,297
	Forrest Michael (Ind.)	17,756
4	**Tom Cole* (R)**	180,080
	Blake Cummings (D)	79,674
	David Joyce (Ind.)	13,027
5	**Mary Fallin* (R)**	171,925
	Steven Perry (D)	88,996

Oregon

Dist.	Representative (Party)	2008 election
1	**David Wu* (D)**	237,567
	Joel Haugen (Ind.)	58,279
	Scott Semrau (Constitution)	14,172
	H. Joe Tabor (LB)	10,992
2	**Greg Walden* (R)**	236,560
	Noah Lemas (D)	87,649
3	**Earl Blumenauer* (D)**	254,235
	Delia Lopez (R)	71,063
	Michael Meo (Pacific Green)	15,063
4	**Peter DeFazio* (D)**	275,143
	Jaynee Germond (CP)	43,133
	Mike Beilstein (Pacific Green)	13,162
5	**Kurt Schrader (D)**	181,577
	Mike Erickson (R)	128,297

Pennsylvania

Dist.	Representative (Party)	2008 election
1	**Robert A. Brady* (D)**	242,799
	Mike Muhammad (R)	24,714
2	**Chaka Fattah* (D)**	276,870
	Adam Lang (R)	34,466
3	**Kathy Dahlkemper (D)**	146,846
	Phil English* (R)	139,757
4	**Jason Altmire* (D)**	186,536
	Melissa Hart (R)	147,411
5	**Glenn Thompson (R)**	155,513
	Mark McCracken (D)	112,509
6	**Jim Gerlach* (R)**	179,423
	Bob Roggio (D)	164,952
7	**Joe Sestak* (D)**	209,955
	W. Craig Williams (R)	142,362
8	**Patrick Murphy* (D)**	197,869
	Tom Manion (R)	145,103
9	**Bill Shuster* (R)**	174,951
	Tony Barr (D)	98,735
10	**Christopher Carney* (D)**	160,837
	Chris Hackett (R)	124,681
11	**Paul Kanjorski* (D)**	146,379
	Lou Barletta (R)	137,151
12	**John Murtha* (D)**	155,268
	William Russell (R)	113,120
13	**Allyson Schwartz* (D)**	196,868
	Marina Kats (R)	108,271

Dist.	Representative (Party)	2008 election
14	**Mike Doyle* (D)**	242,326
	Titus North (GR)	23,214
15	**Charles Dent* (R)**	181,433
	Sam Bennett (D)	128,333
16	**Joseph Pitts* (R)**	170,329
	Bruce Slater (D)	120,193
	John A. Murphy (Ind.)	11,768
17	**Tim Holden* (D)**	192,699
	Toni Gilhooley (R)	109,909
18	**Tim Murphy* (R)**	213,349
	Steve O'Donnell (D)	119,661
19	**Todd Platts* (R)**	218,862
	Philip Avillo (D)	109,533

Rhode Island

Dist.	Representative (Party)	2008 election
1	**Patrick Kennedy* (D)**	145,254
	Jonathan Scott (R)	51,340
	Kenneth Capalbo (Ind.)	15,108
2	**James Langevin* (D)**	158,416
	Mark Zaccaria (R)	67,433

South Carolina

Dist.	Representative (Party)	2008 election
1	**Henry Brown* (R)**	177,540
	Linda Ketner (D)	163,724
2	**Joe Wilson* (R)**	184,583
	Rob Miller (D)	158,627
3	**J. Gresham Barrett* (R)**	186,799
	Jane Dyer (D)	101,724
4	**Bob Inglis* (R)**	184,440
	Paul Corden (D)	113,291
5	**John Spratt* (D)**	188,785
	Albert Spencer (R)	113,282
6	**Jim Clyburn* (D)**	193,378
	Nancy Harrelson (R)	93,059

South Dakota

Dist.	Representative (Party)	2008 election
	Stephanie Herseth Sandlin (D)	256,041
	Chris Lien (R)	122,966

Tennessee

Dist.	Representative (Party)	2008 election
1	**Phil Roe (R)**	168,343
	Rob Russell (D)	57,525
2	**John Duncan* (R)**	227,120
	Bob Scott (D)	63,639
3	**Zach Wamp* (R)**	184,964
	Doug Vandagriff (D)	73,059
4	**Lincoln Davis* (D)**	146,776
	Monty Lankford (R)	94,447
5	**Jim Cooper* (D)**	181,467
	Gerard Donovan (R)	85,471
6	**Bart Gordon* (D)**	194,264
	Chris Baker (Ind.)	66,764
7	**Marsha Blackburn* (R)**	217,332
	Randy Morris (D)	99,549
8	**John Tanner* (D)**	Unopposed
	One independent opponent earning fewer than 100 votes	
9	**Steve Cohen* (D)**	198,798
	Jake Ford (Ind.)	11,003
	Dewey Clark (Ind.)	10,047

Texas

Dist.	Representative (Party)	2008 election
1	**Louie Gohmert* (R)**	189,012
	Roger Owen (Ind.)	26,814
2	**Ted Poe* (R)**	175,101
	Craig Wolfe (LB)	21,813
3	**Sam Johnson* (R)**	170,742
	Tom Daley (D)	108,693
4	**Ralph Hall* (R)**	206,906
	Glenn Melancon (D)	88,067
5	**Jeb Hensarling* (R)**	162,894
	Ken Ashby (LB)	31,967
6	**Joe Barton* (R)**	174,008
	Ludwig Otto (D)	99,919
7	**John Culberson* (R)**	162,635
	Michael Skelly (D)	123,242
8	**Kevin Brady* (R)**	207,128
	Kent Hargett (D)	70,758
9	**Al Green* (D)**	143,868
	Brad Walters (LB)	9,760
10	**Michael McCaul* (R)**	179,493
	Larry Joe Doherty (D)	143,719
11	**Mike Conaway* (R)**	189,625
	John Strohm (LB)	25,051
12	**Kay Granger* (R)**	181,662
	Tracey Smith (D)	82,250
13	**Mac Thornberry* (R)**	180,078
	Roger Waun (D)	51,841
14	**Ron Paul* (R)**	Unopposed

Dist.	Representative (Party)	2008 election
15	**Rubén Hinojosa* (D)**	107,578
	Eddie Zamora (R)	52,303
16	**Sylvestre Reyes* (D)**	130,375
	Benjamin Eloy "Ben" Mendoza (Ind.)	16,348
	Mette Baker (LB)	12,000
17	**Chet Edwards* (D)**	134,592
	Rob Curnock (R)	115,581
18	**Sheila Jackson Lee* (D)**	148,617
	John Faulk (R)	39,095
19	**Randy Neugebauer* (R)**	168,501
	Dwight Fullingim (D)	58,030
20	**Charlie Gonzalez* (D)**	127,298
	Robert Litoff (R)	44,585
21	**Lamar Smith* (R)**	243,471
	James Strohm (LB)	60,879
22	**Pete Olson (R)**	161,996
	Nick Lampson* (D)	140,160
23	**Ciro Rodriguez* (D)**	134,090
	Lyle Larson (R)	100,799
24	**Kenny Marchant* (R)**	151,434
	Tom Love (D)	111,089
25	**Lloyd Doggett* (D)**	191,755
	George Morovich (R)	88,693
	Jim Stutsman (LB)	10,848
26	**Michael C. Burgess* (R)**	195,181
	Ken Leach (D)	118,167
	Stephanie B. Weiss (LB)	11,028
27	**Solomon Ortiz* (D)**	104,864
	William Willie Vaden (R)	69,458
28	**Henry Cuellar* (D)**	123,494
	Jim Fish (R)	52,524
29	**Gene Green* (D)**	79,718
	Eric Story (R)	25,512
30	**Eddie Bernice Johnson* (D)**	168,249
	Fred Wood (R)	32,361
31	**John Carter* (R)**	175,563
	Brian Ruiz (D)	106,559
32	**Pete Sessions* (R)**	116,283
	Eric Roberson (D)	82,406
Utah		
1	**Rob Bishop* (R)**	196,799
	Morgan Bowen (D)	92,469
2	**Jim Matheson* (D)**	220,666
	Bill Dew (R)	120,083
3	**Jason Chaffetz (R)**	187,035
	Bennion Spencer (D)	80,626
	Jim Noorlander (Constitution)	17,408
Vermont		
	Peter Welch* (D)	248,203
	Mike Bethel (Ind.)	14,349
	Jerry Trudell (Energy Independence)	10,818
Virginia		
1	**Rob Wittman* (R)**	203,839
	Bill Day (D)	150,432
2	**Glenn Nye (D)**	141,857
	Thelma Drake* (R)	128,486
3	**Bobby Scott* (D)**	Unopposed
4	**Randy Forbes* (R)**	199,075
	Andrea Miller (D)	135,041

Dist.	Representative (Party)	2008 election
5	**Tom Perriello (D)**	158,810
	Virgil Goode* (R)	158,083
6	**Bob Goodlatte* (R)**	192,350
	Sam Rasoul (D)	114,367
7	**Eric Cantor* (R)**	233,531
	Anita Hartke (D)	138,123
8	**Jim Moran* (D)**	222,986
	Mark Ellmore (R)	97,425
9	**Rick Boucher* (D)**	Unopposed
10	**Frank Wolf* (R)**	223,140
	Judy M. Feder (D)	147,357
11	**Gerry Connolly (D)**	196,598
	Keith Fimian (R)	154,758
Washington		
1	**Jay Inslee* (D)**	233,780
	Larry Ishmael (R)	111,240
2	**Rick Larsen* (D)**	217,416
	Rick Bart (R)	131,051
3	**Brian Baird* (D)**	216,701
	Michael Delavar (R)	121,828
4	**Doc Hastings* (R)**	169,940
	George Fearing (D)	99,430
5	**Cathy McMorris Rodgers* (R)**	211,305
	Mark Mays (D)	112,382
6	**Norm Dicks* (D)**	205,991
	Doug Cloud (R)	102,081
7	**Jim McDermott* (D)**	291,963
	Steve Beren (R)	57,054
8	**Dave Reichert* (R)**	191,568
	Darcy Burner (D)	171,358
9	**Adam Smith* (D)**	176,295
	James Postma (R)	93,080
West Virginia		
1	**Alan Mollohan* (D)**	Unopposed
2	**Shelley Moore Capito* (R)**	147,334
	Anne Barth (D)	110,819
3	**Nick Rahall* (D)**	133,522
	Marty Gearhart (R)	66,005
Wisconsin		
1	**Paul Ryan* (R)**	231,009
	Marge Krupp (D)	125,268
2	**Tammy Baldwin* (D)**	277,914
	Peter Theron (R)	122,513
3	**Ron Kind* (D)**	225,208
	Paul Stark (R)	122,760
4	**Gwen Moore* (D)**	222,728
	Michael LaForest (Ind.)	29,282
5	**Jim Sensenbrenner* (R)**	275,271
	Robert Raymond (Ind.)	69,715
6	**Tom Petri* (R)**	221,875
	Roger Kittelson (D)	126,090
7	**David Obey* (D)**	212,666
	Dan Mielke (R)	136,938
8	**Steven Kagen* (D)**	193,662
	John Gard (R)	164,621
Wyoming		
	Cynthia Lummis (R)	131,244
	Gary Trauner (D)	106,758
	W. David Herbert (LB)	11,030

(1) Vacant effective June 27, 2009, following June 26 resignation of Rep. Ellen Tauscher. (2) Rep. Hilda Solis resigned Feb. 24, 2009; Judy Chu (D) was sworn in July 16, 2009, following a special election. (3) Not seated; Mike Quigley (D) was sworn in Apr. 21, 2009, following a special election. (4) Rep. Kirsten Gillibrand resigned on Jan. 26, 2009; Scott Murphy (D) was sworn in Apr. 29, 2009, following a special election. (5) Vacant effective Sept. 22, 2009, following Sept. 21 resignation of Rep. John McHugh.

Nonvoting Members of Congress

Representative (Party)	2008 election
American Samoa	
Eni F.H. Faleomavaega Hunkin* (D)	7,499
Amata Coleman Radewagen (R)	4,350
FualaʻAu Rosie F. Tago Lancaster (Ind.)	570
District of Columbia	
Eleanor Holmes Norton* (D)	228,376
Maude Louise Hills (Statehood Green)	16,693
Guam	
Madeleine Z. Bordallo* (D)	Unopposed

Representative (Party)	2008 election
Puerto Rico—Resident Commissioner	
Pedro Pierluisi (New Progressive Party)	1,010,304
Alfredo Salazar (Popular Dem. Party)	810,111
Carlos A. Velazquez Lopez (Puerto Ricans for Puerto Rico Party)	46,126
Jessica Martinez Birriel (Puerto Rican Independence Party)	37,865
Virgin Islands	
Donna M. Christensen* (D)	Unopposed

STATE GOVERNMENT

Governors of States and Puerto Rico

As of Sept. 2009. Of the 50 state governors, 22 are Republicans and 28 are Democrats.

State	Capital, ZIP Code	Governor	Party	Term years	Term expires	Annual salary
Alabama	Montgomery 36104	Bob Riley	Rep.	4	Jan. 2011	$112,895
Alaska	Juneau 99801	Sean Parnell[1]	Rep.	4	Dec. 2010	125,000
Arizona	Phoenix 85007	Jan Brewer[2]	Rep.	4	Jan. 2011	95,000
Arkansas	Little Rock 72201	Mike Beebe	Dem.	4	Jan. 2011	84,114
California	Sacramento 95814	Arnold Schwarzenegger[3]	Rep.	4	Jan. 2011	173,967
Colorado	Denver 80203	Bill Ritter	Dem.	4	Jan. 2011	90,000
Connecticut	Hartford 06106	M. Jodi Rell	Rep.	4	Jan. 2011	150,000
Delaware	Dover 19901	Jack A. Markell	Dem.	4	Jan. 2013	171,000
Florida	Tallahassee 32399	Charlie Crist	Rep.	4	Jan. 2011	130,273
Georgia	Atlanta 30334	Sonny Perdue	Rep.	4	Jan. 2011	139,340
Hawaii	Honolulu 96813	Linda Lingle	Rep.	4	Dec. 2010	129,660
Idaho	Boise 83702	C. L. "Butch" Otter	Rep.	4	Jan. 2011	115,349
Illinois	Springfield 62706	Patrick Quinn[4]	Dem.	4	Jan. 2011	177,412
Indiana	Indianapolis 46204	Mitch E. Daniels Jr.	Rep.	4	Jan. 2013	95,000
Iowa	Des Moines 50319	Chester J. Culver	Dem.	4	Jan. 2011	130,000
Kansas	Topeka 66612	Mark Parkinson[5]	Dem.	4	Jan. 2011	110,707
Kentucky	Frankfort 40601	Steven L. Beshear	Dem.	4	Dec. 2011	124,497
Louisiana	Baton Rouge 70802	Bobby Jindal	Rep.	4	Jan. 2012	130,000
Maine	Augusta 04330	John E. Baldacci	Dem.	4	Jan. 2011	70,000
Maryland	Annapolis 21401	Martin O'Malley	Dem.	4	Jan. 2011	150,000
Massachusetts	Boston 02133	Deval Patrick	Dem.	4	Jan. 2011	140,535
Michigan	Lansing 48933	Jennifer M. Granholm	Dem.	4	Jan. 2011	177,000
Minnesota	St. Paul 55155	Tim Pawlenty	Rep.	4	Jan. 2011	120,311
Mississippi	Jackson 39201	Haley Barbour	Rep.	4	Jan. 2012	122,160
Missouri	Jefferson City 65101	Jay Nixon	Dem.	4	Jan. 2013	133,821
Montana	Helena 59620	Brian Schweitzer	Dem.	4	Jan. 2013	100,120
Nebraska	Lincoln 68509	David Heineman	Rep.	4	Jan. 2011	105,000
Nevada	Carson City 89701	Jim Gibbons	Rep.	4	Jan. 2011	141,000
New Hampshire	Concord 03301	John H. Lynch	Dem.	2	Jan. 2011	120,095
New Jersey	Trenton 08625	Jon Corzine[3]	Dem.	4	Jan. 2010	175,000
New Mexico	Santa Fe 87501	Bill Richardson	Dem.	4	Jan. 2011	110,000
New York	Albany 12224	David Paterson	Dem.	4	Jan. 2011	179,000
North Carolina	Raleigh 27601	Beverly Purdue	Dem.	4	Jan. 2013	139,590
North Dakota	Bismarck 58501	John Hoeven	Rep.	4	Dec. 2012	105,031
Ohio	Columbus 43215	Ted Strickland	Dem.	4	Jan. 2011	142,057
Oklahoma	Oklahoma City 73105	Brad Henry	Dem.	4	Jan. 2011	147,000
Oregon	Salem 97301	Ted Kulongoski	Dem.	4	Jan. 2011	93,600
Pennsylvania	Harrisburg 17120	Edward G. Rendell	Dem.	4	Jan. 2011	174,914
Rhode Island	Providence 02903	Donald L. Carcieri	Rep.	4	Jan. 2011	117,817
South Carolina	Columbia 29201	Mark Sanford	Rep.	4	Jan. 2011	106,078
South Dakota	Pierre 57501	Mike Rounds	Rep.	4	Jan. 2011	115,331
Tennessee	Nashville 37243	Phil Bredesen[3]	Dem.	4	Jan. 2011	164,292
Texas	Austin 78701	Rick Perry	Rep.	4	Jan. 2011	150,000
Utah	Salt Lake City 84114	Gary R. Herbert[6]	Rep.	4	Jan. 2011	109,900
Vermont	Montpelier 05609	Jim Douglas	Rep.	2	Jan. 2011	142,542
Virginia	Richmond 23219	Timothy M. Kaine	Dem.	4	Jan. 2010	175,000
Washington	Olympia 98501	Christine Gregoire	Dem.	4	Jan. 2013	166,891
West Virginia	Charleston 25301	Joe Manchin III	Dem.	4	Jan. 2013	95,000
Wisconsin	Madison 53704	Jim Doyle	Dem.	4	Jan. 2011	137,092
Wyoming	Cheyenne 82001	Dave Freudenthal	Dem.	4	Jan. 2011	105,000
Puerto Rico	San Juan 00901	Luis Fortuño	PNP[7]	4	Jan. 2013	70,000

(1) Assumed the office July 26, 2009, following resignation of Gov. Sarah Palin. (2) Assumed office Jan. 21, 2009, following Gov. Janet Napolitano's appointment as Secretary of Homeland Security. (3) Does not accept salary. (4) Assumed office Jan. 29, 2009, after Gov. Rod Blagojevich's removal from office. (5) Assumed office Apr. 28, 2009, following Gov. Kathleen Sebelius's appointment as Secretary of Health and Human Services. (6) Assumed office Aug. 11, 2009, following Gov. John Huntsman Jr.'s appointment as U.S. Ambassador to China. (7) New Progressive Party (pro-statehood). Gov. Fortuño is also a registered Republican.

State Elected Officials, Salaries, Party Membership

State officials listed reflect election results of Sept. 2009; legislatures are as of Feb. 2009. Some salaries may be rounded to the nearest dollar.

Alabama

Governor: Bob Riley, R, $112,895
Lt. Gov.: Jim Folsom Jr., D, $12 per day, plus $50 per day, plus $5,458 per mo expenses
Atty. Gen.: Troy King, R, $163,744
Sec. of State: Beth Chapman, R, $79,580
Treasurer: Kay Ivey, R, $79,580
Auditor: Samantha Shaw, R, $79,580
Legislature: Meets annually at Montgomery 1st Tues. in Mar., 1st year of term of office; 1st Tues. in Feb., 2nd and 3rd yrs.; 2nd Tues. in Jan., 4th yr. Members receive $10 per day salary, plus $50 per day and $3,958 per month for expenses.
Senate: Dem., 19; Rep., 13; 3 vacant. Total, 35
House: Dem., 62; Rep., 43. Total, 105

Alaska

Governor: Sean Parnell, R, $125,000
Lt. Gov.: Craig E. Campbell, R, $100,000
Atty. Gen.: Daniel S. Sullivan, R, $135,000
Legislature: Meets annually on 3rd Tues. in Jan. at Juneau for 90 days with a 10-day extension possible upon 2/3 vote. Members receive $24,012 annually, plus $189 or $234 session per diem, depending on season.
Senate: Dem., 10; Rep., 10. Total, 20
House: Dem., 18; Rep., 22. Total, 40

Arizona

Governor: Jan Brewer, R, $95,000
Sec. of State: Ken Bennett, R, $70,000
Atty. Gen.: Terry Goddard, D, $90,000
Treasurer: Dean Martin, R, $70,000
Legislature: Meets annually in Jan. at Phoenix. Each member receives an annual salary of $24,000 plus a per diem.
Senate: Dem., 12; Rep., 18. Total, 30
House: Dem., 24; Rep., 36. Total, 60

Arkansas

Governor: Mike Beebe, D, $84,114
Lt. Gov.: Bill Halter, D, $40,654
Sec. of State: Charlie Daniels, D, $52,570
Atty. Gen.: Dustin McDaniel, D, $70,095
Treasurer: Martha Shoffner, D, $52,570
Auditor: Jim Wood, D, $52,570
General Assembly: Meets annually in Jan. at Little Rock. Members receive an annual salary of $15,362, plus a per diem.
Senate: Dem., 27; Rep., 8. Total, 35
House: Dem., 71; Rep., 28; Green, 1. Total, 100

California

Governor: Arnold Schwarzenegger, R, $173,967[1]
Lt. Gov.: John Garamendi, D, $163,974
Sec. of State: Debra Bowen, R, $159,134
Atty. Gen.: Edmund G. Brown Jr., D, $184,301
Controller: John Chiang, D, $169,743
Treasurer: Bill Lockyer, D, $171,554
Legislature: Meets at Sacramento on the 1st Mon. in Dec. of even-numbered years; each session lasts 2 years. Members receive $116,208 annually, plus $173 per diem.
Senate: Dem., 25; Rep., 14; 1 vacant. Total, 40
House: Dem., 51; Rep., 29. Total, 80
(1) Does not accept salary.

Colorado

Governor: Bill Ritter, D, $90,000
Lt. Gov.: Barbara O'Brien, D, $68,500
Sec. of State: Bernie Buescher, D, $68,500
Atty. Gen.: John W. Suthers, D, $80,000
Treasurer: Cary Kennedy, R, $68,500
General Assembly: Meets annually in Jan. at Denver. Members receive $30,000 annually plus per diem for attendance at interim committee meetings ($45/day for members residing in Denver; $99/day for those residing outside).
Senate: Dem., 21; Rep., 14. Total, 35
House: Dem., 38; Rep., 27. Total, 65

Connecticut

Governor: M. Jodi Rell, R, $150,000
Lt. Gov.: Michael Fedele, R, $110,000
Sec. of State: Susan Bysiewicz, D, $110,000
Treasurer: Denise Nappier, D, $110,000
Comptroller: Nancy S. Wyman, D, $110,000
Atty. Gen.: Richard Blumenthal, D, $110,000
General Assembly: Meets annually odd years in Jan. and even years in Feb., at Hartford. Members receive $28,000 annually, plus $5,500 (senator), $4,500 (representative) per year for expenses.
Senate: Dem., 24; Rep., 12. Total, 36
House: Dem., 114; Rep., 36; 1 vacant. Total, 151

Delaware

Governor: Jack A. Markell, D, $171,000
Lt. Gov.: Matthew Denn, D, $76,250
Sec. of State: Jeffrey W. Bullock, D, $123,850
Atty. Gen.: Joseph R. "Beau" Biden III, D, $140,950
Treasurer: Velda Jones-Potter, D, $110,050
General Assembly: Meets annually the 2nd Tues. in Jan. and continues each Tues., Wed., and Thurs. until June 30, at Dover. Members receive $42,750 annually, plus $7,334 for expenses.
Senate: Dem., 16; Rep., 5. Total, 21
House: Dem., 24; Rep., 17. Total, 41

Florida

Governor: Charlie Crist, R, $130,273
Lt. Gov.: Jeff Kottkamp, R, $124,851
Chief Financial Officer: Alex Sink, D, $128,972
Atty. Gen.: Bill McCollum, R, $128,972
Comm. of Agriculture: Charles H. Bronson, R, $128,972
Legislature: Meets annually at Tallahassee. Members receive $30,336 annually, plus per diem and expense allowance.
Senate: Dem., 14; Rep., 26. Total, 40
House: Dem., 44; Rep., 76. Total, 120

Georgia

Governor: Sonny Perdue, R, $139,340
Lt. Gov.: Casey Cagle, R, $91,609
Sec. of State: Karen Handel, R, $123,637
Atty. Gen.: Thurbert Baker, D, $137,791
General Assembly: Meets annually at Atlanta on 2nd Mon. in Jan. Members receive $17,342 annually plus $173 per diem.
Senate: Dem., 22; Rep., 34. Total, 56
House: Dem., 73; Rep., 107. Total, 180

Hawaii

Governor: Linda Lingle, R, $129,660
Lt. Gov.: James R. Aiona Jr., R, $126,468
Atty. Gen.: Mark J. Bennett, R, $126,468
Comptroller: Russ K. Saito, D, $120,444
Dir. of Budget & Finance: Georgina K. Kawamura, R, $120,444
Legislature: Meets annually on 3rd Wed. in Jan. at Honolulu. Members receive $48,708 annually plus session per diem; presiding officers, $56,208.
Senate: Dem., 23; Rep., 2. Total, 25
House: Dem., 45; Rep., 6. Total, 51

Idaho

Governor: C. L. "Butch" Otter, R, $115,349
Lt. Gov.: Brad Little, R, $30,400
Sec. of State: Ben Ysursa, R, $93,756
Treasurer: Ron Crane, R, $93,756
Atty. Gen.: Lawrence G. Wasden, R, $103,984
Legislature: Meets annually the Mon. on or nearest Jan. 9 at Boise. Members receive $16,116 annually, plus $122 per day during session if required to maintain a 2nd residence, $49 if no 2nd residence; plus $2,200 unvouchered constituent service allowance.
Senate: Dem., 7, Rep., 28. Total, 35
House: Dem., 18; Rep., 52. Total, 70

Illinois

Governor: Patrick Quinn, D, $177,412
Lt. Gov.: Vacant, $135,669
Sec. of State: Jesse White, D, $156,541
Comptroller: Daniel Hynes, D, $135,669
Atty. Gen.: Lisa Madigan, D, $156,541
Treasurer: Alexander Giannoulias, D, $135,669
General Assembly: Meets annually in Nov. and Jan. at Springfield. Members receive $67,836 annually, plus $132 per diem.
Senate: Dem., 37; Rep., 22. Total, 59
House: Dem., 70; Rep., 48. Total, 118

Indiana

Governor: Mitchell E. Daniels Jr., R, $95,000
Lt. Gov.: Becky Skillman, R, $79,192
Sec. of State: Todd Rokita, R, $68,772
Atty. Gen.: Greg Zoeller, R, $100,000
Treasurer: Richard Mourdock, R, $68,772
Auditor: Tim Berry, R, $68,772
Supt. of Public Instruction: Anthony Bennett, R, $79,400
General Assembly: Meets annually on the Tues. after 2nd Mon. in Jan. at Indianapolis. Members receive $22,616 annually, plus $138 per day in session.
Senate: Dem., 17; Rep., 33. Total, 50
House: Dem., 52; Rep., 48. Total, 100

Iowa

Governor: Chester J. Culver, D, $130,000
Lt. Gov.: Patty Judge, D, $103,212
Sec. of State: Michael A. Mauro, D, $103,212
Atty. Gen.: Tom Miller, D, $123,669
Treasurer: Michael L. Fitzgerald, D, $103,212
Auditor: David A. Vaudt, R, $103,212
Sec. of Agriculture: Bill Northey, R, $103,212
General Assembly: Meets annually in Jan. at Des Moines. Members receive $25,000 annually, plus expense allowance and $118 or $88.50 per diem, depending on member's residency.
Senate: Dem., 32; Rep., 18. Total, 50
House: Dem., 56; Rep., 44. Total, 100

Kansas

Governor: Mark Parkinson, D, $110,707
Lt. Gov.: Troy Findley, D, $99,996
Sec. of State: Ron Thornburgh, R, $86,003
Atty. Gen.: Steve Six, D, $98,901
Treasurer: Dennis McKinney, R, $82,563
Insurance Commissioner: Sandy Praeger, R, $86,003
Legislature: Meets annually on the 2nd Mon. of Jan. at Topeka, for a maximum of 90 days. Members receive $89 per day salary, plus $109 per diem in session.
Senate: Dem., 9; Rep., 31. Total, 40
House: Dem., 49; Rep., 76. Total, 125

Kentucky

Governor: Steven L. Beshear, D, $124,497
Lt. Gov.: Daniel Mongiardo, D, $105,840
Sec. of State: Trey Grayson, R, $105,840
Atty. Gen.: John W. Conway, D, $105,840
Treasurer: Todd Hollenbach, D, $105,840
Auditor: Eugenia "Crit" Luallen, D, $105,840
General Assembly: Meets annually on the 1st Tues. after the 1st Mon. in Jan. at Frankfort. Members receive $187 per day, plus $120 per day expenses during session and $1,757 per month for expenses for interim.
Senate: Dem., 15; Rep., 21; 1 ind.; 1 vacant. Total, 38
House: Dem., 65; Rep., 35. Total, 100

Louisiana

Governor: Bobby Jindal, R, $130,000
Lt. Gov.: Mitch Landrieux, D, $115,000
Sec. of State: Jay Dardenne, R, $115,000
Atty. Gen.: James D. "Buddy" Caldwell, D, $115,000
Treasurer: John Kennedy, R, $115,000
Legislature: Meets in even-numbered years at Baton Rouge starting last Mon. in Mar., for 60 legislative days of 85 calendar days; meets in odd-numbered years on last Mon. in Apr. for 45 days of 60 calendar days. Members receive $16,800 annually, plus $500 per month as an unvouchered expense allowance.
Senate: Dem., 22; Rep., 15; 2 vacant. Total, 39
House: Dem., 51; Rep., 50; 3 ind.; 1 vacant. Total, 105

Maine

Governor: John E. Baldacci, D, $70,000
Sec. of State: Matthew Dunlap, D, $83,845
Atty. Gen.: Janet T. Mills, D, $92,248
Treasurer: David G. Lemoine, D, $83,845
State Auditor: Neria R. Douglass, D, $96,782
Legislature: Meets in odd-numbered years at Augusta on first Wed. in Dec.; meets in even-numbered years on Wed. after first Tues. in Jan. Members receive $13,526 for first regular session, $9,874 for 2nd, plus a daily expense allowance.
Senate: Dem., 20; Rep., 15. Total, 35
House: Dem., 95; Rep., 55; 1 unenrolled. Total, 151

Maryland

Governor: Martin O'Malley, D, $150,000
Lt. Gov.: Anthony Brown, D, $125,000
Comptroller: Peter Franchot, D, $125,000
Atty. Gen.: Douglas F. Gansler, D, $125,000
Sec. of State: John P. McDonough, D, $87,500
Treasurer: Nancy Kopp, D, $125,000
General Assembly: Meets 90 consecutive days annually beginning on 2nd Wed. in Jan. at Annapolis. Members receive $43,500 annually, plus expenses.
Senate: Dem., 33; Rep., 14. Total, 47
House: Dem., 104; Rep., 36; 1 ind. Total, 141

Massachusetts

Governor: Deval Patrick, D, $140,535
Lt. Gov.: Timothy Murray, D, $124,920
Sec. of the Commonwealth: William F. Galvin, D, $130,916
Atty. Gen.: Martha Coakley, D, $133,644
Treasurer: Timothy P. Cahill, D, $130,916
State Auditor: A. Joseph DeNucci, D, $130,916
General Court (legislature): Meets Jan. annually in Boston. Members receive $61,440 annually, plus traveling expenses.
Senate: Dem., 35; Rep., 5. Total, 40
House: Dem., 142; Rep., 16; 1 ind.; 1 vacant. Total, 160

Michigan

Governor: Jennifer M. Granholm, D, $177,000
Lt. Gov.: John Cherry, D, $123,900
Sec. of State: Terri Lynn Land, R, $124,900
Atty. Gen.: Michael Cox, R, $124,900
Treasurer: Robert J. Kleine, D, $174,204
Legislature: Meets annually in Jan. at Lansing. Members receive $79,650 annually, plus $12,000 expense allowance.
Senate: Dem., 16; Rep., 21; 1 vacant. Total, 38
House: Dem., 67; Rep., 43. Total, 110

Minnesota

Governor: Tim Pawlenty, R, $120,311
Lt. Gov.: Carol Molnau, R, $78,196
Sec. of State: Mark Ritchie, DFL, $90,222
Atty. Gen.: Lori Swanson, DFL, $114,297
Auditor: Rebecca Otto, DFL, $102,249
Legislature: Meets for up to 120 days total within every 2 years, at St. Paul. Members receive $31,141 annually, plus expense allowance during session.
Senate: DFL, 46; Rep., 21. Total, 67
House: DFL, 87; Rep., 47. Total, 134
Note: DFL = Democratic-Farmer-Labor Party

Mississippi

Governor: Haley Barbour, R, $122,160
Lt. Gov.: Phil Bryant, R, $60,000
Sec. of State: Delbert Hosemann, R, $90,000
Atty. Gen.: Jim Hood, D, $108,960
Treasurer: Tate Reeves, R, $90,000
Auditor: Stacey Pickering, R, $90,000
Legislature: Meets annually in Jan. at Jackson. Members receive $10,000 per year, plus travel allowance, and $1,500 per month when not in session.
Senate: Dem., 27; Rep., 25. Total, 52
House: Dem., 74; Rep., 48. Total, 122

Missouri

Governor: Jay Nixon, D, $133,821
Lt. Gov.: Peter Kinder, R, $86,484
Sec. of State: Robin Carnahan, D, $107,746
Atty. Gen.: Chris Koster, D, $116,437
Treasurer: Clint Zweifel, D, $107,746
State Auditor: Susan Montee, D, $107,746
General Assembly: Meets annually at Jefferson City beginning 1st Wed. after 1st Mon. in Jan. Members receive $35,915 annually.
Senate (2009): Dem., 11; Rep., 23. Total, 34
House (2009): Dem., 74; Rep., 89. Total, 163

Montana

Governor: Brian Schweitzer, D, $100,120
Lt. Gov.: John Bohlinger, R, $79,007
Sec. of State: Linda McCulloch, D, $79,129
Atty. Gen.: Steve Bullocck, D, $89,602
Legislature: Meets odd years in Jan. at Helena. Members receive $83 per legislative day, plus $104 per diem while in session.
Senate (2009): Dem., 23; Rep., 27. Total, 50
House (2009): Dem., 50; Rep., 50. Total, 100

Nebraska

Governor: David Heineman, R, $105,000
Lt. Gov.: Rick Sheehy, R, $75,000
Sec. of State: John A. Gale, R, $85,000
Atty. Gen.: Jon Bruning, R, $95,000
Treasurer: Shane Osborn, R, $85,000
Auditor of Public Accounts: Mike Foley, R, $85,000
Legislature: Unicameral body composed of 49 members who are elected on a nonpartisan ballot and are called senators; meets annually in Jan. at Lincoln. Members receive $12,000 annually, plus expenses.

Nevada

Governor: Jim Gibbons, R, $141,000
Lt. Gov.: Brian Krolicki, R, $60,000
Sec. of State: Ross Miller, D, $97,000
Controller: Kim Wallin, D, $97,000
Atty. Gen.: Catherine Cortez Masto, D, $133,000
Treasurer: Kate Marshall, D, $97,000
Legislature: Meets at Carson City odd years starting on 1st Mon. in Feb. for 120 days. Members receive $138 or $146 per day, plus expenses.
Senate: Dem., 12; Rep., 9. Total, 21
Assembly: Dem., 28; Rep., 14. Total, 42

New Hampshire

Governor: John H. Lynch, D, $120,095
Sec. of State: William M. Gardner, D, $98,923
Atty. Gen.: Kelly A. Ayotte, R, $116,170
Treasurer: Catherine A. Provencher, $98,923
General Court (legis.): Meets every year in Jan. at Concord. Members receive $200, presiding officers $250, biannually.
Senate: Dem., 14; Rep., 10. Total, 24
House: Dem., 224; Rep., 175; 1 ind. Total, 400

New Jersey

Governor: Jon Corzine, D, $175,000[1]
Sec. of State: Nina Mitchell Wells, D, $141,000
Atty. Gen.: Anne Milgram, D, $141,000
Acting Treasurer: R. David Rousseau, D, $141,000
Legislature: Meets throughout the year at Trenton. Members receive $49,000 annually, except president of Senate and speaker of Assembly, who receive 1/3 more.
Senate: Dem., 23; Rep., 17. Total, 40
Assembly: Dem., 48; Rep., 32. Total, 80
(1) Does not accept salary.

New Mexico

Governor: Bill Richardson, D, $110,000
Lt. Gov.: Diane D. Denish, D, $85,000
Sec. of State: Mary Herrera, D, $85,000
Atty. Gen.: Gary King, D, $95,000
Treasurer: James B. Lewis, D, $85,000
Auditor: Hector H. Balderas, D, $85,000
Commissioner of Public Lands: Patrick Lyons, R, $90,000
Legislature: Meets starting on the 3rd Tues. in Jan. at Santa Fe; odd years for 60 days, even years for 30 days. Members receive $144 per day while in session.
Senate: Dem., 27; Rep., 15. Total, 42
House: Dem., 45; Rep., 25 Total, 70

New York

Governor: David Paterson, D, $179,000
Lt. Gov.: Richard Ravitch, D, $151,500
Sec. of State: Lorraine A. Cortés-Vásquez, D, $120,800
Comptroller: Thomas Dinapoli, D, $151,500
Atty. Gen.: Andrew Cuomo, D, $151,500
Legislature: Meets annually on the 1st Wed. after the 1st Mon. in Jan. at Albany. Members receive $79,500 annually, plus per diem.
Senate: Dem., 32; Rep., 30. Total, 62
Assembly: Dem., 108; Rep., 41; 1 ind. Total, 150

North Carolina

Governor: Beverly Perdue, D, $139,590[1]
Lt. Gov.: Walter H. Dalton, D, $123,198[1]
Sec. of State: Elaine F. Marshall, D, $123,198[1]
Atty. Gen.: Roy Cooper, D, $123,198[1]
Treasurer: Janet Cowell, D, $123,198[1]
General Assembly: Meets odd years starting on the 3rd Wed. following the 2nd Mon. in Jan. at Raleigh. Members receive $13,951 annually[1] and a $559 monthly expense allowance, plus travel and other allowances in session. Also meets in even years for a short session (about 6-8 weeks), usually in May.
Senate: Dem., 30; Rep., 20. Total, 50
House: Dem., 68; Rep., 52. Total, 120
(1) In 2009, elected officials accepted voluntary furlough that reduced their earnings by 0.5%.

North Dakota

Governor: John Hoeven, R, $105,031
Lt. Gov.: Jack Dalrymple III, R, $81,537
Sec. of State: Alvin A. Jaeger, R, $83,550
Atty. Gen.: Wayne Stenehjem, R, $91,719
Treasurer: Kelly L. Schmidt, R, $78,904
Legislative Assembly: Meets odd years in Jan. at Bismarck. Members receive $396 per month salary, plus $141 per calendar day salary during session and expenses for housing and lodging.
Senate: Dem., 21; Rep., 26. Total, 47
House: Dem., 36; Rep., 58. Total, 94

Ohio

Governor: Ted Strickland, D, $142,057
Lt. Gov.: Lee Fisher, D, $74,463
Sec. of State: Jennifer Brunner, D, $108,929
Atty. Gen.: Richard Cordray, D, $107,880
Treasurer: Kevin L. Boyce, D, $107,786
Auditor: Mary Taylor, R, $107,874
General Assembly: Meets odd years at Columbus starting on 1st Mon. in Jan. Members receive $60,584 annually.
Senate: Dem., 12; Rep., 21. Total, 33
House: Dem., 53; Rep., 46. Total, 99

Oklahoma

Governor: Brad Henry, D, $147,000
Lt. Gov.: Jari Askins, D, $114,713
Sec. of State: M. Susan Savage, D, $65,000
Atty. Gen.: Drew Edmondson, D, $132,825
Treasurer: Scott Meacham, D, $114,713
Auditor: Steve Burrage, D, $114,713
Legislature: Meets annually the first Mon. in Feb. at Oklahoma City. Members receive $38,400 annually, plus per diem.
Senate: Dem., 22; Rep., 26. Total, 48
House: Dem., 40; Rep., 61. Total, 101

Oregon

Governor: Ted Kulongoski, D, $93,600
Sec. of State: Kate Brown, D, $72,000
Atty. Gen.: John Kroger, D, $77,200
Treasurer: Bem Westlund, D, $72,000
Legislative Assembly: Meets odd years in Jan. at Salem. Members receive $21,612 per year, $109 expenses per diem, plus $450-$750 expense account during interim.
Senate: Dem., 18; Rep., 12. Total, 30
House: Dem., 36; Rep., 24. Total, 60

Pennsylvania

Governor: Edward G. Rendell, D, $174,914
Lt. Gov.: Catherine Baker Knoll, D, $145,529
Sec. of the Commonwealth: Pedro A. Cortés, D, $125,939
Atty. Gen.: Tom Corbett, R, $145,529
Auditor: Jack Wagner, D, $145,529
Treasurer: Rob McCord, D, $145,529
General Assembly: Convenes annually on the 1st Tues. in Jan. at Harrisburg. Members receive $78,315 annually, plus expenses and $158 per diem.
Senate: Dem., 21; Rep., 29. Total, 50
House: Dem., 104; Rep., 99. Total, 203

Rhode Island

Governor: Donald L. Carcieri, R, $117,817
Lt. Gov.: Elizabeth H. Roberts, D, $99,214
Sec. of State: A. Ralph Mollis, D, $99,214
Atty. Gen.: Patrick C. Lynch, D, $141,435
Treasurer: Frank D. Caprio, D, $99,214
General Assembly: Meets annually in Jan. at Providence. Members receive $13,089, plus mileage.
Senate: Dem., 33; Rep., 4; 1 ind. Total, 38
House: Dem., 69; Rep., 6. Total, 75

South Carolina

Governor: Mark Sanford, R, $106,078
Lt. Gov.: R. André Bauer, R, $46,545
Sec. of State: Mark Hammond, R, $92,007
Comptroller: Richard A. Eckstrom, R, $92,007
Atty. Gen.: Henry McMaster, R, $92,007
Treasurer: Converse A. Chellis III, R, $92,007
General Assembly: Meets annually on 2nd Tues. in Jan. at Columbia. Members receive $10,400 annually, plus $119 per diem.
Senate: Dem., 19; Rep., 27. Total, 46
House: Dem., 52; Rep., 71; 1 vacant. Total, 124

South Dakota

Governor: Mike Rounds, R, $115,331
Lt. Gov.: Dennis M. Daugaard, R, $17,699
Sec. of State: Chris Nelson, R, $78,363
Atty. Gen.: Larry Long, R, $97,928
Treasurer: Vernon L. Larson, R, $78,363
Auditor: Rich Sattgast, R, $78,363
Legislature: Meets annually the 2nd Tues. in Jan. at Pierre, for 40-day session in odd-numbered years, and 35-day session in even-numbered years. Members receive $12,000 per 2-year term, plus $110 per diem for days in session.
Senate: Dem., 14; Rep., 21. Total, 35
House: Dem., 24; Rep., 46. Total, 70

Tennessee

Governor: Phil Bredesen, D, $164,292[1]
Lt. Gov./Speaker of the Senate: Ronald Ramsey, R, $75,290
Sec. of State: Tre Hargett, R, $164,964
Treasurer: David H. Lillard, Jr., R, $83,182
Comptroller: Justin Wilson, R, $83,882
Atty. Gen.: Robert E. Cooper Jr., D, $160,688
General Assembly: Meets annually on the 2nd Tues. in Jan. at Nashville. Members receive $19,009 annual salary, plus $171 per diem while in session and $1,000 monthly office allowance.
Senate: Dem., 14; Rep., 19. Total, 33
House: Dem., 49; Rep., 50. Total, 99
(1) Does not accept salary.

Texas

Governor: Rick Perry, R, $150,000
Lt. Gov.: David Dewhurst, R, $7,200 (plus $139 per day during legislative sessions)
Sec. of State: Hope Andrade, R, $125,880
Comptroller: Susan Combs, R, $150,000
Atty. Gen.: Greg W. Abbott, R, $150,000
Railroad Commissioners: Victor G. Carrillo, R, Chair; Elizabeth Jones, R; Michael L. Williams, R; $137,500
Legislature: Meets odd years in Jan. at Austin. Members receive $7,200 annually, plus $139 per diem while in session.
Senate: Dem., 12; Rep., 19. Total, 31
House: Dem., 74; Rep., 76. Total, 150

Utah

Governor: Gary R. Herbert, R, $109,900
Lt. Gov.: Greg Bell, R, $104,405
Atty. Gen.: Mark Shurtleff, R, $104,405
Auditor: Auston G. Johnson, R, $104,405
Treasurer: Richard K. Ellis, R, $104,405
Legislature: Convenes for 45 days, starting on 3rd Mon. in Jan. each year at Salt Lake City. Members receive $130 per day, plus expenses for lodging and meals.
Senate: Dem., 8; Rep., 21. Total, 29
House: Dem., 22; Rep., 53. Total, 75

Vermont

Governor: Jim Douglas, R, $142,542
Lt. Gov.: Brian E. Dubie, R, $60,507
Sec. of State: Deborah L. Markowitz, D, $90,376
Atty. Gen.: William H. Sorrell, D, $108,202
Treasurer: George B. "Jeb" Spaulding, D, $90,376
Auditor: Thomas M. Salmon, D, $95,139
General Assembly: Meets in Jan. at Montpelier. Members receive $625 per 4-day week, plus $118 per day for special session and per diem for lodging and meals.
Senate: Dem., 23; Rep., 7. Total, 30
House: Dem., 95; Rep., 48; VT Progressive, 5; 2 ind. Total, 150

Virginia

Governor: Timothy M. Kaine, D, $175,000
Lt. Gov.: Bill Bolling, R, $36,321
Atty. Gen.: Bill Mims, R, $150,000
Sec. of the Commonwealth: Katherine Hanley, D, $152,793
Treasurer: Manju Ganeriwala, D, $133,506
General Assembly: Meets annually in Jan. at Richmond. Members receive $18,000 (senate) or $17,640 (house) annually, plus expense and mileage allowances.
Senate: Dem., 21; Rep., 19. Total, 40
House: Dem., 45; Rep., 53; 2 ind. Total, 100

Washington

Governor: Christine Gregoire, D, $166,891
Lt. Gov.: Brad Owen, D, $93,948
Sec. of State: Sam Reed, R, $116,950
Atty. Gen.: Rob McKenna, R, $151,718
Treasurer: Jim McIntire, D, $116,950
Auditor: Brian Sonntag, D, $116,950
Legislature: Meets annually in Jan. at Olympia. Members receive $42,106 annually, plus $90 per diem.
Senate: Dem., 31; Rep., 18. Total, 49
House: Dem., 61; Rep., 36; 1 vacant. Total, 98

West Virginia

Governor: Joe Manchin III, D, $95,000
Sec. of State: Natalie Tennant, D, $75,000
Atty. Gen.: Darrell V. McGraw Jr., D, $80,000
Treasurer: John D. Perdue, D, $75,000
Comm. of Agric.: Gus R. Douglass, D, $75,000
Auditor: Glen B. Gainer III, D, $75,000
Legislature: Meets annually in Jan. at Charleston, except after gubernatorial elections, when the legislature meets in Feb. Members receive $20,000 annually and $131 per diem.
Senate: Dem., 26; Rep., 8. Total, 34
House: Dem., 71; Rep., 29. Total, 100

Wisconsin

Governor: Jim Doyle, D, $137,092
Lt. Gov.: Barbara Lawton, D, $72,394
Sec. of State: Douglas La Follette, D, $65,079
Treasurer: Dawn Marie Sass, D, $65,079
Atty. Gen.: J. B. VanHollen, R, $133,033
Legislature: Meets in Jan. of odd-numbered years for a 2-year session. Members receive $49,943 annually, plus $88 per diem.
Senate: Dem., 18; Rep., 15. Total, 33
Assembly: Dem., 52; Rep., 46; 1 ind. Total, 99

Wyoming

Governor: Dave Freudenthal, D, $105,000
Sec. of State: Max Maxfield, R, $92,000
Atty. Gen.: Bruce A. Salzburg, D, $137,000
Treasurer: Joseph B. Meyer, R, $92,000
State Auditor: Rita C. Meyer, R, $92,000
Legislature: Meets odd years in Jan., even years in Feb., at Cheyenne. Members receive $150 per day while in session, plus $85 per diem.
Senate: Dem., 7; Rep., 23. Total, 30
House: Dem., 19; Rep., 41. Total, 60

UNITED STATES FACTS

Superlative U.S. Statistics[1]

Source: U.S. Geological Survey, Dept. of the Interior; U.S. Bureau of the Census, Dept. of Commerce; World Almanac research

Total area for 50 states and Washington, DC (land, 3,537,440 sq mi; water, 256,648 sq mi)		3,794,085 sq mi[2]
Largest state	Alaska	663,267 sq mi
Smallest state	Rhode Island	1,545 sq mi
Largest county (excluding Alaska)	San Bernardino County, CA	20,105 sq mi
Smallest county	Arlington County, VA[3]	26 sq mi
Largest incorporated city	Sitka, AK	4,812 sq mi
Northernmost city	Barrow, AK	71°17′ N
Northernmost point	Point Barrow, AK	71°23′ N
Southernmost city	Hilo, HI	19°44′ N
Southernmost settlement	Naalehu, HI	19°03′ N
Southernmost point	Ka Lae (South Cape), island of Hawaii	18° 55′ N (155°41′ W)
Easternmost city	Eastport, ME	66° 59′05′′ W
Easternmost settlement[4]	Amchitka Isl., AK	179°15′ E
Easternmost point[4]	Pochnoi Point, on Semisopochnoi Isl., AK	179°46′ E
Westernmost city	Atka, AK	174° 12′ W
Westernmost settlement	Adak Station, AK	176° 39′ W
Westernmost point	Amatignak Isl., AK	179° 06′ W
Highest settlement	Climax, CO	11,360 ft
Lowest settlement	Bombay Beach, CA	−223 ft
Highest point on Atlantic coast	Cadillac Mountain, Mount Desert Isl., ME	1,530 ft
Oldest national park	Yellowstone National Park (1872), WY-MT-ID	2,219,791 acres
Largest national park	Wrangell-St. Elias, AK	8,323,148 acres
Highest waterfall	Yosemite Falls—total in 3 sections	2,425 ft
	(Upper Yosemite Fall, 1,430 ft; Cascades, 675 ft; Lower Yosemite Fall, 320 ft)	
Longest river system	Mississippi-Missouri-Red Rock	3,710 mi
Highest mountain	Mount McKinley (Denali), AK	20,320 ft
Lowest point	Death Valley, CA	−282 ft
Deepest lake	Crater Lake, OR	1,932 ft
Rainiest spot	Mount Waialeale, HI	annual avg. rainfall 426 in.
Largest gorge	Grand Canyon, Colorado River, AZ	277 mi long, 600 ft to 18 mi wide, 1 mi deep
Deepest gorge	Hells Canyon, Snake River, OR-ID	7,900 ft
Largest dam	New Cornelia Tailings, Ten Mile Wash, AZ[5]	274,026,000 cu yds material used
Tallest building	Willis Tower, Chicago, IL[6]	1,451 ft
Largest building	Boeing Manufacturing Plant, Everett, WA	472,000,000 cu ft; covers 98 acres
Largest office building	Pentagon, Arlington, VA	77,025,000 cu ft; covers 29 acres
Tallest structure	TV tower, Blanchard, ND	2,063 ft
Longest bridge span	Verrazano-Narrows, NY	4,260 ft
Highest bridge	Royal Gorge, CO	1,053 ft above water
Deepest well	Bertha Rogers gas well (inactive), Washita County, OK	31,441 ft

The 48 Contiguous States

Total Area for 48 states and Washington, DC (Land, 2,959,066 sq mi; Water, 160,824 sq mi)		3,119,887 sq mi[2]
Largest state	Texas	268,581 sq mi
Northernmost city	Bellingham, WA	48°46′ N
Northernmost settlement	Angle Inlet, MN	49°21′ N
Northernmost point	Northwest Angle, MN	49°23′ N
Southernmost city	Key West, FL	24°33′ N
Southernmost mainland city	Florida City, FL	25°27′ N
Southernmost point	Key West, FL	24°33′ N
Easternmost settlement	Lubec, ME	66°58′49′′ W
Easternmost point	West Quoddy Head, ME	66°57′ W
Westernmost town	La Push, WA	124°38′ W
Westernmost point	Cape Alava, WA	124°44′ W
Highest mountain	Mount Whitney, CA	14,494 ft

(1) All areas are total area, including water, unless otherwise noted. (2) Does not add, because of rounding. (3) Smallest county by land area is New York County (Manhattan) at 23 sq mi; its total area including water is 34 square miles. Superlative shown is for smallest total area. (4) Alaska's Aleutian Islands extend into the eastern hemisphere (across 180° longitude) and thus technically contain the easternmost point and settlement in the U.S. (5) The New Cornelia Tailings Dam is a privately owned industrial dam composed of tailings, remnants of a mining process. (6) The former Sears Tower became formally known as the Willis Tower as of July 16, 2009.

Geodetic Datum of North America

In July 1986, the National Oceanic and Atmospheric Administration's National Geodetic Survey (NGS), in cooperation with Canada and Mexico, completed readjustment and redefinition of the system of latitudes and longitudes. The resulting North American Datum of 1983 (NAD 83) replaces the North American Datum of 1927, as well as local reference systems for Hawaii, Puerto Rico, and the Virgin Islands. The change was prompted by Hawaii's increased need for accurate coordinate information. To facilitate use of satellite surveying and navigation systems, such as the Global Positioning System (GPS), the new datum was redefined using the Geodetic Reference System 1980 as the reference ellipsoid because this model more closely approximates the true size and shape of the earth. In addition, the origin of the coordinate system is referenced to the mass center of the Earth to coincide with the orbital orientation of the GPS satellites. Positional changes resulting from the datum redefinition can reach 330 ft in the continental U.S., Canada, and Mexico. Changes that exceed 660 ft can be expected in Alaska, Puerto Rico, and the Virgin Islands. Hawaii's coordinates changed about 1,300 ft.

Additional Statistical Information About the U.S.

The annual *Statistical Abstract of the United States*, published by the U.S. Commerce Dept., Bureau of the Census, contains additional data. For information, write Supt. of Documents, P.O. Box 371954, Pittsburgh, PA 15250-7954, call 1-866-512-1800, or e-mail ContactCenter@gpo.gov. The *Statistical Abstract* can be viewed online at www.census.gov/compendia/statab

Highest and Lowest Altitudes in U.S. States and Territories

Source: U.S. Geological Survey, Dept. of the Interior
(negative sign means below sea level)

State/Territory	HIGHEST POINT Name	County	Elev. (ft)	LOWEST POINT Name	County	Elev. (ft)
Alabama	Cheaha Mountain	Cleburne	2,407	Gulf of Mexico		Sea level
Alaska	Mount McKinley	Denali	20,320	Pacific Ocean		Sea level
American Samoa	Lata Mountain	Tau Island	3,160	Pacific Ocean		Sea level
Arizona	Humphreys Peak	Coconino	12,633	Colorado R.	Yuma	70
Arkansas	Magazine Mountain	Logan	2,753	Ouachita R.	Ashley-Union	55
California	Mount Whitney	Inyo-Tulare	14,494	Death Valley	Inyo	−282
Colorado	Mount Elbert	Lake	14,433	Arikaree R.	Yuma	3,315
Connecticut	S. slope of Mt. Frissell	Litchfield	2,380	Long Island Sound		Sea level
Delaware	Ebright Azimuth	New Castle	448	Atlantic Ocean		Sea level
Dist. of Columbia	Tenleytown	NW part	410	Potomac R.		1
Florida	Britton Hill	Walton	345	Atlantic Ocean		Sea level
Georgia	Brasstown Bald	Towns-Union	4,784	Atlantic Ocean		Sea level
Guam	Mount Lamlam	Agat District	1,332	Pacific Ocean		Sea level
Hawaii	Mauna Kea	Hawaii	13,796	Pacific Ocean		Sea level
Idaho	Borah Peak	Custer	12,662	Snake R.	Nez Perce	710
Illinois	Charles Mound	Jo Daviess	1,235	Mississippi R.	Alexander	279
Indiana	Hoosier Hill	Wayne	1,257	Ohio R.	Posey	320
Iowa	Hawkeye Point	Osceola	1,670	Mississippi R.	Lee	480
Kansas	Mount Sunflower	Wallace	4,039	Verdigris R.	Montgomery	679
Kentucky	Black Mountain	Harlan	4,145	Mississippi R.	Fulton	257
Louisiana	Driskill Mountain	Bienville	535	New Orleans	Orleans	−8
Maine	Mount Katahdin	Piscataquis	5,268	Atlantic Ocean		Sea level
Maryland	Hoye Crest	Garrett	3,360	Atlantic Ocean		Sea level
Massachusetts	Mount Greylock	Berkshire	3,491	Atlantic Ocean		Sea level
Michigan	Mount Arvon	Baraga	1,979	Lake Erie		571
Minnesota	Eagle Mountain	Cook	2,301	Lake Superior		601
Mississippi	Woodall Mountain	Tishomingo	806	Gulf of Mexico		Sea level
Missouri	Taum Sauk Mountain	Iron	1,772	St. Francis R.	Dunklin	230
Montana	Granite Peak	Park	12,799	Kootenai R.	Lincoln	1,800
Nebraska	Panorama Point	Kimball	5,424	Missouri R.	Richardson	840
Nevada	Boundary Peak	Esmeralda	13,147	Colorado R.	Clark	479
New Hampshire	Mount Washington	Coos	6,288	Atlantic Ocean		Sea level
New Jersey	High Point	Sussex	1,803	Atlantic Ocean		Sea level
New Mexico	Wheeler Peak	Taos	13,161	Red Bluff Res.	Eddy	2,842
New York	Mount Marcy	Essex	5,344	Atlantic Ocean		Sea level
North Carolina	Mount Mitchell	Yancey	6,684	Atlantic Ocean		Sea level
North Dakota	White Butte	Slope	3,506	Red R. of the North	Pembina	750
Ohio	Campbell Hill	Logan	1,550	Ohio R.	Hamilton	455
Oklahoma	Black Mesa	Cimarron	4,973	Little R.	McCurtain	289
Oregon	Mount Hood	Clackamas-Hood R.	11,239	Pacific Ocean		Sea level
Pennsylvania	Mount Davis	Somerset	3,213	Delaware R.	Delaware	Sea level
Puerto Rico	Cerro de Punta	Ponce District	4,390	Atlantic Ocean		Sea level
Rhode Island	Jerimoth Hill	Providence	812	Atlantic Ocean		Sea level
South Carolina	Sassafras Mountain	Pickens	3,560	Atlantic Ocean		Sea level
South Dakota	Harney Peak	Pennington	7,242	Big Stone Lake	Roberts	966
Tennessee	Clingmans Dome	Sevier	6,643	Mississippi R.	Shelby	178
Texas	Guadalupe Peak	Culberson	8,749	Gulf of Mexico		Sea level
Utah	Kings Peak	Duchesne	13,528	Beaver Dam Wash	Washington	2,000
Vermont	Mount Mansfield	Chittenden	4,393	Lake Champlain		95
Virginia	Mount Rogers	Grayson-Smyth	5,729	Atlantic Ocean		Sea level
Virgin Islands	Crown Mountain	St. Thomas Island	1,556	Atlantic Ocean		Sea level
Washington	Mount Rainier	Pierce	14,411	Pacific Ocean		Sea level
West Virginia	Spruce Knob	Pendleton	4,863	Potomac R.	Jefferson	240
Wisconsin	Timms Hill	Price	1,951	Lake Michigan		579
Wyoming	Gannett Peak	Fremont	13,804	Belle Fourche R.	Crook	3,099

U.S. Coastline by States

Source: National Oceanic and Atmospheric Administration, U.S. Dept. of Commerce
(in statute miles)

	Coastline[1]	Shoreline[2]		Coastline[1]	Shoreline[2]
ATLANTIC COAST	2,069	28,673	**GULF COAST**	1,631	17,141
Connecticut	0	618	Alabama	53	607
Delaware	28	381	Florida	770	5,095
Florida	580	3,331	Louisiana	397	7,721
Georgia	100	2,344	Mississippi	44	359
Maine	228	3,478	Texas	367	3,359
Maryland	31	3,190			
Massachusetts	192	1,519	**PACIFIC COAST**	7,623	40,298
New Hampshire	13	131	Alaska	5,580	31,383
New Jersey	130	1,792	California	840	3,427
New York	127	1,850	Hawaii	750	1,052
North Carolina	301	3,375	Oregon	296	1,410
Pennsylvania	0	89	Washington	157	3,026
Rhode Island	40	384			
South Carolina	187	2,876	**ARCTIC COAST**	1,060	2,521
Virginia	112	3,315	**UNITED STATES**	12,383	88,633

(1) Figures are lengths of general outline of seacoast. Measurements were made with a unit measure of 30 minutes of latitude on charts as near the scale of 1:1,200,000 as possible. Coastline of sounds and bays is included to a point where they narrow to width of unit measure, and includes the distance across at such point. (2) Figures obtained in 1939-40 with a recording instrument on the largest-scale charts and maps then available. Shoreline of outer coast, offshore islands, sounds, bays, rivers, and creeks is included to the head of tidewater or to a point where tidal waters narrow to a width of 100 ft.

States: Capitals, Key Dates, Geographic Data

The 13 colonies that declared independence from Great Britain and fought the War of Independence (American Revolution) became the 13 original states. They were (in the order in which they ratified the Constitution): Delaware, Pennsylvania, New Jersey, Georgia, Connecticut, Massachusetts, Maryland, South Carolina, New Hampshire, Virginia, New York, North Carolina, and Rhode Island.

State	Settled[1]	Capital	Entered Union Date	Order	Long (approx. mean)	Wide	Land	Water	Total	Rank in area[2]
AL	1702	Montgomery	Dec. 14, 1819	22	330	190	50,744	1,675	52,419	30
AK	1784	Juneau	Jan. 3, 1959	49	1,480[3]	810	571,951	91,316	663,267	1
AZ	1776	Phoenix	Feb. 14, 1912	48	400	310	113,635	364	113,998	6
AR	1686	Little Rock	June 15, 1836	25	260	240	52,068	1,110	53,179	29
CA	1769	Sacramento	Sept. 9, 1850	31	770	250	155,959	7,736	163,696	3
CO	1858	Denver	Aug. 1, 1876	38	380	280	103,718	376	104,094	8
CT	1634	Hartford	Jan. 9, 1788	5	110	70	4,845	699	5,543	48
DE	1638	Dover	Dec. 7, 1787	1	100	30	1,954	536	2,489	49
DC	NA	NA	NA	NA	NA	NA	61	7	68	51
FL	1565	Tallahassee	Mar. 3, 1845	27	500	160	53,927	11,828	65,755	22
GA	1733	Atlanta	Jan. 2, 1788	4	300	230	57,906	1,519	59,425	24
HI	1820	Honolulu	Aug. 21, 1959	50	NA	NA	6,423	4,508	10,931	43
ID	1842	Boise	July 3, 1890	43	570	300	82,747	823	83,570	14
IL	1720	Springfield	Dec. 3, 1818	21	390	210	55,584	2,331	57,914	25
IN	1733	Indianapolis	Dec. 11, 1816	19	270	140	35,867	551	36,418	38
IA	1788	Des Moines	Dec. 28, 1846	29	310	200	55,869	402	56,272	26
KS	1727	Topeka	Jan. 29, 1861	34	400	210	81,815	462	82,277	15
KY	1774	Frankfort	June 1, 1792	15	380	140	39,728	681	40,409	37
LA	1699	Baton Rouge	Apr. 30, 1812	18	380	130	43,562	8,278	51,840	31
ME	1624	Augusta	Mar. 15, 1820	23	320	190	30,862	4,523	35,385	39
MD	1634	Annapolis	Apr. 28, 1788	7	250	90	9,774	2,633	12,407	42
MA	1620	Boston	Feb. 6, 1788	6	190	50	7,840	2,715	10,555	44
MI	1668	Lansing	Jan. 26, 1837	26	490	240	56,804	39,912	96,716	11
MN	1805	St. Paul	May 11, 1858	32	400	250	79,610	7,329	86,939	12
MS	1699	Jackson	Dec. 10, 1817	20	340	170	46,907	1,523	48,430	32
MO	1735	Jefferson City	Aug. 10, 1821	24	300	240	68,886	818	69,704	21
MT	1809	Helena	Nov. 8, 1889	41	630	280	145,552	1,490	147,042	4
NE	1823	Lincoln	Mar. 1, 1867	37	430	210	76,872	481	77,354	16
NV	1849	Carson City	Oct. 31, 1864	36	490	320	109,826	735	110,561	7
NH	1623	Concord	June 21, 1788	9	190	70	8,968	382	9,350	46
NJ	1660	Trenton	Dec. 18, 1787	3	150	70	7,417	1,304	8,721	47
NM	1610	Santa Fe	Jan. 6, 1912	47	370	343	121,356	234	121,589	5
NY	1614	Albany	July 26, 1788	11	330	283	47,214	7,342	54,556	27
NC	1660	Raleigh	Nov. 21, 1789	12	500	150	48,711	5,108	53,819	28
ND	1812	Bismarck	Nov. 2, 1889	39	340	211	68,976	1,724	70,700	19
OH	1788	Columbus	Mar. 1, 1803	17	220	220	40,948	3,877	44,825	34
OK	1889	Oklahoma City	Nov. 16, 1907	46	400	220	68,667	1,231	69,898	20
OR	1811	Salem	Feb. 14, 1859	33	360	261	95,997	2,384	98,381	9
PA	1682	Harrisburg	Dec. 12, 1787	2	283	160	44,817	1,239	46,055	33
RI	1636	Providence	May 29, 1790	13	40	30	1,045	500	1,545	50
SC	1670	Columbia	May 23, 1788	8	260	200	30,109	911	32,020	40
SD	1859	Pierre	Nov. 2, 1889	40	380	210	75,885	1,232	77,116	17
TN	1769	Nashville	June 1, 1796	16	440	120	41,217	926	42,143	36
TX	1682	Austin	Dec. 29, 1845	28	790	660	261,797	6,784	268,581	2
UT	1847	Salt Lake City	Jan. 4, 1896	45	350	270	82,144	2,755	84,899	13
VT	1724	Montpelier	Mar. 4, 1791	14	160	80	9,250	365	9,614	45
VA	1607	Richmond	June 25, 1788	10	430	200	39,594	3,180	42,774	35
WA	1811	Olympia	Nov. 11, 1889	42	360	240	66,544	4,756	71,300	18
WV	1727	Charleston	June 20, 1863	35	240	130	24,078	152	24,230	41
WI	1766	Madison	May 29, 1848	30	310	260	54,310	11,188	65,498	23
WY	1834	Cheyenne	July 10, 1890	44	360	280	97,100	713	97,814	10

Note: Land and water areas may not add to totals because of rounding. NA = Not applicable. (1) First permanent settlement by Europeans. (2) Rank is based on total area as shown. (3) Aleutian Islands and Alexander Archipelago not included.

The Continental Divide of the U.S.

The Continental Divide of the U.S., also known as the Great Divide, is located at the watershed created by the mountain ranges, or tablelands, of the Rocky Mountains. This watershed separates the waters that drain easterly into the Atlantic Ocean and its marginal seas, such as the Gulf of Mexico, from those waters that drain westerly into the Pacific Ocean. The majority of easterly flowing water in the U.S. drains into the Gulf of Mexico before reaching the Atlantic Ocean. The majority of westerly flowing water, before reaching the Pacific Ocean, drains either through the Columbia River or through the Colorado River, which flows into the Gulf of California before reaching the Pacific Ocean.

The location and route of the Continental Divide across the U.S. can briefly be described as follows:

Beginning at the U.S.-Mexican boundary, near long. 108° 45′ W, the Divide, in a northerly direction, crosses New Mexico along the W edge of the Rio Grande drainage basin, entering Colorado near long. 106° 41′ W.

From there by a very irregular route north across Colorado along the W summits of the Rio Grande and of the Arkansas, the South Platte, and the North Platte river basins, and across Rocky Mountain National Park, entering Wyoming near long. 106° 52′ W.

From there in a northwesterly direction, forming the W rims of the North Platte, the Big Horn, and the Yellowstone river basins, crossing the SW portion of Yellowstone National Park.

From there in a westerly and then a northerly direction forming the common boundary of Idaho and Montana, to a point on said boundary near long. 114° 00′ W.

From there northeasterly and northwesterly through Montana and the Glacier National Park, entering Canada near long. 114° 04′ W.

Chronological List of Territories, With State Admissions to Union

Source: National Archives and Records Service

Name of territory	Date of act creating territory	When act took effect	Admission as state	Years as terr.
Northwest Territory[1]	July 13, 1787	No fixed date	Mar. 1, 1803[2]	16
Territory southwest of Ohio River	May 26, 1790	No fixed date	June 1, 1796[3]	6
Mississippi	Apr. 7, 1798	When president acted	Dec. 10, 1817	19
Indiana	May 7, 1800	July 4, 1800	Dec. 11, 1816	16
Orleans	Mar. 26, 1804	Oct. 1, 1804	Apr. 30, 1812[4]	7
Michigan	Jan. 11, 1805	June 30, 1805	Jan. 26, 1837	31
Louisiana-Missouri[5]	Mar. 3, 1805	July 4, 1805	Aug. 10, 1821	16
Illinois	Feb. 3, 1809	Mar. 1, 1809	Dec. 3, 1818	9
Alabama	Mar. 3, 1817	When MS became a state	Dec. 14, 1819	2
Arkansas	Mar. 2, 1819	July 4, 1819	June 15, 1836	17
Florida	Mar. 30, 1822	No fixed date	Mar. 3, 1845	23
Wisconsin	Apr. 20, 1836	July 3, 1836	May 29, 1848	12
Iowa	June 12, 1838	July 3, 1838	Dec. 28, 1846	8
Oregon	Aug. 14, 1848	Date of act	Feb. 14, 1859	10
Minnesota	Mar. 3, 1849	Date of act	May 11, 1858	9
New Mexico	Sept. 9, 1850	On president's proclamation	Jan. 6, 1912	61
Utah	Sept. 9, 1850	Date of act	Jan. 4, 1896	46
Washington	Mar. 2, 1853	Date of act	Nov. 11, 1889	36
Nebraska	May 30, 1854	Date of act	Mar. 1, 1867	12
Kansas	May 30, 1854	Date of act	Jan. 29, 1861	6
Colorado	Feb. 28, 1861	Date of act	Aug. 1, 1876	15
Nevada	Mar. 2, 1861	Date of act	Oct. 31, 1864	3
Dakota	Mar. 2, 1861	Date of act	Nov. 2, 1889	28
Arizona	Feb. 24, 1863	Date of act	Feb. 14, 1912	49
Idaho	Mar. 3, 1863	Date of act	July 3, 1890	27
Montana	May 26, 1864	Date of act	Nov. 8, 1889	25
Wyoming	July 25, 1868	When officers were qualified	July 10, 1890	22
Alaska[6]	May 17, 1884	No fixed date	Jan. 3, 1959	75
Oklahoma	May 2, 1890	Date of act	Nov. 16, 1907	17
Hawaii	Apr. 30, 1900	June 14, 1900	Aug. 21, 1959	59

(1) Included what is now Ohio, Indiana, Illinois, Michigan, E Minnesota, Wisconsin. (2) Ohio was the first state of NW territory admitted. (3) Admitted as the state of Tennessee. (4) Admitted as the state of Louisiana. (5) The act creating Missouri Territory (June 4, 1812) became effective Dec. 7, 1812. (6) Although the May 17, 1884, act actually constituted Alaska as a district, it was often referred to as a territory, and administered as such. The Territory of Alaska was formally organized by an act of Aug. 24, 1912.

Geographic Centers, U.S. and Each State

Source: U.S. Geological Survey, Dept. of the Interior

There is no generally accepted definition of geographic center and no uniform method for determining it. Following the U.S. Geological Survey, the geographic center of an area is defined here as the center of gravity of the surface, or that point on which the surface would balance if it were a plane of uniform thickness. All locations in the following list are approximate.

No marked point has been officially established by any government agency as the geographic center of the 50 states, the conterminous U.S. (48 states), or the North American continent. A group of private citizens erected a monument in Lebanon, KS, marking it as geographic center of the conterminous U.S., and a cairn erected in Rugby, ND, asserts that location as the center of the North American continent.

Geographic centers as reported by the U.S. Geological Survey are indicated below:

United States, including Alaska and Hawaii: W of Castle Rock, Butte County, SD; lat. 44° 58′ N, long. 103° 46′ W
Conterminous U.S. (48 states): Near Lebanon, Smith Co., Kansas; lat. 39° 50′ N, long. 98° 35′ W
North American continent: 6 mi W of Balta, Pierce County, North Dakota; lat. 48° 10′ N, long. 100° 10′ W
Alabama: Chilton, 12 mi SW of Clanton
Alaska: approx. 60 mi NW of Mt. McKinley; lat. 63° 50′ N, long. 152° W;
Arizona: Yavapai, 55 mi E-SE of Prescott
Arkansas: Pulaski, 12 mi NW of Little Rock
California: Madera, 38 mi E of Madera
Colorado: Park, 30 mi NW of Pikes Peak
Connecticut: Hartford, at East Berlin
Delaware: Kent, 11 mi S of Dover
District of Columbia: Near 4th and L Sts. NW
Florida: Hernando, 12 mi N-NW of Brooksville
Georgia: Twiggs, 18 mi SE of Macon
Hawaii: off Maui; lat. 20° 15′ N, long. 156° 20′ W
Idaho: Custer, SW of Challis
Illinois: Logan, 28 mi NE of Springfield
Indiana: Boone, 14 mi N-NW of Indianapolis
Iowa: Story, 5 mi NE of Ames
Kansas: Barton, 15 mi NE of Great Bend
Kentucky: Marion, 3 mi N-NW of Lebanon
Louisiana: Avoyelles, 3 mi SE of Marksville
Maine: Piscataquis, 18 mi N of Dover
Maryland: Prince George's, 4.5 mi NW of Davidsonville
Massachusetts: Worcester, N part of city
Michigan: Wexford, 5 mi N-NW of Cadillac
Minnesota: Crow Wing, 10 mi SW of Brainerd
Mississippi: Leake, 9 mi W-NW of Carthage
Missouri: Miller, 20 mi SW of Jefferson City
Montana: Fergus, 11 mi W of Lewistown
Nebraska: Custer, 10 mi NW of Broken Bow
Nevada: Lander, 26 mi SE of Austin
New Hampshire: Belknap, 3 mi E of Ashland
New Jersey: Mercer, 5 mi SE of Trenton
New Mexico: Torrance, 12 mi S-SW of Willard
New York: Madison, 12 mi S of Oneida and 26 mi SW of Utica
North Carolina: Chatham, 10 mi NW of Sanford
North Dakota: Sheridan, 5 mi SW of McClusky
Ohio: Delaware, 25 mi N-NE of Columbus
Oklahoma: Oklahoma, 8 mi N of Oklahoma City
Oregon: Crook, 25 mi S-SE of Prineville
Pennsylvania: Centre, 2.5 mi SW of Bellefonte
Rhode Island: Kent, 1 mi S-SW of Crompton
South Carolina: Richland, 13 mi SE of Columbia
South Dakota: Hughes, 8 mi NE of Pierre
Tennessee: Rutherford, 5 mi NE of Murfreesboro
Texas: McCulloch, 15 mi NE of Brady
Utah: Sanpete, 3 mi N of Manti
Vermont: Washington, 3 mi E of Roxbury
Virginia: Buckingham, 5 mi SW of Buckingham
Washington: Chelan, 10 mi W-SW of Wenatchee
West Virginia: Braxton, 4 mi E of Sutton
Wisconsin: Wood, 9 mi SE of Marshfield
Wyoming: Fremont, 58 mi E-NE of Lander

International Boundary Lines of the U.S.

The length of the N boundary of the conterminous U.S.—the U.S.-Canadian border, excluding Alaska—is 3,987 mi according to the U.S. Geological Survey, Dept. of the Interior. The length of the Alaskan-Canadian border is 1,538 mi. The U.S.-Mexican border, from the Gulf of Mexico to the Pacific Ocean, is about 1,933 mi (1963 boundary agreement).

Origins of the Names of U.S. States

Source: State officials, Smithsonian Institution, and Topographic Division, U.S. Geological Survey, Dept. of the Interior

Alabama: Indian for tribal town, later a tribe (Alabamas or Alibamons) of the Creek confederacy.

Alaska: Russian version of Aleutian (Eskimo) word, *alakshak*, for "peninsula," "great lands," or "land that is not an island."

Arizona: Spanish version of Pima Indian word for "little spring place," or Aztec *arizuma*, meaning "silver-bearing."

Arkansas: Algonquin name for the Quapaw Indians, meaning "south wind."

California: Bestowed by the Spanish conquistadors (possibly by Cortez). It was the name of an imaginary island, an earthly paradise, in *Las Serges de Esplandian*, a Spanish romance written by Montalvo in 1510. *Baja California* (Lower California, in Mexico) was first visited by Spanish in 1533. The present U.S. state was called *Alta* (Upper) *California*.

Colorado: From Spanish for "red," first applied to Colorado River.

Connecticut: From Mohican and other Algonquin words meaning "long river place."

Delaware: Named for Lord De La Warr, early governor of Virginia; first applied to river, then to Indian tribe (Lenni-Lenape), and the state.

District of Columbia: For Christopher Columbus, 1791.

Florida: Named by Ponce de León *Pascua Florida*, "Flowery Easter," on Easter Sunday, 1513.

Georgia: For King George II of England, by James Oglethorpe, colonial administrator, 1732.

Hawaii: Possibly derived from native word for homeland, *Hawaiki* or *Owhyhee*.

Idaho: Said to be a coined name with the invented meaning "gem of the mountains"; originally suggested for the Pikes Peak mining territory (Colorado), then applied to the new mining territory of the Pacific Northwest. Another theory suggests *Idaho* may be a Kiowa Apache term for the Comanche.

Illinois: French for *Illini* or "land of *Illini*," Algonquin word meaning "men" or "warriors."

Indiana: Means "land of the Indians."

Iowa: Indian word variously translated as "here I rest" or "beautiful land." Named for the Iowa R., which was named for the Iowa Indians.

Kansas: Sioux word for "south wind people."

Kentucky: Indian word that is variously translated as "dark and bloody ground," "meadowland," and "land of tomorrow."

Louisiana: Part of territory called Louisiana by Sieur de La Salle for French King Louis XIV.

Maine: From Maine, ancient French province. Also descriptive, referring to the mainland as distinct from the many coastal islands.

Maryland: For Queen Henrietta Maria, wife of Charles I of England.

Massachusetts: From Indian tribe whose name meant "at or about the Great Hill" in Blue Hills region south of Boston.

Michigan: From Chippewa words, *mici gama*, meaning "great water," after the lake of the same name.

Minnesota: From Dakota Sioux word meaning "cloudy water" or "sky-tinted water" of the Minnesota River.

Mississippi: Probably Chippewa; *mici zibi*, "great river" or "gathering-in of all the waters." Also: Algonquin word, *messipi*.

Missouri: An Algonquin Indian term meaning "river of the big canoes."

Montana: Latin or Spanish for "mountainous."

Nebraska: From Omaha or Otos Indian word meaning "broad water" or "flat river," describing the Platte River.

Nevada: Spanish, meaning "snow-clad."

New Hampshire: Named, 1629, by Capt. John Mason of Plymouth Council for his home county in England.

New Jersey: The Duke of York, 1664, gave a patent to John Berkeley and Sir George Carteret to be called Nova Caesaria, or New Jersey, after England's Isle of Jersey.

New Mexico: Spaniards in Mexico applied term to land north and west of Rio Grande in the 16th century.

New York: For Duke of York and Albany, who received patent to New Netherland from his brother Charles II and sent an expedition to capture it, 1664.

North Carolina: In 1619 Charles I gave a large patent to Sir Robert Heath to be called Province of Carolana, from *Carolus*, Latin name for Charles. A new patent was granted by Charles II to Earl of Clarendon and others. Divided into North and South Carolina, 1710.

North Dakota: *Dakota* is Sioux for "friend" or "ally."

Ohio: Iroquois word for "fine or good river."

Oklahoma: Choctaw word meaning "red man," proposed by Rev. Allen Wright, Choctaw-speaking Indian.

Oregon: Origin unknown. One theory holds that the name possibly derives from *wauregan*, meaning "beautiful," term used by Indians in New England.

Pennsylvania: William Penn, the Quaker who was made full proprietor of this area by King Charles II in 1681, suggested "Sylvania," or "woodland," for his tract. The king's government owed Penn's father, Admiral William Penn, 16,000 pounds, and the land was granted as partial settlement. Charles II added the "Penn" to Sylvania, against the desires of the modest proprietor, in honor of the admiral.

Puerto Rico: Spanish for "rich port."

Rhode Island: Exact origin is unknown. One theory notes that Giovanni de Verrazano recorded an island about the size of Rhodes in the Mediterranean in 1524, but others believe the state was named *Roode Eylandt* by Adriaen Block, Dutch explorer, because of its red clay.

South Carolina: See North Carolina.

South Dakota: See North Dakota.

Tennessee: *Tanasi* was the name of Cherokee villages on the Little Tennessee River. From 1784 to 1788 this was the State of Franklin, or Frankland.

Texas: Variant of word used by Caddo and other Indians meaning "friends" or "allies," and applied to them by the Spanish in eastern Texas. Also written *Texias, Tejas, Teysas*.

Utah: From a Navajo word meaning "upper," or "higher up," as applied to a Shoshone tribe called Ute. Spanish form is *Yutta*. The English is *Uta* or *Utah*. Proposed name *Deseret*, "land of honeybees," from Book of Mormon, was rejected by Congress.

Vermont: From French words *vert* (green) and *mont* (mountain). The Green Mountains were said to have been named by Samuel de Champlain. When the state was formed, 1777, Dr. Thomas Young suggested combining *vert* and *mont* into Vermont.

Virginia: Named by Sir Walter Raleigh, who fitted out the expedition of 1584, in honor of Queen Elizabeth, the Virgin Queen of England.

Washington: Named after George Washington. When the bill creating the Territory of Columbia was introduced in the 32nd Congress, the name was changed to Washington because of the existence of the District of Columbia.

West Virginia: So named when western counties of Virginia refused to secede from the U.S. in 1863.

Wisconsin: An Indian name, spelled *Ouisconsin* and *Mesconsing* by early chroniclers. Believed to mean "grassy place" in Chippewa. Congress made it *Wisconsin*.

Wyoming: From the Algonquin words for "large prairie place," "at the big plains," or "on the great plain."

AFGHANISTAN ALBANIA ALGERIA ANDORRA ANGOLA

ANTIGUA AND BARBUDA ARGENTINA ARMENIA AUSTRALIA AUSTRIA

AZERBAIJAN THE BAHAMAS BAHRAIN BANGLADESH BARBADOS

BELARUS BELGIUM BELIZE BENIN BHUTAN

BOLIVIA BOSNIA AND HERZEGOVINA BOTSWANA BRAZIL BRUNEI

BULGARIA BURKINA FASO BURUNDI CAMBODIA CAMEROON

CANADA CAPE VERDE CENTRAL AFRICAN REPUBLIC CHAD CHILE

CHINA COLOMBIA COMOROS CONGO, DEM. REP. OF THE CONGO REPUBLIC

COSTA RICA CÔTE D'IVOIRE CROATIA CUBA CYPRUS

CZECH REPUBLIC DENMARK DJIBOUTI DOMINICA DOMINICAN REPUBLIC

ECUADOR EGYPT EL SALVADOR EQUATORIAL GUINEA ERITREA

Note: Flag proportions have been standardized to fit page.

457

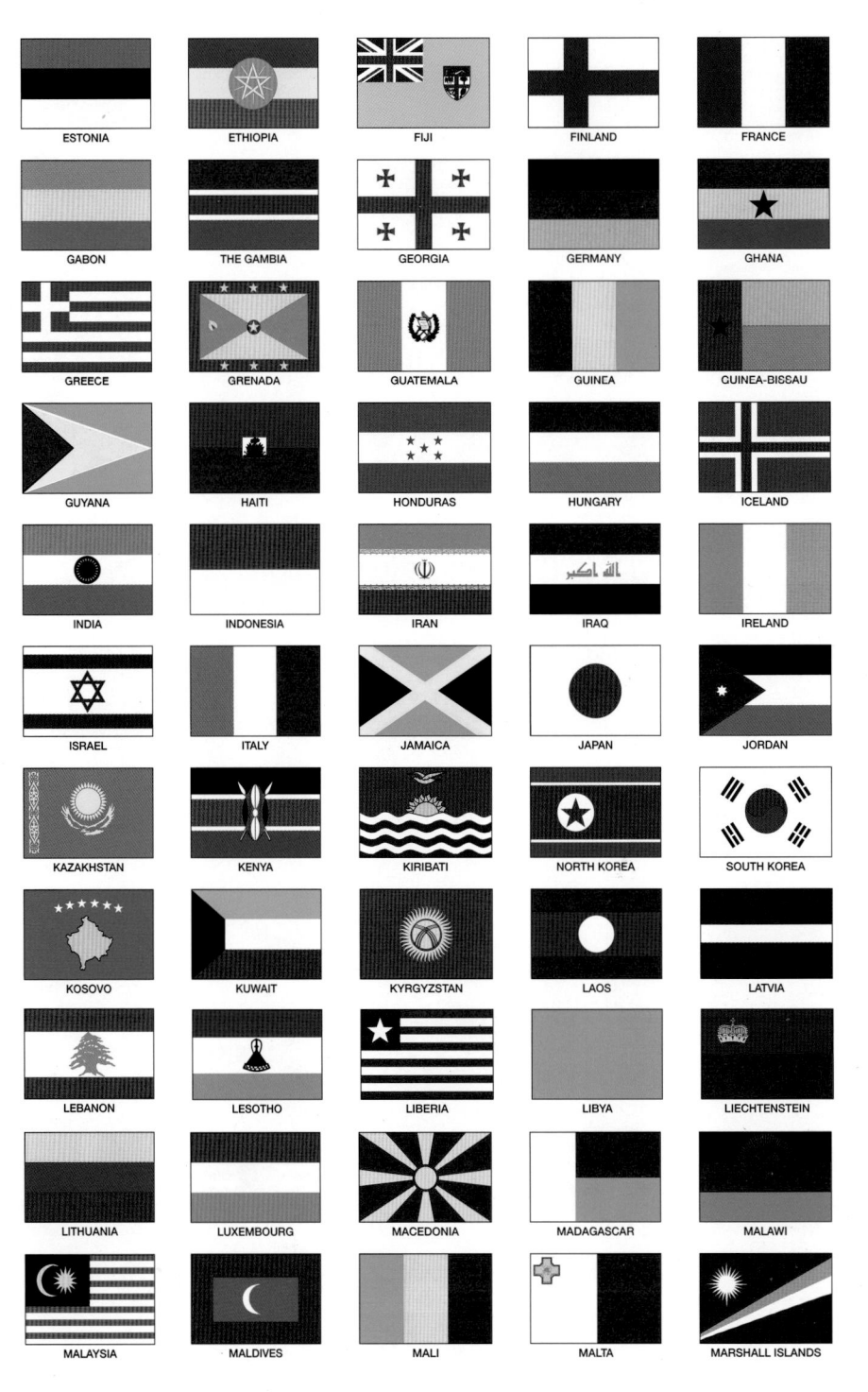

ESTONIA   ETHIOPIA   FIJI   FINLAND   FRANCE

GABON   THE GAMBIA   GEORGIA   GERMANY   GHANA

GREECE   GRENADA   GUATEMALA   GUINEA   GUINEA-BISSAU

GUYANA   HAITI   HONDURAS   HUNGARY   ICELAND

INDIA   INDONESIA   IRAN   IRAQ   IRELAND

ISRAEL   ITALY   JAMAICA   JAPAN   JORDAN

KAZAKHSTAN   KENYA   KIRIBATI   NORTH KOREA   SOUTH KOREA

KOSOVO   KUWAIT   KYRGYZSTAN   LAOS   LATVIA

LEBANON   LESOTHO   LIBERIA   LIBYA   LIECHTENSTEIN

LITHUANIA   LUXEMBOURG   MACEDONIA   MADAGASCAR   MALAWI

MALAYSIA   MALDIVES   MALI   MALTA   MARSHALL ISLANDS

Note: Flag proportions have been standardized to fit page.

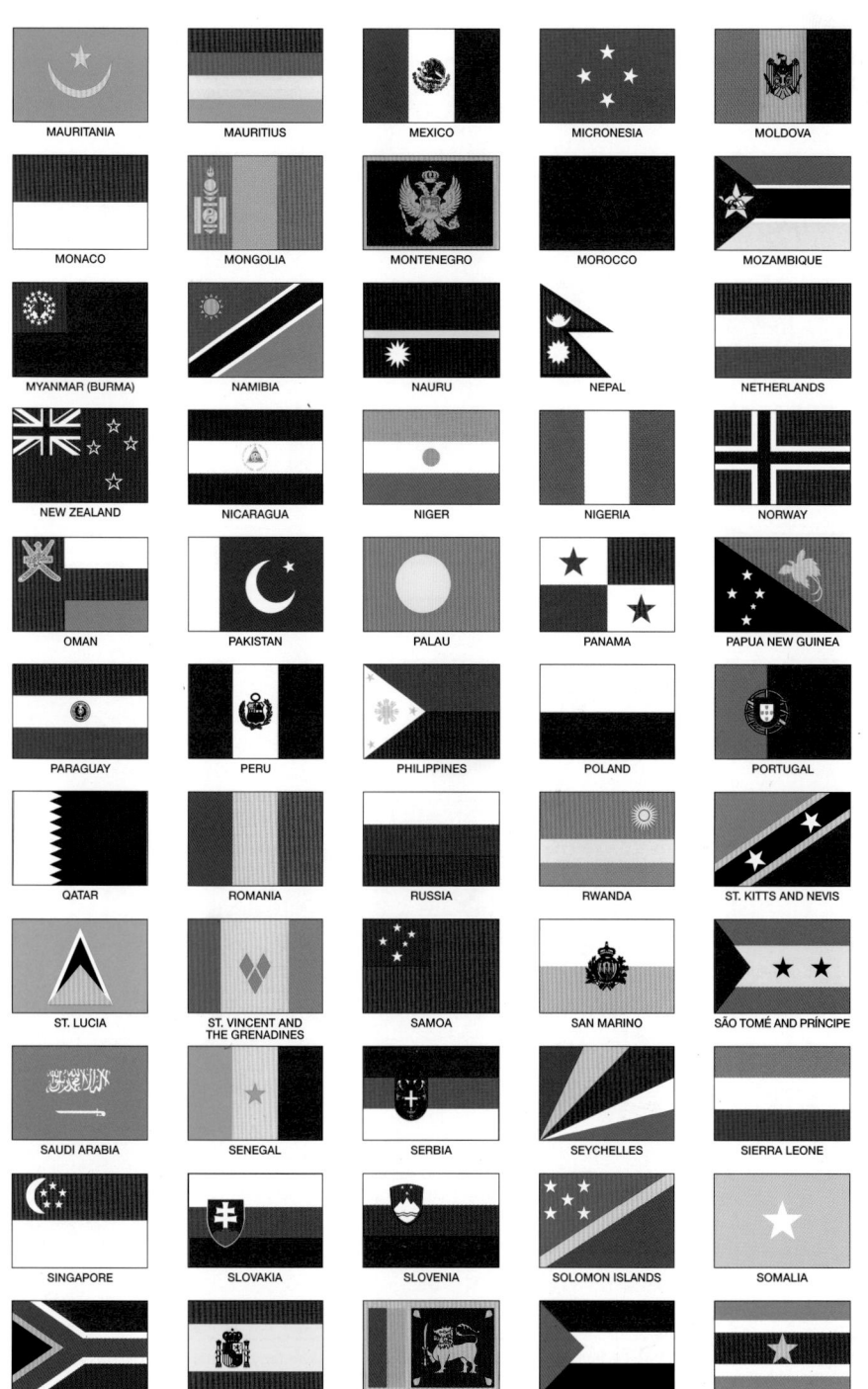

MAURITANIA   MAURITIUS   MEXICO   MICRONESIA   MOLDOVA

MONACO   MONGOLIA   MONTENEGRO   MOROCCO   MOZAMBIQUE

MYANMAR (BURMA)   NAMIBIA   NAURU   NEPAL   NETHERLANDS

NEW ZEALAND   NICARAGUA   NIGER   NIGERIA   NORWAY

OMAN   PAKISTAN   PALAU   PANAMA   PAPUA NEW GUINEA

PARAGUAY   PERU   PHILIPPINES   POLAND   PORTUGAL

QATAR   ROMANIA   RUSSIA   RWANDA   ST. KITTS AND NEVIS

ST. LUCIA   ST. VINCENT AND THE GRENADINES   SAMOA   SAN MARINO   SÃO TOMÉ AND PRÍNCIPE

SAUDI ARABIA   SENEGAL   SERBIA   SEYCHELLES   SIERRA LEONE

SINGAPORE   SLOVAKIA   SLOVENIA   SOLOMON ISLANDS   SOMALIA

SOUTH AFRICA   SPAIN   SRI LANKA   SUDAN   SURINAME

Note: Flag proportions have been standardized to fit page.

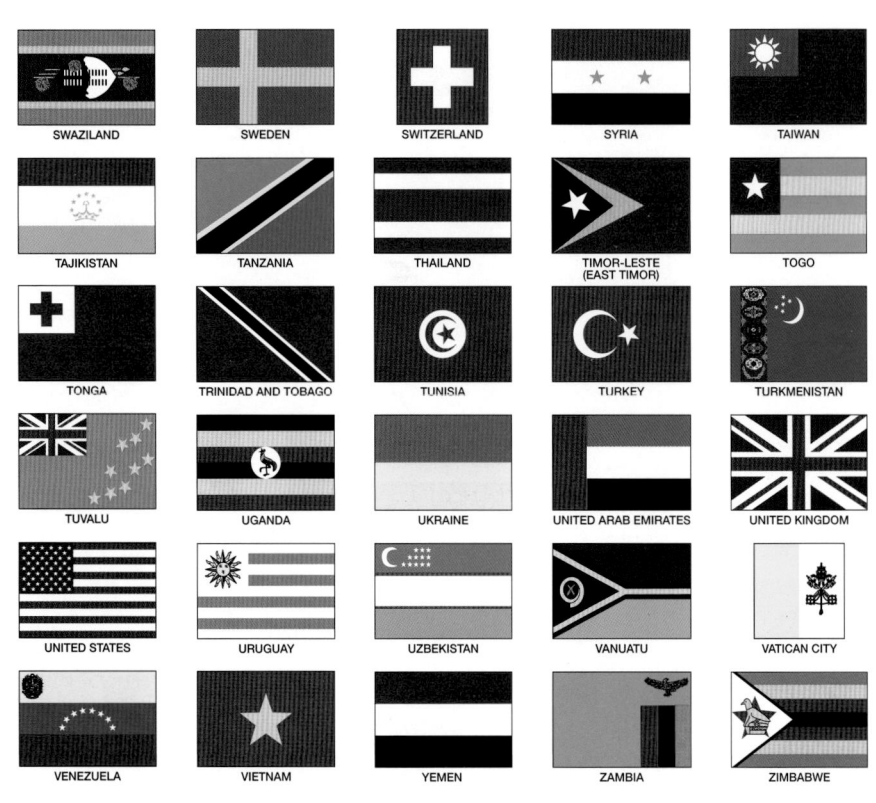

| SWAZILAND | SWEDEN | SWITZERLAND | SYRIA | TAIWAN |

| TAJIKISTAN | TANZANIA | THAILAND | TIMOR-LESTE (EAST TIMOR) | TOGO |

| TONGA | TRINIDAD AND TOBAGO | TUNISIA | TURKEY | TURKMENISTAN |

| TUVALU | UGANDA | UKRAINE | UNITED ARAB EMIRATES | UNITED KINGDOM |

| UNITED STATES | URUGUAY | UZBEKISTAN | VANUATU | VATICAN CITY |

| VENEZUELA | VIETNAM | YEMEN | ZAMBIA | ZIMBABWE |

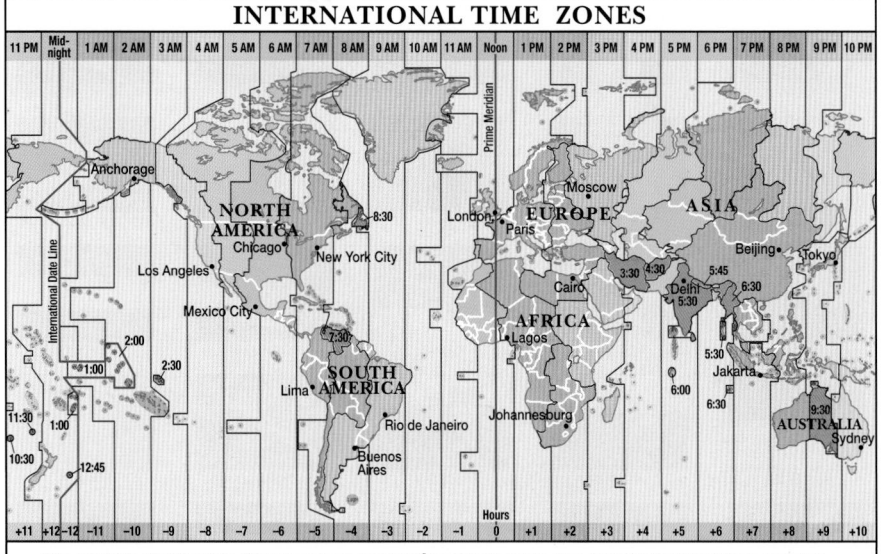

INTERNATIONAL TIME ZONES

The world is divided into 24 time zones, each 15° longitude wide. The longitudinal meridian passing through Greenwich, England, is the starting point, and is called the *prime meridian*. The 12th zone is divided by the 180th meridian (International Date Line). When the line is crossed going west, the date is advanced one day; when crossed going east, the date becomes a day earlier.

© GeoNova

Note: Flag proportions have been standardized to fit page.

460

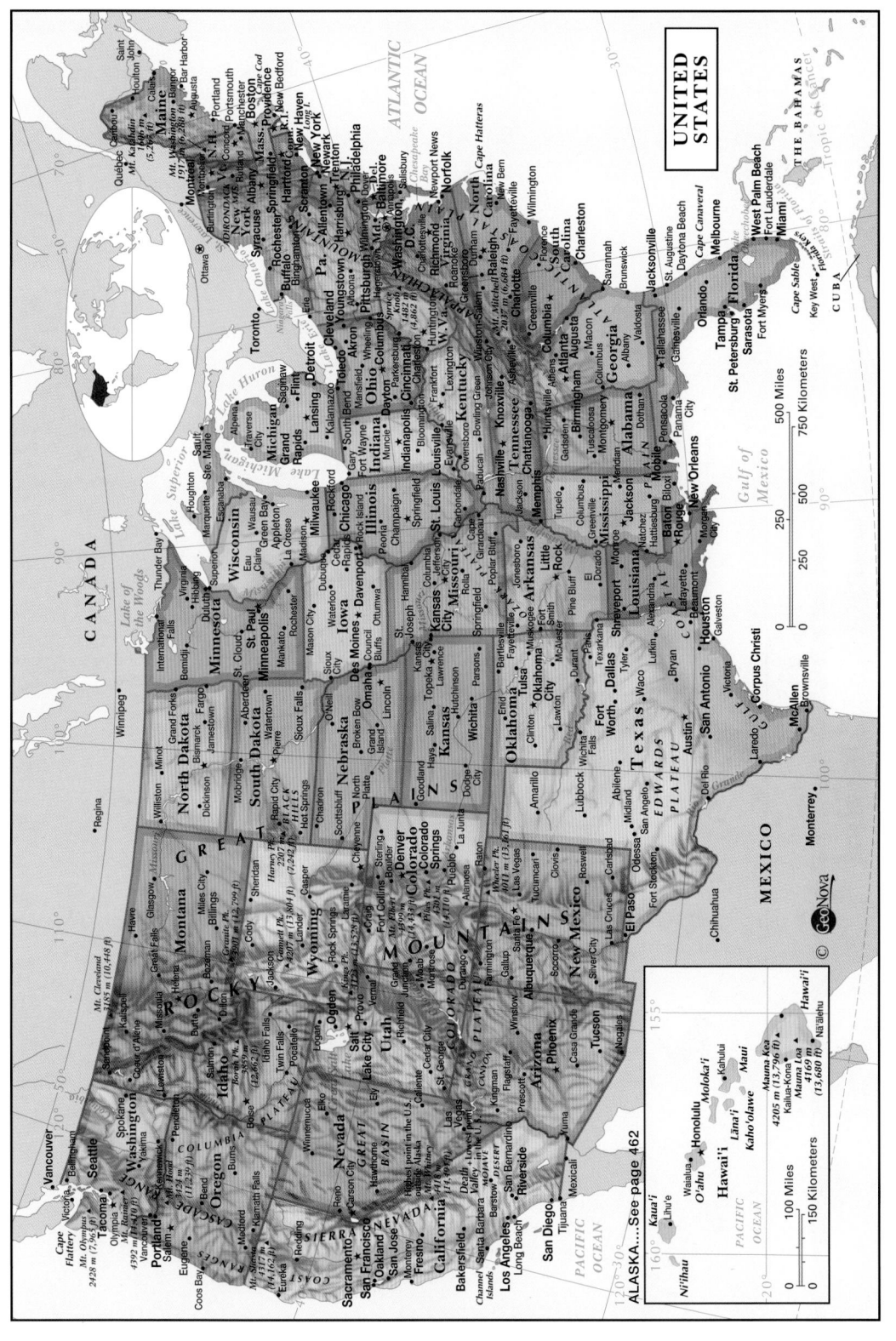

© GeoNova

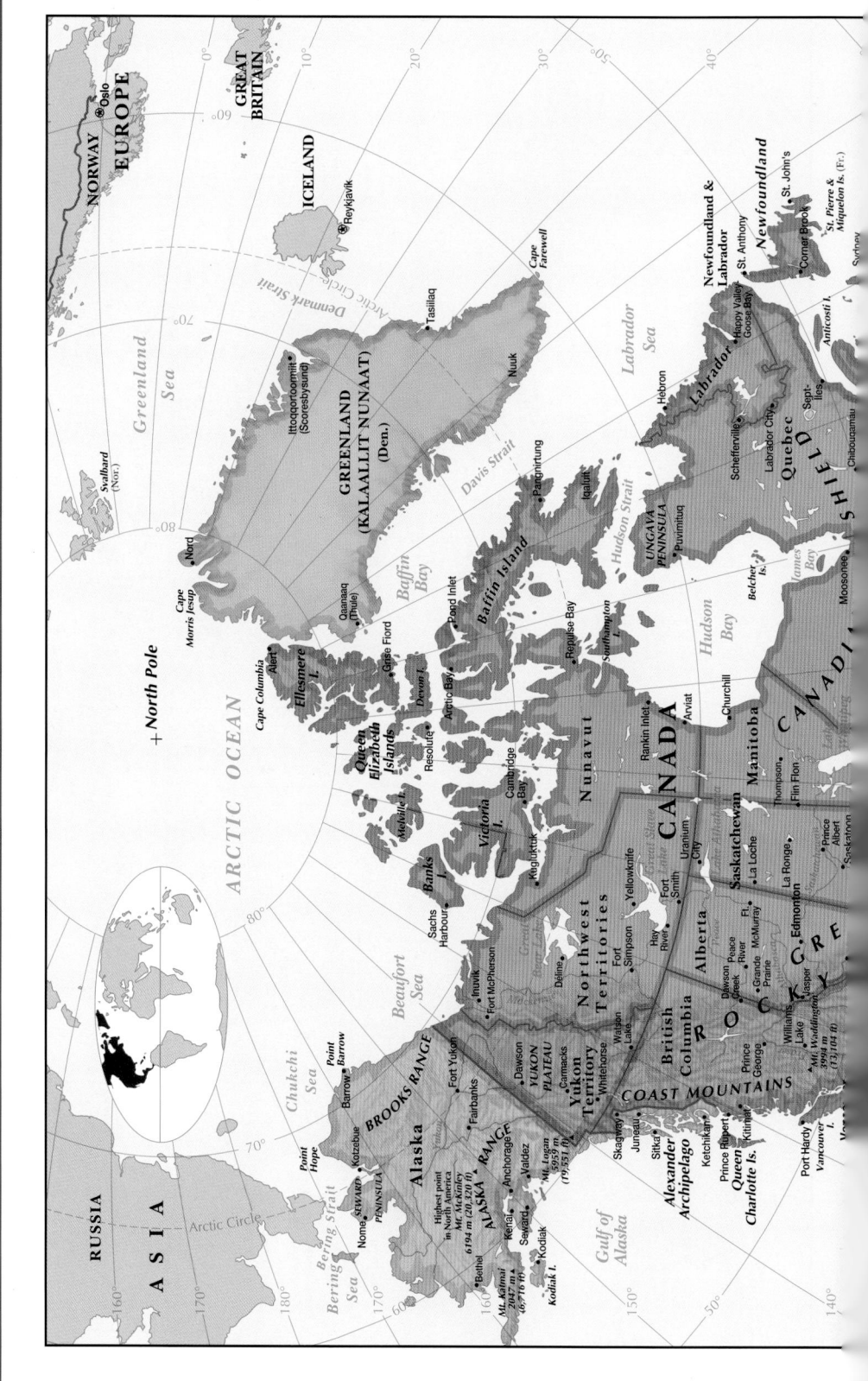

RUSSIA

ASIA

NORWAY ⊛Oslo
EUROPE

GREAT BRITAIN

ICELAND
⊛Reykjavík

Svalbard (Nor.)

Greenland Sea

Denmark Strait

Arctic Circle

Cape Farewell

Tasiilaq

GREENLAND (KALAALLIT NUNAAT) (Den.)

Ittoqqortoormiit (Scoresbysund)

Nuuk

Qaanaaq (Thule)

Nord

Cape Morris Jesup

North Pole

Cape Columbia

Alert

Ellesmere I.

ARCTIC OCEAN

Baffin Bay

Davis Strait

Gase Fjord

Dundas

Arctic Bay

Pangnirtung

Iqaluit

Baffin Island

Pond Inlet

Newfoundland & Labrador
St. Anthony

Newfoundland
Corner Brook
St. John's

St. Pierre & Miquelon Is. (Fr.)
Sydney

Anticosti I.

Labrador Sea

Labrador

Hebron

Happy Valley-Goose Bay

Schefferville

Chibougamau

Labrador City
Sept-Îles

Quebec

CANADIAN SHIELD

Moosonee

James Bay

Belcher Is.

Puvirnituq

UNGAVA PENINSULA

Repulse Bay

Southampton I.

Hudson Strait

Hudson Bay

Churchill

Arviat

Rankin Inlet

Queen Elizabeth Islands

Melville I.

Resolute

Cambridge Bay

Victoria I.

Banks I.

Sachs Harbour

Beaufort Sea

Point Barrow

Barrow

Chukchi Sea

Point Hope

Bering Strait

SEWARD PENINSULA

Kotzebue

Nome

Bethel

Mt. Katmai 2047 m (6,716 ft)

Kodiak I.

Kodiak

Kenai

Seward

Valdez

Anchorage

Highest point in North America Mt. McKinley 6,194 m (20,320 ft)

Mt. Logan 5959 m (19,551 ft)

ALASKA RANGE

BROOKS RANGE

Fairbanks

Fort Yukon

Alaska

Gulf of Alaska

Sitka

Juneau

Skagway

Alexander Archipelago

Ketchikan

Prince Rupert

Kitimat

Queen Charlotte Is.

COAST MOUNTAINS

Prince George

Port Hardy

Vancouver I.

Williams Lake

Mt. Waddington 3994 m (13,104 ft)

British Columbia

ROCKY

Dawson

YUKON PLATEAU

Carmacks

Whitehorse

Yukon Territory

Watson Lake

Inuvik

Fort McPherson

Fort Simpson

Déline

Hay River

Northwest Territories

Fort Smith

Yellowknife

Nunavut

CANADA

Uranium City

Fort Nelson

Jasper

Grande Prairie

Peace River

Dawson Creek

Prince George

Grande Cache

McMurray

Edmonton

Alberta

La Loche

La Ronge

Saskatchewan

Prince Albert

Saskatoon

Flin Flon

Thompson

Manitoba

Kugluktuk

Arctic Circle

90°

80°

70°

60°

50°

40°

30°

20°

10°

0°

140°

150°

160°

170°

180°

70°

80°

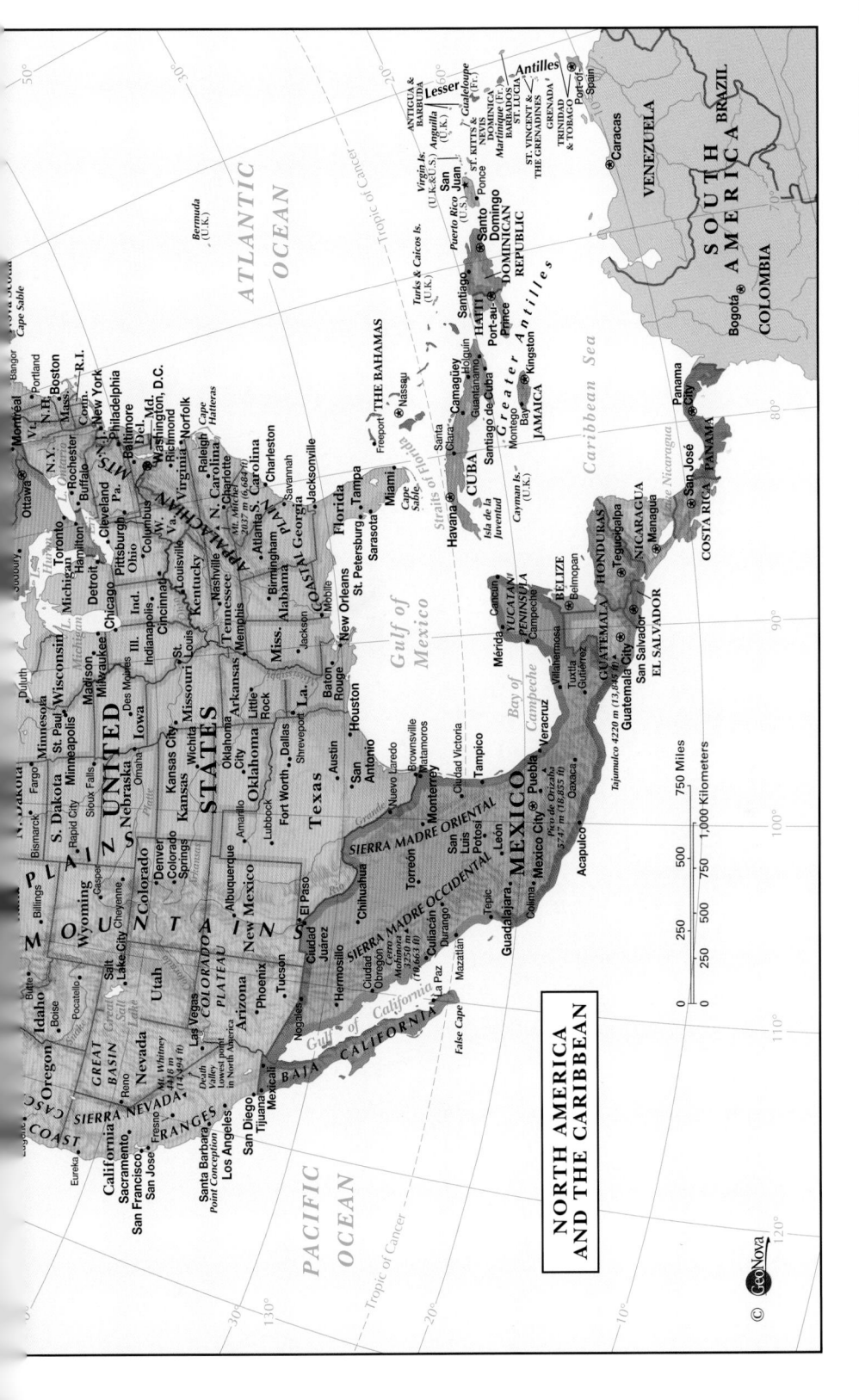

NORTH AMERICA AND THE CARIBBEAN

© GeoNova

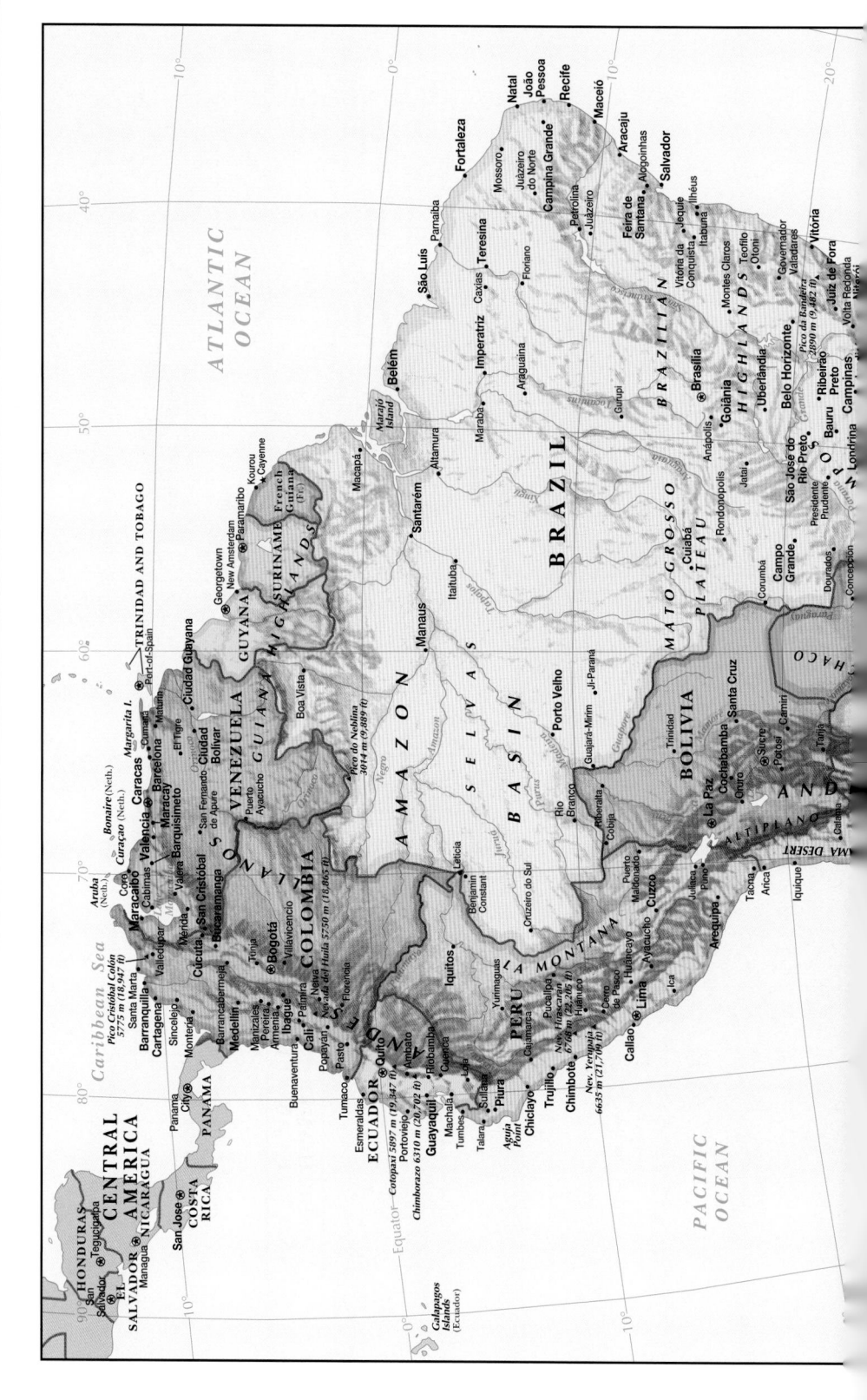

464

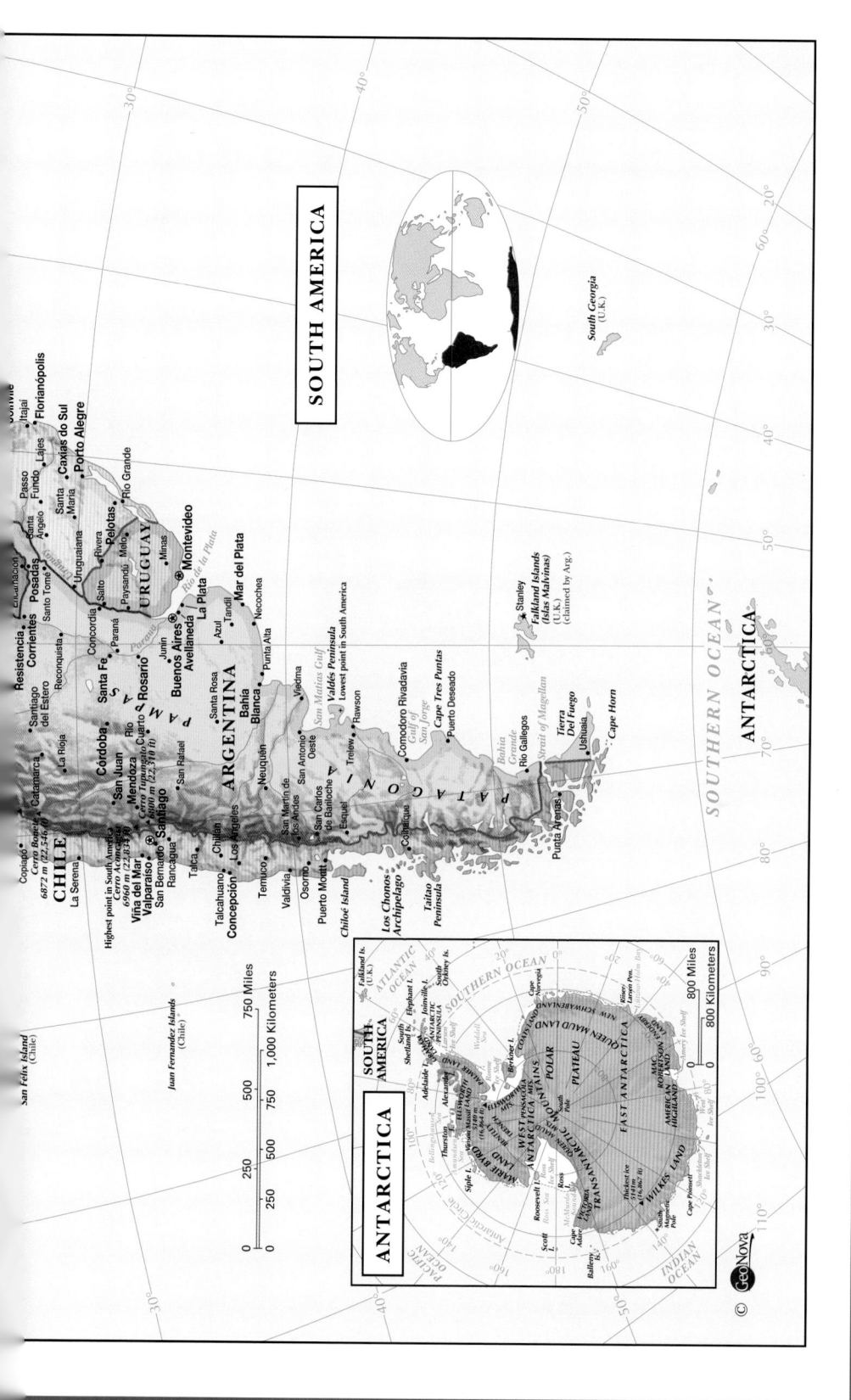

SOUTH AMERICA

ANTARCTICA

EUROPE

GREENLAND
(KALAALLIT NUNAAT)
(Denmark)

Ísafjördur

Akureyri
Keflavík
ICELAND
Reykjavík
Seydhisfjördhur

Arctic Circle

Bodø

Norwegian Sea

Namsos

Torshavn *Faroe*
Islands
(Den.)

Trondheim
Molde
Ålesund

Øst

Shetland
Islands
(U.K.)

Bergen

NORWAY **SWED**

Sund

Orkney
Islands
Thurso

Haugesund
Stavanger
Skien
Drammen
Kristiansand

Oslo
Karlstad
Upp
Örebro
Stock

Hebrides

Inverness

Scotland
Aberdeen
Dundee

ATLANTIC
OCEAN

Londonderry
Northern
Ireland
Belfast

Glasgow
Ayr
Edinburgh

North

Göteborg

Vänern

Norrköping

Vättern

Jönköp

Newcastle

Sea

Ålborg
Jutland
Halmstad
Växjö

Galway
IRELAND
Limerick
Waterford
Cork

UNITED
KINGDOM
Dublin
Liverpool
Manchester
Birmingham

Leeds
Kingston upon Hull
Sheffield

Esbjerg
Århus
DENMARK Odense

Helsingborg
Malmö

Borr
(De

Kiel
Lübeck
Rostock

Wales Swansea
Cardiff
Bristol

Coventry
England
London

Norwich

Groningen
Amsterdam

Hamburg

NORTH

Szcze

Plymouth
Land's End

Portsmouth

The Hague
Dover

Bremen
Hannover
Bielefeld

Madgeburg

Berlin

Oder

PO

Brest

Channel Is.
(U.K.)
Le Havre
Caen
Rouen

Brussels
Lille
BELGIUM
LUXEMBOURG
Luxembourg

Antwerp
Liège
Bonn

Essen
Cologne
Wiesbaden

GERMANY

Kassel
Erfurt
Dresden
Chemnitz

Leipzig

Liberec

Rennes

Paris
Le Mans
Orleans
Nancy
Strasbourg

Saarbrucken
Frankfurt
Mannheim

Nürnberg
Pizen
Prague

CZECH R

Nantes

Loire
Tours

Dijon

Augsburg
Munich
Regensburg

Linz

Bay
of
Biscay

FRANCE
Limoges

Basel
Bern

Zürich
Salzburg
Innsbruck

Vienna

AUSTRIA

A Coruña

Gijón

Santander
Bilbao
Vitoria-Gastéiz
Pamplona

Clermont-Ferrand
Saint-Etienne

Lyon
Geneva
Mt. Blanc
4807 m (15,771 ft)

SWITZERLAND
LIECHTENSTEIN

Matterhorn
4505 m (14,690 ft)

Graz

Klagenfurt

Udine
Trieste

SLOVENIA

Vigo
Leon

Bordeaux

Grenoble

Bergamo
Milan
Verona

Ljubljana

CR

Porto
Braga

Donostia-
San Sebastián
Toulouse

Duero

Valladolid
IBERIAN
Salamanca

Montpellier
Avignon

Torino

Parma

Venice
Rijeka

DINA

Coimbra

PYRENEES
Pico de Aneto
3404 m
(11,169 ft)

Marseille
Toulon

Nice

Genoa

APENNINES

Bologna

Ancona

SAN
MARINO

Split

Adriatic

PORTUGAL
Lisbon
Setubal
Badajoz

Tagus

Zaragoza
ANDORRA

Madrid
Toledo

MONACO

Pisa
Florence

Perugia

SPAIN

Barcelona
Tarragona
Castellon de la Plana

Corsica
(Fr.)
Ajaccio

Elba

VATICAN CITY

Rome

ITALY

Fog

Cape
St. Vincent

PENINSULA
Cordoba

Valencia

Majorca
Palma de
Mallorca

Minorca

Balearic Is.
(Sp.)

Sassari

Sardinia
(It.)

Naples
Vesuvius
1277 m (4,190 ft)

Salerno

Cádiz
Seville
Málaga
Granada

Alicante
Murcia
Cartagena

Almería

Strait of
Gibraltar
GIBRALTAR
(U.K.)

Cagliari

Tyrrhenian

Sea

Palermo
Etna
3369 m (11,053 ft)

Messina

Rabat

Algiers

Mediterranean

Tunis

Sicily
Catani

Reg
Cal

AFRICA

0   250   500 Miles

0   250   500   750 Kilometers

TUNISIA

MALTA Valletta

MOROCCO

ALGERIA

Barents Sea

North Cape

Novaya Zemlya

mmerfest
mso
Kiruna

Vardø

Murmansk

Nar'yan-Mar

Pechora

Ukhta

ASIA

RUSSIA

Ivalo
LAPLAND

Apatity

KOLA PENINSULA

Rovaniemi

White Sea

Arkhangel'sk

Syktyvkar

Bereznïki

URAL

Oulu

Belomorsk

Dvina

Kotlas

Perm'

Skelleftea

FINLAND

Lake Onega

Petrozavodsk

Kirov

Izhevsk

Ufa

MOUNTAINS

Vaasa
Kuopio

Lake Ladoga

Cherepovets

Vologda

Yoshkar Ola

Naberezhnye Chelny

Sterlitamak

Jyvaskyla
ori

Tampere
Lahti
Kotka
Turku

Helsinki

St. Petersburg

Rybinsk
Yaroslavl'

Kostroma

Nizhniy Novgorod

Kazan

Cheboksary

Kama

Gulf of Finland

Tallinn

Velikiy Novgorod

Ivanovo

Ul'yanovsk

Orsk

land Is.
in.)

ESTONIA

Tartu

Tver'

Vladimir

Saransk

Tol'yatti

Samara

Orenburg

Volga

Pskov

Riga

Moscow

Kaluga

Ryazan'

Penza

Ural

LATVIA

Daugavpils

Smolensk

Tula

Liepaja
Klaipeda

LITHUANIA
Kaunas
Vilnius

Vitsyebsk

Orsha

Lipetsk

Tambov

Saratov

KAZAKHSTAN

RUSSIA
Kaliningrad

PLAIN

Minsk

Mahilyow

Bryansk

ROPEAN

Hrodna

Babruysk

Voronezh

Bialystok

BELARUS

Homyel'

Kursk

Warsaw
Brest
Pinsk

Chernihiv

Sumy

Belgorod

Kyiv
(Kiev)

Kharkiv

Volgograd

Lublin
Kielce
ice

Zhytomyr

Cherkasy

Poltava

L'viv

UKRAINE

Vinnytsia

Dnipropetrovs'k

Luhans'k

Horlivka

Don

Astrakhan'

ków

Donets'k

ARTHIAN MOUNTAINS
Kosice
Miskolc
est

Chernivtsi

MOLDOVA

Kryvyy Rih

Mariupol'

Rostov-na-Donu

Prut

Zaporizhzhia

Caspian

Debrecen
Oradea
cskemet
eged

Iasi

Chisinau

Mykolaiv

Sea of Azov

Krasnodar

Stavropol'

Grozny

Makhachkala

Cluj-Napoca

Odesa

Nal'chik

Vladikavkaz

Sea

ROMANIA
Timisoara
Sad

Galati
Brasov
Ploiesti

CRIMEA PENINSULA

Sevastopol'

Simferopol'

Mt. Elbrus 5642 m (18,510 ft) Highest point in Europe

CAUCASUS MTS.

Baku

Bucharest

Constanta

GEORGIA

Tbilisi

AZERBAIJAN

RBIA
Belgrade
Craiova

Ruse

Danube

Black Sea

ARMENIA

Yerevan

AZER.

Nis

Varna

Pleven

BULGARIA

Sofia

Stara Zagora

Burgas

Plovdiv

Pristina
Skopje
ca
BALKAN

MACEDONIA
PENINSULA
ANIA
Kavala

Istanbul

Olympus 2917 m (9,570 ft)

Larisa
Ioannina

Volos

Aegean Sea

Ankara

TURKEY

IRAN

ASIA

GREECE
Patras
Corinth
Peloponnese
alamata
Sparta

Thessaloniki

Athens

Cyclades

Dardanelles

Rhodes (Gr.)

SYRIA

Baghdad

IRAQ

Sea of Crete
Crete
Hania (Gr.)
Iraklion

Nicosia

CYPRUS

LEBANON

Beirut

Damascus

© GeoNova

467

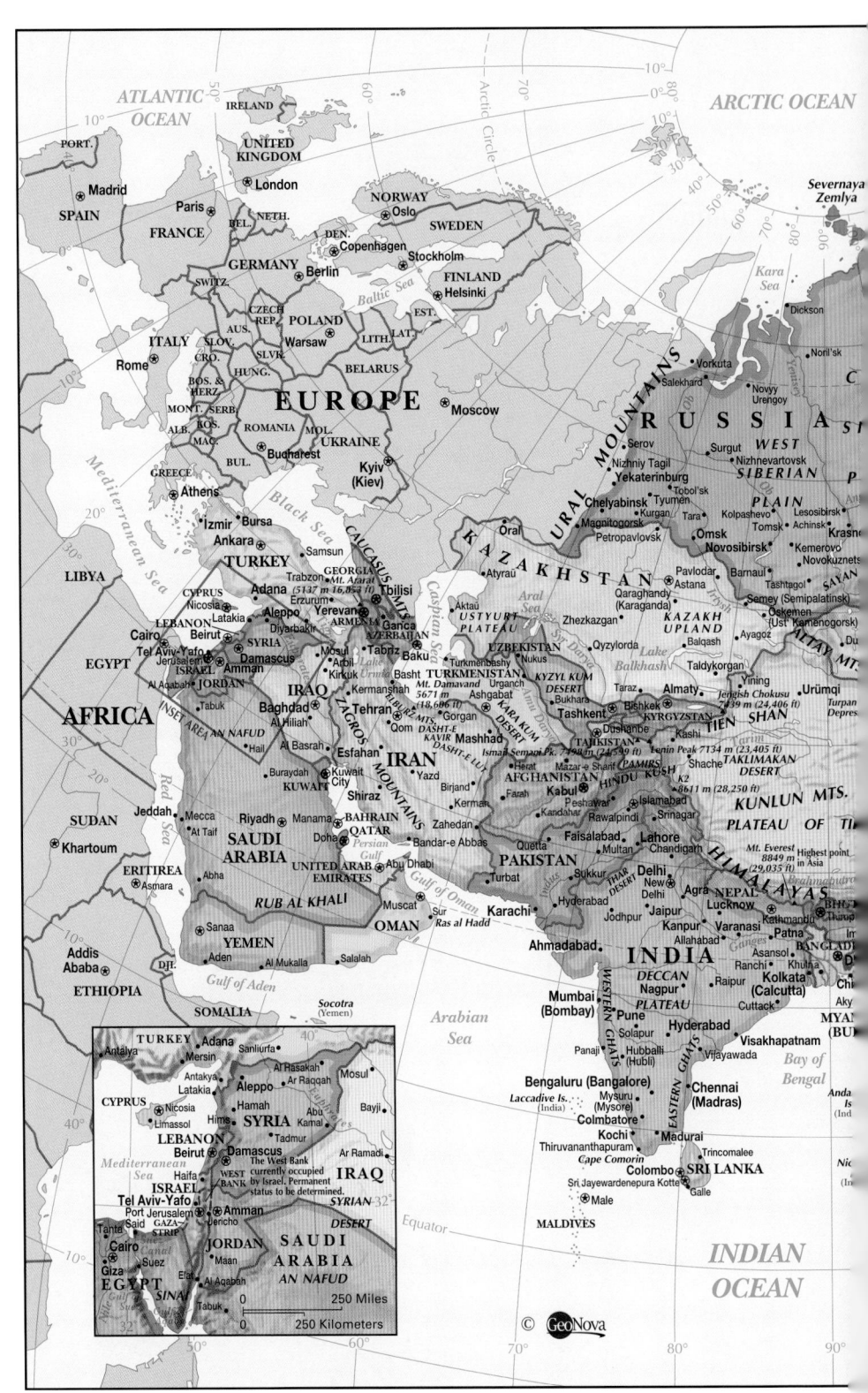

ATLANTIC OCEAN

ARCTIC OCEAN

IRELAND

UNITED KINGDOM
⊛ London

PORT.
⊛ Madrid
SPAIN
Paris ⊛
FRANCE
BEL.
NETH.

NORWAY
⊛ Oslo
DEN. Copenhagen
SWEDEN

GERMANY ⊛ Berlin
SWITZ.
CZECH REP.
AUS.
ITALY SLOV.
CRO.
Rome ●
BOS. & HERZ.
MONT. SERB.
ALB. BOS.
MAC.
GREECE
⊛ Athens
● Izmir ● Bursa
Ankara ⊛
TURKEY
Samsun

POLAND
⊛ Warsaw
SLVK.
HUNG.
ROMANIA MOL.
⊛ Bucharest
BUL.

FINLAND
⊛ Helsinki
Stockholm ⊛
EST.
LITH. LAT.
BELARUS

EUROPE
⊛ Moscow
UKRAINE
⊛ Kyiv (Kiev)

Baltic Sea

Black Sea

Severnaya Zemlya

Kara Sea
● Dickson
● Noril'sk

● Vorkuta
● Salekhard
Novyy Urengoy ●
RUSSIA
SI

URAL MOUNTAINS
● Serov
WEST SIBERIAN
Nizhniy Tagil ● Surgut ● Nizhnevartovsk
Yekaterinburg
Chelyabinsk ● Tyumen ● Tobol'sk
Kurgan ● Tara ● Kolpashevo ● Lesosibirsk
Magnitogorsk ● Omsk ● Tomsk ● Achinsk ● Kras
Petropavlovsk ● Novosibirsk ● Kemerovo
PLAIN
Pavlodar ● Barnaul ● Novokuznets
Astana ● Tashtagol ● SAYAN
Semey (Semipalatinsk)
Öskemen (Ust' Kamenogorsk)
● Ayagoz ● Du
ALTAY MTS.

Mediterranean Sea
LIBYA

CYPRUS
Nicosia ●
Latakia ●
Aleppo ●
CAUCASUS MTS.
Trabzon GEORGIA
Mt. Ararat
(5137 m 16,853 ft)
Erzurum ● ARMENIA
Tbilisi ⊛
Yerevan ⊛
AZERBAIJAN
Ganca ●
Baku ●

Caspian Sea
KAZAKHSTAN
Oral ●
Atyrau ●
Aktaü ●
USTYURT PLATEAU
Aral Sea
KAZAKH UPLAND
Qaraghandy (Karaganda)
Zhezkazgan ●
Balqash ●
Qyzylorda ●
Taldyqorgan ●
Lake Balkhash
Yining ●
Almaty ●
Jenish Chokusu
7439 m (24,406 ft)
Urümqi ●
Turpan Depres

LEBANON
Beirut ⊛ Diyarbakir ●
Tel Aviv-Yafo ● SYRIA
Damascus ⊛
Adana ●
Mosul ●
Arbil ●
Kirkuk ●

Sir Darya
UZBEKISTAN
Nukus ●
Turkmenbashy ●
Urganch ●
KYZYL KUM DESERT
Bukhara ●
Tashkent ●
KYRGYZSTAN
Bishkek ⊛
Kashi ●
TIEN SHAN
TAKLIMAKAN DESERT
Shache ●

Cairo ⊛
EGYPT
AFRICA

Jerusalem ⊛
Amman ⊛
Al 'Aqabah ●
Tabuk ●
ISRAEL JORDAN
IRAQ
Baghdad ⊛
Al Hillah ●
● Hail
Al Basrah ●
Buraydah ●
KUWAIT
Kuwait City ⊛
Jeddah ●
Mecca ⊛
At Taif ●
Riyadh ⊛ Manama ⊛
SAUDI ARABIA
Abha ●
Doha ⊛
QATAR
BAHRAIN
UNITED ARAB EMIRATES
Abu Dhabi ⊛
Bandar-e Abbas ●

ZAGROS MOUNTAINS
Kermanshah ●
Mt. Damavand
5671 m (18,606 ft)
Ashgabat ⊛
Tehran ⊛
Qom ●
Esfahan ●
IRAN
KAVIR
DASHT-E KAVIR
DASHT-E LUT
Yazd ●
Shiraz ●
Kerman ●
Zahedan ●

TURKMENISTAN
KARA KUM DESERT
Dushanbe ⊛
TAJIKISTAN
PAMIRS
Lenin Peak 7134 m (23,405 ft)
Ismail Samani Pk. 7495 m (24,549 ft)
K2 8611 m (28,250 ft)
HINDU KUSH
Mazar-e Sharif ●
Herat ●
AFGHANISTAN
Kabul ⊛
Kandahar ●
Farah ●
Peshawar ●
Islamabad ⊛
Rawalpindi ●
Srinagar ●
Quetta ●
KUNLUN MTS.
PLATEAU OF TI

Mt. Everest
8849 m (29,035 ft)
Highest point in Asia

SUDAN
⊛ Khartoum
ERITREA
Asmara ⊛

Red Sea

RUB AL KHALI

Gulf of Oman
Muscat ⊛
OMAN
Ras al Hadd

Persian Gulf

Faisalabad ●
Lahore ●
Multan ●
Chandigarh ●
PAKISTAN
Turbat ●
Sukkur ●
Karachi ●
Hyderabad ●
THAR DESERT
Indus
Delhi ⊛
New Delhi
Jodhpur ●
Jaipur ●
Agra ●
NEPAL
Kathmandu ⊛
Lucknow ●
Kanpur ●
Allahabad ●
Varanasi ●
Patna ●
HIMALAYAS
PLATEAU OF TI
Ganges
BANGLADESH
D
BHU
Thimp

Jeddah ●

Addis Ababa ⊛
ETHIOPIA
● Sanaa ⊛
YEMEN
Aden ●
Al Mukalla ●
Salalah ●
DJI.

Gulf of Aden
SOMALIA

Socotra (Yemen)

Arabian Sea

Ahmadabad ●
Mumbai (Bombay) ●
INDIA
DECCAN PLATEAU
Nagpur ●
Pune ●
Solapur ●
Hyderabad ●
Raipur ●
Ranchi ●
Asansol ●
Kolkata (Calcutta) ●
Cuttack ●
Visakhapatnam ●
Aky
WESTERN GHATS
Vijayawada ●
Panaji ●
Bengaluru (Bangalore) ●
Laccadive Is. (India)
Mysuru (Mysore) ●
Chennai (Madras) ●
Bay of Bengal
Anda Is (Ind
Colbatore ●
Kochi ●
Madurai ●
Thiruvananthapuram ●
Cape Comorin
EASTERN GHATS
Trincomalee ●
SRI LANKA
Colombo ⊛
Sri Jayewardenepura Kotte
Galle ●
⊛ Male
MALDIVES
MYAN (BU
Nic (Ind

INDIAN OCEAN

Equator

© GeoNova

Inset map (lower left):

TURKEY
Antalya ●
Adana ●
Sanliurfa ●
Mersin ●
Al Hasakah ●
Antakya ●
Ar Raqqah ●
Mosul ●
CYPRUS
Latakia ●
Aleppo ●
Nicosia ⊛
Limassol ●
Hims ●
Hamah ●
SYRIA
Abu Kamal ●
Bayji ●
LEBANON
Beirut ⊛
Tadmur ●
Damascus ⊛
The West Bank currently occupied by Israel. Permanent status to be determined.
Haifa ●
ISRAEL
Port ● Jerusalem ⊛
Said
Tel Aviv-Yafo ●
WEST BANK
Jericho ●
GAZA STRIP
Ar Ramadi ●
IRAQ
SYRIAN DESERT
Mediterranean Sea
Amman ⊛
JORDAN
SAUDI ARABIA
AN NAFUD
Tanta ●
Cairo ⊛
Giza ●
Suez ●
EGYPT
SINAI
Efat ●
Al 'Aqabah ●
Ma'an ●
Tabuk ●

0   250 Miles
0   250 Kilometers

NORTH AMERICA

ASIA

Chukchi
Sea
Bering Strait
Wrangel I.
Providentya
Anadyr
East
Siberian
Sea
New Siberian
Islands
Cherskiy
Bering
Sea

Laptev
Sea
KOLYMA MOUNTAINS
Tiksi
Zyryanka
Shiveluch
3168 m (10,771 ft)
Klyuchevskaya
4750 m (15,584 ft)
Karymsky
1536 m (5,039 ft)
Petropavlovsk-Kamchatskiy

VERKHOYANSK RA.
Verkhoyansk
Susuman
Magadan
KAMCHATKA PEN.

AL
AN
AU
Vilyuysk
Yakutsk
Lensk
Okhotsk
Sea of
Okhotsk
Alaid
2339 m
(7,674 ft)
Aldan

Ust'-Kut
Bodaybo
Berkakit
Aldan
STANOVOY
RANGE
Tynda
Komsomol'sk-
na-Amure
Okha
Sakhalin
Sarycheva
1496 m
(4,908 ft)
Kuril
Is.
(Russia)

Lake
Baykal
Chita
YABLONOVIY RANGE
Svobodnyy
Blagoveshchensk
Khabarovsk
Yuzhno-
Sakhalinsk
Tiatia
1819 m
(5,968 ft)

Ulan-
Ude
Hailar
GREATER KHINGAN RANGE
Yichun
Qiqihar
Harbin
Ussuriysk
Vladivostok
Hokkaido
Sapporo
Hakodate

Darhan
Choybalsan
Ulaanbaatar
Changchun
Jilin
Jixi
Chongjin
Akita
Sendai
Sea of Japan
(East Sea)
Niigata
Honshu
Tokyo

NGOLIA
MONGOLIAN
PLATEAU
Shenyang
Anshan
Fushun
N. KOREA
Hamhung
Pyongyang
JAPAN
Kyoto
Nagoya
Yokohama
Mt. Fuji 3776 m (12,388 ft)

GOBI DESERT
Hohhot
Beijing
Baotou
Dalian
Tianjin
Incheon
Seoul
Daegu
Busan
S. KOREA
Hiroshima
Osaka
Kobe
Shikoku
Kitakyushu
Fukuoka

Yinchuan
Shijiazhuang
Taiyuan
Jinan
Qingdao
Nagasaki
Kagoshima
Kyushu

Xining
Lanzhou
Handan
Luoyang
Xuzhou
Zhengzhou
Nanjing
Yellow
Sea
Ryukyu Is.
(Japan)

Xi'an
Huainan
Hefei
Shanghai
Hangzhou

HINA
Wuhan
Jingdezhen
East China Sea
Okinawa
Naha
PACIFIC
OCEAN

Chengdu
Chongqing
Zigong
Nanchang
Changsha
Shaoyang
Ganzhou
Wenzhou
Fuzhou

Northern
Mariana
Islands
(U.S.)

unming
Gulyang
Guilin
Liuzhou
Xiamen
Taipei
TAIWAN
Kaohsiung

Nanning
Macao
Guangzhou
Hong Kong

honssen
Haiphong
Zhanjiang
Haikou
Laoag
Luzon
Philippine
Sea

LAOS
Hanoi
Louangphabang
Vientiane
Vinh
Hainan
(China)
Baguio
PHILIPPINES
Quezon City
Manila
Naga

Taw
hiang Mai
gon THAILAND
ngoon)
Nakhon
Ratchasima
Hue
Da Nang
South
China
Sea
Mindoro
Panay
Iloilo
Samar
Tacloban
Leyte
Cebu
Butuan

awlamyine
ngkok
CAMBODIA
Batdambang
VIETNAM
Nha Trang
Puerto
Princesa
Negros
Mindanao
Davao

Phnom Penh
Kompong Som
Can Tho
Ho Chi Minh City
Palawan
Sulu
Sea
Zamboanga

Gulf of
Thailand
Kota Kinabalu
Bandar Seri Begawan
BRUNEI
Sandakan
Tarakan
Celebes
Sea
Temate
Halmahera
Manado
Jayapura
New
Guinea
PAPUA
NEW GUINEA
Port Moresby

aman
ea
Hat Yai
George
Town
MALAYSIA
Natuna Is.
Kuching
Gorontalo
Ceram
Ambon
Moluccas

Aceh
Kuala
Kelang
Lumpur
Pontianak
Samainda
Celebes
Banda
Sea
Arafura
Sea

Sibolga
Singapore
SINGAPORE
Balikpapan
Palopo
Baubau

Pekanbaru
Padang
Jambi
Borneo
Sampit
Banjarmasin
Parepare
Makassar

Sumatra
Palembang
Java Sea
INDONESIA
TIMOR LESTE
AUSTRALIA

Bengkulu
Bandar Lampung
Jakarta
Semarang
Surabaya
Malang
Bali
Ende
Dili
Timor
Sumba
Timor
Sea

Bandung
Yogyakarta
Java
Mataram
Kupang

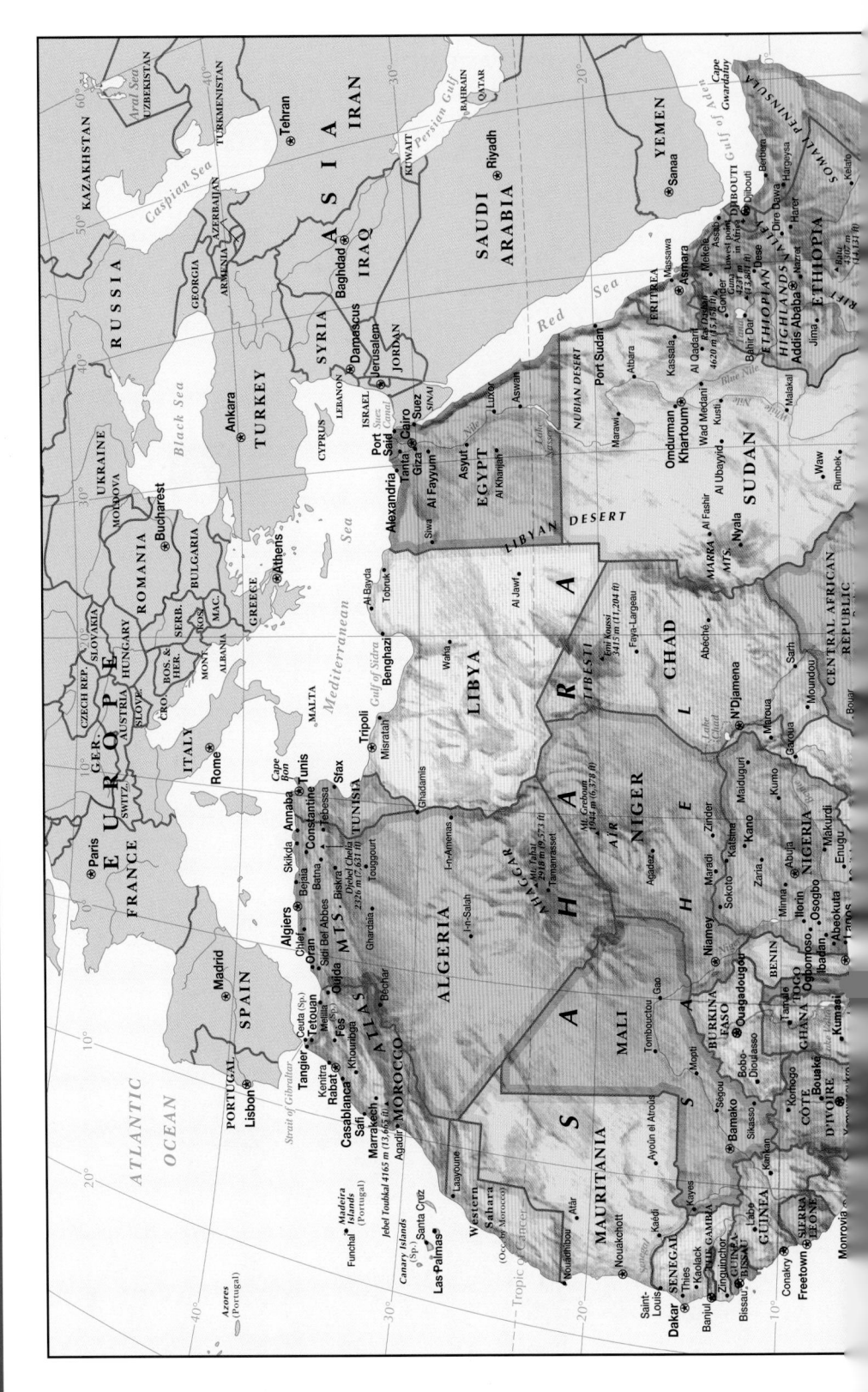

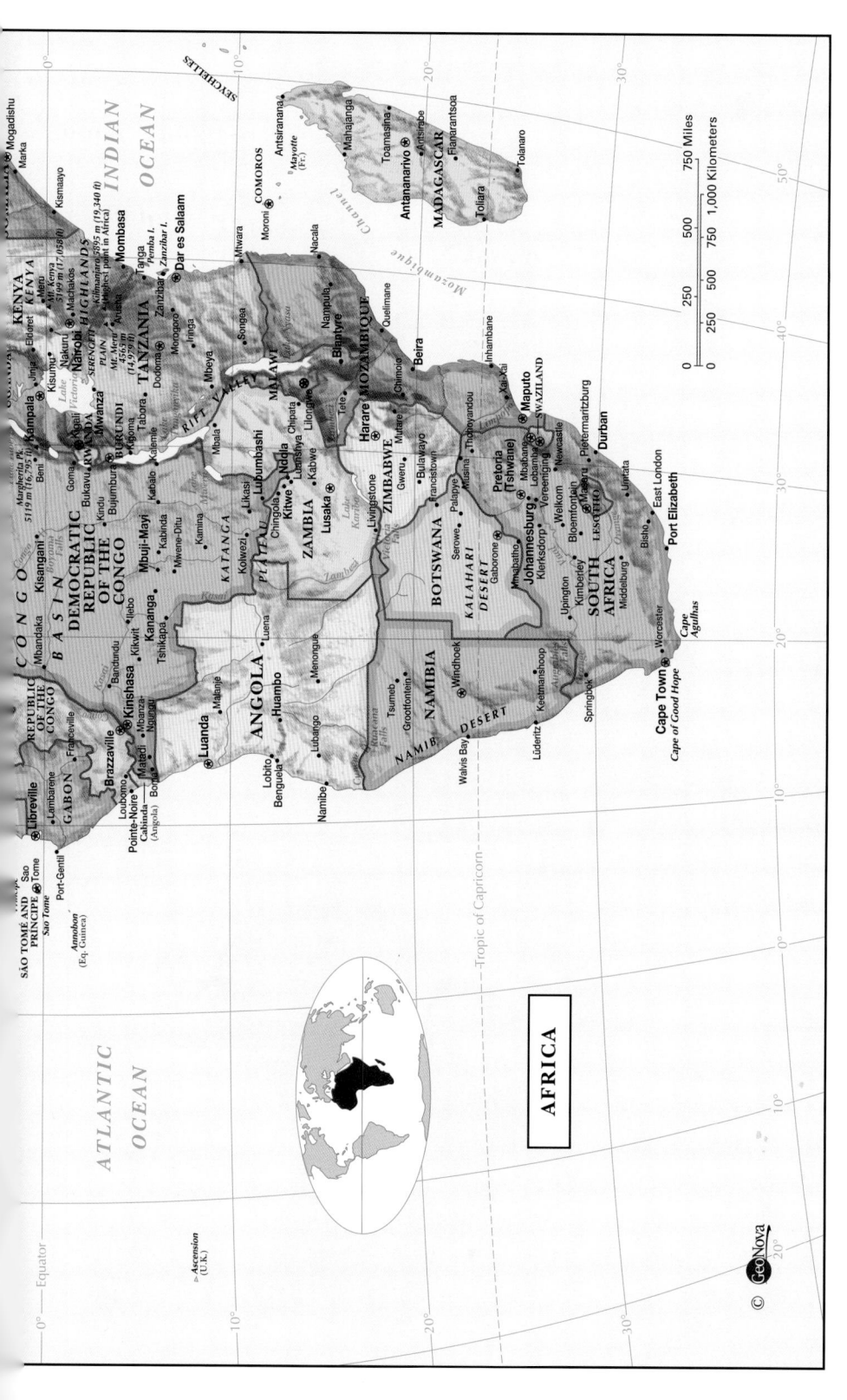

AFRICA

ATLANTIC OCEAN

INDIAN OCEAN

SEYCHELLES

COMOROS

MADAGASCAR

Mozambique Channel

Equator

Tropic of Capricorn

KENYA
SOMALIA
UGANDA
RWANDA
BURUNDI
TANZANIA
DEMOCRATIC REPUBLIC OF THE CONGO
REPUBLIC OF THE CONGO
GABON
SÃO TOMÉ AND PRINCIPE
ANGOLA
ZAMBIA
MALAWI
MOZAMBIQUE
ZIMBABWE
NAMIBIA
BOTSWANA
SOUTH AFRICA
LESOTHO
SWAZILAND

CONGO BASIN
RIFT VALLEY
SERENGETI PLAIN
KATANGA
PLATEAU
KALAHARI DESERT
NAMIB DESERT

Mogadishu
Marka
Kismaayo

Mt. Kenya 5199 m (17,058 ft)
Mt. Kilimanjaro 5895 m (19,340 ft) (highest point in Africa)
Mt. Meru 4565 m (14,979 ft)

Margherita Pk. 5119 m (16,795 ft)

Antsiranana
Mahajanga
Toamasina
Antananarivo
Fianarantsoa
Antsirabe
Toliara
Tolanaro
Nacala
Mayotte (Fr.)
Moroni

Nairobi
Kisumu
Eldoret
Nakuru
Machakos
Meru
Mombasa
Arusha
Tanga
Pemba I.
Zanzibar I.
Zanzibar
Dar es Salaam
Dodoma
Morogoro
Mbeya
Iringa
Songea
Mtwara
Nampula
Quelimane
Blantyre
Beira
Chimoio
Inhambane
Xai-Xai

Mwanza
Tabora
Kigoma
Kampala
Jinja
Bukavu
Bujumbura
Goma
Beni
Kindu
Uvira
Kalemie
Kabalo

Kisangani
Mbandaka
Kananga
Mbuji-Mayi
Ilebo
Likasi
Kolwezi
Lubumbashi
Ndola
Kitwe
Chingola
Kabwe
Kapiri Mposhi
Lusaka
Livingstone
Chipata
Lilongwe
Tete
Harare
Mutare
Bulawayo
Francistown

Kananga
Tshikapa
Kikwit
Bandundu
Kinshasa
Mbanza-Ngungu
Matadi
Boma

Brazzaville
Libreville
Franceville
Lambaréné
Port-Gentil
Pointe-Noire
Loubomo
Cabinda (Angola)
São Tomé
Annobón (Eq. Guinea)
Ascension (U.K.)

Luanda
Malanje
Huambo
Benguela
Lobito
Namibe
Lubango
Menongue

Windhoek
Tsumeb
Grootfontein
Walvis Bay
Lüderitz
Keetmanshoop
Springbok

Gaborone
Serowe
Ghanzi

Johannesburg
Pretoria (Tshwane)
Vereeniging
Klerksdorp
Welkom
Kimberley
Upington
Bloemfontein
Kuruman
Worcester
Cape Town
Cape of Good Hope
Cape Agulhas
Port Elizabeth
East London
Umtata
Durban
Pietermaritzburg
Newcastle
Ladysmith
Maseru
Bisho
Middelburg

Maputo
Mbabane
Lobamba
Manzini
Palapye
Mochudi

Lake Victoria
Lake Tanganyika
Lake Malawi
Lake Kariba

GeoNova

0 250 500 750 Miles
0 250 500 750 1,000 Kilometers

© GeoNova

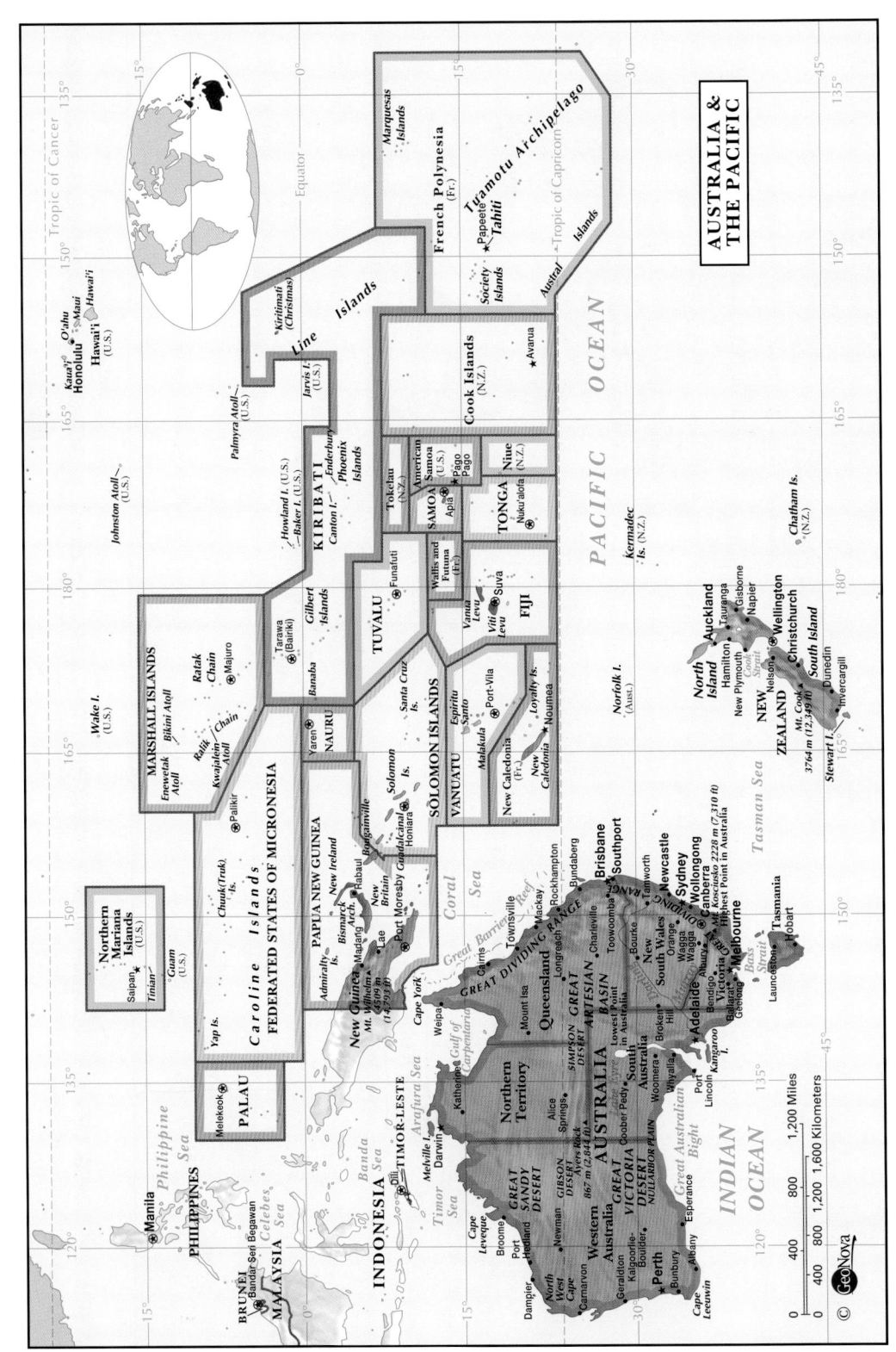

AUSTRALIA &
THE PACIFIC

472

Territorial Sea of the U.S.

According to a Dec. 27, 1988, proclamation by Pres. Ronald Reagan, "The territorial sea of the United States henceforth extends to 12 nautical miles from the baselines of the United States determined in accordance with international law. In accordance with international law, as reflected in the applicable provisions of the 1982 United Nations Convention on the Law of the Sea, within the territorial sea of the United States, the ships of all countries enjoy the right of innocent passage and the ships and aircraft of all countries enjoy the right of transit passage through international straits."

Major Accessions of Territory by the U.S.

Source: U.S. Dept. of the Interior; Bureau of the Census, U.S. Dept. of Commerce

Not including territories such as Panama Canal Zone and the Philippines which are no longer under U.S. jurisdiction; area figures are for total area and may differ from figures for current areas given elsewhere.

Accession	Date	Area (sq mi)	Accession	Date	Area (sq mi)	Accession	Date	Area (sq mi)
Territory in 1790[1]	NA	888,685	Mexican Cession	1848	529,017	Guam[3]	1899	212
Louisiana Purchase	1803	827,192	Gadsden Purchase	1853	29,640	American Samoa[4]	1900	76
Treaty of Florida	1819	72,003	Alaska	1867	586,412	U.S. Virgin Islands	1917	133
Texas	1845	390,143	Hawaii	1898	6,450	Northern Marianas[5]	1986	179
Oregon Territory	1846	285,680	Puerto Rico[2]	1899	3,435			

NA = Not applicable. (1) Includes that part of a drainage basin of Red River of the North, S of 49th parallel, sometimes considered part of Louisiana Purchase. (2) Ceded by Spain in 1898, ratified in 1899, and became the Commonwealth of Puerto Rico by Act of Congress on July 25, 1952. (3) Acquired in 1898; ratified 1899. (4) Acquired in 1899; ratified 1900. (5) Formerly a part of the U.S. administered Trust Territory of the Pacific Islands; became a U.S. commonwealth, Nov. 3, 1986.

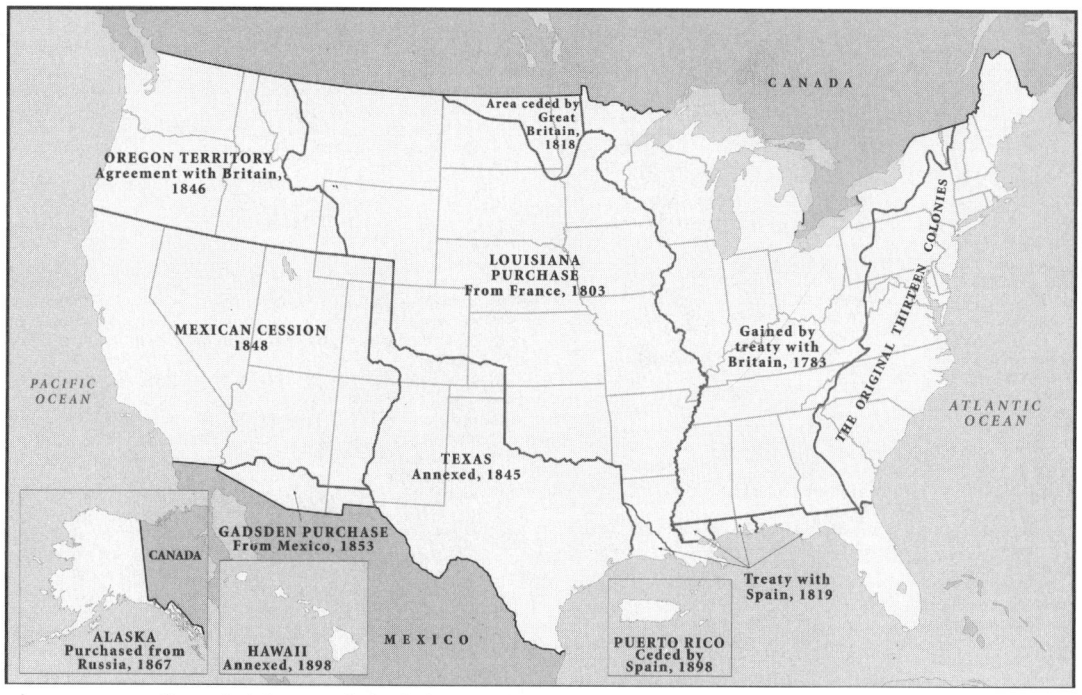

Special Areas Administered by the U.S. Forest Service, 2008

Source: U.S. Forest Service, Dept. of Agriculture

NHL = National Historic Landmark; NS(A) = Nat. Scenic (Area); NM = National Monument; NP = National Preserve; NRA = National Recreation Area; NVM = Nat. Volcanic Monument; SRA = Scenic Recreation Area

Area name	Location	Estab.	Acres[1]	Area name	Location	Estab.	Acres[1]
Admiralty Island NM	AK	1980	974,278	Mount Pleasant NSA	VA	1994	7,580
Allegheny NRA	PA	1984	24,145	Mount Rogers NRA	VA	1966	118,509
Arapaho NRA	CO	1978	32,414	Mount St. Helens NVM	WA	1989	112,605
Beech Creek NS & Botanic Area	OK	1988	6,200	Newberry NVM	OR	1990	54,822
Cascade Head NS Research Area	OR	1974	6,637	North Cascades NSA	WA	1984	87,600
Columbia River Gorge NSA	OR-WA	1986	70,890	Opal Creek SRA	OR	1996	12,645
Coosa Bald NSA	GA	1991	7,100	Oregon Dunes NRA	OR	1972	27,212
Ed Jenkins NRA	GA	1991	23,166	Pine Ridge NRA	NE	1986	6,600
Flaming Gorge NRA	UT-WY	1968	189,825	Rattlesnake NRA	MT	1980	59,119
Giant Sequoia NM	CA	2000	327,769	Santa Rosa and			
Grand Island NRA	MI	1990	12,973	San Jacinto Mts. NM	CA	2000	64,400
Grey Towers NHL	PA	1963	102	Sawtooth NRA	ID	1972	729,428
Hells Canyon NRA	OR-ID	1975	537,770	Smith River NRA	CA	1990	305,169
Indian Nations NS & Wildlife Area	OK	1988	39,171	Spring Mt. NRA	NV	1993	314,367
Jemez NRA	NM	1993	44,670	Spruce Knob-Seneca Rocks NRA	WV	1965	57,232
Land Between the Lakes NRA	KY-TN	1998	170,310	Valles Caldera NP	NM	2000	89,716
Misty Fiords NM	AK	1980	2,293,760	Whiskeytown-Shasta-Trinity NRA	CA	1965	176,367
Mono Basin NSA	CA	1984	128,303	Robert T. Stafford White Rocks NRA	VT	1984	36,561
Mount Baker NRA	WA	1984	8,473	Winding Stair Mt. NRA	OK	1988	25,890

(1) Area administered by the Forest Service or federally owned.

20 Most-Visited Sites in the National Park System, 2008

Source: National Park Service, Dept. of the Interior

Attendance at all areas administered by the National Park Service in 2008 totaled 274,852,949 recreation visits.

Site (location)	Recreation visits	Site (location)	Recreation visits
Blue Ridge Parkway (NC-VA)	16,309,307	Grand Canyon National Park (AZ)	4,425,314
Golden Gate Natl. Recreation Area (CA)	14,554,750	Vietnam Veterans Memorial (DC)	4,243,573
Gateway Natl. Recreation Area (NJ-NY)	9,431,021	World War II Memorial (DC)	4,153,749
Great Smoky Mountains National Park (NC-TN)	9,044,010	San Francisco Maritime Natl. Historical Park (CA)	4,086,211
Lake Mead Natl. Recreation Area (AZ-NV)	7,601,863	Independence National Historical Park (PA)	4,076,638
George Washington Memorial Pkwy. (VA-MD-DC)	7,009,630	Castle Clinton National Monument (NY)	3,727,030
Natchez Trace Parkway (MS-AL-TN)	5,747,235	Korean War Veterans Memorial (DC)	3,654,976
Delaware Water Gap Natl. Recreation Area (NJ-PA)	5,127,074	Statue of Liberty National Monument (NY-NJ)	3,555,244
Lincoln Memorial (DC)	4,678,861	Yosemite National Park (CA)	3,431,514
Cape Cod National Seashore (MA)	4,644,235	Colonial National Historical Park (VA)	3,332,039

National Parks, Other Areas Administered by National Park Service

As of December 2008, the National Park Service administered 84,331,948 acres of federal land across 391 sites. Dates when sites were authorized for initial protection by Congress or by presidential proclamation are given in parentheses. If different, the date the area got its current designation, or was transferred to the National Park Service, follows. Gross area in acres, as of Dec. 31, 2008, follows date(s). Some parks, trails, and other areas are not listed.

National Parks

Acadia, ME (1916/1929): 47,400. Includes Mount Desert Isl., half of Isle au Haut, Schoodic Peninsula on mainland. Highest elevation on Eastern seaboard.

American Samoa, AS (1988): 9,000. Features a paleotropical rain forest and a coral reef.

Arches, UT (1929/1971): 76,679. Contains giant red sandstone arches and other products of erosion.

Badlands, SD (1929/1978): 242,756. Reformations and native prairie. Animal fossils 23-37 mil years old.

Big Bend, TX (1935): 801,163. Rio Grande, Chisos Mts.

Biscayne, FL (1968/1980): 172,971. Aquatic park encompassing chain of islands south of Miami.

Black Canyon of the Gunnison, CO (1933/1999): 30,750. Has a canyon 2,900 ft deep and 40 ft wide at its narrowest part.

Bryce Canyon, UT (1923/1928): 35,835. Spectacularly colorful and unusual display of erosion effects.

Canyonlands, UT (1964): 337,598. At junction of Colorado and Green rivers; extensive evidence of prehistoric Indians.

Capitol Reef, UT (1937/1971): 241,904. A 70-mi uplift of sandstone cliffs dissected by high-walled gorges.

Carlsbad Caverns, NM (1923/1930): 46,766. Largest known caverns; not yet fully explored.

Channel Islands, CA (1938/1980): 249,561. Sea lion breeding place, nesting sea birds, unique plants.

Congaree, SC (1976/1988): 26,546. Last significant tract of southern bottomland hardwood forest in the U.S.

Crater Lake, OR (1902): 183,224. Extraordinary blue lake in the crater of Mt. Mazama, a volcano that erupted about 7,700 years ago; deepest U.S. lake.

Cuyahoga Valley, OH (1974/2000): 32,856. Rural landscape along Ohio and Erie Canal system between Akron and Cleveland.

Death Valley, CA-NV (1933/1994): 3,373,042. Large desert area. Includes the lowest point in the Western Hemisphere; also includes Scotty's Castle.

Denali, AK (1917/1980): 4,740,912. Name changed from Mt. McKinley National Park. Has highest mountain in U.S.; wildlife.

Dry Tortugas, FL (1935/1992): 64,701. Ft. Jefferson and seven coral reef and sand islands near Key West.

Everglades, FL (1934): 1,398,893. Largest remaining subtropical wilderness in continental U.S.

Gates of the Arctic, AK (1978/1984): 7,523,898. Vast wilderness in north central region. Limited federal facilities.

Glacier, MT (1910): 1,013,322. Superb Rocky Mt. scenery, numerous glaciers and glacial lakes. Part of Waterton-Glacier Intl. Peace Park established by U.S. and Canada in 1932.

Glacier Bay, AK (1925/1986): 3,224,841. Great tidewater glaciers that move down mountainsides and break up into the sea; much wildlife.

Grand Canyon, AZ (1893/1919): 1,217,403. Most spectacular part of Colorado River's greatest canyon.

Grand Teton, WY (1929): 310,044. Most impressive part of the Teton Mts., winter feeding ground of largest American elk herd.

Great Basin, NV (1922/1986): 77,180. Includes Wheeler Pk., Lexington Arch, and Lehman Caves.

Great Sand Dunes, CO (1932/2000): 44,246. North America's tallest dunes.

Great Smoky Mountains, NC-TN (1926/1934): 522,051. Largest Eastern U.S. mountain range, magnificent forests.

Guadalupe Mountains, TX (1966): 86,416. Extensive Permian limestone fossil reef; tremendous earth fault.

Haleakala, HI (1916/1960): 33,223. Dormant volcano on Maui with large colorful craters.

Hawaii Volcanoes, HI (1916/1961): 323,431. Contains Kilauea and Mauna Loa, active volcanoes.

Hot Springs, AR (1832/1921): 5,550. Bathhouses are furnished with thermal waters from the park's 47 hot springs; these waters are used for bathing and drinking.

Isle Royale, MI (1931): 571,790. Largest island in Lake Superior, noted for its wilderness area and wildlife.

Joshua Tree, CA (1936/1994): 789,866. Desert region includes Joshua trees, other plant and animal life.

Katmai, AK (1918/1980): 3,674,540. "Valley of Ten Thousand Smokes," scene of 1912 volcanic eruption.

Kenai Fjords, AK (1978/1980): 669,983. Abundant marine mammals, birdlife; Harding Icefield, one of 4 major icecaps in U.S.

Kings Canyon, CA (1890/1940): 461,901. Mountain wilderness, dominated by Kings River Canyons and High Sierra; contains giant sequoias.

Kobuk Valley, AK (1978/1980): 1,750,717. Contains geological and recreational sites. Limited federal facilities.

Lake Clark, AK (1978/1980): 2,619,733. Across Cook Inlet from Anchorage. A scenic wilderness rich in fish and wildlife. Limited federal facilities.

Lassen Volcanic, CA (1907/1916): 106,372. Contains Lassen Peak, recently active volcano, and other volcanic phenomena.

Mammoth Cave, KY (1926/1941): 52,830. 365 mi of explored underground passages, beautiful natural formations, river 300 ft below surface.

Mesa Verde, CO (1906): 52,485. Most notable and best preserved prehistoric cliff dwellings in the U.S.

Mount Rainier, WA (1899): 236,381. Greatest single-peak glacial system in the U.S.

North Cascades, WA (1968): 504,781. Spectacular mountainous region with many glaciers, lakes.

Olympic, WA (1909/1938): 922,651. Mountain wilderness containing finest remnant of Pacific Northwest rainforest, active glaciers, Pacific shoreline, rare elk.

Petrified Forest, AZ (1906/1962): 221,621. Extensive petrified wood and Indian artifacts. Contains part of Painted Desert.

Redwood, CA (1968): 112,582. 40 mi of Pacific coastline, groves of ancient redwoods and world's tallest trees.

Rocky Mountain, CO (1915): 265,758. On the Continental Divide; includes peaks over 14,000 ft.

Saguaro, AZ (1933/1994): 91,440. Part of the Sonoran Desert; includes the giant saguaro cacti, unique to the region.

Sequoia, CA (1890): 404,063. Groves of giant sequoias, highest mountain in conterminous U.S.: Mt. Whitney (14,494 ft). World's largest tree.

Shenandoah, VA (1926): 199,100. Portion of the Blue Ridge Mts.; overlooks Shenandoah Valley; Skyline Drive.

Theodore Roosevelt, ND (1947/1978): 70,447. Contains part of Roosevelt's ranch and scenic badlands.

Virgin Islands, VI (1956): 15,006. Authorized to cover 75% of St. John Isl. and Hassel Isl.; lush growth, lovely beaches, Carib Indian petroglyphs, evidence of colonial Danes.

Voyageurs, MN (1971): 218,200. Abundant lakes, forests, wildlife, canoeing, boating.

Wind Cave, SD (1903): 28,295. Limestone caverns in Black Hills. Extensive wildlife includes a herd of bison.

Wrangell-St. Elias, AK (1978/1980): 8,323,043. Largest area in park system, most peaks over 16,000 ft, abundant wildlife; day's drive east of Anchorage. No federal facilities.

Yellowstone, ID-MT-WY (1872): 2,219,791. World's first national park. World's greatest geyser area has about 10,000 geysers and hot springs; spectacular falls and impressive canyons of the Yellowstone River; grizzly bear, moose, and bison.

Yosemite, CA (1890): 761,268. Yosemite Valley, the nation's highest waterfall, grove of sequoias, and mountains.

Zion, UT (1909/1919): 146,597. Unusual shapes and landscapes resulting from erosion and faulting; evidence of past volcanic activity; contains the "Great White Throne," 2,394-ft. monolith.

National Historical Parks

Adams, MA (1946/1998): 24. Home of Pres. John Adams, John Quincy Adams, and celebrated descendants.

Appomattox Court House, VA (1930/1954): 1,774. Where Lee surrendered to Grant.

Boston, MA (1974): 44. Includes Faneuil Hall, Old North Church, Bunker Hill, Paul Revere House.

Cane River Creole (and heritage area), LA (1994): 207. Preserves the Creole culture as it developed along the Cane R.

Cedar Creek & Belle Grove, VA (2002): 3,712. Civil War battle site and an antebellum plantation in the Shenandoah Valley.

Chaco Culture, NM (1907/1980): 33,960. Ruins of pueblos built by prehistoric Indians including the Pueblo, Hopi, and Navajo.

Chesapeake and Ohio Canal, MD-DC-WV (1938/1971): 19,616. 184-mi historic canal; DC to Cumberland, MD.

Colonial, VA (1930/1936): 8,677. Includes most of Jamestown Isl., site of first successful English colony; Yorktown, site of Cornwallis's surrender to George Washington; and Colonial Parkway.

Cumberland Gap, KY-TN-VA (1940): 22,366. Mountain pass of the Wilderness Road, which carried the first great migration of pioneers into America's interior.

Dayton Aviation Heritage, OH (1992): 86. Commemorates the area's aviation heritage.

George Rogers Clark, IN (1966): 26. Commemorates American defeat of British in West during Revolution.

Harpers Ferry, MD-VA-WV (1944/1963): 3,647. At the confluence of the Shenandoah and Potomac rivers, the site of John Brown's 1859 raid on the Army arsenal.

Hopewell Culture, OH (1923/1992): 1,170. Remains of ceremonial mounds built in the Ohio River Valley, 200 BCE-500 CE.

Independence, PA (1948): 45. Contains several properties associated with the American Revolution and the founding of the U.S. Includes Independence Hall and the Liberty Bell Center.

Jean Lafitte (and preserve), LA (1907/1978): 20,001. Includes Chalmette, site of 1815 Battle of New Orleans; French Quarter.

Kalaupapa, HI (1980): 10,779. Molokai's former leper colony.

Kaloko-Honokohau, HI (1978): 1,161. Preserves the native culture of Hawaii.

Keweenaw, MI (1992): 1,870. Site of first significant copper mine in U.S.

Klondike Gold Rush, AK-WA (1976): 12,996. Preserves Chilkoot Trail used in 1898 Gold Rush. Museum in Seattle.

Lewis & Clark, OR-WA (1958/2004): 1,584. Lewis and Clark encampment, 1805-06. Incorporates former Fort Clatsop Natl. Mem. Park and OR-WA state parks.

Lowell, MA (1978): 141. Textile mills, canal, 19th-cent. structures; park shows planned city of Industrial Revolution.

Lyndon B. Johnson, TX (1969/1980): 1,570. President's birthplace, boyhood home, ranch.

Marsh-Billings-Rockefeller, VT (1992): 643. Boyhood home of conservationist George Perkins Marsh.

Minute Man, MA (1959): 961. Where the Minute Men battled the British, Apr. 19, 1775. Also contains Nathaniel Hawthorne's home.

Morristown, NJ (1933): 1,711. Sites of important military encampments during the American Revolution; Washington's headquarters, 1779-80.

Natchez, MS (1988): 108. Mansions, townhouses, and villas related to history of Natchez.

New Bedford Whaling, MA (1996): 34. Preserves structures and relics associated with the city's 19th-cent. whaling industry.

New Orleans Jazz, LA (1994): 5. Preserves, educates, and interprets jazz as it has evolved in New Orleans.

Nez Perce, ID-MT-OR-WA (1965): 4,570. Illustrates the history and culture of the Nez Perce Indian country (38 separate sites).

Pecos, NM (1965/1990): 6,669. Ruins of ancient Pueblo of Pecos, archaeological sites, and 2 associated Spanish colonial missions from the 17th and 18th centuries.

Pu'uhonua o Honaunau, HI (1955/1978): 420. Until 1819, a sanctuary for Hawaiians vanquished in battle and for those guilty of crimes or breaking taboos.

Rosie the Riveter/WWII Home Front, CA (2000): 145. Site of a shipyard that employed thousands of women in WWII; commemorates women who worked in wartime industries.

Salt River Bay (and ecological preserve), St. Croix, VI (1992): 982. The only known site where, in 1493, members of a Columbus party landed on what is now territory of the U.S.

San Antonio Missions, TX (1978): 826. Four of finest Spanish missions in U.S., 18th-cent. irrigation system.

San Francisco Maritime, CA (1988): 50. Artifacts, photographs, and historic vessels related to the development of the Pacific Coast.

San Juan Island, WA (1966): 1,752. Commemorates peaceful relations between the U.S., Canada, and Great Britain since the 1872 boundary disputes.

Saratoga, NY (1938): 3,394. Scene of a major 1777 battle that became a turning point in the American Revolution.

Sitka, AK (1910/1972): 112. Scene of last major resistance of the Tlingit Indians to the Russians, 1804.

Tumacacori, AZ (1908/1990): 360. Historic Spanish mission building stands near site first visited by Father Kino in 1691.

Valley Forge, PA (1976): 3,466. Continental Army campsite in 1777-78 winter.

War in the Pacific, GU (1978): 2,037. Seven distinct units illustrating the Pacific theater of WWII. Limited federal facilities.

Women's Rights, NY (1980): 7. Seneca Falls site where Lucretia Mott, Elizabeth Cady Stanton organized movement in 1848.

National Battlefields/Parks/Sites

Antietam, MD (1890/1978): 3,230. Battle here ended first Confederate invasion of North, Sept. 17, 1862.

Big Hole, MT (1910/1963): 1,011. Site of major battle with Nez Perce Indians, Aug. 9-10, 1877.

Brices Cross Roads Site, MS (1929): 1. Site of the Confederate victory, June 10, 1864.

Cowpens, SC (1929/1972): 842. American Revolution battlefield, Jan. 17, 1781.

Fort Donelson, TN-KY (1928/1985): 1,006. Site of first major Union victory, Feb. 14-16, 1862.

Fort Necessity, PA (1931/1961): 903. Site of first battle of French and Indian War, July 3, 1754.

Kennesaw Mountain Park, GA (1917/1935): 2,853. Site of major battle of Atlanta campaign in Civil War.

Manassas Park, VA (1940): 5,073. Scene of two battles in Civil War, 1861 and 1862.

Monocacy, MD (1934/1976): 1,647. Civil War battle in defense of Washington, DC, fought here, July 9, 1864.

Moores Creek, NC (1926/1980): 88. Feb. 27, 1776 battle between Patriots and Loyalists commemorated here.

Petersburg, VA (1926/1962): 2,740. Scene of 10-month Union campaigns, 1864-65.

Richmond Park, VA (1936): 7,131. Site of battles defending Confederate capital.

Stones River, TN (1927/1960): 709. Scene of battle that began federal offensive to trisect Confederacy, Dec. 31, 1862-Jan. 2, 1863.

Tupelo, MS (1929/1961): 1. Site of crucial battle over Sherman's supply line, July 14-15, 1865.

Wilson's Creek, MO (1960/1970): 2,369. Scene of Civil War battle for control of Missouri, Aug. 10, 1861.

National Military Parks

Chickamauga and Chattanooga, GA-TN (1890): 9,036. Site where Gen. Sherman and Union armies gained control of TN, 1863.

Fredericksburg and Spotsylvania County, VA (1927/1933): 8,382. Sites of several major Civil War battles and campaigns.

Gettysburg, PA (1895/1933): 5,990. Site of decisive Confederate defeat in North, July 1863, and of Gettysburg Address.

Guilford Courthouse, NC (1917/1933): 230. American Revolution battle site.

Horseshoe Bend, AL (1956): 2,040. On Tallapoosa River, where Gen. Andrew Jackson's forces broke the power of the Upper Creek Indian Confederacy on March 27, 1814.

Kings Mountain, SC (1931/1933): 3,945. Site of American Revolution battle, fought on Oct. 7, 1780.

Pea Ridge, AR (1956): 4,300. Scene of Civil War battle, fought Mar. 7-8, 1862.

Shiloh, TN (1894/1933): 6,181. Major Civil War battle site; includes some well-preserved Indian burial mounds.

Vicksburg, MS (1899/1933): 1,795. Union victory gave North control of the Mississippi and split the Confederate forces.

National Memorials

Arkansas Post, AR (1960): 758. First permanent French settlement in the lower Mississippi River valley.

Arlington House, The Robert E. Lee Memorial, VA (1925/1972): 28. Lee's home overlooking the Potomac River.

Chamizal, El Paso, TX (1966/1974): 55. Commemorates 1963 settlement of 99-year border dispute with Mexico.

Coronado, AZ (1941/1952): 4,750. Commemorates first European exploration of the Southwest.

De Soto, FL (1948): 30. Commemorates 16th-cent. Spanish explorations.

Federal Hall, NY (1939/1955): 0.45. First seat of U.S. government under the Constitution.

Flight 93, Shanksville, PA (2002): 2,262. Commemorates the passengers and crew of Flight 93, who died thwarting an attack on Sept. 11, 2001. Permanent memorial expected for completion in 2011.

Fort Caroline, FL (1950): 138. On St. Johns River, overlooks site of a former French Huguenot colony.

Franklin Delano Roosevelt, DC (1982): 8. Statues of Pres. Roosevelt and Eleanor Roosevelt; waterfalls and gardens.

General Grant, NY (1958): 0.76. Tomb of Ulysses Grant and wife.

Hamilton Grange, NY (1962): 1. Home of Alexander Hamilton.

Jefferson National Expansion, MO (1935): 91. Commemorates westward expansion.

Johnstown Flood, PA (1964): 178. Commemorates 1889 flood.

Korean War Veterans, DC (1986): 2. Dedicated in 1995; honors those who served in the Korean War.

Lincoln Boyhood, IN (1962): 200. Site of Lincoln cabin, Lincoln's boyhood home, and grave site of Lincoln's mother.

Lincoln Memorial, DC (1911/1933): 107. Marble statue of the 16th U.S. president.

Lyndon Baines Johnson Memorial Grove on the Potomac, DC (1973): 17. Overlooks the Potomac R.; vista of the Capitol.

Mount Rushmore, SD (1925): 1,278. World-famous sculpture of 4 presidents: Washington, Jefferson, Lincoln, T. Roosevelt.

Perry's Victory and International Peace Memorial, Put-in-Bay, OH (1936/1972): 25. The world's most massive Doric column, constructed 1912-15, promotes pursuit of peace through arbitration and disarmament.

Roger Williams, Providence, RI (1965): 5. Memorial to founder of Rhode Island.

Thaddeus Kosciuszko, PA (1972): 0.02. Memorial to Polish hero of American Revolution.

Theodore Roosevelt Island, DC (1932/1933): 89. Statue of Roosevelt in wooded island sanctuary.

Thomas Jefferson, DC (1934): 18. Statue of Jefferson in an inscribed circular, colonnaded structure.

USS Arizona, HI (1980): 11. Memorializes American losses at Pearl Harbor.

Vietnam Veterans, DC (1980): 2. Black granite wall inscribed with names of those missing or killed in action in Vietnam War.

Washington Monument, DC (1848/1933): 106. Obelisk honoring the first U.S. president.

World War II, DC (1994/2004): 7. Oval plaza with central pool commemorating those who fought and died.

Wright Brothers, NC (1927/1953): 428. Site of first powered flight.

National Historic Sites

Abraham Lincoln Birthplace, Hodgenville, KY (1916/1959): 345. Memorial building, sinking spring.

Allegheny Portage Railroad, PA (1964): 1,284. Linked the Pennsylvania Canal system and the West.

Andersonville, GA (1970): 515. Noted Civil War prisoner-of-war camp.

Andrew Johnson, Greeneville, TN (1935/1963): 17. Two homes and the tailor shop of the 17th U.S. president.

Bent's Old Fort, CO (1960): 799. Replica of S. Plains outpost.

Boston African-American, MA (1980): 0.59. Pre-Civil War black-owned structures.

Brown v. Board of Education, KS (1992): 2. Commemorates the landmark 1954 U.S. Supreme Court decision, which ended legal segregation in schools.

Carl Sandburg Home, Flat Rock, NC (1968): 264.

Charles Pinckney, SC (1988): 28. Statesman's farm. Pinckney was a principal author and signer of the Constitution.

Christiansted, St. Croix, VI (1952/1961): 27. Commemorates Danish colony.

Clara Barton, MD (1974): 9. Home of founder of American Red Cross.

Edgar Allan Poe, Philadelphia, PA (1978/1980): 0.52. Writer's home, where he wrote short stories.

Edison, West Orange, NJ (1955/1962): 21. Inventor's home and laboratory.

Eisenhower, Gettysburg, PA (1967): 690. Home of 34th president.

Eleanor Roosevelt, Hyde Park, NY (1977): 181. The former first lady's personal retreat.

Eugene O'Neill, Danville, CA (1976): 13. Playwright's home where he wrote his final plays, including *The Iceman Cometh.*

First Ladies, Canton, OH (2000): 0.33. Home of first lady Ida Sexton McKinley. Library now devoted to America's first ladies.

Ford's Theatre, DC (1866/1970): 0.30. Includes theater, now restored, where Lincoln was assassinated, house where he died, and Lincoln Museum.

Fort Bowie, AZ (1964): 999. Focal point of operations against Geronimo and the Apaches.

Fort Davis, TX (1961): 474. Frontier outpost in West Texas. Established to guard the San Antonio-El Paso Road.

Fort Laramie, WY (1938/1960): 833. Military post on Oregon Trail.

Fort Larned, KS (1964/1966): 718. Military post on Santa Fe Trail.

Fort Point, San Francisco, CA (1970): 29. West Coast fortification. Protected San Francisco during and after Civil War.

Fort Raleigh, NC (1941): 513. First attempted English settlement in North America.

Fort Scott, KS (1965/1978): 17. Commemorates U.S. frontier of 1840s and '50s. Was a major focal point of black troop activity and training during Civil War.

Fort Smith, AR-OK (1961): 75. One of the earliest U.S. posts in Missouri Territory, active 1817-90.

Fort Union Trading Post, MT-ND (1966): 444. Principal fur-trading post on upper Missouri, 1829-67.

Fort Vancouver, WA-OR (1948/1961): 194. Headquarters for Hudson's Bay Company in 1825. Early political seat.

Frederick Douglass, DC (1962/1988): 9. Home of famous black abolitionist, writer, and orator.

Frederick Law Olmsted, MA (1979): 7. Home of city planner, famous for designing Central Park in NYC.

Friendship Hill, PA (1978): 675. Home of Albert Gallatin, Jefferson's and Madison's secretary of treasury.

Golden Spike, UT (1957): 2,735. Commemorates completion of first transcontinental railroad in 1869.

Grant-Kohrs Ranch, MT (1972): 1,618. Ranch house owned by John Grant, a 19th-cent. range-cattle industry pioneer.

Hampton, MD (1948): 62. 18th-cent. Georgian mansion, which in 1790 was the largest house in the U.S.

Harry S. Truman, MO (1983): 7. Home of pres. after 1919.

Herbert Hoover, West Branch, IA (1965): 187. Birthplace and boyhood home of 31st president.

Home of Franklin D. Roosevelt, Hyde Park, NY (1944): 792. FDR's birthplace, home, and "summer White House."

Hopewell Furnace, PA (1938/1985): 848. 19th-cent. iron-making village.

Hubbell Trading Post, AZ (1965): 160. Trading post that allowed interaction between the Navajo and white traders in the late 19th and 20th century. Still active today.

James A. Garfield, Mentor, OH (1980): 8. Home of 20th president. Site of his front-porch campaign.

Jimmy Carter, GA (1987): 72. Birthplace and home of 39th president.

John Fitzgerald Kennedy, Brookline, MA (1967): 0.09. Birthplace and childhood home of 35th president.

John Muir, Martinez, CA (1964): 345. Home of Sierra Club founder and "Father of the National Park Service."

Knife River Indian Villages, ND (1974): 1,758. Remnants of villages last occupied by Hidatsa and Mandan Indians.

Lincoln Home, Springfield, IL (1971): 12. Lincoln's residence at the time he was elected 16th president, 1860.

Little Rock Central High School, AR (1998): 27. Commemorates 1957 desegregation during which federal troops had to be called in to protect 9 black students.

Longfellow, Cambridge, MA (1972): 2. Poet's home, 1837-82; Washington's headquarters during Boston siege, 1775-76.

Maggie L. Walker, VA (1978): 1. Richmond home of black leader and first female bank president, daughter of a former slave.

Manzanar, Lone Pine, CA (1992): 814. Commemorates Manzanar War Relocation Ctr., a Japanese-American internment camp during WWII.

Martin Luther King Jr., Atlanta, GA (1980): 39. Birthplace, grave, church of the civil rights leader.

Martin Van Buren, NY (1974): 40. Lindenwald, home of 8th president, near Kinderhook.

Mary McLeod Bethune Council House, DC (1982/1991): 0.07. Commemorates Bethune's leadership in the black women's movement.

Minuteman Missile, SD (1999): 15. Missile launch facilities dating back to the Cold War era.

Nicodemus, KS (1996): 5. Only remaining Western town established by African Americans during Reconstruction.

Ninety Six, SC (1976): 1,022. Colonial trading village and the site of Gen. Nathanael Greene's siege in 1781.

Palo Alto Battlefield, TX (1978): 3,407. Scene of first battle of the Mexican War.

Pennsylvania Avenue, DC (1965): 0.26 Includes area between Capitol and White House, encompassing the U.S. Navy Memorial, Freedom Plaza, the Old Post Office Pavilion, and other sites.

Puukohola Heiau, HI (1972): 86. Ruins of temple built by King Kamehameha, first king of united Hawaiian islands.

Sagamore Hill, Oyster Bay, NY (1962): 83. Home of Pres. Theodore Roosevelt from 1885 until his death in 1919.

Saint-Gaudens, Cornish, NH (1964): 148. Home, studio, and gardens of American sculptor Augustus Saint-Gaudens.

Saint Paul's Church, New York, NY (1943): 6. Site associated with John Peter Zenger's "freedom of press" trial.

Salem Maritime, MA (1938): 9. Major fishing and whaling port famous for 1692 witchcraft trials.

San Juan, PR (1949): 75. 16th-cent. Span. fortifications.

Sand Creek Massacre, CO (2000): 12,583. Site where more than 160 Cheyenne and Arapaho Indians were killed by U.S. soldiers in 1864.

Saugus Iron Works, MA (1974): 9. Reconstructed 17th-cent. colonial ironworks.

Springfield Armory, MA (1974): 55. Small-arms manufacturing center for nearly 200 years.

Steamtown, PA (1986): 62. Railyard, roadhouse, repair shops of former Delaware, Lackawanna & Western Railroad.

Theodore Roosevelt Birthplace, New York, NY (1962): 0.11. Reconstructed brownstone where the president was born.

Theodore Roosevelt Inaugural, Buffalo, NY (1966): 1. Wilcox House where he took oath of office, 1901.

Thomas Stone, MD (1978): 328. Home of signer of Declaration of Independence.

Tuskegee Airmen, AL (1998): 90. Airfield where pilots of all-black air corps unit of WWII received flight training.

Tuskegee Institute, AL (1974): 58. College founded by Booker T. Washington in 1881 for blacks.

Ulysses S. Grant, St. Louis Co., MO (1989): 10. Home of Grant during pre-Civil War years.

Vanderbilt Mansion, Hyde Park, NY (1940): 212. Mansion of 19th-cent. financier.

Washita Battlefield, OK (1996): 315. Scene of Nov. 27, 1868, battle between Plains tribes and the U.S. army.

Weir Farm, Wilton, CT (1990): 74. Home and studio of American impressionist painter J. Alden Weir.

Whitman Mission, WA (1936/1963): 139. Site of Protestant Missionaries to the Cayuse Indians during the mid-19th cent.

William Howard Taft, Cincinnati, OH (1969): 3. Birthplace and early home of the 27th president.

Name	State	Year[1]	Acreage
National Monuments			
African Burial Ground[4]	NY	2006	0.35
Agate Fossil Beds	NE	1965	3,058
Alibates Flint Quarries	TX	1965	1,371
Aniakchak[2]	AK	1978	137,176
Aztec Ruins	NM	1923	318
Bandelier	NM	1916	33,677
Booker T. Washington	VA	1956	239
Buck Island Reef	VI	1961	19,015
Cabrillo	CA	1913	160
Canyon de Chelly	AZ	1931	83,840
Cape Krusenstern[3]	AK	1978	649,085
Capulin Volcano	NM	1916	793
Casa Grande Ruins	AZ	1889	473
Castillo de San Marcos	FL	1924	18
Castle Clinton	NY	1946	1
Cedar Breaks	UT	1933	6,155
Chiricahua	AZ	1924	11,985
Colorado	CO	1911	20,534
Craters of the Moon	ID	1924	53,571
Devils Postpile	CA	1911	798
Devils Tower	WY	1906	1,347
Dinosaur	CO-UT	1915	210,278
Effigy Mounds	IA	1949	2,526
El Malpais	NM	1987	114,277
El Morro	NM	1906	1,279
Florissant Fossil Beds	CO	1969	5,998
Fort Frederica	GA	1936	284
Fort Matanzas	FL	1924	300
Fort McHenry (and Historic Shrine)	MD	1925	43
Fort Pulaski	GA	1924	5,623
Fort Stanwix	NY	1935	16
Fort Sumter	SC	1948	235
Fort Union	NM	1954	721
Fossil Butte	WY	1972	8,198
George Washington Birthplace	VA	1930	662
George Washington Carver	MO	1943	210
Gila Cliff Dwellings	NM	1907	533
Governors Island	NY	2001	23
Grand Portage	MN	1951	710
Hagerman Fossil Beds	ID	1988	4,351
Hohokam Pima[4]	AZ	1972	1,690
Homestead NM of America	NE	1936	211
Hovenweep	CO-UT	1923	785
Jewel Cave	SD	1908	1,274
John Day Fossil Beds	OR	1974	13,944
Lava Beds	CA	1925	46,560
Little Bighorn Battlefield	MT	1879	765
Minidoka Internment [2]	ID	2001	73
Montezuma Castle	AZ	1906	859
Muir Woods	CA	1908	554
Natural Bridges	UT	1908	7,636
Navajo	AZ	1909	360
Ocmulgee	GA	1934	702
Oregon Caves	OR	1909	488
Organ Pipe Cactus	AZ	1937	330,689
Papahanaumokuakea Marine	HI	2006	88,190,080
Petroglyph	NM	1990	7,232
Pinnacles	CA	1908	26,491
Pipe Spring	AZ	1923	40
Pipestone	MN	1937	282
Poverty Point[2]	LA	1988	911
Rainbow Bridge[3]	UT	1910	160
Russell Cave	AL	1961	310
Salinas Pueblo Missions	NM	1909	1,071
Scotts Bluff	NE	1919	3,005
Statue of Liberty	NJ-NY	1924	61
Sunset Crater Volcano	AZ	1930	3,040
Timpanogos Cave	UT	1922	250
Tonto	AZ	1907	1,120
Tuzigoot	AZ	1939	812
Virgin Islands Coral Reef	VI	2001	13,893
Walnut Canyon	AZ	1915	3,529
White Sands	NM	1933	143,733
Wupatki	AZ	1924	35,422
Yucca House[2]	CO	1919	34
National Preserves			
Aniakchak	AK	1978	464,118
Bering Land Bridge	AK	1978	2,697,392
Big Cypress	FL	1974	574,448
Big Thicket	TX	1974	99,404
Craters of the Moon	ID	2002	410,733
Denali	AK	1917	1,334,118
Gates of the Arctic	AK	1978	948,608
Glacier Bay	AK	1925	58,406
Great Sand Dunes	CO	2000	41,686
Katmai	AK	1918	418,699
Lake Clark	AK	1978	1,410,292
Little River Canyon[3]	AL	1992	13,633
Mojave	CA	1994	1,533,563
Noatak	AK	1978	6,569,904
Tallgrass Prairie	KS	1996	10,894
Timucuan Ecological & Historic	FL	1988	46,295
Wrangell-St. Elias	AK	1978	4,852,753
Yukon-Charley Rivers[3]	AK	1978	2,526,512
National Seashores			
Assateague Island	MD-VA	1965	39,727
Canaveral	FL	1975	57,662
Cape Cod	MA	1961	43,609
Cape Hatteras	NC	1937	30,351
Cape Lookout	NC	1966	28,243
Cumberland Island	GA	1972	36,347
Fire Island	NY	1964	19,580
Gulf Islands	FL-MS	1971	137,991
Padre Island	TX	1962	130,434
Point Reyes	CA	1962	71,070
National Parkways			
Blue Ridge	NC-VA	1933	94,250
George Washington Memorial	VA-MD-DC	1930	6,997
John D. Rockefeller Jr. Mem.	WY	1972	23,777
Natchez Trace	MS-AL-TN	1938	52,316
National Lakeshores			
Apostle Islands	WI	1970	69,372
Indiana Dunes	IN	1966	15,096
Pictured Rocks	MI	1966	73,236
Sleeping Bear Dunes	MI	1970	71,291
National Reserves			
City of Rocks	ID	1988	14,407
Ebey's Landing Historical	WA	1978	19,333
National Rivers			
Big South Fork (& Recreation Area)	KY-TN	1976	125,310
Buffalo	AR	1972	94,293
Mississippi (& Recreation Area)	MN	1988	53,775
New River Gorge	WV	1978	72,186
Ozark Riverways	MO	1964	80,785
National Wild and Scenic Rivers			
Alagnak Wild	AK	1980	30,665
Bluestone Scenic[2]	WV	1978	4,310
Delaware Scenic	NY-NJ-PA	1978	1,973
Great Egg Harbor Wild & Scenic	NJ	1992	43,311
Missouri Recreational	NE-SD	1991	34,159
Niobrara Scenic	NE	1991	23,074
Obed Wild & Scenic	TN	1976	5,073
Rio Grande Wild & Scenic[3]	TX	1978	9,600
Saint Croix Scenic	MN-WI	1968	67,469
Upper Delaware Scenic/Recreational	NY-PA	1978	75,000
National Recreation Areas			
Amistad	TX	1965	58,500
Bighorn Canyon	MT-WY	1966	120,296
Boston Harbor Islands	MA	1996	1,482
Chattahoochee R.	GA	1978	9,354
Chickasaw	OK	1902	9,899
Curecanti	CO	1965	41,972
Delaware Water Gap	NJ-PA	1965	66,741
Gateway	NJ-NY	1972	26,607
Gauley R.[3]	WV	1988	11,560
Glen Canyon	AZ-UT	1958	1,254,117
Golden Gate	CA	1972	80,020
Lake Chelan	WA	1968	61,947
Lake Mead	AZ-NV	1936	1,495,664
Lake Meredith	TX	1965	44,978
Lake Roosevelt[5]	WA	1946	100,390
Ross Lake	WA	1968	117,575
Santa Monica Mts.[3]	CA	1978	156,673
Whiskeytown-Shasta-Trinity	CA	1965	42,503
Other Designations			
Catoctin Mountain	MD	1954	5,810
Constitution Gardens	DC	1974	52
Fort Washington	MD	1930	341
Greenbelt	MD	1950	1,175
National Capital	DC	1933	6,726
National Mall	DC	1933	146
Piscataway	MD	1961	4,626
Prince William Forest	VA	1948	16,047
Rock Creek	DC	1890	1,755
White House	DC	1933	18
Wolf Trap Farm Park for Perf. Arts	VA	1966	130
International Historic Site			
Saint Croix Island[3]	ME	1949	45
National Scenic Trails			
Appalachian	ME to GA	1968	2,175
Ice Age	WI	1980	1,000
Natchez Trace	MS-TN	1983	64
North Country	NY to ND	1980	3,200
Potomac Heritage	VA to PA	1983	520

(1) Year first designated. (2) No federal facilities. (3) Limited federal facilities. (4) Not open to the public. (5) Formerly Coulee Dam National Recreation Area.

UNITED STATES HISTORY

Chronology of Events

1492 Christopher Columbus and crew sighted land Oct. 12 in present-day Bahamas.

1513 Juan Ponce de León explored Florida coast.

1524 Giovanni da Verrazano led French expedition along coast from Carolina north to Nova Scotia; entered New York Harbor.

1526 San Miguel de Guadalupe, **first European settlement** in what became U.S. territory, was established in the summer off South Carolina coast; abandoned in October.

1539 Hernando de Soto landed in Florida May 28; crossed Mississippi River, **1541**.

1539: Spanish explorer Hernando de Soto lands in Florida.

1540 Francisco Vásquez de Coronado explored Southwest north of Rio Grande. **Hernando de Alarcón** reached Colorado River; **García López de Cárdenas** reached Grand Canyon. Others explored California coast.

1562 First French colony in what became U.S. territory founded on Parris Island off South Carolina coast; abandoned, **1564**.

1565 St. Augustine, FL, oldest continuously occupied European settlement in U.S., founded Sept. 8 by Pedro Menéndez de Avilés. Spain ceded settlement to U.S. in **1821**.

1579 Sir Francis Drake entered San Francisco Bay and claimed region for Britain.

1585 First English colony in America, sponsored by Sir Walter Raleigh, founded on **Roanoke Island**, off North Carolina coast; colony failed.

1587 Second colony attempted on Roanoke Island. Virginia Dare of colony became **first English infant born** in the New World. Settlers of second colony found to have vanished, **1590**.

1607 Capt. **John Smith** and 105 cavaliers in 3 ships landed on Virginia coast, started Jamestown, **first permanent English settlement** in New World.

1609 Henry Hudson, English explorer of Northwest Passage, employed by Dutch, sailed into New York Harbor in September and up Hudson to Albany. **Samuel de Champlain** explored Lake Champlain, to the north. Spaniards settled **Santa Fe, NM**.

1619 House of Burgesses, **first representative assembly** in New World, elected July 30 at Jamestown, VA. **First black laborers**—indentured servants—in English North American colonies, brought by Dutch to Jamestown in August. Chattel slavery legally recognized, **1650**.

1620 Pilgrims, Puritan separatists, left Plymouth, England, Sept. 16 on *Mayflower*; reached Cape Cod Nov. 19; 103 passengers landed at Plymouth, Dec. 26. **Mayflower Compact**, signed Nov. 11, was agreement to form a self-government. Half of colony died during harsh winter.

1624 Dutch colonies started in Albany and in New York area, where **New Netherland** was established in May.

1626 Peter Minuit bought **Manhattan** for Dutch West India Co. from Manahatta Indians during summer for goods valued at $24; named island **New Amsterdam**.

1630 Settlement of **Boston** established by Massachusetts colonists led by John Winthrop; Winthrop began *The History of New England*. **William Bradford**, a governor of Plym-

outh Colony, began his chronicle *History of Plymouth Plantation (1620-1647)*, first published in entirety in **1856**.

1634 Maryland founded as Catholic colony under charter to Lord Baltimore. Act of Toleration passed **1649** provided for religious tolerance.

1635 Boston Latin School, **oldest public school** in continuous existence in U.S., founded Apr. 23.

1636 Roger Williams founded **Providence, RI**, in June, as a democratically ruled colony with separation of church and state. Charter granted, **1644**. **Harvard College** founded; **oldest institution of higher learning** in U.S.

1640 First book printed in America, the so-called *Bay Psalm Book*.

1647 Liberal constitution drafted in Rhode Island. First law in America providing for **free compulsory basic education** enacted in Massachusetts.

1660 British Parliament passed first **Navigation Act** Dec. 1, regulating colonial commerce to suit English needs.

1661 A version of the New Testament translated into Algonquian became the **first Bible printed** in the colonies.

1664 British troops Sept. 8 seized New Netherland from Dutch. Charles II granted New Netherland and city of New Amsterdam to brother, Duke of York; both renamed **New York**. Dutch recaptured colony **1673**, but ceded it to Britain Nov. 10, **1674**.

1670 Charles Town, SC, founded by English colonists in April.

1673 Regular mail service on horseback instituted Jan. 1 between New York and Boston. **Jacques Marquette** and **Louis Jolliet** reached the upper Mississippi and traveled down it.

1674 Future **Salem witch trial** judge Samuel Sewall began renowned diary covering events through **1729**.

1676 Bloody **Indian war** in New England ended Aug. 12. King Philip, Wampanoag chief, and Narragansett Indians killed. **Nathaniel Bacon** led planters against autocratic British Gov. Sir William Berkeley, burned Jamestown, VA, Sept. 19. Rebellion collapsed when Bacon died; 23 followers executed.

1678 A book of poetry by **Anne Bradstreet** (first published in Britain) revised and expanded for posthumous publication in Massachusetts. Considered first female poet in American colonies.

1679 Fire destroyed 150 houses in Boston. City imported **first fire engines** from England.

1681 John Bunyan's *The Pilgrim's Progress* published in America; became best seller.

1682 Robert Cavelier, Sieur de La Salle, claimed lower Mississippi River country for France and called it **Louisiana** Apr. 9. Had French outposts built in Illinois and Texas, **1684**. Killed during mutiny, **1687**. Spanish colonists became the **first Europeans to settle Texas**, at site of present-day El Paso.

1683 William Penn signed treaty with Delaware Indians Apr. 23 and made payment for **Pennsylvania** lands. The **first German colonists** in America settled near Philadelphia.

1689 New York's English colonial governor, **Sir Edmund Andros**, resigned after armed uprising in Boston on Apr. 18.

1690 First colonial newspaper, *Publick Occurrences*, published by Benjamin Harris but promptly shut down for lack of official permission. Harris also published *New England Primer* for use as elementary school textbook. Large-scale **whaling** operations began in Nantucket, MA.

1692 Witchcraft hysteria began in Salem Village (now Danvers), MA; 20 men and women convicted of witchcraft executed by special court.

1697 *The Essays* of **Sir Francis Bacon**, first published in England in **1597**, was published in America; it became a best seller.

1699 Former privateer Capt. **William Kidd** arrested and sent to England; hanged for piracy, **1701**. French settlements made in **Mississippi, Louisiana**.

1765: Demonstrations erupt in Boston in response to the Stamp Act proclamations.

1702 Legislation enacted making **Church of England** the established church in Maryland.

1704 Indians attacked Deerfield, MA, Feb. 28-29; killed 40, carried off 100. *Boston News Letter*, **first regular newspaper**, started by postmaster John Campbell.

1710 British-colonial troops captured French fort, Port Royal, Nova Scotia, in **Queen Anne's War, 1702-13**. France yielded Nova Scotia by treaty, **1713**.

1712 Slaves revolted in New York Apr. 6; 21 were executed. Second uprising, **1741**; 13 slaves hanged, 13 burned, 71 deported.

1716 First theater in colonies opened in Williamsburg, VA.

1726 Great Awakening, general revival of evangelical religion, began in colonies.

1731 America's **first circulating library** founded in Philadelphia by Benjamin Franklin.

1732 Benjamin Franklin published the **first** *Poor Richard's Almanack*; published annually until **1757**. Last of 13 colonies, **Georgia**, chartered.

1733 Influenza epidemic swept through New York City and Philadelphia.

1735 Editor **John Peter Zenger** was acquitted of libel Aug. 5 in New York after criticizing the British governor's conduct in office.

1739 A series of **slave uprisings** put down in South Carolina.

1741 Famous sermon "Sinners in the Hands of an Angry God," delivered July 8 at Enfield, MA, by Jonathan Ed-

1692: Witch trials begin in Salem Village; 20 men and women are executed.

wards, one of the most important preachers in the **Great Awakening** religious revival. Danish navigator **Vitus Bering**, commanding Russian expedition, reached Alaska.

1744 King George's War pitted British and colonials versus French. Colonials captured Louisbourg, Cape Breton Isl., Nova Scotia, June 17, **1745**. Returned to France **1748** by Treaty of Aix-la-Chapelle.

1752 Benjamin Franklin, flying kite in thunderstorm, proved lightning is electricity, June 15; invented lightning rod. **Liberty Bell**, cast in England, was delivered to Pennsylvania.

1754 French and Indian War began with Ft. Necessity campaign in Pennsylvania. Skirmish May 28, battle at fort July 3-4. British moved Acadian French from Nova Scotia to Louisiana Oct. 8, **1755**. British captured Québec Sept. 18, **1759**, in battles in which French Gen. Joseph de Montcalm and British Gen. James Wolfe were killed. Peace pact signed Feb. 10, **1763**. French lost Canada and Midwest. Delegates from 7 colonies to New York for **Albany Congress**, July 19, approved plan of union by Benjamin Franklin; plan rejected by the colonies.

1757 First streetlights appeared in Philadelphia.

1764 Sugar Act, Apr. 5, placed duties on lumber, foodstuffs in colonies. First law passed by Parliament to specifically raise revenue from colonies, alleviate French and Indian War debts. British enforced this act, unlike with **Molasses Act** of 1733.

1765 Stamp Act, enacted by Parliament Mar. 22, required revenue stamps to help fund royal troops. Nine colonies, at Stamp Act Congress in New York Oct. 7-25, adopted Declaration of Rights. Stamp Act repealed Mar. 17, **1766**. **Quartering Act**, requiring colonists to house British troops, went into effect Mar. 24.

1767 Townshend Acts levied taxes on glass, painter's lead, paper, and tea. In **1770** all duties except on tea were repealed.

1770 British troops fired Mar. 5 into Boston mob, killed 5 including **Crispus Attucks**, a black man, reportedly leader of group; later called **Boston Massacre**.

1773 East India Co. tea ships turned back at Boston, New York, and Philadelphia in May. Cargo ship burned at Annapolis, Oct. 14; cargo thrown overboard at **Boston Tea Party**, Dec. 16, to protest the tea tax. **First museum** in the colonies was officially established in Charleston, SC; later named the Charleston Museum.

1774 "Intolerable Acts" of Parliament curtailed Massachusetts self-rule; barred use of Boston Harbor until tea was paid for. **First Continental Congress** held in Philadelphia Sept. 5-Oct. 26; called for civil disobedience against British. Rhode Island **abolished slavery**.

1775 Patrick Henry addressed Virginia convention, Mar. 23, said, "Give me liberty or give me death!" **Paul Revere, William Dawes**, and Dr. **Samuel Prescott**, Apr. 18, rode to alert patriots that British were on their way to Concord to destroy arms. At **Lexington**, MA, Apr. 19, Minutemen lost 8. On return from **Concord**, British suffered 273 casualties. Col. Ethan Allen (joined by Col. Benedict Arnold) captured **Ft. Ticonderoga** in New York, May 10, also Crown Point. Colonials headed for **Bunker Hill**, fortified Breed's Hill, Charlestown, MA. Repulsed British under Gen. William Howe twice before retreating, June 17. Continental Congress June 15 named **George Washington** commander in chief. Established a postal system, July 26; Benjamin Franklin became the **first postmaster general**.

1776 Thomas Paine's *Common Sense*, famous pro-independence pamphlet, published Jan. 10; quickly sold some 100,000 copies. **France and Spain** agreed May 2 to provide arms to U.S. In Continental Congress June 7, Richard Henry Lee (VA) moved "that these united colonies are, and of right ought to be, free and independent states." Resolution adopted July 2. **Declaration of Independence** approved July 4, signed Aug. 2. Col. William Moultrie's batteries at **Charleston, SC**, repulsed British sea attack June 28. Washington lost **Battle of Long Island** Aug. 27; evacuated New York. **Nathan Hale** executed as spy by British Sept. 22. Brig. Gen. Arnold's **Lake Champlain** fleet was defeated at Valcour Oct. 11, but British returned to Canada. Howe failed to destroy Washington's army at White Plains, Oct. 28. Hessians captured Ft. Washington, Manhattan, and 3,000 men, Nov. 16; captured Ft. Lee, NJ, Nov. 20. Washington, in Pennsylvania, recrossed **Delaware River** Dec. 25-26, defeated Hessians at Trenton, NJ, Dec. 26.

1777 Washington defeated Lord Charles Cornwallis at **Princeton** Jan. 3. Continental Congress, June 14, authorized an **American flag**, the Stars and Stripes. Maj. Gen. John Burgoyne's force of 8,000 from Canada, captured **Ft. Ticonderoga**, July 6. Americans beat back Burgoyne at Bemis Heights, Oct. 7, cut off British escape route. Burgoyne surrendered 5,000 men at Saratoga, NY, Oct. 17. **Articles of Confederation** adopted by Continental Congress, Nov. 15; took effect Mar. 1, **1781**.

1778 France signed treaty of aid with U.S. Feb. 6. Sent fleet; British evacuated Philadelphia, June 18.

1779 George Rogers Clark took Ft. Vincennes in what is now Indiana in February. **John Paul Jones** on the *Bonhomme Richard* defeated *Serapis* in British North Sea waters, Sept. 23.

1780 Charleston, SC, fell to the British May 12, but a British force was defeated near **Kings Mountain, NC**, Oct. 7 by militia. **Benedict Arnold** found to be a traitor Sept. 23. Arnold escaped, made brigadier general in British army.

1781 Bank of North America, **first commercial bank**, incorporated May 26. Cornwallis retired to **Yorktown, VA**. Adm. Francois Joseph de Grasse landed 3,000 French and stopped British fleet in **Hampton Roads**. Washington and Jean Baptiste de Rochambeau joined forces, arrived near Williamsburg, Sept. 26. Siege of Cornwallis began, Oct. 6; **Cornwallis surrendered** Oct. 19.

1782 New British cabinet agreed in March to **recognize U.S. independence**. Preliminary agreement signed in Paris, Nov. 30. Use of **scarlet letter A**, sewn on clothing or branded on skin of adulterers, discontinued in New England.

1783 Massachusetts Supreme Court decision in final Quock Walker trial **legally ended slavery**. Newspapers typically published weekly; **first regular daily newspaper**, *Pennsylvania Evening Post*, went on sale in Philadelphia, May 30. Britain, U.S. signed **Paris peace treaty**, Sept. 3, recognizing American independence; Congress ratified it Jan. 14, **1784**. **Washington ordered army disbanded** Nov. 3, bade farewell to his officers at Fraunces Tavern, New York City, Dec. 4.

1784 Thomas Jefferson's proposal to **ban slavery in new territories** after **1802** was narrowly defeated, Mar. 1.

1776: George Washington's army crosses the Delaware River to defeat Hessian forces in the Battle of Trenton.

1785 Regular stagecoach routes established between Albany, New York City, and Philadelphia.

1786 Delegates from 5 states at Annapolis, MD, Sept. 11-14 asked Congress to call a **constitutional convention**.

1787 Shays's Rebellion of debt-ridden farmers in Massachusetts failed, Jan. 25. **Constitutional convention** opened in Philadelphia, May 25, with Washington presiding. Constitution accepted by delegates, Sept. 17; Delaware became first state to ratify it, Dec. 7; Pennsylvania and New Jersey followed. **Northwest Ordinance** adopted July 13 by Continental Congress for Northwest Territory, north of Ohio River, west of New York; made rules for statehood. Guaranteed freedom of religion, support for schools, no slavery. *Federalist Papers* first appeared in *NY Independent Journal*.

1788 A **large fire in New Orleans**, then a Spanish territory, destroyed much of the city, Mar. 21. **Constitution adopted** June 21 after being ratified by the requisite ninth state (New Hampshire); also ratified by **Georgia, Connecticut, Massachusetts, Maryland, South Carolina, Virginia, and New York** throughout the year. **First U.S. senators elected** Sept. 30, from Pennsylvania.

1789 George Washington chosen president by all electors voting (73 eligible, 69 voting, 4 absent); **John Adams**, vice president, got 34 votes. **First Congress** met at Federal Hall, New York City, and declared Constitution in effect, Mar. 4; Washington inaugurated there Apr. 30; **first inaugural ball** held May 7. U.S. **State Dept.** established by Congress July 27. (Thomas Jefferson installed as first secretary of state Feb. **1790**.) **War Dept.** created Aug. 7, with Henry Knox as secretary; **Treasury Dept.** created Sept. 2, with Alexander Hamilton to be secretary. **Supreme Court** created by Federal Judiciary Act, Sept. 24; **John Jay** confirmed by Congress as **first Supreme Court chief justice**, Sept. 26.

1790 First Supreme Court session held Feb. 2 in New York City. Congress, Mar. 1, authorized decennial **U.S. census**. Collection of data took 18 months. **Naturalization Act** (2-year residency) passed Mar. 26. John Carroll consecrated as **first American Catholic bishop**, Aug. 15. Congress met in **Philadelphia**, new temporary capital, Dec. 6.

1791 Bill of Rights, submitted to states, Sept. 25, **1789**, went into effect Dec. 15. First Bank of the United States, **first bank to be chartered by federal government**, established in Philadelphia.

1792 Coinage Act established **U.S. Mint** in Philadelphia, Apr. 2. Gen. **"Mad" Anthony Wayne** made commander in Ohio-Indiana area, trained American Legion, established string of forts. Routed Indians at Fallen Timbers on Maumee River, Aug. 20, **1794**, checked British at Fort Miami, OH, same year. **White House** cornerstone laid Oct. 13.

1793 Washington inaugurated for second term, Mar. 4, having received 132 electoral votes; **John Adams** again became vice president, having received second highest total, 77. Washington declared **U.S. neutrality**, Apr. 22, in war between Britain and France. Eli Whitney invented **cotton gin**, reviving Southern slavery.

1794 Whiskey Rebellion, western Pennsylvania farmers protesting liquor tax of **1791**, suppressed by federal militia in September. **Jay's Treaty**, controversial treaty with Britain negotiated by John Jay, signed Nov. 19, ratified June 24, **1795**. This treaty intended to settle long-standing differences between U.S. and Britain.

1795 U.S. bought peace from **Algerian pirates** by paying $1 mil ransom for 115 seamen Sept. 5, followed by annual tributes. Gen. Wayne signed **Treaty of Greenville** with Indians, opening Northwest Territory to settlers. Univ. of North Carolina became **first operating state university**.

1796 Washington's farewell address as president delivered Sept. 17. Warned against permanent alliances with foreign powers, big public debt, large military establishment, and devices of "small, artful, enterprising minority."

1797 John Adams inaugurated as second president Mar. 4, having received 71 electoral votes; **Thomas Jefferson** became vice president, having received 68. U.S. frigate *United States* launched at Philadelphia, July 10; *Constellation* at Baltimore, Sept. 7; *Constitution* (Old Ironsides) at Boston, Sept. 20.

1798 Alien and Sedition Acts passed by Federalists June-July; intended to silence political opposition. **War with France threatened** over French raids on U.S. shipping and rejection of U.S. diplomats. Navy (45 ships) and 365 privateers captured 84 French ships. USS *Constellation* took French warship *Insurgente*, **1799**. Napoleon stopped French raids after becoming first consul.

1800 Federal government moved to **Washington, DC**.

1801 John Marshall named Supreme Court chief justice, Jan. 20. **Thomas Jefferson**, who had received same number of electoral votes as Aaron Burr in **1800** election, won out over Burr in House vote reached Feb. 17; Burr named vice president. **Tripoli declared war** June 10 against U.S., which refused added tribute to commerce-raiding Arab corsairs. Land and naval campaigns forced Tripoli to negotiate peace, June 4, **1805**. **Oldest U.S. art institution**, Pennsylvania Academy of Fine Arts, founded in Philadelphia.

1802 Congress established U.S. Military Academy at **West Point, NY**.

1803 Supreme Court, in *Marbury v. Madison*, overturned U.S. law for first time, Feb. 24. Napoleon sold all of Louisiana, stretching to Canadian border, to U.S. for $11,250,000 in bonds, plus $3,750,000 indemnities to American citizens with claims against France. U.S. took title Dec. 20. **Louisiana Purchase** doubled U.S. area.

1804 Meriwether Lewis and **William Clark** expedition ordered by Pres. Thomas Jefferson to explore what is now Northwest U.S. Started from St. Louis May 14; ended Sept. 23, **1806**, back in St. Louis. Vice Pres. **Aaron Burr** shot Alexander Hamilton in duel July 11 in Weehawken, NJ; Hamilton died next day.

1805 U.S. Marines aided by Arab mercenaries, Apr. 27, captured Tripolitan port of Derna. Major victory in war against **Barbary pirates**; inspiration for "to the shores of Tripoli" in Marines Corps song.

1807 Robert Fulton made **first practical steamboat trip**; left New York City Aug. 17, reached Albany, 150 mi away, in 32 hrs. **Embargo Act** banned all trade with foreign countries, forbidding ships to set sail for foreign ports Dec. 22.

1808 Slave importation outlawed. Some 250,000 slaves were illegally imported **1808-60**.

1810 Third U.S. Census found population of 7,239,814. The slave population was put at 1,191,364, and the population of all other non-white free persons at 186,446.

1811 Indiana Territory governor William Henry Harrison defeated Indians led by Tenskwatawa, called the Prophet, in **Battle of Tippecanoe**, Nov. 7. Construction began on **Cumberland Road** in Cumberland, MD; road became important route to West. About 400 **slaves revolted** in Louisiana, killing the son of a plantation owner and marching on New Orleans. The insurrection was suppressed; some 75 slaves killed.

1812 War of 1812 had 3 main causes: Britain seized U.S. ships trading with France; Britain had seized 4,000 naturalized U.S. sailors by **1810**; Britain armed Indians, who raided Western border. U.S. stopped trade with Europe **1807** and **1809**. Trade with Britain only was stopped **1810**. Unaware that Britain had raised blockade against France two days before, **Congress declared war** June 18. British took **Detroit** Aug. 16.

1813 Oliver H. Perry defeated British fleet at **Battle of Lake Erie**, Sept. 10. U.S. won **Battle of the Thames**, Ontario, Oct. 5, but failed in Canadian invasion attempts. York (Toronto) and Buffalo were burned.

1814 Troops under Andrew Jackson defeated Creek Indians led by Chief Weatherford at **Battle of Horseshoe Bend** in Alabama, Mar. 29, ending **Creek Indian War**, begun a year earlier. British landed in Maryland in August, defeated U.S. force Aug. 24, **burned Capitol and White House**.

1793: Eli Whitney patents the cotton gin; massive growth in U.S. cotton production and expansion of Southern slavery follows.

Maryland militia stopped British advance, Sept. 12. British bombardment of Ft. McHenry, Baltimore, for 25 hours, Sept. 13-14, failed, inspiring **Francis Scott Key** to write the words to **"The Star-Spangled Banner."** U.S. won naval **Battle of Lake Champlain** Sept. 11. Peace treaty with Great Britain signed at Ghent, Dec. 24.

1815 Some 5,300 British, unaware of peace treaty, attacked U.S. entrenchments near **New Orleans**, Jan. 8. British had more than 2,000 casualties; Americans lost 71. U.S. flotilla finally ended attacks by **pirates** from Ottoman states of Algiers, Tunis, Tripoli.

1816 Second Bank of the U.S. chartered Apr. 10. The **American Colonization Society**, which sought to address slavery issue by transporting freed blacks to Africa, formed in Washington, DC, Dec. **1816**-Jan. **1817**.

1817 Thomas Hopkins Gallaudet established the **first free public school for the deaf** in Hartford, CT.

1818 Connecticut **expanded suffrage** among white male voters. Massachusetts followed suit in **1820**, and New York in **1821**, reducing or eliminating property qualifications.

1819 Spain ceded **Florida** to U.S. Feb. 22. American steamship *Savannah* made **first part-steam-powered, part-sail-powered crossing of Atlantic**, traveling from Savannah, GA, to Liverpool, England, in 29 days. **Washington Irving**'s *Sketch Book* became best seller.

1820 First organized immigration of blacks to Africa from U.S. began with 86 free blacks sailing to Sierra Leone in February. Henry Clay's **Missouri Compromise** bill passed by Congress, Mar. 3. Slavery was allowed in Missouri but not west of the Mississippi River, north of 36° 30´ (the southern line of Missouri). Repealed **1854**.

1821 Emma Willard founded Troy Female Seminary, **first U.S. women's college**. Stephen Austin established **first American community in Texas**, San Felipe de Austin. **James Fenimore Cooper**'s *The Spy*, novel set during American Revolution, published and became a best seller.

1822 Tension between sports and academics surfaced when Yale College Pres. Timothy Dwight **banned a primitive form of football**, setting fines for violators.

1823 Monroe Doctrine, opposing European intervention in the Americas, enunciated by Pres. James Monroe Dec. 2. The **Hudson River School**, painters who focused on the beauties of nature, began to come to public attention.

1824 Pawtucket, RI, **weavers strike**, first such action by women workers. **Slavery abolished** in state of Illinois Aug. 2.

1825 After a deadlocked election, **John Quincy Adams** was elected president by the House, Feb. 9. **Erie Canal** opened; first boat left Buffalo Oct. 26, reached New York City Nov. 4. John Stevens of Hoboken, NJ, built and operated **first experimental steam locomotive** in U.S.

1826 Thomas Jefferson and **John Adams** both died July 4. **James Fenimore Cooper**'s *The Last of the Mohicans* published.

1827 Massachusetts became first state to pass a law providing for **tax-supported public high schools**.

1828 Baltimore & Ohio, the **first U.S. passenger railroad**, began operations July 4. South Carolina Dec. 19 declared right of **state nullification of federal laws**, opposing the "Tariff of Abominations." **Noah Webster** published his *American Dictionary of the English Language*.

1829 Andrew Jackson inaugurated as president, Mar. 4.

1830 Famous **debate** Jan. 27 between Sen. **Daniel Webster** (MA) and Robert Hayne (SC), on state right to nullify federal law. **Mormon church** organized by Joseph Smith in Fayette, NY, Apr. 6. Pres. Jackson, May 28, signed **Indian Removal Act**, providing land and some pay to Indians who agree to resettle in West.

1831 William Lloyd Garrison began **abolitionist newspaper** *The Liberator* Jan. 1. **Nat Turner**, black slave in Virginia, led local slave rebellion, starting Aug. 21; 57 whites killed. Troops called in, 100 slaves killed. Turner captured, tried, hanged Nov. 11.

1832 Black Hawk War in Illinois and Wisconsin Apr.-Sept. pushed Sauk and Fox Indians west across Mississippi.

1833 American Anti-Slavery Society founded in Philadelphia, Dec. 4. **Oberlin College** became **first to adopt coeducation** in U.S.

1835 Liberty Bell cracked July 8 while tolling death of Chief Justice John Marshall. **Seminole Indians** in Florida under Osceola began attacks Nov. 1, protesting forced removal. The unpopular war ended Aug. 14, **1842**; most of the Indians sent to Oklahoma. **Texas** proclaimed right to secede from Mexico; **Sam Houston** put in command of Texas army, Nov. 2-4. **Gold** discovered on Cherokee land in Georgia. Indians forced to cede lands, Dec. 20, and to cross Mississippi.

1836 Texans besieged at **Alamo** in San Antonio by Mexicans under Santa Anna, Feb. 23-Mar. 6; entire garrison killed. Texas independence declared, Mar. 2. At San Jacinto Apr. 21, Sam Houston and Texans defeated Mexicans. **Ralph Waldo Emerson** published his first work, *Nature*, espousing his philosophy of **transcendentalism**. Marcus Whitman, H. H. Spaulding, and wives reached Fort Walla Walla on Columbia River, OR, **first white women to cross the Continental Divide**, in the Rocky Mountains.

1838 Cherokee Indians forced to walk **"Trail of Tears"** from Georgia to Oklahoma starting in October.

1841 First emigrant wagon train bound for California, 47 persons, left Independence, MO, May 1, reached California Nov. 4. **Edgar Allan Poe** published one of the **first American detective stories**, *The Murders in the Rue Morgue*.

1842 Webster-Ashburton Treaty signed Aug. 9, fixing U.S.-Canada border in Maine and Minnesota. **First use of anesthetic** (sulfuric ether gas).

1843 More than 1,000 settlers left Independence, MO, for Oregon May 22, arriving in October via **Oregon Trail**.

1844 First message over first telegraph line sent May 24 by inventor Samuel F. B. Morse from Washington to Baltimore: "What hath God wrought?"

1845 Congress **overrode a presidential veto for the first time**, Mar. 3, after Pres. John Tyler vetoed a tariff bill. Congress of **Texas voted for annexation** by U.S., July 4. Texas

admitted to Union, Dec. 29. **Edgar Allan Poe**'s poem "The Raven" published.

1846 Mexican War began after Pres. James K. Polk ordered Gen. Zachary Taylor to seize disputed Texan land settled by Mexicans. After border clash, U.S. declared war May 13; Mexico declared war May 23. About 12,000 U.S. troops took Vera Cruz Mar. 27, **1847**, and Mexico City Sept. 14, **1847**. Treaty signed Feb. 2, **1848**, ended war, and Mexico ceded claims to Texas, California, and other territory. Bear flag of **Republic of California** raised by American settlers at Sonoma, June 14. Treaty with Britain June 15 set **Oregon territory boundary** at 49th parallel (extension of existing line). Expansionists had used slogan "54° 40´ or fight." The term **"manifest destiny,"** coined by journalist in **1845**, also came into play. **Mormons**, after violent clashes with settlers over polygamy, left Nauvoo, IL, for West under Brigham Young. They settled July **1847** at Salt Lake City, UT. Elias Howe invented **sewing machine**.

1847 First adhesive U.S. postage stamps—Benjamin Franklin 5¢, Washington 10¢—sold July 1. **Henry Wadsworth Longfellow**'s *Evangeline* published.

1848 Gold discovered Jan. 24 in California; 80,000 prospectors emigrated in **1849**. **Lucretia Mott** and **Elizabeth Cady Stanton** led Seneca Falls, NY, **Women's Rights Convention** July 19-20.

1850 Sen. Henry Clay's **Compromise of 1850** admitted California as 31st state Sept. 9, with slavery forbidden; made Utah and New Mexico territories; made **Fugitive Slave Law** more harsh; and ended District of Columbia slave trade. **Nathaniel Hawthorne**'s *The Scarlet Letter* published.

1851 Herman Melville's *Moby-Dick* published.

1852 Harriet Beecher Stowe's *Uncle Tom's Cabin* published.

1853 Japan receives Comm. Matthew C. Perry, July 14. He negotiated **treaty to open Japan** to U.S. ships. New York City hosted **first World's Fair** in the U.S., beginning July 14. **Stephen Foster** published "My Old Kentucky Home."

1854 Republican Party formed at Ripon, WI, Feb. 28. Opposed Kansas-Nebraska Act, which left issue of slavery to vote of settlers. Act became law May 30. Treaty ratified with Mexico Apr. 25, providing for **Gadsden Purchase** of a strip of land. **Henry David Thoreau**'s *Walden* published.

1855 First railroad train crossed Mississippi River on river's first bridge, between Rock Island, IL, and Davenport, IA, Apr. 21. **Walt Whitman**'s *Leaves of Grass* published.

1856 Republican Party's **first presidential nominee**, John C. Fremont, defeated. Abraham Lincoln made 50 speeches for him. Proslavery group sacked **Lawrence, KS**, May 21; abolitionist John Brown led antislavery contingent against Missourians at Osawatomie, KS, Aug. 30. **First U.S. kindergarten** opened in Watertown, WI.

1857 In **Dred Scott** case, which involved determination of constitutionality of already-repealed Missouri Compromise, Supreme Court decided Mar. 6 that slaves did not become free in a free state, and blacks were not and could not be citizens. **Currier & Ives**, firm of American lithographers, issued their first print.

1858 First Atlantic cable completed, by Cyrus W. Field Aug. 5. **Lincoln-Douglas debates** in Illinois, Aug. 21-Oct. 15.

1859 Edwin L. Drake drilled the **first commercially productive oil well** near Titusville, PA, Aug. 27. Abolitionist **John Brown**, with 21 men, seized U.S. Armory at **Harpers Ferry**, WV, Oct. 16. U.S. Marines captured raiders, killing several. Brown was hanged for treason Dec. 2.

1860 Shoeworkers in Lynn, MA, went on strike Feb. 22. Within a week, strike spread to include 20,000 shoeworkers throughout New England in country's **largest strike to date**. **First Pony Express** between Sacramento, CA, and St. Joseph, MO, started Apr. 3. Republican **Abraham Lincoln** elected president Nov. 6 in 4-way race.

1838: Cherokee Indians are marched from their homes in Georgia to Oklahoma on the "Trail of Tears."

1863: President Abraham Lincoln's Emancipation Proclamation frees slaves in seceding states.

1861 Seven southern states set up **Confederate States of America** Feb. 8, with **Jefferson Davis** as president. **Civil War** began as Confederates fired on **Ft. Sumter** in Charleston, SC, Apr. 12. They captured it Apr. 14. Pres. Lincoln called for 75,000 volunteers Apr. 15. By May, 11 states had **seceded**. Lincoln blockaded Southern ports Apr. 19, cutting off vital exports and aid. Confederates repelled Union forces at first **Battle of Bull Run**, July 21. **First transcontinental telegraph line** put in operation.

1862 Union forces were victorious in Western campaigns, took New Orleans May 1. Battles in East were largely inconclusive despite heavy casualties. The **Battle of Antietam**, in western Maryland Sept. 17, was bloodiest one-day battle of war; each side lost more than 2,000 men. **Homestead Act**, which granted free farms to settlers, approved May 20. **Land Grant Act**, which provided for public land sale to benefit agricultural education, approved July 7. It eventually led to establishment of state university systems.

1863 Pres. Lincoln issued **Emancipation Proclamation** Jan. 1, freeing "all slaves in areas still in rebellion." Entire Mississippi River was in Union hands by July 4. Union forces won major victory at Gettysburg, PA, July 1-3. Pres. Lincoln gave his **Gettysburg Address** Nov. 19. Confederate forces under siege surrendered **Vicksburg, MS**, to Union forces under Gen. Ulysses S. Grant, July 4. About 1,000 were killed or wounded in **draft riots** in New York City; some blacks were hanged by mobs July 13-16. Pres. Lincoln declared **Thanksgiving** a national holiday.

1864 Gen. **William Tecumseh Sherman** marched through Georgia, taking Atlanta Sept. 1 and Savannah Dec. 22. **Sand Creek massacre** of Cheyenne and Arapaho Indians Nov. 29. Soldiers drove Indians out of village; about 150 killed.

1865 Gen. **Robert E. Lee surrendered** 27,800 Confederate troops to Gen. Grant at Appomattox Court House in VA, Apr. 9. J. E. Johnston surrendered 31,200 to Sherman at Durham Station, NC, Apr. 18. Last rebel troops surrendered May 26. Pres. Lincoln shot Apr. 14 by **John Wilkes Booth** in Ford's Theater, Washington, DC. Died the following morning. Vice Pres. **Andrew Johnson** was sworn in as president. Booth was hunted down and fatally wounded, perhaps by his own hand, Apr. 26. Four co-conspirators were hanged July 7. **13th Amendment**, abolishing slavery, ratified Dec. 6.

1866 Congress took control of Southern **Reconstruction**, backed freedmen's rights in legislation vetoed by Johnson; veto overridden by Congress, Apr. 9. **Ku Klux Klan** formed secretly in South to terrorize blacks who voted. Disbanded **1869-71**.

1867 Alaska sold to U.S. by Russia for $7.2 mil Mar. 30, through efforts of Sec. of State William H. Seward. Fraternal society the **Grange** was organized Dec. 4 to protect farmer interests. **Horatio Alger**'s *Ragged Dick* published.

1868 Pres. Johnson again dismissed Sec. of War Edwin M. Stanton after first dismissing him in **1867**. **Johnson impeached** by the House Feb. 24 for violation of Tenure of Office Act but actually in response to his opposition to congressional Reconstruction. He was acquitted by the Senate March-May. **14th Amendment**, providing for citizenship of all persons born or naturalized in U.S. and subject to the jurisdiction thereof, ratified July 9. **Louisa May Alcott**'s *Little Women* published. *The World Almanac*, a publication of the *New York World*, appeared for first time.

1869 Transcontinental railroad completed; golden spike driven at Promontory Summit, UT, May 10, marking junction of Central Pacific and Union Pacific lines. Attempt to "corner" gold led to financial **"Black Friday"** in New York Sept. 24. **Woman suffrage law** passed in Wyoming Territory Dec. 10. **Knights of Labor** labor union formed in Philadelphia. By **1886**, it had 700,000 members nationally.

1870 15th Amendment, making race no bar to voting rights, ratified Feb. 8. **First U.S. boardwalk** completed, in Atlantic City, NJ. **U.S. Weather Bureau** founded.

1871 Great Chicago fire destroyed city Oct. 8-11. **National Rifle Association (NRA)** founded.

1872 Amnesty Act May 22 restored civil rights to citizens of the South, except for 500 Confederate leaders. Congress established Yellowstone, **first national park**. James McNeill Whistler painted famous portrait known informally as **"Whistler's Mother."**

1873 First U.S. postal card issued May 1. **Jesse James** and his gang robbed their first passenger train July 21. Banks failed, panic began in September. **Depression** lasted 5 years. **"Boss" William Tweed** of New York City was convicted Nov. 19 of stealing public funds. He died in jail in **1878**. New York's Bellevue Hospital started **first nursing school**.

1874 Women's Christian Temperance Union established in Cleveland. **First public zoo** in U.S. established in Philadelphia.

1875 Congress passed **Civil Rights Act** Mar. 1, giving equal rights to blacks in public accommodations and jury duty. Act invalidated in **1883** by Supreme Court. **First Kentucky Derby** held May 17. First **Jim Crow segregation law** enacted, in Tennessee.

1876 Democrat **Samuel J. Tilden** received majority of popular votes for president over Republican **Rutherford B. Hayes**, but 22 electoral votes were in dispute. Congress agreed to certify Hayes as winner in Feb. **1877** after Republicans agreed to end federal Reconstruction of South. **Alexander Graham Bell** patented the telephone Mar. 7. Col. **George A. Custer** and 264 soldiers of the 7th Cavalry were killed June 25 in "last stand," **Battle of the Little Bighorn**, MT, in Sioux Indian War.

1877 Molly Maguires—Irish terrorist society in mining areas of Scranton, PA—was broken up by hanging, June 21, of 11 leaders for murders of mine officials and police. Pres. Rutherford B. Hayes sent federal troops to control violent national **railroad strike**.

1869: The golden spike is driven at Promontory Summit, UT, marking the completion of the transcontinental railroad.

1881: Civil War nurse Clara Barton founds the American Red Cross.

1878 First commercial telephone exchange opened, New Haven, CT, Jan. 28. **Thomas A. Edison** founded Edison Electric Light Co. on Oct. 15.

1879 F. W. Woolworth opened his first five-and-ten store, in Utica, NY, Feb. 22. French actress **Sarah Bernhardt** made her U.S. debut Nov. 8 at New York City's Booth Theater. Economist and social philosopher **Henry George** published *Progress & Poverty*, advocating single tax on land.

1880 Chinese Exclusion Treaty signed with China, Nov. 17, providing for restitution of Chinese nationals entering U.S.

1881 Clara Barton founded **American Red Cross** May 21. Pres. **James A. Garfield** shot in Washington, DC, July 2; died Sept. 19. Famous gun battle between the Earp brothers and outlaw rustlers Oct. 26 near the **OK Corral**, Tombstone, AZ. **Booker T. Washington** founded Tuskegee Institute for blacks. **Helen Hunt Jackson**'s *A Century of Dishonor*, about mistreatment of Indians, published.

1882 Chinese Exclusion Act, barring Chinese immigration, passed by Congress May 6.

1883 Civil Service Act, or **Pendleton Act**, passed Jan. 16, created foundations of American civil service system. The **Brooklyn Bridge** opened May 24 as world's longest suspension bridge. The **Northern Pacific Railroad** was completed Sept. 8. **Buffalo Bill Cody**'s Wild West Show began its 30-year touring run.

1884 First long-distance telephone call completed, Mar. 27, between Boston and New York. Switchback Railway—**first U.S. roller coaster** built as amusement park ride—opened at Coney Island in New York City. **Mark Twain**'s *The Adventures of Huckleberry Finn* published.

1885 Washington Monument dedicated Feb. 21.

1886 Haymarket riot and bombing, May 4, followed labor battles for 8-hour day in Chicago; 7 police and 4 workers died. Eight anarchists found guilty Aug. 20; 4 hanged Nov. 11. **Coca-Cola** first sold, May 8, at Jacob's Pharmacy in Atlanta. Apache Indian **Geronimo** surrendered Sept. 4, ending last major Indian war. **Statue of Liberty** dedicated Oct. 28. **American Federation of Labor** (AFL) formed Dec. 8 by 25 craft unions.

1887 Interstate Commerce Act enacted Feb. 4, created Interstate Commerce Commission.

1888 Great blizzard struck Eastern U.S. Mar. 11-14, causing about 400 deaths. Ernest Thayer's poem **"Casey at the Bat"** recited for first time in public at New York City theater in May.

1889 U.S. opened **Oklahoma** to white settlement Apr. 22; within 24 hours claims for 2 mil acres were staked by 50,000 "sooner" settlers. More than 2,200 lives lost in **Johnstown, PA, flood** May 31. **Electric lights** installed at White House.

1890 Sherman Antitrust Act passed July 2, began federal effort to curb monopolies. Massacre at **Wounded Knee**, SD, Dec. 29, the last major conflict between Indians and U.S. troops; about 200 Indian men, women and children and 29 soldiers were killed. **Jacob Riis**'s *How the Other Half Lives*, about city slums, published, instigating reform legislation in New York City. **Emily Dickinson**'s poems published, 4 years after her death.

1891 Forest Reserve Act, Mar. 3, let president close public forest land to settlement for establishment of national parks. **Carnegie Hall**, in New York City, opened May 5.

1892 Ellis Island, in New York Bay, opened Jan. 1 to receive immigrants; closed **1954**. **Homestead, PA, strike** at Carnegie steel mills; 7 guards and 11 strikers and spectators shot to death July 6. James J. Corbett defeated John L. Sullivan Sept. 7 to become **first world heavyweight champion** under Marquess of Queensbury rules.

1893 Columbian Exposition world's fair held May-Oct. in Chicago. Financial panic led to 4-year **depression**. **Mormon Temple** dedicated in Salt Lake City, UT.

1894 Thomas A. Edison's **kinetoscope**, for motion pictures (invented **1887**), given first public showing Apr. 14. **Jacob S. Coxey** led army of unemployed from the Midwest, reaching Washington, DC, Apr. 30. Coxey arrested May 1 for trespassing on Capitol grounds; his army disbanded. **Pullman strike** began May 11 at railroad car plant in Chicago. Milton Hershey started **Hershey Chocolate Company**.

1895 "America, the Beautiful" appeared for first time, in church publication, July 4. **Stephen Crane**'s *The Red Badge of Courage* published.

1896 Supreme Court, in *Plessy v. Ferguson*, May 18, approved racial segregation under the **"separate but equal"** doctrine. **William Jennings Bryan** delivered "Cross of Gold" speech July 9; won Democratic Party nomination. **John Philip Sousa** composed "Stars and Stripes Forever" on Dec. 25.

1897 Olney-Pauncefote Treaty with Britain, Jan. 11, gave wide scope to arbitration in settling disputes; never ratified by U.S. John J. McDermott won **first Boston Marathon** Apr. 19. First Klondike gold arrived in San Francisco July 14, helping set off **Klondike gold rush**. **First subway service** in country opens to public in Boston, Sept. 1.

1898 U.S. battleship *Maine* blown up Feb. 15 in Havana, Cuba; 260 killed. U.S. blockaded Cuba Apr. 22 in aid of independence forces. U.S. declared **war on Spain** Apr. 24; destroyed Spanish fleet in Philippines May 1; took Guam June 20. U.S. took **Puerto Rico** July 25-Aug. 12. Spain agreed Dec. 10 to cede Philippines, Puerto Rico, and Guam, and approved independence for Cuba. Annexation of **Hawaii** signed by Pres. William McKinley, July 7.

1899 Filipino insurgents, unable to get recognition of independence from U.S., started guerrilla war Feb. 4. Their leader, Emilio Aguinaldo, captured May 23, **1901. Philippine insurrection** ended **1902**. Killed were 20,000 Filipino troops and some 200,000 civilians, mostly from disease and starvation. Pres. McKinley signed treaty officially ending **Spanish-American War**, Feb. 10. U.S. declared **Open Door Policy** Sept. 6, to make China an open international market. Philosopher **John Dewey**'s *School and Society*, advocating progressive education ("learn by doing"), published. Pianist Scott Joplin's "Maple Leaf Rag" published, popularizing **ragtime music**.

1890: Jacob Riis's *How the Other Half Lives* documents urban slums and tenements, instigating reform.

1900 International Ladies' Garment Workers Union founded in New York City June 3. Fought sweatshop working conditions. **Carry Nation**, Kansas temperance leader, began raiding saloons with a hatchet. U.S. helped suppress **Boxer Rebellion** in Beijing. Eastman Kodak Co. introduced the **Brownie camera**, popularizing picture-taking.

1901 Texas had first significant oil strike at **Spindletop** well near Beaumont, Jan. 10. Pres. **McKinley** shot Sept. 6 in Buffalo, NY, by anarchist Leon Czolgosz; died Sept. 14. Vice Pres. **Theodore Roosevelt** sworn in as **youngest-ever president**, at age 42 years, 11 months. **Booker T. Washington**'s *Up from Slavery* published. U.S. withdrew troops from **Cuba** May 20, and Cuba became independent.

1902 Permanent **Bureau of the Census** established Mar. 6. **Helen Keller** autobiography appeared in serial form.

1903 Treaty between U.S. and Colombia to have U.S. dig **Panama Canal** signed Jan. 22, rejected by Colombia. Panama declared independence from Colombia with U.S. support Nov. 3; recognized by Pres. Theodore Roosevelt Nov. 6. U.S., Panama signed canal treaty Nov. 18. Wisconsin set first **direct primary voting system**, May 23. **Henry Ford** founded Ford Motor Co., June 16. Boston defeated Pittsburgh, 5 games to 3, Oct. 13 in **first modern World Series**. **First successful flight** in heavier-than-air mechanically propelled airplane by **Orville Wright** Dec. 17 near Kitty Hawk, NC, 120 ft. in 12 secs. Later flight same day by **Wilbur Wright**, 852 ft. in 59 secs. Improved plane patented, 1906. **Iroquois Theater fire** in Chicago killed about 600 out of 1,900 in audience, Dec. 30. Pioneering film *Great Train Robbery* produced.

1904 St. Louis hosted **first Olympics in U.S.**, July 1-Nov. 23. **First section of New York subway** system opened, Oct. 27. **Ida Tarbell** published muckraking *The History of the Standard Oil Company*. **Henry James**'s last great novel, *The Golden Bowl*, published.

1905 Industrial Workers of the World, which advocated Marxian theory of class struggle between workers and capitalists, founded in Chicago, June 27. **Rotary**, oldest service club organization in U.S., founded in Chicago.

1906 San Francisco earthquake and fire, Apr. 18-19, caused more than 3,000 deaths and $400 mil in damages. **Upton Sinclair**'s *The Jungle*, which exposed working conditions in meat-packing industry, published. Helped spur passage of the **Pure Food and Drug Act** and **Meat Inspection Act** June 30.

1907 Financial panic and **depression** started Mar. 13. Pres. Roosevelt sent **"Great White Fleet"** of 16 U.S. battleships around the world in show of power.

1908 Springfield, IL, torn by **anti-black rioting**, Aug. 14-15. Henry Ford introduced **Model T** car, priced at $850, Oct. 1.

1909 Adm. Robert E. Peary claimed to have reached **North Pole** Apr. 6 on sixth attempt, accompanied by black explorer Matthew Henson and 4 Inuit; may have fallen short. National Conference on the Negro convened May 30, leading to founding of **National Association for the Advancement of Colored People** (NAACP).

1910 Boy Scouts of America founded Feb. 8. Former Pres. Roosevelt called for **"new nationalism"** in famous speech in Kansas, Aug. 10.

1911 Building with New York City's **Triangle Shirtwaist Co.** factory caught fire Mar. 25; 146 died. Supreme Court ruled May 15 that **Standard Oil Co.** must be dissolved because it unreasonably restrained trade. **First transcontinental airplane flight** (with numerous stops) by C. P. Rodgers, from New York to Pasadena, CA, Sept. 17-Nov. 5; time in air 82 hrs., 4 mins.

1912 American Girl Guides founded Mar. 12; name changed in **1913** to **Girl Scouts**. U.S. Marines, Aug. 14, sent to **Nicaragua**, which was in default of loans to U.S. and Europe.

1913 16th Amendment, authorizing federal income tax, ratified Feb. 3. The **Armory Show** in New York City brought modern art to U.S. for first time, Feb. 17. **17th Amendment**, providing for direct popular election of U.S. senators, ratified Apr. 8. **Federal Reserve System** authorized Dec. 23, in major reform of U.S. banking and finance.

1914 Ford Motor Co. raised basic wage rates from $2.40 for 9-hr. day to $5 for 8-hr. day, Jan. 5, increasing stability in labor force. When U.S. sailors were arrested in Tampico, Mexico, Apr. 9, Atlantic fleet was sent to **Veracruz**, occupied city. Pres. Woodrow Wilson proclaimed **U.S. neutrality** in the European war, Aug. 4. The **Panama Canal** officially opened Aug. 15. The **Clayton Antitrust Act** passed Oct. 15, strengthening federal antimonopoly powers.

1920: Prohibition of alcoholic beverages goes into effect, but homemade stills are widely in use.

1915 First transcontinental telephone call, New York to San Francisco, completed Jan. 25 by Alexander Graham Bell and Thomas A. Watson. British ship *Lusitania* sunk May 7 by German submarine; 1,198 passengers died, including 128 Americans. (In notice in morning newspapers the day *Lusitania* set sail, Germany had warned Americans against taking passage on British vessels.) As result of U.S. campaign, Germany issued apology and promise of payments, Oct. 5. Pres. Wilson asked for a military fund increase, Dec. 7. U.S. troops landed in **Haiti**, July 28. Haiti became virtual U.S. protectorate under Sept. 16 treaty. D. W. Griffith's film *The Birth of a Nation* released. William J. Simmons partly inspired by film to revive **Ku Klux Klan**, which peaks in 1920s.

1916 Gen. **John J. Pershing** entered Mexico to pursue **Francisco (Pancho) Villa**, who had raided U.S. border areas. Forces withdrew Feb. 5, **1917**. **Rural Credits Acts** passed July 17, followed by **Warehouse Act** Aug. 11; both provided financial aid to farmers. Bomb exploded during **San Francisco Preparedness Day parade** July 22, killed 10. Thomas J. Mooney, labor organizer, and Warren K. Billings, shoeworker, convicted **1917**; both later pardoned. U.S. bought **Virgin Islands** from Denmark Aug. 4. U.S. established military government in the **Dominican Republic** Nov. 29. **Jeannette Rankin** (R, MT) elected to House of Representatives, **first female member of Congress**.

1917 Germany, suffering from British blockade, declared almost unrestricted **submarine warfare** Jan. 31. U.S. cut diplomatic ties with Germany Feb. 3 and formally **declared war** Apr. 6. Jones Act, passed Mar. 2, made **Puerto Rico** a U.S. territory, its inhabitants U.S. citizens. **Conscription law** passed May 18. First U.S. troops arrived in Europe June 26.

1918 Pres. Wilson set out his **14 Points** as basis for peace, Jan. 8. More than 1 mil American troops were in Europe by July. Allied counteroffensive launched at Château-Thierry July 18. War ended with signing of **armistice** Nov. 11. **Influenza epidemic** killed an estimated 20 mil worldwide, 548,000 in U.S.

1919 18th Amendment, providing for prohibition of manufacture, sale, or transfer of alcoholic beverages, ratified Jan. 16, to take effect on Jan. 16, **1920**. **First**

transatlantic flight, by U.S. Navy seaplane, left Rockaway, NY, May 8, stopped at Newfoundland, Azores, Lisbon May 27. **Boston police strike** Sept. 9, earliest strike conducted by government employees. About 250 **foreign-born radicals** deported Dec. 21 to Soviet Union. **Sherwood Anderson**'s *Winesburg, Ohio* published.

1920 In national **Red Scare**, some 2,700 Communists, anarchists, and other radicals were arrested Jan.-May. **League of Women Voters** founded Feb. 14. Senate refused Mar. 19 to ratify **League of Nations Covenant**. **Nicola Sacco** and **Bartolomeo Vanzetti** accused of killing 2 men in Massachusetts payroll holdup Apr. 15. Found guilty **1921**. A 7-year campaign for their release failed; both executed Aug. 23, **1927**. Verdict repudiated **1977** by proclamation of Massachusetts Gov. Michael Dukakis. **19th Amendment** ratified Aug. 18, giving women the vote. **First regular licensed radio broadcasting** began Aug. 20. **Wall St. bombing** in New York City killed 30, injured 100, did $2 mil damage, Sept. 16. **Sinclair Lewis**'s *Main Street*, **F. Scott Fitzgerald**'s *This Side of Paradise*, and **Edith Wharton**'s *The Age of Innocence* published.

1921 Congress sharply curbed immigration, set **national quota system** May 19. Joint congressional resolution declaring **peace with Germany, Austria, and Hungary** signed July 2 by Pres. Warren G. Harding; treaties were signed in Aug. In so-called **Black Sox scandal**, 8 Chicago White Sox players were banned from baseball Aug. 4 for conspiring with gamblers to throw the **1919 World Series**. **Limitation of Armaments Conference** met in Washington, DC, Nov. 12-Feb. 6, **1922**. Major powers agreed to curtail naval construction, outlaw poison gas, restrict submarine attacks on merchant vessels, and respect China's integrity.

1922 During nationwide coal strike, union miners killed some 21 strike-breakers at Herrin, IL, June 21-22, in incident referred to as the **Herrin Massacre**. *Reader's Digest* founded. **T. S. Eliot**'s *The Waste Land* published in London.

1923 First sound-on-film motion picture, *Phonofilm*, shown at Rivoli Theater, New York City, beginning in April. Pres. Calvin Coolidge addressed Congress, Dec. 6; **first radio broadcast of president's annual speech**.

1924 Law approved by Congress June 15 made all **Native Americans U.S. citizens**. **Nellie Tayloe Ross** elected governor of Wyoming and **Miriam (Ma) Ferguson** elected governor of Texas Nov. 9. Ross inaugurated as nation's **first female governor** Jan. 5, **1925**. Ferguson installed Jan. 20, **1925**. **George Gershwin** wrote "Rhapsody in Blue."

1925 John T. Scopes found guilty of having taught **evolution** in Dayton, TN, high school, fined $100 and costs, July 24. **F. Scott Fitzgerald**'s *The Great Gatsby* published.

1926 Dr. Robert H. Goddard demonstrated practicality of rockets Mar. 16 in Auburn, MA, with **first liquid-fuel rocket**; rocket traveled 184 ft. in 2.5 secs. Congress established **Army Air Corps** July 2. **Air Commerce Act** passed Nov. 2, established government agencies for development of airports, radio navigation, and other services. **Ernest Hemingway**'s *The Sun Also Rises* published.

1927 Capt. **Charles A. Lindbergh** left Roosevelt Field, NY, May 20 alone in *Spirit of St. Louis* on first New York-Paris nonstop flight. Reached Le Bourget airfield May 21, 3,610 mi. in 33½ hrs. *The Jazz Singer*, **first feature-length film** in which **spoken dialogue was part of narrative action**, released Oct. 6. Noted for line, "You ain't heard nothin' yet!" *Show Boat*, Jerome Kern and Oscar Hammerstein II's adaptation of Edna Ferber's novel, opened in New York

1929: The Great Depression devastates Americans nationwide; Dorothea Lange's iconic photo, taken in 1936, comes to represent the desperation.

Dec. 27. Considered musical with first serious libretto.

1928 Amelia Earhart became first woman to fly across the Atlantic, June 17. **Herbert Hoover** elected president Nov. 6, defeating New York Gov. Alfred E. Smith, a Catholic.

1929 Gangsters killed 7 rivals in Chicago **St. Valentine's Day massacre** Feb. 14, which won Al Capone control of Chicago's underworld. Stock market crash Oct. 29 marked end of past prosperity as stock prices plummeted. Stock losses for **1929-31** estimated at $50 bil; beginning of **Great Depression**. Albert B. Fall, former secretary of the interior, was convicted of accepting $10,000 bribe in leasing of the **Elk Hills (Teapot Dome)** naval oil reserve; sentenced Nov. 1 to a year in prison and fined. **Thomas Wolfe**'s *Look Homeward, Angel* and **William Faulkner**'s *The Sound and the Fury* published.

1930 London **Naval Reduction Treaty** signed by U.S., Britain, Italy, France, and Japan Apr. 22; in effect Jan. 1, **1931**; expired Dec. 31, **1936**. **Hawley-Smoot Tariff** signed; rate hikes slash world trade. **Sinclair Lewis** became first American to win a **Nobel Prize in literature**. **Dashiell Hammett**'s *The Maltese Falcon*, which introduced detective Sam Spade, published.

1931 Empire State Building opened in New York City May 1, displacing Chrysler Building as world's tallest. **Al Capone** convicted of tax evasion Oct. 17. **Pearl Buck**'s *The Good Earth* published. **Charlie Chaplin** film *City Lights* released.

1932 Reconstruction Finance Corp. established Jan. 22 to stimulate banking and business. Unemployment at 12 mil. Twenty-month-old **Charles Lindbergh Jr.** kidnapped Mar. 1; found dead May 12. Bruno Hauptmann found guilty Feb. **1935**; executed Apr. 3, **1936**. Unemployed World War I veterans demanding Congress pay promised bonus early launched **Bonus March** on Washington, DC, May 29. **Franklin D. Roosevelt** elected president for first time in Democratic landslide, Nov. 8. Chicago Bears won **first NFL title game** Dec. 18, defeating the Portsmouth (OH) Spartans, 9-0.

1933 Pres. Roosevelt named **Frances Perkins** U.S. secretary of labor; **first woman in U.S. cabinet**. Pres. Roosevelt ordered **all U.S. banks closed** Mar. 6. In a "100 days" special session, Mar. 9-June 16, Congress passed **New Deal**, including measures to regulate banks, distribute funds to the jobless, create jobs, raise agricultural prices, and set wage and production standards for industry. **Gold standard** dropped by U.S. in favor of "modified gold bullion standard"; announced by Pres. Roosevelt Apr. 19, ratified by Congress June 5. **Tennessee Valley Authority (TVA)** created by act of Congress, May 18. Prohibition ended in the U.S. as 36th state ratified **21st Amendment** Dec. 5. Pres. Roosevelt foreswore armed intervention in **Western Hemisphere** nations, Dec. 26.

1934 Pres. Roosevelt signed law creating **Securities and Exchange Commission**, June 6. U.S. troops pulled out of **Haiti**, Aug. 6.

1935 Works Progress Administration (WPA) instituted May 6. Rural Electrification Administration created May 11. National Industrial Recovery Act struck down by Supreme Court May 27. **Boulder Dam** (later renamed **Hoover Dam**) completed, May 29. **Social Security Act** passed by Congress Aug. 14. Comedian **Will Rogers** and aviator Wiley Post killed Aug. 15 in Alaska plane crash. **Huey Long**, Louisiana senator and national political leader, shot Sept. 8; died Sept. 10. George Gershwin's jazz opera *Porgy and Bess* opened Oct. 10 in New York. **Committee for Industrial Organization** (later Congress of Industrial Organizations) formed to expand industrial unionism Nov. 9.

1936 Jesse Owens won 4 gold medals at the **Berlin Olympics** in August, first American to do so in track-and-field events at single Olympics. **Baseball Hall of Fame** founded in Cooperstown, NY. **Margaret Mitchell**'s *Gone with the Wind* published.

1937 Airship *Hindenburg* caught fire, was destroyed May 6 as it was landing in Lakehurst, NJ. **Golden Gate Bridge** opened May 27, becoming suspension bridge with world's longest span. **Joe Louis** knocked out James J. Braddock to become world heavyweight champ June 22. Aviator **Amelia Earhart** and copilot Fred Noonan disappeared July 2 near Howland Island, in the Pacific. Pres. Roosevelt asked for 6 additional Supreme Court justices; **"packing" plan** defeated. **Auto, steel labor unions** won first big contracts. **Zora Neale Hurston**'s *Their Eyes Were Watching God* published.

1938 National minimum wage enacted June 25. Orson Welles's radio dramatization of H. G. Wells's *War of the Worlds*, Oct. 30, caused Martian invasion scare. **Seabiscuit** beat War Admiral in match race of the century, at Pimlico track, MD, Nov. 1. Artist Anna Mary Robertson, **"Grandma Moses,"** discovered. **Thornton Wilder**'s *Our Town* produced on Broadway.

1939 Opera singer **Marian Anderson** performed for integrated crowd of 75,000 at Lincoln Memorial Apr. 9. First Lady Eleanor Roosevelt had quit Daughters of the American Revolution after organization refused to let Anderson sing in DC's Constitution Hall. **New York World's Fair**—theme: "The World of Tomorrow"—opened Apr. 30, closed Oct. 31. Reopened for second season May 11, **1940**, ended Oct. 27. **Lou Gehrig**, seriously ill, said farewell to fans at Yankee Stadium, July 4. Albert Einstein alerted Pres. Roosevelt to **A-bomb possibilities** in Aug. 2 letter. **U.S. declared its neutrality** in European war Sept. 5. Pres. Roosevelt proclaimed limited **national emergency** Sept. 8, unlimited emergency May 27, **1941**. Both ended by Pres. Harry Truman, Apr. 28, **1952**. Pocket Books, **first paperback publisher** in U.S., established. **John Steinbeck**'s *The Grapes of Wrath* published. Film versions of *Gone with the Wind*—which went on to win a record 8 Academy Awards—and *The Wizard of Oz* released.

1940 U.S. OK'd sale of **surplus war material** to Britain June 3; announced transfer of 50 overaged destroyers Sept. 3. **First peacetime military draft** in U.S. history approved, Sept. 14. **Forty-hour work week** went into effect, Oct. 24. Pres. **Roosevelt** elected Nov. 5 to third presidential term. **Carson McCullers**'s *The Heart Is a Lonely Hunter* and **Richard Wright**'s *Native Son* published.

1941 Four Freedoms—freedom of speech and religion, freedom from want and fear—termed essential by Pres. Roosevelt in speech to Congress Jan. 6. **Lend-Lease Act** signed Mar. 11 provided $7 bil in military credits for Britain. Lend-lease for USSR approved in Nov. Pres. Roosevelt signed executive order June 25 barring federal government and war contractors from **racial discrimination**. Order also established Fair Employment Practice Committee. The **Atlantic Charter**, 8-point declaration of principles, issued by Pres. Roosevelt and British Prime Min. Winston Churchill, Aug. 14. Japan attacked **Pearl Harbor**, Hawaii, 7:55 AM Hawaiian time, Dec. 7; 19 ships sunk or damaged, 2,300 dead. Pres. Roosevelt called it "a date which will live in infamy." U.S. declared war on Japan Dec. 8. Germany and Italy declared war on U.S. Dec. 11. U.S. responded with declaration of war later on same day. Japanese invaded **Philippines**, Dec. 22; Wake Island fell, Dec. 23. *Citizen Kane*, directed by Orson Welles, released.

1942 Japanese troops took **Bataan** peninsula Apr. 8, took **Corregidor** May 6. Federal government began forcibly moving 110,000 Japanese-Americans from West Coast to **detention camps**. Exclusion lasted 3 years. **Battle of Midway** June 4-7 was Japan's first major defeat. Marines landed on **Guadalcanal** Aug. 7; last Japanese not expelled until Feb. 9, **1943**. U.S., Britain invaded **North Af-**

rica Nov. 8. **First nuclear chain reaction** (fission of uranium isotope U-235) produced at Univ. of Chicago under physicists Arthur Compton, Enrico Fermi, others, Dec. 2. The movie *Casablanca*, starring Humphrey Bogart and Ingrid Bergman, released.

1943 *Oklahoma!* opened Mar. 31 on Broadway. Pres. Roosevelt signed June 10 pay-as-you-go income tax bill. Starting July 1, wage and salary earners were subject to **paycheck withholding tax**. **Detroit race riot** June 21 left 34 dead, 700 injured. Six killed in riot in New York City's **Harlem** section Aug. 2. U.S., Britain invaded **Sicily** July 9, Italian **mainland** Sept. 3. Marines in Nov. recaptured the **Gilbert Islands**, captured by Japan in **1941** and **1942**.

1944 U.S., Allied forces invaded Europe at Normandy, France, on **"D Day,"** June 6, in greatest amphibious landing in history. **Battle of the Bulge**, failed Nazi counteroffensive, waged Dec. 16 to Jan. 28, **1945**. **GI Bill of Rights**, providing benefits to veterans, signed by Pres. Roosevelt June 22. Representatives of the U.S. and other major powers met at **Dumbarton Oaks**, Washington, DC, Aug. 21-Oct. 7, to work out formation of postwar world organization that became the **United Nations**. U.S. forces landed on **Leyte**, Philippines, Oct. 20. Pres. **Roosevelt** elected to fourth term as president Nov. 7.

1945 Yalta Conference met in the Crimea, USSR, Feb. 4-11. Pres. Roosevelt, Prime Min. Churchill, and Soviet leader Joseph Stalin agreed that their 3 countries, plus France, would occupy Germany and that the Soviet Union would enter war against Japan. Marines landed on **Iwo Jima** Feb. 19, won control Mar. 16 after heavy casualties. U.S. forces invaded **Okinawa** Apr. 1, captured it June 21. Pres. **Roosevelt** died in Warm Springs, GA, Apr. 12; Vice Pres. **Harry S. Truman** became president. Germany surrendered May 7; May 8 proclaimed **V-E Day**. **First atomic bomb**, produced at Los Alamos, NM, exploded at Alamogordo, NM, July 16. Bomb dropped on **Hiroshima** Aug. 6, killing about 75,000; bomb dropped on **Nagasaki** Aug. 9, killing about 40,000. Japan agreed to surrender Aug. 14; formally surrendered Sept. 2. At **Potsdam Conference**, July 17-Aug. 2, leaders of U.S., USSR, and Britain agreed on disarmament of Germany, occupation zones, war crimes trials. **Empire State Building** struck accidentally by Army B-25 bomber, July 28, killing 14. U.S. forces entered **Korea** south of 38th parallel to displace Japanese Sept. 8. Gen. **Douglas MacArthur** took over supervision of Japan Sept. 9.

1946 Steel strike by 750,000 started Jan. 21, settled in 4 weeks. Strike by 400,000 **mine workers** began Apr. 1 (settled May 29); other industries (including rail, maritime) followed. Winston Churchill employed the phrase **"Iron Curtain"** in Mar. 5 speech at Westminster College in Fulton, MO. Atomic bomb tested off **Bikini Atoll** in Pacific, July 1. In all, U.S. conducted 23 nuclear tests between 1946 and **1958**. **Philippines** given independence by U.S. July 4. Mother Frances Xavier Cabrini **first American to be canonized**, July 7. Dr. Benjamin Spock's *Baby and Child Care* published as **baby boom** began. **John Hersey**'s *Hiroshima* published.

Dec. 7, 1941: Japan attacks Pearl Harbor, HI; Pres. Roosevelt declares it "a date which will live in infamy."

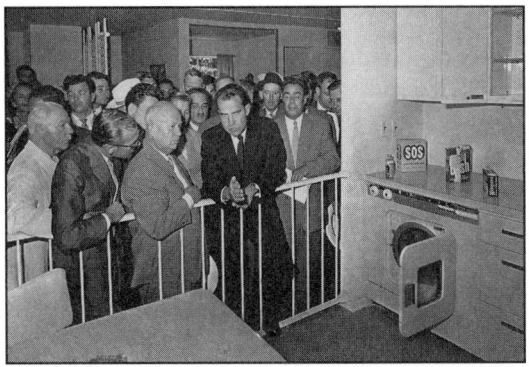

1959: Soviet Premier Nikita Khrushchev and Vice President Richard Nixon engage in famous "Kitchen Debate" in Moscow.

1947 Pres. Truman asked Congress for financial and military aid for Greece and Turkey to help combat Communist subversion (**Truman Doctrine**), Mar. 12. Approved May 15. UN Security Council voted Apr. 2 to place under U.S. trusteeship the **Pacific islands** formerly mandated to Japan. **Jackie Robinson** joined Brooklyn Dodgers Apr. 11, breaking color barrier in major league baseball. The **Marshall Plan** for U.S. aid to European countries proposed by Sec. of State George C. Marshall June 5. Congress authorized some $12 bil in next 4 years. **Taft-Hartley Labor Act** restricting labor union power vetoed by Pres. Truman June 20; Congress overrode veto. Air Force Capt. **Chuck Yeager** broke sound barrier, Oct. 14, in X-1 rocket plane.

1948 Organization of American States founded Apr. 30 by 21 countries. USSR halted all surface traffic into **West Berlin** June 24; in response, U.S. and British troops launched an **airlift**. Soviet blockade halted May 12, **1949**; airlift ended Sept. 30. Pres. **Truman** elected Nov. 2, defeating Gov. Thomas E. Dewey in historic upset. **Alger Hiss** indicted Dec. 15 for perjury, after denying he had passed secret documents to Whittaker Chambers to go to a Communist spy ring. Convicted Jan. 21, **1950**. **Kinsey Report** on sexuality in the human male published.

1949 North Atlantic Treaty Organization (**NATO**) established Aug. 24 by U.S., Canada, and 10 Western European nations, agreeing that an armed attack against one would be considered an attack against all. Eleven leaders of U.S. **Communist Party** convicted Oct. 14 of advocating violent overthrow of U.S. government; sentenced to prison. Supreme Court upheld convictions, **1951**. Pres. Truman, Oct. 26, signed legislation raising **federal minimum wage** from 40¢ an hour to 75¢. **Arthur Miller**'s *Death of a Salesman* opened on Broadway.

1950 Masked bandits robbed **Brink's, Inc.**, Boston express office, Jan. 17 of $2.8 mil. Case solved **1956**; 8 sentenced to life. Pres. Truman authorized production of **H-bomb** Jan. 31. Sen. **Estes Kefauver** (D, TN) chaired Special Committee to Investigate Organized Crime in Interstate Commerce, organized May 3. Also known as Kefauver Committee.

North Korean forces **invaded South Korea** June 25. UN asked for troops to restore peace. Pres. Truman ordered Air Force and Navy to Korea June 27. Truman approved ground forces, air strikes against North Korea June 30. U.S. sent 35 military advisers to **South Vietnam** June 27 and agreed to aid anti-Communist government. U.S. forces landed at **Inchon**, South Korea, Sept. 15. UN forces took Pyongyang Oct. 20, reached China border Nov. 20; China sent troops across border Nov. 26. U.S. banned shipments Dec. 8 to **Communist China** and to Asiatic ports trading with it.

Army **seized all railroads** Aug. 27 on Truman's order to prevent general strike; returned to owners in **1952**. Charles Schulz's *Peanuts* comic strip first appeared in newspapers, Oct. 2. Two members of **Puerto Rican nationalist movement** tried to kill Pres. Truman Nov. 1. Variety show *Your Show of Shows* debuted on TV. David Riesman's *The Lonely Crowd* published.

1951 22nd Amendment, limiting presidential term of office, ratified Feb. 27. **Julius Rosenberg**, his wife, **Ethel Rosenberg**, and **Morton Sobell** found guilty Mar. 29 of conspiracy to commit wartime espionage. Rosenbergs received death penalty. Sobell sentenced to 30 years; released **1969**.

Pres. Truman removed Gen. **Douglas MacArthur** from Korea command Apr. 11 for unauthorized policy statements. **Korea cease-fire talks** began in July; lasted 2 years. Fighting ended July 27, **1953**.

Transcontinental TV began Sept. 4 with Pres. Truman's address at Japanese Peace Treaty Conference in San Francisco. **Japanese peace treaty** signed in San Francisco Sept. 8 by U.S., Japan, and 47 other nations. **J. D. Salinger**'s *Catcher in the Rye* published.

1952 Pres. Truman ordered **seizure of nation's steel mills** Apr. 8 to avert strike. Ruled illegal by Supreme Court June 2. **Peace contract** between West Germany, U.S., Great Britain, and France signed May 26. Last racial and ethnic barriers to naturalization removed, June 26-27, with passage of **Immigration and Naturalization Act of 1952**. **Puerto Rico** proclaimed commonwealth July 25, after referendum Mar. 3. Richard Nixon, as vice-pres. candidate, gave **"Checkers" speech**, so called because of sentimental reference to his dog Checkers, Sept. 23. **First hydrogen device explosion** Nov. 1 in Pacific. **Ralph Ellison**'s *Invisible Man* published.

1953 Federal jury in New York convicted 13 **Communist** leaders on conspiracy charges, Jan. 20. **Julius and Ethel Rosenberg** executed in Sing Sing Prison electric chair, Ossining, NY, June 19, for relaying nuclear secrets to Soviet Union. **Korean War armistice** signed July 27. California Gov. **Earl Warren** sworn in Oct. 5 as 14th chief justice of U.S. Supreme Court.

1954 *Nautilus*, **first atomic-powered submarine**, launched at Groton, CT, Jan. 21. Five members of Congress were wounded in the House Mar. 1 by 4 **Puerto Rican independence supporters** who fired at random from a spectators' gallery.

At televised Army-McCarthy hearings, Apr. 22-June 17, before a Senate subcommittee, Army officials accused Sen. **Joseph McCarthy** (R, WI) of seeking preferential treatment for a draftee, and McCarthy accused Army of hindering probe of Communist infiltration into Army. McCarthy was cleared in the hearings, but the Senate later voted to condemn him, 67-22, for his abuse of the Senate during hearings and debates.

Supreme Court ruled unanimously May 17 that racial segregation in public schools was unconstitutional, in *Brown v. Board of Education of Topeka*. **Ernest Hemingway** won Nobel Prize in literature for *The Old Man and the Sea*.

1955 U.S. agreed Feb. 12 to help train **South Vietnamese army**. Supreme Court ordered "all deliberate speed" in **integration** of public schools, May 31. A summit meeting of leaders of **Big 4**—U.S., Britain, France, and USSR—took place July 18-23 in Geneva, Switzerland.

Rosa Parks refused Dec. 1 to give her seat to white man on bus in Montgomery, AL. Her arrest, detention, and conviction sparked boycott of bus system, organized by Rev. **Martin Luther King Jr.**, by Montgomery's black community, Dec. 5. Bus segregation ordinance declared unconstitutional by federal court in **1956**. Boycott ended Dec. 23 of that year.

America's 2 largest labor organizations merged Dec. 5, creating **AFL-CIO**. Russian-born U.S. citizen **Vladimir Nabokov**'s *Lolita* published.

1956 Massive resistance to **Supreme Court desegregation rulings** was called for Mar. 12 by 101 Southern congressmen. U.S. Supreme Court, Apr. 23, unanimously ruled against **racial segregation** on intrastate buses.

Federal-Aid Highway Act signed June 29, creating **interstate highway system**. **First transatlantic telephone cable** activated Sept. 25. On Oct. 8, in Game 5, Yankee righthander Don Larsen pitched **only perfect World Series game**. **Eugene O'Neill**'s *Long Day's Journey into Night*, autobiographical play about dissolution of his family, opened in November on Broadway.

1957 Congress approved **Civil Rights Act of 1957**, Apr. 29, first such bill since Reconstruction to protect voting rights. The U.S. surgeon general July 12 said studies showed "direct link" between cigarette **smoking and lung cancer**.

Arkansas Gov. Orval Faubus called National Guardsmen Sept. 4 to bar 9 black students from entering all-white high school in **Little Rock**. Faubus complied Sept. 21 with federal court order to remove Guardsmen, but local authorities ordered black students to withdraw. Pres. Eisenhower sent troops Sept. 24 to enforce court order. Pres. Eisenhower signed **Civil Rights Act** into law Sept. 9; provided for creation of Civil Rights Commission.

Jack Kerouac's *On the Road* published.

1958 Army launched **first U.S. Earth-orbiting satellite**, *Explorer I*, Jan. 31 from Cape Canaveral, FL; discovered Van Allen radiation belt. U.S. Marines sent to **Lebanon** to protect elected government from threatened overthrow July-Oct. Nuclear sub *Nautilus* made **first undersea crossing of North Pole** Aug. 5. Presidential aide **Sherman Adams** resigned Sept. 22 over scandal involving alleged improper gifts. **First domestic jet airline passenger service** in U.S. opened by National Airlines Dec. 10 between New York and Miami.

1959 Alaska admitted as 49th state, Jan. 3; **Hawaii** admitted as 50th, Aug. 21. Completion of **St. Lawrence Seaway** Apr. 25 allowed passage of oceangoing vessels between Atlantic Ocean and Great Lakes.

Vice Pres. Richard Nixon, on tour of USSR, held **"kitchen debate,"** July 24, with Soviet Prem. Nikita Khrushchev at U.S. exhibit in Moscow. Prem. **Khrushchev** paid unprecedented visit to U.S. Sept. 15-27; made transcontinental tour.

Pres. Eisenhower issued injunction Oct. 12, upheld and made effective by Supreme Court Nov. 7, ending **record 116-day steel strike**. In **quiz show scandal**, Columbia Univ. Prof. Charles Van Doren admitted to U.S. House subcommittee Nov. 2 that he had been coached before appearances on NBC-TV's *21* in **1956**; he had won $129,000. William Wyler's *Ben-Hur* released; the movie won a record 11 Academy Awards the following year.

1960 Sit-ins began Feb. 1 when 4 black college students in Greensboro, NC, refused to move from a Woolworth lunch counter after being denied service. By Sept. **1961**, more than 70,000 students, whites and blacks, had participated in sit-ins. Pres. Eisenhower signed **Civil Rights Act** May 6.

A U.S. **U-2 reconnaissance plane** was shot down in the Soviet Union May 1; pilot Gary Powers captured. The incident led to cancellation of a Paris summit conference. A **birth control pill** approved as safe for first time by Food and Drug Administration May 9. Vice Pres. **Richard Nixon** and Sen. **John F. Kennedy** faced each other Sept. 26 in first in series of televised debates. Kennedy defeated Nixon to win presidency, Nov. 8. U.S. announced Dec. 15 its backing of rightist group in **Laos**, which took power the next day. Alfred Hitchcock film *Psycho* released.

1961 U.S. severed diplomatic and consular relations with Cuba Jan. 3, after disputes over nationalizations of U.S. firms, U.S. military presence at Guantanamo base. U.S.-directed invasion of Cuba's **Bay of Pigs** Apr. 17 by Cuban exiles unsuccessfully attempted to overthrow the regime of Prem. Fidel Castro.

Peace Corps created by executive order, Mar. 1. **23rd Amendment**, giving DC citizens the right to vote in presidential elections, ratified Mar. 29. Comdr. Alan B. Shepard Jr. rocketed from Cape Canaveral, FL, in a Mercury capsule May 5, in **first U.S.-crewed suborbital space flight**.

"Freedom Rides" from Washington, DC, across Deep South were launched May 20 to protest segregation in interstate transportation.

Joseph Heller's *Catch-22*, **Harper Lee**'s *To Kill a Mockingbird*, and **John Updike**'s *Rabbit, Run* published.

1962 Pres. Kennedy said Feb. 14 that U.S. military advisers in **Vietnam** would fire if fired upon. Lt. Col. John H. Glenn Jr. became **first American in orbit** Feb. 20 when he circled the Earth 3 times in the Mercury capsule *Friendship 7*.

In *Baker v. Carr*, Mar. 26, Supreme Court ruled that constitutional challenges to unequal distribution of voters among legislative districts could be resolved by federal courts. **James Meredith** became first black student at Univ. of Mississippi Oct. 1 after 3,000 troops put down riots.

A Soviet **offensive missile buildup** in Cuba was revealed Oct. 22 by Pres. Kennedy, who ordered naval and air quarantine on shipment of offensive military equipment to the island. He and Soviet Prem. Khrushchev agreed Oct. 28 on formula to end crisis. Kennedy announced Nov. 2 that missile bases in Cuba were being dismantled.

Rachel Carson's *Silent Spring* launched environmentalist movement.

1963 In *Gideon v. Wainwright*, Mar. 18, Supreme Court ruled that all criminal defendants must have counsel.

March for civil rights began May 2 in Birmingham, AL, led to desegregation accord, which in turn sparked rioting and violence. University of Alabama **desegregated** after Gov. George Wallace stepped aside when confronted by federally deployed National Guard troops June 11. Civil rights leader **Medgar Evers** assassinated June 12. On Aug. 28, 200,000 joined in **March on Washington** in support of black demands for equal rights led by Rev. Martin Luther King Jr.; highlight was King's **"I have a dream" speech**. Four black girls killed in bombing of **16th St. Baptist Church** in Birmingham, AL, Sept. 15.

Supreme Court ruled June 17 that laws requiring **recitation of Lord's Prayer or Bible verses** in public schools were unconstitutional. Pres. Kennedy, on Europe trip, addressed huge crowd in **West Berlin**, June 23. Limited **nuclear test-ban treaty** agreed upon July 25 by the U.S., the Soviet Union, and Britain.

South Vietnam Pres. **Ngo Dinh Diem** assassinated Nov. 2; U.S. had earlier withdrawn support. Pres. **Kennedy** shot and fatally wounded Nov. 22 as he rode in motorcade through downtown Dallas, TX. Vice Pres. **Lyndon B. Johnson** sworn in as president. **Lee Harvey Oswald** arrested and charged with murder but was himself shot and fatally wounded Nov. 24. Nightclub owner **Jack Ruby** convicted of Oswald's murder; Ruby died in **1967** while awaiting retrial following reversal of his conviction. **Betty Friedan**'s feminist work *The Feminine Mystique* published.

1964 Panama suspended relations with U.S. Jan. 9 after riots. U.S. offered Dec. 18 to negotiate new canal treaty. **The Beatles** arrived in U.S. for first time; appeared Feb. 9 on *The Ed Sullivan Show*. Supreme Court ruled Feb. 17 in *Wesberry v. Sanders* that **congressional districts** as near as practicable be equal in population so that "one man's vote in a Congressional election is to be worth as much as another's." U.S. reported May 27 it was sending military planes to **Laos**.

Three **civil rights workers** reported missing in Mississippi June 22; bodies found Aug. 4. Eighteen white men tried. On Oct. 20, **1967**, an all-white federal jury convicted 7 of conspiracy in the slayings. Omnibus **civil rights bill** signed by Pres. Johnson July 2, banning discrimination in voting, jobs, public accommodations.

Congress Aug. 7 passed **Tonkin Gulf Resolution**, authorizing presidential action in Vietnam, after North Vietnamese boats reportedly attacked 2 U.S. destroyers Aug. 2. Congress approved War on Poverty bill Aug. 11, providing for a domestic Peace Corps (**VISTA**), **Job Corps**, and antipoverty funding. The **Warren Commission** released a report Sept. 27 concluding that Lee Harvey Oswald was solely responsible for the Kennedy assassination. Pres. **Johnson** elected to full term, Nov. 3, defeating Sen. **Barry Goldwater** (R, AZ) in landslide. **Verrazano-Narrows Bridge** opened in New York City Nov. 21, with world's longest suspension span.

1965 In State of the Union address Jan. 4, Pres. Johnson outlined plans for **"Great Society,"** program of civil rights, antipoverty, and health-care legislation. Pres. Johnson in Feb. ordered continuous bombing of **North Vietnam** below 20th parallel.

Malcolm X assassinated Feb. 21 at New York City rally. **March from Selma to Montgomery**, AL, Mar. 21-25, by Rev. Martin Luther King Jr. to demand federal protection of blacks' voting rights. New **Voting Rights Act**, which banned literacy tests and other voter qualification tests, signed Aug. 6. Arrest of black motorist by white police officers precipitated **Watts riot** in predominantly-black Los Angeles neighborhood Aug. 11-16. Riots resulted in 34 deaths and $200 mil in property damage.

1969: Americans protest the ongoing war in Vietnam in marches and demonstrations nationwide.

Some 14,000 U.S. troops sent to **Dominican Republic** during civil war Apr. 28. All troops withdrawn by next year. Bill establishing **Medicare**, government health insurance program for elderly, signed by Pres. Johnson July 30.

National **immigration quota system** abolished Oct. 3. **Electric power failure** blacked out most of northeastern U.S., parts of 2 Canadian provinces the night of Nov. 9-10.

1966 U.S. forces began firing into **Cambodia** May 1. Bombing of **Hanoi** area of North Vietnam by U.S. planes began June 29. By Dec. 31, 385,300 U.S. troops were stationed in South Vietnam, plus 60,000 offshore and 33,000 in Thailand.

Supreme Court ruled June 13, in *Miranda v. Arizona*, that suspects must be read their rights before police questioning. **Medicare** began July 1. In 96-minute shooting rampage, 25-year-old student **Charles Whitman** killed 15 and wounded 31 from atop a tower at the Univ. of Texas, Austin, Aug. 1; shot dead by police. Whitman had earlier killed his mother and wife.

Dept. of Transportation created, Oct. 15. Edward Brooke (R, MA) elected Nov. 8 as **first black U.S. senator** in 85 years. Robert C. Weaver named secretary of newly created Dept. of Housing and Urban Development, becoming **first black cabinet member**.

1967 Green Bay Packers beat Kansas City Chiefs, 35-10, in **first Super Bowl**, Jan. 15, in Los Angeles. Three astronauts died Jan. 27 in *Apollo 1* fire on ground at Cape Canaveral, FL. **25th Amendment**, providing for presidential succession, ratified Feb. 10. Rep. **Adam Clayton Powell** (D, NY) was denied seat Mar. 1 because of charges he misused government funds. Seated following reelection in **1968** but was fined and stripped of seniority. Pres. **Johnson** and Soviet Prem. **Aleksei Kosygin** met June 23 and 25 at Glassboro State College in New Jersey; agreed not to let any crisis push them into war.

Riots erupted among residents of predominantly black **Newark**, NJ, July 12-17; 26 killed, 1,500 injured, more than 1,000 arrested. In **Detroit**, MI, July 23-30, 43 died, 2,000 injured; 5,000 left homeless by rioting, looting, and burning in city's black neighborhoods. **Thurgood Marshall** sworn in Oct. 2 as **first black Supreme Court justice**. Antiwar march on Washington, DC, Oct. 21-22, drew 50,000 participants. Carl B. Stokes (D, Cleveland) and Richard G. Hatcher (D, Gary, IN) elected **first black mayors** of major U.S. cities Nov. 7.

1968 In **"Tet offensive,"** Communist troops attacked several provincial capitals and other major cities, including Saigon, Jan. 30, but suffered heavy casualties. Pres. Johnson **curbed bombing** of North Vietnam Mar. 31. Peace talks began in Paris May 10. All bombing of North halted Oct. 31.

Rev. **Martin Luther King Jr.** assassinated Apr. 4 in Memphis, TN. **James Earl Ray**, an escaped convict, pleaded guilty to slaying, was sentenced to 99 years. Students at **Columbia Univ.**, Apr. 23-24, seized school buildings in protest demonstrations. Sen. **Robert F. Kennedy** (D, NY) shot June 5 in Los Angeles after celebrating presidential primary victories, died June 6. **Sirhan Bishara Sirhan** convicted of murder, **1969**; death sentence com-

muted to life in prison, **1972**.

Vice Pres. Hubert Humphrey nominated for president at **Democratic National Convention** in Chicago, marked by clash between police and antiwar protestors, Aug. 26-29. Republican nominee **Richard Nixon** won presidency, defeating Humphrey in close race Nov. 5.

Apollo 8 **orbited moon** in 5-day mission, Dec. 21-27. **USS** *Pueblo* and 83-man crew seized in Sea of Japan Jan. 23 by North Koreans; 82 men released Dec. 22.

1969 Expanded 4-party **Vietnam peace talks** began Jan. 18. U.S. force peaked at 543,400 in April. Withdrawal started July 8. Pres. Nixon set Vietnamization policy Nov. 3. Earl Warren retired upon swearing in **Warren Burger**, June 23, as Supreme Court chief justice. In incident that marked birth of gay rights movement, police clashed with patrons of gay bar, the **Stonewall Inn**, in New York City June 27.

U.S. astronaut **Neil Armstrong**, commander of the *Apollo 11* mission, became the **first person to set foot on the moon**, July 20, followed by astronaut **Edwin "Buzz" Aldrin**. Astronaut **Michael Collins** remained aboard command module.

Woodstock rock music festival near Bethel, NY, drew 300,000-500,000 people, Aug. 15-18. **Anti-Vietnam War demonstrations** held in cities across the U.S., marking Vietnam Moratorium day, Oct. 15; on Nov. 15, some 250,000 marched in Washington, DC. Massacre of hundreds of civilians by U.S. troops at **My Lai**, South Vietnam, in **1968** reported Nov. 16. **Kurt Vonnegut Jr.**'s *Slaughterhouse Five* published. *Sesame Street* launched on public TV.

1970 A federal jury Feb. 18 found the **"Chicago 7"** antiwar activists innocent of conspiring to incite riots during **1968** Democratic National Convention. However, 5 were convicted of crossing state lines with intent to incite riots.

Three astronauts safely returned to Earth Apr. 17 after oxygen tank on *Apollo 13* ruptured. Lunar landing cancelled. Millions of Americans participated in antipollution demonstrations Apr. 22 to mark **first Earth Day**.

U.S. and South Vietnamese forces crossed **Cambodian** borders Apr. 30 to get at enemy bases. Four students killed May 4 at **Kent State Univ.** in Ohio by National Guardsmen during war protest. In protest at **Jackson State Univ.** in Mississippi, 2 killed when police fired on protesters.

Anna Mae Hayes of Army Nurse Corps and Elizabeth P. Hoisington, director of Women's Army Corps, became **first female generals** June 11. **Postal reform** measure signed Aug. 12 created an independent U.S. Postal Service. Pres. Nixon, Dec. 31, signed **clean air bill** calling for development of cleaner auto engine and national air quality standards for 10 major pollutants. Garry Trudeau's *Doonesbury* comic strip launched in 30 papers.

1971 Charles Manson and 3 of his cult followers found guilty Jan. 25 of first-degree murder in **1969** slaying of actress Sharon Tate and 6 others. A court-martial jury Mar. 29 convicted Lt. William L. Calley Jr. in murder of 22 South Vietnamese at **My Lai** on Mar. 16, **1968**. He was sentenced to life in prison Mar. 31, later reduced to 20 years.

Pres. Nixon, Apr. 14, relaxed 20-year **trade embargo with China**. **26th Amendment**, lowering the minimum voting age to 18 in all elections, ratified June 30. *New York Times* began publishing June 13 classified **Pentagon Papers**, secret Pentagon study on U.S. involvement in Vietnam. Supreme Court June 30 upheld, 6-3, right of the *Times* and *Washington Post* to publish the documents. Pres. Nixon, Aug. 15, instituted 90-day **wage and price freeze**.

U.S. bombers initiated massive 5-day strike Dec. 26 in North Vietnam in retaliation for alleged violations of agreements reached prior to **1968** bombing halt.

1972 Pres. Nixon arrived in **Beijing** Feb. 21 for 8-day visit to China, in "journey for peace." Joint communiqué released Feb. 27 called for increased Sino-U.S. contacts. Senate, Mar. 22, approved **Equal Rights Amendment** banning discrimination on basis of sex; sent measure to states for ratification.

North Vietnamese forces launched biggest attacks in 4 years across the demilitarized zone Mar. 30. The U.S. responded Apr. 15 with **resumption of bombing** of Hanoi and Haiphong after 4-year lull. Pres. Nixon announced May 8 the mining of North Vietnam ports. Last U.S. combat troops left Aug. 11.

Gov. **George C. Wallace** (D, AL), campaigning for president at Laurel, MD, shopping center May 15, shot and seriously wounded. **Arthur Bremer** convicted Aug. 4, sentenced to 63 years for shooting Wallace and 3 others. In **first visit of U.S. president to Moscow**, Pres. Nixon arrived May 22 for summit talks with Kremlin leaders that culminated in landmark strategic arms pact (**SALT I**). Five men arrested June 17 for breaking into Democratic National Committee offices in **Watergate** office complex in Washington, DC. Supreme Court in *Furman v. Georgia* June 29 ruled **capital punishment** as currently practiced was unconstitutional.

Mark Spitz won 7 gold medals in world record times at the Munich Olympics in Aug.-Sept. **Billie Jean King** defeated Bobby Riggs in 3 straight sets in tennis's nationally televised "Battle of the Sexes," Sept. 20.

Pres. **Nixon** reelected Nov. 7 in landslide, carrying 49 states to defeat Sen. George McGovern (D, SD). Three astronauts, part of *Apollo 17*, made sixth and last lunar landing on Dec. 11. Full-scale **bombing of North Vietnam** resumed after Paris peace negotiations reached impasse Dec. 18. *The Godfather*, directed by Francis Ford Coppola and based on a Mario Puzo novel, is released.

1973 In *Roe v. Wade*, Supreme Court ruled, 7-2, Jan. 22, fetus not a person with constitutional rights and that right to privacy protected woman's decision to have abortion; states may not ban abortions during first 3 months of pregnancy and may regulate, but not ban, abortions during second trimester.

1974: Pres. Richard Nixon resigns from office and departs the White House.

Four-party **Vietnam peace pacts** signed in Paris Jan. 27, and North Vietnam released some 590 U.S. prisoners by Apr. 1. Last U.S. troops left Mar. 29. **End of military draft** announced Jan. 27. Pres. Nixon announced, Apr. 30, resignation of top Nixon aides H. R. Haldeman and John D. Ehrlichman and Attorney Gen. Richard G. Kleindienst, firing of White House Counsel John W. Dean III, as a consequence of the widening **Watergate** scandal. John Dean told Senate hearings June 25 that Pres. Nixon, his staff and campaign aides, and Justice Dept. had conspired to cover up Watergate facts. The U.S. officially ceased bombing in **Cambodia** at midnight Aug. 14 in accord with June congressional action.

Vice Pres. **Spiro Agnew**, Oct. 10, resigned and pleaded no contest to charge of tax evasion on payments made to him by contractors when he was Maryland governor. **Gerald R. Ford**, Oct. 12, became **first appointed vice president** under 25th Amendment; sworn in Dec. 6. The **"Saturday Night Massacre"** occurred Oct. 20, when Pres. Nixon ordered Attorney Gen. Elliot Richardson to fire Watergate special prosecutor Archibald Cox, who had sought handover of Nixon's subpoenaed White House tapes. Richardson refused to comply and resigned; Dep. Attorney Gen. William Ruckelshaus refused and was fired. Solicitor Gen. Robert Bork, as acting attorney gen.,

then fired Cox. Nixon administration named Leon Jaworski, Nov. 1, to succeed Cox.

Skylab, **first U.S. space station**, launched May 14. **Secretariat** became first Triple Crown winner since **Citation** in **1948** by winning Belmont Stakes June 9 in record time. Total **ban on oil exports** to U.S. imposed by Arab oil-producing nations Oct. 19-21 after outbreak of an Arab-Israeli war. Ban was lifted Mar. 18, **1974**. Congress overrode Nov. 7 Pres. Nixon's veto of **war powers bill**, which curbed president's power to commit forces to hostilities abroad without congressional approval.

1974 On Apr. 8, **Hank Aaron** of the Atlanta Braves hit his 715th career home run to break Babe Ruth's record.

House Judiciary Committee opened **impeachment** hearings May 9 against Pres. Nixon. John D. Ehrlichman and 3 **White House "plumbers"** found guilty July 12 of conspiring to violate the civil rights of the psychiatrist of Pentagon Papers leaker Daniel Ellsberg by breaking into psychiatrist's office. Supreme Court ruled, 8-0, July 24 that Pres. Nixon had to turn over 64 **tapes of White House conversations**. House Judiciary Committee, in televised hearings July 24-30, recommended 3 **articles of impeachment** against Pres. Nixon, involving conspiracy to obstruct justice in Watergate cover-up, abuses of power, and defiance of committee subpoenas. The House voted Aug. 20, 412-3, to accept the committee report, which included the impeachment articles.

Pres. Nixon announced his **resignation**, Aug. 8, and stepped down the next day. His support in Congress had begun to collapse Aug. 5, after release of tapes appearing to implicate him in Watergate cover-up. Vice Pres. **Ford** sworn in Aug. 9 as 38th U.S. president. Pres. Ford, Aug. 20, nominated **Nelson Rockefeller** to be vice president; Rockefeller sworn in Dec. 10. Pres. Ford, Sept. 8, issued **pardon to Nixon** for any federal crimes he committed while president.

New York Times published article Dec. 22 on CIA engagement in illegal domestic surveillance. Release of article led to revelation of **"family jewels,"** compilation of CIA reports on activities it engaged in between 1950s and 1970s possibly "outside the legislative charter of this Agency."

1975 Former Atty. Gen. John Mitchell and ex-presidential advisers H. R. Haldeman and John Ehrlichman found guilty Jan. 1 of **Watergate cover-up** charges. Mitchell released **1979**, last of 25 jailed over scandal to leave prison.

U.S. launched **evacuation from Saigon** of Americans and some South Vietnamese Apr. 29 as Communist forces completed takeover of South Vietnam; **South Vietnamese** government officially surrendered Apr. 30. U.S. merchant ship *Mayaguez* and its crew of 39 seized by Cambodian forces in Gulf of Siam May 12. In rescue operation, U.S. Marines attacked Tang Island, planes bombed air base; Cambodia surrendered ship and crew. Congress voted $405 mil for **South Vietnam refugees** May 16; 140,000 flown to U.S.

Publishing heiress **Patricia (Patty) Hearst**, kidnapped Feb. 5, **1974**, by Symbionese Liberation Army, captured in San Francisco Sept. 18 with other militants. She was convicted Mar. 20, **1976**, of bank robbery.

1976 In **"right to die"** case, New Jersey Supreme Court, Mar. 31, allowed comatose Karen Ann Quinlan to be removed from respirator. She survived, dying in nursing home in **1985**. Supreme Court reinstated **death penalty**, July 2, subject to conditions.

U.S. celebrated **200th anniversary of independence** July 4 with festivals, parades, and New York City's Operation Sail, gathering of tall ships from around the world. **"Legionnaire's disease"** killed 29 people who attended American Legion convention July 21-24 in Philadelphia.

Viking II set down on Utopia Plains of **Mars** Sept. 3, following successful landing by *Viking I* on Chryse Plains, July 20. Two U.S. officers on routine mission near DMZ slain by **North Korean soldiers** Aug. 18; North Korea stated "regret," Aug. 21.

1977 Convicted murderer Gary Gilmore executed by Utah firing squad Jan. 17; **first use of capital punishment** in U.S. since **1967**. Pres. Jimmy Carter Jan. 21 pardoned most **Vietnam War draft evaders**.

Natural gas shortage caused by severe winter weather led Congress Feb. 2 to approve emergency gas bill temporarily authorizing reallocation of interstate gas from surplus areas to shortage areas. Pres. Carter signed act Aug. 4 creating new cabinet-level **energy department**.

FBI Dec. 7 released 40,000 pages of previously secret files relating to **Kennedy assassination**. George Lucas's **first** *Star Wars* **film** produced.

1978 Senate voted, Apr. 18 to turn over **Panama Canal** to Panama on Dec. 31, **1999**; Mar. 16 vote had given approval to treaty guaranteeing area's neutrality after the year 2000. Californians, June 6, approved **Proposition 13**, state constitutional amendment slashing property taxes.

Supreme Court, June 28, ruled that special admissions program—under which set number of places reserved for minorities—violated civil rights act, which forbids anyone from being excluded from federally funded program because of race, in *Regents of the Univ. of California v. Bakke*.

Egyptian Pres. **Anwar al-Sadat** and Israeli Prem. **Menachem Begin** reached accord on "framework for peace," Sept. 17, after Pres. Carter-mediated talks at Camp David. New York's Chemical Bank Dec. 20 initiated industry-wide move to raise **lending rate** to near-record 11.75%.

1979 Partial meltdown released radioactive material Mar. 28 at nuclear reactor on **Three Mile Island** near Middletown, PA. American Airlines DC-10 **jetliner crashed** May 25 after takeoff from Chicago, killing 275 people.

In speech July 15, Pres. Carter spoke of national "crisis of confidence" and outlined proposed 10-year $140 bil program to **reduce dependence on foreign oil**. Militant followers of **Ayatollah Khomeini** took hostage some 90 people, including 66 Americans, Nov. 4 at **American embassy in Tehran**, Iran. Khomeini demanded return of former Shah Muhammad Reza Pahlavi, who was undergoing medical treatment in New York City.

1980 Pres. Carter announced, Jan. 4, economic sanctions against USSR in retaliation for Soviet invasion of Afghanistan. At Carter's request, U.S. Olympic Committee voted, Apr. 12, against U.S. participation in **Moscow Summer Olympics**. **Lake Placid**, NY, hosted **Winter Olympics** for second time. The U.S. hockey team defeated heavily favored Russian team Feb. 22 en route to winning gold medal in what was called a "miracle on ice."

Eight Americans killed and 5 wounded, Apr. 24, in **ill-fated hostage rescue attempt** held by Iranian militants. **Mt. St. Helens**, in Washington state, erupted May 18. The blast, with others May 25 and June 12, left 57 dead. In sweeping victory, Nov. 4, **Ronald Reagan** (R) was elected 40th president, defeating incumbent Pres. Carter. Republicans gained control of Senate. Former Beatle **John Lennon** was shot and killed by Mark David Chapman, Dec. 8, in New York City.

1981 Minutes after Reagan's inauguration Jan. 20, 52 **American hostages in Iran** were freed after being held for 444 days. Pres. **Reagan** was shot and seriously wounded, Mar. 30, in Washington, DC; also seriously wounded were a Secret Service agent, a policeman, and Press Sec. **James Brady**. **John W. Hinckley Jr.** arrested, found not guilty by reason of insanity in **1982**, committed to mental institution.

1985: Pres. Ronald Reagan is inaugurated for a second term after winning a record 49 states and 525 electoral votes.

World's **first reusable spacecraft**, space shuttle *Columbia*, sent into space, Apr. 12. It performed its first operational mission in **1982**. Members of the **Professional Air Traffic Controllers Organization**, Aug. 3, went on strike. Most defied a back-to-work order and were dismissed by Pres. Reagan Aug. 5 for violating federal law. Pres. Reagan signed into law Aug. 13 **tax-cut legislation**, expected to save taxpayers $750 bil over 5 years, largest tax cut to date. The Senate confirmed, Sept. 21, appointment of **Sandra Day O'Connor** as **first female Supreme Court justice**.

1982 The 13-year-old Justice Dept. lawsuit against **AT&T** was settled Jan. 8. AT&T agreed to give up 22 Bell System companies and was allowed to expand. **Equal Rights Amendment**, sent to states in **1972**, defeated when deadline for ratification passed June 30 with only 35 of 38 necessary number of states supporting amendment. Centers for Disease Control, July 16, reported evidence of growing **AIDS epidemic**, responsible for 184 deaths in country since first reported in U.S. in June **1981**. The economy showed signs of recovery from **recession** that began in mid-**1981**, as Dow Jones Industrial Average hit 1016.93 Oct. 13, its highest level in 18 months.

NFL strike ended Nov. 16 after 57 days when players and team owners settled with $1.6 bil pact. Retired dentist Dr. Barney B. Clark became **first permanent artificial heart recipient**, Dec. 2; he died Mar. 23, **1983**. The House, Dec. 16, cited EPA administrator Anne Gorsuch for contempt after refusing to produce certain documents concerning the **Superfund**, law that established fund for cleanup and authorized prosecution of hazardous waste dumpers. Singer **Michael Jackson**'s *Thriller* released; eventually considered bestselling album of all time.

1983 Pres. Reagan, Jan. 3, declared Times Beach, MO, a federal disaster area because of toxic **dioxin** in soil. Harold Washington elected Apr. 12 as **first black mayor of Chicago**. On Apr. 20, Pres. Reagan signed compromise bipartisan bill designed to save **Social Security** from bankruptcy.

Sally Ride became **first American woman to travel in space**, June 18, when space shuttle *Challenger* launched from Cape Canaveral, FL. On Sept. 1, **South Korean passenger jet** infringing on Soviet air space and apparently misidentified was shot down; 269 people, including 61 Americans, killed.

On Oct. 23, 241 U.S. Marines and sailors were killed when TNT-laden **suicide truck bomb** blew up Marine barracks at Beirut International Airport in Lebanon. U.S. troops, with small force from 6 Caribbean nations, invaded **Grenada** Oct. 25. After a few days, Grenadian militia and Cuban "construction workers" were overcome, U.S. citizens were evacuated, and the Marxist regime was deposed.

1984 Seven regional companies took over **local telephone service** from AT&T, Jan. 1. On space shuttle *Challenger*'s fourth trip, launched Feb. 3, two astronauts became **first humans to fly free of a spacecraft**. On May 7, Vietnam War veterans reached out-of-court settlement with 7 chemical companies in class-action suit over the herbicide **Agent Orange**.

Former Vice Pres. **Walter Mondale** won Democratic presidential nomination, June 6. He chose Rep. **Geraldine Ferraro** (D, NY) as vice presidential candidate, first woman to be nominated for position by major political party. Pres. Reagan signed bill July 17 cutting federal transportation aid to states that keep their **drinking age** under 21. Pres. **Reagan** reelected Nov. 6 in Republican landslide, carrying 49 states for record 525 electoral votes. **Bernhard Goetz** shot and wounded 4 allegedly menacing teenage boys on NYC subway train, Dec. 22; later acquitted of major charges but was successfully sued.

1985 Visiting Germany, Pres. Reagan, May 5, laid wreath at Bergen-Belsen Nazi concentration camp site and also at military cemetery at **Bitburg**, where some Nazis were buried. Philadelphia police bombed a rowhouse occupied by **MOVE radical group**, May 13; 11 killed, and fire damaged 2 blocks of houses. On June 14, **terrorists seized TWA jet** after takeoff from Athens, Greece, with 153 passengers and crew. Thirty-nine Americans held hostage for 17 days; 1 U.S. service member killed.

Reversing an earlier decision to market "new" Coke, the **Coca-Cola Co.** said, July 10, it would resume marketing soda made under its original "Classic" formula. **Live Aid** rock concert broadcast around the world July 13, raised $70 mil for famine relief in Ethiopia.

On Oct. 7, 4 **Palestinian hijackers** seized Italian cruise ship *Achille Lauro* in the Mediterranean for 2 days. One American, Leon Klinghoffer, killed. For first time in 6 years U.S. and Soviet leaders met at **summit in Geneva**, Nov. 19-20. **General Electric** agreed Dec. 11 to buy RCA Corp. for $6.28 bil, largest merger to date outside oil industry.

1986 The U.S. officially observed **Martin Luther King Jr. Day** for first time Jan. 20. Space shuttle *Challenger* exploded 73 seconds after liftoff, Jan. 28, killing 6 astronauts and Teacher in Space Project participant Christa McAuliffe. In 4-day extravaganza in July, the U.S. celebrated 100th birthday of the **Statue of Liberty**.

The Senate confirmed, Sept. 17, Reagan's nomination of **William Rehnquist** as chief justice and **Antonin Scalia** as associate justice of Supreme Court. Congress completed action Oct. 2 overriding a veto to place economic sanctions on **South Africa**. Lebanese newspaper first broke news of **Iran-Contra scandal** Nov. 3, involving secret U.S. sale of arms to Iran and use of some proceeds to support right-wing Nicaraguan guerrilla movement.

Ivan Boesky, accused of **insider trading**, agreed Nov. 14 to pay $100 million in fines and illicit profits and to plead guilty to an unspecified criminal count. Largest penalty to date imposed for insider trading. Robert Penn Warren named America's **first poet laureate** by the Library of Congress.

1987 Pres. Reagan produced nation's **first trillion-dollar budget**, Jan. 5. **Dow Jones** closed above 2,000 for first time, Jan. 8. The FDA approved, Mar. 20, AZT—first drug shown to be effective in **fight against AIDS**. Nearly 1.4 mil **illegal aliens** met May 4 deadline for applying for amnesty under new federal policy.

Joint public hearings by Senate and House committees investigating **Iran-Contra affair** opened May 5. Lt. Col. **Oliver North**, former National Security Council staff member, said he had believed all his activities were authorized by his superiors. Hearings end Aug. 3. Pres. Reagan, Aug. 12, denied knowing of diversion of funds to contras.

An **Iraqi missile** killed 37 sailors on the USS *Stark* in the Persian Gulf, May 17. Iraq called it an accident. The 200th anniversary of **U.S. Constitution** signing was observed, Sept. 17, in Philadelphia and around the U.S. **Stock market crashed**, Oct. 19, with the Dow Jones plummeting a record 508 points to 1,738, ending bull market that began mid-**1982**. Pres. Reagan and Soviet leader Mikhail Gorbachev Dec. 8, signed **pact to dismantle** all 1,752 U.S. and 859 Soviet missiles with 300- to 3,400-mi. range.

1988 In report issued May 16, Surgeon Gen. C. Everett Koop declared **cigarettes addictive**. Congress approved, in June, greatest expansion yet of **Medicare** benefits, to protect the elderly and disabled against "catastrophic" medical costs. The act was repealed in November **1989**. Much of U.S. suffered **worst drought** in over 50 years; by late June half the nation's agricultural counties had been declared disaster areas.

A missile, fired from U.S. Navy warship *Vincennes* in the Persian Gulf, mistakenly struck a commercial **Iranian airliner**, July 3, killing all 290 aboard. **George H. W. Bush** (R) elected 41st U.S. president, Nov. 8, decisively defeating Massachusetts Gov. **Michael Dukakis** (D). **Pan Am Flight 103** exploded and

crashed, due to terrorist bomb, into town of Lockerbie, Scotland, Dec. 21, killing all 259 people aboard and 11 on the ground. **Drexel Burnham Lambert** agreed, Dec. 21, to plead guilty to insider trading and other violations, and pay penalties of $650 mil, largest such settlement ever.

1989 Major oil spill occurred when *Exxon Valdez* struck Bligh Reef in Alaska's Prince William Sound, Mar. 24. Oliver North convicted, May 4, on charges related to **Iran-Contra scandal**. Conviction thrown out on appeal in **1991** because of his immunized testimony. A measure to rescue **savings and loan industry** signed into law, Aug. 9, by Pres. Bush, launching largest federal rescue to date. Army Gen. **Colin Powell** became **first black chairman of Joint Chiefs of Staff** after being nominated Aug. 10 by Pres. Bush.

Baseball legend **Pete Rose** banned from game for life Aug. 24 for involvement with gamblers. **Hurricane Hugo** swept through the Caribbean and the Carolinas Sept. 10-22, causing at least 86 deaths and $7 bil in damage in the Carolinas alone. Just before a World Series game, Oct. 17, an **earthquake** struck the San Francisco Bay area, causing 63 deaths. L. Douglas Wilder (D) declared governor of Virginia Nov. 27, **first elected black governor** in U.S. history. U.S. troops invaded Panama, Dec. 20, overthrowing the government of **Manuel Noriega**. Noriega, wanted by U.S. authorities on drug charges, surrendered Jan. 3, **1990**.

1990 Junk bond financier **Michael Milken** pleaded guilty to fraud-related charges, Apr. 14; agreed to pay $500 mil in restitution; sentenced Nov. 21 to 10 years in prison. Justice **William Brennan** announced, July 20, resignation from U.S. Supreme Court. His replacement, Judge **David Souter**, confirmed Sept. 27. Pres. Bush signed **Americans with Disabilities Act**, barring discrimination against the disabled, July 26. **Operation Desert Shield** forces left for Saudi Arabia Aug. 7, to defend that country following invasion of **Kuwait** by Iraq, Aug. 2. Pres. Bush Nov. 15 signed into law **Clean Air Act**, strengthened version of Clean Air Act of 1970; focus on urban pollution, cancer-causing emissions from industrial sources.

1991 The U.S. and its allies defeated Iraq in **Persian Gulf War** and liberated Kuwait, which Iraq had invaded the previous year. On Jan. 17, the allies launched a devastating air attack. In rapid ground war starting Feb. 24, which lasted just 100 hours, U.S.-led forces killed or captured thousands of Iraqi soldiers and sent the rest into retreat before Pres. Bush ordered cease-fire Feb. 27.

An 8-month **recession** showed signs of having ended in Mar. The **Dow Jones** Industrial Average closed above 3,000 for first time, Apr. 17. House Speaker announced Oct. 3 closure of **House Bank** by end of year after revelations that House members had written 8,331 bad checks worth hundreds of thousands of dollars. Justice **Thurgood Marshall**, first black to sit on U.S. Supreme Court, announced, June 17, plans to retire. Senate approved, Oct. 15, nomination of **Clarence Thomas** to replace Marshall, despite allegations of sexual harassment against him by former aide Anita Hill. Thomas became second black person to serve on Court.

1989: The *Exxon Valdez* oil spill causes environmental devastation in Alaska's Prince William Sound.

1992 Retail giant **R.H. Macy & Co.** filed for bankruptcy, Jan. 27. Major U.S. carrier Trans World Airlines (**TWA**), filed for bankruptcy, Jan. 31. **Riots** swept South Central Los Angeles Apr. 29 after jury acquitted 4 white police officers on all but one count in 1991 videotaped beating of black motorist **Rodney King**. Death toll in L.A. violence was put at 53. **27th Amendment**, regarding congressional pay raises, ratified May 7.

Hurricane **Andrew** ravaged South Florida and Louisiana Aug. 24-26, causing 65 deaths. White supremacist and fugitive Randall Weaver surrendered Aug. 31 after 11-day **FBI siege** at his **Ruby Ridge**, ID, cabin, during which his wife, son, and a deputy sheriff were killed in exchanges of gunfire. **Bill Clinton** (D) elected 42nd president, Nov. 3, defeating Pres. Bush (R) and independent Ross Perot. A UN-sanctioned military force, led by U.S. troops, arrived in **Somalia** Dec. 9. Presidents of U.S., Canada, and Mexico Dec. 17 signed **North American Free Trade Agreement** (NAFTA), which took effect Jan. 1, 1994. More than 1.1 mil votes were cast to choose portrait of the late **Elvis Presley** for **postage stamp**, first in the U.S. to honor a rock performer.

1996: Pres. Clinton appoints Madeleine Albright first woman secretary of state; she is sworn in, 1997.

1993 A bomb exploded in a parking garage beneath the **World Trade Center** in New York City, Feb. 26, killing 6 people. Four men found guilty, Mar. 4, 1994. Four federal agents killed, Feb. 28, during an unsuccessful raid on **Branch Davidian** compound near **Waco**, TX. A 51-day siege by agents ended Apr. 19, when the compound burned down, leaving more than 70 cult members dead. Eleven cult members acquitted Feb. 26, 1994, of charges in deaths of the federal agents. U.S. agents cleared of wrongdoing in 2000.

Janet Reno became **first female attorney general** Mar. 12. Federal jury, Apr. 17, found 2 Los Angeles police officers guilty and 2 not guilty of violating civil rights of motorist **Rodney King** in 1991 videotaped beating. Mostly white state jury had acquitted the officers on all charges in 1992, sparking riots in L.A. and other cities.

Defense Sec. Les Aspin, Apr. 28, removed restrictions on **aerial combat roles for women** in the armed forces. In a May 14 plebiscite, voters in **Puerto Rico** supported continuing commonwealth status with U.S. **"Motor-voter" bill** was signed by Pres. Clinton, May 20, allowing citizens to register to vote by mail when applying for a driver's license or certain benefits. The **"Great Flood of 1993"** inundated at least 15 mil acres in 9 Midwestern states in summer, leaving about 50 dead as direct result of flood and $15 bil in damages.

Pres. Clinton, July 2, approved recommendations that 33 major U.S. military bases be closed. On July 19 he announced **"don't ask, don't tell, don't pursue"** policy for homosexuals in the military. Judge **Ruth Bader Ginsburg** sworn in, Aug. 10, as 107th justice and second woman on Supreme Court. Pres. Clinton, Aug. 10, signed measure designed to **cut federal budget deficits** by $496 bil over 5 years, through spending cuts and new taxes. **Brady Bill**, a major gun-control measure named after Sarah Brady and former Reagan press sec. James Brady, was signed into law by Pres. Clinton Nov. 30.

1994 A predawn **earthquake** in the Los Angeles area, Jan. 17, claimed 61 lives and caused widespread devastation. Pres. Clinton Feb. 3 lifted 19-year ban on U.S. trade with **Vietnam**. Byron De La Beckwith convicted Feb. 5 of 1963 murder of civil rights leader **Medgar Evers**. Longtime CIA officer **Aldrich Ames** and his wife charged, Feb. 21, with spying. Under plea bargain, he received life in prison, while she drew 63 months.

U.S. troops, Mar. 25, officially ended peacekeeping and humanitarian aid mission in **Somalia**, begun in 1992. Congressional committees, late July, began **Whitewater hearings**. Kenneth Starr named Aug. 5 as independent counsel

to probe Whitewater affair. Major league **baseball players** went on **strike** following Aug. 11 games. World Series canceled; strike ended Apr. 25, 1995. Senate Majority Leader George Mitchell (D, ME), Sept. 26, dropped efforts to pass Pres. Clinton's **health-care reform** package.

1995 104th Congress opened, Jan. 4. A bill to end Congress's exemption from federal labor laws, first in series of measures in Republicans' **"Contract with America,"** cleared Congress Jan. 17; signed into law Jan. 23. Pres. Clinton invoked emergency authority, Jan. 31, to extend $20 bil **loan to Mexico** to help it avert financial collapse. Last UN peacekeeping troops withdrew from **Somalia** Feb. 28-Mar. 3, with aid of U.S. Marines. In Haiti, peacekeeping responsibilities were transferred from U.S. to UN forces Mar. 31, with the U.S. providing 2,400 soldiers.

A truck bomb exploded outside an Oklahoma City federal office building Apr. 19, on 2-year anniversary of end of Waco siege, killing 168 people in deadliest terrorist attack yet on U.S. soil. **Timothy McVeigh** was first and key suspect arrested, Apr. 21. The U.S. space shuttle *Atlantis* made first in series of dockings with Russian space station Mir, June 29-July 4. The U.S. announced July 11 it was reestablishing diplomatic relations with **Vietnam**. Shannon Faulkner won legal fight to gain admission to previously all-male cadet corps of **The Citadel** in South Carolina, Aug. 11, though she dropped out after a few days of training.

Ten Muslim militants convicted, Oct. 1, in failed **plot to blow up UN Headquarters** and other buildings and assassinate political leaders. Former football star **O. J. Simpson** found not guilty Oct. 3 of June 1994 murders of his former wife, Nicole Brown Simpson, and her friend Ron Goldman. Hundreds of thousands of black men participated in **Million Man March** and rally in Washington, DC, Oct. 16, organized by Rev. Louis Farrakhan.

Five Americans among 7 killed, Nov. 13, in bombing of U.S. military post in **Riyadh, Saudi Arabia**. A budget impasse between Congress and Pres. Clinton led to a partial government shutdown beginning Nov. 14. Operations resumed Nov. 20 under continuing resolutions. After talks outside Dayton, OH, warring parties in **Bosnia and Herzegovina** reached agreement Nov. 21 to end their conflict; treaty signed Dec. 14, after which first of some 20,000 U.S. peacekeeping troops arrived in Bosnia. 1973 federal law imposing **55-mph speed limit** was repealed by measure signed Nov. 28, returning authority to states.

1996 Senate, Jan. 26, approved, 87-4, **Second Strategic Arms Reduction Treaty** (START II). Congress, in March, approved **line item veto** bill, giving president power to delete from spending bills any items containing expenditures he or she disapproves of, but it was struck down by Supreme Court, June 25, 1998.

James and Susan McDougal convicted May 28 of fraud and conspiracy in **Whitewater** case. Arkansas Gov. Jim Guy Tucker convicted of similar charges by same jury. The antitax **Freemen** surrendered to federal authorities June 13 after 81-day standoff near Jordan, MT; 4 were convicted, July 8, 1998, of conspiring to defraud banks. A bomb exploded at **Khobar Towers** military complex near Dhahran, Saudi Arabia, June 25, killing 19 American service personnel. Homemade **pipe bomb** exploded July 27 in Atlanta, GA, during Summer Olympics. One person killed by blast. Eric Robert Rudolph pleaded guilty to bombing in 2005.

Major welfare reform bill signed into law, Aug. 22. U.S. signed **Comprehensive Test Ban Treaty**, Sept. 24, which banned all nuclear weapons tests and other nuclear explosions. Senate failed to ratify treaty in 1999. Shannon Lucid, Sept. 26, completed record space voyage of 188 days, longest by woman and by U.S. astronaut. Pres. Clinton reelected to second term, Nov. 5.

1997 **Bombs detonated** at Atlanta, GA, women's clinic that performed abortions, Jan. 16, and at gay nightclub, Feb. 21. Eric Robert Rudolph pleaded guilty in 2005 to both bombings as well as Jan. 1998 bombing of women's clinic in Birmingham, AL, which killed 1.

Madeleine Albright sworn in as secretary of state Jan. 23, becoming **first female State Dept. head**. Former CIA official Harold Nicholson pleaded guilty, Mar. 3, to **spying for Russia**.

Thirty-nine members of **Heaven's Gate** religious cult found dead in Rancho Santa Fe, CA, house Mar. 26, in apparent mass suicide. **Timothy McVeigh** convicted of conspiracy and murder, June 2, in 1995 Oklahoma City bombing; Terry Nichols convicted Dec. 23 on related charges. Islamic militants Ramzi Ahmed Yousef and Eyad Ismoil Yousef convicted, Nov. 12, in 1993 bombing of **World Trade Center**.

1998 After *Drudge Report* website broke the news on alleged affair, several media outlets reported Jan. 21 on evidence of **sexual relationship** between Pres. Clinton and former White House intern **Monica Lewinsky**. Clinton denied affair. Lewinsky, Aug. 6, testified to having had a sexual relationship with Pres. Clinton, but said she was never asked to lie. In grand jury testimony and address to the nation, Aug. 17, Clinton acknowledged an inappropriate relationship with Lewinsky. On Sept. 9, independent counsel **Kenneth Starr** sent the House what he called "credible information that may constitute grounds" for impeachment. House Judiciary Committee, Oct. 5, voted 21-16 along party lines to recommend that President **impeachment** investigation proceed. The House concurred Oct. 8, voting 258-176; 31 Democrats voted yes. The House, Dec. 19, approved 2 articles of **impeachment** charging Pres. Clinton with grand jury **perjury** and **obstruction of justice** in cover-up of his sexual relationship with Lewinsky; 2 other impeachment articles failed.

"Unabomber" Theodore Kaczynski, arrested in Montana in 1993, pleaded guilty Jan. 22 to California and New Jersey bombings that killed 3 people and injured 2. The state of Texas, Feb. 3, **executed its first female convict** in 135 years—Karla Faye Tucker.

Mark McGwire, Sept. 8, hit his 62nd **home run** of the season, breaking Roger Maris's 1961 season record. On Sept. 30, Pres. Clinton announced federal **budget surplus** of $70 bil for fiscal year 1998, the first since 1969. Terrorist **bombs in U.S. embassies** in Nairobi, Kenya, and Dar-es-Salaam, Tanzania, killed at least 257, Aug. 7. The U.S. launched retaliatory strikes, Aug. 20, against alleged terrorist-related targets in Afghanistan and Sudan. **John Glenn**, first U.S. astronaut to orbit Earth, returned to space at age 77 aboard shuttle *Discovery*, Oct. 29-Nov. 7.

Pres. **Clinton**, Nov. 13, settled suit by agreeing to pay $850,000 to **Paula Jones**, who had alleged that he had made an unwanted sexual advance on her in 1991. Country's 4 largest **tobacco companies**, in settlement, Nov. 23, with 46 states, DC, and 4 territories, agreed to pay $206 bil over 25 years to cover public health costs related to smoking.

1999 Pres. **Clinton's impeachment trial**—second such trial in U.S. history—began in GOP-controlled Senate Jan. 7. He was acquitted, Feb. 12. Perjury article failed with 45 votes; obstruction of justice article drew 50-50 vote, with two-thirds vote needed for conviction.

Dr. **Jack Kevorkian**, who claimed to have helped 130 people kill themselves, convicted of 2nd-degree murder Mar. 26 in one death; sentenced to 10-25 years in prison. One man pleaded guilty in April, another convicted in November in 1998 kidnapping and beating death of **Matthew Shepard**, an openly gay student at the Univ. of Wyoming. Eric Harris, 18, and Dylan Klebold, 17, killed 12 fellow students and a teacher Apr. 20 at **Columbine High School** in Littleton, CO, then fatally shot themselves. One NYC police officer pleaded guilty to 6 charges, May 25, and another was convicted on an assault charge, June 8, in connection with 1997 torture of Haitian immigrant **Abner Louima** in police station. **John F. Kennedy Jr.**, son of former president, died in a plane crash, July 16, along with his wife and sister-in-law.

2000 Across U.S., midnight celebrations marked changeover to the year 2000 on Jan. 1; feared **Y2K** computer glitch caused only minor problems. Vermont Gov. Howard Dean (D) signed legislation Apr. 26 allowing same-sex couples in **civil unions** to gain same legal rights as heterosexual married couples. Teams of scientists from U.S. and Britain announced jointly, June 26, that they had determined structure of the **human genome**.

Following bitter international custody dispute, 6-year-old **Elián González** was returned to father in Cuba June 28, 7 months after his rescue from a boat wreck in which his mother and other refugees had drowned off the Florida coast. **Tiger Woods** became youngest player, at age 24, to win all 4 of golf's majors, with record score in the British Open, July 23.

The Food and Drug Administration announced, Sept. 28, approval of **RU-486**, a pill that induces abortions. Seventeen U.S. sailors died Oct. 12 in terrorist bombing of **USS Cole**, which was refueling in Aden, Yemen.

On **election night**, Nov. 7, winner of Florida's 25 deciding electoral votes remained uncertain. Florida Supreme Court, Dec. 8, ordered manual recount of all ballots that did not have a vote for president recorded by machine. On Dec. 12, U.S. Supreme Court reversed that decision. Vice Pres. **Gore** conceded the presidential election to Texas Gov. **George W. Bush** (R) in televised address, Dec. 13.

2001 Congress, Jan. 6, certified **George W. Bush** as president by electoral vote of 271-266 (1 Gore elector abstained). He was sworn in as 43rd president Jan. 20. **AOL-Time Warner** merger completed Jan. 11 after Federal Trade Commission approved it Dec. 2000. Outgoing Pres. Clinton issued 176 pardons and commutations, Jan. 20, including one to **Marc Rich**, fugitive commodities trader whose ex-wife was a Clinton financial backer.

FBI agent **Robert Hanssen** arrested Feb. 20 charged with spying for Soviet Union and Russia over a 20-year period; under plea bargain, sentenced in 2002 to life in prison. **U.S. Navy spy plane** collided with Chinese fighter plane over South China Sea Apr. 1, killing the fighter pilot; 24 U.S. crew members were detained in Hainan until U.S. officials expressed apology, Apr. 12.

Sen. **James Jeffords** (R, VT) announced May 24 he was leaving his party, giving Democrats control of Senate. Pres. Bush signed, June 7, **$1.35 tril tax-cut package**. Oklahoma City bomber **Timothy McVeigh** executed June 11 by lethal injection in Terre Haute, IN. Bush announced Aug. 9 he would allow federal funding of limited **stem-cell research** using human embryos.

On morning of **Sept. 11**, 2 hijacked commercial airliners struck **World Trade Center twin towers** in New York City in **worst-ever terrorist attack** on American soil. A third hijacked plane destroyed a portion of the **Pentagon**; a fourth crashed in a field in Somerset County, Pennsylvania. Some 3,000 people were killed, including about 2,800 at the World Trade Center. U.S. observed a national day of mourning, Sept. 14. Congress, Sept. 21, approved $15 bil **bailout package for airline industry**. Five people died, and 14 became ill, from exposure to **anthrax** traveling through the U.S. postal system, Oct. 4-Nov. 21; former Army microbiologist Bruce Ivins, later suspected of the crime, apparently committed suicide in July 2008.

On Oct. 7, San Francisco Giants outfielder **Barry Bonds** hit his 73rd **home run** for a single-season record.

The U.S. and Britain, Oct. 7, launched sustained **air-strike campaign** against Afghan-based terrorist organization al-Qaeda and the country's ruling Taliban militia. Pres. Bush created **Office of Homeland Security**, Oct. 8, and signed a federal **antiterrorism bill**, Oct. 26. **Taliban** surrendered Kabul, the Afghan capital, Nov. 13, and fled from Kandahar, their stronghold, Dec. 7. Taliban member and U.S. citizen **John Walker Lindh** captured Dec. 2 by U.S. forces in Afghanistan; under plea bargain sentenced in Oct. 2002 to 20 years in prison. U.S. government, Dec. 11, indicted al Qaeda member **Zacarias Moussaoui** as Sept. 11 co-conspirator; he pleaded guilty, was sentenced in May 2006 to life in prison.

Leading energy-trading company **Enron** filed for bankruptcy, Dec. 2. Pres. Bush announced Dec. 13 U.S. withdrawal from **1972 Antiballistic Missile Treaty**.

2002 Taliban and al-Qaeda fighters captured in Afghanistan flown to U.S. naval base at **Guantánamo Bay** in Cuba, with first 20 arriving Jan. 11.

A House committee, Jan. 14, released parts of a letter from Enron employee Sherron Watkins to CEO **Kenneth Lay**, warning him company could "implode" in scandal. Lay resigned Jan. 23. Congress, Jan. 24, began public hearings into **Enron bankruptcy**.

In his first State of the Union address, Jan. 29, Pres. Bush called Iran, Iraq, and North Korea part of an **"axis of evil."** Eight U.S. troops killed Mar. 2-4 in assault against Taliban and al-Qaeda forces in eastern Afghanistan. By Mar. 6, 1,200 U.S. troops were involved in **Operation Anaconda**, which ended Mar. 12.

Final independent prosecutor's report, Mar. 20, found insufficient evidence that Pres. Clinton or his wife had committed any crime in connection with **Whitewater**. Pres. Bush, Mar. 27, signed into law McCain-Feingold **campaign-finance reform bill** that banned unregulated, unrestricted "soft money" donations; part of bill struck down by Supreme Court, June 2007.

Ceremonial last girder removed May 30 from site of **World Trade Center** towers, signaling end of massive clean-up and recovery operation. **Coleen Rowley** testified before congressional committee June 6 that Washington FBI agents had stymied investigative efforts in Minneapolis prior to Sept. 11.

WorldCom announced June 25 it had overstated its cash flow by billions; filed for bankruptcy, July 21.

Pres. Bush told UN General Assembly Sept. 12 that he would work with Security Council to deal with threat posed by Iraq's **weapons of mass destruction**.

Richard Reid pleaded guilty Oct. 4 to all charges stemming from incident aboard a Paris-to-Miami flight in Dec. 2001, when he tried to ignite explosives in his shoes; sentenced Jan. 2003 to life in prison.

Former Pres. **Jimmy Carter** named Oct. 10 as winner of Nobel Peace Prize. On Oct. 10-11 the House, 296-133, and Senate, 77-23, gave Bush backing to use military force against **Iraq**. The Bush administration revealed Oct. 16 that **North Korea** had acknowledged it was developing **nuclear arms**.

Republicans emerged from elections, Nov. 5, with majority in Senate and increased margin in House.

Pres. Bush, Nov. 25, signed legislation creating **Dept. of Homeland Security**.

U.S. Roman Catholic bishops, Nov. 13, approved revised, Vatican-vetted policies dealing with priests who sexually abuse minors. Cardinal **Bernard Law**, Dec. 13, resigned as archbishop of Boston after being criticized for allegedly covering up sexual abuse by Catholic priests. **Trent Lott** (R, MS) bowed out as new Senate majority leader Dec. 20 shortly after being chosen amid furor over comment apparently supporting segregation; Sen. **Bill Frist** (R, TN) elected as leader Dec. 23.

2003 On Jan. 10-11, shortly before leaving office, Gov. **George Ryan** (R, IL) **pardoned or commuted death sentences** of 171 Illinois death row convicts. U.S. Senate, Jan. 22, approved Pres. Bush's nomination of **Tom Ridge** to be **first secretary of homeland security**.

Space shuttle *Columbia* broke apart Feb. 1 over southwestern U.S. during descent toward planned landing; all 7 crew members killed. Official report issued Aug. 26 blamed

2001: The attacks of Sept. 11, 2001, kill more than 2,600 people in New York, including 343 firefighters.

damage sustained during liftoff when chunk of foam came loose and hit the left wing; also cited a "broken safety culture" at NASA.

Senate, Mar. 6, approved the **Strategic Offensive Reductions Treaty**, or **Moscow Treaty**, signed in **2002** by U.S. and Russian leaders. Both sides required to reduce deployed nuclear warheads to 1,700-2,200 by **2012**.

A U.S.-led military offensive aimed at ousting **Saddam Hussein** got underway Mar. 19, when 40 Tomahawk cruise missiles hit targets in Baghdad; strikes continued in succeeding nights. U.S. forces Mar. 21 seized major oil fields near Basra. On Apr. 3, U.S. Marines crossed the Tigris River and moved close to **Baghdad**. By Apr. 8, major government buildings had been occupied and organized resistance had dropped. U.S. forces report control over much of Baghdad, Apr. 9. With collapse of regime, services in major cities were disrupted, and looting became widespread.

Pres. Bush, speaking from the aircraft carrier *Abraham Lincoln*, declared on May 1 the **end of major combat operations**; insurgents continued to mount attacks against both military and civilian targets. Pres. Bush signed a major bill May 28 providing $330 bil in **tax cuts** over several years. Under settlement in private antitrust suit brought by Netscape (unit of AOL), **Microsoft** agreed May 29 to pay **AOL Time Warner** $750 mil.

On June 23, U.S. Supreme Court upheld **affirmative action program** providing preference to minorities for admission to Univ. of Michigan law school, but rejected an undergraduate affirmative action program at the university that employed numerical formulas.

A **power failure** spread rapidly through Ohio, Michigan, and the Northeast, as well as eastern Canada, on Aug. 14. Some 50 mil people in 8 states and Ontario left without electricity for as long as 2 days.

On Sept. 9, Roman Catholic archdiocese of Boston and lawyers representing about 550 victims of **sexual abuse by priests** announced settlement worth up to $85 mil.

California voters, Oct. 7, voted to recall Democratic Gov. Gray Davis from office and replace him with Republican actor-turned-politician **Arnold Schwarzenegger**.

Rev. V. Gene Robinson consecrated Nov. 2 as Episcopal bishop of New Hampshire, the church's **first openly gay bishop**.

The Senate, Nov. 3, approved by voice vote the $87.5 bil for **U.S. military forces in Iraq** and for help rebuilding the country Nov. 3. A Virginia jury, Nov. 17, found **John Muhammad** guilty in 2002 Washington, DC, area **sniper attacks** that killed 10 people; he was sentenced to death. Another Virginia jury found **Lee Malvo** guilty of murder in the attacks, Dec. 18; sentenced to life in prison without parole. Massachusetts Supreme Judicial Court decided 4-3, Nov. 18, that **gay couples had right to marry** under state constitution.

Pres. Bush signed a bill Dec. 8 overhauling **Medicare**. The program would offer in 2006 its first-ever prescription drug benefit, and private insurance companies would have larger role in covering Medicare beneficiaries. **Saddam Hussein** captured by U.S. military forces Dec. 13, in underground hideout southeast of Tikrit. The Bush administration announced Dec. 23 that a Holstein in Washington state had tested positive for **mad-cow disease**; the animal, first in U.S. to be so identified, had already been slaughtered.

2004 On Feb. 12, San Francisco began issuing **marriage licenses to same-sex couples**. On Mar. 11, state supreme court issued stay blocking the practice.

Photos showing abuse of **Abu Ghraib prison inmates** in Iraq by American soldiers emerged Apr. 3. The **National World War II Memorial** in Washington, DC, opened to the public Apr. 29, was dedicated May 29.

Ronald Reagan, 40th U.S. president, died in Los Angeles, June 5. The U.S.-led coalition formally transferred power to an **interim Iraqi government** on June 28. U.S. Supreme Court, June 28, issued three separate decisions regarding **rights of terrorism detainees** that generally curtailed sweeping powers claimed by Pres. Bush as military commander in chief.

The **9/11 Commission Report**, released to the public July 22, summarized what was known about events of that day and called for restructuring of U.S. intelligence operations. In Boston, July 26-29, Democrats nominated Sen. **John Kerry** (MA) for president and Sen. **John Edwards** (NC) for vice president.

Four hurricanes—Charley, Frances, Ivan, and Jeanne—hit Florida and surrounding states Aug. 13-Sept. 25. Storms blamed for over 50 deaths and more than $20 bil in damage in U.S.

Pres. **Bush** and Vice Pres. **Cheney** renominated Sept. 1 on **Republican ticket** at party convention in New York. Number of **U.S. soldiers killed** in the Iraqi conflict reached 1,000 on Sept. 7, including 755 in combat.

The **Boston Red Sox** swept their last 8 games to win **World Series** Oct. 27, for first time since 1918.

Pres. **Bush** reelected Nov. 2, capturing 31 states with 286 electoral votes. Republicans gained 4 Senate seats for new 55-44 majority, won majority in House for sixth consecutive election. After a week-long campaign, U.S. forces took control of the Iraqi city of **Fallujah** from insurgents, Nov. 14, Pres. Bush signed intelligence reform bill Dec. 17, based on 9/11 Commission's findings: bill created **director of national intelligence** to oversee nation's intelligence agencies.

2005 Army Reserve Spec. **Charles Graner Jr.** found guilty, Jan. 14, in connection with **Abu Ghraib** prisoner abuses in Iraq, sentenced to 10 years in prison. Army Reserve Pfc. **Lynndie England**, who had been photographed posing with prisoners, convicted Sept. 26 and sentenced to 3 years. Pres. **Bush** inaugurated for second term, Jan. 20. **Condoleezza Rice** became **first black woman secretary of state**, Jan. 26. **Alberto Gonzales** became **first Hispanic U.S. attorney general**, Feb. 3.

2005: Hurricane Katrina and subsequent failure of levees cause unprecedented destruction in New Orleans.

Supreme Court, Mar. 1, ruled that **executing** convicts who committed their crimes **before age 18** was unconstitutional. **Terri Schiavo**, in a persistent vegetative state since 1990, died Mar. 31, 13 days after feeding tube was removed.

Bipartisan group of 14 senators reached compromise, May 23, averting a **filibuster** that would have derailed nominations of judges. *Vanity Fair* article revealed May 31 that former FBI official **W. Mark Felt** was **"Deep Throat"**—key source for *Washington Post* reporters Bob Woodward and Carl Bernstein when they investigated 1972 Watergate break-in.

Lance Armstrong won record 7th straight Tour de France, July 24. *Discovery* blasted off from Cape Canaveral, FL, July 26, in first shuttle launch since the 2003 *Columbia* disaster.

After striking Florida's Atlantic coast, Aug. 26, **Hurricane Katrina** struck the Gulf coast, Aug. 29, causing devastation in Louisiana, Mississippi, and Alabama. Breech in a levee on Lake Pontchartrain, Aug. 30, flooded **New Orleans**. Relief efforts widely criticized as insufficient.

Chief Justice **William H. Rehnquist** died Sept. 3. Bush Sept. 5 nominated as successor **John G. Roberts Jr.**, whom Bush had earlier nominated to replace retiring Justice O'Connor. On Sept. 29 he was confirmed by Senate, 78-22, and sworn in as 17th chief justice: at 50, the **youngest chief justice** since 1801. White House counsel **Harriet Miers**, nominated Oct. 3 to Supreme Court, withdrew Oct. 27. In her place, Bush, Oct. 31, nominated **Samuel A. Alito Jr.**; confirmed Jan. 31, 2006. House Majority Leader **Tom DeLay** (R, TX) indicted in Texas Sept. 28 for allegedly conspiring to launder illegal contributions; he stepped down from his leadership post.

Civil rights icon **Rosa Parks** died Oct. 24: became 31st person and first woman to lie in honor in Capitol rotunda. **Chicago White Sox**, Oct. 26, defeated the Houston Astros to win their first World Series title since 1917.

New York Times, Dec. 16, reported that Pres. Bush in 2002 had secretly authorized National Security Agency to **eavesdrop** without court warrant on people in the U.S. suspected of terrorist activities. Senate, Dec. 21, passed $453 bil defense appropriations bill after inclusion of **anti-torture amendment**; provision allowing oil drilling in Alaska's **Arctic National Wildlife Refuge** removed from Senate's draft. Tropical Storm Zeta, Dec. 29, the season's 28th ended the **most active hurricane season** on record.

2006 Former top Republican lobbyist **Jack Abramoff** pleaded guilty Jan. 3 to conspiracy to bribe public officials, fraud, and tax evasion. In plea agreement, he promised to cooperate with investigation into his dealings with members of Congress.

Former Enron CEO **Jeffrey Skilling** convicted May 25 of fraud, conspiracy, and insider trading related to Enron's 2001 bankruptcy. **Kenneth Lay**, Enron's founder and Skilling's successor as CEO, found guilty same day of fraud and conspiracy; died July 15.

Pres. Bush, June 13, made unannounced **visit to Baghdad** to demonstrate support for new Iraqi government led by Prem. Nouri Kamel al-Maliki. U.S. Supreme Court ruled June 29 that Pres. Bush's system for trying **terrorism detainees** at Guantánamo Bay, Cuba, military base was unauthorized under federal law and Geneva Conventions.

Bush, July 19, issued his **first veto**, rejecting bill to end federal funding constraints on human embryonic **stem cell research**.

British authorities announced Aug. 10 they had foiled terrorist plot to use **liquid explosives** on passenger flights between Britain and U.S.; new security restrictions prohibited passengers in U.S. from transporting most liquids in carry-on luggage.

In speech Sept. 6 Bush confirmed existence of **secret overseas prisons** for terrorism suspects run by CIA. Defense Dept. same day released new Army Field Manual delimiting permissible interrogation methods.

Pres. Bush signed bill Oct. 26 authorizing construction of 700-mi fence along U.S.-Mexico border: a broader immigration bill that he favored—approved by the Senate but not the House—would have given many **illegal immigrants** a chance to gain citizenship.

Democrats won control of House and Senate in **midterm congressional elections** Nov. 7; Republican majority had ruled House and, with brief exception, the Senate, since 1995 elections. Pres. Bush announced Nov. 8 that Defense Sec. **Donald Rumsfeld**, a focus of criticism over Iraq war, had resigned.

Gerald R. Ford, 38th U.S. president, died Dec. 26 at age 93: had been the oldest-ever living president.

2007 Rep. Nancy Pelosi (D, CA) chosen Jan. 4 as **first woman Speaker of the House**. Pres. Bush announced Jan. 10 he was sending more than 20,000 additional troops to Iraq, in a troop "**surge**" backed by Lt. Gen. David Petraeus, new top U.S. commander in Iraq. Bush administration announced Jan. 17 that a court established under the 1978 **Foreign Intelligence Surveillance Act** (FISA) would have jurisdiction over a National Security Agency program monitoring international communications between people in the U.S. and suspected terrorists.

Reports of substandard conditions at **Walter Reed Army Medical Center** in Washington, DC, resulted in the dismissal of leading military officials involved, Mar. 1-2. A U.S. District Court jury found **I. Lewis "Scooter" Libby**, former chief of staff for Vice Pres. Dick Cheney, guilty Mar. 6 of perjury and obstructing justice in the federal investigation into the leak exposing undercover CIA agent Valerie Plame Wilson. Libby was sentenced to 30 months in prison and fined $250,000 on June 5; Pres. Bush commuted the sentence July 2.

A senior at **Virginia Tech** killed 27 students and 5 faculty members on Apr. 16 before he shot himself fatally on campus in Blacksburg, VA. On Apr. 18 the Supreme Court upheld, 5-4, a federal law enacted in 2003 that banned so-called **partial birth abortion**.

The Senate and House May 24 approved an Iraq and Afghanistan **war-funding bill** without any timetable for withdrawal of U.S. troops from Iraq; as part of the agreement, Congress also approved an increase in the **national minimum wage** from $5.15 to $7.25 per hour in 3 stages over 2 years.

On Wall Street, the **Dow Jones** closed at 14,000.41 July 19, just 59 trading days after passing 13,000. *Harry Potter and the Deathly Hallows*, 7th and final novel in J. K. Rowling's phenomenally successful series, was released July 21, earning record U.S. sales. Pres. Bush issued an executive order July 20 requiring that **imprisoned terror suspects** receive "the basic necessities of life" and barring cruel, inhuman, or degrading treatment or punishment.

A **Minneapolis highway bridge collapsed** Aug. 1, causing the deaths of 13 people. Congress, Aug. 4, cleared a measure allowing the National Security Agency to monitor communications without court warrants, if believed related to terrorism. Barry Bonds tied Major League Baseball's all-time career **home-run record** at 755—set by Hank Aaron—on Aug. 4 in San Diego; Bonds hit No. 756 on Aug. 7. **Karl Rove**, Bush's chief political strategist, announced Aug. 13 that he was resigning. **José Padilla** convicted of conspiracy in terrorism case, Aug. 16, sentenced in Jan. 2008 to 17 years, 4 months in prison. Atty. Gen. **Alberto Gonzales**, blamed for alleged firing of several U.S. attorneys, announced his resignation Aug. 27. Mattel, world's largest toy company, said Aug. 14 that it was recalling nearly 19 mil toys made in China, about half of which had been distributed in the U.S.

Sprinter **Marion Jones** admitted Oct. 5 that she had taken performance-enhancing drugs and agreed to forfeit results dating back to 2000, including 5 Olympic medals.

Congress voted, Nov. 6 and 8, to **overturn a veto** by Pres. Bush for the first time: the bill included projects for hurricane recovery, wetlands restoration, and flood control. On Nov. 7, the cargo ship *Cosco Busan* scraped against the base of the San Francisco-Oakland Bay Bridge, **leaking heavy fuel oil** into the bay. A federal grand jury probing athletes' use of steroids and other performance-enhancing drugs indicted slugger **Barry Bonds** Nov. 15, for allegedly lying to the grand jury in 2003 about his use of steroids and human growth hormone.

On Dec. 6 Pres. Bush announced an accord among mortgage lenders that would impose a 5-year **freeze on interest rates** for some mortgage holders and provide options for some homeowners to refinance mortgages through the Federal Housing Administration. Former U.S. Sen. **George J. Mitchell** (D, ME) presented evidence Dec. 13 concerning alleged use of banned performance-enhancing drugs by 86 current and former Major League Baseball players.

Under a law signed Dec. 17 New Jersey became the **first state to repeal the death penalty** since Supreme Court reinstated it under certain conditions in 1976. An energy bill mandating an increase in automobile **fuel-economy standards** to 35 miles per gallon by 2030 was signed by Pres. Bush Dec. 19; it also set a timetable for the replacement of incandescent light bulbs with more energy-efficient bulbs and required a major increase in the use of biofuels.

2008 In **Iowa caucuses** Jan. 3, former Gov. **Mike Huckabee** (AR) captured 34% of the Republican vote; Gov. **Mitt Romney** (MA) and Sen. **John McCain** (AZ) were among those trailing. Among leading Democrats, Sen. **Barack Obama** (IL) won 38% of delegates; Sen. **Hillary Rodham Clinton** (NY), was behind, tied with former Sen. **John Edwards** (NC). In the Jan. 8 **New Hampshire primary**, however McCain won among Republicans, taking 37% of the vote, and Clinton bounced back to defeat Obama, 39% to 37%. McCain won again in **South Carolina**, while Democrats Jan. 26 delivered a strong win to Obama over Clinton. On Jan. 29, McCain won the **Florida** Republican primary. Edwards left the race the same day.

The Federal Reserve **cut key interest rates** in two stages, Jan. 22 and 30, lowering target for the federal funds rate to 3.0% and the discount rate to 3.5%. The Fed cited "a weakening of the economic outlook," including slow job growth and deterioration in housing and credit markets.

Pres. Bush submitted fiscal 2009 **budget** to Congress Feb. 4 that called for expenditures of $3.107 tril, forecasting a $407 bil deficit.

On **Super Tuesday**, Feb. 5, McCain won 9 states—including California and New York—while Romney won 7 and Huckabee 5. Romney withdrew Feb. 7. Among Democrats, Obama won his home state of Illinois and 12 others, some by large margins; Clinton won in California, New York (her home state), and 7 others, plus American Samoa. McCain and Obama gained in subsequent primaries and caucuses.

A $168 bil **economic stimulus package**, signed Feb. 13 by Pres. Bush, provided tax rebates of up to $600 for individuals and $1,200 for couples, plus $300 per child, with a minimum rebate for certain filers having no tax liability. **McCain locked up GOP nomination** with victories in 4 states, Mar. 4; Huckabee conceded nomination. New York Gov. **Eliot Spitzer** (D) left office Mar. 17, after revelations that he had been a client of a high-priced prostitution service. Obama, in a speech in Philadelphia, Mar. 18, discussed America's racial divide and condemned inflammatory statements by his former longtime pastor, Rev. **Jeremiah Wright**.

Justice Dept. declassified Apr. 1 a 2003 legal brief that had given military interrogators authority to use extreme methods when **questioning detainees** linked to al-Qaeda. **Benedict XVI** made his first papal visit to the U.S., Apr. 15-20. U.S. Supreme Court held Apr. 16 that Kentucky's method of **execution by lethal injection** did not violate constitutional prohibition against cruel and unusual punishment. Clinton defeated Obama, 55%-45%, in **Pennsylvania**'s Democratic primary Apr. 22, but remained behind in delegates and fund-raising; Obama expanded delegate lead in following weeks. On Apr. 23 the Bush administration announced that Gen. **David Petraeus** would be promoted to head Central Command, overseeing military affairs in Middle East and Central Asia.

Interior Dept. announced May 14 that the U.S. was listing the **polar bear as a threatened species** because of shrinking sea ice attributable to global warming. NASA's Phoenix spacecraft landed on Mars May 25, ending a journey of over 9 months and 420 mil miles.

After **final Democratic primaries** June 3, dozens of Democratic superdelegates moved to endorse **Obama**, who **claimed victory** at a rally in St. Paul, MN. Clinton suspended her campaign and **endorsed** him, June 7. Obama announced June 19, that he would forgo public funding (and its associated spending limits), relying on his own fundraising.

U.S. **Supreme Court** ruled June 12 that foreign prisoners at Guantánamo Bay could challenge their detention by filing a writ of **habeas corpus**. The court held June 26 that individuals have a constitutional **right to own a gun**. **Floods** along rivers throughout the Midwest in mid-June claimed at least 24 lives and devastated crops. **Oil prices** spiked above $140 per barrel in June; the national average price for a gallon of regular unleaded gasoline reached $4.087 by July 1.

U.S. Sec. of State **Condoleezza Rice** signed agreement in Czech Republic, July 8, and Poland, Aug. 20, allowing U.S. to place components of a **missile defense system** in those countries. A measure signed July 10 by Pres. Bush expanded federal government's power to spy on suspected terrorists. Nearly 2,100 **wildfires** charred some 1.2 mil acres in northern and central California, starting mostly in late June. U.S. military deaths in Iraq dropped to 13 in July, lowest monthly total since the war began.

Meeting Aug. 25-28 in Denver, CO, Democratic National Convention **nominated Obama for president** and Sen. Joe Biden (DE) for vice president. In acceptance speech Aug. 28, Obama denounced "failed policies" of the Bush administration. On Aug. 29 at a rally in Dayton, OH, McCain introduced his surprise pick for vice president, Gov. **Sarah Palin** of Alaska.

At the XXIX **Summer Olympic Games**, hosted Aug. 8-24 by Beijing, the U.S. won 110 medals—the most of any nation—and American swimmer **Michael Phelps** won the most gold medals, 8.

A **U.S. air strike** against reputed Taliban activity in the Afghanistan village of Azizabad, Aug. 22, caused as many as 90 civilian deaths according to Afghan sources. The U.S., Sept. 1, transferred to Iraqi forces security responsibilities in **Anbar province**, formerly the center of a Sunni insurgency.

Hurricane Gustav hit Louisiana Sept. 1, flooding much of the coastline, but the New Orleans levee system, strengthened since Hurricane Katrina, held up. Some 2 mil people were evacuated beforehand. More than 1 mil people fled the Texas coast in advance of **Hurricane Ike**, which battered Galveston Island and Houston Sept. 13, claiming 37 lives in Texas. On Sept. 12, 25 people were killed when a commuter train ran through a red signal near Chatsworth, CA, and hit an oncoming freight train.

Meeting Sept. 3 in St. Paul, MN, Republican National Convention **nominated McCain for president** and Palin for vice president. Palin's nomination marked only the 2nd time a major U.S. political party had a woman on its national presidential ticket. With financial system in crisis, the federal government Sept. 7 took control of the nation's two largest mortgage finance companies, commonly called **Fannie Mae and Freddie Mac**. On Wall Street a week later, investment titan **Merrill Lynch** agreed to sell itself to Bank of America for $50 bil, and **Lehman Brothers** declared bankruptcy, the largest U.S. bankruptcy to date, after failing to find a buyer.

The Federal Reserve Sept. 16 took control of **American International Group** (AIG), one of the world's largest insurance firms, taking a 79.9% equity stake and giving it a credit line that expanded to $144 bil by Oct. 31. The Fed disclosed Sept. 21 that Wall Street's last two major independent investment banks, **Goldman Sachs and Morgan Stanley**, would restructure themselves as bank holding companies and submit to more rigorous government regulation.

On Sept. 20 a Treasury plan was introduced to purchase up to $700 bil of **"toxic" mortgage-backed securities** to restore confidence among investors and banks reluctant to make loans. The first of several **campaign debates** between Obama and McCain held Sept. 26 in Oxford, MS, focused in large part on the economy. On Sept. 29 a measure covering the so-called **bailout** failed in the House by a vote of 228-205; about two-thirds of Republicans rejected it. The **Dow Jones closed down 778 points**, for a loss in wealth estimated at $1.2 tril. A substantially revised version of the **bailout plan passed** the Senate Oct. 1, 74-25, and the House Oct. 3, 263-171.

A Las Vegas jury Oct. 3 found former football star **O. J.**

2008: Sen. Barack Obama is elected the first African American president.

Simpson and a co-defendant guilty in robbery and kidnapping of two sports memorabilia dealers; Simpson sentenced Dec. 5 to at least 9 years in prison. The Fed announced Oct. 7 that it would begin lending directly to U.S. corporations, and Treasury Sec. **Henry Paulson** said Oct. 13 that the government would apply part of the $700 bil bailout to purchase an equity stake in banks. Concerned about **money-market mutual funds**, the Fed Oct. 21 pledged $540 bil to ease credit flows and bolster investor confidence.

Two separate "**troopergate**" investigations reached differing conclusions, Oct. 10 and Nov. 3, as to Gov. Sarah Palin's actions. Bush administration announced Oct. 11 it had removed **North Korea** from its list of countries that sponsor terrorism, as part of a June agreement for North Korea to begin dismantling its nuclear weapons program.

A federal jury in Washington, DC, found veteran **Sen. Ted Stevens** (R, AK) guilty Oct. 27 of accepting and failing to report some $250,000 in gifts from an oil services firm; he was narrowly defeated for reelection in Nov. Conviction later voided because of prosecutorial misconduct. **Dow Jones** closed Oct. 31 at 9,325,01, for a one-month decline of 14.1%.

Barack Obama elected, Nov. 4, as **first African American president** in U.S. history. The Obama-Biden ticket earned 53% of the popular vote, versus 46% for McCain-Palin, with an electoral vote margin of 365 to 173. Democrats increased their majorities in House and Senate, coming close to veto-proof Senate majority of 60. A key holdout was the Senate race in **Minnesota**, where the outcome was undetermined for months. Election gave Democrats control of both White House and Congress for first time since 1995. **California** voters approved **Proposition 8**, overturning state Supreme Court decision affirming a constitutional right for same-sex couples to marry.

Oct. **unemployment rate** reported, Nov. 7, at 6.5%. **Dow Jones fell 427** points, or 5.1%, Nov. 19, going below 8,000 for first time since 2003. U.S. government Nov. 23 announced plan to provide $20 bil in cash and up to $306 bil more as backup to protect **Citigroup** from potential losses from commercial and residential mortgages; **volatile Dow Jones** responded by rising 397 points.

Preparing to deal with economic crisis and recession, Pres.-elect Obama Nov. 24 named **Timothy Geithner**, president of the Federal Reserve Bank of New York, as his choice for treasury secretary and former treasury secretary **Lawrence Summers** to head White House Economic Council. Obama also said he would promote a **stimulus package** aimed at saving or creating 2.5 mil jobs, especially in infrastructure and alternative energy projects.

Dow dropped 680 points Dec. 1 after reports that U.S. manufacturing had hit a 26-year low and that U.S economy officially fell into **recession** starting in Dec. 2007. Obama named former rival **Hillary Clinton**, Dec. 1, as his choice for **secretary of state**.

Illinois Gov. Rod Blagojevich (D) arrested Dec. 9 on corruption charges arising from FBI recordings of his phone conversations; he was also accused of seeking financial compensation for his choice of a replacement to fill U.S. Senate seat being vacated by Obama. Illinois legislators voted Dec. 15 to **impeach Blagojevich**; he asserted innocence, Dec. 19, and made a Senate appointment, Dec. 30, choosing former state Atty. Gen. **Roland Burris**.

Investment manager **Bernard Madoff** arrested Dec. 11 on charges he had defrauded clients of tens of billions of dollars in what officials said was a massive **Ponzi scheme**.

The Fed Dec. 16 cut **benchmark interest rate** to near zero. Bush announced plans Dec. 19 to lend **General Motors and Chrysler** $17.4 bil to help them survive over the next 3 months.

For events of 2009, see Year in Review—Chronology (pp. 18-39).

Patrick Henry's Speech to the Virginia Convention

The following is an excerpt from Patrick Henry's speech to the Virginia Convention, which met at St. John's Church in Richmond, on Mar. 23, 1775, to react to British oppression.

Gentlemen may cry, peace, peace—but there is no peace. The war is actually begun! The next gale that sweeps from the north will bring to our ears the clash of resounding arms! Our brethren are already in the field! Why stand we here idle? What is it that gentlemen wish? What would they have? Is life so dear, or peace so sweet, as to be purchased at the price of chains and slavery? Forbid it, Almighty God! I know not what course others may take; but as for me, give me liberty, or give me death!

Adoption of the Declaration of Independence

On June 7, 1776, Richard Henry Lee, who had issued the first call for a congress of the colonies, introduced in the Continental Congress at Philadelphia a resolution declaring "that these United Colonies are, and of right ought to be, free and independent states, that they are absolved from all allegiance to the British Crown, and that all political connection between them and the state of Great Britain is, and ought to be, totally dissolved."

The resolution, seconded by John Adams on behalf of the Massachusetts delegation, came up again on June 11 when a committee of five, headed by Thomas Jefferson, was appointed to express the purpose of the resolution in a declaration of independence. The other four were John Adams, Benjamin Franklin, Robert R. Livingston, and Roger Sherman.

Drafting the Declaration was assigned to Jefferson, who worked on a portable desk of his own construction in a room at Market and 7th St. The committee reported the result on June 28, 1776. The members of the Congress suggested a number of changes, which Jefferson called "deplorable." They did not approve Jefferson's arraignment of the British people and King George III for encouraging and fostering the slave trade, which Jefferson called "an execrable commerce." They eliminated 630 words and added 146, leaving 1,322 words in the final draft. In its final form, capitalization was erratic. Jefferson had written that men were endowed with "inalienable" rights; in the final copy it came out as "unalienable" and has been thus ever since.

The Lee-Adams resolution of independence was adopted by 12 "yeas" on July 2—the actual date of the act of independence. The Declaration, which explains the act, was adopted July 4.

After the Declaration was adopted, July 4, 1776, it was turned over to John Dunlap, printer, to be printed on broadsides. The original copy was lost and one of his broadsides was attached to a page in the journal of the Congress. It was read aloud July 8 in Philadelphia, PA, Easton, PA, and Trenton, NJ. On July 9, it was read by order of Gen. George Washington to the troops assembled on the Common in New York City (City Hall Park).

The Continental Congress of July 19, 1776, adopted the following resolution:

"Resolved, That the Declaration passed on the 4th, be fairly engrossed on parchment with the title and stile of 'The Unanimous Declaration of the thirteen United States of America' and that the same, when engrossed, be signed by every member of Congress."

Not all delegates who signed the engrossed Declaration were present on July 4. Robert Morris (PA), William Williams (CT), and Samuel Chase (MD) signed on Aug. 2; Oliver Wolcott (CT), George Wythe (VA), Richard Henry Lee (VA), and Elbridge Gerry (MA) signed in August and September; Matthew Thornton (NH) joined the Congress Nov. 4 and signed later. Thomas McKean (DE) rejoined Washington's army before signing and said later that he signed in 1781.

Charles Carroll of Carrollton was appointed a delegate by Maryland on July 4, 1776, presented his credentials July 18, and signed the engrossed Declaration on Aug. 2. Born Sept. 19, 1737, he was 95 years old and the last surviving signer when he died on Nov. 14, 1832.

Two Pennsylvania delegates who did not support the Declaration on July 4 were replaced. The four New York delegates did not have authority from their state to vote on July 4. On July 9, the New York state convention authorized its delegates to approve the Declaration, and the Congress was so notified on July 15, 1776. The four signed the Declaration on Aug. 2.

The original engrossed Declaration is preserved at the National Archives in Washington, DC.

Declaration of Independence

The Declaration of Independence was adopted by the Continental Congress in Philadelphia on July 4, 1776. John Hancock was president of the Congress, and Charles Thomson was secretary. A copy of the Declaration, engrossed on parchment, was signed by members of Congress on and after Aug. 2, 1776. On Jan. 18, 1777, Congress ordered that "an authenticated copy, with the names of the members of Congress subscribing the same, be sent to each of the United States, and that they be desired to have the same put on record." Authenticated copies were printed in broadside form in Baltimore, where the Continental Congress was then in session. The following text is that of the original printed by John Dunlap at Philadelphia for the Continental Congress. The original is on display at the National Archives.

IN CONGRESS, July 4, 1776.

A DECLARATION

By the REPRESENTATIVES of the

UNITED STATES OF AMERICA,

In GENERAL CONGRESS assembled

When in the Course of human Events, it becomes necessary for one People to dissolve the Political Bands which have connected them with another, and to assume among the Powers of the Earth, the separate and equal Station to which the Laws of Nature and of Nature's God entitle them, a decent Respect to the Opinions of Mankind requires that they should declare the causes which impel them to the Separation.

We hold these Truths to be self-evident, that all Men are created equal, that they are endowed by their Creator with certain unalienable Rights, that among these are Life, Liberty, and the Pursuit of Happiness—That to secure these Rights, Governments are instituted among Men, deriving their just Powers from the Consent of the Governed, that whenever any Form of Government becomes destructive of these Ends, it is the Right of the People to alter or to abolish it, and to institute new Government, laying its Foundation on such Principles, and organizing its Powers in such Form, as to them shall seem most likely to effect their Safety and Happiness. Prudence, indeed, will dictate that Governments long established should not be changed for light and transient Causes; and accordingly all Experience hath shewn, that Mankind are more disposed to suffer, while Evils are sufferable, than to right themselves by abolishing the Forms to which they are accustomed. But when a long Train of Abuses and Usurpations, pursuing invariably the same Object, evinces a Design to reduce them under absolute Despotism, it is their Right, it is their Duty, to throw off such Government, and to provide new Guards for their future Security. Such has been the patient Sufferance of these Colonies; and such is now the Necessity which constrains them to alter their former Systems of Government. The History of the present King of Great-Britain is a History of repeated Injuries and Usurpations, all having in direct Object the Establishment of an absolute Tyranny over these States. To prove this, let Facts be submitted to a candid World.

He has refused his Assent to Laws, the most wholesome and necessary for the public Good.

He has forbidden his Governors to pass Laws of immediate and pressing Importance, unless suspended in their Operation till his Assent should be obtained; and when so suspended, he has utterly neglected to attend to them.

He has refused to pass other Laws for the Accommodation of large Districts of People, unless those People would relinquish the Right of Representation in the Legislature, a Right inestimable to them, and formidable to Tyrants only.

He has called together Legislative Bodies at Places unusual, uncomfortable, and distant from the Depository of their Public Records, for the sole Purpose of fatiguing them into Compliance with his Measures.

He has dissolved Representative Houses repeatedly, for opposing with manly Firmness his Invasions on the Rights of the People.

He has refused for a long Time, after such Dissolutions, to cause others to be elected; whereby the Legislative Powers, incapable of Annihilation, have returned to the People at large for their exercise; the State remaining in the mean time exposed to all the Dangers of Invasion from without, and Convulsions within.

He has endeavoured to prevent the Population of these States; for that Purpose obstructing the Laws for Naturalization of Foreigners; refusing to pass others to encourage their Migrations hither, and raising the Conditions of new Appropriations of Lands.

He has obstructed the Administration of Justice, by refusing his Assent to Laws for establishing Judiciary Powers.

He has made Judges dependent on his Will alone, for the Tenure of their Offices, and the Amount and payment of their Salaries.

He has erected a Multitude of new Offices, and sent hither Swarms of Officers to harrass our People, and eat out their Substance.

He has kept among us, in Times of Peace, Standing Armies, without the consent of our Legislatures.

He has affected to render the Military independent of, and superior to the Civil Power.

He has combined with others to subject us to a Jurisdiction foreign to our Constitution, and unacknowledged by our Laws; giving his Assent to their Acts of pretended Legislation:

For quartering large Bodies of Armed Troops among us:

For protecting them, by a mock Trial, from Punishment for any Murders which they should commit on the Inhabitants of these States:

For cutting off our Trade with all Parts of the World:

For imposing Taxes on us without our Consent:

For depriving us, in many Cases, of the Benefits of Trial by Jury:

For transporting us beyond Seas to be tried for pretended Offences:

For abolishing the free System of English Laws in a neighbouring Province, establishing therein an arbitrary Government, and enlarging its Boundaries, so as to render it at once an Example and fit Instrument for introducing the same absolute Rule into these Colonies:

For taking away our Charters, abolishing our most valuable Laws, and altering fundamentally the Forms of our Governments:

For suspending our own Legislatures, and declaring themselves invested with Power to legislate for us in all Cases whatsoever.

He has abdicated Government here, by declaring us out of his Protection and waging War against us.

He has plundered our Seas, ravaged our Coasts, burnt our towns, and destroyed the Lives of our People.

He is, at this Time, transporting large Armies of foreign Mercenaries to complete the works of Death, Desolation, and Tyranny, already begun with circumstances of Cruelty

and Perfidy, scarcely paralleled in the most barbarous Ages, and totally unworthy the Head of a civilized Nation.

He has constrained our fellow Citizens taken Captive on the high Seas to bear Arms against their Country, to become the Executioners of their Friends and Brethren, or to fall themselves by their Hands.

He has excited domestic Insurrections amongst us, and has endeavoured to bring on the Inhabitants of our Frontiers, the merciless Indian Savages, whose known Rule of Warfare, is an undistinguished Destruction, of all Ages, Sexes and Conditions.

In every stage of these Oppressions we have Petitioned for Redress in the most humble Terms: Our repeated Petitions have been answered only by repeated Injury. A Prince, whose Character is thus marked by every act which may define a Tyrant, is unfit to be the Ruler of a free People.

Nor have we been wanting in Attentions to our British Brethren. We have warned them from Time to Time of Attempts by their Legislature to extend an unwarrantable Jurisdiction over us. We have reminded them of the Circumstances of our Emigration and Settlement here. We have appealed to their native Justice and Magnanimity, and we have conjured them by the Ties of our common Kindred to disavow these Usurpations, which, would inevitably interrupt our Connections and Correspondence. They too have been deaf to the Voice of Justice and of Consanguinity. We must, therefore, acquiesce in the Necessity, which denounces our Separation, and hold them, as we hold the rest of Mankind, Enemies in War, in Peace, Friends.

We, therefore, the Representatives of the UNITED STATES OF AMERICA, in General Congress, Assembled, appealing to the Supreme Judge of the World for the Rectitude of our Intentions, do, in the Name, and by Authority of the good People of these Colonies, solemnly Publish and Declare, That these United Colonies are, and of Right ought to be, Free and Independent States; that they are absolved from all Allegiance to the British Crown, and that all political Connection between them and the State of Great-Britain, is and ought to be totally dissolved; and that as Free and Independent States, they have full Power to levy War, conclude Peace, contract Alliances, establish Commerce, and to do all other Acts and Things which Independent States may of right do. And for the support of this declaration, with a firm Reliance on the Protection of Divine Providence, we mutually pledge to each other our lives, our Fortunes, and our sacred Honor.

JOHN HANCOCK, President
Attest.
CHARLES THOMSON, Secretary.

Signers of the Declaration of Independence

Delegate (state)	Occupation	Birthplace	Born	Died
Adams, John (MA)	Lawyer	Braintree (Quincy), MA	Oct. 30, 1735	July 4, 1826
Adams, Samuel (MA)	Political leader	Boston, MA	Sept. 27, 1722	Oct. 2, 1803
Bartlett, Josiah (NH)	Physician, judge	Amesbury, MA	Nov. 21, 1729	May 19, 1795
Braxton, Carter (VA)	Farmer	Newington Plantation, VA	Sept. 10, 1736	Oct. 10, 1797
Carroll, Charles of Carrollton (MD)	Merchant	Annapolis, MD	Sept. 19, 1737	Nov. 14, 1832
Chase, Samuel (MD)	Judge	Princess Anne, MD	Apr. 17, 1741	June 19, 1811
Clark, Abraham (NJ)	Surveyor	Elizabethtown, NJ	Feb. 15, 1726	Sept. 15, 1794
Clymer, George (PA)	Merchant	Philadelphia, PA	Mar. 16, 1739	Jan. 23, 1813
Ellery, William (RI)	Lawyer	Newport, RI	Dec. 22, 1727	Feb. 15, 1820
Floyd, William (NY)	Soldier	Brookhaven, NY	Dec. 17, 1734	Aug. 4, 1821
Franklin, Benjamin (PA)	Printer, publisher	Boston, MA	Jan. 17, 1706	Apr. 17, 1790
Gerry, Elbridge (MA)	Merchant	Marblehead, MA	July 17, 1744	Nov. 23, 1814
Gwinnett, Button (GA)	Merchant	Gloucester, England	c. 1735	May 19, 1777
Hall, Lyman (GA)	Physician	Wallingford, CT	Apr. 12, 1724	Oct. 19, 1790
Hancock, John (MA)	Merchant	Braintree (Quincy), MA	Jan. 12, 1737	Oct. 8, 1793
Harrison, Benjamin (VA)	Farmer	Charles City County, VA	Apr. 5, 1726	Apr. 24, 1791
Hart, John (NJ)	Farmer	Stonington, CT	c. 1711	May 11, 1779
Hewes, Joseph (NC)	Merchant	Kingston, NJ	Jan. 23, 1730	Nov. 10, 1779
Heyward, Thos. Jr. (SC)	Lawyer, farmer	St. Luke's Parish, SC	July 28, 1746	Mar. 6, 1809
Hooper, William (NC)	Lawyer	Boston, MA	June 17, 1742	Oct. 14, 1790
Hopkins, Stephen (RI)	Judge, educator	Providence, RI	Mar. 7, 1707	July 13, 1785
Hopkinson, Francis (NJ)	Judge, author	Philadelphia, PA	Oct. 2, 1737	May 9, 1791
Huntington, Samuel (CT)	Judge	Windham, CT	July 3, 1731	Jan. 5, 1796
Jefferson, Thomas (VA)	Lawyer	Shadwell, VA	Apr. 13, 1743	July 4, 1826
Lee, Francis Lightfoot (VA)	Farmer	Westmoreland County, VA	Oct. 14, 1734	Jan. 11, 1797
Lee, Richard Henry (VA)	Farmer	Westmoreland County, VA	Jan. 20, 1732	June 19, 1794
Lewis, Francis (NY)	Merchant	Llandaff, Wales	Mar. 21, 1713	Dec. 31, 1802
Livingston, Philip (NY)	Merchant	Albany, NY	Jan. 15, 1716	June 12, 1778
Lynch, Thomas Jr. (SC)	Farmer	Winyah, SC	Aug. 5, 1749	(at sea) 1779
McKean, Thomas (DE)	Lawyer	New London, PA	Mar. 19, 1734	June 24, 1817
Middleton, Arthur (SC)	Farmer	Charleston, SC	June 26, 1742	Jan. 1, 1787
Morris, Lewis (NY)	Farmer	Morrisania (Bronx County), NY	Apr. 8, 1726	Jan. 22, 1798
Morris, Robert (PA)	Merchant	Liverpool, England	Jan. 31, 1734	May 8, 1806
Morton, John (PA)	Judge	Ridley, PA	c. 1724	Apr. 1777
Nelson, Thos. Jr. (VA)	Farmer	Yorktown, VA	Dec. 26, 1738	Jan. 4, 1789
Paca, William (MD)	Judge	Abingdon, MD	Oct. 31, 1740	Oct. 23, 1799
Paine, Robert Treat (MA)	Judge	Boston, MA	Mar. 11, 1731	May 12, 1814
Penn, John (NC)	Lawyer	Caroline County, VA	May 17, 1741	Sept. 14, 1788
Read, George (DE)	Judge	Cecil County, MD	Sept. 18, 1733	Sept. 21, 1798
Rodney, Caesar (DE)	Judge	Dover, DE	Oct. 7, 1728	June 29, 1784
Ross, George (PA)	Judge	New Castle, DE	May 10, 1730	July 14, 1779
Rush, Benjamin (PA)	Physician	Byberry, PA (Philadelphia)	Jan. 4, 1746	Apr. 19, 1813
Rutledge, Edward (SC)	Lawyer	Charleston, SC	Nov. 23, 1749	Jan. 23, 1800
Sherman, Roger (CT)	Lawyer	Newton, MA	Apr. 19, 1721	July 23, 1793
Smith, James (PA)	Lawyer	Northern Ireland	c. 1719	July 11, 1806
Stockton, Richard (NJ)	Lawyer	Princeton, NJ	Oct. 1, 1730	Feb. 28, 1781
Stone, Thomas (MD)	Lawyer	Charles County, MD	c. 1743	Oct. 5, 1787
Taylor, George (PA)	Ironmaster	Ireland	c. 1716	Feb. 23, 1781
Thornton, Matthew (NH)	Physician	Ireland	c. 1714	June 24, 1803
Walton, George (GA)	Judge	Cumberland County, VA	c. 1741	Feb. 2, 1804
Whipple, William (NH)	Merchant, judge	Kittery, ME	Jan. 14, 1730	Nov. 28, 1785
Williams, William (CT)	Merchant	Lebanon, CT	Apr. 8, 1731	Aug. 2, 1811
Wilson, James (PA)	Judge	Carskerdo, Scotland	Sept. 14, 1742	Aug. 21, 1798
Witherspoon, John (NJ)	Clergyman, educator	Gifford, Scotland	Feb. 5, 1723	Nov. 15, 1794
Wolcott, Oliver (CT)	Judge	Windsor, CT	Nov. 20, 1726	Dec. 1, 1797
Wythe, George (VA)	Lawyer	Elizabeth City Co., VA	c. 1726	June 8, 1806

Origin of the Constitution

The War of Independence was conducted by delegates from the original 13 states, who comprised the Congress of the United States of America, known as the Continental Congress. In 1777 the Congress submitted to the legislatures of the states the Articles of Confederation and Perpetual Union, which were ratified by New Hampshire, Massachusetts, Rhode Island, Connecticut, New York, New Jersey, Pennsylvania, Delaware, Virginia, North Carolina, South Carolina, Georgia, and finally, in 1781, Maryland.

The first article read: "The stile of this confederacy shall be the United States of America." This did not signify a sovereign nation, because the states delegated only those powers they could not handle individually, such as to wage war, make treaties, and contract debts for general expenses (e.g., paying the army). Taxes for payment of such debts were lev-ied by the individual states. The president signed himself "President of the United States in Congress assembled," but here the United States were considered in the plural, a cooperating group.

When the war was won, it became evident that a stronger federal union was needed. The Congress left the initiative to the legislatures. Virginia in Jan. 1786 appointed commissioners to meet with representatives of other states; delegates from Virginia, Delaware, New York, New Jersey, and Pennsylvania met at Annapolis. Alexander Hamilton prepared their call asking delegates from all states to meet in Philadelphia in May 1787 "to render the Constitution of the federal government adequate to the exigencies of the union." Congress endorsed the plan on Feb. 21, 1787. Delegates were appointed by all states except Rhode Island.

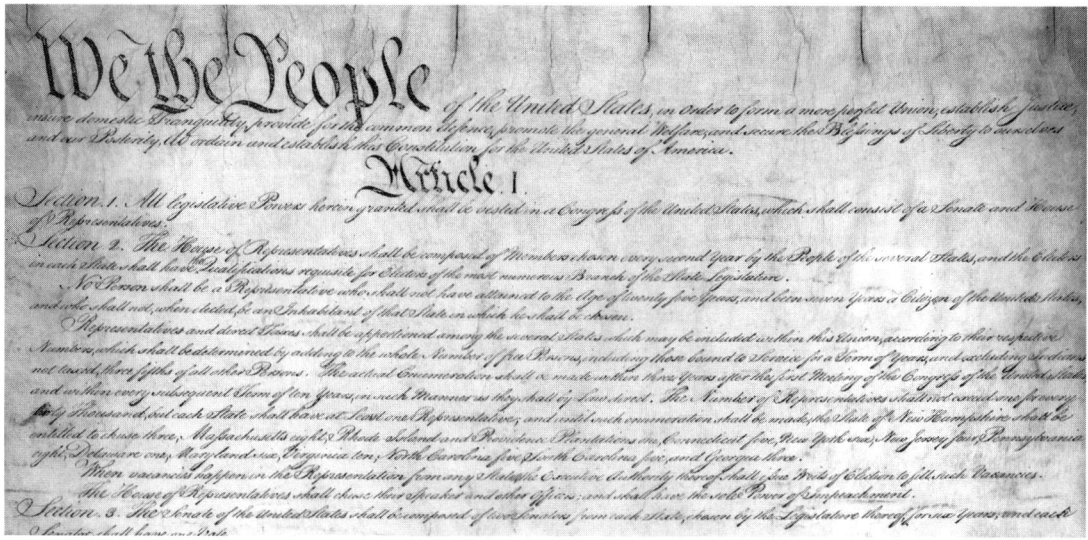

The convention was called for May 14, 1787, but a quorum was not present until May 25. George Washington was chosen president (presiding officer). The states certified 65 delegates, but 10 did not attend. The work was done by 55, not all of whom were present at all sessions. Of the 55 attending delegates, 16 failed to sign, and 39 actually signed Sept. 17, 1787, some with reservations. Some historians have said 74 delegates (9 more than the 65 actually certified) were named, and 19 failed to attend. These 9 additional persons refused the appointment, were never delegates, and were never counted as absentees. Washington sent the Constitution to Congress, and that body, Sept. 28, 1787, ordered it sent to the legislatures, "in order to be submitted to a convention of delegates chosen in each state by the people thereof."

The Constitution was ratified by votes of state conventions as follows: Delaware, Dec. 7, 1787, unanimous; Pennsylvania, Dec. 12, 1787, 46 to 23; New Jersey, Dec. 18, 1787, unanimous; Georgia, Jan. 2, 1788, unanimous; Connecticut, Jan. 9, 1788, 128 to 40; Massachusetts, Feb. 6, 1788, 187 to 168; Maryland, Apr. 28, 1788, 63 to 11; South Carolina, May 23, 1788, 149 to 73; New Hampshire, June 21, 1788, 57 to 46; Virginia, June 25, 1788, 89 to 79; New York, July 26, 1788, 30 to 27. Nine states were needed to establish the operation of the Constitution "between the states so ratifying the same," and New Hampshire was the 9th state. The government did not declare the Constitution in effect until the first Wednesday in Mar. 1789, which was Mar. 4. After that, North Carolina ratified it on Nov. 21, 1789, 194 to 77; and Rhode Island, May 29, 1790, 34 to 32. Vermont in convention ratified it on Jan. 10, 1791, and by act of Congress approved on Feb. 18, 1791, was admitted into the Union as the 14th state, Mar. 4, 1791.

Constitution of the United States

The Original 7 Articles

The text of the Constitution given here (except for Amendment XXVII) is from the pocket-size edition of the Constitution published by the U.S. Government Printing Office as a result of a congressional resolution to print the Constitution in its original form as amended through July 5, 1971. *Text in brackets* indicates that an item has been superseded or amended, or provides background information. **Boldface text preceding** an article, section, or amendment is a brief summary, added by *The World Almanac.*

PREAMBLE

We, the People of the United States, in Order to form a more perfect Union, establish Justice, insure domestic Tranquility, provide for the common defence, promote the general Welfare, and secure the Blessings of Liberty to ourselves and our Posterity, do ordain and establish this Constitution for the United States of America.

ARTICLE I.

Section 1—Legislative powers; in whom vested.

All legislative Powers herein granted shall be vested in a Congress of the United States, which shall consist of a Senate and House of Representatives.

Section 2—House of Representatives, how and by whom chosen. Qualifications of a Representative. Representatives and direct taxes, how apportioned. Enumeration. Vacancies to be filled. Power of choosing officers, and of impeachment.

The House of Representatives shall be composed of Members chosen every second Year by the People of the several States, and the Electors in each State shall have the Qualifications requisite for Electors of the most numerous Branch of the State Legislature.

No person shall be a Representative who shall not have attained to the Age of twenty-five Years, and been seven Years a Citizen of the United States, and who shall not, when elected, be an Inhabitant of that State in which he shall be chosen.

[Representatives and direct taxes shall be apportioned among the several States which may be included within this Union, according to their respective Numbers, which shall be determined by adding to the whole Number of free Persons, including those bound to Service for a Term of Years, and excluding Indians not taxed, three-fifths of all other persons.] [The previous sentence was superseded by Amendment XIV, section 2.] The actual Enumeration shall be made within three Years after the first Meeting of the Congress of the United States, and within every subsequent Term of ten Years, in such Manner as they shall by Law direct. The Number of Representatives shall not exceed one for every thirty Thousand, but each State shall have at Least one Representative; and until such enumeration shall be made, the State of New Hampshire shall be entitled to chuse three, Massachusetts eight, Rhode-Island and Providence Plantations one, Connecticut five, New-York six, New Jersey four, Pennsylvania eight, Delaware one, Maryland six, Virginia ten, North Carolina five, South Carolina five, and Georgia three.

When vacancies happen in the Representation from any State, the Executive Authority thereof shall issue Writs of Election to fill such Vacancies.

The House of Representatives shall chuse their Speaker and other Officers; and shall have the sole Power of Impeachment.

Section 3—Senators, how and by whom chosen. How classified. Qualifications of a Senator. President of the Senate, his right to vote. President pro tem., and other officers of the Senate, how chosen. Power to try impeachments. When President is tried, Chief Justice to preside. Sentence.

The Senate of the United States shall be composed of two Senators from each State, *[chosen by the Legislature thereof]* *[The preceding five words were superseded by Amendment XVII.]* for six Years; and each Senator shall have one Vote.

Immediately after they shall be assembled in Consequence of the first Election, they shall be divided as equally as may be into three Classes. The Seats of the Senators of the first Class shall be vacated at the Expiration of the second Year, of the second Class at the Expiration of the fourth Year, and of the third Class at the Expiration of the Sixth year, so that one-third may be chosen every second Year; *[and if Vacancies happen by Resignation, or otherwise, during the Recess of the Legislature of any State, the Executive thereof may make temporary Appointments until the next Meeting of the Legislature, which shall then fill such Vacancies.]* *[The words in brackets were superseded by Amendment XVII.]*

No person shall be a Senator who shall not have attained to the Age of thirty Years, and been nine Years a Citizen of the United States, and who shall not, when elected, be an Inhabitant of that State for which he shall be chosen.

The Vice President of the United States shall be President of the Senate, but shall have no Vote, unless they be equally divided.

The Senate shall chuse their other Officers, and also a President pro tempore, in the absence of the Vice President, or when he shall exercise the Office of President of the United States.

The Senate shall have the sole Power to try all Impeachments. When sitting for that Purpose, they shall be on Oath or Affirmation. When the President of the United States is tried, the Chief Justice shall preside: And no Person shall be convicted without the Concurrence of two thirds of the Members present.

Judgment in Cases of Impeachment shall not extend further than to removal from Office, and disqualification to hold and enjoy any Office of honor, Trust or Profit under the United States: but the Party convicted shall nevertheless be liable and subject to Indictment, Trial, Judgment and Punishment, according to Law.

Section 4—Times, etc., of holding elections, how prescribed. One session each year.

The Times, Places and Manner of holding Elections for Senators and Representatives, shall be prescribed in each State by the Legislature thereof; but the Congress may at any time by Law make or alter such Regulations, except as to the Place of Chusing Senators.

The Congress shall assemble at least once in every Year, and such Meeting shall be *[on the first Monday in December,]* *[The words in brackets were superseded by Amendment XX, section 2.]* unless they shall by Law appoint a different Day.

Section 5—Membership, quorum, adjournments, rules. Power to punish or expel. Journal. Time of adjournments, how limited, etc.

Each House shall be the Judge of the Elections, Returns and Qualifications of its own Members, and a Majority of each shall constitute a Quorum to do Business; but a smaller number may adjourn from day to day, and may be authorized to compel the Attendance of absent Members, in such manner, and under such Penalties as each House may provide.

Each House may determine the Rules of its Proceedings, punish its members for disorderly Behavior, and, with the Concurrence of two thirds, expel a Member.

Each House shall keep a Journal of its Proceedings, and from time to time publish the same, excepting such Parts as may in their Judgment require Secrecy; and the Yeas and Nays of the Members of either House on any question shall, at the Desire of one fifth of those Present, be entered on the Journal.

Neither House, during the Session of Congress, shall, without the Consent of the other, adjourn for more than three days, nor to any other Place than that in which the two Houses shall be sitting.

Section 6—Compensation, privileges, disqualifications in certain cases.

The Senators and Representatives shall receive a Compensation for their Services, to be ascertained by Law, and paid out of the Treasury of the United States. They shall in all Cases, except Treason, Felony and Breach of the Peace, be privileged from Arrest during their Attendance at the Session of their respective Houses, and in going to and returning from the same; and for any Speech or Debate in either House, they shall not be questioned in any other Place.

No Senator or Representative shall, during the Time for which he was elected, be appointed to any civil Office under the Authority of the United States, which shall have been created, or the Emoluments whereof shall have been encreased during such time; and no Person holding any Office under the United States, shall be a Member of either House during his Continuance in Office.

Section 7—House to originate all revenue bills. Veto. Bill may be passed by two-thirds of each House, notwithstanding, etc. Bill, not returned in ten days, to become a law. Provisions as to orders, concurrent resolutions, etc.

All bills for raising Revenue shall originate in the House of Representatives; but the Senate may propose or concur with Amendments as on other Bills.

Every Bill which shall have passed the House of Representatives and the Senate, shall, before it become a Law, be presented to the President of the United States; If he approve he shall sign it, but if not he shall return it, with his Objections to that House in which it shall have originated, who shall enter the Objections at large on their Journal, and proceed to reconsider it. If after such Reconsideration two thirds of that House shall agree to pass the Bill, it shall be sent, together with the Objections, to the other House, by which it shall likewise be reconsidered, and if approved by two thirds of that House, it shall become a Law. But in all such Cases the Votes of both Houses shall be determined by Yeas and Nays, and the Names of the Persons voting for and against the Bill shall be entered on the Journal of each House respectively. If any Bill shall not be returned by the President within ten Days (Sundays excepted) after it shall have been presented to him, the Same shall be a Law, in like Manner as if he had signed it, unless the Congress by their Adjournment prevent its Return, in which Case it shall not be a Law.

Every order, Resolution, or Vote to which the Concurrence of the Senate and House of Representatives may be necessary (except on a question of Adjournment) shall be presented to the President of the United States; and before the Same shall take Effect, shall be approved by him, or being disapproved by him, shall be repassed by two thirds of the Senate and House of Representatives, according to the Rules and Limitations prescribed in the Case of a Bill.

Section 8—Powers of Congress.

The Congress shall have Power To lay and collect Taxes, Duties, Imposts and Excises, to pay the Debts and provide for the common Defence and general Welfare of the United States; but all Duties, Imposts and Excises shall be uniform throughout the United States;

To borrow money on the credit of the United States;

To regulate Commerce with foreign Nations, and among the several States, and with the Indian Tribes;

To establish an uniform Rule of Naturalization, and uniform Laws on the subject of Bankruptcies throughout the United States;

To coin Money, regulate the Value thereof, and of foreign Coin, and fix the Standard of Weights and Measures;

To provide for the Punishment of counterfeiting the Securities and current Coin of the United States;

To establish Post Offices and post Roads;

To promote the Progress of Science and useful Arts, by securing for limited Times to Authors and Inventors the exclusive Right to their respective Writings and Discoveries;

To constitute Tribunals inferior to the supreme Court;

To define and punish Piracies and Felonies committed on the high Seas, and Offenses against the Law of Nations;

To declare War, grant Letters of Marque and Reprisal, and make Rules concerning Captures on Land and Water;

To raise and support Armies, but no Appropriation of Money to that Use shall be for a longer Term than two Years;

To provide and maintain a Navy;

To make Rules for the Government and Regulation of the land and naval Forces;

To provide for calling forth the Militia to execute the Laws of the Union, suppress Insurrections and repel Invasions;

To provide for organizing, arming, and disciplining the Militia, and for governing such Part of them as may be employed in the Service of the United States, reserving to the States respectively, the Appointment of the Officers, and the Authority of training the Militia according to the discipline prescribed by Congress;

To exercise exclusive Legislation in all Cases whatsoever, over such District (not exceeding ten Miles square) as may, by Cession of particular States, and the acceptance of Congress, become the Seat of the Government of the United States, and to exercise like Authority over all Places purchased by the Consent of the Legislature of the State in which the Same shall be, for the Erection of Forts, Magazines, Arsenals, dock-Yards, and other needful Buildings;—And

To make all Laws which shall be necessary and proper for carrying into Execution the foregoing Powers, and all other Powers vested by this Constitution in the Government of the United States, or in any Department or Officer thereof.

Section 9—Provision as to migration or importation of certain persons. Habeas corpus, bills of attainder, etc. Taxes, how apportioned. No export duty. No commercial preference. Money, how drawn from Treasury, etc. No titular nobility. Officers not to receive presents, etc.

The Migration or Importation of such Persons as any of the States now existing shall think proper to admit, shall not be prohibited by the Congress prior to the Year one thousand eight hundred and eight, but a tax or duty may be imposed on such Importation, not exceeding ten dollars for each Person.

The privilege of the Writ of Habeas Corpus shall not be suspended, unless when in Cases of Rebellion or Invasion the public Safety may require it.

No Bill of Attainder or ex post facto Law shall be passed.

[No capitation, or other direct, Tax shall be laid, unless in Proportion to the Census or Enumeration herein before directed to be taken.] *[Words in brackets modified by Amendment XVI.]*

No Tax or Duty shall be laid on Articles exported from any State.

No Preference shall be given by any Regulation of Commerce or Revenue to the Ports of one State over those of another: nor shall Vessels bound to, or from, one State, be obliged to enter, clear, or pay Duties in another.

No Money shall be drawn from the Treasury, but in Consequence of Appropriations made by Law; and a regular Statement and Account of the Receipts and Expenditures of all public Money shall be published from time to time.

No Title of Nobility shall be granted by the United States: and no Person holding any Office of Profit or Trust under them, shall, without the Consent of the Congress, accept of any present, Emolument, Office, or Title, of any kind whatever, from any King, Prince, or foreign State.

Section 10—States prohibited from the exercise of certain powers.

No State shall enter into any Treaty, Alliance, or Confederation; grant Letters of Marque and Reprisal; coin Money; emit Bills of Credit; make any Thing but gold and silver Coin a Tender in Payment of Debts; pass any Bill of Attainder, ex post facto Law, or Law impairing the Obligation of Contracts, or grant any Title of Nobility.

No State shall, without the Consent of the Congress, lay any Imposts or Duties on Imports or Exports, except what may be absolutely necessary for executing its inspection Laws: and the net Produce of all Duties and Imposts, laid by any State on Imports or Exports, shall be for the Use of the Treasury of the United States; and all such Laws shall be subject to the Revision and Control of the Congress.

No State shall, without the Consent of Congress, lay any duty of Tonnage, keep Troops, or Ships of War in time of Peace, enter into any Agreement or Compact with another State, or with a foreign Power, or engage in War, unless actually invaded, or in such imminent Danger as will not admit of delay.

ARTICLE II.

Section 1—President: his term of office. Electors of President; number and how appointed. Electors to vote on same day. Qualification of President. On whom his duties devolve in case of his removal, death, etc. President's compensation. His oath of office.

The executive Power shall be vested in a President of the United States of America. He shall hold his Office during the Term of four Years, and, together with the Vice President, chosen for the same Term, be elected, as follows.

Each State shall appoint, in such Manner as the Legislature thereof may direct, a Number of Electors, equal to the whole Number of Senators and Representatives to which the State may be entitled in the Congress: but no Senator or Representative, or Person holding an Office of Trust or Profit under the United States, shall be appointed an Elector.

[The Electors shall meet in their respective States, and vote by Ballot for two persons, of whom one at least shall not be an Inhabitant of the same State with themselves. And they shall make a List of all the Persons voted for, and of the Number of Votes for each; which List they shall sign and certify, and transmit sealed to the Seat of the Government of the United States, directed to the President of the Senate. The President of the Senate shall, in the Presence of the Senate and House of Representatives, open all the Certificates, and the Votes shall then be counted. The Person having the greatest Number of Votes shall be the President, if such Number be a Majority of the whole Number of Electors appointed; and if there be more than one who have such Majority, and have an equal Number of Votes, then the House of Representatives shall immediately chuse by Ballot one of them for President; and if no Person have a Majority, then from the five highest on the List the said House shall in like Manner chuse the President. But in chusing the President,

the Votes shall be taken by States, the Representation from each State having one Vote; a quorum for this Purpose shall consist of a Member or Members from two thirds of the States, and a Majority of all the States shall be necessary to a Choice. In every Case, after the Choice of the President, the Person having the greatest Number of Votes of the Electors shall be the Vice President. But if there should remain two or more who have equal Votes, the Senate shall chuse from them by Ballot the Vice-President.] [This clause was superseded by Amendment XII.]

The Congress may determine the Time of chusing the Electors, and the Day on which they shall give their Votes; which Day shall be the same throughout the United States.

No person except a natural born Citizen, or a Citizen of the United States, at the time of the Adoption of this Constitution, shall be eligible to the Office of President; neither shall any Person be eligible to that Office who shall not have attained to the Age of thirty-five Years, and been fourteen Years a Resident within the United States. [For qualification of the Vice President, see Amendment XII.]

[In Case of the Removal of the President from Office, or of his Death, Resignation, or Inability to discharge the Powers and Duties of the said Office, the same shall devolve on the Vice President, and the Congress may by Law, provide for the Case of Removal, Death, Resignation or Inability, both of the President and Vice President, declaring what Officer shall then act as President, and such Officer shall act accordingly, until the Disability be removed, or a President shall be elected.] [This clause was superseded by Amendments XXV.]

The President shall, at stated Times, receive for his Services, a Compensation, which shall neither be encreased nor diminished during the Period for which he shall have been elected, and he shall not receive within that Period any other Emolument from the United States, or any of them.

Before he enter on the Execution of his Office, he shall take the following Oath or Affirmation:—"I do solemnly swear (or affirm) that I will faithfully execute the Office of President of the United States, and will to the best of my Ability, preserve, protect and defend the Constitution of the United States."

Section 2—President to be Commander-in-Chief. He may require opinions of cabinet officers, etc., may pardon. Treaty-making power. Nomination of certain officers. When President may fill vacancies.

The President shall be Commander in Chief of the Army and Navy of the United States, and of the Militia of the several States, when called into the actual Service of the United States; he may require the Opinion in writing, of the principal Officer in each of the executive Departments, upon any subject relating to the Duties of their respective Offices, and he shall have Power to Grant Reprieves and Pardons for Offenses against the United States, except in Cases of Impeachment.

He shall have Power, by and with the Advice and Consent of the Senate, to make Treaties, provided two-thirds of the Senators present concur; and he shall nominate, and by and with the Advice and Consent of the Senate, shall appoint Ambassadors, other public Ministers and Consuls, Judges of the supreme Court, and all other Officers of the United States, whose Appointments are not herein otherwise provided for, and which shall be established by Law: but the Congress may by Law vest the Appointment of such inferior Officers, as they think proper, in the President alone, in the Courts of Law, or in the Heads of Departments.

The President shall have Power to fill up all Vacancies that may happen during the Recess of the Senate, by granting Commissions which shall expire at the End of their next Session.

Section 3—President shall communicate to Congress. He may convene and adjourn Congress, in case of disagreement, etc. Shall receive ambassadors, execute laws, and commission officers.

He shall from time to time give to the Congress Information of the State of the Union, and recommend to their Consideration such Measures as he shall judge necessary and expedient; he may, on extraordinary Occasions, convene both Houses, or either of them, and in Case of Disagreement between them, with Respect to the Time of Adjournment, he may adjourn them to such Time as he shall think proper; he shall receive Ambassadors and other public Ministers; he shall take Care that the Laws be faithfully executed, and shall Commission all the Officers of the United States.

Section 4—All civil offices forfeited for certain crimes.

The President, Vice President and all civil Officers of the United States, shall be removed from Office on Impeachment for, and Conviction of, Treason, Bribery, or other high Crimes and Misdemeanors.

ARTICLE III.

Section 1—Judicial powers, tenure. Compensation.

The judicial Power of the United States, shall be vested in one supreme Court, and in such inferior Courts as the Congress may from time to time ordain and establish. The Judges, both of the supreme and inferior Courts, shall hold their Offices during good Behaviour, and shall, at stated Times, receive for their Services, a Compensation, which shall not be diminished during their Continuance in Office.

Section 2—Judicial power; to what cases it extends. Original jurisdiction of Supreme Court; appellate jurisdiction. Trial by jury, etc. Trial, where.

The judicial Power shall extend to all Cases, in Law and Equity, arising under this Constitution, the Laws of the United States, and Treaties made, or which shall be made, under their Authority;–to all Cases affecting Ambassadors, other public Ministers and Consuls;–to all Cases of admiralty and maritime Jurisdiction;–to Controversies to which the United States shall be a Party;–to Controversies between two or more States; [–between a State and Citizens of another State;–] between Citizens of different States; –between Citizens of the same State claiming Lands under Grants of different States, [and between a State, or the Citizens thereof, and foreign States, Citizens or Subjects.] [This section is modified by Amendment XI.]

In all Cases affecting Ambassadors, other public Ministers and Consuls, and those in which a State shall be Party, the supreme Court shall have original Jurisdiction. In all the other Cases before mentioned, the supreme Court shall have appellate Jurisdiction, both as to Law and Fact, with such Exceptions, and under such Regulations as the Congress shall make.

The trial of all Crimes, except in Cases of Impeachment, shall be by Jury; and such Trial shall be held in the State where the said Crimes shall have been committed; but when not committed within any State, the Trial shall be at such Place or Places as the Congress may by Law have directed.

Section 3—Treason Defined. Proof of. Punishment of.

Treason against the United States, shall consist only in levying War against them, or in adhering to their Enemies, giving them Aid and Comfort. No Person shall be convicted of Treason unless on the Testimony of two Witnesses to the same overt Act, or on Confession in open Court.

The Congress shall have Power to declare the Punishment of Treason, but no Attainder of Treason shall work Corruption of Blood, or Forfeiture except during the Life of the Person attainted.

ARTICLE IV.

Section 1—Each State to give credit to the public acts, etc., of every other State.

Full Faith and Credit shall be given in each State to the public Acts, Records, and judicial Proceedings of every other State. And the Congress may by general Laws prescribe the Manner in which such Acts, Records and Proceedings shall be proved, and the Effect thereof.

Section 2—Privileges of citizens of each State. Fugitives from justice to be delivered up. Persons held to service having escaped, to be delivered up.

The Citizens of each State shall be entitled to all Privileges and Immunities of Citizens in the several States.

A Person charged in any State with Treason, Felony, or other Crime, who shall flee from Justice, and be found in another State, shall on demand of the executive Authority of the State from which he fled, be delivered up, to be removed to the State having Jurisdiction of the Crime.

[No Person held to Service or Labour in one State, under the Laws thereof, escaping into another, shall, in Consequence of any Law or Regulation therein, be discharged from such Service or Labour, but shall be delivered up on Claim of the Party to whom such Service or Labour may be due.] [This clause was superseded by Amendment XIII.]

Section 3—Admission of new States. Power of Congress over territory and other property.

New States may be admitted by the Congress into this Union; but no new State shall be formed or erected within the Jurisdiction of any other State; nor any State be formed by the Junction of two or more States, or parts of States, without the Consent of the Legislatures of the States concerned as well as of the Congress.

The Congress shall have Power to dispose of and make all needful Rules and Regulations respecting the Territory or other Property belonging to the United States; and nothing in this Constitution shall be so construed as to Prejudice any Claims of the United States, or of any particular State.

Section 4—Republican form of government guaranteed. Each State to be protected.

The United States shall guarantee to every State in this Union a Republican Form of Government, and shall protect each of them against Invasion; and on Application of the Legislature, or of the Executive (when the Legislature cannot be convened) against domestic Violence.

ARTICLE V.

Constitution: how amended; proviso.

The Congress, whenever two-thirds of both Houses shall deem it necessary, shall propose Amendments to this Constitution, or, on the Application of the Legislatures of two-thirds of the several States, shall call a Convention for proposing Amendments, which, in either Case, shall be valid to all Intents and Purposes, as part of this Constitution, when ratified by the Legislatures of three-fourths of the several States, or by Conventions in three-fourths thereof, as the one or the other Mode of Ratification may be proposed by the Congress: Provided that no Amendment which may be made prior to the Year One thousand eight hundred and eight shall in any Manner affect the first and fourth Clauses in the Ninth Section of the first Article; and that no State, without its Consent, shall be deprived of its equal Suffrage in the Senate.

ARTICLE VI.

Certain debts, etc., declared valid. Supremacy of Constitution, treaties, and laws of the United States. Oath to support Constitution, by whom taken. No religious test.

All Debts contracted and Engagements entered into, before the Adoption of this Constitution, shall be as valid against the United States under this Constitution, as under the Confederation.

This Constitution, and the Laws of the United States which shall be made in Pursuance thereof; and all Treaties made, or which shall be made, under the Authority of the United States, shall be the supreme Law of the Land; and the Judges in every State shall be bound thereby, any Thing in the Constitution or Laws of any State to the Contrary notwithstanding.

The Senators and Representatives before mentioned, and the Members of the several State Legislatures, and all executive and judicial Officers, both of the United States and of the several States, shall be bound by Oath or Affirmation, to support this Constitution; but no religious Test shall ever be required as a Qualification to any Office or public Trust under the United States.

ARTICLE VII.

What ratification shall establish Constitution.

The Ratification of the Conventions of nine States shall be sufficient for the Establishment of this Constitution between the States so ratifying the Same.

Done in Convention by the Unanimous Consent of the States present the Seventeenth Day of September in the Year of our Lord one thousand seven hundred and Eighty seven and of the Independence of the United States of America the Twelfth.

In Witness whereof We have hereunto subscribed our Names.

G⁰. Washington, Presidt and deputy from Virginia

New Hampshire—John Langdon, Nicholas Gilman

Massachusetts—Nathaniel Gorham, Rufus King

Connecticut—Wm. Saml. Johnson, Roger Sherman

New York—Alexander Hamilton

New Jersey—Wil: Livingston, David Brearley, Wm. Paterson, Jona: Dayton

Pennsylvania—B Franklin, Thomas Mifflin, Robt. Morris, Geo. Clymer, Thos. FitzSimons, Jared Ingersoll, James Wilson, Gouv Morris

Delaware—Geo: Read, Gunning Bedford jun, John Dickinson, Richard Bassett, Jaco: Broom

Maryland—James McHenry, Dan of St Thos. Jenifer, Danl Carroll

Virginia—John Blair, James Madison Jr.

North Carolina—Wm. Blount, Rich'd Dobbs Spaight, Hu Williamson

South Carolina—J. Rutledge, Charles Cotesworth Pinckney, Charles Pinckney, Pierce Butler

Georgia—William Few, Abr Baldwin

Attest: William Jackson, Secretary.

Ten Original Amendments: The Bill of Rights
In force Dec. 15, 1791

[The First Congress, at its first session in the City of New York, Sept. 25, 1789, submitted to the states 12 amendments to clarify certain individual and state rights not named in the Constitution. They are generally called the Bill of Rights.

Influential in framing these amendments was the Declaration of Rights of Virginia, written by George Mason (1725-92) in 1776. Mason, a Virginia delegate to the Constitutional Convention, did not sign the Constitution and opposed its ratification on the ground that it did not sufficiently oppose slavery or safeguard individual rights.

In the preamble to the resolution offering the proposed amendments, Congress said: "The conventions of a number of the States having at the time of their adopting the Constitution, expressed a desire, in order to prevent misconstruction or abuse of its powers, that further declaratory and restrictive clauses should be added, and as extending the ground of public confidence in the government will best insure the beneficent ends of its institution, be it resolved," etc.

Ten of these amendments, now commonly known as one to 10 inclusive, but originally 3 to 12 inclusive, were ratified by the states as follows: New Jersey, Nov. 20, 1789; Maryland, Dec. 19, 1789; North Carolina, Dec. 22, 1789; South Carolina, Jan. 19, 1790; New Hampshire, Jan. 25, 1790; Delaware, Jan. 28, 1790; New York, Feb. 27, 1790; Pennsylvania, Mar. 10, 1790; Rhode Island, June 7, 1790; Vermont, Nov. 3, 1791; Virginia, Dec. 15, 1791; Massachusetts, Mar. 2, 1939; Georgia, Mar. 18, 1939; Connecticut, Apr. 19, 1939. These original 10 ratified amendments follow as Amendments I to X inclusive.

Of the two original proposed amendments that were not ratified promptly by the necessary number of states, the first related to apportionment of Representatives; the second, relating to compensation of members of Congress, was ratified in 1992 and became Amendment 27.]

AMENDMENT I.

Religious establishment prohibited. Freedom of speech, of press, right to assemble and to petition.

Congress shall make no law respecting an establishment of religion, or prohibiting the free exercise thereof; or abridging the freedom of speech, or of the press; or the right of the people peaceably to assemble, and to petition the Government for a redress of grievances.

AMENDMENT II.

Right to keep and bear arms.

A well regulated Militia, being necessary to the security of a free State, the right of the people to keep and bear Arms, shall not be infringed.

AMENDMENT III.

Conditions for quarters for soldiers.

No Soldier shall, in time of peace be quartered in any house, without the consent of the Owner, nor in time of war, but in a manner to be prescribed by law.

AMENDMENT IV.

Protection from unreasonable search and seizure.

The right of the people to be secure in their persons, houses, papers, and effects, against unreasonable searches and seizures, shall not be violated, and no Warrants shall issue, but upon probable cause, supported by Oath or affirmation, and particularly describing the place to be searched, and the persons or things to be seized.

AMENDMENT V.

Provisions concerning prosecution and due process of law. Double jeopardy restriction. Private property not to be taken without compensation.

No person shall be held to answer for a capital, or otherwise infamous crime, unless on a presentment or indictment of a Grand Jury, except in cases arising in the land or naval forces, or in the Militia, when in actual service in time of War or public danger; nor shall any person be subject for the same offence to be twice put in jeopardy of life or limb; nor shall be compelled in any criminal case to be a witness against himself, nor be deprived of life, liberty, or property, without due process of law; nor shall private property be taken for public use, without just compensation.

AMENDMENT VI.

Right to speedy trial, witnesses, etc.

In all criminal prosecutions, the accused shall enjoy the right to a speedy and public trial, by an impartial jury of the State and district wherein the crime shall have been committed, which district shall have been previously ascertained by law, and to be informed of the nature and cause of the accusation; to be confronted with the witnesses against him; to have compulsory process for obtaining witnesses in his favor, and to have the Assistance of Counsel for his defence.

AMENDMENT VII.

Right of trial by jury.

In suits at common law, where the value in controversy shall exceed twenty dollars, the right of trial by jury shall be preserved, and no fact tried by a jury, shall be otherwise reexamined in any Court of the United States, than according to the rules of the common law.

AMENDMENT VIII.

Excessive bail or fines; cruel and unusual punishment.

Excessive bail shall not be required, nor excessive fines imposed, nor cruel and unusual punishments inflicted.

AMENDMENT IX.

Rule of construction of Constitution.

The enumeration in the Constitution, of certain rights, shall not be construed to deny or disparage others retained by the people.

AMENDMENT X.

Rights of States under Constitution.

The powers not delegated to the United States by the Constitution, nor prohibited by it to the States, are reserved to the States respectively, or to the people.

Amendments Since the Bill of Rights

AMENDMENT XI.

Judicial powers construed.

The Judicial power of the United States shall not be construed to extend to any suit in law or equity, commenced or prosecuted against one of the United States by Citizens of another State, or by Citizens or Subjects of any Foreign State.

[This amendment was proposed to the Legislatures of the several States by the Third Congress on March 4, 1794, and was declared to have been ratified in a message from the President to Congress, dated Jan. 8, 1798.

[It was on Jan. 5, 1798, that Secretary of State Pickering received from 12 of the States authenticated ratifications, and informed President John Adams of that fact.

[As a result of later research in the Department of State, it is now established that Amendment XI became part of the Constitution on Feb. 7, 1795, for on that date it had been ratified by 12 States as follows:

[1. New York, Mar. 27, 1794. 2. Rhode Island, Mar. 31, 1794. 3. Connecticut, May 8, 1794. 4. New Hampshire, June 16, 1794. 5. Massachusetts, June 26, 1794. 6. Vermont, between Oct. 9, 1794, and Nov. 9, 1794. 7. Virginia, Nov. 18, 1794. 8. Georgia, Nov. 29, 1794. 9. Kentucky, Dec. 7, 1794. 10. Maryland, Dec. 26, 1794. 11. Delaware, Jan. 23, 1795. 12. North Carolina, Feb. 7, 1795]

[On June 1, 1796, more than a year after Amendment XI had become a part of the Constitution—but before anyone was officially aware of this—Tennessee had been admitted as a State; but not until Oct. 16, 1797, was a certified copy of the resolution of Congress proposing the amendment sent to the Governor of Tennessee, John Sevier, by Secretary of State Pickering, whose office was then at Trenton, New Jersey, because of the epidemic of yellow fever at Philadelphia; it seems, however, that the Legislature of Tennessee took no action on Amendment XI, owing doubtless to the fact that public announcement of its adoption was made soon thereafter.]

[Besides the necessary 12 States, one other, South Carolina, ratified Amendment XI, but this action was not taken until Dec. 4, 1797; the two remaining States, New Jersey and Pennsylvania, failed to ratify.]

AMENDMENT XII.

Manner of choosing President and Vice-President.

[Proposed by Congress Dec. 9, 1803; ratified June 15, 1804.]

The Electors shall meet in their respective states and vote by ballot for President and Vice-President, one of whom, at least, shall not be an inhabitant of the same state with themselves; they shall name in their ballots the person voted for as President, and in distinct ballots the person voted for as Vice-President, and they shall make distinct lists of all persons voted for as President, and of all persons voted for as Vice-President, and of the number of votes for each, which lists they shall sign and certify, and transmit sealed to the seat of the government of the United States, directed to the President of the Senate;—the President of the Senate shall, in presence of the Senate and House of Representatives, open all the certificates and the votes shall then be counted;—The person having the greatest number of votes for President, shall be the President, if such number be a majority of the whole number of Electors appointed; and if no person have such majority, then from the persons having the highest numbers not exceeding three on the list of those voted for as President, the House of Representatives shall choose immediately, by ballot, the President. But in choosing the President, the votes shall be taken by states, the representation from each state having one vote; a quorum for this purpose shall consist of a member or members from two-thirds of the states, and a majority of all the states shall be necessary to a choice. [And if the House of Representatives shall not choose a President whenever the right of choice shall devolve upon them, before the fourth day of March next following, then the Vice-President shall act as President, as in the case of the death or other constitutional disability of the President.] [The words in brackets were superseded by Amendment XX, section 3.] The person having the greatest number of votes as Vice-President, shall be the Vice-President, if such number be a majority of the whole number of Electors appointed, and if no person have a majority, then from the two highest numbers on the list, the Senate shall choose the Vice-President; a quorum for the purpose shall consist of two-thirds of the whole number of Senators, and a majority of the whole number shall be necessary to a choice. But no person constitutionally ineligible to the office of President shall be eligible to that of Vice-President of the United States.

THE RECONSTRUCTION AMENDMENTS

[Amendments XIII, XIV, and XV are commonly known as the Reconstruction Amendments, inasmuch as they followed the Civil War, and were drafted by Republicans who were bent on imposing their own policy of reconstruction on the South. Postbellum legislatures there—Mississippi, South Carolina, Georgia, for example—had set up laws which, it was charged, were contrived to perpetuate Negro slavery under other names.]

AMENDMENT XIII.

Slavery abolished.

[Proposed by Congress Jan. 31, 1865; ratified Dec. 6, 1865. The amendment, when first proposed by a resolution in Congress, was passed by the Senate, 38 to 6, on Apr. 8, 1864, but was defeated in the House, 95 to 66 on June 15, 1864. On reconsideration by the House, on Jan. 31, 1865, the resolution passed, 119 to 56. It was approved by President Lincoln on Feb. 1, 1865, although the Supreme Court had decided in 1798 that the President has nothing to do with the proposing of amendments to the Constitution, or their adoption.]

1. Neither slavery nor involuntary servitude, except as a punishment for crime whereof the party shall have been duly convicted, shall exist within the United States, or any place subject to their jurisdiction.

2. Congress shall have power to enforce this article by appropriate legislation.

AMENDMENT XIV.

Citizenship rights not to be abridged.

[The following amendment was proposed to the Legislatures of the several states by the 39th Congress, June 13, 1866, ratified July 9, 1868, and declared to have been ratified in a proclamation by the Secretary of State, July 28, 1868.]

[The 14th amendment was adopted only by virtue of ratification subsequent to earlier rejections. Newly constituted legislatures in both North Carolina and South Carolina (respectively July 4 and 9, 1868), ratified the proposed amendment, although earlier legislatures had rejected the proposal. The Secretary of State issued a proclamation, which, though doubtful as to the effect of attempted withdrawals by Ohio and New Jersey, entertained no doubt as to the validity of the ratification by North and South Carolina. The following day (July 21, 1868), Congress passed a resolution which declared the 14th Amendment to be a part of the Constitution and directed the Secretary of State so to promulgate it. The Secretary waited, however, until the newly constituted Legislature of Georgia had ratified the amendment, subsequent to an earlier rejection, before the promulgation of the ratification of the new amendment.]

1. All persons born or naturalized in the United States, and subject to the jurisdiction thereof, are citizens of the United States and of the State wherein they reside. No State shall make or enforce any law which shall abridge the privileges or immunities of citizens of the United States; nor shall any State deprive any person of life, liberty, or property, without due process of law; nor deny to any person within its jurisdiction the equal protection of the laws.

2. Representatives shall be apportioned among the several States according to their respective numbers, counting the whole number of persons in each State, excluding Indians not taxed. But when the right to vote at any election for the choice of electors for President and Vice-President of the United States, Representatives in Congress, the Executive and Judicial officers of a State, or the members of the Legislature thereof, is denied to any of the male inhabitants of such State, being [twenty-one] [The words in brackets were changed by Amendment XXVI.] years of age, and citizens of the United States, or in any way abridged, except

for participation in rebellion, or other crime, the basis of representation therein shall be reduced in the proportion which the number of such male citizens shall bear to the whole number of male citizens twenty-one years of age in such State.

3. No person shall be a Senator or Representative in Congress, or elector of President and Vice-President, or hold any office, civil or military, under the United States, or under any State, who, having previously taken an oath, as a member of Congress, or as an officer of the United States, or as a member of any State legislature, or as an executive or judicial officer of any State, to support the Constitution of the United States, shall have engaged in insurrection or rebellion against the same, or given aid or comfort to the enemies thereof. But Congress may by a vote of two-thirds of each House, remove such disability.

4. The validity of the public debt of the United States, authorized by law, including debts incurred for payment of pensions and bounties for services in suppressing insurrection or rebellion, shall not be questioned. But neither the United States nor any State shall assume or pay any debt or obligation incurred in aid of insurrection or rebellion against the United States, or any claim for the loss or emancipation of any slave; but all such debts, obligations and claims shall be held illegal and void.

5. The Congress shall have power to enforce, by appropriate legislation, the provisions of this article.

AMENDMENT XV.

Race no bar to voting rights.

[The following amendment was proposed to the legislatures of the several States by the 40th Congress, Feb. 26, 1869, and ratified Feb. 3, 1870.]

1. The right of citizens of the United States to vote shall not be denied or abridged by the United States or by any State on account of race, color, or previous condition of servitude–

2. The Congress shall have power to enforce this article by appropriate legislation.

AMENDMENT XVI.

Income taxes authorized.

[Proposed by Congress July 12, 1909; ratified Feb. 3, 1913.]

The Congress shall have power to lay and collect taxes on incomes, from whatever source derived, without apportionment among the several States, and without regard to any census or enumeration.

AMENDMENT XVII.

United States Senators to be elected by direct popular vote.

[Proposed by Congress May 13, 1912; ratified Apr. 8, 1913.]

The Senate of the United States shall be composed of two Senators from each State, elected by the people thereof, for six years; and each Senator shall have one vote. The electors in each State shall have the qualifications requisite for electors of the most numerous branch of the State legislatures.

When vacancies happen in the representation of any State in the Senate, the executive authority of such State shall issue writs of election to fill such vacancies: *Provided,* That the legislature of any State may empower the executive thereof to make temporary appointments until the people fill the vacancies by election as the legislature may direct.

This amendment shall not be so construed as to affect the election or term of any Senator chosen before it becomes valid as part of the Constitution.

AMENDMENT XVIII.

Liquor prohibition amendment.

[Proposed by Congress Dec. 18, 1917; ratified Jan. 16, 1919. Repealed by Amendment XXI, effective Dec. 5, 1933.]

1. After one year from the ratification of this article the manufacture, sale, or transportation of intoxicating liquors within, the importation thereof into, or the exportation thereof from the United States and all territory subject to the jurisdiction thereof for beverage purposes is hereby prohibited.

2. The Congress and the several States shall have concurrent power to enforce this article by appropriate legislation.

3. This article shall be inoperative unless it shall have been ratified as an amendment to the Constitution by the legislatures of the several States as provided in the Constitution, within seven years from the date of the submission hereof to the States by the Congress.

[The total vote in the Senates of the various States was 1,310 for, 237 against—84.6% dry. In the lower houses of the States the vote was 3,782 for, 1,035 against—78.5% dry.

[The amendment ultimately was adopted by all the States except Rhode Island.]

AMENDMENT XIX.

Giving nationwide suffrage to women.

[Proposed by Congress June 4, 1919; ratified Aug. 18, 1920.]

The right of citizens of the United States to vote shall not be denied or abridged by the United States or by any State on account of sex.

Congress shall have power to enforce this Article by appropriate legislation.

AMENDMENT XX.

Terms of President and Vice President to begin on Jan. 20; those of Senators, Representatives, Jan. 3.

[Proposed by Congress Mar. 2, 1932; ratified Jan. 23, 1933.]

1. The terms of the President and Vice President shall end at noon on the 20th day of January, and the terms of Senators and Representatives at noon on the 3d day of January, of the years in which such terms would have ended if this article had not been ratified; and the terms of their successors shall then begin.

2. The Congress shall assemble at least once in every year, and such meeting shall begin at noon on the 3d day of January, unless they shall by law appoint a different day.

3. If, at the time fixed for the beginning of the term of the President, the President elect shall have died, the Vice President elect shall become President. If a President shall not have been chosen before the time fixed for the beginning of his term, or if the President elect shall have failed to qualify, then the Vice President elect shall act as President until a President shall have qualified; and the Congress may by law provide for the case wherein neither a President elect nor a Vice President elect shall have qualified, declaring who shall then act as President, or the manner in which one who is to act shall be selected, and such person shall act accordingly until a President or Vice President shall have qualified.

4. The Congress may by law provide for the case of the death of any of the persons from whom the House of Representatives may choose a President whenever the right of choice shall have devolved upon them, and for the case of the death of any of the persons from whom the Senate may choose a Vice President whenever the right of choice shall have devolved upon them.

5. Sections 1 and 2 shall take effect on the 15th day of October following the ratification of this article (Oct. 1933).

6. This article shall be inoperative unless it shall have been ratified as an amendment to the Constitution by the legislatures of three-fourths of the several States within seven years from the date of its submission.

AMENDMENT XXI.

Repeal of Amendment XVIII.

[Proposed by Congress Feb. 20, 1933; ratified Dec. 5, 1933.]

1. The eighteenth article of amendment to the Constitution of the United States is hereby repealed.

2. The transportation or importation into any State, Territory, or possession of the United States for delivery or use therein of intoxicating liquors, in violation of the laws thereof, is hereby prohibited.

3. This article shall be inoperative unless it shall have been ratified as an amendment to the Constitution by conventions in the several States, as provided in the Constitution, within seven years from the date of the submission hereof to the States by the Congress.

AMENDMENT XXII.

Limiting Presidential terms of office.

[Proposed by Congress Mar. 24, 1947; ratified Feb. 27, 1951.]

1. No person shall be elected to the office of the President more than twice, and no person who has held the office of President, or acted as President, for more than two years of a term to which some other person was elected President shall be elected to the office of the President more than once. But this Article shall not apply to any person holding the office of President when this Article was proposed by the Congress, and shall not prevent any person who may be holding the office of President, or acting as President, during the term within which this Article becomes operative from holding the office of President or acting as President during the remainder of such term.

2. This article shall be inoperative unless it shall have been ratified as an amendment to the Constitution by the legislatures of three-fourths of the several States within seven years from the date of its submission to the States by the Congress.

AMENDMENT XXIII.

Presidential vote for District of Columbia.

[Proposed by Congress June 16, 1960; ratified Mar. 29, 1961.]

1. The District constituting the seat of Government of the United States shall appoint in such manner as the Congress may direct:

A number of electors of President and Vice President equal to the whole number of Senators and Representatives in Congress to which the District would be entitled if it were a State, but in no event more than the least populous State; they shall be in addition to those appointed by the States, but they shall be considered, for the purposes of the election of President and Vice President, to be electors appointed by a State; and they shall meet in the District and perform such duties as provided by the twelfth article of amendment.

2. The Congress shall have power to enforce this article by appropriate legislation.

AMENDMENT XXIV.

Barring poll tax in federal elections.

[Proposed by Congress Sept. 14, 1962; ratified Jan. 23, 1964.]

1. The right of citizens of the United States to vote in any primary or other election for President or Vice President, for electors for President or Vice President, or for Senator or Representative in Congress, shall not be denied or abridged by the United States or any State by reason of failure to pay any poll tax or other tax.

2. The Congress shall have power to enforce this article by appropriate legislation.

AMENDMENT XXV.

Presidential disability and succession.

[Proposed by Congress July 6, 1965; ratified Feb. 10, 1967.]

1. In case of the removal of the President from office or of his death or resignation, the Vice President shall become President.

2. Whenever there is a vacancy in the office of the Vice President, the President shall nominate a Vice President who shall take office upon confirmation by a majority vote of both houses of Congress.

3. Whenever the President transmits to the President pro tempore of the Senate and the Speaker of the House of Representatives his written declaration that he is unable to discharge the powers and duties of his office, and until he transmits to them a written declaration to the contrary, such powers and duties shall be discharged by the Vice President as Acting President.

4. Whenever the Vice President and a majority of either the principal officers of the executive departments or of such other body as Congress may by law provide, transmit to the President pro tempore of the Senate and the Speaker of the House of Representatives their written declaration that the President is unable to discharge the powers and duties of his office, the Vice President shall immediately assume the powers and duties of the office as Acting President.

Thereafter, when the President transmits to the President pro tempore of the Senate and the Speaker of the House of Representatives his written declaration that no inability exists, he shall resume the powers and duties of his office unless the Vice President and a majority of either the principal officers of the executive department or of such other body as Congress may by law provide, transmit within four days to the President pro tempore of the Senate and the Speaker of the House of Representatives their written declaration that the President is unable to discharge the powers and duties of his office. Thereupon Congress shall decide the issue, assembling within forty-eight hours for that purpose if not in session. If the Congress, within twenty-one days after receipt of the latter written declaration, or, if Congress is not in session, within twenty-one days after Congress is required to assemble, determines by two-thirds vote of both Houses that the President is unable to discharge the powers and duties of his office, the Vice President shall continue to discharge the same as Acting President; otherwise, the President shall resume the powers and duties of his office.

AMENDMENT XXVI.

Lowering voting age to 18 years.

[Proposed by Congress Mar. 23, 1971; ratified July 1, 1971.]

1. The right of citizens of the United States, who are eighteen years of age or older, to vote shall not be denied or abridged by the United States or by any State on account of age.

2. The Congress shall have the power to enforce this article by appropriate legislation.

AMENDMENT XXVII.

Congressional pay.

[Proposed by Congress Sept. 25, 1789; ratified May 7, 1992.]

No law, varying the compensation for the services of the Senators and Representatives, shall take effect, until an election of Representatives shall have intervened.

How a Bill Becomes a Law

A senator or representative introduces a bill in Congress by sending it to the clerk of the House or the Senate, who assigns it a number and title. This procedure is termed the first reading. The clerk then refers the bill to the appropriate committee of the Senate or House.

If the committee opposes the bill, it will table, or kill, it. Otherwise, the committee holds hearings to listen to opinions and facts offered by members and other interested people. The committee then debates the bill and possibly offers amendments. A vote is taken, and if favorable, the bill is sent back to the clerk of the House or Senate.

The clerk reads the bill to the house—the second reading. Members may then debate the bill and suggest amendments.

After debate and possibly amendment, the bill is given a third reading, simply of the title, and put to a voice or roll-call vote.

If passed, the bill goes to the other house, where it may be defeated or passed, with or without amendments. If defeated, the bill dies. If passed with amendments, a conference committee made up of members of both houses works out the differences and arrives at a compromise.

After passage of the final version by both houses, the bill is sent to the president. If the president signs it, the bill becomes a law. The president may, however, veto the bill by refusing to sign it and sending it back to the house where it originated, with reasons for the veto.

The president's objections are then read and debated, and a roll-call vote is taken. If the bill receives less than a two-thirds majority, it is defeated. If it receives at least two-thirds, it is sent to the other house. If that house also passes it by at least a two-thirds majority, the one veto is overridden, and the bill becomes a law.

If the president neither signs nor vetoes the bill within 10 days—not including Sundays—it automatically becomes a law even without the president's signature. However, if Congress has adjourned within those 10 days, the bill is automatically killed; this indirect rejection is termed a pocket veto.

Note: Under the Line Item Veto Act, effective Jan. 1, 1997, the president was authorized, under certain circumstances, to veto a bill in part, but the legislation was found unconstitutional by the Supreme Court, June 25, 1998.

Confederate States and Secession

The American Civil War (1861-65) grew out of sectional disputes over the continued existence of slavery in the South and the contention of Southern legislators that the states retained many rights, including the right to secede.

The war was not fought by state against state but by one federal regime against another, the Confederate government in Richmond assuming control over the economic, political, and military life of the South, under protest from Georgia and South Carolina.

South Carolina voted an ordinance of secession from the Union, repealing its 1788 ratification of the U.S. Constitution on Dec. 20, 1860, to take effect on Dec. 24. Other states seceded in 1861. Their votes in conventions were: Mississippi, Jan. 9, 84-15; Florida, Jan. 10, 62-7; Alabama, Jan. 11, 61-39; Georgia, Jan. 19, 208-89; Louisiana, Jan. 26, 113-17; Texas, Feb. 1, 166-7, ratified by popular vote on Feb. 23 (for 34,794, against 11,325); Virginia, Apr. 17, 88-55, ratified by popular vote on May 23 (for 128,884;

against 32,134); Arkansas, May 6, 69-1; Tennessee, May 7, ratified by popular vote on June 8 (for 104,019, against 47,238); North Carolina, May 20.

Missouri Unionists stopped secession in conventions Feb. 28 and Mar. 9. The legislature condemned secession Mar. 7. Under the protection of Confederate troops, secessionist members of the legislature adopted a resolution of secession at Neosho, Oct. 31. The Confederate Congress seated the secessionists' representatives.

Kentucky did not secede, and its government remained Unionist. In a part of the state occupied by Confederate troops, Kentuckians approved secession, and the Confederate Congress admitted their representatives.

The Maryland legislature voted against secession Apr. 27, 53-13. Delaware did not secede. Western Virginia held conventions at Wheeling, named a pro-Union governor on June 11, 1861, and was admitted to the Union as West Virginia on June 20, 1863. Its constitution provided for gradual abolition of slavery.

Confederate Government

Forty-two delegates from South Carolina, Georgia, Alabama, Mississippi, Louisiana, and Florida met in convention at Montgomery, AL, on Feb. 4, 1861. They adopted a provisional constitution of the Confederate States of America and elected Jefferson Davis (MS) as provisional president and Alexander H. Stephens (GA) as provisional vice president.

A permanent constitution was adopted Mar. 11. It abolished the African slave trade, but it did not bar interstate

commerce in slaves. On July 20 the Congress moved to Richmond, VA. Davis was elected president in November and was inaugurated on Feb. 22, 1862.

The Congress adopted a flag, consisting of a red field with a white stripe, and a blue jack with a circle of white stars. Later the more popular flag was the red field with blue diagonal crossbars that held 13 white stars, for the 11 states in the Confederacy plus Kentucky and Missouri.

The Gettysburg Address

Delivered by Pres. Abraham Lincoln at Gettysburg, PA, on Nov. 19, 1863.

Fourscore and seven years ago our fathers brought forth on this continent a new nation, conceived in liberty and dedicated to the proposition that all men are created equal.

Now we are engaged in a great civil war, testing whether that nation or any nation so conceived and so dedicated can long endure. We are met on a great battle field of that war. We have come to dedicate a portion of that field, as a final resting-place for those who here gave their lives that this nation might live. It is altogether fitting and proper that we should do this.

But, in a larger sense, we can not dedicate—we can not consecrate—we can not hallow—this ground. The brave men, living and dead, who struggled here, have consecrated

it, far above our poor power to add or detract. The world will little note, nor long remember, what we say here, but it can never forget what they did here. It is for us the living, rather, to be dedicated here to the unfinished work which they who fought here have thus far so nobly advanced. It is rather for us to be here dedicated to the great task remaining before us—that from these honored dead we take increased devotion to that cause for which they gave the last full measure of devotion—that we here highly resolve that these dead shall not have died in vain—that this nation, under God, shall have a new birth of freedom—and that government of the people, by the people, for the people, shall not perish from the earth.

Selected Landmark Decisions of the U.S. Supreme Court, 1803-2008

See also Year in Review: Notable Supreme Court Decisions, 2008-09.

1803: *Marbury v. Madison.* The Court ruled that Congress exceeded its power in the Judiciary Act of 1789; the Court thus established its power to review acts of Congress and declare invalid those it found in conflict with the Constitution.

1819: *McCulloch v. Maryland.* The Court ruled that Congress had the authority to charter a national bank, under the Constitution's granting of the power to enact all laws "necessary and proper" to responsibilities of government.

1819: *Trustees of Dartmouth College v. Woodward.* The Court ruled that a state could not arbitrarily alter the terms of a college's contract. (The Court later used a similar principle to limit the states' ability to interfere with business contracts.)

1857: *Dred Scott v. Sanford.* The Court declared unconstitutional the already-repealed Missouri Compromise of 1820 because it deprived a person of his or her property—a slave—without due process of law. The Court also ruled that slaves were not citizens of any state nor of the U.S. (The latter part of the decision was overturned by ratification of the 14th Amendment in 1868.)

1896: *Plessy v. Ferguson.* The Court ruled that a state law requiring federal railroad trains to provide separate but equal facilities for black and white passengers neither infringed upon federal authority to regulate interstate commerce nor violated the 13th and 14th Amendments. (The "separate but equal" doctrine remained effective until the 1954 *Brown v. Board of Education* decision.)

1904: *Northern Securities Co. v. U.S.* The Court ruled that a holding company formed solely to eliminate competition between two railroad lines was a combination in restraint of trade, violating the federal antitrust act.

1908: *Muller v. Oregon.* The Court upheld a state law limiting the working hours of women. (Louis D. Brandeis, counsel for the state, cited evidence from social workers, physicians, and factory inspectors that the number of hours women worked affected their health and morals.)

1911: *Standard Oil Co. of New Jersey et al. v. U.S.* The Court ruled that the Standard Oil Trust must be dissolved because of its unreasonable restraint of trade.

1919: *Schenck v. U.S.* The Court sustained the Espionage Act of 1917, maintaining that freedom of speech and press could be constrained if "the words used . . . create a clear and present danger."

1925: *Gitlow v. New York.* The Court ruled that the 1st Amendment prohibition against government abridgment of the freedom of speech applied to the states as well as to the federal government. The decision was the first of a number of rulings holding that the 14th Amendment extended the guarantees of the Bill of Rights to state action.

1935: *Schechter Poultry Corp. v. U.S.* The Court ruled that Congress exceeded its authority to delegate legislative powers and to regulate interstate commerce when it enacted the National Industrial Recovery Act, which afforded the U.S. president too much discretionary power.

1951: *Dennis et al. v. U.S.* The Court upheld convictions under the Smith Act of 1940 for invoking Communist theory advocating the forcible overthrow of the government. (In *Yates v. U.S.* [1957], the Court moderated this ruling by allowing such advocacy in the abstract, if not connected to action to achieve the goal.)

1954: *Brown v. Board of Education of Topeka.* The Court ruled that separate public schools for black and white students were inherently unequal, so that state-sanctioned segregation in public schools violated the equal protection guarantee of the 14th Amendment. And in *Bolling v. Sharpe* the same year, the Court ruled that the congressionally mandated segregated public school system in the District of Columbia violated the 5th Amendment's due process guarantee of personal liberty. (The Brown ruling also led to abolition of state-sponsored segregation in other public facilities.)

1957: *Roth v. U.S.; Alberts v. California.* The Court ruled obscene material was not protected by 1st Amendment guarantees of freedom of speech and press, defining obscene

as "utterly without redeeming social value" and appealing to "prurient interests" in the average person's view. This definition was modified in later decisions, and the "average person" standard was replaced by the "local community" standard in *Miller v. California* (1973).

1961: *Mapp v. Ohio.* The Court ruled that evidence obtained in violation of the 4th Amendment guarantee against unreasonable search and seizure must be excluded from use at state as well as federal trials.

1962: *Engel v. Vitale.* The Court held that government bodies could not encourage the recitation of a state-composed prayer in public schools, even if nondenominational, because this would be an unconstitutional attempt to establish religion.

1962: *Baker v. Carr.* The Court held that the constitutional challenges to the unequal distribution of voters among legislative districts could be resolved by federal courts.

1963: *Gideon v. Wainwright.* The Court ruled that state and federal defendants charged with serious crimes must have access to an attorney, at state expense if necessary.

1964: *New York Times Co. v. Sullivan.* The Court ruled that the 1st Amendment protected the press from libel suits for defamatory reports about public officials unless an injured party could prove that a defamatory report was made out of malice or "reckless disregard" for the truth.

1965: *Griswold v. Connecticut.* The Court ruled that a state unconstitutionally interfered with personal privacy in the marriage relationship when it prohibited anyone, including married couples, from using contraceptives.

1966: *Miranda v. Arizona.* The Court ruled that, under the guarantee of due process, suspects in custody, before being questioned, must be informed that they have the right to remain silent, that anything they say may be used against them, and that they have the right to counsel.

1973: *Roe v. Wade; Doe v. Bolton.* The Court ruled that the fetus was not a "person" with constitutional rights and that a right to privacy inherent in the 14th Amendment's due process guarantee of personal liberty protected a woman's decision to have an abortion. During the 1st trimester of pregnancy, the Court maintained, the decision should be left entirely to a woman and her physician. Some regulation of abortion procedures was allowed in the 2nd trimester, and some restriction of abortion in the 3rd.

1974: *U.S. v. Nixon.* The Court ruled that neither the separation of powers nor the need to preserve the confidentiality of presidential communications could alone justify an absolute executive privilege of immunity from judicial demands for evidence to be used in a criminal trial.

1976: *Gregg v. Georgia; Profitt v. Florida; Jurek v. Texas.* The Court held that death, as a punishment for persons convicted of 1st degree murder, was not in and of itself cruel and unusual punishment in violation of the 8th Amendment. But the Court ruled that the sentencing judge and jury must consider the individual character of the offender and the circumstances of the particular crime.

1978: *Regents of the Univ. of Calif. v. Bakke.* The Court ruled that a special admissions program for a state medical school, under which a set number of places were reserved for minorities, violated the 1964 Civil Rights Act, which forbids excluding anyone, because of race, from a federally funded program. However, the Court ruled that race could be considered as one of a complex of factors.

1986: *Bowers v. Hardwick.* The Court refused to extend any constitutional right of privacy to homosexual activity, upholding a Georgia antisodomy law that in effect made such activity a crime. However, the law was struck down by the state supreme court in 1998, and in *Lawrence v. Texas* (2003), the U.S. Supreme Court struck down all state antisodomy laws, as violations of liberty prohibited in the 14th Amendment's due process clause. Also, in *Romer v. Evans* (1996), the Court struck down a Colorado constitutional provision that it ruled violated the 14th Amendment's Equal Protection Clause because it barred legislation whereby "homosexual orientation, conduct, practices, or relationships" granted a person "minority status, quota preferences, protected status, or claim of discrimination."

1990: *Cruzan v. Missouri.* The Court ruled that a person had the right to refuse life-sustaining medical treatment. However, the Court also ruled that, before treatment could be withheld from a comatose patient, a state could require "clear and convincing evidence" that the patient would not have wanted to live. In two **1997** rulings, ***Washington v. Glucksberg*** and ***Vacco v. Quill****, the Court ruled that states could ban doctor-assisted suicide.

1995: *Adarand Constructors, Inc., v. Peña.* The Court held that federal programs that classify people by race, unless "narrowly tailored" to accomplish a "compelling governmental interest," may violate the right to equal protection.

1995: *U.S. Term Limits Inc. v. Thornton.* The Court ruled that neither states nor Congress could limit terms of members of Congress, since the Constitution reserves to the people the right to choose federal lawmakers.

1997: *Clinton v. Jones.* Rejecting an appeal by Pres. Clinton in a sexual harassment suit, the Court ruled that a sitting president did not have temporary immunity from a lawsuit for actions outside the realm of official duties.

1997: *City of Boerne v. Flores.* The Court overturned a 1993 law banning enforcement of laws that "substantially burden" religious practice unless there is a "compelling need" to do so. The Court held that the act was an unwarranted intrusion by Congress on states' prerogatives and an infringement of the judiciary's role.

1997: *Reno v. ACLU.* Citing the right to free expression, the Court overturned a provision making it a crime to display or distribute "indecent" or "patently offensive" material on the Internet. The Court ruled, however, in ***NEA v. Finley*** **(1998)** that "general standards of decency" may be used as a criterion in federal arts funding.

1998: *Clinton v. City of New York.* The Court struck down the Line-Item Veto Act (1996), holding that it unconstitutionally gave the president "the unilateral power to change the text of duly enacted statutes."

1998: *Faragher v. City of Boca Raton*; *Burlington Industries, Inc. v. Ellerth.* The Court issued new guidelines for workplace sexual harassment suits, holding employers responsible for misconduct by supervisory employees. And in ***Oncale v. Sundowner Offshore Services***, the Court ruled that the law against sexual harassment applies regardless of whether harasser and victim are the same sex.

1999: *Dept. of Commerce v. U.S. House.* Upholding a challenge to plans for the 2000 census, the Court prohibited statistical sampling, favored by Democrats, in the apportioning of seats in the U.S. House of Representatives. The Court maintained that an actual head count was required.

1999: *Alden v. Maine*; *Florida Prepaid v. College Savings Bank*; *College Savings Bank v. Florida.* In a series of rulings, the Court applied the principle of "sovereign immunity" to shield states in large part from being sued under federal law.

2000: *Boy Scouts of America v. Dale.* The Court ruled that the Boy Scouts could dismiss a troop leader after learning he was gay, holding that the right to freedom of association outweighed a New Jersey antidiscrimination statute.

2000: *Stenberg v. Carhart.* The Court struck down a Nebraska law that banned so-called partial-birth abortion. It argued that the law could be interpreted as banning other abortion procedures and that it should have made exception for reasons of health. (*See* **1973: *Roe v. Wade.***)

2000: *Bush v. Gore.* The Court ruled that manual recounts of presidential ballots in the Nov. 2000 election could not proceed because inconsistent evaluation standards in different counties violated the equal protection clause. In effect, the ruling meant existing official results leaving George W. Bush as narrow winner of the election would prevail.

2001: *Easley v. Cromartie.* The Court ruled that North Carolina's 12th Congressional District, whose irregular shape had been challenged as an unconstitutional racial gerrymander, was the permissible result of attempts to create a majority-Democrat district.

2001: *Good News Club v. Milford Central School.* The justices found that religious and secular organizations were entitled to equal access to public elementary school grounds for after-school meetings.

2002: *Atkins v. Virginia.* The Court ruled that the execution of mentally retarded felons violated the 8th Amendment ban on "cruel and unusual punishment."

2002: *Ring v. Arizona.* The Court found that only a jury, not a judge, could decide to impose the death penalty.

2002: *Zelman v. Simmons-Harris.* The Court ruled that publicly funded tuition vouchers could be used at religious schools without violating the separation of church and state.

2002: *Federal Maritime Commission v. South Carolina State Ports Authority.* The Court ruled that the 11th Amendment gave states immunity from private lawsuits involving federal agencies.

2003: *Grotter v. Bollinger*; *Gratz v. Bollinger.* The Court upheld affirmative action in admission policies at the Univ. of Michigan Law School. However, in a second decision, the Court ruled against a strict point system based on racial and ethnic backgrounds, as used in the university's undergraduate admissions process.

2004: *Tennessee v. Lane.* The Court ruled that disabled individuals could sue states under the Americans with Disabilities Act for failing to provide adequate access to state courthouses, despite states' usual immunity from private lawsuits in federal court.

2004: *Locke v. Davey.* The justices decided that a scholarship program provided by the state of Washington did not violate the right to free exercise of religion in denying aid to students preparing for the clergy.

2004: *Ashcroft v. ACLU et al.* The Court struck down the Child Online Protection Act, which Congress passed in 1998 to restrict access to online pornography by minors, on the basis that the law, as written, violated the 1st Amendment right of free speech.

2005: *Kelo v. City of New London.* The Court ruled that local governments could force property owners to sell their land in order to facilitate private development projects deemed to be economically beneficial to the community.

2005: *Roper v. Simmons.* The Court ruled that executions of convicts who committed their crimes before age 18 were prohibited under the 8th Amendment ban on cruel and unusual punishment.

2006: *Garcetti v. Ceballos.* The Court ruled that the 1st Amendment guarantee of free speech did not protect statements made by public employees in the course of their official duties.

2006: *Hamdan v. Rumsfeld.* The Court ruled that Pres. George W. Bush's system for trying terrorism detainees at the U.S. military base in Guantanamo Bay, Cuba, was unauthorized under both federal law and the international Geneva Conventions.

2007: *Gonzales v. Carhart et al.*; *Gonzales v. Planned Parenthood Federation of America.* The Court upheld a 2003 federal law prohibiting the abortion procedure known as intact dilation and extraction, or "partial-birth" abortion.

2007: *Parents Involved in Community Schools v. Seattle School District No. 1*; *Madison v. Jefferson County Board of Education.* The Court ruled that two school districts could not, to encourage diversity, use "racial classifications in making school assignments."

2008: *Boumediene v. Bush.* The Court ruled that the guarantee of habeas corpus applied at the U.S. naval base at Guantanamo Bay, Cuba, and that detainees had a constitutional right to challenge their detention in federal court.

2008: *Kennedy v. Louisiana.* The Court ruled that death was a disproportionate penalty, and prohibited by the Constitution, in cases of child rape that did not result in the death of the victim.

2008: *District of Columbia vs. Heller.* The Court overturned DC's handgun ban, ruling that the 2nd Amendment protected individuals' right to own guns for personal use.

Presidential Oath of Office

The Constitution (Article II) directs that the president-elect shall take the following oath or affirmation to be inaugurated as president: "I do solemnly swear [affirm] that I will faithfully execute the office of President of the United States, and will, to the best of my ability, preserve, protect, and defend the Constitution of the United States." (Custom decrees the addition of the words "So help me God" at the end of the oath when taken by the president-elect, with the left hand on the Bible for the duration of the oath, and the right hand slightly raised.)

Law on Succession to the Presidency

If by reason of death, resignation, removal from office, inability, or failure to qualify there is neither a president nor vice president to discharge the powers and duties of the office of president, then the speaker of the House of Representatives shall upon his resignation as speaker and as representative, act as president. The same rule shall apply in the case of the death, resignation, removal from office, or inability of an individual acting as president.

If at the time when a speaker is to begin the discharge of the powers and duties of the office of president there is no speaker, or the speaker fails to qualify as acting president, then the president pro tempore of the Senate, upon his resignation as president pro tempore and as senator, shall act as president.

An individual acting as president shall continue to act until the expiration of the then current presidential term, except that (1) if his discharge of the powers and duties of the office is founded in whole or in part in the failure of both the president-elect and the vice president-elect to qualify, then he shall act only until a president or vice president qualifies, and (2) if his discharge of the powers and duties of the office is founded in whole or in part on the inability of the president or vice president, then he shall act only until the removal of the disability of one of such individuals.

If, by reason of death, resignation, removal from office, or failure to qualify, there is no president pro tempore to act as president, then the officer of the United States who is highest on the following list, and who is not under any disability to discharge the powers and duties of president shall act as president: the secretaries of state, treasury, defense, attorney general, secretaries of interior, agriculture, commerce, labor, health and human services, housing and urban development, transportation, energy, education, veterans affairs, homeland security.

[Legislation approved July 18, 1947; amended Sept. 9, 1965, Oct. 15, 1966, Aug. 4, 1977, and Sept. 27, 1979. See also Constitutional Amendment XXV.]

Origin of the United States National Motto

In God We Trust, designated as the U.S. National Motto by Congress in 1956, originated during the Civil War as an inscription for U.S. coins, although it was used by Francis Scott Key in a slightly different form when he wrote "The Star-Spangled Banner" in 1814. On Nov. 13, 1861, when Union morale had been shaken by battlefield defeats, the Rev. M. R. Watkinson, of Ridleyville, PA, wrote to Sec. of the Treasury Salmon P. Chase. "From my heart I have felt our national shame in disowning God as not the least of our present national disasters," the minister wrote, suggesting "recognition of the Almighty God in some form on our coins." Sec. Chase ordered designs prepared with the inscription *In God We Trust* and backed coinage legislation that authorized use of this slogan. The motto first appeared on some U.S. coins in 1864, and disappeared and reappeared on various coins until 1955, when Congress ordered it placed on all paper money and all coins.

The Great Seal of the U.S.

On July 4, 1776, the Continental Congress appointed a committee consisting of Benjamin Franklin, John Adams, and Thomas Jefferson "to bring in a device for a seal of the United States of America." The designs submitted by this and a subsequent committee were considered unacceptable. After many delays, a third committee, appointed early in 1782, presented a design prepared by lawyer William Barton. Charles Thomson, the secretary of Congress, suggested certain changes, and Congress finally approved the design on June 20, 1782. The obverse side of the seal shows an American bald eagle. In its mouth is a ribbon bearing the motto *E Pluribus Unum* (out of many, one). In the eagle's talons are 13 arrows of war and an olive branch of peace. The reverse side shows an unfinished pyramid with an eye (the Eye of Providence) above it.

The Flag of the U.S.—The Stars and Stripes

The 50-star flag of the United States was raised for the first time officially at 12:01 AM on July 4, 1960, at Fort McHenry National Monument in Baltimore, MD. The 50th star had been added for Hawaii; a year earlier the 49th, for Alaska. Before that, no star had been added since 1912, when New Mexico and Arizona were admitted to the Union.

The true history of the Stars and Stripes has become so cluttered by myth and tradition that the facts are difficult, and in some cases impossible, to establish. For example, it is not certain who designed the Stars and Stripes, who made the first such flag, or even whether it ever flew in any sea fight or land battle of the American Revolution.

All agree, however, that the Stars and Stripes originated as the result of a resolution offered by the Marine Committee of the Second Continental Congress at Philadelphia and adopted on June 14, 1777. It read:

Resolved: that the flag of the United States be thirteen stripes, alternate red and white; that the union be thirteen stars, white in a blue field, representing a new constellation.

Congress gave no hint as to the designer of the flag, no instructions as to the arrangement of the stars, and no information on its appropriate uses. Historians have been unable to find the original flag law.

The resolution establishing the flag was not even published until Sept. 2, 1777. Despite repeated requests, Washington did not get the flags until 1783, after the American Revolution was over. And there is no certainty that they were the Stars and Stripes.

Early Flags

Many historians consider the first flag of the U.S. to have been the Grand Union (sometimes called Great Union) flag, although the Continental Congress never officially adopted it. This flag was a modification of the British Meteor flag, which had the red cross of St. George and the white cross of St. Andrew combined in the blue canton. For the Grand Union flag, 6 horizontal stripes were imposed on the red field, dividing it into 13 alternating red and white stripes. On

Jan. 1, 1776, when the Continental Army came into formal existence, this flag was unfurled on Prospect Hill, Somerville, MA. Washington wrote that "we hoisted the Union Flag in compliment to the United Colonies."

One of several flags about which controversy has raged for years is at Easton, PA. Containing the devices of the national flag in reversed order, this flag has been in the public library at Easton for more than 150 years. Some contend that this flag was actually the first Stars and Stripes, first displayed on July 8, 1776. This flag has 13 red and white stripes in the canton, 13 white stars centered in a blue field.

A flag was hastily improvised from garments by the defenders of Ft. Schuyler at Rome, NY, Aug. 3-22, 1777. Historians believe it was the Grand Union Flag.

The Sons of Liberty had a flag of 9 red and white stripes, to signify 9 colonies, when they met in New York in 1765 to oppose the Stamp Tax. By 1775, the flag had grown to 13 red and white stripes, with a rattlesnake on it.

At Concord, Apr. 19, 1775, the minutemen from Bedford, MA, are said to have carried a flag having a silver arm with sword on a red field. At Cambridge, MA, the Sons of Liberty used a plain red flag with a green pine tree on it.

In June 1775, Washington went from Philadelphia to Boston to take command of the army, escorted to New York by the Philadelphia Light Horse Troop. It carried a yellow flag that had an elaborate coat of arms—the shield charged with 13 knots, the motto "For These We Strive"—and a canton of 13 blue and silver stripes.

In Feb. 1776, Col. Christopher Gadsden, a member of the Continental Congress, gave the South Carolina Provincial Congress a flag "such as is to be used by the commander-in-chief of the American Navy." It had a yellow field, with a rattlesnake about to strike and the words "Don't Tread on Me."

At the Battle of Bennington, Aug. 16, 1777, patriots used a flag of 7 white and 6 red stripes with a blue canton extending down 9 stripes and showing an arch of 11 white stars over the figure 76 and a star in each of the upper corners. The stars are 7-pointed. This flag is preserved in the historical museum in Bennington, VT.

At the Battle of Cowpens, Jan. 17, 1781, the 3d Maryland Regiment is said to have carried a flag of 13 red and white stripes, with a blue canton containing 12 stars in a circle around one star.

Who Designed the Flag? No one knows for certain. Francis Hopkinson, designer of a naval flag, declared he also had designed the flag and in 1781 asked Congress to reimburse him for his services. Congress did not do so. Dumas Malone of Columbia University wrote: "This talented man . . . designed the American flag."

Who Called the Flag "Old Glory"? The flag is said to have been named Old Glory by William Driver, a sea captain of Salem, MA. One legend has it that when he raised the flag on his brig, the *Charles Doggett*, in 1824, he said: "I name thee Old Glory." But his daughter, who presented the flag to the Smithsonian Institution, said he named it at his 21st birthday celebration on Mar. 17, 1824, when his mother presented the homemade flag to him.

The Betsy Ross Legend. The widely publicized legend that Betsy Ross made the first Stars and Stripes in June 1776, at the request of a committee composed of George Washington, Robert Morris, and George Ross, an uncle, was first made public in 1870, by a grandson of Ross. Historians have been unable to find a historical record of such a meeting or committee.

Adding New Stars

The flag of 1777 was used until 1795. Then, on the admission of Vermont and Kentucky to the Union, Congress passed and Pres. Washington signed an act that after May 1, 1795, the flag should have 15 stripes, alternating red and white, and 15 white stars on a blue field.

When new states were admitted, it became evident that the flag would become burdened with stripes. Congress thereupon ordered that after July 4, 1818, the flag should have 13 stripes, symbolizing the 13 original states; that the union have 20 stars, and that whenever a new state was admitted a new star should be added on the July 4 following admission.

No law designates the permanent arrangement of the stars. However, since 1912, when a new state has been admitted, the new design has been announced by executive order. No star is specifically identified with any state.

Code of Etiquette for Display and Use of the U.S. Flag

Reviewed by National Flag Foundation

Although the Stars and Stripes originated in 1777, it was not until 146 years later that there was a serious attempt to establish a uniform code of etiquette for the U.S. flag. On Feb. 15, 1923, the War Department issued a circular on the rules of flag usage. These rules were adopted almost in their entirety June 14, 1923, by a conference of 68 patriotic organizations in Washington, DC. Finally, on June 22, 1942, a joint resolution of Congress, amended by Public Law 94-344, July 7, 1976, codified "existing rules and customs pertaining to the display and use of the flag."

When to Display the Flag—The flag should be displayed on all days, especially on legal holidays and other special occasions, on official buildings when in use, in or near polling places on election days, and in or near schools when in session. Citizens may fly the flag at any time. It is customary to display it only from sunrise to sunset on buildings and on stationary flagstaffs in the open. It may be displayed at night, however, on special occasions, preferably lighted. The flag now flies over the White House both day and night. It flies over the Senate wing of the Capitol when the Senate is in session and over the House wing when that body is in session. It flies day and night over the east and west fronts of the Capitol, without floodlights at night but receiving illumination from the Capitol Dome. It flies 24 hours a day at several other places, including the Ft. McHenry National Monument in Baltimore, where it inspired Francis Scott Key to write "The Star Spangled Banner." The flag also flies 24 hours a day, properly illuminated, at U.S. Customs ports of entry.

Flying the Flag at Half-Staff—Flying the flag at half-staff, that is, halfway up the staff, is a signal of mourning. The flag should be hoisted to the top of the staff for an instant before being lowered to half-staff. It should be hoisted to the peak again before being lowered for the day or night.

As provided by presidential proclamation, the flag should fly at half-staff for 30 days from the day of death of a president or former president; for 10 days from the day of death of a vice president, chief justice or retired chief justice of the U.S., or speaker of the House of Representatives; from day of death until burial of an associate justice of the Supreme Court, cabinet member, former vice president, Senate president pro tempore, or majority or minority Senate or House leader; for a U.S. senator, representative, territorial delegate, or the resident commissioner of Puerto Rico, on day of death and the following day within the metropolitan area of the District of Columbia and from day of death until burial within the decedent's state, congressional district, territory or commonwealth; and for the death of the governor of a state, territory, or possession of the U.S., from day of death until burial.

On Memorial Day, the flag should fly at half-staff until noon and then be raised to the peak. The flag should also fly at half-staff on Korean War Veterans Armistice Day (July 27), National Pearl Harbor Remembrance Day (Dec. 7), and Peace Officers Memorial Day (May 15).

How to Fly the Flag—The flag should be hoisted briskly and lowered ceremoniously and should never be allowed to touch the ground or the floor. When the flag is hung over a sidewalk from a rope extending from a building to a pole, the union should be away from the building. When the flag is hung over the center of a street the union should be to the north in an east-west street and to the east in a north-south street. No other flag may be flown above or, if on the same level, to the right of the U.S. flag, except that at the United Nations Headquarters the UN flag may be placed above flags of all member nations and other national flags may be flown with equal prominence or honor with the flag of the U.S. At services by Navy chaplains at sea, the church pennant may be flown above the flag.

When two flags are placed against a wall with crossed staffs, the U.S. flag should be at right—its own right, and its staff should be in front of the staff of the other flag; when a number of flags are grouped and displayed from staffs, it should be at the center and highest point of the group.

Church and Platform Use—In an auditorium, the flag may be displayed flat, above and behind the speaker. When displayed from a staff in a church or in a public auditorium, the flag should hold the position of superior prominence, in advance of the audience, and in the position of honor at the speaker's right as she or he faces the audience. Any other flag so displayed should be placed on the left of the speaker or to the right of the audience.

When the flag is displayed horizontally or vertically against a wall, the stars should be uppermost and at the observer's left.

When used to cover a casket, the flag should be placed so that the union is at the head and over the left shoulder. It should not be lowered into the grave nor touch the ground.

How to Dispose of Worn Flags—When the flag is in such condition that it is no longer a fitting emblem for display, it should be destroyed in a dignified way, preferably by burning.

When to Salute the Flag—All persons present should face the flag, stand at attention, and salute on the following occasions: (1) when the flag is passing in a parade or in a review, (2) during the ceremony of hoisting or lowering, (3) when the national anthem is played, and (4) during the Pledge of Allegiance. Those present in uniform should render the military salute. Those not in uniform should place the right hand over the heart. A man wearing a hat should remove it with his right hand and hold it to his left shoulder during the salute.

Prohibited Uses of the Flag—The flag should not be dipped to any person or thing. (An exception—customarily, ships salute by dipping their colors.) It should never be displayed with the union down save as a distress signal. It

should never be carried flat or horizontally, but always aloft and free.

It should not be displayed on a float, an automobile, or a boat except from a staff. It should never be used as a covering for a ceiling, nor have placed on it any word, design, or drawing. It should never be used as a receptacle for carrying anything. It should not be used to cover a statue or a monument.

The flag should never be used for advertising purposes, nor be embroidered on such articles as cushions or handkerchiefs, printed or otherwise impressed on boxes or anything that is designed for temporary use and discard; or used as a costume or athletic uniform. Advertising signs should not be fastened to its staff or halyard.

The flag should never be used as drapery of any sort, never festooned, drawn back, nor up, in folds, but always allowed to fall free. Bunting of blue, white, and red, always arranged with the blue above and the white in the middle, should be used for covering a speaker's desk, draping the front of a platform, and for decoration in general.

An act of Congress approved on Feb. 8, 1917, provided certain penalties for the desecration, mutilation, or improper use of the flag within the District of Columbia. A 1968 federal law provided penalties of as much as a year's imprisonment or a $1,000 fine or both for publicly burning or otherwise desecrating any U.S. flag. In addition, many states have laws against flag desecration. In 1989, the Supreme Court ruled that no laws could prohibit political protesters from burning the flag. The decision had the effect of declaring unconstitutional the flag desecration laws of 48 states, as well as a similar federal statute, in cases of peaceful political expression.

The Supreme Court, in June 1990, declared that a new federal law making it a crime to burn or deface the American flag violated the free-speech guarantee of the First Amendment. The 5-4 Court decision led to renewed calls in Congress for a constitutional amendment to make it possible to prosecute flag burners.

Pledge of Allegiance to the Flag

I pledge allegiance to the flag of the United States of America and to the republic for which it stands, one nation under God, indivisible, with liberty and justice for all.

This, the current official version of the Pledge of Allegiance, has developed from the original pledge, which was first published in the Sept. 8, 1892, issue of *Youth's Companion*, a weekly magazine then published in Boston. The original pledge contained the phrase "my flag," which was changed more than 30 years later to "flag of the United States of America." A 1954 act of Congress added the words "under God." (In 2002, the 9th Circuit U.S. Court of Appeals ruled that recitation of the pledge in public schools could not include that phrase. In 2004, however, the U.S. Supreme Court voted to decline to decide the case on a technicality. The lower court's decision was thus overturned.)

The authorship of the pledge was in dispute for many years. The *Youth's Companion* stated in 1917 that the original draft was written by James B. Upham, an executive of the magazine who died in 1910. A leaflet circulated by the magazine later named Upham as the originator of the draft "afterwards condensed and perfected by him and his associates of the Companion force."

Francis Bellamy, a former member of *Youth's Companion* editorial staff, publicly claimed authorship of the pledge in 1923. In 1939, the United States Flag Association, acting on the advice of a committee named to study the controversy, upheld the claim of Bellamy, who had died 8 years earlier. In 1957 the Library of Congress issued a report attributing the authorship to Bellamy.

The History of the National Anthem

"The Star-Spangled Banner" was ordered played by the military and naval services by Pres. Woodrow Wilson in 1916. It was designated the national anthem by Act of Congress, Mar. 3, 1931. The words were written by Francis Scott Key, of Georgetown, MD, during the bombardment of Fort McHenry, Baltimore, Sept. 13-14, 1814. Key was a lawyer, a graduate of St. John's College, Annapolis, and a volunteer in a light artillery company. When a friend, Dr. Beanes, a Maryland physician, was taken aboard Admiral Cockburn's British squadron for interfering with ground troops, Key and J. S. Skinner, carrying a note from Pres. Madison, went to the fleet under a flag of truce on a cartel ship to ask Beanes's release. Cockburn consented, but as the fleet was about to sail up the Patapsco to bombard Fort McHenry, he detained them, first on HMS *Surprise* and then on a supply ship.

Key witnessed the bombardment from his own vessel. It began at 7 AM, Sept. 13, 1814, and lasted, with intermissions, for 25 hrs. The British fired more than 1,500 shells, each weighing as much as 220 lbs. They were unable to approach closely because the U.S. had sunk 22 vessels. Only 4 Americans were killed and 24 wounded. A British bomb-ship was disabled.

During the event, Key wrote a stanza on the back of an envelope. Next day at Indian Queen Inn, Baltimore, he wrote out the poem and gave it to his brother-in-law, Judge J. H. Nicholson. Nicholson suggested use of the tune, "Anacreon in Heaven" (attributed to a British composer named John Stafford Smith), and had the poem printed on broadsides, of which 2 survive. On Sept. 20 it appeared in the *Baltimore American*. Later Key made 3 copies; one is in the Library of Congress, and one in the Pennsylvania Historical Society. The copy Key wrote on Sept. 14 remained in the Nicholson family for 93 years. In 1907 it was sold to Henry Walters of Baltimore. In 1934 it was bought at auction by the Walters Art Gallery, Baltimore, for $26,400. In 1953 it was sold to the Maryland Historical Society for the same price.

The flag that Key saw during the bombardment is preserved in the Smithsonian Institution, Washington, DC. It measures 30 by 42 ft and has 15 alternating red and white stripes and 15 stars, for the original 13 states plus Kentucky and Vermont. It was made by Mary Young Pickersgill. The Baltimore Flag House, a museum, occupies her premises, which were restored in 1953.

The Star-Spangled Banner

Note: The 2nd and 3rd stanzas are commonly omitted as a courtesy to the British.

I

Oh, say can you see by the dawn's early light
What so proudly we hailed at the twilight's last gleaming?
Whose broad stripes and bright stars thru the perilous fight,
O'er the ramparts we watched were so gallantly streaming?
And the rocket's red glare, the bombs bursting in air,
Gave proof through the night that our flag was still there.
Oh, say does that star-spangled banner yet wave
O'er the land of the free and the home of the brave?

II

On the shore, dimly seen through the mists of the deep,
Where the foe's haughty host in dread silence reposes,
What is that which the breeze, o'er the towering steep,
As it fitfully blows, half conceals, half discloses?
Now it catches the gleam of the morning's first beam,
In full glory reflected now shines in the stream:
'Tis the star-spangled banner! Oh long may it wave
O'er the land of the free and the home of the brave!

III

And where is that band who so vauntingly swore
That the havoc of war and the battle's confusion,
A home and a country should leave us no more!
Their blood has washed out their foul footsteps' pollution.
No refuge could save the hireling and slave
From the terror of flight, or the gloom of the grave:
And the star-spangled banner in triumph doth wave
O'er the land of the free and the home of the brave!

IV

Oh! thus be it ever, when freemen shall stand
Between their loved home and the war's desolation!
Blest with victory and peace, may the heav'n rescued land
Praise the Power that hath made and preserved us a nation.
Then conquer we must, when our cause it is just,
And this be our motto: "In God is our trust."
And the star-spangled banner in triumph shall wave
O'er the land of the free and the home of the brave!

America (My Country 'Tis of Thee)

First sung in public on July 4, 1831, at a service in the Park Street Church, Boston, the words were written by Rev. Samuel Francis Smith, a Baptist clergyman, who set them to a melody he found in a German songbook, unaware that it was the tune for the British anthem, "God Save the King/Queen."

My country, 'tis of thee,
Sweet land of liberty,
Of thee I sing.
Land where my fathers died!
Land of the Pilgrims' pride!
From ev'ry mountainside,
Let freedom ring!

My native country, thee,
Land of the noble free,
Thy name I love.
I love thy rocks and rills,
Thy woods and templed hills;
My heart with rapture thrills
Like that above.

Let music swell the breeze,
And ring from all the trees
Sweet freedom's song.
Let mortal tongues awake;
Let all that breathe partake;
Let rocks their silence break,
The sound prolong.

Our fathers' God, to Thee,
Author of liberty,
To Thee we sing.
Long may our land be bright
With freedom's holy light;
Protect us by Thy might,
Great God, our King!

America, the Beautiful

Words composed by Katharine Lee Bates, a Massachusetts educator and author, in 1893, inspired by the view she experienced atop Pikes Peak in Colorado. The final form was established in 1911, and it is set to the music of Samuel A. Ward's "Materna."

O beautiful for spacious skies.
For amber waves of grain,
For purple mountain majesties
Above the fruited plain.
America! America!
God shed His grace on thee,
And crown thy good with brotherhood
From sea to shining sea.

O beautiful for pilgrim feet
Whose stern impassion'd stress
A thorough-fare for freedom beat
Across the wilderness.
America! America!
God mend thine ev'ry flaw,
Confirm thy soul in self control,
Thy liberty in law.

O beautiful for heroes prov'd
In liberating strife,
Who more than self their country lov'd
And mercy more than life.
America! America!
May God thy gold refine
Till all success be nobleness,
And ev'ry gain divine.

O beautiful for patriot dream
That sees beyond the years,
Thine alabaster cities gleam,
Undimmed by human tears.
America! America!
God shed His grace on thee,
And crown thy good with brotherhood
From sea to shining sea.

The Liberty Bell: Its History and Significance

The Liberty Bell is housed in the Liberty Bell Center, located in Philadelphia's National Historical Park.

The original bell was ordered by Assembly Speaker and Chairman of the State House Superintendents Isaac Norris and was ordered from Thomas Lester, Whitechapel Foundry, London. It reached Philadelphia at the end of August 1752. It bore an inscription from Leviticus 25:10: "PROCLAIM LIBERTY THROUGHOUT ALL THE LAND UNTO ALL THE INHABITANTS THEREOF."

The bell was cracked by a stroke of its clapper in Sept. 1752 while it hung on a truss in the State House yard for testing. Pass & Stow, Philadelphia founders, recast the bell, adding 1½ ounces of copper to a pound of the original "Whitechapel" metal to reduce its high tone and brittleness. It was found that the bell contained too much copper, injuring its tone, so Pass & Stow recast it again, this time successfully.

In June 1753 the bell was hung in the old wooden steeple of the State House. In use while the Continental Congress was in session in the State House, it rang out in defiance of British tax and trade restrictions, and it proclaimed the Boston Tea Party and, on July 8, 1776, the first public reading of the Declaration of Independence.

On Sept. 18, 1777, when the British Army was about to occupy Philadelphia, the Liberty Bell was moved in a baggage train of the American Army to Allentown, PA, where it was hidden until June 27, 1778. The bell was moved back to Philadelphia after the British left the city.

In July 1781 the wooden steeple became insecure and had to be taken down. The bell was lowered into the brick section of the tower, where it remained until 1828. Between 1828 and 1844 the old State House bell continued to ring during special occasions. According to tradition, it cracked in 1835 as it tolled the death of Chief Justice John Marshall. It rang for the last time on Feb. 23, 1846. In 1852 it was placed on exhibition in the Declaration Chamber of Independence Hall.

In 1876, when thousands of Americans visited Philadelphia for the Centennial Exposition, the bell was placed in its old wooden support in the tower hallway. In 1877 it was hung from the ceiling of the tower by a chain of 13 links. It was returned again to the Declaration Chamber and in 1896 taken back to the tower hall, where it occupied a glass case. In 1915 the case was removed so that the public might touch it. On Jan. 1, 1976, just after midnight to mark the opening of the Bicentennial Year, the bell was moved to a new glass and steel pavilion behind Independence Hall for easier viewing.

On Oct. 9, 2003, the bell was transferred from Liberty Bell Pavilion to its present location, where exhibits and displays explain the history of the bell.

The measurements of the bell are as follows: circumference around the lip, 12 ft ½ in.; circumference around the crown, 6 ft 11¼ in.; lip to the crown, 3 ft; height over the crown, 2 ft 3 in.; thickness at lip, 3 in.; thickness at crown, 1¼ in.; weight, 2,080 lbs; length of clapper, 3 ft 2 in.

Statue of Liberty National Monument

Since 1886, the Statue of Liberty, formally known as "Liberty Enlightening the World," has stood as a symbol of freedom in New York harbor. It also commemorates French-American friendship, for it was given by the people of France and designed by French sculptor Frederic Auguste Bartholdi (1834-1904).

On Washington's Birthday, Feb. 22, 1877, Congress approved the use of a site on Bedloe's Island suggested by Bartholdi. This island of 12 acres had been owned in the 17th century by a Walloon named Isaac Bedloe. It was called Bedloe's until Aug. 3, 1956, when Pres. Dwight Eisenhower approved a measure changing the name to Liberty Island.

The statue was finished on May 21, 1884, and presented to the U.S. minister to France, Levi Parsons Morton, July 4, 1884, by Ferdinand de Lesseps, head of the Franco-Ameri-

can Union, promoter of the Panama Canal, and builder of the Suez Canal.

On Aug. 5, 1884, the Americans laid the cornerstone for the pedestal, to be built on the foundations of Fort Wood, erected by the government in 1811. The American committee had raised $125,000, but this was inadequate. Joseph Pulitzer, owner of the *New York World*, appealed on Mar. 16, 1885, for general donations. By Aug. 11, 1885, he had raised $100,000. The statue itself arrived dismantled, in 214 packing cases, from Rouen, France, in June 1885. The last rivet of the statue was driven on Oct. 28, 1886, when Pres. Grover Cleveland dedicated the monument.

The Statue of Liberty National Monument was designated as such in 1924. It is administered by the National Park Service. A $2.5-mil building housing the American Museum of Immigration was opened by Pres. Richard Nixon on Sept.

26, 1972, at the base of the statue. It houses a permanent exhibition tracing the history of American immigration.

Four years of restoration work funded and led by the Statue of Liberty-Ellis Island Foundation were completed before the statue's 1986 centennial. Among other repairs, the $87-million project included replacing the 1,600 wrought iron bands that hold the statue's copper skin to its frame, replacing its torch, and installing an elevator. A 4-day "Liberty Weekend" extravaganza of concerts, tall ships, ethnic festivals, and fireworks, July 3-6, 1986, celebrated the 100th anniversary. Chief Justice Warren E. Burger swore in 5,000 new citizens on Ellis Island, while 20,000 others across the country were sworn in through a satellite telecast. Other ceremonies followed on Oct. 28, 1986, the statue's exact 100th birthday.

Following the Sept. 11 terrorist attacks, Liberty Island was closed to visitors. On Dec. 20, 2001, the secretary of the interior reopened the island after installing airport-type screening facilities at passenger embarkation areas at Battery Park in Manhattan and Liberty State Park in New Jersey.

To open the statue, the federal government needed to increase security throughout the park. In addition to federally funded security upgrades, significant safety improvements were made to meet building codes. The National Park Service turned to the Statue of Liberty-Ellis Island Foundation, which began a fund-raising campaign to help finance safety renovations inside the statue, additional exits, improved handicapped access, and upgraded fire suppression and emergency warning systems. The federal investment in upgrades amounted to about $30 million, with the private sector contributing an additional $7 million. Access to the statue was finally restored on Aug. 3, 2004. The crown of the statue reopened July 4, 2009; visitors must make a reservation to visit the top of the pedestal or the statue's crown.

Reservations are available by visiting www.statue cruises.com or by calling 1-877-LADY-TIX. A limited number of "walk up" reservations may also be available at ferry embarkation areas. Free, ranger-guided tours are available daily. Monument pass holders can visit the original torch, taken down during renovation in the 1980s, and the museum. For more information, visit www.nps.gov/stli and www.statueofliberty.org

Statue Statistics

The statue weighs 450,000 lbs., or 225 tons. The copper sheeting weighs 200,000 lbs. There are 167 steps from the land level to the top of the pedestal, 168 steps inside the statue to the head, and 54 rungs on the ladder leading to the arm that holds the torch.

	Ft	In		Ft	In
Height from base to torch tip	151	1	Nose, length	4	6
Foundation of pedestal to torch tip	305	1	Right arm, length	42	0
Heel to top of head	111	1	Right arm, max. thickness	12	0
Hand, length	16	5	Thickness of waist	35	0
Index finger, length	8	0	Mouth, width	3	0
Size of fingernail		13x10	Tablet, length	23	7
Head from chin to cranium	17	3	Tablet, width	13	7
Head thickness, ear to ear	10	0			

Emma Lazarus's Famous Poem

Engraved on pedestal below the statue.

The New Colossus

Not like the brazen giant of Greek fame,
With conquering limbs astride from land to land;
Here at our sea-washed, sunset gates shall stand
A mighty woman with a torch, whose flame
Is the imprisoned lightning, and her name
Mother of Exiles. From her beacon-hand
Glows world-wide welcome; her mild eyes command

The air-bridged harbor that twin cities frame.
"Keep ancient lands, your storied pomp!" cries she
With silent lips. "Give me your tired, your poor,
Your huddled masses yearning to breathe free,
The wretched refuse of your teeming shore.
Send these, the homeless, tempest-tost to me,
I lift my lamp beside the golden door!"

Ellis Island

Ellis Island was the gateway to America for over 12 mil immigrants between 1892 and 1924. In the late 18th century, Samuel Ellis, a New York City merchant, purchased the island and gave it his name. From Ellis, it passed to New York State, and the U.S. government bought it in 1808. On Jan. 1, 1892, the government opened the first federal immigration center in the U.S. there. The 27½-acre site eventually supported more than 35 buildings, including the Main Building with its Great Hall, in which as many as 5,000 people a day were processed.

Closed as an immigration station in 1954, Ellis Island was proclaimed part of the Statue of Liberty National Monument in 1965 by Pres. Lyndon B. Johnson. After a 6-year, $170 million restoration project funded by the Statue of Liberty-Ellis Island Foundation, Ellis Island was reopened as a museum in 1990. Artifacts, historic photographs and documents, oral histories, and ethnic music depicting 400 years of American immigration are housed in the museum. The museum also in-

cludes The American Immigrant Wall of Honor (www.wall ofhonor.com), which is inscribed with more than 600,000 names that have been placed in tribute. Registrations are still being accepted for inclusion in the memorial.

The American Family Immigration History Center® opened in April 2001. It contains an electronic database of ship passenger arrival information through the Port of New York and Ellis Island from 1892 to 1924. Data on over 25 million individuals are available, as well as an interactive database which features a Living Family Archive, multimedia presentations on various immigration groups and patterns, reproductions of original ships' passenger manifests, and pictures of over 800 immigrant ships (www.ellisis land.org).

In 1998, the Supreme Court ruled that nearly 90% of the island (the 24.2 acres which are landfill) lies in New Jersey, while the original 3.3 acres, on which the museum is located, are in New York.

PRESIDENTS OF THE UNITED STATES

U.S. Presidents

Name	Politics	Born	Birthplace	Inaug.	Age at inaug.	Died	Age at death
1. George Washington	Fed.	1732, Feb. 22	VA	1789	57	1799, Dec. 14	67
2. John Adams	Fed.	1735, Oct. 30	MA	1797	61	1826, July 4	90
3. Thomas Jefferson	Dem.-Rep.	1743, Apr. 13	VA	1801	57	1826, July 4	83
4. James Madison	Dem.-Rep.	1751, Mar. 16	VA	1809	57	1836, June 28	85
5. James Monroe	Dem.-Rep.	1758, Apr. 28	VA	1817	58	1831, July 4	73
6. John Quincy Adams	Dem.-Rep.	1767, July 11	MA	1825	57	1848, Feb. 23	80
7. Andrew Jackson	Dem.	1767, Mar. 15	SC	1829	61	1845, June 8	78
8. Martin Van Buren	Dem.	1782, Dec. 5	NY	1837	54	1862, July 24	79
9. William Henry Harrison	Whig	1773, Feb. 9	VA	1841	68	1841, Apr. 4	68
10. John Tyler	Whig	1790, Mar. 29	VA	1841	51	1862, Jan. 18	71
11. James Knox Polk	Dem.	1795, Nov. 2	NC	1845	49	1849, June 15	53
12. Zachary Taylor	Whig	1784, Nov. 24	VA	1849	64	1850, July 9	65
13. Millard Fillmore	Whig	1800, Jan. 7	NY	1850	50	1874, Mar. 8	74
14. Franklin Pierce	Dem.	1804, Nov. 23	NH	1853	48	1869, Oct. 8	64
15. James Buchanan	Dem.	1791, Apr. 23	PA	1857	65	1868, June 1	77
16. Abraham Lincoln	Rep.	1809, Feb. 12	KY	1861	52	1865, Apr. 15	56
17. Andrew Johnson	(1)	1808, Dec. 29	NC	1865	56	1875, July 31	66
18. Ulysses S. Grant	Rep.	1822, Apr. 27	OH	1869	46	1885, July 23	63
19. Rutherford Birchard Hayes	Rep.	1822, Oct. 4	OH	1877	54	1893, Jan. 17	70
20. James Abram Garfield	Rep.	1831, Nov. 19	OH	1881	49	1881, Sept. 19	49
21. Chester Alan Arthur	Rep.	1829, Oct. 5	VT	1881	51	1886, Nov. 18	57
22. Grover Cleveland	Dem.	1837, Mar. 18	NJ	1885	47	1908, June 24	71
23. Benjamin Harrison	Rep.	1833, Aug. 20	OH	1889	55	1901, Mar. 13	67
24. Grover Cleveland	Dem.	1837, Mar. 18	NJ	1893	55	1908, June 24	71
25. William McKinley	Rep.	1843, Jan. 29	OH	1897	54	1901, Sept. 14	58
26. Theodore Roosevelt	Rep.	1858, Oct. 27	NY	1901	42	1919, Jan. 6	60
27. William Howard Taft	Rep.	1857, Sept. 15	OH	1909	51	1930, Mar. 8	72
28. (Thomas) Woodrow Wilson	Dem.	1856, Dec. 28	VA	1913	56	1924, Feb. 3	67
29. Warren Gamaliel Harding	Rep.	1865, Nov. 2	OH	1921	55	1923, Aug. 2	57
30. (John) Calvin Coolidge	Rep.	1872, July 4	VT	1923	51	1933, Jan. 5	60
31. Herbert Clark Hoover	Rep.	1874, Aug. 10	IA	1929	54	1964, Oct. 20	90
32. Franklin Delano Roosevelt	Dem.	1882, Jan. 30	NY	1933	51	1945, Apr. 12	63
33. Harry S. Truman	Dem.	1884, May 8	MO	1945	60	1972, Dec. 26	88
34. Dwight David Eisenhower	Rep.	1890, Oct. 14	TX	1953	62	1969, Mar. 28	78
35. John Fitzgerald Kennedy	Dem.	1917, May 29	MA	1961	43	1963, Nov. 22	46
36. Lyndon Baines Johnson	Dem.	1908, Aug. 27	TX	1963	55	1973, Jan. 22	64
37. Richard Milhous Nixon[2]	Rep.	1913, Jan. 9	CA	1969	56	1994, Apr. 22	81
38. Gerald Rudolph Ford	Rep.	1913, July 14	NE	1974	61	2006, Dec. 26	93
39. James Earl (Jimmy) Carter	Dem.	1924, Oct. 1	GA	1977	52		
40. Ronald Wilson Reagan	Rep.	1911, Feb. 6	IL	1981	69	2004, June 5	93
41. George Herbert Walker Bush	Rep.	1924, June 12	MA	1989	64		
42. Wm. Jefferson (Bill) Clinton	Dem.	1946, Aug. 19	AR	1993	46		
43. George Walker Bush	Rep.	1946, July 6	CT	2001	54		
44. Barack Hussein Obama	Dem.	1961, Aug. 4	HI	2009	47		

(1) Andrew Johnson, a Democrat, was nominated vice president by Republicans and elected with Lincoln on National Union ticket.
(2) Resigned Aug. 9, 1974.

U.S. Presidents, Vice Presidents, Congresses

President	Service	Vice President	Congresses
1. George Washington	Apr. 30, 1789-Mar. 3, 1797	1. John Adams	1, 2, 3, 4
2. John Adams	Mar. 4, 1797-Mar. 3, 1801	2. Thomas Jefferson	5, 6
3. Thomas Jefferson	Mar. 4, 1801-Mar. 3, 1805	3. Aaron Burr	7, 8
	Mar. 4, 1805-Mar. 3, 1809	4. George Clinton	9, 10
4. James Madison	Mar. 4, 1809-Mar. 3, 1813	George Clinton[1]	11, 12
	Mar. 4, 1813-Mar. 3, 1817	5. Elbridge Gerry[2]	13, 14
5. James Monroe	Mar. 4, 1817-Mar. 3, 1825	6. Daniel D. Tompkins	15, 16, 17, 18
6. John Quincy Adams	Mar. 4, 1825-Mar. 3, 1829	7. John C. Calhoun	19, 20
7. Andrew Jackson	Mar. 4, 1829-Mar. 3, 1833	John C. Calhoun[3]	21, 22
	Mar. 4, 1833-Mar. 3, 1837	8. Martin Van Buren	23, 24
8. Martin Van Buren	Mar. 4, 1837-Mar. 3, 1841	9. Richard M. Johnson	25, 26
9. William Henry Harrison[4]	Mar. 4, 1841-Apr. 4, 1841	10. John Tyler	27
10. John Tyler	Apr. 6, 1841-Mar. 3, 1845	(None)	27, 28
11. James K. Polk	Mar. 4, 1845-Mar. 3, 1849	11. George M. Dallas	29, 30
12. Zachary Taylor[4]	Mar. 5, 1849-July 9, 1850	12. Millard Fillmore	31
13. Millard Fillmore	July 10, 1850-Mar. 3, 1853	(none)	31, 32
14. Franklin Pierce	Mar. 4, 1853-Mar. 3, 1857	13. William R. King[5]	33, 34
15. James Buchanan	Mar. 4, 1857-Mar. 3, 1861	14. John C. Breckinridge	35, 36
16. Abraham Lincoln	Mar. 4, 1861-Mar. 3, 1865	15. Hannibal Hamlin	37, 38
(4)	Mar. 4, 1865-Apr. 15, 1865	16. Andrew Johnson	39
17. Andrew Johnson	Apr. 15, 1865-Mar. 3, 1869	(None)	39, 40
18. Ulysses S. Grant	Mar. 4, 1869-Mar. 3, 1873	17. Schuyler Colfax	41, 42
	Mar. 4, 1873-Mar. 3, 1877	18. Henry Wilson[6]	43, 44
19. Rutherford B. Hayes	Mar. 4, 1877-Mar. 3, 1881	19. William A. Wheeler	45, 46
20. James A. Garfield[4]	Mar. 4, 1881-Sept. 19, 1881	20. Chester A. Arthur	47
21. Chester A. Arthur	Sept. 20, 1881-Mar. 3, 1885	(None)	47, 48
22. Grover Cleveland[7]	Mar. 4, 1885-Mar. 3, 1889	21. Thomas A. Hendricks[8]	49, 50
23. Benjamin Harrison	Mar. 4, 1889-Mar. 3, 1893	22. Levi P. Morton	51, 52
24. Grover Cleveland[7]	Mar. 4, 1893-Mar. 3, 1897	23. Adlai E. Stevenson	53, 54
25. William McKinley	Mar. 4, 1897-Mar. 3, 1901	24. Garret A. Hobart[9]	55, 56
(4)	Mar. 4, 1901-Sept. 14, 1901	25. Theodore Roosevelt	57
26. Theodore Roosevelt	Sept. 14, 1901-Mar. 3, 1905	(None)	57, 58
	Mar. 4, 1905-Mar. 3, 1909	26. Charles W. Fairbanks	59, 60
27. William H. Taft	Mar. 4, 1909-Mar. 3, 1913	27. James S. Sherman[10]	61, 62

President	Service	Vice President	Congresses
28. Woodrow Wilson	Mar. 4, 1913-Mar. 3, 1921	28. Thomas R. Marshall	63, 64, 65, 66
29. Warren G. Harding[4]	Mar. 4, 1921-Aug. 2, 1923	29. Calvin Coolidge	67
30. Calvin Coolidge	Aug. 3, 1923-Mar. 3, 1925	(None)	68
	Mar. 4, 1925-Mar. 3, 1929	30. Charles G. Dawes	69, 70
31. Herbert C. Hoover	Mar. 4, 1929-Mar. 3, 1933	31. Charles Curtis	71, 72
32. Franklin D. Roosevelt[11]	Mar. 4, 1933-Jan. 20, 1941	32. John N. Garner	73, 74, 75, 76, 77
	Jan. 20, 1941-Jan. 20, 1945	33. Henry A. Wallace	77, 78, 79
(4)	Jan. 20, 1945-Apr. 12, 1945	34. Harry S. Truman	79
33. Harry S. Truman	Apr. 12, 1945-Jan. 20, 1949	(None)	79, 80, 81
	Jan. 20, 1949-Jan. 20, 1953	35. Alben W. Barkley	81, 82, 83
34. Dwight D. Eisenhower	Jan. 20, 1953-Jan. 20, 1961	36. Richard M. Nixon	83, 84, 85, 86, 87
35. John F. Kennedy[4]	Jan. 20, 1961-Nov. 22, 1963	37. Lyndon B. Johnson	87, 88
36. Lyndon B. Johnson	Nov. 22, 1963-Jan. 20, 1965	(None)	88, 89
	Jan. 20, 1965-Jan. 20, 1969	38. Hubert H. Humphrey	89, 90, 91
37. Richard M. Nixon	Jan. 20, 1969-Jan. 20, 1973	39. Spiro T. Agnew[12]	91, 92, 93
(13)	Jan. 20, 1973-Aug. 9, 1974	40. Gerald R. Ford[14]	93
38. Gerald R. Ford[15]	Aug. 9, 1974-Jan. 20, 1977	41. Nelson A. Rockefeller[16]	93, 94, 95
39. Jimmy Carter	Jan. 20, 1977-Jan. 20, 1981	42. Walter F. Mondale	95, 96, 97
40. Ronald W. Reagan	Jan. 20, 1981-Jan. 20, 1989	43. George H. W. Bush	97, 98, 99, 100, 101
41. George H. W. Bush	Jan. 20, 1989-Jan. 20, 1993	44. Dan Quayle	101, 102, 103
42. Bill Clinton	Jan. 20, 1993-Jan. 20, 2001	45. Al Gore	103, 104, 105, 106, 107
43. George W. Bush	Jan. 20, 2001-Jan. 20, 2009	46. Dick Cheney	107, 108, 109, 110
44. Barack H. Obama	Jan. 20, 2009-	47. Joe Biden	111

(1) Died Apr. 20, 1812. (2) Died Nov. 23, 1814. (3) Resigned Dec. 28, 1832, to become U.S. senator. (4) Died in office. (5) Died Apr. 18, 1853. (6) Died Nov. 22, 1875. (7) Terms not consecutive. (8) Died Nov. 25, 1885. (9) Died Nov. 21, 1899. (10) Died Oct. 30, 1912. (11) First president to be inaugurated under 20th Amendment, Jan. 20, 1937. (12) Resigned Oct. 10, 1973. (13) Resigned Aug. 9, 1974. (14) First nonelected vice president, chosen under 25th Amendment procedure. (15) First president never elected president or vice president. (16) Second nonelected vice president, chosen under 25th Amendment. Confirmed Dec. 19, 1974.

Vice Presidents of the U.S.

The numerals given vice presidents do not coincide with those given presidents, because some presidents (Tyler, Fillmore, A. Johnson, Arthur) had none, and some had more than one.

Name	Birthplace	Year	Home	Inaug.	Politics	Place of death	Year	Age at death
1. John Adams	Quincy, MA	1735	MA	1789	Fed.	Quincy, MA	1826	90
2. Thomas Jefferson	Shadwell, VA	1743	VA	1797	Dem.-Rep.	Monticello, VA	1826	83
3. Aaron Burr	Newark, NJ	1756	NY	1801	Dem.-Rep.	Staten Island, NY	1836	80
4. George Clinton	Little Britain, NY	1739	NY	1805	Dem.-Rep.	Washington, DC	1812	73
5. Elbridge Gerry	Marblehead, MA	1744	MA	1813	Dem.-Rep.	Washington, DC	1814	70
6. Daniel D. Tompkins	Scarsdale, NY	1774	NY	1817	Dem.-Rep.	Staten Island, NY	1825	51
7. John C. Calhoun[1]	Abbeville, SC	1782	SC	1825	Dem.-Rep.	Washington, DC	1850	68
8. Martin Van Buren	Kinderhook, NY	1782	NY	1833	Dem.	Kinderhook, NY	1862	79
9. Richard M. Johnson[2]	Louisville, KY	1780	KY	1837	Dem.	Frankfort, KY	1850	70
10. John Tyler	Greenway, VA	1790	VA	1841	Whig	Richmond, VA	1862	71
11. George M. Dallas	Philadelphia, PA	1792	PA	1845	Dem.	Philadelphia, PA	1864	72
12. Millard Fillmore	Cayuga Co., NY	1800	NY	1849	Whig	Buffalo, NY	1874	74
13. William R. King	Sampson Co., NC	1786	AL	1853	Dem.	Cahaba, AL	1853	67
14. John C. Breckinridge	Lexington, KY	1821	KY	1857	Dem.	Lexington, KY	1875	54
15. Hannibal Hamlin	Paris, ME	1809	ME	1861	Rep.	Bangor, ME	1891	81
16. Andrew Johnson	Raleigh, NC	1808	TN	1865	(3)	Carter Co., TN	1875	66
17. Schuyler Colfax	New York, NY	1823	IN	1869	Rep.	Mankato, MN	1885	62
18. Henry Wilson	Farmington, NH	1812	MA	1873	Rep.	Washington, DC	1875	63
19. William A. Wheeler	Malone, NY	1819	NY	1877	Rep.	Malone, NY	1887	68
20. Chester A. Arthur	Fairfield, VT	1829	NY	1881	Rep.	New York, NY	1886	57
21. Thomas A. Hendricks	Zanesville, OH	1819	IN	1885	Dem.	Indianapolis, IN	1885	66
22. Levi P. Morton	Shoreham, VT	1824	NY	1889	Rep.	Rhinebeck, NY	1920	96
23. Adlai E. Stevenson[4]	Christian Co., KY	1835	IL	1893	Dem.	Chicago, IL	1914	78
24. Garret A. Hobart	Long Branch, NJ	1844	NJ	1897	Rep.	Paterson, NJ	1899	55
25. Theodore Roosevelt	New York, NY	1858	NY	1901	Rep.	Oyster Bay, NY	1919	60
26. Charles W. Fairbanks	Unionville Centre, OH	1852	IN	1905	Rep.	Indianapolis, IN	1918	66
27. James S. Sherman	Utica, NY	1855	NY	1909	Rep.	Utica, NY	1912	57
28. Thomas R. Marshall	N. Manchester, IN	1854	IN	1913	Dem.	Washington, DC	1925	71
29. Calvin Coolidge	Plymouth Notch, VT	1872	MA	1921	Rep.	Northampton, MA	1933	60
30. Charles G. Dawes	Marietta, OH	1865	IL	1925	Rep.	Evanston, IL	1951	85
31. Charles Curtis	Topeka, KS	1860	KS	1929	Rep.	Washington, DC	1936	76
32. John Nance Garner	Red River Co., TX	1868	TX	1933	Dem.	Uvalde, TX	1967	98
33. Henry A. Wallace	Adair County, IA	1888	IA	1941	Dem.	Danbury, CT	1965	77
34. Harry S. Truman	Lamar, MO	1884	MO	1945	Dem.	Kansas City, MO	1972	88
35. Alben W. Barkley	Graves County, KY	1877	KY	1949	Dem.	Lexington, VA	1956	78
36. Richard M. Nixon	Yorba Linda, CA	1913	CA	1953	Rep.	New York, NY	1994	81
37. Lyndon B. Johnson	Stonewall, TX	1908	TX	1961	Dem.	San Antonio, TX	1973	64
38. Hubert H. Humphrey	Wallace, SD	1911	MN	1965	Dem.	Waverly, MN	1978	66
39. Spiro T. Agnew[5]	Baltimore, MD	1918	MD	1969	Rep.	Berlin, MD	1996	77
40. Gerald R. Ford[6]	Omaha, NE	1913	MI	1973	Rep.	Rancho Mirage, CA	2006	93
41. Nelson A. Rockefeller[7]	Bar Harbor, ME	1908	NY	1974	Rep.	New York, NY	1979	70
42. Walter F. Mondale	Ceylon, MN	1928	MN	1977	Dem.			
43. George H. W. Bush	Milton, MA	1924	TX	1981	Rep.			
44. James Danforth (Dan) Quayle Jr.	Indianapolis, IN	1947	IN	1989	Rep.			
45. Albert A. Gore	Washington, DC	1948	TN	1993	Dem.			
46. Richard B. Cheney	Lincoln, NE	1941	WY	2001	Rep.			
47. Joseph R. Biden Jr.	Scranton, PA	1942	DE	2009	Dem.			

(1) Resigned Dec. 28, 1832, having been elected to the Senate to fill a vacancy. (2) Richard M. Johnson was the only vice president to be chosen by the Senate because of a tied vote in the Electoral College. (3) Andrew Johnson was a Democrat, nominated vice president by Republicans, and elected with Lincoln on the National Union Ticket. (4) Grandfather of Democratic candidate for president in 1952 and 1956. (5) Resigned Oct. 10, 1973. (6) First nonelected vice president, chosen under 25th Amendment procedure. (7) Second nonelected vice president, chosen under 25th Amendment.

Biographies of the Presidents

George Washington (1789-97), 1st president, Federalist, was born on Feb. 22, 1732, in Wakefield on Pope's Creek, Westmoreland Co., VA, the son of Augustine and Mary Ball Washington. He spent his early childhood on a farm near Fredericksburg. His father died when Washington was 11. He studied mathematics and surveying, and at 16, he went to live with his elder half brother, Lawrence, who built and named Mount Vernon in Virginia. Washington surveyed the lands of Thomas Fairfax in the Shenandoah Valley. He accompanied Lawrence to Barbados, West Indies, where he contracted smallpox and was deeply scarred. Lawrence died in 1752, and Washington inherited his property. He valued land, and when he died, he owned 70,000 acres in Virginia and 40,000 acres in what is now West Virginia.

Washington's military service began in 1753, when Lt. Gov. Robert Dinwiddie of Virginia sent him on missions deep into Ohio country. He clashed with the French and had to surrender Fort Necessity on July 3, 1754. He was an aide to the British general Edward Braddock and was at his side when the army was ambushed and defeated (July 9, 1755) on a march to Fort Duquesne. He helped take Fort Duquesne from the French in 1758.

After Washington's marriage to Martha Dandridge Custis, a widow, in 1759, he managed his family estate at Mount Vernon. Although not at first for independence, he opposed the repressive measures of the British crown and took charge of the Virginia troops before war broke out. He was made commander of the newly created Continental Army by the Continental Congress on June 15, 1775.

The American victory was due largely to Washington's leadership. He was resourceful, a disciplinarian, and the one dependable force for unity. Washington favored a federal government. He became chairman of the Constitutional Convention of 1787 and helped get the Constitution ratified. Unanimously elected president by the electoral college, he was inaugurated Apr. 30, 1789, on the balcony of New York's Federal Hall. He was reelected in 1792. Washington made an effort to avoid partisan politics as president.

Refusing to consider a 3rd term, Washington retired to Mount Vernon in March 1797. A ride in snow and rain around his estate led to what present-day doctors believe to have been an attack of acute epiglottitis. Doctors were unsuccessful in treating the inflammation in his throat, and Washington died Dec. 14, 1799.

John Adams (1797-1801), 2nd president, Federalist, was born on Oct. 30, 1735, in Braintree (now Quincy), MA, the son of John and Susanna Boylston Adams. He was a great-grandson of Henry Adams, who came from England in 1636. He graduated from Harvard in 1755, then taught school and studied law. He married Abigail Smith in 1764. In 1765 he argued against taxation without representation before the royal governor. In 1770, he successfully defended in court the British soldiers who fired on civilians in the Boston Massacre. He was a delegate to the Continental Congress and a signer of the Declaration of Independence. In 1778, Congress sent Adams and John Jay to join Benjamin Franklin as diplomatic representatives in Europe. Because he ran second to Washington in electoral college balloting in Feb. 1789, Adams became the nation's first vice president, a post he characterized as highly insignificant; he was reelected in 1792.

In 1796 Adams was chosen president by the electors. His administration was marked by growing conflict with fellow Federalist Alexander Hamilton and with others in his own cabinet who supported Hamilton's strongly anti-French position. Adams avoided full-scale war with France but became unpopular, especially after securing passage of the Alien and Sedition Acts in 1798. His foreign policy contributed significantly to the election of Thomas Jefferson in 1800.

Adams lived for a quarter century after he left office, during which time he wrote extensively. He died July 4, 1826, on the same day as his rival Thomas Jefferson (the 50th anniversary of the Declaration of Independence).

Thomas Jefferson (1801-09), 3rd president, Democratic-Republican, was born on Apr. 13, 1743, in Shadwell in Goochland (now Albemarle) Co., VA, the son of Peter and Jane Randolph Jefferson. His father died when Jefferson was 14, leaving him 2,750 acres and his slaves. Jefferson attended (1760-62) the College of William and Mary, read Greek and Latin classics, and played the violin. In 1769 he was elected to the Virginia House of Burgesses. In 1770 he began building his home, Monticello, and in 1772 he married Martha Wayles Skelton, a wealthy widow. Jefferson helped establish the Virginia Committee of Correspondence. As a member of the 2nd Continental Congress he drafted the Declaration of Independence. He also was a member of the Virginia House of Delegates (1776-79) and was elected governor of Virginia in 1779, succeeding Patrick Henry. He was reelected in 1780 but resigned in 1781 after British troops invaded Virginia. During his term he wrote the statute on religious freedom. After his wife's death in 1782, Jefferson again became a delegate to the Congress, and in 1784 he drafted the report that was the basis for the Ordinances of 1784, 1785, and 1787. He was minister to France from 1785 to 1789, when George Washington appointed him secretary of state.

Jefferson's strong faith in the consent of the governed conflicted with the emphasis on executive control, favored by Sec. of the Treasury Alexander Hamilton, and Jefferson resigned on Dec. 31, 1793. In the 1796 election Jefferson was the Democratic-Republican candidate for president; John Adams won the election, and Jefferson became vice president. In 1800, Jefferson and Aaron Burr received equal electoral college votes; the House of Representatives elected Jefferson president. Jefferson was a strong advocate of westward expansion; major events of his first term were the Louisiana Purchase (1803) and the Lewis and Clark expedition. An important development during his second term was passage of the Embargo Act, barring U.S. ships from setting sail to foreign ports. Jefferson established the Univ. of Virginia and designed its buildings. He died July 4, 1826, on the same day as John Adams (the 50th anniversary of the Declaration of Independence).

Analysis of DNA taken from descendants of Jefferson and Sally Hemings, one of his slaves, revealed a very high probability of Jefferson fathering at least one, perhaps all, of her six known children.

James Madison (1809-17), 4th president, Democratic-Republican, was born on Mar. 16, 1751, in Port Conway, King George Co., VA, the son of James and Eleanor Rose Conway Madison. Madison graduated from the College of New Jersey in 1771. He served in the Virginia Constitutional Convention (1776), and, in 1780, became a delegate to the 2nd Continental Congress. He was chief recorder at the Constitutional Convention in 1787 and supported ratification in the *Federalist Papers*, written with Alexander Hamilton and John Jay. In 1789, Madison was elected to the House of Representatives, where he helped frame the Bill of Rights and fought against passage of the Alien and Sedition Acts. In the 1790s, he helped found the Democratic-Republican Party, which ultimately became the Democratic Party. He became Jefferson's secretary of state in 1801.

Madison was elected president in 1808. His first term was marked by tensions with Great Britain, and his conduct of foreign policy was criticized by the Federalists and by his own party. Nevertheless, he was reelected in 1812, the year war was declared on Great Britain. The war that many considered a second American revolution ended with a treaty that did not settle any of the issues. Madison's most important action after the war was demilitarizing the U.S.-Canadian border.

In 1817, Madison retired to his estate, Montpelier, where he served as an elder statesman. He edited his famous papers on the Constitutional Convention and helped found the Univ. of Virginia, of which he became rector in 1826. He died June 28, 1836.

James Monroe (1817-25), 5th president, Democratic-Republican, was born on Apr. 28, 1758, in Westmoreland Co., VA, the son of Spence and Elizabeth Jones Monroe. He entered the College of William and Mary in 1774 but left to serve in the 3rd Virginia Regiment during the American Revolution. After the war, he studied law with Thomas Jefferson. In 1782 he was elected to the Virginia House of Delegates, and he served (1783-86) as a delegate to the Continental Congress. He opposed ratification of the Constitution because it lacked a bill of rights. Monroe was elected to the U.S. Senate in 1790. In 1794, Pres. Washington appointed Monroe minister to France. He served twice as governor of Virginia (1799-1802, 1811). Pres. Jefferson also sent him to France as minister (1803), and from 1803 to 1807, he served as minister to Great Britain.

In 1816 Monroe was elected president; he was reelected in 1820 with all but one electoral college vote. His administration became known as the Era of Good Feeling. He obtained Florida from Spain, settled boundary disputes with Britain over Canada, and eliminated border forts. He supported the antislavery position that led to the Missouri Compromise. His most significant contribution was the Monroe Doctrine, which opposed European intervention in the Western Hemisphere and became a cornerstone of U.S. foreign policy.

Although Monroe retired to Oak Hill, VA, financial problems forced him to sell his property and move to New York City. He died there on July 4, 1831.

John Quincy Adams (1825-29), 6th president, independent Federalist, later Democratic-Republican, was born on July 11, 1767, in Braintree (now Quincy), MA, the son of John and Abigail Adams. His father was the 2nd president. He studied abroad and at Harvard College, from which he graduated in 1787. In 1803, he was elected to the U.S. Senate. President Monroe chose him as his secretary of state in 1817. In this capacity he negotiated the cession of Florida from Spain, supported exclusion of slavery in the Missouri Compromise, and helped formulate the Monroe Doctrine. In 1824, Adams was elected president by the House of Representatives after he failed to win an electoral college majority. His expansion of executive powers was strongly opposed, and in the 1828 election he lost to Andrew Jackson. In 1831 he entered the House of Representatives and served 17 years with distinction. He opposed slavery, the annexation of Texas, and the Mexican War. He helped establish the Smithsonian Institution.

Adams suffered a stroke in the House and died in the Speaker's Room on Feb. 23, 1848.

Andrew Jackson (1829-37), 7th president, Democratic-Republican, later a Democrat, was born on Mar. 15, 1767, in the Waxhaw district, on the border of North and South Carolina, the son of Andrew and Elizabeth Hutchinson Jackson. At the age of 13, he joined the militia to fight in the American Revolution and was captured. Orphaned at age 14, Jackson was brought up by a well-to-do uncle. By age 20, he was practicing law, and later served as prosecuting attorney in Nashville, TN. In 1796 he helped draft the constitution of Tennessee, and for a year he occupied its one seat in the House of Representatives. The next year he served in the U.S. Senate.

In the War of 1812, Jackson crushed the Creek Indians at Horseshoe Bend, AL (1814), and, with a greatly outnumbered army consisting chiefly of backwoods militia members and volunteers, defeated Gen. Edward Pakenham's British troops at the Battle of New Orleans (1815). Nicknamed "Old Hickory" for his toughness, he emerged a national hero.

In 1818 Jackson briefly invaded Spanish Florida to quell Seminoles and outlaws who harassed frontier settlements. He ran for president against John Quincy Adams in 1824, but, although he won the most popular and electoral votes, he did not have a majority. The House of Representatives decided the election and chose Adams. In the 1828 election, however, Jackson defeated Adams, carrying the West and the South.

As president, Jackson introduced what became known as the spoils system—rewarding party members with government posts. Perhaps his most controversial act, however, was depositing federal funds in so-called pet banks, those directed by Democratic bankers, rather than in the Bank of the United States. "Let the people rule" was his slogan. In 1832, Jackson killed the congressional caucus for nominating presidential candidates and substituted the national convention. When South Carolina refused to collect imports under his protective tariff, he ordered army and naval forces to Charleston. After leaving office in 1837, he retired to the Hermitage, outside Nashville, where he died on June 8, 1845.

Martin Van Buren (1837-41), 8th president, Democrat, was born on Dec. 5, 1782, in Kinderhook, NY, the son of Abraham and Maria Hoes Van Buren. After attending local schools, he studied law and became a lawyer at the age of 20. A consummate politician, Van Buren began his career in the New York state senate and then served as state attorney general from 1816 to 1819. He was elected to the U.S. Senate in 1821. He helped swing Eastern support to Andrew Jackson in the 1828 election and then served as Jackson's secretary of state from 1829 to 1831. In 1832 he was elected vice president. Known as the "Little Magician," Van Buren was extremely influential in Jackson's administration.

In 1836, Van Buren defeated William Henry Harrison for president and took office as the financial panic of 1837 initiated a nationwide depression. Although he instituted the independent treasury system, his refusal to spend land revenues led to his defeat by William Henry Harrison in 1840. In 1844 he lost the Democratic nomination to James K. Polk. In 1848 he again ran for president on the Free Soil ticket but lost. He died in Kinderhook on July 24, 1862.

William Henry Harrison (1841), 9th president, Whig, who served only 31 days, was born on Feb. 9, 1773, in Berkeley, Charles City Co., VA, the son of Benjamin Harrison, a signer of the Declaration of Independence, and of Elizabeth Bassett Harrison. He attended Hampden-Sydney College. Harrison served as secretary of the Northwest Territory in 1798 and was its delegate to the House of Representatives in 1799. He was the first governor of Indiana Territory and served as superintendent of Indian affairs. With 900 men he put down a Shawnee uprising at Tippecanoe, IN, on Nov. 7, 1811. A generation later, in 1840, he waged a rousing presidential campaign, using the slogan "Tippecanoe and Tyler Too." The Tyler of the slogan was his running mate, John Tyler.

Although born to one of the wealthiest, most prestigious, and most influential families in Virginia, Harrison was elected president with the slogan, "Log Cabin and Hard Cider." He caught pneumonia during his inauguration and died Apr. 4, 1841, after only one month in office.

John Tyler (1841-45), 10th president, independent Whig, was born on Mar. 29, 1790, in Greenway, Charles City Co., VA, the son of John and Mary Armistead Tyler. His father was governor of Virginia (1808-11). Tyler graduated from the College of William and Mary in 1807 and in 1811 was elected to the Virginia legislature. In 1816 he was chosen for the U.S. House of Representatives. He served in the Virginia legislature again from 1823 to 1825, when he was elected governor of Virginia. After a stint in the U.S. Senate (1827-36), he was elected vice president (1840).

When William Henry Harrison died only a month after taking office, Tyler succeeded him. Because he was the first person to occupy the presidency without having been elected to that office, he was referred to as "His Accidency." He gained passage of the Preemption Act of 1841, which gave squatters on government land the right to buy 160 acres at the minimum auction price. His last act as president was to sign a resolution annexing Texas. Tyler accepted renomination in 1844 from some Democrats but withdrew in favor of the official party candidate, James K. Polk. A strong advocate of states' rights, he served briefly in the Confederate House of Representatives before he died in Richmond, VA, on Jan. 18, 1862.

James Knox Polk (1845-49), 11th president, Democrat, was born on Nov. 2, 1795, in Mecklenburg Co., NC, the son of Samuel and Jane Knox Polk. He graduated from the Univ. of North Carolina in 1818 and served in the Tennessee state legislature from 1823 to 1825. He served in the U.S. House of Representatives from 1825 to 1839, the last 4 years as Speaker. He was governor of Tennessee from 1839 to 1841. In 1844, after the Democratic National Convention became deadlocked, it nominated Polk, who became the first "dark horse" candidate for president. He was nominated primarily because he favored annexation of Texas.

As president, Polk reestablished the independent treasury system originated by Van Buren. He was so intent on acquiring California from Mexico that he sent troops to the Mexican border and, when Mexicans attacked, declared that a state of war existed. The Mexican War ended with the annexation of California and much of the Southwest as part of America's "manifest destiny." Polk compromised on the Oregon boundary ("54-40 or fight!") by accepting the 49th parallel and yielding Vancouver Island to the British. Polk died in Nashville, TN, on June 15, 1849, a few months after leaving office.

Zachary Taylor (1849-50), 12th president, Whig, who served only 16 months, was born on Nov. 24, 1784, in Orange Co., VA, the son of Richard and Sarah Strother Taylor. He grew up on his father's plantation near Louisville, KY, where he was educated by private tutors. In 1808 Taylor joined the regular army and was commissioned first lieutenant. He fought in the War of 1812, the Black Hawk War (1832), and the second Seminole War (beginning in 1837). He was called "Old Rough and Ready." In 1846 Pres. Polk sent him with an army to the Rio Grande. When the Mexicans attacked him, Polk declared war. Outnumbered 4-1, Taylor defeated Antonio López de Santa Anna at Buena Vista (1847).

A national hero, Taylor received the Whig nomination in 1848 and was elected president, even though he had never bothered to vote. He resumed the spoils system and, though a slaveholder, worked to admit California as a free state. He fell ill, likely from a case of acute gastroenteritis, and died in office on July 9, 1850.

Millard Fillmore (1850-53), 13th president, Whig, was born on Jan. 7, 1800, in Cayuga Co., NY, the son of Nathaniel and Phoebe Millard Fillmore. Although he had little schooling, he became a law clerk at the age of 22 and a year later was admitted to the bar. He was elected to the New York state assembly in 1828 and served until 1831. From 1833 until 1835 and again from 1837 to 1843, he represented his district in the U.S. House of Representatives. He opposed the entrance of Texas as a slave state and voted for a protective tariff. In 1844 he was defeated for governor of New York.

In 1848 he was elected vice president, and he succeeded as president after Taylor's death. Fillmore favored the Compromise of 1850 and signed the Fugitive Slave Law. His policies pleased neither expansionists nor slaveholders, and he was not renominated in 1852. In 1856 he was nominated by the American (Know-Nothing) Party, but despite the support of the Whigs, he was defeated by James Buchanan. He died in Buffalo, NY, on Mar. 8, 1874.

Franklin Pierce (1853-57), 14th president, Democrat, was born on Nov. 23, 1804, in Hillsboro, NH, the son of Benjamin Pierce, Revolutionary War general and governor of New Hampshire, and Anna Kendrick. He graduated from Bowdoin College in 1824 and was admitted to the bar in 1827. He was elected to the New Hampshire state legislature in 1829 and was chosen Speaker in 1831. He went to the U.S. House in 1833 and was elected a U.S. senator in 1837. He enlisted in the Mexican War and became brigadier general under Gen. Winfield Scott.

In 1852 Pierce was nominated as the Democratic presidential candidate on the 49th ballot. He decisively defeated Gen. Scott, his Whig opponent, in the election. Although he was against slavery, Pierce was influenced by proslavery Southerners. He supported the controversial Kansas-Nebraska Act, which left the question of slavery in the new territories of Kansas and Nebraska to popular vote. Pierce signed a reciprocity treaty with Canada and approved the Gadsden Purchase of a border area on a proposed railroad route, from Mexico. Denied renomination, he spent most of his remaining years in Concord, NH, where he died on Oct. 8, 1869.

James Buchanan (1857-61), 15th president, Federalist, later Democrat, was born on Apr. 23, 1791, near Mercersburg, PA, the son of James and Elizabeth Speer Buchanan. He graduated from Dickinson College in 1809 and was admitted to the bar in 1812. He fought in the War of 1812 as a volunteer. He was twice elected to the Pennsylvania general assembly, and in 1821 he entered the U.S. House of Representatives. After briefly serving (1832-33) as minister to Russia, he was elected U.S. senator from Pennsylvania. As Polk's secretary of state (1845-49), he ended the Oregon dispute with Britain and supported the Mexican War and annexation of Texas. As minister to Great Britain, he signed the Ostend Manifesto (1854), declaring a U.S. right to take Cuba by force should efforts to purchase it fail.

Nominated by Democrats, Buchanan was elected president in 1856. On slavery he favored popular sovereignty and choice by state constitutions but did not consistently uphold this position. He denied the right of states to secede but opposed coercion and attempted to keep peace by not provoking secessionists. Buchanan left office having failed to deal decisively with the situation. He died at Wheatland, his estate, near Lancaster, PA, on June 1, 1868.

Abraham Lincoln (1861-65), 16th president, Whig, then Republican, was born on Feb. 12, 1809, in a log cabin on a farm in Hardin (now Larue) Co., KY, the son of Thomas and Nancy Hanks Lincoln. The Lincolns moved to Spencer Co., IN, near Gentryville, when Lincoln was 7. After Lincoln's mother died, his father married Mrs. Sarah Bush Johnston in 1819. In 1830 the family moved to Macon Co., IL.

Defeated in 1832 in a race for the state legislature, Lincoln was elected on the Whig ticket two years later and served in the lower house from 1834 to 1842. In 1837 Lincoln was admitted to the bar and became partner in a Springfield, IL, law office. He soon won recognition as an effective and resourceful attorney. In 1846, he was elected to the U.S. House of Representatives, where he attracted attention during a single term for his opposition to the Mexican War and his position on slavery. In 1856 he campaigned for the newly founded Republican Party, and in 1858 he became its senatorial candidate against Stephen A. Douglas. Although he lost the election, Lincoln gained national recognition from his debates with Douglas.

In 1860, Lincoln was nominated for president by the Republican Party on a platform of restricting slavery. He ran against Douglas, a northern Democrat; John C. Breckinridge, a southern proslavery Democrat; and John Bell, of the Constitutional Union Party. As a result of Lincoln's winning the election, South Carolina seceded from the Union on Dec. 20, 1860, followed in 1861 by 10 other Southern states.

The Civil War erupted when Fort Sumter, which Lincoln decided to resupply, was attacked by Confederate forces on Apr. 12, 1861. Lincoln called successfully for recruits from the North. On Sept. 22, 1862, five days after the Battle of Antietam, Lincoln announced that slaves in territory then in rebellion would be free Jan. 1, 1863, the date of the Emancipation Proclamation. His speeches, including his Gettysburg and inaugural addresses, are remembered for their eloquence.

Lincoln was reelected, in 1864, over Gen. George B. McClellan, Democrat. Gen. Robert E. Lee surrendered on Apr. 9, 1865. On Apr. 14, Lincoln was shot by actor John Wilkes Booth in Ford's Theater, in Washington, DC. He died the next day.

Andrew Johnson (1865-69), 17th president, Democrat, was born on Dec. 29, 1808, in Raleigh, NC, the son of Jacob and Mary McDonough Johnson. He was apprenticed to a tailor as a youth, but ran away after two years and eventually settled in Greeneville, TN. He became popular with the townspeople and in 1829 was elected councilman and later mayor. In 1835 he was sent to the state general assembly. In 1843 he was elected to the U.S. House of Representatives, where he served for 10 years. Johnson was also governor of Tennessee from 1853 to 1857, when he was elected to the U.S. Senate. He supported John C. Breckinridge against Lincoln in the 1860 election. Although Johnson had held slaves, he opposed secession and tried to prevent Tennessee from seceding. In Mar. 1862, Lincoln appointed him military governor of occupied Tennessee.

In 1864, in order to balance Lincoln's ticket with a Southern Democrat, the Republicans nominated Johnson for vice president. He was elected vice president with Lincoln and then succeeded to the presidency upon Lincoln's death. Soon afterward, in a controversy with Congress over the president's power over the South, he proclaimed an amnesty to all Confederates, except certain leaders, if they would ratify the 13th Amendment abolishing slavery. States doing so added anti-Negro provisions that enraged Congress, which restored military control over the South. When Johnson removed Sec. of War Edwin M. Stanton, without notifying the Senate, the House impeached him in Feb. 1868. Charging him with thereby having violated the Tenure of Office Act, the House was actually responding to his opposition to harsh congressional Reconstruction, expressed in repeated vetoes. He was tried by the Senate, and in May, in two separate votes on different counts, Johnson was acquitted, both times by only one vote.

Johnson was denied renomination but remained politically active. He was reelected to the Senate in 1874. Johnson died July 31, 1875, at Carter Station, TN.

Ulysses S. Grant (1869-77), 18th president, Republican, was born on Apr. 27, 1822, in Point Pleasant, OH, the son of Jesse R. and Hannah Simpson Grant. The next year the family moved to Georgetown, OH. Grant was named Hiram Ulysses. Upon entering West Point in 1839, he found his name had been put down as Ulysses S. Grant, with his middle name first and his mother's maiden name as his middle name. He eventually adopted it as his true name but maintained the "S" did not stand for anything. Grant graduated in 1843. During the Mexican War, Grant served under both Gen. Zachary Taylor and Gen. Winfield Scott. In 1854, he resigned his commission because of loneliness and drinking problems, and in the following years he engaged in generally unsuccessful farming and business ventures. With the start of the Civil War, he was named colonel and then brigadier general of the Illinois Volunteers. He took Forts Henry and Donelson and fought at Shiloh. His brilliant campaign against Vicksburg and his victory at Chattanooga made him so prominent that Lincoln placed him in command of all Union armies. Grant accepted Lee's surrender at Appomattox Court House on Apr. 9, 1865. Pres. Johnson appointed Grant secretary of war when he suspended Stanton, but Grant was not confirmed.

Grant was nominated for president by the Republicans in 1868 and elected over Democrat Horatio Seymour. The 15th Amendment, the amnesty bill, and peaceful settlement of disputes with Great Britain were events of his administration. The Liberal Republicans and Democrats opposed him with Horace Greeley in the 1872 election, but Grant was reelected. His second administration was marked by scandals, including the Crédit Mobelier affair, the Whiskey Ring, in which high-ranked officials conspired to defraud the government of taxes, and the impeachment of his Secretary of War. An attempt by the Stalwarts (Old Guard Republicans) to nominate him in 1880 failed. In 1884 the collapse of an investment firm in which he was a partner left Grant penniless. He wrote his personal memoirs while ill with cancer and completed them shortly before his death at Mt. McGregor, NY, on July 23, 1885.

Rutherford Birchard Hayes (1877-81), 19th president, Republican, was born on Oct. 4, 1822, in Delaware, OH, the son of Rutherford and Sophia Birchard Hayes. He was reared by his uncle, Sardis Birchard. Hayes graduated from Kenyon College in 1842 and from Harvard Law School in 1845. He practiced law in Lower Sandusky (now Fremont), OH, and was city solicitor of Cincinnati from 1858 to 1861. During the Civil War, he was major of the 23rd Ohio Volunteers. He was wounded several times, and by the end of the war he had risen to the rank of brevet major general. While serving (1865-67) in the U.S. House of Representatives, Hayes supported Reconstruction and Johnson's impeachment. He was twice elected governor of Ohio (1867, 1869). After losing a race for the U.S. House in 1872, he was reelected governor of Ohio in 1875.

In 1876, Hayes was nominated for president and believed he had lost the election to Democrat Samuel J. Tilden. But a few Southern states submitted two sets of electoral votes, and the result was in dispute. An electoral commission, consisting of 8 Republicans and 7 Democrats, awarded all disputed votes to Hayes, allowing him to become president by one electoral vote. Hayes, keeping a promise to Southerners, withdrew troops from areas still occupied in the South, ending the era of Reconstruction. He proposed civil service reforms, alienating those favoring the spoils system, and advocated repeal of the Tenure of Office Act restricting presidential power to dismiss officials. He supported sound money and specie payments.

Hayes died in Fremont, OH, on Jan. 17, 1893.

James Abram Garfield (1881), 20th president, Republican, was born on Nov. 19, 1831, in Orange, Cuyahoga Co., OH, the son of Abram and Eliza Ballou Garfield. His father died in 1833, and he was reared in poverty by his mother. He worked as a canal bargeman, a farmer, and a carpenter. He attended Western Reserve Eclectic Institute and graduated from Williams College in 1856. He returned to Western Reserve to teach and in 1857, at age 25, he became the school's president. In 1859 he was elected to the Ohio legislature. Antislavery and antisecession, he volunteered for military service in the Civil War, becoming colonel of the 42nd Ohio Infantry and brigadier in 1862. He fought at Shiloh, TN, was chief of staff for Gen. William Starke Rosecrans, and was made major general for gallantry at Chickamauga, GA. He entered Congress as a radical Republican in 1863, calling for execution or exile of Confederate leaders, but he moderated his views after the Civil War. On the electoral commission in 1877 he voted for Hayes against Tilden on strict party lines.

Garfield was a senator-elect in 1880 when he became the Republican nominee for president. He was chosen as a compromise over Gen. Grant, James G. Blaine, and John Sherman, and won election despite some bitterness among Grant's supporters. For much of his brief tenure as president, Garfield was concerned with a fight with New York Sen. Roscoe Conkling, who opposed two major appointments made by Garfield. On July 2, 1881, Garfield was shot and seriously wounded by a mentally disturbed office seeker, Charles J. Guiteau, while entering a railroad station in Washington, DC. He lingered on in the White House before finally succumbing on Sept. 19, 1881, in Elberon, NJ.

Chester Alan Arthur (1881-85), 21st president, Republican, was born on Oct. 5, 1829, in Fairfield, VT, to William and Malvina Stone Arthur. He graduated from Union College in 1848, taught school in Vermont, then studied law and practiced in New York City. In 1853, he argued in a fugitive slave case that slaves transported through New York State were thereby freed. In 1871, he was appointed collector of the Port of New York. Pres. Hayes, an opponent of the spoils system, forced him to resign in 1878. This made the New York machine enemies of Hayes. Arthur and the Stalwarts (Old Guard Republicans) tried to nominate Grant for a 3rd term as president in 1880. When Garfield was nominated, Arthur was nominated for vice president in the interests of harmony.

Upon Garfield's assassination, Arthur became president. Despite his past connections, he signed major civil service reform legislation. Arthur tried to dissuade Congress from enacting the high protective tariff of 1883. He was defeated for renomination in 1884 by James G. Blaine. He died in New York City on Nov. 18, 1886.

Grover Cleveland (1885-89; 1893-97)

(According to a State Dept. ruling, Grover Cleveland should be counted as both the 22nd and the 24th president, because his two terms were not consecutive),

Democrat, was born Stephen Grover Cleveland on Mar. 18, 1837, in Caldwell, NJ, the son of Richard F. and Ann Neal Cleveland. When he was a small boy, his family moved to New York. Prevented by his father's death from attending college, he studied by himself and was admitted to the bar in Buffalo, NY, in 1859. In succession he became assistant district attorney (1863), sheriff (1871), mayor (1881), and governor of New York (1882). He was an independent, honest administrator who hated corruption. Cleveland was nominated for president over Tammany Hall opposition in 1884 and defeated Republican James G. Blaine.

As president, he enlarged the civil service and vetoed many pension raids on the Treasury. In the 1888 election he was defeated by Benjamin Harrison, although his popular vote was larger. Reelected over Harrison in 1892, he faced a money crisis brought about by a lowered gold reserve, circulation of paper, and exorbitant silver purchases under the Sherman Silver Purchase Act. He obtained a repeal of the Sherman Act but was unable to secure effective tariff reform. A severe economic depression and labor troubles racked his administration, but he refused to interfere in business matters and rejected Jacob Coxey's demand for unemployment relief. In 1894, he broke the Pullman strike. Cleveland was not renominated in 1896.

He died in Princeton, NJ, on June 24, 1908.

Benjamin Harrison (1889-93),

23rd president, Republican, was born on Aug. 20, 1833, in North Bend, OH, the son of John Scott and Elizabeth Irwin Harrison. His great-grandfather, Benjamin Harrison, was a signer of the Declaration of Independence; his grandfather, William Henry Harrison, was 9th president; his father was a member of Congress. He attended school on his father's farm and graduated from Miami University in Oxford, OH, in 1852. He was admitted to the bar in 1854 and practiced in Indianapolis, IN. During the Civil War, he rose to the rank of brevet brigadier general and fought at Kennesaw Mountain, Peachtree Creek, Nashville, and in the Atlanta campaign. He lost the 1876 gubernatorial election in Indiana but succeeded in becoming a U.S. senator in 1881.

In 1888 he defeated Cleveland for president despite receiving fewer popular votes. As president, he expanded the pension list and signed the McKinley high tariff bill, the Sherman Antitrust Act, and the Sherman Silver Purchase Act. During his administration, six states were admitted to the Union. He was defeated for reelection in 1892. He died in Indianapolis, IN, on Mar. 13, 1901.

William McKinley (1897-1901),

25th president, Republican, was born on Jan. 29, 1843, in Niles, OH, the son of William and Nancy Allison McKinley. McKinley briefly attended Allegheny College. When the Civil War broke out in 1861, he enlisted and served for the duration. He rose to captain and in 1865 was made brevet major. After studying law in Albany, NY, he opened a law office in Canton, OH (1867). He served twice in the U.S. House (1877-83; 1885-91) and led the fight there for the McKinley Tariff, passed in 1890; he was not reelected to the House as a result. He served two terms (1892-96) as governor of Ohio.

In 1896 he was elected president as a proponent of a protective tariff and sound money (gold standard) over William Jennings Bryan, the Democrat and a proponent of free silver. McKinley was reluctant to intervene in Cuba, but the loss of the battleship *Maine* at Havana crystallized opinion. He demanded

Spain's withdrawal from Cuba; Spain made some concessions, but Congress announced a state of war as of Apr. 21, 1898. He was reelected in the 1900 campaign, defeating Bryan's anti-imperialist arguments with the promise of a "full dinner pail." McKinley was respected for his conciliatory nature and for his conservative stance on business issues. On Sept. 6, 1901, while welcoming citizens at the Pan-American Exposition, in Buffalo, NY, he was shot by Leon Czolgosz, an anarchist. He died Sept. 14.

Theodore Roosevelt (1901-09),

26th president, Republican, was born on Oct. 27, 1858, in New York City, the son of Theodore and Martha Bulloch Roosevelt. He was a 5th cousin of Franklin D. Roosevelt and an uncle of Eleanor Roosevelt. Roosevelt graduated from Harvard University in 1880. He attended Columbia Law School briefly but abandoned law to enter politics. He was elected to the New York State Assembly in 1881 and served until 1884. He spent the next two years ranching and hunting in the Dakota Territory. In 1886, he ran unsuccessfully for mayor of New York City. He was civil service commissioner in Washington, DC, from 1889 to 1895. From 1895 to 1897, he served as New York City's police commissioner. He was assistant secretary of the Navy under McKinley. The Spanish-American War made him nationally known. He organized the 1st U.S. Volunteer Cavalry (Rough Riders) and, as lieutenant colonel, led the charge up Kettle Hill in San Juan. Elected New York governor in 1898, he fought the spoils system and achieved taxation of corporation franchises.

Nominated for vice president in 1900, Roosevelt became the nation's youngest president when McKinley was assassinated. He was reelected in 1904. As president he fought corruption of politics by big business, dissolved the Northern Securities Co. and others for violating antitrust laws, intervened in the 1902 coal strike on behalf of the public, obtained the Elkins Law (1903) forbidding rebates to favored corporations, and helped pass the Hepburn Railway Rate Act of 1906 (extending jurisdiction of the Interstate Commerce Commission). He helped obtain passage of the Pure Food and Drug Act (1906) and of employers' liability laws. Roosevelt vigorously organized conservation efforts. He mediated the peace between Japan and Russia in 1905, for which he won the Nobel Peace Prize. He abetted the 1903 revolution in Panama that led to U.S. acquisition of territory for the Panama Canal.

In 1908 Roosevelt obtained the nomination of William H. Taft, who was elected. Feeling that Taft had abandoned his policies, he unsuccessfully sought the nomination in 1912. He then ran on the Progressive "Bull Moose" ticket against Taft and Woodrow Wilson, splitting the Republicans and ensuring Wilson's election. During the campaign he was shot by a mentally deranged man but was not seriously wounded. In 1916, after unsuccessfully seeking the presidential nomination, he supported the Republican candidate, Charles E. Hughes. A strong friend of Britain, he fought for U.S. intervention in World War I.

Roosevelt was a voracious reader and wrote some 40 books, including *The Winning of the West*. He died Jan. 6, 1919, at Sagamore Hill, his home in Oyster Bay, NY.

William Howard Taft (1909-13),

27th president, Republican, and 10th chief justice of the U.S., was born on Sept. 15, 1857, in Cincinnati, OH, the son of Alphonso and Louisa Maria Torrey Taft. His father was secretary of war and attorney general in Grant's cabinet and minister to Austria and Russia under Arthur. Taft graduated from Yale in 1878 and from Cincinnati Law School in 1880. After working as a law reporter for Cincinnati newspapers, he served as assistant prosecuting attorney (1881-82), assistant county solicitor (1885), superior court judge (1887), U.S. solicitor-general (1890), and federal circuit judge (1892). In 1900 he became head of the U.S. Philippines Commission and was the first civil governor of the Philippines (1901-04). In 1904 he served as secretary of war, and in 1906 he was sent to Cuba to help avert a threatened revolution.

Taft was groomed for the presidency by Theodore Roosevelt and elected over William Jennings Bryan in 1908. Taft vigorously continued Roosevelt's trust-busting, instituted the Dept. of Labor, and drafted the amendments calling for direct election of senators and the income tax. However, his tariff and conservation policies angered progressives. Although renominated in 1912, he was opposed by Roosevelt, who ran on the Progressive Party ticket; the result was Democrat Woodrow Wilson's election.

Taft, with some reservations, supported the League of Nations. After leaving office, he was professor of constitutional law at Yale (1913-21) and chief justice of the U.S. (1921-30). Taft was the only person in U.S. history to have been both president and chief justice. He died in Washington, DC, on Mar. 8, 1930.

(Thomas) Woodrow Wilson (1913-21), 28th president, Democrat, was born on Dec. 28, 1856, in Staunton, VA, the son of Joseph Ruggles and Janet (Jessie) Woodrow Wilson. He grew up in Georgia and South Carolina. He attended Davidson College in North Carolina before graduating from Princeton University in 1879. He studied law at the Univ. of Virginia and political science at Johns Hopkins Univ., where he received his PhD in 1886. He taught at Bryn Mawr (1885-88) and at Wesleyan (1888-90) before joining the faculty at Princeton. He was president of Princeton from 1902 until 1910, when he was elected governor of New Jersey. In 1912 he was nominated for president with the aid of William Jennings Bryan, who sought to block James "Champ" Clark and Tammany Hall. Wilson won because the Republican vote for Taft was split by the Progressives.

As president, Wilson protected American interests in revolutionary Mexico and fought for American rights on the high seas. He oversaw the creation of the Federal Reserve system, cut the tariff, and developed a reputation as a reformer. His sharp warnings to Germany led to the resignation of his secretary of state, Bryan, a pacifist. In 1916 he was reelected by a slim margin with the slogan, "He kept us out of war," although his attempts to mediate in the war failed. After several American ships were sunk by the Germans, he secured a declaration of war against Germany on Apr. 6, 1917.

Wilson outlined his peace program on Jan. 8, 1918, in the Fourteen Points, a state paper that had worldwide influence. He enunciated a doctrine of self-determination for the settlement of territorial disputes. The Germans accepted his terms and an armistice on Nov. 11, 1918.

Wilson went to Paris to help negotiate the peace treaty, the crux of which he considered the League of Nations. The Senate demanded reservations that would not make the U.S. subordinate to the votes of other nations in case of war. Wilson refused and toured the country to get support. He suffered a stroke in Oct. 1919. An invalid, he clung to his office while his wife and doctors effectively functioned as president.

Wilson was awarded the 1919 Nobel Peace Prize, but the treaty embodying the League of Nations was ultimately rejected by the Senate in 1920. He left the White House in Mar. 1921. He died in Washington, DC, on Feb. 3, 1924.

Warren Gamaliel Harding (1921-23), 29th president, Republican, was born on Nov. 2, 1865, near Corsica (now Blooming Grove), OH, the son of George Tyron and Phoebe Elizabeth Dickerson Harding. He attended Ohio Central College, studied law, and became editor and publisher of a county newspaper. He entered the political arena as state senator (1901-04) and then served as lieutenant governor (1904-06). In 1910 he ran unsuccessfully for governor of Ohio; in 1914 he was elected to the U.S. Senate. In the Senate he voted for antistrike legislation, women's suffrage, and the Volstead Prohibition Enforcement Act over Pres. Wilson's veto. He opposed the League of Nations.

In 1920 he was nominated for president and defeated James M. Cox in the election. The Republicans capitalized on war weariness and fear that Wilson's League of Nations would curtail U.S. sovereignty. Harding stressed a return to "normalcy" and worked for tariff revision and the repeal of excess profits law and high income taxes. His secretary of the interior, Albert B. Fall, became involved in the Teapot Dome scandal, over the illegal leasing of U.S. government-owned oil reserves.

As rumors began to circulate about the corruption in his administration, Harding fell ill after a trip to Alaska, and he died suddenly in San Francisco on Aug. 2, 1923.

(John) Calvin Coolidge (1923-29), 30th president, Republican, was born on July 4, 1872, in Plymouth Notch, VT, the son of John Calvin and Victoria J. Moor Coolidge. Coolidge graduated from Amherst College in 1895. He entered Republican state politics and served as mayor of Northampton, MA, as state senator, as lieutenant governor, and, in 1919, as governor. In Sept. 1919, Coolidge attained national prominence by calling out the state guard in the Boston police strike. He declared, "There is no right to strike against the public safety by anybody, anywhere, anytime." This brought his name before the Republican convention of 1920, where he was nominated for vice president.

Coolidge succeeded to the presidency on Harding's death. As president, he opposed the League of Nations and the soldiers' bonus bill, which was passed over his veto. In 1924 he was elected to the presidency by a huge majority. He substantially reduced the national debt. He twice vetoed the McNary-Haugen farm bill, which would have provided relief to financially hard-pressed farmers.

With Republicans eager to renominate him, Coolidge simply announced on Aug. 2, 1927, "I do not choose to run for president in 1928." He died in Northampton, MA, on Jan. 5, 1933.

Herbert Clark Hoover (1929-33), 31st president, Republican, was born on Aug. 10, 1874, in West Branch, IA, the son of Jesse Clark and Hulda Randall Minthorn Hoover. Hoover grew up in Indian Territory (now Oklahoma) and Oregon and graduated from Stanford University with a degree in geology in 1895. He worked briefly with the U.S. Geological Survey and then managed mines in Australia, Asia, Europe, and Africa. While chief engineer of imperial mines in China, he directed food relief for victims of the Boxer Rebellion. He gained a reputation not only as an engineer but as a humanitarian as he directed the American Relief Committee, London (1914-15) and the U.S. Commission for Relief in Belgium (1915-19). He was U.S. Food Administrator (1917-19), American Relief Administrator (1918-23), and in charge of Russian Relief (1918-23). He served as secretary of commerce under both Harding and Coolidge. Some historians believe that he was the most effective secretary of commerce ever to hold that office.

In 1928 Hoover was elected president over Alfred E. Smith. In 1929 the stock market crashed, and the economy collapsed. During the Great Depression, Hoover inaugurated some government assistance programs, but he was opposed to administration of aid through a federal bureaucracy. As the effects of the depression continued, he was defeated in the 1932 election by Franklin D. Roosevelt. Hoover remained active after leaving office. President Truman named him coordinator of the European Food Program (1946) and chairman of the Commission on Organization of the Executive Branch (1947-49; 1953-55).

Hoover died in New York City on Oct. 20, 1964.

Franklin Delano Roosevelt (1933-45), 32nd president, Democrat, was born on Jan. 30, 1882, in Hyde Park, NY, the son of James and Sara Delano Roosevelt. He graduated from Harvard University in 1903. He attended Columbia University Law School without taking a degree and was admitted to the New York State bar in 1907. His political career began when he was elected to the New York State senate in 1910. In 1913 Pres. Wilson appointed him assistant secretary of the navy, a post he held during World War I.

In 1920 Roosevelt ran for vice president with James Cox and was defeated. From 1921 to 1928 he worked in his New York law office and was also vice president of a bank. In Aug. 1921, he was stricken with poliomyelitis, which left his legs paralyzed. As a result of therapy he was able to stand, or walk a few steps, with the aid of leg braces.

Roosevelt served two terms as governor of New York (1929-33). In 1932, Democratic convention delegate W. G. McAdoo, pledged to nominee John N. Garner, threw his votes to Roosevelt, who was nominated for president. The Depression and the promise to repeal Prohibition ensured his election. He asked for emergency powers, proclaimed the New Deal, and put into effect a vast number of administrative changes. Foremost was the use of public funds for relief and public works, resulting in deficit financing. He greatly expanded the federal government's regulation of business and by an excess profits tax and progressive income taxes produced a redistribution of earnings on an unprecedented scale. He also promoted legislation establishing the Social Security system. He was the last president inaugurated on Mar. 4 (1933) and the first inaugurated on Jan. 20 (1937).

Roosevelt was the first president to use radio for "fireside chats." When the Supreme Court nullified some New Deal laws, he sought power to "pack" the Court with additional justices, but Congress refused to give him the authority. He was the first president to break the "no 3rd term" tradition (1940) and was elected to a 4th term in 1944, despite failing health.

Roosevelt was openly hostile to fascist governments before World War II and launched a lend-lease program on behalf of the Allies. With British Prime Min. Winston Churchill he wrote a declaration of principles to be followed after Nazi defeat (the Atlantic Charter of Aug. 14, 1941) and urged the Four Freedoms (freedom of speech, of worship, from want, from fear) Jan. 6, 1941. When Japan attacked Pearl Harbor on Dec. 7, 1941, the U.S. entered the war. Roosevelt guided the nation through the war and conferred with allied heads of state at Casablanca, Morocco (Jan. 1943), Quebec, Canada (Aug. 1943), Tehran, Iran (Nov.-Dec. 1943), Cairo, Egypt (Nov. and Dec. 1943), and Yalta, Ukraine (Feb. 1945).

Roosevelt did not live to see the end of the war. He died of a cerebral hemorrhage in Warm Springs, GA, on Apr. 12, 1945.

Harry S. Truman (1945-53), 33rd president, Democrat, was born on May 8, 1884, in Lamar, MO, the son of John Anderson and Martha Ellen Young Truman. A family disagreement on whether his middle name should be Shipp or Solomon, after his two grandfathers, resulted in his using only the middle initial S. After graduating from high school in Independence, MO, he worked for the *Kansas City Star* (1901) as a railroad timekeeper and as a clerk in Kansas City banks until about 1905. He ran his family's farm from 1906 to 1917, then served in France during World War I. After the war he opened a haberdashery, was a judge on the Jackson Co. Court (1922-24), and attended Kansas City School of Law (1923-25).

Truman was elected to the U.S. Senate in 1934 and reelected in 1940. In 1944, with Roosevelt's backing, he was nominated for vice president and elected. On Roosevelt's death in 1945, Truman became president. In 1948, in a famous upset victory, he defeated Republican Thomas E. Dewey to win election to a new term.

Truman authorized the first uses of the atomic bomb (Hiroshima and Nagasaki, Aug. 6 and 9, 1945), bringing World War II to a rapid end. He was responsible for what came to be called the Truman Doctrine to aid nations such as Greece and Turkey, threatened by Communist takeover, and his strong commitment to NATO and to the Marshall Plan helped bring the two about. In 1948-49, he broke a Soviet blockade of West Berlin with a massive airlift. When Communist North Korea invaded South Korea (June 1950), he won UN approval for a "police action" and, without prior congressional consent, sent in forces under Gen. Douglas MacArthur. When MacArthur opposed his policy of limited objectives, Truman removed him.

He died in Kansas City, MO, on Dec. 26, 1972.

Dwight David Eisenhower (1953-61), 34th president, Republican, was born on Oct. 14, 1890, in Denison, TX, the son of David Jacob and Ida Elizabeth Stover Eisenhower. He grew up on a small farm in Abilene, KS, and graduated from West Point in 1915. He was on the staff of Gen. Douglas MacArthur in the Philippines from 1935 to 1939. In 1942, he was made commander of Allied forces landing in North Africa; the next year he was made full general. He became supreme Allied commander in Europe that same year and as such led the Normandy invasion (June 6, 1944). On Dec. 20, 1944, he was given the rank of general of the Army, which was made permanent in 1946.

On May 7, 1945, Eisenhower received the surrender of Germany at Rheims, France. He returned to the U.S. to serve as chief of staff (1945-48). His memoir, *Crusade in Europe* (1948), was a best-seller. In 1948 he became president of Columbia University; in 1950 he became commander of NATO forces.

Eisenhower resigned from the army and was nominated for president by the Republicans in 1952. He defeated Adlai E. Stevenson in the 1952 election and again in 1956. Eisenhower called himself a moderate, favored the "free market system" versus government price and wage controls, kept government out of labor disputes, reorganized the defense establishment, and promoted missile programs. He continued foreign aid, helped negotiate a cease fire truce in the Korean War, endorsed Taiwan and SE Asia defense treaties, backed the UN in condemning the Anglo-French raid on Egypt, and advocated the "open skies" policy of mutual inspection with the USSR. He sent U.S. troops into Little Rock, AR, in Sept. 1957, to enforce school integration.

Eisenhower died on Mar. 28, 1969, in Washington, DC.

John Fitzgerald Kennedy (1961-63), 35th president, Democrat, was born on May 29, 1917, in Brookline, MA, the son of Joseph P. and Rose Fitzgerald Kennedy. He graduated from Harvard University in 1940. While serving in the Navy (1941-45), he commanded a patrol torpedo (PT) boat in the Solomons and won the Navy and Marine Corps Medal. In 1956, while recovering from spinal surgery, he wrote *Profiles in Courage*, which won a Pulitzer Prize in 1957. He served in the House of Representatives from 1947 to 1953 and was elected to the Senate in 1952 and 1958. In 1960, he won the Democratic nomination for president and narrowly defeated Republican Vice Pres. Richard M. Nixon. Kennedy was the youngest president ever elected to the office and the first Catholic.

Despite the image of youth and vigor he conveyed to the public, Kennedy suffered from serious medical problems, including Addison's disease and severe chronic back pain that required him to wear a back brace. The public was not aware of the extent of these problems, or of his many marital infidelities, including an affair with a young White House press aide that only became known in 2003.

In Apr. 1961, the new Kennedy administration suffered a severe setback when an invasion force of anti-Castro Cubans, trained and directed by the CIA, failed to establish a beachhead at the Bay of Pigs in Cuba. One of Kennedy's most important acts as president was his successful demand on Oct. 22, 1962, that the Soviet Union dismantle its missile bases in Cuba. Kennedy also defied Soviet attempts to force the Allies out of Berlin. He started the Peace Corps, backed civil rights, and expanded medical care for the aged. Space exploration was greatly developed during his administration.

On Nov. 22, 1963, President Kennedy was assassinated while riding in a motorcade in Dallas, TX. A commission chaired by Chief Justice Earl Warren concluded in Sept. 1964 that the sole assassin had been Lee Harvey Oswald, a former U.S. Marine and, at the time of the shooting, an ardent Marxist. Oswald was captured a short time after the assassination and charged with the crime. Two days after the assassination, before he could go on trial, he was shot dead by nightclub owner Jack Ruby while being moved to a county jail.

Lyndon Baines Johnson (1963-69), 36th president, Democrat, was born on Aug. 27, 1908, near Stonewall, TX, the son of Sam Ealy and Rebekah Baines Johnson. He graduated from Southwest Texas State Teachers College in 1930 and attended Georgetown University Law School. He taught public speaking in Houston (1930-31) and then served as secretary to Rep. R. M. Kleberg (1931-35). In 1937 Johnson won an election to fill the vacancy caused by the death of a U.S. representative and in 1938 was elected to the full term, after which he returned for four terms. During 1941 and 1942 he also served in the Navy in the Pacific, earning a Silver Star for bravery. He was elected U.S. senator in 1948 and reelected in 1954. He became Democratic leader of the Senate in 1953. Johnson had strong support for the Democratic presidential nomination at the 1960 convention, where the nominee, John F. Kennedy, asked him to run for vice president. His campaigning helped overcome religious bias against Kennedy in the South.

Johnson became president when Kennedy was assassinated. He was elected to a full term in 1964. Johnson's domestic program was of considerable importance. He won passage of major civil rights, anti-poverty, aid to education, and health-care (Medicare, Medicaid) legislation—the "Great Society" program. However, his escalation of the war in Vietnam came to overshadow the achievements of his administration. In the face of increasing division in the nation and in his own party over his handling of the war, Johnson declined to seek another term.

Johnson died on Jan. 22, 1973, in San Antonio, TX.

Richard Milhous Nixon (1969-74), 37th president, Republican, was born on Jan. 9, 1913, in Yorba Linda, CA, the son of Francis Anthony and Hannah Milhous Nixon. He graduated from Whittier College in 1934 and from Duke University Law School in 1937. After practicing law in Whittier, CA, and serving briefly in the Office of Price Administration in 1942, he entered the Navy and served in the South Pacific. Nixon was elected to the House of Representatives in 1946 and 1948. He achieved prominence as the House Un-American Activities Committee member who forced the showdown leading to the Alger Hiss perjury conviction. In 1950 he was elected to the Senate.

Nixon was elected vice president in the Eisenhower landslides of 1952 and 1956. He won the Republican nomination for president in 1960 but was narrowly defeated by John F. Kennedy. He ran unsuccessfully for governor of California in 1962. In 1968 he again won the GOP presidential nomination, then defeated Hubert Humphrey for the presidency.

As president, Nixon appointed four Supreme Court justices, including the chief justice, moving the court to the right. As a "new federalist," he sought to shift responsibility to state and local governments. He dramatically altered relations with China, which he visited in 1972—the first U.S. president to do so. With foreign affairs adviser Henry Kissinger, he pursued détente with the Soviet Union, signing major arms limitation and other treaties and increasing trade. He began a gradual withdrawal from Vietnam, but U.S. troops remained there through his first term. He ordered an incursion into Cambodia (1970) and the bombing of Hanoi and mining of Haiphong Harbor (1972). Reelected by a large majority in Nov. 1972, he secured a Vietnam cease-fire in Jan. 1973.

Nixon's 2nd term was cut short by scandal, after disclosures relating to a June 1972 burglary of Democratic Party headquarters in the Watergate office complex in DC. The courts and Congress sought tapes of Nixon's office conversations and called for criminal proceedings against former White House aides and for a House inquiry into possible impeachment. Nixon claimed executive privilege, but the Supreme Court ruled against him. In July 1974, the House Judiciary Committee recommended adoption of three impeachment articles charging him with obstruction of justice, abuse of power, and contempt of Congress. On Aug. 5, he released transcripts of conversations that linked him to cover-up activities. He resigned on Aug. 9, becoming the first president ever to do so.

In later years, Nixon emerged as an elder statesman. He died Apr. 22, 1994, in New York City.

Gerald Rudolph Ford (1974-77), 38th president, Republican, was born on July 14, 1913, in Omaha, NE, the son of Leslie and Dorothy Gardner King, and was named Leslie Lynch King Jr. When he was 2, his parents divorced, and he and his mother moved to Grand Rapids, MI. There she met and married Gerald R. Ford, who formally adopted him and gave him his name. Ford graduated from the Univ. of Michigan in 1935 and from Yale Law School in 1941. He began practicing law in Grand Rapids, but in 1942, he joined the Navy and served in the Pacific, leaving the service in 1946 as a lieutenant commander. He entered the House of Representatives in 1949 and spent 25 years in the House, eight of them as Republican leader.

On Oct. 12, 1973, after Vice Pres. Spiro T. Agnew resigned, Pres. Nixon nominated Ford to replace him. It was the first use of the procedures set out in the 25th Amendment. When Nixon resigned, Aug. 9, 1974, because of the Watergate scandal, Ford became president; he was the only president who was never elected either to the presidency or to the vice presidency.

Ford was widely credited with having contributed to rebuilding morale after the Nixon presidency. But he was also criticized by many when, in a controversial move, he pardoned Nixon for any federal crimes he might have committed as pres-

ident. Ford vetoed 48 bills in his first 21 months in office, mostly in the interest of fighting high inflation; he was less successful in curbing high unemployment. In foreign policy, Ford continued to pursue détente.

Ford was narrowly defeated in the 1976 election. In 1999, he received the Medal of Freedom, the country's highest civilian award, and the Congressional Gold Medal, in recognition of his public service.

Ford died Dec. 26, 2006, at home in Rancho Mirage, CA.

James Earl (Jimmy) Carter (1977-81), 39th president, Democrat, was the first president from the Deep South since before the Civil War. He was born on Oct. 1, 1924, in Plains, GA, the son of James and Lillian Gordy Carter. Carter graduated from the U.S. Naval Academy in 1946 and in 1952 entered the Navy's nuclear submarine program as an aide to Capt. (later Adm.) Hyman Rickover. He studied nuclear physics at Union College.

Carter's father died in 1953, and he left the Navy to take over the family peanut farming businesses. He served in the Georgia state senate (1963-67) and as governor of Georgia (1971-75). In 1976, Carter won the Democratic nomination and defeated Pres. Gerald R. Ford.

On his first full day in office, Carter pardoned all Vietnam draft evaders. He played a major role in the negotiations leading to the 1979 peace treaty between Israel and Egypt, and he won passage of new treaties with Panama providing for U.S. control of the Panama Canal to end in 2000. Carter was widely criticized, however, for the poor state of the economy and was viewed by some as weak in his handling of foreign policy. In Nov. 1979, Iranian student militants attacked the U.S. embassy in Tehran and held members of the embassy staff hostage. Efforts to obtain release of the hostages were a major preoccupation during the rest of his term. He reacted to the Soviet invasion of Afghanistan by imposing a grain embargo and boycotting the Moscow Olympic Games.

Carter was defeated by Ronald Reagan in the 1980 election. The 52 American hostages in Iran were finally released on Inauguration Day, 1981, just after Reagan officially became president. In 2007, the Carter Center celebrated its 25th anniversary. Since its founding by Carter and his wife, Rosalynn Carter, in 1982, the Center has observed more than 67 elections in 26 countries with struggling democracies and reduced incidents of Guinea worm disease. In large part for his diplomatic efforts in office and subsequently, he was awarded the Nobel Peace Prize in 2002.

Ronald Wilson Reagan (1981-89), 40th president, Republican, was born on Feb. 6, 1911, in Tampico, IL, the son of John Edward and Nellie Wilson Reagan. Reagan graduated from Eureka College in 1932, after which he worked as a sports announcer in Des Moines, IA. He began a successful career as an actor in 1937, starring in numerous movies, and later in television, until the 1960s. During World War II Reagan served in the Army Air Force, making training films. He was president of the Screen Actors Guild in 1947-52 and in 1959-60. Reagan was elected governor of California in 1966 and reelected in 1970.

In 1980, Reagan gained the Republican presidential nomination and won a landslide victory over Jimmy Carter. He was easily reelected in 1984. Reagan forged a bipartisan coalition in Congress, which led to enactment of his program of large-scale tax cuts, cutbacks in many government programs, and a major defense buildup. He signed a Social Security reform bill designed to provide for the long-term solvency of the system. In 1986, he signed into law a major tax-reform bill. He was shot and seriously wounded in 1981 by a would-be assassin who was later declared insane.

In 1982, the U.S. joined France and Italy in maintaining a peacekeeping force in Beirut, Lebanon, and the next year Reagan sent a task force to invade Grenada after two Marxist coups on the island. Reagan's opposition to international terrorism led to the U.S. bombing of Libyan military installations in 1986. He strongly supported El Salvador, the Nicaraguan contras, and other anticommunist governments and forces throughout the world. He also held four summit meetings with Soviet leader Mikhail Gorbachev. At the 1987 meeting in Washington, DC, a historic treaty eliminating short- and medium-range missiles from Europe was signed.

Reagan faced a crisis in 1986-87. It was revealed that the U.S. had sold weapons through Israeli brokers to Iran in exchange for the release of U.S. hostages being held in Lebanon and that subsequently some of the money had been diverted to the Nicaraguan contras (Congress had barred U.S. aid to the contras). The scandal led to the resignation of leading White House aides. As Reagan left office in Jan. 1989, the nation was experiencing its 6th consecutive year of economic prosperity. Over the same period, however, the federal government recorded large budget deficits.

In 1994, in a letter to the American people, Reagan revealed that he was suffering from Alzheimer's disease. He died on June 5, 2004, in Los Angeles, CA, from complications of the disease.

George Herbert Walker Bush (1989-93),
41st president, Republican, was born on June 12, 1924, in Milton, MA, the son of Prescott and Dorothy Walker Bush. He served as a U.S. Navy pilot in World War II. After graduating from Yale University in 1948, he settled in Texas, where, in 1953, he helped found an oil company. After losing a bid for a U.S. Senate seat in 1964, he was elected to the House of Representatives in 1966 and 1968. He lost a second U.S. Senate race in 1970. Subsequently he served as U.S. ambassador to the United Nations (1971-73), headed the U.S. Liaison Office in Beijing (1974-75), and was director of the CIA (1976-77).

Following an unsuccessful bid for the 1980 Republican presidential nomination, Bush became Ronald Reagan's running mate, and served as vice president from 1981 to 1989.

In 1988, Bush gained the GOP presidential nomination and defeated Michael Dukakis. Bush took office faced with U.S. budget and trade deficits, and insolvent U.S. savings and loan institutions. He faced a severe budget deficit annually, struggled with military cutbacks, and vetoed abortion-rights legislation. In 1990 he agreed to a budget deficit-reduction plan that included tax hikes.

Bush supported Soviet reforms, Eastern Europe democratization, and good relations with Beijing. In Dec. 1989, Bush sent troops to Panama; they overthrew the government and captured military dictator Gen. Manuel Noriega.

Bush reacted to Iraq's Aug. 1990 invasion of Kuwait by sending U.S. forces to the Persian Gulf area and assembling a UN-backed coalition, including NATO and Arab League members. After a month-long air war, in Feb. 1991, Allied forces retook Kuwait in a 4-day ground assault. The quick victory, with extremely light casualties on the U.S. side, gave Bush at that time one of the highest presidential approval ratings in history. His popularity plummeted by the end of 1991, however, as the economy slipped into recession. He was defeated by Bill Clinton in the 1992 election. In 2005, he led campaigns with former Pres. Clinton to raise money for the victims of the Indian Ocean tsunami and Hurricane Katrina.

William Jefferson (Bill) Clinton (1993-2001),
42nd president, Democrat, was born Aug. 19, 1946, in Hope, AR, son of William Blythe and Virginia Cassidy Blythe, and was named William Jefferson Blythe IV. Blythe died in an auto accident before his son was born. His widow married Roger Clinton, whose last name Bill Clinton then took.

Clinton became interested in politics and went to Georgetown University, where he graduated with high honors in 1968. He attended Oxford University for 2 years as a Rhodes scholar. During that time he legally avoided the draft and possible service in Vietnam, according to some critics, by misleading his draft board. Clinton worked on George McGovern's 1972 presidential campaign and earned a degree from Yale Law School in 1973. He taught at the University of Arkansas law school from 1973 to 1976, when he was elected state attorney general. In 1978 he was elected governor, becoming the nation's youngest at the time. Defeated for reelection in 1980, he was returned to office several times thereafter. He married law school classmate Hillary Rodham in 1975. They had a daughter, Chelsea, in 1980.

Clinton won most of the 1992 presidential primaries, moving his party toward the center as he tried to broaden his appeal; as the Democratic nominee he defeated Pres. George H. W. Bush

and Reform Party candidate Ross Perot in the Nov. election. In 1993, Clinton won passage of a measure to reduce the federal budget deficit and won congressional approval of the North American Free Trade Agreement. However, his administration's plan for major health-care reform legislation died in Congress. After 1994 midterm elections, Clinton faced Republican majorities in both houses of Congress. He followed a centrist course at home, sent troops to Bosnia to help implement a peace settlement, and cultivated relations with Russia and China.

Though accused of improprieties in his involvement in the Whitewater Development Corp., an Arkansas land-development venture, Clinton won reelection with 49% of the vote in 1996. Independent prosecutor Kenneth Starr did not find substantial and credible evidence of impeachable wrongdoing by the Clintons. He submitted a report to Congress, however, providing evidence of an affair between Clinton and former White House intern Monica Lewinsky. In 1998, Clinton became only the 2nd U.S. president to be impeached by the House of Representatives. He was charged with perjury and obstruction of justice in connection with his attempted cover-up of the affair but was acquitted by the Senate the following year. He retained wide popularity, aided by a strong economy.

In 1999 the United States joined other NATO nations in an aerial bombing campaign that induced Serbia to withdraw troops from Kosovo, where they had been terrorizing ethnic Albanians. In 2000 he became the first president since the Vietnam War to visit Vietnam. On Clinton's last full day in office, Starr's successor as independent counsel agreed to conclude the Whitewater investigation. As part of the deal, Clinton acknowledged giving false testimony about his affair with Lewinsky, gave up his law license for 5 years, and paid a $25,000 fine.

After leaving office, Clinton remained active in public life, starting the Clinton Global Initiative in 2005, and promoted his wife's career. Hillary Clinton was elected in 2000 to the U.S. Senate from New York; reelected in 2006, she ran unsuccessfully for the 2008 Democratic presidential nomination. In 2009, she became secretary of state under her former rival Barack Obama.

George Walker Bush (2001-09),
43rd president, Republican, was born on July 6, 1946, in New Haven, CT. He was the first of six children born to George Herbert Walker Bush and his wife, the former Barbara Pierce, a close collateral descendant of Pres. Franklin Pierce. Bush was the first son of a former president to win the White House since John Quincy Adams took office in 1825.

Bush grew up in Midland and Houston, TX, and attended Andover Prep in Massachusetts. In 1968 he graduated from Yale; eligible for the draft and possible Vietnam service, he fulfilled his military service requirement with the Texas Air National Guard. After earning a master's degree from Harvard Business School, he returned to Midland in 1975 and went into the oil business. Two years later he married Laura Welch, a librarian; in 1981 she gave birth to twin daughters, Barbara and Jenna. Bush lost a race for Congress in 1978 and returned to the oil business, but success proved elusive. After aiding in his father's successful 1988 presidential campaign, he became managing partner of the Texas Rangers baseball team. Bush ran for governor in 1994, defeating popular incumbent Ann Richards. He won reelection by a landslide in 1998.

Campaigning as a "compassionate conservative" in 2000, Bush won the Republican presidential nomination and, with running mate Dick Cheney, defeated the Democratic ticket led by Al Gore in one of the closest-ever U.S. presidential elections. The victory was not sealed until a mid-Dec. ruling by the U.S. Supreme Court left Florida's crucial electoral votes in Bush's column.

In May 2001, Bush won approval from Congress for a major tax cut package projected to amount to $1.35 tril over the next decade. After the Sept. 11, 2001, terrorist attacks, Bush's presidency was transformed as he declared a "war against terrorism." By Dec. the U.S. military, aided by forces from other nations, had deposed Afghanistan's Taliban regime, which was sheltering al-Qaeda terrorists. The new Afghan government was weak, however, and unable to maintain control over much of the countryside. In March 2003, the U.S., aided mainly by UK military forces, launched an air and ground war against Iraq and deposed Saddam Hussein. However, no evidence was found that his regime had developed weapons of mass destruction, the key rationale for the war. A new Iraqi government was formed in June 2004, but insurgent violence and U.S. troop casualties continued.

Bush was reelected in Nov. 2004 with 51% of the popular vote, but his popularity declined in his 2nd term. His push for Social Security reform, a key initiative, failed in Congress, and his administration was criticized for its response to Hurricane Katrina, which devastated New Orleans and the Gulf Coast in Aug.-Sept. 2005. He also failed to win passage of a broad immigration proposal for granting legal status to many illegal immigrants. But the Senate confirmed his nominees for chief justice and associate justice of the Supreme Court, John G. Roberts Jr., 2005, and Samuel A. Alito Jr., 2006. In 2006, he exercised his veto for the first time, preventing legislation that would have eased restrictions on federal funding for stem cell research.

After Democrats won majorities in House and Senate 2006 midterm elections, Bush accepted the resignation of Defense Sec. Donald Rumsfeld, a target of widespread criticism over the Iraq war. Two months later, he announced a "surge" in U.S. troop strength in Iraq, from around 130,000 to 160,000 by mid-2007. A sharp drop in casualties ensued, aided also by a shift in alliances. But the Taliban was gaining strength in Afghanistan and Pakistan. The administration was also damaged by revelations of prisoner abuse by some, and attracted controversy after memos that had given legal sanction to extreme interrogation methods surfaced. U.S. military deaths in Iraq passed the 4,000 mark in Mar. 2008. North Korea emerged as an increasing threat, announcing that it would resume operations at its main nuclear reactor.

The U.S. economy fell into recession in Dec. 2007; Bush and congressional leaders responded in Feb. 2008 with a $168 billion stimulus plan that provided rebates for taxpayers. The cost of oil passed $140 a barrel and gas prices passed $4 a gallon in summer 2008. Problems in home finance and credit markets triggered a deeper crisis in Sept. The Treasury Dept. announced a bailout of mortgage finance firms Fannie Mae and Freddie Mac. Lehman Bros. filed for bankruptcy, while the Fed rescued insurance giant AIG with a line of credit reaching $144 billion. A Bush administration-backed plan to buy up to $700 billion in devalued mortgage-related assets, opposed by many Republicans and rejected by Congress in late Sept., cleared Congress Oct. 3, after a severe stock market plunge bolstered support. The economic crisis added to Bush's unpopularity and contributed to the Nov. defeat of GOP presidential candidate Sen. John McCain (AZ).

Barack Hussein Obama (2009-), 44th president, Democrat, was born Aug. 4, 1961, in Honolulu, HI. Barack Obama Sr., Obama's father, was a black Kenyan, and Stanley Ann Dunham, his mother, a white American from Kansas. By the time Obama was 6, his parents had divorced and his mother had married an Indonesian man and moved to Indonesia. Returning to Hawaii, he lived with his grandparents while attending high school. He received a bachelor's degree (1983) from Columbia Univ., worked from the mid-1980s as a community organizer in impoverished areas of Chicago's South Side, and earned a law degree (1991) from Harvard Univ., where he was elected the first African American president of the Harvard Law Review. He then practiced civil rights law in Chicago and taught at the Univ. of Chicago Law School. In 1992, he married attorney and later hospital administrator Michelle Robinson (1964-). They have 2 daughters, Malia (1998-) and Natasha (Sasha) (2001-).

Obama won election to the Illinois state senate in 1996 and was twice reelected. He failed to capture the Democratic nomination for a U.S. House seat in 2000, but took 53% of the vote in a 7-candidate primary to win nomination for a U.S. Senate seat in Mar. 2004. Obama was already known to many through his 1995 memoir, *Dreams From My Father: A Story of Race and Inheritance*, and he gained national attention when he delivered the keynote address at the Democratic National Convention in July 2004. He earned 70% of the vote in Nov. to defeat conservative radio talk show host Alan Keyes, also an African American. Obama became the lone African American in the Senate, and only the 3rd since Reconstruction. His 2nd book, *The Audacity of Hope: Thoughts on Reclaiming the American Dream* (2006), rose to the top of best-seller lists.

In early 2007 Obama announced his candidacy for the 2008 Democratic presidential nomination. He stressed his long-standing opposition to the Iraq war and a determination to bring change to Washington, and used the Internet as a key means to raise funds and gather supporters, especially among young voters. He gained momentum with a 1st-place finish in the Jan. 2008 Iowa caucuses, ahead of the former First Lady and expected front-runner Sen. Hillary Clinton (NY), among others. Though he came in 2nd to Clinton in the New Hampshire primary, Obama rebounded to win in South Carolina. With the withdrawal of other rivals, Obama competed head to head with Clinton on "Super Tuesday," Feb. 5, emerging with a slight lead in pledged delegates. He went on to win a string of 11 caucuses and primaries. In Mar., videos were circulated of his longtime former pastor, the Rev. Jeremiah Wright, an African American, making inflammatory racial statements; Obama responded with a well-received speech on race relations, in which he condemned Wright's rhetoric. He later cut ties with the Chicago clergyman. Although Obama lost some later primaries to Clinton by large margins, he had a clear majority of delegates and superdelegates by the end of primary season. He was nominated at the party convention in Aug., becoming the 1st African American presidential candidate of a major American political party. His choice for vice president, Sen. Joe Biden (DE), was nominated as his running mate.

In the fall campaign, Republican presidential nominee Sen. John McCain (AZ) and his vice-presidential pick, Alaska Gov. Sarah Palin, portrayed Obama as inexperienced and devoted to higher taxes and big government. Obama drew strength from an exceptionally smooth-running campaign organization and fundraising apparatus, the unpopularity of the Iraq war and Republican Pres. George W. Bush, and an economic crisis that came to dominate the campaign. He won the election on Nov. 4, with 53% of the vote, the biggest proportion for a Democratic national ticket in 44 years.

Obama acted quickly as president-elect to promise an economic stimulus package and name an economic team, announcing Timothy Geithner as his choice for treasury secretary. He named former rival Hillary Clinton to be secretary of state and said he would retain Robert Gates as defense secretary. While most of his cabinet choices were easily confirmed, former Sen. Tom Daschle (SD), Obama's 1st choice for secretary of health and human services, withdrew his name after revelations of unpaid back taxes

Obama was inaugurated Jan. 20, 2009, becoming the first African American president. He promptly issued orders to promote transparency in government, lift restrictions on federal funding for programs abroad providing abortion services or counseling, and reverse Bush-era policies on interrogation of detainees suspected of terrorism. In particular, he mandated that the U.S. military detention facility at Guantánamo Bay be closed within a year. While vowing that the U.S. "will not torture" detainees, he sought to reassure the intelligence community that interrogators who had acted under past guidelines would not be penalized, but his attorney general, Eric Holder, named a special prosecutor to probe cases of possible prisoner abuse.

The administration won passage Feb. 13 of a $787 bil economic stimulus package providing for tax cuts and some $575 bil in new spending, although it did not receive significant bipartisan support as sought by Obama. The administration also unveiled a $2 tril financial rescue plan and won congressional approval for a $3.4 tril fiscal 2010 budget plan that expanded spending in key areas and increased taxes on the wealthy. An administration task force rejected proposed rescue plans by General Motors and Chrysler, leaving these automakers to file for bankruptcy. While the economy continued to shed jobs, the stock market made rebounds, aided by optimism that the economy might recover before long. But Obama had difficulty gaining momentum in Congress for a major health reform program.

In Feb. 2009 Obama announced an Iraq withdrawal plan under which most U.S. troops would remain through 2009, with all combat troops leaving by Aug. 2010. He called for narrower U.S. goals but increased U.S. troop strength in Afghanistan, where troop and civilian casualties continued to rise. Obama made overtures to improve relations with the Muslim world and with the nation of Iran, but progress appeared difficult. He achieved an important victory at home when Sonia Sotomayor, his nominee to replace retiring Supreme Court Justice David Souter, was confirmed in Aug. 2009 in a 68-31 Senate vote.

Wives and Children of the Presidents

Name (born-died; married)	State	Sons/daughters	Name (born-died; married)	State	Sons/daughters
Martha Dandridge Custis Washington (1731-1802; 1759)	VA	None	Mary Scott Lord Dimmick Harrison (1858-1948; 1896)	PA	0/1
Abigail Smith Adams (1744-1818; 1764)	MA	3/2	Ida Saxton McKinley (1847-1907; 1871)	OH	0/2
Martha Wayles Skelton Jefferson (1748-82; 1772)	VA	1/5	Alice Hathaway Lee Roosevelt (1861-84; 1880)	MA	0/1
Dolley Payne Todd Madison (1768-1849; 1794)	NC	None	Edith Kermit Carow Roosevelt (1861-1948; 1886)	CT	4/1
Elizabeth Kortright Monroe (1768-1830; 1786)	NY	1/2	Helen Herron Taft (1861-1943; 1886)	OH	2/1
Louisa Catherine Johnson Adams (1775-1852; 1797)	MD[1]	3/1	Ellen Louise Axson Wilson (1860-1914; 1885)	GA	0/3
Rachel Donelson Robards Jackson (1767-1828; 1791)	VA	1[2]	Edith Bolling Galt Wilson (1872-1961; 1915)	VA	None
Hannah Hoes Van Buren (1783-1819; 1807)	NY	4/0	Florence Kling De Wolfe Harding (1860-1924; 1891)	OH	None
Anna Tuthill Symmes Harrison (1775-1864; 1795)	NJ	6/4	Grace Anna Goodhue Coolidge (1879-1957; 1905)	VT	2/0
Letitia Christian Tyler (1790-1842; 1813)	VA	3/5	Lou Henry Hoover (1875-1944; 1899)	IA	2/0
Julia Gardiner Tyler (1820-89; 1844)	NY	5/2	Anna Eleanor Roosevelt (1884-1962; 1905)	NY	5/1
Sarah Childress Polk (1803-91; 1824)	TN	None	Elizabeth Virginia (Bess) Wallace Truman (1885-1982; 1919)	MO	0/1
Margaret (Peggy) Mackall Smith Taylor (1788-1852; 1810)	MD	1/5	Mamie Geneva Doud Eisenhower (1896-1979; 1916)	IA	2/0
Abigail Powers Fillmore (1798-1853; 1826)	NY	1/1	Jacqueline Lee Bouvier Kennedy (1929-94; 1953)	NY	2/1
Caroline Carmichael McIntosh Fillmore (1813-81; 1858)	NJ	None	Claudia (Lady Bird) Alta Taylor Johnson (1912-2007; 1934)	TX	0/2
Jane Means Appleton Pierce (1806-63; 1834)	NH	3/0	Thelma Catherine Patricia Ryan Nixon (1912-93; 1940)	NV	0/2
Mary Todd Lincoln (1818-82; 1842)	KY	4/0	Elizabeth (Betty) Bloomer Warren Ford (1918; 1948)	IL	3/1
Eliza McCardle Johnson (1810-76; 1827)	TN	3/2	Eleanor Rosalynn Smith Carter (1927; 1946)	GA	3/1
Julia Boggs Dent Grant (1826-1902; 1848)	MO	3/1	Anne Frances (Nancy) Robbins Davis Reagan (1921; 1952)	NY	1/1[3]
Lucy Ware Webb Hayes (1831-89; 1852)	OH	7/1	Barbara Pierce Bush (1925; 1945)	NY	4/2
Lucretia Rudolph Garfield (1832-1918; 1858)	OH	5/2	Hillary Diane Rodham Clinton (1947; 1975)	IL	0/1
Ellen Lewis Herndon Arthur (1837-80; 1859)	VA	2/1	Laura Lane Welch Bush (1946; 1977)	TX	0/2
Frances Folsom Cleveland (1864-1947; 1886)	NY	2/3	Michelle LaVaughn Robinson Obama (1964; 1992)	IL	0/2
Caroline Lavinia Scott Harrison (1832-92; 1853)	OH	1/1			

Note: Pres. Buchanan was unmarried. (1) Born in London, father a MD citizen. (2) Adopted son. (3) Pres. Reagan's first wife, whom he later divorced, was Jane Wyman. They had a daughter who died in infancy, a daughter who lived past infancy, and an adopted son.

First Lady Michelle Obama

Michelle Robinson Obama was born in Chicago, IL, Jan. 17, 1964. She graduated from Princeton University, 1985, earned a law degree from Harvard University, 1988, and joined Chicago law firm Sidley & Austin. She served as assistant commissioner of planning and development for Chicago, then as founding executive director of the Chicago chapter of Public Allies, an AmeriCorps program. She began working for the Univ. of Chicago in 1996, first as associate dean of student services, then as the Univ. of Chicago Medical Center's VP of community and external affairs. Michelle and Barack Obama were married in 1992; in 1998, their daughter Malia was born, followed by Natasha (Sasha) in 2001.

As First Lady, Michelle Obama planned to focus on issues related to supporting military families, helping women balance career and family, and encouraging national service.

Burial Places of the Presidents

President	Burial place	President	Burial place	President	Burial place
Washington	Mt. Vernon, VA	Pierce	Concord, NH	Wilson	Wash. Natl. Cathedral, DC
J. Adams	Quincy, MA	Buchanan	Lancaster, PA	Harding	Marion, OH
Jefferson	Charlottesville, VA	Lincoln	Springfield, IL	Coolidge	Plymouth Notch, VT
Madison	Montpelier Station, VA	A. Johnson	Greeneville, TN	Hoover	West Branch, IA
Monroe	Richmond, VA	Grant	New York, NY	F. Roosevelt	Hyde Park, NY
J. Q. Adams	Quincy, MA	Hayes	Fremont, OH	Truman	Independence, MO
Jackson	Nashville, TN	Garfield	Cleveland, OH	Eisenhower	Abilene, KS
Van Buren	Kinderhook, NY	Arthur	Albany, NY	Kennedy	Arlington Natl. Cem., VA
W. H. Harrison	North Bend, OH	Cleveland	Princeton, NJ	L. B. Johnson	Stonewall, TX
Tyler	Richmond, VA	B. Harrison	Indianapolis, IN	Nixon	Yorba Linda, CA
Polk	Nashville, TN	McKinley	Canton, OH	Ford	Grand Rapids, MI
Taylor	Louisville, KY	T. Roosevelt	Oyster Bay, NY	Reagan	Simi Valley, CA
Fillmore	Buffalo, NY	Taft	Arlington Natl. Cem., VA		

Presidential Facts

Oldest president: Ronald Reagan, who was 77 when he left office

Youngest president: Theodore Roosevelt, who was 42 when sworn in after McKinley's death

Youngest person elected president: John F. Kennedy, who was 43 when elected in 1960

Tallest president: Abraham Lincoln, who was 6 feet, 4 inches

Shortest president: James Madison, who was 5 feet, 4 inches

Heaviest president: William Howard Taft, who was 332 pounds in 1911

First president to live in the White House: John Adams, who moved there in 1800

First president inaugurated in Washington, DC: Thomas Jefferson, in 1801

First president whose parents were immigrants: Andrew Jackson; his parents immigrated from Ireland in 1765

First president born a U.S. citizen: Martin Van Buren, in Kinderhook, NY, 1782

First president born outside the original colonies: Abraham Lincoln, in Kentucky, 1809

Most common presidential home state: Virginia, with 8 presidents

First president of all 50 states: Dwight D. Eisenhower, first inaugurated in 1953

First president born in the 20th century: John F. Kennedy, in 1917

First president to be photographed while in office: James K. Polk, in 1849

First president to have a telephone in the White House: Rutherford B. Hayes, in 1879

First president to address the nation on radio: Warren G. Harding, in 1922

First president to appear on TV: Franklin D. Roosevelt, at opening ceremonies for the 1939 World's Fair

First president to give a live, televised news conference: John F. Kennedy, in 1961

First president to hold an Internet chat: Bill Clinton, in 1999

Only presidents who lost the popular vote while winning election: John Quincy Adams, in 1824 (elected by the House after general election failed to produce a majority); Rutherford B. Hayes, in 1876; Benjamin Harrison, in 1888; George W. Bush, in 2000. Popular vote totals before 1824 are unknown.

Only presidents chosen by the House of Representatives: Thomas Jefferson (1st term) and John Quincy Adams

Most common Alma Mater (undergraduate): Harvard, with 5 presidents

Only left-handed presidents: James Garfield, Herbert Hoover, Harry Truman, Gerald Ford, Ronald Reagan, George H. W. Bush, Bill Clinton, and Barack Obama

Only Catholic elected president: John F. Kennedy; the most common religious affiliations have been Episcopalian (11) and Presbyterian (7)

Only bachelor presidents: James Buchanan, who never married, and Grover Cleveland, who married Frances Folsom in the White House in 1886

Only divorced president: Ronald Reagan; divorced from actress Jane Wyman in 1948, married Nancy Davis in 1952

Presidents who died on July 4: John Adams and Thomas Jefferson (both 1826) and James Monroe (1831)

Only president buried in Washington, DC: Woodrow Wilson, who was interred at the Washington National Cathedral

Presidential Libraries

Presidential libraries are coordinated by the National Archives and Records Administration (www.archives.gov/presidential-libraries). Materials for presidents before Herbert Hoover are held by private institutions.

Herbert Hoover Library and Museum
210 Parkside Dr.
West Branch, IA 52358
PHONE: 319-643-5301
E-MAIL: hoover.library@nara.gov
WEBSITE: hoover.archives.gov

Franklin D. Roosevelt Library and Museum
4079 Albany Post Rd.
Hyde Park, NY 12538-1990
PHONE: 800-FDR-VISIT
E-MAIL: roosevelt.library@nara.gov
WEBSITE: www.fdrlibrary.marist.edu

Harry S. Truman Library and Museum
500 West U.S. Hwy. 24
Independence, MO 64050-2481
PHONE: 800-833-1225
E-MAIL: truman.library@nara.gov
WEBSITE: www.trumanlibrary.org

Dwight D. Eisenhower Library
200 SE 4th St.
Abilene, KS 67410-2900
PHONE: 877-RING-IKE
E-MAIL: eisenhower.library@nara.gov
WEBSITE: eisenhower.archives.gov

John F. Kennedy Library and Museum
Columbia Pt.
Boston, MA 02125-3312
PHONE: 866-JFK-1960
E-MAIL: kennedy.library@nara.gov
WEBSITE: www.jfklibrary.org

Lyndon Baines Johnson Library and Museum
2313 Red River St.
Austin, TX 78705-5737
PHONE: 512-721-0200
E-MAIL: johnson.library@nara.gov
WEBSITE: www.lbjlib.utexas.edu

Richard Nixon Library and Museum
18001 Yorba Linda Blvd.
Yorba Linda, CA 92886-3903
714-983-9120
E-MAIL: nixon@nara.gov
WEBSITE: www.nixonarchives.gov
MD OFFICE: Natl. Archives at College Park
8601 Adelphi Rd.
College Park, MD 20740-6001
PHONE: 301-837-3290

Gerald R. Ford Library and Museum
LIBRARY: 1000 Beal Ave.
Ann Arbor, MI 48109-2109
PHONE: 734-205-0555
MUSEUM: 303 Pearl St. NW

Grand Rapids, MI 49504-5353
PHONE: 616-254-0400
E-MAIL: ford.library@nara.gov
WEBSITE: www.fordlibrarymuseum.gov

Jimmy Carter Library and Museum
441 Freedom Pkwy.
Atlanta, GA 30307-1498
PHONE: 404-865-7100
E-MAIL: carter.library@nara.gov
WEBSITE: www.jimmycarterlibrary.gov

Ronald Reagan Library and Museum
40 Presidential Dr.
Simi Valley, CA 93065-0600
PHONE: 800-410-8354
E-MAIL: reagan.library@nara.gov
WEBSITE: www.reagan.utexas.edu

George Bush Library and Museum
1000 George Bush Dr. West
College Station, TX 77845
PHONE: 979-691-4000
E-MAIL: library.bush@nara.gov
WEBSITE: bushlibrary.tamu.edu

William J. Clinton Library and Museum
1200 President Clinton Ave.
Little Rock, AR 72201
PHONE: 501-374-4242
E-MAIL: clinton.library@nara.gov
WEBSITE: www.clintonlibrary.gov

Presidential Impeachment in U.S. History

The U.S. Constitution provides for impeachment and removal from office of federal officials on grounds of "Treason, Bribery, or other high Crimes and Misdemeanors" (Article II, Sect. 4). Impeachment is the bringing of charges by the House of Representatives. It is followed by a Senate trial; a two-thirds majority vote of Senators present is needed for conviction and removal from office.

In 1868, **Andrew Johnson** became the first president impeached by the House, for his removal of Sec. of War Edwin

M. Stanton without first notifying the Senate. He was tried but not convicted. In 1974, impeachment articles against Pres. **Richard Nixon**, in connection with the Watergate scandal, were adopted by the House Judiciary Committee. He resigned Aug. 9, and the House accepted the committee report without taking further action. In 1998, Pres. **Bill Clinton** was impeached by the House in connection with covering up a sexual relationship with former White House intern Monica Lewinsky. He was tried in the Senate in 1999 and acquitted.

PRESIDENTIAL ELECTIONS

Electoral and Popular Vote, 2008 and 2004

Source: Federal Election Commission

State	2008 Electoral Vote Obama	2008 Electoral Vote McCain	2008 Electoral Vote Nader	Democrat Obama	Republican McCain	Indep.[1] Nader	2004 Electoral Vote Kerry	2004 Electoral Vote Bush	2004 Electoral Vote Nader	Democrat Kerry	Republican Bush	Indep.[1] Nader	State
AL	0	9	0	813,479	1,266,546	6,788	0	9	0	691,830	1,174,278	6,777	AL
AK	0	3	0	123,594	193,841	3,783	0	3	0	85,819	151,498	3,884	AK
AZ	0	10	0	1,034,707	1,230,111	11,301	0	10	—	724,589	905,379	—	AZ
AR	0	6	0	422,310	638,017	12,882	0	6	0	464,156	566,676	6,031	AR
CA	55	0	0	8,274,473	5,011,781	108,381	55	0	—	5,427,055	4,403,495	—	CA
CO	9	0	0	1,288,633	1,073,629	13,352	0	9	0	898,566	1,017,322	11,426	CO
CT	7	0	0	997,772	629,428	19,162	7	0	0	847,666	686,923	12,708	CT
DE	3	0	0	255,459	152,374	2,401	3	0	0	199,887	171,531	2,151	DE
DC	3	0	0	245,800	17,367	958	3	0	0	183,876	19,007	1,318	DC
FL	27	0	0	4,282,074	4,045,624	28,124	0	27	0	3,460,923	3,838,432	32,048	FL
GA	0	15	—	1,844,123	2,048,759	1,158	0	15	—	1,302,703	1,867,988	—	GA
HI	4	0	0	325,871	120,566	3,825	4	0	—	231,318	194,109	—	HI
ID	0	4	0	236,440	403,012	7,175	0	4	—	180,920	408,254	—	ID
IL	21	0	0	3,419,348	2,031,179	30,948	21	0	—	2,826,757	2,313,415	—	IL
IN	11	0	—	1,374,039	1,345,648	909	0	11	—	960,899	1,474,475	—	IN
IA	7	0	0	828,940	682,379	8,014	0	7	0	732,483	745,734	5,806	IA
KS	0	6	0	514,765	699,655	10,527	0	6	0	416,905	711,083	8,955	KS
KY	0	8	0	751,985	1,048,462	15,378	0	8	0	709,072	1,064,504	8,807	KY
LA	0	9	0	782,989	1,148,275	6,997	0	9	0	818,211	1,101,710	7,015	LA
ME	4	0	0	421,923	295,273	10,636	4	0	0	364,153	308,997	7,476	ME
MD	10	0	0	1,629,467	959,862	14,713	10	0	0	1,209,827	936,505	10,573	MD
MA	12	0	0	1,904,097	1,108,854	28,841	12	0	—	1,793,916	1,067,163	—	MA
MI	17	0	0	2,872,579	2,048,639	33,085	17	0	0	2,471,402	2,306,259	23,914	MI
MN	10	0	0	1,573,354	1,275,409	30,152	10	0	0	1,443,564	1,345,168	18,537	MN
MS	0	6	0	554,662	724,597	4,011	0	6	0	435,584	657,920	2,995	MS
MO	0	11	0	1,441,911	1,445,814	17,813	0	11	—	1,253,879	1,452,715	—	MO
MT	0	3	0	231,667	242,763	3,686	0	3	0	170,172	261,939	6,074	MT
NE[2]	1	4	0	333,319	452,979	5,406	0	5	0	234,303	486,025	5,292	NE[2]
NV	5	0	0	533,736	412,827	6,150	0	5	0	393,372	414,939	4,785	NV
NH	4	0	0	384,826	316,534	3,503	4	0	0	340,019	330,848	4,447	NH
NJ	15	0	0	2,215,422	1,613,207	21,298	15	0	0	1,799,320	1,587,494	18,614	NJ
NM	5	0	0	472,422	346,832	5,327	0	5	0	353,788	364,569	3,898	NM
NY	31	0	0	4,804,945	2,752,771	41,249	31	0	0	3,967,047	2,780,749	103,310	NY
NC	15	0	—	2,142,651	2,128,474	1,448	0	15	0	1,488,278	1,919,903	—	NC
ND	0	3	0	141,278	168,601	4,189	0	3	0	110,662	195,998	3,741	ND
OH	20	0	0	2,940,044	2,677,820	42,337	0	20	—	2,659,664	2,796,147	—	OH
OK	0	7	—	502,496	960,165	—	0	7	—	504,077	959,655	—	OK
OR	7	0	0	1,037,291	738,475	18,614	7	0	—	888,544	818,792	—	OR
PA	21	0	0	3,276,363	2,655,885	42,977	21	0	—	2,877,351	2,754,689	—	PA
RI	4	0	0	296,571	165,391	4,829	4	0	0	247,071	161,345	3,976	RI
SC	0	8	0	862,449	1,034,896	5,053	0	8	0	647,998	920,321	5,410	SC
SD	0	3	0	170,924	203,054	4,267	0	3	0	149,225	232,545	4,317	SD
TN	0	11	0	1,087,437	1,479,178	11,560	0	11	0	1,033,030	1,381,852	8,832	TN
TX	0	34	—	3,528,633	4,479,328	5,751	0	34	—	2,816,501	4,495,797	—	TX
UT	0	5	0	327,670	596,030	8,416	0	5	0	226,456	608,851	10,815	UT
VT	3	0	0	219,262	98,974	3,339	3	0	0	183,621	120,710	4,426	VT
VA	13	0	0	1,959,532	1,725,005	11,483	0	13	—	1,396,233	1,662,439	—	VA
WA	11	0	0	1,750,848	1,229,216	29,489	11	0	0	1,068,762	921,543	14,704	WA
WV	0	5	0	303,857	397,466	7,219	0	5	0	321,641	418,151	3,951	WV
WI	10	0	0	1,677,211	1,262,393	17,605	10	0	0	1,488,935	1,477,122	16,324	WI
WY	0	3	0	82,868	164,958	2,525	0	3	0	70,620	167,129	2,734	WY
Total	**365**	**173**	**0**	**69,498,516**	**59,948,323**	**739,034**	**252**	**286**	**0**	**55,572,650**	**59,130,092**	**396,071**	**Total**

(—) = Not listed on state's ballot. (1) Listed on the ballot in some states as particular party. (2) Nebraska is one of two states (the other is Maine) that may split its electoral votes between candidates.

2008 Presidential Popular Vote

Candidate (Party)	Vote total	Percent of vote
Barack Obama (Democrat)	69,498,516	52.93%
John McCain (Republican)	59,948,323	45.65
Ralph Nader (Independent, Peace and Freedom)	739,034	0.56
Bob Barr (Libertarian)	523,715	0.40
Chuck Baldwin (Constitution/Reform/ U.S. Taxpayers)	199,750	0.15
Cynthia McKinney (Green, Independent, Mountain)	161,797	0.12
Alan Keyes (America's Independent)	47,746	0.04
Ron Paul (Constitution, Louisiana Taxpayers)	42,426	0.03
Gloria La Riva (Socialism and Liberation)	6,818	0.01
Brian Moore (Liberty Union, Socialist)	6,538	<0.01
Róger Calero (Socialist Workers)	5,151	<0.01
Richard Duncan (Independent)	3,905	<0.01
James Harris (Socialist Workers)	2,424	<0.01

Candidate (Party)	Vote total	Percent of vote
Charles Jay (Boston Tea Party/ Independent)	2,422	<0.01%
John Joseph Polachek (New)	1,149	<0.01
Frank Edward McEnulty (Unaffiliated)	829	<0.01
Jeffrey J. Wamboldt (Independent)	764	<0.01
Thomas Robert Stevens (Objectivist)	755	<0.01
Gene C. Amondson (Prohibition)	653	<0.01
Jeffrey "Jeff" Boss (Vote Here)	639	<0.01
George Phillies (Libertarian)	531	<0.01
Ted Weill (Reform)	481	<0.01
Jonathan E. Allen (Heartquake '08)	480	<0.01
Bradford Lyttle (U.S. Pacifist)	110	<0.01
Write-In (Miscellaneous)	112,597	0.09
None of These Candidates (Nevada)	6,267	<0.01
Total votes cast	**131,313,820**	
Voting age population, Nov. 2008	225,499,000	
Percentage casting vote for president		58.23%

Note: Party designations vary from one state to another. Vote totals for the candidates listed above include any write-in votes they received.

PRESIDENTIAL ELECTION RESULTS BY STATE AND COUNTY

All results are official. Results for Connecticut, Maine, Massachusetts, and Rhode Island are for selected cities or towns. All totals statewide.

Source: Alaska district results, Alaska Div. of Elections; New Hampshire and Vermont county results, respective secretary of state's office; Alaska totals and all other state results, Federal Election Commission.

Alabama

County	2008 Obama (D)	McCain (R)	2004 Kerry (D)	Bush (R)
Autauga	6,091	17,398	4,758	15,196
Baldwin	19,362	61,192	15,599	52,971
Barbour	5,685	5,862	4,832	5,899
Bibb	2,289	6,247	2,089	5,472
Blount	3,518	20,362	3,938	17,386
Bullock	4,001	1,389	3,210	1,494
Butler	4,174	5,472	3,413	4,979
Calhoun	16,325	32,326	15,083	29,814
Chambers	6,782	8,060	5,347	7,622
Cherokee	2,299	7,285	3,040	5,923
Chilton	3,666	13,934	3,778	12,829
Choctaw	3,633	4,220	3,303	3,897
Clarke	5,907	7,455	4,627	6,730
Clay	1,722	4,946	1,893	4,624
Cleburne	1,166	5,204	1,391	4,370
Coffee	5,068	14,909	4,480	13,019
Colbert	9,698	14,729	10,598	13,188
Conecuh	3,411	3,461	2,719	3,271
Coosa	2,269	3,245	2,055	2,905
Covington	3,238	12,431	3,423	11,119
Crenshaw	1,938	4,316	1,698	3,777
Cullman	5,855	28,837	8,045	26,818
Dale	5,257	13,873	4,484	13,621
Dallas	13,958	6,791	11,175	7,335
DeKalb	5,654	17,951	7,092	16,904
Elmore	8,268	25,695	6,471	22,056
Escambia	5,176	9,365	3,814	8,513
Etowah	13,480	30,562	15,328	26,999
Fayette	1,988	5,875	2,408	5,534
Franklin	3,469	8,048	4,514	7,690
Geneva	2,106	9,314	2,113	8,342
Greene	4,402	876	3,764	958
Hale	4,969	3,196	4,631	3,281
Henry	2,990	5,558	2,452	4,881
Houston	12,194	29,205	9,144	26,874
Jackson	6,367	14,068	8,635	11,534
Jefferson	166,015	149,843	132,286	158,680
Lamar	1,614	5,419	1,956	4,894
Lauderdale	13,318	24,050	14,628	22,161
Lawrence	5,159	9,269	6,155	7,730
Lee	21,410	32,344	16,227	27,972
Limestone	9,530	23,588	9,126	19,702
Lowndes	5,447	1,807	4,233	1,786
Macon	9,444	1,396	7,800	1,570
Madison	64,062	86,910	52,644	77,173
Marengo	5,925	5,511	5,037	5,255
Marion	2,597	9,530	3,808	8,983
Marshall	7,021	25,680	8,452	22,783
Mobile	81,741	97,670	63,732	92,014
Monroe	5,023	6,173	3,666	5,831
Montgomery	61,999	41,972	45,160	44,097
Morgan	13,882	35,986	14,131	32,477
Perry	4,423	1,676	3,767	1,738
Pickens	4,584	5,426	3,915	5,170
Pike	5,856	7,981	4,334	7,483
Randolph	3,062	7,169	2,817	6,127
Russell	10,078	8,700	8,375	8,337
St. Clair	6,088	27,630	5,456	23,500
Shelby	20,575	68,945	14,850	63,435
Sumter	5,218	1,723	4,527	1,880
Talladega	13,769	20,109	11,374	18,331
Tallapoosa	6,052	13,105	5,451	12,392
Tuscaloosa	32,738	45,351	26,447	42,877
Walker	7,418	20,719	9,016	19,167
Washington	3,032	5,592	3,145	5,060
Wilcox	4,553	1,849	3,838	1,834
Winston	1,756	8,099	2,236	8,130
Totals	**813,479**	**1,266,546**	**693,933**	**1,176,394**

Alabama Vote Since 1952

2008: McCain, Rep., 1,266,546; Obama, Dem., 813,479; Nader, Ind., 6,788; Barr, Ind., 4,991; Baldwin, Ind., 4,310.

2004: Bush, R., 1,176,394; Kerry, D., 693,933; Nader, Ind., 6,701; Badnarik, Ind., 3,529; Peroutka, Ind., 1,994.

2000: Bush, R., 941,173; Gore, D., 692,611; Nader, Ind., 18,323; Buchanan, Ind., 6,351; Browne, LB., 5,893; Phillips, Ind., 775; Hagelin, Ind., 447.

1996: Dole, R., 769,044; Clinton, D., 662,165; Perot, Ind. (Ref.), 92,149; Browne, LB., 5,290; Phillips, Ind., 2,365; Hagelin, Natural Law, 1,697; Harris, Ind., 516.

1992: Bush, R., 804,283; Clinton, D., 690,080; Perot, Ind., 183,109; Marrou, LB., 5,737; Fulani, New Alliance, 2,161.

1988: Bush, R., 815,576; Dukakis, D., 549,506; Paul, Lib., 8,460; Fulani, Ind., 3,311.

1984: Reagan, R., 872,849; Mondale, D., 551,899; Bergland, LB., 9,504.

1980: Reagan, R., 654,192; Carter, D., 636,730; Anderson, Independent, 16,481; Rarick, Amer. Ind., 15,010; Clark, LB., 13,318; Bubar, Statesman, 1,743; Hall, Com., 1,629; DeBerry, Soc. Workers, 1,303; McReynolds, Socialist, 1,006; Commoner, Citizens, 517.

1976: Carter, D., 659,170; Ford, R., 504,070; Maddox, Amer. Ind., 9,198; Bubar, Proh., 6,669; Hall, Com., 1,954; MacBride, LB., 1,481.

1972: Nixon, R., 728,701; McGovern, D., 219,108 plus 37,815 Natl. Dem. Party of Alabama; Schmitz, Conservative, 11,918; Munn, Proh., 8,551.

1968: Wallace, 3rd Party, 691,425; Humphrey, D., 196,579; Nixon, R., 146,923; Munn, Proh., 4,022.

1964: Goldwater, R., 479,085; Dem. (electors unpledged), 209,848; scattered, 105.

1960: Kennedy, D., 324,050; Nixon, R., 237,981; Faubus, States' Rights, 4,367; Decker, Proh., 2,106; King, Afro-Americans, 1,485; scattered, 236.

1956: Stevenson, D., 290,844; Eisenhower, R., 195,694; Ind. electors, 20,323.

1952: Stevenson, D., 275,075; Eisenhower, R., 149,231; Hamblen, Proh., 1,814.

Alaska

District	2008 Obama (D)	McCain (R)	2004 Kerry (D)	Bush (R)
No. 1	2,957	4,149	1,949	4,522
No. 2	3,468	4,029	3,248	4,162
No. 3	5,657	2,828	4,808	3,031
No. 4	4,161	4,302	3,063	4,043
No. 5	3,339	3,426	2,974	3,674
No. 6	2,351	4,234	2,105	3,746
No. 7	4,283	6,297	3,259	5,272
No. 8	4,995	4,983	4,009	4,194
No. 9	2,805	4,141	2,232	3,909
No. 10	2,074	3,392	1,725	3,720
No. 11	1,924	7,736	1,523	6,416
No. 12	1,914	5,467	1,766	5,679
No. 13	2,800	8,432	2,325	6,489
No. 14	2,132	8,108	1,909	6,504
No. 15	2,510	8,227	2,331	6,030
No. 16	2,636	7,774	2,356	6,559
No. 17	2,645	6,621	2,190	6,366
No. 18	2,046	4,252	1,632	4,400
No. 19	3,095	4,106	2,521	4,087
No. 20	2,474	2,536	1,925	2,705
No. 21	3,647	4,837	2,917	4,836
No. 22	3,337	3,109	2,855	3,225
No. 23	4,075	2,808	3,449	2,789
No. 24	3,380	4,127	2,684	3,835
No. 25	3,233	3,042	2,837	3,062
No. 26	4,472	4,037	3,878	3,946
No. 27	3,130	5,159	2,670	4,713
No. 28	3,642	5,953	2,679	5,271
No. 29	2,684	4,127	2,058	3,874
No. 30	3,486	5,500	2,693	4,864
No. 31	3,596	6,419	2,853	5,803
No. 32	5,176	6,867	4,118	5,981
No. 33	2,089	6,571	1,879	5,523
No. 34	1,920	7,358	1,720	6,065
No. 35	4,959	4,254	3,780	4,442
No. 36	2,264	4,201	1,985	4,080
No. 37	1,868	2,661	1,587	2,591
No. 38	2,056	2,549	1,983	2,004
No. 39	2,323	2,695	1,963	2,407
No. 40	2,686	2,137	1,926	2,743
Totals	**123,594**	**193,841**	**111,025**	**190,889**

Alaska Vote Since 1960

2008: McCain, Rep., 193,841; Obama, Dem., 123,594; Nader, Ind., 3,783; Baldwin, Alaskan Independence, 1,660; Barr, Lib., 1,589.

2004: Bush, R., 190,889; Kerry, D., 111,025; Nader, Populist, 5,069; Peroutka, AK Ind., 2,092; Badnarik, LB., 1,675; Cobb, Green, 1,058.

2000: Bush, R., 167,398; Gore, D., 79,004; Nader, Green, 28,747; Buchanan, Reform, 5,192; Browne, LB., 2,636; Hagelin, Natural Law, 919; Phillips, Constitution, 596.

1996: Dole, R., 122,746; Clinton, D., 80,380; Perot, Ref., 26,333; Nader, Green, 7,597; Browne, LB., 2,276; Phillips, U.S. Taxpayers, 925; Hagelin, Natural Law, 729.

1992: Bush, R., 102,000; Clinton, D., 78,294; Perot, Ind., 73,481; Gritz, Populist/America First, 1,379; Marrou, LB., 1,378.

1988: Bush, R., 119,251; Dukakis, D., 72,584; Paul, Lib., 5,484; Fulani, New Alliance, 1,024.

1984: Reagan, R., 138,377; Mondale, D., 62,007; Bergland, LB., 6,378.

1980: Reagan, R., 86,112; Carter, D., 41,842; Clark, LB., 18,479; Anderson, Ind., 11,155; write-in, 857.
1976: Ford, R., 71,555; Carter, D., 44,058; MacBride, LB., 6,785.
1972: Nixon, R., 55,349; McGovern, D., 32,967; Schmitz, Amer., 6,903.
1968: Nixon, R., 37,600; Humphrey, D., 35,411; Wallace, 3rd Party, 10,024.
1964: Johnson, D., 44,329; Goldwater, R., 22,930.
1960: Nixon, R., 30,953; Kennedy, D., 29,809.

Arizona

County	2008		2004	
	Obama (D)	McCain (R)	Kerry (D)	Bush (R)
Apache	15,141	8,381	15,658	8,384
Cochise	18,526	28,360	17,514	26,556
Coconino	27,064	19,449	29,243	22,526
Gila	7,566	13,425	8,314	12,343
Graham	3,487	8,375	3,185	7,467
Greenlee	1,165	1,711	1,146	1,899
La Paz	1,794	3,302	1,849	3,158
Maricopa	542,206	675,027	504,849	679,455
Mohave	21,286	42,729	20,503	36,794
Navajo	14,953	19,199	14,815	17,277
Pima	191,465	168,670	193,128	171,109
Pinal	42,905	57,714	27,252	37,006
Santa Cruz	8,680	4,517	6,909	4,668
Yavapai	34,731	58,043	33,127	53,468
Yuma	17,679	23,658	16,032	22,184
Totals	**1,034,707**	**1,230,111**	**893,524**	**1,104,294**

Arizona Vote Since 1952

2008: McCain, Rep., 1,230,111; Obama, Dem., 1,034,707; Barr, Lib., 12,555; Nader, New Progressive, 11,301, McKinney, Green, 3,406.
2004: Bush, R., 1,104,294; Kerry, D., 893,524; Badnarik, LB., 11,856.
2000: Bush, R., 781,652; Gore, D., 685,341; Nader, Green, 45,645; Buchanan, R., 12,373; Smith, LB., 5,775; Hagelin, Natural Law, 1,120.
1996: Clinton, D., 653,288; Dole, R., 622,073; Perot, Ref., 112,072; Browne, LB., 14,358.
1992: Bush, R., 572,086; Clinton, D., 543,050; Perot, Ind., 353,741; Gritz, Populist/America First, 8,141; Marrou, LB., 6,759; Hagelin, Natural Law, 2,267.
1988: Bush, R., 702,541; Dukakis, D., 454,029; Paul, Lib., 13,351; Fulani, New Alliance, 1,662.
1984: Reagan, R., 681,416; Mondale, D., 333,854; Bergland, LB., 10,585.
1980: Reagan, R., 529,688; Carter, D., 246,843; Anderson, Ind., 76,952; Clark, LB., 18,784; De Berry, Soc. Workers, 1,100; Commoner, Citizens, 551; Hall, Com., 25; Griswold, Workers World, 2.
1976: Ford, R., 418,642; Carter, D., 295,602; McCarthy, Ind., 19,229; MacBride, LB., 7,647; Camejo, Soc. Workers, 928; Anderson, Amer., 564; Maddox, Amer. Ind., 85.
1972: Nixon, R., 402,812; McGovern, D., 198,540; Jenness, Soc. Workers, 30,945; Schmitz, Amer., 21,208.
1968: Nixon, R., 266,721; Humphrey, D., 170,514; Wallace, 3rd Party, 46,573; McCarthy, New Party, 2,751; Cleaver, Peace and Freedom, 217; Halstead, Soc. Workers, 85; Blomen, Soc. Labor, 75.
1964: Goldwater, R., 242,535; Johnson, D., 237,753; Hass, Soc. Labor, 482.
1960: Nixon, R., 221,241; Kennedy, D., 176,781; Hass, Soc. Labor, 469.
1956: Eisenhower, R., 176,990; Stevenson, D., 112,880; Andrews, Ind., 303.
1952: Eisenhower, R., 152,042; Stevenson, D., 108,528.

Arkansas

County	2008		2004	
	Obama (D)	McCain (R)	Kerry (D)	Bush (R)
Arkansas	2,616	4,184	3,110	3,789
Ashley	2,883	5,166	3,881	4,567
Baxter	6,531	12,841	7,129	11,128
Benton	23,412	50,855	20,756	46,571
Boone	4,429	10,559	4,640	9,793
Bradley	1,673	2,259	2,206	2,011
Calhoun	690	1,459	939	1,340
Carroll	4,160	6,070	4,161	6,184
Chicot	2,927	1,935	2,993	1,725
Clark	4,265	4,608	4,990	4,144
Clay	2,245	3,032	3,264	2,759
Cleburne	2,951	7,962	4,517	7,107
Cleveland	909	2,443	1,450	2,009
Columbia	3,496	5,711	4,108	5,729
Conway	3,144	4,687	3,982	4,009
Craighead	11,229	18,859	13,665	15,818
Crawford	5,265	14,746	6,764	13,391
Crittenden	9,361	7,420	8,277	6,930
Cross	2,580	4,393	3,135	3,864
Dallas	1,470	1,756	1,671	1,700
Desha	2,546	1,977	2,851	1,729
Drew	2,598	3,860	2,952	3,262
Faulkner	14,099	25,310	14,538	21,514
Franklin	1,868	4,407	3,008	4,181

County	2008		2004	
	Obama (D)	McCain (R)	Kerry (D)	Bush (R)
Fulton	1,818	2,700	2,370	2,522
Garland	14,987	25,011	18,040	21,734
Grant	1,562	5,022	2,524	4,205
Greene	4,541	8,578	6,564	7,237
Hempstead	2,861	4,252	3,817	3,580
Hot Spring	4,216	7,014	5,901	5,960
Howard	1,745	2,956	2,166	2,736
Independence	3,551	8,023	5,443	7,430
Izard	1,767	3,141	2,586	2,833
Jackson	2,220	3,146	3,515	2,624
Jefferson	18,272	10,614	19,675	10,218
Johnson	3,043	4,911	3,622	4,311
Lafayette	1,133	1,685	1,567	1,604
Lawrence	2,136	3,357	3,544	2,951
Lee	2,263	1,455	2,548	1,492
Lincoln	1,709	2,513	2,149	1,921
Little River	1,752	3,247	2,677	2,575
Logan	2,196	5,136	3,361	5,076
Lonoke	5,880	17,046	7,454	14,398
Madison	2,142	3,970	2,421	3,873
Marion	2,379	4,510	2,602	4,127
Miller	4,866	9,913	6,139	8,448
Mississippi	6,638	6,967	7,593	6,121
Monroe	1,505	1,602	2,049	1,586
Montgomery	1,090	2,359	1,524	2,367
Nevada	1,471	2,061	1,694	1,752
Newton	740	1,716	1,506	2,779
Ouachita	4,598	5,602	5,188	5,345
Perry	1,351	2,743	1,921	2,435
Phillips	5,687	3,094	5,642	3,161
Pike	1,087	2,727	1,310	2,013
Poinsett	2,740	4,900	4,069	3,555
Polk	1,955	5,470	2,473	5,192
Pope	5,986	15,535	7,100	13,614
Prairie	1,048	2,223	1,562	2,030
Pulaski	88,632	70,094	84,532	67,903
Randolph	2,460	3,601	3,412	3,158
St. Francis	5,371	3,910	5,684	3,815
Saline	12,657	30,842	14,153	24,864
Scott	1,052	2,790	1,473	2,514
Searcy	1,161	2,726	1,370	2,565
Sebastian	13,592	28,404	16,479	27,303
Sevier	1,254	3,052	2,035	2,516
Sharp	2,436	4,535	3,265	4,097
Stone	1,756	3,810	2,255	3,188
Union	6,177	10,657	7,071	10,502
Van Buren	2,145	4,269	3,310	3,988
Washington	28,965	37,915	27,597	35,726
White	6,708	19,429	9,129	17,001
Woodruff	1,350	1,135	1,972	1,021
Yell	2,001	3,805	2,913	3,678
Totals	**422,310**	**638,017**	**469,953**	**572,898**

Arkansas Vote Since 1952

2008: McCain, Rep., 638,017; Obama, Dem., 422,310; Nader, Ind., 12,882; Barr, Lib., 4,776; Baldwin, Const., 4,023; McKinney, Green, 3,470; LaRiva, Socialism/Liberation, 1,139.
2004: Bush, R., 572,898; Kerry, D., 469,953; Nader, Populist, 6,171; Badnarik, LB., 2,352; Peroutka, Constitution, 2,083; Cobb, Green, 1,488.
2000: Bush, R., 472,940; Gore, D., 422,768; Nader, Green, 13,421; Buchanan, Reform, 7,358; Browne, LB., 2,781; Phillips, Constitution, 1,415; Hagelin, Natural Law, 1,098.
1996: Clinton, D., 475,171; Dole, R., 325,416; Perot, Ref., 69,884; Nader, Ind., 3,649; Browne, Ind., 3,076; Phillips, Ind., 2,065; Forbes, Ind., 932; Collins, Ind., 823; Masters, Ind., 749; Moorehead, Ind., 747; Hagelin, Ind., 729; Hollis, Ind., 538; Dodge, Ind., 483.
1992: Clinton, D., 505,823; Bush, R., 337,324; Perot, Ind., 99,132; Phillips, U.S. Taxpayers, 1,437; Marrou, LB., 1,261; Fulani, New Alliance, 1,022.
1988: Bush, R., 466,578; Dukakis, D., 349,237; Duke, Chr. Pop., 5,146; Paul, Lib., 3,297.
1984: Reagan, R., 534,774; Mondale, D., 338,646; Bergland, LB., 2,220.
1980: Reagan, R., 403,164; Carter, D., 398,041; Anderson, Ind., 22,468; Clark, LB., 8,970; Commoner, Citizens, 2,345; Bubar, Statesman, 1,350; Hall, Com., 1,244.
1976: Carter, D., 498,604; Ford, R., 267,903; McCarthy, Ind., 639; Anderson, Amer., 389.
1972: Nixon, R., 445,751; McGovern, D., 198,899; Schmitz, Amer., 3,016.
1968: Wallace, 3rd Party, 235,627; Nixon, R., 189,062; Humphrey, D., 184,901.
1964: Johnson, D., 314,197; Goldwater, R., 243,264; Kasper, Natl. States' Rights, 2,965.
1960: Kennedy, D., 215,049; Nixon, R., 184,508; Faubus, Natl. States' Rights, 28,952.
1956: Stevenson, D., 213,277; Eisenhower, R., 186,287; Andrews, Ind., 7,008.
1952: Stevenson, D., 226,300; Eisenhower, R., 177,155; Hamblen, Proh., 886; MacArthur, Christian Nat., 458; Hass, Soc. Labor, 1.

California

County	2008		2004	
	Obama (D)	McCain (R)	Kerry (D)	Bush (R)
Alameda	489,102	119,553	422,585	130,911
Alpine	422	252	373	311
Amador	7,813	10,561	6,541	11,107
Butte	41,474	39,954	42,448	51,662
Calaveras	8,464	10,979	8,286	13,601
Colusa	2,206	3,273	1,947	4,142
Contra Costa	292,620	132,215	257,254	150,608
Del Norte	3,869	4,429	3,892	5,356
El Dorado	39,442	49,349	32,242	52,878
Fresno	127,093	124,990	103,154	141,988
Glenn	3,693	5,874	2,995	6,308
Humboldt	30,807	16,704	37,988	25,714
Imperial	17,791	10,850	17,964	15,890
Inyo	3,208	3,833	3,350	5,091
Kern	87,806	129,290	68,603	140,417
Kings	14,747	19,710	10,833	21,003
Lake	11,986	8,034	13,141	11,093
Lassen	3,586	7,483	3,158	8,126
Los Angeles	2,162,842	915,763	1,907,736	1,076,225
Madera	14,997	20,251	13,481	24,871
Marin	101,638	26,912	99,070	34,378
Mariposa	3,766	4,880	3,251	5,215
Mendocino	15,963	6,256	24,385	12,955
Merced	34,031	28,704	24,491	32,773
Modoc	1,311	2,980	1,149	3,235
Mono	2,827	2,159	2,628	2,621
Monterey	81,282	36,364	75,241	47,838
Napa	38,703	19,413	33,666	22,059
Nevada	28,037	25,211	24,220	28,790
Orange	527,334	562,211	419,239	641,832
Placer	64,460	80,209	55,573	95,969
Plumas	4,715	6,039	4,129	6,905
Riverside	210,905	197,517	228,806	322,473
Sacramento	293,516	202,433	236,657	235,539
San Benito	11,413	7,167	9,851	8,698
San Bernardino	291,717	263,044	227,789	289,306
San Diego	653,037	531,732	526,437	596,033
San Francisco	311,714	51,070	296,772	54,355
San Joaquin	105,932	87,279	87,012	100,978
San Luis Obispo	66,978	60,253	58,742	67,995
San Mateo	222,767	75,006	197,922	83,315
Santa Barbara	102,424	64,508	90,314	76,806
Santa Clara	386,279	158,630	386,100	209,094
Santa Cruz	78,495	20,063	89,102	30,354
Shasta	24,322	41,482	24,339	52,249
Sierra	743	1,157	646	1,249
Siskiyou	7,575	9,288	7,880	12,673
Solano	98,775	54,736	85,096	62,301
Sonoma	144,399	47,184	148,261	68,204
Stanislaus	75,106	74,025	58,829	85,407
Sutter	7,360	10,445	9,602	20,254
Tehama	8,801	14,618	7,504	15,572
Trinity	3,233	2,940	2,782	3,560
Tulare	33,491	46,047	32,494	65,399
Tuolumne	11,532	14,988	10,104	15,745
Ventura	164,699	130,485	148,859	160,314
Yolo	53,488	24,592	42,885	28,005
Yuba	7,107	9,608	5,687	12,076
Totals	8,274,473	5,011,781	6,745,485	5,509,826

California Vote Since 1952

2008: Obama, Dem., 8,274,473; McCain, Rep., 5,011,781; Nader, Peace/Freedom, 108,381; Barr, Lib., 67,582; Alan Keyes, American Ind., 40,673; McKinney, Green, 38,774.

2004: Kerry, D., 6,745,485; Bush, R., 5,509,826; Badnarik, LB., 50,165; Cobb, Green, 40,771; Peltier, Peace & Freedom, 27,607; Peroutka, Amer. Ind., 26,645.

2000: Gore, D., 5,861,203; Bush, R., 4,567,429; Nader, Green, 418,707; Browne, LB., 45,520; Buchanan, Reform, 44,987; Phillips, Amer. Ind., 17,042; Hagelin, Natural Law, 10,934.

1996: Clinton, D., 5,119,835; Dole, R., 3,828,380; Perot, Ref., 697,847; Nader, Green, 237,016; Browne, LB., 73,600; Feinland, Peace & Freedom, 25,332; Phillips, Amer. Ind., 21,202; Hagelin, Natural Law, 15,403.

1992: Clinton, D., 5,121,325; Bush, R., 3,630,575; Perot, Ind., 2,296,006; Marrou, LB., 48,139; Daniels, Ind., 18,597; Phillips, U.S. Taxpayers, 12,711.

1988: Bush, R., 5,054,917; Dukakis, D., 4,702,233; Paul, Lib., 70,105; Fulani, Ind., 31,181.

1984: Reagan, R. 5,305,410; Mondale, D., 3,815,947; Bergland, LB., 48,400.

1980: Reagan, R. 4,524,858; Carter, D., 3,083,661; Anderson, Ind., 739,833; Clark, LB., 148,434; Commoner, Ind., 61,063; Smith, Peace and Freedom, 18,116; Rarick, Amer. Ind., 9,856.

1976: Ford, R., 3,882,244; Carter, D., 3,742,284; McCarthy, write-in, 58,412; MacBride, LB., 56,388; Maddox, Amer. Ind., 51,098; Wright, People's, 41,731; Camejo, Soc. Workers, 17,259; Hall, Com., 12,766; write-in, 4,935.

1972: Nixon, R., 4,602,096; McGovern, D., 3,475,847; Schmitz, Amer. Ind., 232,554; Spock, Peace and Freedom, 55,167; Hospers, LB., 980; Jenness, Soc. Workers, 574; Hall, Com., 373; Fisher, Soc. Labor, 197; Munn, Proh., 53; Green, Universal, 21.

1968: Nixon, R., 3,467,664; Humphrey, D., 3,244,318; Wallace, 3rd Party, 487,270; Peace and Freedom, 27,707; McCarthy, Alternative, 20,721; Gregory, write-in, 3,230; Blomen, Soc. Labor, 341; Mitchell, Com., 260; Munn, Proh., 59; Soeters, Defense, 17.

1964: Johnson, D., 4,171,877; Goldwater, R., 2,879,108; Hass, Soc. Labor, 489; DeBerry, Soc. Workers, 378; Munn, Proh., 305; Hensley, Universal, 19.

1960: Nixon, R., 3,259,722; Kennedy, D., 3,224,099; Decker, Proh., 21,706; Hass, Soc. Labor, 1,051.

1956: Eisenhower, R., 3,027,668; Stevenson, D., 2,420,136; Holtwick, Proh., 11,119; Andrews, Constitution, 6,087; Hass, Soc. Labor, 300; Hoopes, Soc., 123; Dobbs, Soc. Workers, 96; Smith, Christian Natl., 8.

1952: Eisenhower, R., 2,897,310; Stevenson, D., 2,197,548; Hallinan, Prog., 24,106; Hamblen, Proh., 15,653; MacArthur, (Tenny Ticket), 3,326; Hass, Soc. Labor, 273; Hoopes, Soc., 206; (Kellems Ticket) 178; scattered, 3,249.

Colorado

County	2008		2004	
	Obama (D)	McCain (R)	Kerry (D)	Bush (R)
Adams	90,113	62,321	69,122	65,912
Alamosa	3,521	2,635	3,017	3,179
Arapahoe	128,366	100,409	110,262	119,475
Archuleta	2,822	3,618	2,141	3,601
Baca	532	1,568	483	1,680
Bent	799	1,077	785	1,338
Boulder	115,339	41,644	105,564	51,586
Broomfield	16,031	12,675	10,935	12,007
Chaffee	4,827	4,832	3,766	4,875
Cheyenne	198	890	198	923
Clear Creek	3,295	2,278	2,989	2,522
Conejos	2,106	1,616	1,894	1,864
Costilla	1,236	411	1,170	566
Crowley	552	976	478	1,006
Custer	914	1,668	739	1,657
Delta	5,007	9,905	4,224	9,722
Denver	195,499	60,226	166,135	69,903
Dolores	356	803	333	785
Douglas	51,813	73,225	39,661	80,651
Eagle	13,055	8,112	9,744	8,533
Elbert	3,775	9,030	2,834	8,389
El Paso	104,670	155,914	77,648	161,361
Fremont	6,801	12,595	5,933	12,313
Garfield	10,847	10,932	9,228	11,123
Gilpin	1,944	1,249	1,807	1,329
Grand	3,961	4,088	3,243	4,260
Gunnison	5,512	3,112	4,782	3,479
Hinsdale	239	343	236	355
Huerfano	1,989	1,582	1,663	1,700
Jackson	277	624	210	710
Jefferson	155,020	129,291	126,558	140,644
Kiowa	172	630	172	712
Kit Carson	898	2,420	729	2,721
Lake	1,847	1,076	1,623	1,261
La Plata	15,422	11,170	13,409	11,704
Larimer	84,461	68,932	68,266	75,884
Las Animas	3,483	3,033	3,300	3,196
Lincoln	543	1,683	503	1,819
Logan	2,837	5,986	2,491	6,168
Mesa	23,470	43,669	19,564	41,539
Mineral	270	334	227	383
Moffat	1,566	4,101	1,355	4,247
Montezuma	4,619	6,913	3,867	6,988
Montrose	6,115	11,525	4,776	11,218
Morgan	3,762	6,222	3,039	6,787
Otero	3,454	4,324	3,164	4,947
Ouray	1,629	1,360	1,278	1,402
Park	4,196	4,835	3,445	4,781
Phillips	587	1,513	582	1,717
Pitkin	7,260	2,448	6,335	2,784
Prowers	1,464	3,026	1,308	3,392
Pueblo	38,074	28,523	35,369	31,117
Rio Blanco	654	2,425	566	2,403
Rio Grande	2,427	2,916	2,006	3,448
Routt	8,133	4,634	6,392	5,199
Saguache	1,620	913	1,594	1,163
San Juan	264	218	253	216
San Miguel	3,345	930	2,876	1,079
Sedgwick	468	857	374	971
Summit	9,700	4,845	8,144	5,370
Teller	4,370	7,939	3,556	8,094
Washington	518	1,935	455	2,050
Weld	46,644	55,913	31,868	55,591
Yuma	1,105	3,238	1,064	3,456
Totals	1,288,633	1,073,629	1,001,732	1,101,255

Colorado Vote Since 1952

2008: Obama, Dem., 1,288,633; McCain, Rep., 1,073,629; Nader, Unaff., 13,352; Barr, Lib., 10,898; Baldwin, Const., 6,233; Alan Keyes, American Ind., 3,051; McKinney, Green, 2,822; McEnulty, unaff., 829; Jay, Boston Tea, 598; Allen, HeartQuake '08, 348; Stevens, Objectivist, 336; Moore, Socialist USA, 226; LaRiva, Socialism/Liberation, 158; Harris, Socialist Wkrs., 154; Lyttle, U.S. Pacifist, 110; Amondson, Prohib., 85.

2004: Bush, R., 1,101,255; Kerry, D., 1,001,732; Nader, Ref., 12,718; Badnarik, LB., 7,664; Peroutka, Amer. Const., 2,562; Cobb, Green, 1,591; Andress, Ind., 804; Amondson, Concerns of People, 378; Van Auken, Soc. Equal., 329; Harris, Soc. Wkrs., 241; Brown, Soc., 216; Dodge, Prohib., 140.

2000: Bush, R., 883,748; Gore, D., 738,227; Nader, Green, 91,434; Browne, LB., 12,799; Buchanan, Reform, 10,465; Hagelin, Reform, 2,240; Phillips, Amer. Constitution, 1,319; McReynolds, Soc., 712; Harris, Soc. Workers, 216; Dodge, Proh., 208.

1996: Dole, R., 691,848; Clinton, D., 671,152; Perot, Ref., 99,629; Nader, Green, 25,070; Browne, LB., 12,392; Phillips, Amer. Constitution, 2,813; Collins, Ind., 2,809; Hagelin, Natural Law, 2,547; Hollis, Soc., 669; Moorehead, Workers World, 599; Templin, Amer., 557; Dodge, Proh., 375; Harris, Soc. Workers, 244.

1992: Clinton, D., 629,681; Bush, R., 562,850; Perot, Ind., 366,010; Marrou, LB., 8,669; Fulani, New Alliance, 1,608.

1988: Bush, R., 728,177; Dukakis, D., 621,453; Paul, Lib., 15,482; Dodge, Proh., 4,604.

1984: Reagan, R., 821,817; Mondale, D., 454,975; Bergland, LB., 11,257.

1980: Reagan, R., 652,264; Carter, D., 367,973; Anderson, Ind., 130,633; Clark, LB., 25,744; Commoner, Citizens, 5,614; Bubar, Statesman, 1,180; Pulley, Socialist, 520; Hall, Com., 487.

1976: Ford, R., 584,367; Carter, D., 460,353; McCarthy, Ind., 26,107; MacBride, LB., 5,330; Bubar, Proh., 2,882.

1972: Nixon, R., 597,189; McGovern, D., 329,980; Schmitz, Amer., 17,269; Fisher, Soc. Labor, 4,361; Spock, People's, 2,403; Hospers, LB., 1,111; Jenness, Soc. Workers, 555; Munn, Proh., 467; Hall, Com., 432.

1968: Nixon, R., 409,345; Humphrey, D., 335,174; Wallace, 3rd Party, 60,813; Blomen, Soc. Labor, 3,016; Gregory, New-party, 1,393; Munn, Proh., 275; Halstead, Soc. Workers, 235.

1964: Johnson, D., 476,024; Goldwater, R., 296,767; DeBerry, Soc. Workers, 2,537; Munn, Proh., 1,356; Hass, Soc. Labor, 302.

1960: Nixon, R., 402,242; Kennedy, D., 330,629; Hass, Soc. Labor, 2,803; Dobbs, Soc. Workers, 572.

1956: Eisenhower, R., 394,479; Stevenson, D., 263,997; Hass, Soc. Lab., 3,308; Andrews, Ind., 759; Hoopes, Soc., 531.

1952: Eisenhower, R., 379,782; Stevenson, D., 245,504; MacArthur, Constitution, 2,181; Hallinan, Prog., 1,919; Hoopes, Soc., 365; Hass, Soc. Labor, 352.

Connecticut

City	2008		2004	
	Obama (D)	McCain (R)	Kerry (D)	Bush (R)
Bridgeport	33,941	6,501	26,280	10,326
Bristol	15,774	9,467	14,201	10,619
Danbury	15,962	10,697	13,477	12,399
Fairfield	17,236	13,071	15,068	14,706
Greenwich	16,233	13,937	14,334	15,830
Hartford	31,741	2,686	22,595	4,623
New Britain	16,742	5,442	14,122	6,560
New Haven	38,452	5,017	30,979	7,175
Norwalk	24,489	12,651	20,615	14,201
Stamford	31,733	17,510	27,588	18,866
Waterbury	22,594	12,821	16,122	15,961
West Hartford	23,576	10,021	21,612	11,641
Other	705,847	507,867	620,495	550,919
Totals	**997,772**	**629,428**	**857,488**	**693,826**

Connecticut Vote Since 1952

2008: Obama, Dem., 997,772; McCain, Rep., 629,428; Nader, Ind., 19,162.

2004: Kerry, D., 857,488; Bush, R., 693,826; Nader, Petitioning Cand., 12,969; Cobb, Green, 9,564; Badnarik, LB., 3,367; Peroutka, Concerned Citizens, 1,543.

2000: Gore, D., 816,015; Bush, R., 561,094; Nader, Green, 64,452; Phillips, Concerned Citizens, 9,695; Buchanan, Reform, 4,731; Browne, LB., 3,484.

1996: Clinton, D., 735,740; Dole, R., 483,109; Perot, Ref., 139,523; Nader, Green, 24,321; Browne, LB., 5,788; Phillips, Concerned Citizens, 2,425; Hagelin, Natural Law, 1,703.

1992: Clinton, D., 682,318; Bush, R., 578,313; Perot, Ind., 348,771; Marrou, LB., 5,391; Fulani, New Alliance, 1,363.

1988: Bush, R., 750,241; Dukakis, D., 676,584; Paul, Lib., 14,071; Fulani, New Alliance, 2,491.

1984: Reagan, R., 890,877; Mondale, D., 569,597.

1980: Reagan, R., 677,210; Carter, D., 541,732; Anderson, Ind., 171,807; Clark, LB., 8,570; Commoner, Citizens, 6,130; scattered, 836.

1976: Ford, R., 719,261; Carter, D., 647,895; Maddox, George Wallace Party, 7,101; LaRouche, U.S. Labor, 1,789.

1972: Nixon, R., 810,763; McGovern, D., 555,498; Schmitz, Amer., 17,239; scattered, 777.

1968: Humphrey, D., 621,561; Nixon, R., 556,721; Wallace, 3rd Party, 76,650; scattered, 1,300.

1964: Johnson, D., 826,269; Goldwater, R., 390,996; scattered, 1,313.

1960: Kennedy, D., 657,055; Nixon, R., 565,813.

1956: Eisenhower, R., 711,837; Stevenson, D., 405,079; scattered, 205.

1952: Eisenhower, R., 611,012; Stevenson, D., 481,649; Hoopes, Soc., 2,244; Hallinan, People's, 1,466; Hass, Soc. Labor, 535; write-in, 5.

Delaware

County	2008		2004	
	Obama (D)	McCain (R)	Kerry (D)	Bush (R)
Kent	36,383	29,822	23,875	31,578
New Castle	178,712	74,595	146,179	93,079
Sussex	40,299	47,939	30,098	47,003
Totals	**255,459**	**152,374**	**200,152**	**171,660**

Delaware Vote Since 1952

2008: Obama, Dem., 255,459; McCain, Rep., 152,374; Nader, Ind. (Delaware), 2,401; Barr, Lib., 1,109; Baldwin, Const., 626; McKinney, Green, 385; Calero, Socialist Wkrs., 58.

2004: Kerry, D., 200,152; Bush, R., 171,660; Nader, Ind., 2,153; Badnarik, LB., 586; Peroutka, Constitution, 289; Cobb, Green, 250; Brown, Nat. Law, 100.

2000: Gore, D., 180,068; Bush, R., 137,288; Nader, Green, 8,307; Buchanan, Reform, 777; Browne, LB., 774; Phillips, Constitution, 208; Hagelin, Natural Law, 107.

1996: Clinton, D., 140,355; Dole, R., 99,062; Perot, Ind. (Ref.), 28,719; Browne, LB., 2,052; Phillips, U.S. Taxpayers, 348; Hagelin, Natural Law, 274.

1992: Clinton, D., 126,054; Bush, R., 102,313; Perot, Ind., 59,213; Fulani, New Alliance, 1,105.

1988: Bush, R., 139,639; Dukakis, D., 108,647; Paul, Lib., 1,162; Fulani, New Alliance, 443.

1984: Reagan, R., 152,190; Mondale, D., 101,656; Bergland, LB., 268.

1980: Reagan, R., 111,252; Carter, D., 105,754; Anderson, Ind., 16,288; Clark, LB., 1,974; Greaves, Amer., 400.

1976: Carter, D., 122,596; Ford, R., 109,831; McCarthy, non-partisan, 2,437; Anderson, Amer., 645; LaRouche, U.S. Labor, 136; Bubar, Proh., 103; Levin, Soc. Labor, 86.

1972: Nixon, R., 140,357; McGovern, D., 92,283; Schmitz, Amer., 2,638; Munn, Proh., 238.

1968: Nixon, R., 96,714; Humphrey, D., 89,194; Wallace, 3rd Party, 28,459.

1964: Johnson, D., 122,704; Goldwater, R., 78,078; Munn, Proh., 425; Hass, Soc. Labor, 113.

1960: Kennedy, D., 99,590; Nixon, R., 96,373; Faubus, States' Rights, 354; Decker, Proh., 284; Hass, Soc. Labor, 82.

1956: Eisenhower, R., 98,057; Stevenson, D., 79,421; Oltwick, Proh., 400; Hass, Soc. Labor, 110.

1952: Eisenhower, R., 90,059; Stevenson, D., 83,315; Hass, Soc. Lab., 242; Hamblen, Proh., 234; Hallinan, Prog., 155; Hoopes, Soc., 20.

District of Columbia

	2008		2004	
	Obama (D)	McCain (R)	Kerry (D)	Bush (R)
Totals	245,800	17,367	202,970	21,256

District of Columbia Vote Since 1964

2008: Obama, Dem., 245,800; McCain, Rep., 17,367; Nader, Ind., 958; McKinney, Green, 590.

2004: Kerry, D., 202,970; Bush, R., 21,256; Nader, Ind., 1,485; Cobb, DC Statehood Green, 737; Badnarik, LB., 502; Harris, Soc. Wkrs., 130.

2000: Gore, D., 171,923; Bush, R., 18,073; Nader, Green, 10,576; Browne, LB., 669; Harris, Soc. Workers, 114.

1996: Clinton, D., 158,220; Dole, R., 17,339; Nader, Green, 4,780; Perot, Ref., 3,611; Browne, LB., 588; Hagelin, Natural Law, 283; Harris, Soc. Workers, 257.

1992: Clinton, D., 192,619; Bush, R., 20,698; Perot, Ind., 9,681; Fulani, New Alliance, 1,459; Daniels, Ind., 1,186.

1988: Dukakis, D., 159,407; Bush, R., 27,590; Fulani, New Alliance, 2,901; Paul, Lib., 554.

1984: Mondale, D., 180,408; Reagan, R., 29,009; Bergland, LB., 279.

1980: Carter, D., 130,231; Reagan, R., 23,313; Anderson, Ind., 16,131; Commoner, Citizens, 1,826; Clark, LB., 1,104; Hall, Com., 369; DeBerry, Soc. Workers, 173; Griswold, Workers World, 52; write-in, 690.

1976: Carter, D., 137,818; Ford, R., 27,873; Camejo, Soc. Workers, 545; MacBride, LB., 274; Hall, Com., 219; LaRouche, U.S. Labor, 157.

1972: McGovern, D., 127,627; Nixon, R., 35,226; Reed, Soc. Workers, 316; Hall, Com., 252.

1968: Humphrey, D., 139, 566; Nixon, R., 31,012.

1964: Johnson, D., 169,796; Goldwater, R., 28,801.

Florida

County	2008		2004	
	Obama (D)	McCain (R)	Kerry (D)	Bush (R)
Alachua	73,134	47,025	62,504	47,762
Baker	2,326	8,672	2,180	7,738
Bay	23,603	56,597	21,068	53,404
Bradford	3,430	8,135	3,244	7,557
Brevard	127,400	157,402	110,309	153,068
Broward	487,638	234,690	453,873	244,674
Calhoun	1,821	4,344	2,116	3,782
Charlotte	39,006	45,180	34,256	44,428
Citrus	31,428	43,666	29,277	39,500
Clay	26,635	66,847	18,971	62,078
Collier	52,710	83,238	43,892	83,631
Columbia	9,171	18,668	8,031	16,758
DeSoto	4,378	5,625	3,913	5,524
Dixie	1,921	5,188	1,960	4,434
Duval	192,173	197,171	158,610	220,190
Escambia	61,152	90,826	48,329	93,566
Flagler	24,682	23,931	18,578	19,633
Franklin	2,122	3,799	2,401	3,472
Gadsden	15,566	6,805	14,629	6,253
Gilchrist	1,993	5,654	2,017	4,936
Glades	1,674	2,533	1,718	2,443
Gulf	2,144	4,971	2,407	4,805
Hamilton	2,360	3,179	2,260	2,792
Hardee	2,561	4,758	2,149	5,049
Hendry	4,998	5,779	3,960	5,757
Hernando	18,980	25,220	37,187	42,635
Highlands	17,913	25,903	15,347	25,878
Hillsborough	219,580	209,503	214,132	245,576
Holmes	1,443	7,023	1,810	6,412
Indian River	29,565	39,972	23,956	36,938
Jackson	7,632	13,695	7,555	12,122
Jefferson	4,082	3,794	4,135	3,298
Lafayette	640	2,677	845	2,460
Lake	62,710	82,512	48,221	74,389
Lee	117,878	145,624	93,860	144,176
Leon	91,356	55,521	83,873	51,615
Levy	6,707	11,751	6,074	10,410
Liberty	892	2,337	1,070	1,927
Madison	4,270	4,544	4,050	4,191
Manatee	67,785	78,040	61,262	81,318
Marion	70,771	89,571	57,271	81,283
Martin	33,474	44,110	30,208	41,362
Miami-Dade	491,195	351,462	409,732	361,095
Monroe	20,868	18,906	19,654	19,467
Nassau	10,577	27,326	8,573	23,783
Okaloosa	25,623	68,181	19,368	69,693
Okeechobee	5,102	7,551	5,153	6,978
Orange	271,866	186,079	193,354	192,539
Osceola	59,081	39,489	38,633	43,117
Palm Beach	342,527	211,163	328,687	212,688
Pasco	102,217	109,902	84,749	103,230
Pinellas	243,994	206,909	225,460	225,686
Polk	113,552	128,658	86,009	123,559
Putnam	13,201	19,586	12,412	18,311
St. Johns	35,578	68,800	26,399	59,196
St. Lucie	66,830	52,323	51,835	47,592
Santa Rosa	19,394	55,843	14,659	52,059
Sarasota	102,413	102,650	88,442	104,692
Seminole	99,140	104,885	76,971	108,172
Sumter	17,644	30,859	11,584	19,800
Suwannee	4,572	11,672	4,522	11,153
Taylor	2,787	6,446	3,049	5,467
Union	1,299	3,933	1,251	3,396
Volusia	127,474	113,716	115,519	111,924
Wakulla	5,303	8,869	4,896	6,777
Walton	7,158	19,527	6,213	17,555
Washington	2,858	8,165	2,912	7,369
Totals	**4,282,074**	**4,045,624**	**3,583,544**	**3,964,522**

Florida Vote Since 1952

2008: Obama, Dem., 4,282,074; McCain, Rep., 4,045,624; Nader, Ecology (Florida), 28,124; Barr, Lib., 17,218; Baldwin, Const., 7,915; McKinney, Green, 2,887; Keyes, American Ind., 2,550; LaRiva, Socialism/Liberation, 1,516; Jay, Boston Tea, 795; Harris, Socialist Wkrs., 533; Stevens, Objectivist, 419; Moore, Socialist USA, 405; Amondson, Prohib., 293.

2004: Bush, R., 3,964,522; Kerry, D., 3,583,544; Nader, Ref., 32,971; Badnarik, LB., 11,996; Peroutka, Constitution, 6,626; Cobb, Green, 3,917; Brown, Soc., 3,502; Harris, Soc. Wkrs., 2,732.

2000: Bush, R., 2,912,790; Gore, D., 2,912,253; Nader, Green, 97,488; Buchanan, Reform, 17,484; Browne, LB., 16,415; Hagelin, Nat. Law, 2,281; Moorehead, Wkrs. World, 1,804; Phillips, Constit., 1,371; McReynolds, Soc., 622; Harris, Soc. Wkrs., 562.

1996: Clinton, D., 2,545,968; Dole, R., 2,243,324; Perot, Ref., 483,776; Browne, LB., 23,312.

1992: Bush, R., 2,171,781; Clinton, D., 2,071,651; Perot, Ind., 1,052,481; Marrou, LB., 15,068.

1988: Bush, R., 2,616,597; Dukakis, D., 1,655,851; Paul, Lib., 19,796, Fulani, New Alliance, 6,655.

1984: Reagan, R., 2,728,775; Mondale, D., 1,448,344.

1980: Reagan, R., 2,046,951; Carter, D., 1,419,475; Anderson, Ind., 189,692; Clark, LB., 30,524; write-in, 285.

1976: Carter, D., 1,636,000; Ford, R., 1,469,531; McCarthy, Ind., 23,643; Anderson, Amer., 21,325.

1972: Nixon, R., 1,857,759; McGovern, D., 718,117; scattered, 7,407.

1968: Nixon, R., 886,804; Humphrey, D., 676,794; Wallace, 3rd Party, 624,207.

1964: Johnson, D., 948,540; Goldwater, R., 905,941.

1960: Nixon, R., 795,476; Kennedy, D., 748,700.

1956: Eisenhower, R., 643,849; Stevenson, D., 480,371.

1952: Eisenhower, R., 544,036; Stevenson, D., 444,950; scattered, 351.

Georgia

County	2008		2004	
	Obama (D)	McCain (R)	Kerry (D)	Bush (R)
Appling	1,846	5,085	1,848	4,494
Atkinson	938	1,941	799	1,666
Bacon	817	3,089	930	2,853
Baker	846	828	936	821
Baldwin	8,587	7,823	6,775	7,709
Banks	1,027	5,120	1,149	4,410
Barrow	6,657	17,625	4,095	13,520
Bartow	9,662	25,976	7,741	22,311
Ben Hill	2,590	3,417	2,180	3,331
Berrien	1,468	4,889	1,638	3,917
Bibb	38,851	26,981	29,322	28,107
Bleckley	1,380	3,657	1,281	3,167
Brantley	1,119	5,080	1,258	4,333
Brooks	2,669	3,507	2,193	2,912
Bryan	3,630	9,105	2,590	7,363
Bulloch	9,586	14,174	6,840	12,252
Burke	5,233	4,344	4,213	4,232
Butts	3,064	5,944	2,572	5,119
Calhoun	1,342	862	1,119	890
Camden	6,482	10,502	4,637	9,488
Candler	1,209	2,286	1,096	2,048
Carroll	14,334	28,661	10,224	24,837
Catoosa	6,025	18,218	5,807	16,406
Charlton	1,193	2,458	1,064	2,311
Chatham	62,755	46,829	45,630	45,484
Chattahoochee	830	811	773	905
Chattooga	2,591	5,564	2,809	4,992
Cherokee	22,350	70,279	14,824	58,238
Clarke	29,513	15,309	21,718	15,052
Clay	879	558	798	509
Clayton	82,527	16,506	56,113	23,106
Clinch	989	1,678	750	1,501
Cobb	141,216	170,957	103,955	173,467
Coffee	4,811	8,872	3,979	8,306
Colquitt	4,139	9,185	3,378	8,296
Columbia	15,703	39,322	11,442	35,549
Cook	2,075	3,782	1,733	3,065
Coweta	15,521	37,571	10,647	31,682
Crawford	1,832	3,358	1,552	2,830
Crisp	3,078	4,423	2,357	3,865
Dade	1,608	4,698	1,823	4,368
Dawson	1,632	8,242	1,407	6,649
Decatur	4,424	5,890	3,577	5,348
DeKalb	254,594	65,581	200,787	73,570
Dodge	2,595	5,543	2,384	4,584
Dooly	2,138	1,991	1,973	1,853
Dougherty	26,135	12,547	19,805	13,711
Douglas	27,825	26,812	15,997	25,846
Early	2,602	2,709	1,701	2,495
Echols	201	981	231	757
Effingham	4,936	15,230	3,613	12,503
Elbert	3,366	4,868	2,984	4,626
Emanuel	3,068	5,110	2,774	4,666
Evans	1,374	2,462	1,213	2,291
Fannin	2,611	7,807	2,727	6,862
Fayette	20,313	38,501	14,887	37,346
Floyd	10,691	23,132	10,038	21,400
Forsyth	15,406	59,166	9,201	47,267
Franklin	1,910	6,054	2,245	5,218
Fulton	272,000	130,136	199,436	134,372
Gilmer	2,614	8,408	2,510	7,414
Glascock	210	1,202	250	1,016
Glynn	12,676	20,479	8,962	18,608
Gordon	4,268	13,113	4,028	11,671
Grady	3,539	5,775	3,092	5,068
Greene	3,339	4,532	2,774	4,069
Gwinnett	129,025	158,746	81,708	160,445
Habersham	2,900	11,766	2,750	10,434
Hall	14,457	44,962	10,514	38,883
Hancock	3,535	795	2,715	822
Haralson	2,248	8,658	2,434	7,703
Harris	4,179	10,645	3,400	8,878
Hart	3,365	6,537	3,479	5,500
Heard	1,042	3,133	1,148	2,788
Henry	40,527	47,115	21,096	42,759

County	2008 Obama (D)	McCain (R)	2004 Kerry (D)	Bush (R)
Houston	22,094	33,392	15,054	29,862
Irwin	1,197	2,605	1,051	2,347
Jackson	4,950	17,776	3,468	12,611
Jasper	1,935	3,916	1,558	3,157
Jeff Davis	1,350	3,847	1,277	3,549
Jefferson	4,149	3,061	3,447	3,066
Jenkins	1,482	1,936	1,494	1,898
Johnson	1,198	2,426	1,263	2,279
Jones	4,572	7,782	3,855	6,939
Lamar	2,745	4,871	2,432	4,027
Lanier	1,062	1,787	931	1,641
Laurens	7,769	12,052	6,281	10,883
Lee	3,100	9,923	2,182	8,201
Liberty	10,474	5,828	6,619	6,131
Lincoln	1,650	2,731	1,337	2,309
Long	1,288	2,119	1,033	1,994
Lowndes	17,405	21,085	12,516	18,981
Lumpkin	2,586	8,326	2,091	6,690
Macon	3,251	1,712	2,906	1,851
Madison	2,957	8,224	2,527	7,254
Marion	1,381	1,772	1,275	1,670
McDuffie	3,989	5,400	2,899	4,846
McIntosh	2,905	3,282	2,523	2,837
Meriwether	4,465	4,982	3,709	4,402
Miller	809	1,897	736	1,694
Mitchell	3,872	4,201	3,360	3,885
Monroe	4,106	7,933	3,216	6,522
Montgomery	1,045	2,521	1,007	2,150
Morgan	3,091	5,987	2,304	4,902
Murray	3,026	8,180	2,899	7,745
Muscogee	44,158	29,568	32,867	30,850
Newton	20,827	20,337	10,939	18,095
Oconee	4,825	12,120	3,789	10,276
Oglethorpe	2,232	4,144	1,899	3,688
Paulding	17,229	39,192	9,420	30,843
Peach	5,927	5,173	3,961	4,554
Pickens	2,595	10,004	2,444	8,115
Pierce	1,253	5,500	1,234	4,680
Pike	1,574	6,542	1,506	5,193
Polk	4,052	9,850	3,868	8,467
Pulaski	1,377	2,553	1,294	2,202
Putnam	3,102	5,966	2,880	5,188
Quitman	597	509	543	409
Rabun	2,001	5,487	1,918	4,650
Randolph	1,833	1,370	1,612	1,418
Richmond	52,100	26,842	39,262	29,764
Rockdale	20,421	16,860	12,136	18,856
Schley	479	1,252	464	1,063
Screven	3,024	3,423	2,534	3,360
Seminole	1,657	2,315	1,278	1,977
Spalding	10,141	14,885	7,460	13,461
Stephens	2,705	7,689	2,714	6,904
Stewart	1,305	783	1,220	797
Sumter	6,444	5,713	5,562	5,688
Talbot	2,367	1,300	1,830	1,103
Taliaferro	643	339	612	335
Tattnall	1,932	4,730	1,787	4,657
Taylor	1,533	2,019	1,458	1,912
Telfair	1,862	2,486	1,590	2,171
Terrell	2,501	1,890	1,951	1,859
Thomas	7,720	10,642	5,997	9,659
Tift	4,749	9,431	3,864	8,619
Toombs	2,964	6,658	2,567	6,196
Towns	1,391	4,292	1,430	3,823
Treutlen	1,112	1,826	1,052	1,691
Troup	10,438	15,374	7,630	14,183
Turner	1,427	2,096	1,135	1,815
Twiggs	2,402	2,087	2,220	2,112
Union	2,486	8,007	2,327	6,847
Upson	4,050	7,282	3,424	6,634
Walker	6,094	17,101	5,986	15,340
Walton	8,469	27,253	5,887	21,594
Ware	4,034	8,311	3,449	7,790
Warren	1,554	1,087	1,360	1,121
Washington	4,607	4,216	3,733	4,081
Wayne	2,858	7,601	2,683	6,819
Webster	515	588	515	485
Wheeler	794	1,408	847	1,192
White	2,174	8,467	2,016	7,403
Whitfield	8,167	19,230	6,933	19,297
Wilcox	978	2,159	902	1,705
Wilkes	2,315	2,705	2,028	2,490
Wilkinson	2,298	2,349	2,235	2,261
Worth	2,540	5,777	2,219	5,105
Totals	**1,844,123**	**2,048,759**	**1,366,149**	**1,914,254**

Georgia Vote Since 1952

2008: McCain, Rep., 2,048,759; Obama, Dem., 1,844,123; Barr, Lib., 28,731.
2004: Bush, R., 1,914,254; Kerry, D., 1,366,149; Badnarik, LB., 18,387.
2000: Bush, R., 1,419,720; Gore, D., 1,116,230; Browne, LB., 36,332; Buchanan, Independent, 10,926.

1996: Dole, R., 1,080,843; Clinton, D., 1,053,849; Perot, Ref., 146,337; Browne, LB., 17,870.
1992: Clinton, D., 1,008,966; Bush, R., 995,252; Perot, Ind., 309,657; Marrou, LB., 7,110.
1988: Bush, R., 1,081,331; Dukakis, D., 714,792; Paul, Lib., 8,435; Fulani, New Alliance, 5,099.
1984: Reagan, R., 1,068,722; Mondale, D., 706,628.
1980: Carter, D., 890,955; Reagan, R., 654,168; Anderson, Ind., 36,055; Clark, LB., 15,627.
1976: Carter, D., 979,409; Ford, R., 483,743; write-in, 4,306.
1972: Nixon, R., 881,496; McGovern, D., 289,529; Schmitz, Amer., 812; scattered, 2,935.
1968: Wallace, 3rd Party, 535,550; Nixon, R., 380,111; Humphrey, D., 334,440; write-in, 162.
1964: Goldwater, R., 616,600; Johnson, D., 522,557.
1960: Kennedy, D., 458,638; Nixon, R., 274,472; write-in, 239.
1956: Stevenson, D., 444,388; Eisenhower, R., 222,778; Andrews, Ind., write-in, 1,754.
1952: Stevenson, D., 456,823; Eisenhower, R., 198,979; Liberty Party, 1.

Hawaii

County	2008 Obama (D)	McCain (R)	2004 Kerry (D)	Bush (R)
Hawaii	50,808	14,865	35,116	22,032
Honolulu	213,977	88,049	152,873	144,232
Kauai	20,408	6,243	14,916	9,740
Maui	39,725	11,152	28,803	18,187
Totals	**325,871**	**120,566**	**231,708**	**194,191**

Hawaii Vote Since 1960

2008: Obama, Dem., 325,871; McCain, Rep., 120,566; Nader, Ind. (Hawaii), 3,825; Barr, Lib., 1,314 Baldwin, Const., 1,013; McKinney, Green, 979.
2004: Kerry, D., 231,708; Bush, R., 194,191; Cobb, Green, 1,737; Badnarik, LB., 1,377.
2000: Gore, D., 205,286; Bush, R., 137,845; Nader, Green, 21,623; Browne, LB., 1,477; Buchanan, Reform, 1,071; Phillips, Constitution, 343; Hagelin, Natural Law, 306.
1996: Clinton, D., 205,012; Dole, R., 113,943; Perot, Ref., 27,358; Nader, Green, 10,386; Browne, LB., 2,493; Hagelin, Natural Law, 570; Phillips, Taxpayers, 358.
1992: Clinton, D., 179,310; Bush, R., 136,822; Perot, Ind., 53,003; Gritz, Populist/America First, 1,452; Marrou, LB., 1,119.
1988: Dukakis, D., 192,364; Bush, R., 158,625; Paul, Lib., 1,999; Fulani, New Alliance, 1,003.
1984: Reagan, R., 184,934; Mondale, D., 147,098; Bergland, LB., 2,167.
1980: Carter, D., 135,879; Reagan, R., 130,112; Anderson, Ind., 32,021; Clark, LB., 3,269; Commoner, Citizens, 1,548; Hall, Com., 458.
1976: Carter, D., 147,375; Ford, R., 140,003; MacBride, LB., 3,923.
1972: Nixon, R., 168,865; McGovern, D., 101,409.
1968: Humphrey, D., 141,324; Nixon, R., 91,425; Wallace, 3rd Party, 3,469.
1964: Johnson, D., 163,249; Goldwater, R., 44,022.
1960: Kennedy, D., 92,410; Nixon, R., 92,295.

Idaho

County	2008 Obama (D)	McCain (R)	2004 Kerry (D)	Bush (R)
Ada	82,023	92,879	58,523	94,641
Adams	728	1,515	555	1,468
Bannock	14,792	19,356	12,903	21,479
Bear Lake	502	2,377	494	2,506
Benewah	1,407	2,646	1,148	2,823
Bingham	4,424	12,230	3,605	12,734
Blaine	6,947	3,439	5,992	4,034
Boise	1,240	2,433	970	2,501
Bonner	7,840	11,145	6,649	10,697
Bonneville	11,415	29,324	8,356	30,048
Boundary	1,474	3,098	1,268	3,012
Butte	318	1,056	321	1,077
Camas	187	422	139	450
Canyon	20,147	42,752	13,415	41,599
Caribou	553	2,656	491	2,753
Cassia	1,305	6,240	1,153	6,562
Clark	64	305	46	302
Clearwater	1,211	2,569	1,117	2,839
Custer	620	1,704	559	1,762
Elmore	2,523	5,571	1,959	6,011
Franklin	599	4,231	456	4,527
Fremont	1,065	4,700	741	4,965
Gem	2,166	5,585	1,628	5,416
Gooding	1,485	3,764	1,278	3,973
Idaho	1,935	5,895	1,689	6,017
Jefferson	1,641	8,540	1,084	7,703
Jerome	1,794	4,897	1,344	5,177
Kootenai	22,120	38,387	17,584	36,173
Latah	9,191	7,984	8,430	8,686
Lemhi	796	2,938	915	3,079
Lewis	479	1,275	440	1,359
Lincoln	497	967	466	1,388
Madison	1,625	11,120	826	10,693
Minidoka	1,137	3,976	1,331	5,797

County	2008 Obama (D)	McCain (R)	2004 Kerry (D)	Bush (R)
Nez Perce	7,123	10,357	6,476	11,009
Oneida	381	1,724	304	1,789
Owyhee	944	3,024	685	2,859
Payette	2,415	5,988	1,848	6,256
Power	1,027	1,754	829	2,105
Shoshone	2,521	2,953	2,331	2,922
Teton	2,302	2,263	1,416	2,235
Twin Falls	8,621	19,032	6,458	19,672
Valley	2,394	2,750	1,843	2,863
Washington	1,241	3,168	1,033	3,274
Totals	**236,440**	**403,012**	**181,098**	**409,235**

Idaho Vote Since 1952

2008: McCain, Rep., 403,012; Obama, Dem., 236,440; Nader, Ind., 7,175; Baldwin, Const., 4,747; Barr, Lib., 3,658.
2004: Bush, R., 409,235; Kerry, D., 181,098; Badnarik, LB., 3,844; Peroutka, Constitution, 3,084.
2000: Bush, R., 336,937; Gore, D., 138,637; Buchanan, Reform, 7,615; Browne, LB., 3,488; Phillips, Constitution, 1,469; Hagelin, Natural Law, 1,177.
1996: Dole, R., 256,595; Clinton, D., 165,443; Perot, Ref., 62,518; Browne, LB., 3,325; Phillips, U.S. Taxpayers, 2,230; Hagelin, Natural Law, 1,600.
1992: Bush, R., 202,645; Clinton, D., 137,013; Perot, Ind., 130,395; Gritz, Populist/America First, 10,281; Marrou, LB., 1,167.
1988: Bush, R., 253,881; Dukakis, D., 147,272; Paul, Lib., 5,313; Fulani, Ind., 2,502.
1984: Reagan, R., 297,523; Mondale, D., 108,510; Bergland, LB., 2,823.
1980: Reagan, R., 290,699; Carter, D., 110,192; Anderson, Ind., 27,058; Clark, LB., 8,425; Rarick, Amer., 1,057.
1976: Ford, R., 204,151; Carter, D., 126,549; Maddox, Amer., 5,935; MacBride, LB., 3,558; LaRouche, U.S. Labor, 739.
1972: Nixon, R., 199,384; McGovern, D., 80,826; Schmitz, Amer., 28,869; Spock, People's, 903.
1968: Nixon, R., 165,369; Humphrey, D., 89,273; Wallace, 3rd Party, 36,541.
1964: Johnson, D., 148,920; Goldwater, R., 143,557.
1960: Nixon, R., 161,597; Kennedy, D., 138,853.
1956: Eisenhower, R., 166,979; Stevenson, D., 105,868; Andrews, Ind., 126; write-in, 16.
1952: Eisenhower, R., 180,707; Stevenson, D., 95,081; Hallinan, Prog., 443; write-in, 23.

Illinois

County	2008 Obama (D)	McCain (R)	2004 Kerry (D)	Bush (R)
Adams	11,700	18,592	10,511	20,834
Alexander	2,189	1,692	2,016	1,831
Bond	3,832	3,938	3,228	4,068
Boone	11,324	10,396	8,286	11,132
Brown	985	1,541	895	1,679
Bureau	8,872	7,902	7,961	9,822
Calhoun	1,421	1,221	1,367	1,317
Carroll	3,956	3,589	3,537	4,534
Cass	2,690	2,617	2,492	3,163
Champaign	48,351	33,748	41,524	39,896
Christian	6,912	7,869	6,112	9,044
Clark	3,737	4,406	2,877	5,082
Clay	2,423	3,924	2,101	4,416
Clinton	7,653	9,348	6,797	10,219
Coles	11,704	10,962	9,566	13,015
Cook	1,608,870	482,395	1,439,724	597,405
Crawford	3,877	5,067	3,194	6,083
Cumberland	2,052	3,155	1,862	3,497
DeKalb	25,765	18,260	19,263	21,095
DeWitt	3,299	4,345	2,836	4,920
Douglas	3,226	5,001	2,767	5,702
DuPage	227,416	182,860	180,097	218,902
Edgar	3,737	4,393	3,093	5,258
Edwards	1,140	2,136	930	2,412
Effingham	5,256	11,313	4,388	11,774
Fayette	3,963	5,493	3,571	5,880
Ford	2,226	4,075	1,912	4,511
Franklin	8,873	9,390	8,816	10,388
Fulton	9,722	6,244	9,080	7,818
Gallatin	1,587	1,211	1,573	1,619
Greene	2,617	3,048	2,457	3,559
Grundy	9,134	9,144	8,463	11,198
Hamilton	1,794	2,353	1,814	2,653
Hancock	3,753	4,778	3,975	5,837
Hardin	892	1,330	923	1,501
Henderson	2,213	1,540	2,269	1,857
Henry	13,177	11,247	11,877	13,212
Iroquois	4,640	8,686	3,832	9,914
Jackson	15,199	9,665	14,300	11,190
Jasper	2,063	2,963	1,781	3,529
Jefferson	7,460	9,293	6,713	10,160
Jersey	5,036	5,320	4,597	5,435
Jo Daviess	6,392	5,163	5,311	6,174
Johnson	1,477	3,138	1,813	3,997
Kane	105,592	84,223	73,813	92,065
Kankakee	24,719	22,508	20,003	24,739

County	2008 Obama (D)	McCain (R)	2004 Kerry (D)	Bush (R)
Kendall	23,529	20,675	12,497	19,776
Knox	14,165	9,396	13,403	11,111
Lake	111,051	85,284	134,352	139,081
LaSalle	27,415	21,855	24,263	26,101
Lawrence	3,013	3,401	2,518	4,162
Lee	7,757	8,243	6,416	9,307
Livingston	6,184	9,180	5,632	10,316
Logan	5,245	7,424	4,273	9,112
Macon	6,780	6,047	23,341	28,118
Macoupin	71,976	64,595	11,193	11,413
Madison	37,551	36,657	63,399	59,384
Marion	25,419	24,901	7,694	9,413
Marshall	12,071	9,879	2,806	3,734
Mason	68,836	57,059	3,215	3,907
Massac	8,334	8,687	2,805	4,578
McDonough	3,078	3,142	7,119	7,656
McHenry	3,540	3,139	50,330	76,412
McLean	2,693	4,371	29,877	41,276
Menard	2,704	3,672	2,137	4,408
Mercer	4,885	3,830	4,512	4,405
Monroe	7,943	9,870	6,788	9,468
Montgomery	6,486	6,141	5,979	6,851
Morgan	7,458	7,585	5,650	9,392
Moultrie	2,663	3,466	2,388	4,028
Ogle	11,247	13,131	9,018	14,918
Peoria	44,396	33,018	41,121	41,051
Perry	4,697	5,077	4,770	5,589
Piatt	3,856	4,988	3,124	5,392
Pike	3,021	4,451	2,849	5,032
Pope	842	1,339	918	1,500
Pulaski	1,636	1,592	1,372	1,720
Putnam	1,900	1,376	1,704	1,623
Randolph	7,387	7,536	6,771	8,076
Richland	3,177	4,320	2,529	5,153
Rock Island	42,175	25,338	39,880	29,663
St. Clair	77,896	47,005	62,410	50,203
Saline	5,082	6,096	4,697	7,057
Sangamon	51,176	46,857	38,630	55,904
Schuyler	1,896	1,830	1,594	2,403
Scott	1,090	1,453	927	1,696
Shelby	4,236	6,390	3,744	6,753
Stark	1,357	1,513	1,189	1,841
Stephenson	11,010	9,686	8,913	12,212
Tazewell	29,335	33,203	25,814	36,058
Union	3,916	4,999	3,735	5,333
Vermilion	16,228	16,046	14,726	18,731
Wabash	2,462	3,252	1,752	4,212
Warren	4,286	3,637	3,938	4,474
Washington	3,338	4,468	2,986	5,072
Wayne	2,545	5,381	2,139	6,102
White	3,315	3,985	3,071	5,180
Whiteside	15,587	10,867	13,723	12,959
Will	154,691	119,049	117,172	130,728
Williamson	12,893	17,351	11,685	18,086
Winnebago	69,903	53,806	59,740	60,782
Woodford	6,969	12,137	6,005	12,698
Totals	**3,419,348**	**2,031,179**	**2,891,550**	**2,345,946**

Illinois Vote Since 1952

2008: Obama, Dem., 3,419,348; McCain, Rep., 2,031,179; Nader, Ind., 30,948; Barr, Lib., 19,642; McKinney, Green, 11,838; Baldwin, Const., 8,256; Polachek, New, 1,149.
2004: Kerry, D., 2,891,550; Bush, R., 2,345,946; Badnarik, LB., 32,442.
2000: Gore, D., 2,589,026; Bush, R., 2,019,421; Nader, Green, 103,759; Buchanan, Ind., 16,106; Browne, LB., 11,623; Hagelin, Reform, 2,127.
1996: Clinton, D., 2,341,744; Dole, R., 1,587,021; Perot, Ref., 346,408; Browne, LB., 22,548; Phillips, U.S. Taxpayers, 7,606; Hagelin, Natural Law, 4,606.
1992: Clinton, D., 2,453,350; Bush, R., 1,734,096; Perot, Ind., 840,515; Marrou, LB., 9,218; Fulani, New Alliance, 5,267; Gritz, Populist/America First, 3,577; Hagelin, Natural Law, 2,751; Warren, Soc. Workers, 1,361.
1988: Bush, R., 2,310,939; Dukakis, D., 2,215,940; Paul, Lib., 14,944; Fulani, Solid., 10,276.
1984: Reagan, R., 2,707,103; Mondale, D., 2,086,499; Bergland, LB., 10,086.
1980: Reagan, R., 2,358,049; Carter, D., 1,981,413; Anderson, Ind., 346,754; Clark, LB., 38,939; Commoner, Citizens, 10,692; Hall, Com., 9,711; Griswold, Workers World, 2,257; DeBerry, Soc. Workers, 1,302; write-in, 604.
1976: Ford, R., 2,364,269; Carter, D., 2,271,295; McCarthy, Ind., 55,939; Hall, Com., 9,250; MacBride, LB., 8,057; Camejo, Soc. Workers, 3,615; Levin, Soc. Labor, 2,422; LaRouche, U.S. Labor, 2,018; write-in, 1,968.
1972: Nixon, R. 2,788,179; McGovern, D., 1,913,472; Fisher, Soc. Labor, 12,344; Hall, Com., 4,541; Schmitz, Amer., 2,471; others, 2,229.
1968: Nixon, R., 2,174,774; Humphrey, D., 2,039,814; Wallace, 3rd Party, 390,958; Blomen, Soc. Labor, 13,878; write-in, 325.
1964: Johnson, D., 2,796,833; Goldwater, R., 1,905,946; write-in, 62.

1960: Kennedy, D., 2,377,846; Nixon, R., 2,368,988; Hass, Soc. Labor, 10,560; write-in, 15.
1956: Eisenhower, R., 2,623,327; Stevenson, D., 1,775,682; Hass, Soc. Labor, 8,342; write-in, 56.
1952: Eisenhower, R., 2,457,327; Stevenson, D., 2,013,920; Hass, Soc. Labor, 9,363; write-in, 448.

Indiana

County	2008 Obama (D)	McCain (R)	2004 Kerry (D)	Bush (R)
Adams	4,928	8,402	3,512	9,734
Allen	71,083	77,668	46,710	82,013
Bartholomew	13,555	17,061	9,191	19,093
Benton	1,563	2,180	1,135	2,797
Blackford	2,677	2,690	1,903	3,447
Boone	9,744	16,616	5,636	17,055
Brown	3,852	4,060	2,730	4,512
Carroll	3,733	4,845	2,689	5,868
Cass	6,995	8,339	4,315	9,480
Clark	21,918	25,299	17,648	24,495
Clay	4,954	6,264	3,333	7,361
Clinton	5,306	6,915	3,335	8,471
Crawford	2,286	2,393	1,932	2,609
Daviess	3,369	7,096	2,573	7,936
Dearborn	7,123	14,886	6,596	14,231
Decatur	3,890	6,443	2,621	7,499
DeKalb	7,169	9,771	4,810	10,468
Delaware	28,356	20,904	20,436	27,064
Dubois	8,748	9,526	5,210	11,726
Elkhart	31,289	39,344	17,966	42,967
Fayette	4,387	4,917	3,626	5,761
Floyd	16,248	19,944	13,857	19,877
Fountain	3,094	4,151	2,477	5,260
Franklin	3,404	7,017	2,925	6,977
Fulton	3,700	5,145	2,607	6,027
Gibson	6,455	8,449	5,378	9,133
Grant	11,291	14,726	8,509	18,769
Greene	5,709	7,689	4,606	8,609
Hamilton	49,691	78,391	26,388	77,887
Hancock	11,869	21,991	6,912	20,771
Harrison	7,271	10,529	6,171	11,015
Hendricks	24,394	39,578	13,548	38,430
Henry	10,058	10,894	7,176	13,137
Howard	17,803	20,207	12,998	23,714
Huntington	5,842	10,289	3,877	11,617
Jackson	7,445	9,852	5,092	11,083
Jasper	5,044	7,669	3,678	8,056
Jay	3,746	4,400	2,740	5,427
Jefferson	6,255	7,052	5,117	7,763
Jennings	5,302	6,257	3,538	6,864
Johnson	21,536	36,417	13,109	37,765
Knox	7,569	8,639	5,649	9,990
Kosciusko	9,229	20,484	5,977	22,136
LaGrange	3,659	5,697	21,114	20,916
Lake	138,603	67,417	114,743	71,903
LaPorte	28,247	17,911	21,114	20,916
Lawrence	7,208	11,018	5,346	12,207
Madison	30,152	26,403	21,882	32,526
Marion	237,275	131,459	162,249	156,072
Marshall	7,880	10,401	5,593	12,074
Martin	1,706	3,112	1,522	3,414
Miami	5,559	8,305	3,886	9,600
Monroe	41,332	21,083	26,965	22,834
Montgomery	6,005	9,055	3,536	10,901
Morgan	10,314	18,105	6,650	19,197
Newton	2,623	3,300	2,032	3,757
Noble	7,063	9,671	4,703	10,859
Ohio	1,158	1,712	1,139	1,796
Orange	3,390	4,536	2,885	5,683
Owen	3,570	4,415	2,536	5,000
Parke	2,913	3,900	2,362	4,550
Perry	5,140	3,201	4,131	4,137
Pike	2,700	3,221	2,418	3,745
Porter	39,046	33,796	29,388	34,794
Posey	5,820	6,794	4,085	7,833
Pulaski	2,466	3,368	1,750	3,797
Putnam	6,331	8,085	4,103	8,908
Randolph	4,839	5,787	3,812	7,172
Ripley	4,187	7,794	3,510	8,224
Rush	3,228	4,270	2,000	5,363
St. Joseph	68,700	48,510	52,637	55,254
Scott	4,268	4,443	3,822	4,793
Shelby	6,983	10,330	4,519	11,397
Spencer	5,037	4,998	3,920	5,934
Starke	4,778	4,473	3,987	4,846
Steuben	6,283	7,670	4,345	8,433
Sullivan	4,282	4,341	3,341	4,999
Switzerland	1,638	1,940	1,479	2,161
Tippecanoe	37,709	29,789	20,818	30,897
Tipton	3,250	4,452	2,203	5,628
Union	1,220	2,058	1,045	2,266
Vanderburgh	39,368	37,449	28,767	41,463
Vermillion	4,002	3,004	3,424	3,536
Vigo	25,023	18,111	18,426	20,988
Wabash	5,455	8,238	3,920	9,607
Warren	1,753	2,164	1,356	2,565
Warrick	12,329	16,013	8,980	16,930
Washington	4,561	6,512	3,879	6,915
Wayne	13,459	14,558	10,775	16,586
Wells	4,403	8,503	3,112	9,168
White	4,839	5,730	3,277	6,974
Whitley	5,861	9,122	3,880	9,512
Totals	1,374,039	1,345,648	969,011	1,479,438

Indiana Vote Since 1952

2008: Obama, Dem., 1,374,039; McCain, Rep., 1,345,648; Barr, Lib., 29,257.
2004: Bush, R., 1,479,438; Kerry, D., 969,011; Badnarik, LB., 18,058.
2000: Bush, R., 1,245,836; Gore, D., 901,980; Buchanan, Ind., 16,959; Browne, LB., 15,530.
1996: Dole, R., 1,006,693; Clinton, D., 887,424; Perot, Ref., 224,299; Browne, LB., 15,632.
1992: Bush, R., 989,375; Clinton, D., 848,420; Perot, Ind., 455,934; Marrou, LB., 7,936; Fulani, New Alliance, 2,583.
1988: Bush, R., 1,297,763; Dukakis, D., 860,643; Fulani, New Alliance, 10,215.
1984: Reagan, R., 1,377,230; Mondale, D., 841,481; Bergland, LB., 6,741.
1980: Reagan, R., 1,255,656; Carter, D., 844,197; Anderson, Ind., 111,639; Clark, LB., 19,627; Commoner, Citizens, 4,852; Greaves, Amer., 4,750; Hall, Com., 702; DeBerry, Soc., 610.
1976: Ford, R., 1,185,958; Carter, D., 1,014,714; Anderson, Amer., 14,048; Camejo, Soc. Workers, 5,695; LaRouche, U.S. Labor, 1,947.
1972: Nixon, R., 1,405,154; McGovern, D., 708,568; Reed, Soc. Workers, 5,575; Spock, Peace and Freedom, 4,544; Fisher, Soc. Labor, 1,688.
1968: Nixon, R., 1,067,885; Humphrey, D., 806,659; Wallace, 3rd Party, 243,108; Munn, Proh., 4,616; Halstead, Soc. Workers, 1,293; Gregory, write-in, 36.
1964: Johnson, D., 1,170,848; Goldwater, R., 911,118; Munn, Proh., 8,266; Hass, Soc. Labor, 1,374.
1960: Nixon, R., 1,175,120; Kennedy, D., 952,358; Decker, Proh., 6,746; Hass, Soc. Labor, 1,136.
1956: Eisenhower, R., 1,182,811; Stevenson, D., 783,908; Holtwick, Proh., 6,554; Hass, Soc. Labor, 1,334.
1952: Eisenhower, R., 1,136,259; Stevenson, D., 801,530; Hamblen, Proh., 15,335; Hallinan, Prog., 1,222; Hass, Soc. Labor, 979.

Iowa

County	2008 Obama (D)	McCain (R)	2004 Kerry (D)	Bush (R)
Adair	1,920	2,059	1,844	2,402
Adams	1,113	1,039	977	1,317
Allamakee	3,962	2,961	3,449	3,530
Appanoose	2,964	3,081	3,063	3,340
Audubon	1,731	1,631	1,608	1,958
Benton	7,035	6,431	6,747	6,658
Black Hawk	38,564	24,467	35,392	28,046
Boone	7,333	6,265	7,027	6,870
Bremer	6,870	5,704	6,025	6,665
Buchanan	6,037	4,131	5,608	4,797
Buena Vista	4,065	4,217	3,520	4,887
Butler	3,348	3,686	3,001	4,417
Calhoun	2,335	2,747	2,243	3,255
Carroll	5,284	4,905	4,689	5,762
Cass	3,201	3,990	2,679	4,796
Cedar	5,201	4,278	4,747	4,869
Cerro Gordo	14,305	9,344	13,372	10,960
Cherokee	2,883	3,365	2,988	3,758
Chickasaw	3,897	2,536	3,708	3,040
Clarke	2,214	2,112	2,323	2,200
Clay	3,908	4,345	3,547	4,898
Clayton	5,174	3,640	4,736	4,312
Clinton	14,733	9,068	13,813	10,666
Crawford	3,697	3,338	3,220	3,955
Dallas	15,101	16,904	10,917	15,183
Davis	2,262	2,553	1,731	2,148
Decatur	1,983	2,019	1,859	2,088
Delaware	4,630	4,108	4,227	4,908
Des Moines	12,396	7,687	12,456	8,221
Dickinson	4,609	5,150	4,140	5,337
Dubuque	23,791	16,694	26,561	20,100
Emmet	2,565	2,366	2,405	2,697
Fayette	5,889	4,199	5,185	5,128
Floyd	4,797	3,044	4,349	3,745
Franklin	2,566	2,495	2,340	3,128
Fremont	2,490	2,708	1,510	2,362
Greene	2,359	2,340	2,459	2,618
Grundy	2,774	3,936	2,386	4,429
Guthrie	2,603	3,025	2,614	3,325
Hamilton	3,999	3,909	3,895	4,367
Hancock	2,790	3,008	2,484	3,368
Hardin	4,368	4,301	4,015	4,875
Harrison	3,549	3,906	2,906	4,680
Henry	5,306	5,582	4,127	5,220
Howard	2,933	1,721	2,614	2,028

County	2008 Obama (D)	McCain (R)	2004 Kerry (D)	Bush (R)
Humboldt	2,151	2,881	2,146	3,162
Ida	1,455	2,025	1,415	2,342
Iowa	4,173	4,173	3,841	4,544
Jackson	6,069	3,662	5,656	4,242
Jasper	10,195	8,750	10,430	9,462
Jefferson	5,028	3,321	4,490	3,648
Johnson	50,708	20,639	41,847	22,715
Jones	5,431	4,398	5,054	4,834
Keokuk	2,508	2,703	2,294	3,119
Kossuth	4,609	4,310	4,132	5,042
Lee	9,470	6,724	10,152	7,472
Linn	67,476	43,384	60,442	49,442
Louisa	2,520	2,310	2,297	2,572
Lucas	2,024	2,329	1,987	2,543
Lyon	1,673	4,461	1,303	4,751
Madison	3,702	4,525	3,380	4,538
Mahaska	4,450	6,249	3,790	6,858
Marion	7,408	9,232	6,574	9,990
Marshall	9,918	8,229	9,443	9,557
Mills	2,970	4,177	2,308	4,556
Mitchell	3,175	2,465	2,785	2,646
Monona	2,284	2,407	2,397	2,575
Monroe	1,793	1,997	1,855	2,067
Montgomery	2,318	2,878	1,899	3,601
Muscatine	10,850	7,907	9,542	9,020
O'Brien	2,333	4,883	2,330	5,328
Osceola	1,037	2,027	934	2,295
Page	2,892	4,344	2,211	5,243
Palo Alto	2,420	2,290	2,482	2,674
Plymouth	4,564	7,744	4,278	7,810
Pocahontas	1,794	2,131	1,822	2,441
Polk	119,569	88,983	105,218	95,828
Pottawattamie	20,226	21,161	16,906	24,558
Poweshiek	5,441	4,331	5,043	4,965
Ringgold	1,236	1,401	1,286	1,466
Sac	2,237	2,699	2,215	3,128
Scott	48,675	36,239	42,122	39,958
Shelby	2,847	3,472	2,355	4,256
Sioux	3,010	13,440	2,259	14,229
Story	26,268	18,812	23,296	20,819
Tama	4,859	3,813	4,487	4,456
Taylor	1,344	1,602	1,252	1,908
Union	2,990	2,774	2,747	3,165
Van Buren	1,540	1,980	1,568	2,211
Wapello	8,481	6,466	9,125	7,403
Warren	12,261	12,112	10,730	12,160
Washington	5,140	5,228	4,595	5,977
Wayne	1,356	1,563	1,379	1,733
Webster	9,847	8,299	9,561	8,959
Winnebago	3,236	2,726	2,707	3,175
Winneshiek	6,808	4,260	5,354	5,324
Woodbury	20,290	20,798	21,455	22,451
Worth	2,560	1,612	2,286	1,795
Wright	3,087	3,187	2,930	3,631
Totals	828,940	682,379	741,898	751,957

Iowa Vote Since 1952

2008: Obama, Dem., 828,940; McCain, Rep., 682,379; Nader, Peace/Freedom, 8,014; Barr, Lib., 4,590; Baldwin, Const., 4,445; McKinney, Green, 1,423; Harris, Socialist Wkrs., 292; Moore, Socialist USA, 182; LaRiva, Socialism/Liberation, 121.

2004: Bush, R., 751,957; Kerry, D., 741,898; Nader, Petitioning Cand., 5,973; Badnarik, LB., 2,992; Peroutka, Constitution, 1,304; Cobb, Green, 1,141; Harris, Soc. Wkrs., 373; Van Auken, Petitioning Cand., 176.

2000: Gore, D., 638,517; Bush, R., 634,373; Nader, Green, 29,374; Buchanan, Reform, 5,731; Browne, LB., 3,209; Hagelin, Ind., 2,281; Phillips, Constitution, 613; Harris, Soc. Workers, 190; McReynolds, Soc., 107.

1996: Clinton, D., 620,258; Dole, R., 492,644; Perot, Ref., 105,159; Nader, Green, 6,550; Hagelin, Natural Law, 3,349; Browne, LB., 2,315; Phillips, Taxpayers, 2,229; Harris, Soc. Workers, 331.

1992: Clinton, D., 586,353; Bush, R., 504,891; Perot, Ind., 253,468; Hagelin, Natural Law, 3,079; Gritz, Populist/America First, 1,177; Marrou, LB., 1,076.

1988: Dukakis, D., 670,557; Bush, R., 545,355; LaRouche, Ind., 3,526; Paul, Lib., 2,494.

1984: Reagan, R., 703,088; Mondale, D., 605,620; Bergland, LB., 1,844.

1980: Reagan, R., 676,026; Carter, D., 508,672; Anderson, Ind., 115,633; Clark, LB., 13,123; Commoner, Citizens, 2,273; McReynolds, Socialist, 534; Hall, Com., 298; DeBerry, Soc. Wkrs., 244; Greaves, Amer., 189; Bubar, Statesman, 150; scattered, 519.

1976: Ford, R., 632,863; Carter, D., 619,931; McCarthy, Ind., 20,051; Anderson, Amer., 3,040; MacBride, LB., 1,452.

1972: Nixon, R., 706,207; McGovern, D., 496,206; Schmitz, Amer., 22,056; Jenness, Soc. Workers, 488; Hall, Com., 272; Green, Universal, 199; Fisher, Soc. Labor, 195; scattered, 321.

1968: Nixon, R., 619,106; Humphrey, D., 476,699; Wallace, 3rd Party, 66,422; Halstead, Soc. Workers, 3,377; Cleaver, Peace and Freedom, 1,332; Munn, Proh., 362; Blomen, Soc. Labor, 241.

1964: Johnson, D., 733,030; Goldwater, R., 449,148; Munn, Proh., 1,902; Hass, Soc. Labor, 182; DeBerry, Soc. Workers, 159.

1960: Nixon, R., 722,381; Kennedy, D., 550,565; Hass, Soc. Labor, 230; write-in, 634.

1956: Eisenhower, R., 729,187; Stevenson, D., 501,858; Andrews (A.C.P. of Iowa), 3,202; Hoopes, Soc., 192; Hass, Soc. Labor, 125.

1952: Eisenhower, R., 808,906; Stevenson, D., 451,513; Hallinan, Prog., 5,085; Hamblen, Proh., 2,882; Hoopes, Soc., 219; Hass, Soc. Labor, 139; scattered, 29.

Kansas

County	2008 Obama (D)	McCain (R)	2004 Kerry (D)	Bush (R)
Allen	2,130	3,481	1,922	3,867
Anderson	1,161	2,329	1,295	2,500
Atchison	3,157	3,717	3,120	3,880
Barber	585	1,794	588	1,782
Barton	2,967	7,636	2,874	8,666
Bourbon	2,343	4,159	2,216	4,372
Brown	1,284	2,926	1,268	3,092
Butler	8,942	17,756	7,495	18,438
Chase	371	934	418	1,055
Chautauqua	385	1,396	404	1,529
Cherokee	3,366	5,750	3,726	6,083
Cheyenne	432	1,247	320	1,353
Clark	241	870	257	1,014
Clay	982	2,919	793	3,174
Cloud	1,213	3,070	1,210	3,221
Coffey	1,105	3,008	1,093	3,259
Comanche	194	756	200	770
Cowley	4,859	8,263	4,818	9,407
Crawford	7,646	7,453	7,617	8,626
Decatur	340	1,189	355	1,355
Dickinson	2,353	5,961	2,364	6,295
Doniphan	1,077	2,336	1,065	2,491
Douglas	33,141	17,475	28,634	20,544
Edwards	326	979	386	1,084
Elk	359	1,035	369	1,119
Ellis	3,917	8,037	4,033	7,891
Ellsworth	838	1,996	801	2,259
Finney	3,188	6,776	2,351	7,479
Ford	2,848	5,587	2,286	6,632
Franklin	4,366	6,969	3,921	7,391
Geary	3,368	4,376	2,531	4,703
Gove	257	1,120	247	1,196
Graham	323	1,043	334	1,082
Grant	616	1,941	561	2,169
Gray	416	1,585	408	1,816
Greeley	150	587	138	584
Greenwood	916	2,087	911	2,282
Hamilton	233	836	229	888
Harper	740	1,960	727	2,154
Harvey	6,185	8,865	5,331	9,534
Haskell	265	1,216	227	1,356
Hodgeman	202	836	223	953
Jackson	2,266	3,770	2,064	3,730
Jefferson	3,450	5,058	3,253	5,408
Jewell	312	1,229	385	1,495
Johnson	124,142	149,816	97,866	158,103
Kearny	302	1,138	272	1,177
Kingman	918	2,468	904	2,801
Kiowa	197	903	256	1,275
Labette	3,782	4,955	3,615	5,400
Lane	187	786	181	823
Leavenworth	12,749	16,387	11,039	15,949
Lincoln	334	1,175	391	1,368
Linn	1,401	3,029	1,631	3,048
Logan	222	1,171	248	1,255
Lyon	5,661	6,468	5,234	7,951
Marion	4,113	8,732	1,536	4,516
Marshall	1,607	3,695	1,789	3,261
McPherson	1,779	3,150	3,589	9,595
Meade	369	1,527	356	1,748
Miami	5,644	9,229	4,838	9,013
Mitchell	692	2,405	693	2,609
Montgomery	4,203	9,142	4,338	9,598
Morris	897	1,858	931	1,961
Morton	225	1,129	276	1,287
Nemaha	1,405	3,761	1,355	4,027
Neosho	2,496	4,372	2,424	4,705
Ness	283	1,197	382	1,407
Norton	488	1,836	473	2,092
Osage	2,508	4,768	2,537	4,800
Osborne	391	1,441	454	1,587
Ottawa	703	2,304	595	2,333
Pawnee	869	1,923	773	2,172
Phillips	516	2,066	557	2,256
Pottawatomie	2,552	6,816	2,176	6,326
Pratt	1,265	2,765	1,200	3,121
Rawlins	270	1,243	289	1,414
Reno	9,711	15,858	9,114	17,748
Republic	627	1,949	607	2,238
Rice	1,137	2,746	1,130	3,182
Riley	10,033	11,729	7,908	12,672
Rooks	467	2,054	534	2,121
Rush	498	1,217	517	1,226
Russell	719	2,470	810	2,671

County	2008 Obama (D)	2008 McCain (R)	2004 Kerry (D)	2004 Bush (R)
Saline	7,897	13,754	7,524	15,111
Scott	311	1,788	347	1,924
Sedgwick	79,175	104,119	64,839	110,381
Seward	1,376	3,620	1,122	4,272
Shawnee	40,072	40,806	36,264	44,188
Sheridan	252	1,068	239	1,144
Sherman	677	1,932	632	2,088
Smith	437	1,695	540	1,803
Stafford	535	1,483	506	1,649
Stanton	187	625	165	796
Stevens	277	1,770	310	1,936
Sumner	3,304	6,637	3,217	7,092
Thomas	761	2,762	816	3,007
Trego	415	1,215	434	1,225
Wabaunsee	1,020	2,375	1,001	2,531
Wallace	96	690	112	742
Washington	640	2,193	643	2,498
Wichita	163	835	183	869
Wilson	1,218	2,927	1,060	3,263
Woodson	507	1,045	530	1,204
Wyandotte	38,482	16,211	34,923	17,919
Totals	**514,765**	**699,655**	**434,993**	**736,456**

Kansas Vote Since 1952

2008: McCain, Rep., 699,655; Obama, Dem., 514,765; Nader, Ind., 10,527; Barr, Lib., 6,706; Baldwin, Reform, 4,148.

2004: Bush, R., 736,456; Kerry, D., 434,993; Nader, Ref., 9,348; Badnarik, LB., 4,013; Peroutka, Ind., 2,899.

2000: Bush, R., 622,332; Gore, D., 399,276; Nader, Ind., 36,086; Buchanan, Reform, 7,370; Browne, LB., 4,525; Hagelin, Ind., 1,373; Phillips, Constitution, 1,254.

1996: Dole, R., 583,245; Clinton, D., 387,659; Perot, Ref., 92,639; Browne, LB., 4,557; Phillips, Ind., 3,519; Hagelin, Ind., 1,655.

1992: Bush, R., 449,951; Clinton, D., 390,434; Perot, Ind., 312,358; Marrou, LB., 4,314.

1988: Bush, R., 554,049; Dukakis, D., 422,636; Paul, Ind.,12,553; Fulani, Ind., 3,806.

1984: Reagan, R., 674,646; Mondale, D., 332,471; Bergland, LB., 3,585.

1980: Reagan, R., 566,812; Carter, D., 326,150; Anderson, Ind., 68,231; Clark, LB., 14,470; Shelton, Amer., 1,555; Hall, Com., 967; Bubar, Statesman, 821; Rarick, Conservative, 789.

1976: Ford, R., 502,752; Carter, D., 430,421; McCarthy, Ind., 13,185; Anderson, Amer., 4,724; MacBride, LB., 3,242; Maddox, Conservative, 2,118; Bubar, Proh., 1,403.

1972: Nixon, R., 619,812; McGovern, D., 270,287; Schmitz, Conservative, 21,808; Munn, Proh., 4,188.

1968: Nixon, R., 478,674; Humphrey, D., 302,996; Wallace, 3rd Party, 88,921; Munn, Proh., 2,192.

1964: Johnson, D., 464,028; Goldwater, R., 386,579; Munn, Proh., 5,393; Hass, Soc. Labor, 1,901.

1960: Nixon, R., 561,474; Kennedy, D., 363,213; Decker, Proh., 4,138.

1956: Eisenhower, R., 566,878; Stevenson, D., 296,317; Holtwick, Proh., 3,048.

1952: Eisenhower, R., 616,302; Stevenson, D., 273,296; Hamblen, Proh., 6,038; Hoopes, Soc., 530.

Kentucky

County	2008 Obama (D)	2008 McCain (R)	2004 Kerry (D)	2004 Bush (R)
Adair	1,888	5,512	1,764	5,628
Allen	2,023	5,258	1,923	5,202
Anderson	3,461	6,884	3,141	6,363
Ballard	1,427	2,537	1,759	2,389
Barren	5,434	11,133	5,216	10,822
Bath	2,210	2,234	2,608	2,269
Bell	2,718	9,519	4,210	6,722
Boone	16,292	33,812	12,391	32,329
Bourbon	3,385	4,820	3,198	4,953
Boyd	8,886	11,429	10,132	11,501
Boyle	4,764	7,697	4,646	7,764
Bracken	1,241	2,066	1,213	2,363
Breathitt	2,205	2,671	3,327	2,542
Breckinridge	3,110	5,281	2,884	5,580
Bullitt	10,056	19,857	9,043	19,433
Butler	1,555	3,696	1,436	4,109
Caldwell	2,212	3,866	2,245	4,066
Calloway	6,165	8,991	5,728	9,293
Campbell	15,619	24,045	14,253	25,540
Carlisle	879	1,699	1,102	1,734
Carroll	1,716	2,032	1,688	2,175
Carter	4,314	5,252	5,577	5,422
Casey	1,219	4,679	1,174	5,109
Christian	8,822	13,515	6,970	13,935
Clark	5,749	9,664	5,661	9,540
Clay	1,552	5,710	1,901	5,726
Clinton	761	3,366	952	3,369
Crittenden	1,254	2,604	1,438	2,726
Cumberland	697	2,056	848	2,356
Daviess	19,282	23,692	15,788	25,372
Edmonson	1,652	3,562	1,856	3,595
Elliott	1,535	902	2,064	871
Estill	1,555	3,685	1,907	3,633
Fayette	66,040	59,884	57,994	66,406
Fleming	2,279	3,432	2,406	3,749
Floyd	7,530	7,741	11,132	6,612
Franklin	11,767	11,911	11,620	12,281
Fulton	1,226	1,530	1,340	1,527
Gallatin	1,278	1,840	1,188	1,869
Garrard	2,012	5,117	1,841	4,784
Grant	3,109	5,605	2,818	5,951
Graves	5,843	10,056	6,206	9,903
Grayson	3,154	6,605	2,905	7,170
Green	1,204	3,785	1,312	3,866
Greenup	6,621	8,449	7,630	8,696
Hancock	2,128	1,924	1,709	2,286
Hardin	15,650	23,896	11,507	24,627
Harlan	2,586	7,165	4,332	6,659
Harrison	2,916	4,520	2,807	4,855
Hart	2,290	4,397	2,470	4,269
Henderson	10,049	9,523	8,101	10,467
Henry	2,724	4,081	2,366	4,094
Hickman	812	1,406	926	1,395
Hopkins	7,104	11,916	6,420	12,314
Jackson	743	4,407	769	4,369
Jefferson	196,272	153,865	170,158	164,566
Jessamine	6,236	13,710	5,476	12,972
Johnson	2,413	5,964	3,288	5,940
Kenton	26,465	40,706	22,834	43,664
Knott	2,523	2,950	4,685	2,648
Knox	3,074	8,150	3,822	8,108
LaRue	1,913	4,153	1,823	4,111
Laurel	4,593	17,563	5,297	16,819
Lawrence	2,036	3,503	2,705	3,755
Lee	752	1,978	878	2,018
Leslie	766	3,574	1,266	3,661
Letcher	2,623	5,367	4,192	4,801
Lewis	1,510	3,213	1,667	3,778
Lincoln	2,752	6,273	2,796	5,996
Livingston	1,622	2,890	2,007	2,675
Logan	3,811	6,925	3,768	6,815
Lyon	1,577	2,220	1,769	2,132
Madison	11,285	19,043	11,525	18,922
Magoffin	1,258	4,078	2,843	2,836
Marion	1,963	2,386	3,399	3,905
Marshall	12,392	19,694	6,383	9,049
Martin	2,105	2,434	1,504	2,996
Mason	3,596	3,842	2,644	4,381
McCracken	5,593	9,463	11,361	18,218
McCreary	808	2,824	1,530	4,121
McLean	2,891	4,102	1,823	2,584
Meade	4,343	6,691	3,724	7,152
Menifee	1,276	1,155	1,284	1,215
Mercer	3,159	6,781	3,224	6,745
Metcalfe	1,350	2,734	1,472	2,645
Monroe	1,067	3,537	1,158	4,657
Montgomery	4,234	5,947	4,506	5,647
Morgan	1,858	2,377	2,532	2,682
Muhlenberg	6,221	6,447	6,636	6,749
Nelson	7,654	10,139	6,524	10,161
Nicholas	1,272	1,634	1,332	1,700
Ohio	4,059	5,781	3,627	6,311
Oldham	9,996	18,992	8,080	18,801
Owen	1,694	2,969	1,615	3,084
Owsley	381	1,279	430	1,558
Pendleton	2,027	3,676	1,940	4,045
Perry	3,444	6,762	5,400	6,187
Pike	9,525	12,665	14,002	12,611
Powell	2,065	2,867	2,249	2,687
Pulaski	5,590	19,862	5,829	19,535
Robertson	451	533	413	670
Rockcastle	1,410	4,757	1,320	4,804
Rowan	4,074	3,907	4,556	4,063
Russell	1,579	5,702	1,772	6,009
Scott	7,712	11,782	6,325	10,600
Shelby	6,871	11,451	5,277	10,909
Simpson	2,775	4,437	2,730	4,273
Spencer	2,519	5,378	1,970	4,816
Taylor	3,165	7,568	2,979	7,247
Todd	1,543	3,336	1,491	3,242
Trigg	2,246	4,189	2,046	4,023
Trimble	1,484	2,239	1,428	2,332
Union	2,804	3,120	2,398	3,534
Warren	17,650	25,957	14,326	25,100
Washington	1,890	3,305	1,724	3,479
Wayne	2,201	4,868	2,616	5,027
Webster	2,390	3,037	2,304	3,207
Whitley	3,484	10,014	3,985	9,559
Wolfe	1,493	1,408	1,744	1,385
Woodford	5,027	7,130	4,480	6,937
Totals	**751,985**	**1,048,462**	**712,733**	**1,069,439**

Kentucky Vote Since 1952

2008: McCain, Rep., 1,048,462; Obama, Dem., 751,985; Nader, Ind., 15,378; Barr, Lib., 5,989; Baldwin, Constitution, 4,694.
2004: Bush, R., 1,069,439; Kerry, D., 712,733; Nader, Ind., 8,856; Badnarik, LB., 2,619; Peroutka, Constitution, 2,213.
2000: Bush, R., 872,520; Gore, D., 638,923; Nader, Green, 23,118; Buchanan, Reform, 4,152; Browne, LB., 2,885; Hagelin, Natural Law, 1,513; Phillips, Constitution, 915.
1996: Clinton, D., 636,614; Dole, R., 623,283; Perot, Ref., 120,396; Browne, LB., 4,009; Phillips, U.S. Taxpayers, 2,204; Hagelin, Natural Law, 1,493.
1992: Clinton, D., 665,104; Bush, R., 617,178; Perot, Ind., 203,944; Marrou, LB., 4,513.
1988: Bush, R., 734,281; Dukakis, D., 580,368; Duke, Pop., 4,494; Paul, Lib., 2,118.
1984: Reagan, R., 815,345; Mondale, D., 536,756.
1980: Reagan, R., 635,274; Carter, D., 616,417; Anderson, Ind., 31,127; Clark, LB., 5,531; McCormack, Respect For Life, 4,233; Commoner, Citizens, 1,304; Pulley, Socialist, 393; Hall, Com., 348.
1976: Carter, D., 615,717; Ford, R., 531,852; Anderson, Amer., 8,308; McCarthy, Ind., 6,837; Maddox, Amer. Ind., 2,328; MacBride, LB., 814.
1972: Nixon, R., 676,446; McGovern, D., 371,159; Schmitz, Amer., 17,627; Spock, People's, 1,118; Jenness, Soc. Workers, 685; Hall, Com., 464.
1968: Nixon, R., 462,411; Humphrey, D., 397,547; Wallace, 3rd Party, 193,098; Halstead, Soc. Workers, 2,843.
1964: Johnson, D., 669,659; Goldwater, R., 372,977; Kasper, Natl. States Rights, 3,469.
1960: Nixon, R., 602,607; Kennedy, D., 521,855.
1956: Eisenhower, R., 572,192; Stevenson, D., 476,453; Byrd, States' Rights, 2,657; Holtwick, Proh., 2,145; Hass, Soc. Labor, 358.
1952: Stevenson, D., 495,729; Eisenhower, R., 495,029; Hamblen, Proh., 1,161; Hass, Soc. Labor, 893; Hallinan, Proh., 336.

Louisiana

Parish	2008		2004	
	Obama (D)	McCain (R)	Kerry (D)	Bush (R)
Acadia	7,028	19,228	8,937	16,083
Allen	2,891	6,333	3,791	5,140
Ascension	14,620	31,225	13,955	24,661
Assumption	4,756	5,981	5,585	4,966
Avoyelles	6,327	10,234	6,976	8,302
Beauregard	3,071	10,718	3,666	9,470
Bienville	3,589	3,776	3,399	3,612
Bossier	12,701	32,706	12,317	30,040
Caddo	55,220	52,105	51,739	54,292
Calcasieu	30,227	50,431	32,864	46,075
Caldwell	1,118	3,696	1,384	3,308
Cameron	613	3,089	1,367	3,190
Catahoula	1,659	3,486	1,673	3,219
Claiborne	3,025	3,750	2,854	3,704
Concordia	3,766	5,668	3,446	5,427
DeSoto	5,241	6,882	5,026	6,211
E. Baton Rouge	99,431	95,297	82,298	99,943
East Carroll	2,267	1,254	1,980	1,357
East Feliciana	4,383	5,431	4,091	5,021
Evangeline	5,852	9,792	5,757	7,949
Franklin	2,959	6,278	2,828	6,141
Grant	1,474	6,906	1,977	5,911
Iberia	12,492	20,123	12,426	19,420
Iberville	9,023	7,185	8,259	6,333
Jackson	2,456	5,190	2,525	5,038
Jefferson	64,853	113,008	72,136	117,882
Jefferson Davis	3,923	9,277	4,745	8,055
Lafayette	32,145	62,055	31,210	57,732
Lafourche	9,662	27,089	14,417	22,734
LaSalle	860	5,601	1,155	5,015
Lincoln	8,267	10,676	7,242	10,791
Livingston	6,674	43,247	9,895	33,976
Madison	3,100	2,152	2,334	2,291
Morehouse	5,789	7,258	5,336	7,471
Natchitoches	7,801	9,054	7,398	9,261
Orleans	116,042	28,041	152,610	42,847
Ouachita	24,769	41,708	22,016	41,750
Plaquemines	3,378	6,889	4,181	7,866
Pointe Coupee	5,516	6,702	5,712	5,429
Rapides	20,109	36,605	18,904	34,492
Red River	2,080	2,484	2,140	2,507
Richland	3,311	5,751	3,082	5,471
Sabine	2,245	7,226	2,743	6,711
St. Bernard	3,491	9,642	9,956	19,597
St. Charles	8,519	16,456	8,856	14,747
St. Helena	3,567	2,522	3,173	2,235
St. James	6,993	5,432	6,407	4,545
St. John the Baptist	12,420	8,908	10,305	9,039
St. Landry	20,267	21,647	18,166	18,315
St. Martin	9,419	14,443	10,321	12,095
St. Mary	9,342	13,181	9,547	12,877
St. Tammany	24,589	83,047	24,665	75,139
Tangipahoa	16,427	31,421	15,345	26,181
Tensas	1,646	1,367	1,469	1,453
Terrebonne	11,579	28,208	13,684	26,358

Parish	2008		2004	
	Obama (D)	McCain (R)	Kerry (D)	Bush (R)
Union	3,103	7,619	3,089	7,457
Vermilion	6,261	18,069	9,085	15,069
Vernon	3,534	11,946	4,035	11,032
Washington	6,122	12,215	6,554	11,006
Webster	6,610	11,417	6,833	11,070
W. Baton Rouge	5,043	6,654	4,932	5,822
West Carroll	878	4,045	1,231	3,740
W. Feliciana	2,414	3,149	2,214	2,932
Winn	2,044	4,628	2,056	4,366
Totals	**782,989**	**1,148,275**	**820,299**	**1,102,169**

Louisiana Vote Since 1952

2008: McCain, Rep., 1,148,275; Obama, Dem., 782,989; Paul, Louisiana Taxpayers, 9,368; McKinney, Green, 9,187; Nader, Ind., 6,997; Baldwin, Const., 2,581; Harris, Socialist Wkrs., 735; LaRiva, Socialism/Liberation, 354; Amondson, Prohib., 275.
2004: Bush, R., 1,102,169; Kerry, D., 820,299; Nader, Better Life, 7,032; Peroutka, Constitution, 5,203; Badnarik, LB., 2,781; Brown, Protect Wking Fam., 1,795; Amondson, Prohib., 1,566; Cobb, Green, 1,276; Harris, Soc. Wkrs., 985.
2000: Bush, R., 927,871; Gore, D., 792,344; Nader, Green, 20,473; Buchanan, Reform, 14,356; Phillips, Constitution, 5,483; Browne, LB., 2,951; Harris, Soc. Workers, 1,103; Hagelin, Natural Law, 1,075.
1996: Clinton, D., 927,837; Dole, R., 712,586; Perot, Ref., 123,293; Browne, LB., 7,499; Nader, Liberty, Ecology, Community, 4,719; Phillips, Taxpayers, 3,366; Hagelin, Natural Law, 2,981; Moorehead, Workers World, 1,678.
1992: Clinton, D., 815,971; Bush, R., 733,386; Perot, Ind., 211,478; Gritz, Populist/America First, 18,545; Marrou, LB., 3,155; Daniels, Ind., 1,663; Phillips, U.S. Taxpayers, 1,552; Fulani, New Alliance, 1,434; LaRouche, Ind., 1,136.
1988: Bush, R., 883,702; Dukakis, D., 717,460; Duke, Pop., 18,612; Paul, Lib., 4,115.
1984: Reagan, R., 1,037,299; Mondale, D., 651,586; Bergland, LB., 1,876.
1980: Reagan, R., 792,853; Carter, D., 708,453; Anderson, Ind., 26,345; Rarick, Amer. Ind., 10,333; Clark, LB., 8,240; Commoner, Citizens, 1,584; DeBerry, Soc. Work., 783.
1976: Carter, D., 661,365; Ford, R., 587,446; Maddox, Amer., 10,058; Hall, Com., 7,417; McCarthy, Ind., 6,588; MacBride, LB., 3,325.
1972: Nixon, R., 686,852; McGovern, D., 298,142; Schmitz, Amer., 52,099; Jenness, Soc. Workers, 14,398.
1968: Wallace, 3rd Party, 530,300; Humphrey, D., 309,615; Nixon, R., 257,535.
1964: Goldwater, R., 509,225; Johnson, D., 387,068.
1960: Kennedy, D., 407,339; Nixon, R., 230,890; States' Rights (unpledged), 169,572.
1956: Eisenhower, R., 329,047; Stevenson, D., 243,977; Andrews, States' Rights, 44,520.
1952: Stevenson, D., 345,027; Eisenhower, R., 306,925.

Maine

County	2008		2004	
	Obama (D)	McCain (R)	Kerry (D)	Bush (R)
Auburn	6,866	4,686	6,869	5,219
Augusta	5,418	3,637	5,543	4,149
Bangor	9,405	6,257	9,162	7,135
Biddeford	6,839	2,903	6,520	3,756
Brunswick	6,502	3,371	7,288	4,248
Gorham	5,190	3,599	4,393	4,133
Lewiston	10,258	5,898	11,021	6,523
Orono	4,244	1,416	3,649	1,578
Portland	28,272	7,833	26,800	9,455
Presque Isle	2,420	2,094	2,309	2,268
Saco	6,457	3,444	5,892	3,948
Sanford	5,953	3,607	5,582	4,634
Scarborough	6,750	4,866	5,651	5,569
S. Portland	9,911	4,011	8,965	4,882
Waterville	5,070	2,109	5,056	2,413
Westbrook	5,446	3,024	5,047	3,744
Windham	5,069	3,989	4,400	4,553
Other	291,414	229,451	272,695	251,994
Totals	**421,923**	**295,273**	**396,842**	**330,201**

Maine Vote Since 1952

2008: Obama, Dem., 421,923; McCain, Rep., 295,273; Nader, Ind., 10,636; McKinney, Green, 2,900.
2004: Kerry, D., 396,842; Bush, R., 330,201; Nader, Better Life, 8,069; Cobb, Green, 2,936; Badnarik, LB., 1,965; Peroutka, Constitution, 735.
2000: Gore, D., 319,951; Bush, R., 286,616; Nader, Green, 37,127; Buchanan, Reform, 4,443; Browne, LB., 3,074; Phillips, Constitution, 579.
1996: Clinton, D., 312,788; Dole, R., 186,378; Perot, Ref., 85,970; Nader, Green, 15,279; Browne, LB., 2,996; Phillips, Taxpayers, 1,517; Hagelin, Natural Law, 825.
1992: Clinton, D., 263,420; Perot, Ind., 206,820; Bush, R., 206,504; Marrou, LB., 1,681.
1988: Bush, R., 307,131; Dukakis, D., 243,569; Paul, Lib., 2,700; Fulani, New Alliance, 1,405.
1984: Reagan, R., 336,500; Mondale, D., 214,515.

1980: Reagan, R., 238,522; Carter, D., 220,974; Anderson, Ind., 53,327; Clark, LB., 5,119; Commoner, Citizens, 4,394; Hall, Com., 591; write-in, 84.
1976: Ford, R., 236,320; Carter, D., 232,279; McCarthy, Ind., 10,874; Bubar, Proh., 3,495.
1972: Nixon, R., 256,458; McGovern, D., 160,584; scattered, 229.
1968: Humphrey, D., 217,312; Nixon, R., 169,254; Wallace, 3rd Party, 6,370.
1964: Johnson, D., 262,264; Goldwater, R., 118,701.
1960: Nixon, R., 240,608; Kennedy, D., 181,159.
1956: Eisenhower, R., 249,238; Stevenson, D., 102,468.
1952: Eisenhower, R., 232,353; Stevenson, D., 118,806; Hallinan, Prog., 332; Hass, Soc. Labor, 156; Hoopes, Soc., 138; scattered, 1.

Maryland

County	2008		2004	
	Obama (D)	McCain (R)	Kerry (D)	Bush (R)
Allegany	10,693	18,405	10,576	18,980
Anne Arundel	125,015	129,682	103,324	133,231
Baltimore	214,151	158,714	182,474	166,051
Calvert	20,299	23,095	15,967	23,017
Caroline	4,971	8,015	3,810	7,396
Carroll	28,060	54,503	22,974	55,275
Cecil	17,665	23,855	14,680	22,556
Charles	42,635	25,732	29,354	28,442
Dorchester	6,912	8,168	5,411	7,801
Frederick	54,013	55,170	39,503	59,934
Garrett	3,736	8,903	3,291	9,085
Harford	48,552	71,751	39,685	71,565
Howard	87,120	55,393	72,257	59,724
Kent	4,953	4,905	4,278	4,900
Montgomery	307,960	116,273	273,936	136,334
Prince George's	323,105	37,969	260,532	55,532
Queen Anne's	8,575	15,087	7,070	14,489
St. Mary's	19,023	24,705	13,776	23,725
Somerset	4,779	5,037	4,034	4,884
Talbot	9,035	10,995	7,367	11,288
Washington	26,245	34,169	20,387	36,917
Wicomico	19,436	21,849	15,137	21,998
Worcester	11,374	15,607	9,648	15,349
City				
Baltimore	214,385	28,681	175,022	36,230
Totals	**1,629,467**	**959,862**	**1,334,493**	**1,024,703**

Maryland Vote Since 1952
2008: Obama, Dem., 1,629,467; McCain, Rep., 959,862; Nader, Maryland Ind., 14,713; Barr, Lib., 9,842; McKinney, Green, 4,747; Baldwin, Reform, 3,760.
2004: Kerry, D., 1,334,493; Bush, R., 1,024,703; Nader, Populist, 11,854; Badnarik, LB., 6,094; Cobb, Green, 3,632; Peroutka, Constitution, 3,421.
2000: Gore, D., 1,144,008; Bush, R., 813,827; Nader, Green, 53,768; Browne, LB., 5,310; Buchanan, Reform., 4,248; Phillips, Constitution, 918.
1996: Clinton, D., 966,207; Dole, R., 681,530; Perot, Ref., 115,812; Browne, LB., 8,765; Phillips, Taxpayers, 3,402; Hagelin, Natural Law, 2,517.
1992: Clinton, D., 988,571; Bush, R., 707,094; Perot, Ind., 281,414; Marrou, LB., 4,715; Fulani, New Alliance, 2,786.
1988: Bush, R., 876,167; Dukakis, D., 826,304; Paul, Lib., 6,748; Fulani, New Alliance, 5,115.
1984: Reagan, R., 879,918; Mondale, D., 787,935; Bergland, LB., 5,721.
1980: Carter, D., 726,161; Reagan, R., 680,606; Anderson, Ind., 119,537; Clark, LB., 14,192.
1976: Carter, D., 759,612; Ford, R., 672,661.
1972: Nixon, R., 829,305; McGovern, D., 505,781; Schmitz, Amer., 18,726.
1968: Humphrey, D., 538,310; Nixon, R., 517,995; Wallace, 3rd Party, 178,734.
1964: Johnson, D., 730,912; Goldwater, R., 385,495; write-in, 50.
1960: Kennedy, D., 565,800; Nixon, R., 489,538.
1956: Eisenhower, R., 559,738; Stevenson, D., 372,613.
1952: Eisenhower, R., 499,424; Stevenson, D., 395,337; Hallinan, Prog., 7,313.

Massachusetts

City	2008		2004	
	Obama (D)	McCain (R)	Kerry (D)	Bush (R)
Boston	184,320	45,248	160,884	44,518
Brockton	23,206	9,611	20,091	10,058
Brookline	22,269	4,788	21,256	5,269
Cambridge	40,464	4,662	35,886	5,338
Chicopee	14,160	8,259	14,642	7,957
Fall River	22,431	7,892	23,859	7,369
Framingham	17,731	8,430	17,239	8,448
Lawrence	15,567	3,620	11,547	4,796
Lowell	20,576	10,363	18,195	10,554
Lynn	20,223	8,703	19,372	8,373
Medford	17,507	8,627	17,737	7,932
New Bedford	24,881	8,201	25,551	7,328
Newton	33,075	10,208	32,061	10,025
Quincy	22,775	15,536	24,173	13,373
Somerville	26,450	5,197	24,300	5,232
Springfield	38,228	10,976	33,583	13,028

City	2008		2004	
	Obama (D)	McCain (R)	Kerry (D)	Bush (R)
Waltham	15,233	8,372	14,517	8,228
Weymouth	14,681	12,331	15,367	10,912
Worcester	40,925	18,333	38,264	17,648
Other	1,279,365	896,551	1,227,624	858,194
Totals	**1,904,097**	**1,108,854**	**1,803,800**	**1,071,109**

Massachusetts Vote Since 1952
2008: Obama, Dem., 1,904,097; McCain, Rep., 1,108,854; Nader, Ind., 28,841; Barr, Lib., 13,189; McKinney, Green, 6,550; Baldwin, Reform, 4,971.
2004: Kerry, D., 1,803,800; Bush, R., 1,071,109; Badnarik, LB., 15,022; Cobb, Green, 10,623.
2000: Gore, D., 1,616,487; Bush, R., 878,502; Nader, Green, 173,564; Browne, LB., 16,366; Buchanan, Reform, 11,149; Hagelin, Natural Law, 2,884.
1996: Clinton, D., 1,571,509; Dole, R., 718,058; Perot, Ref., 227,206; Browne, LB., 20,424; Hagelin, Natural Law, 5,183; Moorehead, Workers World, 3,276.
1992: Clinton, D., 1,318,639; Bush, R., 805,039; Perot, Ind., 630,731; Marrou, LB., 9,021; Fulani, New Alliance, 3,172; Phillips, U.S. Taxpayers, 2,218; Hagelin, Natural Law, 1,812; LaRouche, Ind., 1,027.
1988: Dukakis, D., 1,401,415; Bush, R., 1,194,635; Paul, Lib., 24,251; Fulani, New Alliance, 9,561.
1984: Reagan, R., 1,310,936; Mondale, D., 1,239,606.
1980: Reagan, R., 1,057,631; Carter, D., 1,053,802; Anderson, Ind., 382,539; Clark, LB., 22,038; DeBerry, Soc. Workers, 3,735; Commoner, Citizens, 2,056; McReynolds, Soc., 62; Bubar, Statesman, 34; Griswold, Workers World, 19; scattered, 2,382.
1976: Carter, D., 1,429,475; Ford, R., 1,030,276; McCarthy, Ind., 65,637; Camejo, Soc. Workers, 8,138; Anderson, Amer., 7,555; LaRouche, U.S. Labor, 4,922; MacBride, LB., 135.
1972: McGovern, D., 1,332,540; Nixon, R., 1,112,078; Jenness, Soc. Workers, 10,600; Schmitz, Amer., 2,877; Fisher, Soc. Labor, 129; Spock, People's, 101; Hall, Com., 46; Hospers, LB., 43; scattered, 342.
1968: Humphrey, D., 1,469,218; Nixon, R., 766,844; Wallace, 3rd Party, 87,088; Blomen, Soc. Labor, 6,180; Munn, Proh., 2,369; scattered, 53; blank, 25,394.
1964: Johnson, D., 1,786,422; Goldwater, R., 549,727; Hass, Soc. Labor, 4,755; Munn, Proh., 3,735; scattered, 159; blank, 48,104.
1960: Kennedy, D., 1,487,174; Nixon, R., 976,750; Hass, Soc. Labor, 3,892; Decker, Proh., 1,633; others, 31; blank and void, 26,024.
1956: Eisenhower, R., 1,393,197; Stevenson, D., 948,190; Hass, Soc. Labor, 5,573; Holtwick, Proh., 1,205; others, 341.
1952: Eisenhower, R., 1,292,325; Stevenson, D., 1,083,525; Hallinan, Prog., 4,636; Hass, Soc. Labor, 1,957; Hamblen, Proh., 886; scattered, 69; blank, 41,150.

Michigan

County	2008		2004	
	Obama (D)	McCain (R)	Kerry (D)	Bush (R)
Alcona	2,896	3,404	2,871	3,592
Alger	2,472	2,188	2,395	2,318
Allegan	23,526	29,526	19,355	34,022
Alpena	7,705	7,125	7,407	7,665
Antrim	6,079	7,506	5,072	8,379
Arenac	4,155	3,807	4,076	4,071
Baraga	1,725	1,846	1,660	1,977
Barry	13,449	16,431	11,312	18,638
Bay	32,589	23,794	31,049	25,448
Benzie	5,461	4,687	4,383	5,284
Berrien	40,376	36,128	32,846	41,076
Branch	8,412	9,534	7,004	10,784
Calhoun	34,550	28,538	29,891	32,093
Cass	12,080	11,112	9,537	12,964
Charlevoix	6,817	7,306	5,729	8,214
Cheboygan	6,721	6,919	5,941	7,798
Chippewa	8,169	8,249	7,203	9,122
Clare	7,496	6,793	6,984	7,088
Clinton	20,001	19,724	15,483	21,989
Crawford	3,440	3,558	3,126	4,017
Delta	9,976	8,763	9,381	9,680
Dickinson	5,995	7,049	5,650	7,734
Eaton	30,736	25,898	25,411	29,781
Emmet	8,515	9,315	6,846	10,332
Genesee	143,919	72,445	128,334	83,870
Gladwin	6,590	6,391	6,343	6,770
Gogebic	4,757	3,330	4,421	3,935
Grand Traverse	23,255	24,713	18,256	27,446
Gratiot	9,102	8,324	7,377	9,834
Hillsdale	8,765	11,221	7,123	12,804
Houghton	7,473	8,100	6,731	8,889
Huron	8,367	8,434	7,629	9,671
Ingham	95,698	47,143	76,877	54,734
Ionia	14,808	15,850	10,647	16,621
Iosco	7,307	6,583	6,557	7,301
Iron	3,080	2,947	3,215	3,224
Isabella	16,679	11,220	12,334	11,754
Jackson	37,480	35,692	31,025	40,029
Kalamazoo	73,407	48,411	61,462	57,147
Kalkaska	3,780	4,527	3,189	5,084
Kent	149,855	148,305	116,909	171,201

County	2008 Obama (D)	McCain (R)	2004 Kerry (D)	Bush (R)
Keweenaw	610	756	630	781
Lake	2,919	2,269	2,675	2,503
Lapeer	21,457	22,831	18,086	25,556
Leelanau	7,354	6,937	6,048	7,733
Lenawee	24,638	22,223	20,787	25,675
Livingston	42,346	55,581	33,991	58,860
Luce	1,191	1,490	1,045	1,749
Mackinac	3,027	3,268	2,819	3,706
Macomb	223,754	187,645	196,160	202,166
Manistee	7,234	5,506	6,272	6,295
Marquette	19,630	12,902	17,412	14,690
Mason	7,816	7,146	6,333	8,124
Mecosta	9,099	9,235	7,730	9,710
Menominee	5,980	4,855	5,326	5,942
Midland	20,742	22,285	18,355	24,369
Missaukee	2,898	4,469	2,319	5,055
Monroe	39,180	35,852	36,089	37,470
Montcalm	13,208	13,291	11,471	14,968
Montmorency	2,403	2,841	2,196	3,300
Muskegon	53,400	28,855	44,282	35,302
Newaygo	10,788	11,862	9,057	13,608
Oakland	372,694	276,881	319,387	316,633
Oceana	6,405	5,860	5,441	6,677
Ogemaw	5,391	5,133	5,215	5,454
Ontonagon	1,966	1,823	1,863	2,262
Osceola	4,848	5,966	4,467	6,599
Oscoda	1,887	2,320	1,792	2,570
Otsego	5,634	6,752	4,674	7,470
Ottawa	51,925	84,823	35,552	92,048
Presque Isle	3,719	3,605	3,432	3,982
Roscommon	7,082	6,727	6,810	7,364
Saginaw	60,260	42,218	54,887	47,165
Sanilac	40,676	38,555	7,883	12,632
Schoolcraft	12,311	12,876	2,137	2,267
Shiawassee	9,047	10,678	16,881	19,407
St. Clair	2,184	2,058	36,174	42,740
St. Joseph	18,015	15,054	9,648	15,340
Tuscola	13,503	13,739	12,631	15,389
Van Buren	18,589	15,535	16,151	17,634
Washtenaw	130,547	53,943	109,953	61,455
Wayne	656,303	216,880	600,047	257,750
Wexford	7,357	8,044	6,034	8,966
Totals	**2,872,579**	**2,048,639**	**2,479,183**	**2,313,746**

Michigan Vote Since 1952

2008: Obama, Dem., 2,872,579; McCain, Rep., 2,048,639; Nader, Natural Law, 33,085; Barr, Lib., 23,716; Baldwin, US Taxpayers, 14,685; McKinney, Green, 8,892.

2004: Kerry, D., 2,479,183; Bush, R., 2,313,746; Nader, Ind., 24,035; Badnarik, LB., 10,552; Cobb, Green, 5,325; Peroutka, U.S. Taxpayers, 4,980; Brown, Nat. Law, 1,431.

2000: Gore, D., 2,170,418; Bush, R., 1,953,139; Nader, Green, 84,165; Browne, LB., 16,711; Phillips, U.S. Taxpayers, 3,791; Hagelin, Natural Law, 2,426.

1996: Clinton, D., 1,989,653; Dole, R., 1,481,212; Perot, Ref., 336,670; Browne, LB., 27,670; Hagelin, Natural Law, 4,254; Moorehead, Workers World, 3,153; White, Soc. Equality, 1,554.

1992: Clinton, D., 1,871,182; Bush, R., 1,554,940; Perot, Ind., 824,813; Marrou, LB., 10,175; Phillips, U.S. Taxpayers, 8,263; Hagelin, Natural Law, 2,954.

1988: Bush, R., 1,965,486; Dukakis, D., 1,675,783; Paul, Lib., 18,336; Fulani, Ind., 2,513.

1984: Reagan, R., 2,251,571; Mondale, D., 1,529,638; Bergland, LB., 10,055.

1980: Reagan, R., 1,915,225; Carter, D., 1,661,532; Anderson, Ind., 275,223; Clark, LB., 41,597; Commoner, Citizens, 11,930; Hall, Com., 3,262; Griswold, Workers World, 30; Greaves, Amer., 21; Bubar, Statesman, 9.

1976: Ford, R., 1,893,742; Carter, D., 1,696,714; McCarthy, Ind., 47,905; MacBride, LB., 5,406; Wright, People's, 3,504; Camejo, Soc. Workers, 1,804; LaRouche, U.S. Labor, 1,366; Levin, Soc. Labor, 1,148; scattered, 2,160.

1972: Nixon, R., 1,961,721; McGovern, D., 1,459,435; Schmitz, Amer., 63,321; Fisher, Soc. Labor, 2,437; Jenness, Soc. Workers, 1,603; Hall, Com., 1,210.

1968: Humphrey, D., 1,593,082; Nixon, R., 1,370,665; Wallace, 3rd Party, 331,968; Halstead, Soc. Workers, 4,099; Blomen, Soc. Labor, 1,762; Cleaver, New Politics, 4,585; Munn, Proh., 60; scattered, 29.

1964: Johnson, D., 2,136,615; Goldwater, R., 1,060,152; DeBerry, Soc. Workers, 3,817; Hass, Soc. Labor, 1,704; Proh. (no candidate listed), 699; scattered, 145.

1960: Kennedy, D., 1,687,269; Nixon, R., 1,620,428; Dobbs, Soc. Workers, 4,347; Decker, Proh., 2,029; Daly, Tax Cut, 1,767; Hass, Soc. Labor, 1,718; Ind. Amer. (unpledged), 539.

1956: Eisenhower, R., 1,713,647; Stevenson, D., 1,359,898; Holtwick, Proh., 6,923.

1952: Eisenhower, R., 1,551,529; Stevenson, D., 1,230,657; Hamblen, Proh., 10,331; Hallinan, Prog., 3,922; Hass, Soc. Labor, 1,495; Dobbs, Soc. Workers, 655; scattered, 3.

Minnesota

County	2008 Obama (D)	McCain (R)	2004 Kerry (D)	Bush (R)
Aitkin	4,595	4,589	4,539	4,768
Anoka	86,976	91,357	80,226	91,853
Becker	7,687	8,851	6,756	9,795
Beltrami	12,019	9,762	10,592	10,237
Benton	8,454	10,338	8,059	10,043
Big Stone	1,552	1,362	1,536	1,483
Blue Earth	19,325	14,782	16,865	15,737
Brown	5,809	7,456	5,158	8,395
Carlton	11,501	6,549	11,462	6,642
Carver	20,654	28,156	16,456	28,510
Cass	7,276	8,660	6,835	8,875
Chippewa	3,280	2,907	3,424	3,089
Chisago	12,783	15,789	12,219	15,705
Clay	16,666	11,978	12,989	14,365
Clearwater	1,877	2,291	1,871	2,438
Cook	2,019	1,240	1,733	1,489
Cottonwood	2,759	3,157	2,726	3,557
Crow Wing	15,859	18,567	14,005	19,106
Dakota	116,778	104,364	104,635	108,959
Dodge	4,463	5,468	4,117	5,593
Douglas	9,256	11,241	8,219	11,793
Faribault	3,736	4,196	3,767	4,794
Fillmore	5,921	4,993	5,825	5,694
Freeborn	9,915	6,955	9,733	7,681
Goodhue	12,420	12,775	12,103	13,134
Grant	1,850	1,646	1,856	1,893
Hennepin	420,958	231,054	383,841	255,133
Houston	5,906	4,743	5,276	5,631
Hubbard	4,872	6,558	4,741	6,444
Isanti	8,248	11,324	7,883	11,190
Itasca	13,460	10,309	13,290	10,705
Jackson	2,618	2,858	2,652	3,024
Kanabec	3,743	4,479	3,592	4,527
Kandiyohi	10,125	11,319	9,337	11,704
Kittson	1,492	1,016	1,333	1,307
Koochiching	3,649	2,962	3,662	3,539
Lac Qui Parle	2,160	1,912	2,390	2,093
Lake	4,174	2,636	4,212	2,769
Lake of the Woods	971	1,278	921	1,428
Le Sueur	6,994	7,636	6,466	7,746
Lincoln	1,517	1,491	1,558	1,736
Lyon	6,110	6,315	5,292	7,203
Mahnomen	7,505	10,993	1,339	1,132
Marshall	1,436	843	2,308	3,187
Martin	2,311	2,285	4,590	6,311
McLeod	4,413	6,053	6,712	11,407
Meeker	5,380	6,737	5,292	6,854
Mille Lacs	6,072	7,049	5,677	7,194
Morrison	6,547	9,735	6,794	9,698
Mower	11,605	7,075	12,334	7,591
Murray	2,345	2,320	2,218	2,719
Nicollet	9,887	7,968	8,797	8,689
Nobles	4,244	4,368	3,898	5,159
Norman	2,129	1,204	1,954	1,794
Olmsted	38,711	36,202	33,285	37,371
Otter Tail	13,856	18,077	12,038	19,734
Pennington	3,394	3,248	3,117	3,767
Pine	7,084	6,862	7,228	7,033
Pipestone	2,023	2,652	1,900	3,066
Polk	7,850	7,148	6,729	8,724
Pope	3,317	3,069	3,301	3,303
Ramsey	182,974	88,942	171,846	97,096
Red Lake	1,120	983	963	1,164
Redwood	3,250	4,308	3,104	4,898
Renville	3,904	3,956	3,787	4,430
Rice	17,381	13,723	16,425	13,881
Rock	2,079	2,775	2,000	3,111
Roseau	3,097	4,438	2,442	5,355
Scott	77,351	38,742	23,958	36,055
Sherburne	29,208	36,724	15,816	25,182
Sibley	17,957	26,140	3,109	4,669
St. Louis	2,998	4,492	77,958	40,112
Stearns	35,690	41,194	32,659	41,726
Steele	9,016	10,068	7,994	10,389
Stevens	2,781	2,710	2,821	3,030
Swift	2,907	2,184	3,165	2,481
Todd	5,277	6,637	5,034	6,945
Traverse	1,043	933	1,026	1,076
Wabasha	5,646	5,935	5,548	6,120
Wadena	2,882	4,128	2,791	4,214
Waseca	4,401	5,211	4,179	5,457
Washington	70,277	64,334	61,395	65,751
Watonwan	2,562	2,526	2,514	2,970
Wilkin	1,550	1,786	1,169	2,303
Winona	16,308	10,975	14,231	12,686
Wright	26,343	37,779	22,618	36,176
Yellow Medicine	2,816	2,579	2,799	2,878
Totals	**1,573,354**	**1,275,409**	**1,445,014**	**1,346,695**

Minnesota Vote Since 1952

2008: Obama, Dem., 1,573,354; McCain, Rep., 1,275,409; Nader, Ind., 30,152; Barr, Lib., 9,174; Baldwin, Const., 6,787; McKinney, Green, 5,174; Calero, Socialist Wkrs., 790.

2004: Kerry, D., 1,445,014; Bush, R., 1,346,695; Nader, Better Life, 18,683; Badnarik, LB., 4,639; Cobb, Green, 4,408; Peroutka, Constitution, 3,074; Harens, other, 2,387; Van Auken, Soc. Equal., 539; Calero, Soc. Wkrs., 416.

2000: Gore, D., 1,168,266; Bush, R., 1,109,659; Nader, Green, 126,696; Buchanan, Reform Minnesota, 22,166; Browne, LB., 5,282; Phillips, Constitution, 3,272; Hagelin, Reform, 2,294; Harris, Soc. Workers, 1,022.

1996: Clinton, D., 1,120,438; Dole, R., 766,476; Perot, Ref., 257,704; Nader, Green, 24,908; Browne, LB., 8,271; Peron, Grass Roots, 4,898; Phillips, U.S. Taxpayers, 3,416; Hagelin, Natural Law, 1,808; Birrenbach, Ind. Grass Roots, 787; Harris, Soc. Workers, 684; White, Soc. Equality, 347.

1992: Clinton, D., 1,020,997; Bush, R., 747,841; Perot, Ind., 562,506; Marrou, LB., 3,373; Gritz, Populist/America First, 3,363; Hagelin, Natural Law, 1,406.

1988: Dukakis, D., 1,109,471; Bush, R., 962,337; McCarthy, Minn. Prog., 5,403; Paul, Lib., 5,109.

1984: Mondale, D., 1,036,364; Reagan, R., 1,032,603; Bergland, LB., 2,996.

1980: Carter, D., 954,173; Reagan, R., 873,268; Anderson, Ind., 174,997; Clark, LB., 31,593; Commoner, Citizens, 8,406; Hall, Com., 1,117; DeBerry, Soc. Workers, 711; Griswold, Workers World, 698; McReynolds, Soc., 536; write-in, 281.

1976: Carter, D., 1,070,440; Ford, R., 819,395; McCarthy, Ind., 35,490; Anderson, Amer., 13,592; Camejo, Soc. Workers, 4,149; MacBride, LB., 3,529; Hall, Com., 1,092.

1972: Nixon, R., 898,269; McGovern, D., 802,346; Schmitz, Amer., 31,407; Fisher, Soc. Labor, 4,261; Spock, People's, 2,805; Jenness, Soc. Workers, 940; Hall, Com., 662; scattered, 962.

1968: Humphrey, D., 857,738; Nixon, R., 658,643; Wallace, 3rd Party, 68,931; Cleaver, Peace and Freedom, 935; Halstead, Soc. Workers, 808; McCarthy, write-in, 585; Mitchell, Com., 415; Blomen, Ind. Gov., 285; scattered, 2,613.

1964: Johnson, D., 991,117; Goldwater, R., 559,624; Hass, Industrial Gov., 2,544; DeBerry, Soc. Workers, 1,177.

1960: Kennedy, D., 779,933; Nixon, R., 757,915; Dobbs, Soc. Workers, 3,077; Hass, Industrial Gov., 962.

1956: Eisenhower, R., 719,302; Stevenson, D., 617,525; Hass, Soc. Labor (Ind. Govt.), 2,080; Dobbs, Soc. Workers, 1,098.

1952: Eisenhower, R., 763,211; Stevenson, D., 608,458; Hallinan, Prog., 2,666; Hass, Soc. Labor, 2,383; Hamblen, Proh., 2,147; Dobbs, Soc. Workers, 618.

Mississippi

County	2008		2004	
	Obama (D)	McCain (R)	Kerry (D)	Bush (R)
Adams	7,630	5,300	8,423	6,996
Alcorn	3,701	9,752	5,454	8,634
Amite	3,320	4,214	3,012	4,147
Attala	3,739	5,209	3,145	5,014
Benton	2,224	2,329	2,245	1,969
Bolivar	9,471	4,487	9,631	5,535
Calhoun	2,242	4,068	2,234	4,131
Carroll	2,027	3,886	1,900	3,664
Chickasaw	4,053	3,934	4,078	4,193
Choctaw	1,459	2,624	1,366	2,694
Claiborne	3,561	632	4,362	950
Clarke	2,727	4,679	2,402	5,068
Clay	6,424	4,412	4,753	4,342
Coahoma	6,947	2,502	6,805	3,676
Copiah	7,640	6,683	4,961	6,374
Covington	3,826	5,503	3,158	5,044
DeSoto	19,265	43,510	13,255	36,306
Forrest	11,622	15,296	10,220	16,318
Franklin	1,722	2,896	1,574	2,893
George	1,398	7,050	1,724	6,223
Greene	1,362	4,358	1,421	3,850
Grenada	4,995	6,215	4,180	5,872
Hancock	3,195	11,614	5,107	12,581
Harrison	22,175	37,927	23,076	39,703
Hinds	68,794	29,187	54,845	36,975
Holmes	6,945	1,504	6,366	1,961
Humphreys	3,180	1,243	3,168	1,679
Issaquena	523	322	516	439
Itawamba	1,938	7,240	2,802	6,833
Jackson	15,534	32,959	15,572	35,134
Jasper	4,476	3,660	4,117	3,855
Jefferson	3,295	450	2,821	630
Jefferson Davis	3,924	2,512	2,959	2,668
Jones	8,089	18,726	7,398	19,125
Kemper	2,876	1,694	2,465	2,109
Lafayette	7,997	10,278	6,218	9,004
Lamar	4,694	16,969	3,923	16,410
Lauderdale	13,048	19,368	10,292	19,736
Lawrence	2,513	4,318	2,308	3,956
Leake	3,575	4,509	3,212	4,962
Lee	11,769	22,403	10,127	20,254
Leflore	8,914	4,105	7,566	4,635
Lincoln	5,505	10,781	4,418	10,008
Lowndes	13,110	13,934	10,408	13,690

County	2008		2004	
	Obama (D)	McCain (R)	Kerry (D)	Bush (R)
Madison	18,034	24,781	13,268	24,257
Marion	3,764	7,350	3,888	7,999
Marshall	9,573	6,650	8,591	5,975
Monroe	7,137	10,165	6,237	9,308
Montgomery	2,244	2,638	2,473	3,002
Neshoba	2,584	7,205	2,600	7,780
Newton	3,063	6,338	2,280	6,165
Noxubee	4,970	1,507	4,346	1,723
Oktibbeha	9,326	9,320	7,015	9,068
Panola	8,370	7,515	6,615	6,769
Pearl River	3,727	16,156	4,472	14,896
Perry	1,521	4,040	1,261	3,747
Pike	7,958	7,441	7,881	8,660
Pontotoc	2,951	9,656	2,660	8,480
Prentiss	3,020	7,703	3,327	6,538
Quitman	2,797	1,334	2,032	1,360
Rankin	14,235	47,645	11,005	43,054
Scott	4,709	6,205	3,802	6,395
Sharkey	1,722	784	1,560	1,120
Simpson	4,393	6,660	3,272	7,138
Smith	1,821	5,715	1,496	5,577
Stone	1,746	4,661	1,528	4,146
Sunflower	7,158	2,900	6,359	3,534
Tallahatchie	3,646	2,435	3,420	2,737
Tate	4,951	7,639	4,347	6,760
Tippah	2,514	6,809	3,016	6,174
Tishomingo	1,941	6,195	2,846	5,379
Tunica	2,917	864	2,140	950
Union	2,727	8,302	2,839	7,906
Walthall	3,421	4,244	2,435	3,888
Warren	9,502	9,953	8,224	11,356
Washington	12,884	6,274	11,569	7,731
Wayne	3,860	6,056	3,193	5,562
Webster	1,321	4,032	1,341	3,708
Wilkinson	3,498	1,556	2,794	1,563
Winston	4,606	5,473	3,978	5,386
Yalobusha	3,104	3,604	2,656	3,278
Yazoo	5,725	4,219	5,013	5,672
Totals	**554,662**	**724,597**	**457,766**	**684,981**

Mississippi Vote Since 1952

2008: McCain, Rep., 724,597; Obama, Dem., 554,662; Nader, Ind., 4,011; Baldwin, Const., 2,551; Barr, Lib., 2,529; McKinney, Green, 1,034; Weill, Reform, 481.

2004: Bush, R., 684,981; Kerry, D., 458,094; Nader, Ref., 3,177; Badnarik, LB., 1,793; Peroutka, Constitution, 1,759; Harris, Ind., 1,268; Cobb, Green, 1,073.

2000: Bush, R., 572,844; Gore, D., 404,614; Nader, Ind., 8,122; Phillips, Constitution, 3,267; Buchanan, Reform, 2,265; Browne, LB., 2,009; Harris, Ind., 613; Hagelin, Natural Law, 450.

1996: Dole, R., 439,838; Clinton, D., 394,022; Perot, Ind. (Ref.), 52,222; Browne, LB., 2,809; Phillips, Taxpayers, 2,314; Hagelin, Natural Law, 1,447; Collins, Ind., 1,205.

1992: Bush, R., 487,793; Clinton, D., 400,258; Perot, Ind., 85,626; Fulani, New Alliance, 2,625; Marrou, LB., 2,154; Phillips, U.S. Taxpayers, 1,652; Hagelin, Natural Law, 1,140.

1988: Bush, R., 557,890; Dukakis, D., 363,921; Duke, Ind., 4,232; Paul, Lib., 3,329.

1984: Reagan, R., 582,377; Mondale, D., 352,192; Bergland, LB., 2,336.

1980: Reagan, R., 441,089; Carter, D., 429,281; Anderson, Ind., 12,036; Clark, LB., 5,465; Griswold, Workers World, 2,402; Pulley, Soc. Workers, 2,347.

1976: Carter, D., 381,309; Ford, R., 366,846; Anderson, Amer., 6,678; McCarthy, Ind., 4,074; Maddox, Ind., 4,049; Camejo, Soc. Workers, 2,805; MacBride, LB., 2,609.

1972: Nixon, R., 505,125; McGovern, D., 126,782; Schmitz, Amer., 11,598; Jenness, Soc. Workers, 2,458.

1968: Wallace, 3rd Party, 415,349; Humphrey, D., 150,644; Nixon, R., 88,516.

1964: Goldwater, R., 356,528; Johnson, D., 52,618.

1960: Democratic unpledged electors, 116,248; Kennedy, D., 108,362; Nixon, R., 73,561. Mississippi's victorious slate of 8 unpledged Democratic electors cast their votes for Sen. Harry F. Byrd (D, VA).

1956: Stevenson, D., 144,498; Eisenhower, R., 56,372; Black and Tan Grand Old Party, 4,313; total, 60,685; Byrd, Ind., 42,966.

1952: Stevenson, D., 172,566; Eisenhower, Ind., vote pledged to Rep. candidate, 112,966.

Missouri

County	2008		2004	
	Obama (D)	McCain (R)	Kerry (D)	Bush (R)
Adair	5,735	5,891	4,938	6,367
Andrew	3,345	5,279	3,069	5,135
Atchison	1,000	1,936	1,005	2,137
Audrain	4,434	6,167	4,318	6,294
Barry	4,630	9,758	4,223	9,599
Barton	1,455	4,414	1,373	4,572
Bates	3,271	4,833	3,398	5,004
Benton	3,629	5,759	3,381	5,575
Bollinger	1,690	3,972	1,754	4,102
Boone	47,062	36,849	37,643	37,801

County	2008 Obama (D)	McCain (R)	2004 Kerry (D)	Bush (R)
Buchanan	19,164	19,110	17,799	19,812
Butler	5,316	11,805	4,666	11,696
Caldwell	1,814	2,654	1,645	2,593
Callaway	7,580	11,389	6,559	11,108
Camden	7,773	14,074	6,296	13,122
Cape Girardeau	12,208	24,768	10,568	23,814
Carroll	1,535	2,955	1,568	3,155
Carter	984	1,840	964	1,797
Cass	19,844	29,695	16,681	27,253
Cedar	2,060	4,194	1,910	4,238
Chariton	1,799	2,339	1,892	2,421
Christian	11,883	25,382	9,059	22,102
Clark	1,572	1,782	1,794	1,899
Clay	53,761	54,516	44,670	51,193
Clinton	4,545	5,709	4,165	5,287
Cole	13,959	24,385	11,753	24,752
Cooper	2,996	4,902	2,400	5,058
Crawford	3,911	6,007	3,632	5,686
Dade	1,184	2,864	1,104	2,963
Dallas	2,656	4,895	2,407	4,788
Daviess	1,400	2,263	1,402	2,351
DeKalb	1,692	2,889	1,707	2,941
Dent	2,056	4,655	1,865	4,369
Douglas	2,140	4,405	1,741	4,498
Dunklin	4,540	7,044	4,901	6,720
Franklin	21,256	27,355	18,556	26,429
Gasconade	2,899	4,763	2,355	4,753
Gentry	1,235	1,964	1,201	2,085
Greene	56,181	77,683	46,657	77,885
Grundy	1,580	3,006	1,561	3,172
Harrison	1,287	2,512	1,279	2,729
Henry	4,869	6,095	4,461	6,361
Hickory	2,171	2,850	2,043	2,791
Holt	802	1,794	811	1,864
Howard	2,036	2,708	1,972	2,915
Howell	5,736	10,982	5,118	11,097
Iron	2,213	2,090	2,157	2,477
Jackson	210,824	124,687	183,654	130,500
Jasper	15,730	31,667	13,002	31,846
Jefferson	53,467	50,804	46,057	46,624
Johnson	9,480	12,183	7,790	12,257
Knox	759	1,212	761	1,207
Laclede	5,218	10,875	4,213	10,578
Lafayette	6,902	9,442	6,412	9,656
Lawrence	5,097	11,263	4,506	11,194
Lewis	1,837	2,594	1,754	2,862
Lincoln	10,234	12,924	8,368	11,316
Linn	2,638	3,140	2,440	3,422
Livingston	2,435	3,993	2,278	4,029
Macon	2,454	5,499	2,856	4,673
Madison	2,784	4,586	1,972	2,905
Maries	2,042	2,897	1,563	2,825
Marion	1,599	2,853	4,568	7,815
McDonald	4,703	7,705	2,215	5,443
Mercer	519	1,169	582	1,207
Miller	3,553	7,797	2,959	7,797
Mississippi	2,247	3,034	2,374	2,903
Moniteau	2,084	4,467	1,913	4,743
Monroe	1,703	2,533	1,647	2,632
Montgomery	2,347	3,428	2,147	3,563
Morgan	3,565	5,451	3,053	5,657
New Madrid	3,370	4,593	3,716	4,154
Newton	7,450	17,637	6,564	17,187
Nodaway	4,493	5,568	3,830	6,226
Oregon	1,811	2,652	1,823	2,769
Osage	1,907	5,062	1,673	4,975
Ozark	1,661	2,918	1,561	3,083
Pemiscot	3,029	3,954	3,381	3,398
Perry	3,005	5,527	2,621	5,583
Pettis	6,932	11,018	5,801	11,603
Phelps	7,394	11,706	6,666	11,874
Pike	3,487	4,268	3,670	4,314
Platte	21,459	24,460	18,412	23,302
Polk	4,553	8,956	3,775	8,586
Pulaski	5,249	9,552	3,551	8,618
Putnam	695	1,591	772	1,660
Ralls	2,041	2,987	2,031	2,986
Randolph	3,984	6,457	3,586	6,551
Ray	5,241	5,593	5,034	5,673
Reynolds	1,417	1,780	1,449	1,896
Ripley	1,795	3,447	1,907	3,693
Saline	84,183	102,550	4,479	5,389
Schuyler	1,886	2,981	894	1,124
Scotland	11,540	12,660	828	1,352
Scott	333,123	221,705	6,057	11,330
Shannon	4,979	3,732	1,618	2,511
Shelby	4,712	4,962	1,201	2,280
St. Charles	775	1,139	66,855	95,826
St. Clair	793	1,249	1,841	3,098
St. Francois	6,258	11,563	10,748	12,087

County	2008 Obama (D)	McCain (R)	2004 Kerry (D)	Bush (R)
St. Louis	1,637	2,075	295,284	244,969
Ste. Genevieve	1,114	2,166	4,281	3,791
Stoddard	3,899	9,172	3,946	9,242
Stone	5,029	11,147	4,578	10,534
Sullivan	1,173	1,607	1,178	1,880
Taney	6,683	14,736	5,601	13,578
Texas	3,410	7,215	3,664	7,234
Vernon	3,381	5,334	3,206	5,732
Warren	6,705	8,675	5,461	7,883
Washington	4,711	4,706	4,459	4,641
Wayne	2,243	3,784	2,250	3,919
Webster	5,685	10,431	4,657	10,194
Worth	427	707	436	691
Wright	2,557	5,784	2,188	6,090
City				
St. Louis	132,925	24,662	116,133	27,793
Totals	**1,441,911**	**1,445,814**	**1,259,171**	**1,455,713**

Missouri Vote Since 1952

2008: McCain, Rep., 1,445,814; Obama, Dem., 1,441,911; Nader, Ind., 17,813; Barr, Lib., 11,386; Baldwin, Const., 8,201.

2004: Bush, R., 1,455,713; Kerry, D., 1,259,171; Badnarik, LB., 9,831; Peroutka, Constitution, 5,355.

2000: Bush, R., 1,189,924; Gore, D., 1,111,138; Nader, Green, 38,515; Buchanan, Reform, 9,818; Browne, LB., 7,436; Phillips, Constitution, 1,957; Hagelin, Natural Law, 1,104.

1996: Clinton, D., 1,025,935; Dole, R., 890,016; Perot, Ref., 217,188; Phillips, U.S. Taxpayers, 11,521; Browne, LB., 10,522; Hagelin, Natural Law, 2,287.

1992: Clinton, D., 1,053,873; Bush, R., 811,159; Perot, Ind., 518,741; Marrou, LB., 7,497.

1988: Bush, R., 1,084,953; Dukakis, D., 1,001,619; Fulani, New Alliance, 6,656; Paul, write-in, 434.

1984: Reagan, R., 1,274,188; Mondale, D., 848,583.

1980: Reagan, R., 1,074,181; Carter, D., 931,182; Anderson, Ind., 77,920; Clark, LB., 14,422; DeBerry, Soc. Workers, 1,515; Commoner, Citizens, 573; write-in, 31.

1976: Carter, D., 999,163; Ford, R., 928,808; McCarthy, Ind., 24,329.

1972: Nixon, R., 1,154,058; McGovern, D., 698,531.

1968: Nixon, R., 811,932; Humphrey, D., 791,444; Wallace, 3rd Party, 206,126.

1964: Johnson, D., 1,164,344; Goldwater, R., 653,535.

1960: Kennedy, D., 972,201; Nixon, R., 962,221.

1956: Stevenson, D., 918,273; Eisenhower, R., 914,299.

1952: Eisenhower, R., 959,429; Stevenson, D., 929,830; Hallinan, Prog., 987; Hamblen, Proh., 885; MacArthur, Christian Nationalist, 302; America First, 233; Hoopes, Soc., 227; Hass, Soc. Labor, 169.

Montana

County	2008 Obama (D)	McCain (R)	2004 Kerry (D)	Bush (R)
Beaverhead	1,611	2,983	1,103	3,067
Big Horn	3,490	1,622	2,215	2,028
Blaine	1,711	1,138	1,300	1,424
Broadwater	854	1,853	533	1,778
Carbon	2,431	3,093	1,847	3,342
Carter	111	573	76	623
Cascade	17,486	16,675	13,701	19,028
Chouteau	1,118	1,625	946	1,913
Custer	2,262	3,040	1,630	3,297
Daniels	343	692	326	764
Dawson	1,587	2,626	1,494	2,884
Deer Lodge	3,341	1,481	2,700	1,725
Fallon	318	1,082	289	1,178
Fergus	1,921	4,100	1,582	4,425
Flathead	15,976	25,361	11,587	26,019
Gallatin	23,984	22,375	16,405	22,392
Garfield	109	595	52	590
Glacier	3,361	1,443	2,641	1,828
Golden Valley	122	342	119	396
Granite	601	1,013	404	1,144
Hill	3,563	2,763	2,997	3,505
Jefferson	2,574	3,525	1,881	3,844
Judith Basin	396	799	322	944
Lake	6,693	6,463	4,960	7,245
Lewis & Clark	16,939	14,794	12,717	16,494
Liberty	367	594	281	734
Lincoln	3,018	5,699	2,320	5,889
Madison	321	726	983	2,868
McCone	1,596	2,803	320	791
Meagher	298	624	247	698
Mineral	844	1,051	542	1,242
Missoula	35,701	20,266	26,983	23,989
Musselshell	615	1,552	538	1,663
Park	4,140	4,349	3,199	4,771
Petroleum	68	227	55	228
Phillips	638	1,423	456	1,677
Pondera	1,224	1,583	956	1,853
Powder River	207	797	154	856
Powell	1,021	1,679	761	1,993

County	2008 Obama (D)	McCain (R)	2004 Kerry (D)	Bush (R)
Prairie	211	503	181	546
Ravalli	8,332	12,922	6,144	13,279
Richland	1,196	3,158	1,120	3,110
Roosevelt	2,527	1,455	2,195	1,762
Rosebud	1,898	1,739	1,520	1,982
Sanders	1,964	3,556	1,502	3,461
Sheridan	953	987	846	1,159
Silver Bow	11,651	4,806	9,307	6,381
Stillwater	1,512	2,989	1,025	3,090
Sweet Grass	552	1,433	445	1,509
Teton	1,291	1,873	1,047	2,232
Toole	736	1,321	690	1,583
Treasure	154	310	121	348
Valley	1,616	2,099	1,431	2,476
Wheatland	286	632	250	706
Wibaux	146	379	144	407
Yellowstone	31,740	36,225	24,120	40,903
Totals	231,667	242,763	173,710	266,063

Montana Vote Since 1952

2008: McCain, Rep., 242,763; Obama, Dem., **231,667**; Paul, Const., 10,638; Nader, Ind., 3,686; Barr, Lib., 1,355.

2004: Bush, R., 266,063; Kerry, D., 173,710; Nader, Ind., 6,168; Peroutka, Constitution, 1,764; Badnarik, LB., 1,733; Cobb, Green, 996.

2000: Bush, Rep, 240,178; Gore, D., 137,126; Nader, Green, 24,437; Buchanan, Reform, 5,697; Browne, LB., 1,718; Phillips, Constitution, 1,155; Hagelin, Natural Law, 675.

1996: Dole, R., 179,652; Clinton, D., 167,922; Perot, Ref., 55,229; Browne, LB., 2,526; Hagelin, Natural Law, 1,754.

1992: Clinton, D., 154,507; Bush, R., 144,207; Perot, Ind., 107,225; Gritz, Populist/America First, 3,658.

1988: Bush, R., 190,412; Dukakis, D., 168,936; Paul, Lib., 5,047; Fulani, New Alliance, 1,279.

1984: Reagan, R., 232,450; Mondale, D., 146,742; Bergland, LB., 5,185.

1980: Reagan, R., 206,814; Carter, D., 118,032; Anderson, Ind., 29,281; Clark, LB., 9,825.

1976: Ford, R., 173,703; Carter, D., 149,259; Anderson, Amer., 5,772.

1972: Nixon, R., 183,976; McGovern, D., 120,197; Schmitz, Amer., 13,430.

1968: Nixon, R., 138,835; Humphrey, D., 114,117; Wallace, 3rd Party, 20,015; Munn, Proh., 510; Caton, New Reform, 470; Halstead, Soc. Workers, 457.

1964: Johnson, D., 164,246; Goldwater, R., 113,032; Kasper, Natl. States' Rights, 519; Munn, Proh., 499; DeBerry, Soc. Workers, 332.

1960: Nixon, R., 141,841; Kennedy, D., 134,891; Decker, Proh., 456; Dobbs, Soc. Workers, 391.

1956: Eisenhower, R., 154,933; Stevenson, D., 116,238.

1952: Eisenhower, R., 157,394; Stevenson, D., 106,213; Hallinan, Prog., 723; Hamblen, Proh., 548; Hoopes, Soc., 159.

Nebraska

County	2008 Obama (D)	McCain (R)	2004 Kerry (D)	Bush (R)
Adams	4,624	8,163	3,791	9,233
Antelope	754	2,367	613	2,761
Arthur	39	217	24	240
Banner	61	341	56	379
Blaine	43	266	38	301
Boone	742	2,042	546	2,309
Box Butte	1,844	2,888	1,657	3,396
Boyd	250	839	228	911
Brown	311	1,208	268	1,426
Buffalo	5,768	12,920	4,100	14,222
Burt	1,406	1,895	1,272	2,349
Butler	1,175	2,534	1,068	3,016
Cass	4,709	7,076	3,619	7,763
Cedar	1,187	2,912	1,083	3,387
Chase	341	1,466	302	1,652
Cherry	599	2,360	483	2,509
Cheyenne	1,064	3,284	893	3,791
Clay	761	2,134	743	2,543
Colfax	1,125	2,014	990	2,589
Cuming	1,255	2,701	966	3,330
Custer	1,178	4,220	1,040	4,518
Dakota	2,966	3,255	3,027	3,526
Dawes	1,245	2,330	1,119	2,809
Dawson	2,352	5,368	1,728	6,149
Deuel	243	732	222	820
Dixon	946	1,785	938	2,028
Dodge	6,587	8,482	5,250	10,716
Douglas	116,893	106,419	83,330	120,813
Dundy	218	783	186	858
Fillmore	953	1,907	828	2,314
Franklin	442	1,078	412	1,277
Frontier	348	1,030	275	1,160
Furnas	556	1,725	492	1,950
Gage	4,405	5,389	3,655	6,575
Garden	283	844	201	970

County	2008 Obama (D)	McCain (R)	2004 Kerry (D)	Bush (R)
Garfield	212	800	196	806
Gosper	260	771	222	890
Grant	41	321	41	352
Greeley	457	714	361	865
Hall	7,687	12,788	6,228	14,592
Hamilton	1,322	3,362	1,012	3,785
Harlan	399	1,327	398	1,467
Hayes	85	460	66	524
Hitchcock	346	997	296	1,171
Holt	1,065	3,663	894	4,217
Hooker	75	355	64	392
Howard	1,083	1,847	900	2,020
Jefferson	1,504	2,091	1,352	2,600
Johnson	914	1,139	885	1,470
Kearney	870	2,217	707	2,621
Keith	965	2,917	743	3,356
Keya Paha	115	409	98	442
Kimball	427	1,328	366	1,491
Knox	1,248	2,724	1,086	3,062
Lancaster	63,464	57,925	52,747	69,764
Lincoln	4,937	10,609	4,905	11,056
Logan	81	327	67	357
Loup	86	302	68	314
Madison	45	240	2,934	10,981
McPherson	4,076	9,542	49	259
Merrick	978	2,356	833	2,771
Morrill	546	1,700	495	1,755
Nance	540	1,110	459	1,237
Nemaha	1,207	2,090	1,066	2,595
Nuckolls	692	1,607	541	1,884
Otoe	2,893	3,991	2,275	5,018
Pawnee	481	857	481	986
Perkins	310	1,086	262	1,285
Phelps	1,043	3,340	830	3,872
Pierce	781	2,372	546	2,824
Platte	3,734	9,279	2,657	11,130
Polk	665	1,810	549	2,146
Red Willow	1,216	3,748	1,055	4,129
Richardson	1,121	1,880	1,297	2,924
Rock	136	635	130	740
Saline	2,597	2,373	2,420	3,071
Sarpy	28,010	38,816	17,455	40,163
Saunders	3,739	6,132	2,884	6,441
Scotts Bluff	4,645	9,575	3,843	10,378
Seward	2,671	4,596	2,114	5,353
Sheridan	451	1,934	430	2,136
Sherman	583	940	541	1,072
Sioux	116	600	123	677
Stanton	657	1,772	559	2,159
Thayer	850	1,729	764	2,075
Thomas	51	331	60	378
Thurston	1,108	970	1,212	1,154
Valley	704	1,647	564	1,801
Washington	3,681	6,409	2,754	7,083
Wayne	1,249	2,503	1,059	2,971
Webster	550	1,323	557	1,403
Wheeler	96	334	81	366
York	1,594	4,807	1,304	5,393
Totals	333,319	452,979	254,328	512,814

Nebraska Vote Since 1952

2008: McCain, Rep., 452,979; Obama, Dem., 333,319; Nader, Petitioning Candidate, 5,406; Baldwin, Nebraska, 2,972; Barr, Lib., 2,740; McKinney, Green, 1,028.

2004: Bush, R., 512,814; Kerry, D., 254,328; Nader, Petitioning Cand., 5,698; Badnarik, LB., 2,041; Peroutka, Nebraska, 1,314; Cobb, Green, 978; Calero, Petitioning Cand., 82.

2000: Bush, R., 433,862; Gore, D., 231,780; Nader, Green, 24,540; Buchanan, Ind., 3,646; Browne, LB., 2,245; Hagelin, Natural Law, 478; Phillips, Ind., 468.

1996: Dole, R., 363,467; Clinton, D., 236,761; Perot, Ref., 71,278; Browne, LB., 2,792; Phillips, Ind., 1,928; Hagelin, Natural Law, 1,189.

1992: Bush, R., 343,678; Clinton, D., 216,864; Perot, Ind., 174,104; Marrou, LB., 1,340.

1988: Bush, R., 397,956; Dukakis, D., 259,235; Paul, Lib., 2,534; Fulani, New Alliance, 1,740.

1984: Reagan, R., 459,135; Mondale, D., 187,475; Bergland, LB., 2,075.

1980: Reagan, R., 419,214; Carter, D., 166,424; Anderson, Ind., 44,854; Clark, LB., 9,041.

1976: Ford, R., 359,219; Carter, D., 233,287; McCarthy, Ind., 9,383; Maddox, Amer. Ind., 3,378; MacBride, LB., 1,476.

1972: Nixon, R., 406,298; McGovern, D., 169,991; scattered, 817.

1968: Nixon, R., 321,163; Humphrey, D., 170,784; Wallace, 3rd Party, 44,904.

1964: Johnson, D., 307,307; Goldwater, R., 276,847.

1960: Nixon, R., 380,553; Kennedy, D., 232,542.

1956: Eisenhower, R., 378,108; Stevenson, D., 199,029.

1952: Eisenhower, R., 421,603; Stevenson, D., 188,057.

Nevada

| County | 2008 | | 2004 | |
	Obama (D)	McCain (R)	Kerry (D)	Bush (R)
Churchill	3,494	6,831	2,705	7,335
Clark	379,204	256,401	281,767	255,337
Douglas	10,671	14,645	8,275	15,192
Elko	4,537	10,958	3,050	11,938
Esmeralda	104	303	99	367
Eureka	144	564	144	571
Humboldt	1,909	3,584	1,361	3,896
Lander	574	1,462	414	1,602
Lincoln	518	1,498	418	1,579
Lyon	8,405	12,154	5,637	11,136
Mineral	1,082	1,131	931	1,336
Nye	7,223	9,535	5,616	8,487
Pershing	673	1,075	538	1,341
Storey	1,099	1,245	871	1,253
Washoe	99,395	76,743	74,841	81,545
White Pine	1,230	2,440	1,082	2,604
City				
Carson City	11,622	11,419	9,441	13,171
Totals	**533,736**	**412,827**	**397,190**	**418,690**

Nevada Vote Since 1952

2008: Obama, Dem., 533,736; McCain, Rep., 412,827; Nader, Ind., 6,150; Barr, Lib., 4,263; Baldwin, Const., 3,194; McKinney, Green, 1,411; None of these candidates, 6,267.

2004: Bush, R., 418,690; Kerry, D., 397,190; Nader, Ind., 4,838; None of These Candidates, Ind., 3,688; Badnarik, LB., 3,176; Peroutka, Indep. Amer., 1,152; Cobb, Green, 853.

2000: Bush, R., 301,575; Gore, D., 279,978; Nader, Green, 15,008; Buchanan, Citizens First, 4,747; None of These Candidates, 3,315; Browne, LB., 3,311; Phillips, Ind. Amer., 621; Hagelin, Natural Law, 415.

1996: Clinton, D., 203,974; Dole, R., 199,244; Perot, Ref., 43,986; None of These Candidates, 5,608; Nader, Green, 4,730; Browne, LB., 4,460; Phillips, Ind. Amer., 1,732; Hagelin, Natural Law, 545.

1992: Clinton, D., 189,148; Bush, R., 175,828; Perot, Ind., 132,580; Gritz, Populist/America First, 2,892; Marrou, LB., 1,835.

1988: Bush, R., 206,040; Dukakis, D., 132,738; Paul, Lib., 3,520; Fulani, New Alliance, 835.

1984: Reagan, R., 188,770; Mondale, D., 91,655; Bergland, LB., 2,292.

1980: Reagan, R., 155,017; Carter, D., 66,666; Anderson, Ind., 17,651; Clark, LB., 4,358.

1976: Ford, R., 101,273; Carter, D., 92,479; MacBride, LB., 1,519; Maddox, Amer. Ind., 1,497; scattered, 5,108.

1972: Nixon, R., 115,750; McGovern, D., 66,016.

1968: Nixon, R., 73,188; Humphrey, D., 60,598; Wallace, 3rd Party, 20,432.

1964: Johnson, D., 79,339; Goldwater, R., 56,094.

1960: Kennedy, D., 54,880; Nixon, R., 52,387.

1956: Eisenhower, R., 56,049; Stevenson, D., 40,640.

1952: Eisenhower, R., 50,502; Stevenson, D., 31,688.

New Hampshire

| County | 2008 | | 2004 | |
	Obama (D)	McCain (R)	Kerry (D)	Bush (R)
Belknap	16,796	16,402	14,080	17,920
Carroll	15,221	13,387	13,319	14,614
Cheshire	26,971	15,205	24,438	16,463
Coos	9,532	6,558	8,585	8,143
Grafton	31,446	17,687	26,180	20,277
Hillsborough	104,820	97,178	94,121	99,724
Merrimack	45,078	34,010	39,975	36,060
Rockingham	83,723	81,917	75,437	82,069
Strafford	37,990	25,021	32,942	25,825
Sullivan	13,249	9,169	11,434	10,142
Totals	**384,826**	**316,534**	**340,511**	**331,237**

New Hampshire Vote Since 1952

2008: Obama, Dem., 384,826; McCain, Rep., 316,534; Nader, Ind., 3,503; Barr, Lib., 2,217; Phillies, Lib., 531.

2004: Kerry, D., 340,511; Bush, R., 331,237; Nader, Ind., 4,479.

2000: Bush, R., 273,559; Gore, D., 266,348; Nader, Green, 22,198; Browne, LB., 2,757; Buchanan, Independence, 2,615; Phillips, Constitution, 328.

1996: Clinton, D., 246,166; Dole, R., 196,486; Perot, Ref., 48,387; Browne, LB., 4,214; Phillips, Taxpayers, 1,344.

1992: Clinton, D., 209,040; Bush, R., 202,484; Perot, Ind., 121,337; Marrou, LB., 3,548.

1988: Bush, R., 281,537; Dukakis, D., 163,696; Paul, Lib., 4,502; Fulani, New Alliance, 790.

1984: Reagan, R., 267,051; Mondale, D., 120,377; Bergland, LB., 735.

1980: Reagan, R., 221,705; Carter, D., 108,864; Anderson, Ind., 49,693; Clark, LB., 2,067; Commoner, Citizens, 1,325; Hall, Com., 129; Griswold, Workers World, 76; DeBerry, Soc. Workers, 72; scattered, 68.

1976: Ford, R., 185,935; Carter, D., 147,645; McCarthy, Ind., 4,095; MacBride, LB., 936; Reagan, write-in, 388; LaRouche, U.S. Labor, 186; Camejo, Soc. Workers, 161; Levin, Soc. Labor, 66; scattered, 215.

1972: Nixon, R., 213,724; McGovern, D., 116,435; Schmitz, Amer., 3,386; Jenness, Soc. Workers, 368; scattered, 142.

1968: Nixon, R., 154,903; Humphrey, D., 130,589; Wallace, 3rd Party, 11,173; New Party, 421; Halstead, Soc. Workers, 104.

1964: Johnson, D., 182,065; Goldwater, R., 104,029.

1960: Nixon, R., 157,989; Kennedy, D., 137,772.

1956: Eisenhower, R., 176,519; Stevenson, D., 90,364; Andrews, Const., 111.

1952: Eisenhower, R., 166,287; Stevenson, D., 106,663.

New Jersey

| County | 2008 | | 2004 | |
	Obama (D)	McCain (R)	Kerry (D)	Bush (R)
Atlantic	62,498	46,244	55,746	49,487
Bergen	208,410	174,526	207,666	189,833
Burlington	121,222	83,078	110,411	95,936
Camden	142,433	68,072	137,765	81,427
Cape May	20,510	24,591	21,475	28,832
Cumberland	34,355	22,238	27,875	24,362
Essex	228,944	72,370	203,681	83,374
Gloucester	76,789	60,017	66,835	60,033
Hudson	141,557	51,478	127,447	60,646
Hunterdon	29,637	38,966	26,050	39,888
Mercer	99,719	47,196	91,580	56,604
Middlesex	179,924	115,969	166,628	126,492
Monmouth	147,424	159,461	133,773	163,650
Morris	101,245	122,706	98,066	135,241
Ocean	109,240	159,480	99,839	154,204
Passaic	110,331	71,850	94,962	75,200
Salem	15,909	14,763	13,749	15,721
Somerset	73,785	67,221	66,476	72,508
Sussex	28,692	43,998	23,990	44,506
Union	132,006	73,967	119,372	82,517
Warren	20,421	27,304	18,044	29,542
Totals	**2,215,422**	**1,613,207**	**1,911,430**	**1,670,003**

New Jersey Vote Since 1952

2008: Obama, Dem., 2,215,422; McCain, Rep., 1,613,207; Nader, Ind., 21,298; Barr, Ind., 8,441; Baldwin, Ind., 3,956; McKinney, Ind., 3,636; Moore, Ind., 699; Boss, Ind., 639; Calero, Ind., 523; LaRiva, Ind., 416.

2004: Kerry, D., 1,911,430; Bush, R., 1,670,003; Nader, Ind., 19,418; Badnarik, Ind., 4,514; Peroutka, Ind., 2,750; Cobb, Ind., 1,807; Brown, Ind., 664; Van Auken, Ind., 575; Calero, Ind., 530.

2000: Gore, D., 1,788,850; Bush, R., 1,284,173; Nader, Ind., 94,554; Buchanan, Ind., 6,989; Browne, Ind., 6,312; Hagelin, Ind., 2,215; McReynolds, Ind., 1,880; Phillips, Ind., 1,409; Harris, Ind., 844.

1996: Clinton, D., 1,652,361; Dole, R., 1,103,099; Perot, Ref., 262,134; Nader, Green, 32,465; Browne, LB., 14,763; Hagelin, Natural Law, 3,887; Phillips, Taxpayers, 3,440; Harris, Soc. Workers, 1,837; Moorehead, Workers World, 1,337; White, Soc. Equality, 537.

1992: Clinton, D., 1,436,206; Bush, R., 1,356,865; Perot, Ind., 521,829; Marrou, LB., 6,822; Fulani, New Alliance, 3,513; Phillips, U.S. Taxpayers, 2,670; LaRouche, Ind., 2,095; Warren, Soc. Workers, 2,011; Daniels, Ind., 1,996; Gritz, Populist/America First, 1,867; Hagelin, Natural Law, 1,353.

1988: Bush, R., 1,740,604; Dukakis, D., 1,317,541; Lewin, Peace and Freedom, 9,953; Paul, Lib., 8,421.

1984: Reagan, R., 1,933,630; Mondale, D., 1,261,323; Bergland, LB., 6,416.

1980: Reagan, R., 1,546,557; Carter, D., 1,147,364; Anderson, Ind., 234,632; Clark, LB., 20,652; Commoner, Citizens, 8,203; McCormack, Right to Life, 3,927; Lynen, Middle Class, 3,694; Hall, Com., 2,555; Pulley, Soc. Workers, 2,198; McReynolds, Soc., 1,973; Gahres, Down With Lawyers, 1,718; Griswold, Workers World, 1,288; Wendelken, Ind., 923.

1976: Ford, R., 1,509,688; Carter, D., 1,444,653; McCarthy, Ind., 32,717; MacBride, LB., 9,449; Maddox, Amer., 7,716; Levin, Soc. Labor, 3,686; Hall, Com., 1,662; LaRouche, U.S. Labor, 1,650; Camejo, Soc. Workers, 1,184; Wright, People's, 1,044; Bubar, Proh., 554; Zeidler, Soc., 469.

1972: Nixon, R., 1,845,502; McGovern, D., 1,102,211; Schmitz, Amer., 34,378; Spock, People's, 5,355; Fisher, Soc. Labor, 4,544; Jenness, Soc. Workers, 2,233; Mahalchik, Amer. First, 1,743; Hall, Com., 1,263.

1968: Nixon, R., 1,325,467; Humphrey, D., 1,264,206; Wallace, 3rd Party, 262,187; Halstead, Soc. Workers, 8,667; Gregory, Peace and Freedom, 8,084; Blomen, Soc. Labor, 6,784.

1964: Johnson, D., 1,867,671; Goldwater, R., 963,843; DeBerry, Soc. Workers, 8,181; Hass, Soc. Labor, 7,075.

1960: Kennedy, D., 1,385,415; Nixon, R., 1,363,324; Dobbs, Soc. Workers, 11,402; Lee, Cons., 8,708; Hass, Soc. Labor, 4,262.

1956: Eisenhower, R., 1,606,942; Stevenson D., 850,337; Holtwick, Proh., 9,147; Hass, Soc. Labor, 6,736; Andrews, Cons., 5,317; Dobbs, Soc. Workers, 4,004; Krajewski, Amer. Third Party, 1,829.

1952: Eisenhower, R., 1,373,613; Stevenson, D., 1,015,902; Hoopes, Soc., 8,593; Hass, Soc. Labor, 5,815; Hallinan, Prog., 5,589; Krajewski, Poor Man's, 4,203; Dobbs, Soc. Workers, 3,850; Hamblen, Proh., 989.

New Mexico

County	2008 Obama (D)	McCain (R)	2004 Kerry (D)	Bush (R)
Bernalillo	168,406	109,212	132,252	121,454
Catron	659	1,396	551	1,427
Chaves	8,160	13,630	6,726	14,773
Cibola	3,176	1,717	3,913	3,477
Colfax	3,465	2,800	2,824	3,082
Curry	4,655	9,585	3,541	10,649
De Baca	358	676	281	706
Dona Ana	38,574	27,211	31,762	29,548
Eddy	7,289	12,468	6,880	13,268
Grant	8,092	5,381	7,095	6,135
Guadalupe	1,541	615	1,340	914
Harding	256	357	259	380
Hidalgo	990	934	861	1,081
Lea	5,084	13,301	3,646	14,430
Lincoln	3,482	5,906	2,822	6,070
Los Alamos	5,709	4,986	5,206	5,810
Luna	4,289	3,857	3,340	4,164
McKinley	15,993	6,183	13,051	7,351
Mora	2,156	565	1,876	928
Otero	8,602	12,791	6,433	14,066
Quay	1,546	2,363	1,422	2,661
Rio Arriba	11,245	3,648	9,753	5,149
Roosevelt	2,270	4,285	2,082	4,997
Sandoval	32,102	24,887	21,421	22,628
San Juan	17,645	27,418	14,843	29,525
San Miguel	10,128	2,421	8,683	3,313
Santa Fe	53,802	15,443	47,074	18,466
Sierra	2,351	3,011	1,926	3,162
Socorro	4,643	3,011	4,025	3,696
Taos	13,384	2,827	10,987	3,666
Torrance	3,068	3,721	2,386	4,026
Union	492	1,218	411	1,454
Valencia	15,142	13,033	11,270	14,474
Totals	**472,422**	**346,832**	**370,942**	**376,930**

New Mexico Vote Since 1952

2008: Obama, Dem., 472,422; McCain, Rep., 346,832; Nader, Ind., 5,327; Barr, Lib., 2,428; Baldwin, Const., 1,597; McKinney, Green, 1,552.

2004: Bush, R., 376,930; Kerry, D., 370,942; Nader, Ind., 4,053; Badnarik, Libert., 2,382; Cobb, Green, 1,226; Peroutka, Constitution, 771.

2000: Gore, D., 286,783; Bush, R., 286,417; Nader, Green, 21,251; Browne, LB., 2,058; Buchanan, Reform, 1,392; Hagelin, Natural Law, 361; Phillips, Constitution, 343.

1996: Clinton, D., 273,495; Dole, R., 232,751; Perot, Ref., 32,257; Nader, Green, 13,218; Browne, LB., 2,996; Phillips, Taxpayers, 713; Hagelin, Natural Law, 644.

1992: Clinton, D., 261,617; Bush, R., 212,824; Perot, Ind., 91,895; Marrou, LB., 1,615.

1988: Bush, R., 270,341; Dukakis, D., 244,497; Paul, Lib., 3,268; Fulani, New Alliance, 2,237.

1984: Reagan, R., 307,101; Mondale, D., 201,769; Bergland, LB., 4,459.

1980: Reagan, R., 250,779; Carter, D., 167,826; Anderson, Ind., 29,459; Clark, LB., 4,365; Commoner, Citizens, 2,202; Bubar, Statesman, 1,281; Pulley, Soc. Workers, 325.

1976: Ford, R., 211,419; Carter, D., 201,148; Camejo, Soc. Wkrs., 2,462; MacBride, Lib., 1,110; Zeidler, Soc., 240; Bubar, Proh., 211.

1972: Nixon, R., 235,606; McGovern, D., 141,084; Schmitz, Amer., 8,767; Jenness, Soc. Workers, 474.

1968: Nixon, R., 169,692; Humphrey, D., 130,081; Wallace, 3rd Party, 25,737; Chavez, 1,519; Halstead, Soc. Workers, 252.

1964: Johnson, D., 194,017; Goldwater, R., 131,838; Hass, Soc. Labor, 1,217; Munn, Proh., 543.

1960: Kennedy, D., 156,027; Nixon, R., 153,733; Decker, Proh., 777; Hass, Soc. Labor, 570.

1956: Eisenhower, R., 146,788; Stevenson, D., 106,098; Holtwick, Proh., 607; Andrews, Ind., 364; Hass, Soc. Labor, 69.

1952: Eisenhower, R., 132,170; Stevenson, D., 105,661; Hamblen, Proh., 297; Hallinan, Ind. Prog., 225; MacArthur, Christian National, 220; Hass, Soc. Labor, 35.

New York

County	2008 Obama (D)	McCain (R)	2004 Kerry (D)	Bush (R)
Albany	86,096	47,629	89,323	54,872
Allegany	6,396	10,308	6,566	12,310
Bronx[1]	300,327	38,560	283,994	56,701
Brooklyn[1]	545,785	139,594	514,973	167,149
Broome	43,510	37,773	46,281	43,568
Cattaraugus	13,858	16,975	13,514	20,051
Cayuga	16,667	14,283	17,534	17,743
Chautauqua	26,936	26,593	27,257	32,434
Chemung	17,706	18,793	17,080	21,321
Chenango	9,256	9,708	9,277	11,582
Clinton	18,232	11,535	17,624	15,330
Columbia	15,536	12,851	15,929	14,457
Cortland	10,616	8,970	10,670	11,613
Delaware	8,562	9,765	8,724	11,958
Dutchess	64,759	55,601	58,232	63,372

County	2008 Obama (D)	McCain (R)	2004 Kerry (D)	Bush (R)
Erie	218,645	154,716	251,090	184,423
Essex	9,531	7,189	8,768	9,869
Franklin	9,593	6,245	9,543	8,383
Fulton	9,147	11,537	9,202	12,570
Genesee	10,029	14,573	10,331	16,725
Greene	9,611	11,992	8,933	12,996
Hamilton	1,060	1,903	1,145	2,475
Herkimer	10,920	13,213	11,675	16,024
Jefferson	16,222	18,593	16,860	21,231
Lewis	4,813	5,700	4,546	6,624
Livingston	13,446	15,906	11,504	17,729
Madison	13,299	13,560	13,121	16,537
Manhattan[1]	490,634	79,448	526,765	107,405
Monroe	196,564	139,001	173,497	163,545
Montgomery	8,592	10,428	9,449	11,338
Nassau	316,523	272,765	323,070	288,355
Niagara	44,105	43,748	47,602	47,111
Oneida	45,531	46,555	40,792	52,392
Onondaga	118,390	80,476	116,381	94,006
Ontario	22,797	23,000	21,166	27,999
Orange	73,299	68,896	63,394	79,089
Orleans	6,142	9,166	5,959	10,317
Oswego	23,192	21,991	24,133	26,325
Otsego	12,072	11,059	12,723	13,342
Putnam	19,371	23,545	19,575	26,356
Queens[1]	436,398	144,362	433,835	165,954
Rensselaer	36,550	31,126	36,075	34,734
Rockland	65,134	58,199	64,191	65,130
St. Lawrence	21,642	15,972	22,857	18,029
Saratoga	51,932	49,734	48,730	56,158
Schenectady	35,529	28,172	35,971	32,066
Schoharie	5,760	7,520	5,630	8,591
Schuyler	3,792	4,431	3,445	4,960
Seneca	6,903	6,556	6,979	7,981
Staten Island[1]	73,192	80,853	68,448	90,325
Steuben	15,823	22,690	14,523	26,980
Suffolk	318,920	289,236	315,909	309,949
Sullivan	15,850	13,312	15,034	15,319
Tioga	9,702	12,077	9,694	13,762
Tompkins	26,401	11,004	27,229	13,994
Ulster	50,300	31,394	47,602	37,821
Warren	14,416	14,422	13,405	16,969
Washington	11,867	11,717	10,624	13,827
Wayne	16,831	21,083	15,709	24,709
Westchester	248,249	143,086	229,849	159,628
Wyoming	6,035	10,487	6,134	11,745
Yates	4,390	4,784	4,205	6,309
Totals	**4,804,945**	**2,752,771**	**4,314,280**	**2,962,567**

(1) Borough of New York City.

New York Vote Since 1952

2008: Obama, Dem., 4,804,945; McCain, Rep., 2,752,771; Nader, Populist, 41,249; Barr, Lib., 19,596; McKinney, Green, 12,801; Calero, Socialist Wkrs., 3,615; LaRiva, Socialism/Liberation, 1,639.

2004: Kerry, D., 4,314,280; Bush, R., 2,962,567; Nader, Ind., 99,873; Badnarik, LB., 11,607; Calero, Soc. Wkrs., 2,405.

2000: Gore, D., 4,112,965; Bush, R., 2,405,570; Nader, Green, 244,360; Buchanan, Reform, 31,554; Hagelin, Independence, 24,369; Browne, LB., 7,664; Harris, Soc. Workers, 1,790; Phillips, Constitution, 1,503.

1996: Clinton, D., 3,756,177; Dole, R., 1,933,492; Perot, Ind. (Ref.), 503,458; Nader, Green, 75,956; Phillips, Right to Life, 23,580; Browne, LB., 12,220; Hagelin, Natural Law, 5,011; Moorehead, Workers World, 3,473; Harris, Soc. Workers, 2,762.

1992: Clinton, D., 3,444,450; Bush, R., 2,346,649; Perot, Ind., 1,090,721; Warren, Soc. Workers, 15,472; Marrou, LB., 13,451; Fulani, New Alliance, 11,318; Hagelin, Natural Law, 4,420.

1988: Dukakis, D., 3,347,882; Bush, R., 3,081,871; Marra, Right to Life, 20,497; Fulani, New Alliance, 15,845.

1984: Reagan, R., 3,664,763; Mondale, D., 3,119,609; Bergland, LB., 11,949.

1980: Reagan, R., 2,893,831; Carter, D., 2,728,372; Anderson, Ind., 467,801; Clark, LB., 52,648; McCormack, Right To Life, 24,159; Commoner, Citizens, 23,186; Hall, Com., 7,414; DeBerry, Soc. Wkrs., 2,068; Griswold, Wkrs. World, 1,416; scattered, 1,064.

1976: Carter, D., 3,389,558; Ford, R., 3,100,791; MacBride, LB., 12,197; Hall, Com., 10,270; Camejo, Soc. Workers, 6,996; LaRouche, U.S. Labor, 5,413; blank, void, or scattered, 143,037.

1972: Nixon, R., 3,824,642; McGovern, D., 2,767,956; Lib., 183,128; total, 2,951,084; Reed, Cons., 368,136; Soc. Wkrs., 7,797; Fisher, Soc. Labor, 4,530; Hall, Com., 5,641; blank, void, or scattered, 161,641.

1968: Humphrey, D., 3,378,470; Nixon, R., 3,007,932; Wallace, 3rd Party, 358,864; Gregory, Freedom and Peace, 24,517; Halstead, Soc. Workers, 11,851; Blomen, Soc. Labor, 8,432; blank, void, and scattered, 171,164.

1964: Johnson, D., 4,913,156; Goldwater, R., 2,243,559; Hass, Soc. Labor, 6,085; DeBerry, Soc. Workers, 3,215; scattered, 188; blank and void, 151,383.

1960: Kennedy, D., 3,423,909; Liberal, 406,176; total, 3,830,085; Nixon, R., 3,446,419; Dobbs, Soc. Workers, 14,319; scattered, 256; blank and void, 88,896.

1956: Eisenhower, R., 4,340,340; Stevenson, D., 2,458,212, Liberal, 292,557, total, 2,750,769; write-in votes for Andrews, 1,027; Werdel, 492; Hass, 150; Hoopes, 82; others, 476.
1952: Eisenhower, R., 3,952,815; Stevenson, D., 2,687,890; Liberal, 416,711; total, 3,104,601; Hallinan, Amer. Lab., 64,211; Hoopes, Soc., 2,664; Dobbs, Soc. Workers, 2,212; Hass, Ind. Gov't., 1,560; scattered, 178; blank and void, 87,813.

North Carolina

	2008		2004	
County	Obama (D)	McCain (R)	Kerry (D)	Bush (R)
Alamance	28,590	34,501	20,686	33,302
Alexander	5,153	11,747	4,618	10,928
Alleghany	2,017	3,117	1,922	2,883
Anson	6,293	4,067	5,413	3,796
Ashe	4,861	7,885	4,477	7,292
Avery	2,163	5,617	1,805	5,678
Beaufort	9,426	13,437	7,025	12,432
Bertie	6,248	3,338	4,938	3,057
Bladen	7,846	7,530	6,109	6,174
Brunswick	21,280	30,662	14,903	22,925
Buncombe	69,415	52,236	51,868	52,491
Burke	14,623	21,766	11,728	18,922
Cabarrus	31,191	45,340	19,803	40,780
Caldwell	12,007	22,397	9,999	21,186
Camden	1,587	3,118	1,339	2,480
Carteret	11,079	22,868	7,732	17,716
Caswell	5,466	5,177	4,539	4,868
Catawba	25,535	42,843	18,858	39,602
Chatham	17,783	14,591	12,897	12,892
Cherokee	3,748	8,591	3,635	7,517
Chowan	3,652	3,751	2,406	2,967
Clay	1,731	3,692	1,628	3,209
Cleveland	17,274	25,950	14,215	22,750
Columbus	11,088	12,998	10,343	10,773
Craven	17,335	23,163	14,019	23,575
Cumberland	73,926	51,596	45,788	49,139
Currituck	3,685	7,159	2,909	6,013
Dare	7,760	9,621	6,136	9,345
Davidson	22,192	45,135	17,191	42,075
Davie	6,102	13,846	4,233	12,372
Duplin	8,866	10,734	6,923	9,611
Durham	102,237	32,040	74,524	34,614
Edgecombe	17,365	8,416	12,877	8,163
Forsyth	90,712	73,304	63,340	75,294
Franklin	13,022	13,183	9,286	11,540
Gaston	31,247	52,220	20,254	43,252
Gates	2,827	2,546	2,121	1,924
Graham	1,265	2,824	1,272	2,693
Granville	13,010	11,373	9,057	9,491
Greene	3,774	4,258	2,665	3,800
Guilford	141,680	97,511	100,042	98,254
Halifax	15,726	8,867	11,528	8,088
Harnett	16,519	23,311	11,563	20,922
Haywood	12,724	14,902	11,237	14,545
Henderson	20,062	30,903	15,003	28,025
Hertford	7,479	3,083	5,141	2,942
Hoke	9,133	6,197	5,794	5,257
Hyde	1,225	1,203	1,048	1,235
Iredell	27,201	44,979	18,065	38,675
Jackson	8,671	7,793	6,737	7,351
Johnston	26,475	43,164	17,266	36,903
Jones	2,364	2,807	1,893	2,607
Lee	10,703	12,652	7,657	11,834
Lenoir	13,157	13,281	10,207	12,939
Lincoln	11,674	23,561	9,434	20,052
Macon	6,514	11,382	5,489	9,448
Madison	6,603	10,262	4,234	5,175
Martin	5,011	5,175	5,102	5,334
McDowell	6,488	5,914	5,330	10,590
Mecklenburg	252,642	152,957	166,828	155,084
Mitchell	2,220	5,472	2,080	5,686
Montgomery	4,870	6,125	4,313	5,745
Moore	17,534	27,165	13,555	24,714
Nash	23,013	23,660	15,693	21,902
New Hanover	48,588	50,004	35,572	45,351
Northampton	6,893	3,662	5,584	3,176
Onslow	19,296	29,942	11,250	25,890
Orange	53,712	20,226	42,910	20,771
Pamlico	2,820	3,809	2,335	3,679
Pasquotank	10,170	7,720	6,984	6,609
Pender	9,832	13,517	6,999	10,037
Perquimans	2,761	3,674	1,971	2,965
Person	8,410	10,007	6,198	8,973
Pitt	39,763	33,429	24,924	28,590
Polk	4,394	5,986	3,787	5,140
Randolph	16,280	40,644	12,966	37,771
Richmond	9,586	9,316	8,383	7,709
Robeson	22,315	16,883	17,868	15,909
Rockingham	16,730	22,435	14,430	22,840
Rowan	23,272	37,284	16,735	34,915
Rutherford	9,595	18,631	8,184	16,343

	2008		2004	
County	Obama (D)	McCain (R)	Kerry (D)	Bush (R)
Sampson	11,753	13,952	9,649	12,600
Scotland	8,105	5,972	6,386	5,141
Stanly	8,815	19,193	7,650	17,814
Stokes	6,816	14,335	5,767	13,583
Surry	10,399	18,574	8,304	17,587
Swain	2,803	2,896	2,419	2,593
Transylvania	7,203	9,299	6,097	9,386
Tyrrell	932	960	731	855
Union	31,038	53,882	17,974	42,820
Vance	13,095	7,584	8,762	6,884
Wake	247,914	183,291	169,909	177,324
Warren	6,663	2,992	5,171	2,840
Washington	3,734	2,667	2,969	2,484
Watauga	14,513	13,300	11,232	12,659
Wayne	22,507	26,800	15,076	24,883
Wilkes	8,889	20,152	7,862	19,197
Wilson	19,754	18,338	14,206	16,264
Yadkin	4,501	12,355	3,451	11,816
Yancey	4,470	5,021	4,434	4,940
Totals	**2,142,651**	**2,128,474**	**1,525,849**	**1,961,166**

North Carolina Vote Since 1952
2008: Obama, Dem., 2,142,651; McCain, Rep., 2,128,474; Barr, Lib., 25,722.
2004: Bush, R., 1,961,166; Kerry, D., 1,525,849; Badnarik, LB., 11,731.
2000: Bush, R., 1,631,163; Gore, D., 1,257,692; Browne, LB., 13,891; Buchanan, Reform, 8,874.
1996: Dole, R., 1,225,938; Clinton, D., 1,107,849; Perot, Ref., 168,059; Browne, LB., 8,740; Hagelin, Natural Law, 2,771.
1992: Bush, R., 1,134,661; Clinton, D., 1,114,042; Perot, Ind., 357,864; Marrou, LB., 5,171.
1988: Bush, R., 1,237,258; Dukakis, D., 890,167; Fulani, New Alliance, 5,682; Paul, write-in, 1,263.
1984: Reagan, R., 1,346,481; Mondale, D., 824,287; Bergland, LB., 3,794.
1980: Reagan, R., 915,018; Carter, D., 875,635; Anderson, Ind., 52,800; Clark, LB., 9,677; Commoner, Citizens, 2,287; DeBerry, Soc. Workers, 416.
1976: Carter, D., 927,365; Ford, R., 741,960; Anderson, Amer., 5,607; MacBride, LB., 2,219; LaRouche, U.S. Labor, 755.
1972: Nixon, R., 1,054,889; McGovern, D., 438,705; Schmitz, Amer., 25,018.
1968: Nixon, R., 627,192; Wallace, 3rd Party, 496,188; Humphrey, D., 464,113.
1964: Johnson, D., 800,139; Goldwater, R., 624,844.
1960: Kennedy, D., 713,136; Nixon, R., 655,420.
1956: Stevenson, D., 590,530; Eisenhower, R., 575,062.
1952: Stevenson, D., 652,803; Eisenhower, R., 558,107.

North Dakota

	2008		2004	
County	Obama (D)	McCain (R)	Kerry (D)	Bush (R)
Adams	434	785	353	915
Barnes	2,723	2,808	2,186	3,541
Benson	1,566	772	1,196	1,002
Billings	114	375	99	449
Bottineau	1,384	2,046	1,168	2,468
Bowman	478	1,106	397	1,280
Burke	285	639	336	808
Burleigh	15,524	25,381	11,621	26,577
Cass	37,577	32,515	26,010	39,619
Cavalier	930	1,125	887	1,522
Dickey	1,039	1,517	883	1,890
Divide	461	629	487	751
Dunn	526	1,078	571	1,178
Eddy	582	548	534	655
Emmons	545	1,226	611	1,449
Foster	687	913	518	1,219
Golden Valley	209	640	195	719
Grand Forks	16,079	14,498	12,646	17,298
Grant	402	869	264	952
Griggs	597	682	505	907
Hettinger	406	892	405	1,044
Kidder	421	751	433	902
LaMoure	868	1,307	712	1,592
Logan	299	725	265	844
McHenry	980	1,371	1,030	1,744
McIntosh	579	914	436	1,254
McKenzie	932	1,730	847	1,897
McLean	1,858	2,762	1,664	3,014
Mercer	1,472	2,788	1,245	3,285
Morton	5,073	7,853	4,073	8,325
Mountrail	1,476	1,403	1,465	1,527
Nelson	904	797	778	1,107
Oliver	332	680	310	790
Pembina	1,486	1,710	1,321	2,466
Pierce	792	1,300	686	1,475
Ramsey	2,311	2,358	1,885	2,943
Ransom	1,369	993	1,199	1,352
Renville	505	796	497	953

County	2008 Obama (D)	McCain (R)	2004 Kerry (D)	Bush (R)
Richland	3,510	3,892	2,821	5,264
Rolette	3,403	1,042	2,564	1,392
Sargent	1,112	774	1,021	1,147
Sheridan	227	550	200	727
Sioux	1,144	215	804	319
Slope	106	297	89	335
Stark	3,794	7,019	3,013	7,220
Steele	612	404	616	586
Stutsman	4,042	5,484	3,438	6,517
Towner	620	536	606	754
Traill	2,135	1,839	1,651	2,543
Walsh	2,323	2,410	1,905	3,194
Ward	10,125	15,038	8,236	17,008
Wells	840	1,468	858	1,654
Williams	2,915	6,273	2,512	6,278
Totals	**141,278**	**168,601**	**111,052**	**196,651**

North Dakota Vote Since 1952

2008: McCain, Rep., 168,601; Obama, Dem., 141,278; Nader, Ind., 4,189; Barr, Lib., 1,354; Baldwin, Const., 1,199.

2004: Bush, R., 196,651; Kerry, D., 111,052; Nader, Ind., 3,756; Badnarik, LB., 851; Peroutka, Constitution, 514.

2000: Bush, R., 174,852; Gore, D., 95,284; Nader, Ind., 9,486; Buchanan, Reform, 7,288; Browne, Ind., 660; Phillips, Constitution, 373; Hagelin, Ind., 313.

1996: Dole, R., 125,050; Clinton, D., 106,905; Perot, Ref., 32,515; Browne, LB., 847; Phillips, Ind., 745; Hagelin, Natural Law, 349.

1992: Bush, R., 136,244; Clinton, D., 99,168; Perot, Ind., 71,084.

1988: Bush, R., 166,559; Dukakis, D., 127,739; Paul, Lib., 1,315; LaRouche, Natl. Econ. Recovery, 905.

1984: Reagan, R., 200,336; Mondale, D., 104,429; Bergland, LB., 703.

1980: Reagan, R., 193,695; Carter, D., 79,189; Anderson, Ind., 23,640; Clark, LB., 3,743; Commoner, LB., 429; McLain, Natl. People's League, 296; Greaves, Amer., 235; Hall, Com., 93; DeBerry, Soc. Workers, 89; McReynolds, Soc., 82; Bubar, Statesman, 54.

1976: Ford, R., 153,470; Carter, D., 136,078; Anderson, Amer., 3,698; McCarthy, Ind., 2,952; Maddox, Amer. Ind., 269; MacBride, LB., 256; scattered, 371.

1972: Nixon, R., 174,109; McGovern, D., 100,384; Schmitz, Amer., 5,646; Jenness, Soc. Workers, 288; Hall, Com., 87.

1968: Nixon, R., 138,669; Humphrey, D., 94,769; Wallace, 3rd Party, 14,244; Halstead, Soc. Workers, 128; Munn, Prohibition, 38; Troxell, Ind., 34.

1964: Johnson, D., 149,784; Goldwater, R., 108,207; DeBerry, Soc. Workers, 224; Munn, Proh., 174.

1960: Nixon, R., 154,310; Kennedy, D., 123,963; Dobbs, Soc. Workers, 158.

1956: Eisenhower, R., 156,766; Stevenson, D., 96,742; Andrews, Amer., 483.

1952: Eisenhower, R., 191,712; Stevenson, D., 76,694; MacArthur, Christian Nationalist, 1,075; Hallinan, Prog., 344; Hamblen, Proh., 302.

Ohio

County	2008 Obama (D)	McCain (R)	2004 Kerry (D)	Bush (R)
Adams	4,041	6,725	4,281	7,653
Allen	16,575	26,167	16,470	32,580
Ashland	9,027	14,788	8,576	16,209
Ashtabula	24,233	18,464	24,060	21,038
Athens	19,258	9,107	18,998	10,847
Auglaize	6,492	15,938	5,903	17,016
Belmont	15,986	15,127	17,576	15,589
Brown	7,280	11,873	7,140	12,647
Butler	62,871	101,537	56,243	109,872
Carroll	6,302	6,952	6,300	7,695
Champaign	7,161	10,919	6,968	11,718
Clark	29,122	31,821	33,535	34,941
Clermont	30,124	60,287	25,887	62,949
Clinton	6,267	12,037	5,417	12,938
Columbiana	21,222	24,891	23,429	25,753
Coshocton	7,580	8,583	7,378	9,839
Crawford	8,045	12,050	7,773	13,885
Cuyahoga	441,836	196,369	448,503	221,600
Darke	7,456	17,226	7,846	18,306
Defiance	7,394	9,334	6,975	11,397
Delaware	35,848	53,670	27,048	53,143
Erie	22,277	17,080	21,421	18,597
Fairfield	28,487	40,708	24,783	42,715
Fayette	4,199	6,931	4,334	7,376
Franklin	305,144	205,338	285,801	237,253
Fulton	9,627	11,414	8,224	13,640
Gallia	4,616	8,047	5,366	8,576
Geauga	20,692	28,314	19,850	30,370
Greene	27,162	39,252	30,531	48,388
Guernsey	7,369	8,950	7,768	9,962
Hamilton	208,802	187,862	199,679	222,616
Hancock	13,357	21,898	10,352	25,105
Hardin	4,847	7,553	4,891	8,441
Harrison	3,495	3,717	3,780	4,274
Henry	6,163	8,091	5,111	9,902

County	2008 Obama (D)	McCain (R)	2004 Kerry (D)	Bush (R)
Highland	6,437	11,390	6,194	12,211
Hocking	6,083	6,201	6,175	6,936
Holmes	3,074	7,590	2,697	8,468
Huron	9,461	10,001	10,568	14,817
Jackson	5,108	7,837	5,700	8,585
Jefferson	17,266	17,216	19,024	17,185
Knox	10,702	16,207	9,820	17,068
Lake	54,786	54,441	59,049	62,193
Lawrence	10,956	15,055	12,118	15,454
Licking	19,768	30,545	30,053	49,016
Logan	7,615	13,440	6,825	14,471
Lorain	77,719	55,031	78,970	61,203
Lucas	134,729	70,865	132,715	87,160
Madison	6,193	10,178	6,203	11,117
Mahoning	76,356	44,339	83,194	48,761
Marion	12,016	14,840	11,930	17,171
Medina	24,614	31,785	36,272	48,196
Meigs	3,990	5,891	4,438	6,272
Mercer	5,636	14,730	5,118	15,650
Miami	10,739	22,217	17,606	33,992
Monroe	3,623	2,973	4,243	3,424
Montgomery	136,110	123,040	142,997	138,371
Morgan	2,921	3,387	2,875	3,758
Morrow	5,960	9,787	5,775	10,474
Muskingum	17,209	20,174	16,421	22,254
Noble	2,419	3,387	2,654	3,841
Ottawa	11,760	10,417	11,118	12,073
Paulding	4,043	5,204	3,610	6,206
Perry	7,128	7,585	7,257	7,856
Pickaway	8,229	13,087	8,579	14,161
Pike	5,833	6,005	5,989	6,520
Portage	32,160	26,959	40,675	35,583
Preble	6,846	13,340	7,274	13,734
Putnam	5,169	12,855	4,392	14,370
Richland	24,473	32,590	24,638	36,872
Ross	13,636	16,027	13,978	17,231
Sandusky	15,101	13,935	12,686	16,221
Scioto	14,470	16,472	16,827	18,259
Seneca	12,751	13,588	10,957	15,886
Shelby	6,777	15,005	6,535	16,204
Stark	66,712	63,283	95,337	92,215
Summit	151,932	107,937	156,587	118,558
Trumbull	62,254	39,319	66,673	40,977
Tuscarawas	20,957	19,940	18,853	23,829
Union	8,348	15,049	6,665	15,870
Van Wert	5,046	8,993	4,095	10,678
Vinton	2,405	2,962	2,651	3,249
Warren	32,372	69,741	26,044	68,037
Washington	12,082	16,638	12,538	17,532
Wayne	21,144	28,730	19,786	31,879
Williams	7,892	9,618	6,481	12,040
Wood	32,956	28,819	29,401	33,592
Wyandot	4,362	6,190	3,708	7,254
Totals	**2,940,044**	**2,677,820**	**2,741,165**	**2,859,764**

Ohio Vote Since 1952

2008: Obama, Dem., 2,940,044; McCain, Rep., 2,677,820; Nader, Ind., 42,337; Barr, Lib., 19,917; Baldwin, Const., 12,565; McKinney, Green, 8,518;.Duncan, Ind., 3,905; Moore, Socialist, 2,735.

2004: Bush, R., 2,859,768; Kerry, D., 2,741,167; Badnarik, nonpartisan, 14,676; Peroutka, nonpartisan, 939.

2000: Bush, R., 2,351,209; Gore, D., 2,186,190; Nader, Ind., 117,857; Buchanan, Ind., 26,724; Browne, LB., 13,475; Hagelin, Natural Law, 6,169; Phillips, Ind., 3,823.

1996: Clinton, D., 2,148,222; Dole, R., 1,859,883; Perot, Ref., 483,207; Browne, Ind., 12,851; Moorehead, Ind., 10,813; Hagelin, Natural Law, 9,120; Phillips, Ind., 7,361.

1992: Clinton, D., 1,984,942; Bush, R., 1,894,310; Perot, Ind., 1,036,426; Marrou, LB., 7,252; Fulani, New Alliance, 6,413; Gritz, Populist/America First, 4,699; Hagelin, Natural Law, 3,437; LaRouche, Ind., 2,446.

1988: Bush, R., 2,416,549; Dukakis, D., 1,939,629; Fulani, Ind., 12,017; Paul, Ind., 11,926.

1984: Reagan, R., 2,678,559; Mondale, D., 1,825,440; Bergland, LB., 5,886.

1980: Reagan, R., 2,206,545; Carter, D., 1,752,414; Anderson, Ind., 254,472; Clark, LB., 49,033; Commoner, Citizens, 8,564; Hall, Com., 4,729; Congress, Ind., 4,029; Griswold, Workers World, 3,790; Bubar, Statesman, 27.

1976: Carter, D., 2,011,621; Ford, R., 2,000,505; McCarthy, Ind., 58,258; Maddox, Amer. Ind., 15,529; MacBride, LB., 8,961; Hall, Com., 7,817; Camejo, Soc. Workers, 4,717; LaRouche, U.S. Labor, 4,335; scattered, 130.

1972: Nixon, R., 2,441,827; McGovern, D., 1,558,889; Schmitz, Amer., 80,067; Fisher, Soc. Labor, 7,107; Hall, Com., 6,437; Wallace, Ind., 460.

1968: Nixon, R., 1,791,014; Humphrey, D., 1,700,586; Wallace, 3rd Party, 467,495; Gregory, 372; Blomen, Soc. Labor, 120; Halstead, Soc. Workers, 69; Mitchell, Com., 23; Munn, Proh., 19.

1964: Johnson, D., 2,498,331; Goldwater, R., 1,470,865.

1960: Nixon, R., 2,217,611; Kennedy, D., 1,944,248.

1956: Eisenhower, R., 2,262,610; Stevenson, D., 1,439,655.

1952: Eisenhower, R., 2,100,391; Stevenson, D., 1,600,367.

Oklahoma

County	2008 Obama (D)	McCain (R)	2004 Kerry (D)	Bush (R)
Adair	2,049	4,636	2,562	4,971
Alfalfa	411	2,023	470	2,201
Atoka	1,370	3,509	1,946	3,142
Beaver	265	2,197	297	2,272
Beckham	1,625	5,769	1,931	5,454
Blaine	1,011	3,100	1,222	3,199
Bryan	4,423	9,295	5,745	8,615
Caddo	3,395	6,401	3,916	6,491
Canadian	11,422	36,411	9,712	33,297
Carter	5,603	13,241	6,466	12,178
Cherokee	7,193	9,182	8,623	9,569
Choctaw	1,859	3,729	2,639	3,168
Cimarron	152	1,119	184	1,242
Cleveland	39,673	64,730	34,007	65,720
Coal	570	1,609	1,203	1,396
Comanche	14,120	20,127	12,022	21,170
Cotton	690	1,793	898	1,742
Craig	2,072	3,858	2,504	3,894
Creek	8,318	20,181	9,929	18,848
Custer	2,660	7,842	2,801	7,839
Delaware	5,084	10,274	5,591	10,017
Dewey	346	1,857	408	1,843
Ellis	282	1,627	395	1,685
Garfield	5,545	17,066	5,586	17,685
Garvin	3,028	7,708	3,707	7,610
Grady	5,516	15,187	5,970	14,136
Grant	514	1,836	571	1,950
Greer	566	1,548	719	1,529
Harmon	333	757	354	838
Harper	221	1,342	268	1,397
Haskell	1,474	3,206	2,378	2,946
Hughes	1,705	3,132	2,283	3,066
Jackson	2,263	6,716	2,232	7,024
Jefferson	805	1,649	1,057	1,546
Johnston	1,246	2,707	1,713	2,635
Kay	5,462	13,229	5,957	14,121
Kingfisher	1,009	5,372	1,022	5,630
Kiowa	1,226	2,536	1,413	2,610
Latimer	1,313	2,857	1,945	2,535
Le Flore	5,136	11,603	6,741	10,683
Lincoln	3,503	10,468	4,041	10,149
Logan	5,716	12,555	4,869	11,474
Love	1,257	2,589	1,538	2,295
Major	3,550	11,184	537	3,122
Marshall	2,792	7,744	2,088	3,363
Mayes	3,318	4,903	6,933	9,946
McClain	515	2,955	3,742	10,041
McCurtain	1,642	3,729	3,684	7,472
McIntosh	5,749	10,231	4,488	4,692
Murray	1,592	3,746	2,130	3,665
Muskogee	11,286	15,276	12,585	15,124
Noble	1,174	3,881	1,335	3,993
Nowata	1,411	3,029	1,660	2,805
Okfuskee	1,478	2,642	1,743	2,542
Oklahoma	116,133	163,099	97,298	174,741
Okmulgee	6,187	8,724	7,367	8,363
Osage	7,493	12,150	8,068	11,467
Ottawa	4,266	6,904	5,086	7,443
Pawnee	2,063	4,533	2,564	4,412
Payne	10,601	18,435	10,101	19,560
Pittsburg	5,454	11,739	7,452	11,134
Pontotoc	4,511	9,749	5,165	9,647
Pottawatomie	7,906	17,728	8,638	17,215
Pushmataha	1,265	3,208	1,934	2,863
Roger Mills	286	1,502	382	1,388
Rogers	10,770	27,732	11,918	24,976
Seminole	2,977	5,599	3,648	5,624
Sequoyah	4,454	9,465	5,910	8,865
Stephens	4,538	14,392	5,515	13,646
Texas	923	5,332	1,016	5,450
Tillman	1,042	2,195	1,175	2,273
Tulsa	96,106	158,322	90,220	163,452
Wagoner	8,805	21,426	9,157	19,081
Washington	6,308	16,457	6,862	16,551
Washita	1,050	3,716	1,340	3,705
Woods	870	3,043	932	3,166
Woodward	1,348	6,402	1,458	6,193
Totals	**502,496**	**960,165**	**503,966**	**959,792**

Oklahoma Vote Since 1952
2008: McCain, Rep., 960,165; Obama, Dem., 502,496.
2004: Bush, R., 959,792; Kerry, D., 503,966.
2000: Bush, R., 744,337; Gore, D., 474,276; Buchanan, Reform, 9,014; Browne, LB., 6,602.
1996: Dole, R., 582,315; Clinton, D., 488,105; Perot, Ref., 130,788; Browne, LB., 5,505.
1992: Bush, R., 592,929; Clinton, D., 473,066; Perot, Ind., 319,878; Marrou, LB., 4,486.
1988: Bush, R., 678,367; Dukakis, D., 483,423; Paul, Lib., 6,261; Fulani, New Alliance, 2,985.
1984: Reagan, R., 861,530; Mondale, D., 385,080; Bergland, LB., 9,066.

1980: Reagan, R., 695,570; Carter, D., 402,026; Anderson, Ind., 38,284; Clark, LB., 13,828.
1976: Ford, R., 545,708; Carter, D., 532,442; McCarthy, Ind., 14,101.
1972: Nixon, R., 759,025; McGovern, D., 247,147; Schmitz, Amer., 23,728.
1968: Nixon, R., 449,697; Humphrey, D., 301,658; Wallace, 3rd Party, 191,731.
1964: Johnson, D., 519,834; Goldwater, R., 412,665.
1960: Nixon, R., 533,039; Kennedy, D., 370,111.
1956: Eisenhower, R., 473,769; Stevenson, D., 385,581.
1952: Eisenhower, R., 518,045; Stevenson, D., 430,939.

Oregon

County	2008 Obama (D)	McCain (R)	2004 Kerry (D)	Bush (R)
Baker	2,795	5,643	2,616	6,253
Benton	29,421	15,036	26,515	18,460
Clackamas	95,237	76,161	95,129	97,691
Clatsop	10,579	7,113	10,461	8,503
Columbia	13,253	10,351	12,563	11,868
Coos	14,270	15,236	14,393	18,291
Crook	3,623	6,348	3,024	6,830
Curry	5,216	6,626	5,220	7,332
Deschutes	38,612	38,918	31,179	41,757
Douglas	19,153	28,635	18,089	35,956
Gilliam	429	642	370	755
Grant	980	2,670	780	3,204
Harney	946	2,592	839	2,815
Hood River	6,229	3,240	5,587	4,124
Jackson	47,664	47,806	44,366	56,519
Jefferson	3,648	4,360	3,243	4,762
Josephine	17,338	22,926	15,214	26,241
Klamath	9,115	18,682	8,264	22,733
Lake	954	2,631	802	3,039
Lane	104,010	58,149	107,769	75,007
Lincoln	13,991	8,649	13,753	10,160
Linn	21,702	27,576	19,940	31,260
Malheur	2,922	7,099	2,577	8,123
Marion	55,610	53,174	57,671	69,900
Morrow	1,398	2,501	1,361	2,732
Multnomah	264,741	71,084	259,585	98,439
Polk	17,046	17,272	15,484	19,508
Sherman	382	632	390	694
Tillamook	7,018	5,732	6,750	7,003
Umatilla	9,400	15,126	8,884	17,068
Union	4,612	7,563	4,428	8,879
Wallowa	1,490	2,832	1,269	3,132
Wasco	5,649	4,900	5,691	6,119
Washington	128,402	80,203	121,140	107,223
Wheeler	276	497	245	612
Yamhill	20,494	21,068	17,572	23,839
Totals	**1,037,291**	**738,475**	**943,163**	**866,831**

Oregon Vote Since 1952
2008: Obama, Dem., 1,037,291; McCain, Rep., 738,475; Nader, Peace Party of Oregon, 18,614; Baldwin, Const., 7,693; Barr, Lib., 7,635; McKinney, Pacific Green, 4,543.
2004: Kerry, D., 943,163; Bush, R., 866,831; Badnarik, LB., 7,260; Cobb, Pac. Green, 5,315; Peroutka, Constitution, 5,257.
2000: Gore, D., 720,342; Bush, R., 713,577; Nader, Green, 77,357; Browne, LB., 7,447; Buchanan, Ind., 7,063; Hagelin, Reform, 2,574; Phillips, Constitution, 2,189.
1996: Clinton, D., 649,641; Dole, R., 538,152; Perot, Ref., 121,221; Nader, Pacific, 49,415; Browne, LB., 8,903; Phillips, Taxpayers, 3,379; Hagelin, Natural Law, 2,798; Hollis, Soc., 1,922.
1992: Clinton, D., 621,314; Bush, R., 475,757; Perot, Ind., 354,091; Marrou, LB., 4,277; Fulani, New Alliance, 3,030.
1988: Dukakis, D., 616,206; Bush, R., 560,126; Paul, Lib., 14,811; Fulani, Ind., 6,487.
1984: Reagan, R., 658,700; Mondale, D., 536,479.
1980: Reagan, R., 571,044; Carter, D., 456,890; Anderson, Ind., 112,389; Clark, LB., 25,838; Commoner, Citizens, 13,642; scattered, 1,713.
1976: Ford, R., 492,120; Carter, D., 490,407; McCarthy, Ind., 40,207; write-in, 7,142.
1972: Nixon, R., 486,686; McGovern, D., 392,760; Schmitz, Amer., 46,211; write-in, 2,289.
1968: Nixon, R., 408,433; Humphrey, D., 358,866; Wallace, 3rd Party, 49,683; write-in, McCarthy, 1,496; N. Rockefeller, 69; others, 1,075.
1964: Johnson, D., 501,017; Goldwater, R., 282,779; write-in, 2,509.
1960: Nixon, R., 408,060; Kennedy, D., 367,402.
1956: Eisenhower, R., 406,393; Stevenson, D., 329,204.
1952: Eisenhower, R., 420,815; Stevenson, D., 270,579; Hallinan, Ind., 3,665.

Pennsylvania

County	2008 Obama (D)	McCain (R)	2004 Kerry (D)	Bush (R)
Adams	17,475	26,134	13,764	28,247
Allegheny	368,453	269,819	368,912	271,925
Armstrong	10,729	17,715	12,025	18,925
Beaver	39,738	42,358	42,146	39,916
Bedford	6,001	15,928	6,016	16,606
Berks	91,803	75,868	76,309	87,122

County	2008 Obama (D)	McCain (R)	2004 Kerry (D)	Bush (R)
Blair	18,798	30,812	18,105	35,751
Bradford	10,202	14,911	8,590	16,942
Bucks	178,345	149,860	163,438	154,469
Butler	29,882	52,294	30,090	54,959
Cambria	30,697	29,981	32,591	34,048
Cameron	802	1,239	794	1,599
Carbon	13,235	12,646	12,223	12,519
Centre	41,141	32,543	30,733	33,133
Chester	135,150	112,266	109,708	120,036
Clarion	6,415	10,126	6,049	11,063
Clearfield	14,549	18,656	13,518	20,533
Clinton	6,799	7,126	5,823	8,035
Columbia	12,597	13,704	10,679	16,052
Crawford	15,684	19,265	16,013	21,965
Cumberland	45,355	59,693	37,928	67,648
Dauphin	69,352	57,964	55,299	65,296
Delaware	170,949	109,766	162,601	120,425
Elk	6,910	6,252	6,602	7,872
Erie	74,206	49,284	67,921	57,372
Fayette	25,509	25,669	29,120	25,045
Forest	1,014	1,366	989	1,571
Franklin	21,052	41,711	16,562	41,817
Fulton	1,562	4,612	1,475	4,772
Greene	7,365	7,451	7,674	7,786
Huntingdon	6,611	11,724	5,879	12,126
Indiana	16,964	19,617	15,831	20,254
Jefferson	6,132	11,248	6,073	13,371
Juniata	3,055	6,463	2,797	7,144
Lackawanna	67,112	39,198	59,573	44,766
Lancaster	97,290	124,475	74,328	145,591
Lawrence	19,371	21,496	21,387	21,938
Lebanon	22,004	32,325	18,109	37,089
Lehigh	86,226	62,668	73,940	70,160
Luzerne	71,903	60,512	69,573	64,953
Lycoming	18,335	30,215	15,681	33,961
McKean	6,186	8,835	6,294	10,941
Mercer	24,319	24,321	24,833	26,311
Mifflin	5,364	10,904	4,889	11,726
Monroe	36,655	25,892	27,967	27,971
Montgomery	249,949	163,030	222,048	175,741
Montour	3,347	4,555	2,666	4,903
Northampton	74,956	58,352	63,446	62,102
Northumberland	13,555	18,012	14,602	22,262
Perry	6,384	13,032	5,423	13,919
Philadelphia	574,930	113,260	542,205	130,099
Pike	11,448	12,456	8,656	12,444
Potter	2,277	5,073	2,268	5,640
Schuylkill	28,187	33,682	29,231	35,640
Snyder	5,375	9,895	4,348	10,566
Somerset	12,437	20,925	12,842	23,802
Sullivan	1,228	1,840	1,213	2,056
Susquehanna	8,314	10,551	7,351	11,573
Tioga	6,012	10,542	5,437	12,019
Union	7,207	9,720	5,700	10,334
Venango	8,708	12,817	9,024	14,472
Warren	8,669	9,824	8,044	10,999
Washington	44,286	48,753	48,225	47,673
Wayne	9,824	12,618	8,060	13,713
Westmoreland	69,004	96,786	77,774	100,087
Wyoming	5,631	6,494	4,982	7,782
York	81,748	107,367	63,701	114,270
Totals	**3,276,363**	**2,655,885**	**2,938,095**	**2,793,847**

Pennsylvania Vote Since 1952

2008: Obama, Dem., 3,276,363; McCain, Rep., 2,655,885; Nader, Ind., 42,977; Barr, Lib., 19,912.

2004: Kerry, D., 2,938,095; Bush, R., 2,793,847; Badnarik, LB., 21,185; Cobb, Green, 6,319; Peroutka, Constitution, 6,318.

2000: Gore, D., 2,485,967; Bush, R., 2,281,127; Nader, Green, 103,392; Buchanan, Reform, 16,023; Phillips, Constitution, 14,428; Browne, LB., 11,248.

1996: Clinton, D., 2,215,819; Dole, R., 1,801,169; Perot, Ref., 430,984; Browne, LB., 28,000; Phillips, Constitutional, 19,552; Hagelin, Natural Law, 5,783.

1992: Clinton, D., 2,239,164; Bush, R., 1,791,841; Perot, Ind., 902,667; Marrou, LB., 21,477; Fulani, New Alliance, 4,661.

1988: Bush, R., 2,300,087; Dukakis, D., 2,194,944; McCarthy, Consumer, 19,158; Paul, Lib., 12,051.

1984: Reagan, R., 2,584,323; Mondale, D., 2,228,131; Bergland, LB., 6,982.

1980: Reagan, R., 2,261,872; Carter, D., 1,937,540; Anderson, Ind., 292,921; Clark, LB., 33,263; DeBerry, Soc. Workers, 20,291; Commoner, Consumer, 10,430; Hall, Com., 5,184.

1976: Carter, D., 2,328,677; Ford, R., 2,205,604; McCarthy, Ind., 50,584; Maddox, Const., 25,344; Camejo, Soc. Workers, 3,009; LaRouche, U.S. Labor, 2,744; Hall, Com., 1,891; others, 2,934.

1972: Nixon, R., 2,714,521; McGovern, D., 1,796,951; Schmitz, Amer., 70,593; Jenness, Soc. Workers, 4,639; Hall, Com., 2,686; others, 2,715.

1968: Humphrey, D., 2,259,405; Nixon, R., 2,090,017; Wallace, 3rd Party, 378,582; Gregory, Peace and Freedom, 7,821; Blomen, Soc. Labor, 4,977; Halstead, Soc. Workers, 4,862; others, 2,264.

1964: Johnson, D., 3,130,954; Goldwater, R., 1,673,657; DeBerry, Soc. Workers, 10,456; Hass, Soc. Labor, 5,092; scattered, 2,531.

1960: Kennedy, D., 2,556,282; Nixon, R., 2,439,956; Hass, Soc. Labor, 7,185; Dobbs, Soc. Workers, 2,678; scattered, 440.

1956: Eisenhower, R., 2,585,252; Stevenson, D., 1,981,769; Hass, Soc. Labor, 7,447; Dobbs, Militant Workers, 2,035.

1952: Eisenhower, R., 2,415,789; Stevenson, D., 2,146,269; Hamblen, Proh., 8,771; Hallinan, Prog., 4,200; Hoopes, Soc., 2,684; Dobbs, Militant Workers, 1,502; Hass, Ind. Govt., 1,347; scattered, 155.

Rhode Island

County	2008 Obama (D)	McCain (R)	2004 Kerry (D)	Bush (R)
Cranston	22,520	13,981	20,331	14,471
East Providence	15,380	6,216	13,655	6,359
Pawtucket	18,486	6,098	15,567	6,394
Providence	46,252	8,545	35,917	9,787
Warwick	25,802	16,541	23,164	16,640
Other	168,107	114,008	151,126	115,395
Totals	**296,571**	**165,391**	**259,760**	**169,046**

Rhode Island Vote Since 1952

2008: Obama, Dem., 296,571; McCain, Rep., 165,391; Nader, Ind., 4,829; Barr, Lib., 1,382; McKinney, Green, 797; Baldwin, Const., 675; LaRiva, Socialism/Liberation, 122.

2004: Kerry, D., 259,765; Bush, R., 169,046; Nader, Ref., 4,651; Cobb, Green, 1,333; Badnarik, LB., 907; Peroutka, Constitution, 339; Parker, Workers World, 253.

2000: Gore, D., 249,508; Bush, R., 130,555; Nader, Ind., 25,052; Buchanan, Reform, 2,273; Browne, Ind., 742; Hagelin, Ind., 271; Moorehead, Ind., 199; Phillips, Ind., 97; McReynolds, Ind., 52; Harris, Ind., 34.

1996: Clinton, D., 233,050; Dole, R., 104,683; Perot, Ref., 43,723; Nader, Green, 6,040; Browne, Lib., 1,109; Phillips, U.S. Taxpayers, 1,021; Hagelin, Natural Law, 435; Moorehead, Workers World, 186.

1992: Clinton, D., 213,299; Bush, R., 131,601; Perot, Ind., 105,045; Fulani, New Alliance, 1,878.

1988: Dukakis, D., 225,123; Bush, R., 177,761; Paul, Lib., 825; Fulani, New Alliance, 280.

1984: Reagan, R., 212,080; Mondale, D., 197,106; Bergland, LB., 277.

1980: Carter, D., 198,342; Reagan, R., 154,793; Anderson, Ind., 59,819; Clark, LB., 2,458; Hall, Com., 218; McReynolds, Soc., 170; DeBerry, Soc. Workers, 90; Griswold, Workers World, 77.

1976: Carter, D., 227,636; Ford, R., 181,249; MacBride, LB., 715; Camejo, Soc. Workers, 462; Hall, Com., 334; Levin, Soc. Labor, 188.

1972: Nixon, R., 220,383; McGovern, D., 194,645; Jenness, Soc. Workers, 729.

1968: Humphrey, D., 246,518; Nixon, R., 122,359; Wallace, 3rd Party, 15,678; Halstead, Soc. Workers, 383.

1964: Johnson, D., 315,463; Goldwater, R., 74,615.

1960: Kennedy, D., 258,032; Nixon, R., 147,502.

1956: Eisenhower, R., 225,819; Stevenson, D., 161,790.

1952: Eisenhower, R., 210,935; Stevenson, D., 203,293; Hallinan, Prog., 187; Hass, Soc. Labor, 83.

South Carolina

County	2008 Obama (D)	McCain (R)	2004 Kerry (D)	Bush (R)
Abbeville	4,593	6,264	4,389	5,436
Aiken	26,101	42,849	19,799	39,077
Allendale	3,029	947	2,565	985
Anderson	24,132	48,690	20,697	43,355
Bamberg	4,426	2,309	3,841	2,138
Barnwell	4,931	4,769	3,982	4,606
Beaufort	30,396	37,821	21,505	33,331
Berkeley	27,755	36,205	20,142	32,104
Calhoun	3,970	3,695	3,393	3,448
Charleston	82,698	69,822	63,758	70,297
Cherokee	7,215	13,305	6,466	12,090
Chester	7,071	5,922	5,790	5,798
Chesterfield	7,842	8,325	6,729	7,252
Clarendon	8,673	6,758	7,087	6,061
Colleton	8,616	8,525	6,699	7,264
Darlington	14,505	14,544	11,829	13,416
Dillon	7,408	5,874	4,832	4,301
Dorchester	21,806	29,929	14,733	26,006
Edgefield	5,075	6,334	4,051	5,611
Fairfield	7,591	3,912	5,764	3,531
Florence	28,012	29,861	21,442	27,689
Georgetown	14,199	15,790	10,602	12,606
Greenville	70,886	116,363	55,347	111,481
Greenwood	12,348	16,995	8,954	14,264
Hampton	5,816	3,439	4,832	3,097
Horry	38,879	64,609	29,547	50,447
Jasper	5,389	3,365	3,840	2,933
Kershaw	11,226	16,466	8,515	14,160
Lancaster	12,139	16,441	7,631	12,916
Laurens	10,578	15,334	9,205	14,466
Lee	5,960	3,074	4,960	2,901
Lexington	33,303	74,960	25,393	67,132
Marion	2,755	2,437	7,767	5,589
Marlboro	9,608	5,416	4,984	3,423

County	2008 Obama (D)	McCain (R)	2004 Kerry (D)	Bush (R)
McCormick	6,794	3,996	2,648	2,396
Newberry	6,708	9,616	4,483	7,654
Oconee	9,481	21,164	8,395	18,811
Orangeburg	27,263	12,115	24,698	12,695
Pickens	11,691	32,552	10,287	29,759
Richland	105,656	57,941	76,283	56,212
Saluda	3,323	5,191	3,001	4,537
Spartanburg	41,632	65,042	33,633	62,004
Sumter	25,431	18,581	18,695	18,074
Union	5,935	7,449	5,236	6,592
Williamsburg	11,279	5,004	9,044	4,795
York	37,918	54,500	24,226	45,234
Totals	**862,449**	**1,034,896**	**661,699**	**937,974**

South Carolina Vote Since 1952

2008: McCain, Rep., 1,034,896; Obama, Dem., 862,449; Barr, Lib., 7,283; Baldwin, Const., 6,827; Nader, Petitioning Candidate, 5,053; McKinney, Green, 4,461.

2004: Bush, R., 937,974; Kerry, D., 661,699; Nader, Ind., 5,520; Peroutka, Constitution, 5,317; Badnarik, LB., 3,608; Brown, United Citizen, 2,124; Cobb, Green, 1,488.

2000: Bush, R., 786,892; Gore, D., 566,039; Nader, United Citizens, 20,279; Browne, LB., 4,898; Buchanan, Reform, 3,309; Phillips, Constitution, 1,682; Hagelin, Natural Law, 943.

1996: Dole, R., 573,458; Clinton, D., 506,283; Perot, Ref./Patriot, 64,386; Browne, LB., 4,271; Phillips, U.S. Taxpayers, 2,043; Hagelin, Natural Law, 1,248.

1992: Bush, R., 577,507; Clinton, D., 479,514; Perot, Ind., 138,872; Marrou, LB., 2,719; Phillips, U.S. Taxpayers, 2,680; Fulani, New Alliance, 1,235.

1988: Bush, R., 606,443; Dukakis, D., 370,554; Paul, Lib., 4,935; Fulani, United Citizens, 4,077.

1984: Reagan, R., 615,539; Mondale, D., 344,459; Bergland, LB., 4,359.

1980: Reagan, R., 439,277; Carter, D., 428,220; Anderson, Ind., 13,868; Clark, LB., 4,807; Rarick, Amer. Ind., 2,086.

1976: Carter, D., 450,807; Ford, R., 346,149; Anderson, Amer., 2,996; Maddox, Amer. Ind., 1,950; write-in, 681.

1972: Nixon, R., 477,044; McGovern, D., 184,559; Schmitz, Amer., 10,075; United Citizens, 2,265; write-in, 17.

1968: Nixon, R., 254,062; Wallace, 3rd Party, 215,430; Humphrey, D., 197,486.

1964: Goldwater, R., 309,048; Johnson, D., 215,700; write-in: Wallace, 5; Nixon, 1; Powell, 1; Thurmond, 1.

1960: Kennedy, D., 198,129; Nixon, R., 188,558; write-in, 1.

1956: Stevenson, D., 136,372; Byrd, Ind., 88,509; Eisenhower, R., 75,700; Andrews, Ind., 2.

1952: Stevenson, D., 173,004. Under state law votes cast for 2 Eisenhower slates of electors could not be combined. Eisenhower, Ind., 158,289; R., 9,793; total, 168,082. Hamblen, Proh., 1.

South Dakota

County	2008 Obama (D)	McCain (R)	2004 Kerry (D)	Bush (R)
Aurora	655	794	620	1,009
Beadle	3,493	4,054	3,443	4,917
Bennett	557	614	759	833
Bon Homme	1,367	1,712	1,293	2,063
Brookings	7,207	6,431	5,443	7,662
Brown	9,041	8,067	7,943	10,386
Brule	965	1,407	1,040	1,544
Buffalo	454	156	603	223
Butte	1,306	2,821	1,009	3,166
Campbell	243	591	239	708
Charles Mix	1,807	2,109	2,155	2,556
Clark	830	1,065	875	1,435
Clay	3,808	2,296	3,315	2,692
Codington	5,595	6,374	4,803	7,778
Corson	837	535	972	720
Custer	1,475	2,909	1,272	2,922
Davison	3,554	4,731	3,263	5,561
Day	1,785	1,372	1,817	1,671
Deuel	1,054	1,088	961	1,406
Dewey	1,326	921	1,606	921
Douglas	424	1,293	393	1,596
Edmunds	819	1,213	765	1,434
Fall River	1,338	2,348	1,326	2,413
Faulk	426	739	418	945
Grant	1,786	1,951	1,633	2,392
Gregory	771	1,423	813	1,685
Haakon	186	938	219	1,007
Hamlin	1,043	1,661	1,015	1,946
Hand	718	1,247	668	1,482
Hanson	961	1,426	745	1,379
Harding	135	575	94	704
Hughes	3,037	5,298	2,697	6,017
Hutchinson	1,242	2,285	1,177	2,899
Hyde	226	547	259	631
Jackson/ Washabaugh	435	668	508	726
Jerauld	535	535	482	736
Jones	147	463	134	565
Kingsbury	1,277	1,435	1,163	1,804

County	2008 Obama (D)	McCain (R)	2004 Kerry (D)	Bush (R)
Lake	3,033	2,993	2,509	3,359
Lawrence	4,932	6,787	3,857	7,489
Lincoln	8,642	11,803	5,703	11,161
Lyman	710	894	872	1,029
Marshall	1,219	1,646	1,099	1,242
McCook	441	915	1,201	2,017
McPherson	1,261	900	369	1,180
Meade	3,749	7,515	2,941	8,347
Mellette	373	445	361	553
Miner	605	577	641	810
Minnehaha	39,831	39,241	32,314	44,189
Moody	1,663	1,508	1,609	1,790
Pennington	17,787	27,592	14,213	29,976
Perkins	499	1,102	418	1,329
Potter	482	937	463	1,143
Roberts	2,672	1,781	2,527	2,396
Sanborn	500	669	581	817
Shannon	2,967	330	3,566	526
Spink	1,550	1,660	1,478	2,259
Stanley	510	1,017	464	1,129
Sully	233	581	201	702
Todd	2,208	571	2,543	889
Tripp	914	1,859	972	2,230
Turner	1,681	2,538	1,646	3,084
Union	3,244	4,310	3,000	3,987
Walworth	923	1,668	878	1,967
Yankton	4,838	5,039	4,237	6,003
Ziebach	554	312	641	447
Totals	**170,924**	**203,054**	**149,244**	**232,584**

South Dakota Vote Since 1952

2008: McCain, Rep., 203,054; Obama, Dem., 170,924; Nader, Ind., 4,267; Baldwin, Const., 1,895; Barr, Lib., 1,835.

2004: Bush, R., 232,584; Kerry, D., 149,244; Nader, Ind., 4,320; Peroutka, Constitution, 1,103; Badnarik, LB., 964.

2000: Bush, R., 190,700; Gore, D., 118,804; Buchanan, Reform, 3,322; Phillips, Ind., 1,781; Browne, LB., 1,662.

1996: Dole, R., 150,543; Clinton, D., 139,333; Perot, Ref., 31,250; Browne, LB., 1,472; Phillips, Taxpayers, 912; Hagelin, Natural Law, 316.

1992: Bush, R., 136,718; Clinton, D., 124,888; Perot, Ind., 73,295.

1988: Bush, R., 165,415; Dukakis, D., 145,560; Paul, Lib., 1,060; Fulani, New Alliance, 730.

1984: Reagan, R., 200,267; Mondale, D., 116,113.

1980: Reagan, R., 198,343; Carter, D., 103,855; Anderson, Ind., 21,431; Clark, LB., 3,824; Pulley, Soc. Workers, 250.

1976: Ford, R., 151,505; Carter, D., 147,068; MacBride, LB., 1,619; Hall, Com., 318; Camejo, Soc. Workers, 168.

1972: Nixon, R., 166,476; McGovern, D., 139,945; Jenness, Soc. Workers, 994.

1968: Nixon, R., 149,841; Humphrey, D., 118,023; Wallace, 3rd Party, 13,400.

1964: Johnson, D., 163,010; Goldwater, R., 130,108.

1960: Nixon, R., 178,417; Kennedy, D., 128,070.

1956: Eisenhower, R., 171,569; Stevenson, D., 122,288.

1952: Eisenhower, R., 203,857; Stevenson, D., 90,426.

Tennessee

County	2008 Obama (D)	McCain (R)	2004 Kerry (D)	Bush (R)
Anderson	11,385	19,614	12,896	18,510
Bedford	5,026	10,215	5,268	8,351
Benton	2,644	3,695	3,869	3,161
Bledsoe	1,517	3,166	1,927	2,849
Blount	15,252	35,553	15,047	33,241
Bradley	9,353	28,324	9,431	25,951
Campbell	3,866	6,535	6,163	7,859
Cannon	2,010	3,320	2,515	2,931
Carroll	3,980	7,454	5,070	6,605
Carter	5,587	15,849	6,395	15,768
Cheatham	5,497	10,697	5,918	9,676
Chester	1,794	4,586	2,242	4,086
Claiborne	3,078	7,174	4,034	6,448
Clay	1,248	1,674	1,675	1,650
Cocke	3,340	8,945	3,935	8,297
Coffee	7,131	13,244	8,243	11,793
Crockett	1,818	3,749	2,459	3,242
Cumberland	7,889	17,436	8,327	15,144
Davidson	158,032	102,702	132,737	107,839
Decatur	1,595	3,178	2,268	2,566
DeKalb	2,832	4,085	3,445	3,685
Dickson	7,504	11,672	8,597	10,567
Dyer	4,411	9,859	5,287	8,447
Fayette	6,888	12,158	5,696	8,962
Fentress	1,831	4,789	2,371	4,293
Franklin	6,609	10,533	7,800	9,129
Gibson	7,406	13,516	8,511	10,596
Giles	4,614	6,902	5,273	6,163
Grainger	2,065	5,297	2,569	4,907
Greene	7,107	17,148	7,635	16,382
Grundy	1,969	2,561	2,789	2,107
Hamblen	6,804	15,501	7,433	14,742
Hamilton	64,205	81,666	57,302	78,547

County	2008 Obama (D)	McCain (R)	2004 Kerry (D)	Bush (R)
Hancock	604	1,587	777	1,756
Hardeman	5,919	5,225	5,685	4,704
Hardin	2,794	7,076	3,834	6,087
Hawkins	5,924	14,745	6,684	13,447
Haywood	4,891	3,165	4,359	3,140
Henderson	3,021	7,669	3,448	6,585
Henry	5,152	8,182	5,732	7,340
Hickman	3,563	4,784	4,263	4,359
Houston	1,678	1,608	2,126	1,440
Humphreys	3,600	3,818	4,485	3,261
Jackson	2,284	2,185	2,998	2,026
Jefferson	5,177	13,092	5,469	11,625
Johnson	1,837	4,620	1,812	4,634
Knox	67,923	109,847	66,013	110,803
Lake	1,024	1,175	2,634	2,078
Lauderdale	4,322	4,933	4,474	4,164
Lawrence	5,160	10,565	6,592	9,959
Lewis	1,803	2,951	2,192	2,819
Lincoln	3,694	9,226	4,546	7,829
Loudon	6,058	15,815	5,708	14,041
Macon	5,539	12,984	2,738	4,670
Madison	3,131	7,134	16,840	21,679
Marion	2,060	5,145	5,548	5,862
Marshall	20,027	23,289	4,722	5,825
Maury	4,506	6,746	12,379	17,505
McMinn	4,319	6,755	5,891	11,980
McNairy	13,057	20,282	4,101	5,787
Meigs	1,371	2,795	1,595	2,500
Monroe	5,049	11,478	5,354	10,123
Montgomery	25,634	30,103	20,070	28,627
Moore	881	2,010	1,084	1,668
Morgan	1,969	4,717	2,924	4,401
Obion	4,308	8,873	5,549	7,859
Overton	3,418	4,495	4,518	3,941
Perry	1,329	1,596	1,579	1,522
Pickett	854	1,786	1,033	1,600
Polk	2,124	4,267	2,724	3,924
Putnam	9,735	17,098	10,566	15,637
Rhea	2,905	8,033	3,665	7,301
Roane	7,222	15,643	8,706	14,467
Robertson	9,318	17,903	9,865	15,331
Rutherford	40,412	59,850	31,647	52,200
Scott	1,720	4,931	3,086	4,509
Sequatchie	1,717	3,606	1,986	2,951
Sevier	8,597	24,915	8,621	22,143
Shelby	253,633	143,422	216,945	158,137
Smith	2,990	4,561	4,044	3,739
Stewart	2,470	2,956	2,860	2,675
Sullivan	18,346	44,802	19,637	42,555
Sumner	21,486	44,947	21,458	40,181
Tipton	7,911	17,114	7,379	14,178
Trousdale	1,474	1,687	1,851	1,314
Unicoi	2,106	5,011	2,374	5,030
Union	1,828	4,461	2,524	4,145
Van Buren	849	1,293	1,209	1,120
Warren	17,650	25,957	6,808	7,503
Washington	15,894	32,216	14,944	29,735
Wayne	1,355	4,075	1,951	3,999
Weakley	4,594	8,853	5,588	7,817
White	3,369	6,100	4,147	5,269
Williamson	27,879	64,843	21,732	57,451
Wilson	15,462	33,767	15,277	28,924
Totals	**1,087,437**	**1,479,178**	**1,036,477**	**1,384,375**

Tennessee Vote Since 1952

2008: McCain, Rep., 1,479,178; Obama, Dem., 1,087,437; Nader, Ind., 11,560; Barr, Ind., 8,547; Baldwin, Ind., 8,191; McKinney, Ind., 2,499; Moore, Ind., 1,326; Jay, Ind., 1,011.

2004: Bush, R., 1,384,375; Kerry, D., 1,036,477; Nader, Ind., 8,992; Badnarik, Ind., 4,866; Peroutka, Ind., 2,570.

2000: Bush, R., 1,061,949; Gore, D., 981,720; Nader, Green, 19,781; Browne, LB., 4,284; Buchanan, Reform, 4,250; Brown, Ind., 1,606; Phillips, Ind., 1,015; Hagelin, Reform, 613; Venson, Ind., 535.

1996: Clinton, D., 909,146; Dole, R., 863,530; Perot, Ind. (Ref.), 105,918; Nader, Ind., 6,427; Browne, Ind., 5,020; Phillips, Ind., 1,818; Collins, Ind., 688; Hagelin, Ind., 636; Michael, Ind., 408; Dodge, Ind., 324.

1992: Clinton, D., 933,521; Bush, R., 841,300; Perot, Ind., 199,968; Marrou, LB., 1,847.

1988: Bush, R., 947,233; Dukakis, D., 679,794; Paul, Ind., 2,041; Duke, Ind., 1,807.

1984: Reagan, R., 990,212; Mondale, D., 711,714; Bergland, LB., 3,072.

1980: Reagan, R., 787,761; Carter, D., 783,051; Anderson, Ind., 35,991; Clark, LB., 7,116; Commoner, Citizens, 1,112; Bubar, Statesman, 521; McReynolds, Soc., 519; Hall, Com., 503; DeBerry, Soc. Workers, 490; Griswold, Workers World, 400; write-in, 152.

1976: Carter, D., 825,879; Ford, R., 633,969; Anderson, Amer., 5,769; McCarthy, Ind., 5,004; Maddox, Amer. Ind., 2,303; MacBride, LB., 1,375; Hall, Com., 547; LaRouche, U.S. Labor, 512; Bubar, Proh., 442; Miller, Ind., 316; write-in, 230.

1972: Nixon, R., 813,147; McGovern, D., 357,293; Schmitz, Amer., 30,373; write-in, 369.

1968: Nixon, R., 472,592; Wallace, 3rd Party, 424,792; Humphrey, D., 351,233.

1964: Johnson, D., 635,047; Goldwater, R., 508,965; write-in, 34.

1960: Nixon, R., 556,577; Kennedy, D., 481,453; Faubus, States' Rights, 11,304; Decker, Proh., 2,458.

1956: Eisenhower, R., 462,288; Stevenson, D., 456,507; Andrews, Ind., 19,820; Holtwick, Proh., 789.

1952: Eisenhower, R., 446,147; Stevenson, D., 443,710; Hamblen, Proh., 1,432; Hallinan, Prog., 885; MacArthur, Christian Nationalist, 379.

Texas

County	2008 Obama (D)	McCain (R)	2004 Kerry (D)	Bush (R)
Anderson	4,624	11,855	4,678	11,525
Andrews	790	3,815	677	3,837
Angelina	9,377	19,569	9,302	18,932
Aransas	3,005	6,691	2,640	6,569
Archer	739	3,591	878	3,556
Armstrong	128	856	170	830
Atascosa	4,400	5,546	4,421	7,635
Austin	2,819	8,777	2,582	8,072
Bailey	680	1,618	525	1,882
Bandera	2,248	6,934	1,738	6,933
Bastrop	11,678	13,797	9,794	13,290
Baylor	366	1,262	467	1,169
Bee	3,645	4,467	4,045	5,428
Bell	40,185	49,066	27,165	52,135
Bexar	275,023	245,932	210,976	260,698
Blanco	1,466	3,417	1,267	3,277
Borden	40	316	55	303
Bosque	1,796	5,760	1,815	5,737
Bowie	10,801	24,136	11,880	21,791
Brazoria	36,461	67,444	28,904	63,662
Brazos	20,459	37,403	16,128	37,594
Brewster	1,819	1,781	1,729	1,980
Briscoe	205	616	191	620
Brooks	1,747	556	1,823	845
Brown	2,819	12,049	2,523	11,640
Burleson	2,053	4,546	2,276	4,405
Burnet	4,596	12,034	4,147	11,456
Caldwell	5,385	6,084	5,052	6,436
Calhoun	2,727	4,106	2,561	4,348
Callahan	1,063	4,589	1,073	4,542
Cameron	48,401	26,641	33,998	34,801
Camp	1,733	2,794	1,778	2,638
Carson	406	2,547	485	2,450
Cass	3,489	8,276	4,630	7,383
Castro	719	1,561	631	1,794
Chambers	3,185	9,966	2,953	8,618
Cherokee	4,605	11,693	4,439	11,329
Childress	497	1,782	511	1,629
Clay	1,085	4,213	1,299	3,971
Cochran	284	758	249	856
Coke	297	1,252	266	1,338
Coleman	643	3,011	778	3,035
Collin	108,200	184,116	68,935	174,435
Collingsworth	292	1,052	346	1,051
Colorado	2,503	5,790	2,161	5,488
Comal	12,365	35,203	9,153	31,574
Comanche	1,339	3,807	1,431	3,813
Concho	257	807	270	911
Cooke	3,051	11,871	3,142	11,908
Coryell	6,611	11,537	5,122	12,421
Cottle	187	509	214	549
Crane	319	1,119	254	1,314
Crockett	512	1,026	473	1,248
Crosby	684	1,221	622	1,647
Culberson	510	267	375	407
Dallam	302	1,267	305	1,473
Dallas	424,468	309,477	336,641	346,246
Dawson	1,135	2,894	1,114	3,419
De Witt	1,246	3,456	1,610	5,100
Deaf Smith	589	1,580	1,133	4,139
Delta	90,830	149,592	627	1,447
Denton	1,715	4,888	59,346	140,891
Dickens	234	730	245	815
Dimmit	2,692	874	2,365	1,188
Donley	291	1,370	349	1,429
Duval	3,298	1,076	2,916	1,160
Eastland	1,271	5,163	1,582	5,249
Ector	9,118	26,190	8,579	27,502
Edwards	346	673	217	745
El Paso	15,315	38,046	95,142	73,261
Ellis	121,589	61,598	11,640	34,602
Erath	3,126	10,757	2,710	9,506
Falls	1,958	2,975	2,427	3,454
Fannin	3,464	8,090	4,001	7,893
Fayette	3,009	7,572	2,803	7,527
Fisher	687	1,083	758	1,161

County	2008 Obama (D)	McCain (R)	2004 Kerry (D)	Bush (R)
Floyd	729	1,784	545	2,032
Foard	208	327	235	347
Fort Bend	98,136	102,846	68,722	93,625
Franklin	1,094	3,394	1,011	3,185
Freestone	2,032	5,201	2,070	5,057
Frio	2,405	1,644	1,931	1,991
Gaines	650	3,385	608	3,540
Galveston	41,543	61,844	43,919	61,290
Garza	375	1,355	326	1,480
Gillespie	2,570	9,559	2,104	9,297
Glasscock	52	502	44	488
Goliad	1,329	2,298	1,219	2,267
Gonzales	2,158	4,062	1,709	4,291
Gray	1,153	6,920	1,289	7,260
Grayson	13,892	31,122	13,452	30,777
Gregg	13,130	29,159	12,306	29,939
Grimes	2,704	5,561	2,713	5,263
Guadalupe	16,070	30,750	10,290	28,208
Hale	2,693	7,139	2,078	8,025
Hall	324	930	413	860
Hamilton	862	2,875	845	2,856
Hansford	239	1,847	240	1,903
Hardeman	373	1,199	480	1,214
Hardin	3,935	16,589	5,608	15,030
Harris	588,611	570,143	475,865	584,723
Harrison	8,874	17,085	9,642	16,473
Hartley	250	1,711	315	1,736
Haskell	699	1,388	867	1,539
Hays	28,416	29,624	20,110	27,021
Hemphill	216	1,342	257	1,380
Henderson	7,890	20,810	8,505	20,210
Hidalgo	90,122	39,614	62,369	50,931
Hill	3,802	9,220	3,751	9,225
Hockley	1,794	5,789	1,385	6,160
Hood	5,078	17,269	4,865	16,280
Hopkins	3,528	9,297	3,443	8,582
Houston	2,653	5,869	2,921	5,848
Howard	2,539	7,020	2,663	7,480
Hudspeth	430	458	302	577
Hunt	8,591	20,571	7,971	20,065
Hutchinson	1,321	7,358	1,503	7,839
Irion	164	644	141	684
Jack	470	2,527	643	2,470
Jackson	1,251	3,560	1,296	3,766
Jasper	3,636	8,960	4,471	8,347
Jeff Davis	467	746	378	764
Jefferson	44,854	42,877	47,066	44,423
Jim Hogg	1,336	472	1,344	712
Jim Wells	6,683	4,825	6,824	5,817
Johnson	12,903	36,683	12,325	34,818
Jones	1,525	4,197	1,658	4,254
Karnes	1,710	2,658	1,543	3,114
Kaufman	11,157	23,727	8,947	21,304
Kendall	3,591	12,960	2,532	11,434
Kenedy	108	93	85	82
Kent	99	342	138	382
Kerr	5,564	16,729	4,557	16,538
Kimble	341	1,487	324	1,482
King	8	151	18	137
Kinney	633	907	542	1,051
Kleberg	5,251	4,539	4,550	5,366
Knox	366	986	464	1,081
La Salle	5,240	12,940	1,229	989
La Vaca	1,156	3,344	2,152	5,974
Lamar	1,895	5,628	5,338	12,054
Lamb	1,051	713	857	3,410
Lampasas	1,867	6,286	1,593	5,422
Lee	2,000	4,312	1,899	4,160
Leon	1,415	5,563	1,754	5,023
Liberty	5,980	15,417	6,780	14,821
Limestone	2,515	5,062	2,752	5,028
Lipscomb	155	1,092	184	1,147
Live Oak	1,038	3,079	1,036	3,147
Llano	2,250	7,279	2,257	7,241
Loving	12	67	12	65
Lubbock	30,295	66,022	22,472	70,135
Lynn	623	1,469	490	1,776
Madison	1,144	2,883	1,235	2,837
Marion	1,644	2,566	1,884	2,441
Martin	314	1,389	288	1,514
Mason	546	1,543	459	1,600
Matagorda	6,682	11,929	4,355	8,119
Maverick	8,554	2,316	5,948	4,025
McCulloch	728	2,263	745	2,465
McLennan	29,959	49,005	26,760	52,090
McMullen	131	400	95	467
Medina	5,119	10,404	4,322	10,389
Menard	295	712	331	761
Midland	9,672	36,135	8,005	36,585
Milam	3,040	5,215	3,445	5,291
Mills	398	1,753	416	1,794
Mitchell	586	1,814	639	1,912
Montague	1,594	6,235	1,946	5,910
Montgomery	36,530	119,542	28,628	104,654
Moore	1,123	4,282	1,009	4,601
Morris	2,054	3,157	2,437	2,818
Motley	67	522	113	564
Nacogdoches	8,393	14,828	7,152	14,160
Navarro	5,399	10,803	5,259	10,715
Newton	1,750	3,440	2,513	3,159
Nolan	1,521	3,485	1,541	3,722
Nueces	47,811	52,264	44,439	59,359
Ochiltree	243	2,851	251	2,922
Oldham	102	813	108	733
Orange	7,646	21,509	11,476	20,292
Palo Pinto	2,499	7,264	2,816	7,137
Panola	2,586	7,582	2,958	7,021
Parker	10,429	36,646	8,966	31,795
Parmer	719	2,969	389	2,375
Pecos	1,476	2,480	1,242	3,167
Polk	6,215	13,703	6,964	13,778
Potter	8,932	20,741	7,489	21,401
Presidio	1,250	489	1,159	715
Rains	1,041	3,130	1,213	2,998
Randall	9,461	41,895	7,849	40,520
Reagan	197	795	184	956
Real	375	1,237	325	1,314
Red River	1,538	3,461	2,097	3,379
Reeves	1,605	1,444	1,600	1,777
Refugio	1,382	1,853	1,232	2,212
Roberts	41	477	46	461
Robertson	2,674	3,979	2,979	3,792
Rockwall	8,468	23,243	5,320	20,120
Runnels	720	3,118	792	3,239
Rusk	4,983	13,641	4,899	13,390
Sabine	1,077	3,749	1,476	3,138
San Augustine	1,327	2,338	1,506	2,235
San Jacinto	2,721	6,151	2,688	5,394
San Patricio	8,842	12,390	7,764	13,474
San Saba	487	1,941	529	1,894
Schleicher	322	969	312	1,012
Scurry	1,088	4,414	981	4,576
Shackelford	208	1,284	229	1,292
Shelby	2,546	6,629	2,951	6,295
Sherman	78	493	124	942
Smith	23,628	54,995	19,970	53,392
Somervell	798	2,675	831	2,701
Starr	8,233	1,488	7,199	2,552
Stephens	626	2,869	703	2,803
Sterling	97	520	71	544
Stonewall	206	524	250	499
Sutton	381	1,189	280	1,173
Swisher	812	1,676	626	1,487
Tarrant	274,101	347,843	207,286	349,462
Taylor	12,658	34,265	10,648	37,197
Terrell	186	323	159	306
Terry	1,379	2,863	794	3,166
Throckmorton	166	671	202	656
Titus	3,140	6,023	3,173	5,709
Tom Green	11,068	27,201	9,007	28,185
Travis	253,278	136,671	197,235	147,885
Trinity	1,924	4,091	2,204	3,985
Tyler	2,159	5,633	2,659	5,043
Upshur	2,106	5,871	4,225	10,232
Upton	288	898	185	1,009
Uvalde	4,120	4,585	3,298	5,148
Val Verde	6,982	5,752	4,757	6,968
Van Zandt	4,503	15,727	4,822	14,976
Victoria	9,829	19,876	8,553	20,875
Walker	7,323	11,610	5,977	11,710
Waller	7,107	8,238	6,145	7,679
Ward	899	2,667	901	2,856
Washington	4,031	10,173	3,389	9,597
Webb	33,435	13,111	23,654	17,753
Wharton	4,935	9,427	4,702	9,288
Wheeler	314	1,916	420	1,960
Wichita	13,828	31,673	12,819	32,472
Wilbarger	1,196	3,279	1,284	3,685
Willacy	3,405	1,454	2,734	2,209
Williamson	67,347	87,938	43,117	83,284
Wilson	5,360	10,903	4,409	10,400
Winkler	477	1,529	391	1,604
Wise	4,469	15,967	4,783	15,177
Wood	3,996	13,638	4,034	12,831
Yoakum	450	1,989	376	2,228
Young	1,302	5,938	1,511	5,874
Zapata	1,939	918	1,662	1,228
Zavala	3,263	596	2,332	777
Totals	**3,528,633**	**4,479,328**	**2,832,704**	**4,526,917**

Texas Vote Since 1952

2008: McCain, Rep., 4,479,328; Obama, Dem., 3,528,633 Barr, Lib., 56,116.

2004: Bush, R., 4,526,917; Kerry, D., 2,832,704; Badnarik, LB., 38,787.

2000: Bush, R., 3,799,639; Gore, D., 2,433,746; Nader, Green, 137,994; Browne, LB., 23,160; Buchanan, Ind., 12,394.

1996: Dole, R., 2,736,167; Clinton, D., 2,459,683; Perot, Ind. (Ref.), 378,537; Browne, LB., 20,256; Phillips, U.S. Taxpayers, 7,472; Hagelin, Natural Law, 4,422.

1992: Bush, R., 2,496,071; Clinton, D., 2,281,815; Perot, Ind., 1,354,781; Marrou, LB., 19,699.

1988: Bush, R., 3,036,829; Dukakis, D., 2,352,748; Paul, Lib., 30,355; Fulani, New Alliance, 7,208.

1984: Reagan, R., 3,433,428; Mondale, D., 1,949,276.

1980: Reagan, R., 2,510,705; Carter, D., 1,881,147; Anderson, Ind., 111,613; Clark, LB., 37,643; write-in, 528.

1976: Carter, D., 2,082,319; Ford, R., 1,953,300; McCarthy, Ind., 20,118; Anderson, Amer., 11,442; Camejo, Soc. Workers, 1,723; write-in, 2,982.

1972: Nixon, R., 2,298,896; McGovern, D., 1,154,289; Jenness, Soc. Workers, 8,664; Schmitz, Amer., 6,039; others, 3,393.

1968: Humphrey, D., 1,266,804; Nixon, R., 1,227,844; Wallace, 3rd Party, 584,269; write-in, 489.

1964: Johnson, D., 1,663,185; Goldwater, R., 958,566; Lightburn, Constitution, 5,060.

1960: Kennedy, D., 1,167,932; Nixon, R., 1,121,699; Sullivan, Constitution, 18,169; Decker, Proh., 3,870; write-in, 15.

1956: Eisenhower, R., 1,080,619; Stevenson, D., 859,958; Andrews, Ind., 14,591.

1952: Eisenhower, R., 1,102,878; Stevenson, D., 969,228; Hamblen, Proh., 1,983; MacArthur, Christian Nationalist, 833; MacArthur, Constitution, 730; Hallinan, Prog., 294.

Utah

County	2008		2004	
	Obama (D)	McCain (R)	Kerry (D)	Bush (R)
Beaver	509	1,786	493	2,023
Box Elder	3,080	14,340	2,244	15,751
Cache	9,806	27,799	6,375	32,486
Carbon	3,368	3,960	3,415	4,950
Daggett	129	294	108	380
Davis	28,831	73,317	20,893	86,187
Duchesne	897	4,592	738	4,742
Emery	965	3,338	831	3,781
Garfield	402	1,663	264	1,848
Grand	1,981	1,787	1,858	2,130
Iron	3,078	11,786	2,267	12,815
Juab	730	2,647	605	2,681
Kane	850	2,194	576	2,414
Millard	733	3,565	626	4,084
Morgan	674	3,219	472	3,301
Piute	141	635	123	646
Rich	154	829	109	922
Salt Lake	176,988	176,932	135,949	215,728
San Juan	2,322	2,586	1,906	2,971
Sanpete	1,449	6,036	1,189	7,004
Sevier	1,320	6,222	920	6,597
Summit	9,194	6,691	6,977	7,936
Tooele	5,349	10,201	4,130	12,181
Uintah	1,407	8,113	1,266	8,518
Utah	26,276	111,273	17,357	128,269
Wasatch	2,818	5,271	1,854	5,503
Washington	9,251	33,594	7,513	35,633
Wayne	333	930	279	1,062
Weber	24,028	43,250	19,862	51,199
Totals	**327,670**	**596,030**	**241,199**	**663,742**

Utah Vote Since 1952

2008: McCain, Rep., 596,030; Obama, Dem., 327,670; Baldwin, Const., 12,012; Nader, unaff., 8,416; Barr, Lib., 6,966; McKinney, unaff., 982; LaRiva, unaff., 262.

2004: Bush, R., 663,742; Kerry, D., 241,199; Nader, Ind., 11,305; Peroutka, Constitution, 6,841; Badnarik, LB., 3,375; Jay, Pers. Choice, 946; Harris, Soc. Wkrs., 393.

2000: Bush, R., 515,096; Gore, D., 203,053; Nader, Green, 35,850; Buchanan, Reform, 9,319; Browne, LB., 3,616; Phillips, Ind. Amer., 2,709; Hagelin, Natural Law, 763; Harris, Soc. Workers, 186; Youngkeit, Ind., 161.

1996: Dole, R., 361,911; Clinton, D., 221,633; Perot, Ref., 66,461; Nader, Green, 4,615; Browne, LB., 4,129; Phillips, Taxpayers, 2,601; Templin, Ind. Amer., 1,290; Crane, Ind., 1,101; Hagelin, Natural Law, 1,085; Moorehead, Workers World, 298; Harris, Soc. Workers, 235; Dodge, Proh., 111.

1992: Bush, R., 322,632; Perot, Ind., 203,400; Clinton, D., 183,429; Gritz, Populist/America First, 28,602; Marrou, LB., 1,900; Hagelin, Natural Law, 1,319; LaRouche, Ind., 1,089.

1988: Bush, R., 428,442; Dukakis, D., 207,352; Paul, Lib., 7,473; Dennis, Amer., 2,158.

1984: Reagan, R., 469,105; Mondale, D., 155,369; Bergland, LB., 2,447.

1980: Reagan, R., 439,687; Carter, D., 124,266; Anderson, Ind., 30,284; Clark, LB., 7,226; Commoner, Citizens, 1,009; Greaves, Amer., 965; Rarick, Amer. Ind., 522; Hall, Com., 139; DeBerry, Soc. Workers, 124.

1976: Ford, R., 337,908; Carter, D., 182,110; Anderson, Amer., 13,304; McCarthy, Ind., 3,907; MacBride, LB., 2,438; Maddox, Amer. Ind., 1,162; Camejo, Soc. Workers, 268; Hall, Com., 121.

1972: Nixon, R., 323,643; McGovern, D., 126,284; Schmitz, Amer., 28,549.

1968: Nixon, R., 238,728; Humphrey, D., 156,665; Wallace, 3rd Party, 26,906; Peace and Freedom, 180; Halstead, Soc. Workers, 89.

1964: Johnson, D., 219,628; Goldwater, R., 181,785.

1960: Nixon, R., 205,361; Kennedy, D., 169,248; Dobbs, Soc. Workers, 100.

1956: Eisenhower, R., 215,631; Stevenson, D., 118,364.

1952: Eisenhower, R., 194,190; Stevenson, D., 135,364.

Vermont

County	2008		2004	
	Obama (D)	McCain (R)	Kerry (D)	Bush (R)
Addison	13,202	5,667	11,147	7,077
Bennington	12,524	6,133	11,069	7,616
Caledonia	8,900	5,472	7,106	6,765
Chittenden	59,611	22,237	49,369	26,422
Essex	1,733	1,284	1,276	1,591
Franklin	13,179	7,853	10,598	8,936
Grand Isle	2,694	1,490	2,246	1,754
Lamoille	8,914	3,515	7,636	4,260
Orange	9,799	5,047	8,159	6,421
Orleans	7,998	4,482	6,330	5,666
Rutland	19,355	11,584	15,904	14,440
Washington	22,324	9,129	19,177	11,461
Windham	17,585	5,997	15,489	7,280
Windsor	21,444	9,084	18,561	11,491
Totals	**219,262**	**98,974**	**184,067**	**121,180**

Vermont Vote Since 1952

2008: Obama, Dem., 219,262; McCain, Rep., 98,974; Nader, Ind., 3,339; Barr, Lib., 1,067; Baldwin, Const., 500; Calero, Socialist Wkrs., 150; LaRiva, Socialism/Liberation, 149; Moore, Liberty Union, 141.

2004: Kerry, D., 184,067; Bush, R., 121,180; Nader, Ind., 4,494; Badnarik, LB., 1,102; Parker, Liberty Union, 265; Calero, Soc. Wkrs., 244.

2000: Gore, D., 149,022; Bush, R., 119,775; Nader, Green, 20,374; Buchanan, Reform, 2,192; Lane, Grass Roots, 1,044; Browne, LB., 784; Hagelin, Natural Law, 219; McReynolds, Liberty Union, 161; Phillips, Constitution, 153; Harris, Soc. Workers, 70.

1996: Clinton, D., 137,894; Dole, R., 80,352; Perot, Ref., 31,024; Nader, Green, 5,585; Browne, LB., 1,183; Hagelin, Natural Law, 498; Peron, Grass Roots, 480; Phillips, Taxpayers, 382; Hollis, Liberty Union, 292; Harris, Soc. Workers, 199.

1992: Clinton, D., 133,590; Bush, R., 88,122; Perot, Ind., 65,985.

1988: Bush, R., 124,331; Dukakis, D., 115,775; Paul, Lib., 1,000; LaRouche, Ind., 275.

1984: Reagan, R., 135,865; Mondale, D., 95,730; Bergland, LB., 1,002.

1980: Reagan, R., 94,598; Carter, D., 81,891; Anderson, Ind., 31,760; Commoner, Citizens, 2,316; Clark, LB., 1,900; McReynolds, Liberty Union, 136; Hall, Com., 118; DeBerry, Soc. Workers, 75; scattered, 413.

1976: Ford, R., 100,387; Carter, D., 77,798; Carter, Ind. Vermonter, 991; total, 79,789; McCarthy, Ind., 4,001; Camejo, Soc. Workers, 430; LaRouche, U.S. Labor, 196; scattered, 99.

1972: Nixon, R., 117,149; McGovern, D., 68,174; Spock, Liberty Union, 1,010; Jenness, Soc. Workers, 296; scattered, 318.

1968: Nixon, R., 85,142; Humphrey, D., 70,255; Wallace, 3rd Party, 5,104; Gregory, New Party, 579; Halstead, Soc. Workers, 295.

1964: Johnson, D., 107,674; Goldwater, R., 54,868.

1960: Nixon, R., 98,131; Kennedy, D., 69,186.

1956: Eisenhower, R., 110,390; Stevenson, D., 42,549; scattered, 39.

1952: Eisenhower, R., 109,717; Stevenson, D., 43,355; Hallinan, Prog., 282; Hoopes, Soc., 185.

Virginia

County	2008		2004	
	Obama (D)	McCain (R)	Kerry (D)	Bush (R)
Accomack	7,607	7,833	5,518	7,726
Albemarle	29,792	20,576	22,088	21,189
Alleghany	3,553	3,715	3,203	3,962
Amelia	2,488	3,970	1,862	3,499
Amherst	6,094	8,470	4,866	7,758
Appomattox	2,641	4,903	2,191	4,366
Arlington	78,994	29,876	63,987	29,635
Augusta	9,825	23,120	7,019	22,100

County	2008 Obama (D)	McCain (R)	2004 Kerry (D)	Bush (R)
Bath	1,043	1,349	828	1,432
Bedford	11,017	24,420	9,102	21,925
Bland	864	2,031	846	1,962
Botetourt	5,693	11,471	4,801	10,865
Brunswick	4,973	2,877	4,062	2,852
Buchanan	4,063	4,541	5,275	4,507
Buckingham	3,489	3,428	2,789	3,185
Campbell	8,091	17,444	6,862	15,891
Caroline	7,163	5,617	4,878	4,999
Carroll	4,108	8,186	3,888	8,173
Charles City	2,838	1,288	2,155	1,254
Charlotte	2,705	3,372	2,223	3,166
Chesterfield	74,310	86,413	49,346	83,745
Clarke	3,457	3,840	2,699	3,741
Craig	876	1,695	901	1,706
Culpeper	8,802	10,711	5,476	10,026
Cumberland	2,255	2,418	1,721	2,377
Dickenson	3,278	3,324	3,761	3,591
Dinwiddie	6,246	6,526	4,569	6,193
Essex	2,934	2,379	2,007	2,304
Fairfax	310,359	200,994	245,671	211,980
Fauquier	14,616	19,227	10,712	19,011
Floyd	2,937	4,441	2,488	4,162
Fluvanna	6,185	6,420	4,415	6,458
Franklin	9,618	15,414	8,002	14,048
Frederick	12,961	20,149	8,853	19,386
Giles	3,192	4,462	3,047	4,320
Gloucester	6,916	12,089	5,105	11,084
Goochland	4,813	7,643	3,583	6,668
Grayson	2,480	4,540	2,430	4,655
Greene	3,174	4,980	2,240	4,570
Greensville	3,122	1,729	2,514	1,732
Halifax	8,126	8,600	6,220	8,363
Hanover	18,447	37,344	13,941	35,404
Henrico	86,262	67,340	60,864	71,809
Henry	11,118	13,758	9,851	13,358
Highland	590	930	522	982
Isle of Wight	8,573	11,258	5,871	9,929
James City	17,352	20,912	11,934	18,949
King and Queen	1,918	1,763	1,506	1,737
King George	4,473	5,888	2,739	5,124
King William	3,344	4,966	2,436	4,397
Lancaster	3,235	3,647	2,477	3,724
Lee	3,219	5,825	4,005	5,664
Loudoun	74,607	63,328	47,271	60,382
Louisa	6,978	8,182	4,844	7,083
Lunenburg	2,703	2,900	2,362	2,858
Madison	2,862	3,758	2,176	3,556
Mathews	1,943	3,456	1,589	3,497
Mecklenburg	7,127	7,817	5,293	7,319
Middlesex	2,391	3,545	1,914	3,336
Montgomery	21,027	19,026	14,128	17,000
Nelson	4,391	3,647	3,543	3,539
New Kent	3,493	6,385	2,443	5,414
Northampton	3,800	2,713	2,775	2,669
Northumberland	3,312	4,041	2,548	3,832
Nottoway	3,413	3,499	2,635	3,303
Orange	7,107	8,506	5,015	7,749
Page	4,235	6,041	3,324	6,221
Patrick	2,879	5,491	2,572	5,507
Pittsylvania	11,401	18,724	9,274	17,673
Powhatan	4,237	10,088	3,112	8,955
Prince Edward	5,101	4,174	3,632	3,571
Prince George	7,130	8,752	5,066	8,131
Prince William	93,386	67,589	61,271	69,776
Pulaski	5,918	8,857	5,310	8,769
Rappahannock	2,105	2,227	1,837	2,172
Richmond	1,618	2,092	1,243	2,082
Roanoke	19,812	30,571	16,082	30,596
Rockbridge	4,347	5,732	3,627	5,412
Rockingham	10,453	22,468	7,273	21,737
Russell	4,931	6,389	5,167	6,077
Scott	2,725	6,980	3,324	6,479
Shenandoah	6,903	11,995	5,186	11,820
Smyth	4,239	7,817	4,143	7,906
Southampton	4,402	4,583	3,431	4,018
Spotsylvania	24,897	28,610	16,623	28,527
Stafford	25,716	29,221	17,208	28,500
Surry	2,626	1,663	1,954	1,543
Sussex	3,301	2,026	2,420	1,890
Tazewell	5,596	11,201	7,184	10,039

County	2008 Obama (D)	McCain (R)	2004 Kerry (D)	Bush (R)
Warren	6,997	8,879	5,241	8,600
Washington	8,063	16,077	7,339	14,749
Westmoreland	4,577	3,719	3,370	3,433
Wise	4,995	8,914	5,802	8,330
Wythe	4,107	8,207	3,581	7,911
York	13,700	19,833	10,276	19,396
Cities				
Alexandria	50,473	19,181	41,116	19,844
Bedford	1,208	1,497	1,042	1,472
Bristol	2,665	4,579	2,400	4,275
Buena Vista	1,108	1,282	936	1,417
Charlottesville	15,705	4,078	11,088	4,172
Chesapeake	53,993	52,624	38,744	52,283
Colonial Heights	2,562	6,161	2,061	6,129
Covington	1,304	1,020	1,179	1,104
Danville	12,352	8,361	9,436	9,399
Emporia	1,702	897	1,247	970
Fairfax	6,571	4,686	5,395	5,045
Falls Church	4,695	1,970	3,944	2,074
Franklin	2,817	1,575	1,910	1,613
Fredericksburg	6,155	3,413	4,085	3,390
Galax	1,052	1,317	987	1,336
Hampton	46,917	20,476	32,016	23,399
Harrisonburg	8,444	6,048	4,726	6,165
Hopewell	5,285	4,149	3,573	4,251
Lexington	1,540	914	1,340	982
Lynchburg	16,269	17,638	11,727	14,400
Manassas	7,518	5,975	5,562	7,257
Manassas Park	2,463	1,634	1,498	1,807
Martinsville	4,139	2,311	3,036	2,538
Newport News	51,972	28,667	35,319	32,208
Norfolk	62,819	24,814	43,518	26,401
Norton	743	744	725	768
Petersburg	13,774	1,583	9,682	2,238
Poquoson	1,748	5,229	1,424	5,004
Portsmouth	32,322	13,983	24,112	15,212
Radford	2,930	2,418	2,244	2,564
Richmond	73,180	18,472	52,167	21,637
Roanoke	24,934	15,394	18,862	16,661
Salem	5,164	7,088	4,254	7,115
Staunton	5,569	5,330	3,756	5,805
Suffolk	22,233	18,592	15,233	16,763
Virginia Beach	98,763	100,225	70,666	103,752
Waynesboro	3,906	4,815	2,792	5,092
Williamsburg	4,328	2,353	2,216	2,064
Winchester	5,268	4,725	3,967	5,283
Totals	1,959,532	1,725,005	1,454,742	1,716,959

Virginia Vote Since 1952

2008: Obama, Dem., 1,959,532; McCain, Rep., 1,725,005; Nader, Ind., 11,483; Barr, Lib., 11,067; Baldwin, Ind. Green, 7,474; McKinney, Green, 2,344.

2004: Bush, R., 1,716,959; Kerry, D., 1,454,742; Badnarik, LB., 11,032; Peroutka, Constitution, 10,161.

2000: Bush, R., 1,437,490; Gore, D., 1,217,290; Nader, Green, 59,398; Browne, LB., 15,198; Buchanan, Reform, 5,455; Phillips, Constitution, 1,809.

1996: Dole, R., 1,138,350; Clinton, D., 1,091,060; Perot, Ref., 159,861; Phillips, Taxpayers, 13,687; Browne, LB., 9,174; Hagelin, Natural Law, 4,510.

1992: Bush, R., 1,150,517; Clinton, D., 1,038,650; Perot, Ind., 348,639; LaRouche, Ind., 11,937; Marrou, LB., 5,730; Fulani, New Alliance, 3,192.

1988: Bush, R., 1,309,162; Dukakis, D., 859,799; Fulani, Ind., 14,312; Paul, LB., 8,336.

1984: Reagan, R., 1,337,078; Mondale, D., 796,250.

1980: Reagan, R., 989,609; Carter, D., 752,174; Anderson, Ind., 95,418; Commoner, Citizens, 14,024; Clark, LB., 12,821; DeBerry, Soc. Workers, 1,986.

1976: Ford, R., 836,554; Carter, D., 813,896; Camejo, Soc. Workers, 17,802; Anderson, Amer., 16,686; LaRouche, U.S. Labor, 7,508; MacBride, LB., 4,648.

1972: Nixon, R., 988,493; McGovern, D., 438,887; Schmitz, Amer., 19,721; Fisher, Soc. Labor, 9,918.

1968: Nixon, R., 590,319; Humphrey, D., 442,387; Wallace, 3rd Party, 320,272; Blomen, Soc. Labor, 4,671; Gregory, Peace and Freedom, 1,680; Munn, Proh., 601. *10,561 votes for Wallace were omitted in the count.

1964: Johnson, D., 558,038; Goldwater, R., 481,334; Hass, Soc. Labor, 2,895.

1960: Nixon, R., 404,521; Kennedy, D., 362,327; Coiner, Cons., 4,204; Hass, Soc. Labor, 397.

1956: Eisenhower, R., 386,459; Stevenson, D., 267,760; Andrews, States' Rights, 42,964; Hoopes, Soc. D., 444; Hass, Soc. Labor, 351.

1952: Eisenhower, R., 349,037; Stevenson, D., 268,677; Hass, Soc. Labor, 1,160; Hoopes, Soc. D., 504; Hallinan, Prog., 311.

Washington

County	2008 Obama (D)	McCain (R)	2004 Kerry (D)	Bush (R)
Adams	1,346	2,822	1,315	3,751
Asotin	4,114	5,407	3,319	5,320
Benton	23,366	40,244	21,549	44,350
Chelan	13,678	17,484	10,471	18,482
Clallam	17,512	15,978	17,049	18,871
Clark	93,541	82,631	79,538	88,646
Columbia	667	1,447	605	1,470
Cowlitz	18,944	13,969	21,589	20,217
Douglas	4,631	7,048	4,306	8,900
Ferry	1,386	1,817	1,201	2,019
Franklin	6,536	10,787	5,188	10,757
Garfield	384	966	365	935
Grant	9,364	16,756	7,779	17,799
Grays Harbor	15,759	11,614	14,583	12,871
Island	21,688	19,070	18,216	19,754
Jefferson	12,914	6,195	11,610	6,650
King	545,329	217,589	580,378	301,043
Kitsap	61,255	47,456	60,796	55,608
Kittitas	7,887	9,320	6,731	9,052
Klickitat	4,871	4,868	4,036	5,016
Lewis	11,719	17,293	10,726	21,042
Lincoln	2,024	3,794	1,706	4,015
Mason	14,934	12,512	12,894	11,987
Okanogan	6,163	6,942	6,309	9,636
Pacific	6,066	4,531	5,570	4,634
Pend Oreille	2,546	3,704	2,310	3,693
Pierce	143,491	111,851	158,231	150,783
San Juan	7,172	2,889	6,589	3,290
Skagit	28,145	23,031	25,131	26,139
Skamania	2,797	2,513	2,374	2,695
Snohomish	177,471	120,064	156,468	134,317
Spokane	102,164	105,059	87,490	111,606
Stevens	6,386	9,308	6,822	13,015
Thurston	69,999	44,565	62,650	47,992
Wahkiakum	1,112	1,100	1,021	1,171
Walla Walla	7,539	10,632	8,257	14,323
Whatcom	53,313	36,635	48,268	40,296
Whitman	7,957	7,304	8,287	9,397
Yakima	32,484	40,877	28,474	43,352
Totals	1,750,848	1,229,216	1,510,201	1,304,894

Washington Vote Since 1952

2008: Obama, Dem., 1,750,848; McCain, Rep., 1,229,216; Nader, Ind., 29,489; Barr, Lib., 12,728; Baldwin, Const., 9,432; McKinney, Green, 3,819; LaRiva, Socialism/Liberation, 705; Harris, Socialist Wkrs., 641.

2004: Kerry, D., 1,510,201; Bush, R., 1,304,894; Nader, Ind., 23,283; Badnarik, LB., 11,955; Peroutka, Constitution, 3,922; Cobb, Green, 2,974; Parker, Workers World, 1,077; Harris, Soc. Wkrs., 547; Van Auken, Soc. Equal., 231.

2000: Gore, D., 1,247,652; Bush, R., 1,108,864; Nader, Green, 103,002; Browne, LB., 13,135; Buchanan, Freedom, 7,171; Hagelin, Natural Law, 2,927; Phillips, Constitution, 1,989; Moorehead, Wkrs. World, 1,729; McReynolds, Soc., 660; Harris, Soc. Wkrs., 304.

1996: Clinton, D., 1,123,323; Dole, R., 840,712; Perot, Ref., 201,003; Nader, Ind., 60,322; Browne, LB., 12,522; Hagelin, Natural Law, 6,076; Phillips, Taxpayers, 4,578; Collins, Ind., 2,374; Moorehead, Workers World, 2,189; Harris, Soc. Workers, 738.

1992: Clinton, D., 993,037; Bush, R., 731,234; Perot, Ind., 541,780; Marrou, LB., 7,533; Gritz, Populist/America First, 4,854; Hagelin, Natural Law, 2,456; Phillips, U.S. Taxpayers, 2,354; Fulani, New Alliance, 1,776; Daniels, Ind., 1,171.

1988: Dukakis, D., 933,516; Bush, R., 903,835; Paul, Lib., 17,240; LaRouche, Ind., 4,412.

1984: Reagan, R., 1,051,670; Mondale, D., 798,352; Bergland, LB., 8,844.

1980: Reagan, R., 865,244; Carter, D., 650,193; Anderson, Ind., 185,073; Clark, LB., 29,213; Commoner, Citizens, 9,403; DeBerry, Soc. Workers, 1,137; McReynolds, Soc., 956; Hall, Com., 834; Griswold, Workers World, 341.

1976: Ford, R., 777,732; Carter, D., 717,323; McCarthy, Ind., 36,986; Maddox, Amer., 8,585; Anderson, Amer., 5,046; MacBride, LB., 5,042; Wright, People's, 1,124; Camejo, Soc. Workers, 905; LaRouche, U.S. Labor, 903; Hall, Com., 817; Levin, Soc. Labor, 713; Zeidler, Soc., 358.

1972: Nixon, R., 837,135; McGovern, D., 568,334; Schmitz, Amer., 58,906; Spock, Ind., 2,644; Hospers, LB., 1,537; Fisher, Soc. Labor, 1,102; Jenness, Soc. Workers, 623; Hall, Com., 566.

1968: Humphrey, D., 616,037; Nixon, R., 588,510; Wallace, 3rd Party, 96,990; Cleaver, Peace and Freedom, 1,609; Blomen, Soc. Labor, 488; Mitchell, Free Ballot, 377; Halstead, Soc. Workers, 270.

1964: Johnson, D., 779,699; Goldwater, R., 470,366; Hass, Soc. Labor, 7,772; DeBerry, Freedom Soc., 537.

1960: Nixon, R., 629,273; Kennedy, D., 599,298; Hass, Soc. Labor, 10,895; Curtis, Constitution, 1,401; Dobbs, Soc. Workers, 705.

1956: Eisenhower, R., 620,430; Stevenson, D., 523,002; Hass, Soc. Labor, 7,457.

1952: Eisenhower, R., 599,107; Stevenson, D., 492,845; MacArthur, Christian Nationalist, 7,290; Hallinan, Prog., 2,460; Hass, Soc. Labor, 633; Hoopes, Soc., 254; Dobbs, Soc. Workers, 119.

West Virginia

County	2008 Obama (D)	McCain (R)	2004 Kerry (D)	Bush (R)
Barbour	2,415	3,678	2,610	4,004
Berkeley	15,945	20,779	12,244	21,293
Boone	4,490	3,603	5,933	4,207
Braxton	2,691	2,618	3,035	2,986
Brooke	4,666	4,932	5,493	5,189
Cabell	15,110	18,571	16,583	21,035
Calhoun	976	1,345	1,266	1,588
Clay	1,417	1,748	1,835	2,198
Doddridge	732	2,205	800	2,362
Fayette	7,134	7,578	8,971	7,881
Gilmer	1,117	1,578	1,159	1,665
Grant	987	3,150	963	4,063
Greenbrier	5,561	7,347	6,084	8,358
Hampshire	2,968	5,197	2,455	5,489
Hancock	5,285	7,257	6,906	7,298
Hardy	1,880	3,360	1,617	3,635
Harrison	13,488	17,715	13,238	17,111
Jackson	4,821	7,066	5,384	7,686
Jefferson	11,606	10,526	9,301	10,539
Kanawha	40,148	40,588	43,010	44,430
Lewis	2,096	4,312	2,475	4,445
Lincoln	2,972	3,556	4,048	4,102
Logan	4,862	6,297	7,877	7,047
Marion	11,507	11,389	12,771	12,150
Marshall	5,943	7,709	6,435	8,516
Mason	4,444	5,822	5,408	6,487
McDowell	3,410	2,852	4,501	2,762
Mercer	7,388	13,167	9,178	13,057
Mineral	3,717	7,546	3,518	7,854
Mingo	3,567	4,565	5,983	4,612
Monongalia	16,853	15,612	16,313	17,670
Monroe	1,969	3,344	2,311	3,590
Morgan	2,704	4,408	2,272	4,511
Nicholas	6,007	6,115	4,788	5,485
Ohio	8,481	10,590	8,543	11,694
Pendleton	1,049	1,605	1,381	2,146
Pleasants	1,127	1,753	1,349	2,061
Pocahontas	1,538	1,993	1,573	2,295
Preston	4,190	7,299	3,963	7,855
Putnam	9,424	15,295	9,301	15,716
Raleigh	10,115	17,358	11,815	18,519
Randolph	4,527	6,051	4,892	6,512
Ritchie	989	2,753	1,070	3,086
Roane	2,506	2,936	2,612	3,440
Summers	2,276	2,875	2,504	2,978
Taylor	2,420	3,518	2,617	3,893
Tucker	1,280	2,118	1,400	2,179
Tyler	1,234	2,390	1,401	2,798
Upshur	2,896	5,870	3,034	6,191
Wayne	6,101	8,890	8,411	10,070
Webster	1,543	1,374	1,965	1,724
Wetzel	2,919	3,318	3,330	3,656
Wirt	777	1,482	896	1,727
Wood	12,446	22,670	14,025	24,948
Wyoming	2,724	4,605	3,694	4,985
Totals	303,857	397,466	326,541	423,778

West Virginia Vote Since 1952

2008: McCain, Rep., 397,466; Obama, Dem., 303,857; Nader, unaff., 7,219; Baldwin, Const., 2,465; McKinney, Mountain, 2,355.

2004: Bush, R., 423,778; Kerry, D., 326,541; Nader, Ind., 4,063; Badnarik, LB., 1,405.

2000: Bush, R., 336,475; Gore, D., 295,497; Nader, Green, 10,680; Buchanan, Reform, 3,169; Browne, LB., 1,912; Hagelin, Natural Law, 367.

1996: Clinton, D., 327,812; Dole, R., 233,946; Perot, Ref., 71,639; Browne, LB., 3,062.

1992: Clinton, D., 331,001; Bush, R., 241,974; Perot, Ind., 108,829; Marrou, LB., 1,873.

1988: Dukakis, D., 341,016; Bush, R., 310,065; Fulani, New Alliance, 2,230.

1984: Reagan, R., 405,483; Mondale, D., 328,125.

1980: Carter, D., 367,462; Reagan, R., 334,206; Anderson, Ind., 31,691; Clark, LB., 4,356.

1976: Carter, D., 435,864; Ford, R., 314,726.

1972: Nixon, R., 484,964; McGovern, D., 277,435.

1968: Humphrey, D., 374,091; Nixon, R., 307,555; Wallace, 3rd Party, 72,560.

1964: Johnson, D., 538,087; Goldwater, R., 253,953.

1960: Kennedy, D., 441,786; Nixon, R., 395,995.

1956: Eisenhower, R., 449,297; Stevenson, D., 381,534.

1952: Stevenson, D., 453,578; Eisenhower, R., 419,970.

Wisconsin

County	2008 Obama (D)	McCain (R)	2004 Kerry (D)	Bush (R)
Adams	5,808	3,976	5,447	4,890
Ashland	5,697	2,507	5,805	3,313
Barron	12,076	10,456	11,696	12,030
Bayfield	5,978	3,316	5,845	3,754
Brown	67,241	55,827	54,935	67,173
Buffalo	3,979	2,946	3,998	3,502
Burnett	4,337	4,200	4,499	4,743
Calumet	13,296	12,720	10,290	14,721
Chippewa	16,236	13,489	14,751	15,450
Clark	7,450	6,337	6,966	7,966
Columbia	16,658	12,189	14,300	14,956
Crawford	5,124	2,905	4,656	3,680
Dane	202,812	71,829	181,052	90,369
Dodge	19,178	23,013	16,690	27,201
Door	10,142	7,112	8,367	8,910
Douglas	15,827	7,833	16,537	8,448
Dunn	13,055	9,616	12,039	10,879
Eau Claire	33,143	20,944	30,068	24,653
Florence	1,134	1,512	993	1,703
Fond du Lac	23,457	28,155	19,216	33,291
Forest	2,671	1,960	2,509	2,608
Grant	14,911	9,109	12,864	12,208
Green	11,499	6,730	9,575	8,497
Green Lake	3,998	5,392	3,605	6,472
Iowa	8,076	3,915	7,122	5,348
Iron	1,915	1,470	1,956	1,884
Jackson	5,572	3,550	5,249	4,387
Jefferson	21,448	21,095	17,925	23,776
Juneau	6,209	5,187	5,734	6,473
Kenosha	45,615	31,237	40,107	35,587
Kewaunee	5,902	4,711	5,175	5,970
La Crosse	38,514	23,698	33,170	28,289
Lafayette	4,732	2,984	4,402	3,929
Langlade	5,182	5,081	4,751	6,235
Lincoln	8,419	6,510	7,484	8,024
Manitowoc	22,421	19,231	20,652	23,027
Marathon	36,363	30,339	30,899	36,394
Marinette	11,124	9,705	10,190	11,866
Marquette	4,051	3,625	3,785	4,604
Menominee	1,257	185	1,412	288
Milwaukee	316,916	147,573	297,653	180,287
Monroe	10,178	8,657	8,973	10,375
Oconto	9,926	8,754	8,534	11,043
Oneida	11,905	9,627	10,464	11,351
Outagamie	50,255	39,641	40,169	48,903
Ozaukee	20,570	32,160	17,714	34,904
Pepin	2,101	1,615	2,181	1,853
Pierce	11,695	9,715	11,176	10,437
Polk	10,876	11,282	11,173	12,095
Portage	24,815	13,807	21,861	16,546
Price	4,559	3,458	4,349	4,312
Racine	53,405	45,941	48,229	52,456
Richland	5,072	3,348	4,501	4,836
Rock	50,515	27,356	46,598	33,151
Rusk	3,855	3,253	3,820	3,985
Sauk	20,989	22,657	15,708	14,415
Sawyer	18,606	11,567	4,411	4,951
Shawano	4,763	4,199	8,657	12,150
Sheboygan	10,192	9,381	27,608	34,458
St. Croix	30,392	30,796	18,784	22,679
Taylor	4,560	4,586	3,829	5,582
Trempealeau	8,320	4,807	8,075	5,878
Vernon	8,478	5,377	7,924	6,774
Vilas	6,490	7,054	5,713	8,155
Walworth	24,176	25,482	19,177	28,754
Washburn	4,716	4,259	4,705	4,762
Washington	25,713	47,725	21,234	50,641
Waukesha	85,248	145,089	73,626	154,926
Waupaca	12,952	12,131	10,792	15,941
Waushara	5,868	5,769	5,257	6,888
Winnebago	48,156	37,943	40,943	46,542
Wood	21,705	16,576	18,950	20,592
Totals	**1,677,211**	**1,262,393**	**1,489,504**	**1,478,120**

Wisconsin Vote Since 1952

2008: Obama, Dem., 1,677,211; McCain, Rep., 1,262,393; Nader, Ind., 17,605; Barr, Lib., 8,858; Baldwin, Ind., 5,072; McKinney, Green, 4,216; Wamboldt, Ind., 764; Moore, Ind., 540; LaRiva, Ind., 237.
2004: Kerry, D., 1,489,504; Bush, R., 1,478,120; Nader, Ind., 16,390; Badnarik, LB., 6,464; Cobb, Green, 2,661; Brown, Ind., 471; Harris, Ind., 411.
2000: Gore, D., 1,242,987; Bush, R., 1,237,279; Nader, Green, 94,070; Buchanan, Reform, 11,446; Browne, LB., 6,640; Phillips, Constitution, 2,042; Moorehead, Workers World, 1,063; Hagelin, Reform, 878; Harris, Soc. Workers, 306.
1996: Clinton, D., 1,071,971; Dole, R., 845,029; Perot, Ref., 227,339; Nader, Green, 28,723; Phillips, Taxpayers, 8,811; Browne, LB.,

7,929; Hagelin, Natural Law, 1,379; Moorehead, Workers World, 1,333; Hollis, Soc., 848; Harris, Soc. Workers, 483.
1992: Clinton, D., 1,041,066; Bush, R., 930,855; Perot, Ind., 544,479; Marrou, LB., 2,877; Gritz, Populist/America First, 2,311; Daniels, Ind., 1,883; Phillips, U.S. Taxpayers, 1,772; Hagelin, Natural Law, 1,070.
1988: Dukakis, D., 1,126,794; Bush, R., 1,047,499; Paul, Lib., 5,157; Duke, Pop., 3,056.
1984: Reagan, R., 1,198,584; Mondale, D., 995,740; Bergland, LB., 4,883.
1980: Reagan, R., 1,088,845; Carter, D., 981,584; Anderson, Ind., 160,657; Clark, LB., 29,135; Commoner, Citizens, 7,767; Rarick, Constitution, 1,519; McReynolds, Soc., 808; Hall, Com., 772; Griswold, Workers World, 414; DeBerry, Soc. Workers, 383; scattered, 1,337.
1976: Carter, D., 1,040,232; Ford, R., 1,004,987; McCarthy, Ind., 34,943; Maddox, Amer. Ind., 8,552; Zeidler, Soc., 4,298; MacBride, LB., 3,814; Camejo, Soc. Workers, 1,691; Wright, People's, 943; Hall, Com., 749; LaRouche, U.S. Lab., 738; Levin, Soc. Labor, 389; scattered, 2,839.
1972: Nixon, R., 989,430; McGovern, D., 810,174; Schmitz, Amer., 47,525; Spock, Ind., 2,701; Fisher, Soc. Labor, 998; Hall, Com., 663; Reed, Ind., 506; scattered, 893.
1968: Nixon, R., 809,997; Humphrey, D., 748,804; Wallace, 3rd Party, 127,835; Blomen, Soc. Labor, 1,338; Halstead, Soc. Workers, 1,222; scattered, 2,342.
1964: Johnson, D., 1,050,424; Goldwater, R., 638,495; DeBerry, Soc. Workers, 1,692; Hass, Soc. Labor, 1,204.
1960: Nixon, R., 895,175; Kennedy, D., 830,805; Dobbs, Soc. Workers, 1,792; Hass, Soc. Labor, 1,310.
1956: Eisenhower, R., 954,844; Stevenson, D., 586,768; Andrews, Ind., 6,918; Hoopes, Soc., 754; Hass, Soc. Labor, 710; Dobbs, Soc. Workers, 564.
1952: Eisenhower, R., 979,744; Stevenson, D., 622,175; Hallinan, Ind., 2,174; Dobbs, Ind., 1,350; Hoopes, Ind., 1,157; Hass, Ind., 770.

Wyoming

County	2008 Obama (D)	McCain (R)	2004 Kerry (D)	Bush (R)
Albany	8,618	7,981	7,117	9,006
Big Horn	1,108	4,043	960	4,232
Campbell	2,986	13,001	2,464	12,415
Carbon	2,336	4,331	2,158	4,758
Converse	1,380	4,924	1,184	4,447
Crook	612	2,967	501	2,836
Fremont	6,016	11,082	5,338	11,429
Goshen	1,832	3,942	1,566	4,114
Hot Springs	618	1,834	623	1,812
Johnson	908	3,334	676	3,231
Laramie	16,070	24,549	13,171	25,951
Lincoln	1,823	6,485	1,364	6,423
Natrona	8,144	17,573	9,863	21,512
Niobrara	244	1,017	230	1,064
Park	3,757	10,838	3,007	10,917
Platte	1,407	2,993	1,328	3,149
Sheridan	4,450	10,169	4,066	9,689
Sublette	936	3,316	730	2,847
Sweetwater	5,762	10,360	5,208	10,653
Teton	7,472	4,567	5,972	5,124
Uinta	2,317	5,759	1,815	6,081
Washakie	1,042	2,956	855	3,200
Weston	658	2,618	580	2,739
Totals	**82,868**	**164,958**	**70,776**	**167,629**

Wyoming Vote Since 1952

2008: McCain, Rep., 164,958; Obama, Dem., 82,868; Nader, Ind., 2,525; Barr, Lib., 1,594; Baldwin, Ind., 1,192.
2004: Bush, R., 167,629; Kerry, D., 70,776; Nader, Ind., 2,741; Badnarik, LB., 1,171; Peroutka, Ind., 631.
2000: Bush, R., 147,947; Gore, D., 60,481; Buchanan, Reform, 2,724; Browne, LB., 1,443; Phillips, Ind., 720; Hagelin, Natural Law, 411.
1996: Dole, R., 105,388; Clinton, D., 77,934; Perot, Ind. (Ref.), 25,928; Browne, LB., 1,739; Hagelin, Natural Law, 582.
1992: Bush, R., 79,347; Clinton, D., 68,160; Perot, Ind., 51,263.
1988: Bush, R., 106,867; Dukakis, D., 67,113; Paul, Lib., 2,026; Fulani, New Alliance, 545.
1984: Reagan, R., 133,241; Mondale, D., 53,370; Bergland, LB., 2,357.
1980: Reagan, R., 110,700; Carter, D., 49,427; Anderson, Ind., 12,072; Clark, LB., 4,514.
1976: Ford, R., 92,717; Carter, D., 62,239; McCarthy, Ind., 624; Reagan, Ind., 307; Anderson, Amer., 290; MacBride, LB., 89; Brown, Ind., 47; Maddox, Amer. Ind., 30.
1972: Nixon, R., 100,464; McGovern, D., 44,358; Schmitz, Amer., 748.
1968: Nixon, R., 70,927; Humphrey, D., 45,173; Wallace, 3rd Party, 11,105.
1964: Johnson, D., 80,718; Goldwater, R., 61,998.
1960: Nixon, R., 77,451; Kennedy, D., 63,331.
1956: Eisenhower, R., 74,573; Stevenson, D., 49,554.
1952: Eisenhower, R., 81,047; Stevenson, D., 47,934; Hamblen, Proh., 194; Hoopes, Soc., 40; Haas, Soc. Labor, 36.

The Electoral College

The president and the vice president are the only elective federal officials not chosen by direct vote of the people. They are elected by the members of the Electoral College, an institution provided for in the U.S. Constitution.

On presidential election day, the first Tuesday after the first Monday in November of every 4th year, each state chooses as many electors as it has senators and representatives in Congress. In 1964, for the first time, as provided by the 23rd Amendment to the Constitution, the District of Columbia voted for 3 electors. Thus, with 100 senators and 435 representatives, there are 538 members of the Electoral College, with a majority of 270 electoral votes needed to elect the president and vice president.

Although political parties were not part of the original plan created by the Founding Fathers, today political parties customarily nominate their lists of electors at their respective state conventions. Some states print names of the candidates for president and vice president at the top of the Nov. ballot; others list only the electors' names. In either case, the electors of the party receiving the highest vote are elected. Two states, Maine and Nebraska, allow for proportional allocation.

The electors meet on the first Monday after the 2nd Wednesday in December in their respective state capitals or in some other place prescribed by state legislatures. By long-established custom, they vote for their party nominees, although this is not required by federal law; some states do require it.

The Constitution requires electors to cast a ballot for at least one person who is not an inhabitant of that elector's home state. This ensures that presidential and vice presidential candidates from the same party will not be from the same state. (In 2000, Republican vice presidential nominee Dick Cheney changed his voter registration to Wyoming, where he grew up and which he'd once represented in Congress, from Gov. George W. Bush's home state of Texas.) Also, an elector cannot be a member of Congress or hold federal office.

Certified and sealed lists of the votes of the electors in each state are sent to the president of the U.S. Senate, who then opens them in the presence of the members of the Senate and House of Representatives in a joint session held in early Jan., and the electoral votes of all the states are then officially counted.

If no candidate for president has a majority, the House of Representatives chooses a president from the top 3 candidates, with all representatives from each state combining to cast one vote for that state. The House decided the outcome of the 1800 and 1824 presidential elections. If no candidate for vice president has a majority, the Senate chooses from the top 2, with the senators voting as individuals. The Senate chose the vice president following the 1836 election.

Under the electoral college system, a candidate who fails to be the top vote getter in the popular vote still may win a majority of electoral votes. This happened in the elections of 1876, 1888, and 2000.

Electoral Votes for President, 2008

Electoral votes based on the 2000 Census were in force beginning with the 2004 elections.

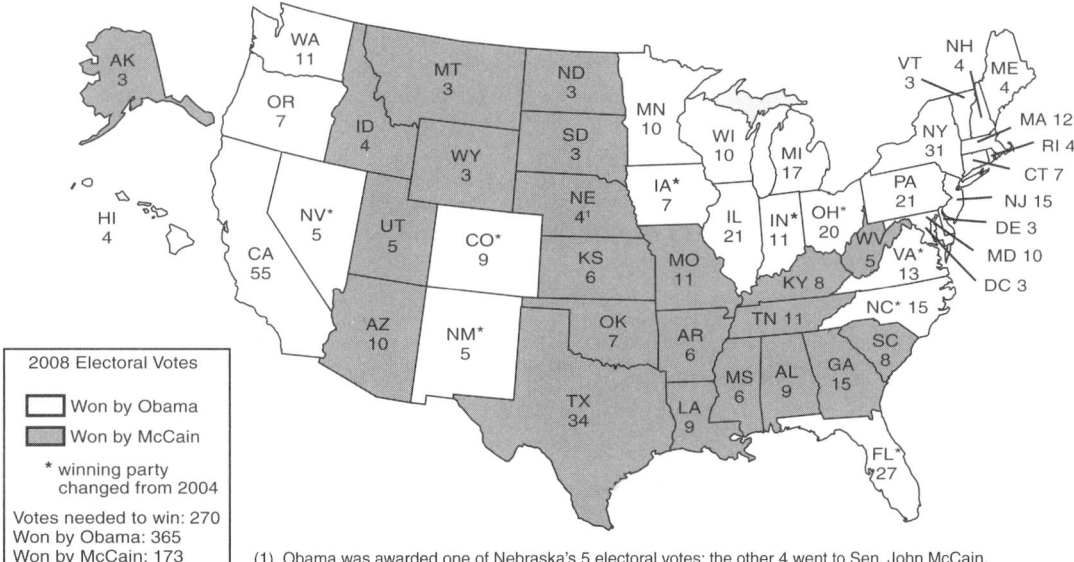

2008 Electoral Votes

☐ Won by Obama

▨ Won by McCain

* winning party changed from 2004

Votes needed to win: 270
Won by Obama: 365
Won by McCain: 173

(1) Obama was awarded one of Nebraska's 5 electoral votes; the other 4 went to Sen. John McCain.

Voter Turnout in Presidential Elections, 1932-2008

Source: Federal Election Commission; Commission for Study of American Electorate; *Congressional Quarterly*

	Candidates	Voter participation (% of voting-age population)		Candidates	Voter participation (% of voting-age population)
1932	Roosevelt-Hoover	52.4%	1972	Nixon-McGovern	55.2%[1]
1936	Roosevelt-Landon	56.0	1976	Carter-Ford	53.5
1940	Roosevelt-Willkie	58.9	1980	Reagan-Carter	54.0
1944	Roosevelt-Dewey	56.0	1984	Reagan-Mondale	53.1
1948	Truman-Dewey	51.1	1988	Bush-Dukakis	50.2
1952	Eisenhower-Stevenson	61.6	1992	Clinton-Bush-Perot	55.9
1956	Eisenhower-Stevenson	59.3	1996	Clinton-Dole-Perot	49.0
1960	Kennedy-Nixon	62.8	2000	Bush-Gore	51.3
1964	Johnson-Goldwater	61.9	2004	Bush-Kerry	60.7
1968	Nixon-Humphrey	60.9	2008	Obama-McCain	58.2

(1) The sharp drop in 1972 followed the expansion of eligibility with the enfranchisement of 18- to 20-year-olds.

Major-Party Nominees for President and Vice President, 1856-2008

Asterisk (*) denotes winning ticket

	Democratic			Republican	
Year	President	Vice President	Year	President	Vice President
1856	James Buchanan	John Breckinridge	1856	John Frémont	William Dayton
1860	Stephen A. Douglas[1]	Herschel V. Johnson	1860	Abraham Lincoln*	Hannibal Hamlin
1864	George McClellan	G. H. Pendleton	1864	Abraham Lincoln*	Andrew Johnson
1868	Horatio Seymour	Francis Blair	1868	Ulysses S. Grant*	Schuyler Colfax
1872	Horace Greeley	B. Gratz Brown	1872	Ulysses S. Grant*	Henry Wilson
1876	Samuel J. Tilden	Thomas Hendricks	1876	Rutherford B. Hayes*	William Wheeler
1880	Winfield Hancock	William English	1880	James A. Garfield*	Chester A. Arthur
1884	Grover Cleveland*	Thomas Hendricks	1884	James G. Blaine	John Logan
1888	Grover Cleveland	A. G. Thurman	1888	Benjamin Harrison*	Levi Morton
1892	Grover Cleveland*	Adlai Stevenson	1892	Benjamin Harrison	Whitelaw Reid
1896	William J. Bryan	Arthur Sewall	1896	William McKinley*	Garret Hobart
1900	William J. Bryan	Adlai Stevenson	1900	William McKinley*	Theodore Roosevelt
1904	Alton Parker	Henry Davis	1904	Theodore Roosevelt*	Charles Fairbanks
1908	William J. Bryan	John Kern	1908	William H. Taft*	James Sherman
1912	Woodrow Wilson*	Thomas Marshall	1912	William H. Taft	James Sherman[2]
1916	Woodrow Wilson*	Thomas Marshall	1916	Charles E. Hughes	Charles Fairbanks
1920	James M. Cox	Franklin D. Roosevelt	1920	Warren G. Harding*	Calvin Coolidge
1924	John W. Davis	Charles W. Bryan	1924	Calvin Coolidge*	Charles G. Dawes
1928	Alfred E. Smith	Joseph T. Robinson	1928	Herbert Hoover*	Charles Curtis
1932	Franklin D. Roosevelt*	John N. Garner	1932	Herbert Hoover	Charles Curtis
1936	Franklin D. Roosevelt*	John N. Garner	1936	Alfred M. Landon	Frank Knox
1940	Franklin D. Roosevelt*	Henry A. Wallace	1940	Wendell L. Willkie	Charles McNary
1944	Franklin D. Roosevelt*	Harry S. Truman	1944	Thomas E. Dewey	John W. Bricker
1948	Harry S. Truman*	Alben W. Barkley	1948	Thomas E. Dewey	Earl Warren
1952	Adlai E. Stevenson	John J. Sparkman	1952	Dwight D. Eisenhower*	Richard M. Nixon
1956	Adlai E. Stevenson	Estes Kefauver	1956	Dwight D. Eisenhower*	Richard M. Nixon
1960	John F. Kennedy*	Lyndon B. Johnson	1960	Richard M. Nixon	Henry Cabot Lodge
1964	Lyndon B. Johnson*	Hubert H. Humphrey	1964	Barry M. Goldwater	William E. Miller
1968	Hubert H. Humphrey	Edmund S. Muskie	1968	Richard M. Nixon*	Spiro T. Agnew
1972	George S. McGovern	R. Sargent Shriver Jr.[3]	1972	Richard M. Nixon*	Spiro T. Agnew
1976	Jimmy Carter*	Walter F. Mondale	1976	Gerald R. Ford	Bob Dole
1980	Jimmy Carter	Walter F. Mondale	1980	Ronald Reagan*	George H. W. Bush
1984	Walter F. Mondale	Geraldine Ferraro	1984	Ronald Reagan*	George H. W. Bush
1988	Michael S. Dukakis	Lloyd Bentsen	1988	George H. W. Bush*	Dan Quayle
1992	Bill Clinton*	Al Gore	1992	George H. W. Bush	Dan Quayle
1996	Bill Clinton*	Al Gore	1996	Bob Dole	Jack Kemp
2000	Al Gore	Joseph Lieberman	2000	George W. Bush*	Richard Cheney
2004	John Kerry	John Edwards	2004	George W. Bush*	Richard Cheney
2008	Barack Obama*	Joseph Biden	2008	John McCain	Sarah Palin

(1) Douglas and Johnson were nominated at the Baltimore convention. An earlier convention in Charleston, SC, failed to reach a consensus and resulted in a split in the party. The Southern faction of the Democrats nominated John Breckinridge for president and Joseph Lane for vice president. (2) Died Oct. 30; replaced on ballot by Nicholas Butler. (3) Chosen by Democratic National Committee after Thomas Eagleton withdrew because of controversy over past treatments for depression.

Third-Party and Independent Presidential Candidates

Although many "third party" candidates or independents have pursued the presidency, only 10 of these from 1832 to 2000 have polled more than a million votes. In most elections since 1860, fewer than one vote in 20 has been cast for a third-party candidate. Major vote getters among third-party and independent candidates include James B. Weaver (People's Party), 1892; former Pres. Theodore Roosevelt (Progressive Party), 1912; Robert M. La Follette (Progressive Party), 1924; George C. Wallace (American Independent Party), 1968; and H. Ross Perot, as an independent in 1992 and with the Reform Party in 1996. In these 6 elections non-major-party candidates combined polled at least 10% of the vote.

Roosevelt outpolled the Republican candidate, William Howard Taft, in 1912, capturing 28% of the popular vote and 88 electoral votes. In 1948, Strom Thurmond was able to capture 39 electoral votes (from 5 Southern states); however, all third parties received only 5.75% of the popular vote in the election. Twenty years later, George Wallace's popularity in the same region allowed him to get 46 electoral votes and 13.5% of the popular vote.

In 1992 Perot captured 19% of the popular vote; however, he did not win a single state. In 1996, Perot won 8% of the popular vote; all third-party candidates combined won just over 10%. In 2000, Ralph Nader won about 3% of the vote.

Despite the difficulty in winning the presidency, independent and third-party candidates often bring attention to their most prominent issues. They can also affect the outcome between major-party candidates.

Notable Third Party and Independent Campaigns by Year

Party	Presidential nominee	Year	Issues	Strength in
Anti-Masonic	William Wirt	1832	Against secret societies and oaths	PA, VT
Liberty	James G. Birney	1844	Anti-slavery	North
Free Soil	Martin Van Buren	1848	Anti-slavery	NY, OH
American (Know-Nothing)	Millard Fillmore	1856	Anti-immigrant	Northeast, South
Greenback	Peter Cooper	1876	For "cheap money," labor rights	National
Greenback	James B. Weaver	1880	For "cheap money," labor rights	National
Prohibition	John P. St. John	1884	Anti-liquor	National
People's (Populists)	James B. Weaver	1892	For "cheap money," end of national banks	South, West
Socialist	Eugene V. Debs	1900-12; 1920	For public ownership	National
Progressive (Bull Moose)	Theodore Roosevelt	1912	Against high tariffs	Midwest, West
Progressive	Robert M. La Follette	1924	Farmer and labor rights	Midwest, West
Socialist	Norman Thomas	1928-48	Liberal reforms	National
Union	William Lemke	1936	Anti-New Deal	National
States' Rights (Dixiecrats)	Strom Thurmond	1948	For states' rights	South
Progressive	Henry A. Wallace	1948	Anti-Cold War	NY, CA
American Independent	George C. Wallace	1968	For states' rights	South
American	John G. Schmitz	1972	For "law and order"	Far West, OH, LA
None (Independent)	John B. Anderson	1980	A 3rd choice	National
None (Independent)	H. Ross Perot	1992	Federal budget deficit	National
Reform	H. Ross Perot	1996	Deficit; campaign finance	National
Green, Independent	Ralph Nader	2000-08	Corporate power; domestic priorities	National

Popular and Electoral Vote for President, 1789-2008

(D) Democrat; (DR) Democratic Republican; (F) Federalist; (LR) Liberal Republican; (NR) National Republican;
(P) People's; (PR) Progressive; (R) Republican; (RF) Reform; (SR) States' Rights; (W) Whig; Asterisk (*)–See notes at bottom.

Year	President elected	Popular	Elec.	Major losing candidate(s)	Popular	Elec.
1789	George Washington (F)	Unknown	69	No opposition	—	—
1792	George Washington (F)	Unknown	132	No opposition	—	—
1796	John Adams (F)	Unknown	71	Thomas Jefferson (DR)	Unknown	68
1800*	Thomas Jefferson (DR)	Unknown	73	Aaron Burr (DR)	Unknown	73
1804	Thomas Jefferson (DR)	Unknown	162	Charles Pinckney (F)	Unknown	14
1808	James Madison (DR)	Unknown	122	Charles Pinckney (F)	Unknown	47
1812	James Madison (DR)	Unknown	128	DeWitt Clinton (F)	Unknown	89
1816	James Monroe (DR)	Unknown	183	Rufus King (F)	Unknown	34
1820	James Monroe (DR)	Unknown	231	John Quincy Adams (DR)	Unknown	1
1824*	John Quincy Adams (DR)	113,122	84	Andrew Jackson (DR)	151,271	99
				Henry Clay (DR)	46,587	37
				William H. Crawford (DR)	44,282	41
1828	Andrew Jackson (D)	642,553	178	John Quincy Adams (NR)	500,897	83
1832	Andrew Jackson (D)	701,780	219	Henry Clay (NR)	484,205	49
1836	Martin Van Buren (D)	764,176	170	William H. Harrison (W)	550,816	73
1840	William H. Harrison (W)	1,275,390	234	Martin Van Buren (D)	1,128,854	60
1844	James K. Polk (D)	1,339,494	170	Henry Clay (W)	1,300,004	105
1848	Zachary Taylor (W)	1,361,393	163	Lewis Cass (D)	1,223,460	127
				Martin Van Buren (Free Soil)	291,501	—
1852	Franklin Pierce (D)	1,607,510	254	Winfield Scott (W)	1,386,942	42
1856	James Buchanan (D)	1,836,072	174	John C. Fremont (R)	1,342,345	114
				Millard Fillmore (American)	873,053	8
1860	Abraham Lincoln (R)	1,865,908	180	Stephen A. Douglas (D)	848,019	12
				John C. Breckinridge (D)	845,763	72
				John Bell (Const. Union)	589,581	39
1864	Abraham Lincoln (R)	2,218,388	212	George McClellan (D)	1,812,807	21
1868	Ulysses S. Grant (R)	3,013,650	214	Horatio Seymour (D)	2,708,744	80
1872*	Ulysses S. Grant (R)	3,598,235	286	Horace Greeley (D-LR)*	2,834,671	—
1876*	Rutherford B. Hayes (R)	4,034,311	185	Samuel J. Tilden (D)	4,288,546	184
1880	James A. Garfield (R)	4,446,158	214	Winfield S. Hancock (D)	4,444,260	155
1884	Grover Cleveland (D)	4,874,621	219	James G. Blaine (R)	4,848,936	182
1888	Benjamin Harrison (R)	5,443,892	233	Grover Cleveland (D)	5,534,488	168
1892	Grover Cleveland (D)	5,551,883	277	Benjamin Harrison (R)	5,179,244	145
				James Weaver (P)	1,027,329	22
1896	William McKinley (R)	7,108,480	271	William J. Bryan (D-P)	6,511,495	176
1900	William McKinley (R)	7,218,039	292	William J. Bryan (D)	6,358,345	155
1904	Theodore Roosevelt (R)	7,626,593	336	Alton B. Parker (D)	5,082,898	140
1908	William H. Taft (R)	7,676,258	321	William J. Bryan (D)	6,406,801	162
1912	Woodrow Wilson (D)	6,293,152	435	Theodore Roosevelt (PR)	4,119,207	88
				William H. Taft (R)	3,483,922	8
1916	Woodrow Wilson (D)	9,126,300	277	Charles E. Hughes (R)	8,546,789	254
1920	Warren G. Harding (R)	16,153,115	404	James M. Cox (D)	9,133,092	127
1924	Calvin Coolidge (R)	15,719,921	382	John W. Davis (D)	8,386,704	136
				Robert M. La Follette (PR)	4,822,856	13
1928	Herbert Hoover (R)	21,437,277	444	Alfred E. Smith (D)	15,007,698	87
1932	Franklin D. Roosevelt (D)	22,829,501	472	Herbert Hoover (R)	15,760,684	59
1936	Franklin D. Roosevelt (D)	27,757,333	523	Alfred Landon (R)	16,684,231	8
1940	Franklin D. Roosevelt (D)	27,313,041	449	Wendell Willkie (R)	22,348,480	82
1944	Franklin D. Roosevelt (D)	25,612,610	432	Thomas E. Dewey (R)	22,117,617	99
1948	Harry S. Truman (D)	24,179,345	303	Thomas E. Dewey (R)	21,991,291	189
				Strom Thurmond (SR)	1,169,021	39
				Henry A. Wallace (PR)	1,157,172	—
1952	Dwight D. Eisenhower (R)	33,936,234	442	Adlai E. Stevenson (D)	27,314,992	89
1956*	Dwight D. Eisenhower (R)	35,590,472	457	Adlai E. Stevenson (D)	26,022,752	73
1960*	John F. Kennedy (D)	34,226,731	303	Richard M. Nixon (R)	34,108,157	219
1964	Lyndon B. Johnson (D)	43,129,566	486	Barry M. Goldwater (R)	27,178,188	52
1968	Richard M. Nixon (R)	31,785,480	301	Hubert H. Humphrey (D)	31,275,166	191
				George C. Wallace (3rd party)	9,906,473	46
1972*	Richard M. Nixon (R)	47,169,911	520	George S. McGovern (D)	29,170,383	17
1976*	Jimmy Carter (D)	40,830,763	297	Gerald R. Ford (R)	39,147,793	240
1980	Ronald Reagan (R)	43,904,153	489	Jimmy Carter (D)	35,483,883	49
				John B. Anderson (independent)	5,719,437	—
1984	Ronald Reagan (R)	54,455,075	525	Walter F. Mondale (D)	37,577,185	13
1988*	George H. W. Bush (R)	48,886,097	426	Michael S. Dukakis (D)	41,809,074	111
1992	Bill Clinton (D)	44,908,254	370	George H. W. Bush (R)	39,102,343	168
				H. Ross Perot (independent)	19,741,065	—
1996	Bill Clinton (D)	45,590,703	379	Bob Dole (R)	37,816,307	159
				H. Ross Perot (RF)	7,866,284	—
2000*	George W. Bush (R)	50,459,211	271	Al Gore (D)	51,003,894	266
				Ralph Nader (Green)	2,834,410	—
2004*	George W. Bush (R)	62,040,610	286	John Kerry (D)	59,028,444	251
2008	Barack H. Obama (D)	69,498,459	365	John McCain (R)	59,948,283	173

*1800—Elected by House of Representatives because of tied electoral vote. 1824—Elected by House of Representatives because no candidate had polled a majority. By 1824, the Democratic Republicans had become a loose coalition of competing political groups. By 1828, the supporters of Jackson were known as Democrats, and the John Q. Adams and Henry Clay supporters as National Republicans. 1872—Greeley died Nov. 29, 1872. His electoral votes were split among 4 individuals. 1876—FL, LA, OR, and SC election returns were disputed. Congress in joint session (Mar. 2, 1877) declared Hayes and Wheeler elected president and vice president. 1956—Democrats elected 74 electors, but one from Alabama refused to vote for Stevenson. 1960—Sen. Harry F. Byrd (D, VA) received 15 electoral votes. 1972—John Hospers of California received one vote from an elector of Virginia. 1976—Ronald Reagan of CA received one vote from an elector of Washington. 1988—Sen. Lloyd Bentsen (D, TX) received 1 vote from an elector of West Virginia. 2000—One Gore elector from Washington, DC, abstained. Nader was listed as "Independent" on the ballot in some states, and was not on the ballot in all states. 2004—One Minnesota elector voted for VP candidate John Edwards for both president and vice president.

100 MOST POPULOUS U.S. CITIES

Source: Bureau of Labor Statistics: employment; Bureau of Econ. Analysis: per cap. income; other data U.S. Census Bureau

Included here are the 100 most populous U.S. cities, using 2008 Census Bureau estimates. Population rank indicated by figure in parentheses. Most data are for the city proper. Some statistics, where noted, apply to the whole Metropolitan Statistical Area (MSA). Employment figures are for 2008 unless noted otherwise; per capita income figures are for 2007. Mayors are as of Sept. 2009. Inc.=Incorporated; est.=Established. **Note:** Websites are as of Sept. 2009 and subject to change. For a listing of the 100 largest U.S. cities, ranked by population, *see* p. 618.

Akron, Ohio

Population (2008): 207,510 (97); **Pop. density:** 3,342; **Pop. change (2000-08):** –4.4%. **Area:** 62.1 sq mi. **Employment (2008):** 100,958 employed; 6.7% unemployed. **Per capita income (MSA):** $36,563; increase (2006-07): 4.5%.
Mayor: Donald L. Plusquellic, Democrat
History: settled 1825; inc. as city 1865; located on Ohio-Erie Canal and is a port of entry; polymer center of the Americas.
Transportation: 1 intl., 1 regional airport; major trucking industry; Conrail, Amtrak; metro transit system. **Communications:** 1 daily newspaper; 6 TV, 8 radio stations. **Medical facilities:** 6 hosp. **Educational facilities:** 1 univ. and college; 57 pub. schools. **Further information:** Greater Akron Chamber, One Cascade Plz., 17th Floor, Akron, OH 44308; www.greaterakronchamber.org; www.ci.akron.oh.us

Albuquerque, New Mexico

Population (2008): 521,999 (34); **Pop. density:** 2,890; **Pop. change (2000-08):** 16.2%. **Area:** 180.6 sq mi. **Employment (2008):** 257,388 employed; 3.8% unemployed. **Per capita income (MSA):** $33,305; increase (2006-07): 2.9%.
Mayor: Martin J. Chávez, Democrat
History: founded 1706 by the Spanish; inc. 1890.
Transportation: 1 intl. airport; 1 railroad; bus system. **Communications:** 1 daily newspaper; 11 TV, 40 radio stations. **Medical facilities:** 19 major hosp. **Educational facilities:** 1 univ., 25 colleges; 132 pub. schools. **Further information:** Albuquerque Convention & Visitors Bureau, PO Box 26866, Albuquerque, NM 87125-6866; www.itsatrip.org; www.cabq.gov

Anaheim, California

Population (2008): 335,288 (55); **Pop. density:** 6,857; **Pop. change (2000-08):** 2.0%. **Area:** 48.9 sq mi. **Employment (2008):** 165,954 employed; 6.8% unemployed. **Per capita income (MSA):** $42,278; increase (2006-07): 4.3%.
Mayor: Curt Pringle, Republican
History: founded 1857; inc. 1870; home of Disneyland Resort, the Mighty Ducks of Anaheim, and the Los Angeles Angels of Anaheim.
Transportation: Amtrak; Metrolink (2 stns.), OCTA bus service. **Communications:** 1 daily newspaper; 2 TV, 2 radio stations (MSA). **Medical facilities:** 5 hosp.; 5 medical centers. **Educational facilities:** 11 colleges and trade schools; 65 pub. schools, 33 private schools. **Further information:** City Hall, 200 South Anaheim Blvd., Ste. 733, Anaheim, CA 92805; www.anaheimoc.org; www.anaheim.net

Anchorage, Alaska

Population (2008): 279,243 (67); **Pop. density:** 165; **Pop. change (2000-08):** 7.3%. **Area:** 1,697 sq mi. **Employment (2008):** 146,259 employed; 5.3% unemployed. **Per capita income (MSA):** $43,515; increase (2006-07): 4.8%.
Mayor: Dan Sullivan, Republican
History: founded 1914 as a construction camp for railroad; HQ of Alaska Defense Command, WWII; severely damaged in earthquake 1964, now rebuilt; current population center of Alaska.
Transportation: 1 intl., 1 regional airport, 2 seaplane bases, 2 airfields; 1 railroad; transit system; 1 port. **Communications:** 1 daily newspaper; 13 TV, 25 radio stations. **Medical facilities:** 5 hosp. **Educational facilities:** 2 univ., 8 trade schools/colleges; 96 pub. schools. **Further information:** Anchorage Chamber of Commerce, 1016 W 6th Ave., Ste. 303, Anchorage, AK, 99501; www.anchoragechamber.org; www.muni.org

Arlington, Texas

Population (2008): 374,417 (50); **Pop. density:** 3,908; **Pop. change (2000-08):** 10.8%. **Area:** 95.8 sq mi. **Employment (2008):** 194,371 employed; 4.6% unemployed. **Per capita income (MSA):** $41,499; increase (2006-07): 4.0%.
Mayor: Robert N. Cluck, Republican
History: settled in 1840s; inc. 1884.
Transportation: 1 muni. airport; freight railways. **Communications:** 2 TV, 1 radio stations. **Medical facilities:** 7 hosp.

Educational facilities: 1 univ., 8 colleges and trade schools; 74 pub. schools. **Further information:** Arlington Chamber of Commerce, 505 E. Border St., Arlington, TX 76010; City of Arlington, 101 W. Abram, Arlington, TX 76010; www.arlington tx.com; www.ci.arlington.tx.us

Arlington, Virginia

Population (2008): 209,969 (96); **Pop. density:** 8,107; **Pop. change (2000-08):** 12.4%. **Area:** 25.9 sq mi. **Employment (2008):** NA. **Per capita income (MSA):** $54,971; increase (2006-07): 4.7%.
Chairman: Barbara Favola, Democrat
History: originally part of the U.S. capital, the area west of the Potomac was returned to Virginia in 1846; it was known as Alexandria until 1920, when the county was renamed Arlington.
Transportation: 1 natl. airport, 2 intl. airports nearby; Metro connecting with Washington, DC; VA Railway Express connecting with outer suburbs; Amtrak. **Communications:** 21 TV, 44 radio stations. **Medical facilities:** 1 major hosp.; numerous urgent care centers. **Educational facilities:** 5 univ., 5 coll. and trade schools; 35 pub. schools: 22 elem., 6 middle, 4 high. **Further information:** Arlington County Government, 2300 Clarendon Blvd., Arlington, VA 22201; www.arlingtonvirginia.com; www.arlingtonva.us

Atlanta, Georgia

Population (2008): 537,958 (33); **Pop. density:** 4,085; **Pop. change (2000-08):** 28.7%. **Area:** 131.7 sq mi. **Employment (2008):** 220,899 employed; 7.1% unemployed. **Per capita income (MSA):** $37,744; increase (2006-07): 3.4%.
Mayor: Shirley Franklin, Democrat
History: founded as Terminus 1837; renamed Atlanta 1845; inc. 1847; played major role in Civil War; became permanent state capital 1877; birthplace of civil rights movement; host to 1996 Centennial Olympic Games.
Transportation: 1 intl., 1 regional airport; 3 railroad lines; MARTA bus and rapid rail service. **Communications:** 3 daily newspapers; 21 TV, 24 radio stations. **Medical facilities:** 19 hosp.; VA hosp.; U.S. Centers for Disease Control and Prevention; American Cancer Society. **Educational facilities:** 6 univ., 10 colleges; 89 pub. schools. **Further information:** Metro Atlanta Chamber of Commerce, 235 Andrew Young Intl. Blvd. NW, Atlanta, GA 30303; www.metroatlantachamber.com; www.atlantaga.gov

Aurora, Colorado

Population (2008): 319,057 (58); **Pop. density:** 2,238; **Pop. change (2000-08):** 15.4%. **Area:** 142.5 sq mi. **Employment (2008):** 164,653 employed; 6.1% unemployed. **Per capita income (MSA):** $46,682; increase (2006-07): 3.6%.
Mayor: Ed Tauer, Republican
History: founded in 1891 and originally called Fletcher; renamed Aurora in 1907; inc. 1929. Early growth stimulated by presence of military bases; fast-growing trade, technology, and medical science center.
Transportation: adjacent to Denver Intl. Airport; bus system. **Communications:** 1 daily newspaper; 2 TV, 3 radio stations. **Medical facilities:** 3 hosp. **Educational facilities:** 2 univ., 6 colleges and technical schools; 49 pub. schools, 4 private schools. **Further information:** Aurora Planning Dept., 15151 E. Alameda Pkwy., Aurora, CO 80012; www.aurora chamber.org; www.auroragov.org;

Austin, Texas

Population (2008): 757,688 (15); **Pop. density:** 3,013; **Pop. change (2000-08):** 15.0%. **Area:** 251.5 sq mi. **Employment (2008):** 400,719 employed; 4.1% unemployed. **Per capita income (MSA):** $37,238; increase (2006-07): 2.2%.
Mayor: Lee Leffingwell, Non-Partisan
History: first permanent settlement 1835; capital of Rep. of Texas 1839; named after Stephen Austin; inc. 1840.
Transportation: 1 intl. airport; 2 railroads; bus system. **Communications:** 1 daily, 2 weekly newspapers; 15 TV, 12 radio stations. **Medical facilities:** 26 hosp. **Educational facili-**

ties: 8 4-year univ. (6 public, 2 private), 14 2-year colleges (2 public, 12 private), 17 colleges and trade schools. **Further information:** Greater Austin Chamber, 210 Barton Springs Rd., Ste. 400, Austin, TX 78704; www.austinchamber.com; www.austintexas.org; www.ci.austin.tx.us

Bakersfield, California

Population (2008): 321,078 (57); **Pop. density:** 2,839; **Pop. change (2000-08):** 31.8%. **Area:** 113.1 sq mi. **Employment (2008):** 143,849 employed; 6.8% unemployed. **Per capita income (MSA):** $27,090; increase (2006-07): 4.7%.

Mayor: Harvey L. Hall, Non-Partisan

History: named after Col. Thomas Baker, an early settler; inc. 1898.

Transportation: 2 airports; Amtrak; Greyhound; 3 local bus systems. **Communications:** 1 daily newspaper; 7 TV, 29 radio stations. **Medical facilities:** 7 hosp. **Educational facilities:** 4 univ., 5 colleges/technical schools; 43 public schools. **Further information:** Greater Bakersfield Chamber of Commerce, 1725 Eye St., Bakersfield, CA 93301; www.bakersfieldchamber.org; www.bakersfieldcity.us

Baltimore, Maryland

Population (2008): 636,919 (20); **Pop. density:** 7,883; **Pop. change (2000-08):** −2.2%. **Area:** 80.8 sq mi. **Employment (2008):** 259,710 employed; 6.7% unemployed. **Per capita income (MSA):** $45,887; increase (2006-07): 6.0%.

Mayor: Sheila Dixon, Democrat

History: founded by Maryland legislature 1729; inc. 1797; War of 1812 British artillery barrage of Ft. McHenry (1814) inspired Francis Scott Key to write "Star-Spangled Banner"; birthplace of America's railroads 1828; rebuilt after fire 1904; site of National Aquarium 1981.

Transportation: 1 intl. airport; 3 railroads; subway system; light rail system; bus system; Inner Harbor water taxi system; 2 underwater tunnels. **Communications:** 4 daily newspapers; 8 TV, 21 radio stations. **Medical facilities:** 23 hosp. **Educational facilities:** 12 univ., 18 colleges and trade schools; 203 pub. schools. **Further information:** Greater Baltimore Committee, 111 S. Calvert St., Ste. 1700, Baltimore, MD 21202-6180; www.gbc.org; www.baltimore.org; www.ci.baltimore.md.us

Baton Rouge, Louisiana

Population (2008): 223,689 (84); **Pop. density:** 2,913; **Pop. change (2000-08):** −2.2%. **Area:** 76.8 sq mi. **Employment (2008):** 105,571 employed; 4.9% unemployed. **Per capita income (MSA):** $34,236; increase (2006-07): 6.4%.

Mayor-President: Melvin "Kip" Holden, Democrat

History: claimed by Spain at time of Louisiana Purchase 1803; est. independence by rebellion 1810; inc. as town 1817; became state capital 1849; Union-held most of Civil War.

Transportation: 1 airport; 3 railroad trunk lines; 1 bus line. **Communications:** 1 daily newspaper; 13 TV, 18 radio stations. **Medical facilities:** 17 hosp. **Educational facilities:** 2 univ., 24 colleges and trade schools; 94 pub., 52 priv. schools. **Further information:** The Chamber of Greater Baton Rouge, 564 Laurel St., Baton Rouge, LA, 70801; www.brac.org; www.brgov.com

Birmingham, Alabama

Population (2008): 228,798 (83); **Pop. density:** 1,526; **Pop. change (2000-08):** −5.6%. **Area:** 149.9 sq mi. **Employment (2008):** 93,314 employed; 6.0% unemployed. **Per capita income (MSA):** $39,401; increase (2006-07): 5.6%.

Mayor: Larry P. Langford, Democrat

History: settled 1871 at the intersection of 2 major railroads, within proximity of elements needed for iron and steel production.

Transportation: 1 intl. airport; 4 major rail freight lines; Amtrak; 1 bus line; 75 truck line terminals; 5 air cargo cos.; 7 barge lines. **Communications:** 1 daily newspaper; 9 TV, 21 radio stations; 1 educational TV, 1 educational radio station. **Medical facilities:** 16 hosp.; VA hosp. **Educational facilities:** 7 univ., 16 colleges; 66 pub. schools. **Further information:** Birmingham Area Chamber of Commerce, 505 N. 20th St., Birmingham, AL 35203; www.birminghamchamber.com; www.informationbirmingham.com

Boise, Idaho

Population (2008): 205,314 (100); **Pop. density:** 3,218; **Pop. change (2000-08):** 5.3%. **Area:** 63.8 sq mi. **Employment**

(MSA; 2008): 104,943 employed; 4.6% unemployed. **Per capita income (MSA; 2007):** $35,737; increase (2006-07): 2.3%.

Mayor: David H. Bieter, Non-Partisan

History: Gold discovered in area, 1862; inc., proclaimed capital of Idaho Terr., 1864; on Oregon Trail.

Transportation: 1 regional airport; 1 bus line; 1 intercity bus line. **Communications:** 2 daily, 1 weekly newspapers; 6 TV, 23 radio stns. **Medical facilities:** 9 hosp. **Educational facilities:** 1 univ. and 6 colleges; 53 pub. schools. **Further information:** P.O. Box 2368, Boise, Idaho 83701; www.boise.org; www.boise chamber.org; www.cityofboise.org

Boston, Massachusetts

Population (2008): 609,023 (22); **Pop. density:** 12,583; **Pop. change (2000-08):** 3.4%. **Area:** 48.4 sq mi. **Employment (2008):** 292,221 employed; 5.1% unemployed. **Per capita income (MSA):** $53,443; increase (2006-07): 5.8%.

Mayor: Thomas M. Menino, Democrat

History: settled 1630 by John Winthrop; capital of Mass. Bay Colony; figured strongly in Am. Revolution, earning distinction as the "Cradle of Liberty"; inc. 1822.

Transportation: 1 intl. airport; 2 railroads; city rail and subway system; 3 underwater tunnels; port. **Communications:** 3 daily newspapers; 11 TV, 21 radio stations. **Medical facilities:** 39 hosp. **Educational facilities:** 31 univ. and colleges. **Further information:** Greater Boston Convention and Visitors Bureau, 2 Copley Pl., Suite 105, Boston, MA 02116; www.boston usa.com; www.cityofboston.gov

Buffalo, New York

Population (2008): 270,919 (69); **Pop. density:** 6,673; **Pop. change (2000-08):** −7.4%. **Area:** 40.6 sq mi. **Employment (2008):** 113,913 employed; 7.2% unemployed. **Per capita income (MSA):** $35,038; increase (2006-07): 4.2%.

Mayor: Byron W. Brown, Democrat

History: settled 1780 by Seneca Indians; raided twice by British, War of 1812; served as western terminus for Erie Canal, became a center for trade and manufacturing; inc. 1832; last stop on the Underground Railroad; key point for Canada-U.S. political, trade, and social relations.

Transportation: 1 intl. airport; 4 Class I railroads; Amtrak metro rail system; water service to Great Lakes-St. Lawrence Seaway system and Atlantic seaboard. **Communications:** 12 TV, 18 radio stations. **Medical facilities:** 16 hosp.; 40 research centers. **Educational facilities:** 15 colleges and univ.; 71 pub. schools. **Further information:** Buffalo Niagara Visitor Center, Market Arcade/Walden Galleria, 617 Main St., Ste. 200, Buffalo, NY 14203; www.buffaloniagara.org; www.ci.buffalo.ny.us

Chandler, Arizona

Population (2008): 247,140 (76); **Pop. density:** 4,268; **Pop. change (2000-08):** 39.5%. **Area:** 57.9 sq mi. **Employment (2008):** 123,867 employed; 3.7% unemployed. **Per capita income (MSA):** $35,185; increase (2006-07): 1.0%.

Mayor: Boyd W. Dunn, Non-Partisan

History: town formed 1912; population doubled in 1990s as "the high-tech oasis of the Silicon Desert."

Transportation: 1 muni.; 1 private airport; mass transit system. **Communications:** 1 government access cable channel. **Medical facilities:** 2 hosp. **Educational facilities:** 2 univ., 1 community coll.; 26 elem., 6 junior high, 3 high schools; 13 charter schools. **Further information:** Chandler Chamber, 25 South Arizona Pl., Suite 201, Chandler, AZ 85225; www.chandler chamber.com; www.chandleraz.gov

Charlotte, North Carolina

Population (2008): 687,456 (18); **Pop. density:** 2,837; **Pop. change (2000-08):** 21.3%. **Area:** 242.3 sq mi. **Employment (2008):** 336,774 employed; 5.5% unemployed. **Per capita income (MSA):** $39,231; increase (2006-07): 2.2%.

Mayor: Patrick McCrory, Republican

History: settled by Scotch-Irish immigrants 1740s; inc. 1768 and named after Queen Charlotte, George III's wife; scene of first major U.S. gold discovery 1799.

Transportation: 1 intl. airport; 2 major railway lines; 1 bus line; 605 trucking firms. **Communications:** 2 daily newspapers; 8 TV, 13 radio stations. **Medical facilities:** 8 hosp. **Educational facilities:** 9 univ., 9 colleges; 94 elem. schools, 32 middle schools, 25 high schools. **Further information:** Charlotte Chamber of Commerce, 330 S. Tryon St., Charlotte, NC 28202; www.charlottechamber.com; www.charmeck.org

Chesapeake, Virginia

Population (2008): 220,111 (88); **Pop. density:** 646; **Pop. change (2000-08):** 10.5%. **Area:** 340.7 sq mi. **Employment (2008):** 111,340 employed; 3.9% unemployed. **Per capita income (MSA):** $36,837; increase (2006-07): 4.6%.

Mayor: Alan P. Krasnoff, Independent

History: region settled in 1620s with first English colonies on banks of Elizabeth River; home to Great Dismal Swamp Canal, first envisioned by George Washington in 1763; Battle of Great Bridge fought here Dec. 1775; inc. as a city 1963. **Transportation:** 2 regional airports; freight rail service; bus service. **Communications:** 3 TV, 5 radio stations. **Medical facilities:** 1 hosp. **Educational facilities:** 9 colleges and univ.; 56 pub. schools and educational centers. **Further information:** City of Chesapeake, Public Communications Dept., 306 Cedar Rd., Chesapeake, VA 23322; www.chesapeake.va.us

Chicago, Illinois

Population (2008): 2,853,114 (3); **Pop. density:** 12,563; **Pop. change (2000-08):** −1.5%. **Area:** 227.1 sq mi. **Employment (2008):** 1,237,430 employed; 7.0% unemployed. **Per capita income (MSA):** $44,346; increase (2006-07): 6.5%.

Mayor: Richard M. Daley, Democrat

History: site acquired from Indians 1795; significant white settlement began with Erie Canal 1825; chartered as city 1837; boomed with arrival of railroads and canal to Mississippi R.; one-third of city destroyed by fire 1871; major grain and livestock market. **Transportation:** 2 intl. airports; major railroad system; trucking industry. **Communications:** 16 TV, 38 radio stations. **Medical facilities:** 44 hosp. **Educational facilities:** 63 insts. of higher learning; 623 pub. schools. **Further information:** Chicagoland Chamber of Commerce, Aon Center, 200 E. Randolph St., Ste. 2200, Chicago, IL 60601-6436; www.chicagoland chamber.org; www.cityofchicago.org

Chula Vista, California

Population (2008): 219,318 (89); **Pop. density:** 4,485; **Pop. change (2000-08):** 26.4%. **Area:** 48.9 sq mi. **Employment (2008):** 85,048 employed; 7.0% unemployed. **Per capita income (MSA):** $44,430; increase (2006-07): 4.0%.

Mayor: Cheryl Cox, Republican

History: visited by Spanish in 1542; became part of Spanish land grant in 1795; came into the U.S. during the Mexican War in 1847; inc. 1911. WWII brought aircraft industry and growth. **Transportation:** bus system, DART paratransit. **Communications:** See San Diego, CA. **Medical facilities:** 2 hosp. **Educational facilities:** 5 colleges; 65 pub. schools. **Further Information:** Chula Vista Chamber of Commerce, 233 Fourth Ave., Chula Vista, CA 91910. www.chulavistachamber.org; www.chulavista ca.gov

Cincinnati, Ohio

Population (2008): 333,336 (56); **Pop. density:** 4,274; **Pop. change (2000-08):** 0.6%. **Area:** 78.0 sq mi. **Employment (2008):** 154,811 employed; 6.1% unemployed. **Per capita income (MSA):** $37,782; increase (2006-07): 4.1%.

Mayor: Mark Mallory, Democrat

History: founded 1788 and named after the Society of Cincinnati, an organization of Revolutionary War officers; chartered as village 1802; inc. as city 1819. **Transportation:** 1 intl., 2 muni. airports; 3 railroads; 2 bus systems. **Communications:** 3 daily newspapers; 9 TV, 17 radio stations. **Medical facilities:** 28 hosp.; Cincinnati Children's Hosp. Medical Ctr.; VA hosp. **Educational facilities:** 4 univ., 12 colleges, 8 technical and 2-year colleges; 65 pub. schools. **Further information:** Chamber of Commerce, 441 Vine St., Ste. 300, Cincinnati, OH 45202; www.cincinnatichamber.com; www.cincinnati-oh.gov

Cleveland, Ohio

Population (2008): 433,748 (41); **Pop. density:** 5,590; **Pop. change (2000-08):** −9.2%. **Area:** 77.6 sq mi. **Employment (2008):** 168,307 employed; 8.5% unemployed. **Per capita income (MSA):** $38,963; increase (2006-07): 5.1%.

Mayor: Frank G. Jackson, Democrat

History: surveyed in 1796; given recognition as village 1815, inc. as city 1836; annexed Ohio City 1854. **Transportation:** 1 intl., 2 muni. airports; rail service; rapid transit system; major port. **Communications:** 10 TV, 23 radio stations. **Medical facilities:** 14 hosp. **Educational facilities:** 8 univ. and colleges; 127 pub. schools. **Further information:**

Greater Cleveland Partnership, The Highbee Building, 100 Public Sq., Ste. 210, Cleveland, OH 44113-2291; www.gcpartner ship.com; www.city.cleveland.oh.us

Colorado Springs, Colorado

Population (2008): 80,307 (48); **Pop. density:** 2,048; **Pop. change (2000-08):** 5.3%. **Area:** 185.7 sq mi. **Employment (2008):** 204,785 employed; 5.6% unemployed. **Per capita income (MSA):** $35,717; increase (2006-07): 3.7%.

Mayor: Lionel Rivera, Republican

History: founded at the foot of Pike's Peak; inc. 1872. **Transportation:** 2 muni. airports; 1 bus line. **Communications:** 7 TV, 17 radio stations. **Medical facilities:** 6 hosp. **Educational facilities:** 11 univ., 5 colleges; 185 public schools. **Further information:** Chamber of Commerce, 2 N. Cascade Ave., Ste. 110, Colorado Springs, CO 80903; www.colorado springschamber.org; www.springsgov.com

Columbus, Ohio

Population (2008): 754,885 (16); **Pop. density:** 3,590; **Pop. change (2000-08):** 5.9%. **Area:** 210.3 sq mi. **Employment (2008):** 398,894 employed; 5.5% unemployed. **Per capita income (MSA):** $37,428; increase (2006-07): 4.4%.

Mayor: Michael B. Coleman, Democrat

History: first settlement 1797; laid out as new capital 1812 with current name; became city 1834. **Transportation:** 2 intl., 2 muni. airports, 2 airfields; 3 railroads; 3 intercity bus lines. **Communications:** 13 TV, 20 radio stations. **Medical facilities:** 17 hosp. **Educational facilities:** 11 univ. and colleges, 8 technical and 2-year schools; 128 pub. schools. **Further information:** Greater Columbus Chamber of Commerce, 150 S. Front St. Ste. 200, Columbus, OH 43215. Experience Columbus, Administrative Office and Columbus Visitor Center, 277 W. Nationwide Blvd., Ste. 125, Columbus, OH 43215; www.columbus.org; www.experiencecolumbus.org; www.cityofcolumbus.org

Corpus Christi, Texas

Population (2008): 286,462 (64); **Pop. density:** 1,853; **Pop. change (2000-08):** 3.2%. **Area:** 154.6 sq mi. **Employment (2008):** 140,237 employed; 4.5% unemployed. **Per capita income (MSA):** $33,171; increase (2006-07): 6.5%.

Mayor: Joe Adame, Non-Partisan

History: settled 1839 and inc. 1852. **Transportation:** 1 intl. airport; 3 freight railroads; 2 bus lines, metro bus system. **Communications:** 23 TV, 15 radio stations. **Medical facilities:** 8 hosp. **Educational facilities:** 2 univ., 1 college; 60 pub. schools. **Further information:** Corpus Christi Regional Economic Development Corp., One Shoreline Plz., 800 N. Shoreline Blvd., Ste. 1300 South, Corpus Christi, TX 78401; www.ccredc.com; www.cctexas.com

Dallas, Texas

Population (2008): 1,279,910 (8); **Pop. density:** 3,737; **Pop. change (2000-08):** 7.7%. **Area:** 342.5 sq mi. **Employment (2008):** 556,600 employed; 5.5% unemployed. **Per capita income (MSA):** $41,499; increase (2006-07): 4.0%.

Mayor: Tom Leppert, Republican

History: first settled 1841; platted 1846; inc. 1871; developed as the financial and commercial center of Southwest; headquarters of regional Federal Reserve Bank; major center for distribution and high-tech manufacturing. **Transportation:** 1 intl., 1 natl., 1 muni. airport, 1 charter/corp. airport, 2 airfields; Amtrak; transit system. **Communications:** 11 TV, 19 radio stations. **Medical facilities:** 33 hosp. **Educational facilities:** 12 univ. and colleges, 3 community college campuses; 225 pub. schools. **Further information:** Greater Dallas Chamber, Resource Center, 700 N. Pearl St., Ste. 1200, Dallas, TX 75201; www.dallaschamber.org; www.dallascityhall.com

Denver, Colorado

Population (2008): 598,707 (24); **Pop. density:** 3,903; **Pop. change (2000-08):** 8.1%. **Area:** 153.4 sq mi. **Employment (2008):** 306,900 employed; 5.5% unemployed. **Per capita income (MSA):** $46,682; increase (2006-07): 3.6%.

Mayor: John W. Hickenlooper, Democrat

History: settled 1858 by gold prospectors and miners; inc. 1861; became territorial capital 1867; growth spurred by gold and silver boom; became financial, industrial, cultural center of Rocky Mt. region. **Transportation:** 1 intl., 1 regional, 2 muni. airports; 5 rail freight lines, Amtrak; 1 bus line. **Communications:** 22 TV, 23 radio stations. **Medical facilities:** 15 hosp. **Educational facilities:** 15 four-yr. colleges and univ., 8 two-yr. and community colleges; 151 pub. schools. **Further information:** Denver Metro Chamber of Commerce, 1445 Market St., Denver, CO 80202-1729; www.denverchamber.org; www.denvergov.org

Detroit, Michigan

Population (2008): 912,062 (11); **Pop. density:** 6,571; **Pop. change (2000-08):** –4.1%. **Area:** 138.8 sq mi. **Employment (2008):** 303,186 employed; 16.0% unemployed. **Per capita income (MSA):** $39,009; increase (2006-07): 4.6%.

Mayor: Dave Bing, Democrat

History: founded by French 1701; controlled by British 1760; acquired by U.S. 1796; destroyed by fire 1805; fought over during War of 1812; inc. as city 1815; capital of state 1837-47; auto manufacturing began 1890.

Transportation: 1 intl., 1 muni. airport; 10 railroads (4 Class I); pub. transit system; major intl. port. **Communications:** 11 TV, 23 radio stations. **Medical facilities:** 14 hosp. **Educational facilities:** 2 univ., 3 colleges, 1 community college; 227 pub. schools. **Further information:** Detroit Regional Chamber, One Woodward Ave., Ste. 1900, PO Box 33840, Detroit, MI 48232-0840; www.detroitchamber.com, www.detroitmi.gov

Durham, North Carolina

Population (2008): 223,284 (85); **Pop. density:** 2,360; **Pop. change (2000-08):** 18.9%. **Area:** 94.6 sq mi. **Employment (2008):** 112,440 employed; 4.6% unemployed. **Per capita income (MSA):** $38,845; increase (2006-07): 5.2%.

Mayor: William V. Bell, Democrat

History: inc. 1869; Trinity College moved to Durham in 1892, renamed Duke Univ. in 1924.

Transportation: 1 intl. airport; 1 train station; 2 area bus systems. **Communications:** 5 TV, 8 radio stations. **Medical facilities:** 5 hosp. **Educational facilities:** 2 univ., 1 comm. coll., school of nursing; 52 pub. schools. **Further information:** Durham Convention and Visitors Bureau, 101 E. Morgan St., Durham, NC 2770-3333; www.durhamchamber.org; www.durham-nc.com; www.ci.durham.nc.us

El Paso, Texas

Population (2008): 613,190 (21); **Pop. density:** 2,462; **Pop. change (2000-08):** 8.7%. **Area:** 249.1 sq mi. **Employment (2008):** 240,180 employed; 5.9% unemployed. **Per capita income (MSA):** $26,585; increase (2006-07): 5.6%.

Mayor: John Cook, Non-Partisan

History: first settled 1598; inc. 1873; arrival of railroad 1881 boosted city's population and industries.

Transportation: 1 intl. airport, 1 airfield; 2 rail providers; 4 intl. ports of entry. **Communications:** 9 TV, 22 radio stations. **Medical facilities:** 16 hosp. **Educational facilities:** 5 univ., 2 colleges, 2 grad. and doctoral programs; 92 pub. schools. **Further information:** Greater El Paso Chamber of Commerce, 10 Civic Center Plz., El Paso, TX 79901; www.elpaso.org; www.elpasotexas.gov

Fort Wayne, Indiana

Population (2008): 251,591 (73); **Pop. density:** 3,185; **Pop. change (2000-08):** <0.05%. **Area:** 79.0 sq mi. **Employment (2008):** 119,826 employed; 6.4% unemployed. **Per capita income (MSA):** $33,173; increase (2006-07): 3.6%.

Mayor: Tom Henry, Democrat

History: French fort 1680; U.S. fort 1794; settled by 1832; inc. 1840 prior to Wabash-Erie canal completion 1843.

Transportation: 1 intl. airport, 1 airfield; 3 railroads; 6 bus lines. **Communications:** 11 newspapers; 6 TV, 26 radio stations. **Medical facilities:** 9 hosp. **Educational facilities:** 8 univ., 5 colleges, 3 bus. schools; 53 pub. schools. **Further information:** Chamber of Commerce, 826 Ewing St., Fort Wayne, IN 46802-2182; www.fwchamber.org; www.ci.ft-wayne.in.us

Fort Worth, Texas

Population (2008): 703,073 (17); **Pop. density:** 2,404; **Pop. change (2000-08):** 29.9%. **Area:** 292.5 sq mi. **Employment (2008):** 304,280 employed; 5.2% unemployed. **Per capita income (MSA):** $41,499; increase (2006-07): 4.0%.

Mayor: Mike J. Moncrief, Democrat

History: established as military post 1849; inc. 1873; oil discovered 1917.

Transportation: 2 intl., 2 muni., 1 industrial airport, 4 airfields; 4 major railroads, Amtrak; local bus service; 1 transcontinental, 1 intrastate bus line. **Communications:** 7 TV, 11 radio stations. **Medical facilities:** 15 hosp. **Educational facilities:** 5 univ. and colleges; 144 pub. schools. **Further information:** Chamber of Commerce, 777 Taylor St. #900, Fort Worth, TX 76102; www.fortworthchamber.com; www.fortworthgov.org;

Fresno, California

Population (2008): 476,050 (35); **Pop. density:** 4,560; **Pop. change (2000-08):** 10.8%. **Area:** 104.4 sq mi. **Employment (2008):** 206,560 employed; 9.9% unemployed. **Per capita income (MSA):** $28,181; increase (2006-07): 3.7%.

Mayor: Ashley Swearengin, Non-Partisan

History: founded 1872; inc. as city 1885.

Transportation: 1 intl., 1 corp./charter, 1 muni. airport; Amtrak; 1 bus line; intracity bus system. **Communications:** 16 TV, 26 radio stations. **Medical facilities:** 9 hosp. **Educational facilities:** 9 colleges; 88 pub. schools. **Further information:** Greater Fresno Area Chamber of Commerce, 2331 Fresno St., Fresno, CA 93721; www.fresnochamber.com; www.fresno.gov

Garland, Texas

Population (2008): 218,577 (90); **Pop. density:** 3,828; **Pop. change (2000-08):** 1.3%. **Area:** 57.1 sq mi. **Employment (2008):** 104,539 employed; 5.3% unemployed. **Per capita income (MSA):** $41,499; increase (2006-07): 4.0%.

Mayor: Ronald Jones, Non-Partisan

History: settled 1850s; inc. 1891.

Transportation: 30 min. from Dallas/Ft. Worth Intl. Airport; 2 railroads. **Communications:** 2 TV, 2 radio stations. **Medical facilities:** 2 hosp. **Educational facilities:** 3 univ., 2 community colleges; 67 pub. schools. **Further information:** Chamber of Commerce, 914 S. Garland Ave., Garland, TX 75040; www.garlandchamber.com; www.ci.garland.tx.us

Gilbert, Arizona

Population (2008): 216,449 (94); **Pop. density:** 5,034; **Pop. change (2000-08):** 88.7%. **Area:** 43.0 sq. mi. **Employment:** 113,486 employed; 2.7% unemployed. **Per capita income (MSA):** $35,185; increase (2006-07): 1.0%.

Mayor: John Lewis, Non-Partisan

History: est. 1891; inc. 1920.

Transportation: 1 intl., 1 muni. airport, 1 airfield nearby. **Communications:** 2 daily newspapers; 20 TV, 48 radio stations. **Medical facilities:** 5 hosp. **Educational facilities:** several colleges in immediate area; 42 public schools. **Further information:** Gilbert Chamber of Commerce, 119 North Gilbert Rd., Ste. 101, P.O. Box 527, Gilbert, AZ 85299-0527; www.gilbertaz.com; www.ci.gilbert.az.us

Glendale, Arizona

Population (2008): 251,522 (74); **Pop. density:** 4,516; **Pop. change (2000-08):** 14.5%. **Area:** 55.7 sq mi. **Employment (2008):** 138,266 employed; 5.0% unemployed. **Per capita income (MSA):** $35,185; increase (2006-07): 1.0%.

Mayor: Elaine M. Scruggs, Non-Partisan

History: est. 1892; inc. 1910.

Transportation: 1 muni. airport. **Communications:** 1 TV, 4 radio stations. **Medical facilities:** 4 hosp. **Educational facilities:** 12 institutes of higher education; 82 pub. schools. **Further information:** City of Glendale Marketing/Communications Department, 5850 W. Glendale Ave., Glendale, AZ 85301; www.glendaleazchamber.org; www.glendaleaz.com

Greensboro, North Carolina

Population (2008): 250,642 (75); **Pop. density:** 2,394; **Pop. change (2000-08):** 9.8%. **Area:** 104.7 sq mi. **Employment (2008):** 122,877 employed; 5.9% unemployed. **Per capita income (MSA):** $33,783; increase (2006-07): 3.6%.

Mayor: Yvonne J. Johnson, Democrat

History: settled 1749; site of Revolutionary War conflict 1781 between Generals Nathanael Greene and Cornwallis; inc. 1807, origin of civil rights sit-in movement.

Transportation: 1 intl. airport, 2 airfields; 2 railroads; Trailways/Greyhound bus service. **Communications:** 3 TV, 10 radio stations. **Medical facilities:** 2 hosp. **Educational facilities:** 3 univ., 4 colleges; 94 pub. schools. **Further information:** Chamber of Commerce, 342 N. Elm St., Greensboro, NC 27401; www.greensboro.org; www.greensboro-nc.gov

Henderson, Nevada

Population (2008): 252,064 (71); **Pop. density:** 3,163; **Pop. change (2000-08):** 43.8%. **Area:** 79.7 sq mi. **Employment (2008):** 137,906 employed; 5.1% unemployed. **Per capita income (MSA):** $39,188; increase (2006-07): 2.3%.

Mayor: Andy A. Hafen, Democrat

History: early growth spurred by World War II magnesium mining; inc. 1953.

Transportation: Henderson Executive Airport; Citizens Area Transit (CAT) public transportation. **Communications:** 2 TV, 8 radio stations. **Medical facilities:** 3 hosp. **Educational facilities:** 5 coll., 2 vocational schools; 29 elem., 9 middle, 9 high schools. **Further information:** City of Henderson Public Information Office, 240 Water St., Henderson, NV 89015; www.hendersonchamber.com; www.cityofhenderson.com

Hialeah, Florida

Population (2008): 210,542 (95); **Pop. density:** 10,966; **Pop. change (2000-08):** –7.0%. **Area:** 19.2 sq mi. **Employment (2008):** 90,316 employed; 8.0% unemployed. **Per capita income (MSA):** $43,123; increase (2006-07): 4.7%.

Mayor: Julio Robaina, Republican

History: founded 1917, inc. 1925; industrial and residential city NW of Miami; Hialeah Park Horse Racing Track.

Transportation: 5 mi from Miami Intl. Airport; Amtrak; 2 rail freight lines; Metrorail, Metrobus systems; access to Port of Miami. **Communications:** 2 radio stations. **Medical facilities:** 3 hosp. **Educational facilities:** 8 univ. and colleges; 25 pub., 39 private schools. **Further information:** Hialeah-Dade Development, Inc., 501 Palm Ave., Hialeah, FL 33010; www.hialeahchamber.org; www.hialeahfl.gov

Honolulu, Hawaii

Population (2008): 374,676 (49); **Pop. density:** 4,372; **Pop. change (2000-08):** 0.8%. **Area:** 85.7 sq mi. **Employment (2008):** 438,069 employed; 3.5% unemployed (CDP). **Per capita income (MSA):** $42,015; increase (2006-07): 6.2%.

Mayor: Mufi Hannemann, Non-Partisan

History: harbor entered by Europeans 1778; declared capital of kingdom by King Kamehameha III 1850; Pearl Harbor naval base attacked by Japanese Dec. 7, 1941.

Transportation: 1 intl. airport; 2 commercial harbors. **Communications:** 14 TV, 39 radio stations. **Medical facilities:** 6 hosp. **Educational facilities:** 7 univ., 2 community colleges; 60 pub. schools. **Further information:** Hawaii Visitors and Convention Bureau, 2270 Kalakaua Ave., Ste. 801, Honolulu, HI 96815; www.gohawaii.com; www.visit-oahu.com; www.honolulu.gov

Houston, Texas

Population (2008): 2,242,193 (4); **Pop. density:** 3,870; **Pop. change (2000-08):** 13.6%. **Area:** 579.4 sq mi. **Employment (2008):** 1,003,849 employed; 4.7% unemployed. **Per capita income (MSA):** $46,471; increase (2006-07): 6.8%.

Mayor: Bill White, Democrat

History: founded 1836; inc. 1837; capital of Repub. of Texas 1837-39; developed rapidly after construction of channel to Gulf of Mexico 1914; world center of oil and natural gas technology.

Transportation: 1 intl., 1 natl., 1 regional, 4 muni., 2 corp./ charter airports, 6 airfields; 4 mainline railroads; major bus and rail transit system; major intl. port. **Communications:** 17 TV, 70 radio stations. **Medical facilities:** 111 hosp. **Educational facilities:** 11 univ., 10 comm. colleges, 6 med. schools, 27 spec. schools; 293 pub. schools. **Further information:** Greater Houston Partnership, 1200 Smith St., Ste. 700, Houston, TX 77002-4400; www.houston.org; www.houstontx.gov

Indianapolis, Indiana

Population (2008): 798,382 (14); **Pop. density:** 2,209; **Pop. change (2000-08):** 2.1%. **Area:** 361.5 sq mi. **Employment (2008):** 397,581 employed; 5.6% unemployed (city balance). **Per capita income (MSA):** $38,455; increase (2006-07): 3.0%.

Mayor: Gregory A. Ballard, Republican

History: settled 1820; became capital 1825.

Transportation: 1 intl., 4 muni., 1 corp./charter airport, 2 airfields; 5 railroads; 3 interstate bus lines. **Communications:** 14 TV, 21 radio stations. **Medical facilities:** 17 hosp. **Educational facilities:** 8 univ. and colleges; 80 pub. schools. **Further information:** Greater Indianapolis Chamber of Commerce, 111 Monument Cir., Ste. 1950, Indianapolis, IN 46204; www.indy chamber.com; www.indygov.org

Irvine, California

Population (2008): 207,500 (98); **Pop. density:** 4,491; **Pop. change (2000-08):** 44.0%. **Area:** 46.2 sq mi. **Employment (MSA; 2008):** 82,516 employed; 3.9% unemployed. **Per capita income (MSA; 2007):** $42,278; increase (2006-07): 4.3%.

Mayor: Sukhee Kang, Non-Partisan

History: Univ. of Calif., Irvine campus announced, 1959; planned city developed around campus, 1960s; inc. 1971.

Transportation: 1 regional airport; Amtrak; 1 intercounty bus line. **Communications:** 2 daily, 1 weekly newspapers; 28 TV, 74 radio stations.. **Medical facilities:** 1 hosp. **Educational facilities:** 3 univ. and 1 college; 57 pub. schools. **Further information:** Irvine Chamber of Commerce, 2485 McCabe Way, Ste. 150, Irvine, California 92614; www.irvine cvb.org; www.irvinechamber.com; www.cityofirvine.org

Jacksonville, Florida

Population (2008): 807,815 (13); **Pop. density:** 1,066; **Pop. change (2000-08):** 9.8%. **Area:** 757.7 sq mi. **Employment (2008):** 395,226 employed; 6.0% unemployed. **Per capita income (MSA):** $39,191; increase (2006-07): 3.0%.

Mayor: John Peyton, Republican

History: settled 1816 as Cowford; renamed after Andrew Jackson 1822; inc. 1832; rechartered 1851; scene of conflicts in Seminole and Civil wars.

Transportation: 1 intl., 3 muni. airports; 3 railroads; 2 interstate bus lines; 2 seaports. **Communications:** 15 TV, 22 radio stations. **Medical facilities:** 9 hosp. **Educational facilities:** 7 univ., 5 colleges, 1 community college; 278 pub. schools, 114 private schools. **Further information:** Chamber of Commerce, 3 Independent Dr., Jacksonville, FL 32202; www.myjaxchamber. com; www.expandinjax.com; www.coj.net

Jersey City, New Jersey

Population (2008): 241,114 (78); **Pop. density:** 16,182; **Pop. change (2000-08):** 0.4%. **Area:** 14.9 sq mi. **Employment (2008):** 107,680 employed; 6.7% unemployed. **Per capita income (MSA):** $52,855; increase (2006-07): 6.5%.

Mayor: Jerramiah Healy, Democrat

History: site bought from Indians 1630; chartered as town by British 1668; scene of Revolutionary War conflict 1779; chartered under present name 1838; important station on Underground Railroad.

Transportation: intercity bus and subway system; ferry service to Manhattan. **Communications:** 3 radio stations. **Medical facilities:** 3 hosp. **Educational facilities:** 1 univ., 2 colleges; 38 pub. schools. **Further information:** Hudson County Chamber of Commerce, 660 Newark Ave., Ste. 220, Jersey City, NJ 07306; www.cityofjerseycity.com

Kansas City, Missouri

Population (2008): 451,572 (39); **Pop. density:** 1,440; **Pop. change (2000-08):** 2.3%. **Area:** 313.5 sq mi. **Employment (2008):** 216,991 employed; 7.6% unemployed. **Per capita income (MSA):** $39,222; increase (2006-07): 4.4%.

Mayor: Mark Funkhouser, Democrat

History: settled by 1838 at confluence of the Missouri and Kansas rivers; inc. 1850.

Transportation: 1 intl., 1 muni. airport; a major rail center; more than 300 motor freight carriers; 7 barge lines. **Communications:** 11 TV, 17 radio stations. **Medical facilities:** 17 hosp. **Educational facilities:** 22 univ. and colleges. **Further information:** Greater Kansas City Chamber of Commerce, 911 Main St., Ste. 2600, Kansas City, MO 64105; www.kcchamber.com; www.kcmo.org

Laredo, Texas

Population (2008): 221,659 (86); **Pop. density:** 2,824; **Pop. change (2000-08):** 24.6%. **Area:** 78.5 sq mi. **Employment (2008):** 82,990 employed; 5.2% unemployed. **Per capita income (MSA):** $21,423; increase (2006-07): 5.7%.

Mayor: Raul G. Salinas, Non-Partisan

History: founded by Spanish colonists in 1755; part of U.S. from 1848; fast growth fueled by immigration; became principal port of entry into Mexico.

Transportation: 1 intl. airport; 2 railroads; 3 interstate bus lines, 2 local bus lines. **Communications:** 8 TV, 9 radio stations. **Medical facilities:** 4 hosp. **Educational facilities:** 1 univ., 1 community college, 7 vocational training centers; 62 public schools, 29 private schools. **Further information:** Laredo Chamber of Commerce, P.O. Box 790, Laredo, TX 78042; www.laredochamber.com; www.cityoflaredo.com

Las Vegas, Nevada

Population (2008): 558,383 (28); **Pop. density:** 4,928; **Pop. change (2000-08):** 16.3%. **Area:** 113.3 sq mi. **Employment (2008):** 272,182 employed; 6.7% unemployed. **Per capita income (MSA):** $39,188; increase (2006-07): 2.3%.

Mayor: Oscar B. Goodman, Democrat

History: occupied by Mormons 1855-57; bought by railroad 1903; city of Las Vegas inc. 1911; gambling legalized 1931.

Transportation: 1 intl., 1 muni. airport; 1 railroad; monorail; bus system. **Communications:** 19 TV, 27 radio stations. **Medical facilities:** 21 hosp. **Educational facilities:** 1 univ., 2 state colleges; 277 pub. schools in area. **Further information:** Las Vegas Chamber of Commerce, 3720 Howard Hughes Pkwy., Las Vegas, NV 89169-0916; www.lvchamber.com; www.lasvegasnevada.gov

Lexington, Kentucky

Population (2008): 282,114 (65); **Pop. density:** 992; **Pop. change (2000-08):** 8.3%. **Area:** 284.5 sq mi. **Employment (2008):** 144,068 employed; 4.8% unemployed (county). **Per capita income (MSA):** $37,253; increase (2006-07): 4.8%.

Mayor: Jim Newberry, Democrat

History: site was founded and named in 1775 by hunters after the site of the opening battle of the Revolutionary War at Lexington, Mass.; settled 1779; chartered 1782; inc. as a city 1832.

Transportation: 1 regional airport; 2 railroads; city buses. **Communications:** 5 TV, 9 radio stations. **Medical facilities:** 13 hosp. **Educational facilities:** 2 univ., 4 colleges; 53 public schools: 35 elem., 10 middle, 6 high, 2 technology schools. **Further information:** Commerce Lexington, 330 E. Main St., Lexington, KY 40507; www.commercelexington.com; www.lexingtonky.com

Lincoln, Nebraska

Population (2008): 251,624 (72); **Pop. density:** 3,373; **Pop. change (2000-08):** 11.0%. **Area:** 74.6 sq mi. **Employment (2008):** 140,333 employed; 3.0% unemployed. **Per capita income (MSA):** $35,254; increase (2006-07): 4.6%.

Mayor: Chris Beutler, Democrat

History: originally called Lancaster; chosen state capital 1867, renamed after Abraham Lincoln; inc. 1869.

Transportation: 1 regional airport; Amtrak, 2 railroads; Greyhound. **Communications:** 6 TV, 14 radio stations. **Medical facilities:** 8 hosp. **Educational facilities:** 3 univ., 3 voc.-tech./business colleges; 55 pub., 30 private schools, 3 focus programs. **Further information:** Chamber of Commerce, PO Box 83006, Lincoln, NE 68501-3006; www.lcoc.com; www.lincoln.org; www.lincoln.ne.gov

Long Beach, California

Population (2008): 463,789 (37); **Pop. density:** 9,202; **Pop. change (2000-08):** 0.5%. **Area:** 50.4 sq mi. **Employment (2008):** 220,257 employed; 8.3% unemployed. **Per capita income (MSA):** $42,278; increase (2006-07): 4.3%.

Mayor: Bob Foster, Democrat

History: settled as early as 1784 by Spanish; by 1884 present site developed on harbor; inc. 1888; oil discovered 1921.

Transportation: 1 natl. airport; 3 railroads; 4 bus co. with 40 bus lines, light rail services; major intl. port. **Communications:** 1 TV, 3 radio stations. **Medical facilities:** 7 hosp. **Educational facilities:** 1 univ., 1 community college (2 campuses); 87 pub. schools in district. **Further information:** Long Beach City Hall, 333 W. Ocean Blvd., Long Beach, CA 90802; www.lbchamber.com; www.longbeach.gov

Los Angeles, California

Population (2008): 3,833,995 (2); **Pop. density:** 8,173; **Pop. change (2000-08):** 3.8%. **Area:** 469.1 sq mi. **Employment (2008):** 1,777,775 employed; 8.3% unemployed. **Per capita income (MSA):** $42,278; increase (2006-07): 4.3%.

Mayor: Antonio Villaraigosa, Democrat

History: founded by Spanish 1781; captured by U.S. 1846; inc. 1850; grew rapidly after coming of railroads, 1876 and 1885; Hollywood a district of L.A.

Transportation: 1 intl., 1 muni. airport; 3 railroads; major freeway system; intracity bus and rail system. **Communications:** 20 TV, 32 radio stations. **Medical facilities:** 30 hosp. **Educational facilities:** 158 univ. and colleges (incl. junior, community, and other); 1,858 pub. schools, 1,120 private schools. **Further information:** Los Angeles Area Chamber of Commerce, 350 S. Bixel St., Los Angeles, CA 90017; www.lachamber.org; www.ci.la.ca.us

Louisville, Kentucky

Population (2008): 557,224 (30); **Pop. density:** 8,973; **Pop. change (2000-08):** 1.1%. **Area:** 62.1 sq mi. **Employment (2008):** 335,398 employed; 6.4% unemployed (metro-gov. area balance). **Per capita income (MSA):** $37,473; increase (2006-07): 4.5%.

Mayor: Jerry E. Abramson, Democrat

History: settled 1778; named for Louis XVI of France; inc. 1828; base for Union forces in Civil War.

Transportation: 1 intl., 1 regional airport; 1 terminal, 4 trunk-line railroads; metro bus line; Greyhound station; 5 barge lines. **Communications:** 9 TV, 19 radio stations. **Medical facilities:** 16 hosp. **Educational facilities:** 10 univ. and colleges, 32 business and vocational schools. **Further information:** Greater Louisville, Inc. Metro Chamber of Commerce, 614 W. Main St., Ste. 6000, Louisville, KY 40202; www.greaterlouisville.com; www.gotolouisville.com; www.louisvilleky.gov

Lubbock, Texas

Population (2008): 220,483 (87); **Pop. density:** 1,921; **Pop. change (2000-08):** 10.4%. **Area:** 114.8 sq mi. **Employment (2008):** 111,614 employed; 3.7% unemployed. **Per capita income (MSA):** $30,234; increase (2006-07): 4.4%.

Mayor: Tom Martin, Republican

History: settled 1879; laid out 1891; inc. 1909 through merger of two towns.

Transportation: 1 intl. airport, 1 airfield; 2 railroads; bus line. **Communications:** 16 TV, 18 radio stations. **Medical facilities:** 7 hosp. **Educational facilities:** 3 univ., 1 junior college; 51 pub. schools. **Further information:** Chamber of Commerce, 1301 Broadway, Ste. 101, Lubbock, TX 79401; www.lubbockchamber.com; www.ci.lubbock.tx.us

Madison, Wisconsin

Population (2008): 231,916 (81); **Pop. density:** 3,376; **Pop. change (2000-08):** 10.7%. **Area:** 68.7 sq mi. **Employment (2008):** 138,337 employed; 3.2% unemployed. **Per capita income (MSA):** $42,557; increase (2006-07): 4.6%.

Mayor: Dave Cieslewicz, Democrat

History: settled 1832; selected as site for state capital, named after James Madison, 1836; chartered 1856.

Transportation: 1 natl. airport, 1 airfield; 3 freight rail lines; 1 intracity, 3 intercity bus systems. **Communications:** 6 TV, 15 radio stations. **Medical facilities:** 5 hosp. **Educational facilities:** 7 colleges and univ., including main branch of Univ. of Wisconsin; 30 elem., 11 middle, 5 high schools. **Further information:** Greater Madison Chamber of Commerce, PO Box 71, Madison, WI 53701-0071; www.greatermadisonchamber.com; www.ci.madison.wi.us

Memphis, Tennessee

Population (2008): 669,651 (19); **Pop. density:** 2,398; **Pop. change (2000-08):** –3.0%. **Area:** 279.3 sq mi. **Employment (2008):** 289,772 employed; 7.5% unemployed. **Per capita income (MSA):** $37,147; increase (2006-07): 4.5%.

Mayor: Myron Lowery, Democrat

History: French, Spanish, and U.S. forts by 1797; settled by 1819; inc. as town 1826, as city 1840; surrendered charter to state 1879 after yellow fever epidemics; rechartered as city 1893.

Transportation: 1 intl. airport; 5 railroads; 1 bus system. **Communications:** 9 TV, 20 radio stations. **Medical facilities:** 15 hosp. **Educational facilities:** 17 univ. and colleges; 191 public schools. **Further information:** Memphis Regional Chamber, 22 N. Front St., 2nd Floor, Memphis, TN 38101; www.memphischamber.com; www.ci.memphis.tn.us

Mesa, Arizona

Population (2008): 463,552 (38); **Pop. density:** 3,708; **Pop. change (2000-08):** 16.4%. **Area:** 125.0 sq mi. **Employment (2008):** 247,707 employed; 4.4% unemployed. **Per capita income (MSA):** $35,185; increase (2006-07): 1.0%.

Mayor: Scott Smith, Republican

History: founded by Mormons 1878; inc. 1883; population boomed fivefold 1960-80.

Transportation: 1 muni. airport, 1 airfield; metro bus service. **Communications:** 3 TV, 4 radio stations. **Medical facilities:** 7 hosp. **Educational facilities:** 5 univ., 7 colleges; 82 pub. schools. **Further information:** Convention and Visitor's Bureau and Mesa Chamber of Commerce, 120 N. Center, Mesa, AZ 85201; www.visitmesa.com; www.mesachamber.org; www.mesaaz.gov

Miami, Florida

Population (2008): 413,201 (43); **Pop. density:** 11,574; **Pop. change (2000-08):** 14.0%. **Area:** 35.7 sq mi. **Employment (2008):** 172,126 employed; 6.2% unemployed. **Per capita income (MSA):** $43,123; increase (2006-07): 4.7%.

Mayor: Manuel A. Diaz, Independent

History: site of fort 1836; settlement began 1870; inc. 1896, modern city developed into financial and recreation center; land speculation in 1920s added to city's growth, as did Cuban, Central and South American, and Haitian immigration since 1960.

Transportation: 1 intl., 1 regional, 1 corp. airport, 2 airfields, 1 seaplane base; Amtrak, transit rail system; 2 bus lines; 65 truck lines; seaport. **Communications:** 23 TV, 21 radio stations. **Medical facilities:** 19 hosp. **Educational facilities:** 6 univ. and colleges. **Further information:** Greater Miami Chamber of Commerce, Omni Intl. Complex, 1601 Biscayne Blvd., Miami, FL 33132; www.greatermiami.com; www.miami gov.com

Milwaukee, Wisconsin

Population (2008): 604,477 (23); **Pop. density:** 6,290; **Pop. change (2000-08):** 1.3%. **Area:** 96.1 sq mi. **Employment (2008):** 258,655 employed; 6.6% unemployed. **Per capita income (MSA):** $41,774; increase (2006-07): 5.2%.

Mayor: Tom Barrett, Democrat

History: Indian trading post by 1674; settlement began 1835; inc. as city 1848; famous beer industry.

Transportation: 1 intl. airport, 1 airfield; 3 railroads; 4 bus lines; major port. **Communications:** 14 TV, 19 radio stations. **Medical facilities:** 17 hosp. **Educational facilities:** 7 univ. and colleges, 182 pub. schools. **Further information:** Visit Milwaukee, 648 N. Plankinton Ave., Ste. 425, Milwaukee, WI 53203-2917; www.visitmilwaukee.org; www.city.milwaukee.gov

Minneapolis, Minnesota

Population (2008): 382,605 (47); **Pop. density:** 6,969; **Pop. change (2000-08):** <0.05%. **Area:** 54.9 sq mi. **Employment (2008):** 204,704 employed; 5.1% unemployed. **Per capita income (MSA):** $46,752; increase (2006-07): 5.5%.

Mayor: R. T. Rybak, Democrat

History: site visited by Hennepin 1680; included in area of military reservations 1819; inc. 1867.

Transportation: 1 intl., 2 regional, 1 muni. airports, 1 airfield; 5 railroads. **Communications:** 10 TV, 17 radio stations. **Medical facilities:** 7 hosp. **Educational facilities:** 10 univ. and colleges; 121 pub., 28 private schools. **Further information:** City of Minneapolis Office of Pub. Affairs, 301M City Hall, 350 S. Fifth St., Minneapolis, MN 55415; www.minneapolischamber.org; www.minneapolis.mn.us

Nashville, Tennessee

Population (2008): 596,462 (26); **Pop. density:** 1,260; **Pop. change (2000-08):** 9.3%. **Area:** 473.3 sq mi. **Employment (2008):** 307,290 employed; 5.2% unemployed (metro-gov. balance). **Per capita income (MSA):** $38,851; increase (2006-07): 3.4%.

Mayor: Karl Dean, Democrat

History: settled 1779; first chartered 1806; became permanent state capital 1843; home of Grand Ole Opry.

Transportation: 1 intl. airport, 2 airfields; 1 railroad; bus line; transit system of buses and trolleys. **Communications:** 15 TV, 18 radio stations. **Medical facilities:** 14 hosp. **Educational facilities:** 17 universities and colleges; 130 pub. schools. **Further information:** Chamber of Commerce, 211 Commerce St., Ste 100, Nashville, TN 37201; www.nashvillechamber.com; www.nashville.gov

Newark, New Jersey

Population (2008): 278,980 (68); **Pop. density:** 11,722; **Pop. change (2000-08):** 2.4%. **Area:** 23.8 sq mi. **Employment (2008):** 97,328 employed; 9.6% unemployed. **Per capita income (MSA):** $52,855; increase (2006-07): 6.5%.

Mayor: Cory Booker, Democrat

History: settled by Puritans 1666; used as supply base by Washington 1776; inc. as town 1833, as city 1836.

Transportation: 1 intl. airport; 4 railroads; bus system; subways; 1 intl. seaport. **Communications:** 1 daily, 8 weekly newspapers; 3 TV, 5 radio stations. **Medical facilities:** 6 hosp.

Educational facilities: 5 univ. and colleges; 58 elem., 13 junior and senior high schools, 10 special schools, 2 vocational schools, 40 private schools. **Further information:** Newark Public Information Office, City of Newark, 920 Broad St. #214, Newark, NJ 07102; www.rbp.org; www.ci.newark.nj.us

New Orleans, Louisiana

Population (2008): 311,853 (59); **Pop. density:** 1,727; **Pop. change (2000-08):** −35.7%. **Area:** 180.6 sq mi. **Employment (2008):** 105,559 employed; 6.1% unemployed. **Per capita income (MSA):** $44,295; increase (2006-07): 4.5%.

Mayor: C. Ray Nagin, Democrat

History: founded by French 1718; became major seaport on Mississippi R.; acquired by U.S. as part of Louisiana Purchase 1803; inc. as city 1805; Americans defeated British forces at the Battle of New Orleans in 1815.

Transportation: 1 intl., 1 regional airport; major railroad center; street car and bus lines. **Communications:** 15 TV, 43 radio stations. **Medical facilities:** 13 hosp. **Educational facilities:** 6 univ. and 4 colleges. **Further information:** New Orleans Metropolitan Convention & Visitors Bureau, Inc., 2020 St. Charles Ave., New Orleans, LA 70130; www.neworleans chamber.org; www.neworleanscvb.com; www.cityofno.com

New York, New York

Population (2008): 8,363,710 (1); **Pop. density:** 27,576; **Pop. change (2000-08):** 4.4%. **Area:** 303.3 sq mi. **Employment (2008):** 3,730,777 employed; 5.5% unemployed. **Per capita income (MSA):** $52,855; increase (2006-07): 6.5%.

Mayor: Michael R. Bloomberg, Independent

History: trading post established 1624; British took control from Dutch 1664 and named city New York; briefly U.S. capital; Washington inaugurated as president 1789; under new charter, 1898, city expanded to include 5 boroughs: The Bronx, Brooklyn, Queens, and Staten Island, as well as Manhattan; Sept. 11, 2001, terrorist attack destroyed World Trade Center, killed more than 2,600.

Transportation: 3 intl. airports serve area; 2 seaplane bases; 2 rail terminals; major subway network that includes 26 routes; 244 bus routes; ferry system; 4 underwater tunnels. **Communications:** 13 TV, 38 radio stations. **Medical facilities:** 70 hosp.; 6 academic medical centers. **Educational facilities:** 54 univ. and colleges; 1,198 pub. schools. **Further information:** Convention and Visitors Bureau, 810 Seventh Ave., New York, NY 10019; www.manhattancc.org; www.nyc visit.com; www.nyc.gov

Norfolk, Virginia

Population (2008): 234,220 (80); **Pop. density:** 4,362; **Pop. change (2000-08):** −0.1%. **Area:** 53.7 sq mi. **Employment (2008):** 96,041 employed; 5.3% unemployed. **Per capita income (MSA):** $36,837; increase (2006-07): 4.6%.

Mayor: Paul D. Fraim, Non-Partisan

History: founded 1682; burned by patriots to prevent capture by British during Revolutionary War; rebuilt and inc. as town 1805, as city 1845; site of world's largest naval base; major east coast commercial port and cruise terminal.

Transportation: 1 intl., 1 charter/corp. airport, 1 airfield; 2 railroads; Amtrak; bus system; free downtown shuttle. **Communications:** 5 TV, 15 radio stations. **Medical facilities:** 8 hosp. **Educational facilities:** 2 univ., 2 colleges, 1 medical school; 59 pub. schools. **Further information:** Norfolk Convention and Visitors Bureau, 232 E. Main St., Norfolk, VA 23510; www.norfolkcvb.com; www.norfolk.gov

North Las Vegas, Nevada

Population (2008): 217,253 (92); **Pop. density:** 2,768; **Pop. change (2000-08):** 88.0%. **Area:** 78.5 sq mi. **Employment (2008):** 91,342 employed; 7.3% unemployed. **Per capita income (MSA):** $39,188; increase (2006-07): 2.3%.

Mayor: Shari L. Buck, Non-Partisan

History: inc. 1946.

Transportation: 1 regional airport, near 1 intl. airport. **Communications:** 15 TV, 45 radio stations. **Medical facilities:** 1 hosp. **Educational facilities:** 39 pub. schools. **Further information:** North Las Vegas Chamber of Commerce, 3345 W. Craig Rd., Ste. B, North Las Vegas, NV 89032; www.northlas vegaschamber.com; www.cityofnorthlasvegas.com

Oakland, California

Population (2008): 404,155 (44); **Pop. density:** 7,204; **Pop. change (2000-08):** 1.2%. **Area:** 56.1 sq mi. **Employment (2008):** 181,166 employed; 9.5% unemployed. **Per capita income (MSA):** $60,983; increase (2006-07): 5.4%.

Mayor: Ron Dellums, Democrat

History: area settled by Spanish 1820; inc. as city under present name 1854.

Transportation: 1 intl. airport; western terminus for 2 railroads; underground, 75-mi underwater subway. **Communications:** 1 TV, 3 radio stations. **Medical facilities:** 4 hosp. **Educational facilities:** 12 East Bay colleges and univ.; 81 pub. schools. **Further information:** Oakland Metropolitan Chamber of Commerce, 475 14th St., Oakland, CA 94612-1903; www.oaklandchamber.com; www.oaklandnet.com

Oklahoma City, Oklahoma

Population (2008): 551,789 (31); **Pop. density:** 909; **Pop. change (2000-08):** 9.0%. **Area:** 607.0 sq mi. **Employment (2008):** 245,820 employed; 3.8% unemployed. **Per capita income (MSA):** $38,834; increase (2006-07): 6.8%.

Mayor: Mick Cornett, Republican

History: settled during land rush in Midwest 1889; inc. 1890; became capital 1910; oil discovered 1928. Bomb in 1995 destroyed federal office bldg., killed 168 people.

Transportation: 1 intl., 1 regional airport, 2 airfields; 2 railroad; pub. transit system; 1 major bus line. **Communications:** 18 TV, 17 radio stations. **Medical facilities:** 23 hosp. **Educational facilities:** 20 univ. and colleges; 83 pub., 37 private schools. **Further information:** Chamber of Commerce, Economic Development Division, 123 Park Ave., Oklahoma City, OK 73102; www.okccvb.org; www.greateroklahomacity.com; www.okc.gov

Omaha, Nebraska

Population (2008): 438,646 (40); **Pop. density:** 3,791; **Pop. change (2000-08):** 9.7%. **Area:** 115.7 sq mi. **Employment (2008):** 224,504 employed; 3.6% unemployed. **Per capita income (MSA):** $41,655; increase (2006-07): 5.1%.

Mayor: Jim Suttle, Democrat

History: founded 1854; inc. 1857; large food-processing, telecommunications, information-processing center.

Transportation: 1 natl. airport, 1 airfield; 3 major railroads; intercity bus line. **Communications:** 10 TV, 17 radio stations. **Medical facilities:** 12 hosp. **Educational facilities:** 5 univ., 6 colleges; 243 pub., 78 private schools. **Further information:** Greater Omaha Chamber of Commerce, 1301 Harney St., Omaha, NE 68102; www.omahachamber.org; www.ci.omaha.ne.us

Orlando, Florida

Population (2008): 230,519 (82); **Pop. density:** 2,465; **Pop. change (2000-08):** 19.7%. **Area:** 93.5 sq mi. **Employment (2008):** 127,064 employed; 5.6% unemployed. **Per capita income (MSA):** $34,528; increase (2006-07): 2.6%.

Mayor: Buddy Dyer, Democrat

History: Fort Gatlin built just south of present-day Orlando in 1838; name changed from Jernigan to Orlando, 1856; inc. 1875; Walt Disney World opened in 1971.

Transportation: 2 intl., 1 regional, 1 corp./charter airport; 2 bus lines. **Communications:** 18 TV, 11 radio stations. **Medical facilities:** 3 hosp. **Educational facilities:** 3 colleges and univ.; 153 public schools, 4 tech schools. **Further Information:** Orlando/Orange County Convention and Visitors Bureau, 6700 Forum Dr., Ste. 100, Orlando, FL 32821-8087; www.orlando.org; www.orlandoinfo.com; www.ci.orlando.fl.us

Philadelphia, Pennsylvania

Population (2008): 1,447,395 (6); **Pop. density:** 10,714; **Pop. change (2000-08):** −4.6%. **Area:** 135.1 sq mi. **Employment (2008):** 582,321 employed; 7.2% unemployed. **Per capita income (MSA):** $45,499; increase (2006-07): 5.1%.

Mayor: Michael A. Nutter, Democrat

History: first settled by Swedes 1638; Swedes surrendered to Dutch 1654; settled by English and Scottish Quakers 1678; named Philadelphia 1682; chartered 1701; Continental Congresses convened 1774, 1775; Declaration of Independence signed here 1776; national capital 1790-1800; state capital 1683-1799.

Transportation: 1 intl., 2 muni. airports; 3 railroads;; subway, El, rail commuter, bus, and streetcar system major freshwater ports. **Communications:** 4 major daily newspapers; 12 TV, 42 radio stations. **Medical facilities:** 39 hosp. **Educational facilities:** 29 univ. and colleges. **Further information:** Greater Philadelphia Chamber of Commerce, Business Information Center, 200 S. Broad St., Ste. 700, Philadelphia PA 19102; www.philachamber.com; www.phila.gov

Phoenix, Arizona

Population (2008): 1,567,924 (5); **Pop. density:** 3,302; **Pop. change (2000-08):** 18.6%. **Area:** 474.9 sq mi. **Employment (2008):** 815,225 employed; 5.7% unemployed. **Per capita income (MSA):** $35,185; increase (2006-07): 1.0%.

Mayor: Phil Gordon, Democrat

History: founded 1867; inc. as city 1881; became territorial capital 1889.

Transportation: 1 intl., 2 muni. airports; 2 transcontinental and 10 intrastate railroads; transcontinental bus line; pub. transit system. **Communications:** 22 TV, 22 radio stations. **Medical facilities:** 24 hosp. **Educational facilities:** 36 institutions of higher learning; 380 pub. schools: 247 elem. and junior, 35 senior high, 98 charter schools. **Further information:** Greater Phoenix Chamber of Commerce, 201 N. Central Ave., 27th Fl., Phoenix, AZ 85004; www.phoenixchamber.com; www.phoenix.gov

Pittsburgh, Pennsylvania

Population (2008): 310,037 (60); **Pop. density:** 5,576; **Pop. change (2000-08):** −7.3%. **Area:** 55.6 sq mi. **Employment (2008):** 145,224 employed; 5.2% unemployed. **Per capita income (MSA):** $41,206; increase (2006-07): 6.2%.

Mayor: Luke Ravenstahl, Democrat

History: settled around Ft. Pitt 1758; inc. as city 1816; became an inland port; by Civil War, already a center for iron production.

Transportation: 1 intl., 1 regional airport, 1 airfield; 20 railroads; trolley/subway system; 2 bus lines. **Communications:** 12 TV, 22 radio stations. **Medical facilities:** 18 hosp. **Educational facilities:** 3 univ., 6 colleges; 93 pub. schools. **Further information:** Greater Pittsburgh Convention & Visitors Bureau, Regional Enterprise Tower, 30th Floor, 425 Sixth Ave., Pittsburgh, PA 15219; Pittsburgh Regional Alliance, Regional Enterprise Tower, Ste. 1100, 425 Sixth Ave., Pittsburgh, PA 15219; www.visitpittsburgh.com; www.alleghenyconference.org/chamber; www.pghgov.com

Plano, Texas

Population (2008): 267,480 (70); **Pop. density:** 3,736; **Pop. change (2000-08):** 20.3%. **Area:** 71.6 sq mi. **Employment (2008):** 138,608 employed; 4.5% unemployed. **Per capita income (MSA):** $41,499; increase (2006-07): 4.0%.

Mayor: Phil Dyer, Non-Partisan

History: settled 1846; inc. as city 1873.

Transportation: DART bus line and 2 DART light rail stations. **Communications:** 1 TV, 2 radio stations. **Medical facilities:** 7 hosp. **Educational facilities:** 5 institutions of higher learning, 68 pub. schools. **Further information:** City of Plano Public Information Dept. 1520 K Ave., Ste. 320, Plano, TX 75074; Plano Chamber of Commerce, 1200 E. 15th St., Plano, TX 75074; www.planochamber.org; www.plano.gov

Portland, Oregon

Population (2008): 557,706 (29); **Pop. density:** 4,153; **Pop. change (2000-08):** 5.4%. **Area:** 134.3 sq mi. **Employment (2008):** 289,318 employed; 5.7% unemployed. **Per capita income (MSA):** $38,842; increase (2006-07): 4.5%.

Mayor: Sam Adams, Democrat

History: settled by pioneers 1845; developed as trading center, aided by California Gold Rush 1849; city chartered 1851.

Transportation: 1 intl. airport; 2 major rail freight lines, Amtrak; mass transit bus, light rail, and street car system; marine port. **Communications:** 11 TV, 25 radio stations. **Medical facilities:** 8 hosp. **Educational facilities:** 25 univ. and colleges, 1 community college. **Further information:** Portland Business Alliance, 200 SW Market St., Ste. 1770, Portland, OR 97201; www.portlandalliance.com; www.portlandonline.com

Raleigh, North Carolina

Population (2008): 392,552 (45); **Pop. density:** 3,425; **Pop. change (2000-08):** 36.1%. **Area:** 114.6 sq mi. **Employment (2008):** 198,398 employed; 4.4% unemployed. **Per capita income (MSA):** $39,373; increase (2006-07): 4.7%.

Mayor: Charles Meeker, Democrat

History: named after Sir Walter Raleigh; site chosen for capital 1788; laid out 1792; inc. 1795; occupied by Gen. Sherman 1865.

Transportation: 1 intl. airport, 1 airfield; 3 railroads; 2 bus lines. **Communications:** 8 TV, 13 radio stations. **Medical facilities:** 7 hosp. **Educational facilities:** 6 univ. and colleges, 1 community college; 140 pub. schools (county). **Further information:** Chamber of Commerce, 800 S. Salisbury St., Raleigh, NC 27602; www.raleigh-wake.org; www.raleighchamber.org, www.raleigh-nc.org

Reno, Nevada

Population (2008): 217,016 (93); **Pop. density:** 3,141; **Pop. change (2000-08):** 18.4%. **Area:** 69.1 sq mi. **Employment (2008):** 110,016 employed; 6.7% unemployed. **Per capita income (MSA):** $45,332; increase (2006-07): 3.0%.

Mayor: Robert Cashell, Republican

History: Founded in 1857. Originally named Lakes Crossing. Name changed to Reno, after a Union Civil War general, in 1868 with the arrival of the transcontinental railroad.

Transportation: 1 intl. airport, 1 airfield; Amtrak, Union Pacific Railroad; local and national bus lines. **Communications:** 11 TV, 14 radio stations. **Medical facilities:** 8 hosp. **Educational facilities:** 1 univ., 58 public schools. **Further information:** City of Reno, NV, PO Box 1900, Reno, NV 89505; www.reno-sparkschamber.org; www.cityofreno.com

Riverside, California

Population (2008): 295,357 (61); **Pop. density:** 3,782; **Pop. change (2000-08):** 15.5%. **Area:** 78.1 sq mi. **Employment (2008):** 147,537 employed; 8.7% unemployed. **Per capita income (MSA):** $28,804; increase (2006-07): 2.6%.

Mayor: Ronald O. Loveridge, Non-Partisan

History: founded 1870; inc. 1886; known for its citrus industry; home of the parent navel orange tree and the historic Mission Inn.

Transportation: intl. airport nearby, 1 muni. airport; rail freight lines, commuter line; trolley/bus system; interstate freeways. **Communications:** 3 TV, 7 radio stations. **Medical facilities:** 3 hosp. **Educational facilities:** 3 univ., 1 community college. **Further information:** Chamber of Commerce, 3985 University Ave., Riverside, CA 92501; www.riverside-chamber.com; www.riversideca.gov

Rochester, New York

Population (2008): 206,886 (99); **Pop. density:** 5,779; **Pop. change (2000-08):** −5.9%. **Area:** 35.8 sq mi. **Employment (2008):** 88,140 employed; 7.5% unemployed. **Per capita income (MSA):** $37,028; increase (2006-07): 4.0%.

Mayor: Robert Duffy, Democrat

History: first permanent settlement 1812; inc. as village 1817, as city 1834; developed as Erie Canal town.

Transportation: 1 intl. airport; Amtrak; 2 bus lines; intracity transit service; Port of Rochester. **Communications:** 10 TV, 17 radio stations. **Medical facilities:** 5 hosp. **Educational facilities:** 11 colleges, 3 community colleges. **Further information:** Rochester Business Alliance, 150 State St., Ste. 400, Rochester, NY 14614; www.rochesterbusinessalliance.com; www.cityofrochester.gov

Sacramento, California

Population (2008): 463,794 (36); **Pop. density:** 4,772; **Pop. change (2000-08):** 13.9%. **Area:** 97.2 sq mi. **Employment (2008):** 199,085 employed; 8.5% unemployed. **Per capita income (MSA):** $38,424; increase (2006-07): 3.2%.

Mayor: Kevin Johnson, Democrat

History: settled 1839; important trading center during California Gold Rush 1840s; became state capital 1854.

Transportation: 1 intl., 1 corp./charter, 2 muni. airports; 2 mainline transcontinental rail carriers; bus and light rail system; Port of Sacramento. **Communications:** 15 TV, 21 radio stations. **Medical facilities:** 10 hosp. **Educational facilities:** 7 colleges and univ., 5 community colleges; 81 pub. schools. **Further information:** Sacramento Metropolitan Chamber of Commerce, One Capitol Mall, Ste. 300, Sacramento, CA 95814; www.metrochamber.org; www.cityofsacramento.org

St. Louis, Missouri

Population (2008): 354,361 (52); **Pop. density:** 5,725; **Pop. change (2000-08):** 1.8%. **Area:** 61.9 sq mi. **Employment (2008):** 143,183 employed; 7.8% unemployed. **Per capita income (MSA):** $39,278; increase (2006-07): 5.2%.

Mayor: Francis Slay, Democrat

History: founded 1764 as a fur trading post by French; acquired by U.S. 1803; chartered as city 1822; became independent city 1876; lies on Mississippi R., near confluence with Missouri R.

Transportation: 1 intl., 1 muni. airport; 1 airfield; 2nd largest rail center, 7 trunk-line railroads; bus and light rail; 32 barge lines; 550 motor freight carriers; 2nd largest inland port in nation. **Communications:** 2 TV, 2 radio stations. **Medical facilities:** 23 hosp. **Educational facilities:** 8 univ., 13 colleges and seminaries; 63 public schools, 29 parochial schools, 5 magnet/charter high schools. **Further information:** St. Louis Planning & Urban Design Agency, 1015 Locust St., Ste. 1200, St. Louis, MO 63101; www.stlrcga.org; www.explorestlouis.com; www.stlouis.missouri.org

St. Paul, Minnesota

Population (2008): 279,590 (66); **Pop. density:** 5,295; **Pop. change (2000-08):** −2.5%. **Area:** 52.8 sq mi. **Employment (2008):** 136,611 employed; 5.5% unemployed. **Per capita income (MSA):** $46,752; increase (2006-07): 5.5%.

Mayor: Chris Coleman, Democrat

History: founded in early 1840s as Pig's Eye Landing; became capital of the Minnesota territory 1849 and chartered as St. Paul 1854.

Transportation: 1 intl., 2 muni. airports; 6 major rail lines; 2 interstate bus lines; pub. transit system. **Communications:** 7 TV, 2 radio stations. **Medical facilities:** 7 hosp. **Educational facilities:** 5 univ., 5 colleges, 1 technical, 3 law schools, 1 art and design college; 65 public, 39 private schools. **Further information:** St. Paul Area Chamber of Commerce, 401 N. Robert St., Ste. 150, St. Paul, MN 55101; www.saintpaulchamber.com; www.ci.stpaul.mn.us

St. Petersburg, Florida

Population (2008): 245,314 (77); **Pop. density:** 4,116; **Pop. change (2000-08):** −1.4%. **Area:** 59.6 sq mi. **Employment (2008):** 118,694 employed; 6.1% unemployed. **Per capita income (MSA):** $36,554; increase (2006-07): 3.0%.

Mayor: Rick Baker, Democrat

History: founded 1888; inc. 1903.

Transportation: 1 intl., 1 regional airport; Amtrak bus connection; county-wide public bus system; downtown "Looper" bus service; has largest muni. marina in Florida; 1 cruise port. **Communications:** 2 daily newspapers; 1 radio station. **Medical facilities:** 8 hosp. **Educational facilities:** 1 univ., 1 college, 1 law school, 27 elem., 9 middle, 5 high schools, 3 alternative/vocational schools; 100 private schools. **Further information:** City of St. Petersburg, 175 5th St. N., St. Petersburg, FL 33701; www.stpete.com; www.stpete.org

San Antonio, Texas

Population (2008): 1,351,305 (7); **Pop. density:** 3,315; **Pop. change (2000-08):** 16.5%. **Area:** 407.6 sq mi. **Employment (2008):** 596,205 employed; 4.5% unemployed. **Per capita income (MSA):** $33,845; increase (2006-07): 3.9%.

Mayor: Julián Castro, Non-Partisan

History: first Spanish garrison 1718; Battle at the Alamo in 1836; city subsequently captured by Texans; inc. 1837; 1st town meeting in Texas took place here in 1845.

Transportation: 1 intl., 1 muni. airport, 6 airfields; 2 railroads; 3 bus lines; pub. transit system. **Communications:** 27 TV, 26 radio stations. **Medical facilities:** 31 hosp. **Educational facilities:** 18 univ. and colleges; 16 pub. school districts. **Further information:** The Greater San Antonio Chamber of Commerce, 602 E. Commerce St., San Antonio, TX 78205; www.sachamber.org; www.sanantonio.gov

San Diego, California

Population (2008): 1,279,329 (9); **Pop. density:** 3,945; **Pop. change (2000-08):** 4.6%. **Area:** 324.3 sq mi. **Employment (2008):** 657,314 employed; 6.0% unemployed. **Per capita income (MSA):** $44,430; increase (2006-07): 4.0%.

Mayor: Jerry Sanders, Republican

History: claimed by the Spanish 1542; first mission est. 1769; scene of conflict during Mexican-American War 1846; inc. 1850.

Transportation: 1 intl., 2 muni. airports; 1 railroad; major freeway system; bus system; trolley system. **Communications:** 13 TV, 23 radio stations. **Medical facilities:** 15 hosp. **Educational facilities:** 25 colleges and univ.; 177 pub. schools. **Further information:** San Diego Regional Chamber of Commerce, 402 W. Broadway, Ste. 1000, San Diego, CA 92101; www.sdchamber.org; www.sandiego.gov

San Francisco, California

Population (2008): 808,976 (12); **Pop. density:** 17,323; **Pop. change (2000-08):** 4.2%. **Area:** 46.7 sq mi. **Employment (2008):** 426,682 employed; 5.3% unemployed. **Per capita income (MSA):** $60,983; increase (2006-07): 5.4%.

Mayor: Gavin Newsom, Democrat

History: nearby Farallon Islands sighted by Spanish 1542; city settled by 1776; claimed by U.S. 1846; became a major city during California Gold Rush 1849; inc. as city 1850; earthquake devastated city 1906.

Transportation: 1 intl. airport; intracity railway system; 2 railway transit systems; bus and railroad service; ferry system; 1 underwater tunnel. **Communications:** 13 TV, 30 radio stations. **Medical facilities:** 5 hosp. **Educational facilities:** 18 univ. and colleges; 34 preschools, 102 K-12 schools, 8 county/court schools, 9 charter schools. **Further information:** San Francisco Visitors Information Center, 900 Market St., San Francisco, CA 94102; www.sfchamber.com; www.onlyinsanfrancisco.com; www.ci.sf.ca.us

San Jose, California

Population (2008): 948,279 (10); **Pop. density:** 5,422; **Pop. change (2000-08):** 5.9%. **Area:** 174.9 sq mi. **Employment (2008):** 429,359 employed; 6.7% unemployed. **Per capita income (MSA):** $59,338; increase (2006-07): 6.4%.

Mayor: Chuck Reed, Democrat

History: founded by the Spanish 1777 between San Francisco and Monterey; state cap. 1849-51; inc. 1850.

Transportation: 1 intl., 1 muni. airport; 2 railroads; light rail system; bus system. **Communications:** 5 TV, 10 radio stations. **Medical facilities:** 5 hosp. **Educational facilities:** 6 univ. and colleges. **Further information:** San Jose Convention and Visitors Bureau, 408 Almaden Blvd., San Jose, CA 95110; www.sanjose.org; www.sanjoseca.gov

Santa Ana, California

Population (2008): 339,130 (54); **Pop. density:** 12,514; **Pop. change (2000-08):** 0.3%. **Area:** 27.1 sq mi. **Employment (2008):** 148,238 employed; 8.5% unemployed. **Per capita income (MSA):** $42,278; increase (2006-07): 4.3%.

Mayor: Miguel Pulido, Democrat

History: founded 1769; inc. as city 1869.

Transportation: 1 natl. airport; Amtrak; 5 major freeways including main Los Angeles-San Diego artery. **Communications:** 2 TV, 3 radio stations. **Medical facilities:** 3 hosp. **Educational facilities:** 1 community college. **Further information:** Santa Ana Chamber of Commerce, 2020 N. Broadway, 2nd Fl., Santa Ana, CA 92706; www.santaanachamber.com; www.ci.santa-ana.ca.us

Scottsdale, Arizona

Population (2008): 235,371 (79); **Pop. density:** 1,278; **Pop. change (2000-08):** 16.2%. **Area:** 184.2 sq mi. **Employment (2008):** 139,712 employed; 3.6% unemployed. **Per capita income (MSA):** $35,185; increase (2006-07): 1.0%.

Mayor: W. J. Lane, Republican

History: founded 1888 by Army Chaplain Winfield Scott; inc. June 25, 1951; slogan "West's Most Western Town," by Mayor Malcolm White, adopted 1951.

Transportation: 1 muni. airport; regional bus system; local trolley system; taxi system. **Communications:** 5 radio stations. **Medical facilities:** 7 hosp. **Educational facilities:** 1 univ. nearby, 1 community college; 3 unified school districts. **Further information:** Scottsdale Convention and Visitors Bureau, Galleria Corporate Center, 4343 N. Scottsdale Rd., Ste. 170, Scottsdale, AZ 85251; www.scottsdalechamber.com; www.scottsdalecvb.com; www.scottsdaleaz.gov

Seattle, Washington

Population (2008): 598,541 (25); **Pop. density:** 7,134; **Pop. change (2000-08):** 6.2%. **Area:** 83.9 sq mi. **Employment

(2008): 355,184 employed; 4.0% unemployed. **Per capita income (MSA):** $49,401; increase (2006-07): 7.3%.

Mayor: Greg Nickels, Democrat

History: settled 1851; inc. 1869; suffered severe fire 1889; played prominent role during Alaska Gold Rush 1897; growth followed opening of Panama Canal 1914; center of aircraft industry WWII.

Transportation: 2 intl. airports, 2 seaplane bases; 2 railroads; ferries serve Puget Sound, Alaska, Canada; cruise ships to Alaska. **Communications:** 8 TV, 45 radio stations. **Medical facilities:** 12 hosp. **Educational facilities:** 3 univ., 18 community colleges. **Further information:** Greater Seattle Chamber of Commerce, 1301 5th Ave., Ste. 2500, Seattle, WA 98101-2611; www.seattlechamber.com; www.seattle.gov

Stockton, California

Population (2008): 287,037 (63); **Pop. density:** 5,247; **Pop. change (2000-08):** 18.1%. **Area:** 54.7 sq mi. **Employment (2008):** 108,169 employed; 12.7% unemployed. **Per capita income (MSA):** $28,739; increase (2006-07): 4.1%.

Mayor: Ann Johnston, Non-Partisan

History: site purchased 1842; settled 1849; inc. 1850; chief distributing point for agric. products of San Joaquin Valley.

Transportation: 1 muni. airport; 4 railroads; 2 bus lines, county bus system; deepwater inland seaport. **Communications:** 5 TV, 8 radio stations. **Medical facilities:** 4 hosp.; regional burn, cancer, heart centers. **Educational facilities:** 9 univ. and colleges; 58 pub. schools. **Further information:** Chamber of Commerce, 445 W. Weber Ave., Ste. 220, Stockton, CA 95203; www.stocktonchamber.org; www.visitstockton.org; www.stocktongov.com

Tampa, Florida

Population (2008): 340,882 (53); **Pop. density:** 3,041; **Pop. change (2000-08):** 12.3%. **Area:** 112.1 sq mi. **Employment (2008):** 153,359 employed; 6.5% unemployed. **Per capita income (MSA):** $36,554; increase (2006-07): 3.0%.

Mayor: Pam Iorio, Democrat

History: U.S. army fort on site 1824; inc. 1851; Ybor City National Historical Landmark district.

Transportation: 1 intl., 2 muni. airports; CSX rail, Amtrak Rail; bus system; downtown streetcar; Port of Tampa. **Communications:** 16 TV, 11 radio stations. **Medical facilities:** 30 hosp. **Educational facilities:** 10 univ. and colleges; 209 K-12 pub. schools, 60 additional school centers (Hillsborough County). **Further information:** Greater Tampa Chamber of Commerce, 615 Channelside Dr., Ste. 108, PO Box 420, Tampa, FL 33601; www.tampachamber.com; www.tampagov.net

Toledo, Ohio

Population (2008): 293,201 (62); **Pop. density:** 3,638; **Pop. change (2000-08):** −6.6%. **Area:** 80.6 sq mi. **Employment (2008):** 130,508 employed; 9.0% unemployed. **Per capita income (MSA):** $33,316; increase (2006-07): 4.2%.

Mayor: Carleton S. "Carty" Finkbeiner, Democrat

History: site of Ft. Industry 1794; Battles of Ft. Meigs and Ft. Timbers 1812; figured in "Toledo War" 1835-36 between Ohio and Michigan over borders; inc. 1837.

Transportation: 2 muni. airports; 4 railroads; 53 motor freight lines; 16 interstate bus lines. **Communications:** 10 TV, 11 radio stations. **Medical facilities:** 4 hosp. **Educational facilities:** 6 univ. and colleges. **Further information:** Toledo Area Chamber of Commerce, 300 Madison Ave., Ste. 200, Toledo, OH 43604; www.toledochamber.com; www.ci.toledo.oh.us

Tucson, Arizona

Population (2008): 541,811 (32); **Pop. density:** 9,675; **Pop. change (2000-08):** 11.2%. **Area:** 56.0 sq mi. **Employment (2008):** 263,065 employed; 5.7% unemployed. **Per capita income (MSA):** $31,755; increase (2006-07): 2.5%.

Mayor: Robert E. Walkup, Republican

History: settled 1775 by Spanish as a presidio; acquired by U.S. in Gadsden Purchase 1853; inc. 1877.

Transportation: 1 intl. airport; 2 railroads; 1 city bus line, 2 intercity bus lines, 1 trolley. **Communications:** 11 TV, 32 radio stations. **Medical facilities:** 11 hosp. **Educational facilities:** 1 univ., 1 community college; 216 pub. schools. **Further information:** Tucson Metropolitan Chamber of Commerce, 465 St. Mary's Rd., PO Box 991, Tucson, AZ 85701; www.tucsonchamber.org; www.visittucson.org; www.tucsonaz.gov

Tulsa, Oklahoma

Population (2008): 385,635 (46); **Pop. density:** 2,112; **Pop. change (2000-08):** −1.9%. **Area:** 182.6 sq mi. **Employment (2008):** 182,114 employed; 3.7% unemployed. **Per capita income (MSA):** $41,307; increase (2006-07): 6.6%.

Mayor: Kathryn L. Taylor, Democrat

History: settled in 1836 by Creek Indians; modern town founded 1882 and inc. 1898; oil discovered early 20th century; emerging as telecommunications hub.

Transportation: 1 intl., 1 regional airport, 1 airfield; 5 rail lines; 5 bus lines; transit bus system. **Communications:** 25 TV, 15 radio stations. **Medical facilities:** 18 hosp. **Educational facilities:** 8 univ. and colleges; 85 pub., 39 private schools. **Further information:** Tulsa Metro Chamber, 2 West 2nd St., Williams Tower II, Ste. 150, Tulsa, OK 74103; www.tulsachamber.com; www.cityoftulsa.org

Virginia Beach, Virginia

Population (2008): 433,746 (42); **Pop. density:** 1,747; **Pop. change (2000-08):** 2.0%. **Area:** 248.3 sq mi. **Employment (2008):** 217,725 employed; 3.7% unemployed. **Per capita income (MSA):** $36,837; increase (2006-07): 4.6%.

Mayor: William D. Sessoms Jr., Independent

History: area founded by Capt. John Smith 1607; formed by merger with Princess Anne Co. 1963.

Transportation: 1 private airfield; 2 railroads; 1 bus line; pub. transit system. **Communications:** 4 TV, 4 radio stations. **Medical facilities:** 3 hosp. **Educational facilities:** 1 univ., 2 colleges; 87 pub. schools. **Further information:** Virginia Beach Dept. of Economic Development, 222 Central Park Ave., Ste. 1000, Virginia Beach, VA 23462; Virginia Beach Convention and Visitors Bureau, 2100 Parks Ave., Virginia Beach, VA 23451; www.yesvirginiabeach.com; www.vbfun.com; www.vbgov.com

Washington, District of Columbia

Population (2008): 591,833 (27); **Pop. density:** 9,639; **Pop. change (2000-08):** 3.5%. **Area:** 61.4 sq mi. **Employment (2008):** 309,528 employed; 7.0% unemployed. **Per capita income (MSA):** $54,971; increase (2006-07): 4.7%.

Mayor: Adrian M. Fenty, Democrat

History: U.S. capital; site at Potomac R. chosen by George Washington 1790 on land ceded from VA and MD (portion S of Potomac returned to VA 1846); Congress first met 1800; inc. 1802; sacked by British, War of 1812; 125 killed during Sept. 11, 2001 terrorist attack on the Pentagon.

Transportation: 3 intl. airports in area; Amtrak, 6 other passenger and cargo rail lines; Metrobus/Metrorail transit system; bus line. **Communications:** 18 TV, 20 radio stations. **Medical facilities:** 17 hosp. **Educational facilities:** 10 univ. and colleges. **Further information:** DC Chamber of Commerce, 1213 K St. NW, Washington, DC 20005; www.dcchamber.org; www.dc.gov

Wichita, Kansas

Population (2008): 366,046 (51); **Pop. density:** 2,695; **Pop. change (2000-08):** 4.0%. **Area:** 135.8 sq mi. **Employment (2008):** 185,567 employed; 4.6% unemployed. **Per capita income (MSA):** $38,552; increase (2006-07): 3.9%.

Mayor: Carl Brewer, Democrat

History: founded 1864; inc. 1871.

Transportation: 1 natl., 1 muni. airport, 4 airfields; 3 major rail freight lines; 2 bus lines. **Communications:** 8 TV, 15 radio stations. **Medical facilities:** 12 hosp. **Educational facilities:** 3 univ., 1 medical school; 96 pub. schools. **Further information:** Chamber of Commerce, 350 W. Douglas Ave., Wichita, KS 67202; www.wichitakansas.org; www.gwedc.org; www.wichita.gov

Winston-Salem, North Carolina

Population (2008): 217,600 (91); **Pop. density:** 1,998; **Pop. change (2000-08):** 8.0%. **Area:** 108.9 sq mi. **Employment (2008):** 100,061 employed; 5.8% unemployed. **Per capita income (MSA):** $35,481; increase (2006-07): 4.5%.

Mayor: Allen Joines, Democrat

History: founded as Winston in 1851; became Winston-Salem in 1913; the Reynolds Building, completed in 1929, was used as a model for the Empire State Building, which was designed by the same architects.

Transportation: 1 intl., 1 general aviation airport; local and regional mass transit system. **Communications:** 1 daily newspaper, 5 TV, 17 radio stations. **Medical facilities:** 4 hosp., 1 school of medicine. **Educational facilities:** 4 colleges and univ., 1 community college; 74 public, 28 private schools. **Further information:** The Greater Winston-Salem Chamber of Commerce, 601 W. Fourth St., P.O. Box 1408, Winston-Salem, NC 27102; www.winstonsalem.com; www.cityofws.org

Fastest-Growing Big Cities*

City	2008 population	2000 population	% change
1. Gilbert, AZ	216,449	114,701	88.7
2. North Las Vegas, NV	217,253	115,531	88.0
3. Irvine, CA	207,500	144,145	44.0
4. Henderson, NV	252,064	175,273	43.8
5. Chandler, AZ	247,140	177,103	39.5
6. Raleigh, NC	392,552	288,354	36.1
7. Bakersfield, CA	321,078	243,658	31.8
8. Fort Worth, TX	703,073	541,370	29.9
9. Atlanta, GA	537,958	418,109	28.7
10. Chula Vista, CA	219,318	173,553	26.4

Fastest-Shrinking Big Cities*

City	2008 population	2000 population	% change
1. New Orleans, LA	311,853	484,674	−35.7
2. Cleveland, OH	433,748	477,472	−9.2
3. Buffalo, NY	270,919	292,648	−7.4
4. Pittsburgh, PA	310,037	334,563	−7.3
5. Hialeah, Fl	210,542	226,440	−7.0
6. Toledo, Oh	293,201	313,782	−6.6
8. Rochester, NY	206,886	219,774	−5.9
8. Birmingham, AL	228,798	242,452	−5.6
9. Philadelphia, PA	1,447,395	1,517,550	−4.6
10. Akron, OH	207,510	217,106	−4.4

*Among those with populations of 200,000 or more, based on 2008 U.S. Census Bureau estimates.

Percent of Population by Race and Hispanic Origin, 10 Largest Cities[1]

City	White	Black or African-Amer.	Amer. Indian, Alaska Native	Asian	Hawaiian & Other Pacific Isl.	Some other race[2]	Two or more races	Hispanic or Latino (of any race)
1. New York, NY	44.7	26.6	0.5	9.8	0.1	13.4	4.9	27.0
2. Los Angeles, CA	46.9	11.2	0.8	10.0	0.2	25.7	5.2	46.5
3. Chicago, IL	42.0	36.8	0.4	4.3	0.1	13.6	2.9	26.0
4. Houston, TX	49.3	25.3	0.4	5.3	0.1	16.5	3.1	37.4
5. Phoenix, AZ	71.1	5.1	2.0	2.0	0.1	16.4	3.3	34.1
6. Philadelphia, PA	45.0	43.2	0.3	4.5	0	4.8	2.2	8.5
7. San Antonio, TX	67.7	6.8	0.8	1.6	0.1	19.3	3.7	58.7
8. Dallas, TX	50.8	25.9	0.5	2.7	0	17.2	2.7	35.6
9. San Diego, CA	60.2	7.9	0.6	13.6	0.5	12.4	4.8	25.4
10. San Jose, CA	47.5	3.5	0.8	26.9	0.4	15.9	5.0	30.2

(1) City rankings as determined by 2008 Census Bureau estimates; race and Hispanic origin percentages are based on 2000 Census figures. (2) Persons who, instead of choosing a race listed in the questionnaire, filled in a designation under "some other race."

Sources: Population: U.S. Commerce Dept., Bureau of the Census—Census 2000: April 1, 2000, and July 2008 est. **Area:** Bureau of the Census, Geography Division. **Acres forested:** Agriculture Dept., Forest Service. **Chief airports:** Transportation Dept., Federal Aviation Admin. **Chief manuf. goods:** Bureau of the Census, Manufacturing and Construction Division. **Chief crops & Livestock:** Agriculture Dept., Natl. Agricultural Stat. Service. Many states do not separately report hog/pig or broiler stats. **Lumber production:** Bureau of the Census, Industry Division. **Nonfuel minerals:** Dept. of Interior, Office of Mineral Information. **Commercial fishing:** Commerce Dept., Natl. Marine Fisheries Service. **Gross state product & Per capita personal income:** Commerce Dept., Bureau of Economic Analysis. **Sales tax:** Fed. of Tax Admin. **Employment distribution & Unemployment:** Labor Dept., Bureau of Labor Statistics. **New private housing:** Bureau of the Census, Residential Construction Branch. **Finance:** Federal Deposit Insurance Corp. **Lottery figures** (not all states have a lottery): North American Assn. of State and Provincial Lotteries, for local fiscal year. **Federal employees:** Labor Dept., Office of Personnel Management. **Energy:** Energy Dept., Energy Information Administration. Other information from sources in individual states. Some data on Outlying U.S. Areas & Other Islands provided by the CIA World Factbook. For information about tourism earnings, see Transportation and Tourism.

NOTE: Pop. density is for land area only. Categories under racial distribution may not add to 100% due to rounding. "Nat. AK" (Native Alaskans) includes Eskimos and Aleuts. **Hispanic population may be of any race** and is dispersed among racial categories, besides being listed separately. Chief airports had 500,000+ boardings in 2005. Nonfuel mineral values for some states exclude small amounts to avoid disclosing proprietary data. Categories under employment distribution are nonfarm only and are not all-inclusive. Commercial bank and savings institution figures are for FDIC-insured institutions only. Postal Service, TN Valley Auth., and some other agencies are not included in federal govt. numbers. Notable federal facilities marked with an asterisk (*) have been recommended for realignment or closure by the U.S. Dept. of Defense, to be completed by Sept. 15, 2011. Electricity prod. excludes independent power producers; negative power generation denotes that electric power consumed for plant use exceeds gross generation. **Famous Persons lists may include nonnatives** associated with the state as well as persons born there. Websites are subject to change and are not endorsed by *The World Almanac*.

Alabama (AL)
Heart of Dixie, Camellia State

People. Population (2008 est.): 4,661,900; rank: 23; net change (2007-08): 0.8%. **Pop. density:** 92.1 per sq mi. **Racial distribution** (2008): 71.0% white; 26.4% black; 1.0% Asian; 0.5% Native Amer./Nat. AK; <0.05% Hawaiian/Pacific Islander; 2 or more races, 1.1%. **Hispanic pop.** (any race): 2.9%.

Geography. Total area: 52,419 sq mi; rank: 30. **Land area:** 50,744 sq mi; rank: 28. **Acres forested:** 22.7 mil. **Location:** East South Central state extending N-S from Tenn. to the Gulf of Mexico; E of the Mississippi River. **Climate:** long, hot summers; mild winters; generally abundant rainfall. **Topography:** coastal plains, including Prairie Black Belt, give way to hills, broken terrain; highest elevation, 2,407 ft. **Capital:** Montgomery. **Chief airports at:** Birmingham, Huntsville.

Economy. Chief industries: pulp & paper, chemicals, electronics, apparel, textiles, primary metals, lumber and wood products, food processing, fabricated metals, automotive tires, oil and gas exploration. **Chief manuf. goods:** animal slaughtering & processing, chemicals & synthetics, paper & paperboard, iron & steel, petroleum, tires, aerospace, aluminum, auto body & electronics. **Chief crops:** cotton, greenhouse & nursery, hay, peanuts, corn, soy beans. **Livestock** (Jan. 2009): 1.3 mil cattle/calves; (Dec. 2008): 15.7 mil chickens (excl. broilers), 1.1 bil broilers. **Timber/lumber** (est. 2008): 1.8 bil bd. ft; pine, hardwoods. **Nonfuel minerals** (2008 prelim.): $1.2 bil; cement (portland), stone (crushed), lime, sand and gravel (construction), clays (common). **Commercial fishing** (2008): $44.3 mil. **Chief port:** Mobile. **Gross state product** (est. 2008): $170.0 bil. **Sales tax** (2009): 4.0%. **Employment distrib.** (June 2008): 18.9% govt.; 19.7% trade/trans./util.; 14.4% mfg.; 10.3% ed./health; 11.2% prof./bus. serv.; 8.8% leisure/hosp.; 5.0% finance; 5.7% constr.; 4.0% other serv.; 1.4% info. **Unemployment** (2008): 5.0%. **Per cap. pers. income** (2008 prelim.): $33,643. **New private housing** (2008): 17,464 units/$2.1 bil. **Commercial banks** (2008): 170; deposits: $73.0 bil. **Savings institutions** (2008): 17; deposits: $3.5 bil.

Federal govt. Fed. civ. employees (Mar. 2007): 36,487; **avg. salary:** $67,605. **Notable fed. facilities:** Redstone Arsenal; Ft. Rucker; Marshall Space Flight Ctr.; Anniston Army Depot; *Maxwell/Gunter AFB; U.S. Corps of Engineers.

Energy. Electricity production (est. 2007 kWh by source): coal: 77.4 bil; gas: 8.6 bil; nuclear: 34.3 bil; petroleum: 72.0 bil.

State data. Motto: We dare defend our rights. **Flower:** Camellia. **Bird:** Yellowhammer. **Tree:** Southern Longleaf pine. **Song:** Alabama. **Entered union** Dec. 14, 1819; rank, 22nd. **State fair:** no official state fair; regional and county fairs held in Sept. and Oct.

History. Alabama was inhabited by the Creek, Cherokee, Chickasaw, Alabama, and Choctaw peoples when Spanish explorers arrived in the early 1500s. The French made the first permanent settlement at Fort Louis, 1702, and founded Mobile, 1711. France later gave up the entire region to England under the Treaty of Paris, 1763. Spanish forces took control of the Mobile Bay area, 1780, and it remained under Spanish control until seized by U.S. troops, 1813. Most of present-day Alabama was held by the Creeks until Gen. An-drew Jackson broke their power, 1814. When Alabama became a state, 1819, black slaves made up about 1/3 of the population. The Indian Removal Act of 1830 forced most remaining Creeks west. The state seceded, 1861, and the Confederate states were organized Feb. 4, at Montgomery, the first capital; the state was readmitted, 1868. Birmingham, founded 1871, became a center for iron- and steel-making. The Montgomery bus boycott, 1955, sparked by Rosa Parks, helped launch the civil rights movement; other confrontations came at Birmingham, 1963, and Selma, 1965. The leading political figure from the 1960s through the '80s, 4-term Gov. George Wallace, started as a segregationist but later won with black support. Growth in the auto industry boosted the state economy as the 21st cent. began.

Tourist attractions. First White House of the Confederacy, Civil Rights Memorial, Alabama Shakespeare Festival, in Montgomery; Ivy Green (Helen Keller's birthplace), Tuscumbia; Civil Rights Museum, statue of Vulcan, in Birmingham; Carver Museum, Tuskegee; W. C. Handy Home, Museum, & Library, Florence; Alabama Space and Rocket Center, Huntsville; Moundville State Monument; Pike Pioneer Museum, Troy; USS *Alabama* Memorial Park, Mobile; Russell Cave Natl. Monument, near Bridgeport: a detailed record of occupancy by humans from about 10,000 BCE to 1650 CE.

Famous Alabamians. Hank Aaron, Tallulah Bankhead, Hugo L. Black, Paul "Bear" Bryant, George Washington Carver, Nat King Cole, William C. Handy, Bo Jackson, Helen Keller, Coretta Scott King, Harper Lee, Joe Louis, Willie Mays, John Hunt Morgan, Jim Nabors, Jesse Owens, Condoleezza Rice, George Wallace, Booker T. Washington, Hank Williams.

Tourist information. Alabama Tourism Department, 401 Adams Ave., Ste. 126, PO Box 4927, Montgomery, AL 36103; 1-800-ALABAMA, (334) 242-4169; www.alabama.travel

Website. www.alabama.gov

Alaska (AK)
The Last Frontier (unofficial)

People. Population (2008 est.): 686,293; rank: 47; net change (2007-08): 0.8%. **Pop. density:** 1.2 per sq mi. **Racial distribution** (2008): 70.6% white; 4.3% black; 4.5% Asian; 15.3% Native Amer./Nat. AK; 0.7% Hawaiian/Pacific Islander; 2 or more races, 4.6%. **Hispanic pop.** (any race): 6.1%.

Geography. Total area: 663,267 sq mi; rank: 1. **Land area:** 571,951 sq mi; rank: 1. **Acres forested:** 126.9 mil. **Location:** NW corner of North America, bordered on E by Canada. **Climate:** SE, SW, and central regions, moist and mild; far north extremely dry. Extended summer days, winter nights, throughout. **Topography:** includes Pacific and Arctic mountain systems, central plateau, and Arctic slope. Mt. McKinley, 20,320 ft, is the highest point in North America. **Capital:** Juneau. **Chief airport at:** Anchorage.

Economy. Chief industries: petroleum, tourism, fishing, mining, forestry, transportation, aerospace. **Chief manuf. goods:** petroleum, seafood. **Chief crops:** greenhouse products, barley, oats, hay, potatoes, carrots. **Livestock** (Jan. 2009): 14,000 cattle/calves. **Timber/lumber:** figs. withheld; spruce, yellow cedar, hemlock. **Nonfuel minerals** (2008 prelim.): $2.7 bil; zinc, gold, lead, silver, sand and gravel (construction). **Commercial fishing** (2008): $1.7 bil. **Chief ports:**

Anchorage, Dutch Harbor, Kodiak, Seward, Skagway, Juneau, Sitka, Valdez, Wrangell. **Gross state product** (est. 2008): $47.9 bil. **Sales tax** (2009): none. **Employment distrib.** (June 2008): 24.3% govt.; 20.3% trade/trans./util.; 4.6% mfg.; 11.0% ed./health; 8.0% prof./bus. serv.; 11.4% leisure/hosp.; 4.5% finance; 5.9% constr.; 3.5% other serv.; 2.0% info. **Unemployment** (2008): 6.7%. **Per cap. pers. income** (2008 prelim.): $43,321. **New private housing** (2008): 901 units/$209.2 mil. **Commercial banks** (2008): 7; deposits: $13.3 bil. **Savings institutions** (2008): 2; deposits: $370 mil.

Federal govt. Fed. civ. employees (Mar. 2007): 12,446; **avg. salary:** $58,579. **Notable fed. facilities:** *Elmendorf AFB; *Ft. Richardson; Ft. Wainwright; *Eilson AFB; Ft. Greely.

Energy. Electricity production (est. 2007 kWh by source): coal: 211.0 mil; gas: 3.8 bil; petroleum: 1.1 bil.

State data. Motto: North to the future. **Flower:** Forget-Me-Not. **Bird:** Willow ptarmigan. **Tree:** Sitka spruce. **Song:** Alaska's Flag. **Entered union** Jan. 3, 1959; rank, 49th. **State fair** at Palmer; late Aug.-early Sept.

History. Early inhabitants included the Tlingit-Haida and Athabascan peoples. Ancestors of the Aleut and Inuit (Eskimo) probably arrived from Siberia between 10,000 and 6,000 years ago. Vitus Bering, a Dane sailing for Russia, was the first European to land in Alaska, 1741. Russians, pursuing the fur trade, established a permanent settlement on Kodiak Island, 1784. Sec. of State William H. Seward bought Alaska from Russia for $7.2 mil in 1867, a bargain some called "Seward's Folly." Discovery of gold in the Klondike region of Canada's Yukon Territory, 1896, triggered an Alaskan gold rush. Alaska became a territory, 1912, and a state, 1959. A huge oil find at Prudhoe Bay, 1968, led to construction of the Trans-Alaska Pipeline, 1974-77. The *Exxon Valdez* supertanker ran aground, 1989, spilling about 11 mil gallons of crude oil; the cleanup cost more than $2.2 bil. Repeated attempts by Congress members to allow oil and gas drilling in the Arctic National Wildlife Refuge have failed.

Tourist attractions. Inside Passage; Portage Glacier; Mendenhall Glacier; Ketchikan Totems; Glacier Bay Natl. Park and Preserve; Denali Natl. Park, one of N. America's great wildlife sanctuaries, surrounding Mt. McKinley, N. America's highest peak; Mt. Roberts Tramway, Juneau; Pribilof Islands fur seal rookeries; restored St. Michael's Russian Orthodox Cathedral, Sitka; White Pass & Yukon Route railroad; Skagway; Katmai Natl. Park & Preserve.

Famous Alaskans. Tom Bodett, Susan Butcher, Ernest Gruening, Jewel (Kilcher), Gov. Tony Knowles, Sydney Laurence, Libby Riddles, Jefferson "Soapy" Smith.

Tourist information. Alaska Travel Industry Association, 2600 Cordova St., Ste. 201, Anchorage, AK 99503; (800) 327-9372; www.travelalaska.com

Website. www.state.ak.us

Arizona (AZ)
Grand Canyon State

People. Population (2008 est.): 6,500,180; rank: 14; net change (2007-08): 2.3%. **Pop. density:** 57.2 per sq mi. **Racial distribution** (2008): 86.5% white; 4.2% black; 2.5% Asian; 4.9% Native Amer./Nat. AK; 0.2% Hawaiian/Pacific Islander; 2 or more races, 1.8%. **Hispanic pop.** (any race): 30.1%.

Geography. Total area: 113,998 sq mi; rank: 6. **Land area:** 113,635 sq mi; rank: 6. **Acres forested:** 18.7 mil. **Location:** southwestern U.S. **Climate:** clear and dry in the southern regions and northern plateau; high central areas have heavy winter snows. **Topography:** Colorado plateau in the N, containing the Grand Canyon; Mexican Highlands running diagonally NW to SE; Sonoran Desert in the SW. **Capital:** Phoenix. **Chief airports at:** Tucson, Phoenix.

Economy. Chief industries: manufacturing, construction, tourism, mining, agriculture. **Chief manuf. goods:** aerospace, semiconductors, navigational instruments, cement, plastics, structural metals, dairy, printing, furniture. **Chief crops:** cotton, grapes, apples, lettuce, hay, potatoes, sorghum, barley, corn, wheat. **Livestock** (Jan. 2009): 1.0 mil cattle/calves, 150,000 sheep/lambs. **Timber/lumber:** figs. withheld; pine, fir, spruce. **Nonfuel minerals** (2008 prelim.): $7.8 bil; copper, molybdenum concentrates, sand and gravel (construction), cement (portland), stone (crushed). **Gross state product** (est. 2008): $248.9 bil. **Sales tax** (2009): 5.6%. **Employment distrib.** (June 2008): 15.4% govt.; 19.8% trade/trans./util.; 6.8% mfg.; 12.0% ed./health; 15.3% prof./bus. serv.; 10.5% leisure/hosp.; 6.8% finance; 7.5% constr.;

3.8% other serv.; 1.6% info. **Unemployment** (2008): 5.5%. **Per cap. pers. income** (2008 prelim.): $32,953. **New private housing** (2008): 26,082 units/$4.5 bil. **Commercial banks** (2008): 80; deposits: $74.3 bil. **Savings institutions** (2008): 13; deposits: $4.4 bil. **Lottery** (2008): total sales: $472.9 mil; profit: $144.6 mil.

Federal govt. Fed. civ. employees (Mar. 2007): 37,130; **avg. salary:** $58,259. **Notable fed. facilities:** *Luke AFB, Davis-Monthan AFB; *Ft. Huachuca; Yuma Proving Grounds.

Energy. Electricity production (est. 2007 kWh by source): coal: 40.9 bil; gas: 14.3 bil; hydroelectric: 125.0 mil; nuclear: 26.8 bil; petroleum: 44.0 mil.

State data. Motto: Ditat Deus (God enriches). **Flower:** Blossom of the Saguaro cactus. **Bird:** Cactus wren. **Tree:** Paloverde. **Song:** Arizona. **Entered union** Feb. 14, 1912; rank, 48th. **State fair** at Phoenix; Oct.-early Nov.

History. Paleo-Indians hunted large game in the area at least 12,000 years ago. Anasazi, Mogollon, and Hohokam civilizations lived there c. 300 BCE-1300 CE; Navajo and Apache came c. 15th cent. Marcos de Niza, a Franciscan, and Estevanico, a black former slave, explored, 1539; Spanish explorer Francisco Vásquez de Coronado visited, 1540. Eusebio Francisco Kino, a Jesuit missionary, taught Indians 1692-1711, and left missions. Tubac, a Spanish fort, became the first European settlement, 1752. Spain ceded Arizona to Mexico, 1821. The U.S. took over, 1848, after the Mexican War. The area below the Gila River came from Mexico in the Gadsden Purchase, 1853. Arizona became a territory, 1863. Apache wars ended with Geronimo's surrender, 1886. Arizona became a state, 1912, and grew rapidly after 1960 with a fourfold rise in population over the next 4 decades. Barry Goldwater was a leading conservative voice in the U.S. Senate (1953-65, 1969-87). The border with Mexico is a major gateway for illegal immigration to the U.S.

Tourist attractions. The Grand Canyon; Painted Desert; Petrified Forest Natl. Park; Canyon de Chelly; Meteor Crater; London Bridge, Lake Havasu City; Biosphere 2, Oracle; Navajo Natl. Monument.

Famous Arizonans. Bruce Babbitt, Cochise, Alice Cooper, Geronimo, Barry Goldwater, Zane Grey, Carl Hayden, George W. P. Hunt, Helen Jacobs, Bil Keane, Percival Lowell, John McCain, William H. Pickering, John J. Rhodes, Morris Udall, Stewart Udall, Frank Lloyd Wright.

Tourist information. Arizona Office of Tourism, 1110 W. Washington St., Ste. 155, Phoenix, AZ 85007; (866) 275-5816; www.arizonaguide.com

Website. www.az.gov

Arkansas (AR)
Natural State, Razorback State

People. Population (2008 est.): 2,855,390; rank: 32; net change (2007-08): 0.9%. **Pop. density:** 54.9 per sq mi. **Racial distribution** (2008): 80.8% white; 15.8% black; 1.1% Asian; 0.9% Native Amer./Nat. AK; 0.1% Hawaiian/Pacific Islander; 2 or more races, 1.4%. **Hispanic pop.** (any race): 5.6%.

Geography. Total area: 53,179 sq mi; rank: 29. **Land area:** 52,068 sq mi; rank: 27. **Acres forested:** 18.8 mil. **Location:** west south-central U.S. **Climate:** long, hot summers, mild winters; generally abundant rainfall. **Topography:** eastern delta and prairie, southern lowland forests, and the northwestern highlands, which include the Ozark Plateaus. **Capital:** Little Rock. **Chief airports at:** Cave Springs, Little Rock.

Economy. Chief industries: manufacturing, agriculture, tourism, forestry. **Chief manuf. goods:** poultry processing, motor vehicles & parts, iron & steel, paper & paperboard, plastics, preserved fruits & vegetables, aerospace, rubber. **Chief crops:** rice, soybeans, cotton, hay, wheat, corn, sorghum, tomatoes, peaches, watermelons, pecans, blueberries, grapes. **Livestock** (Jan. 2009): 1.8 mil cattle/calves; (Dec. 2008): 280,000 hogs/pigs, 20.7 mil chickens (excl. broilers), 1.2 bil broilers. **Timber/lumber** (est. 2008): 2.0 bil bd. ft; oak, hickory, gum, cypress, pine. **Nonfuel minerals** (2008 prelim.): $843 mil; bromine, stone (crushed), cement (portland), sand and gravel (construction), lime. **Chief ports:** Little Rock, Pine Bluff, Osceola, Helena, Fort Smith, Van Buren, Camden, Dardanelle, North Little Rock, West Memphis, Crossett, McGehee, Morrilton. **Gross state product** (est. 2008): $98.3 bil. **Sales tax** (2009): 6%. **Employment distrib.** (June 2008): 17.3% govt.; 20.6% trade/trans./util.; 15.1% mfg.; 12.9% ed./health; 9.9% prof./bus. serv.; 8.7% leisure/

hosp.; 4.5% finance; 4.7% constr.; 3.8% other serv.; 1.6% info. **Unemployment** (2008): 5.1%. **Per cap. pers. income** (2008 prelim.): $31,266. **New private housing** (2008): 8,810 units/$994.4 mil. **Commercial banks** (2008): 151; deposits: $45.0 bil. **Savings institutions** (2008): 8; deposits: $2.2 bil.

Federal govt. Fed. civ. employees (Mar. 2007): 13,680; **avg. salary:** $57,092. **Notable fed. facilities:** Little Rock AFB; Pine Bluff Arsenal; Natl. Ctr. for Toxicological Research, Jefferson.

Energy. Electricity production (est. 2007 kWh by source): coal: 25.6 bil; gas: 1.5 bil; hydroelectric: 30.0 mil; nuclear: 15.5 bil; petroleum: 140.0 mil.

State data. Motto: Regnat Populus (The people rule). **Flower:** Apple blossom. **Bird:** Mockingbird. **Tree:** Pine. **Song:** Arkansas. **Entered union** June 15, 1836; rank, 25th. **State fair** at Little Rock; mid-Oct.

History. Quapaw, Caddo, Osage, Cherokee, and Choctaw peoples lived in the area at the time of European contact. The first European explorers were de Soto, 1541; Marquette and Jolliet, 1673; and La Salle, 1682. French fur trader Henri de Tonty founded the first settlement, 1686, at Arkansas Post. In 1762, the area was ceded by France to Spain, then given back again, 1800, and was part of the Louisiana Purchase, 1803. It was made a territory, 1819, and entered the Union as a slave state, 1836. Arkansas seceded in 1861, after the Civil War began, and was readmitted, 1868. Pres. Eisenhower sent federal troops, 1957, to keep Gov. Orval Faubus from blocking racial integration at Central High School in Little Rock. Wal-Mart, now the world's leading retailer, opened its first store at Rogers, 1962. Elected 5 times as governor, Bill Clinton later served 2 terms in the White House (1993-2001); his presidential library opened, 2004, in Little Rock.

Tourist attractions. Hot Springs Natl. Park (water ranging from 95°F-147°F); Eureka Springs; Ozark Folk Center; Blanchard Caverns, near Mountain View; Crater of Diamonds (only U.S. diamond mine) near Murfreesboro; Toltec Mounds Archeological State Park, Little Rock; Buffalo Natl. River; Mid-America Museum, Hot Springs; Pea Ridge Natl. Military Park; Tanyard Springs, Morrilton; Wiederkehr Wine Village.

Famous Arkansans. Daisy Bates, Dee Brown, Paul "Bear" Bryant, Glen Campbell, Johnny Cash, Hattie Caraway, Wesley Clark, Bill Clinton, "Dizzy" Dean, Orval Faubus, James W. Fulbright, John Grisham, John H. Johnson, Douglas MacArthur, John L. McClellan, James S. McDonnell, Scottie Pippen, Dick Powell, Brooks Robinson, Billy Bob Thornton, Winthrop Rockefeller, Mary Steenburgen, Edward Durell Stone, Sam Walton, Archibald Yell.

Tourist information. Arkansas Dept. of Parks & Tourism, 1 Capitol Mall, Little Rock, AR 72201; 1-800-NATURAL; www.arkansas.com

Website. www.state.ar.us

California (CA)

Golden State

People. Population (2008 est.): 36,756,666; rank: 1; net change (2007-08): 1.0%. **Pop. density:** 236.0 per sq mi. **Racial distribution** (2008): 76.6% white; 6.7% black; 12.5% Asian; 1.2% Native Amer./Nat. AK; 0.4% Hawaiian/Pacific Islander; 2 or more races, 2.6%. **Hispanic pop.** (any race): 36.6%.

Geography. Total area: 163,696 sq mi; rank: 3. **Land area:** 155,959 sq mi; rank: 3. **Acres forested:** 32.8 mil. **Location:** western coast of U.S. **Climate:** moderate temperatures and rainfall along the coast; extremes in the interior. **Topography:** long mountainous coastline; central valley; Sierra Nevada on the east; desert basins of the southern interior; rugged mountains of the north. **Capital:** Sacramento. **Chief airports at:** Burbank, Fresno, Long Beach, Los Angeles, Oakland, Ontario, Palm Springs, Sacramento, San Diego, San Francisco, San Jose, Santa Ana.

Economy. Chief industries: agriculture, tourism, apparel, electronics, telecommunications, entertainment. **Chief manuf. goods:** petroleum, aerospace, precision instruments, semiconductors, telecom. & broadcasting equip., pharmaceutical, wineries, plastics, medical equip., preserved fruits & vegetables, printing, dairy, cut & sew apparel, motor vehicles. **Chief crops:** grapes, nursery products, almonds, lettuce, hay, strawberries, floriculture, tomatoes, cotton, oranges, pistachios, walnuts, broccoli, carrots, rice, peaches, lemons. **Livestock** (Jan. 2009): 5.3 mil cattle/calves, 660,000 sheep/lambs; (Dec. 2008): 24.2 mil chickens (excl. broilers).

Timber/lumber (est. 2008): 2.4 bil bd. ft; fir, pine, redwood, oak. **Nonfuel minerals** (2008 prelim.): $4.0 bil; sand and gravel (construction), cement (portland), boron minerals, stone (crushed), soda ash. **Commercial fishing** (2008): $113.4 mil. **Chief ports:** Long Beach, Los Angeles, San Diego, Oakland, San Francisco, Sacramento, Stockton. **Gross state product** (est. 2008): $1.8 trillion. **Sales tax** (2009): 7.25%. **Employment distrib.** (June 2008): 16.9% govt.; 19.0% trade/trans./util.; 9.5% mfg.; 11.2% ed./health; 15.0% prof./bus. serv.; 10.5% leisure/hosp.; 5.8% finance; 5.4% constr.; 3.4% other serv.; 3.1% info. **Unemployment** (2008): 7.2%. **Per cap. pers. income** (2008 prelim.): $42,696. **New private housing** (2008): 62,681 units/$12.3 bil. **Commercial banks** (2008): 317; deposits: $627.3 bil. **Savings institutions** (2008): 36; deposits: $135.2 bil. **Lottery** (2008): total sales: $3.0 bil; profit: $1.1 bil.

Federal govt. Fed. civ. employees (Mar. 2007): 152,554; **avg. salary:** $69,844. **Notable fed. facilities:** San Diego; *USMC Camp Pendleton; Naval Base Coronado; Twentynine Palms; Miramar; Travis AFB; Naval Research Lab., Monterey; Lawrence Livermore Natl. Lab; Berkeley Natl. Lab; NASA Jet Propulsion Lab; Edwards AFB (NASA Dryden Flight Research Ctr., AF Flight Test Ctr.); San Francisco Mint.

Energy. Electricity production (est. 2007 kWh by source): gas: 20.7 bil; hydroelectric: 310.0 mil; nuclear: 35.8 bil; petroleum: 61.0 mil.

State data. Motto: Eureka (I have found it). **Flower:** Golden poppy. **Bird:** California valley quail. **Tree:** California redwood. **Song:** I Love You, California. **Entered union** Sept. 9, 1850; rank, 31st. **State fair** at Sacramento; late Aug.-early Sept.

History. Early inhabitants included more than 100 different Native American tribes with multiple dialects. The first European explorers were Cabrillo, 1542, and Drake, 1579. The first settlement was the Spanish Alta California mission at San Diego, 1769, first in a string founded by Franciscan Father Junípero Serra. California became a province of independent Mexico, 1821. U.S. traders and settlers arrived in the 19th cent. and staged the Bear Flag revolt, 1846, in protest against Mexican rule; later that year U.S. forces occupied California. At the end of the Mexican War, Mexico ceded the territory to the U.S., 1848; that same year gold was discovered, and the famed gold rush began. California became a state, 1850. An economic downturn in the 1870s spurred riots against Chinese immigrants, who had come as laborers in the boom years. An earthquake and related fires devastated San Francisco, 1906. During World War II, Japanese Americans, many of them U.S. citizens, were held in detention camps, 1942-45. Ronald Reagan, a former movie actor, became state governor (1967-75) and U.S. president (1981-89). A budget crisis, 2003, resulted in the recall of Gov. Gray Davis and the election of another former actor, Arnold Schwarzenegger. Led by Hollywood in entertainment and Silicon Valley in high-tech, the state's economy dwarfs that of most nations.

Tourist attractions. The *Queen Mary*, Aquarium of the Pacific, in Long Beach; Palomar Mountain; Disneyland, Anaheim; Getty Center, Universal Studios, in Los Angeles; Tournament of Roses & Rose Bowl, Pasadena; Golden State Museum, Sacramento; San Diego Zoo; Yosemite Valley; Lassen and Sequoia-Kings Canyon natl. parks; Lake Tahoe; Mojave and Colorado deserts; San Francisco Bay; Napa Valley; Monterey Peninsula; oldest living things on earth believed to be a stand of Bristlecone pines in the Inyo Natl. Forest, est. 4,700 years old; Redwood Natl. & State Parks.

Famous Californians. Edmund G. (Pat) Brown, Jerry Brown, Luther Burbank, Julia Child, Ted Danson, Cameron Diaz, Leonardo DiCaprio, Joe DiMaggio, Dianne Feinstein, John C. Fremont, Tom Hanks, Bret Harte, William Randolph Hearst, Helen Hunt, Jack Kemp, Monica Lewinsky, Jack London, George Lucas, Mark McGwire, Marilyn Monroe, John Muir, Richard M. Nixon, George S. Patton Jr., Gregory Peck, Nancy Pelosi, Ronald Reagan, Sally K. Ride, William Saroyan, Father Junípero Serra, O. J. Simpson, Kevin Spacey, Leland Stanford, John Steinbeck, Arnold Schwarzenegger, Shirley Temple, Earl Warren, Ted Williams, Serena Williams, Venus Williams, Tiger Woods.

Tourist information. California Tourism, PO Box 1499, Sacramento, CA 95812-1499; (877) 225-4367; www.visitcalifornia.com

Website. www.state.ca.us

Colorado (CO)
Centennial State

People. Population (2008 est.): 4,939,456; rank: 22; net change (2007-08): 2.0%. **Pop. density:** 47.7 per sq mi. **Racial distribution** (2008): 89.7% white; 4.3% black; 2.7% Asian; 1.2% Native Amer./Nat. AK; 0.2% Hawaiian/Pacific Islander; 2 or more races, 2.0%. **Hispanic pop.** (any race): 20.2%.

Geography. Total area: 104,094 sq mi; rank: 8. **Land area:** 103,718 sq mi; rank: 8. **Acres forested:** 22.6 mil. **Location:** W central U.S. **Climate:** low relative humidity, abundant sunshine, wide daily, seasonal temp. ranges; alpine conditions in the high mountains. **Topography:** eastern dry high plains; hilly to mountainous central plateau; western Rocky Mountains of high ranges, with broad valleys, deep, narrow canyons. **Capital:** Denver. **Chief airports at:** Denver, Colorado Springs.

Economy. Chief industries: manufacturing, construction, government, tourism, agriculture, aerospace, electronics equipment. **Chief manuf. goods:** animal slaughtering, beer, petroleum, pharmaceuticals, aerospace, medical equip., precision instruments, printing, semiconductors. **Chief crops:** hay, corn, potatoes, wheat, onions, dry edible beans, sunflowers, sugar beets, barley, proso millet, cabbage, peaches, lettuce, apples, cantaloupes. **Livestock** (Jan. 2009): 2.6 mil cattle/calves, 410,000 sheep/lambs; (Dec. 2008): 720,000 hogs/pigs, 4.76 mil chickens (excl. broilers). **Timber/lumber** (est. 2008): 106 mil bd. ft; oak, ponderosa pine, Douglas fir. **Nonfuel minerals** (2008 prelim.): $2.1 bil; molybdenum concentrates, sand and gravel (construction), gold, cement (portland), stone (crushed). **Gross state product** (est. 2008): $248.6 bil. **Sales tax** (2009): 2.9%. **Employment distrib.** (June 2008): 16.0% govt.; 18.2% trade/trans./util.; 6.0% mfg.; 10.5% ed./health; 15.2% prof./bus. serv.; 11.9% leisure/hosp.; 6.6% finance; 7.2% constr.; 4.0% other serv.; 3.2% info. **Unemployment** (2008): 4.9%. **Per cap. pers. income** (2008 prelim.): $42,377. **New private housing** (2008): 18,998 units/$4.0 bil. **Commercial banks** (2008): 181; deposits: $79.5 bil. **Savings institutions** (2008): 17; deposits: $3.6 bil. **Lottery** (2008): total sales: $505.8 mil; profit: $122.3 mil.

Federal govt. Fed. civ. employees (Mar. 2007): 35,657; **avg. salary:** $70,351. **Notable fed. facilities:** *U.S. Air Force Academy; Peterson AFB; Denver Mint; Ft. Carson; Natl. Renewable Energy Labs; U.S. Rail Transportation Test Ctr.; Cheyenne Mtn. Operations Ctr. (NORAD, U.S. Space Comm.); Denver Federal Ctr.; Natl. Ctr. for Atmospheric Research; Natl. Inst. for Standards & Technology, Boulder; Natl. Wildlife Res. Ctr.; NOAA Env. Technology Lab.

Energy. Electricity production (est. 2007 kWh by source): coal: 35.8 bil; gas: 4.7 bil; hydroelectric: −168.0 mil; petroleum: 27.0 mil.

State data. Motto: Nil Sine Numine (Nothing without Providence). **Flower:** Rocky Mountain columbine. **Bird:** Lark bunting. **Tree:** Colorado blue spruce. **Song:** Where the Columbines Grow. **Entered union** Aug. 1, 1876; rank 38th. **State fair** at Pueblo; mid-Aug.-early Sept.

History. Paleo-Indians hunted big game in the area at least 11,000 years ago. Anasazi cliff dwellers flourished around Mesa Verde until about 1300 CE; other Native Americans were the Ute, Pueblo, Cheyenne, and Arapaho. The region was claimed by Spain, but passed to France, 1800. The U.S. acquired eastern Colorado in the Louisiana Purchase, 1803. Lt. Zebulon M. Pike explored the area, 1806, sighting the peak that bears his name. After the Mexican War, 1846-48, U.S. immigrants settled in the east, former Mexicans in the south. Gold was discovered in 1858, causing a population boom. Congress created Colorado Territory, 1861. Conflict between newcomers and displaced Native Americans led to the Sand Creek Massacre, 1864, in which U.S. soldiers and settlers killed some 150 Cheyenne and Arapaho. Most Native Americans were later removed to Oklahoma Territory. The 1870s brought statehood, 1876, and rich silver finds that turned Leadville into a boomtown. Federal military and civilian employment in Colorado surged in the 1940s and '50s; since then, tourism and high-tech industries have fueled the economy. The state's Hispanic population grew from 5.8% in 1980 to 19.9% in 2007.

Tourist attractions. Rocky Mountain and Black Canyon of the Gunnison natl. parks; Aspen Ski Resort; Garden of the Gods, Colorado Springs; Great Sand Dunes, Dinosaur, and Colorado natl. monuments; Pikes Peak and Mt. Evans highways; Mesa Verde Natl. Park (ancient Anasazi Indian cliff dwellings); Grand Mesa Natl. Forest; mining towns of Central City, Silverton, Cripple Creek; Burlington's Old Town; Bent's Fort, near La Junta; Georgetown Loop Historic Mining Railroad Park, Cumbres & Toltec Scenic Railroad; limited stakes gaming in Central City, Blackhawk, Cripple Creek, Ignacio, and Towaoe.

Famous Coloradans. Tim Allen, Frederick Bonfils, Henry Brown, Molly Brown, William N. Byers, M. Scott Carpenter, Lon Chaney, Jack Dempsey, Mamie Eisenhower, Douglas Fairbanks, Barney Ford, Scott Hamilton, John Kerry, Chief Ourey, "Baby Doe" Tabor, Lowell Thomas, Byron R. White, Paul Whiteman.

Tourist information. Colorado Tourism Office, 1625 Broadway, Ste. 1700, Denver, CO 80202; 1-800-COLORA-DO; www.colorado.com

Website. www.colorado.gov

Connecticut (CT)
Constitution State, Nutmeg State

People. Population (2008 est.): 3,501,252; rank: 29; net change (2007-08): 0.3%. **Pop. density:** 723.3 per sq mi. **Racial distribution** (2008): 84.3% white; 10.3% black; 3.5% Asian; 0.4% Native Amer./Nat. AK; 0.1% Hawaiian/Pacific Islander; 2 or more races, 1.5%. **Hispanic pop.** (any race): 12.0%.

Geography. Total area: 5,543 sq mi; rank: 48. **Land area:** 4,845 sq mi; rank: 48. **Acres forested:** 1.8 mil. **Location:** New England state in NE corner of the U.S. **Climate:** moderate; winters avg. slightly below freezing; warm, humid summers. **Topography:** western upland, the Berkshires, in the NW, highest elevations; narrow central lowland N-S; hilly eastern upland drained by rivers. **Capital:** Hartford. **Chief airport at:** Windsor Locks.

Economy. Chief industries: manufacturing, retail trade, government, services, finances, insurance, real estate. **Chief manuf. goods:** aerospace, chemicals, fabricated metals, precision instruments, toiletries, medical equip., printing, plastics. **Chief crops:** nursery stock, Christmas trees, mushrooms, sweet corn, apples, tobacco, hay. **Livestock** (Jan. 2009): 52,000 cattle/calves; (Dec. 2008): 3.4 mil chickens (excl. broilers). **Timber/lumber** (est. 2008): 20 mil bd. ft; oak, birch, beech, maple. **Nonfuel minerals** (2008 prelim.): $140 mil; stone (crushed), sand and gravel (construction), stone (dimension), clays (common), gemstones (natural). **Commercial fishing** (2008): $17.1 mil. **Chief ports:** New Haven, Bridgeport, New London. **Gross state product** (est. 2008): $216.2 bil. **Sales tax** (2009): 6.0%. **Employment distrib.** (June 2008): 14.7% govt.; 18.1% trade/trans./util.; 11.1% mfg.; 16.9% ed./health; 12.2% prof./bus. serv.; 8.4% leisure/hosp.; 8.4% finance; 4.1% constr.; 3.8% other serv.; 2.2% info. **Unemployment** (2008): 5.7%. **Per cap. pers. income** (2008 prelim.): $56,248. **New private housing** (2008): 5,220 units/$1.2 bil. **Commercial banks** (2008): 35; deposits: $52.2 bil. **Savings institutions** (2008): 38; deposits: $31.0 bil. **Lottery** (2008): total sales: $998.1 mil; profit: $285.1 mil.

Federal govt. Fed. civ. employees (Mar. 2007): 7,923; **avg. salary:** $71,636. **Notable fed. facilities:** U.S. Coast Guard Academy; *Navy Sub Base New London.

Energy. Electricity production (est. 2007 kWh by source): petroleum: 1.0 mil.

State data. Motto: Qui Transtulit Sustinet (He who transplanted still sustains). **Flower:** Mountain laurel. **Bird:** American robin. **Tree:** White oak. **Song:** Yankee Doodle. **Fifth of** the 13 original states to ratify the Constitution, Jan. 9, 1788. **State Fair:** no official state fair; district and local fairs, largest at Durham, late Sept.

History. At the time of European contact, inhabitants of the area were Algonquian peoples, including the Mohegan and Pequot. Dutch explorer Adriaen Block was the first European visitor, 1614. By 1634, settlers from Plymouth Bay had started colonies along the Connecticut River; in 1637 they defeated the Pequots. The Colony of Connecticut was chartered by England, 1662, adding New Haven, 1665. A Patriot stronghold in the American Revolution, the state actively supported the antislavery movement and the Union cause in the Civil War. The state economy prospered in the 20th cent. from insurance- and defense-related industries. *Nautilus*, the first nuclear-powered submarine, was launched at Groton, 1954.

Tourist attractions. Mark Twain House, Hartford; Yale University's Art Gallery, Peabody Museum, in New Haven; Mystic Seaport, Marine Life Aquarium; P. T. Barnum Museum, Bridgeport; Gillette Castle, Hadlyme; USS *Nautilus* Memorial, Groton (1st nuclear-powered submarine); Mashantucket Pequot Museum & Research Ctr., Foxwoods Resort & Casino, in Ledyard; Mohegan Sun, Uncasville; Lake Compounce, Bristol.

Famous "Nutmeggers." Ethan Allen, Phineas T. Barnum, G.W. Bush, Samuel Colt, Jonathan Edwards, Nathan Hale, Katharine Hepburn, Isaac Hull, Robert Mitchum, J. Pierpont Morgan, Ralph Nader, Israel Putnam, Wallace Stevens, Harriet Beecher Stowe, Mark Twain, Noah Webster, Eli Whitney.

Tourist information. Connecticut Commission on Culture and Tourism, One Constitution Plz., 2nd Fl., Hartford, CT 06103; 1-888-CTVISIT, (860) 256-2800; www.ctvisit.com

Website. www.ct.gov

Delaware (DE)
First State, Diamond State

People. Population (2008 est.): 873,092; rank: 45; net change (2007-08): 1.3%. **Pop. density:** 447.9 per sq mi. **Racial distribution** (2008): 74.3% white; 20.9% black; 2.9% Asian; 0.4% Native Amer./Nat. AK; 0.1% Hawaiian/Pacific Islander; 2 or more races, 1.4%. **Hispanic pop.** (any race): 6.8%.

Geography. Total area: 2,489 sq mi; rank: 49. **Land area:** 1,954 sq mi; rank: 49. **Acres forested:** 0.4 mil. **Location:** the Delmarva Peninsula on the Atlantic coastal plain. **Climate:** moderate. **Topography:** Piedmont plateau to the N, sloping to a near sea-level plain. **Capital:** Dover.

Economy. Chief industries: chemicals, agriculture, finance, poultry, shellfish, tourism, auto assembly, food processing, transportation equipment. **Chief manuf. goods:** pharmaceuticals, poultry processing, soap & cleaning compounds, precision instruments, basic chemicals, plastics. **Chief crops:** soybeans, corn, greenhouse & nursery, wheat, potatoes, barley, hay, watermelons, lima beans, green peas, pumpkins, mushrooms, cabbage. **Livestock** (Jan. 2009): 21,000 cattle/calves; (Dec. 2008): 242.9 mil broilers. **Timber/lumber:** figs. withheld; hardwoods and softwoods. **Nonfuel minerals** (2008 prelim.): $21.5 mil; sand and gravel (construction), magnesium compounds, stone (crushed), gemstones (natural). **Commercial fishing** (2008): $6.7 mil. **Chief port:** Wilmington. **Gross state product** (est. 2008): $61.8 bil. **Sales tax** (2009): none. **Employment distrib.** (June 2008): 13.7% govt.; 18.8% trade/trans./util.; 7.6% mfg.; 13.5% ed./health; 13.4% prof./bus. serv.; 10.0% leisure/hosp.; 10.4% finance; 6.2% constr.; 4.8% other serv.; 1.6% info. **Unemployment** (2008): 4.8%. **Per cap. pers. income** (2008 prelim.): $40,852. **New private housing** (2008): 3,346 units/$393.6 mil. **Commercial banks** (2008): 34; deposits: $91.5 bil. **Savings institutions** (2008): 8; deposits: $85.4 bil. **Lottery** (2008): total sales: $736.4 mil; profit: $252.5 mil.

Federal govt. Fed. civ. employees (Mar. 2007): 3,140; **avg. salary:** $61,268. **Notable fed. facilities:** Dover AFB, Federal Wildlife Refuge, Bombay Hook.

Energy. Electricity production (est. 2006 kWh by source): petroleum: 4 mil.

State data. Motto: Liberty and independence. **Flower:** Peach blossom. **Bird:** Blue hen chicken. **Tree:** American holly. **Song:** Our Delaware. **First** of original 13 states to ratify the Constitution, Dec. 7, 1787. **State fair** at Harrington; mid-late July.

History. The Lenni Lenape (Delaware) people lived in the region at the time of European contact. Henry Hudson located the Delaware R., 1609, and in 1610, English explorer Samuel Argall entered Delaware Bay, naming the area after Virginia's governor, Lord De La Warr. Dutch, Swedish, and Finnish settlers were followed by the British, who took control in 1664. After 1682, Delaware became part of Pennsylvania, and in 1704 it was granted its own assembly. It adopted a constitution as the state of Delaware, 1776, and was first to ratify the federal Constitution, 1787. Although it remained in the Union during the Civil War, Delaware retained slavery until the 13th Amendment abolished it in 1865. The DuPont company, founded as a gunpowder mill in 1802, became an industrial giant in the 20th century, making nylon, Teflon, and other synthetics. Pro-business laws drew many out-of-state firms to incorporate in Delaware. In 2000, Ruth Ann Minner was elected Delaware's first woman governor.

Tourist attractions. Ft. Christina Monument, site of founding of New Sweden, Holy Trinity (Old Swedes) Church, erected 1698, the oldest Protestant church in the U.S. still in use, in Wilmington; Hagley Museum, Winterthur Museum and Gardens, near Wilmington; New Castle historic district; John

Dickinson "Penman of the Revolution" home, Dover; Rehoboth Beach; Dover Downs Intl. Speedway.

Famous Delawareans. Thomas F. Bayard, Joseph Biden, Henry Seidel Canby, E. I. du Pont, John P. Marquand, Howard Pyle, Caesar Rodney.

Tourist information. Delaware Tourism Office, 99 Kings Hwy., Dover, DE 19901; 1-866-2VISITDE; www.visitdelaware.com

Website. www.delaware.gov

Florida (FL)
Sunshine State

People. Population (2008 est.): 18,328,340; rank: 4; net change (2007-08): 0.7%. **Pop. density:** 341.9 per sq mi. **Racial distribution** (2008): 79.8% white; 15.9% black; 2.3% Asian; 0.5% Native Amer./Nat. AK; 0.1% Hawaiian/Pacific Islander; 2 or more races, 1.4%. **Hispanic pop.** (any race): 21.0%.

Geography. Total area: 65,755 sq mi; rank: 22. **Land area:** 53,927 sq mi; rank: 26. **Acres forested:** 16.1 mil. **Location:** peninsula jutting southward 500 mi between the Atlantic and the Gulf of Mexico. **Climate:** subtropical N of Bradenton-Lake Okeechobee-Vero Beach line; tropical S of line. **Topography:** land is flat or rolling; highest point is 345 ft in the NW. **Capital:** Tallahassee. **Chief airports at:** Fort Lauderdale, Fort Myers, Jacksonville, Miami, Orlando, Pensacola, Sanford, Sarasota/Bradenton, Tampa, West Palm Beach.

Economy. Chief industries: tourism, agriculture, manufacturing, construction, services, international trade. **Chief manuf. goods:** navigational instruments, medical equip., cement, broadcasting equip., beverages, phosphatic fertilizer, preserved fruits & vegetables, structural metal, printing. **Chief crops:** greenhouse & nursery, oranges, sugarcane, tomatoes, green peppers, grapefruit, strawberries, snap beans, sweet corn, potatoes, cucumbers, tangerines. **Livestock** (Jan. 2009): 1.7 mil cattle/calves; (Dec. 2008): 12.6 mil chickens (excl. broilers), 63.8 mil broilers. **Timber/lumber** (est. 2008): 783 mil bd. ft; pine, cypress, cedar. **Nonfuel minerals** (2008 prelim.): $4.2 bil; phosphate rock, stone (crushed), cement (portland), sand and gravel (construction), zirconium concentrates. **Commercial fishing** (2008): $170.0 mil. **Chief ports:** Pensacola, Tampa, Manatee, Miami, Port Everglades, Jacksonville, St. Petersburg, Canaveral. **Gross state product** (est. 2008): $744.1 bil. **Sales tax** (2009): 6.0%. **Employment distrib.** (June 2008): 13.3% govt.; 20.2% trade/trans./util.; 4.7% mfg.; 13.1% ed./health; 16.5% prof./bus. serv.; 12.1% leisure/hosp.; 6.8% finance; 6.7% constr.; 4.4% other serv.; 2.0% info. **Unemployment** (2008): 6.2%. **Per cap. pers. income** (2008 prelim.): $39,070. **New private housing** (2008): 61,042 units/$10.8 bil. **Commercial banks** (2008): 333; deposits: $325.7 bil. **Savings institutions** (2008): 48; deposits: $54.6. bil. **Lottery** (2008): total sales: 4.2 bil; profit: $1.3 bil.

Federal govt. Fed. civ. employees (Mar. 2007): 78,436; **avg. salary:** $64,438. **Notable fed. facilities:** John F. Kennedy Space Ctr.; Eglin AFB; MacDill AFB; *Pensacola NAS; Jacksonville NAS; Mayport Naval Sta.

Energy. Electricity production (est. 2007 kWh by source): coal: 62.9 bil; gas: 88.6 bil; nuclear: 29.3 bil; petroleum: 15.1 bil.

State data. Motto: In God we trust. **Flower:** Orange blossom. **Bird:** Mockingbird. **Tree:** Sabal palmetto palm. **Song:** Old Folks at Home. **Entered union** Mar. 3, 1845; rank, 27th. **State fair** at Tampa; early-mid Feb.

History. Florida has been inhabited for at least 12,000 years. Timucua, Apalachee, and Calusa peoples were living in the region when the earliest Europeans came; later the Seminole migrated from Georgia to Florida, becoming dominant there in the early 18th cent. The first European to see Florida was Ponce de León, 1513. France established a colony, Fort Caroline, on the St. Johns River, 1564. Spain settled St. Augustine, 1565, and Spanish troops massacred most of the French. Britain's Sir Francis Drake burned St. Augustine, 1586. In 1763, Spain ceded Florida to Great Britain, which held the area 20 years before returning it to Spain. Florida was ceded to the U.S. in the Adams-Onís Treaty, 1819. The Seminole War, 1835-42, resulted in removal of most Native Americans to Indian Territory. Florida joined the Union in 1845, seceded in 1861, and was readmitted in 1868. In the late 19th cent., hotel and railroad builder Henry M. Flagler laid the foundations of the tourism industry. The state experienced phenomenal population growth in the 20th cent., especially after 1950. The first U.S. astronaut was launched into space from Cape Canaveral, 1961. Walt Disney World opened near Orlando, 1971. Hurricane Andrew slammed S. Florida, 1992, causing at least $25 bil in property damage. A dispute over Florida's presidential vote in 2000 led to the U.S. Supreme Court decision awarding the White House to George W. Bush; his brother Jeb was state governor 1999-2007. Cuban expatriates wield major political influence in the Miami area.

Tourist attractions. Miami Beach; Castillo de San Marcos, St. Augustine (oldest permanent European settlement in U.S.); Walt Disney World Resort, Sea World, Universal Studios, near Orlando; Kennedy Space Center & U.S. Astronaut Hall of Fame; Everglades Natl. Park; Ringling Museums of Art & the Circus, in Sarasota; Cypress Gardens, Winter Haven; Busch Gardens, Tampa; Florida Caverns State Park, near Mariana; Church St. Station, Orlando; Silver Springs, Ocala.

Famous Floridians. Edna Buchanan, Jeb Bush, Marjory Stoneman Douglas, Henry M. Flagler, Carl Hiaasen, Zora Neale Hurston, James Weldon Johnson, MacKinlay Kantor, John D. MacDonald, Chief Osceola, Claude Pepper, Henry B. Plant, A. Philip Randolph, Marjorie Kinnan Rawlings, Janet Reno, Joseph W. Stilwell, Charles P. Summerall, Ben Vereen.

Tourist information. Visit Florida, 2540 W. Executive Center Cir., Ste. 200, Tallahassee, FL 32301; 1-888-7FLA-USA; www.visitflorida.com
Website. www.myflorida.com

Georgia (GA)
Empire State of the South, Peach State

People. Population (2008 est.): 9,685,744; rank: 9; net change (2007-08): 1.7%. **Pop. density:** 168.4 per sq mi. **Racial distribution** (2008): 65.4% white; 30.0% black; 2.9% Asian; 0.4% Native Amer./Nat. AK; 0.1% Hawaiian/Pacific Islander; 2 or more races, 1.3%. **Hispanic pop.** (any race): 8.0%.

Geography. Total area: 59,425 sq mi; rank: 24. **Land area:** 57,906 sq mi; rank: 21. **Acres forested:** 24.8 mil. **Location:** South Atlantic state. **Climate:** maritime tropical air masses dominate in summer; polar air masses in winter; E central area drier. **Topography:** most southerly of the Blue Ridge Mts. cover NE and N central; central Piedmont extends to the fall line of rivers; coastal plain levels to the coast flatlands. **Capital:** Atlanta. **Chief airports at:** Atlanta, Savannah.

Economy. Chief industries: services, manufacturing, retail trade. **Chief manuf. goods:** carpet & rugs, animal slaughtering & processing, motor vehicles & parts, plastics, aircrafts, paper, chemicals, food. **Chief crops:** cotton, greenhouse & nursery, peanuts, pecans, corn, tomatoes, cucumbers, onions, watermelons, tobacco, squash, blueberries, hay, cabbage, soybeans, peaches, snap beans, wheat. **Livestock** (Jan. 2009): 1.1 mil cattle/calves; (Dec. 2008): 27.2 mil chickens (excl. broilers), 1.4 bil broilers. **Timber/lumber** (est. 2008): 2.3 bil bd. ft; pine, hardwood. **Nonfuel minerals** (2008 prelim.): $1.9 bil; clays (kaolin), stone (crushed), cement (portland), clays (fuller's earth), sand and gravel (construction). **Commercial fishing** (2008): $12.5 mil. **Chief ports:** Savannah, Brunswick. **Gross state product** (est. 2008): $397.8 bil. **Sales tax** (2009): 4.0%. **Employment distrib.** (June 2008): 16.3% govt.; 21.5% trade/trans./util.; 10.0% mfg.; 11.1% ed./health; 13.6% prof./bus. serv.; 9.9% leisure/hosp.; 5.5% finance; 5.2% constr.; 3.9% other serv.; 2.8% info. **Unemployment** (2008): 6.2%. **Per cap. pers. income** (2008 prelim.): $33,975. **New private housing** (2008): 35,368 units/$5.0 bil. **Commercial banks** (2008): 354; deposits: $179.2 bil. **Savings institutions** (2008): 29; deposits: $5.1bil. **Lottery** (2008): total sales: $3.5 bil; profit: $867.7 mil.

Federal govt. Fed. civ. employees (Mar. 2007): 72,621; **avg. salary:** $64,586. **Notable fed. facilities:** Ft. Benning; Ft. Stewart; Fed. Law Enforcement Training Ctr., Glynco; Robins AFB; Ft. Gordon; King's Bay Naval Base; Moody AFB; *Navy Supply Corps School; *Ft. McPherson; Centers for Disease Control; Marine Corps Logistics.

Energy. Electricity production (est. 2007 kWh by source): coal: 89.6 bil; gas: 8.8 bil; hydroelectric: −322.0 mil; nuclear: 32.5 bil; petroleum: 85.0 mil.

State data. Motto: Wisdom, justice, and moderation. **Flower:** Cherokee rose. **Bird:** Brown thrasher. **Tree:** Live oak. **Song:** Georgia On My Mind. **Fourth** of the 13 original states to ratify the Constitution, Jan. 2, 1788. **State fair** at Macon, late Sept.-Oct.

History. Creek and Cherokee peoples were living in the region when Spaniards founded Santa Catalina mission, 1566, on Saint Catherines Island. Gen. James Oglethorpe established a colony at Savannah, 1733, for the poor and religiously persecuted. Oglethorpe defeated a Spanish army from Florida at Bloody Marsh, 1742. Georgia was a battleground in the American Revolution, with the British finally evacuating Savannah in 1782. When Georgia entered the Union, 1788, its plantation economy relied on slaves for rice and cotton growing. The Cherokee were removed to Indian Territory, 1838-39, and thousands died on the long march, known as the Trail of Tears. By 1860 the number of slaves exceeded 462,000 (44% of the total population). Georgia seceded from the Union, 1861, and was invaded by Union forces, 1864, under Gen. William T. Sherman, who took Atlanta, Sept. 2, and proceeded on his famous "march to the sea," ending in Dec., in Savannah. Georgia was readmitted, 1870. Born 1929 in Atlanta, Martin Luther King Jr., made the city his home base during the civil rights struggles of the 1960s. Atlanta became the leading city of the "New South," world headquarters of Coca-Cola and CNN, and host of the 1996 Summer Olympic Games. Hispanics are a rapidly growing economic and political force in the state.

Tourist attractions. State Capitol, Stone Mt. Park, Six Flags Over Georgia, Kennesaw Mt. Natl. Battlefield Park, Martin Luther King Jr. Natl. Historic Site, Underground Atlanta, Jimmy Carter Library & Museum, all Atlanta; Chickamauga and Chattanooga Natl. Military Park, near Dalton; Chattahoochee Natl. Forest; Helen alpine village; Dahlonega, site of America's first gold rush; Brasstown Bald Mt.; Lake Lanier; Franklin D. Roosevelt's Little White House, Warm Springs; Callaway Gardens, Pine Mt.; Andersonville Natl. Historic Site; Okefenokee Swamp, near Waycross; Jekyll, St. Simons, Cumberland islands; Savannah historic riverfront district.

Famous Georgians. Kim Basinger, Griffin Bell, James Bowie, James Brown, Erskine Caldwell, Jimmy Carter, Ray Charles, Lucius D. Clay, Ty Cobb, James Dickey, John C. Fremont, Newt Gingrich, Joel Chandler Harris, "Doc" Holliday, Holly Hunter, Alan Jackson, Jasper Johns, Martin Luther King Jr., Gladys Knight, Sidney Lanier, Little Richard, Juliette Gordon Low, Margaret Mitchell, Sam Nunn, Flannery O'Connor, Otis Redding, Burt Reynolds, Julia Roberts, Jackie Robinson, Clarence Thomas, Travis Tritt, Ted Turner, Carl Vinson, Alice Walker, Herschel Walker, Joseph Wheeler, Joanne Woodward, Trisha Yearwood, Andrew Young.

Tourist information. Dept. of Economic Development, 75 Fifth St., NW, Ste. 1200, Atlanta, GA 30308; 1-800-VISITGA; www.exploregeorgia.org
Website. www.georgia.gov

Hawai'i (HI)
Aloha State

People. Population (2008 est.): 1,288,198; rank: 42; net change (2007-08): 0.8%. **Pop. density:** 200.4 per sq mi. **Racial distribution** (2008): 29.7% white; 3.1% black; 39.3% Asian; 0.6% Native Amer./Nat. AK; 9.1% Hawaiian/Pacific Islander; 2 or more races, 18.3%. **Hispanic pop.** (any race): 8.7%.

Geography. Total area: 10,931 sq mi; rank: 43. **Land area:** 6,423 sq mi; rank: 47. **Acres forested:** 1.7 mil. **Location:** Hawaiian Islands lie in the North Pacific, 2,397 mi SW from San Francisco. **Climate:** subtropical, with wide variations in rainfall; Waialeale, on Kaua'i, wettest spot in U.S. (annual rainfall 460 in.) **Topography:** islands are tops of a chain of submerged volcanic mountains; active volcanoes: Mauna Loa, Kilauea. **Capital:** Honolulu. **Chief airports at:** Hilo, Honolulu, Kahului, Kailua Kona, Lihue.

Economy. Chief industries: tourism, defense, sugar, pineapples. **Chief manuf. goods:** concrete, printing, baked goods, sugar, preserved fruits & vegetables, apparel. **Chief crops:** flowers & nursery, pineapples, seed crops, sugarcane, macadamia nuts, coffee, algae, papayas, tomatoes, bananas, basil, ginger. **Livestock** (Jan. 2009): 150,000 cattle/calves; (Dec. 2008): 373,000 chickens (excl. broilers). **Timber/lumber:** figs. undisclosed. **Nonfuel minerals** (2008 prelim.): $158 mil; stone (crushed), sand and gravel (construction), gemstones (natural). **Commercial fishing** (2008): $84.9 mil. **Chief ports:** Honolulu, Hilo, Kailua. **Gross state product** (est. 2008): $63.8 bil. **Sales tax** (2009): 4.0%. **Employment distrib.** (June 2008): 20.0% govt.; 18.9% trade/trans./util.; 2.4% mfg.; 12.0% ed./health;

12.3% prof./bus. serv.; 17.3% leisure/hosp.; 4.7% finance; 6.3% constr.; 4.3% other serv.; 1.7% info. **Unemployment** (2008): 3.9%. **Per cap. pers. income** (2008 prelim.): $40,490. **New private housing** (2008): 4,115 units/$1.2 bil. **Commercial banks** (2008): 8; deposits: $20.6 bil. **Savings institutions** (2008): 3; deposits: $5.6 bil.

Federal govt. Fed. civ. employees (Mar. 2007): 22,355; **avg. salary:** $57,163. **Notable fed. facilities:** Pearl Harbor Naval Shipyard; Schofield Barracks; Marine Corps Base-Kaneohe Bay; *Hickam AFB; Tripler Army Med. Ctr.; Ft. Shafter; Wheeler AFB; Prince Kuhio Federal Bldg.

Energy. Electricity production (est. 2007 kWh by source): petroleum: 7.0 bil.

State data. Motto: The life of the land is perpetuated in righteousness. **Flower:** Yellow hibiscus. **Bird:** Hawaiian goose. **Tree:** Kukui (Candlenut). **Song:** Hawai'i Pono'i. **Entered union** Aug. 21, 1959; rank, 50th. **State fair** at Honolulu, late May-June.

History. Polynesians from islands 2,000 mi to the S settled the Hawaiian Islands, probably 300-600 CE. The first European visitor was British captain James Cook, 1778. King Kamehameha I united the islands by 1810. Christian missionaries arrived, 1819, bringing Western culture. Under the reign, 1825-54, of King Kamehameha III, a constitution, legislature, and public school system were instituted. Sugar production began, 1835, and it became the dominant industry. Queen Liliuokalani was deposed, 1893, and a republic was established, 1894, headed by Sanford B. Dole. Annexation by the U.S. came in 1898. The Japanese attack on Pearl Harbor, Dec. 7, 1941, brought the U.S. into World War II. Hawai'i attained statehood, 1959. Hurricane Iniki pounded Kaua'i, 1992, causing about $1 bil in damage. In 2006, Pres. George W. Bush designated the Northwestern Hawaiian Islands National Monument, a marine area of 140,000 sq mi.

Tourist attractions. Hawaii Volcanoes, Haleakala natl. parks; Natl. Memorial Cemetery of the Pacific, Waikiki Beach, Diamond Head, in Honolulu; USS *Arizona* Memorial, Pearl Harbor; Hanauma Bay; Polynesian Cultural Center, Laie; Nu'uanu Pali; Waimea Canyon; Wailoa and Wailuku River state parks.

Famous Islanders. Bernice Pauahi Bishop, Tia Carrere, Father Damien de Veuster, Don Ho, Duke Kahanamoku, King Kamehameha, Brook Mahealani Lee, Daniel K. Inouye, Jason Scott Lee, Queen Liliuokalani, Bette Midler, Ellison Onizuka.

Tourist information. Hawaii Visitors and Conventions Bureau, 2270 Kalakaua Ave., Ste. 801, Honolulu, HI 96815; 1-800-GOHAWAII; www.gohawaii.com

Website. www.ehawaii.gov

Idaho (ID)
Gem State

People. Population (2008 est.): 1,523,816; rank: 39; net change (2007-08): 1.8%. **Pop. density:** 18.4 per sq mi. **Racial distribution** (2008): 94.6% white; 0.9% black; 1.1% Asian; 1.5% Native Amer./Nat. AK; 0.1% Hawaiian/Pacific Islander; 2 or more races, 1.7%. **Hispanic pop.** (any race): 10.2%.

Geography. Total area: 83,570 sq mi; rank: 14. **Land area:** 82,747 sq mi; rank: 11. **Acres forested:** 21.4 mil. **Location:** northwestern Mountain state bordering on British Columbia. **Climate:** tempered by Pacific westerly winds; drier, colder, continental climate in SE; altitude an important factor. **Topography:** Snake R. plains in the S; central region of mountains, canyons, gorges (Hells Canyon, 7,900 ft, deepest in N. America); subalpine northern region. **Capital:** Boise. **Chief airport at:** Boise.

Economy. Chief industries: manufacturing, agriculture, tourism, lumber, mining, electronics. **Chief manuf. goods:** computers & electronics, preserved fruits & vegetables, cheese, lumber. **Chief crops:** potatoes, wheat, hay, sugar beets, barley, greenhouse & nursery, onions, dry beans, corn, mint, apples, hops, peaches, lentils, peas, cherries, plums & prunes, oats. **Livestock** (Jan. 2009): 2.1 mil cattle/calves, 210,000 sheep/lambs; (Dec. 2008): 859,000 chickens (excl. broilers). **Timber/lumber** (est. 2006): 854 mil bd. ft; pine, fir, spruce. **Nonfuel minerals** (2008 prelim.): $1.2 bil; phosphate rock, molybdenum concentrates, sand and gravel (construction), silver, lead. **Chief port:** Lewiston. **Gross state product** (est. 2008): $52.7 bil. **Sales tax** (2009): 6.0%. **Employment distrib.** (June 2008): 18.3% govt.; 19.9% trade/trans./util.; 9.4% mfg.; 11.3% ed./health;

12.8% prof./bus. serv.; 10.1% leisure/hosp.; 4.9% finance; 7.6% constr.; 3.1% other serv.; 1.7% info. **Unemployment** (2008): 4.9%. **Per cap. pers. income** (2008 prelim.): $32,133. **New private housing** (2008): 6,470 units/$1.1 bil. **Commercial banks** (2008): 31; deposits: $14.9 bil. **Savings institutions** (2008): 6; deposits: $2.3 bil. **Lottery** (2008): total sales: $136.8 mil; profit: $36.2 mil.

Federal govt. Fed. civ. employees (Mar. 2007): 8,731; **avg. salary:** $59,223. **Notable fed. facilities:** Idaho Natl. Lab; *Mountain Home AFB.

Energy. Electricity production (est. 2007 kWh by source): gas: 127.0 mil.

State data. Motto: Esto Perpetua (It is perpetual). **Flower:** Syringa. **Bird:** Mountain bluebird. **Tree:** White pine. **Song:** Here We Have Idaho. **Entered union** July 3, 1890; rank, 43rd. **State fair** at Boise, late Aug.; at Blackfoot, early Sept.

History. Paleo-Indian hunters roamed the land over 13,000 years ago; later inhabitants included Shoshone, Northern Paiute, Bannock, and Nez Percé peoples. Lewis and Clark expedition explored, 1805-06. Next came fur traders, 1809-34, and missionaries, 1830s-50s. Mormons made their first permanent settlement at Franklin, 1860. Idaho's gold rush began the same year and brought thousands of permanent settlers. A series of Indian wars followed, including a remarkable campaign by Chief Joseph and the Nez Percé that ended with his surrender in Montana, 1877. Idaho became a territory, 1863, and a state, 1890. In the 20th cent., it emerged as a leader in potato, lumber, and silver output. The Sun Valley ski resort opened in 1936, boosting tourism. Startup of Lewiston's river port, 1975, opened Idaho to oceangoing trade. Fueled by high-tech job growth, the state's population jumped 13.3% in 2000-06.

Tourist attractions. Hells Canyon, deepest gorge in N. America; World Center for Birds of Prey, Boise; Craters of the Moon Natl. Monument; Sun Valley, in Sawtooth Mts.; Shoshone Falls; Lava Hot Springs; Lake Pend Oreille; Lake Coeur d'Alene; Sawtooth Natl. Recreation Area, Redfish Lake; River of No Return Wilderness Area.

Famous Idahoans. William E. Borah, Frank Church, Lou Dobbs, Fred T. Dubois, Chief Joseph, Harmon Killebrew, Ezra Pound, Sacagawea, Picabo Street, Lana Turner.

Tourist information. Idaho Division of Tourism Development, 700 W. State St., PO Box 83720, Boise, ID 83720; 1-800-VISITID; www.visitid.org

Website. www.state.id.us

Illinois (IL)
Prairie State

People. Population (2008 est.): 12,901,563; rank: 5; net change (2007-08): 0.6%. **Pop. density:** 232.4 per sq mi. **Racial distribution** (2008): 79.1% white; 14.9% black; 4.3% Asian; 0.3% Native Amer./Nat. AK; 0.1% Hawaiian/Pacific Islander; 2 or more races, 1.2%. **Hispanic pop.** (any race): 15.2%.

Geography. Total area: 57,914 sq mi; rank: 25. **Land area:** 55,584 sq mi; rank: 24. **Acres forested:** 4.5 mil. **Location:** East North Central state; western, southern, and eastern boundaries formed by Mississippi, Ohio, and Wabash rivers, respectively. **Climate:** temperate; typically cold, snowy winters, hot summers. **Topography:** prairie and fertile plains throughout; open hills in the southern region. **Capital:** Springfield. **Chief airports at:** Chicago (2).

Economy. Chief industries: services, manufacturing, travel, wholesale and retail trade, finance, insurance, real estate, construction, health care, agriculture. **Chief manuf. goods:** food, petroleum, plastics, chemicals, agricultural machinery, pharmaceuticals, motor vehicles, printing. **Chief crops:** corn, soybeans, hay, wheat, greenhouse & nursery, apples, peaches, sorghum. **Livestock** (Jan. 2009): 1.2 mil cattle/calves, 58,000 sheep/lambs; (Dec. 2008): 4.4 mil hogs/pigs, 5.9 mil chickens (excl. broilers). **Timber/lumber** (est. 2008): 142 mil bd. ft; oak, hickory, maple, cottonwood. **Nonfuel minerals** (2008 prelim.): $1.1 bil; stone (crushed), cement (portland), sand and gravel (construction), sand and gravel (industrial), lime. **Chief port:** Chicago. **Gross state product** (est. 2008): $633.7 bil. **Sales tax** (2009): 6.25%. **Employment distrib.** (June 2008): 14.0% govt.; 20.3% trade/trans./util.; 11.1% mfg.; 13.0% ed./health; 14.7% prof./bus. serv.; 9.2% leisure/hosp.; 6.6% finance; 4.6% constr.; 4.4% other serv.; 1.9% info. **Unemployment** (2008): 6.5%. **Per cap. pers. income** (2008 prelim.): $42,397. **New private housing** (2008): 22,528 units/$3.8 bil. **Commercial banks**

(2008): 619; deposits: $319.9 bil. **Savings institutions** (2008): 93; deposits: $24.3 bil. **Lottery** (2008): total sales: $2.1 bil; profit: $657.0 mil.

Federal govt. Fed. civ. employees (Mar. 2007): 46,177; **avg. salary:** $70,807. **Notable fed. facilities:** *Great Lakes Naval Station; Fermi Natl. Accelerator Lab; Argonne Natl. Lab; Scott AFB; *Rock Island Arsenal.

Energy. Electricity production (est. 2007 kWh by source): coal: 9.4 bil; gas: 764.0 mil.

State data. Motto: State sovereignty—national union. **Flower:** Native violet. **Bird:** Cardinal. **Tree:** White oak. **Song:** Illinois. **Entered union** Dec. 3, 1818; rank, 21st. **State fair** at Springfield, mid-Aug.; DuQuoin, late Aug.-Sept.

History. The region has been inhabited for at least 10,000 years; seminomadic Algonquian peoples, including the Peoria, Illinois, Kaskaskia, and Tamaroa, lived there at the time of European contact. Fur traders were the first Europeans in Illinois, followed shortly by Jolliet and Marquette, 1673, and La Salle, 1680, who built a fort near present-day Peoria. French priests established the first permanent settlements, at Cahokia, near present-day St. Louis, 1699, and Kaskaskia, 1703. France ceded the area to Britain, 1763, and in 1778, American Gen. George Rogers Clark took Kaskaskia from the British without a shot. Illinois became a separate territory, 1809, and a state, 1818. Defeat of Native American tribes in the Black Hawk War, 1832, and canal, rail, and road construction brought rapid change. Mormon settlers at Nauvoo, 1839, met with hostility, and a Carthage mob killed Mormon leader Joseph Smith and his brother, 1844. The great Chicago Fire, 1871, destroyed the city's downtown. Illinois became a center for the labor movement, leading to bitter conflicts such as the Haymarket riot, 1886, and Pullman strike, 1894. Social reformer Jane Addams founded Hull House, 1889, to aid immigrants and the poor. During 1900-70, as manufacturing expanded, many African Americans arrived from the southern U.S. Chicago police violently suppressed antiwar protests at the 1968 Democratic National Convention. Dennis Hastert was the longest serving Republican Speaker of the House, 1999-2007. Barack Obama, elected in 2004, was only the fifth African American to serve in the U.S. Senate.

Tourist attractions. Chicago museums and parks; Illinois State Museum, Abraham Lincoln Presidential Library and Museum, in Springfield; Cahokia Mounds, Collinsville; Starved Rock State Park; Crab Orchard Wildlife Refuge; Mormon settlement at Nauvoo; Fts. Kaskaskia, Chartres, Massac (parks); Shawnee Natl. Forest; Dickson Mounds Museum, Lewistown.

Famous Illinoisans. Jane Addams, John Ashcroft, Saul Bellow, Jack Benny, Ray Bradbury, Gwendolyn Brooks, William Jennings Bryan, St. Frances Xavier Cabrini, Hillary Rodham Clinton, Clarence Darrow, John Deere, Stephen A. Douglas, James T. Farrell, George W. Ferris, Marshall Field, Betty Friedan, Benny Goodman, Ulysses S. Grant, Dennis Hastert, Ernest Hemingway, Charlton Heston, Wild Bill Hickok, Henry J. Hyde, Abraham Lincoln, Vachel Lindsay, Edgar Lee Masters, Oscar Mayer, Cyrus McCormick, Ronald Reagan, Donald Rumsfeld, Carl Sandburg, Adlai Stevenson, James Watson, Frank Lloyd Wright, Philip Wrigley.

Tourist information. Illinois Bureau of Tourism, 100 W. Randolph St., Ste. 3-400, Chicago, IL 60601; 1-800-2CONNECT; www.enjoyillinois.com

Website. www.illinois.gov

Indiana (IN)
Hoosier State

People. Population (2008 est.): 6,376,792; rank: 16; net change (2007-08): 0.6%. **Pop. density:** 178.0 per sq mi. **Racial distribution** (2008): 88.0% white; 9.1% black; 1.4% Asian; 0.3% Native Amer./Nat. AK; <0.05% Hawaiian/Pacific Islander; 2 or more races, 1.2%. **Hispanic pop.** (any race): 5.2%.

Geography. Total area: 36,418 sq mi; rank: 38. **Land area:** 35,867 sq mi; rank: 38. **Acres forested:** 4.7 mil. **Location:** East North Central state; Lake Michigan on N border. **Climate:** 4 distinct seasons with a temperate climate. **Topography:** hilly southern region; fertile rolling plains of central region; flat, heavily glaciated north; dunes along Lake Michigan shore. **Capital:** Indianapolis. **Chief airport at:** Indianapolis.

Economy. Chief industries: manufacturing, services, agriculture, government, wholesale and retail trade, transportation and public utilities. **Chief manuf. goods:** motor vehicles & parts, iron & steel mills, pharmaceuticals, petroleum, plas-

tics, medical equipment, printing. **Chief crops:** corn, soybeans, greenhouse & nursery, wheat, hay, tomatoes, watermelons, apples. **Livestock** (Jan. 2009): 860,000 cattle/calves, 50,000 sheep/lambs; (Dec. 2008): 3.5 mil hogs/pigs, 31.0 mil chickens (excl. broilers). **Timber/lumber** (est. 2008): 327 mil bd. ft; oak, tulip, beech, sycamore. **Nonfuel minerals** (2008 prelim.): $932 mil; stone (crushed), cement (portland), sand and gravel (construction), lime, stone (dimension). **Chief ports:** Burns Harbor, Portage; Southwind Maritime, Mt. Vernon; Clark Maritime, Jeffersonville. **Gross state product** (est. 2008): $254.9 bil. **Sales tax** (2009): 7.0%. **Employment distrib.** (June 2008): 14.0% govt.; 19.6% trade/trans./util.; 18.1% mfg.; 13.3% ed./health; 9.8% prof./bus. serv.; 9.9% leisure/hosp.; 4.7% finance; 5.2% constr.; 3.8% other serv.; 1.4% info. **Unemployment** (2008): 5.9%. **Per cap. pers. income** (2008 prelim.): $34,103. **New private housing** (2008): 16,631 units/$2.5 bil. **Commercial banks** (2008): 151; deposits: $81.9 bil. **Savings institutions** (2008): 53; deposits: $8.8 bil. **Lottery** (2008): total sales: $822.8 mil; profit: $217.1 mil.

Federal govt. Fed. civ. employees (Mar. 2007): 22,025; **avg. salary:** $60,837. **Notable fed. facilities:** Nav. Surface Warfare Ctr., Crane Div.

Energy. Electricity production (est. 2007 kWh by source): coal: 115.0 bil; gas: 2.0 bil; petroleum: 142.0 mil.

State data. Motto: Crossroads of America. **Flower:** Peony. **Bird:** Cardinal. **Tree:** Tulip poplar. **Song:** On the Banks of the Wabash, Far Away. **Entered union** Dec. 11, 1816; rank, 19th. **State fair** at Indianapolis; mid-Aug.

History. When the Europeans arrived, Miami, Potawatomi, Kickapoo, Piankashaw, Wea, and Shawnee peoples inhabited the region. La Salle visited the present South Bend area, 1679 and 1681. The first French fort was built near present-day Lafayette, 1717. A French trading post was established, 1731-32, at Vincennes. France ceded the area to Britain, 1763. During the American Revolution, American Gen. George Rogers Clark captured Vincennes, 1778, and defeated British forces, 1779. Indiana became a territory, 1800, and a state, 1816. The Miami were beaten, 1794, at Fallen Timbers, and Gen. William H. Harrison defeated Tecumseh's Indian confederation, 1811, at Tippecanoe. Manufacturing grew rapidly after the Civil War. U.S. Steel founded Gary, 1906. An automotive test track was the site of the first Indianapolis 500 race, 1911. The auto industry remains key to the state economy; in 2006, Honda announced it would build a $550-mil plant near Greensburg.

Tourist attractions. Lincoln Log Cabin Historic Site, near Charleston; George Rogers Clark Park, Vincennes; Wyandotte Caves; Tippecanoe Battlefield Park, near Lafayette; Benjamin Harrison home, Indianapolis 500 raceway and museum, in Indianapolis; Indiana Dunes, Chesterton; National College Football Hall of Fame, South Bend; Hoosier Natl. Forest.

Famous "Hoosiers." Larry Bird, Ambrose Burnside, Hoagy Carmichael, Jim Davis, James Dean, Eugene V. Debs, Theodore Dreiser, Paul Dresser, Jeff Gordon, Benjamin Harrison, Gil Hodges, Michael Jackson, David Letterman, Carole Lombard, John Mellencamp, Jane Pauley, Cole Porter, Gene Stratton Porter, Ernie Pyle, Dan Quayle, James Whitcomb Riley, Oscar Robertson, Red Skelton, Booth Tarkington, Kurt Vonnegut, Lew Wallace, Wendell L. Willkie, Wilbur Wright.

Tourist information. Indiana Office of Tourism Development, 1 North Capital, Ste. 600, Indianapolis, IN 46204; (800) 677-9800; www.visitindiana.com

Website. www.in.gov

Iowa (IA)
Hawkeye State

People. Population (2008 est.): 3,002,555; rank: 30; net change (2007-08): 0.6%. **Pop. density:** 53.8 per sq mi. **Racial distribution** (2008): 94.2% white; 2.7% black; 1.6% Asian; 0.4% Native Amer./Nat. AK; 0.1% Hawaiian/Pacific Islander; 2 or more races, 1.1%. **Hispanic pop.** (any race): 4.2%.

Geography. Total area: 56,272 sq mi; rank: 26. **Land area:** 55,869 sq mi; rank: 23. **Acres forested:** 2.9 mil. **Location:** West North Central state bordered by Mississippi R. on the E and Missouri R. on the W. **Climate:** humid, continental. **Topography:** Watershed from NW to SE; soil especially rich and land level in the N central counties. **Capital:** Des Moines. **Chief airports at:** Cedar Rapids, Des Moines.

Economy. Chief industries: agriculture, communications, construction, finance, insurance, trade, services, manufacturing. **Chief manuf. goods:** machinery, vegetable oils, animal slaughtering & processing, laundry equipment, plastics, motor vehicles & parts. **Chief crops:** corn, soybeans, hay, greenhouse & nursery, oats. **Livestock** (Jan. 2009): 4.0 mil cattle/calves, 200,000 sheep/lambs; (Dec. 2008): 19.8 mil hogs/pigs, 65.4 mil chickens (excl. broilers). **Timber/lumber** (est. 2008): 63 mil bd. ft; red cedar. **Nonfuel minerals** (2008 prelim.): $782 mil; stone (crushed), cement (portland), sand and gravel (construction), lime, gypsum (crude). **Gross state product** (est. 2008): $135.7 bil. **Sales tax** (2009): 6.0%. **Employment distrib.** (June 2008): 16.6% govt.; 20.1% trade/trans./util.; 14.9% mfg.; 13.0% ed./health; 7.9% prof./bus. serv.; 9.5% leisure/hosp.; 6.8% finance; 5.0% constr.; 3.8% other serv.; 2.2% info. **Unemployment** (2008): 4.1%. **Per cap. pers. income** (2008 prelim.): $36,680. **New private housing** (2008): 8,412 units/$1.3 bil. **Commercial banks** (2008): 380; deposits: $54.5 bil. **Savings institutions** (2008): 22; deposits: $5.6 bil. **Lottery** (2008): total sales: $249.0 mil; profit: $57.0 mil.

Federal govt. Fed. civ. employees (Mar. 2007): 8,567; **avg. salary:** $59,369. **Notable fed. facilities:** Ames Lab; Natl. Animal Disease Ctr.

Energy. Electricity production (est. 2007 kWh by source): coal: 36.5 bil; gas: 3.1 bil; petroleum: 182.0 mil.

State data. Motto: Our liberties we prize, and our rights we will maintain. **Flower:** Wild rose. **Bird:** Eastern goldfinch. **Tree:** Oak. **Rock:** Geode. **Entered union** Dec. 28, 1846; rank, 29th. **State fair** at Des Moines; mid-Aug.

History. Early inhabitants were Mound Builders who dwelt on Iowa's fertile plains. Later, Iowa and Yankton Sioux lived in the area. The first Europeans, Marquette and Jolliet, gave France its claim to the area, 1673. In 1762, France ceded the region to Spain, but Napoleon took it back, 1800. It became part of the U.S. through the Louisiana Purchase, 1803. Native American Sauk and Fox tribes moved into the area but relinquished their land in defeat, after the 1832 uprising led by the Sauk chieftain Black Hawk. Iowa became a territory in 1838, and entered as a free state, 1846, strongly supporting the Union. Fertile land lured farmers from eastern states, 1850-1900 and the population rose rapidly. Growth slowed in the 20th cent., as farming became mechanized. Surging demand for ethanol fuel from Iowa corn contributed more than $2.6 bil to the state economy in 2005. Severe flooding in eastern Iowa in June 2008 caused billions of dollars in damages and forced the evacuation of thousands of residents.

Tourist attractions. Herbert Hoover birthplace and library, West Branch; Effigy Mounds Natl. Monument, prehistoric Indian burial site, Marquette; Amana Colonies; Grant Wood's paintings and memorabilia, Davenport Municipal Art Gallery; Living History Farms, Des Moines; Adventureland, Prairie Meadows horse racing, in Altoona; Boone & Scenic Valley Railroad; Greyhound Parks, in Dubuque and Council Bluffs; riverboat cruises and casino gambling, Mississippi and Missouri Rivers; Iowa Great Lakes, Okoboji.

Famous Iowans. Tom Arnold, Johnny Carson, Marquis Childs, Buffalo Bill Cody, Mamie Dowd Eisenhower, Bob Feller, George Gallup, Susan Glaspell, James Norman Hall, Harry Hansen, Herbert Hoover, Ann Landers, Glenn Miller, Lillian Russell, Billy Sunday, James A. Van Allen, Abigail Van Buren, Carl Van Vechten, Henry Wallace, John Wayne, Meredith Willson, Grant Wood.

Tourist information. Iowa Tourism Office, Iowa Dept. of Economic Development, 200 E. Grand Ave., Des Moines, IA 50309; (888) 472-6035; www.traveliowa.com
Website. www.iowa.gov

Kansas (KS)
Sunflower State

People. Population (2008 est.): 2,802,134; rank: 33; net change (2007-08): 0.9%. **Pop. density:** 34.3 per sq mi. **Racial distribution** (2008): 88.7% white; 6.2% black; 2.2% Asian; 1.0% Native Amer./Nat. AK; 0.1% Hawaiian/Pacific Islander; 2 or more races, 1.8%. **Hispanic pop.** (any race): 9.1%.

Geography. Total area: 82,277 sq mi; rank: 15. **Land area:** 81,815 sq mi; rank: 13. **Acres forested:** 2.1 mil. **Location:** West North Central state, with Missouri R. on E. **Climate:** temperate but continental, with great extremes between summer and winter. **Topography:** hilly Osage Plains in the E; central region level prairie and hills; high plains in the W. **Capital:** Topeka. **Chief airport at:** Wichita.

Economy. Chief industries: manufacturing, finance, insurance, real estate, services. **Chief manuf. goods:** animal slaughtering, aerospace, petroleum, plastics, machinery, navigational instruments, printing. **Chief crops:** wheat, corn, soybeans, hay, sorghum, sunflowers, cotton, potatoes. **Livestock** (Jan. 2009): 6.3 mil cattle/calves, 80,000 sheep/lambs; (Dec. 2008): 1.7 mil hogs/pigs. **Timber/lumber:** figs. withheld; oak, walnut. **Nonfuel minerals** (2008 prelim.): $1.1 bil; helium (grade-A), cement (portland), stone (crushed), salt, helium (crude). **Chief port:** Kansas City. **Gross state product** (est. 2008): $122.7 bil. **Sales tax** (2009): 5.3%. **Employment distrib.** (June 2008): 18.5% govt.; 19.0% trade/trans./util.; 13.4% mfg.; 12.4% ed./health; 10.7% prof./bus. serv.; 8.5% leisure/hosp.; 5.3% finance; 4.9% constr.; 3.8% other serv.; 2.9% info. **Unemployment** (2008): 4.4%. **Per cap. pers. income** (2008 prelim.): $37,978. **New private housing** (2008): 8,188 units/$1.2 bil. **Commercial banks** (2008): 359; deposits: $51.1 bil. **Savings institutions** (2008): 19; deposits: $6.8 bil. **Lottery** (2008): total sales: $236.7 mil; profit: $71.0 mil.

Federal govt. Fed. civ. employees (Mar. 2007): 15,168; **avg. salary:** $61,278. **Notable fed. facilities:** Fts. Riley, Leavenworth; Leavenworth Fed. Pen.; McConnell AFB; Colmery-O'Neal Veterans Hospital.

Energy. Electricity production (est. 2007 kWh by source): coal: 36.4 bil; gas: 2.0 bil; nuclear: 10.4 bil; petroleum: 55.0 mil.

State data. Motto: Ad Astra per Aspera (To the stars through difficulties). **Flower:** Native sunflower. **Bird:** Western meadowlark. **Tree:** Cottonwood. **Song:** Home on the Range. **Entered union** Jan. 29, 1861; rank, 34th. **State fair** at Hutchinson; begins Friday after Labor Day.

History. Wichita, Pawnee, Kansa, and Osage peoples lived in the area when Coronado explored it in 1541. These Native Americans—hunters who also farmed—were joined on the Plains by the nomadic Cheyenne, Arapaho, Comanche, and Kiowa about 1800. France claimed the region, 1682, ceded its claim to Spain, 1762, then regained control, 1800, before selling it to the U.S. in the Louisiana Purchase, 1803. After 1830, thousands of Native Americans were removed from more eastern states to Kansas. Organized as a territory, 1854, the area witnessed violent clashes between pro- and antislavery settlers and became known as "Bleeding Kansas." It entered the Union as a free state, 1861. After the Civil War, rail construction and huge cattle drives from Texas turned Abilene and Dodge City into cowboy capitals. Russian Mennonite immigrants brought a new strain of winter wheat, 1874, transforming Kansas agriculture. Carry Nation launched her anti-saloon crusade in the 1890s. Part of the "Dust Bowl," the state experienced drought and depression in the 1930s. Topeka was the focus of the famous *Brown v. Board of Education* decision, 1954, that led to desegregation of U.S. public schools. Bob Dole represented Kansas in the U.S. Senate (1969-96) but failed in several efforts to win higher office.

Tourist attractions. Eisenhower Center, Abilene; Natl. Agricultural Ctr. & Hall of Fame, Bonner Springs; Dodge City-Boot Hill; Old Cowtown Museum, Wichita; Ft. Scott and Ft. Larned, restored 1800s cavalry forts; Kansas Cosmosphere and Space Center, Hutchinson; Woodlands Racetrack, Kansas City; U.S. Cavalry Museum, Ft. Riley; Heartland Park Raceway, Topeka.

Famous Kansans. Kirstie Alley, Roscoe "Fatty" Arbuckle, Ed Asner, Gwendolyn Brooks, John Brown, George Washington Carver, Wilt Chamberlain, Walter P. Chrysler, Glenn Cunningham, John Stuart Curry, Robert Dole, Amelia Earhart, Wyatt Earp, Dwight D. Eisenhower, Ron Evans, Maurice Greene, Wild Bill Hickok, Cyrus Holliday, Dennis Hopper, William Inge, Don Johnson, Walter Johnson, Nancy Landon Kassebaum, Buster Keaton, Emmett Kelly, Alf Landon, Edgar Lee Masters, Hattie McDaniel, Oscar Micheaux, Carry Nation, Georgia Neese-Gray, Charlie Parker, Gordon Parks, Jim Ryun, Barry Sanders, Vivian Vance, William Allen White, Jess Willard.

Tourist information. Kansas Dept. of Commerce, Travel and Tourism Div., 1000 SW Jackson St., Ste. 100, Topeka, KS 66612; (785) 296-2009; www.travelks.com
Website. www.kansas.gov

Kentucky (KY)
Bluegrass State

People. Population (2008 est.): 4,269,245; rank: 26; net change (2007-08): 0.8%. **Pop. density:** 108.1 per sq mi. **Racial distribution** (2008): 89.9% white; 7.7% black; 1.0% Asian; 0.3% Native Amer./Nat. AK; <0.05% Hawaiian/Pacific Islander; 2 or more races, 1.1%. **Hispanic pop.** (any race): 2.4%.

Geography. Total area: 40,409 sq mi; rank: 37. **Land area:** 39,728 sq mi; rank: 36. **Acres forested:** 12.0 mil. **Location:** East South Central state, bordered on N by Illinois, Indiana, Ohio; on E by West Virginia and Virginia; on S by Tennessee; on W by Missouri. **Climate:** moderate, with plentiful rainfall. **Topography:** mountainous in E; rounded hills of the Knobs in the N; Bluegrass, heart of state; wooded rocky hillsides of the Pennyroyal; Western Coal Field; the fertile Purchase in the SW. **Capital:** Frankfort. **Chief airports at:** Covington, Lexington, Louisville.

Economy. Chief industries: manufacturing, services, finance, insurance and real estate, retail trade, public utilities. **Chief manuf. goods:** motor vehicles & parts, aluminum, basic chemicals, plastics, iron & steel, rubber, printing. **Chief crops:** hay, corn, soybeans, tobacco, wheat. **Livestock** (Jan. 2009): 2.3 mil cattle/calves, 40,000 sheep/lambs; (Dec. 2008): 6.7 mil chickens (excl. broilers), 306.1 mil broilers. **Timber/lumber** (est. 2008): 515 mil bd. ft; hardwoods, pines. **Nonfuel minerals** (2008 prelim.): $772 mil; stone (crushed), lime, cement (portland), sand and gravel (construction), clays (common). **Chief ports:** Paducah, Louisville, Covington, Owensboro, Ashland, Henderson County, Lyon County, Hickman-Fulton County. **Gross state product** (est. 2008): $156.4 bil. **Sales tax** (2009): 6.0%. **Employment distrib.** (June 2008): 17.5% govt.; 20.8% trade/trans./util.; 13.2% mfg.; 12.7% ed./health; 9.6% prof./bus. serv.; 9.5% leisure/hosp.; 5.0% finance; 4.8% constr.; 4.1% other serv.; 1.6% info. **Unemployment** (2008): 6.4%. **Per cap. pers. income** (2008 prelim.): $31,826. **New private housing** (2008): 10,494 units/$1.3 bil. **Commercial banks** (2008): 208; deposits: $62.2 bil. **Savings institutions** (2008): 26; deposits: $2.1 bil. **Lottery** (2008): total sales: $778.2 mil; profit: $192.1 mil.

Federal govt. Fed. civ. employees (Mar. 2007): 22,713; **avg. salary:** $54,799. **Notable fed. facilities:** U.S. Gold Bullion Depository, Ft. Knox; Ft. Campbell; Fed. Correctional Institution, Lexington; Army Corps of Engineers, Louisville.

Energy. Electricity production (est. 2007 kWh by source): coal: 82.1 bil; gas: 1.5 bil; petroleum: 98.0 mil.

State data. Motto: United we stand, divided we fall. **Flower:** Goldenrod. **Bird:** Cardinal. **Tree:** Tulip poplar. **Song:** My Old Kentucky Home. **Entered union** June 1, 1792; rank, 15th. **State fair** at Louisville; mid-Aug.

History. Paleo-Indians first arrived about 14,000 years ago. Much later, Shawnee, Wyandot, Delaware, and Cherokee peoples also used the area mostly for hunting. Explored by Thomas Walker and Christopher Gist, 1750-51, Kentucky was the first area W of the Alleghenies settled by American pioneers. The first permanent settlement was Harrodsburg, 1774. Daniel Boone blazed the Wilderness Trail through the Cumberland Gap and founded Ft. Boonesborough, 1775. Clashes with Native Americans were frequent, 1774-94. Virginia dropped its claims to the region, and Kentucky became a state, 1792. Tobacco growing, horse breeding, coal mining, and bourbon whiskey making were major industries in the 19th cent. A slave state, Kentucky tried to stay neutral in the Civil War, but then opted for the Union; many Kentuckians sided with the Confederacy. The U.S. gold depository at Fort Knox opened, 1937. Led by Toyota, Ford, and GM, auto manufacturing has grown in recent decades; about 10% of cars and trucks built in the U.S. each year are made in Kentucky.

Tourist attractions. Churchill Downs (Kentucky Derby), Louisville; Land Between the Lakes Natl. Recreation Area, lakes Kentucky & Barkley; Mammoth Cave Natl. Park; Lake Cumberland; Lincoln's birthplace, Hodgenville; My Old Kentucky Home State Park, Bardstown; Cumberland Gap Natl. Historical Park, Middlesboro; Kentucky Horse Park, Lexington; Shaker Village, Pleasant Hill.

Famous Kentuckians. Muhammad Ali, John James Audubon, Alben W. Barkley, Daniel Boone, Louis D. Brandeis, John C. Breckinridge, Kit Carson, Albert B. "Happy" Chandler, Henry Clay, Jefferson Davis, D. W. Griffith, "Casey" Jones, Abraham Lincoln, Mary Todd Lincoln, Thomas Hunt Morgan, Carry Nation, Col. Harland Sanders, Diane Sawyer, Adlai Stevenson, Jesse Stuart, Zachary Taylor, Hunter S. Thompson, Robert Penn Warren, Whitney Young Jr.

Tourist information. Kentucky Dept. of Travel, Capital Plaza Tower, 22nd Fl., 500 Mero St., Frankfort, KY 40601; (800) 225-8747; www.kentuckytourism.com
Website. www.kentucky.gov

Louisiana (LA)
Pelican State

People. Population (2008 est.): 4,410,796; rank: 25; net change (2007-08): 0.9%. **Pop. density:** 102.1 per sq mi. **Racial distribution** (2008): 64.8% white; 32.0% black; 1.4% Asian; 0.6% Native Amer./Nat. AK; <0.05% Hawaiian/Pacific Islander; 2 or more races, 1.1%. **Hispanic pop.** (any race): 3.4%.

Geography. Total area: 51,840 sq mi; rank: 31. **Land area:** 43,562 sq mi; rank: 33. **Acres forested:** 14.2 mil. **Location:** West South Central state on the Gulf Coast. **Climate:** subtropical, affected by continental weather patterns. **Topography:** lowlands of marshes and Mississippi R. flood plain; Red R. Valley lowlands; upland hills in the Florida Parishes; average elevation, 100 ft. **Capital:** Baton Rouge. **Chief airports at:** Baton Rouge, Metairie.

Economy. Chief industries: wholesale and retail trade, tourism, manufacturing, construction, transportation, communication, public utilities, finance, insurance, real estate, mining. **Chief manuf. goods:** petroleum, chemicals, plastics material & resin, pesticides & fertilizers, cleaning products, paper & paperboard, ships, structural metals. **Chief crops:** sugarcane, cotton, rice, soybeans, corn, sweet potatoes. **Livestock** (Jan. 2009): 890,000 cattle/calves; (Dec. 2008): 2.4 mil chickens (excl. broilers). **Timber/lumber** (est. 2008): 1.2 bil bd. ft; pines, hardwoods, oak. **Nonfuel minerals** (2008 prelim.): $508 mil; salt, sand and gravel (construction), stone (crushed), sand and gravel (industrial), clays (common). **Commercial fishing** (2008): $272.9 mil. **Chief ports:** New Orleans, Baton Rouge, Lake Charles, Port of S. Louisiana (La Place), Shreveport, Plaquemine, St. Bernard, Alexandria. **Gross state product** (est. 2008): $222.2 bil. **Sales tax** (2009): 4.0%. **Employment distrib.** (June 2008): 18.7% govt.; 19.7% trade/trans./util.; 8.1% mfg.; 12.9% ed./health; 10.5% prof./bus. serv.; 10.4% leisure/hosp.; 5.0% finance; 7.1% constr.; 3.6% other serv.; 1.4% info. **Unemployment** (2008): 4.6%. **Per cap. pers. income** (2008 prelim.): $36,271. **New private housing** (2008): 16,305 units/$2.2 bil. **Commercial banks** (2008): 141; deposits: $70.5 bil. **Savings institutions** (2008): 26; deposits: $4.2 bil. **Lottery** (2008): total sales: $373.7 mil; profit: $131.8 mil.

Federal govt. Fed. civ. employees (Mar. 2007): 19,978; **avg. salary:** $60,272. **Notable federal facilities:** Ft. Polk (Joint Readiness Training Ctr.); Barksdale AFB; Strategic petroleum: Reserve, Michoud Assembly Plant, Southern Regional Research Ctr., Army Corps of Engineers, all New Orleans; New Orleans NAS.

Energy. Electricity production (est. 2007 kWh by source): coal: 10.7 bil; gas: 13.9 bil; nuclear: 17.1 bil; petroleum: 232.0 mil.

State data. Motto: Union, justice, and confidence. **Flower:** Magnolia. **Bird:** Eastern brown pelican. **Tree:** Cypress. **Song:** Give Me Louisiana. **Entered union** Apr. 30, 1812; rank, 18th. **State fair** at Shreveport; late Oct.-early Nov.

History. Caddo, Tunica, Choctaw, Chitimacha, and Chawash peoples lived in the region at the time of European contact. Spanish explorers in the early 16th cent. reached the mouth of the Mississippi. La Salle, 1682, claimed the region for France. Early French and Spanish settlers were the ancestors of Louisiana Creoles. Cajuns descended from the Acadians, French settlers expelled by the British from Nova Scotia, Canada, in 1755. France ceded the Louisiana region to Spain, 1762, took it back, 1800, and sold it to the U.S., 1803, in the Louisiana Purchase. Admitted as a state in 1812, Louisiana witnessed the Battle of New Orleans, 1815. Cotton and sugar plantations relied on black slaves, who made up 47% of the population in 1860, on the eve of the Civil War. Louisiana seceded, 1861, and was readmitted, 1868. Jazz was born in New Orleans in the early 20th cent. As governor (1928-32), Huey Long pushed populist programs. The offshore oil and gas industry developed after World War II. Many tropical storms and floods have battered Louisiana, including Hurricane Katrina, 2005, which devastated New Orleans.

Tourist attractions. French Quarter and other New Orleans attractions; Jean Lafitte Natl. Hist. Park, Chalmette;

Longfellow-Evangeline State Hist. Site, St. Martinville; Kent Plantation House, Alexandria; Hodges Gardens, Natchitoches; USS *Kidd* Memorial, Baton Rouge.

Famous Louisianans. Louis Armstrong, Pierre Beauregard, Judah P. Benjamin, Braxton Bragg, Kate Chopin, Johnnie Cochran, Harry Connick Jr., Ellen DeGeneres, Fats Domino, Lillian Hellman, Grace King, Elmore Leonard, Bob Livingston, Huey Long, Eli & Peyton Manning, Wynton Marsalis, Leonidas K. Polk, Anne Rice, Henry Miller Shreve, Britney Spears, Edward D. White Jr.

Tourist information. Louisiana Office of Tourism, PO Box 94291, Baton Rouge, LA 70804-9291; (800) 677-4082; www.louisianatravel.com

Website. www.louisiana.gov

Maine (ME)
Pine Tree State

People. Population (2008 est.): 1,316,456; rank: 40; net change (2007-08): 0.1%. **Pop. density:** 42.7 per sq mi. **Racial distribution** (2008): 96.4% white; 1.0% black; 0.9% Asian; 0.6% Native Amer./Nat. AK; <0.05% Hawaiian/Pacific Islander; 2 or more races, 1.1%. **Hispanic pop.** (any race): 1.3%.

Geography. Total area: 35,385 sq mi; rank: 39. **Land area:** 30,862 sq mi; rank: 39. **Acres forested:** 17.7 mil. **Location:** New England state at northeastern tip of U.S. **Climate:** Southern interior and coastal, influenced by air masses from the S and W; northern clime harsher, avg. over 100 in. snow in winter. **Topography:** Appalachian Mts. extend through state; western borders have rugged terrain; long sand beaches on southern coast; northern coast mainly rocky promontories, peninsulas, fjords. **Capital:** Augusta. **Chief airport at:** Portland.

Economy. Chief industries: manufacturing, agriculture, fishing, services, trade, government, finance, insurance, real estate, construction. **Chief manuf. goods:** paper, ships & boats, cardboard, frozen/canned fruits & vegetables, plastics, baked goods. **Chief crops:** potatoes, greenhouse & nursery, wild blueberries, apples, hay, maple syrup. **Livestock** (Jan. 2009): 89,000 cattle/calves; (Dec. 2008): 5.0 mil chickens (excl. broilers). **Timber/lumber** (est. 2008): 823 mil bd. ft; pine, spruce, fir. **Nonfuel minerals** (2008 prelim.): $229 mil; sand and gravel (construction), cement (portland), stone (crushed), stone (dimension), cement (masonry). **Commercial fishing** (2008): $287.5 mil. **Chief ports:** Searsport, Portland, Eastport. **Gross state product** (est. 2008): $49.7 bil. **Sales tax** (2009): 5.0%. **Employment distrib.** (June 2008): 16.6% govt.; 20.1% trade/trans./util.; 9.4% mfg.; 18.4% ed./health; 8.9% prof./bus. serv.; 10.9% leisure/hosp.; 5.2% finance; 5.0% constr.; 3.2% other serv.; 1.8% info. **Unemployment** (2008): 5.4%. **Per cap. pers. income** (2008 prelim.): $35,381. **New private housing** (2008): 3,615 units/$582.2 mil. **Commercial banks** (2008): 12; deposits: $11.0 bil. **Savings institutions** (2008): 23; deposits: $8.5 bil. **Lottery** (2008): total sales: $228.5 mil; profit: $49.5 mil.

Federal govt. Fed. civ. employees (Mar. 2007): 10,158; **avg. salary:** $59,828. **Notable fed. facilities:** Portsmouth Naval Shipyard; *Brunswick NAS.

Energy. Electricity production (est. 2006 kWh by source): hydroelectric: 6 mil.

State data. Motto: Dirigo (I direct). **Flower:** White pine cone and tassel. **Bird:** Chickadee. **Tree:** Eastern white pine. **Song:** State of Maine Song. **Entered union** Mar. 15, 1820; rank, 23rd. **State fair** at Bangor, late July-early Aug.; at Skowhegan, mid-Aug.

History. Paleo-Indians arrived about 11,500 years ago. Maine was inhabited by Algonquian peoples including the Abnaki, Penobscot, and Passamaquoddy at the time of European contact. French settled, 1604, at the St. Croix River, English, c. 1607, on the Kennebec; both settlements failed. A royal charter, 1691, made Maine part of Massachusetts. Maine broke off, 1819, and became a separate state, 1820. Drawing on vast forest resources, the pulp and paper industry developed after the Civil War. Bath Iron Works began building U.S. Navy vessels and other ships in the 1890s. Mail-order and retail giant L.L. Bean was founded, 1912. Women have fared well in state politics: Margaret Chase Smith became the first woman to serve in both houses of Congress (House, 1940-49; Senate, 1949-73), and Olympia Snowe and Susan Collins have represented Maine in the Senate since the mid-1990s.

Tourist attractions. Acadia Natl. Park, Bar Harbor, on Mt. Desert Island; Old Orchard Beach; Portland's Old Port; Kennebunkport; Common Ground Country Fair, Unity; Portland Head Light; Baxter State Pk.; Freeport/L. L. Bean.

Famous "Down Easters." Leon Leonwood (L.L.) Bean, James G. Blaine, Cyrus H. K. Curtis, Hannibal Hamlin, Sarah Jewett, Stephen King, Henry Wadsworth Longfellow, Sir Hiram and Hudson Maxim, Edna St. Vincent Millay, George Mitchell, Edmund Muskie, Judd Nelson, Edwin Arlington Robinson, Joan Benoit Samuelson, Liv Tyler, Kate Douglas Wiggin, Ben Ames Williams.

Tourist information. Maine Office of Tourism, 59 State House Station, Augusta, ME 04333; (888) 624-6345; www.visitmaine.com

Website. www.state.me.us

Maryland (MD)
Old Line State, Free State

People. Population (2008 est.): 5,633,597; rank: 19; net change (2007-08): 0.3%. **Pop. density:** 580.5 per sq mi. **Racial distribution** (2008): 63.4% white; 29.4% black; 5.1% Asian; 0.4% Native Amer./Nat. AK; 0.1% Hawaiian/Pacific Islander; 2 or more races, 1.6%. **Hispanic pop.** (any race): 6.7%.

Geography. Total area: 12,407 sq mi; rank: 42. **Land area:** 9,774 sq mi; rank: 42. **Acres forested:** 2.6 mil. **Location:** South Atlantic state stretching from the Ocean to the Allegheny Mts. **Climate:** continental in the west; humid subtropical in the east. **Topography:** Eastern Shore of coastal plain and Maryland Main of coastal plain, piedmont plateau, and the Blue Ridge, separated by the Chesapeake Bay. **Capital:** Annapolis. **Chief airport at:** Glen Burnie.

Economy. Chief industries: manufacturing, biotechnology and information technology, services, tourism. **Chief manuf. goods:** navigational instruments, pharmaceutical & medicine, broadcasting equip., plastics, printing, milk & ice cream. **Chief crops:** greenhouse & nursery, corn, soybeans, wheat, hay, tomatoes, watermelons, barley, potatoes, apples. **Livestock** (Jan. 2009): 185,000 cattle/calves, 24,000 sheep/lambs; (Dec. 2008): 2.6 mil chickens (excl. broilers), 298.6 mil broilers. **Timber/lumber** (est. 2008): 245 mil bd. ft; hardwoods. **Nonfuel minerals** (2008 prelim.): $548 mil; cement (portland), stone (crushed), sand and gravel (construction), cement (masonry), stone (dimension). **Commercial fishing** (2008): $73.5 mil. **Chief port:** Baltimore. **Gross state product** (est. 2008): $273.3 bil. **Sales tax** (2009): 6.0%. **Employment distrib.** (June 2008): 18.1% govt.; 18.0% trade/trans./util.; 4.8% mfg.; 14.4% ed./health; 15.4% prof./bus. serv.; 9.6% leisure/hosp.; 5.9% finance; 7.2% constr.; 4.6% other serv.; 1.9% info. **Unemployment** (2008): 4.4%. **Per cap. pers. income** (2008 prelim.): $48,091. **New private housing** (2008): 13,018 units/$2.2 bil. **Commercial banks** (2008): 89; deposits: $79.3 bil. **Savings institutions** (2008): 50; deposits: $17.3 bil. **Lottery** (2008): total sales: $1.7 bil; profit: $529.4 mil.

Federal govt. Fed. civ. employees (Mar. 2007): 111,675; **avg. salary:** $86,088. **Notable fed. facilities:** U.S. Naval Academy; Natl. Agriculture Res. Ctr.; Ft. Meade, Aberdeen Proving Ground; Naval Air Sys. Command; Goddard Space Flight Ctr.; Natl. Inst. of Health; Natl. Inst. of Standards & Technology; Food & Drug Admin.; Bureau of the Census; Natl. Naval Med. Ctr., Bethesda; Natl. Marine Fisheries Serv.; Natl. Oceanic and Atmospheric Admin.

Energy. Electricity production (est. 2007 kWh by source): petroleum: 21.0 mil.

State data. Motto: Fatti Maschii, Parole Femine (Manly deeds, womanly words). **Flower:** Black-eyed Susan. **Bird:** Baltimore oriole. **Tree:** White oak. **Song:** Maryland, My Maryland. **Seventh** of the original 13 states to ratify the U.S. Constitution, Apr. 28, 1788. **State fair** at Timonium; late Aug.-early Sept.

History. Europeans encountered Algonquian-speaking Nanticoke and Piscataway and Iroquois-speaking Susquehannock when they first visited the area. Italian navigator Verrazano reached the Chesapeake region in the early 16th cent. English Capt. John Smith explored and mapped the area, 1608. William Claiborne set up a trading post on Kent Island in Chesapeake Bay, 1631. King Charles I granted land to Cecilius Calvert, Lord Baltimore, 1632; Calvert's brother Leonard, with about 200 settlers, founded St. Marys, 1634. During the Revolutionary War, Baltimore (1776-77) and Annapolis (1783-84) served as temporary capitals of the U.S.

In the War of 1812, when a British fleet tried to take Ft. McHenry, Marylander Francis Scott Key wrote "The Star-Spangled Banner," 1814. Born into slavery at Tuckahoe in 1818, Frederick Douglass became a leading abolitionist. Although a slaveholding state, Maryland stayed in the Union during the Civil War and was the site of the battle of Antietam, 1862. Gov. Spiro Agnew elected U.S. Vice Pres. 1968, 1972; pleaded no contest to tax evasion and resigned 1973. Israeli and Egyptian leaders reached a historic peace accord at the Camp David presidential retreat, 1978. A major effort is under way to clean up pollution in the Chesapeake Bay watershed.

Tourist attractions. Laurel Park (Maryland Million); Ocean City; restored Ft. McHenry—near which Francis Scott Key wrote "The Star-Spangled Banner," Pimlico track (The Preakness), Edgar Allan Poe house, Camden Yards, Natl. Aquarium, Harborplace, all Baltimore; Antietam Battlefield, near Hagerstown; South Mountain Battlefield; U.S. Naval Academy, Maryland State House (oldest still in legislative use in the U.S.), in Annapolis; Natl. Cryptologic Museum, Ft. Meade.

Famous Marylanders. John Astin, Benjamin Banneker, Tom Clancy, Jonathan Demme, Francis Scott Key, H. L. Mencken, Kweisi Mfume, Ogden Nash, Charles Willson Peale, William Pinkney, Edgar Allan Poe, Cal Ripken Jr., Babe Ruth, Upton Sinclair, Roger B. Taney, John Waters, Montel Williams.

Tourist information. Maryland Office of Tourism Development, 401 E. Pratt St., 14th Fl., Baltimore, MD 21202; 1-866-MD-WELCOME; www.visitmaryland.org
Website. www.maryland.gov

Massachusetts (MA)
Bay State, Old Colony

People. Population (2008 est.): 6,497,967; rank: 15; net change (2007-08): 0.5%. **Pop. density:** 833.0 per sq mi. **Racial distribution** (2008): 86.2% white; 7.0% black; 4.9% Asian; 0.3% Native Amer./Nat. AK; 0.1% Hawaiian/Pacific Islander; 2 or more races, 1.4%. **Hispanic pop.** (any race): 8.6%.

Geography. Total area: 10,555 sq mi; rank: 44. **Land area:** 7,840 sq mi; rank: 45. **Acres forested:** 3.2 mil. **Location:** New England state along Atlantic seaboard. **Climate:** temperate, with colder and drier clime in western region. **Topography:** jagged indented coast from Rhode Island around Cape Cod; flat land yields to stony upland pastures near central region and gentle hilly country in west; except in west, land is rocky, sandy, and not fertile. **Capital:** Boston. **Chief airport at:** Boston.

Economy. Chief industries: services, trade, manufacturing. **Chief manuf. goods:** electronics & instruments, pharmaceuticals, telecom. & broadcasting equip., plastics, medical equip., printing. **Chief crops:** greenhouse & nursery, cranberries, tomatoes, sweet corn, apples, hay, tobacco. **Livestock** (Jan. 2009): 43,000 cattle/calves; (Dec. 2008): 129,000 chickens (excl. broilers). **Timber/lumber** (est. 2008): 37 mil bd. ft; white pine, oak, other hard woods. **Nonfuel minerals** (2008 prelim.): $246 mil; stone (crushed), sand and gravel (construction), lime, stone (dimension), clays (common). **Commercial fishing** (2008): $399.6 mil. **Chief ports:** Boston, Fall River, New Bedford, Salem, Gloucester, Plymouth. **Gross state product** (est. 2008): $365.0 bil. **Sales tax** (2009): 5.0%. **Employment distrib.** (June 2008): 13.2% govt.; 17.2% trade/trans./util.; 8.8% mfg.; 18.7% ed./health; 14.9% prof./bus. serv.; 9.8% leisure/hosp.; 6.8% finance; 4.2% constr.; 3.7% other serv.; 2.7% info. **Unemployment** (2008): 5.3%. **Per cap. pers. income** (2008 prelim.): $50,735. **New private housing** (2008): 9,883 units/$1.9 bil. **Commercial banks** (2008): 47; deposits: $114.8 bil. **Savings institutions** (2008): 152; deposits $70.5 bil. **Lottery** (2008): total sales: $4.7 bil; profit: $913.0 mil.

Federal govt. Fed. civ. employees (Mar. 2007): 27,457; **avg. salary:** $70,738. **Notable fed. facilities:** Thomas P. O'Neill Jr. Fed. Bldg.; J.W. McCormack Bldg.; JFK Fed. Bldg.; Hanscom AFB; *Natick Army Soldier Systems Ctr.

Energy. Electricity production (est. 2007 kWh by source): gas: 252.0 mil; petroleum: 60.0 mil.

State data. Motto: Ense Petit Placidam Sub Libertate Quietem (By the sword we seek peace, but peace only under liberty). **Flower:** Mayflower. **Bird:** Chickadee. **Tree:** American elm. **Song:** All Hail to Massachusetts. **Sixth** of the

original 13 states to ratify Constitution, Feb. 6, 1788. **State fair** at West Springfield; mid-Sept.-early Oct.

History. Early inhabitants were Algonquian peoples: Nauset, Wampanoag, Massachuset, Pennacook, Nipmuc, and Pocumtuc. Pilgrims settled in Plymouth, 1620, giving thanks for their survival with the first Thanksgiving Day, 1621. About 20,000 new settlers arrived, 1630-40. Colonist-Native American relations deteriorated, leading to King Philip's War, 1675-76, which the colonists won. Witch trials at Salem, 1692, led to the execution of 20 people. Demonstrations against British restrictions set off the Boston Massacre, 1770, and the Boston Tea Party, 1773. The first bloodshed of American Revolution was at Lexington, 1775. After statehood, Massachusetts prospered from shipbuilding, seafaring, and the making of textiles, shoes, and metal goods, while artists, writers, and social reformers flourished. The controversial Sacco-Vanzetti case, 1920-27, ended with the execution of 2 Italian immigrants on murder and robbery charges. After World War II, old industries declined, knowledge-intensive enterprises thrived, and the Kennedys became a dominant political family. The state's highest court ruled, 2003, that same-sex couples could legally marry.

Tourist attractions. Provincetown arts colony; Cape Cod; Plymouth Rock, Plimoth Plantation, Mayflower II, all Plymouth; Freedom Trail, Museum of Fine Arts, New England Aquarium, and other Boston attractions; Tanglewood, Hancock Shaker Village, Berkshire Scenic Railway Museum, Norman Rockwell Museum, and other Berkshires attractions; Salem; Old Sturbridge Village; Old Deerfield Historic District; Walden Pond, Concord; Naismith Memorial Basketball Hall of Fame, Springfield.

Famous "Bay Staters." John Adams, John Quincy Adams, Samuel Adams, Louisa May Alcott, Horatio Alger, Susan B. Anthony, Crispus Attucks, Clara Barton, Alexander Graham Bell, Stephen Breyer, George H. W. Bush, John Cheever, E. E. Cummings, Emily Dickinson, Charles Eliot, Ralph Waldo Emerson, William Lloyd Garrison, Edward Everett Hale, John Hancock, Nathaniel Hawthorne, Oliver Wendell Holmes, Winslow Homer, Elias Howe, John F. Kennedy, John Kerry, Jack Kerouac, Jack Lemmon, James Russell Lowell, Cotton Mather, Samuel F. B. Morse, Edgar Allan Poe, Paul Revere, Norman Rockwell, Dr. Seuss (Theodor Seuss Geisel), Henry David Thoreau, Barbara Walters, James McNeil Whistler, John Greenleaf Whittier.

Tourist information. Massachusetts Office of Travel & Tourism, 10 Park Plz., Ste. 4510, Boston, MA 02116; 1-800 227-MASS; www.massvacation.com
Website. www.mass.gov

Michigan (MI)
Great Lakes State, Wolverine State

People. Population (2008 est.): 10,003,422; rank: 8; net change (2007-08): –0.5%. **Pop. density:** 177.0 per sq mi. **Racial distribution** (2008): 81.2% white; 14.2% black; 2.4% Asian; 0.6% Native Amer./Nat. AK; <0.05% Hawaiian/Pacific Islander; 2 or more races, 1.5%. **Hispanic pop.** (any race): 4.1%.

Geography. Total area: 96,716 sq mi; rank: 11. **Land area:** 56,804 sq mi; rank: 22. **Acres forested:** 19.5 mil. **Location:** East North Central state bordering on 4 of the 5 Great Lakes, divided into an Upper and Lower Peninsula by the Straits of Mackinac, which link lakes Michigan and Huron. **Climate:** well-defined seasons tempered by the Great Lakes. **Topography:** low rolling hills give way to northern tableland of hilly belts in Lower Peninsula; Upper Peninsula is level in the east, with swampy areas; western region is higher and more rugged. **Capital:** Lansing. **Chief airports at:** Detroit, Flint, Grand Rapids.

Economy. Chief industries: manufacturing, services, tourism, agriculture, forestry/lumber. **Chief manuf. goods:** motor vehicles & parts, plastics, metalworking machinery, non-wood office furniture, fabricated metals. **Chief crops:** greenhouse & nursery, soybeans, corn, wheat, sugar beets, apples, blueberries, potatoes, dry beans, cherries, hay, cucumbers, tomatoes, grapes. **Livestock** (Jan. 2009): 1.1 mil cattle/calves, 78,000 sheep/lambs; (Dec. 2008): 1.0 mil hogs/pigs, 11.5 mil chickens (excl. broilers). **Timber/lumber** (est. 2008): 793 mil bd. ft; maple, oak, aspen. **Nonfuel minerals** (2008 prelim.): $2.1 bil; iron ore (usable shipped), cement (portland), sand and gravel (construction), salt, stone (crushed). **Commercial fishing** (2008):

$14.9 mil. **Chief ports:** Detroit, Saginaw River, Escanaba, Muskegon, Sault Ste. Marie, Port Huron, Marine City. **Gross state product** (est. 2008): $382.5 bil. **Sales tax** (2009): 6.0%. **Employment distrib.** (June 2008): 15.0% govt.; 18.5% trade/trans./util.; 13.9% mfg.; 14.1% ed./health; 13.7% prof./bus. serv.; 10.1% leisure/hosp.; 4.9% finance; 3.8% constr.; 4.2% other serv.; 1.5% info. **Unemployment** (2008): 8.4%. **Per cap. pers. income** (2008 prelim.): $35,299. **New private housing** (2008): 10,911 units/$1.8 bil. **Commercial banks** (2008): 162; deposits: $145.5 bil. **Savings institutions** (2008): 22; deposits: $11.7 bil. **Lottery** (2008): total sales: $2.3 bil; profit: $740.7 mil.

Federal govt. Fed. civ. employees (Mar. 2007): 26,000; **avg. salary:** $68,898. **Notable fed. facilities:** Isle Royal, Sleeping Bear Dunes national parks; Army TACOM Life Cycle Mgmt. Command; Hart-Dole-Inouye Fed. Ctr.

Energy. Electricity production (est. 2007 kWh by source): coal: 69.8 bil; gas: 1.2 bil; hydroelectric: −1.1 bil; nuclear: 27.5 bil; petroleum: 448.0 mil.

State data. Motto: Si Quaeris Peninsulam Amoenam, Circumspice (If you seek a pleasant peninsula, look about you). **Flower:** Apple blossom. **Bird:** Robin. **Tree:** White pine. **Song:** Michigan, My Michigan. **Entered union** Jan. 26, 1837; rank, 26th. **State fair** at Detroit, late Aug.-early Sept.; at Escanaba, mid-Aug.

History. Hunting and fishing peoples lived in the region as early as 11,000 years ago. Ojibwa, Ottawa, Miami, Potawatomi, and Huron inhabited the area at the time of European contact. French fur traders and missionaries arrived in the 17th cent. and established a settlement at Sault Ste. Marie, 1668. British took over, 1763, and crushed a Native American uprising led by Ottawa chieftain Pontiac. Treaty of Paris ceded the area to U.S., 1783, but British remained until 1796. Michigan was organized as a territory, 1805. The British seized Ft. Mackinac and Detroit, 1812, but the U.S. regained control, 1814. The opening of the Erie Canal, 1825, and new land laws and Native American cessions led the way for a flood of settlers. Strongly antislavery, Michigan became a state, 1837, and supplied 90,000 soldiers to the Union army in the Civil War. In the 20th cent., automobile manufacturing was the backbone of the economy. Henry Ford launched the Model T car, 1908; the United Auto Workers union was founded, 1935. Motown music flourished in Detroit in the 1960s, but riots in 1967 dealt the city a heavy blow. As the auto industry faltered, Michigan lost more than 20% of its automotive-related jobs between 2002 and 2007.

Tourist attractions. Henry Ford Museum/Greenfield Village, Dearborn; Frederick Meijer Gardens and Sculpture Park, Grand Rapids; Tahquamenon (Hiawatha) Falls; De Zwaan windmill and Tulip Festival, Holland; "Soo Locks," St. Mary's Falls Ship Canal, Sault Ste. Marie; Air Zoo, Kalamazoo; Mackinac Island; Museum of African-American History, Motown Historical Museum, in Detroit.

Famous Michiganders. Ralph Bunche, Francis Ford Coppola, Paul de Kruif, Thomas Edison, Edna Ferber, Gerald R. Ford, Henry Ford, Aretha Franklin, Edgar Guest, Lee Iacocca, Robert Ingersoll, Magic Johnson, Casey Kasem, Will Kellogg, Ring Lardner, Elmore Leonard, Charles Lindbergh, Joe Louis, Madonna, Malcolm X, Terry McMillan, Michael Moore, Pontiac, Gilda Radner, Diana Ross, Glenn Seaborg, Tom Selleck, Sinbad (David Adkins), John Smoltz, Lily Tomlin, Stewart Edward White, Serena Williams.

Tourist information. Michigan Economic Development Corp., 300 N. Washington Square, Lansing, MI 48913; (888) 784-7328; www.michigan.org

Website. www.michigan.gov

Minnesota (MN)

North Star State, Gopher State

People. Population (2008 est.): 5,220,393; rank: 21; net change (2007-08): 0.7%. **Pop. density:** 65.6 per sq mi. **Racial distribution** (2008): 89.0% white; 4.6% black; 3.5% Asian; 1.2% Native Amer./Nat. AK; 0.1% Hawaiian/Pacific Islander; 2 or more races, 1.5%. **Hispanic pop.** (any race): 4.1%.

Geography. Total area: 86,939 sq mi; rank: 12. **Land area:** 79,610 sq mi; rank: 14. **Acres forested:** 16.4 mil. **Location:** West North Central state bounded on the E by Wisconsin and Lake Superior, on the N by Canada, on the W by the Dakotas, and on the S by Iowa. **Climate:** northern part

of state lies in the moist Great Lakes storm belt; the western border lies at the edge of the semi-arid Great Plains. **Topography:** central hill and lake region covering approx. half the state; to the NE, rocky ridges and deep lakes; to the NW, flat plain; to the S, rolling plains and deep river valleys. **Capital:** St. Paul. **Chief airport** at: Minneapolis.

Economy. Chief industries: agribusiness, forest products, mining, manufacturing, tourism. **Chief manuf. goods:** petroleum & asphalt, computers & electronics, milk & cheese, printing, animal slaughtering, paper & product, medical equip. **Chief crops:** corn, soybeans, hay, sugar beets, wheat, potatoes, greenhouse & nursery, dry edible beans, green peas, sunflowers. **Livestock** (Jan. 2009): 2.4 mil cattle/calves, 140,000 sheep/lambs; (Dec. 2008): 7.5 mil hogs/pigs, 13.4 mil chickens (excl. broilers), 44.9 mil broilers. **Timber/lumber** (est. 2008): 230 mil bd. ft; needleleaves and hardwoods. **Nonfuel minerals** (2008 prelim.): $3.2 bil; iron ore (usable shipped), sand and gravel (construction), stone (crushed), sand and gravel (industrial), stone (dimension). **Commercial fishing** (2008): $304,908. **Chief ports:** Duluth, St. Paul, Minneapolis. **Gross state product** (est. 2008): $262.8 bil. **Sales tax** (2009): 6.5%. **Employment distrib.** (June 2008): 15.2% govt.; 18.9% trade/trans./util.; 12.1% mfg.; 15.4% ed./health; 11.8% prof./bus. serv.; 9.4% leisure/hosp.; 6.5% finance; 4.4% constr.; 4.1% other serv.; 2.1% info. **Unemployment** (2008): 5.4%. **Per cap. pers. income** (2008 prelim.): $42,772. **New private housing** (2008): 11,551 units/$2.2 bil. **Commercial banks** (2008): 435; deposits: $96.5 bil. **Savings institutions** (2008): 33; deposits: $4.6 bil. **Lottery** (2008): total sales: $461.5 mil; profit: $116.3 mil.

Federal govt. Fed. civ. employees (Mar. 2007): 16,723; **avg. salary:** $65,114.

Energy. Electricity production (est. 2007 kWh by source): coal: 31.2 bil; gas: 2.0 bil; nuclear: 13.1 bil; petroleum: 172.0 mil.

State data. Motto: L'Etoile du Nord (The star of the north). **Flower:** Pink and white lady's-slipper. **Bird:** Common loon. **Tree:** Red pine. **Song:** Hail! Minnesota. **Entered union** May 11, 1858; rank, 32nd. **State fair** at St. Paul; late Aug.-early Sept.

History. Inhabited for at least 10,000 years, the region was home to Dakota Sioux when Europeans arrived. French fur traders Pierre Esprit Radisson and Médard Chouart, sieur des Groseilliers, explored in the mid-17th cent. In 1679, Daniel Greysolon, sieur Duluth, claimed the entire region for France. Ojibwa arrived in the 18th cent. and warred with the Sioux for over 100 years. Britain took the area east of the Mississippi, 1763. The U.S. took over that portion after the American Revolution and gained the western area, 1803, in the Louisiana Purchase. The U.S. built Ft. St. Anthony (now Ft. Snelling), 1819, and bought Native American lands, 1837, spurring an influx of settlers from the east. Minnesota became a territory, 1849, and a state, 1858. Sioux staged a bloody uprising, the Battle of Wood Lake, 1862, and were driven from the state. Railroad construction after the Civil War spurred the growth of the grain, timber, and iron mining industries. Opening of the St. Lawrence Seaway, 1959, aided the port of Duluth. Elected as a reformer, colorful former wrestler Jesse Ventura served as governor, 1999-2003. Two-term Sen. Paul Wellstone, one of a long line of liberal Minnesota Democrats, died when his campaign plane crashed, 2002. The I-35W Mississippi River Bridge in Minneapolis collapsed Aug. 1, 2007, killing 13.

Tourist attractions. Minneapolis Institute of Arts, Walker Art Center, Minneapolis Sculpture Garden, Minnehaha Falls (Hiawatha), Guthrie Theater, all Minneapolis; Ordway Theater, Winter Carnival, in St. Paul; Voyageurs Natl. Park; Mayo Clinic, Rochester; North Shore (of Lake Superior).

Famous Minnesotans. Warren Burger, Ethan and Joel Coen, William O. Douglas, Bob Dylan, F. Scott Fitzgerald, Al Franken, Judy Garland, Cass Gilbert, Hubert Humphrey, Garrison Keillor, Sister Elizabeth Kenny, Jessica Lange, Sinclair Lewis, Paul Manship, Roger Maris, E. G. Marshall, William and Charles Mayo, Eugene McCarthy, Walter F. Mondale, Prince (Rodgers Nelson), Charles Schulz, Harold Stassen, Thorstein Veblen, Jesse Ventura, Paul Wellstone.

Tourist information. Explore Minnesota Tourism, Metro Square, 121 7th Pl. E., Ste. 100, St. Paul, MN 55101. 1-888-TOURISM; www.exploreminnesota.com

Website. www.state.mn.us

Mississippi (MS)

Magnolia State

People. Population (2008 est.): 2,938,618; rank: 31; net change (2007-08): 0.6%. **Pop. density:** 62.6 per sq mi. **Racial distribution** (2008): 60.6% white; 37.2% black; 0.8% Asian; 0.5% Native Amer./Nat. AK; <0.05% Hawaiian/Pacific Islander; 2 or more races, 0.9%. **Hispanic pop.** (any race): 2.2%.

Geography. Total area: 48,430 sq mi; rank: 32. **Land area:** 46,907 sq mi; rank: 31. **Acres forested:** 19.6 mil. **Location:** East South Central state bordered on the W by the Mississippi R. and on the S by the Gulf of Mexico. **Climate:** semi-tropical, with abundant rainfall, long growing season, and extreme temperatures unusual. **Topography:** low, fertile delta between the Yazoo and Mississippi rivers; loess bluffs stretching around delta border; sandy gulf coastal terraces followed by piney woods and prairie; rugged, high sandy hills in extreme NE followed by Black Prairie Belt, Pontotoc Ridge, and flatwoods into the north central highlands. **Capital:** Jackson. **Chief airport at:** Jackson.

Economy. Chief industries: warehousing & distribution, services, manufacturing, government, wholesale and retail trade. **Chief manuf. goods:** petroleum, upholstered furniture, poultry processing, motor vehicle parts, plastics, ships & boats, chemicals. **Chief crops:** cotton, soybeans, rice, hay, corn, sweet potatoes. **Livestock** (Jan. 2009): 960,000 cattle/calves; (Dec. 2008): 10.2 mil chickens (excl. broilers), 840.7 mil broilers. **Timber/lumber** (est. 2008): 2.0 bil bd. ft; pine, oak, hardwoods. **Nonfuel minerals** (2008 prelim.): $228 mil; stone (crushed), sand and gravel (construction), clays (fuller's earth), cement (portland), clays (ball). **Commercial fishing** (2008): $43.7 mil. **Chief ports:** Pascagoula, Vicksburg, Gulfport, Natchez, Greenville. **Gross state product** (est. 2008): $91.8 bil. **Sales tax** (2009): 7.0%. **Employment distrib.** (June 2008): 21.2% govt.; 19.7% trade/trans./util.; 14.3% mfg.; 11.0% ed./health; 8.3% prof./bus. serv.; 11.1% leisure/hosp.; 4.1% finance; 5.1% constr.; 3.3% other serv.; 1.2% info. **Unemployment** (2008): 6.9%. **Per cap. pers. income** (2008 prelim.): $29,569. **New private housing** (2008): 11,428 units/$1.3 bil. **Commercial banks** (2008): 102; deposits: $45.0 bil. **Savings institutions** (2008): 6; deposits: $432 mil.

Federal govt. Fed. civ. employees (Mar. 2007): 18,261; **avg. salary:** $60,326. **Notable fed. facilities:** *Keesler AFB; Meridian NAS; Columbus AFB; NASA Stennis Space Ctr.; Army Corps of Engineers Waterways Experiment Sta.; Naval Constr. Battalion Ctr., Gulfport.

Energy. Electricity production (est. 2007 kWh by source): coal: 14.5 bil; gas: 11.8 bil; nuclear: 9.4 bil; petroleum: 397.0 mil.

State data. Motto: Virtute et Armis (By valor and arms). **Flower:** Magnolia. **Bird:** Mockingbird. **Tree:** Magnolia. **Song:** Go, Mississippi! **Entered union** Dec. 10, 1817; rank, 20th. **State fair** at Jackson; begins first Wed. in Oct.

History. Choctaw, Chickasaw, and Natchez peoples were living in the region at the time of European contact. The Spaniard Hernando de Soto explored the area, 1540-41. La Salle traced the Mississippi River from Illinois to its mouth and claimed the entire Mississippi Valley for France, 1682. The first settlement, was the French Ft. Maurepas, 1699, on Biloxi Bay. The region was ceded to Britain, 1763, and claimed by Spain, 1779-98, then became a U.S. territory, 1798, and a state, 1817. Slavery spread along with cotton plantations, and slaves made up 55% of the population, 1860. Mississippi seceded, 1861. In the Civil War, Union forces captured Vicksburg, 1863, and caused extensive damage elsewhere. Mississippi reentered the Union, 1870. For the next 100 years, resistance to desegregation and violence against blacks made the state a battleground for the African American civil rights movement. Hurricanes Camille, 1969, and Katrina, 2005, caused substantial damage to the Gulf Coast. Since the early 1990s, casino gambling has boosted the economy.

Tourist attractions. Vicksburg Natl. Military Park and Cemetery, other Civil War sites; Hattiesburg; Natchez Trace; Indian mounds; Antebellum homes; pilgrimages in Natchez and some 25 other cities; The Elvis Presley Birthplace & Museum, Tupelo; Smith Robertson Museum, Mynelle Gardens, in Jackson; Mardi Gras, Shrimp Festival, in Biloxi; Gulf Islands Natl. Seashore.

Famous Mississippians. Margaret Walker Alexander, Dana Andrews, Jimmy Buffett, Bo Diddley, William Faulkner, Brett Favre, Shelby Foote, Morgan Freeman, John Grisham, Fannie Lou Hamer, Jim Henson, Faith Hill, John Lee Hooker, Robert Johnson, James Earl Jones, B. B. King, L. Q. C. Lamar, Trent Lott, Gerald McRaney, Willie Morris, Walter Payton, Elvis Presley, Leontyne Price, Charley Pride, LeAnn Rimes, Muddy Waters, Eudora Welty, Tennessee Williams, Oprah Winfrey, Johnny Winter, Richard Wright, Tammy Wynette.

Tourist information. Mississippi Division of Tourism. PO Box 849, Jackson, MS 39205; 1-866-SEE-MISS; www.visitmississippi.org

Website. www.ms.gov

Missouri (MO)

Show Me State

People. Population (2008 est.): 5,911,605; rank: 18; net change (2007-08): 0.6%. **Pop. density:** 86.0 per sq mi. **Racial distribution** (2008): 85.0% white; 11.5% black; 1.5% Asian; 0.5% Native Amer./Nat. AK; 0.1% Hawaiian/Pacific Islander; 2 or more races, 1.4%. **Hispanic pop.** (any race): 3.2%.

Geography. Total area: 69,704 sq mi; rank: 21. **Land area:** 68,886 sq mi; rank: 18. **Acres forested:** 15.1 mil. **Location:** West North Central state near the geographic center of the conterminous U.S.; bordered on the E by the Mississippi R., on the NW by the Missouri R. **Climate:** continental, susceptible to cold Canadian air, moist, warm gulf air, and drier SW air. **Topography:** rolling hills, open, fertile plains, and well-watered prairie N of the Missouri R.; south of the river land is rough and hilly with deep, narrow valleys; alluvial plain in the SE; low elevation in the west. **Capital:** Jefferson City. **Chief airports at:** Kansas City, St. Louis.

Economy. Chief industries: agriculture, manufacturing, aerospace, tourism. **Chief manuf. goods:** motor vehicles & parts, aerospace, pharmaceuticals, plastics, soap, animal slaughtering & processing, printing. **Chief crops:** soybeans, corn, hay, cotton & cottonseed, wheat, rice, sorghum. **Livestock** (Jan. 2009): 4.3 mil cattle/calves, 83,000 sheep/lambs; (Dec. 2008): 3.1 mil hogs/pigs, 9.6 mil chickens (excl. broilers). **Timber/lumber** (est. 2008): 432 mil bd. ft; oak, hickory. **Nonfuel minerals** (2008 prelim.): $2.1 bil; stone (crushed), lead, cement (portland), lime, zinc. **Gross state product** (est. 2008): $237.8 bil. **Sales tax** (2009): 4.225%. **Employment distrib.** (June 2008): 15.8% govt.; 19.6% trade/trans./util.; 10.3% mfg.; 13.8% ed./health; 12.1% prof./bus. serv.; 10.4% leisure/hosp.; 5.9% finance; 5.4% constr.; 4.3% other serv.; 2.3% info. **Unemployment** (2008): 6.1%. **Per cap. pers. income** (2008 prelim.): $35,228. **New private housing** (2008): 13,273 units/$1.9 bil. **Commercial banks** (2008): 365; deposits: $105.0 bil. **Savings institutions** (2008): 33; deposits: $5.7 bil. **Lottery** (2008): total sales: $995.5 mil; profit: $266.6 mil.

Federal govt. Fed. civ. employees (Mar. 2007): 37,181; **avg. salary:** $58,211. **Notable fed. facilities:** Federal Reserve banks; *Ft. Leonard Wood; Jefferson Barracks Natl. Cem.; Whiteman AFB.

Energy. Electricity production (est. 2007 kWh by source): coal: 74.8 bil; gas: 4.2 bil; hydroelectric: 383.0 mil; nuclear: 9.4 bil; petroleum: 73.0 mil.

State data. Motto: Salus Populi Suprema Lex Esto (The welfare of the people shall be the supreme law). **Flower:** Hawthorn. **Bird:** Bluebird. **Tree:** Dogwood. **Song:** Missouri Waltz. **Entered union** Aug. 10, 1821; rank, 24th. **State fair** at Sedalia, mid-Aug.; at Bethany, late Aug.-early Sept.

History. In the 17th cent., when French explorers arrived, Algonquian Sauk, Fox, and Illinois and Siouan Osage, Missouri, Iowa, and Kansa peoples were living in the region; few remained by the 1830s. French hunters and lead miners made the first settlement c. 1735, at Ste. Genevieve. The territory was ceded to Spain by the French, 1762, then returned to France, 1800, and acquired by the U.S. in the Louisiana Purchase, 1803. Powerful earthquakes rocked New Madrid, 1811-12. Missouri became a territory, 1812, and entered the Union as a slave state, 1821. St. Louis became the gateway for pioneers heading West. Though Missouri stayed with the Union, pro- and antislavery forces battled there during the Civil War. In the late 19th cent. railroad building and the cattle trade made Kansas City a boomtown. The most notable Missourian of the 20th cent., Harry S. Truman, was U.S. president, 1945-53. The state, a political bellwether, voted for the winner in every presidential election from 1960 to 2004.

Tourist attractions. Silver Dollar City, Branson; Mark Twain Area, Hannibal; Pony Express Museum, St. Joseph; Harry S. Truman Library, Independence; Gateway Arch, St. Louis; Worlds of Fun, Kansas City; Lake of the Ozarks; Churchill Mem., Fulton; State Capitol, Jefferson City.

Famous Missourians. Maya Angelou, Robert Altman, Burt Bacharach, Josephine Baker, Scott Bakula, Thomas Hart Benton, Tom Berenger, Yogi Berra, Chuck Berry, George Caleb Bingham, Daniel Boone, Omar Bradley, William Burroughs, Kate Capshaw, Dale Carnegie, George Washington Carver, Bob Costas, Walter Cronkite, Walt Disney, T. S. Eliot, Richard Gephardt, John Goodman, Betty Grable, Edwin Hubble, Jesse James, Rush Limbaugh, Marianne Moore, Reinhold Niebuhr, J. C. Penney, John J. Pershing, Brad Pitt, Joseph Pulitzer, Ginger Rogers, Bess Truman, Harry S. Truman, Kathleen Turner, Tina Turner, Mark Twain, Dick Van Dyke, Tennessee Williams, Lanford Wilson, Shelley Winters, Jane Wyman.

Tourist information. Missouri Division of Tourism. PO Box 1055, Jefferson City, MO 65102; (800) 519-2100; www.visitmo.com

Website. www.mo.us

Montana (MT)
Treasure State

People. Population (2008 est.): 967,440; rank: 44; net change (2007-08): 1.1%. **Pop. density:** 6.6 per sq mi. **Racial distribution** (2008): 90.5% white; 0.7% black; 0.6% Asian; 6.4% Native Amer./Nat. AK; 0.1% Hawaiian/Pacific Islander; 2 or more races, 1.7%. **Hispanic pop.** (any race): 3.0%.

Geography. Total area: 147,042 sq mi; rank: 4. **Land area:** 145,552 sq mi; rank: 4. **Acres forested:** 25.0 mil. **Location:** Mountain state bounded on the E by the Dakotas, on the S by Wyoming, on the SSW by Idaho, and on the N by Canada. **Climate:** colder, continental climate with low humidity. **Topography:** Rocky Mts. in western third of the state; eastern two-thirds gently rolling northern Great Plains. **Capital:** Helena.

Economy. Chief industries: agriculture, timber, mining, tourism, oil and gas. **Chief manuf. goods:** sawmills, softwood veneer & plywood, petroleum. **Chief crops:** wheat, barley, hay, sugar beets, potatoes, dry beans, flaxseed, cherries, corn, oats. **Livestock** (Jan. 2009): 2.6 mil cattle/calves, 255,000 sheep/lambs; (Dec. 2008): 510,000 chickens (excl. broilers). **Timber/lumber** (est. 2008): 712 mil bd. ft; Douglas fir, pines, larch. **Nonfuel minerals** (2008 prelim.): $1.4 bil; copper, molybdenum, platinum metal, gold, palladium metal. **Gross state product** (est. 2008): $35.9 bil. **Sales tax** (2009): none. **Employment distrib.** (June 2008): 19.0% govt.; 20.7% trade/trans./util.; 4.5% mfg.; 13.1% ed./health; 9.1% prof./bus. serv.; 13.9% leisure/hosp.; 4.9% finance; 7.3% constr.; 3.9% other serv.; 1.7% info. **Unemployment** (2008): 4.5%. **Per cap. pers. income** (2008 prelim.): $34,256. **New private housing** (2008): 2,376 units/$359.2 mil. **Commercial banks** (2008): 80; deposits: $15.3 bil. **Savings institutions** (2008): 2; deposits: $242 mil. **Lottery** (2008): total sales: $43.8 mil; profit: $11.0 mil.

Federal govt. Fed. civ. employees (Mar. 2007): 9,984; **avg. salary:** $57,340. **Notable fed. facilities:** Malmstrom AFB & missile silos; Ft. Peck, Hungry Horse, Libby, Yellowtail, and other dams.

Energy. Electricity production (est. 2007 kWh by source): coal: 352.0 mil.

State data. Motto: Oro y Plata (Gold and silver). **Flower:** Bitterroot. **Bird:** Western meadowlark. **Tree:** Ponderosa pine. **Song:** Montana. **Entered union** Nov. 8, 1889; rank, 41st. **State fair** at Great Falls; late July-early Aug.

History. Paleo-Indian hunters reached the area over 12,000 years ago. Cheyenne, Blackfoot, Crow, Assiniboin, Salish (Flatheads), Kootenai, and Kalispel peoples lived in the region before Europeans arrived. French explorers visited the region, 1742. The U.S. acquired the area partly through the Louisiana Purchase, 1803, partly through explorations of Lewis and Clark, 1805-6. Fur traders and missionaries established posts in the early 19th cent. Gold was discovered on Grasshopper Creek, 1862, and Montana Territory was established, 1864. Indian uprisings reached their peak with the defeat of Gen. George Custer at the Battle of Little Bighorn, 1876. Chief Joseph and the Nez Percé tribe surrendered here, 1877, after a long trek across the state. Mining activity and the coming of the Northern Pacific Railway, 1883, brought population growth. Montana became a state, 1889. Copper wealth from the Butte pits resulted in the turn of the

century "War of Copper Kings" as feuding factions contended for "the richest hill on earth." During the first half of the 20th cent., the Anaconda Copper firm wielded enormous political influence. Jeannette Rankin, a suffragist and pacifist, was the first woman elected to Congress, 1916. Mike Mansfield served 34 years in Congress and was Senate Democratic leader, 1961-77. An 18-year hunt for notorious "Unabomber" Theodore Kaczynski ended with his arrest, 1996, at his cabin near Lincoln.

Tourist attractions. Glacier Natl. Park; Yellowstone Natl. Park; Museum of the Rockies, Bozeman; Museum of the Plains Indian, Blackfeet Reservation, near Browning; Little Bighorn Battlefield Natl. Monument and Custer Natl. Cemetery; Flathead Lake; Helena; Lewis and Clark Caverns State Park, near Whitehall; Lewis and Clark Interpretive Center, Great Falls.

Famous Montanans. Dana Carvey, Gary Cooper, Marcus Daly, Chet Huntley, Will James, Myrna Loy, David Lynch, Mike Mansfield, Brent Musburger, Jeannette Rankin, Charles M. Russell, Lester Thurow.

Tourist information. Travel Montana, Dept. of Commerce, 301 S. Park Ave., PO Box 200533, Helena, MT 59601; 1-800-VISITMT; www.visitmt.org

Website. www.mt.gov

Nebraska (NE)
Cornhusker State

People. Population (2008 est.): 1,783,432; rank: 38; net change (2007-08): 0.8%. **Pop. density:** 23.2 per sq mi. **Racial distribution** (2008): 91.4% white; 4.5% black; 1.7% Asian; 1.1% Native Amer./Nat. AK; 0.1% Hawaiian/Pacific Islander; 2 or more races, 1.3%. **Hispanic pop.** (any race): 7.9%.

Geography. Total area: 77,354 sq mi; rank: 16. **Land area:** 76,872 sq mi; rank: 15. **Acres forested:** 1.2 mil. **Location:** West North Central state with the Missouri R. for a NE and E border. **Climate:** continental semi-arid. **Topography:** till plains of the central lowland in the eastern third rising to the Great Plains and hill country of the north central and NW. **Capital:** Lincoln. **Chief airport at:** Omaha.

Economy. Chief industries: agriculture, manufacturing. **Chief manuf. goods:** animal slaughtering, grain & oilseed, farm machinery, medical equip., motor vehicle parts, printing, structural metals. **Chief crops:** corn, sorghum, soybeans, hay, wheat, dry beans, oats, potatoes, sugar beets. **Livestock** (Jan. 2009): 6.4 mil cattle/calves, 71,000 sheep/lambs; (Dec. 2008): 3.3 mil hogs/pigs, 11.5 mil chickens (excl. broilers), 6.7 mil broilers. **Timber/lumber:** figs. withheld; oak, hickory, and elm. **Nonfuel minerals** (2008 prelim.): $138 mil; cement (portland), stone (crushed), sand and gravel (construction), lime, clays (common). **Chief ports:** Omaha, Sioux City, Brownville, Blair, Plattsmouth, Nebraska City. **Gross state product** (est. 2008): $83.3 bil. **Sales tax** (2009): 5.5%. **Employment distrib.** (June 2008): 16.8% govt.; 21.1% trade/trans./util.; 10.3% mfg.; 13.6% ed./health; 11.2% prof./bus. serv.; 8.8% leisure/hosp.; 7.2% finance; 5.4% constr.; 3.6% other serv.; 1.9% info. **Unemployment** (2008): 3.3%. **Per cap. pers. income** (2008 prelim.): $37,730. **New private housing** (2008): 6,346 units/$859.6 mil. **Commercial banks** (2008): 242; deposits: $35.5 bil. **Savings institutions** (2008): 15; deposits: $3.3 bil. **Lottery** (2008): total sales: $121.9 mil; profit: $31.0 mil.

Federal govt. Fed. civ. employees (Mar. 2007): 9,344; **avg. salary:** $60,450. **Notable fed. facilities:** *Offutt AFB.

Energy. Electricity production (est. 2007 kWh by source): coal: 19.7 bil; gas: 1.0 bil; nuclear: 11.0 bil.

State data. Motto: Equality before the law. **Flower:** Goldenrod. **Bird:** Western meadowlark. **Tree:** Cottonwood. **Song:** Beautiful Nebraska. **Entered union** Mar. 1, 1867; rank, 37th. **State fair** at Lincoln; late Aug.-early Sept.

History. When Europeans arrived, Pawnee, Ponca, Omaha, and Oto peoples lived in the region. Spanish and French explorers visited the area prior to its acquisition in the Louisiana Purchase, 1803. Lewis and Clark passed through, 1804-06. The first permanent settlement was Bellevue, near Omaha, 1823. The 1834 Indian Intercourse Act declared Nebraska Indian country and excluded white settlement, but conflicts with settlers eventually forced Native Americans to move to reservations. Nebraska became a territory, 1854, and a state, 1867. Many Civil War veterans settled under free land terms of the 1862 Homestead Act; as agriculture grew, struggles followed between homesteaders and ranchers. Since the mid-1930s, Nebraska has been the only state with a unicameral legislature. A leader in agribusiness, Nebraska has also become a major telemarketing center. The "Oracle of Omaha," investor Warren Buffett, one of the world's wealthiest men, announced in 2006 he would give most of his $44 bil fortune to charity.

Tourist attractions. State Museum (Elephant Hall), State Capitol, in Lincoln; Stuhr Museum of the Prairie Pioneer, Grand Island; Museum of the Fur Trade, Chadron; Henry Doorly Zoo, Joslyn Art Museum, in Omaha; Ashfall Fossil Beds, Strategic Air and Space Museum, Ashland; Boys Town, Omaha; Arbor Lodge State Park, Nebraska City; Buffalo Bill Ranch State Hist. Park, North Platte; Pioneer Village, Minden; Oregon Trail landmarks; Scotts Bluff Natl. Monument; Chimney Rock Natl. Historic Site; Ft. Robinson; Hastings Museum of Natural & Cultural Hist.

Famous Nebraskans. Grover Cleveland Alexander, Fred Astaire, Marlon Brando, Charles W. Bryan, William Jennings Bryan, Warren Buffett, Johnny Carson, Willa Cather, Dick Cavett, Dick Cheney, William F. "Buffalo Bill" Cody, Loren Eiseley, Rev. Edward J. Flanagan, Henry Fonda, Gerald R. Ford, Bob Gibson, Rollin Kirby, Harold Lloyd, Malcolm X, J. Sterling Morton, John Neihardt, Nick Nolte, George Norris, Tom Osborne, John J. Pershing, Roscoe Pound, Chief Red Cloud, Mari Sandoz, Robert Taylor, Darryl F. Zanuck.

Tourist information. Nebraska Division of Travel and Tourism, PO Box 98907, Lincoln, NE 68509-8907; 1-877-NEBRASKA; www.visitnebraska.gov

Website. www.nebraska.gov

Nevada (NV)
Sagebrush State, Battle Born State, Silver State

People. Population (2008 est.): 2,600,167; rank: 35; net change (2007-08): 1.8%. **Pop. density:** 23.7 per sq mi. **Racial distribution** (2008): 80.9% white; 8.1% black; 6.2% Asian; 1.5% Native Amer./Nat. AK; 0.5% Hawaiian/Pacific Islander; 2 or more races, 2.8%. **Hispanic pop.** (any race): 25.7%.

Geography. Total area: 110,561 sq mi; rank: 7. **Land area:** 109,826 sq mi; rank: 7. **Acres forested:** 11.1 mil. **Location:** Mountain state bordered on N by Oregon and Idaho, on E by Utah and Arizona, on SE by Arizona, and on SW and W by California. **Climate:** semi-arid and arid. **Topography:** rugged N-S mountain ranges; highest elevation, Boundary Peak, 13,140 ft; southern area is within the Mojave Desert; lowest elevation, Colorado River at southern tip of state, 479 ft. **Capital:** Carson City. **Chief airports at:** Las Vegas, Reno.

Economy. Chief industries: gaming, tourism, mining, manufacturing, government, retailing, warehousing, trucking. **Chief manuf. goods:** gaming machines, cement & concrete, plastics, printing, architectural & structural metals, electricity instruments. **Chief crops:** hay, onions, potatoes, alfalfa, wheat, garlic, mint, barley. **Livestock** (Jan. 2009): 450,000 cattle/calves, 67,000 sheep/lambs. **Timber/lumber** (est. 2008): <0.5 mil bd. ft; piñon, juniper, other pines. **Nonfuel minerals** (2008 prelim.): $6.5 bil; gold, copper, sand and gravel (construction), magnesite silver. **Gross state product** (est. 2008): $131.2 bil. **Sales tax** (2009): 6.5%. **Employment distrib.** (June 2008): 12.4% govt.; 18.3% trade/trans./util.; 3.9% mfg.; 7.4% ed./health; 12.0% prof./bus. serv.; 26.5% leisure/hosp.; 4.9% finance; 9.6% constr.; 2.9% other serv.; 1.2% info. **Unemployment** (2008): 6.7%. **Per cap. pers. income** (2008 prelim.): $40,353. **New private housing** (2008): 14,881 units/$1.7 bil. **Commercial banks** (2008): 54; deposits: $118.5 bil. **Savings institutions** (2008):12; deposits: $81.3 bil.

Federal govt. Fed. civ. employees (Mar. 2007): 10,086; **avg. salary:** $61,873. **Notable fed. facilities:** Nevada Test Site; Hawthorne Army Depot; Nellis AFB & Range Complex; Fallon NAS; Natl. Wild Horse & Burro Ctr. at Palomino Valley.

Energy. Electricity production (est. 2007 kWh by source): coal: 7.1 bil; gas: 12.4 bil; petroleum: 12.0 mil.

State data. Motto: All for our country. **Flower:** Sagebrush. **Bird:** Mountain bluebird. **Trees:** Single-leaf piñon and bristlecone pine. **Song:** Home Means Nevada. **Entered union** Oct. 31, 1864; rank, 36th. **State fair** at Reno; late Aug.

History. Shoshone, Paiute, Bannock, and Washoe peoples lived in the area at the time of European contact. Nevada was first explored by Spaniards, 1776. In the 1820s, fur traders Peter Skene Ogden and Jedediah Smith separately explored the area. It was acquired by the U.S., 1848, at the end of the Mexican War. A trading post at Mormon Station, now Genoa, was established, 1850. Discovery of the Comstock Lode, rich in gold and silver, 1859, spurred a population

boom. Nevada became a territory, 1861, and a state, 1864. Hoover Dam was built, 1931-36. WIth gambling legal since 1931, a surge in resort casino construction after World War II turned Las Vegas into one of the nation's most popular tourist destinations. An influx of Hispanics and Asians, attracted by service-industry and construction jobs, helped make Nevada the fastest-growing state in the U.S. during 1990-2005, and again in 2007.

Tourist attractions. Legalized gambling at Lake Tahoe, Reno, Las Vegas, Laughlin, Elko County, and elsewhere; Hoover Dam; Lake Mead; Great Basin Natl. Park; Valley of Fire State Park; Virginia City; Red Rock Canyon Natl. Conservation Area; Liberace Museum, The Strip, Fremont St., Atomic Testing Museum, Pinball Hall of Fame, all Las Vegas; Lamoille Canyon; Pyramid Lake; Lost City Museum, Overton; Skiing near Lake Tahoe.

Famous Nevadans. Andre Agassi, Walter Van Tilburg Clark, George Ferris, Sarah Winnemucca Hopkins, Paul Laxalt, Dat So La Lee, John William Mackay, Anne Martin, Pat McCarran, Key Pittman, William Morris Stewart.

Tourist information. Commission on Tourism, 401 N. Carson St., Carson City, NV 89701; 1-800-NEVADA8; www.travelnevada.com

Website. www.nv.gov

New Hampshire (NH)
Granite State

People. Population (2008 est.): 1,315,809; rank: 41; net change (2007-08): 0.3%. **Pop. density:** 147.0 per sq mi. **Racial distribution** (2008): 95.5% white; 1.2% black; 1.9% Asian; 0.3% Native Amer./Nat. AK; <0.05% Hawaiian/Pacific Islander; 2 or more races, 1.1%. **Hispanic pop.** (any race): 2.6%.

Geography. Total area: 9,350 sq mi; rank: 46. **Land area:** 8,968 sq mi; rank: 44. **Acres forested:** 4.9 mil. **Location:** New England state bounded on S by Massachusetts, on W by Vermont, on N and NW by Canada, on E by Maine and the Atlantic Ocean. **Climate:** highly varied, due to its nearness to high mountains and ocean. **Topography:** low, rolling coast followed by countless hills and mountains rising out of a central plateau. **Capital:** Concord. **Chief airport at:** Manchester.

Economy. Chief industries: tourism, manufacturing, agriculture, trade, mining. **Chief manuf. goods:** navigational instr., circuit boards, electrical equip., fabricated metal, machinery, medical equip., plastics. **Chief crops:** greenhouse & nursery, apples, sweet corn, hay, Christmas trees, berries, maple syrup. **Livestock** (Jan. 2009): 39,000 cattle/calves; (Dec. 2008): 358,000 chickens (excl. broilers). **Timber/lumber** (est. 2008): 217 mil bd. ft; white pine, hemlock, oak, birch. **Nonfuel minerals** (2008 prelim.): $119 mil; stone (crushed), sand and gravel (construction), stone (dimension), gemstones (natural). **Commercial fishing** (2008): $20.8 mil. **Chief ports:** Portsmouth, Hampton, Rye. **Gross state product** (est. 2008): $60.0 bil. **Sales tax** (2009): none. **Employment distrib.** (June 2008): 14.1% govt.; 21.7% trade/trans./util.; 11.7% mfg.; 15.9% ed./health; 10.4% prof./bus. serv.; 10.4% leisure/hosp.; 5.9% finance; 4.4% constr.; 3.4% other serv.; 1.9% info. **Unemployment** (2008): 3.8%. **Per cap. pers. income** (2008 prelim.): $42,830. **New private housing** (2008): 3,234 units/$593.5 mil. **Commercial banks** (2008): 19; deposits: $16.3 bil. **Savings institutions** (2008): 22; deposits: $6.7 bil. **Lottery** (2008): total sales: $261.1 mil; profit: $75.7 mil.

Federal govt. Fed. civ. employees (Mar. 2007): 4,254; **avg. salary:** $73,166. **Notable fed. facilities:** Army Cold Regions Res. & Engineering Lab.

Energy. Electricity production (est. 2007 kWh by source): coal: 3.9 bil; gas: 14.0 mil; petroleum: 303.0 mil.

State data. Motto: Live free or die. **Flower:** Purple lilac. **Bird:** Purple finch. **Tree:** White birch. **Song:** Old New Hampshire. **Ninth** of the original 13 states to ratify the Constitution, June 21, 1788. **State fair:** no official state fair; many agricultural fairs statewide, July through Sept.

History. The area has been inhabited for about 10,000 years. Algonquian-speaking peoples, including the Pennacook, lived in the region when the Europeans arrived. The first explorers to visit the area were England's Martin Pring, 1603, and France's Champlain, 1605. The first settlement was Odiorne's Point (now port of Rye), 1623. Before the American Revolution, New Hampshire residents raided a British fort at Portsmouth, 1774, and drove the royal governor out, 1775. New Hampshire became the first colony to adopt its own constitution, 1776. After statehood, 1788, New Hampshire became a textile manufacturing center. The mill towns declined in the first half of the 20th cent., but tourism and high-technology industries, lured by low taxes, have revived the economy since the 1960s. A state law requires it to hold the first primary of the presidential campaign season.

Tourist attractions. Mt. Washington, highest peak in Northeast; Lake Winnipesaukee; Crawford, Franconia, Pinkham notches, Flume Gorge, Canon Mt. aerial tramway, all White Mt. region; Strawbery Banke, Portsmouth; Canterbury Shaker Village; Saint-Gaudens, Natl. Historic Site, Cornish; Mt. Monadnock.

Famous New Hampshirites. Salmon P. Chase, Ralph Adams Cram, Mary Baker Eddy, Daniel Chester French, Robert Frost, Horace Greeley, Sarah Buell Hale, Franklin Pierce, Augustus Saint-Gaudens, Adam Sandler, Alan Shepard, David H. Souter, Daniel Webster.

Tourist information. Division of Travel & Tourism Development, 172 Pembroke Rd., PO Box 1856; Concord, NH 03302-1856; 1-800-FUNINNH; www.visitnh.gov

Website. www.nh.gov

New Jersey (NJ)
Garden State

People. Population (2008 est.): 8,682,661; rank: 11; net change (2007-08): 0.3%. **Pop. density:** 1,180.7 per sq mi. **Racial distribution** (2008): 76.0% white; 14.5% black; 7.7% Asian; 0.3% Native Amer./Nat. AK; 0.1% Hawaiian/Pacific Islander; 2 or more races, 1.4%. **Hispanic pop.** (any race): 16.3%.

Geography. Total area: 8,721 sq mi; rank: 47. **Land area:** 7,417 sq mi; rank: 46. **Acres forested:** 2.1 mil. **Location:** Middle Atlantic state bounded on N and E by New York and Atlantic Ocean, on S and W by Delaware and Pennsylvania. **Climate:** moderate, with marked difference bet. NW and SE extremities. **Topography:** Appalachian Valley in the NW also has highest elevation, High Pt., 1,801 ft; Appalachian Highlands, flat-topped NE-SW mountain ranges; Piedmont Plateau, low plains broken by high ridges (Palisades) rising 400-500 ft; Coastal Plain, covering three-fifths of state in SE, rises from sea level to gentle slopes. **Capital:** Trenton. **Chief airport at:** Newark.

Economy. Chief industries: pharmaceuticals, telecommunications, biotechnology, printing & publishing. **Chief manuf. goods:** petroleum, pharmaceuticals, toiletries, chemicals, plastics, printing, navigational instr., medical equip., paper prod. **Chief crops:** greenhouse & nursery, blueberries, peaches, corn, hay, tomatoes, bell peppers, cranberries, soybeans, apples. **Livestock** (Jan. 2009): 38,000 cattle/calves; (Dec. 2008): 1.6 mil chickens (excl. broilers). **Timber/lumber** (est. 2008): 34 mil bd. ft; pine, cedar, mixed hardwoods. **Nonfuel minerals** (2008 prelim.): $326 mil; sand and gravel (construction), stone (crushed), sand and gravel (industrial), greensand marl, peat. **Commercial fishing** (2008): $168.7 mil. **Chief ports:** Newark, Elizabeth, Hoboken, Camden. **Gross state product** (est. 2008): $474.9 bil. **Sales tax** (2009): 7.0%. **Employment distrib.** (June 2008): 15.9% govt.; 21.3% trade/trans./util.; 7.4% mfg.; 14.4% ed./health; 15.0% prof./bus. serv.; 8.8% leisure/hosp.; 6.5% finance; 4.2% constr.; 4.1% other serv.; 2.4% info. **Unemployment** (2008): 5.5%. **Per cap. pers. income** (2008 prelim.): $50,919. **New private housing** (2008): 18,363 units/$2.8 bil. **Commercial banks** (2008): 100; deposits: $155.7 bil. **Savings institutions** (2008): 74; deposits: $71.4 bil. **Lottery** (2008): total sales: $2.5 bil; profit: $882.1 mil.

Federal govt. Fed. civ. employees (Mar. 2007): 28,401; **avg. salary:** $76,669. **Notable fed. facilities:** McGuire AFB; *Ft. Monmouth; Picatinny Arsenal; *Lakehurst Naval Air Engineering Ctr.; Ft. Dix; FAA William J. Hughes Technical Ctr.

Energy. Electricity production (est. 2007 kWh by source): coal: 294.0 mil; hydroelectric: −269.0 mil; petroleum: 57.0 mil.

State data. Motto: Liberty and prosperity. **Flower:** Purple violet. **Bird:** Eastern goldfinch. **Tree:** Red oak. **Third** of the original 13 states to ratify the Constitution, Dec. 18, 1787. **State fair** at Augusta; late July-early Aug.

History. The Lenni Lenape (Delaware) peoples lived in the region and had mostly peaceful relations with European colonists, who arrived after the explorers Verrazano, 1524, and Hudson, 1609. The first permanent European settlement was Dutch, at Bergen (now Jersey City), 1660. When the British took New Netherland, 1664, the area between the Delaware and Hudson Rivers was given to Lord John Berkeley and Sir George Carteret. During the American Revolution, New Jer-

sey was the scene of many major battles, including Trenton, 1776; Princeton, 1777; and Monmouth, 1778. New Jersey was the third state to ratify the Constitution, 1787, and the first to approve the Bill of Rights, 1789. In a duel at Weehawken, 1804, Vice Pres. Aaron Burr fatally shot Alexander Hamilton. Canal and railroad building stimulated the growth of cities and industries in the 19th cent. The 20th cent. arrival of large numbers of African Americans, Italians, Irish, European Jews, Puerto Ricans, Asian Indians, and other groups made New Jersey one of the most diverse states in the U.S. Construction of resort casinos in Atlantic City from the late 1970s revitalized tourism. Gov. James McGreevey resigned, 2004, after acknowledging an extramarital affair with a man later identified as his former homeland security adviser.

Tourist attractions. 127 mi of beaches, boardwalks at Atlantic City (with gambling), Seaside Heights, Ocean City, Wildwood; Grover Cleveland birthplace, Caldwell; Cape May Historic District; Edison Natl. Historic Site, W. Orange; Six Flags Great Adventure, Jackson; Liberty State Park, Liberty Science Center, in Jersey City; Pine Barrens wilderness area; Princeton University; Revolutionary War sites; Adventure Aquarium, Battleship NJ, Walt Whitman house, in Camden.

Famous New Jerseyans. Jason Alexander, Samuel Alito, Count Basie, Judy Blume, Jon Bon Jovi, Bill Bradley, Aaron Burr, Grover Cleveland, James Fenimore Cooper, Stephen Crane, Danny DeVito, Thomas Edison, Albert Einstein, James Gandolfini, Allen Ginsberg, Alexander Hamilton, Ed Harris, Whitney Houston, Buster Keaton, Joyce Kilmer, Norman Mailer, Jack Nicholson, Thomas Paine, Dorothy Parker, Joe Pesci, Molly Pitcher, Paul Robeson, Philip Roth, Antonin Scalia, Wally Schirra, H. Norman Schwarzkopf, Frank Sinatra, Bruce Springsteen, Martha Stewart, Meryl Streep, Dave Thomas, John Travolta, Walt Whitman, William Carlos Williams, Woodrow Wilson.

Tourist information. Dept. of State, Division of Travel and Tourism, PO Box 460, Trenton, NJ 08625; 1-800-VISITNJ; www.visitnj.org

Website. www.state.nj.us

New Mexico (NM)
Land of Enchantment

People. Population (2008 est.): 1,984,356; rank: 36; net change (2007-08): 1.0%. **Pop. density:** 16.4 per sq mi. **Racial distribution** (2008): 84.0% white; 3.0% black; 1.4% Asian; 9.7% Native Amer./Nat. AK; 0.1% Hawaiian/Pacific Islander; 2 or more races, 1.8%. **Hispanic pop.** (any race): 44.9%.

Geography. Total area: 121,589 sq mi; rank: 5. **Land area:** 121,356 sq mi; rank: 5. **Acres forested:** 16.7 mil. **Location:** Southwestern state bounded by Colorado on the N, Oklahoma, Texas, and Mexico on the E and S, and Arizona on the W. **Climate:** dry, with temperatures rising or falling 5°F with every 1,000 ft elevation. **Topography:** eastern third, Great Plains; central third, Rocky Mts. (85% of the state is over 4,000-ft elevation); western third, high plateau. **Capital:** Santa Fe. **Chief airport at:** Albuquerque.

Economy. Chief industries: government, services, trade. **Chief manuf. goods:** semiconductors, medical equip., navigational/measuring/medical/control instruments, aircrafts, chemicals, jewelry. **Chief crops:** hay, pecans, corn, greenhouse & nursery, chiles, onions, cotton, wheat, peanuts. **Livestock** (Jan. 2009): 1.5 mil cattle/calves, 120,000 sheep/lambs. **Timber/lumber:** figs. withheld; ponderosa pine, Douglas fir. **Nonfuel minerals** (2008 prelim.): $1.8 bil; copper, potash, sand and gravel (construction), molybdenum concentrates, cement (portland). **Gross state product** (est. 2008): $79.9 bil. **Sales tax** (2009): 5.0%. **Employment distrib.** (June 2008): 22.9% govt.; 17.2% trade/trans./util.; 4.1% mfg.; 13.2% ed./health; 12.8% prof./bus. serv.; 10.6% leisure/hosp.; 4.1% finance; 7.2% constr.; 3.7% other serv.; 2.0% info. **Unemployment** (2008): 4.2%. **Per cap. pers. income** (2008 prelim.): $32,091. **New private housing** (2008): 6,070 units/$1.1 bil. **Commercial banks** (2008): 56; deposits: $20.4 bil. **Savings institutions** (2008): 9; deposits: $1.9 bil. **Lottery** (2008): total sales: $147.1 mil; profit: $40.8 mil.

Federal govt. Fed. civ. employees (Mar. 2007): 24,293; **avg. salary:** $61,521. **Notable fed. facilities:** Kirtland, *Cannon, *Holloman AF bases; Los Alamos Natl. Lab; *White Sands Missile Range; Natl. Solar Observatory; Natl. Radio Astronomy Observatory; Sandia Natl. Labs.

Energy. Electricity production (est. 2007 kWh by source): coal: 27.6 bil; gas: 6.1 bil; petroleum: 41.0 mil.

State data. Motto: Crescit Eundo (It grows as it goes). **Flower:** Yucca. **Bird:** Roadrunner. **Tree:** Piñon. **Song:** O, Fair New Mexico; Asi Es Nuevo Mexico. **Entered union** Jan. 6, 1912; rank, 47th. **State fair** at Albuquerque, mid-Sept.; at Las Cruces, early Oct.; at Roswell, early Oct.; at Deming, early Oct.

History. Inhabited for more than 10,000 years, the region was home to Sandia, Clovis, Folsom, Mogollon, and Anasazi cultures, followed by the Pueblo people, Anasazi descendants; later, nomadic Navajo and Apache came. Franciscan Marcos de Niza and a former black slave, Estevanico, explored the area, 1539, seeking gold; Coronado followed, 1540. First settlements were near San Juan Pueblo, 1598, and at Santa Fe, 1610. Settlers alternately traded and fought with the Apache, Comanche, and Navajo. Trade on the Santa Fe Trail to Missouri started, 1821. After the Mexican War began, 1846, Gen. Stephen Kearny took Santa Fe without firing a shot, and declared New Mexico part of the U.S. All Hispanic New Mexicans and Pueblo became U.S. citizens by terms of the 1848 treaty ending the war. New Mexico became a territory, 1850, but did not attain statehood until 1912. Pancho Villa raided Columbus, 1916, and U.S. troops were sent to the area. The world's first atomic bomb was exploded at a test site near Alamogordo, 1945. An underground nuclear waste depository opened near Carlsbad, 1999. Construction on a "spaceport" for space tourism, partially financed by the state, began June 2009.

Tourist attractions. Carlsbad Caverns Natl. Park, with world's largest natural underground chamber; Santa Fe, oldest capital in U.S.; White Sands Natl. Monument, world's largest gypsum deposit; Chaco Culture Natl. Hist. Park; Acoma Pueblo, "sky city" built atop a 357-ft mesa; Taos Art Colony & Ski Valley; Ute Lake State Park; Shiprock; Roswell.

Famous New Mexicans. Ben Abruzzo, Maxie Anderson, Jeff Bezos, Billy (the Kid) Bonney, Kit Carson, Bob Foster, Peter Hurd, Tony Hillerman, Archbishop Jean Baptiste Lamy, Nancy Lopez, Bill Mauldin, Georgia O'Keeffe, Bill Richardson, Kim Stanley, Al Unser, Bobby Unser, Lew Wallace.

Tourist information. New Mexico Dept. of Tourism, 491 Old Santa Fe Trl., Santa Fe, NM 87501; (800) 733-6396; www.newmexico.org

Website. www.newmexico.gov

New York (NY)
Empire State

People. Population (2008 est.): 19,490,297; rank: 3; net change (2007-08): 0.3%. **Pop. density:** 413.6 per sq mi. **Racial distribution** (2008): 73.4% white; 17.3% black; 7.0% Asian; 0.6% Native Amer./Nat. AK; 0.1% Hawaiian/Pacific Islander; 2 or more races, 1.6%. **Hispanic pop.** (any race): 16.7%.

Geography. Total area: 54,556 sq mi; rank: 27. **Land area:** 47,214 sq mi; rank: 30. **Acres forested:** 18.7 mil. **Location:** Middle Atlantic state, bordered by the New England states, Atlantic Ocean, New Jersey and Pennsylvania, Lakes Ontario and Erie, and Canada. **Climate:** variable; the SE region moderated by the ocean. **Topography:** highest and most rugged mountains in the NE Adirondack upland; St. Lawrence-Champlain lowlands extend from Lake Ontario NE along the Canadian plain; Hudson-Mohawk lowland follows the flows of the rivers N and W, 10-30 mi wide; Atlantic coastal plain in the SE; Appalachian Highlands, covering half the state westward from the Hudson Valley, include the Catskill Mts., Finger Lakes; plateau of Erie-Ontario lowlands. **Capital:** Albany. **Chief airports at:** Albany, Buffalo, Islip, New York (2), Rochester, Syracuse, Westchester County.

Economy. Chief industries: manufacturing, finance, communications, tourism, transportation, services. **Chief manuf. goods:** pharmaceuticals, photographic chemicals, electronics, automotive parts, toiletries, printing, plastics, apparel. **Chief crops:** greenhouse & nursery, apples, corn, hay, cabbage, onions, soybeans, potatoes, snap beans, grapes, squash, pumpkins, tomatoes, wheat, cucumbers, green peas. **Livestock** (Jan. 2009): 1.4 mil cattle/calves, 62,000 sheep/lambs; (Dec. 2008): 5.8 mil chickens (excl. broilers). **Timber/lumber** (est. 2008): 514 mil bd. ft; birch, sugar and red maple, basswood, hemlock, pine, oak, ash. **Nonfuel minerals** (2008 prelim.): $1.5 bil; salt, stone (crushed), sand and gravel (construction), cement (portland), zinc. **Commercial fishing** (2008): $57.3 mil. **Chief ports:** New York, Buffalo, Albany. **Gross state product** (est. 2008): $1.1 trillion. **Sales tax** (2009): 4.0%. **Employment distrib.** (June 2008): 17.3% govt.; 17.3% trade/trans./util.; 6.1% mfg.; 18.2% ed./health; 13.0% prof./bus. serv.; 8.4% leisure/hosp.; 8.2% finance; 4.1% constr.; 4.2% other serv.; 3.0% info. **Unemployment** (2008): 5.4%. **Per cap. pers. income** (2008 prelim.): $48,076. **New private housing** (2008): 51,637 units/$6.3 bil. **Commercial banks** (2008): 160; deposits: $655.2 bil. **Savings institutions** (2008): 78; deposits: $101.6 bil. **Lottery** (2008): total sales: $7.5 bil; profit: $2.6 bil.

Federal govt. Fed. civ. employees (Mar. 2007): 64,042; **avg. salary:** $68,128. **Notable fed. facilities:** Ft. Drum; West Point Military Academy; Merchant Marine Academy; AF Research Labs., Rome; Watervliet Arsenal; Brookhaven Natl. Lab.

Energy. Electricity production (est. 2007 kWh by source): coal: 1.4 bil; gas: 14.7 bil; hydroelectric: –768.0 mil; petroleum: 4.4 bil.

State data. Motto: Excelsior (Ever upward). **Flower:** Rose. **Bird:** Bluebird. **Tree:** Sugar maple. **Song:** I Love New York. **Eleventh** of the original 13 states to ratify the Constitution, July 26, 1788. **State fair** at Syracuse; late Aug.-early Sept.

History. When Europeans arrived, Algonquians including the Mahican, Wappinger, and Lenni Lenape inhabited the region, as did the Iroquoian Mohawk, Oneida, Onondaga, Cayuga, and Seneca tribes, who established the League of the Five Nations. Verrazano entered New York harbor, 1524. In 1609, Henry Hudson visited the river later named for him, and Champlain explored the lake that now bears his name. The first permanent settlement was Dutch, near present-day Albany, 1624. New Amsterdam was settled, 1626, at the S tip of Manhattan island. A British fleet seized New Netherland, 1664. Key battles of the American Revolution included Saratoga, 1777. In the 19th cent., New York City emerged as one of the world's great metropolitan areas, a center for trade, finance, and arts, and a haven for millions of immigrants. Completion of Erie Canal, 1825, established the state as a gateway to the West. The first women's rights convention was held in Seneca Falls, 1848. Although the state backed the Union in the Civil War, the military draft, 1863, triggered 3 days of riots in New York City. Industry declined in the 20th cent., and California and Texas passed New York in population. Attica was the scene of a bloody prison revolt, 1971. New Yorkers, 2000, elected former First Lady Hillary Rodham Clinton to the U.S. Senate. Two jet aircraft hijacked by terrorists on Sept. 11, 2001, destroyed the World Trade Center in lower Manhattan.

Tourist attractions. New York City; Adirondack and Catskill Mts.; Finger Lakes; Great Lakes; Thousand Islands; Niagara Falls; Saratoga Springs; Philipsburg Manor, Sunnyside (Washington Irving's home), Dutch Church of Sleepy Hollow, near Tarrytown; Corning Museum of Glass; Fenimore House, Natl. Baseball Hall of Fame and Museum, in Cooperstown; Ft. Ticonderoga; Empire State Plaza, Albany; Lake Placid; Franklin D. Roosevelt Natl. Historic Site, Hyde Park; Long Island beaches; Theodore Roosevelt estate, Sagamore Hill, Oyster Bay; Turning Stone Casino.

Famous New Yorkers. Woody Allen, Susan B. Anthony, James Baldwin, Lucille Ball, Ann Bancroft, L. Frank Baum, Milton Berle, Humphrey Bogart, Barbara Boxer, Mel Brooks, Benjamin Cardozo, De Witt Clinton, Peter Cooper, Aaron Copland, Tom Cruise, Robert De Niro, George Eastman, Millard Fillmore, Lou Gehrig, George and Ira Gershwin, Ruth Bader Ginsburg, Rudolph Giuliani, Jackie Gleason, Stephen Jay Gould, Julia Ward Howe, Charles Evans Hughes, Washington Irving, Henry and William James, John Jay, Michael Jordan, Edward Koch, Fiorello LaGuardia, Herman Melville, Arthur Miller, J. Pierpont Morgan Jr., Eddie Murphy, Joyce Carol Oates, Carroll O'Connor, Rosie O'Donnell, Eugene O'Neill, Jerry Orbach, George Pataki, Colin Powell, Nancy Reagan, John D. Rockefeller, Nelson Rockefeller, John Roberts, Richard Rodgers, Ray Romano, Eleanor Roosevelt, Franklin D. Roosevelt, Theodore Roosevelt, Tim Russert, J. D. Salinger, Caroline Kennedy Schlossberg, Jerry Seinfeld, Al Sharpton, Paul Simon, Alfred E. Smith, Elizabeth Cady Stanton, Barbra Streisand, Donald Trump, William (Boss) Tweed, Martin Van Buren, Luther Vandross, Gore Vidal, Denzel Washington, Edith Wharton, Walt Whitman.

Tourist information. Empire State Development, Travel Information Center, 30 South Pearl St., Albany, NY 12245; 1-800-CALLNYS; (518) 474-4116; www.iloveny.com

Website. www.state.ny.us

North Carolina (NC)
Tar Heel State, Old North State

People. Population (2008 est.): 9,222,414; rank: 10; net change (2007-08): 2.0%. **Pop. density:** 189.7 per sq mi. **Racial distribution** (2008): 73.9% white; 21.6% black; 1.9% Asian; 1.3% Native Amer./Nat. AK; 0.1% Hawaiian/Pacific Islander; 2 or more races, 1.2%. **Hispanic pop.** (any race): 7.4%.

Geography. Total area: 53,819 sq mi; rank: 28. **Land area:** 48,711 sq mi; rank: 29. **Acres forested:** 18.4 mil. **Location:** South Atlantic state bounded by Virginia, South Carolina, Georgia, Tennessee, and the Atlantic Ocean. **Climate:** sub-tropical in SE, medium-continental in mountain region; tempered by the Gulf Stream and the mountains in W. **Topography:** coastal plain and tidewater, two-fifths of state, extending to the fall line of the rivers; piedmont plateau, another two-fifths, of gentle to rugged hills; southern Appalachian Mts. contains the Blue Ridge and Great Smoky Mts. **Capital:** Raleigh. **Chief airports at:** Charlotte, Greensboro, Raleigh.

Economy. Chief industries: manufacturing, agriculture, tourism. **Chief manuf. goods:** transportation, tobacco, pharmaceuticals, toiletries, plastics, animal slaughtering & processing, household furniture, fabric & apparel. **Chief crops:** greenhouse & nursery, tobacco, cotton, soybeans, corn, Christmas trees, sweet potatoes, wheat, peanuts, blueberries, cucumbers, tomatoes, hay, potatoes. **Livestock** (Jan. 2009): 850,000 cattle/calves, 28,000 sheep/lambs (Dec. 2008): 9.6 mil hogs/pigs, 19.6 mil chickens (excl. broilers), 796.1 mil broilers. **Timber/lumber** (est. 2008): 2.0 bil bd. ft; yellow pine, oak, hickory, poplar, maple. **Nonfuel minerals** (2008 prelim.): $876 mil; stone (crushed), phosphate rock, sand and gravel (industrial), sand and gravel (construction), stone (dimension). **Commercial fishing** (2008): $86.8 mil. **Chief ports:** Morehead City, Wilmington. **Gross state product** (est. 2008): $400.2 bil. **Sales tax** (2009): 4.5%. **Employment distrib.** (June 2008): 16.4% govt.; 18.6% trade/trans./util.; 12.5% mfg.; 12.7% ed./health; 12.1% prof./bus. serv.; 10.0% leisure/hosp.; 5.1% finance; 6.2% constr.; 4.5% other serv.; 1.7% info. **Unemployment** (2008): 6.3%. **Per cap. pers. income** (2008 prelim.): $34,439. **New private housing** (2008): 54,652 units/$8.4 bil. **Commercial banks** (2008): 99; deposits: $213.0 bil. **Savings institutions** (2008): 39; deposits: $6.5 bil. **Lottery** (2008): total sales: $1.1 bil; profit: $350.0 mil.

Federal govt. Fed. civ. employees (Mar. 2007): 37,991; **avg. salary:** $61,158. **Notable fed. facilities:** Ft. Bragg; *Camp LeJeune Marine Base. *Cherry Point Marine Air Station; Natl. Inst. of Environmental Health Sciences, EPA Research & Dev. Labs, all in Research Triangle Park.

Energy. Electricity production (est. 2007 kWh by source): coal: 76.6 bil; gas: 3.4 bil; hydroelectric: 137.0 mil; nuclear: 40.0 bil; petroleum: 228.0 mil.

State data. Motto: Esse Quam Videri (To be rather than to seem). **Flower:** Dogwood. **Bird:** Cardinal. **Tree:** Pine. **Song:** The Old North State. **Twelfth** of the original 13 states to ratify the Constitution, Nov. 21, 1789. **State fair** at Raleigh, mid-Oct.; at Fletcher, mid-Sept.

History. Algonquian, Siouan, and Iroquoian peoples lived in the region at the time of European contact. Sir Walter Raleigh tried to found a colony, 1584-87; the "Lost Colony" on Roanoke Island, 1587, disappeared without a trace. Permanent settlers came from Virginia in the mid-17th cent. The province's congress was the first to vote for independence, 1776. In the Revolutionary War, Cornwallis's forces were defeated at Kings Mountain, 1780, and forced out after Guilford Courthouse, 1781. The state ratified the Constitution, 1789, only after Congress passed the Bill of Rights. North Carolina, with a slave population of 1/3, seceded from the Union,1861, and provided more troops to the Confederacy than any other state; it was readmitted, 1868. The Wright brothers made the first powered airplane flight at Kitty Hawk, 1903. Sit-ins at segregated Greensboro lunch counters, 1960, drew national attention to the civil rights movement. Long reliant on tobacco, textiles, and wood products, North Carolina has prospered since the 1960s from advanced technologies in the Raleigh-Durham-Chapel Hill area and banking in Charlotte. The hurricane-prone state was hit hard by Hazel, 1954, Fran, 1996, and Floyd, 1999.

Tourist attractions. Cape Hatteras and Cape Lookout natl. seashores; Great Smoky Mts.; Guilford Courthouse and Moore's Creek parks; 66 American Revolution battle sites; Bennett Place (where last Confederate army surrendered), near Durham; Ft. Raleigh, Roanoke Island; Wright Brothers Natl. Memorial, Kitty Hawk; Battleship *North Carolina*, Wilmington; NC Zoo, Asheboro; NC Symphony, Exploris, NC museums of Art, Nat. Sciences, History, in Raleigh; Carl Sandburg Home, Hendersonville; Biltmore House & Gardens, Asheville.

Famous North Carolinians. David Brinkley, Shirley Caesar, John Coltrane, Rick Dees, Elizabeth Hanford Dole, John Edwards, Ava Gardner, Richard J. Gatling, Billy Graham, Andy Griffith, O. Henry, Andrew Jackson, Andrew Johnson, Michael Jordan, Wm. Rufus King, Charles Kuralt, Meadowlark Lemon, Dolley Madison, Thelonious Monk, Edward R. Murrow, Arnold Palmer, Richard Petty, James K. Polk, Charlie Rose, Carl Sandburg, Enos Slaughter, Dean Smith, James Taylor, Thomas Wolfe.

Tourist information. North Carolina Division of Tourism, Film and Sports Development, 4324 Mail Service Center, Raleigh, NC 27699; 1-800-VISIT-NC; (919) 733-8372 (local calls); www.visitnc.com

Website. www.nc.gov

North Dakota (ND)
Peace Garden State

People. Population (2008 est.): 641,481; rank: 48; net change (2007-08): 0.6%. **Pop. density:** 9.3 per sq mi. **Racial distribution** (2008): 91.4% white; 1.1% black; 0.7% Asian; 5.6% Native Amer./Nat. AK; 0.1% Hawaiian/Pacific Islander; 2 or more races, 1.2%. **Hispanic pop.** (any race): 2.1%.

Geography. Total area: 70,700 sq mi; rank: 19. **Land area:** 68,976 sq mi; rank: 17. **Acres forested:** 0.7 mil. **Location:** West North Central state, situated exactly in the middle of North America, bounded on the N by Canada, on the E by Minnesota, on the S by South Dakota, on the W by Montana. **Climate:** continental, with a wide range of temperature and moderate rainfall. **Topography:** Central Lowland in the E comprises the flat Red River Valley and the Rolling Drift Prairie; Missouri Plateau of the Great Plains on the W. **Capital:** Bismarck.

Economy. Chief industries: agriculture, mining, tourism, manufacturing, telecommunications, energy, food processing. **Chief manuf. goods:** machinery, wood product, motor vehicles & parts, furniture, processed foods. **Chief crops:** wheat, soybeans, corn, sugar beets, barley, dry beans, sunflowers, canola, potatoes, flaxseed, hay, dry peas, lentils, oats. **Livestock** (Jan. 2009): 1.8 mil cattle/calves, 88,000 sheep/lambs. **Timber/lumber:** figs. withheld; oak, ash, cottonwood, aspen. **Nonfuel minerals** (2008 prelim.): $45.3 mil; sand and gravel (construction), lime, stone (crushed), clays (common), sand and gravel (industrial). **Gross state product** (est. 2008): $31.2 bil. **Sales tax** (2009): 5.0%. **Employment distrib.** (June 2008): 20.3% govt.; 21.3% trade/trans./util.; 7.2% mfg.; 14.2% ed./health; 8.4% prof./bus. serv.; 9.5% leisure/hosp.; 5.5% finance; 5.8% constr.; 4.2% other serv.; 2.1% info. **Unemployment** (2008): 3.2%. **Per cap. pers. income** (2008 prelim.): $39,321. **New private housing** (2008): 2,833 units/$398.8 mil. **Commercial banks** (2008): 102; deposits: $14.4 bil. **Savings institutions** (2008): 2; deposits: $907 mil. **Lottery** (2008): total sales: $22.1 mil; profit: $6.1 mil.

Federal govt. Fed. civ. employees (Mar. 2007): 6,060; **avg. salary:** $56,853. **Notable fed. facilities:** Minot AFB; *Grand Forks AFB; Northern Prairie Wildlife Res. Ctr.; Garrison Dam Nat. Fish Hatchery; Theodore Roosevelt Natl. Park; Grand Forks Human Nutrition Res. Ctr.; Ft. Union Natl. Hist. Site.

Energy. Electricity production (est. 2007 kWh by source): coal: 28.7 bil; petroleum: 47.0 mil.

State data. Motto: Liberty and union, now and forever, one and inseparable. **Flower:** Wild prairie rose. **Bird:** Western meadowlark. **Tree:** American elm. **Song:** North Dakota Hymn. **Entered union** Nov. 2, 1889; rank, 39th. **State fair** at Minot; late July.

History. Paleo-Indian peoples hunted in the area at least 11,000 years ago. At the time of European contact, the Ojibwa, Yanktonai and Teton Sioux, Mandan, Arikara, and Hidatsa peoples lived in the region. Pierre de Varennes, sieur de La Vérendrye, was the first French fur trader in the area, 1738, followed by the English at the end of the 18th cent. Lewis and Clark built Ft. Mandan, near present-day Washburn, 1804-05, and wintered there. The first permanent settlement was at Pembina, 1812. Missouri River steamboats reached the area, 1832. Dakota Territory was organized, 1861. The first railroad arrived, 1872. The "bonanza farm" craze of the 1870s-80s led to statehood, 1889. The Nonpartisan League, a farmers' group favoring state ownership of industries, helped elect Lynn Frazier as governor, 1916, but he and others were ousted in a recall vote, 1921. The predominantly agricultural state had a 6.5% drop in population, 1930-2005.

Tourist attractions. North Dakota Heritage Center, Bismarck; Bonanzaville, Fargo; Ft. Union Trading Post Natl. Historic Site; Lake Sakakawea; Intl. Peace Garden; Theodore Roosevelt Natl. Park, including Elkhorn Ranch, Badlands; Ft. Abraham Lincoln State Park and Museum, near Mandan; Dakota Dinosaur Museum, Dickinson; Knife River Indian Villages-Natl. Hist. Site.

Famous North Dakotans. Maxwell Anderson, Angie Dickinson, John Bernard Flannagan, Phil Jackson, Louis L'Amour, Peggy Lee, Eric Sevareid, Ann Sothern, Vilhjalmur Stefansson, Lawrence Welk.

Tourist information. North Dakota Tourism Division, Century Center, 1600 E. Century Ave., Ste. 2, PO Box 2057, Bismarck, ND 58502; (800) 435-5663; www.ndtourism.com
Website. www.nd.gov

Ohio (OH)
Buckeye State

People. Population (2008 est.): 11,485,910; rank: 7; net change (2007-08): 0.1%. **Pop. density:** 281.1 per sq mi. **Racial distribution** (2008): 84.8% white; 12.0% black; 1.6% Asian; 0.3% Native Amer./Nat. AK; <0.05% Hawaiian/Pacific Islander; 2 or more races, 1.3%. **Hispanic pop.** (any race): 2.6%.

Geography. Total area: 44,825 sq mi; rank: 34. **Land area:** 40,948 sq mi; rank: 35. **Acres forested:** 7.9 mil. **Location:** East North Central state bounded on the N by Michigan and Lake Erie; on the E and S by Pennsylvania, West Virginia, and Kentucky; on the W by Indiana. **Climate:** temperate but variable; weather subject to much precipitation. **Topography:** generally rolling plain; Allegheny plateau in E; Lake Erie plains extend southward; central plains in the W. **Capital:** Columbus. **Chief airports at:** Akron, Cleveland, Columbus, Dayton.

Economy. Chief industries: manufacturing, trade, services. **Chief manuf. goods:** motor vehicles & parts, petroleum, plastics & rubber, iron & steel, aircraft, machinery, fabricated metal, printing. **Chief crops:** corn, soybeans, hay, wheat, grapes, potatoes, tomatoes, apples, strawberries, tobacco. **Livestock** (Jan. 2009): 1.3 mil cattle/calves, 130,000 sheep/lambs; (Dec. 2008): 1.9 mil hogs/pigs, 33.3 mil chickens (excl. broilers), 57.5 mil broilers. **Timber/lumber** (est. 2008): 313 mil bd. ft; oak, ash, maple, walnut, beech. **Nonfuel minerals** (2008 prelim.): $1.1 bil; stone (crushed), salt, sand and gravel (construction), lime, cement (portland). **Commercial fishing** (2008): $10.6 mil. **Chief ports:** Toledo, Conneaut, Cleveland, Ashtabula. **Gross state product** (est. 2008): $471.5 bil. **Sales tax** (2009): 5.5%. **Employment distrib.** (June 2008): 14.5% govt.; 19.3% trade/trans./util.; 14.0% mfg.; 14.5% ed./health; 12.4% prof./bus. serv.; 9.7% leisure/hosp.; 5.5% finance; 4.2% constr.; 4.1% other serv.; 1.6% info. **Unemployment** (2008): 6.5%. **Per cap. pers. income** (2008 prelim.): $35,511. **New private housing** (2008): 17,666 units/$2.9 bil. **Commercial banks** (2008): 182; deposits: $195.4 bil. **Savings institutions** (2008): 105; deposits: $32.5 bil. **Lottery** (2008): total sales: $2.3 bil; profit: $672.2 mil.

Federal govt. Fed. civ. employees (Mar. 2007): 45,685; **avg. salary:** $70,276. **Notable fed. facilities:** Wright-Patterson AFB; Defense Supply Ctr., Columbus; *NASA John H. Glenn Res. Ctr.; *Lima Army Tank Plant.

Energy. Electricity production (est. 2007 kWh by source): coal: 98.8 bil; gas: 1.2 bil; petroleum: 239.0 mil.

State data. Motto: With God, all things are possible. **Flower:** Scarlet carnation. **Bird:** Cardinal. **Tree:** Buckeye. **Song:** Beautiful Ohio. **Entered union** Mar. 1, 1803; rank, 17th. **State fair** at Columbus; early Aug.

History. Paleo-Indians hunted in the area about 11,000 years ago; the Adena and Hopewell cultures followed. Wyandot, Delaware, Miami, and Shawnee peoples sparsely occupied the area when the first Europeans arrived. La Salle visited the region, 1669. France claimed it, 1682, but ceded it to Britain, 1763. After the American Revolution, Ohio became part of the Northwest Territory, 1787. The first permanent settlement was at Marietta, 1788. Cincinnati was also founded, 1788; Cleveland, 1796. Indian warfare abated with the Treaty of Greenville, 1795. Ohio became a state, 1803. In the War of 1812, Oliver Hazard Perry's victory on Lake Erie and William

Henry Harrison's invasion of Canada, 1813, ended British incursions. Columbus, founded 1812, became the state capital, 1816. Before the Civil War, Ohioans aided the Underground Railroad, helping runaway slaves. Agricultural for much of the 19th cent., the state became an industrial powerhouse in the 20th. Manufacturing jobs dropped by 24%, 1998-2007. No Republican has ever won the presidency without carrying Ohio, and the state's 20 electoral votes proved crucial to Pres. George W. Bush in 2004.

Tourist attractions. Mound City Group, Hopewell Culture Natl. Hist. Park; Neil Armstrong Air and Space Museum, Wapakoneta; Air Force Museum, Dayton; Pro Football Hall of Fame, Canton; King's Island amusement park, Mason; Lake Erie Islands, Cedar Point amusement park, in Sandusky; birthplaces, homes of, and memorials to U.S. Pres. W. H. Harrison, Grant, Garfield, Hayes, B. Harrison, McKinley, Harding, Taft; Amish Region, Tuscarawas/Holmes counties; German Village, Columbus; Jack Nicklaus' Golf Center, Mason; Bob Evans Farm, Rio Grande; Rock and Roll Hall of Fame and Museum, Cleveland.

Famous Ohioans. Sherwood Anderson, Neil Armstrong, George Bellows, Halle Berry, Ambrose Bierce, Erma Bombeck, Drew Carey, Hart Crane, George Custer, Clarence Darrow, Paul Laurence Dunbar, Thomas Edison, Clark Gable, John Glenn, Zane Grey, Bob Hope, William Dean Howells, Toni Morrison, Jack Nicklaus, Jesse Owens, Jack Paar, Pontiac, Eddie Rickenbacker, John D. Rockefeller Sr. and Jr., Roy Rogers, Pete Rose, Arthur Schlesinger Jr., Gen. William Sherman, Steven Spielberg, Gloria Steinem, Harriet Beecher Stowe, Charles Taft, Robert A. Taft, William H. Taft, Tecumseh, James Thurber, Ted Turner, Orville and Wilbur Wright.

Tourist information. Division of Travel and Tourism, PO Box 1001, Columbus, OH 43216; 1-800-BUCKEYE; www.discoverohio.com
Website. www.ohio.gov

Oklahoma (OK)
Sooner State

People. Population (2008 est.): 3,642,361; rank: 28; net change (2007-08): 0.9%. **Pop. density:** 53.1 per sq mi. **Racial distribution** (2008): 78.1% white; 8.0% black; 1.7% Asian; 8.0% Native Amer./Nat. AK; 0.1% Hawaiian/Pacific Islander; 2 or more races, 4.1%. **Hispanic pop.** (any race): 7.6%.

Geography. Total area: 69,898 sq mi; rank: 20. **Land area:** 68,667 sq mi; rank: 19. **Acres forested:** 7.7 mil. **Location:** West South Central state bounded on the N by Colorado and Kansas; on the E by Missouri and Arkansas; on the S and W by Texas and New Mexico. **Climate:** temperate; southern humid belt merging with colder northern continental; humid eastern and dry western zones. **Topography:** high plains predominate in the W, hills and small mountains in the E; the east central region is dominated by the Arkansas R. Basin, and the Red R. Plains, in the S. **Capital:** Oklahoma City. **Chief airports at:** Oklahoma City, Tulsa.

Economy. Chief industries: manufacturing, mineral and energy exploration and production, agriculture, services. **Chief manuf. goods:** animal slaughtering & processing, petroleum, plastics & rubber, fabricated metals, machinery, motor vehicles & parts. **Chief crops:** wheat, greenhouse & nursery, hay, cotton, corn, soybeans, pecans, sorghum, peanuts. **Livestock** (Jan. 2009): 5.4 mil cattle/calves, 80,000 sheep/lambs; (Dec. 2008): 2.4 mil hogs/pigs, 4.8 mil chickens (excl. broilers), 237.8 mil broilers. **Timber/lumber** (est. 2008): 307 mil bd. ft; pine, oak, hickory. **Nonfuel minerals** (2008 prelim.): $746 mil; stone (crushed), cement (portland), sand and gravel (construction), iodine (crude), sand and gravel (industrial). **Chief ports:** Catoosa, Muskogee. **Gross state product** (est. 2008): $146.4 bil. **Sales tax** (2009): 4.5%. **Employment distrib.** (June 2008): 19.8% govt.; 18.2% trade/trans./util.; 9.5% mfg.; 12.3% ed./health; 11.6% prof./bus. serv.; 9.2% leisure/hosp.; 5.4% finance; 4.8% constr.; 4.0% other serv.; 1.8% info. **Unemployment** (2008): 3.8%. **Per cap. pers. income** (2008 prelim.): $36,899. **New private housing** (2008): 10,502 units/$1.6 bil. **Commercial banks** (2008): 261; deposits: $56.1 bil. **Savings institutions** (2008): 7; deposits: $6.9 bil. **Lottery** (2008): total sales: $203.8 mil; profit: $71.6 mil.

Federal govt. Fed. civ. employees (Mar. 2007): 34,390; **avg. salary:** $60,413. **Notable fed. facilities:** Tinker AFB; FAA Mike Monroney Aeronautical Ctr.; *Ft. Sill; *Altus AFB;

McAlester Army Ammunition Plant; Vance AFB; Natl. Inst. for petroleum: & Energy Res.; Natl. Severe Storms Lab.

Energy. Electricity production (est. 2007 kWh by source): coal: 31.1 bil; gas: 19.7 bil; hydroelectric: –263.0 mil; petroleum: 156.0 mil.

State data. Motto: Labor Omnia Vincit (Labor conquers all things). **Flower:** Mistletoe. **Bird:** Scissor-tailed flycatcher. **Tree:** Redbud. **Song:** Oklahoma! **Entered union** Nov. 16, 1907; rank, 46th. **State fair** at Oklahoma City, mid-Sept.; at Tulsa, 4th Thursday after Labor Day-2nd Sunday of Oct.

History. Few Native Americans inhabited the region when the Spanish explorer Coronado arrived, 1541; in the 16th and 17th cent., French traders visited. Part of the Louisiana Purchase, 1803, Oklahoma was known as Indian Country and, from 1834, Indian Territory. It became home to the "Five Civilized Tribes"—Cherokee, Choctaw, Chickasaw, Creek, and Seminole—after the forced removal of Indians from the eastern U.S., 1828-46. The land was also used by Comanche, Osage, and other Plains Indians. As white settlers pressed west, land was opened for homesteading by "runs" and lottery. The first run was in 1889; the most famous run, 1893, was to the Cherokee Outlet. Oklahoma became a state, 1907. In the early 20th cent., oil finds brought wealth to the Tulsa area; the Greenwood section of the city, then known as the "Negro Wall Street," was devastated by a white mob, 1921. Depression and drought drove many "Okies" from the Dust Bowl to California in the 1930s. A truck bomb in Oklahoma City, 1995, destroyed a federal office building, killing 168 people; Timothy McVeigh was executed for the crime, 2001.

Tourist attractions. Cherokee Heritage Center, Tahlequah; Oklahoma City Natl. Memorial; Natl. Cowboy Hall of Fame, Remington Park Race Track, White Water Bay and Frontier City theme pks., in Oklahoma City; Will Rogers Memorial, Claremore; Ft. Gibson; Ouachita Natl. Forest; Philbrook Museum of Art, Gilcrease Museum, in Tulsa; Tulsa's art deco district; Wichita Mts. Wildlife Refuge; Woolaroc Museum & Wildlife Preserve, Bartlesville; Sequoyah's Home Site, Sallisaw.

Famous Oklahomans. Troy Aikman, Carl Albert, Gene Autry, Johnny Bench, William "Hopalong Cassidy" Boyd, Garth Brooks, Lon Chaney, L. Gordon Cooper, Walter Cronkite, Jerome "Dizzy" Dean, Ralph Ellison, John Hope Franklin, James Garner, Geronimo, Woody Guthrie, Paul Harvey, Ron Howard, Gen. Patrick J. Hurley, Ben Johnson, Jeane Kirkpatrick, Louis L'Amour, Shannon Lucid, Mickey Mantle, Reba McEntire, Wiley Post, Tony Randall, Oral Roberts, Will Rogers, Sam Snead, Barry Switzer, Maria Tallchief, Jim Thorpe, J.C. Watts Jr.

Tourist information. Travel and Tourism Division, 120 N. Robinson, 6th Fl., PO Box 52002, Oklahoma City, OK 73152-2002; (800) 652-6552; www.travelok.com

Website. www.ok.gov

Oregon (OR)
Beaver State

People. Population (2008 est.): 3,790,060; rank: 27; net change (2007-08): 1.5%. **Pop. density:** 39.5 per sq mi. **Racial distribution** (2008): 90.1% white; 2.0% black; 3.6% Asian; 1.4% Native Amer./Nat. AK; 0.3% Hawaiian/Pacific Islander; 2 or more races, 2.5%. **Hispanic pop.** (any race): 11.0%.

Geography. Total area: 98,381 sq mi; rank: 9. **Land area:** 95,997 sq mi; rank: 10. **Acres forested:** 30.2 mil. **Location:** Pacific state, bounded on N by Washington; on E by Idaho; on S by Nevada and California; on W by the Pacific. **Climate:** coastal mild and humid climate; continental dryness and extreme temperatures in the interior. **Topography:** Coast Range of rugged mountains; fertile Willamette R. Valley to E and S; Cascade Mt. Range of volcanic peaks E of the valley; plateau E of Cascades, remaining two-thirds of state. **Capital:** Salem. **Chief airport at:** Portland.

Economy. Chief industries: manufacturing, services, trade, finance, insurance, real estate, government, construction. **Chief manuf. goods:** wood products, frozen produce, printing, computers & electronics, transportation equipment, industrial machinery. **Chief crops:** greenhouse & nursery, grass seed, hay, wheat, potatoes, Christmas trees, onions, pears, hazelnuts, corn, grapes, cherries, blackberries, blueberries, peppermint, snap beans, apples, hops. **Livestock** (Jan. 2009): 1.2 mil cattle/calves, 220,000 sheep/lambs; (Dec. 2008): 3.0 mil chickens (excl. broilers). **Timber/lumber** (est. 2008): 4.9 bil bd. ft; Douglas fir, hemlock, ponderosa pine. **Nonfuel minerals** (2008 prelim.): $419 mil; stone (crushed), sand and gravel (construction), cement (portland), diatomite, perlite (crude). **Commercial fishing** (2008): $103.1 mil. **Chief ports:** Portland, Astoria, Coos Bay. **Gross state product** (est. 2008): $161.6 bil. **Sales tax** (2009): none. **Employment distrib.** (June 2008): 17.5% govt.; 19.5% trade/trans./util.; 11.3% mfg.; 12.5% ed./health; 11.4% prof./bus. serv.; 10.3% leisure/hosp.; 6.0% finance; 5.6% constr.; 3.5% other serv.; 2.1% info. **Unemployment** (2008): 6.4%. **Per cap. pers. income** (2008 prelim.): $35,956. **New private housing** (2008): 11,676 units/$2.2 bil. **Commercial banks** (2008): 52; deposits: $41.6 bil. **Savings institutions** (2008): 9; deposits: $7.5 bil. **Lottery** (2008): total sales: $1.2 bil; profit: $678.7 mil.

Federal govt. Fed. civ. employees (Mar. 2007): 19,632; **avg. salary:** $63,431. **Notable fed. facilities:** Bonneville Power Administration.

Energy. Electricity production (est. 2007 kWh by source): coal: 4.4 bil; gas: 3.9 bil; petroleum: 5.0 mil.

State data. Motto: She flies with her own wings. **Flower:** Oregon grape. **Bird:** Western meadowlark. **Tree:** Douglas fir. **Song:** Oregon, My Oregon. **Entered union** Feb. 14, 1859; rank, 33rd. **State fair** at Salem; 11 days ending with Labor Day.

History. More than 100 Native American tribes inhabited the area at the time of European contact, including the Chinook, Yakima, Cayuse, Modoc, and Nez Percé. Capt. Robert Gray sighted and sailed into the Columbia River, 1792. Lewis and Clark, traveling overland, wintered at its mouth, 1805-06. Fur traders sent by John Jacob Astor established the Astoria trading post in the Columbia River region, 1811. Settlers arrived in the Willamette Valley, 1834. In 1843, the first large wave of settlers arrived via the Oregon Trail. Oregon became a territory, 1848, and a state, 1859. Early in the 20th cent., the "Oregon System"—political reforms that included initiative, referendum, recall, direct primary, and woman suffrage—was adopted. Originally dominated by forest products, the economy diversified after World War II, with high-tech firms clustering in the "Silicon Forest" area around Portland. Oregonians were the first in the U.S. to pass measures allowing physician-assisted suicide for terminally ill patients, 1994, and establishing an all-mail voting system, 1998.

Tourist attractions. John Day Fossil Beds Natl. Monument; Columbia River Gorge; Timberline Lodge, Mt. Hood Natl. Forest; Crater Lake Natl. Park; Oregon Dunes Natl. Recreation Area; Ft. Clatsop Natl. Memorial; Oregon Caves Natl. Monument; Oregon Museum of Science and Industry, Portland; Shakespeare Festival, Ashland; High Desert Museum, Bend; Multnomah Falls; Diamond Lake; "Spruce Goose," Evergreen Aviation Museum, McMinnville.

Famous Oregonians. Ernest Bloch, Bill Bowerman, Ernest Haycox, Chief Joseph, Ken Kesey, Phil Knight, Ursula K. Le Guin, Edwin Markham, Tom McCall, Dr. John McLoughlin, Joaquin Miller, Bob Packwood, Linus Pauling, Steve Prefontaine, John Reed, Alberto Salazar, Mary Decker Slaney, William Simon U'Ren.

Tourist information. Travel Oregon, 670 Hawthorne SE, Ste. 240, Salem, OR 97301; (800) 547-7842; www.traveloregon.com

Website. www.oregon.gov

Pennsylvania (PA)
Keystone State

People. Population (2008 est.): 12,448,279; rank: 6; net change (2007-08): 0.2%. **Pop. density:** 278.2 per sq mi. **Racial distribution** (2008): 85.4% white; 10.8% black; 2.4% Asian; 0.2% Native Amer./Nat. AK; <0.05% Hawaiian/Pacific Islander; 2 or more races, 1.1%. **Hispanic pop.** (any race): 4.8%.

Geography. Total area: 46,055 sq mi; rank: 33. **Land area:** 44,817 sq mi; rank: 32. **Acres forested:** 16.6 mil. **Location:** Middle Atlantic state, bordered on the E by the Delaware R.; on the S by the Mason-Dixon Line; on the W by West Virginia and Ohio; on the N/NE by Lake Erie and New York. **Climate:** continental with wide fluctuations in seasonal temperatures. **Topography:** Allegheny Mts. run SW to NE, with Piedmont and Coast Plain in the SE triangle; Allegheny Front a diagonal spine across the state's center; N and W rugged plateau falls to Lake Erie Lowland. **Capital:** Harrisburg. **Chief airports at:** Harrisburg, Philadelphia, Pittsburgh.

Economy. Chief industries: agribusiness, advanced manufacturing, health care, travel & tourism, depository institutions, biotechnology, printing & publishing, research & consulting, trucking & warehousing, transportation by air, engineering & management, legal services. **Chief manuf. goods:** petroleum, pharmaceuticals, plastics, iron & steel, printing, paper & paperboard, confectionery & snacks, animal slaughtering & processing. **Chief crops:** greenhouse & nursery, mushrooms, corn, hay, soybeans, apples, tomatoes, wheat, grapes, peaches, potatoes, strawberries, tobacco. **Livestock** (Jan. 2009): 1.6 mil cattle/calves, 100,000 sheep/lambs; (Dec. 2008): 1.1 mil hogs/pigs, 25.8 mil chickens (excl. broilers), 160.9 mil broilers. **Timber/lumber** (est. 2008): 1.0 bil bd. ft; pine, oak, maple. **Nonfuel minerals** (2008 prelim.): $1.7 bil; stone (crushed), cement (portland), sand and gravel (construction), lime, cement (masonry). **Commercial fishing** (2008): $278,690. **Chief ports:** Philadelphia, Pittsburgh, Erie. **Gross state product** (est. 2008): $553.3 bil. **Sales tax** (2009): 6.0%. **Employment distrib.** (June 2008): 12.6% govt.; 19.3% trade/trans./util.; 11.1% mfg.; 18.4% ed./health; 12.3% prof./bus. serv.; 9.2% leisure/hosp.; 5.7% finance; 4.6% constr.; 4.5% other serv.; 1.8% info. **Unemployment** (2008): 5.4%. **Per cap. pers. income** (2008 prelim.): $40,265. **New private housing** (2008): 24,577 units/$4.1 bil. **Commercial banks** (2008): 180; deposits: $204.8 bil. **Savings institutions** (2008): 96; deposits: $66.9 bil. **Lottery** (2008): total sales: $3.1 bil; profit: $928.1 mil.

Federal govt. Fed. civ. employees (Mar. 2007): 64,326; **avg. salary:** $63,627. **Notable fed. facilities:** Army War College, Carlisle Barracks; *Naval Inventory Control Point, Mechanicsburg; Philadelphia Mint, Defense Supply Ctr., Naval Surface Warfare Ctr., in Phila.; Defense Distribution Ctr., New Cumberland; *Tobyhanna Army Depot; *Letterkenny Army Depot; *NAS Willow Grove; *Charles E. Kelly Support Facility.

Energy. Electricity production (est. 2007 kWh by source): petroleum: 4.0 mil.

State data. Motto: Virtue, liberty, and independence. **Flower:** Mountain laurel. **Bird:** Ruffed grouse. **Tree:** Hemlock. **Song:** Pennsylvania. **Second** of the original 13 states to ratify the Constitution, Dec. 12, 1787. **State fair:** no official state fair; county and community fairs, Mar.-Oct.

History. When Europeans came, Algonquian-speaking Lenni Lenape (Delaware) and Shawnee and the Iroquoian Susquehannocks, Erie, and Seneca occupied the region. Swedish explorers made the first permanent settlement, 1643, on Tinicum Island. The Dutch seized the settlement, 1655, but lost it to the British, 1664. The region was given by Charles II to William Penn, 1681. Philadelphia ("brotherly love") was the capital of the colonies during most of the American Revolution, and of the U.S., 1790-1800; the Declaration of Independence, 1776, and Constitution, 1787, were signed here. Philadelphia was taken by the British, 1777; Washington's troops encamped at Valley Forge in the bitter winter of 1777-78. Slavery was abolished, 1780. Union victory at the Battle of Gettysburg, July 1-3, 1863, marked a turning point in the Civil War. A dam collapse at Johnstown, 1889, killed at least 2,200 people. From the late 19th cent. to the mid-20th, Pittsburgh prospered from coal and steel; later, heavy industry declined, but the city revived as a hub of finance, health care, and research. The Three Mile Island nuclear plant near Harrisburg had a near-meltdown, 1979. One of 4 hijacked planes on Sept. 11, 2001, crashed near Shanksville; a national memorial was designated on the site in 2002.

Tourist attractions. Independence Natl. Historic Park, Franklin Institute Science Museum, Philadelphia Museum of Art, in Philadelphia; Valley Forge Natl. Historic Park; Gettysburg Natl. Military Park; Pennsylvania Dutch Country; Hershey; Duquesne Incline, Carnegie Institute, Heinz Hall, in Pittsburgh; Pocono Mts.; Pennsylvania's Grand Canyon, Tioga County; Allegheny Natl. Forest; Laurel Highlands; Presque Isle State Park; Fallingwater, Mill Run; Johnstown; Steamtown, Scranton; U.S. Brig Niagara, Erie; Oil Heritage Region, Northwest PA.

Famous Pennsylvanians. Marian Anderson, Maxwell Anderson, George Blanda, James Buchanan, Andrew Carnegie, Rachel Carson, Perry Como, Bill Cosby, Thomas Eakins, Stephen Foster, Benjamin Franklin, Robert Fulton, Martha Graham, Milton Hershey, Gene Kelly, Grace Kelly (Princess Grace of Monaco), Dan Marino, George C. Marshall, Chris Matthews, John J. McCloy, Margaret Mead, Andrew W. Mellon, Joe Montana, Stan Musial, Joe Namath, John O'Hara, Arnold Palmer, Robert E. Peary, Mike Piazza, Tom Ridge, Mary Roberts Rinehart, Fred Rogers, Betsy Ross, Will Smith,

Jimmy Stewart, Jim Thorpe, Johnny Unitas, John Updike, Honus Wagner, Andy Warhol, Benjamin West.

Tourist information. Pennsylvania Tourism Office, Department of Community and Economic Development, Commonwealth Keystone Building, 4th Fl., 400 North St., Harrisburg, PA 17120-0225; 1-800-VISITPA; www.visitpa.com

Website. www.pa.gov

Rhode Island (RI)
Little Rhody, Ocean State

People. Population (2008 est.): 1,050,788; rank: 43; net change (2007-08): −0.2%. **Pop. density:** 1,016.4 per sq mi. **Racial distribution** (2008): 88.5% white; 6.4% black; 2.8% Asian; 0.6% Native Amer./Nat. AK; 0.1% Hawaiian/Pacific Islander; 2 or more races, 1.6%. **Hispanic pop.** (any race): 11.6%.

Geography. Total area: 1,545 sq mi; rank: 50. **Land area:** 1,045 sq mi; rank: 50. **Acres forested:** 0.4 mil. **Location:** New England state. **Climate:** invigorating and changeable. **Topography:** eastern lowlands of Narragansett Basin; western uplands of flat and rolling hills. **Capital:** Providence. **Chief airport at:** Warwick.

Economy. Chief industries: services, manufacturing. **Chief manuf. goods:** plastics, fabricated metals, electrical equip., jewelry. **Chief crops:** greenhouse & nursery, sweet corn, berries, potatoes, apples, hay. **Livestock** (Jan. 2009): 5,000 cattle/calves. **Timber/lumber:** figs. withheld. **Nonfuel minerals** (2008 prelim.): $55.7 mil; sand and gravel (construction), stone (crushed), sand and gravel (industrial), gemstones (natural). **Commercial fishing** (2008): $66.6 mil. **Chief ports:** Providence, Quonset Point, Newport. **Gross state product** (est. 2008): $47.4 bil. **Sales tax** (2009): 7.0%. **Employment distrib.** (June 2008): 13.3% govt.; 16.0% trade/trans./util.; 9.9% mfg.; 19.9% ed./health; 11.3% prof./bus. serv.; 11.3% leisure/hosp.; 6.9% finance; 4.5% constr.; 4.6% other serv.; 2.3% info. **Unemployment** (2008): 7.8%. **Per cap. pers. income** (2008 prelim.): $41,008. **New private housing** (2008): 1,058 units/$232.3 mil. **Commercial banks** (2008):10; deposits: $25.3 bil. **Savings institutions** (2008): 13; deposits: $4.3 bil. **Lottery** (2008): total sales: $2.4 bil; profit: $355.6 mil.

Federal govt. Fed. civ. employees (Mar. 2007): 6,457; **avg. salary:** $78,042. **Notable fed. facilities:** Naval War College; Naval Underwater Warfare Ctr.; NE Fisheries Science Ctr.; EPA Atlantic Ecology Div. Lab.

Energy. Electricity production (est. 2007 kWh by source): petroleum: 16.0 mil.

State data. Motto: Hope. **Flower:** Violet. **Bird:** Rhode Island red. **Tree:** Red maple. **Song:** Rhode Island. **Thirteenth** of original 13 states to ratify the Constitution, May 29, 1790. **State fair:** no state fair; largest fair at Richmond, mid-Aug.

History. When Europeans arrived, Narragansett, Niantic, Nipmuc, and Wampanoag peoples lived in the region. Verrazano visited the area, 1524. The first permanent settlement was founded at Providence, 1636, by Roger Williams, who was exiled from the Massachusetts Bay Colony; Anne Hutchinson, also exiled, settled Portsmouth, 1638. Quaker and Jewish immigrants seeking freedom of worship began arriving, 1650s-60s. The colonists broke the power of the Narragansett in the Great Swamp Fight, 1675, the decisive battle in King Philip's War. The colony was the first to formally renounce all allegiance to King George III, May 4, 1776. Initially opposed to joining the Union, Rhode Island was the last of the 13 colonies to ratify the Constitution, 1790. Trade, textiles, and metal goods dominated the economy in the 19th cent., and Newport became a fashionable resort after the Civil War. Immigration from Ireland, Italy, Portugal, French Canada, and most recently Latin America have given Rhode Island the highest proportion of Roman Catholics of any state, 64% in 2006.

Tourist attractions. Newport mansions; yachting races including Newport to Bermuda; Block Island; Touro Synagogue (oldest in U.S.) Newport; First Baptist Church in America, Providence; Slater Mill Historic Site, Pawtucket; Gilbert Stuart birthplace, Saunderstown.

Famous Rhode Islanders. Ambrose Burnside, George M. Cohan, Nelson Eddy, Jabez Gorham, Nathanael Greene, Christopher and Oliver La Farge, John McLaughlin, Matthew C. and Oliver Hazard Perry, Gilbert Stuart.

Tourist information. Rhode Island Tourism Division, 315 Iron Horse Way, Ste. 101, Providence, RI 02908; (800) 250-7384; www.visitrhodeisland.com
Website. www.state.ri.us

South Carolina (SC)
Palmetto State

People. Population (2008 est.): 4,479,800; rank: 24; net change (2007-08): 1.7%. **Pop. density:** 149.0 per sq mi. **Racial distribution** (2008): 68.7% white; 28.5% black; 1.2% Asian; 0.4% Native Amer./Nat. AK; 0.1% Hawaiian/Pacific Islander; 2 or more races, 1.1%. **Hispanic pop.** (any race): 4.1%.

Geography. Total area: 32,020 sq mi; rank: 40. **Land area:** 30,109 sq mi; rank: 40. **Acres forested:** 12.7 mil. **Location:** South Atlantic state, bordered by North Carolina on the N; Georgia on the SW and W; the Atlantic Ocean on the E, SE, and S. **Climate:** humid subtropical. **Topography:** Blue Ridge province in NW has highest peaks; piedmont lies between the mountains and the fall line; coastal plain covers two-thirds of the state. **Capital:** Columbia. **Chief airports at:** Charleston, Columbia, Greer, Myrtle Beach.

Economy. Chief industries: tourism, agriculture, manufacturing. **Chief manuf. goods:** chemicals & synthetics, motor vehicles & parts, plastics, paper & paper product, turbines, rubber, textiles. **Chief crops:** greenhouse & nursery, tobacco, soybeans, cotton, corn, peaches, wheat, tomatoes, peanuts. **Livestock** (Jan. 2009): 380,000 cattle/calves; (Dec. 2008): 6.2 mil chickens (excl. broilers), 236.9 mil broilers. **Timber/lumber** (est. 2008): 1.1 bil bd. ft; pine, oak. **Nonfuel minerals** (2008 prelim.): $617 mil; cement (portland), stone (crushed), sand and gravel (construction), cement (masonry), sand and gravel (industrial). **Commercial fishing** (2008): $17.5 mil. **Chief ports:** Charleston, Georgetown, Royal. **Gross state product** (est. 2008): $156.4 bil. **Sales tax** (2009): 6.0%. **Employment distrib.** (June 2008): 17.6% govt.; 19.1% trade/trans./util.; 12.5% mfg.; 10.4% ed./health; 11.6% prof./bus. serv.; 11.9% leisure/hosp.; 5.5% finance; 5.8% constr.; 3.9% other serv.; 1.4% info. **Unemployment** (2008): 6.9%. **Per cap. pers. income** (2008 prelim.): $31,884. **New private housing** (2008): 25,918 units/$4.2 bil. **Commercial banks** (2008): 81; deposits: $61.3 bil. **Savings institutions** (2008): 28; deposits: $5.3 bil. **Lottery** (2008): total sales: $992.5 mil; profit: $263.9 mil.

Federal govt. Fed. civ. employees (Mar. 2007): 19,189; **avg. salary:** $59,864. **Notable fed. facilities:** *Ft. Jackson; *Charleston AFB; *Naval Weapons Station Charleston; Parris Island; Shaw AFB; USMC Air Station Beaufort; Savannah River Site.

Energy. Electricity production (est. 2007 kWh by source): coal: 41.6 bil; gas: 4.6 bil; hydroelectric: –1.2 bil; nuclear: 53.2 bil; petroleum: 175.0 mil.

State data. Motto: Dum Spiro Spero (While I breathe, I hope). **Flower:** Yellow jessamine. **Bird:** Carolina wren. **Tree:** Palmetto. **Song:** Carolina. **Eighth** of the original 13 states to ratify the Constitution, May 23, 1788. **State fair** at Columbia, mid-Oct.; at Aiken, late Oct.

History. When Europeans arrived, Cherokee, Catawba, and Muskogean peoples lived in the area. Spanish and French came in the 16th cent. The first English colonists settled near the Ashley River, 1670, and moved to the site of present-day Charleston, 1680. The colonists seized the government, 1775, and the royal governor fled. The British took Charleston, 1780, but were defeated at Kings Mountain that same year, and at Cowpens, 1781. In the 1830s, South Carolinians, angered by federal protective tariffs, adopted the Nullification Doctrine, holding that a state can void an act of Congress. Plantation agriculture relied on slave labor to cultivate rice and cotton; slaves made up 57% of the population in 1860, when South Carolina was the first state to secede from the Union. Confederate troops fired on and forced the surrender of U.S. troops at Ft. Sumter, in Charleston Harbor, 1861, launching the Civil War. The state was readmitted to the Union,1868. Strom Thurmond, who ran for president as a segregationist in 1948, later served 48 years in the U.S. Senate (1955-2003). Formerly dependent on textiles, the state has attracted new industries by courting foreign investment.

Tourist attractions. Historic Charleston, Charleston Museum (est. 1773, oldest in U.S.); Ft. Sumter Natl. Monument, in Charleston Harbor; Middleton Place, Magnolia Plantation, Cypress Gardens, Drayton Hall, all near Charleston; other gardens at Brookgreen, Edisto, Glencairn; Myrtle Beach; Hilton Head Island; Revolutionary War battle sites; Andrew Jackson State Park; SC State Museum, Riverbanks Zoo, in Columbia.

Famous South Carolinians. Charles Bolden, James F. Byrnes, John C. Calhoun, Joe Frazier, DuBose Heyward, Ernest F. Hollings, Andrew Jackson, Jesse Jackson, "Shoeless" Joe Jackson, James Longstreet, Francis Marion, Andie McDowell, Ronald McNair, Charles Pinckney, John Rutledge, Thomas Sumter, Strom Thurmond, John B. Watson.

Tourist information. SC Dept. of Parks, Recreation, & Tourism, 1205 Pendleton St., Columbia, SC 29201; 1-866-224-9339; (803) 734-1700; www.discoversouthcarolina.com
Website. www.sc.gov

South Dakota (SD)
Coyote State, Mount Rushmore State

People. Population (2008 est.): 804,194; rank: 46; net change (2007-08): 1.1%. **Pop. density:** 10.6 per sq mi. **Racial distribution** (2008): 88.2% white; 1.1% black; 0.7% Asian; 8.5% Native Amer./Nat. AK; 0.1% Hawaiian/Pacific Islander; 2 or more races, 1.4%. **Hispanic pop.** (any race): 2.6%.

Geography. Total area: 77,116 sq mi; rank: 17. **Land area:** 75,885 sq mi; rank: 16. **Acres forested:** 1.7 mil. **Location:** West North Central state bounded on the N by North Dakota; on the E by Minnesota and Iowa; on the S by Nebraska; on the W by Wyoming and Montana. **Climate:** characterized by extremes of temperature, persistent winds, low precipitation and humidity. **Topography:** Prairie Plains in the E; rolling hills of the Great Plains in the W; the Black Hills, rising 3,500 ft, in the SW corner. **Capital:** Pierre.

Economy. Chief industries: agriculture, services, manufacturing. **Chief manuf. goods:** animal slaughtering, machinery, semiconductors, surgical appliances. **Chief crops:** corn, soybeans, wheat, hay, sunflowers, sorghum, oats, barley. **Livestock** (Jan. 2009): 3.7 mil cattle/calves, 305,000 sheep/lambs; (Dec. 2008): 1.3 mil hogs/pigs, 2.8 mil chickens (excl. broilers). **Timber/lumber:** figs. withheld; ponderosa pine. **Nonfuel minerals** (2008 prelim.): $270 mil; cement (portland), stone (crushed), gold, sand and gravel (construction), stone (dimension). **Gross state product** (est. 2008): $37.0 bil. **Sales tax** (2009): 4.0%. **Employment distrib.** (June 2008): 18.4% govt.; 19.6% trade/trans./util.; 10.3% mfg.; 14.5% ed./health; 6.9% prof./bus. serv.; 11.1% leisure/hosp.; 7.6% finance; 6.1% constr.; 3.8% other serv.; 1.7% info. **Unemployment** (2008): 3.0%. **Per cap. pers. income** (2008 prelim.): $37,375. **New private housing** (2008): 3,884 units/$500.5 mil. **Commercial banks** (2008): 90; deposits: $73.5 bil. **Savings institutions** (2008): 6; deposits: $1.4 bil. **Lottery** (2008): total sales: $704.3 mil; profit: $122.6 mil.

Federal govt. Fed. civ. employees (Mar. 2007): 7,907; **avg. salary:** $55,771. **Notable fed. facilities:** *Ellsworth AFB.

Energy. Electricity production (est. 2007 kWh by source): coal: 2.7 bil; gas: 350.0 mil; petroleum: 59.0 mil.

State data. Motto: Under God, the people rule. **Flower:** Pasqueflower. **Bird:** Chinese ring-necked pheasant. **Tree:** Black Hills spruce. **Song:** Hail, South Dakota. **Entered union** Nov. 2, 1889; rank, 40th. **State fair** at Huron; late Aug.-early Sept.

History. Paleo-Indians hunted in the region at least 11,500 years ago. At the time of first European contact, Mandan, Hidatsa, Arikara, and Sioux lived in the area. The French Vérendrye brothers explored the region, 1742-43. The U.S. acquired the territory in the Louisiana Purchase, 1803, and Lewis and Clark passed through, 1804-06. In 1817 a trading post opened at what would become Fort Pierre. Dakota Territory was established, 1861. Gold was discovered, 1874, in the Black Hills on Sioux land; the "Great Dakota Boom" began in 1879. South Dakota became a state, 1889. The massacre of Native American families at Wounded Knee, 1890, ended Sioux resistance; 83 years later, armed supporters of the American Indian Movement, a Native American rights group, occupied the area, leading to a 70-day standoff. Major economic activities include agribusiness and, since the 1980s, credit card services. Republicans scored a key election victory, 2004, with the defeat of 3-term U.S. Sen. Tom Daschle, a national Democratic leader.

Tourist attractions. Black Hills; Mt. Rushmore; Needles Highway; Harney Peak, tallest E. of Rockies; Deadwood, 1876 Gold Rush town; Custer State Park; Jewel Cave Natl. Monument; Badlands Natl. Park "moonscape"; "Great Lakes of S. Dakota"; Ft. Sisseton; Great Plains Zoo & Museum, Sioux Falls; Corn Palace, Mitchell; Wind Cave Natl. Park; Crazy Horse Memorial, mountain carving in progress.

Famous South Dakotans. Sparky Anderson, Black Elk, Bob Barker, Tom Brokaw, Crazy Horse, Thomas Daschle, Myron Floren, Mary Hart, Cheryl Ladd, Dr. Ernest O. Lawrence, George McGovern, Billy Mills, Allen Neuharth, Pat O'Brien, Sitting Bull.

Tourist information. Department of Tourism and State Development, Capitol Lake Plaza, 711 E. Wells Ave., c/o 500 E. Capitol Ave., Pierre, SD 57501-5070; 1-800-SDAKOTA; www.travelsd.com

Website. www.sd.gov

Tennessee (TN)
Volunteer State

People. Population (2008 est.): 6,214,888; rank: 17; net change (2007-08): 1.1%. **Pop. density:** 150.7 per sq mi. **Racial distribution** (2008): 80.4% white; 16.8% black; 1.3% Asian; 0.3% Native Amer./Nat. AK; 0.1% Hawaiian/Pacific Islander; 2 or more races, 1.1%. **Hispanic pop.** (any race): 3.7%.

Geography. Total area: 42,143 sq mi; rank: 36. **Land area:** 41,217 sq mi; rank: 34. **Acres forested:** 14.5 mil. **Location:** East South Central state bounded on the N by Kentucky and Virginia; on the E by North Carolina; on the S by Georgia, Alabama, and Mississippi; on the W by Arkansas and Missouri. **Climate:** humid continental to the N; humid subtropical to the S. **Topography:** rugged country in the E; the Great Smoky Mts. of the Unakas; low ridges of the Appalachian Valley; the flat Cumberland Plateau; slightly rolling terrain and knobs of the Interior Low Plateau, the largest region; Eastern Gulf Coastal Plain to the W, laced with streams; Mississippi Alluvial Plain, a narrow strip of swamp and flood plain in the extreme W. **Capital:** Nashville. **Chief airports at:** Maryville, Memphis, Nashville.

Economy. Chief industries: manufacturing, trade, services, tourism, finance, insurance, real estate. **Chief manuf. goods:** motor vehicles & parts, computers & electronics, food, chemicals, plastics, printing, appliances, aluminum. **Chief crops:** greenhouse & nursery, soybeans, cotton, corn, tobacco, hay, tomatoes, wheat. **Livestock** (Jan. 2009): 2.0 mil cattle/calves, 34,000 sheep/lambs; (Dec. 2008): 2.8 mil chickens (excl. broilers), 199.7 mil broilers. **Timber/lumber:** (est. 2008): 896 mil bd. ft; red oak, white oak, yellow poplar, hickory. **Nonfuel minerals** (2008 prelim.): $856 mil; stone (crushed), cement (portland), zinc, sand and gravel (construction), clays (ball). **Chief ports:** Memphis, Nashville, Chattanooga, Knoxville. **Gross state product** (est. 2008): $252.1 bil. **Sales tax** (2009): 7.0%. **Employment distrib.** (June 2008): 14.7% govt.; 21.9% trade/trans./util.; 13.3% mfg.; 12.8% ed./health; 11.4% prof./bus. serv.; 10.2% leisure/hosp.; 5.1% finance; 5.1% constr.; 3.8% other serv.; 1.8% info. **Unemployment** (2008): 6.4%. **Per cap. pers. income** (2008 prelim.): $34,330. **New private housing** (2008): 22,389 units/$3.1 bil. **Commercial banks** (2008): 212; deposits: $100.1 bil. **Savings institutions** (2008): 22; deposits: $4.7 bil. **Lottery** (2008): total sales: $1.1 bil; profit: $286.1 mil.

Federal govt. Fed. civ. employees (Mar. 2007): 26,187; **avg. salary:** $60,551. **Notable fed. facilities:** Tennessee Valley Authority; Oak Ridge Natl. Lab; Arnold Engineering Development Ctr.; Ft. Campbell; NSA Mid-South, Millington.

Energy. Electricity production (est. 2007 kWh by source): coal: 58.9 bil; gas: 532.0 mil; hydroelectric: −704.0 mil; nuclear: 28.7 bil; petroleum: 140.0 mil.

State data. Motto: Agriculture and commerce. **Flower:** Iris. **Bird:** Mockingbird. **Tree:** Tulip poplar. **Songs:** My Homeland, Tennessee; When It's Iris Time in Tennessee; My Tennessee; Tennessee Waltz; Rocky Top. **Entered union** June 1, 1796; rank, 16th. **State fair** at Nashville, early Sept.; at Clarksville, mid-July; at Jackson, mid-Sept.

History. Inhabited for at least 20,000 years, the region was home to Creek and Yuchi peoples when the first Europeans arrived; the Cherokee moved into the region in the early 18th cent. Spanish explorers visited the area, 1540. English traders crossed the Great Smoky Mtns. from the east, while France's Marquette and Jolliet sailed down the Mississippi on the west, 1673. The first permanent settlement was of Virginians on the Watauga River, 1769. After the American Revolution, in which Tennesseans fought in eastern campaigns, the region became a territory, 1790, and a state, 1796. Slavery was widespread in western Tennessee,

where cotton was the main crop, but much less common in the east. The state seceded, 1861, and saw many Civil War engagements; some 187,000 Tennesseans fought for the Confederacy and 51,000 for the Union. Tennessee was re-admitted in 1866, the only former Confederate state not to have a postwar military government. The famous Scopes trial, 1925, questioned the teaching of evolution in public schools. In the 1930s, the Tennessee Valley Authority, a federal program, brought electric power to rural areas. Nashville became the capital of country music, while Memphis fostered the blues and, with Elvis Presley in the 1950s, rock 'n' roll. Martin Luther King Jr. was assassinated in Memphis, 1968. Since the 1970s, auto plants have become major employers, as has Federal Express. Al Gore Jr., U.S. vice pres. (1993-2001), lost his 2000 presidential bid partly because he failed to carry his home state of Tennessee.

Tourist attractions. Reelfoot Lake; Lookout Mountain, Tennessee Aquarium, in Chattanooga; Fall Creek Falls; Great Smoky Mts. Natl. Park; Lost Sea, Sweetwater; Cherokee Natl. Forest; Cumberland Gap Natl. Park; Andrew Jackson's home, the Hermitage, near Nashville; homes of Pres. Polk and Andrew Johnson; American Museum of Science and Energy, Oak Ridge; Parthenon, Grand Old Opry, Opryland USA, all Nashville; Dollywood theme park, Pigeon Forge; Graceland, home of Elvis Presley, Memphis; Alex Haley Home and Museum, Henning; Casey Jones Village, Jackson.

Famous Tennesseans. Roy Acuff, Davy Crockett, David Farragut, Ernie Ford, Aretha Franklin, Morgan Freeman, Bill Frist, Al Gore Jr., Alex Haley, William C. Handy, Sam Houston, Cordell Hull, Andrew Jackson, Andrew Johnson, Casey Jones, Estes Kefauver, Grace Moore, Dolly Parton, Minnie Pearl, James Polk, Elvis Presley, Dinah Shore, Bessie Smith, Fred Thompson, Hank Williams Jr., Alvin York.

Tourist information. Dept. of Tourist Development, Wm. Snodgrass/Tennessee Tower, 312 Rosa L. Parks Ave., 25th Fl., Nashville, TN 37243; (800) 462-8366; www.tnvacation.com

Website. www.tn.gov

Texas (TX)
Lone Star State

People. Population (2008 est.): 24,326,974; rank: 2; net change (2007-08): 2.0%. **Pop. density:** 93.1 per sq mi. **Racial distribution** (2008): 82.4% white; 11.9% black; 3.5% Asian; 0.8% Native Amer./Nat. AK; 0.1% Hawaiian/Pacific Islander; 2 or more races, 1.3%. **Hispanic pop.** (any race): 36.5%.

Geography. Total area: 268,581 sq mi; rank: 2. **Land area:** 261,797 sq mi; rank: 2. **Acres forested:** 17.3 mil. **Location:** Southwestern state, bounded on the SE by the Gulf of Mexico; on the SW by Mexico, separated by the Rio Grande; surrounding states are Louisiana, Arkansas, Oklahoma, New Mexico. **Climate:** extremely varied; driest region is the Trans-Pecos; wettest is the NE. **Topography:** Gulf Coast Plain in the S and SE; North Central Plains slope upward with some hills; the Great Plains extend over the Panhandle, are broken by low mountains; the Trans-Pecos is the southern extension of the Rockies. **Capital:** Austin. **Chief airports at:** Austin, Dallas, El Paso, Fort Worth, Houston (2), Lubbock, San Antonio.

Economy. Chief industries: manufacturing, trade, oil and gas extraction, services. **Chief manuf. goods:** petroleum, chemicals & resins, computers & electronics, animal slaughtering & processing, plastics, aerospace. **Chief crops:** cotton, greenhouse & nursery, corn, wheat, sorghum, hay, peanuts, onions, rice, pecans, grapefruit. **Livestock** (Jan. 2009): 13.6 mil cattle/calves, 870,000 sheep/lambs; (Dec. 2008): 1.1 mil hogs/pigs, 24.8 mil chickens (excl. broilers), 640.8 mil broilers. **Timber/lumber** (est. 2008): 1.5 bil bd. ft; pine, cypress. **Nonfuel minerals** (2008 prelim.): $3.3 bil; cement (portland), stone (crushed), sand and gravel (construction), salt, lime. **Commercial fishing** (2008): $176.1 mil. **Chief ports:** Houston, Galveston, Brownsville, Beaumont, Port Arthur, Corpus Christi. **Gross state product** (est. 2008): $1.2 trillion. **Sales tax** (2009): 6.25%. **Employment distrib.** (June 2008): 16.2% govt.; 20.1% trade/trans./util.; 8.8% mfg.; 12.1% ed./health; 12.8% prof./bus. serv.; 9.8% leisure/hosp.; 6.2% finance; 6.4% constr.; 3.4% other serv.; 2.1% info. **Unemployment** (2008): 4.9%. **Per cap. pers. income** (2008 prelim.): $38,575. **New private housing** (2008): 129,523 units/$17.6 bil. **Commercial banks** (2008): 644; deposits: $360.6 bil.

Savings institutions (2008): 60; deposits: $123.6 bil. **Lottery** (2008): total sales: $3.7 bil; profit: $1.0 bil.

Federal govt. Fed. civ. employees (Mar. 2007): 124,577; **avg. salary:** $62,482. **Notable fed. facilities:** Forts *Hood, *Bliss, *Sam Houston; *Lackland, *Randolph, *Sheppard, *Dyess, Goodfellow AF Bases; NASA Johnson Space Ctr.; Naval Air Training School, Corpus Christi NAS; Kingsville NAS; Ft. Worth Western Currency Facility.

Energy. Electricity production (est. 2007 kWh by source): coal: 61.7 bil; gas: 34.3 bil; petroleum: 68.0 mil.

State data. Motto: Friendship. **Flower:** Bluebonnet. **Bird:** Mockingbird. **Tree:** Pecan. **Song:** Texas, Our Texas. **Entered union** Dec. 29, 1845; rank, 28th. **State fair** at Dallas, late Sept.-mid-Oct.; at Beaumont, mid-Oct.; at Belton, late Aug.-early Sept.; at Denton, mid-Aug.; at Tyler, late Sept.

History. Humans have lived in the region for at least 12,000 years. Coahuiltecan, Karankawa, Caddo, Jumano, and Tonkawa peoples were in the area when the first Europeans came; later, Apache, Comanche, Cherokee, and Wichita arrived. Early Spanish explorers included Pineda, who sailed along the Texas coast, 1519; Cabeza de Vaca, shipwrecked near Galveston along with the former slave Estevanico, 1528; and Coronado, who crossed the Panhandle, 1541. Spaniards made the first settlement at Ysleta, near El Paso, 1682. Americans moved into the land early in the 19th cent. Mexico, of which Texas was a part, won independence from Spain, 1821. Texans rebelled, 1836, losing to Santa Anna at the Alamo, but winning decisively under Sam Houston at San Jacinto. With Houston as president, 1836-38 and 1841-44, the Republic of Texas functioned as a nation until admitted to the Union. With a slave population of 30%, Texas seceded, 1861; mostly unscathed by the Civil War, it was readmitted, 1870. In 1900 a powerful hurricane lashed Galveston, killing at least 8,000. Cotton and cattle were dominant until 1901, when the Spindletop gusher, near Beaumont, launched the petroleum and petrochemical industries. By 2000 the state population ranked 2nd in the U.S. With wealth and population came political power, notably in the presidencies of Lyndon B. Johnson (1963-69), George H. W. Bush (1989-93), and George W. Bush (2001-09).

Tourist attractions. Padre Island Natl. Seashore; Big Bend, Guadalupe Mts. natl. parks; Ft. Davis; Six Flags Over Texas, Arlington SeaWorld, Six Flags Fiesta Texas, The Alamo, San Antonio Missions Natl. Hist. Park, all San Antonio; Cowgirl Hall of Fame, Kimball Art Museum, in Fort Worth; Lyndon B. Johnson Natl. Historical Park, Johnson City; Lyndon B. Johnson Library and Museum, Austin; Texas State Aquarium, Corpus Christi; George Bush Library, College Station.

Famous Texans. Lance Armstrong, Stephen F. Austin, Lloyd Bentsen, James Bowie, Carol Burnett, George H. W. Bush, George W. Bush, Joan Crawford, J. Frank Dobie, Dwight D. Eisenhower, Morgan Fairchild, Farrah Fawcett, Sam Houston, Howard Hughes, Kay Bailey Hutchison, Molly Ivins, Lyndon B. Johnson, Tommy Lee Jones, Janis Joplin, Barbara Jordan, Mary Martin, Chester Nimitz, Sandra Day O'Connor, H. Ross Perot, Katherine Anne Porter, Dan Rather, Sam Rayburn, Ann Richards, Sissy Spacek, Kenneth Starr, George Strait.

Tourist information. Texas Tourism, PO Box 12428, Austin, TX 78711; (800) 452-9292; www.traveltex.com

Website. www.texasonline.com

Utah (UT)
Beehive State

People. Population (2008 est.): 2,736,424; rank: 34; net change (2007-08): 2.5%. **Pop. density:** 33.3 per sq mi. **Racial distribution** (2008): 92.9% white; 1.3% black; 2.0% Asian; 1.4% Native Amer./Nat. AK; 0.8% Hawaiian/Pacific Islander; 2 or more races, 1.7%. **Hispanic pop.** (any race): 12.0%.

Geography. Total area: 84,899 sq mi; rank: 13. **Land area:** 82,144 sq mi; rank: 12. **Acres forested:** 18.0 mil. **Location:** Middle Rocky Mountain state; its southeastern corner touches Colorado, New Mexico, and Arizona, and is the only spot in the U.S. where 4 states join. **Climate:** arid; ranging from warm desert in SW to alpine in NE. **Topography:** high Colorado plateau is cut by brilliantly colored canyons of the SE; broad, flat, desert-like Great Basin of the W; the Great Salt Lake and Bonneville Salt Flats to the NW; Middle Rockies in the NE run E-W; valleys and plateaus of the Wasatch

Front. **Capital:** Salt Lake City. **Chief airport at:** Salt Lake City.

Economy. Chief industries: services, trade, manufacturing, government, transportation, utilities. **Chief manuf. goods:** food, petroleum, nonferrous metal, motor vehicles & parts, aerospace, sporting goods, fabricated metal, computers & electronics. **Chief crops:** hay, greenhouse & nursery, wheat, cherries, onions, apples, barley, peaches, corn. **Livestock** (Jan. 2009): 810,000 cattle/calves, 290,000 sheep/lambs; (Dec. 2008): 3.9 mil chickens (excl. broilers). **Timber/lumber** (est. 2008): 20 mil bd. ft; aspen, spruce, pine. **Nonfuel minerals** (2008 prelim.): $4.2 bil; copper, molybdenum concentrates, magnesium metal, gold, potash. **Gross state product** (est. 2008): $109.8 bil. **Sales tax** (2009): 4.7%. **Employment distrib.** (June 2008): 16.8% govt.; 19.6% trade/trans./util.; 10.1% mfg.; 11.2% ed./health; 13.1% prof./bus. serv.; 9.2% leisure/hosp.; 5.9% finance; 7.7% constr.; 2.9% other serv.; 2.6% info. **Unemployment** (2008): 3.4%. **Per cap. pers. income** (2008 prelim.): $30,291. **New private housing** (2008): 10,905 units/$1.8 bil. **Commercial banks** (2008): 73; deposits: $211.2 bil. **Savings institutions** (2008): 9; deposits: $18.2 bil.

Federal govt. Fed. civ. employees (Mar. 2007): 28,833; **avg. salary:** $56,946. **Notable fed. facilities:** *Hill AFB; *Tooele Army Depot; Army Dugway Proving Ground.

Energy. Electricity production (est. 2007 kWh by source): coal: 35.9 bil; gas: 5.1 bil; petroleum: 34.0 mil.

State data. Motto: Industry. **Flower:** Sego lily. **Bird:** Seagull. **Tree:** Blue spruce. **Song:** Utah, This is the Place. **Entered union** Jan. 4, 1896; rank, 45th. **State fair** at Salt Lake City; early Sept.

History. Ute, Gosiute, Southern Paiute, and Navajo peoples lived in the region at the time of European contact. Spanish Franciscans visited the area, 1776; American fur traders followed. Permanent settlement began with the arrival of the Latter-day Saints, or Mormons, 1847; they made the arid land bloom and created a prosperous economy. Organized in 1849, the State of Deseret asked admission to the Union; instead, Congress established Utah Territory, 1850, and Brigham Young was appointed governor. The Union Pacific and Central Pacific railroads met near Promontory Point, May 10, 1869, creating the first transcontinental railroad. Statehood was not achieved until 1896, after a long controversy over the Mormon practices of economic isolationism and polygamy, which the church renounced in 1890. The 20th cent. brought expansion in mining, defense-related industries, and, more recently, information technologies. More than 2/3 of Utahans are Mormons; the church has its world headquarters in Salt Lake City. Utah experienced 43% population growth, 1990-2005, and had the highest birthrate and lowest median age of any state in the U.S.

Tourist attractions. Temple Square, Mormon Church headquarters, in Salt Lake City; Great Salt Lake; Zion, Canyonlands, Bryce Canyon, Arches, and Capitol Reef natl. parks; Dinosaur, Rainbow Bridge, Timpanogos Cave, and Natural Bridges natl. monuments; Lake Powell; Flaming Gorge Natl. Recreation Area.

Famous Utahans. Maude Adams, Ezra Taft Benson, John Moses Browning, Mariner Eccles, Philo Farnsworth, James Fletcher, David M. Kennedy, J. Willard Marriott, Merlin Olsen, Osmond family, Ivy Baker Priest, George Romney, Roseanne, Wallace Stegner, Brigham Young, Loretta Young.

Tourist information. Utah Office of Tourism, Council Hall/Capitol Hill, 300 N. State St., Salt Lake City, UT 84114; (800) 200-1160; www.utah.com

Website. www.utah.gov

Vermont (VT)
Green Mountain State

People. Population (2008 est.): 621,270; rank: 49; net change (2007-08): 0.1%. **Pop. density:** 67.4 per sq mi. **Racial distribution** (2008): 96.4% white; 0.9% black; 1.1% Asian; 0.4% Native Amer./Nat. AK; <0.05% Hawaiian/Pacific Islander; 2 or more races, 1.2%. **Hispanic pop.** (any race): 1.4%.

Geography. Total area: 9,614 sq mi; rank: 45. **Land area:** 9,250 sq mi; rank: 43. **Acres forested:** 4.6 mil. **Location:** northern New England state. **Climate:** temperate, with considerable temperature extremes; heavy snowfall in mountains. **Topography:** Green Mts. N-S backbone 20-36 mi wide; avg. altitude 1,000 ft. **Capital:** Montpelier. **Chief airport at:** Burlington.

Economy. Chief industries: manufacturing, tourism, agriculture, trade, finance, insurance, real estate, government. **Chief manuf. goods:** dairy, plastics, printing, wood furniture, sporting goods, metalworking machinery. **Chief crops:** greenhouse & nursery, hay, maple syrup, apples, berries, sweet corn. **Livestock** (Jan. 2009): 270,000 cattle/calves; (Dec. 2008): 250,000 chickens (excl. broilers). **Timber/lumber** (est. 2008): 144 mil bd. ft; pine, spruce, fir, hemlock. **Nonfuel minerals** (2008 prelim.): $98.8 mil; stone (crushed), sand and gravel (construction), stone (dimension), talc (crude), gemstones (natural). **Gross state product** (est. 2008): $25.4 bil. **Sales tax** (2009): 6.0%. **Employment distrib.** (June 2008): 17.4% govt.; 19.1% trade/trans./util.; 11.6% mfg.; 18.5% ed./health; 7.4% prof./bus. serv.; 10.6% leisure/hosp.; 4.3% finance; 5.8% constr.; 3.2% other serv.; 1.9% info. **Unemployment** (2008): 4.8%. **Per cap. pers. income** (2008 prelim.): $38,880. **New private housing** (2008): 1,444 units/$240.7 mil. **Commercial banks** (2008): 12; deposits: $5.7 bil. **Savings institutions** (2008): 10; deposits: $4.3 bil. **Lottery** (2008): total sales: $102.0 mil; profit: $22.6 mil.

Federal govt. Fed. civ. employees (Mar. 2007): 3,929; **avg. salary:** $61,270. **Notable fed. facilities:** Law Enforcement Support Ctr.

Energy. Electricity production (est. 2007 kWh by source): gas: 2.0 mil; petroleum: 9.0 mil.

State data. Motto: Freedom and unity. **Flower:** Red clover. **Bird:** Hermit thrush. **Tree:** Sugar maple. **Song:** These Green Mountains. **Entered union** Mar. 4, 1791; rank, 14th. **State fair** at Rutland; early Sept.

History. Inhabited for 10,000 years or more, the region attracted Abenaki and Mahican peoples before Europeans arrived. Champlain explored the lake that now bears his name, 1609. The first European settlement was on Isle la Motte, in Lake Champlain, 1666. During the American Revolution, Ethan Allen and the Green Mountain Boys captured Ft. Ticonderoga (NY), 1775. Under a constitution that provided for public schools and abolished slavery, settlers declared a republic, 1777. Vermont joined the Union, 1791. Agriculture dominated in the 19th cent. Still mainly rural, the state expanded tourism and manufacturing after World War II, and IBM became the largest private employer. In 2000, with Howard Dean as governor (1991-2003), Vermont became the first state in the U.S. to legalize same-sex civil unions.

Tourist attractions. Shelburne Museum; Rock of Ages Quarry, Graniteville; Vermont Marble Museum, Proctor; Bennington Battle Monument; Pres. Calvin Coolidge homestead, Plymouth; Maple Grove Maple Museum, St. Johnsbury; Ben & Jerry's Factory, N. Waterbury.

Famous Vermonters. Ethan Allen, Chester A. Arthur, Calvin Coolidge, Howard Dean, John Deere, George Dewey, John Dewey, Stephen A. Douglas, Dorothy Canfield Fisher, James Fisk, James Jeffords, Rudy Vallee.

Tourist information. Vermont Dept. of Tourism and Marketing, Ntl. Life Building 6th Floor, Montpelier, VT 05620; (802) 828-3237; 1-800-VERMONT; www.vermontvacation.com

Website. www.vermont.gov

Virginia (VA)
Old Dominion

People. Population (2008 est.): 7,769,089; rank: 12; net change (2007-08): 0.9%. **Pop. density:** 196.7 per sq mi. **Racial distribution** (2008): 73.0% white; 19.9% black; 4.9% Asian; 0.4% Native Amer./Nat. AK; 0.1% Hawaiian/Pacific Islander; 2 or more races, 1.7%. **Hispanic pop.** (any race): 6.8%.

Geography. Total area: 42,774 sq mi; rank: 35. **Land area:** 39,594 sq mi; rank: 37. **Acres forested:** 15.8 mil. **Location:** South Atlantic state bounded by the Atlantic Ocean on the E and surrounded by North Carolina, Tennessee, Kentucky, West Virginia, and Maryland. **Climate:** mild and equable. **Topography:** mountain and valley region in the W, including the Blue Ridge Mts.; rolling piedmont plateau; tidewater, or coastal plain, including the eastern shore. **Capital:** Richmond. **Chief airports at:** Arlington, Dulles, Highland Springs, Newport News, Norfolk.

Economy. Chief industries: services, trade, government, manufacturing, tourism, agriculture. **Chief manuf. goods:** beverages & tobacco, transportation equip., animal slaughtering & processing, plastics, textiles, paper & paper product,

printing, pharmaceuticals, furniture, chemicals. **Chief crops:** greenhouse & nursery, soybeans, tomatoes, corn, tobacco, hay, cotton, apples, wheat, peanuts, potatoes. **Livestock** (Jan. 2009): 1.5 mil cattle/calves, 75,000 sheep/lambs; (Dec. 2008): 4.2 mil chickens (excl. broilers), 250.3 mil broilers. **Timber/lumber** (est. 2008): 1.2 bil bd. ft; pine and hardwoods. **Nonfuel minerals** (2008 prelim.): $1.1 bil; stone (crushed), cement (portland), sand and gravel (construction), lime, zirconium concentrates. **Commercial fishing** (2008): $145.6 mil. **Chief ports:** Hampton Roads, Richmond, Alexandria. **Gross state product** (est. 2008): $397.0 bil. **Sales tax** (2009): 4.0%. **Employment distrib.** (June 2008): 18.3% govt.; 17.5% trade/trans./util.; 7.2% mfg.; 11.3% ed./health; 17.1% prof./bus. serv.; 9.6% leisure/hosp.; 5.1% finance; 6.3% constr.; 5.0% other serv.; 2.4% info. **Unemployment** (2008): 4.0%. **Per cap. pers. income** (2008 prelim.): $42,876. **New private housing** (2008): 27,577units/$4.1 bil. **Commercial banks** (2008): 138; deposits: $155.3 bil. **Savings institutions** (2008): 15; deposits: $38.6 bil. **Lottery** (2008): total sales: $1.4 bil; profit: $455.3 mil.

Federal govt. Fed. civ. employees (Mar. 2007): 127,986; **avg. salary:** $78,654. **Notable fed. facilities:** Pentagon; *Norfolk Naval Sta., Shipyard, & other Hampton Roads; *Ft. Belvoir; *Langley AFB; NASA Langley Res. Ctr.; CIA George Bush Ctr. for Intelligence, Langley; Quantico USMC Base, FBI Academy; *Dahlgren Nav. Surface Warfare Ctr. & Lab; USDA Food and Nutrition Serv.; U.S. Geological Survey Natl. Ctr.

Energy. Electricity production (est. 2007 kWh by source): coal: 29.4 bil; gas: 5.9 bil; hydroelectric: −1.6 bil; nuclear: 27.3 bil; petroleum: 1.6 bil.

State data. Motto: Sic Semper Tyrannis (Thus always to tyrants). **Flower:** Dogwood. **Bird:** Cardinal. **Tree:** Dogwood. **Song Emeritus:** Carry Me Back to Old Virginia. **Tenth** of the original 13 states to ratify the Constitution, June 25, 1788. **State fair** at Richmond; late Sept.-early Oct.

History. Cherokee and Susquehanna peoples and the Algonquians of the Powhatan Confederacy were in the region when Europeans arrived. English settlers founded Jamestown, 1607. Virginians were indispensable to the founding of the American republic, and 4 of the first 5 U.S. presidents—Washington, Jefferson, Madison, and Monroe—came from there. The conclusive battle of the American Revolution took place at Yorktown, 1781. The state profited from tobacco, cotton, and the slave trade; in 1860, slaves made up nearly 1/3 of the population. Virginia seceded from the Union, 1861, and Richmond became the capital of the Confederacy, but Western counties, loyal to the Union, split off to become West Virginia, 1863. The war ended with Lee's surrender to Grant at Appomattox, 1865, and Virginia was readmitted to the Union, 1870. In the 20th cent., expansion of federal civilian jobs and military facilities transformed the economy. State officials pledged "massive resistance" to racial integration in the mid-1950s, but eventually accommodated. In 1989, L. Douglas Wilder became the first elected black governor in U.S. history. On Sept. 11, 2001, terrorist hijackers crashed a jet into U.S. defense headquarters at the Pentagon, in Arlington.

Tourist attractions. Colonial Williamsburg; Busch Gardens Williamsburg; Wolf Trap Farm, near Vienna; Arlington Natl. Cemetery; Mt. Vernon, home of George Washington; Jamestown Settlement; Yorktown; Jefferson's Monticello, Charlottesville; Robert E. Lee's birthplace, Stratford Hall, and grave, Lexington; Appomattox; Shenandoah Natl. Park; Blue Ridge Parkway; Virginia Beach; Kings Dominion, near Richmond.

Famous Virginians. Richard E. Byrd, James B. Cabell, Henry Clay, Katie Couric, Jubal Early, Jerry Falwell, William Henry Harrison, Patrick Henry, A.P. Hill, Thomas Jefferson, Joseph E. Johnston, Robert E. Lee, Meriwether Lewis and William Clark, James Madison, John Marshall, George Mason, James Monroe, George Pickett, Pocahontas, Edgar Allan Poe, John Randolph, Walter Reed, Rev. Pat Robertson, John Smith, J.E.B. Stuart, William Styron, Zachary Taylor, John Tyler, Maggie Walker, Booker T. Washington, George Washington, L. Douglas Wilder, Woodrow Wilson.

Tourist Information. Virginia Tourism Corp., 901 E. Byrd St., Richmond, VA 23219; 1-800-VISITVA; www.virginia.org

Website. www.virginia.gov

Washington (WA)
Evergreen State

People. Population (2008 est.): 6,549,224; rank: 13; net change (2007-08): 1.5%. **Pop. density:** 98.6 per sq mi. **Racial distribution** (2008): 84.3% white; 3.7% black; 6.7% Asian; 1.7% Native Amer./Nat. AK; 0.5% Hawaiian/Pacific Islander; 2 or more races, 3.1%. **Hispanic pop.** (any race): 9.8%.

Geography. Total area: 71,300 sq mi; rank: 18. **Land area:** 66,544 sq mi; rank: 20. **Acres forested:** 22.3 mil. **Location:** Pacific state bordered by Canada on the N; Idaho on the E; Oregon on the S; and the Pacific Ocean on the W. **Climate:** mild, dominated by the Pacific Ocean and protected by the Cascades. **Topography:** Olympic Mts. on NW peninsula; open land along coast to Columbia R.; flat terrain of Puget Sound Lowland; Cascade Mts. region's high peaks to the E; Columbia Basin in central portion; highlands to the NE; mountains to the SE. **Capital:** Olympia. **Chief airports at:** Seattle, Spokane.

Economy. Chief industries: advanced technology, aerospace, biotechnology, intl. trade, forestry, tourism, recycling, agriculture & food processing. **Chief manuf. goods:** aerospace, petroleum, food, paper, milled lumber, plastics, structural metals, computers & electronics. **Chief crops:** apples, potatoes, wheat, hay, cherries, greenhouse & nursery, forest products, pears, grapes, onions, hops, sweet corn, Christmas trees, mint, raspberries. **Livestock** (Jan. 2009): 1.1 mil cattle/calves, 53,000 mil sheep/lambs; (Dec. 2008): 6.8 mil chickens (excl. broilers). **Timber/lumber** (est. 2008): 3.5 bil bd. ft; Douglas fir, hemlock, cedar, pine. **Nonfuel minerals** (2008 prelim.): $619 mil; sand and gravel (construction), stone (crushed), cement (portland), zinc, gold. **Commercial fishing** (2008): $230.5 mil. **Chief ports:** Seattle, Tacoma, Vancouver, Kelso-Longview. **Gross state product** (est. 2008): $322.8 bil. **Sales tax** (2009): 6.5%. **Employment distrib.** (June 2008): 18.3% govt.; 18.6% trade/trans./util.; 10.0% mfg.; 11.7% ed./health; 11.9% prof./bus. serv.; 10.0% leisure/hosp.; 5.1% finance; 7.0% constr.; 3.6% other serv.; 3.5% info. **Unemployment** (2008): 5.3%. **Per cap. pers. income** (2008 prelim.): $42,356. **New private housing** (2008 prelim.): 28,919 units/$5.1 bil. **Commercial banks** (2008): 103; deposits: $89.0 bil. **Savings institutions** (2008):19; deposits: $23.3 bil. **Lottery** (2008): total sales: $521.1 mil; profit: $130.3 mil.

Federal govt. Fed. civ. employees (Mar. 2007): 50,052; **avg. salary:** $66,363. **Notable fed. facilities:** Bonneville Power Admin.; *Ft. Lewis; *McChord AFB; DOE Hanford Nuclear Site; Naval Base Kitsap (Bremerton & Bangor); Whidbey Island NAS; Naval Sta., Everett; Pacific Northwest Natl. Lab.

Energy. Electricity production (est. 2007 kWh by source): gas: 2.5 bil; hydroelectric: 45.0 mil; nuclear: 8.1 bil.

State data. Motto: Alki (By and by). **Flower:** Western rhododendron. **Bird:** Willow goldfinch. **Tree:** Western hemlock. **Song:** Washington, My Home. **Entered union** Nov. 11, 1889; rank, 42nd. **State fairs:** no official state fair; county and area fairs, April-Sept.

History. People of the Clovis culture lived in the region 11,000 years ago. At the time of European contact, Native Americans in the area included Nez Percé, Spokane, Yakima, Cayuse, Okanogan, Walla Walla, and Colville peoples in the interior and Nooksak, Chinook, Nisqually, Clallam, Makah, Quinault, and Puyallup peoples along the coast. Spain's Bruno Hezeta sailed the coast, 1775. In 1792, British naval officer George Vancouver mapped the Puget Sound area, and American Capt. Robert Gray sailed up the Columbia River. Fur traders and missionaries arrived in the first half of the 19th cent. Final agreement on the border of Washington and Canada was made with Britain, 1846. Completion in 1883 of a transcontinental rail link between Puget Sound and the eastern U.S. aided immigration, and Washington became a state in 1889. In the 20th cent., cheap hydroelectric power spurred growth in the aluminum and aircraft industries; founded in 1975, Microsoft became a computer software giant. Mt. St. Helens erupted, 1980. With grunge music, Starbucks coffee, and Amazon.com, Seattle became a national trendsetter in the 1990s; violent street protests disrupted a World Trade Organization meeting there in 1999. Gary Locke, in office 1997-2005, was the first U.S. governor of Chinese ancestry.

Tourist attractions. Seattle Center, Space Needle, waterfront, Museum of Flight, Underground Tour, all Seattle; Mt. Rainier, Olympic, and North Cascades natl. parks; Mt. St. Helens; Puget Sound; San Juan Islands; Grand Coulee Dam; Columbia R. Gorge Natl. Scenic Area; Spokane's Riverfront Park.

Famous Washingtonians. Raymond Carver, Kurt Cobain, Bing Crosby, William O. Douglas, Bill Gates, Jimi Hendrix, Henry M. Jackson, Gary Larson, Mary McCarthy, Robert Motherwell, Edward R. Murrow, Theodore Roethke, Ann Rule, Hilary Swank, Julia Sweeney, Adam West, Marcus Whitman, Minoru Yamasaki.

Tourist information. WA State Tourism Office, 128 10th Ave. SW, PO Box 42525, Olympia, WA 98504; (800) 544-1800; www.experiencewa.com

Website. access.wa.gov

West Virginia (WV)
Mountain State

People. Population (2008 est.): 1,814,468; rank: 37; net change (2007-08): 0.3%. **Pop. density:** 75.5 per sq mi. **Racial distribution** (2008): 94.5% white; 3.6% black; 0.7% Asian; 0.2% Native Amer./Nat. AK; <0.05% Hawaiian/Pacific Islander; 2 or more races, 1.0%. **Hispanic pop.** (any race): 1.1%.

Geography. Total area: 24,230 sq mi; rank: 41. **Land area:** 24,078 sq mi; rank: 41. **Acres forested:** 12.0 mil. **Location:** South Atlantic state bounded on the N by Ohio, Pennsylvania, Maryland; on the S and W by Virginia, Kentucky, Ohio; on the E by Maryland and Virginia. **Climate:** humid continental climate except for marine modification in the lower panhandle. **Topography:** ranging from hilly to mountainous; Allegheny Plateau in the W, covers two-thirds of the state; mountains here are the highest in the state, over 4,000 ft. **Capital:** Charleston.

Economy. Chief industries: manufacturing, services, mining, tourism. **Chief manuf. goods:** chemicals, aluminum, motor vehicle parts, lumber & plywood, primary & fabricated metals. **Chief crops:** hay, apples, corn, peaches, soybeans, tobacco, wheat. **Livestock** (Jan. 2009): 415,000 cattle/calves, 33,000 sheep/lambs; (Dec. 2008): 1.7 mil chickens (excl. broilers), 85.7 mil broilers. **Timber/lumber** (est. 2008): 518 mil bd. ft; oak, yellow poplar, hickory, walnut, cherry. **Nonfuel minerals** (2008 prelim.): $276 mil; stone (crushed), cement (portland), lime, sand and gravel (industrial), sand and gravel (construction). **Chief port:** Huntington. **Gross state product** (est. 2008): $61.7 bil. **Sales tax** (2009): 6.0%. **Employment distrib.** (June 2008): 19.0% govt.; 18.6% trade/trans./util.; 7.6% mfg.; 15.1% ed./health; 8.1% prof./bus. serv.; 9.8% leisure/hosp.; 3.9% finance; 5.1% constr.; 7.4% other serv.; 1.5% info. **Unemployment** (2008): 4.3%. **Per cap. pers. income** (2008 prelim.): $30,831. **New private housing** (2008): 3,481 units/$483.4 mil. **Commercial banks** (2008): 80; deposits: $26.1 bil. **Savings institutions** (2008): 7; deposits: $805 mil. **Lottery** (2008): total sales: $1.5 bil; profit: $579.0 mil.

Federal govt. Fed. civ. employees (Mar. 2007): 14,728; **avg. salary:** $62,569. **Notable fed. facilities:** Natl. Radio Astronomy Observatory, Green Bank; Bureau of Public Debt Bldg.; Harpers Ferry Natl. Park; Alderson Fed. Prison for Women; FBI Natl. Crime Info. Ctr.

Energy. Electricity production (est. 2007 kWh by source): coal: 68.5 bil; gas: 136.0 mil; petroleum: 190.0 mil.

State data. Motto: Montani Semper Liberi (Mountaineers are always free). **Flower:** Big rhododendron. **Bird:** Cardinal. **Tree:** Sugar maple. **Songs:** The West Virginia Hills; This Is My West Virginia; West Virginia, My Home, Sweet Home. **Entered union** June 20, 1863; rank, 35th. **State fair** at Lewisburg; mid-Aug.

History. Sparsely inhabited at the time of European contact, the area was primarily Native American hunting grounds. British explorers Thomas Batts and Robert Fallam reached the New River, 1671. Coal, discovered in 1742, was mined extensively by the mid-19th cent. White settlement led to conflicts with Native Americans, including a major battle in which frontiersmen defeated an Indian confederacy at Point Pleasant, 1774. The region joined the Union as part of Virginia, 1788. Longstanding tensions between the E and W parts of the state came to a head in 1861, when Virginia seceded. Delegates of W counties, meeting at Wheeling, repudiated the act and created a new state, Kanawha, later renamed West Virginia, which was admitted to the Union in 1863. Poverty has been a problem for much of the state's subsequent history. West Virginia continues to rank low in per capita personal income, despite billions of dollars in federal contracts brought to the state by 9-term U.S. Sen. Robert Byrd; in 2006 he became the longest-serving member in Senate history.

Tourist attractions. Harpers Ferry Natl. Historic Park; Clay Center & Avampato Discovery Museum, Charleston; White Sulphur Springs (The Greenbrier) and Berkeley Springs mineral water spas; New River Gorge Natl. River; Beckley Exhibition Coal Mine; Monongahela Natl. Forest; Fenton Glass, Williamstown; Blenko Glass, Milton; Sternwheel Regatta, Charleston; Mountain State Forest Festival, Elkins; skiing at Canaan Valley, Snowshoe, Timberline, Winterplace; Mountain State Art & Craft Festival, Ripley; Oglebay Resort, Wheeling; white water rafting on New and Gauley rivers.

Famous West Virginians. Newton D. Baker, Pearl Buck, Robert Byrd, John W. Davis, Thomas "Stonewall" Jackson, Don Knotts, Dwight Whitney Morrow, Michael Owens, Mary Lou Retton, Walter Reuther, Cyrus Vance, Jerry West, Charles "Chuck" Yeager.

Tourist information. West Virginia Division of Tourism, 90 MacCorkle Ave., SW, South Charleston, WV 25303; 1-800-CALLWVA; www.escape2wv.com

Website. www.wv.gov

Wisconsin (WI)
Badger State

People. Population (2008 est.): 5,627,967; rank: 20; net change (2007-08): 0.5%. **Pop. density:** 103.9 per sq mi. **Racial distribution** (2008): 89.7% white; 6.1% black; 2.0% Asian; 1.0% Native Amer./Nat. AK; <0.05% Hawaiian/Pacific Islander; 2 or more races, 1.2%. **Hispanic pop.** (any race): 5.1%.

Geography. Total area: 65,498 sq mi; rank: 23. **Land area:** 54,310 sq mi; rank: 25. **Acres forested:** 16.3 mil. **Location:** East North Central state, bounded on the N by Lake Superior and Upper Michigan; on the E by Lake Michigan; on the S by Illinois; on the W by the St. Croix and Mississippi rivers. **Climate:** long, cold winters and short, warm summers tempered by the Great Lakes. **Topography:** narrow Lake Superior Lowland plain met by Northern Highland, which slopes gently to the sandy crescent Central Plain; Western Upland in the SW; 3 broad parallel limestone ridges running N-S are separated by wide and shallow lowlands in the SE. **Capital:** Madison. **Chief airports at:** Madison, Milwaukee.

Economy. Chief industries: services, manufacturing, trade, government, agriculture, tourism. **Chief manuf. goods:** transportation, dairy, animal slaughtering & processing, paper, printing, plastics, computers & electronics. **Chief crops:** corn, greenhouse & nursery, soybeans, potatoes, cranberries, hay, wheat, snap beans, apples, peas. **Livestock** (Jan. 2009): 3.4 mil cattle/calves, 85,000 mil sheep/lambs; (Dec. 2008): 360,000 hogs/pigs, 6.0 mil chickens (excl. broilers), 51.7 mil broilers. **Timber/lumber** (est. 2008): 452 mil bd. ft; maple, birch, oak, evergreens. **Nonfuel minerals** (2008 prelim.): $575 mil; sand and gravel (construction), stone (crushed), sand and gravel (industrial), lime, stone (dimension). **Commercial fishing** (2008): $5.6 mil. **Chief ports:** Superior, Ashland, Milwaukee, Green Bay, Kewaunee, Pt. Washington, Manitowoc, Sheboygan, Marinette, Kenosha. **Gross state product** (est. 2008): $240.4 bil. **Sales tax** (2009): 5.0%. **Employment distrib.** (June 2008): 14.4% govt.; 18.7% trade/trans./util.; 17.0% mfg.; 14.0% ed./health; 9.6% prof./bus. serv.; 9.5% leisure/hosp.; 5.6% finance; 4.5% constr.; 4.8% other serv.; 1.7% info. **Unemployment** (2008): 4.7%. **Per cap. pers. income** (2008 prelim.): $37,314. **New private housing** (2008): 15,509 units/$2.5 bil. **Commercial banks** (2008): 268; deposits: $99.9 bil. **Savings institutions** (2008): 39; deposits: $14.9 bil. **Lottery** (2008): total sales: $494.7 mil; profit: $140.0 mil.

Federal govt. Fed. civ. employees (Mar. 2007): 13,620; **avg. salary:** $61,835. **Notable fed. facilities:** *Ft. McCoy; USDA Forest Products Lab.

Energy. Electricity production (est. 2007 kWh by source): coal: 38.9 bil; gas: 3.2 bil; nuclear: 12.1 bil; petroleum: 122.0 mil.

State data. Motto: Forward. **Flower:** Wood violet. **Bird:** Robin. **Tree:** Sugar maple. **Song:** On, Wisconsin! **Entered union** May 29, 1848; rank, 30th. **State fair** at West Allis; early Aug.

History. At the time of European contact, Ojibwa, Menominee, Winnebago, Kickapoo, Sauk, Fox, and Potawatomi peoples inhabited the area. French explorer Jean Nicolet reached Green Bay, 1634; French missionaries and fur traders followed. The British took over, 1763. The U.S. won the land after the American Revolution but did not wield control until forts were established at Green Bay and Prairie du Chien, 1816. Native Americans rebelled against the seizure of tribal lands in the Black Hawk War, 1832, but were defeated and relocated to reservations. Wisconsin became a territory, 1836, and a state, 1848. Some 96,000 soldiers served the Union cause during the Civil War. Many immigrants arrived from Germany, Poland, and Scandinavia. Wisconsin agriculture focused on dairy; Milwaukee became a manufacturing center. As gov., 1901-06, Robert La Follette pushed Progressive reforms such as direct primary voting and consumer protection laws. An era of "McCarthyism" ended when anti-Communist crusader Sen. Joseph McCarthy (R, WI) was censured by the U.S. Senate, 1954.

Tourist attractions. Old Wade House & Carriage Museum, Greenbush; Villa Louis, Prairie du Chien; Circus World Museum, Baraboo; Wisconsin Dells; Old World Wisconsin, Eagle; Door County peninsula; Chequamegon and Nicolet natl. forests; Lake Winnebago; House on the Rock, Dodgeville; Monona Terrace, Madison.

Famous Wisconsinites. Don Ameche, Carrie Chapman Catt, Willem Dafoe, Edna Ferber, Hamlin Garland, King Camp Gillette, Harry Houdini, Robert La Follette, Alfred Lunt, Pat O'Brien, Georgia O'Keeffe, William H. Rehnquist, John Ringling, Donald K. "Deke" Slayton, Spencer Tracy, Thorstein Veblen, Orson Welles, Laura Ingalls Wilder, Thornton Wilder, Frank Lloyd Wright.

Tourist information. Wisconsin Dept. of Tourism, 201 W. Washington Ave., PO Box 8690, Madison, WI 53708-8690; 1-800-432-TRIP; www.travelwisconsin.com

Website. www.wisconsin.gov

Wyoming (WY)
Equality State, Cowboy State

People. Population (2008 est.): 532,668; rank: 51; net change (2007-08): 1.8%. **Pop. density:** 5.5 per sq mi. **Racial distribution** (2008): 93.9% white; 1.3% black; 0.7% Asian; 2.5% Native Amer./Nat. AK; 0.1% Hawaiian/Pacific Islander; 2 or more races, 1.5%. **Hispanic pop.** (any race): 7.7%.

Geography. Total area: 97,814 sq mi; rank: 10. **Land area:** 97,100 sq mi; rank: 9. **Acres forested:** 11.4 mil. **Location:** Mountain state lying in the high western plateaus of the Great Plains. **Climate:** semi-desert conditions throughout; true desert in the Big Horn and Great Divide basins. **Topography:** eastern Great Plains rise to the foothills of the Rocky Mts.; the Continental Divide crosses the state from the NW to the SE. **Capital:** Cheyenne.

Economy. Chief industries: mineral extraction, oil, natural gas, tourism and recreation, agriculture. **Chief manuf. goods:** petroleum, chemicals, fabricated metal, beet sugar, lumber. **Chief crops:** hay, sugar beets, barley, dry beans, wheat, corn, greenhouse & nursery, oats. **Livestock** (Jan. 2009): 1.4 mil cattle/calves; 420,000 mil sheep/lambs; (Dec. 2008): 13,000 chickens (excl. broilers). **Timber/lumber** (est. 2008): 111 mil bd. ft; ponderosa & lodgepole pine, Douglas fir, Engelmann spruce. **Nonfuel minerals** (2008 prelim.): $1.9 bil; soda ash, clays (bentonite), helium (grade-A), sand and gravel (construction), cement (portland). **Gross state product** (est. 2008): $35.3 bil. **Sales tax** (2009): 4.0%. **Employment distrib.** (June 2008): 23.0% govt.; 18.6% trade/trans./util.; 3.2% mfg.; 7.8% ed./health; 6.5% prof./bus. serv.; 12.5% leisure/hosp.; 3.9% finance; 9.9% constr.; 3.9% other serv.; 1.3% info. **Unemployment** (2008): 3.1%. **Per cap. pers. income** (2008 prelim.): $49,719. **New private housing** (2008): 2,669 units/$557.5 mil. **Commercial banks** (2008): 49; deposits: $10.6 bil. **Savings institutions** (2008): 4; deposits: $441 mil.

Federal govt. Fed. civ. employees (Mar. 2007): 5,344; **avg. salary:** $56,839. **Notable fed. facilities:** Warren AFB.

Energy. Electricity production (est. 2007 kWh by source): coal: 42.3 bil; petroleum: 45.0 mil.

State data. Motto: Equal rights. **Flower:** Indian paintbrush. **Bird:** Western meadowlark. **Tree:** Plains Cottonwood. **Song:** Wyoming. **Entered union** July 10, 1890; rank, 44th. **State fair** at Douglas; mid-Aug.

History. Inhabited for at least 12,000 years, the region supported Shoshone, Crow, Cheyenne, Oglala Sioux, and Arapaho peoples when Europeans arrived. France's Vérendrye brothers were the first Europeans to see the region, 1742-43. John Colter, an American, traversed the Yellowstone area, 1807-08. Trappers and fur traders followed in the 1820s. Forts Laramie and Bridger became important stops on trails to the West Coast. Population grew after the Union Pacific crossed the state, 1867-68. Wyoming became a territory, 1868, and the first to extend full voting rights to women, 1869. Statehood was attained, 1890. Disputes between large landowners and small ranchers culminated in the Johnson County Cattle War, 1892; federal troops were called in to restore order. Nellie Tayloe Ross was the first woman governor to take office in the U.S., 1925. Wyoming, the least populous state, has relied on the energy, tourism, and ranching industries in recent decades. Dick Cheney, Wyoming's representative in the U.S. House, 1979-89, served as U.S. vice pres. (2001-09).

Tourist attractions. Yellowstone Natl. Park, the first U.S. national park, est. 1872; Grand Teton Natl. Park; Natl. Elk Refuge; Devils Tower Natl. Monument; Ft. Laramie Natl. Hist. Site and nearby pioneer trail ruts; Buffalo Bill Historical Center, Cody; Cheyenne Frontier Days.

Famous Wyomingites. James Bridger, William F. "Buffalo Bill" Cody, Curt Gowdy, Esther Hobart Morris, Jackson Pollock, Nellie Tayloe Ross.

Tourist information. Wyoming Travel and Tourism, 1520 Etchepare Cir., Cheyenne, WY 82007; (800) 225-5996; www.wyomingtourism.org

Website. www.wyoming.gov

District of Columbia (DC)

People. Population (2008 est.): 591,833; rank: 50; net change (2008-09): 0.7%. **Pop. density:** 9,687.0 per sq mi. **Racial distribution** (2008): 40.1% white; 54.4% black; 3.4% Asian; 0.4% Native Amer./Nat. AK; 0.1% Hawaiian/Pacific Islander; 2 or more races, 1.6%. **Hispanic pop.** (any race): 8.6%.

Geography. Total area: 68 sq mi; rank: 51. **Land area:** 61 sq mi; rank: 51. **Location:** at the confluence of the Potomac and Anacostia rivers, flanked by Maryland on the N, E, and SE and by Virginia on the SW. **Climate:** hot humid summers, mild winters. **Topography:** low hills rise toward the N away from the Potomac R. and slope to the S; highest elevation, 410 ft, lowest Potomac R., 1 ft.

Economy. Chief industries: government, legal, publishing, medical, service, tourism. **Gross product** (est. 2008): $97.2 bil. **Sales tax** (2009): 5.75%. **Employment distrib.** (June 2008): 33.2% govt.; 4.0% trade/trans./util.; 0.2% mfg.; 13.9% ed./health; 22.5% prof./bus. serv.; 8.0% leisure/hosp.; 4.0% finance; 1.8% constr.; 9.3% other serv.; 3.0% info. **Unemployment** (2008): 7.0%. **Per cap. pers. income** (2008 prelim.): $64,991. **New private housing** (2008): 536 units/$67.1 mil. **Commercial banks** (2008): 25; deposits: $22.6 bil. **Savings institutions** (2008): 9; deposits: $811 mil. **Lottery** (2008): total sales: $252.3 mil; profit: $70.4 mil.

Federal govt. Fed. civ. employees (Mar. 2007): 149,034; **avg. salary:** $94,527.

District data. Motto: Justitia omnibus (Justice for all). **Flower:** American beauty rose. **Tree:** Scarlet oak. **Bird:** Wood thrush.

History. The District of Columbia, coextensive with the city of Washington, is the seat of the U.S. federal government. It lies on the west central edge of Maryland on the Potomac River, opposite Virginia. The Piscataway, an Algonquian-speaking people, were living in the region when Europeans arrived in the 17th cent. Proposals for a "federal town" for the deliberations of the Continental Congress were made in 1783. Authorized by Congress, 1790, Pres. George Washington chose the Potomac site and persuaded landowners to sell their holdings to the government. Its area was originally 100 sq mi taken from the sovereignty of Maryland and Virginia. Virginia's portion south of the Potomac was given back to that state in 1846.

Pres. Washington chose Pierre Charles L'Enfant, a Frenchman, to plan the capital. Surveyor Andrew Ellicott finished the official map and design of the city, assisted by Benjamin Banneker, a black architect and astronomer. Pres. Washington laid the cornerstone of the north wing of the Capitol building, 1793, and Pres. John Adams moved to the new national capital, 1800. The City of Washington was incorporated, 1802. British troops invaded, 1814, setting fire to the Capitol, the President's House (as the White House was then called), and other buildings. Pres. Lincoln ended slavery in the district, 1862. Many African Americans arrived after the Civil War, but racial segregation remained legal until the mid-20th cent. After federal government expansion spurred population growth, 1930-50, an exodus to the suburbs shrank the city's population, 1950-2005.

The 23rd Amendment (1961) granted residents the right to vote for president and vice president. Congress, which has legislative authority over the District under the Constitution, approved legislation in 1970 giving the District one delegate to the House of Representatives, who could vote in committee but not on the floor. Voters approved, 1974, a congressionally drafted charter giving them the right to elect their own mayor and city council. The district won the right to levy taxes, but Congress retained power to veto council actions and approve the city budget. Security measures were dramatically increased after terrorists attacked the U.S. on Sept. 11, 2001. After a 34-year absence, major league baseball returned to the city in 2005.

Tourist attractions. See Washington, DC, Capital of the U.S.

Famous Washingtonians. Edward Albee, Frederick Douglass, John Foster Dulles, Duke Ellington, Katherine Graham, Goldie Hawn, J. Edgar Hoover, Pete Sampras, John Philip Sousa.

Tourist information. Destination DC, 901 7th St. NW, 4th Fl., Washington, DC, 20001-3719; (800) 422-8644, (202) 789-7000; www.washington.org

Website. www.dc.gov

OUTLYING U.S. AREAS

American Samoa (AS)

People. Population (July 2009 est.): 65,628. **Population growth rate** (2008-09 est.): 1.2%. **Pop. density:** 852 per sq mi. **Ethnic distrib.** (est. 2008): 91.6% Pacific Islander; 2.8% Asian; 1.1% white; 2 or more races, 4.2%. **Languages:** Samoan, English, Tongan.

Geography. Total area: 77 sq mi. **Land area:** 77 sq mi. **Location:** American Samoa is the most southerly of all lands under U.S. sovereign, about 2,300 mi. SW of Honolulu. It is an unincorporated territory consisting of 7 small islands of the Samoan group: **Tutuila** (52.59 sq mi), **Aunu'u** (0.59 sq mi), **Manu'a Group: Ta'u** (17.57 sq mi), **Olosega** (2.03 sq mi), **Ofu** (2.83 sq mi), and the atolls **Rose** (0.03 sq mi) and **Swains** (1.38 sq mi). **Climate:** marine tropical, avg. temp 82°F with little seasonal variation; avg. annual rainfall about 36 in. **Topography:** volcanic islands, rugged peaks, and limited coastal plains. About 70% of the land is bush and mountains. **Capital:** Pago Pago on Tutuila. **Chief airport at:** Pago Pago.

Economy. Chief industries: tuna fishing and processing, trade, services, tourism. **Chief crops:** giant taro, taro, yams,

coconuts, breadfruits, bananas, papayas. **Livestock** (2003): 300 cattle; 68,372 chickens; 64,208 hogs/pigs. **Commercial fishing** (2008): $11.7 mil. **Fed. employees** (2005): 70. **Unemployment** (2005): 29.8%. **Gross domestic product** (2007 est.): $75.3 mil. **Commercial banks** (2008): 2; deposits: $188 mil.

Energy. Electricity production (2006): 180 mil. kWh.

Misc. data. Motto: Samoa Muamua le Atua (In Samoa, God is first). **Flower:** Paogo (Ula-fala). **Plant:** Ava. **Song:** Amerika Samoa.

History. A tripartite agreement between Great Britain, Germany, and the U.S. in 1899 gave the U.S. sovereignty over the eastern islands of the Samoan group; these islands became American Samoa. Local chiefs ceded Tutuila and Aunu'u to the U.S. in 1900, and the Manu'a group and Rose Island in 1904; Swains Island was annexed in 1925. Samoa (Western), comprising the larger islands of the Samoan group, was a New Zealand mandate and UN Trusteeship until it became independent Jan. 1, 1962 (now called Samoa).

From 1900 to 1951, American Samoa was under the jurisdiction of the U.S. Navy. Since 1951, it has been under the Interior Dept. On Jan. 3, 1978, the first popularly elected

Samoan governor and lieutenant governor were inaugurated. Previously, the governor was appointed by the Sec. of the Interior. American Samoa has a bicameral legislature and elects a delegate to the U.S. House of Representatives who has a voice but no vote, except in committees.

Hurricane Val, 1991, caused $80 mil in damages. Scientists discovered a rapidly growing volcano, Vailulu'u, between Ta'u and Rose in 1975.

American Samoans are of Polynesian origin. They are nationals of the U.S.; as of 2000, 91,029 lived in the U.S., including 16,166 in Hawaii, 37,498 in California, and 8,049 in Washington.

Tourist attractions. Rose Atoll; Vaitogi coast; Natl. Park of American Samoa; tropical rainforest.

Tourist information. Office of Tourism, Dept. of Commerce, American Samoa Govt., PO Box 1147, Pago Pago, AS 96799; (684) 699-9411; www.amsamoatourism.com

Website. www.americansamoa.gov

Guam (GU)

People. Population (July 2009 est.): 178,430. **Population growth rate** (2008-09 est.): 1.4%. **Pop. density:** 842 per sq mi. **Ethnic distrib.** (2000): 37.1% Chamorro; 26.3% Filipino; 11.3% other Pacific Islander; 6.9% white; 6.3% other Asian; 2.3% other; 9.8% two or more race/ethnicities. **Languages:** English, Chamorro, Philippine/other Pacific Island languages.

Geography. Total area: 212 sq mi. **Land area:** 212 sq mi. **Location:** largest and southernmost of the Mariana Islands in the West Pacific, 3,700 mi W of Hawaii. **Climate:** tropical, with temperatures from 70° to 90° F; rainy July to Nov., avg. annual rainfall, about 80 to 100 in. **Topography:** coralline limestone plateau in the N; southern chain of low volcanic mountains sloping gently to the W, more steeply to coastal cliffs on the E; general elevation, 500 ft; highest point, Mt. Lamlam, 1,334 ft. **Capital:** Hagåtña. **Chief airport at:** Hagåtña.

Economy. Chief industries: U.S. military, tourism, construction, shipping, concrete products, printing & publishing. **Chief manuf. goods:** textiles, foods. **Chief crops:** watermelons, cucumbers, eggplant, long beans, bananas, bitter melons, taro, squash. **Livestock** (2002): 154 cattle; 675 hogs/pigs; 2,703 chickens. **Commercial fishing:** $722,466. **Nonfuel minerals** (est. 2004): $13 mil; crushed stone. **Chief port:** Apra Harbor. **Gross domestic product** (2005 est.): $2.5 bil. **Employment distrib.** (Dec. 2005): 33.1% trade/trans; 26.2% serv.; 25.5% govt.; 7.7% constr.; 2.9% mfg.; 0.3% agric. **Unemployment** (2005): 7.0%. **Mean earner's income** (2003): $21,778. **Commercial banks** (2008): 6; deposits: $1.8 bil. **Savings institutions** (2008): 1; deposits: $54 mil.

Energy. Electricity production (2006): 1.8 bil. kWh.

Federal govt. Fed. employees (2005): 3,300. **Notable fed. facilities:** *Anderson AFB.

Misc. data. Motto: Where America's day begins. **Flower:** Puti Tai Nobio (Bougainvillea). **Bird:** Ko'ko (Guam Rail). **Tree:** Ifit (Intsia bijuga). **Song:** Stand Ye Guamanians.

History. Guam was probably settled by voyagers from the Indonesian-Philippine archipelago by 3rd cent. BCE. Pottery, rice cultivation, and megalithic technology show strong East Asian cultural influence. Centralized, village clan-based communities engaged in agriculture and offshore fishing. The estimated population by the early 16th cent. was 50,000-75,000. Magellan arrived in the Marianas Mar. 6, 1521. They were colonized in 1668 by Spanish missionaries, who named them the Mariana Islands in honor of Maria Anna, queen of Spain. When Spain ceded Guam to the U.S., it sold the other Marianas to Germany. Japan obtained a League of Nations mandate over the German islands in 1919; in Dec. 1941 it seized Guam, which was retaken by the U.S. in July-August 1944.

Guam is a self-governing organized unincorporated U.S. territory. The Organic Act of 1950 provided for a governor, elected to a 4-year term, and a 21-member unicameral legislature, elected biennially by the residents, who are American citizens. In 1970, the first governor was elected. In 1972, a U.S. law gave Guam one delegate to the U.S. House of Representatives who has a voice but no vote, except in committees.

Guam's quest to change its status to a U.S. Commonwealth began in the late 1970s. The Guam Commission on Self-Determination, created in 1984, developed a draft Commonwealth Act. In 1993, legislation proposing a change of status was submitted to the U.S. Congress. In 1994, the U.S. Congress passed legislation transferring 3,200 acres of land on Guam from federal to local control.

Typhoon Omar damaged 75-90% of the island's buildings, 1992. A Korean Air jetliner crashed and burned near Agana, 1997, killing 228 of 254 aboard.

Tourist attractions. Tropical climate, oceanic marine environment; Tarzan Falls; Plaza de España; beaches; water sports; duty-free port shopping.

Tourist information. Guam Visitors Bureau, 401 Pale San Vitores Rd., Tumon, Guam 96913; (671) 646-5278; www.visitguam.org

Website. www.guam.gov

Commonwealth of the Northern Mariana Islands (MP)

People. Population (July 2009 est.): 88,662. **Population growth rate** (2008-09 est.): 2.3%. **Pop. density:** 481 per sq mi. **Ethnic distrib.** (2000): 56.3% Asian; 36.3% Pacific Islander; 1.8% white; 0.8% other; 4.8% two or more races/ethnicities. **Languages:** Philippine languages, Chinese, Chamorro, English.

Geography. Total area: 184.2 sq mi. **Land area:** 184.2 sq mi. **Location:** between Guam and the Tropic of Cancer, the 14 islands of the Northern Marianas form a 300-mi. long archipelago. The indigenous population is concentrated on the 3 largest of the 6 inhabited islands: **Saipan**, the seat of government and commerce, **Rota**, and **Tinian**. **Climate:** tropical, with avg. temperature around 82°F, moderated by northeast trade winds; avg. annual rainfall, 80-100 in. **Topography:** Limestone S islands with even terraces and coral reefs; volcanic N isles. **Capital:** Saipan. **Chief airport at:** Saipan.

Economy. Chief industries: mining, tourism, apparel mfg., retail. **Chief manuf. goods:** apparel, stone, clay and glass products. **Chief crops:** bananas, cucumbers, sweet potatoes, chinese cabbage, taro. **Livestock** (2002): 1,319 cattle; 2,242 hogs/pigs; 7,027 chickens. **Commercial fishing:** $815,108. **Chief port:** Saipan. **Gross domestic product** (2005): $900 mil. **Fed. employees** (2005): 124. **Unemployment** (2005): 8.0%. **Commercial banks** (2008): 3; deposits: $450 mil. **Savings institutions** (2008): 1; deposits: $11 mil.

Energy. Electricity production (2009): 60,600 kWh.

Misc. data. Flower: Plumeria. **Bird:** Mariana Fruit-dove. **Tree:** Flame Tree. **Song:** Gi Talo Gi Halom Tasi (In the middle of the sea).

History. The people of the Northern Marianas are predominantly of Chamorro cultural extraction, although Carolinians and immigrants from other areas of E. Asia and Micronesia have also settled in the islands. English is among the several languages commonly spoken.

The German-controlled Northern Marianas were placed under Japanese control by a League of Nations mandate after World War I. The U.S. captured the islands during World War II. From July 18, 1947, the U.S. had administered the Northern Marianas under a trusteeship agreement with the UN Security Council. In 1975, the residents voted to become a U.S. commonwealth.

The Northern Mariana Islands has been self-governing since 1978, when a constitution drafted and adopted by the people became effective and a popularly elected bicameral legislature (2-year term), with offices of governor (4-year term) and lieut. governor, was inaugurated. Pres. Ronald Reagan proclaimed the Northern Marianas a commonwealth, 1986, and the UN formally ended its trusteeship, 1990.

Under the 1976 Commonwealth Covenant with the U.S., the islands are exempt from federal immigration and import laws, and minimum wage is lower than on the mainland. The garment making industry, which has since boomed, has drawn accusations of sweatshop conditions from some critics. Legislation passed in 2007 will raise the minimum wage to the federal rate by 2015.

Tourist attractions. WWII sites; House of Taga; beaches, water sports; resorts; gambling.

Tourist information. Marianas Visitors Authority, PO Box 500861, Saipan, MP 96950; (670) 664-3200; www.mymarianas.com

Website. www.gov.mp

Commonwealth of Puerto Rico (PR)
(Estado Libre Asociado de Puerto Rico)

People. Population (2009 est.): 3,971,020 (about 4.1 mil. more Puerto Ricans reside in the mainland U.S.). **Population growth rate:** (2008-09): 0.3%. **Pop. density:** 1,129 per sq mi. **Racial distribution** (2007): 76.2% white; 6.9% black; 0.3% Asian; 0.2% Native American/Nat. AK; 12% other; 2 or more races, 4.4%. **Hispanic pop.** (any race): 98.8%. **Languages:** Spanish and English are joint official languages.

Geography. Total area: 3,515 sq mi. **Land area:** 3,459 sq mi. **Location:** island lying between the Atlantic to the N and the Caribbean to the S; it is easternmost of the West Indies group called the Greater Antilles, of which Cuba, Hispaniola, and Jamaica are the larger islands. **Climate:** mild, with a mean temperature of 77°F. **Topography:** mountainous throughout three-fourths of its rectangular area, surrounded by a broken coastal plain; highest peak, Cerro de Punto, 4,390 ft. **Capital:** San Juan. **Chief airport at:** San Juan.

Economy. Chief industries: manufacturing, service, tourism. **Chief manuf. goods:** pharmaceuticals, medical equip., electronics, apparel, food products. **Chief crops:** pineapples, pumpkins, coffee, watermelons, plantains, bananas. **Livestock** (2005): 420,000 cattle; 16,000 sheep; 100,000 hogs/pigs; (Dec. 2008) 1.4 mil. chickens;. **Commercial fishing:** $3.8 mil. **Nonfuel minerals** (est. 2004): $187 mil; mostly crushed stone, portland cement. **Chief port:** San Juan. **Gross domestic product** (est. 2008): $88.0 bil. **Employment distrib.** (June 2008): 30.8% govt.; 17.2% trade/trans./util.; 9.9% mfg.; 9.8% ed./health; 10.1% prof./bus. serv.; 7.0% leisure/hosp.; 4.7% finance; 6.7% constr.; 1.6% other serv.; 2.1% info. **Unemployment** (2008): 11.5%. **Per capita pers. income** (est. 2006): $12,997. **Commercial banks** (2008): 12; deposits: $64.5 bil. **Lottery** (2008): total sales: $364.0 mil; profit: $126.5 mil.

Federal govt. Fed. civ. employees (2005): 11,308. **Notable fed. facilities:** P.R. Natl. Guard Training Area at Camp Santiago, and at Ft. Allen, Juana Diaz; *U.S. Army Station at Ft. Buchanan; Intl. Inst. of Tropical Forestry; Vieques Natl. Wildlife Ref.; USGS Caribbean Water Science Ctr.

Energy. Electricity production (2006): 23.8 bil kWh.

Misc. data. Motto: Joannes Est Nomen Eius (John is his name). **Flower:** Maga. **Bird:** Reinita. **Tree:** Ceiba. **National anthem:** La Borinqueña.

History. Puerto Rico (or Borinquen, after the original Arawak Indian name, Boriquen) was visited by Columbus on his second voyage, Nov. 19, 1493. In 1508, the Spanish arrived.

Sugarcane was introduced, 1515, and slaves were imported 3 years later. Gold mining petered out, 1570. Spaniards fought off a series of British and Dutch attacks; slavery was abolished, 1873. Under the treaty of Paris, Puerto Rico was ceded to the U.S. after the Spanish-American War, 1898. In 1952 the people voted in favor of Commonwealth status.

The Commonwealth of Puerto Rico is a self-governing part of the U.S. with a primarily Hispanic culture. The island's citizens have virtually the same control over their internal affairs as do the 50 states of the U.S. However, they do not vote in national general elections, only in national primaries.

Puerto Rico is represented in the U.S. House of Representatives by a Resident Commissioner who has a voice but no vote, except in committees.

No federal income tax is collected from residents on income earned from local sources in Puerto Rico. Nevertheless, as part of the U.S. legal system, Puerto Rico is subject to the provisions of the U.S. Constitution; most federal laws apply as they do in the 50 states.

Puerto Rico's famous "Operation Bootstrap," begun in the late 1940s, succeeded in changing the island from "The Poorhouse of the Caribbean" to an area with the highest per capita income in Latin America. This program encouraged manufacturing and development of the tourist trade by selective tax exemption, low-interest loans, and other incentives. Despite the marked success of Puerto Rico's development efforts over an extended period of time, per capita income in Puerto Rico is low in comparison to that of the 50 states.

In plebiscites held in 1967, 1993, and 1998, voters chose to retain Commonwealth status. Protests mounted in the late-1990s over the U.S. Navy's use of Vieques Island for live ammunition training; official military exercises there were terminated, 2003.

Tourist attractions. Ponce Museum of Art; Forts El Morro and San Cristobal; Old Walled City of San Juan; Arecibo Observatory; Cordillera Central and state parks; El Yunque Rain Forest; San Juan Cathedral; Porta Coeli Chapel and Museum of Religious Art, Interamerican Univ., San Germán; Condado Convention Center; Casa Blanca, Ponce de León family home, Puerto Rican Family Museum of 16th and 17th centuries, and Fine Arts Center, all in San Juan.

Cultural facilities and events. Festival Casals classical music concerts, mid-June; Puerto Rico Symphony Orchestra at Music Conservatory; Botanical Garden and Museum of Anthropology, Art, and History at the University of Puerto Rico; Institute of Puerto Rican Culture, at the Dominican Convent.

Famous Puerto Ricans. Julia de Burgos, Marta Casals Istomin, Pablo Casals, José Celso Barbosa, Orlando Cepeda, Roberto Clemente, José de Diego, José Feliciano, Doña Felisa Rincón de Gautier, Luis A. Ferré, José Ferrer, Commodore Diégo E. Hernández, Miguel Hernández Agosto, Rafael Hernández (El Jibarito), Rafael Hernández Colón, Raúl Julía, René Marqués, Ricky Martin, Concha Meléndez, Rita Moreno, Luis Muñoz Marín, Luis Palés Matos, Adm. Horacio Rivero.

Tourist information. The Puerto Rico Tourism Company, La Princesa Bldg. #2, Paseo La Princesa, Old San Juan, PR 00902; (800) 866-7827; www.gotopuertorico.com

Website. www.gobierno.pr (site is in Spanish)

Virgin Islands (VI)
St. John, St. Croix, St. Thomas

People. Population (July 2009 est.): 109,825. **Population growth rate** (2008-09 est.): –0.03%. **Pop. density:** 808 per sq mi. **Ethnic distrib.** (2000): 76.2% black; 13.1% white; 1.1% Asian; 6.1% other races; 2 or more races, 3.5%. **Languages:** English (official), Spanish, Creole.

Geography. Total area: 136 sq mi. **Land area:** 135 sq mi. **Location:** 3 larger and 50 smaller islands and cays in the S and W of the V.I. group (British V.I. colony to the N and E), which is situated 70 mi E of Puerto Rico, located W of the Anegada Passage, a major channel connecting the Atlantic Ocean and the Caribbean Sea. **Climate:** subtropical; the sun tempered by gentle trade winds; humidity is low; average temperature, 78° F. **Topography:** St. Thomas is mainly a ridge of hills running E and W, and has little tillable land; St. Croix rises abruptly in the N but slopes to the S to flatlands and lagoons; St. John has steep, lofty hills and valleys with little level tillable land. **Capital:** Charlotte Amalie on St. Thomas. **Chief airport at:** Charlotte Amalie.

Economy. Chief industries: retail, petroleum, tourism, prof. consulting. **Chief manuf. goods:** rum, stone, glass & clay products, electronics, textiles. **Chief crops:** cucumbers, mangoes, tomatoes, bananas, lettuce. **Livestock** (2002): 2,223 cattle; 2,389 sheep; 2,223 goats; 1,085 hogs/pigs; 1,830 chickens. **Commercial fishing:** $10.7 mil. **Minerals:** stone, crushed limestone, traprock. **Chief port:** Charlotte Amalie. **Gross domestic product** (2004 est.): $1.6 bil. **Fed. employees** (2005): 690. **Unemployment** (2006 est.): 6.2%. **Per capita income** (2001 est.): $19,000. **Commercial banks** (2008): 4; deposits: $2.0 bil.

Energy. Electricity production (2006): 960 mil. kWh.

Misc. data. Motto: United in Pride and Hope. **Flower:** Yellow cedar. **Bird:** Yellow breast. **Song:** Virgin Islands March.

History. The islands were visited by Columbus in 1493. Spanish forces, 1555, defeated the Caribes and claimed the territory; by 1596 the native population was annihilated. First permanent settlement in the U.S. territory, 1672, by the Danes; U.S. purchased the islands, 1917, for defense purposes.

The Virgin Islands has a republican form of government, headed by a governor and lieut. governor elected, since 1970, by popular vote for 4-year terms. There is a 15-member unicameral legislature, elected by popular vote for a 2-year term. Residents of the V.I. have been U.S. citizens since 1927. Since 1973 they have elected a delegate to the U.S. House of Representatives, who has a voice but no vote, except in committees.

Hurricane Hugo, 1989, caused $500 mil in damages; U.S. troops were deployed to suppress looting and unrest.

Tourist attractions. Magens Bay, St. Thomas; duty-free shopping; Virgin Islands Natl. Park; beaches, Indian relics, and evidence of colonial Danes.

Tourist information. USVI Division of Tourism, PO Box 6400, St. Thomas 00804; 1-800-372-USVI; www.usvitourism.vi

Website. ltg.gov.vi

Other Islands

Navassa lies between Haiti and Jamaica, 100 mi S of Guantanamo Bay, Cuba, in the Caribbean; it covers 1,147 acres, and is uninhabited. Claimed 1857, USCG lighthouse built 1917, now inoperative. Natl. Wildlife Refuge since 1999. Administered by the Dept. of Interior.

The three coral islands of **Wake Atoll**—**Wake, Wilkes,** and **Peale**—lie in the Pacific Ocean on the direct route from Hawaii to Hong Kong, about 2,300 mi W of Honolulu and 1,500 mi NE of Guam. The group is 4.5 mi long, 1.5 mi wide. Land area totals 2.5 sq mi. The U.S. annexed Wake Atoll Jan. 17, 1899. Japan occupied Wake 1941-45. Designated a Natl. Hist. Landmark in 1985. Wake is owned by the U.S. Air Force, administered by the Dept. of Interior, but used by the Army as a missile launch facility. The population consists of military personnel and contractors. Most infrastructure damaged by super typhoon Ioke in 2006.

The following mostly uninhabited islands are part of the **Pacific/Remote Islands Natl. Wildlife Refuge Complex** administered by the Dept. of Interior: **Midway Atoll**, acquired in 1867, has 3 main islands—Sand, Spit, and Eastern—1,250 mi WNW of Honolulu, with an area of about 1,500 acres. Naval activity ended in 1997. Has the world's largest colony of Laysan albatross. **Johnston Atoll**, 800 mi WSW of Honolulu, is 2 natural & 2 man-made islands across 107 sq mi administered by the Navy. Johnston was a nuclear test site in 1958, 1962; the Army disposed of chemical weapons 1990-2000. Cleanup ended in 2005. **Kingman Reef** is a barren, coral atoll 932 mi S of Hawaii, annexed 1922. **Palmyra Atoll** is 54 islets over 753 sq mi, 1,052 mi S of Hawaii; annexed with Hawaii in 1898. Part privately owned by the Nature Conservancy. **Jarvis Island** covers 1,086 acres, 1,300 mi S of Honolulu near the equator. West of Jarvis are **Howland and Baker Islands,** 36 mi apart and about 1,600 mi SW of Honolulu.

WASHINGTON, DC, CAPITAL OF THE U.S.

Most attractions are free. All times are subject to change. For more details call the Washington, DC, Convention and Visitors Association at 1-800-422-8644, or visit www.washington.org

Bureau of Engraving and Printing

The **Bureau of Engraving and Printing** of the U.S. Treasury Dept. is the headquarters for the making of U.S. paper money. Public tours are offered Mon.-Fri., 9-10:45 AM, 12:30-2 PM (later in summer), except on federal holidays. 14th and C Sts. SW; (866) 874-2330. **Website:** www.money factory.gov

Capitol

The **United States Capitol** was originally designed by Dr. William Thornton, an amateur architect, who submitted a plan in 1793 that won him $500 and a city lot. Three other architects designed or supervised the construction of the Capitol before its completion.

The present cast iron dome at its greatest exterior height measures 135 ft, 5 in. and is topped by the bronze Statue of Freedom, which stands 19½ ft and weighs 14,985 lb. On its base are the words *E Pluribus Unum* ("Out of Many, One").

The Capitol is open to the public Mon.-Sat., 8:30 AM-4:30 PM. It is closed Jan. 1, Inauguration Day, Thanksgiving Day, and Dec. 25.

To observe debate while Congress is in session, those living in the U.S. may obtain tickets from their U.S. representative or senator. Visitors from other countries may obtain passes at the Capitol. Between Constitution & Independence Aves., at Pennsylvania Ave.; (202) 225-6827. **Website:** www.visitthecapital.gov

Federal Bureau of Investigation

The **Federal Bureau of Investigation** offers guided one-hour tours of its headquarters. Visitors learn about the history of the FBI and see weapons confiscated from famous gangsters, photos of most-wanted fugitives, the DNA laboratory, goods forfeited/seized in narcotics operations, and a sharpshooting demonstration.

Tours have been suspended for building renovation. J. Edgar Hoover Bldg., Pennsylvania Ave., between 9th and 10th Sts. NW; (202) 324-3447. **Website:** www.fbi.gov

Folger Shakespeare Library

The **Folger Shakespeare Library**, on Capitol Hill, is a research institution holding rare books and manuscripts of the Renaissance period and the largest collection of Shakespearean materials in the world. Exhibit may be visited Mon.-Sat., 10 AM-5 PM, except federal holidays. 201 E. Capitol St. SE; (202) 544-4600. **Website:** www.folger.edu

Holocaust Memorial Museum

The **U.S. Holocaust Memorial Museum** opened on Apr. 21, 1993. The museum documents the events of the Holocaust through permanent and temporary displays, interactive videos, and special lectures. The permanent exhibition is not recommended for children under age 11.

The museum is open daily, 10 AM-5:20 PM, except Yom Kippur and Dec. 25; extended hours Mon.-Thurs. (10 AM-6:20 PM) from Apr.-June. A limited number of free tickets are available at the door; advance tickets may be ordered for a small fee at 1-800-400-9373. Tickets are needed only for the permanent

exhibition, only March through August. 100 Raoul Wallenberg Pl. SW; (202) 488-0400. **Website:** www.ushmm.org

Jefferson Memorial

Dedicated Apr. 13, 1943, the **Thomas Jefferson Memorial** stands on the south shore of the Tidal Basin in West Potomac Park. It is a circular stone structure that combines architectural elements of the dome of the Pantheon in Rome and the rotunda designed by Jefferson for the Univ. of Virginia.

The memorial is open daily, 24 hrs., staffed 9:30 AM-11:30 PM. Has elevator and curb ramps for handicapped; (202) 426-6841. **Website:** www.nps.gov/thje

John F. Kennedy Center

The **John F. Kennedy Center for the Performing Arts** opened Sept. 8, 1971. Designed by Edward Durell Stone, it includes an opera house, a concert hall, several theaters, 2 restaurants, and a library. Free tours are available Mon.-Fri., 10 AM-5 PM and Sat. & Sun., 10 AM-1 PM. 2700 F St. NW; (202) 467-4600; (800) 444-1324. **Website:** www.kennedy-center.org

Korean War Veterans Memorial

Dedicated on July 27, 1995, the **Korean War Veterans Memorial** honors Americans who served in the war. Situated at the west end of the Mall, the triangular-shaped stone and steel memorial features a multiservice formation of 19 combat-ready troops clad in ponchos with the wind at their back. A granite wall, with images of men and women who served, juts into a pool of water, the Pool of Remembrance.

The memorial is open daily, 24 hrs., staffed 9:30 AM-11:30 PM. French Dr. SW across from Lincoln Memorial; (202) 426-6841. **Website:** www.nps.gov/kowa

Library of Congress

Established by and for Congress in 1800, the **Library of Congress** extends its services to other government agencies and libraries, scholars, and the general public. It contains more than 134 mil. items in some 460 languages.

Exhibit halls are open to the public Mon.-Fri., 8:30 AM-9:30 PM; Sat., 8:30 AM-5 PM. A few areas are open on most federal holidays; all are closed Jan. 1, Thanksgiving, and Dec. 25. 101 Independence Ave. SE; (202) 707-8000. **Website:** www. loc.gov

Lincoln Memorial

Designed by Henry Bacon, the **Lincoln Memorial** in West Potomac Park is a large marble hall enclosing a statue of Abraham Lincoln seated on an armchair. The memorial was dedicated May 30, 1922. The statue was designed by Daniel Chester French and sculpted by French and the Piccirilli brothers. The text of the Gettysburg Address is in the south chamber; that of Lincoln's Second Inaugural speech is in the north chamber. Each is engraved on a stone tablet.

The memorial is open daily, 24 hrs., staffed 9:30 AM-11:30 PM, and is wheelchair-accessible. W. Potomac Park at 23rd St. NW; (202) 426-6841. **Website:** www.nps.gov/linc

National Archives and Records

Original copies of the Declaration of Independence, the Constitution, and the Bill of Rights are on display in the **National Archives** Exhibition Hall. The National Archives also holds other valuable U.S. government records and historic maps, photographs, and manuscripts. Central Research and Microfilm Research Rooms are also available to the public for genealogical research.

Exhibition Hall open daily 10 AM-5:30PM (later in spring and summer). 7th & Pennsylvania Ave. NW; (202) 357-5000. **Website:** www.archives.gov

National Gallery of Art

The **National Gallery of Art** was established by Congress, Mar. 24, 1937, and opened Mar. 17, 1941. The original West building was designed by John Russell Pope. The East building, opened in 1978, was designed by I. M. Pei. Open daily, Mon.-Sat. 10 AM-5 PM, Sunday 11 AM-6 PM. Closed Jan. 1 and Dec. 25. 4th & Constitution Ave NW; (202) 737-4215.**Website:** www.nga.gov

Franklin Delano Roosevelt Memorial

Opened May 2, 1997, the **FDR Memorial** features 9 bronze sculptural ensembles depicting FDR, Eleanor Roosevelt, and events from the Great Depression and World War II. This 7.5-acre memorial is located near the Tidal Basin in a park-like setting and is wheelchair accessible.

Grounds, staffed daily, 8 AM-11:45 PM, except Dec. 25. 1850 W. Basin Dr. SW; (202) 426-6841. **Website:** www.nps.gov/fdrm

Smithsonian Institution

The **Smithsonian Institution**, established in 1846, is the world's largest museum complex. It holds some 144 mil artifacts and specimens in its trust. There are 15 museums and the National Zoo in the D.C. area. The **Smithsonian Information Center** is located in "the Castle" on the Mall. Also on the Mall are the **National Museum of American History**, the **National Museum of Natural History**, the **National Air and Space Museum**, the **National Museum of the American Indian**, the **Hirshhorn Museum and Sculpture Garden**, the **Arthur M. Sackler & Freer Galleries of Art**, the **National Museum of African Art**, and the **Arts and Industries Building**(closed for renovation). Located nearby are the **National Postal Museum**, the **National Museum of American Art**, the **National Portrait Gallery**, and the **Renwick Gallery**. Farther away, at 1901 Fort Pl. SE, is the **Anacostia Museum**. The **Air and Space Museum's Udvar-Hazy Center** is near Dulles Airport in Virginia.

Most museums are open daily, except Dec. 25, 10 AM-5:30 PM (later in summer); (202) 633-1000. **Website:** www.si.edu

Vietnam Veterans Memorial

Originally dedicated Nov. 13, 1982, the **Vietnam Veterans Memorial** recognizes the men and women who served in the armed forces in the Vietnam War. The names of more than 58,000 Americans who lost their lives or remain missing are inscribed on a V-shaped black-granite wall, designed by Maya Ying Lin.

Since 1982, 2 additions have been made to the Memorial. The 1st, dedicated on Nov. 11, 1984, is the Frederick Hart sculpture *Three Servicemen*. On Nov. 11, 1993, the Vietnam Women's Memorial, designed by Glenna Goodacre, was dedicated, honoring the more than 11,500 women who served in Vietnam.

The memorial is open daily, 24 hrs., staffed 9:30 AM-11:30 PM. Constitution Ave. & Bacon Dr. NW; (202) 426-6841. **Website:** www.nps.gov/vive

Washington Monument

The **Washington Monument**, dedicated in 1885, is a tapering shaft, or obelisk, of white marble, 555 ft, 5 $\frac{1}{8}$ inches in height and 55 ft, 1½ in. square at base. Eight small windows, 2 on each side, are located at the 500-ft level.

Open daily, 9 AM-5 PM (later in summer), except July 1, Dec. 25. Free timed passes are available; advance passes are available for a small fee. 15th & Constitution Ave. NW; (202) 426-6841. **Website:** www.nps.gov/wash

White House

The **White House**, the President's residence, stands on 18 acres on the south side of Pennsylvania Ave., between the Treasury and the old Executive Office Building. The walls are of sandstone, quarried at Aquia Creek, VA. The building was first made white with lime-based whitewash in 1798, but the name did not become official until 1901.

The White House is normally open for free self-guided tours of 10 or more Tues.-Thurs., 7:30-11 AM; Fri., 7:30 AM-noon; Sat., 7:30 AM-1 PM. (Tour requests must be made at least one month in advance through your member of Congress.) Only the public rooms on the ground floor and state floor may be visited. 1600 Pennsylvania Ave. The White House Visitor Center at 1450 Pennsylvania Ave. is open daily 7:30 AM-4 PM; (202) 456-7041. **Website:** www.whitehouse.gov

National World War II Memorial

The **National WWII Memorial** is dedicated to the approx. 16 mil. veterans who served and the more than 400,000 who died in the war. It rests on 7.4 acres of land at the east end of the reflecting pool on the Mall. The memorial opened on April 29, 2004, and was dedicated on May 29.

At the north and south entrances are 43-ft archways, representing the Atlantic and Pacific theaters. Inside the grounds is a large, oval plaza with a wall of 4,000 gold stars; each represents 100 American deaths. Fifty-six pillars ringing the center represent the states, territories, and District of Columbia. There is also a garden enclosed by a stone wall, the Circle of Remembrance.

The memorial is wheelchair-accessible and open daily, 24 hrs., staffed 9:30 AM-11:30 PM. Located on 17th St. between Constitution and Independence Aves.; (202) 426-6841. **Website:** www.nps.gov/nwwm

Attractions Near Washington, DC

Arlington National Cemetery

Arlington National Cemetery, on the former Custis-Lee estate in Arlington, VA, is the site of the **Tomb of the Unknowns** and is the final resting place of Pres. W.H. Taft, John F. Kennedy and his wife, Jacqueline Bouvier Kennedy Onassis. An eternal flame burns over the grave site. Many other famous Americans are buried at Arlington, as well as more than 300,000 U.S. military personnel, from every major war.

North of the National Cemetery stands the **U.S. Marine Corps War Memorial**, also known as Iwo Jima. The memorial is a bronze statue of the raising of the U.S. flag on Mt. Suribachi, Feb. 23, 1945, during World War II, executed by Felix de Weldon from the photograph by Joe Rosenthal.

On the southern side of the Memorial Bridge, near the cemetery entrance, a memorial honoring the women in the military was dedicated Oct. 18, 1997. The **Women in Military Service for America Memorial** is a semicircular retaining wall 226 ft long with a central niche 30 ft high.

Open daily, 8 AM-5 PM (8 AM-7 PM, Apr.-Sept.), Arlington, VA; (703) 607-8000. **Website:** www.arlingtoncemetery.org

Mount Vernon

Mount Vernon, George Washington's estate, is on the south bank of the Potomac R., 16 mi from Washington, DC, in northern Virginia. The present house is believed to be an enlargement of one built by Augustine Washington in 1735. His son Lawrence renamed the estate after British Navy Adm. Edward Vernon. George Washington, Lawrence's half brother, inherited it in 1761. The estate has been restored to its 18th-century appearance and includes many original furnishings. Washington and his wife, Martha, are buried on the grounds.

Open 365 days, Apr.-Aug. 8 AM-5 PM; Mar., Sept.-Oct. 9 AM-5 PM; Nov.-Feb. 9 AM-4 PM; (703) 780-2000; (800) 429-1520. Admission: adults $15, seniors (62+) $14, children (6-11) $7, age 5 and under free. **Website:** www.mountvernon.org

The Pentagon

The **Pentagon**, headquarters of the Dept. of Defense, is the largest office building in the U.S. It houses more than 23,000 employees in offices occupying 3,705,793 sq ft. The building was severely damaged when struck by a plane Sept. 11, 2001.

Group tours available to government agencies, educational institutions, or military units by reservation only. General public must use the Pentagon website or contact their member of Congress to request a tour. Non U.S. citizens must contact their national embassy. Arlington, VA (I-395 South to Boundary Channel Drive exit); (703) 697-1776. **Website:** pentagon.afis.osd.mil

UNITED STATES POPULATION

Census Origins and Methods

The U.S. census is conducted every 10 years as mandated by the Constitution, Article 1, Section 2. The primary purpose is to apportion seats in the House of Representatives and determine state legislative district boundaries. The data are also critical for a vast array of government programs and for providing demographic information to individuals and businesses.

The first U.S. census was conducted in 1790, a little more than a year after George Washington became president. It counted the number of free white males age 16 and over (to measure how many men might be available for military service), the number under 16, the number of free white females, all other free persons (including any American Indians who paid taxes), and slaves. It took 18 months to collect the data, at a cost of about $1 million in today's dollars. Census results from each enumeration district were required to be publicly displayed within that district, a practice that lasted through the 1840 census. The 1790 census, which counted a total of 3.9 million people, resulted in an increase of 41 seats (65 to 106) in the House of Representatives.

As the nation expanded, so did the scope of the census data. The first inquiry on manufacturing industries was made in 1810. Questions on agriculture, mining, and fisheries were added in 1840. In 1850, the census included questions on social issues—taxation, churches, poverty, and crime.

The 1880 census had so many questions that it took the full 10 years between censuses to publish all the results. Because of this delay, Congress limited the 1900 census to questions on population, manufactures, agriculture, and mortality. Many of the dropped topics reappeared in later censuses.

Today, the secretary of commerce and the Census Bureau are directed by law to take censuses of population, housing, agriculture, irrigation, manufactures, mineral industries, other businesses (wholesale trade, retail trade, services), construction, transportation, and governments at stated intervals. They also conduct smaller-scale surveys on behalf of other federal agencies.

U.S. marshals supervised the first 9 censuses and reported to the president (1790), the secretary of state (1800-40), or the secretary of the interior (1850-70). There was no continuity of personnel from one census to the next. In 1902, Congress authorized a permanent Census Office in the Interior Dept. In 1903, the agency was transferred to the new Dept. of Commerce and Labor, and when the department split in 1913, the Bureau of the Census was placed in the Commerce Dept.

The Census Bureau began using statistical sampling techniques in the 1940s, computers in the 1950s, and mail enumeration in the 1960s, all in an effort to publish more data sooner and at a lower cost, and with less burden on the public. For the 2010 Census, the Census Bureau plans to continue mailing questionnaires to most housing units in the country, but to use handheld computers, rather than paper and pencil, in doing follow-up interviews at nonresponding households.

The 2010 Census will focus on counting the population through use of a short-form questionnaire. In previous censuses, about 5 in 6 households received the short form while 1 in 6 households received the long-form questionnaire, which asked questions about details such as ancestry, marital status, and occupation. The American Community Survey (ACS) replaces the need in 2010 for the long form. First implemented nationwide in 2005 and conducted yearly on a random sample of the population, the ACS gathers detailed demographic, economic, and housing information about America's communities.

Population by State, 2000, 2008

Source: Population Estimates Program, 2000 Census, U.S. Census Bureau, U.S. Dept. of Commerce
(ranked by 2008 population counts)

Rank	State	2008 population[1]	2000 population[2]	% change 2000-08	Rank	State	2008 population[1]	2000 population[2]	% change 2000-08
1.	California	36,756,666	33,871,648	8.5%	29.	Connecticut	3,501,252	3,405,565	2.8%
2.	Texas	24,326,974	20,851,820	16.7	30.	Iowa	3,002,555	2,926,324	2.6
3.	New York	19,490,297	18,976,457	2.7	31.	Mississippi	2,938,618	2,844,658	3.3
4.	Florida	18,328,340	15,982,378	14.7	32.	Arkansas	2,855,390	2,673,400	6.8
5.	Illinois	12,901,563	12,419,293	3.9	33.	Kansas	2,802,134	2,688,418	4.2
6.	Pennsylvania	12,448,279	12,281,054	1.4	34.	Utah	2,736,424	2,233,169	22.5
7.	Ohio	11,485,910	11,353,140	1.2	35.	Nevada	2,600,167	1,998,257	30.1
8.	Michigan	10,003,422	9,938,444	0.7	36.	New Mexico	1,984,356	1,819,046	9.1
9.	Georgia	9,685,744	8,186,453	18.3	37.	West Virginia	1,814,468	1,808,344	0.3
10.	North Carolina	9,222,414	8,049,313	14.6	38.	Nebraska	1,783,432	1,711,263	4.2
11.	New Jersey	8,682,661	8,414,350	3.2	39.	Idaho	1,523,816	1,293,953	17.8
12.	Virginia	7,769,089	7,078,515	9.8	40.	Maine	1,316,456	1,274,923	3.3
13.	Washington	6,549,224	5,894,121	11.1	41.	New Hampshire	1,315,809	1,235,786	6.5
14.	Arizona	6,500,180	5,130,632	26.7	42.	Hawaii	1,288,198	1,211,537	6.3
15.	Massachusetts	6,497,967	6,349,097	2.3	43.	Rhode Island	1,050,788	1,048,319	0.2
16.	Indiana	6,376,792	6,080,485	4.9	44.	Montana	967,440	902,195	7.2
17.	Tennessee	6,214,888	5,689,283	9.2	45.	Delaware	873,092	783,600	11.4
18.	Missouri	5,911,605	5,595,211	5.7	46.	South Dakota	804,194	754,844	6.5
19.	Maryland	5,633,597	5,296,486	6.4	47.	Alaska	686,293	626,932	9.5
20.	Wisconsin	5,627,967	5,363,675	4.9	48.	North Dakota	641,481	642,200	-0.1
21.	Minnesota	5,220,393	4,919,479	6.1	49.	Vermont	621,270	608,827	2.0
22.	Colorado	4,939,456	4,301,261	14.8	50.	District of Columbia	591,833	572,059	3.5
23.	Alabama	4,661,900	4,447,100	4.8	51.	Wyoming	532,668	493,782	7.9
24.	South Carolina	4,479,800	4,012,012	11.7		**Total resident pop.[3]**	**304,059,724**	**281,421,906**	**8.0**
25.	Louisiana	4,410,796	4,468,976	-1.3		Northeast	54,924,779	53,594,378	2.5
26.	Kentucky	4,269,245	4,041,769	5.6		Midwest	66,561,448	64,392,776	3.4
27.	Oregon	3,790,060	3,421,399	10.8		South	111,718,549	100,236,820	11.5
28.	Oklahoma	3,642,361	3,450,654	5.6		West	70,854,948	63,197,932	12.1

(1) Population estimates are for July 1. (2) Population figures are for April 1 of decennial census year. (3) Resident population excludes military personnel and civilian U.S. citizens living abroad.

Density of Population by State, 1930-2000

Source: Decennial Censuses, U.S. Census Bureau, U.S. Dept. of Commerce

(per square mile, land area only)

State	1930	1960	1980	1990	2000	State	1930	1960	1980	1990	2000
AL.......	51.8	6.4	76.7	79.6	87.6	MT......	3.7	4.6	5.4	5.5	6.2
AK	0.1	0.4	0.7	1.0	1.1	NE	18.0	18.4	20.4	20.5	22.3
AZ.......	3.8	11.5	23.9	32.3	45.2	NV	0.8	2.6	7.3	10.9	18.2
AR	35.2	34.3	43.9	45.1	51.3	NH......	51.6	67.7	102.7	123.7	137.8
CA	36.2	100.8	151.8	191.1	217.2	NJ	537.3	817.8	992.9	1,044.5	1,134.4
CO	10.0	16.9	27.9	31.8	41.5	NM......	3.5	7.8	10.7	12.5	15.0
CT	328.0	523.2	641.4	678.5	702.9	NY	262.6	355.4	371.9	381.0	401.9
DE	120.5	228.3	304.2	341.0	401.1	NC	64.5	93.5	120.7	136.2	165.2
DC	7,981.5	12,440.3	10,396.3	9,884.4	9,316.4	ND......	9.7	9.2	9.5	9.3	9.3
FL.......	27.1	91.7	180.7	239.9	296.4	OH......	161.6	237.0	263.7	264.9	277.3
GA	49.7	68.1	94.3	111.9	141.4	OK......	34.6	33.9	44.1	45.8	50.3
HI	57.5	98.5	150.2	172.6	188.6	OR......	9.9	18.4	27.4	29.6	35.6
ID	5.4	8.1	11.4	12.2	15.6	PA	213.8	252.6	264.7	265.1	274.0
IL	136.4	181.3	205.6	205.6	223.4	RI.......	649.8	822.5	906.4	960.3	1,003.2
IN	89.4	130.0	153.1	154.6	169.5	SC	56.8	79.1	103.7	115.8	133.2
IA	44.1	49.4	52.2	49.7	52.4	SD......	9.1	9.0	9.1	9.2	9.9
KS	22.9	26.6	28.9	30.3	32.9	TN	62.4	86.5	111.4	118.3	138.0
KY	65.2	76.5	92.1	92.8	101.7	TX	22.1	36.6	54.4	64.9	79.6
LA.......	46.5	74.8	96.6	96.9	102.6	UT	6.2	10.8	17.8	21.0	27.2
ME	25.7	31.4	36.4	39.8	41.3	VT	38.8	42.2	55.3	60.8	65.8
MD	165.0	317.2	431.5	489.1	541.9	VA	60.7	100.2	135.0	156.3	178.8
MA	537.4	656.9	731.8	767.4	809.8	WA......	23.3	42.9	62.1	73.1	88.6
MI.......	84.9	137.7	163.1	163.6	175.0	WV......	71.8	77.2	81.0	74.5	75.1
MN	32.0	42.9	51.2	55.0	61.8	WI	53.7	72.8	86.6	90.1	98.8
MS	42.4	46.4	53.7	54.9	60.6	WY......	2.3	3.4	4.8	4.7	5.1
MO	52.4	62.7	71.4	74.3	81.2	U.S.	41.2	50.7	64.0	70.3	79.6

Note: For purposes of comparison, Alaska and Hawaii are included in above tabulation for 1930, though they were not yet states.

U.S. Area and Population, 1790-2000

Source: Decennial Censuses, U.S. Census Bureau, U.S. Dept. of Commerce

Census date	AREA (square miles)			POPULATION			
	Gross area[1]	Land area	Water area[1]	Number	Per sq mi of land	Increase over preceding census Number	%
1790 (Aug. 2)	891,364	864,746	24,065	3,929,214	4.5	—	—
1800 (Aug. 4)	891,364	864,746	24,065	5,308,483	6.1	1,379,269	35.1%
1810 (Aug. 6)	1,722,685	1,681,828	34,175	7,239,881	4.3	1,931,398	36.4
1820 (Aug. 7)	1,792,552	1,749,462	38,544	9,638,453	5.5	2,398,572	33.1
1830 (June 1)	1,792,552	1,749,462	38,544	12,866,020	7.4	3,227,567	33.5
1840 (June 1)	1,792,552	1,749,462	38,544	17,069,453	9.8	4,203,433	32.7
1850 (June 1)	2,991,655	2,940,042	52,705	23,191,876	7.9	6,122,423	35.9
1860 (June 1)	3,021,295	2,969,640	52,747	31,443,321	10.6	8,251,445	35.6
1870 (June 1)	3,612,299	3,540,705	68,082	39,818,449[2]	11.2	8,375,128	26.6
1880 (June 1)	3,612,299	3,540,705	68,082	50,189,209	14.2	10,370,760	26.0
1890 (June 1)	3,612,299	3,540,705	68,082	62,979,766	17.8	12,790,557	25.5
1900 (June 1)	3,618,770	3,547,314	67,901	76,212,168	21.5	13,232,402	21.0
1910 (Apr. 15)	3,618,770	3,547,045	68,170	92,228,496	26.0	16,016,328	21.0
1920 (Jan. 1)	3,618,770	3,546,931	68,284	106,021,537	29.9	13,793,041	15.0
1930 (Apr. 1)	3,618,770	3,554,608	60,607	123,202,624	34.7	17,181,087	16.2
1940 (Apr. 1)	3,618,770	3,554,608	60,607	132,164,569	37.2	8,961,945	7.3
1950 (Apr. 1)	3,618,770	3,552,206	63,005	151,325,798	42.6	19,161,229	14.5
1960 (Apr. 1)	3,618,770	3,540,911	74,212	179,323,175	50.6	27,997,377	18.5
1970 (Apr. 1)	3,618,770	3,536,855	78,444	203,302,031	57.5	23,978,856	13.4
1980 (Apr. 1)	3,618,770	3,539,289	79,481	226,542,199	64.0	23,240,168	11.4
1990 (Apr. 1)	3,717,796	3,536,278	181,518	248,718,302	70.3	22,176,103	9.8
2000 (Apr. 1)	3,794,083	3,537,438	256,645	281,424,603	79.6	32,706,301	13.1

Note: Percent changes are computed on the basis of change in population since the preceding census date, so the period covered is not always exactly 10 years. Population density figures given for various years represent the area within the boundaries of the U.S. under its jurisdiction on the date in question—including, in some cases, considerable areas not organized or settled and not actually covered by the census. In 1870, for example, Alaska was not covered by the census, but its area is included in density calculations. Population figures may reflect corrections made to initial tabulated census counts. (1) Figures for 1790 to 1980 cover inland water only. Figure for 1990 includes inland, coastal, and Great Lakes water. Figure for 2000 includes additional territorial water as determined by presidential decree in Dec. 1998. (2) Revised to include adjustments for underenumeration in Southern states; unrevised number is 38,558,371. (3) Census count includes count question resolution corrections processed through Dec. 1997 and does not include adjustments for census coverage errors. (4) Total pop. count reflects modifications to the 2000 census population as documented in the Count Question Resolution program.

U.S. Population by Official

Source: Decennial Censuses, U.S. Census Bureau

State[2]	1790[1]	1800[1]	1810[1]	1820[1]	1830[1]	1840[1]	1850[1]	1860	1870	1880	1890	1900	1910
AL[2]		1	9	128	310	591	772	964,201	996,992	1,262,505	1,513,401	1,828,697	2,138,093
AK										33,426	32,052	63,592	64,356
AZ	......	......	......	......	......	......	......		9,658	40,440	88,243	122,931	204,354
AR	......	......	1	14	30	98	210	435,450	484,471	802,525	1,128,211	1,311,564	1,574,449
CA	......	......	......	......	......	......	93	379,994	560,247	864,694	1,213,398	1,485,053	2,377,549
CO	......	......	......	......	......	......	......	34,277	39,864	194,327	413,249	539,700	799,024
CT	238	251	262	275	298	310	371	460,147	537,454	622,700	746,258	908,420	1,114,756
DE	59	64	73	73	77	78	92	112,216	125,015	146,608	168,493	184,735	202,322
DC	......	8	16	23	30	34	52	75,080	131,700	177,624	230,392	278,718	331,069
FL	......	......	......	......	35	54	87	140,424	187,748	269,493	391,422	528,542	752,619
GA	83	163	252	341	517	69	906	1,057,286	1,184,109	1,542,180	1,837,353	2,216,331	2,609,121
HI												154,001	191,909
ID	......	......	......	......	......	......	......		14,999	32,610	88,548	161,772	325,594
IL	......	......	12	55	157	476	851	1,711,951	2,539,891	3,077,871	3,826,352	4,821,550	5,638,591
IN	......	6	25	147	343	686	988	1,350,428	1,680,637	1,978,301	2,192,404	2,516,462	2,700,876
IA	......	......	......	......	......	43	192	674,913	1,194,020	1,624,615	1,912,297	2,231,853	2,224,771
KS	......	......	......	......	......	......	......	107,206	364,399	996,096	1,428,108	1,470,495	1,690,949
KY	74	221	407	564	688	780	982	1,155,684	1,321,011	1,648,690	1,858,635	2,147,174	2,289,905
LA	......	......	77	153	216	352	518	708,002	726,915	939,946	1,118,588	1,381,625	1,656,388
ME[3]	97	152	229	298	399	502	583	628,279	626,915	648,936	661,086	694,466	742,371
MD	320	342	381	407	447	470	583	687,049	780,894	934,943	1,042,390	1,188,044	1,295,346
MA[3]	379	423	472	523	610	738	995	1,231,066	1,457,351	1,783,085	2,238,947	2,805,346	3,366,416
MI	......	......	5	9	32	212	398	749,113	1,184,059	1,636,937	2,093,890	2,420,982	2,810,173
MN	......	......	......	......	......	......	6	172,023	439,706	780,773	1,310,283	1,751,394	2,075,708
MS[2]	......	8	31	75	137	376	607	791,305	827,922	1,131,597	1,289,600	1,551,270	1,797,114
MO	......	......	20	67	140	384	682	1,182,012	1,721,295	2,168,380	2,679,185	3,106,665	3,293,335
MT	......	......	......	......	......	......	......		20,595	39,159	142,924	243,329	376,053
NE	......	......	......	......	......	......	......	28,841	122,993	452,402	1,062,656	1,066,300	1,192,214
NV	......	......	......	......	......	......	......	6,857	42,491	62,266	47,355	42,335	81,875
NH	142	184	214	244	269	285	318	326,073	318,300	346,991	376,530	411,588	430,572
NJ	184	211	246	278	321	373	490	672,035	906,096	1,131,116	1,444,933	1,883,669	2,537,167
NM[4]	......	......	......	......	......	......	62	93,516	91,874	119,565	160,282	195,310	327,301
NY	340	589	959	1,373	1,919	2,429	3,097	3,880,735	4,382,759	5,082,871	6,003,174	7,268,894	9,113,614
NC	394	478	556	639	736	753	869	992,622	1,071,361	1,399,750	1,617,949	1,893,810	2,206,287
ND[5]	......	......	......	......	......	......	......			2,405	36,909	190,983	577,056
OH	......	45	231	581	938	1,519	1,980	2,339,511	2,665,260	3,198,062	3,672,329	4,157,545	4,767,121
OK[6]	......	......	......	......	......	......	......				258,657	790,391	1,657,155
OR[6]	......	......	......	......	......	......	12	52,465	90,923	174,768	317,704	413,536	672,765
PA	434	602	810	1,049	1,348	1,724	2,312	2,906,215	3,521,951	4,282,891	5,258,113	6,302,115	7,665,111
RI	69	69	77	83	97	109	148	174,620	217,353	276,531	345,506	428,556	542,610
SC	249	346	415	503	581	594	669	703,708	705,606	995,577	1,151,149	1,340,316	1,515,400
SD[5]	......	......	......	......	......	......	......	4,837	11,776	98,268	348,600	401,570	583,888
TN	36	106	262	423	682	829	1,003	1,109,801	1,258,520	1,542,359	1,767,518	2,020,616	2,184,789
TX	......	......	......	......	......	......	213	604,215	818,579	1,591,749	2,235,527	3,048,710	3,896,542
UT	......	......	......	......	......	......	11	40,273	86,786	143,963	210,779	276,749	373,351
VT	85	154	218	236	281	292	314	315,098	330,551	332,286	332,422	343,641	355,956
VA[7]	692	808	878	938	1,044	1,025	1,120	1,219,630	1,225,163	1,512,565	1,655,980	1,854,184	2,061,612
WA[6,8]	......	......	......	......	......	......	1	11,594	23,955	75,116	357,232	518,103	1,141,990
WV[7]	56	79	105	137	177	225	302	376,688	442,014	618,457	762,794	958,800	1,221,119
WI	......	......	......	......	......	31	305	775,881	1,054,670	1,315,497	1,693,330	2,069,042	2,333,860
WY	......	......	......	......	......	......	......		9,118	20,789	62,555	92,531	145,965
U.S.[9]	**3,929**	**5,308**	**7,240**	**9,638**	**12,866**	**17,063**	**23,192**	**31,443,321**	**38,558,371**	**50,189,209**	**62,979,766**	**76,212,168**	**92,228,531**

Note: Where possible, population shown is that of the 2000 area of the state. Members of the Armed Forces overseas or other U.S. nationals abroad are not included. Totals revised to include corrections of initial tabulated counts. (1) Totals for 1790 through 1850 are in thousands. (2) 1800 and 1810 figures are for those parts of Mississippi Territory now part of present-day states of AL and MS. (3) 1790-1810 figures for MA do not include the pop. of the district taken from MA to form the state of ME in 1820. (4) 1850 figure incl. pop. for parts of Territory of New Mexico now part of present-day states of AZ, NM, CO, and NV. 1860 figure incl. pop. in parts taken to form part of Arizona Territory in 1863. (5) 1860 figure is for Dakota Territory, which comprised the present-day states of ND and SD. 1870 and 1880 figures are for parts of Dakota Territory that became the two states in 1889. (6) 1850 pop. figure for parts of Oregon Territory taken to form part of Washington Territory in 1853 and 1859 are listed under WA. (7) 1790-1860 figures for VA do not include the pop. of areas taken from VA to form the state of WV in 1863. (8) 1860 figure incl. pop. in present-day ID and parts of MT and WY. (9) 1830 and 1840 pop. totals incl. persons (5,318 in 1830; 6,100 in 1840) on public ships in the service of the U.S. not credited to any region, division, or state.

Estimated Population of American Colonies, 1630-1780

Source: U.S. Census Bureau, U.S. Dept. of Commerce
(numbers in thousands)

Colony	1630	1650	1670	1690	1700	1720	1740	1750	1770	1780
Total	4.6	50.4	111.9	210.4	250.9	466.2	905.6	1,170.8	2,148.1	2,780.4
Maine (counties)[1]	0.4	1.0	...	...	...	...	...	...	31.3	49.1
New Hampshire[2]	0.5	1.3	1.8	4.2	5.0	9.4	23.3	27.5	62.4	87.8
Vermont[3]	...	...	...	...	...	...	...	...	10.0	47.6
Plymouth and Massachusetts[1,2,4]	0.9	15.6	35.3	56.9	55.9	91.0	151.6	188.0	235.3	268.6
Rhode Island[2]	...	0.8	2.2	4.2	5.9	11.7	25.3	33.2	58.2	52.9
Connecticut[2]	...	4.1	12.6	21.6	26.0	58.8	89.6	111.3	183.9	206.7
New York[2]	0.4	4.1	5.8	13.9	19.1	36.9	63.7	76.7	162.9	210.5
New Jersey[2]	...	...	1.0	8.0	14.0	29.8	51.4	71.4	117.4	139.6
Pennsylvania[2]	...	...	...	11.4	18.0	31.0	85.6	119.7	240.1	327.3
Delaware[2]	...	0.2	0.7	1.5	2.5	5.4	19.9	28.7	35.5	45.4
Maryland[2]	...	4.5	13.2	24.0	29.6	66.1	116.1	141.1	202.6	245.5
Virginia[2]	2.5	18.7	35.3	53.0	58.6	87.8	180.4	231.0	447.0	538.0
North Carolina[2]	...	...	3.9	7.6	10.7	21.3	51.8	73.0	197.2	270.1
South Carolina[2]	...	...	0.2	3.9	5.7	17.0	45.0	64.0	124.2	180.0
Georgia[2]	...	...	...	...	...	...	...	2.0	23.4	56.1
Kentucky[5]	...	...	...	...	...	...	...	...	15.7	45.0
Tennessee[6]	...	...	...	...	...	...	...	...	1.0	10.0

(1) For 1660-1750, Maine counties are included with Massachusetts. Maine was part of Massachusetts until it became a separate state in 1820. (2) One of the original 13 states. (3) Admitted to statehood in 1791. (4) Plymouth became a part of the Province of Massachusetts in 1691. (5) Admitted to statehood in 1792. (6) Admitted to statehood in 1796.

Census, 1790-2000
U.S. Dept. of Commerce

1920	1930	1940	1950	1960	1970	1980	1990	2000	State
2,348,174	2,646,248	2,832,961	3,061,743	3,266,740	3,444,165	3,893,888	4,040,587	4,447,100	AL
55,036	59,278	72,524	128,643	226,167	300,382	401,851	550,043	626,932	AK
334,162	435,573	499,261	749,587	1,302,161	1,770,900	2,718,215	3,665,228	5,130,632	AZ
1,752,204	1,854,482	1,949,387	1,909,511	1,786,272	1,923,295	2,286,435	2,350,725	2,673,400	AR
3,426,861	5,677,251	6,907,387	10,586,223	15,717,204	19,953,134	23,667,902	29,760,021	33,871,648	CA
939,629	1,035,791	1,123,296	1,325,089	1,753,947	2,207,259	2,889,964	3,294,394	4,301,261	CO
1,380,631	1,606,903	1,709,242	2,007,280	2,535,234	3,031,709	3,107,576	3,287,116	3,405,565	CT
223,003	238,380	266,505	318,085	446,292	548,104	594,338	666,168	783,600	DE
437,571	486,869	663,091	802,178	763,956	756,510	638,333	606,900	572,059	DC
968,470	1,468,211	1,897,414	2,771,305	4,951,560	6,789,443	9,746,324	12,937,926	15,982,378	FL
2,895,832	2,908,506	3,123,723	3,444,578	3,943,116	4,589,575	5,463,105	6,478,216	8,186,453	GA
255,912	368,336	422,330	499,794	632,772	768,561	964,691	1,108,229	1,211,537	HI
431,866	445,032	524,873	588,637	667,191	712,567	943,935	1,006,749	1,293,953	ID
6,485,280	7,630,654	7,897,241	8,712,176	10,081,158	11,113,976	11,426,518	11,430,602	12,419,293	IL
2,930,390	3,238,503	3,427,796	3,934,224	4,662,498	5,193,669	5,490,224	5,544,159	6,080,485	IN
2,404,021	2,470,939	2,538,268	2,621,073	2,757,537	2,824,376	2,913,808	2,776,755	2,926,324	IA
1,769,257	1,880,999	1,801,028	1,905,299	2,178,611	2,246,578	2,363,679	2,477,574	2,688,418	KS
2,416,630	2,614,589	2,845,627	2,944,806	3,038,156	3,218,706	3,660,777	3,685,296	4,041,769	KY
1,798,509	2,101,593	2,363,880	2,683,516	3,257,022	3,641,306	4,205,900	4,219,973	4,468,976	LA
768,014	797,423	847,226	913,774	969,265	992,048	1,124,660	1,227,928	1,274,923	ME
1,449,661	1,631,526	1,821,244	2,343,001	3,100,689	3,922,399	4,216,975	4,781,468	5,296,486	MD
3,852,356	4,249,614	4,316,721	4,690,514	5,148,578	5,689,170	5,737,037	6,016,425	6,349,097	MA
3,668,412	4,842,325	5,256,106	6,371,766	7,823,194	8,875,083	9,262,078	9,295,297	9,938,444	MI
2,387,125	2,563,953	2,792,300	2,982,483	3,413,864	3,804,971	4,075,970	4,375,099	4,919,479	MN
1,790,618	2,009,821	2,183,796	2,178,914	2,178,141	2,216,912	2,520,638	2,573,216	2,844,658	MS
3,404,055	3,629,367	3,784,664	3,954,653	4,319,813	4,676,501	4,916,686	5,117,073	5,595,211	MO
548,889	537,606	559,456	591,024	674,767	694,409	786,690	799,065	902,195	MT
1,296,372	1,377,963	1,315,834	1,325,510	1,411,330	1,483,493	1,569,825	1,578,385	1,711,263	NE
77,407	91,058	110,247	160,083	285,278	488,738	800,493	1,201,833	1,998,257	NV
443,083	465,293	491,524	533,242	606,921	737,681	920,610	1,109,252	1,235,786	NH
3,155,900	4,041,334	4,160,165	4,835,329	6,066,782	7,168,164	7,364,823	7,730,188	8,414,350	NJ
360,350	423,317	531,818	681,187	951,023	1,016,000	1,302,894	1,515,069	1,819,046	NM
10,385,227	12,588,066	13,479,142	14,830,192	16,782,304	18,236,967	17,558,072	17,990,455	18,976,457	NY
2,559,123	3,170,276	3,571,623	4,061,929	4,556,155	5,082,059	5,881,766	6,628,637	8,049,313	NC
646,872	680,845	641,935	619,636	632,446	617,761	652,717	638,800	642,200	ND
5,759,394	6,646,697	6,907,612	7,946,627	9,706,397	10,652,017	10,797,630	10,847,115	11,353,140	OH
2,028,283	2,396,040	2,336,434	2,233,351	2,328,284	2,559,229	3,025,290	3,145,585	3,450,654	OK
783,389	953,786	1,089,684	1,521,341	1,768,687	2,091,385	2,633,105	2,842,321	3,421,399	OR
8,720,017	9,631,350	9,900,180	10,498,012	11,319,366	11,793,909	11,863,895	11,881,643	12,281,054	PA
604,397	687,497	713,346	791,896	859,488	949,723	947,154	1,003,464	1,048,319	RI
1,683,724	1,738,765	1,899,804	2,117,027	2,382,594	2,590,516	3,121,820	3,486,703	4,012,012	SC
636,547	692,849	642,961	652,740	680,514	665,507	690,768	696,004	754,844	SD
2,337,885	2,616,556	2,915,841	3,291,718	3,567,089	3,923,687	4,591,120	4,877,185	5,689,283	TN
4,663,228	5,824,715	6,414,824	7,711,194	9,579,677	11,196,730	14,229,191	16,986,510	20,851,820	TX
449,396	507,847	550,310	688,862	890,627	1,059,273	1,461,037	1,722,850	2,233,169	UT
352,428	359,611	359,231	377,747	389,881	444,330	511,456	562,758	608,827	VT
2,309,187	2,421,851	2,677,773	3,318,680	3,966,949	4,648,494	5,346,818	6,187,358	7,078,515	VA
1,356,621	1,563,396	1,736,191	2,378,963	2,853,214	3,409,169	4,132,156	4,866,692	5,894,121	WA
1,463,701	1,729,205	1,901,974	2,005,552	1,860,421	1,744,237	1,949,644	1,793,477	1,808,344	WV
2,632,067	2,939,006	3,137,587	3,434,575	3,951,777	4,417,731	4,705,767	4,891,769	5,363,675	WI
194,402	225,565	250,742	290,529	330,066	332,416	469,557	453,588	493,782	WY
106,021,568	123,202,660	132,164,569	151,325,798	179,323,175	203,211,926	226,545,805	248,709,873	281,421,906	U.S.

U.S. Center of Population, 1790-2000

Source: Decennial Censuses, U.S. Census Bureau, U.S. Dept. of Commerce

The **U.S. center of population (mean)** is considered here to be the center of population gravity, or that point upon which the U.S. would balance if it were a rigid plane without weight and the population distributed thereon, with each individual assumed to have equal weight and to exert an influence on a central point proportional to his or her distance from that point.

Census year	N Lat °	′	″	W Long °	′	″	Approximate location
1790	39	16	30	76	11	12	Kent Co., MD, 23 miles east of Baltimore
1800	39	16	6	76	56	30	Howard Co., MD, 18 miles west of Baltimore
1810	39	11	30	77	37	12	Loudoun Co., VA, 40 miles northwest by west of Washington, DC
1820	39	5	42	78	33	0	Hardy Co., WV, 16 miles east of Moorefield[1]
1830	38	57	54	79	16	54	Grant Co., WV, 19 miles west-southwest of Moorefield[1]
1840	39	2	0	80	18	0	Upshur Co., WV, 16 miles south of Clarksburg[1]
1850	38	59	0	81	19	0	Wirt Co., WV, 23 miles southeast of Parkersburg[1]
1860	39	0	24	82	48	48	Pike Co., OH, 20 miles south by east of Chillicothe
1870	39	12	0	83	35	42	Highland Co., OH, 48 miles east by north of Cincinnati
1880	39	4	8	84	39	40	Boone Co., KY, 8 miles west by south of Cincinnati, OH
1890	39	11	56	85	32	53	Decatur Co., IN, 20 miles east of Columbus
1900	39	9	36	85	48	54	Bartholomew Co., IN, 6 miles southeast of Columbus
1910	39	10	12	86	32	20	Monroe Co., IN, in the city of Bloomington
1920	39	10	21	86	43	15	Owen Co., IN, 8 miles south-southeast of Spencer
1930	39	3	45	87	8	6	Greene Co., IN, 3 miles northeast of Linton
1940	38	56	54	87	22	35	Sullivan Co., IN, 2 miles southeast by east of Carlisle
1950[2]	38	48	15	88	22	8	Clay Co., IL, 3 miles northeast of Louisville
1960	38	35	58	89	12	35	Clinton Co., IL, 6½ miles northwest of Centralia
1970	38	27	47	89	42	22	St. Clair Co., IL, 5 miles east-southeast of Mascoutah
1980	38	8	13	90	34	26	Jefferson Co., MO, ¼ mile west of DeSoto
1990	37	52	20	91	12	55	Crawford Co., MO, 9.7 miles southeast of Steelville
2000	37	41	49	91	48	34	Phelps Co., MO, 2.8 miles east of Edgar Springs

(1) West Virginia was set off from Virginia on Dec. 31, 1862, and was admitted as a state on June 20, 1863. (2) Incl. Alaska and Hawaii.

Congressional Apportionment

Source: Decennial Censuses, U.S. Census Bureau, U.S. Dept. of Commerce

The Constitution, in Article 1, Section 2, provided for a census of the population every 10 years to serve as a basis for apportionment of representatives among the states. This apportionment largely determines the number of electoral votes allotted to each state.

The number of representatives each state in Congress is determined by the state's population, though each state is entitled to one representative regardless of population size. A congressional apportionment has been made after each decennial census except that of 1920. (The year above each column is the year of the census on which apportionment for the next election year is based.) Prior to 1870, $3/5$ the number of slaves were added to the total free population. Indians "not taxed" were excluded until 1940.

Under provisions of a law that became effective Nov. 15, 1941, representatives are apportioned by the method of equal proportions. In the application of this method, the apportionment is made so that the average population per representative has the least possible variation between one state and any other.

The first House of Representatives, in 1789, had 65 members, as provided by the Constitution. Of these, the largest numbers were from Virginia (10), Massachusetts (8), and Pennsylvania (8).

As the nation's population grew, the number of representatives was increased, but the total membership has been fixed at 435 since the apportionment based on the 1910 census.

State	2000	1990	1980	1970	1950	1900	1850	State	2000	1990	1980	1970	1950	1900	1850
AL	7	7	7	7	9	9	7	NE	3	3	3	3	4	6	NA
AK	1	1	1	1	1	NA	NA	NV	3	2	2	1	1	1	NA
AZ	8	6	5	4	2	NA	NA	NH	2	2	2	2	2	2	3
AR	4	4	4	4	6	7	2	NJ	13	13	14	15	14	10	5
CA	53	52	45	43	30	8	2	NM	3	3	3	2	2	NA	NA
CO	7	6	6	5	4	3	NA	NY	29	31	34	39	43	37	33
CT	5	6	6	6	6	5	4	NC	13	12	11	11	12	10	8
DE	1	1	1	1	1	1	1	ND	1	1	1	1	2	2	NA
FL	25	23	19	15	8	3	1	OH	18	19	21	23	23	21	21
GA	13	11	10	10	10	11	8	OK	5	6	6	6	6	5	NA
HI	2	2	2	2	1	NA	NA	OR	5	5	5	4	4	2	1
ID	2	2	2	2	2	1	NA	PA	19	21	23	25	30	32	25
IL	19	20	22	24	25	25	9	RI	2	2	2	2	2	2	2
IN	9	10	10	11	11	13	11	SC	6	6	6	6	6	7	6
IA	5	5	6	6	8	11	2	SD	1	1	1	2	2	2	NA
KS	4	4	5	5	6	8	NA	TN	9	9	9	8	9	10	10
KY	6	6	7	7	8	11	10	TX	32	30	27	24	22	16	2
LA	7	7	8	8	8	7	4	UT	3	3	3	2	2	1	NA
ME	2	2	2	2	3	4	6	VT	1	1	1	1	1	2	3
MD	8	8	8	8	7	6	6	VA	11	11	10	10	10	10	13
MA	10	10	11	12	14	14	11	WA	9	9	8	7	7	3	NA
MI	15	16	18	19	18	12	4	WV	3	3	4	4	6	5	NA
MN	8	8	8	8	9	9	2	WI	8	9	9	9	10	11	3
MS	4	5	5	5	6	8	5	WY	1	1	1	1	1	1	NA
MO	9	9	9	10	11	16	7								
MT	1	1	2	2	2	1	NA	**Total**	**435**	**435**	**435**	**435**	**435**	**391**	**237**

NA = Not applicable.

U.S. Slave and "Free Colored" Population, 1790, 1820, 1860[1]

Source: Decennial Censuses, U.S. Census Bureau, U.S. Dept. of Commerce

	1790 Census			1820 Census			1860 Census		
	Slaves	% slaves	Free colored	Slaves	% slaves	Free colored	Slaves	% slaves	Free colored
Northern states[2]	**40,370**	**2.1**	**33,016**	**18,001**	**0.3**	**92,351**	**18**	**0**	**225,224**
Connecticut	2,759	1.2	2,801	97	0	7,844	0	0	8,627
New Jersey	11,423	6.2	2,762	7,557	2.7	12,460	18	0	25,318
New York	21,324	6.3	4,654	10,088	0.7	29,279	0	0	49,005
Pennsylvania	3,737	0.9	6,537	211	0	30,202	0	0	56,949
Border/disputed states ..	**123,753**	**27.4**	**12,056**	**248,860**	**22.4**	**55,794**	**429,403**	**20.6**	**118,652**
Delaware	8,887	15.0	3,899	4,509	6.2	12,958	1,798	1.6	19,829
Kansas..............	—	—	—	—	—	—	2	0	625
Kentucky	11,830	16.2	114	126,732	22.5	2,759	225,483	19.5	10,684
Maryland	103,036	32.2	8,043	107,397	26.4	39,730	87,189	12.7	83,942
Missouri	—	—	—	10,222	15.4	347	114,931	9.7	3,572
Southern states	**533,774**	**35.4**	**20,301**	**1,263,780**	**37.8**	**74,381**	**3,521,110**	**34.3**	**132,760**
Alabama	—	—	—	41,879	32.7	571	435,080	45.1	2,690
Arkansas	—	—	—	1,617	11.3	59	111,115	25.5	144
Florida	—	—	—	—	—	—	61,745	44.0	932
Georgia	29,264	35.5	398	149,654	43.9	1,763	462,198	43.7	3,500
Louisiana	—	—	—	69,064	45.2	10,476	331,726	46.9	18,647
Mississippi	—	—	—	32,814	43.5	458	436,631	55.2	773
North Carolina	100,572	25.5	4,975	205,017	32.1	14,612	331,059	33.4	30,463
South Carolina	107,094	43.0	1,801	258,475	51.4	6,826	402,406	57.2	9,914
Tennessee	3,417	9.5	361	80,107	18.9	2,727	275,719	24.8	7,300
Texas..............	—	—	—	—	—	—	182,566	30.2	355
Virginia..............	293,427	39.2	12,766	425,153	39.9	36,889	490,865	30.7	58,042
Total territories[3]	**—**	**—**	**—**	**6,377**	**19.3**	**4,048**	**3,229**	**1.1**	**11,434**
Total states and territories	**697,897**	**17.8**	**59,466**	**1,538,125**	**16.0**	**233,504**	**3,953,760**	**12.6**	**488,070**

(1) "Free colored" was an official Census Bureau designation in these decades. All pop. figures for slaves and free colored include both blacks and those of mixed-race background. (2) Some states had negligible slave populations that are not listed separately but are included in regional totals (relevant census years in parentheses): California (1860), Illinois (1820, 1860), Indiana (1820, 1860), Iowa (1860), Maine (1820, 1860), Massachusetts (1790, 1820, 1860), Michigan (1860), Minnesota (1860), New Hampshire (1790, 1820, 1860), Ohio (1820, 1860), Oregon (1860), Rhode Island (1790, 1820, 1860), Vermont (1820, 1860), and Wisconsin (1860). (3) Incl. Colorado (1860), Dakota (1860), the District of Columbia (1820, 1860), Nebraska (1860), Nevada (1860), New Mexico (1860), Utah (1860), and Washington (1860).

Metropolitan Area Populations, 1990-2008

Source: Population Estimates Program, Decennial Censuses, U.S. Census Bureau, U.S. Dept. of Commerce

(ranked by 2008 population counts)

Metropolitan Statistical Areas (MSAs) are defined, or delineated geographically, for federal statistical use by the Office of Management and Budget (OMB), with technical assistance from the U.S. Census Bureau. The standards used to define metropolitan areas are reviewed and revised before each decennial census. The standards currently in use were published in 2000. Geographic areas are generally redefined following a decennial census. Other Census data may be used between Census years to update area boundaries.

MSAs have at least one urbanized area of 50,000 or more inhabitants, plus an adjacent area closely integrated socially and economically with the core as measured by commuting ties. Micropolitan Statistical Areas, which are not included in the rankings below, have at least one urban cluster with a population of at least 10,000 but no more than 50,000.

About 83.9% of the total U.S. population, resided in an MSA in 2000. This number represented an increase of 28.9 mil (13.9%) since 1990. The OMB has designated 366 MSAs in the U.S. and 8 MSAs in Puerto Rico as of Nov. 2008.

		Population			Percent change	
Rank	Metropolitan Statistical Area (MSA)	2008[1]	2000	1990	2000-08	1990-2008
1.	New York-Northern New Jersey-Long Island, NY-NJ-PA	19,006,798	18,323,002	16,846,046	3.7%	12.8%
2.	Los Angeles-Long Beach-Santa Ana, CA	12,872,808	12,365,627	11,273,720	4.1	14.2
3.	Chicago-Naperville-Joliet, IL-IN-WI	9,569,624	9,098,316	8,182,076	5.2	17.0
4.	Dallas-Fort Worth-Arlington, TX	6,300,006	5,161,544	3,989,294	22.1	57.9
5.	Philadelphia-Camden-Wilmington, PA-NJ-DE-MD	5,838,471	5,687,147	5,435,550	2.7	7.4
6.	Houston-Sugar Land-Baytown, TX	5,728,143	4,715,407	3,767,233	21.5	52.1
7.	Miami-Fort Lauderdale-Pompano Beach, FL	5,414,772	5,007,564	4,056,228	8.1	33.5
8.	Atlanta-Sandy Springs-Marietta, GA	5,376,285	4,247,981	3,068,975	26.6	75.2
9.	Washington-Arlington-Alexandria, DC-VA-MD-WV	5,358,130	4,796,183	4,122,259	11.7	30.0
10.	Boston-Cambridge-Quincy, MA-NH	4,522,858	4,391,344	4,133,895	3.0	9.4
11.	Detroit-Warren-Livonia, MI	4,425,110	4,452,557	4,248,699	-0.6	4.2
12.	Phoenix-Mesa-Scottsdale, AZ	4,281,899	3,251,876	2,238,498	31.7	91.3
13.	San Francisco-Oakland-Fremont, CA	4,274,531	4,123,740	3,684,112	3.7	16.0
14.	Riverside-San Bernardino-Ontario, CA	4,115,871	3,254,821	2,588,793	26.5	59.0
15.	Seattle-Tacoma-Bellevue, WA	3,344,813	3,043,878	2,559,136	9.9	30.7
16.	Minneapolis-St. Paul-Bloomington, MN-WI	3,229,878	2,968,806	2,538,776	8.8	27.2
17.	San Diego-Carlsbad-San Marcos, CA	3,001,072	2,813,833	2,498,016	6.7	20.1
18.	St. Louis, MO-IL	2,816,710	2,698,687	2,580,720	4.4	9.1
19.	Tampa-St. Petersburg-Clearwater, FL	2,733,761	2,395,997	2,067,959	14.1	32.2
20.	Baltimore-Towson, MD	2,667,117	2,552,994	2,382,172	4.5	12.0
21.	Denver-Aurora, CO	2,506,626	2,179,240	1,650,489	15.0	51.9
22.	Pittsburgh, PA	2,351,192	2,431,087	2,468,289	-3.3	-4.7
23.	Portland-Vancouver-Beaverton, OR-WA	2,207,462	1,927,881	1,523,741	14.5	44.9
24.	Cincinnati-Middletown, OH-KY-IN	2,155,137	2,009,632	1,844,915	7.2	16.8
25.	Sacramento–Arden-Arcade–Roseville, CA	2,109,832	1,796,857	1,481,220	17.4	42.4
26.	Cleveland-Elyria-Mentor, OH	2,088,291	2,148,143	2,102,248	-2.8	-0.7
27.	Orlando-Kissimmee, FL	2,054,574	1,644,561	1,224,844	24.9	67.7
28.	San Antonio, TX	2,031,445	1,711,703	1,407,745	18.7	44.3
29.	Kansas City, MO-KS	2,002,047	1,836,038	1,636,527	9.0	22.3
30.	Las Vegas-Paradise, NV	1,865,746	1,375,765	741,368	35.6	151.7
31.	San Jose-Sunnyvale-Santa Clara, CA	1,819,198	1,735,819	1,534,274	4.8	18.6
32.	Columbus, OH	1,773,120	1,612,694	1,405,168	9.9	26.2
33.	Indianapolis-Carmel, IN	1,715,459	1,525,104	1,294,217	12.5	32.5
34.	Charlotte-Gastonia-Concord, NC-SC	1,701,799	1,330,448	1,024,690	27.9	66.1
35.	Virginia Beach-Norfolk-Newport News, VA-NC	1,658,292	1,576,370	1,450,855	5.2	14.3
36.	Austin-Round Rock, TX	1,652,602	1,249,763	846,227	32.2	95.3
37.	Providence-New Bedford-Fall River, RI-MA	1,596,611	1,582,997	1,509,789	0.9	5.8
38.	Nashville-Davidson–Murfreesboro–Franklin, TN	1,550,733	1,311,789	1,048,216	18.2	47.9
39.	Milwaukee-Waukesha-West Allis, WI	1,549,308	1,500,741	1,432,149	3.2	8.2
40.	Jacksonville, FL	1,313,228	1,122,750	925,213	17.0	41.9
41.	Memphis, TN-MS-AR	1,285,732	1,205,204	1,067,263	6.7	20.5
42.	Louisville-Jefferson County, KY-IN	1,244,696	1,161,975	1,056,156	7.1	17.9
43.	Richmond, VA	1,225,626	1,096,957	949,244	11.7	29.1
44.	Oklahoma City, OK	1,206,142	1,095,421	971,042	10.1	24.2
45.	Hartford-West Hartford-East Hartford, CT	1,190,512	1,148,618	1,123,678	3.6	5.9
46.	New Orleans-Metairie-Kenner, LA	1,134,029	1,316,510	1,264,383	-13.9	-10.3
47.	Buffalo-Niagara Falls, NY	1,124,309	1,170,111	1,189,340	-3.9	-5.5
48.	Birmingham-Hoover, AL	1,117,608	1,052,238	956,646	6.2	16.8
49.	Salt Lake City, UT	1,115,692	968,858	768,075	15.2	45.3
50.	Raleigh-Cary, NC	1,088,765	797,071	544,020	36.6	100.1
51.	Rochester, NY	1,034,090	1,037,831	1,002,410	-0.4	3.2
52.	Tucson, AZ	1,012,018	843,746	666,957	19.9	51.7
53.	Tulsa, OK	916,079	859,532	761,019	6.6	20.4
54.	Fresno, CA	909,153	799,407	667,490	13.7	36.2
55.	Honolulu, HI	905,034	876,156	836,231	3.3	8.2
56.	Bridgeport-Stamford-Norwalk, CT	895,030	882,567	827,645	1.4	8.1
57.	Albany-Schenectady-Troy, NY	853,919	825,875	809,642	3.4	5.5
58.	New Haven-Milford, CT	846,101	824,008	804,219	2.7	5.2
59.	Albuquerque, NM	845,913	729,649	599,416	15.9	41.1
60.	Omaha-Council Bluffs, NE-IA	837,925	767,041	685,797	9.2	22.2
61.	Dayton, OH	836,544	848,153	843,835	-1.4	-0.9
62.	Allentown-Bethlehem-Easton, PA-NJ	808,210	740,395	686,688	9.2	17.7
63.	Bakersfield, CA	800,458	661,645	544,981	21.0	46.9
64.	Oxnard-Thousand Oaks-Ventura, CA	797,740	753,197	669,016	5.9	19.2
65.	Worcester, MA	783,806	750,963	709,705	4.4	10.4
66.	Grand Rapids-Wyoming, MI	776,833	740,482	645,918	4.9	20.3
67.	Baton Rouge, LA	774,327	705,973	623,850	9.7	24.1
68.	El Paso, TX	742,062	679,622	591,610	9.2	25.4
69.	Columbia, SC	728,063	647,158	548,936	12.5	32.6
70.	McAllen-Edinburg-Mission, TX	726,604	569,463	383,545	27.6	89.4

(1) Population estimates are for July 1.

Population of 100 Largest U.S. Cities, 1850-2008[1]

Source: Population Estimates Program, Decennial Censuses, U.S. Census Bureau, U.S. Dept. of Commerce
(ranked by 2008 population counts)

Rank City	2008	2000	1990	1980	1970	1950	1900	1850
1. New York, NY	8,363,710	8,008,278	7,322,564	7,071,639	7,895,563	7,891,957	3,437,202	696,115
2. Los Angeles, CA	3,833,995	3,694,820	3,485,398	2,968,528	2,811,801	1,970,358	102,479	1,610
3. Chicago, IL	2,853,114	2,896,016	2,783,726	3,005,072	3,369,357	3,620,962	1,698,575	29,963
4. Houston, TX	2,242,193	1,953,631	1,630,553	1,595,138	1,233,535	596,163	44,633	2,396
5. Phoenix, AZ	1,567,924	1,321,045	983,403	789,704	584,303	106,818	5,544	...
6. Philadelphia, PA	1,447,395	1,517,550	1,585,577	1,688,210	1,949,996	2,071,605	1,293,697	121,376
7. San Antonio, TX	1,351,305	1,144,646	935,933	785,940	654,153	408,442	53,321	3,488
8. Dallas, TX	1,279,910	1,188,580	1,006,877	904,599	844,401	434,462	42,638	...
9. San Diego, CA	1,279,329	1,223,400	1,110,549	875,538	697,471	334,387	17,700	...
10. San Jose, CA	948,279	894,943	782,248	629,400	459,913	95,280	21,500	...
11. Detroit, MI	912,062	951,270	1,027,974	1,203,368	1,514,063	1,849,568	285,704	21,019
12. San Francisco, CA	808,976	776,733	723,959	678,974	715,674	775,357	342,782	34,776
13. Jacksonville, FL	807,815	735,617	635,230	540,920	504,265	204,517	28,429	1,045
14. Indianapolis, IN[2]	798,382	781,870	741,952	700,807	736,856	427,173	169,164	8,091
15. Austin, TX	757,688	656,562	465,622	345,890	253,539	132,459	22,258	629
16. Columbus, OH	754,885	711,470	632,910	565,021	540,025	375,901	125,560	17,882
17. Fort Worth, TX	703,073	534,694	447,619	385,164	393,455	278,778	26,688	...
18. Charlotte, NC	687,456	540,828	395,934	315,474	241,420	134,042	18,091	1,065
19. Memphis, TN	669,651	650,100	610,337	646,174	623,988	396,000	102,320	8,841
20. Baltimore, MD	636,919	651,154	736,014	786,741	905,787	949,708	508,957	169,054
21. El Paso, TX	613,190	563,662	515,342	425,259	322,261	130,485	15,906	...
22. Boston, MA	609,023	589,141	574,283	562,994	641,071	801,444	560,892	136,881
23. Milwaukee, WI	604,477	596,974	628,088	636,297	717,372	637,392	285,315	20,061
24. Denver, CO	598,707	554,636	467,610	492,686	514,678	415,786	133,859	...
25. Seattle, WA	598,541	563,374	516,259	493,846	530,831	467,591	80,671	...
26. Nashville-Davidson, TN[2]	596,462	545,524	510,784	455,651	426,029	174,307	80,865	10,165
27. Washington, DC	591,833	572,059	606,900	638,432	756,668	802,178	278,718	40,001
28. Las Vegas, NV	558,383	478,434	258,295	164,674	125,787	24,624	...	...
29. Portland, OR	557,706	529,121	437,319	368,148	379,967	373,628	90,426	...
30. Louisville-Jefferson, KY[2]	557,224	256,231	269,063	298,694	361,706	369,129	204,731	43,194
31. Oklahoma City, OK	551,789	506,132	444,719	404,014	368,164	243,504	10,037	...
32. Tucson, AZ	541,811	486,699	405,390	330,537	262,933	45,454	7,531	...
33. Atlanta, GA	537,958	416,474	394,017	425,022	495,039	331,314	89,872	2,572
34. Albuquerque, NM	521,999	448,607	384,736	332,920	244,501	96,815	6,238	...
35. Fresno, CA	476,050	427,652	354,202	217,491	165,655	91,669	12,470	...
36. Sacramento, CA	463,794	407,018	369,365	275,741	257,105	137,572	29,282	6,820
37. Long Beach, CA	463,789	461,522	429,433	361,498	358,879	250,767	2,252	...
38. Mesa, AZ	463,552	396,375	288,091	152,404	63,049	16,790	722	...
39. Kansas City, MO	451,572	441,545	435,146	448,028	507,330	456,622	163,752	...
40. Omaha, NE	438,646	390,007	335,795	313,939	346,929	251,117	102,555	...
41. Cleveland, OH	433,748	478,403	505,616	573,822	750,879	914,808	381,768	17,034
42. Virginia Beach, VA	433,746	425,257	393,069	262,199	172,106	5,390	...	...
43. Miami, FL	413,201	362,470	358,548	346,681	334,859	249,276	1,681	...
44. Oakland, CA	404,155	399,484	372,242	339,337	361,561	384,575	66,960	...
45. Raleigh, NC	392,552	276,093	207,951	150,255	122,830	65,679	13,643	4,518
46. Tulsa, OK	385,635	393,049	367,302	360,919	330,350	182,740	1,390	...
47. Minneapolis, MN	382,605	382,618	368,383	370,951	434,400	521,718	202,718	...
48. Colorado Springs, CO	380,307	360,890	281,140	215,105	135,517	45,472	21,085	...
49. Honolulu, HI[3]	374,676	371,657	365,272	365,048	324,871	248,034	39,306	...
50. Arlington, TX	374,417	332,969	261,721	160,113	90,229	7,692	1,079	...
51. Wichita, KS	366,046	344,284	304,011	279,838	276,554	168,279	24,671	...
52. St. Louis, MO	354,361	348,189	396,685	452,801	622,236	856,796	575,238	77,860
53. Tampa, FL	340,882	303,447	280,015	271,577	277,714	124,681	15,839	...
54. Santa Ana, CA	339,130	337,977	293,742	204,023	155,710	45,533	4,933	...
55. Anaheim, CA	335,288	328,014	266,406	219,494	166,408	14,556	1,456	...
56. Cincinnati, OH	333,336	331,285	364,040	385,409	453,514	503,998	325,902	115,435
57. Bakersfield, CA	321,078	247,057	174,820	105,611	69,515	34,784	4,836	...
58. Aurora, CO	319,057	276,393	222,103	158,588	74,974	11,421	202	...
59. New Orleans, LA	311,853	484,674	496,938	557,927	593,471	570,445	287,104	116,375
60. Pittsburgh, PA	310,037	334,563	369,879	423,959	520,089	676,806	321,616	46,601
61. Riverside, CA	295,357	255,166	226,505	170,591	140,089	46,764	7,973	...
62. Toledo, OH	293,201	313,619	332,943	354,635	383,062	303,616	131,822	3,829
63. Stockton, CA	287,037	243,771	210,943	148,283	109,963	70,853	17,506	...
64. Corpus Christi, TX	286,462	277,454	257,453	232,134	204,525	108,287	4,703	...
65. Lexington-Fayette, KY	282,114	260,512	225,366	204,165	108,137	55,534	26,369	8,159
66. St. Paul, MN	279,590	287,151	272,235	270,230	309,866	311,349	163,065	1,112
67. Anchorage, AK	279,243	260,283	226,338	174,431	48,081	11,254	...	...
68. Newark, NJ	278,980	273,546	275,221	329,248	381,930	438,776	246,070	38,894
69. Buffalo, NY	270,919	292,648	328,123	357,870	462,768	580,132	352,387	42,261
70. Plano, TX	267,480	222,030	128,713	72,331	17,872	2,126	1,304	...
71. Henderson, NV	252,064	175,381	64,942	23,376	16,400	5,717	...	...
72. Lincoln, NE	251,624	225,581	191,972	171,932	149,518	98,884	40,169	...
73. Fort Wayne, IN	251,591	205,727	173,072	172,391	178,269	133,607	45,115	4,282
74. Glendale, AZ	251,522	218,812	148,134	96,988	36,228	8,179	...	...
75. Greensboro, NC	250,642	223,891	183,521	155,642	144,076	74,389	10,035	...
76. Chandler, AZ	247,140	176,581	89,862	29,673	13,763	3,799	...	...
77. St. Petersburg, FL	245,314	248,232	238,629	238,647	216,159	96,738	1,575	...
78. Jersey City, NJ	241,114	240,055	228,537	223,532	260,350	299,017	206,433	6,856
79. Scottsdale, AZ	235,371	202,705	130,069	88,364	67,823	2,032	...	...
80. Norfolk, VA	234,220	234,403	261,229	266,979	307,951	213,513	46,624	14,326

Rank City	2008	2000	1990	1980	1970	1950	1900	1850
81. Madison, WI	231,916	208,054	191,262	170,616	171,809	96,056	19,164	1,525
82. Orlando, FL	230,519	185,951	164,693	128,394	99,006	52,367	2,481	...
83. Birmingham, AL	228,798	242,820	265,968	284,413	300,910	326,037	38,415	...
84. Baton Rouge, LA	223,689	227,818	219,531	220,394	165,921	125,629	11,269	3,905
85. Durham, NC	223,284	187,035	136,611	100,831	95,438	71,311	6,679	...
86. Laredo, TX	221,659	176,576	122,899	91,449	69,024	51,910	13,429	...
87. Lubbock, TX	220,483	199,564	186,206	174,361	149,101	71,747	...	...
88. Chesapeake, VA	220,111	199,184	151,976	114,486	89,580	...	...	...
89. Chula Vista, CA	219,318	173,556	135,163	83,927	67,901	31,339	...	...
90. Garland, TX	218,577	215,768	180,650	138,857	81,437	10,571	819	...
91. Winston-Salem, NC ...	217,600	185,776	143,485	131,885	133,683	87,811	13,650	...
92. North Las Vegas, NV ..	217,253	115,488	47,707	42,739	46,067	...	...	...
93. Reno, NV	217,016	180,480	134,230	100,756	72,863	32,497	4,500	...
94. Gilbert, AZ	216,449	109,697	29,188	5,717	1,971	...	...	...
95. Hialeah, FL	210,542	226,419	188,004	145,254	102,452	19,676	...	...
96. Arlington, VA[3]	209,969	189,453	170,936	152,599	174,284	135,449	6,430	...
97. Akron, OH	207,510	217,074	223,019	237,177	275,425	274,605	42,728	3,266
98. Irvine, CA	207,500	143,072	110,330	62,134	...	...	...	...
99. Rochester, NY	206,886	219,773	231,636	241,741	295,011	332,488	162,608	36,403
100. Boise City, ID	205,314	185,787	125,738	102,249	74,990	34,393	5,957	...

(1) 2008 population estimates are for July 1. Population figures for census years 1950-2000 are for April 1; census years 1850 and 1900 are for June 1. (2) Part of a consolidated city-county government. The populations of other incorporated places within the county have been excluded from population totals shown here. For years that predate the establishment of a consolidated city-county government, city population is shown. (3) Census designated place, or CDP. Although not incorporated, CDPs are recognized as statistical equivalents for census purposes. Honolulu CDP is coextensive with Honolulu Judicial District within the city and county of Honolulu. Arlington CDP is coextensive with Arlington Co.

Largest Counties by Population, 2000, 2008

Source: Population Estimates Program, 2000 Census, U.S. Census Bureau, U.S. Dept. of Commerce
(ranked by 2008 population counts)

Rank County	2008 population[1]	2000 population[2]	% change	Rank County	2008 population[1]	2000 population[2]	% change
1. Los Angeles Co., CA	9,862,049	9,519,338	3.6%	13. Wayne Co., MI	1,949,929	2,061,162	−5.4%
2. Cook Co., IL	5,294,664	5,376,741	−1.5	14. King Co., WA	1,875,519	1,737,034	8
3. Harris Co., TX	3,984,349	3,400,578	17.2	15. Clark Co., NV	1,865,746	1,375,765	35.6
4. Maricopa Co., AZ ..	3,954,598	3,072,149	28.7	16. Santa Clara Co., CA	1,764,499	1,682,585	4.9
5. Orange Co., CA	3,010,759	2,846,289	5.8	17. Broward Co., FL ...	1,751,234	1,623,018	7.9
6. San Diego Co., CA..	3,001,072	2,813,833	6.7	18. Tarrant Co., TX	1,750,091	1,446,219	21
7. Kings Co., NY	2,556,598	2,465,326	3.7	19. New York Co., NY ..	1,634,795	1,537,195	6.3
8. Dallas Co., TX	2,412,827	2,218,899	8.7	20. Bexar Co., TX	1,622,899	1,392,931	16.5
9. Miami-Dade Co., FL	2,398,245	2,253,362	6.4	21. Suffolk Co., NY	1,512,224	1,419,369	6.5
10. Queens Co., NY	2,293,007	2,229,379	2.9	22. Middlesex Co., MA	1,482,478	1,465,396	1.2
11. Riverside Co., CA...	2,100,516	1,545,387	35.9	23. Alameda Co., CA...	1,474,368	1,443,741	2.1
12. San Bernardino Co., CA	2,015,355	1,709,434	17.9	24. Philadelphia Co., PA	1,447,395	1,517,550	−4.6
				25. Sacramento Co., CA	1,394,154	1,223,499	13.9

Note: 10 smallest counties by mid-year 2008 population estimates: Loving Co., TX (42); Kalawao Co., HI (117); King Co., TX (281); Arthur Co., NE (338); Kenedy Co., TX (388); Blaine Co., NE (428); Petroleum Co., MT (436); McPherson Co., NE (514); San Juan Co., CO (552); Thomas Co., NE (583). (1) Population estimates are for July 1. (2) Census population figures are for April 1.

Mobility, by Selected Characteristics, 2007-08

Source: Annual Social and Economic Supplement, Current Population Survey, U.S. Census Bureau, U.S. Dept. of Commerce
(numbers in thousands)

	Total	Location of new residence Same county	Diff. county, same state	Diff. state	Abroad		Total	Location of new residence Same county	Diff. county, same state	Diff. state	Abroad
Age						**Marital status[1]**					
Ages 1 to 14..........	7,613	5,345	1,124	944	200	Married, spouse present	9,292	5,567	1,781	1,542	402
Ages 15 and older	27,554	17,668	5,158	3,783	945	Married, spouse absent	656	385	87	105	79
Ages 25 and older	19,555	12,395	3,706	2,800	654	Widowed	731	448	154	117	12
Ages 65 and older	1,361	767	321	223	50	Divorced	3,237	2,232	580	377	48
						Separated	1,155	861	179	101	14
Income[1]						Never married	12,485	8,175	2,377	1,543	390
Without income	3,736	2,372	564	438	362	**Educational attainment[2]**					
Under $5,000 or loss ...	2,435	1,423	468	430	114	Not high school graduate	3,069	2,247	470	254	98
$5,000 to $9,999	2,624	1,821	408	321	74	High school graduate ..	5,773	3,842	1,074	712	145
$10,000 to $19,999	5,138	3,419	901	680	138	Some college or associate degree....	5,158	3,319	1,020	707	112
$20,000 to $29,999	4,239	2,851	800	523	65	Bachelor's degree	3,681	2,072	760	667	182
$30,000 to $39,999	3,305	2,190	701	364	50	Prof. or graduate degree	1,875	913	383	461	118
$40,000 to $49,999	1,976	1,223	454	276	23	**Ownership status**					
$50,000 to $59,999	1,331	802	289	205	35	In owner-occupied unit	11,158	6,850	2,306	1,719	283
$60,000 to $74,999	1,064	626	241	172	25	In renter-occupied unit[3]	24,011	16,163	3,976	3,009	863
$75,000 to $99,999	797	455	162	162	18	**Total movers[4].......**	**35,167**	**23,013**	**6,282**	**4,727**	**1,145**
$100,000 and over.....	910	485	171	212	42						

Note: Total movers consists of people who moved to a new residence in the 12 months preceding the March survey. Numbers may not add up totals because of rounding. (1) Ages 15 and older. (2) Ages 25 and older. (3) Includes units occupied without payment of cash rent. (4) Ages 1 and older.

U.S. Foreign-Born Population

Source: Annual Social and Economic Supplements, Current Population Surveys, U.S. Census Bureau, U.S. Dept. of Commerce

Percentage of Population That Is Foreign-Born, 1900-2007

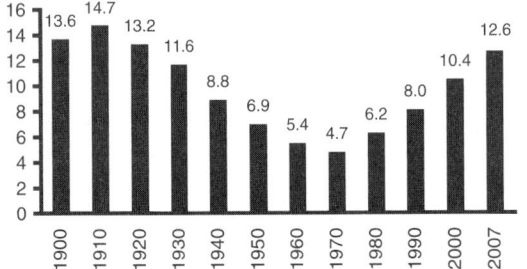

Foreign-Born Population by Regional Origin, 1995-2007
(numbers in thousands)

Region	2007[1]	%	2000	1995
Europe	4,635	12.4%	4,355	3,937
Under 18	263	18.7	250	232
Asia	9,746	26.1	7,246	6,121
Under 18	665	22.0	657	767
Latin America	20,267	54.4	14,477	11,777
Under 18	1,583	52.4	1,684	1,481
Other	2,632	7.1	2,301	2,658
Under 18	510	16.9	245	275
All Regions	**37,279**	**100.0**	**28,379**	**24,493**
Under 18	**3,021**	**100.0**	**2,837**	**2,726**

(1) Figures for Under 18 are as of 2006

Foreign-Born Population: Top Countries of Origin, 1880-2008

Source: American Community Survey, Decennial Censuses, U.S. Census Bureau, U.S. Dept. of Commerce

(numbers in thousands; % is of all foreign-born)

1880 Country	No.	%	1920 Country	No.	%	1960 Country	No.	%	2000 Country	No.	%	2008 Country	No.	%
Germany	1,967	29.4	Germany	1,686	12.1	Italy	1,257	12.9	Mexico	9,177	29.5	Mexico	11,413	30.1
Ireland	1,855	27.8	Italy	1,610	11.6	Germany	990	10.2	China[2]	1,519	4.9	China[2]	1,913	5.0
Gr. Britain	918	13.7	U.S.S.R.	1,400	10.1	Canada	953	9.8	Philippines	1,369	4.4	Philippines	1,685	4.4
Canada	717	10.7	Poland	1,140	8.2	Gr. Britain	765	7.9	India	1,023	3.3	India	1,623	4.3
Sweden	194	2.9	Canada	1,138	8.2	Poland	748	7.7	Vietnam	988	3.2	Vietnam	1,138	3.0
Norway	182	2.7	Gr. Britain	1,135	8.2	U.S.S.R.	691	7.1	Cuba	873	2.8	El Salvador	1,095	2.9
France	107	1.6	Ireland	1,037	7.5	Mexico	576	5.9	Korea[3]	864	2.8	Korea[3]	1,031	2.7
China[1]	104	1.6	Sweden	626	4.5	Ireland	339	3.5	Canada	821	2.6	Cuba	975	2.6
Switzerland	89	1.3	Austria	576	4.1	Austria	305	3.1	El Salvador	817	2.6	Canada	819	2.2
Czech.	85	1.3	Mexico	486	3.5	Hungary	245	2.5	Germany	707	2.3	Dominican Republic	772	2.0
Total	**6,680**	**100.0**	**Total**	**13,921**	**100.0**	**Total**	**9,738**	**100.0**	**Total**	**31,108**	**100.0**	**Total**	**37,961**	**100.0**

Note: Data based on sample and subject to sampling variability. (1) Includes Taiwan. (2) Includes Hong Kong and Taiwan. (3) Includes North and South Korea.

Languages Spoken at Home by the U.S. Population, 2008

Source: American Community Survey, U.S. Census Bureau, U.S. Dept. of Commerce

(ranked by numbers of speakers)

Language	Number (thous.)	% of total pop.	% English ability[1]
Total population[2]	283,149.5	100.00%	NA
Speak only English	227,365.5	80.30	NA
Speak another language[3]	55,784.0	19.70	NA
Spanish or Spanish Creole	34,559.9	12.21	46.7%
Chinese	2,465.8	0.87	56.2
Tagalog	1,488.4	0.53	32.1
French (incl. Patois, Cajun)	1,332.6	0.47	20.9
Vietnamese	1,225.0	0.43	60.2
German	1,122.0	0.40	17.7
Korean	1,051.6	0.37	58.6
Russian	864.1	0.31	51.0
Arabic	786.2	0.28	35.4
Italian	782.1	0.28	29.1
African languages	742.4	0.26	31.9
Other Asian languages	705.2	0.25	30.6
Portuguese or Portuguese Creole	661.4	0.23	40.6
Other Indic languages	652.9	0.23	38.8
French Creole	646.1	0.23	44.9
Polish	619.6	0.22	43.8
Hindi	560.1	0.20	23.0
Other Indo-European languages	446.7	0.16	37.1
Japanese	439.9	0.16	45.4
Persian	379.4	0.13%	38.5%
Other Pacific Island languages	354.8	0.13	39.7
Urdu	352.6	0.12	31.0
Greek	337.3	0.12	26.6
Gujarathi	332.8	0.12	35.5
Other Slavic languages	332.4	0.12	36.5
Other West Germanic languages	277.5	0.10	23.0
Serbo-Croatian	274.0	0.10	42.2
Armenian	231.5	0.08	43.8
Hebrew	213.0	0.08	18.9
Other Native North American languages	192.7	0.07	14.8
Hmong	189.7	0.07	48.1
Mon-Khmer, Cambodian	183.4	0.06	55.1
Navajo	170.6	0.06	26.5
Yiddish	169.2	0.06	32.8
Laotian	146.8	0.05	51.6
Thai	140.9	0.05	53.6
Scandinavian languages	133.9	0.05	12.1
Other and unspecified languages	125.5	0.04	37.9
Hungarian	93.8	0.03	28.6

NA = Not applicable or available. **Note:** Data based on sample and subject to sampling variability. (1) Speakers of other languages were asked how well they spoke English: "very well," "well," "not well," or "not at all." Figures shown here are percentage of speakers of an individual language who indicated they spoke English less than "very well." (2) 5 years and older.

Persons Granted Legal Permanent Resident Status by State of Residence, 2008[1]

Source: Office of Immigration Statistics, U.S. Dept. of Homeland Security
(ranked by fiscal year 2008 counts)

State	Number	State	Number	State	Number	State	Number
Total	1,107,126	Michigan	17,947	Kansas	5,344	New Hampshire	2,466
California	238,444	Minnesota	15,832	Kentucky	5,315	Delaware	2,295
New York	143,679	North Carolina	15,174	Oklahoma	4,306	Mississippi	1,679
Florida	133,445	Ohio	14,595	South Carolina	4,241	Maine	1,617
Texas	89,811	Colorado	12,741	Louisiana	4,011	Alaska	1,534
New Jersey	53,997	Connecticut	12,190	Alabama	3,877	Guam	1,305
Illinois	42,723	Nevada	11,768	Rhode Island	3,735	West Virginia	798
Massachusetts	30,369	Oregon	9,028	Iowa	3,696	South Dakota	773
Virginia	30,257	Tennessee	8,348	Nebraska	3,668	Vermont	771
Georgia	27,769	Indiana	8,028	New Mexico	3,509	North Dakota	662
Maryland	27,062	Wisconsin	7,306	Puerto Rico	3,287	Montana	543
Pennsylvania	23,646	Missouri	7,078	Arkansas	2,997	Wyoming	458
Washington	23,170	Hawaii	6,572	Idaho	2,766	Other[2]	1,117
Arizona	20,638	Utah	6,087	District of Columbia	2,652		

(1) Applicants for legal permanent resident (LPR) status, or "green cards," may already live in the U.S. These applicants include refugees, some temporary workers, foreign students, family members, and certain undocumented immigrants. Applicants from outside the U.S. enter the country on a visa, and are granted LPR status upon admittance. (2) Includes U.S. dependencies and armed forces posts.

Persons Granted Legal Permanent Resident Status by Top Areas of Residence, 2008[1]

Source: Office of Immigration Statistics, U.S. Dept. of Homeland Security
(ranked by fiscal year 2008 counts)

Core Based Statistical Area (CBSA)[2]	Number	% of total	Core Based Statistical Area (CBSA)[2]	Number	% of total
Total	1,107,126	100.0%	Baltimore-Towson, MD	8,217	0.7%
New York-Northern New Jersey-Long Island, NY-NJ-PA	179,981	16.3	Portland-Vancouver-Beaverton, OR-WA	7,604	0.7
Los Angeles-Long Beach-Santa Ana, CA	96,492	8.7	Austin-Round Rock, TX	5,797	0.5
Miami-Fort Lauderdale-Pompano Beach, FL	87,787	7.9	Columbus, OH	5,401	0.5
Washington-Arlington-Alexandria, DC-VA-MD-WV	42,827	3.9	Honolulu, HI	5,026	0.5
			San Antonio, TX	4,865	0.4
Chicago-Naperville-Joliet, IL-IN-WI	39,826	3.6	El Paso, TX	4,746	0.4
San Francisco-Oakland-Fremont, CA	36,120	3.3	Providence-New Bedford-Fall River, RI-MA	4,689	0.4
Houston-Sugar Land-Baytown, TX	30,514	2.8	Bridgeport-Stamford-Norwalk, CT	4,662	0.4
Dallas-Fort Worth-Arlington, TX	26,451	2.4	Fresno, CA	4,472	0.4
Boston-Cambridge-Quincy, MA-NH	24,691	2.2	Charlotte-Gastonia-Concord-Rock Hill, NC-SC	4,262	0.4
Atlanta-Sandy Springs-Marietta, GA	22,329	2.0	Oxnard-Thousand Oaks-Ventura, CA	3,884	0.4
San Jose-Sunnyvale-Santa Clara, CA	21,022	1.9	Nashville-Davidson–Murfreesboro–Franklin, TN	3,871	0.3
San Diego-Carlsbad-San Marcos, CA	20,491	1.9	Saint Louis, MO-IL	3,798	0.3
Philadelphia-Camden-Wilmington, PA-NJ-DE-MD	18,914	1.7	Kansas City, MO-KS	3,773	0.3
Riverside-San Bernardino-Ontario, CA	17,792	1.6	Hartford-West Hartford-East Hartford, CT	3,754	0.3
Seattle-Tacoma-Bellevue, WA	17,090	1.5	Salt Lake City, UT	3,668	0.3
Phoenix-Mesa-Scottsdale, AZ	14,228	1.3	Bakersfield, CA	3,524	0.3
Orlando-Kissimmee, FL	13,956	1.3	Stockton, CA	3,510	0.3
Minneapolis-St. Paul-Bloomington, MN-WI	13,372	1.2	Jacksonville, FL	3,475	0.3
Detroit-Warren-Livonia, MI	11,801	1.1	Raleigh-Cary, NC	3,432	0.3
Tampa-St. Petersburg-Clearwater, FL	10,089	0.9	Indianapolis-Carmel, IN	3,386	0.3
Las Vegas-Paradise, NV	9,507	0.9	McAllen-Edinburg-Mission, TX	3,229	0.3
Sacramento–Arden-Arcade–Roseville–Woodland, CA	9,440	0.9	Cleveland-Elyria-Mentor, OH	3,084	0.3
			Louisville-Jefferson County, KY-IN	2,977	0.3
Denver-Aurora, CO	8,408	0.8	Naples-Marco Island, FL	2,967	0.3
			Milwaukee-Waukesha-West Allis, WI	2,949	0.3

(1) Applicants for legal permanent resident (LPR) status, or "green cards," may already live in the U.S. These applicants include refugees, some temporary workers, foreign students, family members, and certain undocumented immigrants. Applicants from outside the U.S. enter the country on a visa, and are granted LPR status upon admittance. (2) CBSAs refer collectively to metropolitan and micropolitan statistical areas. These areas are defined for federal statistical use by the Office of Management and Budget, with technical assistance from the U.S. Census Bureau.

Unauthorized Immigrant Population, 2000, 2008

Source: Office of Immigration Statistics, U.S. Dept. of Homeland Security
(ranked by 2008 population counts)

Country of Birth				State of Residence			
	Est. population[1]		% change		Est. population[1]		% change
Country of birth	2008	2000	2000-08	State of residence	2008	2000	2000-08
All countries	11,600,000	8,460,000	37%	All states	11,600,000	8,460,000	37%
Mexico	7,030,000	4,680,000	50	California	2,850,000	2,510,000	14
El Salvador	570,000	430,000	35	Texas	1,680,000	1,090,000	54
Guatemala	430,000	290,000	48	Florida	840,000	800,000	5
Philippines	300,000	200,000	51	New York	640,000	540,000	19
Honduras	300,000	160,000	81	Arizona	560,000	330,000	70
Korea[2]	240,000	180,000	37	Illinois	550,000	440,000	25
China	220,000	190,000	14	Georgia	460,000	220,000	109
Brazil	180,000	100,000	72	New Jersey	400,000	350,000	14
Ecuador	170,000	110,000	50	North Carolina	380,000	260,000	46
India	160,000	120,000	29	Nevada	280,000	170,000	65
Other countries	2,000,000	2,000,000	0	Other states	2,950,000	1,760,000	68

Note: Unauthorized immigrant pop. estimates are made using the "residual" method. The estimated size of the legally resident foreign-born pop. (i.e., legal permanent residents; asylees; refugees; nonimmigrant students, temporary workers, and exchange visitors) is subtracted from the estimated size of the total foreign-born pop. Figures may not add up to totals because of rounding. (1) Pop. estimates are for January of year listed. (2) Includes North and South Korea.

U.S. Population by Age, Sex, and Household, 2008

Source: American Community Survey, U.S. Census Bureau, U.S. Dept. of Commerce

	Number	%		Number	%
Total population[1]	**304,059,728**	**100.0%**	Sex		
Age			Male.	149,863,485	49.3%
Under 5 years.	20,910,221	6.9	Female	154,196,243	50.7
5 to 14 years	40,196,100	13.2	**Total households[2]**	**113,101,329**	**100.0**
15 to 17 years	12,815,575	4.2	Family households.	75,030,551	66.3
18 to 24 years	30,107,814	9.9	2-person household	32,146,737	28.4
25 to 34 years	40,319,446	13.3	3-person household	17,112,133	15.1
35 to 44 years	42,744,592	14.1	4-person household	14,852,392	13.1
45 to 54 years	44,435,652	14.6	5-or-more-person household	10,919,289	9.7
55 to 64 years	33,718,075	11.1	Married-couple family	55,692,103	49.2
65 years and over	38,812,253	12.8	Female HH, no husband present	14,171,071	12.5
15 to 44 years	125,987,427	41.4	Male HH, no wife present	5,167,377	4.6
18 years and over	230,137,832	75.7	Nonfamily households (total HHs). . .	38,070,778	33.7
Male.	112,009,961	36.8	Householder living alone.	31,406,497	27.8
Female.	118,127,871	38.9	65 years and over.	10,631,504	9.4
75 years and over	18,646,653	6.1	2-person household	5,452,165	4.8
85 years and over	5,385,787	1.8	3-or-more-person household	1,212,116	1.1
Median age (years)	36.9	NA	Average household size	2.62	NA

NA = Not applicable. HH = Householder. **Note:** Data based on sample and subject to sampling variability. (1) Beginning in 2006, people living in group quarters (both institutional and noninstitutional, e.g., correctional facilities, military barracks, university housing) included in population universe. (2) Data limited to household population; does not include people living in group quarters.

Elderly U.S. Population, 1900-2050

Source: Decennial Censuses, Population Estimates Program, Population Projections Program, U.S. Census Bureau, U.S. Dept. of Commerce
(numbers in thousands)

	65 and over		85 and over			65 and over		85 and over	
Year	Number	% tot. pop.	Number	% tot. pop.	Year	Number	% tot. pop.	Number	% tot. pop.
1900[1]	3,080	4.1%	122	0.2%	2008[2]	38,870	12.8%	5,722	1.0%
1920[1]	4,933	4.7	210	0.2	2010[3]	40,229	13.0	5,751	1.9
1940[1]	9,019	6.8	365	0.3	2020[3]	54,804	16.1	6,597	1.9
1960	16,560	9.2	929	0.5	2030[3]	72,092	19.3	8,745	2.3
1980	25,549	11.3	2,240	1.0	2040[3]	81,238	20.0	14,198	3.5
2000	34,992	12.4	4,240	1.5	2050[3]	88,547	20.2	19,041	4.3

(1) Excludes Alaska and Hawaii. (2) Population estimate is for July 1. (3) Projections are for July 1 of the given year.

Projections of Total U.S. Population by Age, 2010-50

Source: Population Projections Program, U.S. Census Bureau, U.S. Dept. of Commerce
(numbers in thousands; % distribution may not add to totals due to overlapping categories and rounding)

	2010		2020		2030		2040		2050	
Age	No.	% distrib.	No.	% distrib.	No.	% distrib.	No.	% distrib.	No.	% distrib.
Total.	310,233	100.0	341,387	100.0	373,504	100.0	405,655	100.0	439,010	100.0
Under 5 years.	21,100	6.8%	22,846	6.7%	24,161	6.5%	26,117	6.4%	28,148	6.4%
5-14 years	41,281	13.3	45,303	13.3	48,799	13.1	51,998	12.8	56,370	12.8
15-24 years	43,549	14.0	44,353	13.0	48,914	13.1	52,909	13.0	56,593	12.9
25-34 years	41,818	13.5	46,061	13.5	47,020	12.6	51,847	12.8	56,165	12.8
35-44 years	41,277	13.3	43,664	12.8	48,223	12.9	49,545	12.2	54,696	12.5
45-54 years	44,705	14.4	41,354	12.1	44,030	11.8	48,784	12.0	50,378	11.5
55-64 years	36,275	11.7	43,003	12.6	40,266	10.8	43,216	10.7	48,111	11.0
65 years and over . .	40,229	13.0	54,805	16.1	72,094	19.3	81,239	20.0	88,548	20.2
85 years and over . .	5,751	1.9	6,597	1.9	8,746	2.3	14,198	3.5	19,042	4.3

Note: Interim projections of U.S. population consistent with Census 2000, as enumerated. Projections are for July 1, exclude Armed Forces and U.S. citizens residing outside of the U.S., and are based on middle series projections for births, deaths, and net migration.

Disability Status by Age, 2008

Source: American Community Survey, U.S. Census Bureau, U.S. Dept. of Commerce
(numbers in thousands)

Disability type	Number	% of pop.	Disability type	Number	% of pop.
Total population	**298,575**	**100.0%**	**Total population (5 and over)**	**277,667**	**100.0**
With a disability[1]	36,072	12.1	With a cognitive difficulty[2]	13,425	4.8%
5 to 17 years	2,741	0.9	5 to 17 years	2,069	0.7
Under 18 years	2,897	1.0	18 to 64 years	7,695	2.8
18 to 64 years	18,995	6.4	65 years and over	3,661	1.3
65 years and over	14,180	4.7	With an ambulatory difficulty[3]	19,189	6.9
With a hearing difficulty	10,362	3.5	5 to 17 years	365	0.1
Under 18 years	454	0.2	18 to 64 years	9,629	3.5
18 to 64 years	4,054	1.4	65 years and over	9,196	3.3
65 years and over	5,854	2.0	With a self-care difficulty[4]	7,203	2.6
With a vision difficulty.	6,781	2.3	5 to 17 years	365	0.1
Under 18 years	506	0.2	18 to 64 years	3,333	1.2
18 to 64 years	3,427	1.1	65 years and over	3,419	1.2
65 years and over	2,847	1.0	**Total population (18 and over)**	**224,788**	**100.0**
			With an independent living difficulty[5]	12,915	5.8
			18 to 64 years	6,531	2.9
			65 years and over	6,384	2.8

Note: Data based on sample and subject to sampling variability. Does not include population in the armed forces and civilian institutions (i.e., facilities in which population under formal supervision or custody). (1) Defined by the Census Bureau as the "restriction in participation that results from a lack of fit between the individual's functional limitations and the characteristics of the physical and social environment." (2) Concentrating, remembering, or making decisions. (3) Walking or climbing stairs. (4) Dressing or bathing. (5) Doing errands alone, such as visiting a doctor's office or shopping.

Marital Status of the U.S. Population[1], 1960-2008

Source: Annual Social and Economic Supplements, Current Population Surveys, U.S. Census Bureau, U.S. Dept. of Commerce

(numbers in millions; figures may not add up to totals due to rounding)

Marital status	Total				Male				Female			
	2008	2000	1980	1960[2]	2008	2000	1980	1960[2]	2008	2000	1980	1960[2]
Total	238.0	213.8	171.9	124.9	115.6	103.1	81.9	60.3	122.4	110.7	89.9	64.6
Married	128.9	120.2	104.8	84.4	64.2	59.7	51.8	41.8	64.6	60.5	53.0	42.6
Never married	71.5	60.0	44.5	27.5	38.7	32.3	24.2	15.3	32.8	27.8	20.2	12.3
Divorced	23.3	19.9	9.9	2.8	9.8	8.6	3.9	1.1	13.6	11.3	6.0	1.7
Widowed	14.3	13.7	12.7	10.2	2.9	2.6	2.0	2.1	11.4	11.1	10.8	8.1
% of total, subset pops.												
Married	54.1	56.2	61.0	67.6	55.6	57.9	63.2	69.3	52.8	54.7	58.9	65.9
Never married	30.0	28.1	25.9	22.0	33.5	31.3	29.6	25.3	26.8	25.1	22.5	19.0
Divorced	9.8	9.3	5.8	2.3	8.5	8.3	4.8	1.8	11.1	10.2	6.6	2.6
Widowed	6.0	6.4	7.4	8.1	2.5	2.5	2.4	3.5	9.3	10.0	12.0	12.5

(1) Ages 15 and older. (2) Ages 14 and older.

Living Arrangements of Children[1], 1970-2008

Source: Annual Social and Economic Supplements, Current Population Surveys, U.S. Census Bureau, U.S. Dept. of Commerce

% of children (with selected characteristic at left) living with—

Race, Hispanic origin, and year	No. of children (thous.)	Both parents[2]	Mother only—		Married spouse absent	Never remarried	Widowed	Father only	Neither parent
			Total	Divorced					
White alone[3]									
1970	58,791	90%	8%	3%	3%	Z	2%	1%	2%
1980	52,242	83	14	7	4	1%	2	2	2
1990	51,390	79	16	8	4	3	1	3	2
2000	56,455	75	17	NA	NA	NA	NA	4	3
2008	56,482	76	17	7	1	5	1	4	3
Black alone[3]									
1970	9,422	59	30	5	16	4	4	2	10
1980	9,375	42	44	11	16	13	4	28	12
1990	10,018	38	51	10	12	27	2	4	8
2000	11,412	38	49	NA	NA	NA	NA	4	9
2008	11,342	38	51	9	2	33	2	3	8
Hispanic[4]									
1970	4,006	78	NA	NA	NA	NA	NA	NA	NA
1980	5,459	75	20	6	8	4	2	2	4
1990	7,174	67	27	7	10	8	2	3	3
2000	11,613	65	25	NA	NA	NA	NA	4	5
2008	15,644	70	24	6	2	11	1	2	4

NA = Not available. Z = Less than 0.5%. (1) Under 18 years of age, not including those in group quarters and those who are a family reference person or spouse. (2) Married and not married to each other. (3) Not in combination with another race. (4) Hispanics may be of any race.

Children[1] by Presence and Type of Parent(s), 2008

Source: Annual Social and Economic Supplements, Current Population Surveys, U.S. Census Bureau, U.S. Dept. of Commerce
(numbers in thousands)

	Number	% of tot.		Number	% of tot.
Total children	74,104	100.0%	Living with one parent	19,501	26.3%
			Mother only	16,888	22.8
Living with two parents	51,785	69.9	Biological mother	16,610	22.4
Married parents	49,426	66.7	Father only	2,613	3.5
Unmarried parents	2,360	3.2	Biological father	2,524	3.4
			Living with no parents	2,818	3.8
Biological mother and father	46,427	62.7	Grandparents only	1,510	2.0
Married parents	44,376	59.9	Other relatives only	705	1.0
Biological mother and stepfather	3,183	4.3	Nonrelatives only	479	0.6
Biological father and stepmother	930	1.3	Other arrangement	124	0.2
Biological mother and adoptive father	195	0.3			
Biological father and adoptive mother	42	0.1	Living with at least 1 biological parent	69,911	94.3
Adoptive mother and father	795	1.1	Living with at least 1 stepparent	4,468	6.0
Other[2]	213	0.3	Living with at least 1 adoptive parent	1,274	1.7

(1) Excludes children living in group quarters, and those who are a family reference person or spouse. (2) Includes children living with one adoptive parent and one stepparent, or two stepparents.

Unmarried-Partner Households by Sex of Partners, 2008

Source: American Community Survey, U.S. Census Bureau, U.S. Dept. of Commerce

Household[1]	Number	% of tot.	% of cat.	Household[1]	Number	% of tot.	% of cat.
Total households	113,101,329	100.0%	NA	Female HH, female partner	294,143	0.3%	4.7%
Unmarried-partner households	6,213,542	5.5%	100.0%	Male HH, male partner	270,608	0.2	4.4
Male HH, female partner	2,903,211	2.6	46.7	All other households	106,887,787	94.5	100.0
Female HH, male partner	2,745,580	2.4	44.2				

HH = Householder. **Note:** Data based on sample and subject to sampling variability. (1) Not including people living in group quarters (both institutional and noninstitutional, e.g., correctional facilities, military barracks, university housing).

Population, by Sex, Race, Residence, and Median Age, 1790-2008

Source: Decennial Censuses, Population Estimates, U.S. Census Bureau, U.S. Dept. of Commerce

(numbers in thousands, except as indicated)

	SEX		RACE				RESIDENCE		MEDIAN AGE (years)		
				Black							
					% tot.						
	Male	Female	White	Number	pop	Other	Urban[2]	Rural	All races	White	Black
Conterminous U.S.[1]											
1790 (Aug. 2)	NA	NA	3,172	757	19.3%	NA	202	3,728	NA	NA	NA
1810 (Aug. 6)	NA	NA	5,862	1,378	19.0	NA	525	6,714	NA	16.0	NA
1820 (Aug. 7)	4,897	4,742	7,867	1,772	18.4	NA	693	8,945	16.7	16.6	17.2
1840 (June 1)	8,689	8,381	14,196	2,874	16.8	NA	1,845	15,218	17.8	17.9	17.6
1860 (June 1)	16,085	15,358	26,923	4,442	14.1	79	6,217	25,227	19.4	19.7	17.5
1870 (June 1)	19,494	19,065	33,589	4,880	12.7	89	9,902	28,656	20.2	20.4	18.5
1880 (June 1)	25,519	24,637	43,403	6,581	13.1	172	14,130	36,059	20.9	21.4	18.0
1890 (June 1)	32,237	30,711	55,101	7,489	11.9	358	22,106	40,874	22.0	22.5	17.8
1900 (June 1)	38,816	37,178	66,809	8,834	11.6	351	30,215	45,997	22.9	23.4	19.4
1920 (Jan. 1)	53,900	51,810	94,821	10,463	9.9	427	54,253	51,768	25.3	25.5	22.3
1930 (Apr. 1)	62,137	60,638	110,287	11,891	9.7	597	69,161	54,042	26.5	26.9	23.5
1940 (Apr. 1)	66,062	65,608	118,215	12,866	9.8	589	74,705	57,459	29.0	29.5	25.3
United States											
1950 (Apr. 1)	74,833	75,864	135,150	15,045	10.0	713	96,847	54,479	30.2	30.8	26.1
1960 (Apr. 1)	88,331	90,992	158,832	18,872	10.5	1,620	125,269	54,054	29.5	30.3	23.5
1970 (Apr. 1)	98,926	104,309	178,098	22,581	11.1	2,557	149,647	53,565	28.1	28.9	22.4
1980 (Apr. 1)	110,053	116,493	194,713	26,683	11.8	5,150	167,051	59,495	30.0	30.9	24.9
1990 (Apr. 1)	121,284	127,507	208,741	30,517	12.3	9,533	187,053	61,656	32.8	33.7	27.9
2000 (Apr. 1)[3]	138,054	143,368	195,575	35,704	12.7	13,716	222,361	59,061	36.5	38.6	30.0
2008 (July 1, est.)[3] . . .	149,925	154,135	199,491	39,059	12.8	17,195	NA	NA	36.8	38.2	31.4

NA = Not available. (1) Excludes Alaska and Hawaii. (2) Unlike in previous Census years, residents of urban areas (densely settled areas with 50,000 or more inhabitants) and urban clusters (densely settled areas with at least 2,500 but fewer than 50,000) were counted in the 2000 census. (3) Race data are for one race alone, not in combination with one or more other race. The category "white" does not include people who reported being white alone, of Hispanic origin. Because new race categories were introduced in the 2000 census, race data are not comparable to figures from previous years. "Other" consists of American Indians and Alaska Natives, Asians, and Native Hawaiians and other Pacific Islanders.

U.S. Population by Race and Hispanic Origin, 1990-2000

Source: Decennial Censuses, U.S. Census Bureau, U.S. Dept. of Commerce

	2000 Census		1990 Census		% change, 1990-2000[5]	
					Using one race only	Using one or more races
	One race only	One or more races[4]	Number	% of total pop.	data from 2000 Census	data from 2000 Census
Race[1,2]						
Total population	274,595,678	281,421,906	248,709,873	100.0%	10.4%	13.2%
White	211,460,626	216,930,975	199,686,070	80.3	5.9	8.6
Black or African American	34,658,190	36,419,434	29,986,060	12.1	15.6	21.5
American Indian and Alaska Native . .	2,475,956	4,119,301	1,959,234	0.8	26.4	110.3
Asian	10,242,998	11,898,828	7,273,662	2.9	40.8	63.6
Native Hawaiian and other Pac. Isl. . . .	398,835	874,414	NA	NA	NA	NA
Some other race	15,359,073	18,521,486	9,804,847	3.9	56.6	88.9
Hispanic origin and race[2]						
Hispanic or Latino (any race)	33,081,736	35,305,818	22,354,059	9.0	48.0	57.9
Not Hispanic or Latino	241,513,942	246,116,088	226,355,814	91.0	6.7	8.7
White	194,552,774	198,177,900	188,128,296	75.6	3.4	5.3
Black or African American	33,947,837	35,383,751	29,216,293	11.7	16.2	21.1
American Indian and Alaska Native . .	2,068,883	3,444,700	1,793,773	0.7	15.3	92.0
Asian[3]	10,123,169	11,579,494	6,968,359	2.8	45.3	66.2
Native Hawaiian and other Pac. Isl.[3] . .	353,509	748,149	NA	NA	NA	NA
Some other race[4]	467,770	1,770,645	249,093	0.1	87.8	610.8

NA = Not applicable. (1) Because individuals could report only one race in 1990 could report more than one race in 2000, and because of other changes in the census questionnaire, the race data for 1990 and 2000 are not directly comparable. (2) Hispanic or Latino persons may be of any race. (3) The "Asian or Pacific Islander" category was used in the 1990 Census. It was split into two categories—"Asian" and "Native Hawaiian and other Pacific Islander"—in the 2000 Census. (4) Alone or in combination with one or more of the other race categories listed. (5) Columns 5 and 6 provide, respectively, a minimum-maximum range for the percent change in population of each race between 1990 and 2000.

U.S. Population by Ancestry Reported, 2008

Source: American Community Survey, U.S. Census Bureau, U.S. Dept. of Commerce

(numbers in thousands; ranked by number self-identifying)

Ancestry reported[1]	Number	% of tot.	Ancestry reported[1]	Number	% of tot.	Ancestry reported[1]	Number	% of tot.
Total population	304,060	100.0%	Scottish	5,827	1.9%	West Indian (except		
German	50,272	16.5	Dutch	4,9296	1.6	Hispanic groups)[4]	2,532	0.8%
Irish	36,279	11.9	Norwegian	4,643	1.5	French Canadian	2,079	0.7
English	27,516	9.0	Swedish	4,390	1.4	Welsh	1,980	0.7
American	17,927	5.9	Scotch-Irish[2]	3,538	1.2	Czech	1,594	0.5
Italian	17,749	5.8	Russian	3,130	1.0	Other groups not listed		
Polish	9,887	3.3	European	3,006	1.0	here	133,269	43.8
French (except			Sub-Saharan African[3]	2,891	1.0	Unclassified or not		
Basque)	9,447	3.1				reported	35,057	11.5

Note: Data based on sample and subject to sampling variability. (1) Single ancestry or multiple ancestries with which people self-identified. Official data for race and Hispanic origin groups are not included here as they are tracked elsewhere by the Census Bureau. (2) As of 2008, people who reported Irish-Scotch ancestry are no longer classified as being "Scotch-Irish" but included instead in the "Other groups" category. (3) Incl. Cape Verdean, Ethiopian, Ghanian, Kenyan, Liberian, Nigerian, Senegalese, Sierra Leonean, Somalian, South African, Sudanese, Ugandan, Zimbabwean, African, and other sub-Saharan African. (4) Incl. Bahamian, Barbadian, Belizean, Bermudan, British West Indian, Dutch West Indian, Haitian, Jamaican, Trinidadian and Tobagonian, U.S. Virgin Islander, West Indian, and other West Indian.

Race and Minority Group Populations by Age, 2008

Source: American Community Survey, U.S. Census Bureau, U.S. Dept. of Commerce

Race/age	Number	% of race	Race/age	Number	% of race
White (not Hispanic or Latino)	**198,942,886**	**100.0%**	**American Indian and Alaska Native**	**2,443,422**	**100.0%**
Under 5 years.	11,001,726	5.5	Under 5 years	191,036	7.8
Under 18 years.	41,379,056	20.8	Under 18 years	690,965	28.3
18 to 64 years	126,350,264	63.5	18 to 64 years	1,572,057	64.3
65 years and over.	31,213,566	15.7	65 years and over	180,400	7.4
85 years and over.	4,570,411	2.3	85 years and over	16,675	0.7
Black or African American	**37,586,050**	**100.0**	**Some other race**	**14,992,188**	**100.0**
Under 5 years.	2,835,910	7.5	Under 5 years	1,594,154	10.6
Under 18 years.	10,556,005	28.1	Under 18 years	4,968,910	33.1
18 to 64 years	23,768,599	63.2	18 to 64 years	9,426,108	62.9
65 years and over.	3,261,446	8.7	65 years and over	597,170	4.0
85 years and over.	379,834	1.0	85 years and over	53,529	0.4
Asian	**13,413,976**	**100.0**	**Two or more races**.	**7,013,872**	**100.0**
Under 5 years.	854,481	6.4	Under 5 years	1,176,676	16.8
Under 18 years.	2,951,479	22.0	Under 18 years	3,400,285	48.5
18 to 64 years	9,168,105	68.3	18 to 64 years	3,293,338	47.0
65 years and over.	1,294,392	9.6	65 years and over	320,249	4.6
85 years and over.	128,097	1.0	85 years and over	32,764	0.5
Native Hawaiian or Pacific Islander	**427,810**	**100.0**	**Hispanic or Latino (any race)**.	**46,891,456**	**100.0**
Under 5 years.	30,099	7.0	Under 5 years	5,252,921	11.2
Under 18 years.	113,232	26.5	Under 18 years	16,051,868	34.2
18 to 64 years	286,426	67.0	18 to 64 years	28,209,081	60.2
65 years and over.	28,152	6.6	65 years and over	2,630,507	5.6
85 years and over.	3,144	0.7	85 years and over	264,562	0.6

Note: Data based on sample and subject to sampling variability.

Educational Attainment of the U.S. Population[1], 2008

Source: American Community Survey, U.S. Census Bureau, U.S. Dept. of Commerce

(numbers in thousands)

Race/highest schooling completed	Number	% of race	Race/highest schooling completed	Number	% of race
White (not Hispanic or Latino)	**139,290**	**100.0%**	**American Indian and Alaska Native**.	**1,455**	**100.0%**
Less than high school diploma.	13,833	9.9	Less than high school diploma	355	24.4
High school graduate[2]	40,877	29.3	High school graduate[2].	442	30.4
Some college or associate's degree	41,817	30.0	Some college or associate's degree	474	32.6
Bachelor's degree or higher.	42,763	30.7	Bachelor's degree or higher	184	12.7
Black or African-American	**22,611**	**100.0**	**Some other race**	**8,232**	**100.0**
Less than high school diploma.	4,374	19.3	Less than high school diploma	3,607	43.8
High school graduate[2]	7,110	31.4	High school graduate[2].	2,146	26.1
Some college or associate's degree	7,161	31.7	Some college or associate's degree	1,653	20.1
Bachelor's degree or higher.	3,966	17.5	Bachelor's degree or higher	825	10.0
Asian	**9,189**	**100.0**	**Two or more races**	**2,811**	**100.0**
Less than high school diploma.	1,368	14.9	Less than high school diploma	434	15.4
High school graduate[2]	1,468	16.0	High school graduate[2].	703	25.0
Some college or associate's degree	1,788	19.5	Some college or associate's degree	991	35.2
Bachelor's degree or higher.	4,565	49.7	Bachelor's degree or higher	683	24.3
Native Hawaiian or Pacific Islander	**247**	**100.0**	**Hispanic or Latino (any race)**.	**25,558**	**100.0**
Less than high school diploma.	33	13.4	Less than high school diploma	10,028	39.2
High school graduate[2]	84	33.7	High school graduate[2].	6,641	26.0
Some college or associate's degree	94	37.9	Some college or associate's degree	5,588	21.9
Bachelor's degree or higher.	37	14.9	Bachelor's degree or higher	3,300	12.9

Note: Data based on sample and subject to sampling variability. (1) Adults age 25 and older. (2) Incl. equivalency.

U.S. Population Growth by Race and Hispanic Origin, 1970-2020[1]
Source: Decennial Censuses, American Community Survey, Population Projections Program, U.S. Census Bureau, U.S. Dept. of Commerce
(figures in millions)

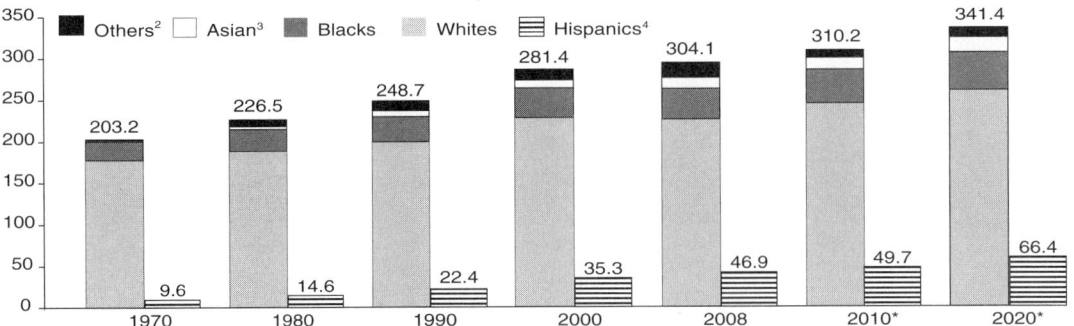

*Projected. (1) Because of changes in census questions and methods, data on race and Hispanic origin may not be wholly comparable over time. (2) Includes American Indians and Alaska Natives, and other races. From 2000 on, this category also includes Native Hawaiians and other Pacific Islanders, and persons reporting 2 or more races. (3) Figures for 1970-90 include Pacific Islanders. (4) May be of any race.

Race and Minority Groups, Percentage by State, 2008
Source: American Community Survey, U.S. Census Bureau, U.S. Dept. of Commerce

State	White (%)	Black or African American (%)	Asian (%)	American Indian and Alaska Native (%)	Native Hawaiian and other Pacific Islander (%)	Some other race (%)	Two or more races (%)	Hispanic or Latino, any race (%)
Alabama	68.4%	26.1%	1.0%	0.5%	0.02%	0.07%	1.2%	2.8%
Alaska	65.6	3.4	4.6	12.5	0.54	0.14	7.1	6.2
Arizona	58.2	3.5	2.3	4.1	0.13	0.14	1.6	30.1
Arkansas	75.6	15.5	1.0	0.5	0.06	0.07	1.7	5.5
California	42.0	5.9	12.2	0.4	0.33	0.29	2.2	36.6
Colorado	70.8	3.6	2.5	0.6	0.10	0.20	2.0	20.2
Connecticut	73.6	9.0	3.4	0.2	0.03	0.30	1.5	12.0
Delaware	68.2	20.2	2.9	0.3	0.01	0.20	1.5	6.8
District of Columbia	32.8	52.8	3.3	0.3	0.10	0.33	1.7	8.6
Florida	60.1	14.8	2.2	0.2	0.04	0.29	1.3	21.0
Georgia	57.9	29.6	2.8	0.2	0.03	0.29	1.2	7.9
Hawaii	24.8	2.3	37.6	0.1	8.57	0.08	17.8	8.7
Idaho	85.1	0.5	1.2	0.9	0.07	0.07	2.0	10.2
Illinois	64.5	14.4	4.2	0.1	0.02	0.27	1.3	15.3
Indiana	83.1	8.5	1.3	0.2	0.02	0.15	1.6	5.2
Iowa	90.2	2.5	1.5	0.2	0.05	0.08	1.2	4.1
Kansas	80.2	5.5	2.1	0.6	0.07	0.11	2.3	9.1
Kentucky	87.8	7.4	1.0	0.1	0.06	0.09	1.3	2.3
Louisiana	61.8	31.7	1.5	0.6	0.02	0.14	1.0	3.4
Maine	95.2	0.9	0.8	0.5	0.02	0.05	1.6	1.0
Maryland	57.5	28.5	5.0	0.2	0.03	0.28	1.8	6.6
Massachusetts	78.5	5.7	4.9	0.2	0.01	0.75	1.3	8.6
Michigan	77.3	13.8	2.3	0.5	0.03	0.12	1.8	4.1
Minnesota	85.3	4.4	3.5	1.0	0.01	0.11	1.6	4.1
Mississippi	58.6	37.4	0.8	0.4	0.02	0.07	0.8	2.0
Missouri	82.1	11.1	1.4	0.3	0.07	0.08	1.8	3.2
Montana	87.9	0.5	0.6	5.9	0.07	0.10	2.1	2.8
Nebraska	84.2	4.0	1.5	0.7	0.04	0.07	1.7	7.8
Nevada	57.0	7.1	5.9	1.1	0.42	0.29	2.4	25.7
New Hampshire	93.0	0.9	2.0	0.1	0.02	0.08	1.2	2.6
New Jersey	61.4	13.0	7.6	0.1	0.02	0.39	1.1	16.3
New Mexico	41.6	1.9	1.3	8.6	0.02	0.19	1.5	44.9
New York	59.7	14.7	6.9	0.3	0.03	0.50	1.2	16.7
North Carolina	67.1	21.0	1.8	1.0	0.04	0.22	1.4	7.4
North Dakota	89.8	0.9	0.8	5.2	0.01	0.03	1.2	2.0
Ohio	82.4	11.6	1.5	0.2	0.01	0.12	1.6	2.6
Oklahoma	71.3	7.1	1.7	6.2	0.09	0.09	6.0	7.7
Oregon	79.9	1.7	3.4	0.9	0.25	0.09	2.8	11.0
Pennsylvania	81.2	10.1	2.4	0.1	0.02	0.19	1.2	4.8
Rhode Island	78.4	4.7	2.8	0.4	0.03	0.75	1.3	11.6
South Carolina	65.1	27.9	1.1	0.2	0.02	0.17	1.4	4.1
South Dakota	86.0	0.9	0.8	7.9	0.01	0.17	1.8	2.4
Tennessee	77.0	16.3	1.3	0.2	0.05	0.12	1.4	3.7
Texas	47.2	11.2	3.4	0.3	0.07	0.17	1.1	36.5
Utah	81.7	1.0	1.9	1.0	0.75	0.10	1.6	12.0
Vermont	95.0	0.7	1.2	0.2	0.01	0.16	1.5	1.2
Virginia	66.8	19.3	4.8	0.2	0.05	0.22	1.8	6.8
Washington	75.3	3.3	6.4	1.2	0.43	0.26	3.4	9.8
West Virginia	93.5	3.3	0.5	0.1	0.01	0.07	1.3	1.1
Wisconsin	84.9	5.7	2.0	0.8	0.02	0.12	1.3	5.1
Wyoming	86.7	1.0	0.7	1.7	0.03	0.14	2.0	7.7
Total U.S.	**65.4**	**12.1**	**4.4**	**0.7**	**0.13**	**0.23**	**1.7**	**15.4**

Note: Data based on sample and subject to sampling variability. (1) Not Hispanic or Latino.

American Indian and Alaska Native Population, by State, 2000

Source: 2000 Census, U.S. Census Bureau, U.S. Dept. of Commerce

Rank	State	One race only[1]	More than one race[2]	Rank	State	One race only[1]	More than one race[2]
1.	California	333,346	294,216	27.	Georgia	21,737	31,460
2.	Oklahoma	273,230	118,719	28.	Virginia	21,172	31,692
3.	Arizona	255,879	36,673	29.	New Jersey	19,492	29,612
4.	New Mexico	173,483	17,992	30.	Pennsylvania	18,348	34,302
5.	Texas	118,362	97,237	31.	Arkansas	17,808	19,194
6.	North Carolina	99,551	32,185	32.	Idaho	17,645	9,592
7.	Alaska	98,043	21,198	33.	Indiana	15,815	23,448
8.	Washington	93,301	65,639	34.	Maryland	15,423	24,014
9.	New York	82,461	89,120	35.	Tennessee	15,152	24,036
10.	South Dakota	62,283	5,998	36.	Massachusetts	15,015	23,035
11.	Michigan	58,479	65,933	37.	Nebraska	14,896	7,308
12.	Montana	56,068	10,252	38.	South Carolina	13,718	13,738
13.	Minnesota	54,967	26,107	39.	Mississippi	11,652	7,903
14.	Florida	53,541	64,339	40.	Wyoming	11,133	3,879
15.	Wisconsin	47,228	22,158	41.	Connecticut	9,639	14,849
16.	Oregon	45,211	40,456	42.	Iowa	8,989	9,257
17.	Colorado	44,241	35,448	43.	Kentucky	8,616	15,936
18.	North Dakota	31,329	3,899	44.	Maine	7,098	6,058
19.	Illinois	31,006	42,155	45.	Rhode Island	5,121	5,604
20.	Utah	29,684	10,761	46.	West Virginia	3,606	7,038
21.	Nevada	26,420	15,802	47.	Hawaii	3,535	21,347
22.	Louisiana	25,477	17,401	48.	New Hampshire	2,964	4,921
23.	Missouri	25,076	35,023	49.	Delaware	2,731	3,338
24.	Kansas	24,936	22,247	50.	Vermont	2,420	3,976
25.	Ohio	24,486	51,589	51.	District of Columbia	1,713	3,062
26.	Alabama	22,430	22,019		**United States**	**2,475,956**	**1,643,345**

(1) Respondents self-identified as American Indian and Alaska Native only on the 2000 Census. (2) Respondents self-identified as American Indian and Alaska Native in combination with one or more other races.

Largest American Indian and Alaska Native Tribal Groupings, 2000

Source: 2000 Census, U.S. Census Bureau, U.S. Dept. of Commerce

Tribal grouping	American Indian and Alaska Native alone		American Indian and Alaska Native in combination with one or more races		American Indian and Alaska Native tribal grouping alone or in any combination
	One tribal grouping	More than one tribal grouping	One tribal grouping	More than one tribal grouping	
Cherokee	281,069	18,793	390,902	38,769	729,533
Navajo	269,202	6,789	19,491	2,715	298,197
Sioux	108,272	4,794	35,179	5,115	153,360
Chippewa	105,907	2,730	38,635	2,397	149,669
Latin American	104,354	1,850	73,042	1,694	180,940
Choctaw	87,349	9,552	50,123	11,750	158,774
Pueblo	59,533	3,527	9,943	1,082	74,085
Apache	57,060	7,917	24,947	6,909	96,833
Lumbee	51,913	642	4,934	379	57,868
Eskimo	45,919	1,418	6,919	505	54,761
Iroquois	45,212	2,318	29,763	3,529	80,822
Creek	40,223	5,495	21,652	3,940	71,310
Blackfeet	27,104	4,358	41,389	12,899	85,750
Chickasaw	20,887	3,014	12,025	2,425	38,351
Tohono O'odham	17,466	714	1,748	159	20,087
Inupiat Eskimo	16,047	845	2,282	191	19,365
Potawatomi	15,817	592	8,602	584	25,595
Yaqui	15,224	1,245	5,184	759	22,412
Tlingit-Haida	14,825	1,059	6,047	434	22,365
Alaskan Athabascan	14,520	815	3,218	285	18,838
Seminole	12,431	2,982	9,505	2,513	27,431
Aleut	11,941	832	3,850	355	16,978
Cheyenne	11,191	1,365	4,655	993	18,204
Puget Sound Salish	11,034	226	3,212	159	14,631
Comanche	10,120	1,568	6,120	1,568	19,376
Paiute	9,705	1,163	2,315	349	13,532
Total American Indian/Alaska Native[4]	**2,423,531**	**52,425**	**1,585,396**	**57,949**	**4,119,301**

(1) Respondents self-identified as American Indian and Alaska Native and as members of one or more tribal groupings. (2) Respondents self-identified as American Indian and Alaska Native in combination with one or more other races and as members of one or more tribal groupings. (3) Sum of preceding columns. (4) Includes tribal groupings not listed separately.

U.S. Places of 10,000 or More Population—With ZIP and Area Codes

Source: U.S. Bureau of the Census, Dept. of Commerce; NeuStar Inc.

The following is a list of places of 10,000 or more inhabitants recognized by the Bureau of the Census, U.S. Dept. of Commerce, based on July 1, 2008, Census Bureau estimates. Also given are 2000 census populations. This list includes **places that are incorporated** under the laws of their respective states as cities, boroughs, towns, and villages, as well as boroughs in Alaska and towns in the 6 New England states, New York, and Wisconsin. Townships are not included.

Places that the Census Bureau designates as **"census designated places" (CDPs)** are also included; these are marked (c). The Census Bureau does not calculate estimates for CDPs. CDP boundaries can change from one census to another, or between censuses.

This list also includes, in *italics*, **minor civil divisions (MCDs)** for Connecticut, Maine, Massachusetts, New Hampshire, Rhode Island, and Vermont. MCDs are not incorporated and not recognized as CDPs, but are often the primary political or administrative divisions of a county.

An **asterisk** (*) denotes that the ZIP code given is for general delivery; named streets and/or P.O. boxes within the community may differ; consult www.usps.com. Telephone **area codes** are given in parentheses. Some regions have 2 or more area codes intermixed (where new customers receive the newer area code); these are known as **overlays**, which are also noted. When 2 or more area codes are listed for one place, consult local operators for assistance. Area codes based on latest information as of Aug. 2009. For a listing in numerical order of specific area codes in the U.S., Canada, and the Caribbean, see Computers and Telecommunications chapter, page 370.

For some places listed, no area code and/or ZIP code is available. — = Not available.

Alabama

As of July 10, 2010, area code (938) overlays area code (256).

ZIP	Place	Area Code	2008	2000
*35007	Alabaster	(205)	29,352	22,619
*35950	Albertville	(256)	19,794	17,247
*35010	Alexander City	(256)	15,080	15,008
*36201	Anniston	(256)	23,662	24,276
*35611	Athens	(256)	23,715	18,967
*36830	Auburn	(334)	56,088	42,987
*35020	Bessemer	(205)	28,542	29,672
*35201	Birmingham	(205)	228,798	242,820
35040	Calera	(205)	10,742	3,158
*35215	Center Point (c)	(205)	15,408	22,784
*35055	Cullman	(256)	15,295	13,995
36526	Daphne	(251)	19,093	16,581
*35601	Decatur	(256)	56,068	53,929
*36301	Dothan	(334)	66,505	57,737
*36330	Enterprise	(334)	25,351	21,178
*36027	Eufaula	(334)	14,502	13,908
35064	Fairfield	(205)	11,316	12,381
*36532	Fairhope	(251)	17,147	12,480
*35630	Florence	(256)	37,877	36,264
*36535	Foley	(251)	13,807	7,590
35214	Forestdale (c)	(205)	—	10,509
*35967	Fort Payne	(256)	14,061	12,938
*35901	Gadsden	(256)	36,816	38,978
35071	Gardendale	(205)	13,665	11,626
*36542	Gulf Shores	(251)	10,248	5,044
35640	Hartselle	(256)	13,888	12,019
35080	Helena	(205)	14,639	10,296
*35209	Homewood	(205)	23,840	25,043
*35244	Hoover	(205)	71,020	62,742
*35023	Hueytown	(205)	15,751	15,364
*35801	Huntsville	(256)	176,645	158,216
36265	Jacksonville	(256)	10,077	8,404
*35501	Jasper	(205)	14,131	14,052
35094	Leeds	(205)	11,312	10,455
*35758	Madison	(256)	38,714	29,329
36054	Millbrook	(334)	16,640	10,386
*36601	Mobile	(251)	191,022	198,915
*36104	Montgomery	(334)	202,696	201,568
35004	Moody	(205)	13,400	8,053
*35223	Mountain Brook	(205)	21,061	20,604
*35661	Muscle Shoals	(256)	13,032	11,924
*35476	Northport	(205)	23,118	19,435
*35801	Opelika	(334)	26,808	23,498
36203	Oxford	(256)	20,622	14,592
*36360	Ozark	(334)	14,711	15,119
35124	Pelham	(205)	21,266	14,369
*35125	Pell City	(205)	12,841	9,565
*36867	Phenix City	(334)	31,125	28,265
35127	Pleasant Grove	(205)	10,254	9,983
*36067	Prattville	(334)	32,480	24,303
36610	Prichard	(251)	27,662	28,633
36206	Saks (c)	(256)	—	10,698
36571	Saraland	(251)	12,946	12,288
*35768	Scottsboro	(256)	14,994	14,762
*36701	Selma	(334)	18,847	20,512
*35150	Sylacauga	(256)	12,843	12,616
*35160	Talladega	(256)	16,943	15,143
*36081	Troy	(334)	15,148	13,935
35173	Trussville	(205)	18,985	12,924
*35401	Tuscaloosa	(205)	90,221	77,906
36083	Tuskegee	(334)	11,357	11,846
*35216	Vestavia Hills	(205)	30,892	24,476

Alaska (907)

ZIP	Place	2008	2000
*99501	Anchorage	279,243	260,283
*99708	College (c)	—	11,402
*99701	Fairbanks	35,132	30,224
*99801	Juneau	30,988	30,711
*99654	Wasilla	10,256	5,469

Arizona

ZIP	Place	Area Code	2008	2000
*85220	Apache Junction	(480)	32,776	31,814
85323	Avondale	(623)	81,299	35,883
*85326	Buckeye	(623)	47,261	6,537
*86442	Bullhead City	(928)	40,868	33,769
86322	Camp Verde	(928)	10,849	9,451
85704	Casas Adobes (c)	(520)	—	54,011
*85222	Casa Grande	(520)	41,152	25,224
*85225	Chandler	(480)	247,140	176,581
86323	Chino Valley	(928)	11,078	7,835
85228	Coolidge	(520)	10,261	7,786
86326	Cottonwood	(928)	11,412	9,179
86326	Cottonwood-Verde Village (c)	(928)	—	10,610
*85607	Douglas	(520)	17,515	14,312
85746	Drexel Heights (c)	(520)	—	23,849
85335	El Mirage	(623)	24,751	7,609
85231	Eloy	(520)	12,750	10,375
*86004	Flagstaff	(928)	60,222	52,894
*85232	Florence	(520)	20,781	17,054
85705	Flowing Wells (c)	(520)	—	15,050
85367	Fortuna Foothills (c)	(928)	—	20,478
*85268	Fountain Hills	(480)	25,227	20,235
*85234	Gilbert	(480)	216,449	109,697
*85301	Glendale	(623)	251,522	218,812
85338	Goodyear	(623)	59,508	18,911
*86401	Kingman	(928)	27,817	20,069
*86403	Lake Havasu City	(928)	56,553	41,938
85653	Marana	(520)	34,466	13,556
*85238	Maricopa	(520)	45,571	—
*85201	Mesa	(480)	463,552	396,375
*86440	Mohave Valley (c)	(928)	—	13,694
86401	New Kingman-Butler (c)	(928)	—	14,810
*85087	New River (c)	(623)	—	10,740
*85621	Nogales	(520)	19,573	20,878
*85737	Oro Valley	(520)	43,465	29,700
85253	Paradise Valley	(480)	14,990	13,664
*85541	Payson	(928)	15,486	13,620
*85345	Peoria	(623)	157,960	108,364
*85034	Phoenix	(602)	1,567,924	1,321,045
*86301	Prescott	(928)	42,697	33,938
*86314	Prescott Valley	(928)	38,535	23,535
85242	Queen Creek	(480)	24,361	4,316
85629	Sahuarita	(520)	22,913	3,242
85349	San Luis	(928)	24,909	15,322
*85251	Scottsdale	(480)	235,371	202,705
*86336	Sedona	(928)	11,599	10,192
*85901	Show Low	(928)	12,324	7,695
*85635	Sierra Vista	(520)	43,320	37,775
85350	Somerton	(928)	12,346	7,266
*85351	Sun City (c)	(623)	—	38,309
*85375	Sun City West (c)	(623)	—	26,344
85248	Sun Lakes (c)	(480)	—	11,936
*85374	Surprise	(623)	92,897	30,848
85749	Tanque Verde (c)	(520)	—	85,749
*85282	Tempe	(480)	175,523	158,625
*85726	Tucson	(520)	541,811	486,699
*85364	Yuma	(928)	90,041	77,515

Arkansas

ZIP	Place	Area Code	2008	2000
*71923	Arkadelphia	(870)	11,130	10,912
*72714	Bella Vista (c)	(479)	16,388	16,582
*72015	Benton	(501)	29,452	21,906
72712	Bentonville	(479)	35,526	19,730
*72315	Blytheville	(870)	16,105	18,272
*72022	Bryant	(501)	15,040	9,764
72023	Cabot	(501)	23,614	15,261
*71701	Camden	(870)	11,512	13,154
*72032	Conway	(501)	57,544	43,167
*71730	El Dorado	(870)	19,905	21,530
*72701	Fayetteville	(479)	73,372	58,047
*72335	Forrest City	(870)	13,281	14,774

ZIP	Place	Area Code	2008	2000
*72901	Fort Smith	(479)	84,716	80,268
*72601	Harrison	(870)	13,200	12,152
72342	Helena-West Helena	(870)	12,190	—
*71801	Hope	(870)	10,378	10,616
*71901	Hot Springs	(501)	39,467	35,750
*72076	Jacksonville	(501)	31,351	29,916
*72401	Jonesboro	(870)	63,960	55,515
*72201	Little Rock	(501)	189,515	183,133
*71753	Magnolia	(870)	11,081	10,858
72364	Marion	(870)	12,217	8,901
*72113	Maumelle	(501)	16,201	10,557
*72653	Mountain Home	(870)	12,592	11,012
*72114	North Little Rock	(501)	59,430	60,433
*72450	Paragould	(870)	24,800	22,017
*71601	Pine Bluff	(870)	50,408	55,085
*72756	Rogers	(479)	56,726	38,829
*72801	Russellville	(479)	27,602	23,682
*72143	Searcy	(501)	22,299	18,928
*72120	Sherwood	(501)	24,542	21,511
72761	Siloam Springs	(479)	14,825	10,843
*72764	Springdale	(479)	68,180	45,798
71854	Texarkana	(870)	30,087	26,448
*72956	Van Buren	(479)	22,543	18,986
*72301	West Memphis	(870)	27,070	27,666

California

Area code (707) overlays area code (714). Area code (747) overlays area code (818). Area code (442) overlays area code (760).

ZIP	Place	Area Code	2008	2000
92301	Adelanto	(760)	28,553	18,130
*91376	Agoura Hills	(818)	22,283	20,537
*94501	Alameda	(510)	70,580	72,259
94507	Alamo (c)	(925)	—	15,626
94706	Albany	(510)	16,004	16,444
*91802	Alhambra	(626)	85,953	85,804
92656	Aliso Viejo	(949)	41,572	—
*91901	Alpine (San Diego Co.) (c)	(619)	—	13,143
*91003	Altadena (c)	(626)	—	42,610
95127	Alum Rock (c)	(408)	—	13,479
94589	American Canyon	(707)	16,315	9,774
*92803	Anaheim	(714)	335,288	328,014
96007	Anderson	(530)	10,538	9,022
*94509	Antioch	(925)	100,219	90,532
*92307	Apple Valley	(760)	70,200	54,239
*91006	Arcadia	(626)	56,248	53,054
*95521	Arcata	(707)	17,044	16,651
95825	Arden-Arcade (c)	(916)	—	96,025
*93420	Arroyo Grande	(805)	17,180	15,851
*90701	Artesia	(562)	16,244	16,380
93203	Arvin	(661)	15,070	12,956
94577	Ashland (c)	(510)	—	20,793
*93422	Atascadero	(805)	28,452	26,411
95301	Atwater	(209)	26,565	23,113
*95603	Auburn	(530)	13,219	12,462
93204	Avenal	(559)	17,147	14,674
91746	Avocado Heights (c)	(626)	—	15,148
91702	Azusa	(626)	46,847	44,712
*93302	Bakersfield	(661)	321,078	247,057
91706	Baldwin Park	(626)	77,380	75,837
92220	Banning	(951)	28,917	23,562
*92312	Barstow	(760)	24,596	21,119
94565	Bay Point (c)	(925)	—	21,534
93402	Baywood-Los Osos (c)	(805)	—	14,351
92223	Beaumont	(951)	32,663	11,384
*90201	Bell	(323)	36,657	36,664
*90202	Bell Gardens	(213)/(323)/(562)	44,692	44,054
*90706	Bellflower	(562)	73,033	72,878
94002	Belmont	(650)	24,776	25,123
94510	Benicia	(707)	26,174	26,865
*94704	Berkeley	(510)	101,371	102,743
*90210	Beverly Hills	(213)/(310)/(323)	34,445	33,784
94526	Blackhawk-Camino Tassajara (c)	(925)	—	10,048
92316	Bloomington (c)	(951)	—	19,318
*92225	Blythe	(760)	21,727	12,155
*91902	Bonita (c)	(619)	—	12,401
92227	Brawley	(760)	22,725	22,052
*92822	Brea	(562)/(714)	38,314	35,410
*94513	Brentwood	(925)	49,480	23,302
*90622	Buena Park	(714)	79,379	78,282
*91510	Burbank (Los Angeles Co.)	(818)	102,968	100,316
*94010	Burlingame	(650)	27,706	28,158
*91372	Calabasas	(818)	22,185	20,033
*92231	Calexico	(760)	38,344	27,109
*93504	California City	(760)	14,556	8,385
*93010	Camarillo	(805)	63,324	57,077
95682	Cameron Park (c)	(530)	—	14,549
*95008	Campbell	(408)	38,617	38,138
92587	Canyon Lake	(951)	11,243	9,952
*92008	Carlsbad	(760)	96,374	78,247
*95608	Carmichael (c)	(916)	—	49,742
*93013	Carpinteria	(805)	13,655	14,194
*90745	Carson	(310)	92,366	89,730
92077	Casa de Oro-Mt. Helix (c)	(619)	—	18,874
*94546	Castro Valley (c)	(510)	—	57,292
*92235	Cathedral City	(760)	52,095	42,647
95307	Ceres	(209)	42,690	34,609
*90703	Cerritos	(562)	51,326	51,488
94541	Cherryland (c)	(510)	—	13,837
*95926	Chico	(530)	83,791	59,954
*91708	Chino	(909)	83,031	67,168
91709	Chino Hills	(909)	73,879	66,787
93610	Chowchilla	(559)	19,193	11,127
*91910	Chula Vista	(619)	219,318	173,556
91702	Citrus (c)	(626)	—	10,581
*95621	Citrus Heights	(916)	84,432	85,071
91711	Claremont	(909)	35,470	33,998
94517	Clayton	(925)	11,278	10,762
95422	Clearlake	(707)	15,040	13,142
*93612	Clovis	(559)	92,318	68,468
92236	Coachella	(760)	39,391	22,724
93210	Coalinga	(559)	18,974	11,668
*92324	Colton	(909)	50,517	47,662
90040	Commerce	(323)	13,435	12,568
*90221	Compton	(310)	93,851	93,493
*94520	Concord	(925)	121,160	121,780
*93212	Corcoran	(559)	25,139	14,458
92877	Corona	(951)	149,923	124,966
*92118	Coronado	(619)	22,633	24,100
*92628	Costa Mesa	(714)/(949)	110,080	108,724
92679	Coto de Caza (c)	(949)	—	13,057
*91722	Covina	(626)	46,944	46,837
90201	Cudahy	(323)	24,334	24,208
*90230	Culver City	(310)	38,580	38,816
*95014	Cupertino	(408)	53,637	50,546
90630	Cypress	(714)	47,123	46,229
*94015	Daly City	(415)/(650)	101,514	103,621
*92629	Dana Point	(949)	35,700	35,110
*94526	Danville	(925)	41,182	41,715
*95616	Davis	(530)	62,593	60,308
*93215	Delano	(661)	53,051	38,824
*92240	Desert Hot Springs	(760)	24,489	16,582
91765	Diamond Bar	(909)	57,235	56,287
93618	Dinuba	(559)	20,335	16,844
95620	Dixon	(707)	17,412	16,103
90239	Downey	(562)	107,587	107,323
*91009	Duarte	(626)	21,839	21,486
94568	Dublin	(925)	44,297	29,973
92343	East Hemet (c)	(951)	—	14,823
90022	East Los Angeles (c)	(323)	—	124,283
94303	East Palo Alto	(650)	33,575	29,506
91775	East San Gabriel (c)	(626)	—	14,512
*92020	El Cajon	(619)	92,718	94,869
*92244	El Centro	(760)	40,083	37,835
94530	El Cerrito	(510)	22,222	23,171
95762	El Dorado Hills (c)	(916)	—	18,016
*91734	El Monte	(626)	121,791	115,965
*93446	El Paso de Robles (Paso Robles)	(805)	28,715	24,297
90245	El Segundo	(310)	16,217	16,033
*94803	El Sobrante (c)	(510)	—	12,260
*95624	Elk Grove	(916)	133,003	—
*92024	Encinitas	(760)	60,372	58,014
*92025	Escondido	(760)	137,103	133,559
*95501	Eureka	(707)	25,300	26,128
94533	Fairfield	(707)	103,683	96,178
95628	Fair Oaks (c)	(916)	—	28,008
*92028	Fallbrook (c)	(760)	—	29,100
93223	Farmersville	(559)	10,056	8,737
*95015	Fillmore	(805)	15,053	13,643
90001	Florence-Graham (c)	(323)	—	60,197
95828	Florin (c)	(916)	—	27,653
*95630	Folsom	(916)	67,788	51,884
95841	Foothill Farms (c)	(916)	—	17,426
92610	Foothill Ranch (c)	(949)	—	10,899
*92334	Fontana	(909)	184,984	128,929
95540	Fortuna	(707)	11,329	10,497
94404	Foster City	(650)	29,089	28,803
*92728	Fountain Valley	(714)	55,516	54,978
*94537	Fremont	(510)	202,867	203,413
*93706	Fresno	(559)	476,050	427,652
*92834	Fullerton	(714)	131,868	126,003
95632	Galt	(209)	24,026	19,472
*92842	Garden Grove	(714)	165,796	165,196
*90247	Gardena	(310)	58,554	57,746
*95020	Gilroy	(408)	49,934	41,464
92509	Glen Avon (c)	(951)	—	14,853
*91209	Glendale	(818)	197,176	194,973
*91741	Glendora	(626)	49,410	49,415
*93116	Goleta	(805)	29,404	—
92324	Grand Terrace	(951)	12,204	11,626
95746	Granite Bay (c)	(916)	—	19,388
*95945	Grass Valley	(530)	12,232	10,922
93927	Greenfield	(831)	15,222	12,583

ZIP	Place	Area Code	2008	2000
93433	Grover Beach	(805)	13,131	13,067
91745	Hacienda Heights (c)	(626)	—	53,122
94019	Half Moon Bay	(650)	12,449	11,842
*93230	Hanford	(559)	50,103	41,686
90716	Hawaiian Gardens	(562)	15,229	14,779
*90250	Hawthorne	(310)/(323)	84,305	84,112
*94544	Hayward	(510)	142,061	140,030
95448	Healdsburg	(707)	10,971	10,722
92546	Hemet	(951)	70,991	58,812
94547	Hercules	(510)	24,484	19,488
90254	Hermosa Beach	(310)	19,350	18,566
*92340	Hesperia	(760)	85,883	62,582
92346	Highland	(909)	51,096	44,605
94010	Hillsborough	(650)	10,844	10,825
*95023	Hollister	(831)	34,877	34,413
*92647	Huntington Beach	(714)	192,620	189,594
90255	Huntington Park	(323)	60,898	61,348
92251	Imperial	(760)	13,648	7,560
*91932	Imperial Beach	(619)	26,543	26,992
*92201	Indio	(760)	84,443	49,116
*90301	Inglewood	(310)/(323)	112,714	112,580
*92619	Irvine	(714)/(949)	207,500	143,072
93117	Isla Vista (c)	(805)	—	18,344
93630	Kerman	(559)	12,737	8,551
93930	King City	(831)	11,627	11,094
93631	Kingsburg	(559)	11,064	9,199
*91011	La Cañada Flintridge	(818)	20,671	20,318
94549	Lafayette	(925)	25,011	23,908
95758	Laguna (c)	(916)	—	34,309
*92652	Laguna Beach	(949)	23,995	23,727
*92654	Laguna Hills	(949)	31,838	31,178
*92607	Laguna Niguel	(949)	64,469	61,891
*92654	Laguna Woods	(949)	18,170	16,507
*90631	La Habra	(562)/(949)	59,155	58,974
*92531	Lake Elsinore	(951)	50,952	28,928
92630	Lake Forest	(949)	75,566	58,707
*93535	Lake Los Angeles (c)	(661)	—	11,523
92040	Lakeside(c)	(619)	—	19,560
*90714	Lakewood	(562)	78,444	79,345
*91941	La Mesa	(619)	54,673	54,749
*90638	La Mirada	(562)/(714)	49,809	46,783
93241	Lamont (c)	(661)	—	13,296
*93539	Lancaster	(661)	145,469	118,718
90623	La Palma	(562)/(714)	15,603	15,408
91977	La Presa (c)	(619)	—	32,721
*91747	La Puente	(626)	40,642	41,063
*92253	La Quinta	(760)	43,865	23,694
95401	La Riviera (c)	(916)	—	10,273
*94939	Larkspur	(415)	11,693	12,014
95330	Lathrop	(209)	17,197	10,445
91750	La Verne	(909)	33,623	31,638
*90260	Lawndale	(310)	31,346	31,711
*91945	Lemon Grove	(619)	24,089	24,918
93245	Lemoore	(559)	23,873	19,712
90304	Lennox (c)	(310)	—	22,950
95648	Lincoln	(916)	43,602	11,205
95901	Linda (c)	(530)	—	13,474
93247	Lindsay	(559)	10,571	10,297
95062	Live Oak (Santa Cruz Co.) (c)	(831)	—	16,628
*94550	Livermore	(925)	80,188	73,345
95334	Livingston	(209)	13,400	10,473
*95240	Lodi	(209)	61,301	56,999
92354	Loma Linda	(951)	21,601	18,681
90717	Lomita	(310)	20,156	20,046
*93436	Lompoc	(805)	41,099	41,103
*90801	Long Beach	(310)/(562)	463,789	461,522
*90720	Los Alamitos	(562)/(949)	11,656	11,536
*94022	Los Altos	(650)	28,349	27,693
*90086	Los Angeles	(213)/(310)/(323)/(818)	3,833,995	3,694,820
93635	Los Banos	(209)	34,968	25,869
*95030	Los Gatos	(408)	29,320	28,592
90262	Lynwood	(213)/(310)/(323)	70,025	69,845
93250	McFarland	(661)	12,098	9,618
95521	McKinleyville (c)	(707)	—	13,599
*93638	Madera	(559)	56,700	43,207
95954	Magalia (c)	(530)	—	10,569
*90265	Malibu	(310)	13,009	12,575
*90266	Manhattan Beach	(310)	36,605	33,852
*95336	Manteca	(209)	65,028	49,258
93933	Marina	(831)	17,943	25,101
94553	Martinez	(925)	35,145	35,866
95901	Marysville	(530)	11,700	12,268
90270	Maywood	(323)	28,224	28,083
93640	Mendota	(559)	10,339	7,890
*94025	Menlo Park	(650)	30,087	30,785
*95340	Merced	(209)	77,160	63,893
94030	Millbrae	(650)	20,800	20,718
*94941	Mill Valley	(415)	13,268	13,600
*95035	Milpitas	(408)	67,503	62,698
91752	Mira Loma (c)	(951)	—	17,617
*92690	Mission Viejo	(949)	94,461	93,102
*95350	Modesto	(209)	202,967	188,856
*91017	Monrovia	(626)	37,651	36,929
91763	Montclair	(909)	36,530	33,049
90640	Montebello	(323)	61,906	62,150
*93940	Monterey	(831)	27,763	29,674
*91754	Monterey Park	(323)/(626)/(818)	61,234	60,051
*93021	Moorpark	(805)	36,372	31,415
*94556	Moraga	(925)	17,050	—
*92552	Moreno Valley	(951)	190,871	142,381
*95037	Morgan Hill	(408)	38,096	33,556
*93442	Morro Bay	(805)	10,333	10,350
*94041	Mountain View	(650)	71,348	70,708
*92564	Murrieta	(951)	97,918	44,282
*94558	Napa	(707)	74,547	72,585
*91950	National City	(619)	58,680	54,260
*94560	Newark	(510)	41,781	42,471
95360	Newman	(209)	10,226	7,093
*92658	Newport Beach	(949)	79,661	70,032
93444	Nipomo (c)	(805)	—	12,626
91760	Norco	(951)	26,659	24,157
*90650	Norwalk	(562)	102,982	103,298
95603	North Auburn (c)	(530)	—	11,847
94025	North Fair Oaks (c)	(650)	—	15,440
95660	North Highlands (c)	(916)	—	44,187
*94947	Novato	(415)	52,785	47,630
95361	Oakdale	(209)	20,299	15,503
*94617	Oakland	(510)	404,155	399,484
94561	Oakley	(925)	32,035	25,619
*92056	Oceanside	(760)	169,684	161,029
93308	Oildale (c)	(661)	—	27,885
95961	Olivehurst (c)	(530)	—	11,061
*91761	Ontario	(909)	171,691	158,007
*92863	Orange	(714)	136,392	128,821
93646	Orange Cove	(559)	10,641	7,722
95662	Orangevale (c)	(916)	—	26,705
*93457	Orcutt (c)	(805)	—	28,830
94563	Orinda	(925)	18,445	17,599
*95965	Oroville	(530)	14,684	13,004
*93030	Oxnard	(805)	185,717	170,358
94044	Pacifica	(650)	37,739	38,390
93950	Pacific Grove	(831)	14,601	15,522
*93590	Palmdale	(661)	143,197	116,670
*92260	Palm Desert	(760)	50,876	41,155
*92262	Palm Springs	(760)	47,952	42,807
*94303	Palo Alto	(650)	59,395	58,598
*90274	Palos Verdes Estates	(310)	13,585	13,340
*95969	Paradise	(530)	26,469	26,408
90723	Paramount	(562)	55,236	55,266
95823	Parkway-So. Sacramento (c)	(916)	—	36,468
93648	Parlier	(559)	13,273	11,145
*91109	Pasadena	(323)/(626)/(818)	143,080	133,936
	Paso Robles. See El Paso de Robles			
95363	Patterson	(209)	19,034	11,606
92509	Pedley (c)	(951)	—	11,207
*92572	Perris	(951)	55,643	36,189
*94952	Petaluma	(707)	54,666	54,548
*90660	Pico Rivera	(562)	63,138	63,428
*94611	Piedmont	(510)	10,481	10,952
94564	Pinole	(510)	18,808	19,039
94565	Pittsburg	(925)	64,148	56,769
*92871	Placentia	(714)	49,692	46,488
94523	Pleasant Hill	(925)	32,862	32,837
*94566	Pleasanton	(925)	66,828	63,654
*91769	Pomona	(909)	152,699	149,473
*93257	Porterville	(559)	51,830	39,615
*93041	Port Hueneme	(805)	21,478	21,845
*92064	Poway	(858)	48,858	48,044
93907	Prunedale (c)	(831)	—	16,432
92065	Ramona (c)	(760)	—	15,691
*95670	Rancho Cordova	(916)	62,265	—
*91729	Rancho Cucamonga	(909)	171,176	127,743
*92270	Rancho Mirage	(760)	16,714	13,249
90275	Rancho Palos Verdes	(310)	41,106	41,145
91941	Rancho San Diego (c)	(619)	—	20,155
92688	Rancho Santa Margarita	(949)	49,591	47,214
96080	Red Bluff	(530)	14,025	13,147
*96049	Redding	(530)	90,201	80,865
*92373	Redlands	(909)	69,689	63,591
*90277	Redondo Beach	(310)	66,882	63,261
*94063	Redwood City	(650)	74,060	75,402
93654	Reedley	(559)	23,439	20,756
*92377	Rialto	(909)	98,700	91,873
*94802	Richmond	(510)	102,285	99,216
*93556	Ridgecrest	(760)	25,638	24,927
95673	Rio Linda (c)	(916)	—	10,466
95366	Ripon	(209)	14,473	10,146
95367	Riverbank	(209)	20,606	15,826
*92502	Riverside	(951)	295,357	255,166
*95677	Rocklin	(916)	52,811	36,330
*94928	Rohnert Park	(707)	40,496	42,236
93560	Rosamond (c)	(661)	—	14,349

ZIP	Place	Area Code	2008	2000
*91770	Rosemead	(626)	54,412	53,505
95826	Rosemont (c)	(916)	—	22,904
*95678	Roseville	(916)	112,660	79,921
90720	Rossmoor (c)	(714)	—	10,298
91748	Rowland Heights (c)	(626)	—	48,553
*92519	Rubidoux (c)	(951)	—	29,180
*95814	Sacramento	(916)	463,794	407,018
95368	Salida (c)	(209)	—	12,560
*93907	Salinas	(831)	143,640	151,060
*94960	San Anselmo	(415)	11,986	12,378
*92401	San Bernardino	(909)	198,580	185,401
*94066	San Bruno	(650)	40,315	40,165
*93001	San Buenaventura (Ventura)	(805)	103,706	100,916
*94070	San Carlos	(650)	27,238	27,718
*92674	San Clemente	(949)	61,465	49,936
*92138	San Diego	(619)/(858)	1,279,329	1,223,400
91773	San Dimas	(909)	35,043	34,980
*91341	San Fernando	(818)	23,833	23,564
*94142	San Francisco	(415)	808,976	776,733
*91778	San Gabriel	(626)	40,445	39,804
93657	Sanger	(559)	25,447	18,931
*92581	San Jacinto	(951)	37,842	23,779
*95113	San Jose	(408)	948,279	894,943
*92690	San Juan Capistrano	(949)	34,793	33,826
*94577	San Leandro	(510)	77,880	79,452
*93401	San Luis Obispo	(805)	43,636	44,174
*92069	San Marcos	(760)	79,114	54,977
*91108	San Marino	(626)	12,808	12,945
*94402	San Mateo	(650)	92,256	92,482
94806	San Pablo	(510)	30,729	30,215
*94915	San Rafael	(415)	55,602	56,063
94583	San Ramon	(925)	49,161	44,722
*92711	Santa Ana	(714)/(949)	339,130	337,977
*93102	Santa Barbara	(805)	86,093	92,325
*95050	Santa Clara	(408)	110,200	102,361
*91380	Santa Clarita	(661)	169,500	151,088
*95060	Santa Cruz	(831)	56,124	54,593
90670	Santa Fe Springs	(562)	17,159	17,438
*93454	Santa Maria	(805)	86,356	77,423
*90401	Santa Monica	(310)	87,664	84,084
*93060	Santa Paula	(805)	28,618	28,598
*95402	Santa Rosa	(707)	155,796	147,595
*92071	Santee	(619)	53,860	52,975
*95070	Saratoga	(408)	30,445	29,843
*95066	Scotts Valley	(831)	11,128	11,385
90740	Seal Beach	(562)	24,127	24,157
93955	Seaside	(831)	33,797	31,696
93662	Selma	(559)	22,807	19,444
*93263	Shafter	(661)	15,800	12,736
*96019	Shasta Lake	(916)	10,192	9,008
*91025	Sierra Madre	(626)	10,834	10,578
*90806	Signal Hill	(562)	10,882	9,333
*93065	Simi Valley	(805)	120,543	111,351
92075	Solana Beach	(858)	12,825	12,979
93960	Soledad	(831)	28,124	11,263
91733	South El Monte	(626)	21,397	21,144
*90280	South Gate	(323)/(562)	96,640	96,375
*96151	South Lake Tahoe	(530)	23,333	23,609
*91030	So. Pasadena	(213)/(323)/626)/(818)	24,446	24,292
*94080	South San Francisco	(650)	62,502	60,552
91744	South San Jose Hills (c)	(626)	—	20,218
90605	South Whittier (c)	(562)	—	55,193
95991	South Yuba City (c)	(530)	—	12,651
*91977	Spring Valley (c)	(619)	—	26,663
*94309	Stanford (c)	(650)	—	13,315
90680	Stanton	(714)	37,589	37,403
*95208	Stockton	(209)	287,037	243,771
*94585	Suisun City	(707)	26,977	26,118
*92586	Sun City (c)	(951)	—	17,773
*94086	Sunnyvale	(408)	132,109	131,760
*96130	Susanville	(530)	17,336	13,541
94941	Tamalpais-Homestead Val. (c)	(415)	—	10,691
*93581	Tehachapi	(661)	11,736	10,957
*92589	Temecula	(951)	97,100	57,716
91780	Temple City	(626)	38,341	33,377
*91359	Thousand Oaks	(805)	123,091	117,005
*90503	Torrance	(310)	140,820	137,946
95376	Tracy	(209)	79,196	56,929
*96161	Truckee	(916)	16,185	13,864
*93274	Tulare	(559)	56,654	43,994
*95380	Turlock	(209)	68,404	55,810
*92781	Tustin	(714)/(949)	71,814	67,504
92705	Tustin Foothills (c)	(714)	—	24,044
*92277	Twentynine Palms	(760)	33,480	14,764
*95482	Ukiah	(707)	14,956	15,497
94587	Union City	(510)	72,123	66,869
*91785	Upland	(909)	72,091	68,393
*95687	Vacaville	(707)	92,219	88,625
91744	Valinda (c)	(626)	—	21,776
*94590	Vallejo	(707)	114,729	116,760
92343	Valle Vista (c)	(951)	—	10,488
*92393	Victorville	(760)	110,318	64,029
90043	View Park-Windsor Hills (c)	(310)	—	10,958
91722	Vincent (c)	(925)	—	15,097
95829	Vineyard (c)	(916)	—	10,109
*93291	Visalia	(559)	121,040	91,565
*92083	Vista	(760)	91,144	89,857
*91788	Walnut	(626)	30,744	30,004
*94596	Walnut Creek	(925)	63,486	64,296
90255	Walnut Park (c)	(213)	—	16,180
93280	Wasco	(661)	24,628	21,263
*95076	Watsonville	(831)	50,442	44,265
90502	West Carson (c)	(310)	—	21,138
*91790	West Covina	(626)	105,790	105,080
90069	West Hollywood	(310)/(323)	36,005	35,716
*92685	Westminster	(714)	88,975	88,207
*90047	Westmont (c)	(323)	—	31,623
91746	West Puente Valley (c)	(626)	—	22,589
*95691	West Sacramento	(916)	47,511	31,615
*90606	West Whittier-Los Nietos (c)	(562)	—	24,164
*90605	Whittier	(562)	82,267	83,680
92595	Wildomar (c)	(951)	—	14,064
90222	Willowbrook (c)	(323)	—	34,138
95492	Windsor	(707)	25,362	22,744
92040	Winter Gardens (c)	(619)	—	19,771
*95695	Woodland	(530)	54,567	49,151
*92885	Yorba Linda	(714)	65,717	58,918
*95991	Yuba City	(530)	61,226	36,758
92399	Yucaipa	(909)	49,750	41,207
*92286	Yucca Valley	(760)	20,375	16,865

Colorado

Area code (720) overlays area code (303).

ZIP	Place	Area Code	2008	2000
*80004	Arvada	(303)	107,361	102,153
*80017	Aurora	(303)	319,057	276,393
80221	Berkley (c)	(970)	—	10,743
*80908	Black Forest (c)	(719)	—	8,143
*80302	Boulder	(303)	94,171	94,673
*80601	Brighton	(303)	31,380	20,905
*80020	Broomfield	(303)	54,858	38,272
*81212	Cañon City	(719)	15,889	15,431
*80104	Castle Rock	(303)	44,369	20,224
80120	Castlewood (c)	(303)	—	25,567
*80015	Centennial	(303)	99,680	—
81222	Cimarron Hills (c)	(719)	—	15,194
81520	Clifton (c)	(970)	—	17,345
*80903	Colorado Springs	(719)	380,307	360,890
80120	Columbine (c)	(303)	—	24,095
80022	Commerce City	(303)	42,473	20,991
*80202	Denver	(303)	598,707	554,636
*81301	Durango	(970)	16,416	13,922
*80110	Englewood	(303)	32,669	31,727
80516	Erie	(303)	16,432	6,291
80620	Evans	(970)	18,842	9,514
80221	Federal Heights	(303)	11,732	12,065
80913	Fort Carson (c)	(719)	—	10,566
*80525	Fort Collins	(970)	136,509	118,652
*80701	Fort Morgan	(970)	10,539	11,034
80817	Fountain	(719)	19,669	15,197
*80401	Golden	(303)	17,321	17,159
*81501	Grand Junction	(970)	49,688	41,986
*80631	Greeley	(970)	91,492	76,930
*80111	Greenwood Village	(303)	14,230	11,035
80163	Highlands Ranch (c)	(303)	—	70,931
80127	Ken Caryl (c)	(303)	—	30,887
80026	Lafayette	(303)	25,065	23,197
*80226	Lakewood	(303)	140,989	144,126
*80126	Littleton	(303)	40,777	40,340
*80501	Longmont	(303)	85,928	71,093
80027	Louisville	(303)	19,133	18,937
*80538	Loveland	(970)	65,587	50,608
*81401	Montrose	(970)	17,989	12,344
*80233	Northglenn	(303)	33,697	31,575
*80134	Parker	(303)	43,767	23,558
*81003	Pueblo	(719)	104,951	102,121
81007	Pueblo West (c)	(719)	—	16,899
80911	Security-Widefield (c)	(719)	—	29,845
80221	Sherrelwood (c)	(303)	—	17,657
80122	Southglenn (c)	(303)	—	43,520
80751	Sterling	(970)	12,800	11,360
80027	Superior	(303)	10,549	9,011
*80229	Thornton	(303)	113,429	82,384
80229	Welby (c)	(303)	—	12,973
*80030	Westminster	(303)	107,056	100,940
*80033	Wheat Ridge	(303)	30,894	32,913
*80550	Windsor	(970)	18,058	9,896

Connecticut

As of Dec. 12, 2009, area code (745) overlays area code (203). See introductory note.

ZIP	Place	Area Code	2008	2000
06401	Ansonia	(203)	18,503	18,554
06001	Avon	(860)	17,328	15,832
06037	Berlin	(860)	20,364	18,215
06801	Bethel	(203)	18,438	18,067
06002	Bloomfield	(860)	20,727	19,587
06405	Branford	(203)	28,969	28,683
*06602	Bridgeport	(203)	136,405	139,529
*06010	Bristol	(860)	60,927	60,062
06804	Brookfield	(203)	16,657	15,664
06019	Canton	(860)	10,104	8,840
06040	Central Manchester (c)	(860)	—	30,595
*06410	Cheshire	(203)	29,066	28,543
06413	Clinton	(860)	13,554	13,094
*06415	Colchester	(860)	15,578	14,551
06340	Conning Towers-Nautilus Pk. (c)	(860)	—	10,241
06238	Coventry	(860)	12,207	11,504
06416	Cromwell	(860)	13,600	12,871
*06810	Danbury	(203)	79,256	74,848
06820	Darien	(203)	20,177	19,607
06418	Derby	(203)	12,393	12,391
*06424	East Hampton	(860)	12,685	13,352
*06108	East Hartford	(860)	48,571	49,575
*06512	East Haven	(203)	28,590	28,189
06333	East Lyme	(860)	19,022	18,118
*06088	East Windsor	(860)	10,822	9,818
06029	Ellington	(860)	14,568	12,921
*06082	Enfield	(860)	44,895	45,212
*06825	Fairfield	(203)	57,345	57,340
*06032	Farmington	(860)	25,116	23,641
06033	Glastonbury	(860)	33,263	31,876
*06035	Granby	(860)	11,219	10,347
*06830	Greenwich	(203)	61,937	61,101
06351	Griswold	(860)	11,398	10,807
06340	Groton	(860)	39,167	39,907
06437	Guilford	(203)	22,398	21,398
*06514	Hamden	(203)	57,862	56,913
*06101	Hartford	(860)	124,062	121,578
*06239	Killingly	(860)	17,826	16,472
06339	Ledyard	(860)	15,078	14,687
06443	Madison	(203)	18,803	17,858
*06040	Manchester	(860)	56,385	54,740
*06250	Mansfield	(860)	24,622	20,720
*06450	Meriden	(203)	59,186	58,244
06457	Middletown	(860)	48,030	43,167
*06460	Milford	(203)	54,136	50,594
06461	Milford	(203)	55,907	52,305
06468	Monroe	(203)	19,359	19,247
06353	Montville	(860)	19,612	18,546
06770	Naugatuck	(203)	31,931	30,989
*06050	New Britain	(860)	70,486	71,538
*06840	New Canaan	(203)	19,912	19,395
06812	New Fairfield	(203)	14,059	13,953
*06511	New Haven	(203)	123,669	123,626
*06101	Newington	(860)	29,699	29,306
06320	New London	(860)	25,891	25,671
06776	New Milford	(860)	28,338	27,121
06470	Newtown	(203)	26,737	25,031
06471	North Branford	(203)	14,374	13,906
06473	North Haven	(203)	23,961	23,035
*06856	Norwalk	(203)	83,185	82,951
06360	Norwich	(860)	36,388	36,117
06475	Old Saybrook	(860)	10,521	10,367
06477	Orange	(203)	13,781	13,233
06478	Oxford	(203)	12,734	9,821
06374	Plainfield	(860)	15,430	14,619
06062	Plainville	(860)	17,221	17,328
06782	Plymouth	(860)	11,969	11,634
06877	Ridgefield	(203)	24,011	23,643
06067	Rocky Hill	(860)	18,852	17,350
*06483	Seymour	(203)	16,251	15,454
06484	Shelton	(203)	39,991	38,101
*06070	Simsbury	(860)	23,615	23,234
06071	Somers	(860)	10,984	10,417
06488	Southbury	(203)	19,702	18,567
06489	Southington	(860)	42,250	39,728
*06074	South Windsor	(860)	25,966	24,412
*06075	Stafford	(860)	11,773	11,307
*06904	Stamford	(203)	119,303	117,083
06378	Stonington	(860)	18,371	17,906
*06268	Storrs (c)	(860)	—	10,996
*06602	Stratford	(203)	48,853	49,976
*06078	Suffield	(860)	15,136	13,552
06084	Tolland	(860)	14,705	13,146

ZIP	Place	Area Code	2008	2000
*06790	Torrington	(860)	35,312	35,202
06611	Trumbull	(203)	34,688	34,243
06066	Vernon	(860)	29,839	28,063
*06492	Wallingford	(203)	44,859	43,026
06492	Wallingford Center (c)	(203)	—	17,509
*06702	Waterbury	(203)	107,037	107,271
*06385	Waterford	(860)	18,794	19,152
06795	Watertown	(860)	22,095	21,661
*06101	West Hartford	(860)	60,495	63,589
06516	West Haven	(203)	52,420	52,360
06883	Weston	(203)	10,183	10,037
*06880	Westport	(203)	26,592	25,749
*06101	Wethersfield	(860)	25,719	26,271
06226	Willimantic (c)	(860)	—	15,823
06897	Wilton	(203)	17,698	17,633
*06094	Winchester	(860)	10,716	10,664
*06280	Windham	(860)	23,609	22,857
*06095	Windsor	(860)	28,851	28,237
06096	Windsor Locks	(860)	12,495	12,043
*06716	Wolcott	(203)	16,434	15,215

Delaware (302)

ZIP	Place	2008	2000
19701	Bear (c)	—	17,593
19713	Brookside (c)	—	14,806
*19901	Dover	36,107	32,135
19702	Glasgow (c)	—	12,840
19707	Hockessin (c)	—	12,902
19709	Middletown	12,152	6,161
*19711	Newark	29,886	28,547
19800	Pike Creek (c)	—	19,751
*19899	Wilmington	72,592	72,664

District of Columbia (202)

ZIP	Place	2008	2000
*20090	Washington	591,833	572,059

Florida

Area code (321) overlays area code (407). Area code (754) overlays area code (954). Area code (786) overlays area code (305).

ZIP	Place	Area Code	2008	2000
*32714	Altamonte Springs	(407)	39,947	41,200
*32712	Apopka	(407)	37,935	26,642
*32233	Atlantic Beach	(904)	13,147	13,368
33823	Auburndale	(863)	14,353	11,032
*33160	Aventura	(305)	29,254	25,267
32807	Azalea Park (c)	(407)	—	11,073
*33830	Bartow	(863)	16,919	15,340
34667	Bayonet Point (c)	(727)	—	23,577
33507	Bayshore Gardens (c)	(941)	—	17,350
*33756	Bellair-Meadowbrook Terrace (c)	(904)	—	16,539
33430	Belle Glade	(561)	16,681	14,906
*34420	Belleview	(352)	—	21,201
*33509	Bloomingdale (c)	(813)	—	19,839
33433	Boca Del Mar (c)	(561)	—	21,832
*33431	Boca Raton	(561)	85,670	74,764
*34135	Bonita Springs	(239)	42,730	32,797
33547	Boyette (c)	(813)	—	64,775
*33436	Boynton Beach	(561)	68,291	60,389
*34206	Bradenton	(941)	53,513	49,504
*33509	Brandon (c)	(813)	—	77,895
32503	Brent (c)	(850)	—	22,257
33317	Broadview Park (c)	(954)	—	6,798
33142	Brownsville (c)	(305)	—	14,393
32404	Callaway	(850)	13,899	14,233
32920	Cape Canaveral	(321)	10,147	8,829
*33920	Cape Coral	(239)	156,835	102,286
*33055	Carol City (c)	(305)	—	59,443
*32707	Casselberry	(407)	24,759	22,629
33624	Citrus Park (c)	(813)	—	20,226
*32966	Citrus Ridge (c)	(772)	—	12,015
*33758	Clearwater	(727)	105,774	108,787
*34711	Clermont	(352)	13,100	9,333
*32922	Cocoa	(321)	16,478	16,412
*32931	Cocoa Beach	(321)	11,920	12,482
*33097	Coconut Creek	(954)	50,436	43,566
32809	Conway (c)	(407)	—	14,394
*33328	Cooper City	(954)	29,422	27,939
*33114	Coral Gables	(305)	42,781	42,249
*33075	Coral Springs	(954)	125,783	117,549
33157	Coral Terrace (c)	(305)	—	24,380
33015	Country Club (c)	(305)	—	36,310
33196	Country Walk (c)	(305)	—	10,653
*32536	Crestview	(850)	19,444	14,766
*33157	Cutler (c)	(305)	—	17,390
33189	Cutler Bay (c)	(305)	29,070	
*33157	Cutler Ridge (c)	(305)	—	24,781
33919	Cypress Lake (c)	(239)	—	12,072
*33004	Dania Beach	(954)	28,093	—

ZIP	Place	Area Code	2008	2000
*33329	Davie	(954)	90,238	75,720
*32114	Daytona Beach	(386)	64,211	64,112
*32713	DeBary	(386)	16,303	15,559
*33441	Deerfield Beach	(954)	74,584	64,583
*32720	De Land	(386)	27,243	20,904
*33444	Delray Beach	(561)	64,092	60,020
*32783	Deltona	(407)	84,408	69,543
*32541	Destin	(850)	12,563	11,119
*33178	Doral	(305)	23,974	—
*34698	Dunedin	(727)	35,988	35,691
33610	East Lake (c)	(813)	—	29,394
*32132	Edgewater	(386)	21,415	18,668
33614	Egypt Lake-Leto (c)	(813)	—	32,782
34680	Elfers (c)	(727)	—	13,161
*34295	Englewood (c)	(941)	—	16,196
32534	Ensley (c)	(850)	—	18,752
*32726	Eustis	(352)	19,129	15,106
32804	Fairview Shores (c)	(305)	—	13,898
*32034	Fernandina Beach	(904)	11,610	10,549
32514	Ferry Pass (c)	(850)	—	27,176
32960	Florida Ridge (c)	(772)	—	15,217
32714	Forest City (c)	(407)	—	12,612
*33310	Fort Lauderdale	(954)	183,126	152,397
*33902	Fort Myers	(239)	65,394	48,208
*34981	Fort Pierce	(772)	40,885	37,516
*32548	Fort Walton Beach	(850)	18,880	19,973
33172	Fountainbleau (c)	(305)	—	59,549
*32259	Fruit Cove (c)	(904)	—	16,077
34232	Fruitville (c)	(941)	—	12,741
*32602	Gainesville	(352)	114,916	95,447
33138	Gladeview (c)	(954)	—	14,468
33143	Glenvar Heights (c)	(305)	—	16,243
34116	Golden Gate (c)	(239)	—	20,951
33055	Golden Glades (c)	(305)	—	32,623
32733	Goldenrod (c)	(407)	—	12,871
32560	Gonzalez (c)	(850)	—	11,365
33624	Greater Carrollwood (c)	(813)	—	33,519
33624	Greater Northdale (c)	(813)	—	20,461
33573	Greater Sun Center (c)	(813)	—	16,321
*33454	Greenacres	(561)	32,174	27,569
33581	Gulf Gate Estates (c)	(941)	—	11,647
*33737	Gulfport	(727)	12,327	12,527
*33844	Haines City	(863)	19,056	13,174
*33009	Hallandale Beach	(305)/(954)	38,683	—
33434	Hamptons at Boca Raton (c)	(561)	—	11,306
*33010	Hialeah	(305)	210,542	226,419
*33016	Hialeah Gardens	(305)	19,631	19,297
*33455	Hobe Sound (c)	(772)	—	11,376
*34690	Holiday (c)	(727)	—	21,904
*32125	Holly Hill	(386)	13,199	12,119
*33022	Hollywood	(954)	141,740	139,357
*33030	Homestead	(305)	57,936	31,909
34447	Homosassa Springs (c)	(352)	—	12,458
*34667	Hudson (c)	(727)	—	12,765
*34142	Immokalee (c)	(239)	—	19,763
33908	Iona (c)	(239)	—	11,756
33162	Ives Estates (c)	(305)	—	17,586
*32203	Jacksonville	(904)	807,815	735,617
*32250	Jacksonville Beach	(904)	21,673	20,990
33568	Jasmine Estates (c)	(727)	—	18,213
*34957	Jensen Beach (c)	(772)	—	11,100
*33458	Jupiter	(561)	48,879	39,328
*33183	Kendale Lakes (c)	(305)	—	56,901
*33256	Kendall (c)	(305)	—	75,226
33193	Kendall West (c)	(305)	—	38,034
33037	Key Largo (c)	(305)	—	11,886
33556	Keystone (c)	(813)	—	14,627
*33040	Key West	(305)	22,364	25,478
*33573	Kings Point (c)	(305)	—	12,207
*34744	Kissimmee	(407)	62,291	47,814
*32159	Lady Lake	(352)	14,940	11,828
*32055	Lake City	(386)	12,427	9,980
*33804	Lakeland	(863)	93,333	78,452
33801	Lakeland Highlands (c)	(863)	—	12,557
33612	Lake Magdalene (c)	(813)	—	28,755
*32746	Lake Mary	(407)	15,143	11,458
32073	Lakeside (c)	(904)	—	30,927
*33853	Lake Wales	(863)	14,474	10,194
34951	Lakewood Park (c)	(772)	—	10,458
*33461	Lake Worth	(561)	35,513	35,133
33461	Lake Worth Corridor (c)	(561)	—	18,663
*34639	Land O'Lakes (c)	(813)	—	20,971
*33465	Lantana	(561)	10,071	9,437
*33770	Largo	(727)	72,732	69,371
*33313	Lauderdale Lakes	(954)	31,004	31,705
*33313	Lauderhill	(954)	67,007	57,585
*34748	Leesburg	(352)	22,113	15,956
*33936	Lehigh Acres (c)	(239)	—	33,430
*33033	Leisure City (c)	(305)	—	22,152
*33074	Lighthouse Point	(954)	11,118	10,767
32810	Lockhart (c)	(407)	—	12,944
*32750	Longwood	(407)	13,493	13,745

ZIP	Place	Area Code	2008	2000
*33549	Lutz (c)	(813)	—	17,081
32444	Lynn Haven	(850)	15,254	12,451
*32751	Maitland	(407)	14,931	12,019
*34145	Marco Island	(239)	15,634	—
*33093	Margate	(954)	54,086	53,909
32824	Meadow Woods (c)	(407)	—	11,286
*32901	Melbourne	(321)	77,351	71,382
*32953	Merritt Island (c)	(321)	—	36,090
*33101	Miami	(305)	413,201	362,470
*33152	Miami Beach	(305)	84,633	87,933
33023	Miami Gardens	(305)	109,346	—
*33014	Miami Lakes	(305)	21,727	—
*33266	Miami Springs	(305)	12,534	13,712
*32068	Middleburg (c)	(904)	—	10,338
*33023	Miramar	(954)	108,484	72,739
*32757	Mount Dora	(352)	12,869	9,418
32526	Myrtle Grove (c)	(850)	—	17,211
*34102	Naples	(239)	21,532	20,976
*34653	New Port Richey	(727)	17,578	16,117
*32168	New Smyrna Beach	(386)	23,325	20,048
*32578	Niceville	(850)	12,313	11,684
33269	Norland (c)	(305)	—	22,995
*33918	North Fort Myers (c)	(239)	—	40,214
*33068	North Lauderdale	(954)	41,772	32,264
*33261	North Miami	(305)	55,908	59,880
*33160	North Miami Beach	(305)	37,997	40,786
*33408	North Palm Beach	(561)	12,149	12,064
*34287	North Port	(941)	54,907	22,797
33307	Oakland Park	(305)	42,293	30,966
*33860	Oak Ridge (c)	(407)	—	22,349
*34478	Ocala	(352)	54,801	45,943
*34761	Ocoee	(407)	32,290	24,391
*33163	Ojus (c)	(305)	—	16,642
34677	Oldsmar	(813)	13,401	11,910
*33265	Olympia Heights (c)	(305)	—	13,452
*33054	Opa-Locka	(305)	15,287	14,951
*32802	Orlando	(407)	230,519	185,951
*32174	Ormond Beach	(386)	37,984	36,301
*32765	Oviedo	(407)	32,606	26,316
*32177	Palatka	(386)	10,813	10,033
*32905	Palm Bay	(321)	100,786	79,413
*33408	Palm Beach Gardens	(561)	49,227	35,058
*34990	Palm City (c)	(772)	—	20,097
*32135	Palm Coast	(386)	72,316	32,732
*34221	Palmetto	(941)	14,284	12,571
33157	Palmetto Bay	(305)/(786)	22,666	—
33157	Palmetto Estates (c)	(305)	—	13,675
*34683	Palm Harbor (c)	(727)	—	59,248
*33601	Palm River-Clair Mel (c)	(813)	—	17,589
*33406	Palm Springs	(561)	16,442	11,699
32082	Palm Valley (c)	(904)	—	19,860
*32401	Panama City	(850)	36,644	36,417
*32417	Panama City Beach	(850)	14,642	7,671
*33067	Parkland	(954)	24,017	13,835
*33029	Pembroke Pines	(954)	145,661	137,427
*32502	Pensacola	(850)	53,820	56,255
33156	Pinecrest	(305)	18,614	19,055
32858	Pine Hills (c)	(407)	—	41,764
*33781	Pinellas Park	(727)	47,173	45,658
33168	Pinewood (c)	(305)	—	16,523
*33318	Plantation	(954)	83,628	82,934
*33566	Plant City	(813)	32,761	29,915
*34758	Poinciana (c)	(407)	—	13,647
*33060	Pompano Beach	(954)	101,943	78,191
*33952	Port Charlotte (c)	(941)	—	46,451
*32129	Port Orange	(904)	54,616	45,823
32927	Port St. John (c)	(321)	—	12,112
*34981	Port St. Lucie	(772)	154,353	88,769
34992	Port Salerno (c)	(772)	—	10,141
*33032	Princeton (c)	(305)	—	10,090
*33950	Punta Gorda	(941)	16,343	14,344
33177	Richmond West (c)	(305)	—	28,082
33569	Riverview (c)	(813)	—	12,035
*33419	Riviera Beach	(561)	36,430	29,884
*32955	Rockledge	(321)	24,747	20,170
*33411	Royal Palm Beach	(561)	30,312	21,523
*34695	Safety Harbor	(727)	17,089	17,203
*32084	Saint Augustine	(904)	12,404	11,592
*34769	Saint Cloud	(407)	28,745	20,074
*33733	Saint Petersburg	(727)	245,314	248,232
33912	San Carlos Park (c)	(239)	—	16,317
33432	Sandalfoot Cove (c)	(305)	—	16,582
*32771	Sanford	(407)	50,634	38,291
*34230	Sarasota	(941)	52,340	52,715
33577	Sarasota Springs (c)	(941)	—	15,875
32937	Satellite Beach	(321)	11,762	9,577
33055	Scott Lake (c)	(305)	—	14,401
*32958	Sebastian	(772)	20,265	16,181
*33870	Sebring	(863)	10,714	9,667
*33770	Seminole	(813)	19,002	10,890
33505	South Bradenton (c)	(941)	—	21,587

ZIP	Place	Area Code	2008	2000
32121	South Daytona	(386)	13,662	13,177
*33243	South Miami	(305)	10,707	10,741
33157	South Miami Heights (c)	(305)	—	33,522
33595	South Venice (c)	(941)	—	13,539
*34604	Spring Hill (c)	(352)	—	69,078
*34994	Stuart	(772)	15,858	14,633
33160	Sunny Isles Beach	(305)	16,317	—
*33325	Sunrise	(954)	89,026	85,779
*33283	Sunset (c)	(305)	—	17,150
33144	Sweetwater	(305)	13,072	—
*32301	Tallahassee	(850)	171,922	150,624
*33320	Tamarac	(954)	59,340	55,588
33144	Tamiami (c)	(305)	—	54,788
*33601	Tampa	(813)	340,882	303,447
*34689	Tarpon Springs	(727)	23,369	21,003
32778	Tavares	(352)	13,746	9,700
*33687	Temple Terrace	(813)	22,619	20,918
33186	The Crossings (c)	(305)	—	23,557
33196	The Hammocks (c)	(305)	—	47,379
*32780	Titusville	(321)	44,756	40,670
32615	Town 'n' Country (c)	(813)	—	72,523
32817	Union Park (c)	(407)	—	10,191
33024	University (c)	(813)	—	30,736
33165	University Park (c)	(305)	—	26,538
32401	Upper Grand Lagoon (c)	(850)	—	10,889
*34285	Venice	(941)	20,946	17,764
*32960	Vero Beach	(772)	16,982	17,705
32960	Vero Beach South (c)	(772)	—	20,362
33901	Villas (c)	(239)	—	11,346
32507	Warrington (c)	(850)	—	15,207
32791	Wekiva Springs (c)	(407)	—	23,169
*33414	Wellington	(561)	54,530	38,216
33714	West and East Lealman (c)	(727)	—	21,753
33626	Westchase (c)	(813)	—	11,116
33165	Westchester (c)	(305)	—	30,271
33138	West Little River (c)	(305)	—	32,498
*32912	West Melbourne	(321)	15,328	9,824
*33326	Weston	(954)	63,628	49,286
*33416	West Palm Beach	(561)	98,779	82,103
33023	West Park	(954)	14,432	—
32505	West Pensacola (c)	(850)	—	21,939
33165	Westwood Lakes (c)	(305)	—	12,005
*33305	Wilton Manors	(954)	12,616	12,697
*34787	Winter Garden	(407)	29,385	14,351
*33880	Winter Haven	(863)	33,353	26,487
*32789	Winter Park	(407)	27,909	24,090
*32707	Winter Springs	(407)	32,667	31,666
32547	Wright (c)	(850)	—	21,697
34972	Yeehaw Junction (c)	(407)	—	21,778
*33540	Zephyrhills	(813)	13,152	10,833

Georgia

Area code (678) overlays area code (770). Area code (762) overlays area code (706).

ZIP	Place	Area Code	2008	2000
*30101	Acworth	(770)	19,476	13,422
*31706	Albany	(229)	75,831	76,939
*30004	Alpharetta	(770)	49,903	34,854
*31709	Americus	(229)	16,524	17,013
*30603	Athens-Clarke County	(706)	113,398	100,266
*30301	Atlanta	(404)	537,958	416,474
*30903	Augusta-Richmond County	(706)	194,149	195,182
*39818	Bainbridge	(229)	12,337	11,722
30032	Belvedere Park (c)	(404)	—	18,945
*31520	Brunswick	(912)	16,269	15,600
*30518	Buford	(404)	11,780	10,668
*30701	Calhoun	(706)	14,807	10,667
30032	Candler-McAfee (c)	(404)	—	28,294
*30114	Canton	(770)	22,724	7,709
*30117	Carrollton	(770)	23,291	19,843
*30120	Cartersville	(770)	19,010	15,925
30125	Cedartown	(770)	10,123	9,470
30366	Chamblee	(404)	11,200	9,552
30337	College Park	(404)	19,969	20,382
*31908	Columbus	(706)	186,984	—
*30013	Conyers	(404)	13,545	10,689
*31015	Cordele	(229)	11,518	11,608
*30014	Covington	(770)	14,980	11,547
31805	Cusseta-Chattahoochee County	(706)	13,754	—
*30132	Dallas	(770)	10,584	5,056
*30720	Dalton	(706)	33,648	27,912
*30030	Decatur	(404)	18,986	18,147
*30362	Doraville	(404)	10,268	9,862
*31533	Douglas	(912)	11,413	10,639
*30134	Douglasville	(404)	31,035	20,065
30333	Druid Hills (c)	(404)	—	12,741
*31021	Dublin	(478)	17,509	15,857
*30096	Duluth	(404)	26,125	22,122
*30356	Dunwoody (c)	(404)	—	32,808
30364	East Point	(404)	43,418	39,595
30809	Evans (c)	(706)	—	17,727

ZIP	Place	Area Code	2008	2000
30213	Fairburn	(770)	11,024	5,464
*30214	Fayetteville	(404)	15,136	11,148
*30297	Forest Park	(404)	21,726	21,447
31905	Fort Benning South (c)	(706)	—	11,737
*31313	Fort Stewart (c)	(912)	—	11,205
*30501	Gainesville	(770)	35,668	25,578
31754	Georgetown (c)	(912)	—	10,599
30316	Gresham Park (c)	(404)	—	9,215
*30223	Griffin	(770)	23,719	23,451
*31313	Hinesville	(912)	30,152	30,392
*31546	Jesup	(912)	10,459	9,279
30097	Johns Creek	(770)	59,431	—
*30144	Kennesaw	(404)	31,628	21,675
31548	Kingsland	(912)	13,659	10,506
*30240	LaGrange	(706)	28,401	25,998
*30045	Lawrenceville	(404)	29,258	22,397
*30047	Lilburn	(404)	11,599	11,307
*30052	Loganville	(770)	10,562	5,435
30126	Mableton (c)	(404)	—	29,733
*30253	McDonough	(770)	19,768	8,493
*31201	Macon	(478)	92,775	97,255
*30060	Marietta	(404)	67,562	58,748
30907	Martinez (c)	(706)	—	27,749
*31061	Milledgeville	(478)	20,703	18,757
30004	Milton	(770)	15,156	—
*30655	Monroe	(770)	13,381	11,407
*31768	Moultrie	(229)	15,409	14,387
30087	Mountain Park (c)	(404)	—	11,753
*30263	Newnan	(770)	30,474	16,242
*30071	Norcross	(404)	10,737	8,410
30319	North Atlanta (c)	(404)	—	38,579
30033	North Decatur (c)	(404)	—	15,270
30033	North Druid Hills (c)	(404)	—	18,852
30032	Panthersville (c)	(404)	—	11,791
*30269	Peachtree City	(404)	34,788	31,580
31069	Perry	(478)	12,990	9,602
31322	Pooler	(912)	14,875	6,239
30127	Powder Springs	(404)	15,614	12,481
30074	Redan (c)	(404)	—	33,841
31324	Richmond Hill	(912)	10,571	6,959
*30274	Riverdale	(404)	15,279	12,478
*30161	Rome	(706)	36,041	34,980
*30077	Roswell	(404)	87,657	79,334
31558	Saint Marys	(912)	16,763	13,761
31522	Saint Simons (c)	(912)	—	13,381
30358	Sandy Springs	(404)	82,674	—
*31402	Savannah	(912)	132,410	131,510
30079	Scottdale (c)	(404)	—	9,803
*30080	Smyrna	(404)	49,854	40,999
*30078	Snellville	(404)	20,112	15,351
*30458	Statesboro	(912)	27,158	22,698
30281	Stockbridge	(404)	14,360	9,853
30518	Sugar Hill	(404)	17,204	11,399
30024	Suwanee	(770)	16,277	8,725
*31792	Thomasville	(229)	19,286	18,162
*31794	Tifton	(229)	17,284	15,060
*30084	Tucker (c)	(404)	—	26,532
30291	Union City	(404)	16,961	11,621
*31603	Valdosta	(229)	48,547	43,724
*30474	Vidalia	(912)	11,355	10,491
30180	Villa Rica	(770)	12,838	4,134
*31088	Warner Robins	(478)	61,336	48,804
*31501	Waycross	(912)	14,774	15,333
31410	Wilmington Island (c)	(912)	—	14,213
30680	Winder	(770)	14,064	10,201
*30188	Woodstock	(770)	23,141	10,050

Hawaii (808)

ZIP	Place	2008	2000
96706	Ewa Beach (c)	—	14,650
96701	Halawa (c)	—	13,891
*96720	Hilo (c)	—	40,759
*96820	Honolulu (c)	374,676	371,657
*96732	Kahului (c)	—	20,146
96863	Kailua (Honolulu Co.) (c)	—	36,513
96744	Kaneohe (c)	—	34,970
96863	Kaneohe Station (c)	—	11,827
96753	Kihei (c)	—	16,749
96706	Makakilo (c)	—	13,156
96789	Mililani Town (c)	—	28,608
96792	Nanakuli (c)	—	10,814
96782	Pearl City (c)	—	30,976
96857	Schofield Barracks (c)	—	14,428
*96786	Wahiawa (c)	—	16,151
96792	Waianae (c)	—	10,506
96793	Wailuku (c)	—	12,296
96701	Waimalu (c)	—	29,371
96797	Waipahu (c)	—	33,108
96797	Waipio (c)	—	11,672

Idaho (208)

ZIP	Place	2008	2000
*83401	Ammon	13,646	6,187
83221	Blackfoot	11,012	10,419
*83707	Boise	205,314	185,787
*83605	Caldwell	42,331	25,967

ZIP	Place	2008	2000
83202	Chubbuck	11,828	9,700
*83814	Coeur d'Alene	43,360	34,514
83616	Eagle	19,471	11,085
*83714	Garden City	11,713	10,624
83835	Hayden	12,873	9,159
*83402	Idaho Falls	54,334	50,730
*83634	Kuna	13,354	5,382
83501	Lewiston	31,764	30,904
*83642	Meridian	66,916	34,919
*83843	Moscow	22,798	21,291
*83647	Mountain Home	12,382	11,143
*83653	Nampa	80,362	51,867
*83201	Pocatello	54,901	51,466
*83854	Post Falls	26,460	17,247
*83440	Rexburg	28,028	17,257
*83301	Twin Falls	42,197	34,469

Illinois

Area code (224) overlays area code (847). Area code (331) overlays area code (630). Area code (779) overlays area code (815). Area code (872) overlays area code (312).

ZIP	Place	Area Code	2008	2000
60101	Addison	(630)	36,917	35,914
*60102	Algonquin	(847)	30,352	23,276
60803	Alsip	(708)	18,692	19,725
62002	Alton	(618)	29,393	30,496
60002	Antioch	(847)	13,892	8,788
*60005	Arlington Heights	(847)	73,399	76,031
*60505	Aurora	(630)	171,782	142,990
*60010	Barrington	(847)	10,374	10,168
*60103	Bartlett	(630)	42,209	36,706
*60510	Batavia	(630)	27,502	23,866
*60083	Beach Park	(847)	13,119	10,072
*62220	Belleville	(618)	41,097	41,410
60104	Bellwood	(708)	18,973	20,535
61008	Belvidere	(815)	26,461	20,820
*60106	Bensenville	(630)	20,138	20,703
60402	Berwyn	(708)	49,919	54,016
*60108	Bloomingdale	(630)	21,848	21,675
*61701	Bloomington	(309)	73,026	64,808
*60406	Blue Island	(708)	22,325	23,463
*60440	Bolingbrook	(630)	70,823	56,321
60914	Bourbonnais	(815)	19,024	15,256
60915	Bradley	(815)	14,964	12,784
60455	Bridgeview	(708)	14,991	15,335
60513	Brookfield	(708)	18,077	19,085
60089	Buffalo Grove	(847)	42,972	42,909
60459	Burbank	(708)	27,567	27,902
60527	Burr Ridge	(630)	11,398	10,408
62206	Cahokia	(618)	15,103	16,391
60409	Calumet City	(708)	36,800	39,071
60175	Campton Hills	(630)	11,031	—
61520	Canton	(309)	14,545	15,288
*62901	Carbondale	(618)	26,231	20,681
*60188	Carol Stream	(630)	40,004	40,438
60110	Carpentersville	(847)	37,741	30,586
60013	Cary	(847)	19,559	15,531
62801	Centralia	(618)	13,569	14,136
*61821	Champaign	(217)	79,389	67,518
60410	Channahon	(815)	14,030	7,344
61920	Charleston	(217)	21,715	21,039
62629	Chatham	(217)	10,676	8,583
*60411	Chicago Heights	(708)	30,586	32,776
60415	Chicago Ridge	(708)	13,366	14,127
*60607	Chicago	(312)/(773)	2,853,114	2,896,016
60804	Cicero	(708)	80,414	85,616
62234	Collinsville	(618)	25,960	24,707
60478	Country Club Hills	(708)	16,723	16,169
60435	Crest Hill	(815)	20,451	13,329
60445	Crestwood	(708)	11,051	11,251
*60014	Crystal Lake	(815)	41,797	38,000
*61832	Danville	(217)	32,248	33,904
60561	Darien	(630)	22,370	22,860
*62525	Decatur	(217)	76,256	81,860
60015	Deerfield	(847)	19,667	18,420
60115	DeKalb	(815)	45,497	39,018
*60018	Des Plaines	(847)	57,062	58,720
61021	Dixon	(815)	15,033	15,941
60419	Dolton	(708)	23,889	25,614
*60515	Downers Grove	(630)	49,250	48,724
61244	East Moline	(309)	20,892	20,333
*61611	East Peoria	(309)	22,760	22,638
*62201	East St. Louis	(618)	28,773	31,542
*62025	Edwardsville	(618)	24,557	21,491
62401	Effingham	(217)	12,489	12,384
*60120	Elgin	(847)	106,330	94,487
*60009	Elk Grove Village	(847)	33,320	34,727
60126	Elmhurst	(630)	46,013	42,762
60707	Elmwood Park	(708)	24,052	25,405
*60201	Evanston	(847)	77,693	74,239
60805	Evergreen Park	(708)	19,359	20,821
*62208	Fairview Heights	(618)	16,643	15,034
*60130	Forest Park	(708)	15,224	15,688
60020	Fox Lake	(847)	11,087	9,178
60423	Frankfort	(815)	17,981	10,391
*60131	Franklin Park	(847)	17,965	19,434
61032	Freeport	(815)	24,615	26,443
60030	Gages Lake (c)	(847)	—	10,415
*61401	Galesburg	(309)	31,181	33,706
60134	Geneva	(630)	24,302	19,515
62034	Glen Carbon	(618)	12,607	10,425
*60137	Glen Ellyn	(630)	27,142	26,999
*60139	Glendale Heights	(630)	31,847	31,765
*60025	Glenview	(847)	46,180	41,847
62035	Godfrey	(618)	17,524	16,286
60441	Goodings Grove (c)	(815)	—	17,084
62040	Granite City	(618)	30,703	31,301
60030	Grayslake	(847)	21,735	18,506
60031	Gurnee	(847)	30,608	28,834
60133	Hanover Park	(630)	36,777	38,278
*60426	Harvey	(708)	28,056	30,000
60429	Hazel Crest	(708)	14,075	14,816
62948	Herrin	(618)	12,337	11,298
*60457	Hickory Hills	(708)	13,326	13,926
*60035	Highland Park	(847)	31,449	31,365
*60521	Hinsdale	(630)	18,439	17,349
*60195	Hoffman Estates	(847)	53,641	49,495
*60491	Homer Glen	(708)	26,111	—
*60430	Homewood	(708)	18,475	19,543
60142	Huntley	(847)	22,923	5,730
*62650	Jacksonville	(217)	19,415	18,940
*60436	Joliet	(815)	146,125	106,221
60458	Justice	(708)	12,452	12,193
60901	Kankakee	(815)	26,710	27,491
61443	Kewanee	(309)	12,302	12,944
60526	La Grange Park	(708)	12,404	13,295
60525	La Grange	(708)	15,244	15,608
60045	Lake Forest	(847)	20,990	20,059
*60102	Lake in the Hills	(847)	29,698	23,152
*60047	Lake Zurich	(847)	20,610	18,104
60438	Lansing	(708)	26,672	28,332
*60439	Lemont	(630)	16,176	13,098
*60048	Libertyville	(847)	21,843	20,742
62656	Lincoln	(217)	14,541	15,369
*60645	Lincolnwood	(847)	11,810	12,359
60046	Lindenhurst	(847)	14,695	12,539
60532	Lisle	(630)	23,135	21,182
*60441	Lockport	(815)	24,810	15,191
60148	Lombard	(630)	42,890	42,322
*61130	Loves Park	(815)	24,457	20,044
60534	Lyons	(708)	10,250	10,255
*61115	Machesney Park	(815)	22,815	20,759
61455	Macomb	(309)	19,736	18,558
62959	Marion	(618)	17,388	16,035
*60426	Markham	(708)	12,248	12,620
*60443	Matteson	(708)	17,420	12,928
61938	Mattoon	(217)	17,177	18,291
*60153	Maywood	(708)	25,035	26,987
*60050	McHenry	(815)	26,862	21,501
*60160	Melrose Park	(708)	21,853	23,171
60445	Midlothian	(708)	13,657	14,315
60447	Minooka	(815)	10,514	3,971
60448	Mokena	(708)	19,236	14,583
*61265	Moline	(309)	43,088	43,768
60538	Montgomery	(630)	15,229	5,471
60450	Morris	(815)	13,812	11,928
61550	Morton	(309)	16,039	15,198
60053	Morton Grove	(847)	22,478	22,451
60056	Mount Prospect	(847)	53,338	56,265
62864	Mount Vernon	(618)	16,298	16,269
60060	Mundelein	(847)	33,717	30,935
*60540	Naperville	(630)	143,117	128,358
60451	New Lenox	(815)	24,137	17,771
60714	Niles	(847)	28,666	30,068
*61761	Normal	(309)	52,056	45,386
*60634	Norridge	(708)	13,954	14,582
60542	North Aurora	(630)	15,812	10,585
*60064	North Chicago	(847)	32,608	35,918
*60062	Northbrook	(708)	33,936	33,435
60164	Northlake	(708)	11,462	11,878
62269	O'Fallon	(618)	27,540	21,910
60452	Oak Forest	(708)	27,740	28,051
*60303	Oak Lawn	(708)	53,244	55,245
*60303	Oak Park	(708)	49,557	52,524
*60462	Orland Park	(708)	55,514	51,077
60543	Oswego	(630)	31,504	13,326
61350	Ottawa	(815)	19,419	18,307
*60067	Palatine	(847)	67,080	65,479
60463	Palos Heights	(708)	12,469	11,260
60465	Palos Hills	(708)	16,924	17,665
60466	Park Forest	(708)	22,583	23,462
60068	Park Ridge	(847)	36,927	37,775

ZIP	Place	Area Code	2008	2000
*61554	Pekin	(309)	33,430	33,857
*61601	Peoria	(309)	114,114	112,936
*60544	Plainfield	(815)	36,507	13,038
60545	Plano	(630)	11,886	5,633
61764	Pontiac	(815)	11,258	11,864
60070	Prospect Heights	(847)	16,047	17,081
*62301	Quincy	(217)	39,983	40,366
61866	Rantoul	(217)	12,189	12,857
60471	Richton Park	(708)	12,842	12,533
60827	Riverdale	(708)	14,163	15,055
60305	River Forest	(708)	11,176	11,635
*61125	Rockford	(815)	157,272	150,115
*61201	Rock Island	(309)	38,139	39,684
60008	Rolling Meadows	(847)	23,463	24,604
*60446	Romeoville	(815)	38,028	21,153
60172	Roselle	(630)	23,209	23,115
60073	Round Lake	(847)	16,748	5,842
60073	Round Lake Beach	(847)	27,855	25,859
*60174	Saint Charles	(630)	32,829	27,896
60411	Sauk Village	(708)	10,254	10,411
*60194	Schaumburg	(847)	71,716	75,386
*60176	Schiller Park	(847)	11,573	11,850
*62269	Shiloh	(618)	11,173	7,643
*60436	Shorewood	(815)	15,521	7,686
*60077	Skokie	(847)	66,620	63,348
60177	South Elgin	(847)	21,131	16,100
60473	South Holland	(708)	21,083	22,147
*62703	Springfield	(217)	117,352	111,454
60475	Steger	(708)	10,421	9,682
61081	Sterling	(815)	15,124	15,451
60107	Streamwood	(630)	37,119	36,407
61364	Streator	(815)	13,780	14,190
60501	Summit	(708)	10,223	10,637
*62221	Swansea	(618)	12,927	10,579
60178	Sycamore	(815)	17,679	12,020
62568	Taylorville	(217)	12,238	11,427
60477	Tinley Park	(708)	59,198	48,401
*61801	Urbana	(217)	39,641	36,395
60061	Vernon Hills	(847)	24,462	20,120
60181	Villa Park	(630)	22,198	22,075
60555	Warrenville	(630)	13,033	13,363
61571	Washington	(309)	13,942	10,841
60084	Wauconda	(847)	12,219	9,448
*60085	Waukegan	(847)	90,788	87,901
60154	Westchester	(708)	15,710	16,824
*60185	West Chicago	(630)	26,454	23,469
60558	Western Springs	(708)	12,690	12,493
60559	Westmont	(630)	24,979	24,554
*60187	Wheaton	(630)	54,465	55,416
60090	Wheeling	(847)	36,063	34,496
60091	Wilmette	(847)	26,418	27,651
60093	Winnetka	(847)	12,371	12,419
*60191	Wood Dale	(630)	13,855	13,535
62095	Wood River	(618)	10,973	11,296
60517	Woodridge	(630)	34,130	30,934
60098	Woodstock	(815)	23,930	20,151
60482	Worth	(708)	10,426	11,047
60560	Yorkville	(630)	16,505	6,189
60099	Zion	(847)	25,161	22,866

Indiana

ZIP	Place	Area Code	2008	2000
*46011	Anderson	(765)	57,282	59,734
46706	Auburn	(260)	13,026	12,074
46123	Avon	(317)	12,238	6,248
47421	Bedford	(812)	13,486	13,768
46107	Beech Grove	(317)	14,316	14,880
*47408	Bloomington	(812)	71,819	69,291
46112	Brownsburg	(317)	19,994	14,520
*46032	Carmel	(317)	66,769	37,733
46303	Cedar Lake	(219)	10,981	9,279
46304	Chesterton	(219)	12,705	10,488
*47129	Clarksville	(812)	21,873	21,400
*47201	Columbus	(812)	40,001	39,059
47331	Connersville	(765)	13,931	15,411
*47933	Crawfordsville	(765)	15,043	15,243
*46307	Crown Point	(219)	24,376	19,806
*46311	Dyer	(219)	15,913	13,895
46312	East Chicago	(219)	29,978	32,414
*46515	Elkhart	(574)	52,653	51,874
*47708	Evansville	(812)	116,309	121,582
*46038	Fishers	(317)	69,011	37,835
*46802	Fort Wayne	(260)	251,591	205,727
*46041	Frankfort	(765)	16,394	16,662
46131	Franklin	(317)	23,258	19,463
*46401	Gary	(219)	95,920	102,746
*46526	Goshen	(574)	32,630	29,383
46530	Granger (c)	(574)	—	28,284
46135	Greencastle	(765)	10,145	9,880
46140	Greenfield	(317)	18,787	14,600
47240	Greensburg	(812)	10,730	10,260

ZIP	Place	Area Code	2008	2000
*46142	Greenwood	(317)	47,720	36,037
46319	Griffith	(219)	16,311	17,334
*46320	Hammond	(219)	76,732	83,048
*46322	Highland	(219)	22,641	23,546
46342	Hobart	(219)	27,891	25,363
46750	Huntington	(260)	16,521	17,450
*46206	Indianapolis	(317)	798,382	781,870
*47546	Jasper	(812)	14,116	12,100
*47130	Jeffersonville	(812)	30,479	27,362
46755	Kendallville	(260)	10,452	9,616
*46902	Kokomo	(765)	45,694	46,113
*46350	La Porte	(219)	21,174	21,621
*47901	Lafayette	(765)	64,049	56,397
46405	Lake Station	(219)	13,246	13,948
*46226	Lawrence	(317)	43,247	38,915
46052	Lebanon	(765)	15,400	14,222
46947	Logansport	(574)	18,663	19,684
47250	Madison	(812)	12,716	12,004
*46952	Marion	(765)	30,212	31,320
46151	Martinsville	(765)	11,800	11,698
*46401	Merrillville	(219)	33,057	30,560
*46360	Michigan City	(219)	32,405	32,900
*46544	Mishawaka	(574)	50,026	46,557
46158	Mooresville	(317)	11,763	9,273
*47302	Muncie	(765)	64,975	67,430
46321	Munster	(219)	22,105	21,511
*47150	New Albany	(812)	37,296	37,603
47362	New Castle	(765)	18,339	17,780
46774	New Haven	(260)	13,685	12,406
*46060	Noblesville	(317)	42,155	28,590
*46970	Peru	(765)	12,301	12,994
46168	Plainfield	(317)	27,832	18,396
46563	Plymouth	(574)	11,038	9,840
46368	Portage	(219)	36,976	33,496
*47374	Richmond	(765)	36,733	39,124
46373	Saint John	(219)	12,999	8,382
46375	Schererville	(219)	28,886	24,851
47274	Seymour	(812)	19,223	18,101
46176	Shelbyville	(765)	18,516	17,951
*46624	South Bend	(574)	103,807	107,789
46224	Speedway	(317)	12,594	12,881
*47808	Terre Haute	(812)	60,007	59,614
*46383	Valparaiso	(219)	30,429	27,428
47591	Vincennes	(812)	17,976	18,701
46992	Wabash	(260)	10,815	11,743
*46580	Warsaw	(574)	13,627	12,415
47501	Washington	(812)	11,397	11,380
*46580	West Lafayette	(765)	30,847	28,778
46074	Westfield	(317)	21,171	9,293
46077	Zionsville	(317)	13,655	8,775

Iowa

ZIP	Place	Area Code	2008	2000
50009	Altoona	(515)	13,854	10,345
*50010	Ames	(515)	56,510	50,731
*50021	Ankeny	(515)	42,287	27,117
52722	Bettendorf	(563)	32,584	31,275
*50036	Boone	(515)	12,614	12,803
52601	Burlington	(319)	25,327	26,839
*50613	Cedar Falls	(319)	38,059	36,145
*52401	Cedar Rapids	(319)	128,056	120,758
*52732	Clinton	(563)	26,407	27,772
50325	Clive	(515)	15,234	12,855
52241	Coralville	(319)	18,478	15,123
*51501	Council Bluffs	(712)	59,536	58,268
*52802	Davenport	(563)	100,827	98,359
*50318	Des Moines	(515)	197,052	198,682
*52001	Dubuque	(563)	57,250	57,686
50501	Fort Dodge	(515)	25,180	25,136
52627	Fort Madison	(319)	10,897	10,715
50125	Indianola	(515)	14,361	12,998
*52240	Iowa City	(319)	67,831	62,220
50131	Johnston	(515)	15,691	8,649
52632	Keokuk	(319)	10,387	11,427
52302	Marion	(319)	32,821	26,294
50158	Marshalltown	(641)	25,850	26,009
*50401	Mason City	(641)	27,337	29,172
52761	Muscatine	(563)	22,504	22,697
50208	Newton	(641)	15,042	15,579
52317	North Liberty	(319)	11,561	5,367
52577	Oskaloosa	(641)	11,069	10,938
52501	Ottumwa	(641)	24,342	24,998
50219	Pella	(641)	10,208	9,832
*51101	Sioux City	(712)	82,807	85,013
51301	Spencer	(712)	10,986	11,317
*50322	Urbandale	(515)	38,369	29,072
*50701	Waterloo	(319)	66,662	68,747
50263	Waukee	(515)	12,367	5,126
*50265	West Des Moines	(515)	55,426	46,403

Kansas

ZIP	Place	Area Code	2008	2000
67002	Andover	(316)	10,351	6,698
67005	Arkansas City	(620)	11,070	11,963
66002	Atchison	(913)	10,402	10,232
67337	Coffeyville	(620)	10,312	11,021
67037	Derby	(316)	22,517	17,807
*67801	Dodge City	(620)	25,689	25,176
67042	El Dorado	(316)	12,591	12,057
66801	Emporia	(620)	26,380	26,760
*67846	Garden City	(620)	28,557	28,451
*66030	Gardner	(913)	17,462	9,396
67530	Great Bend	(620)	15,564	15,345
*67601	Hays	(785)	20,368	20,013
67060	Haysville	(316)	10,364	8,502
*67501	Hutchinson	(620)	40,889	40,787
*66441	Junction City	(785)	20,671	18,886
*66102	Kansas City	(913)	142,562	146,866
66043	Lansing	(913)	10,691	9,199
*66044	Lawrence	(785)	90,520	80,098
*66048	Leavenworth	(913)	34,729	35,420
*66209	Leawood	(913)	31,342	27,656
*66214	Lenexa	(913)	46,822	40,238
*67901	Liberal	(620)	20,074	19,666
*66502	Manhattan	(785)	52,284	44,831
67460	McPherson	(620)	13,396	13,770
*66202	Merriam	(913)	10,814	11,008
*67114	Newton	(316)	18,133	17,190
*66061	Olathe	(913)	119,993	92,962
66067	Ottawa	(785)	12,850	11,921
*66204	Overland Park	(913)	171,231	149,080
67357	Parsons	(620)	11,065	11,514
*66762	Pittsburg	(620)	19,669	19,243
*66208	Prairie Village	(913)	21,479	22,072
*67401	Salina	(785)	46,483	45,679
*66203	Shawnee	(913)	60,954	47,996
*66601	Topeka	(785)	123,446	122,377
*67202	Wichita	(316)	366,046	344,284
67156	Winfield	(620)	11,497	12,206

Kentucky

ZIP	Place	Area Code	2008	2000
*41101	Ashland	(606)	21,346	21,981
40004	Bardstown	(502)	11,242	10,374
*40403	Berea	(859)	14,431	9,851
42101	Bowling Green	(270)	55,097	49,296
41005	Burlington (c)	(859)	—	10,779
42718	Campbellsville	(270)	11,010	10,498
41011	Covington	(859)	43,235	43,370
40422	Danville	(859)	15,524	15,477
*42701	Elizabethtown	(270)	24,144	22,542
*41018	Erlanger	(859)	17,188	16,676
40291	Fern Creek (c)	(502)	—	17,870
*41042	Florence	(859)	27,745	23,551
42223	Fort Campbell North (c)	(270)	—	14,338
40121	Fort Knox (c)	(270)	—	12,377
41075	Fort Thomas	(859)	15,222	16,495
*40601	Frankfort	(502)	27,322	27,741
40324	Georgetown	(502)	21,589	18,080
*42141	Glasgow	(270)	14,302	13,019
*42420	Henderson	(270)	27,933	27,373
40228	Highview (c)	(502)	—	15,161
*42240	Hopkinsville	(270)	32,076	30,089
41051	Independence	(859)	21,694	14,982
*40269	Jeffersontown	(502)	26,226	26,633
*40507	Lexington-Fayette	(859)	282,114	260,512
*40232	Louisville/Jefferson County[1]	(502)	557,224	—
*40252	Lyndon	(502)	11,242	9,369
42431	Madisonville	(270)	19,106	19,307
42066	Mayfield	(270)	10,186	10,349
40047	Mount Washington	(502)	11,980	8,485
42071	Murray	(270)	16,557	14,950
40219	Newburg (c)	(502)	—	20,636
*41071	Newport	(859)	15,766	17,048
*40356	Nicholasville	(859)	26,444	19,680
*40259	Okolona (c)	(502)	—	17,807
*42301	Owensboro	(270)	55,516	54,067
*42003	Paducah	(270)	25,521	26,307
*40268	Pleasure Ridge Park (c)	(502)	—	25,776
*40160	Radcliff	(502)	22,013	21,961
*40475	Richmond	(859)	32,895	27,152
*40207	Saint Matthews	(502)	18,709	15,852
*40066	Shelbyville	(502)	11,294	10,085
40256	Shively	(502)	16,641	15,157
*42501	Somerset	(606)	12,449	11,352
*40272	Valley Station (c)	(502)	—	22,946
*40391	Winchester	(859)	16,598	16,724

(1) Louisville merged with Jefferson County in 2003. The 2008 and 2000 populations are for all of Jefferson County except the separate incorporated places of Anchorage, Middletown, and Jeffersontown.

Louisiana

ZIP	Place	Area Code	2008	2000
*70510	Abbeville	(337)	12,103	11,887
*71301	Alexandria	(318)	48,639	46,342
70714	Baker	(225)	13,360	13,793
71220	Bastrop	(318)	11,814	12,988
*70821	Baton Rouge	(225)	223,689	227,818
*70364	Bayou Cane (c)	(985)	—	17,046
*70427	Bogalusa	(985)	12,607	13,365
*71111	Bossier City	(318)	62,384	56,461
*70043	Chalmette (c)	(504)	—	32,069
*70526	Crowley	(337)	13,922	14,225
*70726	Denham Springs	(225)	10,308	8,757
*70634	DeRidder	(337)	10,008	9,808
70047	Destrehan (c)	(985)	—	11,260
70072	Estelle (c)	(504)	—	15,880
70535	Eunice	(337)	11,500	11,499
71459	Fort Polk South (c)	(337)	—	11,000
*70053	Gretna	(504)	16,399	17,423
*70401	Hammond	(985)	19,803	17,639
*70058	Harvey (c)	(504)	—	22,226
*70360	Houma	(985)	32,512	32,393
70121	Jefferson (c)	(504)	—	11,843
70546	Jennings	(337)	10,529	10,986
*70062	Kenner	(504)	66,942	70,517
70445	Lacombe (c)	(985)	—	112,030
*70501	Lafayette	(337)	113,656	110,257
*70601	Lake Charles	(337)	71,061	71,757
*70068	Laplace (c)	(985)	—	27,684
70070	Luling (c)	(985)	—	1,512
*70471	Mandeville	(985)	12,421	10,489
*70072	Marrero (c)	(504)	—	36,165
70075	Meraux (c)	(504)	—	10,192
*70812	Merrydale (c)	(225)	—	10,427
*70009	Metairie (c)	(504)	—	146,136
*71055	Minden	(318)	12,962	13,027
*71207	Monroe	(318)	51,215	53,107
*70380	Morgan City	(985)	11,604	12,703
70611	Moss Bluff (c)	(337)	—	10,535
*71457	Natchitoches	(318)	18,241	17,865
*70560	New Iberia	(337)	32,959	32,623
*70140	New Orleans	(504)	311,853	484,674
*70570	Opelousas	(337)	23,220	22,860
*71360	Pineville	(318)	14,776	13,829
70394	Raceland (c)	(985)	—	10,224
70123	River Ridge (c)	(504)	—	14,588
*71270	Ruston	(318)	21,123	20,546
70817	Shenandoah (c)	(318)	—	17,070
*71102	Shreveport	(318)	199,729	200,145
*70458	Slidell	(985)	27,183	25,695
*70663	Sulphur	(337)	19,450	20,512
70056	Terrytown (c)	(504)	—	25,430
*70301	Thibodaux	(985)	14,052	14,431
70056	Timberlane (c)	(504)	—	11,405
*71291	West Monroe	(318)	12,899	13,250
*70094	Westwego	(504)	10,098	10,763
70791	Zachary	(225)	14,252	11,275

Maine (207)
See introductory note.

ZIP	Place	2008	2000
*04210	Auburn	23,177	23,203
*04330	Augusta	18,282	18,560
*04401	Bangor	31,756	31,473
*04005	Biddeford	21,435	20,942
04011	Brunswick	21,720	21,172
04011	Brunswick (c)	—	14,816
04105	Falmouth	10,724	10,310
04038	Gorham	15,563	14,141
04043	Kennebunk	11,448	10,476
03904	Kittery	10,427	9,543
*04240	Lewiston	35,131	35,690
*04101	Portland	62,561	64,249
04072	Saco	18,125	16,822
04073	Sanford	21,156	20,806
04073	Sanford (c)	—	10,133
*04074	Scarborough	19,054	16,970
*04106	South Portland	23,803	23,324
*04901	Waterville	16,016	15,605
*04092	Westbrook	16,534	16,142
*04062	Windham	16,715	14,904
03909	York	14,064	12,854

Maryland
Area code (240) overlays area code (301). Area code (443) overlays area code (410).

ZIP	Place	Area Code	2008	2000
21001	Aberdeen	(410)	13,993	13,842
*20783	Adelphi (c)	(301)	—	14,998
*21401	Annapolis	(410)	36,524	35,838
21227	Arbutus (c)	(410)	—	20,116
*21012	Arnold (c)	(410)	—	23,422

ZIP	Place	Area Code	2008	2000
*20916	Aspen Hill (c)	(301)	—	50,228
21220	Ballenger Creek (c)	(410)	—	13,518
*21203	Baltimore	(410)	636,919	651,154
21050	Bel Air North (c)	(410)	—	25,798
21014	Bel Air South (c)	(410)	—	39,711
*20705	Beltsville (c)	(301)	—	15,690
*20814	Bethesda (c)	(301)	—	55,277
*20715	Bowie	(301)	52,544	50,269
21225	Brooklyn Park (c)	(410)	—	10,938
20705	Calverton (c)	(301)	—	12,610
21613	Cambridge	(410)	11,752	10,911
*20748	Camp Springs (c)	(301)	—	17,968
21234	Carney (c)	(410)	—	28,264
*21228	Catonsville (c)	(410)	—	39,820
20657	Chesapeake Ranch Estates-Drum Point (c)	(301)	—	11,503
20782	Chillum (c)	(301)	—	34,252
20735	Clinton (c)	(301)	—	26,064
21030	Cockeysville (c)	(410)	—	19,388
*20914	Colesville (c)	(301)	—	19,810
*20740	College Park	(301)	26,925	24,657
*21045	Columbia (c)	(410)/(301)	—	88,254
20743	Coral Hills (c)	(301)	—	10,720
21114	Crofton (c)	(410)	—	20,091
*21502	Cumberland	(301)	20,495	21,518
20872	Damascus (c)	(301)	—	11,430
21222	Dundalk (c)	(410)	—	62,306
20737	East Riverdale (c)	(301)	—	14,961
*21601	Easton	(410)	14,677	11,708
21040	Edgewood (c)	(410)	—	23,378
21784	Eldersburg (c)	(410)	—	27,741
21075	Elkridge (c)	(410)	—	22,042
*21921	Elkton	(410)	14,842	11,893
*21043	Ellicott City (c)	(410)	—	56,397
21221	Essex (c)	(410)	—	39,078
20904	Fairland (c)	(301)	—	21,738
21061	Ferndale (c)	(410)	—	16,056
*20747	Forestville (c)	(301)	—	12,707
*20744	Fort Washington (c)	(301)	—	23,845
*21701	Frederick	(301)	59,213	52,767
20744	Friendly (c)	(301)	—	10,938
*20877	Gaithersburg	(301)	58,744	52,613
*20874	Germantown (c)	(301)	—	55,419
*21061	Glen Burnie (c)	(410)	—	38,922
20769	Glenn Dale (c)	(301)	—	12,609
20785	Greater Landover (c)	(301)	—	22,900
20772	Greater Upper Marlboro (c)	(301)	—	18,720
21122	Green Haven (c)	(410)	—	17,415
21771	Green Valley (c)	(301)	—	12,262
*20770	Greenbelt	(301)	21,098	21,456
*21740	Hagerstown	(301)	39,728	36,687
21740	Halfway (c)	(301)	—	10,065
21078	Havre de Grace	(410)	13,085	11,331
20748	Hillcrest Heights (c)	(301)	—	16,359
*20780	Hyattsville	(301)	15,376	14,733
21085	Joppatowne (c)	(410)	—	11,391
*20772	Kettering (c)	(301)	—	11,008
*21122	Lake Shore (c)	(410)	—	13,065
*20787	Langley Park (c)	(301)	—	16,214
20706	Lanham-Seabrook (c)	(301)	—	18,190
21227	Lansdowne-Baltimore Highlands (c)	(410)	—	15,724
*20707	Laurel	(301)	22,329	19,960
20653	Lexington Park (c)	(410)	—	11,021
21701	Linganore-Bartonsville (c)	(301)	—	12,529
21207	Lochearn (c)	(410)	—	25,269
*21093	Lutherville-Timonium (c)	(410)	—	15,814
21093	Mays Chapel (c)	(410)	—	11,427
21220	Middle River (c)	(410)	—	23,958
21207	Milford Mill (c)	(410)	—	26,527
*20886	Montgomery Village (c)	(301)	—	38,051
20784	New Carrollton (c)	(301)	12,460	12,589
*20815	North Bethesda (c)	(301)	—	38,610
20707	North Laurel (c)	(301)	—	20,468
20878	North Potomac (c)	(301)	—	23,044
21811	Ocean Pines (c)	(410)	—	10,496
21113	Odenton (c)	(410)	—	20,534
*20832	Olney (c)	(301)	—	31,438
21206	Overlea (c)	(410)	—	12,148
21117	Owings Mills (c)	(410)	—	20,193
*20750	Oxon Hill-Glassmanor (c)	(301)	—	35,355
21234	Parkville (c)	(410)	—	31,118
21401	Parole (c)	(410)	—	14,031
*21122	Pasadena (c)	(410)	—	12,093
21128	Perry Hall (c)	(410)	—	28,705
*21282	Pikesville (c)	(410)	—	29,123
*20850	Potomac (c)	(301)	—	44,822
21133	Randallstown (c)	(301)	—	30,870
20855	Redland (c)	(301)	—	16,998
*21136	Reisterstown (c)	(410)	—	22,438
*21122	Riviera Beach (c)	(410)	—	12,695
*20850	Rockville	(301)	60,734	47,388

ZIP	Place	Area Code	2008	2000
20772	Rosaryville (c)	(301)	—	12,322
21237	Rosedale (c)	(410)	—	19,199
21221	Rossville (c)	(410)	—	11,515
*20602	Saint Charles (c)	(301)	—	33,379
*21801	Salisbury	(410)	28,200	23,743
*20763	Savage-Guilford (c)	(410)	—	12,918
21144	Severn (c)	(410)	—	35,076
21146	Severna Park (c)	(410)	—	28,507
*20907	Silver Spring (c)	(301)	—	76,540
21061	South Gate (c)	(410)	—	28,672
20707	South Laurel (c)	(301)	—	20,479
*20752	Suitland-Silver Hills (c)	(301)	—	33,515
*20913	Takoma Park	(301)	17,701	17,299
*21204	Towson (c)	(410)	—	51,793
*20602	Waldorf (c)	(301)	—	22,312
20743	Walker Mill (c)	(301)	—	11,104
*21157	Westminster	(410)	17,689	16,731
*20902	Wheaton-Glenmont (c)	(301)	—	57,694
20903	White Oak (c)	(301)	—	20,973
21207	Woodlawn (c) (Baltimore Co.)	(410)	—	36,079

Massachusetts

Area code (339) overlays area code (781). Area code (351) overlays area code (978). Area code (774) overlays area code (508). Area code (857) overlays area code (617). See introductory note.

ZIP	Place	Area Code	2008	2000
02351	Abington	(781)	16,689	14,605
*01720	Acton	(978)	20,797	20,331
*02743	Acushnet	(508)	10,368	10,161
01001	Agawam	(413)	28,091	28,144
01913	Amesbury (c)	(978)	—	12,327
01913	Amesbury	(978)	16,584	16,450
*01002	Amherst	(413)	35,565	34,874
*01002	Amherst Center (c)	(413)	—	17,050
*01810	Andover	(978)	33,418	31,247
*02205	Arlington	(781)	40,993	42,389
01721	Ashland	(508)	15,807	14,674
*01331	Athol	(978)	11,570	11,299
02703	Attleboro	(508)	42,833	42,068
01501	Auburn	(508)	16,222	15,901
*02630	Barnstable Town	(508)	46,184	—
*01730	Bedford	(781)	13,545	12,595
01007	Belchertown	(413)	14,233	12,968
02019	Bellingham	(508)	15,900	15,314
*02478	Belmont	(781)	23,291	24,194
01915	Beverly	(978)	39,343	39,862
*01821	Billerica	(978)	41,844	38,981
*02205	Boston	(617)	609,023	589,141
*02532	Bourne	(508)	19,392	18,721
*02185	Braintree	(781)	35,294	33,828
*02324	Bridgewater	(508)	25,774	25,185
*02303	Brockton	(508)	93,007	94,304
*02446	Brookline	(617)	54,896	57,107
*01803	Burlington	(781)	24,985	22,876
*02139	Cambridge	(617)	105,596	101,355
*02021	Canton	(781)	22,048	20,775
*02330	Carver	(508)	11,574	11,163
01507	Charlton	(508)	12,585	11,263
01824	Chelmsford	(978)	34,409	33,858
02150	Chelsea	(617)	41,577	35,080
*01020	Chicopee	(413)	54,941	54,653
01510	Clinton	(978)	13,965	13,435
01742	Concord	(978)	17,450	16,993
01923	Danvers	(978)	26,762	25,212
*02714	Dartmouth	(508)	33,899	30,666
*02026	Dedham	(781)	24,630	23,464
02638	Dennis	(508)	15,349	15,973
01826	Dracut	(978)	29,501	28,562
01571	Dudley	(508)	11,073	10,036
*02332	Duxbury	(781)	14,496	14,248
02333	East Bridgewater	(508)	13,996	12,974
*01028	East Longmeadow	(413)	15,332	14,100
01027	Easthampton	(413)	16,195	15,994
*02334	Easton	(508)	23,209	22,299
02149	Everett	(617)	37,353	38,037
02719	Fairhaven	(508)	16,112	16,159
*02722	Fall River	(508)	90,931	91,938
*02540	Falmouth	(508)	33,123	32,660
01420	Fitchburg	(978)	40,239	39,102
02035	Foxborough	(508)	16,347	16,246
*01701	Framingham	(508)	64,885	66,910
02038	Franklin	(508)	32,148	29,560
*01440	Gardner	(978)	20,682	20,770
*01930	Gloucester	(978)	30,243	30,273
01519	Grafton	(508)	17,553	14,894
*01301	Greenfield	(413)	17,828	18,168
*01301	Greenfield (c)	(413)	—	13,716
*01450	Groton	(978)	10,632	9,547
*02339	Hanover	(781)	13,995	13,164
*02341	Hanson	(781)	10,019	9,495
02645	Harwich	(508)	12,298	12,386
*01830	Haverhill	(978)	61,275	58,969

ZIP	Place	Area Code	2008	2000
*02043	Hingham	(781)	22,561	19,882
02343	Holbrook	(781)	10,644	10,785
01520	Holden	(508)	16,608	15,621
01746	Holliston	(508)	13,901	13,801
*01040	Holyoke	(413)	39,947	39,838
01748	Hopkinton	(508)	14,338	13,346
01749	Hudson	(978)	19,597	18,113
01749	Hudson (c)	(978)	—	14,388
02045	Hull	(781)	11,041	11,050
02601	Hyannis (c)	(508)	—	11,050
01938	Ipswich	(978)	13,219	12,987
02364	Kingston	(781)	12,328	11,780
02347	Lakeville	(508)	10,515	9,821
*01842	Lawrence	(978)	70,014	72,043
01524	Leicester	(508)	10,990	10,471
01453	Leominster	(978)	41,055	41,303
*02420	Lexington	(781)	30,272	30,355
*01028	Longmeadow	(413)	15,329	15,633
*01853	Lowell	(978)	103,615	105,167
01056	Ludlow	(413)	22,410	21,209
*01901	Lynn	(781)	86,957	89,050
01940	Lynnfield	(781)	11,412	11,542
02148	Malden	(781)	55,597	56,340
*02048	Mansfield	(508)	23,969	22,414
01945	Marblehead	(781)	19,951	20,377
01752	Marlborough	(508)	37,932	36,255
*02050	Marshfield	(781)	24,735	24,324
02649	Mashpee	(508)	14,227	12,946
01754	Maynard	(978)	10,182	10,433
02052	Medfield	(508)	12,275	12,273
*02155	Medford	(781)	55,573	55,765
02053	Medway	(508)	12,785	12,448
02176	Melrose	(781)	26,708	27,134
01844	Methuen	(978)	44,055	43,789
*02346	Middleborough	(508)	21,117	19,941
01757	Milford	(508)	27,246	26,799
01757	Milford (c)	(508)	—	24,230
*01527	Millbury	(508)	13,401	12,784
02186	Milton	(617)	26,187	26,062
*02584	Nantucket	(508)	11,215	9,520
01760	Natick	(508)	31,880	32,170
*02494	Needham	(781)	28,560	28,911
*02740	New Bedford	(508)	91,365	93,768
01950	Newburyport	(978)	17,542	17,189
*02456	Newton	(617)	82,139	83,829
02056	Norfolk	(508)	11,029	10,460
01247	North Adams	(413)	13,711	14,681
01845	North Andover	(978)	27,522	27,202
*02760	North Attleborough	(508)	27,794	27,143
02760	North Attleborough Center (c)	(508)	—	16,796
*01864	North Reading	(978)	17,272	13,837
*01060	Northampton	(413)	28,379	28,978
01532	Northborough	(508)	14,646	14,013
01534	Northbridge	(508)	14,383	13,182
*02766	Norton	(508)	19,186	18,036
02061	Norwell	(781)	10,293	9,765
02062	Norwood	(781)	28,211	28,587
01540	Oxford	(508)	13,615	13,352
01069	Palmer	(413)	12,933	12,497
*01960	Peabody	(978)	51,331	48,129
*02359	Pembroke	(781)	18,714	16,927
01463	Pepperell	(978)	11,382	11,142
*01201	Pittsfield	(413)	42,652	45,793
*02360	Plymouth	(508)	55,705	51,701
*02169	Quincy	(617)	92,339	88,025
02368	Randolph	(781)	30,082	30,963
*02767	Raynham	(508)	13,566	11,739
01867	Reading	(781)	23,052	23,708
02769	Rehoboth	(508)	11,474	10,172
02151	Revere	(781)	60,204	47,283
02370	Rockland	(781)	17,883	17,670
*01970	Salem	(978)	41,256	40,407
*02563	Sandwich	(508)	20,129	20,136
01906	Saugus	(781)	27,478	26,078
*02066	Scituate	(781)	17,926	17,863
02771	Seekonk	(508)	13,575	13,425
02067	Sharon	(781)	17,373	17,408
*01545	Shrewsbury	(508)	33,435	31,640
*02725	Somerset	(508)	18,055	18,234
*02143	Somerville	(617)	75,662	77,478
01075	South Hadley	(413)	17,241	17,196
01550	Southbridge	(508)	16,852	17,214
01550	Southbridge (c)	(508)	—	12,878
01562	Spencer	(508)	11,922	11,691
*01101	Springfield	(413)	150,640	152,082
02180	Stoneham	(781)	21,471	22,219
02072	Stoughton	(781)	26,927	27,149
01776	Sudbury	(978)	17,207	16,841
01907	Swampscott	(781)	13,944	14,412
02777	Swansea	(508)	16,155	15,901
*02780	Taunton	(508)	55,702	55,976

ZIP	Place	Area Code	2008	2000
01876	Tewksbury	(978)	29,543	28,851
01879	Tyngsborough	(978)	12,019	11,081
01569	Uxbridge	(508)	12,672	11,156
01880	Wakefield	(781)	24,717	24,804
02081	Walpole	(508)	23,133	22,824
*02451	Waltham	(781)	60,236	59,226
02571	Wareham	(508)	21,221	20,335
*02471	Watertown	(781)	32,365	32,986
01778	Wayland	(508)	12,996	13,100
01570	Webster	(508)	16,655	16,415
01570	Webster (c)	(508)	—	11,600
*02457	Wellesley	(781)	27,244	26,613
*01089	West Springfield	(413)	27,459	—
*01581	Westborough	(508)	18,467	17,997
*01085	Westfield	(413)	40,608	40,072
01886	Westford	(978)	22,066	20,754
02493	Weston	(781)	11,711	11,469
02790	Westport	(508)	15,417	14,183
02090	Westwood	(781)	14,189	14,117
*02188	Weymouth	(781)	53,261	53,988
02382	Whitman	(781)	14,447	13,882
01095	Wilbraham	(413)	13,970	13,473
01887	Wilmington	(978)	21,649	21,363
01475	Winchendon	(978)	10,164	9,611
01890	Winchester	(781)	21,090	20,810
02152	Winthrop	(617)	21,880	18,303
*01801	Woburn	(781)	36,871	37,258
*01613	Worcester	(508)	175,011	172,648
*02093	Wrentham	(508)	11,133	10,554
*02675	Yarmouth	(508)	23,778	24,807

Michigan

Area code (947) overlays area code (248).

ZIP	Place	Area Code	2008	2000
49221	Adrian	(517)	21,391	21,574
*48101	Allen Park	(313)	26,014	29,376
49401	Allendale (c)	(616)	—	11,555
49707	Alpena	(989)	10,465	11,304
*48106	Ann Arbor	(734)	114,386	114,024
*48321	Auburn Hills	(248)	20,931	19,837
*49016	Battle Creek	(269)	52,053	53,364
*48707	Bay City	(989)	33,874	36,817
48505	Beecher (c)	(810)	—	12,793
*49022	Benton Harbor	(269)	10,814	11,182
48072	Berkley	(248)	14,787	15,531
49307	Big Rapids	(231)	10,257	10,849
*48012	Birmingham	(248)	18,932	19,291
*48301	Bloomfield (c)	(248)	—	43,021
48509	Burton	(810)	29,845	30,308
49601	Cadillac	(231)	10,245	10,000
*48184	Canton (c)	(734)	—	76,366
*48017	Clawson	(248)	12,157	12,732
48046	Clinton (c)	(517)	—	95,648
49036	Coldwater	(517)	10,514	12,697
49321	Comstock Park (c)	(616)	—	10,674
49508	Cutlerville (c)	(616)	—	15,114
*48120	Dearborn	(313)	86,477	97,775
*48127	Dearborn Heights	(313)	51,972	58,264
*48231	Detroit	(313)	912,062	951,270
*49506	East Grand Rapids	(616)	10,467	10,764
*48826	East Lansing	(517)	45,857	46,525
48021	Eastpointe	(586)	32,497	34,077
49829	Escanaba	(906)	12,214	13,140
*48333	Farmington Hills	(248)	78,522	82,111
48430	Fenton	(810)	11,678	10,582
48220	Ferndale	(248)	21,112	22,105
*48501	Flint	(810)	112,900	124,943
49506	Forest Hills (c)	(616)	—	20,942
48026	Fraser	(586)	14,902	15,297
*48135	Garden City	(734)	26,743	30,047
49417	Grand Haven	(616)	10,608	11,168
*49501	Grand Rapids	(616)	193,396	197,800
*49418	Grandville	(616)	16,718	16,263
48138	Grosse Ile (c)	(734)	—	10,894
48230	Grosse Pointe Park	(313)	10,956	12,443
48230	Grosse Pointe Woods	(313)	15,154	17,080
*48212	Hamtramck	(313)	20,512	22,976
48225	Harper Woods	(313)	12,584	14,254
48625	Harrison (c)	(989)	—	24,461
48840	Haslett (c)	(517)	—	11,283
48030	Hazel Park	(248)	17,955	18,963
48203	Highland Park	(313)	14,153	16,746
*49423	Holland	(616)	34,076	35,048
48842	Holt (c)	(517)	—	11,315
48141	Inkster	(313)/(734)	26,621	30,115
48846	Ionia	(616)	12,589	10,569
*49204	Jackson	(517)	33,518	36,316
*49428	Jenison (c)	(616)	—	17,211
*49001	Kalamazoo	(269)	72,179	77,145
*49518	Kentwood	(616)	47,419	45,255
*48901	Lansing	(517)	113,968	119,128

ZIP	Place	Area Code	2008	2000
48146	Lincoln Park	(313)	35,317	40,008
*48150	Livonia	(734)	91,220	100,545
48071	Madison Heights	(248)	29,531	31,101
49855	Marquette	(906)	20,916	19,661
*48640	Midland	(989)	40,917	41,685
*48161	Monroe	(734)	21,374	22,076
*48046	Mount Clemens	(586)	16,781	17,312
*48804	Mount Pleasant	(989)	26,675	25,946
49444	Muskegon Heights	(231)	11,623	12,049
*49440	Muskegon	(231)	39,401	40,105
*48047	New Baltimore	(586)	11,346	7,405
*49120	Niles	(269)	11,258	12,204
49505	Northview (c)	(616)	—	14,730
*49441	Norton Shores	(231)	23,307	22,527
*48376	Novi	(248)	54,054	47,386
48237	Oak Park	(248)	30,547	29,793
*48805	Okemos (c)	(517)	—	20,216
*48867	Owosso	(989)	14,963	15,713
48170	Plymouth Township (c)	(734)	—	27,798
*48343	Pontiac	(248)	66,095	66,337
*48061	Port Huron	(810)	30,869	32,338
*49081	Portage	(269)	46,133	44,897
*48239	Redford (c)	(313)	—	51,622
*48192	Riverview	(734)	11,817	13,272
*48308	Rochester	(248)	11,002	10,467
*48306	Rochester Hills	(248)	69,014	68,825
48174	Romulus	(313)/(734)	22,963	22,979
48066	Roseville	(586)	46,782	48,129
*48068	Royal Oak	(248)	57,110	60,062
48604	Saginaw Township North (c)	(989)	—	24,994
48603	Saginaw Township South (c)	(989)	—	13,801
*48605	Saginaw	(989)	55,620	61,799
*48080	Saint Clair Shores	(313)	60,364	63,096
*49783	Sault Sainte Marie	(906)	14,087	16,542
49455	Shelby (c)	(231)	—	65,159
*48037	Southfield	(248)	75,392	78,296
48195	Southgate	(734)	27,739	30,136
48178	South Lyon	(248)	10,959	10,036
*48311	Sterling Heights	(586)	127,160	124,471
49091	Sturgis	(269)	10,916	11,285
48180	Taylor	(313)/(734)	60,619	65,868
*49684	Traverse City	(231)	14,398	14,532
48183	Trenton	(734)	17,965	19,584
*48099	Troy	(248)	80,264	80,959
49534	Walker	(616)	23,722	21,842
*48090	Warren	(586)	133,939	138,247
*48329	Waterford (c)	(248)	—	73,150
48917	Waverly (c)	(517)	—	16,194
48184	Wayne	(734)	17,186	19,051
*48323	West Bloomfield Township (c)	(248)	—	64,862
*48185	Westland	(313)/(734)	78,961	86,602
48393	Wixom	(248)	13,425	13,263
48183	Woodhaven	(734)	12,634	12,530
*48192	Wyandotte	(734)	24,739	28,006
*49509	Wyoming	(616)	70,462	69,368
*48197	Ypsilanti	(734)	21,464	22,362

Minnesota

Area codes (651), (763), and (952) overlay area code (612).

ZIP	Place	Area Code	2008	2000
56007	Albert Lea	(507)	17,389	18,356
56308	Alexandria	(320)	11,237	8,820
*55304	Andover	(763)	30,442	26,588
*55303	Anoka	(612)	17,289	18,076
55124	Apple Valley	(952)	50,004	45,527
55912	Austin	(507)	22,800	23,314
*56601	Bemidji	(218)	13,541	11,917
*55014	Blaine	(651)	55,042	44,942
*55420	Bloomington	(952)	81,280	85,172
*56401	Brainerd	(218)	13,691	13,178
*55429	Brooklyn Center	(763)	27,402	29,172
*55443	Brooklyn Park	(763)	71,308	67,388
55313	Buffalo	(763)	14,222	10,097
*55337	Burnsville	(651)	59,139	60,220
55316	Champlin	(763)	23,503	22,193
55317	Chanhassen	(952)	23,480	20,321
55318	Chaska	(952)	24,116	17,449
55720	Cloquet	(218)	11,387	11,201
55421	Columbia Heights	(612)	18,210	18,520
*55433	Coon Rapids	(763)	61,832	61,607
55016	Cottage Grove	(651)	33,623	30,582
*55428	Crystal	(763)	21,707	22,698
*55806	Duluth	(218)	84,284	86,918
*55121	Eagan	(651)	63,985	63,557
*55005	East Bethel	(763)	11,895	10,941
*55344	Eden Prairie	(612)	61,191	54,901
*55424	Edina	(952)	45,608	47,425
55330	Elk River	(763)	23,194	16,447
*56031	Fairmont	(507)	10,221	10,889
55021	Faribault	(507)	22,009	20,818
55024	Farmington	(651)	19,057	12,365

ZIP	Place	Area Code	2008	2000
*56537	Fergus Falls	(218)	13,636	13,471
55025	Forest Lake	(651)	17,373	6,798
*55432	Fridley	(763)	25,868	27,449
*55427	Golden Valley	(763)	20,344	20,281
*55304	Ham Lake	(763)	15,020	12,710
55033	Hastings	(651)	22,126	18,204
*55746	Hibbing	(218)	16,209	17,071
*55343	Hopkins	(952)	16,961	17,145
*55038	Hugo	(651)	13,139	6,363
55350	Hutchinson	(320)	13,913	13,080
*55076	Inver Grove Heights	(651)	33,383	29,751
*55044	Lakeville	(952)	54,542	43,128
*55014	Lino Lakes	(651)	20,174	16,791
*56001	Mankato	(507)	36,245	32,427
*55311	Maple Grove	(763)	61,542	50,365
*55109	Maplewood	(651)	36,087	34,947
56258	Marshall	(507)	12,647	12,735
*55118	Mendota Heights	(651)	11,594	11,434
*55440	Minneapolis	(612)	382,605	382,618
*55345	Minnetonka	(952)	50,081	51,301
*55362	Monticello	(763)	11,780	7,868
*56560	Moorhead	(218)	36,012	32,177
55112	Mounds View	(763)	12,005	12,738
55112	New Brighton	(651)	21,563	22,206
*54427	New Hope	(763)	20,428	20,873
56073	New Ulm	(507)	13,048	13,594
55056	North Branch	(651)	10,417	8,023
55057	Northfield	(507)	19,633	17,147
*56002	North Mankato	(507)	12,530	11,798
55109	North Saint Paul	(651)	11,247	11,929
*55128	Oakdale	(651)	27,034	26,653
*55330	Otsego	(763)	13,874	6,389
55060	Owatonna	(507)	24,855	22,434
*55446	Plymouth	(763)	71,486	65,894
55372	Prior Lake	(952)	23,836	15,917
55303	Ramsey	(763)	23,734	18,510
55066	Red Wing	(651)	15,687	16,116
55423	Richfield	(612)	32,728	34,439
55422	Robbinsdale	(763)	13,518	14,123
*55901	Rochester	(507)	100,413	85,806
55068	Rosemount	(651)	21,197	14,619
*55113	Roseville	(651)	32,815	33,690
*56301	Saint Cloud	(320)	66,948	59,107
*55426	Saint Louis Park	(952)	45,465	44,126
55376	Saint Michael	(763)	15,278	9,099
*55101	Saint Paul	(651)	279,590	287,151
56082	Saint Peter	(507)	10,971	9,747
56377	Sartell	(320)	13,915	9,641
56379	Sauk Rapids	(320)	12,013	10,213
55378	Savage	(952)	27,692	21,115
*55379	Shakopee	(612)	33,455	20,568
55126	Shoreview	(651)	25,111	25,924
*55075	South Saint Paul	(651)	19,552	20,167
*55082	Stillwater	(651)	17,896	15,143
*55127	Vadnais Heights	(651)	12,506	13,069
*55118	West Saint Paul	(651)	18,935	19,405
*55110	White Bear Lake	(651)	24,095	24,325
56201	Willmar	(320)	17,774	18,351
*55987	Winona	(507)	26,785	27,069
*55125	Woodbury	(651)	56,128	46,463
56187	Worthington	(507)	11,036	11,283

Mississippi

Area code (769) overlays area code (601).

ZIP	Place	Area Code	2008	2000
*39530	Biloxi	(228)	45,670	50,644
*39042	Brandon	(601)	22,160	16,436
*39601	Brookhaven	(601)	13,296	9,861
39046	Canton	(601)	12,520	12,911
*38614	Clarksdale	(662)	18,006	20,645
*38732	Cleveland	(662)	12,218	13,841
*39056	Clinton	(601)	26,313	23,347
*39701	Columbus	(662)	23,798	25,944
*38834	Corinth	(662)	14,253	14,054
39553	Gautier	(228)	16,306	11,681
*38701	Greenville	(662)	35,764	41,633
*38930	Greenwood	(662)	16,084	18,425
*38901	Grenada	(662)	14,664	14,879
*39501	Gulfport	(228)	70,055	71,127
*39401	Hattiesburg	(601)	51,993	44,779
38632	Hernando	(662)	12,318	6,812
38637	Horn Lake	(662)	24,669	14,099
*38751	Indianola	(662)	10,805	12,066
*39205	Jackson	(601)	173,861	184,256
*39440	Laurel	(601)	18,693	18,393
39560	Long Beach	(228)	12,234	17,320
*39110	Madison	(601)	17,681	14,692
*39648	McComb	(601)	13,684	13,337
*39302	Meridian	(601)	38,232	39,968
*39563	Moss Point	(228)	13,951	15,851
*39120	Natchez	(601)	16,413	18,464

ZIP	Place	Area Code	2008	2000
*39564	Ocean Springs	(228)	17,149	17,225
38654	Olive Branch	(662)	31,830	21,054
38655	Oxford	(662)	17,265	11,756
*39567	Pascagoula	(228)	23,609	26,200
*39288	Pearl	(601)	24,400	21,961
39465	Petal	(601)	10,575	7,579
39466	Picayune	(601)	11,787	10,535
*39157	Ridgeland	(601)	21,509	20,173
*38671	Southaven	(662)	44,076	28,977
*39759	Starkville	(662)	24,187	21,869
*38801	Tupelo	(662)	36,233	34,211
*39180	Vicksburg	(601)	24,974	26,407
39773	West Point	(662)	11,292	12,145
39194	Yazoo City	(662)	11,425	14,550

Missouri

ZIP	Place	Area Code	2008	2000
63123	Affton (c)	(314)	—	20,535
63010	Arnold	(636)	20,603	19,965
*63011	Ballwin	(636)	30,033	31,283
63137	Bellefontaine Neighbors	(314)	10,241	11,271
64012	Belton	(816)	24,591	21,730
*64015	Blue Springs	(816)	55,698	48,080
*65613	Bolivar	(417)	11,013	9,143
*63044	Bridgeton	(314)	15,028	15,550
*63701	Cape Girardeau	(573)	37,370	35,349
64836	Carthage	(417)	13,916	12,668
*63017	Chesterfield	(636)	46,064	46,802
*63105	Clayton	(314)	16,088	12,825
*65201	Columbia	(573)	100,733	84,531
*63128	Concord (c)	(314)	—	16,689
63126	Crestwood	(314)	11,408	11,863
63141	Creve Coeur	(314)	16,868	16,500
64024	Excelsior Springs	(816)	12,002	10,847
63640	Farmington	(573)	16,097	13,924
*63135	Ferguson	(314)	20,964	22,406
63028	Festus	(636)	11,246	9,660
*63033	Florissant	(314)	50,561	50,497
65473	Fort Leonard Wood (c)	(573)		13,666
65251	Fulton	(573)	12,707	12,128
*64118	Gladstone	(816)	28,243	26,365
64029	Grain Valley	(816)	10,352	5,160
64030	Grandview	(816)	24,033	24,881
63401	Hannibal	(573)	17,432	17,757
*63042	Hazelwood	(314)	25,345	26,206
*64050	Independence	(816)	110,440	113,288
63755	Jackson	(573)	13,744	11,947
*65101	Jefferson City	(573)	40,771	39,636
63136	Jennings	(314)	14,625	15,469
*64801	Joplin	(417)	49,775	45,504
*64108	Kansas City	(816)	451,572	441,545
63857	Kennett	(573)	10,707	11,260
*63501	Kirksville	(660)	17,368	16,988
63122	Kirkwood	(314)	26,760	27,324
63367	Lake Saint Louis	(636)	14,160	10,169
65536	Lebanon	(417)	14,336	12,155
*64063	Lee's Summit	(816)	84,208	70,700
63125	Lemay (c)	(314)	—	17,215
*64068	Liberty	(816)	30,568	26,232
*63011	Manchester	(636)	18,569	19,161
65340	Marshall	(660)	12,118	12,433
63043	Maryland Heights	(314)	25,949	25,756
64468	Maryville	(816)	10,800	10,581
63129	Mehlville (c)	(314)	—	28,822
65265	Mexico	(573)	11,074	11,320
65270	Moberly	(660)	14,227	11,945
*64850	Neosho	(417)	11,317	10,505
65714	Nixa	(417)	18,829	12,124
63366	O'Fallon	(636)	76,819	46,169
63129	Oakville (c)	(314)	—	35,309
63114	Overland	(314)	15,632	16,838
65721	Ozark	(417)	18,095	9,665
*63901	Poplar Bluff	(573)	17,096	16,651
64083	Raymore	(816)	17,703	11,146
*64133	Raytown	(816)	28,194	30,388
65738	Republic	(417)	13,715	8,438
*65401	Rolla	(573)	18,438	16,367
63074	Saint Ann	(314)	12,766	13,607
*63301	Saint Charles	(636)	64,386	60,321
*64501	Saint Joseph	(816)	76,197	73,990
*63166	Saint Louis	(314)	354,361	348,189
*63376	Saint Peters	(636)	55,500	51,381
*65301	Sedalia	(660)	20,990	20,339
63801	Sikeston	(573)	17,053	16,992
63138	Spanish Lake (c)	(314)	—	21,337
*65801	Springfield	(417)	156,206	151,580
63011	Town and Country	(314)	10,710	10,894
63379	Troy	(314)	12,270	6,737
63130	University City	(314)	36,289	37,428
64093	Warrensburg	(660)	19,034	16,340
63090	Washington	(636)	14,392	13,243
64870	Webb City	(417)	11,532	9,812

ZIP	Place	Area Code	2008	2000
63119	Webster Groves	(314)	22,335	23,230
63385	Wentzville	(636)	23,768	6,896
*65775	West Plains	(417)	12,045	10,866
*63011	Wildwood	(314)	34,195	32,884

Montana (406)

ZIP	Place	2008	2000
*59101	Billings	103,994	89,847
*59718	Bozeman	39,442	27,509
*59701	Butte–Silver Bow	32,119	33,892
*59401	Great Falls	59,251	56,690
*59601	Helena	29,351	25,780
*59901	Kalispell	21,182	14,223
*59801	Missoula	68,202	57,053

Nebraska

ZIP	Place	Area Code	2008	2000
68310	Beatrice	(402)	12,769	12,496
*68108	Bellevue	(402)	49,699	44,382
68108	Chalco (c)	(402)	—	10,736
*68601	Columbus	(402)	21,595	20,971
*68025	Fremont	(402)	25,224	25,174
*68802	Grand Island	(308)	45,801	42,940
*68901	Hastings	(402)	25,394	24,064
*68847	Kearney	(308)	30,417	27,431
68128	La Vista	(402)	16,643	11,699
68850	Lexington	(308)	10,126	10,011
*68501	Lincoln	(402)	251,624	225,581
*68701	Norfolk	(402)	22,940	23,516
*69101	North Platte	(308)	24,107	23,878
*68005	Omaha	(402)	438,646	390,007
*68046	Papillion	(402)	23,739	16,363
*69361	Scottsbluff	(308)	14,785	14,732
68776	South Sioux City	(402)	11,936	11,925

Nevada

ZIP	Place	Area Code	2008	2000
*89005	Boulder City	(702)	14,720	14,966
*89701	Carson City	(775)	54,867	52,457
*89801	Elko	(775)	17,156	16,708
89139	Enterprise (c)	(702)	—	14,676
89408	Fernley	(775)	12,942	
89410	Gardnerville Ranchos (c)	(775)	—	11,054
*89015	Henderson	(702)	252,064	175,381
*89125	Las Vegas	(702)	558,383	478,434
*89024	Mesquite	(702)	16,444	9,389
*89030	North Las Vegas	(702)	217,253	115,488
*89041	Pahrump (c)	(775)	—	24,631
89109	Paradise (c)	(775)	—	186,070
*89501	Reno	(775)	217,016	180,480
*89431	Sparks	(775)	88,602	66,346
89815	Spring Creek (c)	(702)	—	10,548
*89147	Spring Valley (c)	(702)	—	117,390
89433	Sun Valley (c)	(775)	—	19,461
89110	Sunrise Manor (c)	(702)	—	156,120
89101	Winchester (c)	(702)	—	26,958

New Hampshire (603)
See introductory note.

ZIP	Place	2008	2000
03031	Amherst	11,801	10,769
03110	Bedford	21,122	18,274
03743	Claremont	12,968	13,151
*03301	Concord	42,255	40,687
03038	Derry	34,242	34,021
03038	Derry (c)	—	22,661
*03820	Dover	28,609	26,884
03824	Durham	13,667	12,664
03824	Durham (c)	—	12,904
03833	Exeter	14,762	14,058
03045	Goffstown	17,567	16,929
*03842	Hampton	15,367	14,937
03755	Hanover	11,068	10,850
03106	Hooksett	13,783	11,721
03051	Hudson	24,771	22,928
*03431	Keene	22,407	22,563
*03246	Laconia	17,065	16,411
*03766	Lebanon	12,806	12,568
03053	Londonderry	25,016	23,236
03053	Londonderry (c)	—	11,417
*03103	Manchester	108,586	107,006
03054	Merrimack	26,457	25,119
03055	Milford	14,972	13,535
*03060	Nashua	86,576	86,605
03076	Pelham	12,581	10,914
*03801	Portsmouth	20,443	20,784
03077	Raymond	10,234	9,674
*03867	Rochester	30,654	28,461
03079	Salem	29,414	28,112
03878	Somersworth	11,967	11,477
03087	Windham	13,230	10,709

New Jersey

Area code (551) overlays area code (201). Area code (848) overlays area code (732). Area code (862) overlays area code (973).

ZIP	Place	Area Code	2008	2000
07712	Asbury Park	(732)	16,546	16,930
*08401	Atlantic City	(609)	39,408	40,517
07001	Avenel (c)	(732)	—	17,552
08034	Barclay-Kingston (c)	(856)	—	10,728
07002	Bayonne	(201)	57,448	61,842
08722	Beachwood	(732)	10,835	10,375
07109	Belleville (c)	(973)	—	35,928
*08031	Bellmawr	(856)	11,176	11,262
07621	Bergenfield	(201)	25,611	26,247
07922	Berkeley Heights (c)	(908)	—	13,407
08805	Bound Brook	(732)	10,365	10,155
08302	Bridgeton	(856)	24,742	22,771
08203	Brigantine	(609)	12,647	12,594
08015	Browns Mills (c)	(609)	—	11,257
*08101	Camden	(856)	79,383	79,904
07008	Carteret	(732)	23,367	20,709
07009	Cedar Grove (c)	(973)	—	12,300
08002	Cherry Hill Mall (c)	(856)	—	13,238
07066	Clark (c)	(732)/(908)	—	14,597
07010	Cliffside Park	(201)	22,863	23,007
*07015	Clifton	(973)	78,219	78,672
08108	Collingswood	(856)	13,817	14,326
07067	Colonia (c)	(732)	—	17,811
07016	Cranford (c)	(908)	—	22,578
*07801	Dover	(973)	17,860	18,188
07628	Dumont	(201)	16,968	17,503
08816	East Brunswick (c)	(732)	—	46,756
*07019	East Orange	(973)	65,390	69,824
07073	East Rutherford	(201)/(973)	10,074	8,716
*07724	Eatontown	(732)	14,195	14,008
08043	Echelon (c)	(856)	—	10,440
*08818	Edison (c)	(732)/(908)	—	97,687
*07207	Elizabeth	(908)	124,755	120,568
*07407	Elmwood Park	(201)	18,634	18,925
*07631	Englewood	(201)	29,112	26,203
08618	Ewing (c)	(609)	—	35,707
07410	Fair Lawn	(201)/(973)	30,521	31,637
07022	Fairview (Bergen Co.)	(201)	13,540	13,255
07932	Florham Park	(973)	12,389	8,857
08863	Fords (c)	(732)	—	15,032
07024	Fort Lee	(201)	36,275	35,461
07417	Franklin Lakes	(201)	11,619	10,422
07728	Freehold	(732)	11,425	10,976
07026	Garfield	(862)/(973)	28,971	29,786
08028	Glassboro	(856)	19,751	19,068
07452	Glen Rock	(201)	11,131	11,546
*08030	Gloucester City	(856)	11,503	11,484
08053	Greentree (c)	(856)	—	11,536
07093	Guttenberg	(201)	10,528	10,807
*07602	Hackensack	(201)	42,804	42,677
08033	Haddonfield	(856)	11,442	11,659
08037	Hammonton	(609)	13,424	12,604
07029	Harrison	(973)	15,201	14,424
07604	Hasbrouck Heights	(201)	11,410	11,662
*07506	Hawthorne	(973)	17,997	18,218
08904	Highland Park	(732)	14,245	13,999
07205	Hillside (c)	(908)/(973)	—	21,747
07030	Hoboken	(201)	40,577	38,577
08753	Holiday City-Berkeley (c)	(732)	—	13,884
07843	Hopatcong	(973)	15,491	15,888
07111	Irvington (c)	(973)	—	60,695
08830	Iselin (c)	(732)	—	16,698
*07303	Jersey City	(201)	241,114	240,055
07734	Keansburg	(732)	10,550	10,732
*07032	Kearny	(201)/(973)	36,746	40,513
08701	Lakewood (c)	(732)	—	36,065
*08733	Leisure Village West-Pine Lake Park (c)	(732)	—	11,085
07035	Lincoln Park	(973)	10,635	10,930
07036	Linden	(732)/(908)	39,162	39,394
08021	Lindenwold	(856)	17,485	17,414
07424	Little Falls (c)	(973)	—	10,855
07643	Little Ferry	(201)	10,477	10,800
07039	Livingston (c)	(973)	—	27,391
07644	Lodi	(201)/(973)	23,776	23,971
07740	Long Branch	(732)	32,622	31,340
07071	Lyndhurst (c)	(201)	—	19,383
07940	Madison	(973)	16,009	16,530
08835	Manville	(908)	10,800	10,343
07040	Maplewood (c)	(973)	—	23,868
08053	Marlton (c)	(856)	—	10,260
08619	Mercerville-Hamilton Sq. (c)	(609)	—	26,419
08840	Metuchen	(732)	13,098	12,840
08846	Middlesex	(732)	13,644	13,717
07041	Millburn (c)	(973)	—	19,765
08332	Millville	(856)	28,930	26,847

ZIP	Place	Area Code	2008	2000
*07042	Montclair (c)	(973)	—	38,977
08057	Moorestown-Lenola (c)	(856)	—	13,860
07751	Morganville (c)	(732)	—	11,255
*07960	Morristown	(973)	19,268	18,544
*08901	New Brunswick	(732)	51,149	48,573
07646	New Milford	(201)	15,947	16,400
07974	New Providence	(908)	11,905	11,907
*07102	Newark	(973)	278,980	273,546
07031	North Arlington	(201)	14,701	15,181
08902	North Brunswick Twp. (c)	(732)	—	36,287
*07060	North Plainfield	(908)	21,143	21,103
07110	Nutley (c)	(973)	—	27,362
07436	Oakland	(201)	13,312	12,466
*08050	Ocean Acres (c)	(609)	—	13,155
08226	Ocean City	(609)	14,756	15,378
08857	Old Bridge (c)	(732)	—	22,833
*07051	Orange (c)	(973)	—	32,868
07650	Palisades Park	(201)	19,375	17,073
*07652	Paramus	(201)	26,128	25,737
07055	Passaic	(973)	66,884	67,861
*07510	Paterson	(973)	145,643	149,222
*08110	Pennsauken (c)	(856)	—	35,737
08070	Pennsville (c)	(856)	—	11,657
*08861	Perth Amboy	(732)	48,742	47,303
08865	Phillipsburg	(908)	14,528	15,166
08021	Pine Hill	(856)	11,308	10,880
*07061	Plainfield	(908)	46,126	47,829
*08232	Pleasantville	(609)	18,853	19,012
08742	Point Pleasant Beach	(732)	20,139	19,306
07442	Pompton Lakes	(973)	11,031	10,640
08536	Princeton Meadows (c)	(609)	—	13,436
*08540	Princeton	(609)	13,391	14,203
07065	Rahway	(732)	28,624	26,500
07446	Ramsey	(201)	14,595	14,351
*07701	Red Bank	(732)	11,866	11,844
07657	Ridgefield	(201)	10,851	10,830
07660	Ridgefield Park	(201)	12,370	12,873
*07451	Ridgewood	(201)/(973)	24,163	24,936
07456	Ringwood	(973)	12,681	12,396
07661	River Edge	(201)	10,674	10,946
07203	Roselle	(908)	20,599	21,274
07204	Roselle Park	(908)	12,802	13,281
07070	Rutherford	(201)	17,454	18,110
*08872	Sayreville	(732)	42,208	40,377
*07094	Secaucus	(201)	15,372	15,931
08244	Somers Point	(609)	11,343	11,614
08876	Somerville	(908)	12,637	12,423
07080	South Plainfield	(732)/(908)	22,623	21,810
*08882	South River	(732)	15,682	15,322
*07901	Summit	(908)	20,557	21,131
07670	Tenafly	(201)	14,662	13,806
*07724	Tinton Falls	(732)	19,703	15,053
*07512	Totowa	(973)	10,621	9,892
*08650	Trenton	(609)	82,883	85,403
07083	Union (Union Co.) (c)	(908)	—	66,167
*07087	Union City	(201)	62,183	67,088
08406	Ventnor City	(609)	12,187	12,910
*08360	Vineland	(856)	58,780	56,271
07057	Wallington	(201)/(973)	11,296	11,583
07465	Wanaque	(201)/(973)	12,195	10,266
07093	West New York	(201)	46,472	45,768
07424	West Paterson	(973)	11,908	10,987
*07091	Westfield	(732)/(908)	29,450	29,644
*07675	Westwood	(201)	10,699	10,999
*08096	Woodbury	(856)	10,450	10,307

New Mexico (505)

ZIP	Place	2008	2000
*88310	Alamogordo	35,757	35,582
*87101	Albuquerque	521,999	448,607
*88210	Artesia	10,994	10,692
*88220	Carlsbad	25,629	25,625
*88101	Clovis	32,352	32,667
*88030	Deming	15,480	14,116
*87401	Farmington	42,637	37,844
*87301	Gallup	19,979	20,209
*88240	Hobbs	30,476	28,657
*88001	Las Cruces	91,865	74,267
*87701	Las Vegas	13,818	14,565
87544	Los Alamos (c)	—	11,909
87031	Los Lunas	14,153	10,034
87107	North Valley (c)	—	11,923
*88130	Portales	12,215	11,131
*87124	Rio Rancho	79,655	51,765
*88201	Roswell	46,198	45,293
*87501	Santa Fe	71,831	62,203
*88061	Silver City	10,329	10,545
87105	South Valley (c)	—	39,060
*88063	Sunland Park	14,453	13,309

New York

Area code (347) overlays area code (718). Area codes (646) and (917) overlay area code (212).

ZIP	Place	Area Code	2008	2000
*12201	Albany	(518)	93,539	95,658
12010	Amsterdam	(518)	17,533	18,355
12603	Arlington (c)	(845)	—	12,481
*13021	Auburn	(315)	27,138	28,574
11702	Babylon	(631)	12,760	12,615
11510	Baldwin (c)	(516)	—	23,455
*14020	Batavia	(585)	15,202	16,256
11706	Bay Shore (c)	(631)	—	23,852
12508	Beacon	(845)	14,566	13,808
11710	Bellmore (c)	(516)	—	16,441
11714	Bethpage (c)	(516)	—	16,543
*13902	Binghamton	(607)	44,729	47,380
11717	Brentwood (c)	(631)	—	53,917
14610	Brighton (c)	(585)	—	35,584
*14240	Buffalo	(716)	270,919	292,648
*14424	Canandaigua	(585)	11,168	11,264
11720	Centereach (c)	(631)	—	27,285
11722	Central Islip (c)	(516)	—	31,950
14225	Cheektowaga (c)	(716)	—	79,988
12047	Cohoes	(518)	15,025	15,521
11725	Commack (c)	(631)	—	36,367
11726	Copiague (c)	(631)	—	21,922
11727	Coram (c)	(631)	—	34,923
*14830	Corning	(607)	10,281	10,842
13045	Cortland	(607)	18,434	18,740
11729	Deer Park (c)	(631)	—	28,316
14043	Depew	(716)	15,307	16,629
11746	Dix Hills (c)	(631)	—	26,024
10522	Dobbs Ferry	(914)	11,134	10,622
*14048	Dunkirk	(716)	12,085	13,131
11730	East Islip (c)	(631)	—	14,078
11758	East Massapequa (c)	(516)	—	19,565
11554	East Meadow (c)	(516)	—	37,461
11731	East Northport (c)	(631)	—	20,845
11772	East Patchogue (c)	(631)	—	20,824
11518	East Rockaway	(516)	10,438	10,414
10709	Eastchester (c)	(914)	—	18,564
*14901	Elmira	(607)	29,271	30,940
11003	Elmont (c)	(516)	—	32,657
11731	Elwood (c)	(631)	—	10,916
*13760	Endicott	(607)	12,411	13,038
13762	Endwell (c)	(607)	—	11,706
13219	Fairmount (c)	(315)	—	10,795
*11001	Floral Park	(516)	15,846	15,967
13603	Fort Drum (c)	(315)	—	12,123
11010	Franklin Square (c)	(516)	—	29,342
14063	Fredonia	(716)	11,064	10,706
11520	Freeport	(516)	43,881	43,783
13069	Fulton	(315)	11,219	11,855
*11530	Garden City	(516)	22,275	21,672
14624	Gates-North Gates (c)	(585)	—	15,138
*14456	Geneva	(315)	13,216	13,617
11542	Glen Cove	(516)	26,895	26,622
12801	Glens Falls	(518)	13,877	14,354
12078	Gloversville	(518)	14,990	15,413
14616	Greece (c)	(585)	—	14,614
11740	Greenlawn (c)	(631)	—	13,286
11946	Hampton Bays (c)	(631)	—	12,236
10528	Harrison	(914)	26,665	24,154
*11788	Hauppauge (c)	(631)	—	20,100
10927	Haverstraw	(845)	11,029	10,117
*11551	Hempstead	(516)	53,915	56,554
*11802	Hicksville (c)	(516)	—	41,260
*11743	Huntington (c)	(631)	—	18,403
11746	Huntington Station (c)	(631)	—	29,910
14617	Irondequoit (c)	(585)	—	52,354
11751	Islip (c)	(631)	—	20,575
*14850	Ithaca	(607)	29,763	29,287
*14702	Jamestown	(716)	29,463	31,730
10535	Jefferson Valley-Yorktown (c)	(914)	—	14,891
11753	Jericho (c)	(516)	—	13,045
13790	Johnson City	(607)	14,727	15,535
*14217	Kenmore	(716)	15,002	16,426
11754	Kings Park (c)	(631)	—	16,146
*12401	Kingston	(845)	22,441	23,456
10950	Kiryas Joel	(845)	21,793	13,138
14218	Lackawanna	(716)	17,588	19,064
11755	Lake Grove	(631)	10,948	10,250
11779	Lake Ronkonkoma (c)	(631)	—	19,701
*14086	Lancaster	(716)	11,108	11,188
11756	Levittown (c)	(516)	—	53,067
11757	Lindenhurst	(631)	28,824	27,819
*14094	Lockport	(716)	20,630	22,279
11561	Long Beach	(516)	35,698	35,462
11563	Lynbrook	(516)	19,852	19,911
10543	Mamaroneck	(914)	18,413	18,752
11949	Manorville (c)	(631)	—	11,131
11758	Massapequa (c)	(516)	—	22,652
11762	Massapequa Park	(516)	17,385	17,499
13662	Massena	(315)	10,539	11,209
11950	Mastic (c)	(631)	—	15,436
11951	Mastic Beach (c)	(631)	—	11,543
11763	Medford (c)	(631)	—	21,985
11747	Melville (c)	(631)	—	14,533
11566	Merrick (c)	(516)	—	22,764
*10940	Middletown	(845)	25,865	25,388
11764	Miller Place (c)	(631)	—	10,580
11501	Mineola	(516)	19,108	19,234
10952	Monsey (c)	(845)	—	14,504
10549	Mount Kisco	(914)	10,393	9,983
*10551	Mount Vernon	(914)	68,653	68,381
10954	Nanuet (c)	(845)	—	16,707
11767	Nesconset (c)	(631)	—	11,992
11590	New Cassel (c)	(516)	—	13,298
10956	New City (c)	(845)	—	34,038
*10802	New Rochelle	(914)	74,115	72,182
*10001	New York	(212)/(718)	8,363,710	8,008,278
*12550	Newburgh	(845)	28,101	28,259
*14302	Niagara Falls	(716)	51,345	55,593
11701	North Amityville (c)	(631)	—	16,572
11703	North Babylon (c)	(631)	—	17,877
11706	North Bay Shore (c)	(631)	—	14,992
11710	North Bellmore (c)	(516)	—	20,079
11757	North Lindenhurst (c)	(631)	—	11,767
11758	North Massapequa (c)	(516)	—	19,152
11566	North Merrick (c)	(516)	—	11,844
11040	North New Hyde Park (c)	(516)	—	14,542
14120	North Tonawanda	(716)	31,222	33,262
11580	North Valley Stream (c)	(516)	—	15,789
11793	North Wantagh (c)	(516)	—	12,156
11572	Oceanside (c)	(516)	—	32,733
13669	Ogdensburg	(315)	11,119	12,364
14760	Olean	(585)/(716)	14,149	15,347
13421	Oneida	(315)	10,723	10,987
13820	Oneonta	(607)	13,208	13,292
10562	Ossining	(914)	23,798	24,010
13126	Oswego	(315)	17,351	17,954
11772	Patchogue	(631)	12,194	11,919
10965	Pearl River (c)	(845)	—	15,553
10566	Peekskill	(914)	24,484	22,441
11803	Plainview (c)	(516)	—	25,637
*12901	Plattsburgh	(518)	19,393	18,816
10573	Port Chester	(914)	28,171	27,867
11050	Port Washington (c)	(516)	—	15,215
*12601	Poughkeepsie	(845)	29,654	29,871
11961	Ridge (c)	(631)	—	13,380
11901	Riverhead (c)	(631)	—	10,513
*14692	Rochester	(585)	206,886	219,773
*11571	Rockville Centre	(516)	24,414	24,568
11778	Rocky Point (c)	(631)	—	10,185
*13440	Rome	(315)	33,673	34,950
11779	Ronkonkoma (c)	(631)	—	20,029
11575	Roosevelt (c)	(516)	—	15,854
12303	Rotterdam (c)	(518)	—	20,536
10580	Rye	(914)	15,060	14,955
11780	Saint James (c)	(631)	—	13,268
13454	Salisbury (c)	(315)	—	12,341
12866	Saratoga Springs	(518)	28,844	26,186
11782	Sayville (c)	(631)	—	16,735
10583	Scarsdale	(914)	17,695	17,823
*12301	Schenectady	(518)	61,152	61,821
11783	Seaford (c)	(516)	—	15,791
11784	Selden (c)	(631)	—	21,861
10591	Sleepy Hollow	(914)	10,212	9,212
11787	Smithtown (c)	(631)	—	26,901
11735	South Farmingdale (c)	(516)	—	15,061
10977	Spring Valley	(845)	26,291	25,464
*11790	Stony Brook (c)	(631)	—	13,727
10980	Stony Point (c)	(845)	—	11,744
*10901	Suffern	(845)	11,088	11,006
11791	Syosset (c)	(516)	—	18,544
*13220	Syracuse	(315)	138,068	147,306
10591	Tarrytown	(914)	11,031	11,090
11776	Terryville (c)	(631)	—	10,589
*14150	Tonawanda	(716)	14,819	16,136
*12180	Troy	(518)	47,459	49,170
11553	Uniondale (c)	(516)	—	23,011
*13504	Utica	(315)	58,082	60,651
*11582	Valley Stream	(516)	36,007	36,368
11793	Wantagh (c)	(516)	—	18,971
*13601	Watertown	(315)	27,310	26,705
*11704	West Babylon (c)	(631)	—	43,452
10993	West Haverstraw	(845)	10,252	10,295
11795	West Islip (c)	(631)	—	28,907
14224	West Seneca (c)	(716)	—	45,943
*11590	Westbury (c)	(516)	15,065	14,263
*10602	White Plains	(914)	57,342	53,077
11598	Woodmere (c)	(516)	—	16,447
11798	Wyandach (c)	(631)	—	10,546
*10702	Yonkers	(914)	201,588	196,086

North Carolina

Area code (980) overlays area code (704).

ZIP	Place	Area Code	2008	2000
28315	Albemarle	(910)	15,522	15,680
*27502	Apex	(919)	33,075	20,212
*27203	Asheboro	(336)	24,609	21,672
*28802	Asheville	(828)	74,543	68,889
*28607	Boone	(828)	13,945	13,472
*27215	Burlington	(336)	50,857	44,917
27510	Carrboro	(919)	18,162	16,782
*27511	Cary	(919)	129,545	94,536
*27514	Chapel Hill	(919)	52,542	48,715
*28204	Charlotte	(704)	687,456	540,828
*27520	Clayton	(919)	15,841	6,973
27012	Clemmons	(336)	17,234	13,827
*28025	Concord	(704)	66,311	55,977
28031	Cornelius	(704)	24,487	11,969
*28036	Davidson	(704)	10,305	7,139
*28334	Dunn	(910)	10,029	9,196
*27701	Durham	(919)	223,284	187,035
*27288	Eden	(336)	15,469	15,908
*27909	Elizabeth City	(252)	20,025	17,188
*28302	Fayetteville	(910)	174,091	121,015
*28307	Fort Bragg (c)	(910)	—	29,183
27526	Fuquay-Varina	(919)	17,002	7,898
27529	Garner	(919)	27,138	17,757
*28052	Gastonia	(704)	72,505	66,277
*27530	Goldsboro	(919)	37,597	39,043
27253	Graham	(336)	14,533	12,833
*27420	Greensboro	(336)	250,642	223,891
*27834	Greenville	(252)	79,629	60,476
*28532	Havelock	(252)	21,764	22,442
*27536	Henderson	(252)	15,850	16,095
*28739	Hendersonville	(828)	12,005	10,420
*28603	Hickory	(828)	41,305	37,222
*27260	High Point	(336)	101,835	85,839
27540	Holly Springs	(919)	20,870	9,192
28348	Hope Mills	(910)	13,262	11,237
*28070	Huntersville	(704)	44,054	24,960
28079	Indian Trail	(704)	18,976	11,905
*28540	Jacksonville	(910)	76,233	66,715
*28081	Kannapolis	(704)	42,521	36,910
*27284	Kernersville	(336)	22,392	17,126
28086	Kings Mountain	(704)	11,175	9,693
*28502	Kinston	(252)	22,360	23,688
*28352	Laurinburg	(910)	15,548	15,874
*28645	Lenoir	(828)	17,890	16,793
27023	Lewisville	(336)	12,878	8,826
*27292	Lexington	(336)	20,407	19,953
*28092	Lincolnton	(704)	10,859	9,965
*28358	Lumberton	(910)	22,006	20,795
28403	Masonboro (c)	(910)	—	11,812
*28105	Matthews	(704)	26,901	22,127
27302	Mebane	(919)	10,624	7,284
28227	Mint Hill	(704)	20,369	14,922
*28110	Monroe	(704)	32,543	26,228
*28115	Mooresville	(704)	21,954	18,823
*28655	Morganton	(828)	17,194	17,310
27560	Morrisville	(919)	13,699	5,208
28120	Mount Holly	(704)	10,081	9,618
*28562	New Bern	(252)	28,586	23,128
28658	Newton	(828)	13,372	12,560
*28374	Pinehurst	(910)	12,331	9,706
28399	Piney Green (c)	(910)	—	11,658
*27611	Raleigh	(919)	392,552	276,093
*27320	Reidsville	(336)	14,871	14,485
27870	Roanoke Rapids	(252)	16,403	16,957
*27801	Rocky Mount	(252)	57,010	55,893
*28144	Salisbury	(704)	28,972	26,462
*27330	Sanford	(919)	29,284	23,220
*28150	Shelby	(704)	21,449	19,477
27577	Smithfield	(919)	12,965	11,510
*28387	Southern Pines	(910)	12,675	10,918
*28677	Statesville	(704)	26,414	23,320
27886	Tarboro	(252)	10,257	11,138
*27360	Thomasville	(336)	26,526	19,788
*27587	Wake Forest	(919)	27,068	12,588
27889	Washington	(252)	10,112	9,583
*28402	Wilmington	(910)	100,192	75,838
*27893	Wilson	(252)	48,433	44,405
*27102	Winston-Salem	(336)	217,600	185,776

North Dakota (701)

ZIP	Place	2008	2000
*58501	Bismarck	60,389	55,532
*58601	Dickinson	16,035	16,010
*58102	Fargo	93,531	90,599
*58201	Grand Forks	51,313	49,321
*58401	Jamestown	14,630	15,527
58554	Mandan	18,091	16,718
*58701	Minot	35,419	36,567
58078	West Fargo	23,708	14,940
*58801	Williston	12,641	12,512

Ohio

Area code (234) overlays area code (330). Area code (567) overlays area code (419).

ZIP	Place	Area Code	2008	2000
*44309	Akron	(330)	207,510	217,074
*44601	Alliance	(330)	22,476	23,253
44001	Amherst	(440)	11,724	11,797
44805	Ashland	(419)	21,850	21,249
*44004	Ashtabula	(440)	19,689	20,962
45701	Athens	(740)	22,088	21,342
44202	Aurora	(330)	14,548	13,556
44515	Austintown (c)	(330)	—	31,627
44012	Avon Lake	(440)	23,996	18,145
44011	Avon	(440)	17,086	11,446
44203	Barberton	(330)	26,581	27,899
44140	Bay Village	(440)	14,606	16,087
44122	Beachwood	(216)	11,108	12,186
45434	Beavercreek	(937)	39,909	37,984
44146	Bedford	(216)/(440)	12,965	14,214
*44146	Bedford Heights	(216)/(440)	10,485	11,375
43311	Bellefontaine	(937)	12,665	13,069
44017	Berea	(440)	17,987	18,970
43209	Bexley	(614)	12,507	13,203
*45242	Blue Ash	(513)	12,783	12,513
44513	Boardman (c)	(330)	—	37,215
*43402	Bowling Green	(419)	29,542	29,636
44141	Brecksville	(440)	12,851	13,382
45211	Bridgetown North (c)	(513)	—	12,569
44147	Broadview Heights	(440)	17,274	15,967
44144	Brooklyn	(216)	10,410	11,586
44142	Brook Park	(216)/(440)	19,194	21,218
44212	Brunswick	(330)	34,711	33,388
44820	Bucyrus	(419)	12,252	13,224
*43725	Cambridge	(740)	11,192	11,520
*44711	Canton	(330)	78,362	80,806
*45822	Celina	(419)	10,255	10,303
*45458	Centerville (Montgomery Co.)	(937)	22,904	23,024
45601	Chillicothe	(740)	22,296	21,796
*45202	Cincinnati	(513)	333,336	331,285
43113	Circleville	(740)	13,681	13,485
45315	Clayton	(937)	12,906	13,347
*44101	Cleveland	(216)	433,748	478,403
*44118	Cleveland Heights	(216)	45,827	49,958
*43216	Columbus	(614)	754,885	711,470
44030	Conneaut	(440)	12,355	12,485
43812	Coshocton	(740)	11,353	11,682
*44222	Cuyahoga Falls	(330)	51,090	49,374
*45401	Dayton	(937)	154,200	166,179
43512	Defiance	(419)	16,063	16,465
43015	Delaware	(740)	33,719	25,243
44622	Dover	(330)	12,466	12,210
*43016	Dublin	(614)/(740)	38,536	31,392
*44112	East Cleveland	(216)	24,507	27,217
*44095	Eastlake	(440)	19,520	20,255
43920	East Liverpool	(330)	11,996	13,089
*44035	Elyria	(440)	54,979	55,953
*45322	Englewood	(937)	12,686	12,235
*44117	Euclid	(216)	47,415	52,717
45324	Fairborn	(937)	32,366	32,052
*45011	Fairfield	(513)	42,384	42,097
44126	Fairview Park	(440)	15,762	17,572
*45839	Findlay	(419)	36,987	38,967
45224	Finneytown (c)	(513)	—	13,492
45240	Forest Park	(513)	18,514	19,463
45230	Forestville (c)	(513)	—	10,978
44830	Fostoria	(419)	13,000	13,931
45005	Franklin	(513)	12,941	11,396
43420	Fremont	(419)	16,655	17,375
43230	Gahanna	(614)	33,892	32,636
44833	Galion	(419)	10,737	11,341
*44125	Garfield Heights	(216)	27,734	30,734
44420	Girard	(330)	10,069	10,902
44232	Green	(330)	23,404	22,817
45331	Greenville	(937)	12,983	13,294
43123	Grove City	(614)	33,829	27,075
*45011	Hamilton	(513)	62,477	60,690
43026	Hilliard	(614)/(740)	27,901	24,230
45424	Huber Heights	(937)	37,148	38,212
*44236	Hudson	(330)	23,037	22,439
45638	Ironton	(740)	11,307	11,211
*44240	Kent	(330)	27,983	27,906
*45429	Kettering	(937)	53,708	57,502
44107	Lakewood	(216)	50,704	56,646
43130	Lancaster	(740)	36,976	35,335
45039	Landen (c)	(513)	—	12,766
45036	Lebanon	(513)	20,535	16,962
*45802	Lima	(419)	37,829	40,081
*44052	Lorain	(440)	70,239	68,652
*45140	Loveland	(513)	11,734	11,677
44124	Lyndhurst	(216)/(440)	13,848	15,279
*44056	Macedonia	(330)	10,435	9,224
*44901	Mansfield	(419)	49,579	49,346

ZIP	Place	Area Code	2008	2000
44137	Maple Heights	(216)	23,667	26,156
45750	Marietta	(740)	14,307	14,515
*43302	Marion	(740)	35,841	35,318
*43040	Marysville	(937)	18,212	15,942
45040	Mason	(513)	29,682	22,016
*44646	Massillon	(330)	32,613	31,325
43537	Maumee	(419)	13,856	15,237
44124	Mayfield Heights	(440)	17,737	19,386
*44256	Medina	(330)	26,011	25,139
*44060	Mentor	(440)	51,825	50,278
*45343	Miamisburg	(937)	19,793	19,489
44130	Middleburg Heights	(216)/(440)	14,928	15,542
*45042	Middletown	(513)	51,422	51,605
*45050	Monroe	(513)	12,178	7,133
45242	Montgomery	(513)	10,458	10,163
43050	Mount Vernon	(740)	16,037	14,375
44657	New Franklin	(330)	14,937	2,191
44663	New Philadelphia	(330)	17,319	17,056
*43055	Newark	(740)	47,236	46,279
44446	Niles	(330)	19,268	20,932
45239	Northbrook (c)	(513)	—	11,076
*44720	North Canton	(330)	16,925	16,369
44070	North Olmsted	(440)	31,319	34,113
*44039	North Ridgeville	(440)	28,153	22,338
44133	North Royalton	(440)	29,331	28,648
44203	Norton	(330)	11,472	11,523
44857	Norwalk	(419)	16,637	16,238
*45212	Norwood	(513)	20,341	21,675
*43616	Oregon	(419)	18,921	19,355
45056	Oxford	(513)	22,887	21,943
44077	Painesville	(440)	18,474	17,503
*44129	Parma	(216)/(440)	77,947	85,655
44130	Parma Heights	(216)/(440)	19,757	21,659
43062	Pataskala	(740)	12,683	10,249
*43551	Perrysburg	(419)	17,049	16,945
43147	Pickerington	(614)/(740)	17,531	9,792
45356	Piqua	(937)	20,582	20,738
*45662	Portsmouth	(740)	20,297	20,909
43065	Powell	(614)	12,814	6,247
44266	Ravenna	(330)	11,381	11,771
*45215	Reading	(513)	10,523	11,292
43068	Reynoldsburg	(614)/(740)	33,657	32,069
44143	Richmond Heights	(216)/(440)	10,174	10,944
45431	Riverside	(937)	25,327	23,545
44116	Rocky River	(440)	18,900	20,735
44460	Salem	(330)	11,781	12,197
*44870	Sandusky	(419)	25,688	27,844
44131	Seven Hills	(216)/(440)	11,616	12,080
*44122	Shaker Heights	(216)	26,460	29,405
*45241	Sharonville	(513)	13,377	13,804
44878	Shiloh (c)	(419)	—	11,272
*45365	Sidney	(937)	19,944	20,211
44139	Solon	(440)	21,866	21,802
*44121	South Euclid	(216)	21,209	23,537
45066	Springboro	(513)	17,551	12,380
45246	Springdale	(513)	10,384	10,563
*45501	Springfield	(937)	62,269	65,358
*43952	Steubenville	(740)	18,820	19,015
44224	Stow	(330)	33,899	32,139
44241	Streetsboro	(330)	14,488	12,311
*44136	Strongsville	(440)	42,617	43,858
44471	Struthers	(330)	10,734	11,756
43560	Sylvania	(419)	19,185	18,670
44278	Tallmadge	(330)	17,293	16,390
44883	Tiffin	(419)	17,347	18,135
*43601	Toledo	(419)	293,201	313,619
45067	Trenton	(513)	10,866	8,746
*45426	Trotwood	(937)	26,039	27,420
*45373	Troy	(937)	21,975	21,999
44087	Twinsburg	(330)	17,394	17,006
*44122	University Heights	(216)	12,519	14,146
*43221	Upper Arlington	(614)	31,878	33,686
43078	Urbana	(937)	11,442	11,613
45377	Vandalia	(937)	14,124	14,603
45891	Van Wert	(419)	10,211	10,690
*44089	Vermilion	(440)	10,754	10,927
*44281	Wadsworth	(330)	20,696	18,437
*44481	Warren	(330)	43,789	46,832
*44122	Warrensville Heights	(216)	13,618	15,109
*43160	Washington	(740)	13,654	—
*45449	West Carrollton City	(937)	12,761	13,818
*43081	Westerville	(614)	36,231	35,318
44145	Westlake	(440)	30,546	31,719
45239	White Oak (c)	(513)	—	13,277
43213	Whitehall	(614)	18,180	19,201
44092	Wickliffe	(440)	12,983	13,484
*44094	Willoughby	(440)	22,561	22,621
*44095	Willowick	(440)	13,727	14,361
45177	Wilmington	(937)	12,603	11,921
44691	Wooster	(330)	26,212	24,811
43085	Worthington	(614)	13,314	14,125

ZIP	Place	Area Code	2008	2000
45385	Xenia	(937)	27,357	24,164
*44501	Youngstown	(330)	72,925	82,026
*43701	Zanesville	(740)	25,129	25,586

Oklahoma

ZIP	Place	Area Code	2008	2000
*74820	Ada	(580)	16,729	15,691
*73521	Altus	(580)	18,912	21,447
*73401	Ardmore	(580)	24,810	23,711
*74003	Bartlesville	(918)	35,914	34,748
73008	Bethany	(405)	19,729	20,307
74008	Bixby	(918)	20,678	13,336
*74012	Broken Arrow	(918)	92,931	74,859
*73018	Chickasha	(405)	17,062	15,850
73020	Choctaw	(405)	11,354	9,377
*74017	Claremore	(918)	17,458	15,873
*73115	Del City	(405)	22,067	22,128
*73533	Duncan	(580)	22,617	22,505
74701	Durant	(580)	16,450	13,549
*73034	Edmond	(405)	79,559	68,315
*73644	Elk City	(580)	11,311	10,510
*73036	El Reno	(405)	16,545	16,212
*73701	Enid	(580)	47,396	47,045
73044	Guthrie	(405)	11,043	9,925
73942	Guymon	(580)	10,702	10,472
74037	Jenks	(918)	15,590	9,557
*73501	Lawton	(580)	90,091	92,757
*74501	McAlester	(918)	18,388	17,783
*74354	Miami	(918)	13,027	13,704
*73140	Midwest City	(405)	56,394	54,088
*73153	Moore	(405)	52,615	41,138
*74401	Muskogee	(918)	40,099	38,310
73064	Mustang	(405)	17,727	13,156
*73069	Norman	(405)	106,957	95,694
*73125	Oklahoma City	(405)	551,789	506,132
74447	Okmulgee	(918)	12,634	13,022
*74055	Owasso	(918)	27,467	18,502
*74601	Ponca City	(580)	24,507	25,919
74063	Sand Springs	(918)	18,489	17,451
*74066	Sapulpa	(918)	21,173	19,166
*74801	Shawnee	(405)	30,562	28,692
*74074	Stillwater	(405)	47,653	39,065
*74464	Tahlequah	(918)	16,623	14,458
*74103	Tulsa	(918)	385,635	393,049
73096	Weatherford	(580)	10,185	9,859
*73801	Woodward	(580)	12,299	11,853
*73099	Yukon	(405)	22,849	21,043

Oregon

Area code (971) overlays area code (503). As of Feb. 10, 2010, area code (458) overlays area code (541).

ZIP	Place	Area Code	2008	2000
*97321	Albany	(541)	48,081	40,852
*97006	Aloha (c)	(503)	—	41,741
97601	Altamont (c)	(541)	—	19,603
97520	Ashland	(541)	21,390	19,522
*97005	Beaverton	(503)	91,757	76,129
*97701	Bend	(541)	77,181	52,029
97013	Canby	(503)	15,637	12,790
*97291	Cedar Mill (c)	(503)	—	12,597
97502	Central Point	(541)	16,503	12,493
97058	City of the Dalles	(541)	11,897	—
97420	Coos Bay	(541)	15,665	15,374
97113	Cornelius	(503)	11,464	9,652
*97333	Corvallis	(541)	51,110	49,322
97338	Dallas	(503)	15,892	12,459
*97440	Eugene	(541)	150,104	137,893
97116	Forest Grove	(503)	20,985	17,708
97301	Four Corners (c)	(503)	—	13,922
97027	Gladstone	(503)	12,079	11,438
*97526	Grants Pass	(541)	33,217	23,003
*97030	Gresham	(503)	101,221	90,205
*97015	Happy Valley	(503)	12,643	4,519
97303	Hayesville (c)	(503)	—	18,222
97838	Hermiston	(541)	15,297	13,154
*97123	Hillsboro	(503)	93,638	70,186
97307	Keizer	(503)	35,864	32,203
*97601	Klamath Falls	(541)	20,276	19,462
97850	La Grande	(541)	12,682	12,327
*97034	Lake Oswego	(503)	36,926	35,278
97355	Lebanon	(541)	15,397	12,950
97741	McMinnville	(503)	31,185	26,499
*97501	Medford	(541)	73,212	63,154
*97269	Milwaukie	(503)	20,707	20,490
97132	Newberg	(503)	22,953	18,064
97268	Oak Grove (c)	(503)	—	12,808
97267	Oatfield (c)	(503)	—	15,750
97914	Ontario	(541)	10,991	10,985
97045	Oregon City	(503)	31,404	25,754
97801	Pendleton	(541)	16,380	16,354

ZIP	Place	Area Code	2008	2000
*97208	Portland	(503)	557,706	529,121
97754	Prineville	(541)	10,085	7,356
97756	Redmond	(541)	24,551	13,481
97470	Roseburg	(541)	20,681	20,017
97051	Saint Helens	(503)	12,510	10,019
*97309	Salem	(503)	153,435	136,924
97140	Sherwood	(503)	17,373	11,791
*97477	Springfield	(541)	57,224	52,864
*97281	Tigard	(503)	48,713	41,223
97060	Troutdale	(503)	15,438	13,777
97062	Tualatin	(503)	26,476	22,791
97068	West Linn	(503)	25,236	22,261
97070	Wilsonville	(503)	19,055	13,991
*97071	Woodburn	(503)	22,728	20,100

Pennsylvania

Area code (267) overlays area code (215). Area code (484) overlays area code (610). Area code (878) overlays area code (412).

ZIP	Place	Area Code	2008	2000
15001	Aliquippa	(724)	10,631	11,734
*18105	Allentown	(610)	107,250	106,632
*16603	Altoona	(814)	46,144	49,523
19003	Ardmore (c)	(610)	—	12,616
18612	Back Mountain (c)	(570)	—	26,690
15234	Baldwin	(412)	18,562	19,999
18603	Berwick	(570)	10,216	10,774
15102	Bethel Park	(412)	31,562	33,556
*18016	Bethlehem	(610)	72,241	71,329
*17815	Bloomsburg	(570)	12,772	12,375
19008	Broomall (c)	(610)	—	11,046
*16001	Butler	(724)	13,933	15,121
*17013	Carlisle	(717)	18,379	17,970
15108	Carnot-Moon (c)	(412)	—	10,637
17201	Chambersburg	(717)	18,302	17,862
*19013	Chester	(610)	36,564	36,854
19320	Coatesville	(610)	11,624	10,838
17109	Colonial Park (c)	(717)	—	13,259
17512	Columbia	(717)	10,033	10,311
19026	Drexel Hill (c)	(610)	—	29,364
*18512	Dunmore	(570)	13,978	14,018
19401	East Norriton (c)	(610)	—	13,211
18301	East Stroudsburg	(570)	10,390	9,888
*18042	Easton	(610)	26,080	26,263
17022	Elizabethtown	(717)	12,069	11,887
*18049	Emmaus	(610)	11,349	11,313
17522	Ephrata	(717)	13,074	13,213
*16501	Erie	(814)	103,817	103,717
16063	Fernway (c)	(724)	—	12,188
15237	Franklin Park	(412)	12,172	11,364
18052	Fullerton (c)	(610)	—	14,268
*15601	Greensburg	(724)	15,249	15,889
15101	Hampton Twp. (c) (Allegheny Co.)	(412)	—	17,526
*17331	Hanover	(717)	15,025	14,535
*17105	Harrisburg	(717)	47,148	48,950
15065	Harrison Twp. (c) (Allegheny Co.)	(412)	—	10,934
*18201	Hazleton	(570)	21,732	23,329
16148	Hermitage	(724)	16,327	16,157
17033	Hershey (c)	(717)	—	12,771
19044	Horsham (c)	(215)	—	14,779
*15701	Indiana	(724)	14,754	14,895
*15907	Johnstown	(814)	21,641	23,906
19406	King of Prussia (c)	(610)	—	18,511
18704	Kingston	(570)	12,943	13,855
*17604	Lancaster	(717)	54,626	56,348
19446	Lansdale	(215)	15,526	16,071
19050	Lansdowne	(610)	10,638	11,044
*17042	Lebanon	(717)	24,097	24,461
*19055	Levittown (c)	(215)	—	53,966
15068	Lower Burrell	(724)	12,087	12,608
15237	McCandless Twp. (c)	(412)	—	29,022
*15134	McKeesport	(412)	22,130	24,040
*16335	Meadville	(814)	13,233	13,685
18936	Montgomeryville (c)	(215)	—	12,031
15228	Mount Lebanon (c)	(412)	—	33,017
18707	Mountain Top (c)	(570)	—	15,269
15120	Munhall	(412)	11,199	12,264
*15146	Municipality of Monroeville	(412)	27,639	—
15668	Municipality of Murrysville	(724)	19,488	—
18634	Nanticoke	(570)	10,199	10,955
19086	Nether Providence Twp. (c)	(610)	—	13,456
*16108	New Castle	(724)	24,212	26,309
*15068	New Kensington	(724)	13,667	14,701
*19403	Norristown	(610)	31,843	31,282
15137	North Versailles (c)	(412)	—	11,125
16301	Oil City	(814)	10,598	11,504
15235	Penn Hills (c)	(412)	—	46,809
*19104	Philadelphia	(215)	1,447,395	1,517,550
*19460	Phoenixville	(610)	16,382	14,788
*15233	Pittsburgh	(412)	310,037	334,563
15239	Plum	(412)	26,198	26,940

ZIP	Place	Area Code	2008	2000
*19464	Pottstown	(610)	21,288	21,859
17901	Pottsville	(570)	14,405	15,549
19087	Radnor Twp. (c)	(610)	—	30,878
*19612	Reading	(610)	80,506	81,207
15237	Ross Twp. (c)	(412)	—	32,551
15857	Saint Marys	(814)	13,409	14,502
15106	Scott Twp. (c)	(412)	—	17,288
*18505	Scranton	(570)	72,233	76,415
15116	Shaler Twp. (c)	(412)	—	29,757
*16146	Sharon	(724)	14,869	16,328
17404	Shiloh (c)	(717)	—	10,192
15129	South Park Twp. (c)	(814)	—	14,340
19064	Springfield (c) (Delaware Co.)	(610)	—	23,677
*16804	State College	(814)	39,419	38,420
15401	Uniontown	(724)	11,682	12,422
19063	Upper Providence Twp. (c)	(610)	—	10,509
15241	Upper Saint Clair (c)	(412)	—	20,053
15301	Washington (Wash. Co.)	(724)	14,754	15,268
17315	Weigelstown (c)	(717)	—	10,117
*19380	West Chester	(610)	18,315	17,861
*15122	West Mifflin	(412)	20,669	22,464
19401	West Norriton (c)	(610)	—	14,901
18052	Whitehall (Allegheny Co.)	(412)	13,400	14,444
*18703	Wilkes-Barre	(570)	40,932	43,123
15221	Wilkinsburg	(412)	17,522	19,196
*17701	Williamsport	(570)	29,456	30,706
19090	Willow Grove (c)	(215)	—	16,234
19094	Woodlyn (c)	(610)	—	10,036
19610	Wyomissing	(610)	10,399	8,587
19050	Yeadon	(610)	11,367	11,762
*17405	York	(717)	40,097	40,862

Rhode Island (401)
See introductory note.

ZIP	Place	2008	2000
02806	*Barrington*	16,368	16,819
02809	*Bristol*	22,465	22,469
02830	*Burrillville*	16,480	15,796
02863	Central Falls	18,683	18,928
02816	*Coventry*	34,660	33,668
*02905	Cranston	79,980	79,269
02864	Cumberland	34,209	31,840
02818	*East Greenwich*	13,293	12,948
02914	East Providence	48,480	48,688
02814	Glocester	10,499	9,948
02919	*Johnston*	28,524	28,195
02865	Lincoln	21,996	20,898
02842	Middletown	16,108	17,334
02882	Narragansett	16,436	16,361
02840	Newport	23,523	26,475
02843	Newport East (c)	—	11,463
02852	North Kingstown	26,539	26,326
02908	North Providence	32,695	32,411
02896	North Smithfield	11,513	10,618
*02860	Pawtucket	71,765	72,958
02871	Portsmouth	16,909	17,149
*02904	Providence	171,557	173,618
02857	Scituate	10,817	10,324
02917	Smithfield	21,181	20,613
02879	South Kingstown	29,082	27,921
02878	Tiverton	14,951	15,260
02864	Valley Falls (c)	—	11,599
02885	Warren	11,005	11,360
*02886	Warwick	84,483	85,808
02893	West Warwick	29,255	29,581
02891	Westerly	23,377	22,966
02891	Westerly (c)	—	17,682
02895	Woonsocket	43,268	43,224

South Carolina

ZIP	Place	Area Code	2008	2000
*29801	Aiken	(803)	29,434	25,337
*29621	Anderson	(864)	27,027	25,514
29920/29906	Beaufort	(843)	11,755	12,950
29611	Berea (c)	(864)	—	14,158
29033	Cayce	(803)	12,646	12,150
*29402	Charleston	(843)	111,978	96,650
29631	Clemson	(864)	13,012	11,939
*29201	Columbia	(803)	127,029	116,278
*29526	Conway	(843)	15,894	11,788
29204	Dentsville (c)	(803)	—	13,009
29640	Easley	(864)	20,325	17,754
*29501	Florence	(843)	31,570	30,248
*29715	Fort Mill	(803)	10,032	7,587
*29341	Gaffney	(864)	13,200	12,968
29605	Gantt (c)	(864)	—	13,962
29445	Goose Creek	(843)	37,900	29,208
*29602	Greenville	(864)	59,988	56,002
29646	Greenwood	(864)	22,533	22,071
*29650	Greer	(864)	24,557	16,843
*29406	Hanahan	(843)	16,065	12,937

ZIP	Place	Area Code	2008	2000
*29928	Hilton Head Island	(843)	33,913	33,862
29063	Irmo	(803)	11,684	11,039
29456	Ladson (c)	(843)	—	13,264
*29072	Lexington	(803)	15,901	9,793
29662	Mauldin	(864)	21,784	15,224
*29465	Mount Pleasant	(843)	65,472	47,609
*29575	Myrtle Beach	(803)	30,596	22,759
29108	Newberry	(803)	10,907	10,580
*29841	North Augusta	(803)	20,712	17,574
*29410	North Charleston	(843)	94,407	79,641
*29582	North Myrtle Beach	(843)	15,816	10,974
*29115	Orangeburg	(803)	13,224	12,765
29611	Parker (c)	(864)	—	10,760
29935	Port Royal	(843)	11,064	3,950
29020	Red Hill (c)	(843)	—	10,509
*29730	Rock Hill	(803)	67,339	49,765
29417	Saint Andrews (c)	(843)	—	21,814
29210	Seven Oaks (c)	(803)	—	15,755
*29681	Simpsonville	(864)	17,144	14,352
*29577	Socastee (c)	(843)	—	14,295
*29306	Spartanburg	(864)	39,584	39,673
*29483	Summerville	(843)	45,193	27,752
*29150	Sumter	(803)	38,625	39,643
29687	Taylors (c)	(864)	—	20,125
29607	Wade Hampton (c)	(864)	—	20,458
*29169	West Columbia	(803)	13,914	13,064

South Dakota (605)

ZIP	Place	2008	2000
*57401	Aberdeen	24,460	24,658
*57006	Brookings	19,865	18,504
*57350	Huron	11,033	11,893
57301	Mitchell	14,752	14,558
57501	Pierre	13,899	13,876
*57701	Rapid City	65,491	59,607
*57701	Rapid Valley (c)	—	61,459
*57101	Sioux Falls	154,997	123,975
*57783	Spearfish	10,010	8,606
57069	Vermillion	10,495	9,765
57201	Watertown	20,488	20,237
*57078	Yankton	13,798	13,528

Tennessee

ZIP	Place	Area Code	2008	2000
*37303	Athens	(423)	14,275	13,220
*38184	Bartlett	(901)	47,501	40,543
37660	Bloomingdale (c)	(423)	—	10,350
*37027	Brentwood	(615)	36,176	23,445
*37621	Bristol	(423)	25,817	24,821
38012	Brownsville	(731)	10,316	10,748
*37401	Chattanooga	(423)	170,880	155,554
*37040	Clarksville	(931)	119,735	103,455
*37311	Cleveland	(423)	39,753	37,192
*38017	Collierville	(901)	39,211	31,872
*38401	Columbia	(931)	34,402	33,055
*38501	Cookeville	(931)	29,234	23,923
*38555	Crossville	(931)	11,599	8,981
*37055	Dickson	(615)	13,972	12,244
*38024	Dyersburg	(731)	17,126	17,452
37411	East Brainerd (c)	(423)	—	14,132
37412	East Ridge	(423)	19,642	20,640
*37643	Elizabethton	(423)	13,955	13,372
*37922	Farragut	(865)	20,350	17,720
*37064	Franklin	(615)	58,481	41,842
37066	Gallatin	(615)	29,343	23,230
*38138	Germantown	(901)	37,251	37,348
*37072	Goodlettsville	(615)	17,075	13,780
*37743	Greeneville	(423)	15,440	15,198
*37075	Hendersonville	(615)	47,725	40,620
*38301	Jackson	(731)	63,158	59,643
*37601	Johnson City	(423)	61,990	55,469
*37662	Kingsport	(423)	44,473	44,905
*37950	Knoxville	(865)	184,802	173,890
*37086	La Vergne	(615)	30,034	18,687
37087	Lebanon	(615)	24,648	20,235
37091	Lewisburg	(931)	11,003	10,413
*37110	McMinnville	(931)	13,270	12,749
37355	Manchester	(931)	10,012	8,294
38237	Martin	(731)	10,208	10,515
37801	Maryville	(865)	27,156	23,120
*38101	Memphis	(901)	669,651	650,100
37343	Middle Valley (c)	(423)	—	11,854
*38053	Millington	(901)	10,165	10,433
*37813	Morristown	(423)	27,636	24,965
*37122	Mount Juliet	(615)	21,718	12,366
*37130	Murfreesboro	(615)	101,753	68,816
*37202	Nashville-Davidson	(615)	596,462	545,524
*37830	Oak Ridge	(865)	27,677	27,387
37148	Portland	(615)	11,154	8,458
37415	Red Bank	(423)	11,573	12,418

ZIP	Place	Area Code	2008	2000
*37862	Sevierville	(865)	16,846	11,757
*37160	Shelbyville	(931)	19,669	16,105
37167	Smyrna	(615)	37,867	25,569
*37379	Soddy-Daisy	(423)	12,511	11,530
37174	Spring Hill	(931)	26,230	7,715
*37172	Springfield	(615)	17,261	14,329
*37388	Tullahoma	(931)	18,579	17,994
*38261	Union City	(731)	10,569	10,876
37188	White House	(615)	10,048	7,220

Texas

Area codes (281) and (832) overlay area code (713). Area code (430) overlays area code (903). Area code (682) overlays area code (817). Area codes (972) and (469) overlay area code (214).

ZIP	Place	Area Code	2008	2000
*79604	Abilene	(325)	116,484	115,930
75001	Addison	(214)	14,964	14,166
78516	Alamo	(956)	16,608	14,760
77039	Aldine (c)	(713)	—	13,979
*78332	Alice	(361)	19,797	19,010
*75002	Allen	(214)	81,268	43,554
78574	Alton	(956)	11,523	4,384
*77511	Alvin	(713)	22,853	21,413
*79105	Amarillo	(806)	187,236	173,627
79714	Andrews	(432)	10,142	9,652
*77515	Angleton	(979)	18,613	18,130
*76004	Arlington	(817)	374,417	332,969
77346	Atascocita (c)	(281)	—	35,757
*75751	Athens	(903)	12,320	11,297
*78712	Austin	(512)	757,688	656,562
*76020	Azle	(817)	11,347	9,600
77518	Bacliff (c)	(409)	—	19,343
75180	Balch Springs	(214)	20,003	19,375
*77414	Bay City	(979)	17,891	18,667
*77520	Baytown	(713)	70,330	66,430
*77707	Beaumont	(409)	110,553	113,866
*76021	Bedford	(817)	49,155	47,152
*78102	Beeville	(361)	12,682	13,129
*77401	Bellaire	(713)	18,197	15,642
76513	Belton	(254)	17,876	14,623
*76126	Benbrook	(817)	22,957	20,208
*79720	Big Spring	(432)	24,270	25,233
*78006	Boerne	(830)	10,283	6,178
75418	Bonham	(903)	10,660	9,990
*79007	Borger	(806)	12,677	14,302
*77833	Brenham	(979)	15,270	13,507
*78520	Brownsville	(956)	175,494	139,722
*76801	Brownwood	(325)	19,140	18,813
78717	Brushy Creek (c)	(903)	—	15,371
*77801	Bryan	(979)	72,357	65,660
76354	Burkburnett	(940)	10,418	10,927
*76028	Burleson	(817)	34,908	20,976
78130	Canyon Lake (c)	(830)	—	16,870
*79015	Canyon	(806)	14,602	12,875
*75006	Carrolton	(214)	125,595	109,576
*75104	Cedar Hill	(214)	44,786	32,093
*78613	Cedar Park	(512)	62,308	26,049
77530	Channelview (c)	(713)	—	29,685
78108	Cibolo	(210)	14,555	3,035
77450	Cinco Ranch (c)	(281)	—	11,196
*76031	Cleburne	(817)	29,889	26,005
77015	Cloverleaf (c)	(713)	—	23,508
77531	Clute	(979)	10,765	10,424
*77840	College Station	(979)	84,128	67,890
76034	Colleyville	(817)	24,428	19,636
*77301	Conroe	(936)	55,429	36,811
78109	Converse	(210)	17,510	11,508
*75019	Coppell	(214)	39,154	35,958
76522	Copperas Cove	(254)	30,710	29,592
*76205	Corinth	(940)	20,773	11,325
*78469	Corpus Christi	(361)	286,462	277,454
*75110	Corsicana	(903)	26,459	24,485
76036	Crowley	(817)	12,368	7,467
*75221	Dallas	(214)	1,279,910	1,188,580
77536	Deer Park	(713)	30,890	28,520
*78840	Del Rio	(830)	36,682	33,867
*75020	Denison	(903)	24,001	22,773
*76201	Denton	(940)	119,454	80,537
*75115	DeSoto	(214)	47,568	37,646
77539	Dickinson	(281)	17,886	17,093
78537	Donna	(956)	17,094	14,768
79029	Dumas	(806)	13,916	13,747
*75138	Duncanville	(214)	36,109	36,081
*78852	Eagle Pass	(830)	26,668	22,413
*78539	Edinburg	(956)	71,520	48,465
77437	El Campo	(979)	10,773	10,945
*79910	El Paso	(915)	613,190	563,662
*75119	Ennis	(214)	19,506	16,045
*76039	Euless	(817)	52,579	46,005
*75381	Farmers Branch	(214)	26,455	27,508
*75022	Flower Mound	(214)	69,307	50,702

ZIP	Place	Area Code	2008	2000
76119	Forest Hill	(817)	13,858	12,949
75126	Forney	(214)	15,223	5,588
76544	Fort Hood (c)	(254)	—	33,711
*76161	Fort Worth	(817)	703,073	534,694
78624	Fredericksburg	(830)	11,098	8,911
*77541	Freeport	(979)	12,494	12,708
*77546	Friendswood	(281)	33,979	29,037
*75034	Frisco	(214)	96,676	33,714
*76240	Gainesville	(940)	16,452	15,538
77547	Galena Park	(713)	10,207	10,592
*77550	Galveston	(409)	57,086	57,247
*75040	Garland	(214)	218,577	215,768
*76528	Gatesville	(254)	15,252	15,591
*78626	Georgetown	(512)	49,618	28,339
75154	Glenn Heights	(214)	11,078	7,224
*75051	Grand Prairie	(214)	160,641	127,427
*76051	Grapevine	(817)	50,471	42,059
*75401	Greenville	(903)	25,676	23,960
77619	Groves	(409)	14,393	15,733
*76117	Haltom City	(817)	40,181	39,018
*76548	Harker Heights	(254)	25,417	17,308
*78550	Harlingen	(956)	64,843	57,564
*75652	Henderson	(903)	11,631	11,273
*79045	Hereford	(806)	14,499	14,597
76643	Hewitt	(254)	13,561	11,085
78557	Hidalgo	(956)	11,984	7,322
75067	Highland Village	(214)	16,737	12,173
*79927	Horizon City	(915)	13,043	5,233
*77052	Houston	(713)	2,242,193	1,953,631
*77338	Humble	(713)	14,899	14,579
*77340	Huntsville	(936)	38,480	35,078
*76053	Hurst	(817)	38,550	36,273
78634	Hutto	(512)	13,599	1,250
*75015	Irving	(214)	201,358	191,615
75766	Jacksonville	(903)	14,367	13,868
78729	Jollyville (c)	(512)	—	15,813
*77449	Katy	(713)	13,913	11,775
*76248	Keller	(817)	38,951	27,345
*78028	Kerrville	(830)	22,821	20,425
*75662	Kilgore	(903)	12,010	11,301
*76540	Killeen	(254)	116,934	86,911
*78363	Kingsville	(361)	24,702	25,575
78640	Kyle	(512)	26,103	5,314
78572	La Homa (c)	(956)	—	10,433
77566	Lake Jackson	(979)	27,417	26,386
*78734	Lakeway	(512)	11,193	8,002
*77568	La Marque	(409)	14,236	13,682
*75146	Lancaster	(214)	35,761	25,894
*77571	La Porte	(713)	34,274	31,880
*78041	Laredo	(956)	221,659	176,576
*77573	League City	(281)	71,222	45,444
*78641	Leander	(512)	25,424	7,596
*78268	Leon Valley	(210)	10,269	9,239
*79336	Levelland	(806)	12,450	12,866
*75067	Lewisville	(214)	101,624	77,737
75068	Little Elm	(214)	24,947	3,646
*78233	Live Oak	(210)	13,142	9,156
78644	Lockhart	(512)	13,661	11,615
*75606	Longview	(903)	77,211	73,344
*79408	Lubbock	(806)	220,483	199,564
*75901	Lufkin	(936)	34,530	32,709
77657	Lumberton	(409)	10,354	8,731
*78501	McAllen	(956)	129,776	106,414
*75070	McKinney	(214)	121,211	54,369
76063	Mansfield	(817)	46,142	28,031
*75670	Marshall	(903)	23,798	23,935
78570	Mercedes	(956)	15,131	13,649
*75149	Mesquite	(214)	132,123	124,523
*79701	Midland	(432)	106,561	94,996
76065	Midlothian	(214)	16,478	7,480
*76067	Mineral Wells	(940)	16,880	16,946
*78572	Mission	(956)	67,119	45,408
77083	Mission Bend (c)	(713)	—	30,831
*77489	Missouri City	(713)	74,723	52,913
*75455	Mount Pleasant	(903)	15,011	13,935
*75094	Murphy	(214)	14,779	3,099
*75961	Nacogdoches	(936)	32,205	29,914
77627	Nederland	(409)	16,096	17,422
*78130	New Braunfels	(830)	53,547	36,494
77479	New Territory (c)	(281)	—	13,861
*76161	North Richland Hills	(817)	65,078	55,635
*79761	Odessa	(432)	98,801	90,943
*77630	Orange	(409)	19,494	18,643
*75801	Palestine	(903)	18,390	17,598
*79065	Pampa	(806)	17,382	17,887
*75460	Paris	(903)	26,050	25,898
*77501	Pasadena	(713)	146,439	141,674
*77581	Pearland	(713)	82,903	37,640
78721	Pecan Grove (c)	(254)	—	13,551
*78660	Pflugerville	(512)	39,653	16,335
78577	Pharr	(956)	65,258	46,660
*79072	Plainview	(806)	21,334	22,336
*75074	Plano	(214)	267,480	222,030
*77640	Port Arthur	(409)	55,910	57,755
78374	Portland	(361)	16,490	14,827
*77979	Port Lavaca	(361)	11,432	12,035
77651	Port Neches	(409)	12,604	13,601
*75080	Richardson	(214)	101,589	91,802
*77469	Richmond	(713)	13,493	11,081
78582	Rio Grande City	(956)	13,950	11,923
76701	Robinson	(254)	10,327	7,845
78380	Robstown	(361)	12,179	12,727
*75087	Rockwall	(214)	35,247	17,976
78584	Roma	(956)	11,257	9,617
77471	Rosenberg	(713)	33,595	24,043
*78681	Round Rock	(512)	104,446	61,136
*75088	Rowlett	(214)	55,780	44,503
75048	Sachse	(214)	18,688	9,751
*76179	Saginaw	(817)	20,295	12,374
*76902	San Angelo	(325)	91,880	88,439
*78265	San Antonio	(210)	1,351,305	1,144,646
78586	San Benito	(956)	25,072	23,444
79849	San Elizario (c)	(915)	—	11,046
78589	San Juan	(956)	33,970	26,229
*78666	San Marcos	(512)	52,927	34,733
*77510	Santa Fe	(409)	10,479	9,548
*78154	Schertz	(210)	30,669	18,694
77586	Seabrook	(281)	11,525	9,443
75159	Seagoville	(214)	11,998	10,823
*78155	Seguin	(830)	26,394	22,011
*75090	Sherman	(903)	38,077	35,082
*79549	Snyder	(325)	10,406	10,783
79927	Socorro	(915)	32,007	27,152
77587	South Houston	(713)	16,351	15,833
76092	Southlake	(817)	26,595	21,519
*77373	Spring (c)	(713)	—	36,385
*77477	Stafford	(713)	19,541	15,681
*76401	Stephenville	(254)	16,921	14,921
*77478	Sugar Land	(713)	80,704	63,328
*75482	Sulphur Springs	(903)	15,473	14,551
79556	Sweetwater	(325)	10,657	11,415
76574	Taylor	(512)	16,090	13,575
*76501	Temple	(254)	59,654	54,514
*75160	Terrell	(214)	19,527	13,606
*75501	Texarkana	(903)	36,611	34,782
*77590	Texas City	(409)	44,491	41,521
*75056	The Colony	(214)	42,281	26,531
77387	The Woodlands (c)	(713)	—	55,649
*77375	Tomball	(713)	10,234	9,089
*75702	Tyler	(903)	97,705	83,650
*78148	Universal City	(830)	18,376	14,849
75205	University Park	(214)	24,853	23,324
*78801	Uvalde	(830)	16,142	14,929
*76384	Vernon	(940)	10,924	11,660
*77901	Victoria	(361)	62,558	60,603
*77662	Vidor	(409)	11,063	11,440
*76702	Waco	(254)	124,009	113,726
76148	Watauga	(817)	24,005	21,908
*75165	Waxahachie	(214)	28,668	21,426
*76086	Weatherford	(817)	26,686	19,000
77598	Webster	(281)	10,665	9,083
78728	Wells Branch (c)	(512)	—	11,271
*78596	Weslaco	(956)	33,354	26,935
79764	West Odessa (c)	(432)	—	17,799
77005	West University Place	(713)	15,583	14,211
*76108	White Settlement	(817)	16,301	14,831
*76307	Wichita Falls	(940)	101,202	104,197
75098	Wylie	(214)	37,861	15,132

Utah
Area code (385) overlays area code (801).

ZIP	Place	Area Code	2008	2000
84003	American Fork	(801)	27,064	21,941
*84010	Bountiful	(801)	44,473	41,301
84302	Brigham City	(435)	18,709	17,411
84109	Canyon Rim (c)	(801)	—	10,428
*84720	Cedar City	(435)	28,667	20,527
84014	Centerville	(801)	15,720	14,585
*84015	Clearfield	(801)	27,851	25,974
84015	Clinton	(801)	19,855	12,585
84121	Cottonwood Heights[1]	(801)	35,418	—
84121	Cottonwood West (c)	(801)	—	18,727
84020	Draper	(801)	42,317	25,220
84043	Eagle Mountain	(801)	22,309	2,157
84109	East Millcreek (c)	(801)	—	21,385
84025	Farmington	(801)	17,217	12,081
84065	Herriman	(801)	17,689	1,523
84003	Highland	(801)	16,189	8,172
*84117	Holladay	(801)	25,676	14,561
84737	Hurricane	(435)	13,321	8,250
84037	Kaysville	(801)	25,820	20,351
84118	Kearns (c)	(801)	—	33,659
*84041	Layton	(801)	65,514	58,474
84043	Lehi	(801)	46,802	19,028
84042	Lindon	(801)	10,466	8,363
*84321	Logan	(435)	48,657	42,670

ZIP	Place	Area Code	2008	2000
84044	Magna (c)	(801)	—	22,770
84047	Midvale	(801)	28,129	27,029
84109	Millcreek (c)	(801)	—	30,377
*84157	Murray	(801)	46,201	34,024
*84404	North Ogden	(801)	17,682	15,026
84054	North Salt Lake	(801)	13,446	8,749
*84401	Ogden	(801)	82,865	77,226
84084	Oquirrh (c)	(801)	—	10,390
*84057	Orem	(801)	93,250	84,324
*84651	Payson	(801)	17,429	12,716
84062	Pleasant Grove	(801)	33,798	23,468
*84601	Provo	(801)	118,581	105,166
*84065	Riverton	(801)	39,751	25,011
*84067	Roy	(801)	35,672	32,885
*84770	Saint George	(435)	72,718	49,663
*84101	Salt Lake City	(801)	181,698	181,743
*84070	Sandy	(801)	96,660	88,418
84043	Saratoga Springs	(801)	16,053	1,003
84095	South Jordan	(801)	51,131	29,437
84403	South Ogden	(801)	15,891	14,377
84165	South Salt Lake	(801)	21,607	22,038
84660	Spanish Fork	(801)	31,538	20,246
84663	Springville	(801)	28,520	20,424
84075	Syracuse	(801)	22,195	9,398
84118	Taylorsville	(801)	58,785	57,439
84074	Tooele	(435)	30,120	22,502
84780	Washington	(435)	17,716	8,186
*84084	West Jordan	(801)	104,447	68,336
*84170	West Valley City	(801)	123,447	108,896

(1) Cottonwood Heights CDP was incorporated as a city in 2005.

Vermont (802)
See introductory note.

ZIP	Place	2008	2000
05201	Bennington	15,093	15,737
*05301	Brattleboro	11,491	12,005
*05401	Burlington	38,897	38,889
*05446	Colchester	17,237	16,986
*05451	Essex	19,649	18,626
05047	Hartford	10,696	10,367
05468	Milton	10,714	9,479
*05701	Rutland	16,742	17,292
*05403	South Burlington	17,574	15,814

Virginia
Area code (571) overlays area code (703).

ZIP	Place	Area Code	2008	2000
*22313	Alexandria	(703)	143,885	128,283
22003	Annandale (c)	(703)	—	54,994
*22210	Arlington	(703)	209,969	189,453
*22041	Bailey's Crossroads (c)	(703)	—	23,166
*24060	Blacksburg	(540)	41,796	39,573
23235	Bon Air (c)	(804)	—	16,213
*24203	Bristol	(276)	17,424	17,367
20109	Bull Run (c)	(703)	—	11,337
*22150	Burke (c)	(703)	—	57,737
24018	Cave Spring (c)	(540)	—	24,941
*20120	Centreville (c)	(703)	—	48,661
*20151	Chantilly (c)	(703)	—	41,041
*22906	Charlottesville	(434)	41,487	45,049
*23320	Chesapeake	(757)	220,111	199,184
*23831	Chester (c)	(804)	—	17,890
*24073	Christiansburg	(540)	19,477	16,947
23834	Colonial Heights	(804)	17,768	16,897
*22701	Culpeper	(540)	13,977	9,664
22193	Dale City (c)	(703)	—	55,971
*24541	Danville	(434)	44,660	48,411
23222	East Highland Park (c)	(804)	—	12,488
*22030	Fairfax	(703)	23,844	21,498
*22046	Falls Church	(703)	11,169	10,377
22308	Fort Hunt (c)	(703)	—	12,923
22310	Franconia (c)	(703)	—	31,907
*22404	Fredericksburg	(540)	22,818	19,279
22630	Front Royal	(540)	14,616	13,589
*23060	Glen Allen (c)	(804)	—	12,562
22306	Groveton (c)	(703)	—	21,296
*23670	Hampton	(757)	145,494	146,437
*22801	Harrisonburg	(540)	44,015	40,468
*20170	Herndon	(703)	22,045	21,655
23075	Highland Springs (c)	(804)	—	15,137
24019	Hollins (c)	(540)	—	14,309
23860	Hopewell	(804)	23,142	22,354
22306	Hybla Valley (c)	(703)	—	16,721
22043	Idylwood (c)	(703)	—	16,005
22042	Jefferson (c)	(703)	—	27,422
22191	Lake Ridge (c)	(540)	—	30,404
23228	Lakeside (c)	(804)	—	11,157
23060	Laurel (c)	(804)	—	14,875
*20175	Leesburg	(703)	39,641	28,311
22312	Lincolnia (c)	(703)	—	15,788
*22079	Lorton (c)	(703)	—	17,786

ZIP	Place	Area Code	2008	2000
*24506	Lynchburg	(434)	72,596	65,269
24572	Madison Heights (c)	(434)	—	11,584
*20110	Manassas	(703)	35,205	35,135
20113	Manassas Park	(703)	11,319	10,290
*24112	Martinsville	(276)	14,543	15,416
*22101	McLean (c)	(703)	—	38,929
*23111	Mechanicsville (c)	(804)	—	30,464
*22116	Merrifield (c)	(703)	—	11,170
22026	Montclair (c)	(703)	—	15,728
22121	Mount Vernon (c)	(703)	—	28,582
22122	Newington (c)	(703)	—	19,784
*23607	Newport News	(757)	179,614	180,150
*23501	Norfolk	(757)	234,220	234,403
22124	Oakton (c)	(703)	—	29,348
*23804	Petersburg	(804)	32,916	33,740
*23662	Poquoson	(757)	11,829	11,566
*23707	Portsmouth	(757)	100,577	100,565
*24141	Radford	(540)	16,125	15,859
*20190	Reston (c)	(703)	—	56,407
*23232	Richmond	(804)	202,002	197,790
*24022	Roanoke	(540)	92,967	94,911
24281	Rose Hill (c)	(276)	—	15,058
*24153	Salem	(540)	25,449	24,747
*22150	Springfield (c)	(703)	—	30,417
*24402	Staunton	(540)	23,967	23,853
*23434	Suffolk	(757)	82,302	63,677
24502	Timberlake (c)	(434)	—	10,683
23229	Tuckahoe (c)	(804)	—	43,242
22101	Tysons Corner (c)	(703)	—	18,540
*22180	Vienna	(703)	14,903	14,453
*23450	Virginia Beach	(757)	433,746	425,257
22980	Waynesboro	(540)	21,953	19,520
22152	West Springfield (c)	(703)	—	28,378
*23185	Williamsburg	(757)	12,481	11,998
*22601	Winchester	(540)	25,897	23,585
24592	Wolf Trap (c)	(703)	—	14,001
*22191	Woodbridge (c)	(703)	—	31,941

Washington

ZIP	Place	Area Code	2008	2000
98520	Aberdeen	(360)	16,042	16,461
98036	Alderwood Manor (c)	(425)	—	15,329
*98221	Anacortes	(360)	16,798	14,557
98223	Arlington	(360)	16,810	11,713
*98002	Auburn	(253)	55,426	40,314
98110	Bainbridge Island	(206)	21,890	20,308
98604	Battle Ground	(360)	16,812	9,296
*98009	Bellevue	(425)	123,771	109,569
*98225	Bellingham	(360)	78,905	67,171
*98390	Bonney Lake	(360)	16,809	9,687
*98011	Bothell	(425)	32,307	30,150
*98337	Bremerton	(360)	36,006	37,259
98178	Bryn Mawr-Skyway (c)	(206)	—	13,977
*98166	Burien	(206)	31,316	31,881
98292	Camano (c)	(360)	—	13,347
*98607	Camas	(360)	17,950	12,534
98055	Cascade-Fairwood (c)	(425)	—	34,580
98531	Centralia	(360)	15,710	14,742
99004	Cheney	(509)	10,385	8,832
98072	Cottage Lake (c)	(206)	—	24,330
98042	Covington	(253)	18,115	13,783
*98198	Des Moines	(206)	28,755	29,267
99213	Dishman (c)	(509)	—	10,031
98031	East Hill-Meridian (c)	(253)/(425)	—	29,308
98056	East Renton Highlands (c)	(425)	—	13,264
98802	East Wenatchee	(509)	12,286	5,757
98801	East Wenatchee Bench (c)	(509)	—	13,658
*98020	Edmonds	(425)	40,158	39,515
98387	Elk Plain (c)	(253)	—	15,697
*98926	Ellensburg	(509)	17,141	15,414
98022	Enumclaw	(360)	10,684	11,116
*98201	Everett	(425)	98,212	91,488
*98002	Federal Way	(253)	84,309	83,259
98248	Ferndale	(360)	11,359	8,758
98597	Five Corners (c)	(360)	—	12,207
98433	Fort Lewis (c)	(253)	—	19,089
98011	Inglewood-Finn Hill (c)	(425)	—	22,661
*98027	Issaquah	(425)	24,057	11,212
98626	Kelso	(360)	12,188	11,895
*98028	Kenmore	(425)	20,374	18,678
*99336	Kennewick	(509)	63,216	54,693
*98031	Kent	(253)/(425)	83,978	79,524
98033	Kingsgate (c)	(425)	—	12,222
*98033	Kirkland	(425)	47,303	45,054
*98509	Lacey	(360)	40,702	31,226
98155	Lake Forest Park	(206)	12,438	13,142
98002	Lakeland North (c)	(253)	—	15,085
98002	Lakeland South (c)	(253)	—	11,436
98258	Lake Stevens	(425)	13,599	6,361
*98498	Lakewood	(253)	56,983	58,211

ZIP	Place	Area Code	2008	2000
98092	Lea Hill (c)	(253)	—	10,871
*98632	Longview	(360)	36,562	34,660
98264	Lynden	(360)	11,737	9,020
*98046	Lynnwood	(425)	33,572	33,847
98038	Maple Valley	(425)	19,929	14,209
*98012	Martha Lake (c)	(425)	—	12,633
*98270	Marysville	(360)	34,482	25,315
98040	Mercer Island	(206)	24,163	22,036
*98082	Mill Creek	(425)	16,907	11,525
*98272	Monroe	(360)	17,059	13,795
98837	Moses Lake	(509)	18,800	14,953
98043	Mountlake Terrace	(425)	19,912	20,362
*98273	Mount Vernon	(360)	31,513	26,232
98275	Mukilteo	(425)	20,742	18,019
98012	North Creek (c)	(425)	—	25,742
98270	North Marysville (c)	(425)	—	21,161
*98277	Oak Harbor	(360)	22,744	19,795
*98501	Olympia	(360)	45,322	42,514
99214	Opportunity (c)	(509)	—	25,065
98662	Orchards (c)	(360)	—	17,852
98204	Paine Field-Lake Stickney (c)	(425)	—	24,383
98444	Parkland (c)	(253)	—	24,053
*99301	Pasco	(509)	55,246	32,066
98037	Picnic Point-North Lynnwood (c)	(425)	—	22,953
*98362	Port Angeles	(360)	18,982	18,397
98390	Prairie Ridge (c)	(360)	—	11,688
*99163	Pullman	(509)	26,920	24,675
*98371	Puyallup	(253)	36,330	33,011
*98052	Redmond	(425)	49,548	45,256
*98058	Renton	(425)	62,266	50,052
*99352	Richland	(509)	46,155	38,708
98188	Riverton-Boulevard Park (c)	(206)	—	11,188
98686	Salmon Creek (c)	(360)	—	16,767
*98074	Sammamish	(425)	40,179	34,104
*98148	SeaTac	(206)	25,840	25,496
98208	Seattle Hill-Silver Firs (c)	(425)	598,541	563,374
*98101	Seattle	(206)/(425)	598,541	563,374
98284	Sedro-Woolley	(360)	10,871	8,658
*98133	Shoreline	(206)	52,005	53,025
*98315	Silverdale (c)	(360)	—	15,816
98373	South Hill (c)	(253)	—	31,623
98387	Spanaway (c)	(253)	—	21,588
*99211	Spokane Valley	(509)	86,144	—
*99210	Spokane	(509)	202,319	195,629
98944	Sunnyside	(509)	14,949	13,905
*98402	Tacoma	(253)	197,181	193,556
*98138	Tukwila	(206)	17,092	17,181
*98501	Tumwater	(360)	14,100	12,698
98053	Union Hill-Novelty Hill (c)	(425)	—	11,265
98467	University Place	(253)	30,345	29,933
*98661	Vancouver	(360)	163,186	143,560
*98013	Vashon (c)	(206)	—	10,123
99362	Walla Walla	(509)	30,643	29,686
98671	Washougal	(360)	13,509	8,595
*98801	Wenatchee	(509)	29,898	27,856
98258	West Lake Stevens (c)	(425)	—	18,071
*99353	West Richland	(509)	10,857	8,385
99181	West Valley (c)	(509)	—	10,433
98166	White Center (c)	(206)	—	20,975
*98072	Woodinville	(425)	11,240	9,194
*98903	Yakima	(509)	84,074	71,845

West Virginia (304)

Area code (681) overlays area code (304).

ZIP	Place	2008	2000
*25801	Beckley	16,832	17,254
24701	Bluefield	11,093	11,451
*25301	Charleston	50,302	53,421
*26301	Clarksburg	16,441	16,743
25301	Cross Lanes (c)	—	10,353
*26554	Fairmont	19,024	19,097
*25704	Huntington	49,185	51,475
*25401	Martinsburg	17,020	14,972
*26505	Morgantown	29,642	26,809
*26101	Parkersburg	31,611	33,099
25177	Saint Albans	10,996	11,567
*25303	South Charleston	12,427	13,390
25569	Teays Valley (c)	—	12,704
*26105	Vienna	10,536	10,861
26062	Weirton	18,748	20,411
26003	Wheeling	28,913	31,419

Wisconsin

As of Aug. 14, 2010, area code (534) overlays area code (715).

ZIP	Place	Area Code	2008	2000
54301	Allouez	(920)	14,718	15,443
*54911	Appleton	(920)	70,305	70,087
*54304	Ashwaubenon	(920)	17,235	17,634
53913	Baraboo	(608)	11,244	10,711
53916	Beaver Dam	(920)	15,133	15,169
54311	Bellevue	(920)	15,031	—

ZIP	Place	Area Code	2008	2000
*53511	Beloit	(608)	36,160	35,775
*53045	Brookfield	(262)	39,020	38,649
*53209	Brown Deer	(414)	11,716	12,170
53105	Burlington	(262)	10,930	9,936
53108	Caledonia	(262)	24,220	—
53012	Cedarburg	(262)	11,101	10,908
*54729	Chippewa Falls	(715)	12,929	12,925
53110	Cudahy	(414)	18,809	18,429
54115	De Pere	(920)	24,779	20,559
*54703	Eau Claire	(715)	65,426	61,704
*53711	Fitchburg	(608)	23,344	20,501
*54935	Fond du Lac	(920)	42,025	42,203
53538	Fort Atkinson	(920)	11,895	11,621
53132	Franklin	(414)	35,500	29,494
53022	Germantown	(262)	19,594	18,260
*53209	Glendale	(414)	12,992	13,367
53024	Grafton	(262)	11,613	10,312
*54303	Green Bay	(920)	101,025	102,313
53129	Greendale	(414)	13,978	14,405
*53220	Greenfield	(414)	36,075	35,476
53027	Hartford	(262)	13,853	10,905
*54303	Howard	(920)	16,753	13,546
*54016	Hudson	(715)	12,196	8,775
*53545	Janesville	(608)	62,516	59,498
54130	Kaukauna	(920)	15,414	12,983
*53140	Kenosha	(262)	96,950	90,352
*54601	La Crosse	(608)	50,902	51,818
54140	Little Chute	(920)	11,121	10,476
*53714	Madison	(608)	231,916	208,054
*54220	Manitowoc	(920)	33,169	34,053
54143	Marinette	(715)	10,800	11,749
*54449	Marshfield	(715)	18,267	18,800
54952	Menasha	(920)	16,627	16,331
*53051	Menomonee Falls	(262)	34,607	32,647
54751	Menomonie	(715)	15,581	14,937
*53097	Mequon	(262)	23,584	21,823
53562	Middleton	(608)	16,244	15,770
*53201	Milwaukee	(414)	604,477	596,974
53566	Monroe	(608)	10,481	10,843
53406	Mount Pleasant	(262)	26,572	—
53150	Muskego	(414)	23,234	21,397
*54956	Neenah	(920)	25,060	24,507
*53186	New Berlin	(262)	38,649	38,220
53154	Oak Creek	(414)	33,482	28,456
53066	Oconomowoc	(262)	14,172	12,382
54650	Onalaska	(608)	16,778	14,839
*54901	Oshkosh	(920)	63,679	62,916
53072	Pewaukee (city)	(262)	12,494	11,783
53818	Platteville	(608)	10,297	9,989
*53158	Pleasant Prairie	(262)	19,847	16,136
54467	Plover	(715)	11,720	10,520
53074	Port Washington	(262)	11,174	10,467
*53401	Racine	(262)	82,196	81,855
54022	River Falls	(715)	14,352	12,560
*53081	Sheboygan	(920)	47,895	50,792
53211	Shorewood	(414)	13,226	13,763
53172	South Milwaukee	(414)	21,129	21,256
*54481	Stevens Point	(715)	25,327	24,551
53589	Stoughton	(608)	12,966	12,354
*54173	Suamico	(920)	10,881	—
*53590	Sun Prairie	(608)	28,322	20,369
54880	Superior	(715)	26,223	27,368
53089	Sussex	(262)	10,048	8,828
*54241	Two Rivers	(920)	11,807	12,639
53593	Verona	(608)	11,486	7,052
*53094	Watertown	(920)	22,930	21,598
*53186	Waukesha	(262)	68,008	64,825
53597	Waunakee	(608)	11,290	8,995
53963	Waupun	(920)	10,469	10,718
*54403	Wausau	(715)	37,576	38,426
*53213	Wauwatosa	(414)	45,004	47,271
53214	West Allis	(414)	59,416	61,254
*53095	West Bend	(262)	29,894	28,152
*54476	Weston	(715)	13,447	12,079
*53217	Whitefish Bay	(414)	13,584	14,163
53190	Whitewater	(262)	14,291	13,437
*54494	Wisconsin Rapids	(715)	17,164	18,435

Wyoming (307)

ZIP	Place	2008	2000
*82609	Casper	54,047	49,644
*82009	Cheyenne	56,915	53,011
*82930	Evanston	11,781	11,507
*82716	Gillette	26,871	19,646
*82935	Green River	12,149	11,808
*82072	Laramie	27,664	27,204
82501	Riverton	10,032	9,310
*82901	Rock Springs	20,200	18,708
82801	Sheridan	17,197	15,804

Note: In this section, the notation BCE (before the common era) is applied to years dating to the traditional BC (before Christ) era, and CE (common era) is applied to AD (anno domini) dates. This notation is now preferred in scientific and academic publications. The traditional Gregorian Calendar system and its dates and years are unaltered except by these labels.

Other abbreviations used in this chapter include: KYA = thousand years ago, MYA = million years ago, BP = years before the present, c. = circa, fl. = flourished, r. = ruled, b. = born, d. = died.

Prehistory: Our Ancestors Emerge
Reviewed by G. A. Clark, Ph.D., Sept. 2008

Evidence of the origins of *Homo sapiens sapiens*, the genus, species and subspecies to which all living humans belong, comes from a small, but increasing, number of fossils, from genetic and anatomical studies, and from interpretation of the geological and archaeological records. The latest evidence suggests that humans evolved from apelike primate ancestors that lived in eastern and central Africa 7-5 million years ago (MYA). Although all humans living today are members of a single species, the fossil record confirms that our ancestors coexisted with a number of similar species throughout our evolutionary history. Current theories trace the first hominin (upright, bipedal, humanlike primate)[1] to Africa, where several distinct genera appeared 6-4 MYA. They lived in a variety of environments throughout most of the continent, including swampy forest margins, woodlands, and open savannas (usually near lakes or springs). In addition to *Australopithecus afarensis*—better known as "Lucy," a 3.2 MYA Ethiopian specimen found in 1974—these earliest hominins include such recent discoveries as *Sahelanthropus* (c. 6.5 MYA, from Chad), *Ardipithecus* (c. 5 MYA, Kenya), *Kenyanthropus* (c. 3.5 MYA, Kenya), and *Orrorin* (c. 5 MYA, Kenya). Later, between 4 and 3 MYA, these earliest hominins gave rise to at least two groups of savanna/lake-edge adapted "man-apes." Called australopithecines, they are divided into "gracile" and "robust" lineages, both containing a number of species. The robust australopithecines were characterized by enormous molar and premolar teeth; they probably went extinct around 1 MYA, or slightly thereafter. Although it is uncertain from which australopithecine species humans descended, the most likely species are usually assigned to the gracile lineage.

Cave paintings in Lascaux, France, discovered in 1940, have been carbon-dated to 11,000 to 30,000 years BP.

Our genus, *Homo*, arose 3-2 MYA, when hominins began to produce primitive stone tools. The oldest tools are dated to c. 2.5 MYA from the Kada Gona site, in Ethiopia, and were used for scraping and cutting meat, sinew, and wood. It is not known whether these early hominins had the ability to speak, but they were social animals, lived in groups of c. 12-20 individuals, aggregated and dispersed seasonally, had campsites, and subsisted by gathering plants and small animals and by scavenging other kills. A closer ancestor, *Homo ergaster*, appeared in E Africa around 1.9 MYA and was the first to leave the continent, spreading throughout Eurasia by c. 1.8 MYA. *H. ergaster* is sometimes grouped with *H. erectus*, a species first identified in the 1890s on the island of Java. It was capable of hunting large and medium-sized hoofed animals, such as antelopes and horses, learned to make and control fire—by c. 500 KYA (thousand years ago) in Europe, possibly earlier in Africa—and almost certainly had primitive language skills.

After about 350 KYA, Europe provides a particularly rich set of fossil evidence usually assigned to *H. erectus*. By a near-universal consensus, this species gave rise to the Neanderthals, who appeared c. 200 KYA. Neanderthals were human-like in most respects: they could speak, were proficient hunters of large game, had sophisticated tools and weapons and a developed social organization, and were well adapted to the harsh climates of Ice Age Europe. Recent advances in molecular biology support the theory that Neanderthals were a distinct population or species that in some places coexisted, but evidently did not interbreed with early modern humans (also called Crô-Magnons). *H. antecessor*, a new species (c. 870 KYA) identified at the Trinchera Dolina site in north-central Spain, might help clarify the relationship between the earliest representatives of *Homo* in western Europe, and the Neanderthals. A similar situation may have occurred in E Asia, where more primitive *Homo* species coexisted with early modern humans after c. 40 KYA, and possibly as recently as 18 KYA, on the island of Flores, in Indonesia.

Since 2004, excavations at Liang Bua cave on Flores have recovered the remains of 12-15 tiny hominins dated between c. 95-18 KYA. Popularly called "hobbits" because of their diminutive stature (c. 3.5 ft. tall at adulthood) and large, broad feet, they had brains averaging less than one-third the size of even the smallest modern human brains, yet were accompanied by thousands of stone artifacts, evidence for the hunting of stegodonts (dwarfed elephants), and clear signs of fire. Dubbed *H. floresiensis*, they probably represent a normal-sized *H. erectus* population that colonized Flores some 800 KYA and subsequently became dwarfed because of limited habitat. One probable implication is that the cognitive capacities of Middle Pleistocene hominins have been seriously underestimated.

Genetic evidence indicates that the first *Homo sapiens* originated in E Africa between 200 and 100 KYA. The oldest modern human fossils are dated to c. 160 KYA and were found at the Herto site in Ethiopia's Middle Awash valley. The species quickly spread, displacing, extinguishing, outcompeting, and/or genetically "swamping" the archaic humans it encountered. Modern humans were living in Israel by c. 100 KYA, and in Romania by c. 35 KYA. Migration from Asia to Australia took place as early as 60 KYA. First confirmation for the crossing from Asia to the Americas by the Bering land bridge dates to the end of the last Ice Age, at 14 KYA. However, genetic data suggests that small, isolated groups of hunter-gatherers arrived in the Americas up to 4,000 years earlier, settling in both continents. Their arrival was rapidly followed by the extinction of the indigenous Pleistocene "megafauna" (e.g. mammoths, mastodons), due either to overexploitation by humans, an extraterrestrial impact c. 12,900 years ago, or a combination of both.

As human cognitive capacities slowly expanded over the Pleistocene (1.7-0.01 MYA), a variety of behavioral modes—in toolmaking, diet, shelter, social arrangements, and spiritual expression—arose as humans adapted to different geographic and climatic zones. By about 13,000 years ago, sites from all over the world show seasonal migration patterns and efficient exploitation of a wide range of plant and animal foods, some of which were eventually domesticated.

The ability to make fire at will enormously expanded the human food niche. Fire-making possibly began as early as 1 MYA in Africa and is clearly documented in throughout Eurasia after c. 500 KYA. Hearths were found in northern Israel by c. 750 KYA, and by 465 KYA in southwestern France. Fire-hardened wooden throwing spears c. 3 m long were fashioned by big-game hunters c. 400 KYA at the Schoeningen lignite mine in Germany. Scraping tools, dated after 750 KYA in Europe, N Africa, the Middle East, and Central Asia, suggest the preparation of hides for clothing. The oldest relatively unambiguous evidence of personal adornment, perforated shell beads, dates to c. 120 KYA at Skhul Cave on

Mount Carmel in Israel. Although they were probably invented much earlier, impressions in burnt clay from the Czech Republic document the ability to weave cloth baskets and nets by 28 KYA. By the time Australia was settled, human ancestors had learned to navigate in boats over considerable distances in open water. The earliest-known bone tools were fashioned some 90 KYA at Semliki, in the Congo basin, by fishermen who crafted sophisticated bone harpoons to catch giant catfish.

About 60 KYA, the earliest immigrants to Australia carved and painted designs on rocks. Although the painted caves of Cosquer and Chauvet in southern France have (contested) radiocarbon dates of c. 32 KYA, painting, engraving and bodily decoration flourished in Europe 15 KYA, along with stone and ivory sculpture. More than 200 western European caves show remarkable examples of naturalistic wall painting. A few musical instruments—bone flutes with precisely bored holes—have been found in sites dated after 40 KYA. Over the course of the Upper Pleistocene (c. 130-12 KYA), the number of people surviving long enough to become grandparents slowly increased. With more adults available to provide child care, humans began to develop more complex, multigenerational social systems. The "reach" of social memory increased accordingly. Shortly after 12 KYA, among widely separated foraging communities in both hemispheres, a series of dramatic technological and social changes occurred, marking the Neolithic, or New Stone, Age. As the world climate became drier and warmer, population/resource imbalances ensued, creating the conditions that selected for increased human interference in the life cycles of certain plants and animals. This interference ultimately resulted in the appearance of domestication economies. Domesticated plants and animals encouraged population growth and the appearance of permanent settlements, which in turn reduced birth spacing and spurred more population growth. Reliance upon domesticated plants and animals, coupled with technological advances like pottery-making, precipitated a dramatic increase in world population and social complexity. Genetic research suggests that mutations related to traits currently found in some human populations, such as Europeans' unusually light skin pigmentation and ability to process lactose, arose after c. 12 KYA.

Sites in the Americas, southeast Europe, and the Middle East show roughly contemporaneous (12-10 KYA) evidence of Neolithic domestication economies; similar evidence of E and S Asian, W European, and sub-Saharan African Neolithic adaptations dates to 10-7 KYA. From W Asian sources, farming and the herding of sheep and goats spread rapidly throughout the Mediterranean basin, perhaps in as short a time interval as 100-200 years. The variety of crops—wheat, barley, rice, maize, squash, beans and tubers—and a mix of other characteristics suggest that this adaptation occurred independently in as many as 12 or 13 places in both hemispheres. Evidence for fermented beverages likewise coincides with the early Neolithic settled farming lifestyle. Northern Chinese farmers concocted a wine-like drink from rice, honey, and fruit between 9,000 and 8,000 years ago. In highland W Asia, in what is today Iran, vintners were fermenting grapes and making wine by c. 7400 KYA. The plants and animals associated with the Neolithic Revolution provided the basis for all subsequent social and cultural evolution worldwide.

(1) Although "hominid" was standard usage several decades ago, "hominin" is now more commonly used in reference to human ancestors because of new developments in the interpretation of primate evolution.

Earliest Civilizations: 4000-1000 BCE

Mesopotamia. If history began with writing, the first chapter opened in Mesopotamia, the Tigris-Euphrates river valley. The Sumerians used clay tablets with pictographs to keep records after 4000 BCE. A **cuneiform** (wedge-shaped) script evolved by 3000 BCE as a full syllabic alphabet. Neighboring peoples adapted the script for their own use.

Sumerian life centered, from 4000 BCE, on large cities (Eridu, Ur, Uruk, Nippur, Kish, and Lagash) organized around temples and priestly bureaucracies, with surrounding plains watered by vast irrigation works and worked with traction plows. Sailboats, wheeled vehicles, potter's wheels, and kilns were used. Copper was smelted and tempered from c. 4000 BCE; bronze was produced not long after. Ores, as well as precious stones and metals, were obtained through long-distance ship and caravan trade. Iron was used from c. 2000 BCE. Improved ironworking, developed partly by the Hittites, became widespread by 1200 BCE.

Sumerian political primacy passed among cities and their kingly dynasties. Semitic-speaking peoples, with cultures

The Pyramids of Giza, including the Great Pyramid, were built during Egypt's 4th dynasty (c. 2575-2465).

derived from the Sumerian, founded a succession of dynasties that ruled in Mesopotamia and neighboring areas for most of 1,800 years; among them were the **Akkadians** (first under Sargon I, c. 2350 BCE), the Amorites (whose laws, codified by **Hammurabi**, c. 1792-1750 BCE, have biblical parallels), and the Assyrians, with interludes of rule by the Hittites, Kassites, and Mitanni.

Mesopotamian learning, preserved in vast libraries, was practically oriented. Scribes maintained lists of astronomical phenomena, plants, animals, and stones were maintained; medical texts listed ailments and herbal cures. The Sumerians worshiped anthropomorphic gods representing natural forces. Sacrifices were made at **ziggurats**—huge stepped temples.

The Syria-Palestine area, site of some of the earliest urban remains (Jericho, 7000 BCE), and of the recently uncovered **Ebla** civilization (fl. 2500 BCE), experienced Egyptian cultural and political influence along with Mesopotamian. The **Phoenician** coast was an active commercial center. A phonetic alphabet was invented here before 1600 BCE. It became the ancestor of many other alphabets.

Egypt. Agricultural villages along the Nile River were united by around 3300 BCE into 2 kingdoms, Upper and Lower Egypt, unified (c. 3100 BCE) under the pharaoh Menes. A bureaucracy supervised construction of canals and monuments (**pyramids** starting 2700 BCE). Control over Nubia to the S was asserted from 2600 BCE. Brilliant **Old Kingdom** Period achievements in architecture, sculpture, and painting reached their height during the 3rd and 4th Dynasties. **Hieroglyphic writing** appeared by 3200 BCE, recording a sophisticated literature that included religious writings, philosophy, history, and science. An ordered hierarchy of gods, including totemistic animal elements, was served by a powerful priesthood in Memphis. The pharaoh was identified with the falcon god Horus. Other trends included belief in an afterlife and short-lived quasi-monotheistic reforms introduced by the pharaoh **Akhenaton** (c. 1379-1362 BCE), also the husband of Nefertiti.

After a period of dominance by Semitic Hyksos from Asia (c. 1700-1550 BCE), the **New Kingdom** established an empire in Syria. Egypt became increasingly embroiled in Asiatic wars and diplomacy. Conquered by Persia in 525 BCE, it eventually faded away as an independent culture.

India. An urban civilization with an as-yet undeciphered writing system stretched across the Indus Valley and along the Arabian Sea c. 3000-1500 BCE. Major sites are Harappa and **Mohenjo-Daro** in Pakistan, well-planned geometric cities with underground sewers and vast granaries. The entire region may have been ruled as a single state. Bronze was used, and arts and crafts were well developed. Religious life apparently took the form of fertility cults. Indus civilization was probably in decline when it was destroyed by **Aryans** who arrived from the NW, speaking an Indo-European language. Led by a warrior aristocracy whose legendary deeds are in the **Rig Veda**, the Aryans spread E and S, bringing their sky gods, priestly (Brahman) ritual, and the beginnings of the caste system; local customs and beliefs were assimilated by the conquerors.

Europe. On Crete, the Bronze Age **Minoan civilization** emerged c. 2500 BCE. A prosperous economy and richly decorative art was supported by seaborne commerce. Mycenae and other cities in mainland Greece and Asia Minor (e.g., **Troy**) preserved elements of the culture until c. 1200 BCE. Cretan Linear A script (c. 2000-1700 BCE) remains undeciphered; Linear B script (c. 1300-1200 BCE) records an early Greek dialect. The possible connection between Mycenaean monumental stonework and the megalithic monuments of W Europe, Iberia, and Malta (c. 4000-1500 BCE) is unclear.

China. Proto-Chinese neolithic cultures had long covered N and SE China when the first large political state was organized in the N by the **Shang dynasty** (c. 1523 BCE). Shang kings called themselves Sons of Heaven, and they presided over a cult of human and animal sacrifice to ancestors and nature gods. The Chou dynasty, starting c. 1027 BCE, expanded the area of the Son of Heaven's dominion, but feudal states exercised most temporal power. A writing system with 2,000 characters was already in use under the Shang, with **pictographs** later supplemented by phonetic characters. Many of its principles and symbols, despite changes in spoken Chinese, were preserved in later writing systems. Technical advances allowed urban specialists to create fine ceramic and jade products, and bronze casting after 1500 BCE was the most advanced in the world. Bronze artifacts discovered in N Thailand date from 3600 BCE, hundreds of years before similar Middle Eastern finds.

Americas. **Olmecs** settled (1500 BCE) on the Gulf coast of Mexico and developed the first known civilization in the western hemisphere. Temple cities and huge stone sculpture date from 1200 BCE. A rudimentary calendar and writing system existed. Olmec religion, centering on a jaguar god, and Olmec art forms influenced later Meso-American cultures.

Formation of Classical Societies: 1000 BCE-400 BCE

Greece. After a period of decline during the Dorian Greek invasions (1200-1000 BCE), the Aegean area developed a unique civilization. Drawing on Mycenaean traditions, Mesopotamian learning (weights and measures, lunisolar calendar, astronomy, musical scales), the Phoenician alphabet (modified for Greek), and Egyptian art, Greek city-states saw a rich elaboration of intellectual life. The two great epic poems attributed to Homer, the *Iliad* and the *Odyssey*, were probably composed around the 8th cent. BCE. Long-range commerce was aided by metal coinage (introduced by the Lydians in Asia Minor before 700 BCE); colonies were founded around the Mediterranean (Cumae in Italy in 760 BCE; Massalia in France c. 600 BCE) and Black Sea shores.

Philosophy, starting with Ionian speculation on the nature of matter (Thales, c. 634-546 BCE), continued by other "Pre-Socratics" (e.g., Heraclitus, c. 535-415 BCE; Parmenides, b. c. 515 BCE), reached a high point in Athens in the rationalist idealism of **Plato** (c. 428-347 BCE), a disciple of **Socrates** (c. 469-399 BCE; executed for alleged impiety), and in **Aristotle** (384-322 BCE), a pioneer in many fields, from natural sciences to logic, ethics, and metaphysics. The **arts** were highly valued. Architecture culminated in the **Parthenon** (438 BCE) by Phidias (fl. 490-430 BCE). Poetry (Sappho, c. 610-580 BCE; Pindar, c. 518-438 BCE) and **drama** (Aeschylus, 525-456 BCE; Sophocles, c. 496-406 BCE; Euripides, c. 484-406 BCE) thrived. Male beauty and strength, a chief artistic theme, were celebrated at the national games at Olympia.

Ruled by local tyrants or **oligarchies**, the Greeks were not politically united, but managed to resist inclusion in the Persian Empire—Persian king Darius was defeated at Marathon (490 BCE), his son Xerxes at Salamis (480 BCE), and the Persian army at Plataea (479 BCE). Democracy sprouted in Athens as statesman Pericles (495-429 BCE) sought participation in government from all citizens. Local warfare was common; the **Peloponnesian Wars** (431-404 BCE) ended in Sparta's victory over Athens. Greek political power subsequently waned, but Greek cultural forms spread far and wide.

Hebrews. Nomadic Hebrew tribes entered Canaan before 1200 BCE, settling among other Semitic peoples speaking the same language. They brought from the desert a **monotheistic** faith said to have been revealed to Abraham in Canaan c. 1800 BCE and Moses at Mt. Sinai c. 1250 BCE, after the Hebrews' escape from bondage in Egypt. David (r. 1000-961 BCE) and Solomon (r. 961-922 BCE) united them in a kingdom that briefly dominated the area. **Phoeni-**cians to the N founded Mediterranean colonies (Carthage, c. 814 BCE) and sailed into the Atlantic.

A temple in Jerusalem became the national religious center, with sacrifices performed by a hereditary priesthood. Polytheistic influences, especially of the fertility cult of Baal, were opposed by **prophets** (Elijah, Amos, Isaiah).

Divided into **two kingdoms** after Solomon, the Hebrews were unable to resist the revived Assyrian empire, which conquered Israel, the N kingdom, in 722 BCE. Judah, the S kingdom, was conquered in 586 BCE by the Babylonians under Nebuchadnezzar II. With the fixing of most of the biblical canon by the mid-4th cent. BCE and the emergence of rabbis, Judaism successfully survived the loss of Hebrew autonomy. A Jewish kingdom was revived under the Hasmoneans (168-42 BCE).

China. During the **Eastern Chou** dynasty (770-256 BCE), Chinese culture spread E to the sea and S to the Yangtze R. Large feudal states on the periphery of the empire contended for preeminence, but continued to recognize the Son of Heaven (king), who retained a purely ritual role enriched with courtly music and dance. In the Age of Warring States (403-221 BCE), when the first sections of the **Great Wall** were built, the Ch'in state in the W gained supremacy and finally united all of China.

Iron tools entered China c. 500 BCE, and casting techniques were advanced, aiding agriculture. Peasants owned their land and owed civil and military service to nobles. China's cities grew in number and size; barter remained the chief trade medium.

Intellectual ferment among noble scribes and officials produced the Classical Age of Chinese literature and philosophy. **Confucius** (551-479 BCE) urged a restoration of a supposedly harmonious social order of the past through proper conduct in accordance with one's station and through filial and ceremonial piety. The *Analects* attributed to him are revered throughout E Asia.

Among other thinkers, **Mencius** (d. 289 BCE) added the view that the Mandate of Heaven can be removed from an unjust dynasty. The Legalists sought to curb the supposed natural wickedness of people through new institutions and harsh laws. The Naturalists emphasized the balance of opposites—yin, yang—in the world. **Taoists** sought mystical knowledge through meditation and disengagement.

India. The political and cultural center of India shifted from the Indus to the Ganges River Valley. Buddhism, Jainism, and mystical revisions of orthodox Vedism all developed c. 500-300 BCE. The *Upanishads,* last part of the *Veda*, urged escape from the cycle of rebirth into the physical world. Vedism remained the preserve of the Brahman caste.

China's Great Wall, first built during the Age of Warring States (403-221 BCE), was rebuilt, extended, and modified for thousands of years to protect China from outside invaders.

In contrast, **Buddhism**, founded by Siddhartha Gautama (c. 563-c. 483 BCE)—Buddha ("Enlightened One")—appealed to merchants in the urban centers and took hold at first (and most lastingly) on the geographic fringes of Indian civilization. The classic Indian epics were composed in this era: the **Ramayana** perhaps c. 300 BCE, the **Mahabharata** over a period starting around 400 BCE.

N India was divided into a large number of monarchies and aristocratic republics, probably derived from tribal groupings, when the Magadha kingdom was formed in Bihar c. 542 BCE. It soon became the dominant power. The

Maurya dynasty, founded by Chandragupta c. 321 BCE, expanded the kingdom, uniting most of N India in a centralized bureaucratic empire. The third Mauryan king, **Asoka** (reigned c. 274-236 BCE), conquered most of the subcontinent. He converted to Buddhism and inscribed its tenets on pillars throughout India. He downplayed the caste system.

Before its final decline in India, Buddhism developed into a popular worship of heavenly Bodhisattvas ("enlightened beings"), and it produced a refined architecture (the Great Stupa [shrine] at Sanchi, 100 CE) and sculpture (Gandhara reliefs, 1-400) CE.

Persia. Aryan peoples (Persians, Medes) dominated the area of present Iran by the beginning of the 1st millennium BCE. The prophet **Zoroaster** (born c. 628 BCE) introduced a dualistic religion in which the forces of good (Ahura Mazda, "Lord of Wisdom") and evil (Ahriman) battle for dominance; individuals are judged by their actions and earn damnation or salvation. Zoroaster's hymns (*Gathas*) are included in the *Avesta*, the Zoroastrian scriptures. A version of this faith became the established religion of the Persian Empire.

Africa. Nubia, periodically occupied by Egypt since about 2600 BCE, ruled Egypt c. 750-661 BCE and survived as an independent Egyptianized kingdom (**Kush**; capital Meroe) for 1,000 years. The Iron Age Nok culture flourished c. 500 BCE- 200 CE on the Benue Plateau of **Nigeria**.

Americas. The Chavin culture controlled N Peru c. 900 BCE to 200 BCE. Its ceremonial centers, featuring the jaguar god, survived long after. Its architecture, ceramics, and textiles had influenced other Peruvian cultures. **Mayan civilization** began to develop in Central America as early as 1500 BCE.

Great Empires Unite the Classical World: 400 BCE-400 CE

Persia and Alexander the Great. Cyrus, ruler of a small kingdom in Persia from 559 BCE, united the Persians and Medes within 10 years and conquered Asia Minor and Babylonia in another 10. His son Cambyses, followed by **Darius** (r. 522-486 BCE), added vast lands to the E and N as far as the Indus Valley and Central Asia, as well as Egypt and Thrace. The whole empire was ruled by an international bureaucracy and army, with Persians holding the chief positions. The resources and styles of all the subject civilizations were exploited to create a rich syncretic art.

The kingdom of Macedon, which under Philip II dominated the Greek world and Egypt, was passed on to his son **Alexander** in 336 BCE. Within 13 years, Alexander had conquered all the Persian dominions. Imbued by his tutor Aristotle with Greek ideals, Alexander encouraged colonization, and Greek-style cities were founded. After his death in 323 BCE, wars of succession divided the empire into 3 significant dynasties—the Antigonids in Asia Minor and **Macedon,** the Ptolemies in Egypt, and the **Seleucids** in Mesopotamia. In the ensuing 300 years (the **Hellenistic Era**), a cosmopolitan Greek-oriented culture permeated the ancient world from W Europe to the borders of India, absorbing native elites everywhere.

Hellenistic philosophy stressed the private individual's search for happiness. The Cynics followed Diogenes (c. 372-287 BCE), who stressed self-sufficiency and restriction of desires and expressed contempt for luxury and social convention. Zeno (c. 335-c.263 BCE) and the **Stoics** exalted reason, identified it with virtue, and counseled an ascetic disregard for misfortune. The **Epicureans** tried to build lives of moderate pleasure without political or emotional involvement. Hellenistic arts imitated life realistically, especially in sculpture and literature (comedies of Menander, 342-292 BCE).

The sciences thrived, especially at Alexandria, where the Ptolemies financed a great library and museum. Fields of study included mathematics (**Euclid**'s geometry, c. 300 BCE); astronomy (heliocentric theory of Aristarchus, 310-230 BCE; Julian calendar, 45 BCE; **Ptolemy**'s *Almagest*, c. 150 CE); geography (world map of Eratosthenes, 276-194 BCE); hydraulics (**Archimedes**, 287-212 BCE); medicine (Galen, 130-200 CE); and chemistry. Inventors refined uses for siphons, valves, gears, springs, screws, levers, cams, and pulleys.

A restored Persian empire under the **Parthians** (northern Iranian tribesmen) controlled the eastern Hellenistic world from 250 BCE to 229 CE. The Parthians and the succeeding **Sassanian dynasty** (c. 224-651 CE) fought with Rome periodically. The Sassanians revived Zoroastrianism as a state religion and patronized a nationalistic artistic and scholarly renaissance.

Rome. The city of Rome was founded, according to legend, by Romulus in 753 BCE. Through military expansion and colonization, and by granting citizenship to conquered tribes, the city annexed all of Italy S of the Po in the 100-year period before 268 BCE. The Latin and other Italic tribes were annexed first, followed by the **Etruscans** (founders of a great civilization, N of Rome) and the Greek colonies in the S. With a large standing army and reserve forces of several hundred thousand, Rome was able to defeat **Carthage** in the 3 **Punic Wars** (264-241, 218-201, 149-146 BCE), despite the invasion of Italy by **Hannibal** (218 BCE), thus gaining Sicily and territory in Spain and N Africa.

Rome exploited local disputes to conquer Greece and Asia Minor in the 2nd cent. BCE, and Egypt in the 1st (after the defeat and suicide of **Antony and Cleopatra**, 30 BCE). The Mediterranean civilized world, up to the disputed Parthian border, was now Roman and remained so for 500 years. Less civilized regions were added to the Empire: Gaul (conquered by **Julius Caesar**, 58-51 BCE), Britain (43 CE), and Dacia NE of the Danube (107 CE).

The original aristocratic republican government, with democratic features added in the 5th and 4th cent. BCE, deteriorated under the pressures of empire and class conflict (**Gracchus** brothers, social reformers, murdered in 133 BCE and 121 BCE; slave revolts in 135 BCE and 73 BCE). After a series of civil wars (Marius vs. Sulla, 88-82 BCE; Caesar vs. **Pompey**, 49-45 BCE; triumvirate vs. Caesar's assassins, 44-43 BCE; Antony vs. Octavian, 32-30 BCE), the empire came under the rule of a deified monarch (first emperor, **Augustus**, 27 BCE-14 CE).

Provincials (nearly all granted citizenship by Caracalla, 212 CE) came to dominate the army and civil service. Traditional **Roman law,** systematized and interpreted by independent jurists, and local self-rule in provincial cities were supplanted by a vast tax-collecting bureaucracy in the 3rd and 4th cent. The legal rights of women, children, and slaves were strengthened.

Roman innovations in **civil engineering** included water mills, windmills, and rotary mills and use of cement that hardened under water. Monumental architecture (baths, theaters, temples) relied on the arch and the dome. The network of roads (some still standing) stretched 53,000 mi, passing through mountain tunnels as long as 3.5 mi. Aqueducts brought water to cities; underground sewers removed waste.

Roman art and literature were derivative of Greek models. Innovations were made in sculpture (naturalistic busts, equestrian statues), decorative wall painting (as at Pompeii), satire (**Juvenal**, 60-127 CE), history (**Tacitus**, 56-120 CE), prose romance (Petronius, d. 66 CE). Gladiatorial contests dominated public amusements, which were supported by the state.

India. The **Gupta** monarchs reunited N India c. 320 CE. Their peaceful and prosperous reign saw a revival of Hindu religious thought and Brahman power. The old Vedic traditions were combined with devotion to many indigenous deities (who were seen as manifestations of Vedic gods). Caste lines were reinforced, and Buddhist practices gradually disappeared or were integrated with **Hindu** traditions. The art (often erotic), architecture, and literature of the period, patronized by the Gupta court, are considered among India's finest achievements (Kalidasa, poet and dramatist, fl. c. 400 CE). Mathematical innovations included use of the zero and decimal numbers. Invasions by White Huns from the NW destroyed the empire c. 550 CE. Rich cultures also developed in S India during this period. Emotional Tamil religious poetry contributed to the Hindu revival. The Pallava kingdom controlled much of S India c. 350-880 CE and helped to spread Indian civilization to SE Asia.

China. The Ch'in ruler Shih Huang Ti (r. 221-210 BCE), known as the First Emperor, centralized political authority. standardized the written language, laws, weights, measures, and coinage, and conducted a census, but tried to destroy most philosophical texts. The **Han dynasty** (202 BCE-220 CE) instituted the Mandarin bureaucracy, which lasted 2,000 years. Local officials were selected by examination in Confucian classics and trained at the imperial university and provincial schools.

The invention of **paper** facilitated this bureaucratic system. Agriculture was promoted, but peasants bore most of the tax burden. Irrigation was improved, water clocks and sundials were used, astronomy and mathematics thrived, and landscape painting was perfected.

With the expansion S and W (to nearly the present borders of today's China), trade was opened with India, SE Asia, and the Middle East, over sea and caravan routes. Indian missionaries brought Mahayana Buddhism to China by the 1st cent. CE and spawned a variety of sects. Taoism was revived and merged with popular superstitions. **Taoist and Buddhist monasteries** and convents multiplied in the turbulent centuries after the collapse of the Han dynasty.

Monotheism Spreads: 1-750 CE

Roman Empire. Polytheism was practiced in the Roman Empire, and religions indigenous to particular Middle Eastern nations became international. Roman citizens worshiped **Isis** of Egypt, **Mithras** of Persia, **Demeter** of Greece, and the great mother **Cybele** of Phrygia. Their cults centered on mysteries (secret ceremonies) and the promise of an afterlife, symbolized by the death and rebirth of the god. The Jews of the empire preserved their monotheistic religion, Judaism, the world's oldest (c. 1300 BCE) continuous religion. Its teachings are contained in the Bible (the Old Testament). 1st-cent. Judaism embraced several sects, including the **Sadducees**, mostly drawn from the Temple priesthood, who were culturally Hellenized; the **Pharisees**, who upheld the full range of traditional customs and practices as of equal weight to literal scriptural law and elaborated synagogue worship; and the **Essenes**, an ascetic, millenarian sect. Messianic fervor led to repeated, unsuccessful rebellions against Rome (66-70, 135). As a result, the Temple in Jerusalem was destroyed and the population decimated; this event marked the beginning of the Diaspora (living in exile). To preserve the faith, a program of codification of law was begun at the academy of Yavneh. The work continued for some 500 years in Palestine and in Babylonia, ending in the final redaction (c. 600) of the **Talmud**, a huge collection of legal and moral debates, rulings, liturgy, biblical exegesis, and legendary materials.

Christianity, which emerged as a distinct sect by the 2nd half of the 1st cent., is based on the teachings of **Jesus**, whom believers considered the Savior (Messiah or Christ) and son of God. Missionary activities of the Apostles and such early leaders as **Paul of Tarsus** spread the faith. Intermittent persecution, as in Rome under Nero in 64 CE, on grounds of suspected disloyalty, failed to disrupt the Christian communities. Each congregation, generally urban and of plebeian character, was tightly organized under a leader (bishop), elders (presbyters or priests), and assistants (deacons). The four **Gospels** (accounts of the life and teachings of Jesus) and the Acts of the Apostles were written down in the late 1st and early 2nd cent. and circulated along with letters of Paul and other Christian leaders. An authoritative canon of these writings was not fixed until the 4th cent.

A school for priests was established at Alexandria in the 2nd cent. Its teachers (**Origen** c. 182-251) helped define doctrine and promote the faith in Greek-style philosophical works. Neoplatonism underwent Christian coloration in the writings of Church Fathers such as **Augustine** (354-430). Christian hermits began to associate in monasteries, first in Egypt (St. Pachomius c. 290-345), then in other eastern lands, then in the W (**St. Benedict's rule**, 529). Devotion to saints, especially Mary, mother of Jesus, spread. Under **Constantine** (r. 306-37), Christianity became in effect the established religion of the Empire. Pagan temples were expropriated, state funds were used to build churches and support the hierarchy, and laws were adjusted in accordance with Christian ideas. Pagan worship was banned by the end of the 4th cent., and severe restrictions were placed on Judaism.

The newly established church was rocked by doctrinal disputes, often exacerbated by regional rivalries. Chief heresies (as defined by church councils, backed by imperial authority) were **Arianism**, which denied the divinity of Jesus; **Monophysitism**, denying the human nature of Christ; **Donatism**, which regarded as invalid any sacraments administered by sinful clergy; and **Pelagianism**, which denied the necessity of unmerited divine aid (grace) for salvation.

Islam. The earliest Arab civilization emerged by the end of the 2nd millennium BCE in the watered highlands of Yemen. Seaborne and caravan trade in frankincense and myrrh connected the area with the Nile and Fertile Crescent. The Minaean, Sabean (Sheba), and Himyarite states successively held sway. By Muhammad's time (7th cent. CE), the region was a province of Sassanian Persia. In the N, the Nabataean kingdom at Petra and the kingdom of Palmyra were Aramaicized, Romanized, and finally absorbed, as neighboring Judea had been, into the Roman Empire. Nomads shared the central region with a few trading towns and oases. Wars between tribes and raids on communities were common and were celebrated in a poetic tradition that by the 6th cent. helped establish a classic literary Arabic.

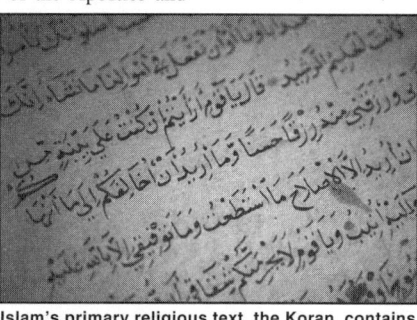
Islam's primary religious text, the Koran, contains 114 chapters, or sura.

About 610, **Muhammad**, a 40-year-old Arab man of Mecca, emerged as a prophet. He proclaimed a revelation from the one true God, calling on contemporaries to abandon idolatry and restore the faith of Abraham. He introduced his religion as "Islam," meaning "submission" to the one God, Allah, as a continuation of the biblical faith of Abraham, Moses, and Jesus, all respected as prophets in this system. His teachings, recorded in the **Koran** (*al-Qur'an* in Arabic), in many ways were inclusive of Abrahamic monotheistic ideas known to the Jews and Christians in Arabia. A key aspect of the Abrahamic connection was insistence on justice in society, which led to severe opposition among the aristocrats in Mecca. As conditions worsened for Muhammad and his followers, he decided in 622 to make a *hegira* ("flight") to Medina, 200 mi to the N. This event marks the beginning of the Muslim lunar calendar. Hostilities between Mecca and Medina increased, and in 629 Muhammad conquered Mecca. By the time he died in 632, nearly all the Arabian peninsula accepted his political and religious leadership.

After his death the majority of Muslims (later known as **Sunni** Muslims) recognized the leadership of the **caliph** ("successor") Abu Bakr (632-34), followed by Umar (634-44), Uthman (644-56), and Ali (656-60). A minority, the **Shiites**, insisted instead on the leadership of Ali, Muhammad's cousin and son-in-law. By 644, **Muslim rule** over Arabia was confirmed. Muslim armies had threatened the Byzantine and Persian empires, which were weakened by wars and disaffection among subject peoples (including Coptic and Syriac Christians opposed to the Byzantine Orthodox establishment). Syria, Palestine, Egypt, Iraq, and Persia fell to Muslim armies. The new administration assimilated existing systems in the region; hence the conquered peoples participated in running the empire. The Koran recognized the so-called Peoples of the Book, i.e., Christians, Jews, and Zoroastrians, as tolerated monotheists, and Muslim policy was relatively tolerant to minorities living as "protected" peoples. An expanded tax system, based on conquests of the Persian and Byzantine empires, provided revenue to organize campaigns against neighboring non-Muslim regions.

Under the **Umayyads** (661-750) and **Abbasids** (750-1256), territorial expansion led Muslim armies across N Africa and into Spain (711). Muslim armies in the W were stopped at Tours (France) in 732 by the Frankish ruler **Charles Martel**. Asia Minor, the Indus Valley, and Transoxiana were conquered in the E. The conversion of conquered peoples to Islam was gradual. In many places the official Arabic language supplanted the local tongues. But in the eastern regions the Arab rulers and their armies adopted Persian cultures and language as part of their Muslim identity.

Disputes over succession, and pious opposition to injustices in society, led to a number of oppositional movements, which also led to the factionalization of Muslim community. The **Shiites** supported leadership candidates descended from Muhammad, believing them to be carriers of some kind of divine authority. The **Kharijites** supported an egalitarian system derived from the Koran, opposing and even engaging in battle against those who did not agree with them.

New Peoples Enter World History: 400-900 CE

Barbarian invasions. Germanic tribes infiltrated S and E from their Baltic homeland during the 1st millennium BCE, reaching S Germany by 100 BCE and the Black Sea by 214 CE. Organized into large federated tribes under elected kings, most resisted Roman domination and raided the empire in time of civil war (Goths took Dacia in 214, raided Thrace in 251-69). Germanic troops and commanders dominated the Roman armies by the end of the 4th cent. **Huns**, invaders from Asia, entered Europe in 372, driving more Germans into the W empire. Emperor Valens allowed Visigoths to cross the Danube in 376. Huns under Attila (d. 453) raided Gaul, Italy, and the Balkans.

The W empire, weakened by overtaxation and social stagnation, was overrun in the 5th cent. Gaul was effectively lost in 406-7, Spain in 409, Britain in 410, Africa in 429-39. Rome was sacked in 410 by Visigoths under Alaric and in 455 by Vandals. The **last western emperor**, Romulus Augustulus, was deposed in 476 by the Germanic chief Odovacar.

Celts. Celtic cultures, which in pre-Roman times covered most of W Europe, were confined almost entirely to the British Isles after the Germanic invasions. **St. Patrick** completed (c. 457-92) the conversion of Ireland and a strong monastic tradition took hold. Irish monastic missionaries in Scotland, England, and the continent (Columba c. 521-97; Columbanus c. 543-615) helped restore Christianity after the Germanic invasions. **Monasteries** became centers of classic and Christian learning and presided over the recording of a Christianized Celtic mythology, elaborated by secular writers and bards. An intricate decorative art style developed, especially in book illumination (Lindisfarne Gospels, c. 700; Book of Kells, 8th cent.).

Successor states. The Visigothic kingdom in Spain (from 419) and much of France (to 507) saw continuation of Roman administration, language, and law (Breviary of Alaric, 506) until its destruction by the Muslims (711). The Vandal kingdom in Africa (from 429) was conquered by the Byzantines in 533. Italy was ruled successively by an Ostrogothic kingdom under Byzantine suzerainty (489-554), direct Byzantine government, and German Lombards (568-774). The Lombards divided the peninsula with the Byzantines and papacy under the dynamic reformer **Pope Gregory the Great** (590-604) and successors.

King Clovis (r. 481-511) united the Franks on both sides of the Rhine and, after his conversion to Christianity, defeated the Arian heretics, Burgundians (after 500), and Visigoths (507) with the support of native clergy and the papacy. Under the **Merovingian** kings, a feudal system emerged: power was fragmented among hierarchies of military landowners. Social stratification, which in late Roman times had acquired legal, hereditary sanction, was reinforced.

The Carolingians (747-987) expanded the kingdom and restored central power. **Charlemagne** (r. 768-814) conquered nearly all the Germanic lands, including Lombard Italy, and was crowned Emperor by Pope Leo III in Rome in 800. A centuries-long decline in commerce and arts was reversed under Charlemagne's patronage. He welcomed Jews to his kingdom, which became a center of Jewish learning (Rashi, 1040-1105). He sponsored the Carolingian Renaissance of learning under the Anglo-Latin scholar Alcuin (c. 732-804), who reformed church liturgy.

Byzantine Empire. Under **Diocletian** (r. 284-305) the Roman empire had been divided into 2 parts to facilitate administration and defense. **Constantine** founded (330) **Constantinople** (at old Byzantium) as a fully Christian city. Commerce and taxation financed a sumptuous, orientalized court, a class of hereditary bureaucratic families, and magnificent urban construction (Hagia Sophia, 532-37). The city's fortifications and naval innovations repelled assaults by Goths, Huns, Slavs, Bulgars, Avars, Arabs, and Scandinavians. Greek replaced Latin as the official language by c. 700. **Byzantine art**, a solemn, sacral, and stylized variation of late classical styles (mosaics at the Church of San Vitale, Ravenna, Italy 526-48), was a starting point for medieval art in E and W Europe.

Justinian (r. 527-65) reconquered parts of Spain, N Africa, and Italy, codified **Roman law** (Codex Justinianus [529] was medieval Europe's chief legal text), closed the Platonic Academy at Athens, and ordered all pagans to convert. Lombards in Italy and Arabs in Africa retook most of his conquests. The Isaurian dynasty from Anatolia (from 717) and the Macedonian dynasty (867-1054) restored military and commercial power. The Iconoclast controversy (726-843) over the permissibility of images helped alienate the Eastern Church from the papacy.

Abbasid Empire. Baghdad (est. 762), became seat of the **Abbasid dynasty** (est. 750), while Umayyads continued to rule in Spain. A brilliant cosmopolitan civilization emerged, inaugurating a Muslim-Arab golden age. Arabic was the lingua franca of the empire; intellectual sources from Persian, Sanskrit, Greek, and Syriac were rendered into Arabic. Christians and Jews equally participated in this translation movement, which also involved interaction between Jewish legal thought and Islamic law, as much as between Christian theology and Muslim scholasticism. Persian-style court life, with art and music, flourished at the court of **Harun al-Rashid** (786-809), celebrated in the masterpiece known to English readers as *The Arabian Nights*. The sciences, medicine, and mathematics were pursued at Baghdad, Cordova, and Cairo (est. 969). The culmination of this intellectual synthesis in Islamic civilization came with the scientific and philosophical works of **Avicenna** (Ibn Sina, 980-1037), **Averroes** (Ibn Rushd, 1126-98), and **Maimonides** (1135-1204), a Jew who wrote in Arabic. This intellectual tradition was translated into Latin and opened a new period in Christian thought.

The Mayan calendar, developed in pre-Columbian Mesoamerica, is considered extremely sophisticated.

The decentralization of the **Abbasid** empire, from 874, led to establishment of various Muslim dynasties under different ethnic groups. Persians, Berbers, and Turks ruled different regions, retaining connection with the Abbasid caliph at the religious level. The Abbasid period also saw various religious movements against the orthodox position held by governing authorities. This situation in Muslim religion led to the establishment of different legal, theological, and mystical schools of thought. The most influential mass movement was **Sufism**, which aimed at the reaching out of the average individual in quest of a spiritual path. Al-Ghazali (1058-1111) is credited with reconciling personal Sufism with orthodox Sunni tradition.

Africa. Immigrants from Saba in S Arabia helped set up the **Axum** kingdom in Ethiopia in the 1st cent. (their language, Ge'ez, is preserved by the Ethiopian Church). In the 3rd cent., when the kingdom became Christianized, it defeated Kushite Meroe and expanded its influence into Yemen. Axum was the center of a vast ivory trade and controlled the Red Sea coast until c. 1100. Arab conquest in Egypt cut Axum's political and economic ties with Byzantium.

The Iron Age entered W Africa by the end of the 1st millennium BCE. **Ghana**, the first known sub-Saharan state, ruled in the upper Senegal-Niger region c. 400-1240, controlling the trade of gold from mines in the S to trans-Sahara caravan routes to the N. The **Bantu** peoples, probably of W African origin, began to spread E and S perhaps 2,000 years ago, displacing the Pygmies and Bushmen of central and S Africa during a 1,500-year period.

Japan. The advanced Neolithic Yayoi period, when irrigation, rice farming, and iron and bronze casting techniques were introduced from China or Korea, persisted to c. 400 CE. The myriad Japanese states were then united by the **Yamato** clan, under an emperor who acted as chief priest of the animistic Shinto cult. Japanese political and military intervention by the 6th cent. in Korea, then under strong Chinese influence, quickened a Chinese cultural invasion of Japan, bringing Buddhism, the Chinese language (which long remained a literary and governmental medium), Chinese ideographs, and Buddhist styles in paint-

ing, sculpture, literature, and architecture (7th cent., Horyu-ji temple at Nara). The Taika Reforms (646) tried unsuccessfully to centralize Japan according to Chinese bureaucratic and Buddhist philosophical values.

A nativist reaction against the Buddhist **Nara period** (710-94) ushered in the **Heian period** (794-1185) centered at the new capital, Kyoto. Japanese elegance and simplicity modified Chinese styles in architecture, scroll painting, and literature; the writing system was also simplified. The courtly novel *Tale of Genji* (1010-20) testifies to the enhanced role of women in medieval Japanese literature and culture.

Southeast Asia. The historic peoples of SE Asia began arriving some 2,500 years ago from China and Tibet, displacing scattered aborigines. Their agriculture relied on rice and yams. Indian cultural influences were strongest; literacy and Hindu and Buddhist ideas followed the S India-China trade route. From the S tip of Indochina, the kingdom of **Funan** (1st-7th cent.) traded as far W as Persia. It was absorbed by Chenla, itself conquered by the **Khmer Empire** (600-1300). The Khmers, under Hindu god-kings (Suryavarman II, 1113-c. 1150), built the monumental Angkor Wat temple center for the royal phallic cult. The **Nam-Viet** kingdom in Annam, dominated by China and Chinese culture for 1,000 years, emerged in the 10th cent., growing at the expense of the Khmers, who also lost ground in the NW to the new, highly organized **Thai** kingdom. On Sumatra, the **Srivijaya** Empire controlled vital sea lanes (7th to 10th cent.). A Buddhist dynasty, the Sailendras, ruled central **Java** (8th-9th cent.), building at Borobudur one of the largest stupas in the world.

China. The Sui dynasty (581-618) ushered in a period of commercial, artistic, and scientific achievement in China, continuing under the **Tang** dynasty (618-906). Inventions like the magnetic compass, gunpowder, the abacus, and printing were introduced or perfected. Medical innovations included cataract surgery. The state, from its cosmopolitan capital, Chang-an, supervised foreign trade, which exchanged Chinese silks, porcelains, and art for spices, ivory, etc., over Central Asian caravan routes and sea routes reaching Africa. A golden age of poetry bequeathed valuable works to later generations (Tu Fu, 712-70; Li Po, 701-62). Landscape painting flourished.

Commercial and industrial expansion continued under the **Northern Sung** dynasty (960-1126), facilitated by paper money and credit notes. But commerce never achieved respectability; government monopolies expropriated successful merchants. The population, long stable at 50 million, doubled in 200 years with the introduction of early-ripening rice and the double harvest. In art, native Chinese styles were revived.

Americas. From 300 to 600 a Native American empire stretched from the Valley of Mexico to Guatemala, centering on the huge city **Teotihuacán** (founded 100 BCE). To the S, in Guatemala, a high **Mayan** civilization developed (150-900) around hundreds of rural ceremonial centers. The Mayans improved on Olmec writing and the calendar and pursued astronomy and mathematics. In South America, a widespread pre-Inca culture grew from **Tiahuanacu**, Bolivia, near Lake Titicaca (Gateway of the Sun, c. 700).

Christian Europe Regroups and Expands: 900-1300

Scandinavians. Pagan Danish and Norse (Viking) adventurers, traders, and pirates raided the coasts of the British Isles (Dublin, est. c. 831), France, and even the Mediterranean for over 200 years beginning in the late 8th cent. Inland settlement in the W was limited to Great Britain (King Canute, 994-1035) and Normandy, settled (911) under Rollo, as a fief of France. Vikings also reached Iceland (874), Greenland (c. 986), and North America (**Leif Ericson** and others, c. 1000).

Norse traders (**Varangians**) developed Russian river commerce from the 8th to the 11th cent. and helped set up a state at Kiev in the late 9th cent. Conversion to Christianity occurred in the 10th cent., reaching Sweden 100 years later. In the 11th cent. Norman bands conquered S Italy and Sicily, and Duke **William of Normandy** conquered (1066) England, bringing feudal government and the French language, essential elements in later English civilization.

Central and East Europe. Slavs began to expand from about 150 CE in all directions in Europe, and by the 7th cent. they reached as far S as the Adriatic and Aegean seas. In the Balkan Peninsula they dislocated Romanized local populations or assimilated newcomers (Bulgarians, a Turkic people). The first **Slavic states** were Moravia (628) in Central Europe and the Bulgarian state (680) in the Balkans. Missions of St. Methodius and Cyril (whose Greek-based cyrillic alphabet is still used by some S and E Slavs) converted (863) Moravia.

The Eastern Slavs, part-civilized under the overlordship of the Turkish-Jewish **Khazar** trading empire (7th-10th cent.), gravitated toward Constantinople by the 9th cent. The **Kievan state** adopted (989) Eastern Christianity under Prince Vladimir. King Boleslav I (992-1025) began **Poland**'s long history of conquest. The

Construction on Piazza del Duomo began in 1063 in Pisa; the cathedral is one of the best standing examples of Romanesque architecture.

Magyars (**Hungarians**), in present-day Hungary since 896, accepted (1001) Latin Christianity.

Germany. The German kingdom that emerged after the breakup of Charlemagne's W Empire remained a confederation of largely autonomous states. Otto I, a Saxon who was king from 936, established the **Holy Roman Empire**—a union of Germany and N Italy—in alliance with Pope John XII, who crowned (962) him emperor; he defeated (955) the Magyars. Imperial power was greatest under the **Hohenstaufens** (1138-1254), despite the growing opposition of the papacy, which ruled central Italy, and the Lombard League cities. Frederick II (1194-1250) improved administration and patronized the arts; after his death, German influence was removed from Italy.

Christian Spain. From its N mountain redoubts, Christian rule slowly migrated S through the 11th cent., when Muslim unity collapsed. After the capture (1085) of **Toledo**, the kingdoms of Portugal, Castile, and Aragon undertook repeated crusades of reconquest, finally completed in 1492. Elements of Islamic civilization persisted in recaptured areas, influencing all Western Europe.

Crusades. Pope Urban II called for a crusade (1095) to restore Asia Minor to Byzantium and the Holy Land to Christendom, respectively. This first crusade captured Jerusalem and led to the foundation of 4 Frankish states in the Levant. The defeat inflicted upon crusaders at the Battle of Hattin (1187) by **Saladin** (c. 1137-93), the Kurdish ruler of Egypt and Syria, effectively negated territorial gains. Many

crusades followed until 1291. The 4th crusade sacked Constantinople (1204). Other crusades were launched against Christian heretics (Albigensian Crusade, 1229), pagans, and enemies of the papacy.

Economy. The agricultural base of European life benefited from improvements in **plow design** (c. 1000) and by draining of lowlands and clearing of forests, leading to a rural population increase. Towns grew in N Italy, Flanders, and N Germany (Hanseatic League). Improvements in **loom design** permitted factory textile production. **Guilds** dominated urban trades from the 12th cent. Banking (centered in Italy, 12th-15th cent.) facilitated long-distance trade.

The Church. The split between the Eastern and Western churches was formalized in 1054. Western and Central Europe was divided into 500 bishoprics under one united hierarchy, but conflicts between secular and church authorities were frequent (German **Investiture Controversy**, 1075-1122). Clerical power was first strengthened through the international monastic reform begun at Cluny in 910. Popular religious enthusiasm often expressed itself in heretical movements (Waldensians from 1173), but was channeled by the **Dominican** (1215) and **Franciscan** (1223) friars into the religious mainstream.

Arts. Romanesque architecture (9th-mid-12th cent.) expanded on late Roman models, using the rounded arch and massed stone to support enlarged basilicas. Painting and sculpture followed Byzantine models. The literature of **chivalry** was exemplified by the epic (*Chanson de Roland*, c. 1100) and by courtly love poems of the troubadours of Provence and minnesingers of Germany. **Gothic** architecture emerged in France (choir of St. Denis, c. 1140) and spread along with French cultural influence. Rib vaulting and pointed arches were used to combine soaring heights with delicacy, and they freed walls for display of stained glass. Exteriors were covered with painted relief sculpture and embellished with elaborate architectural detail.

Learning. Law, medicine, and philosophy were advanced at independent **universities** (Bologna, Paris, 12th cent.), originally corporations of students and masters. Twelfth-cent. translations of Greek classics, especially Aristotle, encouraged an analytic approach. Scholastic philosophy, from Anselm (1033-1109) to **Aquinas** (1225-74), attempted to understand revelation through reason.

Apogee of Central Asian Power and the Spread of Islam: 1250-1500

Turks. Turkic peoples, of Central Asian ancestry, were a military threat to the Byzantine and Persian Empires from the 6th cent. After several waves of invasions, during which most of the Turks adopted Islam, the **Seljuk Turks** took (1055) Baghdad. They ruled Persia, Iraq and, after 1071, Asia Minor, where massive numbers of Turks settled. The empire was divided in the 12th cent. into smaller states ruled by Seljuks, Kurds, and Mamluks (a military caste of former Turk, Kurd, and Circassian slaves), which governed Egypt and the Middle East until the Ottoman era (c. 1290-1922).

Osman I (r. c. 1290-1326) and succeeding sultans united Anatolian Turkish warriors in a militaristic state that waged holy war against Byzantium and Balkan Christians. Most of the Balkans had been subdued, and Anatolia united, when Constantinople fell (1453). By the mid-16th cent., Hungary, the Middle East, and N Africa had been conquered. The Turkish advance was stopped at Vienna (1529) and at the naval battle of Lepanto (1571) by Spain, Venice, and the papacy.

The **Ottoman state** was governed in accordance with orthodox Muslim law. Greek, Armenian, and Jewish communities were segregated and were ruled by religious leaders responsible for taxation; they dominated trade. State offices

and most army ranks were filled by slaves through a system of child conscription among Christians.

India. Mahmud of Ghazni (971-1030) led repeated Turkish raids into N India. Turkish power was consolidated in 1206 with the start of the **Sultanate at Delhi**. Centralization of state power under the early Delhi sultans went far beyond traditional Indian practice. Muslim rule of most of the subcontinent lasted until the British conquest about 600 years later.

Mongols. Genghis Khan (c. 1167-1227) first united the feuding Mongol tribes, and built their armies into an effective offensive force around a core of highly mobile cavalry. He and his immediate successors created the largest land empire in history; by 1279 it stretched from the E coast of Asia to the Danube, from the Siberian steppes to the Arabian Sea. East-West trade and contacts were facilitated (Marco Polo, c. 1254-1324). The western Mongols were Islamized by 1295; successor states soon lost their Mongol character by assimilation. They were briefly reunited under the Turk Tamerlane (1336-1405).

Kublai Khan ruled China from his new capital Beijing (est. c. 1264). Naval campaigns against Japan (1274, 1281) and Java (1293) were defeated, the latter by the Hindu-Buddhist maritime kingdom of Majapahit. The **Yuan** dynasty used Mongols and other foreigners (including Europeans) in official posts and tolerated the return of Nestorian Christianity (suppressed 841-45) and the spread of Islam in the S and W. A native reaction expelled the Mongols in 1367-68.

Russia. The Kievan state in Russia, weakened by the decline of Byzantium and the rise of the Catholic Polish-Lithuanian state, was overrun (1238-40) by the Mongols. Only the northern trading republic of Novgorod remained independent. The grand dukes of Moscow emerged as leaders of a coalition of princes that eventually (by 1481) defeated the Mongols. After the fall of Constantinople in 1453, the **Tsars** (Caesars) at Moscow (from Ivan III, r. 1462-1505) set up an independent Russian Orthodox Church. Commerce failed to revive. The isolated Russian state remained agrarian, with the peasant class falling into serfdom.

Persia. A revival of Persian literature, making use of the Arab alphabet and literary forms, began in the 10th cent. (epic of Firdausi, 935-1020). An art revival, influenced by Chinese styles introduced after the Mongols came to power in Iran, began in the 13th cent. Persian cultural and political forms, and often the Persian language, were used for centuries by Turkish and Mongol elites from the Balkans to India. Persian mystics from Rumi (1207-73) to Jami (1414-92) promoted **Sufism** in their poetry.

Africa. Two militant Islamic Berber dynasties emerged from the Sahara to carve out empires from the Sahel to central Spain—the **Almoravids** (c. 1050-1140) and the fanatical **Almohads** (c. 1125-1269). The Ghanaian empire was replaced in the upper Niger by Mali (c. 1230-1340), whose Muslim rulers imported Egyptians to help make **Timbuktu** a center of commerce (in gold, leather, and slaves) and learning. The Songhay empire (to 1590) replaced Mali. To the S, forest kingdoms produced refined artworks (Ife terra cotta, **Benin** bronzes).

Other **Muslim states** in Nigeria (Hausas) and Chad originated in the 11th cent. and continued in some form until the 19th-cent. European conquest. Less-developed Bantu kingdoms existed across central Africa.

Some 40 Muslim Arab-Persian trading colonies and city-states were established all along the E African coast from the 10th cent. (Kilwa, Mogadishu). The interchange with Bantu peoples produced the **Swahili** language and culture. Gold, palm oil, and slaves were brought from the interior, stimulating the growth of the Monamatapa kingdom of the Zambezi (15th cent.). The Christian Ethiopian empire (from 13th cent.) continued the traditions of Axum.

Southeast Asia. Islam was introduced into Malaya and the Indonesian islands by Arab, Persian, and Indian traders. Coastal Muslim cities and states (starting before 1300) soon dominated the interior. Chief among these was the **Malacca** state (c. 1400-1511), on the Malay peninsula.

Arts and Statecraft Thrive in Europe: 1350-1600

Italy. Distinctive Italian achievements in literature and fine arts during the late Middle Ages (**Dante**, 1265-1321; Giotto, 1276-1337) led to the vigorous new styles of the Renaissance (14th-16th cent.). Patronized by the rulers of the quarreling petty states of Italy (**Medicis** in Florence and the papacy, c. 1400-1737), the plastic arts perfected realistic techniques, including **perspective** (Masaccio, 1401-28, **Leonardo da Vinci**, 1452-1519). Classical motifs were used in architecture, and increased talent and expense were put into secular buildings. The Florentine dialect was refined as a national literary language (**Petrarch**, 1304-74). Greek refugees from the E strengthened the respect of humanist scholars for the classic sources. Soon an international movement aided by the spread of **printing** (Gutenberg, c. 1397-1468), **humanism** was optimistic about the power of human reason (Erasmus of Rotterdam, 1466-1536, **More**'s *Utopia*, 1516) and valued individual effort in the arts and in politics (**Machiavelli**, 1469-1527).

France. The French monarchy, strengthened in its repeated struggles with powerful nobles (Burgundy, Flanders, Aquitaine) by alliances with the growing commercial towns, consolidated bureaucratic control under Philip IV (r. 1285-1314) and extended French influence into Germany and Italy (popes at Avignon, France, 1309-1417). The **Hundred Years War** (1337-1453) ended English dynastic claims in France (battles of Crécy, 1346, and Poitiers, 1356; Joan of Arc executed, 1431). A French Renaissance, dating from royal invasions (1494, 1499) of Italy, was encouraged at the court of Francis I (r. 1515-47), who centralized taxation and law. French vernacular literature consciously asserted its independence (La Pléiade, 1549).

England. The evolution of England's unique political institutions began with the **Magna Carta** (1215), by which King John guaranteed the privileges of nobles and church against the monarchy and assured jury trial. After the **Wars of the Roses** (1455-85), the **Tudor dynasty** reasserted royal prerogatives (Henry VIII, r. 1509-47), but the trend toward independent departments and ministerial government also continued. English trade (wool exports from c. 1340) was protected by the nation's growing maritime power (**Spanish Armada** destroyed, 1588).

English replaced French and Latin in the late 14th cent. in law and literature (**Chaucer**, c. 1340-1400) and English translation of the Bible began (Wycliffe, 1380s). **Elizabeth I** (r. 1558-1603) presided over a confident flowering of poetry (Spenser, 1552-99), drama (**Shakespeare**, 1564-1616), and music.

German Empire. From among a welter of minor feudal states, church lands, and independent cities, the **Habsburgs** assembled a far-flung territorial domain, based in Austria from 1276. Family members held the title of Holy Roman Emperor from 1438 to the Empire's dissolution in 1806, but failed to centralize its domains, leaving Germany disunited for centuries. Resistance to Turkish expansion brought Hungary under Austrian control from the 16th cent. The Netherlands, Luxembourg, and Burgundy were added in 1477, curbing French expansion.

The archetypal **Renaissance man, Leonardo da Vinci** innovated in art, science, anatomy, and engineering.

The Flemish painting tradition of naturalism, technical proficiency, and bourgeois subject matter began in the 15th cent. (**Jan Van Eyck**, c. 1390-1441), the earliest northern manifestation of the Renaissance. Albrecht **Dürer** (1471-1528) typified the merging of late Gothic and Italian trends in 16th-cent. German art. Imposing civic architecture flourished in the prosperous commercial cities.

Black Death. The bubonic plague reached Europe from the E in 1348, killing up to half the population by 1350 (and recurring periodically in most areas until the early 18th cent. Labor scarcity forced wages to rise and brought greater freedom to the peasantry, making possible **peasant uprisings** (Jacquerie in France, 1358; Wat Tyler's rebellion in England, 1381).

Spain. Despite the unification of Castile and Aragon in 1479, the 2 countries retained separate governments, and the nobility, especially in Aragon and Catalonia, retained many privileges. Spanish lands in Italy (Naples, Sicily) and the Netherlands entangled the country in European wars through the mid-17th cent., while explorers, traders, and conquerors built up a Spanish empire in the Americas and the Philippines.

From the late 15th cent., a **golden age** of literature and art produced works of social satire (plays of Lope de Vega, 1562-1635; **Cervantes**, 1547-1616), as well as spiritual intensity (**El Greco**, 1541-1614; **Velazquez**, 1599-1660).

Explorations. Organized European maritime exploration began, seeking to evade the Venice-Ottoman monopoly of E trade and to promote Christianity. Beginning in 1418, expeditions from Portugal explored the W coast of Africa, until Vasco da Gama rounded the Cape of Good Hope in 1497 and reached India. A Portuguese trading empire was consolidated by the seizure of Goa (1510) and Malacca (1551). Japan was reached in 1542. The voyages of Christopher **Columbus** (1492-1504) uncovered a world new to Europeans, which Spain hastened to subdue. Navigation schools in Spain and Portugal, the development of large sailing ships (carracks) mounted with cannons, and the invention (c. 1475) of the rifle aided European penetration.

Mughals and Safavids. E of the Ottoman Empire, 2 Muslim dynasties ruled unchallenged in the 16th and 17th cent. The Mughal dynasty of India, founded by Persianized Turkish invaders from the NW under Babur, dates from their 1526 conquest of the Delhi Sultanate. The dynasty ruled most of India for more than 200 years, surviving nominally until 1857. **Akbar** (r. 1556-1605) consolidated administration at his glorious court, where the Urdu language (Persian-influenced Hindi) developed. Trade relations with Europe increased. Under Shah Jahan (1629-58), a secularized art fusing Hindu and Muslim elements flourished in miniature painting and in architecture (**Taj Mahal**). **Sikhism** (founded c. 1519) combined elements of both faiths. Suppression of Hindus and Shi'ite Muslims in S India in the late 17th cent. weakened the empire.

Fanatical devotion to the Shi'ite sect characterized the Safavids (1502-1736) of Persia and led to hostilities with the Sunni Ottomans for more than a century. The prosperity and the strength of the empire are evidenced by the mosques at its capital city, **Isfahan**. The Safavids enhanced Iranian national consciousness.

China. The **Ming** emperors (1368-1644), the last native dynasty in China, wielded unprecedented personal power, while the Confucian bureaucracy began to suffer from inertia. European trade (Portuguese monopoly through **Macao** from 1557) was strictly controlled. Jesuit scholars and scientists (Matteo Ricci, 1552-1610) introduced some Western science; their writings familiarized the West with China. Chinese technological inventiveness declined from this era, but the arts thrived, especially in the areas of painting and ceramics.

Japan. After the decline of the first hereditary shogunate (chief generalship) at **Kamakura** (1185-1333), fragmentation of power accelerated, as did the consequent social mobility. Under Kamakura and the Ashikaga shogunate (1338-1573), the daimyos (lords) and samurai (warriors) grew more powerful and promoted a martial ideology. Japanese pirates and traders plied the China coast. Popular Buddhist movements included the nationalist Nichiren sect (from c. 1250) and **Zen** (brought from China, 1191), which stressed meditation and a disciplined esthetic (tea ceremony, gardening, martial arts, *No* drama).

Reformed Europe Expands Overseas: 1500-1700

Reformation. Theological debate and protests against real and perceived clerical corruption existed in the medieval Christian world, expressed by such dissenters as John **Wycliffe** (c. 1320-84) and his followers (the Lollards) in England, and **Huss** (burned as a heretic, 1415) in Bohemia.

Martin **Luther** (1483-1546) preached that faith alone leads to salvation, without the mediation of clergy or good works. He attacked the authority of the pope, rejected priestly celibacy, and recommended individual study of the Bible (which he translated into German c. 1525). His 95 Theses (1517) led to his excommunication (1521). John **Calvin** (1509-64) said that God's elect were predestined for salvation and all others for damnation; good conduct and success were signs of election. Calvin in Geneva and John **Knox** (1505-72) in Scotland established theocratic states.

Henry VIII asserted English national authority and secular power by breaking away (1534) from the Catholic Church, creating what would become the Anglican Church. Monastic property was confiscated, and some Protestant doctrines given official sanction.

Religious wars, A century and a half of religious wars began with a S German peasant uprising (1524), repressed with Luther's support. Radical sects—democratic, pacifist, millenarian—arose (Anabaptists ruled Münster in 1534-35) and were suppressed violently. Civil war in France from 1562 between **Huguenots** (Protestant nobles and merchants) and Catholics ended with the 1598 **Edict of Nantes**, tolerating Protestants (revoked 1685). Habsburg attempts to restore Catholicism in Germany were resisted in 25 years of fighting; the 1555 Peace of Augsburg guarantee of religious independence to local princes and cities was confirmed only after the **Thirty Years War** (1618-48), when much of Germany was devastated by local and foreign armies (Sweden, France).

A Catholic Reformation, or **Counter Reformation**, met the Protestant challenge, defining an official theology at the Council of Trent (1545-63). The **Jesuit** order (Society of Jesus), founded in 1534 by Ignatius Loyola (1491-1556), helped reconvert large areas of Poland, Hungary, and S Germany and sent missionaries to the New World, India, and China, while the **Inquisition** suppressed heresy in Catholic countries. A revival of religious fervor appeared in devotional literature (Teresa of Avila, 1515-82) and in grandiose **Baroque** art (Bernini, 1598-1680).

Scientific Revolution. The late nominalist thinkers (Ockham, c. 1300-49) of Paris and Oxford challenged Aristotelian orthodoxy, allowing for a freer scientific approach. At the same time, metaphysical values, such as the Neoplatonic faith in an orderly, mathematical cosmos, still motivated and directed inquiry. Nicolaus **Copernicus** (1473-1543) promoted the heliocentric theory, which was confirmed when Johannes **Kepler** (1571-1630) discovered the mathematical laws describing the elliptical orbits of the planets. The traditional Christian-Aristotelian belief that the heavens and the earth were fundamentally different collapsed when **Galileo Galilei** (1564-1642) discovered moving sunspots, irregular moon topography, and moons around Jupiter, though he did face religious opposition (Galileo's retraction, 1633). He and Sir Isaac **Newton** (1642-1727) developed a mechanics that unified cosmic and earthly phenomena. Newton and Gottfried von **Leibniz** (1646-1716) invented calculus. René **Descartes** (1596-1650), best known for his influential philosophy, also invented analytic geometry.

An explosion of **observational science** included the discovery of blood circulation (Harvey, 1578-1657) and microscopic life (Leeuwenhoek, 1632-1723), and advances in anatomy (Vesalius, 1514-64, dissected corpses) and chemistry (Boyle, 1627-91). Scientific research institutes were founded: Florence (1657), London (**Royal Society**, 1660), Paris (1666). Inventions proliferated (Savery's steam engine, 1696).

Arts. Mannerist trends of the High Renaissance (**Michelangelo**, 1475-1564) exploited virtuosity, grace, novelty, and exotic subjects and poses. The notion of artistic genius was promoted. Private connoisseurs entered the art market. These trends were elaborated in the 17th cent. **Baroque** era on a grander scale. Dynamic movement in painting and sculpture was emphasized by sharp lighting effects, rich materials (colored marble, gilt), and realistic details. Curved facades, broken lines, rich detail, and ceiling decoration characterized Baroque architecture. Monarchs, princes, and prelates, usually Catholic, used Baroque art to enhance and embellish their authority, as in royal portraits (Velazquez, 1599-1660; Van Dyck, 1599-1641).

National styles emerged. In France, a taste for rectilinear order and serenity (Poussin, 1594-1665), linked to the new rational philosophy, was expressed in classical forms. The influence of **classical values** in French literature (tragedies of **Racine**, 1639-99) gave rise to the "battle of the Ancients and Moderns." New forms included the essay (**Montaigne**, 1533-92) and novel (*Princesse de Cleves*, La Fayette, 1678).

Dutch painting of the 17th cent. was unique in its wide social distribution. The Flemish tradition of undemonstrative realism reached its peak in **Rembrandt** (1606-69) and Jan Vermeer (1632-75).

Economy. European economic expansion, known as the **commercial revolution**, was stimulated by new trade with the East, by New World gold and silver, and by a doubling of population (50 million in 1450, 100 million in 1600). **New business and financial techniques** were developed and refined, such as joint-stock companies, insurance, and letters of credit and exchange. The Bank of Amsterdam (1609) and the Bank of England (1694) broke the old monopoly of private banking families. The rise of a business mentality was typified by the spread of clock towers in cities in the 14th cent. By the mid-15th cent., portable clocks were available; the first watch was invented in 1502.

By 1650, most governments had adopted the **mercantile system**, in which they sought to amass metallic wealth by protecting merchants' foreign and colonial trade monopolies. The rise in prices and the new coin-based economy undermined craft guild and feudal manorial systems. Expanding industries (clothweaving, mining) benefited from technical advances. Coal replaced wood as the chief fuel; it was used to fuel new 16th-cent. blast furnaces making cast iron.

New World. The **Aztecs** united much of the Meso-American area in a militarist empire by 1519, from their capital, Tenochtitlán (pop. 300,000), which was the center of a cult requiring ritual human sacrifice. Most of the civilized areas of South America were ruled by the centralized Inca Empire (1476-1534), stretching 2,000 mi from Ecuador to NW Argentina. Lavish and sophisticated traditions in pottery, weaving, sculpture, and architecture were maintained in both regions.

These empires, beset by revolts, fell in 2 short campaigns to gold-seeking Spanish forces based in the Antilles and Panama. Hernán **Cortés** took Mexico (1519-21); Francisco **Pizarro,** Peru (1532-35). From these centers, land and sea expeditions claimed most of North and South America for Spain. The indigenous high cultures did not survive the impact of **Christian missionaries** and the new upper class of whites and mestizos. Although the Spanish administration intermittently concerned itself with their welfare, the population was reduced by European diseases and remained impoverished at most levels. New World silver and such native products as potatoes, tobacco, corn, peanuts, chocolate, and rubber exercised a major economic influence on Europe.

Brazil, which the Portuguese reached in 1500 and settled after 1530, and the Caribbean colonies of several European nations developed a plantation economy where sugarcane, tobacco, cotton, coffee, rice, indigo, and lumber were grown by slaves. From the early 16th to late 19th cent., 10 million Africans were transported to **slavery** in the Americas and Caribbean islands.

Netherlands. The urban, Calvinist N provinces of the Netherlands rebelled (1568) against Habsburg Spain and founded an oligarchic mercantile republic. Their control of the Baltic grain market enabled them to exploit Mediterranean food shortages. Religious refugees—French and Belgian Protestants, Iberian Jews—added to the commercial talent pool. After Spain absorbed Portugal (1580), the Dutch seized

Portuguese possessions and created a vast but short-lived commercial empire in Brazil, the Antilles, Africa, Ceylon, Malacca, Indonesia, and Taiwan. The Dutch also challenged or supplanted Portuguese traders in China and Japan. Revolution in 1640 restored Portuguese independence.

England. Anglicanism became firmly established under **Elizabeth I** after a brief Catholic interlude under "Bloody Mary" (1553-58). But religious and political conflicts led to a rebellion (1642) by Parliament. Forces of the Roundheads (Puritans) defeated the Cavaliers (Royalists); Charles I was beheaded (1649). The new Commonwealth was ruled as a military dictatorship by Oliver **Cromwell**, who also brutally crushed (1649-51) an Irish rebellion. Conflicts within the Puritan camp (democratic Levelers defeated, 1649) aided the Stuart restoration (1660), but Parliament was strengthened and the peaceful **"Glorious Revolution"** (1688) advanced political and religious liberties (writings of **Locke**, 1632-1704). British privateers (Drake, 1540-96) challenged Spanish control of the New World and penetrated Asian trade routes (Madras taken, 1639). North American colonies (Jamestown, 1607; Plymouth, 1620) provided an outlet for private enterprise and religious dissenters from Europe.

France. Emerging from the religious civil wars in 1628, France regained military and commercial great power status (under the ministries of **Richelieu**, Mazarin, and Colbert). Under **Louis XIV** (reigned 1643-1715), royal absolutism triumphed over nobles and local *parlements* (defeat of Fronde, 1648-53). Permanent colonies were founded in Canada (1608), the Caribbean (1626), and India (1674).

Martin Luther, one of the primary catalysts of Protestantism, was excommunicated by Pope Leo X in 1521 over his "95 Theses" (1517).

Sweden. Sweden seceded from the Scandinavian Union in 1523. The thinly populated agrarian state (with copper, iron, and timber exports) was united by the Vasa kings, whose conquests by the mid-17th cent. made Sweden the dominant Baltic power. The empire collapsed in the Great Northern War (1700-21).

Poland. After the union with Lithuania in 1447, Poland ruled vast territories from the Baltic to the Black Sea, resisting German and Turkish incursions. Catholic nobles failed to gain the loyalty of their Orthodox Christian subjects in the E; commerce and trades were practiced by German and Jewish immigrants. The bloody 1648-49 Cossack uprising began the kingdom's dismemberment.

China. A new dynasty, the **Manchus**, invaded from the NE, seized power in 1644, and expanded Chinese control to its greatest extent in Central and SE Asia. Trade and diplomatic contact with Europe grew, carefully controlled by China. New crops (sweet potato, maize, peanut) allowed economic and population growth (pop. 300 million, in 1800). Traditional arts and literature were pursued with increased sophistication (*Dream of the Red Chamber*, novel, mid-18th cent.).

Japan. Tokugawa Ieyasu, shogun from 1603, finally unified and pacified feudal Japan. Hereditary nobles (daimyos and samurai) monopolized government office and the professions. An urban merchant class grew, literacy spread, and a cultural renaissance occurred (**haiku**, a verse innovation of the poet Basho, 1644-94). Fear of European domination led to persecution of Christian converts from 1597 and to stringent isolation from outside contact from 1640.

Philosophy, Industry, and Revolution: 1700-1800

Science and Reason. Greater faith in reason and empirical observation, instead of tradition and religious beliefs, espoused since the Renaissance (Francis Bacon, 1561-1626), was bolstered by scientific discoveries. René **Descartes** (1596-1650) used a rationalistic approach modeled on geometry and introspection to discover "self-evident" truths as a foundation of knowledge. Sir Isaac **Newton** emphasized induction from experimental observation. Baruch

de **Spinoza** (1632-77), who called for political and intellectual freedom, developed a systematic rationalistic philosophy in his classic work *Ethics*.

French philosophers assumed leadership of the **Enlightenment** in the 18th cent. Montesquieu (1689-1755) used British history to support his notions of limited government. **Voltaire**'s (1694-1778) diaries and novels of exotic travel illustrated the intellectual trends toward secular ethics and

The storming of the Bastille fortress (1789) marked the beginning of the French Revolution.

relativism. Jean-Jacques **Rousseau**'s (1712-78) radical concepts of the **social contract** and of the inherent goodness of the common man gave impetus to antimonarchical republicanism. The *Encyclopedia* (1751-72, edited by Diderot and d'Alembert), designed as a monument to reason, was largely devoted to practical technology.

In England, ideals of liberty were connected with empiricist philosophy and science in the followers of John **Locke**. But British empiricism, especially as developed by the skeptical David **Hume** (1711-76), radically reduced the role of reason in philosophy, as did the evolutionary approach to law and politics of Edmund Burke (1729-97) and the utilitarian ethics of Jeremy Bentham (1748-1832). Adam Smith (1723-90) and other **physiocrats** called for a rationalization of economic activity by removing artificial barriers to a supposedly natural free exchange of goods known as **laissez-faire**.

German writers participated in the new philosophical trends popularized by Christian von Wolff (1679-1754). Immanuel **Kant**'s (1724-1804) transcendental idealism, unifying an empirical epistemology with a priori moral and logical concepts, directed German thought away from skepticism. Italian contributions included work on electricity (Galvani, 1737-98; Volta, 1745-1827), the pioneer historiography of Vico (1668-1744), and writings on penal reform (Beccaria, 1738-94). Benjamin Franklin (1706-90) was celebrated in Europe for his varied achievements.

The growth of the **press** (*Spectator*, 1711-12) and the wide distribution of realistic but sentimental **novels** attested to the increase of a large bourgeois public.

Arts. **Rococo** art, characterized by extravagant decorative effects, asymmetries copied from organic models, and artificial pastoral subjects, was favored by the continental aristocracy for most of the cent. (Watteau, 1684-1721) and had musical analogies in the ornamentalized polyphony of late Baroque. The **Neoclassical** art after 1750, associated with the new scientific archaeology, was more streamlined and was infused with the supposed moral and geometric rectitude of the Roman Republic (David, 1748-1825). In England, **town planning** on a grand scale began.

Industrial Revolution in England. Agricultural improvements, such as the sowing drill (1701) and livestock breeding, were implemented on the large fields provided by enclosure of common lands by private owners. Profits from agriculture and from colonial and foreign trade (1800 volume, £54 million) were channeled through hundreds of banks and the **Stock Exchange** (est. 1773) into new industrial processes.

The Newcomen steam pump (1712) aided coal mining. Coal fueled the new efficient steam engines patented by James Watt in 1769, and coke-smelting produced cheap, sturdy iron for machinery by the 1730s. The **flying shuttle** (1733) and **spinning jenny** (c. 1764) were used in the large new cotton textile factories, where women and children were much of the work force. Goods were transported cheaply over **canals** (2,000 mi; built 1760-1800).

American Revolution. The British colonies in North America attracted a mass immigration of religious dissenters and poor people throughout the 17th and 18th cent., coming from the British Isles, Germany, the Netherlands, and other countries. The population reached 3 million non-natives by the 1770s. The small native population was greatly reduced by European diseases and by wars with the various colonies. British attempts to control colonial trade and to tax the colonists to pay for the costs of colonial administration and defense clashed with local self-government and eventually provoked the colonies to a successful rebellion.

Central and East Europe. The monarchs of the three states that dominated E Europe—Austria, Prussia, and Russia—accepted the advice and legitimacy of philosophes in creating modern, centralized institutions in their kingdoms, which were enlarged by the division (1772-95) of Poland.

Under **Frederick II** (called the Great) (r. 1740-86) Prussia, with its efficient modern army, doubled in size. State monopolies and tariff protection fostered industry, and some legal reforms were introduced. Austria's heterogeneous realms were unified under **Maria Theresa** (r. 1740-80) and **Joseph II** (r. 1780-90). Reforms in education, law, and religion were enacted, and the Austrian serfs were freed (1781). With its defeat in the Seven Years' War in 1763, Austria failed to regain Silesia, which had been seized by Prussia, but it was compensated by expansion to the E and S (Hungary, Slavonia, 1699; Galicia, 1772).

Russia, whose borders continued to expand, adopted some Western bureaucratic and economic policies under **Peter I** (r. 1682-1725) and **Catherine II** (r. 1762-96). Trade and cultural contacts with the West multiplied from the new Baltic Sea capital, **St. Petersburg** (est. 1703).

French Revolution. The growing French middle class lacked political power and resented aristocratic tax privileges, especially in light of the successful American Revolution. Peasants lacked adequate land and were burdened with feudal obligations to nobles. War with Britain led to the loss of French Canada and drained the treasury, finally forcing the king to call the **Estates-General** in 1789 (first time since 1614), in an atmosphere of food riots (poor crop in 1788).

Aristocratic resistance to absolutism was soon overshadowed by the reformist Third Estate (middle class), which proclaimed itself the **National Constituent Assembly** June 17 and took the "Tennis Court oath" on June 20 to secure a constitution. The storming of the **Bastille** on July 14, 1789, by Parisian artisans was followed by looting and seizure of aristocratic property throughout France. Assembly reforms included abolition of class and regional privileges, a Declaration of Rights, suffrage by taxpayers (75% of males), and the **Civil Constitution of the Clergy** providing for election and loyalty oaths for priests. A republic was declared Sept. 22, 1792, in spite of royalist pressure from Austria and Prussia, which had declared war in April (joined by Britain the next year). Louis XVI was beheaded Jan. 21, 1793, and Queen Marie Antoinette was beheaded Oct. 16, 1793.

Royalist uprisings in La Vendée and military reverses led to institution of a **reign of terror** in which tens of thousands of opponents of the Revolution and criminals were executed. Radical reforms in the **Convention** period (Sept. 1793-Oct. 1795) included the abolition of colonial slavery, economic measures to aid the poor, support of public education, and a short-lived de-Christianization.

Division among radicals (execution of Hebert, Danton, and Robespierre, 1794) aided the ascendancy of a moderate **Directory**, which consolidated military victories. **Napoleon Bonaparte** (1769-1821), a popular young general, exploited political divisions and participated in a coup Nov. 9, 1799, making himself first consul (dictator).

India. Sikh and Hindu rebels (Rajputs, Marathas) and Afghans destroyed the power of the Mughals during the 18th cent. After France's defeat (1763) in the Seven Years' War, Britain was the primary European trade power in India. Its control of inland **Bengal and Bihar** was recognized (1765) by the Mughal shah, who granted the **British East India Co.** (under Clive, 1725-74) the right to collect land revenue there. Despite objections from Parliament (1784 India Act), the company's involvement in local wars and politics led to repeated acquisitions of new territory. The company exported Indian textiles, sugar, and indigo.

Nationalism Gathers Momentum: 1800-40

French ideals and empire spread. Inspired by the ideals of the French Revolution, and supported by the expanding French armies, new republican regimes arose near France: the **Batavian** Republic in the Netherlands (1795-1806), the **Helvetic** Republic in Switzerland (1798-1803), the **Cisalpine** Republic in N Italy (1797-1805), the **Ligurian** Republic in Genoa (1797-1805), and the **Parthenopean** Republic in S Italy (1799). A Roman Republic existed briefly in 1798 after Pope Pius VI was arrested by French troops. In Italy and Germany, new nationalist sentiments were stimulated both in imitation of and in reaction to developments in France (anti-French and anti-Jacobin peasant uprisings in Italy, 1796-99).

From 1804, when Napoleon declared himself emperor, to 1812, a succession of military victories (Austerlitz, 1805; Jena, 1806) extended his control over most of Europe, through puppet states (**Confederation of the Rhine** united W German states for the first time and **Grand Duchy of Warsaw** revived Polish national hopes), expansion of the empire, and alliances.

Among the lasting reforms initiated under Napoleon's absolutist reign were: establishment of the Bank of France, centralization of tax collection, codification of law along Roman models (Code Napoléon), and reform and extension of secondary and university education. In an 1801 concordat, the papacy recognized the effective autonomy of the French Catholic Church.

Napoleon's continental successes were offset by British victory under Adm. Horatio Nelson in the **Battle of Trafalgar** (1805). In all, some 400,000 French soldiers were killed in the Napoleonic Wars, along with about 600,000 foreign troops.

Last gasp of old regime. The disastrous 1812 invasion of Russia exposed Napoleon's overextension. After Napoleon's 1814 exile at Elba, his armies were defeated (1815) at **Waterloo**, by British and Prussian troops.

At the **Congress of Vienna**, the monarchs and princes of Europe redrew their boundaries, to the advantage of Prussia (in Saxony and the Ruhr), Austria (in Illyria and Venetia), and Russia (in Poland and Finland). British conquest of Dutch and French colonies (S Africa, Ceylon, Mauritius) was recognized, and France, under the restored Bourbons, retained its expanded 1792 borders. The settlement brought 50 years of international peace to Europe.

But the Congress was unable to check the advance of liberal ideals and of nationalism among the smaller European nations. The 1825 **Decembrist uprising** by liberal officers in Russia was easily suppressed. But an independence movement in **Greece**, stirred by commercial prosperity and a cultural revival, succeeded in expelling Ottoman rule by 1831, with the aid of Britain, France, and Russia.

A constitutional monarchy was secured in France by the **1830 Revolution**; Louis Philippe became king. The revolutionary contagion spread to **Belgium**, which gained its independence (1830) from the Dutch monarchy, to **Poland**, whose rebellion was defeated (1830-31) by Russia, and to Germany.

Romanticism. A new style in intellectual and artistic life replaced Neoclassicism and Rococo after the mid-18th cent. By the early 19th cent., Romanticism prevailed in Europe.

Rousseau had begun the reaction against rationalism; in education (*Émile*, 1762) he stressed subjective spontaneity over regularized instruction. German writers (Lessing, 1729-81; Herder, 1744-1803) favorably compared the German folk song to classical forms and began a cult of Shakespeare, whose passion and "natural" wisdom was a model for the romantic *Sturm und Drang* (Storm and Stress) movement. **Goethe**'s *Sorrows of Young Werther* (1774) set the model for the tragic, passionate genius.

A new interest in **Gothic architecture** in England after 1760 (Walpole, 1717-97) spread through Europe, associated with an aesthetic Christian and mystic revival (**Blake,** 1757-1827). Celtic, Norse, and German mythology and folk tales were revived or imitated (Grimm's Fairy Tales, 1812-22). The medieval revival (Scott's *Ivanhoe,* 1819) led to a new interest in history, stressing national differences and organic growth (**Carlyle,** 1795-1881; Michelet, 1798-1874), corresponding to theories of natural evolution (Lamarck's *Philosophie Zoologique,* 1809; Lyell's *Geology,* 1830-33). A reaction against classicism characterized the English **romantic poets** (beginning with **Wordsworth,** 1770-1850). Revolution and war fed an emphasis on freedom and conflict, expressed by both poets (**Byron,** 1788-1824; **Hugo,** 1802-85) and philosophers (**Hegel,** 1770-1831).

Wild gardens replaced the formal French variety, and painters favored rural, stormy, and mountainous landscapes (**Turner,** 1775-1851; **Constable,** 1776-1837). Clothing became freer, with wigs, hoops, and ruffles discarded. Originality and genius were expected in the life and work of inspired artists (Murger's *Scenes from Bohemian Life,* 1847-49). Exotic locales and themes (as in Gothic horror stories) were used in art and literature (Delacroix, 1798-1863; **Poe,** 1809-49).

Music exhibited the new dramatic style and a breakdown of classical forms (**Beethoven,** 1770-1827). The use of folk melodies and modes aided the growth of distinct national traditions (Glinka in Russia, 1804-57).

Latin America. Francois **Toussaint L'Ouverture** led a successful slave revolt in Haiti, which subsequently became the first Latin American state to achieve independence (1804). The mainland Spanish colonies won their independence (1810-24), under such leaders as Simón **Bolívar** (1783-1830). Brazil became an independent empire (1822) under the Portuguese prince regent. A new class of military officers divided power with large landholders and the church.

United States. Territory under U.S. control nearly doubled in size with the **Louisiana Purchase** (1803). Heavy immigration and exploitation of ample natural resources fueled rapid economic growth. The spread of the franchise, public education, and antislavery sentiment were signs of a widespread democratic ethic.

China. Failure to keep pace with Western arms technology exposed China to greater European influence and hampered efforts to bar imports of opium, which had damaged Chinese society and drained wealth overseas. In the **Opium War** (1839-42), Britain forced China to expand trade opportunities and to cede Hong Kong.

Triumph of Progress: 1840-80

Idea of Progress. As a result of the cumulative scientific, economic, and political changes of the preceding eras, the idea took hold among literate people in the West that continuing growth and improvement was the usual state of human and natural life.

Charles **Darwin**'s statement of the **theory of evolution** and survival of the fittest (On the Origin of Species, 1859), defended by intellectuals and scientists against theological objections, was taken as confirmation that progress was the natural direction of life. The controversy helped define popular ideas of the dedicated scientist and of science's increasing control over the world (Foucault's demonstration of earth's rotation, 1851; **Pasteur**'s germ theory, 1861).

Liberals following Ricardo (1772-1823) in their faith that unrestrained competition would bring continuous economic expansion sought to adjust political life to new social realities and believed that unregulated competition of ideas would yield truth (**Mill,** 1806-73). In England, successive reform bills (1832, 1867, 1884) gave representation to the new industrial towns and extended the franchise to the middle and lower classes and to Catholics, Dissenters, and Jews. On both sides of the Atlantic, reformists tried to improve conditions for the mentally ill (**Dix**, 1802-87), women (Anthony, 1820-1906), and prisoners. Slavery was barred in the British Empire (1833), the U.S. (1865), and Brazil (1888).

Socialist theories based on ideas of human perfectibility or progress were widely disseminated. Utopian socialists such as Saint-Simon (1760-1825) envisaged an orderly, just society directed by a technocratic elite. A model factory town, New Lanark, Scotland, was set up by utopian Robert Owen (1771-1858), and communal experiments were tried in the U.S. (Brook Farm, Mass., 1841-47). Bakunin's (1814-76) anarchism represented the opposite extreme of total freedom. Karl **Marx** (1818-83) posited the inevitable triumph of socialism in industrial countries through a dialectical process of class conflict.

"What Hath God Wrought" was the first message sent on Samuel Morse's telegraph in 1844.

Spread of industry. The technical processes and managerial innovations of the English industrial revolution spread to Europe (especially Germany) and the U.S., causing an explosion of industrial production, demand for raw materials, and competition for markets. Inventors, both trained and self-taught, provided means for larger-scale production (Bessemer steel, 1856; sewing machine, 1846). Many inventions were shown at the universal prosperity-themed 1851 London Great Exhibition at the **Crystal Palace**.

Local specialization and long-distance trade were aided by a revolution in transportation and communication. Railroads were first introduced in the 1820s in England and the U.S. Over 150,000 mi of track had been laid worldwide by 1880, with another 100,000 mi laid in the next decade. Steamships were improved (*Savannah* crossed Atlantic, 1819). The **telegraph**, perfected by 1844 (Morse), connected the Old and New Worlds by cable in 1866 and quickened the pace of international commerce and politics. The first commercial **telephone** exchange went into operation in the U.S. in 1878.

The new class of industrial workers, uprooted from their rural homes, lacked job security and suffered from dangerous overcrowding at work and at home. Many responded by organizing **trade unions** (legalized in England, 1824; France, 1884). The U.S. Knights of Labor had 700,000 members by 1886. The First International (1864-76) tried to unite workers worldwide around a Marxist program. The quasi-Socialist Paris Commune uprising (1871) was violently suppressed. Acts to reduce child labor and regulate conditions were passed (1833-50 in England). Social security measures were introduced by the Bismarck regime (1883-89) in Germany.

Revolutions of 1848. Among the causes of the continent-wide revolutions were an international collapse of credit and resulting unemployment, bad harvests in 1845-47, and a cholera epidemic. The new urban proletariat and expanding bourgeoisie demanded greater political roles. Republics were proclaimed in France, Rome, and Venice. Nationalist feelings reached fever pitch in the Habsburg empire, as Hungary declared independence under Kossuth, as a Slav Congress demanded equality, and as Piedmont tried to drive Austria from Lombardy. A national liberal assembly at Frankfurt called for German unification.

But riots fueled bourgeois fear of socialism (**Marx** and **Engels**, *Communist Manifesto*, 1848), and peasants remained conservative. The old establishment—the Papacy, the Habsburgs with the help of the Czarist Russian army—was able to rout the revolutionaries by 1849. The French Republic succumbed to a renewed monarchy by 1852 (Emperor Napoleon III).

Great nations unified. Using the "blood and iron" tactics of Bismarck from 1862, Prussia controlled N Germany by 1867 (war with Denmark, 1864; Austria, 1866). After defeating France in 1870 (annexation of Alsace-Lorraine), it won the allegiance of S German states. A new **German Empire** was proclaimed (1871). **Italy**, inspired by Giuseppe Mazzini (1805-72) and Giuseppe Garibaldi (1807-82), was unified by the reformed Piedmont kingdom through uprisings, plebiscites, and war.

The **U.S.**, its area expanded after the 1846-48 Mexican War, defeated (1861-65) a secession attempt by southern states in the **Civil War**. Canadian provinces were united in an autonomous **Dominion of Canada** (1867). Control in **India** was removed from the East India Co. and centralized under British administration after the 1857-58 Sepoy rebellion, laying the groundwork for the modern Indian State. Queen Victoria was named Empress of India (1876).

Europe dominates Asia. The Ottoman Empire began to collapse in the face of Balkan nationalisms and European imperial incursions in N Africa (**Suez Canal**, 1869). The Turks had lost control of most of both regions by 1882. Russia completed its expansion S by 1884 (despite the temporary setback of the **Crimean War** with Turkey, Britain, and France, 1853-56), taking Turkestan, all the Caucasus, and Chinese areas in the E and sponsoring Balkan Slavs against the Turks. A succession of reformist and reactionary regimes presided over a slow modernization (serfs freed, 1861). Persian independence suffered as Russia and British India competed for influence.

China was forced to sign a series of unequal treaties with European powers and Japan. Overpopulation and an inefficient dynasty brought misery and caused rebellions (Taiping, Muslims) leaving tens of millions dead. **Japan** was forced by the U.S. (Commodore Perry's visits, 1853-54) and Europe to end its isolation. The Meiji restoration (1868) gave power to a Westernizing oligarchy. Intensified empire-building gave Burma to Britain (1824-85) and Indochina to France (1862-95). Christian missionary activity followed imperial and trade expansion in Asia.

Respectability. Fine arts were expected to reflect and encourage the good morals and manners among the Victorians. Prudery, exaggerated delicacy, and familial piety were heralded by **Bowdler's** expurgated Shakespeare edition (1818). Government-supported mass education sought to inculcate a work ethic as a means to escape poverty (**Horatio Alger**, 1832-99).

The official **Beaux Arts** school in Paris set an international style of imposing public buildings (Paris Opera, 1861-74; Vienna Opera, 1861-69) and uplifting statues (Bartholdi's Statue of Liberty, 1884). Realist painting, influenced by photography (Daguerre, 1837), appealed to a new mass audience with social or historical narrative (Wilkie, 1785-1841; Poynter, 1836-1919) or with serious religious, moral, or social messages (pre-Raphaelites, Millet's *Angelus*, 1858), often drawn from ordinary life. The **Impressionists** (Monet, 1840-1926; Pissarro, 1830-1903; Renoir, 1841-1919) rejected the formalism, sentimentality, and precise techniques of academic art in favor of a spontaneous, undetailed rendering of the world through careful representation of the effect of natural light on objects.

Realistic **novelists** presented the full panorama of social classes and personalities, but retained sentimentality and moral judgment (**Dickens**, 1812-70; **Eliot**, 1819-80; **Tolstoy**, 1828-1910; **Balzac**, 1799-1850).

Veneer of Stability: 1880-1900

Imperialism triumphant. The vast **African** interior, visited by European explorers (Barth, 1821-65; Livingstone, 1813-73), was conquered by the European powers in rapid, competitive thrusts from their coastal bases after 1880, mostly for domestic political and international strategic reasons. W African Muslim kingdoms (Fulani), Arab slave traders (Zanzibar), and Bantu military confederations (Zulu) were alike subdued. Only Christian Ethiopia (defeat of Italy, 1896) and Liberia resisted successfully. France (W Africa) and Britain ("Cape to Cairo," **Boer War,** 1899-1902) were the major beneficiaries. The ideology of "the white man's burden" (Kipling, *Barrack Room Ballads,* 1892) or of a "civilizing mission" (France) justified the conquests.

W European foreign capital investment soared to nearly $40 billion by 1914, but most was in E Europe (France, Germany), the Americas (Britain), and Europe's colonies. The foundation of the modern interdependent world economy was laid, with cartels dominating raw material trade.

An industrious world. Industrial and technological proficiency characterized the 2 new great powers—Germany and the U.S. Coal and iron deposits enabled Germany to reach 2nd or 3rd place status in iron, steel, and shipbuilding by the 1900s. German electrical and chemical industries were world leaders. The U.S. post-Civil War boom (interrupted by "panics"—1884, 1893, 1896) was shaped by massive immigration from S and E Europe from 1880, government subsidy of railroads, and huge private monopolies (Standard Oil, 1870; U.S. Steel, 1901). The **Spanish-American War,** 1898 (Philippine Insurrection, 1899-1902), and the **Open Door policy** in China (1899) made the U.S. a world power.

England led in **urbanization,** with **London** the world capital of finance, insurance, and shipping. Sewer systems (Paris, 1850s), electric subways (London, 1890), parks, and bargain department stores helped improve living standards for most of the urban population of the industrial world.

Westernization of Asia. Asian reaction to European economic, military, and religious incursions took the form of imitation of Western techniques and adoption of Western ideas of progress and freedom. The Chinese "self-strengthening" movement of the 1860s and 1870s included rail, port, and arsenal improvements and metal and textile mills. Reformers such as **K'ang Yu-wei** (1858-1927) won liberalizing reforms in 1898, right after the European and Japanese "scramble for concessions."

A universal education system in Japan and importation of foreign industrial, scientific, and military experts aided Japan's rapid modernization after 1868, under the authoritarian Meiji regime. Japan's victory in the **Sino-Japanese War** (1894-95) put Formosa and Korea in its power.

In India, the British alliance with the remaining princely states masked reform sentiment among the Westernized urban elite; higher education had been conducted largely in English for 50 years. The **Indian National Congress,** founded in 1885, demanded a larger government role for Indians.

***Fin-de-siècle* sophistication.** **Naturalist** writers pushed realism to its extreme limits, adopting a quasi-scientific attitude and writing about formerly taboo subjects such as sex, crime, extreme poverty, and corruption (Flaubert, 1821-80; Zola, 1840-1902; Hardy, 1840-1928). Unseen or repressed psychological motivations were explored in the clinical and theoretical works of Sigmund **Freud** (1856-1939) and in works of fiction (**Dostoyevsky,** 1821-81; James, 1843-1916; Schnitzler, 1862-1931).

A contempt for bourgeois life or a desire to shock a complacent audience was shared by the French **symbolist** poets (Verlaine, 1844-96; Rimbaud, 1854-91), by neopagan English writers (Swinburne, 1837-1909), by continental dramatists (**Ibsen,** 1828-1906), and by satirists (**Wilde,** 1854-1900). The German philosopher Friedrich **Nietzsche** (1844-1900) was influential in his elitism and pessimism.

Postimpressionist art neglected long-cherished conventions of representation (Cézanne, 1839-1906) and showed a willingness to learn from primitive and non-European art (Gauguin, 1848-1903; Japanese prints).

Racism. Gobineau (1816-82) gave a pseudobiological foundation to modern racist theories, which spread in Europe in the latter 19th cent., along with **Social Darwinism,** the belief that societies are and should be organized as a struggle for survival of the fittest. The medieval period was interpreted as an era of natural Germanic rule (Chamberlain, 1855-1927), and notions of racial superiority were associated with German national aspirations (Treitschke, 1834-96). **Anti-Semitism,** with a new racist rationale, became a significant political force in Germany (Anti-Semitic Petition, 1880), Austria (Lueger, 1844-1910), and France (**Dreyfus affair,** 1894-1906).

Last Respite: 1900-09

Alliances. While the peace of Europe (and its dependencies) continued to hold (1907 **Hague Conference** extended the rules of war and international arbitration procedures), imperial rivalries, protectionist trade practices (in Germany and France), and the escalating arms race (British *Dreadnought* battleship launched; Germany widens Kiel canal, 1906) exacerbated minor disputes (German-French Moroccan "crises," 1905, 1911).

Security was sought through balance-of-power alliances: **Triple Alliance** (Germany, Austria-Hungary, Italy; renewed in 1902 and 1907); Anglo-Japanese Alliance (1902), Franco-Russian Alliance (1899), **Entente Cordiale** (Britain, France, 1904), Anglo-Russian Treaty (1907), German-Ottoman friendship.

Ottomans decline. The inefficient, corrupt Ottoman government was unable to resist further loss of territory. Nearly all European lands were lost in 1912 to Serbia, Greece, Montenegro, and Bulgaria. Italy took Libya and the Dodecanese islands the same year, and Britain took Kuwait (1899) and the Sinai (1906). The **Young Turk** revolution in 1908 forced the sultan to restore a constitution, and it introduced some social reform, industrialization, and secularization.

British Empire. British trade and cultural influence remained dominant in the empire, but constitutional reforms presaged its eventual dissolution: The colonies of **Australia** were united in 1901 under a self-governing commonwealth. **New Zealand** acquired dominion status in 1907. The old Boer republics joined Cape Colony and Natal in the self-governing Union of **South Africa** in 1910.

The 1909 Indian Councils Act enhanced the role of elected province legislatures in **India.** The Muslim League (founded 1906) sought separate communal representation.

East Asia. Japan exploited its growing industrial power to expand its empire. Victory in the 1904-5 war against Russia (naval battle of Tsushima, 1905) assured Japan's domination of **Korea** (annexed 1910) and Manchuria (Port Arthur taken, 1905).

In China, central authority began to crumble (empress died, 1908). Reforms (Confucian exam system ended 1905, modernization of the army, building of railroads) were inadequate, and secret societies of reformers and nationalists, inspired by the Westernized **Sun Yat-sen** (1866-1925) fomented periodic uprisings in the S.

Siam, whose independence had been guaranteed by Britain and France in 1896, was split into spheres of influence by those countries in 1907.

Russia. The population of the Russian Empire approached 150 million in 1900. Reforms in education, in law, and in local institutions (*zemstvos*) and an industrial boom starting in the 1880s (oil, railroads) created the beginnings of a modern state, despite the autocratic tsarist regime. Liberals (1903 Union of Liberation), Socialists (Social Democrats founded 1898, Bolsheviks split off 1903), and populists (Social Revolutionaries founded 1901) were periodically repressed, and national minorities were persecuted (anti-Jewish pogroms, 1903, 1905-06).

An industrial crisis after 1900 and harvest failures aggravated poverty among urban workers, and the 1904-05 defeat by Japan (which checked Russia's Asian expansion) sparked the **Revolution of 1905-06**. A **Duma** (parliament) was created, and an agricultural reform (under Stolypin, prime minister 1906-11) created a large class of land-owning peasants (*kulaks*).

The world shrinks. Developments in transportation and communication and mass population movements helped create an awareness of an interdependent world. Early **automobiles** (Daimler, Benz, 1885) were experimental or were designed as luxuries. Assembly-line mass production (Ford Motor Co., 1903) made the invention practical, and by 1910 nearly 500,000 motor vehicles were registered in the U.S. alone. **Heavier-than-air flights** began in 1903 in the U.S. (Wright brothers' *Flyer*), preceded by glider, balloon, and model plane advances in several countries. Trade was advanced by improvements in **ship design** (gyrocompass, 1910), speed (*Lusitania* crossed Atlantic in 5 days, 1907), and reach (Panama Canal begun, 1904).

Henry Ford's factories developed the moving assembly line for production of the Ford Model T.

The first transatlantic **radio** telegraphic transmission occurred in 1901, 6 years after Marconi discovered radio. Radio transmission of human speech had been made in 1900. Telegraphic transmission of photos was achieved in 1904, lending immediacy to news reports. **Phonographs**, popularized by Caruso's recordings (starting 1902), made for quick international spread of musical styles (ragtime). **Motion pictures**, perfected in the 1890s (Dickson, Lumière brothers), became a popular and artistic medium after 1900; newsreels appeared in 1909.

Emigration from crowded European centers soared in the decade: 9 million migrated to the U.S., and millions more went to Siberia, Canada, Argentina, Australia, South Africa, and Algeria. Some 70 million Europeans emigrated in the cent. before 1914. Several million Chinese, Indians, and Japanese migrated to SE Asia, where their urban skills often enabled them to take a predominant economic role.

Social reform. The social and economic problems of the poor were kept in the public eye by realist fiction writers (Dreiser's *Sister Carrie*, 1900; Gorky's *Lower Depths*, 1902; Sinclair's *The Jungle*, 1906; journalists (U.S. **muckrakers**—Steffens, Tarbell), and artists (Ashcan school). Frequent labor strikes and occasional assassinations by anarchists or radicals (Empress Elizabeth of Austria, 1898; King Umberto I of Italy, 1900; U.S. Pres. McKinley, 1901; Russian Interior Minister Plehve, 1904; Portugal's King Carlos, 1908) added to social tension and fear of revolution.

But democratic reformism prevailed. In Germany, Bernstein's (1850-1932) **revisionist Marxism**, downgrading revolution, was accepted by the powerful Social Democrats and trade unions. The British Fabian Society (the Webbs, Shaw) and the Labour Party (founded 1906) worked for reforms such as social security and union rights (1906), while woman suffragists grew more militant. U.S. **progressives** fought big business (Pure Food and Drug Act, 1906). In France, the 10-hour work day (1904) and separation of church and state (1905) were reform victories, as was universal suffrage in Austria (1907).

Arts. An unprecedented period of experimentation, centered in France, produced several **new painting styles**: Fauvism exploited bold color areas (Matisse, *Woman With Hat*, 1905); expressionism reflected powerful inner emotions (the Brücke group, 1905); cubism combined several views of an object on one flat surface (Picasso's *Demoiselles*, 1906-7); futurism tried to depict speed and motion (Italian Futurist Manifesto, 1910). **Architects** explored new uses of steel structures, with facades either neoclassical (Adler and Sullivan in U.S.); curvilinear Art Nouveau (Gaudi's Casa Mila, 1905-10); or functionally streamlined (Wright's Robie House, 1909).

Music and dance shared the experimental spirit. Ruth St. Denis (1877-1968) and Isadora Duncan (1878-1927) pioneered modern dance, while Sergei Diaghilev in Paris revitalized classic ballet from 1909. Composers explored atonal music (Debussy, 1862-1918) or dissonance (Schoenberg, 1874-1951) or revolutionized classical forms (Stravinsky, 1882-1971), often showing jazz or folk music influences.

War and Revolution: 1910-19

War threatens. Germany under Wilhelm II sought a political and imperial role consonant with its industrial strength, challenging Britain's world supremacy and threatening France, which was still resenting the loss (1871) of Alsace-Lorraine. Austria wanted to curb an expanded Serbia (after 1912) and the threat it posed to its own Slav lands. Russia feared Austrian and German political and economic aims in the Balkans and Turkey.

An accelerated arms race resulted from these circumstances. The German standing army rose to more than 2 million men by 1914. Russia and France had more than a million each, and Austria and the British Empire nearly a million each. Dozens of enormous battleships were built by the powers after 1906.

The **assassination of Austrian Archduke Franz Ferdinand** by a Serbian, June 28, 1914, was the pretext for war. The system of alliances made the conflict Europe-wide; Germany's invasion of Belgium to outflank France forced Britain to enter the war. Patriotic fervor was nearly unanimous among all classes in most countries.

World War I. German forces were stopped in France in one month. The rival armies dug **trench networks**. Artillery and improved machine guns prevented either side from any lasting advance despite repeated assaults (600,000 dead at **Verdun**, Feb.-July 1916). Poison gas, used by Germany in 1915, proved ineffective. The entrance of more than 1 million U.S. troops tipped the balance after mid-1917, forcing Germany to sue for peace the next year. The formal armistice was signed on Nov. 11, 1918.

In the E, the Russian armies were thrown back (battle of **Tannenberg**, Aug. 20, 1914), and the war grew unpopular in Russia. An allied attempt to relieve Russia through Turkey failed (**Gallipoli**, 1915). The **Russian Revolution** (1917) abolished the monarchy. The new Bolshevik regime signed the capitulatory Brest-Litovsk peace in March 1918. Italy entered the war on the allied side in May 1915 but was pushed back by Oct. 1917. A renewed offensive with Allied aid in Oct.-Nov. 1918 forced Austria to surrender.

The British Navy successfully blockaded Germany, which responded with submarine U-boat attacks; **unrestricted submarine warfare** against neutrals after Jan. 1917 helped bring the U.S. into the war. Other battlefields included Palestine and Mesopotamia, both of which Britain wrested from the Turks in 1917, and the African and Pacific colonies of Germany, most of which fell to Britain, France, Australia, Japan, and South Africa.

Settlement. At the **Paris Peace Conference** (Jan.-June 1919), concluded by the **Treaty of Versailles**, and in subsequent negotiations and local wars (Russian-Polish War, 1920), the **map of Europe** was redrawn with a nod to U.S. Pres. Woodrow Wilson's principle of self-determination. Austria and Hungary were separated, and much of their land was given to Yugoslavia (formerly Serbia), Romania, Italy, and the newly independent Poland and Czechoslovakia. Germany lost territory in the W, N, and E, while Finland and the Baltic states were detached from Russia. Turkey lost nearly all its Arab lands to British-sponsored Arab states or to direct French and British rule. Belgium's sovereignty was recognized.

From 1916, the civilian populations and economies of both sides were mobilized to an unprecedented degree. Hardships intensified among fighting nations in 1917 (French mutiny crushed in May). More than 10 million soldiers died in the war.

A huge **reparations** burden and partial demilitarization were imposed on Germany. Pres. Wilson obtained approval for a League of Nations, but the U.S. Senate refused to allow the U.S. to join.

Both sides in World War I developed elaborate networks of dug-in trenches from which to fight.

Russian revolution. Military defeats and high casualties caused a contagious lack of confidence in Tsar Nicholas, who was forced to abdicate Mar. 1917. A liberal provisional government failed to end the war, and massive desertions, riots, and fighting between factions followed. A moderate socialist government under Aleksandr Kerensky was overthrown (Nov. 1917) in a violent coup by the **Bolsheviks** in Petrograd under **Lenin,** who later disbanded the elected Constituent Assembly.

The Bolsheviks brutally suppressed all opposition and ended the war with Germany in Mar. 1918. **Civil war** broke out in the summer between the Red Army (the Bolsheviks and their supporters), and monarchists, anarchists, minority nationalities (Ukrainians, Georgians, Poles), and others. Small U.S., British, French, and Japanese units also opposed the Bolsheviks (1918-19; Japan in Vladivostok to 1922). The civil war, anarchy, and pogroms devastated the country until the 1920 Red Army victory. The **Communist Party** leadership retained absolute power.

Other European revolutions. An unpopular monarchy in **Portugal** was overthrown in 1910. The new republic took severe anticlerical measures in 1911.

After a century of Home Rule agitation, during which **Ireland** was devastated by famine (1 million dead, 1846-47) and emigration, republican militants staged an unsuccessful uprising in Dublin during **Easter 1916.** The execution of the leaders and mass arrests by the British won popular support for the rebels. The **Irish Free State**, comprising all but the 6 N counties, achieved dominion status in 1922.

In the aftermath of the world war, radical revolutions were attempted in Germany (**Spartacist** uprising, Jan. 1919), **Hungary** (Kun regime, 1919), and elsewhere. All were suppressed or failed for lack of support.

Chinese revolution. The Manchu Dynasty was overthrown and a republic proclaimed in Oct. 1911. First Pres. Sun Yat-sen resigned in favor of strongman Yuan Shih-k'ai. Sun organized the parliamentarian **Kuomintang** party.

Students launched protests on May 4, 1919, against League of Nations concessions in China to Japan. Nationalist, liberal, and socialist ideas and political groups spread. The **Communist Party** was founded in 1921. A Communist regime took power in Mongolia with Soviet support in 1921.

India restive. Indian objections to British rule erupted in nationalist riots as well as in the nonviolent tactics of Mahatma **Gandhi** (1869-1948). Nearly 400 unarmed demonstrators were shot at **Amritsar** in Apr. 1919. Britain approved limited self-rule that year.

Mexican revolution. Under the long Diaz dictatorship (1877-1911) the economy advanced, but Indian and mestizo lands were confiscated, and concessions to foreigners (mostly U.S.) damaged the middle class. A **revolution in 1910** led to civil wars and U.S. intervention (1914, 1916-17). Land reform and a more democratic constitution (1917) were achieved.

Sciences. Scientific specialization prevailed by the 20th cent. Advances in knowledge and technological aptitude increased with the geometric rise in the number of practitioners. Physicists challenged common-sense views of causality, observation, and a mechanistic universe, putting science further beyond popular grasp (**Einstein's** general theory of relativity, 1916; Bohr's quantum mechanics, 1913; Heisenberg's uncertainty principle, 1927).

Aftermath of War: 1920-29

U.S. Easy credit, technological ingenuity, and war-related industrial decline in Europe caused a long economic boom, in which ownership of new products—**autos, phones, radios**—became more democratized. **Prosperity**, an increase in women workers, women's suffrage (19th Amendment ratified, 1920), and drastic change in fashion (flappers, mannish bob for women, clean-shaven men) created a wide perception of social change, despite prohibition of alcoholic beverages (1919-33). Union membership and strikes increased. Fear of radicals led to Palmer raids (1919-20) and the Sacco/Vanzetti case (1921-27).

Europe sorts itself out. Germany's liberal **Weimar constitution** (1919) could not guarantee a stable government in the face of rightist violence (Rathenau assassinated, 1922) and Communist refusal to cooperate with Socialists. Reparations and Allied occupation of the Rhineland caused staggering inflation that destroyed middle-class savings, but economic expansion resumed after mid-decade, aided by U.S. loans. A sophisticated, **innovative culture** developed in architecture and design (Bauhaus, 1919-28), film (Lang, *M*, 1931), painting (Grosz), music (Weill, *Threepenny Opera*, 1928), theater (Brecht, *A Man's a Man*, 1926), criticism (Benjamin), philosophy (Jung), and fashion. This culture was considered decadent and socially disruptive by rightists.

England elected its first Labour governments (Jan. 1924, June 1929). A 10-day general strike in support of coal miners failed in May 1926. In **Italy**, strikes, political chaos, and violence by small Fascist bands culminated in the Oct. 1922 Fascist March on Rome, which established **Mussolini's** dictatorship. Strikes were outlawed (1926), and Italian influence was pressed in the Balkans (Albania a protectorate, 1926). A conservative dictatorship was also established in **Portugal** in a 1926 military coup.

Czechoslovakia, the only stable democracy to emerge from the war in Central or E Europe, faced opposition from Germans (in the Sudetenland), Ruthenians, and some Slovaks. As the industrial heartland of the old Habsburg empire, it remained fairly prosperous. With French backing, it formed the Little Entente with Yugoslavia (1920) and **Romania** (1921) to block Austrian or Hungarian irredentism. Croats and Slovenes in **Yugoslavia** demanded a federal state until King Alexander I proclaimed (1929) a royal dictatorship. Poland faced internal nationality problems as well (Germans, Ukrainians, Jews); Pilsudski ruled as dictator from 1926. The Baltic states were threatened by traditionally dominant ethnic Germans and by Soviet-supported Communists.

An economic collapse and famine in **Russia** (1921-22) claimed 5 million lives. The New Economic Policy (1921) allowed land ownership by peasants and some private commerce and industry. **Stalin** was absolute ruler within 4 years of Lenin's death (1924). He inaugurated a brutal collectivization program (1929-32) and used foreign Communist parties for Soviet state advantage.

Internationalism. Revulsion against World War I led to pacifist agitation, to the Kellogg-Briand Pact renouncing aggressive war (1928), and to **naval disarmament** pacts (Washington, 1922; London, 1930). But the League of Nations was able to arbitrate only minor disputes (Greece-Bulgaria, 1925).

Middle East. Mustafa Kemal (**Ataturk**) led **Turkish** nationalists in resisting Italian, French, and Greek military advances (1919-23). The sultanate was abolished (1922), and elaborate reforms were passed, including secularization of law and adoption of the Latin alphabet. Ethnic conflict led to persecution of **Armenians** (more than 1 million dead in 1915, 1 million expelled), Greeks (forced Greek-Turk population exchange, 1923), and Kurds (1925 uprising).

With evacuation of the Turks from **Arab** lands, the puritanical Wahabi dynasty of E Arabia conquered (1919-25) what is now Saudi Arabia. British, French, and Arab dynastic and nationalist maneuvering resulted in the creation of 2 more Arab monarchies in 1921—Iraq and Transjordan (both under British control)—and 2 French mandates—Syria and Lebanon. Jewish immigration into British-mandated **Palestine**, inspired by the Zionist movement, was resisted by Arabs, at times violently (1921, 1929 massacres).

Reza Khan ruled **Persia** after his 1921 coup (shah from 1925), centralized control, and created the trappings of a modern secular state.

In 1922, English archaeologist Howard Carter discovered the **tomb** of the boy pharaoh **Tutankhamen** in the Valley of the Kings in Egypt.

China. The Kuomintang under **Chiang Kai-shek** (1887-1975) subdued the warlords by 1928. The Communists were brutally suppressed after their alliance with the Kuomintang was broken in 1927. Relative peace thereafter allowed for industrial and financial improvements, with some Russian, British, and U.S. cooperation.

Arts. Nearly all bounds of subject matter, style, and attitude were broken in the arts of the period. **Abstract** art first took inspiration from natural forms or narrative themes (Kandinsky from 1911) and then worked free of any representational aims (Malevich's suprematism, 1915-19; Mondrian's geometric style from 1917). The **Dada** movement (from 1916) mocked artistic pretension with absurd collages and constructions. Paradox, illusion, and psychological taboos were exploited by **surrealists** by the late 1920s (Dali, Magritte). Architectural schools celebrated industrial values, whether vigorous abstract constructivism (Tatlin, *Monument to 3rd International*, 1919) or the machined, streamlined **Bauhaus** style, which was extended to many design fields (Helvetica typeface).

Prose writers explored revolutionary narrative modes related to dreams (Kafka's *Trial*, 1925), internal monologue (Joyce's *Ulysses*, 1922), and word play (Stein's *Making of Americans*, 1925). Poets and novelists wrote of modern alienation (Eliot's *Waste Land*, 1922) and aimlessness ("The Lost Generation").

Rise of Totalitarians: 1930-39

Depression. A worldwide financial panic and economic depression began with the Oct. 1929 U.S. stock market crash and the May 1931 failure of the Austrian Credit-Anstalt. A credit crunch caused international bankruptcies and **unemployment**: 12 million jobless by 1932 in the U.S., 5.6 million in Germany, 2.7 million in England. Governments responded with **tariff restrictions** (Smoot-Hawley Act, 1930; Ottawa Imperial Conference, 1932), which dried up world trade. Government public works programs were vitiated by deflationary budget balancing.

Germany. Years of agitation by violent extremists were brought to a head by the Depression. Nazi leader Adolf Hitler was named chancellor in Jan. 1933 and given dictatorial power by the Reichstag in March. Opposition parties were disbanded, strikes banned, and all aspects of economic, cultural, and religious life were brought under central government and Nazi party control and manipulated by sophisticated propaganda. Severe persecution of Jews began (**Nuremberg Laws**, Sept. 1935). Many Jews, political opponents, and others were sent to concentration camps (Dachau, 1933), where thousands died or were killed. Public works, renewed conscription (1935), arms production, and a 4-year plan (1936) all but ended unemployment.

Hitler's expansionism started with reincorporation of the Saar (1935), occupation of the **Rhineland** (Mar. 1936), and annexation of Austria (Mar. 1938). At **Munich** (Sept. 1938) Britain and France attempted to appease Hitler and avoid war by successfully encouraging Czechoslovakia's surrender of the Sudetenland territory.

Russia. Rapid industrialization was achieved through successive **5-year plans** starting in 1928, using severe labor discipline and mass forced labor. Industry was financed by a decline in living standards and exploitation of agriculture, which was almost totally collectivized by the early 1930s (*kolkhoz*, collective farm; *sovkhoz*, state farm, often in newly worked lands). Successive **purges** increased the role of professionals and management at the expense of workers. Millions perished in a series of manufactured disasters: extermination (1929-34) of kulaks (peasant landowners), severe famine (1932-33), party purges and show trials (Great Purge, 1936-38), suppression of nationalities, and poor conditions in labor camps.

Spain. An industrial revolution during World War I created an urban proletariat, which was attracted to socialism and anarchism; Catalan nationalists challenged central authority. The 5 years after King Alfonso left Spain in Apr. 1931 were dominated by tension between intermittent leftist and anticlerical governments and clericals, monarchists, and other rightists. Anarchist and Communist rebellions were crushed, but a July 1936 extreme right rebellion led by Gen. Francisco **Franco** and aided by Nazi Germany and Fascist Italy succeeded, after a 3-year **civil war** (more than 1 million dead in battles and atrocities). The war polarized international public opinion.

Italy. Despite propaganda for the ideal of the Corporate State, few domestic reforms were attempted. An entente with Hungary and Austria (Mar. 1934), a pact with Germany and Japan (Nov. 1937), and intervention by 50,000-75,000 troops in Spain (1936-39) sealed Italy's identification with the fascist bloc (anti-Semitic laws after Mar. 1938). Ethiopia was conquered (1935-36), and Albania annexed (Jan. 1939) in conscious imitation of ancient Rome.

Eastern Europe. Repressive regimes fought for power against an active opposition (liberals, socialists, Communists, peasants, Nazis). Minority groups and Jews were restricted within national boundaries that did not coincide with ethnic population patterns. In the destruction of **Czechoslovakia**, Hungary occupied S Slovakia (Nov. 1938) and Ruthenia (Mar. 1939), and a pro-Nazi regime took power in the rest of Slovakia. Other boundary disputes (e.g., Poland-Lithuania, Yugoslavia-Bulgaria, and Romania-Hungary) doomed attempts to build joint fronts against Germany or Russia. Economic depression was severe.

East Asia. After a period of liberalism in **Japan**, nativist militarists dominated the government with peasant support. Manchuria was seized (Sept. 1931-Feb. 1932), and a puppet state was set up (Manchukuo). Adjacent Jehol (Inner Mongolia) was occupied in 1933. China proper was invaded in July 1937; large areas were conquered by Oct. 1938. Hundreds of thousands of rapes, murders, and other atrocities were attributed to the Japanese.

In **China** Communist forces left Kuomintang-besieged strongholds in the S in a Long March (1934-35) to the N.

Italy's Benito Mussolini and Germany's Adolf Hitler affirmed their full political and military alliance with the Pact of Steel (1939).

The Kuomintang-Communist civil war was suspended in Jan. 1937 in the face of threatening Japan.

Democracies. The Roosevelt Administration, in office Mar. 1933, embarked on an extensive program of **New Deal** social reform and economic stimulation, including protection for labor unions (heavy industries organized), Social Security, public works, wage-and-hour laws, and assistance to farmers. Isolationist sentiment (1937 Neutrality Act) prevented U.S. intervention in Europe, but military expenditures were increased in 1939.

French political instability and polarization prevented resolution of economic and international security questions. The **Popular Front** government under Leon Blum (June 1936-Apr. 1938) passed social reforms (40-hr week) and raised arms spending. National coalition governments, which ruled Britain from Aug. 1931, brought economic recovery but failed to define a consistent international policy until Chamberlain's government (from May 1937), which practiced **appeasement** of Germany and Italy.

India. Twenty years of agitation for autonomy and then for independence (Gandhi's **salt march**, 1930) achieved some constitutional reform (extended provincial powers, 1935) despite Muslim-Hindu strife. Social issues assumed prominence with peasant uprisings (1921), strikes (1928), Gandhi's efforts for untouchables (1932 "fast unto death"), and social and agrarian reform by the provinces after 1937.

Arts. The streamlined, geometric design motifs of Art Deco (from 1925) prevailed through the 1930s. **Abstract art** flourished (Moore sculptures from 1931) alongside a new **realism** related to social and political concerns (Socialist Realism, the official Soviet style from 1934; Mexican muralist Rivera, 1886-1957; and Orozco, 1883-1949), which were also expressed in fiction and poetry (Steinbeck's *Grapes of Wrath*, 1939; Sandburg's *The People, Yes*, 1936). Modern architecture (International Style, 1932) was unchallenged in its use of artificial materials (concrete, glass), lack of decoration, and monumentality (Rockefeller Center, 1929-40). Larger-than-life U.S.-made films captured a worldwide audience *(Gone With the Wind, The Wizard of Oz,* both 1939).

War, Hot and Cold: 1940-49

War in Asia-Pacific. Japan occupied Indochina in Sept. 1940, dominated Thailand in Dec. 1941, and attacked Hawaii (**Pearl Harbor**), the Philippines, Hong Kong, and Malaya on Dec. 7, 1941 (precipitating U.S. entrance into the war). Indonesia was attacked in Jan. 1942, and Burma was conquered in Mar. 1942. The Battle of **Midway** (June 1942) turned back the Japanese advance. "Island-hopping" battles (**Guadalcanal**, Aug. 1942-Jan. 1943; **Leyte Gulf**, Oct. 1944; **Iwo Jima**, Feb.-Mar. 1945; **Okinawa**, Apr. 1945) and massive bombing raids on Japan from June 1944 wore out Japanese defenses. U.S. atom bombs, dropped Aug. 6 and 9 on **Hiroshima** and Nagasaki, forced Japan to agree, on Aug. 14, to surrender; formal surrender was on Sept. 2, 1945.

War in Europe. The Nazi-Soviet nonaggression pact (Aug. 1939) freed Germany to attack Poland (Sept. 1939). Britain and France, which had guaranteed Polish independence, declared war on Germany. Russia seized E Poland (Sept. 1939), attacked Finland (Nov. 1939), and took the Baltic states (July 1940). Mobile German forces staged *blitzkrieg* attacks during Apr.-June 1940, conquering neutral Denmark, Norway, and the Low Countries and defeating France; 350,000 British and French troops were evacuated at **Dunkirk** (May). The **Battle of Britain** (June-Dec. 1940) denied Germany air superiority. German-Italian campaigns won the Balkans by Apr. 1941. Three million Axis troops **invaded Russia** in June 1941, marching through Ukraine to the Caucasus, and through White Russia and the Baltic republics to Moscow and Leningrad.

Russian winter counterthrusts (1941-42 and 1942-43) stopped the German advance (**Stalingrad**, Sept. 1942-Feb. 1943). Sustaining great casualties, the Russians drove the Axis from all E Europe and the Balkans in the next 2 years. Invasions of N Africa (Nov. 1942), Italy (Sept. 1943), and **Normandy** (launched on D-Day, June 6, 1944) brought U.S., British, Free French, and allied troops to Germany by spring 1945. In Feb. 1945, the 3 Allied leaders, Winston **Churchill** (Britain), Joseph **Stalin** (USSR), and Franklin D. Roosevelt (U.S.), met in Yalta to discuss strategy and resolve political issues, including the postwar Allied occupation of Germany. Germany surrendered May 7, 1945.

Atrocities. The war brought 20th-cent. cruelty to its peak. The Nazi regime systematically killed an estimated 5-6 million Jews, including some 3 million who died in death camps (e.g., **Auschwitz**). Gypsies, political opponents, people with mental or physical disabilities, and others deemed undesirable were also murdered by the Nazis, as were vast numbers of Slavs.

Civilian deaths. German bombs killed 70,000 British civilians. More than 100,000 Chinese civilians were killed by Japanese forces in the capture and occupation of Nanking. Severe retaliation by the Soviet army, E European partisans, Free French, and others took a heavy toll. U.S. and British bombing of Germany killed hundreds of thousands,

More than 160,000 Allied troops stormed a highly fortified 50-mile stretch of French coastline on D-Day (June 6, 1944).

as did U.S. bombing of Japan (80,000-200,000 at Hiroshima alone). Some 45 million people died in the war.

Settlement. The **United Nations** charter was signed in San Francisco on June 26, 1945, by 50 nations. The International Tribunal at **Nuremberg** convicted 22 German leaders for war crimes in Sept. 1946; 23 Japanese leaders were convicted in Nov. 1948. Postwar border changes included large gains in territory for the USSR, losses for Germany, a shift to the W in Polish borders, and minor losses for Italy. Communist regimes, supported by Soviet troops, took power in most of E Europe, including Soviet-occupied Germany (GDR, aka East Germany, proclaimed Oct. 1949). Japan lost all overseas lands.

Recovery. Basic political and social changes were imposed on Japan and W Germany by the western allies (Japan constitution adopted, Nov. 1946; W German basic law, May 1949). U.S. **Marshall Plan** aid ($12 billion, 1947-51) spurred W European economic recovery after a period of severe inflation and strikes in Europe and the U.S. The British Labour Party introduced a national health service and nationalized basic industries in 1946.

Cold War. Western fears of further Soviet advances (Cominform formed in Oct. 1947; Czechoslovakia coup, Feb. 1948; Berlin blockade, Apr. 1948-Sept. 1949) led to the formation of **NATO**. Civil War in Greece and Soviet pressure on Turkey led to U.S. aid under the **Truman Doctrine** (Mar. 1947). Other anti-Communist security pacts were the Organization of American States (Apr. 1948) and the SE Asia Treaty Organization (Sept. 1954). A new wave of **Soviet purges** and repression intensified in the last years of Stalin's rule, extending to E Europe (Slansky trial in Czechoslovakia, 1951). Only

Yugoslavia resisted Soviet control (expelled by Cominform, June 1948; U.S. aid, June 1949).

China, Korea. Communist forces emerged from World War II strengthened by the Soviet takeover of industrial Manchuria. In 4 years of fighting, the Kuomintang was driven from the mainland; the People's Republic of China was proclaimed Oct. 1, 1949. Korea was divided by USSR and U.S. occupation forces. Separate republics were proclaimed in the 2 zones in Aug.-Sept. 1948.

India. India and Pakistan became independent dominions on Aug. 15, 1947. Millions of Hindu and Muslim refugees were created by the partition; riots (1946-47) took hundreds of thousands of lives; Mahatma **Gandhi** was assassinated in Jan. 1948. Burma became completely independent in Jan. 1948; Ceylon took dominion status in Feb.

Middle East. The UN approved partition of Palestine into Jewish and Arab states. **Israel** was proclaimed a state, May 14, 1948. Arabs rejected partition, but failed to defeat Israel in war (May 1948-July 1949). Immigration from Europe and the Middle East swelled Israel's Jewish population.

Mahatma Gandhi led efforts for Indian autonomy and independence for more than 25 years.

British and French forces left Lebanon and Syria in 1946. Transjordan occupied most of Arab Palestine.

Southeast Asia. Communists and others fought against restoration of French rule in **Indochina** from 1946; a non-Communist government was recognized by France in Mar. 1949, but fighting continued. Both Indonesia and the Philippines became independent; the former in 1949 after 4 years of war with Netherlands, the latter in 1946. Philippine economic and military ties with the U.S. remained strong; a Communist-led peasant rising was checked in 1948.

Arts. New York became the center of the world art market; **abstract expressionism** was the chief mode (Pollock from 1943, de Kooning from 1947). Literature and philosophy explored **existentialism** (Camus's *The Stranger*, 1942; Sartre's *Being and Nothingness*, 1943). Non-Western attempts to revive or create regional styles (Senghor's Négritude, Mishima's novels) only confirmed the emergence of a universal culture. Radio and phonograph records spread American popular music (swing, bebop) around the world.

The American Decade: 1950-59

Polite decolonization. The peaceful decline of European political and military power in Asia and Africa accelerated in the 1950s. Nearly all of **N Africa** was freed by 1956, but France fought a bitter war to retain Algeria, with its large European minority, until 1962. **Ghana**, independent in 1957, led a parade of new black African nations (more than 2 dozen by 1962), which altered the political character of the UN. Ethnic disputes often exploded in the new nations after decolonization (UN troops in Cyprus, 1964; **Nigerian civil war**, 1967-70). Leaders of the new states, mostly sharing socialist ideologies, tried to create an Afro-Asian bloc (Bandung Conference, 1955), but Western economic influence and U.S. political ties remained strong (Baghdad Pact, 1955).

Trade. World trade volume soared, in an atmosphere of monetary stability assured by international accords (**Bretton Woods**, 1944). In Europe, economic integration advanced (**European Economic Community**, 1957; European Free Trade Association, 1960). Comecon (1949) coordinated the economies of Soviet-bloc countries.

U.S. Economic growth produced an abundance of consumer goods (9.3 million motor vehicles sold, 1955). Suburban housing changed life patterns for middle and working classes (Levittown, 1947-51). Pres. Dwight **Eisenhower's** landslide election victories (1952, 1956) reflected consensus politics. A system of alliances and military bases bolstered U.S. influence on all continents. Trade and payments surpluses were balanced by overseas investments and foreign aid ($50 billion, 1950-59).

USSR. In the "thaw" after Stalin's death in 1953, relations with the West improved (evacuation of Vienna, Geneva summit conference, both 1955). Repression of scientific and cultural life eased, and many prisoners were freed culminating in **de-Stalinization** (1956). **Nikita Khrushchev's** leadership aimed at consumer sector growth, but farm production lagged, despite the virgin lands program (from 1954). Soviet crushing of the 1956 Hungarian revolution, the 1960 U-2 spy plane episode, and other incidents renewed East-West tension and domestic curbs.

Eastern Europe. Resentment of Russian domination and Stalinist repression combined with nationalist, economic, and religious factors to produce periodic violence. E Berlin workers rioted (1953), Polish workers rioted in Poznan (June 1956), and a broad-based **revolution** broke out in **Hungary** (Oct. 1956). All were suppressed by Soviet

force or threats (at least 7,000 dead in Hungary), but Poland was allowed to restore private ownership of farms, and a degree of personal and economic freedom returned to Hungary. Yugoslavia experimented with worker self-management and a market economy.

Korea. The 1945 division of Korea along the 38th parallel left industry in the N, which was organized into a militant regime and armed by the USSR. The S was politically disunited. More than 60,000 N Korean troops invaded the S on June 25, 1950. The U.S., backed by the UN Security Council, sent troops. **UN troops** reached the Chinese border in Nov. Some 200,000 Chinese troops crossed the Yalu R. and drove back UN forces. By spring 1951 battle lines had become stabilized near the original 38th parallel border, but heavy fighting continued. Finally, an armistice was signed on July 27, 1953. U.S. troops remained in the S, and U.S. economic and military aid continued. The war stimulated rapid economic recovery in Japan.

China. Starting in 1952, industry, agriculture, and social institutions were forcibly collectivized. In a massive purge, as many as several million people were executed as Kuomintang supporters or as class and political enemies. The **Great Leap Forward** (1958-60) unsuccessfully tried to force the pace of development by substituting labor for investment.

Indochina. Ho Chi Minh's forces, aided by the USSR and the new Chinese Communist government, fought French and pro-French Vietnamese forces to a standstill and captured the strategic **Dien Bien Phu** camp in May 1954. The Geneva Agreements divided Vietnam in half pending elections (never held) and recognized Laos and Cambodia as independent. The U.S. aided the anti-Communist Republic of Vietnam in the S.

Middle East. Arab revolutions placed leftist, militantly nationalist regimes in power in Egypt (1952) and Iraq (1958). But Arab unity attempts failed (United Arab Republic joined Egypt, Syria, Yemen, 1958-61). Arab refusal to recognize Israel (Arab League economic blockade began Sept. 1951) led to a permanent **state of war**, with repeated incidents (Gaza, 1955). Israel occupied Sinai, and Britain and France took (Oct. 1956) the Suez Canal, but were replaced by the UN Emergency Force. The Mossadegh government in Iran nationalized (May 1951) the British-owned oil industry in May, but was overthrown (Aug. 1953) in a U.S.-aided coup.

Latin America. Argentinian dictator Juan **Perón**, in office 1946, crushed opposition and enforced land reform, some nationalization, welfare state measures, and curbs on the Roman Catholic Church. A Sept. 1955 coup deposed Perón. The 1952 revolution in Bolivia brought land reform, nationalization of tin mines, and improvement in the status of Native Americans, who nevertheless remained poor. The Batista regime in Cuba was overthrown (Jan. 1959) by Fidel **Castro**, who imposed a Communist dictatorship, aligned Cuba with the USSR and improved education and health care. A U.S.-backed anti-Castro invasion (**Bay of Pigs**, Apr. 1961) was crushed. Self-government advanced in the British Caribbean.

Technology. Large outlays on research and development in the U.S. and the USSR focused on military appli-

cations (H-bomb in U.S., 1952; USSR, 1953; Britain, 1957; intercontinental missiles, late 1950s). Soviet launching of the **Sputnik** satellite (Oct. 4, 1957) spurred increases in U.S. science education funds (National Defense Education Act).

Literature and film. Alienation from social and literary conventions reached an extreme in the theater of the absurd (Beckett's *Waiting for Godot,* 1952), the "new novel" (Robbe-Grillet's *Voyeur,* 1955), and avant-garde film (Antonioni's *L'Avventura,* 1960). U.S. beatniks (Kerouac's *On the Road,* 1957) and others rejected the supposed conformism of Americans (Riesman's *The Lonely Crowd,* 1950).

Rising Expectations: 1960-69

Economic boom. The longest sustained economic boom on record spanned almost the entire decade in the capitalist world; the closely watched GNP figure doubled (1960-70) in the U.S., fueled by Vietnam War-related budget deficits. The **General Agreement on Tariffs and Trade** (1967) stimulated W European prosperity, which spread to peripheral areas (Spain, Italy, E Germany). Japan became a top economic power. Foreign investment aided the industrialization of Brazil. There were limited Soviet economic reform attempts.

Reform and radicalization. Pres. John F. **Kennedy**, inaugurated 1961, emphasized youthful idealism and vigor; his assassination Nov. 22, 1963, was a national trauma. A series of political and social reform movements took root in the U.S. and other countries. Blacks demonstrated nonviolently and with partial success against segregation and poverty (1963 March on Washington; 1964 **Civil Rights Act**), but some urban areas erupted in extensive riots (Watts, 1965; Detroit, 1967; **Martin Luther King** assassination, Apr. 4, 1968). New concern for the poor (Harrington's *Other America,* 1963) helped lead to Pres. Lyndon Johnson's **"Great Society"** programs (Medicare, Water Quality Act, Higher Education Act, all 1965). Concern for the **environment** surged (Carson's *Silent Spring,* 1962).

Feminism revived as a cultural and political movement (Friedan's *Feminine Mystique,* 1963; National Organization for Women founded 1966), a movement for homosexual rights emerged (Stonewall riot in NYC, 1969). Pope John XXIII called the **Second Vatican Council** (1962-65), which liberalized Roman Catholic liturgy and some other aspects of Catholicism.

Opposition to U.S. involvement in Vietnam, especially among university students (**Moratorium** protest, Nov. 1969), turned violent (Weatherman Chicago riots, Oct. 1969). **New Left** and Marxist theories became popular, and membership in radical groups (Students for a Democratic Society, Black Panthers) increased. Maoist groups, especially in Europe, called for total transformation of society. In France, students sparked a nationwide strike affecting 10 million workers in May-June 1968, but an electoral reaction barred revolutionary change.

China. China's revolutionary militancy under **Mao** Zedong caused disputes with the USSR under "revisionist" Khrushchev, starting in 1960. The 2 powers exchanged fire in 1969 border disputes. China used force to capture (1962) areas disputed with India. The **"Great Proletarian Cultural Revolution"** tried to impose a utopian egalitarian program in China and spread revolution abroad; political struggle, often violent, convulsed China in 1965-68.

Indochina. Communist-led guerrillas aided by N Vietnam fought from 1960 against the S Vietnam government of Ngo Dinh Diem (killed 1963). The U.S. military role increased after the 1964 **Tonkin Gulf** incident. U.S. forces

peaked at 543,400 in Apr. 1969. Massive numbers of N Vietnamese troops also fought. Laotian and Cambodian neutrality were threatened by Communist insurgencies, with N Vietnamese aid, and U.S. intrigues.

Developing World. A bloc of authoritarian leftist regimes among the newly independent nations emerged in political opposition to the U.S.-led Western alliance and came to dominate the conference of nonaligned nations (Belgrade, 1961; Cairo, 1964; Lusaka, 1970). Soviet political ties and military bases were established in Cuba, Egypt, Algeria, Guinea, and other countries whose leaders were regarded as revolutionary heroes by opposition groups in pro-Western or colonial countries. Some leaders were ousted in coups by pro-Western groups—Zaire's Patrice Lumumba (killed 1961), Ghana's Kwame Nkrumah (exiled 1966), and Indonesia's Sukarno (effectively ousted in 1965 after a Communist coup failed).

Middle East. Arab-Israeli tension erupted into a brief war June 1967. Israel emerged from the war as a major regional power. Military shipments before and after the war brought much of the Arab world into the Soviet political sphere. Most Arab states broke U.S. diplomatic ties, while Communist countries cut their ties to Israel. Intra-Arab disputes continued: Egypt and Saudi Arabia supported rival factions in a bloody Yemen civil war 1962-70; Lebanese troops fought Palestinian commandos 1969.

The botched Bay of Pigs invasion (1961) unsuccessfully attempted to overthrow the government of Fidel Castro.

East Europe. To stop the large-scale exodus of citizens, E German authorities built (Aug. 1961) a **fortified wall across Berlin.** Soviet sway in the Balkans was weakened by Albania's support of China (USSR broke ties in Dec. 1961) and Romania's assertion (1964) of industrial and foreign policy autonomy. Liberalization (spring 1968) in Czechoslovakia was crushed by massive force by troops of 5 Warsaw Pact countries. W German treaties (1970) with the USSR and Poland facilitated the transfer of German technology and confirmed postwar boundaries.

Arts and styles. The boundary between fine and popular arts was blurred to some extent by Pop Art (Warhol) and rock musicals (*Hair,* 1968). Informality and exaggeration prevailed in fashion (beards, miniskirts). A nonpolitical "counterculture" developed, rejecting traditional bourgeois life goals and personal habits, and use of marijuana and hallucinogens spread (**Woodstock** festival, Aug. 1969). Indian influence was felt in religion (Ram Dass) and fashion, and **The Beatles,** who brought unprecedented sophistication to rock music, became for many a symbol of the decade.

Science. Achievements in space (**humans on the moon,** July 1969) and electronics (lasers, integrated circuits) encouraged a faith in scientific solutions to problems in agriculture ("green revolution"), medicine (heart transplants, 1967), and other areas. Harmful technology, it was believed, could be controlled (1963 nuclear weapon test ban treaty, 1968 nonproliferation treaty).

Disillusionment: 1970-79

U.S.: Caution and neoconservatism. A relatively sluggish economy, energy shortages, and environmental problems contributed to a **"limits of growth"** philosophy. Suspicion of science and technology killed or delayed major projects (supersonic transport dropped, 1971; Seabrook nuclear power plant protests, 1977-78) and was fed by the Three Mile Island nuclear reactor accident (Mar. 1979).

There were signs of growing mistrust of big government and less support for new social policies. School busing and racial quotas were opposed (Bakke decision, June 1978); the proposed Equal Rights Amendment for women languished; civil rights legislation aimed at protecting homosexuals was opposed (Dade County referendum, June 1977).

Completion of Communist forces' takeover of **South Vietnam** (evacuation of U.S. civilians, Apr. 1975), revelations of Central Intelligence Agency misdeeds (Rockefeller Commission report, June 1975), and **Watergate** scandals (Nixon resigned in Aug. 1974) reduced faith in U.S. moral and material capacity to influence world affairs. Revelations of Soviet crimes (Solzhenitsyn's *Gulag Archipelago,* 1974) and Soviet intervention in Africa helped foster a revival of anti-Communist sentiment.

More than 8.7 million members of the U.S. military served in the divisive Vietnam War (1964-73). The only conflict to require more American military service was World War II, when more than 16 million were called to active duty.

Economy sluggish. The 1960s boom faltered in the 1970s; a severe recession in the U.S. and Europe (1974-75) followed a huge oil price hike (Dec. 1973). Monetary instability (U.S. cut ties to gold in Aug. 1971), the decline of the dollar, and protectionist moves by industrial countries (1977-78) threatened trade. Business investment and spending for research declined. Severe inflation plagued many countries (25% in Britain, 1975; 18% in U.S., 1979).

China picks up pieces. After the 1976 deaths of Mao Zedong and Zhou Enlai, struggle for the leadership succession was won by pragmatists. A nationwide purge of orthodox Maoists was carried out, and the **Gang of Four**, led by Mao's widow, Chiang Ching, arrested. The new leaders freed more than 100,000 political prisoners and reduced public adulation of Mao. Political and trade ties were expanded with Japan, Europe, and the U.S. in the late 1970s, as relations worsened with the USSR, Cuba, and Vietnam (4-week invasion by China, 1979). Ideological guidelines in industry, science, education, and the armed forces, which the ruling faction said had caused chaos and decline, were reversed (bonuses to workers, Dec. 1977; exams for college entrance, Oct. 1977). Severe restrictions on cultural expression were eased.

Europe. European unity moves (EEC-EFTA trade accord, 1972) faltered as economic problems appeared (Britain floated pound, 1972; France floated franc, 1974). Germany and Switzerland curbed guest workers from southern Europe. Greece and Turkey quarreled over Cyprus and Aegean oil rights.

All non-Communist Europe was under democratic rule after free elections (June 1976) in **Spain** 7 months after the death of Franco. The conservative, colonialist regime in **Portugal** was overthrown in Apr. 1974. In **Greece** the 7-year-old military dictatorship yielded power in 1974. Northern Europe, though ruled mostly by Socialists (**Swedish** Socialists unseated in 1976 after 44 years in power), turned more conservative. The **British** Labour government imposed (1975) wage curbs and suspended nationalization schemes. Terrorism in **Germany** (1972 Munich Olympics killings) led to laws curbing some civil liberties. **French** "new philosophers" rejected leftist ideologies, and the Socialist-Communist coalition lost a 1978 election bid.

Religion and politics. The improvement in **Muslim** countries' political fortunes by the 1950s (with the exception of Central Asia under Soviet and Chinese rule) and the growth of Arab oil wealth were followed by a resurgence of traditional religious fervor. Libyan dictator Muammar al-Qaddafi mixed Islamic laws with socialism and called for Muslim return to Spain and Sicily. The illegal Muslim Brotherhood in **Egypt** was accused of violence, while extreme groups bombed (1977) theaters to protest Western and secular values.

In **Turkey**, the National Salvation Party was the first Islamic group to share (1974) power since secularization in the 1920s. In **Iran, Ayatollah Ruhollah Khomeini** led a revolution that deposed the secular shah (Jan. 1979) and created an Islamic republic there. Religiously motivated Muslims took part in an insurrection in Saudi Arabia that briefly seized (1979) the Grand Mosque in Mecca. Muslim puritan opposition to **Pakistan** Pres. Zulfikar Ali-Bhutto helped lead to his overthrow in July 1977. Muslim solidarity, however, could not prevent Pakistan's eastern province (**Bangladesh**) from declaring (Dec. 1971) independence after a bloody civil war.

Muslim and Hindu resentment of coerced sterilization in **India** helped defeat the Indira Gandhi government, which was replaced (Mar. 1977) by a coalition including religious Hindu parties. Muslims in the S **Philippines**, aided by Libya, rebelled against central rule from 1973.

The Buddhist Soka Gakkai movement launched (1964) the Komeito party in **Japan**, which became a major opposition party in 1972 and 1976 elections.

Evangelical Protestant groups grew in the U.S. A revival of interest in Orthodox Christianity occurred among **Russian** intellectuals (Solzhenitsyn). The secularist **Israeli** Labor party, after decades of rule, was ousted in 1977 by conservatives led by Menachem Begin; religious militants founded settlements on the disputed West Bank, part of biblically promised Israel. U.S. Reform Judaism revived many previously discarded traditional practices.

Religious wars raged intermittently in **Northern Ireland** (Catholic vs. Protestant, 1969-97) and **Lebanon** (Christian vs. Muslim, 1975-90), while religious militancy complicated the Israel-Arab dispute (1973 Israel-Arab war). The Camp David Accords in 1978, negotiated by Egyptian Pres. Anwar al-Sadat, Israeli Prime Min. Menachem Begin, and U.S. Pres. Jimmy Carter, facilitated the landmark 1979 **Egypt-Israel peace treaty**, but increased militancy on the West Bank impeded further progress.

Latin America. Repressive conservative regimes strengthened their hold on most of the continent, with a violent coup against the elected (Sept. 1973) Allende government in **Chile**, a 1976 military coup in **Argentina**, and coups against reformist regimes in **Bolivia** (1971, 1979) and **Peru** (1976). In Central America increasing liberal and leftist militancy led to the ouster (1979) of the Somoza regime of **Nicaragua** and to civil conflict in **El Salvador**.

Indochina. Communist victories in Vietnam, Cambodia, and Laos by May 1975 led to new turmoil. The **Pol Pot regime** ordered millions of city-dwellers to resettle in rural areas, in a program of forced labor and terrorism that cost more than 1 million lives (1975-79) and caused hundreds of thousands of ethnic Chinese and others to flee. The Vietnamese invasion of Cambodia (1979) swelled the refugee population and contributed to widespread starvation.

Russian expansion. Soviet influence, checked in some countries (troops ousted by Egypt, 1972), was projected farther afield, often with the use of Cuban troops (Angola, 1975-89; Ethiopia, 1977-88) and aided by a growing navy, a merchant fleet, and international banking ability. **Détente** with the West—1972 Berlin pact, 1972 strategic arms pact (**SALT**)—gave way to a more antagonistic relationship in the late 1970s, exacerbated by the Soviet invasion (1979) of **Afghanistan**.

Africa. The last remaining European colonies were granted independence (**Spanish Sahara**, 1976; **Djibouti**, 1977) and, after 10 years of civil war and many negotiation sessions, a black government took over (1979) in Zimbabwe (Rhodesia); white domination remained in **South Africa**. Great power involvement in local wars (Russia in **Angola**, Ethiopia; France in **Chad, Zaire, Mauritania**) and the use of tens of thousands of Cuban troops were denounced by some African leaders. Ethnic or tribal clashes made Africa a locus of sustained warfare during the late 1970s.

Arts. Traditional modes of painting, architecture, and music received increased popular and critical attention in the 1970s. These more conservative styles coexisted with modernist works in an atmosphere of increased variety and tolerance.

Revitalization of Capitalism, Demand for Democracy: 1980-89

USSR, Eastern Europe. A troublesome 1980-85 for the USSR was followed by 5 years of astonishing change: the surrender of the Communist monopoly, the remaking of the Soviet state, and the beginning of the disintegration of the Soviet empire. After the deaths of Gen. Sec. Leonid **Brezhnev** (1982) and 2 successors (Andropov in 1984 and Chernenko in 1985), the harsh treatment of dissent and restriction of emigration, and the Soviet invasion (Dec. 1979) of Afghanistan, Gen. Sec. Mikhail **Gorbachev** (in office 1985-1991) promoted *glasnost* and *perestroika*—economic, political, and social reform. Supported by the Communist Party (July 1988), he signed (Dec. 1987) the INF disarmament treaty, and he pledged (1988) to cut the military budget. Military withdrawal from Afghanistan was completed in Feb. 1989, the process of democratization went ahead unhindered in Poland and Hungary, and the Soviet people chose (Mar. 1989) part of the new Congress of People's Deputies from competing candidates. By decade's end the **Cold War** appeared to be fading away.

In **Poland, Solidarity**, the labor union founded (1980) by Lech **Walesa**, was outlawed in 1982 and then legalized in 1988, after years of unrest. Poland's first free election since the Communist takeover brought Solidarity victory (June 1989); Tadeusz Mazowiecki, a Walesa adviser, became (Aug. 1989) prime minister in a government with the Communists. In the fall of 1989 the failure of Marxist economies in **Hungary, East Germany, Czechoslovakia, Bulgaria**, and **Romania** brought the collapse of the Communist monopoly and a demand for democracy. In a historic step, the **Berlin Wall** was opened in Nov. 1989.

U.S. "The Reagan Years" (1981-88) brought the **longest economic boom** yet in U.S. history via budget and tax cuts, deregulation, "junk bond" financing, leveraged buyouts, and mergers and takeovers. However, there was a stock market crash (Oct. 1987), and federal budget deficits and the trade deficit increased. Foreign policy showed a **strong anti-Communist stance**, via increased defense spending, aid to anti-Communists in Central America, invasion of Cuba-threatened Grenada, and championing of the MX missile system and "Star Wars" missile defense program. Four Reagan-Gorbachev summits (1985-88) climaxed in the INF treaty (1987), as the Cold War began to wind down. The Iran-contra affair (Oliver North's TV testimony, July 1987) was a major political scandal. Homelessness and drug abuse (especially "crack" cocaine) were growing social problems. In 1988, Vice Pres. George H. W. Bush was elected to succeed Ronald Reagan as president.

Middle East. The Middle East remained militarily unstable, with sharp divisions along economic, political, racial, and religious lines. In **Iran**, the Islamic revolution of 1979 created a strong anti-U.S. stance (hostage crisis, Nov. 1979-Jan. 1981). In Sept. 1980, **Iraq** repudiated its border agreement with Iran and began major hostilities that led to an 8-year war in which millions were killed.

Libya's support for international terrorism induced the U.S. to close (May 1981) its diplomatic mission there and embargo (Mar. 1982) Libyan oil. The U.S. accused Libyan leader Muammar al-Qaddafi of aiding (Dec. 1985) terrorists in Rome and of Vienna airport attacks, and retaliated by bombing Libya (Apr. 1986).

Israel affirmed (July 1980) all Jerusalem as its capital, destroyed (1981) an Iraqi atomic reactor, and invaded (1982) Lebanon, forcing the PLO to agree to withdraw. A **Palestinian uprising**, including women and children hurling rocks and bottles at troops, began (Dec. 1987) in Israeli-occupied Gaza and spread to the West Bank; troops responded with force, killing 300 by the end of 1988, with 6,000 more in detention camps.

Israeli withdrawal from **Lebanon** began in Feb. 1985 and ended in June 1985, as Lebanon continued to be torn by military and political conflict. Artillery duels (Mar.-Apr. 1989) between Christian East Beirut and Muslim West Beirut left 200 dead and 700 wounded. At decade's end, violence still dominated.

Latin America. In **Nicaragua**, the leftist Sandinista National Liberation Front, in power after the 1979 civil war, faced problems as a result of Nicaragua's military aid to leftist guerrillas in El Salvador and U.S. backing of anti-government contras. The U.S. CIA admitted (1984) having directed the mining of Nicaraguan ports, and the U.S. sent humanitarian (1985) and military (1986) aid. Profits from secret arms sales to Iran were found (1987) diverted to contras. Cease-fire talks between the Sandinista government and contras came in 1988, and elections were held in Nicaragua in Feb. 1990.

In **El Salvador**, a military coup (Oct. 1979) failed to halt extreme right-wing violence and left-wing terrorism. Archbishop Oscar Romero was assassinated in Mar. 1980; from Jan. to June some 4,000 civilians were killed in the civil unrest. In 1984, newly elected Pres. José Napoleon Duarte worked to stem human rights abuses, but violence continued.

In **Chile**, Gen. Augusto Pinochet yielded the presidency after a democratic election (Dec. 1989), but remained as head of the army. He had ruled the country since 1973, imposing harsh measures against leftists and dissidents; at the same time he introduced economic programs that restored prosperity to Chile.

Black September, a militant terrorist group, wreaked havoc on the 1972 Olympic Games in Munich, murdering 11 members of the Israeli Olympic delegation after a hostage standoff.

Africa. 1980-85 marked a rapid decline in the economies of virtually all African countries, a result of accelerating desertification, the world economic recession, heavy indebtedness to overseas creditors, rapid population growth, and political instability. Some 60 million Africans faced prolonged hunger in 1981; much of Africa had one of the worst droughts ever in 1983, and by year's end, one-third of the population, or about 150 million, were near **famine**. "Live Aid," a marathon rock concert, was presented in July 1985, and the U.S. and Western nations sent aid in Sept. 1985. Economic hardship fueled political unrest and coups. Wars in Ethiopia and Sudan and military strife in several other nations continued. AIDS took a heavy toll.

South Africa. Anti-apartheid sentiment gathered force in South Africa as demonstrations and violent police response grew. White voters approved (Nov. 1983) the first constitution to give "Coloureds" and Asians a voice, while still excluding blacks (70% of the population). The U.S. imposed economic sanctions in Aug. 1985, and 11 Western nations followed in September. P. W. **Botha**, 1980s president, was succeeded by F. W. **de Klerk**, in Sept. 1989, who promised "evolutionary" change via negotiation with the black population.

Asia. Benazir Bhutto became the first woman to lead a majority-Muslim nation as prime minister of Pakistan (Dec. 1988). The "people power" revolt in the Philippines ousted Ferdinand Marcos (Feb. 1986) after 2 decades as president.

Ayatollah Ruhollah Khomeini returned to Iran after a 14-year exile to take control of the country after the fall of the Shah (1979).

China. During the 1980s the Communist government and paramount leader **Deng Xiaoping** pursued far-reaching changes, expanding commercial and technical ties to the industrialized world and increasing the role of market forces in stimulating urban development. Apr. 1989 brought new demands for political reforms; student demonstrators camped out in Tiananmen Square, Beijing, in a massive peaceful protest. Some 100,000 students and workers marched, and at least 20 other cities saw protests. In response, martial law was imposed; army troops crushed the demonstration in and around Tiananmen Square on June 3-4, with death toll estimates at 500-7,000, up to 10,000 dissidents arrested, 31 people tried and executed. The conciliatory Communist Party chief was ousted; the Politburo adopted (July 1989) reforms against official corruption.

Japan. Japan's relations with other nations, especially the U.S., were dominated by **trade imbalances favoring Japan**.

In 1985, the U.S. trade deficit with Japan was $49.7 billion, one-third of the total U.S. trade deficit. After Japan was found (Apr. 1986) to sell semiconductors and computer memory chips below cost, the U.S. was assured a "fair share" of the market, but charged (Mar. 1987) Japan with failing to live up to the agreement.

European Community. With the addition of Greece, Portugal, and Spain, the EC became a common market of more than 300 million people, the West's largest trading entity. Margaret Thatcher became the first British prime minister in the 20th century to win a 3rd consecutive term (1987). France elected (1981) its first socialist president, François Mitterrand, who was reelected in 1988. Italy elected (1983) its first socialist premier, Bettino Craxi.

International terrorism. With the 1979 overthrow of the shah of Iran, terrorism became a prominent tactic. It increased through the 1980s, but with fewer high-profile attacks after 1985. In 1979-81, Iranian militants held 52 **U.S. hostages in Iran** for 444 days; in 1983 a TNT-laden suicide terrorist blew up U.S. Marine headquarters in Beirut, killing 241 Americans, and a truck bomb blew up a French paratroop barracks, killing 58. The *Achille Lauro* cruise ship was hijacked in 1986, and an American passenger killed; the U.S. subsequently intercepted the Egyptian plane flying the terrorists to safety. Incidents rose to 700 in 1985, and to 1,000 in 1988. **Assassinated leaders** included Egypt's Pres. Anwar al-**Sadat** (1981), India's Prime Min. Indira **Gandhi** (1984), and Lebanese Premier Rashid **Karami** (1987).

Post-Cold War World: 1990-99

Soviet Empire breakup. The world community witnessed the extraordinary disintegration of the **Soviet Union** into 15 independent states. The 1980s had already seen internal reforms and a decline of Communist power both within the Soviet Union and in Eastern Europe. The Soviet breakup began in earnest with declarations of independence adopted by the Baltic republics of **Lithuania, Latvia**, and **Estonia** during an abortive coup against reformist leader Mikhail **Gorbachev** (Aug. 1991). Other republics soon took the same step. In Dec. 1991, **Russia, Ukraine**, and **Belarus** declared the Soviet Union dead; Gorbachev resigned, and the Soviet Parliament went out of existence. The Warsaw Pact and the Council for Mutual Economic Assistance (Comecon) were disbanded. Most of the former Soviet republics joined in a loose confederation called the **Commonwealth of Independent States**. Russia remained the predominant country after the breakup, but its people soon suffered severe economic hardship as the nation, under Pres. Boris **Yeltsin**, moved to revamp the economy and adopt a free market system. In Oct. 1993, **anti-Yeltsin forces** occupied the Parliament building and were ousted by the army; about 140 people died in the fighting.

The Muslim republic of **Chechnya** declared independence from the rest of Russia, but this was met with an invasion by Russian troops (Dec. 1994). After almost 21 months of vicious fighting, a cease-fire took hold in 1996, and the Russians withdrew. In 1999 Russia forcibly suppressed Muslim insurgents in Dagestan and entered neighboring Chechnya, again fighting to gain control over separatist rebels there. Yeltsin resigned office Dec. 31, 1999, to be replaced by Vladimir **Putin** (elected in his own right, Mar. 2000).

Europe. **Yugoslavia** broke apart, and hostilities ensued among the republics along ethnic and religious lines. **Croatia, Slovenia**, and **Macedonia** declared independence (1991), followed by **Bosnia-Herzegovina** (1992). **Serbia** and **Montenegro** remained as the republic of Yugoslavia. Bitter fighting followed, especially in Bosnia, where Serbs reportedly engaged in **"ethnic cleansing"** of the Muslim population; a peace plan (Dayton accord), brokered by the United States, was signed by **Bosnia, Serbia**, and **Croatia**

(Dec. 1995), with **NATO** responsible for policing its implementation. In spring 1999, NATO conducted a bombing campaign aimed at stopping Yugoslavia from its campaign to drive out ethnic Albanians from the Kosovo region; a peace accord was reached in June under which NATO peacekeeping troops entered Kosovo.

The two **Germanys** were reunited after 45 years (Oct. 1990). The union was greeted with jubilation, but stresses became apparent when free market principles were applied to the aging East German industries, resulting in many plant closings and rising unemployment. West German chancellor Helmut **Kohl**, a Christian Democrat, took power after 16 years, in Sept. 1998 elections; Gerhard **Schroeder**, a Social Democrat, took over. Czechoslovakia broke apart peacefully (Jan. 1993), becoming the **Czech Republic** and **Slovakia**. In **Poland**, Lech **Walesa** was elected president (Dec. 1991) but was defeated in his bid for a 2nd term (Nov. 1995).

NATO approved the **Partnership for Peace** Program (Jan. 1994) coordinating the defense of **Eastern** and **Central European** countries; Russia joined the program later that year. NATO signed a pact with **Russia** (1997) providing for NATO expansion into the former Soviet-bloc countries; a similar treaty was set up with **Ukraine**. The **Czech Republic, Hungary**, and **Poland** became members in Jan. 1999; in that year **NATO** celebrated its 50th anniversary. Efforts toward European unity continued with adoption of a single market (Jan. 1993) and conversion of the European Community to the **European Union** as the Maestricht Treaty took effect (Nov. 1993). Agreement was reached for 11 EU members to participate in Economic and Monetary Union, adopting a common currency **(euro)** in Jan. 1999.

An intraparty revolt forced Margaret **Thatcher** out as prime minister of **Great Britain**, to be succeeded by John **Major** (Nov. 1990); 7 years later, Major suffered an overwhelming defeat at the hands of new Labour Party leader, Tony **Blair** (May 1997). The divorce of Prince **Charles and Diana**, followed by the death of Diana in a car accident (Aug. 1997), made headlines around the world. Talks on **peace** in **Northern Ireland** that included participation of Sinn Fein, political arm of the IRA, led to a ground-breaking peace plan, approved in an all-Ireland vote (May 1998). In Dec. 1999, Northern Ireland was granted home rule under a power-sharing cabinet. In **Scotland** voters overwhelmingly approved establishment of a regional legislature (1997), and in **Wales** voters narrowly approved establishment of a local assembly (1997). In a historic innovation, the Church of England **ordained 32 women** as priests (Mar. 1994).

Middle East. In Aug. 1990, **Iraq's Saddam Hussein** ordered his troops to invade **Kuwait.** The UN approved military action in response (Nov. 1990), and an international military force, led by the U.S., bombed Iraq (Jan. 1991) and launched a land attack, crushing the invasion (Feb. 1991). After Iraq accepted the allied terms of the formal cease-fire (Apr. 1991), U.S. troops withdrew, but "no-fly" zones were set up over northern Iraq to protect the Kurds and over southern Iraq to protect Shiite Muslims. The **UN** imposed **sanctions** on Iraq for failure to abide by the cease-fire. Iraq's reported failure to cooperate with UN arms inspectors seeking to eliminate "weapons of mass destruction" led to repeated air strikes by the U.S. and Britain (1998, 2001).

The last Western hostages were freed in **Lebanon,** June 1992. **Israel** and the **Palestine Liberation Organization** signed a peace accord (Sept. 1993) providing for Palestinian self-government in the West Bank and Gaza Strip. Prime Min. Yitzhak **Rabin** and Foreign Min. Shimon **Peres** of Israel and Yasir **Arafat** of the PLO received the Nobel Peace Prize for their efforts (1994). Six Arab nations relaxed their boycott against Israel (1994), and Israel and **Jordan** signed a peace treaty (Oct. 1994). **Rabin was assassinated** (Nov. 1995) by an Israeli opponent of the peace process. After new elections (May 1996), Benjamin Netanyahu as prime minister adopted a harder line in peace negotiations. **Arafat** was elected to the presidency of the Palestinian Authority (Jan. 1996). A Labour government under Ehud **Barak** took power after May 1999 elections.

King **Hussein** of Jordan died (Feb. 1999), to be succeeded by his son Abdullah.

Asia and the Pacific. Hong Kong was returned to **China** (July 1997) after 156 years as a British colony, and **Macao** reverted to Chinese sovereignty (Dec. 1999) after over 400 years of Portuguese rule. Both were to retain their legal and capitalist economic systems for 50 years. **Jiang Zemin**, general secretary of the Chinese Communist Party, assumed the additional post of president of China (Mar. 1993) and emerged as the key leader after the death of leader **Deng Xiaoping** (Feb. 1997). China released from prison—and exiled—some well-known dissidents but continued to be criticized for detentions and other alleged widespread **human rights abuses**. In Nov. 1999 the U.S. and China signed a landmark pact normalizing trade relations.

After years of prosperity, **Thailand, Indonesia,** and **South Korea** in 1997 began to suffer economic reverses that had a worldwide ripple effect. These countries received billion-dollar IMF bailout packages. In **Indonesia**, protests over mismanagement led to the resignation of Pres. **Suharto** (May 1998) after 32 years of nearly autocratic rule. Abdurraham Wahid was elected (Oct. 1999) in the country's first fully democratic elections. In a referendum (Aug. 1999), **East Timor** voted overwhelmingly for independence from Indonesia; pro-Indonesian militias then rampaged through the territory, but a multinational peacekeeping force was allowed in (Sept. 1999) to help restore order. In **South Korea**, former dissident **Kim Dae Jung** was elected president (Dec. 1997). Two previous presidents, Roh Tae Woo and Chun Doo Hwan, were convicted of crimes committed in office but were given amnesty by the new president.

In **Japan** members of a religious cult released the nerve gas sarin on 5 Tokyo subway cars, killing 12 people and injuring more than 5,500 (Mar. 1995). Tamil rebels continued their armed conflict in **Sri Lanka**. In **Afghanistan** the **Taliban**, an extreme Islamic fundamentalist group, gained control of Kabul (Sept. 1996) and, eventually, most of the country. In **North Korea**, longtime dictator **Kim Il Sung** died (July 1994), to be succeeded by his son, **Kim Jong Il**. In the same year the country signed an agreement with the U.S. setting a timetable for North Korea to eliminate its nuclear program. The country also suffered a severe drought, and widespread starvation was feared.

India was beset by riots following destruction of a mosque by Hindu militants (Dec. 1992); Indian army troops repeatedly clashed with pro-independence demonstrators in the disputed Muslim region of **Kashmir**, exacerbating relations with **Pakistan**. Uneasy relations between India and Pakistan reached a new level when both nations conducted nuclear tests in 1998. Conflict in Pakistan between government and the military led to a bloodless coup (Oct. 1999).

British Prime Min. Margaret Thatcher and Pres. Ronald Reagan led according to similar neoconservative political philosophies during the 1980s.

Africa. South Africa was transformed as the white-dominated government abandoned **apartheid** and the country made the transition to a nonracial democratic government. Pres. F. W. **de Klerk** released Nelson **Mandela** from prison (Feb. 1990), after he had been held by the government for 27 years, and lifted a ban on the African National Congress. The white government repealed its apartheid laws (1990, 1991). **Mandela** was elected **president** (Apr. 1994), and a new constitution became law (Dec. 1996). Thabo **Mbeki**, the ANC's candidate to succeed Mandela, was overwhelmingly elected president in June 1999. In **Nigeria**, Gen. Olusegun **Obasanjo** was elected president (Feb. 1999), to become the country's first civilian leader in 15 years.

The decades-long rule of **Mobutu** Sese Seko in **Zaire** came to an end (May 1997) at the hands of rebel forces led by Laurent **Kabila**; an ailing Mobutu fled the country and soon after died. Kabila changed the country's name back to **Democratic Republic of the Congo**; conditions remained unstable.

After the presidents of **Burundi** and **Rwanda** were killed in an airplane crash (Apr. 1994), violence erupted in Rwanda between Hutu and Tutsi factions; hundreds of thousands were slain in genocidal fashion. The conflict spread to refugee camps in neighboring Zaire and Burundi. Factional fighting also erupted in **Somalia** after Pres. Muhammad Siad Barre was ousted (Jan. 1991). The UN sent a U.S.-led **peacekeeping force**, but it was unsuccessful in restoring order. Some soldiers of the peacekeeping force were killed, including 23 Pakistanis (June 1993) and 18 U.S. Rangers (Oct. 1993). The UN ended its mission (Mar. 1995) with no durable government in place. **Liberia** endured factional fighting that lasted almost 5 years and claimed over 150,000 lives; a cease-fire was concluded in Aug. 1995. The World Health Organization reported (1995) that Africa accounted for 70% of **AIDS** cases worldwide.

A 16-year civil war appeared to end in **Angola** (May 1991) when the government signed a peace accord with the rebel UNITA faction. But despite the inauguration of a national unity government (Apr. 1997), insurgents continued to fight and gain territory. **Namibia** officially became independent in Mar. 1990. Claimed by South Africa since 1919 and placed under UN authority in 1971, it had long been a focus of colonial rivalries. In **Algeria**, the army cancelled a 2nd round of parliamentary elections (Jan. 1992) after the Islamic party won a first round. Islamic fundamentalists then began a terrorist campaign that, along with killings by progovernment squads, eventually claimed thousands of lives. A peace plan was worked out with the militants in 1999.

North America. The **North American Free Trade Agreement** (NAFTA), liberalizing trade between the United States, Canada, and Mexico, went into effect Jan. 1, 1994. In **Canada**, the Progressive Conservative Party suffered a crushing defeat in general elections (Oct. 1993), and liberal Jean **Chrétien** became prime minister. The map of Canada was altered in Apr. 1999 to create a new territory, **Nunavut**, out of an area that had been part of Northwest Territories.

In the **United States'** 1992 presidential election, Democrat Bill **Clinton** defeated Pres. George H. W. Bush, but in 1994 congressional elections Republicans gained control of Congress. Clinton won reelection in 1996; the new administration was plagued by scandals but remained popular amid continued economic prosperity. Clinton proposed (Feb. 1998) the first balanced federal budget in nearly 30 years. In Dec. 1998 Clinton was **impeached** by the U.S. House on charges related to the Monica Lewinsky scandal; he was **acquitted** by the Senate in Feb. 1999.

The U.S. Army and Navy were torn by sexual scandals involving abuse of women personnel. The **United States** suffered embarrassment with the discovery of espionage by CIA agents (Aldrich Ames, Harold Nicholson).

In **Mexico**, Ernesto **Zedillo** of the ruling PRI party was elected president (July 1994) after the party's first candidate was assassinated. The country soon faced a crisis affecting the value of the peso, but recovered with the help of a bailout package from the U.S. A peasant revolt spearheaded by the **Zapatista National Liberation Army** erupted in the state of Chiapas (Jan. 1994) and was suppressed.

Central America and the Caribbean.
In **Haiti**, Jean-Bertrand **Aristide** was elected president (Dec. 1990) but was ousted in a military coup after 9 months in office. The UN approved a U.S.-led invasion to restore the elected leader; shortly before troops arrived, a delegation headed by former U.S. Pres. Jimmy Carter arranged (Sept. 1994) for the junta to step aside for Aristide, who served until 1996. In **Nicaragua**, Violetta Chamarro defeated Daniel **Ortega** in the presidential election (Feb. 1990), thus ousting the Sandinistas. In **Panama**, U.S. troops invaded and overthrew the government of Manuel **Noriega** (Dec. 1989), who was wanted on drug charges; Noriega was captured Jan. 1990. On Dec. 31, 1999, Panama assumed full control of the **Panama Canal**, in accord with a treaty with the U.S. In **El Salvador** (1992) and **Guatemala** (1996) the governments signed agreements with rebel factions aimed at ending long-running civil conflicts.

South America.
Alberto **Fujimori** was elected president of **Peru** in June 1990 and, despite his suppression of the constitution (1992), was reelected in 1995. Peru succeeded in capturing (Sept. 1992) the leader of the **Shining Path** guerrilla movement. Leftist guerrillas took hostages at an ambassador's residence in Lima (Dec. 1996); one hostage

was killed during a government assault rescuing the rest (Apr. 1997). Peronist Pres. Carlos Saúl **Menem** served as **Argentina**'s president for much of the decade (elected 1989, reelected 1995), imposing stringent economic measures; he was succeeded in 1999 by Fernando de la **Rúa**.

Former Chilean Pres. Gen. Augusto **Pinochet** continued to head the army until Mar. 1998; he was arrested in London (Oct. 1998) on human rights charges but was judged medically unfit for trial and returned to Chile (Mar. 2000).

In **Brazil**, Fernando Henrique **Cardoso** was elected president (Oct. 1994) and reelected in 1998 amid a growing economic slump; the IMF announced a $42 billion aid package (Nov. 1998). The first UN Conference on Environment and Development, or **Earth Summit**, was held (June 1992) in **Rio de Janeiro**, with delegates from 178 nations.

Terrorism and Crime.
Terrorism, often linked to Mideastern sources continued to target the U.S. and Europe. A terrorist bomb exploded in a garage beneath New York City's **World Trade Center**, killing 6 people (Feb. 1993). Bombings of a U.S. military training center (Nov. 1995) and a barracks holding U.S. airmen (June 1996), both in **Saudi Arabia**, killed 7 and 19, respectively. Bombs exploded outside **U.S. embassies** in Kenya and Tanzania, Aug. 1998, killing over 220 people; the U.S. retaliated with missiles fired at alleged terrorist-linked sites in Afghanistan and Sudan. The Alfred P. Murrah Federal Building in **Oklahoma City**, OK, was destroyed by a bomb that killed 168 people (Apr. 1995).

Science and Technology.
The powerful **Hubble Space Telescope** was launched in Apr. 1990; flaws in its mirrors and solar panels were repaired by space-walking astronauts (Dec. 1993). U.S. space shuttle *Atlantis* docked with the orbiting Russian space station *Mir* (June 1995) in first of several joint missions in a spirit of post-Cold-War cooperation. In Nov. 1998 the first component for a new **International Space Station** was launched into space from Kazakhstan.

Scottish scientist Ian Wilmut announced (Feb. 1997) the **cloning** of a sheep, nicknamed Dolly—the first mammal successfully cloned from a cell from an adult animal.

Tim Berners-Lee launched the first **World Wide Web** server (1990) from the European Center for Nuclear Research (CERN) in Switzerland; CERN announced (1993) that the technology could be used for free. User-friendly graphical browsers (Mosaic, 1993; Netscape, 1994) and affordable Internet service providers (America Online for Macs, 1989, and Windows, 1993) rapidly expanded the reach of the **Internet**.

Opening a New Century: 2000-08

Terrorism. In Oct. 2000, 17 American sailors were killed aboard the **USS** *Cole* in Aden, **Yemen**, when a small boat exploded alongside it in a terrorist attack. On **Sept. 11, 2001**, hijackers crashed 2 jetliners into the twin towers of the **World Trade Center** in New York City and another into the **Pentagon** outside Washington, DC; a 4th crashed in a field in Pennsylvania. The attacks, which destroyed both towers and damaged the Pentagon, killed about 3,000 people, including all 265 aboard the planes. Saudi exile Osama bin Laden and his **al-Qaeda** terrorist network, based in **Afghanistan** and backed by the Taliban government there, emerged as responsible for the attacks. A U.S.-led military campaign launched in Oct. 2001 **ousted the Taliban**, and a transitional government was installed (Dec. 2001), although bin Laden remained at large. Conspirator Zacarias Moussaoui was tried and sentenced to life in prison (May 2006) for his role in the attacks. Khalid Shaikh Mohammed confessed (March 2007) that he was responsible for planning the attacks of Sept. 11, 2001, as well as several other acts of terrorism.

Among incidents elsewhere, a bomb exploded in a truck outside a synagogue in **Tunisia** (Apr. 2002), killing 17 (including the driver). A car bomb on the Indonesian island of **Bali** (Oct. 2002) killed about 200, mostly foreign tourists; Muslim extremists were arrested. Chechen guerrillas

seized a Moscow movie theater (Oct. 2002); more than 100 hostages were killed in a subsequent raid by Russian troops. A terrorist explosion in **Moscow subways** killed 39 (Feb. 2004), and 89 died when 2 Russian planes were destroyed apparently by bombs (Aug. 2004). Chechen guerrillas took over a **Beslan, Russia, school**; 330 hostages, many students, and 31 guerrillas were killed in the standoff (Sept. 2004). The bombing of an Israeli-owned **hotel in Kenya** (Nov. 2002) killed 13 (including the 3 bombers). Suicide attacks against Western targets in **Riyadh**, Saudi Arabia (May 2003), killed 34 people (including 9 attackers). Suicide bombings in **Istanbul**, Turkey (Nov. 2003), hit two Jewish synagogues and British targets, killing about 60 people in all.

Four **commuter trains were bombed** in Madrid, Spain, killing 191 (Mar. 2004); elections held a week later ousted Spain's premier. Three subway trains and a bus were **bombed in London** during rush hour (June 2005); 56 people were killed, including 4 bombers. Three suicide bombers killed 20 others on Indonesian resort island **Bali** (Oct. 2005). Al-Qaeda in Iraq claimed responsibility (Nov. 2005) for **hotel bombings** in Jordan that killed 59, excluding the suicide bombers. Eight explosions killed 207 on commuter trains in Mumbai, India (July 2006); the attacks were tied to an Islamic separatist organization. Another 166 people were killed when Mumbai was again attacked (Nov. 2008) in co-ordinated attacks on sites commonly populated by foreigners, including 2 hotels and a train station. British authorities thwarted (Aug. 2006) an alleged terrorist plot to detonate **liquid explosives** on transatlantic flights.

The U.S. Supreme Court struck down attempts to use military tribunals to try suspected terrorists (June 2006); Pres. Bush acknowledged (Sept. 2006) the existence of CIA-run overseas prisons for terrorism suspects.

War in Iraq. The U.S., with Great Britain, launched an **invasion of Iraq** (Mar. 2003), aimed at ousting the regime of **Saddam Hussein**. Troops took control of Baghdad and other cities, and Pres. Bush declared major combat ended, May 1, but **insurgents** caused continuing casualties among troops and civilians. Searches for **weapons of mass destruction**, cited as major grounds for the invasion, yielded no evidence. **Saddam Hussein** was captured by U.S. troops (Dec. 2003), put on trial by Iraqis, sentenced to death, and **executed** (Dec. 2006).

An interim government was installed (June 2004). Photographic evidence that U.S. soldiers at **Abu Ghraib** prison in Iraq abused detainees arose in Apr. 2004. Despite threats by insurgents, Iraqis turned out in large numbers to vote in national elections (Jan. 2005). In a referendum, **Iraqis approved a constitution** (Oct. 2005), and voted again in parliamentary elections (Dec. 2005). Sectarian violence in Iraq between the **Sunni and Shiite** factions continued to raise fears of civil war; in late 2006, at least 100 people were dying each day. Violent demonstrations followed an attack (Feb. 2006) on Iraq's "**Golden Mosque**" shrine, one of the holiest sites in Shia Islam. The elected government of Premier Nouri Kamel al-Maliki took office (May 2006) representing a Shiite coalition.

U.S. military deaths topped 3,000 (Dec. 2006). To address ongoing sectarian and **insurgent violence**, Pres. Bush announced (Jan. 2007) a so-called "surge," sending an additional 30,000 troops to Iraq. Four truck bombs in Nineveh province (Aug. 2007) killed at least 500 people in the deadliest attack since the war began in 2003. The Iraqi cabinet approved (Nov. 2008) U.S. troop presence after its UN mandate expired in 2008; withdrawal from cities was set for mid-2009, with troops leaving the county entirely by 2011.

The attacks of Sept. 11, 2001, killed more than 2,600 people in New York.

Middle East. The peace process languished early in the decade as **violence between Israelis and Palestinians** escalated, with **suicide bombings** by Palestinians and retaliation by Israeli armed forces. In response to Palestinian suicide attacks, Israeli forces stormed the compound of Palestinian leader Yasir Arafat (Mar. 2002), confining him until early May. **Arafat died** in a Paris hospital (Nov. 2004) and was succeeded by Mahmoud Abbas following elections. The U.S., Russia, UN, and European Union (EU) formally initiated (Apr. 2003) a "**road map**" plan for Israeli-Palestinian **peace negotiations**, but little progress was made. Israel completed (Aug. 2005) evacuation of 25 Jewish settlements in the **West Bank** and **Gaza Strip**. Israeli Prime Min. Ariel Sharon suffered a severe stroke (Jan. 2006); leadership was passed to Ehud Olmert, who went on to lead a coalition government following elections (Apr. 2006). The militant Palestinian political party **Hamas**, which did not acknowledge the right of Israel to exist, won a majority of parliamentary seats over the long-ruling Fatah party (Jan. 2006), casting the peace process

into greater doubt, though talks with other parties, including U.S. Sec. of State Condoleezza Rice, continued.

Israel launched air and ground **attacks on Lebanon** (July 2006) in response to a raid into northern Israel by Lebanon-based **Hezbollah** guerrillas; a ceasefire was declared a month later. Shortly after Hamas announced an end to a 6-month-long ceasefire, Israel launched a 22-day aerial and ground offensive on the Gaza Strip (Dec. 2008), which killed an estimated 1,300 Palestinians.

Iran was censured (Dec. 2003) by the UN Intl. Atomic Energy Agency for covering up aspects of its nuclear weapons program, which it claimed was for peaceful purposes. In spite of escalating international sanctions, **Iran continued to enrich uranium** in defiance of several IAEA deadlines (2006-07) and tested missiles said to be capable of reaching Israel (July 2008).

Europe. In Oct. 2000, Yugoslav strongman Slobodan **Milosevic yielded power** to Vojislav Kostunica, who had declared himself president in the face of anti-Milosevic protests after a disputed election. Milosevic surrendered to Serbian authorities; he went on trial (Feb. 2002) for **war crimes** allegedly committed during 1990s ethnic conflicts in the Balkans but died (Mar. 2006) before a verdict was reached. Former Bosnian Serb leader Radovan Karadzic was also arraigned on war crimes charges (July 2008). Kosovo unilaterally declared independence (Feb. 2008).

By early 2002 the **euro** was the common currency in 12 European Union nations. The EU admitted 10 Eastern European nations (May 2004); 2 more joined in Jan. 2007. The deadline to ratify the EU constitution was extended (June 2005) after voters defeated referenda in France and the Netherlands. Germany elected its first East German chancellor (Nov. 2005), Angela Merkel, also the first woman head of state in Germany.

The first-ever **Concorde jet crash**, near Paris, killed 113 people (July 2000). The Russian nuclear sub *Kursk* **sank** (Aug. 2000) in the Barents Sea, killing 118 crew members. Some 35,000 people across Europe, including over 11,000 in France, reportedly died in 2003 **summer heat waves**.

Pope **John Paul II**, the leader of the world's Roman Catholics, died (Apr. 2005); German cardinal Joseph Ratzinger was elected his successor, taking the name Pope Benedict XVI.

Rioting shook France's immigrant communities in 300 cities and towns (Nov. 2005); over 3,000 arrests were made. A Danish newspaper's publication of cartoon **caricatures of the Prophet Muhammad** sparked violent worldwide protests by Muslims (Jan.-Feb. 2006).

Great Britain and France each underwent leadership changes for the first time in over a decade, replacing their prime minister and president, respectively (May-June 2007). Dmitri Medvedev became Russia's 3rd president (May 2008) and nominated predecessor **Vladimir Putin** as prime minister. Russian troops invaded the Georgian province of South Ossetia (Aug. 2008); a cease-fire was negotiated by French Pres. Nicholas Sarkozy.

Asia. South Korean Pres. **Kim Dae Jung** and North Korean ruler **Kim Jong Il** held a summit meeting and agreed to seek peace and reunification (June 2000), but tensions rose after North Korea admitted conducting a covert nuclear weapons development program (Oct. 2002). **North Korea withdrew** (Jan. 2003) from the Nuclear Nonproliferation Treaty; multi-nation talks were held in

Beijing (Aug. 2003) about the status of its **nuclear program**. Apparent nuclear (Oct. 2006) and missile (July 2006) testing in North Korea continued to cause alarm, tempered when a multiparty agreement was reached (Feb. 2007) and North Korea agreed to end its nuclear program in exchange for an aid package.

Chinese Pres. Jiang Zemin and **Russian** Pres. Vladimir Putin signed a **friendship treaty** (July 2001). With Jiang's retirement **Hu Jintao** was named as China's new Communist party chief (Nov. 2002) and president (Mar. 2003). China's rapidly expanding economy took a hit with several product recall scandals (pet food, Mar. 2007; toys, Aug.-Sept. 2007; infant formula, Sept. 2008). A massive earthquake killed nearly 70,000 people in **Sichuan** province, China (May 2008).

A massive **tsunami** in the Indian Ocean (Dec. 2004) devastated parts of Indonesia, Thailand, India, Sri Lanka, and other Asian and African nations and left some 200,000 dead. An **earthquake** struck the disputed territory of Kashmir and parts of N. Pakistan and India (Oct. 2005); nearly 80,000 were killed.

Pakistan and India **restored diplomatic ties** (May 2003) and declared a **ceasefire** in disputed territory (Nov. 2003). Pakistani Pres. Gen. Pervez Musharraf, in power since a 1999 coup, declared a state of emergency and suspended the constitution (Nov. 2007). Former Prime Min. Benazir **Bhutto was assassinated** (Dec. 2007); her Pakistan Peoples Party (PPP) won the most seats in parliamentary elections (Feb. 2008) and Bhutto's widower, Asif Ali Zardari, was elected president (Sept. 2008) following **Musharraf's resignation** (Aug. 2008).

One of the deadliest natural disasters in recorded history, the 2004 tsunami killed more than 200,000 people in 11 countries.

Afghanistan held its first presidential elections since the fall of the Taliban regime, selecting Hamid Karzai (Oct.-Nov. 2004). The U.S. responded to **escalating violence in Afghanistan** in 2008—the deadliest year of the conflict to date—by announcing plans to double U.S. troop strength there to 68,000.

The military carried out a bloodless coup in Thailand (Sept. 2006), ousting the premier and dissolving the government. **Myanmar's military junta** cracked down on hundreds of thousands of antigovernment protesters (Sept. 2007). More than 80,000 people were killed in a tropical cyclone in Myanmar (May 2008); the regime thwarted aid agencies' efforts.

Africa. The 13th International **AIDS Conference**, held in Durban, South Africa (July 2000), focused on ways of controlling surging AIDS rates in developing countries. Worldwide AIDS estimates were revised downward (Nov. 2007); estimates now showed that the epidemic of new infections had peaked in the late-1990s. **Ethiopia** and **Eritrea** signed a **peace treaty** (Dec. 2000). Laurent **Kabila**, president of the Democratic Republic of the **Congo**, was **shot to death** by a bodyguard (Jan. 2001). Liberian Pres. Charles Taylor went into voluntary exile (Aug. 2003) as part of a deal to end a 14-year-old civil war; other accords were reached aimed at **ending civil wars** in Angola (Apr. 2002) and Côte d'Ivoire (Jan. 2003). **Libya** agreed (Dec. 2003) to abandon programs pursuing weapons of mass destruction.

A peace agreement in the Dem. Rep. of **Congo** (Apr. 2003) did not end violence there; the nation agreed to work with Rwanda to disarm Hutu rebels (Nov. 2007). Civil war between the Muslim-led government and rebels from Christian areas in **Sudan** continued, with massive casualties. Sudanese government-backed militias (**janjaweed**) in the **Darfur** region were accused of displacing 2 mil. people in acts bordering on **genocide**; it was estimated in 2008 that more than 300,000 had been killed there since 2003. Violence was ongoing despite a peace deal (May 2006); the U.N. authorized a 26,000-member peacekeeping force (July 2007), with which Sudan pledged to cooperate. Zimbabwean Pres. Robert Mugabe pulled his country out of the **Commonwealth** (Dec. 2003) after the group reaffirmed suspension of **Zimbabwe** for alleged fraud in the 2002 election. Violence sparked in Kenya (Jan. 2008) and Zimbabwe (Apr. 2008) after **disputed elections** in each nation.

Americas and the Caribbean. Vicente **Fox** of the center-right National Action Party (PAN) was elected **president of Mexico** (July 2000), in a historic defeat for the long-supreme Institutional Revolutionary Party (PRI). Peruvian Pres. Alberto **Fujimori stepped down** during his 3rd term (Nov. 2000), amid scandal, and did not seek reelection. In Jan. 2001, George W. **Bush was inaugurated** as U.S. president, after one of the most controversial elections in U.S. history; he was reelected in Nov. 2004. Power in both houses of the U.S. Congress was transferred to the Democratic Party following Nov. 2006 elections. Democratic Sen. Barack Obama was elected the **first black U.S. president** (Nov. 2008).

Venezuelan Pres. **Hugo Chavez** regained power after a 48-hr coup (Dec. 2002); Chavez's attempt to amend the constitution to eliminate presidential term limits and expand his powers was narrowly rejected by Venezuelans (Dec. 2007). Argentina's **record default** on International Monetary Fund loans resulted (Sept. 2003) in a **$12.5 billion debt-refinancing** agreement. **Haiti** was wracked by anti-government protests, leading to the resignation of Jean-Bertrand **Aristide** in Feb. 2004. Tropical storm Jeanne caused mudslides and flooding that killed more than 1,500 in Haiti, Sept. 2004.

Hurricanes and subsequent flooding and landslides in 2005 killed thousands in the U.S. and abroad: **Katrina**, U.S. Gulf Coast (Aug.); Stan, S. Mexico and N. Central America (Oct.). An earthquake struck south-central Peru (Aug. 2007), killing at least 500 people.

For the first time in 12 years, the Liberal Party handed control of Canada's government to the Conservative Party, led by Prime Minister Stephen Harper (Jan. 2006). Cuban Pres. Fidel **Castro** ceded power for the first time in 47 years to undergo surgery (July 2006), giving his brother, Raul Castro, administrative powers; he formally resigned in Feb. 2008.

Global Economic Crisis. Soaring **food and fuel prices** in the first half of 2008 combined with a financial meltdown (Sept. 2008) sent economic shockwaves through industrialized and developing countries alike. Rising food costs led to an attempted general strike in Egypt and riots in Haiti (Apr. 2008). The price of oil dropped from a high of $137 per barrel to a low of $36 (Dec. 2008).

Space. The U.S. space shuttle *Columbia* broke up on re-entering Earth's atmosphere Feb. 1, 2003, killing all 7 crew members. The NASA space shuttle program resumed with the July 2005 launch of *Discovery*. The Phoenix Mars Lander verified the presence of **water ice in Mars's soil** (June 2008).

Environment. Negotiators from 178 countries agreed to adopt the Kyoto Protocol July 2001, calling for a reduction of greenhouse gases in developed nations; 141 nations had ratified the treaty when it took effect (Feb. 2005). The Intergovernmental Panel on Climate Change called (Feb. 2007) global warming "unequivocal," declaring man-made greenhouse gases a "very likely" cause.

For events of 2009, *see* Year in Review—Chronology (pp. 18-39).

HISTORICAL FIGURES

Note: Information accurate as of Aug. 2009.

Ancient Greeks and Romans

Greeks

Aeschines, orator, 389-314 BCE
Aeschylus, dramatist, 525-456 BCE
Aesop, fableist, c. 620-c. 560 BCE
Alcibiades, politician, 450-404 BCE
Anacreon, poet, c. 582-c. 485 BCE
Anaxagoras, philosopher, c. 500-428 BCE
Anaximander, philosopher, 611-546 BCE
Anaximenes, philosopher, c. 570-500 BCE
Antiphon, speechwriter, c. 480-411 BCE
Apollonius, mathematician, c. 265-170 BCE
Archimedes, mathematician, 287-212 BCE
Aristophanes, dramatist, c. 448-380 BCE
Aristotle, philosopher, 384-322 BCE
Athenaeus, scholar, fl. c. 200
Callicrates, architect, fl. 5th cent. BCE
Callimachus, poet, c. 305-240 BCE
Cratinus, comic dramatist, 520-421 BCE
Democritus, philosopher, c. 460-370 BCE
Demosthenes, orator, 384-322 BCE
Diodorus, historian, fl. 20 BCE
Diogenes, philosopher, 372-c. 287 BCE
Dionysius, historian, d. c. 7 BCE
Empedocles, philosopher, c. 490-430 BCE
Epicharmus, dramatist, c. 530-440 BCE
Epictetus, philosopher, c. 55-c. 135
Epicurus, philosopher, 341-270 BCE
Eratosthenes, scientist, 276-194 BCE
Euclid, mathematician, fl. c. 300 BCE
Euripides, dramatist, c. 484-406 BCE
Galen, physician, 129-216
Heraclitus, philosopher, c. 540-c. 475 BCE
Herodotus, historian, c. 484-420 BCE

Hesiod, poet, 8th cent. BCE
Hippocrates, physician, c. 460-377 BCE
Homer, poet, fl. c. 8th cent. BCE
Isocrates, orator, 436-338 BCE
Menander, dramatist, 342-292 BCE
Parmenides, philosopher, b. c. 515 BCE
Pericles, statesman, c. 495-429 BCE
Phidias, sculptor, c. 500-435 BCE
Pindar, poet, c. 518-c. 438 BCE
Plato, philosopher, c. 428-347 BCE
Plutarch, biographer, c. 46-120
Polybius, historian, c. 200-c. 118 BCE
Praxiteles, sculptor, 400-330 BCE
Pythagoras, phil., math., c. 580-c. 500 BCE
Sappho, poet, c. 610-c. 580 BCE
Simonides, poet, 556-c. 468 BCE
Socrates, philosopher, 469-399 BCE
Solon, statesman, 640-560 BCE
Sophocles, dramatist, c. 496-406 BCE
Strabo, geographer, c. 63 BCE-24 CE
Thales, philosopher, c. 634-546 BCE
Themistocles, politician, c. 524-c. 460 BCE
Theocritus, poet, c. 310-250 BCE
Theophrastus, phil., c. 372-c. 287 BCE
Thucydides, historian, fl. 5th cent. BCE
Timon, philosopher, c. 320-c. 230 BCE
Xenophon, historian, c. 434-c. 355 BCE
Zeno, philosopher, c. 335-c. 263 BCE

Romans

Ammianus, historian, c. 330-395
Apuleius, satirist, c. 124-c. 170
Boethius, scholar, c. 480-524
Caesar, Julius, leader, 100-44 BCE

Catiline, politician, c. 108-62 BCE
Cato (Elder), statesman, 234-149 BCE
Catullus, poet, c. 84-54 BCE
Cicero, orator, 106-43 BCE
Claudian, poet, c. 370-c. 404
Ennius, poet, 239-170 BCE
Gellius, author, c. 130-c. 165
Horace, poet, 65-8 BCE
Juvenal, satirist, 60-127
Livy, historian, 59 BCE-17 CE
Lucan, poet, 39-65
Lucilius, poet, c. 180-c.102 BCE
Lucretius, poet, c. 99-c. 55 BCE
Martial, epigrammatist, c. 38-c. 103
Nepos, historian, c. 100-c. 25 BCE
Ovid, poet, 43 BCE-17 CE
Persius, satirist, 34-62
Plautus, dramatist, c. 254-c. 184 BCE
Pliny the Elder, scholar, 23-79
Pliny the Younger, author, 62-113
Quintilian, rhetorician, c. 35-c. 97
Sallust, historian, 86-34 BCE
Seneca, philosopher, 4 BCE-65 CE
Silius, poet, c. 25-101
Statius, poet, c. 45-c. 96
Suetonius, biographer, c. 69-c. 122
Tacitus, historian, 56-120
Terence, dramatist, 185-c. 159 BCE
Tibullus, poet, c. 55-c. 19 BCE
Vergil, poet, 70-19 BCE
Vitruvius, architect, fl. 1st cent. BCE

Roman Rulers

From Romulus to the end of the Empire in the West. Rulers in the East sat in Constantinople and, for a brief period, in Nicaea, until the capture of Constantinople by the Turks in 1453, when Byzantium was succeeded by the Ottoman Empire.

The Kingdom

BCE
753 Romulus (Quirinus)
716 Numa Pompilius
673 Tullus Hostilius
640 Ancus Marcius
616 L. Tarquinius Priscus
578 Servius Tullius
534 L. Tarquinius Superbus

The Republic

509 Consulate established
509 Quaestorship instituted
498 Dictatorship introduced
494 Plebeian Tribunate created
494 Plebeian Aedileship created
444 Consular Tribunate organized
435 Censorship instituted
366 Praetorship established
366 Curule Aedileship created
362 Military Tribunate elected
326 Proconsulate introduced
311 Naval Duumvirate elected
217 Dictatorship of Fabius Maximus
133 Tribunate of Tiberius Gracchus
123 Tribunate of Gaius Gracchus
 82 Dictatorship of Sulla
 60 First Triumvirate formed (Caesar, Pompeius, Crassus)
 46 Dictatorship of Caesar
 43 Second Triumvirate formed (Octavianus, Antonius, Lepidus)

The Empire

 27 Augustus (Octavian)
CE
 14 Tiberius I
 37 Caligula
 41 Claudius I
 54 Nero
 68 Galba
 69 Galba; Otho, Vitellius
 69 Vespasianus

 79 Titus
 81 Domitianus
 96 Nerva
 98 Trajanus
117 Hadrianus
138 Antoninus Pius
161 Marcus Aurelius and Lucius Verus
169 Marcus Aurelius (alone)
180 Commodus
193 Pertinax; Julianus I
193 Septimius Severus
211 Caracalla and Geta
212 Caracalla (alone)
217 Macrinus
218 Elagabalus (Heliogabalus)
222 Alexander Severus
235 Maximinus I (the Thracian)
238 Gordianus I and Gordianus II; Pupienus and Balbinus
238 Gordianus III
244 Philippus (the Arabian)
249 Decius
251 Gallus and Volusianus
253 Aemilianus
253 Valerianus and Gallienus
258 Gallienus (alone)
268 Claudius Gothicus
270 Quintillus
270 Aurelianus
275 Tacitus
276 Florianus
276 Probus
282 Carus
283 Carinus and Numerianus
286 Diocletianus and Maximianus
305 Galerius and Constantius I
306 Galerius, Maximinus II, Severus I
307 Galerius, Maximinus II, Constantinus I, Licinius, Maxentius
311 Maximinus II, Constantinus I, Licinius, Maxentius
314 Maximinus II, Constantinus I, Licinius
314 Constantinus I and Licinius
324 Constantinus I (the Great)

337 Constantius II, Constans I, Constantius II
340 Constantius II and Constans I
350 Constantius II (alone)
361 Julianus II (the Apostate)
363 Jovianus

West (Rome) and East (Constantinople)

364 Valentinianus I (West), Valens (East)
367 Valentinianus I with Gratianus (West), Valens (East)
375 Gratianus with Valentinianus II (West), Valens (East)
378 Gratianus with Valentinianus II (West), Theodosius I (East)
383 Valentinianus II (West), Theodosius I (East)
394 Theodosius I (the Great)
395 Honorius (West), Arcadius (East)
408 Honorius (West), Theodosius II (East)
423 Valentinianus III (West), Theodosius II (East)
450 Valentinianus III (West), Marcianus (East)
455 Maximus (West), Avitus (West); Marcianus (East)
456 Avitus (West), Marcianus (East)
457 Majorianus (West), Leo I (East)
461 Severus II (West), Leo I (East)
467 Anthemius (West), Leo I (East)
472 Olybrius (West), Leo I (East)
473 Glycerius (West), Leo I (East)
474 Julius Nepos (West), Leo II (East)
475 Romulus Augustulus (West), Zeno (East)
476 End of Empire in West with deposing of Romulus Augustulus by Germanic chief Odovacar, who proclaimed self king. Odovacar murdered by King Theodoric of Ostrogoths, 493

Rulers of England and Great Britain

Reign began	Name	ENGLAND	Age at death[1]

Saxons and Danes

829	Egbert, King of Wessex, won allegiance of all English	NA
839	Ethelwulf, son of Egbert, King of Wessex, Sussex, Kent, Essex	NA
858	Ethelbald, son of Ethelwulf, displaced father in Wessex	NA
860	Ethelbert, 2nd son of Ethelwulf, united Kent and Wessex	NA
866	Ethelred I, 3rd son of Ethelwulf, King of Wessex, fought Danes	NA
871	Alfred (the Great), 4th son of Ethelwulf, defeated Danes, fortified London	52
899	Edward (the Elder), son of Alfred, united English, claimed Scotland	55
924	Athelstan (the Glorious), son of Edward, King of Mercia, Wessex	45
940	Edmund, 3rd son of Edward, King of Wessex, Mercia	25
946	Edred, 4th son of Edward	32
955	Edwy (the Fair), eldest son of Edmund, King of Wessex	18
959	Edgar (the Peaceful), 2nd son of Edmund, ruled all English	32
975	Edward (the Martyr), eldest son of Edgar, murdered by stepmother	17
978; 1014[2]	Ethelred II (the Unready), 2nd son of Edgar, married Emma of Normandy	48
1016	Edmund II (Ironside), son of Ethelred II, King of London	27
1016	Canute (the Dane), gave Wessex to Edmund, married Emma, Ethelred II's widow	40
1035	Harold I (Harefoot), illegitimate son of Canute	NA
1040	Hardecanute, son of Canute by Emma, also King of Denmark	24
1042	Edward (the Confessor), son of Ethelred II, canonized 1161	62
1066	Harold II, Edward's brother-in-law, last Saxon King	44

House of Normandy

1066	William I (the Conqueror), defeated Harold II at Hastings	60
1087	William II (Rufus), 3rd son of William I, killed by arrow	43
1100	Henry I (Beauclerc), youngest son of William I	67

House of Blois

1135	Stephen, son of Adela, daughter of William I, and Count of Blois	50

House of Plantagenet

1154	Henry II, son of Geoffrey Plantagenet (Angevin) by Matilda, daughter of Henry I	56
1189	Richard I (Coeur de Lion), son of Henry II, crusader	42
1199	John (Lackland), son of Henry II, approved Magna Carta, 1215	50
1216	Henry III, son of John, acceded at 9, under regency until 1227	65
1272	Edward I, son of Henry III	68
1307	Edward II, son of Edward I, deposed by Parliament	43
1327	Edward III (of Windsor), son of Edward II	65
1377	Richard II, grandson of Edward III, minor until 1389, deposed	33

House of Lancaster

1399	Henry IV, son of John of Gaunt, Duke of Lancaster, son of Edward III	47
1413	Henry V, son of Henry IV, victor of Agincourt	34
1422; 1470	Henry VI, son of Henry V, overthrown by Edward IV in 1461 but was returned to throne in 1470. Deposed, died in Tower of London, 1471	49

House of York

1461; 1471	Edward IV, great-great-grandson of Edward III, son of Duke of York. Acclaimed king by Parliament, 1461. Driven into exile in 1470 but defeated enemies to regain throne, 1471	40
1483	Edward V, son of Edward IV, murdered in Tower of London	13
1483	Richard III, brother of Edward IV, fell at Bosworth Field	32

House of Tudor

1485	Henry VII, son of Edmund Tudor, Earl of Richmond, whose father had married the widow of Henry V. Descended from Edward III through mother, Margaret Beaufort, via John of Gaunt. By marrying daughter of Edward IV, united Lancaster and York	53
1509	Henry VIII, son of Henry VII, by Elizabeth, daughter of Edward IV	56
1547	Edward VI, son of Henry VIII, by Jane Seymour, his 3rd queen. Ruled under regents, was forced to name Lady Jane Grey his successor. Council of State proclaimed her queen, July 10, 1553. Mary Tudor won Council, was proclaimed queen, July 19. Mary had Lady Jane Grey beheaded for treason, 1554	16
1553	Mary I, daughter of Henry VIII, by Catherine of Aragon	43
1558	Elizabeth I, daughter of Henry VIII, by Anne Boleyn	69

GREAT BRITAIN

House of Stuart

1603	James I (James VI of Scotland), son of Mary, Queen of Scots. First to call self King of Great Britain; this became official with Act of Union, 1707	59
1625	Charles I, only surviving son of James I	48

Commonwealth

1649	Declared upon execution of Charles I	

Protectorate

1653	Oliver Cromwell, served on Council of State, executive body of Commonwealth, following overthrow of monarchy. Named Lord Protector upon creation of Protectorate by 1653 Instrument of Government	59
1658	Richard Cromwell, 3rd son of Oliver Cromwell. Resigned as Lord Protector amid civil war, 1659. Died 1712	86

House of Stuart (restored)

1660	Charles II, eldest son of Charles I, Restoration put him back on throne, died without issue	55
1685	James II, second son of Charles I, deposed, 1688	68
1689	William III, son of William, Prince of Orange, by Mary, daughter of Charles I. Offered joint rule of throne with wife by Parliament	51
1689	Mary II, eldest daughter of James II, wife of William III, died 1694	33
1702	Anne, second daughter of James II, assumed throne on William III's death	49

House of Hanover

1714	George I, son of Elector of Hanover, by Sophia, granddaughter of James I	67
1727	George II, only son of George I, married Caroline of Brandenburg	77
1760	George III, grandson of George II, married Charlotte of Mecklenburg	81
1820	George IV, eldest son of George III, Prince Regent from Feb. 1811	67
1830	William IV, 3rd son of George III, married Adelaide of Saxe-Meiningen	71
1837	Victoria, daughter of Edward, 4th son of George III; married Prince Albert of Saxe-Coburg and Gotha, 1840, who became Prince Consort	81

House of Saxe-Coburg and Gotha

| 1901 | Edward VII, eldest son of Victoria, married Alexandra, Princess of Denmark | 68 |

House of Windsor[3]

1910	George V, 2nd son of Edward VII, married Princess Mary of Teck	70
1936	Edward VIII, eldest son of George V, acceded Jan. 20, abdicated Dec. 11	77
1936	George VI, 2nd son of George V, married Lady Elizabeth Bowes-Lyon	56
1952	Elizabeth II, elder daughter of George VI, acceded Feb. 6	

NA = Age/birth date not certain. (1) Except where noted, year of death is year of accession of succeeding ruler. (2) King Sweyn I of Denmark invaded England in 1013 and declared himself king. Ethelred II reclaimed the throne upon Sweyn's death in 1014. (3) Name adopted by proclamation of George V, July 17, 1917.

Rulers of Scotland

Reign began	Name
846	Kenneth I MacAlpin, first Scot to rule both Scots and Picts
1005	Malcolm II Mackenneth
1034	Duncan I, first general ruler
1040	Macbeth, seized kingdom, slain by Malcolm III MacDuncan
1057	Malcolm III MacDuncan (Canmore), son of Duncan I. Married Margaret, Saxon princess who had fled from Normans
1093	Donald Bane
1094	Duncan II
1095	Donald Bane (restored)
1097	Edgar, son of Queen Margaret, moved court to Edinburgh
1107	Alexander I, brother of Edgar
1124	David I, brother of Edgar
1153	Malcolm IV (the Maiden), grandson of David I
1165	William (the Lion), brother of Malcolm IV
1214	Alexander II, son of William
1249	Alexander III, son of Alexander II, defeated Norse, regained the Hebrides
1286	Margaret (Maid of Norway), granddaughter of Alexander III, child of Eric of Norway, grandniece of Edward I of England. Died 1290 at age 8. (Interregnum, 1290-92)
1292	John Balliol, proclaimed king of Scotland by Edward I of England. (Interregnum, 1296-1306[1])
1306	Robert Bruce (the Bruce), victor at Bannockburn, 1314. Treaty with England and secured throne, 1328
1329	David II, only son of Robert Bruce
1371	Robert II (the Steward), grandson of Robert Bruce, son of Walter, the steward of Scotland. First of so-called Stuart line
1390	Robert III, son of Robert II
1406	James I, son of Robert III
1437	James II, son of James I
1460	James III, eldest son of James II
1488	James IV, eldest son of James III
1513	James V, eldest son of James IV
1542	Mary (Queen of Scots), daughter of James V, became queen before she was 1 week old. Married Francis II, son of Henry II of France, 1558. Francis died in 1560. Married her cousin, Henry Stewart, Lord Darnley, 1565; married James Hepburn, Earl of Bothwell, 1567. Imprisoned by Elizabeth I; beheaded, 1587
1567	James VI, son of Mary and Lord Darnley, became James I, king of England on death of Elizabeth, 1603. Although thrones were thus united, legislative union of Scotland and England did not become official until the Act of Union, 1707

(1) Edward I decreed annexation of Scotland to England, 1296. William Wallace led resistance, 1297-1305.

Prime Ministers of Great Britain

Designations in parentheses describe each government.

W=Whig; T=Tory; Cl=Coalition; P=Peelite; Li=Liberal; C=Conservative[1]; La=Labour

Entered office	Name	Entered office	Name	Entered office	Name
1721	Sir Robert Walpole (W)[2]	1828	Duke of Wellington (T)	1908	Herbert H. Asquith (Li)
1742	Earl of Wilmington (W)	1830	Earl Grey (W)	1915	Herbert H. Asquith (Cl)
1743	Henry Pelham (W)	1834	Viscount Melbourne (W)	1916	David Lloyd George (Cl)
1754	Duke of Newcastle (W)	1834	Sir Robert Peel (C)	1922	Andrew Bonar Law (C)
1756	Duke of Devonshire (W)	1835	Viscount Melbourne (W)	1923	Stanley Baldwin (C)
1757	Duke of Newcastle (W)	1841	Sir Robert Peel (C)	1924	James Ramsay MacDonald (La)
1762	Earl of Bute (T)	1846	Lord (later Earl) John Russell (W)	1924	Stanley Baldwin (C)
1763	George Grenville (W)	1852	Earl of Derby (C)	1929	James Ramsay MacDonald (La)
1765	Marquess of Rockingham (W)	1852	Earl of Aberdeen (P)	1931	James Ramsay MacDonald (Cl)
1766	William Pitt the Elder (Earl of Chatham) (W)	1855	Viscount Palmerston (Li)	1935	Stanley Baldwin (Cl)
		1858	Earl of Derby (C)	1937	Neville Chamberlain (Cl)
1768	Duke of Grafton (W)	1859	Viscount Palmerston (Li)	1940	Winston Churchill (Cl)
1770	Frederick North (Lord North) (T)	1865	Earl Russell (Li)	1945	Winston Churchill (C)
1782	Marquess of Rockingham (W)	1866	Earl of Derby (C)	1945	Clement Attlee (La)
1782	Earl of Shelburne (W)	1868	Benjamin Disraeli (C)	1951	Sir Winston Churchill (C)
1783	Duke of Portland (Cl)	1868	William E. Gladstone (Li)	1955	Sir Anthony Eden (C)
1783	William Pitt the Younger (T)	1874	Benjamin Disraeli (C)	1957	Harold Macmillan (C)
1801	Henry Addington (T)	1880	William E. Gladstone (Li)	1963	Sir Alec Douglas-Home (C)
1804	William Pitt the Younger (T)	1885	Marquess of Salisbury (C)	1964	Harold Wilson (La)
1806	William Wyndham Grenville, Baron Grenville (W)	1886	William E. Gladstone (Li)	1970	Edward Heath (C)
		1886	Marquess of Salisbury (C)	1974	Harold Wilson (La)
1807	Duke of Portland (T)	1892	William E. Gladstone (Li)	1976	James Callaghan (La)
1809	Spencer Perceval (T)	1894	Earl of Rosebery (Li)	1979	Margaret Thatcher (C)
1812	Earl of Liverpool (T)	1895	Marquess of Salisbury (C)	1990	John Major (C)
1827	George Canning (T)	1902	Arthur J. Balfour (C)	1997	Tony Blair (La)
1827	Viscount Goderich (T)	1905	Sir Henry Campbell Bannerman (Li)	2007	Gordon Brown (La)

(1) The Conservative Party was formed in 1834, an outgrowth of the Tory party. (2) Walpole is commonly regarded as the first prime minister of Britain, though the title was not commonly used then and did not become official until 1905.

Rulers of France: Kings, Queens, Presidents

Caesar to Charlemagne

Julius Caesar subdued the Gauls, native tribes of Gaul (France), 58 to 51 BCE. The Romans ruled 500 years. The Franks, a Teutonic tribe, reached the Somme from the East c. 250 CE. By the 5th century the Merovingian Franks ousted the Romans. In 451, with the help of Visigoths, Burgundians, and others, they defeated Attila and the Huns at Chalons-sur-Marne.

Childeric I became leader of the Merovingians, 458. His son Clovis I (Chlodwig, Ludwig, Louis), crowned 481, founded the dynasty. After defeating the Alemanni (Germans), 496, he was baptized a Christian and made Paris his capital. His line ruled until Childeric III was deposed, 751.

The West Merovingians were called Neustrians, the eastern Austrasians. Pepin of Herstal (687-714), major domus, or head of the palace, of Austrasia, took over Neustria as dux (leader) of the Franks. Pepin's son, Charles, called Martel (the Hammer), defeated the Saracens at Tours-Poitiers, 732; was succeeded by his son, Pepin the Short, 741, who deposed Childeric III and ruled as king until 768.

His son, Charlemagne, or Charles the Great (742-814), became king of the Franks, 768, with his brother Carloman, who died 771. Charlemagne ruled France, Germany, parts of Italy, Spain, and Austria, and enforced Christianity. Crowned Emperor of the Romans by Pope Leo III in St. Peter's, Rome, Dec. 25, 800. Succeeded by son, Louis the Pious, 814. At death, 840, Louis left empire to sons, Lothair (Roman emperor); Pepin I (king of Aquitaine); Louis II (of Germany); Charles the Bald (France). They quarreled and, by the Treaty of Verdun, 843, divided the empire.

The date preceding each entry is year of accession.

The Carolingians

843 Charles I (the Bald), Roman Emperor, 875
877 Louis II (the Stammerer), son
879 Louis III (d. 882) and Carloman, brothers
885 Charles II (the Fat), Roman Emperor, 881
888 Eudes (Odo), elected by nobles
898 Charles III (the Simple), son of Louis II, defeated by Robert
922 Robert, brother of Eudes, killed in war
923 Rudolph (Raoul), Duke of Burgundy
936 Louis IV, son of Charles III
954 Lothair, son, aged 13, defeated by Capet
986 Louis V (the Sluggard), left no heirs

The Capets

987 Hugh Capet, son of Hugh the Great
996 Robert II (the Pious), his son
1031 Henry I, son
1060 Philip I (the Fair), son
1108 Louis VI (the Fat), son
1137 Louis VII (the Younger), son
1180 Philip II (Augustus), son, crowned at Reims
1223 Louis VIII (the Lion), son
1226 Louis IX, son, crusader; Louis IX (1214-70) arbitrated disputes with English King Henry III, led crusades, 1248 (captured in Egypt, 1250) and 1270, when he died of plague in Tunis. Canonized 1297 as St. Louis.
1270 Philip III (the Hardy), son
1285 Philip IV (the Fair), son, king at 17
1314 Louis X (the Headstrong), son. His posthumous son, John I, lived only 7 days.
1316 Philip V (the Tall), brother of Louis X
1322 Charles IV (the Fair), brother of Louis X

House of Valois

1328 Philip VI (of Valois), grandson of Philip III
1350 John II (the Good), his son, retired to England
1364 Charles V (the Wise), son
1380 Charles VI (the Beloved), son
1422 Charles VII (the Victorious), son. In 1429 Joan of Arc (Jeanne d'Arc) defeated English at Orleans and Patay and had Charles crowned at Reims, July 17, 1429. Joan was captured May 24, 1430, and executed May 30, 1431, at Rouen for heresy. Charles ordered her rehabilitation, effected 1455.
1461 Louis XI (the Cruel), son, civil reformer
1483 Charles VIII (the Affable), son
1498 Louis XII, great-grandson of Charles V
1515 Francis I, of Angouleme, nephew, son-in-law. Fought 4 major wars, was patron of the arts
1547 Henry II, son, killed at a joust. He was husband of Catherine de Médicis (1519-89) and lover of Diane de Poitiers (1499-1566). Catherine was born in Florence, daughter of Lorenzo de Medici. By marriage to Henry II she became the mother of Francis II, Charles IX, Henry III, and Queen Margaret (Reine Margot), wife of Henry IV (of Navarre).

1559 Francis II, son. Betrothed in 1548 at age 4 to Mary, Queen of Scots, aged 6. They were married 1558. Francis died 1560, aged 16; Mary ruled Scotland, abdicated 1567
1560 Charles IX, brother
1574 Henry III, brother, assassinated

House of Bourbon

1589 Henry IV, of Navarre, assassinated. Henry IV made enemies when he gave tolerance to Protestants by Edict of Nantes, 1598. He was grandson of Queen Margaret of Navarre, literary patron. He married Margaret of Valois, daughter of Henry II and Catherine de Médicis; was divorced. In 1600 married Marie de Médicis, who became Regent of France, 1610-17, for her son, Louis XIII, but was exiled by Richelieu, 1631
1610 Louis XIII (the Just), son. Louis XIII (1601-43) married Anne of Austria. He came to be dominated by his chief minister (1622-42), Cardinal Richelieu.
1643 Louis XIV (the Sun King), son. Louis XIV was king 72 years. Until 1661, Anne of Austria was regent, with Cardinal Mazarin as chief minister; after that, Louis ruled absolutely. Known for his lavish court and patronage of the arts, he exhausted a prosperous country in wars for thrones and territory.
1715 Louis XV, great-grandson. Louis XV married a Polish princess, lost Canada to the English. His favorites, Mme. Pompadour and Mme. Du Barry, influenced policies. Mme. Pompadour's saying "Après moi, le déluge" (After me, the deluge) often incorrectly attributed to Louis XV
1774 Louis XVI, grandson; married Marie Antoinette, daughter of Empress Maria Therese of Austria. King and queen beheaded by Revolution, 1793. Their son, called Louis XVII, died in prison, never ruled

First Republic

1792 National Convention of the French Revolution
1795 Directory, under Barras and others
1799 Consulate, Napoleon Bonaparte, first consul. Elected consul for life, 1802

First Empire

1804 Napoleon I (Napoleon Bonaparte), emperor. Josephine (de Beauharnais), empress, 1804-09; Marie Louise, empress, 1810-14. Her son, Francois (1811-32), titular King of Rome, later Duke de Reichstadt and "Napoleon II," never ruled. Napoleon abdicated 1814, died 1821

Bourbons Restored

1814 Louis XVIII, king, brother of Louis XVI
1824 Charles X, brother, reactionary, deposed by the July Revolution, 1830

House of Orleans

1830 Louis-Philippe (the Citizen King)

Second Republic

1848 Louis Napoleon Bonaparte, president, nephew of Napoleon I

Second Empire

1852 Napoleon III (Louis Napoleon Bonaparte), emperor, Eugenie (de Montijo), empress. Lost Franco-Prussian war, deposed 1870. Son, Prince Imperial (1856-79), died in Zulu War. Eugenie died 1920.

Third Republic—Presidents

1871 Thiers, Louis Adolphe (1797-1877)
1873 MacMahon, Marshal Patrice M. de (1808-93)
1879 Grevy, Paul J. (1807-91)
1887 Sadi-Carnot, M. (1837-94), assassinated
1894 Casimir-Perier, Jean P. P. (1847-1907)
1895 Faure, François Felix (1841-99)
1899 Loubet, Emile (1838-1929)
1906 Fallieres, C. Armand (1841-1931)
1913 Poincare, Raymond (1860-1934)
1920 Deschanel, Paul (1856-1922)
1920 Millerand, Alexandre (1859-1943)
1924 Doumergue, Gaston (1863-1937)
1931 Doumer, Paul (1857-1932), assassinated
1932 Lebrun, Albert (1871-1950), resigned 1940
1940 Vichy govt. under German armistice: Henri Philippe Petain (1856-1951), Chief of State, 1940-44
Provisional govt. after liberation: Charles de Gaulle (1890-1970), Oct. 1944-Jan. 21, 1946; Felix Gouin (1884-1977), Jan. 23, 1946; Georges Bidault (1899-1983), June 24, 1946

Fourth Republic—Presidents

1947 Auriol, Vincent (1884-1966)
1954 Coty, Rene (1882-1962)

Fifth Republic—Presidents

1959 De Gaulle, Charles Andre J. M. (1890-1970)
1969 Pompidou, Georges (1911-74)
1974 Giscard d'Estaing, Valery (1926-)
1981 Mitterrand, François (1916-96)
1995 Chirac, Jacques (1932-)
2007 Sarkozy, Nicolas (1955-)

Rulers of Middle Europe; Rise and Fall of Dynasties; Rulers of Germany

Carolingian Dynasty

Charles the Great, or Charlemagne, ruled France, Italy, and Middle Europe; established Ostmark (later Austria); crowned Roman emperor by pope in Rome, 800 CE; died 814.

Louis I (Ludwig) the Pious, son, crowned by Charlemagne 814; died 840.

Louis II, the German, son, succeeded to East Francia (Germany) 843-76.

Charles the Fat, son, inherited East Francia and West Francia (France) 876, reunited empire, crowned emperor by pope, 881; deposed 887.

Arnulf, nephew, 887-99, partition of empire.

Louis the Child, 899-911, last direct descendant of Charlemagne.

Conrad I, duke of Franconia, first elected German king, 911-18, founded House of Franconia.

Saxon Dynasty; First Reich

Henry I, the Fowler, duke of Saxony, 919-36.

Otto I, the Great, 936-73, son; crowned Holy Roman Emperor by pope, 962.

Otto II, 973-83, son; failed to oust Greeks and Arabs from Sicily.

Otto III, 983-1002, son; crowned emperor at 16.

Henry II, the Saint, duke of Bavaria, 1002-24, great-grandson of Otto the Great.

House of Franconia

Conrad II, 1024-39, elected king of Germany.

Henry III, the Black, 1039-56, son; deposed 3 popes, annexed Burgundy.

Henry IV, 1056-1106, son; regency by his mother, Agnes of Poitou. Banned by Pope Gregory VII, he did penance at Canossa.

Henry V, 1106-25, son; last of Salian Dynasty.

Lothair, duke of Saxony, 1125-37. Crowned emperor in Rome, 1134.

House of Hohenstaufen

Conrad III, duke of Swabia, 1138-52, in 2nd Crusade.

Frederick I, Barbarossa, 1152-90; Conrad's nephew.

Henry VI, 1190-96, took lower Italy from Normans. Son became king of Sicily.

Philip of Swabia, 1197-1208, brother.

Otto IV, of House of Welf, 1198-1215, deposed.

Frederick II, 1215-50, son of Henry VI; king of Sicily; crowned king of Jerusalem in 5th Crusade.

Conrad IV, 1250-54, son; lost lower Italy to Charles of Anjou.

Conradin, 1252-68, son, king of Jerusalem and Sicily, beheaded. Last Hohenstaufen.

Interregnum, 1254-73. Rise of the Electors.

Transition

Rudolph I, of Hapsburg, 1273-91, defeated King Ottocar II of Bohemia. Bequeathed duchy of Austria to eldest son, Albert.

Adolph of Nassau, 1292-98, killed in war with Albert of Austria.

Albert I, king of Germany, 1298-1308, son of Rudolph.

Henry VII, of Luxemburg, 1308-13, crowned emperor in Rome; seized Bohemia, 1310.

Louis IV, of Bavaria (Wittelsbach), 1314-47. Also elected was Frederick of Austria, 1314-30 (Hapsburg). Abolition of papal sanction for election of Holy Roman Emperor.

Charles IV, of Luxemburg, 1347-78, grandson of Henry VII, German emperor and king of Bohemia, Lombardy, Burgundy, took Mark of Brandenburg.

Wenceslaus, 1378-1400, deposed.

Rupert, Duke of Palatine, 1400-10.

Sigismund, 1411-37.

Hungary

Stephen I, House of Arpad, 997-1038. Crowned king, 1000; converted Magyars; canonized 1083. After several centuries of feuds Charles Robert of Anjou became Charles I, 1308-42.

Louis I, the Great, son, 1342-82, joint ruler of Poland with Casimir III, 1370. Defeated Turks.

Mary, daughter, 1382-95, ruled with husband, Sigismund of Luxemburg, 1387-1437, also king of Bohemia. As brother of Wenceslaus he succeeded Rupert as Holy Roman Emperor, 1410.

Albert, 1438-39, son-in-law of Sigismund, also Roman emperor as Albert II (see under Hapsburg).

Ulaszlo I of Poland, 1440-44.

Ladislaus V, posthumous son of Albert II, 1444-57. John Hunyadi (Janos Hunyadi), governor (1446-52), fought Turks, Czechs; died 1456.

Matthias I (Corvinus), son of Hunyadi, 1458-90. Shared rule of Bohemia, captured Vienna, 1485, annexed Austria, Styria, Carinthia.

Ulaszlo II (king of Bohemia), 1490-1516.

Louis II, son, aged 10, 1516-26. Wars with Suleiman, Turk. In 1527, Hungary split between Ferdinand I, Archduke of Austria, brother-in-law of Louis II, and John Zapolya of Transylvania. After Turkish invasion, 1547, Hungary split between Ferdinand, Prince John Sigismund (Transylvania), and the Turks.

House of Hapsburg

Albert V, of Austria, Hapsburg, crowned king of Hungary, Jan. 1438; Roman emperor, March 1438, as Albert II; died 1439.

Frederick III, cousin, 1440-93, fought Turks.

Maximilian I, son, 1493-1519, assumed title of Holy Roman Emperor (German), 1493.

Charles V, grandson, 1519-56. King of Spain with mother co-regent, crowned Roman emperor at Aix, 1520. Confronted Luther at Worms; attempted church reform and religious conciliation; abdicated 1556.

Ferdinand I, king of Bohemia, 1526; of Hungary, 1527; disputed. German king, 1531. Crowned Roman emperor on abdication of brother Charles V, 1556.

Maximilian II, son, 1564-76.

Rudolph II, son, 1576-1612.

Matthias, brother, 1612-19, king of Bohemia and Hungary.

Ferdinand II, of Styria, king of Bohemia, 1617; of Hungary, 1618; Roman emperor, 1619. Bohemian Protestants deposed him, elected Frederick V of Palatine, starting Thirty Years War.

Ferdinand III, son, king of Hungary, 1625, Bohemia, 1627; Roman emperor, 1637. Peace of Westphalia, 1648, ended war.

Leopold I, son, 1658-1705.

Joseph I, son, 1705-11.

Charles VI, brother, 1711-40.

Maria Theresa, daughter, 1740-80, archduchess of Austria, queen of Hungary and Bohemia; ousted pretender, Charles VII, crowned 1742; in 1745 obtained election of her husband Francis I as Roman emperor and co-regent (d. 1765). Fought Seven Years' War with Frederick II of Prussia. Mother of Marie Antoinette.

Joseph II, son, 1765-90, Roman emperor, reformer; powers restricted by Empress Maria Theresa until her death, 1780. First partition of Poland.

Leopold II, brother, 1790-92.

Francis II, son, 1792-1835. Fought Napoleon. Proclaimed first hereditary emperor of Austria, 1804. Forced to abdicate as Roman, 1806; last use of title.

Ferdinand I, son, 1835-48, abdicated during revolution.

Austro-Hungarian Monarchy

Francis Joseph I, nephew, 1848-1916, emperor of Austria, king of Hungary. Dual monarchy of Austria-Hungary formed, 1867. After assassination of heir, Archduke Francis Ferdinand, June 28, 1914, Austrian diplomacy precipitated World War I.

Charles I, grand-nephew, 1916-18, last emperor of Austria and king of Hungary. Abdicated Nov. 11-13, 1918, died 1922.

Rulers of Prussia

Nucleus of Prussia was the Mark of Brandenburg. First margrave Albert the Bear (Albrecht), 1134-70. First Hohenzollern margrave was Frederick, burgrave of Nuremberg, 1417-40.

Frederick William, 1640-88, the Great Elector. Son, Frederick III, 1688-1713, crowned King Frederick of Prussia, 1701.

Frederick William I, son, 1713-40.

Frederick II, the Great, son, 1740-86, annexed Silesia, part of Austria.

Frederick William II, nephew, 1786-97.

Frederick William III, son, 1797-1840, Napoleonic wars.

Frederick William IV, son, 1840-61. Uprising of 1848 and first parliament and constitution.

Second and Third Reich

William I, 1861-88, brother. Annexation of Schleswig and Hanover; Franco-Prussian war, 1870-71; proclamation of German Reich, Jan. 18, 1871, at Versailles; William, German emperor (Deutscher Kaiser); Bismarck, chancellor.

Frederick III, son, 1888.

William II, son, 1888-1918, led Germany in World War I, abdicated as German emperor and king of Prussia, Nov. 9, 1918. Died in exile in Netherlands, June 4, 1941. Minor rulers of Bavaria, Saxony, Wurttemberg also abdicated.

Germany proclaimed republic at Weimar, July 1, 1919. Presidents included Frederick Ebert, 1919-25; Paul von Hindenburg-Beneckendorff, 1925, reelected 1932, died Aug. 2, 1934. Adolf Hitler, chancellor, chosen successor as Leader-Chancellor (Fuehrer-Reichskanzler) of Third Reich. Annexed Austria, Mar. 1938. Precipitated World War II, 1939-45. Suicide Apr. 30, 1945.

Germany After 1945

Following World War II, Germany was split between democratic West and Soviet-dominated East. West German chancellors: Konrad Adenauer, 1949-63; Ludwig Erhard, 1963-66; Kurt Georg Kiesinger, 1966-69; Willy Brandt, 1969-74; Helmut Schmidt, 1974-82; Helmut Kohl, 1982-90. East German Communist party leaders: Walter Ulbricht, 1946-71; Erich Honecker, 1971-89; Egon Krenz, 1989-90.

Germany reunited Oct. 3, 1990. Post-reunification chancellors: Helmut Kohl, 1990-98; Gerhard Schröder, 1998-2005; Angela Merkel, 2005- .

Rulers of Poland

House of Piasts

Mieszko I, 963-92; Poland Christianized 966. Expansion under 3 Boleslavs: I, 992-1025, son, crowned king 1024; II, 1058-79, great-grandson, exiled after killing bishop Stanislav, who became chief patron saint of Poland; III, 1106-38, nephew, divided Poland among 4 sons, eldest suzerain.

Feudal division, 1138-1306. Founding in Prussia of military order Teutonic Knights, 1226. Invasion by Tartars/Mongols, 1226.

Vladislav I, 1306-33, reunited most Polish territories, crowned king 1320. Casimir III the Great, 1333-70, son, developed economy, cultural life, foreign policy.

House of Anjou

Louis I, 1370-82, nephew, was also Louis I of Hungary.

Jadwiga, 1384-99, daughter, married Jagiello, Grand Duke of Lithuania, 1386.

House of Jagiellonians

Vladislav II, 1386-1434, Christianized Lithuania, founded personal union between Poland and Lithuania. Defeated 1410 Teutonic Knights at Grunwald.

Vladislav III, 1434-44, son, simultaneously king of Hungary. Fought Turks, killed 1444 in battle of Varna.

Casimir IV, 1446-92, brother, competed with Hapsburgs, put son Vladislav on throne of Bohemia, later also of Hungary (Ulaszlo II).

Sigismund I, 1506-48, son, patronized science and arts, his and son's reign "Golden Age."

Sigismund II, 1548-72, son, established 1569 real union of Poland and Lithuania (lasted until 1795).

Elective Kings

Polish nobles in 1572 proclaimed Poland a republic headed by king to be elected by whole nobility.

Stephen Batory, 1576-86, duke of Transylvania, married Ann, sister of Sigismund II August. Fought Russians.

Sigismund III Vasa, 1587-1632, nephew of Sigismund II. 1592-98 also king of Sweden. Generals fought Russians, Turks.

Vladislav II Vasa, 1632-48, son. Fought Russians.

John II Casimir Vasa, 1648-68 (abdicated), brother. Fought Cossacks, Swedish (the "Deluge"), Russians, Turks, Tatars.

John III Sobieski, 1674-96. Won Vienna from besieging Turks, 1683.

Stanislav II, 1764-95, last king. Encouraged reforms; first modern constitution in Europe, 1791. Poland partitioned among Russia, Prussia, Austria, 1772, 1793, 1795. Unsuccessful insurrection against foreign invasion, 1794, under Kosciusko, American-Polish general.

1795-1918: Poland Under Foreign Rule

Grand Duchy of Warsaw created by Napoleon I, Frederick August of Saxony grand duke, 1807-15.

Congress of Vienna proclaimed part of Poland "Kingdom" in personal union with Russia, 1815.

Polish uprisings: against Russia, 1830; against Austria, 1846, 1848; against Russia, 1863—all repressed.

1918-39: Second Republic

Head of State Jozef Pilsudski, 1918-22. Presidents: Gabriel Narutowicz, 1922, assassinated; Stanislav Wojciechowski, 1922-26, had to abdicate after Pilsudski's coup d'état; Ignacy Moscicki, 1926-39, ruled (with Pilsudski until his death, 1935) as virtual dictator.

1939-45: Poland Under Foreign Occupation

Nazi and Soviet invasion, Sept. 1939. Polish government-in-exile, first in France, then in England. Vladislav Raczkiewicz, president; Gen. Vladislav Sikorski, then Stanislav Mikolajczyk, prime ministers. Soviet-sponsored Polish Committee of National Liberation proclaimed at Lublin, July 1944, transformed into government Jan. 1, 1945.

Poland After 1945

In the late 1940s, Poland came increasingly under Soviet control. Communist party ruled in Poland until Aug. 1989, when democratic Solidarity party, led by Lech Walesa, gained control of government. Walesa was elected president in 1990, but lost the office to former communist Aleksander Kwasniewski in 1995. The government remained democratic, and Kwasniewski was reelected in Oct. 2000. He was succeeded by Lech Kaczynski, 2005. Donald Tusk was sworn in as prime minister in Nov. 2007, taking over from Jaroslaw Kaczynski, the president's identical twin.

Rulers of Denmark, Sweden, Norway

Denmark

Earliest rulers invaded Britain. King Canute, who ruled in London 1016-35, was most famous. The Valdemars furnished kings until the 15th century. In 1282 the Danes won the first national assembly, Danehof, from King Erik V.

Most redoubtable medieval character was Margaret, daughter of Valdemar IV, born 1353, married at 10 to King Haakon VI of Norway. In 1376 she had her first infant son, Olaf, made king of Denmark. After his death, 1387, she was regent of Denmark and Norway. In 1388, Sweden accepted her as sovereign. In 1389, she made her grand-nephew, Duke Erik of Pomerania, titular king of Denmark, Sweden, and Norway, with herself as regent. In 1397, she effected the Union of Kalmar of the three kingdoms and had Erik VII crowned. In 1439, the three kingdoms deposed him and elected, 1440, Christopher of Bavaria king (Christopher III). On his death, 1448, the union broke up.

Succeeding rulers were unable to enforce their claims as rulers of Sweden until 1520, when Christian II conquered Sweden. He was thrown out 1522, and in 1523, Gustavus Vasa united Sweden. Denmark continued to dominate Norway until the Napoleonic wars, when Frederick VI, 1808-39, joined the Napoleonic cause after Britain destroyed the Danish fleet, 1807. In 1814, he was forced to cede Norway to Sweden and Helgoland to Britain, receiving Lauenburg. Successors Christian VIII, 1839; Frederick VII, 1848; Christian IX, 1863; Frederick VIII, 1906; Christian X, 1912; Frederick IX, 1947; Margrethe II, 1972.

Sweden

Early kings ruled at Uppsala, but did not dominate the country. Sverker, c. 1130-c. 1156, united the Swedes and Goths. In 1435 Sweden obtained the Riksdag, or parliament. After the Union of Kalmar, 1397, the Danes either ruled or harried the country until Christian II of Denmark conquered it anew, 1520. This led to a rising under Gustavus Vasa, who ruled Sweden 1523-60, and established an independent kingdom. Charles IX, 1599-1611, crowned 1604, conquered Moscow. Gustavus II Adolphus, 1611-32, was called the Lion of the North. Later rulers: Christina, 1632; Charles X Gustavus, 1654; Charles XI, 1660; Charles XII (invader of Russia and

Poland, defeated at Poltava, June 28, 1709), 1697; Ulrika Eleanora, sister, elected queen, 1718; Frederick I (of Hesse), her husband, 1720; Adolphus Frederick, 1751; Gustavus III, 1771; Gustavus IV Adolphus, 1792; Charles XIII, 1809. (Union with Norway began 1814.) Charles XIV John, 1818 (he was Jean Bernadotte, Napoleon's Prince of Pontecorvo, elected 1810 to succeed Charles XIII). Charles XIV John founded the present dynasty, the House of Bernadotte: Oscar I, 1844; Charles XV, 1859; Oscar II, 1872; Gustavus V, 1907; Gustav VI Adolf, 1950; Carl XVI Gustaf, 1973.

Norway

Overcoming many rivals, Harald Haarfager, 872-930, conquered Norway, Orkneys, and Shetlands. Olaf I, great-grandson, 995-1000, brought Christianity into Norway, Iceland, and Greenland. In 1035 Magnus the Good also became king of Denmark. Haakon V, 1299-1319, had married his daughter to Erik of Sweden. Their son, Magnus, became ruler of Norway and Sweden at 6. His son, Haakon VI, married Margaret of Denmark; their son Olaf IV became king of Norway and Denmark, followed by Margaret's regency and the Union of Kalmar, 1397.

In 1450, Norway became subservient to Denmark. Christian IV, 1588-1648, founded Christiania, now Oslo. After Napoleonic wars, when Denmark ceded Norway to Sweden, a strong nationalist movement forced recognition of Norway as an independent kingdom united with Sweden under the Swedish kings, 1814-1905. In 1905, the union was dissolved, and Prince Charles of Denmark became Haakon VII. He died Sept. 21, 1957; succeeded by son, Olav V. Olav V died Jan. 17, 1991; succeeded by son, Harald V.

Rulers of the Netherlands and Belgium

The Netherlands (Holland)

William Frederick, Prince of Orange, led a revolt against French rule, 1813; crowned king, 1815. Belgium seceded Oct. 4, 1830, after a revolt. The secession was ratified by the two kingdoms by treaty, Apr. 19, 1839.

Succession: William II, son, 1840; William III, son, 1849; Wilhelmina, daughter of William III and his 2nd wife, Princess Emma of Waldeck, 1890; Wilhelmina abdicated, Sept. 4, 1948, in favor of daughter, Juliana. Juliana abdicated, Apr. 30, 1980, in favor of daughter, Beatrix.

Belgium

A national congress elected Prince Leopold of Saxe-Coburg as king; he took the throne July 21, 1831, as Leopold I.

Succession: Leopold II, son, 1865; Albert I, nephew of Leopold II, 1909; Leopold III, son of Albert, 1934; Prince Charles, Regent 1944; Leopold returned 1950, yielded powers to son Baudouin, Prince Royal, Aug. 6, 1950, abdicated July 16, 1951. Baudouin I took throne July 17, 1951, died July 31, 1993; succeeded by brother, Albert II.

Rulers of Modern Italy

After the fall of Napoleon in 1814, the Congress of Vienna, 1815, restored Italy as a political patchwork, comprising the Kingdom of Naples and Sicily, the Papal States, and smaller units. Piedmont and Genoa were awarded to Sardinia, ruled by King Victor Emmanuel I of Savoy.

United Italy emerged under the leadership of Camillo, Count di Cavour (1810-61), Sardinian prime minister. Agitation was led by Giuseppe Mazzini (1805-72) and Giuseppe Garibaldi (1807-82), soldier; Victor Emmanuel I abdicated 1821. After a brief regency for a brother, Charles Albert was king, 1831-49, abdicating when defeated by the Austrians at Novara. Succeeded by Victor Emmanuel II, 1849-61.

In 1859 France forced Austria to cede Lombardy to Sardinia, which gave rights to Savoy and Nice to France. In 1860, Garibaldi led 1,000 volunteers in a campaign, took Sicily and expelled the King of Naples. In 1860 the House of Savoy annexed Tuscany, Parma, Modena, Romagna, the Two Sicilys, the Marches, and Umbria. Victor Emmanuel assumed the title of King of Italy at Turin Mar. 17, 1861.

In 1866, Victor Emmanuel allied with Prussia in the Austro-Prussian War, and with Prussia's victory, received Venetia. On Sept. 20, 1870, his troops under Gen. Raffaele Cadorna entered Rome and took over the Papal States, ending the temporal power of the Roman Catholic Church.

Succession: Umberto I, 1878, assassinated 1900; Victor Emmanuel III, 1900, abdicated 1946, died 1947; Humbert II, 1946, ruled a month. In 1921 Benito Mussolini (1883-1945) formed the Fascist party; he became prime minister Oct. 31, 1922. He entered World War II as an ally of Hitler. He was deposed July 25, 1943.

At a plebiscite June 2, 1946, Italy voted for a republic; Premier Alcide de Gasperi became chief of state June 13, 1946. On June 28, 1946, the Constituent Assembly elected Enrico de Nicola, Liberal, provisional president. Successive presidents: Luigi Einaudi, elected May 11, 1948; Giovanni Gronchi, Apr. 29, 1955; Antonio Segni, May 6, 1962; Giuseppe Saragat, Dec. 28, 1964; Giovanni Leone, Dec. 29, 1971; Alessandro Pertini, July 9, 1978; Francesco Cossiga, July 3, 1985; Oscar Luigi Scalfaro, May 28, 1992; Carlo Azeglio Ciampi, May 18, 1999; Giorgio Napolitano, May 15, 2006.

Rulers of Spain

From 8th to 11th centuries Spain was dominated by the Moors (Arabs and Berbers). The Christian reconquest established small kingdoms (Asturias, Aragon, Castile, Catalonia, Leon, Navarre, and Valencia). In 1474 Isabella, b. 1451, became Queen of Castile and Leon. Her husband, Ferdinand, b. 1452, inherited Aragon, 1479, with Catalonia, Valencia, and the Balearic Islands, became Ferdinand V of Castile. By Isabella's request Pope Sixtus IV established the Inquisition, 1478. Last Moorish kingdom, Granada, fell 1492. Columbus opened New World of colonies, 1492. Isabella died 1504, succeeded by her daughter, Juana "the Mad," but Ferdinand ruled until his death in 1516.

Charles I, b. 1500, son of Juana, grandson of Ferdinand and Isabella, and of Maximilian I of Hapsburg, succeeded later as Holy Roman Emperor, Charles V, 1520; abdicated 1556. Philip II, son, 1556-98, inherited only Spanish throne; conquered Portugal, fought Turks, sent Armada vs. England. Married to Mary I of England, 1554-58. Succession: Philip III, 1598-1621; Philip IV, 1621-65; Charles II, 1665-1700, left Spain to Philip of Anjou, grandson of Louis XIV, who as Philip V, 1700-46, founded Bourbon dynasty; Ferdinand VI, 1746-59; Charles III, 1759-88; Charles IV, 1788-1808, abdicated.

Napoleon now dominated politics and made his brother Joseph King of Spain, 1808, but the Spanish ousted him in 1813. Ferdinand VII, 1808, 1814-33, lost American colonies (except Cuba, Puerto Rico); succeeded by daughter Isabella II, aged 3, with wife Maria Christina of Naples regent until 1843. Isabella deposed by revolution, 1868. Elected king by the Cortes (parliament), Amadeo of Savoy, 1870, abdicated 1873. First republic, 1873-74. Alfonso XII, son of Isabella, 1875-85. His posthumous son was Alfonso XIII, with his mother, Queen Maria Christina regent. Spanish-American War, 1898, Spain lost Cuba, gave up Puerto Rico, Philippines, Sulu Isls., Marianas. Alfonso took throne, 1902, aged 16, married British Princess Victoria Eugenia of Battenberg, 1906. Dictatorship of Primo de Rivera, 1923-30, precipitated revolution of 1931. Alfonso agreed to leave without formal abdication. Monarchy abolished; the second republic established, with socialist backing. Niceto Alcala Zamora was president until 1936, when Manuel Azaña was chosen.

In July 1936, the army in Morocco revolted against the government and General Francisco Franco led the troops into Spain. The revolution succeeded by Feb. 1939, when Azaña resigned. Franco became chief of state, with provisions that if he was incapacitated, the Regency Council by two-thirds vote could propose a king to the Cortes, which needed to have a two-thirds majority to elect him.

Alfonso XIII died in Rome, 1941, aged 54. His property and citizenship had been restored.

A law restoring the monarchy was approved in a 1947 referendum. Prince Juan Carlos, b. 1938, grandson of Alfonso XIII, was designated by Franco and the Cortes in 1969 as future king and chief of state. Franco died in office, Nov. 20, 1975; Juan Carlos I proclaimed king, Nov. 22.

Rulers of Russia; Leaders of the USSR and Russian Federation

First ruler to consolidate Slavic tribes was Rurik, leader of the Russians who established himself at Novgorod, 862 CE. He and his immediate successors had Scandinavian affiliations. They moved to Kiev after 972 and ruled as Dukes of Kiev. In 988, Vladimir was converted and adopted the Byzantine Greek Orthodox service, later modified by Slav influences. Important as organizer and lawgiver was Yaroslav, 1019-54, whose daughters married kings of Norway, Hungary, and France. His grandson, Vladimir II (Monomakh), 1113-25, was progenitor of several rulers, but in 1169, Andrew Bogolubski overthrew Kiev and began the line known as Grand Dukes of Vladimir.

Of the Grand Dukes of Vladimir, Alexander Nevsky, 1246-63, had a son, Daniel, first to be called Duke of Muscovy (Moscow), who ruled 1263-1303. His successors became Grand Dukes of Muscovy. After Dmitri III Donskoi defeated the Tatars in 1380, they also became Grand Dukes of all Russia. Tatar independence and considerable territorial expansion were achieved under Ivan III, 1462-1505.

Tsars of Muscovy: Ivan III was referred to in church ritual as Tsar. He married Sofia, niece of the last Byzantine emperor. His successor, Basil III, died in 1533 when Basil's son Ivan was only 3. He became Ivan IV, "the Terrible," crowned 1547 as Tsar of all the Russias, ruled until 1584. Under the weak rule of his son, Feodor I, 1584-98, Boris Godunov had control. The dynasty died, and after years of tribal strife and intervention by Polish and Swedish armies, the Russians united under 17-year-old Michael Romanov, distantly related to Ivan IV's first wife. He ruled 1613-45, established the Romanov line. Fourth ruler after Michael was Peter I.

Tsars, or Emperors, of Russia (Romanovs): Peter I, 1682-1725, known as Peter the Great, took title of Emperor in 1721. His successors and dates of accession were Catherine, his widow, 1725; Peter II, his grandson, 1727; Anne, Duchess of Courland, 1730, daughter of Peter the Great's brother, Tsar Ivan V; Ivan VI, 1740, great-grandson of Ivan V, while still a child, kept in prison and murdered, 1764; Elizabeth, daughter of Peter I, 1741; Peter III, grandson of Peter I, 1761, deposed 1762 for his consort, Catherine II, former princess of Anhalt Zerbst (Germany), who is known as Catherine the Great; Paul I, her son, 1796, killed 1801; Alexander I, son of Paul, 1801, defeated Napoleon; Nicholas I, his brother, 1825; Alexander II, son of Nicholas, 1855, assassinated 1881 by terrorists; Alexander III, son, 1881. Nicholas II, son, 1894-1917, last Tsar of Russia, was forced to abdicate by the March 1917 Revolution that followed losses to Germany in WWI. The Tsar, Empress, Tsarevich (Crown Prince), and Tsar's 4 daughters were murdered by the Bolsheviks in Yekaterinburg, July 16, 1918.

Provisional Government: premiers, Prince Georgi Lvov, followed by Alexander Kerensky, 1917.

Union of Soviet Socialist Republics

Bolshevik Revolution, Nov. 7, 1917, removed Kerensky from power; council of People's Commissars formed; Lenin (Vladimir Ilyich Ulyanov) became premier. Lenin died Jan. 21, 1924. Aleksei Rykov (executed 1938) and V. M. Molotov held the office, but actual ruler was Joseph Stalin (Joseph Vissarionovich Dzhugashvili), general secretary of the Central Committee of the Communist Party. Stalin became president of the Council of Ministers (premier) May 7, 1941; died Mar. 5, 1953. Succeeded by Georgi M. Malenkov, as head of the Council and premier. Malenkov also briefly served as first secretary of Central Committee before giving up position to Nikita S. Khrushchev. Malenkov resigned Feb. 8, 1955, became deputy premier, was dropped July 3, 1957. Marshal Nikolai A. Bulganin became premier Feb. 8, 1955, was demoted, and Khrushchev became premier Mar. 27, 1958.

Khrushchev was ousted Oct. 14-15, 1964, replaced by Leonid I. Brezhnev as first secretary of the party and by Aleksei N. Kosygin as premier. On June 16, 1977, Brezhnev also took office as president. He died Nov. 10, 1982; 2 days later the Central Committee elected former KGB head Yuri V. Andropov president. Andropov died Feb. 9, 1984; on Feb. 13, Konstantin U. Chernenko chosen by Central Committee as its general secretary. Chernenko died Mar. 10, 1985; Mar. 11, he was succeeded as general secretary by Mikhail Gorbachev, who replaced Andrei Gromyko as president on Oct. 1, 1988. Gorbachev resigned Dec. 25, 1991, and the Soviet Union officially disbanded the next day. Each of the 15 former Soviet constituent republics became independent.

Post-Soviet Russia

Boris Yeltsin was sworn in July 10, 1991, as Russia's first elected president. With the Dec. 1991 dissolution of the Soviet Union, Russia (officially Russian Federation) became a founding member of the Commonwealth of Independent States. On Dec. 31, 1999, Yeltsin stepped down as president; he named Vladimir Putin his interim successor. Putin won a presidential election Mar. 26, 2000, and was reelected Mar. 14, 2004. Because Russia's constitution limits presidents to two terms of rule, Putin had to relinquish his office in 2008. His successor, Dmitry Medvedev, was sworn in May 7, 2008. A day later, Medvedev's nomination of Putin as prime minister was confirmed.

Leaders in the South American Wars of Liberation

Francisco Antonio Gabriel Miranda (1750-1816), Jose Francisco de San Martin (1778-1850), and Simon Bolivar (1783-1830) led early 19th-century struggles of South American nations to free themselves from Spain. All three, and their contemporaries, operated in periods of factional strife, during which soldiers and civilians suffered.

Miranda, a Venezuelan who had served with the French in the American Revolution and commanded parts of the French Revolutionary armies in the Netherlands, attempted to start a revolt in Venezuela in 1806 and failed. In 1810, with British and American backing, he returned and was briefly dictator, until the British withdrew their support. In 1812 he was overcome by the royalists in Venezuela and taken prisoner, dying in a Spanish prison in 1816.

San Martin was born in Argentina and during 1789-1811, served in campaigns of the Spanish armies in Europe and Africa. He first joined the independence movement in Argentina in 1812 and in 1817 invaded Chile with 4,000 men over the mountain passes. Here he and Gen. Bernardo O'Higgins (1778-1842) defeated the Spaniards at Chacabuco, 1817; O'Higgins was named Liberator and became first director of Chile, 1817-23. In 1821 San Martin occupied Lima and Callao, Peru, and became protector of Peru.

Bolivar was born in Venezuela, the son of an aristocratic family. He first served under Miranda in 1812 and in 1813 captured Caracas, where he was named Liberator. Forced out next year by civil strife, he led a campaign that captured Bogota in 1814. In 1817 he was again in control of Venezuela and was named dictator. He organized Nueva Granada with the help of General Francisco de Paula Santander (1792-1840). By joining Nueva Granada, Venezuela, and the area that is now Panama and Ecuador, the republic of Colombia was formed, with Bolivar president. After numerous setbacks he decisively defeated the Spaniards in the second battle of Carabobo, Venezuela, June 24, 1821.

In May 1822, Gen. Antonio Jose de Sucre, Bolivar's lieutenant, took Quito. Bolivar went to Guayaquil to confer with San Martin, who resigned as protector of Peru. With a new army of Colombians and Peruvians, Bolivar defeated the Spaniards in a battle at Junin in 1824 and cleared Peru.

De Sucre organized Charcas (Upper Peru) as Republica Bolivar (now Bolivia) and acted as president in place of Bolivar, who wrote its constitution. De Sucre defeated the Spanish faction of Peru at Ayacucho, Dec. 19, 1824.

Continued civil strife finally caused the Colombian federation to break apart. Santander turned against Bolivar, but the latter defeated him and banished him. In 1828 Bolivar gave up the presidency he had held precariously for 14 years. He became ill from tuberculosis and died Dec. 17, 1830. He is buried in the national pantheon in Caracas.

Governments of China

Where dynastic dates overlap, the rulers or events referred to appeared in different areas of China.

c. 1994-c. 1766 BCE	Hsia dynasty, first hereditary Chinese dynasty
c. 1766-c. 1027 BCE	Shang dynasty
c. 1027-770 BCE	Western Chou dynasty, capital near site of present-day Xi'an
770-256 BCE	Eastern Chou dynasty, new capital established at Luoyang
403-221 BCE	Period of the Warring States
221-206 BCE	Ch'in dynasty, quasi-feudal states unified for first time; name of China derived from this dynasty
206 BCE-9 CE	Earlier, or Western Han dynasty, founded by rebel leader Liu Pang, zenith of power under Emperor Wu Ti, 140-87 BCE, Chinese state expanded
9-23	Hsin dynasty, established by courtier Wang Mang, who deposed infant emperor for whom he had been acting as regent
25-220	Later, or Eastern Han dynasty
220-265[1]	Wei dynasty, established by son of Han general Ts'ao Ts'ao
221-263[1]	Shu Han dynasty in southwest China
222-280[1]	Wu dynasty in southeast China
265-317	Western Chin dynasty, established by Ssu-ma Yen, Wei dynasty general
317-420	Eastern Chin dynasty, established by prince of Ssu-ma family
420-589	Southern dynasties, four short-lived dynasties with capital at Chien-k'ang (present-day Nanjing)
589-618	Sui dynasty, reunified China; first emperor was Yang Chien, military servant who usurped throne of non-Chinese Northern Chou, 581
618-906	T'ang dynasty, founded by Li Yuan, who led rebellion against the Sui. Early rulers included former imperial concubine Empress Wu, 683-705; Hsuan Tsung, 712-56
907-960	Five Dynasties, period of disunion with short-lived dynasties in North China, 10 independent states mostly in South China
907-1125	Liao dynasty, of Khitan Mongols, capital at Yen-ching (present-day Beijing)
960-1126	Northern Sung dynasty, established by military leader Chao K'uang-yin, capital at Kaifeng
1122-1234	Chin dynasty, of Juchen people of Manchuria; drove Sung out of northern China
1127-1279	Southern Sung dynasty, capital at Lin-an (present-day Hangzhou)
1279-1368	Yuan dynasty, of Mongols; Kublai Khan, grandson of Genghis Khan, high point of Mongol power
1368-1644	Ming dynasty, founded by rebel leader Chu Yuan-chang, former Buddhist monk. Country again under Chinese rule, capital in present-day Nanjing, then Beijing after defeat of Mongolian tribes
1644-1912	Manchu, or Ch'ing dynasty, under Manchu rule with capital at Chiang-ning (present-day Nanjing). Power of Chinese empire reached highest point in its 2,000-year history. Last imperial dynasty; Hsuan T'ung, or Pu Yi, last emperor. Sun Yat-sen led revolution, 1911. Republic of China formed, 1912
1912-1949	Rep. of China, Gen. Yüan Shih-k'ai elected first president. Power passed to provincial warlords with Yüan's death, 1916. Gen. Chiang Kai-shek sought to reunify China under Kuomintang (Nationalist party) rule, 1926; Kuomintang established new national government at Nanjing, 1928. War with Japan, then civil war, led to Nationalist authority collapse, Communist declaration of People's Rep. of China, 1949

(1) Also known as the period of the Three Kingdoms because of warfare between the Wei, Shu Han, and Wu dynasties.

Leaders of People's Republic of China Since 1949

Mao Zedong	Chairman, 1949-59; Chinese Communist Party (CPC) Chairman, 1949-76
Zhou Enlai	Premier, 1949-76; foreign minister, 1949-76
Deng Xiaoping	Deputy Premier, 1952-66, 1973-76; "paramount leader," 1977-97
Liu Shaoqi	Chairman, 1959-68
Hua Guofeng	Premier, 1976-80; CPC Chairman, 1976-81
Hu Yaobang	CPC General Secretary, 1980-87; CPC Chairman 1981-82
Zhao Ziyang	Premier, 1980-87; CPC General Secretary, 1987-89
Li Xiannian	President, 1983-88
Yang Shangkun	President, 1988-93
Li Peng	Premier, 1988-98
Jiang Zemin	CPC General Secretary, 1989-2002; President, 1993-2003
Zhu Rongji	Premier, 1998-2003
Hu Jintao	CPC General Secretary, 2002- ; President, 2003-
Wen Jiabao	Premier, 2003-

Historical Periods of Japan

c. 300-592	Yamato	Conquest of Yamato plain, c. 300 CE
592-710	Asuka	Accession of Empress Suiko, 592
710-794	Nara	Heijo (Nara) completed, 710; capital moved to Nagaoka, 784
794-1185	Heian	Heian (Kyoto) completed, 794
858-1160	Fujiwara	Fujiwara-no-Yoshifusa became regent, 858
1160-1185	Taira	Taira-no-Kiyomoro assumed control, 1160; Minamoto-no-Yoritomo victor over Taira, 1185
1192-1333	Kamakura	Yoritomo became shogun, 1192
1334-1392	Namboku	Emperor Godaigo restored, 1334; Godaigo established Southern Court at Yoshino, 1336
1392-1573	Muromachi	Unification of Southern and Northern Courts, 1392
1467-1600	Sengoku	Onin war began, 1467
1573-1603	Momoyama	Oda Nobunaga entered Kyoto, 1568, deposes last Ashikaga shogun, 1573. Tokugawa Ieyasu victor at Sekigahara, 1600
1603-1867	Edo	Ieyasu became shogun, 1603
1868-1912	Meiji	Emperor Mutsuhito (Meiji) ascended throne, 1867; Meiji Restoration and Charter Oath, 1868
1912-1926	Taisho	Accession of Emperor Yoshihito, 1912
1926-1989	Showa	Accession of Emperor Hirohito, 1926
1989-	Heisei	Accession of Emperor Akihito, 1989

WORLD EXPLORATION AND GEOGRAPHY

Early Explorers of the Western Hemisphere

Reviewed by G. A. Clark, Ph.D., Aug. 2008

In the light of recent discoveries, theories about how and when the first people arrived in the western hemisphere are being reconsidered. Genetic evidence suggests that beginning around 14,000 years before the present (BP), the earliest immigrants crossed a 1,000-km wide "land bridge" between Siberia and Alaska in small groups and spread rapidly south through the Americas, arriving at S America's southern tip by c. 10,700 BP. Kennewick Man, found in 1996 in Washington's Columbia River gorge, dates to 9,600-9,200 BP, and Luzia, dating to 11,500 BP from Brazil, are examples of these early arrivals. Modern Native Americans appear to be descended from peoples indigenous to N and central Asia who arrived in subsequent waves of migration. A growing body of genetic, skeletal, and linguistic evidence documents their migration throughout the Americas.

Archaeologists have confirmed evidence of habitation by 12,900 BP at sites located on the shores of ancient lakes at an elevation of 17,400 feet in Chile's Atacama Desert. There is also growing support for the settlement of Chile's Monte Verde site, dated to c. 12,500 BP, and eight other 13th millennium sites in Brazil, Chile, and Argentina. One theory on their migration holds that a glacier covered much of N America from c. 20,000 to 13,000 BP, so those who settled in S America might have traveled there in small boats skirting the pack ice along the west coast, or spread from N to S America through a controversial 'ice-free corridor' in what today is western Canada. Other theories hold that they arrived before continental glaciation blocked migration from the north, or migrated from Iberia in skin boats. Controversial skeletal evidence from a burial at Santana do Riacho in Brazil (9,460 BP) suggests that some of the early immigrants who came via the land bridge from Siberia may have originated in Africa.

Long before Europeans arrived, the Americas were—for the most part—populated by hunter-gatherers and small-scale horticulturalists. In a few areas (SE U.S., Mesoamerica, coastal Peru and Chile), complex chiefdoms and state-level societies had appeared. Irrigation canals dating to 4,700 BP provide evidence for the origins of large-scale agriculture along the western slopes of Peru's Andes Mountains. The earliest known state in the Americas occupied a 700-sq. mi. area spanning four river valleys in coastal Peru between 3,500 and 500 BP.

Norsemen (Vikings sailing out of Iceland and Greenland), led by Leif Ericson, are usually credited with having been the first Europeans to reach America, with at least five voyages occurring about 1000 CE to areas they called Helluland, Markland, and Vinland—possibly what are known today as Baffin Island, Labrador, and either Newfoundland or further S in New England. L'Anse aux Meadows, on the N tip of Newfoundland, is the only documented settlement, with evidence of a small village with a church dating to c. 1000 CE. The Norsemen tried to import farming and herding economies, but these efforts failed after a few centuries, and Greenland and Newfoundland were abandoned by Europeans.

Sustained contact between the hemispheres began with the first voyage of Christopher Columbus (born Cristoforo Colombo, c. 1451, near Genoa, Italy). Columbus made four voyages to the New World while sailing for the Spanish monarchs Ferdinand II and Isabella. He left Palos, Spain, Aug. 3, 1492, with 88 men and landed at San Salvador (Watling Islands, Bahamas), Oct. 12, 1492. His fleet included three vessels, the *Niña*, *Pinta*, and *Santa María*. He also visited Cuba, Hispaniola, and many smaller Caribbean islands, then populated by the now-extinct Taino Indians. A second expedition left Cadíz, Spain, Sept. 25, 1493, with 17 ships and 1,400 men, reaching the island of Dominica, in the Lesser Antilles, on Nov. 3rd. His third voyage took him from Sanlucar, Spain (May 30, 1498, with 6 ships), to the island of Trinidad and to the adjacent coast of S America, where he made landfall at the mouth of the Orinoco River. A fourth voyage departed Cadíz on May 9, 1502, and reached the E coast of Mexico, Honduras, Panama, and what he christened Santiago (the present day island of Jamaica). Columbus died in Valladolid, Spain, on May 20, 1506, still convinced he had reached Asia by sailing west.

In N America, John and Sebastian Cabot, Italian explorers sailing for the English crown, reached Newfoundland and possibly Nova Scotia in 1497. John's second voyage (1498), seeking the fabled Northwest Passage, a new trade route to Asia, resulted in the loss of his entire fleet. For most of the 16th century, exploration of the New World was dominated by the empires of Spain and Portugal.

In 1497 and 1499 Amerigo Vespucci (for whom the Americas are named), an Italian explorer sailing for Spain, passed along the N and E coasts of South America. He was the first to argue that these lands were previously unknown, and not part of Asia.

Other early explorations are listed below.

Year	Explorer	Nationality (sponsor, if different)	Area reached or explored
1497-98	Vasco da Gama	Portuguese	Cape of Good Hope (Africa), India
1499	Alonso de Ojeda	Spanish	N South American coast, Venezuela
1500, Feb.	Vicente Yañez Pinzon	Spanish	S American coast, Amazon R.
1500, Apr.	Pedro Álvarez Cabral	Portuguese	Brazil
1501	Rodrigo de Bastidas	Spanish	Central America
1513	Vasco Núñez de Balboa	Spanish	Panama, Pacific Ocean
1513	Juan Ponce de León	Spanish	Florida, Yucatán Peninsula
1515	Juan de Solis	Spanish	Río de la Plata
1519	Alonso de Pineda	Spanish	Mouth of Mississippi R.
1519	Hernán Cortés	Spanish	Mexico
1519-20	Ferdinand Magellan	Portuguese (Spanish)	Straits of Magellan, Tierra del Fuego
1524	Giovanni da Verrazano	Italian (French)	Atlantic coast, incl. New York harbor
1528	Cabeza de Vaca	Spanish	Texas coast and interior
1532	Francisco Pizarro	Spanish	Peru
1534	Jacques Cartier	French	Canada, Gulf of St. Lawrence
1536	Pedro de Mendoza	Spanish	Buenos Aires
1539	Francisco de Ulloa	Spanish	California coast
1539-41	Hernando de Soto	Spanish	Mississippi R., near Memphis, TN
1539	Marcos de Niza	Italian (Spanish)	SW United States
1540	Francisco de Coronado	Spanish	SW United States
1540	Hernando Alarcon	Spanish	Colorado R.
1540	Garcia de Lopez Cardenas	Spanish	Colorado, Grand Canyon
1541	Francisco de Orellana	Spanish	Amazon R.
1542	Juan Rodriguez Cabrillo	Portuguese (Spanish)	W Mexico, San Diego harbor
1565	Pedro Menéndez de Aviles	Spanish	St. Augustine, FL
1576	Sir Martin Frobisher	English	Frobisher Bay, Canada
1577-80	Sir Francis Drake	English	California coast
1582	Antonio de Espejo	Spanish	Southwest U.S. (New Mexico)
1584	Amadas & Barlow (for Raleigh)	English	Virginia
1585-87	Sir Walter Raleigh's men	English	Roanoke Isl., NC
1595	Sir Walter Raleigh	English	Orinoco R.
1603-09	Samuel de Champlain	French	Canadian interior, Lake Champlain
1607	Capt. John Smith	English	Atlantic coast
1609-10	Henry Hudson	English (Dutch)	Hudson R., Hudson Bay
1634	Jean Nicolet	French	Lake Michigan, Wisconsin
1673	Jacques Marquette, Louis Jolliet	French	Mississippi R., S to Arkansas
1682	Robert Cavelier, sieur de La Salle	French	Mississippi R., S to Gulf of Mexico
1727-29	Vitus Bering	Danish (Russian)	Bering Strait and Alaska
1789	Sir Alexander Mackenzie	Canadian	NW Canada
1804-06	Meriwether Lewis and William Clark	American	Missouri R., Rocky Mts., Columbia R.

Arctic Exploration

Early Explorers

1587: John Davis (Eng.). Davis Strait to Sanderson's Hope, 72°12′N.

1596: Willem Barents and Jacob van Heemskerck (Holland). Discovered Bear Isl., touched NW tip of Spitsbergen, 79°49′N, rounded Novaya Zemlya, wintered at Ice Haven.

1607: Henry Hudson (Eng.). North along Greenland's E coast to Cape Hold-with-Hope, 73°30′, then N of Spitsbergen to 80°23′. Explored Hudson's Touches (Jan Mayen).

1616: William Baffin and Robert Bylot (Eng.). Baffin Bay to Smith Sound.

1728: Vitus Bering (Dan.). Sailed through strait (Bering) proving Asia and America are separate.

1733-40: Great Northern Expedition (Russ.). Surveyed Siberian Arctic coast.

1741: Vitus Bering (Russ.). Sighted Alaska, named Mount St. Elias. His lieutenant, Chirikof, explored coast.

1771: Samuel Hearne (Brit., Hudson's Bay Co.). Overland from Prince of Wales Fort (Churchill) on Hudson Bay to mouth of Coppermine R.

1778: James Cook (Brit.). Through Bering Strait to Icy Cape, AK, and North Cape, Siberia.

1789: Alexander Mackenzie (North West Co., Brit.). Montreal to mouth of Mackenzie River.

1806: William Scoresby (Brit.). N of Spitsbergen to 81°30′.

1820-23: Ferdinand von Wrangel (Russ.). Surveyed Siberian Arctic coast. His exploration joined James Cook's at North Cape, confirming separation of the continents.

1878-79: (Nils) Adolf Erik Nordenskjöld (Swed.). The 1st to navigate the Northeast Passage—an ocean route connecting Europe's North Sea, along the Arctic coast of Asia and through the Bering Sea, to the Pacific Ocean.

1881: The U.S. steamer *Jeannette*, led by Lt. Cmdr. George W. DeLong, was trapped in ice and crushed, June 1881. DeLong and 11 others died; 12 survived.

1888: Fridtjof Nansen (Nor.) crossed Greenland icecap.

1893-96: Nansen in *Fram* drifted from New Siberian Isls. to Spitsbergen; tried polar dash in 1895, reached Franz Josef Land, 86°14′N.

1897: Salomon A. Andrée (Swed.) and 2 others started in balloon from Spitsbergen, July 11, to drift across pole to U.S., and disappeared. Aug. 6, 1930, their bodies were found on White Isl., 82°57′N, 29°52′E.

1903-06: Roald Amundsen (Nor.) 1st sailed the Northwest Passage—an ocean route linking the Atlantic Ocean to the Pacific via Canada's marine waterways.

North Pole Exploration

Robert E. Peary explored Greenland's coast, 1891-92; tried for North Pole, 1893. In 1900 he reached N limit of Greenland and 83°50′N; in 1902 he reached 84°17′N; in 1906 he went from Ellesmere Isl. to 87°06′N. He sailed in the *Roosevelt*, July 1908, to winter off Cape Sheridan, Grant Land. The dash for the North Pole began Mar. 1 from Cape Columbia, Ellesmere Isl. Peary reportedly reached the pole, 90°N, Apr. 6, 1909; however, later research suggests he may have fallen short of his goal by c. 30-60 mi. The first surface expedition independently confirmed to have reached the N Pole was that of Ralph Plaisted in 1968 (see below).

Peary had several support groups carrying supplies until the last group turned back at 87°47′N. Peary, Matthew Henson, and 4 Eskimos proceeded with dog teams and sleds. They were said to have crossed the pole several times, then built an igloo there and remained 36 hours. Started south, Apr. 7 at 4 PM, for Cape Columbia.

1914: Donald MacMillan (U.S.). Northwest, 200 mi, from Axel Heiberg Is. to seek Peary's Crocker Land.

1915-17: Vihjalmur Stefansson (Can.). Discovered Borden, Brock, Meighen, and Lougheed Isls.

1918-20: Roald Amundsen (Nor.) sailed the Northeast Passage.

1925: Amundsen and Lincoln Ellsworth (U.S.) reached 87°44′N in attempt to fly to N Pole from Spitsbergen.

1926: Richard E. Byrd and Floyd Bennett (U.S.) reputedly flew over North Pole, May 9. (Claim to have reached the pole is in dispute, however.)

1926: Amundsen, Ellsworth, and Umberto Nobile (It.) flew from Spitsbergen over N Pole May 12, to Teller, AK, in dirigible *Norge.*

1928: Nobile crossed N Pole in airship, May 24; crashed, May 25. Amundsen died attempting a rescue.

North Pole Exploration Records

1958: On Aug. 3, submarine *Nautilus,* under Comdr. William R. Anderson, crossed the N Pole beneath the ice.

1960: In Aug., the nuclear-powered U.S. submarine *Seadragon* (Comdr. George P. Steele 2nd) made the 1st E-W underwater transit through the Northwest Passage. Traveling submerged for the most part, it took 6 days to make the 850-mi trek from Baffin Bay to the Beaufort Sea.

1968: On Apr. 19, Ralph Plaisted (U.S.) and 3 amateur explorers on snowmobiles became the first independently confirmed surface expedition to reach the N Pole.

1977: On Aug. 16, the Soviet nuclear icebreaker *Arktika* became the 1st surface ship to reach the N Pole.

1978: On Apr. 30, Naomi Uemura (Jap.) became the 1st person to reach the N Pole alone, traveling by dog sled in a 54-day, 600-mi trek over the frozen Arctic.

1982: In Apr., Sir Ranulph Fiennes and Charles Burton, Brit. explorers, reached the N Pole and became the 1st to circle the earth from pole to pole. They had reached the S Pole 16 months earlier. The 52,000-mi trek took 3 years, involved 23 people, and cost an estimated $18 mil.

1986: On May 2, 6 explorers reached the N Pole assisted only by dogs. They became the 1st to reach the pole without aerial logistics support since at least 1909. The explorers, Amer. Will Steger, Paul Schurke, Ann Bancroft, and Geoff Carroll, and Can. Brent Boddy and Richard Weber, completed the 500-mi journey in 56 days.

1995: On June 15, Weber and Russ. Mikhail Malakhov became the 1st pair to make it to the N Pole and back without any mechanical assistance. The 940-mi trip, made entirely on skis, took 121 days.

2003: On May 20, Pen Hadow (Brit.) became the 1st to reach the N Pole from Canada, solo and without resupply. The 377-mile journey across the ice took 64 days.

2006: On April 16, Prince Albert II of Monaco became the first royal to reach the N Pole.

Antarctic Exploration

Antarctica has been approached since 1773-75, when Capt. James Cook (Brit.) reached 71°10′S. Many sea and landmarks bear names of early explorers. Fabian von Bellingshausen (Russ.) discovered Peter I and Alexander I Isls., 1819-21. Nathaniel Palmer (U.S.) traveled throughout Palmer Peninsula, 60°W, 1820, without realizing that this was a continent. Capt. John Davis (U.S.) made the 1st known landing on the continent on Feb. 7, 1821. Later, in 1823, James Weddell (Brit.) found Weddell Sea, 74°15′S, the southernmost point that had been reached.

First to announce existence of the continent of Antarctica was Charles Wilkes (U.S.), who followed the coast for 1,500 mi, 1840. Adelie Coast, 140°E, was found by Dumont d'Urville (Fr.), 1840. Ross Ice Shelf was found by James Clark Ross (Brit.), 1841-42.

1895: Leonard Kristensen (Nor.) landed a party on the coast of Victoria Land. They were the 1st ashore on the main continental mass. C. E. Borchgrevink, a member of that party, returned in 1899 with a Brit. expedition, 1st to winter on Antarctica.

1902-04: Robert Falcon Scott (Brit.) explored Edward VII Peninsula to 82°17′S, 146°33′E from McMurdo Sound.

1908-09: Ernest Shackleton (Brit.) 1st to use Manchurian ponies in Antarctic sledging. He reached 88°23′S, discovering a route on to the plateau by way of the Beardmore Glacier and pioneering the way to the pole.

1911: Roald Amundsen (Nor.) with 4 men and dog teams reached the S Pole, Dec. 14.

1912: Scott reached the pole from Ross Isl., Jan. 18, with 4 companions. None of Scott's party survived. Their bodies and expedition notes were found, Nov. 12.

1928: 1st person to use an airplane over Antarctica was Sir George Hubert Wilkins (Austral.).

1929: Richard E. Byrd (U.S.) established Little America on Bay of Whales. On 1,600-mi airplane flight begun Nov. 28, he crossed S Pole, Nov. 29, with 3 others.

1934-35: Byrd led 2nd expedition to Little America, explored 450,000 sq mi, wintered alone at 80°04´S.

1934-37: John Rymill led British Graham Land expedition; discovered Palmer Penin. is part of mainland.

1935: Lincoln Ellsworth (U.S.) flew S along E Coast of Palmer Penin., then crossed continent to Little America, making 4 landings.

1939-41: U.S. Navy plane flights discovered about 150,000 sq mi of new land.

1940: Byrd charted most of coast between Ross Sea and Palmer Penin.

1946-47: U.S. Navy undertook Operation Highjump, commanded by Byrd, included 13 ships and 4,000 men. Airplanes photomapped coastline and penetrated beyond pole.

1946-48: Ronne Antarctic Research Expedition Comdr., Finn Ronne, USNR, determined the Antarctic to be only one continent with no strait between Weddell Sea and Ross Sea; explored 250,000 sq mi of land by flights to 79°S.

1955-57: U.S. Navy's Operation Deep Freeze led by Adm. Byrd. Supporting U.S. scientific efforts for the International Geophysical Year (IGY), the operation established 5 coastal stations fronting the Indian, Pacific, and Atlantic oceans and also 3 interior stations; explored more than 1,000,000 sq mi in Wilkes Land.

1957-58: During the IGY, July 1957 through Dec. 1958, scientists from 12 countries conducted Antarctic research at a network of some 60 stations on Antarctica.
Dr. Vivian E. Fuchs (Brit.) led a 12-person Trans-Antarctic Expedition on the 1st land crossing of Antarctica. Starting from the Weddell Sea, they reached Scott Station, Mar. 2, 1958, after traveling 2,158 mi in 98 days.

1958: A group of 5 U.S. scientists led by Edward C. Thiel, seismologist, moving by tractor from Ellsworth Station on Weddell Sea, identified a huge mountain range, 5,000 ft above the ice sheet and 9,000 ft above sea level. The range, originally seen by a Navy plane, was named the Dufek Massif, for Rear Adm. George Dufek.

1959: Argentina, Australia, Belgium, Chile, France, Japan, New Zealand, Norway, South Africa, USSR, UK, and U.S. signed a treaty suspending territorial claims for 30 yrs. and reserving the continent, S of 60°S, for research.

1961-62: Scientists discovered the Bentley Trench, running from Ross Ice Shelf into Marie Byrd Land, near the end of the Ellsworth Mts., toward the Weddell Sea.

1962: Nuclear power plant online at McMurdo Sound.

1963: On Feb. 22, a U.S. plane made the region's longest nonstop flight from McMurdo Station S past the pole to Shackleton Mts., SE to the "Area of Inaccessibility," and back to McMurdo Station covering 3,600 mi in 10 hrs.

1964: New Zealanders mapped the mountain area from Cape Adare W some 400 mi to Pennell Glacier.

1985: Igor A. Zotikov, a Russian researcher, discovered sediments in the Ross Ice Shelf that seem to support the continental drift theory. Ocean Drilling Project finds that the ice sheets of E Antarctica are 37 million yrs. old.

1989: Victoria Murden and Shirley Metz became both the 1st women and the 1st Americans to reach the S Pole overland when they arrived with 9 others on Jan. 17, 1989.

1991: 24 nations approved a protocol to the 1959 Antarctica Treaty, Oct. 4. New conservation provisions, including banning oil and other mineral exploration for 50 yrs.

1994: On Dec. 25, after 50-day trek, Liv Arnesen (Nor.) became 1st woman to ski alone and unaided to the S Pole.

1995: On Dec. 22, a Norwegian, Borge Ousland, reached the S Pole in the fastest time on skis: 44 days.

1996-97 Ousland became 1st person to traverse Antarctica alone; reached S Pole Dec. 19, 1996; traveled 1,675 mi in 64 days, ending Jan. 18, 1997.

2000-01: On Feb. 11, Ann Bancroft and Arnesen became 1st women to ski unaided across Antarctica. The 1,717-mile journey took 94 days.

Volcanoes

Sources: *Volcanoes of the World*, Geoscience Press; Global Volcanism Network, Smithsonian Institution

Roughly 540 volcanoes are known to have erupted during historical times. Nearly 75% of these historically active volcanoes lie along the so-called **Ring of Fire**, running along the W coast of the Americas from the southern tip of Chile to Alaska, down the E coast of Asia from Kamchatka to Indonesia, and continuing from New Guinea to New Zealand. The Ring of Fire marks the boundary between the mobile tectonic plates underlying the Pacific Ocean and those of the surrounding continents. Other active regions occur along rift zones, where plates pull apart, as in Iceland, or where molten material moves up from the mantle over local "hot spots," as in Hawaii. The vast majority of the earth's volcanism occurs at submarine rift zones. For more information on volcanoes, see the Smithsonian Institution's global volcanism website at www.volcano.si.edu

Notable Volcanic Eruptions

Approximately 7,000 years ago, Mazama, a 9,900-ft volcano in southern Oregon, erupted violently, ejecting large amounts of ash and pumice and voluminous pyroclastic flows. The ash spread over the entire northwestern U.S. and as far away as Saskatchewan, Can. During the eruption, the top of the mountain collapsed, leaving a caldera 6 mi across and about a half mile deep, which filled with rainwater to form what is now called Crater Lake.

In 79 CE, Vesuvio, or Vesuvius, a 4,190-ft volcano overlooking Naples Bay, became active after several centuries of apparent inactivity. On Aug. 24 of that year, a heated mud and ash flow swept down the mountain, engulfing the cities of Pompeii, Herculaneum, and Stabiae with debris more than 60 ft deep. About 10% of the population of the 3 towns were killed.

In 1883, an eruption similar to the Mazama eruption occurred on the island of Krakatau. At least 2,000 people died in pyroclastic flows on Aug. 26. The next day, the 2,640-ft peak of the volcano collapsed to 1,000 ft below sea level, sinking most of the island and killing over 3,000. A tsunami (tidal wave) generated by the collapse killed more than 31,000 people in Java and Sumatra, and eventually reached England. Ash from the eruption colored sunsets around the world for 2 years. A similar, even more powerful eruption had taken place 68 years earlier at Mt. Tambora on the Indonesian island of Sumbawa.

Date	Volcano	Deaths (est.)	Date	Volcano	Deaths (est.)
Aug. 24, 79 CE	Mt. Vesuvius, Italy	16,000	May 8, 1902	Mt. Pelée, Martinique	28,000
1586	Kelut, Java, Indon.	10,000	Jan. 30, 1911	Mt. Taal, Phil.	1,400
Dec. 15, 1631	Mt. Vesuvius, Italy	4,000	May 19, 1919	Mt. Kelut, Java, Indon.	5,000
Aug. 12, 1772	Mt. Papandayan, Java, Indon.	3,000	Jan. 17-21, 1951	Mt. Lamington, New Guinea	3,000
June 8, 1783	Laki, Iceland	9,350	May 18, 1980	Mt. St. Helens, U.S.	57
May 21, 1792	Mt. Unzen, Japan	14,500	Mar. 28, 1982	El Chichon, Mex.	1,880
Apr. 10-12, 1815	Mt. Tambora, Sumbawa, Indon.	92,000[1]	Nov. 13, 1985	Nevado del Ruiz, Colombia	23,000
Aug. 26-28, 1883	Krakatau, Indon.	36,000	Aug. 21, 1986	Lake Nyos, Cameroon	1,700
Apr. 24, 1902	Santa María, Guatemala	1,000[2]	June 15, 1991	Mt. Pinatubo, Luzon, Phil.	800[3]

(1) Of these, 10,000 were directly related to the eruption; an additional 82,000 were the result of starvation and disease brought on by the event. (2) An additional 3,000 deaths due to a malaria outbreak are sometimes attributed to the eruption. (3) Of these, about 500 were associated with post-eruption lahars (volcanic mudflows), in addition to the 300 deaths caused directly by the eruption.

Notable Active Volcanoes

Active volcanoes display a wide range of activity. In this table, years are given for last display of eruptive activity, as of mid-2009; the list does not include submarine volcanoes. An eruption may involve explosive ejection of new or old fragmental material, escape of liquid lava, or both. Volcanoes are listed by height, which does not reflect eruptive magnitude.

Name (latest eruption)	Location	Height (ft)
Africa		
Mt. Cameroon (2000)	Cameroon	13,435
Nyiragongo (2009)	Congo	11,384
Nyamuragira (2006)	Congo	10,033
Mt. Oku [Lake Nyos] (1986)	Cameroon	9,878
Ol Doinyo Lengai (2009)	Tanzania	9,718
Fogo (1995)	Cape Verde Isls.	9,281
Piton de la Fournaise (2009)	Réunion Isl., Indian O.	8,635
Karthala (2007)	Comoros	7,746
Erta Ale (2009)	Ethiopia	2,011
Antarctica		
Erebus (2009)	Ross Isl.	12,447
Deception Island (1970)	S. Shetland Isl.	1,890
Asia and Oceania		
Kliuchevskoi (2009)	Kamchatka, Russia	15,863
Kerinci (2009)	Sumatra, Indon.	12,467
Fuji (1708)	Honshu, Japan	12,388
Tolbachik (1976)	Kamchatka, Russia	12,080
Semeru (2009)	Java, Indon.	12,060
Slamet (2009)	Java, Indon.	11,247
Raung (2008)	Java, Indon.	10,932
Shiveluch (2009)	Kamchatka, Russia	10,771
On-take (1980)	Honshu, Japan	10,049
Merapi (2007)	Java, Indon.	9,737
Bezymianny (2009)	Kamchatka, Russia	9,455
Peuet Sague (2000)	Sumatra, Indon.	9,190
Ruapehu (2007)	New Zealand	9,176
Heard (2008)	Indian Ocean	9,006
Changbaishan (1903)	China/Korea	9,003
Asama (2009)	Honshu, Japan	8,425
Mayon (2008)	Luzon, Phil.	8,077
Kanlaon (2006)	Negros Isl., Phil.	7,989
Niigata-Yake-yama (1998)	Honshu, Japan	7,874
Alaid (1996)	Kuril Isls., Russia	7,674
Ulawun (2007)	Papua New Guinea	7,657
Chokai (1974)	Honshu, Japan	7,326
Galunggung (1984)	Java, Indon.	7,113
Azuma (1977)	Honshu, Japan	6,676
Tongariro (Ngauruhoe) (1977)	New Zealand	6,489
Sangeang Api (1988)	Lesser Sunda Isl., Indon.	6,394
Nasu (1963)	Honshu, Japan	6,283
Karkar (1979)	Papua New Guinea	6,033
Bandai (1888)	Honshu, Japan	5,968
Tiatia (1981)	Kuril Isls., Russia	5,968
Manam (2009)	Papua New Guinea	5,928
Kuju (1996)	Kyushu, Japan	5,876
Karangetang (Api Siau) (2009)	Sangihe Isls., Indon.	5,853
Soputan (2008)	Sulawesi, Indon.	5,853
Bagana (2009)	Papua New Guinea	5,741
Kelut (2008)	Java, Indon.	5,679
Adatara (1996)	Honshu, Japan	5,636
Gamalama (2003)	Halmahera, Indon.	5,627
Kirishima (2008)	Kyushu, Japan	5,577
Gamkonora (2007)	Halmahera, Indon.	5,364
Aso (2005)	Kyushu, Japan	5,223
Lokon-Empung (2003)	Sulawesi, Indon.	5,184
Bulusan (2007)	Luzon, Phil.	5,134
Karymsky (2009)	Kamchatka, Russia	5,039
Unzen (1996)	Kyushu, Japan	4,921
Akan (2008)	Hokkaido, Japan	4,918
Sarychev Peak (2009)	Kuril Isls., Russia	4,908
Pinatubo (1993)	Luzon, Phil.	4,875
Lopevi (2008)	Vanuatu	4,636
Akita-Yake-yama (1997)	Honshu, Japan	4,482
Dukono (2009)	Halmahera, Indon.	4,380
Ambrym (2009)	Vanuatu	4,377
Langila (2008)	Papua New Guinea	4,363
Awu (2004)	Sangihe Isls., Indon.	4,331
Akademia Nauk (1996)	Kamchatka, Russia	3,871
Komaga-take (2000)	Hokkaido, Japan	3,711
Sakura-jima (2009)	Kyushu, Japan	3,665
Miyake-jima (2008)	Izu Isl., Japan	2,674
Krakatau (2009)	Indonesia	2,667
Suwanose-jima (2009)	Ryukyu Isls., Japan	2,621
Gaua (1982)	Vanuatu	2,615
Oshima (1990)	Izu Isls., Japan	2,507
Usu (2001)	Hokkaido, Japan	2,418
Rabaul (2009)	Papua New Guinea	2,257
Pagan (2006)	N. Mariana Isl.	1,870
Yasur (2009)	Tanna Island, Vanuatu	1,184
White Island (2001)	Bay of Plenty, New Zealand	1,053

Name (latest eruption)	Location	Height (ft)
Central America and Caribbean		
Tacaná (1986)	Guatemala	13,320
Acatenango (1972)	Guatemala	13,044
Santa María (2009)	Guatemala	12,375
Fuego (2009)	Guatemala	12,346
Irazú (1994)	Costa Rica	11,260
Turrialba (1866)	Costa Rica	10,958
Poás (2009)	Costa Rica	8,884
Pacaya (2009)	Guatemala	8,373
San Miguel (2002)	El Salvador	6,988
Rincón de la Vieja (1998)	Costa Rica	6,286
San Cristóbal (2008)	Nicaragua	5,725
Concepción (2007)	Nicaragua	5,577
Arenal (2009)	Costa Rica	5,479
Soufrière Guadeloupe (1977)	Guadeloupe Isl.	4,813
Pelée (1932)	Martinique	4,583
Momotombo (1905)	Nicaragua	4,255
Soufrière St. Vincent (1979)	St. Vincent	4,003
Soufrière Hills (2009)	Montserrat	3,002
Masaya (2008)	Nicaragua	2,083
North America		
Pico de Orizaba (1846)	Mexico	18,619
Popocatépetl (2009)	Mexico	17,802
Rainier (1894)	Washington	14,409
Wrangell (2002)	Alaska	14,163
Shasta (1786)	California	14,163
Colima (2009)	Mexico	12,631
Lassen Peak (1917)	California	10,456
Redoubt (2009)	Alaska	10,197
Iliamna (1876)	Alaska	10,016
Shishaldin (2004)	Aleutian Isl., AK	9,373
St. Helens (2008)	Washington	8,363
Pavlof (2007)	Alaska	8,264
Veniaminof (2008)	Alaska	8,225
Katmai (1912)	Alaska	6,716
Makushin (1995)	Aleutian Isl., AK	5,905
Great Sitkin (1974)	Aleutian Isl., AK	5,709
Cleveland (2009)	Aleutian Isl., AK	5,676
Gareloi (1989)	Aleutian Isl., AK	5,161
Korovin [Atka complex] (2007)	Aleutian Isl., AK	5,029
Akutan (1992)	Aleutian Isl., AK	4,275
Augustine (2006)	Alaska	4,108
Kiska (1990)	Aleutian Isl., AK	4,003
El Chichón (1982)	Mexico	3,773
Okmok (2008)	Aleutian Isl., AK	3,520
Seguam (1993)	Aleutian Isl., AK	3,458
South America		
Llullaillaco (1877)	Argentina-Chile	22,109
Guallatiri (1960)	Chile	19,918
Tupungatito (1987)	Argentina-Chile	19,685
Cotopaxi (1940)	Ecuador	19,393
El Misti (1985)	Peru	19,101
Láscar (2007)	Chile	18,346
Nevado del Ruiz (1991)	Colombia	17,457
Sangay (2009)	Ecuador	17,159
Irruputuncu (1995)	Chile-Bolivia	16,939
Tungurahua (2009)	Ecuador	16,479
Guagua Pichincha (2009)	Ecuador	15,695
Puracé (1977)	Colombia	15,226
Galeras (2009)	Colombia	14,029
Llaima (2009)	Chile	10,253
Villarrica (2008)	Chile	9,340
Cerro Hudson (1991)	Chile	6,250
Fernandina (2009)	Galápagos Isls., Ecuador	4,842
Europe		
Etna (2009)	Italy	10,925
Vesuvius (1944)	Italy	4,203
Stromboli (2009)	Italy	3,031
Santorini (1950)	Greece	1,204
Mid-Atlantic		
Jan Mayen (1985)	N Atlantic O., Norway	7,470
Grímsvötn (2004)	Iceland	5,659
Hekla (2000)	Iceland	4,892
Krafla (1984)	Iceland	2,694
Mid-Pacific		
Mauna Loa (1984)	Hawaii, HI	13,681
Haleakala (1750)	Maui, HI	10,023
Kilauea (2009)	Hawaii, HI	4,009

Mountains
United States, Canada, Mexico

Peak, state/country	Height (ft)	Peak, state/country	Height (ft)	Peak, state/country	Height (ft)
McKinley (Denali), Alaska	20,320	Alverstone, Alaska-Yukon	14,565	Shavano, Colorado	14,229
Logan, Yukon	19,551	Browne Tower, Alaska	14,530	Belford, Colorado	14,197
Pico de Orizaba, Mexico	18,855	Whitney, California	14,494	Princeton, Colorado	14,197
St. Elias, Alaska-Yukon	18,008	Elbert, Colorado	14,433	Crestone Needle, Colorado	14,197
Popocatépetl, Mexico	17,930	Massive, Colorado	14,421	Yale, Colorado	14,196
Foraker, Alaska	17,400	Harvard, Colorado	14,420	Bross, Colorado	14,172
Iztaccihuatl, Mexico	17,343	Rainier, Washington	14,410	Kit Carson, Colorado	14,165
Lucania, Yukon	17,147	University Peak, Alaska	14,410	Wrangell, Alaska	14,163
King, Yukon	16,971	Williamson, California	14,375	Shasta, California	14,162
Steele, Yukon	16,644	La Plata Peak, Colorado	14,361	El Diente Peak, Colorado	14,159
Bona, Alaska	16,550	Blanca Peak, Colorado	14,345	Point Success, Washington	14,158
Blackburn, Alaska	16,390	Uncompahgre Peak, Colorado	14,309	Maroon Peak, Colorado	14,156
Kennedy, Alaska	16,286	Crestone Peak, Colorado	14,294	Tabeguache, Colorado	14,155
Sanford, Alaska	16,237	Lincoln, Colorado	14,286	Oxford, Colorado	14,153
Vancouver, Alaska-Yukon	15,979	Grays Peak, Colorado	14,270	Sill, California	14,153
South Buttress, Alaska	15,885	Antero, Colorado	14,269	Sneffels, Colorado	14,150
Wood, Yukon	15,885	Torreys Peak, Colorado	14,267	Democrat, Colorado	14,148
Churchill, Alaska	15,638	Castle Peak, Colorado	14,265	Capitol Peak,Colorado	14,130
Fairweather, Alaska-Brit. Columb.	15,300	Quandary Peak, Colorado	14,265	Liberty Cap, Washington	14,112
Zinantecatl (Toluca), Mexico	15,016	Evans, Colorado	14,264	Pikes Peak, Colorado	14,110
Hubbard, Alaska-Yukon	15,015	Longs Peak, Colorado	14,255	Snowmass, Colorado	14,092
Bear, Alaska	14,831	McArthur, Yukon	14,253	Russell, California	14,088
Walsh, Yukon	14,780	Wilson, Colorado	14,246	Eolus, Colorado	14,083
East Buttress, Alaska	14,730	White Mt. Peak, California	14,246	Windom, Colorado	14,082
Matlalcueyetl, Mexico	14,636	North Palisade, California	14,242	Columbia, Colorado	14,073
Hunter, Alaska	14,753	Cameron, Colorado	14,238	Augusta, Alaska	14,070

The highest point in the West Indies is in the Dominican Republic, Pico Duarte (10,417 ft).

Other Notable U.S. Mountains

Peak, state	Height (ft)	Peak, state	Height (ft)	Peak, state	Height (ft)
Gannett Peak, WY	13,804	Adams, WA	12,277	Clingmans Dome, NC-TN	6,643
Grand Teton, WY	13,766	San Gorgonio, CA	11,502	Washington, NH	6,288
Kings, UT	13,528	Hood, OR	11,239	Rogers, VA	5,729
Cloud, WY	13,175	Lassen, CA	10,457	Marcy, NY	5,344
Wheeler, NM	13,161	Granite, CA	10,321	Katahdin, ME	5,268
Boundary, NV	13,140	Guadalupe, TX	8,749	Spruce Knob, WV	4,861
Granite, MT	12,799	Olympus, WA	7,965	Mansfield, VT	4,393
Borah, ID	12,662	Harney, SD	7,242	Black Mountain, KY	4,145
Humphreys, AZ	12,633	Mitchell, NC	6,684		

South America

Peak, country	Height (ft)	Peak, country	Height (ft)	Peak, country	Height (ft)
Aconcagua, Argentina	22,834	Coropuna, Peru	21,083	Solo, Argentina	20,492
Ojos del Salado, Arg.-Chile	22,572	Laudo, Argentina	20,997	Polleras, Argentina	20,456
Bonete, Argentina	22,546	Ancohuma, Bolivia	20,958	Pular, Chile	20,423
Tupungato, Argentina-Chile	22,310	Ausangate, Peru	20,945	Chani, Argentina	20,341
Pissis, Argentina	22,241	Toro, Argentina-Chile	20,932	Aucanquilcha, Chile	20,295
Mercedario, Argentina	22,211	Illampu, Bolivia	20,873	Juncal, Argentina-Chile	20,276
Huascaran, Peru	22,205	Tres Cruces, Argentina-Chile	20,853	Negro, Argentina	20,184
Llullaillaco, Argentina-Chile	22,109	Huandoy, Peru	20,852	Quela, Argentina	20,128
El Libertador, Argentina	22,047	Parinacota, Bolivia-Chile	20,768	Condoriri, Bolivia	20,095
Cachi, Argentina	22,047	Tortolas, Argentina-Chile	20,745	Palermo, Argentina	20,079
Incahuasi, Argentina-Chile	21,720	Ampato, Peru	20,702	Solimana, Peru	20,068
Yerupaja, Peru	21,709	El Condor, Argentina	20,669	San Juan, Argentina-Chile	20,049
Galan, Argentina	21,654	Salcantay, Peru	20,574	Sierra Nevada, Argentina-Chile	20,023
El Muerto, Argentina-Chile	21,457	Chimborazo, Ecuador	20,561	Antofalla, Argentina	20,013
Sajama, Bolivia	21,391	Huancarhuas, Peru	20,531	Marmolejo, Argentina-Chile	20,013
Nacimiento, Argentina	21,302	Famatina, Argentina	20,505	Chachani, Peru	19,931
Illimani, Bolivia	21,201	Pumasillo, Peru	20,492		

Africa

Peak, country	Height (ft)	Peak, country	Height (ft)	Peak, country	Height (ft)
Kilimanjaro, Tanzania	19,340	Meru, Tanzania	14,979	Guna, Ethiopia	13,881
Kenya, Kenya	17,058	Karisimbi, Congo-Rwanda	14,787	Gughe, Ethiopia	13,780
Margherita Pk., Uganda-Congo	16,763	Elgon, Kenya-Uganda	14,178	Toubkal, Morocco	13,661
Ras Dashan, Ethiopia	15,158	Batu, Ethiopia	14,131	Cameroon, Cameroon	13,435

Australia, New Zealand, SE Asian Islands

Peak, country	Height (ft)	Peak, country	Height (ft)	Peak, country	Height (ft)
Jaya, New Guinea	16,500	Wilhelm, New Guinea	14,793	Cook, New Zealand	12,349
Trikora, New Guinea	15,585	Kinabalu, Malaysia	13,455	Semeru, Java, Indonesia	12,060
Mandala, New Guinea	15,420	Kerinci, Sumatra, Indon.	12,467	Kosciusko, Australia	7,310

Height of Mount Everest

Mt. Everest, the world's highest mountain, was considered 29,002 ft when Edmund Hillary and Tenzing Norgay became the 1st climbers to scale it, in 1953. This triangulation figure had been accepted since 1850. In 1954 the Surveyor General of the Republic of India set the height at 29,028 ft, plus or minus 10 ft because of snow; this figure was also accepted by the National Geographic Society.

In 1999, a team of climbers sponsored by Boston's Museum of Science and the National Geographic Society measured the height at the summit using sophisticated satellite-based technology. This new measurement, of 29,035 ft, was accepted by the National Geographic Society and other authorities, including the U.S. National Imagery and Mapping Agency.

As of Sept. 2009, more than 55 years after the 1st climbers had reached the summit, some 3,100 more had followed, and about 206 had died in the attempt.

Europe

Peak, country	Height (ft)	Peak, country	Height (ft)	Peak, country	Height (ft)
Alps		Dent D'Herens, Switzerland	13,686	Schalihorn, Switzerland	13,040
		Breithorn, It.-Switzerland	13,665	Scerscen, Switzerland	13,028
Mont Blanc, France-Italy	15,771	Bishorn, Switzerland	13,645	Eiger, Switzerland	13,025
Monte Rosa (highest peak		Jungfrau, Switzerland	13,642	Jagerhorn, Switzerland	13,024
of group), Switzerland	15,203	Ecrins, France	13,461	Rottalhorn, Switzerland	13,022
Dom, Switzerland	14,911	Monch, Switzerland	13,448		
Liskamm, It.-Switzerland	14,852	Pollux, Switzerland	13,422	**Pyrenees**	
Weisshorn, Switzerland	14,780	Schreckhorn, Switzerland	13,379	Aneto, Spain	11,168
Taschhorn, Switzerland	14,733	Ober Gabelhorn, Switzerland	13,330	Posets, Spain	11,073
Matterhorn, It.-Switzerland	14,690	Gran Paradiso, Italy	13,323	Perdido, Spain	11,007
Dent Blanche, Switzerland	14,293	Bernina, It.-Switzerland	13,284	Vignemale, France-Spain	10,820
Nadelhorn, Switzerland	14,196	Fiescherhorn, Switzerland	13,283	Long, Spain	10,479
Grand Combin, Switzerland	14,154	Grunhorn, Switzerland	13,266	Estats, Spain	10,304
Lenzpitze, Switzerland	14,088	Lauteraarhorn, Switzerland	13,261	Montcalm, Spain	10,105
Finsteraarhorn, Switzerland	14,022	Durrenhorn, Switzerland	13,238		
Castor, Switzerland	13,865	Allalinhorn, Switzerland	13,213	**Caucasus (Europe-Asia)**	
Zinalrothorn, Switzerland	13,849	Weissmies, Switzerland	13,199	Elbrus, Russia	18,510
Hohberghorn, Switzerland	13,842	Lagginhorn, Switzerland	13,156	Shkhara, Georgia	17,064
Alphubel, Switzerland	13,799	Zupo, Switzerland	13,120	Dykh Tau, Russia	17,054
Rimpfischhom, Switzerland	13,776	Fletschhorn, Switzerland	13,110	Kashtan Tau, Russia	16,877
Aletschorn, Switzerland	13,763	Adlerhorn, Switzerland	13,081	Janqi, Georgia	16,565
Strahlhorn, Switzerland	13,747	Gletscherhorn, Switzerland	13,068	Kazbek, Georgia	16,558

Asia (Mainland)

Peak, country/region	Height (ft)	Peak, country/region	Height (ft)	Peak, country/region	Height (ft)
Everest, Nepal-Tibet	29,035	Kungur, Xinjiang, China	25,325	Badrinath, India	23,420
K2 (Godwin Austen), Kashmir	28,250	Tirich Mir, Pakistan	25,230	Nunkun, Kashmir	23,410
Kanchenjunga, India-Nepal	28,208	Makalu II, Nepal-Tibet	25,120	Lenin Peak, Tajikistan	23,405
Lhotse I (Everest), Nepal-Tibet	27,923	Minya Konka, China	24,900	Pyramid, India-Nepal	23,400
Makalu I, Nepal-Tibet	27,824	Kula Gangri, Bhutan-Tibet	24,784	Api, Nepal	23,399
Lhotse II (Everest), Nepal-Tibet	27,560	Changtzu (Everest), Nepal-Tibet	24,780	Pauhunri, India-Tibet	23,385
Dhaulagiri, Nepal	26,810	Muz Tagh Ata, Xinjiang, China	24,757	Trisul, India	23,360
Manaslu I, Nepal	26,760	Skyang Kangri, Kashmir	24,750	Kangto, India-Tibet	23,260
Cho Oyu, Nepal-Tibet	26,750	Ismail Semani Peak,Tajikistan	24,590	Nyenchhe Thanglha, Tibet	23,255
Nanga Parbat, Kashmir	26,660	Jongsang Peak, India-Nepal	24,472	Trisuli, India	23,210
Annapurna I, Nepal	26,504	Jengish Chokusu, Xinjiang, China-		Pumori, Nepal-Tibet	23,190
Gasherbrum, Kashmir	26,470	Kyrgyzstan	24,406	Dunagiri, India	23,184
Broad, Kashmir	26,400	Sia Kangri, Kashmir	24,350	Lombo Kangra, Tibet	23,165
Gosainthan Nepal-Tibet	26,287	Haramosh Peak, Pakistan	24,270	Saipal, Nepal	23,100
Annapurna II, Nepal	26,041	Istoro Nal, Pakistan	24,240	Macha Pucchare, Nepal	22,958
Gyachung Kang, Nepal-Tibet	25,910	Tent Peak, India-Nepal	24,165	Numbar, Nepal	22,817
Disteghil Sar, Kashmir	25,868	Chomo Lhari, Bhutan-Tibet	24,040	Kanjiroba, Nepal	22,580
Himalchuli, Nepal	25,801	Chamlang, Nepal	24,012	Ama Dablam, Nepal	22,350
Nuptse (Everest), Nepal-Tibet	25,726	Kabru, India-Nepal	24,002	Cho Polu, Nepal	22,093
Masherbrum, Kashmir	25,660	Alung Gangri, Tibet	24,000	Lingtren, Nepal-Tibet	21,972
Nanda Devi, India	25,645	Baltoro Kangri, Kashmir	23,990	Khumbutse, Nepal-Tibet	21,785
Rakaposhi, Kashmir	25,550	Mussu Shan, Xinjiang, China	23,890	Hlako Gangri, Tibet	21,266
Kamet, India-Tibet	25,447	Mana, India	23,860	Mt. Grosvenor, China	21,190
Namcha Barwa, Tibet	25,445	Baruntse, Nepal	23,688	Thagchhab Gangri, Tibet	20,970
Gurla Mandhata, Tibet	25,355	Nepal Peak, India-Nepal	23,500	Damavand, Iran	18,606
Ulugh Muz Tagh, Xinjiang, China-		Amne Machin, China	23,490	Ararat, Turkey	16,804
Tibet	25,340	Gauri Sankar, Nepal-Tibet	23,440		

Antarctica

Peak	Height (ft)	Peak	Height (ft)	Peak	Height (ft)
Vinson Massif	16,864	Miller	13,650	Falla	12,549
Tyree	16,290	Long Gables	13,620	Rucker	12,520
Shinn	15,750	Dickerson	13,517	Goldthwait	12,510
Gardner	15,375	Giovinetto	13,412	Morris	12,500
Epperly	15,100	Wade	13,400	Erebus	12,450
Kirkpatrick	14,855	Fisher	13,386	Campbell	12,434
Elizabeth	14,698	Fridtjof Nansen	13,350	Don Pedro Christophersen	12,355
Markham	14,290	Wexler	13,202	Lysaght	12,326
Bell	14,117	Lister	13,200	Huggins	12,247
Mackellar	14,098	Shear	13,100	Sabine	12,200
Anderson	13,957	Odishaw	13,008	Astor	12,175
Bentley	13,934	Donaldson	12,894	Mohl	12,172
Kaplan	13,878	Ray	12,808	Frankes	12,064
Andrew Jackson	13,750	Sellery	12,779	Jones	12,040
Sidley	13,720	Waterman	12,730	Gjelsvik	12,008
Ostenso	13,710	Anne	12,703	Coman	12,000
Minto	13,668	Press	12,566		

Important Islands and Their Areas

Figures are for total areas in square miles. Boldface figure in parentheses shows rank among the world's 10 largest individual islands. Because some islands have not been surveyed accurately, some areas shown are estimates. Some "islands" listed are island groups. Only the largest islands in a group are listed individually. Only islands over 10 sq mi in area are listed.

Antarctica

Adelaide	1,400
Alexander	16,700
Berkner	18,500
Roosevelt	2,900

Arctic Ocean

Akimski, Nunavut	1,159
Amund Ringnes, Nun.	2,029
Axel Heiberg, Nun.	16,671
Baffin, Nun. **(5)**	195,928
Banks, Northwest Territories	27,038
Bathurst, Nun.	6,194
Bolshevik, Russia	4,368
Bolshoy Lyakhovsky, Russia	1,776
Borden, NWT-Nun.	1,079
Bylot, Nun.	4,273
Coats, Nun.	2,123
Cornwallis, Nun.	2,701
Devon, Nun.	21,331
Disko, Greenland	3,312
Ellef Ringnes, Nun.	4,361
Ellesmere, Nun. **(10)**	75,767
Faddayevskiy, Russia	1,930
Franz Josef Land, Russia	8,000
Iturup (Etorofu), Russia	2,596
King William, Nun.	5,062
Komsomolets, Russia	3,477
Mackenzie King, NWT	1,949
Mansel, Nun.	1,228
Melville, NWT-Nun.	16,274
Milne Land, Greenland	1,400
New Siberian Islands, Russia	14,500
Kotelnyy, Russia	4,504
Novaya Zemlya, Russia (2 isls.)	31,730
Oktyabrskoy, Russia	5,471
Prince Charles, NWT	3,676
Prince of Wales, Nun.	12,872
Prince Patrick, NWT	6,119
Somerset, Nun.	9,570
Southampton, Nun.	15,913
Svalbard (tot. group)	23,957
Nordaustlandet	5,410
Spitsbergen	15,060
Traill, Greenland	1,300
Victoria, NWT-Nun. **(9)**	83,897
Wrangel, Russia	2,800

Atlantic Ocean

Anticosti, Canada	3,068
Ascension, UK	34
Azores, Portugal (tot. group)	868
Faial	67
San Miguel	291
Bahama Isls. (tot. group)	5,382
Andros, Bahamas	2,300
Bermuda Isls., UK (tot. group)	21
Bioko Isl., Equatorial Guinea	785
Block Island, RI, U.S.	21
Canary Islands, Spain (tot. group)	2,807
Fuerteventura	688
Gran Canaria	592
Tenerife	795
Cape Breton, Canada	3,981
Cape Verde Islands	1,557
Caviana, Para, Brazil	1,918
Channel Isls., UK (tot. group)	75
Guernsey	24
Jersey	45
Faroe Islands, Denmark	540
Falkland Isls., UK (tot. group)	4,700
East Falkland	2,550
West Falkland	1,750
Great Britain, UK **(8)**	88,407
Greenland, Denmark **(1)**	840,000
Gurupa, Para, Brazil	1,878
Hebrides, Scotland	2,744
Iceland	39,699
Ireland (tot. group)	32,589
Irish Republic	27,137
Northern Ireland (UK)	5,452
Isle of Man, UK	227
Isle of Wight, England	147
Long Island, NY, U.S.	1,320
Madeira Islands, Portugal	306

Atlantic Ocean

Marajo, Brazil	15,444
Martha's Vineyard, MA, U.S.	89
Mount Desert, ME, U.S.	104
Nantucket, MA, U.S.	45
Newfoundland, Canada	42,031
Orkney Islands, Scotland	390
Prince Edward, Canada	2,185
St. Helena, UK	47
Shetland Islands, Scotland	587
Skye, Scotland	670
South Georgia, UK	1,450
Tierra del Fuego, Chile, Arg.	18,800
Tristan da Cunha, UK	40

Baltic Sea

Aland Islands, Finland	590
Bornholm, Denmark	227
Gotland, Sweden	1,159

Caribbean Sea

Antigua	108
Aruba, Netherlands	75
Barbados	166
Cuba	42,804
Isle of Youth	926
Cayman Islands, UK	100
Curacao, Netherlands	171
Dominica	290
Guadeloupe, France	687
Hispaniola (Haiti and Dominican Rep.)	29,389
Jamaica	4,244
Martinique, France	436
Puerto Rico, U.S.	3,339
Tobago	116
Trinidad	1,864
Virgin Islands, UK	59
Virgin Islands, U.S.	134

East Indies

Bali, Indonesia	2,171
Bangka, Indonesia	4,375
Borneo, Indonesia-Malaysia-Brunei **(3)**	280,100
Bougainville, Papua New Guinea	3,880
Buru, Indonesia	3,670
Celebes, Indonesia	69,000
Flores, Indonesia	5,500
Halmahera, Indonesia	6,865
Java (Jawa), Indonesia	48,900
Madura, Indonesia	2,113
Moluccas, Indonesia	32,307
New Britain, Papua New Guinea	14,093
New Guinea, Indon.-PNG **(2)**	306,000
New Ireland, PNG	3,707
Seram, Indonesia	6,621
Sumba, Indonesia	4,306
Sumbawa, Indonesia	5,965
Sumatra, Indonesia **(6)**	165,000
Timor, Indonesia	13,094
Yos Sudarsa, Indonesia	4,500

Indian Ocean

Andaman Isls., India	2,500
Kerguelen, France	2,247
Madagascar **(4)**	226,658
Mauritius	720
Pemba, Tanzania	380
Reunion, France	970
Seychelles	176
Sri Lanka	25,332
Zanzibar, Tanzania	640

Mediterranean Sea

Balearic Isls., Spain	1,927
Corfu, Greece	229
Corsica, France	3,369
Crete, Greece	3,189
Cyprus	3,572
Elba, Italy	86
Euboea, Greece	1,411
Malta	95
Rhodes, Greece	540
Sardinia, Italy	9,301
Sicily, Italy	9,926

Pacific Ocean

Admiralty, AK, U.S.	1,709
Aleutian Isls., AK, U.S. (tot. group)	6,912
Adak	275
Amchitka	116
Attu	350
Kanaga	142
Kiska	106
Tanaga	195
Umnak	686
Unalaska	1,051
Unimak	1,571
Baranof, AK, U.S.	1,636
Chichagof, AK, U.S.	2,062
Chiloe, Chile	3,241
Christmas, Kiribati	94
Diomede, Big, Russia	11
Easter Isl., Chile	69
Fiji (tot. group)	7,056
Vanua Levu	2,242
Viti Levu	4,109
Galapagos Isls., Ecuador	3,043
Graham Isl., British Columbia	2,456
Guadalcanal, Solomon Isls.	2,180
Guam, U.S.	210
Hainan, China	13,000
Hawaiian Isls., HI, U.S. (tot. group)	6,428
Hawaii	4,028
Oahu	600
Hong Kong, China	31
Hoste, Chile	1,590
Japan (tot. group)	145,850
Hokkaido	30,144
Honshu **(7)**	87,805
Kyushu	14,114
Okinawa	459
Shikoku	7,049
Kangaroo, South Australia	1,680
Kodiak, AK, U.S.	3,485
Kupreanof, AK, U.S.	1,084
Marquesas Isls., France	492
Marshall Isls.	70
Melville, N Terr., Australia	2,240
Micronesia	271
New Caledonia, France	6,530
New Zealand (tot. group)	104,454
Chatham Isls.	372
North	44,204
South	58,384
Stewart	674
North Mariana Isls., U.S.	179
Nunivak, AK, U.S.	1,600
Palau	188
Philippines (tot. group)	115,860
Leyte	2,787
Luzon	40,680
Mindanao	36,775
Mindoro	3,690
Negros	4,907
Palawan	4,554
Panay	4,446
Samar	5,050
Prince of Wales, AK, U.S.	2,770
Revillagigedo, AK, U.S.	1,134
Riesco, Chile	1,973
St. Lawrence, AK, U.S.	1,780
Sakhalin, Russia	29,500
Samoa Isls. (tot. group)	1,177
American Samoa, U.S.	77
Tutuila, U.S.	55
Savail, Samoa	659
Upolu, Samoa	432
Santa Catalina, CA, U.S.	75
Santa Ines, Chile	1,407
Tahiti, France	402
Taiwan, China (tot. group)	13,969
Jinmen Dao (Quemoy)	56
Tasmania, Australia	26,178
Tonga Isls.	290
Vancouver Isl., Brit. Columbia	12,079
Vanuatu	4,707
Wellington, Chile	2,549

Persian Gulf

Bahrain	217

Notable Deserts of the World

Deserts are defined as regions of the Earth receiving less than 10 in. of precipitation annually, usually in combination with an evaporation rate exceeding precipitation.

In addition to areas listed below, the continent of Antarctica, with an area of about 5.4 mil square miles (roughly doubled by ice in winter), is generally considered a desert. Annual precipitation averages 8 in. along the coast and far less in the deep interior; however, there is little evaporation.

Arabian (Eastern), 86,000 sq mi in Egypt between the Nile R. and Red Sea, extending southward into Sudan

Atacama, 600-mi-long area rich in nitrate and copper deposits in N Chile

Chihuahuan, 140,000 sq mi in TX, NM, AZ, and Mexico

Dasht-e Kavir, approx. 500 mi long by approx. 200 mi wide in N central Iran

Dasht-e Lut, approx. 300 mi long by 200 mi wide in S central Iran

Death Valley, 3,300 sq mi in CA and NV

Gibson, 120,000 sq mi in the interior of W Australia

Gobi, 500,000 sq mi in Mongolia and China

Great Sandy, 150,000 sq mi in W Australia

Great Victoria, 150,000 sq mi in SW Australia

Kalahari, 100,000 sq mi in S Africa

Kara Kum, 115,000 sq mi in Turkmenistan

Kyzyl Kum, 115,000 sq mi in Kazakhstan and Uzbekistan

Libyan, 425,000 sq mi in the Sahara, extending from Libya through SW Egypt into Sudan

Mojave, 15,000 sq mi in southern CA

Namib, long narrow area (varies from 30-100 mi wide) extending 800 mi along SW coast of Africa

Nubian, 157,000 sq mi in the Sahara in NE Sudan

Painted Desert, section of high plateau in northern AZ extending 200 mi SE from Grand Canyon

Patagonia, 300,000 sq mi in S Argentina

Rub al-Khali (Empty Quarter), 225,000 sq mi in the S Arabian Peninsula

Sahara, 3,500,000 sq mi in N Africa, extending westward to the Atlantic. Largest desert in the world.

Sonoran, 70,000 sq mi in southwestern AZ and southeastern CA extending into NW Mexico

Syrian, 100,000-sq mi area extending over much of N Saudi Arabia, E Jordan, S Syria, and W Iraq

Taklamakan, 140,000 sq mi in Xinjiang Prov., China

Thar (Great Indian), 100,000-sq-mi arid area extending 400 mi along India-Pakistan border

Areas and Average Depths of Oceans, Seas, and Gulfs

Geographers and mapmakers recognize at least 4 major bodies of water: the Pacific, Atlantic, Indian, and Arctic oceans. The Atlantic and Pacific oceans are considered divided at the equator into the N and S Atlantic and the N and S Pacific. The Arctic Ocean is the name for waters N of the continental landmasses in the region of the Arctic Circle. The International Hydrographic Organization delimited a fifth world ocean in 2000. The Southern Ocean extends from the coast of Antarctica north to 60° south latitude, encompassing portions of the Atlantic, Indian, and Pacific oceans.

Name of area	Area (sq mi)	Avg. depth (ft)	Name of area	Area (sq mi)	Avg. depth (ft)
Pacific Ocean	60,060,869	14,040	Sea of Japan	391,100	5,468
Atlantic Ocean	29,637,962	11,810	Hudson Bay	281,900	305
Indian Ocean	26,469,609	12,800	East China Sea	256,600	620
Southern Ocean	7,848,295	14,450	Andaman Sea	218,100	3,667
Arctic Ocean	5,427,050	4,300	Black Sea	196,100	3,906
South China Sea	1,148,500	4,802	Red Sea	174,900	1,764
Caribbean Sea	971,400	8,448	North Sea	164,900	308
Mediterranean Sea	969,100	4,926	Baltic Sea	147,500	180
Bering Sea	873,000	4,893	Yellow Sea	113,500	121
Gulf of Mexico	582,100	5,297	Persian Gulf	88,800	328
Sea of Okhotsk	537,500	3,192	Gulf of California	59,100	2,375

Principal Ocean Depths

Source: National Imagery and Mapping Agency, U.S. Dept. of Defense

Name of area	Location (lat.)	(long.)	Depth (meters)	(fathoms)	(ft)
Pacific Ocean					
Marianas Trench	11°22′ N	142°36′ E	10,924	5,973	35,840
Tonga Trench	23°16′ S	174°44′ W	10,800	5,906	35,433
Philippine Trench	10°38′ N	126°36′ E	10,057	5,499	32,995
Kermadec Trench	31°53′ S	177°21′ W	10,047	5,494	32,963
Bonin Trench	24°30′ N	143°24′ E	9,994	5,464	32,788
Kuril Trench	44°15′ N	150°34′ E	9,750	5,331	31,988
Izu Trench	31°05′ N	142°10′ E	9,695	5,301	31,808
New Britain Trench	06°19′ S	153°45′ E	8,940	4,888	29,331
Yap Trench	08°33′ N	138°02′ E	8,527	4,663	27,976
Japan Trench	36°08′ N	142°43′ E	8,412	4,600	27,599
Peru-Chile Trench	23°18′ S	71°14′ W	8,064	4,409	26,457
Palau Trench	07°52′ N	134°56′ E	8,054	4,404	26,424
Aleutian Trench	50°51′ N	177°11′ E	7,679	4,199	25,194
New Hebrides Trench	20°36′ S	168°37′ E	7,570	4,139	24,836
North Ryukyu Trench	24°00′ N	126°48′ E	7,181	3,927	23,560
Mid. America Trench	14°02′ N	93°39′ W	6,662	3,643	21,857
Atlantic Ocean					
Puerto Rico Trench	19°55′ N	65°27′ W	8,605	4,705	28,232
S Sandwich Trench	55°42′ S	25°56′ W	8,325	4,552	27,313
Romanche Gap	0°13′ S	18°26′ W	7,728	4,226	25,354
Cayman Trench	19°12′ N	80°00′ W	7,535	4,120	24,721
Brazil Basin	09°10′ S	23°02′ W	6,119	3,346	20,076
Indian Ocean					
Java Trench	10°19′ S	109°58′ E	7,125	3,896	23,376
Ob′ Trench	09°45′ S	67°18′ E	6,874	3,759	22,553
Diamantina Trench	35°50′ S	105°14′ E	6,602	3,610	21,660
Vema Trench	09°08′ S	67°15′ E	6,402	3,501	21,004
Agulhas Basin	45°20′ S	26°50′ E	6,195	3,387	20,325
Arctic Ocean					
Eurasia Basin	82°23′ N	19°31′ E	5,450	2,980	17,881
Mediterranean Sea					
Ionian Basin	36°32′ N	21°06′ E	5,150	2,816	16,896

Note: Greater depths have been reported in some areas but have not been officially confirmed by research vessels.

Principal World Rivers

For N American rivers, see separate table.

River	Source or upper limit of length	Outflow	Length (mi)
Africa			
Chari	Bamingui-Bangoran region, Central African Republic	Lake Chad	650
Congo	Junction of Lualaba and Luava Rivers, Congo	Atlantic Ocean	2,720
Cubango (fmr. Okavango)	Central Angola	Okavango Delta	1,000
Gambia	Fouta Djallon massif, Guinea	Atlantic Ocean	700
Kasai	Central Angola	Congo River	1,100
Limpopo	Junction of Marico and Ngotwane Rivers, South Africa	Indian Ocean	1,100
Lualaba	SE Congo	Congo River	1,100
Niger	Fouta Djallon plateau, Guinea	Gulf of Guinea	2,600
Nile	Luvironza River, Burundi	Mediterranean Sea	4,160
Orange	Maluti mountains, N Lesotho	Atlantic Ocean	1,300
Sénégal	Junction of Bafing and Bakoy Rivers, Mali	Atlantic Ocean	1,000
Ubangi	Junction of Uele and Bomu Rivers, Congo	Congo River	700
Zambezi	NW Zambia	Indian Ocean	1,700
Asia			
Amu Darya	Junction of Wakhsh and Panj Rivers, Tajikistan	Aral Sea	1,660
Amur	Junction of Shilka and Argun Rivers, China-Russia	Tartar Strait	1,780
Angara	Lake Baykal, Russia	Yenisei River	1,150
Ayeyarwady (fmr. Irrawaddy)	Junction of Mali and Nmai Rivers, Myanmar	Andaman Sea	1,000
Brahmaputra	Kailas range, Himalayas, SW Tibet	Bay of Bengal	1,800
Chang-Jiang	Tibetan plateau, SW Qinghai, China	East China Sea	3,450
Euphrates	Junction of Kara (Sarasu) and Murat Rivers, Turkey	Shatt al-Arab	1,700
Ganges	Gangotri glacier, Himalayas, India	Bay of Bengal	1,560
Godavari	W Ghats, Maharashtra, India	Bay of Bengal	900
Hsi (see Xi He)			
Huang-He	Kunlun mountains, Qinghai, China	Yellow Sea	3,000
Indus	Kailas range, Himalayas, Tibet	Arabian Sea	1,900
Irtysh	Kazakhstan-Russia	Ob River	2,650
Jordan	Junction of Dan, Banias, and Hazbani streams, Israel	Dead Sea	200
Kolyma	Kolyma and Cherskogo ranges, Russia	Arctic Ocean	1,500
Krishna	W Ghats, Maharashtra, India	Bay of Bengal	800
Kura	NE Turkey	Caspian Sea	950
Lena	W Baikal range, Russia	Laptev Sea	2,648
Mekong	E Tibetan Plateau, China	South China Sea	2,700
Narmada	Madhya Pradesh, India	Arabian Sea	775
Ob	Junction of Biya and Katun Rivers, Russia	Gulf of Ob	2,300
Salween	E. Tibet, China	Gulf of Martaban	1,750
Songhua Jiang	Changbai mountains, Jilin, China	Amur River	1,150
Sungari (see Songhua Jiang)			
Sutlej	Kailas range, Himalayas, Tibet	Indus River	900
Syr	Junction of Naryn and Kara Darya Rivers, Uzbekistan	Aral Sea	1,380
Tarim	Junction of Kashi and Yarkant Rivers, China	Lop Nor	1,300
Tigris	Taurus mountains, Turkey	Shatt al-Arab	1,150
Xi He	E Yunnan, China	South China Sea	1,250
Yamuna	Uttarkashi dist., Uttar Pradesh, India	Ganges River	850
Yangtze (see Chang-Jiang)			
Yellow (see Huang-He)			
Yenisei	Kyzyl, Tuva Republic, Russia	Kara Sea	2,500
Australia			
Darling	Eastern Highlands, NE New South Wales/SE Queensland	Murray River	1,702
Murray	Australian Alps, SE New South Wales	Indian Ocean	1,609
Murrumbidgee	Australian Alps, SE New South Wales	Murray River	1,050
Europe			
Buh, Southern	NW of Khmel'nyts'kyy, Ukraine	Black Sea	532
Buh, Western	ENE of Zolochiv, Ukraine	Wisla River	500
Danube	Brege and Brigach Rivers, Black Forest, SW Germany	Black Sea	1,770
Dnieper	W of Sychevka, Smolensk, Russia	Black Sea	1,420
Dniester	Carpathian mountains, Ukraine	Black Sea	850
Don	SE of Tula, Russia	Sea of Azov	1,200
Drava	Carnic Alps, N Italy	Danube River	450
Dvina, North	Near Veliki Ustyug, Vologda, Russia	White Sea	465
Dvina, West	Valdai Hills, Russia	Gulf of Riga	635
Ebro	Cantabrian mountains, N Spain	Mediterranean Sea	575
Elbe	Giant mountains, NW Czech Republic	North Sea	725
Garonne	Central Pyrenees, Spain	Bay of Biscay	402
Kama	Ural mountains, N of Kuliga, Russia	Volga River	1,260
Loire	Mt. Gerbier-de-Jonc, Vivrais mountains, France	Atlantic Ocean	630
Marne	Langres plateau, NE France	Seine River	325
Meuse	Langres plateau, NE France	North Sea	560
Oder	Sudetes mountains, NE Czech Republic	Baltic Sea	562
Oka	S of Orël, Russia	Volga River	925
Pechora	N Ural mountains, Russia	Barents Sea	1,120
Po	Cottian Alps, Piedmont, NW Italy	Adriatic Sea	405
Rhine	Swiss Alps	North Sea	820

River	Source or upper limit of length	Outflow	Length (mi)
Rhône.	Rhône glacier, NE Valais, Switzerland.	Mediterranean Sea	505
Seine	Langres Plateau, N Burgundy, France	English Channel	480
Shannon.	Near Cuilcagh Mountain, NW Cavan County, Ireland	Atlantic Ocean	240
Tagus.	E of Madrid, Spain	Atlantic Ocean	585
Thames	4 headstreams in the Cotswold Hills, Gloucestershire, England.	North Sea	210
Tiber.	Etruscan Apennines, Italy	Tyrrhenian Sea.	251
Tisza.	N of Rakhiv, W Ukraine	Danube River.	700
Ural.	S Ural mountains, NE Bashkortostan, Russia	Caspian Sea.	1,580
Volga	Valday Hills, Smolensk, Russia	Caspian Sea.	2,290
Weser.	Junction of Fulda and Werra Rivers, Germany	North Sea	273
Wisla	W Beskid range, Carpathian mountains, SW Poland.	Gulf of Gdansk	665

South America

River	Source or upper limit of length	Outflow	Length (mi)
Amazon	Junction of Ucayali and Marañón Rivers, Andes mountains, Peru	Atlantic Ocean	3,900
Araguaía.	Serra des Araras, Goiás-Mato Grosso, Brazil	Tocantins River.	1,100
Beni	Cordillera Real, La Paz, Bolivia	Madeira River.	1,000
Caquetá-Japura	Andes mountains, SW Colombia	Amazon River.	1,750
Juruá	Cerros de Canchyuaya, E Peru	Amazon River.	1,500
Madeira	Junction of Beni and Mamoré Rivers, Bolivia.	Amazon River.	2,100
Magdalena	Cordillera Central, SW Colombia	Caribbean Sea.	1,000
Negro	SE Colombia	Amazon River.	1,400
Orinoco.	Near Mt. Delgado Chalbaud, Guiana Highlands, S Venezuela	Atlantic Ocean	1,600
Paraguay	Central Mato Grosso highlands, Brazil.	Paraná River.	1,584
Paraná	Junction of Paranaíba and Rio Grande, SE Brazil.	Rio de la Plata	2,485
Pilcomayo.	E of Lake Poopó, Bolivia	Paraguay River.	1,000
Purus	Andes mountains, E Peru	Amazon River.	2,100
Putumayo.	Andes mountains, S Colombia.	Amazon River.	1,000
Rio de la Plata	Estuary of Paraná and Uruguay Rivers, Argentina-Uruguay	Atlantic Ocean	170
São Francisco	Serra de Canastra, SW Minas Gerais, Brazil.	Atlantic Ocean	1,800
Tocantins	S central Goiás, Brazil	Para River.	1,640
Ucayali	Junction of Apurímac and Urubamba Rivers, E Peru	Marañón River	1,000
Uruguay	S Brazil.	Rio de la Plata	1,000
Xingu	Central Mato Grosso, Brazil.	Amazon River.	1,230

Major Rivers in North America

River	Source or upper limit of length	Outflow	Length (mi)
Alabama.	Gilmer County, GA.	Mobile River	729
Albany	Lake St. Joseph, Ontario	James Bay	610
Allegheny	Potter County, PA	Ohio River.	325
Altamaha-Ocmulgee	Junction of Yellow and South Rivers, Newton County, GA	Atlantic Ocean	392
Apalachicola-Chattahoochee.	Towns County, GA.	Gulf of Mexico.	524
Arkansas	Lake County, CO	Mississippi River.	1,459
Assiniboine.	Eastern Saskatchewan	Red River.	450
Attawapiskat.	Attawapiskat, Ontario.	James Bay	465
Back (NWT)	Contwoyto Lake, NWT.	Chantrey Inlet, Arctic Ocean	605
Big Black (MS)	Webster County, MS	Mississippi River.	330
Brazos	Junction of Salt and Double Mountain Forks, Stonewall County, TX.	Gulf of Mexico.	950
Canadian	Las Animas County, CO.	Arkansas River.	906
Cedar (IA)	Dodge County, MN.	Iowa River.	329
Cheyenne.	Junction of Antelope Creek and Dry Fork, Converse County, WY	Missouri River.	290
Churchill, Lab.	Lake Ashuanipi, Newfoundland and Labrador	Atlantic Ocean	532
Churchill, Man.	Methy Lake, Saskatchewan	Hudson Bay	1,000
Cimarron	Colfax County, NM.	Arkansas River.	600
Colorado (AZ).	Rocky Mountain Natl. Park, CO (90 mi in Mexico).	Gulf of California.	1,450
Colorado (TX).	West Texas	Matagorda Bay	862
Columbia	Columbia Lake, British Columbia.	Pacific Ocean, bet. OR and WA.	1,243
Columbia, Upper	Columbia Lake, British Columbia.	Mouth of Snake River	890
Connecticut	Third Connecticut Lake, NH.	Long Island Sound, CT.	407
Coppermine (NWT)	Lac de Gras, NWT	Coronation Gulf, Arctic Ocean.	525
Cumberland	Letcher County, KY	Ohio River.	720
Delaware	Schoharie County, NY	Liston Point, Delaware Bay	390
Fraser.	Near Mount Robson (on Continental Divide)	Strait of Georgia	850
Gila.	Catron County, NM	Colorado River.	649
Green (UT-WY)	Junction of Wells and Trail Creeks, Sublette County, WY.	Colorado River.	730
Hudson	Henderson Lake, Essex County, NY	Upper NY Bay.	306
Illinois.	St. Joseph County, IN	Mississippi River.	420
James (ND-SD)	Wells County, ND.	Missouri River.	710
James (VA)	Junction of Jackson and Cowpasture Rivers, Botetourt County, VA.	Hampton Roads	340
Kanawha-New	Junction of North and South Forks of New River, NC	Ohio River.	352
Kentucky	Junction of North and Middle Forks, Lee County, KY	Ohio River.	259
Klamath	Lake Ewauna, Klamath Falls, OR	Pacific Ocean	250

River	Source or upper limit of length	Outflow	Length (mi)
Kootenay	Kootenay Lake, British Columbia	Columbia River	485
Koyukuk	Endicott Mountains, AK	Yukon River	470
Kuskokwim	Alaska Range	Kuskokwim Bay	724
Liard	Southern Yukon, AK	Mackenzie River	693
Little Missouri	Crook County, WY	Missouri River	560
Mackenzie	Great Slave Lake, NWT	Arctic Ocean	1,060
Milk	Junction of North and South Forks, Alberta	Missouri River	625
Minnesota	Big Stone Lake, MN	Mississippi River	332
Mississippi	Lake Itasca, MN	Gulf of Mexico	2,340
Mississippi-Missouri-Red Rock	Source of Red Rock, Beaverhead Co., MT	Gulf of Mexico	3,710
Missouri	Junction of Jefferson, Madison, and Gallatin Rivers, Gallatin County, MT	Mississippi River	2,315
Missouri-Red Rock	Source of Red Rock, Beaverhead Co., MT	Mississippi River	2,540
Mobile-Alabama-Coosa	Gilmer County, GA	Mobile Bay	774
Nelson (MB)	Lake Winnipeg, Manitoba	Hudson Bay	410
Neosho	Morris County, KS	Arkansas River, OK	460
Niobrara	Niobrara County, WY	Missouri River, NE	431
North Canadian	Union County, NM	Canadian River, OK	800
North Platte	Junction of Grizzly and Little Grizzly Creeks, Jackson County, CO	Platte River, NE	618
Ohio	Junction of Allegheny and Monongahela Rivers, Pittsburgh, PA	Mississippi River	981
Ohio-Allegheny	Potter County, PA	Mississippi River	1,310
Osage	East-central Kansas	Missouri River	500
Ottawa	Lake Capimitchigama, Quebec	St. Lawrence River	790
Ouachita	Polk County, AR	Black River	605
Peace	Junction of Finlay and Parsnip Rivers, BC	Slave River	1,210
Pearl	Neshoba County, MS	Gulf of Mexico	411
Pecos	Mora County, NM	Rio Grande	926
Pee Dee-Yadkin	Watauga County, NC	Winyah Bay	435
Pend Oreille-Clark Fork	Near Butte, MT	Columbia River	531
Platte	Junction of North and South Platte Rivers, NE	Missouri River	310
Porcupine	Ogilvie Mountains, AK	Yukon River, AK	569
Potomac	Garrett County, MD	Chesapeake Bay	383
Powder	Junction of South and Middle Forks, WY	Yellowstone River	375
Red (OK-TX-LA)	Curry County, NM	Mississippi River	1,290
Red River of the North	Junction of Otter Tail and Bois de Sioux Rivers, Wilkin County, MN	Lake Winnipeg	545
Republican	Junction of North Fork and Arikaree River, NE	Kansas River	445
Rio Grande	San Juan County, CO	Gulf of Mexico	1,900
Roanoke	Junction of N and S Forks, Montgomery Co., VA	Albemarle Sound	380
Rock (IL-WI)	Dodge County, WI	Mississippi River	300
Sabine	Junction of S and Caddo Forks, Hunt County, TX	Sabine Lake	380
Sacramento	Siskiyou County, CA	Suisun Bay	377
St. Francis	Iron County, MO	Mississippi River	425
St. John	Northwestern Maine	Bay of Fundy	418
St. Lawrence	Lake Ontario, Ontario-NY	Gulf of St. Lawrence, Atlantic Ocean	800
Saguenay	Lake St. John, Quebec	St. Lawrence River	434
Salmon (ID)	Custer County, ID	Snake River	420
San Joaquin	Junction of S and Middle Forks, Madera Co., CA	Suisun Bay	350
San Juan	Silver Lake, Archuleta County, CO	Colorado River	360
Santee-Wateree-Catawba	McDowell County, NC	Atlantic Ocean	538
Saskatchewan, North	Rocky Mountains, Alberta	Saskatchewan R.	800
Saskatchewan, South	Rocky Mountains, Alberta	Saskatchewan R.	865
Savannah	Junction of Seneca and Tugaloo Rivers, Anderson County, SC	Atlantic Ocean, GA-SC	314
Severn (ON)	Sandy Lake, Ontario	Hudson Bay	610
Smoky Hill	Cheyenne County, CO	Kansas River, KS	540
Snake	Teton County, WY	Columbia River, WA	1,038
South Platte	Junction of S and Middle Forks, Park County, CO	Platte River	424
Susitna	Alaska Range	Cook Inlet	313
Susquehanna	Huyden Creek, Otsego County, NY	Chesapeake Bay	447
Tallahatchie	Tippah County, MS	Yazoo River	301
Tanana	Wrangell Mountains, AK	Yukon River	659
Tennessee	Junction of French Broad and Holston Rivers, TN	Ohio River	652
Tennessee-French Broad	Courthouse Creek, Transylvania County, NC	Ohio River	886
Tombigbee	Prentiss County, MS	Mobile River	525
Trinity	North of Dallas, TX	Galveston Bay	360
Wabash	Darke County, OH	Ohio River	512
Washita	Hemphill County, TX	Red River, OK	500
White (AR-MO)	Madison County, AR	Mississippi River	722
Willamette	Douglas County, OR	Columbia River	309
Wind-Bighorn	Junction of Wind and Little Wind Rivers, Fremont Co., WY (Source of Wind R. is Togwotee Pass, Teton Co., WY)	Yellowstone River	338
Wisconsin	Lac Vieux Desert, Vilas County, WI	Mississippi River	430
Yellowstone	Park County, WY	Missouri River	682
Yukon	McNeil R., Yukon	Bering Sea	1,979

Major Natural Lakes of the World

Source: Geological Survey, U.S. Dept. of the Interior; GeoAccess Division, Natural Resources Canada

A lake is generally defined as a body of water surrounded by land. By this definition some bodies of water that are called seas, such as the Caspian Sea and the Aral Sea, are really lakes. In the following table, the word *lake* is omitted when it is part of the name.

Name	Continent	Area (sq mi)	Length (mi)	Maximum depth (ft)	Elevation (ft)
Caspian Sea[1]	Asia-Europe	143,244	760	3,363	−92
Superior	North America	31,700	350	1,330	600
Victoria	Africa	26,828	250	270	3,720
Huron	North America	23,000	206	750	579
Michigan	North America	22,300	307	923	579
Aral Sea[1]	Asia	13,000[2]	260	180	125
Tanganyika	Africa	12,700	420	4,823	2,534
Baykal	Asia	12,162	395	5,315	1,493
Great Bear	North America	12,096	192	1,463	512
Nyasa (Malawi)	Africa	11,150	360	2,280	1,550
Great Slave	North America	11,031	298	2,015	513
Erie	North America	9,910	241	210	570
Winnipeg	North America	9,417	266	200	713
Ontario	North America	7,340	193	802	245
Balkhash[1]	Asia	7,115	376	85	1,115
Ladoga	Europe	6,835	124	738	13
Maracaibo	South America	5,217	133	115	sea level
Onega	Europe	3,710	145	328	108
Eyre[1]	Australia	3,600[3]	90	4	−52
Titicaca	South America	3,200	122	922	12,500
Nicaragua	North America	3,100	102	230	102
Athabasca	North America	3,064	208	407	700
Reindeer	North America	2,568	143	720	1,106
Tonle Sap	Asia	2,500[3]	70	45	NA
Turkana (Rudolf)	Africa	2,473	154	240	1,230
Issyk Kul[1]	Asia	2,355	115	2,303	5,279
Torrens[1]	Australia	2,230[3]	130	(3)	92
Vanern	Europe	2,156	91	328	144
Nettilling	North America	2,140	67	(3)	95
Winnipegosis	North America	2,075	141	38	830
Albert	Africa	2,075	100	168	2,030
Nipigon	North America	1,872	72	540	1,050
Gairdner[1]	Australia	1,840[3]	90	(3)	112
Urmia[1]	Asia	1,815	90	49	4,180
Manitoba	North America	1,799	140	21	813
Chad	Africa	500+[4]	175	24	787

NA = Not available (1) Salt lake. (2) The diversion of feeder rivers since the 1960s has devastated the Aral—once the world's 4th-largest lake (26,000 sq miles). By 2000, the Aral had effectively become three lakes, with the total area shown. (3) Subject to great seasonal variation. (4) Once 4th-largest lake in Africa (about 10,000 sq mi in the 1960s), Chad had shrunk to around 5% of its original size as of 2006 as a result of irrigation and long-term drought.

The Great Lakes

Source: National Ocean Service, U.S. Dept. of Commerce

The Great Lakes form the world's **largest body of fresh water** (in surface area), and with their connecting waterways are the largest inland water transportation unit. Draining the great North Central basin of the U.S., they enable shipping to reach the Atlantic via their outlet, the St. Lawrence R., and to reach the Gulf of Mexico via the Illinois Waterway, from Lake Michigan to the Mississippi R. A 3rd outlet connects with the Hudson R. and then the Atlantic via the New York State Barge Canal System. Traffic on the Illinois Waterway and the N.Y. State Barge Canal System is limited to recreational boating and small shipping vessels.

Only one of the lakes, Lake Michigan, is wholly in the U.S.; the others are shared with Canada. Ships move from the shores of Lake Superior to Whitefish Bay at the E end of the lake, then through the Soo locks, in Sault Ste. Marie, MI, through the St. Mary's R. and into Lake Huron. To reach Gary and the Port of Indiana and South Chicago, IL, ships move W from Lake Huron to Lake Michigan through the Straits of Mackinac. Lake Superior is 601 ft above low water datum at Rimouski, Quebec, on the International Great Lakes Datum (1985). From Duluth, MN, to the E end of Lake Ontario is 1,156 mi.

	Superior	Michigan	Huron	Erie	Ontario
Length in mi	350	307	206	241	193
Breadth in mi	160	118	183	57	53
Deepest soundings in ft	1,333	923	750	210	802
Volume of water in cu mi	2,935	1,180	850	116	393
Area (sq mi) water surface—U.S.	20,600	22,300	9,100	4,980	3,460
Canada	11,100	NA	13,900	4,930	3,880
Area (sq mi) entire drainage basin—U.S.	16,900	45,600	16,200	18,000	15,200
Canada	32,400	NA	35,500	4,720	12,100
TOTAL AREA (sq mi) U.S. and Canada	**81,000**	**67,900**	**74,700**	**32,630**	**34,850**
Low water datum above mean water level at Rimouski, Quebec, avg. level in ft (1985)	601.10	577.50	577.50	569.20	243.30
Latitude, N	46°25′	41°37′	43°00′	41°23′	43°11′
	49°00′	46°06′	46°17′	42°52′	44°15′
Longitude, W	84°22′	84°45′	79°43′	78°51′	76°03′
	92°06′	88°02′	84°45′	83°29′	79°53′
National boundary line in mi	282.8	None	260.8	251.5	174.6
United States shoreline (mainland only) mi	863	1,400	580	431	300

NA = Not applicable.

Famous Waterfalls

Source: National Geographic Society

The earth has thousands of waterfalls, some of considerable magnitude. Their magnitude is determined not only by height but also by volume of flow, steadiness of flow, crest width, whether the water drops sheerly or over a sloping surface, and whether it descends in one leap or in a succession of leaps. A series of low falls flowing over a considerable distance is known as a **cascade**.

Estimated mean annual flow, in cubic feet per second, of major waterfalls is as follows: Niagara, 212,200; Paulo Afonso, 100,000; Urubupunga, 97,000; Iguazu, 61,000; Patos-Maribondo, 53,000; Victoria, 35,400; and Kaieteur, 23,400.

Height = total drop in feet in one or more leaps. # = falls of more than one leap; * = falls that diminish greatly seasonally; ** = falls that reduce to a trickle or are dry for part of each year. If the river names are not shown, they are same as the falls. R. = river; (C) = cascade.

Name, location	Height (ft)
Africa	
Angola	
Ruacana, Cunene R.	406
Lesotho	
Maletsunyane*	630
Zimbabwe-Zambia	
Victoria, Zambezi R.*	343
South Africa	
Augrabies, Orange R.*	480
Tugela#	2,800
Tanzania-Zambia	
Kalambo*	704
Asia	
India	
Kaveri*	320
Gersoppa, Sharavati R.*	830
Japan	
Kegon, L. Chuzenji*	350
Australia	
New South Wales	
Wentworth	614
Wollomombi	722
Queensland	
Tully**	984
Wallaman, Stony Cr.#	1,137
New Zealand	
Helena	722
Sutherland, Arthur R.#	1,904
Europe	
Austria	
Gastein#	487
Krimml#	1,246
France	
Gavarnie*	1,385
Great Britain	
Scotland	
Glomach	370
Wales	
Pistyll Rhaeadr	240
Italy	
Toce (C)	470

Name, location	Height (ft)
Norway	
Mardalsfossen#**	2,154
Skykje**	984
Vetti, Morka-Koldedola R.	900
Sweden	
Handol#	345
Switzerland	
Giessbach (C)	984
Reichenbach#	820
Staubbach	984
Trümmelbach#	1,312
North America	
Canada	
Alberta	
Panther, Nigel Cr.	600
British Columbia	
Della#	1,444
Takakkaw, Daly Glacier#	833
Quebec	
Montmorency	276
Canada-United States	
Niagara (American)	194
Niagara (Horseshoe)	187
United States	
Alabama	
Noccalula Falls	90
California	
Feather*	640
Yosemite National Park	
Bridalveil*	620
Illilouette*	370
Nevada, Merced R.*	594
Ribbon**	1,612
Silver Strand, Meadow Br.**	574
Vernal, Merced R.*	317
Yosemite#**	2,425
Colorado	
Seven Falls, S. Cheyenne Cr.#	300
Hawaii	
Akaka, Kolekole Str.	420
Idaho	
Shoshone, Snake R.**	212

Name, location	Height (ft)
Kentucky	
Cumberland	68
Maryland	
Great, Potomac R. (C)*	76
Minnesota	
Minnehaha**	53
New Jersey	
Passaic	70
New York	
Taughannock*	215
Oregon	
Multnomah#	850
Tennessee	
Fall Creek	256
Washington	
Sluiskin, Paradise R.	300
Snoqualmie**	268
Wisconsin	
Big Manitou, Black R. (C)*	165
Wyoming	
Tower	132
Yellowstone (upper)*	109
Yellowstone (lower)*	308
South America	
Argentina-Brazil	
Iguazú	269
Brazil	
Cachoeira da Fumaça*	1,312
Paulo Afonso, São Francisco R.	275
Colombia	
Tequendama, Bogota R.*	482
Ecuador	
Agoyan, Pastaza R.*	200
Guyana	
Kaieteur, Potaro R.	741
King George VI, Kamarang R.	1,600
Marina, Ipobe R.#	500
Venezuela	
Angel#*	3,212
Cuquenan	2,000

Latitude, Longitude, and Altitude of U.S. and Canadian Cities

Source: U.S. geographic positions, U.S. altitudes provided by Geological Survey, U.S. Dept. of the Interior. Canadian geographic positions and altitudes provided by Natural Resources Canada.

City, State/Province	Lat. N °	′	″	Long. W °	′	″	Elev. (ft)
Abilene, TX	32	26	55	99	43	58	1,718
Akron, OH	41	4	53	81	31	9	1,050
Albany, NY	42	39	9	73	45	24	20
Albuquerque, NM	35	5	4	106	39	2	4,955
Alert, N.W.T.	82	30	0	62	22	0	100
Allentown, PA	40	36	30	75	29	26	350
Amarillo, TX	35	13	19	101	49	51	3,685
Anchorage, AK	61	13	5	149	54	1	101
Ann Arbor, MI	42	16	15	83	43	35	880
Asheville, NC	35	36	3	82	33	15	2,134
Ashland, KY	38	28	42	82	38	17	558
Atlanta, GA	33	44	56	84	23	17	1,050
Atlantic City, NJ	39	21	51	74	25	24	8
Augusta, GA	33	28	15	81	58	30	414
Augusta, ME	44	18	38	69	46	48	45
Austin, TX	30	16	1	97	44	34	501
Bakersfield, CA	35	22	24	119	1	4	408
Baltimore, MD	39	17	25	76	36	45	100
Bangor, ME	44	48	4	68	46	42	158
Baton Rouge, LA	30	27	2	91	9	16	53
Battle Creek, MI	42	19	16	85	10	47	820
Bay City, MI	43	35	40	83	53	20	595
Beaumont, TX	30	5	9	94	6	6	20
Belleville, Ont.	44	14	0	77	21	0	320
Bellingham, WA	48	45	35	122	29	13	100

City, State/Province	Lat. N °	′	″	Long. W °	′	″	Elev. (ft)
Berkeley, CA	37	52	18	122	16	18	150
Billings, MT	45	47	0	108	30	0	3,124
Biloxi, MS	30	23	45	88	53	7	25
Binghamton, NY	42	5	55	75	55	6	865
Birmingham, AL	33	31	14	86	48	9	600
Bismarck, ND	46	48	30	100	47	0	1,700
Bloomington, IL	40	29	3	88	59	37	829
Boise, ID	43	36	49	116	12	9	2,730
Boston, MA	42	21	30	71	3	37	20
Bowling Green, KY	36	59	25	86	26	37	510
Brandon, Man.	49	54	35	99	57	03	1,343
Brantford, Ont.	43	08	0	80	16	0	815
Brattleboro, VT	42	51	3	72	33	30	240
Bridgeport, CT	41	10	1	73	12	19	10
Brockton, MA	42	5	0	71	1	8	112
Buffalo, NY	42	53	11	78	52	43	585
Burlington, Ont.	43	23	10	79	50	15	640
Burlington, VT	44	28	33	73	12	45	113
Butte, MT	46	0	14	112	32	2	5,549
Calgary, Alta.	51	03	0	114	05	0	3,557
Cambridge, MA	42	22	30	71	6	22	30
Canton, OH	40	47	56	81	22	43	1,100
Carson City, NV	39	9	50	119	45	59	4,730
Cedar Rapids, IA	42	0	30	91	38	38	730
Central Islip, NY	40	47	26	73	12	8	88

City, State/Province	Lat. N °	'	"	Long. W °	'	"	Elev. (ft)	City, State/Province	Lat. N °	'	"	Long. W °	'	"	Elev. (ft)
Champaign, IL	40	6	59	88	14	36	740	Kenosha, WI	42	35	5	87	49	16	610
Charleston, SC	32	46	35	79	55	52	118	Key West, FL	24	33	19	81	46	58	8
Charleston, WV	38	20	59	81	37	58	606	Kingston, Ont.	44	18	0	76	28	0	305
Charlotte, NC	35	13	37	80	50	36	850	Kitchener, Ont.	43	27	0	80	29	0	1,040
Charlottetown, P.E.I.	46	14	25	63	08	05	160	Knoxville, TN	35	57	38	83	55	15	889
Chattanooga, TN	35	2	44	85	18	35	685								
Cheyenne, WY	41	8	24	104	49	11	6,067	Lafayette, IN	40	25	0	86	52	31	567
Chicago, IL	41	51	0	87	39	0	596	Lancaster, PA	40	2	16	76	18	21	368
Churchill, Man.	58	43	30	94	07	0	94	Lansing, MI	42	43	57	84	33	20	830
Cincinnati, OH	39	9	43	84	27	25	683	Laredo, TX	27	30	22	99	30	26	414
Cleveland, OH	41	29	58	81	41	44	690	Las Vegas, NV	36	10	30	115	8	11	2,000
Colorado Springs, CO	38	50	2	104	49	15	6,008	Lawrence, MA	42	42	25	71	9	49	50
Columbia, MO	38	57	6	92	20	2	758	Lethbridge, Alta.	49	42	0	112	49	0	3,047
Columbia, SC	34	0	2	81	2	6	314	Lexington, KY	37	59	19	84	28	40	955
Columbus, GA	32	27	39	84	59	16	300	Lihue, HI	21	58	52	159	22	16	206
Columbus, OH	39	57	40	82	59	56	800	Lima, OH	40	44	33	84	6	19	875
Concord, NH	43	12	29	71	32	17	288	Lincoln, NE	40	48	0	96	40	0	1,150
Corpus Christi, TX	27	48	1	97	23	46	35	Little Rock, AR	34	44	47	92	17	22	350
								London, Ont.	42	59	0	81	14	0	875
Dallas, TX	32	47	0	96	48	0	463	Los Angeles, CA	34	3	8	118	14	34	330
Dawson, Yukon	64	03	45	139	25	50	1,214	Louisville, KY	38	15	15	85	45	34	462
Dayton, OH	39	45	32	84	11	30	750	Lowell, MA	42	38	0	71	19	0	102
Daytona Beach, FL	29	12	38	81	1	23	10	Lubbock, TX	33	34	40	101	51	17	3,195
Decatur, IL	39	50	25	88	57	17	670								
Denver, CO	39	44	21	104	59	3	5,260	Macon, GA	32	50	26	83	37	57	400
Des Moines, IA	41	36	2	93	36	32	803	Madison, WI	43	4	23	89	24	4	863
Detroit, MI	42	19	53	83	2	45	585	Manchester, NH	42	59	44	71	27	19	175
Dodge City, KS	37	45	10	100	1	0	2,550	Marshall, TX	32	32	41	94	22	2	410
Dubuque, IA	42	30	2	90	39	52	620	Medicine Hat, Alta.	50	03	0	110	40	0	2,352
Duluth, MN	46	47	0	92	6	23	610	Memphis, TN	35	8	58	90	2	56	254
Durham, NC	35	59	38	78	53	56	394	Meriden, CT	41	32	17	72	48	27	190
								Miami, FL	25	46	26	80	11	38	11
Eau Claire, WI	44	48	41	91	29	54	850	Milwaukee, WI	43	2	20	87	54	23	634
Edmonton, Alta.	53	33	0	113	28	0	2,200	Minneapolis, MN	44	58	48	93	15	49	815
Elizabeth, NJ	40	39	50	74	12	40	38	Minot, ND	48	13	57	101	17	45	1,555
El Paso, TX	31	45	31	106	29	11	3,695	Mobile, AL	30	41	39	88	2	35	16
Enid, OK	36	23	44	97	52	41	1,246	Moncton, N.B.	46	06	57	64	48	11	232
Erie, PA	42	7	45	80	5	7	650	Montgomery, AL	32	22	0	86	18	0	250
Eugene, OR	44	3	8	123	5	8	419	Montpelier, VT	44	15	36	72	34	33	525
Eureka, CA	40	48	8	124	9	45	44	Montréal, Que.	45	31	0	73	39	0	221
Evansville, IN	37	58	29	87	33	21	388	Moose Jaw, Sask.	50	24	0	105	32	0	1,892
								Muncie, IN	40	11	36	85	23	11	952
Fairbanks, AK	64	50	16	147	42	59	440								
Fall River, MA	41	42	5	71	9	20	200	Nashville, TN	36	9	57	86	47	4	440
Fargo, ND	46	52	38	96	47	22	900	Natchez, MS	31	33	37	91	24	11	230
Flagstaff, AZ	35	11	53	111	39	2	6,900	Newark, NJ	40	44	8	74	10	22	95
Flint, MI	43	0	45	83	41	15	750	New Britain, CT	41	39	40	72	46	48	200
Ft. Smith, AR	35	23	9	94	23	54	446	New Haven, CT	41	18	29	72	55	43	40
Ft. Wayne, IN	41	7	50	85	7	44	781	New Orleans, LA	29	57	16	90	4	30	11
Ft. Worth, TX	32	43	31	97	19	14	670	New York, NY	40	42	51	74	0	23	55
Fredericton, N.B.	45	56	43	66	40	0	67	Niagara Falls, Ont.	43	06	0	79	04	0	589
Fresno, CA	36	44	52	119	46	17	296	Nome, AK	64	30	4	165	24	23	25
								Norfolk, VA	36	50	48	76	17	8	10
Gadsden, AL	34	0	51	86	0	24	554	North Bay, Ont.	46	19	0	79	28	0	1,200
Gainesville, FL	29	39	5	82	19	30	183								
Gallup, NM	35	31	41	108	44	31	6,508	Oakland, CA	37	48	16	122	16	11	42
Galveston, TX	29	18	4	94	47	51	10	Ogden, UT	41	13	23	111	58	23	4,299
Gary, IN	41	35	36	87	20	47	600	Oklahoma City, OK	35	28	3	97	30	58	1,195
Grand Junction, CO	39	3	50	108	33	0	4,597	Omaha, NE	41	15	31	95	56	15	1,040
Grand Rapids, MI	42	57	48	85	40	5	610	Orlando, FL	28	32	17	81	22	46	106
Great Falls, MT	47	30	1	111	18	0	3,334	Ottawa, Ont.	45	16	0	75	45	0	382
Green Bay, WI	44	31	9	88	1	11	594								
Greensboro, NC	36	4	21	79	47	32	770	Paducah, KY	37	5	0	88	36	0	345
Greenville, SC	34	51	9	82	23	39	966	Pasadena, CA	34	8	52	118	8	37	865
Guelph, Ont.	43	33	0	80	15	0	1,100	Paterson, NJ	40	55	0	74	10	20	70
Gulfport, MS	30	22	2	89	5	34	25	Pensacola, FL	30	25	16	87	13	1	32
								Peoria, IL	40	41	37	89	35	20	470
Halifax, N.S.	44	52	0	63	43	0	477	Peterborough, Ont.	44	18	0	78	19	0	628
Hamilton, OH	39	23	58	84	33	41	600	Philadelphia, PA	39	57	8	75	9	51	40
Hamilton, Ont.	43	14	0	79	57	0	780	Phoenix, AZ	33	26	54	112	4	24	1,090
Harrisburg, PA	40	16	25	76	53	5	320	Pierre, SD	44	22	6	100	21	2	1,484
Hartford, CT	41	45	49	72	41	8	40	Pittsburgh, PA	40	26	26	79	59	46	770
Helena, MT	46	35	34	112	2	7	4,090	Pittsfield, MA	42	27	0	73	14	45	1,039
Hilo, HI	19	43	47	155	5	24	38	Pocatello, ID	42	52	17	112	26	41	4,464
Honolulu, HI	21	18	25	157	51	30	18	Pt. Arthur, TX	29	53	55	93	55	43	10
Houston, TX	29	45	47	95	21	47	40	Portland, ME	43	39	41	70	15	21	25
Huntsville, AL	34	43	49	86	35	10	641	Portland, OR	45	31	25	122	40	30	50
								Portsmouth, NH	43	4	18	70	45	47	21
Indianapolis, IN	39	46	6	86	9	29	717	Portsmouth, VA	36	50	7	76	17	55	10
Iowa City, IA	41	39	40	91	31	48	685	Prince Rupert, B.C.	54	19	0	130	19	0	116
								Providence, RI	41	49	26	71	24	48	80
Jackson, MI	42	14	45	84	24	5	940	Provo, UT	40	14	2	111	39	28	4,549
Jackson, MS	32	17	55	90	11	5	294	Pueblo, CO	38	15	16	104	36	31	4,662
Jacksonville, FL	30	19	55	81	39	21	12								
Jersey City, NJ	40	43	41	74	4	41	83	Québec City, Que.	46	49	0	71	13	0	244
Johnstown, PA	40	19	36	78	55	20	1200	Racine, WI	42	43	34	87	46	58	630
Joplin, MO	37	5	3	94	30	47	990	Raleigh, NC	35	46	19	78	38	20	350
Juneau, AK	58	18	7	134	25	11	50	Rapid City, SD	44	4	50	103	13	50	3,247
								Reading, PA	40	20	8	75	55	38	266
Kalamazoo, MI	42	17	30	85	35	14	755	Regina, Sask.	50	27	0	104	37	0	1,894
Kansas City, KS	39	6	51	94	37	38	750								
Kansas City, MO	39	5	59	94	34	42	740								

City, State/Province	Lat. N °	'	"	Long. W °	'	"	Elev. (ft)	City, State/Province	Lat. N °	'	"	Long. W °	'	"	Elev. (ft)
Reno, NV	39	31	47	119	48	46	4,498	Stockton, CA	37	57	28	121	17	23	15
Richmond, VA	37	33	13	77	27	38	190	Sudbury, Ont.	46	31	0	80	54	0	1,140
Roanoke, VA	37	16	15	79	56	30	940	Superior, WI.	46	43	15	92	6	14	642
Rochester, MN	44	1	18	92	28	11	990	Sydney, N.S.	46	09	0	60	11	0	203
Rochester, NY	43	9	17	77	36	57	515	Syracuse, NY	43	2	53	76	8	52	400
Rockford, IL	42	16	16	89	5	38	715								
								Tacoma, WA	47	15	11	122	26	35	380
Sacramento, CA	38	34	54	121	29	36	20	Tallahassee, FL	30	26	17	84	16	51	188
Saginaw, MI	43	25	10	83	57	3	595	Tampa, FL	27	56	50	82	27	31	48
St. Catharines, Ont.	43	10	0	79	15	0	321	Terre Haute, IN	39	28	0	87	24	50	501
St. Cloud, MN	45	33	39	94	9	44	1,040	Texarkana, TX	33	25	30	94	2	51	324
St. John, N.B.	45	15	33	66	02	20	357	Thunder Bay, Ont.	48	24	0	89	19	0	653
St. John's, Nfld.	47	34	0	52	44	0	461	Timmins, Ont.	48	28	0	81	20	0	967
St. Joseph, MO	39	46	7	94	50	47	850	Toledo, OH	41	39	50	83	33	19	615
St. Louis, MO	38	37	38	90	11	52	455	Topeka, KS	39	2	54	95	40	40	1,000
St. Paul, MN	44	56	40	93	5	35	780	Toronto, Ont.	43	37	39	79	23	46	251
St. Petersburg, FL	27	46	14	82	40	46	44	Trenton, NJ	40	13	1	74	44	36	54
Salem, OR	44	56	35	123	2	2	154	Trois-Rivières, Que.	46	21	0	72	33	0	198
Salina, KS	38	50	25	97	36	40	1,225	Troy, NY	42	43	42	73	41	32	35
Salt Lake City, UT	40	45	39	111	53	25	4,266	Tucson, AZ	32	13	18	110	55	33	2,390
San Antonio, TX	29	25	26	98	29	36	650	Tulsa, OK	36	9	14	95	59	33	804
San Bernardino, CA.	34	6	30	117	17	20	1,200								
San Diego, CA	32	42	55	117	9	23	40	Urbana, IL	40	6	38	88	12	26	725
San Francisco, CA.	37	46	30	122	25	6	63	Utica, NY	43	6	3	75	13	59	415
San Jose, CA.	37	20	22	121	53	38	87								
San Juan, P.R.	18	28	6	66	6	22	8	Vancouver, B.C.	49	15	0	123	7	0	14
Santa Barbara, CA	34	25	15	119	41	50	50	Victoria, B.C.	48	26	0	123	22	0	63
Santa Cruz, CA	36	58	27	122	1	47	20								
Santa Fe, NM	35	41	13	105	56	14	6,989	Waco, TX	31	32	57	97	8	47	405
Sarasota, FL	27	20	10	82	31	51	27	Walla Walla, WA	46	3	53	118	20	31	1,000
Saskatoon, Sask.	52	07	0	106	38	0	1,653	Washington, DC	38	53	42	77	2	12	25
Sault Ste. Marie, Ont.	46	31	0	84	20	0	630	Waterloo, IA	42	29	34	92	20	34	850
Savannah, GA	32	5	0	81	6	0	42	West Palm Beach, FL	26	42	54	80	3	13	21
Schenectady, NY.	42	48	51	73	56	24	245	Wheeling, WV	40	3	50	80	43	16	672
Seattle, WA	47	36	23	122	19	51	350	Whitehorse, Yukon	60	43	0	135	03	0	2,305
Sheboygan, WI	43	45	3	87	42	52	630	White Plains, NY	41	2	2	73	45	48	220
Sherbrooke, Que.	45	24	0	71	54	0	792	Wichita, KS	37	41	32	97	20	14	1,305
Sheridan, WY	44	47	50	106	57	20	3,742	Wilkes-Barre, PA	41	14	45	75	52	54	550
Shreveport, LA	32	31	30	93	45	0	209	Wilmington, DE	39	44	45	75	32	49	100
Sioux City, IA	42	30	0	96	24	0	1,117	Wilmington, NC	34	13	32	77	56	42	50
Sioux Falls, SD	43	32	48	96	43	48	1,442	Windsor, Ont.	42	18	0	83	01	0	622
South Bend, IN	41	41	0	86	15	0	725	Winnipeg, Man.	49	54	39	97	14	36	783
Spartanburg, SC	34	56	58	81	55	56	816	Winston-Salem, NC.	36	5	59	80	14	40	912
Spokane, WA	47	39	32	117	25	30	2,000	Worcester, MA	42	15	45	71	48	10	480
Springfield, IL	39	48	6	89	38	37	610								
Springfield, MA	42	6	5	72	35	25	70	Yakima, WA	46	36	8	120	30	17	1,066
Springfield, MO	37	12	55	93	17	53	1,300	Yellowknife, N.W.T.	62	27	20	114	21	0	675
Springfield, OH	39	55	27	83	48	32	1,000	Youngstown, OH	41	5	59	80	38	59	861
Stamford, CT	41	3	12	73	32	21	35	Yuma, AZ	32	43	31	114	37	25	160
Steubenville, OH	40	22	11	80	38	3	1,060	Zanesville, OH	39	56	25	82	0	48	710

Latitude and Longitude of World Cities

Source: National Imagery Mapping Agency, U.S. Dept. of Defense

City, Country	Lat. °	'	Long. °	'	City, Country	Lat. °	'	Long. °	'
Athens, Greece	37	59 N	23	44 E	Moscow, Russia	55	45 N	37	35 E
Bangkok, Thailand	13	45 N	100	31 E	Mumbai (Bombay), India	18	58 N	72	50 E
Beijing, China	39	56 N	116	24 E	New Delhi, India	28	36 N	77	12 E
Berlin, Germany	52	31 N	13	25 E	Panama City, Panama	08	58 N	79	32 W
Bogotá, Colombia	04	36 N	74	05 W	Paris, France	48	52 N	02	20 E
Buenos Aires, Argentina	34	36 S	58	28 W	Quito, Ecuador	00	13 S	78	30 W
Cairo, Egypt	30	03 N	31	15 E	Rio de Janeiro, Brazil	22	43 S	43	13 W
Jakarta, Indonesia	06	10 S	106	48 E	Rome, Italy	41	53 N	12	30 E
Jerusalem, Israel	31	46 N	35	14 E	Santiago, Chile	33	27 S	70	40 W
Johannesburg, South Africa	26	12 S	28	05 E	Seoul, South Korea	37	34 N	127	00 E
Kathmandu, Nepal	27	43 N	85	19 E	Sydney, Australia	33	53 S	151	12 E
Kiev, Ukraine	50	26 N	30	31 E	Tehran, Iran	35	40 N	51	26 E
London, UK (Greenwich)	51	30 N	00	00	Tokyo, Japan	35	42 N	139	46 E
Manila, Philippines	14	35 N	121	00 E	Warsaw, Poland	52	15 N	21	00 E
Mexico City, Mexico	19	24 N	99	09 W	Wellington, New Zealand	41	18 S	174	47 E

Highest and Lowest Continental Altitudes

Source: National Geographic Society

Continent	Highest point	Elev. (ft)	Continent	Lowest point	Ft below sea level
Asia	Mount Everest, Nepal-Tibet	29,035	Asia	Dead Sea, Israel-Jordan	1,348
South America	Mount Aconcagua, Argentina	22,834	South America	Valdes Peninsula, Argentina	131
North America	Mount McKinley, Alaska	20,320	North America	Death Valley, California	282
Africa	Kilimanjaro, Tanzania	19,340	Africa	Lake Assal, Djibouti	512
Europe	Mount Elbrus, Russia	18,510	Europe	Caspian Sea, Russia, Azerbaijan	92
Antarctica	Vinson Massif	16,864	Antarctica	Bentley Subglacial Trench	8,327[1]
Australia	Mount Kosciusko, New South Wales	7,310	Australia	Lake Eyre, South Australia	52

(1) Estimated level of the continental floor. Lower points that have yet to be discovered may exist further beneath the ice.

Membership of Religious Groups in the U.S.

Sources: 2009 *Yearbook of American & Canadian Churches*, © National Council of the Churches of Christ in the USA; World Christian Database; *World Almanac* research

These membership figures are the latest available and generally are based on reports made by officials of each group. Figures from other sources may vary. Many groups keep careful records; others only estimate. Not all groups report annually. Church membership figures vary from one denomination to another, but generally the figures reported in this table are inclusive and do not refer simply to full communicants or confirmed members.

The number of houses of worship appears in parentheses. * indicates that the group declines to make membership figures public. Groups reporting fewer than 5,000 members are not included; where membership numbers are not available, only those groups with 50 or more houses of worship are listed.

Religious group (Houses of Worship)	Members
Adventist Churches	
Advent Christian Ch. (294)	23,629
Ch. of God General Conf. (Oregon, IL/Morrow, GA) (80)	7,000
Seventh-day Adventist Ch. (4,833)	1,000,472
Agnostic (NA)	**33,569,331[1]**
American Catholic Church (Syro-Antiochian) (100)	**30,000[1]**
American Evangelical Christian Chs. (192)	**17,400**
Apostolic Catholic Orthodox Ch. (10)	**8,500**
Apostolic Orthodox Catholic Ch. of N.A. (25)	**15,900**
Apostolic Christian Churches of America (87)	**12,880**
Apostolic Episcopal Church (200)	**12,000**
Apostolic Faith Mission Church of God (18)	**9,120**
Atheist (NA)	**1,175,472[1]**
Baha'i Faith	**456,767[1]**
Baptist Churches	
Alliance of Baptists (127)	65,000
American Baptist Assn. (1,760)	275,000
American Baptist Chs. in the U.S.A. (5,558)	1,358,351
Baptist Bible Fellowship Intl. (4,500)	1,200,000
Baptist General Conference (1,071)	147,500
Baptist Missionary Assn. of America (1,306)	177,463
Conservative Baptist Assn. of America (12,000)	200,000
Free Will Baptists, National Assn. of (2,369)	185,798
General Baptists, General Assn. of (840)	52,279
Natl. Baptist Convention of America, Inc. (NA)	3,500,000
Natl. Baptist Convention, U.S.A., Inc. (9,000)	5,000,000
North American Baptist Conference (272)	47,150
Progressive National Baptist Convention, Inc. (2,000)	2,500,000
Regular Baptist Chs., General Assn. of (1,321)	132,700
Seventh Day Baptist General Conf., USA/Canada (96)	6,200
Southern Baptist Convention (44,696)	16,266,920
Berean Fellowship of Chs. (56)	**12,000**
Brethren in Christ Church (232)	**20,739**
Brethren (German Baptists)	
Brethren Ch. (Ashland, OH) (119)	10,387
Church of the Brethren (1,055)	125,418
Old German Baptist Brethren Ch. (56)	6,229
Buddhists	**2,824,397[1]**
Christian Brethren (Plymouth Brethren) (1,150)	**86,000**
Christian Church (Disciples of Christ) (3,731)	**689,507**
Christian Congregation, Inc. (1,496)	**122,181**
Christian and Missionary Alliance (2,009)	**420,006**
Christian Union (NA)	6,034
Churches of Christ in Christian Union (227)	**11,164**
Church of Christ (Holiness) U.S.A. (148)	**11,468**
Church of Christ, Scientist (2,240)	**865,000[1]**
Church of the Living God (170)	**42,000**
Church of the United Brethren in Christ, USA (215)	**23,000**
Churches of Christ (13,000)	**1,639,495**
Christian Chs. and Chs. of Christ (5,579)	1,071,616
Churches of God	
Chs. of God, General Conference (321)	33,083
Ch. of God (Anderson, IN) (2,248)	252,905
Ch. of God (Seventh Day), Denver, CO (200)	11,000
Ch. of God by Faith, Inc. (149)	35,000
Ch. of God, Mountain Assembly, Inc. (120)	7,200
Church of the Nazarene (5,096)	**642,523**
Community Churches, Intl. Council of (155)	**73,174**
Natl. Assn. of Congregational Christian Chs. (432)	**65,392**
Conservative Congregational Christian Conf. (284)	**41,772**
Eastern Catholic Churches	
Armenian Catholic Church (9)	36,000
Chaldean Catholic Church (14)	120,000
Maronite Catholic Church (59)	75,232
Melkite Catholic Church (35)	27,207
Romanian Greek Catholic Church (15)	5,000
Ruthenian Byzantine Catholic Church (223)	99,288
Syrian Catholic Church (12)	13,270
Syro-Malabar Catholic Church (8)	100,000
Ukranian Greek Catholic Church (200)	102,632

Religious group (Houses of Worship)	Members
Eastern Orthodox Churches	
American Carpatho-Russian Orthodox Greek Catholic Ch. (78)	14,011
Antiochian Orthodox Christian Archdiocese of North America (256)	430,000
Armenian Apostolic Ch. of America (36)	360,000
Armenian Apostolic Ch., Dioceses of America (72)	650,000
Coptic Orthodox Ch. (100)	300,000
Greek Orthodox Archdiocese of America (560)	1,500,000
Malankara Orthodox Syrian Ch., Diocese of America (80)	30,000
Mar Thoma Syrian Ch. of India (74)	40,000
Orthodox Ch. in America (737)	1,064,000
Patriarchal Parishes of the Russian Orthodox Ch. in the U.S.A. (31)	17,000
Russian Orthodox Ch. Outside of Russia (190)	480,000
Serbian Orthodox Ch. in the U.S.A. and Canada (68)	67,000
Syrian (Syriac) Orthodox Ch. of Antioch (31)	32,500
Syro-Russian Orthodox Catholic Ch. (180)	26,200
Ukrainian Orthodox Ch. of the U.S.A. (118)	50,000
Episcopal Church (7,055)	**2,116,749**
Ethnoreligionists	**1,422,825[1]**
Evangelical Church Alliance (NA)	**293,375**
Evangelical Congregational Church (139)	**19,339**
Evangelical Covenant Church (783)	**114,283**
Evangelical Free Church of America (1,420)	**350,000**
Friends	
Evangelical Friends Intl. – North American Region (281)	38,844
Friends General Conference (832)	32,000
Friends United Meeting (611)	43,647
Philadelphia Yearly Meeting of the Religious Society of Friends (104)	11,681
Religious Society of Friends (Conservative) (1,200)	104,000
Full Gospel Fellowship of Churches and Ministers Intl. (1,273)	**432,632**
General Church of the New Jerusalem (37)	**6,760**
Hindus	**1,337,734[1]**
Independent Fundamental Churches of America Intl. Inc. (IFCA) (659)	**61,655**
Jains	**79,459[1]**
Jehovah's Witnesses (12,487)	**1,092,169**
Jews	**5,302,245[1]**
Jewish Organizations[2]	
Union for Reform Judaism (900+)	1,500,000
Union of Orthodox Jewish Congregations of America (1,000)	*
The United Synagogue of Conservative Judaism (760)	1,500,000
Jewish Reconstructionist Federation (103)	180,000
Latter-Day Saints	
Ch. of Jesus Christ of Latter-day Saints (13,201)	5,873,408
Community of Christ (935)	178,328
Reorg. Ch. of Jesus Christ of Latter-Day Saints (1,350)	247,000[1]
Liberal Catholic Church (Intl.) (11)	**6,500**
The Liberal Catholic Church—Province of the United States of America (21)	**5,800**
Lutheran Churches	
American Assn. of Lutheran Chs. (70)	16,000
Apostolic Lutheran Ch. of America (58)	7,500[1]
Ch. of the Lutheran Brethren of America (110)	14,427
Ch. of the Lutheran Confession (87)	8,390
Evangelical Lutheran Ch. in America (10,448)	4,709,956
Evangelical Lutheran Synod (131)	19,945
Free Lutheran Congregations, Assn. of (274)	43,428
Independent Evangelical Lutheran Chs., Assn of (35)	6,318
Latvian Evangelical Lutheran Ch. in America (60)	12,100
Lutheran Ch.—Missouri Synod (LCMS) (6,167)	2,383,084
Wisconsin Evangelical Lutheran Synod (1,276)	394,241
Mennonite Churches	
Beachy Amish Mennonite Chs. (207)	11,487
Ch. of God in Christ (Mennonite) (141)	14,262
Fellowship of Evangelical Chs. (42)	6,621
Hutterian Brethren (444)	43,000
Mennonite Ch. USA (935)	109,174
Old Order Amish Ch. (898)	80,820
Old Order (Wisler) Mennonite Church (47)	7,100

Religious group (Houses of Worship)	Members
Methodist Churches	
African Methodist Episcopal Ch. (4,174)	2,500,000
African Methodist Episcopal Zion Ch. (3,337)	1,400,000
Christian Methodist Episcopal Ch. (3,500)	850,000
Evangelical Methodist Ch. (108)	7,348
Free Methodist Ch. of North America (1,030)	75,150
Primitive Methodist Ch. in the U.S.A. (72)	3,984
Southern Methodist Ch. (101)	6,000
United Methodist Ch. (34,398)	7,931,733
Wesleyan Ch. (1,626)	138,164
Messianic Jews	**c. 75,000**
Metropolitan Community Churches, Universal	
Fellowship of (115)	**15,666**
Missionary Church (423)	**43,026**
Moravian Church in America (Northern Prov.) (88)	**21,987**
Muslims	**4,745,054[1]**
National Organization of the New Apostolic Church	
of North America (314)	**38,778**
Old Catholic Orthodox Ch. (11)	**11,470**
Pentecostal Churches	
Apostolic Faith Mission Ch. of God (18)	9,120
Assemblies of God (12,362)	2,863,265
Bible Fellowship Ch. (60)	7,605
Ch. of God (Cleveland, Tennessee) (6,588)	1,053,642
Ch. of God in Christ (15,300)	5,499,875
Ch. of God of Prophecy (1,860)	89,674
Congregational Holiness Ch. (225)	25,000
Elim Assemblies Fellowship (220)	37,000[1]
Intl. Ch. of the Foursquare Gospel (1,875)	353,995
Intl. Pentecostal Holiness Ch. (2,010)	320,135
Open Bible Standard Chs. (302)	45,000
Pentecostal Assemblies of the World, Inc. (1,750)	1,500,000
Pentecostal Ch. of God (1,158)	90,030

Religious group (Houses of Worship)	Members
Pentecostal Free Will Baptist Ch., Inc. (200)	20,000[1]
United House of Prayer (150)	1,515,000[1]
United Pentecostal Ch. Intl. (4,358)	646,304
United Pentecostal Chs. of Christ (62)	7,059
Polish National Catholic Ch. of America (126)	**60,000**
Presbyterian Churches	
Associate Reformed Presbyterian Ch. (General	
Synod) (283)	44,988
Cumberland Presbyterian Ch. (730)	78,451
Evangelical Presbyterian Ch. (207)	89,190
Korean Presbyterian Ch. in America, General	
Assembly of the (302)	55,000
Orthodox Presbyterian Ch. (263)	28,780
Presbyterian Ch. in America (1,645)	340,736
Presbyterian Ch. (U.S.A.) (10,820)	2,941,412
Reformed Presbyterian Ch. of North America (80)	6,347
Reformed Catholic Ch. (100)	**57,000**
Reformed Churches	
Christian Reformed Ch. in North America (776)	191,000
Hungarian Reformed Ch. in America (27)	6,000
Netherlands Reformed Congregations (28)	10,080
Protestant Reformed Chs. in America (29)	7,630
Reformed Ch. in America (891)	264,863
United Church of Christ (5,377)	1,145,281
Reformed Episcopal Church (142)	**11,281**
Roman Catholic Church (18,479)	**67,117,016**
Romanian Orthodox Church in America (30)	**9,000**
Salvation Army (1,438)	**413,028**
Shintoists	**60,560[1]**
Sikhs	**269,862[1]**
Vineyard Chs., Assn. of (592)	**188,000**
Unitarian Universalist Assn. of Congregations	
(1,046)	**221,476**

(1) Source: World Christian Database. (2) From American Jewish Committee.

Adherents of All Religions by Six Continental Areas, Mid-2007

Source: *2008 Encyclopædia Britannica Book of the Year; figures rounded*

Religion (No. of countries)	Africa	Asia	Europe	Latin America	Northern America	Oceania	World
Baha'is (219)	2,135,000	3,677,000	139,000	891,000	718,000	137,000	7,697,000
Buddhists (136)	158,000	379,080,000	1,775,000	743,000	3,288,000	565,000	385,609,000
Chinese Universists (96)	37,500	384,206,000	309,000	183,000	740,000	146,000	385,621,500
Christians (239)	441,184,000	359,614,000	565,254,700	533,386,000	273,388,400	26,990,300	2,199,817,400
Roman Catholics (236)	155,246,000	127,074,000	274,865,000	472,317,000	83,377,000	8,637,000	1,121,516,000
Independents (222)	96,011,000	189,463,000	24,252,000	46,013,000	75,627,000	1,730,000	433,096,000
Protestants (233)	125,152,000	59,201,000	70,345,000	58,130,000	61,077,000	7,906,000	381,811,000
Orthodox (136)	40,651,000	13,700,000	170,468,000	973,000	6,524,000	830,000	233,146,000
Anglicans (165)	47,036,000	845,000	26,070,000	853,000	2,836,000	4,946,000	82,586,000
Marginal (215)	3,615,000	3,310,000	4,523,000	11,526,000	11,755,000	692,000	35,421,000
Unaffiliated (232)	25,252,000	5,628,000	24,428,700	6,004,000	53,937,400	4,249,300	119,499,400
Doubly affiliated (181)	*-51,779,000*	*-39,607,000*	*-29,697,000*	*-62,430,000*	*-21,745,000*	*-2,000,000*	*-207,258,000*
Confucianists (15)	300	6,373,000	18,000	800	0	52,200	6,444,300
Ethnic religionists (145)	113,605,000	145,997,000	1,152,000	3,733,000	1,579,000	339,000	266,405,000
Hindus (126)	2,757,000	868,348,000	1,680,000	760,000	1,715,000	466,000	875,726,000
Jains (11)	82,400	5,173,000	0	0	8,400	700	5,264,500
Jews (135)	129,000	5,718,000	1,840,000	971,000	6,191,000	107,000	14,956,000
Muslims (210)	378,135,700	961,961,000	39,691,800	1,777,000	5,450,600	438,400	1,387,454,500
Neoreligionists (107)	123,000	103,548,000	380,000	800,000	1,594,000	88,300	106,533,300
Shintoists (8)	0	2,732,000	0	7,600	61,800	0	2,801,400
Sikhs (44)	62,900	21,701,000	478,000	6,600	630,000	49,000	22,927,500
Spiritists (56)	3,200	2,000	139,000	13,193,000	164,000	7,400	13,508,600
Taoists (5)	0	3,392,000	0	0	12,200	0	3,404,200
Zoroastrians (24)	1,000	152,000	5,500	0	20,600	1,700	180,800
Other religionists (79)	80,000	75,000	260,000	110,000	670,000	10,000	1,205,000
Nonreligious (238)	6,246,000	615,877,000	94,750,000	17,092,000	38,821,000	4,040,000	776,826,000
Atheists (220)	606,000	128,048,000	19,787,000	2,829,000	1,779,000	416,000	153,465,000

Note: Continental Areas. Following current UN demographic terminology, which divides the world into the 6 major areas shown above. Note that "Asia" includes the former Soviet Central Asian states and "Europe" includes all of Russia, extending eastward to the Pacific. **Countries.** Numbers in parentheses are sovereign and nonsovereign countries in which each religion has a statistically significant and organized following. **Adherents.** As defined in the 1948 Universal Declaration of Human Rights, a person's religion is what he or she says it is. Totals are enumerated following the methodology of the *World Christian Encyclopedia*, 2nd ed. (2001) and *World Christian Trends* (2001), using recent censuses, polls, literature, and other data. Totals may conflict with some estimates for total populations. **Buddhists.** 56% Mahayana, 38% Theravada (Hinayana), 6% Tantrayana (Lamaism). **Chinese Universists.** Followers of traditional Chinese religion (may include worship of local deities, ancestor veneration, Confucian ethics, universism, divination, and some Buddhist elements, among other beliefs and practices). **Christians.** Followers of Jesus Christ. Unaffiliated Christians profess Christian beliefs but are not named on specific church rolls; Independents follow Christian churches and networks that regard themselves as independent from historic, mainstream Christianity; Marginal Christians belong to churches on the margins of mainstream Christianity, including Unitarians, Mormons, Jehovah's Witnesses, Christian Science, and Religious Science; Doubly-affiliated Christians are baptized members of two denominations. **Confucianists.** Non-Chinese followers of Confucius and Confucianism, mostly Koreans in Korea. **Ethnic religionists.** Followers of local, tribal, animistic, or shamanistic religions, with members restricted to one ethnic group. **Hindus.** 68% Vaishnavites, 27% Shaivites, 2% neo-Hindus and reform Hindus. **Jews.** Adherents of Judaism. **Muslims.** 84% Sunni Muslims, 14% Shia Muslims (Shi'ites), 2% other schools. **Neoreligionists.** Followers of Asian 20th-cent. New Religions, New Religious movements, radical new crisis religions, and non-Christian syncretistic mass religions. **Other religionists.** Including a handful of religions, quasi-religions, pseudoreligions, pararreligions, religious or mystic systems, and religious and semireligious brotherhoods of numerous varieties.

Episcopal Church Liturgical Colors and Calendar, 2009-2013

Source: The Rt. Rev. Barry E. Yingling, Editor, the *Churchman's Ordo Kalendar*

The most common liturgical colors in the Episcopal Church are: **White**—Christmas Day through First Sunday after Epiphany; Maundy Thursday (as an alternative to crimson at the Eucharist); from the Vigil of Easter to the Day of Pentecost (Whitsunday); Trinity Sunday; Feasts of the Lord (except Holy Cross Day); the Confession of St. Peter; the Conversion of St. Paul; St. Joseph; St. Mary Magdalene; St. Mary the Virgin; St. Michael and All Angels; All Saints' Day; St. John the Evangelist; memorials of other saints who were not martyred; Independence Day and Thanksgiving Day; weddings and funerals. **Red**—the Day of Pentecost; Holy Cross Day; feasts of apostles and evangelists (except those listed above); feasts and memorials of martyrs (including Holy Innocents' Day). **Violet**—Advent and Lent. **Crimson** or oxblood (dark red)—Holy Week. **Green**—the seasons after Epiphany and after Pentecost. **Black**—optional alternative for funerals and Good Friday.

The days of fasting are Ash Wednesday and Good Friday. Other days of special devotion (penitence) include the 40 days of Lent. Ember Days are days of prayer for the church's ministry. They fall on the Wednesday, Friday, and Saturday after the first Sunday in Lent, the Day of Pentecost, Holy Cross Day, and December 13. Rogation Days, the 3 days before Ascension Day, are days of prayer for God's blessing on the crops, on commerce and industry, and for conservation of the earth's resources.

Days, etc.	2009	2010	2011	2012	2013
Golden Number	15	16	17	18	19
Sunday Letter	D	C	b	A/g	f
Sundays after Epiphany	7	6	9	7	5
Ash Wednesday	Feb. 25	Feb. 17	Mar. 9	Feb. 22	Feb. 13
First Sunday in Lent	Mar. 1	Feb. 21	Mar. 13	Feb. 26	Feb. 17
Passion/Palm Sunday	Apr. 5	Mar. 28	Apr. 17	Apr. 1	Mar. 24
Good Friday	Apr. 10	Apr. 2	Apr. 22	Apr. 6	Mar. 29
Easter Day	Apr. 12	Apr. 4	Apr. 24	Apr. 8	Mar. 31
Ascension Day	May 21	May 13	June 2	May 17	May 9
The Day of Pentecost	May 31	May 23	June 12	May 27	May 19
Trinity Sunday	June 7	May 30	June 19	June 3	May 26
Numbered Proper of 2 Pentecost	#6	#5	#8	#5	#4
First Sunday of Advent	Nov. 29	Nov. 28	Nov. 27	Dec. 2	Dec. 1

Greek Orthodox Movable Ecclesiastical Dates, 2009-2013

Feast days and fasting days are determined annually on the basis of the date of Holy Pascha (Easter). This ecclesiastical cycle begins with the first day of the Triodion and ends with the Sunday of All Saints, a total of 18 weeks.

	2009	2010	2011	2012	2013
Triodion begins	Feb. 8	Jan. 24	Feb. 13	Feb. 5	Feb. 24
1st Sat. of Souls	Feb. 21	Feb. 6	Feb. 26	Feb. 18	Mar. 9
Meat Fare	Feb. 22	Feb. 7	Feb. 27	Feb. 19	Mar. 10
2nd Sat. of Souls	Feb. 28	Feb. 13	Mar. 5	Feb. 25	Mar. 16
Lent Begins	Mar. 2	Feb. 15	Mar. 7	Feb. 27	Mar. 18
St. Theodore—3rd Sat. of Souls	Mar. 7	Feb. 20	Mar. 12	Mar. 3	Mar. 23
Sunday of Orthodoxy	Mar. 8	Feb. 21	Mar. 13	Mar. 4	Mar. 24
Sat. of Lazarus	Apr. 11	Mar. 27	Apr. 16	Apr. 7	Apr. 27
Palm Sunday	Apr. 12	Mar. 28	Apr. 17	Apr. 8	Apr. 28
Holy (Good) Friday	Apr. 17	Apr. 2	Apr. 22	Apr. 13	May 3
Western Easter	Apr. 12	Apr. 4	Apr. 24	Apr. 8	Mar. 31
Orthodox Easter	Apr. 19	Apr. 4	Apr. 24	Apr. 15	May 5
Ascension	May 28	May 13	June 2	May 24	June 13
Sat. of Souls	June 6	May 22	June 11	June 2	June 22
Pentecost	June 7	May 23	June 12	June 3	June 23
All Saints	June 14	May 30	June 19	June 10	June 30
Fast of Holy Apostles (First day)	June 15	May 31	June 20	June 11	—

Important Islamic Dates, 1430-1434 AH (2009-2013)

Source: Imad-ad-Dean, Inc., Bethesda, MD 20814

The Islamic calendar is a strict lunar calendar reckoned from the year of the Hijra (Anno Hegirae, or AH)—Muhammad's flight from Mecca to Medina, in 622 CE. Each year consists of 12 lunar months of 29 or 30 days beginning and ending with each new moon's visible crescent. Common years have 354 days; leap years have 355 days. Some Muslim countries employ a conventionalized calendar with the leap day added to the last month, Dhûl Hijah, but for religious purposes the leap date is taken into account by tracking each new moon sighting. The dates given below are based on the convention that the first new moon must be seen before the following dawn on the East Coast of the Americas. Actual (local) Western Hemisphere sightings may occur a day later, but never a day earlier, than these dates reflect. Holy days begin at sunset on the previous day.

	(1430) 2008-09	(1431) 2009-2010	(1432) 2010-2011	(1433) 2011-2012	(1434) 2012-2013
New Year's Day (Muharram 1)	Dec. 28, 2008	Dec. 17, 2009	Dec. 7, 2010	Nov. 26, 2011	Nov. 15, 2012
Ashura (Muharram 10)	Jan. 6, 2009	Dec. 26, 2009	Dec. 16, 2010	Dec. 5, 2011	Nov. 24, 2012
Mawlid (Rabi'I 12)	Mar. 9, 2009	Feb. 26, 2010	Feb. 15, 2011	Feb. 4, 2012	Jan. 24, 2013
Ramadan 1	Aug. 21, 2009	Aug. 11, 2010	Aug. 1, 2011	July 20, 2012	July 9, 2013
Eid al-Fitr (Shawwal 1)	Sept. 20, 2009	Sept. 9, 2010	Aug. 30, 2011	Aug. 19, 2012	Aug. 8, 2013
Eid al-Adha (Dhûl-Hijjah 10)	Nov. 27, 2009	Nov. 16, 2010	Nov. 6, 2011	Oct. 26, 2012	Oct. 15, 2013

Jewish Holy Days, Festivals, and Fasts, 5769-5773 (2008-2013)

The Jewish calendar consists of 12 lunar months, alternating between 29 and 30 days. It is lunisolar, and adjusts for the solar cycle by adding an extra month (Adar II) in the 3rd, 6th, 8th, 11th, 14th, 17th, and 19th years of a 19-year cycle. The calendar started on the day of Creation, reckoned in the 2nd-3rd cent. BCE as Tishrei 1, 3,761 years before the common era.

The religious calendar begins with the month Nisan, from which all other months are counted, and the civil calendar with Tishrei. The months are 1) Nisan; 2) Iyar; 3) Sivan; 4) Tammuz; 5) Av (also Abh); 6) Elul; 7) Tishrei; 8) Cheshvan (also Marcheshvan); 9) Kislev; 10) Tevet (also Tebeth); 11) Shevat (also Shebhat); 12) Adar; 12a) Adar Sheni (II), added in leap years. The names are Aramaic versions of the Babylonian months, adopted during the Jews' exile in Babylon in the 4th century BCE. Rosh Hashanah, the New Year, begins on Tishrei 1 (Sept.-Oct.). Yom Kippur is the holiest day of the year. All holidays listed below begin at sunset on the previous day, except where noted.

Holiday	Date on Jewish Cal.	(5769) 2008-09		(5770) 2009-10		(5771) 2010-11		(5772) 2011-12		(5773) 2012-13	
Rosh Hashanah (New Year) ...	Tishrei 1	Sept. 30	Tue.	Sept. 19	Sat.	Sept. 9	Thu.	Sept. 29	Thu.	Sept. 17	Mon.
	Tishrei 2	Oct. 1	Wed.	Sept. 20	Sun.	Sept. 10	Fri.	Sept. 30	Fri.	Sept. 18	Tue.
Fast of Gedalya[1]	Tishrei 3	Oct. 2	Thu.	Sept. 21	Mon.	Sept. 12	Sun.*	Oct. 2	Sun.*	Sept. 19	Wed.
Yom Kippur (Day of Atonement)	Tishrei 10	Oct. 9	Thu.	Sept. 28	Mon.	Sept. 18	Sat.	Oct. 8	Sat.	Sept. 26	Wed.
Sukkot	Tishrei 15	Oct. 14	Tue.	Oct. 3	Sat.	Sept. 23	Thu.	Oct. 13	Thu.	Oct. 1	Mon.
	Tishrei 21	Oct. 20	Mon.	Oct. 9	Fri.	Sept. 29	Wed.	Oct. 19	Wed.	Oct. 7	Sun.
Shemini Atzeret	Tishrei 22	Oct. 21	Tue.	Oct. 10	Sat.	Sept. 30	Thu.	Oct. 20	Thu.	Oct. 8	Mon.
Simchat Torah	Tishrei 23	Oct. 22	Wed.	Oct. 11	Sun.	Oct. 1	Fri.	Oct. 21	Fri.	Oct. 9	Tue.
Hanukkah..................	Kislev 25	Dec. 22	Mon.	Dec. 12	Sat.	Dec. 2	Thu.	Dec. 21	Wed.	Dec. 9	Sun.
	Tevet 2 or 3	Dec. 29	Mon.	Dec. 19	Sat.	Dec. 9	Thu.	Dec. 28	Wed.	Dec. 16	Sun.
Fast of the 10th of Tevet[1]......	Tevet 10	Jan. 6	Tue.	Dec. 27	Sun.	Dec. 17	Fri.	Jan. 5	Thu.	Dec. 23	Sun.
Tu B'Shevat	Shevat 15	Feb. 9	Mon.	Jan. 30	Sat.	Jan. 20	Thu.	Feb. 8	Wed.	Jan. 26	Sat.
Ta'anis Esther (Fast of Esther)[1].	Adar 13	Mar. 9	Mon.	Feb. 25	Thu.*	Mar. 17	Thu.*	Mar. 7	Wed.	Feb. 21	Thu.*
Purim	Adar 14	Mar. 10	Tue.	Feb. 28	Sun.	Mar. 20	Sun.	Mar. 8	Thu.	Feb. 24	Sun.
Pesach (Passover)..........	Nisan 15	Apr. 9	Thu.	Mar. 30	Tue.	Apr. 19	Tue.	Apr. 7	Sat.	Mar. 26	Tue.
	Nisan 22	Apr. 16	Thu.	Apr. 6	Tue.	Apr. 26	Tue.	Apr. 14	Sat.	Apr. 2	Tue.
Lag B'Omer	Iyar 18	May 12	Tue.	May 2	Sun.	May 22	Sun.	May 10	Thu.	Apr. 28	Sun.
Shavuot (Pentecost).........	Sivan 6	May 29	Fri.	May 19	Wed.	June 8	Wed.	May 27	Sun.	May 15	Wed.
	Sivan 7	May 30	Sat.	May 20	Thu.	June 9	Thu.	May 28	Mon.	May 16	Thu.
Fast of the 17th Day of Tammuz[1]	Tammuz 17	July 9	Thu.	June 29	Tue.	July 19	Tue.	July 8	Sun.	June 25	Tue.
Fast of the 9th Day of Av	Av 9	July 30	Thu.	July 20	Tue.	Aug. 9	Tue.	July 29	Sun.	July 16	Tue.

*Date changed to avoid Sabbath. (1) "Minor fasts" begin at dawn.

Ash Wednesday and Easter Sunday (Western churches), 1901-2100

Year	Ash Wed.	Easter Sunday	Year	Ash Wed.	Easter Sunday	Year	Ash Wed.	Easter Sunday	Year	Ash Wed.	Easter Sunday	Year	Ash Wed.	Easter Sunday
1901	Feb. 20	Apr. 7	1941	Feb. 26	Apr. 13	1981	Mar. 4	Apr. 19	2021	Feb. 17	Apr. 4	2061	Feb. 23	Apr. 10
1902	Feb. 12	Mar. 30	1942	Feb. 18	Apr. 5	1982	Feb. 24	Apr. 11	2022	Mar. 2	Apr. 17	2062	Feb. 8	Mar. 26
1903	Feb. 25	Apr. 12	1943	Mar. 10	Apr. 25	1983	Feb. 16	Apr. 3	2023	Feb. 22	Apr. 9	2063	Feb. 28	Apr. 15
1904	Feb. 17	Apr. 3	1944	Feb. 23	Apr. 9	1984	Mar. 7	Apr. 22	2024	Feb. 14	Mar. 31	2064	Feb. 20	Apr. 6
1905	Mar. 8	Apr. 23	1945	Feb. 14	Apr. 1	1985	Feb. 20	Apr. 7	2025	Mar. 5	Apr. 20	2065	Feb. 11	Mar. 29
1906	Feb. 28	Apr. 15	1946	Mar. 6	Apr. 21	1986	Feb. 12	Mar. 30	2026	Feb. 18	Apr. 5	2066	Feb. 24	Apr. 11
1907	Feb. 13	Mar. 31	1947	Feb. 19	Apr. 6	1987	Mar. 4	Apr. 19	2027	Feb. 10	Mar. 28	2067	Feb. 16	Apr. 3
1908	Mar. 4	Apr. 19	1948	Feb. 11	Mar. 28	1988	Feb. 17	Apr. 3	2028	Mar. 1	Apr. 16	2068	Mar. 7	Apr. 22
1909	Feb. 24	Apr. 11	1949	Mar. 2	Apr. 17	1989	Feb. 8	Mar. 26	2029	Feb. 14	Apr. 1	2069	Feb. 27	Apr. 14
1910	Feb. 9	Mar. 27	1950	Feb. 22	Apr. 9	1990	Feb. 28	Apr. 15	2030	Mar. 6	Apr. 21	2070	Feb. 12	Mar. 30
1911	Feb. 1	Apr. 16	1951	Feb. 7	Mar. 25	1991	Feb. 13	Mar. 31	2031	Feb. 26	Apr. 13	2071	Mar. 4	Apr. 19
1912	Feb. 21	Apr. 7	1952	Feb. 27	Apr. 13	1992	Mar. 4	Apr. 19	2032	Feb. 11	Mar. 28	2072	Feb. 24	Apr. 10
1913	Feb. 5	Mar. 23	1953	Feb. 18	Apr. 5	1993	Feb. 24	Apr. 11	2033	Mar. 2	Apr. 17	2073	Feb. 8	Mar. 26
1914	Feb. 25	Apr. 12	1954	Mar. 3	Apr. 18	1994	Feb. 16	Apr. 3	2034	Feb. 22	Apr. 9	2074	Feb. 28	Apr. 15
1915	Feb. 17	Apr. 4	1955	Feb. 23	Apr. 10	1995	Mar. 1	Apr. 16	2035	Feb. 7	Mar. 25	2075	Feb. 20	Apr. 7
1916	Mar. 8	Apr. 23	1956	Feb. 15	Apr. 1	1996	Feb. 21	Apr. 7	2036	Feb. 27	Apr. 13	2076	Mar. 4	Apr. 19
1917	Feb. 21	Apr. 8	1957	Mar. 6	Apr. 21	1997	Feb. 12	Mar. 30	2037	Feb. 18	Apr. 5	2077	Feb. 24	Apr. 11
1918	Feb. 13	Mar. 31	1958	Feb. 19	Apr. 6	1998	Feb. 25	Apr. 12	2038	Mar. 10	Apr. 25	2078	Feb. 16	Apr. 3
1919	Mar. 5	Apr. 20	1959	Feb. 11	Mar. 29	1999	Feb. 17	Apr. 4	2039	Feb. 23	Apr. 10	2079	Mar. 8	Apr. 23
1920	Feb. 18	Apr. 4	1960	Mar. 2	Apr. 17	2000	Mar. 8	Apr. 23	2040	Feb. 15	Apr. 1	2080	Feb. 21	Apr. 7
1921	Feb. 9	Mar. 27	1961	Feb. 15	Apr. 2	2001	Feb. 28	Apr. 15	2041	Mar. 6	Apr. 21	2081	Feb. 12	Mar. 30
1922	Mar. 1	Apr. 16	1962	Mar. 7	Apr. 22	2002	Feb. 13	Mar. 31	2042	Feb. 19	Apr. 6	2082	Mar. 4	Apr. 19
1923	Feb. 14	Apr. 1	1963	Feb. 27	Apr. 14	2003	Mar. 5	Apr. 20	2043	Feb. 11	Mar. 29	2083	Feb. 17	Apr. 4
1924	Mar. 5	Apr. 20	1964	Feb. 12	Mar. 29	2004	Feb. 25	Apr. 11	2044	Mar. 2	Apr. 17	2084	Mar. 9	Apr. 26
1925	Feb. 25	Apr. 12	1965	Mar. 3	Apr. 18	2005	Feb. 9	Mar. 27	2045	Feb. 22	Apr. 9	2085	Feb. 28	Apr. 15
1926	Feb. 17	Apr. 4	1966	Feb. 23	Apr. 10	2006	Mar. 1	Apr. 16	2046	Feb. 7	Mar. 25	2086	Feb. 13	Mar. 31
1927	Mar. 2	Apr. 17	1967	Feb. 8	Mar. 26	2007	Feb. 21	Apr. 8	2047	Feb. 27	Apr. 14	2087	Mar. 5	Apr. 20
1928	Feb. 22	Apr. 8	1968	Feb. 28	Apr. 14	2008	Feb. 6	Mar. 23	2048	Feb. 19	Apr. 5	2088	Feb. 25	Apr. 11
1929	Feb. 13	Mar. 31	1969	Feb. 19	Apr. 6	2009	Feb. 25	Apr. 12	2049	Mar. 3	Apr. 18	2089	Feb. 16	Apr. 3
1930	Mar. 5	Apr. 20	1970	Feb. 11	Mar. 29	2010	Feb. 17	Apr. 4	2050	Feb. 23	Apr. 10	2090	Mar. 1	Apr. 16
1931	Feb. 18	Apr. 5	1971	Feb. 24	Apr. 11	2011	Mar. 9	Apr. 24	2051	Feb. 15	Apr. 2	2091	Feb. 21	Apr. 8
1932	Feb. 10	Mar. 27	1972	Feb. 16	Apr. 2	2012	Feb. 22	Apr. 8	2052	Mar. 6	Apr. 21	2092	Feb. 13	Mar. 30
1933	Mar. 1	Apr. 16	1973	Mar. 7	Apr. 22	2013	Feb. 13	Mar. 31	2053	Feb. 19	Apr. 6	2093	Feb. 25	Apr. 12
1934	Feb. 14	Apr. 1	1974	Feb. 27	Apr. 14	2014	Mar. 5	Apr. 20	2054	Feb. 11	Mar. 29	2094	Feb. 17	Apr. 4
1935	Mar. 6	Apr. 21	1975	Feb. 12	Mar. 30	2015	Feb. 18	Apr. 5	2055	Mar. 3	Apr. 18	2095	Mar. 9	Apr. 24
1936	Feb. 26	Apr. 12	1976	Mar. 3	Apr. 18	2016	Feb. 10	Mar. 27	2056	Feb. 16	Apr. 2	2096	Feb. 29	Apr. 15
1937	Feb. 10	Mar. 28	1977	Feb. 23	Apr. 10	2017	Mar. 1	Apr. 16	2057	Mar. 7	Apr. 22	2097	Feb. 13	Mar. 31
1938	Mar. 2	Apr. 17	1978	Feb. 8	Mar. 26	2018	Feb. 14	Apr. 1	2058	Feb. 27	Apr. 14	2098	Mar. 5	Apr. 20
1939	Feb. 22	Apr. 9	1979	Feb. 28	Apr. 15	2019	Mar. 6	Apr. 21	2059	Feb. 12	Mar. 30	2099	Feb. 25	Apr. 12
1940	Feb. 7	Mar. 24	1980	Feb. 20	Apr. 6	2020	Feb. 26	Apr. 12	2060	Mar. 3	Apr. 18	2100	Feb. 10	Mar. 28

Roman Catholic Hierarchy

Source: U.S. Catholic Conference; Holy See Press

Supreme Pontiff

At the head of the Roman Catholic Church is the supreme pontiff, Pope Benedict XVI, Joseph Ratzinger, born in Marktl am Inn, in Bavaria, Germany, on April 16, 1927; ordained priest on June 29, 1951, named archbishop of Munich and Feising in March 1977 and elevated to Cardinal three months later. In 1981, he was appointed prefect of the Congregation for the Doctrine of the Faith, and confirmed as dean of the College of Cardinals on November 30, 2002. He was elected pope by the College of Cardinals on April 19, 2005.

Chronological List of Popes

Source: Annuario Pontificio. Table lists year of accession of each pope.

The Roman Catholic Church named the Apostle Peter as founder of the church in Rome and the first pope. He arrived there c. 42, was martyred there c. 67, and was ultimately canonized as a saint. **The pope's temporal title is:** Sovereign of the State of Vatican City. **The pope's spiritual titles are:** Bishop of Rome, Vicar of Jesus Christ, Successor of St. Peter, Prince of the Apostles, Supreme Pontiff of the Universal Church, Patriarch of the West, Primate of Italy, Archbishop and Metropolitan of the Roman Province.

The names of antipopes are *in italics* and followed by an *. Antipopes were illegitimate claimants to the papal throne.

Year	Pope	Year	Pope	Year	Pope	Year	Pope	Year	Pope
	St. Peter	526	St. Felix IV (III)	872	John VIII	1100	*Theodoric**	1417	Martin V
67	St. Linus	530	Boniface II	882	Marinus I	1102	*Albert**	1431	Eugene IV
76	St. Anacletus	530	*Dioscorus**	884	St. Adrian III	1105	*Sylvester IV**	1439	*Felix V**
	or Cletus	533	John II	885	Stephen V (VI)	1118	Gelasius II	1447	Nicholas V
88	St. Clement I	535	St. Agapitus I	891	Formosus	1118	*Gregory VIII**	1455	Callistus III
97	St. Evaristus	536	St. Silverius, Martyr	896	Boniface VI	1119	Callistus II	1458	Pius II
105	St. Alexander I	537	Vigilius	896	Stephen VI (VII)	1124	Honorius II	1464	Paul II
115	St. Sixtus I	556	Pelagius I	897	Romanus	1124	*Celestine II**	1471	Sixtus IV
125	St. Telesphorus	561	John III	897	Theodore II	1130	Innocent II	1484	Innocent VIII
136	St. Hyginus	575	Benedict I	898	John IX	1130	*Anacletus II**	1492	Alexander VI
140	St. Pius I	579	Pelagius II	900	Benedict IV	1138	*Victor IV**	1503	Pius III
155	St. Anicetus	590	St. Gregory I	903	Leo V	1143	Celestine II	1503	Julius II
166	St. Soter	604	Sabinian	903	*Christopher**	1144	Lucius II	1513	Leo X
175	St. Eleutherius	607	Boniface III	904	Sergius III	1145	Bl. Eugene III	1522	Adrian VI
189	St. Victor I	608	St. Boniface IV	911	Anastasius III	1153	Anastasius IV	1523	Clement VII
199	St. Zephyrinus	615	St. Deusdedit or	913	Landus	1154	Adrian IV	1534	Paul III
217	St. Callistus I		Adeodatus	914	John X	1159	Alexander III	1550	Julius III
217	*St. Hippolytus**	619	Boniface V	928	Leo VI	1159	*Victor IV**	1555	Marcellus II
222	St. Urban I	625	Honorius I	928	Stephen VII(VIII)	1164	*Paschal III**	1555	Paul IV
230	St. Pontian	640	Severinus	931	John XI	1168	*Callistus III**	1559	Pius IV
235	St. Anterus	640	John IV	936	Leo VII	1179	*Innocent III**	1566	St. Pius V
236	St. Fabian	642	Theodore I	939	Stephen VIII(IX)	1181	Lucius III	1572	Gregory XIII
251	St. Cornelius	649	St. Martin I, Martyr	942	Marinus II	1185	Urban III	1585	Sixtus V
251	*Novatian**	654	St. Eugene I	946	Agapitus II	1187	Clement III	1590	Urban VII
253	St. Lucius I	657	St. Vitalian	955	John XII	1187	Gregory VIII	1590	Gregory XIV
254	St. Stephen I	672	Adeodatus II	963	Leo VIII	1191	Celestine III	1591	Innocent IX
257	St. Sixtus II	676	Donus	964	Benedict V	1198	Innocent III	1592	Clement VIII
259	St. Dionysius	678	St. Agatho	965	John XIII	1216	Honorius III	1605	Leo XI
269	St. Felix I	682	St. Leo II	973	Benedict VI	1227	Gregory IX	1605	Paul V
275	St. Eutychian	684	St. Benedict II	974	*Boniface VII**	1241	Celestine IV	1621	Gregory XV
283	St. Caius	685	John V	974	Benedict VII	1243	Innocent IV	1623	Urban VIII
296	St. Marcellinus	686	Conon	983	John XIV	1254	Alexander IV	1644	Innocent X
308	St. Marcellus I	687	*Theodore**	985	John XV	1261	Urban IV	1655	Alexander VII
309	St. Eusebius	687	*Paschal**	996	Gregory V	1265	Clement IV	1667	Clement IX
311	St. Melchiades	687	St. Sergius I	997	*John XVI**	1271	Bl. Gregory X	1670	Clement X
314	St. Sylvester I	701	John VI	999	Sylvester II	1276	Bl. Innocent V	1676	Bl. Innocent XI
336	St. Marcus	705	John VII	1003	John XVII	1276	Adrian V	1689	Alexander VIII
337	St. Julius I	708	Sisinnius	1004	John XVIII	1276	John XXI	1691	Innocent XII
352	Liberius	708	Constantine	1009	Sergius IV	1277	Nicholas III	1700	Clement XI
355	*Felix II**	715	St. Gregory II	1012	Benedict VIII	1281	Martin IV	1721	Innocent XIII
366	St. Damasus I	731	St. Gregory III	1012	*Gregory**	1285	Honorius IV	1724	Benedict XIII
366	*Ursinus**	741	St. Zachary	1024	John XIX	1288	Nicholas IV	1730	Clement XII
384	St. Siricius	752	Stephen II (III)[1]	1032	Benedict IX	1294	St. Celestine V	1740	Benedict XIV
399	St. Anastasius I	757	St. Paul I	1045	Sylvester III	1294	Boniface VIII	1758	Clement XIII
401	St. Innocent I	767	*Constantine**	1045	Benedict IX	1303	Bl. Benedict XI	1769	Clement XIV
417	St. Zosimus	768	*Philip**	1045	Gregory VI	1305	Clement V	1775	Pius VI
418	St. Boniface I	768	Stephen III (IV)	1046	Clement II	1316	John XXII	1800	Pius VII
418	*Eulalius**	772	Adrian I	1047	Benedict IX	1328	*Nicholas V**	1823	Leo XII
422	St. Celestine I	795	St. Leo III	1048	Damasus II	1334	Benedict XII	1829	Pius VIII
432	St. Sixtus III	816	Stephen IV (V)	1049	St. Leo IX	1342	Clement VI	1831	Gregory XVI
440	St. Leo I	817	St. Paschal I	1055	Victor II	1352	Innocent VI	1846	Pius IX
461	St. Hilary	824	Eugene II	1057	Stephen IX (X)	1362	Bl. Urban V	1878	Leo XIII
468	St. Simplicius	827	Valentine	1058	*Benedict X**	1370	Gregory XI	1903	St. Pius X
483	St. Felix III (II)	827	Gregory IV	1059	Nicholas II	1378	Urban VI	1914	Benedict XV
492	St. Gelasius I	844	*John**	1061	Alexander II	1378	*Clement VII**	1922	Pius XI
496	Anastasius II	844	Sergius II	1061	*Honorius II**	1389	Boniface IX	1939	Pius XII
498	St. Symmachus	847	St. Leo IV	1073	St. Gregory VII	1394	*Benedict XIII**	1958	John XXIII
498	*Lawrence** (501–505)	855	Benedict III	1080	*Clement III**	1404	Innocent VII	1963	Paul VI
		855	*Anastasius**	1086	Bl. Victor III	1406	Gregory XII	1978	John Paul I
514	St. Hormisdas	858	St. Nicholas I	1088	Bl. Urban II	1409	*Alexander V**	1978	John Paul II
523	St. John I, Martyr	867	Adrian II	1099	Paschal II	1410	*John XXIII**	2005	Benedict XVI

(1) After St. Zachary, a Roman priest named Stephen was elected, but died before assuming the papacy. Another Stephen was then elected to succeed Zachary as Stephen II. He is sometimes listed as Stephen III.

College of Cardinals

Source: U.S. Conference of Catholic Bishops

Members of the Sacred College of Cardinals are chosen by the pope to be his chief assistants and advisers in the administration of the church. Among their duties is the election of the pope.

In its present form, the College of Cardinals dates from the 12th century. The first cardinals, from about the 6th century, were deacons and priests of the leading churches of Rome and were bishops of neighboring dioceses. The title of cardinal was limited to members of the college in 1567. The number of cardinals was set at 70 in 1586 by Pope Sixtus V. From 1959 Pope John XXIII began to increase the number; however, the number eligible to participate in papal elections was limited to 120. Previous limitations were set aside by Pope John Paul II when he created new cardinals. In 1918 the Code of Canon Law specified that all cardinals must be priests. Pope John XXIII in 1962 established that all cardinals must be bishops, but this can be dispensed with, as in the case of Cardinal Avery Dulles. In 1971, Pope Paul VI decreed that at age 80 cardinals must retire from curial departments and offices and from participation in papal elections.

As of Sept. 2009, there were 185 members of the College, of whom 113 remained eligible to vote.

North American Cardinals

Name	Office	Born	Named Cardinal
Aloysius M. Ambrozic	Archbishop emeritus of Toronto	1930	1998
Javier Lozano Barragan	Pres. Pontifical Council for Health Care Workers, Mexico	1933	2003
William W. Baum[1]	Major Penitentiary emeritus of the Apostolic Penitentiary	1926	1976
Anthony J. Bevilacqua[1]	Archbishop emeritus of Philadelphia	1923	1991
Ernesto Corripio Ahumada[1]	Archbishop emeritus of Mexico City	1919	1979
Daniel N. DiNardo	Archbishop of Galveston-Houston	1949	2007
Edward M. Egan	Archbishop emeritus of New York	1932	2001
John Patrick Foley	Grand Master of the Knights of the Holy Sepulcher	1935	2007
Francis E. George	Archbishop of Chicago	1937	1998
William Henry Keeler	Archbishop emeritus of Baltimore	1931	1994
Bernard F. Law	Archbishop emeritus of Boston	1931	1985
William Levada	Prefect of the Congregation for the Doctrine of the Faith	1936	2006
Roger Mahony	Archbishop of Los Angeles	1936	1991
Adam Joseph Maida	Archbishop emeritus of Detroit	1930	1994
Luis Aponte Martinez[1]	Archbishop emeritus of San Juan	1922	1973
Theodore McCarrick	Archbishop emeritus of Washington, DC	1930	2001
Sean O'Malley	Archbishop of Boston	1944	2006
Marc Ouellet	Archbishop of Quebec	1944	2003
Justin F. Rigali	Archbishop of Philadelphia	1935	2003
Norberto Rivera Carrera	Archbishop of Mexico City	1942	1998
Juan Sandoval Iniguez	Archbishop of Guadalajara	1933	1994
James F. Stafford	Major Penitentiary emeritus of the Apostolic Penitentiary	1932	1998
Jean-Claude Turcotte	Archbishop of Montreal	1936	1994

(1) Ineligible to take part in papal elections (as of Sept. 2009).

The Ten Commandments

In the Hebrew Bible (Old Testament) the Ten Commandments (also called the Decalogue, from the Greek meaning "ten words") were revealed by God to Moses on Mt. Sinai. They form the covenant between God and the Israelites and the moral code that is the basis for the Jewish and Christian religions. The Ten Commandments appear in 2 places in the Old Testament—Exodus 20:1-17 and Deuteronomy 5:6-21.

Most Protestant, Anglican, and Orthodox Christians follow Jewish tradition, as here, which considers the introduction ("I am the Lord . . .") the first commandment and makes the prohibition against idolatry the second. Roman Catholic and Lutheran traditions combine I and II and split the last commandment into 2 that separately prohibit coveting of a neighbor's wife and a neighbor's goods. This arrangement alters the numbering of the other commandments by one.

Following is the text of the Ten Commandments as it appears in Exodus 20:1-17, in the King James version of the Bible [Roman numerals added]:

And God spake all these words, saying,

I. I *am* the LORD thy God, which have brought thee out of the land of Egypt, out of the house of bondage. Thou shalt have no other gods before me.

II. Thou shalt not make unto thee any graven image, or any likeness of *any thing* that *is* in heaven above, or that *is* in the earth beneath, or that *is* in the water under the earth. Thou shalt not bow down thyself to them, nor serve them: for I the LORD thy God *am* a jealous God, visiting the iniquity of the fathers upon the children unto the third and fourth *generation* of them that hate me; and shewing mercy unto thousands of them that love me, and keep my commandments.

III. Thou shalt not take the name of the LORD thy God in vain: for the LORD will not hold him guiltless that taketh his name in vain.

IV. Remember the sabbath day, to keep it holy. Six days shalt thou labour, and do all thy work: but the seventh day *is* the sabbath of the LORD thy God: *in it* thou shalt not do any work, thou, nor thy son, nor thy daughter, thy manservant, nor thy maidservant, nor thy cattle, nor thy stranger that *is* within thy gates: for *in* six days the LORD made heaven and earth, the sea, and all that in them *is*, and rested the seventh day: wherefore the LORD blessed the sabbath day, and hallowed it.

V. Honour thy father and thy mother: that thy days may be long upon the land which the LORD thy God giveth thee.

VI. Thou shalt not kill.

VII. Thou shalt not commit adultery.

VIII. Thou shalt not steal.

IX. Thou shalt not bear false witness against thy neighbour.

X. Thou shalt not covet thy neighbour's house, thou shalt not covet thy neighbour's wife, nor his manservant, nor his maidservant, nor his ox, nor his ass, nor any thing that *is* thy neighbour's.

Books of the Bible

Old Testament—Standard Protestant List

Genesis	I Kings	Ecclesiastes	Obadiah
Exodus	II Kings	Song of Solomon	Jonah
Leviticus	I Chronicles	Isaiah	Micah
Numbers	II Chronicles	Jeremiah	Nahum
Deuteronomy	Ezra	Lamentations	Habakkuk
Joshua	Nehemiah	Ezekiel	Zephaniah
Judges	Esther	Daniel	Haggai
Ruth	Job	Hosea	Zechariah
I Samuel	Psalms	Joel	Malachi
II Samuel	Proverbs	Amos	

New Testament List

Matthew	Ephesians	Hebrews
Mark	Philippians	James
Luke	Colossians	I Peter
John	I Thessalonians	II Peter
Acts	II Thessalonians	I John
Romans	I Timothy	II John
I Corinthians	II Timothy	III John
II Corinthians	Titus	Jude
Galatians	Philemon	Revelation

The standard Protestant Old Testament consists of the same 39 books as in the Bible of Judaism, but the latter is organized differently. The Old Testament used by Roman Catholics has 7 additional "deuterocanonical" books, plus some additional parts of books. The 7 are: **Tobit, Judith, Wisdom, Sirach (Ecclesiasticus), Baruch, I Maccabees,** and **II Maccabees.** Both Catholic and Protestant versions of the New Testament have 27 books, with the same names.

Figures in the Hebrew Bible (Old Testament)

Aaron: First of Hebrew high priests; brother of Moses and Miriam.
Abel: Second son of Adam and Eve; slain by Cain.
Abraham: Founder of monotheism; patriarch; also called Abram.
Adam: First human according to Genesis.
Amos: Herdsman; prophesized against social injustice and oppression of the poor.
Bathsheba: Seduced by King David; mother of King Solomon.
Cain: Tiller of the soil; son of Adam and Eve; killed his brother Abel.
Cyrus: Persian ruler; sent Jews home from exile.
Daniel: Cast into lion's den by Nebuchadnezzer; saved.
David: Israel's greatest king; shepherd, warrior, musician, psalmist.
Deborah: Prophet and judge; ruled over Israel.
Elijah: Great prophet; was victorious over the priests of the Phoenician god, Baal.
Elisha: Prophet; successor to Elijah.
Esther: Jewish wife of the king of Persia; saved Jews from annihilation.
Eve: First woman according to Genesis.
Ezekiel: Visionary; prophesized hope to exiled Jews in Babylon.
Ezra: Great Jewish leader; rededicated worship and Torah law after exile.
Goliath: Giant Philistine warrior; slain by David.
Hannah: Childless; promised child to God; mother to the prophet Samuel.
Hosea: Enacted prophecy; asked God's forgiveness for Israel's unfaithfulness.
Isaac: Son of Abraham and Sarah; saved from sacrificial altar.
Isaiah: Highly educated prophet; avoided war with Assyria. Israel destroyed. Jerusalem survived.
Jacob: Son of Isaac; father of the Twelve Tribes; renamed "Israel" by angel.
Jeremiah: Confronted leaders; urged surrender to Babylon.
Jezebel: Phoenician queen of King Ahab; had Israelite prophets killed.
Job: "Blameless" man; lost family and possessions but not his faith.
Jonah: Swallowed by a great fish; prophesized repentance in Nineveh.
Jonathan: Son of King Saul; friend of David.
Joseph: Favorite of Jacob; interprets Pharaoh's dreams; brings Hebrews to Egypt.
Josiah: Reformist king; repaired Temple; restored worship; reintroduced Passover.
Joshua: Successor of Moses; led Hebrews into Canaan.
Leah: Matriarch; older sister of Rachel; Jacob's wife.
Micah: Prophet; predicted the end of war and beginning of peace.
Miriam: Prophet and great leader of the Hebrews; sister to Moses and Aaron.
Moses: Most important Hebrew prophet; leader of the Israelites; received the Torah.
Nathan: Prophet; confronted King David over his seduction of Bathsheba.
Nebuchadnezzer: Babylonian king; destroyed Jerusalem.
Nehemiah: Led Jews back to Jerusalem from Babylonian exile.
Noah: A man of great faith who, according to *Genesis*, saved his family and two of every living thing on Earth from a great flood.
Rachel: Matriarch; younger sister of Leah; Jacob's wife; Joseph's mother.
Rebecca: Matriarch; wife of Isaac; mother of Jacob.
Ruth: Moabite convert; ancestor of David.
Samuel: Prophet; anointed Saul king of Israel and later anointed David to succeed him.
Samson: Judge and military leader of Israel, possessed super-human strength .
Sarah: First matriarch of Israel; wife of Abraham; mother of Isaac.
Saul: First king of Israel; father of Jonathan.
Solomon: King of Israel at its zenith; known for great wisdom.
Zachariah: Prophet; encouraged rebuilding of Temple destroyed by Babylonians.

Figures in the New Testament

Andrew: One of the Twelve Apostles; brother of Peter and former fisherman; one of the earlier disciples.
Barabbas: Imprisoned with Jesus; set free by Pilate on Passover.
Barnabas: Disciple of Jesus; closely connected with Paul.
Bartholomew: A lesser known member of the Twelve Apostles; cheerful and prayed often.
Cornelius: A Roman convert defended by Peter, allowing Gentiles to become Christians.
Elizabeth: Mother of John the Baptist; relation of the Virgin Mary.
Gabriel: Archangel; appeared to the Virgin Mary to announce that she was to give birth to the messiah.
Herod: Two Herods appear in the New Testament: Herod the Great ordered the death of children around the time of Jesus's birth; his son, Herod, imprisoned John the Baptist, leading to his beheading.
James: One of the Twelve; brother of John the apostle.
Jesus: Central figure of the Gospels; believed to be the messiah and son of God; crucified by the Romans.
John (Baptist): Known as "John the Baptist"; important prophet and forerunner to Jesus; relation of the Virgin Mary.
John (Apostle): Beloved disciple of Jesus; one of the Twelve; possible author of 4th Gospel; brother of James.
Joseph: Husband of the Virgin Mary; descendant of King David.
Judas Iscariot: Betrayer of Jesus; prominent member of the apostles; committed suicide.
Judas Thaddeus: One of the Twelve; also called "Jude" to distinguish him from Judas Iscariot.
Lazarus: Brother of the disciples Martha and Mary of Bethany; raised from the dead at their request; possibly the same Lazarus who appears in Jesus's parable of the rich man.
Luke: Traditional author of the Gospel of Luke; possibly a follower of Paul.
Mark: Traditional author of the Gospel of Mark; possibly a disciple of Peter.
Matthew: One of the Twelve; possible author of the Gospel of Matthew; a former tax collector.
Mary Magdalene: Important female disciple of Jesus; witness to his death and resurrection.
Mary, the mother of Jesus: traditionally believed to be a virgin and conceived without sin; wife of Joseph.
Matthias: Often included on lists of the Twelve Apostles as the apostle who replaced Judas Iscariot after his betrayal.
Paul (Saul): Writer of nearly a quarter of the New Testament; a former persecutor of Christians, converted after a vision; played a significant role in spreading Christianity.
Peter: Considered to be the foremost of the Twelve Apostles; traditionally the first pope and "rock" of the Christian church; author of epistles; also called Simon and Simon Peter.
Philip: One of the Twelve; considered pragmatic and sensible.
Pilate, Pontius: A Roman prefect; played large role in the trial and crucifixion of Jesus.
Simon: One of the Twelve; known as "the Zealot" to distinguish from Simon Peter.
Stephen: Fervently preached that Jesus was the Messiah; stoned to death by angry mob, including Saul; important figure in Saul's conversion.
Thomas: One of the Twelve; known as "Doubting Thomas" because he did not believe Jesus was risen until he could touch him.
Timothy: A disciple closely connected with Paul; recipient of epistles.
Zacharias: Father of John the Baptist; husband of Elizabeth; struck dumb when he doubted his barren wife could become pregnant.

Major Christian Denominations:

Brackets indicate some features that tend to

Denom-ination	Origins	Organization	Authority	Special rites
Baptists	In radical Reformation, objections to infant baptism, demands for church and state separation; John Smyth, English Separatist, in 1609; Roger Williams, 1638, Providence, RI.	Congregational; each local church is autonomous.	Scripture; some Baptists, particularly in the South, interpret the Bible literally.	[Baptism, usually early teen years and after, by total immersion;] Lord's Supper.
Church of Christ (Disciples)	Among evangelical Presbyterians in KY (1804) and PA (1809), in distress over Protestant factionalism and decline of fervor; organized in 1832.	Congregational.	["Where the Scriptures speak, we speak; where the Scriptures are silent, we are silent."]	Adult baptism; Lord's Supper (weekly).
Episco-palians	Henry VIII separated English Catholic Church from Rome, 1534, for political reasons; Protestant Episcopal Church in U.S. founded in 1789.	[Diocesan bishops, in apostolic succession, are elected by parish representatives; the national Church is headed by General Convention and Presiding Bishop; part of the Anglican Communion.]	Scripture as interpreted by tradition, especially 39 Articles (1563); tri-annual convention of bishops, priests, and lay people.	Infant baptism, Eucharist, and other sacraments; sacrament taken to be symbolic, but as having real spiritual effect.
Jehovah's Witnesses	Founded in 1870 in PA by Charles Taze Russell; incorporated as Watch Tower Bible and Tract Society of PA, 1884; name Jehovah's Witnesses adopted in 1931.	A governing body located in NY coordinates worldwide activities; each congregation cared for by a body of elders; each Witness considered a minister.	The Bible.	Baptism by immersion; annual Lord's Meal ceremony.
Latter-day Saints (Mormons)	In a vision of the Father and the Son reported by Joseph Smith (1820s) in NY. Smith also reported receiving new scripture on golden tablets: The Book of Mormon.	Theocratic; 1st Presidency (church president, 2 counselors), 12 Apostles preside over international church. Local congregations headed by lay priesthood leaders.	Revelation to living prophet (church president). The Bible, Book of Mormon, and other revelations to Smith and his successors.	Baptism, at age 8; laying on of hands (which confers the gift of the Holy Ghost); Lord's Supper; temple rites: baptism for the dead, marriage for eternity, others.
Lutherans	Begun by Martin Luther in Wittenberg, Germany, in 1517; objection to Catholic doctrine of salvation and sale of indulgences; break complete, 1519.	Varies from congregational to episcopal; in U.S., a combination of regional synods and congregational polities is most common.	Scripture alone. The Book of Concord (1580), which includes the three Ecumenical Creeds, is subscribed to as a correct exposition of Scripture.	Infant baptism; Lord's Supper; Christ's true body and blood present "in, with, and under the bread and wine."
Methodists	Rev. John Wesley began movement in 1738, within Church of England; first U.S. denomination, Baltimore (1784).	Conference and superintendent system; [in United Methodist Church, general superintendents are bishops—not a priestly order, only an office—who are elected for life.]	Scripture as interpreted by tradition, reason, and experience.	Baptism of infants or adults; Lord's Supper commanded; other rites: marriage, ordination, solemnization of personal commitments.
Orthodox	Developed in original Christian proselytizing; broke with Rome in 1054, after centuries of doctrinal disputes and diverging traditions.	Synods of bishops in autonomous, usually national, churches elect a patriarch, archbishop, or metropolitan; these men, as a group, are the heads of the church.	Scripture, tradition, and the first 7 church councils up to Nicaea II in 787; bishops in council have authority in doctrine and policy.	Seven sacraments: infant baptism and anointing, Eucharist, ordination, penance, marriage, and anointing of the sick.
Pentecostal	In Topeka, KS (1901) and Los Angeles (1906), in reaction to perceived loss of evangelical fervor among Methodists and others.	Originally a movement, not a formal organization, Pentecostalism now has a variety of organized forms and continues also as a movement.	Scripture; individual charismatic leaders, the teachings of the Holy Spirit.	[Spirit baptism, especially as shown in "speaking in tongues"; healing and sometimes exorcism;] adult baptism; Lord's Supper.
Presby-terians	In 16th-cent. Calvinist reformation; differed with Lutherans over sacraments, church government; John Knox founded Scotch Presbyerian church about 1560.	[Highly structured representational system of ministers and lay persons (presbyters) in local, regional, and national bodies (synods).]	Scripture.	Infant baptism; Lord's Supper; bread and wine symbolize Christ's spiritual presence.
Roman Catholics	Traditionally, founded by Jesus who named St. Peter the 1st vicar; developed in early Christian proselytizing, especially after the conversion of imperial Rome in the 4th cent.	[Hierarchy with supreme power vested in pope elected by cardinals;] councils of bishops advise on matters of doctrine and policy.	[The pope, when speaking for the whole church in matters of faith and morals; and tradition (which is expressed in church councils and in part contained in Scripture).]	Mass; 7 sacraments: baptism, reconciliation, Eucharist, confirmation, marriage, ordination, and anointing of the sick (unction).
United Church of Christ	[By ecumenical union, in 1957, of Congregationalists and Evangelical & Reformed, representing both Calvinist and Lutheran traditions.]	Congregational; a General Synod, representative of all congregations, sets general policy.	Scripture.	Infant baptism; Lord's Supper.

How Do They Differ?

distinguish a denomination sharply from others.

Practice	Ethics	Doctrine	Other	Denom-ination
Worship style varies from staid to evangelistic; extensive missionary activity.	Usually opposed to alcohol and tobacco; some tendency toward a perfectionist ethical standard.	*[No creed; true church is of believers only, who are all equal.]*	Believing no authority can stand between the believer and God, the Baptists are strong supporters of church and state separation.	**Baptists**
Tries to avoid any rite not considered part of the 1st-century church; some congregations may reject instrumental music.	Some tendency toward perfectionism; increasing interest in social action programs.	Simple New Testament faith; avoids any elaboration not firmly based on Scripture.	Highly tolerant in doctrinal and religious matters; strongly supportive of scholarly education.	**Church of Christ (Disciples)**
Formal, based on "Book of Common Prayer," updated 1979; services range from austerely simple to highly liturgical.	Tolerant, sometimes permissive; some social action programs.	Scripture; the "historic creeds," which include the Apostles, Nicene, and Athanasian, and the "Book of Common Prayer"; ranges from Anglo-Catholic to low church, with Calvinist influences.	Strongly ecumenical, holding talks with many branches of Christendom.	**Episcopalians**
Meetings are held in Kingdom Halls and members' homes for study and worship; [extensive door-to-door visitations.]	High moral code; stress on marital fidelity and family values; avoidance of tobacco and blood transfusions.	*[God, by his first creation, Christ, will soon destroy all wickedness; 144,000 faithful ones will rule in heaven with Christ over others on a paradise earth.]*	Total allegiance proclaimed only to God's kingdom or heavenly government by Christ; main periodical, *The Watchtower,* is printed in 115 languages.	**Jehovah's Witnesses**
Simple service with prayers, hymns, sermon; private temple ceremonies may be more elaborate.	Temperance; strict moral code; *[tithing];* a strong work ethic with communal self-reliance; *[strong missionary activity];* family emphasis.	Jesus Christ is the Son of God, the Eternal Father. Jesus' atonement saves all humans; those who are obedient to God's laws may become joint-heirs with Christ in God's kingdom.	Mormons believe theirs is the true church of Jesus Christ, restored by God through Joseph Smith. Official name: The Church of Jesus Christ of Latter-day Saints.	**Latter-day Saints (Mormons)**
Relatively simple, formal liturgy with emphasis on the sermon.	Generally conservative in personal and social ethics; doctrine of "2 kingdoms" (worldly and holy) supports conservatism in secular affairs.	Salvation by grace alone through faith; Lutheranism has made major contributions to Protestant theology.	Though still somewhat divided along ethnic lines (German, Swedish, etc.), main divisions are between fundamentalists and liberals.	**Lutherans**
Worship style varies widely by denomination, local church, geography.	Originally pietist and perfectionist; always strong social activist elements.	No distinctive theological development; 25 Articles abridged from Church of England's 39, not binding.	In 1968, The United Methodist Church was formed by the union of The Methodist Church and The Evangelical United Brethren Church.	**Methodists**
Elaborate liturgy, usually in the vernacular, though extremely traditional; the liturgy is the essence of Orthodoxy; veneration of icons.	Tolerant; little stress on social action; divorce, remarriage permitted in some cases; bishops are celibate; priests need not be.	Emphasis on Christ's resurrection, rather than crucifixion; the Holy Spirit proceeds from God the Father only.	Orthodox Church in America originally under Patriarch of Moscow, was granted autonomy in 1970; Greek Orthodox do not recognize this autonomy.	**Orthodox**
Loosely structured service with rousing hymns and sermons, culminating in spirit baptism.	Usually, emphasis on perfectionism, with varying degrees of tolerance.	Simple traditional beliefs, usually Protestant, with emphasis on the immediate presence of God in the Holy Spirit.	Once confined to lower-class "holy rollers," Pentecostalism now appears in mainline churches and has established middle-class congregations.	**Pentecostal**
A simple, sober service in which the sermon is central.	Traditionally, a tendency toward strictness, with firm church- and self-discipline; otherwise tolerant.	Emphasizes the sovereignty and justice of God; no longer dogmatic.	Although traces of belief in predestination (that God has foreordained salvation for the "elect") remain, this idea is no longer a central element in Presbyterianism.	**Presbyterians**
Relatively elaborate ritual centered on the Mass; also rosary recitation, novenas, etc.	Traditionally strict, but increasingly tolerant in practice; divorce and remarriage not accepted, but annulments sometimes granted; celibate clergy, except in Eastern rite.	Highly elaborated; salvation by merit gained through grace; dogmatic; special veneration of Mary, the mother of Jesus.	Relatively rapid change followed Vatican Council II; Mass now in vernacular; more stress on social action, tolerance, ecumenism.	**Roman Catholics**
Usually simple services with emphasis on the sermon.	Tolerant; some social action emphasis.	Standard Protestant; "Statement of Faith" (1959) is not binding.	The 2 main churches in the 1957 union represented earlier unions with small groups of almost every Protestant denomination.	**United Church of Christ**

Major Non-Christian World Religions

Sources: Hinduism and Judaism reviewed by Anthony Padovano, PhD, STD, Prof. of Literature & Relig. Studies, Ramapo College, NJ, Adj. Prof. of Theol., Fordham U., NYC; Bahai reviewed by the Bahai Community Relations Center; Sikhism reviewed by The Sikh Coalition of New York, NY; Islam reviewed by Natana Delong-Bas, Lecturer in Islamic Studies, Boston College.

Islam

Founded: Muhammad received his first revelation in 610 CE.

Founder: Muhammad (c. 570-632), the Prophet.

Sacred texts: Two texts constitute the Muslim sacred canon, the Qur'an and the *Hadith*. The *Qur'an* provides the foundation for Islamic religion and culture. Regarded as the final, perfect, and complete word of God as revealed to Muhammad over the course of his life. Received by Muhammad in the Arabic language, it is memorized in Arabic by adherents regardless of their native language. It is divided into 114 chapters of unequal length, the shortest containing only three verses, and the longest containing 306 verses. The Qur'an is the ultimate source of everything Islamic, from metaphysics to theology to sacred history, to ethics and law, to art. The Hadith, which describes Muhammad's actions, attitudes and teachings, complements the Qur'an. Due to its long history of oral transmission, the Hadith's lessons are seen as somewhat vulnerable to human error; it does not contain God's unadulterated voice as does the Qur'an, but functions as a powerful spiritual and behavioral code nonetheless.

Divisions: There are 2 major groups: the majority Sunni (84% of the worldwide Muslim population) and the minority Shiites (14%). Sects first appeared in Islam at the time of Muhammad's death. The group that came to be known as Sunni accepted Abu Bakr, an early convert, as his successor (caliph), while a smaller number, which became the Shi'a, believed that Ali ibn Abi Talib, the son-in-law and first cousin of the prophet, should have become his successor (Imam). The Sunni successor is called a Caliph, while the Shiite successor is an Imam. Imams are believed to interpret the Qur'an infallibly. **Shiites** fall into 3 major branches: Fivers, Seveners, and Twelvers, reflecting the number of Imams they recognize. Twelvers believe that the 12th Imam has lived an invisible existence since 874, and will return as the Mahdi (a messiah figure) who will usher in a 1,000-year reign of peace and justice. **Sufism** (mystical dimension of Islam) emphasizes personal relation to God and obedience informed by love of God; it is prevalent among both Sunni and Shiites.

Organization: Muhammad was both the last prophet and a statesman. Muslim leaders have often assumed both civil and moral functions within Islamic states. Within the larger community, there are cultural and national groups, held together by a common religious law, the *Shari'a*. Muslims believe that God is the ultimate law giver and that human beings cannot devise laws that oppose divine laws; still the Shari'a is approached differently in different parts of the Islamic world. Over the centuries, Sunnis have developed 4 major schools of law: the Hanafi, the Shafi'i, the Hanbali, and the Maliki schools. The Ja'fari school is the most important and well-known Shiite school. Before the 20th century, religious scholars known as the ulama held much legal power. Judges (qadis) and law-interpreters (muftis) are people learned in religious law who lead congregational prayers in mosques and perform other religious duties.

Practice: Five duties (of both men and women), known as the "Pillars of Islam," are regarded as cardinal in Islam and as central to the life of the Islamic community. In accordance with Islam's absolute commitment to monotheism, the first duty is the profession of faith (the *Shahadah*): "There is no God but Allah and Muhammad is his Prophet." A Muslim must profess this belief publicly at least once in his or her lifetime; it defines the membership of an individual in the Islamic community. The second duty is that of five daily prayers organized in intervals throughout the day: sunrise, early afternoon, late afternoon, immediately after sunset, and before midnight. During prayer, Muslims face the *Kaaba*, a small, cube-shaped structure in the courtyard toward *al-Haram* (the "inviolate place"), at the great mosque of Mecca. All five prayers in Islam are congregational and are to be offered in a mosque, but they may be offered individually if one cannot be present with a congregation. Congregational prayer is required only at the early afternoon prayer on Friday for men. The third cardinal duty of a Muslim is to pay alms, or *zakat*, which should be 2.5% of one's total wealth. This was originally the tax levied by Muhammad on the wealthy members of the community, primarily to help the poor. Only when zakat has been paid is the rest of a Muslim's property considered purified and legitimate. The fourth duty is the fast of the lunar month of Ramadan. During the fasting month, one must abstain from eating, drinking, smoking, impure thoughts, and sexual intercourse from dawn until sunset, and feed at least one poor person, if able. The fifth duty is the pilgrimage to the Kaaba in the Grand Mosque at Mecca, which a Muslim must undertake, with exceptions for poverty and ill health, at least once during his or her lifetime.

Location: W Africa to Philippines, across a band including E Africa, Central Asia and W China, India, Malaysia, Indonesia. Islam has several million adherents in North America and about 30 mil in Europe.

Beliefs: Strictly monotheistic. God is creator of the universe, omnipotent, omniscient, just, forgiving, and merciful. God revealed the Qur'an to Muhammad to guide humanity to truth and justice. Those who sincerely "submit" (literal meaning of "islam") to God attain salvation.

World's Largest Muslim Populations, 2005
Source: World Christian Database

Rank	Country	Muslim population	% of total pop.
1.	Indonesia*	177,790,964	78.7%
2.	India	155,997,935	13.8
3.	Pakistan	151,803,178	96.0
4.	Bangladesh	135,783,807	88.6
5.	Turkey	71,063,349	97.4
6.	Iran	68,480,915	98.7
7.	Nigeria	64,216,116	45.4
8.	Egypt	62,528,782	85.8
9.	Algeria	32,198,945	98.0
10.	Morocco	29,991,256	98.8
11.	Iraq	27,173,698	97.1
12.	Ethiopia	26,744,388	33.9
13.	Sudan	26,292,910	71.3
14.	Afghanistan	24,997,546	99.7
15.	Saudi Arabia	21,924,162	92.9
16.	Uzbekistan	21,916,551	82.4
17.	Yemen	20,901,246	99.1
18.	China	20,318,204	1.6
19.	Syria	17,418,887	92.2
20.	Russia	14,956,494	10.4

*Includes about 50 million persons classified as Muslim by the Indonesian government, but sometimes classified as New Religionists.

Baha'i

Founded: Mid-19th century

Founder: Mirza Husayn-Ali Nuri (1817-1892), later known as Baha'u'llah (Arabic for "Glory of God")

Sacred Texts: The writings of Baha'u'llah and of his herald the Bab (Siyyid Ali-Muhammad, 1819-1850). The primary text is *Kitab-i-Aqdas* (the Most Holy Book).

Organization: The Baha'i administrative system consists of elected nine-member councils at the local, national, and international levels. There are also more than 180 National Spiritual Assemblies and an elected, international governing body known as the Universal House of Justice

Practice: Prayer, meditation, and fasting are key components of Baha'i faith. Work performed in a spirit of service to humanity is considered an important form of worship.

The Baha'i Faith has no clergy and minimal ritual and congregational worship.

Divisions: In a religion in which unity is perhaps the central spiritual value, the Baha'i Faith has avoided separating into sects with differentiated theologies and practices.

Location: Worldwide, with practitioners in 236 countries.

Beliefs: God has progressively revealed His will and purpose through a series of Divine manifestations including Jesus, Buddha, Muhammad, Zoroaster, and Baha'u'llah. Baha'u'llah's teachings include the oneness of humanity, the equality of men and women, the harmony of science and religion, the abandonment of all forms of prejudice, and the elimination of extremes of poverty and wealth.

Buddhism

Founded: About 525 BCE, reportedly near Benares, India.

Founder: Gautama Siddhartha (c. 563-483 BCE), the Buddha, who achieved enlightenment through intense meditation.

Sacred Texts: The *Tripitaka*, a collection of the Buddha's teachings, rules of monastic life, and philosophical commentaries on the teachings; also a vast body of Buddhist teachings and commentaries, many of which are called *sutras*.

Organization: The basic institution is the *sangha*, or monastic order, through which traditions are passed down. Monastic life tends to be democratic and anti-authoritarian.

Practice: Varies widely according to the sect, and ranges from austere meditation to magical chanting and elaborate temple rites. Many practices, such as exorcism of devils, reflect pre-Buddhist beliefs.

Divisions: A variety of sects grouped into 3 primary branches: Theravada, which emphasizes the importance of pure thought and deed; Mahayana (includes Zen and Sokagakkai), which ranges from philosophical schools to belief in the saving grace of higher beings or ritual practices and to practical meditative disciplines; and Vajrayana, or Tantrism, a combination of belief in ritual magic and sophisticated philosophy.

Location: Mainly in Asia, from Sri Lanka to Japan.

Beliefs: Life is suffering, and there is no ultimate reality behind it. The cycle of birth and rebirth continues because of desire and attachment to the unreal "self." Meditation and deeds will end the cycle and achieve Nirvana (nothingness, enlightenment).

Hinduism

Founded: About 1500 BCE by Aryans who migrated to India, where their Vedic religion intermixed with the practices and beliefs of the natives.

Sacred texts: The *Veda,* including the *Upanishads,* a collection of rituals and commentaries; a vast number of epic stories about gods, heroes, and saints, including the *Bhagavadgita,* a part of the *Mahabharata,* and the *Ramayana.*

Organization: None, strictly speaking. Generally, rituals should be performed or assisted by Brahmins, the priestly caste, but in practice, simpler rituals can be performed by anyone. Brahmins are the final judges of ritual purity, the vital element in Hindu life. Temples and religious organizations are usually presided over by Brahmins.

Practice: Primarily passage rites (e.g., initiation, marriage, death, etc.) and daily devotions. Of the public rites, the *puja,* a ceremonial dinner for a god, is the most common.

Divisions: There is no concept of orthodoxy in Hinduism, which presents a variety of sects. The 3 major living traditions are those devoted to the gods Vishnu and Shiva and to the goddess Shakti. Numerous folk beliefs and practices, often in amalgamation with the above groups, exist side by side with philosophical schools.

Location: Mainly India, Nepal, Malaysia, Guyana, Suriname, and Sri Lanka.

Beliefs: There is only one divine principle; the many gods are only aspects of that unity. Life in all its forms is an aspect of the divine, but it appears as a separation from the divine, a meaningless cycle of birth and rebirth (*samsara*) determined by the purity or impurity of past deeds (*karma*). To improve one's *karma* or escape *samsara* by pure acts, thought, and/or devotion is the aim of every Hindu.

Judaism

Founded: About 2000 BCE.

Founder: Abraham is regarded as the founding patriarch, The Torah of Moses is the basic source of the teachings.

Sacred Texts: The 5 books of Moses (the Torah).

Organization: Originally theocratic, Judaism has evolved into a congregational polity. The basic institution is the local synagogue or temple, operated by the congregation and led by a rabbi of their choice. Chief rabbis in France and Great Britain have authority only over those who accept it; in Israel, the 2 chief rabbis have civil authority in family law.

Practice: Among traditional practicioners, almost all areas of life are governed by strict discipline. Sabbath and holidays are marked by observances, and attendance at public worship is considered especially important. Chief annual observances are Passover, celebrating liberation of the Israelites from Egypt and marked by the Seder meal in homes, and the 10 days from Rosh Hashanah (New Year) to Yom Kippur (Day of Atonement), a period of penitence.

Divisions: Judaism is an unbroken spectrum from ultraconservative to ultraliberal, largely reflecting different points of view regarding the binding character of the prohibitions and duties—particularly the dietary and Sabbath observations—traditionally prescribed for the daily life of the Jew.

Location: Mainly in Israel and the U.S.

Beliefs: Strictly monotheistic. God is the creator and ruler of the universe. God established a particular relationship with the Hebrew people: by obeying a divine law God gave them, they would be a special witness to God's mercy and justice. Judaism stresses ethical behavior (and, among the traditional, careful ritual obedience) as true worship of God.

Sikhism

Founded: Late 15th century in South Asia.

Founder: Guru Nanak Dev ji, Sikhism's first Guru.

Sacred Texts: The *Guru Granth Sahib* was compiled by the Sikh Gurus and contains their experiences of the Divine. It also contains writing by other saintly figures of different faiths.

Organization: Each Sikh must make her or his own spiritual journey and not depend on clergy. Congregational prayer led by both men and women takes place in local *Gurudwaras.* Harmandir Sahib in Amritsar, Punjab (Northern India) is the central place of worship.

Practice: Prayers are required in the morning, evening, and before sleeping. The most important mode of congregational prayer is the singing of hymns from the *Guru Granth Sahib.* The "Five Ks" are five articles of faith required of all Sikhs: *Kes* (uncut hair), *Kangha* (comb), *Kara* (steel bracelet), *Kirpan* (sword), and *Kaccha* (short pants).

Divisions: The last living Guru, Guru Gobind Singh (1666-1708) crystallized the practices and beliefs of the faith and determined that no future living Guru was needed. Today the religion is guided by joint sovereignty of Guru Granth and Guru Panth. Guru Granth is the Sikh scripture, as the spiritual manifestation of the Guru, while the Guru Panth is the collectivity of all initiated Sikhs worldwide, as the physical manifestation of the Guru.

Location: Many Sikhs are from Punjabi backgrounds. Punjab is divided between India and Pakistan.

Beliefs: Sikhism preaches a message of devotion, remembrance of God at all times, truthful living, equality between all human beings, and social justice, while emphatically denouncing superstitions and blind rituals. Sikhism is a monotheistic religion based on revelation.

Gods and Goddesses in Egyptian, Norse, and Classical Mythology

Source: World Almanac Research

Major Gods & Goddesses of Ancient Egypt

Name	Relations	Sphere or Position	Emblem/Attribute
Ra (Re)/Atum/Amon	Self-created	The sun, creation	Hawk
Thoth (Djeheuty)	Son of Ra	The moon, wisdom, writing	Ibis/baboon
Ptah	Creator of Atum	Creation, craftsmen	——
Osiris	Brother of Set(h) & Isis	The underworld (dead), fertility, resurrection, vegetation	Bull
Isis	Sister/consort of Osiris	The underworld (dead)	——
Set(h)	Brother of Osiris	Evil, trickery, chaos	Boar, pig
Horus (several)	Sons of Osiris & Isis and Ra & Hathor	The earth	Falcon
Hathor	Consort of Ra	Motherhood, love	Cow
Anubis	Son of Osiris	Embalmer & judge of the dead	Jackal/dog

Major Norse Gods & Goddesses

Name	Relations	Sphere or Position	Emblem/Attribute
Odin	Father of the Aesir (gods)	War and death, poetry, wisdom, magic	Spear, mead, ring/One-eyed
Thor	Son of Odin	Thunder, lightning, rain; champion of the gods	Hammer, belt
Njord	Father of Freyja & Freyr	Wind and sea, wealth and prosperity	——
Frigg	Wife of Odin	Marriage and motherhood, home	——
Freyja (Freya)	Daughter of Njord	Fertility, birth, crops	Necklace
Freyr	Son of Njord	Agriculture, sun, rain	Magic ship, golden boar
Tyr	Son of Odin[1]	Justice, war	Spear/One-handed
Heimdall	Son of nine giantesses	Watchman of the gods; keen sight & hearing	Horn
Balder (Baldur)	Son of Odin	Light, purity	——
Loki	Son of giants; father of Hel (goddess of death), Jormungand (serpent encompassing the world), Fenrir (the wolf).	Malicious trickster	——

(1) Referred to as the son of Hymir in some mythologies.

Major Gods & Goddesses of the Classical World

Greek	Roman	Relations	Sphere or Position
Aphrodite	Venus	Daughter of Zeus & Dione	Love
Apollo	——	Son of Zeus & Leto	Healing, poetry, light
Ares	Mars	Son of Zeus & Hera	War
Artemis	Diana	Daughter of Zeus & Leto	Hunting, chastity
Athena	Minerva	Daughter of Zeus & Metis	Wisdom, crafts, war
Cronus	Saturn	Father of Zeus	Titans' ruler
Demeter	Ceres	Sister of Zeus	Agriculture, fertility
Dionysus	Bacchus	Son of Zeus & Semele	Wine, fertility, ecstasy
Eros	Cupid	Son of Ares & Aphrodite	Love
Hades	Pluto	Brother of Zeus	The underworld, death
Hephaestus	Vulcan	Son of Zeus & Hera	Fire
Hera	Juno	Wife & sister of Zeus	Earth
Hermes	Mercury	Son of Zeus & Maia	Travel, commerce, gods' messenger
Hestia	Vesta	Sister of Zeus	The hearth
Pan	——	Son of Hermes & a wood nymph	Forests, flocks, shepherds
Persephone	Proserpina	Daughter of Zeus & Demeter	Grain
Poseidon	Neptune	Brother of Zeus	The sea
Rhea	Ops	Mother of Zeus	The earth
Uranus	Uranus	Father of Titans (elder gods)	The heavens
Zeus	Jupiter	Son of Cronus & Rhea	Ruler of the gods

LANGUAGE

New Words in English

The following words and definitions were provided by Merriam-Webster Inc., publishers of *Merriam-Webster's Collegiate Dictionary, Eleventh Edition*, released in 2003. The words or meanings are among those that the Merriam-Webster editors decided had achieved enough currency in English to be added to the 2009 printing of the dictionary.

acai: a small dark purple fleshy berrylike fruit of a tall slender palm (*Euterpe oleracea*) of tropical Central and South America that is often used in beverages; *also*: the palm

Anglosphere: the countries of the world in which the English language and cultural values predominate

bodywash: a liquid product for cleansing the body

carbon footprint: the negative impact that something (as a person or business) has on the environment; *specifically*: the amount of carbon emitted by something during a given period

celebutante: a debutante who has attracted such media attention as to be considered a celebrity

ciabatta: a flat oblong bread having a moist interior and a crispy crust

docusoap: a TV series in which the real-life activities of a group of people are presented in soap-opera style

dry-erase board: a hard smooth white surface used for writing or drawing on with markers

flash mob: a group of people summoned (as by e-mail or text message) to a designated location at a specified time to perform an indicated action before dispersing

frenemy: one who pretends to be a friend but is actually an enemy

germophobe: a person who has an abnormal fear of germs

green-collar: of, relating to, or involving actions for protecting the natural environment

guilty pleasure: something pleasurable that induces a usually minor feeling of guilt

locavore: one who eats foods grown locally whenever possible

memory foam: a dense polyurethane foam that becomes more pliable when in contact with heat

mixed martial arts: a contact sport that allows a wide range of fighting techniques including striking, kicking, and grappling

mixtape: a compilation of songs recorded (as onto a cassette tape or a CD) from various sources

polypharmacy: the practice of administering or using multiple medications especially concurrently (as in the treatment of a single disease or of several coexisting conditions)

reggaeton: popular music of Puerto Rican origin that combines rap with Caribbean rhythms

shawarma: a sandwich especially of sliced lamb or chicken, vegetables, and often tahini wrapped in pita bread

SIM card: a card that is inserted into a device (as a cell phone) and that is used to store data (as phone numbers or contact information)

softscape: vegetation (as shrubs and flowers) that is incorporated into a landscape

staycation: a vacation spent at home or nearby

superdelegate: a political party leader or an elected official selected to vote at a presidential nominating convention who may or may not be pledged to support a particular candidate

tase: to shoot with a Taser gun

vlog: a blog that contains video material

waterboarding: an interrogation technique in which water is forced into a detainee's mouth and nose so as to induce the sensation of drowning

webisode: an episode especially of a TV show that may or may not have been telecast but can be viewed at a Web site

woo-hoo or whoo-hoo: used to express exuberant delight or approval

zip line: a cable suspended above an incline to which a pulley and harness are attached for a rider

Words About Words

allegory: extended use of symbols, in the form of characters, animals, or events, that represent ideas or themes. Ex.: John Bunyan, *Pilgrim's Progress*

alliteration: repetition of same, initial consonant sounds of two or more words in sequence or in short intervals. Ex.: "I have stood still and stopped the sound of feet." —Robert Frost, "Acquainted with the Night"

anagram: a word or phrase made by rearranging letters from another word or phrase. Ex.: Clint Eastwood=Old West Action

antithesis: an expression in which contrasting ideas are intentionally juxtaposed, usually in parallel structure. Ex.: "The world will little note, nor long remember, what we say here, but it can never forget what they did here." —Abraham Lincoln, Gettysburg Address

assonance: repetition of same or similar vowel sounds in words located near each other. Ex.: "Green as a dream, and deep as death." —Rupert Brooke, "The Old Vicarage, Grantchester"

back-formation: creation of a word from an existing word, whose forms seem to suggest that the previously existing word derived from the newer word. Ex.: The verb "edit" is a back-formation of the word "editor."

cliché: a saying or expression that has been used so often it has lost its effect. Ex.: work like a dog

euphemism: a mild, indirect expression used instead of a plainer one that might be harsh, unpleasant, or offensive. Ex.: restroom instead of toilet; pass away instead of die

hyperbole: exaggeration for emphasis or effect. Ex.: "And fired the shot heard round the world." —Ralph Waldo Emerson, "Concord Hymn"

irony: an expression in which the intended meaning is contrary to its literal meaning; the words say one thing but mean another. Ex.: "Yet Brutus says he was ambitious; / And Brutus is an honorable man." —Shakespeare, *Julius Caesar*

litotes: intentional understatement made by negating the opposite of what is meant. Ex.: This was no small matter.

metonymy: substitution of one word for another that it suggests. Ex.: The pen is mightier than the sword.

onomatopoeia: words that imitate the sounds they describe. Ex.: buzz, murmur

oxymoron: juxtaposition of contradictory words. Ex.: deafening silence

palindrome: a type of anagram in which a word, phrase, or sentence reads the same backward and forward. Ex.: Ma is a nun as I am.

paradox: a statement that is seemingly contradictory, odd, or opposed to common sense or expectation and yet is presented as true. Ex.: "What a pity that youth must be wasted on the young." —George Bernard Shaw

personification: treating ideas or objects as though they were persons. Ex.: "Because I could not stop for Death— / He kindly stopped for me." —Emily Dickinson, "Because I Could Not Stop for Death"

simile: a comparison between two dissimilar things using the words "like" or "as." Ex.: "My love is like a red, red rose" —Robert Burns, "A Red, Red Rose"

spoonerism: play on words in which the initial sounds of two or more words are transposed, creating different phrases whose meanings when compared can be humorous. Ex.: a blushing crow, a crushing blow

synecdoche: (a form of metonymy) the use of a part for the whole, or the whole for the part. Ex.: All hands on deck!

tautology: unnecessary repetition of an idea in different words, phrases, or sentences. Ex.: close proximity

National Spelling Bee

The annual Scripps National Spelling Bee competition, conducted by The E.W. Scripps Company and other newspapers since 1941, was instituted by *The Courier-Journal* of Louisville, KY, in 1925. Students under 16 who are not beyond the 8th grade are eligible to compete at the local level for a chance to advance to the national competition in Washington, DC. The 2009 winners were Kavya Shivashankar (1st place), of Olathe, KS; Tim Ruiter (2nd place), of Centreville, VA; and Aishwarya Pastapur (3rd place) of Springfield, IL.

Here are the last words given, and spelled correctly, in each of the years from 1981 to 2009 at the National Spelling Bee.

1981	sarcophagus	1987	staphylococci	1993	kamikaze	1999	logorrhea	2005	appoggiatura
1982	psoriasis	1988	elegiacal	1994	antediluvian	2000	demarche	2006	Ursprache
1983	Purim	1989	spoliator	1995	xanthosis	2001	succedaneum	2007	serrefine
1984	luge	1990	fibranne	1996	vivisepulture	2002	prospicience	2008	guerdon
1985	milieu	1991	antipyretic	1997	euonym	2003	pococurante	2009	Laodicean
1986	odontalgia	1992	lyceum	1998	chiaroscurist	2004	autochthonous		

Names of the Days

ENGLISH	RUSSIAN	HEBREW	FRENCH	ITALIAN	SPANISH	GERMAN	JAPANESE
Sunday	voskresenye	yom rishon	dimanche	domenica	domingo	Sonntag	nichiyoubi
Monday	ponedelnik	yom sheni	lundi	lunedì	lunes	Montag	getsuyoubi
Tuesday	vtornik	yom shlishi	mardi	martedì	martes	Dienstag	kayoubi
Wednesday	sreda	yom ravii	mercredi	mercoledì	miércoles	Mittwoch	suiyoubi
Thursday	chetverg	yom hamishi	jeudi	giovedì	jueves	Donnerstag	mokuyoubi
Friday	pyatnitsa	yom shishi	vendredi	venerdì	viernes	Freitag	kinyoubi
Saturday	subbota	shabbat	samedi	sabato	sábado	Samstag	doyoubi

Foreign Words and Phrases

(A=Arabic; F=French; Ger=German; Gr=Greek; I=Italian; J=Japanese; L=Latin; R=Russian; S=Spanish; Y=Yiddish)

à bientôt (F; ah-bee-en-TOH): so long; see you soon

ad hoc (L; ad-HOK): for the end or purpose at hand; impromptu

ad hominem (L; ad-HOH-mee-nem): emotional rather than intellectual; in a dispute, using slander to obscure issues

al fresco (I; ahl-FRAYS-koh): outdoors

anime (J; A-nuh-may): Japanese-style animation

antebellum (L; AHN-teh-BEL-lum): pre-war

apercu(s) (F; ah-per-SOO): first perception or insight; outline

belles lettres (F; bel-LET-truh): writing aspiring to artistic merit

bête noire (F; bet-NWAHR): a thing or person viewed with particular dislike or fear

Bildungsroman (Ger; BIL-doongs-roh-mahn): novel embodying coming-of-age story

bodega (S; boh-DAY-gah): grocery store

bonhomie (F; boh-noh-MEE): friendliness

bon vivant (F; bon-vee-VAHN): a person with refined tastes, espec. for food and drink

boondocks (Tagalog; BUHN-dahks): rural

bourgeois (F; boo-ZHWAH): middle-class; conventional; materialistic

carte blanche (F; kahrt-BLANSH): full discretionary power

casus belli (L; KAH-soos-BEL-lee): reason for going to war

cause célèbre (F; kawz-suh-LEB): a notorious incident

cognoscenti (I; kahn-yuh-SHEN-tee): experts; connoisseurs

contretemps (F; kon-truh-TAHN): awkward situation

coup de grâce (F; kooh-duh-GRAHS): the final blow

cum laude/magna cum laude/summa cum laude (L; kuhm-LOU-day; MAG-na ...; SOO-ma ...): with praise or honor/with great praise or honor/with the highest praise or honor

de facto (L; day-FAK-toh): in fact, if not by law

de jure (L; dee-JOOR-ee, day-YOOR-ay): in accordance with right or law; officially

de rigueur (F; duh-ree-GUR): necessary according to convention or etiquette

détente (F; day-TAHNT): an easing of strained relations

deus ex machina (L; DAY-uhs-eks-MAH-keh-nah): person/event that provides a solution unexpectedly or suddenly, espec. (in literature) a contrived solution to a plot

double entendre (F; DOO-blahn-TAHN-druh): expression with a double meaning, one meaning of which is often risqué

éminence grise (F; ay-meh-nahns-GREEZ): one who wields power behind the scenes

enfant terrible (F; ahn-FAHN-te-REE-bluh): one who is noteworthy for embarrassing or unconventional behavior

ennui (F; ah-NOOEE): boredom; world-weariness; annoyance

e pluribus unum (L; eh-PLOO-ree-boos-OO-noom): out of many, one (U.S. motto)

ersatz (Ger; EHR-zats): artificial; being a (usually inferior) substitute

ex post facto (L; eks-pohst-FAK-toh): retroactive(ly)

fait accompli (F; fayt-uh-kom-PLEE): an accomplished fact

fatwa (A; FAHT-wah): in Islam, a legal or religious decree

faux pas (F; foh-PAH): false step; a social blunder or breach of etiquette

habeas corpus (L; HAY-bee-ahs-KOR-pus): an order for an accused person to be brought to court

hoi polloi (Gr; hoy-puh-LOY): the masses

impresario (I; im-prah-SAH-ri-oh): manager, promoter, or sponsor of a muscial or theatrical program or company

imprimatur (L; im-prah-MAH-toor): approval or official permission to print, espec. by the Roman Catholic church

in loco parentis (L; in-LOH-koh-puh-REN-tis): in place of parent

in medias res (L; in-MAY-dee-oos-rays): into the middle of things

in omnibus (L; in-AHM-ni-buhs): in all things; in all ways

intelligentsia (R; in-te-luh-JEN-see-uh): elite class of society made up of intellectuals and educated people

je ne sais quoi (F; zhuh-nuh-say-KWAH): I don't know what; the little something that eludes description

joie de vivre (F; zhwah-duh-VEEV-ruh): zest for life

leitmotif (Ger; lyt-moh-TEEF): the central theme or idea, particularly in art and literature

mano a mano (S; MAH-noh-ah-MAH-noh): hand to hand; in direct combat

mea culpa (L; MAY-uh-CUL-puh): through my fault

mensch (Y; MENTSCH): an upright, noble, admirable person

modus operandi (L; MOH-duhs-op-uh-RAN-dee): method of operation

mujahideen (A; moo-jah-ha-DEEN): Islamic holy fighters; shares root with the word jihad, which means "a struggle"

noblesse oblige (F; noh-BLES-oh-BLEEZH): the obligation of nobility to help the less fortunate

nolo contendere (L; NOH-loh-kohn-TEN-duh-ree): a plea of no contest whereby a person does not admit guilt but is subject to punishment

non compos mentis (L; non-KOM-puhs-MEN-tis): not of sound mind

non sequitur (L; non-SEH-kwi-tour): a conclusion that does not logically follow from what preceded it

nouveau riche (F; noo-voh-REESH): a newly rich person, espec. one who spends money conspicuously

ombudsman (Swedish; AHM-budz-muhn): person who receives, investigates, and settles complaints

par excellence (F; par-ek-seh-LANS): best of all; incomparable

parvenu (F; par-vuh-NOO): upstart

persona non grata (L; per-SOH-nah-non-GRAH-tah): unwelcome person

pièce de résistance (F; pee-es-duh-ray-ZEES-tonz): the outstanding item in a series or group

pro bono (L; proh-BOH-noh): (legal work) donated for the public good

quid pro quo (L; kwid-proh-KWOH): something given or received for something else

raison d'être (F; RAY-zohnn-DET-ruh): reason for being

savoir faire (F; sav-wahr-FAIR): dexterity in social affairs

Schadenfreude (Ger; SHAH-duhn-froy-deh): joy at another's misfortune

schlemiel (Y; shleh-MEEL): an unlucky, bungling person

schlepp (Y; SHLEP): move slowly, tediously, drag oneself along

semper fidelis (L; SEM-puhr-fee-DAY-lis): always faithful

sobriquet (F; SOH-bri-kay): nickname

terra firma (L; TER-uh-FUR-muh): solid ground

troika (R; TROY-kuh): group of three, espec. a ruling group

vis-à-vis (F; vee-zuh-VEE): compared with; with regard to

voir dire (F; vwar-DEER): examination by lawyers or judge to determine the suitability of a witness or a prospective juror

zeitgeist (Ger; ZITE-gyste): the general intellectual, moral, and cultural climate of an era

Names for Animal Young

calf: cattle, elephant, hippo, camel, others

cheeper: grouse, partridge, quail

chick: chicken, penguin, other birds

cockerel: rooster

codling, sprag: codfish

colt: horse, zebra (male)

cria: llama, alpaca

cub: lion, bear, shark, fox, others

cygnet: swan

duckling: duck

elver: eel

ephyra: jellyfish

eyas: hawk, others

fawn: deer, antelope

filly: horse, zebra (female)

fingerling, fry: fish generally

fledgling, nestling: birds generally

foal: horse, zebra, others

gosling: goose

heifer: cow

hoglet: hedgehog

joey: kangaroo, opossum, wombat, other marsupials

kid: goat

kit: beaver, rabbit, ferret, wolverine, others

kitten, kitty: cat, other small mammals

lamb: sheep

larva: frog, sea urchin, insects generally

parr, smolt, grilse: salmon

peachick: peafowl

piglet, shoat, farrow, suckling: pig

polliwog, tadpole: frog

poult: turkey

puggle: echidna

pullet: hen

pup: dog, fox, seal, rat

spat: oyster, other bivalves

spiderling: spider

spike, blinker, tinker: mackerel

squab: pigeon

whelp: dog, tiger, other carnivorous mammals

yearling: cattle, sheep, horse, others

Names for Animal Collectives

alligators: congregation
ants: army, colony, swarm
apes: shrewdness, troop
bats: colony
bears: sleuth, sloth
bees: colony, swarm, hive, grist
birds: flight, volery
boars/swine: singular, sounder
buffalo: gang, obstinacy
butterflies: flutter
buzzards: wake
camels: caravan, flock, train
cats: clowder, cluster, glaring, pounce
cattle: drove
cheetahs: coalition
clams, oysters: bed
cockroaches: intrusion
cranes: sedge, siege
crocodiles: bask, nest, float
crows: murder, horde
dolphins: pod
doves: dule, pitying
ducks: brace, team
eagles: convocation, aerie
ferrets: business
finches: charm

fish: school, shoal
flamingos: stand, flamboyance
foxes: skulk
geese: flock, gaggle, skein
giraffes: corps, herd, tower
goats: tribe, trip
gorillas: band, whoop
grasshoppers: cloud
hares: down, husk, trip
hawks: cast, kettle
hedgehogs: array, prickle
hippopotami: bloat
horses: pair, team
hounds: cry, mute, pack
hyenas: cackle
iguanas: mess
jellyfish: smack
kangaroos: mob, troop
larks: exaltation
leopards: leap
lions: pride
locusts: plague, swarm
moles: labor
monkeys: troop
mules: barren, span
nightingales: watch

otters: romp
owls: parliament
oxen: yoke
peacocks: muster
pheasants: nest, nide, bouquet
ponies: string
raccoons: gaze
ravens: unkindness
rhinoceroses: crash
seals: pod
sheep: flock, drove, hurtle
snakes: nest
squirrels: dray, scurry
starlings: flock, murmuration
swans: bevy
tigers: streak
toads: knot
trout: hover
turkeys: rafter
turtles: bale
vultures: committee
whales: gam, herd, pod
woodchucks: fall
woodpeckers: descent
zebras: herd, zeal

Some Common Abbreviations and Acronyms

Acronyms are pronounceable words formed from first letters (or syllables) of other words. Some **abbreviations** below (e.g., AIDS, NATO) are thus acronyms. Some acronyms are words coined as abbreviations and written in lower case (e.g., sonar, yuppie). Acronyms do not have periods; usage for other abbreviations varies, but periods have become less common. Capitalization usage may vary from what is shown here. Italicized words preceding parenthetical definitions below are Latin unless otherwise noted. See also other chapters, including Computers and Telecommunications; Weights and Measures.

AA: Alcoholics Anonymous; Associate in Arts; administrative assistant
AAA: American Automobile Association
ABA: American Bar Association
abr.: abridged
AC: alternating current; air-conditioning
AD: *anno Domini* (in the year of the Lord)
ADD: Attention Deficit Disorder
AFL-CIO: American Federation of Labor and Congress of Industrial Organizations
AI: artificial intelligence
AIDS: acquired immune deficiency syndrome
a.m. or **AM:** *ante meridiem* (before noon)
anon: anonymous
APO: army post office
APR: annual percentage rate
ARM: adjustable rate mortgage
ASCAP: American Society of Composers, Authors, and Publishers
ASCII: American Standard Code for Information Interchange
ATM: automated teller machine
AWOL: absent without leave
BA: Bachelor of Arts
bbl: barrel(s)
BC: before Christ
BCE: before the Common Era
bpd: barrels per day
BS: Bachelor of Science
Btu: British thermal unit(s)
bu: bushel(s)
BYOB: bring your own bottle
C: Celsius, centigrade
c: *circa* (about); copyright
CAFTA: Central American Free Trade Agreement
CAT: computerized axial tomography
CBD: Central Business District
CDC: Centers for Disease Control and Prevention; Community Development Corporation
CE: Common Era
CEO: chief executive officer
cf.: *confer* (compare)
CFO: chief financial officer
CIA: Central Intelligence Agency
CIF: cost, insurance, and freight

CIO: chief information officer
CNM: Certified Nurse Midwife
COD: cash (or collect) on delivery
COL or **Col.:** Colonel
COLA: cost of living adjustment
colloq.: colloquial
COO: chief operating officer
CPA: certified public accountant
CPI: Consumer Price Index
CPL or **Cpl.:** Corporal
CPR: cardiopulmonary resuscitation
CPU: central processing unit
CST: Central Standard Time
DA: district attorney
DC: direct current
DD: Doctor of Divinity
DDS: Doctor of Dental Surgery
DHS: Dept. of Homeland Security
DMD: Doctor of Dental Medicine
DMZ: demilitarized zone
DNA: deoxyribonucleic acid
DNR: do not resuscitate
DOA: dead on arrival
DOB: date of birth
dpi: dots per inch
DPT: diphtheria, pertussis, tetanus
DUI: driving under the influence
DVD: digital video disc
DVM: Doctor of Veterinary Medicine
DWI: driving while intoxicated
ed.: edited, edition, editor
EEG: electroencephalogram
e.g.: *exempli gratia* (for example)
EKG: electrocardiogram
EOE: equal opportunity employer
EP: extended play
EPA: Environmental Protection Agency
ERA: Equal Rights Amendment; earned run average
ESL: English as a second language
ESP: extrasensory perception
Esq.: esquire
EST: eastern standard time
et al.: *et alii* (and others)
etc.: *et cetera* (and so forth)
EU: European Union
F: Fahrenheit
FBI: Federal Bureau of Investigation
FDA: Food and Drug Administration

FDIC: Federal Deposit Insurance Corporation
FEMA: Federal Emergency Management Agency
ff.: and those following
FICA: Federal Insurance Contributions Act (Social Security)
fl.: *floruit* (flourished), used for hist. figures when life dates uncertain
FY: fiscal year
FYI: for your information
GATT: General Agreement on Tariffs and Trade
GB: gigabyte(s)
GDP: gross domestic product
GED: general equivalency diploma (for high school)
GIS: geographic information system
GMT: Greenwich mean time
GOP: Grand Old Party (Republican Party)
GPS: Global Positioning System
GUI: graphical user interface
hazmat: HAZardous MATerial
HDTV: high-definition television
HIV: human immunodeficiency virus
HMO: health maintenance organization
HMS: His/Her Majesty's Ship (UK)
Hon.: the Honorable
HOV: high-occupancy vehicle
HRH: her (his) royal highness (UK)
HTML: hypertext markup language
HTTP: hypertext transfer protocol
HVAC: heating, ventilating, and air-conditioning
Hz: hertz
ibid: *ibidem* (in the same place)
i.e.: *id est* (that is)
IMF: International Monetary Fund
IPO: initial public offering
IQ: intelligence quotient
IRA: individual retirement account; Irish Republican Army
IRS: Internal Revenue Service
ISBN: International Standard Book Number
JD: *Juris Doctor* (Doctor of Law)
k: karat
K: kelvin
kWh: kilowatt-hour(s)

laser: Light Amplification by Stimulated Emission of Radiation
LLP: limited licensed partnership
loc. cit.: *loco citato* (in the place cited)
LSAT: Law School Admission Test
LT or **Lt.:** Lieutenant
MA: Master of Arts
MB: megabyte(s)
MBA: Master of Business Administration
MCAT: Medical College Admission Test
MD: *Medicinae Doctor* (Doctor of Medicine)
MIA: missing in action
modem: MOdulator-DEModulator
MP: member of Parliament (UK)
mph: miles per hour
MRI: magnetic resonance imaging
ms, mss: manuscript(s)
MS: Master of Science; multiple sclerosis
MSG: monosodium glutamate
MST: mountain standard time
MVP: most valuable player
NA: not applicable; not available
NAACP: National Association for the Advancement of Colored People
NAFTA: North American Free Trade Agreement
NASA: National Aeronautics and Space Administration
NATO: North Atlantic Treaty Organization
NB or **n.b.:** *nota bene* (note carefully)
NCAA: National Collegiate Athletic Association
NIH: National Institutes of Health
NOW: National Organization for Women
NPR: National Public Radio
NRA: National Rifle Association

obs.: obsolete
OED: Oxford English Dictionary
op: *opus* (work)
OPEC: Organization of Petroleum Exporting Countries
OTC: over the counter
p, pp: page(s)
PA: public address
PAC: political action committee
PC: personal computer; politically correct
pd.: paid; *per diem*
PDA: Personal Digital Assistant
PhD: *Philosophiae Doctor* (doctor of philosophy)
PIN: personal identification number
p.m. or **PM:** *post meridiem* (afternoon)
PS: *post scriptum* (postscript)
PST: Pacific standard time
pt: part(s); pint(s); point(s)
PVT or **Pvt.:** Private
QC: Queen's Counsel (UK)
QED: *quod erat demonstrandum* (which was to be demonstrated)
q.v.: *quod vide* (which see)
radar: RAdio Detecting And Ranging
RCMP: Royal Canadian Mounted Police
REM: rapid eye movement
Rev.: Reverend
rev.: revised; reviewed
RIP: *requiescat in pace* (may he/she rest in peace)
RN: Registered Nurse
RNA: ribonucleic acid
ROTC: Reserve Officers' Training Corps
rpm: revolutions per minute
RSVP: *répondez s'il vous plaît* (Fr.) (please reply)

SARS: severe acute respiratory syndrome
SASE: self-addressed stamped envelope
SETI: Search for Extraterrestrial Intelligence
SGT or **Sgt.:** Sergeant
SIDS: suddent infant death syndrome
SJ: Society of Jesus (Jesuits)
sonar: SOund NAvigation and Ranging
SOP: standard operating procedure
SPCA: Society for the Prevention of Cruelty to Animals
SSI: Supplementary Security Income
TBA: to be announced
TBD: to be determined
TEFL: teaching English as a foreign language
UFO: unidentified flying object
UPC: Universal Product Code
URL: Univeral Resource Locator
USS: United States ship
UTC: coordinated universal time
var.: variant
VCR: videocassette recorder
viz: *videlicet* (namely)
VP: vice president
W: watt(s)
WHO: World Health Organization
WMD: weapons of mass destruction
WPM: words per minute
YMCA: Young Men's Christian Association
YTD: year to date
yuppie: young urban professional
ZIP: zone improvement plan (U.S. Postal Service)

Eponyms
(words named for people)

boycott: to avoid trade or dealings with, as a protest; after Charles C. Boycott, an English land agent in County Mayo, Ireland, ostracized in 1880 for refusing to reduce rents

derby: a stiff felt hat with a dome-shaped crown and narrow rolled brim; after Edward Stanley, 12th Earl of Derby, who in 1780 founded the Derby horse race, to which these hats are worn

derrick: a type of crane consisting of a boom connected to the base of an upright mast; after Derrick, early 17th-cent. English hangman who used a gallows that operated via cables and pulleys

draconian: harsh or severe; after Draco, statesman who codified the laws in Athens in 621 BCE

galvanize: to shock with an electric current, to energize or spur; from Luigi Galvano, Italian physicist who invented a process to cover metals with electrons for protection against rust

gerrymander: to draw an election district in such a way as to favor a political party; after Elbridge Gerry, who created (1812) just such an election district (shaped like a salamander) during his governorship of Massachusetts

guillotine: a machine for beheading; after Joseph Guillotin, French physician who proposed its use in 1789 as more humane than hanging

Luddite: one who opposes new technology; from Ned Ludd, leader of a group of textile workers in England who destroyed machinery in the early 1800s

maudlin: excessively sentimental; from Scriptural figure Mary Magdalene, who is often shown weeping in depictions

mesmerize: to hypnotize or enthrall; from Franz Mesmer, 18th-cent. German physicist who developed therapy using magnetism that led to hypnosis

milquetoast: a timid, unassertive person; after Caspar Milquetoast, comic strip character created by American Harold Tucker Webster in 1924

Pollyanna: an overly optimistic person; based on the title character of a novel (1913) by American writer Eleanor Porter

ritzy: opulent; after the elegant Ritz Hotel, which Swiss-born César Ritz opened in Paris in 1898

salmonella: group of bacteria that can cause infections when contaminated food or water is consumed; named after discoverer Daniel Elmer Salmon, American veterinarian and public health official

sandwich: two or more slices of bread with a filling in between; after John Montagu, 4th Earl of Sandwich (1718-92), who supposedly ate these at the gaming table

shrapnel: originally, a projectile with lead balls designed to inflict maximum damage in explosions, later pieces of shell casings; from Henry Shrapnel (1761-1842), British artillery officer who designed the projectile

silhouette: an outline image; from Étienne de Silhouette (1709-67), a stingy French finance minister

Sisyphean: of, or relating to, futile exertions; from Sisyphus, a king in Greek mythology who was eternally condemned to roll a stone to the top of a hill, only to have it roll back down

Zamboni: an ice resurfacing machine; after American inventor Frank Zamboni, who owned an ice skating rink

Contranyms

Words that can have opposite meanings depending on their usage are known as **contranyms** or self-antonyms. They are also called Janus words, after the Roman god of doors and gates, who is often depicted with two faces looking in opposite directions. Contranyms are produced in various ways: For example, two words with different origins and contradictory meanings might acquire the same spelling, or a word's archaic meaning might be the opposite of the word's meaning in current usage. Here are a few examples of contranyms:

cleave:	to split apart	*or*	to stick together
clip:	to cut	*or*	to fasten
sanction:	approval	*or*	punishment
screen:	to shield	*or*	to present
trim:	to cut away	*or*	to ornament

Contranyms may also have similar sounds but different spellings (e.g., *raise* and *raze*).

Top 10 First Names of Americans by Decade of Birth

Source: U.S. Social Security Administration

BOYS

1880-1889 . . . . John, William, Charles, George, James, Frank, Joseph, Harry, Henry, Edward
1890-1899 . . . . John, William, George, James, Charles, Joseph, Frank, Robert, Harry, Henry
1900-1909 . . . . John, William, James, George, Joseph, Charles, Robert, Frank, Edward, Henry
1910-1919 . . . . John, William, James, Robert, Joseph, Charles, George, Edward, Frank, Walter
1920-1929 . . . . John, Robert, James, William, Charles, George, Joseph, Richard, Edward, Donald
1930-1939 . . . . Robert, James, John, William, Richard, Charles, Donald, George, Thomas, Joseph
1940-1949 . . . . James, Robert, John, William, Richard, David, Charles, Thomas, Michael, Ronald
1950-1959 . . . . Michael, James, Robert, John, David, William, Steven, Richard, Thomas, Mark
1960-1969 . . . . Michael, John, David, James, Robert, Mark, Steven, William, Jeffrey, Richard
1970-1979 . . . . Michael, Christopher, Jason, David, James, John, Brian, Robert, Steven, William
1980-1989 . . . . Michael, Christopher, Matthew, Joshua, David, Daniel, James, John, Robert, Brian
1990-1999 . . . . Michael, Christopher, Matthew, Joshua, Nicholas, Jacob, Andrew, Daniel, Brandon, Tyler
2008 . . . . Jacob, Michael, Ethan, Joshua, Daniel, Alexander, Anthony, William, Christopher, Matthew

GIRLS

1880-1889 . . . . Mary, Anna, Elizabeth, Catherine, Margaret, Emma, Bertha, Minnie, Florence, Clara
1890-1899 . . . . Mary, Anna, Margaret, Helen, Catherine, Elizabeth, Florence, Ruth, Rose, Ethel
1900-1909 . . . . Mary, Helen, Margaret, Anna, Ruth, Catherine, Elizabeth, Dorothy, Marie, Mildred
1910-1919 . . . . Mary, Helen, Dorothy, Margaret, Ruth, Catherine, Mildred, Anna, Elizabeth, Frances
1920-1929 . . . . Mary, Dorothy, Betty, Helen, Margaret, Ruth, Virginia, Catherine, Doris, Frances
1930-1939 . . . . Mary, Betty, Barbara, Shirley, Patricia, Dorothy, Joan, Margaret, Carol, Nancy
1940-1949 . . . . Mary, Linda, Barbara, Patricia, Carol, Sandra, Nancy, Sharon, Judith, Susan
1950-1959 . . . . Deborah, Mary, Linda, Patricia, Susan, Barbara, Karen, Nancy, Donna, Catherine
1960-1969 . . . . Lisa, Deborah, Mary, Karen, Michelle, Susan, Kimberly, Lori, Teresa, Linda
1970-1979 . . . . Jennifer, Michelle, Amy, Melissa, Kimberly, Lisa, Angela, Heather, Kelly, Sarah
1980-1989 . . . . Jessica, Jennifer, Ashley, Sarah, Amanda, Stephanie, Nicole, Melissa, Katherine, Megan
1990-1999 . . . . Ashley, Jessica, Sarah, Brittany, Emily, Kaitlyn, Samantha, Megan, Brianna, Katherine
2008 . . . . Emma, Isabella, Emily, Madison, Ava, Olivia, Sophia, Abigail, Elizabeth, Chloe

Origins of Popular American Given Names

Source: Dr. Cleveland Kent Evans, Bellevue University, Bellevue, NE; World Almanac research

Boys

Alexander: Gr. *Alexandros*, "defender of man"
Andrew: possibly Gr. *andreia*, "manly," or Eng. form of Gr. *Andreas*
Anthony: Roman *Antonius*, possibly from Gr. *anthos*, "flower"
Benjamin: Heb. *Binyamin*, "son of the right hand"
Brandon: Eng. place name, "gorse-covered hill"
Brian: Irish, perhaps Celtic *Brigonos*, "high, noble"
Charles: Ger. *ceorl*, "free man"
Christopher: Gr. *Khristophoros*, "bearing Christ [in one's heart]"
Daniel: Heb. "God is my judge"
David: Heb. *Dodavehu*, perhaps "darling"
Edward: Old Eng. *Eadweard*, "wealth-guard"

Ethan: Heb. "solid," "firm"
Frank: Ger. "Frenchman"
George: Gr. *georgos*, "soil tiller, farmer"
Henry: Ger. *Haimric*, "home-power"
Jack: nickname for John
Jacob: Heb. *Yaakov*, "God protects" or "supplanter"
James: Late Lat. *Iacomus*, form of Jacob
Jason: Gr. *Iason*, "healer"
Jeffrey: Norman Fr., from Ger. *Gaufrid*, "land-peace," or *Gisfrid*, "pledge-peace"
John: Heb. *Yohanan*, "God is gracious"
Jonathan: Heb. "God has given"
Jose: Heb. and Aramaic *Yose*, variant of Joseph
Joseph: Heb. *Yosef*, "[God] shall add"
Joshua: Heb. *Yoshua*, "God saves"
Mark: Lat. *Marcus*, perhaps from Mars, god of war

Matthew: Heb. *Mattathia*, "gift of God"
Michael: Heb. "Who could ever be like God?"
Nathan: Heb. "God has given"; modern short form of Nathaniel or Jonathan
Nicholas: Gr. *Nikolaos*, "victory-people"
Patrick: Lat. *Patricius*, "belonging to the noble class"
Richard: Ger. "power-hardy"
Robert: Ger. *Hrodberht*, "fame-bright"
Ryan: prob. from Irish surname, Gaelic "king"
Samuel: Heb. *Shemuel*, "God heard"
Sean: Gaelic form of John
Steven: Gr. *stephanos*, "crown, garland"
Thomas: Aramaic "twin"
Tyler: Old Eng. *tigeler*, "tile layer"
William: Ger. *Wilhelm*, "will-helmet"

Girls

Abigail: Heb. "My father is joy"
Alexis: Gr. "helper" or "defender"
Amanda: 17th-cent. invention from Lat. "lovable"
Amy: Old Fr. *Amee*, "beloved"
Andrea: possibly Gr. *andreia*, "manly," or fem. form of Andrew or Andreas
Angela: Gr. *angelos*, "messenger [of God]"
Ann Eng. form, **Anne:** Eng., Fr., Ger. form of Hannah
Anna: Lat. and Gr. form of Hannah
Ashley: Eng. place name, "ash grove"
Ava: prob. modern form of Eva, Lat. form of Heb. *Eve*, "to breathe"
Barbara: Gr. *barbarus*, "foreign"
Betty: 18th-cent. nickname for Elizabeth
Brianna: modern fem. form of Brian
Brittany: place name, Fr. province settled by Britons

Carol: form of Charles
Clara: Lat. *clarus*, "famous"
Deborah: Heb. "bee"
Donna: Ital. "lady"
Dorothy: Gr. *Dorothea*, "gift of God"
Elizabeth: Heb. *Elisheba*, perhaps "God is my oath" or "God is good fortune"
Ella: prob. variant or nickname for Eleanor or Ellen
Emily: Roman *Aemilia*, possibly from Lat. *aemulus*, "rival"
Emma: Ger. *ermen*, "whole, entire"
Frances: fem. form of Francis, "a Frenchman"
Haley: Eng. place name, "hay clearing"
Hannah: Heb. "He has favored me"
Heather: Middle Eng. *hathir*, "heather"
Helen: Gr. *Helene*, possibly "sunbeam"
Isabella, Isabel: Lat., Sp. variant of Elizabeth

Jennifer: Cornish form of Welsh *Gwenhwyfar*, "fair-smooth"
Jessica: Shakesp. invention, prob. fem. form of Jesse, Heb. "God exists"
Judith: Heb. "Jewish woman"
Julia: fem. form of Julius, Roman family name, or Lat. "youthful"
Kaitlyn: American spelling of Caitlin, the Irish form of Katherine
Karen: Danish form of Katherine
Katherine: Egyptian *Aikaterine*, later modified to resemble Gr. *katharos*, "pure"
Kelly: Irish Gaelic *Ceallagh*, perhaps "churchgoer" or "bright-headed"
Kimberly: Eng. place name, "Cyneburgh's clearing"
Laura: Lat. *laurus*, "laurel"
Linda: Sp. "pretty" or Ger. "tender"

Lisa: nickname for Elizabeth

Lori: nickname for Lorraine (Fr. "land of Lothar's people") or Laura

Madison: Middle Eng. surname, "son of Madeline or Maud"

Margaret: Gr. *margaron,* "pearl"

Maria: Lat. form of Mary

Marie: Fr. form of Mary

Mary: Eng. form of Heb. *Maryam,* perhaps "seeress" or "wished-for child"

Megan: Welsh form of Margaret

Melissa: Gr. "bee"

Michelle: Fr. fem. form of Michael

Nancy: medieval Eng. nickname for Agnes, Gr. *hagnos,* "holy"; later also nickname for Ann

Nicole: Fr. fem. form of Nicholas

Olivia: Lat. *oliva,* "olive tree"

Patricia: Lat. fem. form of Patrick

Rachel: Heb. "ewe"

Rose: Ger. *hros,* "horse," or Lat. *rosa,* "rose"

Ruth: Heb., perhaps "companion"

Samantha: colonial American invention, prob. combining Sam from Samuel (Heb. "God heard") with *-antha* from Gr. *anthos,* "flower"

Sandra: short form of Alessandra, Ital. fem. form of Alexander

Sarah: Heb. "princess"

Sharon: Biblical place name, Heb. "plain"

Sophia: Gr. "wisdom"

Stephanie: Fr. fem. form of Steven

Susan: Eng. form of Heb. *Shoshana,* "lily"

Teresa: Sp., perhaps "woman from Therasia"

Victoria: fem. form of Victor, from Lat. *vincere,* "to conquer"

30 Most Common Last Names in the U.S. Population

Source: 2000 Census, U.S. Census Bureau, U.S. Dept. of Commerce

Rank	Name	Frequency[1] (%)	Rank	Name	Frequency[1] (%)	Rank	Name	Frequency[1] (%)	Rank	Name	Frequency[1] (%)
1.	Smith	0.881	9.	Rodriguez	0.298	17.	Martin	0.249	24.	Harris	0.220
2.	Johnson	0.688	10.	Wilson	0.290	18.	Jackson	0.247	25.	Clark	0.203
3.	Williams	0.569	11.	Martinez	0.287	19.	Thompson	0.239	26.	Lewis	0.189
4.	Brown	0.512	12.	Anderson	0.283	20.	White	0.237	27.	Robinson	0.186
5.	Jones	0.505	13.	Taylor	0.267	21.	Lopez	0.230	28.	Walker	0.186
6.	Miller	0.418	14.	Thomas	0.263	22.	Lee	0.225	29.	Perez	0.181
7.	Davis	0.398	15.	Hernandez	0.262	23.	Gonzalez	0.222	30.	Hall	0.176
8.	Garcia	0.318	16.	Moore	0.259						

(1) Percent of people in the sample population (269,762,087) with the name shown.

Pen Names

Woody Allen	Allen Stewart Konigsberg
Maya Angelou	Marguerite Johnson
Currer, Ellis, and Acton Bell	Charlotte, Emily, and Anne Brontë
Nellie Bly	Elizabeth Jane Cochrane Seaman
John le Carré	David John Moore Cornwell
Lewis Carroll	Charles Lutwidge Dodgson
Colette	Sidonie Gabrielle Colette
George Eliot	Mary Ann or Marian Evans
Maksim Gorky	Aleksey Maksimovich Peshkov
O. Henry	William Sydney Porter
Hergé	Georges Rémi
P. D. James	Phyllis Dorothy James White
Ann Landers	Esther Pauline Lederer
J. T. LeRoy	Laura Albert
André Maurois	Émile Herzog
Molière	Jean Baptiste Poquelin
Toni Morrison	Chloe Anthony Wofford
Pablo Neruda	Neftalí Ricardo Reyes Basoalto
Frank O'Connor	Michael Donovan
George Orwell	Eric Arthur Blair
Ouida	Marie Louise de la Ramée
Ellery Queen	Frederic Dannay and Manfred B. Lee
Ayn Rand	Alice Rosenbaum
Anne Rice	Howard Allen O'Brien
Saki	Hector Hugh Munro
George Sand	Amandine Lucie Aurore Dupin
Dr. Seuss	Theodor Seuss Geisel
Lemony Snicket	Daniel Handler
Stendhal	Marie-Henri Beyle
Mark Twain	Samuel Clemens
Voltaire	François Marie Arouet

American Manual Alphabet

In the American Manual Alphabet, each letter of the alphabet is represented by a position of the fingers. This system was originally developed in France by Charles Michel de l'Epee in the 1700s. Laurent Clerc and Thomas Gallaudet further refined it into the American Manual Alphabet.

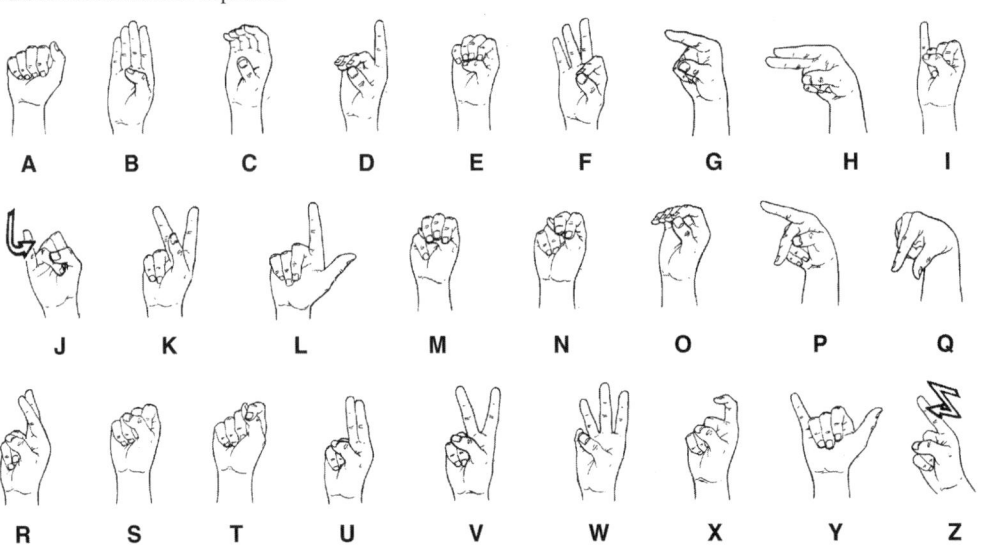

Commonly Misspelled English Words

accidentally
accommodate
accumulate
acknowledgment
acquainted
acquire
a lot
already
amateur
appearance
appropriate
assimilate
bureau
business
calendar
canceled
Caribbean

cemetery
changeable
collectible
commitment
committee
connoisseur
conscience
conscientious
conscious
convenience
deceive
defendant
definitely
desirable
desperate
deterrent
eighth

eligible
eliminate
embarrass
environment
existence
fascinating
February
fluorescent
forty
gauge
government
grammar
harass
humorous
incidentally
independent
indispensable

innocuous
innovative
inoculate
irresistible
jewelry
judgment
laboratory
leisure
license
liaison
lieutenant
lightning
liquefy
maintenance
marriage
medieval
millennium

miniature
miscellaneous
Mississippi
misspelled
mnemonic
mysterious
necessary
noticeable
occasionally
occurrence
omitted
opportunity
optimistic
parallel
patience
performance
permanent

permissible
perseverance
personnel
possess
potatoes
prescient
privilege
propaganda
questionnaire
receipt
receive
recommend
rhythm
ridiculous
sacrilegious
seize
sergeant

separate
sheriff
sincerely
stubbornness
supersede
temperament
temperature
transferred
truly
twelfth
vaccinate
vacillate
vacuum
vicious
Wednesday
weird
wholly

The Principal Languages of the World

Source: Database of *Ethnologue: Languages of the World, 16th Edition.* www.ethnologue.com. M. Paul Lewis, editor.
Copyright © 2009, SIL International. Used by permission.
The following tables count only first language (or mother tongue) speakers. All figures are estimates, as of July 2008.

Languages Spoken by the Most People

This table combines macrolanguages and individual languages, e.g., the Chinese and Arabic macrolanguages combine all the individual varieties listed in the next table. Ranked by millions of speakers.

Language	Speakers (millions)	Language	Speakers (millions)	Language	Speakers (millions)
Chinese	1,213	Russian	144	Vietnamese	69
Spanish	329	Japanese	122	French	68
English	328	German	90	Marathi	68
Arabic	221	Javanese	85	Korean	66
Hindi	182	Abaza	83	Tamil	66
Bengali	181	Lahnda	78	Italian	62
Portuguese	178	Telugu	70	Urdu	61

Individual Languages Spoken by at Least 2 Million People

A "hub" country is the country of origin, not necessarily the country where the most speakers reside (e.g., Portugal is the "hub" country of Portuguese, although more Portuguese speakers live in Brazil). Number of speakers listed is worldwide total for each language. Hub countries are listed alphabetically; within a hub, individual languages are ranked by millions of speakers.

Hub	Language	Countries	Speakers (millions)	Hub	Language	Countries	Speakers (millions)
Afghanistan	Farsi, Eastern	3	8	China (cont'd)	Chinese, Pu-Xian	3	3
	Hazaragi	4	2		Nuosu	1	2
Albania	Albanian, Tosk	10	3	Congo, Dem. Rep.	Luba-Kasai	1	6
Algeria	Arabic, Algerian Spoken	6	22		Koongo	3	5
	Kabyle	3	3		Kituba	1	4
Angola	Umbundu	2	4		Lingala	3	2
	Kimbundu	1	3	Côte d'Ivoire	Baoulé	1	2
Armenia	Armenian	30	6	Croatia	Croatian	14	6
Austria	Bavarian	4	13	Czech Republic	Czech	12	9
Azerbaijan	Azerbaijani, North	10	7	Denmark	Danish	8	6
Bangladesh	Bengali	10	181	Egypt	Arabic, Egyptian Spoken	10	54
	Rangpuri	2	15		Arabic, Sa'idi Spoken	1	19
	Chittagonian	1	13	Ethiopia	Amharic	6	18
	Sylheti	10	10		Oromo, West Central	2	9
Belarus	Belarusan	16	9		Tigrigna	6	6
Belgium	Vlaams	5	6		Oromo, Eastern	1	5
Bolivia	Quechua, South Bolivian	2	4		Oromo, Borana-Arsi-Guji	3	4
	Aymara, Central	4	2		Sidamo	1	3
Bosnia and					Sebat Bet Gurage	1	2
Herzegovina	Bosnian	4	2	Finland	Finnish	7	5
Botswana	Tswana	4	5	France	French	60	68
Brazil	Hunsrik	5	3		Occitan	4	2
Bulgaria	Bulgarian	16	9	Georgia	Georgian	13	4
Burkina Faso	Mòoré	7	5	Germany	German, Standard	43	90
Burundi	Rundi	4	5		Mainfränkisch	1	5
Cambodia	Khmer, Central	7	14		Saxon, Upper	1	2
Cameroon	Beti	1	2	Ghana	Abron	2	23
China	Chinese, Mandarin	20	845		Akan	1	8
	Chinese, Wu	2	77		Éwé	2	3
	Chinese, Yue	20	56	Greece	Greek	38	13
	Chinese, Min Nan	10	47	Guinea	Pular	6	3
	Chinese, Jinyu	1	45		Maninkakan, Eastern	3	2
	Chinese, Xiang	2	36	Haiti	Haitian	10	8
	Chinese, Hakka	17	30	Hungary	Hungarian	14	13
	Chinese, Gan	1	21	India	Hindi	20	182
	Chinese, Min Bei	2	10		Telugu	10	70
	Chinese, Min Dong	7	9		Marathi	5	68
	Uighur	15	9		Tamil	17	66
	Chinese, Huizhou	1	5		Gujarati	20	47
	Chinese, Min Zhong	1	3		Bhojpuri	3	39
	Bouyei	4	3		Awadhi	2	38
					Malayalam	11	36

Hub	Language	Countries	Speakers (millions)
India (cont'd)	Kannada	3	35
	Maithili	2	35
	Oriya	2	32
	Panjabi, Eastern	12	28
	Assamese	4	17
	Chhattisgarhi	1	15
	Haryanvi	1	13
	Magahi	1	13
	Deccan	1	13
	Degaru	1	13
	Malvi	1	10
	Kanauji	1	10
	Dhundari	1	9
	Bagheli	2	8
	Varhadi-Nagpuri	1	7
	Santali	4	6
	Lambadi	1	6
	Kashmiri	4	6
	Marwari	3	6
	Mewati	1	5
	Hadothi	1	5
	Konkani	2	4
	Merwari	1	4
	Mina	1	4
	Konkani, Goan	3	4
	Godwari	1	3
	Shekhawati	1	3
	Garhwali	1	3
	Indian Sign Language	3	3
	Kumaoni	1	2
	Dogri	1	2
	Bagri	2	2
	Kurux	3	2
	Mewari	1	2
Indonesia	Javanese	5	85
	Sunda	1	34
	Indonesian	6	23
	Madura	2	14
	Minangkabau	1	6
	Musi	1	4
	Aceh	1	4
	Banjar	2	4
	Bugis	2	4
	Bali	1	3
	Betawi	1	3
	Malay, Central	1	2
	Sasak	1	2
	Batak Toba	1	2
Iran	Farsi, Western	27	24
	Azerbaijani, South	8	13
	Domari	14	4
	Gilaki	1	3
	Mazanderani	1	3
	Kurdish, Southern	2	3
Iraq	Arabic, Mesopotamian Spoken	5	15
	Arabic, North Mesopotamian Spoken	4	6
	Kurdish, Central	2	4
	Arabic, Gulf Spoken	10	4
Israel	Hebrew	8	5
Italy	Italian	34	62
	Lombard	3	9
	Napoletano-Calabrese	1	7
	Venetian	4	6
	Sicilian	1	5
	Piemontese	3	3
	Emiliano-Romagnolo	2	2
Jamaica	Jamaican Creole English	7	3
Japan	Japanese	25	122
Jordan	Arabic, South Levantine Spoken	9	6
Kazakhstan	Kazakh	14	8
Kenya	Gikuyu	1	7
	Dholuo	2	4
	Kamba	1	4
	Ekegusii	2	2
Korea, South	Korean	33	66
Kyrgyzstan	Kyrgyz	9	3
Laos	Lao	7	3
Lesotho	Sotho, Southern	4	6
Libya	Arabic, Libyan Spoken	3	4
Lithuania	Lithuanian	19	3
Macedonia	Macedonian	9	2
Madagascar	Malagasy, Plateau	4	8
Malawi	Nyanja	6	9
Malaysia	Malay	7	9
	Malay, Kedah	2	3

Hub	Language	Countries	Speakers (millions)
Mali	Bamanankan	7	3
Mauritania	Hassaniyya	8	3
Mongolia	Mongolian, Halh	5	2
Morocco	Arabic, Moroccan Spoken	10	21
	Tamazight, Central Atlas	3	3
	Tachelhit	3	3
Mozambique	Makhuwa	1	3
	Ndau	2	2
Myanmar (Burma)	Burmese	5	32
	Shan	3	3
Nepal	Nepali	5	14
Netherlands	Dutch	12	22
Niger	Zarma	4	2
Nigeria	Hausa	13	25
	Yoruba	6	19
	Igbo	1	18
	Kanuri, Central	6	3
	Tiv	2	2
Norway	Norwegian	1	5
Pakistan	Panjabi, Western	7	63
	Urdu	23	61
	Sindhi	8	21
	Seraiki	3	14
	Pashto, Northern	7	10
	Pashto, Central	1	8
	Balochi, Southern	4	3
	Pashto, Southern	6	3
	Brahui	4	2
Paraguay	Guaraní, Paraguayan	2	5
Philippines	Filipino	1	25
	Tagalog	8	24
	Cebuano	2	16
	Ilocano	2	7
	Hiligaynon	2	6
	Waray-Waray	1	3
	Bicolano, Central	1	3
Poland	Polish	23	40
Portugal	Portuguese	37	178
Romania	Romanian	20	23
Russia	Russian	33	144
	Abaza	3	83
	Tatar	19	7
Rwanda	Rwanda	4	8
Saudi Arabia	Arabic, Najdi Spoken	7	10
	Arabic, Hijazi Spoken	2	6
Senegal	Wolof	6	4
	Pulaar	6	4
Serbia	Serbian	22	7
	Albanian, Gheg	9	4
Slovakia	Slovak	12	5
Somalia	Somali	13	14
South Africa	Zulu	6	10
	Xhosa	3	8
	Afrikaans	12	5
	Sotho, Northern	2	4
	Tsonga	4	4
Spain	Spanish	44	329
	Catalan-Valencian-Balear	18	12
	Galician	2	3
Sri Lanka	Sinhala	8	16
Sudan	Arabic, Sudanese Spoken	6	17
Swaziland	Swati	4	2
Sweden	Swedish	8	8
Switzerland	German, Swiss	5	6
Syria	Arabic, North Levantine Spoken	16	14
Tajikistan	Tajiki	8	4
Tanzania	Sukuma	1	5
Thailand	Thai	5	20
	Thai, Northeastern	1	15
	Thai, Northern	2	6
	Thai, Southern	1	5
Tunisia	Arabic, Tunisian Spoken	5	9
Turkey	Turkish	36	51
	Kurdish, Northern	32	9
Turkmenistan	Turkmen	14	7
Uganda	Ganda	1	4
	Nyankore	1	2
	Soga	1	2
Ukraine	Ukrainian	27	37
United Kingdom	English	112	328
Uzbekistan	Uzbek, Northern	12	19
Vietnam	Vietnamese	23	69
Yemen	Arabic, Sanaani Spoken	1	8
	Arabic, Ta'izzi-Adeni Spoken	8	7
Zambia	Bemba	4	4
Zimbabwe	Shona	5	11

BUILDINGS, BRIDGES, AND TUNNELS

Tallest Buildings in the World

Source: Council on Tall Buildings and Urban Habitat, Illinois Inst. of Technology, www.ctbuh.com; Emporis.com, www.emporis.com

Structures under construction as of mid-2009 are denoted by an asterisk (*). Year in parentheses is date of completion or projected completion; UC = under construction with no projected completion date. Only completed buildings and ones under construction that have "topped out" are included here.

Building	Ht. (ft.)	Stories	Building	Ht. (ft.)	Stories
*Burj Dubai, Dubai (2009)	2,600+	160+	Kingdom Centre, Riyadh (2002)	992	41
Taipei 101, Taipei (2004)	1,670	101	Arraya 2, Kuwait City (2009)	984	56
Shanghai World Financial Center, Shanghai (2008)	1,614	101	Aspire Tower, Doha (2006)	984	36
*International Commerce Centre, Hong Kong (2010)	1,585	107	One Island East, Hong Kong (2008)	979	69
Petronas Tower 1, Kuala Lumpur (1998)	1,483	88	First Bank Tower, Toronto (1975)	978	72
Petronas Tower 2, Kuala Lumpur (1998)	1,483	88	Shanghai Wheelock Square, Shanghai (2009)	978	59
*Nanjing Greenland Financial Center, Nanjing (2009)	1,476	69	Eureka Tower, Melbourne (2006)	975	91
Willis Tower[1], Chicago (1974)	1,451	108	Comcast Center, Philadelphia (2008)	974	57
*West Tower, Guangzhou (2009)	1,435	103	Landmark Tower, Yokohama (1993)	972	73
Jin Mao Building, Shanghai (1999)	1,381	88	Emirates Crown, Dubai (2008)	971	63
Trump International Hotel & Tower, Chicago (2009)	1,362	96	311 South Wacker Drive, Chicago (1990)	961	66
Two International Finance Centre, Hong Kong (2003)	1,362	88	SEG Plaza, Shenzhen (2000)	957	71
*Al Hamra Tower, Kuwait City (2010)	1,354	77	American International Building, New York (1932)	952	67
CITIC Plaza, Guangzhou (1996)	1,283	80	Key Tower, Cleveland (1991)	947	57
Shun Hing Square, Shenzhen (1996)	1,260	69	Plaza 66, Shanghai (2001)	945	66
Empire State Building, New York (1931)	1,250	102	One Liberty Place, Philadelphia (1987)	945	61
Central Plaza, Hong Kong (1992)	1,227	78	Millennium Tower, Dubai (2006)	935	59
Bank of China, Hong Kong (1989)	1,205	70	Tomorrow Square, Shanghai (2003)	934	55
Bank of America Tower, New York (2009)	1,200	54	Columbia Center, Seattle (1984)	933	76
Almas Tower, Dubai (2008)	1,191	68	Chongqing World Trade Center, Chongqing (2005)	929	60
Emirates Tower One, Dubai (1999)	1,165	54	Cheung Kong Centre, Hong Kong (1999)	928	63
Tuntex Sky Tower, Kaohsiung (1997)	1,140	85	The Trump Building, New York (1930)	927	71
Aon Centre, Chicago (1973)	1,136	83	Bank of America Plaza, Dallas (1985)	921	72
The Center, Hong Kong (1998)	1,135	73	United Overseas Bank Plaza, Singapore (1992)	919	66
John Hancock Center, Chicago (1969)	1,127	100	Republic Plaza, Singapore (1995)	919	66
*Wenzhou Trade Center, Wenzhou (2009)	1,094	72	Overseas Union Bank Centre, Singapore (1986)	919	63
Rose Rotana Tower, Dubai (2007)	1,093	72	Citigroup Center, New York (1977)	915	59
Shimao International Plaza, Shanghai (2006)	1,093	60	Hong Kong New World Tower, Shanghai (2002)	913	61
Minsheng Bank Building, Wuhan (2008)	1,087	68	Diwang International Commerce Center, Nanning (2006)	906	54
*Ryugyong Hotel, Pyongyang (UC)	1,083	105	Scotia Plaza, Toronto (1989)	902	68
China World Trade Center Tower III, Beijing (2009)	1,083	74	Williams Tower, Houston (1983)	901	64
The Index, Dubai (2009)	1,076	80	Wuhan World Trade Tower, Wuhan (1998)	896	60
Q1, Gold Coast (2005)	1,058	78	The Cullinan I, Hong Kong (2008)	886	68
Burj al Arab Hotel, Dubai (1999)	1,053	60	The Cullinan II, Hong Kong (2008)	886	68
Nina Tower I, Hong Kong (2006)	1,046	80	Renaissance Tower, Dallas (1975)	886	56
Chrysler Building, New York (1930)	1,046	77	China International Center Tower B, Guangzhou (2007)	884	62
New York Times Tower, New York (2007)	1,046	52	Dapeng International Plaza, Guangzhou (2006)	883	56
*HHHR Tower, Dubai (2009)	1,040	62	21st Century Tower, Dubai (2003)	883	55
Bank of America Plaza, Atlanta (1993)	1,039	55	One Lujiazui, Shanghai (2008)	883	47
U.S. Bank Tower, Los Angeles (1990)	1,018	73	Naberezhnaya Tower C, Moscow (2007)	881	61
*Sky Tower, Abu Dhabi (2010)	1,017	74	*Lanko International Complex Yage Tower, Chongqing (2009)	879	54
Menara Telekom Headquarters, Kuala Lumpur (1999)	1,017	55	Al Faisaliah Center, Riyadh (2000)	876	30
Emirates Tower Two, Dubai (2000)	1,014	56	900 North Michigan Avenue, Chicago (1989)	871	66
AT&T Corporate Center, Chicago (1989)	1,007	60	Bank of America Corporate Center, Charlotte (1992)	871	60
The Address Downtown Burj Dubai, Dubai (2008)	1,004	63	Al Kazim Tower 1, Dubai (2008)	869	53
JP Morgan Chase Tower, Houston (1982)	1,002	75	Al Kazim Tower 2, Dubai (2008)	869	53
*NE Asia Trade Tower, Incheon (2010)	1,001	70	BOCOM Financial Towers, Shanghai (1999)	869	52
Baiyoke Tower II, Bangkok (1997)	997	85	120 Collins St., Melbourne (1991)	869	52
Two Prudential Plaza, Chicago (1990)	995	64	SunTrust Plaza, Atlanta (1992)	867	60
Wells Fargo Plaza, Houston (1983)	992	71			
*Capital City Moscow Tower, Moscow (2010)	989	76			

(1) Willis Group Holdings, the former Sears Tower's largest tenant, changed the name of the building July 16, 2009.

World's 10 Tallest Free-Standing Towers

Structures under construction as of mid-2009 are denoted by an asterisk (*). Year is date of completion or projected completion.

Name	City	Country	Ht. (ft.)	Year	Name	City	Country	Ht. (ft.)	Year
*Guangzhou TV Tower	Guangzhou	China	2,001	2010	Manara Kuala Lumpur	Kuala Lumpur	Malaysia	1,379	1996
CN Tower	Toronto	Canada	1,815	1976	Tianjin Radio & TV Tower	Tianjin	China	1,362	1991
Ostankino Tower	Moscow	Russia	1,772	1967	Central Radio & TV Tower	Beijing	China	1,268	1992
Oriental Pearl TV Tower	Shanghai	China	1,535	1995	Kiev TV Tower	Kiev	Ukraine	1,263	1974
Milad Tower	Tehran	Iran	1,427	2008	Tashkent TV Tower	Tashkent	Uzbekistan	1,230	1985

Tall Buildings in Selected North American Cities

Source: Emporis.com, www.emporis.com; Council on Tall Buildings and Urban Habitat, Illinois Inst. of Technology, www.ctbuh.org

Lists include freestanding towers and other structures that do not have stories and are not technically considered buildings. Structures still under construction as of mid-2009 are denoted by an asterisk (*). Year in parentheses is date of completion or projected completion. Height is generally measured from sidewalk to roof, including penthouse and tower if enclosed as integral part of structure; stories generally counted from street level. NA = Not available or not applicable.

Building	Ht. (ft.)	Stories	Building	Ht. (ft.)	Stories
Atlanta, GA			Park Avenue Condominiums, 750 Park Ave. NE (2000)	486	42
Bank of America Plaza (incl. spire), 600 Peachtree St. NE (1992)	1,039	55	Terminus 100, 3280 Peachtree Rd. NE, Buckhead (2007)	485	27
SunTrust Plaza, 303 Peachtree St. NE (1993)[1]	867	60	Paramount at Buckhead, 3445 Stratford Rd. NE (2004)	478	40
One Atlantic Center, 1201 W. Peachtree St. (1987)	820	50	3630 Peachtree Rd. (2009)	469	40
191 Peachtree Tower (1991)	770	50	Centennial Tower, 101 Marietta St. (1976)	459	36
Westin Peachtree Plaza, 210 Peachtree St. NW (1976)[2]	723	73	Equitable Bldg., 100 Peachtree St. NW (1967)	453	34
Georgia Pacific Tower, 133 Peachtree St. NE (1981)	697	51	Spire, 860 Peachtree St. (2005)	453	28
Promenade II (incl. spire), 1230 Peachtree St. NE (1989)	691	40	Buckhead Grand, 3338 Peachtree Rd. NE (2004)	451	38
AT&T Bldg., 675 W. Peachtree St. (1980)	677	47	One Park Tower, 34 Peachtree St. (1961)	439	32
Sovereign, 3344 Peachtree (2008)	665	48	1100 Peachtree St. NE (1990)	428	28
1180 Peachtree (2006)	657	41	Atlanta Plaza I, 950 E. Paces Ferry Rd. (1986)	425	32
GLG Grand/Four Seasons Hotel, 75 14th St. NE (1992)	609	53	Park Place on Peachtree, 2660 Peachtree Rd. NW (1986)	420	40
The Mansion on Peachtree, 3376 Peachtree Rd. NE (2008)	580	42	2828 Peachtree Luxury Condominiums (2002)	420	33
The Atlantic, 270 17th St. NW (2009)	577	46	1280 West, 1280 W. Peachtree St. NW (1989)	410	38
State of Georgia Bldg., 2 Peachtree St. NW (1967)[3]	556	44	1010 Peachtree (2008)	407	36
Marriott Marquis, 265 Peachtree Center Ave NE (1985)	554	52	Peachtree Summit No. 1, 401 W. Peachtree NE (1975)	406	31
Viewpoint, 855 Peachtree St. NE (2008)	501	36	One Coca Cola Plaza, 310 North Ave. NW (1979)	403	29
Twelve Centennial Park Tower I (incl. spire), 400 W. Peachtree St. NW (2007)	491	39	Tower Place 100, 3340 Peachtree Rd. NE (1974)	401	29

(1) 902 ft. with antenna. (2) 883 ft. with antenna. (3) 599 ft. with antenna.

Building	Ht. (ft.)	Stories
Atlantic City, NJ		
Harrah's Waterfront Tower, 777 Harrah's Blvd. (2008)	525	44
Trump Taj Mahal - Chairman Tower, 1000 Boardwalk (2008)	470	41
The Water Club at Borgata (2008)	457	39
Borgata Hotel & Casino, 1 Borgata Way (2003)	431	42
Trump Taj Mahal I, 1000 Boardwalk (1990)	429	42
Austin, TX		
*Austonian, 200 Congress Ave. (2010)	683	56
360 (incl. spire), 360 Nueces St. (2008)	563	44
Frost Bank Tower, 401 N. Congress Ave. (2004)	516	33
*W Hotel & Residences (2010)	478	37
Spring (2009)	433	43
Ashton, 101 Colorado St. (2009)	416	37
Baltimore, MD		
Legg Mason Bldg., 100 Light St. (1973)	529	40
Bank of America, 10 Light St. (1924)	509	37
*Four Seasons Baltimore & Residences (2010)	494	44
William Donald Schaefer Tower, 6 St. Paul Pl. (1992)	493	29
Commerce Place, 1 South St. (1992)	454	31
Marriott Baltimore Inner Harbor E, 700 Aliceanna St. (2001)	430	32
100 E. Pratt St. (1992)	418	28
Boston, MA		
Hancock Place, 200 Clarendon St. (1976)	790	62
Prudential Tower, 800 Boylston St. (1964)[1]	750	52
Federal Reserve Bldg., 600 Atlantic Ave. (1978)	604	32
Boston Company Bldg., 1 Boston Place (1970)	602	41
One International Place, 100 Oliver St. (1987)	600	46
100 Federal St. (1971)	591	37
One Financial Center, 10 Dewey Square (1984)	590	46
111 Huntington Ave. (2002)	564	36
Two International Place (1993)	538	35
One Post Office Square (1981)	525	40
1 Federal St. (1975)	520	38
Exchange Place, 53 State St. (1984)	510	39
Sixty State St. (1977)	509	38
1 Beacon St. (1972)	507	36
State Street Financial Center (incl. spire), 1 Lincoln St. (2003)	503	36
28 State St. (1970)	500	40
Marriott's Custom House, 3 Mckinley Square (1915)	496	32
*One Franklin, 426 Washington St. (2011)	495	38
John Hancock Bldg., 175 Berkeley St. (1949)	495	26
33 Arch St. (2003)	489	31
225 Franklin St. (1966)	477	33
Millennium Place 1, 10 Avery St. (2001)	475	38
125 High St. (1990)	452	30
100 Summer St. (1975)	450	33
Millennium Place 2, 3 Avery St. (2001)	445	36
McCormack Bldg., I Ashburton Pl. (1975)	401	22
Harbor Towers I, 85 E. India (1971)	400	40
Keystone Bldg., 99 High St. (1971)	400	32

(1) 836 ft. with antenna.

Building	Ht. (ft.)	Stories
Calgary, Alberta		
*The Bow (2011)	774	58
Petro Canada Centre West Tower, 150 6th Ave. SW (1984)	705	53
*Eight Avenue Place East Tower, 8th Ave. & 5th St. SW (2011)	700	49
Bankers Hall East Tower, 855 2nd St. SW (1989)	645	50
Bankers Hall West Tower, 888 3rd St. SW (2000)	645	50
Calgary Tower, 101 9th Ave. SW (1967)	626	Tower
TransCanada Tower, 450 1st St. SW (2001)	581	38
Canterra Tower, 400 3rd Ave. SW (1988)	580	46
*Centennial Place 1 (2009)	578	40
*Jamieson Place (incl. spires), 302 4th Ave. SW (2009)	568	38
First Canadian Centre, 350 7th Ave. SW (1982)	547	41
Western Canadian Place-N. Tower, 707 6th St. SW (1983)	538	41
Canada Trust, Calgary Eatons Centre, 421 7th Ave. SW (1991)	530	40
Scotia Square, 700 2nd St. SW (1976)	509	41
Nexen Bldg., 801 7th Ave. SW (1982)	500	37
Two Bow Valley Square, 205 5th Ave. SW (1974)	468	39
Dome Tower, 333 7th Ave. SW (1976)	463	34
5th & 5th Bldg., 605 5th Ave. SW (1980)	460	35
Shell Centre, 400 4th Ave. SW (1977)	460	34
Home Oil Tower, 324 8th Ave. SW (1976)	449	33
Four Bow Valley Square, 250 6th Ave. SW (1982)	441	37
Fifth Avenue Place East Tower, 425 1st St. SW (1981)	435	35
Fifth Avenue Place West Tower, 237 4th Ave. SW (1981)	435	35
Petro-Canada Tower, East Tower, 111 5th Ave. SW (1983)	427	33
Calgary Courts Centre-North Tower (2007)	423	24
Western Canadian Place-S. Tower, 801 6th St. SW (1983)	420	32
arriVa Tower 1, 411 11th Ave. SE (2008)	418	34
Altius Centre, 500 4th Ave. SW (1972)	415	32
EnCana Place, 150 9th Ave. SW (1982)	410	28
Hewlett Packard Tower, 715 5th Ave. SW (1975)	408	31
Alberta Stock Exchange, 300 5th Ave. (1979)	407	33
Charlotte, NC		
Bank of America Corporate Center, 100 N. Tryon St. (1992)	871	60
*Duke Energy Center, 534 S. Tryon St. (2009)	764	48
*The Vue (2010)	677	50
Hearst Tower, 214 N. Tryon St. (2002)	659	47
One Wachovia Center, 301 S. College St. (1988)	588	42
Bank of America Plaza, 101 S. Tryon St. (1974)	503	40
Interstate Tower, 121 W. Trade St. (1990)	462	32
201 N. Tryon St. (1997)	447	30

Building	Ht. (ft.)	Stories
Three Wachovia Center, 401 S. Tryon St. (2000)	440	29
Two Wachovia Plaza, 301 S. Tryon St. (1971)	433	32
Avenue, 128 W. 5th St. (2007)	425	36
400 S. Tryon St. (1974)	420	32
*Wachovia Condo Tower (2010)	NA	42
Chicago, IL		
Willis Tower, 233 S. Wacker Dr. (1974)[1]	1451	108
Trump International Hotel & Tower (incl. spire), 401 N. Wabash Ave. (2009)	1362	96
Aon Center, 200 E. Randolph St. (1973)	1136	83
John Hancock Center, 875 N. Michigan Ave. (1969)[2]	1127	100
AT&T Corporate Center (incl. spires), 227 W. Monroe St. (1989)	1007	60
Two Prudential Plaza (incl. spire), 180 N. Stetson Ave. (1990)	995	64
311 S. Wacker Drive (1990)	961	66
900 N. Michigan Ave. (1989)	871	66
Water Tower Place, 845 N. Michigan Ave. (1976)	859	74
Chase Tower, 21 S. Clark St. (1969)	850	60
Park Tower, 800 N. Michigan Ave. (2000)	844	67
Aqua, 211 N. Columbus Dr. (2009)	819	82
*The Legacy at Millennium Park, 21-39 S. Wabash (2009)	819	71
300 N. LaSalle (2009)	785	60
3 First National Plaza, 70 W. Madison St. (1981)	767	57
Chicago Title & Trust Center, 161 N. Clark St. (1992)	756	50
*Blue Cross Headquarters, 300 E. Randolph St. (2010)	743	54
One Museum Park, 1215 S. Prairie Ave. (2009)	726	62
Olympia Centre, 737 N. Michigan Ave. (1986)	725	63
330 N. Wabash Ave. (1973)	695	52
*Elysian, 940 N. Rush St. (2009)	686	60
111 S. Wacker Dr. (2005)	681	51
181 W. Madison St. (1990)	680	50
Hyatt Center, 71 S. Wacker (2005)	679	48
One Magnificent Mile, 980 N. Michigan Ave. (1983)	673	57
340 on the Park, 340 W. Randolph St. (2007)	672	64
R.R. Donnelley Center, 77 W. Wacker Dr. (1992)	668	49
UBS Tower, 1 N. Wacker Dr. (2001)	652	50
Daley Center, 55 W. Washington St. (1965)	648	32
55 E. Erie St. (2004)	647	56
Lake Point Tower, 505 N. Lake Shore Dr. (1968)	645	70
River East Center, 350 E. Illinois St. (2001)	644	58
Grand Plaza I (incl. spire), 540 N. State St. (2003)	641	57
155 N. Wacker Dr. (2009)	638	45
Leo Burnett Bldg., 35 W. Wacker Dr. (1989)	635	46
*One Museum Park West, 201 E. Roosevelt Rd. (2010)	633	54
The Heritage at Millennium Park, 125 N. Wabash Ave. (2005)	631	57
NBC Tower (incl. spire), 455 N. Cityfront Plaza Dr. (1989)	627	37
353 N. Clark (2009)	624	44
Millennium Centre, 33 W. Ontario St. (2003)	610	58
Chicago Place, 700 N. Michigan Ave. (1991)	608	49
Board of Trade (incl. statue), 141 W. Jackson Blvd. (1930)	605	44
CNA Plaza, 325 S. Wabash St. (1972)	601	44
Prudential Bldg., 130 E. Randolph St. (1955)[3]	601	41
Heller International Tower, 500 W. Monroe St. (1992)	600	45
One Madison Plaza, 200 W. Madison St. (1982)	599	44
1000 Lake Shore Plaza (1964)	590	55
The Clare at Water Tower, 55 East Pearson St. (2008)	589	52
Citigroup Center, 500 W. Madison St. (1987)	588	42
Mid Continental Plaza, 55 E. Monroe St. (1972)	583	49
Smurfit-Stone Bldg., 150 N. Michigan Ave. (1983)	582	41
North Pier Apts., 474 N. Lake Shore Dr. (1990)	581	61
Citadel Center, 131 S. Dearborn St. (2003)	580	39
The Fordham, 25 E. Superior St. (2003)	574	52
190 S. LaSalle St. (1987)	573	40
One S. Dearborn (2005)	571	39
Onterie Center, 446 E. Ontario St. (1986)	570	58
Chicago Temple, 77 W. Washington St. (1924)	568	23
Palmolive Bldg. (incl. beacon), 919 N. Michigan Ave. (1929)	565	37
Huron Plaza Apts., 30 E. Huron St. (1983)	560	56
Boeing International Headquarters, 100 N. Riverside Plaza (1990)	560	36
The Parkshore, 195 N. Harbor Dr. (1991)	556	56
North Harbor Tower, 175 N. Harbor Dr. (1988)	556	55
Marina City 1, 300 N. State St. (1964)	555	61
Marina City 2, 300 N. State St. (1964)	555	61
Civic Opera Bldg., 20 N. Wacker Dr. (1929)	555	45
Streeter Place, 351 E. Ohio St. (2009)	554	55
Newberry Plaza, 1000 N. State St. (1974)	553	53
Michigan Plaza South, 205 N. Michigan Ave. (1985)	553	46
30 N. LaSalle St. (1975)	553	44
Pittsfield Bldg., 55 E. Washington St. (1927)	551	38
Harbor Point, 155 N. Harbor Dr. (1975)	550	54
One S. Wacker Dr. (1982)	550	40
Kluczynski Federal Bldg., 230 S. Dearborn St. (1975)	545	45
Park Millennium, 222 N. Columbus Dr. (2002)	544	57
USG Bldg., 125 S. Franklin St. (1992)	538	35
The Pinnacle, 21 E. Huron St. (2004)	535	48
LaSalle National Bank, 135 S. LaSalle St. (1934)	535	45
Park Place Tower, 655 W. Irving Park Rd. (1971)	531	56
One N. LaSalle St. (1930)	530	48
The Elysees, 111 E. Chestnut St. (1973)	529	56
River Plaza, 405 N. Wabash St. (1977)	524	56
35 E. Wacker Drive (1927)	523	40
Unitrin Bldg., 1 E. Wacker Dr. (1962)	522	41
Mather Tower, 75 E. Wacker Dr. (1928)	521	41
Chicago Mercantile Exchange, 30 S. Wacker Dr. (1983)	520	40
Chicago Mercantile Exchange, 10 S. Wacker Dr. (1987)	520	40
The Columbian, 1180 S. Michigan Ave. (2008)	517	47

Building	Ht. (ft.)	Stories
191 N. Wacker Drive (2002)	516	37
401 E. Ontario St. (1990)	515	51
One Financial Place, 440 S. LaSalle St. (1985)	515	39
The Streeter, 345 E. Ohio St. (2006)	514	50
5415 N. Sheridan Rd. (1973)	513	54
600 N. Lake Shore Dr. (2009)	513	47
LaSalle-Wacker Bldg., 221 N. LaSalle St. (1930)	512	41
Harris Bank III, 115 S. LaSalle St. (1974)	510	38
321 N. Clark St. (1987)	510	35
*215 W. Washington St. (2010)	509	44
400 E. Ohio St. (1982)	505	50
Carbide & Carbon Bldg., 230 N. Michigan Ave. (1929)	503	37
1 Superior Place, 1 W. Superior St. (1999)	502	52
120 N. LaSalle St. (1992)	501	39
10 South LaSalle St. (1986)	501	37
The Tides, 360 E. South Water St. (2008)	500	51
200 S. Wacker Drive (1981)	500	41

(1) Former Sears Tower; 1,729 ft. with antenna. (2) 1,499 ft. with antenna. (3) 912 ft. with antenna.

Cincinnati, OH

Building	Ht. (ft.)	Stories
*Great American Bldg., 4th & Sycamore St. (2011)	660	41
Carew Tower, 441 Vine St. (1931)[1]	574	49
PNC Tower, 1 W. 4th St. (1913)	495	31
Scripps Center, 312 Walnut St. (1990)	468	36
Fifth Third Tower, 511 Walnut St. (1969)	423	32
Chemed Center, 255 5th St. (1990)	410	32
The Center at 600 Vine (1984)	418	29

(1) 623 ft. with antenna.

Cleveland, OH

Building	Ht. (ft.)	Stories
Key Tower (incl. spire), 127 Public Square (1991)	947	57
Terminal Tower, 50 Public Square (1930)[1]	708	52
200 Public Square (1985)	658	46
100 Erieview, 1801 E. 9th St. (1964)	529	40
One Cleveland Center, 1375 E. 9th St. (1983)	450	31
Fifth Third Center, 600 Superior Ave. (1991)	446	28
Carl B. Stokes Federal Courthouse, 801 W. Superior Ave. (2002)	430	24
Justice Center, 1250 Ontario St. (1976)	420	26
Federal Bldg., 1240 E. 9th St. (1967)	419	32
National City Center, 1900 E. 9th St. (1980)	410	35

(1) 771 ft. with flagpole.

Columbus, OH

Building	Ht. (ft.)	Stories
James A. Rhodes State Office Tower, 30 E. Broad St. (1973)	624	41
Leveque-Lincoln Tower, 50 W. Broad St. (1927)	555	47
William Green Bldg., 30 W. Spring St. (1990)	530	33
Huntington Center, 41 S. High St. (1983)	512	37
Vern Riffe State Office Tower, 77 S. High St. (1988)	503	33
One Nationwide Plaza (1976)	485	40
Franklin County Courthouse, 373 S. High St. (1991)	464	27
AEP Bldg., One Riverside Plaza (1983)	456	31
Borden Bldg., 180 E. Broad St. (1974)	438	34
Three Nationwide Plaza (1989)	408	27

Dallas, TX

Building	Ht. (ft.)	Stories
Bank of America Plaza, 901 Main St. (1985)	921	72
Renaissance Tower (incl. spire), 1201 Elm St. (1974)	886	56
Comerica Bank Tower, 1717 Main St. (1987)	787	60
JP Morgan Chase Tower, 2200 Ross Ave. (1987)	738	55
Fountain Place, 1445 Ross Ave. (1986)	720	58
Trammel Crow Tower, 2001 Ross Ave. (1984)	686	50
1700 Pacific Ave. (1983)	655	50
Thanksgiving Tower, 1600 Pacific Ave. (1982)	645	50
Energy Plaza, 1601 Bryan St. (1983)	629	49
Elm Place, 1401 Elm St. (1965)	628	52
Republic Center Tower I (incl. spire), 300 N. Ervay (1954)	602	36
Republic Center Tower II, 325 N. St. Paul (1964)	598	50
One AT&T Plaza, 208 S. Akard St. (1984)	580	37
One Lincoln Plaza, 500 Akard St. (1984)	579	45
Cityplace Center East, 2711 N. Haskell Ave. (1989)	560	42
Reunion Tower, 300 Reunion Blvd. (1976)	560	Tower
Sheraton Dallas Hotel Center Tower, 400 Olive St. (1959)	550	42
Mercantile Bldg. (incl. spire), 1700 Main St. (1943)	523	31
2001 Bryan St. (1973)	512	40
Harwood Center, 1999 Bryan St. (1982)	483	36
KMPG Centre, 717 N. Harwood St. (1980)	481	34
San Jacinto Tower, 2121 San Jacinto St. (1982)	456	33
Renaissance Hotel, 2222 Stemmons Fwy. (1983)	451	29

Denver, CO

Building	Ht. (ft.)	Stories
Republic Plaza, 330 17th St. (1984)	714	56
1801 California Street (1982)	709	52
Wells Fargo Center, 1700 Lincoln Ave. (1983)	698	50
*Four Seasons Hotel & Tower, 1101 14th St. (2009)	639	45
1999 Broadway (1985)	544	43
707 17th St. (1981)	522	42
555 17th St. (1978)	507	40
Spire, 1434 Champa St. (2009)	483	41
1670 Broadway (1980)	448	36
Hyatt Regency Denver at the Colorado Convention Center, 650 15th St. (2005)	439	37
17th St. Plaza, 1225 17th St. (1982)	438	32
First Interstate Tower North, 633 17th St. (1974)	434	32
Brooks Towers, 1020 15th St. (1968)	420	42
Denver Place South Tower, 999 18th St. (1981)	416	34
One Tabor Center, 1200 17th St. (1984)	408	32
Johns Manville Plaza, 717 17th St. (1984)	404	29

Detroit, MI

Building	Ht. (ft.)	Stories
Marriott Hotel, Renaissance Center I (1977)[1]	727	70
One Detroit Center, 500 Woodward Ave. (1991)[2]	619	45

Building	Ht. (ft.)	Stories
Penobscot Bldg., 633 Griswold Ave. (1928)	566	46
Renaissance Center 100 Tower (1976)	508	39
Renaissance Center 200 Tower (1976)	508	39
Renaissance Center 300 Tower (1976)	508	39
Renaissance Center 400 Tower (1976)	508	39
Guardian Bldg., 500 Griswold Ave. (1929)	489	36
Book Tower, 1249 Washington Blvd. (1925)	472	35
150 W. Jefferson Ave. (1988)	470	29
Fisher Bldg., 3011 W. Grand Blvd. (1928)	444	28
Cadillac Tower, 65 Cadillac Sq. (1928)	437	40
David Stott Bldg., 1150 Griswold St. (1928)	436	38
One Woodward Ave. (1963)	430	30

(1) 755 ft. with antenna. (2) 665 ft. with antenna.

Edmonton, Alberta

Building	Ht. (ft.)	Stories
Manulife Place, 10170-101 St. (1983)	480	36
*Epcor Tower (2010)	450	28
Telus Plaza South, 10020-100 St. (1971)	441	34
Bell Tower, 10104-103 Ave. (1982)	426	34

Fort Worth, TX

Building	Ht. (ft.)	Stories
Burnett Plaza, 801 Cherry St. (1983)	567	40
D.R. Horton Tower, 301 Commerce St. (1984)	547	38
Carter Burgess Plaza, 777 Main St. (1982)	525	40
The Tower, 400 Throckmorton St. (1974)	488	36
Wells Fargo Tower, 201 Main St. (1982)	477	33
Omni Convention Center Hotel, 1300 Houston St. (2009)	447	33

Hartford, CT

Building	Ht. (ft.)	Stories
City Place I, 185 Asylum St. (1980)	535	38
Travelers Tower, 26 Grove St. (1919)	527	24
Goodwin Square, 225 Asylum St. (1990)	522	30
Hartford 21, 221 Trumbull St. (2006)	440	36

Honolulu, HI

Building	Ht. (ft.)	Stories
First Hawaiian Center, 999 Bishop St. (1996)	429	30
Moana Pacific East Tower, 1288 Kapiolani Blvd. (2008)	422	46
Moana Pacific West Tower, 1288 Kapiolani Blvd. (2008)	422	46
Nauru Tower, 1330 Ala Moana Blvd. (1991)	418	44
Hokua Tower, 1288 Ala Moana Blvd. (2006)	418	40
Ko'olani (2006)	400	47
One Waterfront Tower - Makai, 425 South King St. (1990)	400	45
One Waterfront Tower - Mauka, 415 South King St. (1990)	400	45
Hawaiki Tower, 88 Piikoi St. (1999)	400	45
One Archer Lane, 801 S. King St. (1998)	400	41
Imperial Plaza, 725 Kapiolani Blvd. (1992)	400	40

Houston, TX

Building	Ht. (ft.)	Stories
JPMorgan Chase Tower, 600 Travis St. (1982)	1002	75
Wells Fargo Plaza, 1000 Louisiana St. (1983)	992	71
Williams Tower, 2800 Post Oak Blvd. (1983)	901	64
Bank of America Center, 700 Louisiana St. (1983)	780	56
Texaco Heritage Plaza, 1111 Bagby St. (1987)	762	53
Enterprise Plaza, 1100 Louisiana St. (1980)[1]	756	55
Centerpoint Energy Plaza, 1111 Louisiana St. (1996)	741	47
Continental Center I, 1600 Smith St. (1984)	732	55
Fulbright Tower, 1301 McKinney St. (1982)	725	52
One Shell Plaza, 900 Louisiana St. (1970)[2]	714	50
1400 Smith St. (1983)	691	50
3 Allen Center, 333 Clay St. (1980)	685	50
One Houston Center, 1221 McKinney St. (1978)	678	47
First City Tower, 1001 Fannin St. (1984)	662	47
*MainPlace, 811 Main St. (2011)	630	46
San Felipe Plaza, 5847 San Felipe Blvd. (1984)	625	45
ExxonMobile Bldg., 800 Bell Ave. (1962)	606	44
1500 Louisiana St. (2002)	600	40
America General Center, 2929 Allen Parkway (1983)	590	42
Two Houston Center, 909 Fannin St. (1974)	579	40
San Jacinto Column (1939)[3]	570	NA
Marathon Oil Tower, 5555 San Felipe Blvd. (1983)	562	41
Wedge International Tower, 1415 Louisiana St. (1983)	550	44
KBR Tower, 601 Jefferson St. (1973)	550	40
Pennzoil Place I, 700 Milam St. (1976)	523	36
Pennzoil Place II, 700 Louisiana St. (1976)	523	36
Devon Energy Center, 1200 Smith St. (1978)	521	36
Reliant Energy Plaza, 1000 Main St. (2003)	518	36
Total Plaza, 1201 Louisiana St. (1971)	518	35
The Huntington, 2121 Kirby Dr. (1982)	503	34
El Paso Energy Bldg, 1010 Milam St. (1962)	502	33
One Park Place, 1500 McKinney St. (2009)	501	37
Memorial Hermann Tower, 929 Gessner Rd. (2009)	500	35
*Hess Tower, 1501 McKinney St. (2010)	490	29
O'Quinn Medical Tower, 6624 Fannin St. (1991)	477	29
5 Greenway Plaza (1973)	465	31
717 Texas Ave. (2003)	453	34
One Allen Center, 500 Dallas St. (1974)	452	34

(1) 782 ft. with antenna. (2) 999 ft. with antenna. (3) Monument; world's tallest memorial column. Located in La Porte, TX, near Houston.

Indianapolis, IN

Building	Ht. (ft.)	Stories
Chase Tower (incl. spires), 111 Monument Circle (1990)	811	49
One America Tower, 200 N. Illinois St. (1982)	533	38
One Indiana Square, 200 N. Delaware St. (1970)	504	36
Market Tower, 10 W. Market St. (1988)	421	32
300 N. Meridian Bldg. (1988)	408	28
First Indiana Plaza, 135 N. Pennsylvania St. (1988)	401	29

Jacksonville, FL

Building	Ht. (ft.)	Stories
Bank of America Tower, 50 N. Laura St. (1990)	617	42
Modis Tower, 1 Independent Dr. (1975)	535	37
The Peninsula, 1357 Riverplace Blvd. (2006)	437	38
AT&T Tower, 424 N. Pearl St. (1983)	435	27
Riverplace Tower, 1301 Riverplace Blvd. (1967)	433	28

Building	Ht. (ft.)	Stories
Jersey City, NJ		
30 Hudson St. (2004)	781	42
101 Hudson St. (1992)	548	42
Trump Plaza I, 88 Morgan St. (2008).	532	55
Newport Tower, 525 Washington Blvd. (1990).	528	37
Exchange Place Center, 10 Exchange Pl. (1990)	516	32
Hudson Green East Tower, 77 Hudson St. (2009).	500	48
Hudson Green West Tower, 77 Hudson St. (2009)	500	48
Harborside Financial Plaza V, 160 Greene St. (2002).	480	34
Southampton Apts., 20 River Ct. (2000)	450	36
Crystal Point, 2 2nd St. (2009)	436	42
Marbella Apts., 425 Washington Blvd. (2003)	427	40
Kansas City, MO		
One Kansas City Place, 1200 Main St. (1988)	623	42
Town Pavilion, 1111 Main St. (1986)	591	38
Power & Light Bldg., 1330 Baltimore Ave. (1931)	481	34
909 Walnut St. (1931)	454	35
City Hall, 414 E. 12th St. (1937)	443	29
1201 Walnut St. (1991)	427	30
Hyatt Regency Crown Center, 2345 McGee St. (1980).	425	45
Commerce Tower, 911 Main St. (1965)	407	32
City Center Square, 1100 Main St. (1977)	404	30
Las Vegas, NV		
Stratosphere Tower, 2000 Las Vegas Blvd. S. (1996)	1149	Tower
*Fontainebleau Resort Hotel, 2755 Las Vegas Blvd. S. (2009)	735	63
The Palazzo, 3339 Las Vegas Blvd. S. (2007)	642	53
Encore at Wynn Las Vegas, 3145 Las Vegas Blvd. S. (2008)	631	52
Trump International Hotel and Tower 1, 3128 Las Vegas Blvd. S. (2008)	622	64
Wynn Las Vegas, 3145 Las Vegas Blvd. S. (2005)	613	45
*Cosmopolitan Casino Spa Tower, Las Vegas Blvd, & Harmon Ave. (2010)	603	53
*Cosmopolitan Beach Resort Tower, Las Vegas Blvd, & Harmon Ave. (2010)	603	51
*Aria Resort & Casino (2009)	600	60
*Planet Hollywood Towers (2009)	597	50
*VDARA, 2551 W. Harmon Ave. (2009).	554	50
Eiffel Tower, Paris Hotel and Casino, 3645 Las Vegas Blvd. S. (1998)	540	Tower
*Mandarin Oriental Hotel Las Vegas, 3750 Las Vegas Blvd. S. (2009)	539	56
New York, New York Hotel & Casino, 3790 Las Vegas Blvd. S. (1997)	529	48
Palms Place, 4321 W. Flamingo Rd. (2008)	518	50
Bellagio Hotel & Casino, 3600 Las Vegas Blvd. S. (1998)	508	36
Sky Las Vegas, 2780 Las Vegas Blvd. S. (2007)	500	45
Panorama Tower III, 4631 Industrial Blvd. (2009)	494	44
THEhotel, Mandalay Bay, 3950 S. Las Vegas Blvd. (2003)	485	43
Mandalay Bay Hotel & Casino, 3950 S. Las Vegas Blvd. (1999)	480	43
Turnberry Place I, 2777 Paradise Rd. (2001)	477	38
Turnberry Place II, 2777 Paradise Rd. (2002)	477	38
Turnberry Place III, 2777 Paradise Rd. (2004)	477	38
Turnberry Place IV, 2777 Paradise Rd. (2006)	477	38
The Signature at MGM Grand Tower I, 155 E. Harmon Ave. (2006)	475	38
The Signature at MGM Grand Tower II, 155 E. Harmon Ave. (2006)	475	38
The Signature at MGM Grand Tower III, 155 E. Harmon Ave. (2007)	475	38
The Venetian, 3355 Las Vegas Blvd. W. (1999)	475	35
Allure Las Vegas I (2007)	466	41
Palms Resort - Fantasy Tower, 4321 W. Flamingo Rd. (2006)	457	40
Turnberry Towers West Tower, 222 Karen Ave. (2008)	453	45
Turnberry Towers East Tower, 222 Karen Ave. (2009).	453	45
Caesars Palace Tower, 3570 S. Las Vegas Blvd. (1998).	435	29
*VEER I, 3600 S. Las Vegas Blvd. (2009).	432	37
*VEER II, 3600 S. Las Vegas Blvd. (2009)	432	37
Rio Masquerade Tower, 3700 W. Flamingo Rd. (1997)	423	42
Los Angeles, CA		
US Bank Tower, 633 W. 5th St. (1990)	1018	73
Aon Center, 707 Wilshire Blvd. (1974)	858	62
Two California Plaza, 350 S. Grand Ave. (1992)	750	52
Gas Company Tower, 555 W. 5th St. (1991)	749	52
Bank of America Plaza, 333 South Hope St. (1975)	735	55
777 Tower, 777 S. Figueroa St. (1991)	725	53
Wells Fargo Tower, 333 S. Grand Ave. (1983)	723	54
Figueroa at Wilshire, 601 S. Figueroa St. (1989)	717	52
Paul Hastings Tower, 515 S. Flower St. (1971)	699	52
City National Tower, 555 S. Flower St. (1971)	699	52
*L.A. Live Hotel & Condominiums, S. Figueroa & W. Olympic (2010)	667	54
Citigroup Center, 444 S. Flower St. (1979)	625	48
611 Place, 611 W. 6th St. (1969)	620	42
One California Plaza, 300 S. Grand Ave. (1985)	578	42
Century Plaza Tower 1, 2029 Century Park East (1973)	571	44
Century Plaza Tower 2, 2049 Century Park East (1973)	571	44
KPMG Tower, 355 S. Grand Ave. (1984)	560	45
Ernst & Young, LLP Plaza, 725 S. Figueroa St. (1986)	534	41
AIG-SunAmerica Center, 1999 Ave. of the Stars (1989)	533	39
TCW Tower, 865 S. Figueroa St. (1990)	517	37
Union Bank Plaza, 445 S. Figueroa St. (1968)	516	40
10 Universal City Plaza (1984)	506	36
1100 Wilshire (1987)	496	36
Fox Plaza, 2121 Ave. of the Stars (1987)	492	34
Constellation Place, 10250 Constellation Blvd. (2003)	491	35

Building	Ht. (ft.)	Stories
*The Century, 2055 Avenue of the Stars (2009)	478	42
Arco Tower, 1055 W. 7th St. (1987)	462	33
Equitable Bldg., 3435 Wilshire Blvd. (1969)	454	34
City Hall, 200 N. Spring St. (1927)	454	28
AT&T Center, 1150 Olive St. (1965)	452	32
Louisville, KY		
AEGON Center, 400 W. Market St. (1992)	549	35
National City Tower, 101 S. 5th St. (1972)	512	40
PNC Plaza, 5th & Jefferson (1971)	420	30
Humana Center, 500 W. Main St. (1985)	417	27
Mexico City, Mexico		
Torre Mayor, Paseo de la Reforma 505 (2003)	738	55
Torre Ejecutiva Pemex, Marina Nacional 329 Col. Huasteca (1984)	702	52
Torre Altus, Paseo de los Laureles 416 (1999)	640	42
Torre Latino Americana (incl. spire), Eje Central Lazaro Cardenas 2 (1956)	597	45
World Trade Center, Montecito 38 Col. Napoles (1972)[1]	565	50
Arcos Torre I, Paeo de los Tamarindos 400 (1997)	529	35
Arcos Torre II, Paeo de los Tamarindos 400 (2008)	529	35
*Torre Altaire I (2009)	498	42
St. Regis Residences, Paseo de la Reforma 439 (2008)	492	32
*Torre Altaire II (2009)	486	44
*Torre Altaire III (2009)	486	44
Torre Lomas, Paseo de las Palmas 800 (1988)	481	36
*Ritz-Carlton Mexico City, Paseo de la Reforma 342 (2010)	466	34
Santa Fe Flats, Av. Sante Fe 443 (2005)	461	37
(1) 682 ft. with antenna.		
Miami, FL		
*The Capital at Brickell North Tower (incl. spire), 1420 S. Miami Ave. (2011)	806	57
Four Seasons Hotel & Tower, 1441 Brickell Ave (2003)	789	64
Wachovia Financial Center, 200 S. Biscayne Blvd. (1983)	764	55
*The Capital at Brickell South Tower (incl. spire), 1420 S. Miami Ave. (2011)	756	52
900 Biscayne Bay, 900 Biscayne Blvd. (2008)	712	65
Marquis, 1100 Biscayne Blvd. (2009)	679	63
*Met 2 Office Tower, 200 SE 3rd St. (2010)	647	46
Mint at Riverfront, 90 SW 3rd St. (2009)	631	55
Infinity at Brickell, 60 W. 13th St. (2008)	630	52
Bank of America Tower, 100 S.E. Second St. (1987)	625	47
Marinablue, 888 Biscayne Blvd. (2007)	615	57
Plaza on Brickell Tower I, 901 Brickell Ave. (2007)	610	56
Icon Brickell North Tower, 495 Brickell Ave. (2008)	586	58
Icon Brickell South Tower, 495 Brickell Ave. (2008)	586	58
Ten Museum Park, 1040 Biscayne Blvd. (2007)	585	50
Paramount at Edgewater Square, 2066 N. Bayshore Dr. (2009)	555	47
50 Biscayne Blvd. (2007)	554	55
Quantum on the Bay South Tower, 1900 N. Bayshore Dr. (2008)	554	51
Opera Tower, 1750 N. Bayshore Dr. (2007)	543	56
*Park Place at Brickell (incl. spire), 1450 Brickell Ave. (2009)	540	40
Everglades on the Bay North Tower, 244 Biscayne Blvd. (2008)	538	49
Everglades on the Bay South Tower, 244 Biscayne Blvd. (2008)	538	49
Quantum on the Bay North Tower, 1900 N. Bayshore Dr. (2008)	536	44
Jade at Brickell Bay, 1331 Brickell Bay Dr. (2004).	528	49
Plaza on Brickell Tower II, 901 Brickell Ave. (2007).	525	48
Santa Maria, 1643 Brickell Ave. (1997)	520	51
The Ivy, 90-95 SW 3rd St. (2008)	512	45
Stephen P. Clark Center, 111 NW 1 St. (1985)	510	28
Wind, 330 S. Miami Ave. (2008)	501	41
Avenue Brickell Tower, 1060 Brickell Ave. (2007)	495	47
One Biscayne Tower, 2 S. Biscayne Blvd. (1973)	492	39
Espirito Santo Plaza, 1301 Brickell Ave. (2004)	487	36
Brickell Financial Centre Phase I, 680 Brickell Ave. (2009)	484	40
Miami Center, 201 S. Biscayne Blvd. (1983)	484	34
Asia, 900 Brickell Key Blvd. (2007)	483	36
Brickell on the River North, 27 SE 5th St. (2005)	482	42
Three Tequesta Point, 848 Brickell Key Dr. (2001)	480	46
Latitude on the River, 615 SW 2nd Ave. (2007)	476	44
Viceroy, 495 Brickell Ave. (2009)	465	46
One Miami East Tower, 205 S. Brickell Ave. (2005)	460	44
701 Brickell Ave. (1986)	450	33
Miami Beach, FL		
Blue Diamond Tower, 4779 Collins Ave. (2000)	559	44
Green Diamond Tower, 4775 Collins Ave. (2000)	559	44
Akoya, 6365 Collins Ave. (2004)	492	47
Portofino Tower, 300 South Pointe Drive (1997)	484	44
The Continuum on South Beach, South Tower, 1 South Pointe Dr. (2002).	474	40
ICON at South Beach, 450 Alton Rd. (2004).	423	43
The Continuum on South Beach, North Tower, 200 South Pointe Dr. (2008).	415	37
Murano Grande at Portofino, 400 Alton Rd. (2003)	407	37
Murano at Portofino, 1000 South Pointe Dr. (2001)	402	38
Milwaukee, WI		
U.S. Bank Center, 777 E. Wisconsin Ave. (1973)	601	42
100 E. Wisconsin Ave. (1989)	549	37
University Club Tower, 825 N. Prospect Ave. (2007)	446	36
Milwaukee Center. 111 E. Kilbourn Ave. (1987)	426	29
411 Bldg., 411 E. Wisconsin Ave. (1989)	408	30
Minneapolis, MN		
IDS Tower, 80 8th St. South (1973)[1]	792	57
Capella Tower, 225 6th St. South (1992).	776	56

Building	Ht. (ft.)	Stories
Wells Fargo Center, 90 7th St. South (1988)	775	56
33 South 6th St. (1983)	668	52
Campbell Mithun Tower, 222 9th St. South (1984)	582	42
US Bank Plaza I, 200 6th St. South (1981)	561	41
RBC Plaza, 60 6th St. South (1992)	539	40
Fifth Street Towers II, 150 5th St. South (1988)	503	36
Ameriprise Financial Center, 707 2nd Ave. South (2000)	498	31
Target Plaza South, 1020 Nicollet Mall (2001)	492	33
Plaza VII, 45 7th St. South (1987)	475	36
The Carlyle, 220 2nd St. South (2007)	469	41
US Bancorp Center, 800 Nicollet Mall (2000)	468	32
AT&T Tower, 901 Marquette Ave. (1991)	464	34
Accenture Tower, 333 7th St. South (1987)	455	33
Foshay Tower, 821 Marquette Ave. (1929)	448	32
Qwest Bldg., 224 5th St. South (1931)	416	26
Fifty South Sixth (2001)	404	30
Hennepin Co. Government Center, 300 6th St. South (1977)	403	24
(1) 910 ft. with antenna.		

Montréal, Quebec

Building	Ht. (ft.)	Stories
1250 Boulevard Rene Levesque (incl. spire) (1992)	743	47
1000 Rue de la Gauchetiere (1992)	673	51
Tour de la Bourse, 800 Place Victoria (1964)	624	47
1 Place Villa Marie (1962)	616	43
La Tour CIBC, 1155 Rene Levesque Blvd. (1962)	604	43
Montreal Tower (1987)	574	Tower
Tour McGill College, 1501 McGill College (1992)	519	38
Le Complexe Desjardins Sud (1975)	498	40
Tour KMPG, 600 Maisonneuve (1987)	479	34
Place Montreal Trust, 1800 McGill College (1988)	440	30
500 Place d'Armes (1968)	435	32
Tour TELUS, 630 Rene Levesque Blvd. (1962)	429	32
Le Complexe Desjardins Est (1975)	428	32
Port Royal Apts., 1455 Sherbrooke Ouest (1964)	424	33
Marriott Hotel, 1 Place du Canada (1967)	420	38
Tour de la Banque Nationale, 600 Rue de la Gauchetiere (1983)	420	28
Tour Bell, 700 Rue de la Gauchetiere (1983)	420	28
Centre Mount Royal, 1000 Sherbrooke Ouest (1974)	420	28
Le 800, 800 Rene Levesque Blvd. Ouest (1966)	400	30

Nashville, TN

Building	Ht. (ft.)	Stories
BellSouth Tower, 333 Commerce St. (1994)	617	33
Financial Center, 424 Church St. (1986)	490	31
William R. Snodgrass Tennessee Tower, 311 7th Ave. North (1970)	452	31
*The Pinnacle, 150 3rd Ave. South (2010)	435	29
Nashville Life & Casualty Tower, 401 Church St. (1957)	409	30
City Center, 511 Union St. (1987)	402	27

New Orleans, LA

Building	Ht. (ft.)	Stories
One Shell Square, 701 Poydras St. (1972)	697	51
CapitalOne Center, 201 St. Charles Ave. (1985)	645	53
Plaza Tower, 1001 Howard Ave. (1969)	531	45
Energy Centre, 1100 Poydras St. (1984)	530	39
First Bank & Trust Tower, 909 Poydras St. (1987)	481	36
Sheraton Hotel, 500 Canal St. (1985)	478	47
Marriott Hotel, 555 Canal St. (1972)	450	42
Texaco Center, 400 Poydras St. (1983)	442	33
Canal Place One, 365 Canal St. (1979)	439	32
1010 Common St. (1971)	438	31
World Trade Center, 2 Canal St. (1965)	407	33
1450 Poydras St. (1989)	406	26

New York, NY

Building	Ht. (ft.)	Stories
*One World Trade Center (incl. spire) (2013)	1,776	105
Empire State Building, 350 5th Ave. (1931)[1]	1,250	102
Bank of America (incl. spire), One Bryant Park (2009)	1,198	54
Chrysler Building. (incl. spire), 405 Lexington Ave. (1930)	1,046	77
New York Times Tower (incl. spire), 620 8th Ave. (2007)	1,046	52
*Four World Trade Center, 150 Greenwich St. (2012)	975	64
American International Bldg. (incl. spire), 70 Pine St. (1932)	952	67
The Trump Bldg., 40 Wall St. (1930)	927	71
Citigroup Center, 153 E. 53rd St. (1977)	915	59
*Four Seasons Hotel and Condominiums, 99 Church St. (2011)	912	68
*Beekman Place, 8 Spruce St. (2011)	876	76
Trump World Tower, 845 UN Plaza (2001)	861	72
G. E. Bldg., 30 Rockefeller Center (1933)	850	70
Cityspire Center, 150 W. 56th St. (1989)	814	75
One Chase Manhattan Plaza (1960)	813	60
4 Times Square (1999)[2]	809	48
MetLife Bldg., 200 Park Ave. (1963)	808	59
Bloomberg Tower, 731 Lexington Ave. (2005)[3]	806	54
Woolworth Building, 233 Broadway (1913)	792	57
1 Worldwide Plaza, 935 8th Ave. (1989)	778	47
Carnegie Hall Tower, 152 W. 57th St. (1991)	757	60
Bear Stearns World Headquarters, 383 Madison Ave. (2001)	755	47
AXA Center, 787 7th Ave. (1985)	752	51
One Penn Plaza, 250 W. 34th St. (1972)	750	57
Time Warner Center South Tower, 10 Columbus Circle (2004)	750	55
Time Warner Center North Tower, 10 Columbus Circle (2004)	750	55
1251 Ave. of the Americas (1971)	750	54
*Goldman Sachs HQ, 200 Murray St. (2009)	749	44
J.P. Morgan Headquarters, 60 Wall St. (1989)	745	55
One Astor Plaza, 1515 Broadway (1970)	745	54
1 Liberty Plaza, 165 Broadway (1973)	743	54
20 Exchange Place (1931)	741	57
7 World Trade Center (2006)	741	52
Three World Financial Center, 200 Vesey St. (1986)	739	51
Bertelsmann Building (incl. spire), 1540 Broadway (1990)	732	42
Times Square Tower, 1459 Broadway (2004)	726	47
Metropolitan Tower, 142 W. 57th St. (1985)	716	68
JPMorgan Chase World Headquarters, 270 Park Ave. (1960)	707	52
General Motors Bldg., 767 5th Ave. (1968)	705	50
Metropolitan Life Tower, 1 Madison Ave. (1909)	700	50
500 5th Ave. (1931)	697	60
Americas Tower, 1177 Ave. of the Americas (1992)	692	48
Solow Bldg. 9 W. 57th St. (1974)	689	49
HSBC Bank Bldg., 140 Broadway (1967)	688	52
55 Water St. (1972)	687	53
277 Park Ave. (1963)	687	50
1585 Broadway (1989)	685	42
Random House/Park Imperial, 1739 Broadway (2003)	684	52
Four Seasons Hotel, 57 E. 57th St. (1993)	682	52
McGraw Hill, 1221 Ave. of the Americas (1972)	674	51
Barclay Tower, 10 Barclay St. (2007)	673	56
Lincoln Bldg., 60 E. 42nd St. (1930)	673	53
Paramount Plaza, 1633 Broadway (1970)	670	48
Trump Tower, 725 5th Ave. (1982)	664	58
Citicorp, Queens (1990)	658	50
Bank of New York Bldg., 1 Wall St. (1932)	654	50
Silver Towers East, 600 W. 42nd St. (2009)	653	58
Silver Towers West, 600 W. 42nd St. (2009)	653	58
599 Lexington Ave. (1986)	653	51
712 5th Ave. (1990)	650	53
Chanin Bldg., 122 E. 42nd St. (1929)	649	56
245 Park Ave. (1967)	648	47
Sony Bldg., 550 Madison Ave. (1983)	647	37
Two World Financial Center, 225 Liberty St. (1986)	645	44
570 Lexington Ave. (1931)	642	50
1 New York Plaza, 1 Water St. (1969)	640	50
1 Dag Hammarskjold Plaza, 885 2nd Ave. (1972)	637	48
345 Park Ave. (1968)	634	44
*400 5th Ave. (2010)	632	58
Mercantile Bldg., 10 E. 40th St. (1929)	632	48
*W New York Downtown Hotel & Residences, 4 Albany St. (2009)	631	57
Grace Plaza, 1114 Ave. of Amer. (1972)	630	50
Home Insurance Co., 59 Maiden Ln. (1966)	630	44
1095 Ave. of the Americas (1970)	630	40
101 Park Ave. (1982)	629	49
Central Park Place, 301 W. 57th St. (1988)	628	56
888 7th Ave. (1971)	628	45
Burlington House, 1345 Ave. of the Americas (1969)	625	50
Waldorf-Astoria, 301 Park Ave. (1931)	625	47
Olympic Tower, 645 5th Ave. (1976)	620	51
425 Fifth Avenue (2003)	618	55
One Madison Park, 20 E. 23rd St. (2009)	618	51
The Epic, 125 W. 31st St. (2007)	615	58
919 3rd Ave. (1970)	615	47
750 7th Ave. (incl. spire) (1989)	615	35
New York Life, 51 Madison Ave. (1928)	615	33
*Eventi, 835 6th Ave. (2009)	614	46
Tower 49, 12 E. 49th St. (1985)	614	44
Credit Lyonnais Bldg., 1301 Ave. of the Americas (1964)	609	46
The Orion, 350 W. 42nd St. (2006)	604	58
590 Madison Ave. (1983)	603	41
*Times Square Plaza, 644 8th Ave. (2010)	601	40
Marsh & McLennan Headquarters, 1166 Ave. of the Americas (1974)	600	44
Hearst Magazine Tower, 959 8th Ave. (2006)	597	46
3 Lincoln Center, 160 W. 66th St. (1993)	595	60
Trump Palace, 200 E. 69th St. (1991)	594	54
Celanese Bldg., 1211 Ave. of the Americas (1973)	592	45
The London NYC, 151 W. 54th St. (1990)	590	54
Thurgood Marshall U. S. Court House, 505 Pearl St. (1927)	590	37
The Millennium Hilton Hotel, 55 Church St. (1992)	588	58
Sky House, 11 E. 29th St. (2008)	588	55
Museum Tower Apts. 21 W. 53rd St. (1985)	588	52
Time-Life Bldg., 1271 Ave. of the Americas (1959)	587	48
Jacob K. Javits Federal Bldg., 26 Federal Plaza (1967)	587	41
W Times Square, 1567 Broadway (2000)	584	53
Trump International Hotel & Tower, 15 Columbus Circle (1970)	583	44
Stevens Tower, 1185 Ave. of the Americas (1971)	580	42
Municipal Bldg., 1 Centre St. (1914)	580	34
520 Madison Ave. (1981)	577	43
One World Financial Center, 200 Liberty St. (1985)	577	37
Merchandise Mart, 41 Madison Ave. (1973)	576	42
Park Ave. Plaza, 55 E. 52nd St. (1981)	575	44
Lehman Bldg., 745 7th Ave. (2001)	575	38
One Financial Square, 33 Old Slip (1987)	575	37
Marriot Marquis Times Square, 1531 Broadway (1985)	574	50
299 Park Ave. (1967)	574	42
Ernst & Young Tower, 5 Times Square, 590 7th Ave. (2002)	574	40
Socony Mobil Bldg., 150 E. 42nd St. (1956)	572	42
AXA Finance Center, 1290 Ave. of the Americas (1963)	571	43
780 3rd Ave. (1983)	570	49
600 3rd Ave. (1971)	570	42
450 Lexington Ave. (1991)	568	38
Paramount Tower, 240 E. 39th St. (1998)	567	51
785 8th Ave. (2009)	566	42
230 Park Ave. (1928)	565	35
New York Palace Hotel, 455 Madison Ave. (1980)	563	51
Continental Bank Bldg., 30 Broad St. (1932)	562	48
Park Ave. Tower, 65 E. 55th St. (1986)	561	36

Building	Ht. (ft.)	Stories
Nelson Tower, 450 7th Ave. (1931)	560	46
Sherry-Netherland, 781 5th Ave. (1927)	560	40
Swiss Bank Tower, 10 E. 50th St. (1990)	560	36
100 UN Plaza, 327 E. 48th St. (1986)	557	52
Continental Can, 633 3rd Ave. (1962)	557	39
3 Park Ave. (1975)	556	42
Continental Corp., 180 Maiden Lane (1983)	555	41
Sperry & Hutchinson Bldg., 330 Madison Ave. (1964)	555	41
Reuters Bldg., 3 Times Square (2001)[4]	555	30
Madison Belvedere, 14 E. 29th St. (1999)	554	48
*Tower 111, 885 6th Ave. (NA)	554	47
Inmont Bldg., 1133 Ave. of the Americas (1970)	552	45
Downtown by Philippe Starck, 15 Broad St. (1927)	551	42
Biltmore Tower, 267 W. 47th St. (2003)	550	51
Unisys, 605 3rd Ave. (1963)	550	44
2 Grand Central Tower, 140 E. 45th St. (1982)	550	43
The Tower at 15 Central Park West (2008)	550	35
Bell Atlantic, 33 Thomas St. (1974)	550	29

(1) 1,455 ft. with antenna. (2) 1,118 ft. with antenna. (3) 941 ft. with antenna. (4) 659 ft. with antenna.

Oklahoma City, OK

Building	Ht. (ft.)	Stories
Chase Tower, 100 N. Broadway Ave. (1971)	500	36
First National Center (incl. spire), 120 N. Robinson St. (1931)	493	33
City Place, 204 N. Robinson St. (1931)	440	32
Oklahoma Tower, 210 Park Ave. (1982)	434	31

Orlando, FL

Building	Ht. (ft.)	Stories
SunTrust Center Tower, 200 S. Orange Ave. (1988)	441	31
Vue at Lake Eola, 136 E. Robinson St. (2007)	426	35
Orange County Courthouse, 425 N. Orange Ave. (1997)	416	24
Bank of America Center, 390 N. Orange Ave. (1988)	409	28

Philadelphia, PA

Building	Ht. (ft.)	Stories
Comcast Center, 1701 JFK Blvd. (2008)	974	57
One Liberty Place (incl. spire), 1650 Market St. (1987)	945	61
Two Liberty Place (incl. spire), 1601 Chestnut St. (1989)	848	58
Mellon Bank Center, 1735 Market St. (1990)	792	54
Bell-Atlantic Tower, 1717 Arch St. (1991)	725	53
G. Fred DiBona Jr. Bldg., 1901 Market St. (1990)	625	45
Commerce Square #1, 2005 Market St. (1990)	572	40
Commerce Square #2, 2001 Market St. (1992)	572	40
City Hall (incl. statue) (1901)	548	7
Residences at Ritz-Carlton, 1416 S. Penn Square (2009)	518	48
1818 Market St. (1974)	500	40
The St. James, 700 Walnut St. (2004)	498	45
Loews Philadelphia Hotel, 12 S. 12th St. (1932)[1]	492	39
PNC Bank Bldg., 1600 Market St. (1983)	491	40
Centre Square II, 1542 Market St. (1973)	490	38
5 Penn Center, 1601 Market St. (1970)	488	36
1700 Market St. (1969)	482	32
The Murano, 2101 Market St. (2008)	475	42
1 South Broad St. (1930)	472	28
Cira Centre, 2929 Arch St. (2005)	437	29
Two Logan Square, 100 N. 18th St. (1988)	435	34
1835 Market St. (1985)	430	29
Aramark Tower, 1101 Market St. (1984)	417	31
Centre Square I, 1500 Market St. (1973)	416	32
Wachovia Bldg., 123 S. Broad St. (1927)	405	30
Ritz Carlton Hotel, 28 S. Broad St. (1930)	404	30
One Logan Square, 130 N. 18th St. (1982)	400	32

(1) 748 ft. with antenna.

Pittsburgh, PA

Building	Ht. (ft.)	Stories
US Steel Tower, 600 Grant St. (1970)	841	64
One Mellon Bank Center, 500 Grant St. (1983)	725	54
One PPG Place (1984)	635	40
Fifth Ave. Place, 120 5th Ave. (1987)	616	32
One Oxford Centre, 301 Grant St. (1982)	615	46
Gulf Tower, 707 Grant St. (1932)	582	44
University of Pittsburgh Cathedral of Learning, 4200 5th Ave. (1936)	535	42
3 Mellon Bank Center, 525 Wm. Penn Way (1951)	520	41
Freemarkets Center, 210 6th Ave. (1968)	511	39
Grant Bldg., 330 Grant St. (1928)	485	40
Koppers Bldg., 436 7th Ave. (1929)	475	34
Two PNC Plaza, 620 Liberty Ave. (1975)	445	34
Dominion Tower, 625 Liberty Ave. (1987)	430	32
One PNC Plaza, 249 5th Ave. (1972)	424	30
Regional Enterprise Tower, 425 6th Ave. (1953)	410	30

Portland, OR

Building	Ht. (ft.)	Stories
Wells Fargo Center, 1300 SW 5th Ave. (1973)	546	40
U.S. Bancorp Tower, 111 SW 5th Ave. (1983)	536	42
Koin Plaza, 222 SW Columbia St. (1984)	509	31
Pacwest Center, 1211 SW 5th Ave. (1984)	418	30

Raleigh, NC

Building	Ht. (ft.)	Stories
RBC Plaza (incl. spire), 300 Fayetteville St. (2008)	538	32
2 Hanover Square, 434 Fayetteville St. Mall (1991)	431	29
Wachovia Capitol Center, 150 Fayetteville St. Mall (1991)	400	30

St. Louis, MO

Building	Ht. (ft.)	Stories
Gateway Arch (1965)[1]	630	NA
Metropolitan Square Tower, 211 N. Broadway (1988)	593	42
AT&T Center, 909 Pine St. (1984)	588	44
Thomas F. Eagleton Federal Courthouse, 111 S. 10th St. (2000)	557	29
One U.S. Bank Plaza, 505 N. 7th St. (1976)	484	35
Laclede Gas Bldg., 720 Olive St. (1969)	400	31

(1) Monument.

St. Paul, MN

Building	Ht. (ft.)	Stories
Wells Fargo Place, 30 E. 7th St. (1987)	471	36
Galtier Plaza Jackson Tower, 168 E. 6th St. (1986)	443	46
First National Bank, 332 Minnesota St. (1930)	417	32

San Antonio, TX

Building	Ht. (ft.)	Stories
Tower of the Americas, 600 Hemisphere Way (1968)	622	Tower
Marriott Rivercenter, 101 Bowie St. (1988)	546	38
Weston Centre, 112 Pecan St. (1988)	444	32
Grand Hyatt San Antonio, 600 E. Market St. (2008)	424	34
Tower Life, 310 S. St. Mary's St. (1929)	404	30

San Diego, CA

Building	Ht. (ft.)	Stories
One American Plaza, 600 W. Broadway (1991)	500	34
Symphony Tower, 759 B St. (1989)	499	34
Manchester Grand Hyatt, One Market Place (1992)	497	40
Electra, 701 W. Broadway (2008)	475	43
Pinnacle Museum Tower, 500 Front St. (2005)	455	35
Emerald Plaza, 400 W. Broadway (1990)	450	30
Manchester Grand Hyatt Tower 2, One Market Place (2003)	446	32
Harbor Club West, 100 Harbor Dr. (1992)	424	41
Harbor Club East, 200 Harbor Dr. (1992)	424	41
Vantage Point, 1200 10th Ave. (2009)	420	41
The Grande North at Sante Fe Place (2005)	420	39
The Grande South at Sante Fe Place, 1199 Pacific Hwy. (2004)	420	39
Advanced Equities Plaza, 655 Broadway (2005)	412	23

San Francisco, CA

Building	Ht. (ft.)	Stories
Sutro Tower (1972)	977	Tower
Transamerica Pyramid, 600 Montgomery St. (1972)	853	48
555 California St. (1969)	779	52
345 California St. (1986)	695	48
Millennium Tower, 301 Mission St. (2009)	645	58
One Rincon Hill South Tower, 425 First St. (2008)	605	54
101 California St. (1982)	600	48
50 Fremont Center (1985)	600	43
Chevron Tower, 575 Market St. (1975)	573	40
Four Embarcadero Center, 55 Clay St. (1984)	570	45
One Embarcadero Center, 355 Clay St. (1970)	569	45
44 Montgomery St. (1967)	565	43
Spear Tower, 1 Market St. (1976)	565	42
One Sansome Street (1984)	550	43
Shaklee Terrace Bldg., 444 Market St. (1982)	537	38
McKeeson Plaza, 1 Post St. (1969)	529	38
525 Market St. (1972)	529	38
425 Market St. (1973)	524	38
Telsis Tower, 1 Montgomery St. (1982)	500	38
333 Bush St. (1986)	495	43
Hilton San Francisco & Towers, 201 Mason St. (1971)	493	46
Pacific Gas & Electric, 77 Beale St. (1971)	492	34
50 California St. (1972)	487	37
555 Mission St. (2008)	487	33
St. Regis San Francisco, 685 Mission St. (2005)	484	42
100 Pine Center (1972)	476	34
45 Fremont Center (1979)	475	34
333 Market Bldg. (1979)	474	33
650 California St. (1965)	465	33
The Infinity II, 300 Spear St. (2009)	450	40

Seattle, WA

Building	Ht. (ft.)	Stories
Columbia Center, 701 5th Ave. (1985)	933	76
Washington Mutual Tower, 1201 3rd Ave. (1988)	772	55
Two Union Square, 601 Union St. (1989)	740	56
Seattle Municipal Tower, 700 5th Ave. (1990)	722	57
Safeco Plaza, 1001 4th Ave. (1969)	630	50
Space Needle, 203 6th Ave. (1962)	605	Tower
WaMu Center, 1301 2nd Ave. (2006)	598	42
City Centre, 1420 5th Ave. (1989)	580	44
Wells Fargo Center, 999 3rd Ave. (1983)	574	47
Bank of America Fifth Avenue Plaza, 800 Fifth Ave. (1981)	543	42
901 5th Ave. (1973)	536	41
Rainier Tower, 1301 5th Ave. (1977)	514	31
IDX Tower at Fourth & Madison, 915 4th Ave. (2003)	512	40
1918 8th Ave. (2009)	500	36
1000 2nd Ave. (1986)	493	40
Henry M. Jackson Bldg., 915 2nd Ave. (1974)	487	37
Qwest Plaza, 1600 7th Ave. (1976)	466	33
Smith Tower, 506 2nd Ave. (1914)	462	36
One Union Square, 600 University Ave. (1981)	456	36
Olive 8 (2009)	455	39
1111 3rd Ave. (1980)	454	34
Westin Hotel North Tower, 1900 5th Ave. (1982)	448	44
Fifteen Twenty-One Second Avenue (2008)	440	38
Westin Bldg., 2001 6th Ave. (1981)	409	34
*Aspira, 1823 Terry (2009)	400	37

(1) 963 ft. with antenna

Sunny Isles Beach, FL

Building	Ht. (ft.)	Stories
*Solis Resort Spa Residences, 15701 Collins Ave. (2010)	583	53
Jade on the Beach Condominiums, 17001 Collins Ave. (2008)	574	51
Trump Palace, 18101 Collins Ave. (2005)	551	43
Trump Royale, 18201 Collins Ave. (2008)	551	43
Aqualina Ocean Residences, 17875 Collins Ave. (2004)	550	51
Jade Ocean, 17121 Collins Ave. (2008)	543	51
The Pinnacle, 17555 Collins Ave. (1999)	476	40

Building	Ht. (ft.)	Stories
La Perla Ocean Residences, 16701 Collins Ave. (2006)	447	42
Ocean Four Condominiums, 17201 Collins Ave. (NA)	446	40
Ocean Two Condominiums I, 19111 Collins Ave. (2001)	426	40
Ocean Two Condominiums II, 19111 Collins Ave. (2001)	426	40

Tampa, FL

Building	Ht. (ft.)	Stories
Regions Bldg, 100 N. Tampa St. (1992)	579	42
Bank of America Plaza, 101 E. Kennedy Blvd. (1986)	577	42
One Tampa City Center, 201 N. Franklin St. (1981)	537	39
Suntrust Financial Center, 401 E. Jackson St. (1992)	525	36
Element, 808 N. Franklin St. (2009)	460	34
Park Tower, 400 N. Tampa St. (1973)	458	36
Rivergate Tower, 400 N. Ashley Dr. (1988)	454	33

Toronto, Ontario

Building	Ht. (ft.)	Stories
CN Tower, 310 Front St. West (1976)	1,815	Tower
First Bank Tower, 100 King St. West (1975)[1]	978	72
*Trump International Hotel & Tower (incl. spire), 333 Bay St. (2011)	922	59
Scotia Plaza, 40 King's St. West (1989)	902	68
BCE Place, Canada Trust Tower (incl. spire), 161 Bay St. (1990)	856	53
Commerce Court West, 199 Bay St. (1973)[2]	784	57
TD Centre - Toronto Dominion Bank Tower, 66 Wellington St. West (1967)	730	56
Bay-Adelaide Center West Tower, 335 Bay St. (2009)	715	50
*Shangri-La Toronto, 180 University Ave. (2011)	702	65
*Ritz-Carlton Hotel and Residences, 185 Wellington St. West (2010)	699	53
BCE Place, Bay-Wellington Tower, 181 Bay St. (1991)	679	49
*Four Seasons Private Residences West, 48 Yorkville Ave. (2011)	623	55
*Maple Leaf Square North Tower, 15 York St. (2009)	610	54
TD Centre - Royal Trust Tower, 77 King St. West (1969)	600	46
RBC Centre, 155 Wellington St. West (2009)	600	42
1 King West (2005)	578	51
*Maple Leaf Square South Tower, 15 York St. (2009)	571	50
Royal Bank Plaza - South Tower, 200 Bay St. (1976)	567	41
44 Charles St. West (1974)	545	51
Quantum 2, 2195 Yonge St. (2008)	541	51
Residences @ College Park I, Bay St. & College St. (2006)	535	51
Success Tower, 18 Harbour St. (2009)	531	45
*Uptown Residences, 35 Balmuto St. (2010)	518	48
*Festival Tower, 330 King St. West (2010)	514	46
TD Centre - 79 Wellington St. West (1985)	504	39
Harbourview Estates Phase 2, 35 Mariner Terrace (2005)	503	49
Montage, 20 Fort York Blvd. (2009)	502	48
*Burano, 832 Bay St. (2010)	502	48

Building	Ht. (ft.)	Stories
The 250, 250 Yonge St. (1991)	494	35
Two Bloor West (1974)	488	34
*X Condominium, 110 Charles St. East (2010)	487	45
West One, 11 Brunel Ct. (2007)	486	49
Simcoe Place, 200 Front St. West (1995)	486	33
The Residences of College Park II, 763 Bay St. (2008)	482	45
Exchange Tower, 130 King St. West (1983)	480	30
The Met, 21 Carlton St. (2007)	479	43
CIBC-Commerce Court North, 25 King St. West (1931)	477	34
Simpson Tower, 401 Bay St. (1968)	473	33
SP!RE, 33 Lombard St. (2007)	469	45
Cadillac-Fairview Tower, 20 Queen St. West (1982)	465	36
*Murano South Tower, 825 Bay St. (2009)	459	41
Pantages Tower, 200 Victoria St. (2003)	458	46
One Palace Pier Court, Etobicoke (1991)	455	46
Three Palace Pier Court, Etobicoke (1978)	453	46
*Casa Condominium, 33 Charles St. East (2009)	453	45
Oxford Tower, 130 Adelaide St. West (1979)	450	33

(1) 1,116 ft. with antenna. (2) 942 ft. with antenna.

Tulsa, OK

Building	Ht. (ft.)	Stories
BOK Tower, 1 E. 2nd St. (1975)	667	52
Cityplex Central Tower, 2448 E 81st St. (1979)	648	60
First Place Tower, 15 E 5th St. (1973)	516	40
Mid-Continent Tower, 401 S. Boston St. (1984)	513	36
Bank of America Center, 15 W. 6th St. (1967)	412	32
320 S. Boston St. (1928)	400	22

Vancouver, British Columbia

Building	Ht. (ft.)	Stories
Living Shangri-La, 1100 W. Georgia St. (2008)	659	62
*The Private Residences, 699 Howe St. (2011)	517	48
One Wall Centre, 1000 Burrard St. (2001)	491	48
Shaw Tower, 298 Thurlow St. (2004)	489	40
Harbour Centre, 555 W. Hastings St. (1977)[1]	481	30
The Melville, 1189 Melville St. (2007)	464	43
Royal Centre, 1055 W. Georgia St. (1973)	461	37
Bentall V, 550 Burrard St. (2007)	460	34
Park Place, 666 Burrard St. (1984)	459	35
Fairmont Pacific Rim Vancouver, 1011 W. Cordova St. (2009)	458	46
Bentall IV, 550 Burrard St. (1981)	454	35
200 Granville Square (1973)	454	30
Scotia Tower, 650 W. Georgia St. (1977)	452	35
*Patina, 955 Burrard St. (2011)	418	42
T-D Bank Tower, 700 W. Georgia St. (1970)	417	30
*Capitol Residences, 833 Seymour St. (2010)	414	42
Bentall III, 595 Burrard St. (1974)	400	31

(1) 581 ft. with antenna.

Other Tall Buildings in North American Cities

Lists include freestanding towers and other structures that do not have stories and are not technically considered buildings. Structures still under construction as of mid-2009 are denoted by an asterisk (*). Year in parentheses is date of completion or projected completion. Height is generally measured from sidewalk to roof, including penthouse and tower if enclosed as integral part of structure; stories generally counted from street level. NA = Not available or not applicable.

Building	City	Ht. (ft.)	Stories
RSA Battle House Tower (incl. spire) (2007)	Mobile, AL	745	35
The Tower at First National Center (2002)	Omaha, NE	634	45
801 Grand (1991)	Des Moines, IA	630	44
Dataflux Tower (2000)	Monterrey, Mex.	597	43
*Centro de Gobierno Plaza Civica (2010)	Monterrey, Mex.	591	36
Erastus Corning II Tower (1973)	Albany, NY	589	44
Niagara Falls Hilton Phase 2 (2009)	Niagara Falls, ON	581	58
Concourse Corporate Center V (1988)	Sandy Springs, GA	570	34
Concourse Corporate Center VI (1991)	Sandy Springs, GA	553	34
*Absolute World Tower 1 (2010)	Mississauga, ON	548	56
Torre Aura Altitude (2008)	Zapopan, Mex.	548	44
Metropolitan Tower (1986)	Little Rock, AK	546	40
One HSBC Center (1970)	Buffalo, NY	529	40
Vehicle Assembly Bldg. (1965)	Cape Canaveral, FL	525	40
Skylon (1965)	Niagara Falls, ON	520	NA
Westin Virginia Beach Town Center and Residences (2007)	Virginia Beach, VA	508	38
The Beach Club Tower 2 (2006)	Hallandale Beach, FL	505	50
*Absolute World Tower 2 (2010)	Mississauga, ON	495	50
Torre Caney (2008)	Santo Domingo, Dominican Republic	492	38
Mohegan Sun Sky Tower (2002)	Montville, CT	487	34
Chase Tower (1972)	Phoenix, AZ	486	40
The Residences at Ritz-Carlton Westchester (2009)	White Plains, NY	484	44
The Residences at Ritz-Carlton Westchester (2008)	White Plains, NY	484	44
Woodmen Tower (1969)	Omaha, NE	478	30
One Park Tower (2008)	Mississauga, ON	466	38

Building	City	Ht. (ft.)	Stories
National Newark Bldg. (1931)	Newark, NJ	465	36
State Capitol (1932)	Baton Rouge, LA	460	34
Wachovia Center (1995)	Winston-Salem, NC	460	34
The Tower (1988)	Burbank, CA	460	32
Ruan Center (1974)	Des Moines, IA	457	36
Wachovia Tower (1986)	Birmingham, AL	454	34
Regions Center (1975)	Little Rock, AK	454	30
Las Olas River House 1 (2004)	Fort Lauderdale, FL	452	42
Bellevue Towers Two (2008)	Bellevue, WA	450	43
Lincoln Tower One (2005)	Bellevue, WA	450	42
James Monroe Bldg. (1981)	Richmond, VA	449	29
1180 Raymond Blvd. (1930)	Newark, NJ	448	34
The Westin Diplomat (2002)	Hollywood, FL	444	39
Ravinia #3 (1991)	Dunwoody, GA	444	33
Trump Hollywood (2009)	Hollywood, FL	443	40
Xerox Tower (1967)	Rochester, NY	443	30
One Summit Square (1981)	Fort Wayne, IN	442	27
The Beach Club Tower 1 (2005)	Hallandale Beach, FL	440	43
The Beach Club Tower 3 (2007)	Hallandale Beach, FL	440	43
Anadarko Tower (2002)	The Woodlands, TX	439	32
Harbert Plaza (1989)	Birmingham, AL	437	32
Trump Plaza (2007)	New Rochelle, NY	435	40
The Palisades (2001)	Fort Lee, NJ	434	41
Bellevue Towers One (2008)	Bellevue, WA	430	42
100 North Main Bldg. (1965)	Memphis, TN	430	38
Bank of America Bldg. (1927)	Providence, RI	428	26
Torre Commercial America (1994)	Monterrey, Mex.	427	35
AmSouth Bank Bldg. (1969)	Mobile, AL	424	33
Wells Fargo Center (1991)	Sacramento, CA	423	30
Wells Fargo Center (1998)	Salt Lake City, UT	422	26
CanWest Global Place (1990)	Winnipeg, MB	420	33
L.D.S. Church Office Bldg. (1972)	Salt Lake City, UT	420	28

Notable Bridges in North America

Source: Office of Bridge Technology, Federal Highway Administration, U.S. Dept. of Transportation; World Almanac research

All bridges accommodate vehicles; vehicles and railroads; or vehicles, railroads, and pedestrians. Asterisk (*) designates a bridge that carries only railroads. Year is date of completion or projected completion. Span of bridge is the distance between its supports. As of Sept. 2008.

Suspension

Year	Bridge	Location	Main span (ft.)
1964	Verrazano-Narrows	New York, NY	4,260
1937	Golden Gate	San Fran. Bay, CA	4,200
1957	Mackinac	Straits of Mackinac, MI	3,800
1931	George Washington	New York, NY–Fort Lee, NJ	3,500
1950	Tacoma Narrows	Tacoma, WA	2,800
2007	Tacoma Narrows (new)	Tacoma, WA	2,800
2003	Carquinez (new) (Al Zampa Mem.)	Carquinez Strait, CA	2,388
1936	San Fran.-Oakland Bay (West Span)[1]	San Fran. Bay, CA	2,310
1939	Bronx-Whitestone	East R., New York, NY	2,300
1970	Pierre Laporte	Quebec City, QC	2,190
1951/68	Del. Memorial (twin)	Pennsville, NJ–New Castle, DE	2,150
1957	Walt Whitman	Philadelphia, PA	2,000
1929	Ambassador	Detroit, MI–Windsor, ON	1,850
1961	Throgs Neck	New York, NY	1,801
1926	Benjamin Franklin	Philadelphia, PA	1,750
1924	Bear Mtn.	Hudson R., Peekskill, NY	1,632
1903	Williamsburg	East R., New York, NY	1,600
1952/73	William Preston Lane Jr. Mem. (twin)	Sandy Point, MD	1,600
1969	Claiborne Pell/Newport	Narragansett Bay, RI	1,600
1883	Brooklyn	East R., New York, NY	1,596
1938	Lions' Gate	Vancouver, BC	1,550
1963	Vincent Thomas	L.A. Harbor, CA	1,500
1930	Mid-Hudson	Poughkeepsie, NY	1,495
1909	Manhattan	East R., New York, NY	1,470
1955	Angus L. Macdonald	Halifax, NS	1,447
1970	A. Murray MacKay	Halifax, NS	1,400
1936	Triborough (Harlem R. Lift/Bronx Crossing/East R. Suspension)	East R., New York, NY	1,380
2013	San Fran.-Oakland Bay (Self-Anchored Suspension [SAS], East Span)	San Fran. Bay, CA	1,263
1931	St. Johns	Portland, OR	1,207
1929	Mount Hope	Portsmouth–Bristol, RI	1,200
1960	Ogdensburg-Prescott	Ogdensburg, NY–Prescott, ON	1,150
1965	Bidwell Bar	Oroville, CA	1,108
1964	Middle Fork Feather	Butte Co., CA	1,105
1939	Deer Isle-Sedgwick	Deer Isle, ME	1,080
1931	Simon Kenton Mem.	Maysville, KY	1,060
1935	Ile d'Orleans	St. Lawrence R., QC	1,059
1866	John A. Roebling/Covington-Cincinnati	Covington, KY–Cincinnati, OH	1,057
1971	Dent	Orofino, ID	1,050
1900	Ojuela	Mapimi, Mex.	1,030
1849	Wheeling	Ohio R., Wheeling, WV	1,010

Cantilever

Year	Bridge	Location	Main span (ft.)
1917	Québec	Québec City, QC	1,800
1974	Commodore Barry	Chester, PA–Bridgeport, NJ	1,644
1988	Greater New Orleans No. 2	Mississippi R., LA	1,594
1958	Greater New Orleans No. 1	Mississippi R., LA	1,575
1995	Gramercy	Mississippi R., Gramercy, LA	1,460
1936	East Span[2]	San Fran. Bay, CA	1,400
1968	Baton Rouge	Mississippi R., LA	1,235
1955	Tappan Zee	Hudson R., Tarrytown, NY	1,212
1930	Lewis and Clark	Longview, WA–Rainier, OR	1,200
1909	Queensboro	East R., New York, NY	1,182
1958	Carquinez Strait (east)	San Fran. Bay, CA	1,100
1930	Jacques Cartier	Montreal, QC	1,097
1968	Isaiah D. Hart	Jacksonville, FL	1,088
1956	Richmond-San Rafael (twin)	San Fran. Bay, CA	1,070
1963	Newburgh-Beacon (north)	Hudson R., NY	1,000
1980	Newburgh-Beacon (south)	Hudson R., NY	1,000
1950	Martin Luther King Jr.	St. Louis, MO	963
1975	Caruthersville	Mississippi R., MO–TN	920
1969	Silver Memorial	Pt. Pleasant, WV–OH	900
1977	Saint Marys	Saint Marys, WV–OH	900
1981	William S. Ritchie	Ohio R., Ravenswood, WV	900
1987	Carl Perkins	Ohio R., OH–KY	900
1941/88	Natchez-Vidalia (twin)	Mississippi R., Natchez, MS	875
1938	Blue Water	Pt. Huron, MI–ON	871
1972	I-20, Mississippi R.	Vicksburg, MS	870
1972	N. Fork American R.	Auburn, CA	862
1940	Baton Rouge	Mississippi R., LA	848
1899	*Cornwall	St. Lawrence R., LA.	843
1940	U.S. 82, Mississippi R.	Greenville, MS	840
1961	U.S. 49, Mississippi R.	Helena, AR	840
1963	Brent Spence	Covington, KY–Cincinnati, OH	830
1930	*Vicksburg (U.S. 80)	Mississippi R., MS	825
1964	Sunshine (LA-70)	Donaldsonville, LA	825
1929	George Rogers Clark Mem. (U.S. 31)	Ohio R., KY–IN	820
1961	J.C. Van Horne Interprovincial	Campbellton, NB–QC	815
1932	Washington Mem.	Seattle, WA	800
1935	Rip Van Winkle	Catskill, NY	800
1938	Cairo Ohio R.	IL–KY	800
1936	McCullough	Coos Bay, OR	793
1949	Memphis	Mississippi R., TN	790
1935	Huey P. Long[3]	New Orleans, LA	790
1949	Memphis-Arkansas (I-55)	Mississippi R., TN–AR	790
1910	*P&LE RR	Ohio R., PA	750
1930	Ashland-Coal Grove	Ohio R., OH	739
1922	Ironton-Russell	Ohio R., OH–KY	725
1932	Bi-State Vietnam Gold Star	Henderson, KY	720
1979	I-275, Ohio R.	Fort Thomas, KY	720
1962	Champlain	Montreal, QC	707
1926	Columbia R.	Cascade Locks, OR	706
1928	Ohio R., B&O RR, HV RR	Pomeroy-Mason, OH	657
1941	*Pit River	Redding, CA	630
1941	Columbia R.	Kettle Falls, WA	600
1954	Columbia R.	Umatilla, OR	600
1965	Bi-State Vietnam Gold Star	Henderson, KY	600
1954	Columbia R.	The Dalles, OR	576
1968	W. 17th St.	Huntington, WV	562

Simple Truss

Year	Bridge	Location	Main span (ft.)
1977	Jennings Randolph	Chester, WV–E Liverpool, OH	745
1929	Irvin S. Cobb (U.S. 45)	Ohio R., Brookport, IL–Paducah, KY	716
1923	*Tanana R.	Nenana, AK	700
1967	Williamstown-Marietta (I-77)	Ohio R., WV–OH	650
1917	*MacArthur	E St. Louis, IL–St. Louis, MO	647
1992	Discovery	Missouri R, MO	625
1958	*Castleton	Hudson R., NY	598
1938	Easton-Phillipsburg	Delaware R., PA	550
1930	Swindell	Pittsburgh, PA	545
1951	Penn. Tpk. Allegheny	Pittsburgh, PA	534
1951	Rankin	Pittsburgh, PA	525
1906	Donora-Webster	Donora-Webster, PA	515
1908	Hulton	Allegheny R., Harmar, PA	505
1967	AK Native Veterans' Honor	Nenana, AK	500

Steel Truss

Year	Bridge	Location	Main span (ft.)
1990	Glade Creek	Raleigh Co., WV	785
1973	U.S. 190, Atchafalaya R.	Krotz Springs, LA	780
1971	I-95, Piscataqua R.	Portsmouth, NH–Kittery, ME	756
1972	Atchafalaya R.	Simmesport, LA	720
1957	Robert O. Norris	Middlesex Co., VA	648
1978	Atchafalaya R.	Morgan City, LA	607
1960	Summit	Summit, DE	600
1968	Reedy Point	Delaware City, DE	600
1910	McKinley	Mississippi R., St. Louis, MO–Venice, IL	517
1972	Mississippi R.	Muscatine, IA.	512
1896	Newport	Ohio R., KY	511
1931	Lucy Jefferson Lewis Mem.	Cumberland R., Smithland, KY	500
1958	Lake Oahe	Gettysburg, SD	500
1958	Lake Oahe	Mobridge, SD	500
1970	Lake Koocanusa	Lincoln Co., MT	500

Continuous Truss

Year	Bridge	Location	Main span (ft.)
1966	Astoria	Columbia R., OR–WA	1,232
1976	Francis Scott Key	Baltimore, MD	1,200
1981	Ravenswood	Ohio R., Ravenswood, WV	902
1995	Taylor-Southgate	Ohio R., KY–OH	850
1943	Julien Dubuque (U.S. 20)	Mississippi R., IA–IL	845
1966	Charles Braga	Fall River, MA	840
1956	Earle C. Clements (twin)(KY 56)	Ohio R., IL–KY	825
1953	John E. Mathews	Jacksonville, FL	810
1940	Gov. Nice Mem.	Potomac R., Newburg, MD–Dahlgren, VA	800
1950	Maurice J. Tobin	Boston, MA	800
1957	Kingston-Rhinecliff	Hudson R., NY	800
1992	Cooper River	Charleston, SC	800
1986	Rochester-Monaca	Rochester-Monaca, PA	780
1917	*Scioptoville (twin)	Sciotoville, OH–KY	775
1940	Glover Cary	Ohio R., Owensboro, KY–IN	750
1974	Carroll C. Cropper (I-275)	Ohio R., IN–KY	750
1981	Sewickley	Sewickley, PA	750
1984	13th St., Ohio R.	Ashland, KY–OH	740
1959	Monaca-E. Rochester	Monaca-E. Rochester, PA	730
1976	Betsy Ross	Philadelphia, PA	729
1929	Milton-Madison	Ohio R., IN–KY	727
1967	Matthew E. Welsh	Ohio R., Mauckport, IN–KY	725
1962	U.S. 41 Twin	Ohio R., Evansville, IN–Henderson, KY	720
1994	Robert C. Byrd	Huntington, WV	720
1970	Vanport	Vanport, PA	715
1962	Champlain	Montreal, QC	707
1963	John F. Kennedy (I-65)	Ohio R., Louisville, KY–Jeffersonville, IN	700
1973	Girard Point	Philadelphia, PA	700
1956	DE R.-PA Turnpike	Delaware R., NJ–PA	682
1938	Rainbow	Port Arthur-Orange, TX	680
1949	George C. Platt Mem.	Philadelphia, PA	680
1946	Chester	Mississippi R., IL–MO	670
1994	Williamstown-Marietta	Ohio R., WV–OH	650
1955	Jefferson City	Missouri R., MO	640
2000	Mark Twain Mem.	Mississippi R., Hannibal, MO–IL	640
1930	Quincy Mem.	Mississippi R., Quincy, IL–MO	628
1959	Harbor	Corpus Christi, TX	620
1961	Shippingport	Shippingport, PA.	620
1935	Bourne and Sagamore (twin)	Cape Cod Canal, MA	616
1965	I-80, Clarion R.	Clarion, PA	612

Year	Bridge	Location	Main span (ft.)
1975	Donora-Monessen	Donora-Monessen, PA	608
1961	John A. Blatnik	Superior, WI–Duluth, MN	600
1965	Rio Grande Gorge	Taos, NM.	600
1991	Hoffstadt Creek	Mt. St. Helens, WA	600
1991	Jefferson City	Missouri R., MO	596
1962	W. Branch Feather R.	Oroville, CA.	576
1966	Glenwood	Pittsburgh, PA	557
1932	Pulaski Skyway (twin)	Newark, NJ	550
1943	Gold Star Mem.	New London, CT.	540
1968	Emlenton	Emlenton, PA	540
1962	Benicia-Martinez	Benicia-Martinez, CA	528
1914	Brownsville	Brownsville, PA	518
1971	Grandad	Elk River, ID	504

Continuous Box and Plate Girder

Year	Bridge	Location	Main span (ft.)
1967	San Mateo-Hayward #2	San Fran. Bay, CA	750
1976	LA 82, Intracoastal Canal.	Forked Isl., LA.	750
1977	LA 27, Intracoastal Canal.	Gibbstown, LA	750
1969	San Diego-Coronado (twin)	San Diego Bay, CA	660
1967	Bernard F. Dickman (Poplar St.)	St. Louis, MO	647
1992/94	Acosta (twin)	Jacksonville, FL	630
1981	Douglas	Juneau, AK.	620
1976	Wax L. Outlet	Calumet, LA	618
1981	Glenn Jackson (I-205)	Columbia R., OR–WA.	600
1976	Archie Stevenot	Stanislaus R., Sonora, CA	550
1982	Illinois R.	Pekin, IL	550
1982	I-440, Arkansas R.	Little Rock, AR	540
1980	Harrison-McGarity, Tenn. R.	Savannah, TN.	525
1965	MacDonald-Cartier.	Ottawa, ON.	520
1988	Mon City.	Monongahela, PA	520
1984	I-182, Columbia R.	Richland, WA	450
1986	Veterans	Pittsburgh, PA	440
1987	SR 76, Cumberland R.	Dover, TN	440
1987	SR 20, Tennessee R.	Perryville, TN	440
1970	Abernathy (I-205)	Willamette R., OR.	430
1974	I-430, Arkansas R.	Little Rock, AR	430
1965	I-24, Tennessee R.	Marion Co., TN	420
1974	Dunbar-S. Charleston	S. Charleston, WV	420
1975	36th St.	Charleston, WV	420
1978	Lewiston-Clarkston	Snake R., Lewiston, ID–Clarkston, WA.	420
1984	FAU 3456, Tennessee. R.	Chattanooga, TN	420

Continuous Plate

Year	Bridge	Location	Main span (ft.)
1973	Sidney Sherman (I-610).	Houston, TX	630
1971	Atchafalaya Basin (I-10)	Henderson, LA	573
1992	SR 76, Tennessee R.	Paris, TN.	525
1997	SR 114, Tennessee R.	Clifton, TN.	525
1981	IL 23.	Illinois R., IL	510
1968	I-45, Trinity R.	Dallas, TX	480
1978	Antioch	San Joaquin R., CA	460
1977	Thomas Johnson Mem.	Solomons, MD	451
1967	I-90, Mississippi R.	La Crosse, WI	450
1975	I-129, Missouri R.	Sioux City, IA–S. Sioux City, NE	450
1979	Lewis (U.S. 67).	Missouri R., St. Louis, MO	450
1992	Cuba Landing.	Tennessee R., TN.	450
1966	I-480, Missouri R.	Omaha, NE–Council Bluffs, IA	425
1972	Whiskey Bay Pilot	Ramah, LA	425
1972	I-80, Missouri R.	Omaha, NE–Council Bluffs, IA	425
1972	I-635, Missouri R.	Kansas City, KS–MO	425
1983	Pony Express (U.S. 36)	Missouri R., KS–MO	425
1987	I-435.	Missouri R., KS–MO	425
1978	I-24.	Cumberland R., KY.	420
1993	Bob Michel (SR 40)	Peoria, IL	360
1999	SR 53, Clear Fork R.	Fentress/Morgan Co., TN	350

Cable-Stayed

Year	Bridge	Location	Main span (ft.)
2010	John James Audubon	Pointe Coupee-West Feliciana, LA.	1,585
2005	Arthur Ravenel Jr.	Charleston, SC	1,546
1986	Alex Fraser.	Vancouver, BC	1,526
2009	U.S. 82, Mississippi R. (new)	Greenville, MS	1,378
1994	Clark	Alton, IL–MO	1,360
1988	Dame Point	Jacksonville, FL	1,300
1995	Fred Hartman.	Houston Ship Channel, Baytown, TX.	1,250
2003	Sidney Lanier.	Brunswick, GA	1,250
1983	Hale Boggs Mem.	Luling, LA	1,222
1987	Sunshine Skyway.	Tampa Bay, FL	1,200
2002	William Natcher	Ohio R., Owensboro, KY–IN	1,200
2009	Margaret Hunt Hill	Trinity R., Dallas, TX	1,198
1988	Tampico	Panuco R., Mex.	1,181
2006	Penobscot Narrows	Bucksport, ME	1,161
2003	Bill Emerson Mem.	Cape Girardeau, MO–IL	1,150
1988	Skybridge (ALRT)	Fraser R., Vancouver, BC	1,115
1991	Talmadge Mem.	Savannah, GA	1,100
1993	Mezcala	Mex. City-Acapulco Hwy., Mex.	1,024
1978	Pasco-Kennewick.	Columbia R., Pasco, WA.	981
1984	Coatzacoalcos	Coatzacoalcos R., Mex.	945
1985	E. Huntington	Huntington, WV–OH	900
1987	Bayview	Quincy, IL	900
2006	U.S. Grant	Portsmouth, OH–South Shore, KY.	876
1990	Weirton-Steubenville	Ohio R., WV–OH	820
1969	Papineau-Leblanc	Montreal, QC	790
1991	Cochrane	Mobile, AL	780
1995	Chesapeake & Delaware Canal.	C&D Canal, St. Georges, DE	750
2003	Leonard Zakim Bunker Hill.	Boston, MA	745
1966	Longs Creek.	New Brunswick, Can.	713
1967	Hawkshaw	Hawkshaw, NB	713

Year	Bridge	Location	Main span (ft.)
1993	Quetzalapa	Quetzalapa, Mex.	699
1996	Burlington	Burlington, IA	660
1991	Veterans Mem.	Neches R., Port Arthur-Bridge City, TX.	640
1990	Varina-Enon.	Richmond, VA.	630

I-Beam Girder

Year	Bridge	Location	Main span (ft.)
1980	I-20	Shreveport, LA	438
2001	Moore Haven	Caloosahatchee Canal, FL	320
1988	Rte. 18	Weston's Mill Pond, NJ	276

Steel Arch

Year	Bridge	Location	Main span (ft.)
1977	New River Gorge	Fayetteville, WV	1,700
1931	Bayonne (Kill Van Kull)	Bayonne, NJ–New York, NY	1,675
1973	Fremont	Portland, OR.	1,255
1964	Port Mann	Vancouver, BC	1,200
1967	Laviolette	Trois-Rivières, QC	1,100
1990	Roosevelt Lake	Roosevelt Lake, AZ	1,080
1959	Glen Canyon	Page, AZ.	1,028
1962	Lewiston-Queenston	Lewiston, NY–Queenston, ON	1,001
1976	Perrine	Twin Falls, ID	993
1916	*Hell Gate	East R., New York, NY	978
1941	Rainbow.	Niagara Falls, NY–ON	950
1997	Blue Water	Port Huron, MI–ON.	922
1977	Moundsville	Ohio R., WV	912
1972	Hernando DeSoto (I-40) (twin)	Mississippi R., AR–TN	900
2008	Blennerhassett (U.S. 50)	Parkersburg, WV–OH	878
1936	Henry Hudson	Harlem R., New York, NY	840
1966	Bob Cummings-Lincoln Trail	Ohio R., IN–KY.	825
1978	I-57, Mississippi R.	Cairo, IL	821
1961	Sherman Minton (I-64).	New Albany, IN–Louisville, KY	800
1980	I-65, Mobile R.	Mobile, AL	800
1932	West End.	Pittsburgh, PA.	780
1978	I-470, Ohio R.	Wheeling, WV.	780
1995	Navajo	Marble Canyon, AZ.	726
1959	Thaddeus Kosciusko (twin)	Mohawk R., Albany, NY	600
1917	Detroit-Superior High Level	Cuyahoga R., Cleveland, OH	591
2004	Gateway Boulevard	Nashville, TN	545
1874	Eads	Mississippi R., St. Louis, MO–IL	520
2000	Paper Mill Road	Baltimore, MD.	500

Concrete Arch

Year	Bridge	Location	Main span (ft.)
2010	Mike O'Callaghan-Pat Tillman Mem. (U.S. 93)	Colorado R., AZ–NV.	1,060
1994	Natchez Trace Pkwy.	Franklin, TN	582
1993	Lake Street	Minneapolis, St. Paul, MN	556
1971	Fred Redmon (twin)	Selah, WA.	549
1968	Cowlitz R.	Mossyrock, WA.	520
1931	George Westinghouse	Pittsburgh, PA.	460
1923	Cappelen Mem.	Minneapolis, MN.	435
2000	Crooked River	Terrebonne, OR	410
1930	Jack's Run	Pittsburgh, PA.	400
1932	Isaac Lee Patterson	Rogue R., Gold Beach, OR	230

Segmental Concrete

Year	Bridge	Location	Main span (ft.)
1997	Confederation	Prince Edward Isl., NB	820
1978	Shubenacadie R.	S. Maitland, NS	790
1982	Jesse H. Jones Mem.	Houston, TX	750
1992	Jamestown-Verrazano	Narragansett Bay, RI	674
2002	Vietnam Veterans Mem.	James R., Richmond, VA	672
1986	Umatilla	Columbia R., OR–WA	660
2007	Benicia-Martinez (new)	Carquinez Strait, CA.	659
1978	Stanislaus R.	Parrots Ferry, CA	640
1981	Juneau-Douglas.	Gastineau Channel, AK	620
1991	Veterans Mem. Centennial	Coeur d'Alene, ID	520
2008	I-35W St. Anthony Falls[4]	Minneapolis, MN.	504
2001	Smart Road	Blacksburg, VA	472
1974	Pine Valley Creek	Pine Valley, CA.	450
1988	Zilwaukee (twin)	Zilwaukee, MI	392
1985	Red River	Boyce, LA.	370

Twin Concrete Trestle[5]

Year	Bridge	Location	Main span (ft.)
1979	I-55/I-10	Manchac, LA	181,157
1956/69	L. Pontchartrain Cswy. (twin)	Nr. New Orleans, LA.	126,720
1972	Atchafalaya Swamp Frwy.	Baton Rouge, LA	93,984
1983	*I-310.	Kenner, LA	25,925

Concrete Slab Dam[5]

Year	Bridge	Location	Main span (ft.)
1927	Conowingo Dam	Susquehanna R., MD	4,611
1952	John H. Kerr.	Mecklenburg Co., VA.	2,785
1936	Hoover Dam.	Lake Mead, NV	1,324

Movable Bridges
Vertical Lift

Year	Bridge	Location	Main span (ft.)
1959	*Arthur Kill	New York, NY–Elizabeth, NJ	558
1965	Pennsylvania Railroad	Kirkwood-Mt. Pleas., DE	548
1935	*Cape Cod Canal	Buzzards Bay, MA	544
1896	*Delair	Pennsauken, NJ–Philadelphia, PA	542
1931	Burlington-Bristol	Delaware R., NJ–PA.	540
1937	Marine Parkway Gil Hodges Mem.	Jamaica Bay, New York, NY	540
1958	Columbia R. Interstate (I-5)	Portland, OR–Vancouver, WA	531
1908	*Willamette R.	Portland, OR.	521
1968	Second Narrows	Vancouver, BC	493
1911	*Armour-Swift-Burlington	Kansas City, MO.	428
1945	*Harry S Truman	Kansas City, MO.	427
1955	Roosevelt Island	East R., New York, NY	418
1980	U.S. 17, James R.	Isle of Wight Co., VA.	415
1932	*M-K-T RR	Missouri R., MO	414
1969	Cape Fear Mem.	Wilmington, NC	408
1930	Aerial Lift	Duluth, MN	386

Year	Bridge	Location	Main span (ft.)
1962	Burlington	Burlington Canal, ON	370
1941	Main Street	Jacksonville, FL	365
1967	SR-156, James R.	Prince George Co., VA	364
1950	Red R.	Moncla, LA	360
1957	Industrial Canal	New Orleans, LA.	360
1936	Triborough	Harlem R., New York, NY	344
1939	U.S. 9, Passaic R.	Newark, NJ	333
1930	*Martinez	Martinez, CA.	328
1960	St. Andrews Bay	Panama City, FL	327
1929	*Penn-Lehigh	Newark Bay, PA	322
1987	Industrial Canal	New Orleans, LA.	320
1920	*Chattanooga	Tennessee R., TN.	310
1960	Broadway	Harlem R., New York, NY	304
1910	Hawthorne	Willamette R., Portland, OR	244

Steel Suspension

Year	Bridge	Location	Main span (ft.)
1931	Maumee R.	Toledo, OH	785

Bascule

Year	Bridge	Location	Main span (ft.)
2006/08	Woodrow Wilson (I-95) (twin)	Potomac R., VA–MD	366
1940	Charles Berry Mem.	Lorain, OH	333
1917	Market Street/Chief John Ross Mem.	Chattanooga, TN	306
2003	*SW 2nd Avenue	Miami, FL	302

Year	Bridge	Location	Main span (ft.)
1956	Duwamish R.	Seattle, WA.	300
1955	Chehalis R.	Aberdeen, WA	288
1968	Elizabeth R.	Chesapeake, VA.	280
1913	Broadway	Portland, OR.	278
1936	Siuslaw River	Florence, OR	154

Swing

Year	Bridge	Location	Main span (ft.)
1927	Santa Fe	Mississippi R., Ft. Madison, IA	525
1952	George P. Coleman Mem.	Yorktown, VA	500
1897	*Duluth	St. Louis Bay, MN.	486
1991	SW Spokane St.	Seattle, WA	480
1899	*C.M.&N. RR.	Chicago, IL.	474
1913	Rt. 82, Conn. R.	E. Haddam, CT	465
1914	*Coos Bay RR	Coos Bay, OR.	458
1936	Umpqua River	Reedsport, OR.	430
1930	Rigolets Pass	New Orleans, LA	400
1949	South Capitol St./Frederick Douglass Mem.	Washington, DC.	387
1945	Lord Delaware	Mattaponi R., VA	252

Floating Pontoon

Year	Bridge	Location	Main span (ft.)
1963	Evergreen Pt.	Seattle, WA.	7,578
1993	Lacey V. Murrow[6]	Seattle, WA.	6,620
1961	Hood Canal	Hood Canal, WA.	6,521
1989	Third Lake Washington	Seattle, WA.	5,811

Miscellaneous Bridges

Year	Bridge	Type	Location	Main span (ft.)
2002	Croatan Sound[5]	Continuous postension girder	Manteo, NC	5.2 mi
1987	Powder Point[5]	Tropical hardwood	Duxbury, MA.	2,200
1997	Second Blue Water	Continuous tied arch	Pt. Huron, MI–ON.	922
1983	Jefferson Barracks (I-255)	Tied arch	Mississippi R., IL–MO.	910
1916	C&O RR.	Steel girder	Portsmouth, OH.	775
1936	Yaquina Bay	Steel braced and concrete tied arches	Newport, OR.	600
1958	John Snodgrass	Through truss	Tenn. R., Stevenson, AL.	500
1962	International	Arch truss	Sault Ste. Marie, MI–ON.	430
1939	O'Neal (U.S. 43)	Through truss	Tenn. R., Florence, AL	420
1958	Tombigbee R.	Steel girder	Choctow Co., AL.	400
1982	SR 193	Seg. box girder	Dauphin Isl., AL	400

(1) Swing span bridge with 2 spans of 2,310 ft. each, which share a common anchor point in the middle of the bay. (2) Will be demolished upon completion of and rerouting of traffic onto the new East Span. (3) Railroad and vehicular bridge. (4) Replaces the bridge that collapsed on Aug. 1, 2007. (5) Length listed is total length of bridge. (6) Replaces the original Lacey V. Murrow bridge, which opened in 1940 and sank in 1990.

Oldest U.S. Bridges in Continuous Use

Built in 1697, the stone-arch Frankford Ave. Bridge crosses Pennypack Creek in Philadelphia, PA. A 3-span bridge with a total length of 75 ft., it was constructed as part of the King's Road, which eventually connected Philadelphia to New York.

The oldest covered bridge, completed in 1829, is the double-span, 278-ft. Bath-Haverhill Bridge, which spans the Ammonoosuc River, between the towns of Bath and Haverhill, NH.

Some Notable International Bridges

Bridges under construction as of mid-2008 denoted by asterisk (*). Year is date of completion or projected completion. Span is distance between its supports.

Year	Bridge	Location	Main span (ft.)
	Suspension		
1998	Akashi Kaikyo	Japan	6,532
NA	*Izmit Bay[1]	Turkey	5,538
2007	Xihoumen	China.	5,413
1998	Storebælt (Great Belt, East Bridge)	Denmark	5,328
2005	Runyang	China.	4,888
1981	Humber	England.	4,626
1999	Jiangyin Yangtze	China.	4,544
1997	Tsing Ma	China.	4,518
2011	*Hardanger	Norway	4,298
1997	Höga Kusten	Sweden.	3,970
1988	Minami Bisan-Seto	Japan.	3,609
1988	Fatih Sultan Mehmet (Bosphorus II)	Turkey	3,576
1973	Bosphorus	Turkey.	3,524
1999	Kurushima III	Japan.	3,379
1999	Kurushima II	Japan.	3,346
1966	Tagus River[2]	Portugal.	3,323
1964	Forth Road	Scotland.	3,300
1988	Kita Bisan-Seto	Japan.	3,248
1966	Severn	England.	3,241
2001	Yichang	China.	3,150

NA = Not available. (1) Project still in planning stages. (2) Railroad and highway bridge.

Year	Bridge	Location	Main span (ft.)
	Steel Arch		
2008	Chaotianmen	China	1,811
2003	Lupu	China	1,804
1932	Sydney Harbour	Australia.	1,650
2005	Wuhan Yangtze River	China	1,614
2009	*Chenab	India	1,575
2007	Xinguang	China	1,404
2007	Caiyuanba	China	1,378
2008	Airport	Japan	1,247
2000	Yajisha	China	1,181
1962	Bridge of the Americas	Panama	1,128
1967	Zdakov	China	1,083
1961	Runcorn-Widnes	England	1,082
1935	Birchenough	Zimbabwe	1,080

Year	Bridge	Location	Main span (ft.)
	Concrete Arch		
1997	Wanxian	China.	1,378
1980	Krk I	Croatia.	1,280
1995	Jiangjiehe	China	1,083
1998	Yijiang	China	1,024
1964	Gladesville	Australia.	1,000
1965	Amizade	Brazil.	951
1984	Bloukrans	South Africa	892

Year	Bridge	Location	Main span (ft.)
1943	Sandö	Sweden	866
1963	Arrabida	Portugal	886
	Cantilever		
1890	Forth (rail)[1]	Scotland	1,710
1974	Minato	Japan	1,673
1943	Howrah	India	1,500

(1) Two spans of 1,710 ft. each.

Year	Bridge	Location	Main span (ft.)
	Steel Plate and Box Girder		
2006	Shibanpo	China	1,083
1974	Rio-Niteroi	Brazil	984
1956	Sava I.	Serbia.	856
1966	Zoobrücke	Germany	850

Year	Bridge	Location	Main span (ft.)
	Cable-Stayed		
2008	Sutong	China	3,570
2009	*Stonecutters	China	3,340
1999	Tatara	Japan	2,920
1995	Pont de Normandie	France	2,808
2009	*Second Incheon	South Korea	2,625
2001	Nanjing Second Yangtze River	China	2,060
2000	Wuhan Baishazhou Yangtze River	China	2,028
1996	Quingzhou Minjang	China	1,985
1993	Yangpu	China	1,975
1997	Xupu	China	1,936
1998	Meiko Chuo	Japan	1,936
2004	Rion-Antirion	Greece	1,837
1991	Skarnsundet	Norway	1,739
1999	Queshi	China	1,699
1995	Tsurumi Tsubasa	Japan	1,673
2008	Tianxingzhou Yangtze River	China	1,654
2002	Jingsha	China	1,640
2000	Oresund	Denmark–Sweden	1,614
1991	Ikuchi	Japan	1,608
1994	Higashi Kobe	Japan	1,591
1998	Zhanjiang	China	1,575
1997	Ting Kau	China	1,558
1992	Arade	Portugal	1,542
1999	Seo Hae Grand	South Korea	1,542
1989	Yokohama Bay	Japan	1,509
1993	Second Hooghly River	India	1,500
1995	Second Severn Crossing	England/Wales	1,496
2008	Hangzhou Bay[1]	China	1,470

(1) Although its main span is not among the world's longest for cable-stayed bridges, Hangzhou Bay is the world's longest (22.4 mi) transoceanic bridge.

World's Longest Railway Tunnels

Source: World Almanac research

Asterisk (*) designates planned or under construction as of mid-2008.

Tunnel	Year	Length (mi)	Operating railway	Country
*Gotthard Base	2016	35.4	Swiss Federal Railways	Switzerland-Italy
*Brenner Base	2015	34.2	Austrian Federal Railways	Austria-Italy
Seikan	1988	33.5	Japan Railways	Japan
*Mont d'Ambin Base	2015	33.0	Réseau Ferré de France (RFF) & Rete Ferroviaria Italiana (RFI)	France-Italy
English Channel	1994	31.1	Eurotunnel	UK-France
Lötschberg Base	2007	21.0	BLS Lötschbergbahn AG	Switzerland
Guadarrama	2007	17.6	Renfe	Spain
*Hakkoda	2010	16.4	Japan Railways	Japan
Iwate-Ichinohe	2002	16.0	Japan Railways	Japan
Daishimizu	1982	13.8	Japan Railways	Japan
Wushaoling	2006	12.5	Chinese state	China
Simplon No. 1 and 2	1906/22	12.3	BLS Lötschbergbahn AG	Switzerland-Italy
Vereina	1999	11.8	Rhätische Bahn (RhB)	Switzerland
London Tunnels (Channel Tunnel Link)	2007	11.8	LCR	UK
Shin-Kanmon	1975	11.6	Japan Railways	Japan
Apennine	1934	11.5	Ferrovie dello Stato (FS)	Italy
Qinling	2002	11.5	Chinese state	China
Vaglia	2006	10.4	Ferrovie dello Stato (FS)	Italy
Rokko	1972	10.1	Japan Railways	Japan
Furka Base	1982	9.6	Matterhorn Gotthard Railway	Switzerland
Haruna	1982	9.6	Japan Railways	Japan
*Ceneri Base	2016	9.6	Swiss Federal Railways	Switzerland
Severomuyskiy	2003	9.5	Russian Railways	Russia
Gorigamine	1997	9.4	Japan Railways	Japan
Firenzuola	2004	9.4	Ferrovie dello Stato (FS)	Italy
Monte Santomarco	1987	9.3	Ferrovie dello Stato (FS)	Italy

Underwater Vehicular Tunnels in North America

Source: World Almanac research

(more than 5,000 ft. in length; year in parentheses is year of completion)

Name	Location	Waterway	Length (ft.)
Brooklyn Battery (twin) (1950)	New York, NY	East River	9,117
Holland (twin) (1927)	New York, NY–Jersey City, NJ	Hudson River	8,558/8,371
Ted Williams (1995)	Boston, MA	Boston Harbor	8,448
Lincoln (center/north/south tubes) (1937/1945/1957)	New York, NY–Weehawken, NJ	Hudson River	8,216/7,482/8,006
Thimble Shoal (1964)	Northampton Co., VA	Chesapeake Bay	5,734
Chesapeake Channel (1964)	Northampton Co., VA	Chesapeake Bay	5,423
Fort McHenry (twin) (1985)	Baltimore, MD	Patapsco River	7,920
Hampton Roads (twin) (1957/1976)	Hampton, VA	Hampton Roads	7,479
Baltimore Harbor (twin) (1957)	Baltimore, MD	Baltimore Harbor	7,392
Queens Midtown (twin) (1940)	New York, NY	East River	6,414
Sumner (1934)	Boston, MA	Boston Harbor	5,653
Detroit-Windsor (1930)	Detroit, MI–Windsor, ON	Detroit River	5,160
Callahan (1961)	Boston, MA	Boston Harbor	5,070

Land Vehicular Tunnels in the U.S.

Source: Federal Highway Administration, U.S. Dept. of Transportation; World Almanac research

(more than 3,000 ft. in length)

Name	Location	Length (ft.)	Name	Location	Length (ft.)
Anton Anderson Mem.[1]	Whittier, AK	13,300	Lehigh (twin)	PA Turnpike, NE Extension	4,461
Edwin Johnson Mem. (eastbound)	I-70, Clear Creek Co., CO	8,960	Blue Mountain (twin)	PA Turnpike	4,339
Eisenhower Mem. (westbound)	I-70, Summit Co., CO	8,939	Wawona	Yosemite Natl. Pk., CA	4,233
Ted Williams[2]	MA Turnpike, Boston, MA	8,448	Big Walker Mt. (twin)	Bland Co., VA	4,229
Thomas P. O'Neill Jr.	I-93, Boston, MA	7,920	Squirrel Hill	Pittsburgh, PA	4,225
Allegheny (twin)	PA Turnpike	6,070	Hanging Lake (twin)	Glenwood Canyon, CO	4,000
Liberty (twin)	Pittsburgh, PA	5,920	Caldecott (3 tubes)[3]	Oakland, CA	3,771/3,610/3,610
Zion-Mt. Carmel	Zion Natl. Park, UT	5,808	Fort Pitt (twin)	Pittsburgh, PA	3,614
East River Mt. (twin)	I-77, VA–Bluefield, WV	5,412	Mount Baker	Seattle, WA	3,456
Tuscarora Mt. (twin)	PA Turnpike	5,326	Dingess	Mingo Co., WV	3,400
Tetsuo Harano (twin)	H-3 Freeway, HI	5,165	Mall	Washington, DC	3,400
Kittatinny Mt. (twin)	PA Turnpike	4,727	Cody	U.S. 14, 16, 20, WY	3,202
Cumberland Gap (twin)	U.S. 25E, KY–TN	4,600			

(1) Tunnel is used for vehicular and railroad traffic. (2) 3,960 ft. of the tunnel is underwater. (3) Construction is scheduled to begin in 2009 on a fourth tube, with an expected completion date in 2013-14.

Major U.S. Dams and Reservoirs

Source: 2007 National Inventory of Dams, U.S. Army Corps of Engineers

Highest U.S. Dams

Rank	Dam	River	State	Type	Height Feet	Height Meters	Year completed
1.	Oroville	Feather	California	E	770	235	1968
2.	Hoover	Colorado	Nevada	A	730	221	1935
3.	Dworshak	N. Fork Clearwater	Idaho	G	717	219	1973
4.	Glen Canyon	Colorado	Arizona	A	710	216	1963
5.	New Bullards Bar	North Yuba	California	A	635	194	1970
6.	New Melones	Stanislaus	California	R	625	191	1979
7.	Mossyrock	Cowlitz	Washington	A	606	185	1968
8.	Shasta	Sacramento	California	G	602	183	1945
9.	Don Pedro	Tuolumne	California	G	568	173	1971
10.	Hungry Horse	S. Fork Flathead	Montana	A	564	172	1952

E = Embankment, Earthfill; R = Embankment, Rockfill; G = Gravity; A = Arch.

Largest U.S. Embankment Dams

Rank	Dam	River	State	Volume Cubic yards (thousands)	Volume Cubic meters (thousands)	Year completed
1.	Fort Peck	Missouri	Montana	125,628	96,049	1957
2.	Diamond Valley Lake	Domenigoni Valley Creek	California	110,551	84,522	2000
3.	Oahe	Missouri	South Dakota	92,000	70,339	1966
4.	Oroville	Feather	California	80,000	61,164	1968
5.	B. F. Sisk	San Luis Creek	California	77,664	59,378	1967
6.	Garrison	Missouri	North Dakota	66,500	50,843	1953
7.	Cochiti	Rio Grande	New Mexico	65,693	50,228	1975
8.	Fort Randall	Missouri	South Dakota	50,200	38,381	1954
9.	Castaic	Castaic Creek	California	44,000	33,640	1973
10.	Mansfield	Colorado	Texas	33,890	25,911	1942

Note: All earthfill.

Largest U.S. Reservoirs

Rank	Dam	Reservoir	State	Max. reservoir capacity Acre feet (thousands)	Max. reservoir capacity Cubic meters (thousands)	Year completed
1.	Hoover	Lake Mead	Nevada	30,237	37,297	1935
2.	Glen Canyon	Lake Powell	Arizona	29,875	36,850	1963
3.	Garrison	Lake Sakakawea	North Dakota	24,500	30,220	1953
4.	Oahe	Lake Oahe	South Dakota	23,600	29,110	1966
5.	Fort Peck	Fort Peck Lake	Montana	19,100	23,560	1957
6.	Grand Coulee	Lake Roosevelt	Washington	9,562	11,795	1941
7.	Sam Rayburn	Sam Rayburn Lake	Texas	6,520	8,042	1965
8.	Wright Patman	Wright Patman Lake	Texas	6,505	8,024	1954
9.	Fort Randall	Lake Francis Case	South Dakota	6,300	7,771	1954
10.	Wolf Creek	Lake Cumberland	Kentucky	6,089	7,511	1951

Major Dams of the World

Source: Intl. Commission on Large Dams, *World Register of Dams*

Asterisk (*) designates planned or under construction.

World's Highest Dams

Rank	Dam	Country	Height above lowest formation (m)
1.	Rogun*	Tajikistan	335
2.	Nurek	Tajikistan	300
3.	Xiaowan (Yunnan Gorge)	China	292
4.	Grand Dixence	Switzerland	285
5.	Inguri	Georgia	272
6.	Vaiont	Italy	262
7.	Manuel M. Torres	Mexico	261
8.	Tehri*	India	261
9.	Alvaro Obregon	Mexico	260
10.	Mauvoisin	Switzerland	250
11.	Mica	Canada	243
12.	Alberto Lleras C.	Colombia	243
13.	Sayano-Shushenskaya	Russia	242
14.	Ertan	China	240
15.	La Esmeralda	Colombia	237
16.	Kishau*	India	236
17.	Oroville	U.S.	235
18.	El Cajón	Honduras	234
19.	Chirkey	Russia	233
20.	Shuibuya	China	233

World's Largest-Volume Embankment Dams

Rank	Dam	Country	Volume cubic meters × 1,000
1.	Tarbela	Pakistan	127,908
2.	Fort Peck	U.S.	96,049
3.	Tucurui	Brazil	85,200
4.	Ataturk	Turkey	84,500
5.	Diamond Valley Lake	U.S.	84,522
6.	Yacyreta	Argentina/Paraguay	81,000
7.	Rogun*	Tajikistan	75,500
8.	Oahe	U.S.	70,339
9.	Guri	Venezuela	70,000
10.	Parambikulam	India	69,165
11.	High Island West	China	67,000
12.	Gardiner	Canada	65,440
13.	Mangla	Pakistan	64,991
14.	Afsluitdijk	Netherlands	63,400
15.	Oroville	U.S.	61,164
16.	B. F. Sisk	U.S.	59,378
17.	Nurek	Tajikistan	58,000
18.	Tanda	Pakistan	57,250
19.	Garrison	U.S.	50,843
20.	Cochiti	U.S.	50,228

World's Largest-Capacity Reservoirs

Source: Intl. Commission on Large Dams, *World Register of Dams*

Rank	Dam	Country	Capacity cubic meters × 1,000,000	Rank	Dam	Country	Capacity cubic meters × 1,000,000
1.	Kariba	Zimbabwe/Zambia	180,600	9.	Zeya	Russia	68,400
2.	Bratsk	Russia	169,000	10.	Robert-Bourassa	Canada	61,715
3.	High Aswan	Egypt	162,000	11.	La Grande 3	Canada	60,020
4.	Akosombo (Lake Volta)	Ghana	150,000	12.	Ust-Ilim	Russia	59,300
5.	Daniel Johnson	Canada	141,851	13.	Boguchany	Russia	58,200
6.	Guri	Venezuela	135,000	14.	Kuibyshev	Russia	58,000
7.	W. A. C. Bennett	Canada	74,300	15.	Serra da Mesa	Brazil	54,400
8.	Krasnoyarsk	Russia	73,300				

World's Largest-Capacity Hydro Plants

Source: Intl. Commission on Large Dams, *World Register of Dams*

Asterisk (*) designates planned or under construction.

Rank[1]	Dam	Country	Rated capacity planned (MW)	Rank[1]	Dam	Country	Rated capacity planned (MW)
1.	Sanxia (Three Gorges Dam)*	China	18,200	11.	Ust-Ilim	Russia	3,840
2.	Itaipu	Brazil-Paraguay	12,600	12.	Ilha Solteira	Brazil	3,444
3.	Guri (Raúl Leoni)	Venezuela	10,000	13.	Ertan	China	3,300
4.	Tucuruí	Brazil	8,370	14.	Yacyreta	Argentina/Paraguay	3,100
5.	Sayano-Shushenskaya	Russia	6,400	15.	Xingo	Brazil	3,000
6.	Itaipu	Paraguay	6,300	16.	Macagua II	Venezuela	2,940
7.	Krasnoyarsk	Russia	6,000	17.	Gezhouba	China	2,715
8.	Bratsk	Russia	4,500	18.	Minamiaiki	Japan	2,700
9.	Longtan (Guangxi, Tian'e)	China	4,200	19.	Volgograd	Russia	2,541
10.	Xiaowan (Yunnan)	China	4,200	20.	Chief Joseph Dam	U.S.	2,512

(1) Ranked by rated capacity planned.

World Population Growth

Although the population of the world in ancient times can only be very roughly estimated, it is believed that there were perhaps 50 mil people in the world in 1000 BCE. The United Nations Population Division estimates a figure of 300 mil for 1 CE; this chart shows estimated population growth from that time onward as estimated by the UN.

While figures for other centuries vary depending on source, all sources indicate that world population began growing more rapidly in the 18th and 19th centuries and grew much more rapidly in the 20th century. According to UN estimates, the world population reached 1 bil in 1804; rose to 2 bil 123 years later, in 1927; to 3 bil 33 years after that, in 1960; to 4 bil in 1974; to 5 bil in 1987; and to 6 bil in 1999. **The UN estimated the total world population in mid-2009 was about 6.83 bil.**

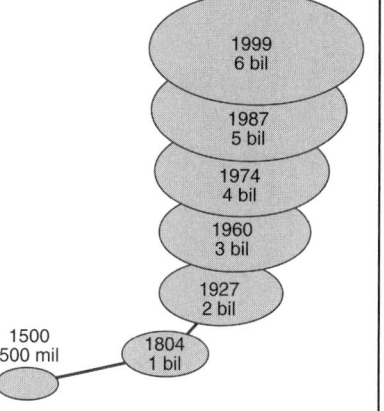

1 CE
300 mil

1250
400 mil

1500
500 mil

1804
1 bil

1927
2 bil

1960
3 bil

1974
4 bil

1987
5 bil

1999
6 bil

Area and Population of the Continents

Source: International Data Base, International Programs Center, Population Division, U.S. Census Bureau, U.S. Dept. of Commerce; *The World Factbook*, Central Intelligence Agency

Continent or region	AREA[1] (sq km)	AREA[1] (sq mi)	% of Earth	% of world, 2009		POPULATION (est., mid-year)			
				2009	2009	1950	1975	2000	2025[2]
Asia	30,938,605	11,945,462	21.1	4,088,647,780	60.4	1,436,631,507	2,411,696,053	3,687,561,791	4,724,949,952
Africa	29,805,695	11,508,043	20.3	990,189,529	14.6	227,958,260	416,244,419	804,093,391	1,382,553,731
N. America. .	23,083,151	8,912,454	15.8	534,051,188	7.9	220,437,787	345,597,198	485,154,091	625,164,920
Europe	22,832,227	8,815,572	15.6	728,227,141	10.8	547,111,554	678,581,833	730,571,148	710,993,295
S. America. .	17,433,220	6,731,004	11.9	392,366,329	5.8	111,359,375	215,785,422	348,080,069	461,956,479
Oceania, incl. Australia. .	8,426,635	3,253,542	5.8	34,685,745	0.5	12,476,128	21,114,852	30,516,253	41,692,136
Antarctica[3] . .	14,000,000	5,405,430	9.6	NA	NA	NA	NA	NA	NA
WORLD	**146,519,533**	**56,571,508**	**100.0**	**6,768,167,712**	**100.0**	**2,555,974,611**	**4,089,019,777**	**6,085,976,743**	**7,947,310,513**

NA = Not applicable. (1) Areas are those used by the U.S. Census Bureau. Figures may not add up to totals due to rounding. (2) Projected. (3) Antarctica has no indigenous inhabitants; researchers stay for various periods of time.

Current Population and Projections for All Countries and Territories

Source: International Data Base, International Programs Center, Population Division, U.S. Census Bureau, U.S. Dept. of Commerce; *The World Factbook*, Central Intelligence Agency

(mid-year figures)

Country/area	2009	2025	2050	Country/area	2009	2025	2050
Afghanistan	28,395,716	39,414,843	53,354,109	Cayman Islands	49,035	67,661	91,118
Albania	3,639,453	3,944,360	4,016,945	Central African			
Algeria	34,178,188	40,290,081	44,163,403	Republic	4,511,488	5,503,035	6,523,563
American Samoa	65,628	79,477	98,269	Chad	10,329,208	13,914,726	20,473,601
Andorra	83,888	85,112	74,765	Chile	16,601,707	18,585,122	19,386,517
Angola	12,799,293	17,418,643	24,746,652	China[1]	1,338,612,968	1,453,123,817	1,424,161,948
Anguilla	14,436	19,739	26,955	Colombia	43,677,372	51,194,904	56,227,630
Antigua and				Comoros	752,438	1,128,278	1,837,671
Barbuda	85,632	103,830	122,930	Congo, Dem.			
Argentina	40,913,584	47,164,630	53,511,279	Rep. of the	68,692,542	109,674,758	189,310,849
Armenia	2,967,004	3,044,164	2,943,441	Congo Rep.	4,012,809	6,161,500	9,598,623
Aruba	103,065	126,130	150,730	Cook Islands	11,870	7,621	5,460
Australia	21,262,641	25,053,669	29,012,740	Costa Rica	4,253,877	5,086,916	5,737,397
Austria	8,210,281	8,189,560	7,520,950	Cote d'Ivoire	20,617,068	27,651,498	37,111,782
Azerbaijan	8,238,672	9,352,531	9,955,428	Croatia	4,489,409	4,374,007	3,864,201
Bahamas, The	307,552	349,116	371,219	Cuba	11,451,652	11,649,747	10,540,567
Bahrain	728,709	868,079	980,431	Cyprus	1,084,748	1,329,908	1,392,078
Bangladesh	156,050,883	192,976,328	233,587,279	Czech Republic	10,211,904	9,844,275	8,540,221
Barbados	284,589	297,015	282,041	Denmark	5,500,510	5,697,913	5,575,147
Belarus	9,648,533	9,033,301	7,738,613	Djibouti	724,622	1,016,919	1,395,810
Belgium	10,414,336	10,453,261	9,882,599	Dominica	72,660	74,374	64,772
Belize	307,899	411,007	543,690	Dominican			
Benin	8,791,832	13,564,964	22,118,545	Republic	9,650,054	11,922,144	14,657,962
Bermuda	67,837	72,862	69,934	Ecuador	14,573,101	17,867,616	21,102,550
Bhutan	691,141	820,143	951,873	Egypt	78,866,635	103,742,157	137,872,522
Bolivia	9,775,246	12,463,434	16,003,638	El Salvador	7,185,218	9,135,049	12,110,592
Bosnia and				Equatorial Guinea	633,441	935,553	1,428,139
Herzegovina	4,613,414	4,535,296	3,891,669	Eritrea	5,647,168	7,987,458	11,381,250
Botswana	1,990,876	2,425,114	2,871,345	Estonia	1,299,371	1,149,245	861,913
Brazil	198,739,269	231,886,946	260,692,493	Ethiopia	85,237,338	140,139,507	278,283,137
Brunei	388,190	498,756	638,157	Faroe Islands	48,856	53,200	57,112
Bulgaria	7,204,687	6,257,716	4,651,477	Fiji	944,720	1,153,311	1,449,492
Burkina Faso	15,746,232	25,384,628	47,429,509	Finland	5,250,275	5,251,272	4,819,615
Burundi	9,511,330	15,464,910	27,148,888	France	64,420,073	68,481,838	69,768,223
Cambodia	14,494,293	18,966,883	23,965,562	French Polynesia	287,032	344,920	393,533
Cameroon	18,879,301	25,522,447	34,908,839	Gabon	1,514,993	2,063,339	3,229,741
Canada	33,487,208	37,558,781	41,135,648	Gambia, The	1,778,081	2,582,098	3,938,007
Cape Verde	429,474	453,544	387,962	Gaza Strip	1,551,859	2,350,255	3,392,849

Country/area	2009	2025	2050
Georgia	4,615,807	4,341,061	3,784,724
Germany	82,329,758	80,637,451	73,607,121
Ghana	23,887,812	30,919,184	40,242,893
Gibraltar	28,796	29,753	28,423
Greece	10,737,428	10,670,697	10,035,935
Greenland	57,600	57,174	49,356
Grenada	90,739	96,320	87,399
Guam	178,430	214,034	243,857
Guatemala	13,276,517	17,564,073	22,995,434
Guernsey	65,484	66,807	60,583
Guinea	10,057,975	15,240,839	26,407,254
Guinea-Bissau	1,533,964	2,061,262	2,894,545
Guyana	752,940	786,286	888,494
Haiti	9,035,536	11,955,107	16,115,229
Honduras	7,833,696	10,143,828	12,948,839
Hong Kong	7,055,071	7,354,531	6,172,725
Hungary	9,905,596	9,437,569	8,374,619
Iceland	306,694	337,632	350,922
India	1,156,897,766	1,396,046,308	1,656,553,632
Indonesia	240,271,522	278,502,882	313,020,847
Iran	66,429,284	76,779,032	81,490,039
Iraq	28,945,569	40,387,147	56,316,329
Ireland	4,203,200	4,842,255	5,396,215
Isle of Man	76,512	81,748	80,338
Israel	7,233,701	8,984,285	10,828,462
Italy	58,126,212	56,234,163	50,389,841
Jamaica	2,825,928	3,151,611	3,554,571
Japan	127,078,679	117,816,135	93,673,826
Jersey	91,626	93,317	84,075
Jordan	6,269,285	7,945,150	11,243,177
Kazakhstan	15,399,437	16,041,146	15,099,700
Kenya	39,002,772	51,261,167	65,175,864
Kiribati	112,850	158,228	235,812
Korea, North	22,665,345	23,579,861	22,926,730
Korea, South	48,508,972	49,372,307	43,368,983
Kosovo	1,804,838	1,999,461	2,222,619
Kuwait	2,692,526	4,179,190	6,382,749
Kyrgyzstan	5,431,747	6,678,722	8,237,623
Laos	6,834,345	9,456,161	13,201,562
Latvia	2,231,503	1,992,516	1,544,073
Lebanon	4,017,095	4,569,812	4,964,025
Lesotho	2,130,819	2,119,170	1,946,586
Liberia	3,441,790	4,753,240	7,091,537
Libya	6,324,357	8,342,156	10,871,760
Liechtenstein	34,761	37,620	35,911
Lithuania	3,555,179	3,355,985	2,787,516
Luxembourg	491,775	586,296	720,603
Macao	559,846	630,434	620,184
Macedonia	2,066,718	2,119,511	1,990,728
Madagascar	20,653,556	32,431,146	56,513,827
Malawi	15,028,757	22,859,677	37,406,745
Malaysia	25,715,819	33,094,692	43,243,714
Maldives	396,334	388,681	444,429
Mali	13,443,225	20,240,154	32,367,436
Malta	405,165	421,239	395,639
Marshall Islands	64,522	83,203	103,092
Mauritania	3,129,486	4,425,089	6,536,272
Mauritius	1,284,264	1,412,384	1,441,100
Mayotte	223,765	356,683	592,046
Mexico	111,211,789	130,198,692	147,907,650
Micronesia	107,434	98,948	74,483
Moldova	4,320,748	4,205,616	3,635,357
Monaco	32,965	34,651	33,042
Mongolia	3,041,142	3,725,352	4,340,496
Montenegro	672,180	635,537	577,654
Montserrat	5,097	5,494	5,582
Morocco	31,285,174	36,484,418	42,026,448
Mozambique	21,669,278	28,893,271	41,842,274
Myanmar (Burma)	48,137,741	52,995,497	54,430,334
Namibia	2,108,665	2,283,845	2,149,815
Nauru	14,019	17,900	22,734
Nepal	28,563,377	36,622,606	45,984,605
Netherlands	16,715,999	17,539,636	17,334,090
Netherlands Antilles	227,049	249,361	254,227
New Caledonia	227,436	263,873	292,299
New Zealand	4,213,418	4,775,930	5,198,992
Nicaragua	5,891,199	7,523,244	9,478,660
Niger	15,306,252	27,062,502	55,304,449
Nigeria	149,229,090	197,222,936	264,262,405
Northern Mariana Islands	51,484	52,564	66,017
Norway	4,660,539	4,916,787	4,966,385
Oman	3,418,085	5,302,131	8,359,218
Pakistan	174,578,558	217,926,995	276,428,758

Country/area	2009	2025	2050
Palau	20,796	22,102	22,894
Panama	3,360,474	4,117,882	4,859,334
Papua New Guinea	5,940,775	7,823,210	10,110,027
Paraguay	6,995,655	9,864,987	14,604,978
Peru	29,546,963	34,678,113	38,638,768
Philippines	97,976,603	128,921,424	171,964,187
Poland	38,482,919	37,349,696	32,084,570
Portugal	10,707,924	10,806,202	9,933,334
Puerto Rico	3,966,213	4,059,331	3,696,940
Qatar	833,285	938,043	1,116,165
Romania	22,215,421	21,260,138	18,678,226
Russia	140,041,247	128,180,396	109,187,353
Rwanda	10,746,311	16,080,729	27,506,207
Saint Barthelemy	7,448	7,056	6,527
Saint Helena	7,637	7,888	7,296
Saint Kitts and Nevis	40,131	46,605	52,661
Saint Lucia	160,267	168,519	162,356
Saint Martin	29,820	33,048	34,601
Saint Pierre and Miquelon	7,063	7,104	6,393
Saint Vincent and the Grenadines	104,574	100,409	93,507
Samoa	219,998	280,753	428,641
San Marino	30,167	34,405	35,263
São Tomé and Principe	212,679	329,651	504,753
Saudi Arabia	28,686,633	35,680,488	49,830,244
Senegal	13,711,597	20,257,238	31,553,295
Serbia	7,379,339	6,845,638	5,869,146
Seychelles	87,476	98,843	100,391
Sierra Leone	5,132,138	7,500,140	13,593,862
Singapore	4,657,542	5,100,929	4,635,110
Slovakia	5,463,046	5,458,581	4,943,616
Slovenia	2,005,692	1,907,560	1,596,947
Solomon Islands	595,613	815,769	1,111,999
Somalia	9,832,017	15,147,912	26,024,500
South Africa	49,052,489	48,714,478	49,400,628
Spain	40,525,002	39,578,066	35,564,293
Sri Lanka	21,324,791	23,707,228	24,920,558
Sudan	41,087,825	57,461,705	88,227,761
Suriname	481,267	560,061	617,249
Swaziland	1,337,186	1,585,439	1,834,151
Sweden	9,059,651	9,315,507	9,084,788
Switzerland	7,604,467	7,774,334	7,296,092
Syria	21,762,978	26,536,400	33,657,629
Taiwan	22,974,347	23,213,741	20,161,286
Tajikistan	7,349,145	9,510,130	12,132,365
Tanzania	41,048,532	53,427,873	66,843,312
Thailand	65,998,436	70,754,525	69,799,501
Timor-Leste	1,131,612	1,498,319	1,954,611
Togo	6,031,808	9,048,532	14,895,142
Tonga	120,898	150,766	188,456
Trinidad and Tobago	1,229,953	1,183,838	1,023,741
Tunisia	10,486,339	11,937,431	12,512,323
Turkey	76,805,524	90,498,016	100,955,188
Turkmenistan	4,884,887	5,800,391	6,607,083
Turks and Caicos Islands	22,942	32,285	42,601
Tuvalu	12,373	15,788	20,010
Uganda	32,369,558	56,744,814	128,007,514
Ukraine	45,700,395	41,037,583	33,573,842
United Arab Emirates	4,798,491	7,063,346	8,018,904
United Kingdom	61,113,205	63,818,586	63,977,435
United States	307,212,123	357,451,620	439,010,253
Uruguay	3,494,382	3,715,772	3,815,368
Uzbekistan	27,606,007	31,823,964	35,116,374
Vanuatu	218,519	264,047	312,153
Vatican City	826	NA	NA
Venezuela	26,814,843	33,188,608	40,255,592
Vietnam	88,576,758	102,458,828	111,173,583
Virgin Islands, British	24,491	30,785	34,333
Virgin Islands, U.S.	109,825	107,163	92,410
Wallis and Futuna	15,289	16,023	15,598
West Bank	2,461,267	3,328,248	4,376,251
Western Sahara	405,210	616,533	996,674
Yemen	22,858,238	32,650,107	45,780,651
Zambia	11,862,740	14,829,985	18,435,053
Zimbabwe	11,392,629	17,370,260	25,198,196
World[2]	6,768,167,712	7,947,310,513	9,316,823,185

NA = Not available. (1) Not including the populations of Hong Kong and Macao, listed separately in this table. (2) Total projected populations do not include countries for which populations are not available.

Population of the World's Largest Cities

Source: *World Population Prospects, World Urbanization Prospects*, Dept. of Economic and Social Affairs, UN Population Division

Pop. figures are UN estimates and projections for "urban agglomerations," i.e., contiguous densely populated urban areas not demarcated by administrative boundaries. The UN releases revised and updated numbers every two years. Data may differ from figures elsewhere in *The World Almanac*.

(ranked by 2007 population counts)

Rank	City, country	Pop. (thousands) 2007	2000	Avg. annual rate of change (%), 2000-05	Pop. (thousands) 1975	2010[1]	2015[1]	Rate of change (%) 1975-2000	2000-15[1]	Pop. of city as % of nation's 2007 pop.
1.	Tokyo, Japan..........	35,676	34,450	0.50%	26,615	36,094	36,371	29.44%	5.58%	27.9%
2.	New York, NY, U.S....	19,040	17,846	0.97	15,880	19,441	19,974	12.38	11.92	6.2
3.	Mexico City (Ciudad de México), Mexico	19,028	18,022	0.78	10,690	19,485	20,189	68.59	12.02	17.9
4.	Bombay (Mumbai), India	18,978	16,086	2.47	7,082	20,072	21,946	127.14	36.43	1.6
5.	São Paulo, Brazil.......	18,845	17,099	1.39	9,614	19,582	20,544	77.86	20.15	9.8
6.	Delhi, India	15,926	12,441	3.81	4,426	17,015	18,669	181.09	50.06	1.4
7.	Shanghai, China	14,987	13,243	1.82	7,326	15,789	17,214	80.77	29.99	1.1
8.	Calcutta (Kolkata), India	14,787	13,058	1.79	7,888	15,577	17,039	65.54	30.49	1.3
9.	Dhaka, Bangladesh.....	13,485	10,285	4.02	2,221	14,796	17,015	363.08	65.44	8.5
10.	Buenos Aires, Argentina	12,795	11,847	1.16	8,745	13,089	13,432	35.47	13.38	32.4
11.	Los Angeles, CA, U.S....	12,500	11,814	0.82	8,926	12,773	13,160	32.35	11.39	4.1
12.	Karachi, Pakistan	12,130	10,019	2.85	3,989	13,052	14,855	151.17	48.27	7.4
13.	Cairo (Al-Qahirah), Egypt	11,893	10,534	1.73	6,450	12,503	13,465	63.32	27.82	15.8
14.	Rio de Janeiro, Brazil ...	11,748	10,803	1.20	7,557	12,171	12,775	42.95	18.25	6.1
15.	Osaka, Japan	11,294	11,165	0.17	9,844	11,337	11,365	13.42	1.79	8.8

(1) Projected.

National Rankings by Population, Area, Population Density, 2009

Source: Population Division/International Programs Center, U.S. Census Bureau, U.S. Dept. of Commerce

As of mid-2009, according to the U.S. Census Bureau, the world had an estimated population of 6,768,167,712. China was the most populous nation, with nearly $1/5$ of the world total.

Largest Populations

Rank	Country	Population
1.	China[1]...........................	1,338,612,968
2.	India	1,156,897,766
3.	United States.....................	307,212,123
4.	Indonesia.........................	240,271,522
5.	Brazil.............................	198,739,269
6.	Pakistan	174,578,558
7.	Bangladesh........................	156,050,883
8.	Nigeria............................	149,229,090
9.	Russia............................	140,041,247
10.	Japan	127,078,679
11.	Mexico............................	111,211,789
12.	Philippines........................	97,976,603
13.	Vietnam...........................	88,576,758
14.	Ethiopia...........................	85,237,338
15.	Germany..........................	82,329,758
16.	Egypt.............................	78,866,635
17.	Turkey............................	76,805,524
18.	Congo, Dem. Rep. of	68,692,542
19.	Iran	66,429,284
20.	Thailand	65,998,436

Smallest Populations

Rank	Country	Population
1.	Vatican City	826
2.	Tuvalu	12,373
3.	Nauru	14,019
4.	Palau	20,796
5.	San Marino........................	30,167
6.	Monaco	32,965
7.	Liechtenstein......................	34,761
8.	Saint Kitts and Nevis	40,131
9.	Marshall Islands...................	64,522
10.	Dominica	72,660
11.	Andorra	83,888
12.	Antigua and Barbuda	85,632
13.	Seychelles	87,476
14.	Grenada..........................	90,739
15.	Saint Vincent and the Grenadines	104,574
16.	Micronesia	107,434
17.	Kiribati	112,850
18.	Tonga............................	120,898
19.	Saint Lucia	160,267
20.	São Tomé and Principe	212,679

Largest Land Areas[2]

Rank	Country	Area (sq mi)	Area (sq km)
1.	Russia.................	6,562,115	16,995,800
2.	China..................	3,600,947	9,326,410
3.	United States	3,537,438	9,161,923
4.	Canada................	3,511,023	9,093,507
5.	Brazil..................	3,265,077	8,456,510
6.	Australia	2,941,299	7,617,930
7.	India	1,147,955	2,973,190
8.	Argentina..............	1,056,642	2,736,690
9.	Kazakhstan.............	1,030,816	2,669,800
10.	Algeria.................	919,595	2,381,740

Smallest Land Areas[2]

Rank	Country	Area (sq mi)	Area (sq km)
1.	Vatican City	0.17	0.44
2.	Monaco	0.75	1.95
3.	Nauru	8.1	21
4.	Tuvalu	10	26
5.	San Marino...........	24	61
6.	Liechtenstein	62	160
7.	Marshall Islands.......	70	181
8.	Saint Kitts and Nevis	101	261
9.	Maldives..............	116	300
10.	Malta	122	316

Most Densely Populated[3]

Rank	Country	Persons per sq mi	Persons per sq km
1.	Monaco.................	43,784.1	16,905.1
2.	Singapore	17,558.9	6,779.5
3.	Vatican City.............	4,862.1	1,877.3
4.	Maldives	3,421.7	1,321.1
5.	Malta	3,320.8	1,282.2
6.	Bangladesh.............	3,018.2	1,165.3
7.	Bahrain	2,834.5	1,094.4
8.	Taiwan	1,844.5	712.2
9.	Nauru	1,729.0	667.6
10.	Barbados...............	1,710.2	660.3

Most Sparsely Populated[3]

Rank	Country	Persons per sq mi	Persons per sq km
1.	Mongolia.................	5.1	2.0
2.	Namibia	6.6	2.6
3.	Australia	7.2	2.8
4.	Suriname	7.7	3.0
5.	Mauritania..............	7.9	3.0
6.	Iceland	7.9	3.1
7.	Botswana	8.8	3.4
8.	Libya...................	9.3	3.6
9.	Canada	9.5	3.7
10.	Guyana	10.2	3.9

(1) Total population does not include mid-2009 population figures for Hong Kong (7,055,071) and Macao (559,846). (2) A country's land area does not include its inland water. Rankings by total area, which includes inland water, may differ. For national total area figures, see the country entries in this chapter. (3) Calculated using land area figures.

Countries Ranked by Gross Domestic Product and Per Capita GDP, 2008[1]

Source: *The World Factbook*, Central Intelligence Agency

GDP (in millions)				Per capita GDP[6]			
Highest		**Lowest**		**Highest**		**Lowest**	
1. U.S.	$14,260,000	1. Tuvalu[3]	$15	1. Liechtenstein[7]	$118,000	1. Zimbabwe	$200
2. China[2]	7,973,000	2. Nauru[4]	60	2. Qatar	110,700	2. Congo, Dem. Rep. of	300
3. Japan	4,329,000	3. Marshall Islands	134	3. Luxembourg	81,000	3. Burundi	400
4. India	3,297,000	4. Palau	164	4. Norway	59,300	4. Liberia	500
5. Germany	2,918,000	5. Micronesia	238	5. Kuwait	57,400	5. Somalia	600
6. Russia	2,266,000	6. São Tomé and Principe	277	6. Brunei	53,100	Guinea-Bissau	600
7. UK	2,226,000	7. Tonga	549	7. Singapore	51,500	7. Central African Republic	700
8. France	2,128,000	8. Kiribati	580	8. U.S.	46,900	Sierra Leone	700
9. Brazil	1,993,000	9. Dominica	720	9. Ireland	45,300	Niger	700
10. Italy	1,823,000	10. Comoros	751	10. Andorra[7]	42,500	Eritrea	700
11. Mexico	1,563,000	11. Saint Kitts and Nevis	778	11. San Marino[7]	41,900	Afghanistan	700
12. Spain	1,403,000	12. Guinea-Bissau	904	12. Iceland	41,800	12. Malawi	800
13. Korea, South	1,335,000	13. Monaco[5]	976	Switzerland	41,800	Ethiopia	800
14. Canada	1,300,000	14. Vanuatu	989	14. Netherlands	40,400	14. Togo	900
15. Indonesia	914,600	15. Samoa	1,049	15. Austria	40,200	Mozambique	900
16. Turkey	902,700	16. St. Vincent and the Grenadines	1,070	16. United Arab Emirates	39,900	16. Rwanda	1,000
17. Iran	841,700	17. Solomon Islands	1,078	17. Canada	39,100	Madagascar	1,000
18. Australia	800,200	18. Grenada	1,161	18. Australia	38,100	Comoros	1,000
19. Taiwan	712,000	19. Liberia	1,526	Sweden	38,100	19. Nepal	1,100
20. Netherlands	672,000	20. Cape Verde	1,626	20. Belgium	37,400	Guinea	1,100

(1) 2008 estimates, unless otherwise indicated. Data may differ from estimates by the U.S. Bureau of Economic Analysis. International GDP estimates are derived from purchasing power parity calculations, which involve the use of international dollar price weights applied to quantities of goods and services produced in a given economy. Countries do not include some territories. (2) Does not include Hong Kong, which had an estimated GDP of $306.6 bil and a per capita GDP of $43,700 in 2008, or Macao, which had an estimated GDP of $18.1 bil and a per capita GDP of $30,000 in 2007. (3) 2002 est. (4) 2005 est. (5) 2006 est. (6) Calculated using population figures for the same year each GDP was available. (7) 2007 est.

Gold Reserves of Central Banks and Governments, 1975-2008

Source: *International Financial Statistics*, International Monetary Fund

(in million fine troy ounces)

Year end	All countries[1]	United States	China[2]	Canada	France	Germany[3]	Italy	Japan	Nether- lands	Switzer- land	United Kingdom
1975	1,018.71	274.71	NA	21.95	100.93	117.61	82.48	21.11	54.33	83.20	21.03
1980	952.99	264.32	12.80	20.98	81.85	95.18	66.67	24.23	43.94	83.28	18.84
1985	949.39	262.65	12.70	20.11	81.85	95.18	66.67	24.33	43.94	83.28	19.03
1990	939.01	261.91	12.70	14.76	81.85	95.18	66.67	24.23	43.94	83.28	18.94
1995	908.79	261.70	12.70	3.41	81.85	95.18	66.67	24.23	34.77	83.28	18.43
2000	952.09	261.61	12.70	1.18	97.25	111.52	78.83	24.55	29.32	77.79	15.67
2001	942.76	262.00	16.10	1.05	97.25	111.13	78.83	24.60	28.44	70.68	11.42
2002	931.18	262.00	19.29	0.60	97.25	110.79	78.83	24.60	27.38	61.62	10.09
2003	913.29	261.55	19.29	0.11	97.25	110.58	78.83	24.60	25.00	52.51	10.07
2004	900.58	261.59	19.29	0.11	95.98	110.38	78.83	24.60	25.00	43.54	10.04
2005	881.69	261.55	19.29	0.11	90.85	110.21	78.83	24.60	22.34	41.48	9.99
2006	867.15	261.50	19.29	0.11	87.44	110.04	78.83	24.60	20.61	41.48	9.97
2007	852.61	261.50	19.29	0.11	83.69	109.87	78.83	24.60	19.98	36.82	9.98
2008	954.61	261.50	NA	0.11	80.13	109.72	78.83	24.60	19.69	33.44	9.98

NA = Not available. (1) Covers IMF members with reported gold holdings. For countries not listed above, see International Monetary Fund's *International Financial Statistics* report. (2) Figures are for mainland China only and do not include Hong Kong or Macao. (3) West Germany prior to 1991.

Consumer Price Changes in Selected Countries, 1975-2008

Source: *International Financial Statistics*, International Monetary Fund

(annual average % change)

Country	1975- 80	1980- 85	1993- 94	1994- 95	1995- 96	1996- 97	1997- 98	1998- 99	1999- 2000	2000- 01	2002- 03	2004- 05	2006- 07	2007- 08
Canada	8.7	7.4	0.2	2.2	1.6	1.6	1.0	1.7	2.7	2.3	2.8	2.2	2.1	2.4
China[1]	NA	NA	24.2	16.9	8.3	2.8	−0.9	−1.4	0.3	0.5	1.2	1.8	4.8	5.9
France	10.5	9.6	1.7	1.8	2.0	1.2	0.7	0.5	1.7	1.6	2.1	1.8	1.5	2.9
Germany	4.1	3.9	3.0	1.8	1.5	1.8	1.0	0.6	1.5	2.0	1.1	2.0	2.1	2.6
Italy	16.3	13.7	4.0	5.2	4.0	2.0	2.0	1.7	2.5	2.8	2.7	2.0	1.8	3.3
Japan	6.5	2.7	0.7	−0.1	0.1	1.7	0.6	−0.3	−0.7	−0.7	−0.3	−0.3	0.1	1.4
Spain	18.6	12.2	4.7	4.7	3.6	2.0	1.8	2.3	3.4	3.6	3.0	3.4	2.8	4.1
Sweden	10.5	9.0	2.2	2.5	0.5	0.5	−0.1	0.5	0.9	2.4	1.9	0.5	2.2	3.4
Switzerland	2.3	4.3	0.8	1.8	0.8	0.5	0.1	0.7	1.5	1.0	0.6	1.2	0.7	2.4
United Kingdom	14.4	7.2	2.5	3.4	2.4	3.1	3.4	1.6	2.9	1.8	2.9	2.8	4.3	4.0
United States	8.9	5.5	2.6	2.8	3.0	2.3	1.6	2.2	3.4	2.8	2.3	3.4	2.9	3.8

NA = Not available. (1) Figures are for mainland China only and do not include Hong Kong or Macao.

Hourly Compensation Costs[1] in Manufacturing in Selected Countries, 1975-2007

Source: Division of Foreign Labor Statistics, Bureau of Labor Statistics, U.S. Dept. of Labor

For production workers only (engaged in assembly, shipping, and maintenance, among other activities) in manufacturing.

(in U.S. dollars)

Country/area	1975	1980	1985	1990	1995	2000	2007	Country/area	1975	1980	1985	1990	1995	2000	2007
Australia	5.75	8.67	8.41	13.45	15.58	14.51	30.17	Luxembourg . . .	6.23	11.52	7.45	15.94	23.54	17.49	30.60
Austria	4.59	9.03	7.71	18.04	25.67	20.13	35.33	Mexico	1.43	2.15	1.55	1.54	1.70	2.07	2.92
Belgium	5.76	11.74	8.21	17.85	25.70	20.15	35.45	Netherlands	6.58	12.05	8.73	17.98	24.02	18.68	34.07
Brazil	—	—	—	—	—	3.50	5.96	New Zealand . . .	3.27	5.44	4.55	8.48	10.35	8.38	17.27
Canada	6.40	9.02	11.39	16.62	16.80	16.78	28.91	Norway	7.20	12.32	10.93	22.71	25.95	23.50	48.56
Czech Republic .	—	—	—	—	2.54	2.85	8.20	Philippines	—	—	—	—	0.94	0.73	1.10
Denmark	6.23	10.83	8.03	18.29	24.87	21.45	42.29	Poland	—	—	—	—	—	2.81	6.17
Finland	5.09	8.66	8.35	20.97	23.05	17.73	34.18	Portugal	1.50	1.96	1.45	3.55	5.09	4.64	8.27
France	5.61	10.06	8.04	16.31	20.06	15.98	28.57	Singapore	0.85	1.55	2.57	3.81	7.72	7.34	8.35
Germany[2]	—	—	—	30.10	22.66	37.66		Spain	2.47	5.75	4.55	11.10	12.47	10.46	20.98
Greece	1.69	3.73	3.66	6.71	9.04	7.63	18.03	Sri Lanka	0.28	0.22	0.28	0.35	0.48	0.48	0.61
Hong Kong[3]	0.75	1.50	1.73	3.22	4.81	5.45	5.78	Sweden	7.12	12.41	9.58	20.75	21.63	20.70	36.03
Hungary	—	—	—	2.98	2.78	7.91		Switzerland	6.09	11.09	9.66	20.85	29.23	21.20	32.88
Ireland	3.66	6.72	6.49	12.63	14.77	13.66	29.04	Taiwan	0.39	1.05	1.51	3.91	5.99	6.19	6.58
Israel	1.99	3.34	3.59	7.56	9.23	11.16	13.91	United Kingdom .	3.21	7.22	5.97	11.95	13.24	16.31	29.73
Italy	4.70	8.21	7.67	17.92	16.69	14.53	28.23	United States . . .	6.24	9.75	12.87	15.00	17.39	19.88	24.59
Japan	2.95	5.43	6.24	12.52	23.34	21.69	19.75	OECD countries[4]	4.32	7.20	7.21	12.86	16.10	14.68	23.68
Korea, South . . .	0.31	0.93	1.20	3.59	7.14	8.08	16.02								

— = Not available. (1) Includes all direct pay (including overtime and bonuses), paid benefits, and social insurance expenditures and other labor taxes. (2) 1975 and 1985 data are for area covered by the former West Germany. 1995-present data are for unified Germany. (3) Part of China since 1997. (4) Organisation for Economic Cooperation and Development (OECD) countries include Canada, Mexico, Australia, Japan, South Korea, New Zealand, and all European countries covered in this table.

Unemployment Rates by Selected Country, 1970-2008[1]

Source: Bureau of Labor Statistics, U.S. Dept. of Labor

Year	U.S.	Australia	Canada	France	Germany[2]	Italy	Japan	Sweden	UK
1970	4.9	1.7	5.7	2.5	0.5	3.2	1.2	1.5	3.1
1975	8.5	4.9	6.9	4.2	3.4	3.4	1.9	1.6	4.5
1980	7.1	6.1	7.3	6.5	2.8	4.4	2.0	2.0	6.9
1985	7.2	8.3	10.2	10.5	7.2	6.0	2.7	2.8	11.4
1990	5.6	6.7	7.7	8.6	5.0	7.0	2.1	1.8	7.1
1991	6.8	9.3	9.8	9.1	5.6	6.9	2.1	3.1	8.9
1992	7.5	10.5	10.6	10.0	6.7	7.3	2.2	5.6	10.0
1993	6.9	10.6	10.8	11.3	8.0	9.8	2.5	9.4	10.4
1994	6.1	9.4	9.6	11.9	8.5	10.7	2.9	9.6	8.7
1995	5.6	8.2	8.6	11.3	8.2	11.3	3.2	9.1	8.7
1996	5.4	8.2	8.8	11.8	8.9	11.3	3.4	9.9	8.1
1997	4.9	8.3	8.4	11.7	9.9	11.4	3.4	10.1	7.0
1998	4.5	7.7	7.7	11.2	9.3	11.5	4.1	8.4	6.3
1999	4.2	6.9	7.0	10.5	8.5	11.0	4.7	7.1	6.0
2000	4.0	6.3	6.1	9.1	7.8	10.2	4.8	5.8	5.5
2001	4.7	6.8	6.5	8.4	7.9	9.2	5.1	5.0	5.1
2002	5.8	6.4	7.0	8.8	8.6	8.7	5.4	5.2	5.2
2003	6.0	5.9	6.9	9.2	9.3	8.5	5.3	5.8	5.0
2004	5.5	5.4	6.4	9.6	10.3	8.1	4.8	6.6	4.8
2005	5.1	5.1	6.0	9.6	11.2	7.8	4.5	7.7	4.9
2006	4.6	4.8	5.5	9.5	10.4	6.9	4.2	7.0	5.5
2007	4.6	4.4	5.3	8.6	8.7	6.2	3.9	6.1	5.4
2008	5.8	4.3	5.3	8.1	7.5	6.8	4.0	6.0	5.7

Note: Civilian labor force, seasonally adjusted. For the sake of comparisons, U.S. unemployment rate concepts were applied to unemployment data for other countries. Previous years' data for some countries have been revised to reflect updated information. (1) As a result of revisions in survey methodology, there are breaks in the data series for the U.S. (1990, 1994); Australia (1986, 2001); Canada (1994); France (1982, 1990); Germany (1983, 1991, 1999, 2005); Italy (1986, 1991, 1993); and Sweden (1987, 2005). Data prior to a survey change are not fully comparable to data after a survey change. (2) For former West Germany only, through 1990; from 1991 on figures are for unified Germany.

Tax Payments[1] in Selected Countries, 2008

Source: *Taxing Wages: 2007/2008*, Organisation for Economic Co-operation and Development

(as % of gross wage earnings; ranked by size of total payment)

Country	Total payment[2]	Income tax	Social security	Gross wage earnings[3]	Country	Total payment[2]	Income tax	Social security	Gross wage earnings[3]
Germany	42.7%	22.2%	20.5%	$51,630	United Kingdom . .	25.6%	16.4%	9.2%	$51,272
Belgium	42.5	28.5	14.0	45,750	United States . . .	24.7	17.0	7.7	40,857
Denmark	40.9	30.3	10.6	41,486	Iceland	24.5	24.3	0.2	33,288
Hungary	38.3	21.3	17.0	16,733	Czech Republic . .	23.6	11.1	12.5	19,029
Netherlands	36.1	15.9	20.2	48,218	Canada	23.4	16.2	7.2	35,253
Austria	33.9	15.9	18.1	43,891	Portugal	22.8	11.8	11.0	24,814
Finland	30.0	23.8	6.2	37,006	Slovak Republic . .	22.8	9.4	13.4	15,182
Norway	29.7	21.9	7.8	47,535	Australia	22.6	22.6	0.0	40,967
Italy	29.3	19.8	9.5	30,245	Switzerland	21.7	10.6	11.1	46,031
Poland	28.6	7.1	21.5	18,227	New Zealand	21.2	21.2	0.0	30,005
France	27.8	14.1	13.7	36,035	Japan	20.3	8.1	12.2	43,211
Turkey	27.5	12.5	15.0	19,112	Spain	19.0	12.7	6.4	30,422
Luxembourg	27.2	15.1	12.1	49,488	Ireland	14.6	9.4	5.2	36,714
Sweden	26.7	19.7	7.0	37,607	Korea	12.5	4.9	7.6	45,613
Greece	26.3	10.3	16.0	35,955	Mexico	5.1	3.7	1.4	10,235

(1) Does not include taxes not listed, such as sales tax or VAT. Rates shown apply to a single person without children with average earnings. (2) Figures may not add up to totals due to rounding. (3) Dollars with equal purchasing power.

Refugees and Asylum Seekers, 2008

Source: *World Refugee Survey 2009*, U.S. Committee for Refugees and Immigrants

These estimates are conservative and have been rounded. Totals include individuals granted asylum and those with pending asylum claims as of year-end 2008. Figures generally do not include those who have achieved permanent resettlement. They also do not include Internally Displaced Persons (IDPs).

(As of Dec. 31, 2008; only countries estimated to host 50,000 or more refugees and asylum seekers are shown below. Region totals include those in countries not listed. Countries of origin are listed in descending order by numbers of refugees and asylum seekers.)

Place of asylum	Origin of most refugees and asylum seekers	Number
AFRICA		**2,692,100**
Cameroon	Central African Republic, Chad, Nigeria	91,900
Chad	Sudan, Central African Republic	330,500
Congo, Dem. Rep.	Angola, Rwanda, Burundi, Uganda, Sudan	192,700
Ethiopia	Somalia, Eritrea, Sudan	135,200
Kenya	Somalia, Ethiopia, Sudan, Congo (Dem. Rep.), Rwanda, Uganda, Eritrea, Burundi	377,400
Rwanda	Congo (Dem. Rep.), Burundi, Senegal, Mauritania	59,000
South Africa	Zimbabwe, Congo (Dem. Rep.), Somalia, Malawi, Ethiopia, Congo Republic, Bangladesh, Pakistan, Tanzania, Mozambique, Uganda, Nigeria, Burundi, India, Uganda	256,200
Sudan	Eritrea, Chad, Ethiopia	233,900
Tanzania	Burundi, Congo (Dem. Rep.)	321,900
Uganda	Congo (Dem. Rep.), Sudan, Rwanda, Somalia, Burundi, Eritrea	155,400
Zambia	Congo (Dem. Rep.), Angola, Zimbabwe, Rwanda	88,900
AMERICAS AND THE CARIBBEAN		**649,500**
Canada	Mexico, Haiti, Colombia, China, Iraq, Afghanistan	72,500
Ecuador	Colombia	135,000
United States	Cuba, China, Myanmar, Iraq, Haiti, Iran, Bhutan, Colombia, Somalia, Burundi, Ethiopia, Indonesia, Russia	161,200
Venezuela	Colombia	211,000
EUROPE		**493,000**
Germany	Serbia, Iraq	54,200
Russia	Afghanistan, Georgia	107,000
Serbia	Croatia, Bosnia and Herzegovina	66,600
MIDDLE EAST AND NORTH AFRICA		**6,343,800**
Algeria	Western Sahara, Former Palestine	96,500
Egypt	Former Palestine, Iraq, Sudan, Somalia	152,400
Gaza Strip	Former Palestine	1,066,100
Iran	Afghanistan, Iraq	993,600
Jordan	Iraq, Former Palestine	621,600
Lebanon	Former Palestine, Iraq, Sudan	333,500
Saudi Arabia	Former Palestine	291,100
Syria	Iraq, Former Palestine, Somalia	1,763,900
West Bank	Former Palestine, Yemen, Somalia, Iraq	762,000
EAST ASIA AND THE PACIFIC		**909,100**
China	Vietnam, North Korea	332,000
Malaysia	Myanmar, Philippines, Indonesia	171,500
Thailand	Myanmar, Laos	368,800
SOUTH AND CENTRAL ASIA		**2,512,400**
Bangladesh	Myanmar	193,100
India	Sri Lanka, China, Myanmar, Afghanistan, Nepal, Bhutan	411,000
Nepal	Bhutan, China	121,300
Pakistan	Afghanistan	1,775,600
TOTAL		**13,599,900**

Internally Displaced Persons

Source: *Global Overview of Trends and Developments*, Internal Displacement Monitoring Centre, Norwegian Refugee Council

Internally displaced persons (IDPs) are people who have been forced to flee their homes due to armed conflict or human rights violations but who have not crossed the border into another country. As such, they are not protected by international refugee law and legally remain under the protection of their home country.

(estimates as of Dec. 31, 2008, unless otherwise noted)

Country	IDPs	Country	IDPs	Country	IDPs
Afghanistan	235,000+	Guatemala	NA	Philippines[1]	259,000-430,000
Algeria	NA	India	500,000+	Russia	82,000-98,000
Angola	19,566	Indonesia[1]	70,000-120,000	Rwanda	NA
Armenia	8,400	Iraq	2.8 mil	Senegal	10,000-70,000
Azerbaijan	603,251	Israel	150,000-420,000	Serbia	247,000
Bangladesh	500,000	Kenya	400,000	Somalia	1.3 mil
Bosnia and Herzegovina	124,593	Kosovo	20,000	Sri Lanka[1]	495,000
Burundi	100,000	Lebanon	90,000-390,000	Sudan	4.9 mil
Central African Republic	108,000	Liberia	23,000	Syria	433,000
Chad[1]	166,718	Macedonia[1]	736	Timor-Leste	30,000
Colombia[2]	2.6 mil-4.4 mil	Mexico	5,500	Togo	1,500
Congo, Dem. Rep.[1]	2 mil	Myanmar	451,000+	Turkey	954,000-1.2 mil
Congo Republic	7,800	Nepal[1]	50,000-70,000	Turkmenistan	NA
Côte d'Ivoire	709,000	Niger	6,500	Uganda[1]	622,000
Croatia[1]	2,402	Nigeria	NA	Uzbekistan	3,400
Cyprus[3]	200,500	Occup. Palestinian Terr.[5]	24,500-115,000	Yemen[1]	100,000
Eritrea[4]	10,000	Pakistan[1]	3 mil	Zimbabwe	570,000-1 mil
Ethiopia	200,000-400,000	Peru	150,000	**Total**	**26 mil**
Georgia	252,000-279,000				

NA = Not available. (1) 2009 est. (2) Lower figure is cumulative since 1994; higher figure is cumulative since 1985. (3) Over 200,000 Greek and Turkish Cypriots displaced in 1974. (4) Government claims all IDPs have been returned or resettled. (5) Higher figure is cumulative since 1967.

Estimated HIV Infection and Reported AIDS Cases, 2007

Source: Joint United Nations Programme on HIV/AIDS (UNAIDS), World Health Organization

While the percentage of people around the world living with HIV/AIDS has stabilized since 2000, the numbers of those with HIV/AIDS continue to rise, in part due to greater access to antiretroviral therapy, particularly in low- and middle-income countries. There were an estimated 2.7 mil new cases of HIV infection and 2 mil AIDS-related deaths in 2007.

About 2 mil of those living with HIV/AIDS in 2007 were children under 15 years of age. 45% of newly-infected adults were between the ages of 15 and 24. Women continued to make up about half of the global HIV/AIDS-infected population. Sub-Saharan Africa remained by far the world's worst affected region. Almost 90% of all children living with HIV/AIDS are in sub-Saharan Africa. The region also accounted for approximately 75% of all AIDS-related deaths in 2007.

Declining rates of new infections in some countries have been offset by increased rates in others. In high-income countries, groups typically most at risk of infection include injecting drug users, men who have sex with men, and sex workers.

Global spending on HIV/AIDS treatment and prevention in 2008 was about $13.7 bil, more than eight times the $1.6 bil spent in 2001. One of the UN's eight Millennium Development Goals is to reverse the epidemic by 2015.

The number of HIV/AIDS cases and deaths are estimated based on all available data, including surveys of pregnant women visiting prenatal clinics, household surveys, monitoring of at-risk population groups, and birth and death records.

Current and New HIV/AIDS Cases and Deaths by Region, 2007

Region	Number living with HIV/AIDS[1]	Percent[2]	New cases	Deaths from AIDS
Sub-Saharan Africa	22,000,000	66.7	1,900,000	1,500,000
South and South-East Asia	4,200,000	12.7	330,000	340,000
Latin America	1,700,000	5.2	140,000	63,000
Eastern Europe and Central Asia	1,500,000	4.5	110,000	58,000
North America	1,200,000	3.6	54,000	23,000
East Asia	740,000	2.2	52,000	40,000
Western and Central Europe	730,000	2.2	27,000	8,000
North Africa and Middle East	380,000	1.2	40,000	27,000
Caribbean	230,000	0.7	20,000	14,000
Oceania	74,000	0.2	13,000	1,000
World[3]	**33,000,000**	**100.0**	**2,700,000**	**2,000,000**

(1) Includes adults (ages 15 and older) and children (under 15). (2) Adults and children within a region living with HIV/AIDS as a percentage of worldwide total living with HIV/AIDS. (3) Figures may not add up to totals because of rounding.

Infectious Disease, Sanitation, and Water Quality

Source: Dept. of Measurement and Health Information, World Health Organization

According to the World Health Organization, 13% of the world's population, or 884 mil people, lacked access to improved water sources (incl. household connections, public standpipes, and dug wells protected from outside contamination) in 2006. WHO estimates that 38% in the same year (more than 2.5 bil people) lacked access to improved sanitation (incl. public sewer connections, septic system connections, and ventilated improved pit latrines). The majority of those without improved water sources or sanitation are in southern Asia and sub-Saharan Africa. As a result, the population in those areas are at increased risk of contracting a variety of infectious and parasitic diseases such as diarrhea, malaria, trachoma, and hepatitis A.

Listed below are nations with the highest death rates from infectious and parasitic diseases, and the poorest access to improved sanitation and water. Rankings and death rates for G-8 countries (plus China) are included for comparison; with the exception of Russia and China, these nations have near-universal (97% or greater) access to improved water and sanitation. In 2006, 65% of China's population had access to improved sanitation, and 88% had access to improved water. In Russia, the figures were 87% and 97%, respectively. (Sanitation figures were not available for France, Italy, or the United Kingdom; water figures were not available for Italy.)

Deaths from Infectious and Parasitic Diseases, 2004

(per 100,000 population; ranked by deaths from infectious and parasitic diseases)

Rank	Country	Infectious and parasitic diseases	Tuberculosis	Diarrheal diseases
1.	Zimbabwe	1,642.6	61.6	58.3
2.	Zambia	1,062.8	60.8	127.8
3.	Swaziland	964.8	81.7	54.2
4.	Botswana	951.1	41.0	56.6
5.	Malawi	948.1	48.4	160.3
6.	Niger	917.2	36.6	350.4
7.	Sierra Leone	895.9	95.9	338.5
8.	Lesotho	882.0	35.1	20.7
9.	Angola	803.4	26.4	345.2
10.	Liberia	801.2	49.8	220.1
114.	Russia	40.6	27.1	0.6
119.	China	33.2	16.6	4.7
132.	United States	23.0	0.3	1.5
137.	France	18.9	1.6	1.6
139.	Japan	17.7	3.3	1.2
151.	Germany	14.3	0.6	1.1
159.	Canada	11.6	0.4	1.8
163.	United Kingdom	10.7	0.8	2.6
166.	Italy	9.5	0.8	0.1

Lowest Access to Improved Sanitation, 2006

Rank	Country	% of total pop. with access
1.	Eritrea	5%
2.	Niger	7
3.	Chad	9
4.	Ghana	10
5.	Ethiopia	11
6.	Sierra Leone	11
7.	Madagascar	12
8.	Togo	12
9.	Burkina Faso	13
10.	Haiti	19

Lowest Access to Improved Water, 2006

Rank	Country	% of total pop. with access
1.	Afghanistan	22%
2.	Somalia	29
3.	Papua New Guinea	40
4.	Ethiopia	42
5.	Mozambique	42
6.	Niger	42
7.	Equatorial Guinea	43
8.	Congo, Dem. Rep. of	46
9.	Madagascar	47
10.	Nigeria	47

Foreign Development Aid Donors, 2007-08[1]

Source: Organisation for Economic Co-operation and Development (OECD)

Development Assistance Committee (DAC) countries are ranked by official development assistance (ODA) as percent of GNI (gross national income) in 2008. In 2008, the U.S. gave the highest total amount of ODA but ranked 22nd among DAC countries in ODA as percent of GNI.

Country/area	ODA as % of GNI 2008	ODA as % of GNI 2007	ODA in current U.S. dollars (millions) 2008	ODA in current U.S. dollars (millions) 2007	Country/area	ODA as % of GNI 2008	ODA as % of GNI 2007	ODA in current U.S. dollars (millions) 2008	ODA in current U.S. dollars (millions) 2007
1. Sweden	0.98%	0.93%	$4,730	$4,339	13. France	0.39%	0.38%	$10,957	$9,884
2. Luxembourg	0.92	0.91	409	376	14. Germany	0.38	0.37	13,910	12,291
3. Norway	0.88	0.95	3,967	3,728	15. Australia	0.34	0.32	3,166	2,669
4. Denmark	0.82	0.81	2,800	2,562	16. Canada	0.32	0.29	4,725	4,080
5. Netherlands	0.80	0.81	6,993	6,224	17. New Zealand	0.30	0.27	346	320
6. Ireland	0.58	0.55	1,325	1,192	18. Portugal	0.27	0.22	614	471
7. Belgium	0.47	0.43	2,381	1,953	19. Greece	0.20	0.16	693	501
8. Finland	0.43	0.39	1,139	981	Italy	0.20	0.19	4,444	3,971
Spain	0.43	0.37	6,686	5,140	21. Japan	0.18	0.17	9,362	7,679
United Kingdom	0.43	0.35	11,409	9,849	United States	0.18	0.16	26,008	21,787
11. Austria	0.42	0.50	1,681	1,808	**Total DAC**	**0.30**	**0.28**	**119,759**	**103,487**
12. Switzerland	0.41	0.37	2,016	1,685	**G7 nations**	**0.25**	**0.23**	**80,815**	**69,539**

(1) 2008 data is preliminary.

Top 10 Recipients of U.S. Development Aid, 2006-07

Source: Development Assistance Committee, Organisation for Economic Co-operation and Development

(in millions of U.S. dollars)

Country	Avg. 2006-07	Country	Avg. 2006-07
1. Iraq	$4,266	6. Nigeria	$514
2. Afghanistan	1,459	7. Congo, Dem. Rep. of	486
3. Sudan	725	8. Pakistan	465
4. Colombia	562	9. Ethiopia	344
5. Egypt	541	10. Kenya	304

Nuclear Powers of the World

As of Sept. 2009, eight countries were acknowledged nuclear powers: the **UK, France, China, India, Pakistan, Russia, North Korea**, and the **U.S.** In addition, **Israel** is suspected of having an arsenal of 100-200 nuclear weapons. **Iran** was suspected of developing nuclear weapons despite the country's claims that it was focusing on nuclear energy. More than 40 nations have the knowledge or technology needed to produce nuclear weapons. All have signed the Nuclear Non-Proliferation Treaty (NPT) except for Israel, India, and Pakistan. N. Korea withdrew Jan. 10, 2003, following its expulsion of Intl. Atomic Energy Agency (IAEA) inspectors in Dec. 2002.

In a draft accord reached at six-party talks with China, Japan, Russia, S. Korea, and the U.S. on Sept. 19, 2005, N. Korea agreed to scrap its nuclear weapons program in exchange for aid. Left unresolved was Pyongyang's continuing demand for international donors to provide light-water nuclear reactors for "peaceful uses."

After further negotiations broke down, N. Korea conducted its first-ever nuclear test Oct. 9, 2006. It returned to a new round of six-party talks in Dec. 2006 and agreed to a deal Feb. 13, 2007: in exchange for closing its main nuclear facility, at Yongbyon, and taking steps toward disabling its nuclear weapons program, the country would receive economic aid and diplomatic recognition. Though N. Korea seemed willing to take conciliatory steps, the next round of talks, in Dec. 2008, ended in deadlock. N. Korea conducted a second nuclear test May 25, 2009, earning it additional UN sanctions.

Despite UN sanctions dating back to Dec. 2006, Iran has refused to suspend its activities in the enrichment of uranium. Iran argued that as an NPT signatory, it had a right to pursue the peaceful application of nuclear technology. The IAEA maintained that Iran has withheld information on the extent of its nuclear activities.

Some countries have offered Iran incentives in return for its cooperation. Iran claimed such demands were "illegitimate." On Sept. 25, 2009, the U.S., along with France and Britain, accused Iran of building a secret uranium enrichment facility. Iran acknowledged the existence of the facility as a backup to its main enrichment site. It disagreed with the IAEA on how much advanced notice it had to give before construction on the plant was completed but said IAEA inspectors would be admitted. International opinion was divided over whether Iran was pursuing enrichment in order to make nuclear weaponry.

Several countries abandoned their nuclear ambitions. **South Africa** announced in 1993 that it had built seven fission weapons (one was under construction) but had dismantled all of them. In the 1980s, **Argentina** and **Brazil** had active nuclear weapons programs but abandoned them by mutual treaty and signed the NPT.

Estimated Numbers of Nuclear Weapons by Country, 1945-2009[1]

Source: *Bulletin of the Atomic Scientists*; Carnegie Endowment for Intl. Peace; Federation of American Scientists; Natural Resources Defense Council; Nuclear Threat Initiative

Year	United States	USSR/Russia	United Kingdom	France	China	India	Pakistan	Total
1945	6	—	—	—	—	—	—	6
1950	369	5	—	—	—	—	—	374
1960	20,434	1,605	30	—	—	—	—	22,069
1970	26,662	11,643	280	36	75	—	—	38,696
1980	24,304	30,062	350	250	280	—	—	55,246
1990	21,004	37,000	300	505	430	—	—	59,239
1995	12,144	27,000	300	500	400	—	—	40,344
2000	10,577	21,000	185	470	400	—	—	32,632
2009	9,420[2]	13,000-14,000[3]	160	300	240	50-60	70-90	23,375

(1) Israel is widely presumed to have a nuclear stockpile, although it has never confirmed nor denied its nuclear status. (2) Only about 2,623 are considered active or operational. Approximately 4,200 have been retired and are awaiting dismantlement. (3) Only about 4,840 are considered operational. The rest are believed to be in reserve or marked for dismantlement.

Nuclear Arms Treaties and Negotiations: A Historical Overview

Aug. 5, 1963: Partial (Limited) Test Ban Treaty signed by U.S., USSR, and Britain in Moscow, went into effect Oct. 10, 1963. Prohibited parties from testing or participating in the testing of nuclear weapons in the atmosphere, in outer space, and under water.

Jan. 27, 1967: Treaty on Principles Governing the Activities of States in the Exploration and Use of Outer Space, including the Moon and Other Celestial Bodies (or the **Outer Space Treaty**) opened to signatures, went into effect Oct. 10, 1967. Banned the introduction of nuclear weapons or any other weapons of mass destruction into space.

July 1, 1968: Nuclear Nonproliferation Treaty (NPT) opened to signatures, went into effect Mar. 5, 1970. With the U.S., USSR, and Great Britain as major signers, the treaty limited the spread of nuclear material for military purposes by agreement not to help non-nuclear nations get or make nuclear weapons.

At an NPT review conference in 1995, the treaty was extended indefinitely. As of Sept. 2009, 190 countries were party to the treaty, not including North Korea, which withdrew in 2003. Israel, India, and Pakistan were not signatories. In Sept. 2009, the UN Security Council unanimously adopted a U.S.-drafted resolution "to create the conditions for a world without nuclear weapons," including strengthening of the NPT.

May 26, 1972: The **Strategic Arms Limitation Talks (SALT I)** led to the signing of two agreements by the U.S. and USSR in Moscow: the **Treaty on the Limitation of Anti-Ballistic Missile Systems** (or the **ABM Treaty**) and the **Interim Agreement on Certain Measures with Respect to the Limitation of Strategic Offensive Arms**. These treaties set a cap on the numbers of intercontinental ballistic missile (ICBM) launchers and submarine-launched ballistic missile (SLBM) launchers.

July 3, 1974: Treaty on the Limitation of Underground Nuclear Weapon Tests (or the **Threshold Test Ban Treaty**) signed by the U.S. and USSR in Moscow. Limited underground testing of nuclear weapons to yields of 150 kilotons or less. On May 28, 1976, U.S. and Russia signed the **Peaceful Nuclear Explosions Treaty**, governing explosions occurring outside of weapons test sites. Both treaties entered into force Dec. 11, 1990.

June 18, 1979: Strategic Offensive Arms Limitation Treaty (or **SALT II**) signed by the U.S. and USSR in Vienna. Limited each side to 2,400 missile launchers and heavy bombers; ceiling to apply until Jan. 1, 1985. Treaty also set a sub-ceiling of 1,320 ICBMs and SLBMs with multiple warheads on each side. Following Dec. 1979 Soviet invasion of Afghanistan, Pres. Jimmy Carter withdrew SALT II from Senate consideration for ratification.

Dec. 8, 1987: Intermediate-Range Nuclear Forces (INF) Treaty signed by the U.S. and USSR in Washington, DC. Eliminated all U.S. and Soviet intermediate- and shorter-range nuclear missiles from Europe and Asia. Entered into force June 1, 1988.

July 31, 1991: Strategic Arms Reduction Treaty (START I) signed by the USSR and U.S. in Moscow, to reduce strategic offensive arms by about 30% in three phases over seven years. START I was the first treaty to mandate reductions by the superpowers.

With the Soviet Union breakup in Dec. 1991, four former republics became independent nations with strategic nuclear weapons: Russia, Ukraine, Kazakhstan, and Belarus. Under the **Lisbon Protocol** of May 1992, Ukraine, Kazakhstan, and Belarus agreed to accede to the NPT as non-nuclear-weapon states, to destroy or transfer their nuclear weapons to Russia, and to ratify START I. As of Sept. 2009, the U.S. and Russia were in talks on a treaty to succeed START I, which was set to expire Dec. 5, 2009.

Jan. 3, 1993: START II signed by the U.S. and Russia in Moscow, ratified by the two countries on Jan. 26, 1996, and Apr. 14, 2000, respectively. Called for reductions in their long-range nuclear arsenals. Both sides withdrew from the treaty before it went into force.

Sept. 24, 1996: Comprehensive Test Ban Treaty (CTBT) signed by the U.S. and Russia in New York City. The CTBT banned all nuclear weapons tests and other nuclear explosions. It was intended to prevent the nuclear powers from developing more advanced weapons, while limiting the ability of other states to acquire such devices. As of Sept. 2009, the CTBT had been signed by 181 nations. It has been ratified by 150, including France, Russia, and the UK but neither the U.S. nor China. It will enter into force after 44 nuclear-capable states ratify it; only 35 have done so.

Dec. 13, 2001: The U.S. announced its intention to withdraw from the **ABM Treaty** in 180 days, arguing that it hindered the government in protecting itself from "future terrorist or rogue state missile attacks." Russia responded by withdrawing from **START II**, stating that U.S. withdrawal from the ABM Treaty effectively invalidated START II.

May 24, 2002: Strategic Offensive Reductions Treaty (SORT or **Moscow Treaty)** signed by the U.S. and Russia in Moscow, entered into force June 1, 2003. Committed both countries to cutting nuclear arsenals to 1,700-2,200 warheads each, down from about 6,000, by Dec. 31, 2012. The U.S. stated it had cut its operationally deployed arsenal to 2,126 by May 2009, three and a half years before the deadline.

Major International Organizations

African Union (AU), inaugurated July 9, 2002, in Durban, South Africa, following disbanding of the Organization of African Unity, and consisting of the same 53 members, i.e., all countries of Africa except Morocco, which left the OAU after it admitted Western Sahara (Sahrawi Arab Dem. Rep.), a territory claimed by Morocco. The new organization is intended to focus on achieving greater socioeconomic integration and unity among its member states. The founders provided for a peer review committee to oversee member states' adherence to standards of good government, respect for human rights, and financial transparency. The AU's founding document authorized the organization to intervene to stop genocide, war crimes, or human rights abuses within individual member nations. **Headquarters:** Addis Ababa, Ethiopia. **Website:** www.africa-union.org

Asia-Pacific Economic Cooperation (APEC), founded Nov. 1989 as a forum to further cooperation on trade and investment between nations of the region and the rest of the world. Its 21 members are Australia, Brunei, Canada, Chile, China, Hong Kong, Indonesia, Japan, Malaysia, Mexico, New Zealand, Papua New Guinea, Peru, Philippines, Russia, Singapore, South Korea, Taiwan, Thailand, the U.S., and Vietnam. **Headquarters:** Singapore. **Website:** www.apec.org

Association of Southeast Asian Nations (ASEAN), formed Aug. 8, 1967, to promote economic, social, and cultural cooperation and development among states of the Southeast Asian region. Its members are Brunei, Cambodia, Indonesia, Laos, Malaysia, Myanmar, Philippines, Singapore, Thailand, and Vietnam. **Headquarters:** Jakarta, Indonesia. **Website:** www.asean sec.org

Caribbean Community and Common Market (CARICOM), established Aug. 1, 1973. Its aim is to increase cooperation in economics, health, education, culture, science and technology, and tax administration, as well as the coordination of foreign policy. Its members are Antigua and Barbuda, The Bahamas, Barbados, Belize, Dominica, Grenada, Guyana, Haiti, Jamaica, Montserrat, St. Kitts and Nevis, St. Lucia, St. Vincent and the Grenadines, Suriname, and Trinidad and Tobago. Anguilla, Bermuda, British Virgin Islands, Cayman Islands, and Turks and Caicos Islands are associate members. **Headquarters:** Georgetown, Guyana. **Website:** www.caricom.org

The Commonwealth, originally called the British Commonwealth of Nations, then the Commonwealth of Nations, is an association of nations and dependencies that were once parts of the former British Empire. The British monarch is the symbolic head of the Commonwealth.

There are 53 independent nations in the Commonwealth. Regular members include the UK and 15 other nations recognizing the British monarch, represented by a governor-general, as their head of state, and member countries in good standing with their own heads of state.

Pakistan was suspended from the councils of the Commonwealth in Oct. 1999, following a military coup, but regained its member status Mar. 2004. Zimbabwe was suspended in Mar. 2002, following election and land redistribution controversies; it withdrew from the Commonwealth in 2003. In Sept. 2009, Fiji's military regime was suspended from full membership. The Commonwealth facilitates consultation among members through meetings of ministers and through a permanent secretariat. **Headquarters:** London, UK. **Website:** www.thecommonwealth.org

Commonwealth of Independent States (CIS), an alliance established in Dec. 1991, made up of former Soviet constituent republics. Its members are Armenia, Azerbaijan, Belarus, Georgia, Kazakhstan, Kyrgyzstan, Moldova, Russia, Tajikistan, Turkmenistan, Ukraine, and Uzbekistan. Georgia withdrew from the organization in Aug. 2009 following fighting with Russia over disputed territory. Policy is set through coordinating bodies such as the Council of the Heads of States and Council of the Heads of Governments. **Headquarters:** Minsk, Belarus. **Website:** www.cis.minsk.by

European Free Trade Association (EFTA), created May 3, 1960, to promote expansion of free trade. By Dec. 31, 1966, tariffs and quotas between member nations had been eliminated. Members entered into free trade agreements with the EU in 1972 and 1973. In 1992, EFTA and EU agreed to create a single market—with free flow of goods, services, capital, and labor—among nations of the two organizations. Its members are Iceland, Liechtenstein, Norway, and Switzerland. **Headquarters:** Geneva, Switzerland. **Website:** www.efta.int

European Union (EU), known as the European Community (EC) until 1994, comprises three organizations with common membership: the European Economic Community (Common Market), the European Coal and Steel Community, and the European Atomic Energy Community (Euratom). A merger of the three communities' executives went into effect July 1, 1967. As of Sept. 2009, there were 27 EU members: the 12 original members (Belgium, Denmark, France, Germany, Greece, Ireland, Italy, Luxembourg, Netherlands, Portugal, Spain, and UK), three that entered Jan. 1, 1995 (Austria, Finland, Sweden), 10 that joined on May 1, 2004 (Cyprus, Czech Republic, Estonia, Hungary, Latvia, Lithuania, Malta, Poland, Slovakia, Slovenia), and two that joined Jan. 1, 2007 (Bulgaria, Romania). Croatia, Macedonia, and Turkey were candidate countries. Some 70 nations in Africa, the Caribbean, and the Pacific are affiliated under the Lomé Convention. **Headquarters:** Brussels, Belgium. **Website:** europa.eu

The EU aims to integrate the economies, coordinate social developments, and bring about political union of the member states. The Council of the Union, European Commission, European Parliament, and European Courts of Justice and of Auditors comprise the permanent structure. Effective Dec. 31, 1992, there are no restrictions on the movement of goods, services, capital, workers, and tourists within the EU. There are also common agricultural, fisheries, and nuclear research policies.

Leaders of the member nations (12 at the time), meeting Dec. 9-11, 1991, in Maastricht, the Netherlands, committed the organization to launching a common currency (the euro) by 1999; sought to establish common foreign policies; laid the groundwork for a common defense policy; gave the organization a leading role in social policy (Britain was not included in this plan); pledged increased aid for poorer member nations; and slightly increased the powers of the 567-member European Parliament. The treaties went into effect Nov. 1, 1993, following ratification by all 12 members.

In June 1998 the European Central Bank was established. In Jan. 1999, 11 of the then-15 EU countries began using the euro for some purposes. By Feb. 2002, national currencies in those 11 countries and Greece were removed from circulation and replaced with the euro as the only currency of legal tender. EU peacekeeping forces replaced NATO troops in Macedonia, Mar. 31, 2003, the first such mission for the organization.

A "Treaty Establishing a Constitution for Europe" was signed Oct. 2004 by EU members but was never ratified. The Treaty of Lisbon, which amends current EU and EC treaties, was signed Dec. 2007 and is awaiting ratification by all member states. As of Sept. 2009, all members except for Ireland have ratified or approved the treaty.

Group of Eight (G-8), established Sept. 22, 1985; forum of seven major industrial democracies (Canada, France, Germany, Italy, Japan, the UK, and U.S.) and (later) Russia, which meet periodically to discuss economic and other issues. At its annual summit in May 1998, the name was changed to G-8 from G-7. The seven were still free to meet without Russia on some issues, especially those relating to global finance. The presidency rotates yearly among members. The 2005 summit was held in Perthshire, Scotland. It was interrupted by the July 7 bombings in London but concluded as scheduled. Since 2005, summits have been held in Russia, Germany, Japan, and Italy.

International Criminal Police Organization (INTERPOL), created 1923 as the International Criminal Police Commission before changing its name in 1956, is the world's largest international police organization. Promotes mutual assistance among all police authorities within the limits of the law existing in different countries. There were 187 member nations as of Sept. 2009. **Headquarters:** Lyon, France. **Website:** www.interpol.int

League of Arab States (Arab League), created Mar. 22, 1945. The League promotes economic, social, political, and military cooperation, mediates disputes, and represents Arab states in certain international negotiations. Its members are Algeria, Bahrain, Comoros, Djibouti, Egypt, Iraq, Jordan, Kuwait, Lebanon, Libya, Mauritania, Morocco, Oman, Palestine (considered an independent state by the League), Qatar, Saudi Arabia, Somalia, Sudan, Syria, Tunisia, United Arab Emirates, and Yemen. **Headquarters:** Cairo, Egypt. **Website:** www.arableagueonline.org

North Atlantic Treaty Organization (NATO), created by treaty (signed Apr. 4, 1949; in effect Aug. 24, 1949). Its 28 members as of Sept. 2009 are Belgium, Bulgaria, Canada, Czech Re-

public, Denmark, Estonia, France, Germany, Greece, Hungary, Iceland, Italy, Latvia, Lithuania, Luxembourg, Netherlands, Norway, Poland, Portugal, Romania, Slovakia, Slovenia, Spain, Turkey, UK, and U.S. Several of these states are former Warsaw Pact Eastern European nations.

Members have agreed to settle disputes by peaceful means, to develop their capacity to resist armed attack, to regard an attack on one as an attack on all, and to take necessary action to repel an attack under Article 51 of the UN Charter. **Headquarters:** Brussels, Belgium. **Website:** www.nato.int

The NATO structure consists of the North Atlantic Council (NAC), the Defense Planning Committee, the Military Committee (realigned in June 2003 and consisting of two commands: Allied Command Operations and Allied Command Transformation), the Nuclear Planning Group, and the Canada-U.S. Regional Planning Group. France detached itself from the military command structure in 1966.

With the end of the cold war in the early 1990s, members put greater stress on political action and on creating a rapid deployment force to react to local crises. By the mid-1990s, 27 nations, including Russia and other former Soviet republics, had joined with NATO in the so-called Partnership for Peace (PfP; drafted Dec. 1993), which provided for limited joint military exercises, peacekeeping missions, and information exchange. NATO has proceeded gradually toward extending full membership to former Eastern bloc nations. On Mar. 12, 1999, three former Warsaw Pact members, Hungary, Poland, and the Czech Republic, formally became members. NATO and Russia signed a cooperation pact May 28, 2002, forming a NATO-Russia Council, and NATO invited seven former eastern-bloc nations to join the alliance, Nov. 21.

A NATO-led multinational force was deployed to help keep the peace in Bosnia and Herzegovina in 1995; in 1999, another force was deployed in Kosovo. Following the terrorist attacks on the U.S., the NATO Council agreed, Sept. 12, 2001, to invoke for the first time Article 5 of the treaty, which stipulates mutual defense of alliance members. NATO assumed control of the International Security Assistance Force in Afghanistan (ISAF), Aug. 2003, marking the first time NATO led a mission outside Europe.

Organization of American States (OAS), formed in Bogotá, Colombia, Apr. 30, 1948. It has a Permanent Council, Inter-American Council for Integral Development, Juridical Committee, and Commission on Human Rights. A general assembly meets annually.

Its 35 members are Antigua and Barbuda, Argentina, The Bahamas, Barbados, Belize, Bolivia, Brazil, Canada, Chile, Colombia, Costa Rica, Dominica, Dominican Republic, Ecuador, El Salvador, Grenada, Guatemala, Guyana, Haiti, Honduras, Jamaica, Mexico, Nicaragua, Panama, Paraguay, Peru, St. Kitts and Nevis, St. Lucia, St. Vincent and the Grenadines, Suriname, Trinidad and Tobago, U.S., Uruguay, and Venezuela. In 1962, the OAS barred the Cuban government from participation though it retains membership. Honduras was suspended in July 2009 because of a coup d'etat in that country. **Headquarters:** Washington, DC. **Website:** www.oas.org

Organization for Economic Cooperation and Development (OECD), established Dec. 14, 1960, to promote the economic and social welfare of all its member countries and to stimulate efforts on behalf of developing nations. The OECD also collects and disseminates economic and environmental information. Its 30 members are Australia, Austria, Belgium, Canada, Czech Republic, Denmark, Finland, France, Germany, Greece, Hungary, Iceland, Ireland, Italy, Japan, Luxembourg, Mexico, Netherlands, New Zealand, Norway, Poland, Portugal, Slovakia, South Korea, Spain, Sweden, Switzerland, Turkey, UK, and the U.S. **Headquarters:** Paris, France. **Website:** www.oecd.org

Organization of Petroleum Exporting Countries (OPEC), created Sept. 14, 1960, by Iran, Iraq, Kuwait, Saudi Arabia, and Venezuela. This group made up of most but not all the major petroleum exporting nations seeks to stabilize the oil market and set world oil prices by controlling production. In addition to the founding countries, members include Algeria, Angola, Ecuador, Indonesia (suspended membership starting in Jan. 2009), Libya, Nigeria, Qatar, and United Arab Emirates. Gabon is a former member. **Headquarters:** Vienna, Austria. **Website:** www.opec.org

Organization for Security and Cooperation in Europe (OSCE), established in 1972 as the Conference on Security and Cooperation in Europe; current name adopted 1995. The group, formed by NATO and Warsaw Pact members, seeks improved East-West relations through a commitment to nonaggression and human rights, and cooperation in economics, science and technology, cultural exchange, and environmental protection. There were 56 member states in 2009, making it the world's largest regional security organization. **Headquarters:** Vienna, Austria. **Website:** www.osce.org

United Nations

The 64th regular session of the United Nations General Assembly opened Sept. 15, 2009, attended by world leaders and other delegates from 192 nations. The UN headquarters is in New York, NY, between First Ave. and Roosevelt Dr. and E. 42nd St. and E. 48th St.

Proposals to establish an organization for maintenance of world peace led to the convening of the United Nations Conference on International Organization in San Francisco, Apr. 25-June 26, 1945, where the UN charter was drawn. It was signed June 26 by 50 nations and by Poland, one of the original 51 members, on Oct. 15, 1945. It went into effect Oct. 24, 1945, upon ratification by the permanent members of the Security Council and a majority of the other signatories.

Purposes. To maintain international peace and security; to develop friendly relations among nations; to achieve international cooperation in solving economic, social, cultural, and humanitarian problems and in promoting respect for human rights and basic freedoms; to be a center for harmonizing the actions of nations in attaining these common ends.

Visitors to the UN. The headquarters is open to the public every day except during the General Debate of the 64th General Assembly Session (Sept. 22-28, 2009), President's Day, Good Friday, Labor Day, Independence Day, Eid al-Fitr, Thanksgiving, Eid al-Adha, Christmas, and New Year's Day.

Guided tours are conducted weekdays from 9:45 PM to 4:45 PM. Tours last approximately 45 mins. Groups of 15 or more require reservations and should e-mail unitg@un.org or telephone (212) 963-4440. Children under 5 not admitted on tours.

United Nations Secretaries General

Took office	Secretary, nation	Took office	Secretary, nation
1946	Trygve Lie, Norway	1982	Javier Pérez de Cuéllar, Peru
1953	Dag Hammarskjöld, Sweden	1992	Boutros Boutros-Ghali, Egypt
1961	U Thant, Burma (Myanmar)	1997	Kofi Annan, Ghana
1972	Kurt Waldheim, Austria	2007	Ban Ki-moon, South Korea

Six Main Organs of the United Nations

The United Nations consists of six principal organs, 15 agencies, and many programs and other bodies. The six principal organs are the General Assembly, the Security Council, the Secretariat, the Economic and Social Council, the Trusteeship Council, and the Intl. Court of Justice.

General Assembly. The General Assembly is composed of representatives of all the member nations. Each nation is entitled to one vote. The General Assembly meets in regular annual sessions and in special session when convoked at the request of the Security Council or a majority of UN members. On important questions a two-thirds majority of members present and voting is required; on other questions a simple majority is sufficient.

The General Assembly must approve the UN budget and apportion expenses among members. A member in arrears can lose its vote if the amount of arrears equals or exceeds the amount of the contributions due for the preceding two full years. The General Assembly proposed a total budget of $4.89 bil for the 2010-2011 biennium. **Website:** www.un.org/ga/

Security Council. The Security Council consists of 15 members, five with permanent seats. The remaining 10 are elected for two-year terms by the General Assembly.

The permanent members of the Council are China, France, Russia, United Kingdom, and the United States. Nonpermanent members with terms expiring Dec. 31, 2009, are Burkina Faso, Costa Rica, Croatia, Libya, and Vietnam; those with terms expiring Dec. 31, 2010, are Austria, Japan, Mexico, Turkey, and Uganda.

The Security Council has the primary responsibility within the UN for maintaining international peace and security. The Council may investigate any dispute that threatens international peace and security.

Any UN member may, if invited by the Council, participate in its discussions, and a nation not a UN member may appear if it is a party to a dispute. Decisions on procedural questions are made by an affirmative vote of nine members. On all other matters the affirmative vote of nine members must include the concurring votes of all permanent members (giving them veto power). A party to a dispute must refrain from voting.

The Security Council directs the various peacekeeping forces deployed throughout the world. **Website:** www.un.org/Docs/sc/

Secretariat. The Secretariat has an international staff (about 40,000 as of 2008) that carries out the day-to-day operations of the UN and is headed by the secretary general. The secretary general is the chief administrative officer of the UN, and is appointed by the General Assembly, on the recommendation of the Security Council, for a five-year, renewable term. The Secretary General reports to the General Assembly and may bring to the attention of the Security Council any matter that threatens international peace. **Website:** www.un.org/en/mainbodies/secretariat/

Economic and Social Council. The Economic and Social Council consists of 54 members elected by the General Assembly for three-year terms. The council is responsible for carrying out UN functions with regard to international economic, social, cultural, educational, health, and related matters. It meets once a year. **Website:** www.un.org/ecosoc/

Trusteeship Council. Made up of the five permanent members of the Security Council. The administration of trust territories was under UN supervision; however, all 11 Trust Territories have attained their right to self-determination. The Council formally suspended its work Nov. 1, 1994. **Website:** www.un.org/en/mainbodies/trusteeship/

International Court of Justice (World Court). The International Court of Justice is the principal judicial organ of the UN. All members are ipso facto parties to the statute of the Court. The Court has jurisdiction over cases the parties submit to it and matters especially provided for in the charter or in treaties. It gives advisory opinions and renders judgments. In disputes between nations, the Court's decisions are binding only between parties concerned and in respect to a particular dispute. If any party to a case fails to heed a judgment, the other party may have recourse to the Security Council.

The 15 judges are elected for nine-year terms by the General Assembly and the Security Council. Retiring judges are eligible for reelection. The Court remains permanently in session, except during vacations. All questions are decided by a majority. The International Court of Justice sits in The Hague, Netherlands. **Website:** www.icj-cij.org

The text of the **UN Charter** may be read online at www.un.org/aboutun/charter/index.html

Selected Specialized and Related Agencies

These specialized and related agencies are autonomous, with their own memberships and organs, and at the same time have a functional relationship or working agreement with the UN (headquarters), except for UNICEF and UNHCR, which report directly to the Economic and Social Council and to the General Assembly.

Food and Agriculture Organization (FAO) helps developing countries modernize farms, forests, and fisheries; improves food distribution and marketing; and educates on nutrition. (Viale delle Terme di Caracalla, 00153 Rome, Italy) **Website:** www.fao.org

International Atomic Energy Agency (IAEA) aims to promote safe, peaceful uses of atomic energy. (P.O. Box 100, Wagramer Strasse 5, A-1400, Vienna, Austria) **Website:** www.iaea.org

International Civil Aviation Org. (ICAO) promotes international civil aviation standards and regulations. (999 University St., Montreal, Quebec H3C 5H7, Canada) **Website:** www.icao.int

International Fund for Agricultural Development (IFAD) seeks to alleviate poverty in rural areas in developing countries. (Via Paolo di Dono, 44, 00142 Rome, Italy) **Website:** www.ifad.org

International Labor Org. (ILO) aims to promote decent and productive employment practices, the improvement of labor conditions, social security, and vocational training. (4 route des Morillons, CH-1211 Geneva 22, Switzerland) **Website:** www.ilo.org

International Maritime Org. (IMO) aims to promote cooperation on technical matters affecting international shipping. (4 Albert Embankment, London, SE1 7SR, UK) **Website:** www.imo.org

International Monetary Fund (IMF) aims to promote international monetary cooperation, currency stabilization, and the expansion of international trade. (700 19th St. NW, Washington, DC 20431) **Website:** www.imf.org

International Telecommunication Union (ITU) regulates all aspects of global communication, including setting standards for radio, telegraph, telephone, and space radio-communications, and allocating radio frequencies. (Place des Nations, 1211 Geneva 20, Switzerland) **Website:** www.itu.int

Office of the High Commissioner for Human Rights (OH-CHR) seeks to uphold human rights standards by monitoring areas of concern, investigating abuses, and working with gov. institutions to improve conditions. (52 Rue des Pâquis, CH-1201 Geneva, Switzerland) **Website:** www.ohchr.org

United Nations Children's Fund (UNICEF) provides financial aid and development assistance to programs for children and mothers in developing countries. (3 United Nations Plaza, New York, NY 10017) **Website:** www.unicef.org

United Nations Educational, Scientific, and Cultural Org. (UNESCO) aims to promote collaboration among nations through education, science, and culture. After a 19-yr boycott, the United States rejoined the organization on Sept. 29, 2003. (7, Place de Fontenoy, 75352 Paris 07 SP, France) **Website:** www.unesco.org

United Nations High Commissioner for Refugees (UNHCR) provides essential assistance for refugees. (Case Postale 2500, CH-1211 Geneva 2 Depot, Switzerland) **Website:** www.unhcr.org

United Nations Industrial Development Org. (UNIDO) helps developing and transitional nations pursue sustainable industrial development while promoting international industrial cooperation. (Vienna Intl. Centre, P.O. Box 300, Wagramerstr. 5, A-1400 Vienna, Austria) **Website:** www.unido.org

Universal Postal Union (UPU) aims to perfect postal services and promote international collaboration. (Case Postale 13, 3000 Berne 15, Switzerland) **Website:** www.upu.int

World Bank Group encompasses two development institutions and three affiliates focused on worldwide poverty reduction. The **International Bank for Reconstruction and Development (IBRD)** provides loans and technical assistance for projects in developing member countries and encourages co-financing for projects from other sources. The **International Development Association (IDA)** provides funds for development projects on concessionary terms to poorer developing member countries. The **International Finance Corporation (IFC)** promotes the growth of the private sector in developing member countries; encourages the development of local capital markets; and stimulates the international flow of private capital. The **Multilateral Investment Guarantee Agency (MIGA)** promotes investment in developing countries; guarantees investments to protect investors from noncommercial risks, such as nationalization; and advises governments on attracting private investment. The **International Center for Settlement of Investment Disputes (IC-SID)** provides conciliation and arbitration services for disputes between foreign investors and host governments that arise out of an investment. (1818 H St. NW, Washington, DC 20433) **Website:** www.worldbank.org

World Health Org. (WHO) aims for the attainment of the highest possible level of health. (Avenue Appia 20, CH-1211 Geneva 27, Switzerland) **Website:** www.who.int

World Intellectual Property Org. (WIPO) seeks to protect, through international cooperation, literary, industrial, scientific, and artistic works. (34, Chemin des Colombettes, CH-1211 Geneva 20, Switzerland) **Website:** www.wipo.int

World Meteorological Org. (WMO) aims to coordinate and improve world meteorological work. (7bis, Avenue de la Paix, Case Postale 2300, CH-1211 Geneva 2, Switzerland) **Website:** www.wmo.int

World Tourism Org. (UNWTO) promotes responsible, sustainable, and universally accessible tourism with the aim of fostering economic development and international understanding. (Capitán Haya 42, 28020 Madrid, Spain) **Website:** www.unwto.org

World Trade Org. (WTO) administers trade agreements and treaties between nations, examines members' trade regimes, keeps track of various trade measures and statistics, and attempts to settle trade disputes. (Centre William Rappard, Rue de Lausanne 154, CH-1211 Geneva 21, Switzerland) **Website:** www.wto.org

Ongoing UN Peacekeeping Missions, 2009

Source: Dept. of Peacekeeping Operations (DPKO), United Nations Secretariat, UN

Numbers listed are peacekeeping personnel as of July 31, 2009, unless otherwise noted. Year given in graphic is the year each mission started.

Uniformed personnel (troops, police, military observers)	93,187[1]	Total personnel serving in 17 DPKO-led peace operations	115,527
Countries contributing uniformed personnel	118	Peacekeeping operations since 1948	63
International civilian personnel (as of June 30, 2009)	5,750[1]	Total fatalities in peacekeeping operations since 1948	2,609[2]
Local civilian personnel (as of June 30, 2009)	12,314[1]	Est. total cost of operations, 1948 to June 30, 2009	$61 bil

(1) Not incl. statistics for two special political and/or peacebuilding missions (BINUB, UNAMA). (2) Incl. fatalities for all UN peace operations.

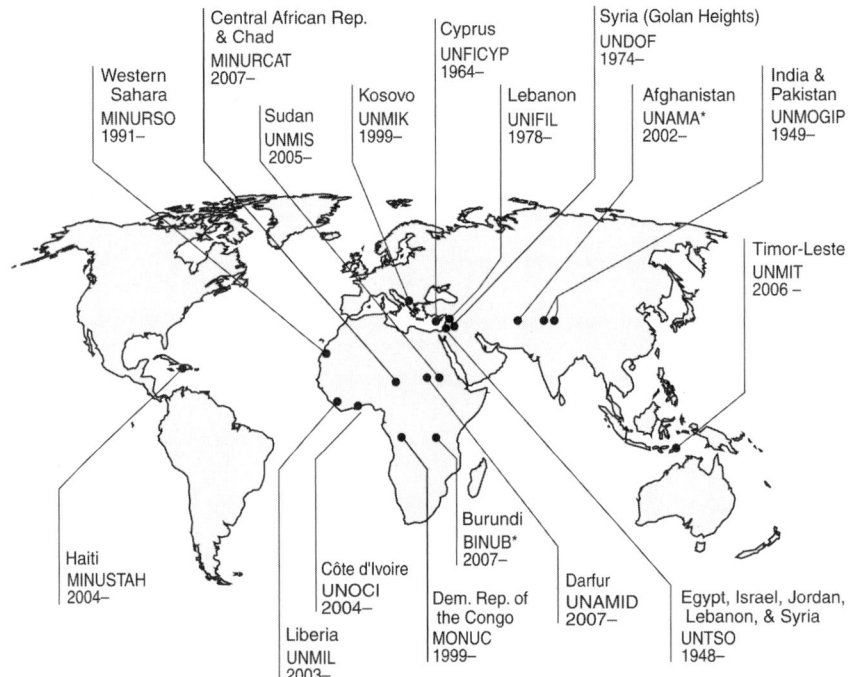

Western Sahara MINURSO 1991–

Central African Rep. & Chad MINURCAT 2007–

Sudan UNMIS 2005–

Kosovo UNMIK 1999–

Cyprus UNFICYP 1964–

Lebanon UNIFIL 1978–

Syria (Golan Heights) UNDOF 1974–

Afghanistan UNAMA* 2002–

India & Pakistan UNMOGIP 1949–

Timor-Leste UNMIT 2006 –

Haiti MINUSTAH 2004–

Côte d'Ivoire UNOCI 2004–

Liberia UNMIL 2003–

Burundi BINUB* 2007–

Dem. Rep. of the Congo MONUC 1999–

Darfur UNAMID 2007–

Egypt, Israel, Jordan, Lebanon, & Syria UNTSO 1948–

*Political or peacebuilding mission directed and supported by the Dept. of Peacekeeping Operations.

Roster of the United Nations

The 192 members of the United Nations, with the years in which they became members (as of Sept. 2009).

Member	Year	Member	Year	Member	Year	Member	Year
Afghanistan	1946	Dominica	1978	Libya	1955	Saint Vincent and the	
Albania	1955	Dominican Republic	1945	Liechtenstein	1990	Grenadines	1980
Algeria	1962	Ecuador	1945	Lithuania	1991	Samoa	1976
Andorra	1993	Egypt[4]	1945	Luxembourg	1945	San Marino	1992
Angola	1976	El Salvador	1945	Macedonia[1,7]	1993	São Tomé and Príncipe	1975
Antigua and Barbuda	1981	Equatorial Guinea	1968	Madagascar	1960	Saudi Arabia	1945
Argentina	1945	Eritrea	1993	Malawi	1964	Senegal	1960
Armenia	1992	Estonia	1991	Malaysia[8]	1957	Serbia[1,9]	2000
Australia	1945	Ethiopia	1945	Maldives	1965	Seychelles	1976
Austria	1955	Fiji	1970	Mali	1960	Sierra Leone	1961
Azerbaijan	1992	Finland	1955	Malta	1964	Singapore[8]	1965
Bahamas, The	1973	France	1945	Marshall Islands	1991	Slovakia[3]	1993
Bahrain	1971	Gabon	1960	Mauritania	1961	Slovenia[1]	1992
Bangladesh	1974	Gambia, The	1965	Mauritius	1968	Solomon Islands	1978
Barbados	1966	Georgia	1992	Mexico	1945	Somalia	1960
Belarus	1945	Germany[5]	1973	Micronesia	1991	South Africa[11]	1945
Belgium	1945	Ghana	1957	Moldova	1992	Spain	1955
Belize	1981	Greece	1945	Monaco	1993	Sri Lanka	1955
Benin	1960	Grenada	1974	Mongolia	1961	Sudan	1956
Bhutan	1971	Guatemala	1945	Montenegro[1,9]	2006	Suriname	1975
Bolivia	1945	Guinea	1958	Morocco	1956	Swaziland	1968
Bosnia and		Guinea-Bissau	1974	Mozambique	1975	Sweden	1946
Herzegovina[1]	1992	Guyana	1966	Myanmar (Burma)	1948	Switzerland	2002
Botswana	1966	Haiti	1945	Namibia	1990	Syria[3]	1945
Brazil	1945	Honduras	1945	Nauru	1999	Tajikistan	1992
Brunei	1984	Hungary	1955	Nepal	1955	Tanzania[12]	1961
Bulgaria	1955	Iceland	1946	Netherlands	1945	Thailand	1946
Burkina Faso	1960	India	1945	New Zealand	1945	Timor-Leste	2002
Burundi	1962	Indonesia[6]	1950	Nicaragua	1945	Togo	1960
Cambodia	1955	Iran	1945	Niger	1960	Tonga	1999
Cameroon	1960	Iraq	1945	Nigeria	1960	Trinidad and Tobago	1962
Canada	1945	Ireland	1955	Norway	1945	Tunisia	1956
Cape Verde	1975	Israel	1949	Oman	1971	Turkey	1945
Central African Rep.	1960	Italy	1955	Pakistan	1947	Turkmenistan	1992
Chad	1960	Jamaica	1962	Palau	1994	Tuvalu	2000
Chile	1945	Japan	1956	Panama	1945	Uganda	1962
China[2]	1945	Jordan	1955	Papua New Guinea	1975	Ukraine	1945
Colombia	1945	Kazakhstan	1992	Paraguay	1945	United Arab Emirates	1971
Comoros	1975	Kenya	1963	Peru	1945	United Kingdom	1945
Congo, Dem. Rep.	1960	Kiribati	1999	Philippines	1945	United States	1945
Congo, Republic of the.	1960	Korea, North	1991	Poland	1945	Uruguay	1945
Costa Rica	1945	Korea, South	1991	Portugal	1955	Uzbekistan	1992
Côte d'Ivoire	1960	Kuwait	1963	Qatar	1971	Vanuatu	1981
Croatia[1]	1992	Kyrgyzstan	1992	Romania	1955	Venezuela	1945
Cuba	1945	Laos	1955	Russia[10]	1945	Vietnam	1977
Cyprus	1960	Latvia	1991	Rwanda	1962	Yemen[13]	1947
Czech Republic[3]	1993	Lebanon	1945	Saint Kitts and Nevis	1983	Zambia	1964
Denmark	1945	Lesotho	1966	Saint Lucia	1979	Zimbabwe	1980
Djibouti	1977	Liberia	1945				

(1) The Socialist Federal Republic of Yugoslavia was an original UN member. After four of its six republics (Bosnia and Herzegovina, Croatia, Macedonia, and Slovenia) declared independence in 1991-92, the two remaining republics, Montenegro and Serbia, reconstituted as the Federal Republic of Yugoslavia. They sought to take over the former Yugoslavia's UN seat in 1992 but were expelled a few months later by General Assembly (GA) vote. It was granted membership in 2000. In 2003, the country changed its name to Serbia and Montenegro. (2) The GA voted in 1971 to expel the Chinese government in Taiwan and admit the government in Beijing. (3) Czechoslovakia, a UN member from 1945 to 1992, was succeeded by the Czech Republic and Slovakia in 1993. (4) Egypt and Syria were original UN members. In 1958, Egypt and Syria established the United Arab Republic and continued under a single UN membership. In 1961, Syria resumed separate membership following independence. (5) The Federal Republic of Germany and the German Democratic Republic became UN members in 1973. In 1990, the two formed one sovereign state. (6) Withdrew from the UN in 1965; rejoined in 1966. (7) Provisionally referred to as The Former Yugoslav Republic of Macedonia when admitted to the UN because Greece objected to its constitutional name. (8) The Federation of Malaya joined the UN in 1957. In 1963, it changed its name to Malaysia following the accession of Singapore, Sabah, and Sarawak. Singapore became an independent UN member in 1965. (9) After Montenegro declared independence in 2006, Serbia continued in the UN as the Republic of Serbia. Montenegro was admitted to the UN as the Republic of Montenegro the same month. (10) The USSR was an original UN member. After the USSR's dissolution in 1991, Russia informed the UN it would continue the Soviet Union's membership in the Security Council and all other UN organs with the support of the Commonwealth of Independent States (comprising most of the former Soviet republics). (11) Readmitted in 1994 after its delegation was suspended from participation in 1974 because of apartheid. (12) Tanganyika was a UN member from 1961 and Zanzibar from 1963. Following the 1964 formation of the United Republic of Tanganyika and Zanzibar, it continued as a single UN member. It later changed its name to the United Republic of Tanzania. (13) The Yemen Arab Republic was admitted in 1947; the People's Democratic Republic of Yemen, in 1967. In 1990, the two nations merged to become the Republic of Yemen. **Note:** Vatican City, Kosovo, and China (Taiwan) are not members. Vatican City is a permanent observer. Taiwan's repeated bids for UN membership have so far been unsuccessful.

U.S. Representatives to the United Nations

The U.S. Representative to the United Nations is the chief of the U.S. Mission to the United Nations in New York and holds the rank and status of Ambassador Extraordinary and Plenipotentiary (A.E.P.). Year given is the year each took office.

Year	Representative	Year	Representative	Year	Representative	Year	Representative
1946	Edward R. Stettinius, Jr.	1968	James Russell Wiggins	1985	Vernon A. Walters	2001	John D. Negroponte
1946	Herschel V. Johnson (act.)	1969	Charles W. Yost	1989	Thomas R. Pickering	2004	John C. Danforth
1947	Warren R. Austin	1971	George H. W. Bush	1992	Edward J. Perkins	2005	Anne W. Patterson (act.)
1953	Henry Cabot Lodge, Jr.	1973	John A. Scali	1993	Madeleine K. Albright		
1960	James J. Wadsworth	1975	Daniel P. Moynihan	1997	Bill Richardson	2005	John R. Bolton
1961	Adlai E. Stevenson	1976	William W. Scranton	1998	A. Peter Burleigh (act.)	2006	Alejandro D. Wolff (act.)
1965	Arthur J. Goldberg	1977	Andrew Young	1999	Richard C. Holbrooke	2007	Zalmay M. Khalilzad
1968	George W. Ball	1979	Donald McHenry	2001	James B. Cunningham (act.)	2009	Susan E. Rice
		1981	Jeane J. Kirkpatrick				

International Criminal Court (ICC)

The International Criminal Court was created when 120 nations signed the Rome Statute on July 17, 1998. Its mission is to try individuals accused of genocide, war crimes, or other crimes against humanity, as has been undertaken in the past by temporary tribunals. The statute came into force July 1, 2002, 60 days after the 60th nation ratified it. As of July 21, 2009, 110 nations were members of the ICC. China, Russia, and the U.S. have not yet joined. The U.S. expressed opposition to some provisions of the ICC, mainly regarding liability of its military in peacekeeping situations.

The ICC, unlike the World Court, is not part of the UN, but an independent international agency with its own administration and budget—made up of funds from member states and voluntary contributions by other institutions, international groups, individuals, and corporations. It consists of 18 judges elected by member nations. An absolute majority of these 18 judges elect three from among themselves to serve as president, first vice president, and second vice president in three-year, renewable terms. A Registry handles the nonjudicial aspects of administration. The Office of the Prosecutor reviews, investigates, and, prosecutes cases referred to it by a state or by the UN Security Council.

Four situations are currently under investigation by the ICC prosecutor: the situation in the Dem. Rep. of the Congo, Uganda, the Central African Republic, and Darfur, Sudan.

Though jurisdiction is limited to member nations, the ICC is a court of last resort. It may also initiate cases involving non-member nations if it deems the country's authorities have not taken steps to investigate or prosecute a case. The ICC is based in The Hague, Netherlands, though it may sit elsewhere. **Website:** www.icc-cpi.int

Geneva Conventions

The Geneva Conventions are four international treaties governing the protection of civilians in time of war, the treatment of prisoners of war, and the care of the wounded and sick in the armed forces. The first convention, covering the sick and wounded in war, was concluded in Geneva, Switzerland, in 1864, at a conference convened by the Swiss government as the urging of the International Committee of the Red Cross. The convention was amended and expanded in 1906. In 1929, two more conventions covering the wounded and prisoners of war were signed. Outrage at the treatment of prisoners and civilians during WWII by some belligerents, notably Germany and Japan, prompted the conclusion, on Aug. 12, 1949, of four new conventions. Three of these restated and strengthened the previous conventions, and the fourth codified general principles of international law governing the treatment of civilians in wartime.

The 1949 convention for civilians provided for special safeguards for wounded persons, children under 15 years of age, pregnant women, and the elderly. Discrimination on racial, religious, national, or political grounds was forbidden. Torture, collective punishment, reprisals, unwarranted destruction of property, and forced use of civilians for an occupier's armed forces were also prohibited. Also included was a pledge to treat prisoners humanely, feed them adequately, and deliver relief supplies to them. They were not to be forced to disclose more than minimal information. Two additional protocols were adopted in June 1977 dealing with the protection of victims, especially civilians, in international and non-international armed conflicts. (A third protocol, adopted in 2005, created the Red Crystal emblem for use along with the Red Cross and Red Crescent.)

Most countries have formally accepted all or most of the humanitarian conventions as binding. As of 2006, all of the then 194 nations had signed onto the 1949 Conventions. However, there is no permanent international machinery in place to enforce these treaties.

Genocide

Source: Convention on the Prevention and Punishment of the Crime of Genocide, United Nations Treaty Series 277; Rome Statute of the International Criminal Court

The term "genocide" (literally "murder of a race") was coined by Prof. Raphael Lemkin (1900-59) in 1944 and refers to the intentional destruction or attempted destruction of a national, ethnic, racial, or religious group, whether in wartime or peacetime. Genocide is defined as killing members of the group, causing serious bodily harm to members of the group, or otherwise attempting to bring about its destruction, including preventing births or transferring children away from the group. Although the legal definition of genocide does not extend to political groups, the term is often used colloquially to refer to large-scale political violence.

The prohibition against genocide is part of customary international law and is codified in the Convention on the Prevention and Punishment of the Crime of Genocide ("Genocide Convention"), entered into force on Jan. 12, 1951. Today, more than 130 nations, including the U.S., are parties to it. Genocide is also prohibited by the domestic laws of many nations.

The first modern trials for genocide were conducted by the Allies after WWII. Although the charter of the Nuremberg Tribunal (the international court set up to try Nazi war criminals) did not use the term "genocide," its definition of "crimes against humanity" included persecution on racial or religious grounds. More recently, the UN Security Council created ad hoc tribunals to try those responsible for genocide and other serious crimes in the former Yugoslavia and in Rwanda. The International Criminal Court (ICC), which began functioning July 1, 2002, also has jurisdiction to try perpetrators of genocide. In Mar. 2005, the Security Council referred the situation in Darfur, Sudan, to the ICC prosecutor. In July 2008, the prosecutor formally accused Sudanese President Omar Hassan al-Bashir of genocide, crimes against humanity, and war crimes, and requested a warrant for his arrest. A three-judge ICC panel upheld the request and indicted al-Bashir in Mar. 2009.

Examples of Genocides Since 1900

Year	Event	Location	Est. deaths
1915	Extermination of Armenians by the Young Turks	Turkey/Ottoman Empire	1,000,000+
1930s	Intentional infliction of famine on Ukraine	Soviet Union (Ukraine)	6,000,000-7,000,000
1933-45	Attempted destruction of European Jewry (Holocaust)	Europe	6,000,000
1975-79	Khmer Rouge campaign of extermination under Pol Pot	Cambodia	1,500,000-2,000,000
1988	Anfal Campaign (named by the Iraqi government) against Iraqi Kurds	Iraq	100,000-200,000
1992-95	Ethnic killings during the breakup of Yugoslavia, chiefly Serbs against Bosnian Muslims	Bosnia-Herzegovina, Serbia, Croatia	200,000
1994	Hutu massacre of Tutsis	Rwanda	800,000
2003-present	Rebel group and government-backed Arab militia attacks on non-Arab southern tribes, black population[1]	Darfur region, Sudan	200,000-400,000

Note: Estimates based on historical evidence. The legal definition of "genocide" does not include politically motivated mass killings. Therefore, instances of mass violence against political or class enemies, such as Josef Stalin's purges in the 1930s, which killed some 20 mil Soviets, and Mao Zedong's Cultural Revolution, which killed several mil Chinese, are not included. The mass killings of an estimated 1.7 mil during Cambodia's Khmer Rouge regime are often spoken of as genocide, despite the fact that many of the murders were politically or class motivated. (1) In 2005, a UN commission concluded that although the "international offenses ... that have been committed in Darfur may be no less serious and heinous than genocide," it did not term the situation there a genocide.

NATIONS OF THE WORLD

As of mid-2009, there were **195 nations** in the world. This number includes three nations that are not members of the United Nations—Kosovo, Taiwan, and Vatican City (the Holy See). The 195 nations are profiled below, in alphabetical order. Certain regions and territories that are not independent nations can be found under the entry for the governing nation.

Sources: Intl. Data Base, U.S. Census Bureau; *The World Factbook*, Central Intelligence Agency; *International Energy Annual*, Energy Information Admin., U.S. Dept. of Energy; *Oil & Gas Journal*, PennWell Corp.; U.S. Dept. of State; United Nations Educational, Scientific, and Cultural Org. (UNESCO); FAO Statistical Database and *Yearbook of Fishery Statistics*, Food and Agriculture Org. of the UN; *Report on the Global AIDS Epidemic*, UNAIDS and World Health Org.; *Intl. Financial Statistics*, Intl. Monetary Fund (IMF); Intl. Telecommunication Union; *World Population Prospects* and *World Urbanization Prospects*, Dept. of Economic and Social Affairs, UN Population Division; *Statistical Yearbook*, UN Statistics Division; *UNWTO World Tourism Barometer*, World Tourism Org.; *The Military Balance*, Intl. Institute for Strategic Studies.

Note: Because of rounding or incomplete enumeration, some percentages may not add up to 100%. FY = Fiscal year. **Population** figures are mid-2009 estimates, unless otherwise noted. Estimated percentage of **urban** population is for 2005. Population figures for **capitals** and **cities (urban aggr.)**, i.e., whole metropolitan areas, are 2007 estimates. Where indicated, the latest available population of the city proper is also given. **Defense budget** and **active troops** figures are from mid-2008 unless otherwise noted. **Crude oil reserves** are Jan. 1, 2009, estimates unless otherwise noted. **Livestock** figures are for 2007 unless otherwise noted. **Fish catch** figures, which include the capture and farming of fish, mollusks, and crustaceans, are for 2007. **Electricity prod.** numbers are for 2006 unless otherwise noted. **GDP** figures are 2008 estimates unless otherwise noted; figures are based on purchasing power parity calculations, involving use of intl. dollar price weights applied to quantities of goods and services produced. **Imports** and **exports** estimates and trade partners are from 2008 unless otherwise noted. **Tourism** figures are latest available and represent receipts from international tourism. **Budget** figures are for expenditures and are 2008 estimates unless otherwise noted. Figures for **intl. reserves less gold, gold,** and changes in **consumer prices** are from 2008 unless otherwise noted. **Railroad** and **motor vehicle** statistics are latest available; comm. (commercial) vehicles include trucks and buses. **Civil aviation** statistics are latest available. Airport figures include total number with paved runways as of 2009. **TV sets, radios,** and **daily newspaper circ.** figures are latest available. **Telephone lines** and **Internet** data are for 2008 unless otherwise noted. **Life expect.** is at birth for persons born in 2008. **Natural inc.** is the difference between the number of births and the number of deaths, in 2008. **Infant mortality** measures the probability of a child dying between birth and exact age 1, in 2008. **HIV rate** is the estimated number of adults, ages 15-49, living with HIV in 2007, divided by the total 2007 population aged 15-49. **Education** figures and **literacy** rates are latest available. Literacy rates, of adults ages 15 or over, generally measure the percent of population able to read and write simple statements on everyday life, not the (smaller) percent able to read and write to carry out effectively activities within the community. **Embassy** addresses are for Wash., DC, area code (202), unless otherwise noted.

For further details and later information on developments around the world, see the Chronology of the Year's Events. See pages 457-72 for full-color maps and flags of all nations.

Afghanistan
Islamic Republic of Afghanistan

People: Population: 33,609,937. **Age distrib.** (%): <15: 44.5; 65+: 2.4. **Pop. density:** 134.4 per sq mi, 51.9 per sq km. **Urban:** 22.9%. **Ethnic groups:** Pashtun 42%, Tajik 27%, Hazara 9%, Uzbek 9%. **Principal languages:** Dari, or Afghan Persian (official), Pashto (official), Turkic (Uzbek, Turkmen), Balochi, Pashai, many others. **Chief religion:** Muslim (official; Sunni 80%, Shi'a 19%).

Geography: Total area: 250,001 sq mi, 647,500 sq km; **Land area:** 250,001 sq mi, 647,500 sq km. **Location:** In SW Asia, NW of the Indian subcontinent. **Neighbors:** Pakistan on E, S; Iran on W; Turkmenistan, Tajikistan, Uzbekistan on N. The NE tip touches China. **Topography:** The country is landlocked and mountainous, much of it over 4,000 ft above sea level. The Hindu Kush Mts. tower 16,000 ft above Kabul and reach a height of 25,000 ft to the E. Trade with Pakistan flows through the 35-mi-long Khyber Pass. The climate is dry, with extreme temperatures, and there are large desert regions. **Capital:** Kabul, 3,277,000.

Government: Type: Islamic republic. **Head of state and gov.:** Pres. Hamid Karzai; b. Dec. 24, 1957; in office: June 19, 2002. **Local divisions:** 32 provinces. **Defense budget:** $153 mil. Active troops: 53,400.

Economy: Industries: textiles, soap, furniture, shoes. **Chief crops:** opium, wheat, fruits, nuts. **Natural resources:** nat. gas, oil, coal, copper, chromite, talc, barites, sulfur, lead, zinc, iron ore, salt, gems. **Arable land:** 12%. **Livestock:** cattle: 4.4 mil; chickens: 9.04 mil; goats: 5.4 mil; sheep: 8.1 mil. **Fish catch** (est.): 1,000 metric tons. **Electricity prod.:** 917 mil kWh. **Labor force** (2004 est.): agric. 80%, industry 10%, services 10%.

Finance: Monetary unit: Afghani (AFN) (Oct. 2009: 47.49 = $1 U.S.). **GDP:** $22.3 bil; **per capita GDP:** $700; **GDP growth:** 3.4%. **Imports** (2007): $4.9 bil; Pakistan 35.8%, U.S. 9.2%, Germany 7.5%, India 4.8%. **Exports** (2007): $327 mil; India 21.1%, Pakistan 20.1%, U.S. 18.8%, Netherlands 7.9%, Tajikistan 6.7%. **Tourism:** NA. **Budget:** $2.6 bil (not incl. $273 mil received from Reconstruction Trust Fund, $63 mil from Law and Order Trust Fund).

Transport: Motor vehicles: 41,000 pass. cars; 100,000 comm. vehicles. **Civil aviation:** 88.9 mil pass.-mi; 16 airports. **Chief ports:** Kheyrabad, Shir Khan.

Communications: TV sets: 14 per 1,000 pop. **Radios:** 136 per 1,000 pop. **Telephone lines:** 101,100. **Internet:** 500,000 users.

Health: Life expect.: 44 male; 44.4 female. **Births** (per 1,000 pop.): 45.8. **Deaths** (per 1,000 pop.): 19.6. **Natural inc.:** 2.63%. **Infant mortality** (per 1,000 live births): 154.7. **HIV rate:** NA.

Education: Compulsory: ages 6-15. **Literacy:** 28%.

Major intl. organizations: UN (FAO, IBRD, ILO, IMF, WHO).

Embassy: 2341 Wyoming Ave. NW 20008; 483-6410.
Website: www.president.gov.af

Afghanistan, occupying a favored invasion route since antiquity, has been variously known as Ariana or Bactria (in ancient times) and Khorasan (in the Middle Ages). Foreign empires alternated rule with local emirs and kings until the 18th cent., when a unified kingdom was established. In 1973, a military coup ushered in a republic.

Pro-Soviet leftists took power in a bloody 1978 coup and concluded an economic and military treaty with the USSR. In Dec. 1979 the USSR began a massive airlift into Kabul and backed a new coup, leading to installation of a more pro-Soviet leader. Soviet forces fanned out over Afghanistan and waged a protracted guerrilla war with Muslim rebels, in which some 15,000 Soviet troops reportedly died.

A UN-mediated agreement was signed Apr. 14, 1988, providing for withdrawal of Soviet troops, a neutral Afghan state, and repatriation of refugees. Afghan rebels rejected the pact. The Soviets completed their troop withdrawal Feb. 15, 1989; fighting between Afghan rebels and government forces ensued. Communist Pres. Najibullah resigned Apr. 16, 1992, as competing guerrilla forces advanced on Kabul. The rebels achieved power Apr. 28, ending 14 years of Soviet-backed regimes. More than 2 mil Afghans had been killed and 6 mil had left the country since 1979.

Following the rebel victory there were clashes between moderates and Islamic fundamentalist forces. Burhanuddin Rabbani, a guerrilla leader, became president June 28, 1992, but fierce fighting continued around Kabul and elsewhere. The Taliban, an insurgent Islamic radical faction, captured Kabul in Sept. 1996. The Taliban executed former Pres. Najibullah and empowered Islamic religious police to enforce codes of dress and behavior that were especially restrictive to women. Rabbani and other ousted leaders fled to the north.

Victories in the northern cities of Mazar-e Sharif, Aug. 8, 1998, and Taloqan, Aug. 8-11, gave the Taliban control over more than 90% of the country. On Aug. 20, U.S. cruise missiles struck southeast of Kabul, hitting facilities the U.S. said were terrorist training camps run by a wealthy Saudi, Osama bin Laden. The UN imposed sanctions Nov. 14, 1999, when Afghanistan refused to turn over bin Laden to the U.S. for prosecution; a UN ban on all military aid to the Taliban took effect Jan. 19, 2001.

After the Sept. 11, 2001, attacks on the World Trade Center and Pentagon, the U.S., blaming bin Laden, demanded that the Taliban surrender him and shut down his al-Qaeda terrorist network. When the Taliban refused, the U.S., with British assistance, began bombing Afghanistan Oct. 7, as part of Operation Enduring Freedom.

Supported by the U.S., the opposition Northern Alliance recaptured Mazar-e Sharif Nov. 9 and took Kabul 4 days later; the Taliban forces abandoned Kandahar, their last stronghold, to southern tribesmen Dec. 7. A power-sharing agreement signed by 4 anti-Taliban factions, including the Northern Alliance, provided for an interim government headed by Hamid Karzai, a Pashtun tribal leader. The UN authorized Dec. 20 a multinational security force. Meanwhile, U.S. and allied forces continued to hunt for bin Laden and other top al-Qaeda and Taliban officials.

Meeting June 13, 2002, in Kabul, a traditional council (*loya jirga*) chose Karzai to head a new transitional government. The U.S. announced the end of major combat operations in Afghanistan, May 1, 2003, but resistance continued, with relief and reconstruction workers targeted. NATO officially assumed control of peacekeeping forces (ISAF) Aug. 11.

A new constitution took effect Jan. 26, 2004. Pres. Karzai won reelection Oct. 9 with 55.4% of the vote. During the campaign, insurgents attempted to kill Pres. Karzai, Sept. 16. U.S. troops launched a new offensive, Dec. 11, but were unable to suppress the insurgency. Violence continued to rise in the run-up to elections Sept. 18, 2005, for a 249-seat national assembly. Millions defied threats of violence to vote; at least 14 people were killed in more than 20 attacks by insurgents.

The most intense fighting in more than 4 years erupted Mar. 2006 with a new wave of suicide bombings, rocket and mortar attacks, and other strikes by Taliban insurgents against military and civilian targets. Erosion of government authority led to an increase in opium growing; the Taliban, local warlords, and some Karzai associates were accused of profiting from the drug trade. A record poppy crop of 8,200 metric tons in 2007 made Afghanistan the source of 93% of the world's illicit opium; drought and local suppression efforts cut estimated output to 7,700 metric tons in 2008 and 6,900 in 2009.

Operating from sanctuaries across the border in Pakistan, Islamist suicide bombers and Taliban insurgents stepped up their activities during 2007-08. A suicide attack in northern Afghanistan, Nov. 6, 2007, killed at least 77 people, including 61 schoolchildren. An apparent attempt to assassinate Pres. Karzai at a military parade in Kabul, Apr. 27, 2008, left 3 people dead and 11 injured. Fighting was especially fierce in the Kandahar area, where a suicide bombing Feb. 17 killed more than 100 people at an outdoor dog-fighting competition, and a daring nighttime raid by Taliban fighters June 13 freed up to 1,200 inmates (including an estimated 350 Taliban members) from Sarposa prison. According to UN statistics, the number of civilian casualties rose from 1,523 in 2007 to 2,118 in 2008.

On Feb. 17, 2009, Pres. Obama announced that "to stabilize a deteriorating situation," the U.S. would send an additional 17,000 troops. By the end of June the U.S. had 58,000 troops in Afghanistan (with the total expected to rise to 68,000 by the end of the year), along with nearly 74,000 military contractors. In a report submitted Aug. 30, Gen. Stanley McChrystal, the top U.S. and NATO commander in Afghanistan, warned that without further troop increases the mission would "likely result in failure."

Violence escalated in the run-up to the presidential election Aug. 20; on that day, Taliban attacks, intended to suppress turnout, killed at least 30 people. Preliminary results released Sept. 8 showed Karzai above 50% of the vote, but a UN-backed commission overseeing the tally ordered a recount, citing "clear and convincing evidence of fraud" at numerous polling stations. Meanwhile, controversy surrounded a NATO air strike Sept. 4 on two hijacked fuel tanker trucks in the northern province of Kunduz; an official investigation found that the attack killed 30 civilians along with 69 Taliban.

From Oct. 2001 through early Sept. 2009, more than 820 U.S. military personnel died in support of Operation Enduring Freedom and the NATO-led, 64,500-member ISAF (to which about 30,000 U.S. troops were assigned); casualties from allied countries totaled about 550, with more than 210 from the U.K. and nearly 130 from Canada. By May 2009, Congress had appropriated more than $189 bil for the Afghanistan war.

Albania
Republic of Albania

People: Population: 3,639,453. **Age distrib.** (%): <15: 23.1; 65+: 9.8. **Pop. density:** 344 per sq mi, 132.8 per sq km. **Urban:** 44.8%. **Ethnic groups:** Albanian 95%, Greek 3%. **Principal languages:** Albanian (official; derived from Tosk dialect), Greek. **Chief religions:** Muslim 70%, Albanian Orthodox 20%, Roman Catholic 10%.

Geography: Total area: 11,100 sq mi, 28,748 sq km; **Land area:** 10,578 sq mi, 27,398 sq km. **Location:** SE Europe, on SE coast of Adriatic Sea. **Neighbors:** Greece on S; Montenegro, Serbia on N; Macedonia on E. **Topography:** Apart from a narrow coastal plain, Albania consists of hills and mountains covered with scrub forest, cut by small E-W rivers. **Capital:** Tirana, 406,000.

Government: Type: Republic. **Head of state:** Pres. Bamir Topi; b. Apr. 24, 1957; in office: July 24, 2007. **Head of gov.:** Prime

Min. Sali Berisha; b. Oct. 15, 1944; in office: Sept. 11, 2005. **Local divisions:** 12 counties divided into 36 districts. **Defense budget:** $198 mil. **Active troops:** 14,295.

Economy: Industries: food proc., textiles & clothing, lumber. **Chief crops:** wheat, corn, potatoes, vegetables, fruits, sugar beets, grapes. **Natural resources:** oil, nat. gas, coal, bauxite, chromite, copper, iron ore, nickel. **Crude oil reserves:** 199.1 mil bbls. **Arable land:** 20%. **Livestock:** cattle: 577,000; chickens: 4.7 mil; goats: 876,000; pigs: 147,000; sheep: 1.9 mil. **Fish catch:** 7,505 metric tons. **Electricity prod.:** 5.5 bil kWh. **Labor force** (2006 est.): agric. 58%, industry 15%, services 27%.

Finance: Monetary unit: Lek (ALL) (Oct. 2009: 91.55 = $1 U.S.). **GDP:** $21.8 bil; **per capita GDP:** $6,000; **GDP growth:** 6.1%. **Imports:** $4.9 bil; Italy 30.7%, Greece 12.5%, Turkey 6.9%, Germany 6.3%, Switzerland 4.6%, Russia 4.2%. **Exports:** $1.3 bil; Italy 57%, Greece 11.8%, China 5.8%. **Tourism:** $1.4 bil. **Budget:** $3.2 bil. **Intl. reserves less gold:** $1.51 bil. **Gold:** 50,000 oz t. **Consumer prices:** 3.4%.

Transport: Railroad: Length: 557 mi. **Motor vehicles:** 174,700 pass. cars; 88,800 comm. vehicles. **Civil aviation:** 92.6 mil pass.-mi; 4 airports. **Chief ports:** Durres, Sarande, Shengjin, Vlore.

Communications: TV sets: 146 per 1,000 pop. **Radios:** 259 per 1,000 pop. **Telephone lines:** 316,400. **Daily newspaper circ.** (2003): 24.4 per 1,000 pop. **Internet:** 471,000 users.

Health: Life expect.: 75.1 male; 80.7 female. **Births** (per 1,000 pop.): 15.2. **Deaths** (per 1,000 pop.): 5.4. **Natural inc.:** 0.98%. **Infant mortality** (per 1,000 live births): 19.3. **HIV rate:** NA.

Major intl. organizations: UN (IBRD, ILO, FAO, IMF, IMO, WHO, WTO), NATO, OSCE.

Education: Compulsory: ages 6-13. **Literacy:** 99%.

Embassy: 2100 S St. NW 20008; 223-4942.

Website: km.gov.al

Ancient Illyria was conquered by Romans, Slavs, and Turks (15th cent.); the Turks Islamized the population. Independent Albania was proclaimed in 1912; the republic was formed in 1920. King Zog I ruled 1925-39, until Italy invaded.

Communist partisans took over in 1944, allied Albania with the USSR, then broke with the USSR in 1960 over de-Stalinization. Later, China provided billions of dollars in assistance, but cut off aid in 1978 when Albania attacked its policies after the death of Chinese ruler Mao Zedong. Large-scale purges of officials occurred during the 1970s.

Enver Hoxha, the nation's ruler for 4 decades, died Apr. 11, 1985. Eventually the new regime introduced some liberalization, including measures in 1990 providing for freedom to travel abroad. Efforts were begun to improve ties with the outside world.

Albania's former Communists were routed in elections Mar. 1992, amid economic collapse and social unrest. Sali Berisha was elected as the first non-Communist president since WWII. Berisha's party claimed a landslide victory in disputed parliamentary elections, May 26 and June 2, 1996. Public protests over the collapse of fraudulent investment schemes in Jan. 1997 led to armed rebellion and anarchy. The UN Security Council, Mar. 28, authorized a 7,000-member force to restore order. Socialists and their allies won parliamentary elections, June 29 and July 6, and international peacekeepers completed their pullout by Aug. 11.

During NATO's air war against Yugoslavia, Mar.-June 1999, Albania hosted some 465,000 Kosovar refugees. Victory by a pro-Berisha coalition in elections July 3, 2005, ended 8 years of Socialist rule. Albania became a full member of NATO Apr. 1, 2009; the nation formally applied for EU membership Apr. 28. Following parliamentary elections June 28, Berisha retained his office as prime minister.

Algeria
People's Democratic Republic of Algeria

People: Population: 34,178,188. **Age distrib.** (%): <15: 25.4; 65+: 5.1. **Pop. density:** 37.2 per sq mi, 14.4 per sq km. **Urban:** 63.3%. **Ethnic groups:** Arab-Berber 99%. **Principal languages:** Arabic (official), French, Berber dialects. **Chief religions:** Sunni Muslim (official) 99%, Christian & Jewish 1%.

Geography: Total area: 919,595 sq mi, 2,381,740 sq km; **Land area:** 919,595 sq mi, 2,381,740 sq km. **Location:** In NW Africa, from Medit. Sea into Sahara Desert. **Neighbors:** Morocco, Western Sahara on W; Mauritania, Mali, Niger on S; Libya, Tunisia on E. **Topography:** The Tell, located on the coast, comprises fertile plains 50-100 mi wide, with a moderate climate and adequate rain. Two major chains of Atlas Mts., running roughly E-W and reaching 7,000 ft, enclose a dry plateau region. Below lies the Sahara, mostly desert with major mineral resources. **Capital:** Algiers (El Djazaïr), 3,354,000. **Cities (urban aggr.):** Oran (Wahran), 798,000.

Government: Type: Republic. **Head of state:** Pres. Abdelaziz Bouteflika; b. Mar. 2, 1937; in office: Apr. 27, 1999. **Head of gov.:** Prime Min. Ahmed Ouyahia; b. July 2, 1952; in office: June 23, 2008. **Local divisions:** 48 provinces. **Defense budget:** $4.3 bil. **Active troops:** 147,000.

Economy: Industries: oil, nat. gas, light industries, mining, electrical, petrochemical, food proc. **Chief crops:** wheat, barley, oats, grapes, olives, citrus. **Natural resources:** oil, nat. gas, iron ore, phosphates, uranium, lead, zinc. **Crude oil reserves:** 12.2 bil bbls. **Arable land:** 3%. **Livestock:** cattle: 1.7 mil; chickens: 125 mil; goats: 3.8 mil; pigs: 5,700; sheep: 19.9 mil. **Fish catch:** 148,842 metric tons. **Electricity prod.:** 33.1 bil kWh. **Labor force** (2003 est.): agric. 14%, industry 13.4%, constr. & public works 10%, trade 14.6%, govt. 32%, other 16%.

Finance: Monetary unit: Dinar (DZD) (Oct. 2009: 72.37 = $1 U.S.). **GDP:** $232.9 bil; **per capita GDP:** $6,900; **GDP growth:** 3.5%. **Imports:** $39.2 bil; France 19.8%, Italy 10.9%, China 9%, Spain 7.6%, Germany 5.4%. **Exports:** $78.2 bil; U.S. 23.9%, Italy 14.9%, Spain 11.1%, Canada 9.6%, France 8.6%, Netherlands 4.5%. **Tourism:** NA. **Budget:** $40.8 bil. **Intl. reserves less gold:** $93 bil. **Gold:** 5.58 mil oz t. **Consumer prices:** 4.4%.

Transport: Railroad: Length: 2,469 mi. **Motor vehicles:** 1.9 mil pass. cars; 1.1 mil comm. vehicles. **Civil aviation:** 1.9 bil pass.-mi; 57 airports. **Chief ports:** Algiers, Annaba, Oran.

Communications: TV sets: 107 per 1,000 pop. **Radios:** 242 per 1,000 pop. **Telephone lines:** 3.3 mil. **Internet:** 4.1 mil users.

Health: Life expect.: 72.1 male; 75.5 female. **Births** (per 1,000 pop.): 17. **Deaths** (per 1,000 pop.): 4.6. **Natural inc.:** 1.24%. **Infant mortality** (per 1,000 live births): 28.8. **HIV rate:** 0.1%.

Education: Compulsory: ages 6-14. **Literacy:** 75.4%.

Major intl. organizations: UN (FAO, IBRD, ILO, IMF, IMO, WHO), AL, AU, OPEC.

Embassy: 2118 Kalorama Rd. NW 20008; 265-2800.

Website: www.premier-ministre.gov.dz or www.algeria-us.org

Earliest known inhabitants were ancestors of Berbers, followed by Phoenicians, Romans, Vandals, and, finally, Arabs. Turkey ruled 1518 to 1830, when France took control. Large-scale European immigration followed. Arab nationalists launched a guerrilla war, 1954, that more than 400,000 French troops were unable to suppress. After French Pres. Charles de Gaulle came to power, 1958, colonial rule ended, nearly all Europeans left, and Algeria declared independence July 5, 1962. Ahmed Ben Bella ruled until 1965, when an army coup installed Col. Houari Boumedienne, a former guerrilla leader who held power until his death in 1978.

Hundreds died in antigovernment riots protesting economic hardship in Oct. 1988. In 1989, voters approved a new constitution, which cleared the way for a multiparty system. The government canceled the Jan. 1992 elections that Islamic fundamentalists were expected to win, and banned all nonreligious activities at Algeria's 10,000 mosques. Pres. Mohammed Boudiaf was assassinated June 29, 1992. Over the next 7 years, Muslim fundamentalists carried out attacks on high-ranking officials, security forces, foreigners, and others; pro-government death squads also were active.

Liamine Zeroual won the presidential election of Nov. 16, 1995. A new constitution banning Islamic political parties and increasing the president's powers passed in a referendum on Nov. 28, 1996. Abdelaziz Bouteflika, who became president after a flawed election on Apr. 15, 1999, made peace with rebels and won approval for an amnesty plan in a referendum on Sept. 16. Some 100 people died and thousands were injured in violent protests Apr.-June 2001, chiefly by Algeria's Berber minority. Bouteflika was reelected Apr. 8, 2004, in a landslide; opponents charged fraud.

An earthquake in northern Algeria, May 21, 2003, claimed over 2,200 lives and left 200,000 people homeless. Under a reconciliation plan approved by referendum Sept. 29, 2005, the government in Mar. 2006 began freeing Islamists jailed for their role in the 1990s civil war, in which up to 200,000 people were killed, and 8,000 "disappeared."

Radical Islamists bombed 2 police stations Oct. 30, 2006, and 7 more police stations Feb. 13, 2007. A group known as al-Qaeda in the Islamic Maghreb (AQIM) carried out suicide bombings Apr. 11 at the Government Palace and a police station in Algiers, killing 33 people; more than 50 died in suicide bombings at Batna, Sept. 6, and Dellys, Sept. 8. Car bombs Dec. 11 killed 17 UN staff members and at least 20 others in Algiers. A surge in AQIM violence in Aug. 2008 left more than 100 people dead. Parliament Nov. 12 amended the constitution to abolish presidential term limits, clearing the way for Bouteflika to run for a 3rd term. He claimed more than 90% of the vote in an election Apr. 9, 2009, denounced as fraudulent by opposition parties.

Andorra
Principality of Andorra

People: Population: 83,888. **Age distrib.** (%): <15: 15.5; 65+: 12.3. **Pop. density:** 464.2 per sq mi, 179.2 per sq km. **Urban:** 90.3%. **Ethnic groups:** Spanish 43%, Andorran 33%, Portuguese 11%, French 7%. **Principal languages:** Catalan (official), French, Castilian, Portuguese. **Chief religion:** Predominantly Roman Catholic.

Geography: Total area: 181 sq mi, 468 sq km; **Land area:** 181 sq mi, 468 sq km. **Location:** SW Europe, in Pyrenees Mts. **Neighbors:** Spain on S, France on N. **Topography:** High mountains and narrow valleys cover the country. **Capital** (2006): Andorra la Vella, 24,211.

Government: Type: Parliamentary co-principality. **Heads of state:** President of France & Bishop of Urgel (Spain), as co-princes. **Head of gov.:** Jaume Bartumeu Cassany; b. Nov. 10, 1954; in office: June 5, 2009. **Local divisions:** 7 parishes. **Defense budget:** Defense is responsibility of France and Spain.

Economy: Industries: tourism, cattle raising, timber, banking, tobacco, furniture. **Chief crops:** rye, wheat, barley, oats. **Natural resources:** hydropower, mineral water, timber, iron ore, lead. **Arable land:** 2%. **Labor force** (2007): agric. 0.3%, industry 20.8%, services 79%.

Finance: Monetary unit: Euro (EUR) (Oct. 2009: 0.68 = $1 U.S.). **GDP** (2007): $3.7 bil; per capita **GDP** (2007): $42,500; **GDP growth:** 2%. **Imports** (2007): $1.8 bil. **Exports** (2007): $117.1 mil. **Tourism:** NA. **Budget** (2005): $386.6 mil.

Transport: Motor vehicles: 49,600 pass. cars; 5,500 comm. vehicles.

Communications: TV sets: 440 per 1,000 pop. **Radios:** 229 per 1,000 pop. **Telephone lines:** 37,400. **Internet:** 59,100 users.

Health: Life expect.: 80.3 male; 85.1 female. **Births** (per 1,000 pop.): 10.6. **Deaths** (per 1,000 pop.): 5.6. **Natural inc.:** 0.5%. **Infant mortality** (per 1,000 live births): 3.7. **HIV rate:** NA.

Education: Compulsory: ages 6-16. **Literacy:** 100%.

Major intl. organizations: UN (WHO), OSCE.

Embassy: 2 UN Plaza, 27th Fl., New York, NY 10017; (212) 750-8064.

Website: www.andorra.ad

France and the bishop of Urgel held joint sovereignty over Andorra from 1278 to 1993. Voters chose to adopt a parliamentary system Mar. 14, 1993, although co-princes remain heads of state.

Tourism, especially skiing, is the economic mainstay. A free port, Andorra attracts more than 10 mil visitors annually.

Angola
Republic of Angola

People: Population: 12,799,293. **Age distrib.** (%): <15: 43.5; 65+: 2.7. **Pop. density:** 26.6 per sq mi, 10.3 per sq km. **Urban:** 54%. **Ethnic groups:** Ovimbundu 37%, Kimbundu 25%, Bakongo 13%. **Principal languages:** Portuguese (official), Bantu, other African languages. **Chief religions:** Indigenous beliefs 47%, Roman Catholic 38%, Protestant 15%.

Geography: Total area: 481,354 sq mi, 1,246,700 sq km; **Land area:** 481,354 sq mi, 1,246,700 sq km. **Location:** In SW Africa on Atlantic coast. **Neighbors:** Namibia on S, Zambia on E, Congo-Kinshasa on N; Cabinda, an enclave separated from rest of country by short Atlantic coast of Congo-Kinshasa, borders Congo-Brazzaville. **Topography:** Mostly plateau elevated 3,000-5,000 ft above sea level, rising from a narrow coastal strip. There is also a temperate highland area in the west-central region, a desert in S, and a tropical rain forest covering Cabinda. **Capital:** Luanda, 4,000,000. **Cities (urban aggr.):** Huambo, 872,000.

Government: Type: Republic. **Head of state:** Pres. José Eduardo dos Santos; b. Aug. 28, 1942; in office: Sept. 20, 1979. **Head of gov.:** Paulo Kassoma; b. June 6, 1951; in office: Sept. 26, 2008. **Local divisions:** 18 provinces. **Defense budget:** $2.3 bil. **Active troops:** 107,000.

Economy: Industries: oil, mining, cement, metal products, fish & food proc. **Chief crops:** bananas, sugarcane, coffee, sisal. **Natural resources:** oil, diamonds, iron ore, phosphates, copper, feldspar, gold, bauxite, uranium. **Crude oil reserves:** 9.04 bil bbls. **Arable land:** 3%. **Livestock:** cattle: 4.2 mil; chickens: 6.9 mil; goats: 2.1 mil; pigs: 782,000; sheep: 340,000. **Fish catch:** 312,440 metric tons. **Electricity prod.:** 3.5 bil kWh. **Labor force** (2003 est.): agric. 85%, industry & services 15%.

Finance: Monetary unit: Kwanza (AOA) (Oct. 2009: 77.81 = $1 U.S.). **GDP:** $110.3 bil; **per capita GDP:** $8,800; **GDP growth:** 13.2%. **Imports:** $17.1 bil; Portugal 19.3%, China 14.7%, U.S. 12.3%, Brazil 8.3%, South Africa 5.4%, France 4.3%. **Exports:** $67.2 bil; China 32.7%, U.S. 26.7%, South Africa 9.6%, France 5.5%. **Tourism:** NA. **Budget:** $15.8 bil. **Intl. reserves less gold:** $11.92 bil. **Gold:** NA. **Consumer prices:** 12.5%.

Transport: Railroad: Length: 1,717 mi. **Motor vehicles:** 117,200 pass. cars; 118,300 comm. vehicles. **Civil aviation:** 375.9 mil pass.-mi; 30 airports. **Chief ports:** Cabinda, Lobito, Luanda, Namibe.

Communications: TV sets: 15 per 1,000 pop. **Radios:** 67 per 1,000 pop. **Telephone lines:** 114,300. **Daily newspaper circ.** (2004): 2.2 per 1,000 pop. **Internet:** 550,000 users.

Health: Life expect.: 37 male; 38.9 female. **Births** (per 1,000 pop.): 44.1. **Deaths** (per 1,000 pop.): 24.4. **Natural inc.:** 1.97%. **Infant mortality** (per 1,000 live births): 182.3. **HIV rate:** 2.1%.

Education: Compulsory: ages 6-9. **Literacy:** 67.4%.

Major intl. organizations: UN (FAO, IBRD, ILO, IMF, IMO, WHO, WTO), AU, OPEC.

Embassy: 2100-2108 16th St. NW 20009; 785-1156.

Website: www.governo.gov.ao or www.angola.org

From the early centuries CE to 1500, Bantu tribes penetrated most of the region. Portuguese came in 1583, allied with the Bakongo kingdom in the north, and developed the slave trade. Large-scale colonization did not begin until the 20th cent, when 400,000 Portuguese immigrated.

A guerrilla war begun in 1961 lasted until 1975, when Portugal granted independence. Fighting then erupted between three rival rebel groups—the National Front, based in Zaire (now Congo), the Soviet-backed Popular Movement for the Liberation of Angola (MPLA), and the National Union for the Total Independence of Angola (UNITA), aided by the U.S. and South Africa.

Cuban troops and Soviet aid helped the MPLA win control of most of the country by 1976, although fighting continued through the 1980s. A peace accord between the MPLA government and UNITA was signed May 1, 1991.

Elections were held in Sept. 1992, but fighting again broke out, as UNITA rejected the results. UNITA signed a new peace treaty with the government, Nov. 20, 1994, but the rebels were slow to demobilize. The UN Security Council voted, Aug. 28, 1997, to impose sanctions on UNITA. The UN ended its mission in Angola in Mar. 1999, as the civil war continued.

As of 2001, the UN estimated that the war with UNITA had claimed some 1 mil lives and left another 2.5 mil people homeless. Rebel leader Jonas Savimbi was killed by government troops Feb. 22, 2002. UNITA agreed to a truce Apr. 4 of that year, ending the 27-year-long civil war. Fighting continued, however, between government forces and separatist guerrillas in oil-rich Cabinda; rebels there agreed to a cease-fire July 2006.

With proven petroleum reserves estimated at 9 bil barrels, Angola is one of Africa's leading oil producers. Mismanagement and corruption led to the diversion of up to $4.2 bil in oil revenues during 1997-2002, according to a Human Rights Watch report. The ruling MPLA claimed victory in voting Sept. 5-6, 2008, in Angola's first parliamentary elections in 16 years. Emblematic of Angola's rising influence were visits in 2009 from Pope Benedict XVI, Mar. 20-22, and U.S. Sec. of State Hillary Clinton, Aug. 9.

Antigua and Barbuda

People: Population: 85,632. **Age distrib.** (%): <15: 26.8; 65+: 6.6. **Pop. density:** 501.1 per sq mi, 193.5 per sq km. **Urban:** 30.7%. **Ethnic groups:** Black 91%, mixed 4%, white 2%. **Principal languages:** English (official), local dialects. **Chief religions:** Anglican 26%, Seventh-Day Adventist 12%, Pentecostal 11%, Moravian 11%, Roman Catholic 10%.

Geography: Total area: 171 sq mi, 443 sq km; **Land area:** 171 sq mi, 443 sq km. **Location:** E Caribbean. **Neighbors:** St. Kitts & Nevis to W, Guadeloupe (Fr.) to S. **Topography:** These are mostly low-lying and limestone coral islands. Antigua is mostly hilly with an indented coast; Barbuda is a flat island with a large lagoon on W. **Capital** (2004): Saint John's, 23,600.

Government: Type: Constitutional monarchy with British-style parliament. **Head of state:** Queen Elizabeth II; represented by Gov.-Gen. Louise Agnetha Lake-Tack; b. July 26, 1944; in office: July 17, 2007. **Head of gov.:** Prime Min. Baldwin Spencer; b. Oct. 8, 1948; in office: Mar. 24, 2004. **Local divisions:** 6 parishes, 2 dependencies. **Defense budget:** $5 mil. **Active troops:** 170.

Economy: Industries: tourism, constr., light mfg. **Chief crops:** cotton, fruits, vegetables. **Arable land:** 18%. **Livestock:** cattle: 14,500; chickens: 110,000; goats: 36,000; pigs: 2,800; sheep: 20,000. **Fish catch:** 3,092 metric tons. **Electricity prod.:** 105 mil kWh. **Labor force** (1983): agric. 7%, industry 11%, services 82%.

Finance: Monetary unit: East Caribbean Dollar (XCD) (Oct. 2009: 2.70 = $1 U.S.). **GDP:** $1.7 bil; **per capita GDP:** $19,600; **GDP growth:** 4.2%. **Imports:** (2007): $522.8 mil. **Exports** (2007): $84.3 mil. **Tourism:** $338 mil. **Budget** (2000 est.): $145.9 mil. **Intl. reserves less gold:** $90 mil. **Gold:** NA. **Consumer prices:** NA.

Transport: Motor vehicles: 24,000 pass. cars; 4,800 comm. vehicles. **Civil aviation:** 76.4 mil pass.-mi; 2 airports. **Chief port:** Saint John's.

Communications: TV sets: 493 per 1,000 pop. **Radios:** 545 per 1,000 pop. **Telephone lines:** 38,000. **Internet:** 65,000 users.

Health: Life expect.: 72.3 male; 76.3 female. **Births** (per 1,000 pop.): 16.8. **Deaths** (per 1,000 pop.): 6.1. **Natural inc.:** 1.06%. **Infant mortality** (per 1,000 live births): 17.5. **HIV rate:** NA.

Education: Compulsory: ages 5-16. **Literacy:** 85.8%.

Major intl. organizations: UN (FAO, IBRD, ILO, IMF, IMO, WHO, WTO), Caricom, the Commonwealth, OAS, OECS.

Embassy: 3216 New Mexico Ave. NW 20016; 362-5122.

Website: www.ab.gov.ag

Columbus landed on Antigua in 1493. The British colonized it in 1632. The British associated state of Antigua achieved independence as Antigua and Barbuda on Nov. 1, 1981. The government maintains close relations with the U.S., the UK, and Venezuela. Tourism, which accounts for more than 50% of GDP, was hit hard by the worldwide recession in 2008-09. The economy suffered a further blow when Robert Allen Stanford, a Texas businessman, was charged by U.S. authorities Feb. 17, 2009, with employing his Antigua-based Stanford International Bank to carry out a fraudulent $8 bil investment scheme.

Argentina
Argentine Republic

People: Population: 40,913,584. **Age distrib.** (%): <15: 25.6; 65+: 10.8. **Pop. density:** 38.7 per sq mi, 15 per sq km. **Urban:** 91.4%. **Ethnic groups:** White (mostly Spanish & Italian) 97%; mestizo (mixed white & Amerindian), Amerindian, other non-white groups 3%. **Principal languages:** Spanish (official), Italian, English, German, French. **Chief religion:** nominally Roman Catholic 92% (less than 20% practicing).

Geography: Total area: 1,068,302 sq mi, 2,766,890 sq km; **Land area:** 1,056,642 sq mi, 2,736,690 sq km. **Location:** Occupies most of southern S. America. **Neighbors:** Chile on W; Bolivia, Paraguay on N; Brazil, Uruguay on NE. **Topography:** Mountains in W are the Andean, Central, Misiones, and Southern ranges. Aconcagua is the highest peak in the Western Hemisphere, alt. 22,834 ft. E of the Andes are heavily wooded plains, called the Gran Chaco in N, and the fertile, treeless Pampas in the central region. Patagonia, in S, is bleak and arid. Rio de la Plata, an estuary in NE, 170 by 140 mi, is mostly fresh water, from 2,485-mi Parana and 1,000-mi Uruguay rivers. **Capital:** Buenos Aires, 12,795,000. (the Senate has approved moving the capital to the Patagonia Region). **Cities (urban aggr.):** Córdoba, 1,452,000; Rosario, 1,203,000.

Government: Type: Republic. **Head of state and gov.:** Pres. Cristina Fernández de Kirchner; b. Feb. 19, 1953; in office: Dec. 10, 2007. **Local divisions:** 23 provinces, 1 federal district. **Defense budget:** $2.1 bil. **Active troops:** 76,000.

Economy: Industries: food proc., vehicles, consumer durables, textiles, chemicals. **Chief crops:** sunflower seeds, lemons, soybeans, grapes, corn. **Natural resources:** lead, zinc, tin, copper, iron ore, mang., oil, uranium. **Crude oil reserves:** 2.6 bil bbls. **Arable land:** 10%. **Livestock:** cattle: 50.8 mil; chickens: 96 mil; goats: 4.3 mil; pigs: 2.3 mil; sheep: 12.5 mil. **Fish catch:** 992,337 metric tons. **Electricity prod.:** 109.4 bil kWh. **Labor force** (2008 est.): agric. 1%, industry 23%, services 76%.

Finance: Monetary unit: Peso (ARS) (Oct. 2009: 3.83 = $1 U.S.). **GDP:** $573.9 bil; **per capita GDP:** $14,200; **GDP growth:** 6.8%. **Imports:** $54.6 bil; Brazil 32.7%, U.S. 15.3%, China 11.5%, Germany 5.5%. **Exports:** $70.6 bil; Brazil 22.3%, China 11.4%, U.S. 7.6%, Chile 6%, Spain 4.1%. **Tourism:** $4.3 bil. **Budget:** $61.3 bil. **Intl. reserves less gold:** $29.12 bil. **Gold:** 1.76 mil oz t. **Consumer prices:** 8.6%.

Transport: Railroad: Length: 19,517 mi. **Motor vehicles:** 5.2 mil pass. cars; 1.8 mil comm. vehicles. **Civil aviation:** 9.3 bil pass.-mi; 156 airports. **Chief ports:** Bahia Blanca, Buenos Aires, La Plata, Punta Colorado.

Communications: TV sets: 293 per 1,000 pop. **Radios:** 681 per 1,000 pop. **Telephone lines:** 9.6 mil. **Daily newspaper circ.** (2004): 35.5 per 1,000 pop. **Internet:** 11.2 mil users.

Health: Life expect.: 73.1 male; 79.8 female. **Births** (per 1,000 pop.): 18.1. **Deaths** (per 1,000 pop.): 7.4. **Natural inc.:** 1.07%. **Infant mortality** (per 1,000 live births): 11.8. **HIV rate:** 0.5%.

Education: Compulsory: ages 5-14. **Literacy:** 97.6%.

Major intl. organizations: UN (FAO, IBRD, ILO, IMF, IMO, WHO, WTO), OAS.

Embassy: 1600 New Hampshire Ave. NW 20009; 238-6401.

Website: www.argentina.ar

Nomadic Indians roamed the Pampas when Spaniards arrived, 1515-16, led by Juan Diaz de Solis. Nearly all the Indians were killed by the late 19th cent. The colonists won independence, 1816, and a long period of disorder ended in a strong centralized government.

Large-scale Italian, German, and Spanish immigration in the decades after 1880 spurred modernization. Social reforms were enacted in the 1920s, but military coups prevailed 1930-46 until the election of Gen. Juan Perón as president.

Perón, with his wife, Eva Duarte (d. 1952), effected labor reforms but also suppressed speech and press freedoms, closed religious schools, and ran the country into debt. A 1955 coup exiled Perón, who was followed by a series of military and civilian regimes. Perón returned in 1973 and was once more elected president. He died 10 months later, succeeded by his wife Isabel, who had been elected vice president, and who became the first woman head of state in the Western Hemisphere.

A military junta ousted Mrs. Perón in 1976 amid charges of corruption. Under a continuing state of siege, the army conducted a "dirty war" against guerrillas and leftists in which an estimated 30,000 people "disappeared." On Dec. 9, 1985, after a trial of 5 months and nearly 1,000 witnesses, 5 former junta members were found guilty of murder and human rights abuses.

Argentine troops seized control of the British-held Falkland Islands (Islas Malvinas) on Apr. 2, 1982. The British imposed an air and sea blockade around the Falklands. Fighting began May 1. British troops landed on East Falkland May 21. Argentine troops surrendered, June 14; Argentine Pres. Leopoldo Galtieri resigned June 17.

Democratic rule returned in 1983 with a victory by Raul Alfonsín's Radical Civic Union party. By 1989 the nation was plagued by severe financial and political problems, as hyperinflation sparked looting and rioting in several cities. The government of Peronist Pres. Carlos Saúl Menem, installed 1989, introduced harsh economic austerity measures.

About 85 people were killed and nearly 300 injured in the terrorist bombing of a Jewish cultural center in Buenos Aires, July 18, 1994. Following passage of a new constitution in Aug. 1994, Menem was reelected president on May 14, 1995.

Buenos Aires Mayor Fernando de la Rúa won the presidential election Oct. 24, 1999. A prolonged recession and a debt of more than $130 bil left Argentina facing an economic crisis in 2001, which austerity measures and IMF aid failed to remedy. After widespread rioting and looting Dec. 19, de la Rúa resigned.

A 2-week period of protests and political upheavals abated when Congress, Jan. 1, 2002, chose a Peronist, Eduardo Alberto Duhalde, to finish de la Rúa's term. Duhalde devalued the peso by cutting its ties with the U.S. dollar. Further economic decline and renewed protests led Duhalde July 2 to schedule an early presidential election for Mar. 2003; another Peronist, Néstor Kirchner, took office May 25, 2003, after Menem pulled out of a runoff election. Kirchner moved to end corruption and human rights abuses among the military and police. A new IMF aid deal, approved Sept. 10, 2003, rescued Argentina from default.

Fire at a Buenos Aires nightclub, Dec. 30, 2004, killed 194 people. The supreme court, June 14, 2005, overturned amnesty laws that had barred prosecution for "dirty war" crimes committed while the military ruled Argentina. Robust economic growth, 2004-05, allowed Argentina to repay its $9.57 bil debt to the IMF, Jan. 3, 2006. After Pres. Kirchner declined to seek a second term, his wife, Cristina Fernández de Kirchner, ran as the Peronist candidate and was elected president Oct. 28, 2007. Responding to mass protests by farmers, Argentina's senate voted July 17, 2008, to block Kirchner's proposed tax increase on agricultural exports. A candidate slate led by Néstor Kirchner suffered a humiliating defeat in legislative elections June 28, 2009, as the Peronists lost control of both houses of Congress.

Armenia
Republic of Armenia

People: Population: 2,967,004. **Age distrib.** (%): <15: 18.2; 65+: 10.6. **Pop. density:** 270.6 per sq mi, 104.5 per sq km. **Urban:** 64.1%. **Ethnic groups:** Armenian 98%, Yezidi (Kurd) 1%, Russian 1%. **Principal languages:** Armenian, Yezidi, Russian. **Chief religions:** Armenian Apostolic 95%, other Christian 4%.

Geography: Total area: 11,484 sq mi, 29,743 sq km; **Land area:** 10,965 sq mi, 28,400 sq km. **Location:** SW Asia. **Neighbors:** Georgia on N, Azerbaijan on E, Iran on S, Turkey on W. **Topography:** Mountainous with many peaks above 10,000 ft. **Capital:** Yerevan, 1,102,000.

Government: Type: Republic. **Head of state:** Pres. Serzh Sargsyan; b. June 30, 1954; in office: Apr. 9, 2008. **Head of gov.:** Prime Min. Tigran Sargsyan; b. Jan. 29, 1960; in office; Apr. 9, 2008. **Local divisions:** 10 provinces, 1 city. **Defense budget:** $296 mil. **Active troops:** 42,080.

Economy: Industries: diamond proc., machine tools & machines, electric motors, tires, knitted wear. **Chief crops:** grapes, vegetables. **Natural resources:** gold, copper, molybd., zinc, bauxite. **Arable land:** 17%. **Livestock:** cattle: 620,200; chickens: 3.9 mil; goats: 42,922; pigs: 152,791; sheep: 589,972. **Fish catch** (est.): 4,566 metric tons. **Electricity prod.:** 5.6 bil kWh. **Labor force** (2006 est.): agric. 46.2%, industry 15.6%, services 38.2%.

Finance: Monetary unit: Dram (AMD) (Oct. 2009: 384.98 = $1 U.S.). **GDP:** $18.8 bil; **per capita GDP:** $6,300; **GDP growth:** 6.8%. **Imports:** $3.8 bil; Russia 19.3%, China 8.7%, Ukraine 7%, Turkey 6.1%, Germany 5.8%, U.S. 4.9%, Iran 4.6%. **Exports:** $1.1 bil; Russia 20.2%, Germany 17.2%, Netherlands 12.2%, Belgium 8.5%, Georgia 7.7%, Bulgaria 5.7%, U.S. 4.9%. **Tourism** (2006): $271 mil. **Budget:** $1.7 bil. **Intl. reserves less gold:** $913 mil. **Gold:** NA. **Consumer prices:** 8.9%.

Transport: Railroad: Length: 525 mi. **Civil aviation:** 665.5 mil pass.-mi; 10 airports.

Communications: TV sets: 241 per 1,000 pop. **Radios:** 239 per 1,000 pop. **Telephone lines:** 650,000. **Daily newspaper circ.** (2004): 7.6 per 1,000 pop. **Internet:** 196,000 users.

Health: Life expect.: 68.8 male; 76.5 female. **Births** (per 1,000 pop.): 12.5. **Deaths** (per 1,000 pop.): 8.3. **Natural inc.:** 0.42%. **Infant mortality** (per 1,000 live births): 20.9. **HIV rate:** 0.1%.

Education: Compulsory: ages 7-14. **Literacy:** 99.5%.

Major intl. organizations: UN (FAO, IBRD, ILO, IMF, WHO, WTO), CIS, OSCE.

Embassy: 2225 R St. NW 20008; 319-1976.

Website: www.gov.am

Ancient Armenia extended into parts of what are now Turkey and Iran. Present-day Armenia was set up as a Soviet republic Apr. 2, 1921. It joined Georgian and Azerbaijan SSRs Mar. 12, 1922, to form the Transcaucasian SFSR, which became part of the USSR Dec. 30, 1922. Armenia became a constituent republic of the USSR Dec. 5, 1936. An earthquake struck Armenia Dec. 7,

1988; approximately 55,000 were killed and several cities and towns were left in ruins.

Armenia declared independence Sept. 23, 1991, and became an independent state when the USSR disbanded Dec. 26, 1991. Both mostly Christian Armenia and mostly Muslim Azerbaijan claimed Nagorno-Karabakh, an enclave in Azerbaijan that has an ethnic Armenian majority; it seceded from Azerbaijan in 1988. A 1992-94 war that cost 30,000 lives ended in a cease-fire with Armenian forces in control of the enclave. Voters in the breakaway region approved a pro-independence constitution Dec. 10, 2006, but the referendum was rejected by the EU and OSCE.

Voters approved, July 5, 1995, a new constitution increasing presidential powers. Pres. Levon Ter-Petrosian won reelection on Sept. 22, 1996, amid claims of fraud; he resigned Feb. 3, 1998, in a conflict over Nagorno-Karabakh. Robert Kocharian, a nationalist born in the disputed region, won the presidency on Mar. 30, 1998. Gunmen stormed Parliament Oct. 27, 1999, killing Prime Min. Vazgen Sarkissian and 7 others. Kocharian won a second term Mar. 5, 2003, in a runoff vote viewed as flawed by opposition groups and Western observers.

An Armenian airliner crashed into the Black Sea, May 3, 2006, killing all 113 people on board. Prime Min. Andranik Margaryan died of a heart attack Mar. 25, 2007, and was replaced by Def. Min. Serzh Sargsyan. He defeated Ter-Petrosian in the presidential election of Feb. 19, 2008; opposition protests in Yerevan were forcibly suppressed Mar. 1, leaving 8 civilians and a police officer dead and 450 injured. A 20-day state of emergency was lifted Mar. 21, and Sargsyan took office Apr. 9. Armenian and Turkish officials established diplomatic ties Oct. 11, 2009, bridging long-standing bitterness over the killing of more than 1 mil Armenians by Ottoman Turks in 1915-18.

Australia
Commonwealth of Australia

People: Population: 21,262,641. **Age distrib.** (%): <15: 18.6; 65+: 13.5. **Pop. density:** 7.2 per sq mi, 2.8 per sq km. **Urban:** 88.2%. **Ethnic groups:** White 92%, Asian 7%, aboriginal & other 1%. **Principal languages:** English, Chinese, Italian, other. **Chief religions:** Roman Catholic 26%, Anglican 21%, other Christian 21%, unspecified 13%, none 15%.

Geography: Total area: 2,967,909 sq mi, 7,686,850 sq km; **Land area:** 2,941,299 sq mi, 7,617,930 sq km. **Location:** SE of Asia, Indian O. is W and S, Pacific O. (Coral, Tasman seas) is E; they meet N of Australia in Timor and Arafura seas. Tasmania lies 150 mi S of Victoria state, across Bass Strait. **Neighbors:** Nearest are Indonesia, Papua New Guinea on N; Solomons, Fiji, and New Zealand on E. **Topography:** An island continent. The Great Dividing Range along the E coast has Mt. Kosciusko, 7,310 ft. The W plateau rises to 2,000 ft, with arid areas in the Great Sandy and Great Victoria deserts. The NW part of Western Australia and Northern Terr. are arid and hot. The NE has heavy rainfall and Cape York Peninsula has jungles. **Capital:** Canberra, 378,000. **Cities (urban aggr.):** Sydney, 4,327,000; Melbourne, 3,728,000; Brisbane, 1,860,000; Perth, 1,532,000; Adelaide, 1,145,000.

Government: Type: Democratic, federal state system. **Head of state:** Queen Elizabeth II, represented by Gov.-Gen. Quentin Bryce; b. Dec. 23, 1942; in office: Sept. 5, 2008. **Head of gov.:** Prime Min. Kevin Rudd; b. Sept. 21, 1957; in office: Dec. 3, 2007. **Local divisions:** 6 states, 2 territories. **Defense budget:** $20.2 bil. **Active troops:** 54,747.

Economy: Industries: mining, industrial & transp. equip., food proc., chemicals, steel. **Chief crops:** wheat, barley, sugarcane, fruits. **Natural resources:** bauxite, coal, iron ore, copper, tin, gold, silver, uranium, nickel, tungsten, mineral sands, lead, zinc, diamonds, nat. gas, oil. **Crude oil reserves:** 1.5 bil bbls. **Other resources:** Wool (world's leading producer), beef. **Arable land:** 6%. **Livestock:** cattle: 28 mil; chickens: 97.4 mil; goats: 518,024; pigs: 2.6 mil; sheep: 85.7 mil. **Fish catch:** 241,735 metric tons. **Electricity prod.:** 237.1 bil kWh. **Labor force** (2005 est.): agric. 3.6%, industry 21.1%, services 75%.

Finance: Monetary unit: Dollars (AUD) (Oct. 2009: 1.12 = $1 U.S.). **GDP:** $800.2 bil; **per capita GDP:** $38,100; **GDP growth:** 2.3%. **Imports:** $193.3 bil; China 15.4%, U.S. 12%, Japan 9.1%, Singapore 7%, Germany 5%, Thailand 4.5%, UK 4.3%, Malaysia 4.1%. **Exports:** $190.2 bil; Japan 22.2%, China 14.6%, S. Korea 8.2%, India 6.1%, U.S. 5.5%, New Zealand 4.3%, UK 4.2%. **Tourism:** $22.3 bil. **Budget:** $309.1 bil. **Intl. reserves less gold:** $19.93 bil. **Gold:** 2.57 mil oz t. **Consumer prices:** 4.4%.

Transport: Railroad: Length: 23,522 mi. **Motor vehicles:** 10.9 mil pass. cars; 2.6 mil comm. vehicles. **Civil aviation:** 561.9 bil pass.-mi; 325 airports. **Chief ports:** Brisbane, Fremantle, Gladstone, Melbourne, Sydney.

Communications: TV sets: 716 per 1,000 pop. **Radios:** 1,391 per 1,000 pop. **Telephone lines:** 9.4 mil. **Daily newspaper circ.** (2004): 155.1 per 1,000 pop. **Internet:** 15.2 mil users.

Health: Life expect.: 79.2 male; 84 female. **Births** (per 1,000 pop.): 12.6. **Deaths** (per 1,000 pop.): 6.7. **Natural inc.:** 0.59%. **Infant mortality** (per 1,000 live births): 4.8. **HIV rate:** 0.2%.

Education: Compulsory: ages 5-15. **Literacy:** 93.4%.

Major intl. organizations: UN and all of its specialized agencies, APEC, the Commonwealth, OECD.
Embassy: 1601 Massachusetts Ave. NW 20036; 797-3000.
Website: www.australia.gov.au

Australia harbors many plant and animal species not found elsewhere, including kangaroos, koalas, platypuses, dingos (wild dogs), Tasmanian devils (raccoon-like marsupials), wombats (bear-like marsupials), and barking and frilled lizards.

Capt. James Cook explored the eastern coast in 1770, when the continent was inhabited by a variety of indigenous peoples. The first European settlers, beginning in 1788, were mostly convicts, soldiers, and government officials. By 1830, Britain had claimed the entire continent, and the immigration of free settlers began to accelerate. The Commonwealth was proclaimed Jan. 1, 1901. Northern Terr. was granted limited self-rule July 1, 1978.

State/territory, capital	Area (sq mi)	Population (Dec. 2008 est.)
New South Wales, Sydney	309,500	7,041,400
Victoria, Melbourne	87,900	5,364,800
Queensland, Brisbane	666,990	4,349,500
Western Australia, Perth	975,100	2,204,000
South Australia, Adelaide	379,900	1,612,000
Tasmania, Hobart	26,200	500,300
Australian Capital Terr., Canberra	900	347,800
Northern Terr., Darwin	519,800	221,700

Racially discriminatory immigration policies were abandoned in 1973, after 3 mil Europeans (half British) had entered since 1945. Indigenous peoples, 90% of them aborigines, number more than 500,000; in the Northern Territory they account for about 28% of the population and hold about 46% of the land. They remain economically disadvantaged.

Australia's agricultural success makes the country among the top exporters of beef, lamb, wool, and wheat. Major mineral deposits have been developed, largely for export. Industrialization has been completed. The nation endured a deep recession 1990-93 but has rebounded strongly.

The Labor Party won a majority in Feb. 1983 general elections and was reelected in 1984, 1987, 1990, and 1993. After an election that focused mainly on economic issues, conservatives swept into power in elections Mar. 2, 1996. Incumbent Prime Min. John Howard retained power in the 1998, 2001, and 2004 elections.

Australia led an international peacekeeping force into Timor in Sept. 1999. In a referendum Nov. 6, voters rejected a proposal that would have made Australia a republic. Sydney hosted the Olympics Sept. 15-Oct. 1, 2000.

Australian troops fought in U.S.-led military operations in Afghanistan (2001) and Iraq (2003). Some 2,000 Australian peacekeepers began arriving in the Solomon Isl., July 24, 2003; nearly all had been withdrawn by mid-2005. In race riots in Sydney suburbs, Dec. 11-12, 2005, thousands of white youths assaulted people of Middle Eastern ancestry, who then retaliated against whites. Australian troops were dispatched, 2006, to suppress disorder in the Solomon Isl. In April and Timor in May; as of mid-2009 about 650 Australian military personnel remained in Timor and 110 in the Solomon Isl.

Pledging to pull combat troops out of Iraq and to ratify the Kyoto Protocol against global warming, Kevin Rudd led the Labor Party to victory in parliamentary elections Nov. 24, 2007. Australia's combat mission in Iraq ended July 31, 2008. Quentin Bryce, the nation's first female governor-general, was sworn in Sept. 5.

Australian External Territories

Norfolk Isl., area 13.4 sq mi, pop. (2009 est.) 2,141, was taken over, 1914. The soil is very fertile, suitable for citrus, bananas, and coffee. Many of the inhabitants are descendants of the *Bounty* mutineers, moved to Norfolk 1856 from Pitcairn Isl. Australia offered the island limited home rule in 1978.

Coral Sea Isls. Territory, area less than 1.2 sq mi, is administered from Norfolk Isl.

Territory of **Ashmore and Cartier Isls.**, area 1.9 sq mi, in the Indian O., came under Australian authority 1934 and are administered as part of Northern Territory. **Heard Isl. and McDonald Isls.**, area 159.1 sq mi, are administered by the Dept. of Science.

Cocos (Keeling) Isls., 27 small coral islands in the Indian O. 1,750 mi NW of Australia. Pop. (2009 est.) 596; area 5.4 sq mi. The residents voted to become part of Australia, Apr. 1984.

Christmas Isl., area 52.1 sq mi (2009 est.) 1,402; 230 mi S of Java, was transferred by Britain in 1958. It has phosphate deposits.

Australian Antarctic Territory was claimed by Australia in 1933, including 2,362,000 sq mi of territory S of 60th parallel S Lat. and between 160th-45th meridians E Long. It does not include Adelie Coast.

Austria
Republic of Austria

People: Population: 8,210,281. **Age distrib.** (%): <15: 14.5; 65+: 18. **Pop. density:** 257.9 per sq mi, 99.6 per sq km. **Urban:** 66.5%. **Ethnic groups:** Austrian 91%, fmr. Yugoslav (incl. Croatian, Slovene, Serb, Bosniak) 4%, Turk 2%. **Principal languages:** German (official), Turkish, Serbian, Croatian (official in Burgenland). **Chief religions:** Roman Catholic 74%, Protestant 5%, Muslim 4%, none 12%.

Geography: Total area: 32,382 sq mi, 83,870 sq km; **Land area:** 31,832 sq mi, 82,444 sq km. **Location:** In S Central Europe. **Neighbors:** Switzerland, Liechtenstein on W; Germany, Czech Rep. on N; Slovakia, Hungary on E; Slovenia, Italy on S. **Topography:** Austria is primarily mountainous, with the Alps and foothills covering the western and southern provinces. The eastern provinces and Vienna are located in the Danube River Basin. **Capital:** Vienna, 2,315,000.

Government: Type: Federal republic. **Head of state:** Pres. Heinz Fischer; b. Oct. 9, 1938; in office: July 8, 2004. **Head of gov.:** Chancellor Werner Faymann; b. May 4, 1960; in office; Dec. 2, 2008. **Local divisions:** 9 bundeslaender (states). **Defense budget:** $3.6 bil. **Active troops:** 34,900.

Economy: Industries: constr., machinery, vehicles & parts, food, metals, chemicals. **Chief crops:** grains, potatoes, sugar beets, wine. **Natural resources:** oil, coal, lignite, timber, iron ore, copper, zinc, antimony. magnesite. **Crude oil reserves:** 50 mil bbls. **Arable land:** 17%. **Livestock:** cattle: 2 mil; chickens: 13.6 mil; goats: 53,108; pigs: 3.1 mil; sheep: 312,375. **Fish catch:** 2,875 metric tons. **Electricity prod.:** 58.8 bil kWh. **Labor force** (2005 est.): agric. 5.5%, industry 27.5%, services 67%.

Finance: Monetary unit: Euro (EUR) (Oct. 2009: 0.68 = $1 U.S.). **GDP:** $329.5 bil; **per capita GDP:** $40,200; **GDP growth:** 1.8%. **Imports:** $168.9 bil; Germany 44.4%, Italy 7.1%, Switzerland 5.2%, Netherlands 4.1%. **Exports:** $163.6 bil; Germany 29.4%, Italy 8.6%, U.S. 4.3%, Switzerland 4.2%. **Tourism:** $18.9 bil. **Budget:** $181.8 bil. **Intl. reserves less gold:** $5.79 bil. **Gold:** 9 mil oz t. **Consumer prices:** 3.2%.

Transport: Railroad: Length: 3,976 mi. **Motor vehicles:** 4.2 mil pass. cars; 367,000 comm. vehicles. **Civil aviation:** 11.7 bil pass.-mi; 25 airports. **Chief ports:** Enns, Krems, Linz, Vienna.

Communications: TV sets: 526 per 1,000 pop. **Radios:** 751 per 1,000 pop. **Telephone lines:** 3.3 mil. **Daily newspaper circ.** (2004): 311.4 per 1,000 pop. **Internet:** 5.4 mil users.

Health: Life expect.: 76.5 male; 82.4 female. **Births** (per 1,000 pop.): 8.7. **Deaths** (per 1,000 pop.): 9.9. **Natural inc.:** −0.12%. **Infant mortality** (per 1,000 live births): 4.5. **HIV rate:** 0.2%.

Education: Compulsory: ages 6-14. **Literacy:** 98%.

Major intl. organizations: UN and all of its specialized agencies, EU, OECD, OSCE.

Embassy: 3524 International Ct. NW 20008; 895-6700.
Website: www.austria.gv.at

Rome conquered Austrian lands from Celtic tribes around 15 BC. In 788 the territory was incorporated into Charlemagne's empire. By 1300, the House of Hapsburg had gained control; they added vast territories in all parts of Europe to their realm in the next few hundred years.

Austrian dominance of Germany was undermined in the 18th cent. and ended by Prussia by 1866. But the Congress of Vienna, 1815, confirmed Austrian control of a large empire in southeast Europe consisting of Germans, Hungarians, Slavs, Italians, and others. The dual Austro-Hungarian monarchy was established in 1867, giving autonomy to Hungary and almost 50 years of peace.

World War I, started after the June 28, 1914, assassination of Archduke Franz Ferdinand, the Hapsburg heir, by a Serbian nationalist, destroyed the empire. By 1918 Austria was reduced to a small republic, with the borders it has today.

Nazi Germany, ruled by the Austrian-born Adolf Hitler, annexed Austria Mar. 13, 1938. The republic was reestablished in 1945, under Allied occupation. Full independence and neutrality were restored in 1955. Austria joined the EU Jan. 1, 1995.

The rise of the right-wing, anti-immigrant Austrian Freedom Party challenged the dominance of the Austrian Social Democratic Party in the late 1990s. When Freedom Party members joined the cabinet, Feb. 4, 2000, the EU imposed political sanctions on Austria for 7 months. Social Democrats won the parliamentary elections of Oct. 1, 2006; they held onto their plurality in elections Sept. 28, 2008, although far-right parties made gains.

Azerbaijan
Republic of Azerbaijan

People: Population: 8,238,672. **Age distrib.** (%): <15: 23.9; 65+: 6.7. **Pop. density:** 247.8 per sq mi, 95.7 per sq km. **Urban:** 51.5%. **Ethnic groups:** Azeri 91%, Dagestani 2%, Russian 2%. **Principal languages:** Azerbaijani (Azeri) (official), Lezgi, Russian. **Chief religions:** Muslim 93%, Russian Orthodox 3%, Armenian Orthodox 2%.

Geography: Total area: 33,436 sq mi, 86,600 sq km; **Land area:** 33,243 sq mi, 86,100 sq km. **Location:** SW Asia. **Neighbors:**

Russia, Georgia on N; Iran on S; Armenia on W; Caspian Sea on E. **Topography:** The Great Caucasus Mts. in N, Karabakh Upland in W border the Kur-Abas lowland; climate is arid except in the subtropical SE. **Capital:** Baku, 1,892,000.

Government: Type: Republic. **Head of state:** Pres. Ilham Aliyev; b. Dec. 24, 1961; in office: Oct. 31, 2003. **Head of gov.:** Prime Min. Artur Rasizade; b. Feb. 26, 1935; in office: Nov. 4, 2003. **Local division:** 59 rayons, 11 cities, 1 autonomous republic. **Defense budget:** $936 mil. **Active troops:** 66,940.

Economy: Industries: oil & nat, gas, oil field equip., steel, iron ore, cement. **Chief crops:** cotton, grain, rice, grapes. **Natural resources:** oil, nat. gas, iron ore, nonferrous metals, bauxite. **Crude oil reserves:** 7 bil bbls. **Arable land:** 21%. **Livestock:** cattle: 2.1 mil; chickens: 18 mil; goats: 577,809; pigs: 21,317; sheep: 7.3 mil. **Fish catch:** 3,056 metric tons. **Electricity prod.:** 21.8 bil kWh. **Labor force** (2005): agric. 39.3%, industry 12.1%, services 48.6%.

Finance: Monetary unit: New Manat (AZN) (Oct. 2009: 0.80 = $1 U.S.). **GDP:** $77.6 bil; **per capita GDP:** $9,500; **GDP growth:** 10.8%. **Imports:** $7.6 bil; Russia 18.9%, Turkey 18.2%, Germany 8.5%, China 6.3%, UK 6.2%, Ukraine 5.3%, Italy 4.5%. **Exports:** $30.6 bil; Italy 24.9%, U.S. 17.6%, Germany 10.8%, France 10.1%, Czech Republic 6.2%, Canada 4.9%. **Tourism:** $178 mil. **Budget:** $9.3 bil. **Intl. reserves less gold:** $4. **Gold:** NA. **Consumer prices:** 53.4%.

Transport: Railroad: Length: 1,319 mi. **Motor vehicles:** 479,000 pass. cars; 126,400 comm. vehicles. **Civil aviation:** 889.2 mil pass.-mi; 27 airports. **Chief port:** Baku.

Communications: TV sets: 257 per 1,000 pop. **Radios:** 23 per 1,000 pop. **Telephone lines:** 1.3 mil. **Daily newspaper circ.** (2001): 16.1 per 1,000 pop. **Internet:** 1.5 mil users.

Health: Life expect.: 62.2 male; 71 female. **Births** (per 1,000 pop.): 17.5. **Deaths** (per 1,000 pop.): 8.3. **Natural inc.:** 0.92%. **Infant mortality** (per 1,000 live births): 56.4. **HIV rate:** 0.2%.

Education: Compulsory: ages 6-16. **Literacy:** 99.4%.

Major intl. organizations: UN (FAO, IBRD, ILO, IMF, IMO, WHO), CIS, OSCE.

Embassy: 2741 34th St. NW 20008; 337-3500.

Website: www.president.az

Azerbaijan was the home of Scythian tribes and part of the Roman Empire. Overrun by Turks in the 11th cent. and conquered by Russia in 1806 and 1813, it joined the USSR Dec. 30, 1922, and became a constituent republic in 1936. Azerbaijan declared independence Aug. 30, 1991, and became an independent state when the Soviet Union disbanded Dec. 26, 1991.

Nagorno-Karabakh, an enclave with a majority population of ethnic Armenians, seceded from Azerbaijan in 1988, triggering a war between mostly Muslim Azerbaijan and most Christian Armenia, 1992-94, in which 30,000 lives were lost (see Armenia).

Voters approved a new constitution expanding presidential powers, Nov. 12, 1995. Pres. Haydar Aliyev, a pro-Russian former Communist, was reelected Oct. 11, 1998, but international monitors called the vote seriously flawed.

The dying Pres. Aliyev named his son Ilham prime minister Aug. 4, 2003. The younger Aliyev won the presidential election of Oct. 15, in a vote considered fraudulent by international observers; he responded to violent protests Oct. 16 by arresting hundreds of opposition leaders and their supporters. Serious abuses also marred the parliamentary elections of Nov. 6, 2005, won by parties loyal to Aliyev. The opening May 25, 2005, of the Baku-Tbilisi-Ceyhan pipeline, providing an outlet for Azerbaijan's vast Caspian oil reserves, transformed the nation's economy.

Pres. Ilham Aliyev won a 2nd term Oct. 15, 2008, in an election boycotted by the main opposition parties. A constitutional amendment abolishing presidential term limits was approved by referendum Mar. 18, 2009.

The Bahamas
Commonwealth of The Bahamas

People: Population: 309,156. **Age distrib.** (%): <15: 25.9; 65+: 6.9. **Pop. density:** 79.5 per sq mi, 30.7 per sq km. **Urban:** 83.1%. **Ethnic groups:** Black 85%, white 12%, Asian & Hispanic 3%. **Principal languages:** English (official), Creole (among Haitian immigrants). **Chief religions:** Baptist 35%, Anglican 15%, Roman Catholic 14%, other Christian 15%.

Geography: Total area: 5,382 sq mi, 13,940 sq km; **Land area:** 3,888 sq mi, 10,070 sq km. **Location:** In Atlantic O., E of Florida. **Neighbors:** Nearest are U.S. on W, Cuba on S. **Topography:** Nearly 700 islands (29 inhabited) and over 2,000 islets in the W Atlantic O. extend 760 mi NW to SE. **Capital:** Nassau, 240,000.

Government: Type: Independent commonwealth. **Head of state:** Queen Elizabeth II, represented by Gov.-Gen. Arthur Dion Hanna; b. Mar. 7, 1928; in office: Feb. 1, 2006. **Head of gov.:** Prime Min. Hubert Alexander Ingraham; b. Aug. 4, 1947; in office: May 4, 2007. **Local divisions:** 21 districts. **Defense budget:** $58 mil. **Active troops:** 860.

Economy: Industries: tourism, banking, cement, oil transshipment, salt, rum. **Chief crops:** citrus, vegetables. **Natural resources:** salt, aragonite, timber. **Arable land:** 1%. **Livestock:** cattle: 750; chickens: 3 mil; goats: 14,500; pigs: 5,000; sheep: 6,500.

Fish catch: 3,815 metric tons. **Electricity prod.:** 1.9 bil kWh. **Labor force** (2005 est.): agric. 5%, industry 5%, tourism 50%, other services 40%.

Finance: Monetary unit: Dollar (BSD) (Oct. 2009: 1.00 = $1 U.S.). **GDP:** $9.1 bil; **per capita GDP:** $29,600; **GDP growth:** –1.5%. **Imports** (2006): $2.4 bil; U.S. 27.1%, Japan 17.8%, S. Korea 14.7%, Singapore 7.9%, Venezuela 5.4%. **Exports** (2006): $674 mil; U.S. 20.8%, Singapore 18.2%, Poland 17.5%, Germany 7.3%, Japan 7.2%, Guatemala 5.5%, Switzerland 4.7%. **Tourism:** $2.2 bil. **Budget** (FY04/05): $1.03 bil. **Intl. reserves less gold:** $369 mil. **Gold:** NA. **Consumer prices:** 4.5%.

Transport: Motor vehicles: 67,100 pass. cars; 13,700 comm. vehicles. **Civil aviation:** 172.1 mil pass.-mi; 23 airports. **Chief ports:** Freeport, Nassau.

Communications: TV sets: 243 per 1,000 pop. **Radios:** 739 per 1,000 pop. **Telephone lines:** 133,000. **Internet:** 142,000 users.

Health: Life expect.: 62.5 male; 69 female. **Births** (per 1,000 pop.): 17.1. **Deaths** (per 1,000 pop.): 9.2. **Natural inc.:** 0.78%. **Infant mortality** (per 1,000 live births): 23.7. **HIV rate:** 3%.

Education: Compulsory: ages 5-16. **Literacy:** 95.6%.

Major intl. organizations: UN (FAO, IBRD, ILO, IMF, IMO, WHO), Caricom, the Commonwealth, OAS.

Embassy: 2220 Massachusetts Ave. NW 20008; 319-2660.

Website: www.bahamas.gov.bs

Christopher Columbus first set foot in the New World on San Salvador (Watling Isl.) in 1492, when Arawak Indians inhabited the islands. British settlement began in 1647; the islands became a British colony in 1783. Internal self-government was granted in 1964; full independence within the Commonwealth was attained July 10, 1973. International banking and investment management have become major industries alongside tourism.

Bahrain
Kingdom of Bahrain

People: Population: 727,785. **Age distrib.** (%): <15: 25.9; 65+: 3.9. **Pop. density:** 2,834.5 per sq mi, 1,094.4 per sq km. **Urban:** 88.4%. **Ethnic groups:** Bahraini 62%, non-Bahraini 38%. **Principal languages:** Arabic, English, Farsi, Urdu. **Chief religions:** Muslim (Shi'a & Sunni) 81%, Christian 9%, other 10%.

Geography: Total area: 257 sq mi, 665 sq km; **Land area:** 257 sq mi, 665 sq km. **Location:** SW Asia, in Persian Gulf. **Neighbors:** Nearest are Saudi Arabia on W, Qatar on E. **Topography:** Bahrain Island, and several adjacent, smaller islands, are flat, hot, and humid, with little rain. **Capital:** Manama (Al-Manamah), 157,000.

Government: Type: Constitutional monarchy. **Head of state:** King Hamad bin Isa al-Khalifa; b. Jan. 28, 1950; in office: as emir Mar. 6, 1999; as king Feb. 14, 2002. **Head of gov.:** Prime Min. Khalifa bin Sulman al-Khalifa; b. Nov. 24, 1936; in office: Jan. 19, 1970. **Local divisions:** 12 municipalities. **Defense budget:** $539 mil. **Active troops:** 8,200.

Economy: Industries: oil proc. & refining, aluminum smelting, iron pelletization, fertilizers, Islamic & offshore banking. **Chief crops:** fruit, vegetables. **Natural resources:** oil, nat. gas, fish, pearls. **Crude oil reserves:** 124.6 mil bbls. **Arable land:** 3%. **Livestock:** cattle: 9,000; chickens: 470,000; goats: 23,000; sheep: 41,000. **Fish catch:** 15,013 metric tons. **Electricity prod.:** 9.2 bil kWh. **Labor force** (1997 est.): agric. 1%, industry 79%, services 20%.

Finance: Monetary unit: Dinar (BHD) (Oct. 2009: 0.38 = $1 U.S.). **GDP:** $26.8 bil; **per capita GDP:** $37,300; **GDP growth:** 6.3%. **Imports:** $14.3 bil; Saudi Arabia 27.5%, Japan 9.1%, U.S. 8.1%, China 5.9%, Germany 5%, UK 4.6%. **Exports:** $17.5 bil; Saudi Arabia 3.5%, UAE 2.3%, U.S. 1.9%. **Tourism:** (2006) $1 bil. **Budget:** $5.2 bil. **Intl. reserves less gold:** NA. **Gold** (2007): 150,000 oz t. **Consumer prices:** 3.5%.

Transport: Motor vehicles: 187,000 pass. cars; 38,400 comm. vehicles. **Civil aviation:** 3.6 bil pass.-mi (incl. Gulf Air traffic apportionment); 3 airports. **Chief ports:** Mina Salman, Sitrah.

Communications: TV sets: 446 per 1,000 pop. **Radios:** 64 per 1,000 pop. **Telephone lines:** 220,000. **Internet:** 402,900 users.

Health: Life expect.: 72.4 male; 77.5 female. **Births** (per 1,000 pop.): 17.3. **Deaths** (per 1,000 pop.): 4.3. **Natural inc.:** 1.3%. **Infant mortality** (per 1,000 live births): 15.6. **HIV rate:** NA.

Education: Compulsory: ages 6-15. **Literacy:** 88.8%.

Major intl. organizations: UN (FAO, IBRD, ILO, IMF, IMO, WHO, WTO), AL.

Embassy: 3502 International Dr. NW 20008; 342-1111.

Website: www.e.gov.bh

Long ruled by the Khalifa family, Bahrain was a British protectorate from 1861 to Aug. 15, 1971, when it regained independence.

Pearls, shrimp, fruits, and vegetables were the mainstays of the economy until oil was discovered in 1932. Crude oil production has declined since the 1970s, but natural gas output has grown and international banking has thrived. Shiite dissidents have clashed with the Sunni-led government since 1996.

Emir Hamad bin Isa al-Khalifa proclaimed himself king Feb. 14, 2002. Local elections in May 2002 marked the first time Bahraini women were allowed to vote and run for office. The first female judge was appointed June 6, 2006.

Bangladesh
People's Republic of Bangladesh
People: Population: 156,050,883. **Age distrib.** (%): <15: 34.6; 65+: 4. **Pop. density:** 3,018.2 per sq mi, 1,165.3 per sq mi, 1,146.6 per sq km. **Urban:** 25.7%. **Ethnic groups:** Bengali 98%. **Principal languages:** Bangla, or Bengali (official), English. **Chief religions:** Muslim 83%, Hindu 16%.

Geography: Total area: 55,599 sq mi, 144,000 sq km; **Land area:** 51,703 sq mi, 133,910 sq km. **Location:** In S Asia, on N bend of Bay of Bengal. **Neighbors:** India nearly surrounds country on W, N, E; Myanmar on SE. **Topography:** The country is mostly a low plain cut by the Ganges and Brahmaputra rivers and their delta. The land is alluvial and marshy along the coast, with hills only in the extreme SE and NE. A tropical monsoon climate prevails, among the rainiest in the world. **Capital:** Dhaka, 13,485,000. **Cities (urban aggr.):** Chittagong, 4,529,000; Khulna, 1,553,000.

Government: Type: Parliamentary democracy. **Head of state:** Pres. Zillur Rahman; b. Mar. 9, 1929; in office: Feb. 12, 2009. **Head of gov.:** Prime Min. Sheikh Hasina Wazed; b. Sept. 28, 1947; in office: Jan. 6, 2009. **Local divisions:** 6 divisions. **Defense budget:** $998 mil. **Active troops:** 157,053.

Economy: Industries: cotton textiles, jute, garments, tea proc., newsprint, cement, chemical fertilizer, light engineering, sugar. **Chief crops:** rice, jute, tea, wheat, sugarcane, potatoes, tobacco. **Natural resources:** nat. gas, timber, coal. **Crude oil reserves:** 28 mil bbls. **Arable land:** 55%. **Livestock:** cattle: 25.3 mil; chickens: 206.9 mil; goats: 52.5 mil; sheep: 1.6 mil. **Fish catch:** 2.44 mil metric tons. **Electricity prod.:** 22.9 bil kWh. **Labor force** (FY95/96): agric. 63%, industry 11%, services 26%.

Finance: Monetary unit: Taka (BDT) (Oct. 2009: 68.70 = $1 U.S.). **GDP:** $224 bil; **per capita GDP:** $1,500; **GDP growth:** 4.9%. **Imports:** $19.6 bil; China 14.7%, India 14.7%, Kuwait 7.5%, Singapore 7.1%, Japan 4.1%. **Exports:** $14 bil; U.S. 21%, Germany 13.2%, UK 8.6%, France 6.3%, Netherlands 4.7%. **Tourism:** $76 mil. **Budget:** $9.8 bil. **Intl. reserves less gold:** $3.69 bil. **Gold:** 110,000 oz t. **Consumer prices:** 8.9%.

Transport: Railroad: Length: 1,720 mi. **Motor vehicles:** 65,000 pass. cars; 145,900 comm. vehicles. **Civil aviation:** 3.3 bil pass.-mi; 15 airports. **Chief ports:** Chittagong, Mongla Port.

Communications: TV sets: 7 per 1,000 pop. **Radios:** 50 per 1,000 pop. **Telephone lines:** 1.3 mil. **Internet:** 556,000 users.

Health: Life expect.: 63.1 male; 63.3 female. **Births** (per 1,000 pop.): 28.9. **Deaths** (per 1,000 pop.): 8. **Natural inc.:** 2.09%. **Infant mortality** (per 1,000 live births): 57.5. **HIV rate:** NA.

Education: Compulsory: ages 6-10. **Literacy:** 53.5%.

Major intl. organizations: UN (FAO, IBRD, ILO, IMF, IMO, WHO, WTO), the Commonwealth.

Embassy: 3510 International Dr. NW 20008; 244-0183.

Website: www.bangladesh.gov.bd

Muslim invaders conquered the formerly Hindu area in the 12th cent. British rule lasted from the 18th cent. to 1947, when East Bengal became part of Pakistan.

Opposing domination by West Pakistan, the Awami League, based in the East, won control of the National Assembly in 1971. Assembly sessions were postponed; riots broke out. Pakistani troops attacked Mar. 25; Bangladesh independence was proclaimed the next day. In the ensuing civil war, 1 mil died and 10 mil fled to India.

War between India and Pakistan broke out Dec. 3, 1971. Pakistan surrendered in the East on Dec. 16. Mujibur Rahman, known as Sheikh Mujib, became prime minister; he was killed in a coup Aug. 15, 1975.

On May 30, 1981, Pres. Ziaur Rahman was killed in an unsuccessful coup attempt by army rivals. Vice Pres. Abdus Sattar assumed the presidency but was ousted in a coup led by army chief of staff Gen. H. M. Ershad, Mar. 1982. Ershad declared Bangladesh an Islamic Republic in 1988; a parliamentary system of government was adopted in 1991. A cyclone struck Apr. 1991, killing over 131,000 people and causing $2.7 bil in damages.

Political turmoil led to the resignation, Mar. 30, 1996, of Prime Min. Khaleda Zia, the widow of Ziaur Rahman. Sheikh Mujib's daughter, Hasina (known as Sheikh Hasina), led the country after the June 12, 1996 election. Floods in July-Sept. 1998 inundated most of the country, killed over 1,400 people (many through disease), and stranded at least 30 mil.

Khaleda Zia returned to power following the parliamentary elections of Oct. 1, 2001. Floods July-Aug. 2004 caused at least 950 deaths and $7 bil in property damage. Militant Islamists set off more than 400 small bombs in over 50 cities and towns, Aug. 17, 2005, killing 3 people. Another wave of jihadist bombings, Nov. 29-Dec. 8, killed 22. A Bangladeshi economist, Muhammad Yunus, and his Grameen Bank won the 2006 Nobel Peace Prize for using very small loans (microcredit) to help alleviate poverty, a severe problem in this densely populated country.

Escalating political violence led Pres. Iajuddin Ahmed to declare a state of emergency Jan. 11, 2007. A military-backed caretaker government filed criminal charges against Khaleda Zia and Sheikh Hasina, but failed in an attempt to force the two former prime ministers into exile. Cyclone Sidr struck Nov. 15, damaging more than 1.5 mil homes and affecting 8.9 mil people; the confirmed death toll reached nearly 3,400.

The Awami League triumphed in parliamentary elections Dec. 29, 2008, and Sheikh Hasina was sworn in as prime minister Jan. 6, 2009, ending 2 years of emergency rule. A mutiny Feb. 25-26 at the Dhaka headquarters of the Bangladesh Rifles, a border force, left 74 people dead, according to official figures.

Barbados
People: Population: 284,589. **Age distrib.** (%): <15: 19.2; 65+: 9.5. **Pop. density:** 1,710.2 per sq mi, 660.3 per sq km. **Urban:** 38.4%. **Ethnic groups:** Black 90%, white 4%, Asian & mixed 6%. **Principal language:** English. **Chief religions:** Protestant 67%, none 17%, other 12%.

Geography: Total area: 166 sq mi, 431 sq km; **Land area:** 166 sq mi, 431 sq km. **Location:** In Atlantic O., farthest E of West Indies. **Neighbors:** Nearest are St. Lucia and St. Vincent & the Grenadines to the W. **Topography:** The island lies alone in the Atlantic almost completely surrounded by coral reefs. Highest point is Mt. Hillaby, 1,115 ft. **Capital:** Bridgetown, 116,000.

Government: Type: Parliamentary democracy. **Head of state:** Queen Elizabeth II, represented by Gov.-Gen. Sir Clifford Husbands; b. Aug. 5, 1926; in office: June 1, 1996. **Head of gov.:** Prime Min. David J. H. Thompson; b. Dec. 25, 1961; in office: Jan. 16, 2008. **Local divisions:** 11 parishes and Bridgetown. **Defense budget:** $28 mil. **Active troops:** 610.

Economy: Industries: tourism, sugar, light mfg., component assembly. **Chief crops:** sugarcane, vegetables, cotton. **Natural resources:** oil, fish, nat. gas. **Crude oil reserves:** 2.2 mil bbls. **Other resources:** Fish. **Arable land:** 37%. **Livestock:** cattle: 11,000; chickens: 3.5 mil; goats: 5,200; pigs: 20,000; sheep: 11,200. **Fish catch** (est.): 1,800 metric tons. **Electricity prod.:** 976 mil kWh. **Labor force** (1996 est.): agric. 10%, industry 15%, services 75%.

Finance: Monetary unit: Dollar (BBD) (Oct. 2009: 2.00 = $1 U.S.). **GDP:** $5.4 bil; **per capita GDP:** $19,100; **GDP growth:** 0.7%. **Imports** (2006): $1.6 bil; U.S. 27.8%, Trinidad and Tobago 26.3%, Russia 7.3%, Germany 4.2%. **Exports** (2006): $385 mil; Trinidad and Tobago 15.5%, Jamaica 13.6%, Brazil 9.9%, U.S. 8.6%, UK 7.8%, St. Lucia 7.2%, St. Vincent and the Grenadines 4.5%. **Tourism:** $1.2 bil. **Budget** (2000 est.): $886 mil. **Intl. reserves less gold** (2007): $531 mil. **Gold:** NA. **Consumer prices:** 8.1%.

Transport: Motor vehicles: 62,100 pass. cars; 9,400 comm. vehicles. **Civil aviation:** 1 airport. **Chief port:** Bridgetown.

Communications: TV sets: 290 per 1,000 pop. **Radios:** 651 per 1,000 pop. **Telephone lines:** 150,000. **Internet:** 188,000 users.

Health: Life expect.: 71.2 male; 75.2 female. **Births** (per 1,000 pop.): 12.5. **Deaths** (per 1,000 pop.): 8.6. **Natural inc.:** 0.39%. **Infant mortality** (per 1,000 live births): 11.1. **HIV rate:** 1.2%.

Education: Compulsory: ages 5-16. **Literacy:** 99.7%.

Major intl. organizations: UN (FAO, IBRD, ILO, IMF, IMO, WHO, WTO), Caricom, the Commonwealth, OAS.

Embassy: 2144 Wyoming Ave. NW 20008; 939-9200.

Website: www.barbados.gov.bb

Barbados was probably named by Portuguese sailors in reference to bearded fig trees. An English ship visited in 1605, and British settlers arrived on the uninhabited island in 1627. Slaves worked the sugar plantations until slavery was abolished in 1834. Self-rule came gradually, with full independence proclaimed Nov. 30, 1966. British traditions have remained.

Belarus
Republic of Belarus
People: Population: 9,648,533. **Age distrib.** (%): <15: 14.3; 65+: 14.5. **Pop. density:** 120.4 per sq mi, 46.5 per sq km. **Urban:** 72.2%. **Ethnic groups:** Belarusian 81%, Russian 11%. **Principal languages:** Belarusian, Russian. **Chief religions:** Eastern Orthodox 80%, other (incl. Roman Catholic, Protestant, Jewish, Muslim) 20%.

Geography: Total area: 80,155 sq mi, 207,600 sq km; **Land area:** 80,155 sq mi, 207,600 sq km. **Location:** E Europe. **Neighbors:** Poland on W; Latvia, Lithuania on N; Russia on E; Ukraine on S. **Topography:** Belarus is a landlocked country consisting mostly of hilly lowland with significant marsh areas in S. **Capital:** Minsk, 1,805,000.

Government: Type: Republic. **Head of state:** Pres. Aleksandr Lukashenko; b. Aug. 30, 1954; in office: July 20,1994. **Head of gov.:** Prime Min. Syarhey Sidorski; b. Mar. 13, 1954; in office: Dec. 19, 2003 (acting from July 10, 2003). **Local divisions:** 6 oblasts and 1 municipality. **Defense budget:** $572 mil. **Active troops:** 72,940.

Economy: Industries: machine tools, tractors, trucks, earthmovers, motorcycles. **Chief crops:** grain, potatoes, vegetables, sugar beets, flax. **Natural resources:** forests, peat, oil, nat. gas, granite, dolomitic limestone, marl, chalk, sand, gravel, clay. **Crude oil reserves:** 198 mil bbls. **Arable land:** 27%. **Livestock:** cattle: 4 mil; chickens: 26.9 mil; goats: 69,600; pigs: 3.6 mil; sheep: 52,200. **Fish catch** (est.): 5,050 metric tons. **Electricity prod.:**

29.9 bil kWh. **Labor force** (2003 est.): agric. 14%, industry 34.7%, services 51.3%.

Finance: Monetary unit: Ruble (BYR) (Oct. 2009: 2,750.00 = $1 U.S.). **GDP:** $114.1 bil; **per capita GDP:** $11,800; **GDP growth:** 10%. **Imports:** $39.2 bil; Russia 59.8%, Germany 7.1%, Ukraine 5.4%. **Exports:** $33 bil; Russia 32.2%, Netherlands 16.9%, Ukraine 8.5%, Latvia 6.6%, Poland 5.5%, UK 4.4%. **Tourism:** $365 mil. **Budget:** $21.2 bil. **Intl. reserves less gold:** $1.74 bil. **Gold:** NA. **Consumer prices:** 14.8%.

Transport: Railroad: Length: 3,441 mi. **Motor vehicles:** 1.8 mil pass. cars; NA comm. vehicles. **Civil aviation:** 238 mil pass.-mi; 35 airports. **Chief port:** Mazyr.

Communications: TV sets: 331 per 1,000 pop. **Radios:** 292 per 1,000 pop. **Telephone lines:** 3.7 mil. **Daily newspaper circ.** (2004): 81.3 per 1,000 pop. **Internet:** 2.9 mil users.

Health: Life expect.: 64.6 male; 76.4 female. **Births** (per 1,000 pop.): 9.6. **Deaths** (per 1,000 pop.): 13.9. **Natural inc.:** −0.43%. **Infant mortality** (per 1,000 live births): 6.5. **HIV rate:** 0.2%.

Education: Compulsory: ages 6-15. **Literacy:** 99.7%.

Major intl. organizations: UN (FAO, IBRD, ILO, IMF, WHO), CIS, OSCE.

Embassy: 1619 New Hampshire Ave. NW 20009; 986-1604. **Website:** www.president.gov.by

Belarus became a constituent republic of the USSR in 1922, although the western region was controlled by Poland. Overrun by German armies in 1941, Belarus was recaptured by Soviet troops in 1944. Following WWII, Belarus increased in area through Soviet annexation of part of NE Poland. Belarus declared independence Aug. 25, 1991. It became an independent state when the Soviet Union disbanded Dec. 26, 1991.

A new constitution was adopted, Mar. 15, 1994, after which Aleksandr Lukashenko was elected president. Russia and Belarus signed a pact Apr. 2, 1996, linking their political and economic systems. An authoritarian constitution enacted in Nov. gave Pres. Lukashenko vast new powers. Opponents charged harassment and fraud in the presidential election of Sept. 9, 2001, won by Lukashenko. In elections on Oct. 17, 2004, considered flawed by foreign observers, nearly all winning candidates were Lukashenko supporters, and a constitutional provision limiting the president to 2 terms was repealed. Lukashenko won a 3rd term, Mar. 19, 2006, in elections criticized by the U.S., EU, and OSCE observers; police in Minsk suppressed postelection protests. The U.S. and EU imposed travel restrictions and financial sanctions on Lukashenko and other top officials.

Lukashenko loyalists swept to victory in parliamentary voting Sept. 28, 2008, after which Aleksandr Lukashenko was reelected president. The IMF agreed Jan. 2009 to extend $2.5 bil in credits to help Belarus weather the global economic downturn.

Belgium
Kingdom of Belgium

People: Population: 10,414,336. **Age distrib.** (%): <15: 16.1; 65+: 17.6. **Pop. density:** 890.8 per sq mi, 344 per sq km. **Urban:** 97.3%. **Ethnic groups:** Fleming 58%, Walloon 31%. **Principal languages:** Dutch, French, German (all official). **Chief religions:** Roman Catholic 75%, other (incl. Protestant) 25%.

Geography: Total area: 11,787 sq mi, 30,528 sq km; **Land area:** 11,690 sq mi, 30,278 sq km. **Location:** In W Europe, on North Sea. **Neighbors:** France on W and S, Luxembourg on SE, Germany on E, Netherlands on N. **Topography:** Mostly flat, the country is trisected by the Scheldt and Meuse, major commercial rivers. The land becomes hilly and forested in the SE (Ardennes) region. **Capital:** Brussels, 1,743,000. **Cities (urban aggr.):** Antwerpen, 920,000.

Government: Type: Parliamentary democracy under a constitutional monarch. **Head of state:** King Albert II; b. June 6, 1934; in office: Aug. 9, 1993. **Head of gov.:** Herman Van Rompuy; b. Oct. 31, 1947; in office: Dec. 30, 2008. **Local divisions:** 10 provinces and Brussels. **Defense budget:** $5 bil. **Active troops:** 38,844.

Economy: Industries: engineering & metal products, motor vehicle assembly, transp. equip., scientific instruments, processed food & beverages, chemicals, metals, textiles, glass, oil. **Chief crops:** sugar beets, vegetables, fruits, grain, tobacco. **Natural resources:** constr. materials, silica sand, carbonates. **Arable land:** 27%. **Livestock:** cattle: 2.6 mil; chickens: 32.8 mil; goats: 26,500; pigs: 6.3 mil; sheep: 150,532. **Fish catch:** 24,669 metric tons. **Electricity prod.:** 79.6 bil kWh. **Labor force** (2007 est.): agric. 2%, industry 25%, services 73%.

Finance: Monetary unit: Euro (EUR) (Oct. 2009: 0.68 = $1 U.S.). **GDP:** $389.3 bil; **per capita GDP:** $37,400; **GDP growth:** 1%. **Imports:** $387.7 bil; Netherlands 19.5%, Germany 17.3%, France 11%, UK 5.7%, U.S. 5.5%, China 4.1%. **Exports:** $371.5 bil; Germany 19.9%, France 17.4%, Netherlands 12.2%, UK 7.2%, U.S. 4.8%, Italy 4.7%. **Tourism:** $10.9 bil. **Budget:** $220.3 bil. **Intl. reserves less gold:** $6.05 bil. **Gold:** 7.32 mil oz t. **Consumer prices:** 4.5%.

Transport: Railroad: Length: 2,009 mi. **Motor vehicles:** 4.9 mil pass. cars; 652,000 comm. vehicles. **Civil aviation:** 3.1 bil

pass.-mi; 27 airports. **Chief ports:** Antwerp (one of the world's busiest), Gent, Liege, Zeebrugge.

Communications: TV sets: 532 per 1,000 pop. **Radios:** 797 per 1,000 pop. **Telephone lines:** 4.5 mil. **Daily newspaper circ.** (2004): 164.7 per 1,000 pop. **Internet:** 7.3 mil users.

Health: Life expect.: 75.9 male; 82.4 female. **Births** (per 1,000 pop.): 10.2. **Deaths** (per 1,000 pop.): 10.4. **Natural inc.:** −0.02%. **Infant mortality** (per 1,000 live births): 4.5. **HIV rate:** 0.2%.

Education: Compulsory: ages 6-18. **Literacy:** 99%.

Major intl. organizations: UN and all of its specialized agencies, EU, NATO, OECD, OSCE.

Embassy: 3330 Garfield St. NW 20008; 333-6900. **Website:** www.belgium.be

Belgium derives its name from the Belgae, the first recorded inhabitants, probably Celts. The land was conquered by Julius Caesar and was ruled for 1800 years by conquerors, including Rome, the Franks, Burgundy, Spain, Austria, and France. After 1815, Belgium was made a part of the Netherlands, but it became an independent constitutional monarchy in 1830.

Belgian neutrality was violated by Germany in both world wars. King Leopold III surrendered to Germany, May 28, 1940. After the war, he was forced by political pressure to abdicate in favor of his son, King Baudouin. Baudouin was succeeded by his brother, Albert II, Aug. 9, 1993.

The Flemings of northern Belgium speak Dutch, while French is the language of the Walloons in the south. The language difference has been a perennial source of controversy between the 2 groups. Parliament has passed measures aimed at transferring power from the central government to 3 regions—Wallonia, Flanders, and Brussels. Constitutional changes in 1993 made Belgium a federal state.

After elections June 10, 2007, rivalries between Flemings and Walloons led to a 9-month political stalemate. Controversy over the sale of troubled bank Fortis NV to BNP Paribas of France led to the resignation of Prime Min. Yves Leterme, Dec. 19, 2008, and his replacement by former Budget Min. Herman Van Rompuy.

Belize

People: Population: 307,899. **Age distrib.** (%): <15: 37.9; 65+: 3.5. **Pop. density:** 35 per sq mi, 13.5 per sq km. **Urban:** 50.2%. **Ethnic groups:** Mestizo 49%, Creole 25%, Maya 11%. **Principal languages:** Spanish, Creole, Mayan dialects, English (official). **Chief religions:** Roman Catholic 50%, Protestant (incl. Pentecostal, Anglican, Seventh-Day Adventist, Mennonite, Methodist) 27%, other 14%, none 9%.

Geography: Total area: 8,867 sq mi, 22,966 sq km; **Land area:** 8,805 sq mi, 22,806 sq km. **Location:** Eastern coast of Central America. **Neighbors:** Mexico on N, Guatemala on W and S. **Topography:** Belize has swampy lowlands in N, Maya Mts. in S, coral reefs and cays near coast. Climate is tropical. **Capital:** Belmopan, 16,000.

Government: Type: Parliamentary democracy. **Head of state:** Queen Elizabeth II, represented by Gov.-Gen. Sir Colville Young; b. Nov. 20, 1932; in office: Nov. 17, 1993. **Head of gov.:** Prime Min. Dean Barrow; b. Mar. 2, 1951; in office: Feb. 8, 2008. **Local divisions:** 6 districts. **Defense budget:** $18 mil. **Active troops:** 1,050.

Economy: Industries: garment prod., food proc., tourism, constr. **Chief crops:** bananas, cacao, citrus, sugar. **Natural resources:** timber, fish, hydropower. **Crude oil reserves:** 6.7 mil bbls. **Arable land:** 3%. **Livestock:** cattle: 72,826; chickens: 1.6 mil; goats: 170; pigs: 21,500; sheep: 6,265. **Fish catch:** 14,382 metric tons. **Electricity prod.:** 208 mil kWh. **Labor force** (2007): agric. 10.2%, industry 18.1%, services 71.7%.

Finance: Monetary unit: Dollar (BZD) (Oct. 2009: 1.95 = $1 U.S.). **GDP:** $2.5 bil; **per capita GDP:** $8,400; **GDP growth:** 3%. **Imports:** $740 mil; U.S. 37.7%, Mexico 12.5%, Cuba 7.8%, Guatemala 7.3%, Russia 5.1%. **Exports:** $458 mil; U.S. 35%, UK 21.1%, Côte d'Ivoire 5.2%, Italy 4.4%. **Tourism:** $291 mil. **Budget:** $344 mil. **Intl. reserves less gold:** $108 mil. **Gold:** NA. **Consumer prices:** 6.4%.

Transport: Motor vehicles: 32,600 pass. cars; 7,800 comm. vehicles. **Civil aviation:** 4 airports. **Chief ports:** Belize City, Big Creek.

Communications: TV sets: 183 per 1,000 pop. **Radios:** 594 per 1,000 pop. **Telephone lines:** 31,100. **Internet:** 34,000 users.

Health: Life expect.: 66.4 male; 70.1 female. **Births** (per 1,000 pop.): 27.8. **Deaths** (per 1,000 pop.): 5.8. **Natural inc.:** 2.21%. **Infant mortality** (per 1,000 live births): 23.6. **HIV rate:** 2.1%.

Education: Compulsory: ages 5-14. **Literacy:** 70.3%.

Major intl. organizations: UN (FAO, IBRD, ILO, IMF, IMO, WHO, WTO), Caricom, the Commonwealth, OAS.

Embassy: 2535 Massachusetts Ave. NW 20008; 332-9636. **Website:** www.governmentofbelize.gov.bz

Belize (formerly British Honduras) was Britain's last colony on the American mainland; independence was achieved Sept. 21, 1981. Relations with neighboring Guatemala, initially tense, have improved in recent years. Belize has become a center for drug trafficking between Colombia and the U.S.

Benin
Republic of Benin

People: Population: 8,791,832. **Age distrib.** (%): <15: 45.2; 65+: 2.6. **Pop. density:** 205.8 per sq mi, 79.5 per sq km. **Urban:** 40%. **Ethnic groups:** Fon & related 39%, Adja & related 15%, Yoruba & related 12%, Bariba & related 9%. **Principal languages:** French (official), Fon, Yoruba, tribal languages. **Chief religions:** Christian (incl. Catholic, Celestial) 43%, Muslim 24%, Vodoun 17%.

Geography: Total area: 43,483 sq mi, 112,620 sq km; **Land area:** 42,711 sq mi, 110,620 sq km. **Location:** In W Africa on Gulf of Guinea. **Neighbors:** Togo on W; Burkina Faso, Niger on N; Nigeria on E. **Topography:** Most of Benin is flat and covered with dense vegetation. The coast is hot, humid, and rainy. **Capital:** Cotonou, 762,000. **Cities (urban aggr.):** Porto-Novo, 257,000.

Government: Type: Republic. **Head of state and gov.:** Pres. Boni Yayi; b. 1952; in office: Apr. 6, 2006. **Local divisions:** 12 departments. **Defense budget:** $55 mil. **Active troops:** 4,750.

Economy: Industries: textiles, food proc., constr. materials, cement. **Chief crops:** cotton, corn, cassava, yams, beans. **Natural resources:** oil, limestone, marble, timber. **Crude oil reserves:** 8 mil bbls. **Arable land:** 24%. **Livestock:** cattle: 1.9 mil; chickens: 14.5 mil; goats: 1.4 mil; pigs: 327,000; sheep: 775,600. **Fish catch:** 30,439 metric tons. **Electricity prod.:** 120 mil kWh. **Labor force:** NA.

Finance: Monetary unit: CFA BCEAO Franc (XOF) (Oct. 2009: 444.97 = $1 U.S.). **GDP:** $12.8 bil; **per capita GDP:** $1,500; **GDP growth:** 4.8%. **Imports:** $1.4 bil; China 39.8%, U.S. 14%, Thailand 6.9%, France 6.9%, Malaysia 4.2%. **Exports:** $894 mil; China 19.7%, Japan 8.9%, India 6.3%, Niger 5.1%, U.S. 4.9%, Nigeria 4.5%, Togo 4.2%. **Tourism:** NA. **Budget:** $1.2 bil. **Intl. reserves less gold:** $818 mil. **Gold:** NA. **Consumer prices:** 7.9%.

Transport: Railroad: Length: 359 mi. **Motor vehicles:** 135,700 pass. cars; 19,200 comm. vehicles. **Civil aviation:** 80.8 mil pass.-mi; 1 airport. **Chief port:** Cotonou.

Communications: TV sets: 44 per 1,000 pop. **Radios:** 448 per 1,000 pop. **Telephone lines:** 159,000. **Daily newspaper circ.** (2004): 0.4 per 1,000 pop. **Internet:** 160,000 users.

Health: Life expect.: 57.4 male; 59.8 female. **Births** (per 1,000 pop.): 39.8. **Deaths** (per 1,000 pop.): 9.7. **Natural inc.:** 3.01%. **Infant mortality** (per 1,000 live births): 66.2. **HIV rate:** 1.2%.

Education: Compulsory: ages 6-11. **Literacy:** 40.5%.

Major intl. organizations: UN (FAO, IBRD, ILO, IMF, IMO, WHO, WTO), AU.

Embassy: 2124 Kalorama Rd. NW 20008; 232-6656.

Website: www.gouv.bz

The Kingdom of Abomey, rising to power in wars with neighboring kingdoms in the 17th cent., came under French domination in the late 19th cent., and was incorporated into French West Africa by 1904. Under the name Dahomey, the country gained independence Aug. 1, 1960; it became Benin in 1975. In the fifth coup since independence Col. Ahmed Kerekou took power in 1972; two years later he declared a socialist state with a "Marxist-Leninist" philosophy. In Dec. 1989, Kerekou announced Marxism-Leninism would no longer be the state ideology.

In Mar. 1991, Kerekou lost to Nicéphore Soglo in Benin's first free presidential election in 30 years. Kerekou defeated Soglo in Mar. 1996 to reclaim the presidency. He won reelection in a runoff Mar. 22, 2001. Boni Yayi, an economist, won a presidential runoff vote, Mar. 19, 2006. He survived an apparent assassination attempt Mar. 15, 2007.

Benin, which in 2006 signed a 5-year, $307 mil aid deal with the U.S., received a visit from Pres. Bush Feb. 16, 2008.

Bhutan
Kingdom of Bhutan

People: Population: 691,141. **Age distrib.** (%): <15: 30.2; 65+: 5.5. **Pop. density:** 38.1 per sq mi, 14.7 per sq km. **Urban:** 31%. **Ethnic groups:** Bhote 50%, ethnic Nepalese 35%, indigenous or migrant tribes 15%. **Principal languages:** Dzongkha (official); various Tibetan & Nepalese dialects. **Chief religions:** Lamaistic Buddhist 75%, Indian- & Nepalese-influenced Hinduism 25%.

Geography: Total area: 18,147 sq mi, 47,000 sq km; **Land area:** 18,147 sq mi, 47,000 sq km. **Location:** S Asia, in eastern Himalayan Mts. **Neighbors:** India on W (Sikkim) and S, China on N. **Topography:** Bhutan is comprised of very high mountains in the N, fertile valleys in the center, and thick forests in the Duar Plain in the S. **Capital:** Thimphu, 83,000.

Government: Type: Constitutional monarchy. **Head of state:** King Jigme Khesar Namgyal Wangchuk; b. Feb. 21, 1980; in office: Dec. 14, 2006. **Head of gov.:** Prime Min. Lyonchen Jigmi Y. Thinley; b. 1952; in office: Apr. 9, 2008. **Local divisions:** 18 districts. **Defense budget/Active troops:** NA.

Economy: Industries: cement, wood products, processed fruits, alcoholic beverages, calcium carbide, tourism. **Chief crops:** rice, corn, root crops, citrus, foodgrains. **Natural resources:** timber, hydropower, gypsum, calcium carbonate. **Arable land:** 2%.

Livestock: cattle: 385,000; chickens: 230,000; goats: 30,000; pigs: 35,000; sheep: 18,000. **Fish catch** (est.): 300 metric tons. **Electricity prod.:** 2.6 bil kWh. **Labor force** (2004 est.): agric. 63%, industry 6%, services 31%.

Finance: Monetary unit: Ngultrum (BTN) (Oct. 2009: 46.90 = $1 U.S.). **GDP:** $3.5 bil; **per capita GDP:** $5,200; **GDP growth:** 21.4%. **Imports** (2006): $320 mil; India 63.9%, Japan 12.1%, China 5.1%. **Exports** (2006): $350 mil; India 94.8%, Italy 1.8%, Japan 0.8%. **Tourism:** $30 mil. **Budget** (2005): $350 mil (nearly three-fifths financed by India's govt.). **Intl. reserves less gold:** $497 mil. **Gold:** NA. **Consumer prices:** 8.4%.

Transport: Civil aviation: 46 mil pass.-mi; 1 airport.

Communications: TV sets: 6 per 1,000 pop. **Radios:** 19 per 1,000 pop. **Telephone lines:** 27,500. **Internet:** 40,000 users.

Health: Life expect.: 64.8 male; 66.3 female. **Births** (per 1,000 pop.): 20.6. **Deaths** (per 1,000 pop.): 7.5. **Natural inc.:** 1.3%. **Infant mortality** (per 1,000 live births): 51.9. **HIV rate:** 0.1%.

Education: Compulsory: ages 6-16. **Literacy:** 55.6%.

Major intl. organizations: UN (FAO, IBRD, IMF, WHO).

Permanent UN mission: 763 United Nations Plz., New York, NY 10017; (212) 490-9660.

Website: www.bhutan.gov.bt

The region came under Tibetan rule in the 16th cent. British influence grew in the 19th cent. A Buddhist monarchy was set up in 1907. According to a 1910 treaty, Britain guided Bhutan's external affairs, while the country remained internally self-governing. Upon independence, India assumed Britain's role in a 1949 revision of the treaty.

Isolated for much of its history, Bhutan has taken steps toward modernization. King Jigme Singye Wangchuk, in power since 1972, stepped down Dec. 14, 2006, in favor of his son, Jigme Khesar Namgyal Wangchuk. Multiparty parliamentary elections took place Mar. 24, 2008, and a new constitution was ratified in July.

Bolivia
Plurinational State of Bolivia

People: Population: 9,775,246. **Age distrib.** (%): <15: 35.5; 65+: 4.5. **Pop. density:** 23.3 per sq mi, 9 per sq km. **Urban:** 64.2%. **Ethnic groups:** Quechua 30%, mestizo (mixed white & Amerindian) 30%, Aymara 25%, white 15%. **Principal languages:** Spanish, Quechua, Aymara (all official). **Chief religions:** Roman Catholic 95%, Protestant (Evangelical Methodist) 5%.

Geography: Total area: 424,164 sq mi, 1,098,580 sq km; **Land area:** 418,685 sq mi, 1,084,390 sq km. **Location:** In W central South America, in the Andes Mts. (one of 2 landlocked countries in South America). **Neighbors:** Peru and Chile on W, Argentina and Paraguay on S, Brazil on E and N. **Topography:** The great central plateau, at an altitude of 12,000 ft, over 500 mi long, lies between two great cordilleras having 3 of the highest peaks in South America. Lake Titicaca, on Peruvian border, is highest lake in world on which steamboats ply (12,506 ft). The E central region has semitropical forests; the llanos, or Amazon-Chaco lowlands are in E. **Capital:** La Paz (admin.), 1,590,000; Sucre (judic.), 243,000. **Cities (urban aggr.):** Santa Cruz, 1,422,000.

Government: Type: Republic. **Head of state and gov.:** Pres. Juan Evo Morales Aima; b. Oct. 26, 1959; in office: Jan. 22, 2006. **Local divisions:** 9 departments. **Defense budget:** $162 mil. **Active troops:** 46,100.

Economy: Industries: mining, smelting, oil, food & beverages, tobacco, handicrafts, clothing. **Chief crops:** soybeans, coffee, coca, cotton, corn, sugarcane, rice, potatoes. **Natural resources:** tin, nat. gas, oil, zinc, tungsten, antimony, silver, iron, lead, gold, timber, hydropower. **Crude oil reserves:** 465 mil bbls. **Other resources:** Timber. **Arable land:** 3%. **Livestock:** cattle: 7.7 mil; chickens: 73.4 mil; goats: 1.8 mil; pigs: 3.6 mil; sheep: 9.1 mil. **Fish catch:** 6,585 metric tons. **Electricity prod.:** 5.2 bil kWh. **Labor force** (2006 est.): agric. 40%, industry 17%, services 43%.

Finance: Monetary unit: Boliviano (BOB) (Oct. 2009: 6.97 = $1 U.S.). **GDP:** $43.3 bil; **per capita GDP:** $4,500; **GDP growth:** 6.1%. **Imports:** $4.7 bil; Brazil 27.8%, Argentina 14.8%, U.S. 10.9%, Chile 9.9%, Peru 7.4%, China 5.1%. **Exports:** $6.5 bil; Brazil 60%, U.S. 8.3%, Japan 4.1%. **Tourism:** $292 mil. **Budget:** $5.5 bil. **Intl. reserves less gold:** $4.5 bil. **Gold:** 910,000 oz t. **Consumer prices:** 14%.

Transport: Railroad: Length: 2,177 mi. **Motor vehicles:** 294,000 pass. cars; 174,000 comm. vehicles. **Civil aviation:** 1.2 bil pass.-mi; 16 airports. **Chief port:** Puerto Aguirre.

Communications: TV sets: 118 per 1,000 pop. **Radios:** 675 per 1,000 pop. **Telephone lines:** 690,000. **Internet:** 1 mil users.

Health: Life expect.: 63.9 male; 69.3 female. **Births** (per 1,000 pop.): 22.3. **Deaths** (per 1,000 pop.): 7.3. **Natural inc.:** 1.5%. **Infant mortality** (per 1,000 live births): 49.1. **HIV rate:** 0.2%.

Education: Compulsory: ages 6-13. **Literacy:** 90.3%.

Major intl. organizations: UN (FAO, IBRD, ILO, IMF, IMO, WHO, WTO), OAS.

Embassy: 3014 Massachusetts Ave. NW 20008; 483-4410.

Website: www.bolivia.gov.bo

The Incas conquered the region's earlier Indian inhabitants in the 13th cent. Spanish rule began in the 1530s and lasted until Aug. 6, 1825. The country is named after Simon Bolivar, independence fighter.

In a series of wars, Bolivia lost its Pacific coast to Chile, the oil-bearing Chaco to Paraguay, and rubber-growing areas to Brazil, 1879-1935.

Economic unrest, especially among militant mine workers, has led to continuing political instability. A reformist government under Victor Paz Estenssoro, 1951-64, nationalized tin mines and attempted to improve conditions for the Indian majority but was overthrown by a military junta. A series of coups and countercoups continued until constitutional government was restored in 1982.

U.S. pressure on the government to reduce the country's coca output, the raw material for cocaine, has led to clashes between police and coca growers and increased anti-U.S. feeling among Bolivians. Gen. Hugo Banzer Suárez, who ruled as a dictator, 1971-78, later governed as president, 1997-2001.

After an inconclusive presidential election June 30, 2002, Congress Aug. 4 chose Gonzalo Sánchez de Lozada, a U.S.-educated mining executive, as head of state. He quit Oct. 17, 2003, after a month of antigovernment protests, led by Bolivian Indians, in which over 70 people died. His successor, Vice Pres. Carlos D. Mesa Gisbert, was embroiled in controversies over energy policy.

Juan Evo Morales Aima, a leftist and coca-farmer advocate, won the presidential election, Dec. 18, 2005. He nationalized the hydrocarbon sector, launched a land-redistribution program to benefit poor farmers, and tightened ties with Venezuela and Cuba; he faced resistance and demands for autonomy from leaders of Bolivia's relatively prosperous lowland provinces. Voters Jan. 25, 2009, approved a new constitution strengthening the rights of Bolivia's indigenous majority and increasing federal control over the country's natural resources. Police Apr. 16 said they had foiled an alleged plot by foreigners to assassinate Pres. Morales.

Bosnia and Herzegovina

People: Population: 4,613,414. **Age distrib.** (%): <15: 14.5; 65+: 14.8. **Pop. density:** 233.7 per sq mi, 90.2 per sq km. **Urban:** 45.7%. **Ethnic groups:** Bosniak 48%, Serb 37%, Croat 14%. **Principal languages:** Bosnian, Croatian, Serbian. **Chief religions:** Muslim 40%, Orthodox 31%, Roman Catholic 15%.

Geography: Total area: 19,772 sq mi, 51,209 sq km; **Land area:** 19,741 sq mi, 51,129 sq km. **Location:** On Balkan Peninsula in SE Europe. **Neighbors:** Serbia, Montenegro on E and SE, Croatia on N and W. **Topography:** Hilly with some mountains. About 36% of the land is forested. **Capital:** Sarajevo, 376,000.

Government: Type: Federal republic. **Heads of state:** Collective presidency with rotating leadership. **Head of gov.:** Prime Min. Nikola Spiric; b. Sept. 4, 1956; in office: Jan. 11, 2007. **Local divisions:** Muslim-Croat Federation, divided into 10 cantons; Serbian-led region (Republika Srpska); internationally supervised Brcko district. **Defense budget:** $196 mil. **Active troops:** 8,543.

Economy: Industries: steel, coal, mining, vehicle assembly, textiles, tobacco products, wooden furniture, tank & aircraft assembly, domestic appliances. **Chief crops:** wheat, corn, fruits, vegetables. **Natural resources:** coal, iron ore, bauxite, copper, lead, zinc, chromite, cobalt, mang. **Arable land:** 20%. **Livestock:** cattle: 467,986; chickens: 13.8 mil; goats: 70,255; pigs: 534,764; sheep: 1.03 mil. **Fish catch:** 9,625 metric tons. **Electricity prod.:** 12.8 bil kWh. **Labor force** (2007): agric. 19.8%, industry 32.6%, services 47.6%.

Finance: Monetary unit: Convertible Marka (BAM) (Oct. 2009: 1.33 = $1 U.S.). **GDP:** $29.7 bil; **per capita GDP:** $6,500; **GDP growth:** 5.5%. **Imports:** $12.3 bil; Croatia 24.8%, Slovenia 12.8%, Germany 12.4%, Italy 10.6%, Hungary 6.6%, Turkey 6.5%, Austria 6.4%. **Exports:** $5.2 bil; Croatia 20.9%, Slovenia 16.8%, Italy 16.8%, Germany 13.1%, Austria 10.4%, Hungary 4.8%. **Tourism:** $728 mil. **Budget:** $7.1 bil. **Intl. reserves less gold:** $2.28 bil. **Gold:** NA. **Consumer prices:** NA.

Transport: Railroad: Length: 621 mi. **Civil aviation:** 29.2 mil pass.-mi; 7 airports. **Chief ports:** Bosanski Samac, Brcko.

Communications: TV sets: 112 per 1,000 pop. **Radios:** 245 per 1,000 pop. **Telephone lines:** 1.03 mil. **Internet:** 1.3 mil users.

Health: Life expect.: 74.7 male; 82.2 female. **Births** (per 1,000 pop.): 8.8. **Deaths** (per 1,000 pop.): 8.5. **Natural inc.:** 0.03%. **Infant mortality** (per 1,000 live births): 9.3. **HIV rate:** <0.1%.

Education: Compulsory: ages 6-15. **Literacy:** 96.7%.

Major intl. organizations: UN (FAO, IBRD, ILO, IMF, IMO, WHO), OSCE.

Embassy: 2109 E St. NW 20037; 337-1500.

Website: www.fbihvlada.gov.ba

Bosnia was ruled by Croatian kings c. 958 CE, and by Hungary 1000-1200. It became organized c. 1200 and later took control of Herzegovina. The kingdom disintegrated from 1391, with the southern part becoming the independent duchy Herzegovina. It was conquered by Turks in 1463 and made a Turkish province. The area was placed under control of Austria-Hungary in 1878 and made part of the province of Bosnia and Herzegovina, which was formally annexed to Austria-Hungary, 1908. Bosnia became a province of Yugoslavia in 1918. It was reunited with Herzegovina as a federated republic in the 1946 Yugoslav constitution.

Bosnia and Herzegovina declared sovereignty Oct. 15, 1991. A referendum for independence was passed Feb. 29, 1992. Ethnic Serbs' opposition to the referendum spurred violent clashes and bombings. The U.S. and EU recognized the republic Apr. 7. Fierce three-way fighting continued between Bosnia's Serbs, Muslims, and Croats. Serb forces massacred thousands of Bosnian Muslims and engaged in "ethnic cleansing" (the expulsion of Muslims and other non-Serbs from areas under Bosnian Serb control). The capital, Sarajevo, was surrounded and besieged by Bosnian Serb forces. Muslims and Croats in Bosnia reached a cease fire Feb. 23, 1994, and signed an accord, Mar. 18, to create a Muslim-Croat confederation in Bosnia. However, by mid-1994, Bosnian Serbs controlled over 70% of the country.

As fighting continued in 1995, the balance of power began to shift toward the Muslim-Croat alliance. Massive NATO air strikes at Bosnian Serb targets beginning Aug. 30 triggered a new round of peace talks, and the siege of Sarajevo was lifted Sept. 15. The new talks produced an agreement in principle to create autonomous regions within Bosnia, with the Serb region (Republika Srpska) constituting 49% of the country. A Croat-Muslim offensive in Sept. recaptured significant territory, leaving Bosnian Serbs in control of approximately half that percentage.

A peace agreement initialed in Dayton, Ohio, Nov. 21, 1995, was signed in Paris, Dec. 14, by leaders of Bosnia, Croatia, and Serbia. Some 60,000 NATO troops (about 20,000 from the U.S.) moved in to police the accord. Meanwhile, a UN tribunal began bringing charges against suspected war criminals. Elections were held Sept. 14, 1996, for a 3-person collective presidency, for seats in a federal parliament, and for regional offices. In Dec. a revamped NATO "stabilization force" (SFOR) of over 30,000 members (more than 8,000 from the U.S.) received an 18-month mandate, which was later extended.

In a landmark verdict Aug. 2, 2001, the UN tribunal found Radislav Krstic, a Bosnian Serb general, guilty in connection with the genocide of thousands of Muslims at Srebrenica in 1995. A European Union peacekeeping force (EUFOR), with 7,000 members, assumed responsibility from SFOR, Dec. 2, 2004. Accused of complicity in the Sarajevo and Srebrenica atrocities, former Bosnian Serb leader Radovan Karadzic was arrested in Serbia, July 21, 2008, and handed over to the UN tribunal. As the security situation in Bosnia improved, EUFOR troop strength dropped below 2,000 by Aug. 2009.

Botswana
Republic of Botswana

People: Population: 1,990,876. **Age distrib.** (%): <15: 34.8; 65+: 3.9. **Pop. density:** 8.8 per sq mi, 3.4 per sq km. **Urban:** 57.3%. **Ethnic groups:** Tswana, or Setswana 79%; Kalanga 11%; Basarwa 3%. **Principal languages:** Setswana, Kalanga, English (official). **Chief religions:** Christian 72%, Badimo 6%, none 21%.

Geography: Total area: 231,804 sq mi, 600,370 sq km; **Land area:** 226,013 sq mi, 585,370 sq km. **Location:** In southern Africa. **Neighbors:** Namibia on N and W, South Africa on S, Zimbabwe on NE; Botswana claims border with Zambia on N. **Topography:** The Kalahari Desert, supporting nomadic Bushmen and wildlife, spreads over SW; there are swamplands and farming areas in N, and rolling plains in E where livestock are grazed. **Capital:** Gaborone, 224,000.

Government: Type: Parliamentary republic. **Head of state and gov.:** Pres. Seretse Khama Ian Khama; b. Feb. 27, 1953; in office: Apr. 1, 2008. **Local divisions:** 10 districts, 4 town councils. **Defense budget:** $317 mil. **Active troops:** 9,000.

Economy: Industries: diamonds, copper, nickel, salt, soda ash, potash. **Chief crops:** livestock, sorghum, maize, millet, beans, sunflowers. **Natural resources:** diamonds, copper, nickel, salt, soda ash, potash, coal, iron ore, silver. **Arable land:** 1%. **Livestock:** cattle: 2.4 mil; chickens: 4 mil; goats: 2 mil; pigs: 5,500; sheep: 300,000. **Fish catch:** 123 metric tons. **Electricity prod.:** 979 mil kWh. **Labor force:** NA.

Finance: Monetary unit: Pula (BWP) (Oct. 2009: 6.75 = $1 U.S.). **GDP:** $27.1 bil; **per capita GDP:** $13,900; **GDP growth:** 2.9%. **Imports:** $4.5 bil. **Exports:** $4.9. **Tourism:** $546 mil. **Budget:** $3.8 bil. **Intl. reserves less gold:** $5.92 bil. **Gold:** NA. **Consumer prices:** 12.7%.

Transport: Railroad: Length: 552 mi. **Motor vehicles:** 83,000 pass. cars; 111,000 comm. vehicles. **Civil aviation:** 64.6 mil pass.-mi; 9 airports.

Communications: TV sets: 21 per 1,000 pop. **Radios:** 154 per 1,000 pop. **Telephone lines:** 142,300. **Daily newspaper circ.** (2004): 41.5 per 1,000 pop. **Internet:** 80,000 users.

Health: Life expect.: 51.3 male; 49 female. **Births** (per 1,000 pop.): 23. **Deaths** (per 1,000 pop.): 14. **Natural inc.:** 0.89%. **Infant mortality** (per 1,000 live births): 44. **HIV rate:** 23.9%.

Education: Compulsory: ages 6-15. **Literacy:** 82.9%.

Major intl. organizations: UN (FAO, IBRD, ILO, IMF, WHO, WTO), the Commonwealth, AU.

Embassy: 1531-1533 New Hampshire Ave. NW 20036; 244-4990.

Website: www.gov.bw

First inhabited by bushmen, then Bantus, the region became the British protectorate of Bechuanaland in 1886. The country became fully independent Sept. 30, 1966, as Botswana.

Cattle raising and mining (diamonds, copper, nickel) have contributed to economic growth; the economy is closely tied to South Africa's. According to the UN, about 15% of the total population has HIV/AIDS. Pres. Festus Mogae transferred power Apr. 1, 2008, to Seretse Khama Ian Khama, son of Botswana's independence leader and first president (1966-80), Sir Seretse Khama.

Brazil
Federative Republic of Brazil

People: Population: 198,739,269. **Age distrib.** (%): <15: 26.7; 65+: 6.4. **Pop. density:** 60.9 per sq mi, 23.5 per sq km. **Urban:** 84.2%. **Ethnic groups:** White 54%, mixed white & black 39%, black 6%. **Principal languages:** Portuguese (official), Spanish, English, minor Amerindian languages. **Chief religions:** Roman Catholic (nominal) 74%, Protestant 15%, none 7%.

Geography: Total area: 3,286,488 sq mi, 8,511,965 sq km; **Land area:** 3,265,077 sq mi, 8,456,510 sq km. **Location:** Occupies E half of South America. **Neighbors:** French Guiana, Suriname, Guyana, Venezuela on N; Colombia, Peru, Bolivia, Paraguay, on W; Argentina, Uruguay on S. **Topography:** Brazil's Atlantic coastline stretches 4,603 mi. In N is the heavily wooded Amazon basin covering half the country. Its network of rivers is navigable for 15,814 mi. The Amazon itself flows 2,093 mi in Brazil, all navigable. The NE region is semiarid scrubland, heavily settled and poor. The S central region, favored by climate and resources, has almost half of the population, produces 75% of farm goods and 80% of industrial output. The narrow coastal belt includes most of the major cities. Almost the entire country has a tropical or semitropical climate. **Capital:** Brasília, 3,599,000. **Cities (urban aggr.):** São Paulo, 18,845,000; Rio de Janeiro, 11,748,000; Belo Horizonte, 5,575,000.

Government: Type: Federal republic. **Head of state and gov.:** Luiz Inacio Lula da Silva; b. Oct. 27, 1945; in office: Jan. 1, 2003. **Local divisions:** 26 states, 1 federal district (Brasília). **Defense budget:** $20.6 bil. **Active troops:** 326,435.

Economy: Industries: textiles, shoes, chemicals, cement, lumber, iron ore, tin, steel, aircraft, motor vehicles & parts. **Chief crops:** coffee, soybeans, wheat, rice, corn, sugarcane, cocoa, citrus. **Natural resources:** bauxite, gold, iron ore, mang., nickel, phosphates, platinum, tin, uranium, oil, hydropower, timber. **Crude oil reserves:** 12.6 bil bbls. **Arable land:** 7%. **Livestock:** cattle: 199.8 mil; chickens: 1.1 bil; goats: 9.5 mil; pigs: 35.9 mil; sheep: 16.2 mil. **Fish catch:** 1.07 mil metric tons. **Electricity prod.:** 411.7 bil kWh. **Labor force** (2003 est.): agric. 20%, industry 14%, services 66%.

Finance: Monetary unit: Real (BRL) (Oct. 2009: 1.75 = $1 U.S.). **GDP:** $2 tril; **per capita GDP:** $10,200; **GDP growth:** 5.1%. **Imports:** $173.1 bil; U.S. 14.9%, China 11.6%, Argentina 7.9%, Germany 7%. **Exports:** $197.9 bil; U.S. 14.6%, China 11.5%, Argentina 8.6%, Netherlands 4.9%, Germany 4.5%. **Tourism:** $5 bil. **Budget** (FY07): $219.9 bil. **Intl. reserves less gold:** $125.2 bil. **Gold:** 1.08 mil oz t. **Consumer prices:** 5.7%.

Transport: Railroad: Length: 17,931 mi. **Motor vehicles:** 16.6 mil pass. cars; 4.5 mil comm. vehicles. **Civil aviation:** 31.5 bil pass.-mi; 721 airports. **Chief ports:** Guaiba, Ilha Grande, Paranagua, Rio Grande, Santos, Sao Sebastiau, Tubarao.

Communications: TV sets: 333 per 1,000 pop. **Radios:** 434 per 1,000 pop. **Telephone lines:** 41.1 mil. **Daily newspaper circ.** (2004): 35.5 per 1,000 pop. **Internet:** 64.9 mil users.

Health: Life expect.: 68.2 male; 75.5 female. **Births** (per 1,000 pop.): 18.7. **Deaths** (per 1,000 pop.): 6.3. **Natural inc.:** 1.24%. **Infant mortality** (per 1,000 live births): 23.3. **AIDS rate:** 0.6%.

Education: Compulsory: ages 7-14. **Literacy:** 90.5%.

Major intl. organizations: UN and most of its specialized agencies, OAS.

Embassy: 3006 Massachusetts Ave. NW 20008; 238-2700.

Website: www.brasil.gov.br

Pedro Alvares Cabral, a Portuguese navigator, is generally credited as the first European to reach Brazil, in 1500. The country was thinly settled by various Indian tribes. Only a few have survived to the present, mostly in the Amazon basin.

In the next centuries, Portuguese colonists gradually pushed inland, bringing along large numbers of African slaves. (Slavery was not abolished until 1888.) The King of Portugal, fleeing before Napoleon's army, moved the seat of government to Brazil in 1808. Brazil thereupon became a kingdom under Dom Joao VI. After his return to Portugal, his son Pedro proclaimed the independence of Brazil, Sept. 7, 1822, and was crowned emperor. The second emperor, Dom Pedro II, was deposed in 1889, and a republic proclaimed, called the United States of Brazil. In 1967 the country was renamed the Federative Republic of Brazil.

A military junta took control in 1930; dictatorial power was assumed by Getulio Vargas, until finally forced out by the military in 1945. A democratic regime prevailed 1945-64, during which time the capital was moved from Rio de Janeiro to Brasília. Military-backed governments ruled Brazil for the next 20 years. Censorship was imposed, and much of the opposition was suppressed amid charges of torture.

Brazil became the leading industrial power of Latin America by the 1970s, while agricultural output soared. By the 1990s, Brazil had one of the world's largest economies; income was poorly distributed, however, and more than one out of four Brazilians continued to survive on less than $1 a day. Despite protective environmental legislation, development has destroyed much of the Amazon ecosystem.

Democratic presidential elections were held in 1985 as the nation returned to civilian rule. Fernando Collor de Mello was elected president in Dec. 1989. In Sept. 1992, Collor was impeached for corruption. He resigned on Dec. 29 as his trial was beginning, and Itamar Franco, who had been acting president, was sworn in as president. In elections held on Oct. 3, 1994, Fernando Henrique Cardoso was elected president. Reelected Oct. 4, 1998, he guided Brazil through a series of financial crises.

A new civil code guaranteeing legal equality for women was enacted Aug. 15, 2001. The IMF approved a $30 bil loan to Brazil Aug. 7, 2002; by then, Brazil's debt already exceeded $260 bil. Luiz Inacio Lula da Silva, a union leader and reformer, won a presidential runoff Oct. 27 with 61% of the vote. Brazil's space program suffered a setback when a rocket exploded on its launchpad Aug. 22, 2003, killing 21 people; the country successfully launched its first rocket into space Oct. 23, 2004.

A top aide to Pres. Lula resigned June 16, 2005, amid allegations the ruling party bribed legislators in exchange for votes; despite this and other scandals, Lula won a 2nd presidential term Oct. 29, 2006. The nation, which already meets much of its energy needs through biofuels, reported huge new offshore oil finds in 2007-08. Floods and mudslides in Santa Catarina, S Brazil, left 135 people dead and 78,000 homeless in Nov. 2008; weeks of heavy rains in N Brazil claimed at least 49 lives and forced more than 400,000 from their homes by late May 2009. The International Olympic Committee Oct. 2 chose Rio de Janeiro to host the 2016 Olympic Games.

Brunei
Brunei Darussalam

People: Population: 388,190. **Age distrib.** (%): <15: 26.6; 65+: 3.3. **Pop. density:** 190.8 per sq mi, 73.7 per sq km. **Urban:** 73.5%. **Ethnic groups:** Malay 66%, Chinese 11%, other 19%. **Principal languages:** Malay (official), English, Chinese. **Chief religions:** Muslim (official) 67%, Buddhist 13%, Christian 10%, other (incl. indigenous beliefs) 10%.

Geography: Total area: 2,228 sq mi, 5,770 sq km; **Land area:** 2,035 sq mi, 5,270 sq km. **Location:** In SE Asia, on the N coast of the island of Borneo; it is surrounded on its landward side by the Malaysian state of Sarawak. **Topography:** Brunei has a narrow coastal plain, with mountains in E, hilly lowlands in W. There are swamps in W and NE. Climate is tropical. **Capital:** Bandar Seri Begawan, 22,000.

Government: Type: Independent sultanate. **Head of state and gov.:** Sultan Sir Muda Hassanal Bolkiah Mu'izzadin Waddaulah; b. July 15, 1946; in office: Jan. 1, 1984 (sultan since Oct. 5, 1967). **Local divisions:** 4 districts. **Defense budget:** $346 mil. **Active troops:** 7,000.

Economy: Industries: oil, oil refining, liquefied nat. gas, constr. **Chief crops:** rice, vegetables, fruits. **Natural resources:** oil, nat. gas, timber. **Crude oil reserves:** 1.1 bil bbls. **Arable land:** 2%. **Livestock:** cattle: 940; chickens: 15.5 mil; goats: 2,720; pigs: 1,800; sheep: 3,000. **Fish catch:** 2,863 metric tons. **Electricity prod.:** 3.1 bil kWh. **Labor force** (2003 est.): agric. 4.5%, industry 63.1%, services 32.4%.

Finance: Monetary unit: Dollar (BND) (Oct. 2009: 1.40 = $1 U.S.). **GDP:** $20.3 bil; **per capita GDP:** $53,100; **GDP growth:** 0.6%. **Imports** (2007): $2.1 bil; Singapore 35.8%, Malaysia 19%, Japan 7.5%, China 6%, Thailand 4.9%, U.S. 4.6%, UK 4.6%. **Exports** (2007): $8.3 bil; Japan 43.8%, Indonesia 23.2%, S. Korea 11.2%, Australia 10.8%. **Tourism:** NA. **Budget** (2004 est.): $4.8 bil. **Intl. reserves less gold:** $486 mil. **Gold:** NA. **Consumer prices:** NA.

Transport: Motor vehicles: 240,000 pass. cars; 22,100 comm. vehicles. **Civil aviation:** 2.3 bil pass.-mi; 2 airport. **Chief ports:** Lumut, Muara, Seria.

Communications: TV sets: 637 per 1,000 pop. **Radios:** 302 per 1,000 pop. **Telephone lines:** 76,600. **Daily newspaper circ.** (2004): 68.4 per 1,000 pop. **Internet:** 217,000 users.

Health: Life expect.: 73.3 male; 77.8 female. **Births** (per 1,000 pop.): 18.4. **Deaths** (per 1,000 pop.): 3.3. **Natural inc.:** 1.51%. **Infant mortality** (per 1,000 live births): 12.7. **HIV rate:** NA.

Education: Compulsory: ages 5-16. **Literacy:** 94.9%.

Major intl. organizations: UN and some of its specialized agencies, APEC, ASEAN, the Commonwealth.

Embassy: 3520 International Ct. NW 20008; 237-1838.

Website: www.brunei.gov.bn

The Sultanate of Brunei was a powerful state in the early 16th cent., with authority over all of the island of Borneo as well as parts of the Sulu Islands and the Philippines. In 1888, a treaty placed the state under the protection of Great Britain.

Brunei became a fully sovereign and independent state on Jan. 1, 1984. Much of the country's oil wealth has been squandered by members of the royal family.

Bulgaria
Republic of Bulgaria

People: Population: 7,204,687. **Age distrib.** (%): <15: 13.8; 65+: 17.7. **Pop. density:** 168.8 per sq mi, 65.2 per sq km. **Urban:** 70.2%. **Ethnic groups:** Bulgarian 84%, Turk 9%, Roma 5%. **Principal languages:** Bulgarian, Turkish, Roma. **Chief religions:** Bulgarian Orthodox 83%, Muslim 12%.

Geography: Total area: 42,823 sq mi, 110,910 sq km; **Land area:** 42,684 sq mi, 110,550 sq km. **Location:** SE Europe, in E Balkan Peninsula on Black Sea. **Neighbors:** Romania on N; Serbia, Macedonia on W; Greece, Turkey on S. **Topography:** The Stara Planina (Balkan) Mts. stretch E-W across the center of the country, with the Danubian plain on N, the Rhodope Mts. on SW, and Thracian Plain on SE. **Capital:** Sofia, 1,185,000.

Government: Type: Republic. **Head of state:** Pres. Georgi Parvanov; b. June 28, 1957; in office: Jan. 22, 2002. **Head of gov.:** Prime Min. Boyko Borisov; b. June 13, 1959; in office: July 27, 2009. **Local divisions:** 28 provinces. **Defense budget:** $881 mil. **Active troops:** 40,747.

Economy: Industries: utilities, food, beverages, tobacco. **Chief crops:** vegetables, fruits, tobacco, wine, wheat, barley, sunflowers, sugar beets. **Natural resources:** bauxite, copper, lead, zinc, coal, timber. **Crude oil reserves:** 15 mil bbls. **Arable land:** 30%. **Livestock:** cattle: 628,271; chickens: 18 mil; goats: 549,076; pigs: 1.01 mil; sheep: 1.6 mil. **Fish catch:** 12,929 metric tons. **Electricity prod.:** 43.2 bil kWh. **Labor force** (2007 est.): agric. 7.5%, industry 35.5%, services 57%.

Finance: Monetary unit: Lev (BGN) (Oct. 2009: 1.33 = $1 U.S.). **GDP:** $93.8 bil; **per capita GDP:** $12,900; **GDP growth:** 6%. **Imports:** $34.9 bil; Russia 14.6%, Germany 11.8%, Italy 7.9%, Ukraine 7.3%, Romania 5.6%, Turkey 5.5%, Greece 5.4%, Austria 4.1%. **Exports:** $22.5 bil; Greece 9.9%, Germany 9.2%, Turkey 8.9%, Italy 8.5%, Romania 7.2%, Belgium 5.9%, France 4.1%. **Tourism:** $3.1 bil. **Budget:** $15.4 bil. **Intl. reserves less gold:** $10.92 bil. **Gold:** 1.28 mil oz t. **Consumer prices:** 12.3%.

Transport: Railroad: Length: 2,668 mi. **Motor vehicles:** 2.5 mil pass. cars; 371,000 comm. vehicles. **Civil aviation:** 697.8 mil pass.-mi; 132 airports. **Chief ports:** Burgas, Varna.

Communications: TV sets: 429 per 1,000 pop. **Radios:** 537 per 1,000 pop. **Telephone lines:** 2.3 mil. **Daily newspaper circ.** (2004): 79 per 1,000 pop. **Internet:** 2.7 mil users.

Health: Life expect.: 69.2 male; 76.7 female. **Births** (per 1,000 pop.): 9.6. **Deaths** (per 1,000 pop.): 14.3. **Natural inc.:** −0.47%. **Infant mortality** (per 1,000 live births): 18.5. **HIV rate:** NA.

Education: Compulsory: ages 7-14. **Literacy:** 98.3%.

Major intl. organizations: UN (FAO, IBRD, ILO, IMF, IMO, WHO, WTO), EU, NATO, OSCE.

Embassy: 1621 22nd St. NW 20008; 387-0174.

Website: www.government.bg

Bulgaria was settled by Slavs in the 6th cent. Turkic Bulgars arrived in the 7th cent., merged with the Slavs, became Christians by the 9th cent., and set up powerful empires in the 10th and 12th centuries. Ottomans prevailed in 1396 and ruled for nearly 500 years.

An 1876 revolt led to an independent kingdom in 1908. Bulgaria expanded after the first Balkan War but lost its Aegean coastline in WWI, when it sided with Germany. Bulgaria joined the Axis in WWII but withdrew in 1944. Communists took power with Soviet aid; monarchy was abolished Sept. 8, 1946.

On Nov. 10, 1989, Communist Party leader and head of state Todor Zhivkov, who had held power for 35 years, resigned. In Jan. 1990, Parliament voted to revoke the constitutionally guaranteed dominant role of the Communist Party. A new constitution took effect July 13, 1991.

Bulgaria's deteriorating economy provoked nationwide strikes and demonstrations in Jan. 1997. The Union of Democratic Forces, an anti-Communist group, won national elections on Apr. 19. The UDF lost the elections of June 17, 2001, to a party headed by the former king, Simeon II. Socialist opposition leader Georgi Parvanov won a presidential runoff vote Nov. 18, 2001; he was re-elected Oct. 29, 2006.

Bulgaria became a full member of NATO, Apr. 2, 2004, and entered the European Union, Jan. 1, 2007. Boyko Borisov, mayor of Sofia, became prime minister after his center-right party won parliamentary elections July 5, 2009.

Burkina Faso

People: Population: 15,746,232. **Age distrib.** (%): <15: 46.2; 65+: 2.5. **Pop. density:** 149 per sq mi, 57.5 per sq km. **Urban:** 18.3%. **Ethnic groups:** Mossi 40%+, other (incl. Gurunsi, Senufo, Lobi, Bobo, Mande, Fulani) approx. 60%. **Principal languages:** French (official), native African Sudanic-family languages. **Chief religions:** Muslim 50%, indigenous beliefs 40%, Christian (mainly Roman Catholic) 10%.

Geography: Total area: 105,869 sq mi, 274,200 sq km; **Land area:** 105,715 sq mi, 273,800 km. **Location:** In W Africa, S of the Sahara. **Neighbors:** Mali on NW; Niger on NE; Benin, Togo, Ghana, Côte d'Ivoire on S. **Topography:** Landlocked Burkina Faso is in the savanna region of W Africa. The N is arid, hot, and thinly populated. **Capital:** Ouagadougou, 1,149,000.

Government: Type: Republic. **Head of state:** Pres. Blaise Compaoré; b. Feb. 3, 1951; in office: Oct. 15, 1987. **Head of gov.:** Prime Min. Tertius Zongo; b. May 18, 1957; in office: June 4, 2007. **Local divisions:** 45 provinces. **Defense budget:** $95 mil. **Active troops:** 10,800.

Economy: Industries: cotton lint, beverages, agric. proc., soap, cigarettes, textiles, gold. **Chief crops:** cotton, peanuts, shea nuts, sesame, sorghum, millet. **Natural resources:** mang., limestone, marble, gold, phosphates, pumice, salt. **Arable land:** 18%. **Livestock:** cattle: 8.8 mil; chickens: 27.2 mil; goats: 11.4 mil; pigs: 2.8 mil; sheep: 7.3 mil. **Fish catch:** 10,500 metric tons. **Electricity prod.:** 548 mil kWh. **Labor force** (2000 est.): agric. 90%, industry & services 10%.

Finance: Monetary unit: CFA BCEAO Franc (XOF) (Oct. 2009: 444.97 = $1 U.S.). **GDP:** $17.8 bil; **per capita GDP:** $1,200; **GDP growth:** 4.5%. **Imports:** $1.3 bil; Côte d'Ivoire 26.4%, France 18.2%, Togo 7.3%, Libya 4.2%. **Exports:** $544 mil; Singapore 16.9%, China 16%, Belgium 12.9%, Thailand 9.1%, Ghana 7%, Niger 5.2%, Denmark 4.9%. **Tourism:** NA. **Budget:** $1.95 bil. **Intl. reserves less gold:** $601 mil. **Gold:** NA. **Consumer prices:** 10.7%.

Transport: Railroad: Length: 386 mi. **Motor vehicles:** 26,500 pass. cars; 22,600 comm. vehicles. **Civil aviation:** 23 mil pass.-mi (incl. Air Afrique traffic apportionment); 2 airports.

Communications: TV sets: 11 per 1,000 pop. **Radios:** 34 per 1,000 pop. **Telephone lines:** 144,000. **Internet:** 140,000 users.

Health: Life expect.: 50.7 male; 54.5 female. **Births** (per 1,000 pop.): 44.7. **Deaths** (per 1,000 pop.): 13.6. **Natural inc.:** 3.11%. **Infant mortality** (per 1,000 live births): 86. **HIV rate:** 1.6%.

Education: Compulsory: ages 6-16. **Literacy:** 28.7%.

Major intl. organizations: UN and many of its specialized agencies, AU.

Embassy: 2340 Massachusetts Ave. NW 20008; 332-5577.

Website: www.gouvernement.gov.bf or www.burkinaembassy-usa.org

The Mossi people entered the area in the 11th to 13th centuries. Their kingdoms ruled until they were defeated by the Mali and Songhai empires.

French control came by 1896, but Upper Volta (renamed Burkina Faso on Aug. 4, 1984) was not established as a separate territory until 1947. Full independence came Aug. 5, 1960, and a pro-French government was elected. The military seized power in 1980. A 1987 coup established the current regime, which instituted a multiparty system in the early 1990s. Pres. Blaise Compaoré won reelection, Nov. 13, 2005, with 80% of the vote. The country, one of the world's poorest, depends heavily on foreign aid.

Burma
See Myanmar.

Burundi
Republic of Burundi

People: Population: 8,988,091. **Age distrib.** (%): <15: 46.2; 65+: 2.5. **Pop. density:** 907.6 per sq mi, 350.4 per sq km. **Urban:** 9.5%. **Ethnic groups:** Hutu (Bantu) 85%, Tutsi (Hamitic) 14%. **Principal languages:** Kirundi, French (both official); Swahili. **Chief religions:** Christian (predominantly Roman Catholic) 67%, indigenous beliefs 23%, Muslim 10%.

Geography: Total area: 10,745 sq mi, 27,830 sq km; **Land area:** 9,904 sq mi, 25,650 sq km. **Location:** In central Africa. **Neighbors:** Rwanda on N, Dem. Rep. of the Congo (formerly Zaire) on W, Tanzania on E and S. **Topography:** Much of the country is grassy highland, with mountains reaching 8,900 ft. The southernmost source of the White Nile is located in Burundi. Lake Tanganyika is the second deepest lake in the world. **Capital:** Bujumbura, 429,000.

Government: Type: Republic. **Head of state and gov.:** Pres. Pierre Nkurunziza; b. Dec. 18, 1963; in office: Aug. 26, 2005. **Local divisions:** 16 provinces. **Defense budget:** $78 mil. **Active troops:** 20,000.

Economy: Industries: light consumer goods, assembly of imported components, public works constr., food proc. **Chief crops:** coffee, cotton, tea, corn, sorghum, sweet potatoes, bananas, manioc. **Natural resources:** nickel, uranium, rare earth oxides, peat, cobalt, copper, platinum, vanadium, hydropower. **Arable land:** 36%. **Livestock:** cattle: 479,106; chickens: 4.7 mil; goats: 1.6 mil; pigs: 189,505; sheep: 292,916. **Fish catch** (est.): 14,200 metric tons. **Electricity prod.:** 87 mil kWh. **Labor force** (2002 est.): agric. 93.6%, industry 2.3%, services 4.1%.

Finance: Monetary unit: Franc (BIF) (Oct. 2009: 1,210.00 = $1 U.S.). **GDP:** $3.1 bil; **per capita GDP:** $400; **GDP growth:** 4.5%. **Imports:** $350 mil; Saudi Arabia 18.3%, Kenya 10.7%, Belgium 7.9%, France 5.8%, Uganda 5.1%, China 4.9%, India 4.5%, Germany 4.3%. **Exports:** $79 mil; Japan 22.3%, Germany 14.4%, Pakistan 7.5%, Rwanda 4.7%, Sudan 4.4%. **Tourism:** NA. **Budget:** $335.4 mil. **Intl. reserves less gold:** $173 mil. **Gold:** NA. **Consumer prices:** 24.1%.

Transport: Motor vehicles: 7,000 pass. cars; 9,300 comm. vehicles. **Civil aviation:** 5 mil pass.-mi; 1 airport. **Chief port:** Bujumbura.

Communications: TV sets: 15 per 1,000 pop. **Radios:** 152 per 1,000 pop. **Telephone lines:** 30,400. **Internet:** 65,000 users.

Health: Life expect.: 50.9 male; 52.6 female. **Births** (per 1,000 pop.): 41.7. **Deaths** (per 1,000 pop.): 12.9. **Natural inc.:** 2.88%. **Infant mortality** (per 1,000 live births): 60.8. **HIV rate:** 2%.

Education: Compulsory: ages 7-12. **Literacy:** 59.3%.

Major intl. organizations: UN (FAO, IBRD, ILO, IMF, WHO, WTO), AU.

Embassy: 2233 Wisconsin Ave. NW, Ste. 212, 20007; 342-2574.

Website: www.burundi-gov.bi or www.burundiembassy-usa.org

The pygmy Twa were the first inhabitants, followed by Bantu Hutus, who were conquered in the 16th cent. by the Tutsi (Watusi), probably from Ethiopia. Under German control in 1899, the area fell to Belgium in 1916, which exercised successively a League of Nations mandate and UN trusteeship over Ruanda-Urundi (now the two countries of Rwanda and Burundi). Burundi became independent July 1, 1962.

An unsuccessful Hutu rebellion in 1972-73 left 10,000 Tutsi and 150,000 Hutu dead. Over 100,000 Hutu fled to Tanzania and Zaire (now Congo). In the 1980s, Burundi's Tutsi-dominated regime pledged itself to ethnic reconciliation and democratic reform. In the nation's first democratic presidential election, in June 1993, a Hutu, Melchior Ndadaye, was elected. He was killed in an attempted coup, Oct. 21, 1993. At least 150,000 Burundians died as a result of ethnic conflict during the next three years. Pres. Cyprien Ntaryamira, elected Jan. 1994, was killed with the president of Rwanda in a mysterious plane crash, Apr. 6. The incident sparked massive carnage in Rwanda; violence in Burundi, initially far more limited, intensified in 1995. Ethnic strife continued after a military coup, July 25, 1996. Former South African Pres. Nelson Mandela mediated peace talks from Dec. 1999; most warring groups signed a draft peace treaty in Arusha, Tanzania, Aug. 28, 2000. Coup attempts were suppressed Apr. 18 and July 23, 2001. A power-sharing government headed by Buyoya was sworn in Nov. 1, but clashes with rebels continued.

Domitien Ndayizeye, a Hutu, became president Apr. 30, 2003. The UN Security Council authorized, May 21, 2004, a 5,650-member peacekeeping force (ONUB) for Burundi. Approval of a power-sharing constitution by referendum, Feb. 28, 2005, paved the way for local and parliamentary elections. Pierre Nkurunziza, former leader of a Hutu rebel group, became president Aug. 26. ONUB was succeeded, Jan. 1, 2007, by the UN Integrated Office in Burundi (BINUB). Under a reconciliation accord reached Dec. 4, 2008, remaining Hutu rebels began to disarm and demobilize.

Cambodia
Kingdom of Cambodia

People: Population: 14,494,293. **Age distrib.** (%): <15: 32.6; 65+: 3.6. **Pop. density:** 212.7 per sq mi, 82.1 per sq km. **Urban:** 19.7%. **Ethnic groups:** Khmer 90%, Vietnamese 5%. **Principal languages:** Khmer (official), French, English. **Chief religion:** Theravada Buddhist 95%.

Geography: Total area: 69,900 sq mi, 181,040 sq km; **Land area:** 68,155 sq mi, 176,520 sq km. **Location:** SE Asia, on Indochina Peninsula. **Neighbors:** Thailand on W and N, Laos on NE, Vietnam on E. **Topography:** The central area, formed by the Mekong R. basin and Tonle Sap lake, is level. Hills and mountains are in SE, a long escarpment separates the country from Thailand on NW. 76% of the area is forested. **Capital:** Phnom Penh, 1,466,000.

Government: Type: Constitutional monarchy. **Head of state:** King Norodom Sihamoni; b. May 14, 1953; in office: Oct. 14, 2004. **Head of gov.:** Prime Min. Samdech Hun Sen; b. Aug. 5, 1952; in office: Nov. 30, 1998. **Local divisions:** 20 provinces and 4 municipalities. **Defense budget:** $137 mil. **Active troops:** 124,300.

Economy: Industries: tourism, garments, rice milling, fishing, wood & wood products, rubber, cement, gem mining, textiles. **Chief crops:** rice, rubber, corn, vegetables. **Natural resources:** oil & gas, timber, gems, iron ore, mang., phosphates. **Arable land:** 20%. **Livestock:** cattle: 3.4 mil; chickens: 15.2 mil; sheep: 2.8 mil.

Fish catch (est.): 530,200 metric tons. **Electricity prod.:** 1.2 bil kWh. **Labor force** (2004 est.): agric. 75%, industry & services NA.

Finance: Monetary unit: Riel (KHR) (Oct. 2009: 4,175.00 = $1 U.S.). **GDP:** $27.9 bil; **per capita GDP:** $2,000; **GDP growth:** 5%. **Imports:** $6.4 bil; Thailand 27.5%, China 16.2%, Vietnam 15.4%, Hong Kong 8.3%, Singapore 7.1%, S. Korea 4.4%. **Exports:** $4.3 bil; U.S. 53.9%, Germany 7.7%, Canada 5.9%, UK 5.4%, Vietnam 4.9%. **Tourism:** $1.1 bil. **Budget:** $1.04 bil. **Intl. reserves less gold:** $1.49 bil. **Gold:** 400,000 oz t. **Consumer prices:** 25%.

Transport: Railroad: Length: 374 mi. **Motor vehicles:** 8,300 pass. cars; 3,100 comm. vehicles. **Civil aviation:** 102.5 mil pass.-mi; 6 airports. **Chief ports:** Phnom Penh, Kampong Saom.

Communications: TV sets: 9 per 1,000 pop. **Radios:** 128 per 1,000 pop. **Telephone lines:** 45,100. **Internet:** 74,000 users.

Health: Life expect.: 59.6 male; 63.8 female. **Births** (per 1,000 pop.): 25.7. **Deaths** (per 1,000 pop.): 8.2. **Natural inc.:** 1.75%. **Infant mortality** (per 1,000 live births): 56.6. **HIV rate:** 0.8%.

Education: Compulsory: ages 6-14. **Literacy:** 76.3%.

Major intl. organizations: UN (FAO, IBRD, ILO, IMF, IMO, WHO, WTO), ASEAN.

Website: www.cambodia.gov.kh

Early kingdoms dating from that of Funan in the 1st cent. CE culminated in the great Khmer empire that flourished from the 9th cent. to the 13th, encompassing present-day Thailand, Cambodia, Laos, and southern Vietnam. The peripheral areas were lost to invading Siamese and Vietnamese, and France established a protectorate in 1863. Independence came in 1953.

Prince Norodom Sihanouk, king 1941-55 and head of state from 1960, tried to maintain neutrality. Relations with the U.S. were broken in 1965, after South Vietnam planes attacked Vietcong forces within Cambodia. Relations were restored in 1969, after Sihanouk charged Viet Communists with arming Cambodian insurgents.

In 1970, pro-U.S. Prem. Lon Nol seized power, demanding removal of 40,000 North Viet troops; the monarchy was abolished. Sihanouk formed a government-in-exile in Beijing, and open war began between the government and Communist Khmer Rouge guerrillas. The U.S. provided heavy military and economic aid.

Khmer Rouge forces captured Phnom Penh Apr. 17, 1975. Cities were depopulated and their residents executed or condemned to forced labor. An estimated 1.7 mil people died in "killing fields" or from other hardships under Khmer Rouge rule, 1975-79.

Severe border fighting broke out with Vietnam in 1978 and developed into a full-fledged Vietnamese invasion. Formation of a Vietnamese-backed government was announced, Jan. 8, 1979, one day after the capture of Phnom Penh. Thousands of refugees fled to Thailand, and widespread starvation was reported. Vietnamese troops remained in Cambodia during the 1980s, meeting resistance from Khmer Rouge guerrillas, especially along the Thai border. Vietnam withdrew nearly all its troops by Sept. 1989.

Following UN-sponsored elections in Cambodia that ended May 28, 1993, the 2 leading parties agreed to share power in an interim government. On Sept. 21, a constitution reestablishing a monarchy was adopted by the National Assembly. It took effect Sept. 24, with Sihanouk as king. The Khmer Rouge, which had boycotted the elections, opposed the new government but the insurgents weakened and splintered by 1996.

Co-Prime Min. Hun Sen staged a coup July 5, 1997, ousting his rival, Prince Norodom Ranariddh. Pol Pot, the Khmer Rouge leader who held power during the late 1970s, was denounced by his former comrades at a show trial, July 25, and sentenced to house arrest; he died Apr. 15, 1998. Sihanouk abdicated because of poor health and was succeeded, Oct. 14, 2004, by his son Norodom Sihamonir.

Arrested in 1999, former Khmer Rouge military chief Ta Mok died July 21, 2006, before he could stand trial for genocide and crimes against humanity. Khieu Samphan, another former Khmer Rouge leader, was arrested Nov. 19, 2007, and charged with crimes against humanity. Hun Sen's party has retained power through a series of flawed elections; the most recent, on July 27, 2008, was described by international observers as a notable improvement over previous votes.

Cameroon
Republic of Cameroon

People: Population: 18,879,301. **Age distrib.** (%): <15: 40.9; 65+: 3.3. **Pop. density:** 104.2 per sq mi, 40.2 per sq km. **Urban:** 54.3%. **Ethnic groups:** Cameroon Highlanders 31%, Equatorial Bantu 19%, Kirdi 11%, Fulani 10%, NW Bantu 8%, E Nigritic 7%, other African 13%. **Principal languages:** English, French (both official); 24 major African lang. groups. **Chief religions:** Indigenous beliefs 40%, Christian 40%, Muslim 20%.

Geography: Total area: 183,568 sq mi, 475,440 sq km; **Land area:** 181,252 sq mi, 469,440 sq km. **Location:** Between W and central Africa. **Neighbors:** Nigeria on NW; Chad, Central African Republic on E; Congo, Gabon, Equatorial Guinea on S. **Topography:** A low coastal plain with rain forests is in S; plateaus in center lead to forested mountains in W, including Mt. Cameroon, 13,435 ft; grasslands in N lead to marshes around Lake Chad. **Capital:** Yaoundé, 1,611,000. **Cities (urban aggr.):** Douala, 1,906,000.

Government: Type: Republic. **Head of state:** Pres. Paul Biya; b. Feb. 13, 1933; in office: Nov. 6, 1982. **Head of gov.:** Prime Min. Philemon Yang; b. June 14, 1947; in office: June 30, 2009. **Local divisions:** 10 provinces. **Defense budget:** $297 mil. **Active troops:** 14,100.

Economy: Industries: oil prod. & refining, aluminum prod., food proc., light consumer goods, textiles, lumber. **Chief crops:** coffee, cocoa, cotton, rubber, bananas, oilseed, grains. **Natural resources:** oil, bauxite, iron ore, timber, hydropower. **Crude oil reserves:** 200 mil bbls. **Arable land:** 13%. **Livestock:** cattle: 6 mil; chickens: 31 mil; goats: 4.4 mil; pigs: 1.4 mil; sheep: 3.8 mil. **Fish catch:** 138,952 metric tons. **Electricity prod.:** 3.9 bil kWh. **Labor force** (2001 est.): agric. 70%, industry 13%, services 17%.

Finance: Monetary unit: CFA BEAC Franc (XAF) (Oct. 2009: 444.97 = $1 U.S.). **GDP:** $42.8 bil; **per capita GDP:** $2,300; **GDP growth:** 3.9%. **Imports:** $4.3 bil; France 21.6%, Nigeria 14.2%, China 9.2%, Belgium 6.2%. **Exports:** $4.8 bil; Spain 18.7%, Italy 12.7%, U.S. 10%, S. Korea 9.3%, France 7.7%, Netherlands 7.6%, China 5.3%. **Tourism:** NA. **Budget:** $3.3 bil. **Intl. reserves less gold:** $2 bil. **Gold:** 30,000 oz t. **Consumer prices:** 5.3%.

Transport: Railroad: Length: 613 mi. **Motor vehicles:** 173,100 pass. cars; 57,400 comm. vehicles. **Civil aviation:** 495.2 mil pass.-mi; 11 airports. **Chief ports:** Douala, Limboh Terminal.

Communications: TV sets: 34 per 1,000 pop. **Radios:** 163 per 1,000 pop. **Telephone lines:** 198,300. **Internet:** 725,000 users.

Health: Life expect.: 52.5 male; 54.1 female. **Births** (per 1,000 pop.): 34.6. **Deaths** (per 1,000 pop.): 12.4. **Natural inc.:** 2.22%. **Infant mortality** (per 1,000 live births): 64.6. **HIV rate:** 5.1%.

Education: Compulsory: ages 6-11. **Literacy:** 67.9%.

Major intl. organizations: UN (FAO, IBRD, ILO, IMF, IMO, WHO, WTO), the Commonwealth, AU.

Embassy: 2349 Massachusetts Ave. NW 20008; 265-8790.

Website: www.spm.gov.cm

Portuguese sailors were the first Europeans to reach Cameroon, in the 15th cent. The European and American slave trade was very active in the area. German control lasted from 1884 to 1916, when France and Britain divided the territory, later receiving League of Nations mandates and UN trusteeships. French Cameroon became independent Jan. 1, 1960; one part of British Cameroon joined Nigeria in 1961, the other part joined Cameroon. Stability has allowed for development of roads, railways, agriculture, and petroleum production.

Pres. Paul Biya has retained power since 1982 in a series of elections that were boycotted by opposition parties or disputed as fraudulent. Rising food and fuel costs and discontent with Biya's continued rule sparked antigovernment riots Feb. 23-29, 2008. The legislature, controlled by Biya loyalists, voted Apr. 10 to abolish a presidential term limit that had been introduced in 1996.

Canada

People: Population: 33,487,208. **Age distrib.** (%): <15: 16.1; 65+: 15.2. **Pop. density:** 9.5 per sq mi, 3.7 per sq km. **Urban:** 80.1%. **Ethnic groups:** British isles origin 28%, French origin 23%, other European 15%, mixed background 26%. **Principal languages:** English, French (both official). **Chief religions:** Roman Catholic 43%, Protestant (incl. United Church, Anglican) 23%, unspecified 12%, none 16%.

Geography: Total area: 3,855,103 sq mi, 9,984,670 sq km; **Land area:** 3,511,023 sq mi, 9,093,507 sq km. The largest country in land size in the Western Hemisphere. **Topography:** Canada stretches 3,426 mi from east to west and extends southward from the North Pole to the U.S. border. Its seacoast includes 36,356 mi of mainland and 115,133 mi of islands, including the Arctic islands almost from Greenland to near the Alaskan border. **Climate:** While generally temperate, varies from freezing winter cold to blistering summer heat. **Capital:** Ottawa-Gatineau, 1,145,000. **Cities**

(urban aggr.): Toronto, 5,213,000; Montréal, 3,678,000; Vancouver, 2,146,000; Calgary, 1,110,000; Edmonton, 1,058,000.

Government: Type: Confederation with parliamentary democracy. **Head of state:** Queen Elizabeth II, represented by Gov.-Gen. Michaëlle Jean; b. Sept. 6, 1957; in office: Sept. 27, 2005. **Head of gov.:** Prime Min. Stephen Harper; b. Apr. 30, 1959; in office: Feb. 6, 2006. **Local divisions:** 10 provinces, 3 territories. **Defense budget:** $18.5 bil. **Active troops:** 64,371.

Economy: Industries: transp. equip., chemicals, minerals, food & fish products, wood & paper products, oil & nat. gas. **Chief crops:** wheat, barley, oilseed, tobacco, fruits, vegetables. **Natural resources:** iron ore, nickel, zinc, copper, gold, lead, molybd., potash, diamonds, silver, fish, timber, wildlife, coal, oil, nat. gas, hydropower. **Crude oil reserves:** 178.1 bil bbls (incl. condensate & oil sands reserves). **Arable land:** 5%. **Livestock:** cattle: 14.2 mil; chickens: 165 mil; goats: 30,000; pigs: 14.9 mil; sheep: 879,100. **Fish catch:** 1.19 mil metric tons. **Electricity prod.:** 594.6 bil kWh. **Labor force** (2006): agric. 2%, mfg. 13%, constr. 6%, services 76%, other 3%.

Finance: Monetary unit: Dollar (CAD) (Oct. 2009: 1.06 = $1 U.S.). **GDP:** $1.3 tril; **per capita GDP:** $39,100; **GDP growth:** 0.4%. **Imports:** $415.2 bil; U.S. 52.4%, China 9.8%, Mexico 4.1%. **Exports:** $459.1 bil; U.S. 77.7%, U.K. 2.7%, Japan 2.3%. **Tourism:** $15.3 bil. **Budget:** $555.2 bil. **Intl. reserves less gold:** $28.42 bil. **Gold:** 110,000 oz t. **Consumer prices:** 2.4%.

Transport: Railroad: Length: 29,011 mi. **Motor vehicles:** 18.1 mil pass. cars; 708,000 comm. vehicles. **Civil aviation:** 58.8 bil pass.-mi; 515 airports. **Chief ports:** Halifax, Hamilton, Montreal, Port-Cartier, Quebec City, Saint John (New Brunswick), Sept-Isles, Vancouver.

Communications: TV sets: 709 per 1,000 pop. **Radios:** 1,038 per 1,000 pop. **Telephone lines:** 18.3 mil. **Daily newspaper circ.** (2004): 174.6 per 1,000 pop. **Internet:** 25.1 mil users.

Health: Life expect.: 78.7 male; 83.8 female. **Births** (per 1,000 pop.): 10.3. **Deaths** (per 1,000 pop.): 7.6. **Natural inc.:** 0.27%. **Infant mortality** (per 1,000 live births): 5.1. **HIV rate:** 0.4%.

Education: Compulsory: ages 6-16. **Literacy:** 99%.

Major intl. organizations: UN and all of its specialized agencies, APEC, the Commonwealth, NAFTA, NATO, OAS, OECD, OSCE.

Embassy: 501 Pennsylvania Ave. NW 20001; 682-1740.

Website: www.canada.gc.ca

French explorer Jacques Cartier, who reached the Gulf of St. Lawrence in 1534, is generally regarded as Canada's founder. But English seaman John Cabot sighted Newfoundland in 1497, and Vikings are believed to have reached the Atlantic coast centuries before either explorer. Canadian settlement was pioneered by the French who established Quebec City (1608) and Montreal (1642) and declared New France a colony in 1663.

Britain acquired Acadia (later Nova Scotia) in 1717 and, through military victory over French forces in Canada, captured Quebec (1759) and obtained control of the rest of New France in 1763. The French, through the Quebec Act of 1774, retained the rights to their own language, religion, and civil law. The British presence in Canada increased during the American Revolution when many colonials, proudly calling themselves United Empire Loyalists, moved north to Canada. Fur traders and explorers led Canadians westward across the continent. Sir Alexander Mackenzie reached the Pacific in 1793 and scrawled on a rock, "From Canada by land."

In Upper and Lower Canada (later called Ontario and Quebec) and in the Maritimes, legislative assemblies appeared in the 18th cent. and reformers called for responsible government. But the War of 1812 intervened. The war, a conflict between Great Britain and the U.S. fought mainly in Upper Canada, ended in a stalemate in 1814.

In 1837 political agitation for more democratic government culminated in rebellions in Upper and Lower Canada. Britain sent Lord Durham to investigate; in a famous report (1839), he recommended union of the 2 parts into one colony called Canada. The union lasted until Confederation, July 1, 1867, when proclamation of the British North America (BNA) Act (now known as the Constitution Act, 1867) launched the Dominion of Canada, consisting of Ontario, Quebec, and the former colonies of Nova Scotia and New Brunswick.

Canada's Provinces and Territories

Provinces/territories	Joined confed.	Area (sq mi)	Population (Apr. 2009 est.)	Capital	Premier	Party	In office
Alberta................	1905	255,287	3,653,840	Edmonton	Ed Stelmach	Prog. Cons.	2006
British Columbia.........	1871	365,948	4,435,344	Victoria	Gordon Campbell	Liberal	2001
Manitoba............	1870	250,947	1,217,163	Winnipeg	Gary Doer	New Democratic	1999
New Brunswick...........	1867	28,355	748,866	Fredericton	Shawn Graham	Liberal	2006
Newfoundland & Labrador ..	1949	156,649	508,726	St. John's	Danny Williams	Prog. Cons.	2003
Nova Scotia...........	1867	21,425	939,475	Halifax	Darrell Dexte	New Democratic	2006
Ontario...............	1867	412,581	13,014,018	Toronto	Dalton McGuinty	Liberal	2003
Prince Edward Island	1873	2,185	140,638	Charlottetown	Robert Ghiz	Liberal	2007
Quebec...............	1867	594,860	7,799,372	Québec	Jean Charest	Liberal	2003
Saskatchewan...........	1905	251,866	1,027,092	Regina	Brad Wall	Saskatchewan	2007
Northwest Territories[1]......	1871	503,951	42,840	Yellowknife	Floyd Roland	non-partisan	2007
Nunavut[1]...............	(2)	818,959	31,762	Iqaluit	Eva Aariak	non-partisan	1999
Yukon[1]	1898	186,661	33,550	Whitehorse	Dennis Fentie	Yukon	2002

(1) Territories also have federally appointed commissioners to represent federal interests. (2) Territory created in 1999 from eastern portion of Northwest Territories.

Since 1840 the Canadian colonies had held the right to internal self-government. The BNA Act, which was the basis for the country's written constitution, established a federal system of government on the model of a British parliament and cabinet structure under the crown. Canada was proclaimed a self-governing Dominion within the British Empire in 1931. With the ratification of the Constitution Act, 1982, Canada severed its last formal legislative link with Britain by obtaining the right to amend its constitution.

The so-called Meech Lake Agreement, 1987, which would have assured constitutional protection for Quebec's efforts to preserve its French language and culture, sparked a separatist revival in Quebec. Subsequently, the Charlottetown agreement called for constitutional changes, such as recognition of Quebec as a "distinct society" within the Canadian confederation. It was defeated by a national referendum Oct. 26, 1992.

Canada became the first nation to ratify the North American Free Trade Agreement between Canada, Mexico, and the U.S. June 23, 1993. It went into effect Jan. 1, 1994.

On Feb. 24, 1993, Brian Mulroney resigned as prime minister after more than 8 years in office; he was succeeded by Kim Campbell. In elections Oct. 25, 1993, the ruling Conservatives were defeated in a landslide that left them only 2 of the 295 seats in the House of Commons. Jean Chrétien became prime minister. In a Quebec referendum held Oct. 30, 1995, proponents of secession lost by a razor-thin margin. The elections of June 2, 1997, left the Liberals with a slim majority.

On Jan. 7, 1998, the government apologized to indigenous peoples for 150 years of mistreatment and pledged to set up a "healing fund." Canada's highest court ruled, Aug. 20, that Quebec cannot secede unilaterally, even if a majority of the province approves. Nunavut ("Our Land"), carved from Northwest Territories as a homeland for the Inuit, was established Apr. 1, 1999. Victory by the Liberals in national elections Nov. 27, 2000, made Chrétien the first Canadian prime minister in over 50 years to head a third successive majority government.

Canada sent 5 warships in Oct. 2001 and 850 troops in Feb. 2002, to join U.S. counterterrorism operations in Afghanistan. Relations between Canada and the U.S. cooled after Prime Min. Chrétien refused to contribute troops to the U.S.-led invasion of Iraq in Mar. 2003.

A SARS outbreak killed more than 40 people in the Toronto area in 2003. Chrétien retired Dec. 12, and Paul Martin became prime minister. Weakened by a scandal involving improper payments to Quebec firms for advertising and sponsorship of cultural and sporting events, the Liberals won only 135 of 308 seats in parliamentary elections June 28, 2004. Martin stayed in office as head of a minority government.

Parliament enacted a bill, July 19, 2005, making same-sex marriage (already permitted in 8 of 10 provinces) legal throughout the country. Michaëlle Jean, a Haitian-born TV journalist, was installed Sept. 27 as Canada's first black governor-general.

Twelve years of Liberal party rule ended when Conservatives won 124 seats to the Liberals' 103 in parliamentary elections, Jan. 23, 2006. Conservative leader Stephen Harper took office Feb. 6 as head of a minority government. Police and intelligence officials in the Toronto area, June 2-3, arrested and charged 17 people with plotting terrorist attacks in Canada; their targets were said to include the House of Commons and the prime minister. The Supreme Court, Feb. 23, 2007, unanimously struck down a law under which foreign-born terrorism suspects had been indefinitely detained without charge. Harper called Sept. 7, 2008, for parliamentary elections Oct. 14, a year earlier than anticipated.

Prime Min. Harper remained in office as head of a minority government after early elections Oct. 14, 2008, as Conservatives increased their plurality to 143 seats in the 308-seat House of Commons. The three main opposition parties—Liberals (77 seats), Bloc Québécois (49), and New Democratic Party (37)—agreed Dec. 1 to form a majority coalition to oust Harper, but he retained power by persuading Gov.-Gen. Michaëlle Jean Dec. 4 to suspend Parliament, thereby avoiding a vote of no-confidence. When Parliament reconvened Jan. 27, 2009, the Liberals agreed to support a Harper budget that included a $32.6 bil stimulus to combat recession. By Aug. 2009, with unemployment at 8.7%, the economy had begun to show signs of an upturn.

Prime Ministers of Canada

Canada is a constitutional monarchy with a parliamentary system of government. It is also a federal state. Canada's official head of state, Queen Elizabeth II, is represented by a resident Governor-General. However, in practice the nation is governed by the Prime Minister, leader of the party that commands the support of a majority of the House of Commons, dominant chamber of Canada's bicameral Parliament.

Name	Party	Term
Sir John A. Macdonald	Conservative	1867-1873
Alexander Mackenzie	Liberal	1873-1878
Sir John A. Macdonald	Conservative	1878-1891

Name	Party	Term
Sir John J. C. Abbott	Conservative	1891-1892
Sir John S. D. Thompson	Conservative	1892-1894
Sir Mackenzie Bowell.	Conservative	1894-1896
Sir Charles Tupper.	Conservative	1896[1]
Sir Wilfrid Laurier	Liberal	1896-1911
Sir Robert Laird Borden	Cons./Union.[2]	1911-1920
Arthur Meighen	Unionist	1920-1921
W. L. Mackenzie King	Liberal	1921-1926
Arthur Meighen	Conservative	1926[3]
W. L. Mackenzie King	Liberal	1926-1930
Richard Bedford Bennett	Conservative	1930-1935
W. L. Mackenzie King	Liberal	1935-1948
Louis St. Laurent	Liberal	1948-1957
John G. Diefenbaker	Prog. Cons.	1957-1963
Lester Bowles Pearson	Liberal	1963-1968
Pierre Elliott Trudeau	Liberal	1968-1979
Joe Clark	Prog. Cons.	1979-1980
Pierre Elliott Trudeau	Liberal	1980-1984
John Napier Turner	Liberal	1984[4]
Brian Mulroney.	Prog. Cons.	1984-1993
Kim Campbell	Prog. Cons.	1993[5]
Jean Chrétien	Liberal	1993-2003
Paul Martin.	Liberal	2003-2006
Stephen Harper	Conservative	2006-

(1) May-July. (2) Conservative 1911-17, Unionist 1917-20. (3) June-Sept. (4) June-Sept. (5) June-Oct.

Cape Verde
Republic of Cape Verde

People: Population: 429,474. **Age distrib.** (%): <15: 35.2; 65+: 6.4. **Pop. density:** 275.8 per sq mi, 106.5 per sq km. **Urban:** 57.4%. **Ethnic groups:** Creole (mulatto) 71%, African 28%. **Principal languages:** Portuguese, Crioulo (blend of Portuguese & W African words). **Chief religions:** Roman Catholic (infused with indigenous beliefs), Protestant (mostly Church of the Nazarene).

Geography: Total area: 1,557 sq mi, 4,033 sq km; **Land area:** 1,557 sq mi, 4,033 sq km. **Location:** In Atlantic O., off W tip of Africa. **Neighbors:** Nearest are Mauritania, Senegal to E. **Topography:** Cape Verde Islands are 15 in number, volcanic in origin (active crater on Fogo). The landscape is eroded and stark, with vegetation mostly in interior valleys. **Capital:** Praia, 125,000.

Government: Type: Republic. **Head of state:** Pres. Pedro Pires; b. Apr. 29, 1934; in office: Mar. 22, 2001. **Head of gov.:** Prime Min. José Maria Neves; b. Mar. 28, 1960; in office: Feb. 1, 2001. **Local divisions:** 17 districts. **Defense budget:** $8 mil. **Active troops:** 1,200.

Economy: Industries food & beverages, fish proc., shoes & garments, salt mining, ship repair. **Chief crops:** bananas, corn, beans, sweet potatoes, sugarcane, coffee, peanuts. **Natural resources:** salt, basalt rock, limestone, kaolin, fish. **Arable land:** 11%. **Livestock:** cattle: 38,100; chickens: 505,000; goats: 188,115; pigs: 217,000; sheep: 14,796. **Fish catch:** 18,328 metric tons. **Electricity prod.:** 47 mil kWh. **Labor force:** NA.

Finance: Monetary unit: Escudo (CVE) (Oct. 2009: 79.42 = $1 U.S.). **GDP:** $1.6 bil; **per capita GDP:** $3,800; **GDP growth:** 5.5%. **Imports:** $866 mil; Portugal 39.5%, Netherlands 11.4%, Spain 6.5%, UK 6.3%, Côte d'Ivoire 4.4%, Brazil 4%. **Exports:** $99 mil; Japan 37.8%, Spain 28.7%, Portugal 17.7%. **Tourism:** $303 mil. **Budget:** $449.7 mil. **Intl. reserves less gold:** $168 mil. **Gold:** NA. **Consumer prices:** 6.8%.

Transport: Motor vehicles: 13,500 pass. cars; 3,100 comm. vehicles. **Civil aviation:** 669.8 mil pass.-mi; 9 airports. **Chief port:** Porto Grande.

Communications: TV sets: 5 per 1,000 pop. **Radios:** NA. **Telephone lines:** 72,000. **Internet:** 102,800 users.

Health: Life expect.: 68 male; 74.8 female. **Births** (per 1,000 pop.): 23.9. **Deaths** (per 1,000 pop.): 6.3. **Natural inc.:** 1.77%. **Infant mortality** (per 1,000 live births): 42.5. **HIV rate:** NA.

Education: Compulsory: ages 6-11. **Literacy:** 83.8%.

Major intl. organizations: UN (FAO, IBRD, ILO, IMF, IMO, WHO), AU.

Embassy: 3415 Massachusetts Ave. NW 20007; 965-6820. **Website:** www.governo.cv

The first Portuguese colonists landed in 1462; African slaves were brought soon after, and most Cape Verdeans descend from both groups. Cape Verde independence came July 5, 1975. Antonio Mascarenhas Monteiro won the nation's first free presidential election Feb. 17, 1991; he was reelected without opposition five years later. Pedro Pires won a presidential runoff election Feb. 25, 2001, and was reelected Feb. 12, 2006. Remittances from Cape Verdean emigrants are a major source of income.

Central African Republic

People: Population: 4,511,488. **Age distrib.** (%): <15: 40.9; 65+: 4.1. **Pop. density:** 18.8 per sq mi, 7.2 per sq km. **Urban:** 38.1%. **Ethnic groups:** Baya 33%, Banda 27%, Mandjia 13%, Sara 10%, Mboum 7%. **Principal languages:** French (official), Sangho (national), tribal languages. **Chief religions:** Indigenous beliefs 35%, Protestant 25%, Roman Catholic 25%, Muslim 15%.

Geography: Total area: 240,535 sq mi, 622,984 sq km; **Land area:** 240,535 sq mi, 622,984 sq km. **Location:** In central Africa. **Neighbors:** Chad on N, Cameroon on W, Congo-Brazzaville and Congo-Kinshasa (formerly Zaire) on S, Sudan on E. **Topography:** Mostly rolling plateau, average altitude 2,000 ft, with rivers draining S to the Congo and N to Lake Chad. Open, well-watered savanna covers most of the area, with an arid area in NE, and tropical rain forest in SW. **Capital:** Bangui, 672,000.

Government: Type: Republic. **Head of state:** Pres. François Bozizé; b. Oct. 14, 1946; in office: Mar. 15, 2003. **Head of gov.:** Prime Min. Faustin Archange Touadéra; b. Apr. 21, 1957; in office: Jan. 22, 2008. **Local divisions:** 14 prefectures, 2 economic prefectures, 1 commune. **Defense budget:** $18 mil. **Active troops:** 3,150.

Economy: Industries: gold & diamond mining, logging, brewing, textiles, footwear, bicycle & motorcycle assembly. **Chief crops:** timber, cotton, coffee, tobacco, manioc, yams, millet, corn, bananas. **Natural resources:** diamonds, uranium, timber, gold, oil, hydropower. **Arable land:** 3%. **Livestock:** cattle: 3.4 mil; chickens: 4.8 mil; goats: 3.1 mil; pigs: 800,000; sheep: 260,000. **Fish catch** (est.): 15,000 metric tons. **Electricity prod.:** 110 mil kWh. **Labor force:** NA.

Finance: Monetary unit: CFA BEAC Franc (XAF) (Oct. 2009: 444.97 = $1 U.S.). **GDP:** $3.2 bil; **per capita GDP:** $700; **GDP growth:** 2.2%. **Imports:** (2007): $237.3 mil; France 17.3%, Cameroon 9.8%, Netherlands 7.3%, U.S. 6.7%. **Exports** (2007): $146.7 mil; Japan 43.2%, Belgium 10.4%, China 8.3%, Indonesia 6%, France 4.7%, Italy 4.3%, Democratic Republic of the Congo 4.3%. **Tourism:** NA. **Budget:** $273 mil. **Intl. reserves less gold:** $79 mil. **Gold:** 10,000 oz t. **Consumer prices:** 9.3%.

Transport: Motor vehicles: 800 pass. cars; 700 comm. vehicles. **Civil aviation:** 80.8 mil pass.-mi (incl. Air Afrique traffic apportionment); 2 airports. **Chief ports:** Bangui, Nola, Nzinga, Salo.

Communications: TV sets: 6 per 1,000 pop. **Radios:** 83 per 1,000 pop. **Telephone lines:** 12,000. **Internet:** 19,000 users.

Health: Life expect.: 44.1 male; 44.3 female. **Births** (per 1,000 pop.): 33.1. **Deaths** (per 1,000 pop.): 18. **Natural inc.:** 1.51%. **Infant mortality** (per 1,000 live births): 82.1. **HIV rate:** 6.3%.

Education: Compulsory: ages 6-15. **Literacy:** 48.6%.

Major intl. organizations: UN (FAO, IBRD, ILO, IMF, WHO, WTO), AU.

Embassy: 1618 22nd St. NW 20008; 483-7800.

Website: www.state.gov/p/af/ci/ct/

Various Bantu peoples migrated through the region for centuries before French control was asserted in the late 19th cent., when the region was named Ubangi-Shari. Complete independence was attained Aug. 13, 1960.

Pres. Jean-Bedel Bokassa, who seized power in a 1965 military coup, proclaimed himself constitutional emperor of the renamed Central African Empire Dec. 1976. Bokassa's rule was characterized by ruthless authoritarianism and human rights violations. He was ousted in a bloodless coup aided by the French government, Sept. 20, 1979. In 1981, Gen. André Kolingba became head of state in another bloodless coup. Multiparty legislative and presidential elections were held in Oct. 1992 but were canceled by the government when Kolingba was losing. New elections, held in Aug. and Sept. 1993, led to the replacement of Kolingba with civilian rule under Pres. Ange-Félix Patassé.

France sent in troops to suppress army mutinies in 1996 and 1997. After thwarting several coup attempts, Patassé was ousted Mar. 15, 2003, by rebels under former army chief François Bozizé. Bozizé won a presidential runoff election May 8, 2005, but insurgent activity by Patassé loyalists and others continued in the north. A national peace conference, Dec. 8-20, 2008, paved the way for the installation of a unity government Jan. 19, 2009.

Chad
Republic of Chad

People: Population: 10,329,208. **Age distrib.** (%): <15: 46.7; 65+: 2.9. **Pop. density:** 21.2 per sq mi, 8.2 per sq km. **Urban:** 25.3%. **Ethnic groups:** Sara 28%, Arab 12%, Mayo-Kebbi 12%, Kanem-Bornou 9%. **Principal languages:** French, Arabic (both official); 120+ diff. languages & dialects. **Chief religions:** Muslim 53%, Catholic 20%, Protestant 14%, animist 7%.

Geography: Total area: 495,750 sq mi, 1,284,000 sq km; **Land area:** 486,180 sq mi, 1,259,200 sq km. **Location:** In central N Africa. **Neighbors:** Libya on N; Niger, Nigeria, Cameroon on W; Central African Republic on S; Sudan on E. **Topography:** Wooded savanna, steppe, and desert in the S; part of the Sahara in the N. Southern rivers flow N to Lake Chad, surrounded by marshland. **Capital:** N'Djaména, 989,000.

Government: Type: Republic. **Head of state:** Pres. Idriss Déby Itno; b. 1952; in office: Dec. 4, 1990. **Head of gov.:** Prime Min. Youssouf Saleh Abbas; b. 1952; in office: Apr. 16, 2008. **Local divisions:** 14 prefectures. **Defense budget:** $70 mil. **Active troops:** 25,350.

Economy: Industries: oil, cotton textiles, meatpacking, brewing, sodium carbonate, soap, cigarettes, constr. materials. **Chief crops:** cotton, sorghum, millet, peanuts, rice, potatoes, manioc. **Natural resources:** oil, uranium, natron, kaolin, fish. **Crude oil reserves:** 1.5 bil bbls. **Arable land:** 3%. **Livestock:** cattle: 6.8 mil; chickens: 5.4 mil; goats: 6.1 mil; pigs: 27,040; sheep: 3 mil. **Fish catch** (est.): 70,000 metric tons. **Electricity prod.:** 95 mil kWh. **Labor force** (2006 est.): agric. 80% (subsistence farming, herding, fishing), industry & services 20%.

Finance: Monetary unit: CFA BEAC Franc (XAF) (Oct. 2009: 444.97 = $1 U.S.). **GDP:** $15.9 bil; **per capita GDP:** $1,600; **GDP growth:** -0.8%. **Imports:** $1.9 bil; France 19.2%, Cameroon 16.2%, China 10.4%, U.S. 8.5%, Germany 6.1%, Saudi Arabia 5.1%, Netherlands 4.4%. **Exports:** $4.5 bil; U.S. 90.7%, China 3.3%, Japan 2.2%. **Tourism:** NA. **Budget:** $1.7 bil. **Intl. reserves less gold:** $874 mil. **Gold:** 10,000 oz t. **Consumer prices:** 10.3%.

Transport: Civil aviation: 80.8 mil pass.-mi (incl. Air Afrique traffic apportionment); 8 airports.

Communications: TV sets: 1 per 1,000 pop. **Radios:** 236 per 1,000 pop. **Telephone lines:** 13,000. **Internet:** 130,000 users.

Health: Life expect.: 46.4 male; 48.5 female. **Births** (per 1,000 pop.): 41.6. **Deaths** (per 1,000 pop.): 16.4. **Natural inc.:** 2.52%. **Infant mortality** (per 1,000 live births): 100.4. **HIV rate:** 3.5%.

Education: Compulsory: ages 6-11. **Literacy:** 25.7%.

Major intl. organizations: UN (FAO, IBRD, ILO, IMF, WHO, WTO), AU.

Embassy: 2002 R St. NW 20009; 462-4009.

Website: www.state.gov/p/af/ci/cd/

Chad was the site of paleolithic and neolithic cultures before the Sahara Desert formed. A succession of kingdoms and Arab slave traders dominated Chad until France took control around 1900. Independence came Aug. 11, 1960. Northern Muslim rebels have fought animist and Christian southern government and French troops from 1966, despite numerous cease-fires and peace pacts.

Rebel forces, led by Hissène Habré, captured the capital and forced Pres. Goukouni Oueddei to flee the country in June 1982. In Dec. 1990, Habré was overthrown by a Libyan-supported insurgent group, the Patriotic Salvation Movement. After approval of a new constitution Mar. 1996, Chad's first multiparty presidential election was held in June and July.

Oil began flowing July 15, 2003, through a 665-mi pipeline that allows landlocked Chad to export via Cameroon. Pres. Idriss Déby Itno won a 3rd term, May 3, 2006, in an election boycotted by major opposition groups. Violence along the Sudan border escalated during the year, as Sudanese *janjaweed* militias and Chadian rebels attacked civilians, and Darfur rebels preyed on refugee camps. Between 140 and 700 civilians died in N'Djamena, Feb. 2-5, 2008, as more than 2,000 Chadian rebels stormed the capital and clashed with government troops in a failed coup attempt. A peace accord with Sudan intended to stop cross-border fighting was signed Mar. 13. In mid-2009, camps in E Chad housed more than 250,000 refugees, most from Darfur, and camps in S Chad held 70,000 refugees, most from the Central African Republic.

Chile
Republic of Chile

People: Population: 16,601,707. **Age distrib.** (%): <15: 23.2; 65+: 9.1. **Pop. density:** 57.4 per sq mi, 22.2 per sq km. **Urban:** 87.6%. **Ethnic groups:** White & white-Amerindian 95%, Mapuche 4%. **Principal languages:** Spanish (official), Mapudungun, German, English. **Chief religions:** Roman Catholic 70%, Evangelical 15%, none 8%.

Geography: Total area: 292,260 sq mi, 756,950 sq km; **Land area:** 289,113 sq mi, 748,800 sq km. **Location:** Occupies western coast of S South America. **Neighbors:** Peru on N, Bolivia on NE, Argentina on E. **Topography:** Andes Mts. on E border incl. some of the world's highest peaks; on W is 2,650-mile Pacific coast. Width varies 100-250 mi. In N is Atacama Desert, in center are agricultural regions, in S, forests and grazing lands. **Capital:** Santiago, 5,720,000. **Cities (urban aggr.):** Valparaíso, 854,000.

Government: Type: Republic. **Head of state and gov.:** Pres. Verónica Michelle Bachelet Jeria; b. Sept. 29, 1951; in office: Mar. 11, 2006. **Local divisions:** 13 regions. **Defense budget:** $5.2 bil. **Active troops:** 60,560.

Economy: Industries: copper, other minerals, foodstuffs, fish proc., iron, steel, wood & wood products, transp. equip., cement, textiles. **Chief crops:** grapes, apples, pears, onions, wheat, corn, oats, peaches, garlic, asparagus, beans. **Natural resources:** copper, timber, iron ore, nitrates, prec. metals, molybd., hydropower. **Crude oil reserves:** 150 mil bbls. **Arable land:** 3%. **Livestock:** cattle: 3.8 mil; chickens: 98 mil; goats: 738,542; pigs: 3 mil; sheep: 3.9 mil. **Fish catch:** 5 mil metric tons. **Electricity prod.:** 50.4 bil kWh. **Labor force** (2005): agric. 13.2%, industry 23%, services 63.9%.

Finance: Monetary unit: Peso (CLP) (Oct. 2009: 553.74 = $1 U.S.). **GDP:** $244.5 bil; **per capita GDP:** $14,900; **GDP growth:** 3.2. **Imports:** $57.6 bil; U.S. 19.1%, China 11.9%, Brazil 9.3%, Argentina 8.8%, S. Korea 5.6%, Japan 4.6%. **Exports:** $66.5 bil; China 15.5%, U.S. 11%, Japan 10.2%, S. Korea 5.9%, Brazil 5.7%, Netherlands 5.1%, Italy 4.3%. **Tourism:** $1.5 bil. **Budget:** $1.5 bil. **Intl. reserves less gold:** $14.98 bil. **Gold:** 10,000 oz t. **Consumer prices:** 8.7%.

Transport: Railroad: Length: 3,406 mi. **Motor vehicles:** 1.6 mil pass. cars; 789,000 comm. vehicles. **Civil aviation:** 8.7 bil pass.-mi; 81 airports. **Chief ports:** Coronel, Huasco, Lirquen, Puerto Ventanas, San Antonio, San Vicente, Valparaiso.

Communications: TV sets: 240 per 1,000 pop. **Radios:** 354 per 1,000 pop. **Telephone lines:** 3.5 mil. **Daily newspaper circ.** (2004): 50.6 per 1,000 pop. **Internet:** 5.5 mil users.

Health: Life expect.: 73.9 male; 80.6 female. **Births** (per 1,000 pop.): 14.8. **Deaths** (per 1,000 pop.): 5.8. **Natural inc.:** 0.91%. **Infant mortality** (per 1,000 live births): 7.9. **HIV rate:** 0.3%.

Education: Compulsory: ages 6-13. **Literacy:** 96.5%.

Major intl. organizations: UN and all of its specialized agencies, APEC, OAS.

Embassy: 1732 Massachusetts Ave. NW 20036; 785-1746.

Website: www.chileangovernment.cl

Northern Chile was under Inca rule before the Spanish conquest, 1536-40. The southern Araucanian Indians resisted until the late 19th cent. Independence was gained 1810-18, under José de San Martin and Bernardo O'Higgins; the latter, as supreme director 1817-23, sought social and economic reforms until deposed. Chile defeated Peru and Bolivia in 1836-39 and 1879-84, gaining mineral-rich northern land.

In 1970, Salvador Allende Gossens, a Marxist, became president with a narrow plurality of the popular vote. His government improved conditions for the poor, but property seizures by left-wing extremists, poorly planned socialist economic programs, and a destabilization campaign backed by the U.S. led to political and financial chaos. A military junta seized power Sept. 11, 1973. With the presidential palace under attack, Allende refused to surrender; police said he killed himself. The junta, headed by Gen. Augusto Pinochet Ugarte, implemented plans to privatize the economy and "exterminate Marxism." Repression continued into the 1980s.

In Dec. 1989 voters elected a civilian president, although Pinochet continued to head the army until Mar. 10, 1998. In Mar. 1994 a Chilean human rights group estimated that human rights violations had claimed more than 3,100 lives during Pinochet's rule. Initial attempts to prosecute him failed when he was declared mentally unfit to stand trial by courts in Britain and Chile.

Ricardo Lagos Escobar, Chile's first Socialist president since the 1973 coup, took office Mar. 11, 2000. Chile and the U.S. signed a free trade accord June 6, 2003. Verónica Michelle Bachelet Jeria, also a Socialist, won a runoff election Jan. 15, 2006, and took office Mar. 11 as Chile's first woman president. Pinochet died Dec. 10, 2006.

Tierra del Fuego is the largest (18,800 sq mi) island in the archipelago of the same name at the southern tip of S. America, an area of majestic mountains, tortuous channels, and high winds. It was visited 1520 by Magellan and named Land of Fire because of its many Indian bonfires. Part of the island is in Chile, part in Argentina. Punta Arenas, on a mainland peninsula, is a center of sheep raising and the world's southernmost city (pop. [2002 census] 116,005); Puerto Williams is the southernmost settlement.

China

People's Republic of China

(Statistical data do not include Hong Kong or Macao.)

People: Population: 1,338,612,968. **Age distrib.** (%): <15: 19.8; 65+: 8.1. **Pop. density:** 371.7 per sq mi, 143.5 per sq km. **Urban:** 40.4%. **Ethnic groups:** Han Chinese 92%; Zhuang, Manchu, Hui, Miao, Uyghur, Tujia, Yi, Mongol, Tibetan, Buyi, Dong, Yao, Korean, other nationalities 9%. **Principal languages:** Standard Chinese or Mandarin (Putonghua, based on Beijing dialect), Yue (Cantonese), Wu (Shanghainese), Minbei (Fuzhou), Minnan (Hokkien-Taiwanese), Xiang, Gan, Hakka dialects, minority languages. **Chief religions:** Officially atheist; Daoist (Taoist), Buddhist, Christian 3%-4%, Muslim 1%-2%.

Geography: Total area: 3,705,407 sq mi, 9,596,960 sq km; **Land area:** 3,600,947 sq mi, 9,326,410 sq km. **Location:** Occupies most of the habitable region of E Asia. **Neighbors:** Mongolia on N; Russia on NE and NW; Afghanistan, Pakistan, Tajikistan, Kyrgystan, Kazakhstan on W; India, Nepal, Bhutan, Myanmar, Laos, Vietnam on S; North Korea on NE. **Topography:** Two-thirds of the vast territory is mountainous or desert; only one-tenth is cultivated. Rolling topography rises to high elevations in the N in the Daxinganlingshanmai separating Manchuria and Mongolia; the Tien Shan in Xinjiang; the Himalayan and Kunlunshanmai in the SW and in Tibet. Length is 1,860 mi from N to S, width E to W is more than 2,000 mi. The eastern half of China is one of the world's best-watered lands. Three great river systems, the

Chang (Yangtze), Huang (Yellow), and Xi, provide water for vast farmlands. **Capital:** Beijing, 11,106,000. **Cities (urban aggr.):** Shanghai, 14,987,000; Guangzhou, Guangdong, 8,829,000; Shenzhen, 7,581,000; Wuhan, 7,243,000; Tianjin, 7,180,000.

Government: Type: Communist Party-led state. **Head of state:** Pres. Hu Jintao; b. Dec. 1942; in office: Mar. 15, 2003 (also gen. secy of Communist Party since Nov. 15, 2002). **Head of gov.:** Premier Wen Jiabao; b. Sept. 1942; in office: Mar. 16, 2003. **Local divisions:** 22 provinces (not including Taiwan), 5 autonomous regions, and 4 municipalities, plus the special administrative regions of Hong Kong (as of July 1, 1997) and Macao (as of Dec. 20, 1999). **Defense budget:** $46.2 bil. **Active troops:** 2,185,000.

Economy: Industries: mining & ore processing, iron, steel, aluminum, coal, machine building, armaments, textiles & apparel, oil, cement, chemicals, fertilizers. **Chief crops:** rice, wheat, potatoes, corn, peanuts, tea, millet, barley, apples, cotton, oilseed. **Natural resources:** coal, iron ore, oil, nat. gas, mercury, tin, tungsten, antimony, mang., molybd., vanadium, magnetite, aluminum, lead, zinc, uranium, hydropower potential. **Crude oil reserves:** 16 bil bbls. **Arable land:** 15%. **Livestock:** cattle: 82.1 mil; chickens: 4.5 bil; goats: 137.9 mil; pigs: 425.7 mil; sheep: 146 mil. **Fish catch:** 56.16 mil metric tons. **Electricity prod.:** 2,717.5 bil kWh. **Labor force** (2006 est.): agric. 43%, industry 25%, services 32%.

Finance: Monetary unit: Yuan Renminbi (CNY) (Oct. 2009: 6.83 = $1 U.S.). **GDP:** $8 tril; **per capita GDP:** $6,000; **GDP growth:** 9%. **Imports:** $1.1 tril; Japan 12.2%, S. Korea 10%, U.S. 6.6%, Hong Kong 4.9%, Germany 4.5%. **Exports:** $1.4 tril; U.S. 18.6%, Hong Kong 12.7%, Japan 8.2%, S. Korea 5.1%, Germany 4.2%. **Tourism:** $37.2 bil. **Budget:** $651.6 bil. **Intl. reserves less gold** (2007): $968.38 bil. **Gold** (2007): 19.29 mil oz t. **Consumer prices:** 5.9%.

Transport: Railroad: Length: 48,364 mi. **Motor vehicles:** 21.3 mil pass. cars; 9.6 mil comm. vehicles. **Civil aviation:** 125.5 bil pass.-mi; 425 airports (not incl. Hong Kong or Macao). **Chief ports:** Dalian, Guangzhou, Ningbo, Qingdao, Qinhuangdao, Shanghai, Shenzhen, Tianjin.

Communications: TV sets: 291 per 1,000 pop. **Radios:** 342 per 1,000 pop. **Telephone lines:** 365.6 mil. **Daily newspaper circ.** (2004): 74.1 per 1,000 pop. **Internet:** 298 mil users.

Health: Life expect.: 71.4 male; 75.2 female. **Births** (per 1,000 pop.): 13.7. **Deaths** (per 1,000 pop.): 7. **Natural inc.:** 0.67%. **Infant mortality** (per 1,000 live births): 21.2. **HIV rate:** 0.1%.

Education: Compulsory: ages 6-14. **Literacy:** 93.3%.

Major intl. organizations: UN (FAO, IBRD, ILO, IMF, IMO, WHO, WTO), APEC.

Embassy: 2300 Connecticut Ave. NW 20008; 328-2500.

Website: english.gov.cn

Remains of various humanlike creatures who lived as early as several hundred thousand years ago have been found in many parts of China. Neolithic agricultural settlements dotted the Huang (Yellow) R. basin from about 5000 BCE. Their language, religion, and art were the sources of later Chinese civilization.

Bronze metallurgy reached a peak and Chinese pictographic writing, similar to today's, was in use in the more developed culture of the Shang Dynasty (c. 1500 BCE-c. 1000 BCE), which ruled much of North China.

A succession of dynasties and interdynastic warring kingdoms ruled China for the next 3,000 years. They expanded Chinese political and cultural domination to the south and west, and developed a society that was technologically and culturally advanced. Rule by foreigners (Mongols in the Yuan Dynasty, 1271-1368, and Manchus in the Ch'ing Dynasty, 1644-1911) did not alter the underlying culture.

A period of relative stagnation left China vulnerable to internal and external pressures in the 19th cent. Rebellions left tens of millions dead, and Russia, Japan, Britain, and other powers exercised political and economic control in large parts of the country. China became a republic Jan. 1, 1912, following the Wuchang Uprising inspired by Dr. Sun Yat-sen, founder of the Kuomintang (Nationalist) party. By 1928, the Kuomintang, led by Chiang Kai-shek, succeeded in nominal reunification of China. About the same time, a bloody purge of Communists from the ranks of the Kuomintang fomented hostilities between the two groups.

For over 50 years, 1894-1945, China was involved in conflicts with Japan. In 1895, China ceded Korea, Taiwan, and other areas. On Sept. 18, 1931, Japan seized the Northeastern Provinces (Manchuria) and set up a puppet state called Manchukuo. Taking advantage of Chinese dissension, Japan invaded China proper July 7, 1937. On Nov. 20 the retreating Nationalist government moved its capital to Chongqing (Chungking) from Nanking (Nanjing), which Japanese troops then ravaged Dec. 13.

From 1939 the Sino-Japanese War (1937-45) became part of the broader world conflict. After its defeat in World War II, Japan gave up all seized land. Within China, conflicts involving the Kuomintang, Communists, and other factions resumed. China came under the domination of Communist armies, 1949-1950. The Kuomintang government fled to Taiwan, Dec. 8, 1949.

The People's Republic of China was proclaimed in Beijing (Peking) Oct. 1, 1949, under Mao Zedong. China and the USSR signed a 30-year treaty of "friendship, alliance, and mutual assistance," Feb. 15, 1950. The U.S. refused recognition of the new regime. On Nov. 26, 1950, the People's Republic sent armies into Korea against U.S. troops and forced a stalemate in the Korean War.

After an initial period of consolidation, 1949-52, industry, agriculture, and social and economic institutions were forcibly molded according to Maoist ideals. However, frequent drastic changes in policy and violent factionalism interfered with economic development. In 1957, Mao admitted an estimated 800,000 people had been executed 1949-54; opponents claimed much higher figures.

The Great Leap Forward, 1958-60, tried to force the pace of economic development through intensive labor on huge new rural communes, and through emphasis on ideological purity. The program caused resistance and was largely abandoned.

By the 1960s, relations with the USSR deteriorated, with disagreements on borders, ideology, and leadership of world Communism. The USSR canceled aid accords, and China, with Albania, launched anti-Soviet propaganda drives.

The Great Proletarian Cultural Revolution, 1965, was an attempt to oppose pragmatism and bureaucratic power and instruct a new generation in revolutionary principles. Massive purges took place. A program of forcibly relocating millions of urban teenagers into the countryside was launched. By 1968 the movement had run its course; many purged officials returned to office in subsequent years, and reforms that had placed ideology above expertise were gradually weakened.

On Oct. 25, 1971, the UN General Assembly ousted the Taiwan government from the UN and seated the People's Republic in its place. The U.S. had supported the mainland's admission but opposed Taiwan's expulsion.

U.S. Pres. Richard Nixon visited China Feb. 21-28, 1972, on invitation from Premier Zhou Enlai, ending years of antipathy between the 2 nations. China and the U.S. opened liaison offices in each other's capitals, May-June 1973. The U.S., Dec. 15, 1978, formally recognized the People's Republic of China as the sole legal government of China; diplomatic relations between the 2 nations were established, Jan. 1, 1979.

Mao died Sept. 9, 1976. By 1978, Vice Premier Deng Xiaoping had consolidated his power, succeeding Mao as "paramount leader" of China. The new ruling group modified Maoist policies in education, culture, and industry, and sought better ties with non-Communist countries. By the mid-1980s, China had enacted far-reaching economic reforms, deemphasizing centralized planning and incorporating market-oriented incentives.

Some 100,000 students and workers staged a march in Beijing to demand political reforms, May 4, 1989. As the unrest spread, martial law was imposed, May 20. Troops entered Beijing, June 3-4, and crushed the pro-democracy protests, as tanks and armored personnel carriers rolled through Tiananmen Square. It is estimated that 5,000 died, 10,000 were injured, and hundreds of students and workers were arrested.

Deng Xiaoping died Feb. 19, 1997, leaving Jiang Zemin in control as president. By agreement with the UK, Hong Kong reverted to Chinese sovereignty July 1 (see below). Portugal returned Macao to China Dec. 20, 1999.

Hu Jintao was named Communist Party general secretary at the 16th party congress, Nov. 15, 2002, and elected president by the 10th National People's Congress, Mar. 15, 2003. A SARS epidemic beginning in late 2002 killed 349 people in mainland China by mid-2003.

In Aug. 2003, China assumed an unprecedented diplomatic role when it hosted multinational talks on N. Korea's nuclear weapons program. With the successful launch and recovery, Oct. 15-16, of the *Shenzhou 5* spacecraft, China became the third nation (after the U.S. and USSR) to send a man into space.

China's industries, exports, and demand for oil have all increased rapidly since the 1980s. Reports in 2007 that China had exported hazardous pet products, toothpaste, tires, and toys focused attention on factories' quality-control problems. Zheng Xiaoyu, the former head of China's food and drug safety agency, was executed July 10 for bribe taking and dereliction of duty.

Bitter cold temperatures and severe blizzards claimed more than 100 lives and caused an estimated $15 bil in economic losses by mid-Feb. 2008. The National People's Congress Mar. 15-16 reelected Pres. Hu Jintao and Premier Wen Jiabao. A powerful earthquake rocked Sichuan Province May 12, leaving 69,226 people dead and 17,923 missing. China reportedly spent $43 bil preparing for the XXIX Summer Olympics, held in Beijing Aug. 8-24, followed by the Paralympic Games, Sept. 6-17. In a new quality-control scandal, China's health ministry reported Sept. 22 that nearly 53,000 babies had been sickened by contaminated milk powder; on Dec. 1, the estimate was raised to 300,000. China has invested heavily in environmental technologies, especially wind and solar power, but illegal mining and ore processing remain major public-health hazards. Propelled by massive government spending, China's GDP grew by 7.1% during Jan.-June 2009, despite the global recession.

Manchuria. Home of the Manchus, rulers of China 1644-1911, Manchuria has accommodated millions of Chinese settlers in the 20th cent. Under Japanese rule 1931-45, the area became industrialized. The region is divided into the 3 northeastern provinces of Heilongjiang, Jilin, and Liaoning.

Autonomous Regions

Guangxi Zhuang is in SE China, bounded on the N by Guizhou and Hunan provinces, E and S by Guangdong, on the SW by Vietnam, and on the W by Yunnan. It produces rice in the river valleys and has valuable forest products. Pop. (2005): 49.25 mil.

Inner Mongolia was organized by the People's Republic in 1947. Its boundaries have undergone frequent changes, reaching its greatest extent in 1956 (and restored in 1979), with an area of 454,600 sq mi, allegedly in order to dilute the minority Mongol population. Chinese settlers outnumber the Mongols more than 10 to 1. Pop. (2005): 23.86 mil. Capital: Hohhot.

Ningxia Hui, in north central China, is about 60,000 sq mi. Pop. (2005): 5.96 mil. Capital: Yinchuan. Situated mainly of the semiarid Inner Mongolian plateau region with desert areas in the N. The Huang He (Yellow R.) flows across the N furnishes water for irrigation. Coal is mined in the E. Modern industry is relatively undeveloped, and only one railroad crosses the region. The majority of the population is Han, and the Hui (Chinese Muslims) constitute about one-third of the population. The region experienced a significant population boom from 1950-80, which has now stabilized.

Xinjiang Uighur, in Central Asia, is 635,900 sq mi, pop. (2004): 19.63 mil (75% Uighurs, a Turkic Muslim group, with a heavy Han Chinese increase in recent years). Capital: Urumqi. It is China's richest region in strategic minerals. China has moved to crack down on Uighur separatists, whom Beijing regards as terrorists. A protest march July 5, 2009, by Uighurs in Urumqi led to violent clashes with Han Chinese; at least 197 people (mostly Han) were killed in the riots. Renewed unrest including protests by Han in early Sept. led to the dismissal of the city's top Communist official.

Tibet, 471,700 sq mi, is a thinly populated region of high plateaus and massive mountains, the Himalayas on the S, the Kunluns on the N. High passes connect with India and Nepal; roads lead into China proper. Capital: Lhasa. Average altitude is 15,000 ft. Jiachan, 15,870 ft, is believed to be the highest inhabited town on earth. Agriculture is primitive. Pop. (2004): 2.74 mil (of whom about 500,000 are Chinese). Another 4 mil Tibetans form the majority of the population of vast adjacent areas that have long been incorporated into China.

China ruled all of Tibet from the 18th cent. Independence came in 1911, but China reasserted control in 1951, and a Communist government was installed in 1953. Serfdom was abolished, but all land remained collectivized.

A Tibetan uprising within China in 1956 spread to Lhasa in 1959. The rebellion was crushed by Chinese troops, and Buddhism was almost totally suppressed. The Dalai Lama and 100,000 Tibetans fled to India.

Rail service from Beijing to Lhasa began July 1, 2006, with completion of the 710-mi Qinghai-Tibet line, the world's highest railway, an ambitious engineering project that cost more than $4 bil. Efforts by Chinese authorities to halt peaceful demonstrations by Tibetan monks led to anti-Chinese riots in Lhasa, Mar. 14, 2008; the Chinese government sent troops into Tibet to crush dissent, sparking international protests.

Hong Kong

Hong Kong (Xianggang), located at the mouth of the Zhu Jiang (Pearl R.) in SE China, 90 mi S of Canton (Guangzhou), was a British dependency from 1842 until July 1, 1997, when it became a Special Administrative Region of China. Its nucleus is Hong Kong Isl., 31 sq mi, occupied by the British in 1841 and formally ceded to them in 1842, on which is located the seat of government. Opposite is Kowloon Peninsula, 3 sq mi, and Stonecutters Isl., added to the territory in 1860. An additional 355 sq mi known as the New Territories, a mainland area and islands, were leased from China, 1898, for 99 years. Area 422 sq mi (total); 402 sq mi (land); pop. (2009 est.) 7,055,071.

Hong Kong is a major center for trade and banking. Per capita GDP, $43,700 (2008 est.), is among the highest in the world. Principal industries are textiles and apparel; also tourism ($11.9 bil expenditures in 2004), electronics, shipbuilding, iron and steel, fishing, cement, and small manufactures. Hong Kong's spinning mills are among the best in the world.

Hong Kong harbor was long an important British naval station and one of the world's great transshipment ports. The colony was often a place of refuge for exiles from mainland China. It was occupied by Japan during WWII.

From 1949 to 1962 Hong Kong absorbed more than a million refugees fleeing Communist China. Starting in the 1950s, cheap labor led to a boom in light manufacturing, while liberal tax policies attracted foreign investment; Hong Kong became one of the wealthiest, most productive areas in the Far East. Poor living and working conditions and low wages for many led to political unrest in the 1960s, but legislation and public works programs raised the standard of living by the 1970s.

With the end of the 99-year lease on the New Territories drawing near, Britain and China signed an agreement, Dec. 19, 1984, under which all of Hong Kong was to be returned to China in 1997; under this agreement Hong Kong was to be allowed to keep its capitalist system for 50 years. In Dec. 1996, an electoral college appointed by China chose a shipping magnate, Tung Chee-hwa, to be Hong Kong's chief executive when it reverted to Chinese control.

Following the transfer of government on July 1, Hong Kong retained its street names and its currency, the Hong Kong dollar (HK$7.75 = $1 U.S.), but without the queen's picture. Official languages remained Chinese (Cantonese dialect) and English. Prodemocracy candidates did well in May 24, 1998, elections, despite having been excluded from the provisional government in 1997. A SARS outbreak in 2003 claimed almost 300 lives and damaged the economy.

Hundreds of thousands of Hong Kong residents turned out July 1, 2003, to protest a proposed anti-subversion law; the bill was withdrawn Sept. 5. Another mass march, July 1, 2004, protested Beijing's refusal to allow greater freedom. Pro-democracy candidates won a majority of the popular vote in elections, Sept. 12, but failed to gain control of the Legislative Council. After Tung Chee-hwa resigned Mar. 10, 2005, Donald Tsang was chosen to serve the remaining 2 years of Tung's term as chief executive; he won a full 5-year term Mar. 25, 2007.

Macao

Macao, area of 11 sq mi, is an enclave, a peninsula and 2 small islands, at the mouth of the Xi (Pearl) R. in China. It was established as a Portuguese trading colony in 1557. In 1849, Portugal claimed sovereignty over the territory; this claim was accepted by China in an 1887 treaty. Portugal granted broad autonomy in 1976. Under a 1987 agreement, Macao reverted to China Dec. 20, 1999. As in the case of Hong Kong, the Chinese government guaranteed Macao it would not interfere in its way of life and capitalist system for a period of 50 years. Tourism is the fastest-growing economic sector; revenues from casinos and other gambling activities reached $13.7 bil in 2008. Pop. (2009 est.): 559,846.

Colombia
Republic of Colombia

People: Population: 45,644,023. **Age distrib.** (%): <15: 28.9; 65+: 5.6. **Pop. density:** 113.8 per sq mi, 43.9 per sq km. **Urban:** 73.6%. **Ethnic groups:** Mestizo 58%, white 20%, mulatto 14%, black 4%, mixed black-Amerindian 3%. **Principal language:** Spanish (official). **Chief religion:** Roman Catholic 90%.

Geography: Total area: 439,736 sq mi, 1,138,910 sq km; **Land area:** 401,044 sq mi, 1,038,700 sq km. **Location:** At the NW corner of South America. **Neighbors:** Panama on NW, Ecuador and Peru on S, Brazil and Venezuela on E. **Topography:** Three ranges of Andes—Western, Central, and Eastern Cordilleras—run through the country from N to S. The eastern range consists mostly of high tablelands, densely populated. The Magdalena R. rises in the Andes, flows N to Caribbean, through a rich alluvial plain. Sparsely settled plains in E are drained by Orinoco and Amazon systems. **Capital:** Bogotá, 7,772,000. **Cities (urban aggr.):** Medellín, 3,297,000; Cali, 2,254,000; Barranquilla, 1,798,000.

Government: Type: Republic. **Head of state and gov.:** Pres. Álvaro Uribe Vélez; b. July 4, 1952; in office: Aug. 7, 2002. **Local divisions:** 32 departments, capital district of Bogotá. **Defense budget:** $6.8 bil. **Active troops:** 267,231.

Economy: Industries: textiles, food proc., oil, clothing & footwear, beverages, chemicals, cement. **Chief crops:** coffee, cut flowers, bananas, rice, tobacco, corn, sugarcane, cocoa beans. **Natural resources:** oil, nat. gas, coal, iron ore, nickel, gold, copper, emeralds, hydropower. **Crude oil reserves:** 1.4 bil bbls. **Arable land:** 2%. **Livestock:** cattle: 26.7 mil; chickens: 150 mil; goats: 1.2 mil; pigs: 1.9 mil; sheep: 3.4 mil. **Fish catch:** 156,102 metric tons. **Electricity prod.:** 51.8 bil kWh. **Labor force** (2005 est.): agric. 22.4%, industry 18.8%, services 58.8%.

Finance: Monetary unit: Peso (COP) (Oct. 2009: 1,925.40 = $1 U.S.). **GDP:** $395.4 bil; **per capita GDP:** $8,800; **GDP growth:** 2.5%. **Imports:** $37.6 bil; U.S. 30.5%, China 8.5%, Mexico 8.5%, Brazil 6.5%, Venezuela 4.3%, Germany 4%. **Exports:** $38.6 bil; U.S. 32.1%, Venezuela 16.8%, Chile 4.8%. **Tourism:** $1.7 bil. **Budget:** $65 bil. **Intl. reserves less gold:** $15.24 bil. **Gold:** 220,000 oz t. **Consumer prices:** 7%.

Transport: Railroad: Length: 2,362 mi. **Motor vehicles:** 2.1 mil pass. cars; 343,500 comm. vehicles. **Civil aviation:** 6.02 bil pass.-mi; 116 airports. **Chief ports:** Barranquilla, Buenaventura, Cartagena, Santa Marta, Turbo.

Communications: TV sets: 279 per 1,000 pop. **Radios:** 539 per 1,000 pop. **Telephone lines:** 6.8 mil. **Daily newspaper circ.** (1999): 26.7 per 1,000 pop. **Internet:** 17.1 mil users.

Health: Life expect.: 68.7 male; 76.5 female. **Births** (per 1,000 pop.): 19.9. **Deaths** (per 1,000 pop.): 5.5. **Natural inc.:** 1.43%. **Infant mortality** (per 1,000 live births): 19.5. **HIV rate:** 0.6%.

Education: Compulsory: ages 5-14. **Literacy:** 93.6%.
Major intl. organizations: UN (FAO, IBRD, ILO, IMF, IMO, WHO, WTO), OAS.
Embassy: 2118 Leroy Pl. NW 20008; 387-8338.
Website: web.presidencia.gov.co

Spain subdued the local Indian kingdoms (Funza, Tunja) by the 1530s and ruled Colombia and neighboring areas as New Granada for 300 years. Independence was won by 1819. Venezuela and Ecuador broke away in 1829-30, and Panama withdrew in 1903.

Colombia is plagued by rural and urban violence. "La Violencia" of 1948-58 claimed 200,000 lives; since 1989, political killings, kidnappings, and "disappearances" have victimized many thousands of civilians, and the internally displaced population has been estimated at up to 3 mil or more. Attempts at land and social reform and progress in industrialization have not reduced massive social problems.

Government activity against local drug traffickers has sparked a series of retaliation killings. On Aug. 18, 1989, Luis Carlos Galán, the ruling party's presidential hopeful for the 1990 election, was assassinated. In 1990, 2 other presidential candidates were assassinated, as drug traffickers carried on a campaign of intimidation.

Right-wing paramilitaries launched a campaign Dec. 22, 2000, against suspected left-wing guerrillas. Legislation expanding the powers of the military was signed Aug. 13, 2001. The collapse of talks with the rebels in Feb. 2002 brought an upsurge of fighting. A hardliner, Álvaro Uribe Vélez, whose father had been killed by leftist rebels in 1983, won a presidential election May 26. A wave of guerrilla violence as he took office led Uribe to declare a "state of unrest" Aug. 12. Police powers were increased Sept. 10 as part of a new government offensive. The constitution was amended, Nov. 30, 2004, to allow the president to seek a second consecutive term; Uribe easily won reelection May 28, 2006. Key political figures, including major allies of Uribe, were arrested in 2007 on charges of colluding with paramilitary death squads. Guerrilla strength has waned in recent years; 15 hostages were freed July 2, 2008, including former presidential candidate Ingrid Betancourt, 3 U.S. defense contractors, and 11 soldiers, in what government leaders called a daring ruse that tricked rebels into giving up their captives.

Relations with Venezuela deteriorated in 2009, as Colombia accused the government of Pres. Hugo Chávez of aiding Colombian guerrillas, and Chávez objected to expanded military cooperation between Colombia and the U.S. Colombia's legislature voted Sept. 1 to authorize a referendum that would allow Pres. Uribe to run for a 3rd term in May 2010.

Colombia produces an estimated 90% of the cocaine reaching the U.S. Since 2000, the U.S. has provided more than $5 bil to Colombia, much of it to combat the drug trade.

Comoros
Union of the Comoros

People: Population: 752,438. **Age distrib.** (%): <15: 42.2; 65+: 3.1. **Pop. density:** 898.1 per sq mi, 346.7 per sq km. **Urban:** 27.9%. **Ethnic groups:** Antalote, Cafre, Makoa, Oimatsaha, Sakalava (all mostly African-Arab mix). **Principal languages:** Arabic, French (both official); Shikomoro (blend of Swahili & Arabic). **Chief religion:** Sunni Muslim 98%.

Geography: Total area: 838 sq mi, 2,170 sq km; **Land area:** 838 sq mi, 2,170 sq km. **Location:** 3 islands—Grande Comore (Njazidja), Anjouan (Nzwani), and Moheli (Mwali)—in the Mozambique Channel between NW Madagascar and SE Africa. **Neighbors:** Nearest are Mozambique on W, Madagascar on E. **Topography:** The islands are of volcanic origin, with an active volcano on Grande Comore. **Capital:** Moroni, 46,000.

Government: Type: Republic. **Head of state and gov.:** Pres. Ahmed Abdallah Mohamed Sambi; b. June 5, 1958; in office: May 26, 2006. **Local divisions:** 3 main islands with 4 municipalities.

Economy: Industries: fishing, tourism, perfume distillation. **Chief crops:** vanilla, cloves, ylang-ylang, perfume essences, copra, coconuts, bananas, cassava. **Arable land:** 36%. **Livestock:** cattle: 47,000; chickens: 500,000; goats: 115,000; sheep: 22,000. **Fish catch** (est.): 16,000 metric tons. **Electricity prod.:** 20 mil kWh. **Labor force** (1996 est.): agric. 80%, industry & services 20%.

Finance: Monetary unit: Franc (KMF) (Oct. 2009: 334.47 = $1 U.S.). **GDP:** $751.2 mil; **per capita GDP:** $1,000; **GDP growth:** 0.5%. **Imports** (2006): $143 mil; Brazil 13.5%, France 13.2%, China 10.5%, UAE 9.2%, South Africa 6.1%, Italy 5.3%, Pakistan 5.3%, Singapore 4.2%, Kenya 4.2%. **Exports** (2006): $32 mil; France 30.5%, Turkey 17.2%, Greece 10.6%, Brazil 10%, Singapore 7.7%, Saudi Arabia 4.9%, India 4.3%. **Tourism:** NA. **Budget:** NA. **Intl. reserves less gold:** $73 mil. **Gold:** NA. **Consumer prices:** NA.

Transport: Civil aviation: 1.9 mil pass.-mi; 4 airports. **Chief ports:** Mayotte, Mutsamudu.

Communications: TV sets: 4 per 1,000 pop. **Radios:** 141 per 1,000 pop. **Telephone lines:** 23,300. **Internet:** 23,000 users.

Health: Life expect.: 60.7 male; 65.5 female. **Births** (per 1,000 pop.): 35.8. **Deaths** (per 1,000 pop.): 7.8. **Natural inc.:** 2.8%. **Infant mortality** (per 1,000 live births): 68.6. **HIV rate:** <0.1%.

Education: Compulsory: ages 6-13. **Literacy:** 75.1%.

Major intl. organizations: UN (FAO, IBRD, ILO, IMF, WHO), AL, AU.

Permanent UN Mission: 866 United Nations Plz., Ste. 418, New York, NY 10017; (212) 750-1637.

Website: www.beit-salam.km

The islands were controlled by Muslim sultans until the French acquired them 1841-1909. They became a French overseas territory in 1947. A 1974 referendum favored independence, with only the Christian island of Mayotte preferring association with France. The French National Assembly decided to allow each of the islands to decide its own fate. The Comore Chamber of Deputies declared independence July 6, 1975, with Ahmed Abdallah as president. In a referendum in 1976, Mayotte voted to remain French.

A leftist regime that seized power from Abdallah in 1975 was deposed in a pro-French 1978 coup in which he regained the presidency. In Nov. 1989, Pres. Abdallah was assassinated; soon after, a multiparty system was instituted. A Sept. 1995 military coup, assisted by French mercenaries, ousted Pres. Said Mohamed Djohar. French troops invaded, Oct. 4, and forced coup leaders to surrender.

Attempts to work out a new constitutional relationship between Grande Comore, Anjouan, and Moheli have been ongoing since Anjouan and Moheli seceded from the Comoros in 1997. Unrest on Grande Comore culminated in a military coup, Apr. 30, 1999. Anjouans endorsed secession in a disputed vote Jan. 23, 2000.

Irregularities marred the presidential runoff election of Apr. 14, 2002, won by Azali Assoumani, who led the 1999 coup. Elections for national and island assemblies took place Mar.-Apr. 2004. Ahmed Abdallah Mohamed Sambi won a presidential runoff vote, May 14, 2006. Each of the 3 islands elected its own president in 2002 and 2007. Anjouan's leader, Col. Mohamed Bacar, who had refused to relinquish power after the central government ruled his 2007 election illegal, was forced to flee when Comorian and African Union troops took control of the island, Mar. 25-26, 2008.

A Yemeni Airbus A310 jetliner en route from Sana'a', Yemen, plunged into rough seas June 30, 2009, while trying to land at Moroni; the crash killed 152 of the 153 people on board.

Congo
Democratic Republic of the Congo

(Congo, officially Democratic Republic of the Congo, is also known as Congo-Kinshasa. It should not be confused with Republic of the Congo, commonly called Congo Republic, and also known as Congo-Brazzaville.)

People: Population: 68,692,542. **Age distrib.** (%): <15: 46.9; 65+: 2.5. **Pop. density:** 78.5 per sq mi, 30.3 per sq km. **Urban:** 32.1%. **Ethnic groups:** 200+ groups, majority Bantu. Four largest tribes (Mongo, Luba, Kongo [all Bantu], Mangbetu-Azande [Hamitic]) 45%. **Principal languages:** French (official), Lingala (lingua franca trade lang.), Kingwana (Kiswahili or Swahili dialect), Kikongo, Tshiluba. **Chief religions:** Roman Catholic 50%, Protestant 20%, Kimbanguist 10%, Muslim 10%.

Geography: Total area: 905,568 sq mi, 2,345,410 sq km. **Land area:** 875,525 sq mi, 2,267,600 sq km. **Location:** In central Africa. **Neighbors:** Congo-Brazzaville on W; Central African Republic, Sudan on N; Uganda, Rwanda, Burundi, Tanzania on E; Zambia, Angola on S. **Topography:** Congo includes the bulk of the Congo R. basin. The vast central region is a low-lying plateau covered by rain forest. Mountainous terraces in the W, savannas in the S and SE, grasslands toward the N, and the high Ruwenzori Mts. on the E surround the central region. A short strip of territory borders the Atlantic O. **Capital:** Kinshasa, 7,843,000. **Cities (urban aggr.):** Lubumbashi, 1,352,000; Mbuji-Mayi, 1,295,000; Kananga, 765,000.

Government: Type: Republic. **Head of state:** Pres. Joseph Kabila; b. June 24, 1971; in office: Jan. 26, 2001. **Head of gov.:** Prime Min. Adolphe Muzito; b. 1957; in office: Oct. 10, 2008. **Local divisions:** 10 provinces, 1 city. **Defense budget:** 166 mil. **Active troops:** 139,251.

Economy: Industries: mining, mineral proc., textiles, footwear, cigarettes, proc. foods & beverages, cement. **Chief crops:** coffee, sugar, palm oil, rubber, tea, quinine, cassava, bananas, root crops, corn, fruits. **Natural resources:** cobalt, copper, oil, diamonds, gold, silver, zinc, mang., tin, uranium, coal, hydropower, timber. **Crude oil reserves:** 180 mil bbls. **Arable land:** 3%. **Livestock:** cattle: 754,060; chickens: 19.8 mil; goats: 4 mil; pigs: 963,110; sheep: 901,370. **Fish catch** (est.): 238,970 metric tons. **Electricity prod.:** 7.2bil kWh. **Labor force:** NA.

Finance: Monetary unit: Franc (CDF) (Oct. 2009: 830.00 = $1 U.S.). **GDP:** $20.6 bil; **per capita GDP:** $300; **GDP growth:** 5.9%. **Imports** (2007): $5.2 bil; South Africa 22.1%, Belgium 11.5%, Zambia 8.3%, Zimbabwe 7%, Kenya 5.9%, China 5.6%, France 5.4%. **Exports** (2007): $6.1 bil; China 44.7%, Belgium 16.9%, Finland 10.5%, U.S. 8.9%, Zambia 4.8%. **Tourism:** NA.

Budget (2006 est.): $2 bil. **Intl. reserves less gold:** 50 mil. **Gold:** NA. **Consumer prices:** NA.

Transport: Railroad: Length: 2,490 mi. **Motor vehicles:** 172,600 pass. cars; 34,600 comm. vehicles. **Civil aviation:** 298.3 mil pass.-mi; 26 airports. **Chief ports:** Boma, Bukavu, Bumba, Goma, Kinshasa, Kisangani, Matadi, Mbandaka.

Communications: TV sets: 2 per 1,000 pop. **Radios:** 376 per 1,000 pop. **Telephone lines:** 37,300. **Internet:** 290,000 users.

Health: Life expect.: 52.2 male; 55.8 female. **Births** (per 1,000 pop.): 43. **Deaths** (per 1,000 pop.): 11.9. **Natural inc.:** 3.11%. **Infant mortality** (per 1,000 live births): 83.1. **HIV rate:** NA.

Education: Compulsory: ages 6-13. **Literacy:** 67.2%.

Major intl. organizations: UN and most of its specialized agencies, AU.

Embassy: 1726 M St. NW 20036; 234-7690.

Website: www.presidentrdc.cd

The earliest inhabitants of Congo may have been the pygmies, followed by Bantus from the east and Nilotic tribes from the north. The large Bantu Bakongo kingdom ruled much of Congo and Angola when Portuguese explorers visited in the 15th cent.

Leopold II, king of the Belgians, formed an international group to exploit the Congo region in 1876. In 1877 Henry M. Stanley explored the Congo, and in 1878 the king's group sent him back to organize the region and win over the native chiefs. The Conference of Berlin, 1884-85, established the Congo Free State with Leopold as king and chief owner. Exploitation of native laborers on the rubber plantations caused international criticism and led to granting of a colonial charter, 1908; the colony became known as the Belgian Congo. Millions of Congolese are believed to have died between 1880 and 1920 as a result of slave labor and other causes under European rule.

Belgian and Congolese leaders agreed Jan. 27, 1960, that Congo would become independent in June. In the first general elections, May 31, the National Congolese movement of Patrice Lumumba won a plurality in the National Assembly. The Republic of the Congo was proclaimed June 30. Widespread violence caused Europeans and others to flee. The UN Security Council, Aug. 9, called on Belgium to withdraw its troops and sent a UN contingent. Lumumba was dismissed as premier Sept. 5, 1960, and was murdered Jan. 17, 1961. The last UN troops left the Congo June 30, 1964.

In late 1965 Gen. Joseph D. Mobutu was named president. He later changed his name to Mobutu Sese Seko and ruled as a dictator. The country became the Democratic Republic of the Congo (1966) and the Republic of Zaire (1971). Under Mobutu, economic decline and government corruption plagued Zaire. He sought to retain power despite mounting international pressure and internal opposition.

During 1994, Zaire was inundated with refugees from the massive ethnic bloodshed in Rwanda. Ethnic violence spread to E Zaire in 1996. In Oct. militant Hutus, who dominated in the refugee camps, fought against rebels (mostly Tutsis) in Zaire, precipitating intervention by government troops. As a result of the fighting, Rwandan refugees abandoned the camps; hundreds of thousands returned to Rwanda, while hundreds of thousands more were dispersed throughout eastern Zaire. The rebels, led by Gen. Laurent Kabila—a former Marxist and longtime opponent of Mobutu—gained momentum and began to move west across Zaire. On May 17, 1997, Kabila's troops entered Kinshasa and Mobutu went into exile. The country again assumed the name Democratic Republic of the Congo. Mobutu died Sept. 7 in Rabat, Morocco.

Kabila, who ruled by decree, alienated UN officials, international aid donors, and former allies. Rebels assisted by Rwanda and Uganda threatened Kinshasa in Aug. 1998, but the assault was turned back with help from Angola, Namibia, and Zimbabwe. Rebel groups agreed to a cease-fire on Aug. 31, 1999, but the truce was widely violated. Kabila was assassinated Jan. 16, 2001, apparently by one of his bodyguards, and was succeeded by his son Joseph.

The overall death toll from the civil war and related causes was estimated at 3.3 mil through Nov. 2002. By then, Rwanda and Uganda had agreed to pull out their remaining troops. A power-sharing accord signed Apr. 2, 2003, led to the installation of a new Congolese government in July. A new constitution won legislative approval May 13, 2005. A UN peacekeeping force (MONUC), established in 1999, remained in the country to oversee elections, held July 30-31, 2006, the nation's first multiparty vote since 1960. Kabila defeated former rebel leader Jean-Pierre Bemba in a presidential runoff election, Oct. 29, 2006.

Hundreds reportedly died in Kinshasa, Mar. 22-23, 2007, in clashes between security forces and a militia loyal to Bemba, who fled to Europe; he was arrested in Belgium May 24, 2008, on war crimes charges. A peace deal with militia groups in eastern Congo, including one led by Tutsi rebel Gen. Laurent Nkunda, was signed Jan. 23, 2008, but Nkunda launched a new offensive Aug. 28; he was arrested by Rwandan authorities Jan. 22, 2009.

MONUC personnel in Congo numbered 18,700 as of July 2009. Visiting eastern Congo Aug. 11, U.S. Sec. of State Hillary Clinton announced a $17 mil program to curb rampant sexual violence in the region; most rapes were reportedly committed by Congolese soldiers.

Congo Republic
Republic of the Congo

(Congo Republic, officially Republic of the Congo, is also known as Congo-Brazzaville. It should not be confused with Democratic Republic of the Congo [formerly Zaire], now commonly called Congo, and also known as Congo-Kinshasa.)

People: Population: 4,012,809. **Age distrib.** (%): <15: 45.9; 65+: 2.8. **Pop. density:** 30.4 per sq mi, 11.8 per sq km. **Urban:** 60.2%. **Ethnic groups:** Kongo 48%, Sangha 20%, Teke 17%, M'Bochi 12%. **Principal languages:** French (official), Lingala & Monokutuba (lingua franca trade languages), many local languages & dialects (Kikongo most widespread). **Chief religions:** Christian 50%, animist 48%, Muslim 2%.

Geography: Total area: 132,047 sq mi, 342,000 sq km; **Land area:** 131,854 sq mi, 341,500 sq km. **Location:** In W central Africa. **Neighbors:** Gabon and Cameroon on W, Central African Republic on N, Congo-Kinshasa (formerly Zaire) on E, Angola on SW. **Topography:** Much of the Congo is covered by thick forests. A coastal plain leads to the fertile Niari Valley. The center is a plateau, the Congo R. basin consists of flood plains in the lower and savanna in the upper portion. **Capital:** Brazzaville, 1,355,000.

Government: Type: Republic. **Head of state:** Pres. Denis Sassou-Nguesso; b. 1943; in office: Oct. 25, 1997. **Head of gov.:** Isidore Mvouba; b. 1954; in office: Jan. 7, 2005. **Local divisions:** 10 regions, 6 communes. **Defense budget:** $94 mil. **Active troops:** 10,000.

Economy: Industries: oil extraction, cement, lumber, brewing, sugar, palm oil. **Chief crops:** cassava, sugar, rice, corn, peanuts, vegetables, coffee, cocoa. **Natural resources:** oil, timber, potash, lead, zinc, uranium, copper, phosphates, gold, magnesium, nat. gas, hydropower. **Crude oil reserves:** 1.6 bil bbls. **Arable land:** 1%. **Livestock:** cattle: 115,000; chickens: 2.4 mil; goats: 295,000; pigs: 47,000; sheep: 99,000. **Fish catch:** 59,966 metric tons. **Electricity prod.:** 444 mil kWh. **Labor force:** NA.

Finance: Monetary unit: CFA BEAC Franc (XAF) (Oct. 2009: 444.97 = $1 U.S.). **GDP:** $15.4 bil; **per capita GDP:** $3,900; **GDP growth:** 6.4%. **Imports:** $3 bil; France 19.1%, China 15.6%, S. Korea 15.2%, U.S. 4.8%, India 4.7%, Italy 4.5%. **Exports:** $10.9 bil; U.S. 44.5%, China 32.8%, France 6%. **Tourism:** NA. **Budget:** $2.4 bil. **Intl. reserves less gold:** $2.51 bil. **Gold:** 10,000 oz t. **Consumer prices:** 7.3%.

Transport: Railroad: Length: 494 mi. **Motor vehicles:** 29,700 pass. cars; 23,100 comm. vehicles. **Civil aviation:** 19.3 mil pass.-mi (incl. Air Afrique traffic apportionment); 6 airports. **Chief ports:** Brazzaville, Djeno, Impfondo, Ouesso, Oyo, Pointe-Noire.

Communications: TV sets: 13 per 1,000 pop. **Radios:** 126 per 1,000 pop. **Telephone lines:** 22,200. **Internet:** 155,000 users.

Health: Life expect.: 52.5 male; 55 female. **Births** (per 1,000 pop.): 41.8. **Deaths** (per 1,000 pop.): 12.3. **Natural inc.:** 2.95%. **Infant mortality** (per 1,000 live births): 81.3. **HIV rate:** 3.5%.

Education: Compulsory: ages 6-16. **Literacy:** 86.8%.

Major intl. organizations: UN (FAO, IBRD, ILO, IMF, IMO, WHO, WTO), AU.

Embassy: 4891 Colorado Ave. NW 20011; 726-5500.

Website: www.presidence.cg

The Loango Kingdom flourished in the 15th cent., as did the Anzico Kingdom of the Batekes; by the late 17th cent. they had weakened. By 1885, France established control of the region, then called the Middle Congo. Republic of the Congo gained independence Aug. 15, 1960.

After a 1963 coup sparked by trade unions, the country adopted a Marxist-Leninist stance, with the USSR and China vying for influence. France remained a dominant trade partner and source of technical assistance, however, and French-owned private enterprise retained a major economic role. In 1970, the country was renamed People's Republic of the Congo. Since the 1980s, oil has come to dominate the economy.

In 1990, Marxism was renounced and opposition parties were legalized. In 1991 the country's name was changed back to Republic of the Congo, and a new constitution was approved. A democratically elected government came into office in 1992. Factional fighting broke out in Brazzaville, June 5, 1997, and intensified during the summer, devastating the capital. Troops loyal to former Marxist dictator Denis Sassou-Nguesso took control of the city Oct. 15, 1997; he claimed lopsided victories in the presidential elections of Mar. 10, 2002, and July 12, 2009.

Costa Rica
Republic of Costa Rica

People: Population: 4,253,877. **Age distrib.** (%): <15: 26.7; 65+: 6.2. **Pop. density:** 217.5 per sq mi, 84 per sq km. **Urban:** 61.7%. **Ethnic groups:** White (incl. mestizo) 94%, black 3%, Amerindian 1%. **Principal languages:** Spanish (official), English spoken around Puerto Limon. **Chief religions:** Roman Catholic 76%, Evangelical 14%.

Geography: Total area: 19,730 sq mi, 51,100 sq km; **Land area:** 19,560 sq mi, 50,660 sq km. **Location:** In Central America. **Neighbors:** Nicaragua on N, Panama on S. **Topography:** Lowlands by the Caribbean are tropical. The interior plateau, with an altitude of about 4,000 ft, is temperate. **Capital:** San José, 1,284,000.

Government: Type: Republic. **Head of state and gov.:** Pres. Óscar Arias Sánchez; b. Sept. 13, 1940; in office: May 8, 2006. **Local divisions:** 7 provinces. **Defense budget:** $159 mil. **Active troops:** 9,800 (paramilitary).

Economy: Industries: microprocessors, food proc., medical equip., textiles & clothing, constr. materials, fertilizer, plastics. **Chief crops:** bananas, pineapples, coffee, melons, ornamental plants, sugar, corn, rice, beans, potatoes. **Natural resources:** hydropower. **Arable land:** 4%. **Livestock:** cattle: 1.2 mil; chickens: 19.5 mil; goats: 5,000; pigs: 676,000; sheep: 2,700. **Fish catch:** 47,500 metric tons. **Electricity prod.:** 8.5 bil kWh. **Labor force** (2006 est.): agric. 14%, industry 22%, services 64%.

Finance: Monetary unit: Colon (CRC) (Oct. 2009: 582.56 = $1 U.S.). **GDP:** $48.3 bil; **per capita GDP:** $11,500; **GDP growth:** 2.7%. **Imports:** $14.6 bil; U.S. 43.3%, Venezuela 6.4%, Mexico 6%, Japan 5.4%, China 5.2%, Brazil 4.2%. **Exports:** $9.7 bil; U.S. 23.4%, China 13.4%, Netherlands 13%, Mexico 5.2%, UK 4.9%. **Tourism:** $2.0 bil. **Budget:** $3.8 bil. **Intl. reserves less gold:** $2.47 bil. **Gold:** NA. **Consumer prices:** 13.4%.

Transport: Railroad: Length: 173 mi. **Motor vehicles:** 669,000 pass. cars; 199,000 comm. vehicles. **Civil aviation:** 1.4 bil pass.-mi; 38 airports. **Chief ports:** Caldera, Puerto Limon.

Communications: TV sets: 229 per 1,000 pop. **Radios:** 774 per 1,000 pop. **Telephone lines:** 1.4 mil. **Daily newspaper circ.** (2004): 64.7 per 1,000 pop. **Internet:** 1.5 mil users.

Health: Life expect.: 74.8 male; 80.1 female. **Births** (per 1,000 pop.): 17.7. **Deaths** (per 1,000 pop.): 4.3. **Natural inc.:** 1.34%. **Infant mortality** (per 1,000 live births): 9. **HIV rate:** 0.4%.

Education: Compulsory: ages 6-15. **Literacy:** 95.9%.

Major intl. organizations: UN (FAO, IBRD, ILO, IMF, IMO, WHO, WTO), OAS.

Embassy: 2114 S St. NW 20008; 234-2945.

Website: www.gobiernofacil.go.cr

Guaymi Indians inhabited the area when Spaniards arrived, 1502. Independence came in 1821. Costa Rica seceded from the Central American Federation in 1838. Since the civil war of 1948-49, there has been little violent social conflict, and free political institutions have been preserved.

Costa Rica, though still a largely agricultural country, has achieved a relatively high standard of living, and land ownership is widespread. Tourism is growing rapidly. Nobel Peace Prize-winner Óscar Arias Sánchez, president 1986-90, won a 2nd term in a close election, Feb. 5, 2006. Corruption charges were filed Aug. 1, 2007, against Miguel Angel Rodríguez, former president of Costa Rica (1998-2002) and OAS secretary-general (2004).

Côte d'Ivoire
Republic of Côte d'Ivoire

People: Population: 20,617,068. **Age distrib.** (%): <15: 40.6; 65+: 2.9. **Pop. density:** 167.9 per sq mi, 64.8 per sq km. **Urban:** 46.8%. **Ethnic groups:** Akan 42%, Voltaiques, or Gur 18%, N Mandes 17%, Krous 11%, S Mandes 10%. **Principal languages:** French (official), 60 native dialects (Dioula most widely spoken). **Chief religions:** Muslim 35%-40%, indigenous 25%-40%, Christian 20%-30%.

Geography: Total area: 124,503 sq mi, 322,460 sq km; **Land area:** 122,780 sq mi, 318,000 sq km. **Location:** On S coast of W Africa. **Neighbors:** Liberia, Guinea on W; Mali, Burkina Faso on N; Ghana on E. **Topography:** Forests cover the W half of the country, and range from a coastal strip to halfway to the N on the E. A sparse inland plain leads to low mountains in NW. **Capital** (2003): Yamoussoukro (official), 668,000; Abidjan (de facto), 3,802,000.

Government: Type: Republic. **Head of state:** Pres. Laurent Gbagbo; b. May 31, 1945; in office: Oct. 26, 2000. **Head of gov.:** Prime Min. Guillaume Soro; b. May 8, 1972; in office: Apr. 4, 2007. **Local divisions:** 58 departments. **Defense budget:** $290 mil. **Active troops:** 17,050.

Economy: Industries: foodstuffs, beverages, wood products, oil refining, truck & bus assembly, textiles, fertilizer. **Chief crops:** coffee, cocoa beans, bananas, palm kernels, corn, rice. **Natural resources:** oil, nat. gas, diamonds, mang., iron ore, cobalt, bauxite, copper, gold. **Crude oil reserves:** 100 mil bbls. **Arable land:** 10%. **Livestock:** cattle: 1.3 mil; chickens: 32.4 mil; goats: 945,000; pigs: 323,500; sheep: 1.2 mil. **Electricity prod.:** 5.3 bil kWh. **Labor force** (2007 est.): agric. 68%, industry & services NA.

Finance: Monetary unit: CFA BCEAO Franc (XOF) (Oct. 2009: 444.97 = $1 U.S.). **GDP:** $33.9 bil; **per capita GDP:** $1,700; **GDP growth:** 2.3%. **Imports:** $7.2 bil; Nigeria 32%, France 15.1%, China 7.8%. **Exports:** $10.4 bil; Germany 11.1%, U.S. 10.3%, Netherlands 9.9%, Nigeria 9.4%, France 6.5%, Burkina

Faso 4.1%. **Tourism:** NA. **Budget:** $3.8 bil. **Intl. reserves less gold:** $1.46 bil. **Gold:** NA. **Consumer prices:** 6.3%.

Transport: Railroad: Length: 410 mi. **Motor vehicles:** 113,900 pass. cars; 54,900 comm. vehicles. **Civil aviation:** 80.8 mil pass.-mi (incl. Air Afrique traffic apportionment); 7 airports. **Chief ports:** Abidjan, Espoir, San-Pédro.

Communications: TV sets: 65 per 1,000 pop. **Radios:** 161 per 1,000 pop. **Telephone lines:** 356,500. **Internet:** 660,000 users.

Health: Life expect.: 54 male; 55.4 female. **Births** (per 1,000 pop.): 32.7. **Deaths** (per 1,000 pop.): 11.2. **Natural inc.:** 2.16%. **Infant mortality** (per 1,000 live births): 69.8. **HIV rate:** 3.9%.

Education: Compulsory: ages 6-15. **Literacy:** 48.7%.

Major intl. organizations: UN and all of its specialized agencies, AU.

Embassy: 3421 Massachusetts Ave. NW 20007; 797-0300. **Website:** www.gouv.ci

A French protectorate from 1842, Côte d'Ivoire became independent in 1960. The name was officially changed from Ivory Coast, Oct. 1985. The country is a leading producer of coffee and cocoa beans.

Students and workers protested, Feb. 1990, demanding the ouster of longtime Pres. Félix Houphouët-Boigny. Côte d'Ivoire held its first multiparty presidential election Oct. 1990, and Houphouët-Boigny retained his office. He died Dec. 7, 1993. The National Assembly named a successor, Henri Konan Bédié, who was reelected Oct. 22, 1995; he was ousted in a military coup Dec. 24, 1999. The coup leader, Robert Guéi, apparently lost a presidential vote Oct. 22, 2000, but claimed victory anyway. After mass protests, he fled, and Laurent Gbagbo became president. Guéi was killed in Abidjan Sept. 19, 2002, after a mutiny broke out there and in Bouaké and Korhogo.

Agreement on power sharing was reached in Mar. 2003, and Gbagbo and former rebel leaders held a ceremony July 5, declaring that the war was over. The country remained divided, however, with rebels holding the north and government forces controlling the south. Under a new accord reached Mar. 4, 2007, rebel leader Guillaume Soro was sworn in as prime min. Apr. 4. An international oil-trading company agreed Sept. 2009 to pay $48.7 mil in compensation for toxic waste dumped in Abidjan by one of the firm's cargo ships in 2006; a UN report said 15 people died and thousands were sickened from chemical exposure.

A UN peacekeeping force for Côte d'Ivoire (UNOCI), authorized in Feb. 2004, included 8,400 uniformed personnel in mid-2008; a small French force is also present. A long-delayed presidential election has been scheduled for Nov. 29, 2009.

Croatia
Republic of Croatia

People: Population: 4,489,409. **Age distrib.** (%): <15: 15.6; 65+: 17. **Pop. density:** 206.1 per sq mi, 79.6 per sq km. **Urban:** 56.5%. **Ethnic groups:** Croat 90%, Serb 5%, other (incl. Bosnian, Hungarian, Slovene, Czech, Roma) 6%. **Principal languages:** Croatian, Serbian. **Chief religions:** Roman Catholic 88%, Orthodox 4%, none 5%.

Geography: Total area: 21,831 sq mi, 56,542 sq km; **Land area:** 21,782 sq mi, 56,414 sq km. **Location:** SE Europe, on the Balkan Peninsula. **Neighbors:** Slovenia, Hungary on N; Bosnia and Herzegovina, Serbia, Montenegro on E. **Topography:** Flat plains in NE; highlands, low mtns. along Adriatic coast. **Capital:** Zagreb, 690,000.

Government: Type: Parliamentary democracy. **Head of state:** Pres. Stipe Mesic; b. Dec. 24, 1934; in office: Feb. 18, 2000. **Head of gov.:** Prime Min. Jadranka Kosor; b. July 1, 1953; in office: July 6, 2009. **Local divisions:** 20 counties and Zagreb. **Defense budget:** $843 mil. **Active troops:** 18,600.

Economy: Industries: chemicals, plastics, machine tools, fabricated metal, electronics. **Chief crops:** wheat, corn, sugar beets, sunflower seed, barley. **Natural resources:** oil, coal, bauxite, iron ore, calcium, gypsum, nat. asphalt, silica, mica, clays, salt, hydropower. **Crude oil reserves:** 79.3 mil bbls. **Arable land:** 26%. **Livestock:** cattle: 482,905; chickens: 6.8 mil; goats: 102,877; pigs: 1.5 mil; sheep: 679,839. **Fish catch:** 53,089 metric tons. **Electricity prod.:** 12.4 bil kWh. **Labor force** (2008): agric. 5%, industry 31.3%, services 63.6%.

Finance: Monetary unit: Kuna (HRK) (Oct. 2009: 4.91 = $1 U.S.). **GDP:** $82.4 bil. **per capita GDP:** $18,300; **GDP growth:** 2.4%. **Imports:** $30.7 bil; Italy 17.1%, Germany 13.4%, Russia 10.5%, China 6.1%, Slovenia 5.6%, Austria 4.9%. **Exports:** $14.7 bil; Italy 18.9%, Bosnia and Herzegovina 15.3%, Germany 10.7%, Slovenia 7.7%, Austria 5.7%. **Tourism:** $9.3 bil. **Budget:** $23.9 bil. **Intl. reserves less gold:** $8.41 bil. **Gold:** NA. **Consumer prices:** 6.1%.

Transport: Railroad: Length: 1,691 mi. **Motor vehicles:** 1.4 mil pass. cars; 168,000 comm. vehicles. **Civil aviation:** 605.2 mil pass.-mi; 23 airports. **Chief ports:** Omisalj, Ploce, Rijeka, Sibenik.

Communications: TV sets: 286 per 1,000 pop. **Radios:** 337 per 1,000 pop. **Telephone lines:** 1.9 mil. **Daily newspaper circ.** (1999): 118.3 per 1,000 pop. **Internet:** 2.2 mil users.

Health: Life expect.: 71.5 male; 79 female. **Births** (per 1,000 pop.): 9.6. **Deaths** (per 1,000 pop.): 11.7. **Natural inc.:** –0.2%. **Infant mortality** (per 1,000 live births): 6.5. **HIV rate:** <0.1%.

Education: Compulsory: ages 7-14. **Literacy:** 98.7%.

Major intl. organizations: UN (FAO, IBRD, ILO, IMF, IMO, WHO, WTO), NATO, OSCE.

Embassy: 2343 Massachusetts Ave. NW 20008; 588-5899. **Website:** www.vlada.hr

From the 7th cent. the area was inhabited by Croats, a south Slavic people. It was formed into a kingdom under Tomislav in 924, and joined with Hungary in 1102. The Croats became westernized and separated from Slavs under Austro-Hungarian influence. Croatia united with other Yugoslav areas to proclaim the Kingdom of Serbs, Croats, and Slovenes in 1918. A nominally independent state between 1941 and 1945, it became a constituent republic in the 1946 constitution.

On June 25, 1991, Croatia declared independence from Yugoslavia. Fighting began between ethnic Serbs and Croats, with the former gaining control of about 30% of Croatian territory. Croatian government troops recaptured most of the Serb-held territory Aug. 1995. Pres. Franjo Tudjman signed a peace accord with leaders of Bosnia and Serbia in Paris, Dec. 14. The last Serb-held enclave, E Slavonia, returned to Croatian control Jan. 15, 1998.

Tudjman died Dec. 10, 1999. Stipe Mesic, a moderate, won a presidential runoff election Feb. 7, 2000, and was reelected Jan. 16, 2005. Talks on EU membership, sought by Croatia, were postponed because of the nation's failure to hand over a suspected war criminal, Gen. Ante Gotovina; he was arrested Dec. 7, 2005, in Spain's Canary Islands. Croatia became a full member of NATO Apr. 1, 2009, but negotiations with the EU were stalled over a border dispute with Slovenia.

Cuba
Republic of Cuba

People: Population: 11,451,652. **Age distrib.** (%): <15: 18.3; 65+: 11.2. **Pop. density:** 267.5 per sq mi, 103.3 per sq km. **Urban:** 75.6%. **Ethnic groups:** White 65%, mulatto & mestizo 25%, black 10%. **Principal language:** Spanish. **Chief religion:** Roman Catholic (nominally, prior to Castro assuming power) 85%.

Geography: Total area: 42,803 sq mi, 110,860 sq km; **Land area:** 42,803 sq mi, 110,860 sq km. **Location:** In Caribbean, westernmost of West Indies. **Neighbors:** Bahamas, U.S. to N; Mexico to W; Jamaica to S; Haiti to E. **Topography:** Coastline is about 2,500 mi. The N coast is steep and rocky, the S coast low and marshy. Low hills and fertile valleys cover more than half the country. Sierra Maestra, in E, is the highest of 3 mountain ranges. **Capital:** Havana, 2,174,000.

Government: Type: Communist state. **Head of state and gov.:** Pres. Raúl Castro Ruz; b. June 3, 1931; in office: Feb. 24, 2008 (acting from July 31, 2006). **Local divisions:** 14 provinces, 1 special municipality. **Defense budget:** NA. **Active troops:** 49,000.

Economy: Industries: sugar, oil, tobacco, constr., nickel. **Chief crops:** sugar, tobacco, citrus, coffee, rice, potatoes, beans. **Natural resources:** cobalt, nickel, iron ore, chromium, copper, salt, timber, silica, oil. **Crude oil reserves:** 124 mil bbls. **Arable land:** 28%. **Livestock:** cattle: 3.8 mil; chickens: 29.4 mil; goats: 1.1 mil; pigs: 1.9 mil; sheep: 2.7 mil. **Fish catch:** 62,144 metric tons. **Electricity prod.:** 15.5 bil kWh. **Labor force** (2005): agric. 20%, industry 19.4%, services 60.6%.

Finance: Monetary unit: Peso (CUP) (Oct. 2009: 26.50 = $1 U.S.). **GDP:** $108.2 bil. **per capita GDP:** $9,500; **GDP growth:** 4.3%. **Imports:** $14.5 bil; Venezuela 31.5%, China 11.8%, Spain 10.6%, Canada 6.7%, U.S. 6.6%. **Exports:** $3.8 bil; China 27.9%, Canada 25.3%, Spain 5.7%, Netherlands 5%, Iran 4.3%. **Tourism:** $2.1 bil. **Budget:** $43.9 bil.

Transport: Railroad: Length: 5,343 mi. **Motor vehicles:** NA pass. cars; 24,000 comm. vehicles. **Civil aviation:** 1.5 bil pass.-mi; 65 airports. **Chief ports:** Cienfuegos, Havana, Matanzas.

Communications: TV sets: 248 per 1,000 pop. **Radios:** 352 per 1,000 pop. **Telephone lines:** 1.1 mil. **Daily newspaper circ.** (2004): 64.7 per 1,000 pop. **Internet:** 1.5 mil users.

Education: Compulsory: ages 6-14. **Literacy:** 99.8%.

Health: Life expect.: 75 male; 79.6 female. **Births** (per 1,000 pop.): 11.3. **Deaths** (per 1,000 pop.): 7.2. **Natural inc.:** 0.41%. **Infant mortality** (per 1,000 live births): 5.9. **HIV rate:** 0.1%.

Major intl. organizations: UN (FAO, ILO, IMO, WHO, WTO). Cuba is an OAS member state, but its current govt. has been excluded from OAS participation since 1962.

Cuban Interests Section: 2630 16th St. NW, 20009; 797-8518.

Website: www.cubagob.cu

Some 50,000 Indians lived in Cuba when it was reached by Columbus in 1492. Its name derives from the Indian Cubanacan. Except for British occupation of Havana, 1762-63, Cuba remained Spanish until 1898. A slave-based sugar plantation economy developed from the 18th cent. Sugar remains the chief product and main export.

A 10-year uprising ended in 1878 with guarantees of rights by Spain, which Spain failed to carry out. A full-scale liberation movement under Jose Martí began Feb. 24, 1895.

The Spanish-American War began Apr. 1898, after the sinking of the USS *Maine* in Havana harbor. Spain, which lost the war, gave up all claims to Cuba. U.S. troops withdrew in 1902, but under 1903 and 1934 agreements, the U.S. continued to lease a site at Guantánamo Bay in the southeast as a naval base (see below). U.S. and other foreign investors acquired a dominant role in the economy. In 1952, former Pres. Fulgencio Batista seized control and established a dictatorship, which grew increasingly harsh and corrupt. Fidel Castro assembled a rebel band in 1956; guerrilla fighting intensified in 1958. Batista fled Jan. 1, 1959, and in the resulting political vacuum Castro took power, becoming premier Feb. 16.

The government began a program of sweeping economic and social changes, without restoring promised liberties. Opponents were imprisoned, and some were executed. Some 700,000 Cubans emigrated in the first years after the Castro takeover, mostly to the U.S. By 1960 all banks and industrial companies had been nationalized, including over $1 bil worth of U.S.-owned properties, mostly without compensation.

In 1961, some 1,400 Cubans, trained and backed by the U.S. Central Intelligence Agency, unsuccessfully tried to invade and overthrow the regime. In the fall of 1962, the U.S. learned the USSR had brought nuclear missiles to Cuba. On Oct. 22, Pres. John F. Kennedy ordered a naval blockade and demanded that the missiles be withdrawn. The crisis ended Oct. 28 when Soviet Prem. Nikita S. Khrushchev agreed to pull out the missiles immediately; in return, the U.S. ended the blockade, pledged not to invade Cuba, and quietly removed its own missiles from Turkey.

In 1977, Cuba and the U.S. signed agreements to exchange diplomats, without restoring full ties, and to regulate offshore fishing. In 1978 and 1980, the U.S. agreed to accept political prisoners released by Cuba, some of whom were criminals and mental patients. A 1987 agreement provided for 20,000 Cubans to emigrate to the U.S. each year; Cuba agreed to take back some 2,500 jailed in the U.S. since 1980. Cuba's support for left-wing regimes and liberation movements in Central America, Africa, and the Caribbean contributed to poor relations with the U.S.

Cuba's economy, hobbled by U.S. sanctions and dependent on aid from other Communist countries, was severely shaken by the collapse of the Communist bloc in the late 1980s. Stiffer trade sanctions enacted by the U.S. in 1992 made things worse. Antigovernment demonstrations in Aug. 1994 prompted Castro to loosen emigration restrictions. A new U.S.-Cuba accord in Sept. ended the exodus of "boat people" after more than 30,000 had left Cuba. In another policy shift, the U.S. announced May 2, 1995, it would admit 20,000 Cuban refugees held at Guantánamo but would send further boat people back to Cuba.

The U.S. imposed additional sanctions after Cuba, Feb. 24, 1996, shot down 2 aircraft operated by anti-Castro exiles. Cuba blamed exile groups for bombings at Havana tourist hotels, July-Sept. 1997. Pope John Paul II visited Cuba, Jan. 21-25, 1998.

On July 31, 2006, the ailing Fidel Castro yielded power to his 75-year-old brother Raúl, who then served as acting president until formally succeeding Fidel Feb. 24, 2008. Hurricanes Gustav and Ike, Aug.-Sept. 2008, devastated the sugar crop and damaged 450,000 homes, causing an estimated $5 bil in losses.

In Apr. 2009, U.S. Pres. Obama called for "a new beginning with Cuba" and eased restrictions on remittances and family travel to the island; on Sept. 14, however, he indicated that a U.S. embargo on trade with Cuba would remain in force.

The U.S., Jan. 11, 2002, began using its naval base at **Guantánamo Bay** to detain prisoners captured in Afghanistan; in Sept. 2009 more than 200 detainees were still being held at the base. The indefinite detention and aggressive interrogation of Afghan prisoners and others at Guantánamo were criticized by human rights groups. Pres. Obama signed Jan. 22, 2009, an executive order calling for the closure of the Guantánamo detention center within a year.

Cyprus
Republic of Cyprus

People: Population: 796,740. **Age distrib.** (%): <15: 19.1; 65+: 12.3. **Pop. density:** 223.3 per sq mi, 86.2 per sq km. **Urban:** 69.3%. **Ethnic groups:** Greek 77%, Turkish 18%. **Principal languages:** Greek, Turkish, English. **Chief religions:** Greek Orthodox 78%, Muslim 18%.

Geography: Total area: 3,571 sq mi, 9,250 sq km; **Land area:** 3,568 sq mi, 9,240 sq km. **Location:** In eastern Mediterranean Sea, off Turkish coast. **Neighbors:** Nearest are Turkey on N, Syria and Lebanon on E. **Topography:** Two mountain ranges run E-W, separated by a wide, fertile plain. **Capital:** Nicosia (Lefkosia), 233,000.

Government: Type: Republic. **Head of state and gov.:** Pres. Dimitris Christofias; b. Aug. 29, 1946; in office; Feb. 28, 2008. **Lo-**

cal divisions: 6 districts. **Defense budget:** $498 mil. **Active troops:** 10,000.

Economy: Industries: tourism, food & beverage proc., cement & gypsum prod., textiles, light chemicals, metal products. **Chief crops:** citrus, vegetables, barley, grapes, olives, vegetables. **Natural resources:** copper, pyrites, asbestos, gypsum, timber, salt, marble, clay earth pigment. **Arable land:** 11%. **Livestock:** cattle: 54,900; chickens: 3.1 mil; goats: 339,000; pigs: 450,300; sheep: 259,400. **Fish catch:** 4,950 metric tons. **Electricity prod.:** 4.4 bil kWh. **Labor force** (2006 est.): agric. 8.5%, industry 20.5%, services 71%.

Finance: Monetary unit: Euro (EUR) (Oct. 2009: 0.68 = $1 U.S.). **GDP:** 22.7 bil; **per capita GDP:** $28,600; **GDP growth:** 3.7%. **Imports:** $9.9 bil; Greece 16.9%, Italy 10.7%, UK 8.7%, Germany 8.3%, Israel 8.2%, China 5.3%, Netherlands 4.1%, France 4%. **Exports:** $1.7 bil; Greece 20.1%, UK 10.8%, Germany 6%. **Tourism:** $2.7 bil. **Budget:** $9.3 bil. **Intl. reserves less gold:** $400 mil. Gold: 450,000 oz t. **Consumer prices:** 4.7%.

Transport: Motor vehicles: 355,000 pass. cars; 126,000 comm. vehicles. **Civil aviation:** 2.6 bil pass.-mi; 13 airports. **Chief ports:** Famagusta (admin. by Turkish Cypriots), Limassol (under govt. control).

Communications: TV sets: 154 per 1000 pop. **Radios:** 406 per 1,000 pop. **Telephone lines:** 413,300. **Daily newspaper circ.** (1999): 124.5 per 1,000 pop. **Internet:** 335,000 users.

Health: Life expect.: 75.8 male; 80.7 female. **Births** (per 1,000 pop.): 12.6. **Deaths** (per 1,000 pop.): 7.8. **Natural inc.:** 0.48%. **Infant mortality** (per 1,000 live births): 6.8. **HIV rate:** NA. **Education:** Compulsory: ages 6-14. **Literacy:** 97.7%.

Major intl. organizations: UN (FAO, IBRD, ILO, IMF, IMO, WHO, WTO), the Commonwealth, EU, OSCE.

Embassy: 2211 R St. NW 20008; 462-5772.

Website: www.cyprus.gov.cy

The Ottoman Empire held Cyprus, 1571-1878, until it yielded control over the island to Britain. Agitation for enosis (union) with Greece increased after WWII, with the Turkish minority opposed, and broke into violence in 1955-56. In 1959, Britain, Greece, Turkey, and Cypriot leaders approved a plan for an independent republic, with constitutional guarantees for the Turkish minority and permanent division of offices on an ethnic basis.

Archbishop Makarios III, formerly the leader of the enosis movement, was elected president, and full independence became final Aug. 16, 1960. Further communal strife led the United Nations to send a peacekeeping force (UNFICYP) in 1964; its mandate has been repeatedly renewed.

The Cypriot National Guard, led by officers from the army of Greece, seized the government July 15, 1974. On July 20, Turkey invaded the island; Greece mobilized its forces but did not intervene. A cease-fire was arranged but collapsed. By Aug. 16, Turkish forces had occupied the northeastern 40% of the island, despite the presence of UN peacekeeping forces.

Face-to-face talks between the Greek and Turkish Cypriot leaders resumed Dec. 4, 2001, for the first time in 4 years. Turkish Cyprus opened its border with Greek Cyprus Apr. 23, 2003, for the first time since partition. In separate referendums Apr. 24, 2004, 65% of Turkish Cypriot voters accepted a UN-sponsored reunification plan, but 76% of Greek Cypriots rejected it. Still divided, Cyprus became a full member of the EU on May 1. Dimitris Christofias won a runoff election Feb. 24, 2008, becoming the country's first Communist president.

Turkish Republic of Northern Cyprus

A declaration of independence was announced by Turkish-Cypriot leader Rauf Denktash, Nov. 15, 1983. The state is not internationally recognized, but has trade relations with some countries. Mehmet Ali Talat succeeded Denktash as president Apr. 24, 2005. Area of TRNC: 1,295 sq mi; pop. (2006 census, prelim.): 264,172, nearly all Turkish. Capital: Lefkosa (Nicosia).

Czech Republic

People: Population: 10,211,904. **Age distrib.** (%): <15: 13.6; 65+: 15.5. **Pop. density:** 342.3 per sq mi, 132.1 per sq km. **Urban:** 73.5%. **Ethnic groups:** Czech 90%, Moravian 4%. **Principal languages:** Czech, Slovak. **Chief religions:** Roman Catholic 27%, Protestant 2%, unaffiliated 59%.

Geography: Total area: 30,450 sq mi, 78,866 sq km; **Land area:** 29,836 sq mi, 77,276 sq km. **Location:** In E central Europe. **Neighbors:** Poland on N, Germany on N and W, Austria on S, Slovakia on E and SE. **Topography:** Bohemia, in W, is a plateau surrounded by mountains; Moravia is hilly. **Capital:** Prague, 1,162,000.

Government: Type: Republic. **Head of state:** Vaclav Klaus; b. June 19, 1941; in office: Mar. 7, 2003. **Head of gov.:** Prime Min. Jan Fischer; b. Jan. 2, 1951; in office: May 8, 2009. **Local divisions:** 13 regions and Prague. **Defense budget:** $2.7 bil. **Active troops:** 24,083.

Economy: Industries: metallurgy, machinery & equip., motor vehicles, glass, armaments. **Chief crops:** wheat, potatoes, sugar beets, hops, fruit. **Natural resources:** coal, kaolin, clay, graphite, timber. **Crude oil reserves:** 15 mil bbls. **Arable land:** 39%. **Livestock:** cattle: 1.4 mil; chickens: 23.6 mil; goats: 16,222; pigs: 2.8 mil; sheep: 168,910. **Fish catch:** 24,723 metric tons. **Electricity prod.:** 79 bil kWh. **Labor force** (2007): agric. 3.6%, industry 40.2%, services 56.2%.

Finance: Monetary unit: Koruna (CZK) (Oct. 2009: 17.35 = $1 U.S.). **GDP:** $265.2 bil; **per capita GDP:** $25,900; **GDP growth:** 3%. **Imports:** $139.4 bil; Germany 30.3%, Slovakia 6.6%, Poland 6.4%, Russia 6.2%, Netherlands 5.6%, Austria 5.2%, China 4.9%, Italy 4.1%. **Exports:** $145.7 bil; Germany 30.6%, Slovakia 9.2%, Poland 6.5%, France 5.3%, UK 4.8%, Austria 4.7%, Italy 4.6%. **Tourism:** $6.6 bil. **Budget:** $76.3 bil. **Intl. reserves less gold:** $23.79 bil. **Gold:** 420,000 oz t. **Consumer prices:** 6.4%.

Transport: Railroad: Length: 5,978 mi. **Motor vehicles:** 3.96 mil pass. cars; 488,400 comm. vehicles. **Civil aviation:** 4.1 bil pass.-mi; 44 airports. **Chief ports:** Decin, Prague, Usti nad Labem.

Communications: TV sets: 487 per 1,000 pop. **Radios:** 803 per 1,000 pop. **Telephone lines:** 2.3 mil. **Daily newspaper circ.** (2004): 182.5 per 1,000 pop. **Internet:** 6 mil users.

Health: Life expect.: 73.3 male; 80.1 female. **Births** (per 1,000 pop.): 8.9. **Deaths** (per 1,000 pop.): 10.7. **Natural inc.:** –0.18%. **Infant mortality** (per 1,000 live births): 3.8. **HIV rate:** NA.

Education: Compulsory: ages 6-15. **Literacy:** 99%.

Major intl. organizations: UN (FAO, IBRD, ILO, IMF, IMO, WHO, WTO), EU, NATO, OECD, OSCE.

Embassy: 3900 Spring of Freedom St. NW 20008; 274-9100.

Website: www.czech.cz

Bohemia and Moravia were part of the Great Moravian Empire in the 9th cent. and later became part of the Holy Roman Empire. Under the kings of Bohemia, Prague in the 14th cent. was the cultural center of Central Europe. Bohemia and Hungary became part of Austria-Hungary.

In 1914-18 Thomas G. Masaryk and Eduard Benes formed a provisional government with the support of Slovak leaders including Milan Stefanik. They proclaimed the Republic of Czechoslovakia Oct. 28, 1918.

Czechoslovakia

By 1938 Nazi Germany had worked up disaffection among German-speaking citizens in Sudetenland and demanded its cession. British Prime Min. Neville Chamberlain, with the acquiescence of France, signed with Hitler at Munich, Sept. 30, 1938, an agreement to the cession, with a guarantee of peace by Hitler and Mussolini. Germany occupied Sudetenland Oct. 1-2.

Hitler on Mar. 15, 1939, dissolved Czechoslovakia, made protectorates of Bohemia and Moravia, and supported the autonomy of Slovakia, proclaimed independent Mar. 14, 1939.

Soviet troops with some Czechoslovak contingents entered eastern Czechoslovakia in 1944 and reached Prague in May 1945; Benes returned as president. In May 1946 elections, the Communist Party won 38% of the votes. In Feb. 1948, the Communists seized power in advance of scheduled elections. The country was renamed the Czechoslovak Socialist Republic. A harsh Stalinist period followed, with complete and violent suppression of all opposition.

In Jan. 1968 a liberalization movement spread through Czechoslovakia. Antonin Novotny, long the Stalinist ruler, was deposed as party leader and succeeded by Alexander Dubcek, a Slovak, who supported democratic reforms. In July, the USSR and 4 Warsaw Pact nations demanded an end to liberalization. On Aug. 20, the Soviet, Polish, East German, Hungarian, and Bulgarian armies invaded Czechoslovakia. Despite demonstrations and riots by students and workers, press censorship was imposed and liberal leaders were ousted. On Apr. 17, 1969, Dubcek resigned as leader of the Communist Party and was succeeded by Gustav Husak. Censorship was tightened, and the Communist Party expelled a third of its members.

More than 700 leading Czechoslovak intellectuals and former party leaders signed a human rights manifesto in 1977, called Charter 77, prompting a renewed crackdown by the regime.

The police crushed the largest antigovernment protests since 1968, when tens of thousands of demonstrators took to the streets of Prague, Nov. 17, 1989. As protesters demanded free elections, the Communist Party leadership resigned Nov. 24; millions went on strike Nov. 27.

On Dec. 10, 1989, the first cabinet in 41 years without a Communist majority took power; Vaclav Havel, playwright and human rights campaigner, was chosen president, Dec. 29. In Mar. 1990 the country was officially renamed the Czech and Slovak Federal Republic. Havel failed to win reelection July 3, 1992; his bid was blocked by a Slovak-led coalition.

Slovakia declared sovereignty, July 17, 1992. Czech and Slovak leaders agreed, July 23, on a basic plan for a peaceful division of Czechoslovakia into 2 independent states.

Czech Republic

Czechoslovakia split into 2 separate states—the Czech Republic and Slovakia—on Jan. 1, 1993. Havel was elected president of the Czech Republic on Jan. 26. Record floods in July 1997 caused more than $1.7 bil in damage. The country became a full member of NATO on Mar. 12, 1999. Floods Aug. 2002 damaged cultural treasures in Prague.

Vaclav Klaus was chosen Feb. 28, 2003, to replace the retiring Havel. After Czech voters June 13-14, 2003, endorsed joining the EU, the nation became a full EU member May 1, 2004. Inconclusive parliamentary elections, June 2-3, 2006, led to a prolonged political deadlock, after which a minority center-right government took office Sept. 4. Addressing as many as 20,000 people in Prague Apr. 5, 2009, Pres. Obama affirmed the U.S. "commitment to seek the peace and security of a world without nuclear weapons."

Denmark
Kingdom of Denmark

People: Population: 5,500,510. **Age distrib.** (%): <15: 18.1; 65+: 16.1. **Pop. density:** 336 per sq mi, 129.7 per sq km. **Urban:** 85.9%. **Ethnic groups:** Scandinavian, Inuit, Faroese, German, Turkish, Iranian, Somali. **Principal languages:** Danish, Faroese, Greenlandic (Inuit dialect), English (predominant second lang.). **Chief religions:** Evangelical Lutheran 95%, other Christian (incl. Protestant, Roman Catholic) 3%, Muslim 2%.

Geography: Total area: 16,639 sq mi, 43,094 sq km; **Land area:** 16,368 sq mi, 42,394 sq km. **Location:** In N Europe, separating North and Baltic seas. **Neighbors:** Germany on S, Norway on NW, Sweden on NE. **Topography:** Consists of the Jutland Peninsula and about 500 islands, 100 inhabited. Land is flat or gently rolling and is almost all in productive use. **Capital:** Copenhagen, 1,085,000.

Government: Type: Constitutional monarchy. **Head of state:** Queen Margrethe II; b. Apr. 16, 1940; in office: Jan. 14, 1972. **Head of gov.:** Prime Min. Lars Løkke Rasmussen; b. May 15, 1964; in office: Apr. 5, 2009; in office: Nov. 27, 2001. **Local divisions:** 5 regions. **Defense budget:** $4 bil. **Active troops:** 29,550.

Economy: Industries: iron, steel, nonferrous metals, chemicals, food proc., machinery & transp. equip., textiles & clothing, electronics, constr., furniture. **Chief crops:** barley, wheat, potatoes, sugar beets. **Natural resources:** oil, nat. gas, fish, salt, limestone, chalk, stone, gravel, sand. **Crude oil reserves:** 1.1 bil bbls. **Arable land:** 53%. **Livestock:** cattle: 1.6 mil; chickens: 16 mil; pigs: 13.7 mil; sheep: 156,503. **Fish catch:** 684,191 metric tons. **Electricity prod.:** 43. bil kWh. **Labor force** (2005 est.): agric. 2.9%, industry 23.8%, services 72.7%.

Finance: Monetary unit: Krone (DKK) (Oct. 2009: 5.05 = $1 U.S.). **GDP:** $203.6 bil; **per capita GDP:** $37,100; **GDP growth:** –1.2%. **Imports:** $116.4 bil; Germany 21%, Sweden 14%, Netherlands 6.7%, Norway 6.2%, China 5.6%, UK 5.1%. **Exports:** $114.9 bil; Germany 17.9%, Sweden 14.5%, UK 8.3%, Norway 5.7%, U.S. 5.3%, France 4.8%, Netherlands 4.6%. **Tourism:** $6.2 bil. **Budget:** $158.8 bil. **Intl. reserves less gold:** $26.27 bil. **Gold:** 2.14 mil oz t. **Consumer prices:** 3.4%.

Transport: Railroad: Length: 1,657 mi. **Motor vehicles:** 1.97 mil pass. cars; 484,000 comm. vehicles. **Civil aviation:** 6.2 bil pass.-mi (incl. Scandinavian Airlines System operations apportionment); 28 airports. **Chief ports:** Aalborg, Aarhus, Copenhagen, Ensted, Esbjerg, Fredericia, Kalundborg.

Communications: TV sets: 776 per 1,000 pop. **Radios:** 1,325 per 1,000 pop. **Telephone lines:** 2.5 mil. **Daily newspaper circ.** (2004): 352.8 per 1,000 pop. **Internet:** 4.6 mil users.

Health: Life expect.: 75.8 male; 80.6 female. **Births** (per 1,000 pop.): 10.7. **Deaths** (per 1,000 pop.): 10.2. **Natural inc.:** 0.05%. **Infant mortality** (per 1,000 live births): 4.4. **HIV rate:** 0.2%.

Education: Compulsory: ages 7-16. **Literacy:** 99%.

Major intl. organizations: UN and all of its specialized agencies, EU, NATO, OECD, OSCE.

Embassy: 3200 Whitehaven St. NW 20008; 234-4300.

Website: www.denmark.dk

The origin of Copenhagen dates back to ancient times, when the fishing and trading place named Havn (port) grew up on a cluster of islets, but Bishop Absalon (1128-1201) is regarded as the actual founder of the city.

Danes formed a large component of the Viking raiders in the early Middle Ages. The Danish kingdom was a major power until the 17th cent., when it lost its land in southern Sweden. Norway was separated in 1815, and Schleswig-Holstein in 1864. Northern Schleswig was returned in 1920. Denmark was occupied by Nazi

Germany, Apr. 1940-May 1945, but Danes helped more than 7,200 Jews escape to safety in Sweden, Sept. 1943.

Voters ratified the Maastricht Treaty, the basic document of the European Union, in May 1993, after rejecting it in 1992. On Sept. 28, 2000, Danes voted not to join the euro currency zone.

The Danish newspaper *Jyllands-Posten* published, Sept. 30, 2005, cartoon images of the prophet Muhammad, offensive to Muslims; the caricatures, republished elsewhere, triggered violent protests and a boycott of Danish products in Islamic countries in early 2006. Raids by Danish police broke up alleged Islamist bomb plots Sept. 2006 and Sept. 2007. A car bomb blast linked to al-Qaeda killed 8 people outside Denmark's embassy in Islamabad, Pakistan, June 2, 2008.

Finance Min. Lars Løkke Rasmussen, deputy leader of the center-right Liberal Party, became prime minister Apr. 5, 2009, replacing Anders Fogh Rasmussen, who had headed the government for 7½ years until he was named NATO secretary general.

The **Faroe Islands** in the North Atlantic, about 300 mi NW of the Shetlands, and 850 mi from Denmark proper, 18 inhabited, have an area of 540 sq mi and pop. (2009 est.) of 48,856. They are an administrative division of Denmark, self-governing in most matters. Torshavn is the capital. Fish is a primary export (292,519 metric tons in 2006).

Greenland (Kalaallit Nunaat)

Greenland, a huge island between the North Atlantic and the Polar Sea, is separated from the North American continent by Davis Strait and Baffin Bay. Its total area is 836,331 sq mi, 81% of which is ice-capped. Most of the island is a lofty plateau 9,000 to 10,000 ft in altitude. The average thickness of the cap is 1,000 ft. Scientists point to accelerated melting of Greenland's ice sheet in recent years as evidence of global warming. The population (2009 est.) is 57,600. Under the 1953 Danish constitution the colony became an integral part of the realm with representatives in the Folketing (Danish legislature). The Danish parliament, 1978, approved home rule for Greenland, effective May 1, 1979. With home rule, Greenlandic place names came into official use. The technically correct name for Greenland is now Kalaallit Nunaat; the official name for its capital is Nuuk, rather than Godthab. Fish is the principal export (120,725 metric tons in 2006).

Djibouti
Republic of Djibouti

People: Population: 516,055. **Age distrib.** (%): <15: 43.3; 65+: 3.7. **Pop. density:** 58.2 per sq mi, 22.5 per sq km. **Urban:** 86.1%. **Ethnic groups:** Somali 60%, Afar 35%. **Principal languages:** French, Arabic (both official); Somali; Afar. **Chief religions:** Muslim 94%, Christian 6%.

Geography: Total area: 8,880 sq mi, 23,000 sq km; **Land area:** 8,873 sq mi, 22,980 sq km. **Location:** On E coast of Africa, separated from Arabian Peninsula by strategically vital strait of Bab el-Mandeb. **Neighbors:** Ethiopia on W and SW, Eritrea on NW, Somalia on SE. **Topography:** The territory, divided into a low coastal plain, mountains behind, and an interior plateau, is arid, sandy, and desolate. Climate is generally hot and dry. **Capital:** Djibouti, 583,000.

Government: Type: Republic. **Head of state:** Pres. Ismail Omar Guelleh; b. Nov. 27, 1947; in office: May 8, 1999. **Head of gov.:** Prime Min. Dileita Mohamed Dileita; b. Mar. 12, 1958; in office: Mar. 7, 2001. **Local divisions:** 5 districts. **Defense budget:** $17 mil. **Active troops:** 10,450.

Economy: Industries: constr., agric. proc. **Chief crops:** fruits, vegetables. **Natural resources:** geothermal areas, gold, clay, granite. **Arable land:** 0.04%. **Livestock:** cattle: 297,000; goats: 512,000; sheep: 466,000. **Fish catch:** 265 metric tons. **Electricity prod.:** 250 mil kWh. **Labor force:** NA.

Finance: Monetary unit: Franc (DJF) (Oct. 2009: 174.23 = $1 U.S.). **GDP:** $1.9 bil; **per capita GDP:** $3,700; **GDP growth:** 5.8%. **Imports** (2006): $1.6 bil; Saudi Arabia 22.1%, India 16.6%, China 9.1%, U.S. 6.5%, Malaysia 4.5%, Ethiopia 4.3%. **Exports** (2006): $340 mil; Somalia 64.6%, Ethiopia 20.9%, UAE 3.3%. **Tourism:** NA. **Budget** (1999 est.): $182 mil. **Intl. reserves less gold:** $114 mil. **Gold:** NA. **Consumer prices:** NA.

Transport: Railroad: Length: 62 mi. **Civil aviation:** 41.6 mil pass.-mi; 3 airports. **Chief port:** Djibouti.

Communications: TV sets: 48 per 1,000 pop. **Radios:** 86 per 1,000 pop. **Telephone lines:** 10,800. **Internet:** 13,000 users.

Health: Life expect.: 41.9 male; 44.8 female. **Births** (per 1,000 pop.): 38.6. **Deaths** (per 1,000 pop.): 19.2. **Natural inc.:** 1.95%. **Infant mortality** (per 1,000 live births): 99.1. **HIV rate:** 3.1%.

Education: Compulsory: ages 6-15. **Literacy:** 67.9%.

Major intl. organizations: UN (FAO, IBRD, ILO, IMF, IMO, WHO, WTO), AL, AU.

Embassy: 1156 15th St. NW, Ste. 515, 20005; 331-0270.

Website: www.presidence.dj

France gained control of the territory in stages between 1862 and 1900. As French Somaliland it became an overseas territory of France in 1945; in 1967 it was renamed the French Territory of the Afars and the Issas.

Ethiopia and Somalia have renounced their claims to the area, but each has accused the other of trying to gain control. There were clashes between Afars (ethnically related to Ethiopians) and Issas (related to Somalis) in 1976. Immigrants from both countries continued to enter the country up to independence, which came June 27, 1977.

French aid is the mainstay of the economy, as well as assistance from Arab countries. A peace accord Dec. 1994 ended a 3-year-long uprising by Afar rebels. An estimated 3,000 French and 1,800 U.S. troops are based in Djibouti.

Dominica
Commonwealth of Dominica

People: Population: 72,660. **Age distrib.** (%): <15: 24; 65+: 10.2. **Pop. density:** 249.6 per sq mi, 96.4 per sq km. **Urban:** 72.9%. **Ethnic groups:** Black 87%, mixed 9%, Carib Amerindian 3%. **Principal languages:** English (official), French patois. **Chief religions:** Roman Catholic 61%, Seventh-Day Adventist 6%, Pentecostal 6%, Baptist 4%, Methodist 4%, other Christian 8%, none 6%.

Geography: Total area: 291 sq mi, 754 sq km; **Land area:** 291 sq mi, 754 sq km. **Location:** In E Caribbean, most northerly Windward Isl. **Neighbors:** Guadeloupe to N, Martinique to S. **Topography:** Mountainous, a central ridge running from N to S, terminating in cliffs; volcanic in origin, with numerous thermal springs; rich deep topsoil on leeward side, red tropical clay on windward coast. **Capital** (2004): Roseau, 20,200.

Government: Type: Parliamentary democracy. **Head of state:** Pres. Nicholas Liverpool; b. Sept. 9, 1934; in office: Oct. 2, 2003. **Head of gov.:** Prime Min. Roosevelt Skerrit; b. June 8, 1972; in office: Jan. 8, 2004. **Local divisions:** 10 parishes. **Defense budget/Active troops:** NA.

Economy: Industries: soap, coconut oil, tourism, copra, furniture, cement blocks, shoes. **Chief crops:** bananas, citrus, mangoes, root crops, coconuts, cocoa. **Natural resources:** timber, hydropower. **Arable land:** 7%. **Livestock:** cattle: 13,500; chickens: 190,000; goats: 9,700; pigs: 5,000; sheep: 7,600. **Fish catch:** 776 metric tons. **Electricity prod.:** 90 mil kWh. **Labor force** (2000 est.): agric. 40%, industry 32%, services 28%.

Finance: Monetary unit: East Caribbean Dollar (XCD) (Oct. 2009: 2.70 = $1 U.S.). **GDP:** $719.6 mil; **per capita GDP:** $9,900; **GDP growth:** 2.6%. **Imports** (2006): $296 mil; Japan 42.5%, U.S. 16.7%, China 13.6%, Trinidad and Tobago 8.3%. **Exports** (2006): $94 mil; Japan 29.8%, China 25.2%, Jamaica 6.2%, Antigua and Barbuda 6%, Guyana 5.1%, UK 4.2%. **Tourism:** $74 mil. **Budget** (2001): $84.4 mil. **Intl. reserves less gold:** $36 mil. **Gold:** NA. **Consumer prices:** 5.1%.

Transport: Motor vehicles: 10,000 pass. cars; 8,000 comm. vehicles. **Civil aviation:** 2 airports. **Chief ports:** Portsmouth, Roseau.

Communications: TV sets: 232 per 1,000 pop. **Radios:** 648 per 1,000 pop. **Telephone lines:** 17,500. **Daily newspaper circ.** (2004): 39.1 per 1,000 pop. **Internet:** 27,500 users.

Health: Life expect.: 72.4 male; 78.4 female. **Births** (per 1,000 pop.): 15.7. **Deaths** (per 1,000 pop.): 8.3. **Natural inc.:** 0.74%. **Infant mortality** (per 1,000 live births): 14.1. **HIV rate:** NA.

Education: Compulsory: ages 5-16. **Literacy:** 94%.

Major intl. organizations: UN (FAO, IBRD, ILO, IMF, IMO, WHO, WTO), Caricom, the Commonwealth, OAS, OECS.

Embassy: 3216 New Mexico Ave. NW 20016; 364-6781.

Website: www.dominica.gov.dm

A British colony since 1805, Dominica was granted self-government in 1967. Independence was achieved Nov. 3, 1978.

Hurricane David struck, Aug. 30, 1979, devastating the island and destroying the banana plantations, Dominica's economic mainstay. Coups were attempted in 1980 and 1981.

Dominica participated in the 1983 U.S.-led invasion of nearby Grenada. Prime Min. Pierre Charles, 49, died of a heart attack Jan. 6, 2004, and was succeeded by Roosevelt Skerrit.

Dominican Republic

People: Population: 9,650,054. **Age distrib.** (%): <15: 31.4; 65+: 5.9. **Pop. density:** 516.6 per sq mi, 199.5 per sq km. **Urban:** 66.8%. **Ethnic groups:** Mixed 73%, white 16%, black 11%. **Principal language:** Spanish (official). **Chief religion:** Roman Catholic 95%.

Geography: Total area: 18,815 sq mi, 48,730 sq km; **Land area:** 18,680 sq mi, 48,380 sq km. **Location:** In W Indies, sharing isl. of Hispaniola with Haiti. **Neighbors:** Haiti on W, Puerto Rico (U.S.) to E. **Topography:** The Cordillera Central range crosses center of the country, rising to over 10,000 ft, highest in the Caribbean. The Cibao Valley to N is major agricultural area. **Capital:** Santo Domingo, 2,154,000.

Government: Type: Republic. **Head of state and gov.:** Pres. Leonel Fernández Reyna; b. Dec. 26, 1953; in office: Aug. 16, 2004. **Local divisions:** 29 provinces and national district. **Defense budget:** $271 mil. **Active troops:** 49,910.

Economy: Industries: tourism, sugar proc., mining, textiles, cement, tobacco. **Chief crops:** sugarcane, coffee, cotton, cocoa, tobacco, rice, beans, potatoes, corn, bananas. **Natural resources:** nickel, bauxite, gold, silver. **Arable land:** 22%. **Livestock:** cattle: 2.2 mil; chickens: 100.5 mil; goats: 187,500; pigs: 580,000; sheep: 123,000. **Fish catch:** 14,689 metric tons. **Electricity prod.:** 13.4 bil kWh. **Labor force** (2005): agric. 14.6%, industry 22.3%, services 63.1%.

Finance: Monetary unit: Peso (DOP) (Oct. 2009: 36.00 = $1 U.S.). **GDP:** $78 bil; **per capita GDP:** $8,200; **GDP growth:** 5.3%. **Imports:** $16.1 bil; U.S. 45.3%, Venezuela 9.6%, Mexico 6.1%, Colombia 4.9%, China 4.6%. **Exports:** $6.9 bil; U.S. 63.1%, Spain 3.7%, Belgium 3.6%. **Tourism:** $4.1 bil. **Budget:** $7.8 bil. **Intl. reserves less gold:** $1.48 bil. **Gold:** 20,000 oz t. **Consumer prices:** 10.6%.

Transport: Railroad: Length: 1,109 mi. **Motor vehicles:** 721,000 pass. cars; 351,000 comm. vehicles. **Civil aviation:** 3.1 mil pass.-mi; 16 airports. **Chief ports:** Boca Chica, Caucedo, Puerto Plata, Rio Haina, Santo Domingo.

Communications: TV sets: 96 per 1,000 pop. **Radios:** 178 per 1,000 pop. **Telephone lines:** 985,700. **Daily newspaper circ.** (2004): 39.1 per 1,000 pop. **Internet:** 2.6 mil users.

Health: Life expect.: 71.6 male; 75.2 female. **Births** (per 1,000 pop.): 22.6. **Deaths** (per 1,000 pop.): 5.3. **Natural inc.:** 1.74%. **Infant mortality** (per 1,000 live births): 26.9. **HIV rate:** 1.1%.

Education: Compulsory: ages 5-13. **Literacy:** 89.1%.

Major intl. organizations: UN (FAO, IBRD, ILO, IMF, IMO, WHO, WTO), OAS.

Embassy: 1715 22nd St. NW 20008; 332-6280.

Website: www.presidencia.gov.do

Carib and Arawak Indians inhabited the island of Hispaniola when Columbus landed in 1492. The city of Santo Domingo, founded 1496, is the oldest settlement by Europeans in the hemisphere.

The western third of the island was ceded to France in 1697. Santo Domingo itself was ceded to France in 1795. Haitian leader Toussaint L'Ouverture seized it, 1801. Spain returned intermittently 1803-21, as several native republics came and went. Haiti ruled again, 1822-44; Spanish occupation occurred 1861-63. The country was occupied by U.S. Marines 1916-24, when a constitutionally elected government was installed.

In 1930, Gen. Rafael Leonidas Trujillo Molina was elected president. Trujillo ruled brutally until his assassination in 1961. Pres. Joaquín Balaguer, appointed by Trujillo in 1960, resigned under pressure in 1962.

Juan Bosch, elected president in the first free elections in 38 years, was overthrown in 1963. On Apr. 24, 1965, Bosch's followers and others, including a few Communists, launched a revolt. Four days later U.S. Marines intervened against pro-Bosch forces. Five S. American countries later sent token units as a peacekeeping force. A provisional government supervised a June 1966 election in which Balaguer defeated Bosch. Balaguer remained in office for most of the next 28 years, but his May 1994 reelection was widely denounced as fraudulent. He cut short his term and on June 30, 1996, Leonel Fernández Reyna was elected.

Hurricane Georges struck Sept. 22, 1998, causing extensive property damage and claiming more than 200 lives. The leftist candidate, Hipólito Mejía, won a presidential vote May 16, 2000. With the nation reeling from a banking scandal and soaring inflation, Fernández defeated Mejía in the election of May 16, 2004. Floods and mudslides in late May killed about 395 people. A fight between rival prison gangs led to a fire, Mar. 7, 2005, in which 136 inmates died. Torrential rains from Tropical Storm Noel, Oct. 28-31, 2007, claimed at least 87 lives. Fernández was reelected May 16, 2008.

East Timor

See Timor-Leste.

Ecuador

Republic of Ecuador

People: Population: 14,573,101. **Age distrib.** (%): <15: 31.1; 65+: 6.2. **Pop. density:** 136.3 per sq mi, 52.6 per sq km. **Urban:** 63.6%. **Ethnic groups:** Mestizo (mixed Amerindian & white) 65%, Amerindian 25%, Spanish & others 7%, black 3%. **Principal languages:** Spanish (official), Amerindian languages (espec. Quechua). **Chief religion:** Roman Catholic 95%.

Geography: Total area: 109,483 sq mi, 283,560 sq km; **Land area:** 106,889 sq mi, 276,840 sq km. **Location:** In NW S. America,

on Pacific coast, astride the Equator. **Neighbors:** Colombia on N, Peru on E and S. **Topography:** Two ranges of Andes run N and S, splitting country into 3 zones: hot, humid lowlands on coast; temperate highlands between ranges; and rainy, tropical lowlands to E. **Capital:** Quito, 1,701,000. **Cities (urban aggr.):** Guayaquil, 2,514,000.

Government: Type: Republic. **Head of state and gov.:** Pres. Rafael Correa; b. Apr. 6, 1963; in office: Jan. 15, 2007. **Local divisions:** 22 provinces. **Defense budget:** $773 mil. **Active troops:** 57,983.

Economy: Industries: oil, food proc., textiles, wood products, chemicals. **Chief crops:** bananas, coffee, cocoa, rice, potatoes, manioc, plantains, sugarcane. **Natural resources:** oil, fish, timber, hydropower. **Crude oil reserves:** 4.7 bil bbls. **Arable land:** 6%. **Livestock:** cattle: 4.7 mil; chickens: 110 mil; goats: 170,750; pigs: 1.3 mil; sheep: 846,435. **Fish catch:** 554,745 metric tons. **Electricity prod.:** 14.8 bil kWh. **Labor force** (2005): agric. 8.3%, industry 21.2%, services 70.4%.

Finance: Monetary unit: Dollar (USD). **GDP:** $107.7 bil; **per capita GDP:** $7,500; **GDP growth:** 6.5%. **Imports:** $17.8 bil; U.S. 22.8%, China 9.7%, Colombia 9.6%, Brazil 5%, Japan 4.6%. **Exports:** $19.2 bil; U.S. 43.8%, Chile 7.3%, Peru 7%, China 4.5%, Russia 4.1%. **Tourism:** $623 mil. **Budget:** $12 bil. **Intl. reserves less gold:** $2.43 bil. **Gold:** 840,000 oz t. **Consumer prices:** 8.4%.

Transport: Railroad: Length: 600 mi. **Motor vehicles:** 411,000 pass. cars; 306,000 comm. vehicles. **Civil aviation:** 538.7 mil pass.-mi; 103 airports. **Chief ports:** Esmeraldas, Guayaquil, Manta, Puerto Bolivar.

Communications: TV sets: 213 per 1,000 pop. **Radios:** 406 per 1,000 pop. **Telephone lines:** 1.9 mil. **Daily newspaper circ.** (2000): 99.1 per 1,000 pop. **Internet:** 1.3 mil users.

Health: Life expect.: 73.9 male; 79.8 female. **Births** (per 1,000 pop.): 21.5. **Deaths** (per 1,000 pop.): 4.2. **Natural inc.:** 1.73%. **Infant mortality** (per 1,000 live births): 21.4. **HIV rate:** 0.3%.

Education: Compulsory: ages 5-14. **Literacy:** 92.6%.

Major intl. organizations: UN (FAO, IBRD, ILO, IMF, IMO, WHO, WTO), OAS, OPEC.

Embassy: 2535 15th St. NW 20009; 234-7200.

Website: www.presidencia.gov.ec

The region, which was the northern Inca empire, was conquered by Spain in 1533. Liberation forces defeated the Spanish May 24, 1822, near Quito. Ecuador became part of the Great Colombia Republic but seceded, May 13, 1830.

Ecuadoran Indians staged protests in the 1990s to demand greater rights. A border war with Peru flared from Jan. 26, 1995, until a truce took effect Mar. 1. Vice Pres. Alberto Dahik resigned and fled Ecuador, Oct. 11, 1995, to avoid arrest on corruption charges. Elected president in a runoff, July 7, 1996, Abdalá Bucaram—a populist known as El Loco, or "The Crazy One"—imposed stiff price increases and other austerity measures. His rising unpopularity and erratic behavior led the National Congress, Feb. 6, 1997, to dismiss him for "mental incapacity."

Jamil Mahuad Witt, mayor of Quito, won a presidential runoff election July 12, 1998. In Sept. 1998 and Mar. 1999 he imposed emergency measures to cope with a continuing economic crisis. Opposed by Indian groups and military leaders, he was ousted Jan. 21, 2000, and succeeded by Vice Pres. Gustavo Noboa Bejarano. Noboa went ahead with a plan introduced by Mahuad to replace the sucre with the U.S. dollar as Ecuador's currency. Lucio Gutiérrez Borbúa, a leader in the 2000 coup, won a presidential runoff Nov. 24, 2002. Noboa, under investigation for financial mismanagement, went into exile Aug. 23, 2003.

Gutiérrez imposed economic austerity measures, purged opponents from the supreme court, Dec. 2004, and then dissolved the court, Apr. 15, 2005. With street protests rising, the military withdrew support of Gutiérrez. Congress ousted him Apr. 20, and Vice Pres. Alfredo Palacio González became president. The U.S. suspended free-trade talks after Ecuador, May 15, 2006, took over oil assets belonging to U.S.-based Occidental Petroleum.

Rafael Correa, a left-wing economist, won a presidential runoff vote Nov. 26, 2006. After a power struggle with the National Congress, Correa scored a major triumph when voters Apr. 15, 2007, approved his plan to convene an assembly to rewrite the constitution. The revised constitution won overwhelming approval in a national referendum Sept. 28, 2008. Early in his term, when oil revenues were high, he boosted development spending and aid to poor families; later, as oil prices dropped, he restricted imports to prevent an outflow of dollars and, in Dec. 2008, allowed Ecuador to default on part of its $10 bil foreign debt. Correa won reelection Apr. 26, 2009.

The **Galápagos Islands**, pop. (2008 est.): 30,000, about 600 mi to the W, are the home of huge tortoises and other unusual animals. The oil tanker *Jessica* ran aground Jan. 16, 2001, off San Cristóbal Isl., spilling some 185,000 gallons of fuel.

Egypt

Arab Republic of Egypt

People: Population: 83,082,869. **Age distrib.** (%): <15: 31.4; 65+: 4.8. **Pop. density:** 216.2 per sq mi, 83.5 per sq km. **Urban:** 42.6%. **Ethnic groups:** Egyptian 99.6%. **Principal languages:** Arabic (official), English & French widely understood by educated classes. **Chief religions:** Muslim (mostly Sunni) 90%, Coptic 9%.

Geography: Total area: 386,662 sq mi, 1,001,450 sq km; **Land area:** 384,345 sq mi, 995,450 sq km. **Location:** NE corner of Africa. **Neighbors:** Libya on W; Sudan on S; Israel, Gaza Strip on E. **Topography:** Almost entirely desolate and barren, with hills and mountains in E and along Nile. The Nile Valley, where most of the people live, stretches 550 mi. **Capital:** Cairo (Al-Qahirah), 11,893,000. **Cities (urban aggr.):** Alexandria, 4,165,000.

Government: Type: Republic. **Head of state:** Pres. Hosni Mubarak; b. May 4, 1928; in office: Oct. 14, 1981. **Head of gov.:** Prime Min. Ahmed Nazif; b. July 8, 1952; in office: July 14, 2004. **Local divisions:** 26 governorates. **Defense budget:** $4.6 bil. **Active troops:** 468,500.

Economy: Industries: textiles, food proc., tourism, chemicals, pharmaceuticals, hydrocarbons, constr., cement, metals. **Chief crops:** cotton, rice, corn, wheat, beans, fruits, vegetables. **Natural resources:** oil, nat. gas, iron ore, phosphates, mang., limestone, gypsum, talc, asbestos, lead, zinc. **Crude oil reserves:** 3.7 bil bbls. **Arable land:** 3%. **Livestock:** cattle: 4.6 mil; chickens: 96 mil; goats: 4 mil; pigs: 30,000; sheep: 5,525. **Fish catch:** 1.01 mil metric tons. **Electricity prod.:** 109.1 bil kWh. **Labor force** (2001 est.): agric. 32%, industry 17%, services 51%.

Finance: Monetary unit: Pound (EGP) (Oct. 2009: 5.48 = $1 U.S.). **GDP:** $443.7 bil; **per capita GDP:** $5,400; **GDP growth:** 7.2%. **Imports:** $56.6 bil; U.S. 10.6%, China 10.2%, Italy 7.5%, Germany 7%, Saudi Arabia 5%. **Exports:** $29.9 bil; Italy 10.3%, U.S. 7.7%, Spain 6.7%, Syria 5.1%, Saudi Arabia 5%, Japan 4.9%, Germany 4.9%, France 4%. **Tourism:** $9.3 bil. **Budget:** $44.9 bil. **Intl. reserves less gold:** $20.92 bil. **Gold:** 2.43 mil oz t. **Consumer prices:** 18.3%.

Transport: Railroad: Length: 3,146 mi. **Motor vehicles:** 2.1 mil pass. cars; 741,000 comm. vehicles. **Civil aviation:** 5.8 bil pass.-mi; 72 airports. **Chief ports:** Alexandria, Damietta, Suez.

Communications: TV sets: 170 per 1,000 pop. **Radios:** 317 per 1,000 pop. **Telephone lines:** 12 mil. **Daily newspaper circ.** (1999): 31.8 per 1,000 pop. **Internet:** 12.6 mil users.

Health: Life expect.: 69.3 male; 74.5 female. **Births** (per 1,000 pop.): 22.1. **Deaths** (per 1,000 pop.): 5.1. **Natural inc.:** 1.7%. **Infant mortality** (per 1,000 live births): 28.4. **HIV rate:** NA.

Education: Compulsory: ages 6-14. **Literacy:** 72%.

Major intl. organizations: UN (FAO, IBRD, ILO, IMF, IMO, WHO, WTO), AL, AU.

Embassy: 3521 International Ct. NW 20008; 895-5400.

Website: www.egypt.gov.eg

Archaeological records of ancient Egyptian civilization date back to 4000 BCE. A unified kingdom arose around 3200 BCE and extended its way south into Nubia and as far north as Syria. A high culture of rulers and priests was built on an economic base of serfdom, fertile soil, and annual flooding of the Nile.

Imperial decline facilitated conquest by Asian invaders (Hyksos, Assyrians). The last native dynasty fell in 341 BCE to the Persians, who were in turn replaced by Greeks (Alexander and the Ptolemies), Romans, Byzantines, and Arabs, who introduced Islam and the Arabic language. The ancient Egyptian language is preserved only in Coptic Christian liturgy.

Egypt was ruled as part of larger Islamic empires for many centuries. Britain intervened in Egypt in 1882 and ruled the country as a protectorate, 1914-22. A 1936 treaty strengthened Egyptian autonomy, but Britain retained bases in Egypt and a condominium over the Sudan. When the state of Israel was proclaimed in 1948, Egypt joined other Arab nations invading Israel and was defeated. In 1951 Egypt abrogated the 1936 treaty; the Sudan became independent in 1956.

An uprising on July 23, 1952, overthrew King Farouk and established a republic. Lt. Col. Gamal Abdel Nasser rose to power, becoming premier in 1954 and president in 1956. Nasser emerged as the most influential leader in the Arab world at the time; within Egypt, he pushed construction of the Aswan High Dam, completed in 1970.

After guerrilla raids across its border, Israel invaded Egypt's Sinai Peninsula, Oct. 29, 1956. Egypt rejected a cease-fire demand by Britain and France; on Oct. 31 the 2 nations dropped bombs and on Nov. 5-6 landed forces. Egypt and Israel accepted a UN cease-fire; fighting ended Nov. 7. Subsequently, a UN Emergency Force guarded the border. Full-scale war with Israel broke out again, June 5, 1967; before it ended under a UN cease-fire June 10, Israel had captured Gaza and the Sinai Peninsula and taken control of the E bank of the Suez Canal.

Nasser died Sept. 28, 1970, and was replaced by Vice Pres. Anwar Sadat. In a surprise attack Oct. 6, 1973, Egyptian forces crossed the Suez Canal into the Sinai. (At the same time, Syrian forces attacked Israelis on the Golan Heights.) Egypt was supplied by a USSR military airlift; the U.S. responded with an airlift to Isra-

el. Israel counterattacked, crossed the canal, and surrounded Suez City. A UN cease-fire took effect Oct. 24. Under an agreement signed Jan. 18, 1974, Israeli forces withdrew from the canal's W bank; limited numbers of Egyptian forces occupied a strip along the E bank. A second accord was signed in 1975, with Israel yielding Sinai oil fields.

Pres. Sadat's surprise visit to Jerusalem, Nov. 1977, opened the prospect of peace with Israel. On Mar. 26, 1979, Egypt and Israel signed a formal peace treaty, ending 30 years of war, and establishing diplomatic relations. On Oct. 6, 1981, Pres. Sadat was assassinated by Muslim extremists within the army; he was succeeded by Hosni Mubarak. Israel returned control of the Sinai to Egypt in Apr. 1982.

Egypt saw a rising tide of Islamic fundamentalist violence in the 1990s. U.S. aid to Egypt, totaling more than $50 bil since 1975, helped to keep Mubarak in power. Egypt supported the U.S.-led coalition against Iraq in the Persian Gulf War, 1991. Egyptian security forces conducted raids against Islamic militants, some of whom were executed for terrorism. Naguib Mahfouz, winner of the 1988 Nobel Prize for literature, was stabbed by Islamic militants Oct. 14, 1994. Pres. Mubarak escaped assassination in Ethiopia, June 26, 1995; Egypt blamed Sudan for the attack. On Nov. 17, 1997, near Luxor, Muslim extremists killed 58 foreign tourists and 4 Egyptians.

Mubarak, who was grazed by a knife-wielding assailant Sept. 6, 1999, was confirmed by popular vote Sept. 26 for a 4th presidential term. An EgyptAir jetliner bound from New York to Cairo plunged into the Atlantic near Nantucket Isl., Oct. 31, 1999, killing all 217 people on board. Fire on a train bound from Cairo to Luxor, Feb. 20, 2002, left more than 360 people dead. An Egyptian charter plane plunged into the Red Sea shortly after takeoff Jan. 3, 2004, killing 148 people, including 133 French tourists.

Terrorists stepped up their campaign against the economically important tourism industry. Bombs Oct. 7, 2004, in and near Taba (a Sinai tourist site popular with Israelis) killed at least 35 people. Another 88 people were killed in bombings July 23, 2005, at Sharm el Sheikh, a Red Sea resort city. Pressured by the U.S., Mubarak agreed to allow opposition candidates in the Sept. 7 presidential election, which he won with an 88.5% majority; turnout was only 23%. Suicide bombings at the Sinai resort town of Dhab, Apr. 24, 2006, killed at least 18 people and injured 85; security forces May 9 killed Nasser Khamis al-Mallahi, leader of the group blamed for the Taba, Sharm el Sheikh, and Dahab attacks. Constitutional amendments expanding presidential powers and barring religiously-based political parties were approved Mar. 26, 2007, in a referendum criticized as fraudulent by opposition groups and human rights observers.

Mubarak announced Apr. 30, 2008, a 30% boost in public-sector salaries to ease widespread anger at rising food prices. At least 95 people died when a rock slide hit a Cairo shantytown Sept. 6. Visiting Cairo University June 4, 2009, Pres. Obama delivered a major speech in which he called for a "new beginning" in relations between the U.S. and the Muslim world.

The **Suez Canal**, 103 mi long, links the Mediterranean and Red seas. It was built by a French corporation 1859-69, but Britain obtained controlling interest in 1875. The last British troops were removed June 13, 1956. On July 26, Egypt nationalized the canal.

El Salvador

Republic of El Salvador

People: Population: 7,185,218. **Age distrib.** (%): <15: 35.4; 65+: 5.3. **Pop. density:** 898.1 per sq mi, 346.8 per sq km. **Urban:** 59.8%. **Ethnic groups:** Mestizo 90%, white 9%, Amerindian 1%. **Principal languages:** Spanish, Nahua. **Chief religions:** Roman Catholic 83%, other 17%.

Geography: Total area: 8,124 sq mi, 21,040 sq km; **Land area:** 8,000 sq mi, 20,720 sq km. **Location:** In Central America. **Neighbors:** Guatemala on W, Honduras on N. **Topography:** A hot Pacific coastal plain in S rises to a cooler plateau and valley region, densely populated. The N is mountainous, including many volcanoes. **Capital:** San Salvador, 1,433,000.

Government: Type: Republic. **Head of state and gov.:** Pres. Mauricio Funes; b. Oct. 18, 1959; in office: June 1, 2009. **Local divisions:** 14 departments. **Defense budget:** $111 mil. **Active troops:** 15,500.

Economy: Industries: food proc., beverages, oil, chemicals, fertilizer, textiles, furniture, light metals. **Chief crops:** coffee, sugar, corn, rice, beans, oilseed, cotton, sorghum. **Natural resources:** hydropower, geothermal power, oil. **Arable land:** 31%. **Livestock:** cattle: 1.4 mil; chickens: 14.7 mil; goats: 11,000; pigs: 441,038; sheep: 5,100. **Fish catch:** 52,368 metric tons. **Electricity prod.:** 5.3 bil kWh. **Labor force** (2006 est.): agric. 19%, industry 23%, services 58%.

Finance: Monetary unit: Colon (SVC) (Oct. 2009: 8.75 = $1 U.S.). **GDP:** $43.6 bil; **per capita GDP:** $6,200; **GDP growth:** 2.5%. **Imports:** $9 bil; U.S. 29.6%, Mexico 10.6%, Guatemala 9.2%, China 4.8%, France 4.3%. **Exports:** $4.6 bil; U.S. 47%, Guatemala 13.8%, Honduras 11.4%, Nicaragua 5.6%. **Tourism:**

$847 mil. **Budget:** $3.7 bil. **Intl. reserves less gold:** $1.59 bil. **Gold:** 230,000 oz t. **Consumer prices:** 6.7%.

Transport: Railroad: Length: 176 mi. **Motor vehicles:** 148,000 pass. cars; 250,800 comm. vehicles. **Civil aviation:** 2.7 bil pass.-mi; 4 airports. **Chief ports:** Acajutla, Puerto Cutuco.

Communications: TV sets: 191 per 1,000 pop. **Radios:** 478 per 1,000 pop. **Telephone lines:** 1.1 mil. **Daily newspaper circ.** (2004): 38 per 1,000 pop. **Internet:** 826,000 users.

Health: Life expect: 68.5 male; 75.8 female. **Births** (per 1,000 pop.): 25.7. **Deaths** (per 1,000 pop.): 5.5. **Natural inc.:** 2.02%. **Infant mortality** (per 1,000 live births): 22.2. **HIV rate:** 0.8%.

Education: Compulsory: ages 7-15. **Literacy:** 85.5%.

Major intl. organizations: UN (FAO, IBRD, ILO, IMF, IMO, WHO, WTO), OAS.

Embassy: 1400 16th St. NW, Ste. 100, 20036; 265-9671.

Website: www.casapres.gob.sv

El Salvador became independent of Spain in 1821, and of the Central American Federation in 1839.

A fight with Honduras in 1969 over the presence of 300,000 Salvadoran workers left 2,000 dead.

A military coup overthrew the government of Pres. Carlos Humberto Romero in 1979, but the ruling military-civilian junta failed to quell a rebellion by leftist insurgents, armed by Cuba and Nicaragua. Extreme right-wing death squads organized to eliminate suspected leftists were blamed for thousands of deaths in the 1980s. The Reagan administration staunchly supported the government with military aid.

After taking the lives of some 75,000 people (with thousands more "disappeared"), the 12-year civil war ended Jan. 16, 1992, as the government and leftist rebels signed a formal peace treaty. Rightist legislators in the National Assembly passed a sweeping amnesty Mar. 20, 1993, for civil war atrocities.

Members of the right-wing ARENA party held the presidency from 1989 to 2009. Mauricio Funes, a leftist and former TV journalist, won the presidential election of Mar. 15, 2009, and took office June 1. Remittances from Salvadorans working in the U.S. are a major source of income.

Equatorial Guinea
Republic of Equatorial Guinea

People: Population: 633,441. **Age distrib.** (%): <15: 41.9; 65+: 4.1. **Pop. density:** 58.5 per sq mi, 22.6 per sq km. **Urban:** 38.9%. **Ethnic groups:** Fang 86%, Bubi 7%, Mdowe 4%. **Principal languages:** Spanish, French (both official); Fang; Bubi. **Chief religions:** Nominally Christian & predominantly Roman Catholic, pagan practices.

Geography: Total area: 10,831 sq mi, 28,051 sq km; **Land area:** 10,831 sq mi, 28,051 sq km. **Location:** Bioko Isl. off W Africa coast in Gulf of Guinea, and Rio Muni, mainland enclave. **Neighbors:** Gabon on S, Cameroon on E and N. **Topography:** Bioko Isl. consists of 2 volcanic mountains and connecting valley. Rio Muni, with over 90% of the area, has coastal plain and low hills beyond. **Capital:** Malabo, 96,000.

Government: Type: Republic. **Head of state:** Pres. Teodoro Obiang Nguema Mbasogo; b. June 5, 1942; in office: Aug. 3, 1979. **Head of gov.:** Prime Min. Ignacio Milam Tang; b. June 20, 1940; in office: July 8, 2008. **Local divisions:** 7 provinces. **Defense budget:** $8 mil. **Active troops:** 1,320.

Economy: Industries: oil, fishing, sawmilling, nat. gas. **Chief crops:** coffee, cocoa, rice, yams, cassava, bananas, palm oil nuts. **Natural resources:** oil, nat. gas, timber, gold. **Crude oil reserves:** 1.1 bil. bbls. **Arable land:** 5%. **Livestock:** cattle: 5,050; chickens: 320,000; goats: 9,000; pigs: 6,100; sheep: 37,600. **Fish catch:** 3,583 metric tons. **Electricity prod.:** 27 mil kWh. **Labor force:** NA.

Finance: Monetary unit: CFA BEAC Franc (XAF) (Oct. 2009: 444.97 = $1 U.S.). **GDP:** $23 bil; **per capita GDP:** $37,200; **GDP growth:** 10.6%. **Imports:** $3.2 bil; Spain 15.2%, U.S. 13.4%, France 12.4%, Côte d'Ivoire 11.9%, China 10.4%, Italy 6.3%, UK 5.8%. **Exports:** $13 bil; U.S. 24%, Spain 19.3%, China 16.2%, France 8.4%, Italy 6.3%. **Tourism:** NA. **Budget:** $2.5 bil. **Intl. reserves less gold:** $2.88 bil. **Gold:** NA. **Consumer prices:** NA.

Transport: Civil aviation: 2.5 mil pass.-mi; 6 airports. **Chief ports:** Bata, Malabo.

Communications: TV sets: 116 per 1,000 pop. **Radios:** 429 per 1,000 pop. **Telephone lines:** 10,000. **Internet:** 12,000 users.

Health: Life expect: 60.4 male; 62.1 female. **Births** (per 1,000 pop.): 37. **Deaths** (per 1,000 pop.): 9.7. **Natural inc.:** 2.73%. **Infant mortality** (per 1,000 live births): 83.8. **HIV rate:** 3.4%.

Education: Compulsory: ages 7-11. **Literacy:** 87%.

Major intl. organizations: UN (FAO, IBRD, ILO, IMF, IMO, WHO), AU.

Embassy: 2020 16th St. NW 20009; 518-5700.

Website: www.equatorialguinea.gq

Fernando Po (now Bioko) Island was reached by Portugal in the late 15th cent. and ceded to Spain in 1778. Independence came

Oct. 12, 1968. Riots occurred in 1969 over disputes between the island and the more backward Rio Muni province on the mainland. Masie Nguema Biyogo, a mainlander, became pres. for life in 1972.

Masie's reign was one of the most brutal in Africa, resulting in a bankrupted nation; most of the nation's 7,000 Europeans emigrated. He was ousted in a military coup, Aug. 1979. Teodoro Obiang Nguema Mbasogo, leader of the coup, became president and installed his family members in key government posts. Multiparty presidential elections, held in 1996 and 2002, were seriously flawed. Oil sales, especially to the U.S., have boomed in recent years. Foreign investment in the oil sector has been extensive, but poverty remains widespread, and health conditions are poor.

Authorities in Zimbabwe and Equatorial Guinea arrested 85 people in Mar. 2004 on charges of plotting to overthrow the Obiang regime. Mark Thatcher, son of the former British prime min., was arrested in South Africa Aug. 25 for alleged involvement; in a plea bargain Jan. 13, 2005, he agreed to pay a $500,000 fine. Pres. Obiang revamped his entire cabinet in Aug. 2006; calling that government "one of the worst ever," he named a new prime minister July 8, 2008. Government officials blamed Nigerian rebels for another apparent coup attempt, suppressed Feb. 17, 2009.

Eritrea
State of Eritrea

People: Population: 5,647,168. **Age distrib.** (%): <15: 42.8; 65+: 3.6. **Pop. density:** 120.6 per sq mi, 46.5 per sq km. **Urban:** 19.4%. **Ethnic groups:** Tigrinya 50%, Tigre & Kunama 40%, Afar 4%. **Principal languages:** Afar, Arabic, Tigre & Kunama, Tigrinya, other Cushitic languages. **Chief religions:** Muslim, Coptic Christian, Roman Catholic, Protestant.

Geography: Total area: 46,842 sq mi, 121,320 sq km; **Land area:** 46,842 sq mi, 121,320 sq km. **Location:** In E Africa, on SW coast of Red Sea. **Neighbors:** Ethiopia on S, Djibouti on SE, Sudan on W. **Topography:** Includes many islands of the Dahlak Archipelago, low coastal plains in S, mountain range with peaks to 9,000 ft in N. **Capital:** Asmara, 601,000.

Government: Type: In transition. **Head of state and gov.:** Pres. Isaias Afwerki; b. Feb. 2, 1946; in office: May 24, 1993. **Local divisions:** 8 provinces. **Defense budget:** NA. **Active troops:** 201,750.

Economy: Industries: food proc., beverages, clothing& textiles. **Chief crops:** sorghum, lentils, vegetables, corn, cotton, tobacco, sisal. **Natural resources:** gold, potash, zinc, copper, salt, poss. oil & nat. gas, fish. **Arable land:** 5%. **Livestock:** cattle: 2 mil; chickens: 1.4 mil; goats: 1.7 mil; sheep: 2.1 mil. **Fish catch:** 1,932 metric tons. **Electricity prod.:** 253 mil kWh. **Labor force** (2004 est.): agric. 80%, industry & services 20%.

Finance: Monetary unit: Nakfa (ERN) (Oct. 2009: 15.11 = $1 U.S.). **GDP:** $3.9 bil; **per capita GDP:** $700; **GDP growth:** 2%. **Imports:** $601 mil; Italy 16.9%, UAE 15.7%, China 13%, India 9.4%, U.S. 6.7%, Germany 6%, Turkey 5%. **Exports:** $13 mil; India 31.7%, Italy 18.6%, Kenya 11.9%, China 11.5%, France 5.4%. **Tourism:** NA. **Budget:** $471.4 mil. **Intl. reserves less gold:** $38 mil. **Gold:** NA. **Consumer prices:** NA.

Transport: Railroad: Length: 190 mi. **Civil aviation:** 4 airports. **Chief ports:** Assab, Massawa.

Communications: TV sets: 16 per 1,000 pop. **Radios:** 484 per 1,000 pop. **Telephone lines:** 40,400. **Internet:** 150,000 users.

Health: Life expect: 59.4 male; 63.5 female. **Births** (per 1,000 pop.): 34.9. **Deaths** (per 1,000 pop.): 8.6. **Natural inc.:** 2.63%. **Infant mortality** (per 1,000 live births): 44.3. **HIV rate:** 1.3%.

Education: Compulsory: ages 7-14. **Literacy:** 58.6%.

Major intl. organizations: UN (FAO, IBRD, ILO, IMF, IMO, WHO), AU.

Embassy: 1708 New Hampshire Ave. NW 20009; 319-1991.

Website: www.shabait.com

Eritrea was part of the Ethiopian kingdom of Aksum. It was an Italian colony from 1890 to 1941, when it was captured by the British. Following a period of British and UN supervision, Eritrea was awarded to Ethiopia as part of a federation in 1952. Ethiopia annexed Eritrea as a province in 1962. This led to a 31-year struggle for independence, which ended when Eritrea formally declared itself an independent nation May 24, 1993. A constitution was ratified in 1997 but not implemented.

A border war with Ethiopia that erupted in June 1998 intensified in May 2000, as Ethiopian troops plunged into western Eritrea; a cease-fire signed June 18 provided for a UN peacekeeping force (UNMEE) to patrol a buffer zone on Eritrean territory. A peace treaty was signed Dec. 12, 2000.

A UN report in July 2007 accused Eritrea of aiding an Islamic insurgency in Somalia. Citing Eritrean obstruction of UNMEE activities, the UN Security Council ended the peacekeeping mission as of July 31, 2008. A report released by Human Rights Watch Apr. 16, 2009, said Eritrea had become "one of the most closed and repressive states in the world."

Estonia
Republic of Estonia

People: Population: 1,299,371. **Age distrib.** (%): <15: 14.9; 65+: 17.6. **Pop. density:** 77.9 per sq mi, 30.1 per sq km. **Urban:** 69.4%. **Ethnic groups:** Estonian 68%, Russian 26%. **Principal languages:** Estonian (official), Russian. **Chief religions:** Evangelical Lutheran 14%, Orthodox 13%, unaffiliated 34%.

Geography: Total area: 17,462 sq mi, 45,226 sq km; **Land area:** 16,684 sq mi, 43,211 sq km. **Location:** E Europe, bordering Baltic Sea and Gulf of Finland. **Neighbors:** Russia on E, Latvia on S. **Topography:** Marshy lowland with numerous lakes and swamps; about 40% forested. Elongated hills show evidence of former glaciation. More than 800 islands on Baltic coast. **Capital:** Tallinn, 397,000.

Government: Type: Republic. **Head of state:** Pres. Toomas Hendrik Ilves; b. Dec. 26, 1953; in office: Oct. 9, 2006. **Head of gov.:** Prime Min. Andrus Ansip; b. Oct. 1, 1956; in office: Apr. 13, 2005. **Local divisions:** 15 counties. **Defense budget:** $344 mil. **Active troops:** 5,300.

Economy: Industries: engineering, electronics, wood products, textiles. **Chief crops:** potatoes, vegetables. **Natural resources:** oil shale, peat, phosphorite, clay, limestone, sand, dolomite, sea mud. **Arable land:** 12%. **Livestock:** cattle: 244,800; chickens: 1.6 mil; goats: 3,300; pigs: 345,800; sheep: 62,700. **Fish catch:** 100,222 metric tons. **Electricity prod.:** 9.2 bil kWh. **Labor force** (2007): agric. 4.7%, industry 33.7%, services 61.6%.

Finance: Monetary unit: Kroon (EEK) (Oct. 2009: 10.61 = $1 U.S.). **GDP:** $27.4 bil; **per capita GDP:** $21,000; **GDP growth:** –3.6%. **Imports:** $15.3 bil; Finland 14.2%, Germany 13.3%, Sweden 10%, Lithuania 8.9%, Latvia 8.9%, Russia 7.4%, Poland 4.6%. **Exports:** $12.6 bil; Finland 18.3%, Sweden 13.8%, Russia 10.3%, Latvia 10%, Lithuania 5.7%, Germany 5.1%, U.S. 4.8%. **Tourism:** $1 bil. **Budget:** $7.2 bil. **Intl. reserves less gold:** $2.57 bil. **Gold:** 10,000 oz t. **Consumer prices:** 10.4%.

Transport: Railroad: Length: 571 mi. **Motor vehicles:** 494,000 pass. cars; 91,000 comm. vehicles. **Civil aviation:** 410.1 mil pass.-mi; 13 airports. **Chief ports:** Kuivastu, Kunda, Muuga, Tallinn, Virtsu.

Communications: TV sets: 567 per 1,000 pop. **Radios:** 191.6 per 1,000 pop. **Telephone lines:** 498,100. **Daily newspaper circ.** (2004): 190.6 per 1,000 pop. **Internet:** 888,000 users.

Health: Life expect.: 67.2 male; 78.3 female. **Births** (per 1,000 pop.): 10.3. **Deaths** (per 1,000 pop.): 13.3. **Natural inc.:** –0.31%. **Infant mortality** (per 1,000 live births): 7.5. **HIV rate:** 1.3%.

Education: Compulsory: ages 7-15. **Literacy:** 99.8%.

Major intl. organizations: UN (FAO, IBRD, ILO, IMF, IMO, WHO, WTO), EU, NATO, OSCE.

Embassy: 2131 Massachusetts Ave. NW 20008; 588-0101.

Website: www.president.ee

Estonia was a province of imperial Russia before World War I, and was independent between World Wars I and II. It was conquered by the USSR in 1940 and incorporated as the Estonian SSR. Estonia declared itself an "occupied territory," and proclaimed itself a free nation Mar. 1990. During an abortive Soviet coup, Estonia declared immediate full independence, Aug. 20, 1991; the Soviet Union recognized its independence in Sept. 1991. The first free elections in over 50 years were held Sept. 20, 1992. The last occupying Russian troops departed by Aug. 31, 1994.

Estonia became a full member of the EU and NATO in 2004. The government accused Russia of orchestrating a cyber attack against Estonia's computer network in Apr.-May 2007. A former high-ranking defense official, Herman Simm, was convicted of treason Feb. 25, 2009, for passing Estonian and NATO security secrets to Russian agents.

Ethiopia
Federal Democratic Republic of Ethiopia

People: Population: 85,237,338. **Age distrib.** (%): <15: 46.1; 65+: 2.7. **Pop. density:** 197.2 per sq mi, 76.1 per sq km. **Urban:** 16.1%. **Ethnic groups:** Oromo 32%, Amara 30%, Tigraway 6%, Somali 6%. **Principal languages:** Amarigna, Oromigna, Tigrigna, Somaligna, English (major foreign lang. taught in schools). **Chief religions:** Christian 61% (Orthodox 51%, Protestant 10%), Muslim 33%, traditional 5%.

Geography: Total area: 435,186 sq mi, 1,127,127 sq km; **Land area:** 432,312 sq mi, 1,119,683 sq km. **Location:** In E Africa. **Neighbors:** Sudan on W; Kenya on S; Somalia, Djibouti on E; Eritrea on N. **Topography:** A high central plateau, 6,000-10,000 ft high, rises to higher mountains near the Great Rift Valley, cutting in from SW. Blue Nile and other rivers cross the plateau, which descends to plains on both W and SE. **Capital:** Addis Ababa, 3,100,000.

Government: Type: Federal republic. **Head of state:** Pres. Girma Wolde Giorgis; b. Dec. 1924; in office: Oct. 8, 2001. **Head of gov.:** Prime Min. Meles Zenawi; b. May 8, 1955; in office: Aug. 23, 1995. **Local divisions:** 9 states, 2 charted cities. **Defense budget:** $336 mil. **Active troops:** 138,000.

Economy: Industries: food proc., beverages, textiles, leather, chemicals, metals proc., cement. **Chief crops:** cereals, pulses, coffee, oilseed, cotton, sugarcane, potatoes. **Natural resources:** gold, platinum, copper, potash, nat. gas, hydropower. **Crude oil reserves:** 0.4 mil bbls. **Arable land:** 10%. **Livestock:** cattle: 43 mil; chickens: 36 mil; goats: 21.7 mil; pigs: 29,000; sheep: 26.1 mil. **Fish catch:** 13,253 metric tons. **Electricity prod.:** 3.3 bil kWh. **Labor force** (2005): agric. 80.2%, industry 6.6%, services 13.2%.

Finance: Monetary unit: Birr (ETB) (Oct. 2009: 12.54 = $1 U.S.). **GDP:** $68.8 bil; **per capita GDP:** $800; **GDP growth:** 11.6. **Imports:** $6.9 bil; China 19.5%, Saudi Arabia 17.9%, India 7.2%, U.S. 5%, Italy 4.4%. **Exports:** $1.6 bil; U.S. 10.1%, Germany 10%, Saudi Arabia 7.6%, Netherlands 7.1%, Djibouti 6.5%, Italy 5.6%, China 4.9%. **Tourism:** $176 mil. **Budget:** $3.7 bil. **Intl. reserves less gold:** $565 mil. **Gold:** NA. **Consumer prices:** 44.4%.

Transport: Railroad: Length: 423 mi. **Motor vehicles:** 81,200 pass. cars; 44,500 comm. vehicles. **Civil aviation:** 3.4 bil pass.-mi; 17 airports.

Communications: TV sets: 5 per 1,000 pop. **Radios:** 185 per 1,000 pop. **Telephone lines:** 908,900. **Daily newspaper circ.** (2004): 4.6 per 1,000 pop. **Internet:** 360,000 users.

Health: Life expect.: 52.5 male; 57.5 female. **Births** (per 1,000 pop.): 44. **Deaths** (per 1,000 pop.): 11.8. **Natural inc.:** 3.21%. **Infant mortality** (per 1,000 live births): 82.6. **HIV rate:** 2.1%.

Education: Compulsory: ages 7-12. **Literacy:** 35.9%.

Major intl. organizations: UN (FAO, IBRD, ILO, IMF, IMO, WHO), AU.

Embassy: 3506 International Dr. NW 20008; 364-1200.

Website: www.moinfo.gov.et

Ethiopian culture was influenced by Egypt and Greece. The ancient monarchy was invaded by Italy in 1880 but maintained its independence until another Italian invasion in 1936. British forces freed the country in 1941.

A series of droughts in the 1970s killed hundreds of thousands. An army mutiny, strikes, and student demonstrations led to the dethronement, Sept. 12, 1974, of Ethiopia's last emperor, Haile Selassie I, ending his 58-year reign; he died Aug. 1975, while being held by the ruling junta, known as the Dergue. The junta dissolved parliament, abolished the monarchy, established a socialist state, redistributed land, curbed the influence of the Coptic Church, and violently suppressed opposition.

The regime, torn by bloody coups, faced uprisings by tribal and political groups aided in part by Sudan and Somalia. Ties with the U.S., once a major ally, deteriorated, while cooperation accords were signed with the USSR in 1977. In 1978, Soviet advisers and Cuban troops helped defeat Somali forces. Ethiopia and Somalia signed a peace agreement in 1988.

A worldwide relief effort began in 1984, as an extended drought threatened the country with famine; up to 1 mil people may have died as a result of starvation and disease.

The Ethiopian People's Revolutionary Democratic Front (EPRDF), an umbrella group of 6 rebel armies, launched a major push against government forces, Feb. 1991. In May, Pres. Mengistu Haile Mariam resigned, finding refuge in Zimbabwe. The EPRDF took over and set up a transitional government. Ethiopia's first multiparty general elections were held in 1995.

Eritrea, a province on the Red Sea, declared its independence May 24, 1993. Fighting along the border with Eritrea, which erupted in June 1998, intensified in May 2000, as Ethiopian forces plunged into Eritrean territory; a cease-fire was signed June 18 and a peace treaty Dec. 12. The war displaced 350,000 Ethiopians and is estimated to have cost the country nearly $3 bil. A collapse of crop prices in 2001, followed by drought in 2002-03, led to severe food shortages. Ethnic clashes Dec. 2003-Jan. 2004 in western Ethiopia left more than 250 people dead; thousands fled to Sudan.

The ruling EPRDF won parliamentary elections May 15, 2005, but opposition parties made big gains. Police opened fire on anti-government protesters in Addis Ababa, June 8, killing at least 36; the government arrested some 3,000 dissidents. Police suppression of further protests in the capital, Nov. 1-4, left at least 46 dead. As part of a crackdown on Oromo Liberation Front rebels, the government rounded up thousands of Oromo, Nov. 2005-Jan. 2006. In July 2006, Ethiopia sent troops into Somalia in response to advances by Islamist militias there. Tried in absentia, former Pres. Mengistu was convicted of genocide Dec. 12, 2006.

Drought and other food supply disruptions led Ethiopia June 2008 to appeal for $325 mil in emergency aid. Ethiopia pulled its troops out of Somalia in Jan. 2009.

Fiji

Republic of the Fiji Islands

People: Population: 944,720. **Age distrib.** (%): <15: 30.3; 65+: 4.8. **Pop. density:** 133.9 per sq mi, 51.7 per sq km. **Urban:** 50.8%. **Ethnic groups:** Fijian (predominantly Melanesian with Polynesian) 57%, Indian 38%. **Principal languages:** English, Fijian (both official); Hindustani. **Chief religions:** Christian (incl. Methodist, Roman Catholic) 53%, Hindu 34%, Muslim 7%.

Geography: Total area: 7,054 sq mi, 18,270 sq km; **Land area:** 7,054 sq mi, 18,270 sq km. **Location:** In western S Pacific O. **Neighbors:** Nearest are Vanuatu to W, Tonga to E. **Topography:** 322 isls. (106 inhabited), many mountainous, with tropical forests and large fertile areas. Viti Levu, the largest isl., has over half the total land area. **Capital:** Greater Suva, 224,000.

Government: Type: In transition. **Head of state:** Acting Pres. Ratu Epeli Nailatikau; b. July 5, 1941; in office: July 30, 2009. **Head of gov.:** Interim Prime Min. Vorege (Frank) Bainimarama; b. Apr. 27, 1954; in office: Jan. 5, 2007. **Local divisions:** 4 divisions comprising 14 provinces and 1 dependency. **Defense budget:** $50 mil. **Active troops:** 3,500.

Economy: Industries: tourism, sugar, clothing, copra, gold, silver. **Chief crops:** sugarcane, coconuts, cassava, rice, sweet potatoes, bananas. **Natural resources:** timber, fish, gold, copper, offshore oil potential, hydropower. **Arable land:** 11%. **Livestock:** cattle: 315,000; chickens: 4.3 mil; goats: 270,000; pigs: 145,000; sheep: 6,000. **Fish catch:** 50,356 metric tons. **Electricity prod.:** 1.1 bil kWh. **Labor force** (2001 est.): agric. 70%, industry & services 30%.

Finance: Monetary unit: Dollar (FJD) (Oct. 2009: 1.93 = $1 U.S.). **GDP:** $3.6 bil; **per capita GDP:** $3,800; **GDP growth:** 0.2%. **Imports** (2006): $3.1 bil; Singapore 30.8%, Australia 20.7%, New Zealand 15.6%, China 5.4%. **Exports** (2006): $1.2 bil; U.S. 15.2%, UK 11.6%, Australia 10.3%, Samoa 5.2%, Tonga 4.6%, Japan 4.1%. **Tourism** (2006): $433 mil. **Budget** (2006): $1.4 bil. **Intl. reserves less gold** (2005): $220 mil. **Gold** (2005): 10,000 oz t. **Consumer prices:** 7.7%.

Transport: Railroad: Length: 371 mi. **Motor vehicles:** 86,600 pass. cars; 59,100 comm. vehicles. **Civil aviation:** 1.5 bil pass.-mi; 4 airports. **Chief ports:** Lautoka, Suva.

Communications: TV sets: 110 per 1,000 pop. **Radios:** 677 per 1,000 pop. **Telephone lines:** 129,100. **Daily newspaper circ.** (2004): 53.5 per 1,000 pop. **Internet:** 103,000 users.

Health: Life expect.: 67.9 male; 73.1 female. **Births** (per 1,000 pop.): 22.1. **Deaths** (per 1,000 pop.): 5.7. **Natural inc.:** 1.65%. **Infant mortality** (per 1,000 live births): 11.9. **HIV rate:** 0.1%.

Education: Compulsory: ages 6-15. **Literacy:** 93.7%.

Major intl. organizations: UN (FAO, IBRD, ILO, IMF, IMO, WHO, WTO).

Embassy: 2000 M St. NW, Ste. 710, 20036; 466-8320.

Website: www.fiji.gov.fj

A British colony since 1874, Fiji became independent Oct. 10, 1970. Cultural differences between the Indian community (descendants of contract laborers brought to the islands in the 19th cent.) and indigenous Fijians have led to political polarization. More than 100,000 Indians have left Fiji since the mid-1980s.

Military coups have been frequent in recent decades. Fiji's first Indian prime minister, Mahendra Chaudhry, took office May 19, 1999. He and other government officials were taken captive May 19, 2000, by indigenous Fijian gunmen led by George Speight. The hostage crisis culminated in a military takeover, May 29, led by Frank Bainimarama. Release of the last remaining hostages in July 2000 coincided with the installation of an interim military-backed government. Speight was later tried for treason; he was sentenced to life in prison, Feb. 18, 2002. Prime Min. Laisenia Qarase headed an elected civilian government, 2001-06. He retained his office in parliamentary voting, May 6-13, 2006, but was ousted in a military coup Dec. 5, and Bainimarama took office as interim prime minister. After a court ruled Apr. 9, 2009, that the 2006 coup was illegal, Pres. Ratu Josefa Iloilo abrogated the constitution, dissolved the judiciary, and reappointed Interim Prime Min. Bainimarama. In July, Bainimarama promised a new constitution by 2013 and legislative elections by 2014; he also named Vice Pres. Ratu Epeli Nailatikau as interim president, to replace the retiring Iloilo.

Finland

Republic of Finland

People: Population: 5,250,275. **Age distrib.** (%): <15: 16.4; 65+: 16.8. **Pop. density:** 44.7 per sq mi, 17.2 per sq km. **Urban:** 62.4%. **Ethnic groups:** Finn 93%, Swede 6%. **Principal languages:** Finnish, Swedish (both official). **Chief religion:** Lutheran Church of Finland 83%, none 15%.

Geography: Total area: 130,559 sq mi, 338,145 sq km; **Land area:** 117,558 sq mi, 304,473 sq km. **Location:** In N Europe. **Neighbors:** Norway on N, Sweden on W, Russia on E. **Topography:** South and central are generally flat areas with low hills and

many lakes. The N has mountainous areas, 3,000-4,000 ft above sea level. **Capital:** Helsinki, 1,115,000.

Government: Type: Constitutional republic. **Head of state:** Pres. Tarja Halonen; b. Dec. 24, 1943; in office: Mar. 1, 2000. **Head of gov.:** Prime Min. Matti Vanhanen; b. Nov. 4, 1955; in office: June 24, 2003. **Local divisions:** 6 laanit (provinces). **Defense budget:** $3.2 bil. **Active troops:** 29,300

Economy: Industries: metals & metal products, electronics, machinery & scientific instruments, shipbuilding, pulp & paper, copper refining, foodstuffs, chemicals, textiles. **Chief crops:** barley, wheat, sugar beets, potatoes. **Natural resources:** timber, iron ore, copper, lead, zinc, chromite. **Arable land:** 7%. **Livestock:** cattle: 926,694; chickens: 5.1 mil; goats: 6,181; pigs: 1.4 mil; sheep: 119,252. **Fish catch:** 177,412 metric tons. **Electricity prod.:** 77.9 bil kWh. **Labor force** (2008): agric. & forestry 4.5%; industry 18.3%; constr. 7.3%; commerce 16%; finance, insurance, & business services 14.5%; transp. & communications 7%; public services 32.4%.

Finance: Monetary unit: Euro (EUR) (Oct. 2009: 0.68 = $1 U.S.). **GDP:** $193.5 bil; **per capita GDP:** $36,900; **GDP growth:** 0.9%. **Imports:** $87.5 bil; Russia 16.3%, Germany 15.7%, Sweden 13.6%, Netherlands 6.3%, China 5.1%, UK 4.2%. **Exports:** $96.6 bil; Russia 11.6%, Sweden 10%, Germany 10%, U.S. 6.4%, UK 5.5%, Netherlands 5.1%. **Tourism:** $2.8 bil. **Budget:** $58.2 bil. **Intl. reserves less gold:** $4.53 bil. **Gold:** 1.58 mil oz t. **Consumer prices:** 4.1%.

Transport: Railroad: Length: 3,600 mi. **Motor vehicles:** 2.4 mil pass. cars; 374,600 comm. vehicles. **Civil aviation:** 7.4 bil pass.-mi; 75 airports. **Chief ports:** Hamina, Helsinki, Kokkola, Kotka, Naantali, Pori, Raahe, Rauma, Turku.

Communications: TV sets: 643 per 1,000 pop. **Radios:** 1,564 per 1,000 pop. **Telephone lines:** 1.7 mil. **Daily newspaper circ.** (2004): 431.1 per 1,000 pop. **Internet:** 4.4 mil users.

Health: Life expect.: 75.3 male; 82.5 female. **Births** (per 1,000 pop.): 10.4. **Deaths** (per 1,000 pop.): 10. **Natural inc.:** 0.04%. **Infant mortality** (per 1,000 live births): 3.5. **HIV rate:** 0.1%.

Education: Compulsory: ages 7-16. **Literacy:** 100%.

Major intl. organizations: UN (FAO, IBRD, ILO, IMF, IMO, WHO, WTO), EU, OECD, OSCE.

Embassy: 3301 Massachusetts Ave. NW 20008; 298-5800.

Website: www.government.fi

The early Finns probably migrated from the Ural area at about the beginning of the Christian era. Swedish settlers brought the country into Sweden, 1154 to 1809, when Finland became an autonomous grand duchy of the Russian Empire. Russian exactions created a strong national spirit; on Dec. 6, 1917, Finland declared its independence, and in 1919 it became a republic.

On Nov. 30, 1939, the Soviet Union invaded, and the Finns were forced to cede 16,173 sq mi of territory. After World War II, further cessions were exacted. In 1948, Finland signed a treaty of mutual assistance with the USSR; Finland and Russia nullified this treaty with a new pact in Jan. 1992.

Following approval by Finnish voters in an advisory referendum Oct. 16, 1994, Finland joined the EU effective Jan. 1, 1995. Pres. Tarja Halonen won a 2nd 6-year term, Jan. 29, 2006. Suicidal rampages by lone gunmen left 9 people dead at a Tuusula high school, Nov. 27, 2007, and claimed 11 lives at a Kauhajoki vocational college, Sept. 23, 2008. Former Pres. Martti Ahtisaari was awarded the Nobel Peace Prize, Oct. 10, 2008, for his efforts in mediating international conflicts.

Aland, or Ahvenanmaa, constituting an autonomous province, is a group of small islands, 590 sq mi, in the Gulf of Bothnia, 25 mi from Sweden, 15 mi from Finland. Mariehamn is the chief port.

France

French Republic

People: Population: 64,057,792. **Age distrib.** (%): <15: 18.6; 65+: 16.4. **Pop. density:** 259.2 per sq mi, 100.1 per sq km. **Urban:** 76.7%. **Ethnic groups:** Celtic & Latin with Teutonic, Slavic, N African, Indochinese, Basque minorities. **Principal languages:** French, rapidly declining regional dialects & languages (incl. Provençal, Breton, Alsatian, Corsican, Catalan, Basque, Flemish). **Chief religions:** Roman Catholic 83%-88%, Muslim 5%-10%.

Geography: Total area: 248,429 sq mi, 643,427 sq km; **Land area:** 247,126 sq mi, 640,053 sq km. **Location:** In W Europe, between Atlantic O. and Medit. Sea. **Neighbors:** Spain, Andorra, Monaco on S; Italy, Switzerland, Germany on E; Luxembourg, Belgium on N. **Topography:** A wide plain covers more than half of the country, in N and W, drained to W by Seine, Loire, Garonne rivers. The Massif Central is a mountainous plateau in center. In E are Alps (Mt. Blanc is tallest in W Europe, 15,771 ft), the lower Jura range, and forested Vosges. The Rhone flows from Lake Geneva to Mediterranean. Pyrenees are in SW, on border with Spain. **Capital:** Paris, 9,904,000. **Cities (urban aggr.):** Lyon, 1,423,000; Marseille-Aix-en-Provence, 1,400,000; Lille, 1,044,000.

Government: Type: Republic. **Head of state:** Pres. Nicolas Sarkozy; b. Jan. 28, 1955; in office: May 16, 2007. **Head of gov.:** Prime Min. François Fillon; b. Mar. 4, 1954; in office: May 17, 2007. **Local divisions:** 22 administrative regions containing 96 departments. **Defense budget:** $60.7 bil. **Active troops:** 352,771.

Economy: Industries: machinery, chemicals, automobiles, metallurgy, aircraft, electronics, tourism. **Chief crops:** wheat, cereals, sugar beets, potatoes, wine grapes. **Natural resources:** coal, iron ore, bauxite, zinc, uranium, antimony, arsenic, potash, feldspar, fluorspar, gypsum, timber, fish. **Crude oil reserves:** 103.3 mil bbls. **Other resources:** Timber, dairy. **Arable land:** 33%. **Livestock:** cattle: 19.4 mil; chickens: 175 mil; goats: 1.3 mil; pigs: 14.7 mil; sheep: 8.5 mil. **Fish catch:** 787,674 metric tons. **Electricity prod.:** 542.4 bil kWh. **Labor force** (2005): agric. 3.8%, industry 24.3%, services 71.8%.

Finance: Monetary unit: Euro (EUR) (Oct. 2009: 0.68 = $1 U.S.). **GDP:** $2.1 tril; **per capita GDP:** $33,200; **GDP growth:** 0.3%. **Imports:** $692 bil; Germany 17.9%, Belgium 11.7%, Italy 8.3%, Spain 6.9%, Netherlands 6.8%, UK 5.1%, U.S. 4.3%. **Exports:** $601.9 bil; Germany 14.3%, Italy 8.7%, Spain 8.3%, UK 7.8%, Belgium 7.6%, U.S. 5.8%, Netherlands 4.2%. **Tourism:** $54.3 bil. **Budget:** $1.4 tril. **Intl. reserves less gold:** $21.83 bil. **Gold:** 80.13 mil oz t. **Consumer prices:** 2.9%.

Transport: Railroad: Length: 18,152 mi. **Motor vehicles:** 29.7 mil pass. cars; 6.4 mil comm. vehicles. **Civil aviation:** 78.7 bil pass.-mi (incl. territories and dependencies); 297 airports. **Chief ports:** Bordeaux, Calais, Dunkerque, Le Havre, Marseille, Nantes, Paris, Rouen, Strasbourg.

Communications: TV sets: 620 per 1,000 pop. **Radios:** 946 per 1,000 pop. **Telephone lines:** 35 mil. **Daily newspaper circ.** (2005): 163.5 per 1,000 pop. **Internet:** 42.3 mil users.

Health: Life expect.: 77.7 male; 84.2 female. **Births** (per 1,000 pop.): 12.7. **Deaths** (per 1,000 pop.): 8.5. **Natural inc.:** 0.42%. **Infant mortality** (per 1,000 live births): 3.4. **HIV rate:** 0.4%.

Education: Compulsory: ages 6-16. **Literacy:** 99%.

Major intl. organizations: UN and most of its specialized agencies, EU, NATO, OECD, OSCE.

Embassy: 4101 Reservoir Rd. NW 20007; 944-6195.

Website: www.premier-ministre.gouv.fr

Celtic Gaul was conquered by Julius Caesar 58-51 BCE; Romans ruled for 500 years. Under Charlemagne, Frankish rule extended over much of Europe. After his death France emerged as one of the successor kingdoms.

The monarchy was overthrown by the French Revolution (1789-93) and succeeded by the First Republic, followed by the First Empire under Napoleon (1804-15), a monarchy (1814-48), the Second Republic (1848-52), the Second Empire (1852-70), the Third Republic (1871-1946), the Fourth Republic (1946-58), and the Fifth Republic (1958 to present).

France suffered severe losses in manpower and wealth in WWI, when it was invaded by Germany. By the Treaty of Versailles, France exacted return of Alsace and Lorraine, provinces seized by Germany in 1871. Germany invaded France again in May 1940, and signed an armistice with a government based in Vichy. After France was liberated by the Allies in Sept. 1944, Gen. Charles de Gaulle became head of the provisional government, serving until 1946. De Gaulle again became premier in 1958, during a crisis over Algeria, and obtained voter approval for a new constitution, ushering in the Fifth Republic. He then became president.

France had withdrawn from Indochina in 1954, and from Morocco and Tunisia in 1956. Most of its remaining African territories, including Algeria, were freed 1958-62.

In May 1968 rebellious students in Paris and other centers rioted, battled police, and were joined by workers who launched nationwide strikes. The government awarded pay increases to the strikers May 26. De Gaulle resigned from office in Apr. 1969, after losing a nationwide referendum on constitutional reform. Georges Pompidou, who was elected to succeed him, continued De Gaulle's emphasis on French independence from the U.S. and Soviet Union. After Pompidou's death, in 1974, Valery Giscard d'Estaing was elected president; he continued the basically conservative policies of his predecessors.

On May 10, 1981, France elected François Mitterrand, a Socialist, president. Under Mitterrand the government nationalized 5 major industries and most private banks. After 1986, however, when rightists won a narrow victory in the National Assembly, Mitterrand chose conservative Jacques Chirac as premier. A 2-year period of "cohabitation" ensued, and France began to pursue a privatization program in which many state-owned companies were sold. After Mitterrand was elected to a 2nd 7-year term in 1988, he appointed a Socialist as premier. The center-right won a large majority in 1993 legislative elections, ushering in another period of "cohabitation" with a conservative premier.

Chirac won the presidency in a runoff election May 7, 1995. He cut government spending to help the French economy meet the budgetary goals set for the introduction of a common European currency. With unemployment at nearly 13%, legislative elections completed June 1, 1997, produced a decisive victory for the leftist

parties. The result was a new period of "cohabitation," this time between a conservative president and a Socialist prime minister, Lionel Jospin. France contributed 7,000 troops to the NATO-led force (KFOR) that entered Kosovo in June 1999.

French voters, disaffected by government scandals, shocked the political establishment in the first round of presidential voting Apr. 21, 2002, by giving Jean-Marie Le Pen, leader of the far-right National Front, a second place finish with 16.9% of the vote; Chirac won only 19.9%, and Jospin was 3rd, with 16.2%. Chirac easily won the May 5 runoff, with 82%, and his center-right allies won parliamentary elections June 9 and 16. Parliament gave final approval Mar. 3, 2004, to a law barring the wearing of Islamic head scarves and other religious symbols in public schools.

Displeased with sluggish economic growth, high unemployment, and budget cuts in entitlement programs, voters showed their discontent by rejecting, May 29, 2005, a proposed EU constitution strongly supported by the Chirac government. A state of emergency was declared Nov. 8 after 12 days of riots that began in Paris and spread to some 300 French cities and towns; rioters were mainly young North and West African immigrants. After a wave of mass protests and strikes, Chirac agreed, Apr. 10, 2006, to rescind a law that made it easier for employers to fire inexperienced young workers.

Campaigning as an economic reformer, the conservative, pro-American Nicolas Sarkozy won a presidential runoff election May 6, 2007. The French bank Société Générale disclosed Jan. 24, 2008, that it had lost more than $7 bil, which it blamed on a "rogue trader," Jerôme Kerviel. Sarkozy responded to the global recession by unveiling Dec. 4 a $33 bil economic stimulus plan focused on infrastructure development; new measures announced Feb. 18, 2009, following labor protests, provided $3.3 bil in aid for lower-income people.

France, a founding member of NATO, formally returned to the alliance's military command structure Apr. 2009 after an absence of 43 years. In mid-2009, France had about 2,900 troops fighting as part of NATO forces in Afghanistan.

The island of **Corsica**, in the Mediterranean W of Italy and N of Sardinia, is a territorial collectivity and region of France comprising 2 departments. It elects a total of 2 senators and 3 deputies to the French Parliament. Area: 3,369 sq mi; pop. (2006 census): 294,118. The capital is Ajaccio, birthplace of Napoleon I. Violence by Corsican separatist groups has hurt tourism, a leading industry on the island. Corsicans rejected, 51-49%, a limited autonomy plan in a referendum July 6, 2003.

Overseas Departments

French Guiana is on the NE coast of South America with Suriname on the W and Brazil on the E and S. Its area is 35,135 sq mi (total); 34,421 sq mi (land); pop. (2007 est.) 203,321. Guiana sends one senator and 2 deputies to the French Parliament. Guiana is administered by a prefect and has a Council General of 16 elected members; capital is Cayenne.

The famous penal colony, Devil's Island, was phased out between 1938 and 1951. The European Space Agency maintains a satellite-launching center (established by France in 1964) in the city of Kourou.

Immense forests of rich timber cover 88% of the land. Fishing (especially shrimp), forestry, and gold mining are the most important industries.

Guadeloupe, in the West Indies' Leeward Islands, consists of 2 large islands, Basse-Terre and Grande-Terre, separated by the Salt River, plus Marie Galante and the Saintes group to the S and, to the N, Desirade. (St. Barthelemy and over half of St. Martin [the Netherlands' portion is called St. Maarten], both formerly part of Guadeloupe, voted for secession in 2003 and became separate overseas territorial collectivities in 2007.) A French possession since 1635, the department is represented in the French Parliament; administration consists of a prefect (governor) as well as an elected general and regional councils.

Area of the islands is 525 sq mi; pop. (2007 est., incl. St. Barthelemy and St. Martin) 456,698, mainly descendants of slaves; capital is Basse-Terre on Basse-Terre Island. The land is fertile; sugar, rum, and bananas are exported. Tourism is an important industry.

Martinique, the northernmost of the Windward Islands, in the West Indies, has been a possession since 1635, and a department since Mar. 1946. It is represented in the French Parliament by 2 senators and 4 deputies. The island was the birthplace of Napoleon's first wife, Empress Josephine.

It has an area of 425 sq mi (total); 409 sq mi (land); pop. (2007 est.) 439,202, mostly descendants of slaves. The capital is Fort-de-France, pop. (2006): 90,347. It is a popular tourist stop. The chief exports are rum, bananas, and petroleum products.

Réunion is a volcanic island in the Indian O. about 420 mi E of Madagascar, and has belonged to France since 1665. Area, 972 sq mi (total); 968 sq mi (land); pop. (2007 est.) 798,094, 30% of French extraction. Capital: Saint-Denis. The chief export is sugar. It elects 5 deputies, 3 senators to the French Parliament.

Overseas Territorial Collectivities

Mayotte, claimed by Comoros and administered by France, voted in 1976 to become a territorial collectivity of France. An island NW of Madagascar, area is 144 sq mi, pop. (2009 est.) 223,765. The capital is Mamoudzou. In Mar. 29, 2009, referendum, 95% of voters endorsed a plan under which Mayotte would become an overseas department of France in 2011.

St. Pierre and Miquelon became a territorial collectivity in 1985. It consists of 2 groups of rocky islands near the SW coast of Newfoundland, inhabited by fishermen. Fish products are the chief export. The St. Pierre group has an area of 10 sq mi; Miquelon, 83 sq mi. Total pop. (2009 est.) 7,051. Capital: Saint-Pierre. Both Mayotte and St. Pierre and Miquelon elect a deputy and a senator to the French Parliament.

St. Barthelemy and **St. Martin** became overseas territorial collectivities in 2007.

Overseas Territories

French Polynesia comprises 130 islands widely scattered among 5 archipelagos in the S Pacific; administered by a Council of Ministers (headed by a president). Territorial Assembly and the Council have headquarters at Papeete, on Tahiti, one of the Society Islands (which include the Windward Isls. and Leeward Isls.). Two deputies and a senator are elected to the French Parliament.

Other groups are the Marquesas Islands; the Tuamotu Archipelago; the Gambier Islands; and the Austral, or Tubuai, Islands.

Total area of the islands administered from Tahiti is 1,609 sq mi (total); 1,413 sq mi (land); pop. (2009 est.) 287,032, more than half on Tahiti. Tahiti is mountainous with a productive coastline bearing coconuts, citrus, pineapples, and vanilla. Cultured pearls are also produced.

Tahiti was visited by Capt. James Cook in 1769 and by Capt. Bligh in the *Bounty*, 1788-89. Its beauty impressed Herman Melville, Paul Gauguin, and Charles Darwin. A coalition favoring independence for French Polynesia within 20 years gained control of the territorial assembly after elections May 23, 2004.

The territory of the **French Southern and Antarctic Lands** comprises Adelie Land, on Antarctica, and island groups in the Indian O. Area: 3,023 sq mi (total); 3,023 sq mi (land).

Adelie, reached 1840, has a 185-mi coastline and tapers 1,240 mi inland to the S Pole. (The U.S. does not recognize national claims in Antarctica.) It has a research station. There are 2 glaciers: Ninnis, 22 mi wide, 99 mi long, and Mentz, 11 mi by 140 mi.

The Indian O. groups are: Kerguelen Archipelago, visited 1772, consists of one large and 300 small islands. The chief is 87 mi long, 74 mi wide, and has Mt. Ross, 6,429 ft tall. Principal research station is Port-aux-Français. Seals often weigh 2 tons; there are blue whales, coal, peat, semiprecious stones. Crozet Archipelago, reached 1772, covers 136 sq mi. Eastern Island rises to 6,560 ft. Saint Paul, in southern Indian O., has warm springs with earth at places heating to 120° to 390°F. Amsterdam is nearby; both produce cod and rock lobster. Military garrisons and meteorological stations are located on the Scattered Isls.

The territory of **New Caledonia** and Dependencies is a group of islands in the Pacific O. about 1,115 mi E of Australia and approx. the same distance NW of New Zealand. Dependencies are the Loyalty Isls., Isle of Pines, Belep Archipelago, and Huon Isls.

The largest island, New Caledonia, is 6,530 sq mi. Total area of the territory is 7,359 sq mi (total); 7,171 sq mi (land); pop. (2009 est.) 227,436. The group was acquired by France in 1853.

The territory is administered by a High Commissioner. There is a popularly elected Territorial Congress. Two deputies and a senator are elected to the French Parliament. Capital: Noumea.

Mining is the chief industry. New Caledonia is one of the world's largest nickel producers. Chrome, iron, cobalt, manganese, silver, gold, lead, and copper are also found. Agric. products include yams, sweet potatoes, potatoes, manioc, corn, and coconuts.

In 1987, New Caledonian voters chose by referendum to remain within the French Republic. There were clashes between French and Melanesians (Kanaks) in 1988. An agreement Apr. 21, 1998, between France and rival New Caledonian factions specified a 15-to 20-year period of "shared sovereignty." The French constitution was amended, July 6, to allow the territory a gradual increase in autonomy; New Caledonian voters approved the plan Nov. 8, 1998, by a 72% majority.

The territory of **Wallis and Futuna** comprises 2 island groups in the SW Pacific S of Tuvalu, N of Fiji, and W of Western Samoa; became an overseas territory July 29, 1961. The islands have a total area of 106 sq mi and population (2009 est.) of 15,289. Alofi, attached to Futuna, is uninhabited. Capital: Mata-Utu. Chief products are copra, yams, taro roots, bananas, and coconuts. A senator and a deputy are elected to the French Parliament.

Gabon
Gabonese Republic

People: Population: 1,514,993. **Age distrib.** (%): <15: 42.1; 65+: 3.9. **Pop. density:** 15.2 per sq mi, 5.9 per sq km. **Urban:** 83.6%. **Ethnic groups:** Bantu tribes (incl. four major groupings of Fang, Bapounou, Nzebi, Obamba), other Africans & Europeans. **Principal languages:** French (official), Fang, Myene, Nzebi, Bapounou/Eschira, Bandjabi. **Chief religions:** Christian 55%-75%, animist.

Geography: Total area: 103,347 sq mi, 267,667 sq km; **Land area:** 99,486 sq mi, 257,667 sq km. **Location:** On Atlantic coast of W central Africa. **Neighbors:** Equatorial Guinea, Cameroon on N; Congo on E and S. **Topography:** Heavily forested, consisting of coastal lowlands; plateaus in N, E, and S; mountains in N, SE, and center. The Ogooue R. system covers most of Gabon. **Capital:** Libreville, 576,000.

Government: Type: Republic. **Head of state:** Pres.-elect Ali Bongo Ondimba; b. Feb. 9, 1959; election held: Aug. 30, 2009. **Head of gov.:** Prime Min. Paul Biyoghé Mba; b. Apr. 18, 1953; in office: July 17, 2009. **Local divisions:** 9 provinces. **Defense budget:** $123 mil. **Active troops:** 4,700.

Economy: Industries: oil extraction & refining, mang., gold, chemicals, ship repair, food & beverages. **Chief crops:** cocoa, coffee, sugar, palm oil, rubber. **Natural resources:** oil, nat. gas, diamonds, niobium, mang., uranium, gold, timber, iron ore, hydropower. **Crude oil reserves:** 2 bil bbls. **Arable land:** 1%. **Livestock:** cattle: 36,000; chickens: 3.1 mil; goats: 91,000; pigs: 213,000; sheep: 196,000. **Fish catch:** 39,124 metric tons. **Electricity prod.:** 1.7 bil kWh. **Labor force** (2000 est.): agric. 60%, industry 15%, services 25%.

Finance: Monetary unit: CFA BEAC Franc (XAF) (Oct. 2009: 444.97 = $1 U.S.). **GDP:** $21.1 bil; **per capita GDP:** $14,200; **GDP growth:** 2%. **Imports:** $2.6 bil; France 32.1%, U.S. 11.1%, China 5.2%, Belgium 4.6%, Cameroon 4.4%, Netherlands 4.2%. **Exports:** $9.3 bil; U.S. 25.4%, China 17.9%, Japan 10.2%, Malaysia 5.8%, France 5.4%, Spain 4%. **Tourism:** NA. **Budget:** $2.3 bil. **Intl. reserves less gold:** $1.25 bil. **Gold:** 10,000 oz t. **Consumer prices:** 5.3%.

Transport: Railroad: Length: 506 mi. **Civil aviation:** 515.1 mil pass.-mi; 13 airports. **Chief ports:** Gamba, Libreville, Lucinda, Port-Gentil.

Communications: TV sets: 251 per 1,000 pop. **Radios:** 501 per 1,000 pop. **Telephone lines:** 26,500. **Internet:** 90,000 users.

Health: Life expect.: 52.5 male; 54.6 female. **Births** (per 1,000 pop.): 35.8. **Deaths** (per 1,000 pop.): 12.6. **Natural inc.:** 2.32%. **Infant mortality** (per 1,000 live births): 52.6. **HIV rate:** 5.9%.

Education: Compulsory: ages 6-16. **Literacy:** 86.2%.

Major intl. organizations: UN (FAO, IBRD, ILO, IMF, IMO, WHO, WTO), AU.

Embassy: 2034 20th St. NW 20009; 797-1000.

Website: www.legabon.ga

France established control over the region in the second half of the 19th cent. Gabon became independent Aug. 17, 1960. Backed by France, Pres. Albert-Bernard Bongo (later Omar Bongo Ondimba) ruled the country 1967-2009, greatly enriching himself and his family. A multiparty political system was introduced in 1990, and a new constitution was enacted Mar. 14, 1991. Bongo's reelection victories in 1993, 1998, and 2003 were faulted by international observers. After he died June 8, 2009, his son Ali Bongo Ondimba, Gabon's defense minister 1999-2009, ran for the presidency. He claimed victory in a disputed election Aug. 30; a court-ordered recount began Sept. 29.

Gabon is one of the most prosperous black African countries, thanks to abundant natural resources, foreign private investment, and government development programs.

The Gambia
Republic of The Gambia

People: Population: 1,782,893. **Age distrib.** (%): <15: 43.6; 65+: 2.8. **Pop. density:** 461.8 per sq mi, 178.3 per sq km. **Urban:** 53.9%. **Ethnic groups:** African 99% (incl. Mandinka 42%, Fula 18%, Wolof 16%). **Principal languages:** English (official), Mandinka, Wolof, Fula, other indigenous vernaculars. **Chief religions:** Muslim 90%, Christian 9%.

Geography: Total area: 4,363 sq mi, 11,300 sq km; **Land area:** 3,861 sq mi, 10,000 sq km. **Location:** On Atlantic coast near W tip of Africa. **Neighbors:** Surrounded on 3 sides by Senegal. **Topography:** A narrow strip of land on each side of lower Gambia R. **Capital:** Banjul, 406,000.

Government: Type: Republic. **Head of state and gov.:** Pres Yahya Jammeh; b. May 25, 1965; in office: July 22, 1994. **Local divisions:** 5 divisions, 1 city. **Defense budget:** $4 mil. **Active troops:** 800.

Economy: Industries: processing peanuts, fish, hides, tourism, beverages, agric. machinery assembly. **Chief crops:** rice, millet, sorghum, peanuts, corn, sesame, cassava, palm kernels. **Natural resources:** fish, titanium, tin, zircon. **Arable land:** 28%. **Livestock:** cattle: 334,000; chickens: 710,000; goats: 280,000;

pigs: 21,700; sheep: 150,000. **Fish catch:** 43,574 metric tons. **Electricity prod.:** 154 mil kWh. **Labor force** (1996): agric. 75%, industry 19%, services 6%.

Finance: Monetary unit: Dalasi (GMD) (Oct. 2009: 26.70 = $1 U.S.). **GDP:** $2.3 bil; **per capita GDP:** $1,300; **GDP growth:** 5.9%. **Imports:** $299 mil; China 22.7%, Senegal 11.7%, Côte d'Ivoire 8.4%, Brazil 7.4%, Netherlands 4.9%. **Exports:** $85 mil; India 32.4%, Japan 22.2%, China 10.7%, Belgium 5.5%, UK 4.7%. **Tourism:** NA. **Budget:** $163.4 mil. **Intl. reserves less gold** (2007): $90 mil. **Gold:** NA. **Consumer prices:** 4.5%.

Transport: Motor vehicles: 6,400 pass. cars; 3,500 comm. vehicles. **Civil aviation:** 1 airport. **Chief port:** Banjul.

Communications: TV Sets: 3 per 1,000 pop. **Radios:** 394 per 1,000 pop. **Telephone lines:** 48,900. **Internet:** 114,200 users.

Health: Life expect.: 53.1 male; 56.9 female. **Births** (per 1,000 pop.): 38.4. **Deaths** (per 1,000 pop.): 11.7. **Natural inc.:** 2.66%. **Infant mortality** (per 1,000 live births): 68.7. **HIV rate:** 0.9%.

Education: Compulsory: ages 7-12. **Literacy:** 40.1%.

Major intl. organizations: UN (FAO, IBRD, ILO, IMF, IMO, WHO, WTO), the Commonwealth, AU.

Embassy: 1156 15th St. NW 20005; 785-1399.

Website: www.gambia.gm

The peoples of Gambia were at one time associated with the West African empires of Ghana, Mali, and Songhai. The area became Britain's first African possession in 1588.

Independence came Feb. 18, 1965; republic status within the Commonwealth was achieved in 1970. The country suffered from severe famine in the 1970s. Senegambia, a confederation with Senegal, lasted from 1982 to 1989.

On July 22, 1994, after 24 years in power, Pres. Dawda K. Jawara was deposed in a bloodless coup by a military officer, Yahya Jammeh. Jammeh barred political activity, detained potential opponents, and governed by decree. Despite a nominal return to constitutional government in 1996, Jammeh has retained a tight grip on power, while Gambia has remained one of the world's poorest countries. Security forces suppressed an alleged coup plot by army officers Mar. 2006. Pres. Jammeh won a 3rd 5-year term Sept. 22, 2006.

Georgia

People: Population: 4,615,807. **Age distrib.** (%): <15: 16.1; 65+: 16.4. **Pop. density:** 171.5 per sq mi, 66.2 per sq km. **Urban:** 52.5%. **Ethnic groups:** Georgian 84%, Azeri 7%, Armenian 6%. **Principal languages:** Georgian (official), Russian, Abkhaz (official in Abkhazia). **Chief religions:** Orthodox Christian 84%, Muslim 10%, Armenian-Gregorian 4%.

Geography: Total area: 26,911 sq mi, 69,700 sq km; **Land area:** 26,911 sq mi, 69,700 sq km. **Location:** SW Asia, on E coast of Black Sea. **Neighbors:** Russia on N and NE, Turkey and Armenia on S, Azerbaijan on SE. **Topography:** Separated from Russia on NE by main range of Caucasus Mts. **Capital:** Tbilisi, 1,100,000.

Government: Type: Republic. **Head of state:** Pres. Mikhail Saakashvili; b. Dec. 21, 1967; in office: Jan. 25, 2004. **Head of gov.:** Prime Min. Nikoloz (Nika) Gilauri; b. Feb., 14, 1975; in office: Feb. 6, 2009. **Local divisions:** 53 rayons, 9 cities, and 2 autonomous republics. **Defense budget:** $573 mil. **Active troops:** 21,150.

Economy: Industries: steel, aircraft, machine tools, elec. appliances, mining, chemicals. **Chief crops:** citrus, grapes, tea, hazelnuts, vegetables. **Natural resources:** forests, hydropower, mang., iron ore, copper, minor coal & oil deposits. **Crude oil reserves:** 35 mil bbls. **Arable land:** 12%. **Livestock:** cattle: 1.1 mil; chickens: 5.1 mil; goats: 92,400; pigs: 343,500; sheep: 696,800. **Fish catch:** 18,377 metric tons. **Electricity prod.:** 7.1 bil kWh. **Labor force** (2006 est.): agric. 55.6%, industry 8.9%, services 35.5%.

Finance: Monetary unit: Lari (GEL) (Oct. 2009: 1.67 = $1 U.S.). **GDP:** $21.5 bil; **per capita GDP:** $4,600; **GDP growth:** 2.1%. **Imports:** $6.3 bil; Turkey 15.1%, Russia 10.9%, U.S. 8.9%, Ukraine 7.1%, Germany 5.9%, Azerbaijan 5.6%, Bulgaria 4.5%, China 4.3%. **Exports:** $2.4 bil; Turkey 19.3%, Bulgaria 17.9%, U.S. 9%, Germany 5.2%, Canada 4.9%, UK 4.3%, Azerbaijan 4.3%. **Tourism:** $384 mil. **Budget:** $3.1 bil. **Intl. reserves less gold:** $961 mil. **Gold:** NA. **Consumer prices:** 10%.

Transport: Railroad: Length: 1,002 mi. **Motor vehicles:** 255,200 pass. cars; 68,600 comm. vehicles. **Civil aviation:** 323.1 mil pass.-mi; 18 airports. **Chief ports:** Batumi, Poti.

Communications: TV sets: 516 per 1,000 pop. **Radios:** 590 per 1,000 pop. **Telephone lines:** 618,000. **Internet:** 1.02 mil users.

Health: Life expect.: 73.2 male; 80.3 female. **Births** (per 1,000 pop.): 10.6. **Deaths** (per 1,000 pop.): 9.5. **Natural inc.:** 0.1%. **Infant mortality** (per 1,000 live births): 16.8. **HIV rate:** 0.1%.

Education: Compulsory: ages 6-14. **Literacy:** 100%.

Major intl. organizations: UN (FAO, IBRD, ILO, IMF, IMO, WHO, WTO), CIS, OSCE.

Embassy: 2209 Massachusetts Ave. NW 20008; 387-2390.

Website: www.government.gov.ge

The region, which contained the ancient kingdoms of Colchis and Iberia, was Christianized in the 4th cent. and conquered by Arabs in the 8th cent. Annexed by Russia in 1801, Georgia was forcibly incorporated into the USSR in 1922.

Georgia declared independence Apr. 9, 1991. It emerged as an independent state when the Soviet Union disbanded Dec. 26. After a power struggle, former Soviet Foreign Min. Eduard A. Shevardnadze became president of Georgia.

He was wounded by a car bomb Aug. 29, 1995, while on his way to Parliament to sign a new constitution. He was reelected president Nov. 5. Shevardnadze escaped another assassination attempt, Feb. 9, 1998, when gunmen ambushed his motorcade. A mutiny by more than 200 soldiers was crushed Oct. 19.

Shevardnadze won another 5-year presidential term Apr. 9, 2000. But parliamentary elections Nov. 2, 2003, denounced as fraudulent by opposition groups and international observers, sparked massive antigovernment protests, causing him to resign Nov. 23. Opposition leader Mikhail Saakashvili won the presidential election of Jan. 4, 2004. He survived an apparent assassination attempt along with U.S. Pres. George W. Bush in Tbilisi May 10, 2005, suppressed an alleged coup plot Sept. 6, 2006, and cracked down violently on antigovernment protests and imposed a state of emergency, Nov. 7-16, 2007; he then called early elections, Jan. 5, 2008, in which he won a renewed mandate.

Since the country gained independence, secessionist movements in the enclaves of South Ossetia and Abkhazia, supported by Russia, have challenged the Tbilisi government. Open warfare between Georgia and Russia erupted when Saakashvili sent troops Aug. 7, 2008, to suppress insurgent activity in Tskhinvali, the South Ossetian capital. Russia retaliated Aug. 8-9 by dispatching its forces to South Ossetia and Abkhazia and launching assaults on key Georgian cities. A cease-fire signed Aug. 15-16 called for withdrawal of Russian forces from Georgia proper, but allowed thousands of Russian troops to remain in the breakaway regions. On Aug. 26, Russian Pres. Dmitri Medvedev formally recognized their independence, a step protested by the U.S. and Georgia's other Western allies. International donors Oct. 22 pledged $4.55 bil in reconstruction aid, including about $1.5 bil from EU members and $1 bil from the U.S.

Germany
Federal Republic of Germany

People: Population: 82,329,758. **Age distrib.** (%): <15: 13.7; 65+: 20.3. **Pop. density:** 610.6 per sq mi, 235.8 per sq km. **Urban:** 73.4%. **Ethnic groups:** German 92%, Turkish 2%, other (incl. Greek, Italian, Polish, Russian, Serbo-Croatian, Spanish) 6%. **Principal language:** German. **Chief religions:** Protestant 34%, Roman Catholic 34%, Muslim 4%, unaffiliated or other 28%.

Geography: Total area: 137,847 sq mi, 357,021 sq km; **Land area:** 134,836 sq mi, 349,223 sq km. **Location:** In central Europe. **Neighbors:** Denmark on N; Netherlands, Belgium, Luxembourg, France on W; Switzerland, Austria on S; Czech Rep., Poland on E. **Topography:** Germany is flat in N, hilly in center and W, and mountainous in Bavaria in the S. Chief rivers are Elbe, Weser, Ems, Rhine, and Main, all flowing toward North Sea, and Danube, flowing toward Black Sea. **Capital:** Berlin, 3,406,000. **Cities (urban aggr.):** Hamburg, 1,757,000; Munich, 1,275,000; Cologne (Köln), 1,004,000.

Government: Type: Federal republic. **Head of state:** Pres. Horst Köhler; b. Feb. 22, 1943; in office: July 1, 2004. **Head of gov.:** Chan. Angela Merkel; b. July 17, 1954; in office: Nov. 22, 2005. **Local divisions:** 16 laender (states). **Defense budget:** $42.1 bil. **Active troops:** 244,324.

Economy: Industries: iron, steel, coal, cement, chemicals, machinery, vehicles, machine tools, electronics, food & beverages, shipbuilding. **Chief crops:** potatoes, wheat, barley, sugar beets, fruit, cabbages. **Natural resources:** coal, lignite, nat. gas, iron ore, copper, nickel, uranium, potash, salt, constr. materials, timber. **Crude oil reserves:** 276 mil bbls. **Arable land:** 33%. **Livestock:** cattle: 12.7 mil; chickens: 114.6 mil; goats: 180,000; pigs: 27.1 mil; sheep: 2.5 mil. **Fish catch:** 293,757 metric tons. **Electricity prod.:** 594.8 bil kWh. **Labor force** (2005): agric. 2.4%, industry 29.7%, services 67.8%.

Finance: Monetary unit: Euro (EUR) (Oct. 2009: 0.68 = $1 U.S.). **GDP:** $2.9 tril; **per capita GDP:** $35,400; **GDP growth:** 1%. **Imports:** $1.2 tril; Netherlands 12.5%, France 8.3%, Belgium 7.5%, China 6.2%, Italy 5.7%, UK 5.4%, Austria 4.3%, Russia 4.2%, U.S. 4.2%. **Exports:** $1.5 tril; France 9.7%, U.S. 7.1%, UK 6.7%, Netherlands 6.6%, Italy 6.4%, Austria 5.4%, Belgium 5.2%, Spain 4.4%, Poland 4%. **Tourism:** $36 bil. **Budget:** $1.5 tril. **Intl. reserves less gold:** $28.01 bil. **Gold:** 109.72 mil oz t. **Consumer prices:** 2.6%.

Transport: Railroad: Length: 26,033 mi. **Motor vehicles:** 45.4 mil pass. cars; 3.5 mil comm. vehicles. **Civil aviation:** 113.4 bil pass.-mi; 330 airports. **Chief ports:** Bremen, Bremerhaven, Duisburg, Hamburg, Karlsruhe, Lubeck, Rostock, Wilhemshaven.

Communications: TV sets: 581 per 1,000 pop. **Radios:** 948 per 1,000 pop. **Telephone lines:** 51.5 mil. **Daily newspaper circ.** (2004): 267.5 per 1,000 pop. **Internet:** 62.5 mil users.

Health: Life expect.: 76.1 male; 82.3 female. **Births** (per 1,000 pop.): 8.2. **Deaths** (per 1,000 pop.): 10.8. **Natural inc.:** –0.26%. **Infant mortality** (per 1,000 live births): 4. **HIV rate:** 0.1%.

Education: Compulsory: ages 6-18. **Literacy:** 99%.

Major intl. organizations: UN and all of its specialized agencies, EU, NATO, OECD, OSCE.

Embassy: 4645 Reservoir Rd. NW 20007; 298-4000.

Website: www.deutschland.de

Germany is a central European nation originally composed of numerous states, with a common language and traditions, that were united in one country in 1871. Germany was split into 2 countries from the end of WWII until 1990, when it was reunified.

History and government. Germanic tribes were defeated by Julius Caesar, 55 and 53 BCE, but Roman expansion north of the Rhine was stopped in 9 CE. Charlemagne, ruler of the Franks, consolidated Saxon, Bavarian, Rhenish, Frankish, and other lands; after him the eastern part became the German Empire. The Thirty Years' War, 1618-48, split Germany into small principalities and kingdoms. After Napoleon, Austria contended with Prussia for dominance, but lost the Seven Weeks' War to Prussia, 1866. Otto von Bismarck, Prussian chancellor, formed the North German Confederation, 1867.

In 1870 Bismarck maneuvered Napoleon III into declaring war. After the quick defeat of France, Bismarck formed the **German Empire** and on Jan. 18, 1871, in Versailles, proclaimed King Wilhelm I of Prussia German emperor (Deutscher kaiser).

The German Empire reached its peak before WWI in 1914, with 208,780 sq mi, plus a colonial empire. After that war Germany ceded Alsace-Lorraine to France; West Prussia and Posen (Poznan) province to Poland; part of Schleswig to Denmark; lost all colonies and ports of Memel and Danzig.

Republic of Germany, 1919-33, adopted the Weimar constitution; met reparation payments and elected Friedrich Ebert and Gen. Paul von Hindenburg presidents.

Third Reich, 1933-45, Adolf Hitler led the National Socialist German Workers' (Nazi) party after WWI. In 1923 he attempted to unseat the Bavarian government and was imprisoned. Pres. von Hindenburg named Hitler chancellor Jan. 30, 1933; on Aug. 3, 1934, the day after Hindenburg's death, the cabinet joined the offices of president and chancellor and made Hitler fuehrer (leader). Hitler abolished freedom of speech and assembly, and began a long series of persecutions climaxed by the murder of millions of Jews and others.

He repudiated the Versailles treaty and reparations agreements, remilitarized the Rhineland (1936), and annexed Austria (Anschluss, 1938). At Munich he made an agreement with Neville Chamberlain, British prime minister, which permitted Germany to annex part of Czechoslovakia. He signed a nonaggression treaty with the USSR, 1939, and declared war on Poland Sept. 1, 1939, precipitating WWII. With total defeat near, Hitler committed suicide in Berlin Apr. 1945. The victorious Allies voided all acts and annexations of Hitler's Reich.

Division of Germany. Germany was sectioned into 4 zones of occupation, administered by the Allied Powers (U.S., USSR, UK, and France). The USSR took control of many E German states. The territory E of the so-called Oder-Neisse line was assigned to, and later annexed by, Poland. Northern East Prussia (now Kaliningrad) was annexed by the USSR. Greater Berlin, within but not part of the Soviet zone, was administered by the 4 occupying powers under the Allied Command. In 1948 the USSR withdrew, established its single command in East Berlin, and cut off supplies. The Western Allies utilized a gigantic airlift to bring food to West Berlin, 1948-49.

In 1949, 2 separate German states were established; in May the zones administered by the Western Allies became West Germany; in Oct. the Soviet sector became East Germany. West Berlin was considered an enclave of West Germany, although its status was disputed by the Soviet bloc.

East Germany. The German Democratic Republic (East Germany) was proclaimed in the Soviet sector of Berlin Oct. 7, 1949. It was declared fully sovereign in 1954, but Soviet troops remained on grounds of security and the 4-power Potsdam agreement.

Coincident with the entrance of West Germany into the European defense community in 1952, the East German government decreed a prohibited zone 3 mi deep along its 600-mi border with West Germany and cut Berlin's telephone lines in two. Berlin was further divided by erection of a fortified wall in 1961, after over 3 mil East Germans had fled to the West.

East Germany suffered severe economic problems at least until the mid-1960s. Then a "new economic system" was introduced, easing central planning controls and allowing factories to make profits provided they were reinvested in operations or redistributed

to workers as bonuses. By the early 1970s, the economy of East Germany was highly industrialized, and the nation was credited with the highest standard of living among Warsaw Pact countries. But growth slowed in the late 1970s, because of shortages of natural resources and labor, and a huge debt to lenders in the West. Comparison with the lifestyle in the West caused many young people to emigrate.

The government firmly resisted following the USSR's policy of *glasnost*, but by Oct. 1989, was faced with nationwide demonstrations demanding reform. Pres. Erich Honecker, in office since 1976, was forced to resign Oct. 18. On Nov. 4, the border with Czechoslovakia was opened and permission granted for refugees to travel to the West. On Nov. 9, the East German government announced its decision to open the border with the West, signaling the end of the "Berlin Wall," which was the supreme emblem of the cold war. On Aug. 23, 1990, the East German parliament agreed to formal unification with West Germany; this occurred Oct. 3.

West Germany. The Federal Republic of Germany (West Germany) was proclaimed May 23, 1949, in Bonn. The occupying powers, the U.S., Britain, and France, restored civil status, Sept. 21. The Western Allies ended the state of war with Germany in 1951 (the U.S. resumed diplomatic relations July 2), while the USSR did so in 1955. The powers lifted controls, and the republic became fully independent May 5, 1955.

Dr. Konrad Adenauer, Christian Democrat, was made chancellor Sept. 15, 1949, and reelected 1953, 1957, 1961. Willy Brandt, heading a coalition of Social Democrats and Free Democrats, became chancellor Oct. 21, 1969, and pursued a policy of *Ostpolitik*, or rapprochement with East Germany and the USSR. Brandt resigned May 1974 because of a spy scandal. Terrorist acts on German soil in the 1970s included activities of the Baader-Meinhof gang and the murder of Israeli athletes by Palestinian commandos at the Olympic Games in Munich, Sept. 5, 1972.

Helmut Kohl became chancellor in 1982 and led Christian Democrats to victory in 1983 and 1987. In 1989, changes in the East German government and the opening of the Berlin Wall sparked talk of reunification of the 2 Germanys. In 1990, under Kohl's leadership, West Germany moved rapidly to reunite with East Germany.

A New Era. In May 1990, NATO ministers adopted a package of proposals on reunification, including the inclusion of the united Germany as a full member of NATO and the barring of the new Germany from having its own nuclear, chemical, or biological weapons. The merger of the 2 Germanys took place Oct. 3, and the first all-German elections since 1932 were held Dec. 2, with West German Chancellor Helmut Kohl confirmed as leader of the unified nation. Eastern Germany received over $1 trillion in public and private funds from western Germany between 1990 and 1995. In 1991, Berlin again became Germany's official capital; the Bundestag (parliament) and parts of the federal executive were relocated from Bonn to Berlin in 1999.

Unemployment hit a postwar high of 12.6% in Jan. 1998. The Kohl era ended after 16 years with the defeat of the Christian Democrats in parliamentary elections Sept. 27; Gerhard Schröder, of the Social Democratic Party, became chancellor. Germany contributed 8,500 troops to the NATO-led security force (KFOR) that entered Kosovo in June 1999.

Despite a stagnant economy, Schröder's coalition of Social Democrats and Greens retained a slim majority in the elections of Sept. 22, 2002. In early 2003, Germany worked with France and Russia to block the UN Security Council from endorsing the U.S.-led invasion of Iraq. When Schröder's party lost its stronghold of North Rhine-Westphalia in regional voting, May 22, 2005, Schröder called early elections for Sept. 18. The Christian Democrats, led by Angela Merkel, won a razor-thin plurality, and after prolonged negotiations she became chancellor Nov. 22, heading a "grand coalition" that included the Socialists.

Germany hosted the G-8 summit in June 2007 but was unable to persuade the U.S. to accept Merkel's plan for a mandatory 50% cut in global emissions of greenhouse gases by 2050. Authorities revealed Sept. 5, 2007, that they had foiled a terrorist bomb plot possibly targeting the U.S. Ramstein Air Base and Frankfurt Intl. Airport. Responding to the global recession, the government passed a 50 bil euro economic stimulus plan in early 2009. Polls showed rising opposition among German voters to the continued deployment of 4,200 German troops with NATO forces in Afghanistan.

Merkel led a center-right coalition to victory in national elections Sept. 27, 2009.

Helgoland, an island of 130 acres in the North Sea, was taken from Denmark by a British Naval Force in 1807 and later ceded to Germany to become part of Schleswig-Holstein province in return for rights in East Africa. The heavily fortified island was surrendered to UK, May 23, 1945, demilitarized in 1947, and returned to West Germany, Mar. 1, 1952. It is a free port.

Ghana

Republic of Ghana

People: Population: 23,832,495. **Age distrib.** (%): <15: 37.3; 65+: 3.6. **Pop. density:** 267.3 per sq mi, 103.2 per sq km. **Urban:** 47.8%. **Ethnic groups:** Akan 45%, Mole-Dagbon 15%, Ewe 12%. **Principal languages:** English (official), Asante, Ewe, Fante. **Chief religions:** Christian (incl. Pentecostal/Charismatic, Protestant, Catholic) 69%, Muslim 16%, traditional 9%, none 6%.

Geography: Total area: 92,456 sq mi, 239,460 sq km; **Land area:** 89,166 sq mi, 230,940 sq km. **Location:** On S coast of W Africa. **Neighbors:** Côte d'Ivoire on W, Burkina Faso on N, Togo on E. **Topography:** Mostly low fertile plains and scrubland, cut by rivers and the artificial Lake Volta. **Capital:** Accra, 2,121,000. **Cities (urban aggr.):** Kumasi, 1,646,000.

Government: Type: Republic. **Head of state and gov.:** Pres. John Atta Mills; b. July 21, 1944; in office: Jan. 7, 2009. **Local divisions:** 10 regions. **Defense budget:** $104 mil. **Active troops:** 13,500.

Economy: Industries: mining, lumbering, light mfg., aluminum smelting, food proc. **Chief crops:** cocoa, rice, cassava, peanuts, corn, shea nuts, bananas. **Natural resources:** gold, timber, industrial diamonds, bauxite, mang., fish, rubber, hydropower. **Crude oil reserves:** 15 mil bbls. **Arable land:** 18%. **Livestock:** cattle: 1.4 mil; chickens: 31 mil; goats: 3.7 mil; pigs: 239,000; sheep: 3.4 mil. **Fish catch:** 321,875 metric tons. **Electricity prod.:** 8.2 bil kWh. **Labor force** (2005 est.): agric. 56%, industry 15%, services 29%.

Finance: Monetary unit: Cedi (GHS) (Oct. 2009: 1.45 = $1 U.S.). **GDP:** $34.2 bil; **per capita GDP:** $1,500; **GDP growth:** 7.3%. **Imports:** $10.2 bil; China 15.9%, Nigeria 15.8%, U.S. 5.9%, France 4.7%, UK 4.7%. **Exports:** $5.2 bil; Netherlands 15.3%, UK 9.1%, France 6.5%, U.S. 5.8%. **Tourism:** NA. **Budget:** $5.5 bil. **Intl. reserves less gold** (2006): $1.39 bil. **Gold:** NA. **Consumer prices:** 16.5.

Transport: Railroad: Length: 588 mi. **Motor vehicles:** 92,000 pass. cars; 124,000 comm. vehicles. **Civil aviation:** 225.6 mil pass.-mi; 7 airports. **Chief port:** Tema.

Communications: TV sets: 115 per 1,000 pop. **Radios:** 680 per 1,000 pop. **Telephone lines:** 143,900. **Internet:** 997,000 users.

Health: Life expect.: 58.6 male; 60.4 female. **Births** (per 1,000 pop.): 29.2. **Deaths** (per 1,000 pop.): 9.4. **Natural inc.:** 1.98%. **Infant mortality** (per 1,000 live births): 52.3. **HIV rate:** 1.9%.

Education: Compulsory: ages 6-14. **Literacy:** 65%.

Major intl. organizations: UN and all of its specialized agencies, the Commonwealth, AU.

Embassy: 3512 International Dr. NW 20008; 686-4520.

Website: www.oop.gov.gh

Named for an African empire along the Niger River, 400-1240 CE, Ghana was ruled by Britain for 113 years as the Gold Coast. The UN in 1956 approved merger with the British Togoland trust territory. Independence came Mar. 6, 1957, and republic status within the Commonwealth in 1960.

Pres. Kwame Nkrumah built hospitals and schools, promoted development projects like the Volta R. hydroelectric and aluminum plants, but ran the country into debt, jailed opponents, and was accused of corruption. A 1964 referendum gave Nkrumah dictatorial powers and set up a one-party socialist state. Nkrumah was overthrown in 1966 by a police-army coup, which expelled Chinese and East German teachers and technicians. Elections were held in 1969, but 4 further coups occurred in 1972, 1978, 1979, and 1981. The 1979 and 1981 coups, led by Flight Lieut. Jerry Rawlings, were followed by suspension of the constitution and banning of political parties. A new constitution, allowing multiparty politics, was approved in Apr. 1992.

In Feb. 1993 more than 1,000 people were killed in ethnic clashes in northern Ghana. Rawlings won the presidential election of Dec. 7, 1996. Kofi Annan, a career UN diplomat from Ghana, served as UN secretary general, 1997-2006.

Opposition leader John Agyekum Kufuor won a runoff vote Dec. 28, 2000, and was sworn in Jan. 7, 2001, marking Ghana's first peaceful transfer of power from one elected president to another. He was reelected Dec. 7, 2004. A major offshore oil find of up to 600 mil barrels was announced in June 2007.

John Atta Mills, a tax law expert who had contended unsuccessfully for the presidency in 2000 and 2004, narrowly defeated the ruling party candidate, Nana Akufo-Addo, in a runoff election Dec. 28, 2008. Pres. Obama chose Ghana for his first official visit to sub-Saharan Africa, July 10-11, 2009.

Greece

Hellenic Republic

People: Population: 10,737,428. **Age distrib.** (%): <15: 14.3; 65+: 19.2. **Pop. density:** 212.6 per sq mi, 82.1 per sq km. **Urban:** 60.4%. **Ethnic groups:** Greek (citizenship) 93%, other (foreign citizenship) 7%. (Greece does not collect ethnicity data.) **Principal language:** Greek (official). **Chief religion:** Greek Orthodox 98%.

Geography: Total area: 50,942 sq mi, 131,940 sq km; **Land area:** 50,502 sq mi, 130,800 sq km. **Location:** Occupies S end of Balkan Peninsula in SE Europe. **Neighbors:** Albania, Macedonia,

Bulgaria on N; Turkey on E. **Topography:** About three-quarters is nonarable, with mountains in all areas. Pindus Mts. run through the country N to S. The heavily indented coastline is 9,385 mi long. Of over 2,000 islands, only 169 are inhabited, among them Crete, Rhodes, Milos, Kerkira (Corfu), Chios, Lesbos, Samos, Euboea, Delos, Mykonos. **Capital:** Athens, 3,242,000. **Cities (urban aggr.):** Thessaloniki, 828,000.

Government: Type: Parliamentary republic. **Head of state:** Pres. Karolos Papoulias; b. June 4, 1929; in office: Mar. 12, 2005. **Head of gov.:** Prime Min. George A. Papandreou; b. June 16, 1952; in office: Oct. 6, 2009. **Local divisions:** 13 regions comprising 51 prefectures. **Defense budget:** $8.7 bil. **Active troops:** 156,600.

Economy: Industries: tourism, food & tobacco proc., textiles, chemicals, metal products. **Chief crops:** wheat, corn, barley, sugar beets, olives, tomatoes, wine, tobacco, potatoes. **Natural resources:** lignite, oil, iron ore, bauxite, lead, zinc, nickel, magnesite. **Crude oil reserves:** 10 mil bbls. **Arable land:** 20%. **Livestock:** cattle: 628,904; chickens: 31.2 mil; goats: 5.4 mil; pigs: 902,305; sheep: 8.8 mil. **Fish catch:** 209,356 metric tons. **Electricity prod.:** 56.9 bil kWh. **Labor force** (2005 est.): agric. 12.4%, industry 22.4%, services 65.1%.

Finance: Monetary unit: Euro (EUR) (Oct. 2009: 0.68 = $1 U.S.). **GDP:** $343 bil; **per capita GDP:** $32,000; **GDP growth:** 2.9%. **Imports:** $93.9 bil; Germany 13.3%, Italy 12.8%, China 6.2%, France 5.6%, Netherlands 5.1%, Russia 4.7%. **Exports:** $29.1 bil; Italy 11.5%, Germany 10.5%, Bulgaria 7%, Cyprus 6.2%, U.S. 5%, UK 4.7%, Romania 4.4%. **Tourism:** $15.5 bil. **Budget:** $120.6 bil. **Intl. reserves less gold:** $223 mil. **Gold:** 3.62 mil oz t. **Consumer prices:** 4.1%.

Transport: Railroad: Length: 1,583 mi. **Motor vehicles:** 4.3 mil pass. cars; 1.2 mil comm. vehicles. **Civil aviation:** 5.8 bil pass.-mi; 67 airports. **Chief ports:** Agioitheodoroi, Aspropyrgos, Pachi, Piraeus, Thessaloníki.

Communications: TV sets: 480 per 1,000 pop. **Radios:** 475 per 1,000 pop. **Telephone lines:** 6 mil. **Internet:** 3.6 mil users.

Health: Life expect.: 77 male; 82.2 female. **Births** (per 1,000 pop.): 9.5. **Deaths** (per 1,000 pop.): 10.4. **Natural inc.:** −0.09%. **Infant mortality** (per 1,000 live births): 5.2. **HIV rate:** 0.2%.

Education: Compulsory: ages 6-14. **Literacy:** 97.1%.

Major intl. organizations: UN (FAO, IBRD, ILO, IMF, IMO, WHO, WTO), EU, NATO, OECD, OSCE.

Embassy: 2217 Massachusetts Ave. NW 20008; 939-1306.

Website: www.primeminister.gr

The achievements of ancient Greece in art, architecture, science, mathematics, philosophy, drama, literature, and democracy became legacies for succeeding ages. Greece reached the height of its glory and power, particularly in the Athenian city-state, in the 5th cent. BCE. Greece fell under Roman rule in the 2nd and 1st centuries BCE. In the 4th cent. CE it became part of the Byzantine Empire and, after the fall of Constantinople to the Turks in 1453, part of the Ottoman Empire.

Greece won its war of independence from Turkey 1821-29, and became a kingdom. A republic was established 1924; the monarchy was restored, 1935. In Oct. 1940, Greece rejected an ultimatum from Italy, but the country was defeated and occupied by Germans, Italians, and Bulgarians. By the end of 1944 the invaders withdrew. Communist resistance forces were overcome by Royalist and British troops. A plebiscite again restored the monarchy.

Communists waged guerrilla war 1947-49 against the government but were defeated with the aid of the U.S. A period of reconstruction and rapid development followed, mainly with conservative governments under Premier Constantine Karamanlis. The Center Union, led by George Papandreou, won elections in 1963 and 1964, but King Constantine, who acceded in 1964, forced Papandreou to resign. A period of political maneuvers ended in the military takeover of Apr. 21, 1967, by Col. George Papadopoulos. King Constantine tried to reverse the consolidation of the harsh dictatorship Dec. 13, 1967, but failed and fled to Italy. Papadopoulos was ousted Nov. 25, 1973.

Greek army officers serving in the National Guard of Cyprus staged a coup on the island July 15, 1974. Turkey invaded Cyprus a week later, precipitating the collapse of the Greek junta, which was implicated in the Cyprus coup. Democratic government returned, and in 1975 the monarchy was abolished.

The 1981 electoral victory of the Panhellenic Socialist Movement (Pasok) of Andreas Papandreou brought substantial changes in Greece's internal and external policies. A scandal centered on George Kostokas, a banker and publisher, led to the arrest or investigation of leading Socialists, implicated Papandreou, and contributed to the defeat of the Socialists at the polls in 1989. However, Papandreou, who was narrowly acquitted Jan. 1992 of corruption charges, led the Socialists to a comeback victory in general elections Oct. 10, 1993.

Tensions between Greece and the Former Yugoslav Republic of Macedonia eased when the 2 countries agreed to normalize relations Sept. 13, 1995. The ailing Papandreou was replaced as prime minister by Costas Simitis, Jan. 18, 1996. Simitis led the Socialists to victory in the election of Sept. 22.

An earthquake that shook Athens Sept. 7, 1999, killed at least 143 people and left more than 60,000 homeless. The Socialists retained power by a narrow margin in the elections of Apr. 9, 2000. Police in 2002 cracked down on the November 17 terrorist movement, blamed for 23 killings since the mid-1970s.

The conservative New Democracy Party won parliamentary elections, Mar. 7, 2004, and Konstantinos (Costas) Karamanlis became prime minister. Athens hosted the Olympic Summer Games, Aug. 13-29, 2004. Rampant wildfires, Aug. 2007, left at least 65 people dead and caused over $1.6 bil in damage. Karamanlis kept his office after early elections Sept. 16. Karamanlis, Jan. 23-25, 2008, became the first Greek government leader in 49 years to pay an official visit to Turkey. Beset by scandals and an ailing economy, he called early elections for Oct. 4, 2009.

Grenada

People: Population: 90,739. **Age distrib.** (%): <15: 32; 65+: 2.8. **Pop. density:** 683.2 per sq mi, 263.8 per sq km. **Urban:** 30.6%. **Ethnic groups:** Black 82%, mixed black & European 13%. **Principal languages:** English (official), French patois. **Chief religions:** Roman Catholic 53%, Anglican 14%, other Protestant 33%.

Geography: Total area: 133 sq mi, 344 sq km; **Land area:** 133 sq mi, 344 sq km. **Location:** In Caribbean, 90 mi N of Venezuela. **Neighbors:** Venezuela, Trinidad & Tobago to S; St. Vincent & the Grenadines to N. **Topography:** Main island is mountainous; country includes Carriacou and Petit Martinique isls. **Capital:** St. George's, 32,000.

Government: Type: Parliamentary democracy. **Head of state:** Queen Elizabeth II, represented by Gov.-Gen. Sir Carlyle Glean; b. Feb. 11, 1932; in office: Nov. 27, 2008. **Head of gov.:** Prime Min. Tillman Thomas; b. June 13, 1945; in office: July 9, 2008. **Local divisions:** 6 parishes, 1 dependency. **Defense budget/Active troops:** NA.

Economy: Industries: food & beverages, textiles, light assembly operations, tourism, constr. **Chief crops:** bananas, cocoa, nutmeg, mace, citrus, avocados. **Natural resources:** timber, tropical fruit. **Arable land:** 6%. **Livestock:** cattle: 4,450; chickens: 270,000; goats: 7,200; pigs: 2,650; sheep: 13,200. **Fish catch:** 2,407 metric tons. **Electricity prod.:** 167 mil kWh. **Labor force** (1999 est.): agric. 24%, industry 14%, services 62%.

Finance: Monetary unit: East Caribbean Dollar (XCD) (Oct. 2009: 2.70 = $1 U.S.). **GDP:** $1.2 bil; **per capita GDP:** $12,900; **GDP growth:** 0.3%. **Imports** (2006): $343 mil; Trinidad and Tobago 40.1%, U.S. 22.8%, Barbados 3.4%. **Exports** (2006): $38 mil; Jamaica 92.2%, St. Lucia 1.3%, U.S. 0.9%. **Tourism:** $110 mil. **Budget** (1997): $102.1 mil. **Intl. reserves less gold:** $68 mil. **Gold:** NA. **Consumer prices:** 8.2%.

Transport: Motor vehicles: 15,800 pass. cars; 4,200 comm. vehicles. **Civil aviation:** 3 airports. **Chief port:** Saint George's. **Communications: TV sets:** 376 per 1,000 pop. **Radios:** 613 per 1,000 pop. **Telephone lines:** 28,600. **Internet:** 24,000 users. **Health: Life expect.:** 63.7 male; 67.5 female. **Births** (per 1,000 pop.): 21.6. **Deaths** (per 1,000 pop.): 6.3. **Natural inc.:** 1.53%. **Infant mortality** (per 1,000 live births): 13.6. **HIV rate:** NA. **Education:** Compulsory: ages 5-16. **Literacy:** 96%. **Major intl. organizations:** UN (FAO, IBRD, ILO, IMF, IMO, WHO, WTO), Caricom, the Commonwealth, OAS, OECS. **Embassy:** 1701 New Hampshire Ave. NW 20009; 265-2561. **Website:** www.gov.gd

Columbus sighted Grenada in 1498. First European settlers were French, 1650. The island was held alternately by France and England until final British occupation, 1784. Grenada became fully independent Feb. 7, 1974, during a general strike.

On Oct. 14, 1983, a military coup ousted Prime Min. Maurice Bishop, who was put under house arrest, later freed by supporters, rearrested, and, finally, on Oct. 19, executed. U.S. forces, with a token force from 6 area nations, invaded Grenada, Oct. 25. Resistance from the Grenadian army and Cuban advisors was quickly overcome as most people welcomed the invading forces. U.S. troops left Grenada in June 1985.

Hurricane Ivan slammed into Grenada, Sept. 7, 2004, killing 39 people and damaging an estimated 90% of the buildings on the island. Tillman Thomas of the National Democratic Congress became prime minister after parliamentary elections July 8, 2008.

Guatemala
Republic of Guatemala

People: Population: 13,276,517. **Age distrib.** (%): <15: 39.4; 65+: 3.8. **Pop. density:** 317.1 per sq mi, 122.4 per sq km. **Urban:** 47.2%. **Ethnic groups:** Mestizo (mixed Amerindian-Spanish) & European 59%, K'iche 9%, Kaqchikel 8%, Mam 8%. **Principal languages:** Spanish, Amerindian languages (23 officially recognized, incl. Quiche, Cakchiquel, Kekchi, Mam, Garifuna, & Xinca). **Chief religions:** Roman Catholic, Protestant, indigenous Mayan beliefs.

Geography: Total area: 42,043 sq mi, 108,890 sq km; **Land area:** 41,865 sq mi, 108,430 sq km. **Location:** In Central America. **Neighbors:** Mexico on N and W, El Salvador on S, Honduras and Belize on E. **Topography:** The central highland and mountain areas are bordered by the narrow Pacific coast and lowlands and fertile river valleys on the Caribbean. Numerous volcanoes in S, more than half a dozen over 11,000 ft. **Capital:** Guatemala City, 1,024,000.

Government: Type: Republic. **Head of state and gov.:** Pres. Álvaro Colom Caballeros; b. June 15, 1951; in office: Jan. 14, 2008. **Local divisions:** 22 departments. **Defense budget:** $166 mil. **Active troops:** 15,500.

Economy: Industries: sugar, textiles& clothing, furniture, chemicals, oil, metals, rubber, tourism. **Chief crops:** sugarcane, corn, bananas, coffee, beans, cardamom. **Natural resources:** oil, nickel, rare woods, fish, chicle, hydropower. **Crude oil reserves:** 83.1 mil bbls. **Arable land:** 13%. **Livestock:** cattle: 3.3 mil; chickens: 31.4 mil; goats: 100,867; pigs: 782,000; sheep: 265,000. **Fish catch:** 33,987 metric tons. **Electricity prod.:** 7.6 bil kWh. **Labor force** (1999 est.): agric. 50%, industry 15%, services 35%.

Finance: Monetary unit: Quetzal (GTQ) (Oct. 2009: 8.32 = $1 U.S.). **GDP:** $68.6 bil; **per capita GDP:** $5,300; **GDP growth:** 4%. **Imports:** $13.4 bil; U.S. 35.7%, Mexico 10%, China 7.3%, El Salvador 4.7%, Costa Rica 4.1%. **Exports:** $7.9 bil; U.S. 41.7%, El Salvador 9.5%, Honduras 8.5%, Mexico 6.4%, Costa Rica 4.4%. **Tourism:** $1.1 bil. **Budget:** $4.9 bil. **Intl. reserves less gold:** $2.9 bil. **Gold:** 220,000 oz t. **Consumer prices:** 12.6%.

Transport: Railroad: Length: 206 mi. **Motor vehicles:** 1.3 mil pass. cars and comm. vehicles. **Civil aviation:** 212.5 mil pass.-mi; 13 airports. **Chief ports:** Puerto Quetzal, Santo Tomas de Castilla. **Communications: TV sets:** 61 per 1,000 pop. **Radios:** 79 per 1,000 pop. **Telephone lines:** 1.4 mil. **Internet:** 2 mil users. **Health: Life expect.:** 68.2 male; 71.9 female. **Births** (per 1,000 pop.): 28.6. **Deaths** (per 1,000 pop.): 5.2. **Natural inc.:** 2.34%. **Infant mortality** (per 1,000 live births): 28.8. **HIV rate:** 0.8%. **Education:** Compulsory: ages 7-15. **Literacy:** 73.2%. **Major intl. organizations:** UN (FAO, IBRD, ILO, IMF, IMO, WHO, WTO), OAS. **Embassy:** 2220 R St. NW 20008; 745-4952. **Website:** www.guatemala.gob.gt

A Mayan Indian empire flourished in what is today Guatemala for over 1,000 years before Spaniards came. Guatemala was a Spanish colony 1524-1821. A republic was established in 1839.

The U.S. intervened in Guatemala in 1954 when the Central Intelligence Agency engineered the overthrow of elected Pres. Jacobo Árbenz Guzmán, a left-wing reformer. Since then, the country has experienced a variety of military and civilian governments and periods of insurgency, repression, and civil war.

Dissident army officers seized power Mar. 23, 1982, denouncing a presidential election as fraudulent and pledging to restore "authentic democracy" to the nation. Political violence caused large numbers of Guatemalans to seek refuge in Mexico. Another military coup occurred Oct. 8, 1983. The nation returned to civilian rule in 1986.

On Sept. 19, 1996, the Guatemalan government and leftist rebels approved a peace accord; the final agreement was signed Dec. 29. During more than 35 years of armed conflict, some 200,000 people were killed or "disappeared" (and are presumed dead); most of these casualties were attributed to the government and its paramilitary allies. U.S. Pres. Bill Clinton, on a visit to Guatemala Mar. 10, 1999, apologized for aid the U.S. had given to forces which he said "engaged in violence and widespread repression."

Drought and weak export prices during 2001-02 worsened the plight of Guatemala's poor, who make up 80% of the population. Oscar Berger Perdomo, the conservative former mayor of Guatemala City, won a presidential runoff election Dec. 28, 2003. Floods and mudslides from Tropical Storm Stan, Oct. 2005, killed at least 669 people; another 844 were missing and presumed dead.

Three Salvadoran lawmakers and their driver were murdered Feb. 19, 2007, while on an official visit to Guatemala; 4 Guatemalan police officers charged with the crime were killed Feb. 25 in the maximum-security prison where they were being held. After a campaign marred by violence, Álvaro Colom Caballeros, a businessman who pledged to fight poverty, won a presidential runoff election Nov. 4, 2007, and took office Jan. 14, 2008. He declared a "state of public calamity" Sept. 8, 2009, to deal with severe food shortages in the "dry corridor" of eastern and central Guatemala.

Guinea
Republic of Guinea

People: Population: 10,057,975. **Age distrib.** (%): <15: 42.8; 65+: 3.5. **Pop. density:** 106 per sq mi, 40.9 per sq km. **Urban:** 33%. **Ethnic groups:** Peuhl 40%, Malinke 30%, Soussou 20%, smaller ethnic groups 10%. **Principal languages:** French (official), each ethnic group's language. **Chief religions:** Muslim 85%, Christian 8%, indigenous beliefs 7%.

Geography: Total area: 94,926 sq mi, 245,857 sq km; **Land area:** 94,926 sq mi, 245,857 sq km. **Location:** On Atlantic coast of W Africa. **Neighbors:** Guinea-Bissau, Senegal, Mali on N; Côte d'Ivoire on E; Liberia, Sierra Leone on S. **Topography:** A narrow coastal belt leads to mountainous middle region, source of the Gambia, Senegal, and Niger rivers. Upper Guinea, farther inland, is cooler upland. The SE is forested. **Capital:** Conakry, 1,494,000.

Government: Type: In transition. **Head of state:** Capt. Moussa Dadis Camara; b. 1964; in office: Dec. 24, 2008. **Head of gov.:** Prime Min. Kabiné Komara; b. 1950; in office: Jan. 2, 2009. **Local divisions:** 33 prefectures, 1 special zone. **Defense budget:** $52 mil. **Active troops:** 12,300.

Economy: Industries: bauxite, gold, diamonds, iron, aluminum refining, light mfg. **Chief crops:** rice, coffee, pineapples, palm kernels, cassava, bananas, sweet potatoes. **Natural resources:** bauxite, iron ore, diamonds, gold, uranium, hydropower, fish, salt. **Arable land:** 4%. **Livestock:** cattle: 4.2 mil; chickens: 17.8 mil; goats: 1.6 mil; pigs: 82,360; sheep: 1.3 mil. **Fish catch** (est.): 100,000 metric tons. **Electricity prod.:** 800 mil kWh. **Labor force** (2006 est.): agric. 76%, industry & services 24%.

Finance: Monetary unit: Franc (GNF) (Oct. 2009: 5,020.00 = $1 U.S.). **GDP:** $10.6 bil; **per capita GDP:** $1,100; **GDP growth:** 4.5%. **Imports:** $1.4 bil; China 10.3%, France 7.8%, Netherlands 7.6%. **Exports:** $1.4 bil; Spain 11.6%, Russia 11%, Ukraine 9.7%, Germany 7.7%, S. Korea 7.2%, U.S. 6.7%, China 5.6%, Ireland 4.8%, France 4.8%. **Tourism:** NA. **Budget:** $802.3 mil. **Intl. reserves less gold** (2005): $67 mil. **Gold:** NA. **Consumer prices:** NA.

Transport: Railroad: Length: 736 mi. **Civil aviation:** 58.4 mil pass.-mi; 5 airports. **Chief ports:** Conakry, Kamsar.

Communications: TV sets: 47 per 1,000 pop. **Radios:** 52 per 1,000 pop. **Telephone lines:** 50,000. **Internet:** 90,000 users.

Health: Life expect.: 55.1 male; 58.1 female. **Births** (per 1,000 pop.): 37.8. **Deaths** (per 1,000 pop.): 11.3. **Natural inc.:** 2.65%. **Infant mortality** (per 1,000 live births): 67.4. **HIV rate:** 1.6%.

Education: Compulsory: ages 7-12. **Literacy:** 29.5%.

Major intl. organizations: UN and most of its specialized agencies, AU.

Embassy: 2112 Leroy Pl. NW 20008; 906-4300.

Website: www.state.gov/p/af/ci/gv/

Guinea, a French colony, attained independence Oct. 2, 1958. Sékou Touré, Guinea's first president (1958-84), turned to Communist nations for support and set up a one-party state. Thousands of opponents were jailed in the 1970s, after an unsuccessful Portuguese invasion. Many were tortured and killed.

The military took control in a bloodless coup after the Mar. 1984 death of Touré. A new constitution was approved in 1991, but movement toward democracy was slow. When presidential elections were finally held, in Dec. 1993, the incumbent, Gen. Lansana Conté, was the official winner; outside monitors called the elections flawed. Conté suppressed an army mutiny in Conakry, Feb. 2-3, 1996, and won reelection in Dec. 1998.

Fighting in early 2001 along the border with Liberia and Sierra Leone created a refugee crisis in Guinea; voluntary repatriation of more than 51,000 Liberian refugees was largely completed in 2007. Major opposition parties boycotted the presidential election Dec. 21, 2003, in which the ailing Conté won 95.6% of the vote. More than 120 died in strikes and protests Jan.-Feb. 2007, until Conté agreed to name a new prime min. from a list approved by union leaders; protests followed his ouster by Conté in May 2008. After Conté's death Dec. 22, 2008, a military junta took power, calling itself the National Council for Democracy and Development. More than 150 people were reportedly killed Sept. 28, 2009, when Guinean troops fired into a crowd of about 50,000 antigovernment protesters in Conakry.

Guinea-Bissau
Republic of Guinea-Bissau

People: Population: 1,533,964. **Age distrib.** (%): <15: 40.8; 65+: 3.1. **Pop. density:** 141.9 per sq mi, 54.8 per sq km. **Urban:** 29.6%. **Ethnic groups:** African 99% (incl. Balanta 30%, Fula 20%, Manjaca 14%, Mandinga 13%). **Principal languages:** Portuguese (official), Crioulo, African languages. **Chief religions:** Indigenous beliefs 50%, Muslim 45%, Christian 5%.

Geography: Total area: 13,946 sq mi, 36,120 sq km; **Land area:** 10,811 sq mi, 28,000 sq km. **Location:** On Atlantic coast of W Africa. **Neighbors:** Senegal on N, Guinea on E and S. **Topography:** A swampy coastal plain covers most of country; to E is a low savanna region. **Capital:** Bissau, 330,000.

Government: Type: Republic. **Head of state:** Pres. Malam Bacai Sanhá; b. May 5, 1947; in office; Sept. 8, 2009. **Head of gov.:** Carlos Gomes Júnior; b. Dec. 19, 1949; in office: Jan. 2, 2009. **Local divisions:** 9 regions. **Defense budget:** $15 mil. **Active troops:** 6,458.

Economy: Industries: agric. products proc., beer, soft drinks. **Chief crops:** rice, corn, beans, cassava, cashew nuts, peanuts, palm kernels, cotton. **Natural resources:** fish, timber, phosphates, bauxite, clay, granite, limestone, unexploited deposits of oil. **Arable land:** 8%. **Livestock:** cattle: 574,060; chickens: 1.7 mil; goats: 370,730; pigs: 2.3 mil; sheep: 358,160. **Fish catch** (est.): 6,200 metric tons. **Electricity prod.:** 6 mil kWh. **Labor force** (2000 est.): agric. 82%, industry & services 18%.

Finance: Monetary unit: CFA BCEAO Franc (XOF) (Oct. 2009: 444.97 = $1 U.S.). **GDP:** $904.2 mil; **per capita GDP:** $600; **GDP growth:** 3.2%. **Imports** (2006): $200 mil; Portugal 24.6%,

Senegal 17.3%, Pakistan 4.8%, France 4.6%, Cuba 4%. **Exports** (2006): $133 mil; India 74.8%, Nigeria 20.5%, Pakistan 0.7%. **Tourism:** NA. **Budget:** NA. **Intl. reserves less gold:** $81 mil. **Gold:** NA. **Consumer prices:** 10.5%.

Transport: Civil aviations: 6.2 mil pass.-mi; 2 airports. **Chief ports:** Bissau, Buba, Cacheu, Farim.

Communications: Radios: 43 per 1,000 pop. **Telephone lines:** 4,600. **Internet:** 37,100 users.

Health: Life expect.: 45.7 male; 49.4 female. **Births** (per 1,000 pop.): 36.4. **Deaths** (per 1,000 pop.): 16.1. **Natural inc.:** 2.04%. **Infant mortality** (per 1,000 live births): 101.6. **HIV rate:** 1.8%.

Education: Compulsory: ages 7-12. **Literacy:** 64.6%.

Major intl. organizations: UN (FAO, IBRD, ILO, IMF, IMO, WHO, WTO), AU.

Permanent UN Mission: 800 Second Ave., Ste. 400F, New York, NY 10017; (917) 770-5598.

Website: www.state.gov/p/af/ci/pu/

Portuguese mariners explored the area in the mid-15th cent.; the slave trade flourished in the 17th and 18th centuries, and colonization began in the 19th.

Beginning in the 1960s, an independence movement waged a guerrilla war and formed a government in the interior that had international support. Independence came Sept. 10, 1974, after the Portuguese regime was overthrown.

A Nov. 1980 coup gave army chief João Bernardo Vieira absolute power. Vieira eventually initiated political liberalization; multiparty elections were held July 3, 1994. An army uprising June 7, 1998, triggered a civil war, with Senegal and Guinea aiding the Vieira regime. After a peace accord signed on Nov. 2 broke down, rebel troops ousted Vieira on May 7, 1999. Elections Nov. 28-29, 1999, and Jan. 16, 2000, brought a return of civilian rule.

Top military officers staged an apparently bloodless coup Sept. 14, 2003. Vieira won a presidential runoff election, July 24, 2005, and returned to power Oct. 1. Gen. Batista Tagme Na Waie, the nation's defense chief, was killed by a bomb Mar. 1, 2009; less than a day later, a group of soldiers murdered Vieira in his presidential palace. Political violence continued as the June 28 presidential election approached; the ruling party candidate, Malam Bacai Sanhá, won a runoff vote July 26 and took office Sept. 8. In recent years, Guinea-Bissau has become an important transit point for cocaine trafficking from Colombia to Europe.

Guyana
Co-operative Republic of Guyana

People: Population: 772,298. **Age distrib.** (%): <15: 25.7; 65+: 5.5. **Pop. density:** 10.2 per sq mi, 3.9 per sq km. **Urban:** 28.2%. **Ethnic groups:** East Indian 44%, black (African) 30%, mixed 17%, Amerindian 9%. **Principal languages:** English, Amerindian dialects, Creole, Caribbean Hindustani, Urdu. **Chief religions:** Hindu 28%, Pentecostal 17%, Roman Catholic 8%, Muslim 7%, Anglican 7%, Seventh-Day Adventist 5%.

Geography: Total area: 83,000 sq mi, 214,970 sq km; **Land area:** 76,004 sq mi, 196,850 sq km. **Location:** On N coast of S. America. **Neighbors:** Venezuela on W, Brazil on S, Suriname on E. **Topography:** Dense tropical forests cover much of land, although flat coastal area up to 40 mi wide, where 90% of the population lives, provides rich alluvial soil for agriculture. A grassy savanna divides the 2 zones. **Capital:** Georgetown, 133,000.

Government: Type: Republic. **Head of state:** Pres. Bharrat Jagdeo; b. Jan. 23, 1964; in office: Aug. 11, 1999. **Head of gov.:** Prime Min. Samuel Hinds; b. Dec. 27, 1943; in office: Dec. 22, 1997. **Local divisions:** 10 regions. **Defense budget:** NA. **Active troops:** 1,100.

Economy: Industries: bauxite, sugar, rice milling, timber, textiles, gold mining. **Chief crops:** sugarcane, rice, shrimp, fish, vegetable oils. **Natural resources:** bauxite, gold, diamonds, hardwood timber, shrimp, fish. **Arable land:** 2%. **Livestock:** cattle: 110,000; chickens: 21.7 mil; goats: 79,000; pigs: 152,791; sheep: 130,000. **Fish catch:** 48,100 metric tons. **Electricity prod.:** 901 mil kWh. **Labor force:** NA.

Finance: Monetary unit: Dollar (GYD) (Oct. 2009: 208.33 = $1 U.S.). **GDP:** $3 bil; **per capita GDP:** $3,800; **GDP growth:** 3%. **Imports:** $1.3 bil; U.S. 23.7%, Trinidad and Tobago 22.5%, Finland 7.8%, Cuba 6.2%, China 5.2%. **Exports:** $800 mil; Canada 21.6%, U.S. 15.8%, UK 12.7%, Netherlands 7.5%, Portugal 4.9%, Trinidad and Tobago 4.9%. **Tourism:** NA. **Budget:** $531.2 mil. **Intl. reserves less gold:** $231 mil. **Gold:** NA. **Consumer prices:** 8.1%.

Transport: Motor vehicles: 61,300 pass. cars; 15,500 comm. vehicles. **Civil aviation:** 108.7 mil pass.-mi; 10 airports. **Chief port:** Georgetown.

Communications: TV sets: 70 per 1,000 pop. **Radios:** 468 per 1,000 pop. **Telephone lines:** 125,000. **Daily newspaper circ.** (2000): 77.3 per 1,000 pop. **Internet:** 205,000 users.

Health: Life expect.: 63.8 male; 69.2 female. **Births** (per 1,000 pop.): 17.9. **Deaths** (per 1,000 pop.): 8.3. **Natural inc.:** 0.96%. **Infant mortality** (per 1,000 live births): 30.4. **HIV rate:** 2.5%.

Education: Compulsory: ages 6-15. **Literacy:** 98.8%.

Major intl. organizations: UN (FAO, IBRD, ILO, IMF, IMO, WHO, WTO), Caricom, the Commonwealth, OAS.

Embassy: 2490 Tracy Pl. NW 20008; 265-6900.

Website: www.gina.gov.gy

Guyana became a Dutch possession in the 17th cent., but sovereignty passed to Britain in 1815. Indentured servants from India soon outnumbered African slaves. Guyana became independent May 26, 1966.

The Port Kaituma ambush of U.S. Rep. Leo J. Ryan and others investigating mistreatment of American followers of the Rev. Jim Jones's People's Temple cult triggered a mass suicide-execution of 911 cultists at Jonestown in the jungle, Nov. 18, 1978.

The People's National Congress, the party in power since Guyana became independent, was voted out of office with the election of Cheddi Jagan in Oct. 1992. When Pres. Jagan died Mar. 6, 1997, Prime Min. Samuel Hinds succeeded him. Jagan's widow, Janet, became prime min. Mar. 17. She won the presidency in a disputed election Dec. 15. She resigned because of ill health Aug. 11, 1999, and was succeeded by Bharrat Jagdeo, then 35, who became the youngest head of state in the Americas. He won re-election Mar. 19, 2001, and Aug. 28, 2006.

Floods from torrential rains, Jan. 2005, affected about 40% of the population. Gunmen in Georgetown killed Agric. Min. Satyadeow Sawh and 2 members of his family, Apr. 22, 2006. Rondell Rawlins, a gang leader suspected in the 2006 assassination plot and accused of ordering massacres in two villages that left 23 dead in early 2008, was killed in a shootout with police Aug. 28, 2008.

Haiti
Republic of Haiti

People: Population: 9,035,536. **Age distrib.** (%): <15: 38.1; 65+: 3.4. **Pop. density:** 849.1 per sq mi, 327.8 per sq km. **Urban:** 42.7%. **Ethnic groups:** Black 95%, mulatto & white 5%. **Principal languages:** French, Creole (both official). **Chief religions:** Roman Catholic 80%, Protestant 16%; roughly half of pop. practices voodoo.

Geography: Total area: 10,714 sq mi, 27,750 sq km; **Land area:** 10,641 sq mi, 27,560 sq km. **Location:** In Caribbean, occupies W third of Isl. of Hispaniola. **Neighbors:** Dominican Republic on E, Cuba to W. **Topography:** About two-thirds is mountainous. Much of rest is semiarid. Coastal areas are warm and moist. **Capital:** Port-au-Prince, 1,998,000.

Government: Type: Republic. **Head of state:** Pres. René Préval; b. Jan. 17, 1943; in office: May 14, 2006. **Head of gov.:** Prime Min. Michèle Pierre-Louis; b. Oct. 5, 1947; in office; Sept. 5, 2008. **Local divisions:** 9 departments. **Defense budget:** NA. **Active troops:** No active armed forces.

Economy: Industries: sugar refining, flour milling, textiles, cement, light assembly of imported parts. **Chief crops:** coffee, mangoes, sugarcane, rice, corn, sorghum. **Natural resources:** bauxite, copper, calcium carbonate, gold, marble, hydropower. **Arable land:** 28%. **Livestock:** cattle: 1.5 mil; chickens: 5.5 mil; goats: 1.9 mil; pigs: 1 mil; sheep: 153,000. **Fish catch** (est.): 10,010 metric tons. **Electricity prod.:** 549 mil kWh. **Labor force** (1995): agric. 66%, industry 9%, services 25%.

Finance: Monetary unit: Gourde (HTG) (Oct. 2009: 39.75 = $1 U.S.). **GDP:** $11.5 bil; **per capita GDP:** $1,300; **GDP growth:** 1.3%. **Imports:** $2.1 bil; U.S. 44.1%, Netherlands Antilles 13.7%, China 5.5%. **Exports:** $490 mil; U.S. 68.8%, Dominican Republic 10.2%, Canada 3%. **Tourism:** NA. **Budget:** $1.05 bil. **Intl. reserves less gold:** $351 mil. **Gold:** NA. **Consumer prices:** 15.5%.

Transport: Motor vehicles: 93,000 pass. cars; 61,600 comm. vehicles. **Civil aviation:** 4 airports. **Chief port:** Cap-Haitien.

Communications: TV sets: 5 per 1,000 pop. **Radios:** 53 per 1,000 pop. **Telephone lines:** 108,000. **Internet:** 1 mil users.

Health: Life expect.: 55.8 male; 59.4 female. **Births** (per 1,000 pop.): 35.7. **Deaths** (per 1,000 pop.): 10.2. **Natural inc.:** 2.55%. **Infant mortality** (per 1,000 live births): 62.3. **HIV rate:** 2.2%.

Education: Compulsory: ages 6-11. **Literacy:** 62.1%.

Major intl. organizations: UN and most of its specialized agencies, OAS, Caricom.

Embassy: 2311 Massachusetts Ave. NW 20008; 332-4090.

Website: www.haiti.org

Haiti, visited by Columbus, 1492, and a French colony from 1697, attained its independence, 1804, following the rebellion led by former slave Toussaint L'Ouverture. After a period of political violence, the U.S. occupied the country 1915-34.

François Duvalier, known as Papa Doc, was elected president in Sept. 1957; in 1964 he was named president for life. Upon his death in 1971, he was succeeded by his son, Jean Claude Duvalier, known as Baby Doc. Following weeks of unrest, Jean Claude fled Haiti aboard a U.S. Air Force jet Feb. 7, 1986. His departure ended the Duvalier family's brutal 28-year dictatorship, but political violence, government corruption, poverty, AIDS and other health problems, and deteriorating environmental quality have continued to plague Haiti.

Father Jean-Bertrand Aristide was elected president Dec. 1990, but in Sept. 1991, he was arrested by the military and expelled from the country. Some 35,000 Haitian refugees were intercepted by the U.S. Coast Guard as they tried to enter the U.S., 1991-92. Most were returned to Haiti. There was a new upsurge of refugees starting in late 1993.

The UN authorized, July 31, 1994, an invasion of Haiti by a multinational force. With U.S. troops already en route, a full-scale invasion was averted, Sept. 18, when military leaders agreed to step down. Aristide returned to Haiti and was restored to office Oct. 15. A UN peacekeeping force exercised responsibility in Haiti from Mar. 31, 1995 to Nov. 30, 1997. Aristide transferred power to his elected successor, René Préval, on Feb. 7, 1996.

At least 140 people died and over 160,000 were left homeless when Hurricane Georges struck Haiti Sept. 22, 1998. Aristide won the presidency Nov. 26, 2000, in an election boycotted by opposition groups. An armed uprising in early 2004 and pressure from France and the U.S. toppled Aristide, who went into exile Feb. 29. A U.S.-led contingent, sent in after the upheaval, yielded authority June 1 to a UN stabilization force (MINUSTAH).

Flooding in late May 2004 killed more than 1,000 people, and more than 2,400 were killed in Tropical Storm Jeanne in Sept. Presidential elections Feb. 7, 2006, restored Préval to power.

Skyrocketing prices for food imports sparked riots and mass protests in Apr. 2008. A succession of hurricanes and tropical storms (Fay, Gustav, Hanna, Ike), Aug.-Sept. 2008, left more than 550 Haitians dead and up to 1 mil homeless. A school collapse near Port-au-Prince Nov. 7 killed 91 students and teachers.

To meet a budget crisis, international donors Apr. 14, 2009, pledged $324 mil for emergency aid and long-term projects. U.S. Sec. of State Hillary Clinton visited the country Apr. 16, and former Pres. Bill Clinton was named special UN envoy to Haiti May 19. MINUSTAH uniformed personnel in Haiti numbered about 9,160 in mid-2009.

Honduras
Republic of Honduras

People: Population: 7,792,854. **Age distrib.** (%): <15: 38.1; 65+: 3.6. **Pop. density:** 180.4 per sq mi, 69.6 per sq km. **Urban:** 46.5%. **Ethnic groups:** Mestizo (mixed Amerindian & European) 90%, Amerindian 7%. **Principal languages:** Spanish, Amerindian dialects. **Chief religions:** Roman Catholic 97%, Protestant 3%.

Geography: Total area: 43,278 sq mi, 112,090 sq km; **Land area:** 43,201 sq mi, 111,890 sq km. **Location:** In Central America. **Neighbors:** Guatemala on W; El Salvador, Nicaragua on S. **Topography:** Caribbean coast is 500 mi long. Pacific coast, on Gulf of Fonseca, is 40 mi long. Country is mountainous, with wide fertile valleys and rich forests. **Capital:** Tegucigalpa, 946,000.

Government: Type: Republic. **Head of state and gov.:** Pres. Roberto Micheletti Bain; b. Aug. 13, 1948; in office: June 28, 2009 (de facto). **Local divisions:** 18 departments. **Defense budget:** $76 mil. **Active troops:** 12,000.

Economy: Industries: sugar, coffee, textiles, clothing, wood products. **Chief crops:** bananas, coffee, citrus. **Natural resources:** timber, gold, silver, copper, lead, zinc, iron ore, antimony, coal, fish, hydropower. **Arable land:** 10%. **Livestock:** cattle: 2.6 mil; chickens: 20.8 mil; goats: 24,500; pigs: 3.1 mil; sheep: 15,000. **Fish catch:** 67,567 metric tons. **Electricity prod.:** 5.8 bil kWh. **Labor force** (2005 est.): agric. 39.2%, industry 20.9%, services 39.8%.

Finance: Monetary unit: Lempira (HNL) (Oct. 2009: 18.90 = $1 U.S.). **GDP:** $10.4 bil; U.S. 51.4%, Guatemala 7.3%, El Salvador 5.4%, Mexico 4.6%, Costa Rica 4.3%. **Exports:** $6 bil; U.S. 64.2%, El Salvador 5.2%, Guatemala 4.2%. **Tourism:** $557 mil. **Budget:** $2.6 bil. **Intl. reserves less gold:** $1.61 bil. **Gold:** 20,000 oz t. **Consumer prices:** 11.4%.

Transport: Railroad: Length: 434 mi. **Motor vehicles:** 46,000 pass. cars; 39,300 comm. vehicles. **Civil aviation:** 246.1 mil pass.-mi; 12 airports. **Chief ports:** La Ceiba, Puerto Cortes, San Lorenzo, Tela.

Communications: TV sets: 95 per 1,000 pop. **Radios:** 410 per 1,000 pop. **Telephone lines:** 825,800. **Internet:** 658,500 users.

Health: Life expect.: 67.8 male; 71 female. **Births** (per 1,000 pop.): 26.9. **Deaths** (per 1,000 pop.): 5.4. **Natural inc.:** 2.16%. **Infant mortality** (per 1,000 live births): 24.6. **HIV rate:** 0.7%.

Education: Compulsory: ages 6-11. **Literacy:** 83.1%.

Major intl. organizations: UN (FAO, IBRD, ILO, IMF, IMO, WHO, WTO), OAS.

Embassy: 3007 Tilden St. NW 20008; 966-7702.

Website: www.gob.hn

Mayan civilization flourished in Honduras in the 1st millennium CE. Columbus arrived in 1502. Honduras became independent after freeing itself from Spain, 1821, and from the Fed. of Central America, 1838.

Gen. Oswaldo Lopez Arellano, president for most of the period 1963-75 by virtue of one election and 2 coups, was ousted by the army in 1975 over charges of pervasive bribery by United Brands Co. of the U.S. An elected civilian government took power in 1982. Some 3,200 U.S. troops were sent to Honduras after the Honduran border was violated by Nicaraguan forces, Mar. 1988.

Already one of the poorest countries in the Western Hemisphere, Honduras was devastated in late Oct. 1998 by Hurricane Mitch, which killed at least 5,600 people and caused more than $850 mil in damage to crops and livestock.

Ricardo Maduro, a businessman who pledged to crack down on crime, won the presidency Nov. 25, 2001. A fire May 17, 2004, killed 104 inmates at an overcrowded prison in San Pedro Sula. Gunmen in that city Dec. 23 killed 28 passengers on a bus. In mid-Nov. 2005, floods and mudslides from Tropical Storm Gamma left 32 dead.

Manuel Zelaya Rosales of the opposition Liberal Party won the presidential election held Nov. 27, 2005. Seeking constitutional changes in his final year in office that would have allowed him to run for a 2nd term, Zelaya lost a political struggle with the Honduran Congress and Supreme Court, and he was ousted by the military June 28, 2009. The U.S. and OAS refused to recognize his successor, congressional leader Roberto Micheletti Bain, and pressed for negotiations that would lead to Zelaya's reinstatement, pending national elections Nov. 29.

Hungary
Republic of Hungary
People: Population: 9,905,596. **Age distrib.** (%): <15: 15; 65+: 15.8. **Pop. density:** 277.8 per sq mi, 107.3 per sq km. **Urban:** 66.3%. **Ethnic groups:** Hungarian 92%, Roma 2%. **Principal language:** Hungarian. **Chief religions:** Roman Catholic 52%, Calvinist 16%, unaffiliated 15%.

Geography: Total area: 35,919 sq mi, 93,030 sq km; **Land area:** 35,653 sq mi, 92,340 sq km. **Location:** In E central Europe. **Neighbors:** Slovakia, Ukraine on N; Austria on W; Slovenia, Serbia, Croatia on S; Romania on E. **Topography:** The Danube R. forms Slovak border in NW, then swings S to bisect the country. Eastern half of Hungary is mainly a great fertile plain, the Alfold; the W and N are hilly. **Capital:** Budapest, 1,679,000.

Government: Type: Parliamentary democracy. **Head of state:** Pres. László Sólyom; b. Jan. 3, 1942; in office: Aug. 5, 2005. **Head of gov.:** Prime Min. Gordon Bajnai; b. Mar. 5, 1968; in office: Apr. 14, 2009. **Local divisions:** 19 counties, 20 urban counties, 1 capital. **Defense budget:** $1.5 bil. **Active troops:** 25,207.

Economy: Industries: mining, metallurgy, constr. materials, processed foods, textiles, chemicals (espec. pharmaceuticals), motor vehicles. **Chief crops:** wheat, corn, sunflower seed, potatoes, sugar beets. **Natural resources:** bauxite, coal, nat. gas, fertile soils. **Crude oil reserves:** 20.2 mil bbls. **Arable land:** 50%. **Livestock:** cattle: 702,000; chickens: 30.3 mil; goats: 70,000; pigs: 4 mil; sheep: 1.3 mil. **Fish catch:** 22,888 metric tons. **Electricity prod.:** 33.9 bil kWh. **Labor force** (2005): agric. 5%, industry 32.4%, services 62.6%.

Finance: Monetary unit: Forint (HUF) (Oct. 2009: 180.67 = $1 U.S.). **GDP:** $196.6 bil; **per capita GDP:** $19,800; **GDP growth:** 0.6%. **Imports:** $106.5 bil; Germany 25.4%, Russia 9%, China 7.6%, Austria 6.1%, Netherlands 4.4%, France 4.4%, Italy 4.3%. **Exports:** $106.6 bil; Germany 26.5%, Italy 5.4%, Romania 5.3%, Austria 4.9%, Slovakia 4.7%, France 4.7%, UK 4.5%, Czech Republic 4%. **Tourism:** $4.7 bil. **Budget:** $71.7 bil. **Intl. reserves less gold:** $21.94 bil. **Gold:** 100,000 oz t. **Consumer prices:** 6.1%.

Transport: Railroad: Length: 5,006 mi. **Motor vehicles:** 2.9 mil pass. cars; 427,000 comm. vehicles. **Civil aviation:** 2.4 bil pass.-mi; 20 airports. **Chief ports:** Baja, Budapest, Csepel, Dunaujvaros, Gyor-Gonyu, Mohacs.

Communications: TV sets: 447 per 1,000 pop. **Radios:** 690 per 1,000 pop. **Telephone lines:** 3.1 mil. **Daily newspaper circ.** (2004): 217 per 1,000 pop. **Internet:** 5.5 mil users.

Health: Life expect.: 69 male; 77.6 female. **Births** (per 1,000 pop.): 9.6. **Deaths** (per 1,000 pop.): 13. **Natural inc.:** −0.34%. **Infant mortality** (per 1,000 live births): 8. **HIV rate:** 0.1%.

Education: Compulsory: ages 7-16. **Literacy:** 98.9%.

Major intl. organizations: UN (FAO, IBRD, ILO, IMF, IMO, WHO, WTO), EU, NATO, OECD, OSCE.

Embassy: 3910 Shoemaker St. NW 20008; 362-6730.

Website: www.hungary.hu

Earliest settlers, chiefly Slav and Germanic, were overrun by Magyars from the E. Stephen I (997-1038) was made king by Pope Sylvester II in 1000 CE. The country suffered repeated Turkish invasions in the 15th-17th centuries. After the defeat of the Turks, 1686-97, Austria dominated, but Hungary obtained concessions until it regained internal independence in 1867, under a dual monarchy with the emperor of Austria. Defeated with the Central Powers in 1918, Hungary lost Transylvania to Romania, Croatia and Bacska to Yugoslavia, and Slovakia and Carpatho-Ruthenia to Czechoslovakia, all of which had large Hungarian minorities. A re-

public under Michael Karolyi and a Bolshevist revolt under Bela Kun were followed by a vote for a monarchy in 1920 with Admiral Nicholas Horthy as regent.

Hungary joined Germany in WWII, and was allowed to annex most of its lost territories. Russian troops captured the country, 1944-45. By terms of an armistice with the Allied powers Hungary agreed to give up territory acquired by the 1938 dismemberment of Czechoslovakia and to return to its borders of 1937.

A republic was declared Feb. 1, 1946. In 1947 a hardline Communist, pro-Soviet government was installed. In 1956, demonstrations against Communist rule developed into open revolt. Soviet forces launched a massive attack Nov. 4 against Budapest with 200,000 troops, 2,500 tanks and armored cars. About 200,000 persons fled the country. Thousands were arrested and executed.

Hungarian troops participated in the 1968 Warsaw Pact invasion of Czechoslovakia. Major economic reforms were launched early in 1968, switching from a central planning system to one based on market forces and profit.

In 1989 Parliament legalized freedom of assembly and association as Hungary shifted away from Communism. In Oct. the Communist Party was formally dissolved. The last Soviet troops left Hungary June 19, 1991. Hungary became a full member of NATO Mar. 12, 1999, and of the EU May 1, 2004.

The IMF, EU, and World Bank agreed Oct. 28, 2008, to extend $25.1 bil to rescue Hungary's economy, which was battered by the global financial crisis. An upsurge in violence against the minority Roma included 6 murders from Nov. 2008 to Sept. 2009.

Iceland
Republic of Iceland
People: Population: 306,694. **Age distrib.** (%): <15: 20.7; 65+: 12.2. **Pop. density:** 7.9 per sq mi, 3.1 per sq km. **Urban:** 92.2%. **Ethnic groups:** Homogeneous mixture of Norse & Celt descendants 94%. **Principal languages:** Icelandic, English, Nordic languages, German widely spoken. **Chief religion:** Lutheran Church of Iceland 86%, unaffiliated 3%.

Geography: Total area: 39,769 sq mi, 103,000 sq km; **Land area:** 38,707 sq mi, 100,250 sq km. **Location:** Isl. at N end of Atlantic O. **Neighbors:** Nearest is Greenland (Den.) to W. **Topography:** Recent volcanic origin. Three-quarters of surface is wasteland: glaciers, lakes, a lava desert. There are geysers and hot springs, and the climate is moderated by the Gulf Stream. **Capital:** Reykjavík, 192,000.

Government: Type: Constitutional republic. **Head of state:** Pres. Olafur Ragnar Grímsson; b. May 14, 1943; in office: Aug. 1, 1996. **Head of gov.:** Prime Min. Jóhanna Sigurdardóttir; b. Oct. 4, 1942; in office: Feb. 1. 2009. **Local divisions:** 23 counties, 14 independent towns. **Defense budget** (2006): $46 mil. **Active troops:** None.

Economy: Industries: fish proc., aluminum smelting, ferrosilicon prod., tourism. **Chief crops:** potatoes, green vegetables. **Natural resources:** fish, hydropower, geothermal power, diatomite. **Arable land:** 0.1%. **Livestock:** cattle: 70,660; chickens: 209,000; goats: 524; pigs: 41,470; sheep: 454,812. **Fish catch:** 1.43 mil metric tons. **Electricity prod.:** 9.7 bil kWh. **Labor force** (2007): agric. 3%, industry 19%, services 78%.

Finance: Monetary unit: Krona (ISK) (Oct. 2009: 123.71 = $1 U.S.). **GDP:** $12.7 bil; **per capita GDP:** $41,800; **GDP growth:** 0.3%. **Imports:** $5.8 bil; Norway 10.9%, Germany 10.4%, Sweden 9%, U.S. 8%, Denmark 7.4%, China 6.8%, Netherlands 6%, UK 4.4%, Japan 4%. **Exports:** $5.7 bil; Netherlands 33.8%, UK 11.7%, Germany 11.5%, U.S. 5.8%, Japan 4.9%, Norway 4.1%. **Tourism:** $539 mil. **Budget:** $8.6 bil. **Intl. reserves less gold:** $2.28 bil. **Gold:** 60,000 oz t. **Consumer prices:** 12.7%.

Transport: Motor vehicles: 187,000 pass. cars; 27,000 comm. vehicles. **Civil aviation:** 2.7 bil pass.-mi; 6 airports. **Chief ports:** Grundartangi, Hafnarfjordur, Reykjavík.

Communications: TV sets: 505 per 1,000 pop. **Radios:** 1,075 per 1,000 pop. **Telephone lines:** 187,000. **Daily newspaper circ.** (2004): 551.6 per 1,000 pop. **Internet:** 284,000 users.

Health: Life expect.: 78.4 male; 82.8 female. **Births** (per 1,000 pop.): 13.5. **Deaths** (per 1,000 pop.): 6.8. **Natural inc.:** 0.67%. **Infant mortality** (per 1,000 live births): 3.4. **HIV rate:** 0.2%.

Education: Compulsory: ages 6-16. **Literacy:** 99%.

Major intl. organizations: UN (FAO, IBRD, ILO, IMF, IMO, WHO, WTO), EFTA, NATO, OECD, OSCE.

Embassy: 1156 15th St. NW, Ste. 1200, 20005; 265-6653.

Website: www.iceland.is

Iceland was an independent republic from 930 to 1262, when it joined with Norway. Its language has maintained its purity for 1,000 years. The Althing, or assembly, established in 930, is the world's oldest surviving parliament.

Danish rule lasted from 1380-1918; the last ties with the Danish crown were severed in 1941. A continuous 55-year U.S. military presence in Iceland ended with the closure of the Keflavík naval air station in Sept. 2006. Iceland's banking system and currency collapsed amid the global financial crisis in Oct. 2008. More than $10 bil in loans from the IMF and European governments restored financial stability; austerity measures were imposed, and the nation entered a deep recession. Political unrest sparked by soaring inflation and unemployment led to the installation Feb. 1, 2009, of a center-left government, which swept to victory in elections Apr. 25. Parliament July 16 approved a plan for Iceland to seek EU membership.

India
Republic of India

People: Population: 1,166,079,217. **Age distrib.** (%): <15: 31.1; 65+: 5.3. **Pop. density:** 1,015.8 per sq mi, 392.2 per sq km. **Urban:** 28.7%. **Ethnic groups:** Indo-Aryan 72%, Dravidian 25%. **Principal languages:** English (most important lang. for national, political, commercial communication); Hindi (nat. lang. & primary tongue); 21 other official languages (incl. Bengali, Gujarati, Kashmiri, Malayalam, Nepali, Punjabi, Sanskrit, Sindhi, Tamil, Urdu; Hindustani, popular variant of Hindi/Urdu widely spoken throughout N. **Chief religions:** Hindu 81%, Muslim 13%, Christian 2%.

Geography: Total area: 1,269,346 sq mi, 3,287,590 sq km; **Land area:** 1,147,955 sq mi, 2,973,190 sq km. **Location:** Occupies most of Indian subcontinent in S Asia. **Neighbors:** Pakistan on W; China, Nepal, Bhutan on N; Myanmar, Bangladesh on E. **Topography:** The Himalaya Mts., highest in world, stretch across India's northern borders. Below, the Ganges Plain is wide, fertile, and among the most densely populated regions of the world. Area below includes Deccan Peninsula. Close to one quarter of area is forested. The climate varies from tropical heat in S to near-Arctic cold in N. Rajasthan Desert is NW; NE Assam Hills get 400 in. of rain a year. **Capital:** Delhi, 15,926,000. **Cities (urban aggr.):** Bombay (Mumbai), 18,978,000; Calcutta (Kolkata), 14,787,000; Madras (Chennai), 7,163,000; Bangalore, 6,787,000; Hyderabad, 6,376,000; Ahmadabad, 5,375,000.

Government: Type: Federal republic. **Head of state:** Pres. Pratibha Patil; b. Dec. 19, 1934; in office: July 25, 2007. **Head of gov.:** Prime Min. Manmohan Singh; b. Sept. 26, 1932; in office: May 22, 2004. **Local divisions:** 28 states, 6 union territories, 1 national capital territory. **Defense budget:** $26.5 bil. **Active troops:** 1,281,200.

Economy: Industries: textiles, chemicals, food proc., steel, transp. equip., cement, mining, oil, machinery, software. **Chief crops:** rice, wheat, oilseed, cotton, jute, tea, sugarcane, potatoes. **Natural resources:** coal, iron ore, mang., mica, bauxite, titanium ore, chromite, nat. gas, diamonds, oil, limestone. **Crude oil reserves:** 5.6 bil bbls. **Arable land:** 49%. **Livestock:** cattle: 176.6 mil; chickens: 560 mil; goats: 125.5 mil; pigs: 14 mil; sheep: 64.3 mil. **Fish catch:** 7.31 mil metric tons. **Electricity prod.:** 703.3 bil kWh. **Labor force** (2003): agric. 60%, industry 12%, services 28%.

Finance: Monetary unit: Rupee (INR) (Oct. 2009: 46.92 = $1 U.S.). **GDP:** $3.3 tril; **per capita GDP:** $2,900; **GDP growth:** 7.4%. **Imports:** $305.5 bil; China 11.8%, U.S. 6.8%, Singapore 4.4%, Germany 4.3%, Australia 4.1%. **Exports:** $176.4 bil; U.S. 12.9%, China 11%, UAE 8.8%, Singapore 4.1%. **Tourism:** $10.7 bil. **Budget:** $178.3 bil. **Intl. reserves less gold:** $160.63 bil. **Gold:** 11.5 mil oz t. **Consumer prices:** 8.3%.

Transport: Railroad: Length: 39,350 mi. **Motor vehicles:** 8.6 mil pass. cars; 10.9 mil comm. vehicles. **Civil aviation:** 29.2 bil pass.-mi; 250 airports. **Chief ports:** Chennai, Jawaharal Nehru, Kandla, Kolkata, Mormugao, Mumbai, New Mangalore, Vishakhapatnam.

Communications: TV sets: 75 per 1,000 pop. **Radios:** 120 per 1,000 pop. **Telephone lines:** 37.9 mil. **Internet:** 81 mil users.

Health: Life expect.: 66.9 male; 71.9 female. **Births** (per 1,000 pop.): 22.2. **Deaths** (per 1,000 pop.): 6.4. **Natural inc.:** 1.58%. **Infant mortality** (per 1,000 live births): 32.3. **HIV rate:** 0.3%.

Education: Compulsory: ages 6-14. **Literacy:** 66%.

Major intl. organizations: UN (FAO, IBRD, ILO, IMF, IMO, WHO, WTO), the Commonwealth.

Embassy: 2107 Massachusetts Ave. NW 20008; 939-7000. **Website:** www.india.gov.in

India has one of the oldest civilizations in the world. Excavations trace the Indus Valley civilization back for at least 5,000 years. Paintings in the mountain caves of Ajanta, richly carved temples, the Taj Mahal in Agra, and the Kutab Minar in Delhi are among relics of the past.

Aryan tribes, speaking Sanskrit, invaded from the northwest around 1500 BCE. Asoka ruled most of the Indian subcontinent in the 3rd cent. BCE, and established Buddhism. But Hinduism revived and eventually predominated. Under the Guptas, 4th-6th cent. CE, science, literature, and the arts enjoyed a "golden age."

Arab invaders established a Muslim foothold in the west in the 8th cent., and Turkish Muslims gained control of North India by 1200. The Mogul emperors ruled 1526-1857.

Vasco da Gama established Portuguese trading posts 1498-1503. The Dutch followed. The British East India Co. sent Capt. William Hawkins, 1609, to get concessions from the Mogul emperor for spices and textiles. Operating as the East India Co. the British gained control of most of India. The British parliament assumed

political direction; under Lord Bentinck, 1828-35, rule by rajahs was curbed. After the Sepoy troops mutinied, 1857-58, the British supported the native rulers.

Nationalism grew rapidly after WWI. The Indian National Congress and the Muslim League demanded constitutional reform. A leader emerged in Mohandas K. Gandhi (called Mahatma, or Great Soul), b. Oct. 2, 1869, assassinated Jan. 30, 1948. He advocated self-rule, nonviolence, and removal of the caste system of untouchability. In 1930 he launched a program of civil disobedience, including a boycott of British goods and rejection of taxes without representation.

In 1935 Britain gave India a constitution providing a bicameral federal congress. Muhammad Ali Jinnah, head of the Muslim League, sought creation of a Muslim nation, Pakistan.

The British government partitioned British India into the dominions of India and Pakistan. India became a member of the UN in 1945, a self-governing member of the Commonwealth in 1947, and a democratic republic, Jan. 26, 1950. More than 12 mil Hindu and Muslim refugees crossed the India-Pakistan borders in a mass transferal of some of the 2 peoples during 1947; about 200,000 were killed in communal fighting.

After Pakistan troops began attacks on Bengali separatists in East Pakistan, Mar. 25, 1971, some 10 mil refugees fled into India. India and Pakistan went to war Dec. 3, 1971, on both the east and west fronts. Pakistan troops in the east surrendered Dec. 16; Pakistan agreed to a cease-fire in the west Dec. 17.

Indira Gandhi, India's prime minister since Jan. 1966, invoked emergency powers in June 1975. Thousands of opponents were arrested and press censorship imposed. These and other actions, including enforcement of coercive birth control measures in some areas, were widely resented. Opposition parties, united in the Janata coalition, turned Gandhi's New Congress Party from power in federal and state parliamentary elections in 1977.

Gandhi became prime minister for the second time, Jan. 14, 1980. She was assassinated by 2 of her Sikh bodyguards Oct. 31, 1984, in response to the government suppression of a Sikh uprising in Punjab in June 1984, which included an assault on the Golden Temple at Amritsar, the holiest Sikh shrine. Widespread rioting followed the assassination; thousands of Sikhs were killed and some 50,000 left homeless. Rajiv, Indira Gandhi's son, replaced her as prime minister. A gas leak at a Union Carbide chemical plant in Bhopal, in Dec. 1984, eventually killed some 14,000 people.

Many died in religious, ethnic, and political conflicts during the late 1980s and early '90s. To suppress the Sikh insurgency in Punjab, Indian government troops attacked the Golden Temple again in 1988. Rajiv Gandhi was swept from office in 1989 amid charges of incompetence and corruption, and assassinated May 21, 1991, while campaigning to regain power. Nationwide riots followed the destruction of a 16th-cent. mosque by Hindu militants in Dec. 1992. Ethnic clashes in Assam, in northwest India, killed thousands in Feb. 1993. Bombs jolted Mumbai and Kolkata, Mar. 12-19, killing over 300.

Mother Teresa, renowned for her work among the poor, died Sept. 5, 1997. India's first lowest-caste president, K. R. Narayanan, took office July 25. India conducted a series of nuclear tests in mid-May 1998, raising tensions with Pakistan. A cyclone that hit the state of Orissa, East India, on Oct. 29, 1999, left some 10,000 people dead. A powerful earthquake in Gujarat state on Jan. 26, 2001, claimed more than 20,000 lives.

India blamed Pakistani-sponsored terrorist groups for an Oct. 1 suicide attack on the state legislature in Jammu and Kashmir (see below), in which at least 40 people died, and a Dec. 13 assault on the Indian parliament in New Delhi Dec. 13, which left 13 people dead. Hindu-Muslim clashes in Gujarat Feb. 27-Mar. 11, 2002, claimed more than 700 lives. A. P. J. Abdul Kalam, a Muslim scientist who spearheaded India's nuclear weapons program, became president July 25.

Led by Rajiv Gandhi's Italian-born widow, Sonia, the Congress Party won the most seats in parliamentary elections Apr.-May 2004. When Hindu nationalists objected to her candidacy, she chose not to become prime minister, and Manmohan Singh, a Sikh economist, took office instead.

The Indian Ocean tsunami of Dec. 26, 2004, left more than 10,700 people dead, some 5,600 missing, and over 647,000 displaced. Islamic extremists were suspected in 7 bombings in Mumbai, July 11, 2006, that killed more than 200 on commuter trains. Pratibha Patil took office July 25, 2007, as India's first female president. Monsoon floods, July-Sept. 2007, killed more than 2,600 people and severely damaged 575,000 homes.

A car bomb July 7, 2008, at India's embassy in Kabul, Afghanistan, left 58 people dead. A wave of bombings July 25-26 killed at least 46 people in Bangalore and Ahmadabad; at least 20 died from bombs in New Delhi Sept. 13. Monsoon floods June-Sept. killed more than 2,200 and affected over 21.8 mil people. At least 224 died in a stampede Sept. 30 at a Hindu temple in Jodhpur. The unmanned Chandrayaan-1, India's first lunar survey mission, was launched into space Oct. 22.

Ten Pakistanis linked to the militant group Lashkar-e-Taiba stormed luxury hotels, a railway station, a Jewish center, and other sites in Mumbai, Nov. 26, 2008; by the time Indian commandos took control 3 days later, the attackers had slaughtered 163 people. Nine of the terrorists were also killed; the lone surviving gunman, Ajmal Kasab, confessed in open court July 20, 2009.

In parliamentary elections Apr. 16-May 13, Prime Min. Manmohan Singh's United Progressive Alliance, led by the Congress party, gained a resounding victory. Despite robust economic growth since the 1990s, especially in high-technology industries, about 40% of India's population earns less than $1.25 per day.

Sikkim, bordered by Tibet, Bhutan, and Nepal, formerly British protected, became a protectorate of India in 1950. Area, 2,740 sq mi; pop. (2001 census): 540,493; capital: Gangtok. In Sept. 1974, India's parliament voted to make Sikkim an associate Indian state, absorbing it into India.

Kashmir is a predominantly Muslim region in the NW that borders India, Pakistan, Afghanistan, and China. Originally a Hindu kingdom, Muslim rule began in 1341; after almost 200 years under the Moguls, the area was incorporated into British India in 1846. Fighting broke out in the region between India and Pakistan in 1947 following independence from Britain. A cease-fire was negotiated by the UN Jan. 1, 1949; it gave Pakistan control of one-third of the area as Azad Kashmir, in the west and northwest, and India the remaining two-thirds, as the Indian state of Jammu and Kashmir. It is India's only Muslim-majority state. Area: 39,146 sq mi; pop. (2001 census): 10,000,000; capitals: Srinagar (summer) and Jammu (winter). Fighting in the area resumed during the 1965 and 1971 wars with Pakistan. China occupied about 14,000 sq mi in the Ladakh district after a war with India in 1962.

In the 1990s there were repeated clashes between Indian army troops and separatist fighters triggered by India's decision to impose central government rule. The clashes strained relations between India and Pakistan, whom India charged with aiding the separatists; fighting was especially heavy in May-June 1999. Tensions escalated in 2002, but U.S. mediation in June helped ease the threat of war.

A cease-fire between Indian and Pakistani troops along the line of control took effect Nov. 25, 2003, but fighting between Indian forces and Islamic militants continued. Estimates of conflict-related deaths since 1989 range from 40,000 to over 80,000. A powerful earthquake Oct. 8, 2005, killed about 80,000 and left up to 3 mil homeless in Pakistani-held Kashmir and northern Pakistan.

France, 1952-54, peacefully yielded to India its 5 colonies, former French India: Pondicherry, Karikal, Mahe, and Yanaon were merged to become Pondicherry, now **Puducherry**, Union Territory, area 190 sq mi; pop. (2001 census): 973,829; the colony of Chandernagor was incorporated into the state of **West Bengal**.

Indonesia
Republic of Indonesia

People: Population: 240,271,522. **Age distrib.** (%): <15: 28.1; 65+: 6. **Pop. density:** 340.7 per sq mi, 131.6 per sq km. **Urban:** 48.1%. **Ethnic groups:** Javanese 41%, Sundanese 15%, Madurese 3%, Minangkabau 3%. **Principal languages:** Bahasa Indonesia (official, modified form of Malay), English, Dutch, local dialects (Javanese most widely spoken). **Chief religions:** Muslim 86%, Protestant 6%, Roman Catholic 3%.

Geography: Total area: 741,100 sq mi, 1,919,440 sq km; **Land area:** 705,192 sq mi, 1,826,440 sq km. **Location:** Archipelago SE of Asian mainland along the Equator. **Neighbors:** Malaysia on N, Papua New Guinea on E, Timor-Leste on S. **Topography:** Indonesia comprises over 13,500 islands (6,000 inhabited), including Java (one of the most densely populated areas in the world with over 2,000 persons per sq mi), Sumatra, Kalimantan (most of Borneo), Sulawesi (Celebes), and West Irian (Irian Jaya, the W half of New Guinea). Also: Bangka, Billiton, Madura, Bali, Timor. The mountains and plateaus on the major islands have a cooler climate than the tropical lowlands. **Capital:** Jakarta, 9,125,000. **Cities (urban aggr.):** Surabaya, 2,845,000.

Government: Type: Republic. **Head of state and gov.:** Susilo Bambang Yudhoyono; b. Sept. 9, 1949; in office: Oct. 20, 2004. **Local divisions:** 30 provinces, 2 special regions, 1 capital district. **Defense budget:** $4.3 bil. **Active troops:** 302,000.

Economy: Industries: oil & nat. gas, textiles, apparel, footwear, mining, cement, chemical fertilizers, plywood, rubber. **Chief crops:** rice, cassava, peanuts, rubber, cocoa, coffee, palm oil, copra. **Natural resources:** oil, tin, nat. gas, nickel, timber, bauxite, copper, coal, gold, silver. **Crude oil reserves:** 3.99 bil bbls. **Arable land:** 11%. **Livestock:** cattle: 11.5 mil; chickens: 1.3 bil; goats: 14.5 mil; pigs: 6.7 mil; sheep: 9.9 mil. **Fish catch:** 8.06 mil metric tons. **Electricity prod.:** 125.7 bil kWh. **Labor force** (2006 est.): agric. 42.1%, industry 18.6%, services 39.3%.

Finance: Monetary unit: Rupiah (IDR) (Oct. 2009: 9,445.72 = $1 U.S.). **GDP:** $914.6 bil; **per capita GDP:** $3,900; **GDP growth:** 6.1%. **Imports:** $116 bil; Singapore 16.9%, China 11.8%, Japan 11.7%, Malaysia 6.9%, U.S. 6.1%, S. Korea 5.4%, Thailand 4.9%. **Exports:** $139.3 bil; Japan 20.2%, U.S. 9.5%, Singapore 9.4%, China 8.5%, S. Korea 6.7%, India 5.2%, Malaysia 4.7%.

Tourism: $5.3 bil. **Budget:** $84.9 bil. **Intl. reserves less gold:** $32.2 bil. **Gold:** 2.35 mil oz t. **Consumer prices:** 10.1%.

Transport: Railroad: Length: 5,300 mi. **Motor vehicles:** 5.5 mil pass. cars; 4.1 mil comm. vehicles. **Civil aviation:** 17.5 bil pass.-mi; 164 airports. **Chief ports:** Banjarmasin, Belawan, Ciwandan, Palembang, Panjang, Sungai Pakning, Tanjung Priok.

Communications: TV sets: 143 per 1,000 pop. **Radios:** 155 per 1,000 pop. **Telephone lines:** 30.4 mil. **Internet:** 30 mil users.

Health: Life expect.: 68 male; 73.1 female. **Births** (per 1,000 pop.): 19.2. **Deaths** (per 1,000 pop.): 6.2. **Natural inc.:** 1.3%. **Infant mortality** (per 1,000 live births): 31. **HIV rate:** 0.2%.

Education: Compulsory: ages 7-15. **Literacy:** 91.4%.

Major intl. organizations: UN and all of its specialized agencies, APEC, ASEAN.

Embassy: 2020 Massachusetts Ave. NW 20036; 775-5200.

Website: www.indonesia.go.id

Hindu and Buddhist civilization from India reached Indonesia nearly 2,000 years ago, taking root especially in Java. Islam spread along the maritime trade routes in the 15th cent., and became predominant by the 16th cent. The Dutch replaced the Portuguese as the area's most important European trade power in the 17th cent., securing territorial control over Java by 1750. The outer islands were not finally subdued until the early 20th cent.

Following Japanese occupation, 1942-45, nationalists led by Sukarno and Hatta declared independence. The Netherlands ceded sovereignty Dec. 27, 1949, after 4 years of fighting. A republic was declared, Aug. 17, 1950, with Sukarno as president. West Irian, on New Guinea, remained under Dutch control but was transferred by the UN to Indonesia in 1963.

Sukarno suspended Parliament in 1960 and was named president for life in 1963. He made close alliances with Communist governments. In Sept. 1965 an attempted coup in which several military officers were murdered was successfully put down, but Sukarno was forced to cede power to the army, led by Gen. Suharto, who became acting president in 1967 and ruled Indonesia for the next 31 years. The regime blamed the coup on the Communist Party; more than 300,000 alleged Communists were killed in army-initiated massacres.

Parliament reelected Suharto to a 7th consecutive 5-year term Mar. 10, 1998, as a severe economic downturn focused public anger on nepotism, cronyism, and corruption in the Suharto regime. Price increases in May sparked mass protests and then mob violence in Jakarta and other cities, claiming some 500 lives. Suharto resigned May 21 and was succeeded by his vice-president, Bacharuddin Jusuf Habibie. Abdurrahman Wahid, leader of Indonesia's largest Muslim organization, was elected president Oct. 20, 1999. In Aug. 2000, under pressure from the legislature, he agreed to share power with Vice Pres. Megawati Sukarnoputri, the daughter of the late Pres. Sukarno. Charging Wahid with incompetence and corruption, the legislature ousted him July 23, 2001, and Megawati became Indonesia's first woman president.

Clashes between Muslims and Christians in the Maluku (Molucca) Isl., 1999-2002, claimed about 5,000 lives. Ethnic violence in Kalimantan, Borneo, killed more than 400 in Feb. 2001. East Timor, a former Portuguese colony that Indonesia invaded in Dec. 1975 and controlled until Oct. 1999, became a fully independent country May 20, 2002, as Timor-Leste. Separatists in Aceh, NW Sumatra, fought repeatedly against government troops during the 1980s and 90s; peace accords were announced in Dec. 2002 and, after that deal unraveled, in July 2005. The last of 24,000 Indonesian government troops pulled out of Aceh, Dec. 29, 2005.

Investigators blamed the Islamic terrorist group Jemaah Islamiyah, an al-Qaeda affiliate, for bombings that killed 202 people, mostly foreign tourists, at nightclubs in Bali, Oct. 12, 2002, and 12 people at a Marriott hotel in Jakarta, Aug. 5, 2003. A car bomb attack outside the Australian embassy in Jakarta, Sept. 9, 2004, killed 9 people and injured more than 180. Susilo Bambang Yudhoyono, a retired general, defeated Megawati Sept. 20 in a direct presidential runoff vote.

A massive earthquake off northwest Sumatra, Dec. 26, 2004, triggered tsunamis that wreaked havoc in the Indian Ocean region. The death toll in Indonesia alone exceeded 125,000, not counting almost 40,000 missing. Another large quake off northwest Sumatra, Mar. 28, 2005, left at least 1,300 dead. On Java in 2006, an earthquake May 27 killed 5,800, left 1.5 mil homeless, and caused damage estimated at $3.1 bil; a tsunami July 17 claimed at least 650 lives.

Two leaders of the Jemaah Islamiyah terror network were arrested in June 2007. Faced with falling oil production, Indonesia left OPEC in 2008. Pres. Yudhoyono won a 2nd 5-year term July 8, 2009, in an election generally praised by international observers. Suicide bombings at 2 Jakarta hotels July 17 left 9 people dead. Police confirmed Sept. 17 that Noordin Muhammad Top, suspected of plotting the recent Jakarta attacks and other terrorist bombings, had been killed in a shootout. Padang, Sumatra, was hit Sept. 30 by a powerful earthquake, which also triggered mudslides in the region; at least 1,100 people were killed, according to preliminary UN estimates.

Iran

Islamic Republic of Iran

People: Population: 66,429,284. **Age distrib.** (%): <15: 21.7; 65+: 5.4. **Pop. density:** 105.2 per sq mi, 40.6 per sq km. **Urban:** 66.9%. **Ethnic groups:** Persian 51%, Azeri 24%, Gilaki & Mazandarani 8%, Kurd 7%, Arab 3%. **Principal languages:** Persian & Persian dialects, Turkic & Turkic dialects, Kurdish, Arabic. **Chief religions:** Muslim (Shi'a 89%, Sunni 9%), other (incl. Zoroastrian, Jewish, Christian, Baha'i) 2%.

Geography: Total area: 636,296 sq mi, 1,648,000 sq km; **Land area:** 631,663 sq mi, 1,636,000 sq km. **Location:** Between the Middle East and S Asia. **Neighbors:** Turkey, Iraq on W; Armenia, Azerbaijan, Turkmenistan on N; Afghanistan, Pakistan on E. **Topography:** Interior highlands and plains surrounded by high mountains, up to 18,000 ft. Large salt deserts cover much of area, but there are many oases and forest areas. Most of population inhabits N and NW. **Capital:** Tehran, 7,873,000. **Cities (urban aggr.):** Mashhad, 2,469,000; Esfahan, 1,628,000.

Government: Type: Islamic republic. **Religious head:** Ayatollah Sayyed Ali Khamenei; b. July 17, 1939; in office: June 4, 1989. **Head of state and gov.:** Pres. Mahmoud Ahmadinejad; b. Oct. 28, 1956; in office: Aug. 3, 2005. **Local divisions:** 28 provinces. **Defense budget:** $7.5 bil. **Active troops:** 523,000.

Economy: Industries: oil, petrochemicals, fertilizers, caustic soda, textiles, cement & other constr. materials, food proc., metal fabrication, armaments. **Chief crops:** wheat, rice, other grains, sugar beets, sugar cane, fruits, nuts, cotton. **Natural resources:** oil, nat. gas, coal, chromium, copper, iron ore, lead, mang., zinc, sulfur. **Crude oil reserves:** 136.2 bil bbls. **Arable land:** 10%. **Livestock:** cattle: 7.6 mil; chickens: 420 mil; goats: 25.5 mil; sheep: 53.8 mil. **Fish catch:** 562,424 metric tons. **Electricity prod.:** 189.9 bil kWh. **Labor force** (2007): agric. 25%, industry 31%, services 45%.

Finance: Monetary unit: Rial (IRR) (Oct. 2009: 9,909.20 = $1 U.S.). **GDP:** $841.7 bil; **per capita GDP:** $12,800; **GDP growth:** 6.5%. **Imports:** $67.3 bil; China 13.5%, UAE 9.8%, Germany 9.1%, S. Korea 6.1%, Russia 5.6%, Italy 5.1%, France 4.2%. **Exports:** $95.1 bil; China 18.5%, Japan 15.4%, Turkey 6.9%, S. Korea 6.8%, Italy 4.9%. **Tourism:** $1.5 bil. **Budget:** $64 bil. **Intl. reserves less gold:** NA. **Gold:** NA. **Consumer prices:** 25.5%.

Transport: Railroad: Length: 5,246 mi. **Motor vehicles:** 1.5 mil pass. cars; 431,200 comm. vehicles. **Civil aviation:** 7.6 bil pass.-mi; 133 airports. **Chief ports:** Assaluyeh, Bandar Abbas, Bandar-e-Eman Khomeyni.

Communications: TV sets: 154 per 1,000 pop. **Radios:** 265 per 1,000 pop. **Telephone lines:** 24.8 mil. **Internet:** 23 mil users.

Health: Life expect.: 69.4 male; 72.4 female. **Births** (per 1,000 pop.): 16.9. **Deaths** (per 1,000 pop.): 5.7. **Natural inc.:** 1.12%. **Infant mortality** (per 1,000 live births): 36.9. **HIV rate:** 0.2%.

Education: Compulsory: ages 6-10. **Literacy:** 84.7%.

Major intl. organizations: UN (FAO, IBRD, ILO, IMF, IMO, WHO), OPEC.

Iranian Interests Section: 2209 Wisconsin Ave. NW 20007; 965-4990.

Website: www.president.ir

Iran, formerly known as Persia, has been settled for thousands of years. Ancestors of the Iranians came from the east during the 2nd millennium BCE; they were an Indo-European group related to the Aryans of India. In 549 BCE Cyrus the Great united the Medes and Persians in the Persian Empire; he conquered Babylonia in 538 BCE, and restored Jerusalem to the Jews. Alexander the Great conquered Persia in 333 BCE, but Persians regained independence in the next century under the Parthians, themselves succeeded by Sassanian Persians in 226 CE. Arabs brought Islam to Persia in the 7th cent., replacing the indigenous Zoroastrian faith. After Persian political and cultural autonomy was reasserted in the 9th cent., arts and sciences flourished.

Turks and Mongols ruled Persia in turn from the 11th cent. to 1502, when Ismael I established the Iranian Safavid dynasty and made Shiite Islam the offical religion. The dynasty lasted until 1722. The British and Russian empires vied for influence in the 19th cent.; Afghanistan was severed from Iran by Britain in 1857.

Reza Khan, a military officer, became prime min., 1923, and shah in 1925. He began modernization, curbed foreign influence, and officially changed the country's name from Persia to Iran in 1935. Fearing the shah's Axis sympathies, British and Soviet troops forced him to abdicate, 1941; he was succeeded by his son, Mohammad Reza Pahlavi. The U.S. Central Intelligence Agency had a major role in the ouster, 1953, of Prime Min. Muhammad Mossadegh, who had nationalized the oil industry.

With U.S. backing, the shah brought economic and social change to Iran (the "White Revolution"), but repression of opposition groups grew severe. Violent protests in 1978 eventually forced the shah to depart, Jan. 16, 1979. Shiite leader Ayatollah Ruhollah Khomeini, exiled by the shah in 1963, returned to Tehran, Feb. 1, and by Feb. 11 pro-Khomeini forces had defeated government troops. Khomeini declared an Islamic theocracy.

Iranian militants seized the U.S. embassy Nov. 4, 1979 and took hostages including 62 Americans. Despite international condemnations and U.S. efforts, including an abortive Apr. 1980 rescue attempt, the crisis continued. The U.S. broke diplomatic relations with Iran, Apr. 7. The shah died in Egypt, July 27. The hostage drama ended Jan. 20, 1981, when an accord, involving the release of frozen Iranian assets, was reached.

A dispute over the Shatt al-Arab waterway situated between Iran and Iraq led to a long and costly war between the 2 countries, 1980-88, killing hundreds of thousands of people. In Nov. 1986 it became known that the U.S., which had generally sided with Iraq during the war, had secretly shipped arms to Iran to gain that country's help in obtaining the release of U.S. hostages held in Lebanon. The revelation sparked a major scandal in the U.S. A U.S. Navy warship shot down an Iranian airliner, July 3, 1988, after mistaking it for an F-14 fighter jet; all 290 aboard the plane died.

An earthquake struck northern Iran June 21, 1990, killing more than 45,000, injuring 100,000, and leaving 400,000 homeless. Some 1 mil Kurdish refugees fled from Iraq to Iran following the Persian Gulf War of 1991. To curb Iran's alleged support for international terrorism, the U.S. in 1996 authorized sanctions on foreign companies that invest there.

Mohammad Khatami, a moderate Shiite Muslim cleric, was elected president on May 23, 1997, winning nearly 70% of the vote. During the next 3 years, hardline Islamists clashed repeatedly and sometimes violently with reformers, who won a majority in parliamentary elections Feb. 18 and May 5, 2000. Inviting rapprochement with Iran, the U.S. eased some sanctions Mar. 18. Khatami was reelected June 8, 2001, with a 77% majority but continued to face resistance from religious conservatives.

The U.S.-led war in Iraq, beginning Mar. 2003, contributed to a new period of instability in Iran. An earthquake Dec. 26 in Bam, southeast Iran, killed about 26,000 people. After the Guardian Council, dominated by religious conservatives, disqualified some 2,400 reformist candidates, hardliners won legislative elections Feb. 20, 2004.

The mayor of Tehran, Mahmoud Ahmadinejad, a religious conservative who campaigned as an economic reformer, defeated former Pres. Hashemi Rafsanjani in a runoff election June 24 and took office Aug. 3. The Bush administration, which in 2002 had called Iran part of an "axis of evil," accused the Iranian regime of seeking to build nuclear weapons, aiding Shiite militias in Iraq, and supplying rockets to Hezbollah fighters in Lebanon for use against Israel.

Seeking to halt Iran's uranium-enrichment program, which could be used for either military or civilian purposes, the UN Security Council imposed sanctions, Dec. 23, 2006, and toughened them, Mar. 24, 2007. After the Guardian Council disqualified about 1,700 reformist candidates, conservative allies of Ahmadinejad won parliamentary elections Mar.-Apr. 2008. Further talks on nuclear enrichment ended in deadlock July 20, and the U.S. imposed additional sanctions Sept. 10.

After a hard-fought campaign, Ahmadinejad claimed victory in the presidential election of June 12, 2009. His main opponent, former Prime Min. Mir Hussein Moussavi, supported by Khatami and Rafsanjani, claimed that the official count, which gave Ahmadinejad more than 62% of the total vote, was fraudulent. Huge protests by Moussavi supporters in Tehran and other major cities were crushed by police and Basij paramilitary forces. A mass trial of more than 100 dissidents, beginning Aug. 1, included confessions that opposition leaders said had been coerced. Tensions with the U.S. and European governments were heightened in late Sept. by disclosures that Iran had been secretly enriching uranium at an underground site near Qom, and by Iranian tests of medium-range missiles capable of reaching Israel or U.S. and European bases in the Persian Gulf region. In direct talks Oct. 1 with the U.S. and other world powers, Iran agreed to allow international inspection of the Qom site and other nuclear safeguards.

Iraq

Republic of Iraq

People: Population: 28,945,657. **Age distrib.** (%): <15: 38.8; 65+: 3. **Pop. density:** 173.5 per sq mi, 67 per sq km. **Urban:** 66.9%. **Ethnic groups:** Arab 75%-80%; Kurdish 15%-20%; Turkoman, Assyrian, or other 5%. **Principal languages:** Arabic, Kurdish (official in Kurdish regions), Turkoman (Turkish dialect), Assyrian, Armenian. **Chief religions:** Muslim (Shi'a 60%-65%, Sunni 32%-37%), Christian or other 3%.

Geography: Total area: 168,754 sq mi, 437,072 sq km; **Land area:** 166,859 sq mi, 432,162 sq km. **Location:** In Middle East, occupying most of historic Mesopotamia. **Neighbors:** Jordan, Syria on W; Turkey on N; Iran on E; Kuwait, Saudi Arabia on S. **Topography:** Mostly an alluvial plain, including the Tigris and Euphrates rivers, descending from mountains in N to desert in SW. Persian Gulf region is marshland. **Capital:** Baghdad, 5,054,000. **Cities (urban aggr.):** Mosul (Al-Mawsil), 1,316,000; Erbil, 926,000; Basra, 870,000.

Government: Type: In transition. **Head of state:** Pres. Jalal Talabani; b. 1933; in office: Apr. 7, 2005. **Head of gov.:** Prime Min.

Nouri Kamel al-Maliki; b. 1950; in office: May 20, 2006. **Local divisions:** 18 governorates (3 in Kurdish Autonomous Region). **Defense budget:** NA. **Active troops:** 577,056.

Economy: Industries: oil, chemicals, textiles, leather, constr. materials, food proc. **Chief crops:** wheat, barley, rice, vegetables, dates, cotton. **Natural resources:** oil, nat. gas, phosphates, sulfur. **Arable land:** 13%. **Crude oil reserves:** 115 bil bbls. **Livestock:** cattle: 1.5 mil; chickens: 33 mil; goats: 1.7 mil; sheep: 6.2 mil. **Fish catch:** 73,589 metric tons. **Electricity prod.:** 30 bil kWh. **Labor force:** NA.

Finance: Monetary unit: Dinar (IQD) (Oct. 2009: 1,153.41 = $1 U.S.). **GDP:** $103.9 bil; **per capita GDP:** $3,700; **GDP growth:** 7.8%. **Imports:** $43.5 bil; Syria 27.6%, Turkey 20.6%, U.S. 11.2%, China 6.2%, Jordan 4.7%. **Exports:** $66.1 bil; U.S. 43.5%, Italy 11%, S. Korea 7.3%, Canada 4.5%, France 4.1%. **Tourism:** NA. **Budget** (FY08 est.): $48.4 bil. **Intl. reserves less gold:** $32.49 bil. **Gold:** 190,000 oz t. **Consumer prices:** NA.

Transport: Railroad: Length: 1,412 mi. **Motor vehicles:** 827,000 pass. cars; 311,000 comm. vehicles. **Civil aviation:** 12.4 mil pass.-mi; 75 airports. **Chief ports:** Al Basrah, Khawr az Zubayr, Umm Qasr.

Communications: TV sets: 82 per 1,000 pop. **Radios:** 229 per 1,000 pop. **Telephone lines:** 1.1 mil. **Internet:** 300,000 users.

Health: Life expect.: 68.3 male; 71 female. **Births** (per 1,000 pop.): 30.8. **Deaths** (per 1,000 pop.): 5.1. **Natural inc.:** 2.56%. **Infant mortality** (per 1,000 live births): 45.4. **HIV rate:** NA.

Education: Compulsory: ages 6-11. **Literacy:** 74.1%.

Major intl. organizations: UN (FAO, IBRD, ILO, IMF, IMO, WHO), AL, OPEC.

Iraqi Interests Section: 1801 P St. NW 20036; 483-7500.

Website: www.cabinet.iq

The Tigris-Euphrates valley, formerly called Mesopotamia, was the site of one of the earliest civilizations in the world. Mesopotamia ceased to be a separate entity after the Persian, Greek, and Arab conquests. The Arabs founded Baghdad, from where the caliph ruled a vast Islamic empire in the 8th and 9th centuries. Mongol and Turkish conquests led to a decline in the region's population, economy, cultural life, and irrigation system.

Britain secured a League of Nations mandate over Iraq after WWI. Independence under a king came in 1932. Rebellious army officers killed King Faisal II, July 14, 1958, and established a leftist, pan-Arab republic, which pursued close ties with the USSR. Successive regimes were increasingly dominated by the Baath Arab Socialist Party. A Baath leader, Saddam Hussein, became president of Iraq, July 16, 1979. After purging his enemies, he ruled as a dictator for more than 2 decades, repressing Iraq's Kurds and Shiites and launching disastrous wars against 2 neighboring nations, Iran and Kuwait. Hussein sought weapons of mass destruction; Israeli planes destroyed a nuclear reactor near Baghdad June 7, 1981, claiming it could be used to produce nuclear weapons.

After skirmishing intermittently for 10 months over the sovereignty of the disputed Shatt al-Arab waterway that divides the two countries, Iraq and Iran entered into open warfare on Sept. 22, 1980. Iran repulsed early Iraqi advances, producing a long and costly stalemate; hundreds of thousands of Iraqis lost their lives during the 8-year conflict. Hussein used poison gas against Iraqi Kurds in 1988, killing up to 5,000 people in Halabja, the first mass use of poison gas against civilians since the Holocaust.

Iraq attacked and overran Kuwait Aug. 2, 1990. Backed by the UN, a U.S.-led coalition launched air and missile attacks on Iraq, Jan. 16, 1991. The coalition began a ground attack to retake Kuwait Feb. 23. Iraqi forces showed little resistance and were soundly defeated in 4 days. Some 175,000 Iraqis were taken prisoner, and Iraqi casualties were estimated at over 85,000. As part of the cease-fire agreement, Iraq agreed to scrap all poison gas and germ weapons and allow UN observers to inspect the sites. UN trade sanctions would remain in effect until Iraq complied with all terms.

In Feb. 1991, Iraqi troops drove Kurdish insurgents and civilians to the borders of Iran and Turkey, causing a refugee crisis. The U.S. and allies established havens inside Iraq for the Kurds. The U.S. launched a missile attack aimed at Iraq's intelligence headquarters in Baghdad June 26, 1993, citing evidence that Iraq had sponsored a plot to kill former Pres. George Bush.

Iraqi cooperation with UN weapons inspection teams was intermittent throughout the 1990s. On Dec. 9, 1996, the UN began a program. An independent panel later concluded that there was massive corruption in UN administration of the program, allowing the Iraqi regime to reap huge profits (aside from the large profits through oil smuggling).

Iraqi resistance to UN access to suspected weapons sites touched off diplomatic crises during 1997-98, culminating in intensive U.S. and British aerial bombardment of Iraqi military targets, Dec. 16-19, 1998. After 2 years of sporadic activity, U.S. and Brit-

ish warplanes struck harder at sites near Baghdad on Feb. 16, 2001.

In a speech before the UN, Sept. 12, 2002, Pres. George W. Bush demanded that Iraq eliminate weapons of mass destruction, refrain from supporting terrorism, and end repression. Despite opposition from some countries, including France, Germany, and Russia, a U.S.-led coalition launched an invasion of Iraq on the evening of Mar. 19, 2003. By Apr. 6 the British controlled Basra and other areas in the south, and the U.S. entered Baghdad Apr. 7. Hussein had disappeared, the Iraqi government had collapsed, and most of Iraq's armed forces had dissolved into the civilian population. On May 1, Pres. Bush declared that major combat there was over. Continuing searches failed to find evidence of usable chemical, biological, or nuclear weapons the U.S. and other countries claimed Iraq had stockpiled.

The U.S. initially governed Iraq through a Coalition Provisional Authority, headed by L. Paul Bremer. A 25-member Iraqi Governing Council was appointed and named a cabinet Sept. 1, 2003. Reconstruction efforts continued but were hampered by guerrilla attacks from Baath remnants, Islamic extremists, and others. Bombings at UN headquarters in Baghdad, Aug. 19 and Sept. 22, led the UN to scale back its presence in Iraq.

Photographs released in Apr. 2004 graphically showed instances of physical abuse and sexual humiliation of Iraqi inmates by U.S. military personnel at Baghdad's Abu Ghraib prison in fall 2003. The images sparked widespread condemnation and U.S. criminal proceedings against some individuals.

Coalition forces succeeded in neutralizing many leaders of the former regime. Two of Hussein's sons, Uday and Qusay, were killed July 22, 2003, by U.S. troops in Mosul. Saddam Hussein was captured in an underground hideout Dec. 13, 2003; tried and convicted for committing crimes against humanity in the 1980s, he was hanged Dec. 30, 2006.

On June 28, 2004, U.S. authorities officially transferred sovereignty to a transitional Iraqi government. Despite threats by insurgents, an estimated 8 mil people in Iraq, mostly Shiites and Kurds, cast ballots Jan. 30, 2005, for a 275-member transitional national assembly. On Apr. 6, the assembly elected Jalal al-Talabani, a Kurd, as president; Ibrahim al-Jaafari, a Shiite, became prime minister. The insurgents launched new waves of attacks, killing hundreds of police and army recruits. Rumors of a suicide bomber set off a stampede by Shiite pilgrims in northern Baghdad Aug. 31, killing close to 1,000 people. The U.S. blamed Jordanian militant Abu Musab al-Zarqawi, leader of the terrorist group Al Qaeda in Iraq, for directing a series of kidnappings, beheadings, and suicide bombings. He was killed by a U.S. air strike, June 7, 2006.

Legislative elections were held Dec. 15, 2005, and official results announced Jan. 20, 2006, but political wrangling delayed installation of a new government, headed by Shiite leader Nouri Kamel al-Maliki, until May 20. Meanwhile, a bomb Feb. 22 that destroyed the dome of Samarra's Golden Mosque, a Shiite shrine, triggered an intensification of sectarian violence between Sunnis and Shiites, much of it in Baghdad. The Iraqi civilian death toll averaged more than 2,800 per month in 2006.

In early 2007, Lt. Gen. David H. Petraeus became the top U.S. military commander in Iraq; a "surge" elevated U.S. troop strength from 132,000 in Jan. to peak of 171,000 in Oct. Many of the reinforcements were sent to the Baghdad area. U.S. troop deaths for all of 2007 totaled 899 (the highest for any year since the war began), but military and civilian casualties dropped steadily from mid-2007 through 2008. Contributing to the reduction in violence were a cease-fire by Shiite militias and a shift by Sunni clan leaders, especially in Anbar Province, against Al Qaeda in Iraq; the U.S. military transferred Anbar to Iraqi government control Sept. 1, 2008.

Parliament approved, Nov. 27, 2008, a status-of-forces agreement calling for the U.S. to withdraw its troops from Iraqi cities and towns by June 30, 2009, and for all U.S. forces to leave Iraq by Dec. 31, 2011. By Sept. 2009 the U.S. troop presence had declined to 130,000, and allied countries had withdrawn nearly all their combat forces. (Also present were tens of thousands of U.S. and other foreign civilian advisers and contractors.) The pullout coincided with an apparent increase in insurgent activities, including truck bombings Aug. 19 that killed at least 95 people and injured nearly 600 at government ministries in central Baghdad.

By Sept. 2009, more than 4,300 U.S. service members had been killed in connection with Operation Iraqi Freedom; about 31,500 had been wounded, many from insurgents' roadside bombs, also known as improvised explosive devices (IEDs). British troop losses totaled more than 170; other allies, over 130. More than 110,000 Iraqi civilians and over 9,100 police and security forces were killed between June 2003 and July 2009, according to a U.S. analysis by the Brookings Institution. Through May 2009, Congress had appropriated more than $642 bil for war-related operations in Iraq.

Ireland

People: Population: 4,203,200. **Age distrib.** (%): <15: 20.9; 65+: 12. **Pop. density:** 158 per sq mi, 61 per sq km. **Urban:** 60.5%. **Ethnic groups:** Irish 87%, other white 8%. **Principal languages:** English (official; generally used), Irish (Gaelic) (official; spoken mainly in W seaboard areas). **Chief religions:** Roman Catholic 87%, Church of Ireland 3%, none 4%.

Geography: Total area: 27,135 sq mi, 70,280 sq km; **Land area:** 26,599 sq mi, 68,890 sq km. **Location:** In Atlantic O. just W of Great Britain. **Neighbors:** United Kingdom (Northern Ireland) on E. **Topography:** Consists of a central plateau surrounded by isolated groups of hills and mountains. Coastline is heavily indented by the Atlantic O. **Capital:** Dublin, 1,059,000.

Government: Type: Parliamentary republic. **Head of state:** Pres. Mary McAleese; b. June 27, 1951; in office: Nov. 11, 1997. **Head of gov.:** Prime Min. Brian Cowen; b. Jan. 10, 1960; in office: May 7, 2008. **Local divisions:** 26 counties. **Defense budget:** $1.3 bil. **Active troops:** 10,460.

Economy: Industries: food products, brewing, textiles, clothing, chemicals, pharmaceuticals, machinery, rail transp. equip. **Chief crops:** turnips, barley, potatoes, sugar beets, wheat. **Natural resources:** nat. gas, peat, copper, lead, zinc, silver, barite, gypsum, limestone, dolomite. **Arable land:** 17%. **Livestock:** cattle: 6.7 mil; chickens: 13 mil; goats: 7,300; pigs: 1.6 mil; sheep: 5.5 mil. **Fish catch:** 313,746 metric tons. **Electricity prod.:** 26.1 bil kWh. **Labor force** (2006 est.): agric. 6%, industry 27%, services 67%.

Finance: Monetary unit: Euro (EUR) (Oct. 2009: 0.68 = $1 U.S.). **GDP:** $188.4 bil; **per capita GDP:** $45,300; **GDP growth:** –3%. **Imports:** $80.9 bil; UK 37.9%, U.S. 11.6%, Germany 8.8%, Netherlands 5.6%. **Exports:** $119.6 bil; UK 18.6%, U.S. 18.3%, Belgium 14.7%, Germany 7%, France 5.9%, Spain 4.2%. **Tourism:** $6.1 bil. **Budget:** $88.3 bil. **Intl. reserves less gold:** $566 mil. **Gold:** 180,000 oz t. **Consumer prices:** 4.1%.

Transport: Railroad: Length: 2,011 mi. **Motor vehicles:** 1.7 mil pass. cars; 300,000 comm. vehicles. **Civil aviation:** 27.8 bil pass.-mi; 17 airports. **Chief ports:** Cork, Dublin, Shannon Foynes.

Communications: TV sets: 406 per 1,000 pop. **Radios:** 697 per 1,000 pop. **Telephone lines:** 2.2 mil. **Daily newspaper circ.** (2004): 182.4 per 1,000 pop. **Internet:** 2.8 mil users.

Health: Life expect.: 75.4 male; 80.9 female. **Births** (per 1,000 pop.): 14.3. **Deaths** (per 1,000 pop.): 7.8. **Natural inc.:** 0.66%. **Infant mortality** (per 1,000 live births): 5.1. **HIV rate:** 0.2%.

Education: Compulsory: ages 6-15. **Literacy:** 99%.

Major intl. organizations: UN (FAO, IBRD, ILO, IMF, IMO, WHO, WTO), EU, OECD, OSCE.

Embassy: 2234 Massachusetts Ave. NW 20008; 462-3939.

Website: www.irlgov.ie

Celtic tribes invaded the islands about the 4th cent. BCE; their Gaelic culture and literature flourished and spread to Scotland and elsewhere in the 5th cent. CE, the same century in which St. Patrick converted the Irish to Christianity. Invasions by Norsemen began in the 8th cent., ended with defeat of the Danes by the Irish King Brian Boru in 1014. English invasions started in the 12th cent.; for over 700 years the Anglo-Irish struggle continued with bitter rebellions and savage repressions.

The Easter Monday Rebellion in 1916 failed but was followed by guerrilla warfare and harsh reprisals by British troops called the "Black and Tans." The Dail Eireann (Irish parliament) reaffirmed independence in Jan. 1919. The British offered dominion status to Ulster (6 counties) and southern Ireland (26 counties) Dec. 1921. The constitution of the Irish Free State, a British dominion, was adopted Dec. 11, 1922. Northern Ireland remained part of the United Kingdom.

A new constitution adopted by plebiscite came into operation Dec. 29, 1937. It declared the name of the state Eire in the Irish language (Ireland in the English) and declared it a sovereign democratic state. On Dec. 21, 1948, an Irish law declared the country a republic rather than a dominion and withdrew it from the Commonwealth. The British Parliament recognized both actions, 1949, but reasserted its claim to incorporate the 6 northeastern counties in the UK.

Irish governments have favored peaceful unification of all Ireland and cooperated with Britain against terrorist groups. After negotiators in Northern Ireland approved a peace settlement on Good Friday, Apr. 10, 1998, voters in the Irish Republic endorsed the accord, on May 22; the agreement required the removal from the Irish constitution of territorial claims on the north.

Expansion of educational opportunities and foreign investment in high-tech industries since the 1990s have boosted Ireland's prosperity. Ireland's first woman president, Mary Robinson, resigned Sept. 12, 1997, to become UN high commissioner for human rights, 1997-2002. She was succeeded as president by Mary McAleese, a law professor from Northern Ireland and the first northerner to hold the office. Implicated in a corruption inquiry, Prime Min. Bertie Ahern announced his resignation Apr. 2, 2008, after 11 years in power; the Dail Eireann May 7 chose Finance Min. Brian Cowen to succeed him. In referendums June 12, 2008, and Oct. 2, 2009, Irish voters first rejected and then approved the Lisbon Treaty, a plan to revamp the EU.

Israel
State of Israel

People: Population: 7,233,701. **Age distrib.** (%): <15: 27.9; 65+: 9.9. **Pop. density:** 921.6 per sq mi, 355.8 per sq km. **Urban:** 91.6%. **Ethnic groups:** Jewish 76% (Israel-born 67%, Europe/American-born 23%, Africa-born 6%), non-Jewish (mostly Arab) 24%. **Principal languages:** Hebrew, Arabic (both official); English (most commonly used foreign lang.). **Chief religions:** Jewish 76%, Muslim 16%, Arab Christian 2%.

Geography: Total area: 8,019 sq mi, 20,770 sq km; **Land area:** 7,849 sq mi, 20,330 sq km. **Location:** Middle East, on E end of Mediterranean Sea. **Neighbors:** Lebanon on N; Syria, West Bank, Jordan on E; Gaza Strip, Egypt on W. **Topography:** The Mediterranean coastal plain is fertile and well-watered. In the center is the Judean Plateau. A triangular-shaped semi-desert region, the Negev, extends from S of Beersheba to an apex at head of the Gulf of Aqaba. The E border drops sharply into the Jordan Rift Valley, including Lake Tiberias (Sea of Galilee) and the Dead Sea, which is c. 1,300 ft below sea level, lowest point on earth's surface. **Capital:** Jerusalem (most countries maintain their embassies in Tel Aviv), 736,000. **Cities (urban aggr.):** Tel Aviv-Jaffa, 3,112,000; Haifa, 1,011,000.

Government: Type: Republic. **Head of state:** Pres. Shimon Peres; b. Aug. 1923; in office: July 15, 2007. **Head of gov.:** Prime Min. Benjamin Netanyahu; b. Oct. 21, 1949; in office; Mar. 31, 2009. **Local divisions:** 6 districts. **Defense budget:** $11.6 bil. **Active troops:** 176,500.

Economy: Industries: high-tech products (incl. aviation, comm., computer-aided design & manufactures, wood & paper products, potash & phosphates, food, beverages, tobacco. **Chief crops:** citrus, vegetables, cotton. **Natural resources:** timber, potash, copper ore, nat. gas, phosphate rock, magnesium bromide, clays, sand. **Crude oil reserves:** 1.9 mil bbls. **Arable land:** 15%. **Livestock:** cattle: 394,000; chickens: 37.1 mil; goats: 87,000; pigs: 21,500; sheep: 433,000. **Fish catch:** 26,236 metric tons. **Electricity prod.:** 48.7 bil kWh. **Labor force** (2008): agric. 2%, industry 16%, services 82%.

Finance: Monetary unit: New Shekel (ILS) (Oct. 2009: 3.72 = $1 U.S.). **GDP:** $201.4 bil; **per capita GDP:** $28,300; **GDP growth:** 4.2%. **Imports:** $64.3 bil; U.S. 12.3%, Belgium 6.5%, China 6.5%, Switzerland 6.1%, Germany 6%. **Exports:** $56.6 bil; U.S. 32.5%, Belgium 7.5%, Hong Kong 6.7%. **Tourism:** $3.1 bil. **Budget:** $53.6 bil. **Intl. reserves less gold:** $27.6 bil. **Gold:** NA. **Consumer prices:** NA.

Transport: Railroad: Length: 567 mi. **Motor vehicles:** 1.7 mil pass. cars; 370,800 comm. vehicles. **Civil aviation:** 10.2 bil pass.-mi; 30 airports. **Chief ports:** Ashdod, Elat, Hadera, Haifa.

Communications: TV sets: 328 per 1,000 pop. **Radios:** 524 per 1,000 pop. **Telephone lines:** 2.9 mil. **Internet:** 2.1 mil users.

Health: Life expect.: 78.5 male; 82.8 female. **Births** (per 1,000 pop.): 20. **Deaths** (per 1,000 pop.): 5.4. **Natural inc.:** 1.46%. **Infant mortality** (per 1,000 live births): 4.3. **HIV rate:** 0.1%.

Education: Compulsory: ages 5-15. **Literacy:** 91.8%.

Major intl. organizations: UN (FAO, IBRD, ILO, IMF, IMO, WHO, WTO).

Embassy: 3514 International Dr. NW 20008; 364-5500.

Website: www.gov.il

Occupying the southwest corner of the ancient Fertile Crescent, Israel contains some of the oldest known evidence of agriculture and of primitive town life. The Hebrews probably arrived early in the 2nd millennium BCE. Under King David and his successors (c. 1000 BCE-597 BCE), Judaism was developed and secured. After conquest by Babylonians, Persians, and Greeks, an independent Jewish kingdom was revived, 168 BCE, but Rome took effective control in the next century, suppressed Jewish revolts in 70 CE and 135 CE, and renamed Judea Palestine, after the earlier coastal inhabitants, the Philistines.

Arab invaders conquered Palestine in 636. The Arabic language and Islam prevailed within a few centuries, but a Jewish minority remained. The land was ruled from the 11th cent. as a part of non-Arab empires by Seljuks, Mamluks, and Ottomans (with a Crusader interval, 1098-1291).

After 4 centuries of Ottoman rule, the land was taken in 1917 by Britain, which pledged in the Balfour Declaration to support a Jewish homeland there. In 1920 a British Palestine Mandate was recognized; in 1922 the land east of the Jordan was detached.

Jewish immigration, begun in the late 19th cent., swelled in the 1930s with refugees from the Nazis; heavy Arab immigration from Syria and Lebanon also occurred. Arab opposition to Jewish immigration turned violent in 1920, 1921, 1929, and 1936. The UN General Assembly voted in 1947 to partition Palestine into an Arab and a Jewish state. Britain withdrew in May 1948.

Israel was declared an independent state May 14, 1948; the Arabs rejected partition. Egypt, Jordan, Syria, Lebanon, Iraq, and Saudi Arabia invaded but failed to destroy the Jewish state, which gained territory. Separate armistices with the Arab nations were signed in 1949; Jordan occupied the West Bank, Egypt occupied Gaza. Neither granted Palestinian autonomy.

After persistent terrorist raids, Israel invaded Egypt's Sinai, Oct. 29, 1956, aided briefly by British and French forces. A UN cease-fire was arranged Nov. 6.

An uneasy truce between Israel and the Arab countries lasted until 1967, when Egypt reoccupied the Gaza Strip and closed the Gulf of Aqaba to Israeli shipping. In a 6-day war that started June 5, the Israelis took the Gaza Strip, occupied the Sinai Peninsula to the Suez Canal, and captured East Jerusalem, Syria's Golan Heights, and Jordan's West Bank. Together, the West Bank and Gaza comprise the Palestinian territories, now represented by the Palestinian Authority (see below).

Egypt and Syria attacked Israel, Oct. 6, 1973 (on Yom Kippur, the most solemn day on the Jewish calendar). Israel counter-attacked, driving the Syrians back, and crossed the Suez Canal. A cease-fire took effect Oct. 24 and a UN peacekeeping force went to the area. Under a disengagement agreement signed Jan. 18, 1974, Israel withdrew from the canal's west bank. Israeli forces raided Entebbe, Uganda, July 3, 1976, and rescued 103 hostages who had been seized by Arab and German terrorists.

Israel's prime ministers, including David Ben-Gurion, Golda Meir, and Yitzhak Rabin, pursued a moderate socialist program, 1948-77. In 1977, the conservative opposition, led by Menachem Begin, was voted into office for the first time. Egypt's Pres. Anwar al-Sadat visited Jerusalem Nov. 1977, and on Mar. 26, 1979, Egypt and Israel signed a formal peace treaty, ending 30 years of war. Israel returned the Sinai to Egypt in 1982.

On June 7, 1981, Israeli jets destroyed an Iraqi atomic reactor near Baghdad that, Israel claimed, would have enabled Iraq to manufacture nuclear weapons. Israeli forces invaded Lebanon, June 6, 1982, to destroy Palestine Liberation Organization (PLO) strongholds there. After massive Israeli bombing of West Beirut, the PLO agreed to evacuate the city. Israeli troops entered West Beirut after newly elected Lebanese Pres. Bashir Gemayel was assassinated on Sept. 14. Israel drew widespread condemnation when Lebanese Christian forces, Sept. 16, entered two West Beirut refugee camps and slaughtered hundreds of Palestinians.

In 1989, violence escalated over the Israeli military occupation of the West Bank and Gaza Strip. In a series of uprisings known as the first intifada, Palestinian protesters defied Israeli troops, who forcibly retaliated. During the Persian Gulf War, 1991, Iraq fired Scud missiles at Israel. The Labor Party of Yitzhak Rabin won parliamentary elections, June 23, 1992.

Ongoing peace talks led to historic agreements between Israel and the PLO, Sept. 1993. The PLO recognized Israel's right to exist; Israel recognized the PLO as the Palestinians' representative. The two sides then signed, Sept. 13, an agreement for limited Palestinian self-rule in the West Bank and Gaza. Israel and Jordan signed, July 25, 1994, in Washington, DC, a declaration ending their 46-year state of war.

Arab and Jewish extremists repeatedly challenged the peace process. A Jewish gunman opened fire on Arab worshippers at a mosque in Hebron, Feb. 25, 1994, killing at least 29 before he himself was killed. On Nov. 4, 1995, an Orthodox Jewish Israeli assassinated Rabin as he left a peace rally in Tel Aviv. Support for Rabin's successor, Shimon Peres, was shaken by a series of suicide bombings and rocket attacks against Israel by Islamic militants. Emphasizing security issues, the candidate of the conservative Likud bloc, Benjamin Netanyahu, was elected prime minister on May 29, 1996.

Under an interim accord brokered by Pres. Bill Clinton and signed by Netanyahu and PLO leader Yasir Arafat at the White House, Oct. 23, 1998, Israel yielded more West Bank territory to the Palestinians, in exchange for new security guarantees. Negotiations bogged down, however, and full implementation did not begin until Sept. 1999. In the interim, Netanyahu lost by a landslide to the Labor candidate, Ehud Barak, in the election of May 17, 1999.

Israel pulled virtually all its troops out of southern Lebanon by May 24, 2000. Marathon summit talks in the U.S. between Barak and Arafat, July 11-25, failed. A second intifada began in late Sept. in Israel and the Palestinian territories. Barak called new elections for prime minister but lost Feb. 6, 2001, to Ariel Sharon, a hardliner. The bloodshed intensified during the summer, as Palestinian suicide bombers launched attacks on Israeli civilians and Israel struck at Palestinian-controlled territory and carried out an assassination campaign against suspected terrorists.

Israel launched a major West Bank offensive Mar. 29, 2002, 2 days after a suicide bomber killed 26 Israeli Jews at a Passover celebration in Netanya. Fighting was particularly fierce at the Jenin refugee camp, where 23 Israeli troops and at least 50 Palestinians were killed. Israel withdrew in early May but, after another wave of suicide bombings, reoccupied much of the West Bank June 21-27.

A U.S.-sponsored "road map" to Middle East peace, unveiled Apr. 30, 2003, made little headway. Israel Sept. 1 vowed "all-out war" against Hamas terrorists. Israeli missile strikes in Gaza City killed Hamas founder and leader Sheikh Ahmed Yassin Mar. 22, 2004, and his successor, Abdel Aziz al-Rantisi, Apr. 17. Hamas suicide bombers Aug. 31 blew up 2 buses in Beersheba, killing 16.

Sharon's decision to pull all Israeli settlers and troops out of Gaza (see below), approved by the cabinet Feb. 20, 2005, led to a realignment in Israeli politics. When right-wing Likud members opposed the plan, Sharon and Deputy Prime Min. Ehud Olmert

broke with them and formed the centrist Kadima Party. Sharon suffered a massive stroke Jan. 4, 2006. With Sharon incapacitated, Olmert became prime minister, led Kadima to victory in Mar. 28 elections, and formed a broad coalition government.

Border clashes in which Hamas militants from Gaza (June 25) and Hezbollah fighters from Lebanon (July 12) killed and captured Israeli soldiers rapidly escalated into full-scale war. Israeli air and ground forces hit hard in Gaza, but the fiercest fighting raged on the northern front. By Aug. 14, when a UN-sponsored cease-fire took hold, the estimated death toll from the war included nearly 1,150 Lebanese, almost 200 Gaza Palestinians, and 150 Israelis.

Israel's inability to gain a decisive victory over Hezbollah led to the resignation of army commander Lt. Gen. Dan Halutz, Jan. 16, 2007; an official report issued Apr. 30 criticized Olmert for a "severe failure" of wartime leadership. Peres became president July 15, 2007, after his predecessor, Moshe Katsav, accused of rape, pleaded guilty to lesser charges, received a suspended sentence, and resigned. Olmert, targeted in multiple corruption inquiries, announced July 30, 2008, that he would resign when his Kadima Party chose a replacement. Foreign Min. Tzipi Livni won a hard-fought party primary Sept. 17.

Unable to form a stable government, Livni called early elections for Feb. 10, 2009. After a campaign overshadowed by a 3-week war between Israel and Hamas in Gaza (see below), both Kadima and Likud fell far short of a majority. On Mar. 31, Netanyahu became prime minister for a 2nd time, heading a coalition that included Likud, Labor, the ultra-nationalist Yisrael Beitenu party, and the ultra-Orthodox Shas party.

Palestinian Territories

The Palestinian territories comprise the Gaza Strip, often called Gaza, and the West Bank, both occupied by Israel in 1967. Since 1996 the Palestinian Authority has been responsible for civil government in the territories. Elected president Jan. 20, 1996, PLO leader Yasir Arafat headed the Palestinian Authority until his death Nov. 11, 2004. Mahmoud Abbas (also called Abu Mazen), who had succeeded Arafat as PLO chairman and leader of the Fatah faction, was elected president Jan. 9, 2005. A victory by Hamas militants in legislative elections Jan. 25, 2006, led to a power struggle with Abbas, who favored a negotiated settlement with Israel. In bitter fighting, Hamas ousted Fatah from Gaza, June 2007, but Abbas retained power in the West Bank. From Sept. 2000, when the second intifada began, the Israeli-Palestinian conflict claimed the lives of more than 1,060 Israelis and at least 4,900 Palestinians; nearly 600 Palestinians were killed by other Palestinians in factional fighting.

The **Gaza Strip** extends northeast from the Sinai Peninsula for 40 km (25 mi), with the Mediterranean Sea to the west and Israel to the east. The Palestinian Authority is responsible for civil government. Nearly all the inhabitants are Palestinian Arabs, more than 35% of whom live in refugee camps. Population (2009 est.) 1,551,859. Area: 139 sq mi.

Israel captured Gaza from Egypt in the 1967 war. It remained under Israeli occupation until May 1994, when the Israeli Defense Forces withdrew. Agreements between Israel and the PLO in 1993 and 1994 provided for interim self-rule in Gaza, but Israel retained control over security. Israel forcibly evacuated all 9,000 Jewish settlers from Gaza by Aug. 22, 2005, and the last remaining Israeli soldiers pulled out Sept. 12. Israel established a fortified barrier on its Gaza border to block Palestinian infiltrators.

After the Hamas takeover, Israel declared Gaza a "hostile entity," Sept. 19, 2007, and intensified military and economic pressures. Hamas thwarted an Israeli blockade, Jan. 2008, by blowing up part of the border wall between Gaza and Egypt. Retaliating for Hamas rocket and mortar attacks, Israel launched an aerial assault and ground offensive in Gaza, Dec. 27, 2008-Jan. 18, 2009; investigators for B'Tselem, an Israeli human rights group, later concluded that the fighting killed 1,387 Palestinians, of whom more than half were civilians. A UN report issued Sept. 15 found evidence of war crimes committed by both sides.

The **West Bank** is located west of the Jordan R. and Dead Sea, bounded by Jordan on the east and by Israel on the north, west, and south. The Palestinian Authority administers several major cities, but Israel retains control over much land, including Jewish settlements. Population (2009 est.): 2,461,267. Area: 2,262.6 sq mi.

Israel captured the West Bank from Jordan in the 1967 war. A 1974 Arab summit conference designated the PLO as sole representative of West Bank Arabs. In 1988 Jordan cut legal and administrative ties with the territory. Jericho was returned to Palestinian control in May 1994. An accord between Israel and the PLO expanding Palestinian self-rule in the West Bank was signed Sept. 28, 1995. Later agreements gave Palestinians full or shared control of 40% of West Bank territory.

In June 2002 the Israeli government began building a controversial security barrier in the West Bank to restrict Palestinian access to Israel and reduce infiltration by suicide bombers. In a nonbinding ruling, July 9, 2004, the World Court said the barrier violated international law. Israel has continued to allow the expansion of Jewish settlements on the West Bank, despite U.S. government calls for a settlement freeze.

Italy
Italian Republic

People: Population: 58,126,212. **Age distrib.** (%): <15: 13.5; 65+: 20.2. **Pop. density:** 512 per sq mi, 197.7 per sq km. **Urban:** 67.6%. **Ethnic groups:** Italian (incl. small clusters of German-, French-, & Slovene-Italians in N; Albanian- & Greek-Italians in S). **Principal languages:** Italian (official), German, French, Slovene. **Chief religions:** Roman Catholic 90%, other (incl. Protestant, Jewish, growing Muslim communities) 10%.

Geography: Total area: 116,306 sq mi, 301,230 sq km; **Land area:** 113,522 sq mi, 294,020 sq km. **Location:** In S Europe, jutting into Mediterranean Sea. **Neighbors:** France on W; Switzerland, Austria on N; Slovenia on E; San Marino, Vatican City. **Topography:** Occupies long boot-shaped peninsula, extending SE from the Alps into Mediterranean, with islands of Sicily and Sardinia offshore. The alluvial Po Valley drains most of N. Rest of the country is rugged and mountainous, except for intermittent coastal plains, like the Campania, S of Rome. Apennine Mts. run down through center of peninsula. **Capital:** Rome, 3,339,000. **Cities (urban aggr.):** Milan, 2,945,000; Naples, 2,250,000; Palermo, 863,000; Turin, 1,652,000.

Government: Type: Republic. **Head of state:** Pres. Giorgio Napolitano; b. June 29, 1925; in office: May 15, 2006. **Head of gov.:** Prime Min. Silvio Berlusconi; b. Sept. 29, 1936; in office: May 8, 2008. **Local divisions:** 20 regions divided into 103 provinces. **Defense budget:** $37.8 bil. **Active troops:** 292,983.

Economy: Industries: tourism, machinery, iron & steel, chemicals, food proc., textiles, motor vehicles. **Chief crops:** fruits, vegetables, grapes, potatoes, sugar beets, soybeans, grain, olives. **Natural resources:** coal, mercury, zinc, potash, marble, pyrite (sulfur); nat. gas& crude oil deposits, fish. **Crude oil reserves:** 406.5 mil bbls. **Arable land:** 26%. **Livestock:** cattle: 6.1 mil; chickens: 100 mil; goats: 955,000; pigs: 9.3 mil; sheep: 8.2 mil. **Fish catch:** 467,043 metric tons. **Electricity prod.:** 291.2 bil kWh. **Labor force** (2005): agric. 4.2%, industry 30.7%, services 65.1%.

Finance: Monetary unit: Euro (EUR) (Oct. 2009: 0.68 = $1 U.S.). **GDP:** $1.8 tril; **per capita GDP:** $31,300; **GDP growth:** −1%. **Imports:** $546.9 bil; Germany 16%, France 8.6%, China 6.2%, Netherlands 5.3%, Libya 4.6%, Russia 4.3%. **Exports:** $546.9 bil; Germany 12.8%, France 11.2%, Spain 6.6%, U.S. 6.3%, UK 5.3%. **Tourism:** $42.7 bil. **Budget:** $1.02 tril. **Intl. reserves less gold:** $24.08 bil. **Gold:** 78.83 mil oz t. **Consumer prices:** 3.3%.

Transport: Railroad: Length: 12,259 mi. **Motor vehicles:** 34.7 mil pass. cars; 4.6 mil comm. vehicles. **Civil aviation:** 31.8 bil pass.-mi; 101 airports. **Chief ports:** Augusta, Genoa, Livorno, Ravenna, Sarroch, Taranto, Trieste, Venice.

Communications: TV sets: 492 per 1,000 pop. **Radios:** 880 per 1,000 pop. **Telephone lines:** 20 mil. **Daily newspaper circ.** (2004): 137.1 per 1,000 pop. **Internet:** 29.1 mil users.

Health: Life expect.: 77.1 male; 83.2 female. **Births** (per 1,000 pop.): 8.4. **Deaths** (per 1,000 pop.): 10.6. **Natural inc.:** −0.23%. **Infant mortality** (per 1,000 live births): 5.6. **HIV rate:** 0.4%.

Education: Compulsory: ages 6-14. **Literacy:** 98.9%.

Major intl. organizations: UN and all of its specialized agencies, EU, NATO, OECD, OSCE.

Embassy: 3000 Whitehaven St. NW 20008; 612-4400.

Website: www.quirinale.it

Rome emerged as the major power in Italy after 500 BCE, dominating the Etruscans to the north and Greeks to the south. Under the Empire, which lasted until the 5th cent. CE, Rome ruled most of Western Europe, the Balkans, the Middle East, and North Africa. After Rome fell, Italy became a patchwork of kingdoms, principalities, and city-states until reunified, 1870.

The Fascist leader Benito Mussolini came to power, 1922, and aligned Italy with Nazi Germany in WWII. After Fascism was overthrown in 1943, Italy declared war on Germany and Japan and contributed to the Allied victory. It surrendered conquered lands and lost its colonies. Mussolini was killed by partisans Apr. 28, 1945. Victor Emmanuel III abdicated May 9, 1946; his son Humbert II was king until June 10, when Italy became a republic after a referendum, June 2-3. In the postwar decades, Italy had a succession of short-lived governments.

Christian Democratic leader and former Prime Min. Aldo Moro was abducted and murdered in 1978 by Red Brigade terrorists. The wave of left-wing political violence, including other kidnappings and assassinations, continued into the 1980s.

In the early 1990s, scandals implicated some of Italy's most prominent politicians. In Mar. 1994 voting, under reformed election rules, right-wing parties won a majority, dislodging Italy's long-powerful Christian Democratic Party. Italy led a 7,000-member peacekeeping force in Albania, Apr.-Aug. 1997, and contributed 2,000 troops to the NATO-led security force (KFOR) that entered Kosovo in June 1999.

Supporters of Silvio Berlusconi, a multibillionaire media magnate, won the parliamentary elections of May 13, 2001. In 2003, Berlusconi backed the U.S.-led war in Iraq, and a force of up to 3,200 Italian troops served in the coalition. Turin hosted the Winter

Olympics, Feb. 10-26, 2006. A coalition of center-left parties led by Romano Prodi scored a narrow win over Berlusconi in parliamentary voting, Apr. 9-10. Italy pulled all its troops out of Iraq by Nov. 2006. Berlusconi returned at the head of a center-right coalition after elections Apr. 13-14, 2008.

An earthquake in the Abruzzo region of central Italy Apr. 6, 2009, battered the town of L'Aquila, killed more than 300 people, and left at least 50,000 homeless. At the G-8 summit in L'Aquila July 8-10, leaders of major industrialized nations agreed on long-term goals for curbing global warming and on a 3-year, $20 bil plan to provide food and agricultural aid to the world's poorest countries. Scandal surrounded Berlusconi's private life throughout the year, especially after his wife announced in early May that she would file for divorce, citing his relationships with much younger women. About 3,300 Italian troops were serving with NATO forces in Afghanistan in mid-2009.

Sicily, 9,926 sq mi, pop. (2007 est.) 5,029,683 is an island 180 by 120 mi, seat of a region that embraces the island of Pantelleria, 32 sq mi, and the Lipari group, 44 sq mi, including 2 active volcanoes: Vulcano, 1,637 ft, and Stromboli, 3,038 ft. From prehistoric times Sicily has been settled by various peoples; a Greek state had its capital at Syracuse. Rome took Sicily from Carthage 215 BCE. **Mt. Etna,** an 11,053-ft active volcano, is its tallest peak.

Sardinia, 9,301 sq mi, pop. (2001 est.) 1,599,500, lies in the Mediterranean, 115 mi W of Italy and 7½ mi S of Corsica. It is 160 mi long, 68 mi wide, and mountainous, with mining of coal, zinc, lead, copper. In 1720 Sardinia was added to the possessions of the Dukes of Savoy in Piedmont and Savoy to form the Kingdom of Sardinia. Giuseppe Garibaldi is buried on the nearby isle of Caprera. **Elba,** 86 sq mi, lies 6 mi W of Tuscany. Napoleon I lived in exile on Elba 1814-15.

Jamaica

People: Population: 2,825,928. **Age distrib.** (%): <15: 31.4; 65+: 7.5. **Pop. density:** 675.8 per sq mi, 260.9 per sq km. **Urban:** 52.7%. **Ethnic groups:** Black 91%, mixed 6%. **Principal languages:** English, English patois. **Chief religion:** Protestant (incl. Seventh-Day Adventist, Pentecostal, Other Church of God, Baptist) 63%, none 21%.

Geography: Total area: 4,244 sq mi, 10,991 sq km; **Land area:** 4,182 sq mi, 10,831 sq km. **Location:** In W Indies. **Neighbors:** Nearest are Cuba to N, Haiti to E. **Topography:** Four-fifths of country covered by mountains. **Capital:** Kingston, 580,000.

Government: Type: Constitutional monarchy with parliamentary system based on UK-model. **Head of state:** Queen Elizabeth II, represented by Patrick Allen; b. Feb. 7, 1951; in office: Feb. 26, 2009. **Head of gov.:** Prime Min. Bruce Golding; b. Dec. 5, 1947; in office: Sept. 11, 2007. **Local divisions:** 14 parishes. **Defense budget:** $108 mil. **Active troops:** 2,830.

Economy: Industries: tourism, bauxite/alumina, agric. proc., light manufactures, rum, cement, metal, paper, chemical products. **Chief crops:** sugarcane, bananas, coffee, citrus, yams. **Natural resources:** bauxite, gypsum, limestone. **Arable land:** 16%. **Livestock:** cattle: 430,000; chickens: 12.5 mil; goats: 440,000; pigs: 35,000; sheep: 1,280. **Fish catch:** 22,164 metric tons. **Electricity prod.:** 7 bil kWh. **Labor force** (2006): agric. 17%, industry 19%, services 64%.

Finance: Monetary unit: Dollar (JMD) (Oct. 2009: 88.53 = $1 U.S.). **GDP:** $20.9 bil; **per capita GDP:** $7,500; **GDP growth:** −0.6%. **Imports:** $7.2 bil; U.S. 34.7%, Trinidad and Tobago 14.4%, Grenada 9.7%, Venezuela 9.5%, Brazil 4.1%. **Exports:** $2.6 bil; U.S. 30.8%, Canada 13.2%, Netherlands 9.8%, UK 9.2%, France 6.7%, Russia 6.6%, Germany 5.5%. **Tourism:** $1.9 bil. **Budget:** $4.3 bil. **Intl. reserves less gold:** $1.15 bil. **Gold:** NA. **Consumer prices:** 22%.

Transport: Motor vehicles: 104,000 pass. cars; 49,000 comm. vehicles. **Civil aviation:** 2.4 bil pass.-mi; 12 airports. **Chief ports:** Kingston, Port Esquivel, Port Kaiser, Port Rhoades, Rocky Point.

Communications: TV sets: 191 per 1,000 pop. **Radios:** 796 per 1,000 pop. **Telephone lines:** 316,600. **Internet:** 1.5 mil users.

Health: Life expect.: 71.9 male; 75.4 female. **Births** (per 1,000 pop.): 20. **Deaths** (per 1,000 pop.): 6.4. **Natural inc.:** 1.37%. **Infant mortality** (per 1,000 live births): 15.6. **HIV rate:** 1.6%.

Education: Compulsory: ages 6-11. **Literacy:** 86%.

Major intl. organizations: UN (FAO, IBRD, ILO, IMF, IMO, WHO, WTO), Caricom, the Commonwealth, OAS.

Embassy: 1520 New Hampshire Ave. NW 20036; 452-0660.

Website: www.jis.gov.jm

Jamaica was visited by Columbus, 1494, and ruled by Spain (under whom Arawak Indians died out) until seized by Britain, 1655. Jamaica won independence Aug. 6, 1962. The island's rich musical innovations include ska and reggae. Rastafarianism is an influential religious movement.

In 1974 Jamaica sought an increase in taxes paid by U.S. and Canadian bauxite mines. The socialist government acquired 50% ownership of the companies' Jamaican interests in 1976, and was reelected that year. Rudimentary welfare state measures were passed. Relations with the U.S. improved in the 1980s when Jamaican politics entered a more conservative phase. Violence between government forces and West Kingston slum residents claimed at least 20 lives July 7-10, 2001.

At least 17 died when Hurricane Ivan hit southern Jamaica Sept. 10-11, 2004. Portia Simpson Miller, leader of the People's National Party, became Jamaica's first female prime minister, Mar. 30, 2006. The opposition Jamaica Labour Party won the parliamentary elections of Sept. 3, 2007.

Japan

People: Population: 127,078,679. **Age distrib.** (%): <15: 13.5; 65+: 22.2. **Pop. density:** 878.3 per sq mi, 339.1 per sq km. **Urban:** 66%. **Ethnic groups:** Japanese 99%. **Principal language:** Japanese. **Chief religions:** Shinto & Buddhist (observed together) 84%, other (incl. Christian) 16%.

Geography: Total area: 145,883 sq mi, 377,835 sq km; **Land area:** 144,689 sq mi, 374,744 sq km. **Location:** Archipelago off E coast of Asia. **Neighbors:** Russia to N, S. Korea to W. **Topography:** Consists of 4 main islands: Honshu ("mainland"), 87,805 sq mi; Hokkaido, 30,144 sq mi; Kyushu, 14,114 sq mi; and Shikoku, 7,049 sq mi. The coast, deeply indented, measures 16,654 mi. The northern islands are continuation of the Sakhalin Mts. The Kunlun range of China continues into southern islands, the ranges meeting in Japanese Alps. In a vast transverse fissure crossing Honshu E-W rises a group of volcanoes, mostly extinct or inactive, including 12,388 ft. Mt. Fuji (Fujiyama) near Tokyo. **Capital:** Tokyo, 35,676,000. **Cities (urban aggr.):** Osaka-Kobe, 11,294,000; Nagoya, 3,230,000; Fukuoka-Kitakyushu, 2,792,000; Sapporo, 2,544,000.

Government: Type: Constitutional monarchy with parliamentary democracy. **Head of state:** Emperor Akihito; b. Dec. 23, 1933; in office: Jan. 7, 1989. **Head of gov.:** Prime Min. Yukio Hatoyama; b. Feb. 11, 1947; in office: Sept. 16, 2009. **Local divisions:** 47 prefectures. **Defense budget:** $41 bil. **Active troops:** 230,300.

Economy: Industries: motor vehicles, electronic equip., machine tools, steel & nonferrous metals, ships, chemicals, textiles, processed foods. **Chief crops:** rice, sugar beets, vegetables, fruit. **Natural resources:** fish. **Crude oil reserves:** 44.1 mil bbls. **Arable land:** 12%. **Livestock:** cattle: 4.4 mil; chickens: 288.5 mil; goats: 32,000; pigs: 9.8 mil; sheep: 10,000. **Fish catch:** 5.6 mil metric tons. **Electricity prod.:** 1,032.7 bil kWh. **Labor force** (2005): agric. 4.4%, industry 27.9%, services 66.4%.

Finance: Monetary unit: Yen (JPY) (Oct. 2009: 88.68 = $1 U.S.). **GDP:** $4.3 tril; **per capita GDP:** $34,000; **GDP growth:** –0.7%. **Imports:** $708.3 bil; China 18.9%, U.S. 10.4%, Saudi Arabia 6.7%, Australia 6.2%, UAE 6.1%, Indonesia 4.3%. **Exports:** $746.5 bil; U.S. 17.8%, China 16%, S. Korea 7.6%, Hong Kong 5.1%. **Tourism:** $9.3 bil. **Budget:** $1.6 tril. **Intl. reserves less gold:** $655.32 bil. **Gold:** 24.6 mil oz t. **Consumer prices:** 1.7%.

Transport: Railroad: Length: 14,606 mi. **Motor vehicles:** 57.1 mil pass. cars; 16.97 mil comm. vehicles. **Civil aviation:** 95.2 bil pass.-mi; 144 airports. **Chief ports:** Chiba, Kawasaki, Kobe, Mizushima, Moji, Nagoya, Osaka, Tokyo, Yokohama.

Communications: TV sets: 719 per 1,000 pop. **Radios:** 956 per 1,000 pop. **Telephone lines:** 47.6 mil. **Daily newspaper circ.** (2004): 551.2 per 1,000 pop. **Internet:** 90.1 mil users.

Health: Life expect.: 78.7 male; 85.6 female. **Births** (per 1,000 pop.): 7.9. **Deaths** (per 1,000 pop.): 9.3. **Natural inc.:** –0.14%. **Infant mortality** (per 1,000 live births): 2.8. **HIV rate:** NA.

Education: Compulsory: ages 6-15. **Literacy:** 99%.

Major intl. organizations: UN and all its specialized agencies, APEC, OECD.

Embassy: 2520 Massachusetts Ave. NW 20008; 238-6700.

Website: www.kantei.go.jp

According to Japanese legend, the empire was founded by Emperor Jimmu, 660 BCE, but earliest records of a unified Japan date from 1,000 years later. Chinese influence was strong in the formation of Japanese civilization. Buddhism was introduced before the 6th cent. CE.

A feudal system, with locally powerful noble families and their samurai warrior retainers, dominated from 1192. Central power was held by successive families of shoguns (military dictators), 1192-1867, until recovered by Emperor Meiji, 1868. The Portuguese and Dutch had minor trade with Japan in the 16th and 17th centuries; U.S. Commodore Matthew C. Perry opened the country to U.S. trade in a treaty ratified 1854. Industrialization was begun in the late 19th cent. Japan fought China, 1894-95, gaining Taiwan. After war with Russia, 1904-05, Russia ceded the southern half of Sakhalin and gave concessions in China. Japan annexed Korea, 1910.

In WWI Japan ousted Germany from Shandong in China and took over German Pacific islands. Japan took Manchuria in 1931 and launched full-scale war in China in 1937. Japan launched war against the U.S. by attacking Pearl Harbor Dec. 7, 1941. The U.S. dropped atomic bombs on Hiroshima, Aug. 6, and Nagasaki, Aug. 9, 1945. Japan surrendered Aug. 14, 1945.

In a new constitution adopted May 3, 1947, Japan renounced the right to wage war; the emperor gave up claims to divinity; the Diet became the sole law-making authority. The U.S. and 48 other non-Communist nations signed a peace treaty and the U.S. a bilateral defense agreement with Japan, in San Francisco Sept. 8, 1951, restoring Japan's sovereignty as of Apr. 28, 1952.

Rebuilding after WWII, Japan emerged as one of the most powerful economies in the world, and as a leader in technology. The U.S. and Western Europe criticized Japan for its restrictive policy on imports, which eventually allowed Japan to accumulate huge trade surpluses.

On June 26, 1968, the U.S. returned to Japanese control the Bonin Isls., Volcano Isls. (including Iwo Jima), and Marcus Isls. On May 15, 1972, Okinawa, the other Ryukyu Isls., and the Daito Isls. were returned by the U.S.; it was agreed the U.S. would continue to maintain military bases on Okinawa.

The Liberal Democratic Party (LDP) governed Japan from the mid-1950s through the early '90s. The Recruit scandal, the nation's worst political scandal since WWII, which involved illegal political donations and stock trading, led to the resignation of LDP Prime Min. Noboru Takeshita in May 1989. Following new political and economic scandals, the LDP was denied a majority in general elections July 18, 1993. On June 29, 1994, Tomiichi Murayama became Japan's first Socialist premier since 1947-48.

An earthquake in the Kobe area in Jan. 1995 claimed more than 5,000 lives, injured nearly 35,000, and caused over $90 bil in property damage. On Mar. 20, a nerve gas attack in the Tokyo subway (blamed on a religious cult) killed 12 and injured thousands. Public anger at the rape of a 12-year-old Okinawa schoolgirl by 3 U.S. servicemen, Sept. 4, led the U.S. to begin reducing its military presence there. Nagano hosted the Winter Olympics, Feb. 7-22, 1998. With the country mired in a lengthy recession, a series of weak LDP governments led Japan.

In Apr. 2001 Junichiro Koizumi, a populist reformer, became LDP leader and prime minister. About 600 noncombatant troops were in Iraq Feb. 2004-July 2006, the first time since WWII that Japanese forces served in an overseas war zone. Koizumi left office in Sept. 2006 and was followed by several short-lived LDP governments. The worldwide recession of 2008-09 hit Japan hard, prompting a series of economic stimulus plans; the largest of these, unveiled Apr. 10, 2009, called for more than $150 bil in spending and tax measures. The LDP suffered a crushing defeat in parliamentary elections Aug. 30, and Yukio Hatoyama of the opposition Democratic Party became prime minister.

Jordan

Hashemite Kingdom of Jordan

People: Population: 6,342,948. **Age distrib.** (%): <15: 31.3; 65+: 4.2. **Pop. density:** 178.6 per sq mi, 69 per sq km. **Urban:** 78.3%. **Ethnic groups:** Arab 98%, Circassian 1%, Armenian 1%. **Principal languages:** Arabic (official), English widely understood among upper & middle classes. **Chief religions:** Sunni Muslim 92%, Christian (majority Greek Orthodox) 6%.

Geography: Total area: 35,637 sq mi, 92,300 sq km; **Land area:** 35,510 sq mi, 91,971 sq km. **Location:** In Middle East. **Neighbors:** Israel, West Bank on W; Saudi Arabia on S; Iraq on E; Syria on N. **Topography:** About 88% is arid. Fertile areas are in W. Only port is on short Aqaba Gulf coast. Country shares Dead Sea (about 1,300 ft below sea level) with Israel. **Capital:** Amman, 1,060,000.

Government: Type: Constitutional monarchy. **Head of state:** King Abdullah II; b. Jan. 30, 1962; in office: Feb. 7, 1999. **Head of gov.:** Prime Min. Nader Dahabi; b. Oct. 7, 1946; in office; Nov. 25, 2007. **Local divisions:** 12 governorates. **Defense budget:** $1.6 bil. **Active troops:** 100,500.

Economy: Industries: clothing, phosphate mining, fertilizers, pharmaceuticals, oil refining, cement, potash, light mfg. **Chief crops:** citrus, tomatoes, cucumbers, olives. **Natural resources:** phosphates, potash, shale oil. **Crude oil reserves:** 1 mil bbls. **Arable land:** 3%. **Livestock:** cattle: 69,100; chickens: 25 mil; goats: 434,000; sheep: 2.5 mil. **Fish catch:** 1,015 metric tons. **Electricity prod.:** 10.9 bil kWh. **Labor force** (2001 est.): agric. 2.7%, industry 20%, services 77.4%.

Finance: Monetary unit: Dinar (JOD) (Oct. 2009: 0.71 = $1 U.S.). **GDP:** $31.6 bil; **per capita GDP:** $5,100; **GDP growth:** 5.6%. **Imports:** $15 bil; Saudi Arabia 20.3%, China 9.7%, Germany 6.5%, U.S. 5.6%. **Exports:** $7.8 bil; U.S. 16%, Iraq 13.4%, UAE 8.1%, India 7.8%, Saudi Arabia 7.8%, Syria 4.6%. **Tourism:** $2.3 bil. **Budget:** $6.5 bil. **Intl. reserves less gold:** $5.56 bil. **Gold:** 410,000 oz t. **Consumer prices:** 14.9%.

Transport: Railroad: Length: 315 mi. **Motor vehicles:** 396,000 pass. cars; 176,000 comm. vehicles. **Civil aviation:** 3.3 bil pass.-mi; 15 airports. **Chief port:** Al Aqabah.

Communications: TV sets: 83 per 1,000 pop. **Radios:** 271 per 1,000 pop. **Telephone lines:** 519,000. **Internet:** 1.5 mil users.

Health: Life expect.: 76.2 male; 81.4 female. **Births** (per 1,000 pop.): 20.1. **Deaths** (per 1,000 pop.): 2.7. **Natural inc.:** 1.74%. **Infant mortality** (per 1,000 live births): 15.6. **HIV rate:** NA.

Education: Compulsory: ages 6-15. **Literacy:** 93.1%.

Major intl. organizations: UN (FAO, IBRD, ILO, IMF, IMO, WHO, WTO), AL.

Embassy: 3504 International Dr. NW 20008; 966-2664.

Website: www.kinghussein.gov.jo

From ancient times to 1922 the lands to the east of the Jordan R. were culturally and politically united with the lands to the W. Arabs conquered the area in the 7th cent.; the Ottomans took control in the 16th. Britain's 1920 Palestine Mandate covered both sides of the Jordan. In 1921, Abdullah, son of the ruler of Hejaz in Arabia, was installed by Britain as emir of an autonomous Transjordan, covering two-thirds of Palestine. An independent kingdom was proclaimed, 1946.

During the 1948 Arab-Israeli war the West Bank and East Jerusalem were added to the kingdom, which changed its name to Jordan. These territories were lost to Israel in the 1967 war, which swelled the number of Arab refugees on the East Bank.

Jordan and Israel officially agreed, July 25, 1994, to end their state of war; a formal peace treaty was signed Oct. 26. Following a prolonged bout with cancer, King Hussein died Feb. 7, 1999, ending a nearly 47-year reign; his eldest son assumed the throne as Abdullah II. From 1991 to 2009, the U.S. provided more than $7.6 bil in economic and military aid to Jordan. About 450,000 refugees from the Iraq war were living in Jordan in mid-2009.

Kazakhstan
Republic of Kazakhstan

People: Population: 15,399,437. **Age distrib.** (%): <15: 21.8; 65+: 7.9. **Pop. density:** 14.9 per sq mi, 5.8 per sq km. **Urban:** 57.1%. **Ethnic groups:** Kazakh (Qazaq) 53%, Russian 30%, Ukrainian 4%. **Principal languages:** Kazakh (Qazaq, state lang.), Russian (official; used in everyday business). **Chief religions:** Muslim 47%, Russian Orthodox 44%.

Geography: Total area: 1,049,155 sq mi, 2,717,300 sq km; **Land area:** 1,030,816 sq mi, 2,669,800 sq km. **Location:** In Central Asia. **Neighbors:** Russia on N; China on E; Kyrgyzstan, Uzbekistan, Turkmenistan on S; Caspian Sea on W. **Topography:** Extends from lower reaches of Volga in Europe to Altay Mts. on Chinese border. **Capital:** Astana, 585,000. **Cities (urban aggr.):** Almaty, 1,209,000.

Government: Type: Republic. **Head of state:** Pres. Nursultan A. Nazarbayev; b. July 6, 1940; in office: Apr. 1990. **Head of gov.:** Prime Min. Karim Masimov; b. 1965; in office: Jan. 10, 2007. **Local divisions:** 14 oblystar, 3 cities. **Defense budget:** $1.2 bil. **Active troops:** 49,000.

Economy: Industries: oil, coal, titanium, phosphates. sulfur, tractors & other agric. machinery, electric motors, constr. materials. **Chief crops:** grain (mostly spring wheat), cotton. **Natural resources:** oil, nat. gas, coal, iron ore, mang., chrome ore, nickel, cobalt, copper, molybd., lead, zinc, bauxite, gold, uranium. **Crude oil reserves:** 30 bil bbls. **Arable land:** 8%. **Livestock:** cattle: 5.7 mil; chickens: 28.1 mil; goats: 2.5 mil; pigs: 1.3 mil; sheep: 12.8 mil. **Fish catch:** 41,628 metric tons. **Electricity prod.:** 67.8 bil kWh. **Labor force** (2006): agric. 31.5%, industry 18.4%, services 50%.

Finance: Monetary unit: Tenge (KZT) (Oct. 2009: 150.90 = $1 U.S.). **GDP:** $175.8 bil; **per capita GDP:** $11,500; **GDP growth:** 2.4%. **Imports:** $38.5 bil; Russia 36.4%, China 24.3%, Germany 6.1%. **Exports:** $72 bil; China 14.3%, Russia 12.2%, Germany 10.8%, Italy 7.1%, Romania 6.7%, France 5.9%, Turkey 4.1%. **Tourism:** $1 bil. **Budget:** $25.3 bil. **Intl. reserves less gold:** $11.6 bil. **Gold:** 2.31 mil oz t. **Consumer prices:** 17.1%.

Transport: Railroad: Length: 8,513 mi. **Motor vehicles:** 1.4 mil pass. cars; 368,000 comm. vehicles. **Civil aviation:** 1.5 bil pass.-mi; 67 airports. **Chief ports:** Aqtau, Atyrau, Oskemen.

Communications: TV sets: 240 per 1,000 pop. **Radios:** 395 per 1,000 pop. **Telephone lines:** 3.4 mil. **Internet:** 2.3 mil users.

Health: Life expect.: 62.2 male; 73.2 female. **Births** (per 1,000 pop.): 16.4. **Deaths** (per 1,000 pop.): 9.4. **Natural inc.:** 0.7%. **Infant mortality** (per 1,000 live births): 26.6. **HIV rate:** 0.1%.

Education: Compulsory: ages 7-17. **Literacy:** 99.6%.

Major intl. organizations: UN (FAO, IBRD, ILO, IMF, IMO, WHO), CIS, OSCE.

Embassy: 1401 16th St. NW 20036; 232-5488.

Website: www.government.kz

The region came under the Mongols' rule in the 13th cent. and gradually came under Russian rule, 1730-1853. It was admitted to the USSR as a constituent republic in 1936.

Kazakhstan declared independence Dec. 16, 1991. It became an independent state when the Soviet Union dissolved Dec. 26, 1991. The Communist Party chief, Nursultan Nazarbayev, was elected president unopposed. He boosted the economy by encouraging Western investment in the oil industry. Dissent was suppressed, and much of the nation's oil wealth was reportedly controlled by the president's family and aides.

Kazakhstan agreed, Feb. 14, 1994, to dismantle nuclear missiles. Private land ownership was legalized Dec. 26, 1995. Astana (formerly Akmola) became the nation's new capital, June 9, 1998. Reelected in 1999 and 2005, Pres. Nazarbayev was authorized to run for an unlimited number of terms under a constitutional amendment passed by parliament May 18, 2007.

Kenya
Republic of Kenya

People: Population: 39,002,772. **Age distrib.** (%): <15: 42.3; 65+: 2.6. **Pop. density:** 177.5 per sq mi, 68.5 per sq km. **Urban:** 20.7%. **Ethnic groups:** Kikuyu 22%, Luhya 14%, Luo 13%, Kalenjin 12%, Kamba 11%, other African 27%. **Principal languages:** English, Kiswahili (both official); numerous indigenous languages. **Chief religions:** Protestant 45%, Roman Catholic 33%, Muslim 10%, indigenous beliefs 10%.

Geography: Total area: 224,962 sq mi, 582,650 sq km; **Land area:** 219,789 sq mi, 569,250 sq km. **Location:** E Africa, on coast of Indian O. **Neighbors:** Uganda on W, Tanzania on S, Somalia on E, Ethiopia on N, Sudan on NW. **Topography:** The northern three-fifths of Kenya is arid. To S, a low coastal area and a plateau varying 3,000-10,000 ft. The Great Rift Valley enters the country N-S, flanked by high mountains. **Capital:** Nairobi, 3,010,000. **Cities (urban aggr.):** Mombasa, 882,000.

Government: Type: Republic. **Head of state:** Pres. Mwai Kibaki; b. Nov. 15, 1931; in office: Dec. 30, 2002. **Head of gov.:** Prime Min. Raila Odinga; b. Jan. 7, 1945; in office: Apr. 17, 2008. **Local divisions:** 7 provinces and Nairobi area. **Defense budget:** $681 mil. **Active troops:** 24,120.

Economy: Industries: small-scale consumer goods (textiles, clothing, soap, cigarettes), agric. proc., oil refining, cement, tourism. **Chief crops:** tea, coffee, corn, wheat, sugarcane, fruit. **Natural resources:** limestone, soda ash, salt, fluorspar, wildlife, hydropower. **Arable land:** 8%. **Livestock:** cattle: 12.9 mil; chickens: 27.5 mil; goats: 14 mil; pigs: 304,200; sheep: 9.4 mil. **Fish catch:** 136,203 metric tons. **Electricity prod.:** 6.3 bil kWh. **Labor force** (2003 est.): agric. 75%, industry & services 25%.

Finance: Monetary unit: Shilling (KES) (Oct. 2009: 75.01 = $1 U.S.). **GDP:** $61.5 bil; **per capita GDP:** $1,600; **GDP growth:** 1.7%. **Imports:** $11.1 bil; UAE 12.5%, China 10.5%, Saudi Arabia 8.7%, India 8.3%, South Africa 6.6%, Japan 5.6%, U.S. 4.2%. **Exports:** $5 bil; Uganda 16.4%, UK 9.1%, Netherlands 8.3%, Tanzania 7.9%, U.S. 5.8%, Pakistan 5.1%. **Tourism:** $917 mil. **Budget:** $6.5 bil. **Intl. reserves less gold:** $1.87 bil. **Gold:** NA. **Consumer prices:** 26.2%.

Transport: Railroad: Length: 1,726 mi. **Motor vehicles:** 324,000 pass. cars; 309,000 comm. vehicles. **Civil aviation:** 4.1 bil pass.-mi; 16 airports. **Chief port:** Mombasa.

Communications: TV sets: 22 per 1,000 pop. **Radios:** 216 per 1,000 pop. **Telephone lines:** 252,300. **Daily newspaper circ.** (1999): 8.2 per 1,000 pop. **Internet:** 3.4 mil users.

Health: Life expect.: 56.4 male; 56.9 female. **Births** (per 1,000 pop.): 37.9. **Deaths** (per 1,000 pop.): 10.3. **Natural inc.:** 2.76%. **Infant mortality** (per 1,000 live births): 56. **HIV rate:** NA.

Education: Compulsory: ages 6-13. **Literacy:** 73.6%.

Major intl. organizations: UN and all of its specialized agencies, the Commonwealth, AU.

Embassy: 2249 R St. NW 20008; 387-6101.

Website: www.kenya.go.ke

Arab colonies exported spices and slaves from the Kenya coast as early as the 8th cent. Britain obtained control in the 19th cent. Kenya won independence Dec. 12, 1963, 4 years after the end of the violent Mau Mau uprising. Jomo Kenyatta, the country's leader since independence, died Aug. 22, 1978. He was succeeded by his vice president, Daniel arap Moi.

During the first half of the 1990s, Kenya suffered widespread unemployment and high inflation. Tribal clashes in the western provinces claimed thousands of lives and left tens of thousands homeless. Pres. Moi won a 3rd term in Dec. 1992 elections, which were marred by violence and fraud. He was reelected Dec. 29, 1997, in an election plagued by irregularities.

A truck bomb explosion at the U.S. embassy in Nairobi, Aug. 7, 1998, killed more than 200 people and injured about 5,000. The U.S. blamed the attack and a near-simultaneous embassy bombing in Tanzania on al-Qaeda. After a trial in New York City, 4 conspirators were convicted May 29, 2001. In Mombasa, Nov. 28, 2002, terrorists linked with al-Qaeda killed 12 Kenyans and 3 Israeli tourists at an Israeli-owned hotel and narrowly missed shooting down an Israeli-bound jet.

Constitutionally barred from seeking another term, Pres. Moi was succeeded Dec. 30, 2002, by Mwai Kibaki, the candidate of the opposition Democratic Party. After a disputed election Dec. 27, 2007, that drew criticism from European and Kenyan monitors, Kenya's Electoral Commission declared Kibaki the winner over challenger Raila Odinga. Weeks of factional violence followed, in which some 1,500 people died and 600,000 were displaced. Under a Feb. 28, 2008, power-sharing deal mediated by former UN Sec. Gen. Kofi Annan, Kibaki remained president and Odinga took the newly created post of prime minister. Drought, corruption, mismanagement, and factional tensions that prevented displaced farmers from returning to their lands contributed to severe food shortages in 2009.

Kiribati
Republic of Kiribati

People: Population: 112,850. **Age distrib.** (%): <15: 37.6; 65+: 3.5. **Pop. density:** 360.4 per sq mi, 139.1 per sq km. **Urban:** 43.6%. **Ethnic groups:** Micronesian 99%. **Principal languages:** English (official), I-Kiribati. **Chief religions:** Roman Catholic 52%, Protestant (Congregational) 40%, other (incl. Seventh-Day Adventist, Muslim, Baha'i, Latter-Day Saints, Church of God) 8%.

Geography: Total area: 313 sq mi, 811 sq km; **Land area:** 313 sq mi, 811 sq km. **Location:** 33 Micronesian islands (the Gilbert, Line, and Phoenix groups) in mid-Pacific scattered in a 2-mil sq mi chain around the point where the International Date Line formerly cut the Equator. In 1997 the Date Line was moved to follow Kiribati's E border. **Neighbors:** Nearest are Nauru to SW, Tuvalu and Tokelau Isls. to S. **Topography:** Except Banaba (Ocean) Isl., all are low-lying, with soil of coral sand and rock fragments, subject to erratic rainfall. **Capital** (2005): Tarawa, 45,989.

Government: Type: Republic. **Head of state and gov.:** Pres. Anote Tong; b. June 11, 1952; in office: July 10, 2003. **Local divisions:** 3 units, 6 districts. **Defense budget/Active troops:** NA.

Economy: Industries: fishing, handicrafts. **Chief crops:** copra, taro, breadfruit, sweet potatoes. **Natural resources:** phosphate. **Arable land:** 3%. **Livestock:** chickens: 480,000; pigs: 12,600. **Fish catch:** 22,715 metric tons. **Electricity prod.:** 10 mil kWh. **Labor force** (2000): agric. 2.7%, industry 32%, services 65.3%.

Finance: Monetary unit: Australia Dollar (AUD) (Oct. 2009: 1.12 = $1 U.S.). **GDP:** $579.5 mil; **per capita GDP:** $5,300; **GDP growth:** 3.4%. **Imports** (2004): $62 mil. **Exports** (2004): $17 mil. **Tourism:** NA. **Budget** (FY05): $59.7 mil.

Transport: Civil aviation: 6.8 mil pass.-mi; 4 airports. **Chief port:** Betio.

Communications: TV sets: 23 per 1,000 pop. **Radios:** 341 per 1,000 pop. **Telephone lines:** 4,000. **Internet:** 2,000 users.

Health: Life expect.: 59.8 male; 66.1 female. **Births** (per 1,000 pop.): 30.3. **Deaths** (per 1,000 pop.): 8. **Natural inc.:** 2.23%. **Infant mortality** (per 1,000 live births): 44.7. **HIV rate:** NA.

Education: Compulsory: ages 6-15. **Literacy:** NA.

Major intl. organizations: UN (FAO, IBRD, ILO, IMF, IMO, WHO), the Commonwealth.

Honorary Consulate: 95 Nakolo Pl., Rm. 265, Honolulu, HI 96819; (808) 834-6775.

Website: www.parliament.gov.ki

A British protectorate since 1892, the Gilbert and Ellice Islands colony was completed with the inclusion of the Phoenix Islands, 1937. Tarawa Atoll was the scene of some of the bloodiest fighting in the Pacific during WWII.

Self-rule was granted 1971; the Ellice Islands separated from the colony in 1975 and became independent Tuvalu, 1978. Kiribati (pronounced *Kiribass*) independence was attained July 12, 1979. Under a treaty of friendship the U.S. relinquished its claims to several Line and Phoenix islands, including Christmas (Kiritimati), Canton, and Enderbury. Kiribati was admitted to the UN Sept. 14, 1999. Pres. Anote Tong won reelection Oct. 17, 2007.

Korea, North
Democratic People's Republic of Korea

People: Population: 22,665,345. **Age distrib.** (%): <15: 21.3; 65+: 9.4. **Pop. density:** 487.5 per sq mi, 188.2 per sq km. **Urban:** 61.6%. **Ethnic group:** Homogeneous, small Chinese community & few ethnic Japanese. **Principal language:** Korean. **Chief religions:** Traditionally Buddhist & Confucianist, some Christian; autonomous religious activities almost nonexistent, government-sponsored religious groups only provide illusion of religious freedom.

Geography: Total area: 46,541 sq mi, 120,540 sq km; **Land area:** 46,491 sq mi, 120,410 sq km. **Location:** In northern E Asia. **Neighbors:** China and Russia on N, S. Korea on S. **Topography:** Mountains and hills cover nearly all the country, with narrow valleys and small plains in between. N and E coasts are most rugged areas. **Capital:** P'yongyang, 3,300,000. **Cities (urban aggr.):** N'ampo, 1,127,000.

Government: Type: Communist state. **Head of state:** Kim Jong Il; b. Feb. 16, 1942; officially assumed post Oct. 8, 1997. **Head of gov.:** Prem. Kim Yong Il; b. May 2, 1944; in office: Apr. 11, 2007. **Local divisions:** 9 provinces, 4 special cities. **Defense budget:** NA. **Active troops:** 1,106,000.

Economy: Industries: military products, machine building, electric power, chemicals, mining, metallurgy, textiles. **Chief crops:** rice, corn, potatoes, soybeans. **Natural resources:** coal, lead, tungsten, zinc, graphite, magnesite, iron ore, copper, gold, pyrites, salt, fluorspar, hydropower. **Arable land:** 22%. **Livestock:** cattle: 576,000; chickens: 17 mil; goats: 3.3 mil; pigs: 2.4 mil; sheep: 168,000. **Fish catch:** 713,000 metric tons. **Electricity prod.:** 21.7 bil kWh. **Labor force** (2004 est.): agric. 37%, industry & services 63%.

Finance: Monetary unit: Won (KPW) (Oct. 2009: 142.45 = $1 U.S.). **GDP:** $40 bil; **per capita GDP:** $1,800; **GDP growth:** 3.7%. **Imports** (2007): $3.1 bil; China 46%, S. Korea 34%, Thailand 6%, Russia 4%. **Exports** (2007): $1.7 bil; S. Korea 45%, China 35%, India 5%. **Tourism:** NA. **Budget:** $2.98 bil.

Transport: Railroad: Length: 3,253 mi. **Civil aviation:** 26.1 mil pass.-mi; 37 airports. **Chief ports:** Chongjin, Haeju, Hungnam, Kimch'aek, Kosong, Najin, Namp'o, Sinuiju, Sonbong, Songnim, Ungsang, Wonsan.

Communications: TV sets: 55 per 1,000 pop. **Radios:** 146 per 1,000 pop. **Telephone lines:** 1.2 mil. **Internet:** NA.

Health: Life expect.: 69.5 male; 75.1 female. **Births** (per 1,000 pop.): 14.6. **Deaths** (per 1,000 pop.): 7.3. **Natural inc.:** 0.73%. **Infant mortality** (per 1,000 live births): 21.9. **HIV rate:** NA.

Labor force: agric. 36%, industry & services 64%.

Education: Compulsory: ages 6-15. **Literacy:** 99%.

Major intl. organizations: UN (FAO, ILO, IMO, WHO).

Permanent UN mission: 820 Second Ave., 13th Fl., New York, NY 10017; (212) 972-3105.

Website: www.naenara.kp or www.korea-dpr.com

The Democratic People's Republic of Korea was founded May 1, 1948, in the zone occupied by Russian troops after WWII. Its armies tried to conquer the south, 1950. After 3 years of fighting, with Chinese and U.S. intervention, a cease-fire was proclaimed.

For the next 4 decades, a hardline Communist regime headed by Kim Il Sung kept tight control over the nation's political, economic, and cultural life. The nation used its abundant mineral and hydroelectric resources to develop its military strength and heavy industry. By the early 1990s, North Korea was widely believed to be developing nuclear weapons. The U.S. and North Korea signed an agreement, Oct. 21, 1994, providing for phased dismantling of North Korea's nuclear development program in return for U.S. energy aid and improved ties with the U.S.

Kim Il Sung died July 8, 1994. He was succeeded by his son, Kim Jong Il. Defections by high officials, a deteriorating economy, and severe food shortages plagued North Korea in the late 1990s.

A first-ever summit conference in Pyongyang between North and South Korean leaders, June 13-15, 2000, marked an improvement in relations between the 2 nations. In a landmark summit, Sept. 2002, North Korea and Japan agreed to normalize relations.

Pres. George W. Bush, in a speech Jan. 31, 2002, included North Korea with Iraq and Iran as part of an "axis of evil." In Oct. 2002, N. Korea admitted to pursuing a secret nuclear weapons program, in violation of past agreements. The U.S. insisted that North Korea end its nuclear weapons program, while North Korea demanded a nonaggression treaty and economic aid from the U.S. During 2003-09, as 6-nation talks sponsored by China sought to resolve the nuclear dispute, North Korea followed a zigzag course, alternately stopping and resuming its nuclear program in order to win further concessions from the U.S.

In Apr.-May 2009, North Korea suspended its participation in the 6-nation talks, expelled IAEA inspectors, tested multiple missiles, and exploded a nuclear device underground. The UN Security Council June 12 toughened sanctions on the North Korean regime. Visiting P'yongyang Aug. 4-5, former U.S. Pres. Bill Clinton met face-to-face with Kim Jong Il and succeeded in freeing two U.S. journalists, Laura Ling and Euna Lee, who had been convicted of illegally entering North Korean territory from China Mar. 17. A series of conciliatory gestures between North and South Korea followed the Clinton mission, including the restoration Sept. 1 of commercial traffic from South Korea to the North Korean border city of Kaesong.

Korea, South
Republic of Korea

People: Population: 48,508,972. **Age distrib.** (%): <15: 16.8; 65+: 10.8. **Pop. density:** 1,279.5 per sq mi, 494 per sq km. **Urban:** 80.8%. **Ethnic group:** Homogeneous, except for some Chinese. **Principal languages:** Korean, English widely taught in school. **Chief religions:** Christian (incl. Protestant, Roman Catholic) 26%, Buddhist 23%, none 49%.

Geography: Total area: 38,023 sq mi, 98,480 sq km; **Land area:** 37,911 sq mi, 98,190 sq km. **Location:** In northern E Asia. **Neighbors:** North Korea on N. **Topography:** Mountainous, with a rugged E coast. W and S coasts are deeply indented, with many islands and harbors. **Capital:** Seoul, 9,796,000. **Cities (urban aggr.):** Busan, 3,480,000; Incheon, 2,550,000.

Government: Type: Republic. **Head of state:** Pres. Lee Myung Bak; b. Dec. 19, 1941; in office: Feb. 25, 2008. **Head of gov.:** Prime Min.-designate Chung Un Chan; b. 1946; appointed: Sept. 3, 2009. **Local divisions:** 9 provinces, 7 special cities. **Defense budget:** $26.6 bil. **Active troops:** 687,000.

Economy: Industries: electronics, telecomm., auto prod., chemicals, shipbuilding, steel. **Chief crops:** rice, root crops, barley, vegetables, fruit. **Natural resources:** coal, tungsten, graphite, molybd., lead, hydropower potential. **Arable land:** 17%. **Live-**

stock: cattle: 2.7 mil; chickens: 119.4 mil; goats: 372,447; pigs: 9.6 mil; sheep: 1,800. **Fish catch:** 3.28 mil metric tons. **Electricity prod.:** 379.7 bil kWh. **Labor force** (2007): agric. 7.2%, industry 25.1%, services 67.7%.

Finance: Monetary unit: Won (KRW) (Oct. 2009: 1,166.32 = $1 U.S.). **GDP:** $1.3 tril; **per capita GDP:** $27,600; **GDP growth:** 2.2%. **Imports:** $427.4 bil; China 19.2%, Japan 15.1%, U.S. 8.8%, Saudi Arabia 6.1%. **Exports:** $433.5 bil; China 25.5%, U.S. 10.9%, Japan 6.4%. **Tourism:** $6.1 bil. **Budget:** $6.1 bil. **Intl. reserves less gold:** $130.59 bil. **Gold:** 460,000 oz t. **Consumer prices:** 4.7%.

Transport: Railroad: Length: 2,101 mi. **Motor vehicles:** 10.6 mil pass. cars; 4.3 mil comm. vehicles. **Civil aviation:** 43.1 bil pass.-mi; 72 airports. **Chief ports:** Inch'on, P'ohang, Pusan, Ulsan.

Communications: TV sets: 364 per 1,000 pop. **Radios:** 1,039 per 1,000 pop. **Telephone lines:** 21.3 mil. **Internet:** 37.5 mil users.

Health: Life expect.: 75.3 male; 82.2 female. **Births** (per 1,000 pop.): 9.1. **Deaths** (per 1,000 pop.): 5.7. **Natural inc.:** 0.34%. **Infant mortality** (per 1,000 live births): 4.3. **HIV rate:** <0.1%.

Education: Compulsory: ages 6-14. **Literacy:** 97.9%.

Major intl. organizations: UN (FAO, IBRD, ILO, IMF, IMO, WHO, WTO), APEC, OECD.

Embassy: 2320 Massachusetts Ave. NW 20008; 939-5663.

Website: www.egov.go.kr

Korea, once called the Hermit Kingdom, has a recorded history since the 1st cent. BCE. It was united in a kingdom under the Silla Dynasty, 668 CE. It was at times associated with the Chinese empire; the treaty that concluded the Sino-Japanese war of 1894-95 recognized Korea's complete independence. In 1910 Japan forcibly annexed Korea as Chosun.

At the Potsdam conference, July 1945, the 38th parallel was designated as the line dividing the Soviet and the American occupation. Russian troops entered Korea Aug. 10, 1945; U.S. troops entered Sept. 8, 1945.

The South Koreans formed the Republic of Korea in May 1948 with Seoul as the capital. Dr. Syngman Rhee was chosen president. A separate, Communist regime was formed in the north; its army attacked the south in June 1950, initiating the Korean War. UN troops, under U.S. command, supported South Korea in the war, which ended in an armistice (July 1953) leaving Korea divided by a demilitarized zone (DMZ) along the 38th parallel.

Rhee's authoritarian rule became increasingly unpopular, and a movement spearheaded by college students forced his resignation Apr. 26, 1960. In an army coup May 16, 1961, Gen. Park Chung Hee became chairman of a ruling junta. He was elected president, 1963; a 1972 referendum allowed him to be reelected for an unlimited series of 6-year terms. Park was assassinated by the chief of the Korean CIA, Oct. 26, 1979.

In May 1980, Gen. Chun Doo Hwan, head of military intelligence, ordered the brutal suppression of pro-democracy demonstrations in Kwangju. On July 1, 1987, following weeks of antigovernment protests, some of them violent, Chun agreed to democratic reforms. In Dec., Roh Tae Woo, a longtime ally of Chun's, was elected president. In 1990, the nation's 3 largest political parties merged; some 100,000 students protested the merger as undemocratic.

Pres. Kim Young Sam took office in 1993. Convicted of mutiny, treason, and corruption, Chun was sentenced to death by a Seoul court, Aug. 26, 1996, for his role in the 1979 coup and 1980 Kwangju massacre; Roh received a 22-1/2 year prison sentence. On Dec. 16, Chun's term was reduced to life in prison, and Roh's to 17 years.

The collapse in Jan. 1997 of the Hanbo steel firm triggered a series of corruption scandals. With currency and stock values plummeting, the nation averted default by agreeing, Dec. 4, on a $57 bil bailout from the IMF. Kim Dae Jung, a longtime dissident, won the presidential election Dec. 18. Chun and Roh were released and pardoned Dec. 22, 1997.

At an unprecedented summit meeting in P'yongyang, June 13-15, 2000, Pres. Kim Dae Jung and North Korean leader Kim Jong Il agreed to work for reconciliation and eventual reunification of their 2 countries. On Oct. 13, 2000, Kim Dae Jung was named the winner of the Nobel Peace Prize. Roh Moo Hyun won a presidential election Dec. 19, 2002.

A subway fire in Taegu, Feb. 18, 2003, killed 198 people; the arsonist was given a life term, and 8 subway officials charged with negligence also received prison sentences. Typhoon Maemi battered Pusan and other areas Sept. 12-13, 2003, leaving about 130 people dead and causing at least $4.1 bil in damage.

The National Assembly, Mar. 12, 2004, impeached Pres. Roh Moo Hyun for violating political neutrality and urging voters to support the Uri Party in upcoming legislative elections; voters backed Roh Apr. 15 by electing a Uri majority, and the Constitutional Court May 14 restored Roh to office. The IAEA Sept. 2 said South Korea had acknowledged having secretly processed a small amount of

uranium to near weapons-grade level in 2000, violating the Nuclear Non-Proliferation Treaty and a bilateral accord with N. Korea.

Ban Ki-Moon, South Korea's foreign minister in 2004-06, took office as UN secretary-general Jan. 1, 2007. Lee Myung Bak, a former construction executive and Seoul mayor nicknamed "The Bulldozer," won the presidential election Dec. 19. Former Pres. Roh Moo Hyun, under investigation for corruption, committed suicide May 23, 2009.

South Korea supplied a 3,600-member force to the U.S.-led coalition in Iraq; by the end of 2008, all Korean troops had been withdrawn. As of Sept. 2009, the U.S. had about 28,500 troops stationed in South Korea.

Kosovo
Republic of Kosovo

People: Population: 1,804,838. **Age distrib.** (%): <15: 27.7; 65+: 6.6. **Pop. density:** 429.4 per sq mi, 165.8 per sq km. **Urban:** NA. **Ethnic groups:** Albanians 88%, Serbs 7%, other (incl. Bosniak, Gorani, Roma) 5%. **Principal languages:** Albanian, Serbian (both official); Bosnian; Turkish; Roma. **Chief religions:** Muslim, Serbian Orthodox, Roman Catholic.

Geography: Total area: 4,203 sq mi, 10,887 sq km. **Land area:** 4,203 sq mi, 10,887 sq km. **Location:** SE Europe between Serbia and Macedonia. **Neighbors:** Serbia on N, Montenegro on NW, Albania on SW, Macedonia on SE. **Topography:** Low flood basins surrounded by several high mountain ranges. **Capital:** Pristina.

Government: Type: Republic. **Head of state:** Pres. Fatmir Sejdiu; b. Oct. 23, 1951; in office: Feb. 10, 2006. **Head of gov.:** Prime Min. Hashim Thaçi; b. Apr. 24, 1968; in office: Jan. 9, 2008. **Local divisions:** 30 municipalities. **Defense budget:** NA. **Active troops:** NA.

Economy: Industries: mineral mining, constr. materials, base metals, leather, machinery, appliances. **Chief crops:** fruits and vegetables (potatoes, berries), wheat, corn, wine, beef. **Natural resources:** nickel, lead, zinc, magnesium, lignite, kaolin, chrome, bauxite. **Crude oil reserves:** NA. **Arable land:** NA. **Livestock:** NA. **Fish catch:** NA. **Electricity prod.** (2006): 4 bil kWh. **Labor force** (2007 est.): agric. 16.5%, industry & services NA.

Finance: Monetary unit: Euro (EUR) (Oct. 2009: 0.68 = $1 U.S.). **GDP:** (2007): $5 bil; **per capita GDP** (2007): $2,300; **GDP growth** (2007): 5.1%. **Imports:**$2.6 bil. **Exports:** $527 mil. **Tourism:** NA. **Budget:** $1 bil. **Intl. reserves less gold:** $416 mil. **Gold:** NA. **Consumer prices:** NA.

Transport: Railroad: Length: 267 mi. **Civil aviation:** 4 airports.

Communications: Telephone lines (2006): 106,300.

Health: Life expect.: 67.3 male; 71.6 female. **Births** (per 1,000 pop.): 19. **Deaths** (per 1,000 pop.): 7. **Natural inc.:** 1.2%. **Infant mortality** (per 1,000 live births): 46.4. **HIV rate:** NA.

Education: NA. **Literacy:** 91.9%.

Major intl. organizations: IMF, ITUC.

Embassy: 900 19th St. NW, Ste. 400, 20006; 380-3581.

Website: www.ks-gov.net

Kosovo was part of the Roman and Byzantine empires before Serbs, a Slavic people, took control in the Middle Ages. After Ottoman Turks defeated Serb forces, 1389, Kosovo's population became predominantly Muslim and Kosovar (ethnic Albanian). Serbia regained control in the First Balkan War (1912-13). Kosovo entered the Kingdom of Serbs, Croats, and Slovenes as part of Serbia after World War I and became an autonomous province of Serbia, a constituent republic of Yugoslavia, after World War II.

Revoking provincial autonomy, Serbia began ruling Kosovo by force in 1989. Albanian secessionists proclaimed an independent Republic of Kosovo in July 1990. As Yugoslavia collapsed, the republics of Serbia (incl. Kosovo) and Montenegro proclaimed a new "Federal Republic of Yugoslavia" in 1992, under Pres. Slobodan Milosevic. Guerrilla attacks by the Kosovo Liberation Army in 1997 brought a ferocious counteroffensive by Serbian authorities.

Fearful that the Serbs were employing "ethnic cleansing" tactics, as they had in Bosnia, the U.S. and its NATO allies sought to pressure the Yugoslav government. When Milosevic refused to comply, NATO launched an air war against Yugoslavia, Mar.-June 1999; the Serbs retaliated by terrorizing the Kosovars and forcing hundreds of thousands to flee, mostly to Albania and Macedonia. A 50,000-member multinational force (KFOR) entered Kosovo in June, and most of the Kosovar refugees had returned by Sept. 1.

From June 1999, Kosovo was administered by a UN mission (UNMIK). When Kosovar and Serbian negotiators were unable to reach agreement on the final status of the region, Kosovo unilaterally declared independence, Feb. 17, 2008. The U.S. and most European allies immediately recognized the new country, but Serbia and Russia refused. As of mid-2009, KFOR had about 13,800 troops in Kosovo; at a June 11 meeting, NATO defense ministers agreed to cut the force to 10,000 by Jan. 2010.

Kuwait
State of Kuwait

People: Population: 2,691,158. **Age distrib.** (%): <15: 26.4; 65+: 2.9. **Pop. density:** 391.1 per sq mi, 151 per sq km. **Urban:** 98.3%. **Ethnic groups:** Kuwaiti 45%, other Arab 35%, South Asian 9%, Iranian 4%. **Principal languages:** Arabic (official), English widely spoken. **Chief religions:** Muslim 85% (Sunni 70%, Shi'a 30%), other (incl. Christian, Hindu, Parsi) 15%.

Geography: Total area: 6,880 sq mi, 17,820 sq km; **Land area:** 6,880 sq mi, 17,820 sq km. **Location:** In Middle East, at N end of Persian Gulf. **Neighbors:** Iraq on N, Saudi Arabia on S. **Topography:** Flat, very dry, and extremely hot. **Capital:** Kuwait City, 2,063,000.

Government: Type: Constitutional monarchy. **Head of state:** Emir Sheikh Sabah al-Ahmad al-Jabir as-Sabah; b. June 6, 1929; in office: Jan. 29, 2006. **Head of gov.:** Prime Min. Sheikh Nasser al-Muhammad al-Ahmad as-Sabah; b. 1940; in office: Feb. 7, 2006. **Local divisions:** 5 governorates. **Defense budget:** $3.8 bil. **Active troops:** 15,500.

Economy: Industries: oil, petrochems., cement, shipbuilding & repair, water desalination, food proc., constr. materials. **Chief crops:** practically none. **Natural resources:** oil, fish, shrimp, nat. gas. **Crude oil reserves:** 104 bil bbls (incl. half of Neutral Zone reserves). **Arable land:** 1%. **Livestock:** cattle: 28,000; chickens: 32.5 mil; goats: 160,000; sheep: 900,000. **Fish catch:** 4,721 metric tons. **Electricity prod.:** 44.8 bil kWh. **Labor force:** NA.

Finance: Monetary unit: Dinar (KWD) (Oct. 2009: 0.29 = $1 U.S.). **GDP:** $149.1 bil; **per capita GDP:** $57,400; **GDP growth:** 8.5%. **Imports:** $24.9 bil; U.S. 11.5%, Japan 8.9%, Germany 7.9%, China 7.1%, Saudi Arabia 6.8%, S. Korea 6.5%, Italy 4.6%, India 4.2%, UK 4.1%. **Exports:** $89.4 bil; Japan 20.9%, S. Korea 15%, U.S. 10.2%, Singapore 9%, China 6.6%, Netherlands 4.2%. **Tourism:** $222 mil. **Budget:** $36.8 bil. **Intl. reserves less gold:** $11.11 bil. **Gold:** 2.54 mil oz t. **Consumer prices:** 10.5%.

Transport: Motor vehicles: 919,000 pass. cars; 215,000 comm. vehicles. **Civil aviation:** 4.5 bil pass.-mi; 4 airports. **Chief ports:** Ash Shu'aybah, Ash Shuwaykh, Mina' al Ahmadi.

Communications: TV sets: 480 per 1,000 pop. **Radios:** 633 per 1,000 pop. **Telephone lines:** 541,000. **Internet:** 1 mil users.

Health: Life expect.: 76.4 male; 78.7 female. **Births** (per 1,000 pop.): 21.9. **Deaths** (per 1,000 pop.): 2.4. **Natural inc.:** 1.95%. **Infant mortality** (per 1,000 live births): 9.2. **HIV rate:** NA.

Education: Compulsory: ages 6-14. **Literacy:** 93.9%.

Major intl. organizations: UN (FAO, IBRD, ILO, IMF, IMO, WHO, WTO), AL, OPEC.

Embassy: 2940 Tilden St. NW 20008; 966-0702.

Website: www.da.gov.kw

Kuwait is ruled by the Sabah dynasty, founded 1759. Britain ran foreign relations and defense from 1899 until independence in 1961. Nearly half the population is non-Kuwaiti, with many Palestinians, and cannot vote.

Oil is the fiscal mainstay, providing most of Kuwait's income. Oil pays for free medical care, education, and social security. There are no taxes, except customs duties.

Kuwait was attacked and overrun by Iraqi forces Aug. 2, 1990. The emir and senior members of the ruling family fled to Saudi Arabia to establish a government in exile. On Aug. 28, Iraq announced that Kuwait was its 19th province. Following several weeks of aerial attacks on Iraq and Iraqi forces in Kuwait, a U.S.-led coalition began a ground attack Feb. 23, 1991. By Feb. 27, Iraqi forces were routed and Kuwait liberated.

Former U.S. Pres. George Bush visited Kuwait, Apr. 14-16, 1993. Kuwaiti authorities arrested 14 Iraqis and Kuwaitis for allegedly plotting to assassinate him during his visit; 13 were convicted and sentenced to prison or death, June 4, 1994. Northern Kuwait was used by U.S. and British troops as a staging area prior to the Mar. 2003 invasion of Iraq.

Political rights were extended to women, May 16, 2005; the first female cabinet member was appointed June 12. Kuwait enacted a $5.2 bil program Mar. 26, 2009, to bail out banks and investment companies battered by the global financial crisis.

Kyrgyzstan
Kyrgyz Republic

People: Population: 5,431,747. **Age distrib.** (%): <15: 29.7; 65+: 5.8. **Pop. density:** 73.5 per sq mi, 28.4 per sq km. **Urban:** 35.8%. **Ethnic groups:** Kyrgyz 65%, Uzbek 14%, Russian 13%. **Principal languages:** Kyrgyz, Russian (both official); Uzbek. **Chief religions:** Muslim 75%, Russian Orthodox 20%.

Geography: Total area: 76,641 sq mi, 198,500 sq km; **Land area:** 73,861 sq mi, 191,300 sq km. **Location:** In Central Asia. **Neighbors:** Kazakhstan on N, China on E, Uzbekistan on W, Tajikistan on S. **Topography:** Landlocked country nearly covered by Tien Shan and Pamir Mts.; avg. elevation 9,020 ft. A large lake, Issyk-Kul, in NE is 1 mi above sea level. **Capital:** Bishkek, 837,000.

Government: Type: Republic. **Head of state:** Pres. Kurmanbek Bakiyev; b. Aug. 1, 1949; in office: Aug. 14, 2005 (acting from Mar. 25). **Head of gov.:** Prime Min. Igor Chudinov; b. Aug. 21, 1961; in office: Dec. 24, 2007. **Local divisions:** 7 oblasts and Bishkek. **Defense budget:** $39 mil. **Active troops:** 10,900.

Economy: Industries: small machinery, textiles, food proc., cement, shoes, sawn logs, refrigerators, furniture, electric motors. **Chief crops:** tobacco, cotton, potatoes, vegetables, grapes, fruits & berries. **Natural resources:** hydropower, gold, rare earth metals, coal, oil, nat. gas, nepheline, mercury, bismuth, lead, zinc. **Crude oil reserves:** 40 mil bbls. **Arable land:** 7%. **Livestock:** cattle: 1.1 mil; chickens: 4.5 mil; goats: 849,873; pigs: 79,567; sheep: 3.2 mil. **Fish catch:** 141 metric tons. **Electricity prod.:** 15.6 bil kWh. **Labor force** (2005 est.): agric. 48%, industry 12.5%, services 39.5%.

Finance: Monetary unit: Som (KGS) (Oct. 2009: 43.59 = $1 U.S.). **GDP:** $11.6 bil; **per capita GDP:** $2,200; **GDP growth:** 7.6%. **Imports:** $3.8 bil; China 70.5%, Russia 13.9%, Kazakhstan 3.4%. **Exports:** $1.8 bil; Russia 29.4%, Switzerland 16.2%, Kazakhstan 15.1%, Afghanistan 12.3%, China 7.6%, Uzbekistan 5.8%. **Tourism:** $346 mil. **Budget:** $993.3 mil. **Intl. reserves less gold:** $748 mil. **Gold:** 80,000 oz t. **Consumer prices:** 24.5%.

Transport: Railroad: Length: 292 mi. **Motor vehicles:** 201,000 pass. cars. **Civil aviation:** 228.7 mil pass.-mi; 18 airports. **Chief port:** Ysyk-Kol.

Communications: TV sets: 49 per 1,000 pop. **Radios:** 113 per 1,000 pop. **Telephone lines:** 494,500. **Daily newspaper circ.** (2004): 0.96 per 1,000 pop. **Internet:** 850,000 users.

Health: Life expect.: 65.1 male; 73.3 female. **Births** (per 1,000 pop.): 23.3. **Deaths** (per 1,000 pop.): 7. **Natural inc.:** 1.63%. **Infant mortality** (per 1,000 live births): 32.3. **HIV rate:** 0.1%.

Education: Compulsory: ages 7-15. **Literacy:** 99.3%.

Major intl. organizations: UN (FAO, IBRD, ILO, IMF, WHO, WTO), CIS, OSCE.

Embassy: 2360 Massachusetts Ave. NW 20008; 338-5141.

Website: www.president.kg

The region was inhabited around the 13th cent. by the Kyrgyz. It was annexed to Russia, 1864, and became a constituent republic of the USSR in 1936. Kyrgyzstan declared independence Aug. 31, 1991. It became an independent state when the USSR disbanded Dec. 26, 1991.

In power since 1990, Pres. Askar Akayev won a 3rd 5-year term in the Oct. 29, 2000, election. Fraud by Akayev loyalists in parliamentary elections Feb.-Mar. 2005 sparked protests. Akayev fled the country, Mar. 24, and formally resigned, Apr. 4. His interim successor, former Prime Min. Kurmanbek Bakiyev, a leader of the "tulip revolution," won by a landslide in the July 10 presidential vote.

After receiving $2 bil in pledges of aid and credits from Russia, Kyrgyzstan in Feb. 2009 ordered the U.S. to close its Manas air base, a key transit point in the U.S.-led war in Afghanistan; the Kyrgyz decision was reversed after the U.S. agreed to pay $180 mil to keep the base open. Official results of the July 23, 2009, election gave Pres. Bakiyev 76% of the vote, but international and local monitors reported numerous irregularities.

Laos
Lao People's Democratic Republic

People: Population: 6,834,942. **Age distrib.** (%): <15: 40.8; 65+: 3.1. **Pop. density:** 76.7 per sq mi, 29.6 per sq km. **Urban:** 27.4%. **Ethnic groups:** Lao 55%, Khmou 11%, Hmong 8%, other (100+ minor ethnic groups) 26%. **Principal languages:** Lao (official), French, English, various ethnic languages. **Chief religions:** Buddhist 667%, other & unspecified 32%.

Geography: Total area: 91,429 sq mi, 236,800 sq km; **Land area:** 89,112 sq mi, 230,800 sq km. **Location:** In Indochina Peninsula in SE Asia. **Neighbors:** Myanmar, China on N; Vietnam on E; Cambodia on S; Thailand on W. **Topography:** Landlocked, dominated by jungle. High mountains along E border are source of the E-W rivers slicing across the country to the Mekong R., which defines most of W border. **Capital:** Vientiane, 745,000.

Government: Type: Communist. **Head of state:** Pres. Choummaly Sayasone; b. Mar. 6, 1936; in office: June 8, 2006. **Head of gov.:** Prime Min. Bouasone Bouphavanh; b. June 3, 1954; in office: June 8, 2006. **Local divisions:** 16 provinces, 1 municipality, 1 special zone. **Defense budget:** $15 mil. **Active troops:** 29,100.

Economy: Industries: mining, timber, electric power, agric. proc., constr., garments, tourism, cement. **Chief crops:** sweet potatoes, vegetables, corn, coffee, sugarcane. **Natural resources:** timber, hydropower, gypsum, tin, gold, gemstones. **Arable land:** 4%. **Livestock:** cattle: 1.3 mil; chickens: 21.9 mil; goats: 230,000; pigs: 2.3 mil. **Fish catch:** 104,925 metric tons. **Electricity prod.:** 1.6 bil kWh. **Labor force** (2005 est.): agric. 80%, industry & services 20%.

Finance: Monetary unit: Kip (LAK) (Oct. 2009: 8,515.00 = $1 U.S. **GDP:** $14 bil; **per capita GDP:** $2,100; **GDP growth:** 7.5%. **Imports:** $1.4 bil; Thailand 68.7%, China 11.3%, Vietnam 4.7%. **Exports:** $1.2 bil; Thailand 34.7%, Vietnam 13.2%, China 8.6%, S. Korea 4.5%. **Tourism** (2005): $146 mil. **Budget:** $646.1 mil. **Intl. reserves less gold:** $408 mil. **Gold:** 280,000 oz t. **Consumer prices:** 7.6%.

Transport: Civil aviation: 77.1 mil pass.-mi; 9 airports.
Communications: TV sets: 10 per 1,000 pop. **Radios:** 145 per 1,000 pop. **Telephone lines:** 97,600. **Daily newspaper circ.** (2004): 2.6 per 1,000 pop. **Internet:** 130,000 users.
Health: Life expect.: 54.2 male; 58.5 female. **Births** (per 1,000 pop.): 34.5. **Deaths** (per 1,000 pop.): 11. **Natural inc.:** 2.34%. **Infant mortality** (per 1,000 live births): 79.6. **HIV rate:** 0.2%.
Education: Compulsory: ages 6-10. **Literacy:** 73.2%.
Major intl. organizations: UN (FAO, IBRD, ILO, IMF, WHO), ASEAN.
Embassy: 2222 S St. NW 20008; 332-6416.
Website: www.na.gov.la

Laos became a French protectorate in 1893, but regained independence as a constitutional monarchy July 19, 1949.

Conflicts among neutralist, Communist, and conservative factions created a chaotic political situation. Armed conflict increased after 1960.

The 3 factions formed a coalition government in June 1962, with neutralist Prince Souvanna Phouma as premier. A 14-nation conference in Geneva signed agreements, 1962, guaranteeing neutrality and independence. By 1964 the Pathet Lao had withdrawn from the coalition, and, with aid from North Vietnamese troops, renewed sporadic attacks. U.S. planes bombed the Ho Chi Minh trail, a supply line from North Vietnam to Communist forces in Laos and South Vietnam.

In 1970 the U.S. stepped up air support and military aid. After Pathet Lao military gains, Souvanna Phouma in May 1975 ordered government troops to cease fighting; the Pathet Lao took control. The Lao People's Democratic Republic was proclaimed Dec. 3, 1975.

From the mid-1970s through the 1980s, Laos relied on Vietnam for military and financial aid. Since easing its foreign investment laws in 1988, Laos has attracted more than $6 bil from Thailand, China, Vietnam, the U.S., and other nations. Laos was admitted to ASEAN on July 23, 1997. The U.S. Congress, Nov. 19, 2004, approved normalization of trade with Laos. The 8th congress of the Communist Party, Mar. 2006, marked the transition to a younger generation of leaders.

Latvia
Republic of Latvia

People: Population: 2,231,503. **Age distrib.** (%): <15: 13.3; 65+: 17. **Pop. density:** 90.9 per sq mi, 35.1 per sq km. **Urban:** 68%. **Ethnic groups:** Latvian 58%, Russian 30%, Belarusian 4%. **Principal languages:** Latvian (official), Russian, Lithuanian. **Chief religions:** Lutheran 20%, Orthodox 15%, unspecified 64%.
Geography: Total area: 24,938 sq mi, 64,589 sq km; **Land area:** 24,552 sq mi, 63,589 sq km. **Location:** E Europe, on Baltic Sea. **Neighbors:** Estonia on N; Lithuania, Belarus on S; Russia on E. **Topography:** Lowland with numerous lakes, marshes, and peat bogs. Principal river, W. Dvina (Daugava), rises in Russia. Glacial hills in E. **Capital:** Riga, 722,000.
Government: Type: Republic. **Head of state:** Pres. Valdis Zatlers; b. Mar. 22, 1955; in office: July 8, 2007. **Head of gov.:** Prime Min. IValdis Dombrovskis; b. Aug. 5, 1971; in office: Mar. 12, 2009. **Local divisions:** 26 counties, 7 municipalities. **Defense budget:** $453 mil. **Active troops:** 5,187.
Economy: Industries: motor vehicles& railroad cars, synthetic fibers, agric. machinery, fertilizers, washing machines, radios, electronics, pharmaceuticals. **Chief crops:** grain, sugar beets, potatoes, vegetables. **Natural resources:** peat, limestone, dolomite, amber, hydropower, wood. **Arable land:** 28%. **Livestock:** cattle: 377,100; chickens: 4.1 mil; goats: 14,300; pigs: 217,000; sheep: 41,300. **Fish catch:** 156,005 metric tons. **Electricity prod.:** 4.7 bil kWh. **Labor force** (2005 est.): agric. 12.1%, industry 25.8%, services 61.8%.
Finance: Monetary unit: Lat (LVL) (Oct. 2009: 0.48 = $1 U.S.). **GDP:** $38.9 bil; **per capita GDP:** $17,300; **GDP growth:** −4.6%. **Imports:** $15.3 bil; Lithuania 16.1%, Germany 12.9%, Russia 10.7%, Poland 7%, Estonia 7%, Sweden 4.4%, Finland 4.3%. **Exports:** $9.6 bil; Lithuania 15.5%, Russia 14.8%, Estonia 13.1%, Germany 7.7%, Sweden 6.2%, Denmark 4.3%. **Tourism:** $671 mil. **Budget:** $10.3 bil. **Intl. reserves less gold:** $3.26 bil. **Gold:** 250,000 oz t. **Consumer prices:** 15.4%.
Transport: Railroad: Length: 1,428 mi. **Motor vehicles:** 742,000 pass. cars; 124,000 comm. vehicles. **Civil aviation:** 721.4 mil pass.-mi; 20 airports. **Chief ports:** Riga, Ventspils.
Communications: TV sets: 757 per 1,000 pop. **Radios:** 701 per 1,000 pop. **Telephone lines:** 644,000. **Daily newspaper circ.** (2004): 154.1 per 1,000 pop. **Internet:** 1.3 mil users.
Health: Life expect.: 66.7 male; 77.3 female. **Births** (per 1,000 pop.): 9.6. **Deaths** (per 1,000 pop.): 13.6. **Natural inc.:** −0.4%. **Infant mortality** (per 1,000 live births): 9. **HIV rate:** 0.8%.
Education: Compulsory: ages 7-15. **Literacy:** 99.8%.
Major intl. organizations: UN (FAO, IBRD, ILO, IMF, IMO, WHO), EU, NATO, OSCE.
Embassy: 2306 Massachusetts Ave. NW 20008; 328-2840.
Website: www.lv

Prior to 1918, Latvia was occupied by the Russians and Germans. It was an independent republic, 1918-39. The Aug. 1939 Soviet-German agreement assigned Latvia to the Soviet sphere of influence. It was officially accepted as part of the USSR on Aug. 5, 1940. It was overrun by the German army in 1941, but retaken in 1945.

During an abortive Soviet coup, Latvia declared independence, Aug. 21, 1991. The Soviet Union recognized Latvia's independence in Sept. 1991. The last Russian troops in Latvia withdrew by Aug. 31, 1994. Responding to international pressure, Latvian voters on Oct. 3, 1998, eased citizenship laws that had discriminated against some 500,000 ethnic Russians. On June 17, 1999, the legislature elected Vaira Vike-Freiberga as Latvia's first woman president. Latvia joined the EU and NATO in 2004. Latvia ratified a proposed EU constitution, June 2, 2005.

Hit hard by recession, Latvia reached agreement Dec. 2008 on a $10.4 bil emergency loan from the EU, IMF, World Bank, and Nordic countries. The economic downturn sparked protests that turned violent Jan. 13, 2009, and led to the fall of the government Feb. 20 and its replacement by a new center-right coalition headed by former Finance Min. Valdis Dombrovskis.

Lebanon
Lebanese Republic

People: Population: 4,017,095. **Age distrib.** (%): <15: 25.8; 65+: 7.2. **Pop. density:** 1,017 per sq mi, 392.7 per sq km. **Urban:** 86.6%. **Ethnic groups:** Arab 95%, Armenian 4%. **Principal languages:** Arabic (official), French, English, Armenian. **Chief religions:** Muslim (incl. Shi'a, Sunni, Druze) 60%, Christian (incl. Maronite Catholic, Greek Orthodox, Assyrian, Protestant) 39%.
Geography: Total area: 4,015 sq mi, 10,400 sq km; **Land area:** 3,950 sq mi, 10,230 sq km. **Location:** In Middle East, on E end of Mediterranean Sea. **Neighbors:** Syria on E, Israel on S. **Topography:** There is a narrow coastal strip, and 2 mountain ranges running N-S enclosing the fertile Beqaa Valley. The Litani R. runs S through the valley, turning W to empty into Mediterranean. **Capital:** Beirut, 1,846,000.
Government: Type: Republic. **Head of state:** Pres. Michel Suleiman; b. Nov. 21, 1948; in office: May 25, 2008. **Head of gov.:** Prime Min.-designate Saad Hariri; b. Apr. 18, 1970; appointed: June 27, 2009. **Local divisions:** 6 governorates. **Defense budget:** $733 mil. **Active troops:** 56,000.
Economy: Industries: banking, tourism, food proc., wine, jewelry, cement, textiles, mineral & chemical products. **Chief crops:** citrus, grapes, tomatoes, apples, vegetables, potatoes, olives, tobacco. **Natural resources:** limestone, iron ore, salt, water (surplus in a water-deficit region). **Arable land:** 16%. **Livestock:** cattle: 77,000; chickens: 35 mil; goats: 495,000; pigs: 800,000; sheep: 340,000. **Fish catch:** 4,614 metric tons. **Electricity prod.:** 8.8 bil kWh. **Labor force:** NA.
Finance: Monetary unit: Pound (LBP) (Oct. 2009: 1,503.44 = $1 U.S.). **GDP:** $44.1 bil; **per capita GDP:** $11,100; **GDP growth:** 6.3%. **Imports:** $16.3 bil; Syria 10.7%, France 9.7%, U.S. 9.5%, Italy 7.4%, China 6.7%, Germany 5%, Saudi Arabia 4.9%, Turkey 4.3%. **Exports:** $5 bil; Syria 23.9%, UAE 12.4%, Switzerland 7.2%, Saudi Arabia 5.9%, Turkey 4%. **Tourism:** NA. **Budget:** $8.4 bil. **Intl. reserves less gold:** $13.14 bil. **Gold:** 9.22 mil oz t. **Consumer prices:** NA.
Transport: Railroad: Length: 249 mi. **Motor vehicles:** 1.4 mil pass. cars; 102,400 comm. vehicles. **Civil aviation:** 1.3 bil pass.-mi; 5 airports. **Chief ports:** Beirut, Tripoli.
Communications: TV sets: 355 per 1,000 pop. **Radios:** 907 per 1,000 pop. **Telephone lines:** 714,000. **Daily newspaper circ.** (2004): 54.2 per 1,000 pop. **Internet:** 2.2 mil users.
Health: Life expect.: 70.9 male; 76 female. **Births** (per 1,000 pop.): 17.6. **Deaths** (per 1,000 pop.): 6.1. **Natural inc.:** 1.16%. **Infant mortality** (per 1,000 live births): 22.6. **HIV rate:** 0.1%.
Education: Compulsory: ages 6-15. **Literacy:** 87.4%.
Major intl. organizations: UN (FAO, IBRD, ILO, IMF, IMO, WHO), AL.
Embassy: 2560 28th St. NW 20008; 939-6300.
Website: www.presidency.gov.lb

Formed from 5 former Turkish Empire districts, Lebanon became an independent state Sept. 1, 1920, administered under French mandate 1920-41. French troops withdrew in 1946.

Under the 1943 National Covenant, all public positions were divided among the various religious communities, with Christians in the majority. By the 1970s, Muslims became the majority and demanded a larger political and economic role.

U.S. Marines intervened, May-Oct. 1958, during a Syrian-aided revolt. Continued raids against Israeli civilians, 1970-75, brought Israeli retaliation in southern Lebanon.

An estimated 60,000 were killed and billions of dollars in damage inflicted in a 1975-76 civil war. Palestinian units and leftist Muslims fought against the Maronite militia, the Phalange, and other Christians. Several Arab countries provided political and arms support to the various factions, while Israel aided Christian forces. Up to 15,000 Syrian troops intervened in 1976 to fight Palestinian groups. A cease-fire was mainly policed by Syria.

Israeli forces invaded Lebanon June 6, 1982, attacking strongholds of the Palestine Liberation Organization (PLO). Israeli and Syrian forces engaged in the Bekaa Valley. On Aug. 21, the PLO evacuated west Beirut after massive Israeli bombings there. Israeli troops entered west Beirut following the Sept. 14 assassination of newly elected Lebanese Pres. Bashir Gemayel. On Sept. 16, Lebanese Christian troops entered the Sabra and Shatila refugee camps and massacred hundreds of Palestinian civilians. An agreement May 17, 1983, between Lebanon, Israel, and the U.S. (but not Syria) provided for the withdrawal of Israeli troops; at least 30,000 Syrian troops remained in Lebanon, and Israel held onto a "security zone" in the south.

In 1983, terrorist bombings became a way of life in Beirut as some 50 people were killed in an explosion at the U.S. Embassy, Apr. 18; 241 U.S. servicemen and 58 French soldiers died in separate Islamist suicide attacks, Oct. 23. The 1980s also witnessed kidnappings of U.S., British, French, and Soviet citizens by Islamic militants. All hostages were released by 1992.

A treaty signed May 22, 1991, between Lebanon and Syria recognized Lebanon as a separate state for the first time since the 2 countries gained independence in 1943.

Israeli forces conducted air raids and artillery strikes against guerrilla bases and villages in southern Lebanon, causing over 200,000 to flee their homes July 25-29, 1993. Some 500,000 civilians fled their homes in Apr. 1996 when Israel again struck suspected guerrilla bases in the south. The economy revived in the 1990s, but Syria continued to dominate Lebanon's political affairs. Israel withdrew virtually all its troops from S Lebanon by May 24, 2000, leaving Hezbollah, an Iranian-backed guerrilla group, in control of much of the region.

Rafik al-Hariri, a former prime minister (1992-98, 2000-04), was killed by a truck bomb, Feb. 14, 2005. Many Lebanese blamed Syria, which denied involvement. As anti-Syrian protests mounted, Syria pulled nearly all its troops out of Lebanon, although some intelligence agents may have remained. An anti-Syrian bloc won parliamentary elections held in May and June. A new cabinet, installed July 19, was headed by Fouad Siniora, a friend and aide to Hariri, and included a Hezbollah member.

A rocket attack and border raid by Hezbollah, July 12, 2006, in which 3 Israeli soldiers were killed and 2 captured, triggered a massive escalation of hostilities. Hezbollah, led by Sheikh Hassan Nasrallah, bombarded northern Israel with nearly 4,000 rockets, while Israeli air and ground forces assaulted suspected Hezbollah strongholds in southern Lebanon and southern Beirut. By Aug. 14, when a UN-sponsored cease-fire took hold, the war dead included nearly 1,150 Lebanese. To enforce the truce, thousands of Lebanese govt. troops began moving into southern Lebanon, and expansion of the small UN force already in Lebanon (UNIFIL) was approved.

Industry Min. Pierre Gemayel, a prominent Christian and critic of Syria, was assassinated Nov. 21, 2006. At an international conference in Paris, Jan. 25, 2007, donor countries pledged more than $7.6 bil in reconstruction aid. After more than 3 months of fighting in which over 400 people died, Lebanese forces Sept. 2 defeated Islamic militants at the Nahr al-Bared Palestinian refugee camp north of Tripoli. A power-sharing accord May 21, 2008, between the Siniora government and Hezbollah eased factional violence and paved the way for Army Chief Gen. Michel Suleiman to become president, ending an 18-month stalemate.

A pro-Western coalition, the March 14 Movement, led by Saad Hariri (son of the slain former prime minister), won a parliamentary majority in elections June 7, 2009. On June 27, Pres. Suleiman designated Hariri to form a new government. Hariri suspended the effort Sept. 10, but was reapppointed by Suleiman the following week. UNIFIL had about 12,130 military personnel in Lebanon in mid-2009.

Lesotho
Kingdom of Lesotho

People: Population: 2,130,819. **Age distrib.** (%): <15: 34.8; 65+: 5. **Pop. density:** 181.8 per sq mi, 70.2 per sq km. **Urban:** 23.3%. **Ethnic groups:** Sotho 99%. **Principal languages:** Sesotho (southern Sotho), English (official), Zulu, Xhosa. **Chief religions:** Christian 80%, indigenous beliefs 20%.

Geography: Total area: 11,720 sq mi, 30,355 sq km; **Land area:** 11,720 sq mi, 30,355 sq km. **Location:** In southern Africa. **Neighbors:** Completely surrounded by Republic of South Africa. **Topography:** Landlocked and mountainous, altitudes from 5,000 to 11,000 ft. **Capital:** Maseru, 210,000.

Government: Type: Modified constitutional monarchy. **Head of state:** King Letsie III; b. July 17, 1963; in office: Feb. 7, 1996. **Head of gov.:** Prime Min. Pakalitha Mosisili; b. Mar. 14, 1945; in office: May 29, 1998. **Local divisions:** 10 districts. **Defense budget:** $40 mil. **Active troops:** 2,000.

Economy: Industries: food, beverages, textiles, apparel assembly, handicrafts. **Chief crops:** corn, wheat, pulses, sorghum, barley. **Natural resources:** water, diamonds, sand, clay, building stone. **Arable land:** 11%. **Livestock:** cattle: 695,000; chickens:

1.9 mil; goats: 715,000; pigs: 27,040; sheep: 1.03 mil. **Fish catch:** 179 metric tons. **Electricity prod.:** 200 mil kWh. **Labor force** (2002 est.): agric. 86% (subsistence); roughly 35% of active male wage earners work in South Africa; industry & services 14%.

Finance: Monetary unit: Loti (LSL) (Oct. 2009: 7.42 = $1 U.S.). **GDP:** $3.3 bil; **per capita GDP:** $1,500; **GDP growth:** 6.8%. **Imports:** $1.9 bil; China 31.1%, Taiwan 23.5%, Hong Kong 19.4%, India 13.8%, Germany 5.2%. **Exports:** $953 mil; U.S. 93.6%, Madagascar 1.7%, Canada 1.5%. **Tourism:** $43 mil. **Budget:** $696.9 mil. **Intl. reserves less gold** (2006): $438 mil. **Gold:** NA. **Consumer prices:** 10.7%.

Transport: Civil aviation: 3 airports.

Communications: TV sets: 16 per 1,000 pop. **Radios:** 52 per 1,000 pop. **Telephone lines:** 65,200. **Internet:** 73,300 users.

Health: Life expect.: 41 male; 39.3 female. **Births** (per 1,000 pop.): 24.4. **Deaths** (per 1,000 pop.): 22.3. **Natural inc.:** 0.21%. **Infant mortality** (per 1,000 live births): 78.6. **HIV rate:** 23.2%.

Education: Compulsory: ages 6-12. **Literacy:** 82.2%.

Major intl. organizations: UN (FOA, IBRD, ILO, IMF, WHO, WTO), the Commonwealth, AU.

Embassy: 2511 Massachusetts Ave. NW 20008; 797-5533.

Website: www.lesotho.gov.ls

Lesotho (once called Basutoland) became a British protectorate in 1868 when Chief Moshesh sought protection against the Boers. Independence came Oct. 4, 1966. Most of Lesotho's GNP is provided by citizens working in South Africa. Livestock raising is the chief industry; diamonds are the chief export.

In Mar. 1990, King Moshoeshoe was exiled by the military government. Letsie III became king Nov. 12. In Mar. 1993, Ntsu Mokhehle, a civilian, was elected prime minister, ending 23 years of military rule. After a series of violent disturbances, the king dismissed the Mokhehle government Aug. 17, 1994; constitutional rule was restored Sept. 14.

Letsie abdicated and Moshoeshoe was reinstated Jan. 25, 1995. Moshoeshoe died in an automobile accident, Jan. 15, 1996. Letsie was reinstated Feb. 7, 1996. South Africa and Botswana sent troops Sept. 22, 1998, to help suppress violent antigovernment protests.

According to UN estimates, more than 20% of the adult population has HIV/AIDS.

Liberia
Republic of Liberia

People: Population: 3,441,790. **Age distrib.** (%): <15: 44.1; 65+: 2.8. **Pop. density:** 92.5 per sq mi, 35.7 per sq km. **Urban:** 58.1%. **Ethnic groups:** Indigenous African (incl. Kpelle, Bassa, Gio) 95%, Americo-Liberians (descended fr. slaves fr. U.S.) 3%, Congo People (descended fr. slaves fr. Caribbean) 3%. **Principal languages:** English (official), about 20 ethnic languages. **Chief religions:** Indigenous beliefs 40%, Christian 40%, Muslim 20%.

Geography: Total area: 43,000 sq mi, 111,370 sq km; **Land area:** 37,189 sq mi, 96,320 sq km. **Location:** On SW coast of W Africa. **Neighbors:** Sierra Leone on W, Guinea on N, Côte d'Ivoire on E. **Topography:** Marshy Atlantic coastline rises to low mountains and plateaus in forested interior; 6 major rivers flow in parallel courses to the ocean. **Capital:** Monrovia, 1,041,000.

Government: Type: Republic. **Head of state and gov.:** Pres. Ellen Johnson-Sirleaf; b. Oct. 29, 1938; in office: Jan. 16, 2006. **Local divisions:** 15 counties. **Defense budget:** NA. **Active troops:** 2,400.

Economy: Industries: rubber & palm oil proc., timber, diamonds. **Chief crops:** rubber, coffee, cocoa, rice, cassava, palm oil, sugarcane, bananas. **Natural resources:** iron ore, timber, diamonds, gold, hydropower. **Arable land:** 3%. **Livestock:** cattle: 38,000; chickens: 5.9 mil; goats: 261,600; pigs: 2.96 mil; sheep: 230,340. **Fish catch:** 16,245 metric tons. **Electricity prod.:** 320 mil kWh. **Labor force** (2000 est.): agric. 70%, industry 8%, services 22%.

Finance: Monetary unit: Dollar (LRD) (Oct. 2009: 71.50 = $1 U.S.). **GDP:** $1.5 bil; **per capita GDP:** $500; **GDP growth:** 7.1%. **Imports** (2006): $7.1 bil; S. Korea 27.5%, Singapore 25.2%, Japan 11.6%, China 11.2%. **Exports** (2006): $1.2 bil; Malaysia 38.2%, U.S. 15.9%, Poland 12.3%, Germany 9%, Belgium 6%. **Tourism:** NA. **Budget:** NA. **Intl. reserves less gold:** $104 mil. **Gold:** NA. **Consumer prices:** NA.

Transport: Railroad: Length: 267 mi. **Motor vehicles:** 17,100 pass. cars; 12,800 comm. vehicles. **Civil aviation:** 4.3 mil pass.-mi; 2 airports. **Chief ports:** Buchanan, Monrovia.

Communications: TV sets: 26 per 1,000 pop. **Radios:** 329 per 1,000 pop. **Telephone lines:** 2,000. **Internet:** 20,000 users.

Health: Life expect.: 39.9 male; 42.5 female. **Births** (per 1,000 pop.): 42.9. **Deaths** (per 1,000 live births): 21.4. **Natural inc.:** 2.15%. **Infant mortality** (per 1,000 live births): 143.9. **HIV rate:** 1.7%.

Education: Compulsory: ages 5-11. **Literacy:** 55.5%.

Major intl. organizations: UN and most of its specialized agencies, AU.

Embassy: 5201 16th St. NW 20011; 723-0437.

Website: www.emansion.gov.lr

Liberia was founded in 1822 by U.S. black freedmen who settled at Monrovia with the aid of colonization societies. It became a republic July 26, 1847, with a constitution modeled on that of the U.S. Descendants of freedmen dominated politics.

Under Pres. William V. S. Tubman, Liberia was a founding member of the UN in 1945. Tubman died in 1971 and was succeeded by his vice president, William R. Tolbert Jr. Charging rampant corruption, an Army Redemption Council of enlisted men staged a bloody predawn coup, Apr. 12, 1980, in which Pres. Tolbert was killed and replaced as head of state by Sgt. Samuel Doe. In 1985, Doe was chosen president in a disputed election.

A civil war began Dec. 1989. In Sept. 1990, Pres. Doe was captured and put to death. Despite the introduction of peacekeeping forces from several countries, the conflict intensified. Factional fighting devastated Monrovia in Apr. 1996. On Sept. 3, Ruth Perry became modern Africa's first female head of state, leading a transitional government. By then, the civil war had claimed more than 150,000 lives and uprooted over half the population.

Former rebel leader Charles Taylor was elected president July 19, 1997, in Liberia's first national election in 12 years. The UN imposed sanctions May 4, 2001, to punish Liberia for aiding the Revolutionary United Front (RUF) insurgency in Sierra Leone. Taylor declared a state of emergency Feb. 8, 2002, after Liberian rebels launched raids near Monrovia.

A UN-sponsored war crimes tribunal indicted Taylor June 4, 2003, for his role in the conflict in Sierra Leone. With rebels again threatening Monrovia, Taylor resigned Aug. 11 and went into exile. The UN authorized a 15,000-member peacekeeping force (UNMIL) Sept. 19 to help stabilize the nation. A businessman, Charles Gyude Bryant, was sworn in Oct. 14 to head a power-sharing interim government. Ellen Johnson-Sirleaf won a presidential runoff election Nov. 8, 2005. Captured Mar. 29, 2006, while trying to flee Nigeria, Taylor was transferred to the Netherlands; his trial at the Hague began June 4, 2007, but was plagued by delays.

In June 2009, Liberia's Truth and Reconciliation Commission, investigating the 1989-2003 wars, listed Pres. Johnson-Sirleaf (who acknowledged having raised money for Taylor in the 1980s) among those it recommended barring from public office for 30 years. Showing support for the Johnson-Sirleaf government, U.S. Secy. of State Hillary Clinton visited Liberia Aug. 13. UNMIL had about 11,500 uniformed personnel in Liberia in mid-2009.

Libya
Great Socialist People's Libyan Arab Jamahiriya
People: Population: 6,310,434. **Age distrib.** (%): <15: 33; 65+: 4.3. **Pop. density:** 9.3 per sq mi, 3.6 per sq km. **Urban:** 77%. **Ethnic groups:** Berber & Arab 97%. **Principal languages:** Arabic, Italian, English all widely understood in major cities. **Chief religion:** Sunni Muslim 97%.

Geography: Total area: 679,362 sq mi, 1,759,540 sq km; **Land area:** 679,362 sq mi, 1,759,540 sq km. **Location:** On Mediterranean coast of N Africa. **Neighbors:** Tunisia, Algeria on W; Niger, Chad on S; Sudan, Egypt on E. **Topography:** Desert and semidesert regions cover 92% of land, with low mountains in S, and a narrow coastal zone. **Capital:** Tripoli (Tarabulus), 2,189,000. **Cities (urban aggr.):** Banghazi, 1,180,000.

Government: Type: Islamic Arabic Socialist "Mass-State." **Head of state and gov.:** Col. Muammar al-Qaddafi; b. Sept. 1942; in power: Sept. 1, 1969. **Local divisions:** 25 municipalities. **Defense budget:** $656 mil. **Active troops:** 76,000.

Economy: Industries: oil, iron & steel, food proc., textiles, handicrafts, cement. **Chief crops:** wheat, barley, olives, dates, citrus, vegetables, peanuts, soybeans. **Natural resources:** oil, nat. gas, gypsum. **Crude oil reserves:** 43.7 bil bbls. **Arable land:** 1%. **Livestock:** cattle: 130,000; chickens: 25 mil; goats: 1.3 mil; sheep: 4.5 mil. **Fish catch:** 32,164 metric tons. **Electricity prod.:** 22.6 bil kWh. **Labor force** (2004 est.): agric. 17%, industry 23%, services 59%.

Finance: Monetary unit: Dinar (LYD) (Oct. 2009: 1.22 = $1 U.S.). **GDP:** $88.8 bil; **per capita GDP:** $14,400; **GDP growth:** 6.3%. **Imports:** $25.3 bil; Italy 22.8%, Germany 8.9%, China 8.5%, Turkey 6.3%, Tunisia 6%, U.S. 4.2%, France 4.2%. **Exports:** $60.3 bil; Italy 39.5%, Germany 12.5%, France 7.7%, Spain 7.1%, U.S. 6.7%, China 4.2%. **Tourism:** NA. **Budget:** $19.5 bil. **Intl. reserves less gold:** $59.93 bil. **Gold:** 4.62 mil oz t. **Consumer prices:** NA.

Transport: Motor vehicles: 552,700 pass. cars; 195,500 comm. vehicles. **Civil aviation:** 976.8 mil pass.-mi; 59 airports. **Chief ports:** Ra's Lanuf, Tripoli, Zawiyah.

Communications: TV sets: 139 per 1,000 pop. **Radios:** 259 per 1,000 pop. **Telephone lines:** 1.03 mil. **Internet:** 323,000 users.

Health: Life expect.: 74.8 male; 79.4 female. **Births** (per 1,000 pop.): 25.6. **Deaths** (per 1,000 pop.): 3.5. **Natural inc.:** 2.22%. **Infant mortality** (per 1,000 live births): 21.9. **HIV rate:** NA.

Education: Compulsory: ages 6-14. **Literacy:** 86.8%.

Major intl. organizations: UN (FAO, IBRD, ILO, IMF, IMO, WHO), AL, AU, OPEC.

Embassy: 2600 Virginia Ave. NW, Ste. 705, 20037; 944-9601. **Website:** www.gpc.gov.ly or www.libyanbureaudc.org

First settled by Berbers, Libya was ruled in succession by Carthage, Rome, the Vandals, and the Ottomans. Italy ruled from 1912, and Britain and France after WWII. Libya became an independent constitutional monarchy Jan. 2, 1952. In 1969 a junta led by Col. Muammar al-Qaddafi seized power.

Libya and Egypt fought several air and land battles along their border in July 1977. Chad charged Libya with military occupation of its uranium-rich northern region in 1977. Libyan troops were driven from their last major stronghold by Chad forces in 1987.

During the 1980s, Libya was accused of aiding terrorists and violent revolutionary groups. The U.S. charged Qaddafi with ordering the Apr. 5, 1986, bombing of a West Berlin discotheque, which killed 3, including a U.S. serviceman. In response, the U.S. sent warplanes to attack what it called "terrorist-related targets" in Libya, Apr. 14, including Qaddafi's barracks.

Libyan agents were accused of planting bombs that blew up Pan Am Flight 103 over Lockerbie, Scotland, killing 270 people Dec. 21, 1988, and UTA Flight 772 over Niger, killing 170 people Sept. 19, 1989. The UN imposed sanctions, Apr. 15, 1992, for Libya's failure to cooperate in the Lockerbie and UTA cases.

Libya agreed in 2003 to renounce terrorism and settle compensation cases for the families of the Lockerbie and UTA bombing victims. The UN lifted sanctions, Sept. 12, 2003. Secret talks with the U.S. and UK led to Libya's announcement Dec. 19 that it would stop developing nuclear, chemical, and biological weapons and long-range missiles. The U.S. ended most economic sanctions Apr. 23, 2004, and restored full diplomatic relations May 15, 2006. Further signs of improved ties with the West included a visit to Benghazi Aug. 30, 2008, by Italian Prime Min. Silvio Berlusconi, who pledged $5 bil in aid projects as reparations for Italy's 32 years of colonial rule; and a Sept. 5 visit by U.S. Secy. of State Condoleezza Rice.

In his 40th year as Libyan leader, Qaddafi was elected Feb. 2, 2009, to a one-year term as head of the African Union. Abdel Basset Ali al-Megrahi, a former Libyan agent sentenced to life in prison in 2001 for his role in the Lockerbie bombing, was freed by Scottish authorities on humanitarian grounds Aug. 20, 2009; British officials differed as to whether a recent UK-Libya oil deal had an impact on the decision to release the ailing Megrahi, who received a jubilant welcome in Libya.

Liechtenstein
Principality of Liechtenstein
People: Population: 34,761. **Age distrib.** (%): <15: 16.6; 65+: 13.9. **Pop. density:** 562.7 per sq mi, 217.3 per sq km. **Urban:** 14.5%. **Ethnic groups:** Liechtensteiner 66%, other 34%. **Principal languages:** German (official), Alemannic dialect. **Chief religions:** Roman Catholic 76%, Protestant 7%.

Geography: Total area: 62 sq mi, 160 sq km; **Land area:** 62 sq mi, 160 sq km. **Location:** Central Europe, in Alps. **Neighbors:** Switzerland on W, Austria on E. **Topography:** Rhine Valley occupies one-third of country, Alps cover the rest. **Capital** (2006): Vaduz, 5,047.

Government: Type: Hereditary constitutional monarchy. **Head of state:** Prince Hans-Adam II; b. Feb. 14, 1945; in office: Nov. 13, 1989. **Head of gov.:** Klaus Tschütscher; b. July 8, 1967; in office: Mar. 25, 2009. **Local divisions:** 11 communes. **Defense budget/Active troops:** NA.

Economy: Industries: electronics, metal mfg., dental products, ceramics, pharmaceuticals, food products, precision instruments, tourism. **Chief crops:** wheat, barley, corn, potatoes. **Natural resources:** hydroelectric potential. **Arable land:** 25%. **Livestock:** cattle: 6,000; goats: 300; pigs: 3,000; sheep: 3,000. **Labor force** (2006): agric. 1.7%, industry 43.5%, services 55.4%.

Finance: Monetary unit: Switzerland Franc (CHF) (Oct. 2009: 1.02 = $1 U.S.). **GDP** (2007): $4.2 bil; **per capita GDP** (2007): $118,000; **GDP growth** (2007): 3.1%. **Imports/Exports:** NA. **Tourism:** NA. **Budget** (1998 est.): $414.1 mil.

Communications: TV sets: 469 per 1,000 pop. **Radios:** 656 per 1,000 pop. **Telephone lines:** 19,600. **Daily newspaper circ.** (2003): 513.6 per 1,000 pop. **Internet:** 23,000.

Health: Life expect.: 76.4 male; 83.5 female. **Births** (per 1,000 pop.): 9.9. **Deaths** (per 1,000 pop.): 7.4. **Natural inc.:** 0.24%. **Infant mortality** (per 1,000 live births): 4.5. **HIV rate:** NA.

Education: Compulsory: ages 6-14. **Literacy:** 100%.

Major intl. organizations: UN (WTO), EFTA, OSCE.

Embassy: 2900 K St. NW, Ste. 602B, 20007; 331-0590. **Website:** www.liechtenstein.li

Liechtenstein became sovereign in 1806. Austria administered Liechtenstein's ports up to 1920; Switzerland has administered its postal services since 1921. Liechtenstein is united with Switzerland by a customs and monetary union. Nearly half of all workers commute daily from Austria, Switzerland, and Germany.

On Aug. 15, 2004, Prince Hans-Adam II assigned day-to-day responsibilities for running the tiny country to his son, Crown Prince Alois. Long regarded as a tax haven, Liechtenstein has recently agreed to ease banking secrecy laws that had impeded international tax fraud investigations.

Lithuania

Republic of Lithuania

People: Population: 3,555,179. **Age distrib.** (%): <15: 14.2; 65+: 16.2. **Pop. density:** 146.9 per sq mi, 56.7 per sq km. **Urban:** 66.6%. **Ethnic groups:** Lithuanian 83%, Polish 7%, Russian 6%. **Principal languages:** Lithuanian (official), Russian, Polish. **Chief religions:** Roman Catholic 79%, Russian Orthodox 4%, none 10%.

Geography: Total area: 25,213 sq mi, 65,300 sq km. **Land area:** 24,201 sq mi, 62,680 sq km. **Location:** In E Europe, on SE coast of Baltic. **Neighbors:** Latvia on N; Belarus on E, S; Poland, Russia on W. **Topography:** Lowland with hills in W and S; fertile soil; many small lakes and rivers, with marshes espec. in N and W. **Capital:** Vilnius, 543,000.

Government: Type: Republic. **Head of state:** Pres. Dalia Grybauskaite; b. Mar. 1, 1956; in office: July 12, 2009. **Head of gov.:** Prime Min. Andrius Kubilius; b. Dec. 8, 1956; in office: Dec. 9, 2008. **Local divisions:** 10 provinces. **Defense budget:** $447 mil. **Active troops:** 8,850.

Economy: Industries: metal-cutting machine tools, electric motors, TVs, refrigerators & freezers, oil refining, textiles. **Chief crops:** grain, potatoes, sugar beets, flax, vegetables. **Natural resources:** peat, amber. **Crude oil reserves:** 12 mil bbls. **Arable land:** 45%. **Livestock:** cattle: 838,800; chickens: 9.2 mil; goats: 20,800; pigs: 1.1 mil; sheep: 36,600. **Fish catch:** 190,890 metric tons. **Electricity prod.:** 11.9 bil kWh. **Labor force** (2005): agric. 14%, industry 29.1%, services 56.9%.

Finance: Monetary unit: Litas (LTL) (Oct. 2009: 2.35 = $1 U.S.). **GDP:** $63.3 bil; **per capita GDP:** $17,800; **GDP growth:** 3.1%. **Imports:** $29.3 bil; Russia 30.2%, Germany 11.7%, Poland 10%, Latvia 5.2%. **Exports:** $23.7 bil; Russia 16%, Latvia 11.6%, Germany 7.2%, Poland 5.8%, Estonia 5.7%, France 4.9%, UK 4.7%, Denmark 4.7%, Belarus 4.5%. **Tourism:** $1.2 bil. **Budget:** $13.6 bil. **Intl. reserves less gold:** $4.08 bil. **Gold:** 190,000 oz t. **Consumer prices:** 10.9%.

Transport: Railroad: Length: 1,097 mi. **Motor vehicles:** 1.5 mil pass. cars; 137,000 comm. vehicles. **Civil aviation:** 435 mil pass.-mi; 32 airports. **Chief port:** Klaipeda.

Communications: TV sets: 422 per 1,000 pop. **Radios:** 502 per 1,000 pop. **Telephone lines:** 784,900. **Daily newspaper circ.** (2004): 107.8 per 1,000 pop. **Internet:** 1.8 mil users.

Health: Life expect.: 69.7 male; 79.9 female. **Births** (per 1,000 pop.): 9. **Deaths** (per 1,000 pop.): 11.1. **Natural inc.:** −0.21%. **Infant mortality** (per 1,000 live births): 6.6. **HIV rate:** 0.1%.

Education: Compulsory: ages 7-15. **Literacy:** 99.7%.

Major intl. organizations: UN (FAO, IBRD, ILO, IMF, IMO, WHO, WTO), EU, NATO, OSCE.

Embassy: 4590 MacArthur Blvd. NW, Ste. 200, 20007; 234-5860. **Website:** www.lrvk.lt

Lithuania was occupied by the German army, 1914-18. It was annexed by the Soviet Russian army, but the Soviets were overthrown, 1919. Lithuania was a democratic republic until 1926, when the regime was ousted by a coup. In 1939 the Soviet-German treaty assigned most of Lithuania to the Soviet sphere of influence. Lithuania was annexed by the USSR Aug. 3, 1940.

Lithuania formally declared its independence from the Soviet Union Mar. 11, 1990. During an abortive Soviet coup in Aug., the Western nations recognized Lithuania's independence, which was ratified by the Soviet Union in Sept. 1991.

The conservative Homeland Union defeated the former Communists in parliamentary elections Oct.-Nov. 1996. A Lithuanian-American, Valdas Adamkus, won the presidency in a runoff election Jan. 4, 1998. He lost to Rolandas Paksas in a runoff, Jan. 5, 2003. After the legislature impeached and removed Paksas from office, Apr. 6, 2004, Adamkus regained the presidency. A plummeting economy spurred popular discontent and brought a rightward shift in parliamentary and presidential elections, 2008-09.

Luxembourg

Grand Duchy of Luxembourg

People: Population: 491,775. **Age distrib.** (%): <15: 18.5; 65+: 14.8. **Pop. density:** 492.5 per sq mi, 190.2 per sq km. **Urban:** 82.8%. **Ethnic groups:** Luxembourger 63%, Portuguese 13%, French 5%, Italian 4%, German 2%. **Principal languages:** Luxembourgish (national); German, French (both administrative). **Chief religions:** Roman Catholic 87%, other (incl. Protestant, Jewish, Muslim) 13%.

Geography: Total area: 998 sq mi, 2,586 sq km; **Land area:** 998 sq mi, 2,586 sq km. **Location:** In W Europe. **Neighbors:** Belgium on W, France on S, Germany on E. **Topography:** Heavy forests (Ardennes) cover N. S is a low, open plateau. **Capital:** Luxembourg-Ville, 84,000.

Government: Type: Constitutional monarchy. **Head of state:** Grand Duke Henri; b. Apr. 16, 1955; in office: Oct. 7, 2000. **Head of gov.:** Prime Min. Jean-Claude Juncker; b. Dec. 9, 1954; in office: Jan. 20, 1995. **Local divisions:** 3 districts. **Defense budget:** $279 mil. **Active troops:** 900.

Economy: Industries: banking & financial services, iron & steel, information tech., telecomm., cargo transport., food proc.,

chemicals, metal products, glass, aluminum. **Chief crops:** wine, grapes, barley, oats, potatoes, wheat, fruits. **Natural resources:** iron ore (no longer exploited). **Arable land:** 27%. **Livestock:** cattle: 191,928; chickens: 81.9 mil; goats: 2,814; pigs: 963,110; sheep: 9,339. **Electricity prod.:** 3.3 bil kWh. **Labor force** (2007 est.): agric. 2.2%, industry 17.2%, services 80.6%.

Finance: Monetary unit: Euro (EUR) (Oct. 2009: 0.68 = $1 U.S.). **GDP:** $39.4 bil; **per capita GDP:** $81,000; **GDP growth:** −0.9%. **Imports:** $27.7 bil; Belgium 28.1%, Germany 23.8%, China 18.8%, France 10%, Netherlands 4.9%. **Exports:** $21.4 bil; Germany 21.7%, France 17.3%, Belgium 10%, Italy 6.9%, UK 6.5%, Netherlands 6%, Spain 5%. **Tourism:** $4 bil. **Budget:** $19.3 bil. **Intl. reserves less gold:** $217 mil. **Gold:** 70,000 oz t. **Consumer prices:** 3.4%.

Transport: Railroad: Length: 171 mi. **Motor vehicles:** 304,000 pass. cars; 41,000 comm. vehicles. **Civil aviation:** 351.7 mil pass.-mi; 1 airport. **Chief port:** Mertert.

Communications: TV sets: 599 per 1,000 pop. **Radios:** 683 per 1,000 pop. **Telephone lines:** 260,600. **Daily newspaper circ.** (2004): 254.5 per 1,000 pop. **Internet:** 387,000 users.

Health: Life expect.: 75.9 male; 82.7 female. **Births** (per 1,000 pop.): 11.8. **Deaths** (per 1,000 pop.): 8.4. **Natural inc.:** 0.33%. **Infant mortality** (per 1,000 live births): 4.6. **HIV rate:** 0.2%.

Education: Compulsory: ages 6-15. **Literacy:** 100%.

Major intl. organizations: UN (FAO, IBRD, ILO, IMF, IMO, WHO, WTO), EU, NATO, OECD, OSCE.

Embassy: 2200 Massachusetts Ave. NW 20008; 265-4171. **Website:** www.gouvernement.lu

Luxembourg, founded about 963, was ruled by Burgundy, Spain, Austria, and France from 1448 to 1815. It left the Germanic Confederation in 1866. Overrun by Germany in 2 world wars, Luxembourg ended its neutrality in 1948, when a customs union with Belgium and Netherlands was adopted.

Luxembourg was one of the 6 founding members (1951) of what became the European Union. Prime Min. Jean-Claude Juncker is the EU's longest-serving head of government.

Macedonia

Former Yugoslav Republic of Macedonia

People: Population: 2,066,718. **Age distrib.** (%): <15: 19.2; 65+: 11.4. **Pop. density:** 215.4 per sq mi, 83.1 per sq km. **Urban:** 65.4%. **Ethnic groups:** Macedonian 64%, Albanian 25%, Turkish 4%, Roma 3%. **Principal languages:** Macedonian, Albanian, Turkish. **Chief religions:** Macedonian Orthodox 65%, Muslim 33%.

Geography: Total area: 9,781 sq mi, 25,333 sq km; **Land area:** 9,597 sq mi, 24,856 sq km. **Location:** In SE Europe. **Neighbors:** Bulgaria on E, Greece on S, Albania on W, Serbia on N. **Topography:** Macedonia is a landlocked, mostly mountainous country, with deep river valleys, 3 large lakes; country is bisected by Vardar R. **Capital:** Skopje, 480,000.

Government: Type: Republic. **Head of state:** Pres. Gjorge Ivanov; b. May 2, 1960; in office: May 12, 2009. **Head of gov.:** Prime Min. Nikola Gruevski; b. Aug. 31, 1970; in office: Aug. 27, 2006. **Local divisions:** 123 municipalities. **Defense budget:** $157 mil. **Active troops:** 10,890.

Economy: Industries: food proc., textiles, chemicals, cement, pharmaceuticals, mining. **Chief crops:** grapes, wine, tobacco, vegetables. **Natural resources:** low-grade iron ore, copper, lead, zinc, mang., nickel, tungsten, gold, silver, asbestos. **Arable land:** 22%. **Livestock:** cattle: 253,766; chickens: 2.3 mil; goats: 126,452; pigs: 47,000; sheep: 817,536. **Fish catch:** 1,218 metric tons. **Electricity prod.:** 6.7 bil kWh. **Labor force** (2007): agric. 19.6%, industry 30.4%, services 50%.

Finance: Monetary unit: Denar (MKD) (Oct. 2009: 41.81 = $1 U.S.). **GDP:** $18.8 bil; **per capita GDP:** $9,100; **GDP growth:** 5.3%. **Imports:** $6.5 bil; Germany 13.3%, Greece 12.4%, Bulgaria 9.9%, Serbia and Montenegro 7%, Italy 6.3%, Turkey 5.6%, Slovenia 5.3%, Poland 4.4%. **Exports:** $4 bil; Serbia and Montenegro 20.5%, Germany 15.5%, Greece 12.5%, Bulgaria 10.2%, Italy 8.9%, Croatia 6.6%. **Tourism:** $185 mil. **Budget:** $2.5 bil. **Intl. reserves less gold:** $1.25 bil. **Gold:** 220,000 oz t. **Consumer prices:** 7.2%.

Transport: Railroad: Length: 434 mi. **Motor vehicles:** 253,000 pass. cars; 28,000 comm. vehicles. **Civil aviation:** 154.7 mil pass.-mi; 10 airports.

Communications: TV sets: 273 per 1,000 pop. **Radios:** 550 per 1,000 pop. **Telephone lines:** 457,100. **Daily newspaper circ.** (2004): 88.8 per 1,000 pop. **Internet:** 875,700 users.

Health: Life expect.: 72 male; 77.1 female. **Births** (per 1,000 pop.): 12. **Deaths** (per 1,000 pop.): 8.8. **Natural inc.:** 0.32%. **Infant mortality** (per 1,000 live births): 9.3. **HIV rate:** <0.1%.

Education: Compulsory: ages 7-14. **Literacy:** 97%.

Major intl. organizations: UN (FAO, IBRD, ILO, IMF, IMO, WHO, WTO, OSCE).

Embassy: 2129 Wyoming Ave. NW 20008; 667-0501. **Website:** www.vlada.mk

Macedonia was ruled by Muslim Turks from 1389 to 1912. In 1913, the area was incorporated into Serbia, which in 1918 became part of the Kingdom of Serbs, Croats, and Slovenes (later Yugoslavia). In 1946, Macedonia became a constituent republic of Yugoslavia.

Macedonia declared its independence Sept. 8, 1991, and was admitted to the UN in 1993. Greece, which objected to Macedonia's use of what it considered a Hellenic name and symbols, imposed a trade blockade on the landlocked nation; the 2 countries agreed to normalize relations Sept. 13, 1995.

By the end of NATO's air war against Yugoslavia, Mar.-June 1999, Macedonia had a Kosovar refugee population of more than 250,000; over 90% had been repatriated by Sept. 1. Boris Trajkovski, candidate of the ruling center-right coalition, won a presidential runoff vote Nov. 14.

Ethnic Albanian guerrillas launched an offensive Mar. 2001 in NW Macedonia. An accord signed Aug. 13 paved the way for the introduction of a NATO peacekeeping force. A law broadening the rights of ethnic Albanians was enacted Jan. 24, 2002. A 320-member EU force replaced the NATO peacekeepers, Mar. -Dec. 2003.

After Trajkovski died in a plane crash Feb. 26, 2004, Prime Min. Branko Crvenkovski won a presidential runoff vote Apr. 28. Prime Min. Nikola Gruevski's governing coalition retained power after parliamentary elections June 1, 2008. Gjorge Ivanov won a presidential runoff vote Apr. 5, 2009, and took office May 12. Greece has blocked Macedonia's bid to join NATO because of the continuing dispute over Macedonia's name.

Madagascar
Republic of Madagascar

People: Population: 20,653,556. **Age distrib.** (%): <15: 43.5; 65+: 3. **Pop. density:** 92 per sq mi, 35.5 per sq km. **Urban:** 28.5%. **Ethnic groups:** Malayo-Indonesian, Cotiers (mixed African, Malayo-Indonesian, & Arab), French, Indian, Creole, Comoran. **Principal languages:** Malagasy, French, English (all official). **Chief religions:** Indigenous beliefs 52%, Christian 41%, Muslim 7%.

Geography: Total area: 226,657 sq mi, 587,040 sq km; **Land area:** 224,534 sq mi, 581,540 sq km. **Location:** In Indian O., off SE coast of Africa. **Neighbors:** Comoro Isls. to NW, Mozambique to W. **Topography:** Humid coastal strip in E, fertile valleys in mountainous center plateau region, and a wider coastal strip on W. **Capital:** Antananarivo, 1,697,000.

Government: Type: In transition. **Head of state:** Pres. Andry Rajoelina; b. May 30, 1974; in office: Mar. 17, 2009. **Head of gov.:** Prime Min. Monja Roindefo; b. 1965; in office: Mar. 17, 2009. **Local divisions:** 6 provinces. **Defense budget:** $82 mil. **Active troops:** 13,500.

Economy: Industries: meat proc., seafood, soap, breweries, tanneries, sugar, textiles, glassware, cement, auto assembly plant. **Chief crops:** coffee, vanilla, sugarcane, cloves, cocoa, rice, cassava, beans, bananas, peanuts. **Natural resources:** graphite, chromite, coal, bauxite, salt, quartz, tar sands, semi-prec. stones, mica, fish, hydropower. **Arable land:** 5%. **Livestock:** cattle: 9.6 mil; chickens: 25 mil; goats: 1.3 mil; pigs: 1.4 mil; sheep: 715,000. **Fish catch:** 162,685 metric tons. **Electricity prod.:** 975 mil kWh. **Labor force:** NA.

Finance: Monetary unit: Ariary (MGA) (Oct. 2009: 2,000.03 = $1 U.S.). **GDP:** $20.1 bil; **per capita GDP:** $1,000; **GDP growth:** 7%. **Imports:** $2.4 bil; China 16.3%, France 12.1%, Iran 8.3%, South Africa 6%, Mauritius 4.3%. **Exports:** $1.2 bil; France 28.8%, U.S. 23.7%, Netherlands 7%, Germany 6.3%, China 4.8%. **Tourism** (2006): $159 mil. **Budget:** $1.6 bil. **Intl. reserves less gold:** $638 mil. **Gold:** NA. **Consumer prices:** 9.2%.

Transport: Railroad: Length: 531 mi. **Civil aviation:** 729.5 mil pass.-mi; 27 airports. **Chief ports:** Antsiranana, Mahajanga, Toamasina, Toliara.

Communications: TV sets: 23 per 1,000 pop. **Radios:** 209 per 1,000 pop. **Telephone lines:** 164,900. **Internet:** 316,100 users.

Health: Life expect.: 60.6 male; 64.5 female. **Births** (per 1,000 pop.): 38.4. **Deaths** (per 1,000 pop.): 8.3. **Natural inc.:** 3.01%. **Infant mortality** (per 1,000 live births): 55.6. **HIV rate:** 0.1%.

Education: Compulsory: ages 6-10. **Literacy:** 70.7%.

Major intl. organizations: UN (FAO, IBRD, ILO, IMF, IMO, WHO, WTO), AU.

Embassy: 2374 Massachusetts Ave. NW 20008; 265-5525. **Website:** www.madagascar.gov.mg

Madagascar was settled 2,000 years ago by Malayan-Indonesian people, whose descendants still predominate. A unified kingdom ruled the 18th and 19th centuries. The island became a French protectorate, 1885, and a colony 1896. Independence came June 26, 1960.

Discontent with inflation and French domination led to a coup in 1972. The new regime nationalized French-owned financial interests, closed French bases and a U.S. space-tracking station, and obtained Chinese aid. The government conducted a program of arrests, expulsion of foreigners, and repression of strikes, 1979.

In 1990, Madagascar ended a ban on multiparty politics that had been in place since 1975. Albert Zafy was elected president in 1993, ending the 17-year rule of Adm. Didier Ratsiraka. After Zafy was impeached by the legislature, Madagascar's constitutional court removed him from office, Sept. 5, 1996. A cholera epidemic, exacerbated by cyclones in Feb. and Apr. 2000, claimed at least 1,600 lives.

Marc Ravalomanana won a power struggle with Ratsiraka that followed a disputed presidential election Dec. 16, 2001; he was re-elected with a 55% majority Dec. 3, 2006. Cyclone Ivan hit Feb. 17, 2008, killing at least 83 people and leaving 145,000 homeless. A power struggle between Ravalomanana and Antananarivo Mayor Andry Rajoelina, backed by the military, culminated in Rajoelina's installation as head of a transitional regime, Mar. 17, 2009. The African Union suspended Madagascar and pushed negotiations for a power-sharing settlement.

Malawi
Republic of Malawi

People: Population: 14,268,711. **Age distrib.** (%): <15: 45.8; 65+: 2.7. **Pop. density:** 392.8 per sq mi, 151.7 per sq km. **Urban:** 17.3%. **Ethnic groups:** Chewa, Nyanja, Tumbuka, Yao, Lomwe, Sena, Tonga, Ngoni, Ngonde. **Principal languages:** Chichewa (official), Chinyanja, Chiyao, Chitumbuka. **Chief religions:** Christian 80%, Muslim 13%.

Geography: Total area: 45,745 sq mi, 118,480 sq km; **Land area:** 36,324 sq mi, 94,080 sq km. **Location:** In SE Africa. **Neighbors:** Zambia on W, Mozambique on S and E, Tanzania on N. **Topography:** Malawi stretches 560 mi N-S along Lake Malawi (Lake Nyasa), most of which belongs to Malawi. High plateaus and mountains line the Rift Valley the length of the nation. **Capital:** Lilongwe, 732,000.

Government: Type: Republic. **Head of state and gov.:** Pres. Bingu wa Mutharika; b. Feb. 24, 1934; in office: May 24, 2004. **Local divisions:** 3 regions, 26 districts. **Defense budget:** $42 mil. **Active troops:** 5,300.

Economy: Industries: tobacco, tea, sugar, sawmill products, cement, consumer goods. **Chief crops:** tobacco, sugarcane, cotton, tea, corn, potatoes, cassava, sorghum. **Natural resources:** limestone, hydropower, unexploited deposits of uranium, coal, & bauxite. **Arable land:** 21%. **Livestock:** cattle: 870,622; chickens: 15.3 mil; goats: 2.7 mil; pigs: 928,952; sheep: 185,609. **Fish catch:** 68,000 metric tons. **Electricity prod.:** 1.1 bil kWh. **Labor force** (2003 est.): agric. 90%, industry & services 10%.

Finance: Monetary unit: Kwacha (MWK) (Oct. 2009: 141.25 = $1 U.S.). **GDP:** $111.8 bil; **per capita GDP:** $800; **GDP growth:** 8.6%. **Imports:** $1.6 bil; South Africa 35.7%, India 8.1%, China 7.2%, Tanzania 5.8%, U.S. 4.5%. **Exports:** $830 mil; South Africa 10.8%, Egypt 9.8%, Zimbabwe 8.7%, U.S. 7.4%, Netherlands 7%, Russia 5.8%, Germany 5.7%. **Tourism:** NA. **Budget:** $1.2 bil. **Intl. reserves less gold** (2007): $137 mil. Gold (2007): 10,000 oz t. **Consumer prices:** 8.7%.

Transport: Railroad: Length: 495 mi. **Motor vehicles:** 2,000 pass. cars; 3,000 comm. vehicles. **Civil aviation:** 113.1 mil pass.-mi; 6 airports. **Chief ports:** Chilumba, Chipoka, Monkey Bay, Nkhata Bay, Nkhotakota.

Communications: TV sets: 3 per 1,000 pop. **Radios:** 476 per 1,000 pop. **Telephone lines:** 236,000. **Internet:** 316,100 users.

Health: Life expect.: 43.7 male; 43.1 female. **Births** (per 1,000 pop.): 41.8. **Deaths** (per 1,000 pop.): 17.9. **Natural inc.:** 2.39%. **Infant mortality** (per 1,000 live births): 90.5. **HIV rate:** 11.9%.

Education: Compulsory: ages 6-13. **Literacy:** 71.8%.

Major intl. organizations: UN (FAO, IBRD, ILO, IMF, IMO, WHO, WTO), the Commonwealth, AU.

Embassy: 1029 Vermont Ave. NW, Ste. 1000, 20005; 721-0270. **Website:** www.malawi.gov.mw

Bantus came to the land in the 16th cent., Arab slavers in the 19th. The area became the British protectorate Nyasaland in 1891. It became independent July 6, 1964, and a republic in 1966.

After 3 decades as a one-party state under Pres. Hastings Kamuzu Banda, Malawi adopted a new constitution and, in multiparty elections held May 17, 1994, chose a new leader, Bakili Muluzi.

Bingu wa Mutharika, candidate of the ruling United Democratic Front, won a disputed presidential election May 20, 2004. In an ongoing power struggle, an effort by Mutharika's former political allies to impeach him was halted by Malawi's Constitutional Court, Oct. 26, 2005. He fired Vice Pres. Cassim Chilumpha but was forced to reinstate him, Feb. 2006; he then had Chilumpha charged with treason, Apr. 28, and held under house arrest. Pres. Mutharika won reelection May 19, 2009.

Malaysia

People: Population: 25,715,819. **Age distrib.** (%): <15: 31.4; 65+: 5. **Pop. density:** 202.7 per sq mi, 78.3 per sq km. **Urban:** 67.6%. **Ethnic groups:** Malay 50%, Chinese 24%, indigenous 11%, Indian 7%. **Principal languages:** Bahasa Malaysia (official), English, Chinese dialects, Panjabi, Thai. **Chief religions:** Muslim 60%, Buddhist 19%, Christian 9%, Hindu 6%.

Geography: Total area: 127,317 sq mi, 329,750 sq km; **Land area:** 126,854 sq mi, 328,550 sq km. **Location:** On SE tip of Asia, plus N coast of the island of Borneo. **Neighbors:** Thailand, Brunei on N; Indonesia on S. **Topography:** Most of W Malaysia is covered by tropical jungle, including the central mountain range that runs N-S through the peninsula. W coast is marshy, the E coast, sandy. E Malaysia has a wide, swampy coastal plain, with interior jungles and mountains. **Capital:** Kuala Lumpur, 1,448,000. **Cities (urban aggr.):** Klang, 956,000; Johore Bharu, 875,000.

Government: Type: Constitutional monarchy. **Head of state:** Paramount Ruler Al-Wathiqu Billah Tuanku Mizan Zainal Abidin ibni al-Marhum Sultan Mahmud al-Muktafi Billah Shah; b. Jan. 22, 1962; in office: Dec. 13, 2006. **Head of gov.:** Prime Min. Najib Razak; b. July 23, 1953; in office: Apr. 3, 2009. **Local divisions:** 13 states, 3 federal territories. **Defense budget:** $4 bil. **Active troops:** 109,000.

Economy: Industries: rubber & palm oil proc., light mfg., electronics, tin mining & smelting, timber, oil. **Chief crops:** rubber, palm oil, cocoa, rice, coconuts, pepper. **Natural resources:** tin, oil, timber, copper, iron ore, nat. gas, bauxite. **Crude oil reserves:** 4 bil bbls. **Arable land:** 5%. **Livestock:** cattle: 785,000; chickens: 190 mil; goats: 285,000; pigs: 2 mil; sheep: 120,000. **Fish catch:** 1.6 mil metric tons. **Electricity prod.:** 99.1 bil kWh. **Labor force** (2005 est.): agric. 13%, industry 36%, services 51%.

Finance: Monetary unit: Ringgit (MYR) (Oct. 2009: 3.43 = $1 U.S.). **GDP:** $384.3 bil; **per capita GDP:** $15,200; **GDP growth:** 4.6%. **Imports:** $154.7 bil; Singapore 23%, China 12.7%, Japan 9.8%, U.S. 7.8%, Thailand 5.7%, S. Korea 4.3%. **Exports:** $198.9 bil; Singapore 15.6%, U.S. 12.9%, China 12.5%, Japan 9.6%, Thailand 4.1%. **Tourism:** $14 bil. **Budget:** $46.7 bil. **Intl. reserves less gold:** $59.18 bil. **Gold:** 1.17 mil oz t. **Consumer prices:** 5.4%.

Transport: Railroad: Length: 1,149 mi. **Motor vehicles** (registration of new vehicles only): 482,000 pass. cars; 53,000 comm. vehicles. **Civil aviation:** 30.8 bil pass.-mi; 38 airports. **Chief ports:** Bintulu, George Town (Penang), Johor Bahru, Kuantan, Labuan, Port Kelang, Tanjung Pelepas.

Communications: TV sets: 174 per 1,000 pop. **Radios:** 434 per 1,000 pop. **Telephone lines:** 4.3 mil. **Daily newspaper circ.** (2004): 109.3 per 1,000 pop. **Internet:** 16.9 mil users.

Health: Life expect.: 70.3 male; 75.9 female. **Births** (per 1,000 pop.): 22.4. **Deaths** (per 1,000 pop.): 5. **Natural inc.:** 1.74%. **Infant mortality** (per 1,000 live births): 16.4. **HIV rate:** 0.5%.

Education: Compulsory: ages 6-11. **Literacy:** 91.9%.

Major intl. organizations: UN (FAO, IBRD, ILO, IMF, IMO, WHO, WTO), APEC, ASEAN, the Commonwealth.

Embassy: 3516 International Ct. NW 20008; 572-9700.

Website: www.gov.my

European traders appeared in the 16th cent.; Britain established control in 1867. Malaysia was created Sept. 16, 1963. It included Malaya (which had become independent in 1957 after the suppression of Communist rebels), plus the formerly British Singapore, Sabah (N Borneo), and Sarawak (NW Borneo). Singapore was separated in 1965, in order to end tensions between Chinese, the majority in Singapore, and Malays in control of the Malaysian government.

A monarch is elected by a council of hereditary rulers of the Malayan states every 5 years.

Abundant natural resources have bolstered prosperity, and foreign investment has aided industrialization and trade. Work on a new federal capital at Putrajaya, south of Kuala Lumpur, began in 1995. However, sagging stock and currency prices forced the postponement of major development projects in Sept. 1997.

Mahathir bin Mohamad dominated Malaysian politics as prime minister, 1981-2003. His successor, Abdullah Ahmad Badawi, took office Oct. 31, 2003, and led his National Front coalition to a resounding win in parliamentary elections Mar. 21, 2004. The Indian Ocean tsunami of Dec. 26, 2004, left at least 68 people dead and 8,000 displaced in Malaysia. Recession and scandals plagued Malaysia as National Front leader Najib Razak took office as prime min. Apr. 3, 2009.

Maldives
Republic of Maldives

People: Population: 396,334. **Age distrib.** (%): <15: 22.3; 65+: 3.9. **Pop. density:** 3,421.7 per sq mi, 1,321.1 per sq km. **Urban:** 33.9%. **Ethnic groups:** South Indian, Sinhalese, Arab. **Principal languages:** Maldivian Dhivehi (Sinhala dialect), English (spoken by most govt. officials). **Chief religion:** Sunni Muslim.

Geography: Total area: 116 sq mi, 300 sq km; **Land area:** 116 sq mi, 300 sq km. **Location:** In Indian O., SW of India. **Neighbors:** Nearest is India on N. **Topography:** 19 atolls with 1,190 islands, 198 inhabited. None of the islands are over 5 sq mi in area, and all are nearly flat. **Capital:** Male, 111,000.

Government: Type: Republic. **Head of state and gov.:** Pres. Mohamed (Anni) Nasheed; b. May 17, 1967; in office: Nov. 11, 2008. **Local divisions:** 19 atolls and Male capital atoll. **Defense budget:** $63 mil. **Active troops:** NA.

Economy: Industries: tourism, fish proc., shipping, boat building, coconut proc., garments. **Chief crops:** coconuts, corn, sweet potatoes. **Natural resources:** fish. **Arable land:** 13%. **Fish catch:** 143,597 metric tons. **Electricity prod.:** 219 mil kWh. **Labor force** (1995): agric. 22%, industry 18%, services 60%.

Finance: Monetary unit: Rufiyaa (MVR) (Oct. 2009: 12.80 = $1 U.S.). **GDP:** $1.7 bil; **per capita GDP:** $4,400; **GDP growth:**

5.7. **Imports** $1.3 bil; Singapore 26.4%, UAE 16.4%, India 10.3%, Malaysia 10%, Thailand 4.7%, Sri Lanka 4.5%. **Exports:** $113 mil; Thailand 32.2%, UK 12.9%, France 11.4%, Italy 8.5%, Algeria 8.4%, Sri Lanka 8%. **Tourism:** $602 mil. **Budget** (2006 est.): $671 mil. **Intl. reserves less gold:** $156 mil. **Gold:** NA. **Consumer prices:** 12%.

Transport: Motor vehicles: 4,200 pass. cars; 300 comm. vehicles. **Civil aviation:** 24.2 mil pass.-mi; 3 airports. **Chief port:** Male.

Communications: TV sets: 38 per 1,000 pop. **Radios:** 129 per 1,000 pop. **Telephone lines:** 46,900. **Internet:** 71,700 users.

Health: Life expect.: 71.5 male; 76 female. **Births** (per 1,000 pop.): 14.8. **Deaths** (per 1,000 pop.): 3.7. **Natural inc.:** 1.12%. **Infant mortality** (per 1,000 live births): 30.6. **HIV rate:** NA.

Education: Compulsory: ages 6-12. **Literacy:** 97%.

Major intl. organizations: UN (FAO, IBRD, IMF, IMO, WHO, WTO), the Commonwealth.

Embassy: 800 2nd Ave., Ste. 400E, New York, NY 10017; (212) 599-6194.

Website: www.maldivesinfo.gov.mv

A British protectorate since 1887, the nation achieved independence July 26, 1965; long a sultanate, the Maldives became a republic in 1968. Tourism and fishing are the most important sectors of the economy. Rising sea levels threaten the country, which comprises at least 1,200 small, low-lying coral islands.

The Indian Ocean tsunami of Dec. 26, 2004, killed at least 82 people and displaced more than 21,600 in Maldives. Pres. Maumoon Abdul Gayoom, in office 1978-2008, lost a runoff vote Oct. 29, 2008, to pro-democracy leader and former political prisoner Mohamed (Anni) Nasheed.

Mali
Republic of Mali

People: Population: 12,666,987. **Age distrib.** (%): <15: 48.3; 65+: 3.1. **Pop. density:** 26.9 per sq mi, 10.4 per sq km. **Urban:** 30.5%. **Ethnic groups:** Mande (incl. Bambara, Malinke, Soninke) 50%, Peul 17%, Voltaic 12%, Tuareg & Moor 10%. **Principal languages:** French (official), Bambara, numerous African languages. **Chief religions:** Muslim 90%, indigenous beliefs 9%.

Geography: Total area: 478,767 sq mi, 1,240,000 sq km; **Land area:** 471,045 sq mi, 1,220,000 sq km. **Location:** In interior of W Africa. **Neighbors:** Mauritania, Senegal on W; Guinea, Côte d'Ivoire, Burkina Faso on S; Niger on E; Algeria on N. **Topography:** Landlocked grassy plain in upper basins of the Senegal and Niger rivers, extending N into the Sahara. **Capital:** Bamako, 1,494,000.

Government: Type: Republic. **Head of state:** Pres. Amadou Toumani Touré; b. Nov. 4, 1948; in office: June 8, 2002. **Head of gov.:** Prime Min. Modibo Sidibé; b. Nov. 7, 1952; in office: Sept. 28, 2007. **Local divisions:** 8 regions, 1 capital district. **Defense budget:** $157 mil. **Active troops:** 7,350.

Economy: Industries: food proc., constr., phosphate & gold mining. **Chief crops:** cotton, millet, rice, corn, vegetables, peanuts. **Natural resources:** gold, phosphates, kaolin, salt, limestone, uranium, gypsum, granite, hydropower. **Arable land:** 4%. **Livestock:** cattle: 7.8 mil; chickens: 33 mil; goats: 9.7 mil; pigs: 71,100; sheep: 8.9 mil. **Fish catch:** 100,640 metric tons. **Electricity prod.:** 505 mil kWh. **Labor force** (2005 est.): agric. 80%, industry & services 20%.

Finance: Monetary unit: CFA BCEAO Franc (XOF) (Oct. 2009: 444.97 = $1 U.S.). **GDP:** $14.6 bil; **per capita GDP:** $1,200; **GDP growth:** 4.2%. **Imports** (2006): $2.4 bil; Senegal 13%, France 11.3%, Côte d'Ivoire 11.1%, China 6%. **Exports** (2006): $294 mil; China 29%, Thailand 9.9%, Denmark 6%, Pakistan 4.8%, Morocco 4%. **Tourism:** NA. **Budget** (2006 est.): $1.8 bil. **Intl. reserves less gold:** $695 mil. **Gold:** NA. **Consumer prices:** 9.2%.

Transport: Railroad: Length: 368 mi. **Motor vehicles:** 72,000 pass. cars; 47,000 comm. vehicles. **Civil aviation:** 80.8 mil pass.-mi (incl. Air Afrique traffic apportionment); 8 airports. **Chief port:** Koulikoro.

Communications: TV sets: 13 per 1,000 pop. **Radios:** 55 per 1,000 pop. **Telephone lines:** 82,800. **Internet:** 125,000 users.

Health: Life expect.: 48 male; 51.9 female. **Births** (per 1,000 pop.): 49.4. **Deaths** (per 1,000 pop.): 16.2. **Natural inc.:** 3.32%. **Infant mortality** (per 1,000 live births): 103.8. **HIV rate:** 1.5%.

Education: Compulsory: ages 7-15. **Literacy:** 23.3%.

Major intl. organizations: UN and most of its specialized agencies, AU.

Embassy: 2130 R St. NW 20008; 332-2249.

Website: www.primature.gov.ml

Until the 15th cent. the area was part of the great Mali Empire. Timbuktu (Tombouctou) was a center of Islamic study. French rule was secured, 1898. The Sudanese Rep. and Senegal became independent as the Mali Federation June 20, 1960, but Senegal withdrew, and the Sudanese Rep. was renamed Mali.

A socialist regime led, 1960-68, by Pres. Modibo Keita, was toppled by a coup. Famine struck in 1973-74, killing as many as 100,000 people. Drought conditions returned in the 1980s.

The military, Mar. 26, 1991, overthrew the government of Pres. Moussa Traoré, who had ruled since 1968. Oumar Konare, a coup leader, was elected president, Apr. 26, 1992. The government and a Tuareg rebel group signed a peace accord June 1994. Twice condemned to death for crimes committed in office, Traoré had his sentences commuted to life imprisonment Dec. 1997 and Sept. 1999; he was pardoned May 2002.

Amadou Toumani Touré, who led the 1991 coup, was elected president May 12, 2002, and reelected Apr. 29, 2007.

Malta
Republic of Malta

People: Population: 405,165. **Age distrib.** (%): <15: 16.1; 65+: 14.5. **Pop. density:** 3,320.8 per sq mi, 1,282.2 per sq km. **Urban:** 93.6%. **Ethnic groups:** Maltese (descendants of ancient Carthaginians & Phoenicians with strong Italian, other Mediterranean elements). **Principal languages:** Maltese, English (both official). **Chief religion:** Roman Catholic 98%.

Geography: Total area: 122 sq mi, 316 sq km; **Land area:** 122 sq mi, 316 sq km. **Location:** In center of Mediterranean Sea. **Neighbors:** Nearest is Italy on N. **Topography:** Isl. of Malta is 95 sq mi; other islands in the group: Gozo, 26 sq mi; Comino, 1 sq mi. Coastline is heavily indented. Low hills cover the interior. **Capital:** Valletta, 199,000.

Government: Type: Parliamentary democracy. **Head of state:** Pres. George Abela; b. Apr. 22, 1948; in office: Apr. 4, 2009. **Head of gov.:** Prime Min. Lawrence Gonzi; b. July 1, 1953; in office: Mar. 23, 2004. **Local divisions:** 3 regions comprising 67 local councils. **Defense budget:** $44 mil. **Active troops:** 1,954.

Economy: Industries: tourism, electronics, shipbuilding & repair, constr., food & beverages, pharmaceuticals. **Chief crops:** potatoes, cauliflower, grapes, wheat, barley, tomatoes, citrus, cut flowers, green peppers. **Natural resources:** limestone, salt. **Arable land:** 31%. **Livestock:** cattle: 19,233; chickens: 1.1 mil; goats: 5,828; pigs: 73,683; sheep: 12,172. **Fish catch:** 3,783 metric tons. **Electricity prod.:** 2.1 bil kWh. **Labor force** (2005 est.): agric. 2.3%, industry 29.6%, services 68%.

Finance: Monetary unit: Euro (EUR) (Oct. 2009: 0.68 = $1 U.S.). **GDP:** $10 bil; **per capita GDP:** $24,700; **GDP growth:** 2.7%. **Imports:** $4.8 bil; Italy 28.1%, UK 13.5%, France 8.2%, Germany 7.4%, Singapore 6.4%. **Exports:** $3.1 bil; Germany 13.5%, Singapore 13%, France 12.2%, U.S. 9.6%, UK 8.2%, Hong Kong 6.7%, Japan 6.4%, Italy 4.7%. **Tourism:** $910 mil. **Budget:** $3.5 bil. **Intl. reserves less gold:** $239 mil. **Gold:** 10,000 oz t. **Consumer prices:** 4.3%.

Transport: Motor vehicles: 235,900 pass. cars; 54,600 comm. vehicles. **Civil aviation:** 1.4 bil pass.-mi; 1 airport. **Chief ports:** Marsaxlokk (Malta Freeport), Valletta.

Communications: TV sets: 549 per 1,000 pop. **Radios:** 669 per 1,000 pop. **Telephone lines:** 241,100. **Internet:** 200,200 users.

Health: Life expect.: 77.1 male; 81.6 female. **Births** (per 1,000 pop.): 10.3. **Deaths** (per 1,000 pop.): 8.3. **Natural inc.:** 0.2%. **Infant mortality** (per 1,000 live births): 3.8. **HIV rate:** 0.1%.

Education: Compulsory: ages 5-15. **Literacy:** 91.6%.

Major intl. organizations: UN (FAO, IBRD, ILO, IMF, IMO, WHO, WTO), the Commonwealth, EU, OSCE.

Embassy: 2017 Connecticut Ave. NW 20008; 462-3611. **Website:** www.gov.mt

Malta was ruled by Phoenicians, Romans, Arabs, Normans, the Knights of Malta, France, and Britain (since 1814). It became independent Sept. 21, 1964. Malta became a republic in 1974. The withdrawal of the last British sailors, Apr. 1, 1979, ended 179 years of British military presence on the island.

From 1971 to 1987 and again from 1996 to 1998, Malta was governed by the socialist Labour Party; the Nationalist Party, which pressed for Malta's entry into the EU, held office 1987-96 and won parliamentary elections in 1998, 2003, and 2008. Malta became a full member of the EU May 1, 2004.

Marshall Islands
Republic of the Marshall Islands

People: Population: 64,522. **Age distrib.** (%): <15: 38.6; 65+: 2.9. **Pop. density:** 923.3 per sq mi, 356.5 per sq km. **Urban:** 70%. **Ethnic groups:** Micronesian. **Principal languages:** English, Marshallese (both official). **Chief religions:** Protestant 55%, Assembly of God 26%, Roman Catholic 8%.

Geography: Total area: 70 sq mi, 181 sq km; **Land area:** 70 sq mi, 181 sq km. **Location:** In N Pacific Ocean; composed of two 800-mi-long parallel chains of coral atolls. **Neighbors:** Nearest are Micronesia to W, Nauru and Kiribati to S. **Topography:** Marshall Islands are low coral limestone and sand islands. **Capital** (2004): Majuro, 20,800.

Government: Type: Republic in free association with the U.S. **Head of state and gov.:** Pres. Litokwa Tomeing; b. Oct. 14, 1939; in office: Jan. 14, 2008. **Local divisions:** 33 municipalities. **Defense budget/Active troops:** NA.

Economy: Industries: copra, tuna proc., tourism, craft items. **Chief crops:** coconuts, tomatoes, melons, taro, breadfruit, fruits. **Natural resources:** coconut products, marine products, deep seabed minerals. **Arable land:** 11%. **Fish catch:** 60,409 metric tons. **Labor force** (2000): agric. 21.4%, industry 20.9%, services 57.7%.

Finance: Monetary unit: Dollar (USD). **GDP:** 133.5 mil; **per capita GDP:** $2,500; **GDP growth:** −0.3%. **Imports:** $79.4 mil. **Exports:** $19.4 mil. **Tourism:** $5 mil. **Budget** (1999): $40 mil.

Transport: Civil aviation: 21.1 mil pass.-mi; 4 airports. **Chief port:** Majuro.

Communications: Telephone lines: 4,400. **Internet:** 2,200 users.

Health: Life expect.: 68.9 male; 73 female. **Births** (per 1,000 pop.): 31.5. **Deaths** (per 1,000 pop.): 4.6. **Natural inc.:** 2.69%. **Infant mortality** (per 1,000 live births): 26.4. **HIV rate:** NA.

Education: Compulsory: ages 6-14. **Literacy:** 93.7%.

Major intl. organizations: UN (FAO, IBRD, IMF, IMO, WHO). **Embassy:** 2433 Massachusetts Ave. NW 20008; 234-5414. **Website:** www.rmigovernment.org

The Marshall Islands were a German possession until WWI and were administered by Japan between the World Wars. After WWII, they were administered by the U.S. as part of the UN Trust Territory of the Pacific Islands. From 1946-58, Bikini and Enewetak atolls were used as test sites for the U.S. nuclear weapons program, including the hydrogen bomb.

The Compact of Free Association, ratified by the U.S. on Oct. 21, 1986, gave the islands their independence. In the compact, the U.S. agreed to provide financial aid to the islands, maintain their defense, and compensate victims of nuclear testing; it was renewed Dec. 2003. The Marshall Islands joined the UN Sept. 17, 1991. Amata Kabua, the islands' first and only president since 1979, died Dec. 19, 1996. His cousin Imata Kabua, elected president Jan. 13, 1997, was succeeded by Kessai Note on Jan. 10, 2000, and by Litokwa Tomeing Jan. 14, 2008.

Mauritania
Islamic Republic of Mauritania

People: Population: 3,129,486. **Age distrib.** (%): <15: 41; 65+: 3.4. **Pop. density:** 7.9 per sq mi, 3 per sq km. **Urban:** 40.4%. **Ethnic groups:** Mixed Moor/black 40%, Moor 30%, black 30%. **Principal languages:** Arabic (official & national); Pulaar, Soninke, Wolof (all national); French. **Chief religion:** Muslim 100%.

Geography: Total area: 397,955 sq mi, 1,030,700 sq km; **Land area:** 397,840 sq mi, 1,030,400 sq km. **Location:** In NW Africa. **Neighbors:** Western Sahara on N; Algeria, Mali on E; Senegal on S. **Topography:** Fertile Senegal R. valley in the S gives way to a wide central region of sandy plains and scrub trees. N is arid and extends into the Sahara. **Capital:** Nouakchott, 673,000.

Government: Type: In transition. **Head of state:** Pres. Mohamed Ould Abdel Aziz; b. 1956; in office: Aug. 5. 2009. **Head of gov.:** Prime Min. Moulaye Ould Mohamed Laghdaf; b. 1957; in office,: Aug. 14, 2008. **Local divisions:** 12 regions, 1 capital district. **Defense budget:** $19 mil. **Active troops:** 15,870.

Economy: Industries: fish proc., iron ore & gypsum mining. **Chief crops:** dates, millet, sorghum, rice, corn. **Natural resources:** iron ore, gypsum, copper, phosphate, diamonds, gold, oil, fish. **Crude oil reserves:** 100 mil bbls. **Arable land:** 0.2%. **Livestock:** cattle: 1.7 mil; chickens: 4.2 mil; goats: 5.6 mil; sheep: 8.9 mil. **Fish catch:** 201,588 metric tons. **Electricity prod.:** 412 mil kWh. **Labor force** (2001 est.): agric. 50%, industry 10%, services 40%.

Finance: Monetary unit: Ouguiya (MRO) (Oct. 2009: 260.50 = $1 U.S.). **GDP:** $6.3 bil; **per capita GDP:** $2,100; **GDP growth:** 3.5%. **Imports** (2006): $1.5 bil; France 16.3%, China 8.4%, Netherlands 6.2%, Spain 5.9%, Belgium 5.2%, U.S. 4.9%, Brazil 4.4%. **Exports** (2006): $1.4 bil; China 39.9%, France 10.4%, Spain 7.1%, Italy 7%, Netherlands 5.5%, Belgium 4.8%, Côte d'Ivoire 4.1%. **Tourism:** NA. **Budget** (2002 est.): $378 mil. **Intl. reserves less gold** (2007): $125 mil. **Gold** (2007): 10,000 oz t. **Consumer prices:** 7.3%.

Transport: Motor vehicles: 12,200 pass. cars; 18,200 comm. vehicles. **Civil aviation:** 37.3 mil pass.-mi (incl. Air Afrique traffic apportionment); 9 airports. **Chief ports:** Nouadhibou, Nouakchott.

Communications: TV sets: 95 per 1,000 pop. **Radios:** 146 per 1,000 pop. **Telephone lines:** 76,400. **Internet:** 45,000 users.

Health: Life expect.: 51.6 male; 56.3 female. **Births** (per 1,000 pop.): 40.1. **Deaths** (per 1,000 pop.): 11.6. **Natural inc.:** 2.85%. **Infant mortality** (per 1,000 live births): 66.7. **HIV rate:** 0.8%.

Education: Compulsory: ages 6-14. **Literacy:** 55.8%.

Major intl. organizations: UN (FAO, IBRD, ILO, IMF, IMO, WHO, WTO), AL, AU.

Embassy: 2129 Leroy Pl. NW 20008; 232-5700. **Website:** www.mauritania.mr

Mauritania was a French protectorate from 1903. It became independent Nov. 28, 1960, and annexed the south of former Spanish Sahara (now Western Sahara) in 1976. Mauritania signed a peace treaty with the Saharan guerrillas of the Polisario Front, 1979, and renounced its own claim to the region.

Maaouiya Ould Sid Ahmed Taya took power in a military coup in 1984. Taya, a U.S. ally, was toppled in a bloodless coup, Aug. 3, 2005. During Jan.-June 2006, up to 10,000 people tried to emigrate in handmade boats from Mauritania to Spain's Canary Islands; more than 1,700 died. Civilian rule was restored, 2006-7, but a military coup, Aug. 6, 2008, toppled the elected government. The coup leader, Gen. Mohamed Ould Abdel Aziz, won a disputed presidential election July 18, 2009, With security declining, the U.S. Peace Corps pulled its volunteers out of Mauritania in Aug.

Major oil finds have recently been developed. Although slavery has been repeatedly abolished, most recently in 1981, thousands of Mauritanians continued to live under conditions of servitude; legislation mandating prison terms for slaveholders was enacted Aug. 8, 2007.

Mauritius
Republic of Mauritius

People: Population: 1,284,264. **Age distrib.** (%): <15: 22.5; 65+: 7.1. **Pop. density:** 1,638.5 per sq mi, 632.6 per sq km. **Urban:** 42.3%. **Ethnic groups:** Indo-Mauritian 68%, Creole 27%. **Principal languages:** English (official; spoken by less than 1% of pop.), Creole, Bhojpuri, French. **Chief religions:** Hindu 48%, Roman Catholic 24%, Muslim 17%.

Geography: Total area: 788 sq mi, 2,040 sq km; **Land area:** 784 sq mi, 2,030 sq km. **Location:** In Indian O., 500 mi E of Madagascar. **Neighbors:** Nearest is Madagascar to W. **Topography:** A volcanic island nearly surrounded by coral reefs. A central plateau is encircled by mountain peaks. **Capital:** Port Louis, 150,000.

Government: Type: Republic. **Head of state:** Pres. Sir Anerood Jugnauth; b. Mar. 29, 1930; in office: Oct. 7, 2003. **Head of gov.:** Prime Min. Navinchandra Ramgoolam; b. July 14, 1947; in office: July 5, 2005. **Local divisions:** 9 districts, 3 dependencies. **Defense budget:** $27 mil. **Active troops:** None.

Economy: Industries: food proc. (largely sugar milling), textiles, clothing, chemicals. **Chief crops:** sugarcane, tea, corn, potatoes, bananas, pulses. **Natural resources:** fish. **Arable land:** 49%. **Livestock:** cattle: 28,500; chickens: 10 mil; goats: 91,500; pigs: 17,413; sheep: 12,000. **Fish catch:** 8,476 metric tons. **Electricity prod.:** 2.2 bil kWh. **Labor force** (2007): agric. & fishing 9%; constr. & industry 30%; transp. & communication 7%; trade, restaurants, hotels 22%; finance 6%, other services 25%.

Finance: Monetary unit: Rupee (MUR) (Oct. 2009: 30.80 = $1 U.S.). **GDP:** $15.3 bil; **per capita GDP:** $12,000; **GDP growth:** 4.6%. **Imports:** $4.4 bil; India 21.3%, France 11.9%, China 9.4%, South Africa 7.6%. **Exports:** $2.4 bil; UK 29.9%, France 14.7%, U.S. 8.3%, Madagascar 7%, Italy 6.4%, Belgium 5%, UAE 4.9%. **Tourism:** $1.3 bil. **Budget:** $1.6 bil. **Intl. reserves less gold:** $1.13 bil. **Gold:** 60,000 oz t. **Consumer prices:** 9.7%.

Transport: Motor vehicles: 124,000 pass. cars; 41,000 comm. vehicles. **Civil aviation:** 3.9 bil pass.-mi; 2 airports. **Chief port:** Port Louis.

Communications: TV sets: 248 per 1,000 pop. **Radios:** 371 per 1,000 pop. **Telephone lines:** 364,500. **Daily newspaper circ.** (2004): 77.2 per 1,000 pop. **Internet:** 380,000 users.

Health: Life expect.: 70.3 male; 77.4 female. **Births** (per 1,000 pop.): 14.6. **Deaths** (per 1,000 pop.): 6.5. **Natural inc.:** 0.81%. **Infant mortality** (per 1,000 live births): 12.6. **HIV rate:** 1.7%.

Education: Compulsory: ages 6-11. **Literacy:** 87.4%.

Major intl. organizations: UN and all of its specialized agencies, the Commonwealth, AU.

Embassy: 4301 Connecticut Ave. NW, Ste. 441, 20008; 244-1491.

Website: www.gov.mu

Mauritius was uninhabited when settled in 1638 by the Dutch, who introduced sugarcane. France took over in 1721, bringing African slaves. Britain ruled from 1810 to Mar. 12, 1968, bringing Indian workers for the sugar plantations.

Mauritius formally severed its association with the British crown Mar. 12, 1992.

Mexico
United Mexican States

People: Population: 111,211,789. **Age distrib.** (%): <15: 29.1; 65+: 6.2. **Pop. density:** 149.8 per sq mi, 57.8 per sq km. **Urban:** 76.3%. **Ethnic groups:** Mestizo (Amerindian-Spanish) 60%, Amerindian 30%, white 9%. **Principal languages:** Spanish; various Mayan, Náhuatl, other regional indigenous languages. **Chief religions:** Roman Catholic 77%, Protestant 6%.

Geography: Total area: 761,606 sq mi, 1,972,550 sq km; **Land area:** 742,490 sq mi, 1,923,040 sq km. **Location:** In southern N. America. **Neighbors:** U.S. on N, Guatemala and Belize on S. **Topography:** The Sierra Madre Occidental Mts. run NW-SE near the west coast; the Sierra Madre Oriental Mts. run near Gulf of Mexico. They join S of Mexico City. Between the 2 ranges lies the dry central plateau, 5,000 to 8,000 ft alt., rising toward the S, with temperate vegetation. Coastal lowlands are tropical. About 45% of land is arid. **Capital:** Mexico City, 19,028,000. **Cities (urban aggr.):** Guadalajara, 4,198,000; Monterrey, 3,712,000; Puebla, 2,195,000; Tijuana, 1,553,000.

Government: Type: Federal republic. **Head of state and gov.:** Pres. Felipe de Jesús Calderón Hinojosa; b. Aug. 18, 1962; in of-

fice: Dec. 1, 2006. **Local divisions:** 31 states, 1 federal district. **Defense budget:** $4 bil. **Active troops:** 255,506.

Economy: Industries: food & beverages, tobacco, chemicals, iron & steel, oil, mining, textiles, clothing, motor vehicles, consumer durables, tourism. **Chief crops:** corn, wheat, soybeans, rice, beans, cotton, coffee, fruit, tomatoes. **Natural resources:** oil, silver, copper, gold, lead, zinc, nat. gas, timber. **Crude oil reserves:** 10.5 bil bbls. **Arable land:** 13%. **Livestock:** cattle: 32 mil; chickens: 496.5 mil; goats: 8.9 mil; pigs: 15.5 mil; sheep: 7.5 mil. **Fish catch** (est.): 1.5 mil metric tons. **Electricity prod.:** 236.4 bil kWh. **Labor force** (2005): agric. 15.1%, industry 25.7%, services 59%.

Finance: Monetary unit: Peso (MXN) (Oct. 2009: 13.46 = $1 U.S.). **GDP:** $1.6 tril; **per capita GDP:** $14,200; **GDP growth:** 1.3%. **Imports:** $308.6 bil; U.S. 55%, China 7.1%, S. Korea 5.2%. **Exports:** $291.3 bil; U.S. 73.1%, Canada 6.2%, Germany 1.9%. **Tourism:** 12.9 bil. **Budget:** $209.2 bil. **Intl. reserves less gold:** $61.76 bil. **Gold:** 120,000 oz t. **Consumer prices:** 5.1%.

Transport: Railroad: Length: 10,884 mi. **Motor vehicles:** 14.7 mil pass. cars; 7.4 mil comm. vehicles. **Civil aviation:** 21.2 bil pass.-mi; 246 airports. **Chief ports:** Altamira, Coatzacoalcos, Manzanillo, Morro Redondo, Salina Cruz, Tampico, Veracruz.

Communications: TV sets: 272 per 1,000 pop. **Radios:** 329 per 1,000 pop. **Telephone lines:** 20.5 mil. **Daily newspaper circ.** (2000): 92.8 per 1,000 pop. **Internet:** 23.3 mil users.

Health: Life expect.: 73 male; 78.8 female. **Births** (per 1,000 pop.): 20. **Deaths** (per 1,000 pop.): 4.8. **Natural inc.:** 1.53%. **Infant mortality** (per 1,000 live births): 19. **HIV rate:** 0.3%.

Education: Compulsory: ages 6-15. **Literacy:** 92.4%.

Major intl. organizations: UN (FAO, IBRD, ILO, IMF, IMO, WHO, WTO), APEC, NAFTA, OAS, OECD.

Embassy: 1911 Pennsylvania Ave. NW 20006; 728-1600.

Website: www.gob.mx

Mexico was the site of advanced Indian civilizations. The Mayans, an agricultural people, moved up from Yucatan, built huge stone pyramids, and invented a calendar. The Toltecs were overcome by the Aztecs, who founded Tenochtitlan 1325 CE, now Mexico City. Hernán Cortés, Spanish conquistador, destroyed the Aztec empire, 1519-21. After 3 centuries of Spanish rule the people rose, under Fr. Miguel Hidalgo y Costilla, 1810, Fr. Morelos y Pavón, 1812, and Gen. Agustín Iturbide, who made himself emperor as Agustín I, 1822. A republic was declared in 1823.

Mexican territory extended into the present American Southwest and California until Texas revolted and established a republic in 1836. The U.S.-Mexican War, 1846-48, resulted in the loss by Mexico of the lands north of the Rio Grande.

French arms supported an Austrian archduke on the throne of Mexico as Maximilian I, 1864-67, but pressure from the U.S. forced France to withdraw. Dictatorial rule by Porfirio Díaz, president 1877-80, 1884-1911, led to a period of rebellion and factional fighting. A new constitution, Feb. 5, 1917, brought reform.

The Institutional Revolutionary Party (PRI) dominated politics from 1929 until the late 1990s. Radical opposition, including some guerrilla activity, was contained by strong measures. Some gains in agriculture, industry, and social services were achieved, but much of the work force remained jobless or underemployed. Although prospects brightened with the discovery of vast oil reserves, inflation and a drop in world oil prices aggravated Mexico's economic problems in the 1980s. Mexico reached agreement with the U.S. and Canada on the North American Free Trade Agreement (NAFTA) Aug. 12, 1992; it took effect Jan. 1, 1994.

Guerrillas of the Zapatista National Liberation Army (EZLN) launched an uprising, Jan. 1, 1994, in southern Mexico. A tentative peace accord was reached Mar. 2. The presidential candidate of the governing PRI, Luis Donaldo Colosio Murrieta, was assassinated at a political rally in Tijuana, Mar. 23. The new PRI candidate, Ernesto Zedillo Ponce de León, won election Aug. 21 and was inaugurated Dec. 1, 1994.

An austerity plan and pledges of aid from the U.S. saved Mexico's currency from collapse in early 1995. Popular Revolutionary Army guerrillas launched coordinated attacks on government targets in Aug. 1996. In elections July 6, 1997, the PRI failed to win a congressional majority for the first time since 1929.

In the presidential election of July 2, 2000, the PRI lost for the first time in over 7 decades; the winner, Vicente Fox Quesada of the National Action Party (PAN), took office Dec. 1, 2000. Hurricane Wilma hit Cancún Oct. 21, 2005, causing $2 bil damage.

Results of the July 2, 2006, presidential vote gave the PAN candidate, conservative Felipe Calderón Hinojosa, a slim margin over former Mexico City mayor Andrés Manuel López Obrador, nominee of the leftist Democratic Revolutionary Party. Claiming vote fraud, López Obrador and his supporters held massive protests, but Calderón was declared the winner and took office Dec. 1, 2006. Torrential rains Oct. 28-Nov. 1, 2007, killed at least 13 people and swamped more than 1 mil homes in Tabasco and Chiapas states. Despite a government crackdown on drug cartels, drug-related violence intensified, claiming more than 13,000 lives from Dec. 2006 to Sept. 2009. The government ordered a shutdown of all nonessential work, May 1-5, 2009, because of an outbreak of the influenza A (H1N1) virus (swine flu).

◀ Changing of the Guard
Iraqi Security Forces in Basra celebrated as U.S. troops completed their withdrawal June 30, 2009, from Iraqi cities. U.S. troops remained a substantial presence in Iraq at forward operating bases.

Election Irregularities

Afghanistan's Electoral Complaints Commission was kept busy following presidential and local elections Aug. 20, 2009, as hundreds of complaints of fraud were submitted.

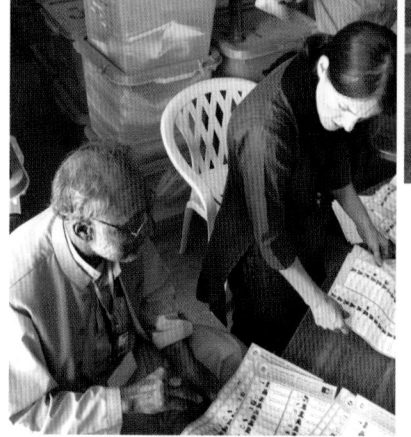

▲ Iran Protests
Hundreds of thousands of Iranians protested, demanded recounts, and alleged fraud in response to Pres. Mahmoud Ahmadinejad's suspicious landslide victory in presidential elections June 12, 2009.

Commitment in Afghanistan

Pres. Barack Obama unveiled his preliminary strategy for fighting the war in Afghanistan Mar. 27, 2009, describing the main goal as defeating the Taliban militia and eliminating safe havens for terrorist networks in Afghanistan and neighboring Pakistan.

Terror in Mumbai

The Taj Mahal luxury hotel was just one of the high-profile targets of terrorist attacks Nov. 26-29, 2008, that left more than 170 dead in Mumbai, India's commercial capital.

▲ War in Gaza

A 22-day-war between Israel and militant Palestinian group Hamas in the Gaza Strip left more than 1,300 Palestinians dead and thousands wounded or homeless by the time a cease-fire had been agreed to, Jan. 18, 2009.

▲ Welcome Home

American journalists Laura Ling (left) and Euna Lee were freed from 12 years "reform through labor" in North Korea after former Pres. Bill Clinton met with Kim Jong-Il Aug. 4, 2009, in Pyongyang.

Nuclear North Korea? ▶

North Korea launched seven short-range missiles July 4, 2009, flouting United Nations Security Council resolutions.

Farewell ▼

Former Philippine President Corazon Aquino died Aug. 1, 2009, in Manila, the Philippines; during Aquino's six years in office, she withstood multiple coup attempts/ revolts.

Honduran Coup d'Etat

The Honduran military stormed the presidential palace early June 28, 2009, and deposed Pres. Manuel Zelaya (seated), hours before a national referendum on constitutional reforms.

▼ Somali Pirates Foiled

Crew members of the *Maersk Alabama* container ship celebrated news that U.S. Navy SEALS had liberated the ship's captain, taken hostage by a band of Somali pirates, in a daring rescue attempt after a 4-day standoff Apr. 12, 2009.

▼ Italy Shaken

A major earthquake struck the Abruzzo region in central Italy Apr. 6, 2009, killing more than 290 people and leaving about 28,000 people homeless.

▲ Guantánamo Closing?

Pres. Barack Obama signed an executive order Jan. 22, 2009, that mandated the closing of the U.S. military prison at Guantánamo Bay, Cuba, by Jan. 22, 2010; another executive order also restricted interrogation techniques approved under former Pres. George W. Bush.

Swine Flu

The World Health Organization (WHO) declared that the A(H1N1) "swine flu" influenza virus had reached global pandemic status June 11, 2009.

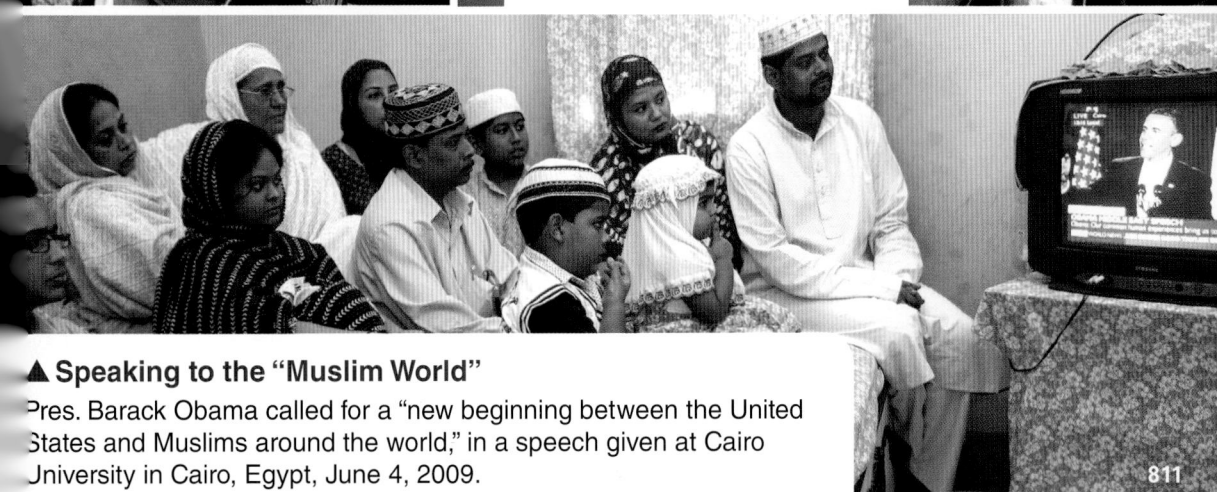

▲ Speaking to the "Muslim World"

Pres. Barack Obama called for a "new beginning between the United States and Muslims around the world," in a speech given at Cairo University in Cairo, Egypt, June 4, 2009.

Last Voyage

NASA astronauts repaired the earth-orbiting Hubble Space Telescope, May 11-24, 2009, installing a new camera, which captured this image from the Carina Nebula. The shuttle fleet was scheduled to be retired in 2010.

Distant Relative? ▶

An international team of paleontologists called "Ida," a 47-million-year-old *Darwinius masillae* primate fossil, "the closest thing we can get to a direct ancestor" to humans in a journal article dated May 19, 2009.

Total Eclipse

People in China, India, and other parts of Asia looked to the sky June 22, 2009, to view the longest total solar eclipse of the 21st century, which lasted 6 minutes, 39 seconds.

New Look ▶

Connie Culp, the recipient of the first face transplant surgery in the U.S., at the Cleveland Clinic in OH, revealed herself to the media May 5, 2009.

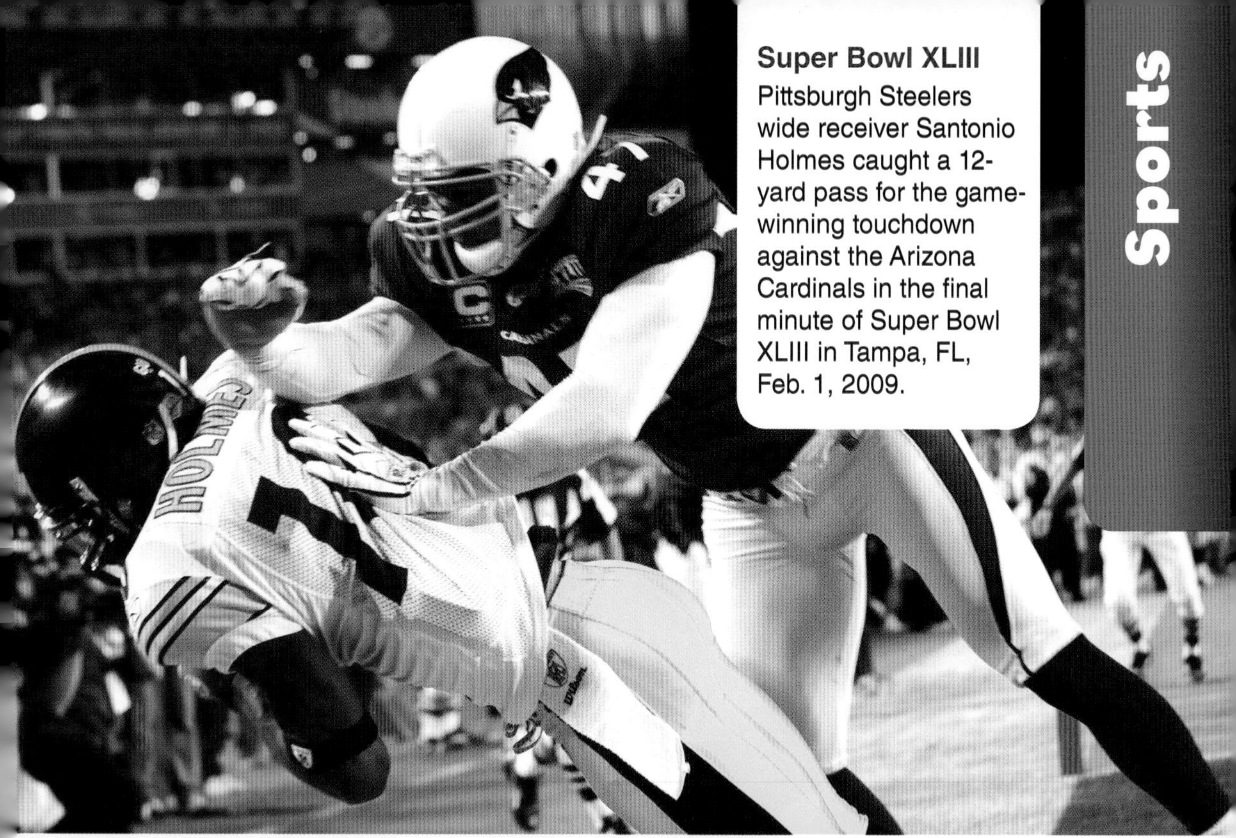

Super Bowl XLIII

Pittsburgh Steelers wide receiver Santonio Holmes caught a 12-yard pass for the game-winning touchdown against the Arizona Cardinals in the final minute of Super Bowl XLIII in Tampa, FL, Feb. 1, 2009.

◀ L.A. Kings

Finals MVP Kobe Bryant led the Los Angeles Lakers to the franchise's 15th NBA championship June 14, 2009, defeating the Orlando Magic in five games.

Unbeatable ▶

The Univ. of Connecticut women's basketball team celebrated their Final Four championship win Apr. 7, 2009, capping off an undefeated season by beating Univ. of Louisville, 76-54.

Wall of Shame, or Hall of Fame?

All-Star sluggers Alex Rodriguez, Manny Ramirez, and David Ortiz were all linked to positive tests for performance-enhancing drugs in 2009, based on the results of anonymous tests administered in 2003; Ramirez was suspended 50 games in 2009 for an unrelated violation of MLB drug policy.

◀ Federer Triumphs, Then Topples

Number-one-ranked Roger Federer Sept. 13, 2009, made the "greatest shot I ever hit in my life"— backwards and between the legs—to earn himself a place in the U.S. Open finals, which he lost for the first time in six years, to underdog Juan Martín del Potro.

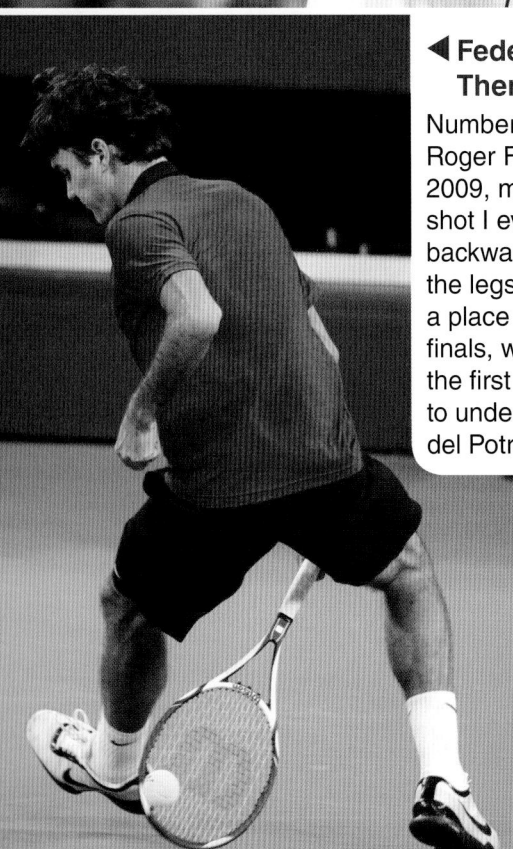

27 Up, 27 Down

White Sox left-hander Mark Buehrle pitched the 18th perfect game in the history of Major League Baseball against the Tampa Bay Rays, July 23, 2009.

Lightning Bolt ▼

Sprinter Usain Bolt of Jamaica Aug. 16 and Aug. 20, 2009, broke his own world records in the men's 100 meters and 200 meters, respectively, at world championships in Berlin, Germany.

Comeback ▲

Alberto Contador of Spain (right) won the 2009 Tour de France July 26, followed by Andy Schleck of Luxembourg (far left); seven-time Tour de France winner Lance Armstrong (center) returned to the Tour after a three-year hiatus, placing third.

So Close ▼

Stewart Cink (below, right) defeated Tom Watson July 19, 2009, in a playoff to win the British Open; the 59-year-old Watson, an eight-time major-tournament winner whose last win was in 1983, came close to becoming the oldest player ever to win a major tournament.

Follow Suit ▲

U.S. teammates Aaron Peirsol, David Walters, Eric Shanteau, and Michael Phelps celebrated winning the 4x100m medley relay at world championships in Rome Aug. 2, 2009; media coverage of the competition focused on some athletes' buoyant performance-enhancing swimsuits, which were to be banned Jan. 1, 2010.

Farewells

Bea Arthur
Apr. 25, 2009

Merce Cunningham
July 26, 2009

Farrah Fawcett
June 25, 2009

John Hope Franklin
Mar. 25, 2009

Paul Harvey
Feb. 28, 2009

Eartha Kitt
Dec. 25, 2008

Frank McCourt
July 19, 2009

Ed McMahon
June 23, 2009

Robert S. McNamara
July 6, 2009

Odetta
Dec. 2, 2008

Les Paul
Aug. 13, 2009

Harold Pinter
Dec. 24, 2008

Natasha Richardson
Mar. 18, 2009

Patrick Swayze
Sept. 14, 2009

John Updike
Jan. 27, 2009

Andrew Wyeth
Jan. 16, 2009

Micronesia
Federated States of Micronesia

People: Population: 107,434. **Age distrib.** (%): <15: 34.8; 65+: 2.9. **Pop. density:** 396.4 per sq mi, 153 per sq km. **Urban:** 66.9%. **Ethnic groups:** Chuukese 49%, Pohnpeian 24%, Kosraean 6%. **Principal languages:** English (official & common lang.), Chuukese, Kosrean, Pohnpeian, Yapese. **Chief religions:** Roman Catholic 50%, Protestant 47%.

Geography: Total area: 271 sq mi, 702 sq km; **Land area:** 271 sq mi, 702 sq km. **Location:** Consists of 607 islands in W Pacific Ocean. **Topography:** Includes both high mountainous islands and low coral atolls; volcanic outcroppings on Pohnpei, Kosrae, and Truk. Climate is tropical. **Capital** (2000): Palikir, 6,444.

Government: Type: Republic in free association with U.S. **Head of state and gov.:** Pres. Emanuel (Manny) Mori; b. Dec. 25, 1948; in office: May 11, 2007. **Local divisions:** 4 states. **Defense budget/Active troops:** NA.

Economy: Industries: tourism, constr., fish proc., specialized aquaculture. **Chief crops:** black pepper, tropical fruits & vegetables, coconuts, bananas, cassava, kava, betel nuts, sweet potatoes. **Natural resources:** forests, marine products, deep seabed minerals. **Arable land:** 6%. **Livestock:** cattle: 14,000; chickens: 190,000; goats: 4,100; pigs: 33,000. **Fish catch:** 17,140 metric tons. **Labor force** (FY05 est.): agric. 0.9%, industry 34.4%, services 64.7% (two-thirds govt. employees).

Finance: Monetary unit: U.S. Dollar (USD). **GDP:** 238.1 mil (supp. by grant aid avg. perhaps $100 mil a year); **per capita GDP:** $2,200; **GDP growth** (2005): 0.3%. **Imports** (2004): $132.7 mil. **Exports** (2004): $14 mil. **Intl. reserves less gold:** $26 mil. **Gold:** NA. **Consumer prices:** NA.

Transport: Civil aviation: 6 airports. **Chief port:** Tomil Harbor. **Communications: TV sets:** 20 per 1,000 pop. **Radios:** 70 per 1,000 pop. **Telephone lines:** 8,700. **Internet:** 16,000 users.

Health: Life expect.: 68.8 male; 72.6 female. **Births** (per 1,000 pop.): 23.7. **Deaths** (per 1,000 pop.): 4.5. **Natural inc.:** 1.91%. **Infant mortality** (per 1,000 live births): 27. **HIV rate:** NA.

Education: Compulsory: ages 6-13. **Literacy:** 89%.

Major intl. organizations: UN (FAO, IBRD, IMF, WHO).

Embassy: 1725 N St. NW 20036; 223-4383.

Website: micronesia.fm

The Federated States of Micronesia, formerly known as the Caroline Islands, was ruled successively by Spain, Germany, Japan, and the U.S. The nation gained independence under a compact of free association with the U.S., Nov. 1986 and was admitted to the UN, Sept. 17, 1991. Tropical Storm Chata'an July 1-2, 2002, left 47 people dead and over 1,000 homeless in Chuuk. Typhoon Sudal battered Yap Apr. 9, 2004, leaving at least 1,500 homeless.

Moldova
Republic of Moldova

People: Population: 4,320,748. **Age distrib.** (%): <15: 15.9; 65+: 10.8. **Pop. density:** 335.3 per sq mi, 129.5 per sq km. **Urban:** 42.6%. **Ethnic groups:** Moldovan/Romanian 78%, Ukrainian 8%, Russian 6%. **Principal languages:** Moldovan (official; virtually same as Romanian lang.), Russian, Gagauz (Turkish dialect). **Chief religions:** Eastern Orthodox 98%, Jewish 2%.

Geography: Total area: 13,067 sq mi, 33,843 sq km; **Land area:** 12,885 sq mi, 33,371 sq km. **Location:** In E Europe. **Neighbors:** Romania on W; Ukraine on N, E, and S. **Topography:** Country is landlocked; mainly hilly plains, with steppelands in S near Black Sea. **Capital:** Chisinau, 592,000.

Government: Type: Republic. **Head of state:** Pres. Mihai Ghimpu; b. Nov. 19, 1951; in office: Sept. 11, 2009 (acting). **Head of gov.:** Prime Min.-designate Vladimir Filat; b. May 6, 1969; appointed: Sept. 17, 2009. **Local divisions:** 9 counties, 1 municipality, 1 autonomous territory. **Defense budget:** $19 mil. **Active troops:** 6,000.

Economy: Industries: sugar, vegetable oil, food proc., agric. machinery, foundry equip. **Chief crops:** vegetables, fruits, wine, grain, sugar beets, sunflower seed, tobacco. **Natural resources:** lignite, phosphorites, gypsum, limestone. **Arable land:** 55%. **Livestock:** cattle: 299,105; chickens: 22.4 mil; goats: 111,935; pigs: 531,818; sheep: 835,077. **Fish catch:** 5,860 metric tons. **Electricity prod.:** 3.8 bil kWh. **Labor force** (2005): agric. 40.6%, industry 16%, services 43.3%.

Finance: Monetary unit: Leu (MDL) (Oct. 2009: 11.15 = $1 U.S.). **GDP:** $10.7 bil; **per capita GDP:** $2,500; **GDP growth:** 7.2%. **Imports:** $4.9 bil; Russia 21%, Romania 15.7%, Ukraine 14.5%, Germany 8.7%, Italy 5.5%, Belarus 4.6%. **Exports:** $1.6 bil; Russia 28.9%, Romania 15.4%, Italy 9.6%, Ukraine 8.4%, Poland 5.5%, Germany 5.1%, Belarus 4%. **Tourism:** $164 mil. **Budget:** $1.8 bil. **Intl. reserves less gold:** $1.09 bil. **Gold:** NA. **Consumer prices:** 12.8%.

Transport: Railroad: Length: 707 mi. **Motor vehicles:** 293,000 pass. cars; 5,000 comm. vehicles. **Civil aviation:** 201.9 mil pass.-mi; 5 airports.

Communications: TV sets: 297 per 1,000 pop. **Radios:** 742 per 1,000 pop. **Telephone lines:** 1.1 mil. **Internet:** 800,000 users.

Health: Life expect.: 66.8 male; 74.4 female. **Births** (per 1,000 pop.): 11. **Deaths** (per 1,000 pop.): 10.8. **Natural inc.:** 0.02%. **Infant mortality** (per 1,000 live births): 13.5. **HIV rate:** 0.4%.

Education: Compulsory: ages 7-15. **Literacy:** 99.2%.

Major intl. organizations: UN (FAO, IBRD, ILO, IMF, IMO, WHO, WTO), CIS, OSCE.

Embassy: 2101 S St. NW 20008; 667-1130.

Website: www.moldova.md

In 1918, Romania annexed all of Bessarabia that Russia had acquired from Turkey in 1812 by the Treaty of Bucharest. In 1924, the Soviet Union established the Moldavian Autonomous Soviet Socialist Republic on the eastern bank of the Dniester. It was merged with the Romanian-speaking districts of Bessarabia in 1940 to form the Moldavian SSR.

During WWII, Romania, allied with Germany, occupied the area. It was recaptured by the USSR in 1944. Moldova declared independence Aug. 27, 1991. It became an independent state when the USSR disbanded Dec. 26, 1991.

Fighting erupted Mar. 1992 in the Trans-Dniester region between Moldovan security forces and Slavic separatists—ethnic Russians and ethnic Ukrainians—who feared Moldova would merge with neighboring Romania. In a plebiscite on Mar. 6, 1994, voters in Moldova supported independence, without unification with Romania.

Defying the Moldovan government, voters in the breakaway Trans-Dniester region held legislative elections and approved a separatist constitution Dec. 24, 1995. A peace accord with Trans-Dniester separatists was signed in Moscow May 8, 1997. In a referendum Sept. 17, 2006, Trans-Dniester voters overwhelmingly supported independence from Moldova and eventual union with Russia. The Communists gained legislative majorities in 2001 and 2005 but were outpolled by a fragile coalition of pro-Western parties, July 29, 2009.

Monaco
Principality of Monaco

People: Population: 32,965. **Age distrib.** (%): <15: 14.6; 65+: 23. **Pop. density:** 43,784.1 per sq mi, 16,905.1 per sq km. **Urban:** 100%. **Ethnic groups:** French 47%, Monegasque 16%, Italian 16%, other 21%. **Principal languages:** French (official), English, Italian, Monegasque. **Chief religion:** Roman Catholic 90%.

Geography: Total area: <1 sq mi, 2 sq km; **Land area:** 0.8 sq mi, 2 sq km. **Location:** On NW Mediterranean coast. **Neighbors:** France to W, N, E. **Topography:** Monaco-Ville sits atop a high promontory, the rest of the principality rises from the port up the hillside. **Capital** (2005): Monaco, 32,409.

Government: Type: Constitutional monarchy. **Head of state:** Prince Albert II; b. Mar. 14, 1958; in office: Apr. 6, 2005. **Head of gov.:** Min. of State Jean-Paul Proust; b. Mar. 3, 1940; in office: June 1, 2005. **Local divisions:** 4 quarters. **Defense budget/Active troops:** NA.

Economy: Industries: tourism, constr., small-scale industrial & consumer products. **Chief crops:** None. **Natural resources:** None. **Arable land:** None. **Fish catch** (est.): 1 metric ton. **Labor force:** NA.

Finance: Monetary unit: Euro (EUR) (Oct. 2009: 0.68 = $1 U.S.). **GDP** (2006): $976.3 mil; **per capita GDP** (2006): $30,000; **GDP growth** (2000): 0.9%. **Imports** (2005): $916.1 mil. **Exports** (2005): $716.3 mil. **Tourism:** NA. **Budget** (2005 est.): $920.6 mil.

Transport: Civil aviation: 3.1 mil pass.-mi. **Chief port:** Monaco.

Communications: TV sets: 758 per 1,000 pop. **Radios:** 1,030 per 1,000 pop. **Telephone lines:** 35,000. **Internet:** 22,000 users.

Health: Life expect.: 76.1 male; 84 female. **Births** (per 1,000 pop.): 9.1. **Deaths** (per 1,000 pop.): 13. **Natural inc.:** −0.39%. **Infant mortality** (per 1,000 live births): 5.2. **HIV rate:** NA.

Education: Compulsory: ages 6-15. **Literacy:** 99%.

Major intl. organizations: UN (FAO, IMO, WHO), OSCE.

Embassy: 2314 Wyoming Ave. NW 20008; 234-1530.

Website: www.gouv.mc

An independent principality for over 300 years, Monaco has belonged to the House of Grimaldi since 1297, except during the French Revolution. It was placed under the protectorate of Sardinia in 1815, and under France, 1861. The Prince of Monaco was an absolute ruler until the 1911 constitution. Monaco was admitted to the UN on May 28, 1993.

Monaco is noted for its mild climate, magnificent scenery, and elegant casinos. Prince Rainier III, who ruled Monaco from 1949 and turned it into one of Europe's top tourist spots, died Apr. 6, 2005, and was succeeded by his son, Albert II.

Mongolia

People: Population: 3,041,142. **Age distrib.** (%): <15: 28.1; 65+: 4. **Pop. density:** 5.1 per sq mi, 2 per sq km. **Urban:** 56.7%. **Ethnic groups:** Mongol (mostly Khalkha) 95%, Turkic (mostly Kazakh) 5%. **Principal languages:** Khalkha Mongol, Turkic, Russian. **Chief religions:** Buddhist Lamaist 50%, Shamanist & Christian 6%, Muslim 4%, none 40%.

Geography: Total area: 603,909 sq mi, 1,564,116 sq km; **Land area:** 599,831 sq mi; 1,553,556 sq km. **Location:** In E Central Asia. **Neighbors:** Russia on N, China on E, W, and S. **Topography:** Mostly a high plateau with mountains, salt lakes, and vast grasslands. Arid lands in S are part of the Gobi Desert. **Capital:** Ulaanbaatar, 885,000.

Government: Type: Republic. **Head of state:** Pres. Tsakhiagiin Elbegdorj; b. Mar. 30, 1963; in office: June 18, 2009. **Head of**

gov.: Prime. Min. Sanjaagiin Bayar; b. 1956; in office: Nov. 22, 2007. **Local divisions:** 18 provinces, 3 municipalities. **Defense budget:** $43 mil. **Active troops:** 10,000.

Economy: Industries: constr. & constr. materials, mining, oil, food & beverages, proc. of animal products. **Chief crops:** wheat, barley, vegetables, forage crops. **Natural resources:** oil, coal, copper, molybd., tungsten, phosphates, tin, nickel, zinc, fluorspar, gold, silver, iron. **Arable land:** 1%. **Livestock:** cattle: 2.2 mil; chickens: 100,000; goats: 15.5 mil; pigs: 7,000; sheep: 14.8 mil. **Fish catch:** 185 metric tons. **Electricity prod.:** 2.9 bil kWh. **Labor force** (2008): agric. 34%, industry 5%, services 61%.

Finance: Monetary unit: Tughrik (MNT) (Oct. 2009: 1,441.50 = $1 U.S.). **GDP:** $9.5 bil; **per capita GDP:** $3,200; **GDP growth:** 9. **Imports:** $3.6 bil; Russia 35.1%, China 28.9%, Japan 7.6%, S. Korea 6.4%. **Exports:** $2.5 bil; China 75.7%, Canada 9%, Russia 3.2%. **Tourism:** NA. **Budget:** $1.5 bil. **Intl. reserves less gold** (2007): $757 mil. **Gold** (2007): 240,000 oz t. **Consumer prices:** 25.1.

Transport: Railroad: Length: 1,125 mi. **Civil aviation:** 467.9 mil pass.-mi; 14 airports.

Communications: TV sets: 58 per 1,000 pop. **Radios:** 142 per 1,000 pop. **Telephone lines:** 165,000. **Daily newspaper circ.** (2004): 19.6 per 1,000 pop. **Internet:** 330,000 users.

Health: Life expect.: 64.9 male; 69.8 female. **Births** (per 1,000 pop.): 21.1. **Deaths** (per 1,000 pop.): 6.2. **Natural inc.:** 1.49%. **Infant mortality** (per 1,000 live births): 41.2. **HIV rate:** 0.1%.

Education: Compulsory: ages 7-15. **Literacy:** 97.3%.

Major intl. organizations: UN (FAO, IBRD, ILO, IMF, IMO, WHO, WTO).

Embassy: 2833 M St. NW 20007; 333-7117.

Website: www.pmis.gov.mn

One of the world's oldest countries, Mongolia reached the zenith of its power in the 13th cent. when Genghis Khan and his successors conquered all of China and extended their influence as far west as Hungary and Poland. In later centuries, the empire dissolved and Mongolia became a province of China.

With the advent of the 1911 Chinese revolution, Mongolia, with Russian backing, declared its independence. A Communist regime was established July 11, 1921.

In 1990, the Mongolian Communist Party yielded its monopoly on power but won election in July. A new constitution took effect Feb. 12, 1992. Natsagiyn Bagabandi, a former Communist, won the presidential election of May 18, 1997. A protracted political crisis took a violent turn Oct. 2, 1998, with the murder of Sanjaasuregiyn Zorig, a popular cabinet member seeking to become prime minister. Pres. Bagabandi was reelected May 20, 2001. Nambaryn Enkhbayar, a former prime minister (2000-04), won the presidential election of May 22, 2005.

Mongolia contributed troops to U.S.-led operations in Afghanistan and Iraq. On Nov. 21, 2005, Pres. George W. Bush became the first sitting U.S. president to visit Mongolia; the U.S. agreed Oct. 22, 2007, to a 5-year, $285-mil aid program. Riots followed parliamentary elections June 29, 2008, won by the ruling Mongolian People's Revolutionary Party (MPRP). In presidential voting May 24, 2009, former Prime Min. Tsakhiagiin Elbergdorj (1998, 2004-06), the Democratic Party candidate, defeated the MPRP's Enkhbayar.

Montenegro

People: Population: 672,180. **Age distrib.** (%): <15: 16; 65+: 13.7. **Pop. density:** 126 per sq mi, 48.7 per sq km. **Urban:** 61.2%. **Ethnic groups:** Montenegrin 43%, Serbian 32%, Bosniak 8%. **Principal languages:** Montenegrin (official), Serbian, Bosnian, Albanian, Croatian. **Chief religions:** Orthodox, Muslim, Roman Catholic.

Geography: Total area: 5,415 sq mi, 14,026 sq km; **Land area:** 5,333 sq mi; 13,812 sq km. **Location:** On Balkan Peninsula in SE Europe. **Neighbors:** Bosnia and Herzegovina on N and W; Serbia on E; Albania on SE; Adriatic Sea on SW; Croatia on W. **Topography:** Most terrain is rugged and mountainous, with few arable regions, mostly along the Zeta R.; narrow coastline is highly indented. **Capital:** Podgorica, 142,000.

Government: Type: Republic. **Head of state:** Pres. Filip Vujanovic; b. Sept. 1, 1954; in office: May 22, 2003. **Head of gov.:** Prime. Min. Milo Djukanovic; b. Feb. 15, 1962; in office: Feb. 29, 2008. **Local divisions:** 21 municipalities. **Defense budget:** $59 mil. **Active troops:** 4,500.

Economy: Industries: steelmaking, aluminum, agric. proc., consumer goods, tourism. **Chief crops:** grains, tobacco, potatoes, citrus fruits, olives, grapes. **Natural resources:** bauxite, hydroelectricity. **Arable land:** 14%. **Livestock:** cattle: 114,922; chickens: 449,000; pigs: 13,294; sheep: 249,281. **Fish catch** (est.): 912 metric tons. **Labor force** (2004 est.): agric. 2%, industry 30%, services 68%.

Finance: Monetary unit: Euro (EUR) (Oct. 2009: 0.68 = $1 U.S.). **GDP:** $6.8 bil; **per capita GDP:** $10,100; **GDP growth:** 7.5%. **Imports** (2003): $601.7 mil. **Exports** (2003): $171.3 mil. **Tourism:** $630 mil. **Budget:** NA. **Intl. reserves less gold:** $311 mil. **Gold:** NA. **Consumer prices:** NA.

Transport: Railroad: Length: 155 mi. **Motor vehicles** (incl. Serbia): 1.6 mil pass. cars; 158,400 comm. cars. **Civil aviation** 726.4 mil pass.-mi (incl. Serbia); 3 airports. **Chief port:** Bar.

Communications: Telephone lines: 362,000. **Internet:** 294,000 users.

Health: Life expect.: 74.2 male; 80.3 female. **Births** (per 1,000 pop.): 11.2. **Deaths** (per 1,000 pop.): 8.5. **Natural inc.:** 0.27%. **Infant mortality** (per 1,000 live births): 10.3. **HIV rate:** NA.

Education: NA. **Literacy:** NA.

Major intl. organizations: UN (FAO, ILO, WHO), OSCE.

Embassy: 1610 New Hampshire Ave. NW 20009; 234-6108.

Website: www.montenegro.yu

Part of the medieval Serbian Kingdom, Montenegro preserved its autonomy for centuries because of its mountainous terrain. After WWI, it was part of the Kingdom of Serbs, Croats, and Slovenes, later renamed Yugoslavia. Italian forces occupied parts of Montenegro during WWII. In 1945, with the establishment of a federal Yugoslavia under Communist rule, Montenegro became one of 6 constituent republics.

In Apr. 1992, after 4 other republics had declared independence, Montenegro and Serbia reconstituted themselves as the Federal Republic of Yugoslavia. Because of its ties with Serbia, Montenegro was a target of NATO air strikes during the Kosovo war, Mar.-June 1999. The republic sought closer ties with the West, however, and worked to reduce its political and economic dependence on Serbia. A referendum on independence passed May 21, 2006, with barely more than the 55% majority required. Montenegro declared independence June 3, 2006, and was admitted as a UN member June 28.

Morocco
Kingdom of Morocco

People: Population: 34,859,364. **Age distrib.** (%): <15: 30; 65+: 5.2. **Pop. density:** 202.3 per sq mi, 78.1 per sq km. **Urban:** 55%. **Ethnic groups:** Arab-Berber 99%. **Principal languages:** Arabic (official), Berber dialects, French (often lang. of business, govt., diplomacy). **Chief religion:** Muslim 99%.

Geography: Total area: 172,414 sq mi, 446,550 sq km; **Land area:** 172,317 sq mi, 446,300 sq km. **Location:** On NW coast of Africa. **Neighbors:** Western Sahara on S, Algeria on E, Spain on N. **Topography:** Consists of 5 natural regions: mountain ranges (Riff in N, Middle Atlas, Upper Atlas, and Anti-Atlas); rich plains in W; alluvial plains in SW; well-cultivated plateaus in the center; a pre-Sahara arid zone extending from SE. **Capital:** Rabat, 1,705,000. **Cities (urban aggr.):** Casablanca (Dar-el-Beida), 3,181,000; Fès, 1,002,000; Marrakech, 872,000.

Government: Type: Constitutional monarchy. **Head of state:** King Mohammed VI; b. Aug. 21, 1963; in office: July 23, 1999. **Head of gov.:** Prime Min. Abbas El Fassi; b. Sept. 18, 1940; in office: Sept. 19, 2007. **Local divisions:** 16 regions. **Defense budget:** $2.4 bil. **Active troops:** 195,800.

Economy: Industries: phosphate rock mining & proc., food proc., leather goods, textiles, constr., tourism. **Chief crops:** barley, wheat, citrus, wine, vegetables, olives. **Natural resources:** phosphates, iron ore, mang., lead, zinc, fish, salt. **Crude oil reserves:** 0.8 mil bbls. **Arable land:** 19%. **Livestock:** cattle: 2.8 mil; chickens: 140 mil; goats: 5.3 mil; pigs: 8,000; sheep: 16.9 mil. **Fish catch:** 894,456 metric tons. **Electricity prod.:** 21.9 bil kWh. **Labor force** (2006 est.): agric. 44.6%, industry 19.8%, services 35.5%.

Finance: Monetary unit: Dirham (MAD) (Oct. 2009: 7.69 = $1 U.S.). **GDP:** $136.6 bil; **per capita GDP:** $4,000; **GDP growth:** 5.4%. **Imports:** $39.2 bil; France 17%, Spain 14.2%, Italy 6.8%, Saudi Arabia 6.8%, China 6.3%, Germany 5.9%, U.S. 4.1%. **Exports:** $20.6 bil; Spain 18.7%, France 17.1%, Brazil 6.9%, U.S. 4.4%, Belgium 4.3%, Italy 4.2%. **Tourism:** $7.2 bil. **Budget:** $21.7 bil. **Intl. reserves less gold:** $14.35 bil. **Gold:** 710,000 oz t. **Consumer prices:** 3.8%.

Transport: Railroad: Length: 1,185 mi. **Motor vehicles:** 1.3 mil pass. cars; 457,000 comm. vehicles. **Civil aviation:** 4.0 bil pass.-mi; 32 airports. **Chief ports:** Agadir, Casablanca, Mohammedia, Safi.

Communications: TV sets: 165 per 1,000 pop. **Radios:** 247 per 1,000 pop. **Telephone lines:** 3 mil. **Daily newspaper circ.** (2003): 11.7 per 1,000 pop. **Internet:** 10.3 mil users.

Health: Life expect.: 69.2 male; 74 female. **Births** (per 1,000 pop.): 21.3. **Deaths** (per 1,000 pop.): 5.5. **Natural inc.:** 1.58%. **Infant mortality** (per 1,000 live births): 38.2. **HIV rate:** 0.1%.

Education: Compulsory: ages 6-14. **Literacy:** 55.6%.

Major intl. organizations: UN (FAO, IBRD, ILO, IMF, IMO, WHO, WTO), AL.

Embassy: 1601 21st St. NW 20009; 462-7979.

Website: www.maroc.ma

Berbers were the original inhabitants, followed by Carthaginians and Romans. Arabs conquered in 683. In the 11th and 12th centuries, a Berber empire ruled all northwest Africa and most of Spain from Morocco.

Part of Morocco came under Spanish rule in the 19th cent.; France controlled the rest in the early 20th. Tribal uprisings lasted from 1911 to 1933. The country became independent Mar. 2, 1956. Tangier, an internationalized seaport, was turned over to Morocco, 1956. Ifni, a Spanish enclave, was ceded in 1969. Morocco annexed the disputed territory of Western Sahara during the second half of the 1970s (see below).

King Hassan II assumed the throne in 1961, reigning until his death on July 23, 1999; he was immediately succeeded by his eldest son. Political reforms in the 1990s included the establishment of a bicameral legislature in 1997.

Five terrorist attacks in Casablanca May 16, 2003, left 45 people dead, including 12 suicide bombers; the government blamed Salafia Jihadia, a group connected with al-Qaeda. An earthquake Feb. 24, 2004, killed at least 629 people in the vicinity of al-Hoceima, northern coastal Morocco. Following a series of suicide bombings in 2007, the government stepped up its campaign against militant Islamists; by Aug. 2009, nearly 1,000 persons considered to be Islamic radicals were in Moroccan prisons.

Western Sahara
Western Sahara, formerly the protectorate of Spanish Sahara, is bounded on the N by Morocco, the NE by Algeria, the E and S by Mauritania, and the W by the Atlantic Ocean. Phosphates are the major resource. Population (2009 est.): 405,210; capital: Laayoune (El Aaiún). Area: 102,703 sq mi.

Spain withdrew from its protectorate in Feb. 1976. On Apr. 14, 1976, Morocco annexed over 70,000 sq mi, with the remainder annexed by Mauritania. The Polisario Front guerrilla movement, which had proclaimed the region independent Feb. 27, launched attacks with Algerian support. After Mauritania signed a treaty with Polisario on Aug. 5, 1979, Morocco occupied Mauritania's portion of Western Sahara.

After years of bitter fighting, Morocco controlled the main urban areas, but Polisario guerrillas moved freely in the vast, sparsely populated deserts. The 2 sides implemented a cease-fire in 1991, when a UN peacekeeping force (MINURSO) was established with a mandate to prepare for a referendum on self-determination as early as 1992; in mid-2009, MINURSO had 235 uniformed personnel in Western Sahara, but no referendum had been held.

Mozambique
Republic of Mozambique
People: Population: 21,669,278. **Age distrib.** (%): <15: 44.3; 65+: 2.9. **Pop. density:** 71.6 per sq mi, 27.6 per sq km. **Urban:** 34.5%. **Ethnic groups:** African (incl. Makhuwa, Tsonga, Lomwe, Sena) 99.7%. **Principal languages:** Portuguese (official; spoken by 27% of pop. as second lang.), Emakhuwa, Xichangana, Elomwe, Cisena. **Chief religions:** Catholic 24%, Muslim 18%, Zionist Christian 18%, none 23%.

Geography: Total area: 309,496 sq mi, 801,590 sq km; **Land area:** 302,739 sq mi, 784,090 sq km. **Location:** On SE coast of Africa. **Neighbors:** Tanzania on N; Malawi, Zambia, Zimbabwe on W; South Africa, Swaziland on S. **Topography:** Coastal lowlands comprise nearly half the country with plateaus rising in steps to the mountains along W border. **Capital:** Maputo, 1,446,000.

Government: Type: Republic. **Head of state:** Pres. Armando Guebuza; b. Jan. 20, 1943; in office Feb. 2, 2005. **Head of gov.:** Prime Min. Luisa Diogo; b. Apr. 11, 1958; in office: Feb. 17, 2004. **Local divisions:** 10 provinces and Maputo municipality. **Defense budget:** $57 mil. **Active troops:** 11,200.

Economy: Industries: food, beverages, chemicals, aluminum, oil products, textiles, cement. **Chief crops:** cotton, cashew nuts, sugarcane, tea, cassava, corn, coconuts, sisal, citrus & tropical fruits, potatoes, sunflowers. **Natural resources:** coal, titanium, nat. gas, hydropower, tantalum, graphite. **Arable land:** 5%. **Livestock:** cattle: 1.4 mil; chickens: 28.5 mil; goats: 5 mil; pigs: 182,000; sheep: 218,882. **Fish catch:** 93,177 metric tons. **Electricity prod.:** 14.6 bil kWh. **Labor force** (1997 est.): agric. 81%, industry 6%, services 13%.

Finance: Monetary unit: Metical (MZN) (Oct. 2009: 27.40 = $1 U.S.). **GDP:** $18.9 bil; **per capita GDP:** $900; **GDP growth:** 6.5%. **Imports:** $3.5 bil; South Africa 34.3%, Australia 8.4%, China 6.1%, U.S. 5%. **Exports:** $2.7 bil; South Africa 17.3%, Italy 14.9%, Spain 11.4%, Belgium 11.1%, UK 5.3%, China 4.9%, Zimbabwe 4.6%. **Tourism:** $163 mil. **Budget:** $2.8 bil. **Intl. reserves less gold:** $1.02 bil. **Gold:** 100,000 oz t. **Consumer prices:** 10.3%.

Transport: Railroad: Length: 2,975 mi. **Motor vehicles:** 112,000 pass. cars; 40,000 comm. vehicles. **Civil aviation:** 276.5 mil pass.-mi; 23 airports. **Chief ports:** Beira, Maputo, Nacala.

Communications: TV sets: 5 per 1,000 pop. **Radios:** 40 per 1,000 pop. **Telephone lines:** 78,300. **Daily newspaper circ.** (2004): 2.7 per 1,000 pop. **Internet:** 350,000 users.

Health: Life expect.: 41.6 male; 40.4 female. **Births** (per 1,000 pop.): 38.2. **Deaths** (per 1,000 pop.): 20.3. **Natural inc.:** 1.79%. **Infant mortality** (per 1,000 live births): 107.8. **HIV rate:** 12.5%.

Education: Compulsory: ages 6-12. **Literacy:** 44.4%.

Major intl. organizations: UN (FAO, IBRD, ILO, IMF, IMO, WHO, WTO), the Commonwealth, AU.

Embassy: 1525 New Hampshire Ave. NW 20036; 293-7146.

Website: www.mozambique.mz

The first Portuguese post on the Mozambique coast was established in 1505, on the trade route to the East. Mozambique became independent June 25, 1975, after a 10-year war against Portuguese colonial domination. The 1974 revolution in Portugal had paved the way for the orderly transfer of power to Frelimo (Front for the Liberation of Mozambique). Frelimo took over local administration Sept. 20, 1974.

The new Frelimo government, headed by Pres. Samora Machel, a former guerrilla commander, provided for a gradual transition to a Communist system. Most of the country's whites emigrated. In the 1980s, severe drought and civil war caused famine and heavy loss of life. Pres. Machel was killed in a plane crash just inside the South African border, Oct. 19, 1986. Frelimo formally abandoned Marxist-Leninism in 1989, and a new constitution, effective Nov. 30, 1990, provided for multiparty elections and a free-market economy.

On Oct. 4, 1992, a peace agreement was signed aimed at ending hostilities between the government and the rebel Mozambique National Resistance (MNR). Repatriation of 1.7 mil Mozambican refugees officially ended June 1995. In Mar. 1999 the heaviest floods in 4 decades left nearly 200,000 people stranded. Even worse flooding in Feb.-Mar. 2000 claimed more than 600 lives, displaced over 1 mil people, and devastated the economy.

Frelimo retained its hold under Pres. Joaquim Chissano (in office 1986-2005) and his successor, Pres. Armando Guebuza, elected Dec. 1-2, 2004. Flooding of the Zambezi River basin, followed by Cyclone Favio, killed at least 45 people and left more than 170,000 people homeless in Feb. 2007. Another flood crisis, Jan.-Mar. 2008, claimed some 700 lives and displaced 650,000 people. Real GDP growth averaged nearly 8% annually during 2000-08 and was expected to remain strong at 4% in 2009.

Myanmar *(formerly Burma)*
Union of Myanmar
People: Population: 48,137,741. **Age distrib.** (%): <15: 25.3; 65+: 5.4. **Pop. density:** 189.6 per sq mi, 73.2 per sq km. **Urban:** 30.6%. **Ethnic groups:** Burman 68%, Shan 9%, Karen 7%. **Principal languages:** Burmese, many ethnic minority languages. **Chief religions:** Buddhist 89%, Christian 4%, Muslim 4%.

Geography: Total area: 261,970 sq mi, 678,500 sq km; **Land area:** 253,955 sq mi, 657,740 sq km. **Location:** Between S and SE Asia, on Bay of Bengal. **Neighbors:** Bangladesh, India on W; China, Laos, Thailand on E. **Topography:** Mountains surround Myanmar on W, N, and E, and dense forests cover much of the nation. N-S rivers provide habitable valleys and communications, especially the Irrawaddy, navigable for 900 mi. Country has a tropical monsoon climate. **Capital:** Yangon, 4,088,000. **Cities (urban agg.):** Mandalay, 961,000; Nay Pyi Taw, 930,000.

Government: Type: Military. **Head of state:** Gen. Than Shwe; b. Feb. 2, 1933; in office: Apr. 23, 1992. **Head of gov.:** Lt. Gen. Thein Sein; b. Apr. 20, 1945; in office: Oct. 24, 2007 (acting from May 18). **Local divisions:** 7 states, 7 divisions. **Defense budget:** $7 bil. **Active troops:** 406,000.

Economy: Industries: agric. proc., wood & wood products, constr. materials, pharmaceuticals, garments. **Chief crops:** rice, pulses, beans, sesame, groundnuts, sugarcane. **Natural resources:** oil, timber, tin, antimony, zinc, copper, tungsten, lead, coal, marble, limestone, prec. stones, nat. gas, hydropower. **Crude oil reserves:** 50 mil bbls. **Arable land:** 15%. **Livestock:** cattle: 12.6 mil; chickens: 107.8 mil; goats: 2.4 mil; pigs: 7 mil; sheep: 497,085. **Fish catch:** 2.84 mil metric tons. **Electricity prod.:** 6 bil kWh. **Labor force** (2001): agric. 70%, industry 7%, services 23%.

Finance: Monetary unit: Kyat (MMK) (Oct. 2009: 6.53 = $1 U.S.). **GDP:** $55.1 bil; **per capita GDP:** $1,200; **GDP growth:** 1.1%. **Imports:** $3.4 bil; China 32%, Thailand 21%, Singapore 20.5%, S. Korea 5.3%, Malaysia 4.2%, Indonesia 4%. **Exports:** $6.3 bil; Thailand 52.6%, India 12%, China 9.2%, Japan 4.4%. **Tourism:** NA. **Budget:** NA. **Intl. reserves less gold** (2006): *$821 mil. **Gold:** NA. **Consumer prices:** 26.8%.

Transport: Railroad: Length: 2,458 mi. **Motor vehicles:** 188,000 pass. cars; 131,000 comm. vehicles. **Civil aviation:** 899.7 mil pass.-mi; 37 airports. **Chief ports:** Moulmein, Rangoon, Sittwe.

Communications: TV sets: 7 per 1,000 pop. **Radios:** 72 per 1,000 pop. **Telephone lines:** 829,000. **Internet:** 46,000 users.

Health: Life expect.: 60.7 male; 65.3 female. **Births** (per 1,000 pop.): 17.2. **Deaths** (per 1,000 pop.): 9.2. **Natural inc.:** 0.8%. **Infant mortality** (per 1,000 live births): 49.1. **HIV rate:** 0.7%.

Education: Compulsory: ages 5-9. **Literacy:** 89.9%.

Major intl. organizations: UN (FAO, IBRD, ILO, IMF, IMO, WHO, WTO), ASEAN.

Embassy: 2300 S St. NW 20008; 332-3344.

Website: www.myanmar.gov.mm

The Burmese arrived from Tibet before the 9th cent., displacing earlier cultures, and a Buddhist monarchy was established by the 11th. Burma was conquered by the Mongol dynasty of China in 1272, then ruled by Shans as a Chinese tributary, until the 16th cent. Britain subjugated Burma in 3 wars, 1824-84, and ruled the country as part of India until 1937, when Burma became self-governing. Independence outside the Commonwealth was achieved Jan. 4, 1948.

Gen. Ne Win dominated politics from 1962 to 1988, first as military ruler, then as constitutional president. His regime drove Indians from the civil service and Chinese from commerce. Economic socialization was advanced, isolation from foreign countries enforced. In 1987 Burma, once the richest nation in Southeast Asia, was granted less-developed status by the UN.

Ne Win resigned July 1988, following antigovernment riots. In Sept. the military seized power, under Gen. Saw Maung. In 1989 the country's name was changed to Myanmar.

The first free multiparty elections in 30 years took place May 27, 1990, with the main opposition party winning a decisive victory, but the military refused to hand over power. A key opposition leader, Aung San Suu Kyi, awarded the Nobel Peace Prize in 1991, was held under house arrest, 1989-95, 2000-02, and again from 2003.

Because of the regime's poor human rights record and continued harassment of Aung San Suu Kyi and her supporters, the U.S. imposed sanctions. The Indian Ocean tsunami of Dec. 26, 2004, killed at least 61 people in Myanmar.

Public anger over soaring fuel costs in Aug. 2007 triggered new challenges to the military regime. In late Sept., thousands of Buddhist monks led mass protests in Yangon; security forces cracked down by raiding monasteries, arresting monks, and firing on demonstrators. On Sept. 25, the U.S. announced tougher sanctions against junta leaders. Cyclone Nargis, May 2-3, 2008, left at least 84,537 people dead, with an estimated 53,836 missing.

An odd episode, May 2009, in which a U.S. citizen, John Yettaw, swam across a Yangon lake and illegally entered Aung San Suu Kyi's home led a Myanmar military court to extend her house arrest by 18 months and sentence him to 7 years in prison. U.S. Sen. Jim Webb (D, VA) gained Yettaw's release during a visit to Myanmar Aug. 14-16. Government forces gained victories over ethnic Karen rebels near the Thailand border in June and against Kokang (ethnic Chinese) insurgents in N Myanmar in Aug.

Namibia
Republic of Namibia
People: Population: 2,108,665. **Age distrib.** (%): <15: 35.9; 65+: 3.9. **Pop. density:** 6.6 per sq mi, 2.6 per sq km. **Urban:** 35.1%. **Ethnic groups:** Black 88%, white 6%, mixed 7%. (About 50% of pop. belong to Ovambo tribe.) **Principal languages:** English (official), Afrikaans (common lang. of most of pop. & about 60% of white pop.), German, indigenous languages. **Chief religions:** Christian 80%-90% (Lutheran at least 50%), indigenous beliefs 10%-20%.

Geography: Total area: 318,696 sq mi, 825,418 sq km; **Land area:** 318,696 sq mi, 825,418 sq km. **Location:** In southern Africa on coast of Atlantic O. **Neighbors:** Angola on N; Botswana, Zambia on E; South Africa on S. **Topography:** Three distinct regions incl. Namib desert along the Atlantic coast, a mountainous central plateau with woodland savanna, and Kalahari desert in E. True forests found in NE. There are 4 rivers, but little other surface water. **Capital:** Windhoek, 313,000.

Government: Type: Republic. **Head of state:** Pres. Hifikepunye Pohamba; b. Aug. 18, 1935; in office: Mar. 21, 2005. **Head of gov.:** Prime Min. Nahas Angula; b. Aug. 22, 1943; in office: Mar. 21, 2005. **Local divisions:** 13 regions. **Defense budget:** $239 mil. **Active troops:** 9,200.

Economy: meatpacking, fish proc., dairy products, mining. **Chief crops:** millet, sorghum, peanuts, grapes. **Natural resources:** diamonds, copper, uranium, gold, silver, lead, tin, lithium, cadmium, tungsten, zinc, salt, hydropower, fish. **Arable land:** 1%. **Livestock:** cattle: 2.5 mil; chickens: 4.7 mil; goats: 2 mil; pigs: 25,000; sheep: 2.7 mil. **Fish catch:** 415,570 metric tons. **Electricity prod.:** 1.6 bil kWh. **Labor force** (1999 est.): agric. 47%, industry 20%, services 33%.

Finance: Monetary unit: Dollar (NAD) (Oct. 2009: 7.42 = $1 U.S.). **GDP:** $13.3 bil; **per capita GDP:** $6,300; **GDP growth:** 2.9%. **Imports:** $3.5 bil. **Exports:** $2.8 bil. **Tourism:** $434 mil. **Budget:** $2.5 bil. **Intl. reserves less gold:** $839 mil. **Gold:** NA. **Consumer prices:** 10.4%.

Transport: Railroad: Length: 1,634 mi. **Civil aviation:** 974.9 mil pass.-mi; 21 airports. **Chief ports:** Luderitz, Walvis Bay.

Communications: TV sets: 38 per 1,000 pop. **Radios:** 143 per 1,000 pop. **Telephone lines:** 140,000. **Daily newspaper circ.** (2004): 28.0 per 1,000 pop. **Internet:** 113,500 users.

Health: Life expect.: 50.4 male; 49.4 female. **Births** (per 1,000 pop.): 23.2. **Deaths** (per 1,000 pop.): 14.1. **Natural inc.:** 0.91%. **Infant mortality** (per 1,000 live births): 45.6. **HIV rate:** 15.3%.

Education: Compulsory: ages 6-15. **Literacy:** 88%.

Major intl. organizations: UN (FAO, IBRD, ILO, IMF, IMO, WHO, WTO), the Commonwealth, AU.

Embassy: 1605 New Hampshire Ave. NW 20009; 986-0540.

Website: www.grnnet.gov.na

Namibia was declared a German protectorate in 1890 and officially called South-West Africa. South Africa seized the territory from Germany in 1915 during WWI; the League of Nations gave South Africa a mandate over the territory in 1920. In 1966, the Marxist South-West Africa People's Organization (SWAPO) launched a guerrilla war for independence. The UN General Assembly named the area Namibia in 1968.

After many years of guerrilla warfare, South Africa, Angola, and Cuba signed a U.S.-mediated agreement Dec. 22, 1988, to end South African administration of Namibia and provide for a ceasefire and transition to independence, in accordance with a 1978 UN plan. A separate accord between Cuba and Angola provided for a phased withdrawal of Cuban troops from Namibia. A constitution providing for multiparty government was adopted Feb. 9, 1990, and Namibia gained independence Mar. 21. SWAPO has remained the dominant political group.

Walvis Bay, the principal deepwater port, had been turned over to South African administration in 1922. It remained in South African hands after independence, but South Africa turned control of the port back to Namibia, as of Mar. 1, 1994. Separatist violence flared in the Caprivi Strip in the late 1990s. In 2009, severe flooding in northern Namibia claimed at least 85 lives by mid-Apr.

Nauru
Republic of Nauru
People: Population: 14,019. **Age distrib.** (%): <15: 34.7; 65+: 2.1. **Pop. density:** 1,729 per sq mi, 667.6 per sq km. **Urban:** 100%. **Ethnic groups:** Nauruan 58%, other Pacific Islander 26%, Chinese 8%, European 8%. **Principal languages:** Nauruan (official; distinct Pacific Isl. lang.), English (widely understood, spoken, used for most govt. & commercial purposes). **Chief religion:** Christian (Protestant 66%, Roman Catholic 33%).

Geography: Total area: 8 sq mi, 21 sq km; **Land area:** 8 sq mi, 21 sq km. **Location:** In W Pacific O. just S of Equator. **Neighbors:** Nearest is Kiribati to E. **Topography:** Mostly a plateau bearing high-grade phosphate deposits, surrounded by a sandy shore and coral reef in concentric rings. **Capital:** Yaren district, 4,616.

Government: Type: Republic. **Head of state and gov.:** Pres. Marcus Stephen; b. Oct. 1, 1969; in office: Dec. 19, 2007. **Local divisions:** 14 districts. **Defense budget/Active troops:** NA.

Economy: Industries: phosphate mining, offshore banking, coconut products. **Chief crops:** coconuts. **Natural resources:** phosphates, fish. **Arable land:** None. **Livestock:** chickens: 5,000; pigs: 2,900. **Fish catch** (est.): 39 metric tons. **Electricity prod.:** 31 mil kWh. **Labor force** (1992): Mining phosphates, public administration, education, transp.

Finance: Monetary unit: Australia Dollar (AUD) (Oct. 2009: 1.12 = $1 U.S.). **GDP** (2005): $60 mil; **per capita GDP** (2005): $5,000; **GDP growth:** NA. **Imports** (2004): $20 mil. **Exports** (2005): $64,000. **Tourism:** NA. **Budget** (2005): $13.5 mil.

Transport: Civil aviation: 224.3 mil pass.-mi; 1 airport. **Chief port:** Nauru.

Communications: TV sets: 1 per 1,000 pop. **Radios:** 45 per 1,000 pop. **Telephone lines:** 1,800. **Internet:** NA.

Health: Life expect.: 60.2 male; 67.6 female. **Births** (per 1,000 pop.): 24.3. **Deaths** (per 1,000 pop.): 6.5. **Natural inc.:** 1.77%. **Infant mortality** (per 1,000 live births): 9.4. **HIV rate:** NA.

Education: Compulsory: ages 6-16. **Literacy:** NA.

Major intl. organizations: UN (FAO, WHO), the Commonwealth.

Permanent UN mission: 800 2nd Ave., Ste. 400A, New York, NY 10017; (212) 937-0074.

Website: gov.nr or www.state.gov/p/eap/ci/nr/

The island was discovered in 1798 by the British but was formally annexed to the German Empire in 1886. After WWI, Nauru became a League of Nations mandate administered by Australia. During WWII the Japanese occupied the island. In 1947 Nauru was made a UN trust territory, administered by Australia. It became an independent republic Jan. 31, 1968, and was admitted to the UN Sept. 14, 1999.

Phosphate exports provided Nauru with per capita revenues that were among the highest in the Third World. Phosphate reserves, however, are nearly depleted, and environmental damage from strip-mining has been severe. Lax banking practices have made Nauru a haven for money laundering; the country has also raised funds by selling passports to noncitizens, possibly to some with terrorist connections. Nauru defaulted on a loan payment for its real estate holdings in Australia and was virtually bankrupt by 2004, when financial reforms were implemented.

Nepal
Federal Democratic Republic of Nepal
People: Population: 28,563,377. **Age distrib.** (%): <15: 36.6; 65+: 4.2. **Pop. density:** 516.7 per sq mi, 199.5 per sq km. **Urban:** 15.8%. **Ethnic groups:** Chhettri 16%, Brahman-Hill 13%, Magar 7%, Tharu 7%. **Principal languages:** Nepali, Maithali, English (spoken by many in govt. & business). **Chief religions:** Hindu 81%, Buddhism 11%, Muslim 4%.

Geography: Total area: 56,827 sq mi, 147,181 sq km; **Land area:** 55,283 sq mi, 143,181 sq km. **Location:** Astride the Himalaya Mts. **Neighbors:** China on N, India on S. **Topography:** The Himalayas stretch across the N, the hill country with its fertile valleys extends across the center, while S border region is part of the flat, subtropical Ganges Plain. **Capital:** Kathmandu, 895,000.

Government: Type: Republic. **Head of state:** Pres. Ram Baran Yadav; b. Feb. 4, 1948; in office: July 23, 2008. **Head of gov.:** Prime Min. Madhav Kumar Nepal; b. Mar. 6, 1953; in office: May 25, 2009. **Local divisions:** 5 regions subdivided into 14 zones. **Defense budget:** $167 mil. **Active troops:** 69,000.

Economy: Industries: tourism; carpets; textiles; small rice, jute, sugar, and oilseed mills. **Chief crops:** rice, corn, wheat, sugarcane, jute, root crops. **Natural resources:** quartz, water, timber, hydropower, lignite, copper, cobalt, iron ore. **Arable land:** 16%. **Livestock:** cattle: 7 mil; chickens: 23.9 mil; goats: 7.8 mil; pigs: 989,429; sheep: 813,621. **Fish catch:** 46,779 metric tons. **Electricity prod.:** 2.7 bil kWh. **Labor force** (2004 est.): agric. 76%, industry 6%, services 18%.

Finance: Monetary unit: Rupee (NPR) (Oct. 2009: 74.70 = $1 U.S.). **GDP:** $31.1 bil; **per capita GDP:** $1,100; **GDP growth:** 4.7%. **Imports:** $3.2 bil; India 59.4%, China 13%, Singapore 1.8%. **Exports:** $868 mil; India 67%, U.S. 7%, Bangladesh 6.7%. **Tourism:** $198 mil. **Budget** (FY06/07): $1.9 bil. **Intl. reserves less gold** (2005): $1.05 bil. **Gold:** NA. **Consumer prices:** 10.9%.

Transport: Railroad: Length: 37 mi. **Motor vehicles:** 63,500 pass. cars; 72,700 comm. vehicles. **Civil aviation:** 542.5 mil pass.-mi; 11 airports.

Communications: TV sets: 6 per 1,000 pop. **Radios:** 38 per 1,000 pop. **Telephone lines:** 805,100. **Internet:** 499,000 users.

Health: Life expect.: 61.1 male; 60.8 female. **Births** (per 1,000 pop.): 29.9. **Deaths** (per 1,000 pop.): 9. **Natural inc.:** 2.1%. **Infant mortality** (per 1,000 live births): 62. **HIV rate:** 0.5%.

Education: Compulsory: ages 5-9. **Literacy:** 56.5%.

Major intl. organizations: UN (FAO, IBRD, ILO, IMF, IMO, WHO, WTO).

Embassy: 2131 Leroy Pl. NW 20008; 667-4550.

Website: www.nepalgov.gov.np

Nepal was originally a group of petty principalities, the inhabitants of one of which, the Gurkhas, became dominant about 1769. In 1951 King Tribhubana Bir Bikram, member of the Shah family, ended the system of rule by hereditary premiers of the Ranas family, who had kept the kings virtual prisoners, and established a cabinet system of government.

Virtually closed to the outside world for centuries, Nepal is now linked to India and Pakistan by roads and air service and to Tibet by road. Polygamy, child marriage, and the caste system were officially abolished in 1963.

The government announced the legalization of political parties in 1990. Elections on Nov. 15, 1994, led to the installation of Nepal's first Communist government, which held power until a no-confidence vote Sept. 10, 1995.

Nine members of Nepal's royal family, including King Birendra and Queen Aishwarya, died as the result of a massacre on the night of June 1, 2001. An official inquiry blamed the carnage on a 10th family member, Crown Prince Dipendra, who reportedly shot himself that night and died 3 days later, allowing Birendra's brother Gyanendra Bir Bikram Shah Dev to take the throne.

Citing the government's failure to stop a Maoist insurgency, King Gyanendra assumed absolute authority, Feb. 1, 2005. After weeks of pro-democracy demonstrations, in which police killed at least 12 protesters, the king agreed Apr. 24, 2006, to reinstate parliament, which had not met for 4 years. A new government, led by Prime Min. Girija Prasad Koirala, signed a peace accord with Maoist rebels Nov. 21, ending a decade-long civil war that had claimed 13,000 lives.

Under a draft constitution that made Koirala acting head of state, Maoists joined an interim parliament Jan. 15, 2007, and entered the cabinet Apr. 1. The king was stripped of most powers. A constituent assembly voted May 28, 2008, to abolish the monarchy and make Nepal a republic. After months of political wrangling, Maoist leader Pushpa Kamal Dahal, popularly known as Prachanda, became prime min. Aug. 18. On May 3, 2009, Prachanda moved to fire Nepal's army chief, who had refused orders to integrate some 19,000 former Maoist rebels into the armed forces; when Pres. Ram Baran Yadav countermanded the firing, Prachanda resigned May 4, and a longtime Communist Party leader, Madhav Kumar Nepal, was sworn in as prime min. May 25.

Netherlands
Kingdom of the Netherlands

People: Population: 16,715,999. **Age distrib.** (%): <15: 17.4; 65+: 14.9. **Pop. density:** 1,277.8 per sq mi, 493.3 per sq km. **Urban:** 80.2%. **Ethnic groups:** Dutch 80%, other 20% (11% of which are non-Western in origin, mainly Turks, Surinamese, Moroccans, Antilleans, Indonesians). **Principal languages:** Dutch, Frisian (both official). **Chief religions:** Roman Catholic 30%, Dutch Reformed 11%, none 42%.

Geography: Total area: 16,033 sq mi, 41,526 sq km; **Land area:** 13,082 sq mi, 33,883 sq km. **Location:** In NW Europe on North Sea. **Neighbors:** Germany on E, Belgium on S. **Topography:** Land is flat, an average alt. of 37 ft above sea level, with much land below sea level reclaimed and protected by some 1,500 mi of dikes. Since 1920 the government has been draining the Ijsselmeer, formerly the Zuider Zee. **Capital:** Amsterdam (official), 1,031,000; The Hague ('s-Gravenhage) (admin.), 624,000. **Cities (urban aggr.):** Rotterdam, 1,005,000.

Government: Type: Parliamentary democracy under a constitutional monarch. **Head of state:** Queen Beatrix; b. Jan. 31, 1938; in office: Apr. 30, 1980. **Head of gov.:** Prime Min. Jan Peter Balkenende; b. May 7, 1956; in office: July 22, 2002. **Seat of govt.:** The Hague. **Local divisions:** 12 provinces. **Defense budget:** $11.1 bil. **Active troops:** 40,537.

Economy: Industries: agroindustries, metal & engineering products, electrical machinery & equip., chemicals, oil, constr., microelectronics, fishing. **Chief crops:** grains, potatoes, sugar beets, fruits, vegetables. **Natural resources:** nat. gas, oil, peat, limestone, salt, sand & gravel. **Crude oil reserves:** 100 mil bbls. **Arable land:** 22%. **Livestock:** cattle: 3.7 mil; chickens: 92.8 mil; goats: 372,600; pigs: 11.6 mil; sheep: 1.4 mil. **Fish catch:** 470,363 metric tons. **Electricity prod.:** 92.6 bil kWh. **Labor force** (2005 est.): agric. 2%, industry 18%, services 80%.

Finance: Monetary unit: Euro (EUR) (Oct. 2009: 0.68 = $1 U.S.). **GDP:** $672 bil; **per capita GDP:** $40,400; **GDP growth:** 2%. **Imports:** $475.9 bil; Germany 17%, China 10.3%, Belgium 9%, U.S. 7.6%, UK 5.8%, Russia 5.2%, France 4.5%. **Exports:** $533.2 bil; Germany 25.2%, Belgium 14.6%, UK 8.9%, France 8.4%, Italy

4.6%. **Tourism:** $13.3 bil. **Budget:** $350.4 bil. **Intl. reserves less gold:** $7.45 bil. **Gold:** 19.69 mil oz t. **Consumer prices:** 2.5%.

Transport: Railroad: Length: 1,747 mi. **Motor vehicles:** 6.99 mil pass. cars; 1.1 mil comm. vehicles. **Civil aviation:** 51.1 bil pass.-mi (incl. territories and dependencies); 20 airports. **Chief ports:** Amsterdam, Ijmuiden, Rotterdam, Terneuzen, Vlissingen.

Communications: TV sets: 540 per 1,000 pop. **Radios:** 980 per 1,000 pop. **Telephone lines:** 7.3 mil. **Daily newspaper circ.** (2004): 307.5 per 1,000 pop. **Internet:** 14.3 mil users.

Health: Life expect.: 76.7 male; 82 female. **Births** (per 1,000 pop.): 10.5. **Deaths** (per 1,000 pop.): 8.7. **Natural inc.:** 0.18%. **Infant mortality** (per 1,000 live births): 4.8. **HIV rate:** 0.2%.

Education: Compulsory: ages 5-17. **Literacy:** 99%.

Major intl. organizations: UN and all of its specialized agencies, EU, NATO, OECD, OSCE.

Embassy: 4200 Linnean Ave. NW 20008; 877-DUTCHHELP.

Website: www.government.nl

Julius Caesar conquered the region in 55 BCE, when it was inhabited by Celtic and Germanic tribes. After the empire of Charlemagne fell apart, the Netherlands (Holland, Belgium, Flanders) split among counts, dukes, and bishops, passed to Burgundy and thence to Spain. William the Silent, prince of Orange, led a confederation of the northern provinces, called Estates, in the Union of Utrecht, 1579; in 1581 they repudiated allegiance to Spain. The rise of the Dutch republic to naval, economic, and artistic eminence came in the 17th cent.

After a period of French hegemony, 1795-1813, the Congress of Vienna in 1815 formed a kingdom of the Netherlands, including Belgium, under William I. In 1830, the Belgians seceded and formed a separate kingdom.

The Netherlands maintained its neutrality in WWI, but was invaded and brutally occupied by Germany, 1940-45. In 1949, after several years of fighting, the Netherlands granted independence to Indonesia.

The murder May 6, 2002, of right-wing populist leader Pim Fortuyn, 9 days before legislative elections, marked the first political assassination in modern Dutch history. The killing of filmmaker Theo van Gogh, Nov. 2, 2004, by an Islamic extremist also shocked many Dutch. Concerns about immigration contributed to the defeat of a proposed EU constitution by 62% to 38% in a referendum, June 1, 2005. On Apr. 30, 2009, the national Queen's Day holiday, a Dutch motorist in Apeldoorn aimed his car at an open-topped bus carrying Queen Beatrix and other royal family members; they were unhurt, but 6 bystanders died, as did the driver.

Netherlands Dependencies

The **Netherlands Antilles**, constitutionally on a level of equality with the Netherlands homeland within the kingdom, consist of 2 island groups in the West Indies. **Curaçao** and **Bonaire** are near the coast of Venezuela; **St. Eustatius, Saba,** and the southern part of **St. Maarten** are southeast of Puerto Rico. The northern two-thirds of St. Maarten belongs to French Guadeloupe; the French call the island St. Martin. Total area of the 2 groups is 371 sq mi, incl. Bonaire (111), Curaçao (171), St. Eustatius (8), Saba (5), St. Maarten (Dutch part) (13). St. Maarten suffered extensive damage from Hurricane Luis, Sept. 1995. Total pop. of the Netherlands Antilles (2009 est.) was 227,049. Willemstad, on Curaçao, is the capital. The principal industry is the refining of crude oil from Venezuela. Tourism is also an important industry, as is shipbuilding.

Aruba, about 26 mi west of Curaçao, was separated from the Netherlands Antilles on Jan. 1, 1986; it is an autonomous member of the Netherlands, the same status as the Netherland Antilles. Area: 75 sq mi; pop. (2009 est.): 103,065; capital: Oranjestad. Chief industries are oil refining and tourism.

New Zealand

People: Population: 4,213,418. **Age distrib.** (%): <15: 20.7; 65+: 12.8. **Pop. density:** 40.7 per sq mi, 15.7 per sq km. **Urban:** 86.2%. **Ethnic groups:** New Zealand European and "New Zealander" 77%, Maori 15%, Asian 10%, Pacific Peoples 7%. **Principal languages:** English, Maori, sign language (all official). **Chief religions:** Anglican 15%, Roman Catholic 12%, Presbyterian 11%, none 26%.

Geography: Total area: 103,738 sq mi, 268,680 sq km. **Land area:** 103,484 sq mi, 268,021 sq km. **Location:** In SW Pacific O. **Neighbors:** Nearest are Australia on W, Fiji and Tonga on N. **Topography:** Each of the 2 main islands (North and South Isls.) is mainly hilly and mountainous. The E coasts consist of fertile plains, especially the broad Canterbury Plains on South Isl. A volcanic plateau is in center of North Isl. South Isl. has glaciers and 15 peaks over 10,000 ft. **Capital:** Wellington, 366,000. **Cities (urban aggr.):** Auckland, 1,245,000.

Government: Type: Parliamentary democracy. **Head of state:** Queen Elizabeth II, represented by Gov.-Gen. Sir Anand Satyanand; b. July 22, 1944; in office: Aug. 23, 2006. **Head of gov.:** Prime Min. John Key; b. Aug. 9, 1961; in office: Nov. 19, 2008. **Local divisions:** 16 regions. **Defense budget:** $1.4 bil. **Active troops:** 9,278.

Economy: Industries: food proc., wood & paper products, textiles, machinery, transp. equip., banking & insurance, tourism, mining. **Chief crops:** dairy products, lamb & mutton, wheat, barley, potatoes, pulses, fruits, vegetables. **Natural resources:** nat. gas, iron ore, sand, coal, timber, hydropower, gold, limestone. **Crude oil reserves:** 60 mil bbls. **Arable land:** 6%. **Livestock:** cattle: 9.7 mil; chickens:

19.8 mil; goats: 111,981; pigs: 366,671; sheep: 38.5 mil. **Fish catch:** 601,060 metric tons. **Electricity prod.:** 42.1 bil kWh. **Labor force** (2006 est.): agric. 7%, industry 19%, services 74%.

Finance: Monetary unit: Dollar (NZD) (Oct. 2009: 1.36 = $1 U.S.). **GDP:** $116.7 bil; **per capita GDP:** $28,000; **GDP growth:** 0.2%. **Imports:** $32.5 bil; Australia 18.1%, China 13.2%, U.S. 9.5%, Japan 8.3%, Singapore 4.7%, Malaysia 4.4%, Germany 4.3%. **Exports:** $30.8 bil; Australia 23.1%, U.S. 10.1%, Japan 8.4%, China 5.8%. **Tourism:** $5.4 bil. **Budget:** $53.7 bil. **Intl. reserves less gold:** $7.24 bil. **Gold:** NA. **Consumer prices:** 4%.

Transport: Railroad: Length: 2,565 mi. **Motor vehicles:** 2.2 mil pass. cars; 490,000 comm. vehicles. **Civil aviation:** 16.2 bil pass.-mi; 41 airports. **Chief ports:** Auckland, Lyttelton, Marsden Point, Tauranga, Wellington, Whangarei.

Communications: TV sets: 516 per 1,000 pop. **Radios:** 997 per 1,000 pop. **Telephone lines:** 1.8 mil. **Daily newspaper circ.** (2004): 182.5 per 1,000 pop. **Internet:** 3 mil users.

Health: Life expect.: 78.3 male; 82.2 female. **Births** (per 1,000 pop.): 14.1. **Deaths** (per 1,000 pop.): 7. **Natural inc.:** 0.71%. **Infant mortality** (per 1,000 live births): 5. **HIV rate:** 0.1%.

Education: Compulsory: ages 5-16. **Literacy:** 99%.

Major intl. organizations: UN (FAO, IBRD, ILO, IMF, IMO, WHO, WTO), APEC, the Commonwealth, OECD.

Embassy: 37 Observatory Cir. NW 20008; 328-4800.

Website: newzealand.govt.nz

The Maori, a Polynesian group from the eastern Pacific, reached New Zealand before and during the 14th cent. The first European to sight New Zealand was Dutch navigator Abel Janszoon Tasman, but the Maori refused to allow him to land. British Capt. James Cook explored the coasts, 1769-70.

British sovereignty was proclaimed and Maori land rights were recognized in the Treaty of Waitangi, 1840, with organized settlement beginning in the same year. Representative institutions were granted in 1853. Maori wars ended in 1870 with British victory. The colony became a dominion in 1907 and gained full independence in 1947. It is a member of the Commonwealth. The Maori make up about 15% of the population; 7 of 122 members of the House of Representatives are directly elected from Maori constituencies, but Maori may also run in other districts.

A progressive tradition in politics dates back to the 19th cent., when New Zealand was internationally known for social experimentation; much of the nation's economy has been deregulated in recent years. Jenny Shipley of the National Party became the nation's first female prime minister, Dec. 8, 1997. The Labour Party, led by Helen Clark, won the general elections of Nov. 27, 1999, and July 27, 2002. New Zealand has supplied small troop contingents to coalition forces in Iraq, 2003-04, and Afghanistan.

The legislature legalized prostitution June 2003. In July, New Zealand contributed troops to the Australian-led force in the Solomon Islands. A measure establishing a Supreme Court and ending appeals to the UK Privy Council passed Oct. 14.

A major settlement of Maori land claims dating from the 19th cent. was signed June 25, 2008. With the country in recession, Clark called new elections Nov. 8, which were won by the National Party, led by John Key.

New Zealand comprises **North Island**, 44,702 sq mi; **South Island**, 58,384 sq mi; **Stewart Island**, 674 sq mi; **Chatham Isls.**, 372 sq mi; and several groups of smaller islands.

In 1965, the **Cook Islands** (pop. [2009 est.]: 11,870; area: 91 sq mi, halfway between New Zealand and Hawaii) became self-governing. New Zealand retains responsibility for defense and foreign affairs. **Niue** attained the same status in 1974; it lies 400 mi W (pop. [2009 est.]: 1,398; area: 100 sq mi). Cyclone Heta devastated Niue Jan. 6, 2004. **Tokelau** (pop. [2009 est.]: 1,416; area: 4 sq mi) comprises 3 atolls 300 mi N of Samoa. Two referendums on Tokelau self-government, held Feb. 13-15, 2006, and Oct. 20-24, 2007, failed to gain the required two-third majority.

Ross Dependency, administered by New Zealand since 1923, comprises 160,000 sq mi of Antarctic territory.

Nicaragua
Republic of Nicaragua

People: Population: 5,891,199. **Age distrib.** (%): <15: 33.8; 65+: 3.3. **Pop. density:** 126.9 per sq mi, 49 per sq km. **Urban:** 55.9%. **Ethnic groups:** Mestizo (mixed Amerindian & white) 69%, white 17%, black 9%, Amerindian 5%. **Principal languages:** Spanish (official); English & indigenous languages on Atlantic coast. **Chief religions:** Roman Catholic 73%, Evangelical 15%, none 9%.

Geography: Total area: 49,998 sq mi, 129,494 sq km; **Land area:** 46,430 sq mi, 120,254 sq km. **Location:** In Central America. **Neighbors:** Honduras on N, Costa Rica on S. **Topography:** Both Caribbean and Pacific coasts are over 200 mi long. Cordillera Mts., with many volcanic peaks, run NW-SE through middle of the country. Between this and a volcanic range to the E lie Lakes Managua and Nicaragua. **Capital:** Managua, 920,000.

Government: Type: Republic. **Head of state and gov.:** Pres. Daniel Ortega Saavedra; b. Nov. 11, 1945; in office: Jan. 10, 2007. **Local divisions:** 15 departments, 2 autonomous regions. **Defense budget:** $37 mil. **Active troops:** 12,000.

Economy: Industries: food proc., chemicals, machinery & metal products, textiles, clothing, oil refining & distribution, beverages, footwear, wood. **Chief crops:** coffee, bananas, sugarcane, cotton, rice, corn, tobacco, sesame, soya. **Natural resources:** gold, silver, copper, tungsten, lead, zinc, timber, fish. **Arable land:** 15%. **Livestock:** cattle: 3.6 mil; chickens: 18 mil; goats: 7,100; pigs: 123,000; sheep: 4,500. **Fish catch:** 37,959 metric tons. **Electricity prod.:** 3 bil kWh. **Labor force** (2006 est.): agric. 29%, industry 19%, services 52%.

Finance: Monetary unit: Cordoba (NIO) (Oct. 2009: 20.60 = $1 U.S.). **GDP:** $16.8 bil; **per capita GDP:** $2,900; **GDP growth:** 3.2%. **Imports:** $5 bil; U.S. 25.1%, Mexico 11.6%, Costa Rica 7.3%, Venezuela 6.4%, Guatemala 5.3%, China 4.3%, El Salvador 4.1%. **Exports:** $2.9 bil; U.S. 60.6%, El Salvador 7.2%, Honduras 4.8%. **Tourism:** $255 mil. **Budget:** $1.3 bil. **Intl. reserves less gold:** $741 mil. **Gold:** NA. **Consumer prices:** 19.8%.

Transport: Motor vehicles: 82,200 pass. cars; 107,700 comm. vehicles. **Civil aviation:** 44.7 mil pass.-mi; 11 airports. **Chief ports:** Bluefields, Corinto, El Bluff.

Communications: TV sets: 69 per 1,000 pop. **Radios:** 270 per 1,000 pop. **Telephone lines:** 312,000. **Internet:** 185,000 users.

Health: Life expect.: 69.1 male; 73.4 female. **Births** (per 1,000 pop.): 23.7. **Deaths** (per 1,000 pop.): 4.3. **Natural inc.:** 1.94%. **Infant mortality** (per 1,000 live births): 25.9. **HIV rate:** 0.2%.

Education: Compulsory: ages 6-12. **Literacy:** 80.5%.

Major intl. organizations: UN and most of its specialized agencies, OAS.

Embassy: 1627 New Hampshire Ave. NW 20009; 939-6570.

Website: www.presidencia.gob.ni

Nicaragua, inhabited by various Indian tribes, was conquered by Spain in 1552. After gaining independence from Spain, 1821, Nicaragua was united for a short period with Mexico, then with the United Provinces of Central America, finally becoming an independent republic, 1838. U.S. Marines occupied the country at times in the early 20th cent., the last time from 1926 to 1933.

Gen. Anastasio Somoza Debayle was elected president in 1967. He resigned in 1972, but was reelected president in 1974. Martial law was imposed in Dec. 1974, after officials were kidnapped by the Marxist Sandinista guerrillas. Violent opposition spread to nearly all classes in 1978; nationwide antigovernment strikes touched off a civil war, which ended when Somoza fled Nicaragua and the Sandinistas took control of Managua in July 1979. Somoza was assassinated in Paraguay, Sept. 17, 1980.

Relations with the U.S. were strained as a result of Nicaragua's aid to leftist guerrillas in El Salvador and U.S. backing of anti-Sandinista contra guerrilla groups. In 1983 the contras launched a major offensive; the Sandinistas imposed rule by decree. In 1985 the U.S. House rejected Pres. Reagan's request for military aid to the contras. The subsequent diversion of funds to the contras from the proceeds of a secret arms sale to Iran caused a major scandal in the U.S.

In a stunning upset, Violeta Barrios de Chamorro defeated Sandinista leader Daniel Ortega Saavedra in national elections, Feb. 25, 1990. Arnoldo Alemán Lacayo, a conservative former mayor of Managua, defeated Ortega in the presidential election of Oct. 20, 1996. Up to 2,000 people died Oct. 30, 1998, in a mudslide caused by rains from Hurricane Mitch.

Drought and a drop in coffee prices plunged Nicaragua into an economic crisis in 2001. Enrique Bolaños Geyer, a conservative businessman, won the presidency that year. The corruption trial of former Pres. Alemán ended with a guilty verdict, Dec. 7, 2003; he was fined $10 mil and sentenced to 20 years in prison. After a medical review, Alemán was allowed to serve the sentence under house arrest. Ortega won the presidential election of Nov. 5, 2006. After taking office Jan. 10, 2007, he irritated the U.S. by cultivating ties with Venezuela and Iran, which offered aid to the financially hard-pressed country. Hurricane Felix, a Category 5 storm that struck Sept. 4, 2007, killed more than 100 people.

Niger
Republic of Niger

People: Population: 15,306,252. **Age distrib.** (%): <15: 49.6; 65+: 2.3. **Pop. density:** 31.3 per sq mi, 12.1 per sq km. **Urban:** 16.3%. **Ethnic groups:** Haoussa 55%, Djerma Sonrai 21%, Tuareg 9%, Peuhl 9%. **Principal languages:** French (official), Hausa, Djerma. **Chief religions:** Muslim 80%, other (incl. indigenous beliefs & Christian) 20%.

Geography: Total area: 489,191 sq mi, 1,267,000 sq km; **Land area:** 489,076 sq mi, 1,266,700 sq km. **Location:** In interior of N Africa. **Neighbors:** Libya, Algeria on N; Mali, Burkina Faso on W; Benin, Nigeria on S; Chad on E. **Topography:** Mostly arid desert and mountains. A narrow savanna in S and Niger R. basin in the SW contain most of the population. **Capital:** Niamey, 915,000.

Government: Type: Republic. **Head of state:** Pres. Mamadou Tandja; b. 1938; in office: Dec. 22, 1999. **Head of gov.:** Prime Min. Ali Badjo Gamatié; in office: Oct. 2, 2009. **Local divisions:** 7 departments, 1 capital district. **Defense budget:** $46 mil. **Active troops:** 5,300.

Economy: Industries: uranium mining, cement, brick, textiles, food proc., chemicals, slaughterhouses. **Chief crops:** cowpeas, cotton, peanuts, millet, sorghum, cassava, rice. **Natural resources:** uranium, coal, iron ore, tin, phosphates, gold, molybd., gypsum, salt, oil. **Arable land:** 11%. **Livestock:** cattle: 8.2 mil; chickens: 11.1 mil; goats: 12.2 mil; pigs: 40,000; sheep: 9.8 mil.

Fish catch: 29,768 metric tons. **Electricity prod.:** 240 mil kWh. **Labor force** (1995): agric. 90%, industry 6%, services 4%.

Finance: Monetary unit: CFA BCEAO Franc (XOF) (Oct. 2009: 444.97 = $1 U.S.). **GDP:** $10 bil; **per capita GDP:** $700; **GDP growth:** 9.5%. **Imports** (2006): $800 mil; France 19.4%, Nigeria 8.6%, China 8.5%, French Polynesia 7.6%, Belgium 5%, Cote d'Ivoire 4.9%. **Exports** (2006): $428 mil; Japan 80.4%, Nigeria 8.5%, France 2.9%. **Tourism:** NA. **Budget** (2002 est.): $320 mil. **Intl. reserves less gold:** $456 mil. **Gold:** NA. **Consumer prices:** 11.3%.

Transport: Motor vehicles: 9,300 pass. cars; 3,800 comm. vehicles. **Civil aviation:** 80.8 mil pass.-mi (incl. Air Afrique traffic apportionment); 10 airports.

Communications: TV sets: 15 per 1,000 pop. **Radios:** 36 per 1,000 pop. **Telephone lines:** 64,700. **Daily newspaper circ.** (2004): 0.2 per 1,000 pop. **Internet:** 80,000 users.

Health: Life expect.: 44.3 male; 44.3 female. **Births** (per 1,000 pop.): 49.6. **Deaths** (per 1,000 pop.): 20.3. **Natural inc.:** 2.94%. **Infant mortality** (per 1,000 live births): 115.4. **HIV rate:** 0.8%.

Education: Compulsory: ages 7-12. **Literacy:** 30.4%.

Major intl. organizations: UN (FAO, IBRD, ILO, IMF, WHO, WTO), AU.

Embassy: 2204 R St. NW 20008; 483-4224.

Website: www.presidence.ne

Niger was part of ancient and medieval African empires. European explorers reached the area in the late 18th cent. The French colony of Niger was established 1900-02, after the defeat of Tuareg fighters, who had invaded the area from the north a century before. The country became independent Aug. 3, 1960.

In 1993, Niger held its first free and open elections since independence; an opposition leader, Mahamane Ousmane, won the presidency. A peace accord Apr. 24, 1995, ended a Tuareg rebellion that began in 1990. A coup, Jan. 27, 1996, followed by a disputed presidential election in July, left the military in control of Niger. On Apr. 9, 1999, Gen. Ibrahim Bare Mainassara, Niger's president since 1996, was assassinated, apparently by members of his security team. Elections were held Oct. 17 and Nov. 24, 1999, under a new constitution, approved by referendum July 18, that restored civilian rule.

One of the world's poorest countries, Niger experienced severe food shortages in 2005 after locusts and drought ruined the grain harvest. A resurgence of Tuareg rebel activity in June 2007 brought a major government counteroffensive. Popularly elected in 1999 and 2004, Pres. Mamadou Tandja invoked emergency powers in 2009, dissolving Niger's parliament and constitutional court in order to push ahead with a referendum on constitutional changes that would allow him to run for a 3rd term; the referendum passed Aug. 4 with a majority officially reported as 92%.

Nigeria
Federal Republic of Nigeria

People: Population: 149,229,090. **Age distrib.** (%): <15: 41.5; 65+: 3.1. **Pop. density:** 424.4 per sq mi, 163.8 per sq km. **Urban:** 46.2%. **Ethnic groups:** 250+ ethnic groups: Hausa & Fulani 29%, Yoruba 21%, Igbo (Ibo) 18%, Ijaw 10%, Kanuri 4%, Ibibio 4%, Tiv 3% most populous, politically influential groups. **Principal languages:** English (official), Hausa, Yoruba, Igbo (Ibo), Fulani. **Chief religions:** Muslim 50%, Christian 40%, indigenous beliefs 10%.

Geography: Total area: 356,669 sq mi, 923,768 sq km; **Land area:** 351,650 sq mi, 910,768 sq km. **Location:** On S coast of W Africa. **Neighbors:** Benin on W, Niger on N, Chad and Cameroon on E. **Topography:** 4 E-W regions divide Nigeria: a coastal mangrove swamp 10-60 mi wide, a tropical rain forest 50-100 mi wide, a plateau of savanna and open woodland, and semi-desert in N. **Capital:** Abuja, 1,576,000. **Cities (urban aggr.):** Lagos, 9,466,000; Kano, 3,140,000; Ibadan, 2,628,000.

Government: Type: Federal republic. **Head of state and gov.:** Pres. Umaru Musa Yar'Adua; b. Aug. 16, 1951; in office: May 29, 2007. **Local divisions:** 36 states, 1 capital territory. **Defense budget:** $980 mil. **Active troops:** 80,000.

Economy: Industries: crude oil, coal, tin, columbite, palm oil, peanuts, cotton, rubber, wood, hides & skins, textiles. **Chief crops:** cocoa, peanuts, palm oil, corn, rice, sorghum, millet, cassava, yams, rubber. **Natural resources:** nat. gas, oil, tin, iron ore, coal, limestone, niobium, lead, zinc. **Crude oil reserves:** 36.2 bil bbls. **Arable land:** 33%. **Livestock:** cattle: 16.2 mil; chickens: 166.1 mil; goats: 52.5 mil; pigs: 6.6 mil; sheep: 33.1 mil. **Fish catch:** 615,507 metric tons. **Electricity prod.:** 22.1 bil kWh. **Labor force** (1999 est.): agric. 70%, industry 10%, services 20%.

Finance: Monetary unit: Naira (NGN) (Oct. 2009: 146.03 = $1 U.S.). **GDP:** $335.4 bil; **per capita GDP:** $2,300; **GDP growth:** 5.3%. **Imports:** $45.5 bil; China 12.7%, Netherlands 10.5%, U.S. 8.2%, S. Korea 5.6%, UK 5.2%, France 4.3%. **Exports:** $76.8 bil; U.S. 45.8%, Brazil 10.4%, Spain 8%, France 5%. **Tourism:** NA. **Budget:** $21.7 bil. **Intl. reserves less gold:** $34.41 bil. **Gold:** 690,000 oz t. **Consumer prices:** 11.6%.

Transport: Railroad: Length: 2,178 mi. **Motor vehicles** (newly registered): 52,300 pass. cars; 13,500 comm. vehicles. **Civil aviation:** 581 mil pass.-mi; 38 airports. **Chief ports:** Calabar, Lagos.

Communications: TV sets: 69 per 1,000 pop. **Radios:** 226 per 1,000 pop. **Telephone lines:** 1.3 mil. **Internet:** 11 mil users.

Health: Life expect.: 45.8 male; 47.3 female. **Births** (per 1,000 pop.): 37.2. **Deaths** (per 1,000 pop.): 16.9. **Natural inc.:** 2.04%. **Infant mortality** (per 1,000 live births): 95.7. **HIV rate:** 3.1%.

Education: Compulsory: ages 6-14. **Literacy:** 72%.

Major intl. organizations: UN (FAO, IBRD, ILO, IMF, IMO, WHO, WTO), the Commonwealth, AU, OPEC.

Embassy: 3519 International Ct. NW 20008; 986-8400.

Website: www.nigeria.gov.ng

Early cultures in Nigeria date back to at least 700 BCE. From the 12th to the 14th centuries, more advanced cultures developed in the Yoruba area, at Ife, and in the north, where Muslim influence prevailed. Portuguese and British slavers appeared from the 15th-16th centuries. Britain seized Lagos, 1861, and gradually extended control inland until 1900. Nigeria became independent Oct. 1, 1960, and a republic Oct. 1, 1963.

On May 30, 1967, the Eastern Region seceded, proclaiming itself the Republic of Biafra, plunging the country into civil war. Casualties in the war were estimated at over 1 mil, including many "Biafrans" (mostly Ibos) who died of starvation despite international efforts to provide relief. The secessionists, after steadily losing ground, capitulated Jan. 12, 1970.

Nigeria emerged as one of the world's leading oil exporters in the 1970s, but much of the revenue has been squandered through corruption and mismanagement. After 13 years of military rule, the nation made a peaceful return to civilian government, Oct. 1979. Military rule resumed, Dec. 31, 1983; a second coup came in 1985.

Headed by Gen. Ibrahim Babangida, the military regime held elections June 12, 1993, but annulled the vote June 23 when it appeared that Moshood Abiola would win. Riots followed and many were killed. Babangida resigned and appointed a civilian to head an interim government, Aug. 26, but that government was ousted Nov. 17 in a coup led by Gen. Sani Abacha. On June 11, 1994, Abiola declared himself president; he was jailed June 23.

Abacha's brutal rule ended June 8, 1998, when he died of an apparent heart attack. Abiola died in prison July 7, as Abacha's successor, Gen. Abdulsalam Abubakar, was reportedly preparing to free him. Abiola's death sparked riots in Lagos and other cities; on July 20, Abubakar promised elections and a return to civilian rule. Olusegun Obasanjo (a former military ruler) won the presidential vote Feb. 27, 1999, Nigeria's first civilian government in 15 years.

An oil fire that exploded from a ruptured pipeline in southern Nigeria, Oct. 17, 1998, killed at least 700 people who were scavenging for fuel. The imposition of strict Islamic law in northern states led to clashes, Jan.-Mar. 2000, in which at least 800 people died. Clashes between Muslims and Christians Sept. 7-12 and Oct. 13-14 claimed an estimated 600 lives; another 200 people died when soldiers went on a rampage in southeast Nigeria Oct. 22-24.

At least 1,000 people were killed Jan. 27, 2002, when an army weapons depot in Lagos exploded; many of the victims drowned in a drainage canal while fleeing the blasts. Controversy over Nigeria's plans to host a Miss World pageant sparked sectarian riots in Kaduna, Nov. 20-24, leaving more than 200 people dead and 1,100 injured. Obasanjo won reelection Apr. 19, 2003.

Christian militia members massacred about 630 Muslims at Yelwa, central Nigeria, May 2, 2004. Obasanjo's chosen successor, Umaru Musa Yar'Adua, won a landslide victory Apr. 21, 2007, in a presidential election marred by violence and described as "not credible" by international monitors. Clashes between government security forces and Boko Haram, a radical Islamist sect in NE Nigeria, killed up to 800 people in late July 2009. Rebel activities in the Niger Delta region in recent years have led to cutbacks in Nigeria's petroleum output and upward pressure on worldwide oil prices.

Norway
Kingdom of Norway

People: Population: 4,660,539. **Age distrib.** (%): <15: 18.5; 65+: 15.2. **Pop. density:** 39.3 per sq mi, 15.2 per sq km. **Urban:** 77.3%. **Ethnic groups:** Norwegian (incl. Sami). **Principal languages:** Bokmal Norwegian, Nynorsk Norwegian (both official); Sami (official in 6 municipalities). **Chief religion:** Church of Norway 86%.

Geography: Total area: 125,021 sq mi, 323,802 sq km; **Land area:** 118,704 sq mi, 307,442 sq km. **Location:** W part of Scandinavian peninsula in NW Europe (extends farther north than any European land). **Neighbors:** Sweden, Finland, Russia on E. **Topography:** Highly indented coast is lined with tens of thousands of islands. Mountains and plateaus cover most of the country, which is only 25% forested. **Capital:** Oslo, 835,000.

Government: Type: Hereditary constitutional monarchy. **Head of state:** King Harald V; b. Feb. 21, 1937; in office: Jan. 17, 1991. **Head of gov.:** Prime Min. Jens Stoltenberg; b. Mar. 16, 1959; in office: Oct. 17, 2005. **Local divisions:** 19 provinces. **Defense budget:** $5.5 bil. **Active troops:** 19,100.

Economy: Industries: oil & gas, food proc., shipbuilding, pulp & paper products, metals, chemicals, timber, mining, textiles, fishing. **Chief crops:** barley, wheat, potatoes. **Natural resources:** oil, nat. gas, iron ore, copper, lead, zinc, titanium, pyrites, nickel, fish, timber, hydropower. **Crude oil reserves:** 6.7 bil bbls. **Arable land:** 3%. **Livestock:** cattle: 905,515; chickens: 3.5 mil; goats: 71,987; pigs: 837,892; sheep: 2.3 mil. **Fish catch:** 3.34 mil metric tons. **Electricity prod.:** 119.9 bil kWh. **Labor force** (2008): agric. 2.9%, industry 21.1%, services 76%.

Finance: Monetary unit: Krone (NOK) (Oct. 2009: 5.67 = $1 U.S.). **GDP:** $275.4 bil; **per capita GDP:** $59,300; **GDP growth:** 2.6%. **Imports:** $86 bil; Sweden 14.4%, Germany 13.4%, Denmark 6.9%, China 6.4%, UK 5.9%, U.S. 5.4%, Netherlands 4.2%. **Exports:** $168.8 bil; UK 27%, Germany 12.8%, Netherlands 10.4%, France 9.4%, Sweden 6.5%, U.S. 4.5%. **Tourism:** $4.5 bil. **Budget:** $158 bil. **Intl. reserves less gold:** $33.08 bil. **Gold:** NA. **Consumer prices:** 3.8%.

Transport: Railroad: Length: 2,556 mi. **Motor vehicles:** 2.03 mil pass. cars; 494,000 comm. vehicles. **Civil aviation:** 5.8 bil pass.-mi (incl. Scandinavian Airlines System operations apportionment); 67 airports. **Chief ports:** Bergen, Borg Havn, Haugesund, Maaloy, Mongstad, Narvik, Oslo, Sture.

Communications: TV sets: 653 per 1,000 pop. **Radios:** 917 per 1,000 pop. **Telephone lines:** 1.9 mil. **Daily newspaper circ.** (2004): 516 per 1,000 pop. **Internet:** 4.2 mil users.

Health: Life expect.: 77.2 male; 82.6 female. **Births** (per 1,000 pop.): 11.1. **Deaths** (per 1,000 pop.): 9.3. **Natural inc.:** 0.18%. **Infant mortality** (per 1,000 live births): 3.6. **HIV rate:** 0.1%.

Education: Compulsory: ages 6-16. **Literacy:** 100%.

Major intl. organizations: UN and all of its specialized agencies, EFTA, NATO, OECD, OSCE.

Embassy: 2720 34th St. NW 20008; 333-6000.

Website: www.norway.no

The first ruler of Norway was Harald the Fairhaired, who came to power in 872 CE. Between 800 and 1000, Norway's Vikings raided and occupied widely dispersed parts of Europe.

The country was united with Denmark 1381-1814, and with Sweden, 1814-1905. In 1905, the country became independent with Prince Charles of Denmark as king.

Norway remained neutral during WWI. Germany attacked Norway Apr. 9, 1940, and held it until liberation May 8, 1945. The country abandoned its neutrality after the war, and joined NATO. In a referendum Nov. 28, 1994, Norwegian voters rejected European Union membership.

Abundant hydroelectric resources provided the base for industrialization, giving Norway one of the highest living standards in the world. The country is a leading producer and exporter of crude oil, with extensive reserves in the North Sea. Norway's merchant marine is one of the world's largest.

A center-left bloc led by Jens Stoltenberg won parliamentary elections Sept. 12, 2005, and remained in power after elections Sept. 13-14, 2009. Norway has provided a force of about 500 soldiers to the NATO command in Afghanistan.

Svalbard is a group of mountainous islands in the Arctic O., area 23,560 sq mi, pop. (2009 est.) 2,116. The largest, Spitsbergen (formerly called West Spitsbergen), 15,060 sq mi, seat of the governor, is about 370 mi N of Norway. By a treaty signed in Paris, 1920, major European powers recognized the sovereignty of Norway, which incorporated it in 1925.

Jan Mayen, area 146 sq mi, is a volcanic island located about 565 mi W-NW of Norway; it was annexed in 1929.

Oman
Sultanate of Oman

People: Population: 3,418,085. **Age distrib.** (%): <15: 42.7; 65+: 2.8. **Pop. density:** 41.7 per sq mi, 16.1 per sq km. **Urban:** 71.5%. **Ethnic groups:** Arab, Baluchi, South Asian (incl. Indian, Pakistani, Sri Lankan, Bangladeshi), African. **Principal languages:** Arabic (official), English, Baluchi, Urdu, Indian dialects. **Chief religions:** Ibadhi Muslim 75%, other (incl. Sunni Muslim, Shi'a Muslim, Hindu) 25%.

Geography: Total area: 82,031 sq mi, 212,460 sq km; **Land area:** 82,031 sq mi, 212,460 sq km. **Location:** On SE coast of Arabian peninsula. **Neighbors:** United Arab Emirates, Saudi Arabia, Yemen on W. **Topography:** A narrow coastal plain up to 10 mi wide, a range of barren mountains reaching 9,900 ft, and a wide, stony, mostly waterless plateau, avg. alt. 1,000 ft. Also, an exclave at the tip of the Musandam peninsula controls access to the Persian Gulf. **Capital:** Masqat, 620,000.

Government: Type: Absolute monarchy. **Head of state and gov.:** Sultan Qabus bin Said; b. Nov. 18, 1940; in office: July 23, 1970 (also prime min. since Jan. 2, 1972). **Local divisions:** 6 regions and 2 governorates. **Defense budget:** 3.2 bil. **Active troops:** 42,600.

Economy: Industries: crude oil production & refining, nat. gas production, constr., cement, copper. **Chief crops:** dates, limes, bananas, alfalfa, vegetables. **Natural resources:** oil, copper, asbestos, marble, limestone, chromium, gypsum, nat. gas. **Crude oil reserves:** 5.5 bil bbls. **Arable land:** 0.1%. **Livestock:** cattle: 313,580; chickens: 4.2 mil; goats: 1.6 mil; sheep: 366,190. **Fish catch:** 151,834 metric tons. **Electricity prod.:** 12.8 bil kWh. **Labor force:** NA.

Finance: Monetary unit: Rial (OMR) (Oct. 2009: 0.38 = $1 U.S.). **GDP:** $67 bil; **per capita GDP:** $20,200; **GDP growth:** 6.4%. **Imports:** $16.7 bil; Japan 19.5%, UAE 17.9%, U.S. 7%, Germany 6.8%. **Exports:** $37.7 bil; China 31.4%, Japan 15.9%, S. Korea 13.6%, Thailand 7.8%, UAE 7.2%. **Tourism:** NA. **Budget:** $13.7 bil. **Intl. reserves less gold:** $7.52 bil. **Gold:** NA. **Consumer prices:** 12.1%.

Transport: Motor vehicles: 324,000 pass. cars; 109,100 comm. vehicles. **Civil aviation:** 4.7 bil pass.-mi (incl. Gulf Air traffic apportionment); 10 airports. **Chief ports:** Mina' Qabus, Salalah.

Communications: TV sets: 575 per 1,000 pop. **Radios:** 607 per 1,000 pop. **Telephone lines:** 274,200. **Internet:** 469,000 users.

Health: Life expect.: 71.6 male; 76.3 female. **Births** (per 1,000 pop.): 35.3. **Deaths** (per 1,000 pop.): 3.7. **Natural inc.:** 3.16%. **Infant mortality** (per 1,000 live births): 17.4. **HIV rate:** NA.

Education: Compulsory: ages 6-15. **Literacy:** 84.4%.

Major intl. organizations: UN (FAO, IBRD, ILO, IMF, IMO, WHO, WTO), AL.

Embassy: 2535 Belmont Rd. NW 20008; 387-1980.

Website: www.omanet.om

Oman was originally called Muscat and Oman. A long history of rule by other lands, including Portugal in the 16th cent., ended with the ouster of the Persians in 1744. By the early 19th cent., Muscat and Oman was one of the most important countries in the region, controlling much of the Persian and Pakistan coasts.

British influence was confirmed in a 1951 treaty, and Britain helped suppress an uprising by traditionally rebellious interior tribes against control by Muscat in the 1950s.

On July 23, 1970, Sultan Said bin Taimur was overthrown by his son, who changed the nation's name to Sultanate of Oman. Petroleum and natural gas are major sources of income. Although Oman has strong military and economic ties to the U.S., it has also cultivated favorable relations with Iran.

Pakistan
Islamic Republic of Pakistan

People: Population: 176,242,949. **Age distrib.** (%): <15: 37.2; 65+: 4.2. **Pop. density:** 586.2 per sq mi, 226.3 per sq km. **Urban:** 34.9%. **Ethnic groups:** Punjabi, Pashtun (Pathan), Sindhi, Sariaki. **Principal languages:** English, Urdu (both official; English lingua franca of elite & most govt. ministries); Punjabi; Sindhi; Siraiki (Punjabi variant); Pashtu. **Chief religion:** Muslim (official; Sunni 77%, Shi'a 20%) 97%.

Geography: Total area: 310,403 sq mi, 803,940 sq km; **Land area:** 300,666 sq mi, 778,720 sq km. **Location:** In W part of South Asia. **Neighbors:** Iran on W, Afghanistan and China on N, India on E. **Topography:** The Indus R. rises in the Hindu Kush and Himalaya Mts. in the N (highest is K2, or Godwin Austen, 28,250 ft, 2nd highest in world), then flows over 1,000 mi through fertile valley and empties into Arabian Sea. Thar Desert, Eastern Plains flank Indus Valley. **Capital:** Islamabad, 780,000. **Cities (urban aggr.):** Karachi, 12,130,000; Lahore, 6,577,000; Faisalabad, 2,617,000.

Government: Type: Republic. **Head of state:** Pres. Asif Ali Zardari; b. July 26, 1955; in office: Sept. 9, 2008. **Head of gov.:** Prime Min. Syed Yousaf Raza Gilani; b. June 9, 1952; in office: Mar. 25, 2008. **Local divisions:** 4 provinces and 1 capital territory, plus federally administered tribal areas. **Defense budget:** $4.5 bil. **Active troops:** 617,000.

Economy: Industries: textiles & apparel, food proc., pharmaceuticals, constr. materials, paper products. **Chief crops:** cotton, wheat, rice, sugarcane, fruits. **Natural resources:** nat. gas reserves, limited oil, poor quality coal, iron ore, copper, salt, limestone. **Crude oil reserves:** 339 mil bbls. **Arable land:** 24%. **Livestock:** cattle: 30.7 mil; chickens: 263 mil; goats: 55.2 mil; sheep: 26.8 mil. **Fish catch:** 570,282 metric tons. **Electricity prod.:** 90.4 bil kWh. **Labor force** (2005 est.): agric. 43%, industry 20.3%, services 36.6%.

Finance: Monetary unit: Rupee (PKR) (Oct. 2009: 83.36 = $1 U.S.). **GDP:** $427.3 bil; **per capita GDP:** $2,500; **GDP growth:** 2.7%. **Imports:** $38.3 bil; China 15.4%, Saudi Arabia 12.2%, UAE 11.3%, Kuwait 5.5%, U.S. 4.8%. **Exports:** $21.9 bil; U.S. 16%, UAE 11.7%, Afghanistan 8.6%, UK 4.4%, China 4.4%. **Tourism:** $276 mil. **Budget:** $27.6 bil. **Intl. reserves less gold:** $4.67 bil. **Gold:** 2.1 mil oz t. **Consumer prices:** 20.3%.

Transport: Railroad: Length: 4,841 mi. **Motor vehicles:** 1.5 mil pass. cars; 663,000 comm. vehicles. **Civil aviation:** 8.9 bil pass.-mi; 98 airports. **Chief ports:** Karachi, Port Muhammad Bin Qasim.

Communications: TV sets: 105 per 1,000 pop. **Radios:** 94 per 1,000 pop. **Telephone lines:** 4.4 mil. **Daily newspaper circ.** (2004): 50.3 per 1,000 pop. **Internet:** 18.5 mil users.

Health: Life expect.: 63.1 male; 65.2 female. **Births** (per 1,000 pop.): 28.4. **Deaths** (per 1,000 pop.): 7.8. **Natural inc.:** 2.05%. **Infant mortality** (per 1,000 live births): 66.9. **HIV rate:** 0.1%.

Education: Compulsory: ages 5-9. **Literacy:** 54.9%.

Major intl. organizations: UN (FAO, IBRD, ILO, IMF, IMO, WHO, WTO), the Commonwealth.

Embassy: 3517 International Ct. NW 20008; 243-6500.

Website: www.pakistan.gov.pk

Pakistan shares the 5,000-year history of the India-Pakistan subcontinent. At present-day Harappa and Mohenjo Daro, the Indus Valley Civilization, with large cities and elaborate irrigation systems, flourished c. 4,000-2,500 BCE. Aryan invaders from the northwest conquered the region around 1,500 BCE, forging the Vedic civilization that dominated the region for over a thousand years. Other invaders from the west followed. The first Arab invasion, 712 CE, introduced Islam. Present-day Pakistan and India were part of the Mogul empire from 1526 to 1857. Muslim power faded by the end of the 19th cent. as the British gained control of the north and northwest areas of the subcontinent.

After WWI, the Muslims of British India began agitation for minority rights in elections. Muhammad Ali Jinnah (1876-1948) was the principal architect of Pakistan. When the British withdrew Aug. 14, 1947, the Islamic majority areas of India acquired self-government as Pakistan, with dominion status in the Commonwealth. Pakistan was divided into 2 sections, West Pakistan and East Pakistan. The 2 areas were nearly 1,000 mi apart on opposite sides of India.

The Awami League, which had sought regional autonomy for East Pakistan for several years, won a majority in Dec. 1970 elections to a constituent assembly. On Mar. 1, 1971, Pakistan's military-dominated government postponed the assembly. Rioting and strikes broke out in the East. On Mar. 25, government troops launched attacks in the East. The Easterners, aided by India, proclaimed the independent nation of Bangladesh. In months of widespread fighting, thousands were killed. Some 10 mil Easterners fled into India. Full-scale war between India and Pakistan had spread to both the East and West fronts by Dec. 3. Pakistan troops in the East surrendered Dec. 16; Pakistan agreed to a cease-fire in the West Dec. 17. On July 3, 1972, Pakistan and India signed a pact agreeing to withdraw troops from their borders and resolve problems peacefully.

Zulfikar Ali Bhutto, leader of the Pakistan People's Party, which had won the most West Pakistan votes in Dec. 1970 elections, became president Dec. 20, 1971. Bhutto was overthrown in a military coup July 1977. Convicted of complicity in a 1974 political murder, he was executed Apr. 4, 1979. Millions of Afghan refugees flooded into Pakistan after the USSR invaded Afghanistan Dec. 1979; by Aug. 2008, some 3.5 mil refugees had been repatriated, but 1.8 mil remained.

Pres. Mohammad Zia ul-Haq was killed when his plane exploded in Aug. 1988. Following Nov. elections, Benazir Bhutto, daughter of Zulfikar Ali Bhutto, was named prime minister, becoming the first woman leader of a Muslim nation. She was accused of corruption and dismissed by the president, Aug. 1990. Bhutto returned to power Oct. 1993 but was dismissed again, Nov. 1996, amid further corruption charges. Responding to nuclear weapons tests by India, Pakistan conducted its own tests in 1998; the U.S. imposed economic sanctions on both countries.

In mid-1999, Muslim infiltrators, apparently including Pakistani troops, seized Indian-held positions in the disputed territory of Kashmir, which witnessed its heaviest fighting in over 2 decades (see Kashmir). After meeting with Pres. Bill Clinton on July 4, Prime Min. Nawaz Sharif agreed to a Pakistani pullback. Growing conflict between Sharif and the military climaxed in his firing on Oct. 12 of army chief Gen. Pervez Musharraf, whose supporters staged a bloodless coup. Musharraf assumed the presidency June 20, 2001.

Following the Sept. 11, 2001, terrorist attacks on the U.S., Pres. Musharraf, Sept. 19, pledged cooperation with the U.S. in fighting Taliban and al-Qaeda militants within its own tribal areas and in neighboring Afghanistan. In return, the U.S. waived its 1998 sanctions and offered Pakistan financial aid and debt relief. A referendum Apr. 30, 2002, extended Musharraf's rule for 5 years; many observers called the vote rigged.

Accused of selling atomic secrets to Iran, Libya, and North Korea, Pakistan's top nuclear scientist, Abdul Qadeer Khan, made a televised apology, Feb. 4, 2004, and said his actions were unauthorized. He received a pardon from Musharraf Feb. 5. An earthquake that rocked Pakistan and the Pakistani-held region of Kashmir Oct. 8, 2005, killed about 80,000 people and left up to 3 mil homeless.

Musharraf's grip weakened in 2007, as his efforts to oust Pakistan's chief justice sparked mass protests by pro-democracy demonstrators. Musharraf survived an assassination attempt (at least the 4th in 5 years) when gunmen fired on his plane July 6. As Taliban and al-Qaeda activity within Pakistan intensified, attacks by Islamic militants and counterattacks by government forces claimed hundreds of lives.

Musharraf retained the presidency in an electoral college vote Oct. 6, 2007, after his main opponents boycotted the election. More than 140 people died Oct. 18 when suicide bombers struck a convoy carrying Benazir Bhutto from the Karachi airport after more than 8 years in exile. Musharraf imposed emergency rule Nov. 3 and suspended the constitution, while Pakistan's Supreme Court debated the constitutionality of his reelection. Musharraf gave up his army post Nov. 25, was sworn in as civilian president the next day, and lifted emergency rule Dec. 16. Bhutto was assassinated Dec. 27 after a rally in Rawalpindi.

Headed by Bhutto's widower, Asif Ali Zardari, the Pakistan Peoples Party led in parliamentary elections Feb. 18, 2008. Musharraf resigned Aug. 18 under threat of impeachment, and Zardari became president Sept. 9. Meanwhile, the security situation continued to deteriorate, as U.S. and Pakistani forces clashed with the Taliban near the Afghan border, and Islamists executed new suicide attacks; a truck bomb at Islamabad's Marriott hotel Sept. 20 killed at least 54 people.

The government announced Feb. 16, 2009, a truce conceding de facto control of the strategic Swat Valley to the Taliban. The cease-fire broke down in May, when government forces launched an offensive that reclaimed most of the region; the fighting displaced nearly 2 mil civilians. A U.S. missile strike Aug. 5 in South Waziristan killed Pakistani Taliban leader Baitullah Mehsud, who was accused of aiding the insurgency in Afghanistan and of plotting Benazir Bhutto's murder, 2007, and the Marriott hotel attack, 2008. The U.S. provided more than $3 bil in aid to Pakistan during Pres. Zardari's first year in office.

Palau
Republic of Palau
People: Population: 20,796. **Age distrib.** (%): <15: 22.9; 65+: 6.2. **Pop. density:** 117.6 per sq mi, 45.4 per sq km. **Urban:** 77.1%. **Ethnic groups:** Palauan (Micronesian with Malayan & Melanesian) 70%, Filipino 15%, Chinese 5%. **Principal languages:** English (official); Palauan, Sonsorolese, Tobi, Angaur, Japanese (all also official in certain states); Filipino, English. **Chief religions:** Roman Catholic 42%, Protestant 23%, Modekngei 9% (indigenous to Palau).
Geography: Total area: 177 sq mi, 458 sq km; **Land area:** 177 sq mi, 458 sq km. **Location:** Archipelago (26 islands, more than 300 islets) in W Pacific Ocean, about 530 mi SE of the Philippines. **Neighbors:** Micronesia to E, Indonesia to S. **Topography:** A mountainous main island and low coral atolls, usually fringed with large barrier reefs. **Capital** (2005): Melekeok, 391.
Government: Type: Republic in free association with the U.S. **Head of state and gov.:** Pres. Johnson Toribiong; b. July 22, 1946; in office: Jan. 15, 2009. **Local divisions:** 16 states. **Defense budget/Active troops:** NA.
Economy: Industries: tourism, craft items, constr., garment making. **Chief crops:** coconuts, copra, cassava, sweet potatoes. **Natural resources:** forests, gold & other minerals, marine products, deep seabed minerals. **Arable land:** 9%. **Fish catch:** 1,003 metric tons. **Labor force** (1990): agric. 20%, industry & services NA.
Finance: Monetary unit: U.S. Dollar (USD). **GDP:** 164 mil (incl. U.S. subsidy); **per capita GDP:** $8,100; **GDP growth** (2005): 5.5%. **Imports** (2004): $107.3 mil. **Exports** (2004): $5.9 mil. **Tourism** (2006): $93 mil. **Budget** (FY04/05 est.): $72.4 mil.
Transport: Civil aviation: 1 airport. **Chief port:** Koror.
Communications: TV sets: 98 per 1,000 pop. **Radios:** 550 per 1,000 pop. **Telephone lines:** 7,500. **Internet:** 5,400 users.
Health: Life expect.: 67.8 male; 74.4 female. **Births** (per 1,000 pop.): 17.4. **Deaths** (per 1,000 pop.): 6.7. **Natural inc.:** 1.07%. **Infant mortality** (per 1,000 live births): 13.7. **HIV rate:** NA.
Education: Compulsory: ages 6-14. **Literacy:** 91.9%.
Major intl. organizations: UN (FAO, IBRD, ILO, IMF, WHO). **Embassy:** 1700 Pennsylvania Ave. NW, Ste. 400, 20006; 452-6814.
Website: www.palaugov.net

Spain acquired the Palau Islands in 1886 and sold them to Germany in 1899. Japan seized them in 1914. American forces occupied the islands in 1944; in 1947, they became part of the U.S.-administered UN Trust Territory of the Pacific Islands. In 1981 Palau became an autonomous republic; the republic ratified a compact of free association with the U.S. in 1993 and became an independent nation on Oct. 1, 1994. The government of Pres. Johnson Toribiong, elected Nov. 4, 2008, agreed in June 2009 to accept 13 Uighur (Chinese Muslim) detainees who had been held by the U.S. at Guantánamo Bay, Cuba, after their capture in Pakistan and Afghanistan in 2001.

Panama
Republic of Panama
People: Population: 3,360,474. **Age distrib.** (%): <15: 29.3; 65+: 6.8. **Pop. density:** 114.5 per sq mi, 44.2 per sq km. **Urban:** 70.8%. **Ethnic groups:** Mestizo (mixed Amerindian & white) 70%, Amerindian & mixed (West Indian) 14%, white 10%, Amerindian 6%. **Principal languages:** Spanish (official), English. **Chief religions:** Roman Catholic 85%, Protestant 15%.
Geography: Total area: 30,193 sq mi, 78,200 sq km; **Land area:** 29,340 sq mi, 75,990 sq km. **Location:** In Central America. **Neighbors:** Costa Rica on W, Colombia on E. **Topography:** 2 mountain ranges run the length of the isthmus. Tropical rain forests cover the Caribbean coast and E Panama. **Capital:** Panama City, 1,281,000.
Government: Type: Republic. **Head of state and gov.:** Pres. Ricardo Martinelli Berrocal; b. Mar. 11, 1952; in office: July 1, 2009. **Local divisions:** 9 provinces, 5 territories. **Defense budget:** $200 mil. **Active troops:** None.
Economy: Industries: constr., brewing, cement & other constr. materials, sugar milling. **Chief crops:** bananas, rice, corn, coffee, sugarcane. **Natural resources:** copper, mahogany forests, shrimp, hydropower. **Arable land:** 7%. **Livestock:** cattle: 1.5 mil; chickens: 15.2 mil; goats: 6,300; pigs: 325,500. **Fish catch:** 215,569 metric tons. **Electricity prod.:** 5.8 bil kWh. **Labor force** (2006): agric. 15%, industry 18%, services 67%.
Finance: Monetary unit: Balboa (PAB) (Oct. 2009: 1.00 = $1 U.S.). **GDP:** $38.8 bil; **per capita GDP:** $11,700; **GDP growth:** 9.2%. **Imports:** $15 bil; Japan 29.5%, Singapore 17.6%, China 15.4%, U.S. 13.2%, France 4.5%. **Exports:** $10.3 bil; U.S. 17.2%, Germany 14.6%, Italy 9%, Greece 6.1%, Netherlands 4.8%, Denmark 4.2%, Spain 4.2%. **Tourism:** $1.2 bil. **Budget:** $4.8 bil. **Intl. reserves less gold** (2007): $1.23 bil. **Gold:** NA. **Consumer prices:** 8.8%.
Transport: Railroad: Length: 47 mi. **Motor vehicles:** 251,000 pass. cars; 79,000 comm. vehicles. **Civil aviation:** 3.2 bil pass.-mi; 54 airports. **Chief ports:** Balboa, Colon, Cristobal.
Communications: TV sets: 192 per 1,000 pop. **Radios:** 299 per 1,000 pop. **Telephone lines:** 495,800. **Daily newspaper circ.** (2004): 65.1 per 1,000 pop. **Internet:** 778,800 users.

Health: Life expect.: 74.1 male; 79.8 female. **Births** (per 1,000 pop.): 20.7. **Deaths** (per 1,000 pop.): 4.7. **Natural inc.:** 1.6%. **Infant mortality** (per 1,000 live births): 13.4. **HIV rate:** 1%.

Education: Compulsory: ages 6-11. **Literacy:** 93.4%.

Major intl. organizations: UN (FAO, IBRD, ILO, IMF, IMO, OAS, WHO, WTO).

Embassy: 2862 McGill Ter. NW 20008; 483-1407.

Website: www.presidencia.gob.pa

The coast of Panama was sighted by Rodrigo de Bastidas, sailing with Columbus for Spain in 1501, and was visited by Columbus in 1502. Vasco Núñez de Balboa crossed the isthmus and "discovered" the Pacific Ocean, Sept. 13, 1513. Spanish colonies were ravaged by Francis Drake, 1572-95, and Henry Morgan, 1668-71. Morgan destroyed the old city of Panama which had been founded in 1519. Freed from Spain, Panama joined Colombia in 1821.

Panama declared independence from Colombia Nov. 3, 1903, with U.S. support. Panama granted use, occupation, and control of the Canal Zone to the U.S. by treaty, ratified Feb. 26, 1904. In 1978, a new treaty provided for a gradual takeover by Panama of the canal, and withdrawal of U.S. troops, to be completed before the end of the century. U.S. payments were substantially increased in the interim.

Pres. Delvalle was ousted by the National Assembly, Feb. 26, 1988, after he tried to fire the head of the Panama Defense Forces, Gen. Manuel Antonio Noriega, who was under U.S. federal indictment on drug charges. U.S. troops invaded Panama Dec. 20, 1989, and Noriega surrendered Jan. 3, 1990.

Mireya Moscoso, widow of former Pres. Arnulfo Arias, was elected president May 2, 1999, becoming Panama's first female head of state. The U.S. handed over control of the Panama Canal to Panama Dec. 31, 1999. Martin Torrijos Espino, son of Brig. Gen. Omar Torrijos Herrera (dictator of Panama, 1968-81), won the presidential election of May 2, 2004. A $5.3-bil plan to widen the canal was approved by national referendum Oct. 22, 2006; construction began Sept. 3, 2007. Ricardo Martinelli Berrocal, a conservative supermarket magnate, was elected president May 3, 2009, and took office July 1.

Papua New Guinea
Independent State of Papua New Guinea

People: Population: 6,057,263. **Age distrib.** (%): <15: 36.9; 65+: 4.1. **Pop. density:** 34.6 per sq mi, 13.4 per sq km. **Urban:** 12.6%. **Ethnic groups:** Melanesian, Papuan, Negrito, Micronesian, Polynesian. **Principal languages:** Melanesian Pidgin (lingua franca), 820 indigenous languages. **Chief religions:** Roman Catholic 27%, Evangelical Lutheran 20%, United Church 12%, Seventh-Day Adventist 10%, Pentecostal 9%.

Geography: Total area: 178,704 sq mi, 462,840 sq km; **Land area:** 174,850 sq mi, 452,860 sq km. **Location:** SE Asia, occupying E half of island of New Guinea and about 600 nearby islands. **Neighbors:** Indonesia on W, Australia on S. **Topography:** Thickly forested mts. cover much of center of the country, with lowlands along the coasts. Included are some islands of Bismarck and Solomon groups, such as Admiralty Isls., New Ireland, New Britain, and Bougainville. **Capital:** Port Moresby, 299,000.

Government: Type: Parliamentary democracy. **Head of state:** Queen Elizabeth II, represented by Gov.-Gen. Sir Paulias Matane; b. 1931; in office: June 29, 2004. **Head of gov.:** Prime Min. Sir Michael Somare; b. Apr. 9, 1936; in office: Aug. 5, 2002. **Local divisions:** 20 provinces. **Defense budget:** $35 mil. **Active troops:** 3,100.

Economy: Industries: copra crushing, palm oil proc., plywood production, mining. **Chief crops:** coffee, cocoa, copra, palm kernels, tea, sugar, rubber, sweet potatoes. **Natural resources:** gold, copper, silver, nat. gas, timber, oil, fisheries. **Crude oil reserves:** 88 mil bbls. **Arable land:** 0.5%. **Livestock:** cattle: 94,000; chickens: 4 mil; goats: 3,000; pigs: 1.8 mil; sheep: 7,000. **Fish catch:** 264,238 metric tons. **Electricity prod.:** 2.9 bil kWh. **Labor force** (2005 est.): agric. 85%, industry & services NA.

Finance: Monetary unit: Kina (PGK) (Oct. 2009: 2.74 = $1 U.S.). **GDP:** $13.2 bil; **per capita GDP:** $2,200; **GDP growth:** 7.2%. **Imports:** $3.1 bil; Australia 43.3%, Singapore 15.9%, China 10.2%, Japan 5.9%. **Exports:** $5.7 bil; Australia 28%, Japan 9.5%, China 5.5%. **Tourism:** NA. **Budget:** $2.2 bil. **Intl. reserves less gold:** $1.27 bil. **Gold:** 60,000 oz t. **Consumer prices:** 10.8%.

Transport: Motor vehicles: 24,900 pass. cars; 87,800 comm. vehicles. **Civil aviation:** 431.9 mil pass.-mi; 21 airports. **Chief ports:** Kimbe, Lae, Madang, Rabaul, Wewak.

Communications: TV sets: 13 per 1,000 pop. **Radios:** 91 per 1,000 pop. **Telephone lines:** 60,000. **Daily newspaper circ.** (2004): 8.6 per 1,000 pop. **Internet:** 120,000 users.

Health: Life expect.: 63.8 male; 68.3 female. **Births** (per 1,000 pop.): 28.1. **Deaths** (per 1,000 pop.): 7. **Natural inc.:** 2.12%. **Infant mortality** (per 1,000 live births): 46.7. **HIV rate:** 1.5%.

Education: Compulsory: ages 6-14. **Literacy:** 57.8%.

Major intl. organizations: UN (FAO, IBRD, ILO, IMF, IMO, WHO, WTO), the Commonwealth, APEC.

Embassy: 1779 Massachusetts Ave. NW, Ste. 805, 20036; 745-3680.

Website: www.pngonline.gov.pg

Human remains have been found in the interior of New Guinea dating back at least 10,000 years and possibly much earlier. Europeans visited in the 15th cent., but actual land claims did not begin until the 19th cent., when the Dutch took control of the island's western half (now part of Indonesia). The southern half of eastern New Guinea was first claimed by Britain in 1884, and transferred to Australia in 1905. The northern half was claimed by Germany in 1884, but captured in WWI by Australia, which received a League of Nations mandate and then a UN trusteeship. The 2 territories were administered jointly after 1949, gained self-government Dec. 1, 1973, and became independent Sept. 16, 1975.

Secessionist rebels clashed with government forces on Bougainville beginning in 1988; a truce signed Oct. 10, 1997, brought a halt to the fighting, which had claimed some 20,000 lives. The country suffered from a severe drought in 1997. A tsunami killed at least 3,000 people July 17, 1998. A Bougainville autonomy agreement was signed Aug. 30, 2001. Army mutinies were suppressed in Mar. 2001 and Mar. 2002. Sir Michael Somare, the nation's 1st prime minister (1975-80, 1982-85), regained the office in 2002 and was reelected by parliament Aug. 13, 2007.

The country has extensive energy resources; a proposed pipeline would transport natural gas to Queensland, Australia.

Paraguay
Republic of Paraguay

People: Population: 6,995,655. **Age distrib.** (%): <15: 36.7; 65+: 5.2. **Pop. density:** 45.6 per sq mi, 17.6 per sq km. **Urban:** 58.5%. **Ethnic groups:** Mestizo (mixed Spanish & Amerindian) 95%. **Principal languages:** Spanish, Guaraní (both official). **Chief religions:** Roman Catholic 90%, Protestant 6%.

Geography: Total area: 157,047 sq mi, 406,750 sq km; **Land area:** 153,398 sq mi, 397,300 sq km. **Location:** Landlocked country in central S. America. **Neighbors:** Bolivia on N, Argentina on S, Brazil on E. **Topography:** Paraguay R. bisects the country. To E are fertile plains, wooded slopes, grasslands. To W is the Gran Chaco plain, with marshes and scrub trees. Extreme W is arid. **Capital:** Asunción, 1,870,000.

Government: Type: Republic. **Head of state and gov.:** Pres. Fernando Armindo Lugo Méndez; b. May 30, 1951; in office: Aug. 15, 2008. **Local divisions:** 17 departments and capital city. **Defense budget:** $100 mil. **Active troops:** 10,650.

Economy: Industries: sugar, cement, textiles, beverages, wood products. **Chief crops:** cotton, sugarcane, soybeans, corn, wheat, tobacco, cassava, fruits, vegetables. **Natural resources:** hydropower, timber, iron ore, mang., limestone. **Arable land:** 7%. **Livestock:** cattle: 10 mil; chickens: 17 mil; goats: 155,000; pigs: 1.6 mil; sheep: 500,000. **Fish catch** (est.): 22,100 metric tons. **Electricity prod.:** 53.2 bil kWh. **Labor force** (2007): agric. 31%, industry 17%, services 52%.

Finance: Monetary unit: Guarani (PYG) (Oct. 2009: 4,910.00 = $1 U.S.). **GDP:** $28.9 bil; **per capita GDP:** $4,200; **GDP growth:** 5.8%. **Imports:** $9.2 bil; Brazil 28.3%, U.S. 22.9%, Argentina 12.7%, China 11.2%. **Exports:** $8.2 bil; Argentina 23.9%, Brazil 17.7%, Uruguay 13%, Chile 7.1%, Russia 6.3%, Spain 4.4%. **Tourism:** $102 mil. **Budget:** $2.5 bil. **Intl. reserves less gold:** $1.85 bil. **Gold:** NA. **Consumer prices:** 10.2%.

Transport: Railroad: Length: 22 mi. **Motor vehicles:** 361,400 pass. cars; 62,400 comm. vehicles. **Civil aviation:** 311.3 mil pass.-mi; 14 airports. **Chief ports:** Asunción, Encarnación, San Antonio, Villeta.

Communications: TV sets: 205 per 1,000 pop. **Radios:** 182 per 1,000 pop. **Telephone lines:** 363,000. **Internet:** 694,000 users.

Health: Life expect.: 73 male; 78.3 female. **Births** (per 1,000 pop.): 28.5. **Deaths** (per 1,000 pop.): 4.5. **Natural inc.:** 2.4%. **Infant mortality** (per 1,000 live births): 25.6. **HIV rate:** 0.6%.

Education: Compulsory: ages 6-14. **Literacy:** 93.7%.

Major intl. organizations: UN (FAO, IBRD, ILO, IMF, IMO, WHO, WTO), OAS.

Embassy: 2400 Massachusetts Ave. NW 20008; 483-6960.

Website: www.embaparusa.gov.py

Guaraní Indians inhabited Paraguay before Europeans came. Visited by Sebastian Cabot in 1527 and settled as a Spanish possession in 1535, Paraguay gained its independence from Spain in 1811. It lost half its population and much of its territory to Brazil, Uruguay, and Argentina in the War of the Triple Alliance, 1865-70. Large areas were won from Bolivia in the Chaco War, 1932-35. Gen. Alfredo Stroessner, a military strongman, held the presidency 1954-89, until his ouster in a military coup.

Although the country returned to civilian rule in 1993, the next 6 years were marked by a protracted power struggle involving a popular military leader, Gen. Lino César Oviedo. Accused of insubordination, he surrendered Dec. 12, 1997, but was freed Aug. 18, 1998, following the inauguration of Pres. Raúl Cubas Grau, Oviedo's successor as Colorado Party nominee. The assassination of Vice Pres. Luis María Argaña, Mar. 23, 1999, by an unidentified gunman, was widely attributed to Cubas and triggered protests and an impeachment vote; Cubas resigned Mar. 28 and was succeeded by Senate leader Luis Angel González Macchi. An attempted military coup was suppressed May 18, 2000.

Mass protests over the depressed economy led to the proclamation of a state of emergency July 15, 2002. Nicanor Duarte Frutos of the Colorado Party won the presidency, Apr. 27, 2003.

Paraguayan authorities blamed a leftist group, Patria Libre, for the Sept. 2004 kidnapping and subsequent murder of Cecilia Cubas, daughter of former Pres. Cubas. Former Pres. González Macchi was convicted of fraud and embezzlement, Dec. 4, 2006, and sentenced to 8 years in prison. Fernando Lugo, a former Catholic cleric known as the "bishop of the poor," won a presidential election Apr. 20, 2008, ending over 6 decades of Colorado rule. On Apr. 13, 2009, he acknowledged, in response to a paternity suit, that he had fathered a child while still a Roman Catholic bishop; within the next 10 days, 2 other women came forward with similar allegations.

Peru
Republic of Peru

People: Population: 29,546,963. **Age distrib.** (%): <15: 29.1; 65+: 5.7. **Pop. density:** 59.8 per sq mi, 23.1 per sq km. **Urban:** 71.1%. **Ethnic groups:** Amerindian 45%, mestizo (mixed Amerindian & white) 37%, white 15%. **Principal languages:** Spanish, Quechua (both official); Aymara; minor Amazonian languages. **Chief religion:** Roman Catholic 81%.

Geography: Total area: 496,226 sq mi, 1,285,220 sq km; **Land area:** 494,211 sq mi, 1,280,000 sq km. **Location:** On Pacific coast of S. America. **Neighbors:** Ecuador, Colombia on N; Brazil, Bolivia on E; Chile on S. **Topography:** An arid coastal strip, 10-100 mi wide, supports much of the population thanks to widespread irrigation. The Andes cover 27% of land area. The uplands are well-watered, as are the eastern slopes reaching the Amazon basin, which covers half the country. **Capital:** Lima, 8,012,000. **Cities (urban aggr.):** Arequipa, 815,000.

Government: Type: Republic. **Head of state:** Pres. Alan García; b. May 23, 1949; in office: July 28, 2006. **Head of gov.:** Prime Min. Javier Velásquez Quesquén; b. Mar. 12, 1960; in office: July 11, 2009. **Local divisions:** 12 regions, 24 departments, 1 constitutional province. **Defense budget:** $1.2 bil. **Active troops:** 114,000.

Economy: Industries: mining & refining of minerals, oil extraction & refining, nat. gas, fishing, textiles, clothing, food proc. **Chief crops:** asparagus, coffee, cotton, sugarcane, rice, potatoes, corn, plantains, grapes, oranges, coca. **Natural resources:** copper, silver, gold, oil, timber, fish, iron ore, coal, phosphate, potash, hydropower, nat. gas. **Crude oil reserves:** 415.8 mil bbls. **Arable land:** 3%. **Livestock:** cattle: 5.4 mil; chickens: 120.2 mil; goats: 1.9 mil; pigs: 3.1 mil; sheep: 14.6 mil. **Fish catch:** 7.26 mil metric tons. **Electricity prod.:** 24.9 bil kWh. **Labor force** (2005): agric. 0.7%, industry 23.8%, services 75.5%.

Finance: Monetary unit: Nuevo Sol (PEN) (Oct. 2009: 2.90 = $1 U.S.). **GDP:** 247.3 bil; **per capita GDP:** $8,500; **GDP growth:** 9.8%. **Imports:** $28.4 bil; U.S. 24.5%, China 10.6%, Brazil 7.8%, Chile 5.3%, Ecuador 5.2%, Argentina 4.7%, Colombia 4.1%. **Exports:** $31.5 bil; U.S. 18.9%, China 14.9%, Canada 7.8%, Japan 6.6%, Chile 5.5%. **Tourism:** $1.7 bil. **Budget:** $29.1 bil. **Intl. reserves less gold:** $19.65 bil. **Gold:** 1.11 mil oz t. **Consumer prices:** 5.8%.

Transport: Railroad: Length: 1,236 mi. **Motor vehicles:** 906,600 pass. cars; 555,300 comm. vehicles. **Civil aviation:** 3.3 bil pass.-mi; 57 airports. **Chief ports:** Callao, Iquitos, Matarani, Paita, Pucallpa, Yurimaguas.

Communications: TV sets: 147 per 1,000 pop. **Radios:** 273 per 1,000 pop. **Telephone lines:** 2.9 mil. **Internet:** 7.1 mil users.

Health: Life expect.: 68.6 male; 72.4 female. **Births** (per 1,000 pop.): 19.8. **Deaths** (per 1,000 pop.): 6.2. **Natural inc.:** 1.36%. **Infant mortality** (per 1,000 live births): 29.5. **HIV rate:** 0.5%.

Education: Compulsory: ages 6-16. **Literacy:** 90.5%.

Major intl. organizations: UN and all of its specialized agencies, APEC, OAS.

Embassy: 1700 Massachusetts Ave. NW 20036; 833-9860. **Website:** www.peru.gob.pe

The powerful Inca empire had its seat at Cuzco in the Andes and covered much of S. America. A civil war had weakened the empire when Francisco Pizarro, Spanish conquistador, began raiding Peru for its wealth, 1532. In 1533 he executed the Inca ruler, Atahualpa, and enslaved the people.

Lima was the seat of Spanish viceroys until the Argentine liberator, José de San Martin, captured it in 1821; Spanish forces were ultimately routed by Simón Bolívar, 1824. For much of the 19th cent., the country was governed by military leaders. Chile defeated Peru in the War of the Pacific, 1879-83. The first half of the 20th cent. was dominated by rivalry between right-wing groups (allied with the military) and the leftist APRA party.

Peru returned to democratic leadership in 1980 but was plagued by economic problems and by leftist Shining Path (Sendero Luminoso) guerrillas. Conflict between guerrillas and government troops, 1980-2000, killed more than 69,000 people, mostly Andean Indians.

Elected president in June 1990, Alberto Fujimori, the son of Japanese immigrants, dissolved the National Congress, suspended parts of the constitution, and initiated press censorship, Apr. 5, 1992. The leader of Shining Path was captured Sept. 12. Fujimori won reelection Apr. 9, 1995, but his repressive antiterrorism tactics drew international criticism.

Fujimori's path to a 3rd term was cleared when his lone remaining challenger withdrew, charging electoral fraud, 6 days before a runoff vote on May 28, 2000. Scandals involving his top aide and intelligence chief, Vladimiro Montesinos, led Fujimori to resign his office Nov. 20 while on a visit to Japan; instead of accepting his resignation, Congress ousted him as "morally unfit."

Alejandro Toledo won a presidential runoff election June 3, 2001. Montesinos was captured in Venezuela June 23; extradited to Peru, he was convicted in a series of criminal trials. Charges were filed Sept. 5, 2001, against the exiled Fujimori, alleging his complicity in the killings by a paramilitary death squad of at least 25 people during 1991-92. Fujimori was arrested in Chile, Nov. 7, 2005, and extradited to Peru, Sept. 22, 2007. He was convicted in 3 separate proceedings: on Dec. 11, 2007, for ordering the illegal search of Montesinos's wife's apartment in 2000; on Apr. 7, 2009, for his role in the 1991-92 killings; and on July 20, 2009, for having paid a $15 mil bribe to Montesinos in 2000. He pleaded guilty Sept. 29 to further charges of bribery and illegal wiretaps.

A sagging economy, resurgent rebel activity, and a series of scandals eroded Toledo's popularity during 2003-05. Alan García, whose 1st term as president, 1985-90, had ended with the country facing hyperinflation and guerrilla war, won a presidential runoff election June 4, 2006. An earthquake rocked SW coastal Peru, Aug. 15, 2007, killing more than 500 people and leaving 200,000 homeless. A kickback scandal involving oil and gas contracts led the cabinet to resign Oct. 10, 2008. Government decrees promoting Amazon resource development triggered violent clashes in June 2009 between government forces and indigenous Peruvians, killing at least 34 people; the cabinet stepped down, and the decrees were repealed.

Philippines
Republic of the Philippines

People: Population: 97,976,603. **Age distrib.** (%): <15: 35.2; 65+: 4.1. **Pop. density:** 851.1 per sq mi, 328.6 per sq km. **Urban:** 62.7%. **Ethnic groups:** Tagalog 28%, Cebuano 13%, Ilocano 9%, Bisaya/Binisaya 8%, Hiligaynon Ilonggo 8%. **Principal languages:** Filipino (based on Tagalog), English (both official); 8 major dialects. **Chief religions:** Roman Catholic 81%, Muslim 5%.

Geography: Total area: 115,831 sq mi, 300,000 sq km; **Land area:** 115,124 sq mi, 298,170 sq km. **Location:** An archipelago off SE coast of Asia. **Neighbors:** Nearest are Malaysia, Indonesia on S; Taiwan on N. **Topography:** The country consists of some 7,100 islands stretching 1,100 mi N-S. About 95% of area and population are on 11 largest islands, which are mountainous, except for the heavily indented coastlines and central plain on Luzon. **Capital:** Manila, 11,100,000. **Cities (urban aggr.):** Davao, 1,402,000; Cebu, 815,000.

Government: Type: Republic. **Head of state and gov.:** Pres. Gloria Macapagal Arroyo; b. Apr. 5, 1947; in office: Jan. 20, 2001. **Local divisions:** 79 provinces. **Defense budget:** $1.1 bil. **Active troops:** 106,000.

Economy: Industries: electronics assembly, garments, footwear, pharmaceuticals, chemicals, wood products, food proc. **Chief crops:** sugarcane, coconuts, rice, corn, bananas, cassavas, pineapples, mangoes. **Natural resources:** timber, oil, nickel, cobalt, silver, gold, salt, copper. **Crude oil reserves:** 138.5 mil bbls. **Arable land:** 19%. **Livestock:** cattle: 2.6 mil; chickens: 135.6 mil; goats: 7.3 mil; pigs: 13.5 mil; sheep: 30,000. **Fish catch:** 4.72 mil metric tons. **Electricity prod.:** 53.9 bil kWh. **Labor force** (2008 est.): agric. 35%, industry 15%, services 50%.

Finance: Monetary unit: Peso (PHP) (Oct. 2009: 46.68 = $1 U.S.). **GDP:** $317.5 bil; **per capita GDP:** $3,300; **GDP growth:** 3.8%. **Imports:** $60.8 bil; Japan 14.2%, U.S. 11.8%, China 11.4%, Singapore 10.3%, Saudi Arabia 6%, S. Korea 4.8%, Thailand 4.7%. **Exports:** $48.2 bil; China 25.7%, U.S. 12.7%, Japan 12.4%, Hong Kong 8.7%, Singapore 6.9%, Malaysia 4.4%. **Tourism:** $4.9 bil. **Budget:** $24.9 bil. **Intl. reserves less gold:** $21.55 bil. **Gold:** 4.95 mil oz t. **Consumer prices:** 9.3%.

Transport: Railroad: Length: 557 mi. **Motor vehicles:** 2.6 mil pass. cars; 297,800 comm. vehicles. **Civil aviation:** 10.6 bil pass.-mi; 85 airports. **Chief ports:** Cagayan de Oro, Cebu, Davao, Liman, Manila, Nasipit Harbor.

Communications: TV sets: 110 per 1,000 pop. **Radios:** 161 per 1,000 pop. **Telephone lines:** 3.9 mil. **Daily newspaper circ.** (2004): 78.6 per 1,000 pop. **Internet:** 5.6 mil users.

Health: Life expect.: 67.9 male; 73.8 female. **Births** (per 1,000 pop.): 26.4. **Deaths** (per 1,000 pop.): 5.2. **Natural inc.:** 2.13%. **Infant mortality** (per 1,000 live births): 21.2. **HIV rate:** NA.

Education: Compulsory: ages 6-12. **Literacy:** 93.4%.

Major intl. organizations: UN (FAO, IBRD, ILO, IMF, IMO, WHO, WTO), APEC, ASEAN.

Embassy: 1600 Massachusetts Ave. NW 20036; 467-9300. **Website:** www.gov.ph

Originally inhabited by Malay peoples, the archipelago was visited by Magellan, 1521. The Spanish founded Manila, 1571. The islands, named for King Philip II of Spain, were ceded by Spain to the U.S. for $20 mil, 1898, following the Spanish-American War. U.S. troops suppressed a guerrilla uprising in a brutal 6-year war, 1899-1905. Japan attacked the Philippines Dec. 8, 1941, and occupied the islands during WWII. On July 4, 1946, independence was proclaimed. A republic was established.

The repressive and corrupt regime of Pres. Ferdinand Marcos and his wife, Imelda, ruled the Philippines 1965-86. The assassination of prominent opposition leader Benigno S. Aquino Jr. Aug. 21, 1983, sparked demonstrations calling for Marcos's resignation. Amid allegations of widespread election fraud, Marcos was declared the victor Feb. 16, 1986, over Corazon Aquino, widow of the slain opposition leader. Mass protests and international pressure forced Marcos to flee the country Feb. 25, and Corazon Aquino became president.

Her government was plagued by a weak economy, widespread poverty, Communist and Muslim insurgencies, and lukewarm military support. Rebel troops seized military bases and TV stations and bombed the presidential palace, Dec. 1, 1989. Government forces, with U.S. air support, defeated the attempted coup. Aquino endorsed Fidel Ramos in the May 1992 presidential election, which he won. The U.S. vacated the Subic Bay Naval Station in late 1992, ending its long military presence in the Philippines. The government signed a cease-fire agreement, Jan. 30, 1994, with Muslim separatist guerrillas, but some rebels refused to abide by the accord. A new treaty providing for expansion and development of an autonomous Muslim region on Mindanao was signed Sept. 2, 1996, formally ending a rebellion that had claimed more than 120,000 lives since 1972.

Running as a populist, Joseph (Erap) Estrada, a former movie actor, won the presidential election of May 11, 1998. Charged with bribery and corruption, he was impeached Nov. 13, 2000. When the Supreme Court ruled the presidency vacant Jan. 20, 2001, Vice Pres. Gloria Macapagal Arroyo became president.

As part of the war on terrorism, the U.S. assisted Filipino troops in combating Abu Sayyaf, an Islamic guerrilla group. Pres. Arroyo won reelection May 10, 2004. Flooding and mudslides from tropical storms, Nov.-Dec. 2004, left at least 1,060 people dead, more than 560 missing, and 880,000 displaced. Former Pres. Estrada was convicted, Sept. 12, 2007, of taking more than $85 mil in bribes and kickbacks while in office; he received a pardon from Pres. Arroyo, Oct. 25. Typhoon Fengshen, June 21-22, 2008, left at least 557 people dead and destroyed more than 90,000 homes; at least 700 more people died when the ferry *Princess of the Stars* capsized and ran aground in the storm. Pres. Arroyo said June 27, 2009, that she would not seek to remain in office beyond May 2010, when new elections are scheduled.

Poland
Republic of Poland

People: Population: 38,482,919. **Age distrib.** (%): <15: 15; 65+: 13.4. **Pop. density:** 327.4 per sq mi, 126.4 per sq km. **Urban:** 61.5%. **Ethnic groups:** Polish 97%. **Principal language:** Polish. **Chief religion:** Roman Catholic 90%.

Geography: Total area: 120,726 sq mi, 312,679 sq km; **Land area:** 117,555 sq mi, 304,465 sq km. **Location:** On Baltic Sea in E central Europe. **Neighbors:** Germany on W; Czech Rep., Slovakia on S; Lithuania, Belarus, Ukraine on E; Russia on N. **Topography:** Mostly lowlands forming part of the Northern European Plain. The Carpathian Mts. along S border rise to 8,200 ft. **Capital:** Warsaw, 1,707,000. **Cities (urban aggr.):** Lódz, 758,000; Kraków, 756,000.

Government: Type: Republic. **Head of state:** Pres. Lech Kaczynski; b. June 18, 1949; in office: Dec. 23, 2005. **Head of gov.:** Prime Min. Donald Tusk; b. Apr. 22, 1957; in office: Nov. 16, 2007. **Local divisions:** 16 provinces. **Defense budget:** $8 bil. **Active troops:** 121,808.

Economy: Industries: machine building, iron & steel, coal mining, chemicals, shipbuilding, food proc., glass, beverages, textiles. **Chief crops:** potatoes, fruits, vegetables, wheat. **Natural resources:** coal, sulfur, copper, nat. gas, silver, lead, salt, amber. **Crude oil reserves:** 96.4 mil bbls. **Arable land:** 40%. **Livestock:** cattle: 5.7 mil; chickens: 133.1 mil; goats: 143,929; pigs: 18.1 mil; sheep: 331,900. **Fish catch:** 187,448 metric tons. **Electricity prod.:** 151.2 bil kWh. **Labor force** (2005): agric. 17.4%, industry 29.2%, services 53.4%.

Finance: Monetary unit: Zloty (PLN) (Oct. 2009: 2.83 = $1 U.S.). **GDP:** $667.9 bil; **per capita GDP:** $17,300; **GDP growth:** 4.8%. **Imports:** $199 bil; Germany 28.3%, Russia 9.9%, Italy 6.2%, Netherlands 5.4%, France 4.8%, China 4.5%, Czech Republic 4%. **Exports:** $175.3 bil; Germany 24.9%, France 6.2%, Italy 6%, UK 5.7%, Czech Republic 5.6%, Russia 5.3%. **Tourism:** $10.5 bil. **Budget:** $91.4 bil. **Intl. reserves less gold:** $38.5 bil. **Gold:** 3.31 mil oz t. **Consumer prices:** 4.3%.

Transport: Railroad: Length: 13,865 mi. **Motor vehicles:** 11.98 mil pass. cars; 2.5 mil comm. vehicles. **Civil aviation:** 3.9 bil pass.-mi; 84 airports. **Chief ports:** Gdansk, Gdynia, Swinoujscie, Szczecin.

Communications: TV sets: 387 per 1,000 pop. **Radios:** 522 per 1,000 pop. **Telephone lines:** 10.3 mil. **Daily newspaper circ.** (2004): 113.6 per 1,000 pop. **Internet:** 18.7 mil users.

Health: Life expect.: 71.4 male; 79.7 female. **Births** (per 1,000 pop.): 10. **Deaths** (per 1,000 pop.): 10. **Natural inc.:** 0%. **Infant mortality** (per 1,000 live births): 6.9. **HIV rate:** 0.1%.

Education: Compulsory: ages 7-15. **Literacy:** 99.3%.

Major intl. organizations: UN (FAO, IBRD, ILO, IMF, IMO, WHO, WTO), EU, NATO, OECD, OSCE.

Embassy: 2640 16th St. NW 20009; 234-3800.

Website: www.poland.gov.pl

Slavic tribes in the area were converted to Latin Christianity in the 10th cent. Poland was a great power from the 14th to the 17th

centuries. In 3 partitions (1772, 1793, 1795) it was apportioned among Prussia, Russia, and Austria. Overrun by the Austro-German armies in WWI, it declared its independence on Nov. 11, 1918, and was recognized as independent by the Treaty of Versailles, June 28, 1919. Large territories to the east were taken in a war with Russia, 1921.

Germany and the USSR invaded Poland Sept. 1939 and divided the country. During the war, some 6 mil Polish citizens, half of them Jews, were killed by the Nazis. In compensation for 69,860 sq mi ceded to the USSR when the war ended, Poland received approx. 40,000 sq mi of German territory east of the Oder-Neisse line comprising Silesia, Pomerania, West Prussia, and part of East Prussia. The election of 1947 was completely dominated by the Communists, who aligned themselves with the USSR.

In 12 years of rule by Stalinists, large estates were abolished, industries nationalized, schools secularized, and Roman Catholic prelates jailed. Farm production fell off. Harsh working conditions caused a riot in Poznan, June 28-29, 1956. A new Politburo, committed to a more independent Polish Communism, was named Oct. 1956, with Wladyslaw Gomulka as first secretary of the party. Collectivization of farms was ended. Gomulka agreed to permit religious liberty and religious publications, provided the church kept out of politics.

In Dec. 1970 workers in port cities rioted because of price rises and new incentive wage rules. On Dec. 20 Gomulka resigned as party leader; he was succeeded by Edward Gierek. The rules were dropped and price rises revoked.

After 2 months of labor turmoil had crippled the country, the Polish government, Aug. 30, 1980, met the demands of striking workers at the Lenin Shipyard, Gdansk. Government concessions included the right to form independent trade unions and the right to strike. By 1981, 9.5 mil workers had joined the independent trade union (Solidarity). As Solidarity's demands grew bolder, the government, spurred by fear of Soviet intervention, imposed martial law Dec. 13. Lech Walesa and other Solidarity leaders were arrested.

On Apr. 5, 1989, an accord was reached between the government and opposition factions on political and economic reforms, including free elections. Candidates endorsed by Solidarity swept the parliamentary elections, June 4. Lech Walesa became president Dec. 22, 1990.

A radical economic program designed to transform the economy into a free-market system led to inflation and unemployment. In Sept. 1993, former Communists and other leftists won a majority in the lower house of Parliament. A former Communist, Aleksander Kwasniewski, defeated Walesa in a presidential election in 1995 and was reelected 5 years later. A new constitution was approved by referendum May 25, 1997. Poland became a full member of NATO, Mar. 12, 1999, and entered the European Union May 1, 2004.

Lech Kaczynski, the conservative mayor of Warsaw, won a presidential runoff election Oct. 23, 2005. In July 2006 he appointed his identical twin brother Jaroslaw as prime min. Poland's governing coalition fell apart in 2007, and the center-right Civic Platform party, led by Donald Tusk, won parliamentary elections Oct. 21. Poland, a close U.S. ally, agreed Aug. 2008 to allow the U.S. to station part of a missile-defense system on Polish soil, but this plan was scrapped by the U.S. 13 months later. Russia, which had opposed the U.S. deployment, said Sept. 19, 2009, that it would drop its threat to deploy missiles in Kaliningrad, on the Polish border.

Poland pulled its final contingent of 900 troops out of Iraq in Oct. 2008. About 2,000 Polish troops were serving in Afghanistan as of mid-2009.

Portugal
Portuguese Republic

People: Population: 10,707,924. **Age distrib.** (%): <15: 16.3; 65+: 17.6. **Pop. density:** 301.6 per sq mi, 116.5 per sq km. **Urban:** 57.6%. **Ethnic groups:** Homogeneous Mediterranean stock. **Principal languages:** Portuguese, Mirandese (both official). **Chief religion:** Roman Catholic 85%.

Geography: Total area: 35,672 sq mi, 92,391 sq km; **Land area:** 35,503 sq mi, 91,951 sq km. **Location:** At SW extreme of Europe. **Neighbors:** Spain on N, E. **Topography:** Portugal N of Tajus R., which bisects country NE-SW, is mountainous, cool and rainy. To the S there are drier, rolling plains, and a warm climate. **Capital:** Lisbon, 2,812,000. **Cities (urban aggr.):** Porto, 1,337,000.

Government: Type: Republic. **Head of state:** Pres. Aníbal Cavaco Silva; b. July 15, 1939; in office: Mar. 9, 2006. **Head of gov.:** Prime Min. José Sócrates Carvalho Pinto de Sousa; b. Sept. 6, 1957; in office: Mar. 12, 2005. **Local divisions:** 18 districts, 2 autonomous regions. **Defense budget:** $3.4 bil. **Active troops:** 42,910.

Economy: Industries: textiles, footwear, wood & cork, paper, chemicals, auto-parts mfg., wine, porcelain & ceramics, ship constr. & refurbishment, tourism. **Chief crops:** grain, potatoes, tomatoes, olives, grapes. **Natural resources:** fish, forests (cork), iron ore, tungsten, uranium, marble, hydropower. **Arable land:** 17%. **Livestock:** cattle: 1.4 mil; chickens: 37 mil; goats: 547,410; pigs: 2.3 mil; sheep: 3.5 mil. **Fish catch:** 260,770 metric tons. **Electricity prod.:** 46.3 bil kWh. **Labor force** (2007 est.): agric. 10%, industry 30%, services 60%.

Finance: Monetary unit: Euro (EUR) (Oct. 2009: 0.68 = $1 U.S.). **GDP:** $236.5 bil; **per capita GDP:** $22,200; **GDP growth:** −0.1%. **Imports:** $87.8 bil; Spain 28.9%, Germany 11.6%, France

8%, Italy 4.9%, Netherlands 4.4%. **Exports:** $56.4 bil; Spain 25.7%, Germany 12.7%, France 11.1%, Angola 5.9%, UK 5.3%. **Tourism:** $10.1 bil. **Budget:** $98 bil. **Intl. reserves less gold:** $850 mil. **Gold:** 12.3 mil oz t. **Consumer prices:** 2.6%.

Transport: Railroad: Length: 1,731 mi. **Motor vehicles:** 6 mil pass. cars; 1.97 mil comm. vehicles. **Civil aviation:** 10.5 bil pass.-mi; 43 airports. **Chief ports:** Leixoes, Lisbon, Setubal, Sines.

Communications: TV sets: 567 per 1,000 pop. **Radios:** 306 per 1,000 pop. **Telephone lines:** 4.1 mil. **Daily newspaper circ.** (1999): 67.4 per 1,000 pop. **Internet:** 4.5 mil users.

Health: Life expect.: 74.8 male; 81.5 female. **Births** (per 1,000 pop.): 10.4. **Deaths** (per 1,000 pop.): 10.6. **Natural inc.:** –0.02%. **Infant mortality** (per 1,000 live births): 4.8. **HIV rate:** 0.5%.

Education: Compulsory: ages 6-14. **Literacy:** 94.9%.

Major intl. organizations: UN (FAO, IBRD, ILO, IMF, IMO, WHO, WTO), EU, NATO, OECD, OSCE.

Embassy: 2012 Massachusetts Ave. NW 20036; 350-5400. **Website:** www.portugal.gov.pt

Portugal, an independent state since the 12th cent., was a kingdom until a revolution in 1910 drove out King Manoel II and a republic was proclaimed. From 1932 a strong, repressive government was headed by Premier Antonio de Oliveira Salazar. Illness forced his retirement in Sept. 1968.

On Apr. 25, 1974, the government was seized by a military junta led by Gen. Antonio de Spinola, who became president. The new government reached agreements providing independence for Guinea-Bissau, Mozambique, Cape Verde Islands, Angola, and São Tomé and Príncipe. Banks, insurance companies, and other industries were nationalized.

Parliament approved, June 1, 1989, a program to denationalize industries. Portugal returned Macao to China on Dec. 20, 1999. With the economy lagging, opposition Socialists won a majority in elections Feb. 20, 2005. The conservative Aníbal Cavaco Silva, a former prime min., 1985-95. defeated two Socialist candidates to win the presidential election of Jan. 22, 2006. After a referendum to ease abortion restrictions failed Feb. 11, 2007, because of low turnout, parliament enacted a similar measure. Socialists won a plurality in legislative elections Sept. 27, 2009.

Azores Isls., in the Atlantic, 740 mi W of Portugal, have an area of 868 sq mi and a pop. (2008 est.) of 244,780. A 1951 agreement gave the U.S. rights to use defense facilities in the Azores. The **Madeira Isls.**, 350 mi off the NW coast of Africa, have an area of 306 sq mi and a pop. (2008 est.) of 247,161. Both groups were offered partial autonomy in 1976.

Qatar
State of Qatar

People: Population: 833,285. **Age distrib.** (%): <15: 21.8; 65+: 1.4. **Pop. density:** 188.7 per sq mi, 72.9 per sq km. **Urban:** 95.4%. **Ethnic groups:** Arab 40%, Indian 18%,Pakistani 18%, Iranian 10%. **Principal languages:** Arabic (official), English commonly used as second lang. **Chief religions:** Muslim 78%, Christian 9%.

Geography: Total area: 4,416 sq mi, 11,437 sq km; **Land area:** 4,416 sq mi, 11,437 sq km. **Location:** Middle East, occupying peninsula on W coast of Persian Gulf. **Neighbors:** Saudi Arabia on S. **Topography:** Mostly flat desert with some limestone ridges; vegetation of any kind is scarce. **Capital:** Doha (Ad-Dawhah), 384,000.

Government: Type: Traditional monarchy. **Head of state:** Emir Sheikh Hamad bin Khalifa al Thani; b. 1952; in office: June 27, 1995. **Head of gov.:** Prime Min. Sheikh Hamad bin Jassim bin Jabr al-Thani; b. 1959; in office: Apr. 3, 2007. **Local divisions:** 9 municipalities. **Defense budget:** $1.1 bil. **Active troops:** 11,800.

Economy: Industries: crude oil prod. & refining, ammonia, fertilizers, petrochems., commercial ship repair. **Chief crops:** fruits, vegetables. **Natural resources:** oil, nat. gas, fish. **Crude oil reserves:** 15.2 bil bbls. **Arable land:** 2%. **Livestock:** cattle: 8,000; chickens: 4.5 mil; sheep: 160,000; goats: 727,000. **Fish catch:** 15,226 metric tons. **Electricity prod.:** 14.4 bil kWh. **Labor force:** NA.

Finance: Monetary unit: Riyal (QAR) (Oct. 2009: 3.64 = $1 U.S.). **GDP:** $91.3 bil; **per capita GDP:** $110,700; **GDP growth:** 13.4%. **Imports:** $21.2 bil; U.S. 12.3%, Germany 9.2%, Italy 9.1%, Japan 8.1%, France 6.3%, UAE 5.6%, S. Korea 5.5%, UK 5%, Saudi Arabia 4.7%, Turkey 4.3%. **Exports:** $55.1 bil; Japan 40.8%, S. Korea 16.3%, Singapore 11.8%, Thailand 4.6%, India 4.4%. **Tourism:** NA. **Budget:** $22.6 bil. **Intl. reserves less gold:** $6.27 bil. **Gold:** 400,000 oz t. **Consumer prices:** 15%.

Transport: Motor vehicles: 267,800 pass. cars; 122,300 comm. vehicles. **Civil aviation:** 11.1 bil pass.-mi (incl. Gulf Air traffic apportionment); 3 airports. **Chief ports:** Doha, Ra's Laffan.

Communications: TV sets: 866 per 1,000 pop. **Radios:** 450 per 1,000 pop. **Telephone lines:** 263,400. **Internet:** 436,000 users.

Health: Life expect.: 73.5 male; 77 female. **Births** (per 1,000 pop.): 15.7. **Deaths** (per 1,000 pop.): 2.5. **Natural inc.:** 1.32%. **Infant mortality** (per 1,000 live births): 13.1. **HIV rate:** NA.

Education: Compulsory: ages 6-17. **Literacy:** 90.2%.

Major intl. organizations: UN (FAO, IBRD, ILO, IMF, IMO, WHO, WTO), AL, OPEC.

Embassy: 2555 M St. NW 20037; 274-1600. **Website:** portal.www.gov.qa

Qatar was under Bahrain's control until the Ottoman Turks took power, 1872 to 1915. In a treaty signed 1916, Qatar gave Great Britain responsibility for its defense and foreign relations. After Britain announced it would remove its military forces from the Persian Gulf area by the end of 1971, Qatar sought a federation with other British-protected states in the area; this failed and Qatar declared itself independent, Sept. 1, 1971. Crown Prince Hamad bin Khalifa al-Thani ousted his father, Emir Khalifa bin Hamad al-Thani, June 27, 1995. In municipal elections held Mar. 8, 1999, women participated for the 1st time as candidates and voters.

Qatar, one of the world's leading exporters of liquefied natural gas, has experienced rapid economic growth in recent years. Military ties with the U.S. have been expanding; Camp As-Sayliyah, a base near Doha, served as a command center for the U.S.-led invasion of Iraq, Mar. 2003. The influential Arab news network Al-Jazeera is based in Qatar.

Romania

People: Population: 22,215,421. **Age distrib.** (%): <15: 15.5; 65+: 14.7. **Pop. density:** 249.8 per sq mi, 96.4 per sq km. **Urban:** 53.7%. **Ethnic groups:** Romanian 90%, Hungarian 7%, Roma 3%. **Principal languages:** Romanian (official), Hungarian, Romany. **Chief religions:** Eastern Orthodox 87%, Protestant 8%, Roman Catholic 5%.

Geography: Total area: 91,699 sq mi, 237,500 sq km; **Land area:** 88,935 sq mi, 230,340 sq km. **Location:** SE Europe, on the Black Sea. **Neighbors:** Moldova on E, Ukraine on N, Hungary and Serbia on W, Bulgaria on S. **Topography:** The Carpathian Mts. encase the north-central Transylvanian plateau. There are wide plains S and E of the mountains, through which flow the lower reaches of the rivers of Danube system. **Capital:** Bucharest, 1,942,000.

Government: Type: Republic. **Head of state:** Pres. Traian Basescu; b. Nov. 4, 1951; in office: Dec. 20, 2004. **Head of gov.:** Prime Min. Emil Boc; b. Sept. 6, 1966; in office: Dec. 22, 2008. **Local divisions:** 41 counties and Bucharest. **Defense budget:** $3 bil. **Active troops:** 73,200.

Economy: Industries: elec. machinery & equip., textiles & footwear, light machinery, auto assembly, mining, timber. **Chief crops:** wheat, corn, barley, sugar beets, sunflower seed, potatoes, grapes. **Natural resources:** oil (reserves declining), timber, nat. gas, coal, iron ore, salt, hydropower. **Crude oil reserves:** 600 mil bbls. **Arable land:** 39%. **Livestock:** cattle: 2.9 mil; chickens: 85 mil; goats: 727,000; pigs: 6.8 mil; sheep: 7.7 mil. **Fish catch:** 16,496 metric tons. **Electricity prod.:** 59.3 bil kWh. **Labor force** (2006): agric. 29.7%, industry 23.2%, services 47.1%.

Finance: Monetary unit: New Leu (RON) (Oct. 2009: 2.89 = $1 U.S.). **GDP:** $271.4 bil; **per capita GDP:** $12,200; **GDP growth:** 7.1%. **Imports:** $76.2 bil; Germany 16.3%, Italy 11.4%, Hungary 7.4%, Russia 6%, France 5.7%, Turkey 4.9%, Austria 4.9%, Kazakhstan 4.6%, China 4.2%. **Exports:** $49.4 bil; Germany 16.5%, Italy 15.6%, France 7.4%, Turkey 6.6%, Hungary 5.1%, Bulgaria 4.2%. **Tourism:** $1.6 bil. **Budget:** $60.4 bil. **Intl. reserves less gold:** $23.94 bil. **Gold:** 3.33 mil oz t. **Consumer prices:** 7.8%.

Transport: Railroad: Length: 6,703 mi. **Motor vehicles:** 3.4 mil pass. cars; 533,000 comm. vehicles. **Civil aviation:** 1.2 bil pass.-mi; 25 airports. **Chief ports:** Braila, Constanta, Galati, Tulcea.

Communications: TV sets: 312 per 1,000 pop. **Radios:** 335 per 1,000 pop. **Telephone lines:** 5 mil. **Daily newspaper circ.** (2004): 70.3 per 1,000 pop. **Internet:** 6.1 mil users.

Health: Life expect.: 68.7 male; 75.9 female. **Births** (per 1,000 pop.): 10.6. **Deaths** (per 1,000 pop.): 11.8. **Natural inc.:** –0.12%. **Infant mortality** (per 1,000 live births): 23.7. **HIV rate:** 0.1%.

Education: Compulsory: ages 7-14. **Literacy:** 97.6%.

Major intl. organizations: UN (FAO, IBRD, ILO, IMF, IMO, WHO, WTO), NATO, OSCE.

Embassy: 1607 23rd St. NW 20008; 332-4846. **Website:** www.guv.ro

Romania's earliest known people merged with invading Proto-Thracians, preceding by centuries the Dacians. The Dacian kingdom was occupied by Rome, 106-271 CE; people and language were Romanized. The principalities of Wallachia and Moldavia, dominated by Turkey, were united in 1859, became Romania in 1861, and gained recognition as an independent kingdom, 1881.

After WWI, Romania acquired Bessarabia, Bukovina, Transylvania, and Banat. In 1940 it ceded Bessarabia and Northern Bukovina to the USSR, part of southern Dobrudja to Bulgaria, and northern Transylvania to Hungary. In 1941, Prem. Marshal Ion Antonescu led Romania in support of Germany against the USSR. In 1944 he was overthrown, and Romania joined the Allies. After occupation by Soviet troops, a People's Republic was proclaimed, Dec. 30, 1947.

On Aug. 22, 1965, a new constitution proclaimed Romania a Socialist Republic. Pres. Nicolae Ceausescu maintained an independent course in foreign affairs, but his domestic policies were repressive. All industry was state-owned, and state farms and cooperatives owned almost all arable land. Ceausescu's security forces fired on antigovernment demonstrators in Dec. 1989, killing hundreds, but when the army sided with the protesters, his regime fell. Ceausescu and his wife were captured and, following a trial in which they were found guilty of genocide, were executed Dec. 25, 1989.

A new constitution providing for a multiparty system took effect Dec. 8, 1991. Many of Romania's state-owned companies were privatized in 1996. Romania became a full NATO member in 2004 and entered the European Union Jan. 1, 2007.

Floods in July-Aug. 2005 left more than 50 people dead. Parliament voted Apr. 19, 2007, to suspend Pres. Traian Basescu, as part of an ongoing political dispute, but 75% of voters in a referendum May 19 refused to support his ouster. The IMF and other donors agreed to provide a $27 bil loan Mar. 25, 2009, to rescue Romania from the global recession. Iraq, a firm U.S. ally, pulled its last remaining troops out of Iraq July 2009; at that time, the country had 1,025 soldiers serving with NATO-led forces in Afghanistan.

Russia
Russian Federation

People: Population: 140,041,247. **Age distrib.** (%): <15: 14.8; 65+: 13.7. **Pop. density:** 21.3 per sq mi, 8.2 per sq km. **Urban:** 72.9%. **Ethnic groups:** Russian 80%, Tatar 4%. **Principal languages:** Russian, many minority languages. **Chief religions:** Russian Orthodox 15%-20%, Muslim 10%-15%.

Geography: Total area: 6,592,772 sq mi, 17,075,200 sq km; **Land area:** 6,562,115 sq mi, 16,995,800 sq km., more than 76% of total area of the former USSR and the largest country in the world. **Location:** Stretches from E Europe across N Asia to the Pacific O. **Neighbors:** Finland, Norway, Estonia, Latvia, Belarus, Ukraine on W; Georgia, Azerbaijan, Kazakhstan, China, Mongolia, N. Korea on S; Kaliningrad exclave bordered by Poland on the S, Lithuania on the N and E. **Topography:** Every type of climate except distinctly tropical. The European portion is a low plain, grassy in S, wooded in N, with Ural Mts. on E, and Caucasus Mts. on S. Urals stretch N-S for 2,500 mi. The Asiatic portion is a vast plain, with mountains on S and in E; tundra covers extreme N, with forest belt below; plains, marshes are in W, desert in SW. **Capital:** Moscow, 10,452,000. **Cities (urban aggr.):** Saint Petersburg, 4,553,000; Novosibirsk, 1,389,000; Yekaterinburg, 1,313,000; Nizhniy Novgorod, 1,278,000.

Government: Type: Federal republic. **Head of state:** Pres. Dmitri Medvedev; b. Sept. 14, 1965; in office: May 7, 2008. **Head of gov.:** Prime Min. Vladimir Putin; b. Oct. 7, 1952; in office: May 8, 2008. **Local divisions:** 7 federal districts incl. 49 provinces, 21 autonomous republics, 6 territories, 1 autonomous region, 10 autonomous districts, 2 federal cities. **Defense budget:** $32.2 bil. **Active troops:** 1,027,000.

Economy: Industries: coal, oil, gas, chemicals, metals; machine building; defense (incl. radar, missiles); transp. equip.; comm. equip.; agric. machinery, constr. equip.; electric power generating & transmitting equip.; medical & scientific instruments; consumer durables, textiles. **Chief crops:** grain, sugar beets, sunflower seed, vegetables, fruits. **Natural resources:** oil, nat. gas, coal, minerals, timber (climate, terrain, & distance are big obstacles to exploitation of nat. resources). **Crude oil reserve:** 60 bil bbls. **Arable land:** 7%. **Livestock:** cattle: 21.5 mil; chickens: 358.3 mil; goats: 2.2 mil; pigs: 15.9 mil; sheep: 17.5 mil. **Fish catch:** 3.59 mil metric tons. **Electricity prod.:** 940.6 bil kWh. **Labor force** (2007 est.): agric. 10.2%, industry 27.4%, services 62.4%.

Finance: Monetary unit: Ruble (RUB) (Oct. 2009: 29.84 = $1 U.S.). **GDP:** $2.3 tril; **per capita GDP:** $16,100; **GDP growth:** 5.6%. **Imports:** $302 bil; Germany 13.4%, China 12.8%, Japan 6.5%, Ukraine 6.3%, U.S. 4.4%, Italy 4.3%, S. Korea 4.1%. **Exports:** $471.6 bil; Netherlands 10.8%, Italy 8%, Germany 7.8%, Turkey 5.9%, Ukraine 5.4%, China 4.5%, Poland 4.4%. **Tourism:** $9.6 bil. **Budget:** $262 bil. **Intl. reserves less gold:** $267.84 bil. **Gold:** 16.71 mil oz t. **Consumer prices:** 14.1%.

Transport: Railroad: Length: 54,157 mi **Motor vehicles:** 25.5 mil pass. cars; 4.6 mil comm. vehicles. **Civil aviation:** 39.3 bil pass.-mi; 595 airports. **Chief ports:** Azov, Kaliningrad, Kavkaz, Nakhodka, Novorossiysk, Primorsk, St. Petersburg, Vostochny.

Communications: TV sets: 421 per 1,000 pop. **Radios:** 417 per 1,000 pop. **Telephone lines:** 44.2 mil. **Daily newspaper circ.** (2004): 91.8 per 1,000 pop. **Internet:** 45.4 mil users.

Health: Life expect.: 59.2 male; 73.1 female. **Births** (per 1,000 pop.): 11. **Deaths** (per 1,000 pop.): 16.1. **Natural inc.:** −0.5%. **Infant mortality** (per 1,000 live births): 10.8. **HIV rate:** 1.1%.

Education: Compulsory: ages 6-15. **Literacy:** 99.5%.

Major intl. organizations: UN (FAO, IBRD, ILO, IMF, IMO, WHO), APEC, CIS, OSCE.

Embassy: 2650 Wisconsin Ave. NW 20007; 298-5700.

Website: www.gov.ru or kremlin.ru

History. Slavic tribes began migrating into Russia from the W in the 5th cent. The first Russian state, centered in Novgorod and Kiev, was founded by Scandinavian chieftains in the 9th cent. In the 13th cent., Mongols overran the country. It recovered under the grand dukes and princes of Muscovy, or Moscow, and by 1480 freed itself from the Mongols. Ivan the Terrible was first formally proclaimed Tsar (1547). Peter the Great (1682-1725) extended the domain and, in 1721, founded the Russian Empire.

Western ideas and the beginnings of modernization spread through the huge Russian empire in the 19th and early 20th centuries, but political evolution failed to keep pace.

Military reverses in the 1905 war with Japan and in WWI led to the breakdown of the Tsarist regime. The 1917 Revolution began in Mar. with a series of sporadic strikes for higher wages by factory workers. A provisional democratic government under Prince Georgi Lvov was established but was followed in May by a second provisional govern-

ment, under Alexander Kerensky. The Kerensky government and the freely-elected Constituent Assembly were overthrown in a Communist coup led by Vladimir Ilyich Lenin Nov. 7.

Soviet Union

Lenin's death Jan. 21, 1924, resulted in an internal power struggle eventually won by Joseph Stalin. He secured his position at first by exiling opponents, but from the 1930s to 1953, he resorted to a series of "purge" trials, mass executions, and mass exiles to work camps. These measures resulted in millions of deaths, according to most estimates.

Germany and the Soviet Union signed a non-aggression pact Aug. 1939; Germany launched a massive invasion of the Soviet Union, June 1941. A notable heroic episode was the "900 days" siege of Leningrad (now St. Petersburg), lasting to Jan. 1944, and causing a million deaths; the city was never taken. Russian winter counterthrusts, 1941-42 and 1942-43, stopped the German advance. Turning point was the failure of German troops to take and hold Stalingrad (now Volgograd), Sept. 1942 to Feb. 1943. With British and U.S. Lend-Lease aid and sustaining great casualties, the Russians drove the German forces from eastern Europe and the Balkans in the next 2 years.

After WWII, Communists took over in countries throughout the region, extending the Soviet sphere of influence. The USSR and the U.S., the world's leading nuclear superpowers, faced off against each other as cold war rivals. After Stalin died, Mar. 5, 1953, Nikita Khrushchev gained power. In 1956 he denounced Stalin and "de-Stalinization" began.

Under Khrushchev the open antagonism of Poles and Hungarians toward domination by Moscow was brutally suppressed in 1956. He aided the Cuban revolution under Fidel Castro but withdrew Soviet missiles from Cuba during a confrontation with U.S. Pres. Kennedy, Sept.-Oct. 1962. Khrushchev was suddenly deposed, Oct. 1964, and replaced by Leonid I. Brezhnev. In Aug. 1968 Soviet forces led an invasion of Czechoslovakia, crushing liberalization there.

Massive Soviet military aid to North Vietnam in the late 1960s and early 1970s helped assure Communist victories throughout Indo-China. In Dec. 1979, Soviet forces entered Afghanistan to support that government against rebels. In Apr. 1988, the Soviets agreed to withdraw their troops, ending a futile 8-year war.

Mikhail Gorbachev was chosen gen. secy. of the Communist Party, Mar. 1985. In 1987 he initiated a program of political and economic reforms, through openness (*glasnost*) and restructuring (*perestroika*). Gorbachev faced economic problems as well as ethnic and nationalist unrest in the republics. An apparent coup by Communist hardliners Aug. 1991, was foiled with help from Russian Republic Pres. Boris Yeltsin. On Aug. 24, Gorbachev resigned as leader of the Communist Party. Several republics declared their independence, including Russia, Ukraine, and Kazakhstan. On Aug. 29, the Soviet Parliament voted to suspend all activities of the Communist Party.

The Soviet Union officially broke up Dec. 26, 1991. The Soviet hammer and sickle flying over the Kremlin was lowered and replaced by the flag of Russia, ending the domination of the Communist Party over all areas of national life since 1917.

Russian Federation

Led by Pres. Yeltsin, Russia took steps toward privatization; immediate effects were inflation and a severe economic downturn. In June 1992, Yeltsin and U.S. Pres. George H. W. Bush agreed to massive arms reductions. Yeltsin prevailed in a power struggle with the Congress of People's Deputies, which was dominated by conservatives and former Communists, and in a referendum Dec. 12, 1993, a new constitution was approved. In Dec. 1994 the Russian government sent troops into the breakaway republic of Chechnya. Grozny, the Chechen capital, fell in Feb. 1995 after heavy fighting, but Chechen rebels continued to resist.

Despite poor health, Yeltsin won a presidential runoff election over a Communist opponent, July 3, 1996. On Aug. 14, after rebels embarrassed the Russian military by retaking Grozny, Yeltsin gave his security chief, Alexander Lebed, broad powers to negotiate an end to the Chechnya war. Lebed and Chechen leaders signed a peace accord Aug. 31. On Oct. 17, Yeltsin dismissed Lebed for insubordination. Russian troops remaining in Chechnya were pulled out Jan. 1997. On May 27, Yeltsin signed a "founding act" increasing cooperation with NATO and paving the way for NATO to admit Eastern European nations.

Russia's economic crisis deepened in the late 1990s, heightening tensions between Yeltsin and parliament. Russia moved forcibly in Aug. 1999 to suppress Islamic rebels in Dagestan; the conflict soon spread to neighboring Chechnya, where Russia launched a full-scale assault.

Yeltsin unexpectedly resigned Dec. 31, 1999, naming Prime Min. Vladimir Putin as his interim successor. Russian troops took control of Grozny in early Feb. 2000. Putin defeated 10 opponents in a presidential election Mar. 26. Russia, which supported the U.S.-led war in Afghanistan in 2001, sided with France and Germany in blocking UN Security Council endorsement of the U.S.-led invasion of Iraq, Mar. 2003.

Putin's allies won legislative elections, Dec. 7, 2003, and the president was reelected Mar. 14, 2004, with 71% of the vote; international election monitors cited flaws on both occasions. Putin blamed Chechen terrorists for a blast on a Moscow subway car,

Feb. 6, that killed at least 39 people. A bomb in Grozny, May 9, killed Chechnya's pro-Moscow president, Akhmad Kadyrov, and at least 6 others. Putin's choice for the Chechen presidency, Maj. Gen. Alu Alkhanov, was elected Aug. 29.

The Chechnya conflict unleashed a wave of terrorism elsewhere during Aug.-Sept. 2004. After taking off the night of Aug. 24 from Moscow's Domodedovo airport, 2 passenger planes exploded in midair, killing 90 people. A suicide bombing in a Moscow subway station Aug. 31 left 11 dead. Chechen rebels Sept. 1 seized control of a school in Beslan, North Ossetia, taking more than 1,100 hostages; Russian troops stormed the school Sept. 3; in the end more than 330 people died, including 186 children. Putin cited the terrorist threat Sept. 13 in proposing a government overhaul that would tighten his control over parliament and regional officeholders.

On Nov. 5, 2004, Russia ratified the Kyoto Protocol, which aims to curb greenhouse gas emissions and global warming. Russian forces killed Chechen rebel leader Aslan Maskhadov, Mar. 8, 2005. Mikhail Khodorkovsky, an oil tycoon whose political agenda had rivaled Putin's, was convicted of fraud and tax evasion, May 31, and sentenced to 9 years in prison. Chechen guerrilla leader Shamil Basayev, who had organized the terrorist attack at Beslan, was killed July 10, 2006. Another Putin opponent, former Russian agent Alexander Litvinenko, was poisoned with radioactive polonium-210 and died in London Nov. 23.

Constitutionally barred from seeking another term, Pres. Putin backed his protégé Dmitri Medvedev, who won the presidential election Mar. 2, 2008, and after taking office May 7 named Putin as prime minister. A long-simmering conflict with Georgia erupted into open warfare Aug. 7-16, as Russia dispatched troops to support secessionists in the enclaves of South Ossetia and Abkhazia and launched assaults on strategic Georgian cities; a cease-fire left thousands of Russian troops in the breakaway regions, which Pres. Medvedev recognized as independent on Aug. 26.

An economic boom fueled by oil and gas sales came to a halt in late 2008. The global financial crisis and a drop in oil prices led to turmoil on Russian financial markets, which were closed Sept. 17-18 as the government put together a $130-bil emergency rescue plan. As the crisis deepened, the government loaned banks $37 bil Oct. 7 and began buying shares to prop up the Russian stock exchange.

Russia declared Apr. 16, 2009, that it had ended counterterrorism operations in Chechnya; from June through August, however, there was a marked upsurge of insurgent violence in Chechnya and neighboring Dagestan and Ingushetia. During a visit to Russia July 6-7, U.S. Pres. Obama met with Pres. Medvedev and Prime Min. Putin. Repairing relations strained since the 2008 Georgia war, Russia and the U.S. agreed on measures to reduce nuclear stockpiles and increase military cooperation.

Rwanda
Republic of Rwanda

People: Population: 10,473,282. **Age distrib.** (%): <15: 42.1; 65+: 2.4. **Pop. density:** 1,087.3 per sq mi, 419.8 per sq km. **Urban:** 17.5%. **Ethnic groups:** Hutu (Bantu) 84%, Tutsi (Hamitic) 15%. **Principal languages:** Kinyarwanda (universal Bantu vernacular), French, English (all official); Swahili used in commercial centers. **Chief religions:** Roman Catholic 57%, Protestant 26%, Adventist 11%, Muslim 5%.

Geography: Total area: 10,169 sq mi, 26,338 sq km; **Land area:** 9,633 sq mi, 24,948 sq km. **Location:** In E central Africa. **Neighbors:** Uganda on N, Congo (formerly Zaire) on W, Burundi on S, Tanzania on E. **Topography:** Grassy uplands and hills cover most of country, with chain of volcanoes in the NW. The source of the Nile R. has been located in headwaters of the Kagera (Akagera) R., SW of Kigali. **Capital:** Kigali, 860,000.

Government: Type: Republic. **Head of state:** Pres. Paul Kagame; b. Oct. 23, 1957; in office: Apr. 22, 2000 (de facto from Mar. 24). **Head of gov.:** Prime Min. Bernard Makuza (b. 1961; in office: Mar. 8, 2000. **Local divisions:** 12 prefectures subdivided into 155 communes. **Defense budget:** $62 mil. **Active troops:** 33,000.

Economy: Industries: cement, agric. products, soap, plastic goods, textiles. **Chief crops:** coffee, tea, pyrethrum (insecticide made from chrysanthemums), bananas, beans, sorghum, potatoes. **Natural resources:** gold, tin ore, tungsten ore, methane, hydropower. **Arable land:** 46%. **Livestock:** cattle: 950,000; chickens: 2 mil; goats: 1.3 mil; pigs: 270,000; sheep: 470,000. **Fish catch:** 13,088 metric tons. **Electricity prod.:** 134 mil kWh. **Labor force** (2000): agric. 90%, industry & services 10%.

Finance: Monetary unit: Franc (RWF) (Oct. 2009: 564.40 = $1 U.S.). **GDP:** $9.7 bil; **per capita GDP:** $1,000; **GDP growth:** 11.2%. **Imports:** $809 mil; Kenya 17.1%, China 6.2%, Uganda 6%, Belgium 5.9%, Germany 5.1%. **Exports:** $213 mil; China 9.1%, Thailand 8.8%, Germany 7.5%, U.S. 4.6%, Belgium 4.2%. **Tourism:** NA. **Budget:** $873.1 mil. **Intl. reserves less gold:** $387 mil. **Gold:** NA. **Consumer prices:** 15.4%.

Transport: Motor vehicles: 10,700 pass. cars; 16,300 comm. vehicles. **Civil aviation:** 1.2 mil pass.-mi; 4 airports. **Chief ports:** Cyangugu, Gisenyi, Kibuye.

Communications: Radios: 101 per 1,000 pop. **Telephone lines:** 16,800. **Internet:** 300,000 users.

Health: Life expect.: 48.6 male; 51 female. **Births** (per 1,000 pop.): 40. **Deaths** (per 1,000 pop.): 14.5. **Natural inc.:** 2.55%. **Infant mortality** (per 1,000 live births): 83.4. **HIV rate:** 2.8%. **Education:** Compulsory: ages 7-12. **Literacy:** 64.9%.

Major intl. organizations: UN (FAO, IBRD, ILO, IMF, WHO, WTO), AU.

Embassy: 1714 New Hampshire Ave. NW 20009; 232-2882. **Website:** www.gov.rw

For centuries, the Tutsi (an extremely tall people) dominated the Hutu (90% of the population). A civil war broke out in 1959 and Tutsi power was ended. Many Tutsi went into exile. Rwanda, which had been part of the Belgian UN trusteeship of Rwanda-Urundi, became independent July 1, 1962.

In 1963 Tutsi exiles unsuccessfully attempted to reseize power; a large-scale massacre of Tutsi followed. Hutu rivalries led to a bloodless coup July 1973 in which Hutu army officer Juvénal Habyarimana took power. After another invasion and coup attempt by Tutsi exiles in 1990, a multiparty democracy was established.

Renewed ethnic strife led to an Aug. 1993 peace accord between the government and rebels of the Tutsi-led Rwandan Patriotic Front (RPF). But after Habyarimana and Burundi Pres. Cyprien Ntaryamira were killed Apr. 6, 1994, in a suspicious plane crash, massive violence broke out. More than 1 mil may have died in massacres, mostly of Tutsi by Hutu militias, and in civil warfare as the RPF sought power. About 2 mil Tutsi and Hutu fled to camps in Zaire (now Dem. Rep. of the Congo) and other countries, where many died of cholera and other diseases. French troops under a UN mandate moved into SW Rwanda June 23 to establish a "safe zone." The RPF claimed victory, installing a government in July led by a moderate Hutu president. French troops pulled out Aug. 22. A UN peacekeeping mission ended Mar. 8, 1996, but the Rwandan government and a UN-sponsored tribunal in Tanzania continued to gather evidence of crimes against humanity. More than 1 mil refugees, mostly Hutu, flooded back to Rwanda from Tanzania and Zaire in Nov. and Dec. 1996.

Firing squads in Rwanda on Apr. 24, 1998, executed 22 people convicted of genocide. Former Prime Min. Jean Kambanda pleaded guilty May 1 before the UN tribunal and received a life sentence Sept. 4, 1998. RPF leader Maj. Gen. Paul Kagame became Rwanda's first Tutsi president Apr. 22, 2000.

Rwandans in 2003 approved a new constitution, May 26, re-elected Pres. Kagame, Aug. 25, and chose a new parliament, Sept. 29-30. Former Pres. Bizimungu was sentenced to 15 years for embezzlement, June 2004; he was pardoned by Kagame and released, Apr. 6, 2007. Rwanda cut diplomatic ties with France Nov. 24, 2006, after a French judge linked Kagame and his close aides to the deaths in 1994 of Habyarimana and Ntaryamira.

Rwanda has experienced steady economic growth in recent years. Pres. Bush visited the country and conferred with Pres. Kagame Feb. 19, 2008. The U.S. has funded efforts to train the Rwandan military and control HIV/AIDS and malaria.

Accused of being one of the architects of the 1994 genocide, Col. Theoneste Bagosora was convicted and sentenced to life in prison by the UN tribunal Dec. 18, 2008. A Rwandan court handed out a life sentence Jan. 20, 2009, to former Justice Min. Agnes Ntamabyariro for her role in inciting the massacres. Up to 4,000 Rwandan troops fought that month alongside Congolese forces against Hutu militias in E Congo. Rwanda had up to 3,200 peacekeepers in the Darfur region of Sudan in 2009.

Saint Kitts and Nevis
Federation of Saint Kitts and Nevis

People: Population: 40,131. **Age distrib.** (%): <15: 26.3; 65+: 7.9. **Pop. density:** 398.2 per sq mi, 153.8 per sq km. **Urban:** 32.2%. **Ethnic group:** Predominantly black; some British, Portuguese, Lebanese. **Principal language:** English. **Chief religions:** Anglican, other Protestant, Roman Catholic.

Geography: Total area: 101 sq mi, 261 sq km; **Land area:** 101 sq mi, 261 sq km. **Location:** In N part of the Leeward group of Lesser Antilles in E Caribbean Sea. **Neighbors:** Antigua and Barbuda to E. **Topography:** St. Kitts has forested volcanic slopes; Nevis rises from beaches to central peak. Climate is tropical moderated by sea breezes. **Capital** (2006): Basseterre, 12,900.

Government: Type: Constitutional monarchy. **Head of state:** Queen Elizabeth II, represented by Gov.-Gen. Sir Cuthbert M. Sebastian; b. Oct. 22, 1921; in office: Jan. 1, 1996. **Head of gov.:** Prime Min. Denzil Llewellyn Douglas; b. Jan. 14, 1953; in office: July 7, 1995. **Local div.:** 14 parishes. **Def. budget/Troops:** NA.

Economy: Industries: tourism, cotton, salt, copra, clothing, footwear, beverages. **Chief crops:** sugarcane, rice, yams, vegetables, bananas. **Arable land:** 19%. **Livestock:** cattle: 6,500; chickens: 70,000; goats: 7,500; sheep: 6,000. **Fish catch** (est.): 450 metric tons. **Electricity prod.:** 130 mil kWh. **Labor force:** NA.

Finance: Monetary unit: East Caribbean Dollar (XCD) (Oct. 2009: 2.70 = $1 U.S.). **GDP:** $777.7 mil; **per capita GDP:** $19,500; **GDP growth:** 3%. **Imports** (2006): $383 mil; U.S. 46.7%, Trinidad and Tobago 14.8%, UK 4.1%. **Exports** (2006): $84 mil; U.S. 40.4%, Malaysia 40.2%, Canada 3.7%. **Tourism:** $126 mil. **Budget** (2003 est.): $128.2 mil. **Intl. reserves less gold:** $72 mil. **Gold:** NA. **Consumer prices:** 5.5%.

Transport: Railroad: Length: 31 mi. **Motor vehicles:** 9,000 pass. cars; 3,000 comm. vehicles. **Civil aviation:** 2 airports. **Chief port:** Basseterre.

Communications: TV sets: 256 per 1,000 pop. **Radios:** 718 per 1,000 pop. **Telephone lines:** 20,400. **Internet:** 16,000 users.

Health: Life expect.: 70.1 male; 76 female. **Births** (per 1,000 pop.): 17.7. **Deaths** (per 1,000 pop.): 8.2. **Natural inc.:** 0.95%. **Infant mortality** (per 1,000 live births): 14.3. **HIV rate:** NA.

Education: Compulsory: ages 5-16. **Literacy:** 97.8%.

Major intl. organizations: UN (FAO, IBRD, ILO, IMF, IMO, WHO, WTO), Caricom, the Commonwealth, OAS, OECS.

Embassy: 3216 New Mexico Ave. NW 20016; 686-2636.

Website: www.gov.kn

St. Kitts (formerly St. Christopher; known by indigenous peoples as Liamuiga) and Nevis were reached and named by Columbus in 1493. They were settled by Britain in 1623, but ownership was disputed with France until 1713. They were part of the Leeward Islands Federation, 1871-1956, and the Federation of the West Indies, 1958-62. The colony achieved self-government as an Associated State of the UK in 1967, and became fully independent Sept. 19, 1983. A secession referendum on Nevis, Aug. 10, 1998, fell short of the two-thirds majority required.

St. Kitts and Nevis is the smallest independent nation in the Western Hemisphere.

Saint Lucia

People: Population: 160,267. **Age distrib.** (%): <15: 24.4; 65+: 9.2. **Pop. density:** 685 per sq mi, 264.5 per sq km. **Urban:** 27.6%. **Ethnic groups:** Black 83%, mixed 12%, East Indian 2%. **Principal languages:** English (official), French patois. **Chief religions:** Roman Catholic 68%, Seventh-Day Adventist 9%, Pentecostal 6%, none 5%.

Geography: Total area: 238 sq mi, 616 sq km; **Land area:** 234 sq mi, 606 sq km. **Location:** In E Caribbean, 2nd largest of Windward Isls. **Neighbors:** Martinique to N, St. Vincent to S. **Topography:** Mountainous, volcanic in origin; Soufriere, a volcanic crater, in S. Wooded mountains run N-S to Mt. Gimie, 3,145 ft, with streams through fertile valleys. **Capital:** Castries, 14,000.

Government: Type: Constitutional monarchy. **Head of state:** Queen Elizabeth II, represented by Gov.-Gen. Dame Calliopa Pearlette Louisy; b. June 8, 1946; in office: Sept. 17, 1997. **Head of gov.:** Prime Min. Stephenson King; b. Nov. 13, 1958; in office: Sept. 9, 2007 (acting from May 1). **Local divisions:** 11 quarters. **Defense budget/Active troops:** NA.

Economy: Industries: clothing, electronic components assembly, beverages, corrugated cardboard boxes, tourism. **Chief crops:** bananas, coconuts, vegetables, citrus, root crops, cocoa. **Natural resources:** forests, pumice, mineral springs, geothermal potential. **Arable land:** 6%. **Livestock:** cattle: 12,500; chickens: 280,000; goats: 8,816; pigs: 19,520; sheep: 7,736. **Fish catch** (est.): 1,556 metric tons. **Electricity prod.:** 331 mil kWh. **Labor force** (2002 est.): agric. 21.4%; industry, commerce, & mfg. 24.7%; services 53.6%.

Finance: Monetary unit: East Caribbean Dollar (XCD) (Oct. 2009: 2.70 = $1 U.S.). **GDP:** $1.8 bil; **per capita GDP:** $11,100; **GDP growth:** 1.7%. **Imports** (2006): $791 mil; Brazil 68.6%, U.S. 11.8%, Trinidad and Tobago 7.5%. **Exports** (2006): $288 mil; UK 28.8%, U.S. 23.5%, Antigua and Barbuda 7.2%, Dominica 7%, Barbados 6.3%, Trinidad and Tobago 5.9%, Grenada 4.8%. **Tourism:** $317 mil. **Budget** (2000 est.): $146.7 mil. **Intl. reserves less gold:** $93 mil. **Gold:** NA. **Consumer prices:** 7.2%.

Transport: Motor vehicles: 23,800 pass. cars; 9,800 comm. vehicles. **Civil aviation:** 2 airports. **Chief ports:** Castries, Cul-de-Sac, Vieux-Fort.

Communications: TV sets: 368 per 1,000 pop. **Radios:** 750 per 1,000 pop. **Telephone lines:** 40,900. **Internet:** 100,000 users.

Health: Life expect.: 73.6 male; 79 female. **Births** (per 1,000 pop.): 15.4. **Deaths** (per 1,000 pop.): 6.7. **Natural inc.:** 0.87%. **Infant mortality** (per 1,000 live births): 13.8. **HIV rate:** NA.

Education: Compulsory: ages 5-15. **Literacy:** 90.1%.

Major intl. organizations: UN (FAO, IBRD, ILO, IMF, IMO, WHO, WTO), Caricom, the Commonwealth, OAS, OECS.

Embassy: 3216 New Mexico Ave. NW 20016; 364-6792.

Website: www.stlucia.gov.lc

St. Lucia was ceded to Britain by France at the Treaty of Paris, 1814. Self-government was granted with the West Indies Act, 1967. Independence was attained Feb. 22, 1979.

Saint Vincent and the Grenadines

People: Population: 104,574. **Age distrib.** (%): <15: 25.9; 65+: 7.8. **Pop. density:** 696.3 per sq mi, 268.8 per sq km. **Urban:** 45.9%. **Ethnic groups:** Black 66%, mixed 19%, East Indian 6%. **Principal languages:** English, French patois. **Chief religions:** Anglican 47%, Methodist 28%, Roman Catholic 13%, other (incl. Hindu, Seventh-Day Adventist, other Protestant) 12%.

Geography: Total area: 150 sq mi, 389 sq km; **Land area:** 150 sq mi, 389 sq km. **Location:** In E Caribbean, St. Vincent (133 sq mi) and the northern islets of the Grenadines form a part of Windward chain. **Neighbors:** St. Lucia to N, Barbados to E, Grenada to S. **Topography:** St. Vincent is volcanic, with a ridge of thickly wooded mountains running its length. **Capital:** Kingstown, 26,000.

Government: Type: Constitutional monarchy. **Head of state:** Queen Elizabeth II, represented by Sir Frederick Ballantyne; b. July 5, 1936; in office: Sept. 2, 2002. **Head of gov.:** Prime Min.

Ralph Gonsalves; b. Aug. 8, 1946; in office: Mar. 29, 2001. **Local divisions:** 6 parishes. **Defense budget/Active troops:** NA.

Economy: Industries: food proc., cement, furniture, clothing, starch. **Chief crops:** bananas, coconuts, sweet potatoes, spices. **Natural resources:** hydropower. **Arable land:** 18%. **Livestock:** cattle: 5,100; chickens: 130,000; goats: 7,300; pigs: 9,180; sheep: 12,000. **Fish catch:** 5,250 metric tons. **Electricity prod.:** 129 mil kWh. **Labor force** (1980 est.): agric. 26%, industry 17%, services 57%.

Finance: Monetary unit: East Caribbean Dollar (XCD) (Oct. 2009: 2.70 = $1 U.S.). **GDP:** $1.1 bil; **per capita GDP:** $10,200; **GDP growth:** 0.9%. **Imports** (2006): $578 mil; Singapore 27.3%, Trinidad and Tobago 13.3%, U.S. 12.2%, China 7.3%, Italy 7.2%, Norway 5.2%. **Exports** (2006): $193 mil; Greece 38.8%, France 23.1%, Italy 9.2%. **Tourism:** $111 mil. **Budget** (2000 est.): $85.8 mil. **Intl. reserves less gold:** $54 mil. **Gold:** NA. **Consumer prices:** 10.1%.

Transport: Motor vehicles: 14,000 pass. cars; 5,000 comm. vehicles. **Civil aviation:** 5 airports. **Chief port:** Kingstown.

Communications: TV sets: 230 per 1,000 pop. **Radios:** 688 per 1,000 pop. **Telephone lines:** 22,800. **Internet:** 66,000 users.

Health: Life expect.: 72.4 male; 76.3 female. **Births** (per 1,000 pop.): 15.8. **Deaths** (per 1,000 pop.): 6. **Natural inc.:** 0.99%. **Infant mortality** (per 1,000 live births): 13.6. **HIV rate:** NA.

Education: Compulsory: ages 5-15. **Literacy:** 96%.

Major intl. organizations: UN (FAO, IBRD, ILO, IMF, IMO, WHO, WTO), Caricom, the Commonwealth, OAS, OECS.

Embassy: 3216 New Mexico Ave. NW 20016; 364-6730.

Website: www.gov.vc

Columbus landed on St. Vincent on Jan. 22, 1498 (St. Vincent's Day). Britain and France both laid claim to the island in the 17th and 18th centuries; the Treaty of Versailles, 1783, finally ceded it to Britain. Associated State status was granted 1969; independence was attained Oct. 27, 1979.

Samoa *(formerly* Western Samoa*)*
Independent State of Samoa

People: Population: 219,998. **Age distrib.** (%): <15: 37.6; 65+: 5.7. **Pop. density:** 194.2 per sq mi, 75 per sq km. **Urban:** 22.4%. **Ethnic groups:** Samoan 93%, Euronesians (mixed European, Polynesian) 7%. **Principal languages:** Samoan (Polynesian), English. **Chief religions:** Congregationalist 35%, Roman Catholic 20%, Methodist 15%, Latter-Day Saints 13%.

Geography: Total area: 1,137 sq mi, 2,944 sq km; **Land area:** 1,133 sq mi, 2,934 sq km. **Location:** In S Pacific O. **Neighbors:** Nearest are Fiji to SW, Tonga to S. **Topography:** Main islands, Savaii (659 sq mi) and Upolu (432 sq mi), both ruggedly mountainous, and small islands Manono and Apolima. **Capital:** Apia, 43,000.

Government: Type: Constitutional monarchy. **Head of state:** Tuiatua Tupua Tamasese Efi; b. Mar. 1, 1938; in office: June 20, 2007. **Head of gov.:** Prime Min. Tuilaepa Sailele Malielegaoi; b. Apr. 14, 1945; in office: Nov. 23, 1998. **Local divisions:** 11 districts. **Defense budget/Active troops:** NA.

Economy: Industries: food proc., building materials, auto parts. **Chief crops:** coconuts, bananas, taro, yams, coffee, cocoa. **Natural resources:** hardwood forests, fish, hydropower. **Arable land:** 21%. **Livestock:** cattle: 29,000; chickens: 450,000; pigs: 202,000. **Fish catch:** 4,609 metric tons. **Electricity prod.:** 109 mil kWh. **Labor force:** NA.

Finance: Monetary unit: Tala (WST) (Oct. 2009: 2.63 = $1 U.S.). **GDP:** $1 bil; **per capita GDP:** $4,800; **GDP growth:** 0.3%. **Imports** (2006): $324 mil; New Zealand 20.8%, Fiji 18.9%, Singapore 18.8%, Australia 6.6%, China 4.4%, U.S. 4%. **Exports** (2006): $131 mil; Australia 36.9%, American Samoa 35.3%, U.S. 2.9%. **Tourism** (2005): $77 mil. **Budget** (FY04/05 est.): $78.1 mil. **Intl. reserves less gold:** $57 mil. **Gold:** NA. **Consumer prices:** 11.5%.

Transport: Motor vehicles: 9,600 pass. cars; 1,200 comm. vehicles. **Civil aviation:** 228.7 mil pass.-mi; 2 airports. **Chief port:** Apia.

Communications: TV sets: 56 per 1,000 pop. **Radios:** 1,035 per 1,000 pop. **Telephone lines:** 28,800. **Internet:** 9,000 users.

Health: Life expect.: 68.8 male; 74.5 female. **Births** (per 1,000 pop.): 28.2. **Deaths** (per 1,000 pop.): 5.8. **Natural inc.:** 2.24%. **Infant mortality** (per 1,000 live births): 25. **HIV rate:** NA.

Education: Compulsory: ages 5-14. **Literacy:** 98.7%.

Major intl. organizations: UN (FAO, IBRD, ILO, IMF, IMO, WHO), the Commonwealth.

Embassy: 800 Second Ave., Ste. 400J, New York, NY 10017; (212) 599-6196.

Website: www.govt.ws

Samoa (formerly known as Western Samoa to distinguish it from American Samoa, a small U.S. territory) was a German colony, 1899 to 1914, when New Zealand landed troops and took over. It became a New Zealand mandate under the League of Nations and, in 1945, a New Zealand UN Trusteeship.

An elected local government took office in Oct. 1959, and the country became fully independent Jan. 1, 1962. Malietoa Tanumafili II, Samoa's head of state since independence, died May 11, 2007, and was succeeded by Tuiatua Tupua Tamasese Efi. An earthquake and tsunami Sept. 29, 2009, left at least 135 people dead in Samoa.

San Marino
Republic of San Marino

People: Population: 30,324. **Age distrib.** (%): <15: 16.8; 65+: 17.4. **Pop. density:** 1,283.3 per sq mi, 495.5 per sq km. **Urban:** 94.1%. **Ethnic groups:** Sammarinese, Italian. **Principal language:** Italian. **Chief religion:** Roman Catholic.

Geography: Total area: 24 sq mi, 61 sq km; **Land area:** 24 sq mi, 61 sq km. **Location:** In N central Italy near Adriatic coast. **Neighbors:** Completely surrounded by Italy. **Topography:** The country lies on slopes of Mt. Titano. **Capital:** San Marino, 4,402.

Government: Type: Republic. **Heads of state and gov.:** Two co-regents appt. every 6 months. **Local divisions:** 9 castelli. **Defense budget/Active troops:** NA.

Economy: Industries: tourism, banking, textiles, electronics, ceramics, cement, wine. **Chief crops:** wheat, grapes, corn, olives. **Natural resources:** building stone. **Arable land:** 17%. **Labor force** (2008 est.): agric. 0.1%, industry 37.7%, services 62.2%.

Finance: Monetary unit: Euro (EUR) (Oct. 2009: 0.68 = $1 U.S.). **GDP** (2007): $1.7 bil; **per capita GDP** (2007): $41,900; **GDP growth** (2007): 4.3%. **Imports** (2007): $3.7 bil. **Exports** (2007): $4.6 bil. **Intl. reserves less gold:** $248 mil. **Tourism:** NA. **Budget** (2004): $672.3 mil. **Intl. reserves less gold:** $459 mil. **Gold:** NA. **Consumer prices:** NA.

Transport: NA.

Communications: TV sets: 875 per 1,000 pop. **Radios:** 1,346 per 1,000 pop. **Telephone lines:** 21,300. **Internet:** 16,000 users.

Health: Life expect.: 78.4 male; 85.6 female. **Births** (per 1,000 pop.): 9.7. **Deaths** (per 1,000 pop.): 8.4. **Natural inc.:** 0.14%. **Infant mortality** (per 1,000 live births): 5.4. **HIV rate:** NA.

Education: Compulsory: ages 6-14. **Literacy:** 96%.

Major intl. organizations: UN (FAO, IBRD, ILO, IMF, IMO, WHO), OSCE.

Honorary Consulate: 1899 L St. NW, Ste. 500, 20036; 223-3517. **Website:** www.visitsanmarino.com or www.esteri.sm

San Marino claims to be the oldest state in Europe and to have been founded in the 4th cent. It has had a treaty of friendship with Italy since 1862. A Communist-led coalition ruled 1947-57; a similar coalition ruled 1978-86. The Pact for San Marino, a center-right coalition, won parliamentary elections Nov. 9, 2008.

São Tomé and Príncipe
Democratic Republic of São Tomé and Príncipe

People: Population: 212,679. **Age distrib.** (%): <15: 46.9; 65+: 3.5. **Pop. density:** 550.3 per sq mi, 212.5 per sq km. **Urban:** 58.1%. **Ethnic groups:** Descendants of Angolan slaves, freed slaves, & contract laborers fr. Angola, Mozambique, Cape Verde; Europeans (primarily Portuguese). **Principal language:** Portuguese (official). **Chief religions:** Catholic 70%, Evangelical 3%, none 19%.

Geography: Total area: 387 sq mi, 1,001 sq km; **Land area:** 386 sq mi, 1,001 sq km. **Location:** In Gulf of Guinea about 125 miles off W central Africa. **Neighbors:** Gabon, Equatorial Guinea to E. **Topography:** São Tomé and Príncipe islands, part of an extinct volcano chain, are both covered by lush forests and croplands. **Capital:** São Tomé, 58,000.

Government: Type: Republic. **Head of state:** Pres. Fradique Melo de Menezes; b. Mar. 21, 1942; in office: Sept. 3, 2001. **Head of gov.:** Prime Min. Joaquím Rafael Branco; b. 1953; in office: June 22, 2008. **Local divisions:** 2 provinces. **Defense budget/Active troops:** NA.

Economy: Industries: light constr., textiles, soap, beer, fish proc., timber. **Chief crops:** cocoa, coconuts, palm kernels, copra, cinnamon, pepper, coffee, bananas, papayas, beans. **Natural resources:** fish, hydropower. **Arable land:** 8%. **Livestock:** cattle: 4,800; chickens: 420,000; goats: 5,200; pigs: 2,620; sheep: 3,000. **Fish catch** (est.): 4,150 metric tons. **Electricity prod.:** 18 mil kWh. **Labor force:** Pop. mainly engaged in subsistence agric. & fishing; shortage of skilled workers.

Finance: Monetary unit: Dobra (STD) (Oct. 2009: 15,525.80 = $1 U.S.). **GDP:** $276.5 mil; **per capita GDP:** $1,300; **GDP growth:** 5.5%. **Imports:** $88 mil; Portugal 55.9%, Belgium 9.6%, Japan 9.3%. **Exports:** $8 mil; Japan 75.5%, Belgium 7.5%, Netherlands 6.2%. **Tourism:** NA. **Budget:** $57.3 mil. **Intl. reserves less gold:** $25 mil. **Gold:** NA. **Consumer prices:** NA.

Transport: Civil aviation: 11.2 mil pass.-mi; 2 airports. **Chief port:** São Tomé.

Communications: TV sets: 229 per 1,000 pop. **Radios:** 319 per 1,000 pop. **Telephone lines:** 7,700. **Internet:** 24,800 users.

Health: Life expect.: 66.3 male; 69.7 female. **Births** (per 1,000 pop.): 39.1. **Deaths** (per 1,000 pop.): 6. **Natural inc.:** 3.31%. **Infant mortality** (per 1,000 live births): 38.4. **HIV rate:** NA.

Education: Compulsory: ages 7-12. **Literacy:** 87.9%.

Major intl. organizations: UN (FAO, IBRD, ILO, IMF, IMO, WHO), AU.

Permanent UN mission: 460 Park Ave., 11th Fl., New York, NY 10022; (212) 317-0533.

Website: www.gov.st

The islands were discovered in 1471 by the Portuguese, who brought the first settlers—convicts and exiled Jews. Sugar planting was replaced by the slave trade as the chief economic activity until coffee and cocoa were introduced in the 19th cent.

Portugal agreed, 1974, to turn the colony over to the Gabon-based Movement for the Liberation of São Tomé and Príncipe, which proclaimed as first president its East German-trained leader, Manuel Pinto da Costa. Independence came July 12, 1975. Democratic reforms were instituted in 1987. In 1991 Miguel Trovoada won the first free presidential election following da Costa's withdrawal. A military coup that ousted Trovoada Aug. 15, 1995, was reversed a week later after Angolan mediation. Trovoada defeated da Costa in a presidential runoff election, July 21, 1996.

Fradique de Menezes, a wealthy cocoa exporter, easily beat da Costa in the presidential election of July 29, 2001. The government was ousted in a military coup July 16, 2003, but was restored to power a week later and reelected July 30, 2006. The country, long one of the world's poorest, has sought to develop large oil deposits in the Gulf of Guinea.

Saudi Arabia
Kingdom of Saudi Arabia

People: Population: 28,686,633. **Age distrib.** (%): <15: 38; 65+: 2.5. **Pop. density:** 34.6 per sq mi, 13.3 per sq km. **Urban:** 81%. **Ethnic groups:** Arab 90%, Afro-Asian 10%. **Principal language:** Arabic. **Chief religion:** Muslim 100%.

Geography: Total area: 830,000 sq mi, 2,149,690 sq km; **Land area:** 830,000 sq mi, 2,149,690 sq km. **Location:** Occupies most of Arabian Peninsula in Mid-East. **Neighbors:** Kuwait, Iraq, Jordan on N; Yemen, Oman on S; United Arab Emirates, Qatar on E. **Topography:** Bordered by Red Sea on W. The highlands on W, up to 9,000 ft, slope as arid, barren desert to the Persian Gulf on E. **Capital:** Riyadh, 4,465,000. **Cities (urban aggr.):** Jiddah, 3,012,000; Mecca (Makkah), 1,385,000; Medina, 1,010,000; Ad-Dammam, 822,000.

Government: Type: Monarchy with council of ministers. **Head of state and gov.:** King Abdullah bin Abdul Aziz; b. Aug. 1, 1924; in office: Aug. 1, 2005. **Local divisions:** 13 provinces. **Defense budget:** $35.4 bil. **Active troops:** 221,500.

Economy: Industries: oil prod. & refining, petrochems., cement, fertilizers, plastics, metals, constr. **Chief crops:** wheat, barley, tomatoes, melons, dates, citrus. **Natural resources:** oil, nat. gas, iron ore, gold, copper. **Crude oil reserves:** 266.7 bil bbls (incl. half of Neutral Zone reserves). **Arable land:** 2%. **Livestock:** cattle: 372,000; chickens: 145 mil; goats: 2.2 mil; sheep: 7 mil. **Fish catch** (est.): 88,410 metric tons. **Electricity prod.:** 169 bil kWh. **Labor force** (2005 est.): agric. 6.7%, industry 21.4%, services 71.9%.

Finance: Monetary unit: Riyal (SAR) (Oct. 2009: 3.75 = $1 U.S.). **GDP:** $576.5 bil; **per capita GDP:** $20,500; **GDP growth:** 4.2%. **Imports:** $108.3 bil; U.S. 12.4%, China 10.6%, Japan 7.8%, Germany 7.5%, Italy 4.9%, S. Korea 4.7%, UK 4.2%. **Exports:** $309.8 bil; U.S. 18.5%, Japan 16.5%, China 10.2%, S. Korea 8.6%, Singapore 4.8%. **Tourism:** $5.2 bil. **Budget:** $118.3 bil. **Intl. reserves less gold:** $19.7 bil. **Gold:** 4.6 mil oz t. **Consumer prices:** 9.9%.

Transport: Railroad: Length: 865 mi. **Motor vehicles:** 9.95 mil pass. cars and comm. vehicles. **Civil aviation:** 14.8 bil pass.-mi; 80 airports. **Chief ports:** Ad Dammam, Al Jubayl, Jiddah, Yanbu' al Sinaiyah.

Communications: TV sets: 263 per 1,000 pop. **Radios:** 321 per 1,000 pop. **Telephone lines:** 4.1 mil. **Internet:** 7.7 mil users.

Health: Life expect.: 74 male; 78.2 female. **Births** (per 1,000 pop.): 28.9. **Deaths** (per 1,000 pop.): 2.5. **Natural inc.:** 2.64%. **Infant mortality** (per 1,000 live births): 11.9. **HIV rate:** NA.

Education: Compulsory: ages 6-11. **Literacy:** 85%.

Major intl. organizations: UN (FAO, IBRD, ILO, IMF, IMO, WHO, WTO), AL, OPEC.

Embassy: 601 New Hampshire Ave. NW 20037; 342-3800.

Website: www.saudi.gov.sa

Before Muhammad, Arabia was divided among numerous warring tribes and small kingdoms. It was united for the first time by Muhammad, in the early 7th cent. His successors conquered the entire Near East and North Africa, bringing Islam and the Arabic language. But Arabia itself soon returned to its former status.

Nejd, in central Arabia, long an independent state and center of the Wahhabi sect, fell under Turkish rule in the 18th cent. In 1913 Ibn Saud, founder of the Saudi dynasty, overthrew the Turks and captured the Turkish province of Hasa in eastern Arabia; he took the Hejaz region in western Arabia in 1925 and most of Asir, in SW Arabia, by 1926. The discovery of oil in the 1930s transformed the nation.

The Hejaz contains the holy cities of Islam—Medina, where the Mosque of the Prophet enshrines the tomb of Muhammad, and Mecca, his birthplace. More than 2 mil Muslims make pilgrimage to Mecca annually. Stampedes and other disasters have killed thousands of pilgrims in recent decades.

Ibn Saud reigned until his death, Nov. 1953. Subsequent kings have been sons of Ibn Saud. The king exercises authority together with a Council of Ministers. The Islamic religious code is the law of the land. Alcohol and public entertainments are restricted, and women have an inferior legal status.

Saudi Arabia has often allied itself with the U.S. and other Western nations, and billions of dollars of advanced arms have been purchased from Britain, France, and the U.S.; however, Western support for Israel has often strained relations. Saudi units fought against Israel in the 1948 and 1973 Arab-Israeli wars. Beginning with the 1967 Arab-Israeli war, Saudi Arabia provided large annual financial gifts to Egypt; aid was later extended to Syria, Jordan, and Palestinian groups.

King Faisal played a leading role in the 1973-74 Arab oil embargo against the U.S. and other nations. Crown Prince Khalid was proclaimed king on Mar. 25, 1975, after the assassination of Faisal. Fahd became king on June 13, 1982, following Khalid's death.

After Iraq invaded Kuwait, Aug. 2, 1990, Saudi Arabia accepted the Kuwait royal family and more than 400,000 Kuwaiti refugees. King Fahd invited Western and Arab troops to deploy on Saudi soil. During the 1991 Persian Gulf War, 28 U.S. soldiers were killed when an Iraqi missile hit their barracks in Dhahran, Feb. 25, 1991. Islamic extremists were blamed for truck bombs that killed 7 (5 from the U.S.) at a military training center in Riyadh, Nov. 13, 1995, and 19 Americans at a base in Dhahran, June 25, 1996.

The presence of 15 Saudis among the 19 al-Qaeda hijackers who took part in the Sept. 11, 2001, attacks on the U.S. raised new tensions between the U.S. and Saudi governments, and some blamed the Saudi government for allowing Muslim extremism to flourish in Saudi Arabia. Policy differences over the Israeli-Palestinian dispute and Iraq (where Saudi jihadists have supported the Sunni cause) were further irritants. The U.S. completed a pullout of its combat forces from Saudi Arabia in Sept. 2003.

Alarmed at guerrilla attacks that killed more than 100 people, mostly foreigners, in Saudi Arabia during 2003-04, the Saudi government stepped up antiterrorist activities in cooperation with the U.S. Islamist candidates on a "golden list" circulated by conservative clerics fared well in municipal council elections, Feb.-Apr. 2005; women were barred from voting in the elections, the country's first since 1963.

King Fahd, on the throne since 1982, died Aug. 1, 2005. He was succeeded by his half-brother, Abdullah, who had in effect ruled the Kingdom since Fahd suffered a stroke in Nov. 1995. Guards thwarted an attack by suicide bombers, Feb. 24, 2006, at the huge Abqaiq oil and gas facility. Security officials, Apr. 27, 2007, announced the arrest of 172 men accused of plotting attacks on oil installations, military posts, and other targets.

King Abdullah conferred at the Vatican Nov. 6, 2007, with Benedict XVI, in the first official meeting between a pope and a Saudi monarch. To combat Islamic extremism, the Saudis disclosed a program Mar. 20, 2008, to retrain 40,000 Muslim clerics. Abdullah sponsored a global interfaith conference in Spain, July 16-18.

Soaring oil revenues in 2004-08 provided funds for more than $500 bil in investments, including plans to diversify the economy and redevelop Mecca. Al-Qaeda claimed responsibility for a suicide attack in Jiddah, Aug. 27, 2009, that slightly injured Deputy Interior Min. Muhammad bin Nayef, the royal family member in charge of Saudi counterterrorism efforts.

Senegal
Republic of Senegal

People: Population: 13,711,597. **Age distrib.** (%): <15: 42.2; 65+: 3. **Pop. density:** 185 per sq mi, 71.4 per sq km. **Urban:** 41.6%. **Ethnic groups:** Wolof 43%, Pular 24%, Serer 15%. **Principal languages:** French (official), Wolof, Pulaar, Jola, Mandinka. **Chief religions:** Muslim 94%, Christian (mostly Roman Catholic) 5%, indigenous beliefs 1%.

Geography: Total area: 75,749 sq mi, 196,190 sq km; **Land area:** 74,132 sq mi, 192,000 sq km. **Location:** At W extreme of Africa. **Neighbors:** Mauritania on N, Mali on E, Guinea and Guinea-Bissau on S; surrounds Gambia on three sides. **Topography:** Low rolling plains cover most of Senegal, rising somewhat in SE. Swamp and jungles are in SW. **Capital:** Dakar, 2,604,000.

Government: Type: Republic. **Head of state:** Pres. Abdoulaye Wade; b. May 29, 1926; in office: Apr. 1, 2000. **Head of gov.:** Prime Min. Souleymane Ndéné Ndiaye; b. Aug. 6, 1958; in office: Apr. 30, 2009. **Local divisions:** 11 regions. **Defense budget:** $193 mil. **Active troops:** 13,620.

Economy: Industries: agric. & fish proc., phosphate mining, fertilizer prod., oil refining. **Chief crops:** peanuts, millet, corn, sorghum, rice, cotton, tomatoes, green vegetables. **Natural resources:** fish, phosphates, iron ore. **Arable land:** 13%. **Livestock:** cattle: 3.2 mil; chickens: 34.9 mil; goats: 4.4 mil; pigs: 319,360; sheep: 5.1 mil. **Fish catch:** 421,517 metric tons. **Electricity prod.:** 2.3 bil kWh. **Labor force** (2007 est.): agric. 77.5%, industry & services 22.5%.

Finance: Monetary unit: CFA BCEAO Franc (XOF) (Oct. 2009: 444.97 = $1 U.S.). **GDP:** $22 bil; **per capita GDP:** $1,600; **GDP growth:** 4.8%. **Imports:** $4.3 bil; France 20%, UK 15.4%, China 7.5%, Belgium 4.6%, Thailand 4.5%, Netherlands 4.1%. **Exports:** $2 bil; Mali 19.5%, India 5.9%, France 5.5%, The Gambia 5.4%, Italy 4.9%. **Tourism:** NA. **Budget:** $3.8 bil. **Intl. reserves less gold:** $1.04 bil. **Gold:** NA. **Consumer prices:** 5.8%.

Transport: Railroad: Length: 563 mi. **Motor vehicles:** 147,000 pass. cars; 46,000 comm. vehicles. **Civil aviation:** 528.8 mil pass.-mi (incl. Air Afrique traffic apportionment); 10 airports. **Chief port:** Dakar.

Communications: TV sets: 41 per 1,000 pop. **Radios:** 141 per 1,000 pop. **Telephone lines:** 237,800. **Daily newspaper circ.** (2004): 8.7 per 1,000 pop. **Internet:** 1.02 mil users.

Health: Life expect.: 55.7 male; 58.5 female. **Births** (per 1,000 pop.): 36.5. **Deaths** (per 1,000 pop.): 10.7. **Natural inc.:** 2.58%. **Infant mortality** (per 1,000 live births): 58.9. **HIV rate:** 1%.
Education: Compulsory: ages 7-12. **Literacy:** 42.6%.
Major intl. organizations: UN and all of its specialized agencies, AU.
Embassy: 2112 Wyoming Ave. NW 20008; 234-0540.
Website: www.gouv.sn

Portuguese settlers arrived in the 15th cent., but French control grew from the 17th cent. The last independent Muslim state was subdued in 1893. Senegal became an independent republic Aug. 20, 1960, but French political and economic influence remained strong. Senegambia, a loose confederation of Senegal and The Gambia, was established in 1982 but dissolved 7 years later.

Forty years of Socialist Party rule ended when Abdoulaye Wade, leader of the Senegalese Democratic Party, won a presidential runoff election Mar. 19, 2000. A Senegalese ferry capsized off the coast of The Gambia Sept. 26, 2002, killing at least 1,863 people. A peace accord signed Dec. 30, 2004, with separatists in Cassamance Province, S Senegal, sought to end a 22-year insurgency. Pres. Wade was reelected Feb. 25, 2007.

Serbia
Republic of Serbia

People: Population: 7,379,339. **Age distrib.** (%): <15: 15.4; 65+: 16.8. **Pop. density:** 246.7 per sq mi, 95.2 per sq km. **Urban:** 51.5%. **Ethnic groups:** Serb 83%, Hungarian 4%, Romany 1%. **Principal languages:** Serbian (official), Hungarian. **Chief religions:** Serbian Orthodox 85%, Catholic 6%, Muslim 3%.

Geography: Total area: 29,913 sq mi, 77,474 sq km; **Land area:** 29,913 sq mi, 77,474 sq km. **Location:** On Balkan Peninsula in SE Europe. **Neighbors:** Croatia, Bosnia and Herzegovina on W; Hungary on N; Romania, Bulgaria on E; Montenegro, Albania, Macedonia on S. **Topography:** Terrain varies widely, with fertile plains drained by Danube and other rivers in N, limestone basins in E, ancient mountains and hills in SE, and very high coastline in Montenegro along SW. **Capital:** Belgrade, 1,099,000.

Government: Type: Republic. **Head of state:** Pres. Boris Tadic; b. Jan. 15, 1958; in office: July 11, 2004. **Head of gov.:** Prime Min. Mirko Cvetkovic; b. Aug. 16, 1950; in office: July 7, 2008. **Local divisions:** 1 republic with 1 autonomous province. **Defense budget:** $985 mil. **Active troops:** 24,257.

Economy: Industries: sugar, agric. machinery, elec. & comm. equip., paper & pulp, transp. equip. **Chief crops:** wheat, maize, sugar beets, sunflower. **Natural resources:** oil, gas, coal, antimony, copper, zinc, gold, pyrite, limestone, marble, salt. **Crude oil reserves:** 77.5 mil bbls. **Arable land:** NA. **Livestock:** cattle: 1.1 mil; chickens: 15.7 mil; goats: 149,000; pigs: 3.8 mil; sheep: 1.6 mil. **Fish catch:** 9,159 metric tons. **Labor force** (2002): agric. 30%, industry 46%, services 24% (not incl. Kosovo & Montenegro).

Finance: Monetary unit: Dinar (RSD) (Oct. 2009: 63.61 = $1 U.S.). **GDP:** $80.3 bil; **per capita GDP:** $10,800; **GDP growth:** 5.4%. **Imports:** (2007) $18.4 bil. **Exports:** $8.8 bil. **Tourism:** $531 mil. **Budget:** $9.8 bil. **Intl. reserves less gold:** $7.22 bil. **Gold:** 410,000 oz t. **Consumer prices:** 12.9%.

Transport: Railroad: Length: 2,100 mi. **Motor vehicles** (incl. Montenegro): 1.6 mil pass. cars; 158,400 comm. cars. **Civil aviation:** 726.4 mil pass.-mi (incl. Montenegro); 10 airports.

Communications: TV sets: 277 per 1,000 pop. **Radios:** 296 per 1,000 pop. **Telephone lines:** 3.1 mil. **Internet:** 2.4 mil users.

Health: Life expect.: 72.7 male; 78.1 female. **Births** (per 1,000 pop.): 12.1. **Deaths** (per 1,000 pop.): 10.8. **Natural inc.:** 0.13%. **Infant mortality** (per 1,000 live births): 11.9. **HIV rate:** 0.1%.
Education: Compulsory: ages 7-14. **Literacy** (incl. Montenegro): 96.4%.
Major intl. organizations: UN (FAO, IBRD, ILO, IMF, IMO, WHO), OSCE.
Embassy: 2134 Kalorama Rd. NW 20008; 332-0333.
Website: www.gov.yu

Serbia, which had since 1389 been a vassal principality of Turkey, was established as an independent kingdom by the Treaty of Berlin, 1878. After the Balkan wars, Serbia's boundaries were enlarged by the annexation of Old Serbia and Macedonia, 1913.

When the Austro-Hungarian empire collapsed after WWI, the Kingdom of Serbs, Croats, and Slovenes was formed from the former provinces of Croatia, Dalmatia, Bosnia, Herzegovina, Slovenia, Vojvodina, and the independent state of Montenegro. The name became Yugoslavia in 1929.

Nazi Germany invaded in 1941. After the Nazis were driven out in 1945, Yugoslavia became a federal republic, headed by Josip Broz, a Communist, known as Marshal Tito. He rejected Stalin's policy of dictating to all Communist nations, and he accepted economic and military aid from the West. Pres. Tito died May 4, 1980. Yugoslavia held together for a decade, then broke apart. Croatia and Slovenia declared independence in 1991. In Croatia, fighting began between Croats and ethnic Serbs. Serbia sent arms and medical supplies to the Serb rebels in Croatia. Croatian forces clashed with Yugoslav army units and their Serb supporters.

The republics of Serbia and Montenegro proclaimed a new "Federal Republic of Yugoslavia" Apr. 17, 1992. Serbia, under Pres. Slobodan Milosevic, was the main arms supplier to ethnic

Serb fighters in Bosnia and Herzegovina. The UN imposed sanctions May 30 on the newly reconstituted Yugoslavia as a means of ending the bloodshed in Bosnia.

A peace agreement initialed in Dayton, OH, Nov. 21, 1995, was signed in Paris, Dec. 14, by Milosevic and leaders of Bosnia and Croatia. In May 1996, a UN tribunal in the Netherlands began trying suspected war criminals from the former Yugoslavia. The UN lifted sanctions against Yugoslavia Oct. 1, 1996, after elections were held in Bosnia. Mass protests erupted when Milosevic refused to accept opposition victories in local elections Nov. 17; non-Communist governments took office in Belgrade and other cities in Feb. 1997. Barred from running for a 3rd term as Serbian president, Milosevic had himself inaugurated as president of Yugoslavia on July 23, 1997.

Efforts by Serbia to suppress a secessionist movement in Kosovo province led in Mar.-June 1999 to a war with the U.S. and its NATO allies; they accused Milosevic of pursuing a policy of ethnic cleansing against the Kosovars (ethnic Albanians), who were predominantly Muslim. NATO stationed a multinational force in Kosovo, which was placed under UN administration.

Defeated in a presidential election Sept. 24, 2000, by opposition leader Vojislav Kostunica, Milosevic initially refused to accept the result. A rising tide of mass demonstrations forced him to resign Oct. 6, and Kostunica was sworn in the next day. Charged with corruption and abuse of power, Milosevic surrendered to Serbian authorities Apr. 1, 2001. He was extradited June 28 to The Hague, Netherlands, where a UN tribunal had indicted him for war crimes. His trial began Feb. 12, 2002, but proceeded slowly. He was found dead in his prison cell Mar. 11, 2006, before a verdict was reached.

A pact to reconstitute Yugoslavia as a new union of Serbia and Montenegro took effect Feb. 4, 2003. Zoran Djindjic, premier of the Republic of Serbia, was assassinated Mar. 12 in Belgrade; the murder triggered a roundup of more than 4,500 people associated with organized crime and the Milosevic regime. Serbia's union with Montenegro disintegrated in 2006, as Montenegrins voted support for separation in a referendum May 21, and Montenegro became an independent republic June 3.

After years of fruitless negotiations, Kosovo unilaterally declared independence from Serbia Feb. 17, 2008; the new country was immediately recognized by the U.S. and most European allies, but not by Serbia and Russia. Following parliamentary elections in Serbia May 11, a pro-Western government under Mirko Cvetkovic took office July 7. Serbia, seeking EU membership, met a key requirement of European leaders July 21 by arresting former Bosnian Serb leader Radovan Karadzic, who was then extradited to the International Criminal Court in the Netherlands on charges of genocide and crimes against humanity. With trade and investment down because of the global recession, the IMF May 15, 2009, increased Serbia's standby credit line to about $4 bil.

Vojvodina is a nominally autonomous province in northern Serbia (8,304 sq mi), with a population (2008 est.) of 1,979,389, mostly Serbian. The capital is Novi Sad.

Seychelles
Republic of Seychelles

People: Population: 87,476. **Age distrib.** (%): <15: 22.8; 65+: 7.1. **Pop. density:** 497.9 per sq mi, 192.3 per sq km. **Urban:** 52.9%. **Ethnic groups:** Mixed French, African, Indian, Chinese, and Arab. **Principal languages:** English, Creole (both official). **Chief religions:** Roman Catholic 82%, Anglican 6%.

Geography: Total area: 176 sq mi, 455 sq km; **Land area:** 176 sq mi, 455 sq km. **Location:** In Indian O. 700 miles NE of Madagascar. **Neighbors:** Nearest are Madagascar on SW, Somalia on NW. **Topography:** A group of 86 islands, about half of them composed of coral, the other half granite, the latter predominantly mountainous. **Capital** (2004): Victoria, 23,200.

Government: Type: Republic. **Head of state and gov.:** Pres. James Michel, b. Aug. 18, 1944; in office: Apr. 14, 2004. **Local divisions:** 23 districts. **Defense budget:** $11 mil. **Active troops:** 200.

Economy: Industries: fishing, tourism, coconuts & vanilla proc., coir (coconut fiber) rope, boat building. **Chief crops:** coconuts, cinnamon, vanilla, sweet potatoes, cassava, bananas. **Natural resources:** fish, copra, cinnamon trees. **Arable land:** 2%. **Livestock:** cattle: 1,420; chickens: 575,000; goats: 5,200; pigs: 18,700. **Fish catch:** 66,239 metric tons. **Electricity prod.:** 208 mil kWh. **Labor force** (2006): agric. 3%, industry 23%, services 74%.

Finance: Monetary unit: Rupee (SCR) (Oct. 2009: 9.80 = $1 U.S.). **GDP:** 1.7 bil; **per capita GDP:** $19,800; **GDP growth:** 0%. **Imports:** $882 mil; Saudi Arabia 18.3%, Singapore 12.9%, France 10.8%, Spain 8.5%, Germany 7.4%, South Africa 5.7%. **Exports:** $475 mil; UK 22.1%, France 20%, Mauritius 10.5%, Japan 8.3%, Italy 8.1%, Netherlands 6.3%, Spain 4%. **Tourism:** $228 mil. **Budget:** $285 mil. **Intl. reserves less gold:** $41 mil. **Gold:** NA. **Consumer prices:** 37%.

Transport: Motor vehicles: 6,200 pass. cars; 2,400 comm. vehicles. **Civil aviation:** 781.7 mil pass.-mi; 8 airports. **Chief port:** Victoria.

Communications: TV sets: 214 per 1,000 pop. **Radios:** 560 per 1,000 pop. **Telephone lines:** 23,200. **Internet:** 32,000 users.

Health: Life expect.: 67.3 male; 78.1 female. **Births** (per 1,000 pop.): 15.6. **Deaths** (per 1,000 pop.): 6.2. **Natural inc.:** 0.94%. **Infant mortality** (per 1,000 live births): 14.4. **HIV rate:** NA.

Education: Compulsory: ages 6-15. **Literacy:** 91.8%.

Major intl. organizations: UN (FAO, IBRD, ILO, IMF, IMO, WHO), the Commonwealth, AU.

Embassy: 800 Second Ave., Ste. 400C, New York, NY 10017; (212) 972-1785.

Website: www.egov.sc

The islands were occupied by France in 1768 and seized by Britain in 1794. Ruled as part of Mauritius from 1814, Seychelles became a separate colony in 1903. Independence was declared June 29, 1976. The first president was ousted in a coup a year later by a socialist leader, France Albert René. A new constitution, approved June 1993, provided for a multiparty state. After nearly 27 years in power, Pres. René resigned Apr. 14, 2004, and was succeeded by Vice Pres. James Michel, who won a full 5-year term in elections July 28-30, 2006.

Sierra Leone
Republic of Sierra Leone

People: Population: 6,440,053. **Age distrib.** (%): <15: 44.5; 65+: 3.2. **Pop. density:** 232.9 per sq mi, 89.9 per sq km. **Urban:** 36.8%. **Ethnic groups:** 20 African ethnic groups 90% (Temne 30%, Mende 30%, other 30%), Creole (Krio; descendants of freed Jamaican slaves) 10%. **Principal languages:** English (official), Mende (principal vernacular in S), Temne (principal vernacular in N), Krio (Eng.-based Creole, a lingua franca). **Chief religions:** Muslim 60%, Christian 10%, indigenous beliefs 30%.

Geography: Total area: 27,699 sq mi, 71,740 sq km; **Land area:** 27,653 sq mi, 71,620 sq km. **Location:** On W coast of W Africa. **Neighbors:** Guinea on N and E, Liberia on S. **Topography:** The heavily-indented, 210-mi coastline has mangrove swamps. Behind are wooded hills, rising to a plateau and mountains in E. **Capital:** Freetown, 827,000.

Government: Type: Republic. **Head of state and gov.:** Pres. Ernest Bai Koroma; b. Oct. 2, 1953; in office: Sept. 17, 2007. **Local divisions:** 3 provinces, 1 area. **Defense budget:** $29 mil. **Active troops:** 10,500.

Economy: Industries: diamonds, small-scale mfg. (beverages, textiles), oil refining. **Chief crops:** rice, coffee, cocoa, palm kernels & palm oil, peanuts. **Natural resources:** diamonds, titanium ore, bauxite, iron ore, gold, chromite. **Arable land:** 8%. **Livestock:** cattle: 350,000; chickens: 7.5 mil; goats: 540,000; pigs: 52,000; sheep: 470,000. **Fish catch:** 144,535 metric tons. **Electricity prod.:** 250 mil kWh. **Labor force:** NA.

Finance: Monetary unit: Leone (SLL) (Oct. 2009: 3,555.12 = $1 U.S.). **GDP:** $4.3 bil; **per capita GDP:** $700; **GDP growth:** 5.5%. **Imports** (2006): $560 mil; China 10.5%, Cote d'Ivoire 8.9%, U.S. 7.9%, Belgium 6.7%, UK 6.7%, Thailand 5.2%, India 4.2%. **Exports** (2006): $216 mil; Belgium 41%, U.S. 23.2%, France 5.7%, Netherlands 4.3%. **Tourism:** $22 mil. **Budget** (2000 est.): $351 mil. **Intl. reserves less gold** (2007): $137 mil. **Gold:** NA. **Consumer prices:** 7.1%.

Transport: Motor vehicles: 7,700 pass. cars; 7,700 comm. vehicles. **Civil aviation:** 58.4 mil pass.-mi; 1 airport. **Chief ports:** Freetown, Pepel.

Communications: TV sets: 13 per 1,000 pop. **Radios:** 274 per 1,000 pop. **Telephone lines:** 31,500. **Internet:** 13,900 users.

Health: Life expect.: 38.6 male; 43.3 female. **Births** (per 1,000 pop.): 45.1. **Deaths** (per 1,000 pop.): 22.3. **Natural inc.:** 2.28%. **Infant mortality** (per 1,000 live births): 156.5. **HIV rate:** 1.7%.

Education: Compulsory: ages 6-12. **Literacy:** 38.1%.

Major intl. organizations: UN (FAO, IBRD, ILO, IMF, IMO, WHO, WTO), the Commonwealth, AU.

Embassy: 1701 19th St. NW 20009; 939-9261.

Website: www.statehouse.gov.sl

Freetown was founded in 1787 by the British government as a haven for freed slaves. Full independence arrived Apr. 27, 1961. Sierra Leone declared itself a republic Apr. 19, 1971. A one-party state was established by referendum in 1978.

Mutinous soldiers ousted Pres. Joseph Momoh Apr. 30, 1992. Another coup, Jan. 16, 1996, paved the way for multiparty elections and a return to civilian rule. A peace accord, signed Nov. 30 with the Revolutionary United Front (RUF), brought a temporary halt to a civil war that had claimed over 10,000 lives in 5 years.

A coup on May 25, 1997, was met with widespread international opposition. Armed intervention by Nigeria restored Pres. Ahmad Tejan Kabbah to power on Mar. 10, 1998, but RUF rebels (who funded their operations through illicit diamond sales) mounted a guerrilla counteroffensive, killing thousands of civilians and mutilating thousands more. The Kabbah government signed a power-sharing agreement with the RUF on July 7, 1999. A UN mission (UNAMSIL) was established in Oct. to help maintain the agreement. The accord collapsed in early May 2000, as RUF guerrillas took more than 500 UN peacekeepers hostage. Rebel leader Foday Sankoh was captured in Freetown May 17. The hostages were freed by the end of May, and 233 more UN personnel behind rebel lines were rescued July 15.

A UN-sponsored disarmament program in 2001 reduced the level of violence. On Jan. 16, 2002, the government and the UN signed an agreement creating the Sierra Leone Special Court to try war crimes that had occurred from Nov. 1996 onwards. Government and rebel leaders declared an official end to the war Jan. 18; by then, the death toll had risen to more than 50,000. Kabbah won the May 14 presidential election.

Sankoh, an indicted war criminal, died in UN custody July 29, 2003. UNAMSIL, which ended Dec. 31, 2005, was succeeded by UNIOSIL, a UN mission intended to strengthen political institutions. Opposition leader Ernest Bai Koroma won a presidential runoff vote, Sept. 8, 2007. Under an anti-corruption law signed Sept. 2, 2008, Koroma became Sierra Leone's first head of state to declare all his assets. Three former RUF leaders were convicted of war crimes Feb. 25, 2009.

Singapore
Republic of Singapore

People: Population: 4,657,542. **Age distrib.** (%): <15: 14.4; 65+: 8.9. **Pop. density:** 17,558.9 per sq mi, 6,779.5 per sq km. **Urban:** 100%. **Ethnic groups:** Chinese 77%, Malay 14%, Indian 8%. **Principal languages:** Mandarin, English, Malay, Hokkien, Cantonese, Teochew. **Chief religions:** Buddhist 43%, Muslim 15%, Taoist 9%, none 15%.

Geography: Total area: 269 sq mi, 697 sq km; **Land area:** 265 sq mi, 687 sq km. **Location:** Off tip of Malayan Peninsula in SE Asia. **Neighbors:** Nearest are Malaysia on N, Indonesia on S. **Topography:** Singapore is a flat, formerly swampy island. The nation includes 40 nearby islets. **Capital:** Singapore, 4,436,000.

Government: Type: Republic. **Head of state:** Pres. S. R. Nathan; b. July 3, 1924; in office: Sept. 1, 1999. **Head of gov.:** Prime Min. Lee Hsien Loong; b. Feb. 10, 1952; in office: Aug. 12, 2004. **Defense budget:** $7 bil. **Active troops:** 72,500.

Economy: Industries: electronics, chemicals, financial services, oil drilling equip., oil refining, rubber proc. & rubber products, proc. food & beverages, offshore platform constr., life sciences. **Chief crops:** rubber, copra, fruit, orchids, vegetables. **Natural resources:** fish. **Arable land:** 1%. **Livestock:** cattle: 200; chickens: 2 mil; goats: 600; pigs: 260,000. **Fish catch:** 8,025 metric tons. **Electricity prod.:** 37.1 bil kWh. **Labor force** (2007): industry 22.6%, services 77.4%.

Finance: Monetary unit: Dollar (SGD) (Oct. 2009: 1.40 = $1 U.S.). **GDP:** $237.3 bil; **per capita GDP:** $51,500; **GDP growth:** 1.1%. **Imports:** $219.5 bil; Malaysia 11.9%, U.S. 11.8%, China 10.5%, Japan 8.1%, S. Korea 5.6%, Indonesia 5.5%, Saudi Arabia 4.6%. **Exports:** $342.7 bil; Malaysia 12.1%, Indonesia 10.5%, Hong Kong 10.3%, China 9.2%, U.S. 7.1%, Japan 4.9%, Australia 4.1%. **Tourism:** $9.2 bil. **Budget:** $21.5 bil. **Intl. reserves less gold:** $113.09 bil. **Gold:** NA. **Consumer prices:** 6.5%.

Transport: Motor vehicles: 463,000 pass. cars; 141,400 comm. vehicles. **Civil aviation:** 51.5 bil pass.-mi; 8 airports. **Chief port:** Singapore.

Communications: TV sets: 341 per 1,000 pop. **Radios:** 744 per 1,000 pop. **Telephone lines:** 1.9 mil. **Daily newspaper circ.** (2004): 360.8 per 1,000 pop. **Internet:** 3.4 mil users.

Health: Life expect.: 79.3 male; 84.7 female. **Births** (per 1,000 pop.): 9. **Deaths** (per 1,000 pop.): 4.5. **Natural inc.:** 0.45%. **Infant mortality** (per 1,000 live births): 2.3. **HIV rate:** 0.2%.

Education: Compulsory: ages 6-16. **Literacy:** 94.4%.

Major intl. organizations: UN (IBRD, ILO, IMF, IMO, WHO, WTO), the Commonwealth, APEC, ASEAN.

Embassy: 3501 International Pl. NW 20008; 537-3100.

Website: www.gov.sg

Founded in 1819 by Sir Thomas Stamford Raffles, Singapore was a British colony until 1959, when it became autonomous within the Commonwealth. On Sept. 16, 1963, it joined with Malaya, Sarawak, and Sabah to form the Federation of Malaysia. Tensions between Malayans, dominant in the federation, and ethnic Chinese, dominant in Singapore, led to an accord under which Singapore became a separate nation, Aug. 9, 1965.

Singapore is one of the world's largest ports and a major center of manufacturing, banking, and commerce. Standards in health, education, and housing are generally high. The government, dominated by a single party, has taken strong actions to keep order and suppress dissent.

Singapore has had only 3 prime mins.: Lee Kuan Yew, who dominated national politics, 1959-90; Goh Chok Tong, 1990-2004; and Lee Kuan Yew's son, Lee Hsien Loong, who took office Aug. 12, 2004. Singapore's export-dependent economy was hit hard by the global downturn but began to recover by mid-2009.

Slovakia
Slovak Republic

People: Population: 5,463,046. **Age distrib.** (%): <15: 15.8; 65+: 12.5. **Pop. density:** 289.9 per sq mi, 111.9 per sq km. **Urban:** 56.2%. **Ethnic groups:** Slovak 86%, Hungarian 10%, Roma 2%. **Principal languages:** Slovak (official), Hungarian. **Chief religions:** Roman Catholic 69%, Protestant 11%, none 13%.

Geography: Total area: 18,859 sq mi, 48,845 sq km; **Land area:** 18,842 sq mi, 48,800 sq km. **Location:** In E central Europe. **Neighbors:** Poland on N, Hungary on S, Austria and Czech Rep. on W, Ukraine on E. **Topography:** Mountains (Carpathians) in N, fertile Danube plane in S. **Capital:** Bratislava, 424,000.

Government: Type: Republic. **Head of state:** Pres. Ivan Gasparovic; b. Mar. 27, 1941; in office: June 15, 2004. **Head of gov.:** Prime Min. Robert Fico; b. Sept. 15, 1964; in office: July 4, 2006. **Local divisions:** 8 departments. **Defense budget:** $1.4 bil. **Active troops:** 17,445.

Economy: Industries: metal & metal products; food & beverages; electricity, gas, coke, oil, nuclear fuels; chems. & manmade fibers; machinery; paper & printing. **Chief crops:** grains, potatoes, sugar beets, hops, fruit. **Natural resources:** brown coal& lignite; small amounts of iron ore, copper, & mang. ore, salt. **Crude oil reserves:** 9 mil bbls. **Arable land:** 29%. **Livestock:** cattle: 507,820; chickens: 12.9 mil; goats: 38,352; pigs: 1.1 mil; sheep: 332,571. **Fish catch:** 4,071 metric tons. **Electricity prod.:** 29.7 bil kWh. **Labor force** (2008): agric. 4%, industry 39%, services 56.9%.

Finance: Monetary unit: Euro (EUR) (Oct. 2009: 0.68 = $1 U.S.). **GDP:** $119.5 bil; **per capita GDP:** $21,900; **GDP growth:** 6.4%. **Imports:** $73.6 bil; Germany 20%, Czech Republic 17.7%, Russia 10.6%, Hungary 6.9%, S. Korea 5.2%, Austria 5%, Poland 4.9%, China 4.1%. **Exports:** $72.6 bil; Germany 20%, Czech Republic 13.1%, France 6.7%, Poland 6.6%, Hungary 6.3%, Austria 5.9%, Italy 5.8%, UK 4.7%. **Tourism:** $2.0 bil. **Budget:** $36 bil. **Intl. reserves less gold:** $11.59 bil. **Gold:** 1.13 mil oz t. **Consumer prices:** 4.6%.

Transport: Railroad: Length: 2,251 mi. **Motor vehicles:** 1.3 mil pass. cars; 197,000 comm. vehicles. **Civil aviation:** 589.7 mil pass.-mi; 20 airports. **Chief ports:** Bratislava, Komarno.

Communications: TV sets: 418 per 1,000 pop. **Radios:** 967 per 1,000 pop. **Telephone lines:** 1.1 mil. **Daily newspaper circ.** (2004): 125.7 per 1,000 pop. **Internet:** 2.8 mil users.

Health: Life expect.: 71.2 male; 79.3 female. **Births** (per 1,000 pop.): 10.6. **Deaths** (per 1,000 pop.): 9.5. **Natural inc.:** 0.11%. **Infant mortality** (per 1,000 live births): 7. **HIV rate:** <0.1%.

Education: Compulsory: ages 6-15. **Literacy:** 99.6%.

Major intl. organizations: UN (FAO, IBRD, ILO, IMF, IMO, WHO, WTO), EU, NATO, OECD, OSCE.

Embassy: 3523 International Ct. NW 20008; 237-1054.

Website: www.government.gov.sk

Slovakia was originally settled by Illyrian, Celtic, and Germanic tribes and was incorporated into Great Moravia in the 9th cent. It became part of Hungary in the 11th cent. Overrun by Czech Hussites in the 15th cent., it was restored to Hungarian rule in 1526. The Slovaks disassociated themselves from Hungary after WWI and joined the Czechs of Bohemia to form the Republic of Czechoslovakia, Oct. 28, 1918.

Germany invaded Czechoslovakia, 1939, and declared Slovakia independent. Slovakia rejoined Czechoslovakia in 1945. Czechoslovakia split into 2 separate states—the Czech Republic and Slovakia—on Jan. 1, 1993.

Slovakia attained full membership in the EU and NATO in 2004. Robert Fico, a leftist, became prime minister July 4, 2006, replacing a center-right coalition government. Slovakia adopted the euro currency as scheduled on Jan. 1, 2009, but its economy, which had been one of Europe's fastest growing, was battered by the global recession. Pres. Ivan Gasparovic won a 2nd 5-year term in a runoff election Apr. 4, 2009.

Slovenia
Republic of Slovenia

People: Population: 2,005,692. **Age distrib.** (%): <15: 13.5; 65+: 16.5. **Pop. density:** 257.8 per sq mi, 99.5 per sq km. **Urban:** 49.5%. **Ethnic groups:** Slovene 83%, Serb 2%, Croat 2%. **Principal languages:** Slovenian, Serbo-Croatian. **Chief religions:** Catholic 58%, Muslim 2%, none 10%.

Geography: Total area: 7,827 sq mi, 20,273 sq km; **Land area:** 7,780 sq mi, 20,151 sq km. **Location:** In SE Europe. **Neighbors:** Italy on W, Austria on N, Hungary on NE, Croatia on SE, S. **Topography:** Mostly hilly; 42% forested. **Capital:** Ljubljana, 244,000.

Government: Type: Republic. **Head of state:** Pres. Danilo Türk; b. Feb. 19, 1952; in office: Dec. 22, 2007. **Head of gov.:** Prime Min. Borut Pahor; b. Nov. 2, 1963; in office: Nov. 21, 2008. **Local divisions:** 183 municipalities, 11 urban municipalities. **Defense budget:** $741 mil. **Active troops:** 7,200.

Economy: Industries: ferrous metallurgy & aluminum products, electronics (incl. military), trucks, electric power equip., wood products, textiles, chemicals, machine tools. **Chief crops:** potatoes, hops, wheat, sugar beets, corn, grapes. **Natural resources:** lignite, lead, zinc, hydropower, forests. **Arable land:** 9%. **Livestock:** cattle: 451,293; chickens: 2.9 mil; goats: 27,798; pigs: 575,120; sheep: 131,528. **Fish catch:** 2,464 metric tons. **Electricity prod.:** 14.2 bil kWh. **Labor force** (2007): agric. 2.5%, industry 36%, services 61.5%.

Finance: Monetary unit: Euro (EUR) (Oct. 2009: 0.68 = $1 U.S.). **GDP:** $59.3 bil; **per capita GDP:** $29,600; **GDP growth:** 3.5%. **Imports:** $33.4 bil; Germany 17.2%, Italy 16.6%, Austria 11.2%, France 4.7%, Croatia 4.1%. **Exports:** $29.6 bil; Germany 18.6%, Italy 11.7%, Croatia 8.3%, Austria 7.5%, France 5.7%, Russia 4.8%. **Tourism:** $2.5 bil. **Budget:** $19 bil. **Intl. reserves less gold:** $564 mil. **Gold:** 100,000 oz t. **Consumer prices:** 5.6%.

Transport: Railroad: Length: 763 mi. **Motor vehicles:** 971,100 pass. cars; 62,700 comm. vehicles. **Civil aviation:** 439.3 mil pass.-mi; 6 airports. **Chief port:** Koper.

Communications: TV sets: 362 per 1,000 pop. **Radios:** 404 per 1,000 pop. **Telephone lines:** 1.01 mil. **Daily newspaper circ.** (2002): 172.8 per 1,000 pop. **Internet:** 992,200 users.

Health: Life expect.: 73 male; 80.7 female. **Births** (per 1,000 pop.): 9. **Deaths** (per 1,000 pop.): 10.5. **Natural inc.:** –0.15%. **Infant mortality** (per 1,000 live births): 4.3. **HIV rate:** <0.1%.

Education: Compulsory: ages 6-14. **Literacy:** 99.7%.

Major intl. organizations: UN (FAO, IBRD, ILO, IMF, IMO, WHO, WTO), EU, NATO, OSCE.

Embassy: 2410 California St. NW 20008; 386-6601.

Website: e-uprava.gov.si

The Slovenes settled in their current territory during the 6th to the 8th cent. They fell under German domination as early as the 9th cent. Modern Slovenian political history began after 1848 when the Slovenes, divided among several Austrian provinces, began their struggle for unification. In 1918 a majority of Slovenes became part of the Kingdom of Serbs, Croats, and Slovenes, later renamed Yugoslavia.

Slovenia declared independence June 25, 1991, and joined the UN May 22, 1992. It attained full membership in the EU and NATO in 2004. Slovenia adopted the euro currency Jan. 1, 2007. On Mar. 5, 2008, it became the first former Yugoslav republic to formally recognize Kosovo's independence from Serbia. A center-left coalition took office following legislative elections Sept. 21 the same year.

Solomon Islands

People: Population: 595,613. **Age distrib.** (%): <15: 39.5; 65+: 3.5. **Pop. dens.:** 56 per sq mi, 21.6 per sq km. **Urban:** 17%. **Ethnic groups:** Melanesian 95%, Polynesian 3%. **Principal languages:** English (official, but spoken by only 1%-2% of pop.), Melanesian pidgin (lingua franca in much of country), 120 indigenous languages. **Chief religions:** Church of Melanesia 33%, Roman Catholic 19%, South Seas Evangelical 17%, Seventh-Day Adventist 11%, United Church 10%.

Geography: Total area: 10,985 sq mi, 28,450 sq km; **Land area:** 10,633 sq mi, 27,540 sq km. **Location:** Melanesian Archipelago in W Pacific O. **Neighbors:** Nearest is Papua New Guinea to W. **Topography:** 10 large volcanic, rugged islands; 4 groups of smaller ones. **Capital:** Honiara, 66,000.

Government: Type: Parliamentary democracy. **Head of state:** Queen Elizabeth II, represented by Gov.-Gen. Frank Ofagioro Kabui; in office; July 7, 2009. **Head of gov.:** Prime Min. David Derek Sikua; b. Sept. 10, 1959; in office: Dec. 20, 2007. **Local divisions:** 9 provinces and Honiara. **Defense budget/Active troops:** NA.

Economy: Industries: fish (tuna), mining, timber. **Chief crops:** cocoa beans, coconuts, palm kernels, rice, potatoes, vegetables, fruit. **Natural resources:** fish, forests, gold, bauxite, phosphates, lead, zinc, nickel. **Arable land:** 1%. **Livestock:** cattle: 13,600; chickens: 235,000; pigs: 54,000. **Fish catch:** 31,410 metric tons. **Electricity prod.:** 64 mil kWh. **Labor force** (2000 est.): agric. 75%, industry 5%, services 20%.

Finance: Monetary unit: Dollar (SBD) (Oct. 2009: 7.99 = $1 U.S.). **GDP:** $1.1 bil; **per capita GDP:** $1,900; **GDP growth:** 7.3%. **Imports** (2006): $256 mil; Singapore 27.7%, Australia 18.7%, Fiji 4.6%, Papua New Guinea 4.4%, New Zealand 4.2%. **Exports** (2006): $237 mil; China 47.5%, Thailand 6.6%, S. Korea 6.3%, Spain 5.3%. **Tourism:** $4 mil. **Budget** (2003): $75.1 mil. **Intl. reserves less gold:** $58 mil. **Gold:** NA. **Consumer prices:** 17.3%.

Transport: Civil aviation: 49.1 mil pass.-mi; 2 airports. **Chief ports:** Honiara, Viru Harbor.

Communications: TV sets: 16 per 1,000 pop. **Radios:** 141 per 1,000 pop. **Telephone lines:** 8,000. **Daily newspaper circ.** (2004): 10.8 per 1,000 pop. **Internet:** 10,000 users.

Health: Life expect.: 70.9 male; 76.1 female. **Births** (per 1,000 pop.): 28.5. **Deaths** (per 1,000 pop.): 3.8. **Natural inc.:** 2.47%. **Infant mortality** (per 1,000 live births): 19.7. **HIV rate:** NA.

Education: NA. **Literary:** NA.

Major intl. organizations: UN (FAO, IBRD, ILO, IMF, IMO, WHO, WTO), the Commonwealth.

Embassy: 800 Second Ave., Ste. 400L, New York, NY 10017; (212) 599-6192.

Website: www.parliament.gov.sb

The Solomon Isls. were sighted 1568 by an expedition from Peru. Britain established a protectorate in the 1890s over most of the group, inhabited by Melanesians. The islands saw major WWII battles. They achieved self-government Jan. 2, 1976, and formal independence July 7, 1978.

A coup attempt June 5, 2000, sparked factional fighting in Honiara. Violence and lawlessness became widespread over the next 3 years. To restore order, a 2,225-member intervention force, led by Australia and authorized by the Pacific Isls. Forum, began arriving in Honiara July 24, 2003; nearly all foreign troops were removed by mid-2005.

Following elections Apr. 5, 2006, parliament's choice of Snyder Rini as prime min. led to 2 days of rioting in Honiara over alleged influence-buying by the ethnic Chinese business community. Rini resigned Apr. 26 rather than face a no-confidence vote, and Manasseh Sogavare replaced him. An earthquake and tsunami Apr. 2, 2007, claimed at least 52 lives. David Derek Sikua became prime min. Dec. 20 after Sogavare lost a no-confidence vote.

Somalia

People: Population: 9,832,017. **Age distrib.** (%): <15: 45; 65+: 2.5. **Pop. density:** 40.6 per sq mi, 15.7 per sq km. **Urban:** 35.2%. **Ethnic groups:** Somali 85%, Bantu & other non-Somali 15%. **Principal languages:** Somali (official), Arabic, Italian, English. **Chief religion:** Sunni Muslim.

Geography: Total area: 246,201 sq mi, 637,657 sq km; **Land area:** 242,216 sq mi, 627,337 sq km. **Location:** Occupies eastern horn of Africa. **Neighbors:** Djibouti, Ethiopia, Kenya on W. **Topography:** The coastline extends for 1,700 mi. Hills cover the N; center and S are flat. **Capital:** Mogadishu, 1,100,000.

Government: Type: In transition. **Head of state:** Pres. Sheikh Sharif Sheikh Ahmed; b. July 25, 1964; in office: Jan. 31, 2009. **Head of gov.:** Prime Min. Omar Abdirashid Ali Sharmarke; b. June 18, 1960; in office: Feb. 14, 2009. **Local divisions:** 18 regions. **Defense budget:** NA. **Active troops:** 2,000 (Ethiopian trained transitional govt.).

Economy: Industries: few light industries, incl. sugar refining, textiles, wireless comm. **Chief crops:** bananas, sorghum, corn, coconuts, rice. **Natural resources:** uranium, largely unexploited iron ore reserves, tin, gypsum, bauxite, copper, salt, nat. gas, likely oil reserves. **Arable land:** 2%. **Livestock:** cattle: 5.4 mil; chickens: 3.4 mil; goats: 12.7 mil; pigs: 4,200; sheep: 13.1 mil. **Fish catch** (est.): 30,000 metric tons. **Electricity prod.:** 280 mil kWh. **Labor force** (1975): agric. 71%, industry & services 29%.

Finance: Monetary unit: Shilling (SOS) (Oct. 2009: 1,401.00 = $1 U.S.). **GDP:** 5.5 bil; **per capita GDP:** $600; **GDP growth:** 2.6%. **Imports** (2006): $798 mil; Djibouti 31.5%, India 8.3%, Kenya 8.2%, U.S. 6.4%, Oman 6.3%, UAE 5.9%, Yemen 5.1%. **Exports** (2006): $300 mil; UAE 53.5%, Yemen 20%, Oman 6.4%. **Tourism:** NA. **Budget:** NA.

Transport: Civil aviation: 81.4 mil pass.-mi; 7 airports. **Chief ports:** Berbera, Kismaayo.

Communications: TV sets: 14 per 1,000 pop. **Radios:** 53 per 1,000 pop. **Telephone lines:** 100,000. **Internet:** 102,000 users.

Health: Life expect.: 47.4 male; 51.1 female. **Births** (per 1,000 pop.): 44.1. **Deaths** (per 1,000 pop.): 15.9. **Natural inc.:** 2.82%. **Infant mortality** (per 1,000 live births): 111. **HIV rate:** 0.5%.

Education: Compulsory: ages 6-13. **Literacy:** 37.8%.

Major intl. organizations: UN (FAO, IBRD, ILO, IMF, IMO, WHO), AL, AU.

Permanent UN mission: 425 E. 61st St., Ste. 702, New York, NY, 10021; (212) 688-9410. (Embassy ceased operation in U.S. in 1991.)

Website: www.state.gov/p/af/ci/so/

British Somaliland (present-day North Somalia) was formed in the 19th cent., as was Italian Somaliland (now central and South Somalia). Italy lost its African colonies in WWII. British Somaliland gained independence, June 26, 1960, and by prearrangement, merged July 1 with the UN Trust Territory of Somalia to create the independent Somali Republic.

On Oct. 15, 1969, Somalia's first civilian president, Abdirashid Ali Sharmarke, was assassinated. Six days later, a military group led by Maj. Gen. Muhammad Siad Barre seized power. In 1970, Barre declared the country a socialist state—the Somali Democratic Republic.

Somalia has laid claim to Ogaden, the huge eastern region of Ethiopia, peopled mostly by Somalis. Ethiopia battled Somali rebels in 1977. Some 11,000 Cuban troops with Soviet arms defeated Somali army troops and ethnic Somali rebels in Ethiopia, 1978. As many as 1.5 mil refugees entered Somalia. Guerrilla fighting in Ogaden continued until 1988, when a peace agreement was reached with Ethiopia.

The civil war intensified again and Barre was forced to flee the capital, Jan. 1991. Fighting between rival factions caused 40,000 casualties in 1991 and 1992, and by mid-1992 the civil war, drought, and banditry combined to produce a famine that threatened some 1.5 mil people with starvation.

In Dec. 1992 the UN accepted a U.S. offer of troops to safeguard food delivery to the starving. The UN took control of the multinational relief effort from the U.S. May 4, 1993. While the operation helped alleviate the famine, there were significant U.S. and other casualties; a failed mission Oct. 3-4 left 18 U.S. troops and more than 500 Somalis dead. The U.S. withdrew its peacekeeping forces Mar. 25, 1994.

When the last UN troops pulled out Mar. 3, 1995, Mogadishu had no functioning central government, and armed factions controlled different regions. By 1999 a joint police force was operating in the capital, but much of the country, especially southern Somalia, faced continued violence and food shortages. After political and factional leaders signed a peace deal Jan. 29, 2004, a transitional parliament, Somalia's first legislature in 13 years, was inaugurated Aug. 22. Meeting in Nairobi, Kenya, the parliament chose Abdullahi Yusuf Ahmed as president; he was sworn in Oct. 14. The Indian Ocean tsunami of Dec. 26, 2004, killed at least 150 people and displaced about 5,000 in Somalia.

Because Mogadishu was held by his rivals, Pres. Yusuf moved, July 26, 2005, to make his transitional capital at Jowhar; an interim parliament convened Feb. 26, 2006, at Baidoa. On June 5, an Islamist militia took over Mogadishu, defeating secular warlords backed by the U.S. The Islamists, calling themselves the Supreme Islamic Courts Council, also held much of the central and southern regions. Pres. Yusuf escaped assassination, Sept. 18, but 8 others died in a car bomb explosion at Baidoa 5 days later.

With aid from Ethiopian troops, transitional govt. forces recaptured Mogadishu in late Dec. 2006. The UN Security Council authorized, Feb. 20, 2007, an African Union peacekeeping mission to Somalia (AMISOM), but the troops were targeted by insurgents. An upsurge of fighting in Mogadishu, Feb.-Apr., killed hundreds of people and caused 350,000 to flee the capital. Bombings and kidnappings escalated in 2007-08, as a series of cease-fires failed; the increasing violence forced international aid workers to pull out, worsening a humanitarian crisis.

After Pres. Yusuf resigned Dec. 29, 2008, the transitional parliament, meeting in Djibouti Jan. 31, 2009, elected a moderate Islamist, Sheikh Sharif Sheikh Ahmed; by then, Ethiopia had completely withdrawn its troops from Somalia. A state of emergency was declared June 22 after Islamist insurgents stepped up their attacks on officials of the UN-backed government. A helicopter strike by U.S. commandos in southern Somalia Sept. 14 killed a top al-Qaeda leader, the Kenyan-born Saleh Ali Saleh Nabhan. Pirates continued to operate in coastal waters, carrying out more than 150 attacks off the Horn of Africa during Jan.-Sept. 2009.

South Africa
Republic of South Africa

People: Population: 49,052,489. **Age distrib.** (%): <15: 28.9; 65+: 5.4. **Pop. density:** 104.1 per sq mi, 40.2 per sq km. **Urban:** 59.3%. **Ethnic groups:** Black African 79%, white 10%. **Principal languages:** IsiZulu, IsiXhosa, Afrikaans, Sepedi, English, Setswana, Sesotho. **Chief religions:** Zion Christian 11%, Pentecostal/Charismatic 8%, Catholic 7%, Dutch Reformed 7%, none 15%.

Geography: Total area: 471,011 sq mi, 1,219,912 sq km; **Land area:** 471,011 sq mi, 1,219,912 sq km. **Location:** At southern extreme of Africa. **Neighbors:** Namibia, Botswana, Zimbabwe on N; Mozambique, Swaziland on E; surrounds Lesotho. **Topography:** Large interior plateau reaches close to the country's 1,739-mi coastline. There are few major rivers or lakes; rainfall sparse in W, more plentiful in E. **Capital:** Cape Town (legis.), 3,215,000; Pretoria (admin.), 1,338,000; Bloemfontein (judic.), 417,000. **Cities (urban aggr.):** Johannesburg, 3,435,000; East Rand (Ekurhuleni), 2,986,000; Durban, 2,729,000.

Government: Type: Republic. **Head of state and gov.:** Pres. Jacob Zuma; b. Apr. 12, 1942; in office: May 9, 2009. **Local divisions:** 9 provinces. **Defense budget:** $3.8 bil. **Active troops:** 62,082.

Economy: Industries: mining (espec. platinum, gold, chromium), auto assembly, metalworking, machinery, textiles, chemicals, fertilizers, foodstuffs. **Chief crops:** corn, wheat, sugarcane, fruits, vegetables. **Natural resources:** gold, chromium, antimony, coal, iron ore, mang., nickel, phosphates, tin, uranium, gem diamonds, platinum, copper, vanadium, salt, nat. gas. **Crude oil reserves:** 15 mil bbls. **Arable land:** 12%. **Livestock:** 13.9 mil; chickens: 126 mil; goats: 6.3 mil; pigs: 1.7 mil; sheep: 25.1 mil. **Fish catch:** 682,960 metric tons. **Electricity prod.:** 227.7 bil kWh. **Labor force** (2007 est.): agric. 9%, industry 26%, services 65%.

Finance: Monetary unit: Rand (ZAR) (Oct. 2009: 7.37 = $1 U.S.). **GDP:** $491 bil; **per capita GDP:** $10,100; **GDP growth:** 3.1%. **Imports:** $90.6 bil; Germany 10.8%, China 10.3%, U.S. 7%, Angola 6.8%, Saudi Arabia 5.7%, Japan 4.9%, UK 4.8%, Iran 4.4%. **Exports:** $86.1 bil; U.S. 11.1%, Japan 9.8%, UK 9.6%, China 8.7%, Germany 6.8%, Netherlands 4.1%. **Tourism:** $8.4 bil. **Budget:** $66.7 bil. **Intl. reserves less gold:** $19.86 bil. **Gold:** 4.01 mil oz t. **Consumer prices:** 9.9%.

Transport: Railroad: Length: 12,969 mi. **Civil aviation:** 18.1 bil pass.-mi; 148 airports. **Chief ports:** Cape Town, Durban, Port Elizabeth, Richards Bay, Saldanha Bay.

Communications: TV sets: 138 per 1,000 pop. **Radios:** 355 per 1,000 pop. **Telephone lines:** 4.4 mil. **Daily newspaper circ.** (2004): 29.6 per 1,000 pop. **Internet:** 4.2 mil users.

Health: Life expect.: 49.6 male; 48.1 female. **Births** (per 1,000 pop.): 20.2. **Deaths** (per 1,000 pop.): 16.9. **Natural inc.:** 0.33%. **Infant mortality** (per 1,000 live births): 45.1. **HIV rate:** 18.1%.

Education: Compulsory: ages 7-15. **Literacy:** 88%.

Major intl. organizations: UN (FAO, IBRD, ILO, IMF, IMO, WHO, WTO), the Commonwealth, AU.

Embassy: 3051 Massachusetts Ave. NW 20008; 232-4400. **Website:** www.gov.za

Bushmen and KhoiKhoi were the original inhabitants. Bantus, including Zulu, Xhosa, Swazi, and Sotho, had occupied the area from northeastern to southern South Africa before the 17th cent.

The Cape of Good Hope area was settled by the Dutch, beginning in the 17th cent. Britain seized the Cape in 1806. Many Dutch trekked north and founded 2 republics, Transvaal and Orange Free State. Diamonds were discovered, 1867, and gold, 1886. The Dutch (Boers) resented encroachments by the British and others; the Anglo-Boer War followed, 1899-1902. Britain won and, effective May 31, 1910, created the Union of South Africa, incorporating 2 British colonies (Cape and Natal) with Transvaal and Orange Free State. After a referendum, the Union became the Republic of South Africa, May 31, 1961, and withdrew from the Commonwealth.

With the election victory of Daniel Malan's National Party in 1948, the policy of separate development of the races, or apartheid, already existing unofficially, became official. Under apartheid, blacks were severely restricted to certain occupations, and paid far lower wages than whites for similar work. Only whites could vote or run for public office. Persons of Asian Indian ancestry and those of mixed race ("coloureds") had limited political rights. In 1959 the government passed acts providing for the eventual creation of several Bantu nations, or Bantustans.

Protests against apartheid were brutally suppressed. At Sharpeville on Mar. 21, 1960, 69 black protesters were killed by government troops. At least 600 persons, mostly Bantus, were killed in 1976 riots protesting apartheid. In 1981, South Africa launched military operations in Angola and Mozambique to combat guerrilla groups. Meanwhile, the apartheid system slowly began to crumble.

In 1986, Nobel Peace Prize winner Bishop Desmond Tutu called for Western nations to apply sanctions against South Africa to force an end to apartheid. Pres. P. W. Botha announced in Apr. the end to the nation's system of racial pass laws and offered blacks an advisory role in government. On May 19, South Africa attacked 3 neighboring countries—Zimbabwe, Botswana, Zambia—to strike at guerrilla strongholds of the black nationalist African National Congress (ANC). A nationwide state of emergency was declared June 12, giving almost unlimited power to the security forces.

Some 2 mil South African black workers staged a massive strike, June 6-8, 1988. Pres. Botha, head of the government since 1978, resigned Aug. 14, 1989, and was replaced by F. W. de Klerk. In 1990 the government lifted its ban on the ANC. Black nationalist leader Nelson Mandela was freed Feb. 11 after more than 27 years in prison. In Feb. 1991, Pres. de Klerk pledged to end all apartheid laws.

In 1993 negotiators agreed on basic principles for a new democratic constitution. South Africa's partially self-governing black territories, or "homelands," were dissolved and incorporated into a national system of 9 provinces. In elections Apr. 26-29, 1994, the ANC won 62.7% of the vote, making Mandela president. The National Party won 20.4%. The Inkatha Freedom Party won 10.5% and control of the legislature in a mainly Zulu province. By then, fighting between the ANC and Inkatha (aided, during the apartheid era, by South African defense forces) had killed more than 14,000 people in the Zulu region since the mid-1980s.

In 1995, Mandela appointed a truth commission, led by Desmond Tutu, to document human rights abuses under apartheid. A post-apartheid constitution became law Dec. 10, 1996. The ANC won a landslide victory in elections held June 2, 1999. ANC leader Thabo Mbeki thus became South Africa's second popularly elected president. South Africa, Nov. 30, 2006, became the 1st country in Africa to legalize same-sex marriage.

After Mbeki's former deputy president, Jacob Zuma, defeated him in a power struggle for the ANC leadership, Mbeki resigned his presidential office, Sept. 21, 2008. He was succeeded by ANC deputy leader Kgalema Motlanthe. Corruption charges against Zuma were dropped Apr. 6, 2009, and he became president after the ANC swept national elections Apr. 22.

Spain
Kingdom of Spain

People: Population: 40,525,002. **Age distrib.** (%): <15: 14.5; 65+: 18.1. **Pop. density:** 210.1 per sq mi, 81.1 per sq km. **Urban:** 76.7%. **Ethnic groups:** mixed Mediterranean & Nordic. **Principal languages:** Castilian Spanish (official); Catalan, Galician, Basque (all official regionally). **Chief religion:** Roman Catholic 94%.

Geography: Total area: 194,897 sq mi, 504,782 sq km; **Land area:** 192,874 sq mi, 499,542 sq km. **Location:** In SW Europe. **Neighbors:** Portugal on W; France, Andorra on N; Morocco to S. **Topography:** The interior is a high, arid plateau broken by mountain ranges and river valleys. The NW is heavily watered, the S has lowlands and a Medit. climate. **Capital:** Madrid, 5,567,000. **Cities (urban aggr.):** Barcelona, 4,920,000; Valencia, 808,000.

Government: Type: Constitutional monarchy. **Head of state:** King Juan Carlos I de Borbon y Borbon; b. Jan. 5, 1938; in office: Nov. 22, 1975. **Head of gov.:** Prime Min. José Luis Rodríguez Zapatero; b. Aug. 4, 1960; in office: Apr. 17, 2004. **Local divisions:** 17 autonomous communities and two autonomous cities. **Defense budget:** $17.5 bil. **Active troops:** 221,750.

Economy: Industries: textiles & apparel, food & beverages, metals, chems., shipbuilding, automobiles, mach. tools, tourism, pharm., med. equip. **Chief crops:** grain, vegetables, olives, wine grapes, sugar beets, citrus. **Natural resources:** coal, lignite, iron ore, copper, lead, zinc, uranium, tungsten, mercury, pyrites, fluorspar, gypsum, kaolin, potash, hydropower. **Crude oil reserves:** 150 mil bbls. **Arable land:** 27%. **Livestock:** cattle: 6.6 mil; chickens: 137 mil; goats: 2.9 mil; pigs: 26.1 mil; sheep: 22.2 mil. **Fish catch:** 1.09 mil metric tons. **Electricity prod.:** 283.4 bil kWh. **Labor force** (2008 est.): agric. 4%, industry 26.4%, services 69.5%.

Finance: Monetary unit: Euro (EUR) (Oct. 2009: 0.68 = $1 U.S.). **GDP:** $1.4 tril; **per capita GDP:** $34,700; **GDP growth:** 1.2%. **Imports:** $414.5 bil; Germany 14.5%, France 11.1%, Italy 7.4%, China 6.3%, UK 4.6%, Neth. 4.4%. **Exports:** $285.4 bil; France 18.4%, Germany 10.6%, Portugal 8.7%, Italy 8%, UK 6.7%, U.S. 4.2%. **Tourism:** $57.6 bil. **Budget:** $556.5 bil. **Intl. reserves less gold:** $8.06 bil. **Gold:** 9.05 mil oz t. **Consumer prices:** 4.1%.

Transport: Railroad: Length: 9,500 mi. **Motor vehicles:** 20.3 mil pass. cars; 4.9 mil comm. vehicles. **Civil aviation:** 44.1 bil pass.-mi; 95 airports. **Chief ports:** Algeciras, Barcelona, Bilbao, Cartagena, Huelva, Tarragona, Valencia.

Communications: TV sets: 555 per 1,000 pop. **Radios:** 331 per 1,000 pop. **Telephone lines:** 20.2 mil. **Daily newspaper circ.** (2004): 144.5 per 1,000 pop. **Internet:** 25.2 mil users.

Health: Life expect.: 76.6 male; 83.5 female. **Births** (per 1,000 pop.): 9.9. **Deaths** (per 1,000 pop.): 9.9. **Natural inc.:** 0%. **Infant mortality** (per 1,000 live births): 4.3. **HIV rate:** 0.5%.

Education: Compulsory: ages 6-16. **Literacy:** 97.4%.

Major intl. organizations: UN and all of its specialized agencies, EU, NATO, OECD, OSCE.

Embassy: 2375 Pennsylvania Ave. NW 20037; 452-0100.

Website: www.la-moncloa.es

Initially settled by Iberians, Basques, and Celts, Spain was successively ruled (wholly or in part) by Carthage, Rome, and the Visigoths. Muslims invaded Iberia from N Africa in 711. Reconquest of the peninsula by Christians from the N laid the foundations of modern Spain. In 1469 the kingdoms of Aragon and Castile were united by the marriage of Ferdinand II and Isabella I. Moorish rule ended with the fall of Granada, 1492. Spain's large Jewish community was expelled the same year.

Spain obtained a colonial empire with the 1492 "discovery" of America by Columbus and the conquest of Mexico by Cortes and of Peru by Pizarro. It also controlled the Netherlands and parts of Italy and Germany. Spain lost its American colonies in the early 19th cent. It lost Cuba, the Philippines, and Puerto Rico during the Spanish-American War, 1898.

Primo de Rivera became dictator, 1923. King Alfonso XIII revoked the dictatorship, 1930, but was forced into exile in 1931. A republic was proclaimed, which disestablished the church, curtailed its privileges, and secularized education. In 1936-39 a Popular Front of socialists, Communists, republicans, and anarchists governed Spain.

Army officers under Francisco Franco revolted, 1936. Franco received help and troops from Italy and Germany, while the USSR, France, and Mexico supported the republic. Some 500,000 to 1 mil died before the war's end Mar. 28, 1939. Franco was named *caudillo*, leader of the nation. Spain was officially neutral in WWII, but its cordial relations with fascist countries prompted its exclusion from the UN until 1955.

In July 1969, Franco and the Cortes (Parliament) designated Prince Juan Carlos future king and chief of state. After Franco's death, Nov. 20, 1975, Juan Carlos was sworn in as king. In free elections June 1977, moderates and democratic socialists emerged as the largest parties.

In 1981 a coup attempt by right-wing military officers was thwarted by the king. The Socialist Workers' Party, under Felipe González Márquez, won 4 consecutive general elections between 1982 and 1993 but lost to a coalition of conservative and regional parties in the Mar. 3, 1996, election. The Popular Party of conservative Prime Min. José María Aznar won a majority in the Mar. 12, 2000, parliamentary election. Aznar, going against Spanish public opinion, openly supported the U.S.-led invasion of Iraq, Mar. 2003.

Four commuter trains were bombed in central Madrid, Mar. 11, 2004, killing 191 people. The opposition Socialist Workers Party won elections 3 days later, and Socialist leader José Luis Rodríguez Zapatero, who became prime min. Apr. 17, fulfilled a campaign pledge to remove all 1,300 Spanish troops from Iraq. Spain legalized same-sex marriage, July 3, 2005. A Spanish tribunal Oct. 31, 2007, convicted 18 Islamic extremists of mass murder in connection with the 2004 train bombings; 7 other suspects (including alleged mastermind Rabei Osman, an Egyptian) were acquitted, and 18 were found guilty on lesser charges.

Prime Min. Zapatero won a 2nd term in elections Mar. 9, 2008. As the financial crisis spread worldwide, Spain's banking, building, and tourism industries suffered; in July 2009, the unemployment rate reached 18.5%.

Catalonia and the **Basque country** were granted autonomy, Jan. 1980, following overwhelming approval in home-rule referendums. But Basque extremists pushed for independence. The Basque separatist group ETA carried out bombings that have killed about 830 since 1968. ETA declared a permanent cease-fire effective Mar. 24, 2006, after which the Spanish govt. agreed to formal peace talks. Negotiations broke down after ETA exploded a car bomb at the Madrid airport, Dec. 30, 2006, killing 2; Basque militants formally rescinded the truce, June 5, 2007. In Catalonia, voters approved a plan for expanded home-rule, June 18, 2006.

The **Balearic Isls.** in the W Mediterranean, 1,927 sq mi, are a province of Spain; they include **Majorca** (Mallorca; capital Palma de Mallorca), **Minorca, Cabrera, Ibiza,** and **Formentera.** The **Canary Isls.**, 2,807 sq mi, in the Atlantic W of Morocco, form 2 provinces, and include the islands of Tenerife, Palma, Gomera, Hierro, Grand Canary, Fuerteventura, and Lanzarote; Las Palmas and Santa Cruz are thriving ports. More than 1,700 people died trying to get from Mauritania to the Canary Islands in rickety boats, Jan.-June 2006.

Ceuta and Melilla, small Spanish enclaves on Morocco's Mediterranean coast, gained limited autonomy in Sept. 1994. Spain has sought the return of Gibraltar, in British hands since 1704.

Sri Lanka
Democratic Socialist Republic of Sri Lanka

People: Population: 21,324,791. **Age distrib.** (%): <15: 23.9; 65+: 8.1. **Pop. density:** 853.1 per sq mi, 329.4 per sq km. **Urban:** 15.1%. **Ethnic groups:** Sinhalese 74%, Sri Lankan Moors 7%. **Principal languages:** Sinhala (official & national), Tamil (national), English (commonly used in govt.). **Chief religions:** Buddhist 69%, Muslim 8%, Hindu 7%, Christian 6%.

Geography: Total area: 25,332 sq mi, 65,610 sq km; **Land area:** 24,996 sq mi, 64,740 sq km. **Location:** In Indian O. off SE coast of India. **Neighbors:** India on NW. **Topography:** Coastal area and N half are flat; S-central area is hilly and mountainous. **Capital:** Colombo, 656,000; Sri Jayewardenepura Kotte (admin.), 120,000.

Government: Type: Republic. **Head of state:** Pres. Mahinda Rajapaksa; b. Nov. 18, 1945; in office: Nov. 19, 2005. **Head of gov.:** Prime Min. Ratnasiri Wickremanayake; b. May 5, 1933; in office: Nov. 21, 2005. **Local divisions:** 9 provinces with 25 districts. **Defense budget:** $975 mil. **Active troops:** 150,900.

Economy: Industries: rubber proc., tea, coconuts, tobacco, telecomm., insurance, banking, clothing, textiles, cement, oil refining. **Chief crops:** rice, sugarcane, grains, pulses, oilseed, spices, tea, rubber. **Natural resources:** limestone, graphite, mineral sands, gems, phosphates, clay, hydropower. **Arable land:** 14%. **Livestock:** cattle: 1.2 mil; chickens: 13.8 mil; goats: 388,600; pigs: 94,210; sheep: 16,480. **Fish catch:** 318,642 metric tons. **Electricity prod.:** 8.3 bil kWh. **Labor force** (2008 est.): agric. 34.7%, industry 26.1%, services 39.2%.

Finance: Monetary unit: Rupee (LKR) (Oct. 2009: 114.82 = $1 U.S.). **GDP:** $91.9 bil; **per capita GDP:** $4,300; **GDP growth:** 6%. **Imports:** $12.3 bil; India 21.2%, China 11.2%, Iran 7.9%, Singapore 7.7%. **Exports:** $7.9 bil; U.S. 21.7%, UK 11.9%, India 6.8%, Germany 5.1%, Belgium 4.8%, Italy 4.7%. **Tourism:** $385 mil. **Budget:** $7.8 bil. **Intl. reserves less gold:** $1.66 bil. **Gold:** 170,000 oz t. **Consumer prices:** 22.6%.

Transport: Railroad: Length: 900 mi. **Motor vehicles:** 507,000 pass. cars; 280,000 comm. vehicles. **Civil aviation:** 5.3 bil pass.-mi; 14 airports. **Chief port:** Colombo.

Communications: TV sets: 102 per 1,000 pop. **Radios:** 211 per 1,000 pop. **Telephone lines:** 3.4 mil. **Daily newspaper circ.** (2002): 26.1 per 1,000 pop. **Internet:** 1.1 mil users.

Health: Life expect.: 73 male; 77.1 female. **Births** (per 1,000 pop.): 16.6. **Deaths** (per 1,000 pop.): 6.1. **Natural inc.:** 1.06%. **Infant mortality** (per 1,000 live births): 19. **HIV rate:** NA.

Education: Compulsory: ages 5-13. **Literacy:** 91.5%.

Major intl. organizations: UN (FAO, IBRD, ILO, IMF, IMO, WHO, WTO), the Commonwealth.

Embassy: 2148 Wyoming Ave. NW 20008; 483-4025.

Website: www.priu.gov.lk

The island was known to the ancient world as Taprobane (Greek for copper-colored) and later as Serendip (from Arabic). Colonists from N India subdued the indigenous Veddahs about 543 BCE; their descendants, the Buddhist Sinhalese, still form most of the population. Hindu descendants of Tamil immigrants from S India account for about one-fifth of the population.

Parts were occupied by the Portuguese in 1505 and the Dutch in 1658. The British seized the island in 1796. As Ceylon it became an independent member of the Commonwealth in 1948, and the Republic of Sri Lanka May 22, 1972.

Prime Min. Solomon W. R. D. Bandaranaike was assassinated Sept. 25, 1959. His widow, Mrs. Sirimavo Bandaranaike, served as prime min. 1960-65, 1970-77, 1994-2000. In 1971 the nation suffered economic problems and terrorist activities by ultra-leftists, thousands of whom were executed. Massive land reform and nationalization of foreign-owned plantations took place in the mid-1970s.

Tensions between Sinhalese and Tamil separatists erupted into violence in the early 1980s. More than 60,000 died in the civil war, which continued for the next 2 decades; another 20,000, mostly young Tamils, "disappeared" after they were taken into custody by government security forces.

Pres. Ranasinghe Premadasa was assassinated May 1, 1993, by a Tamil rebel. Mrs. Bandaranaike's daughter, Chandrika Bandaranaike Kumaratunga, became prime min. after the Aug. 16, 1994, general elections. Elected president Nov. 9, Kumaratunga appointed her mother prime min. Kumaratunga, who was injured in a suicide bomb attack at a campaign rally Dec. 18, 1999, won a second 6-year term 3 days later. In failing health, Mrs. Bandaranaike resigned Aug. 10 and died Oct. 10, 2000.

A truce accord intended to bring an end to the civil war was signed Feb. 22, 2002. The Indian Ocean tsunami of Dec. 26, 2004, left more than 31,100 dead, 4,100 missing, and 519,000 displaced in Sri Lanka.

Prime Min. Mahinda Rajapaksa of the United People's Freedom Alliance won the presidential election of Nov. 17, 2005. A resurgence of fighting by govt. forces, paramilitary groups, and Tamil rebels beginning in Dec. 2005 claimed thousands more lives during the next 3 years. The army launched a fierce offensive, eventually trapping the rebels in a small patch of territory in the northeast and displacing some 265,000 civilians; an estimated 7,000 noncombatants were killed between Jan. 20 and May 7, 2009. On May 18-19, Tamil leader Vellupillai Prabhakaran was killed, and Pres. Rajapaksa formally declared victory.

Sudan
Republic of the Sudan

People: Population: 41,087,825. **Age distrib.** (%): <15: 40.7; 65+: 2.5. **Pop. density:** 44.8 per sq mi, 17.3 per sq km. **Urban:** 40.8%. **Ethnic groups:** Black 52%, Arab 39%, Beja 6%. **Principal languages:** Arabic (official); Nubian; Ta Bedawie; Nilotic, Nilo-Hamitic, Sudanic dialects; English. **Chief religions:** Sunni Muslim 70% (in N), Christian 5% (mostly in S & Khartoum), indigenous beliefs 25%.

Geography: Total area: 967,499 sq mi, 2,505,810 sq km; **Land area:** 917,379 sq mi, 2,376,000 sq km. **Location:** At E end of Sahara desert zone. **Neighbors:** Egypt on N; Libya, Chad, Central African Republic on W; Congo, Uganda, Kenya on S; Ethiopia, Eritrea on E. **Topography:** The N consists of Libyan Desert in W, and the mountainous Nubia Desert in E, with narrow Nile valley between. Center contains large, fertile, rainy areas with fields, pasture, and forest. The S has rich soil, heavy rain. **Capital:** Khartoum, 4,754,000.

Government: Type: Republic with strong military influence. **Head of state and gov.:** Pres. Gen. Omar Hassan Ahmad Al-Bashir; b. Jan. 1, 1944; in office: June 30, 1989. **Local divisions:** 26 states. **Defense budget:** NA. **Active troops:** 109,300.

Economy: Industries: oil, cotton ginning, textiles, cement, edible oils, sugar, pharmaceuticals, armaments. **Chief crops:** cotton, peanuts, sorghum, millet, wheat, gum arabic, sugarcane, cassava, mangos, papaya. **Natural resources:** oil, small reserves of iron ore, copper, chromium ore, zinc, tungsten, mica, silver, gold, hydropower. **Crude oil reserves:** 5 bil bbls. **Arable land:** 7%. **Livestock:** cattle: 41.4 mil; chickens: 35 mil; goats: 43 mil; sheep: 50.9 mil. **Fish catch:** 67,467 metric tons. **Electricity prod.:** 4 bil kWh. **Labor force** (1998 est.): agric. 80%, industry 7%, services 13%.

Finance: Monetary unit: Pound (SDG) (Oct. 2009: 2.31 = $1 U.S.). **GDP:** $88.1 bil; **per capita GDP:** $2,200; **GDP growth:** 6.5%. **Imports:** $9.3 bil; China 24.9%, Saudi Arabia 8%, UAE 5.9%, India 5.8%, Egypt 5.3%. **Exports:** $12.2 bil; China 56.3%, Japan 30%, Indonesia 4.9%. **Tourism:** $262 mil. **Budget:** $10.9 bil. **Intl. reserves less gold:** $908 mil. **Gold:** NA. **Consumer prices:** 14.3%.

Transport: Railroad: Length: 3,715 mi. **Motor vehicles:** 47,300 pass. cars; 62,500 comm. vehicles. **Civil aviation:** 616.4 mil pass.-mi; 19 airports. **Chief port:** Port Sudan.

Communications: TV sets: 173 per 1,000 pop. **Radios:** 480 per 1,000 pop. **Telephone lines:** 356,100. **Internet:** 3.8 mil users.

Health: Life expect.: 49.4 male; 51.2 female. **Births** (per 1,000 pop.): 34.3. **Deaths** (per 1,000 pop.): 13.6. **Natural inc.:** 2.07%. **Infant mortality** (per 1,000 live births): 87. **HIV rate:** 1.4%.

Education: Compulsory: ages 6-13. **Literacy:** 60.9%.

Major intl. organizations: UN (FAO, IBRD, ILO, IMF, IMO, WHO), AL, AU.

Embassy: 2210 Massachusetts Ave. NW 20008; 338-8565.

Website: www.sudan.gov.sd or www.state.gov/p/af/ci/su/

Northern Sudan, ancient Nubia, was settled by Egyptians in antiquity. The population was converted to Coptic Christianity in the 6th cent. Arab conquests brought Islam to the area in the 15th cent. In the 1820s Egypt took over Sudan, defeating the last of earlier empires, including the Fung. In the 1880s a revolution was led by Muhammad Ahmad, who called himself the Mahdi (leader of the faithful), and his followers, the dervishes.

In 1898 an Anglo-Egyptian force crushed the Mahdi's successors. In 1951 the Egyptian Parliament abrogated its 1899 and 1936 treaties with Great Britain and provided for a separate Sudanese constitution. Sudan voted for complete independence effective Jan. 1, 1956. In 1969, a Revolutionary Council took power, led by authoritarian Pres. Gaafar al-Nimeiry.

Economic problems plagued the nation in the 1980s and 1990s, aggravated by civil war and influxes of refugees from neighboring countries. After 16 years in power, Pres. Jaafar al-Nimeiry was overthrown in a bloodless coup, Apr. 6, 1985. Sudan held its first democratic parliamentary elections in 18 years in 1986, but the elected government was toppled in a bloodless coup June 30, 1989.

In the mid-1980s, rebels in the south (populated largely by black Christians and followers of tribal religions) took up arms against government domination by northern Sudan, mostly Arab-Muslim. War and related famine cost an estimated 2 mil lives and displaced millions of southerners. In 1993, Amnesty International accused the Sudanese government of "ethnic cleansing."

A new constitution based on Islamic law took effect June 30, 1998. On Aug. 20, in retaliation for bombings in Kenya and Tanzania, U.S. missiles destroyed a Khartoum pharmaceutical plant the U.S. alleged was associated with terrorist activities; independent inquiries later cast some doubt on the U.S. claim.

An accord to end the rebellion in the south was signed Jan. 9, 2005. Under a power-sharing constitution with autonomy for southern Sudan, former rebel leader John Garang became first vice pres., July 9. His death 3 weeks later in a helicopter crash sparked riots in Khartoum and other cities, Aug. 1-3, killing at least 130. A national unity government was installed Sept. 20.

During 2003-09, a rebellion in the Darfur region of western Sudan led to a new crisis. Marauding Arab militias, known as the *janjaweed*, retaliated by attacking black African villagers, looting and burning homes, and killing inhabitants, reportedly in collusion with Sudanese government troops. The African Union sent more than 7,000 peacekeepers, but fighting continued. Rebel and militia activities in both Sudan and Chad led to border clashes and further attacks on civilians. The UN Security Council voted July 31, 2007, to begin deploying a joint UN-African Union force of up to 26,000 peacekeepers (UNMIS), but fewer than 10,000 uniformed personnel had been sent by mid-2009.

On Mar. 4, 2009, the International Criminal Court in The Hague, Netherlands, issued a warrant for Pres. Bashir's arrest on charges of war crimes and other crimes against humanity in Darfur. Bashir defied the warrant, and the Sudanese government retaliated by ordering 13 of the largest international aid groups to leave Darfur; in June some of these groups were allowed to return. Subsequent months brought an upsurge of fighting both in Darfur and southern Sudan. By Sept. 2009 the Darfur war had killed about 300,000 people and displaced another 2.7 mil.

Suriname
Republic of Suriname

People: Population: 481,267. **Age distrib.** (%): <15: 27.1; 65+: 6.3. **Pop. density:** 7.7 per sq mi, 3 per sq km. **Urban:** 73.9%. **Ethnic groups:** Hindustani, or East Indian 37%, Creole (mixed white & black) 31%, Javanese 15%, Maroon (descendants of escaped slaves) 10%. **Principal languages:** Dutch (official), English widely spoken, Sranang Tongo (Surinamese, native lang. of Creoles & lingua franca among others), Caribbean Hindustani, Javanese. **Chief religions:** Hindu 27%, Protestant (predominantly Moravian) 25%, Roman Catholic 23%, Muslim 20%.

Geography: Total area: 63,039 sq mi, 163,270 sq km; **Land area:** 62,344 sq mi, 161,470 sq km. **Location:** On N shore of S. America. **Neighbors:** Guyana on W, Brazil on S, French Guiana on E. **Topography:** A flat Atlantic coast, where dikes permit agriculture. Inland is forest belt; to S, largely unexplored hills cover 75% of country. **Capital:** Paramaribo, 252,000.

Government: Type: Republic. **Head of state and gov.:** Pres. Runaldo Ronald Venetiaan; b. June 18, 1936; in office: Aug. 12, 2000. **Local divisions:** 10 districts. **Defense budget:** $22 mil. **Active troops:** 1,840.

Economy: Industries: mining, alumina prod., oil, food proc., fishing. **Chief crops:** paddy rice, bananas, palm kernels, coconuts, plantains, peanuts. **Natural resources:** timber, hydropower, fish, kaolin, shrimp, bauxite, gold, small amounts of nickel, copper, platinum, iron ore. **Crude oil reserves:** 79.6 mil bbls. **Arable land:** 0.4%. **Livestock:** cattle: 137,000; chickens: 3.8 mil; goats: 7,100; pigs: 24,500; sheep: 7,700. **Fish catch:** 29,679 metric tons. **Electricity prod.:** 1.6 bil kWh. **Labor force** (2004): agric. 8%, industry 14%, services 78%.

Finance: Monetary unit: Dollar (SRD) (Oct. 2009: 2.72 = $1 U.S.). **GDP:** $4.3 bil; **per capita GDP:** $8,900; **GDP growth:** 6%. **Imports** (2006): $1.3 bil; U.S. 30.8%, Netherlands 15.3%, Trinidad and Tobago 14%, China 7.6%, Japan 6.4%. **Exports** (2006): $1.4 bil; Canada 36.1%, Belgium 12.5%, Norway 12.4%, UAE 8.8%, U.S. 7.7%. **Tourism:** NA. **Budget** (2004): $425.9 mil. **Intl. reserves less gold:** $281 mil. **Gold:** 50,000 oz t. **Consumer prices:** 13.2%.

Transport: Motor vehicles: 76,000 pass. cars; 29,900 comm. vehicles. **Civil aviation:** 1.1 bil pass.-mi; 5 airports. **Chief ports:** Paramaribo, Wageningen.

Communications: TV sets: 241 per 1,000 pop. **Radios:** 728 per 1,000 pop. **Telephone lines:** 81,500. **Daily newspaper circ.** (2005): 80.1 per 1,000 pop. **Internet:** 50,000 users.

Health: Life expect.: 70.8 male; 76.4 female. **Births** (per 1,000 pop.): 17. **Deaths** (per 1,000 pop.): 5.5. **Natural inc.:** 1.15%. **Infant mortality** (per 1,000 live births): 19.4. **HIV rate:** 2.4%.

Education: Compulsory: ages 6-12. **Literacy:** 90.4%.

Major intl. organizations: UN (FAO, IBRD, ILO, IMF, IMO, WHO, WTO), Caricom, OAS.

Embassy: 4301 Connecticut Ave. NW, Ste. 460, 20008; 244-7488.

Website: www.surinameembassy.org

The Netherlands acquired Suriname in 1667 from Britain, in exchange for New Netherlands (New York). The 1954 Dutch constitution raised the colony to a level of equality with the Netherlands and the Netherlands Antilles. Independence was granted Nov. 25, 1975, despite objections from East Indians. Some 40% of the population (mostly East Indians) immigrated to the Netherlands in the months before independence.

The National Military Council took control of the government Feb. 1982. Civilian rule was restored in 1987, but political turmoil continued until 1992, disrupting the nation's economy. A special assembly, convened after parliament deadlocked, reelected Pres. Runaldo Ronald Venetiaan on Aug. 3, 2005.

Swaziland
Kingdom of Swaziland

People: Population: 1,123,913. **Age distrib.** (%): <15: 39.4; 65+: 3.7. **Pop. density:** 169.2 per sq mi, 65.3 per sq km. **Urban:** 24.1%. **Ethnic groups:** African 97%, European 3%. **Principal languages:** English, siSwati (both official; Eng. used in govt.). **Chief religions:** Zionist (blend of Christianity & indigenous ancestral worship) 40%, Roman Catholic 20%, Muslim 10%, other (incl. Anglican, Baha'i, Methodist, Mormon, Jewish) 30%.

Geography: Total area: 6,704 sq mi, 17,363 sq km; **Land area:** 6,642 sq mi, 17,203 sq km. **Location:** In southern Africa, near Indian O. coast. **Neighbors:** South Africa on N, W, S; Mozambique on E. **Topography:** Descends W-E in broad belts, becoming more arid in low veld region, then rising to plateau in E. **Capital:** Mbabane, 78,000.

Government: Type: Constitutional monarchy. **Head of state:** King Mswati III; b. Apr. 19, 1968; in office: Apr. 25, 1986. **Head of gov.:** Prime Min. Barnabas Sibusiso Dlamini; b. May 15, 1942; in office: Oct. 23, 2008. **Local divisions:** 4 districts. **Defense budget/Active troops:** NA.

Economy: Industries: coal, wood pulp, sugar, soft drink concentrates, textiles & apparel. **Chief crops:** sugarcane, cotton, corn, tobacco, rice, citrus, pineapples. **Natural resources:** asbestos, coal, clay, cassiterite, hydropower, forests, small gold & diamond deposits, quarry stone, talc. **Arable land:** 10%. **Livestock:** cattle: 585,000; chickens: 3.2 mil; goats: 276,000; pigs: 30,000; sheep: 28,000. **Fish catch** (est.): 70 metric tons. **Electricity prod.:** 424 mil kWh. **Labor force:** NA.

Finance: Monetary unit: Lilangeni (SZL) (Oct. 2009: 7.42 = $1 U.S.). **GDP:** $5.7 bil; **per capita GDP:** $5,100; **GDP growth:** 2.7%. **Imports:** $1.9 bil. **Exports:** $1.8 bil. **Tourism:** NA. **Budget:** $1.1 bil. **Intl. reserves less gold:** $488 mil. **Gold:** NA. **Consumer prices:** NA.

Transport: Railroad: Length: 187 mi. **Motor vehicles:** 54,900 pass. cars; 66,100 comm. vehicles. **Civil aviation:** 42.3 mil pass.-mi; 1 airport.

Communications: TV sets: 112 per 1,000 pop. **Radios:** 168 per 1,000 pop. **Telephone lines:** 44,000. **Daily newspaper circ.** (2004): 24.2 per 1,000 pop. **Internet:** 48,200 users.

Health: Life expect.: 31.7 male; 32.3 female. **Births** (per 1,000 pop.): 26.6. **Deaths** (per 1,000 pop.): 30.7. **Natural inc.:** −0.41%. **Infant mortality** (per 1,000 live births): 69.6. **HIV rate:** 26.1%.

Education: Compulsory: ages 6-12. **Literacy:** 79.6%.

Major intl. organizations: UN (FAO, IBRD, ILO, IMF, WHO, WTO), the Commonwealth, AU.

Embassy: 1712 New Hampshire Ave. NW 20009; 234-5002. **Website:** www.gov.sz

The royal house of Swaziland traces back 400 years, and is one of Africa's last ruling dynasties. The Swazis, a Bantu people, were driven to Swaziland from lands to the N by the Zulus in 1820. Their autonomy was later guaranteed by Britain and Transvaal (later part of South Africa), with Britain assuming control after 1903. Independence came Sept. 6, 1968. In 1973 the king repealed the constitution and assumed full powers.

A new constitution banning political parties took effect Oct. 13, 1978. Under a revised constitution effective Feb. 8, 2006, nonpartisan parliamentary elections were held Sept. 19, 2008. The AIDS crisis and the huge gap between rich and poor have fueled student and labor unrest in recent years.

Sweden
Kingdom of Sweden

People: Population: 9,059,651. **Age distrib.** (%): <15: 15.7; 65+: 18.8. **Pop. density:** 57.1 per sq mi, 22 per sq km. **Urban:** 84.3%. **Ethnic groups:** Swedes with Finnish & Sami minorities. **Principal language:** Swedish. **Chief religions:** Lutheran 87%, other (incl. Roman Catholic, Orthodox, Baptist, Muslim, Jewish, Buddhist) 13%.

Geography: Total area: 173,732 sq mi, 449,964 sq km; **Land area:** 158,663 sq mi, 410,934 sq km. **Location:** On Scandinavian Peninsula in N Europe. **Neighbors:** Norway on W, Denmark on S (across Kattegat), Finland on E. **Topography:** Mountains along NW border cover 25% of Sweden, flat or rolling terrain covers central and southern areas, which include several large lakes. **Capital:** Stockholm, 1,264,000.

Government: Type: Constitutional monarchy. **Head of state:** King Carl XVI Gustaf; b. Apr. 30, 1946; in office: Sept. 19, 1973. **Head of gov.:** Prime Min. Fredrik Reinfeldt; b. Aug. 4, 1965; in office: Oct. 5, 2006. **Local divisions:** 21 counties. **Defense budget:** $6.8 bil. **Active troops:** 16,900.

Economy: Industries: iron & steel, precision equip. (bearings, radio & phone parts, armaments), wood pulp & paper products, proc. foods, motor vehicles. **Chief crops:** barley, wheat, sugar beets. **Natural resources:** iron ore, copper, lead, zinc, gold, silver, uranium, timber, hydropower. **Arable land:** 6%. **Livestock:** cattle: 1.6 mil; chickens: 7.1 mil; pigs: 1.7 mil; sheep: 508,921. **Fish catch:** 243,618 metric tons. **Electricity prod.:** 138.5 bil kWh. **Labor force** (2008 est.): agric. 1.1%, industry 28.2%, services 70.7%.

Finance: Monetary unit: Krona (SEK) (Oct. 2009: 6.93 = $1 U.S.). **GDP:** $344.3 bil; **per capita GDP:** $38,100; **GDP growth:**

−0.4%. **Imports:** $165.3 bil; Germany 17.5%, Denmark 9.4%, Norway 8.6%, UK 6.2%, Finland 5.7%, Netherlands 5.6%, France 5%, Russia 4.4%, China 4.2%. **Exports:** $183.1 bil; Germany 10.4%, Norway 9.5%, Denmark 7.4%, UK 7.4%, U.S. 6.6%, Finland 6.3%, Netherlands 5.1%, France 4.9%, Belgium 4.4%. **Tourism:** $12 bil. **Budget:** $240.5 bil. **Intl. reserves less gold:** $16.81 bil. **Gold:** 4.4 mil oz t. **Consumer prices:** 3.4%.

Transport: Railroad: Length: 7,228 mi. **Motor vehicles:** 4.2 mil pass. cars; 475,000 comm. vehicles. **Civil aviation:** 7.1 bil pass.-mi (incl. Scandinavian Airlines System operations apportionment); 152 airports. **Chief ports:** Brofjorden, Göteborg, Helsingborg, Lulea, Malmö, Stenungsund, Stockholm, Trelleborg, Visby.

Communications: TV sets: 551 per 1,000 pop. **Radios:** 932 per 1,000 pop. **Telephone lines:** 5.3 mil. **Daily newspaper circ.** (2004): 480.6 per 1,000 pop. **Internet:** 8.1 mil users.

Health: Life expect.: 78.5 male; 83.1 female. **Births** (per 1,000 pop.): 10.2. **Deaths** (per 1,000 pop.): 10.2. **Natural inc.:** −0.01%. **Infant mortality** (per 1,000 live births): 2.8. **HIV rate:** 0.1%.

Education: Compulsory: ages 7-16. **Literacy:** 99%.

Major intl. organizations: UN and all of its specialized agencies, EU, OECD, OSCE.

Embassy: 2900 K St. NW 20007; 467-2600. **Website:** www.sweden.se

The Swedes have lived in present-day Sweden for at least 5,000 years, longer than nearly any other European people. Gothic tribes from Sweden played a major role in the disintegration of the Roman Empire. Other Swedes helped create the first Russian state in the 9th cent.

The Swedes were Christianized from the 11th cent., and a strong centralized monarchy developed. A parliament, the Riksdag, was first called in 1435, the earliest parliament on the European continent, with all classes of society represented.

Swedish independence from rule by Danish kings (dating from 1397) was secured by Gustavus I in a revolt, 1521-23; he built up the government and military and established the Lutheran Church. In the 17th cent. Sweden was a major European power, gaining most of the Baltic seacoast, but its international position subsequently declined. The Napoleonic wars, 1799-1815, in which Sweden acquired Norway (it became independent 1905), were the last in which Sweden participated. Armed neutrality was maintained in both world wars.

More than 4 decades of Social Democratic rule ended in the 1976 parliamentary elections; the party returned to power in the 1982 elections. After Prime Min. Olof Palme was shot to death in Stockholm, Feb. 28, 1986, Ingvar Carlsson took office. Carl Bildt, a non-Socialist, became prime min. Oct. 1991, with a mandate to restore Sweden's economic competitiveness. The Social Democrats returned to power following 1994 elections.

Swedish voters approved membership in the European Union Nov. 13, 1994, and Sweden entered the EU as of Jan. 1, 1995. Carlsson retired and was succeeded by Goran Persson in Mar. 1996. Persson and his Social Democrats led coalition governments after the elections of Sept. 20, 1998, and Sept. 15, 2002. Foreign Min. Anna Lindh died Sept. 11, 2003, after being stabbed in a Stockholm department store. Swedish voters Sept. 14 rejected adoption of the euro currency.

A center-right alliance led by Fredrik Reinfeldt defeated the Social Democrats in the elections of Sept. 17, 2006. Parliament voted Apr. 1, 2009, to legalize same-sex marriage. The global recession of 2008-09 led to a steep drop in orders for Swedish exports, especially cars and trucks, but the economy began to recover in mid-2009.

Switzerland
Swiss Confederation

People: Population: 7,604,467. **Age distrib.** (%): <15: 15.6; 65+: 16.3. **Pop. density:** 495.2 per sq mi, 191.2 per sq km. **Urban:** 73.3%. **Ethnic groups:** German 65%, French 18%, Italian 10%. **Principal languages:** German, French, Italian, Romansch (all national & official). **Chief religions:** Roman Catholic 42%, Protestant 35%, Muslim 4%, none 11%.

Geography: Total area: 15,942 sq mi, 41,290 sq km; **Land area:** 15,355 sq mi, 39,770 sq km. **Location:** In Alps Mts. in central Europe. **Neighbors:** France on W; Italy on S; Liechtenstein, Austria on E; Germany on N. **Topography:** The Alps cover 60% of land area; the Jura, near France, 10%. Running between, NE-SW, are midlands, 30%. **Capital:** Bern, 337,000. **Cities (urban aggr.):** Zürich, 1,108,000.

Government: Type: Federal republic. **Head of state and gov.:** The president is elected by the Federal Assembly to a nonrenewable 1-year term. **Local divisions:** 20 full cantons, 6 half cantons. **Defense budget:** $3.5 bil. **Active troops:** 22,823.

Economy: Industries: machinery, chemicals, watches, textiles, precision instruments, tourism, banking, insurance. **Chief crops:** grains, fruits, vegetables. **Natural resources:** hydropower potential, timber, salt. **Arable land:** 10%. **Livestock:** cattle: 1.6 mil; chickens: 5 mil; goats: 79,081; pigs: 1.6 mil; sheep: 443,584. **Fish catch:** 2,594 metric tons. **Electricity prod.:** 60.2 bil kWh. **Labor force** (2005): agric. 3.9%, industry 22.8%, services 73.2%.

Finance: Monetary unit: Franc (CHF) (Oct. 2009: 1.02 = $1 U.S.). **GDP:** $316.7 bil; **per capita GDP:** $41,800; **GDP growth:** 1.6%. **Imports:** $213 bil; Germany 27.7%, U.S. 10.6%, Italy

10.3%, France 8.4%, Russia 4.4%, UK 4%. **Exports:** $233.1 bil; Germany 21.2%, U.S. 8.7%, France 8.2%, Italy 7.9%, Austria 4.5%. **Tourism:** $12.2 bil. **Budget:** $143.1 bil. **Intl. reserves less gold:** $29.26 bil. **Gold:** 33.44 mil oz t. **Consumer prices:** 2.4%.

Transport: Railroad: Length: 3,037 mi. **Motor vehicles:** 3.9 mil pass. cars; 353,100 comm. vehicles. **Civil aviation:** 12.7 bil pass.-mi; 43 airports. **Chief port:** Basel.

Communications: TV sets: 457 per 1,000 pop. **Radios:** 979 per 1,000 pop. **Telephone lines:** 4.8 mil. **Daily newspaper circ.** (2004): 420 per 1,000 pop. **Internet:** 5.7 mil users.

Health: Life expect.: 77.9 male; 83.7 female. **Births** (per 1,000 pop.): 9.6. **Deaths** (per 1,000 pop.): 8.5. **Natural inc.:** 0.11%. **Infant mortality** (per 1,000 live births): 4.2 **HIV rate:** 0.6%.

Education: Compulsory: ages 7-15. **Literacy:** 99%.

Major intl. organizations: UN and most of its specialized agencies, EFTA, OECD, OSCE.

Embassy: 2900 Cathedral Ave. NW 20008; 745-7900.

Website: www.ch.ch

Switzerland, the former Roman province of Helvetia, traces its modern history to 1291, when 3 cantons created a defensive league. Other cantons were subsequently admitted to the Swiss Confederation, which obtained its independence from the Holy Roman Empire through the Peace of Westphalia (1648). The cantons were joined under a federal constitution in 1848, with large powers of local control retained by each.

Switzerland has maintained an armed neutrality since 1815 and has not been involved in a foreign war since 1515. It is the seat of many UN and other international agencies but did not become a full member of the UN until Sept. 10, 2002.

Switzerland is a world banking center. Stung by charges that assets seized by the Nazis and deposited in Swiss banks in WWII had not been properly returned, the government announced, Mar. 5, 1997, a $4.7 bil fund to compensate victims of the Holocaust and other catastrophies. Swiss banks agreed Aug. 12, 1998, to pay $1.25 bil in reparations. Abortion was decriminalized by a June 2, 2002 referendum. In referendums June 5 and Sept. 25, 2005, voters backed plans harmonizing travel, asylum, law enforcement, and labor policies with the EU; more rights for same-sex couples were also endorsed June 5.

The Swiss government responded to an international financial crisis in Oct. 2008 by bailing out the troubled banking giant UBS. Bowing to pressure from U.S. tax authorities, UBS agreed in Jan. 2009 to close some 19,000 hidden offshore accounts, and pledged Aug. 19 to disclose data on accounts held by over 4,400 U.S. clients. Switzerland's GDP was forecast to shrink by more than 3% in 2009.

Syria
Syrian Arab Republic

People: Population: 20,178,485. **Age distrib.** (%): <15: 35.9; 65+: 3.4. **Pop. density:** 284 per sq mi, 109.6 per sq km. **Urban:** 53.2%. **Ethnic groups:** Arab 90%; Kurds, Armenians, & other 10%. **Principal languages:** Arabic (official), Kurdish, Armenian, Aramaic, Circassian widely understood. **Chief religions:** Sunni Muslim 74%, other Muslim (incl. Alawite, Druze) 16%, Christian (various denominations) 10%.

Geography: Total area: 71,498 sq mi, 185,180 sq km; **Land area:** 71,062 sq mi, 184,050 sq km. **Location:** Middle East, at E end of Medit. Sea. **Neighbors:** Lebanon, Israel on W; Jordan on S; Iraq on E; Turkey on N. **Topography:** Syria has a short Medit. coastline, then stretches E and S with fertile lowlands and plains, alternating with mountains and large desert areas. **Capital:** Damascus (Dimashq), 2,466,000. **Cities (urban aggr.):** Aleppo (Halab), 2,738,000; Homs, 1,005,000.

Government: Type: Republic (under military regime). **Head of state:** Pres. Bashar al-Assad; b. Sept. 11, 1965; in office: July 17, 2000. **Head of gov.:** Prime Min. Muhammad Naji al-Otari; b. 1944; in office: Sept. 10, 2003. **Local divisions:** 14 provinces. **Defense budget:** $1.5 bil. **Active troops:** 292,600.

Economy: Industries: oil, textiles, food proc., beverages, tobacco, phosphate rock mining. **Chief crops:** wheat, barley, cotton, lentils, chickpeas, olives, sugar beets. **Natural resources:** oil, phosphates, chrome & mang. ores, asphalt, iron ore, rock salt, marble, gypsum, hydropower. **Crude oil reserves:** 2.5 bil bbls. **Arable land:** 25%. **Livestock:** cattle: 1.2 mil; chickens: 24.5 mil; goats: 1.6 mil; sheep: 22.9 mil. **Fish catch:** 17,881 metric tons. **Electricity prod.:** 35.3 bil kWh. **Labor force** (2006 est.): agric. 19.2%, industry 14.5%, services 66.3%.

Finance: Monetary unit: Pound (SYP) (Oct. 2009: 46.05 = $1 U.S.). **GDP:** $98.8 bil; **per capita GDP:** $5,000; **GDP growth:** 5.1%. **Imports:** $14.5 bil; Saudi Arabia 11.8%, China 8.8%, Russia 6.5%, Italy 5.9%, Egypt 5.8%, UAE 5.8%, Ukraine 4.6%, Turkey 4.3%, Iran 4.3%. **Exports:** $12.8 bil; Iraq 30.2%, Germany 9.6%, Lebanon 9.5%, Italy 6.2%, France 5.4%, Egypt 5.3%, Saudi Arabia 5%. **Tourism:** NA. **Budget:** $11.2 bil. **Intl. reserves less gold:** NA. **Gold:** 830,000 oz t. **Consumer prices:** 15.%.

Transport: Railroad: Length: 1,275 mi. **Motor vehicles:** 333,000 pass. cars; 442,000 comm. vehicles. **Civil aviation:** 1.6 bil pass.-mi; 29 airports. **Chief ports:** Latakia, Tartus.

Communications: TV sets: 68 per 1,000 pop. **Radios:** 278 per 1,000 pop. **Telephone lines:** 3.6 mil. **Internet:** 3.6 mil users.

Health: Life expect.: 69.5 male; 72.3 female. **Births** (per 1,000 pop.): 26.6. **Deaths** (per 1,000 pop.): 4.7. **Natural inc.:** 2.19%. **Infant mortality** (per 1,000 live births): 26.8. **HIV rate:** NA.

Education: Compulsory: ages 6-14. **Literacy:** 83.1%.

Major intl. organizations: UN (FAO, IBRD, ILO, IMF, IMO, WHO), AL.

Embassy: 2215 Wyoming Ave. NW 20008; 232-6313.

Website: www.mot.gov.sy

Syria was the center of the Seleucid empire, but later became absorbed in the Roman and Arab empires. Ottoman rule prevailed for 4 cents., until the end of WWI.

The state of Syria was formed from former Turkish districts, separated by the Treaty of Sevres, 1920, and divided into the states of Syria and Greater Lebanon. Both were administered under a French League of Nations mandate, 1920-41.

Syria was proclaimed a republic by the occupying French Sept. 16, 1941, and exercised full independence Apr. 17, 1946. Syria joined the Arab invasion of Israel in 1948.

Syria joined Egypt Feb. 1958 in the United Arab Republic but seceded Sept. 1961. The Socialist Baath party and military leaders seized power Mar. 1963. The Baath, a pan-Arab organization, became the only legal party. The government has been dominated by the Alawite minority.

In the Arab-Israeli war of June 1967, Israel seized and occupied the Golan Heights, from which Syria had shelled Israeli settlements. On Oct. 6, 1973, Syria participated with Egypt in an attack on Israel, but failed to recapture the Golan Heights. Syrian troops entered Lebanon in 1976, during the Lebanese civil war, and remained a strong presence in the country. They fought Palestinian guerrillas and, later, Christian militiamen. Syria sided with Iran during the Iran-Iraq war, 1980-88.

Following Israel's invasion of Lebanon, June 6, 1982, Israeli planes destroyed 17 Syrian antiaircraft missile batteries in the Bekaa Valley, June 9. Some 25 Syrian planes were downed during the engagement. Israel and Syria agreed to a cease-fire June 11. Syria's alleged role in promoting international terrorism led to strained relations with the U.S. and Great Britain.

Syria condemned the Aug. 1990 Iraqi invasion of Kuwait and sent troops to help Allied forces in the Gulf War. In 1991, Syria accepted U.S. proposals for the terms of an Arab-Israeli peace conference. Syria subsequently participated in negotiations with Israel, but progress toward peace was slow.

Hafez al-Assad, president of Syria since 1971, died June 10, 2000, and was succeeded by his son Bashar al-Assad. Following the U.S.-led invasion of Iraq, Mar. 2003, the U.S. pressured Syria to rein in extremists and deny safe haven to fugitive Iraqi leaders. Israeli planes hit an alleged terrorist camp near Damascus Oct. 4, 2003. The U.S. imposed limited sanctions on Syria, May 11, 2004.

The killing of former Lebanese Prime Min. Rafik al-Hariri by a truck bomb in Beirut, Feb. 14, 2005, was a catalyst for massive anti-Syrian protests in Lebanon. Syria denied responsibility for the blast but pulled nearly all its troops out of Lebanon by Apr. 26; some Syrian intelligence agents may have remained. Syria aided Hezbollah fighters in their conflict with Israel. When Israeli armed forces struck Lebanon, July-Aug. 2006, in an effort to cripple Hezbollah, about 180,000 Lebanese found temporary refuge in Syria. Four suspected Islamic militants stormed the U.S. embassy in Damascus Sept. 12 but were gunned down by Syrian security guards.

In an uncontested referendum, May 27, 2007, Syrian voters confirmed Pres. Bashar al-Assad for another 7-year term. On Sept. 6, Israel bombed a secret site in N Syria where the Israelis reportedly believed Syria and North Korea were developing a nuclear facility; both countries denied the claim. Violent incidents in 2008 included the Feb. 12 killing of Hezbollah commander Imad Mugniyah, by a car bomb in Damascus; the assassination Aug. 1 of Brig. Gen. Muhammad Suleiman, a close military aide to Pres. Assad, shot by a sniper at a beach resort; and a car bombing Sept. 27 that killed 17 people near a security complex in Damascus. Relations between the U.S. and Syria improved in 2009, and the U.S. pledged in July to ease trade sanctions. About 1.2 mil Iraqi refugees were living in Syria as of Sept. 2009.

Taiwan

People: Population: 22,974,347. **Age distrib.** (%): <15: 16.7; 65+: 10.7. **Pop. density:** 1,844.5 per sq mi, 712.2 per sq km. **Urban:** NA. **Ethnic groups:** Taiwanese (incl. Hakka) 84%, mainland Chinese 14%, indigenous 2%. **Principal languages:** Mandarin Chinese (official), Taiwanese (Min), Hakka dialects. **Chief religions:** Mixture of Buddhist & Taoist 93%, Christian 5%.

Geography: Total area: 13,892 sq mi, 35,980 sq km; **Land area:** 12,456 sq mi, 32,260 sq km. **Location:** Off SE coast of China, between E and S China seas. **Neighbors:** Nearest is China to NW. **Topography:** A mountain range forms backbone of island; the eastern half is very steep and craggy, western slope is flat, fertile, and well cultivated. **Capital:** Taipei, 2,603,000. **Cities (urban aggr.):** Kaohsiung, 1,538,000; Taichung, 1,078,000.

Government: Type: Democracy. **Head of state:** Pres. Ma Ying-jeou; b. July 13, 1950; in office: May 20, 2008. **Head of gov.:** Prime Min. Wu Den-yih; b. Jan. 30, 1948; in office: Sept. 10, 2009. **Local divisions:** 16 counties, 5 municipalities, 2 special municipalities (Taipei, Kaohsiung). **Defense budget:** $9.6 bil. **Active troops:** 290,000.

Economy: Industries: electronics, oil refining, armaments, chemicals, textiles, iron & steel, machinery, cement, food proc., pharmaceuticals. **Chief crops:** rice, corn, vegetables, fruit, tea. **Natural resources:** small deposits of coal, nat. gas, limestone, marble, asbestos. **Crude oil reserves:** 2.4 mil bbls. **Arable land:** 24%. **Fish catch:** 1.5 mil metric tons. **Electricity prod.:** 216.6 bil kWh. **Labor force** (2008 est.): agric. 5.1%, industry 36.8%, services 58%.

Finance: Monetary unit: New Dollar (TWD) (Oct. 2009: 32.12 = $1 U.S.). **GDP:** $712 bil; **per capita GDP:** $31,100; **GDP growth:** 0.1%. **Imports:** $236.7 bil; Japan 19.3%, China 13%, U.S. 10.9%, Saudi Arabia 6.3%, S. Korea 5.5%. **Exports:** $254.9 bil; China 29.2%, U.S. 12%, Hong Kong 9.8%, Japan 6.9%, Singapore 4.6%. **Tourism:** $5.2 bil. **Budget:** $75.7 bil. **Intl. reserves less gold:** $189.39 bil. **Gold:** NA. **Consumer prices:** NA.

Transport: Railroad: Length: 987 mi. **Civil aviation:** 38 airports. **Chief ports:** Chilung (Keelung), Kaohsiung, Taichung.

Communications: TV sets: 327 per 1,000 pop. **Radios:** 402 per 1,000 pop. **Telephone lines:** 14.3 mil. **Internet:** 15.1 mil users.

Health: Life expect.: 74.9 male; 80.9 female. **Births** (per 1,000 pop.): 9. **Deaths** (per 1,000 pop.): 6.7. **Natural inc.:** 0.23%. **Infant mortality** (per 1,000 live births): 5.5. **HIV rate:** NA.

Education: Compulsory: ages 6-14. **Literacy:** 96.1%.

Major intl. organizations: APEC.

Taipei Economic and Cultural Representative Office: 4201 Wisconsin Ave. NW 20016; 895-1800.

Website: english.www.gov.tw

Large-scale Chinese immigration began in the 17th cent. The island came under mainland control after an interval of Dutch rule, 1620-62. Taiwan (also called Formosa) was ruled by Japan 1895-1945. The Kuomintang (Chinese nationalist govt.) fled to Taiwan in 1949 and established the Republic of China under Chiang Kai-shek, who ruled until his death in 1975. The U.S. provided military aid to deter a Communist invasion.

In 1971, the UN expelled Taiwan from its seat and recognized the mainland government. The U.S. officially recognized the People's Republic, Dec. 15, 1978, and severed ties with Taiwan. However, the U.S. and Taiwan have continued a strong trading relationship and maintain contact via quasi-official agencies.

Land reform, government planning, U.S. aid and investment, and free universal education brought huge advances in industry, agriculture, and living standards. In 1987 martial law was lifted after 38 years, and in 1991 the 43-year period of emergency rule ended. Taiwan held its first direct presidential election Mar. 23, 1996. An earthquake on Sept. 21, 1999, killed more than 2,300 people and injured thousands more.

Five decades of Nationalist Party rule ended with the presidential election of Mar. 18, 2000, won by Chen Shui-bian, leader of the pro-independence Democratic Progressive Party. Chen was wounded in an apparent assassination attempt Mar. 19, 2004, one day before he narrowly won a 2nd term as president. Promising increased cooperation with China, Taipei Mayor Ma Ying-jeou, candidate of the opposition Kuomintang, won the presidential election Mar. 22, 2008.

Jailed on corruption charges Nov. 12, 2008, former Pres. Chen Shui-bian was convicted and sentenced to life in prison, Sept. 11, 2009. Flooding and mudslides from Typhoon Morakot, Aug. 7-9, left at least 700 people dead or missing; criticism of the government's disaster response led to a cabinet shake-up a month later.

Since 1949, the People's Republic has considered Taiwan a rebel province of the mainland; until 1991, Taiwan claimed to be the sole government of both. In 2003, China replaced the U.S. as Taiwan's leading trade partner. China has warned that any Taiwan move toward independence could provoke military action.

The **Penghu Isls.** (Pescadores), 49 sq mi, pop. (2006 est.) 91,785, lie between Taiwan and the mainland. **Quemoy,** pop. (2006 est.) 76,491, and **Matsu,** pop. (2006 est.) 9,786, lie just off the mainland.

Tajikistan
Republic of Tajikistan

People: Population: 7,349,145. **Age distrib.** (%): <15: 34.3; 65+: 3.6. **Pop. density:** 133.4 per sq mi, 51.5 per sq km. **Urban:** 26.4%. **Ethnic groups:** Tajik 80%, Uzbek 15%. **Principal languages:** Tajik (official), Russian (widely used in govt. & business). **Chief religions:** Sunni Muslim 85%, Shi'a Muslim 5%.

Geography: Total area: 55,251 sq mi, 143,100 sq km; **Land area:** 55,097 sq mi, 142,700 sq km. **Location:** Central Asia. **Neighbors:** Uzbekistan on N and W, Kyrgyzstan on N, China on E, Afghanistan on S. **Topography:** Mountainous region that contains the Pamirs, Trans-Alai mountain system. **Capital:** Dushanbe, 553,000.

Government: Type: Republic. **Head of state:** Pres. Imomali Rakhmon; b. Oct. 5, 1952; in office: Nov. 6, 1994. **Head of gov.:** Prime Min. Akil Akilov; b. Feb. 2, 1944; in office: Dec. 20, 1999. **Local divisions:** 2 viloyats, 1 autonomous viloyat. **Defense budget:** $87 mil. **Active troops:** 8,800.

Economy: Industries: aluminum, zinc, lead, chemicals & fertilizers, cement, vegetable oil, metal-cutting machine tools. **Chief crops:** cotton, grain, fruits, grapes, vegetables. **Natural resources:** hydropower, some oil, uranium, mercury, lead, zinc, antimony, tungsten, silver, gold. **Crude oil reserves:** 12 mil bbls. **Arable**

land: 7%. **Livestock:** cattle: 1.4 mil; chickens: 2.6 mil; goats: 1.2 mil; pigs: 672; sheep: 2 mil. **Fish catch** (est.): 172 metric tons. **Electricity prod.:** 17 bil kWh. **Labor force** (2000 est.): agric. 67.2%, industry 7.5%, services 25.3%.

Finance: Monetary unit: Somoni (TJS) (Oct. 2009: 4.38 = $1 U.S.). **GDP:** 13.2 bil; **per capita GDP:** $1,800; **GDP growth:** 7.9%. **Imports:** $4.1 bil; China 26%, Russia 24.5%, Kazakhstan 10.6%, Uzbekistan 6.8%, Turkey 5.4%. **Exports:** $1.5 bil; Russia 15.7%, Turkey 13.8%, Italy 11.7%, Norway 11.5%, Uzbekistan 10.2%, Iran 9.8%. **Tourism:** NA. **Budget:** $673 mil. **Intl. reserves less gold** (2006): $116 mil. **Gold:** 70,000 oz t. **Consumer prices:** NA.

Transport: Railroad: Length: 423 mi. **Motor vehicles:** 117,100 pass. cars; 16,800 comm. vehicles. **Civil aviation:** 585.3 mil pass.-mi; 18 airports.

Communications: TV sets: 328 per 1,000 pop. **Radios:** 143 per 1,000 pop. **Telephone lines:** 360,000. **Internet:** 600,000 users.

Health: Life expect.: 62 male; 68.2 female. **Births** (per 1,000 pop.): 27.2. **Deaths** (per 1,000 pop.): 6.9. **Natural inc.:** 2.02%. **Infant mortality** (per 1,000 live births): 42.3. **HIV rate:** 0.3%.

Education: Compulsory: ages 7-15. **Literacy:** 99.6%.

Major International Organizations: UN (FAO, IBRD, ILO, IMF, WHO), CIS, OSCE.

Embassy: 1005 New Hampshire Ave. NW 20037; 223-6090.

Website: www.parlament.tj

There were settled societies in the region from about 3000 BCE. Invaders have included Iranians, Arabs (who converted the population to Islam), Mongols, Uzbeks, Afghans, and Russians. The USSR gained control 1918-25. The region then was part of the Uzbek SSR until the Tajik SSR was proclaimed in 1929.

Tajikistan declared independence Sept. 9, 1991. Factional fighting led to the installation of a pro-Communist regime, Jan. 1993. A new constitution establishing a presidential system was approved by referendum Nov. 6, 1994.

Clashes between Muslim rebels, reportedly armed by Afghanistan, and troops loyal to the government (and supported by Russia) claimed an estimated 55,000 lives by mid-1997, despite a series of peace accords. Constitutional changes including legalization of Islamic political parties were approved by referendum Sept. 26, 1999. Pres. Imomali Rakhmonov won a Nov. 6 election called "a farce" by human-rights observers. Voters approved, June 22, 2003, constitutional changes giving Rakhmonov the right to serve as president until 2020. Leading opposition groups boycotted the election of Nov. 6, 2006, again won by Rakhmonov. He changed his name to Rakhmon in 2007 under a decree that banned Slavic name endings and other Soviet-era practices.

Poverty and corruption are widespread. Much of the nation's income is supplied by international donors and by remittances from young Tajiks working in Russia and Kazakhstan.

Tanzania
United Republic of Tanzania

People: Population: 41,048,532. **Age distrib.** (%): <15: 43; 65+: 2.9. **Pop. density:** 120 per sq mi, 46.3 per sq km. **Urban:** 24.2%. **Ethnic groups:** African 99% (Bantu 95%, 130+ tribes), Arab, African. **Principal languages:** Kiswahili or Swahili, English (both official; Eng. primary lang. of commerce, admin., higher ed.); Arabic widely spoken in Zanzibar; local languages. **Chief religions:** Christian 30%, Muslim 35%, indigenous beliefs 35%; Muslim 99%+ on Zanzibar.

Geography: Total area: 364,900 sq mi, 945,087 sq km; **Land area:** 342,101 sq mi, 886,037 sq km. **Location:** On coast of E Africa. **Neighbors:** Kenya, Uganda on N; Rwanda, Burundi, Congo on W; Zambia, Malawi, Mozambique on S. **Topography:** Hot, arid central plateau, surrounded by lake region in W, temperate highlands in N and S, the coastal plains. Mt. Kilimanjaro, 19,340 ft, is highest in Africa. **Capital:** Dodoma, 183,000. **Cities (urban agr.):** Dar es Salaam, 2,930,000.

Government: Type: Republic. **Head of state:** Pres. Jakaya Mrisho Kikwete; b. Oct. 7, 1950; in office: Dec. 21, 2005. **Head of gov.:** Prime Min. Mizengo Kayanza Peter Pinda; b. Aug. 12, 1948; in office: Feb. 8, 2008. **Local divisions:** 25 regions. **Defense budget:** $162 mil. **Active troops:** 27,000.

Economy: Industries: agric. proc.; diamond, gold, & iron mining; oil refining; apparel. **Chief crops:** coffee, sisal, tea, cotton, pyrethrum (insecticide from chrysanthemums), cashews, tobacco, cloves. **Natural resources:** hydropower, tin, phosphates, iron ore, coal, diamonds, gemstones, gold, nat. gas, nickel. **Arable land:** 4%. **Livestock:** cattle: 18 mil; chickens: 30 mil; goats: 12.6 mil; pigs: 455,000; sheep: 3.6 mil. **Fish catch:** 329,711 metric tons. **Electricity prod.:** 2.7 bil kWh. **Labor force** (2002 est.): agric. 80%, industry & services 20%.

Finance: Monetary unit: Shilling (TZS) (Oct. 2009: 1,305.00 = $1 U.S.). **GDP:** $54.3 bil; **per capita GDP:** $1,300; **GDP growth:** 7.1%. **Imports:** $6.3 bil; China 14.5%, South Africa 7.3%, Kenya 7.2%, India 6.3%, UAE 6.1%. **Exports:** $2.4 bil; India 10.1%, China 7.2%, Japan 6.4%, UAE 5.6%, Netherlands 5.4%, Germany 5%. **Tourism:** NA. **Budget:** $1.86 bil. **Gold:** NA. **Consumer prices:** 10.3%.

Transport: Railroad: Length: 2,292 mi. **Motor vehicles:** 35,600 pass. cars; 98,800 comm. vehicles. **Civil aviation:** 152.9 mil pass.-mi; 9 airports. **Chief port:** Dar es Salaam.

Communications: TV sets: 21 per 1,000 pop. **Radios:** 280 per 1,000 pop. **Telephone lines:** 123,800. **Daily newspaper circ.** (2004): 1.6 per 1,000 pop. **Internet:** 520,000 users.

Health: Life expect.: 50.1 male; 52.9 female. **Births** (per 1,000 pop.): 35.1. **Deaths** (per 1,000 pop.): 12.9. **Natural inc.:** 2.22%. **Infant mortality** (per 1,000 live births): 70.5. **HIV rate:** 6.2%.

Education: Compulsory: ages 7-13. **Literacy:** 72.3%.

Major intl. organizations: UN and all of its specialized agencies, the Commonwealth, AU.

Embassy: 2139 R St. NW 20008; 939-6125.

Website: www.tanzania.go.tz

The Republic of Tanganyika in E Africa and the island Republic of Zanzibar, off Tanganyika's coast, both of which had recently gained independence, joined to form the United Republic of Tanzania, Apr. 26, 1964. Zanzibar retains internal self-government.

Until resigning as president in 1985, Julius K. Nyerere, a former Tanganyikan independence leader, dominated Tanzania's politics, which emphasized government planning and control of the economy, with single-party rule. In 1992 the constitution was amended to establish a multiparty system. Privatization of the economy was undertaken in the 1990s.

At least 500 people died when an overcrowded Tanzanian ferry sank in Lake Victoria, May 21, 1996. A bomb at the U.S. embassy in Dar-es-Salaam, Aug. 7, 1998, killed 11 people and injured at least 70 others. The U.S. blamed the attack and a near-simultaneous embassy bombing in Kenya on Islamic terrorists associated with Osama bin Laden. After a trial in New York City, 4 conspirators were convicted May 29, 2001.

President since 1995, Benjamin Mkapa was reelected Oct. 29, 2000. Over 280 people died in a train wreck June 24, 2002, SE of Dodoma. Jakaya Mrisho Kikwete of the ruling Chama Cha Mapinduzi (Party of the Revolution) won the Dec. 14, 2005, presidential election.

Tanganyika. Arab colonization and slaving began in the 8th cent. CE; Portuguese sailors explored the coast by about 1500. Other Europeans followed.

In 1885 Germany established German East Africa, of which Tanganyika formed the bulk. It became a League of Nations mandate and, after 1946, a UN trust territory, both under Britain. It became independent Dec. 9, 1961, and a republic within the Commonwealth a year later.

Zanzibar, the Isle of Cloves, lies 23 mi off mainland Tanzania; area 640 sq mi and pop. (2002) 622,459. The island of **Pemba,** 25 mi to the NE, area 380 sq mi and pop. (2002) 362,166 is included in the administration.

Chief industry is cloves and clove oil production, of which Zanzibar and Pemba produce most of the world's supply.

Zanzibar was for centuries the center for Arab slave traders. Portugal ruled the region for 2 centuries until ousted by Arabs around 1700. Zanzibar became a British Protectorate in 1890; independence came Dec. 10, 1963. Revolutionary forces overthrew the Sultan Jan. 12, 1964. The new government ousted Western diplomats and newsmen, slaughtered thousands of Arabs, and nationalized farms. Union with Tanganyika followed.

Thailand
Kingdom of Thailand

People: Population: 65,905,410. **Age distrib.** (%): <15: 20.8; 65+: 8.7. **Pop. density:** 333.5 per sq mi, 128.8 per sq km. **Urban:** 32.3%. **Ethnic groups:** Thai 75%, Chinese 14%. **Principal languages:** Thai, English (secondary lang. of elite), ethnic & regional dialects. **Chief religions:** Buddhism 95%, Muslim 5%.

Geography: Total area: 198,457 sq mi, 514,000 sq km; **Land area:** 197,596 sq mi, 511,770 sq km. **Location:** On Indochinese and Malayan peninsulas in SE Asia. **Neighbors:** Myanmar on W and N, Laos on N, Cambodia on E, Malaysia on S. **Topography:** A plateau dominates NE third of Thailand, dropping to the fertile alluvial valley of Chao Phraya R. in center. Forested mountains are in N, with narrow fertile valleys. The S peninsula region is covered by rain forests. **Capital:** Bangkok (Krung Thep), 6,704,000.

Government: Type: Constitutional monarchy. **Head of state:** King Bhumibol Adulyadej; b. Dec. 5, 1927; in office: June 9, 1946. **Head of gov.:** Prime Min. Abhisit Vejjajiva; b. Aug. 3, 1964; in office: Dec. 17, 2008. **Local divisions:** 76 provinces. **Defense budget:** $3.3 bil. **Active troops:** 306,600.

Economy: Industries: tourism, textiles & garments, agric. proc., beverages, tobacco, cement, light mfg. (such as electric appliances, computers & parts, automobiles & automotive parts). **Chief crops:** rice, cassava, rubber, corn, sugarcane, coconuts, soybeans. **Natural resources:** tin, rubber, nat. gas, tungsten, tantalum, timber, lead, fish, gypsum, lignite, fluorite. **Crude oil reserves:** 441 mil bbls. **Arable land:** 28%. **Livestock:** cattle: 6.5 mil; chickens: 209.1 mil; goats: 310,000; pigs: 8.4 mil; sheep: 52,000. **Fish catch:** 3.86 mil metric tons. **Electricity prod.:** 130.7 bil kWh. **Labor force** (2005 est.): agric. 42.6%, industry 20.2%, services 37.1%.

Finance: Monetary unit: Baht (THB) (Oct. 2009: 33.36 = $1 U.S.). **GDP:** $547.4 bil; **per capita GDP:** $8,400; **GDP growth:**

2.6%. **Imports:** $157.3 bil; Japan 18.8%, China 11.2%, U.S. 6.4%, UAE 6%, Malaysia 5.5%, Saudi Arabia 4.1%, Singapore 4%. **Exports:** $174.8 bil; U.S. 11.4%, Japan 11.4%, China 9.2%, Singapore 5.7%, Hong Kong 5.6%, Malaysia 5.6%, Australia 4.3%. **Tourism:** $16.7 bil. **Budget:** $49.8 bil. **Intl. reserves less gold:** $70.55 bil. **Gold:** 2.7 mil oz t. **Consumer prices:** 5.5%.

Transport: Railroad: Length: 2,530 mi. **Motor vehicles:** 3.9 mil pass. cars; 5.7 mil comm. vehicles. **Civil aviation:** 31.6 bil pass.-mi; 64 airports. **Chief ports:** Bangkok, Laem Chabang, Prachuap Port, Si Racha.

Communication: TV sets: 274 per 1,000 pop. **Radios:** 234 per 1,000 pop. **Telephone lines:** 7 mil. **Internet:** 12.1 mil users.

Health: Life expect.: 70.5 male; 75.3 female. **Births** (per 1,000 pop.): 13.6. **Deaths** (per 1,000 pop.): 7.2. **Natural inc.:** 0.64%. **Infant mortality** (per 1,000 live births): 18.2. **HIV rate:** 1.4%.

Education: Compulsory: ages 6-14. **Literacy:** 94.2%.

Major intl. organizations: UN (FAO, IBRD, ILO, IMF, IMO, WHO, WTO), ASEAN, APEC.

Embassy: 1024 Wisconsin Ave. NW, Ste. 401, 20007; 944-3600.

Website: www.thaigov.go.th

Thais began migrating from southern China during the 11th cent. A unified Thai kingdom was established in 1350. Known as Siam until 1939, Thailand is the only country in SE Asia never taken over by a European power, thanks to King Mongkut and his son King Chulalongkorn. Ruling successively from 1851 to 1910, they modernized the country and signed trade treaties with Britain and France. A bloodless revolution in 1932 limited the monarchy. Thailand was an ally of Japan during WWII and of the U.S. during the postwar period. For decades, the military had a dominant role in governing the country.

A steep downturn in the economy forced Thailand to seek more than $15 bil in emergency international loans in Aug. 1997. A new constitution won legislative approval Sept. 27. By the end of the 1990s, according to UN estimates, more than 750,000 people in Thailand had HIV/AIDS; a nationwide prevention campaign has reduced the number of new infections.

Following elections in Jan. 2001, Thaksin Shinawatra, a wealthy former telecommunications executive, became prime min. On Feb. 1, 2003, Thaksin launched a nationwide crackdown on methamphetamines; human rights observers criticized police tactics in the drug war, which killed more than 2,200 people by Apr. 30. The Indian Ocean tsunami of Dec. 26, 2004, left about 5,400 people dead and over 2,800 missing in Thailand.

Elections Feb. 6, 2005, gave Thaksin's party a huge majority in parliament. Facing rising opposition and accused of benefiting improperly from the sale of his family's telecom business, Thaksin called snap elections for Apr. 2, 2006, 3 years ahead of schedule; the vote, which major parties boycotted, was later ruled unconstitutional. A military junta took power in a bloodless coup Sept. 19.

Thaksin supporters won elections Dec. 23, 2007, and Samak Sundaravej became prime min. after civilian rule was restored Jan. 22, 2008. After a series of antigovernment protests paralyzed Bangkok, Prime Min. Samak imposed emergency rule Sept. 2; he was ousted a week later by Thailand's Constitutional Court, ostensibly for getting paid to host TV cooking shows while he held public office. Thaksin's brother-in-law Somchai Wongsawat became prime min. Sept. 18, but a Constitutional Court ruling Dec. 2 barred him from politics and dissolved his People Power Party because of electoral fraud.

The political turmoil continued in 2009, as mass protests by Thaksin supporters led the government to postpone a summit meeting of East Asian leaders planned for Pattaya, Apr. 11, and to declare a state of emergency in Bangkok, Apr. 12-24. Meanwhile, about 60,000 security forces in southern Thailand sought to suppress a Muslim insurgency; from Jan. 2004 to Sept. 2009, more than 3,500 people, mostly civilians, died in the fighting.

Timor-Leste
(East Timor)
Democratic Republic of Timor-Leste

People: Population: 1,131,612. **Age distrib.** (%): <15: 34.7; 65+: 3.4. **Pop. density:** 197 per sq mi, 76.1 per sq km. **Urban:** 26.1%. **Ethnic groups:** Austronesian (Malayo-Polynesian), Papuan. **Principal languages:** Tetum, Portuguese (both official); Indonesian; English; about 16 indigenous languages (incl. Tetum, Galole, Mambae, Kemak). **Chief religion:** Roman Catholic 98%.

Geography: Total area: 5,743 sq mi, 14,874 sq km. **Land area:** 5,743 sq mi, 14,874 sq km. **Location:** E half of Timor Isl. in SW Pacific O. **Neighbors:** Indonesia (West Timor) on W. **Topography:** Terrain is rugged, rising to 9,721 ft at Mt. Ramelau. **Capital:** Dili, 159,000.

Government: Type: Republic. **Head of state:** Pres. José Ramos-Horta; b. Dec. 26, 1949; in office: May 20, 2007. **Head of gov.:** Prime Min. Xanana Gusmão; b. June 20, 1946; in office: Aug. 8, 2007. **Local divisions:** 13 districts. **Defense budget:** NA. **Active troops:** 1,286.

Economy: Industries: printing, soap mfg., handicrafts, woven cloth. **Chief crops:** coffee, rice, corn, cassava, sweet potatoes. **Natural resources:** gold, oil, nat. gas, mang., marble. **Arable land:** 8%. **Livestock:** cattle: 171,000; chickens: 2.2 mil; goats:

80,000; pigs: 346,000; sheep: 25,000. **Fish catch** (est.): 350 metric tons. **Labor force** (2006): agric. 90%.

Finance: Monetary unit: U.S. Dollar (USD). **GDP:** $2.5 bil; **per capita GDP:** $2,300; **GDP growth:** 12.8%. **Imports** (2004): $202 mil. **Exports** (2005): $10 mil. **Tourism:** NA. **Budget** (FY06/07 est.): $309 mil. **Intl. reserves less gold:** $137 mil. **Gold:** NA. **Consumer prices:** 9.1%.

Transport: Civil aviation: 2 airports. **Chief port:** Dili.

Communication: Telephone lines: 2,400. **Internet:** 1,800 users.

Health: Life expect.: 64.6 male; 69.4 female. **Births** (per 1,000 pop.): 26.5. **Deaths** (per 1,000 pop.): 6. **Natural inc.:** 2.05%. **Infant mortality** (per 1,000 live births): 42. **HIV rate:** NA.

Education: Compulsory: ages 7-15. **Literacy:** 58.6%.

Major intl. organizations: UN (FAO, IBRD, ILO, IMF, IMO, WHO).

Embassy: 4201 Connecticut Ave. NW 20008; 966-3202.

Website: www.timor-leste.gov.tl

The collapse of Portuguese rule in East Timor led to an outbreak of factional fighting in Aug. 1975 and an invasion by Indonesia in Dec. Indonesia annexed East Timor as a 27th province in 1976, despite international condemnation. In over 2 decades some 200,000 Timorese died as a result of civil war, famine, and persecution by Indonesian authorities. In a referendum held Aug. 30, 1999, under UN auspices, Timorese voted overwhelmingly for independence. Pro-Indonesian militias then went on a rampage, terrorizing the population. Under pressure, the government allowed entrance of an international peacekeeping force, which began arriving in Sept.; a UN interim administration formally took command Oct. 26, 1999.

Pro-independence forces won elections for a constituent assembly Aug. 30, 2001. Xanana Gusmão, a former guerrilla leader, won the presidential election Apr. 14, 2002. As Timor-Leste, the territory became independent May 20 and entered the UN Sept. 27. Australia and other nations sent peacekeepers to suppress a wave of gang violence that engulfed Dili in May 2006.

Pres. José Ramos-Horta, a Nobel laureate, won a presidential runoff vote May 9, 2007. After inconclusive parliamentary elections June 30, Ramos-Horta ended a political deadlock by choosing Gusmão as prime min. Renegade soldiers shot and seriously wounded Ramos-Horta in a failed coup attempt Feb. 11, 2008.

Togo
Togolese Republic

People: Population: 6,019,877. **Age distrib.** (%): <15: 41.5; 65+: 2.8. **Pop. density:** 286.7 per sq mi, 110.7 per sq km. **Urban:** 39.9%. **Ethnic groups:** African (37 tribes; Ewe, Mina, Kabre largest). **Principal languages:** French (official & lang. of commerce), Ewe & Mina (in S), Kabye & Dagomba (in N). **Chief religions:** Christian 29%, Muslim 20%, indigenous beliefs 51%.

Geography: Total area: 21,925 sq mi, 56,785 sq km; **Land area:** 20,998 sq mi, 54,385 sq km. **Location:** On S coast of W Africa. **Neighbors:** Ghana on W, Burkina Faso on N, Benin on E. **Topography:** A range of hills running SW-NE splits Togo into 2 savanna plains regions. **Capital:** Lomé, 1,452,000.

Government: Type: Republic. **Head of state:** Pres. Faure Gnassingbé; b. June 6, 1966; in office: May 4, 2005. **Head of gov.:** Prime Min. Gilbert Fossoun Houngbo; b. Feb. 4, 1961; in office: Sept. 8, 2008. **Local divisions:** 5 regions. **Defense budget:** $42 mil. **Active troops:** 8,550.

Economy: Industries: phosphate mining, agric. proc., cement, handicrafts. **Chief crops:** coffee, cocoa, cotton, yams, cassava, corn. **Natural resources:** phosphates, limestone, marble. **Arable land:** 44%. **Livestock:** cattle: 355,000; chickens: 15.6 mil; goats: 1.5 mil; pigs: 554,000; sheep: 2 mil. **Fish catch:** 24,905 metric tons. **Electricity prod.:** 203 mil kWh. **Labor force** (1998 est.): agric. 65%, industry 5%, services 30%.

Finance: Monetary unit: CFA BCEAO Franc (XOF) (Oct. 2009: 444.97 = $1 U.S.). **GDP:** $5.1 bil; **per capita GDP:** $900; **GDP growth:** 1.1%. **Imports:** $1.5 bil; China 39.1%, Netherlands 7.9%, France 7.2%, Thailand 5.1%. **Exports:** $782 mil; Ghana 14.3%, Burkina Faso 12.4%, Germany 11%, Benin 7.8%, Brazil 5.6%, Belgium 5.4%, Mali 5%, Netherlands 4.8%. **Tourism:** NA. **Budget:** $427.7 mil. **Intl. reserves less gold:** $377 mil. **Gold:** NA. **Consumer prices:** 8.7%.

Transport: Railroad: Length: 331 mi. **Motor vehicles:** 51,400 pass. cars; 24,500 comm. vehicles. **Civil aviation:** 80.8 mil pass.-mi (incl. Air Afrique traffic apportionment); 2 airports. **Chief ports:** Kpeme, Lomé.

Communications: TV sets: 22 per 1,000 pop. **Radios:** 244 per 1,000 pop. **Telephone lines:** 140,900. **Daily newspaper circ.** (2000): 1.9 per 1,000 pop. **Internet:** 350,000 users.

Health: Life expect.: 56.2 male; 60.4 female. **Births** (per 1,000 pop.): 36.7. **Deaths** (per 1,000 pop.): 9.5. **Natural inc.:** 2.72%. **Infant mortality** (per 1,000 live births): 57.7. **HIV rate:** 3.3%.

Education: Compulsory: ages 6-15. **Literacy:** 53.2%.

Major intl. organizations: UN (FAO, IBRD, ILO, IMF, IMO, WHO, WTO), AU.

Embassy: 2208 Massachusetts Ave. NW 20008; 234-4212.

Website: www.assemblee-nationale.tg or www.state.gov/p/af/ci/to/

Togoland was administered by Germany and then by France and Britain. The French sector became the republic of Togo Apr. 27, 1960. In office since 1967, Pres. Gnassingbé Eyadéma was Africa's longest-serving head of state until his death Feb. 5, 2005. His son, Faure Gnassingbé, was immediately installed as president, but other African leaders pressured Togo to hold an election, which Gnassingbé won Apr. 24. Opposition parties disputed the result, and protests led to violent clashes in Lomé.

After a shootout at his home Apr. 12, 2009, former Defense Min. Kpatcha Gnassingbé, the president's brother, sought refuge Apr. 15 at the U.S. embassy in Lomé; denied asylum, he was arrested by Togolese authorities and accused of plotting a coup.

Tonga
Kingdom of Tonga

People: Population: 120,898. **Age distrib.** (%): <15: 32.8; 65+: 4.3. **Pop. density:** 436.1 per sq mi, 168.4 per sq km. **Urban:** 24%. **Ethnic groups:** Polynesian, Europeans. **Principal languages:** Tongan, English. **Chief religion:** Christian (mostly Free Wesleyan Church).

Geography: Total area: 289 sq mi, 748 sq km; **Land area:** 277 sq mi, 718 sq km. **Location:** In western S Pacific O. **Neighbors:** Nearest are Fiji to W, Samoa to NE. **Topography:** Tonga comprises 170 volcanic and coral islands, 36 inhabited. **Capital:** Nuku'alofa, 25,000.

Government: Type: Constitutional monarchy. **Head of state:** King George Tupou V; b. May 4, 1948; in office: Sept. 11, 2006. **Head of gov.:** Prime Min. Feleti Vaka'uta Sevele; b. July 7, 1944; in office: Mar. 30, 2006 (acting from Feb. 11). **Local divisions:** 3 island groups. **Defense budget/Active troops:** NA.

Economy: Industries: tourism, constr., fishing. **Chief crops:** squash, coconuts, copra, bananas, vanilla beans, cocoa, coffee, ginger, black pepper. **Natural resources:** fish. **Arable land:** 20%. **Livestock:** cattle: 11,250; chickens: 330,000; goats: 12,600; pigs: 81,200. **Fish catch:** 2,656 metric tons. **Electricity prod.:** 43 mil kWh. **Labor force** (2003 est.): agric. 31.8%, industry 30.6%, services 37.6%.

Finance: Monetary unit: Pa'anga (TOP) (Oct. 2009: 1.90 = $1 U.S.). **GDP:** $549 mil; **per capita GDP:** $4,600; **GDP growth:** 1.2%. **Imports** (2006): $139 mil; Fiji 35.9%, New Zealand 23.4%, U.S. 9.1%, Australia 8.6%, China 4.2%. **Exports** (2006): $22 mil; U.S. 29.5%, Japan 12%, New Zealand 12%, Fiji 7.1%, Samoa 6%, Australia 4.8%, Hong Kong 4.3%, S. Korea 4.2%. **Tourism:** $15 mil. **Budget** (FY07/08): $109.8 mil. **Intl. reserves less gold:** $45 mil. **Gold:** NA. **Consumer prices:** 10.4%.

Transport: Motor vehicles: 7,000 pass. cars; 7,000 comm. vehicles. **Civil aviation:** 11.8 mil pass.-mi; 1 airport. **Chief port:** Nuku'alofa.

Communications: TV sets: 61 per 1,000 pop. **Radios:** 663 per 1,000 pop. **Telephone lines:** 25,500. **Internet:** 8,400 users.

Health: Life expect.: 67.9 male; 73.1 female. **Births** (per 1,000 pop.): 21.8. **Deaths** (per 1,000 pop.): 5.1. **Natural inc.:** 1.67%. **Infant mortality** (per 1,000 live births): 11.9. **HIV rate:** NA.

Education: Compulsory: ages 6-14. **Literacy:** 99.2%.

Major intl. organizations: UN (FAO, IBRD, ILO, IMF, IMO, WHO), the Commonwealth.

Embassy: 250 E. 51st St., New York, NY 10022; (917) 369-1025.

Website: pmo.gov.to

The islands were first visited by the Dutch in the early 17th cent. A series of civil wars ended in 1845 with establishment of the Tupou dynasty. In 1900 Tonga became a British protectorate. On June 4, 1970, Tonga became independent and a member of the Commonwealth. It joined the UN on Sept. 14, 1999. George Tupou V became king Sept. 11, 2006, following the death of his father, Taufa'ahau Tupou IV, who had reigned since 1965.

Trinidad and Tobago
Republic of Trinidad and Tobago

People: Population: 1,229,953. **Age distrib.** (%): <15: 19.6; 65+: 7.9. **Pop. density:** 621.2 per sq mi, 239.9 per sq km. **Urban:** 12.2%. **Ethnic groups:** Indian (South Asian) 40%, African 38%, mixed 21%. **Principal languages:** English (official), Caribbean Hindustani, French, Spanish, Chinese. **Chief religions:** Roman Catholic 26%, Hindu 23%, Anglican 8%, Baptist 7%, Pentecostal 7%, Muslim 6%.

Geography: Total area: 1,980 sq mi, 5,128 sq km; **Land area:** 1,980 sq mi, 5,128 sq km. **Location:** In Caribbean, off E coast of Venezuela. **Neighbors:** Nearest is Venezuela to SW. **Topography:** Three low mountain ranges cross Trinidad E-W, with a well-watered plain between N and central ranges. Parts of E and W coasts are swamps. Tobago, 116 sq mi, lies 20 mi NE. **Capital:** Port of Spain, 54,000.

Government: Type: Parliamentary democracy. **Head of state:** Pres. George Maxwell Richards; b. 1931; in office: Mar. 17, 2003. **Head of gov.:** Prime Min. Patrick Augustus Mervyn Manning; b. Aug. 17, 1946; in office: Dec. 24, 2001. **Local div.:** 8 counties, 3 municipalities, 1 ward. **Def. budget:** $55 mil. **Active troops:** 4,063.

Economy: Industries: oil, chemicals, tourism, food proc. **Chief crops:** cocoa, rice, citrus, coffee, vegetables. **Natural resources:** oil, nat. gas, asphalt. **Crude oil reserves:** 728.3 mil bbls. **Arable land:** 15%. **Livestock:** cattle: 30,000; chickens: 28.5 mil; goats: 60,000; pigs: 45,000; sheep: 3,500. **Fish catch:** 8,406 metric tons. **Electricity prod.:** 6.6 bil kWh. **Labor force** (2007 est.): agric. 3.8%; mfg., mining, & quarrying 12.8%; constr. & utilities 20.4%; services 62.9%.

Finance: Monetary unit: Dollar (TTD) (Oct. 2009: 6.23 = $1 U.S.). **GDP:** $29 bil; **per capita GDP:** $23,600; **GDP growth:** 3.5%. **Imports:** $9.8 bil; U.S. 27.4%, Brazil 10%, Venezuela 8.1%, Colombia 4.8%, China 4.2%, Gabon 4.1%. **Exports:** $15.9 bil; U.S. 47.5%, Spain 8.3%, Netherlands 7.4%, Jamaica 6.1%. **Tourism:** NA. **Budget:** $6.2 bil. **Intl. reserves less gold:** $6.13 bil. **Gold:** 60,000 oz t. **Consumer prices:** 12%.

Transport: Motor vehicles: 320,000 pass. cars; 71,000 comm. vehicles. **Civil aviation:** 1.9 bil pass.-mi; 3 airports. **Chief ports:** Point Fortin, Point Lisas, Port-of-Spain.

Communications: TV sets: 337 per 1,000 pop. **Radios:** 532 per 1,000 pop. **Telephone lines:** 307,000. **Daily newspaper circ.** (2003): 149.1 per 1,000 pop. **Internet:** 227,000 users.

Health: Life expect.: 66.1 male; 68 female. **Births** (per 1,000 pop.): 13.2. **Deaths** (per 1,000 pop.): 10.9. **Natural inc.:** 0.23%. **Infant mortality** (per 1,000 live births): 23.6. **HIV rate:** 1.5%.

Education: Compulsory: ages 5-11. **Literacy:** 98.7%.

Major intl. organizations: UN (FAO, IBRD, ILO, IMF, IMO, WHO, WTO), Caricom, the Commonwealth, OAS.

Embassy: 1708 Massachusetts Ave. NW 20036; 467-6490.

Website: www.gov.tt

Columbus sighted Trinidad in 1498. A British possession since 1802, Trinidad and Tobago won independence Aug. 31, 1962. It became a republic in 1976.

The nation is one of the most prosperous in the Caribbean. Oil production has increased with offshore finds. Middle Eastern oil is refined and exported, mostly to the U.S.

In July 1990, some 120 Muslim extremists captured the Parliament building and TV station and took about 50 hostages, including Prime Min. Arthur N. R. Robinson, who was beaten, shot in the legs, and tied to explosives. After a 6-day siege, the rebels surrendered.

Basdeo Panday, the country's first prime min. of East Indian ancestry, took office Nov. 9, 1995. Robinson became president on Mar. 19, 1997. Patrick Manning of the People's National Movement (PNM) became prime min. after elections Dec. 10, 2001. George Maxwell Richards, a former university dean, succeeded Robinson as president, Mar. 17, 2003. The PNM retained power in parliamentary elections Nov. 5, 2007.

Tunisia
Tunisian Republic

People: Population: 10,486,339. **Age distrib.** (%): <15: 22.7; 65+: 7.2. **Pop. density:** 174.8 per sq mi, 67.5 per sq km. **Urban:** 65.3%. **Ethnic groups:** Arab 98%, European 1%, Jewish & other 1%. **Principal languages:** Arabic (official), French (used in commerce). **Chief religions:** Muslim 98%, Christian 1%, Jewish & other 1%.

Geography: Total area: 63,170 sq mi, 163,610 sq km; **Land area:** 59,985 sq mi, 155,360 sq km. **Location:** On N coast of Africa. **Neighbors:** Algeria on W, Libya on E. **Topography:** The N is wooded and fertile. The central coastal plains are given to grazing and orchards. The S is arid, approaching Sahara Desert. **Capital:** Tunis, 745,000.

Government: Type: Republic. **Head of state:** Pres. Gen. Zine al-Abidine Ben Ali; b. Sept. 3, 1936; in office: Nov. 7, 1987. **Head of gov.:** Prime Min. Mohamed Ghannouchi; b. Aug. 18, 1941; in office: Nov. 17, 1999. **Local divisions:** 24 governorates. **Defense budget:** $470 mil. **Active troops:** 35,800.

Economy: Industries: oil, mining, tourism, textiles, footwear, agribusiness. **Chief crops:** olives, olive oil, grain, tomatoes, citrus fruit, sugar beets, dates, almonds. **Natural resources:** oil, phosphates, iron ore, lead, zinc, salt. **Crude oil reserves:** 425 mil bbls. **Arable land:** 17%. **Livestock:** cattle: 710,130; chickens: 64 mil; goats: 1.6 mil; pigs: 6,000; sheep: 7.6 mil. **Fish catch:** 106,561 metric tons. **Electricity prod.:** 12.7 bil kWh. **Labor force** (1995 est.): agric. 55%, industry 23%, services 22%.

Finance: Monetary unit: Dinar (TND) (Oct. 2009: 1.29 = $1 U.S.). **GDP:** $81.7 bil; **per capita GDP:** $7,900; **GDP growth:** 4.4%. **Imports:** $23.2 bil; France 22.4%, Italy 20.1%, Germany 9.4%, Libya 4.8%, Spain 4.6%. **Exports:** $19.2 bil; France 28.4%, Italy 18%, Germany 9.6%, Libya 5.8%, Spain 5%. **Tourism:** $2.6 bil. **Budget:** $9.5 bil. **Intl. reserves less gold:** $5.75 bil. **Gold:** 220,000 oz t. **Consumer prices:** 4.9%.

Transport: Railroad: Length: 1,342 mi. **Motor vehicles:** 552,900 pass. cars; 281,500 comm. vehicles. **Civil aviation:** 1.9 bil pass.-mi; 16 airports. **Chief ports:** Bizerte, Gabes, La Goulette, Rades, Sfax, Skhira.

Communications: TV sets: 190 per 1,000 pop. **Radios:** 158 per 1,000 pop. **Telephone lines:** 1.2 mil. **Daily newspaper circ.** (2001): 22.7 per 1,000 pop. **Internet:** 2.8 mil users.

Health: Life expect.: 73.8 male; 77.5 female. **Births** (per 1,000 pop.): 15.5. **Deaths** (per 1,000 pop.): 5.2. **Natural inc.:** 1.03%. **Infant mortality** (per 1,000 live births): 23.4. **HIV rate:** 0.1%.

Education: Compulsory: ages 6-16. **Literacy:** 77.7%.

Major intl. organizations: UN (FAO, IBRD, ILO, IMF, IMO, WHO, WTO), AL, AU.

Embassy: 1515 Massachusetts Ave. NW 20005; 862-1850.

Website: www.tunisiaonline.com or www.carthage.tn

Site of ancient Carthage and a former Barbary state under the suzerainty of Turkey, Tunisia became a protectorate of France under a treaty signed May 12, 1881. The nation became independent Mar. 20, 1956, and ended the monarchy the following year. Habib Bourguiba, an independence leader, served as president until 1987, when he was deposed by his prime min., Zine al-Abidine Ben Ali, who then won 4 presidential elections, 1989-2004, all tightly controlled by the ruling party. Presidential and parliamentary elections were scheduled for Oct. 25, 2009.

Tunisia has actively repressed Islamic fundamentalism. A synagogue blast on Djerba Isl., Apr. 11, 2002, apparently set off by al-Qaeda, killed 14 Germans, 5 Tunisians, and 2 French tourists.

Turkey
Republic of Turkey

People: Population: 76,805,524. **Age distrib.** (%): <15: 27.2; 65+: 6.1. **Pop. density:** 258.1 per sq mi, 99.6 per sq km. **Urban:** 67.3%. **Ethnic groups:** Turkish 80%, Kurdish 20%. **Principal languages:** Turkish (official); Kurdish; Dimli, or Zaza. **Chief religion:** Muslim (mostly Sunni) 99.8%.

Geography: Total area: 301,384 sq mi, 780,580 sq km; **Land area:** 297,592 sq mi, 770,760 sq km. **Location:** Occupies Asia Minor, stretches into continental Europe; borders on Medit. and Black seas. **Neighbors:** Bulgaria, Greece on W; Georgia, Armenia on N; Iran on E; Iraq, Syria on S. **Topography:** Central Turkey has wide plateaus, with hot, dry summers and cold winters. High mountains ring the interior on all but W, with more than 20 peaks over 10,000 ft. Rolling plains are in W; mild, fertile coastal plains are in S, W. **Capital:** Ankara, 3,716,000. **Cities (urban aggr.):** Istanbul, 10,061,000; Izmir, 2,587,000.

Government: Type: Republic. **Head of state:** Pres. Abdullah Gül; b. Oct. 29, 1950; in office: Aug. 28, 2007. **Head of gov.:** Prime Min. Recep Tayyip Erdogan; b. Feb. 26, 1954; in office: Mar. 14, 2003. **Local divisions:** 81 provinces. **Defense budget:** $13.6 bil. **Active troops:** 510,600.

Economy: Industries: textiles, food proc., autos, electronics, mining, steel, oil, constr. **Chief crops:** tobacco, cotton, grain, olives, sugar beets, pulse, citrus. **Natural resources:** coal, iron ore, copper, chromium, antimony, mercury, gold, barite, borate. **Crude oil reserves:** 300 mil bbls. **Arable land:** 30%. **Livestock:** cattle: 10.9 mil; chickens: 344.8 mil; goats: 6.3 mil; pigs: 1,362; sheep: 25.5 mil. **Fish catch:** 772,471 metric tons. **Electricity prod.:** 167.9 bil kWh. **Labor force** (2005): agric. 29.5%, industry 24.7%, services 45.8%.

Finance: Monetary unit: Lira (TRY) (Oct. 2009: 1.47 = $1 U.S.). **GDP:** $902.7 bil; **per capita GDP:** $11,900; **GDP growth:** 1.1%. **Imports:** $193.9 bil; Russia 15.5%, Germany 9.3%, China 7.8%, U.S. 5.9%, Italy 5.5%, France 4.5%, Iran 4.1%. **Exports:** $140.8 bil; Germany 9.8%, UK 6.2%, UAE 6%, Italy 5.9%, France 5%, Russia 4.9%. **Tourism:** $18.5 bil. **Budget:** $156.1 bil. **Intl. reserves less gold:** $45.72 bil. **Gold:** 3.73 mil oz t. **Consumer prices:** 10.4%.

Transport: Railroad: Length: 5,404 mi. **Motor vehicles:** 5.8 mil pass. cars; 2.7 mil comm. vehicles. **Civil aviation:** 15.1 bil pass.-mi; 90 airports. **Chief ports:** Aliaga, Diliskelesi, Izmir, Kocaeli, Mercin Limani, Nemrut Limani.

Communications: TV sets: 328 per 1,000 pop. **Radios:** 510 per 1,000 pop. **Telephone lines:** 17.5 mil. **Internet:** 24.5 mil users.

Health: Life expect.: 70.7 male; 75.7 female. **Births** (per 1,000 pop.): 16.1. **Deaths** (per 1,000 pop.): 6. **Natural inc.:** 1.01%. **Infant mortality** (per 1,000 live births): 37. **HIV rate:** NA.

Education: Compulsory: ages 6-14. **Literacy:** 88.7%.

Major intl. organizations: UN (FAO, IBRD, ILO, IMF, IMO, WHO, WTO), NATO, OECD, OSCE.

Embassy: 2525 Massachusetts Ave. NW 20008; 612-6700.

Website: www.tccb.gov.tr

Ancient inhabitants of Turkey were among the world's first agriculturalists. Such civilizations as the Hittite, Phrygian, and Lydian flourished in Asiatic Turkey (Asia Minor), as did much of Greek civilization. After the fall of Rome in the 5th cent., Constantinople (now Istanbul) was the capital of the Byzantine Empire for 1,000 years. It fell in 1453 to Ottoman Turks, who ruled a vast empire for over 400 years.

Just before WWI, Turkey, or the Ottoman Empire, ruled what is now Syria, Lebanon, Iraq, Jordan, Israel, Saudi Arabia, Yemen, and islands in the Aegean Sea. Turkey joined Germany and Austria in WWI, and its defeat resulted in the loss of much territory and the fall of the sultanate. A secular republic was established Oct. 29, 1923, with Mustafa Kemal (later Kemal Ataturk) as its first president. Ataturk led Turkey until his death in 1938.

Turkey kept neutral during most of WWII. The country became a full member of NATO in 1952 and remained a Western ally despite domestic political instability. Military coups overthrew civilian governments in 1960 and 1980. Turkey invaded nearby Cyprus July 20, 1974, to prevent that country from being united with Greece; since then, Cyprus has been divided into Greek and Turkish zones.

In recent decades, Turkish governments have contended with Kurdish separatism and the rise of militant Islam. Turkey was a member of the U.S.-led force that ousted Iraq from Kuwait, 1991. In the aftermath of the war, millions of Kurdish refugees fled to Turkey's border to escape Iraqi forces. Turkish offensives against the Kurds caused heavy casualties among guerrillas and civilians. Kurdish militants raided Turkish diplomatic missions in some 25 Western European cities June 24, 1993.

Tansu Ciller officially became Turkey's first woman prime min. July 5, 1993. The Welfare Party, an Islamic group, gained strength in the 1990s but was unable to form a government until June 1996, when it came to power in coalition with Ciller's True Path Party. The pro-Islamic government resigned June 18, 1997, under pressure from the military, which stepped up its campaign against Islamic fundamentalism in 1998.

Kurdish rebel leader Abdullah Öcalan was captured Feb. 15, 1999; convicted of terrorism June 29, he was sentenced to death by a Turkish security court. His organization, the Kurdistan Workers' Party, announced Aug. 5, 1999, that it would abandon its 14-year-old insurgency, in which more than 30,000 people died.

Earthquakes in Apr. and Nov. 1999 killed over 17,000 people. The IMF announced $7.5 bil in emergency loans Dec. 6, 2000, to help Turkey cope with a severe financial crisis. The death penalty was abolished Aug. 3, 2002, and Öcalan's sentence was commuted to life in prison Oct. 3. The Justice and Development Party (AKP), an Islamic group led by Recep Tayyip Erdogan, won elections Nov. 3.

During the U.S.-led invasion of Iraq, Mar.-Apr. 2003, Turkey, a NATO ally, refused to allow coalition forces to launch attacks on N Iraq from Turkish soil. Suicide bombings by Islamic extremists Nov. 15-20, 2003, killed 58 people and wounded about 750 at 2 synagogues, the British consulate, and the offices of a London-based bank, all in Istanbul. Erdogan's party scored a landslide win in national elections, July 22, 2007. Overcoming objections by the military and other secularists, parliament, Aug. 28, chose an Islamic politician, Abdullah Gül, as president. An effort to ban the ruling AKP failed by one vote in Turkey's Constitutional Court July 30, 2008, but the justices cut the party's public funding in half and warned it to restrain Islamic influence on state institutions. An Istanbul court Mar. 25, 2009, approved the indictment of 56 persons, including 2 high-ranking retired generals, accused of taking part in an ultranationalist plot to overthrow the AKP government; they joined 86 defendants already on trial in the same case.

Turkey has long sought to become a full member of the European Union, but the EU has deferred talks on accession until economic, human rights, and immigration issues are resolved.

Turkmenistan

People: Population: 4,884,887. **Age distrib.** (%): <15: 28.9; 65+: 4.3. **Pop. density:** 25.9 per sq mi, 10 per sq km. **Urban:** 47.3%. **Ethnic groups:** Turkmen 85%, Uzbek 5%, Russian 4%. **Principal languages:** Turkmen, Russian, Uzbek. **Chief religions:** Muslim 89%, Eastern Orthodox 9%.

Geography: Total area: 188,456 sq mi, 488,100 sq km; **Land area:** 188,456 sq mi, 488,100 sq km. **Location:** Central Asia bordering Caspian Sea. **Neighbors:** Kazakhstan on N; Uzbekistan on N and E; Afghanistan, Iran on S. **Topography:** The Kara Kum Desert occupies 80% of the area. Bordered on W by Caspian Sea. **Capital:** Ashgabat, 744,000.

Government: Type: Republic with authoritarian rule. **Head of state and gov.:** Pres. Gurbanguly Berdymukhammedov; b. June 29, 1957; in office: Feb. 14, 2007 (acting from Dec. 21, 2006). **Local divisions:** 5 regions. **Defense budget:** $209 mil. **Active troops:** 22,000.

Economy: Industries: nat. gas, oil, oil products, textiles, food proc. **Chief crops:** cotton, grain. **Natural resources:** oil, nat. gas, sulfur, salt. **Crude oil reserves:** 600 mil bbls. **Arable land:** 5%. **Livestock:** cattle: 1.9 mil; chickens: 7 mil; goats: 900,000; pigs: 29,800; sheep: 15.5 mil. **Fish catch** (est.): 15,016 metric tons. **Electricity prod.:** 12.8 bil kWh. **Labor force** (2004 est.): agric. 48.2%, industry 14%, services 37.8%.

Finance: Monetary unit: New Manat (TMT) (Oct. 2009: 2.85 = $1 U.S.). **GDP:** $29.8 bil; **per capita GDP:** $6,200; **GDP growth:** 10.5. **Imports:** $5.7 bil; Russia 16.6%, China 14.7%, Turkey 14.6%, UAE 10.8%, Ukraine 7.2%, Germany 5.8%, Iran 5.3%. **Exports:** $11.9 bil; Ukraine 41.6%, Iran 14%, Poland 9.6%, Hungary 7.8%. **Tourism:** NA. **Budget:** $1.6 bil.

Transport: Railroad: Length: 1,852 mi. **Civil aviation:** 1.2 bil pass.-mi; 22 airports. **Chief port:** Turkmenbasy.

Communications: TV sets: 198 per 1,000 pop. **Radios:** 289 per 1,000 pop. **Telephone lines:** 495,000. **Daily newspaper circ.** (2004): 9.4 per 1,000 pop. **Internet:** 75,000 users.

Health: Life expect.: 65.5 male; 71.8 female. **Births** (per 1,000 pop.): 25.1. **Deaths** (per 1,000 pop.): 6.1. **Natural inc.:** 1.9%. **Infant mortality** (per 1,000 live births): 51.8. **HIV rate:** <0.1%.

Education: Compulsory: ages 7-15. **Literacy:** 99.5%.

Major intl. organizations: UN (FAO, IBRD, ILO, IMF, IMO, WHO), CIS, OSCE.

Embassy: 2207 Massachusetts Ave. NW 20008; 588-1500.

Website: www.turkmenistan.gov.tm

The region has been inhabited by Turkic tribes since the 10th cent. It became part of Russian Turkestan in 1881, and a constituent republic of the USSR in 1925. Turkmenistan declared independence Oct. 27, 1991, and became an independent state when the USSR disbanded Dec. 26, 1991.

Extensive oil and gas reserves place Turkmenistan in a favorable economic position. Political power centered around the former Communist Party apparatus, and authoritarian Pres. Saparmurad Niyazov (also known as Turkmenbashi) became the object of a personality cult. Niyazov died Dec. 21, 2006, and was succeeded by Gurbanguly Berdymukhammedov; he won the presidential election of Feb. 11, 2007, considered neither free nor fair by international observers.

Tuvalu

People: Population: 12,373. **Age distrib.** (%): <15: 29.2; 65+: 5.2. **Pop. density:** 1,232.5 per sq mi, 475.9 per sq km. **Urban:** 48.1%. **Ethnic group:** Polynesian 96%, Micronesian 4%. **Principal languages:** Tuvaluan, English, Samoan. **Chief religion:** Church of Tuvalu (Congregationalist) 97%.

Geography: Total area: 10 sq mi, 26 sq km; **Land area:** 10 sq mi, 26 sq km. **Location:** 9 islands forming NW-SE chain 360 mi long in SW Pacific O. **Neighbors:** Nearest are Kiribati to N, Fiji to S. **Topography:** The islands are all low-lying atolls, nowhere rising more than 15 ft above sea level, composed of coral reefs. **Capital** (2002): Funafuti (atoll), 4,492.

Government: Type: Constitutional monarchy, with a parliamentary democracy. **Head of state:** Queen Elizabeth II, represented by Gov.-Gen. Filoimea Telito; in office: Apr. 15, 2005. **Head of gov.:** Prime Min. Apisai Ielemia; b. 1955; in office: Aug. 14, 2006. **Defense budget/Active troops:** NA.

Economy: Industries: fishing, tourism, copra. **Chief crops:** coconuts. **Natural resources:** fish. **Arable land:** None. **Livestock:** chickens: 45,000; pigs: 13,600. **Fish catch** (est.): 2,201. **Labor force:** People make a living mainly through exploitation of the sea, reefs, and atolls and from wages sent home by those abroad (mostly workers in phosphate industry and sailors).

Finance: Monetary unit: Dollar (TVD) (Oct. 2009: 1.12 = $1 U.S.). **GDP** (2002): $14.9 mil; **per capita GDP** (2002): $1,600; **GDP growth** (2006): 3%. **Imports** (2005): $12.9 mil. **Exports** (2004): $1 mil. **Tourism:** NA. **Budget** (2006): $23.1 mil.

Transport: Civil aviation: NA. **Chief port:** Funafuti.

Communications: TV sets: 9 per 1,000 pop. **Radios:** 364 per 1,000 pop. **Telephone lines:** 1,500. **Internet:** 4,200 users.

Health: Life expect.: 66.7 male; 71.4 female. **Births** (per 1,000 pop.): 22.8. **Deaths** (per 1,000 pop.): 7. **Natural inc.:** 1.58%. **Infant mortality** (per 1,000 live births): 19. **HIV rate:** NA.

Education: Compulsory: ages 7-14. **Literacy:** NA.

Major intl. organizations: UN (FAO, ILO, IMO, WHO), the Commonwealth.

Permanent UN Mission: 800 Second Ave., Ste. 400D, New York, NY 10017; (212) 490-0534.

Website: www.timelesstuvalu.com

The Ellice Islands separated from the British Gilbert and Ellice Islands Colony in 1975 and became Tuvalu; independence came Oct. 1, 1978. In 2000, Tuvalu joined the United Nations.

Uganda
Republic of Uganda

People: Population: 32,369,558. **Age distrib.** (%): <15: 50; 65+: 2.1. **Pop. density:** 419.8 per sq mi, 162.1 per sq km. **Urban:** 12.5%. **Ethnic groups:** Baganda 17%, Banyakole 10%, Basoga 8%, Bakiga 7%. **Principal languages:** English (official; taught in grade schools, used in courts of law, most newspapers, some radio broadcasts), Ganda or Luganda (most widely used of Niger-Congo languages, may be taught in school). **Chief religions:** Roman Catholic 42%, Protestant (incl. Anglican, Pentecostal, Seventh-Day Adventist) 42%, Muslim 12%.

Geography: Total area: 91,136 sq mi, 236,040 sq km; **Land area:** 77,108 sq mi, 199,710 sq km. **Location:** In E Central Africa. **Neighbors:** Sudan on N, Congo (formerly Zaire) on W, Rwanda and Tanzania on S, Kenya on E. **Topography:** Most of Uganda is a high plateau 3,000-6,000 ft high, with high Ruwenzori range in W (Mt. Margherita 16,763 ft), volcanoes in SW; NE is arid, W and SW rainy. Lakes Victoria, Edward, Albert form much of borders. **Capital:** Kampala, 1,420,000.

Government: Type: Republic. **Head of state:** Pres. Yoweri Kaguta Museveni; b. Aug. 15, 1944; in office: Jan. 29, 1986. **Head of gov.:** Prime Min. Apolo Nsibambi; b. Nov. 27, 1938; in office: Apr. 5, 1999. **Local divisions:** 56 districts. **Defense budget:** $232 mil. **Active troops:** 45,000.

Economy: Industries: sugar, brewing, tobacco, cotton textiles. **Chief crops:** coffee, tea, cotton, tobacco, cassava, potatoes, corn, millet, pulses, cut flowers. **Natural resources:** copper, cobalt, hydropower, limestone, salt. **Arable land:** 22%. **Livestock:** cattle: 7.2 mil; chickens: 27 mil; goats: 8.3 mil; pigs: 2.1 mil; sheep: 1.7 mil. **Fish catch:** 551,110 metric tons. **Electricity prod.:** 1.2 bil kWh. **Labor force** (1999 est.): agric. 82%, industry 5%, services 13%.

Finance: Monetary unit: Shilling (UGX) (Oct. 2009: 1,906.00 = $1 U.S.). **GDP:** $39.4 bil; **per capita GDP:** $1,300; **GDP growth:** 6.9%. **Imports:** $3.6 bil; Kenya 31.1%, UAE 8.7%, China 7.6%, Japan 6.2%, South Africa 6%, India 5.1%. **Exports:** $2 bil; Belgium 11.6%, Netherlands 9.8%, Germany 8.5%, Italy 6.6%, Rwanda 5.2%, France 4.9%, U.S. 4.7%, UAE 4%. **Tourism:** NA. **Budget:** $2.5 bil. **Intl. reserves less gold:** $1.49 bil. **Gold:** NA. **Consumer prices:** 12.1%.

Transport: Railroad: Length: 773 mi. **Motor vehicles:** 65,000 pass. cars; 104,000 comm. vehicles. **Civil aviation:** 187.7 mil pass.-mi; 5 airports. **Chief ports:** Entebbe, Jinja, Port Bell.

Communications: TV sets: 28 per 1,000 pop. **Radios:** 130 per 1,000 pop. **Telephone lines:** 168,500. **Internet:** 2.5 mil users.

Health: Life expect.: 51.3 male; 53.4 female. **Births** (per 1,000 pop.): 48.1. **Deaths** (per 1,000 pop.): 12.3. **Natural inc.:** 3.58%. **Infant mortality** (per 1,000 live births): 66. **HIV rate:** 5.4%.

Education: Compulsory: ages 6-12. **Literacy:** 73.6%.

Major intl. organizations: UN (FAO, IBRD, ILO, IMF, WHO, WTO), the Commonwealth, AU.

Embassy: 5911 16th St. NW 20011; 726-7100.

Websites: www.statehouse.go.ug

Britain obtained a protectorate over Uganda in 1894. The country became independent Oct. 9, 1962, and a republic within the Commonwealth a year later. In 1967, the traditional kingdoms, including the powerful Buganda state, were abolished.

Gen. Idi Amin seized power from Prime Min. Milton Obote in 1971. During his 8 years of dictatorial rule, he was responsible for the deaths of up to 300,000 of his opponents. In 1972 he expelled nearly all of Uganda's 45,000 Asians. Tanzanian troops and Ugandan exiles and rebels ousted Amin, Apr. 11, 1979.

Obote held the presidency from Dec. 1980 until his ouster in a military coup July 27, 1985. Guerrilla war and rampant human rights abuses plagued Uganda under Obote's regime.

Conditions improved after Yoweri Museveni took power in Jan. 1986. In 1993 the Buganda and other traditional monarchies were restored, but only for ceremonial purposes. Uganda helped Laurent Kabila seize power in the Congo (formerly Zaire) in 1997 but sent troops in 1998 to aid insurgents seeking his ouster. A withdrawal accord was signed Sept. 6, 2002.

Pres. Museveni won reelection Mar. 12, 2001, and Feb. 23, 2006; opponents disputed the latter result, citing what they claimed were trumped-up charges of treason, terrorism, and rape lodged against Museveni's main rival, Kizza Besigye.

An ongoing insurgency in N Uganda has killed more than 100,000 people and forced up to 2 mil to flee. The Lord's Resistance Army (LRA), a rebel group, has fought the Museveni govt. since 1986 and has abducted some 30,000 children to serve as soldiers and sex slaves. Peace talks brokered by Sudan began July 2006; as talks continued through 2007, the violence diminished, and many refugees returned to their homes. A cease-fire accord was signed Feb. 23, 2008, but Ugandan and Congolese troops (with aid from the U.S.) launched a new offensive against the LRA in late 2008.

Ukraine

People: Population: 45,700,395. **Age distrib.** (%): <15: 13.8; 65+: 15.9. **Pop. density:** 196.1 per sq mi, 75.7 per sq km. **Urban:** 67.8%. **Ethnic groups:** Ukrainian 78%, Russian 17%. **Principal languages:** Ukrainian (official), Russian, Romanian, Polish, Hungarian. **Chief religions:** Ukrainian Orthodox (Kiev patriarchate) 50%, Ukrainian Orthodox (Moscow patriarchate) 26%, Ukrainian Greek Catholic 8%, Ukrainian Autocephalous Orthodox 7%.

Geography: Total area: 233,090 sq mi, 603,700 sq km; **Land area:** 233,090 sq mi, 603,700 sq km. **Location:** In E Europe. **Neighbors:** Belarus on N; Russia on NE and E; Moldova and Romania on SW; Hungary, Slovakia, and Poland on W. **Topography:** Part of the E European plain. Mountainous areas include the Carpathians in the SW and Crimean chain in the S. Arable black soil constitutes a large part of the country. **Capital:** Kiev, 2,709,000. **Cities (urban aggr.):** Kharkiv, 1,461,000; Dnipropetrovs'k, 1,050,000; Odesa, 991,000.

Government: Type: Republic. **Head of state:** Pres. Viktor Andriyovych Yushchenko; b. Feb. 23, 1954; in office: Jan. 23, 2005. **Head of gov.:** Prime Min. Yulia Tymoshenko; b. Nov. 27, 1960; in office: Dec. 18, 2007. **Local divisions:** 24 oblasts, 2 municipalities, 1 autonomous republic. **Defense budget:** $1.8 bil. **Active troops:** 129,925.

Economy: Industries: coal, electric power, metals, machinery & transp. equip., chemicals, food proc. (espec. sugar). **Chief crops:** grain, sugar beets, sunflower seeds, vegetables. **Natural resources:** iron ore, coal, mang., nat. gas, oil, salt, sulfur, graphite, titanium, magnesium, kaolin, nickel, mercury, timber. **Crude oil reserves:** 395 mil bbls. **Arable land:** 54%. **Livestock:** cattle: 6.2 mil; chickens: 145.6 mil; goats: 692,500; pigs: 8.1 mil; sheep: 924,700. **Fish catch:** 243,241 metric tons. **Electricity prod.:** 182.4 bil kWh. **Labor force** (2005): agric. 19.4%, industry 24.2%, services 56.4%.

Finance: Monetary unit: Hryvna (UAH) (Oct. 2009: 8.31 = $1 U.S.). **GDP:** $339.8 bil; **per capita GDP:** $7,400; **GDP growth:** 2.7%. **Imports:** $84.7 bil; Russia 27.4%, Germany 10.5%, China 8.6%, Poland 7.1%, Turkmenistan 4.7%. **Exports:** $67.7 bil; Rus-

sia 23.3%, Turkey 8.2%, Italy 5%. **Tourism:** $4.6 bil. **Budget:** $45.1 bil. **Intl. reserves less gold:** $20 bil. **Gold:** 850,000 oz t. **Consumer prices:** 25.2%.

Transport: Railroad: Length: 13,456 mi. **Motor vehicles:** 5.5 mil pass. cars; 889,000 comm. vehicles. **Civil aviation:** 2.5 bil pass.-mi; 189 airports. **Chief ports:** Feodosiya, Kerch, Kherson, Mariupol, Mykolayiv, Odesa, Yuzhnyy.

Communications: TV sets: 433 per 1,000 pop. **Radios:** 882 per 1,000 pop. **Telephone lines:** 13.2 mil. **Daily newspaper circ.** (2004): 131 per 1,000 pop. **Internet:** 10.4 mil users.

Health: Life expect.: 62.2 male; 74.2 female. **Births** (per 1,000 pop.): 9.6. **Deaths** (per 1,000 pop.): 15.9. **Natural inc.:** –0.64%. **Infant mortality** (per 1,000 live births): 9.2. **HIV rate:** 1.6%.

Education: Compulsory: ages 6-17. **Literacy:** 99.7%.

Major intl. organizations: UN (FAO, IBRD, ILO, IMF, IMO, WHO), CIS, OSCE.

Embassy: 3350 M St. NW 20007; 333-0606.

Website: www.kmu.gov.ua

Ukrainians' Slavic ancestors inhabited the region well before the 1st cent. CE. In the 9th cent., the princes of Kiev established a strong state called Kievan Rus, which included much of present-day Ukraine. Internal conflicts led to the disintegration of the Ukrainian state by the 13th cent. Mongol rule was supplanted by Poland and Lithuania in the 14th and 15th centuries. The N Black Sea coast and Crimea came under Turkish control in 1478. Ukrainian Cossacks, starting in the late 16th cent., rebelled against the occupiers of Ukraine: Russia, Poland, and Turkey.

An independent Ukrainian National Republic was proclaimed on Jan. 22, 1918. But in 1921, Ukraine's neighbors occupied and divided Ukrainian territory. In 1922, Ukraine became a constituent republic of the USSR. In 1932-33, the Soviet government engineered a famine in eastern Ukraine, resulting in the deaths of 6-7 mil Ukrainians. During WWII the Ukrainian nationalist underground fought both Nazi and Soviet forces. Over 5 mil Ukrainians died in the war. With the reoccupation of Ukraine by Soviet troops in 1944 came a renewed wave of repression.

The world's worst nuclear power plant disaster occurred in Chernobyl, Ukraine, in Apr. 1986; many thousands were killed or disabled as a result of the radiation leak. The plant was finally shut down Dec. 15, 2000.

Ukrainian independence was restored in Dec. 1991 with the dissolution of the Soviet Union. In the post-Soviet period Ukraine was burdened with a deteriorating economy. Following a 1994 accord with Russia and the U.S., Ukraine's large nuclear arsenal was transferred to Russia for destruction.

President since 1994, Leonid Kuchma attempted to engineer the election in 2004 of his handpicked successor, Prime Min. Viktor Yanukovych, also favored by Russia. The main challenger, Viktor Yushchenko, a former prime min., was poisoned in Sept. with dioxin, but continued to campaign. Official results of a runoff vote Nov. 21 showed a win for Yanukovych. Yushchenko supporters, calling the election fraudulent, staged massive protests (the "orange revolution"), and the vote was annulled. An election return Dec. 26 gave the victory to Yushchenko. Inaugurated Jan. 23, 2005, he dismissed his cabinet Sept. 8, amid allegations of infighting and corruption among his top aides.

Yushchenko's Our Ukraine party fared poorly in parliamentary elections Mar. 26, 2006, and the resurgent Yanukovych, whose party won the vote, returned as prime min. Aug. 4. The two rivals then engaged in a year-long political struggle. A report released Feb. 19, 2007, by the International Organization for Migration estimated that 117,000 Ukrainians had been trafficked abroad as forced laborers or prostitutes since 1991.

Following elections Sept. 30, 2007, Yulia Tymoshenko, a former "orange revolution" ally of Yushchenko, became prime min. Dec. 18. Russia's war with Georgia in Aug. 2008 led to a split between the anti-Russian Yushchenko and Tymoshenko. But with the country reeling from recession and needing an IMF bailout, agreement on a new governing coalition was reached Dec.10, and parliamentary elections were postponed. A natural-gas price dispute with Russia that had led to a midwinter cutoff of Russian gas supplies to Ukraine and other countries of central and E Europe was resolved Jan. 19, 2009.

United Arab Emirates

People: Population: 4,798,491. **Age distrib.** (%): <15: 20.4; 65+: 0.9. **Pop. density:** 148.7 per sq mi, 57.4 per sq km. **Urban:** 77.7%. **Ethnic groups:** Emirati 19%, other Arab & Iranian 23%, South Asian 50%, other expatriates (incl. Westerners & East Asians) 8%. **Principal languages:** Arabic (official), Persian, English, Hindi, Urdu. **Chief religions:** Muslim 96% (Shi'a 16%), other (incl. Christian, Hindu) 4%.

Geography: Total area: 32,278 sq mi, 83,600 sq km; **Land area:** 32,278 sq mi, 83,600 sq km. **Location:** Middle East, on S shore of the Persian Gulf. **Neighbors:** Saudi Arabia on W and S, Oman on E. **Topography:** A barren, flat coastal plain gives way to uninhabited sand dunes on S. Hajar Mts. on E. **Capital:** Abu Dhabi, 603,000. **Cities (urban aggr.):** Dubai, 1,379,000.

Government: Type: Federation of emirates. **Head of state:** Pres. Sheikh Khalifa ibn Zaid an-Nahayan; b. 1948; in office: Nov. 3, 2004. **Head of gov.:** Prime Min. Sheikh Muhammad ibn Rashid al-Maktum; b. 1949; in office: Jan. 5, 2006. **Local divisions:** 7 autonomous emirates: Abu Dhabi, Ajman, Dubai, Fujaira, Ras al-Khaimah, Sharjah, Umm al-Qaiwain. **Defense budget:** $10.1 bil. **Active troops:** 51,000.

Economy: Industries: oil & petrochems., fishing, aluminum, cement, fertilizers, constr. materials. **Chief crops:** dates, vegetables, watermelons. **Natural resources:** oil, nat. gas. **Crude oil reserves:** 97.8 bil bbls. **Arable land:** 1%. **Livestock:** cattle: 125,000; chickens: 15.5 mil; goats: 1.6 mil; sheep: 615,000. **Fish catch** (est.): 87,570 metric tons. **Electricity prod.:** 62.8 bil kWh. **Labor force** (2000 est.): agric. 7%, industry 15%, services 78%.

Finance: Monetary unit: Dirham (AED) (Oct. 2009: 3.67 = $1 U.S.). **GDP:** $184.3 bil; **per capita GDP:** $39,900; **GDP growth:** 7.4%. **Imports:** $145.8 bil; China 13.5%, India 9.8%, U.S. 9.2%, Germany 6.8%, Japan 6.4%, Turkey 4.7%, Italy 4.5%. **Exports:** $210.5 bil; Japan 25.5%, S. Korea 8.6%, Thailand 5.8%, India 4.8%. **Tourism:** NA. **Budget:** $38.1 bil. **Intl. reserves less gold:** $20.58 bil. **Gold:** NA. **Consumer prices:** NA.

Transport: Motor vehicles: 321,600 pass. cars; 84,200 comm. vehicles. **Civil aviation:** 40.5 bil pass.-mi (incl. Gulf Air traffic apportionment); 24 airports. **Chief ports:** Al Fujayrah, Khawr Fakkan (Sharjah), Mina' Jabal Ali (Dubai), Mina' Rashid (Dubai), Mina Saqr, Mina' Zayid (Abu Dhabi).

Communications: TV sets: 309 per 1,000 pop. **Radios:** 355 per 1,000 pop. **Telephone lines:** 1.5 mil. **Internet:** 2.9 mil users.

Health: Life expect.: 73.3 male; 78.6 female. **Births** (per 1,000 pop.): 16.1. **Deaths** (per 1,000 pop.): 2.1. **Natural inc.:** 1.39%. **Infant mortality** (per 1,000 live births): 13.1. **HIV rate:** NA.

Education: Compulsory: ages 6-14. **Literacy:** 90.4%.

Major intl. organizations: UN (FAO, IBRD, ILO, IMF, IMO, WHO, WTO), AL, OPEC.

Embassy: 3522 International Ct. NW, Ste. 400, 20008; 243-2400.

Website: www.government.ae

The 7 "Trucial Sheikdoms" gave Britain control of defense and foreign relations in the 19th cent. They merged to become an independent state Dec. 2, 1971. The Abu Dhabi Petroleum Co. was fully nationalized in 1975. Oil revenues have made the UAE one of the world's wealthiest countries. International banking, investment, and construction have boomed; holdings of Abu Dhabi's largest government-sponsored investment fund were estimated at $550 bil in Oct. 2008. Foreigners make up more than 80% of the population and nearly all the private work force.

The UAE and U.S. signed a civilian nuclear cooperation agreement Jan. 15, 2009. As the global recession hit Dubai's high-flying economy, the UAE government said Feb. 22 it would provide $10 bil to allow Dubai to meet its international debt obligations.

United Kingdom
United Kingdom of Great Britain and Northern Ireland

People: Population: 61,113,205. **Age distrib.** (%): <15: 16.7; 65+: 16.2. **Pop. density:** 655.2 per sq mi, 253 per sq km. **Urban:** 89.7%. **Ethnic groups:** White 92% (English 84%, Scottish 9%, Welsh 5%, N Irish 3%), Black 2%, Indian 2%. **Principal languages:** English, Welsh, Scottish form of Gaelic. **Chief religions:** Christian (incl. Anglican, Roman Catholic, Presbyterian, Methodist) 72%, Muslim 3%, unspecified or none 23%.

Geography: Total area: 94,526 sq mi, 244,820 sq km; **Land area:** 93,278 sq mi, 241,590 sq km. **Location:** Off NW coast of Europe, across English Channel, Strait of Dover, North Sea. **Neighbors:** Ireland to W, France to SE. **Topography:** England is mostly rolling land, rising to Uplands of southern Scotland. Lowlands are in center of Scotland, granite Highlands are in N. Coast is heavily indented, especially on W. British Isles have milder climate than N Europe due to Gulf Stream and ample rainfall. Severn, 220 mi, and Thames, 215 mi, are longest rivers. **Capital:** London, 8,567,000. **Cities (urban aggr.):** Birmingham, 2,285,000; Manchester, 2,230,000; West Yorkshire, 1,529,000; Glasgow, 1,160,000.

Government: Type: Constitutional monarchy. **Head of state:** Queen Elizabeth II; b. Apr. 21, 1926; in office: Feb. 6, 1952. **Head of gov.:** Prime Min. Gordon Brown; b. Feb. 20, 1951; in office: June 27, 2007. **Local divisions:** 467 local authorities, including England: 387; Wales: 22; Scotland: 32; Northern Ireland: 26. **Defense budget:** $63.3 bil. **Active troops:** 160,280.

Economy: Industries: machine tools, electric power equip., automation equip., railroad equip., shipbuilding, aircraft, motor vehicles & parts, electronics & comm. equip., metals, chemicals, coal, oil, paper & paper products. **Chief crops:** cereals, oilseed, potatoes, vegetables. **Natural resources:** coal, oil, nat. gas, iron ore, lead, zinc, gold, tin, limestone, salt, clay, chalk, gypsum. **Crude oil reserves:** 3.4 bil bbls. **Arable land:** 23%. **Livestock:** cattle: 10.3 mil; chickens: 157.5 mil; goats: 95,000; pigs: 4.8 mil; sheep: 33.9 mil. **Fish catch:** 793,894 metric tons. **Electricity prod.:** 372 bil kWh. **Labor force** (2006 est.): agric. 1.4%, industry 18.2%, services 80.4%.

Finance: Monetary unit: Pound (GBP) (Oct. 2009: 0.63 = $1 U.S.). **GDP:** $2.2 tril; **per capita GDP:** $36,500; **GDP growth:** 0.7%. **Imports:** $636 bil; Germany 13.1%, U.S. 8.7%, China 7.5%,

Netherlands 7.4%, France 6.8%, Norway 6%, Belgium 4.7%, Italy 4.1%. **Exports:** $464.9 bil; U.S. 13.9%, Germany 11.5%, Netherlands 7.8%, France 7.5%, Ireland 7.5%, Belgium 5.2%, Spain 4.1%. **Tourism:** $38.6 bil. **Budget:** $1.2 tril. **Intl. reserves less gold:** $28.79 bil. **Gold:** 9.98 mil oz t. **Consumer prices:** 4%.

Transport: Railroad: Length: 10,224 mi. **Motor vehicles:** 28.3 mil pass. cars; 4.1 mil comm. vehicles. **Civil aviation:** 124.5 bil pass.-mi; 307 airports. **Chief ports:** Dover, Felixstowe, Immingham, Liverpool, London, Southampton, Teesport.

Communications: TV sets: 661 per 1,000 pop. **Radios:** 1,437 per 1,000 pop. **Telephone lines:** 33.2 mil. **Daily newspaper circ.** (2004): 289.8 per 1,000 pop. **Internet:** 48.8 mil users.

Health: Life expect.: 76.4 male; 81.5 female. **Births** (per 1,000 pop.): 10.7. **Deaths** (per 1,000 pop.): 10.1. **Natural inc.:** 0.06%. **Infant mortality** (per 1,000 live births): 4.9. **HIV rate:** 0.2%.

Education: Compulsory: ages 5-16. **Literacy:** 99%.

Major intl. organizations: UN and all of its specialized agencies, the Commonwealth, EU, NATO, OECD, OSCE.

Embassy: 3100 Massachusetts Ave. NW 20008; 588-6500.

Website: www.direct.gov.uk

The United Kingdom of Great Britain and Northern Ireland comprises England, Wales, Scotland, and Northern Ireland.

Queen and Royal Family. The ruling sovereign is Elizabeth II of the House of Windsor, b. Apr. 21, 1926, elder daughter of King George VI. She succeeded to the throne Feb. 6, 1952, and was crowned June 2, 1953. She was married Nov. 20, 1947, to Lt. Philip Mountbatten, b. June 10, 1921, former Prince of Greece. He was created Duke of Edinburgh, and given the title H.R.H., Nov. 19, 1947; he was named Prince of the United Kingdom and Northern Ireland Feb. 22, 1957. Prince Charles Philip Arthur George, b. Nov. 14, 1948, is the Prince of Wales and heir apparent. His first son, William Philip Arthur Louis, b. June 21, 1982, is second in line to the throne.

Parliament is the legislative body for the UK, with certain powers over dependent units. It consists of 2 houses: The **House of Commons** has 646 members, elected by direct ballot and divided as follows: England, 529; Wales, 40; Scotland, 59; Northern Ireland, 18. Following a drastic reduction in 1999 in the number of hereditary peerages, the **House of Lords** (July 2009) comprised 724 active members: 92 hereditary peers, 606 life peers, and 2 archbishops and 24 bishops of the Church of England.

Resources and Industries. Great Britain's major occupations are manufacturing and trade. Metals and metal-using industries contribute more than 50% of exports. Of about 60 mil acres of land in England, Wales, and Scotland, 46 mil are farmed, of which 17 mil are arable, the rest pastures. Large oil and gas fields have been found in the North Sea. Commercial oil production began in 1975. There are large deposits of coal.

Britain imports all of its cotton, rubber, sulphur, about 80% of its wool, half of its food and iron ore, also certain amounts of paper, tobacco, chemicals. Manufactured goods made from these basic materials have been exported since the industrial age began. Main exports are machinery, chemicals, textiles, clothing, autos and trucks, iron and steel, locomotives, ships, jet aircraft, farm machinery, drugs, radio, TV, radar and navigation equipment, scientific instruments, arms, whisky.

Religion and Education. The Church of England is Protestant Episcopal. The queen is its temporal head, with rights of appointments to archbishoprics, bishoprics, and other offices. There are 2 provinces, Canterbury and York, each headed by an archbishop. The most famous church is Westminster Abbey (1050-1760), site of coronations, tombs of Elizabeth I, Mary, Queen of Scots, kings, poets, and of the Unknown Warrior.

The most celebrated British universities are Oxford and Cambridge, each dating to the 13th cent. There are about 70 other universities.

History. Recent research indicates that Britain was separated from the European continent at least 200,000 years ago by a catastrophic flood that created the English Channel. Migrants across the Channel included the Celts, who arrived 2,500 to 3,000 years ago. Their language survives in Welsh and Gaelic enclaves.

England was added to the Roman Empire in 43 CE. After the withdrawal of Roman legions in 410, waves of Jutes, Angles, and Saxons arrived from German lands. They contended with Danish raiders for control from the 8th through 11th centuries. The last successful invasion was by French speaking Normans in 1066, who united the country with their dominions in France.

Opposition by nobles to royal authority forced King John to agree to the Magna Carta in 1215, a guarantee of rights and the rule of law. In the ensuing decades, the foundations of the parliamentary system were laid.

English dynastic claims to large parts of France led to the Hundred Years War, 1338-1453, and the defeat of England. A long civil war, the War of the Roses, lasted 1455-85, and ended with the establishment of the powerful Tudor monarchy. A distinct English civilization flourished. The economy prospered over long periods of domestic peace unmatched in continental Europe. Religious independence was secured when the Church of England was separated from the authority of the pope in 1534.

During the reign of Queen Elizabeth I, 1558-1603, England became a major naval power, leading to the founding of colonies in the new world and the expansion of trade with Europe and the Orient. Scotland was united with England when James VI of Scotland was crowned James I of England in 1603.

A struggle between Parliament and the Stuart kings led to a bloody civil war, 1642-49, and the establishment of a republic under the Puritan Oliver Cromwell. The monarchy was restored in 1660, but the "Glorious Revolution" of 1688 confirmed the sovereignty of Parliament: a Bill of Rights was granted 1689.

In the 18th cent., parliamentary rule was strengthened. Technological and entrepreneurial innovations led to the Industrial Revolution. The 13 N. American colonies were lost but replaced by growing empires in Canada and India. Britain's role in the defeat of Napoleon, 1815, strengthened its position as the leading world power.

The extension of the franchise in 1832 and 1867, the formation of trade unions, and the development of universal public education were among the drastic social changes that accompanied the spread of industrialization and urbanization in the 19th cent. Large parts of Africa and Asia were added to the empire during the reign of Queen Victoria, 1837-1901.

Though victorious in WWI, Britain suffered huge casualties and economic dislocation. Ireland became independent in 1921, and independence movements became active in India and other colonies. The country suffered major bombing damage in WWII but rallied by Prime Min. Winston Churchill, held out against Germany until Allied victory was achieved, 1945.

Industrial growth continued in the postwar period, but Britain lost its leadership position to other powers. Labor governments passed socialist programs nationalizing some basic industries and expanding social security. Prime Min. Margaret Thatcher's Conservative governments, 1979-90, revived the role of private enterprise. Her Conservative successor, John Major, held power 1990-97. The UK sent military forces to the Persian Gulf War, 1991. The Channel Tunnel linking Britain to the Continent was inaugurated May 6, 1994.

On May 1, 1997, the Labour Party swept into power, making Tony Blair, 43, Britain's youngest prime min. since 1812. Diana, Princess of Wales, died in a car crash in Paris, Aug. 31. Britain played a leading role in the NATO air war against Yugoslavia, Mar.-June 1999, and contributed 12,000 troops to the multinational security force in Kosovo (KFOR).

Blair led Labour to another landslide election victory June 7, 2001. After the Sept. 11 attacks on the U.S., Britain took an important role in the U.S.-led war against terrorism. The UK participated in the bombing of Afghanistan that began Oct. 7, 2001; about 9,000 UK troops were serving in Afghanistan as of Sept. 2009, with more than 210 fatalities recorded since the war started.

Overcoming dissent within his own cabinet, Blair committed British troops to the U.S.-led invasion of Iraq, Mar.-Apr. 2003. UK forces, which numbered 46,000 at the height of combat operations, had been almost entirely pulled out by mid-2009, with more than 170 deaths reported.

In elections May 5, 2005, Blair became the first Labour prime min. to win 3 consecutive terms. Suicide bombings on 3 London underground trains and a bus, July 7, left 56 people dead and hundreds injured; police identified the bombers as 4 British Muslim men (3 of Pakistani origin). British authorities announced Aug. 10, 2006, that they had thwarted a plot to use liquid explosives to blow up passenger aircraft flying the UK-U.S. route.

Blair stepped down June 27, 2007, and was succeeded by Gordon Brown. Failed car bombings in London, June 29, and at Glasgow Airport Scotland, June 30, led to the arrest in Britain of 7 suspects, mostly foreign-born medical workers. Severe floods June-Aug. in central England caused at least $2 bil in damage. Responding Oct. 13, 2008, to the worldwide financial crisis, Prime Min. Brown initiated a plan to partially nationalize 3 of Britain's largest banks and support them with a capital infusion of up to $63 bil. Michael Martin, Labour speaker of the House of Commons, resigned May 19, 2009, amid revelations that parliamentarians of all parties had padded their salaries with questionable expense claims. Britain's deepest recession since World War II had begun to ease by midyear, although the unemployment rate continued to climb, reaching 7.9% in July.

Wales

The Principality of Wales in western Britain has an area of 8,019 sq mi and a population (2008 est.) of 2,993,400. Cardiff is the capital, pop. (2005 est., city proper) 319,700.

Less than 20% of Wales residents speak English and Welsh; about 32,000 speak Welsh solely. A 1979 referendum rejected, 4-1, the creation of an elected Welsh assembly; a similar proposal passed by a thin margin on Sept. 18, 1997. Elections for the 60-seat assembly were held in 1997, 2003, and 2007.

Early Anglo-Saxon invaders drove Celtic peoples into the mountains of Wales, terming them Waelise (Welsh, or foreign). There they developed a distinct nationality. Members of the ruling house of Gwynedd in the 13th cent. fought England but were crushed, 1283. Edward of Caernarvon, son of Edward I of England, was created Prince of Wales, 1301.

Scotland

Scotland, a kingdom now united with England and Wales in Great Britain, occupies the northern 37% of the main British island, and the Hebrides, Orkney, Shetland, and smaller islands. Length 275 mi, breadth approx. 150 mi, area 30,418 sq mi, pop. (2008 est.) 5,168,500.

The Lowlands, a belt of land approx. 60 mi wide from the Firth of Clyde to the Firth of Forth, divide the farming region of the Southern Uplands from the granite Highlands of the N; they contain 75% of the population and most of the industry. The Highlands, famous for hunting and fishing, have been opened to industry by many hydroelectric power stations.

Edinburgh, pop. (2006 est., city proper) 463,510, is the capital. Glasgow, pop. (2006 est., city proper) 580,690, is Britain's greatest industrial center. It is a shipbuilding complex on the Clyde and an ocean port. Aberdeen, pop. (2006 est.) 202,090, NE of Edinburgh, is a major port, center of granite industry, fish-processing, and North Sea oil exploration. Dundee, pop. (2006 est.) 142,160, NE of Edinburgh, is an industrial and fish-processing center. About 90,000 persons speak Gaelic as well as English.

History. Scotland was called Caledonia by the Romans who battled early Celtic tribes and occupied southern areas from the 1st to the 4th centuries. Missionaries from Britain introduced Christianity in the 4th cent.; St. Columba, an Irish monk, converted most of Scotland in the 6th cent.

The Kingdom of Scotland was founded in 1018. William Wallace and Robert Bruce both defeated English armies 1297 and 1314, respectively.

In 1603 James VI of Scotland, son of Mary, Queen of Scots, succeeded to the throne of England as James I, and effected the Union of the Crowns. In 1707 Scotland received representation in the British Parliament, resulting from the union of former separate Parliaments. Its executive in the British cabinet is the Secretary of State for Scotland. The growing Scottish National Party urges independence. A 1979 referendum on the creation of an elected Scottish assembly was defeated, but a proposal to create a regional legislature with limited taxing authority passed by a landslide Sept. 11, 1997. Elections for the 129-seat parliament were held 1999, 2003, and 2007; in the 2007 vote, Scottish Nationalist candidates upset the Labour Party.

Memorials of Robert Burns, Sir Walter Scott, John Knox, and Mary, Queen of Scots, draw many tourists, as do the beauties of the Trossachs, Loch Katrine, Loch Lomond, and abbey ruins.

Industries. Engineering products are the most important industry, with growing emphasis on office machinery, autos, electronics, and other consumer goods. Oil has been discovered offshore in the North Sea, stimulating on-shore support industries.

Scotland produces fine woolens, worsteds, tweeds, silks, fine linens, and jute. It is known for its special breeds of cattle and sheep. Fisheries have large hauls of herring, cod, whiting. Whisky is the biggest export.

The Hebrides are a group of c. 500 islands, 100 inhabited, off the W coast. The **Inner Hebrides** include Skye, Mull, and Iona, the last famous for the arrival of St. Columba, 563 CE. The **Outer Hebrides** include Lewis and Harris. Industries include sheep raising and weaving. The **Orkney Isls.**, c. 90, are to the NE. The capital is Kirkwall, on Pomona Isl. Fish curing, sheep raising, and weaving are occupations. NE of the Orkneys are the 200 **Shetland Isls.**, 24 inhabited, home of Shetland ponies. The Orkneys and Shetlands are centers for the North Sea oil industry.

Northern Ireland

Northern Ireland was constituted in 1920 from 6 of the 9 counties of Ulster, the NE corner of Ireland. Area 5,452 sq mi, pop. (2008 est) 1,775,000. Capital and chief industrial center, Belfast, pop. (2006 est., city proper) 267,400.

Industries. Shipbuilding, including large tankers, has long been an important industry, centered in Belfast, the largest port. Linen manufacture is also important, along with apparel, rope, and twine. Growing diversification has added engineering products, synthetic fibers, and electronics. There are large numbers of cattle, hogs, and sheep. Potatoes, poultry, and dairy foods are also produced.

Government. An act of the British Parliament, 1920, divided Northern from Southern Ireland, each with a parliament and government. When Ireland became a dominion, 1921, and later a republic, Northern Ireland chose to remain a part of the United Kingdom. It elects 18 members to the House of Commons.

During 1968-69, large demonstrations were conducted by Roman Catholics who charged they were discriminated against in voting rights, housing, and employment. The Catholics, a minority comprising about a third of the population, demanded abolition of property qualifications for voting in local elections. Violence and terrorism intensified, involving branches of the Irish Republican Army (outlawed in the Irish Republic), Protestant groups, police, and British troops. Between 1969 and 2001 more than 3,500 were killed in sectarian violence in Northern Ireland, Ireland, England, and elsewhere. For most of this period, the Northern Ireland parliament was suspended, and Britain imposed direct rule.

A settlement reached on Good Friday, Apr. 10, 1998, provided for restoration of home rule and election of a 108-member assembly with safeguards for minority rights. Both Ireland and Great Britain agreed to give up their constitutional claims on Northern Ireland. The accord was approved May 22 by voters in Northern Ireland and the Irish Republic, and elections to the assembly were held June 25. IRA dissidents seeking to derail the agreement were responsible for a bomb at Omagh Aug. 15 that killed 29 people and injured over 330.

London transferred authority to a Northern Ireland power-sharing government Dec. 2, 1999. Delays in IRA disarmament led to several suspensions of self-government. The IRA stated July 28, 2005, that it had renounced violence and ordered all units to disarm. In response, the British began reducing their military presence in the region. On Sept. 26, an international monitoring group reported that the IRA had apparently scrapped its entire arsenal. The Northern Ireland legislature, suspended for 3 1/2 years, reconvened May 15, 2006. Elections were held Mar. 7, 2007.

Religion and Education. Northern Ireland is about 58% Protestant, 42% Roman Catholic. Education is compulsory between the ages of 5 and 16 years.

Channel Islands
The Channel Islands, area 75 sq mi, pop. (2003 est.) 145,000, off the NW coast of France, the only parts of the one-time Dukedom of Normandy belonging to England, are Jersey, Guernsey and the dependencies of Guernsey—Alderney, Brechou, Great Sark, Little Sark, Herm, Jethou, and Lihou. **Jersey,** pop. (2009 est.) 91,626, and **Guernsey,** pop. (2009 est.) 65,870, have separate legal existences and lieutenant governors named by the Crown. The islands were the only British soil occupied by German troops in WWII.

Isle of Man
The Isle of Man, area 221 sq mi, pop. (2009 est.) 76,512, is in the Irish Sea, 20 mi from Scotland, 30 mi from Cumberland. It is rich in lead and iron. The island has its own laws and a lieutenant governor appointed by the Crown. The Tynwald (legislature) consists of the Legislative Council, partly elected, and House of Keys, elected. Capital: Douglas. Farming, tourism, and fishing (kippers, scallops) are chief occupations. Man is famous for the Manx tailless cat.

Gibraltar
Gibraltar, a dependency on the S coast of Spain, guards the entrance to the Mediterranean. The Rock of Gibraltar has been in British possession since 1704; it is 2.5 mi long, 3/4 of a mi wide and 1,396 ft in height; a narrow isthmus connects it with the mainland. Pop. (2009 est.) 28,034.

Gibraltar has historically been an object of contention between Britain and Spain. In 1967, residents voted with near unanimity to remain under British rule. A new constitution, May 30, 1969, increased Gibraltarian control of domestic affairs (the UK continues to handle defense and internal security matters). Following a 1984 agreement between Britain and Spain, the border, closed by Spain in 1969, was fully reopened in Feb. 1985. A UN General Assembly resolution requested Britain to end Gibraltar's colonial status by Oct. 1, 1996. A plan for the UK and Spain to share sovereignty was rejected by Gibraltar voters, Nov. 7, 2002. Residents approved a new constitution Nov. 30, 2006.

British West Indies
Swinging in a vast arc from the coast of Venezuela NE, then N and NW toward Puerto Rico are the Leeward Islands, forming a coral and volcanic barrier sheltering the Caribbean from the open Atlantic. Many of the islands are self-governing British possessions. Universal suffrage was instituted 1951-54; ministerial systems were set up 1956-60.

The **Leeward Isls.** still associated with the UK are **Montserrat,** area 40 sq mi, pop. (2009 est.) 5,097, capital Plymouth; the **British Virgin Isls.,** 59.1 sq mi, pop. (2009 est.) 24,491, capital Road Town; and **Anguilla,** the most northerly of Leeward Islands, 40 sq mi, pop. (2009 est.) 14,436, capital The Valley. Montserrat has been devastated by the Soufrière Hills volcano, which began erupting July 18, 1995.

The three **Cayman Isls.,** a dependency, lie S of Cuba, NW of Jamaica. Pop. (2009 est.) 49,035, most of it on Grand Cayman. It is a free port; in the 1970s Grand Cayman became a tax-free refuge for foreign funds and branches of many Western banks were opened there. Total area 101 sq mi, capital George Town.

The **Turks and Caicos Isls.** are a dependency at the SE end of the Bahama Islands. Of about 30 islands, only 6 are inhabited; area 166 sq mi, pop. (2009 est.) 22,942; capital Grand Turk. Salt, shellfish, and conch shells are the main exports.

Bermuda
Bermuda is a British dependency governed by a royal governor and an assembly, dating from 1620, the oldest legislative body among British dependencies. Capital is Hamilton.

It is a group of about 150 small islands of coral formation, 20 inhabited, comprising 21 sq mi in the western Atlantic, 580 mi E of N. Carolina. Pop. (2009 est.) 67,837 (about 55% of African descent). Pop. density is high.

Tourism is the major industry. Bermuda is also a haven for the offshore insurance industry. Exports include petroleum products, medicine. In a referendum Aug. 15, 1995, voters rejected independence by nearly a 3-to-1 majority.

Hurricane Fabian, the most potent storm to reach Bermuda in 50 years, struck Sept. 5, 2003; 4 people were missing and presumed dead, and damage was estimated at over $300 mil.

South Atlantic
The **Falkland Isls.,** a dependency, lie 300 mi E of the Strait of Magellan at the southern end of S. America.

The Falklands, or Islas Malvinas, include 2 large islands and about 200 smaller ones, area 4,700 sq mi, pop. (2008 est.) 3,140, capital Stanley. The licensing of foreign fishing vessels has become the major source of revenue. Sheep-grazing is a main industry; wool is the principal export. There are indications of large oil and gas deposits. The islands are also claimed by Argentina, though 97% of inhabitants are of British origin. Argentina invaded the islands Apr. 2, 1982. The British responded by sending a task force to the area, landing their main force on the Falklands, May 21, and forcing an Argentine surrender at Port Stanley, June 14. A pact resuming commercial air service with Argentina was signed July 14, 1999.

British Antarctic Territory, south of 60° S lat., formerly a dependency of the Falkland Isls., was made a separate colony in 1962 and includes the South Shetland Isls., the South Orkneys, and the Antarctic Peninsula. A chain of meteorological stations is maintained.

South Georgia and the **South Sandwich Isls.,** formerly administered by the Falklands Isls., became a separate dependency in 1985. Total area of 1,507 sq mi. South Georgia, with no permanent population, is about 800 mi SE of the Falklands; the South Sandwich Isls. are uninhabited, about 470 mi SE of South Georgia.

St. Helena, an island 1,200 mi off the W coast of Africa and 1,800 mi E of S. America, 160 sq mi and pop. (2009 est.) 7,637. Flax, lace, and rope-making are the chief industries. After Napoleon Bonaparte was defeated at Waterloo the Allies exiled him to St. Helena, where he lived from Oct. 16, 1815, to his death, May 5, 1821. Capital is Jamestown.

Tristan da Cunha is the principal island in a group of islands of volcanic origin, total area 40 sq mi, halfway between the Cape of Good Hope and S. America. A volcanic peak 6,760 ft high erupted in 1961. The 262 inhabitants were removed to England, but most returned in 1963. The islands are dependencies of St. Helena. Pop. (2002) 284.

Ascension is an island of volcanic origin, 34 sq mi in area, 700 mi NW of St. Helena, through which it is administered. It is a communications relay center for Britain, and has a U.S. satellite tracking center. Pop. (2002) was 1,050, half of them communications workers. The island is noted for sea turtles.

British Indian Ocean Territory
Formed Nov. 1965, embracing islands formerly dependencies of Mauritius or Seychelles: the Chagos Archipelago (including Diego Garcia), Aldabra, Farquhar, and Des Roches. The latter 3 were transferred to Seychelles, which became independent in 1976. Area 23 sq mi. No permanent civilian population remains; the UK and the U.S. maintain a military presence.

Pacific Ocean
Pitcairn Isl. is in the Pacific, halfway between S. America and Australia. The island was discovered in 1767 by Philip Carteret but was not inhabited until 23 years later when the mutineers of the *Bounty* landed there. The area is 18 sq mi and 2009 pop. was 48. It is a British dependency and is administered by a British High Commissioner in New Zealand and a local Council. The uninhabited islands of Henderson, Ducie, and Oeno are in the Pitcairn group.

United States
United States of America
People: Population: 307,212,123. (incl. 50 states & Dist. of Columbia). (Note: U.S. pop. figures may differ elsewhere in *The World Almanac.*) **Age distrib.** (%): <15: 20.2; 65+: 12.8. **Pop. density:** 86.8 per sq mi, 33.5 per sq km. **Urban:** 80.8%. **Ethnic groups:** White 80%, black 13%, Asian 4%, Amerindian & Alaska native 1%. (Hispanic, any race 15%.) **Principal languages:** English, Spanish, Hawaiian (official in Hawaii). **Chief religions:** Protestant 51%, Roman Catholic 24%, Mormon 2%, other Christian 2%, Jewish 2%, none 4%.

Geography: Total area: 3,794,083 sq mi, 9,826,630 sq km; **Land area:** 3,537,438 sq mi, 9,161,923 sq km. **Topography:** Vast central plain, mountains in W, hills and low mountains in E. **Capital:** Washington, DC, 4,338,000.

Government: Federal republic, strong democratic tradition. **Head of state and gov.:** Pres. Barack Obama; b. Aug. 4, 1961; in office: Jan. 20, 2009. **Local divisions:** 50 states and Dist. of Columbia. **Defense budget:** $552.6 bil. **Active troops:** 1,539,587.

Economy: Industries: oil, steel, motor vehicles, aerospace, telecomm., chemicals, electronics, food proc., consumer goods, lumber, mining. **Chief crops:** wheat, corn, fruits, vegetables, cotton. **Natural resources:** coal, copper, lead, molybd., phosphates, uranium, bauxite, gold, iron, mercury, nickel, potash, silver, tungsten, zinc, oil, nat. gas, timber. **Crude oil reserves:** 21.3 bil bbls.

Arable land: 18%. **Livestock:** cattle: 97 mil; chickens: 2.1 bil; goats: 2.9 mil; pigs: 61.9 mil; sheep: 6.2 mil. **Fish catch:** 5.3 mil metric tons. **Electricity prod.:** 4,071.3 bil kWh. **Labor force** (2007): farming, forestry, & fishing 0.6%; mfg., extraction, transp., & crafts 22.6%; managerial, professional, & technical 35.5%; sales & office 24.8%; other services 16.5%.

Finance: Monetary unit: Dollar (USD). **GDP:** $14.3 tril; **per capita GDP:** $46,900; **GDP growth:** 1.1%. **Imports:** $2.1 tril; China 16.5%, Canada 15.7%, Mexico 10.1%, Japan 6.6%, Germany 4.6%. **Exports:** $1.3 tril; Canada 20.1%, Mexico 11.7%, China 5.5%, Japan 5.1%, Germany 4.2%, UK 4.1%. **Tourism:** $96.7 bil. **Budget:** $2.7 tril. **Intl. reserves less gold:** $43.24 bil. **Gold:** 261.5 mil oz t. **Consumer prices:** 3.8%.

Transport: Railroad: Length: 140,695 mi. **Motor vehicles:** 222.7 mil pass. cars; 8.7 mil comm. vehicles. **Civil aviation:** 770.4 bil pass.-mi (incl. territories and dependencies); 5,174 airports.

Communications: TV sets: 844 per 1,000 pop. **Radios:** 2,116 per 1,000 pop. **Telephone lines:** 150 mil. **Daily newspaper circ.** (2004): 193.2 per 1,000 pop. **Internet:** 230.6 mil users.

Health: Life expect.: 75.3 male; 81.1 female. **Births** (per 1,000 pop.): 14.2. **Deaths** (per 1,000 pop.): 8.3. **Natural inc.:** 0.59%. **Infant mortality** (per 1,000 live births): 6.3. **HIV rate:** 0.6%.

Education: Compulsory: ages 6-17. **Literacy:** 99%.

Major intl. organizations: UN (FAO, IBRD, ILO, IMF, IMO, WHO, WTO), APEC, NAFTA, NATO, OAS, OECD, OSCE.

Website: www.usa.gov

See also U.S. History chapter; Chronology of the Year's Events.

Uruguay
Oriental Republic of Uruguay

People: Population: 3,494,382. **Age distrib.** (%): <15: 22.4; 65+: 13.3. **Pop. density:** 52.1 per sq mi, 20.1 per sq km. **Urban:** 92%. **Ethnic groups:** White 88%, mestizo 8%, black 4%. **Principal languages:** Spanish, Portunol, Brazilero (Port.-Span. mix). **Chief religions:** Roman Catholic 66%, Protestant 2%, nonprofessing or other 31%.

Geography: Total area: 68,039 sq mi, 176,220 sq km; **Land area:** 67,035 sq mi, 173,620 sq km. **Location:** In southern S. America, on Atlantic O. **Neighbors:** Argentina on W, Brazil on N. **Topography:** Uruguay is composed of rolling, grassy plains and hills, well watered by rivers flowing W to Uruguay R. **Capital:** Montevideo, 1,513,000.

Government: Type: Republic. **Head of state and gov.:** Pres. Tabaré Ramón Vázquez Rosas; b. Jan. 17, 1940; in office: Mar. 1, 2005. **Local divisions:** 19 departments. **Defense budget:** $304 mil. **Active troops:** 25,382.

Economy: Industries: food proc., elec. machinery, transp. equip., oil products, textiles. **Chief crops:** rice, wheat, soybeans, barley. **Natural resources:** hydropower, minor minerals, fisheries. **Arable land:** 8%. **Livestock:** cattle: 12.4 mil; chickens: 14 mil; goats: 16,000; pigs: 245,000; sheep: 10.3 mil. **Fish catch:** 108,750 metric tons. **Electricity prod.:** 5.3 bil kWh. **Labor force** (2007 est.): agric. 9%, industry 15%, services 76%.

Finance: Monetary unit: Peso (UYU) (Oct. 2009: 20.99 = $1 U.S.). **GDP:** $43.2 bil; **per capita GDP:** $12,400; **GDP growth:** 8.9%. **Imports:** $8.7 bil; Brazil 17.3%, Argentina 16%, China 11.9%, U.S. 10.4%, Paraguay 6.9%, Nigeria 4.8%. **Exports:** $7.1 bil; Brazil 18.2%, China 9%, Argentina 7.1%, Germany 6.3%, Mexico 5.5%, Netherlands 4.4%, Russia 4.2%. **Tourism:** $809 mil. **Budget:** $6.3 bil. **Intl. reserves less gold:** $4.12 bil. **Gold:** 10,000 oz t. **Consumer prices:** 7.9%.

Transport: Railroad: Length: 1,020 mi. **Motor vehicles:** 471,000 pass. cars; 61,000 comm. vehicles. **Civil aviation:** 608.9 mil pass.-mi; 9 airports. **Chief port:** Montevideo.

Communications: TV sets: 531 per 1,000 pop. **Radios:** 603 per 1,000 pop. **Telephone lines:** 959,300. **Internet:** 1.3 mil users.

Health: Life expect.: 72.9 male; 79.5 female. **Births** (per 1,000 pop.): 14.2. **Deaths** (per 1,000 pop.): 9.1. **Natural inc.:** 0.51%. **Infant mortality** (per 1,000 live births): 11.7. **HIV rate:** 0.6%.

Education: Compulsory: ages 6-15. **Literacy:** 98%.

Major intl. organizations: UN (FAO, IBRD, ILO, IMF, IMO, WHO, WTO), OAS.

Embassy: 1913 I St. NW 20006; 331-1313.

Website: www.uruguay.gub.uy or www.uruwashi.org

Spanish settlers began to supplant the indigenous Charrua Indians in 1624. Portuguese from Brazil arrived later, but Uruguay was attached to the Spanish Viceroyalty of Rio de la Plata in the 18th cent. Rebels fought against Spain beginning in 1810. An independent republic was declared Aug. 25, 1825.

Socialist measures were adopted in the early 1900s. The state retains a dominant role in the power, telephone, railroad, cement, oil-refining, and other industries, although some privatization began in the early 2000s. Uruguay's standard of living remains one of the highest in S. America, and political and labor conditions among the freest. A leftist, Tabaré Vázquez, was elected president Oct. 31, 2004, and took office Mar. 1, 2005. Presidential and legislative elections are scheduled for Oct. 25, 2009.

Uzbekistan
Republic of Uzbekistan

People: Population: 27,606,007. **Age distrib.** (%): <15: 28.1; 65+: 4.9. **Pop. density:** 168.1 per sq mi, 64.9 per sq km. **Urban:** 36.7%. **Ethnic groups:** Uzbek 80%, Russian 6%, Tajik 5%. **Principal languages:** Uzbek (official), Russian, Tajik. **Chief religions:** Muslim (mostly Sunni) 88%, Eastern Orthodox 9%.

Geography: Total area: 172,742 sq mi, 447,400 sq km; **Land area:** 164,248 sq mi, 425,400 sq km. **Location:** Central Asia. **Neighbors:** Kazakhstan on N and W; Kyrgyzstan, Tajikistan on E; Afghanistan, Turkmenistan on S. **Topography:** Mostly plains and desert. **Capital:** Tashkent, 2,184,000.

Government: Type: Republic with authoritarian rule. **Head of state:** Pres. Islam A. Karimov; b. Jan. 30, 1938; in office: Mar. 24, 1990. **Head of gov.:** Prime Min. Shavkat Mirziyaev; b 1957; in office: Dec. 11, 2003. **Local divisions:** 12 regions, 1 autonomous republic, 1 city. **Defense budget:** $94 mil. **Active troops:** 67,000.

Economy: Industries: textiles, food proc., machine building, metallurgy, gold, nat. gas, chemicals. **Chief crops:** cotton, vegetables, fruits, grain. **Natural resources:** nat. gas, oil, coal, gold, uranium, silver, copper, lead, zinc, tungsten, molybd. **Crude oil reserves:** 594 mil bbls. **Arable land:** 11%. **Livestock:** cattle: 7 mil; chickens: 24.2 mil; goats: 2 mil; pigs: 92,300; sheep: 10.5 mil. **Fish catch** (est.): 6,226 metric tons. **Electricity prod.:** 46.7 bil kWh. **Labor force** (1995): agric. 44%, industry 20%, services 36%.

Finance: Monetary unit: Som (UZS) (Oct. 2009: 1,514.50 = $1 U.S.). **GDP:** $71.7 bil; **per capita GDP:** $2,600; **GDP growth:** 9%. **Imports:** $7.1 bil; Russia 27.6%, China 16.3%, S. Korea 11.5%, Germany 6.1%, Kazakhstan 5.4%, Turkey 4.5%, U.S. 4%. **Exports:** $10.4 bil; Russia 25.3%, Turkey 9.7%, Kazakhstan 7.6%, Bangladesh 6.5%, China 6.1%, Ukraine 6%, Japan 5.3%, U.S. 4.9%, Tajikistan 4.1%. **Tourism:** NA. **Budget:** $6.5 bil.

Transport: Railroad: Length: 2,265 mi. **Civil aviation:** 2.7 bil pass.-mi; 33 airports. **Chief port:** Termiz.

Communications: TV sets: 280 per 1,000 pop. **Radios:** 465 per 1,000 pop. **Telephone lines:** 1.8 mil. **Internet:** 2.5 mil users.

Health: Life expect.: 68.7 male; 74.9 female. **Births** (per 1,000 pop.): 18. **Deaths** (per 1,000 pop.): 5.3. **Natural inc.:** 1.27%. **Infant mortality** (per 1,000 live births): 24.2. **HIV rate:** 0.1%.

Education: Compulsory: ages 7-15. **Literacy:** 96.9%.

Major intl. organizations: UN (FAO, IBRD, ILO, IMF, WHO), CIS, OSCE.

Embassy: 1746 Massachusetts Ave. NW 20036; 887-5300.

Website: www.uz

The region was overrun by the Mongols under Genghis Khan in 1220. In the 14th cent., Uzbekistan became the center of a native Timurid empire. In later centuries Muslim feudal states emerged. Russian military conquest began in the 19th cent. Uzbek SSR became a Soviet republic in 1925.

Uzbekistan declared independence Aug. 29, 1991. It became an independent republic when the Soviet Union disbanded Dec. 26, 1991. Since then, the authoritarian government of Uzbekistan has been led by a former Communist, Islam A. Karimov.

Attacks by Islamic militants, Mar.-July 2004, killed more than 50 people. In June 2004, Russia's OAO Lukoil signed a $1 bil deal to develop Uzbekistan's natural gas fields. Militants bombed the U.S. and Israeli embassies in Tashkent, July 30.

After armed dissidents at Andizhan, east Uzbekistan, attacked government buildings and freed hundreds of prisoners, May 12-13, 2005, Uzbek security forces opened fire on rebels and unarmed demonstrators, killing many. Karimov then launched a general crackdown on human rights activists. Irritated by U.S. human rights pressures, Karimov ordered the U.S. to vacate an airbase used to support operations in Afghanistan; the U.S. pullout was completed Nov. 21. Meeting in Moscow a week earlier, Karimov and Russian Pres. Vladimir Putin signed a military cooperation agreement.

Karimov remained in office following the formal expiration of his presidential term Jan. 22, 2007; despite a 2-term limit under the constitution, he ran for a 3rd term Dec. 23 and won with an 88.1% majority. Sanctions imposed by the EU on Uzbek officials after the 2005 Andizhan shootings were lifted Oct. 13, 2008.

Vanuatu
Republic of Vanuatu

People: Population: 218,519. **Age distrib.** (%): <15: 30.7; 65+: 4. **Pop. density:** 46.4 per sq mi, 17.9 per sq km. **Urban:** 23.5%. **Ethnic groups:** Ni-Vanuatu 99%. **Principal languages:** Local languages (100+); pidgin, or Bislama; English; French. **Chief religions:** Presbyterian 31%, Anglican 13%, Roman Catholic 13%, other Christian 14%, Seventh-Day Adventist 11%, indigenous beliefs 6%.

Geography: Total area: 4,710 sq mi, 12,200 sq km; **Land area:** 4,710 sq mi, 12,200 sq km. **Location:** SW Pacific, 1,200 mi. NE of Brisbane, Australia. **Neighbors:** Fiji to E, Solomon Isls. to NW. **Topography:** Dense forest with narrow coastal strips of cultivated land. **Capital:** Port Vila, 40,000.

Government: Type: Republic. **Head of state:** Pres. Iolu Johnson Abil; b. 1942; in office: Sept. 2, 2009. **Head of gov.:** Prime Min. Edward Natapei; b. 1954; in office: Sept. 22, 2008. **Local divisions:** 6 provinces. **Defense budget/Active troops:** NA.

Economy: Industries: food & fish freezing, wood proc., meat canning. Chief crops: copra, coconuts, cocoa, coffee, taro, yams, fruits, vegetables. Natural resources: mang., hardwood forests, fish. Arable land: 2%. Livestock: cattle: 156,000; chickens: 360,000; goats: 12,200; pigs: 63,000. Fish catch: 85,442 metric tons. Electricity prod.: 43 mil kWh. Labor force (2000 est.): agric. 65%, industry 5%, services 30%.

Finance: Monetary unit: Vatu (VUV) (Oct. 2009: 96.75 = $1 U.S.). GDP: $988.5 mil; per capita GDP: $4,600; GDP growth: 6.6%. Imports (2006): $156 mil; Australia 18.1%, U.S. 16.4%, Japan 12.3%, Singapore 11.2%, New Zealand 7.7%, Fiji 6.9%, China 6.3%. Exports (2006): $40 mil; Thailand 75.6%, India 10.4%, Japan 5.4%. Tourism: NA. Budget (2005): $72.2 mil. Intl. reserves less gold: $75 mil. Gold: NA. Consumer prices: 4.8%.

Transport: Motor vehicles: 6,000 pass. cars; 4,600 comm. vehicles. Civil aviation: 144.2 mil pass.-mi; 3 airports. Chief ports: Forari, Port-Vila, Santo.

Communications: TV sets: 12 per 1,000 pop. Radios: 350 per 1,000 pop. Telephone lines: 10,400. Daily newspaper circ. (2004): 14.3 per 1,000 pop. Internet: 17,000 users.

Health: Life expect.: 62 male; 65.3 female. Births (per 1,000 pop.): 21.9. Deaths (per 1,000 pop.): 7.6. Natural inc.: 1.43%. Infant mortality (per 1,000 live births): 50.8. HIV rate: NA.

Education: Compulsory: ages 6-12. Literacy: 78.1%.

Major intl. organizations: UN (FAO, IBRD, ILO, IMF, IMO, WHO), the Commonwealth.

Permanent UN mission: 800 Second Ave., Ste. 400B, New York, NY 10017; (212) 661-4323.

Website: www.governmentofvanuatu.gov.vu

The Anglo-French condominium of the New Hebrides, administered jointly by France and Great Britain since 1906, became the independent Republic of Vanuatu on July 30, 1980. Vanuatu is located in the "Ring of Fire," a zone where earthquakes and volcanic eruptions are frequent.

Vatican City (The Holy See)

People: Population: 826. Pop. density: 4,862.1 per sq mi, 1,877.3 per sq km. Urban: 100%. Ethnic groups: Italian, Swiss, other. Principal languages: Italian, Latin, French, various others. Chief religion: Roman Catholic.

Geography: Total area: 0.17 sq mi, 0.44 sq km; Land area: 0.17 sq mi, 0.44 sq km. Location: In Rome, Italy. Neighbors: Completely surrounded by Italy.

Economy: Industries: printing; coins, medals, postage stamps prod.; worldwide banking & financial activities. Labor force: Essentially services with small amount of industry; nearly all dignitaries, priests, nuns, guards, and approx. 3,000 lay workers live outside the Vatican.

Finance: Monetary unit: Euro (EUR) (Oct. 2009: 0.68 = $1 U.S.). Budget (2006): $307 mil.

Apostolic Nunciature: 3339 Massachusetts Ave. NW 20008; 333-7121.

Website: www.vatican.va

The popes for many centuries, with brief interruptions, held temporal sovereignty over mid-Italy (the so-called Papal States), comprising an area of some 16,000 sq mi, with a population in the 19th cent. of more than 3 mil. This territory was incorporated in the new Kingdom of Italy (1861), the sovereignty of the pope being confined to the palaces of the Vatican and the Lateran in Rome and the villa of Castel Gandolfo, by an Italian law, May 13, 1871.

A Treaty of Conciliation, a concordat, and a financial convention were signed Feb. 11, 1929, by Cardinal Gasparri and Premier Mussolini. The documents established the independent state of Vatican City and gave the Roman Catholic church special status in Italy. The treaty (Lateran Agreement) was made part of the Constitution of Italy (Article 7) in 1947. Italy and the Vatican signed an agreement in 1984 on revisions of the concordat; the accord eliminated Roman Catholicism as the state religion and ended required religious education in Italian schools.

Vatican City includes the Basilica of Saint Peter, the Vatican Palace and Museum covering over 13 acres, the Vatican gardens, and neighboring buildings between Viale Vaticano and the church. Thirteen buildings in Rome, outside the boundaries, enjoy extraterritorial rights; these buildings house congregations or officers necessary for the administration of the Holy See.

The legal system is based on the code of canon law, the apostolic constitutions, and laws especially promulgated for the Vatican City by the pope. The Secretariat of State represents the Holy See in its diplomatic relations.

The present sovereign of the State of Vatican City is the Supreme Pontiff Benedict XVI, born Joseph Ratzinger in Marktl am Inn, Germany, Apr. 16, 1927, elected Apr. 19, 2005.

Venezuela

Bolivarian Republic of Venezuela

People: Population: 26,814,843. Age distrib. (%): <15: 30.5; 65+: 5.2. Pop. density: 78.7 per sq mi, 30.4 per sq km. Urban: 92.3%. Ethnic groups: Spanish, Italian, Portuguese, Arab, German, African, indigenous. Principal languages: Spanish (official), indigenous dialects. Chief religion: Roman Catholic 96%.

Geography: Total area: 352,144 sq mi, 912,050 sq km; Land area: 340,561 sq mi, 882,050 sq km. Location: On Carib. coast of S. America. Neighbors: Colombia on W, Brazil on S, Guyana on E. Topography: Flat coastal plain and Orinoco Delta are bordered by Andes Mts. and hills. Plains, called llanos, extend between mountains and Orinoco. Guiana Highlands and plains are S of Orinoco, which stretches 1,600 mi and drains 80% of country. Capital: Caracas, 2,985,000. Cities (urban aggr.): Maracaibo, 2,072,000; Valencia, 1,770,000.

Government: Type: Federal republic. Head of state and gov.: Pres. Hugo Rafael Chávez Frías; b. July 28, 1954; in office: Feb. 2, 1999. Local divisions: 23 states, 1 federal district (Caracas), 1 federal dependency (72 islands). Defense budget: $2.8 bil. Active troops: 115,000.

Economy: Industries: oil, constr. materials, food proc., textiles, iron ore mining, steel, aluminum, motor vehicle assembly. Chief crops: corn, sorghum, sugarcane, rice, bananas, vegetables, coffee. Natural resources: oil, nat. gas, iron ore, gold, bauxite, other minerals, hydropower, diamonds. Crude oil reserves: 99.4 bil bbls. Arable land: 3%. Livestock: cattle: 16.8 mil; chickens: 120 mil; goats: 1.4 mil; pigs: 3 mil; sheep: 563,830. Fish catch (est.): 477,210 metric tons. Electricity prod.: 108.4 bil kWh. Labor force (1997 est.): agric. 13%, industry 23%, services 64%.

Finance: Monetary unit: Bolivar Fuerte (VEF) (Oct. 2009: 2.15 = $1 U.S.). GDP: $357.4 bil; per capita GDP: $13,500; GDP growth: 4.8%. Imports: $48.1 bil; U.S. 24.4%, Colombia 13.9%, Brazil 9.6%, China 6.5%, Mexico 5.3%, Panama 5.1%. Exports: $93.5 bil; U.S. 41.2%, Netherlands Antilles 7.9%, China 4.9%. Tourism: $817 mil. Budget: $58.9 bil. Intl. reserves less gold: $21.49 bil. Gold: 11.46 mil oz t. Consumer prices: 30.4%.

Transport: Railroad: Length: 501 mi. Motor vehicles: 2.5 mil pass. cars; 677,000 comm. vehicles. Civil aviation: 1.6 bil pass.-mi; 131 airports. Chief ports: La Guaira, Maracaibo, Puerto Cabello, Punta Cardon.

Communications: TV sets: 185 per 1,000 pop. Radios: 296 per 1,000 pop. Telephone lines: 6.3 mil. Daily newspaper circ. (2004): 93.3 per 1,000 pop. Internet: 7.2 mil users.

Health: Life expect.: 70.4 male; 76.7 female. Births (per 1,000 pop.): 20.9. Deaths (per 1,000 pop.): 5.1. Natural inc.: 1.58%. Infant mortality (per 1,000 live births): 22. HIV rate: NA.

Education: Compulsory: ages 6-15. Literacy: 93%.

Major intl. organizations: UN (FAO, IBRD, ILO, IMF, IMO, WHO, WTO), OAS, OPEC.

Embassy: 1099 30th St. NW 20007; 342-2214.

Website: www.presidencia.gob.ve or www.embavenez-us.org

Columbus first set foot on the S. American continent on the peninsula of Paria, Aug. 1498. Alonso de Ojeda, 1499, was the first European to see Lake Maracaibo. He called the land Venezuela, or Little Venice, because the Indians had houses on stilts. Spanish colonialists dominated Venezuela until Simón Bolívar's victory near Carabobo in June 1821. The republic was formed after secession from the Colombian Federation in 1830. Military strongmen ruled Venezuela for much of its history. Since 1959, the country has had democratically elected governments.

Oil accounts for more than 75% of export earnings and about half of government revenues. The government, Jan. 1, 1976, nationalized the oil industry with compensation. Attempts to reduce dependence on the hydrocarbon sector have met with limited success. The country has large reserves of natural gas; a large new gas find in the Gulf of Venezuela was announced Sept. 2009.

An attempted coup by midlevel military officers was thwarted by loyalist troops Feb. 4, 1992. A second coup attempt was thwarted in Nov. Pres. Carlos Andrés Pérez was removed from office on corruption charges, May 1993; he was convicted, May 1996, of mismanaging a $17 mil secret government fund.

A 1992 coup leader, Hugo Chávez, who ran as a populist, was elected president Dec. 6, 1998. Voters on Dec. 15, 1999, approved a new constitution greatly increasing his powers.

Popular among the poor, Chávez alienated some middle- and upper-class Venezuelans with his program of economic and political reform, and his foreign policy antagonized the U.S. Gunfire erupted at a mass protest Apr. 11, 2002, in Caracas, killing at least 17 people. Chávez was forced to relinquish power, but when an interim government issued decrees suspending democratic institutions, Chávez loyalists rebelled; the coup fell apart, and the president reclaimed his office Apr. 14. Opponents of Chávez organized strikes and recall efforts, 2003-04, but failed to oust him.

Chávez countered U.S. attempts to isolate him diplomatically and militarily by solidifying ties with other Latin American leftist leaders and with Iran and Russia. With the economy surging, he captured a 63% majority in the Dec. 3, 2006, presidential election. On Jan. 31, 2007, the legislature granted him the power to rule by decree. Constitutional changes abolishing presidential term limits were rejected by Venezuelan voters Dec. 2, 2007, but approved Feb. 15, 2009. Emboldened by the victory, Chávez pressured domestic critics and consolidated his control over the armed forces.

Vietnam

Socialist Republic of Vietnam

People: Population: 86,967,524. **Age distrib.** (%): <15: 24.9; 65+: 5.7. **Pop. density:** 692.3 per sq mi, 267.3 per sq km. **Urban:** 26.4%. **Ethnic groups:** Kinh (Viet) 86%, Tay 2%, Thai 2%, Muong 2%. **Principal languages:** Vietnamese (official), English (increasingly favored as second lang.), French, Chinese, Khmer. **Chief religions:** Buddhist 9%, Catholic 7%, none 81%.

Geography: Total area: 127,244 sq mi, 329,560 sq km; **Land area:** 125,622 sq mi, 325,360 sq km. **Location:** SE Asia, on E coast of Indochinese Peninsula. **Neighbors:** China on N; Laos, Cambodia on W. **Topography:** Vietnam is long and narrow, with 1,400-mi coast. About 22% of country is readily arable, including densely settled Red R. valley in N, narrow coastal plains in center, and the wide, often marshy Mekong R. Delta in S. The rest consists of semi-arid plateaus and barren mountains, with some stretches of tropical rain forest. **Capital:** Hà Noi, 4,378,000. **Cities (urban aggr.):** Hai Phòng, 1,969,000; Ho Chi Minh City, 5,314,000.

Government: Type: Communist. **Head of state:** Pres. Nguyen Minh Triet; b. Oct. 8, 1942; in office: June 27, 2006. **Head of gov.:** Prime Min. Nguyen Tan Dung; b. Nov. 17, 1949; in office: June 27, 2006. **Local divisions:** 58 provinces, 3 cities, 1 capital region. **Defense budget:** $3.7 bil. **Active troops:** 455,000.

Economy: Industries: food proc., garments, shoes, machine-building, mining. **Chief crops:** rice, coffee, rubber, cotton, tea, pepper, soybeans, cashews, sugarcane, peanuts, bananas. **Natural resources:** phosphates, coal, mang., bauxite, chromate, offshore oil & gas deposits, forests, hydropower. **Crude oil reserves:** 600 mil bbls. **Arable land:** 20%. **Livestock:** cattle: 6.7 mil; chickens: 158.2 mil; goats: 1.8 mil; pigs: 26.6 mil. **Fish catch:** 4.32 mil metric tons. **Electricity prod.:** 54.3 bil kWh. **Labor force** (2005): agric. 55.6%, industry 18.9%, services 25.5%.

Finance: Monetary unit: Dong (VND) (Oct. 2009: 17,839.80 = $1 U.S.). **GDP:** $241.7 bil; **per capita GDP:** $2,800; **GDP growth:** 6.2%. **Imports:** $77.6 bil; China 21.3%, Singapore 11.7%, Japan 10.4%, S. Korea 7.4%, Thailand 6.6%. **Exports:** $61.6 bil; U.S. 20.9%, Japan 13.7%, Australia 7.4%, China 6.9%, Germany 4.5%. **Tourism** (2006): $3.2 bil. **Budget:** $19.6 bil. **Intl. reserves less gold:** $15.51 bil. **Gold:** NA. **Consumer prices:** 23.1%.

Transport: Railroad: Length: 1,458 mi. **Motor vehicles:** NA pass. vehicles; 205,900 comm. vehicles. **Civil aviation:** 5.7 bil pass.-mi; 37 airports. **Chief ports:** Da Nang, Hai Phong, Ho Chi Minh City.

Communications: TV sets: 184 per 1,000 pop. **Radios:** 107 per 1,000 pop. **Telephone lines:** 29.6 mil. **Daily newspaper circ.** (1999): 5.8 per 1,000 pop. **Internet:** 20.8 mil users.

Health: Life expect.: 68.5 male; 74.3 female. **Births** (per 1,000 pop.): 16.5. **Deaths** (per 1,000 pop.): 6.2. **Natural inc.:** 1.03%. **Infant mortality** (per 1,000 live births): 23.6. **HIV rate:** 0.5%.

Education: Compulsory: ages 6-14. **Literacy:** 90.3%.

Major intl. organizations: UN (FAO, IBRD, ILO, IMF, IMO, WHO, WTO), APEC, ASEAN.

Embassy: 1233 20th St. NW, Ste. 400, 20036; 861-0737.

Website: www.na.gov.vn

Settled by Viets from central China, Vietnam was held by China, 111 BCE-939 CE, and was a vassal state during subsequent periods. Conquest by France began in 1858 and ended in 1884 with the protectorates of Tonkin and Annam in the N and the colony of Cochin-China in the S.

Japan occupied Vietnam in 1940. A number of groups formed the Vietminh (Independence) League, headed by Ho Chi Minh, Communist guerrilla leader. In Aug. 1945 the Vietminh forced out Bao Dai, former emperor of Annam, head of a Japan-sponsored regime. France, seeking to reestablish colonial control, battled Communist and nationalist forces, 1946-54, and was defeated at Dienbienphu, May 8, 1954.

Separate states formed in N. and S. Vietnam, with Communists under Ho Chi Minh (backed by Russia and China) controlling N. Vietnam and a non-Communist government (backed by the U.S.) established in S. Vietnam, with its capital at Saigon. N. Vietnam aided Vietcong guerrillas who sought to take over S. Vietnam. The U.S. committed hundreds of thousands of troops to defend S. Vietnam and launched massive bombing raids against N. Vietnam and border areas of Laos and Cambodia. Casualties of the war were as follows—Combat deaths: U.S. 47,369; S. Vietnam more than 200,000; other allied forces 5,225. Total U.S. fatalities numbered more than 58,000. Vietnamese civilian casualties were more than 1 mil. The war displaced more than 6.5 mil in S. Vietnam.

A cease-fire agreement was signed in Paris Jan. 27, 1973, by the U.S., N. and S. Vietnam, and the Vietcong. It was never implemented. The Saigon regime surrendered Apr. 30, 1975. N. Vietnam assumed control, and began transforming society along Communist lines. The country was officially reunited July 2, 1976.

Conditions in the region remained unstable after the Vietnam War ended. Heavy fighting with Cambodia took place, 1977-80. Relations with China soured as 140,000 ethnic Chinese left Vietnam charging discrimination; China cut off economic aid. Reacting to Vietnam's invasion of Cambodia, China attacked 4 Vietnamese border provinces, Feb. 1979.

Vietnam announced reforms aimed at reducing central control of the economy in 1987. Citing Hanoi's cooperation in returning re-

mains of U.S. soldiers killed in the Vietnam War, the U.S. announced an end, Feb. 3, 1994, to a 19-year-old U.S. embargo on trade with Vietnam. The U.S. extended full diplomatic recognition to Vietnam July 11, 1995. U.S. Pres. Bill Clinton made a historic visit to Vietnam Nov. 17-19, 2000.

The U.S. and Vietnam agreed June 5, 2006, to strengthen defense ties. Communists reputed to be economic reformers took the top govt. leadership posts June 27. The U.S. has become Vietnam's top export market, with total annual trade over $10 bil; during Jan.-Sept. 2009, U.S. firms invested $4 bil in Vietnam.

Western Samoa

See Samoa.

Yemen

Republic of Yemen

People: Population: 23,822,783. **Age distrib.** (%): <15: 46.2; 65+: 2.5. **Pop. density:** 116.9 per sq mi, 45.1 per sq km. **Urban:** 28.9%. **Ethnic groups:** Predominantly Arab, Afro-Arab, South Asian, European. **Principal language:** Arabic (official). **Chief religion:** Muslim (incl. Sunni and Shi'a).

Geography: Total area: 203,850 sq mi, 527,970 sq km; **Land area:** 203,850 sq mi, 527,970 sq km. **Location:** Middle East, on S coast of the Arabian Peninsula. **Neighbors:** Saudi Arabia on N, Oman on E. **Topography:** A sandy coastal strip leads to well-watered fertile mountains in interior. **Capital:** Sana'a', 2,008,000. **Cities (urban aggr.):** Al-Hudaydah, 780,000; Ta'izz, 751,000.

Government: Type: Republic. **Head of state:** Pres. Ali Abdullah Saleh; b. Mar. 21, 1942; in office: May 22, 1990. **Head of gov.:** Prime Min. Ali Muhammad Mujawar; b. 1953; in office: Apr. 7, 2007. **Local divisions:** 19 governorates and capital region. **Defense budget:** $908 mil. **Active troops:** 66,700.

Economy: Industries: oil prod. & refining, small-scale prod. of cotton textiles & leather goods, food proc. **Chief crops:** grain, fruits, vegetables, pulses, coffee, cotton. **Natural resources:** oil; fish; rock salt; marble; small deposits of coal, gold, lead, nickel, & copper. **Crude oil reserves:** 3 bil bbls. **Arable land:** 3%. **Livestock:** cattle: 1.5 mil; chickens: 51 mil; goats: 8.4 mil; sheep: 8.4 mil. **Fish catch** (est.): 179,916 metric tons. **Electricity prod.:** 5 bil kWh. **Labor force:** Most people employed in agric. & herding; services, constr., industry, & commerce account for less than one-fourth of labor force.

Finance: Monetary unit: Rial (YER) (Oct. 2009: 202.85 = $1 U.S.). **GDP:** $55.3 bil; **per capita GDP:** $2,400; **GDP growth:** 3.2%. **Imports:** $8.8 bil; UAE 16.4%, China 12.4%, Saudi Arabia 7.8%, Kuwait 5.8%, U.S. 4.3%. **Exports:** $9 bil; China 30.9%, Thailand 26.4%, India 17.2%, Japan 5.2%, UAE 4.3%. **Tourism** (2005): $262 mil. **Budget:** $8.2 bil. **Intl. reserves less gold:** $5.27 bil. **Gold:** 50,000 oz t. **Consumer prices:** 19%.

Transport: Motor vehicles: 346,600 pass. cars; 587,900 comm. vehicles. **Civil aviation:** 1.7 bil pass.-mi; 18 airports. **Chief ports:** Aden, Hudaydah, Mukalla.

Communications: TV sets: 286 per 1,000 pop. **Radios:** 64 per 1,000 pop. **Telephone lines:** 1.1 mil. **Daily newspaper circ.** (2004): 4.1 per 1,000 pop. **Internet:** 370,000 users.

Health: Life expect.: 61 male; 64.9 female. **Births** (per 1,000 pop.): 42.4. **Deaths** (per 1,000 pop.): 7.8. **Natural inc.:** 3.46%. **Infant mortality** (per 1,000 live births): 56.3. **HIV rate:** NA.

Education: Compulsory: ages 6-14. **Literacy:** 58.9%.

Major intl. organizations: UN (FAO, IBRD, ILO, IMF, IMO, WHO), AL.

Embassy: 2319 Wyoming Ave. NW 20008; 965-4760.

Website: www.nic.gov.ye

Yemen's territory once was part of the ancient biblical Kingdom of Sheba, or Saba. Yemen became independent in 1918, after centuries of Ottoman Turkish rule.

Imam Yahya ibn Muhammad ruled, 1904-48, and after his assassination was succeeded by his son, Imam Ahmed ruled, 1948-62. Army officers headed by Brig. Gen. Abdullah al-Salal declared the country to be the Yemen Arab Republic, Sept. 1962. Ahmed's heir, the Imam Mohamad al-Badr, fled to the mountains where tribesmen joined royalist forces, aided by the Saudi monarchy. Fighting between royalists and republicans killed about 150,000 people until hostilities ended in 1970.

Meanwhile, South Yemen, formed from the British colony of Aden and the British protectorate of South Arabia, became independent Nov. 1967. A Marxist state and a Soviet ally, it took the name People's Democratic Republic of Yemen in 1970. More than 300,000 Yemenis fled from the S to the N after independence, contributing to 2 decades of hostility between the 2 states.

The 2 countries were formally united May 21, 1990, but regional clan-based rivalries led to full-scale civil war in 1994. Secessionists declared a breakaway state in South Yemen, May 21, 1994, but northern troops captured the former southern capital of Aden in July. A new constitution was approved Sept. 28.

Yemen, the ancestral home of Osama bin Laden, has been caught in a crossfire between the U.S. and Islamic extremists. While on a refueling stop in Aden, Oct. 12, 2000, the destroyer U.S.S. Cole was bombed, leaving 17 Americans dead and more than 3 dozen injured; the U.S. government blamed the attack on terrorists associated with bin Laden. The U.S. sent troops in 2002 to help track down members of al-Qaeda.

Clashes beginning in June 2004 between Yemeni government forces and Shiite rebels led by an anti-U.S. cleric, Hussein al-Houthi, left more than 200 people dead. The government announced Sept. 10 that Yemeni troops had killed al-Houthi. Incumbent Pres. Ali Abdullah Saleh was reelected Sept. 20, 2006. During 2007-09, Shiite rebels in the northwest, secessionists in the south, al-Qaeda militants in the east, and pirates in coastal waters continued to challenge government authority.

Yugoslavia
See Montenegro and Serbia.

Zaire
See Congo.

Zambia
Republic of Zambia
People: Population: 11,862,740. **Age distrib.** (%): <15: 45.1; 65+: 2.3. **Pop. density:** 41.5 per sq mi, 16 per sq km. **Urban:** 35%. **Ethnic groups:** African 99%. **Principal languages:** English (official), major vernaculars (incl. Bemba, Kaonda, Lozi, Lunda, Luvale, Nyanja, Tonga), about 70 other indigenous languages. **Chief religions:** Christian 50%-75%, Muslim & Hindu 24%-49%.

Geography: Total area: 290,586 sq mi, 752,614 sq km; **Land area:** 285,995 sq mi, 740,724 sq km. **Location:** In S central Africa. **Neighbors:** Congo on N; Tanzania, Malawi, Mozambique on E; Zimbabwe, Namibia on S; Angola on W. **Topography:** Mostly high plateau covered with thick forests and drained by several important rivers, including the Zambezi. **Capital:** Lusaka, 1,328,000.

Government: Type: Republic. **Head of state and gov.:** Pres. Rupiah Banda; b. Feb. 1937; in office: Nov. 2, 2008 (acting from June 29, 2008. **Local divisions:** 9 provinces. **Defense budget:** $247 mil. **Active troops:** 15,100.

Economy: Industries: copper mining & proc., constr., foodstuffs. **Chief crops:** corn, sorghum, rice, peanuts, sunflower seeds, vegetables, flowers, tobacco, cotton, sugarcane, cassava, coffee. **Natural resources:** copper, cobalt, zinc, lead, coal, emeralds, gold, silver, uranium, hydropower. **Arable land:** 7%. **Livestock:** cattle: 2.9 mil; chickens: 30 mil; goats: 1.3 mil; pigs: 340,000; sheep: 152,000. **Fish catch** (est.): 70,125 metric tons. **Electricity prod.:** 9.3 bil kWh. **Labor force** (2004): agric. 85%, industry 6%, services 9%.

Finance: Monetary unit: Kwacha (ZMK) (Oct. 2009: 4,659.60 = $1 U.S.). **GDP:** $17.5 bil; **per capita GDP:** $1,500; **GDP growth:** 6%. **Imports:** $4.7 bil; South Africa 49.3%, China 8.2%, UAE 7.9%, India 4.4%. **Exports:** $4.8 bil; Switzerland 36.2%, South Africa 10.5%, China 8.1%, Democratic Republic of the Congo 5%, Saudi Arabia 4.9%, Egypt 4.7%, Italy 4.3%. **Tourism:** NA. **Budget:** $2.7 bil. **Intl. reserves less gold:** $711 mil. **Gold:** NA. **Consumer prices:** 12.4%.

Transport: Railroad: Length: 1,340 mi. **Motor vehicles:** 3,700 pass. cars; 3,900 comm. vehicles. **Civil aviation:** 10.6 mil pass.-mi; 9 airports. **Chief port:** Mpulungu.

Communications: TV sets: 145 per 1,000 pop. **Radios:** 160 per 1,000 pop. **Telephone lines:** 90,600. **Daily newspaper circ.** (2004): 4.9 per 1,000 pop. **Internet:** 700,000 users.

Health: Life expect.: 38.5 male; 38.7 female. **Births** (per 1,000 pop.): 40.5. **Deaths** (per 1,000 pop.): 21.4. **Natural inc.:** 1.92%. **Infant mortality** (per 1,000 live births): 101. **HIV rate:** 15.2%.

Education: Compulsory: ages 7-13. **Literacy:** 68%.

Major intl. organizations: UN (FAO, IBRD, ILO, IMF, WHO, WTO), the Commonwealth, AU.

Embassy: 2419 Massachusetts Ave. NW 20008; 265-9717. **Website:** www.statehouse.gov.zm

Ruled by the British as Northern Rhodesia, the country became the independent republic of Zambia within the Commonwealth Oct. 24, 1964. Independence leader Kenneth Kaunda governed the country as president, 1964-91. A Zambian government corporation in 1970 took over 51% of 2 foreign-owned copper-mining companies. Privately-held land and other enterprises were nationalized in 1975. In the 1980s and 1990s lowered copper prices hurt the economy and severe drought caused famine.

Food riots erupted in June 1990, as the nation suffered its worst violence since independence. Elections held Oct. 1991 brought an end to Kaunda's one-party rule. The new government sought to sell state enterprises, including the copper industry. Pres. Frederick Chiluba won reelection Nov. 18, 1996, but international observers cited harassment of opposition parties. A coup attempt was suppressed Oct. 28, 1997.

Thwarted in his effort to change the constitution to allow himself to run for a 3rd term, Chiluba endorsed Levy Patrick Mwanawasa, who won a disputed election Dec. 27, 2001. Food shortages threatened more than 2 mil Zambians in 2002; the government refused to distribute shipments of U.S. grain because it was genetically modified. In a hard-fought election, Sept. 28, 2006, Mwanawasa won a 2nd term. Accused of embezzling state funds while he was president, Chiluba was ordered to pay $58 mil by a

British court, June 7, 2007; he was acquitted by a Zambian court, Aug. 17, 2009, of misusing $500,000 in public money.

Pres. Mwanawasa suffered a stroke June 29, 2008, and died Aug. 19. Vice-Pres. Rupiah Banda became acting pres. He won the presidency by a narrow margin in an election Oct. 30, 2008.

The country has made progress in treating HIV/AIDS, which afflicts nearly 1 mil adults in Zambia.

Zimbabwe
Republic of Zimbabwe
People: Population: 11,392,629. **Age distrib.** (%): <15: 43.9; 65+: 3.9. **Pop. density:** 76.3 per sq mi, 29.5 per sq km. **Urban:** 35.9%. **Ethnic groups:** African 98% (Shona 82%, Ndebele 14%), mixed & Asian 1%, white <1%. **Principal languages:** English (official), Shona, Sindebele, minor tribal dialects. **Chief religions:** Syncretic (mix of Christian & indigenous beliefs) 50%, Christian 25%, indigenous beliefs 24%.

Geography: Total area: 150,804 sq mi, 390,580 sq km; **Land area:** 149,294 sq mi, 386,670 sq km. **Location:** In southern Africa. **Neighbors:** Zambia on N, Botswana on W, South Africa on S, Mozambique on E. **Topography:** High plateau country, rising to mountains on E border, sloping down on other borders. **Capital:** Harare, 1,572,000.

Government: Type: In transition. **Head of state and gov.:** Pres. Robert Mugabe; b. Feb. 21, 1924; in office: Dec. 31, 1987. **Head of gov.:** Morgan Tsvangirai; b. Mar. 10, 1952; in office: Feb. 11, 2009. **Local divisions:** 8 provinces, 2 cities. **Defense budget:** NA. **Active troops:** 29,000.

Economy: Industries: mining, steel, wood products, cement, chemicals. **Chief crops:** corn, cotton, tobacco, wheat, coffee, sugarcane, peanuts. **Natural resources:** coal, chromium ore, asbestos, gold, nickel, copper, iron ore, vanadium, lithium, tin, platinum group metals. **Arable land:** 8%. **Livestock:** cattle: 5.4 mil; chickens: 23 mil; goats: 3 mil; pigs: 630,000; sheep: 610,000. **Fish catch** (est.): 12,950 metric tons. **Electricity prod.:** 9.5 bil kWh. **Labor force** (1996): agric. 66%, industry 10%, services 24%.

Finance: Monetary unit: Dollar (ZWD) (Oct. 2009: 361.90 = $1 U.S.). **GDP:** $1.9 bil; **per capita GDP:** $200; **GDP growth:** −14.1%. **Imports:** $1.9 bil; South Africa 52.2%, China 7%, Botswana 4.5%. **Exports:** $1.3 bil; South Africa 36.1%, Democratic Republic of the Congo 8.9%, Botswana 8%, China 5.5%, Zambia 4.4%, Japan 4.1%, Italy 4.1%. **Tourism:** NA. **Budget:** $3 bil. **Intl. reserves less gold:** NA. **Gold:** NA. **Consumer prices** (2007): 24,411%.

Transport: Railroad: Length: 1,912 mi. **Motor vehicles:** 598,000 pass. cars; 103,000 comm. vehicles. **Civil aviation:** 343.6 mil pass.-mi; 19 airports. **Chief ports:** Binga, Kariba.

Communications: TV sets: 35 per 1,000 pop. **Radios:** 389 per 1,000 pop. **Telephone lines:** 354,000. **Internet:** 1.4 mil users.

Health: Life expect.: 45.1 male; 43.5 female. **Births** (per 1,000 pop.): 31.6. **Deaths** (per 1,000 pop.): 17.3. **Natural inc.:** 1.43%. **Infant mortality** (per 1,000 live births): 33.9. **HIV rate:** 15.3%.

Education: Compulsory: ages 6-12. **Literacy:** 91.2%.

Major intl. organizations: UN (FAO, IBRD, ILO, IMF, IMO, WHO, WTO), AU.

Embassy: 1608 New Hampshire Ave. NW 20009; 332-7100. **Website:** www.zim.gov.zw

Britain took over the area as Southern Rhodesia in 1923 from the British South Africa Co. (which, under Cecil Rhodes, had conquered it by 1897) and granted internal self-government. Under a 1961 constitution, voting was restricted to keep whites in power.

On Nov. 11, 1965, Prime Min. Ian D. Smith announced his country's unilateral declaration of independence. Britain termed the act illegal and demanded that the country (known as Rhodesia until 1980) enfranchise the black African majority. The UN imposed sanctions and, in May 1968, a trade embargo, as black nationalist groups launched guerrilla attacks.

After the country held its first universal-franchise election, Apr. 21, 1979, all parties accepted a cease-fire, Dec. 5. Independence as Zimbabwe was achieved Apr. 18, 1980. Robert Mugabe, the nation's 1st prime min., became executive president in 1987.

From the late 1990s, Mugabe's rule became increasingly repressive. A land redistribution campaign triggered violent attacks in Apr. 2000 against some white farmers. (Whites made up less than 1% of the population but held 70% of the land.) International observers criticized Mugabe for relying on fraud and intimidation to win the presidential election of Mar. 9-11, 2002. The EU, the U.S., and the Commonwealth imposed sanctions on the Mugabe regime. In May 2005, Mugabe launched Operation Murambatsvina ("Drive out rubbish"), razing shanty dwellings and illegal street markets in urban areas and leaving some 700,000 people homeless. During 2006-08, inflation soared to a yearly rate of more than 100,000%.

Using force to intimidate his opponents, Mugabe clung to power after a widely discredited presidential election, Mar. 29, 2008, and June 27 runoff vote. A power-sharing deal was reached Sept. 15, 2008, and after prolonged and difficult negotiations, opposition leader Morgan Tsvangirai was sworn in as prime min. Feb. 11, 2009. In a car crash Mar. 6 that he described as an accident, Tsvangirai was injured and his wife Susan was killed. The power-sharing deal was threatened when Tsvangirai announced a boycott of the cabinet, Oct. 16.

SPORTS

SPORTS HIGHLIGHTS OF 2009

The **2009 BCS National Championship Game** (held in Miami, FL, on Jan. 8) did little to end calls for a playoff system in college football. 2007 Heisman Trophy-winning quarterback Tim Tebow and the Florida Gators defeated top-ranked Oklahoma and its 2008 Heisman Trophy-winning quarterback Sam Bradford, by a 24-14 score. But several other teams could also claim that they were the best team in the country. USC and Texas both compiled one-loss seasons and Utah went undefeated; all three notched impressive bowl game victories. The ensuing chaos led even Pres. Barack Obama to call for a playoff system.

The Pittsburgh Steelers became the first NFL franchise to win six Super Bowl titles with a thrilling come-from-behind 27-23 win over the underdog Arizona Cardinals in **Super Bowl XLIII**, held Feb. 1, 2009, in Tampa, FL. Pittsburgh wide receiver Santonio Holmes, who leaped over three Cardinals defenders and touched the end zone with both feet before tumbling out of bounds with the winning touchdown catch, was the game's MVP.

Former New York Giants wide receiver Plaxico Burress pleaded guilty Aug. 20 to a reduced charge of attempted criminal possession of a weapon, after accidentally shooting himself with a handgun he was carrying illegally in a New York City nightclub in Nov. 2008. Michael Vick signed with the Philadelphia Eagles and returned to the NFL in Aug. after serving 18 months in prison for running a dog-fighting operation.

Ranked no. 1 at the beginning of the 2008-09 season, the Univ. of North Carolina breezed through the **NCAA men's basketball tournament**. The Tar Heels won all six of their games by double-digit margins and defeated the hometown favorite Michigan State Spartans, 89-72, at Ford Field in Detroit to capture the championship Apr. 6. All-American senior forward Tyler Hansbrough finished his college career with a flourish, scoring 18 points.

The Univ. of Connecticut Huskies had a similarly easy trip through the **NCAA women's basketball tournament**. The Huskies completed an undefeated season, won all of their games in the tournament by double digits, and defeated Louisville 76-54 in the Apr. 7 final in St. Louis. Center Tina Charles was honored as the women's Final Four's most outstanding player.

For the 31st year in a row, thoroughbred horse racing failed to produce a Triple Crown winner. Mine That Bird, a 50-1 longshot, captured the **Kentucky Derby**, but could not catch filly Rachel Alexandra two weeks later in the Preakness Stakes. Summer Bird, who shared a sire with Mine That Bird, outran the Derby winner to claim the Belmont Stakes on June 6.

The 2008-09 **Stanley Cup** championship featured a rematch between the Pittsburgh Penguins and the Detroit Red Wings. This time it was the Penguins who came out on top, winning a decisive seventh game, 2-1, in Detroit on June 12. Pittsburgh center Evgeni Malkin, whose 36 total points led all skaters, won the Conn Smythe Trophy for the most valuable player in the playoffs.

The Los Angeles Lakers won their 15th **NBA Championship** with a decisive 4-1 series win over the Orlando Magic June 14 in Orlando. It was the Lakers' first title in seven years and the first for finals MVP Kobe Bryant without former teammate Shaquille O'Neal's dominating presence.

After failing to make the playoffs for the first time in 14 years, Major League Baseball's New York Yankees went on a spending spree before the 2009 season, doling out more than $400 million in contracts to pitchers CC Sabathia and A. J. Burnett and first baseman Mark Teixeira. The investment paid off, as the "Bronx Bombers" won 103 games in the regular season, more than any other team in baseball. The Yankees also christened new Yankee Stadium, where select tickets sold for more than $1,000. The crosstown New York Mets also inaugurated a **new ballpark**, Citi Field, in 2009. White Sox pitcher Mark Buehrle threw a perfect game—the first in the Major Leagues since 2004—against the Tampa Bay Rays in Chicago July 23, thanks in no small part to a spectacular leaping catch by outfielder Dewayne Wise.

Steroids and other performance-enhancing drugs continued to stain baseball in 2009. Before the season began, Yankees' third baseman Alex Rodriguez admitted to using steroids while a member of the Texas Rangers from 2001-03, after test results from that era surfaced. Sluggers David Ortiz of the Boston Red Sox and Manny Ramirez of the Los Angeles Dodgers were also implicated, though the 2003 test had been administered anonymously. In an unrelated incident May 7, Ramirez was suspended for 50 games for testing positive for a banned substance that athletes often take to counteract the side effects of steroid use.

In professional golf, Argentina's Angel Cabrera won the green jacket at **the Masters** on Apr. 12, outlasting Kenny Perry and Chad Campbell through two sudden-death playoff holes. Unheralded Lucas Glover won the **U.S. Open**, which was held at Bethpage State Park's Black Course in New York, June 15-21. The final round of the **British Open**, held at Scotland's Turnberry on July 19, took four playoff holes to decide, with Stewart Cink denying Tom Watson's surprise bid to become the oldest major champion in history. Y. E. Yang became the first Asian-born player to win a major tournament by capturing the **PGA Championship** Aug. 16 at Hazeltine National Golf Club in Chaska, MN.

Two streaks in men's **tennis** came to an end in 2009: Rafael Nadal's four consecutive French Open titles and Roger Federer's five straight U.S. Open wins. Nadal lost in the fourth round to Robin Soderling, who eventually lost to Federer in the French final; Federer fell in the U.S. final to Argentina's Juan Martin del Potro. Federer also won his sixth Wimbledon championship, beating Andy Roddick in a four-hour match that featured a 30-game final set, the longest in Wimbledon history. The win gave Federer a **record 15 Grand Slam** titles, pushing Federer past Pete Sampras for the most in men's history.

Serena Williams defeated Dinara Safina at the Australian Open, and Safina fell to Svetlana Kuznetsova in an all-Russian final at the French Open. Serena Williams defeated her sister Venus in an all-Williams match at Wimbledon. Belgium's Kim Clijsters won the U.S. Open after taking two years off to get married and have a baby, though the most-talked about incident of the tournament was Serena Williams' expletive-filled tirade at an official for calling a foot fault. The ensuing penalty point caused Williams to lose her semifinal match to Clijsters.

Decade in Review: Memorable Sports Moments (2000-09)

The decade in sports had it all: broken records, miracle comebacks, amazing upsets—even the end of a legendary curse. Here are the top moments of triumph and heartbreak that fans will be talking about for years to come.

The Longest Yard
January 30, 2000

The first major sporting event of the decade was one of the most thrilling. The Tennessee Titans held the high-powered St. Louis Rams offense in check for much of Super Bowl XXXIV. But with less than two minutes to play, Rams quarterback Kurt Warner connected with Isaac Bruce for a 73-yard go-ahead touchdown. Trailing 23-16, quarterback Steve McNair marched the Titans 87 yards to the Rams 10-yard line. With just five seconds left, McNair completed a short pass to Kevin Dyson. Rams linebacker Mike Jones saved the day by tackling Dyson at the one-yard line as he desperately stretched for the end zone and time ran out.

Team of the Decade?
2000, 2002-04, 2009

No team dominated the decade quite like the Univ. of Connecticut women's basketball team. Coach Geno Auriemma led the Huskies to five NCAA championships between 2000 and 2009, including undefeated seasons in 2002 and 2009. The team cruised to the 2000 title, winning its six NCAA tournament games by an average of more than 31 points. High-scoring guard Diana Taurasi helped the Huskies win three straight championships from 2002 to 2004. After a four-year mini-slump, UConn closed the "aughts" on a winning note by crushing Louisville, 76-54, in the 2009 women's NCAA championship game.

The Sox on Top (Finally!)
October 27, 2004; October 26, 2005

After selling Babe Ruth to the rival New York Yankees in 1920, the Boston Red Sox endured decades of heartbreaking losses that convinced many fans that the team was cursed. It looked as if the suffering would continue after Boston dropped the first three games of the 2004 American League Championship Series to the New York Yankees. No baseball team had ever overcome a 3-0 playoff deficit in a seven-game series. Yet the Red Sox did just that, winning four straight games behind the clutch hitting of David Ortiz. Boston completed its miracle postseason run by sweeping the St. Louis Cardinals in the World Series, claiming the team's first championship since 1918.

Another long championship drought ended a year later, when the Chicago White Sox won their first World Series since 1917. Led by timely hitting from Jermaine Dye and Scott Podsednik, Chicago swept the Houston Astros to claim its first title in 88 years. Unfortunately, the same could not be said for the White Sox's crosstown rivals, as the Cubs' World Series drought passed the 100-year mark in 2008.

Living Strong
July 24, 2005

Perhaps no major sporting event requires more physical endurance and mental toughness than the Tour de France. And no athlete embodies those traits better than Lance Armstrong. His promising cycling career appeared to end in 1996, when he was diagnosed with testicular cancer, which had spread to his brain and lungs. Given a slim chance of survival, Armstrong vowed to defy the odds and return to cycling. In 1998, he did just that. He completed his miracle comeback by winning his first Tour de France the following year—and he just kept on winning until he called it quits after his record seventh Tour victory in July 2005. Armstrong came out of retirement in 2009 and finished third at the Tour de France.

Fallen Champion
May 20, 2006

No thoroughbred has won the Triple Crown since Affirmed in 1978. In 2006, an undefeated bay colt named Barbaro seemed poised to break that drought. On May 6, he won the Kentucky Derby by a spectacular 6½ lengths—the largest winning margin in 60 years. But tragedy struck at the Preakness Stakes two weeks later. Early in the race, Barbaro "took a bad step," according to jockey Edgar Prado, and broke three bones in his right hind leg. A record crowd of more than 118,000—and millions of TV viewers—watched in shock. The next day, Barbaro underwent a six-hour operation to repair his life-threatening injuries. His battle for survival made headlines, and gifts and get-well wishes poured in from around the country. Sadly, the horse suffered a number of setbacks over the next several months and he was euthanized on January 29, 2007.

A Perfect Upset
February 3, 2008

In Super Bowl XLII, all that stood between the New England Patriots and the first 19-0 undefeated season in NFL history was the New York Giants—a team they had already defeated to cap an unbeaten regular season. A Super Bowl-record 97.5 million U.S. television viewers watched as the Giants' suffocating defense frustrated New England quarterback Tom Brady for much of the game. However, the Pats seemed to put the game away late in the fourth quarter when a Brady-to-Randy Moss touchdown put the team ahead, 14-10. Quarterback Eli Manning and the Giants had one last chance. An impossible-seeming 32-yard catch by David Tyree—who squeezed the ball against his helmet as he fell backward—kept their final drive alive. Manning's 13-yard touchdown toss to Plaxico Burress with 35 seconds left gave the Giants a 17-14 lead and ended New England's quest for perfection.

Seems Like Old Times
June 17, 2008

The 2008 NBA Finals were a dream matchup for fans of hoop history. The league's two most storied franchises, the Boston Celtics and the Los Angeles Lakers, renewed a championship rivalry that dates back to 1959, when the Lakers were still based in Minneapolis. The 2008 Finals marked the teams' 11th face-off for the championship—but their first since 1987. Kobe Bryant and the Lakers could not contain the Celtics' talented trio of Kevin Garnett, Paul Pierce, and Ray Allen. The six-game series victory gave Boston its record 17th championship—and its ninth over the rival Lakers.

Tiger on the Prowl
June 16, 2008

By June 2008, Tiger Woods had already won 13 major championships and established himself as the best golfer of his generation. But his gritty performance at the 2008 U.S. Open stands out in a career of memorable moments. Playing on an injured knee, Woods stormed into the lead with two eagles and a birdie at the end of the third round. He winced in pain and limped through the fourth round, before sinking a pressure-packed 12-foot putt to force an 18-hole playoff with Rocco Mediate.

In the playoff round, Woods sank a clutch birdie putt to force a sudden-death playoff, which he won on the first hole. After the tournament, Woods had surgery to repair a torn anterior cruciate ligament (ACL) in his left knee and also revealed that he had been playing with two stress fractures in his left leg.

"Rafa" Vs. Roger
July 6, 2008

The growing rivalry between the two best men's tennis players in the world, Spain's Rafael Nadal and Switzerland's Roger Federer, reached its peak in the 2008 Wimbledon final. The match marked their seventh meeting in four years with a Grand Slam title at stake. Federer, who hadn't lost a match on grass since 2002, was seeking his sixth straight Wimbledon title.

Nadal won the first two sets, 6-4, 6-4, before Federer battled back to win third- and fourth-set tiebreakers. That set up an epic back-and-forth fifth set that was finally won by an exhausted Nadal, 9-7. Three-time Wimbledon champ John McEnroe called the grueling 4-hour, 48-minute battle—even longer off-the-court because of multiple rain delays—"the greatest match I've ever seen."

Best of Beijing
August 8-24, 2008

The 2008 Beijing Games saw two of the greatest record-breaking performances in Olympic history. The eyes of the world were on 23-year-old U.S. swimmer Michael Phelps as he reached his lofty goal of a record eight gold medals—one better than the seven won by Mark Spitz at the 1972 Games. Only eight countries won more gold medals in Beijing than Michael Phelps did. The swimmer's incredible performance overshadowed the fleet footwork of Usain Bolt. The Jamaican sprinter seemed to barely break a sweat in winning the 100 meters, 200 meters, and 400-meter relay in record-setting fashion. Bolt became the first sprinter to set world records in all three events at one Olympiad. He then broke his own records in the 100- and 200-meter events at the 2009 World Championships.

OLYMPICS
2008 Summer Olympic Games
Beijing, China, Aug. 8-24, 2008

More than 10,000 athletes from 204 nations met in Beijing, China, to compete in the Summer Olympic Games Aug. 8-24, 2008. The run-up to the games was plagued by concerns over air quality and doping, but neither figured prominently once the Games began. Only six athletes tested positive for performance-enhancing drugs, far fewer than the 26 who had tested positive in Athens, Greece, in 2004.

Thirty-eight new world records were set during the course of the XXIX Olympiad. U.S. swimmer Michael Phelps, who had dazzled at the 2004 Games in Athens, won eight gold medals, breaking the record for most gold medals won at a single Olympiad, held by American swimmer Mark Spitz since 1972. Phelps set seven world records in the process. Jamaican track star Usain Bolt set a new world record in the 100-m sprint, covering the distance in 9.69 seconds; Bolt won two other races in record time.

The NBA-star studded U.S. men's basketball team, known to some as the "Redeem Team" in reference to the 2004 U.S. team's collapse, handily clinched the gold; the U.S. women's basketball team also claimed gold. In a rain-soaked final match, Americans Misty May-Treanor and Kerri Walsh became the first pair to repeat as beach volleyball gold medalists.

The U.S. came out on top of the overall medal count, with 110 medals, but host nation China won more gold medals than any other country for the first time, with 51.

2008 Final Medal Standings

	G	S	B	T		G	S	B	T		G	S	B	T
United States	36	38	36	110	Czech Republic	3	3	0	6	Estonia	1	1	0	2
China	51	21	28	100	Slovakia	3	2	1	6	Portugal	1	1	0	2
Russia	23	21	28	72	Georgia	3	0	3	6	Iran	1	0	1	2
Great Britain	19	13	15	47	North Korea	2	1	3	6	Trinidad & Tobago	0	2	0	2
Australia	14	15	17	46	Argentina	2	0	4	6	Algeria	0	1	1	2
Germany	16	10	15	41	Switzerland	2	0	4	6	Bahamas	0	1	1	2
France	7	16	17	40	Uzbekistan	1	2	3	6	Colombia	0	1	1	2
South Korea	13	10	8	31	Armenia	0	0	6	6	Kyrgyzstan	0	1	1	2
Italy	8	10	10	28	Slovenia	1	2	2	5	Morocco	0	1	1	2
Ukraine	7	5	15	27	Bulgaria	1	1	3	5	Tajikistan	0	1	1	2
Japan	9	6	10	25	Indonesia	1	1	3	5	Bahrain	1	0	0	1
Cuba	2	11	11	24	Sweden	0	4	1	5	Cameroon	1	0	0	1
Belarus	4	5	10	19	Croatia	0	2	3	5	Panama	1	0	0	1
Spain	5	10	3	18	Lithuania	0	2	3	5	Tunisia	1	0	0	1
Canada	3	9	6	18	Mongolia	2	2	0	4	Chile	0	1	0	1
Netherlands	7	5	4	16	Thailand	2	2	0	4	Ecuador	0	1	0	1
Brazil	3	4	8	15	Zimbabwe	1	3	0	4	Iceland	0	1	0	1
Kenya	5	5	4	14	Finland	1	1	2	4	Malaysia	0	1	0	1
Kazakhstan	2	4	7	13	Greece	0	2	2	4	Singapore	0	1	0	1
Jamaica	6	3	2	11	Nigeria	0	1	3	4	South Africa	0	1	0	1
Poland	3	6	1	10	Taiwan	0	0	4	4	Sudan	0	1	0	1
Hungary	3	5	2	10	Mexico	2	0	1	3	Vietnam	0	1	0	1
Norway	3	5	2	10	Latvia	1	1	1	3	Afghanistan	0	0	1	1
New Zealand	3	1	5	9	India	1	0	2	3	Egypt	0	0	1	1
Romania	4	1	3	8	Austria	0	1	2	3	Israel	0	0	1	1
Turkey	1	4	3	8	Ireland	0	1	2	3	Mauritius	0	0	1	1
Ethiopia	4	1	2	7	Serbia	0	1	2	3	Moldova	0	0	1	1
Denmark	2	2	3	7	Belgium	1	1	0	2	Togo	0	0	1	1
Azerbaijan	1	2	4	7	Dominican Rep.	1	1	0	2	Venezuela	0	0	1	1

Summer Olympic Games Champions, 1896-2008
(*Olympic record; (w) wind-aided)

The 1980 games were boycotted by 62 nations, including the U.S. The 1984 games were boycotted by the USSR and most Eastern bloc nations. E and W Germany competed separately, 1968-88. The 1992 Unified Team consisted of 12 former Soviet republics. The 1992 Independent Olympic Participants (I.O.P.) were from Serbia, Montenegro, and Macedonia.

Not all sports are listed here, and many events are omitted, even within listed sports, particularly if the event has not been held in more recent Games.

Baseball (Men)

1992 Cuba, Taiwan, Japan	**2000** United States, Cuba, Korea	**2008** South Korea, Cuba, United States
1996 Cuba, Japan, United States	**2004** Cuba, Australia, Japan	

Boxing
Weight class limits have changed many times since the first Olympic boxing events were held in 1904.
The following were used in the 2008 Olympic Games.

Lt. Flyweight (48 kg/106 lbs)
1968	Francisco Rodriguez, Venezuela
1972	Gyorgy Gedo, Hungary
1976	Jorge Hernandez, Cuba
1980	Shamil Sabyrov, USSR
1984	Paul Gonzalez, United States
1988	Ivailo Hristov, Bulgaria
1992	Rogelio Marcelo, Cuba
1996	Daniel Petrov, Bulgaria
2000	Brahim Asloum, France
2004	Yan Bhartelemy Varela, Cuba
2008	Zou Shiming, China

Flyweight (51 kg/112 lbs)
1904	George Finnegan, United States
1920	William Di Gennara, United States
1924	Fidel LaBarba, United States
1928	Antal Kocsis, Hungary
1932	Istvan Enekes, Hungary
1936	Willi Kaiser, Germany
1948	Pascual Perez, Argentina
1952	Nathan Brooks, United States
1956	Terence Spinks, Great Britain
1960	Gyula Torok, Hungary
1964	Fernando Atzori, Italy
1968	Ricardo Delgado, Mexico
1972	Georgi Kostadinov, Bulgaria
1976	Leo Randolph, United States
1980	Peter Lessov, Bulgaria
1984	Steve McCrory, United States
1988	Kim Kwang Sun, S. Korea
1992	Su Choi Choi, N. Korea
1996	Maikro Romero, Cuba
2000	Wijan Ponlid, Thailand
2004	Yuriorkis Gamboa Toledano, Cuba
2008	Somjit Jongjohor, Thailand

Bantamweight (54 kg /119 lbs)
1904	Oliver Kirk, United States
1908	A. Henry Thomas, Great Britain
1920	Clarence Walker, South Africa
1924	William Smith, South Africa
1928	Vittorio Tamagnini, Italy
1932	Horace Gwynne, Canada
1936	Ulderico Sergo, Italy
1948	Tibor Csik, Hungary
1952	Pentti Hamalainen, Finland
1956	Wolfgang Behrendt, E. Germany
1960	Oleg Grigoryev, USSR
1964	Takao Sakurai, Japan
1968	Valery Sokolov, USSR
1972	Orlando Martinez, Cuba
1976	Yong-Jo Gu, N. Korea
1980	Juan Hernandez, Cuba
1984	Maurizio Stecca, Italy

1988	Kennedy McKinney, United States
1992	Joel Casamayor, Cuba
1996	Istvan Kovacs, Hungary
2000	Guillermo Rigondeaux, Cuba
2004	Guillermo Rigondeaux, Cuba
2008	Badar-Uugan Enkhbat, Mongolia

Featherweight (57 kg/125 lbs)

1904	Oliver Kirk, United States
1908	Richard Gunn, Great Britain
1920	Paul Fritsch, France
1924	John Fields, United States
1928	Lambertus van Klaveren, Netherlands
1932	Carmelo Robledo, Argentina
1936	Oscar Casanovas, Argentina
1948	Ernesto Formenti, Italy
1952	Jan Zachara, Czechoslovakia
1956	Vladimir Safronov, USSR
1960	Francesco Musso, Italy
1964	Stanislav Stephashkin, USSR
1968	Antonin Roldan, Mexico
1972	Boris Kousnetsov, USSR
1976	Angel Herrera, Cuba
1980	Rudi Fink, E. Germany
1984	Meldrick Taylor, United States
1988	Giovanni Parisi, Italy
1992	Andreas Tews, Germany
1996	Somluck Kamsing, Thailand
2000	Bekzat Sattarkhanov, Kazakhstan
2004	Alexei Tichtchenko, Russia
2008	Vasyl Lomachenko, Ukraine

Lightweight (60 kg/132 lbs)

1904	Harry Spanger, United States
1908	Frederick Grace, Great Britain
1920	Samuel Mosberg, United States
1924	Hans Nielsen, Denmark
1928	Carlo Orlandi, Italy
1932	Lawrence Stevens, South Africa
1936	Imre Harangi, Hungary
1948	Gerald Dreyer, South Africa
1952	Aureliano Bolognesi, Italy
1956	Richard McTaggart, Great Britain
1960	Kazimierz Pazdzior, Poland
1964	Jozef Grudzien, Poland
1968	Ronald Harris, United States
1972	Jan Szczepanski, Poland
1976	Howard Davis, United States
1980	Angel Herrera, Cuba
1984	Pernell Whitaker, United States
1988	Andreas Zuelow, E. Germany
1992	Oscar De La Hoya, United States
1996	Hocine Soltani, Algeria
2000	Mario Kindelan, Cuba
2004	Mario Kindelan, Cuba
2008	Alexey Tishchenko, Russia

Lt. Welterweight (64 kg/141 lbs)

1952	Charles Adkins, United States
1956	Vladimir Yengibaryan, USSR
1960	Bohumil Nemecek, Czechoslovakia
1964	Jerzy Kulej, Poland
1968	Jerzy Kulej, Poland
1972	Ray Seales, United States
1976	Ray Leonard, United States
1980	Patrizio Oliva, Italy

1984	Jerry Page, United States
1988	Viatcheslav Janovski, USSR
1992	Hector Vinent, Cuba
1996	Hector Vinent, Cuba
2000	Mahamadkadyz Abdullaev, Uzbekistan
2004	Manus Boonjumnong, Thailand
2008	Felix Diaz, Dominican Republic

Welterweight (69 kg/152 lbs)

1904	Albert Young, United States
1920	Albert Schneider, Canada
1924	Jean Delarge, Belgium
1928	Edward Morgan, New Zealand
1932	Edward Flynn, United States
1936	Sten Suvio, Finland
1948	Julius Torma, Czechoslovakia
1952	Zygmunt Chychia, Poland
1956	Nicolae Linca, Romania
1960	Giovanni Benvenuti, Italy
1964	Marian Kasprzyk, Poland
1968	Manfred Wolke, E. Germany
1972	Emilio Correa, Cuba
1976	Jochen Bachfeld, E. Germany
1980	Andres Aldama, Cuba
1984	Mark Breland, United States
1988	Robert Wangila, Kenya
1992	Michael Carruth, Ireland
1996	Oleg Saitov, Russia
2000	Oleg Saitov, Russia
2004	Artayev Bakhtiyar, Kazakhstan
2008	Bakhyt Sarsekbayev, Kazakhstan

Lt. Middleweight (71 kg/156 lbs)

1952	Laszlo Papp, Hungary
1956	Laszlo Papp, Hungary
1960	Wilbert McClure, United States
1964	Boris Lagutin, USSR
1968	Boris Lagutin, USSR
1972	Dieter Kottysch, W. Germany
1976	Jerzy Rybicki, Poland
1980	Armando Martinez, Cuba
1984	Frank Tate, United States
1988	Park Si Hun, S. Korea
1992	Juan Lemus, Cuba
1996	David Reid, United States
2000	Yermakhan Ibraimov, Kazakhstan

Middleweight (75 kg/165 lbs)

1904	Charles Mayer, United States
1908	John Douglas, Great Britain
1920	Harry Mallin, Great Britain
1924	Harry Mallin, Great Britain
1928	Piero Toscani, Italy
1932	Carmen Barth, United States
1936	Jean Despeaux, France
1948	Laszlo Papp, Hungary
1952	Floyd Patterson, United States
1956	Gennady Schatkov, USSR
1960	Edward Crook, United States
1964	Valery Popenchenko, USSR
1968	Christopher Finnegan, Great Britain
1972	Vyacheslav Lemechev, USSR
1976	Michael Spinks, United States
1980	Jose Gomez, Cuba
1984	Joon-Sup Shin, S. Korea

1988	Henry Maske, E. Germany
1992	Ariel Hernandez, Cuba
1996	Ariel Hernandez, Cuba
2000	Jorge Gutierrez, Cuba
2004	Gaydarbek Gaydarbekov, Russia
2008	James Degale, Great Britain

Lt. Heavyweight (81 kg/178 lbs)

1920	Edward Eagan, United States
1924	Harry Mitchell, Great Britain
1928	Victor Avendano, Argentina
1932	David Carstens, South Africa
1936	Roger Michelot, France
1948	George Hunter, South Africa
1952	Norvel Lee, United States
1956	James Boyd, United States
1960	Cassius Clay, United States
1964	Cosimo Pinto, Italy
1968	Dan Poznyak, USSR
1972	Mate Parlov, Yugoslavia
1976	Leon Spinks, United States
1980	Slobodan Kacar, Yugoslavia
1984	Anton Josipovic, Yugoslavia
1988	Andrew Maynard, United States
1992	Torsten May, Germany
1996	Vassili Jirov, Kazakhstan
2000	Alexander Lebziak, Russia
2004	Andre Ward, United States
2008	Zhang Xiaoping, China

Heavyweight (91 kg/201 lbs)

1984	Henry Tillman, United States
1988	Ray Mercer, United States
1992	Felix Savon, Cuba
1996	Felix Savon, Cuba
2000	Felix Savon, Cuba
2004	Odlanier Solis Fonte, Cuba
2008	Rakhim Chakhkiev, Russia

Super Heavyweight (91+ kg/201+ lbs)

(known as heavyweight, 1904-80)

1904	Samuel Berger, United States
1908	Albert Oldham, Great Britain
1920	Ronald Rawson, Great Britain
1924	Otto von Porat, Norway
1928	Arturo Rodriguez Jurado, Argentina
1932	Santiago Lovell, Argentina
1936	Herbert Runge, Germany
1948	Rafael Iglesias, Argentina
1952	H. Edward Sanders, United States
1956	T. Peter Rademacher, United States
1960	Franco De Piccoli, Italy
1964	Joe Frazier, United States
1968	George Foreman, United States
1972	Teofilo Stevenson, Cuba
1976	Teofilo Stevenson, Cuba
1980	Teofilo Stevenson, Cuba
1984	Tyrell Biggs, United States
1988	Lennox Lewis, Canada
1992	Roberto Balado, Cuba
1996	Vladimir Klitchko, Ukraine
2000	Audley Harrison, Great Britain
2004	Alexander Povetkin, Russia
2008	Roberto Cammarelle, Italy

Gymnastics—Men

Floor Exercises

1932	István Pelle, Hungary
1936	Georges Miez, Switzerland
1948	Ferenc Pataki, Hungary
1952	William Thoresson, Sweden
1956	Valentin Muratov, USSR
1960	Nobuyuki Aihara, Japan
1964	Franco Menichelli, Italy
1968	Sawao Kato, Japan
1972	Nikolay Andrianov, USSR
1976	Nikolay Andrianov, USSR
1980	Roland Brückner, E. Germany
1984	Li Ning, China
1988	Serguei Kharikov, USSR
1992	Xiaosahuang Li, China
1996	Ioannis Melissanidis, Greece

Floor Exercises

2000	Igors Vihrovs, Latvia
2004	Kyle Shewfelt, Canada
2008	Zou Kai, China

Horizontal Bars

1896	Hermann Weingärtner, Germany
1904	Anton Heida, United States; Edward Hennig, United States (tie)
1924	Leon Stukelj, Yugoslavia
1928	Georges Miez, Switzerland
1932	Dallas Denver Bixler, United States
1936	Aleksanteri Saarvala, Finland
1948	Josef Stalder, Switzerland
1952	Jakob (Jack) Günthard, Switzerland
1956	Takashi Ono, Japan

Horizontal Bars

1960	Takashi Ono, Japan
1964	Boris Shakhlin, USSR
1968	Mikhail Voronin, USSR; Akinori Nakayama, Japan (tie)
1972	Mitsuo Tsukahara, Japan
1976	Mitsuo Tsukahara, Japan
1980	Stoyan Deltchev, Bulgaria
1984	Shinji Morisue, Japan
1988	Valeri Lioukine, USSR; Vladimir Artemov, USSR (tie)
1992	Trent Dimas, United States
1996	Andreas Wecker, Germany
2000	Alexei Nemov, Russia
2004	Igor Cassina, Italy
2008	Zou Kai, China

Individual All-Round

1900	Gustave Sandras, France
1904	Julius Lenhart, United States
1908	G. Alberto Braglia, Italy
1912	G. Alberto Braglia, Italy
1920	Giorgio Zampori, Italy
1924	Leon Stukelj, Yugoslavia
1928	Georges Miez, Switzerland
1932	Romeo Neri, Italy
1936	Karl-Alfred Schwarzmann, Germany
1948	Veikko Huhtanen, Finland
1952	Viktor Ivanovich Chukarin, USSR
1956	Viktor Ivanovich Chukarin, USSR
1960	Boris Shakhlin, USSR
1964	Yukio Endo, Japan
1968	Sawao Kato, Japan
1972	Sawao Kato, Japan
1976	Nikolay Andrianov, USSR
1980	Aleksandr Dityatin, USSR
1984	Koji Gushiken, Japan
1988	Vladimir Artemov, USSR
1992	Vitaly Scherbo, Unified Team (Belarus)
1996	Li Xiaosahuang, China
2000	Alexei Nemov, Russia
2004	Paul Hamm, United States
2008	Yang Wei, China

Parallel Bars

1896	Alfred Flatow, Germany
1904	George Eyser, United States
1924	August Güttinger, Switzerland
1928	Ladislav Vacha, Czechoslovakia
1932	Romeo Neri, Italy
1936	Konrad Frey, Germany
1948	Michael Reusch, Switzerland
1952	Hans Eugster, Switzerland
1956	Viktor Ivanovich Chukarin, USSR
1960	Boris Shakhlin, USSR
1964	Yukio Endo, Japan
1968	Akinori Nakayama, Japan
1972	Sawao Kato, Japan
1976	Sawao Kato, Japan
1980	Aleksandr Tkachev, USSR
1984	Barthold Wayne Conner, United States
1988	Vladimir Artemov, USSR
1992	Vitaly Scherbo, Unified Team (Belarus)
1996	Roustam Sharipov, Ukraine
2000	Li Xiaopeng, China
2004	Valeri Goncharov, Ukraine
2008	Li Xiaopeng, China

Pommel Horse

1896	Louis Zutter, Switzerland
1904	Anton Heida, United States
1924	Josef Wilhelm, Switzerland
1928	Hermann Hänggi, Switzerland

Pommel Horse

1932	István Pelle, Hungary
1936	Konrad Frey, Germany
1948	Heikki Savolainen, Finland; Paavo Johannes Aaltonen, Finland; Veikko Huhtanen, Finland (tie)
1952	Viktor Ivanovich Chukarin, USSR
1956	Boris Shakhlin, USSR
1960	Eugen Georg Oskar Ekman, Finland; Boris Shakhlin, USSR (tie)
1964	Miroslav Cerar, Yugoslavia
1968	Miroslav Cerar, Yugoslavia
1972	Viktor Klimenko, USSR
1976	Zoltan Magyar, Hungary
1980	Zoltan Magyar, Hungary
1984	Li Ning, China; Peter Glen Vidmar, United States (tie)
1988	Zsolt Borkai, Hungary; Dmitri Bilozerchev, USSR; Lubomir Geraskov, Bulgaria (tie)
1992	Pae Gil-Su, North Korea; Vitaly Scherbo, Unified Team (Belarus) (tie)
1996	Li Donghua, Switzerland
2000	Marius Daniel Urzica, Romania
2004	Teng Haibin, China
2008	Xiao Qin, China

Rings

1896	Ioannis Mitropoulos, Greece
1904	Hermann Glass, United States
1924	Francesco Martino, Italy
1928	Leon Stukelj, Yugoslavia
1932	George Julius Gulack, United States
1936	Alois Hudec, Czechoslovakia
1948	Karl Frei, Switzerland
1952	Grant Shaginyan, USSR
1956	Albert Azaryan, USSR
1960	Albert Azaryan, USSR
1964	Takuji Hayata, Japan
1968	Akinori Nakayama, Japan
1972	Akinori Nakayama, Japan
1976	Nikolay Andrianov, USSR
1980	Aleksandr Dityatin, USSR
1984	Li Ning, China; Koji Gushiken, Japan (tie)
1988	Holger Behrendt, E. Germany; Dmitri Bilozerchev, USSR (tie)
1992	Vitaly Scherbo, Unified Team (Belarus)
1996	Juri Chechi, Italy
2000	Szilveszter Csollany, Hungary
2004	Dimosthenis Tampakos, Greece
2008	Chen Yibing, China

Team Competition

1904	United States, United States, United States
1908	Sweden, Norway, Finland
1912	Italy, Hungary, Great Britain

Team Competition

1920	Italy, Belgium, France
1924	Italy, France, Switzerland
1928	Switzerland, Czechoslovakia, Yugoslavia
1932	Italy, United States, Finland
1936	Germany, Switzerland, Finland
1948	Finland, Switzerland, Hungary
1952	USSR, Switzerland, Finland
1956	USSR, Japan, Finland
1960	Japan, USSR, Italy
1964	Japan, USSR, Unified Team of Germany
1968	Japan, USSR, E. Germany
1972	Japan, USSR, E. Germany
1976	Japan, USSR, E. Germany
1980	USSR, E. Germany, Hungary
1984	United States, China, Japan
1988	USSR, E. Germany, Japan
1992	Unified Team, China, Japan
1996	Russia, China, Ukraine
2000	China, Ukraine, Russia
2004	Japan, United States, Romania
2008	China, Japan, United States

Trampoline

2000	Alexander Moskalenko, Russia
2004	Yuri Nikitin, Ukraine
2008	Lu Chunlong, China

Vault

1896	Carl Schumann, Germany
1904	George Eyser, United States; Anton Heida, United States (tie)
1924	Frank Kriz, United States
1928	Eugen Mack, Switzerland
1932	Savino Guglielmetti, Italy
1936	Karl-Alfred Schwarzmann, Germany
1948	Paavo Johannes Aaltonen, Finland
1952	Viktor Ivanovich Chukarin, USSR
1956	Helmut Bantz, Unified Team of Germany; Valentin Muratov, USSR (tie)
1960	Takashi Ono, Japan; Boris Shakhlin, USSR (tie)
1964	Haruhiro Yamashita, Japan
1968	Mikhail Voronin, USSR
1972	Klaus Köste, E. Germany
1976	Nikolay Andrianov, USSR
1980	Nikolay Andrianov, USSR
1984	Lou Yun, China
1988	Lou Yun, China
1992	Vitaly Scherbo, Unified Team (Belarus)
1996	Alexei Nemov, Russia
2000	Gervasio Deferr, Spain
2004	Gervasio Deferr, Spain
2008	Leszek Blanik, Poland

Gymnastics—Women

Balance Beam

1952	Nina Bocharova, USSR
1956	Agnes Keleti, Hungary
1960	Eva Vechtova-Bosakova, Czechoslovakia
1964	Vera Caslavska, Czechoslovakia
1968	Natalya Kuchinskaya, USSR
1972	Olga Korbut, USSR
1976	Nadia Comaneci, Romania
1980	Nadia Comaneci, Romania
1984	Ecaterina Szabo, Romania; Simona Pauca, Romania (tie)
1988	Daniela Silivas, Romania
1992	Tatiana Lyssenko, Unified Team (Ukraine)
1996	Shannon Miller, United States
2000	Liu Xuan, China
2004	Catalina Ponor, Romania
2008	Shawn Johnson, United States

Floor Exercises

1952	Agnes Keleti, Hungary
1956	Agnes Keleti, Hungary; Larisa Latynina, USSR (tie)
1960	Larisa Latynina, USSR
1964	Larisa Latynina, USSR
1968	Vera Caslavska, Czechoslovakia; Larisa Petrik, USSR (tie)
1972	Olga Korbut, USSR

Floor Exercises

1976	Nelli Kim, USSR
1980	Nelli Kim, USSR; Nadia Comaneci, Romania (tie)
1984	Ecaterina Szabo, Romania
1988	Daniela Silivas, Romania
1992	Lavinia Corina Milosovici, Romania
1996	Lilia Podkopayeva, Ukraine
2000	Elena Zamolodchikova, Russia
2004	Catalina Ponor, Romania
2008	Sandra Izbasa, Romania

Individual All-Round

1952	Mariya Gorokhovskaya, USSR
1956	Larisa Latynina, USSR
1960	Larisa Latynina, USSR
1964	Vera Caslavska, Czechoslovakia
1968	Vera Caslavska, Czechoslovakia
1972	Lyudmila Turischeva, USSR
1976	Nadia Comaneci, Romania
1980	Elena Davydova, USSR
1984	Mary-Lou Retton, United States
1988	Elena Shushunova, USSR
1992	Tatiana Goutsou, Unified Team
1996	Lilia Podkopayeva, Ukraine
2000	Simona Amanar, Romania
2004	Carly Patterson, United States
2008	Nastia Liukin, United States

Team Competition

1928	Netherlands, Italy, Great Britain
1936	Germany, Czechoslovakia, Hungary
1948	Czechoslovakia, Hungary, United States
1952	USSR, Hungary, Czechoslovakia
1956	USSR, Hungary, Romania
1960	USSR, Czechoslovakia, Romania
1964	USSR, Czechoslovakia, Japan
1968	USSR, Czechoslovakia, E. Germany
1972	USSR, E. Germany, Hungary
1976	USSR, Romania, E. Germany
1980	USSR, Romania, E. Germany
1984	Romania, United States, China
1988	USSR, Romania, E. Germany
1992	Unified Team, Romania, United States
1996	United States, Russia, Romania
2000	Romania, Russia, China
2004	Romania, United States, Russia
2008	China, United States, Romania

Trampoline

2000	Irina Karavaeva, Russia
2004	Anna Dogonadze, Germany
2008	He Wenna, China

Uneven Bars		Uneven Bars		Vault	
1952	Margit Korondi, Hungary	1996	Svetlana Khorkina, Russia	1976	Nelli Kim, USSR
1956	Agnes Keleti, Hungary	2000	Svetlana Khorkina, Russia	1980	Natalia Shaposhnikova, USSR
1960	Polina Astakhova, USSR	2004	Emilie LePennec, France	1984	Ecaterina Szabo, Romania
1964	Polina Astakhova, USSR	2008	He Kexin, China	1988	Svetlana Boginskaya, USSR
1968	Vera Caslavska, Czechoslovakia			1992	Henrietta Onodi, Hungary; Lavinia
1972	Karin Janz, E. Germany		**Vault**		Corina Milosovici, Romania (tie)
1976	Nadia Comaneci, Romania	1952	Ekaterina Kalinchuk, USSR	1996	Simona Amanar, Romania
1980	Maxi Gnauck, E. Germany	1956	Larisa Latynina, USSR	2000	Elena Zamolodchikova, Russia
1984	Julianne Lyn McNamara, United	1960	Margarita Nikolaeva, USSR	2004	Monica Rosu, Romania
	States; Yan-Hong Ma, China (tie)	1964	Vera Caslavska, Czechoslovakia	2008	Hong Un Jong, North Korea
1988	Daniela Silivas, Romania	1968	Vera Caslavska, Czechoslovakia		
1992	Lu Li, China	1972	Karin Janz, E. Germany		

Soccer

Men		Men		Men	
1900	Great Britain, France, Belgium	1956	USSR, Yugoslavia, Bulgaria	1992	Spain, Poland, Ghana
1904	Canada, United States, United	1960	Yugoslavia, Denmark, Hungary	1996	Nigeria, Argentina, Brazil
	States	1964	Hungary, Czechoslovakia, Unified	2000	Cameroon, Spain, Chile
1908	Great Britain, Denmark, Netherlands		Team of Germany	2004	Argentina, Paraguay, Italy
1912	Great Britain, Denmark, Netherlands	1968	Hungary, Bulgaria, Japan	2008	Argentina, Nigeria, Brazil
1920	Belgium, Spain, Netherlands	1972	Poland; Hungary; USSR, E.		
1924	Uruguay, Switzerland, Sweden		Germany (tie for bronze)		**Women**
1928	Uruguay, Argentina, Italy	1976	E. Germany, Poland, USSR	1996	United States, China, Norway
1936	Italy, Austria, Norway	1980	Czechoslovakia, E. Germany, USSR	2000	Norway, United States, Germany
1948	Sweden, Yugoslavia, Denmark	1984	France, Brazil, Yugoslavia	2004	United States, Brazil, Germany
1952	Hungary, Yugoslavia, Sweden	1988	USSR, Brazil, W. Germany	2008	United States, Brazil, Germany

Swimming and Diving—Men

	50-Meter Freestyle	Time		400-Meter Freestyle	Time
1988	Matt Biondi, United States	0:22.14	1960	Murray Rose, Australia	4:18.3
1992	Aleksandr Popov, Unified Team	0:21.91	1964	Don Schollander, United States	4:12.2
1996	Aleksandr Popov, Russia	0:22.13	1968	Mike Burton, United States	4:09.0
2000	Anthony Ervin, United States	0:21.98	1972	Brad Cooper, Australia	4:00.27
2000	Gary Hall Jr., United States	0:21.98	1976	Brian Goodell, United States	3:51.93
2004	Gary Hall Jr., United States	0:21.93	1980	Vladimir Salnikov, USSR	3:51.31
2008	Cesar Cielo Filho, Brazil	0:21.30*	1984	George DiCarlo, United States	3:51.23
			1988	Ewe Dassler, E. Germany	3:46.95
	100-Meter Freestyle	**Time**	1992	Yevgeny Sadovyi, Unified Team	3:45.00
1896	Alfred Hajos, Hungary	1:22.2	1996	Danyon Loader, New Zealand	3:47.97
1904	Zoltan de Halmay, Hungary (100 yards)	1:02.8	2000	Ian Thorpe, Australia	3:40.59*
1908	Charles Daniels, United States	1:05.6	2004	Ian Thorpe, Australia	3:43.10
1912	Duke P. Kahanamoku, United States	1:03.4	2008	Park Taehwan, South Korea	3:41.86
1920	Duke P. Kahanamoku, United States	1:01.4			
1924	John Weissmuller, United States	0:59.0		**1,500-Meter Freestyle**	**Time**
1928	John Weissmuller, United States	0:58.6	1908	Henry Taylor, Great Britain	22:48.4
1932	Yasuji Miyazaki, Japan	0:58.2	1912	George Hodgson, Canada	22:00.0
1936	Ferenc Csik, Hungary	0:57.6	1920	Norman Ross, United States	22:23.2
1948	Wally Ris, United States	0:57.3	1924	Andrew Charlton, Australia	20:06.6
1952	Clark Scholes, United States	0:57.4	1928	Arne Borg, Sweden	19:51.8
1956	Jon Henricks, Australia	0:55.4	1932	Kusuo Kitamura, Japan	19:12.4
1960	John Devitt, Australia	0:55.2	1936	Noboru Terada, Japan	19:13.7
1964	Don Schollander, United States	0:53.4	1948	James McLane, United States	19:18.5
1968	Mike Wenden, Australia	0:52.2	1952	Ford Konno, United States	18:30.3
1972	Mark Spitz, United States	0:51.22	1956	Murray Rose, Australia	17:58.9
1976	Jim Montgomery, United States	0:49.99	1960	Jon Konrads, Australia	17:19.6
1980	Jorg Woithe, E. Germany	0:50.40	1964	Robert Windle, Australia	17:01.7
1984	Rowdy Gaines, United States	0:49.80	1968	Mike Burton, United States	16:38.9
1988	Matt Biondi, United States	0:48.63	1972	Mike Burton, United States	15:52.58
1992	Aleksandr Popov, Unified Team	0:49.02	1976	Brian Goodell, United States	15:02.40
1996	Aleksandr Popov, Russia	0:48.74	1980	Vladimir Salnikov, USSR	14:58.27
2000	Pieter van den Hoogenband, Netherlands	0:48.30	1984	Michael O'Brien, United States	15:05.20
2004	Pieter van den Hoogenband, Netherlands	0:48.17	1988	Vladimir Salnikov, USSR	15:00.40
2008	Alain Bernard, France	0:47:21	1992	Kieren Perkins, Australia	14:43.48
			1996	Kieren Perkins, Australia	14:56.40
	200-Meter Freestyle	**Time**	2000	Grant Hackett, Australia	14:48.33
1968	Mike Wenden, Australia	1:55.2	2004	Grant Hackett, Australia	14:43.40
1972	Mark Spitz, United States	1:52.78	2008	Oussama Mellouli, Tunisia	14:40.84
1976	Bruce Furniss, United States	1:50.29			
1980	Sergei Kopliakov, USSR	1:49.81		**100-Meter Backstroke**	**Time**
1984	Michael Gross, W. Germany	1:47.44	1904	Walter Brack, Germany (100 yds.)	1:16.8
1988	Duncan Armstrong, Australia	1:47.25	1908	Arno Bieberstein, Germany	1:24.6
1992	Yevgeny Sadovyi, Unified Team	1:46.70	1912	Harry Hebner, United States	1:21.2
1996	Danyon Loader, New Zealand	1:47.63	1920	Warren Kealoha, United States	1:15.2
2000	Pieter van den Hoogenband, Netherlands	1:45.35	1924	Warren Kealoha, United States	1:13.2
2004	Ian Thorpe, Australia	1:44.71	1928	George Kojac, United States	1:08.2
2008	Michael Phelps, United States	1:42.96*	1932	Masaji Kiyokawa, Japan	1:08.6
			1936	Adolph Kiefer, United States	1:05.9
	400-Meter Freestyle	**Time**	1948	Allen Stack, United States	1:06.4
1904	C. M. Daniels, United States (440 yards)	6:16.2	1952	Yoshi Oyakawa, United States	1:05.4
1908	Henry Taylor, Great Britain	5:36.8	1956	David Thiele, Australia	1:02.2
1912	George Hodgson, Canada	5:24.4	1960	David Thiele, Australia	1:01.9
1920	Norman Ross, United States	5:26.8	1968	Roland Matthes, E. Germany	0:58.7
1924	John Weissmuller, United States	5:04.2	1972	Roland Matthes, E. Germany	0:56.58
1928	Albert Zorilla, Argentina	5:01.6	1976	John Naber, United States	0:55.49
1932	Clarence Crabbe, United States	4:48.4	1980	Bengt Baron, Sweden	0:56.33
1936	Jack Medica, United States	4:44.5	1984	Rick Carey, United States	0:55.79
1948	William Smith, United States	4:41.0	1988	Daichi Suzuki, Japan	0:55.05
1952	Jean Boiteux, France	4:30.7			
1956	Murray Rose, Australia	4:27.3			

100-Meter Backstroke

Year	Champion	Time
1992	Mark Tewksbury, Canada	0:53.98
1996	Jeff Rouse, United States	0:54.10
2000	Lenny Krayzelburg, United States	0:53.72
2004	Aaron Peirsol, United States	0:54.06
2008	Aaron Peirsol, United States	0:52.54*

200-Meter Backstroke

Year	Champion	Time
1964	Jed Graef, United States	2:10.3
1968	Roland Matthes, E. Germany	2:09.6
1972	Roland Matthes, E. Germany	2:02.82
1976	John Naber, United States	1:59.19
1980	Sandor Wladar, Hungary	2:01.93
1984	Rick Carey, United States	2:00.23
1988	Igor Polianski, USSR	1:59.37
1992	Martin Lopez-Zubero, Spain	1:58.47
1996	Brad Bridgewater, United States	1:58.54
2000	Lenny Krayzelburg, United States	1:56.76
2004	Aaron Peirsol, United States	1:54.95
2008	Ryan Lochte, United States	1:53.94*

100-Meter Breaststroke

Year	Champion	Time
1968	Don McKenzie, United States	1:07.79
1972	Nobutaka Taguchi, Japan	1:04.94
1976	John Hencken, United States	1:03.11
1980	Duncan Goodhew, Great Britain	1:03.44
1984	Steve Lundquist, United States	1:01.65
1988	Adrian Moorhouse, Great Britain	1:02.04
1992	Nelson Diebel, United States	1:01.50
1996	Fred Deburghgraeve, Belgium	1:00.60
2000	Domenico Fioravanti, Italy	1:00.46
2004	Kosuke Kitajima, Japan	1:00.08
2008	Kosuke Kitajima, Japan	0:58.91*

200-Meter Breaststroke

Year	Champion	Time
1908	Frederick Holman, Great Britain	3:09.2
1912	Walter Bathe, Germany	3:01.8
1920	Haken Malmroth, Sweden	3:04.4
1924	Robert Skelton, United States	2:56.6
1928	Yoshiyuki Tsuruta, Japan	2:48.8
1932	Yoshiyuki Tsuruta, Japan	2:45.4
1936	Tetsuo Hamuro, Japan	2:41.5
1948	Joseph Verdeur, United States	2:39.3
1952	John Davies, Australia	2:34.4
1956	Masura Furukawa, Japan	2:34.7
1960	William Mulliken, United States	2:37.4
1964	Ian O'Brien, Australia	2:27.8
1968	Felipe Munoz, Mexico	2:28.7
1972	John Hencken, United States	2:21.55
1976	David Wilkie, Great Britain	2:15.11
1980	Robertas Zhulpa, USSR	2:15.85
1984	Victor Davis, Canada	2:13.34
1988	Jozsef Szabo, Hungary	2:13.52
1992	Mike Barrowman, United States	2:10.16
1996	Norbert Rozsa, Hungary	2:12.57
2000	Domenico Fioravanti, Italy	2:10.87
2004	Kosuke Kitajima, Japan	2:09.44
2008	Kosuke Kitajima, Japan	2:07.64*

100-Meter Butterfly

Year	Champion	Time
1968	Doug Russell, United States	0:55.9
1972	Mark Spitz, United States	0:54.27
1976	Matt Vogel, United States	0:54.35
1980	Par Arvidsson, Sweden	0:54.92
1984	Michael Gross, W. Germany	0:53.08
1988	Anthony Nesty, Suriname	0:53.00
1992	Pablo Morales, United States	0:53.32
1996	Denis Pankratov, Russia	0:52.27
2000	Lars Froelander, Sweden	0:52.00
2004	Michael Phelps, United States	0:51.25
2008	Michael Phelps, United States	0:50.58*

200-Meter Butterfly

Year	Champion	Time
1956	William Yorzyk, United States	2:19.3
1960	Michael Troy, United States	2:12.8
1964	Kevin J. Berry, Australia	2:06.6
1968	Carl Robie, United States	2:08.7
1972	Mark Spitz, United States	2:00.70
1976	Mike Bruner, United States	1:59.23
1980	Sergei Fesenko, USSR	1:59.76
1984	Jon Sieben, Australia	1:57.04
1988	Michael Gross, W. Germany	1:56.94
1992	Mel Stewart, United States	1:56.26
1996	Denis Pankratov, Russia	1:56.51
2000	Tom Malchow, United States	1:55.35
2004	Michael Phelps, United States	1:54.04
2008	Michael Phelps, United States	1:52.03*

200-Meter Individual Medley

Year	Champion	Time
1968	Charles Hickcox, United States	2:12.0
1972	Gunnar Larsson, Sweden	2:07.17
1984	Alex Baumann, Canada	2:01.42
1988	Tamas Darnyi, Hungary	2:00.17
1992	Tamas Darnyi, Hungary	2:00.76
1996	Attila Czene, Hungary	1:59.91
2000	Massimiliano Rosolino, Italy	1:58.98
2004	Michael Phelps, United States	1:57.14
2008	Michael Phelps, United States	1:54.23*

400-Meter Individual Medley

Year	Champion	Time
1964	Dick Roth, United States	4:45.4
1968	Charles Hickcox, United States	4:48.4
1972	Gunnar Larsson, Sweden	4:31.98
1976	Rod Strachan, United States	4:23.68
1980	Aleksandr Sidorenko, USSR	4:22.89
1984	Alex Baumann, Canada	4:17.41
1988	Tamas Darnyi, Hungary	4:14.75
1992	Tamas Darnyi, Hungary	4:14.23
1996	Tom Dolan, United States	4:14.90
2000	Tom Dolan, United States	4:11.76
2004	Michael Phelps, United States	4:08.26
2008	Michael Phelps, United States	4:03.84*

4x100-Meter Freestyle Relay

Year	Champion	Time
1964	United States	3:31.2
1968	United States	3:31.7
1972	United States	3:26.42
1984	United States	3:19.03
1988	United States	3:16.53
1992	United States	3:16.74
1996	United States	3:15.41
2000	Australia	3:13.67
2004	South Africa	3:13.17
2008	United States	3:08.24*

4x200-Meter Freestyle Relay

Year	Champion	Time
1908	Great Britain	10:55.6
1912	Australia	10:11.6
1920	United States	10:04.4
1924	United States	9:53.4
1928	United States	9:36.2
1932	Japan	8:58.4
1936	Japan	8:51.5
1948	United States	8:46.0
1952	United States	8:31.1
1956	Australia	8:23.6
1960	United States	8:10.2
1964	United States	7:52.1
1968	United States	7:52.33
1972	United States	7:35.78
1976	United States	7:23.22
1980	USSR	7:23.50
1984	United States	7:15.69
1988	United States	7:12.51
1992	Unified Team	7:11.95
1996	United States	7:14.84
2000	Australia	7:07.05
2004	United States	7:07.33
2008	United States	6:58.56*

4x100-Meter Medley Relay

Year	Champion	Time
1960	United States	4:05.4
1964	United States	3:58.4
1968	United States	3:54.9
1972	United States	3:48.16
1976	United States	3:42.22
1980	Australia	3:45.70
1984	United States	3:39.30
1988	United States	3:36.93
1992	United States	3:36.93
1996	United States	3:34.84
2000	United States	3:33.73
2004	United States	3:30.68
2008	United States	3:29.34*

10km Marathon

Year	Champion	Time
2008	Maarten van der Weijden, Netherlands	1:51:51.6

Platform Diving

Year	Champion	Points
1904	Dr. G. E. Sheldon, United States	112.75
1908	Hjalmar Johansson, Sweden	183.75
1912	Erik Adlerz, Sweden	73.94
1920	Clarence Pinkston, United States	100.67
1924	Albert White, United States	97.46
1928	Pete Desjardins, United States	98.74
1932	Harold Smith, United States	124.80
1936	Marshall Wayne, United States	113.58
1948	Sammy Lee, United States	130.05
1952	Sammy Lee, United States	156.28
1956	Joaquin Capilla, Mexico	152.44
1960	Robert Webster, United States	165.56

Platform Diving	Points
1964 Robert Webster, United States	148.58
1968 Klaus Dibiasi, Italy	164.18
1972 Klaus Dibiasi, Italy	504.12
1976 Klaus Dibiasi, Italy	600.51
1980 Falk Hoffmann, E. Germany	835.65
1984 Greg Louganis, United States	710.91
1988 Greg Louganis, United States	638.61
1992 Sun Shuwei, China	677.31
1996 Dmitri Sautin, Russia	692.34
2000 Tian Liang, China	724.53
2004 Hu Jia, China	748.08
2008 Matthew Mitcham, Australia	537.95

Springboard Diving	Points
1908 Albert Zurner, Germany	85.50
1912 Paul Guenther, Germany	79.23
1920 Louis Kuehn, United States	675.40
1924 Albert White, United States	97.46
1928 Pete Desjardins, United States	185.04
1932 Michael Galitzen, United States	161.38
1936 Richard Degener, United States	163.57
1948 Bruce Harlan, United States	163.64
1952 David Browning, United States	205.29

Springboard Diving	Points
1956 Robert Clotworthy, United States	159.56
1960 Gary Tobian, United States	170.00
1964 Kenneth Sitzberger, United States	159.90
1968 Bernie Wrightson, United States	170.15
1972 Vladimir Vasin, USSR	594.09
1976 Phil Boggs, United States	619.52
1980 Aleksandr Portnov, USSR	905.02
1984 Greg Louganis, United States	754.41
1988 Greg Louganis, United States	730.80
1992 Mark Lenzi, United States	676.53
1996 Xiong Ni, China	701.46
2000 Xiong Ni, China	708.72
2004 Peng Bo, China	787.30
2008 He Chong, China	572.90

Synchronized Platform	Points
2004 Tian Liang and Yang Jinghui, China	383.88
2008 Lin Yue and Huo Liang, China	468.18

Synchronized Springboard	Points
2004 Nikolaos Siranidis and Thomas Bimis, Greece	353.34
2008 Wang Feng and Qin Kai, China	469.08

Swimming and Diving—Women

50-Meter Freestyle	Time
1988 Kristin Otto, E. Germany	0:25.49
1992 Yang Wenyi, China	0:24.76
1996 Amy Van Dyken, United States	0:24.87
2000 Inge de Bruijn, Netherlands	0:24.32
2004 Inge de Bruijn, Netherlands	0:24.58
2008 Britta Steffen, Germany	0:24.06*

100-Meter Freestyle	Time
1912 Fanny Durack, Australia	1:22.2
1920 Ethelda Bleibtrey, United States	1:13.6
1924 Ethel Lackie, United States	1:12.4
1928 Albina Osipowich, United States	1:11.0
1932 Helene Madison, United States	1:06.8
1936 Hendrika Mastenbroek, Holland	1:05.9
1948 Greta Andersen, Denmark	1:06.3
1952 Katalin Szoke, Hungary	1:06.8
1956 Dawn Fraser, Australia	1:02.0
1960 Dawn Fraser, Australia	1:01.2
1964 Dawn Fraser, Australia	0:59.5
1968 Jan Henne, United States	1:00.0
1972 Sandra Neilson, United States	0:58.59
1976 Kornelia Ender, E. Germany	0:55.65
1980 Barbara Krause, E. Germany	0:54.79
1984 Carrie Steinseifer, United States	0:55.92
Nancy Hogshead, United States (tie)	0:55.92
1988 Kristin Otto, E. Germany	0:54.93
1992 Zhuang Yong, China	0:54.64
1996 Li Jingyi, China	0:54.50
2000 Inge de Bruijn, Netherlands	0:53.83
2004 Jodie Henry, Australia	0:53.84
2008 Britta Steffen, Germany	0:53.12*

200-Meter Freestyle	Time
1968 Debbie Meyer, United States	2:10.5
1972 Shane Gould, Australia	2:03.56
1976 Kornelia Ender, E. Germany	1:59.26
1980 Barbara Krause, E. Germany	1:58.33
1984 Mary Wayte, United States	1:59.23
1988 Heike Friedrich, E. Germany	1:57.65
1992 Nicole Haislett, United States	1:57.90
1996 Claudia Poll, Costa Rica	1:58.16
2000 Susie O'Neill, Australia	1:58.24
2004 Camelia Potec, Romania	1:58.03
2008 Federica Pellegrini, Italy	1:54.82*

400-Meter Freestyle	Time
1924 Martha Norelius, United States	6:02.2
1928 Martha Norelius, United States	5:42.8
1932 Helene Madison, United States	5:28.5
1936 Hendrika Mastenbroek, Netherlands	5:26.4
1948 Ann Curtis, United States	5:17.8
1952 Valerie Gyenge, Hungary	5:12.1
1956 Lorraine Crapp, Australia	4:54.6
1960 Susan Chris von Saltza, United States	4:50.6
1964 Virginia Duenkel, United States	4:43.3
1968 Debbie Meyer, United States	4:31.8
1972 Shane Gould, Australia	4:19.44
1976 Petra Thuemer, E. Germany	4:09.89
1980 Ines Diers, E. Germany	4:08.76
1984 Tiffany Cohen, United States	4:07.10
1988 Janet Evans, United States	4:03.85
1992 Dagmar Hase, Germany	4:07.18
1996 Michelle Smith, Ireland	4:07.25

400-Meter Freestyle	Time
2000 Brooke Bennett, United States	4:05.80
2004 Laure Manaudou, France	4:05.34
2008 Rebecca Adlington, Great Britain	4:03.22

800-Meter Freestyle	Time
1968 Debbie Meyer, United States	9:24.0
1972 Keena Rothhammer, United States	8:53.68
1976 Petra Thuemer, E. Germany	8:37.14
1980 Michelle Ford, Australia	8:28.90
1984 Tiffany Cohen, United States	8:24.95
1988 Janet Evans, United States	8:20.20
1992 Janet Evans, United States	8:25.52
1996 Brooke Bennett, United States	8:27.89
2000 Brooke Bennett, United States	8:19.67
2004 Ai Shibata, Japan	8:24.54
2008 Rebecca Adlington, Great Britain	8:14.10*

100-Meter Backstroke	Time
1924 Sybil Bauer, United States	1:23.2
1928 Marie Braun, Netherlands	1:22.0
1932 Eleanor Holm, United States	1:19.4
1936 Dina Senff, Netherlands	1:18.9
1948 Karen Harup, Denmark	1:14.4
1952 Joan Harrison, South Africa	1:14.3
1956 Judy Grinham, Great Britain	1:12.9
1960 Lynn Burke, United States	1:09.3
1964 Cathy Ferguson, United States	1:07.7
1968 Kaye Hall, United States	1:06.2
1972 Melissa Belote, United States	1:05.78
1976 Ulrike Richter, E. Germany	1:01.83
1980 Rica Reinisch, E. Germany	1:00.86
1984 Theresa Andrews, United States	1:02.55
1988 Kristin Otto, E. Germany	1:00.89
1992 Krisztina Egerszegi, Hungary	1:00.68
1996 Beth Botsford, United States	1:01.19
2000 Diana Mocanu, Romania	1:00.21
2004 Natalie Coughlin, United States	1:00.37
2008 Natalie Coughlin, United States	0:58.96

200-Meter Backstroke	Time
1968 Pokey Watson, United States	2:24.8
1972 Melissa Belote, United States	2:19.19
1976 Ulrike Richter, E. Germany	2:13.43
1980 Rica Reinisch, E. Germany	2:11.77
1984 Jolanda De Rover, Netherlands	2:12.38
1988 Krisztina Egerszegi, Hungary	2:09.29
1992 Krisztina Egerszegi, Hungary	2:07.06
1996 Krisztina Egerszegi, Hungary	2:07.83
2000 Diana Mocanu, Romania	2:08.16
2004 Kirsty Coventry, Zimbabwe	2:09.19
2008 Kirsty Coventry, Zimbabwe	2:05.24*

100-Meter Breaststroke	Time
1968 Djurdjica Bjedov, Yugoslavia	1:15.8
1972 Cathy Carr, United States	1:13.58
1976 Hannelore Anke, E. Germany	1:11.16
1980 Ute Geweniger, E. Germany	1:10.22
1984 Petra Van Staveren, Netherlands	1:09.88
1988 Tania Dangalakova, Bulgaria	1:07.95
1992 Elena Roudkovskaia, Unified Team	1:08.00
1996 Penny Heyns, South Africa	1:07.73
2000 Megan Quann, United States	1:07.05
2004 Luo Xuejuan, China	1:06.64
2008 Leisel Jones, Australia	1:05.17*

200-Meter Breaststroke

Year	Name	Time
1924	Lucy Morton, Great Britain	3:33.2
1928	Hilde Schrader, Germany	3:12.6
1932	Clare Dennis, Australia	3:06.3
1936	Hideko Maehata, Japan	3:03.6
1948	Nelly Van Vliet, Netherlands	2:57.2
1952	Eva Szekely, Hungary	2:51.7
1956	Ursula Happe, Germany	2:53.1
1960	Anita Lonsbrough, Great Britain	2:49.5
1964	Galina Prozumenschikova, USSR	2:46.4
1968	Sharon Wichman, United States	2:44.4
1972	Beverly Whitfield, Australia	2:41.71
1976	Marina Koshevaia, USSR	2:33.35
1980	Lina Kachushite, USSR	2:29.54
1984	Anne Ottenbrite, Canada	2:30.38
1988	Silke Hoerner, E. Germany	2:26.71
1992	Kyoko Iwasaki, Japan	2:26.65
1996	Penny Heyns, South Africa	2:25.41
2000	Agnes Kovacs, Hungary	2:24.35
2004	Amanda Beard, United States	2:23.37
2008	Rebecca Soni, United States	2:20.22*

100-Meter Butterfly

Year	Name	Time
1956	Shelley Mann, United States	1:11.0
1960	Carolyn Schuler, United States	1:09.5
1964	Sharon Stouder, United States	1:04.7
1968	Lynn McClements, Australia	1:05.5
1972	Mayumi Aoki, Japan	1:03.34
1976	Kornelia Ender, E. Germany	1:00.13
1980	Caren Metschuck, E. Germany	1:00.42
1984	Mary T. Meagher, United States	0:59.26
1988	Kristin Otto, E. Germany	0:59.00
1992	Qian Hong, China	0:58.62
1996	Amy Van Dyken, United States	0:59.13
2000	Inge de Bruijn, Netherlands	0:56.61*
2004	Petria Thomas, Australia	0:57.72
2008	Lisbeth Trickett, Australia	0:56.73

200-Meter Butterfly

Year	Name	Time
1968	Ada Kok, Netherlands	2:24.7
1972	Karen Moe, United States	2:15.57
1976	Andrea Pollack, E. Germany	2:11.41
1980	Ines Geissler, E. Germany	2:10.44
1984	Mary T. Meagher, United States	2:06.90
1988	Kathleen Nord, E. Germany	2:09.51
1992	Summer Sanders, United States	2:08.67
1996	Susan O'Neill, Australia	2:07.76
2000	Misty Hyman, United States	2:05.88
2004	Otylia Jedrzejczak, Poland	2:06.05
2008	Liu Zige, China	2:04.18*

200-Meter Individual Medley

Year	Name	Time
1968	Claudia Kolb, United States	2:24.7
1972	Shane Gould, Australia	2:23.07
1984	Tracy Caulkins, United States	2:12.64
1988	Daniela Hunger, E. Germany	2:12.59
1992	Lin Li, China	2:11.65
1996	Michelle Smith, Ireland	2:13.93
2000	Yana Klochkova, Ukraine	2:10.68
2004	Yana Klochkova, Ukraine	2:11.14
2008	Stephanie Rice, Australia	2:08.45*

400-Meter Individual Medley

Year	Name	Time
1964	Donna de Varona, United States	5:18.7
1968	Claudia Kolb, United States	5:08.5
1972	Gail Neall, Australia	5:02.97
1976	Ulrike Tauber, E. Germany	4:42.77
1980	Petra Schneider, E. Germany	4:36.29
1984	Tracy Caulkins, United States	4:39.24
1988	Janet Evans, United States	4:37.76
1992	Krisztina Egerszegi, Hungary	4:36.54
1996	Michelle Smith, Ireland	4:39.18
2000	Yana Klochkova, Ukraine	4:33.59
2004	Yana Klochkova, Ukraine	4:34.83
2008	Stephanie Rice, Australia	4:29.45*

4x100-Meter Freestyle Relay

Year	Name	Time
1912	Great Britain	5:52.8
1920	United States	5:11.6
1924	United States	4:58.8
1928	United States	4:47.6
1932	United States	4:38.0
1936	Netherlands	4:36.0
1948	United States	4:29.2
1952	Hungary	4:24.4
1956	Australia	4:17.1
1960	United States	4:08.9
1964	United States	4:03.8
1968	United States	4:02.5

4x100-Meter Freestyle Relay

Year	Name	Time
1972	United States	3:55.19
1976	United States	3:44.82
1980	East Germany	3:42.71
1984	United States	3:43.43
1988	East Germany	3:40.63
1992	United States	3:39.46
1996	United States	3:39.29
2000	United States	3:36.61
2004	Australia	3:35.94
2008	Netherlands	3:33.76*

4x200-Meter Freestyle Relay

Year	Name	Time
1996	United States	7:59.87
2000	United States	7:57.80
2004	United States	7:53.42
2008	Australia	7:44.31*

4x100-Meter Medley Relay

Year	Name	Time
1960	United States	4:41.1
1964	United States	4:33.9
1968	United States	4:28.3
1972	United States	4:20.75
1976	East Germany	4:07.95
1980	East Germany	4:06.67
1984	United States	4:08.34
1988	East Germany	4:03.74
1992	United States	4:02.54
1996	United States	4:02.88
2000	United States	3:58.30
2004	Australia	3:57.32
2008	Australia	3:52.69*

10km Marathon

Year	Name	Time
2008	Larisa Ilchenko, Russia	1:59:27.7

Platform Diving

Year	Name	Points
1912	Greta Johansson, Sweden	39.90
1920	Stefani Fryland-Clausen, Denmark	34.60
1924	Caroline Smith, United States	33.20
1928	Elizabeth B. Pinkston, United States	31.60
1932	Dorothy Poynton, United States	40.26
1936	Dorothy Poynton Hill, United States	33.93
1948	Victoria M. Draves, United States	68.87
1952	Patricia McCormick, United States	79.37
1956	Patricia McCormick, United States	84.85
1960	Ingrid Kramer, Germany	91.28
1964	Lesley Bush, United States	99.80
1968	Milena Duchkova, Czechoslovakia	109.59
1972	Ulrika Knape, Sweden	390.00
1976	Elena Vaytsekhouskaya, USSR	406.59
1980	Martina Jaschke, E. Germany	596.25
1984	Zhou Jihong, China	435.51
1988	Xu Yanmei, China	445.20
1992	Fu Mingxia, China	461.43
1996	Fu Mingxia, China	521.58
2000	Laura Wilkinson, United States	543.75
2004	Chantelle Newbery, Australia	590.31
2008	Chen Ruolin, China	447.70

Springboard Diving

Year	Name	Points
1920	Aileen Riggin, United States	539.90
1924	Elizabeth Becker, United States	474.50
1928	Helen Meany, United States	78.62
1932	Georgia Coleman United States	87.52
1936	Marjorie Gestring, United States	89.27
1948	Victoria M. Draves, United States	108.74
1952	Patricia McCormick, United States	147.30
1956	Patricia McCormick, United States	142.36
1960	Ingrid Kramer, Germany	155.81
1964	Ingrid Engel-Kramer, Germany	145.00
1968	Sue Gossick, United States	150.77
1972	Micki King, United States	450.03
1976	Jenni Chandler, United States	506.19
1980	Irina Kalinina, USSR	725.91
1984	Sylvie Bernier, Canada	530.70
1988	Gao Min, China	580.23
1992	Gao Min, China	572.40
1996	Fu Mingxia, China	547.68
2000	Fu Mingxia, China	609.42
2004	Guo Jingjing, China	633.15
2008	Guo Jingjing, China	415.35

Synchronized Platform

Year	Name	Points
2004	Lao Lishi and Li Ting, China	352.14
2008	Wang Xin and Chen Ruolin, China	363.54

Synchronized Springboard

Year	Name	Points
2004	Wu Minxia and Guo Jingjing, China	336.90
2008	Guo Jingjing and Wu Minxia, China	343.50

Tennis

Men's Singles

1896	John Boland, Great Britain
1900	Hugh Lawrence Doherty, Great Britain
1904	Beals Coleman Wright, United States
1908	Josiah George Ritchie, Great Britain
1912	Charles Lyndhurst Winslow, South Africa
1920	Louis Raymond, South Africa
1924	Vincent Richards, United States
1988	Miloslav Mecir, Czechoslovakia
1992	Marc Rosset, Switzerland
1996	Andre Agassi, United States
2000	Eugueni Kafelnikov, Russia
2004	Nicolas Massu, Chile
2008	Rafael Nadal, Spain

Men's Doubles

1896	John Boland, Great Britain & Friedrick Traun, Germany
1900	Hugh Lawrence Doherty & Reginald Frank Doherty, Great Britain
1904	Edgar Welch Leonard & Beals Coleman Wright, United States
1908	George Whiteside Hillyard & Reginald Frank Doherty, Great Britain
1912	Harry Austin Kitson & Charles Lyndhurst Winslow, South Africa
1920	Oswald Graham Noel Turnbull & Maxwell Woosnam, Great Britain
1924	Vincent Richards & Francis Townsend Hunter, United States
1988	Kenneth Flach & Robert A. Seguso, United States

Men's Doubles

1992	Boris Franz Becker & Michael Stich, Germany
1996	Mark Woodforde & Todd Woodbridge, Australia
2000	Sebastien Lareau & Daniel Nestor, Canada
2004	Fernando Gonzales & Nicolas Massu, Chile
2008	Roger Federer & Stanislas Wawrinka, Switzerland

Women's Singles

1900	Charlotte Cooper, Great Britain
1908	Dorothy Katherine Chambers, Great Britain
1912	Marguerite Broquedis, France
1920	Suzanne Lenglen, France
1924	Helen Wills, United States
1988	Steffi Graf, W. Germany
1992	Jennifer Capriati, United States
1996	Lindsay Davenport, United States
2000	Venus Williams, United States
2004	Justine Henin-Hardenne, Belgium
2008	Elena Dementieva, Russia

Women's Doubles

1920	Winifred Margaret McNair & Kathleen McKane, Great Britain
1924	Hazel Virginia Wightman & Helen Wills, United States
1988	Pamela Howard Shriver & Zina Garrison, United States
1992	Gigi Fernandez & Mary Joe Fernandez, United States
1996	Gigi Fernandez & Mary Joe Fernandez, United States
2000	Venus Williams & Serena Williams, United States
2004	Ting Li & Tian Tian Sun, China
2008	Serena Williams & Venus Williams, United States

Track and Field—Men

100-Meter Run		Time
1896	Thomas Burke, United States	12.0s
1900	Francis W. Jarvis, United States	11.0s
1904	Archie Hahn, United States	11.0s
1908	Reginald Walker, South Africa	10.8s
1912	Ralph Craig, United States	10.8s
1920	Charles Paddock, United States	10.8s
1924	Harold Abrahams, Great Britain	10.6s
1928	Percy Williams, Canada	10.8s
1932	Eddie Tolan, United States	10.3s
1936	Jesse Owens, United States	10.3s
1948	Harrison Dillard, United States	10.3s
1952	Lindy Remigino, United States	10.4s
1956	Bobby Morrow, United States	10.5s
1960	Armin Hary, Germany	10.2s
1964	Bob Hayes, United States	10.0s
1968	Jim Hines, United States	9.95s
1972	Valery Borzov, USSR	10.14s
1976	Hasely Crawford, Trinidad	10.06s
1980	Allan Wells, Great Britain	10.25s
1984	Carl Lewis, United States	9.99s
1988	Carl Lewis, United States	9.92s
1992	Linford Christie, Great Britain	9.96s
1996	Donovan Bailey, Canada	9.84s
2000	Maurice Greene, United States	9.87s
2004	Justin Gatlin, United States	9.85s
2008	Usain Bolt, Jamaica	9.69s*

200-Meter Run		Time
1900	Walter Tewksbury, United States	22.2s
1904	Archie Hahn, United States	21.6s
1908	Robert Kerr, Canada	22.6s
1912	Ralph Craig, United States	21.7s
1920	Allan Woodring, United States	22.0s
1924	Jackson Scholz, United States	21.6s
1928	Percy Williams, Canada	21.8s
1932	Eddie Tolan, United States	21.2s
1936	Jesse Owens, United States	20.7s
1948	Mel Patton, United States	21.1s
1952	Andrew Stanfield, United States	20.7s
1956	Bobby Morrow, United States	20.6s
1960	Livio Berruti, Italy	20.5s
1964	Henry Carr, United States	20.3s
1968	Tommie Smith, United States	19.83s
1972	Valeri Borzov, USSR	20.00s
1976	Donald Quarrie, Jamaica	20.23s
1980	Pietro Mennea, Italy	20.19s
1984	Carl Lewis, United States	19.80s
1988	Joe DeLoach, United States	19.75s
1992	Mike Marsh, United States	20.01s
1996	Michael Johnson, United States	19.32s
2000	Konstantinos Kenteris, Greece	20.09s
2004	Shawn Crawford, United States	19.79s
2008	Usain Bolt, Jamaica	19.30s*

400-Meter Run		Time
1896	Thomas Burke, United States	54.2s
1900	Maxey Long, United States	49.4s
1904	Harry Hillman, United States	49.2s
1908	Wyndham Halswelle, Great Brit., walkover	50.0s
1912	Charles Reidpath, United States	48.2s
1920	Bevil Rudd, South Africa	49.6s
1924	Eric Liddell, Great Britain	47.6s
1928	Ray Barbuti, United States	47.8s
1932	William Carr, United States	46.2s
1936	Archie Williams, United States	46.5s
1948	Arthur Wint, Jamaica	46.2s
1952	George Rhoden, Jamaica	45.9s
1956	Charles Jenkins, United States	46.7s
1960	Otis Davis, United States	44.9s
1964	Michael Larrabee, United States	45.1s
1968	Lee Evans, United States	43.86s
1972	Vincent Matthews, United States	44.66s
1976	Alberto Juantorena, Cuba	44.26s
1980	Viktor Markin, USSR	44.60s
1984	Alonzo Babers, United States	44.27s
1988	Steven Lewis, United States	43.87s
1992	Quincy Watts, United States	43.50s
1996	Michael Johnson, United States	43.49s*
2000	Michael Johnson, United States	43.84s
2004	Jeremy Wariner, United States	44.00s
2008	LaShawn Merritt, United States	43.75s

800-Meter Run		Time
1896	Edwin Flack, Australia	2m. 11s
1900	Alfred Tysoe, Great Britain	2m. 1.2s
1904	James Lightbody, United States	1m. 56s
1908	Mel Sheppard, United States	1m. 52.8s
1912	James Meredith, United States	1m. 51.9s
1920	Albert Hill, Great Britain	1m. 53.4s
1924	Douglas Lowe, Great Britain	1m. 52.4s
1928	Douglas Lowe, Great Britain	1m. 51.8s
1932	Thomas Hampson, Great Britain	1m. 49.8s
1936	John Woodruff, United States	1m. 52.9s
1948	Mal Whitfield, United States	1m. 49.2s
1952	Mal Whitfield, United States	1m. 49.2s
1956	Thomas Courtney, United States	1m. 47.7s
1960	Peter Snell, New Zealand	1m. 46.3s
1964	Peter Snell, New Zealand	1m. 45.1s
1968	Ralph Doubell, Australia	1m. 44.3s
1972	Dave Wottle, United States	1m. 45.9s
1976	Alberto Juantorena, Cuba	1m. 43.50s
1980	Steve Ovett, Great Britain	1m. 45.40s
1984	Joaquim Cruz, Brazil	1m. 43.00s
1988	Paul Ereng, Kenya	1m. 43.45s
1992	William Tanui, Kenya	1m. 43.66s
1996	Vebjoern Rodal, Norway	1m. 42.58s*
2000	Nils Schumann, Germany	1m. 45.08s
2004	Yuriy Borzakovskiy, Russia	1m. 44.45s
2008	Wilfred Bungei, Kenya	1m. 44.65s

1,500-Meter Run

Year	Champion	Time
1896	Edwin Flack, Australia	4m. 33.2s
1900	Charles Bennett, Great Britain	4m. 6.2s
1904	James Lightbody, United States	4m. 5.4s
1908	Mel Sheppard, United States	4m. 3.4s
1912	Arnold Jackson, Great Britain	3m. 56.8s
1920	Albert Hill, Great Britain	4m. 1.8s
1924	Paavo Nurmi, Finland	3m. 53.6s
1928	Harry Larva, Finland	3m. 53.2s
1932	Luigi Beccali, Italy	3m. 51.2s
1936	Jack Lovelock, New Zealand	3m. 47.8s
1948	Henri Eriksson, Sweden	3m. 49.8s
1952	Joseph Barthel, Luxembourg	3m. 45.2s
1956	Ron Delany, Ireland	3m. 41.2s
1960	Herb Elliott, Australia	3m. 35.6s
1964	Peter Snell, New Zealand	3m. 38.1s
1968	Kipchoge Keino, Kenya	3m. 34.9s
1972	Pekka Vasala, Finland	3m. 36.3s
1976	John Walker, New Zealand	3m. 39.17s
1980	Sebastian Coe, Great Britain	3m. 38.4s
1984	Sebastian Coe, Great Britain	3m. 32.53s
1988	Peter Rono, Kenya	3m. 35.96s
1992	Fermin Cacho Ruiz, Spain	3m. 40.12s
1996	Noureddine Morceli, Algeria	3m. 35.78s
2000	Noah Ngeny, Kenya	3m. 32.07s*
2004	Hicham el-Guerrouj, Morocco	3m. 34.18s
2008	Rashid Ramzi, Bahrain	3m. 32.94s

3,000-Meter Steeplechase

Year	Champion	Time
1920	Percy Hodge, Great Britain	10m. 0.4s
1924	Willie Ritola, Finland	9m. 33.6s
1928	Toivo Loukola, Finland	9m. 21.8s
1932	Volmari Iso-Hollo, Finland	10m. 33.4s
	(About 3,450 m; extra lap by error.)	
1936	Volmari Iso-Hollo, Finland	9m. 3.8s
1948	Thore Sjoestrand, Sweden	9m. 4.6s
1952	Horace Ashenfelter, United States	8m. 45.4s
1956	Chris Brasher, Great Britain	8m. 41.2s
1960	Zdzislaw Krzyszkowiak, Poland	8m. 34.2s
1964	Gaston Roelants, Belgium	8m. 30.8s
1968	Amos Biwott, Kenya	8m. 51s
1972	Kipchoge Keino, Kenya	8m. 23.6s
1976	Anders Garderud, Sweden	8m. 08.2s
1980	Bronislaw Malinowski, Poland	8m. 09.7s
1984	Julius Korir, Kenya	8m. 11.8s
1988	Julius Kariuki, Kenya	8m. 05.51s*
1992	Matthew Birir, Kenya	8m. 08.84s
1996	Joseph Keter, Kenya	8m. 07.12s
2000	Reuben Kosgei, Kenya	8m. 21.43s
2004	Ezekiel Kemboi, Kenya	8m. 05.81s
2008	Brimin Kiprop Kirpruto, Kenya	8m. 10.34s

5,000-Meter Run

Year	Champion	Time
1912	Hannes Kolehmainen, Finland	14m. 36.6s
1920	Joseph Guillemot, France	14m. 55.6s
1924	Paavo Nurmi, Finland	14m. 31.2s
1928	Willie Ritola, Finland	14m. 38s
1932	Lauri Lehtinen, Finland	14m. 30s
1936	Gunnar Hockert, Finland	14m. 22.2s
1948	Gaston Reiff, Belgium	14m. 17.6s
1952	Emil Zatopek, Czechoslovakia	14m. 06.6s
1956	Vladimir Kuts, USSR	13m. 39.6s
1960	Murray Halberg, New Zealand	13m. 43.4s
1964	Bob Schul, United States	13m. 48.8s
1968	Mohamed Gammoudi, Tunisia	14m. 05.0s
1972	Lasse Viren, Finland	13m. 26.4s
1976	Lasse Viren, Finland	13m. 24.76s
1980	Miruts Yifter, Ethiopia	13m. 21.0s
1984	Said Aouita, Morocco	13m. 05.59s
1988	John Ngugi, Kenya	13m. 11.70s
1992	Dieter Baumann, Germany	13m. 12.52s
1996	Venuste Niyongabo, Burundi	13m. 07.96s
2000	Millon Wolde, Ethiopia	13m. 35.49s
2004	Hicham el-Guerrouj, Morocco	13m. 14.39s
2008	Kenenisa Bekele, Ethiopia	12m. 57.82s*

10,000-Meter Run

Year	Champion	Time
1912	Hannes Kolehmainen, Finland	31m. 20.8s
1920	Paavo Nurmi, Finland	31m. 45.8s
1924	Willie Ritola, Finland	30m. 23.2s
1928	Paavo Nurmi, Finland	30m. 18.8s
1932	Janusz Kusocinski, Poland	30m. 11.4s
1936	Ilmari Salminen, Finland	30m. 15.4s
1948	Emil Zatopek, Czechoslovakia	29m. 59.6s
1952	Emil Zatopek, Czechoslovakia	29m. 17.0s
1956	Vladimir Kuts, USSR	28m. 45.6s
1960	Pyotr Bolotnikov, USSR	28m. 32.2s
1964	Billy Mills, United States	28m. 24.4s
1968	Naftali Temu, Kenya	29m. 27.4s
1972	Lasse Viren, Finland	27m. 38.4s

10,000-Meter Run

Year	Champion	Time
1976	Lasse Viren, Finland	27m. 40.4s
1980	Miruts Yifter, Ethiopia	27m. 42.7s
1984	Alberto Cova, Italy	27m. 47.54s
1988	Brahim Boutaib, Morocco	27m. 21.46s
1992	Khalid Skah, Morocco	27m. 46.70s
1996	Haile Gebrselassie, Ethiopia	27m. 07.34s
2000	Haile Gebrselassie, Ethiopia	27m. 18.20s
2004	Kenenisa Bekele, Ethiopia	27m. 05.10s
2008	Kenenisa Bekele, Ethiopia	27m. 01.17s*

Marathon

Year	Champion	Time
1896	Spiridon Loues, Greece	2h. 58m. 50s
1900	Michel Theato, France	2h. 59m. 45s
1904	Thomas Hicks, United States	3h. 28m. 63s
1908	John J. Hayes, United States	2h. 55m. 18.4s
1912	Kenneth McArthur, South Africa	2h. 36m. 54.8s
1920	Hannes Kolehmainen, Finland	2h. 32m. 35.8s
1924	Albin Stenroos, Finland	2h. 41m. 22.6s
1928	A.B. El Ouafi, France	2h. 32m. 57s
1932	Juan Zabala, Argentina	2h. 31m. 36s
1936	Kijung Son, Japan (Korean)	2h. 29m. 19.2s
1948	Delfo Cabrera, Argentina	2h. 34m. 51.6s
1952	Emil Zatopek, Czechoslovakia	2h. 23m. 03.2s
1956	Alain Mimoun, France	2h. 25m.
1960	Abebe Bikila, Ethiopia	2h. 15m. 16.2s
1964	Abebe Bikila, Ethiopia	2h. 12m. 11.2s
1968	Mamo Wolde, Ethiopia	2h. 20m. 26.4s
1972	Frank Shorter, United States	2h. 12m. 19.8s
1976	Waldemar Cierpinski, E. Germany	2h. 09m. 55s
1980	Waldemar Cierpinski, E. Germany	2h. 11m. 03s
1984	Carlos Lopes, Portugal	2h. 09m. 21s
1988	Gelindo Bordin, Italy	2h. 10m. 32s
1992	Hwang Young-Cho, S. Korea	2h. 13m. 23s
1996	Josia Thugwane, South Africa	2h. 12m. 36s
2000	Gezahgne Abera, Ethiopia	2h. 10m. 11s
2004	Stefano Baldino, Italy	2h. 10m. 55s
2008	Samuel Kamau Wansiru, Kenya	2h. 06m. 32s*

4x100-Meter Relay

Year	Team	Time
1912	Great Britain	42.4s
1920	United States	42.2s
1924	United States	41.0s
1928	United States	41.0s
1932	United States	40.0s
1936	United States	39.8s
1948	United States	40.6s
1952	United States	40.1s
1956	United States	39.5s
1960	Germany (U.S. disqualified)	39.5s
1964	United States	39.0s
1968	United States	38.24s
1972	United States	38.19s
1976	United States	38.33s
1980	USSR	38.26s
1984	United States	37.83s
1988	USSR (U.S. disqualified)	38.19s
1992	United States	37.40s
1996	Canada	37.69s
2000	United States	37.61s
2004	Great Britain	38.07s
2008	Jamaica	37.10s*

4x400-Meter Relay

Year	Team	Time
1908	United States	3m. 29.4s
1912	United States	3m. 16.6s
1920	Great Britain	3m. 22.2s
1924	United States	3m. 16s
1928	United States	3m. 14.2s
1932	United States	3m. 08.2s
1936	Great Britain	3m. 9s
1948	United States	3m. 10.4s
1952	Jamaica	3m. 03.9s
1956	United States	3m. 04.8s
1960	United States	3m. 02.2s
1964	United States	3m. 00.7s
1968	United States	2m. 56.16s
1972	Kenya	2m. 59.8s
1976	United States	2m. 58.65s
1980	USSR	3m. 01.1s
1984	United States	2m. 57.91s
1988	United States	2m. 56.16s
1992	United States	2m. 55.74s
1996	United States	2m. 55.99s
2000	United States (a)	2m. 56.35s
2004	United States	2m. 55.91s
2008	United States	2m. 55.39s*

(a) The International Olympic Committee stripped the 2000 U.S. relay team of their medals in Aug. 2008 after one of the team's members, Antonio Pettigrew, admitted to doping.

20-Kilometer Walk	Time
1956 Leonid Spirin, USSR	1h. 31m. 27.4s
1960 Vladimir Golubnichy, USSR	1h. 33m. 7.2s
1964 Kenneth Mathews, Great Britain	1h. 29m. 34.0s
1968 Vladimir Golubnichy, USSR	1h. 33m. 58.4s
1972 Peter Frenkel, E. Germany	1h. 26m. 42.4s
1976 Daniel Bautista, Mexico	1h. 24m. 40.6s
1980 Maurizio Damilano, Italy	1h. 23m. 35.5s
1984 Ernesto Canto, Mexico	1h. 23m. 13.0s
1988 Josef Pribilinec, Czechoslovakia	1h. 19m. 57.0s
1992 Daniel Plaza Montero, Spain	1h. 21m. 45.0s
1996 Jefferson Perez, Ecuador	1h. 20m. 07s
2000 Robert Korzeniowski, Poland	1h. 18m. 59.0s*
2004 Ivano Brugnetti, Italy	1h. 19m. 40s
2008 Valeriy Borchin, Russia	1h. 19m. 01s

50-Kilometer Walk	Time
1932 Thomas W. Green, Great Britain	4h. 50m. 10s
1936 Harold Whitlock, Great Britain	4h. 30m. 41.4s
1948 John Ljunggren, Sweden	4h. 41m. 52s
1952 Giuseppe Dordoni, Italy	4h. 28m. 07.8s
1956 Norman Read, New Zealand	4h. 30m. 42.8s
1960 Donald Thompson, Great Britain	4h. 25m. 30s
1964 Abdon Pamich, Italy	4h. 11m. 12.4s
1968 Christoph Hohne, E. Germany	4h. 20m. 13.6s
1972 Bern Kannenberg, W. Germany	3h. 56m. 11.6s
1980 Hartwig Gauter, E. Germany	3h. 49m. 24.0s
1984 Raul Gonzalez, Mexico	3h. 47m. 26.0s
1988 Vyacheslav Ivanenko, USSR	3h. 38m. 29.0s
1992 Andrei Perlov, Unified Team	3h. 50m. 13.0s
1996 Robert Korzeniowski, Poland	3h. 43m. 30s
2000 Robert Korzeniowski, Poland	3h. 42m. 22s
2004 Robert Korzeniowski, Poland	3h. 38m. 46s
2008 Alex Schwazer, Italy	3h. 37m. 09s*

110-Meter Hurdles	Time
1896 Thomas Curtis, United States	17.6s
1900 Alvin Kraenzlein, United States	15.4s
1904 Frederick Schule, United States	16.0s
1908 Forrest Smithson, United States	15.0s
1912 Frederick Kelly, United States	15.1s
1920 Earl Thomson, Canada	14.8s
1924 Daniel Kinsey, United States	15.0s
1928 Sydney Atkinson, South Africa	14.8s
1932 George Saling, United States	14.6s
1936 Forrest Towns, United States	14.2s
1948 William Porter, United States	13.9s
1952 Harrison Dillard, United States	13.7s
1956 Lee Calhoun, United States	13.5s
1960 Lee Calhoun, United States	13.8s
1964 Hayes Jones, United States	13.6s
1968 Willie Davenport, United States	13.33s
1972 Rod Milburn, United States	13.24s
1976 Guy Drut, France	13.30s
1980 Thomas Munkelt, E. Germany	13.39s
1984 Roger Kingdom, United States	13.20s
1988 Roger Kingdom, United States	12.98s
1992 Mark McCoy, Canada	13.12s
1996 Allen Johnson, United States	12.95s
2000 Anier Garcia, Cuba	13.00s
2004 Liu Xiang, China	12.91s*
2008 Dayron Robles, Cuba	12.93s

400-Meter Hurdles	Time
1900 J. W. B. Tewksbury, United States	57.6s
1904 Harry Hillman, United States	53.0s
1908 Charles Bacon, United States	55.0s
1920 Frank Loomis, United States	54.0s
1924 F. Morgan Taylor, United States	52.6s
1928 Lord Burghley, Great Britain	53.4s
1932 Robert Tisdall, Ireland	51.7s
1936 Glenn Hardin, United States	52.4s
1948 Roy Cochran, United States	51.1s
1952 Charles Moore, United States	50.8s
1956 Glenn Davis, United States	50.1s
1960 Glenn Davis, United States	49.3s
1964 Rex Cawley, United States	49.6s
1968 Dave Hemery, Great Britain	48.12s
1972 John Akii-Bua, Uganda	47.82s
1976 Edwin Moses, United States	47.64s
1980 Volker Beck, E. Germany	48.70s
1984 Edwin Moses, United States	47.75s
1988 Andre Phillips, United States	47.19s
1992 Kevin Young, United States	46.78s*
1996 Derrick Adkins, United States	47.54s

400-Meter Hurdles	Time
2000 Angelo Taylor, United States	47.50s
2004 Felix Sanchez, Dominican Republic	47.63s
2008 Angelo Taylor, United States	47.25s

Discus Throw	Dist.	
1896 Robert Garrett, United States	29.15m	(95' 7")
1900 Rudolf Bauer, Hungary	36.04m	(118' 3")
1904 Martin Sheridan, United States	39.28m	(128' 10")
1908 Martin Sheridan, United States	40.89m	(134' 1")
1912 Armas Taipale, Finland	45.21m	(148' 3")
1920 Elmer Niklander, Finland	44.68m	(146' 7")
1924 Clarence Houser, United States	46.15m	(151' 4")
1928 Clarence Houser, United States	47.32m	(155' 3")
1932 John Anderson, United States	49.49m	(162' 4")
1936 Ken Carpenter, United States	50.48m	(165' 7")
1948 Adolfo Consolini, Italy	52.78m	(173' 2")
1952 Sim Iness, United States	55.03m	(180' 6")
1956 Al Oerter, United States	56.36m	(184' 11")
1960 Al Oerter, United States	59.18m	(194' 2")
1964 Al Oerter, United States	61.00m	(200' 1")
1968 Al Oerter, United States	64.78m	(212' 6")
1972 Ludvik Danek, Czechoslovakia	64.40m	(211' 3")
1976 Mac Wilkins, United States	67.50m	(221' 5")
1980 Viktor Rashchupkin, USSR	66.64m	(218' 8")
1984 Rolf Dannenberg, W. Germany	66.60m	(218' 6")
1988 Jurgen Schult, E. Germany	68.82m	(225' 9")
1992 Romas Ubartas, Lithuania	65.12m	(213' 8")
1996 Lars Riedel, Germany	69.40m	(227' 8")
2000 Virgilijus Alekna, Lithuania	69.30m	(227' 4")
2004 Virgilijus Alekna, Lithuania	69.89m	(228' 9¾")*
2008 Gerd Kanter, Estonia	68.82m	(225' 9½")

Hammer Throw	Dist.	
1900 John Flanagan, United States	49.73m	(163' 1")
1904 John Flanagan, United States	51.22m	(168' 0")
1908 John Flanagan, United States	51.92m	(170' 4")
1912 Matt McGrath, United States	54.74m	(179' 7")
1920 Pat Ryan, United States	52.86m	(173' 5")
1924 Fred Tootell, United States	53.28m	(174' 10")
1928 Patrick O'Callaghan, Ireland	51.38m	(168' 7")
1932 Patrick O'Callaghan, Ireland	53.92m	(176' 11")
1936 Karl Hein, Germany	56.48m	(185' 4")
1948 Imre Németh, Hungary	56.06m	(183' 11")
1952 József Csérmák, Hungary	60.34m	(197' 11")
1956 Harold Connolly, United States	63.18m	(207' 3")
1960 Vasily Rudenkov, USSR	67.10m	(202' 0")
1964 Romuald Klim, USSR	69.74m	(228' 10")
1968 Gyula Zsivótsky, Hungary	73.36m	(240' 8")
1972 Anatoly Bondarchuk, USSR	75.50m	(247' 8")
1976 Yuri Syedykh, USSR	77.52m	(254' 4")
1980 Yuri Syedykh, USSR	81.80m	(268' 4")
1984 Juha Tiainen, Finland	78.08m	(256' 2")
1988 Sergei Litvinov, USSR	84.80m	(278' 2")*
1992 Andrey Abduvaliyev, Unified Team	82.54m	(270' 9")
1996 Balázs Kiss, Hungary	81.24m	(266' 6")
2000 Szymon Ziolkowski, Poland	80.02m	(262' 6")
2004 Koji Murofushi, Japan	82.91m	(272')
2008 Primoz Kozmus, Slovenia	82.02m	(269' 1")

High Jump	Height	
1896 Ellery Clark, United States	1.81m	(5'11¼")
1900 Irving Baxter, United States	1.90m	(6' 2¾")
1904 Samuel Jones, United States	1.80m	(5' 11")
1908 Harry Porter, United States	1.90m	(6' 2¾")
1912 Alma Richards, United States	1.93m	(6' 4")
1920 Richmond Landon, United States	1.93m	(6' 4")
1924 Harold Osborn, United States	1.98m	(6' 6")
1928 Robert W. King, United States	1.94m	(6' 4¼")
1932 Duncan McNaughton, Canada	1.97m	(6' 5½")
1936 Cornelius Johnson, United States	2.03m	(6' 8")
1948 John L. Winter, Australia	1.98m	(6' 6")
1952 Walter Davis, United States	2.04m	(6' 8¼")
1956 Charles Dumas, United States	2.12m	(6' 11½")
1960 Robert Shavlakadze, USSR	2.16m	(7' 1")
1964 Valery Brumel, USSR	2.18m	(7' 1¾")
1968 Dick Fosbury, United States	2.24m	(7' 4¼")
1972 Jüri Tarmak, USSR	2.23m	(7' 3¾")
1976 Jacek Wszola, Poland	2.25m	(7' 4½")
1980 Gerd Wessig, E. Germany	2.36m	(7' 8¾")
1984 Dietmar Mögenburg, W. Germany	2.35m	(7' 8½")
1988 Hennady Avdyeyenko, USSR	2.38m	(7' 9¾")
1992 Javier Sotomayor Sanabria, Cuba	2.34m	(7' 8)
1996 Charles Austin, United States	2.39m	(7' 10")*
2000 Sergey Kliugin, Russia	2.35m	(7' 8½")
2004 Stefen Holm, Sweden	2.36m	(7' 9¾")
2008 Andrey Silnov, Russia	2.36m	(7' 9¾")

Javelin Throw	Dist.	
1908 Erik Lemming, Sweden	54.82m	(179' 10")
1912 Erik Lemming, Sweden	60.64m	(198' 11")
1920 Jonni Myyrä, Finland	64.78m	(215' 10")
1924 Jonni Myyrä, Finland	62.96m	(206' 7")
1928 Eric Lundkvist, Sweden	66.60m	(218' 6")
1932 Matti Järvinen, Finland	72.70m	(238' 6")
1936 Gerhard Stöck, Germany	71.84m	(235' 8")
1948 Kai Tapio Rautavaara, Finland	69.76m	(228' 11")
1952 Cy Young, United States	73.78m	(242' 1")
1956 Egil Danielsen, Norway	85.70m	(281' 2")
1960 Viktor Tsibulenko, USSR	84.64m	(277' 8")
1964 Pauli Nevala, Finland	82.66m	(271' 2")
1968 Janis Lusis, USSR	90.10m	(295' 7")
1972 Klaus Wolfermann, W. Germany	90.48m	(296' 10")
1976 Miklós Németh, Hungary	94.58m	(310' 4")
1980 Dainis Kula, USSR	91.20m	(299' 2")
1984 Arto Härkönen, Finland	86.76m	(284' 8")
1988 Tapio Korjus, Finland	84.28m	(276' 6")
1992 Jan Zelezny, Czechoslovakia	89.66m	(294' 2")
1996 Jan Zelezny, Czech Republic	88.16m	(289' 3")
2000 Jan Zelezny, Czech Republic	90.17m	(295' 9½")
2004 Andreas Thorkildsen, Norway	86.50m	(283' 10")
2008 Andreas Thorkildsen, Norway	90.57m	(297' 1¾")

Note: New records were kept after javelin was modified in 1986.

Long Jump	Dist.	
1896 Ellery Clark, United States	6.35m	(20' 10")
1900 Alvin Kraenzlein, United States	7.18m	(23' 6¾")
1904 Meyer Prinstein, United States	7.34m	(24' 1")
1908 Frank Irons, United States	7.48m	(24' 6½")
1912 Albert Gutterson, United States	7.60m	(24' 11¼")
1920 William Petterssen, Sweden	7.15m	(23' 5½")
1924 William DeHart Hubbard, U.S.	7.44m	(24' 5")
1928 Edward B. Hamm, United States	7.73m	(25' 4½")
1932 Edward Gordon, United States	7.64m	(25' ¾")
1936 Jesse Owens, United States	8.06m	(26' 5½")
1948 Willie Steele, United States	7.82m	(25' 8")
1952 Jerome Biffle, United States	7.57m	(24' 10")
1956 Gregory Bell, United States	7.83m	(25' 8¼")
1960 Ralph Boston, United States	8.12m	(26' 7¾")
1964 Lynn Davies, Great Britain	8.07m	(26' 5¾")
1968 Bob Beamon, United States	8.90m	(29' 2½")*
1972 Randy Williams, United States	8.24m	(27' ½")
1976 Arnie Robinson, United States	8.35m	(27' 4¾")
1980 Lutz Dombrowski, E. Germany	8.54m	(28' ¼")
1984 Carl Lewis, United States	8.54m	(28' ¼")
1988 Carl Lewis, United States	8.72m	(28' 7½")
1992 Carl Lewis, United States	8.67m	(28' 5½")
1996 Carl Lewis, United States	8.50m	(27' 10¾")
2000 Ivan Pedroso, Cuba	8.55m	(28' ¾")
2004 Dwight Phillips, United States	8.59m	(28' 2¼")
2008 Irving Jahir Saladino Aranda, Panama	8.34m	(27' 4¼")

Pole Vault	Height	
1896 William Welles Hoyt, United States	3.30m	(10' 10")
1900 Irving Baxter, United States	3.30m	(10' 10")
1904 Charles Dvorak, United States	3.50m	(11' 6")
1908 A. C. Gilbert, United States; Edward Cooke Jr., United States	3.71m	(12' 2")
1920 Frank Foss, United States	4.09m	(13' 5")
1924 Lee Barnes, United States	3.95m	(12' 11½")
1928 Sabin W. Carr, United States	4.20m	(13' 9¼")
1932 William Miller, United States	4.31m	(14' 1¾")
1936 Earle Meadows, United States	4.35m	(14' 3¼")
1948 Guinn Smith, United States	4.30m	(14' 1¼")
1952 Robert Richards, United States	4.55m	(14' 11¼")
1956 Robert Richards, United States	4.56m	(14' 11½")
1960 Don Bragg, United States	4.70m	(15' 5")
1964 Fred Hansen, United States	5.10m	(16' 8¾")
1968 Bob Seagren, United States	5.40m	(17' 8½")
1972 Wolfgang Nordwig, E. Germany	5.50m	(18' ½")
1976 Tadeusz Slusarski, Poland	5.50m	(18' ½")
1980 Wladyslaw Kozakiewicz, Poland	5.78m	(18' 11½")
1984 Pierre Quinon, France	5.75m	(18' 10¼")
1988 Sergei Bubka, USSR	5.90m	(19' 4¼")
1992 Maksim Tarassov, Unified Team	5.80m	(19' ¼")
1996 Jean Galfione, France	5.92m	(19' 5")
2000 Nick Hysong, United States	5.90m	(19' 4¼")
2004 Timothy Mack, United States	5.95m	(19' 6¼")
2008 Steve Hooker, Australia	5.96m	(19' 6¾")*

Shot Put	Dist.	
1896 Robert Garrett, United States	11.22m	(36' 9¾")
1900 Richard Sheldon, United States	14.10m	(46' 3¼")
1904 Ralph Rose, United States	14.81m	(48' 7")
1908 Ralph Rose, United States	14.21m	(46' 7½")
1912 Pat McDonald, United States	15.34m	(50' 4")
1920 Ville Pörhölä, Finland	14.81m	(48' 7¼")
1924 L. Clarence Houser, United States	14.99m	(49' 2¼")
1928 John Kuck, United States	15.87m	(52' ¾")
1932 Leo Sexton, United States	16.00m	(52' 6")
1936 Hans Woellke, Germany	16.20m	(53' 1¾")
1948 Wilbur Thompson, United States	17.12m	(56' 2")
1952 W. Parry O'Brien, United States	17.41m	(57' 1½")
1956 W. Parry O'Brien, United States	18.57m	(60' 11¼")
1960 William Nieder, United States	19.68m	(64' 6¾")
1964 Dallas Long, United States	20.33m	(66' 8½")
1968 Randy Matson, United States	20.54m	(67' 4¾")
1972 Wladyslaw Komar, Poland	21.18m	(69' 6")
1976 Udo Beyer, E. Germany	21.05m	(69' ¾")
1980 Vladimir Kyselyov, USSR	21.35m	(70' ½")
1984 Alessandro Andrei, Italy	21.26m	(69' 9")
1988 Ulf Timmermann, E. Germany	22.47m	(73' 8¾")*
1992 Michael Stulce, United States	21.70m	(71' 2½")
1996 Randy Barnes, United States	21.62m	(70' 11¼")
2000 Arsi Harju, Finland	21.29m	(69' 10¼")
2004 Yuriy Bilonog, Ukraine	21.16m	(69' 5¼")
2008 Tomasz Majewski, Poland	21.51m	(70' 6¾")

Triple Jump	Dist.	
1896 James Connolly, United States	13.71m	(44' 11¾")
1900 Meyer Prinstein, United States	14.47m	(47' 5¾")
1904 Meyer Prinstein, United States	14.35m	(47' 1")
1908 Timothy Ahearne, G.B.-Ireland	14.92m	(48' 11½")
1912 Gustaf Lindblom, Sweden	14.76m	(48' 5")
1920 Vilho Tuulos, Finland	14.50m	(47' 7")
1924 Anthony Winter, Australia	15.52m	(50' 11")
1928 Mikio Oda, Japan	15.21m	(49' 11")
1932 Chuhei Nambu, Japan	15.72m	(51' 7")
1936 Naoto Tajima, Japan	16.00m	(52' 6")
1948 Arne Ahman, Sweden	15.40m	(50' 6¼")
1952 Adhemar Ferreira da Silva, Brazil	16.22m	(53' 2¾")
1956 Adhemar Ferreira da Silva, Brazil	16.35m	(53' 7¾")
1960 Jozef Schmidt, Poland	16.81m	(55' 1½")
1964 Jozef Schmidt, Poland	16.85m	(55' 3½")
1968 Viktor Saneyev, USSR	17.39m	(57' ¾")
1972 Viktor Saneyev, USSR	17.35m	(56' 11¼")
1976 Viktor Saneyev, USSR	17.29m	(56' 8¾")
1980 Jaak Uudmae, USSR	17.35m	(56' 11")
1984 Al Joyner, United States	17.26m	(56' 7½")
1988 Khristo Markov, Bulgaria	17.61m	(57' 9½")
1992 Mike Conley, United States	18.17m	(59' 7½")(w)
1996 Kenny Harrison, United States	18.09m	(59' 4¼")*
2000 Jonathan Edwards, Britain	17.71m	(58' 1¼")
2004 Christian Olsson, Sweden	17.79m	(58' 4½")
2008 Nelson Evora, Portugal	17.67m	(57' 11¾")

Decathlon (not held 1908)	Points
1904 Thomas Kiely, Ireland	6,036
1912 Hugo Wieslander, Sweden (a)	7,724.49
1920 Helge Lovland, Norway	6,804.35
1924 Harold Osborn, United States	7,710.77
1928 Paavo Yrjola, Finland	8,053.29
1932 James Bausch, United States	8,462.23
1936 Glenn Morris, United States	7,900
1948 Robert Mathias, United States	7,139
1952 Robert Mathias, United States	7,887
1956 Milton Campbell, United States	7,937
1960 Rafer Johnson, United States	8,392
1964 Willi Holdorf, Germany (b)	7,887
1968 Bill Toomey, United States	8,193
1972 Nikolai Avilov, USSR	8,454
1976 Bruce Jenner, United States	8,617
1980 Daley Thompson, Great Britain	8,495
1984 Daley Thompson, Great Britain (c)	8,798
1988 Christian Schenk, E. Germany	8,488
1992 Robert Zmelik, Czechoslovakia	8,611
1996 Dan O'Brien, United States	8,824
2000 Erki Nool, Estonia	8,641
2004 Roman Sebrle, Czech Republic	8,893*
2008 Bryan Clay, United States	8,791

(a) Jim Thorpe of the U.S. won the 1912 Decathlon with 8,413 pts. but was disqualified and had to return his medals because he had played pro baseball prior to the Olympics. The IOC in 1982 posthumously restored his decathlon and pentathlon golds. (b) Former point systems used prior to 1964. (c) Scoring change effective Apr. 1985; Thompson's readjusted score is 8,847 pts.

Track and Field—Women

100-Meter Run

Year	Winner	Time
1928	Elizabeth Robinson, United States	12.2s
1932	Stella Walsh, Poland (a)	11.9s
1936	Helen Stephens, United States	11.5s
1948	Francina Blankers-Koen, Netherlands	11.9s
1952	Marjorie Jackson, Australia	11.5s
1956	Betty Cuthbert, Australia	11.5s
1960	Wilma Rudolph, United States	11.0s
1964	Wyomia Tyus, United States	11.4s
1968	Wyomia Tyus, United States	11.08s
1972	Renate Stecher, E. Germany	11.07s
1976	Annegret Richter, W. Germany	11.08s
1980	Lyudmila Kondratyeva, USSR	11.06s
1984	Evelyn Ashford, United States	10.97s
1988	Florence Griffith-Joyner, United States	10.54s*
1992	Gail Devers, United States	10.82s
1996	Gail Devers, United States	10.94s
2000	Marion Jones, United States (b)	10.75s
2004	Yuliya Nesterenko, Belarus	10.93s
2008	Shelly-Ann Fraser, Jamaica	10.78s

(a) A 1980 autopsy determined that Walsh was a man. (b) Jones's medals were revoked in 2008 due to doping.

200-Meter Run

Year	Winner	Time
1948	Francina Blankers-Koen, Netherlands	24.4s
1952	Marjorie Jackson, Australia	23.7s
1956	Betty Cuthbert, Australia	23.4s
1960	Wilma Rudolph, United States	24.0s
1964	Edith McGuire, United States	23.0s
1968	Irena Szewinska, Poland	22.5s
1972	Renate Stecher, E. Germany	22.40s
1976	Barbel Eckert, E. Germany	22.37s
1980	Barbel Wockel, E. Germany	22.03s
1984	Valerie Brisco-Hooks, United States	21.81s
1988	Florence Griffith-Joyner, United States	21.34s*
1992	Gwen Torrence, United States	21.81s
1996	Marie-Jose Perec, France	22.12s
2000	Marion Jones, United States (a)	21.84s
2004	Veronica Campbell, Jamaica	22.05s
2008	Veronica Campbell-Brown, Jamaica	21.74s

(a) Jones's medals were revoked in 2008 due to doping.

400-Meter Run

Year	Winner	Time
1964	Betty Cuthbert, Australia	52.0s
1968	Colette Besson, France	52.0s
1972	Monika Zehrt, E. Germany	51.08s
1976	Irena Szewinska, Poland	49.29s
1980	Marita Koch, E. Germany	48.88s
1984	Valerie Brisco-Hooks, United States	48.83s
1988	Olga Bryzgina, USSR	48.65s
1992	Marie-Jose Perec, France	48.83s
1996	Marie-Jose Perec, France	48.25s*
2000	Cathy Freeman, Australia	49.11s
2004	Tonique Williams-Darling, Bahamas	49.41s
2008	Christine Ohuruogu, Great Britain	49.62s

800-Meter Run

Year	Winner	Time
1928	Lina Radke, Germany	2m. 16.8s
1960	Ludmila Shevtsova, USSR	2m. 04.3s
1964	Ann Packer, Great Britain	2m. 01.1s
1968	Madeline Manning, United States	2m. 00.9s
1972	Hildegard Falck, W. Germany	1m. 58.6s
1976	Tatyana Kazankina, USSR	1m. 54.94s
1980	Nadezhda Olizarenko, USSR	1m. 53.43s*
1984	Doina Melinte, Romania	1m. 57.60s
1988	Sigrun Wodars, E. Germany	1m. 56.10s
1992	Ellen Van Langen, Netherlands	1m. 55.54s
1996	Svetlana Masterkova, Russia	1m. 57.73s
2000	Maria Mutola, Mozambique	1m. 56.15s
2004	Kelly Holmes, Great Britain	1m. 56.38s
2008	Pamela Jelimo, Kenya	1m. 54.87s

1,500-Meter Run

Year	Winner	Time
1972	Lyudmila Bragina, USSR	4m. 01.4s
1976	Tatyana Kazankina, USSR	4m. 05.48s
1980	Tatyana Kazankina, USSR	3m. 56.6s
1984	Gabriella Dorio, Italy	4m. 03.25s
1988	Paula Ivan, Romania	3m. 53.96s*
1992	Hassiba Boulmerka, Algeria	3m. 55.30s
1996	Svetlana Masterkova, Russia	4m. 00.83s
2000	Nouria Benida Merah, Algeria	4m. 05.10s
2004	Kelly Holmes, Great Britain	3m. 57.90s
2008	Nancy Jebet Langat, Kenya	4m. 00.23s

3,000-Meter Run

Year	Winner	Time
1984	Maricica Puica, Romania	8m. 35.96s
1988	Tatyana Samolenko, USSR	8m. 26.53s*
1992	Elena Romanova, Unified Team	8m. 46.04s

3,000-Meter Steeplechase

Year	Winner	Time
2008	Gulnara Galkina-Samitova, Russia	8m. 58.81s

5,000-Meter Run

Year	Winner	Time
1996	Wang Junxia, China	14m. 59.88s
2000	Gabriela Szabo, Romania	14m. 40.79s*
2004	Meseret Defar, Ethiopia	14m. 45.65s
2008	Tirunesh Dibaba, Ethiopia	15m. 41.40s

10,000-Meter Run

Year	Winner	Time
1988	Olga Boldarenko, USSR	31m. 44.69s
1992	Derartu Tulu, Ethiopia	31m. 06.02s
1996	Fernanda Ribeiro, Portugal	31m. 01.63s
2000	Derartu Tulu, Ethiopia	30m. 17.49s
2004	Xing Huina, China	30m. 24.36s
2008	Tirunesh Dibaba, Ethiopia	29m. 54.66s*

Marathon

Year	Winner	Time
1984	Joan Benoit, United States	2h. 24m. 52s
1988	Rosa Mota, Portugal	2h. 25m. 40s
1992	Valentina Yegorova, Unified Team	2h. 32m. 41s
1996	Fatuma Roba, Ethiopia	2h. 26m. 05s
2000	Naoko Takahashi, Japan	2h. 23m. 14s*
2004	Mizuki Noguchi, Japan	2h. 26m. 20s
2008	Constantina Tomescu, Romania	2h. 26m. 44s

4x100-Meter Relay

Year	Winner	Time
1928	Canada	48.4s
1932	United States	46.9s
1936	United States	46.9s
1948	Netherlands	47.5s
1952	United States	45.9s
1956	Australia	44.5s
1960	United States	44.5s
1964	Poland	43.6s
1968	United States	42.88s
1972	West Germany	42.81s
1976	East Germany	42.55s
1980	East Germany	41.60s*
1984	United States	41.65s
1988	United States	41.98s
1992	United States	42.11s
1996	United States	41.95s
2000	Bahamas	41.95s
2004	Jamaica	41.73s
2008	Russia	42.31s

4x400-Meter Relay

Year	Winner	Time
1972	East Germany	3m. 23s
1976	East Germany	3m. 19.23s
1980	USSR	3m. 20.02s
1984	United States	3m. 18.29s
1988	USSR	3m. 15.17s*
1992	Unified Team	3m. 20.20s
1996	United States	3m. 20.91s
2000	United States	3m. 22.62s
2004	United States	3m. 19.01s
2008	United States	3m. 18.54s

10-Kilometer Walk

Year	Winner	Time
1992	Chen Yueling, China	44m. 32s
1996	Elena Nikolayeva, Russia	41m. 49s*

20-Kilometer Walk

Year	Winner	Time
2000	Wang Liping, China	1h. 29m. 05s
2004	Athanasia Tsoumeleka, Greece	1h. 29m. 12s
2008	Olga Kaniskina, Russia	1h. 26m. 31s*

100-Meter Hurdles

Year	Winner	Time
1972	Annelie Ehrhardt, E. Germany	12.59s
1976	Johanna Schaller, E. Germany	12.77s
1980	Vera Komisova, USSR	12.56s
1984	Benita Brown-Fitzgerald, United States	12.84s
1988	Jordanka Donkova, Bulgaria	12.38s
1992	Paraskevi Patoulidou, Greece	12.64s
1996	Ludmila Enquist, Sweden	12.58s
2000	Olga Shishigina, Kazakhstan	12.65s
2004	Joanna Hayes, United States	12.37s*
2008	Dawn Harper, United States	12.54s

400-Meter Hurdles

Year	Winner	Time
1984	Nawal el Moutawakil, Morocco	54.61s
1988	Debra Flintoff-King, Australia	53.17s
1992	Sally Gunnell, Great Britain	53.23s
1996	Deon Hemmings, Jamaica	52.82s
2000	Irina Privalova, Russia	53.02s
2004	Fani Halkia, Greece	52.82s
2008	Melaine Walker, Jamaica	52.64s*

Discus Throw	Dist.
1928 Halina Konopacka, Poland 39.62m	(130' 0")
1932 Lillian Copeland, United States 40.58m	(133' 2")
1936 Gisela Mauermayer, Germany 47.62m	(156' 3")
1948 Micheline Ostermeyer, France. 41.92m	(137' 6")
1952 Nina Ponomareva, USSR 51.42m	(168' 8")
1956 Olga Fikotová, Czechoslovakia 53.68m	(176' 1")
1960 Nina Ponomareva, USSR 55.10m	(180' 9")
1964 Tamara Press, USSR 57.26m	(187' 10")
1968 Lia Manoliu, Romania 58.28m	(191' 2")
1972 Faina Melnik, USSR 66.62m	(218' 7")
1976 Evelin Jahl, E. Germany 69.00m	(226' 4")
1980 Evelin Jahl, E. Germany 69.96m	(229' 6")
1984 Ria Stalman, Netherlands 65.36m	(214' 5")
1988 Martina Hellmann, E. Germany. 72.30m	(237' 2")*
1992 Maritza Martén Garcia, Cuba 70.06m	(229' 10")
1996 Ilke Wyludda, Germany. 69.66m	(228' 6")
2000 Ellina Zvereva, Belarus 68.40m	(224' 5")
2004 Natalya Sadova, Russia 67.02m	(219' 9")
2008 Stephanie Brown Trafton, United States 64.74m	(212' 4¾")

Hammer Throw	Dist.
2000 Kamila Skolimowska, Poland 71.16m	(233' 5¾")
2004 Olga Kuzenkova, Russia 75.02m	(246' 1")
2008 Aksana Miankova, Belarus. 76.34m	(250' 5½")*

High Jump	Height
1928 Ethel Catherwood, Canada 1.59m	(5' 2½")
1932 Jean Shiley, United States. 1.65m	(5' 5")
1936 Ibolya Csák, Hungary 1.60m	(5' 3")
1948 Alice Coachman, U. S. 1.68m	(5' 6")
1952 Esther Brand, South Africa 1.67m	(5' 5¾")
1956 Mildred L. McDaniel, U. S. 1.76m	(5' 9¼")
1960 Iolanda Balas, Romania 1.85m	(6' ¾")
1964 Iolanda Balas, Romania 1.90m	(6' 2¾")
1968 Miloslava Resková, Czech. 1.82m	(5' 11½")
1972 Ulrike Meyfarth, W. Germany 1.92m	(6' 3½")
1976 Rosemarie Ackermann, E. Ger.. . . . . 1.93m	(6' 4")
1980 Sara Simeoni, Italy 1.97m	(6' 5½")
1984 Ulrike Meyfarth, W. Germany 2.02m	(6' 7½")
1988 Louise Ritter, United States. 2.03m	(6' 8")
1992 Heike Henkel, Germany 2.02m	(6' 7½")
1996 Stefka Kostadinova, Bulgaria 2.05m	(6' 8¾")
2000 Yelena Yelesina, Russia 2.01m	(6' 7")
2004 Yelena Slesarenko, Russia 2.06m	(6' 9")*
2008 Tia Hellebaut, Belgium 2.05m	(6' 8¾")

Javelin Throw	Dist.
1932 "Babe" Didrikson, United States 43.68m	(143' 4")
1936 Tilly Fleischer, Germany 45.18m	(148' 3")
1948 Herma Bauma, Austria 45.56m	(149' 6")
1952 Dana Zátopková, Czechoslovakia. . 50.46m	(165' 7")
1956 Inese Jaunzeme, USSR 53.86m	(176' 8")
1960 Elvira Ozolina, USSR 55.98m	(183' 8")
1964 Mihaela Penes, Romania 60.54m	(198' 7")
1968 Angéla Németh, Hungary 60.36m	(198' 0")
1972 Ruth Fuchs, E. Germany. 63.88m	(209' 7")
1976 Ruth Fuchs, E. Germany. 65.94m	(216' 4")
1980 Maria Colón Ruenes, Cuba 68.40m	(224' 5")
1984 Tessa Sanderson, Great Britain 69.56m	(228' 2")
1988 Petra Felke, E. Germany. 74.68m	(245' 0")

Javelin Throw	Dist.
1992 Silke Renke, Germany 68.34m	(224' 2")
1996 Heli Rantanen, Finland. 67.94m	(222' 11")
2000 Trine Hattestad, Norway 68.91m	(226' 1")
2004 Osleidys Menendez, Cuba 71.53m	(234' 8")*
2008 Barbora Spotakova, Czech Republic 71.42m	(234' ¾")

Note: New records were kept after javelin was modified in 1999.

Long Jump	Dist.
1948 Olga Gyarmati, Hungary. 5.69m	(18' 8")
1952 Yvette Williams, New Zealand 6.24m	(20' 5¼")
1956 Elzbieta Krzeskinska, Poland 6.35m	(20' 10")
1960 Vira Krepkina, USSR 6.37m	(20' 10¾")
1964 Mary Rand, Great Britain 6.76m	(22' 2¼")
1968 Viorica Viscopoleanu, Romania 6.82m	(22' 4½")
1972 Heidemarie Rosendahl, W. Ger. 6.78m	(22' 3")
1976 Angela Voigt, E. Germany 6.72m	(22' ¾")
1980 Tatyana Kolpakova, USSR 7.06m	(23' 2")
1984 Anisoara Cusmir-Stanciu, Rom. 6.96m	(22' 10")
1988 Jackie Joyner-Kersee, United States . 7.40m	(24' 3½")*
1992 Heike Drechsler, Germany 7.14m	(23' 5¼")
1996 Chioma Ajunwa, Nigeria. 7.12m	(23' 4½")
2000 Heike Drechsler, Germany 6.99m	(22' 11¼")
2004 Tatyana Lebedeva, Russia 7.07m	(23' 2½")
2008 Maurren Higa Maggi, Brazil 7.04m	(23' 1¼")

Pole Vault	Height
2000 Stacy Dragila, United States. 4.60m	(15' 1")
2004 Elena Isinbaeva, Russia 4.91m	(16' 1¹/₃")
2008 Elena Isinbaeva, Russia 5.05m	(16' 6¾")*

Shot Put	Dist.
1948 Micheline Ostermeyer, France 13.75m	(45' 1½")
1952 Galina Zybina, USSR 15.28m	(50' 1½")
1956 Tamara Tyshkyevich, USSR 16.59m	(54' 5¼")
1960 Tamara Press, USSR 17.32m	(56' 10")
1964 Tamara Press, USSR 18.14m	(59' 6¼")
1968 Margitta Gummel, E. Germany. 19.61m	(64' 4")
1972 Nadezhda Chizova, USSR 21.03m	(69' 0")
1976 Ivanka Khristova, Bulgaria 21.16m	(69' 5¼")
1980 Ilona Slupianek, E. Germany 22.41m	(73' 6¼")*
1984 Claudia Losch, W. Germany. 20.49m	(67' 2¼")
1988 Natalya Lisovskaya, USSR. 22.24m	(72' 11¾")
1992 Svetlana Krivelyova, Unified Team . . 21.06m	(69' 1¼")
1996 Astrid Kumbernuss, Germany 20.56m	(67' 5½")
2000 Yanina Karolchik, Belarus. 20.56m	(67' 5½")
2004 Yumileidi Cumba Jay, Cuba 19.59m	(64' 3¼")
2008 Valerie Vili, New Zealand 20.56m	(67' 5½")

Triple Jump	Dist.
1996 Inessa Kravets, Ukraine 15.33m	(50' 3½")
2000 Tereza Marinova, Bulgaria 15.20m	(49' 10½")
2004 Francoise Mbango Etone, Cameroon 15.30m	(50' 2¹/₃")
2008 Francoise Mbango Etone, Cameroon 15.39m	(50' 6")*

Heptathlon	Points
1984 Glynis Nunn, Australia	6,390
1988 Jackie Joyner-Kersee, United States	7,291*
1992 Jackie Joyner-Kersee, United States	7,044
1996 Ghada Shouaa, Syria	6,780
2000 Denise Lewis, Great Britain	6,584
2004 Carolina Kluft, Sweden	6,952
2008 Nataliia Dobrynska, Ukraine.	6,733

Winter Olympic Games in 2006—Highlights

Turin (Torino), Italy, Feb. 10-26, 2006

The XX Winter Olympic Games opened Feb. 10, 2006, in Turin—Italy's 4th largest city and the largest ever to host the Winter Games. More than 2,500 athletes from 84 countries competed in 84 medal events over 16 days in Turin. As in 1998 and 2002, Germany led the medal count, with 29, but the U.S. claimed 25 medals, its highest medal count for Winter Games not held in the U.S.

The XXI Winter Olympic Games were scheduled to be held Feb. 12-28, 2010, in Vancouver, Canada.

2006 Final Medal Standings

	Gold	Silver	Bronze	Total		Gold	Silver	Bronze	Total
Germany	11	12	6	29	Czech Republic.	1	2	1	4
United States	9	9	7	25	Estonia	3	0	0	3
Canada	7	10	7	24	Croatia.	1	2	0	3
Austria	9	7	7	23	Australia	1	0	1	2
Russia	8	6	8	22	Poland	0	1	1	2
Norway.	2	8	9	19	Ukraine	0	0	2	2
Sweden	7	2	5	14	Japan.	1	0	0	1
Switzerland.	5	4	5	14	Belarus	0	1	0	1
South Korea	6	3	2	11	Great Britain	0	1	0	1
Italy.	5	0	6	11	Bulgaria	0	1	0	1
China	2	4	5	11	Slovakia.	0	1	0	1
France	3	2	4	9	Latvia.	0	0	1	1
Netherlands	3	2	4	9					
Finland	0	6	3	9	TOTAL	84	84	84	252

Winter Olympic Games Champions, 1924-2006

In 1992, the Unified Team represented the former Soviet republics of Russia, Ukraine, Belarus, Kazakhstan, and Uzbekistan.

Alpine Skiing

Men's Downhill

Year	Champion	Time
1948	Henri Oreiller, France	2:55.0
1952	Zeno Colo, Italy	2:30.8
1956	Toni Sailer, Austria	2:52.2
1960	Jean Vuarnet, France	2:06.0
1964	Egon Zimmermann, Austria	2:18.16
1968	Jean-Claude Killy, France	1:59.85
1972	Bernhard Russi, Switzerland	1:51.43
1976	Franz Klammer, Austria	1:45.73
1980	Leonhard Stock, Austria	1:45.50
1984	Bill Johnson, United States	1:45.49
1988	Pirmin Zurbriggen, Switzerland	1:59.63
1992	Patrick Ortlieb, Austria	1:50.37
1994	Tommy Moe, United States	1:45.75
1998	Jean-Luc Cretier, France	1:50.11
2002	Fritz Strobl, Austria	1:39.13
2006	Antoine Deneriaz, France	1:48.80

Men's Super Giant Slalom

Year	Champion	Time
1988	Franck Piccard, France	1:39.66
1992	Kjetil-Andre Aamodt, Norway	1:13.04
1994	Markus Wasmeier, Germany	1:32.53
1998	Hermann Maier, Austria	1:34.82
2002	Kjetil Andre Aamodt, Norway	1:21.58
2006	Kjetil Andre Aamodt, Norway	1:30.65

Men's Giant Slalom

Year	Champion	Time
1952	Stein Eriksen, Norway	2:25.0
1956	Toni Sailer, Austria	3:00.1
1960	Roger Staub, Switzerland	1:48.3
1964	Francois Bonlieu, France	1:46.71
1968	Jean-Claude Killy, France	3:29.28
1972	Gustavo Thoeni, Italy	3:09.62
1976	Heini Hemmi, Switzerland	3:26.97
1980	Ingemar Stenmark, Sweden	2:40.74
1984	Max Julen, Switzerland	2:41.18
1988	Alberto Tomba, Italy	2:06.37
1992	Alberto Tomba, Italy	2:06.98
1994	Markus Wasmeier, Germany	2:52.46
1998	Hermann Maier, Austria	2:38.51
2002	Stephan Eberharter, Austria	2:23.28
2006	Benjamin Raich, Austria	2:35.00

Men's Slalom

Year	Champion	Time
1948	Edi Reinalter, Switzerland	2:10.3
1952	Othmar Schneider, Austria	2:00.0
1956	Toni Sailer, Austria	3:14.7
1960	Ernst Hinterseer, Austria	2:08.9
1964	Josef Stiegler, Austria	2:11.13
1968	Jean-Claude Killy, France	1:39.73
1972	Francisco Fernandez-Ochoa, Spain	1:49.27
1976	Piero Gros, Italy	2:03.29
1980	Ingemar Stenmark, Sweden	1:44.26
1984	Phil Mahre, United States	1:39.41
1988	Alberto Tomba, Italy	1:39.47
1992	Finn Christian Jagge, Norway	1:44.39
1994	Thomas Stangassinger, Austria	2:02.02
1998	Hans-Petter Buraas, Norway	1:49.31
2002	Jean-Pierre Vidal, France	1:41.06
2006	Benjamin Raich, Austria	1:43.14

Men's Combined

Year	Champion	Time
1936	Franz-Pfnuer, Germany	99.25 (pts.)
1948	Henri Oreiller, France	3.27 (pts.)
1988	Hubert Strolz, Austria	36.55 (pts.)
1992	Josef Polig, Italy	14.58 (pts.)
1994	Lasse Kjus, Norway	3:17.53
1998	Mario Reiter, Austria	3:08.06
2002	Kjetil Andre Aamodt, Norway	3:17.56
2006	Ted Ligety, United States	3:09.35

Women's Downhill

Year	Champion	Time
1948	Hedi Schlunegger, Switzerland	2:28.3
1952	Trude Beiser-Jochum, Austria	1:47.1
1956	Madeleine Berthod, Switzerland	1:40.7
1960	Heidi Biebl, Germany	1:37.6
1964	Christl Haas, Austria	1:55.39
1968	Olga Pall, Austria	1:40.87
1972	Marie-Theres Nadig, Switzerland	1:36.68
1976	Rosi Mittermaier, W. Germany	1:46.16
1980	Annemarie Moser-Proell, Austria	1:37.52
1984	Michela Figini, Switzerland	1:13.36
1988	Marina Kiehl, W. Germany	1:25.86
1992	Kerrin Lee-Gartner, Canada	1:52.55
1994	Katja Seizinger, Germany	1:35.93
1998	Katja Seizinger, Germany	1:28.89
2002	Carole Montillet, France	1:39.56
2006	Michaela Dorfmeister, Austria	1:56.49

Women's Super Giant Slalom

Year	Champion	Time
1988	Sigrid Wolf, Austria	1:19.03
1992	Deborah Compagnoni, Italy	1:21.22
1994	Diann Roffe (Steinrotter), United States	1:22.15
1998	Picabo Street, United States	1:18.02
2002	Daniela Ceccarelli, Italy	1:13.59
2006	Michaela Dorfmeister, Austria	1:32.47

Women's Giant Slalom

Year	Champion	Time
1952	Andrea Mead Lawrence, United States	2:06.8
1956	Ossi Reichert, Germany	1:56.5
1960	Yvonne Ruegg, Switzerland	1:39.9
1964	Marielle Goitschel, France	1:52.24
1968	Nancy Greene, Canada	1:51.97
1972	Marie-Theres Nadig, Switzerland	1:29.90
1976	Kathy Kreiner, Canada	1:29.13
1980	Hanni Wenzel, Liechtenstein (2 runs)	2:41.66
1984	Debbie Armstrong, United States	2:20.98
1988	Vreni Schneider, Switzerland	2:06.49
1992	Pernilla Wiberg, Sweden	2:12.74
1994	Deborah Compagnoni, Italy	2:30.97
1998	Deborah Compagnoni, Italy	2:50.59
2002	Janica Kostelic, Croatia	2:30.01
2006	Julia Mancuso, United States	2:09.19

Women's Slalom

Year	Champion	Time
1948	Gretchen Fraser, United States	1:57.2
1952	Andrea Mead Lawrence, United States	2:10.6
1956	Renee Colliard, Switzerland	1:52.3
1960	Anne Heggtveit, Canada	1:49.6
1964	Christine Goitschel, France	1:29.86
1968	Marielle Goitschel, France	1:25.86
1972	Barbara Ann Cochran, United States	1:31.24
1976	Rosi Mittermaier, W. Germany	1:30.54
1980	Hanni Wenzel, Liechtenstein	1:25.09
1984	Paoletta Magoni, Italy	1:36.47
1988	Vreni Schneider, Switzerland	1:36.69
1992	Petra Kronberger, Austria	1:32.68
1994	Vreni Schneider, Switzerland	1:56.01
1998	Hilde Gerg, Germany	1:32.40
2002	Janica Kostelic, Croatia	1:46.10
2006	Anja Paerson, Sweden	1:29.04

Women's Combined

Year	Champion	Time
1936	Christl Cranz, Germany	97.06 (pts.)
1948	Trude Beiser-Jochum, Austria	6.58 (pts.)
1988	Anita Wachter, Austria	29.25 (pts.)
1992	Petra Kronberger, Austria	2.55 (pts.)
1994	Pernilla Wiberg, Sweden	3:05.16
1998	Katja Seizinger, Germany	2:40.74
2002	Janica Kostelic, Croatia	2:43.28
2006	Janica Kostelic, Croatia	2:51.08

Biathlon

Men's 10 Kilometers

Year	Champion	Time
1980	Frank Ullrich, E. Germany	32:10.69
1984	Eirik Kvalfoss, Norway	30:53.80
1988	Frank-Peter Roetsch, E. Germany	25:08.10
1992	Mark Kirchner, Germany	26:02.30
1994	Serguei Tchepikov, Russia	28:07.00
1998	Ole Einar Bjoerndalen, Norway	27:16.20
2002	Ole Einar Bjoerndalen, Norway	24:51.30
2006	Sven Fischer, Germany	26:11.6

Men's 12.5 Kilometers

Year	Champion	Time
2002	Ole Einar Bjoerndalen, Norway	32:34.6
2006	Vincent Defrasne, France	35:20.2

Men's 15 Kilometers

Year	Champion	Time
2006	Michael Greis, Germany	47:20.0

Men's 20 Kilometers

Year	Champion	Time
1960	Klas Lestander, Sweden	1:33:21.6
1964	Vladimir Melanin, USSR	1:20:26.8
1968	Magnar Solberg, Norway	1:13:45.9
1972	Magnar Solberg, Norway	1:15:55.50
1976	Nikolai Kruglov, USSR	1:14:12.26
1980	Anatoly Aljabiev, USSR	1:08:16.31
1984	Peter Angerer, W. Germany	1:11:52.7
1988	Frank-Peter Roetsch, E. Germany	0:56:33.33
1992	Yevgeny Redkine, Unified Team	0:57:34.4
1994	Serguei Tarasov, Russia	0:57:25.3
1998	Halvard Hanevold, Norway	0:56:16.4
2002	Ole Einar Bjoerndalen, Norway	0:51:03.03
2006	Michael Greis, Germany	0:54:23.0

Men's 30-Kilometer Relay

Year		Time
1968	USSR, Norway, Sweden (40 km)	2:13:02.4
1972	USSR, Finland, E. Germany (40 km)	1:51:44.92
1976	USSR, Finland, E. Germany (40 km)	1:57:55.64
1980	USSR, E. Germany, W. Germany	1:34:03.27
1984	USSR, Norway, W. Germany	1:38:51.70
1988	USSR, W. Germany, Italy	1:22:30.00
1992	Germany, Unified Team, Sweden	1:24:43.50
1994	Germany, Russia, France	1:30:22.1
1998	Germany, Norway, Russia	1:19:43.3
2002	Norway, Germany, France	1:23:42.3
2006	Germany, Russia, France	1:21:51.5

Women's 7.5 Kilometers

Year		Time
1992	Anfissa Restsova, Unified Team	24:29.2
1994	Myriam Bedard, Canada	26:08.8
1998	Galina Koukleva, Russia	23:08.0
2002	Kati Wilhelm, Germany	20:41.4
2006	Florence Baverel-Robert, France	22:31.4

Women's 10 Kilometers

Year		Time
2002	Olga Pyleva, Russia	31:07.7
2006	Kati Wilhelm, Germany	36:43.6

Women's 12.5 Kilometers

Year		Time
2006	Anna Carin Olofsson, Sweden	40:36.5

Women's 15 Kilometers

Year		Time
1992	Antje Misersky, Germany	51:47.2
1994	Myriam Bedard, Canada	52:06.6
1998	Ekaterina Dafovska, Bulgaria	54:52.0
2002	Andrea Henkel, Germany	47:30.0
2006	Svetlana Ishmouratova, Russia	49:24.1

Women's 24-Kilometer Relay

Year		Time
1992	France, Germany, Unified Team (22.5 km)	1:15:55.6
1994	Russia, Germany, France (30 km)	1:47:19.5
1998	Germany, Russia, Norway (30 km)	1:40:13.6
2002	Germany, Norway, Russia (30 km)	1:27:55.0
2006	Russia, Germany, France	1:16:12.5

Bobsledding

(Driver in parentheses.)

4-Man Bob

Year		Time
1924	Switzerland (Eduard Scherrer)	5:45.54
1928	United States (William Fiske) (5-man)	3:20.50
1932	United States (William Fiske)	7:53.68
1936	Switzerland (Pierre Musy)	5:19.85
1948	United States (Francis Tyler)	5:20.10
1952	Germany (Andreas Ostler)	5:07.84
1956	Switzerland (Franz Kapus)	5:10.44
1964	Canada (Victor Emery)	4:14.46
1968	Italy (Eugenio Monti) (2 races)	2:17.39
1972	Switzerland (Jean Wicki)	4:43.07
1976	E. Germany (Meinhard Nehmer)	3:40.43
1980	E. Germany (Meinhard Nehmer)	3:59.92
1984	E. Germany (Wolfgang Hoppe)	3:20.22
1988	Switzerland (Ekkehard Fasser)	3:47.51
1992	Austria (Ingo Appelt)	3:53.90
1994	Germany (Wolfgang Hoppe)	3:27.28
1998	Germany II (Christoph Langen)	2:39.41
2002	Germany II (Andre Lange)	3:07.51
2006	Germany (Andre Lange)	3:40.42

2-Man Bob

Year		Time
1932	United States (Hubert Stevens)	8:14.74
1936	United States (Ivan Brown)	5:29.29
1948	Switzerland (F. Endrich)	5:29.20
1952	Germany (Andreas Ostler)	5:24.54
1956	Italy (Dalla Costa)	5:30.14
1964	Great Britain (Anthony Nash)	4:21.90
1968	Italy (Eugenio Monti)	4:41.54
1972	W. Germany (Wolfgang Zimmerer)	4:57.07
1976	E. Germany (Meinhard Nehmer)	3:44.42
1980	Switzerland (Erich Schaerer)	4:09.36
1984	E. Germany (Wolfgang Hoppe)	3:25.56
1988	USSR (Janis Kipours)	3:54.19
1992	Switzerland (Gustav Weber)	4:03.26
1994	Switzerland (Gustav Weber)	3:30.81
1998	Canada (Pierre Lueders), Italy (Guenther Huber) (tie)	3:37.24
2002	Germany II (Christoph Langen)	3:10.11
2006	Germany (Andre Lange)	3:43.38

2-Woman Bob

Year		Time
2002	United States II (Jill Bakken)	1:37.76
2006	Germany (Sandra Kiriasis)	3:49.98

Curling

Men

1998	Switzerland, Canada, Norway
2002	Norway, Canada, Switzerland
2006	Canada, Finland, United States

Women

1998	Canada, Denmark, Sweden
2002	Britain, Switzerland, Canada
2006	Sweden, Switzerland, Canada

Figure Skating

Men's Singles

1908[1]	Ulrich Salchow, Sweden
1920[1]	Gillis Grafstrom, Sweden
1924	Gillis Grafstrom, Sweden
1928	Gillis Grafstrom, Sweden
1932	Karl Schaefer, Austria
1936	Karl Schaefer, Austria
1948	Richard Button, United States
1952	Richard Button, United States
1956	Hayes Alan Jenkins, United States
1960	David W. Jenkins, United States
1964	Manfred Schnelldorfer, Germany
1968	Wolfgang Schwartz, Austria
1972	Ondrej Nepela, Czechoslovakia
1976	John Curry, Great Britain
1980	Robin Cousins, Great Britain
1984	Scott Hamilton, United States
1988	Brian Boitano, United States
1992	Viktor Petrenko, Unified Team
1994	Aleksei Urmanov, Russia
1998	Ilya Kulik, Russia
2002	Alexei Yagudin, Russia
2006	Yevgeny Plushenko, Russia

(1) Event held during Summer Olympic Games.

Women's Singles

1908[1]	Madge Syers, Great Britain
1920[1]	Magda Julin-Mauroy, Sweden
1924	Herma von Szabo-Planck, Austria
1928	Sonja Henie, Norway
1932	Sonja Henie, Norway
1936	Sonja Henie, Norway
1948	Barbara Ann Scott, Canada
1952	Jeanette Altwegg, Great Britan
1956	Tenley Albright, United States
1960	Carol Heiss, United States
1964	Sjoukje Dijkstra, Netherlands
1968	Peggy Fleming, United States
1972	Beatrix Schuba, Austria
1976	Dorothy Hamill, United States
1980	Anett Poetzsch, E. Germany
1984	Katarina Witt, E. Germany
1988	Katarina Witt, E. Germany
1992	Kristi Yamaguchi, United States
1994	Oksana Baiul, Ukraine
1998	Tara Lipinski, United States
2002	Sarah Hughes, United States
2006	Shizuka Arakawa, Japan

(1) Event held during Summer Olympic Games.

Pairs

1908[1]	Anna Hubler & Heinrich Burger, Germany
1920[1]	Ludovika & Walter Jakobsson, Finland
1924	Helene Engelman & Alfred Berger, Austria
1928	Andree Joly & Pierre Brunet, France
1932	Andree Joly & Pierre Brunet, France
1936	Maxi Herber & Ernst Baier, Germany
1948	Micheline Lannoy & Pierre Baugniet, Belgium
1952	Ria and Paul Falk, Germany
1956	Elisabeth Schwartz & Kurt Oppelt, Austria
1964	Ludmila Beloussova & Oleg Protopopov, USSR
1968	Ludmila Beloussova & Oleg Protopopov, USSR
1972	Irina Rodnina & Alexei Ulanov, USSR
1976	Irina Rodnina & Aleksandr Zaitzev, USSR
1980	Irina Rodnina & Aleksandr Zaitzev, USSR
1984	Elena Valova & Oleg Vassiliev, USSR
1988	Ekaterina Gordeeva & Sergei Grinkov, USSR
1992	Natalia Mishkutienok & Artur Dimitriev, Unified Team
1994	Ekaterina Gordeeva & Sergei Grinkov, Russia
1998	Oksana Kazakova & Artur Dmitriev, Russia
2002	Elena Berezhnaya & Anton Sikharulidze, Russia; Jamie Sale & David Pelletier, Canada (tie)
2006	Tatyana Totmianina & Maxim Marinin, Russia

(1) Event held during Summer Olympic Games.

Ice Dancing

1976	Ludmila Pakhomova & Aleksandr Gorschkov, USSR
1980	Natalya Linichuk & Gennadi Karponosov, USSR
1984	Jayne Torvill & Christopher Dean, Great Britain
1988	Natalia Bestemianova & Andrei Bukin, USSR
1992	Marina Klimova & Sergei Ponomarenko, Unified Team
1994	Pasha Grishuk & Evgeny Platov, Russia
1998	Pasha Grishuk & Evgeny Platov, Russia
2002	Marina Anissina & Gwendal Peizerat, France
2006	Tatyana Navka & Roman Kostomarov, Russia

Freestyle Skiing

Men's Moguls		Points
1992	Edgar Grospiron, France	25.81
1994	Jean-Luc Brassard, Canada	27.24
1998	Jonny Moseley, United States	26.93
2002	Janne Lahtela, Finland	27.97
2006	Dale Begg-Smith, Australia	26.77

Men's Aerials		Points
1994	Andreas Schoenbaechler, Switzerland	234.67
1998	Eric Bergoust, United States	255.64
2002	Ales Valenta, Czech Republic	257.02
2006	Xiaopeng Han, China	250.77

Women's Moguls		Points
1992	Donna Weinbrecht, United States	23.69
1994	Stine Lise Hattestad, Norway	25.97
1998	Tae Satoya, Japan	25.06
2002	Kari Traa, Norway	25.94
2006	Jennifer Heil, Canada	26.50

Women's Aerials		Points
1994	Lina Tcherjazova, Uzbekistan	166.84
1998	Nikki Stone, United States	193.00
2002	Alisa Camplin, Australia	193.47
2006	Evelyne Leu, Switzerland	202.55

Ice Hockey

Men

1920[1]	Canada, United States, Czechoslovakia
1924	Canada, United States, Great Britain
1928	Canada, Sweden, Switzerland
1932	Canada, United States, Germany
1936	Great Britain, Canada, United States
1948	Canada, Czechoslovakia, Switzerland
1952	Canada, United States, Sweden
1956	USSR, United States, Canada
1960	United States, Canada, USSR
1964	USSR, Sweden, Czechoslovakia
1968	USSR, Czechoslovakia, Canada
1972	USSR, United States, Czechoslovakia
1976	USSR, Czechoslovakia, W. Germany
1980	United States, USSR, Sweden
1984	USSR, Czechoslovakia, Sweden
1988	USSR, Finland, Sweden
1992	Unified Team, Canada, Czechoslovakia
1994	Sweden, Canada, Finland
1998	Czech Republic, Russia, Finland
2002	Canada, United States, Russia
2006	Sweden, Finland, Czech Republic

Women

1998	United States, Canada, Finland
2002	Canada, United States, Sweden
2006	Canada, Sweden, United States

(1) Event held during Summer Olympic Games.

Luge

Men's Singles		Time
1964	Thomas Keohler, E. Germany	3:27.77
1968	Manfred Schmid, Austria	2:52.48
1972	Wolfgang Scheidel, E. Germany	3:27.58
1976	Detlef Guenther, E. Germany	3:27.688
1980	Bernhard Glass, E. Germany	2:54.796
1984	Paul Hildgartner, Italy	3:04.258
1988	Jens Mueller, E. Germany	3:05.548
1992	Georg Hackl, Germany	3:02.363
1994	Georg Hackl, Germany	3:21.571
1998	Georg Hackl, Germany	3:18.436
2002	Armin Zoeggeler, Italy	2:57.941
2006	Armin Zoeggeler, Italy	3:26.088

Women's Singles		Time
1964	Ortun Enderlein, Germany	3:24.67
1968	Erica Lechner, Italy	2:28.66
1972	Anna M. Muller, E. Germany	2:59.18
1976	Margit Schumann, E. Germany	2:50.621
1980	Vera Zozulya, USSR	2:36.537
1984	Steffi Martin, E. Germany	2:46.570
1988	Steffi Walter, E. Germany	3:03.973

Women's Singles		Time
1992	Doris Neuner, Austria	3:06.696
1994	Gerda Weissensteiner, Italy	3:15.517
1998	Silke Kraushaar, Germany	3:23.779
2002	Sylke Otto, Germany	2:52.464
2006	Sylke Otto, Germany	3:07.979

Men's Doubles		Time
1964	Austria	1:41.62
1968	E. Germany	1:35.85
1972	Italy, E. Germany (tie)	1:28.35
1976	E. Germany	1:25.604
1980	E. Germany	1:19.331
1984	W. Germany	1:23.620
1988	E. Germany	1:31.940
1992	Germany	1:32.053
1994	Italy	1:36.720
1998	Germany	1:41.105
2002	Germany	1:26.082
2006	Austria	1:34.497

Nordic Skiing

Men's Sprint		Time
2002	Tor Arne Hetland, Norway (1.5 km)	2:56.9
2006	Bjoern Lind, Sweden (1.3 km)	2:26.5

Men's Team Sprint		Time
2006	Bjoern Lind & Thobias Fredriksson, Sweden	17:02.9

Men's 10 Kilometers (6.2 miles)		Time
1992	Vegard Ulvang, Norway	27:36.0
1994	Bjoern Daehlie, Norway	24:20.1
1998	Bjoern Daehlie, Norway	27:24.5
2002	Thomas Alsgaard, Norway; Frode Estil, Norway (tie) (a)	49:48.9

(a) Awarded gold after Johann Muehlegg of Spain was stripped of gold for a drug offense.

Men's 15 Kilometers (9.3 miles)		Time
1924	Thorleif Haug, Norway	1:14:31
1928	Johan Grottumsbraaten, Norway	1:37:01
1932	Sven Utterstrom, Sweden	1:23:07
1936	Erik-August Larsson, Sweden	1:14:38
1948	Martin Lundstrom, Sweden	1:13:50
1952	Hallgeir Brenden, Norway	1:01:34
1956	Hallgeir Brenden, Norway	0:49:39.0
1960	Haakon Brusveen, Norway	0:51:55.5
1964	Eero Maentyranta, Finland	0:50:54.1
1968	Harald Groenningen, Norway	0:47:54.2
1972	Sven-Ake Lundback, Sweden	0:45:28.24
1976	Nikolai Balukov, USSR	0:43:58.47
1980	Thomas Wassberg, Sweden	0:41:57.63
1984	Gunde Svan, Sweden	0:41:25.6
1988	Mikhail Deviatiarov, USSR	0:41:18.9
1992	Bjoern Daehlie, Norway	0:38:01.9
1994	Bjoern Daehlie, Norway	0:35:48.8
1998	Thomas Alsgaard, Norway	1:07:01.7
2002	Andrus Veerpalu, Estonia	0:37:07.4
2006	Andrus Veerpalu, Estonia	0:38:01.3

Note: Approx. 18-km course 1924-52.

Men's 30 Kilometers (18.6 miles)		Time
1956	Veikko Hakulinen, Finland	1:44:06.0
1964	Eero Maentyranta, Finland	1:30:50.7
1968	Franco Nones, Italy	1:35:39.2
1972	Vyacheslav Vedenine, USSR	1:36:31.15
1976	Sergei Saveliev, USSR	1:30:29.38
1980	Nikolai Zimyatov, USSR	1:27:02.80
1984	Nikolai Zimyatov, USSR	1:28:56.3
1988	Aleksei Prokourorov, USSR	1:24:26.3
1992	Vegard Ulvang, Norway	1:22:27.8
1994	Thomas Alsgaard, Norway	1:12:26.4
1998	Mika Myllylae, Finland	1:33:55.8
2002	Christian Hoffmann, Austria (a)	1:11:31.0
2006	Eugeni Dementiev, Russia	1:17:00.8

(a) Awarded gold after Johann Muehlegg of Spain was stripped of gold for a drug offense.

Men's 50 Kilometers (31.2 miles)		Time
1924	Thorleif Haug, Norway	3:44:32.0
1928	Per Erik Hedlund, Sweden	4:52:03.0
1932	Veli Saarinen, Finland	4:28:00.0
1936	Elis Wiklund, Sweden	3:30:11.0
1948	Nils Karlsson, Sweden	3:47:48.0
1952	Veikko Hakulinen, Finland	3:33:33.0
1956	Sixten Jernberg, Sweden	2:50:27.0
1960	Kalevi Hamalainen, Finland	2:59:06.3
1964	Sixten Jernberg, Sweden	2:43:52.6
1968	Ole Ellefsaeter, Norway	2:28:45.8
1972	Paal Tyldum, Norway	2:43:14.75
1976	Ivar Formo, Norway	2:37:30.05

Men's 50 Kilometers (31.2 miles)

		Time
1980	Nikolai Zimyatov, USSR	2:27:24.60
1984	Thomas Wassberg, Sweden	2:15:55.8
1988	Gunde Svan, Sweden	2:04:30.9
1992	Bjoern Daehlie, Norway	2:03:41.5
1994	Vladimir Smirnov, Kazakhstan	2:07:20.3
1998	Bjoern Daehlie, Norway	2:05:08.2
2002	Mikhail Ivanov, Russia	2:06:20.8
2006	Giorgio di Centa, Italy	2:06:11.8

Men's 40-Kilometer Relay

		Time
1936	Finland, Norway, Sweden	2:41:33.0
1948	Sweden, Finland, Norway	2:32:08.0
1952	Finland, Norway, Sweden	2:20:16.0
1956	USSR, Finland, Sweden	2:15:30.0
1960	Finland, Norway, USSR	2:18:45.6
1964	Sweden, Finland, USSR	2:18:34.6
1968	Norway, Sweden, Finland	2:08:33.5
1972	USSR, Norway, Switzerland	2:04:47.94
1976	Finland, Norway, USSR	2:07:59.72
1980	USSR, Norway, Finland	1:57:03.46
1984	Sweden, USSR, Finland	1:55:06.30
1988	Sweden, USSR, Czechoslovakia	1:43:58.60
1992	Norway, Italy, Finland	1:39:26.00
1994	Italy, Norway, Finland	1:41:15.00
1998	Norway, Italy, Finland	1:40:55.70
2002	Norway, Italy, Germany	1:32:45.5
2006	Italy, Germany, Sweden	1:43:45.7

Women's Sprint

		Time
2002	Julia Tchepalova, Russia (1.5 km)	3:10.6
2006	Chandra Crawford, Canada (1.1 km)	2:12.3

Women's Team Sprint

		Time
2006	Lina Andersson & Anna Dahlberg, Sweden	16:36.9

Women's 5 Kilometers (3.1 miles)

		Time
1964	Claudia Boyarskikh, USSR	17:50.5
1968	Toini Gustafsson, Sweden	16:45.2
1972	Galina Koulacova, USSR	17:00.50
1976	Helena Takalo, Finland	15:48.69
1980	Raisa Smetanina, USSR	15:06.92
1984	Marja-Liisa Haemaelainen, Finland	17:04.0
1988	Marjo Matikainen, Finland	15:04.0
1992	Marjut Lukkarinen, Finland	14:13.8
1994	Ljubov Egorova, Russia	14:08.8
1998	Larissa Lazutina, Russia	17:37.9
2002	Beckie Scott, Canada (a)	25:09.9

(a) Awarded gold after Olga Danilova of Russia was stripped of gold and Larissa Lazutina of Russia was stripped of silver for drug offenses.

Women's 10 Kilometers (6.2 miles)

		Time
1952	Lydia Wideman, Finland	41:40.0
1956	Lyubov Kosyreva, USSR	38:11.0
1960	Maria Gusakova, USSR	39:46.6
1964	Claudia Boyarskikh, USSR	40:24.3
1968	Toini Gustafsson, Sweden	36:46.5
1972	Galina Koulacova, USSR	34:17.82
1976	Raisa Smetanina, USSR	30:13.41
1980	Barbara Petzold, E. Germany	30:31.54
1984	Marja-Liisa Haemaelainen, Finland	31:44.2
1988	Vida Ventsene, USSR	30:08.3
1992	Lyubov Egorova, Unified Team	25:53.7
1994	Lyubov Egorova, Russia	27:30.1
1998	Larissa Lazutina, Russia	46.06.9
2002	Bente Skari, Norway	28:05.6
2006	Kristina Smigun, Estonia	27:51.4

Women's 15 Kilometers (9.3 miles)

		Time
1992	Lyubov Egorova, Unified Team	42:20.8
1994	Manuela Di Centa, Italy	39:44.5
1998	Olga Danilova, Russia	46:55.4
2002	Stefania Belmondo, Italy	39:54.4
2006	Kristina Smigun, Estonia	42:48.7

Women's 30 Kilometers (18.6 miles)

		Time
1992	Stefania Belmondo, Italy	1:22:30.1
1994	Manuela Di Centa, Italy	1:25:41.6
1998	Julija Tchepalova, Russia	1:22:01.5
2002	Gabriella Paruzzi, Italy	1:30:57.1
2006	Katerina Neumannova, Czech Republic	1:22:25.4

Women's 20-Kilometer Relay

		Time
1956	Finland, USSR, Sweden (15 km)	1:09:01.0
1960	Sweden, USSR, Finland (15 km)	1:04:21.4
1964	USSR, Sweden, Finland (15 km)	0:59:20.2
1968	Norway, Sweden, USSR (15 km)	0:57:30.0
1972	USSR, Finland, Norway (15 km)	0:48:46.15
1976	USSR, Finland, E. Germany	1:07:49.75
1980	E. Germany, USSR, Norway	1:02:11.1
1984	Norway, Czechoslovakia, Finland	1:06:49.7
1988	USSR, Norway, Finland	0:59:51.1
1992	United Team, Norway, Italy	0:59:34.8

Women's 20-Kilometer Relay

		Time
1994	Russia, Norway, Italy	0:57:12.5
1998	Russia, Norway, Italy	0:55:13.5
2002	Germany, Norway, Switzerland	0:49:30.6
2006	Russia, Germany, Italy	0:54:47.7

Nordic Combined—Men

7.5 Kilometer Nordic Combined

2002	Samppa Lajunen, Finland
2006	Felix Gottwald, Austria

15 Kilometer Nordic Combined

1924	Thorleif Haug, Norway
1928	Johan Grottumsbraaten, Norway
1932	Johan Grottumsbraaten, Norway
1936	Oddbjorn Hagen, Norway
1948	Heikki Hasu, Finland
1952	Simon Slattvik, Norway
1956	Sverre Stenersen, Norway
1960	Georg Thoma, W. Germany
1964	Tormod Knutsen, Norway
1968	Franz Keller, W. Germany
1972	Ulrich Wehling, E. Germany
1976	Ulrich Wehling, E. Germany
1980	Ulrich Wehling, E. Germany
1984	Tom Sandberg, Norway
1988	Hippolyt Kempf, Switzerland
1992	Fabrice Guy, France
1994	Fred Barre Lundberg, Norway
1998	Bjarte Engen Vik, Norway
2002	Samppa Lajunen, Finland
2006	Georg Hettich, Germany

Team Nordic Combined

1988	W. Germany, Switzerland, Austria
1992	Japan, Norway, Austria
1994	Japan, Norway, Switzerland
1998	Norway, Finland, France
2002	Finland, Germany, Austria
2006	Austria, Germany, Finland

Skeleton

	Men	Time
1928	Jennison Heaton, United States	3:01.8
1948	Nino Bibbia, Italy	5:23.2
2002	Jim Shea, United States	1:41.96
2006	Duff Gibson, Canada	1:55.88

	Women	Time
2002	Tristan Gale, United States	1:45.11
2006	Maya Pedersen, Switzerland	1:59.83

Ski Jumping—Men

	Normal Hill	Points
1964	Veikko Kankkonen, Finland	229.9
1968	Jiri Raska, Czechoslovakia	216.5
1972	Yukio Kasaya, Japan	244.2
1976	Hans-Georg Aschenbach, E. Germany	252.0
1980	Toni Innauer, Austria	266.3
1984	Jens Weissflog, E. Germany	215.2
1988	Matti Nykaenen, Finland	230.5
1992	Ernst Vettori, Austria	222.8
1994	Espen Bredesen, Norway	282.0
1998	Jani Soininen, Finland	234.5
2002	Simon Ammann, Switzerland	269.0
2006	Lars Bystoel, Norway	266.5

	Large Hill	Points
1924	Jacob Tullin Thams, Norway	18.960
1928	Alfred Andersen, Norway	19.208
1932	Birger Ruud, Norway	228.1
1936	Birger Ruud, Norway	232.0
1948	Petter Hugsted, Norway	228.1
1952	Arnfinn Bergmann, Norway	226.0
1956	Antti Hyvarinen, Finland	227.0
1960	Helmut Recknagel, E. Germany	227.2
1964	Toralf Engan, Norway	230.7
1968	Vladimir Beloussov, USSR	231.3
1972	Wojciech Fortuna, Poland	219.9
1976	Karl Schnabl, Austria	234.8
1980	Jouko Tormanen, Finland	271.0
1984	Matti Nykaenen, Finland	231.2
1988	Matti Nykaenen, Finland	224.0
1992	Toni Nieminen, Finland	239.5
1994	Jens Weissflog, Germany	274.5
1998	Kazuyoshi Funaki, Japan	272.3
2002	Simon Ammann, Switzerland	281.4
2006	Thomas Morgenstern, Austria	276.9

Team Large Hill

Year		Points
1988	Finland, Yugoslavia, Norway	634.4
1992	Finland, Austria, Czechoslovakia	644.4
1994	Germany, Japan, Austria	970.1
1998	Japan, Germany, Austria	933.0
2002	Germany, Finland, Slovenia	974.1
2006	Austria, Finland, Norway	984.0

Snowboarding

Men's Parallel Giant Slalom

Year		Time
1998	Ross Rebagliati, Canada	2:03.96
2002	Philipp Schoch, Switzerland	NA
2006	Philipp Schoch, Switzerland	NA

Note: In 2002, the Giant Slalom became the Parallel Giant Slalom.

Men's Halfpipe

Year		Points
1998	Gian Simmen, Switzerland	85.2
2002	Ross Powers, United States	46.1
2006	Shaun White, United States	46.8

Men's Snowboard Cross

Year	
2006	Seth Wescott, United States

Women's Parallel Giant Slalom

Year		Time
1998	Karine Ruby, France	2:17.34
2002	Isabelle Blanc, France	NA
2006	Daniela Meuli, Switzerland	NA

Note: In 2002, the Giant Slalom became the Parallel Giant Slalom.

Women's Halfpipe

Year		Points
1998	Nicola Thost, Germany	74.6
2002	Kelly Clark, United States	47.9
2006	Hannah Teter, United States	46.4

Women's Snowboard Cross

Year	
2006	Tanja Frieden, Switzerland

Speed Skating

*Olympic record

Men's 500 Meters

Year		Time
1924	Charles Jewtraw, United States	0:44.0
1928	Thunberg, Finland; Evensen, Norway (tie)	0:43.4
1932	John A. Shea, United States	0:43.4
1936	Ivar Ballangrud, Norway	0:43.4
1948	Finn Helgesen, Norway	0:43.1
1952	Kenneth Henry, United States	0:43.2
1956	Evgeniy Grishin, USSR	0:40.2
1960	Evgeniy Grishin, USSR	0:40.2
1964	Terry McDermott, United States	0:40.1
1968	Erhard Keller, W. Germany	0:40.3
1972	Erhard Keller, W. Germany	0:39.44
1976	Evgeny Kulikov, USSR	0:39.17
1980	Eric Heiden, United States	0:38.03
1984	Sergei Fokichev, USSR	0:38.19
1988	Uwe-Jens Mey, E. Germany	0:36.45
1992	Uwe-Jens Mey, E. Germany	0:37.14
1994	Aleksandr Golubev, Russia	0:36.33
1998	Hiroyasu Shimizu, Japan	0:35.59
2002	Casey FitzRandolph, United States	0:34.42*
2006	Joey Cheek, United States	0:34.82

Men's 1,000 Meters

Year		Time
1976	Peter Mueller, United States	1:19.32
1980	Eric Heiden, United States	1:15.18
1984	Gaetan Boucher, Canada	1:15.80
1988	Nikolai Guiliaev, USSR	1:13.03
1992	Olaf Zinke, Germany	1:14.85
1994	Dan Jansen, United States	1:12.43
1998	Ids Postma, Netherlands	1:10.64
2002	Gerard van Velde, Netherlands	1:07.18*
2006	Shani Davis, United States	1:08.89

Men's 1,500 Meters

Year		Time
1924	Clas Thunberg, Finland	2:20.8
1928	Clas Thunberg, Finland	2:21.1
1932	John A. Shea, United States	2:57.5
1936	Charles Mathiesen, Norway	2:19.2
1948	Sverre Farstad, Norway	2:17.6
1952	Hjalmar Andersen, Norway	2:20.4
1956	Grishin; Mikhailov, both USSR (tie)	2:08.6
1960	Aas, Norway; Grishin, USSR (tie)	2:10.4
1964	Ants Anston, USSR	2:10.3
1968	Cornelis Verkerk, Netherlands	2:03.4
1972	Ard Schenk, Netherlands	2:02.96
1976	Jan Egil Storholt, Norway	1:59.38
1980	Eric Heiden, United States	1:55.44
1984	Gaetan Boucher, Canada	1:58.36
1988	Andre Hoffman, E. Germany	1:52.06
1992	Johann Koss, Norway	1:54.81
1994	Johann Koss, Norway	1:51.29
1998	Aadne Sondral, Norway	1:47.87

Men's 1,500 Meters

Year		Time
2002	Derek Parra, United States	1:43.95*
2006	Enrico Fabris, Italy	1:45.97

Men's 5,000 Meters

Year		Time
1924	Clas Thunberg, Finland	8:39.0
1928	Ivar Ballangrud, Norway	8:50.5
1932	Irving Jaffee, United States	9:40.8
1936	Ivar Ballangrud, Norway	8:19.6
1948	Reidar Liaklev, Norway	8:29.4
1952	Hjalmar Andersen, Norway	8:10.6
1956	Boris Shilkov, USSR	7:48.7
1960	Viktor Kosichkin, USSR	7:51.3
1964	Knut Johannesen, Norway	7:38.4
1968	F. Anton Maier, Norway	7:22.4
1972	Ard Schenk, Netherlands	7:23.61
1976	Sten Stensen, Norway	7:24.48
1980	Eric Heiden, United States	7:02.29
1984	Sven Tomas Gustafson, Sweden	7:12.28
1988	Tomas Gustafson, Sweden	6:44.63
1992	Geir Karlstad, Norway	6:59.97
1994	Johann Koss, Norway	6:34.96
1998	Gianni Romme, Netherlands	6:22.20
2002	Jochem Uytdehaage, Netherlands	6:14.66*
2006	Chad Hedrick, United States	6:14.68

Men's 10,000 Meters

Year		Time
1924	Julius Skutnabb, Finland	18:04.8
1928	Event not held because of thawing of ice	
1932	Irving Jaffee, United States	19:13.6
1936	Ivar Ballangrud, Norway	17:24.3
1948	Ake Seyffarth, Sweden	17:26.3
1952	Hjalmar Andersen, Norway	16:45.8
1956	Sigvard Ericsson, Sweden	16:35.9
1960	Knut Johannesen, Norway	15:46.6
1964	Jonny Nilsson, Sweden	15:50.1
1968	Jonny Hoeglin, Sweden	15:23.6
1972	Ard Schenk, Netherlands	15:01.35
1976	Piet Kleine, Netherlands	14:50.59
1980	Eric Heiden, United States	14:28.13
1984	Igor Malkov, USSR	14:39.90
1988	Tomas Gustafson, Sweden	13:48.20
1992	Bart Veldkamp, Netherlands	14:12.12
1994	Johann Koss, Norway	13:30.55
1998	Gianni Romme, Netherlands	13:15.33
2002	Jochem Uytdehaage, Netherlands	12:58.92*
2006	Bob de Jong, Netherlands	13:01.57

Women's 500 Meters

Year		Time
1960	Helga Haase, Germany	0:45.9
1964	Lydia Skoblikova, USSR	0:45.0
1968	Ludmila Titova, USSR	0:46.1
1972	Anne Henning, United States	0:43.33
1976	Sheila Young, United States	0:42.76
1980	Karin Enke, E. Germany	0:41.78
1984	Christa Rothenburger, E. Germany	0:41.02
1988	Bonnie Blair, United States	0:39.10
1992	Bonnie Blair, United States	0:40.33
1994	Bonnie Blair, United States	0:39.25
1998	Catriona Le May-Doan, Canada	0:38.21
2002	Catriona Le May Doan, Canada	0:37.30*
2006	Svetlana Zhurova, Russia	0:38.23

Women's 1,000 Meters

Year		Time
1960	Klara Guseva, USSR	1:34.1
1964	Lydia Skoblikova, USSR	1:33.2
1968	Carolina Geijssen, Netherlands	1:32.6
1972	Monika Pflug, W. Germany	1:31.40
1976	Tatiana Averina, USSR	1:28.43
1980	Natalya Petruseva, USSR	1:24.10
1984	Karin Enke, E. Germany	1:21.61
1988	Christa Rothenburger, E. Germany	1:17.65
1992	Bonnie Blair, United States	1:21.90
1994	Bonnie Blair, United States	1:18.74
1998	Marianne Timmer, Netherlands	1:16.51
2002	Chris Witty, United States	1:13.83*
2006	Marianne Timmer, Netherlands	1:16.05

Women's 1,500 Meters

Year		Time
1960	Lydia Skoblikova, USSR	2:52.2
1964	Lydia Skoblikova, USSR	2:22.6
1968	Kaija Mustonen, Finland	2:22.4
1972	Dianne Holum, United States	2:20.85
1976	Galina Stepanskaya, USSR	2:16.58
1980	Anne Borckink, Netherlands	2:10.95
1984	Karin Enke, E. Germany	2:03.42
1988	Yvonne van Gennip, Netherlands	2:00.68
1992	Jacqueline Boerner, Germany	2:05.87
1994	Emese Hunyady, Austria	2:02.19
1998	Marianne Timmer, Netherlands	1:57.58
2002	Anni Friesinger, Germany	1:54.02*
2006	Cindy Klassen, Canada	1:55.27

Women's 3,000 Meters	Time
1960 Lydia Skoblikova, USSR	5:14.3
1964 Lydia Skoblikova, USSR	5:14.9
1968 Johanna Schut, Netherlands	4:56.2
1972 Christina Baas-Kaiser, Netherlands	4:52.14
1976 Tatiana Averina, USSR	4:45.19
1980 Bjoerg Eva Jensen, Norway	4:32.13
1984 Andrea Schoene, E. Germany	4:24.79
1988 Yvonne van Gennip, Netherlands	4:11.94
1992 Gunda Niemann, Germany	4:19.90
1994 Svetlana Bazhanova, Russia	4:17.43
1998 Gunda Niemann-Stirnemann, Germany	4:07.29
2002 Claudia Pechstein, Germany	3:57.70*
2006 Ireen Wust, Netherlands	4:02.43

Women's 5,000 Meters	Time
1988 Yvonne van Gennip, Netherlands	7:14.13
1992 Gunda Niemann, Germany	7:31.57
1994 Claudia Pechstein, Germany	7:14.37
1998 Claudia Pechstein, Germany	6:59.61
2002 Claudia Pechstein, Germany	6:46.91*
2006 Clara Hughes, Canada	6:59.07

Men's Team Pursuit	Time
2006 Italy, Canada, Netherlands	3:44.46

Women's Team Pursuit	Time
2006 Germany, Canada, Russia	3:01.25

Short-Track Speed Skating

*Olympic record

Men's 500 Meters	Time
1998 Takafumi Nishitani, Japan	42.862
2002 Marc Gagnon, Canada	41.802*
2006 Apolo Anton Ohno, United States	41.935

Men's 1,000 Meters	Time
1992 Kim Ki-Hoon, S. Korea	1:30.76
1994 Kim Ki-Hoon, S. Korea	1:34.57
1998 Dong-Sung Kim, S. Korea	1:32.375
2002 Steven Bradbury, Australia	1:29.109
2006 Hyun-Soo Ahn, S. Korea	1:26.739*

Men's 1,500 Meters	Time
2002 Apolo Anton Ohno, United States	2:18.541
2006 Hyun-Soo Ahn, S. Korea	2:25.341

Men's 5,000-Meter Relay	Time
1992 S. Korea, Canada, Japan	7:14.02
1994 Italy, United States, Australia	7:11.74
1998 Canada, S. Korea, China	7:06.075
2002 Canada, Italy, China	6:51.579
2006 S. Korea, Canada, United States	6:43.376*

Women's 500 Meters	Time
1992 Cathy Turner, United States	47.04
1994 Cathy Turner, United States	45.98
1998 Annie Perreault, Canada	46.568
2002 Yang Yang (A), China	44.187
2006 Meng Wang, China	44.345

Women's 1,000 Meters	Time
1998 Chun Lee-Kyung, S. Korea	1:42.776
2002 Yang Yang (A), China	1:36.391
2006 Sun-Yu Jin, S. Korea	1:32.859

Women's 1,500 Meters	Time
2002 Gi-Hyun Ko, S. Korea	2:31.581
2006 Sun-Yu Jin, S. Korea	2:23.494

Women's 3,000 Meter Relay	Time
1992 Canada, United States, Unified Team	4:36.62
1994 S. Korea, Canada, United States	4:26.64
1998 S. Korea, China, Canada	4:16.26
2002 S. Korea, China, Canada	4:12.793*
2006 S. Korea, Canada, Italy	4:17.040

Olympic Information

The modern Olympic Games, first held in Athens, Greece, in 1896, were the result of efforts by Baron Pierre de Coubertin, a French educator, to promote interest in education and culture and to foster better international understanding through love of athletics. His inspiration was the ancient Greek Olympic Games, most notable of the 4 Panhellenic celebrations. The games were combined patriotic, religious, and athletic festivals held every 4 years. The first such recorded festival was held in 776 BCE, which the Greeks began to keep their calendar by "Olympiads," or 4-year spans between the games.

Baron de Coubertin enlisted 13 nations to send athletes to the first modern Olympics in 1896; now athletes from nearly 200 nations and territories compete in the Summer Olympics. The Winter Olympic Games were started in 1924.

Symbol: Five rings or circles, linked together to represent the sporting friendship of all peoples. They also symbolize 5 geographic areas—Europe, Asia, Africa, Australia, and America. Each ring is a different color—blue, yellow, black, green, or red.

Flag: The symbol of the 5 rings on a plain white background.

Creed: "The most important thing in the Olympic Games is not to win but to take part, just as the most important thing in life is not the triumph but the struggle. The essential thing is not to have conquered but to have fought well."

Motto: "Citius, Altius, Fortius." Latin meaning "swifter, higher, stronger."

Oath: "In the name of all competitors I promise that we will take part in these Olympic Games, respecting and abiding by the rules which govern them, in the true spirit of sportsmanship for the glory of sport and the honor of our teams."

Flame: The modern version of the flame was adopted in 1936. The torch used to kindle it is first lit by the sun's rays at Olympia, Greece, then carried to the site of the Games by relays of runners. Ships and planes are used when necessary.

Sites of Winter Olympic Games

1924 Chamonix, France	1952 Oslo, Norway	1976 Innsbruck, Austria	1998 Nagano, Japan
1928 St. Moritz, Switzerland	1956 Cortina d'Ampezzo, Italy	1980 Lake Placid, NY	2002 Salt Lake City, UT
1932 Lake Placid, NY	1960 Squaw Valley, CA	1984 Sarajevo, Yugoslavia	2006 Turin, Italy
1936 Garmisch-Partenkirchen, Germany	1964 Innsbruck, Austria	1988 Calgary, AB, Canada	2010 Vancouver, BC, Canada
	1968 Grenoble, France	1992 Albertville, France	2014 Sochi, Russia
1948 St. Moritz, Switzerland	1972 Sapporo, Japan	1994 Lillehammer, Norway	

Sites of Summer Olympic Games

1896 Athens, Greece	1928 Amsterdam, Netherlands	1964 Tokyo, Japan	1992 Barcelona, Spain
1900 Paris, France	1932 Los Angeles, CA	1968 Mexico City, Mexico	1996 Atlanta, GA
1904 St. Louis, MO	1936 Berlin, Germany	1972 Munich, W. Germany	2000 Sydney, Australia
1906 Athens, Greece*	1948 London, England	1976 Montreal, QC, Canada	2004 Athens, Greece
1908 London, England	1952 Helsinki, Finland	1980 Moscow, USSR	2008 Beijing, China
1912 Stockholm, Sweden	1956 Melbourne, Australia	1984 Los Angeles, CA	2012 London, England
1920 Antwerp, Belgium	1960 Rome, Italy	1988 Seoul, South Korea	2016 Rio de Janeiro, Brazil
1924 Paris, France			

*Games not recognized by International Olympic Committee. Games VI (1916), XII (1940), and XIII (1944) were not celebrated.

Paralympics

The first Olympic games for the disabled were held in Rome after the 1960 Summer Olympics; use of the name "paralympic" began with the 1964 games in Tokyo. The Paralympics are held by the Olympic host country in the same year and usually the same city or venue. A goal of the Paralympics is to provide elite competition to athletes with functional disabilities that prevent their involvement in the Olympics. In 1976 the first Winter Paralympics were held, in Ornskoldsvik, Sweden.

The XIII Paralympic Summer Games were held Sept. 6-17, 2008, in Beijing, China. Nearly 4,000 athletes from a record 147 nations competed in 472 events in 20 sports including, for the first time, rowing.

The X Paralympic Winter Games were expected to be held Mar. 12-21, 2010, in Vancouver, Canada. About 650 athletes from 45 nations were expected to compete in 5 sports.

Special Olympics

Special Olympics is an international program of year-round sports training and athletic competition for people with intellectual disabilities. All 50 U.S. states, Washington, DC, and Guam have chapter offices. In addition, there are accredited Special Olympics programs in more than 165 countries. Persons wishing to volunteer or find out more can contact Special Olympics, 1133 19th St. NW, Washington, DC 20036, or access the Special Olympics website at www.specialolympics.org

The 12th Special Olympics World Summer Games were held Oct. 2-11, 2007, in Shanghai, China. Almost 7,500 athletes, 3,500 event officials, and 40,000 volunteers attended the first Special Olympic World Games held in Asia. Twenty-five athletic events were held, including badminton, bocce, bowling, cycling, equestrian sports, golf, gymnastics (artistic and rhythmic), judo, kayaking, powerlifting, roller skating, swimming and diving, table tennis, tennis, and track and field. Scheduled team sports included basketball, cricket, dragon boat racing, handball, lion dancing, sailing, soccer, and volleyball.

The 9th Special Olympics World Winter Games were held in Boise, ID, Feb. 7-13, 2009. More than 2,000 athletes from 113 countries competed in alpine skiing, cross-country skiing, figure skating, floor hockey, snowboarding, snowshoeing, and speed skating events.

TRACK AND FIELD

World Track and Field Outdoor Records

As of Oct. 1, 2009.

The International Association of Athletics Federations, the world body of track and field, recognizes only records in metric distances, except for the mile. *Pending ratification.

Men's Records

Running

Event	Record	Holder	Nationality	Date	Location
100 meters	9.58 s.	Usain Bolt	Jamaica	Aug. 16, 2009	Berlin, Germany
200 meters	19.19 s.	Usain Bolt	Jamaica	Aug. 20, 2009	Berlin, Germany
400 meters	43.18 s.	Michael Johnson	U.S.	Aug. 26, 1999	Seville, Spain
800 meters	1 min, 41.11 s.	Wilson Kipketer	Denmark	Aug. 24, 1997	Cologne, Germany
1,000 meters	2 min, 11.96 s.	Noah Ngeny	Kenya	Sept. 5, 1999	Rieti, Italy
1,500 meters	3 min, 26.00 s.	Hicham El Guerrouj	Morocco	July 14, 1998	Rome, Italy
1 mile	3 min, 43.13 s.	Hicham El Guerrouj	Morocco	July 7, 1999	Rome, Italy
2,000 meters	4 min, 44.79 s.	Hicham El Guerrouj	Morocco	Sept. 7, 1999	Berlin, Germany
3,000 meters	7 min, 20.67 s.	Daniel Komen	Kenya	Sept. 1, 1996	Rieti, Italy
5,000 meters	12 min, 37.35 s.	Kenenisa Bekele	Ethiopia	May 31, 2004	Hengelo, Netherlands
10,000 meters	26 min, 17.53 s.	Kenenisa Bekele	Ethiopia	Aug. 26, 2005	Brussels, Belgium
20,000 meters	56 min, 26.00 s.	Haile Gebrselassie	Ethiopia	June 27, 2007	Ostrava, Czech Rep.
25,000 meters	1 hr., 13 min, 55.80 s.	Toshihiko Seko	Japan	Mar. 22, 1981	Christchurch, NZ
3,000 meter stpl.	7 min, 53.63 s.	Saif Saaeed Shaheen	Qatar	Sept. 3, 2004	Brussels, Belgium
Marathon	2 hr., 3 min, 59.00 s.	Haile Gebrselassie	Ethiopia	Sept. 28, 2008	Berlin, Germany

Hurdles

Event	Record	Holder	Nationality	Date	Location
110 meters	12.87 s.	Dayron Robles	Cuba	June 12, 2008	Ostrava, Czech Rep.
400 meters	46.78 s.	Kevin Young	U.S.	Aug. 6, 1992	Barcelona, Spain

Relay Races

Event	Record	Holder	Nationality	Date	Location
400 mtrs. (4x100)	37.10 s.	(Carter, Frater, Bolt, Powell)	Jamaica	Aug. 22, 2008	Beijing, China
800 mtrs. (4x200)	1 min, 18.68 s.	(Marsh, Burrell, Heard, Lewis)	U.S.	Apr. 17, 1994	Walnut, CA
1,600 mtrs. (4×400)	2 min, 54.29 s.[1]	(Valmon, Watts, Reynolds, Johnson)	U.S.	Aug. 22, 1993	Stuttgart, Germany
3,200 mtrs. (4×800)	7 min, 2.43 s.	(Mutua, Yiampoy, Kombich, Bungei)	Kenya	Aug. 25, 2006	Brussels, Belgium

(1) IAAF voted in Aug. 2008 to revoke a new world record set by the U.S. team in 1998; one of its members, Antonio Pettigrew, admitted to doping in May 2008.

Field Events

Event	Record	Holder	Nationality	Date	Location
High jump	2.45m (8' ½")	Javier Sotomayor	Cuba	July 27, 1993	Salamanca, Spain
Long jump	8.95m (29' 4½")	Mike Powell	U.S.	Aug. 30, 1991	Tokyo, Japan
Triple jump	18.29m (60' ¼")	Jonathan Edwards	Gr. Britain	Aug. 7, 1995	Göteborg, Sweden
Pole vault	6.14m (20' 1¾")	Sergey Bubka	Ukraine	July 31, 1994	Sestriere, Italy
16-lb. shot put	23.12m (75' 10¼")	Randy Barnes	U.S.	May 20, 1990	Westwood, CA
Discus	74.08m (243' 0")	Jürgen Schult	E. Germany	June 6, 1986	Neubrandenburg, E. Germany
Javelin	98.48m (323' 1")	Jan Železný	Czech Rep.	May 25, 1996	Stuttgart, W. Germany
16-lb. hammer	86.74m (284' 7")	Yuriy Sedykh	USSR	Aug. 30, 1986	Jena, Germany
Decathlon	9,026 pts.	Roman Šebrle	Czech Rep.	May 27, 2001	Götzis, Austria

Women's Records

Running

Event	Record	Holder	Nationality	Date	Location
100 meters	10.49 s.	Florence Griffith-Joyner	U.S.	July 16, 1988	Indianapolis, IN
200 meters	21.34 s.	Florence Griffith-Joyner	U.S.	Sept. 29, 1988	Seoul, S. Korea
400 meters	47.60 s.	Marita Koch	E. Germany	Oct. 6, 1985	Canberra, Australia
800 meters	1 min, 53.28 s.	Jarmila Kratochvílová	Czechoslovakia	July 26, 1983	Munich, W. Germany
1,000 meters	2 min, 28.98 s.	Svetlana Masterkova	Russia	Aug. 23, 1996	Brussels, Belgium
1,500 meters	3 min, 50.46 s.	Qu Yunxia	China	Sept. 11, 1993	Beijing, China
1 mile	4 min, 12.56 s.	Svetlana Masterkova	Russia	Aug. 14, 1996	Zurich, Switzerland
2,000 meters	5 min, 25.36 s.	Sonia O'Sullivan	Ireland	July 8, 1994	Edinburgh, Scotland
3,000 meters	8 min, 6.11 s.	Wang Junxia	China	Sept. 13, 1993	Beijing, China
3,000 meter stpl.	8 min, 58.81 s.	Gulnara Galkina-Samitova	Russia	Aug. 17, 2008	Beijing, China

Event	Record	Holder	Nationality	Date	Location
5,000 meters	14 min, 11.15 s.	Tirunesh Dibaba	Ethiopia	June 6, 2008	Oslo, Norway
10,000 meters	29 min, 31.78 s.	Wang Junxia	China	Sept. 8, 1993	Beijing, China
20,000 meters	1 h., 5 min, 26.60 s.	Tegla Loroupe	Kenya	Sept. 3, 2000	Borgholzhausen, Germany
30,000 meters	1 h., 45 min, 50.00 s.	Tegla Loroupe	Kenya	June 6, 2003	Warstein, Germany
Marathon	2 h., 15 min, 25.00 s.	Paula Radcliffe	UK	April 13, 2003	London, England

Hurdles

Event	Record	Holder	Nationality	Date	Location
100 meters	12.21 s.	Yordanka Donkova	Bulgaria	Aug. 20, 1988	Stara Zagora, Bulgaria
400 meters	52.34 s.	Yuliya Pechenkina	Russia	Aug. 8, 2003	Tula, Russia

Relay Races

Event	Record	Holder	Nationality	Date	Location
400 mtrs. (4×100).	41.37 s.	(Gladisch, Rieger, Auerswald, Goehr)	E. Germany	Oct. 6, 1985	Canberra, Australia
800 mtrs. (4×200).	1 min, 27.46 s.	U.S. "Blue" (Jenkins, Colander, Perry, Jones)	U.S.	Apr. 29, 2000	Philadelphia, PA
1,600 mtrs. (4×400)	3 min, 15.17 s.	(Ledovskaya, Nazarova, Pinigina, Bryzgina)	USSR	Oct. 1, 1988	Seoul, S. Korea
3,200 mtrs. (4×800)	7 min, 50.17 s.	(Olizarenko, Gurina, Borisova, Podyalovskaya)	USSR	Aug. 5, 1984	Moscow, USSR

Field Events

Event	Record	Holder	Nationality	Date	Location
High jump	2.09m (6' 10¼")	Stefka Kostadinova	Bulgaria	Aug. 30, 1987	Rome, Italy
Long jump	7.52m (24' 8¼")	Galina Chistyakova	USSR	June 11, 1988	Leningrad, Russia
Triple jump	15.50m (50' 10¼")	Inessa Kravets	Ukraine	Aug. 10, 1995	Göteborg, Sweden
Pole vault	5.06m (16' 7¼")*	Yelena Isinbaeva	Russia	Aug. 28, 2009	Zürich, Switzerland
Shot put	22.63m (74' 3").	Natalya Lisovskaya	USSR	June 7, 1987	Moscow, Russia
Discus	76.80m (252' 0").	Gabriele Reinsch	E. Germany	July 9, 1988	Neubrandenburg, E. Germany
Hammer	77.96m (255' 9¼")	Anita Włodarczyk	Poland	Aug. 22, 2009	Berlin, Germany
Javelin	72.28m (237' 1¾")	Barbora Špotáková	Czech Rep.	Sept. 13, 2008	Stuttgart, Germany
Heptathlon	7,291 pts.	Jackie Joyner-Kersee	U.S.	Sept. 24, 1988	Seoul, S. Korea

World Track and Field Indoor Records

As of Oct. 1, 2009.

The International Association of Athletics Federations first recognized world indoor track and field records on Jan. 1, 1987. World indoor bests set prior to Jan. 1, 1987, were subject to approval as world records providing they met the IAAF world records criteria, including drug testing. Criteria for indoor and outdoor records are the same, except that a track performance cannot be set on an indoor track longer than 200 meters. (a) = altitude.

Men's Records

Event	Record	Holder	Nationality	Date	Location
50 meters	5.56 s. (a)	Donovan Bailey	Canada	Feb. 9, 1996	Reno, NV
60 meters	6.39 s.	Maurice Greene	U.S.	Mar. 3, 2001	Atlanta, GA
	6.39 s.	Maurice Greene	U.S.	Feb. 3, 1998	Madrid, Spain
200 meters	19.92 s.	Frank Fredericks	Namibia	Feb. 18, 1996	Liévin, France
400 meters	44.57 s.	Kerron Clement	U.S.	Mar. 12, 2005	Fayetteville, AR
800 meters	1 min., 42.67 s.	Wilson Kipketer	Denmark	Mar. 9, 1997	Paris, France
1,000 meters	2 min., 14.96 s.	Wilson Kipketer	Denmark	Feb. 20, 2000	Birmingham, England
1,500 meters	3 min., 31.18 s.	Hicham El Guerrouj	Morocco	Feb. 2, 1997	Stuttgart, Germany
1 mile	3 min., 48.45 s.	Hicham El Guerrouj	Morocco	Feb. 12, 1997	Ghent, Belgium
3,000 meters	7 min., 24.90 s.	Daniel Komen	Kenya	Feb. 6, 1998	Budapest, Hungary
5,000 meters	12 min., 49.60 s.	Kenenisa Bekele	Ethiopia	Feb. 20, 2004	Birmingham, England
50-meter hurdles	6.25 s.	Mark McKoy	Canada	Mar. 5, 1986	Kobe, Japan
60-meter hurdles	7.30 s.	Colin Jackson	Gr. Britain	Mar. 6, 1994	Sindelfingen, Germany
High jump	2.43m (7' 11½")	Javier Sotomayor	Cuba	Mar. 4, 1989	Budapest, Hungary
Pole vault	6.15m (20' 2")	Sergey Bubka	Ukraine	Feb. 21, 1993	Donetsk, Ukraine
Long jump	8.79m (28' 10¼")	Carl Lewis	U.S.	Jan. 27, 1984	New York, NY
Triple jump	17.83m (58' 6")	Aliecer Urrutia	Cuba	Mar. 1, 1997	Sindelfingen, Germany
	17.83m (58' 6")	Christian Olsson	Sweden	Mar. 7, 2004	Budapest, Hungary
Shot put	22.66m (74' 4¼")	Randy Barnes	U.S.	Jan. 20, 1989	Los Angeles, CA

Women's Records

Event	Record	Holder	Nationality	Date	Location
50 meters	5.96 s.	Irina Privalova	Russia	Feb. 9, 1995	Madrid, Spain
60 meters	6.92 s.	Irina Privalova	Russia	Feb. 9, 1995	Madrid, Spain
	6.92 s.	Irina Privalova	Russia	Feb. 11, 1993	Madrid, Spain
200 meters	21.87 s.	Merlene Ottey	Jamaica	Feb. 13, 1993	Liévin, France
400 meters	49.59 s.	Jarmila Kratochvílová	Czechoslovakia	Mar. 7, 1982	Milan, Italy
800 meters	1 min., 55.82 s.	Jolanda Ceplak	Slovenia	Mar. 3, 2002	Vienna, Austria
1,000 meters	2 min., 30.94 s.	Maria Mutola	Mozambique	Feb. 25, 1999	Stockholm, Sweden
1,500 meters	3 min., 58.28 s.	Yelena Soboleva	Russia	Feb. 18, 2006	Moscow, Russia
1 mile	4 min., 17.14 s.	Doina Melinte	Romania	Feb. 9, 1990	E. Rutherford, NJ
3,000 meters	8 min., 23.72 s.	Meseret Defar	Ethiopia	Feb. 3, 2007	Stuttgart, Germany
5,000 meters	14 min., 24.37 s.	Meseret Defar	Ethiopia	Feb. 18, 2009	Stockholm, Sweden
50-meter hurdles	6.58 s.	Cornelia Oschkenat	E. Germany	Feb. 20, 1988	Berlin, Germany
60-meter hurdles	7.68 s.	Susanna Kallur	Sweden	Feb. 10, 2008	Karlsruhe, Germany
High jump	2.08m (6' 10")	Kajsa Bergqvist	Sweden	Feb. 4, 2006	Arnstadt, Germany
Pole vault	5.00m (16' 4¾")	Yelena Isinbaeva	Russia	Feb. 15, 2009	Donetsk, Ukraine
Long jump	7.37m (24' 2¼")	Heike Drechsler	E. Germany	Feb. 13, 1988	Vienna, Austria
Triple jump	15.36m (50' 4¾")	Tatyana Lebedeva	Russia	Mar. 3, 2004	Budapest, Hungary
Shot put	22.50m (73' 10")	Helena Fibingerová	Czechoslovakia	Feb. 19, 1977	Jablonec, Czechoslovakia

COLLEGE BASKETBALL
2009 Men's NCAA Tournament: An Old Favorite Dominates

The Univ. of North Carolina Tar Heels defeated Michigan State, 89-72, to win NCAA Men's Division I national basketball title Apr. 6, 2009, in Detroit, MI. The Tar Heels' offense set two records by halftime, leading the Spartans 55-34 for the highest first-half point-total and the biggest halftime lead. With the tournament win, North Carolina became the first team to begin and end the season in first place since 1982, when James Worthy and Michael Jordan led the Tar Heels to the championship.

NCAA Division I Basketball Champions, 1939-2009

Year	Champion	Coach	Final opponent	Score	Most outstanding player	Site
1939	Oregon	Howard Hobson	Ohio St.	46-33	Jimmy Hull, Ohio St.	Evanston, IL
1940	Indiana	Branch McCracken	Kansas	60-42	Marvin Huffman, Indiana	Kansas City, MO
1941	Wisconsin	Harold Foster	Washington St.	39-34	John Kotz, Wisconsin	Kansas City, MO
1942	Stanford	Everett Dean	Dartmouth	53-38	Howard Dallmar, Stanford	Kansas City, MO
1943	Wyoming	Everett Shelton	Georgetown	46-34	Ken Sailors, Wyoming	New York, NY
1944	Utah	Vadal Peterson	Dartmouth	42-40[1]	Arnold Ferrin, Utah	New York, NY
1945	Oklahoma St.[2]	Henry Iba	NYU	49-45	Bob Kurland, Oklahoma St.	New York, NY
1946	Oklahoma St.[2]	Henry Iba	North Carolina	43-40	Bob Kurland, Oklahoma St.	New York, NY
1947	Holy Cross	Alvin Julian	Oklahoma	58-47	George Kaftan, Holy Cross	New York, NY
1948	Kentucky	Adolph Rupp	Baylor	58-42	Alex Groza, Kentucky	New York, NY
1949	Kentucky	Adolph Rupp	Oklahoma St.	46-36	Alex Groza, Kentucky	Seattle, WA
1950	CCNY	Nat Holman	Bradley	71-68	Irwin Dambrot, CCNY	New York, NY
1951	Kentucky	Adolph Rupp	Kansas St.	68-58	Bill Spivey, Kentucky	Minneapolis, MN
1952	Kansas	Forrest Allen	St. John's	80-63	Clyde Lovellette, Kansas	Seattle, WA
1953	Indiana	Branch McCracken	Kansas	69-68	B. H. Born, Kansas	Kansas City, MO
1954	La Salle	Kenneth Loeffler	Bradley	92-76	Tom Gola, La Salle	Kansas City, MO
1955	San Francisco	Phil Woolpert	La Salle	77-63	Bill Russell, San Francisco	Kansas City, MO
1956	San Francisco	Phil Woolpert	Iowa	83-71	Hal Lear, Temple	Evanston, IL
1957	North Carolina	Frank McGuire	Kansas	54-53[1]	Wilt Chamberlain, Kansas	Kansas City, MO
1958	Kentucky	Adolph Rupp	Seattle	84-72	Elgin Baylor, Seattle	Louisville, KY
1959	California	Pete Newell	West Virginia	71-70	Jerry West, West Virginia	Louisville, KY
1960	Ohio St.	Fred Taylor	California	75-55	Jerry Lucas, Ohio St.	San Francisco, CA
1961	Cincinnati	Edwin Jucker	Ohio St.	70-65[1]	Jerry Lucas, Ohio St.	Kansas City, MO
1962	Cincinnati	Edwin Jucker	Ohio St.	71-59	Paul Hogue, Cincinnati	Louisville, KY
1963	Loyola (IL)	George Ireland	Cincinnati	60-58[1]	Art Heyman, Duke	Louisville, KY
1964	UCLA	John Wooden	Duke	98-83	Walt Hazzard, UCLA	Kansas City, MO
1965	UCLA	John Wooden	Michigan	91-80	Bill Bradley, Princeton	Portland, OR
1966	Texas-El Paso[3]	Don Haskins	Kentucky	72-65	Jerry Chambers, Utah	College Park, MD
1967	UCLA	John Wooden	Dayton	79-64	Lew Alcindor, UCLA	Louisville, KY
1968	UCLA	John Wooden	North Carolina	78-55	Lew Alcindor, UCLA	Los Angeles, CA
1969	UCLA	John Wooden	Purdue	92-72	Lew Alcindor, UCLA	Louisville, KY
1970	UCLA	John Wooden	Jacksonville	80-69	Sidney Wicks, UCLA	College Park, MD
1971	UCLA	John Wooden	Villanova*	68-62	Howard Porter, Villanova*	Houston, TX
1972	UCLA	John Wooden	Florida St.	81-76	Bill Walton, UCLA	Los Angeles, CA
1973	UCLA	John Wooden	Memphis[4]	87-66	Bill Walton, UCLA	St. Louis, MO
1974	North Carolina St.	Norm Sloan	Marquette	76-64	David Thompson, NC St.	Greensboro, NC
1975	UCLA	John Wooden	Kentucky	92-85	Richard Washington, UCLA	San Diego, CA
1976	Indiana	Bob Knight	Michigan	86-68	Kent Benson, Indiana	Philadelphia, PA
1977	Marquette	Al McGuire	North Carolina	67-59	Butch Lee, Marquette	Atlanta, GA
1978	Kentucky	Joe Hall	Duke	94-88	Jack Givens, Kentucky	St. Louis, MO
1979	Michigan St.	Jud Heathcote	Indiana St.	75-64	Magic Johnson, Michigan St.	Salt Lake City, UT
1980	Louisville	Denny Crum	UCLA*	59-54	Darrell Griffith, Louisville	Indianapolis, IN
1981	Indiana	Bob Knight	North Carolina	63-50	Isiah Thomas, Indiana	Philadelphia, PA
1982	North Carolina	Dean Smith	Georgetown	63-62	James Worthy, N. Carolina	New Orleans, LA
1983	North Carolina St.	Jim Valvano	Houston	54-52	Hakeem Olajuwon, Houston	Albuquerque, NM
1984	Georgetown	John Thompson	Houston	84-75	Patrick Ewing, Georgetown	Seattle, WA
1985	Villanova	Rollie Massimino	Georgetown	66-64	Ed Pinckney, Villanova	Lexington, KY
1986	Louisville	Denny Crum	Duke	72-69	Pervis Ellison, Louisville	Dallas, TX
1987	Indiana	Bob Knight	Syracuse	74-73	Keith Smart, Indiana	New Orleans, LA
1988	Kansas	Larry Brown	Oklahoma	83-79	Danny Manning, Kansas	Kansas City, MO
1989	Michigan	Steve Fisher	Seton Hall	80-79[1]	Glen Rice, Michigan	Seattle, WA
1990	UNLV	Jerry Tarkanian	Duke	103-73	Anderson Hunt, UNLV	Denver, CO
1991	Duke	Mike Krzyzewski	Kansas	72-65	Christian Laettner, Duke	Indianapolis, IN
1992	Duke	Mike Krzyzewski	Michigan	71-51	Bobby Hurley, Duke	Minneapolis, MN
1993	North Carolina	Dean Smith	Michigan	77-71	Donald Williams, N. Carolina	New Orleans, LA
1994	Arkansas	Nolan Richardson	Duke	76-72	Corliss Williamson, Arkansas	Charlotte, NC
1995	UCLA	Jim Harrick	Arkansas	89-78	Ed O'Bannon, UCLA	Seattle, WA
1996	Kentucky	Rick Pitino	Syracuse	76-67	Tony Delk, Kentucky	E. Rutherford, NJ
1997	Arizona	Lute Olson	Kentucky	84-79[1]	Miles Simon, Arizona	Indianapolis, IN
1998	Kentucky	Tubby Smith	Utah	78-69	Jeff Sheppard, Kentucky	San Antonio, TX
1999	Connecticut	Jim Calhoun	Duke	77-74	Richard Hamilton, Connecticut	St. Petersburg, FL
2000	Michigan St.	Tom Izzo	Florida	89-76	Mateen Cleaves, Michigan St.	Indianapolis, IN
2001	Duke	Mike Krzyzewski	Arizona	82-72	Shane Battier, Duke	Minneapolis, MN
2002	Maryland	Gary Williams	Indiana	64-52	Juan Dixon, Maryland	Atlanta, GA
2003	Syracuse	Jim Boeheim	Kansas	81-78	Carmelo Anthony, Syracuse	New Orleans, LA
2004	Connecticut	Jim Calhoun	Georgia Tech	82-73	Emeka Okafor, Connecticut	San Antonio, TX
2005	North Carolina	Roy Williams	Illinois	75-70	Sean May, North Carolina	St. Louis, MO
2006	Florida	Billy Donovan	UCLA	73-57	Joakim Noah, Florida	Indianapolis, IN
2007	Florida	Billy Donovan	Ohio State	84-75	Corey Brewer, Florida	Atlanta, GA
2008	Kansas	Bill Self	Memphis	75-68[1]	Mario Chalmers, Kansas	San Antonio, TX
2009	North Carolina	Roy Williams	Michigan State	89-72	Wayne Ellington, North Carolina	Detroit, MI

*Declared ineligible after the tournament. (1) Overtime. (2) Then known as Oklahoma A&M. (3) Then known as Texas Western. (4) Then known as Memphis State.

Top Division I Basketball Career Scorers
(Through 2008-09 season. Minimum 1,500 points; ranked by average points per game.)

Player, school	Years	Points	Avg.	Player, school	Years	Points	Avg.
Pete Maravich, LSU	1968-70	3,667	44.2	Dwight Lamar, LA-Lafayette[1]	1972-73	1,862	32.7
Austin Carr, Notre Dame	1969-71	2,560	34.6	Frank Selvy, Furman	1952-54	2,538	32.5
Oscar Robertson, Cincinnati	1958-60	2,973	33.8	Rick Mount, Purdue	1968-70	2,323	32.3
Calvin Murphy, Niagara	1968-70	2,548	33.1	Darrell Floyd, Furman	1954-56	2,281	32.1

(1) Known as SW Louisiana until 1999.

2009 MEN'S NCAA BASKETBALL TOURNAMENT

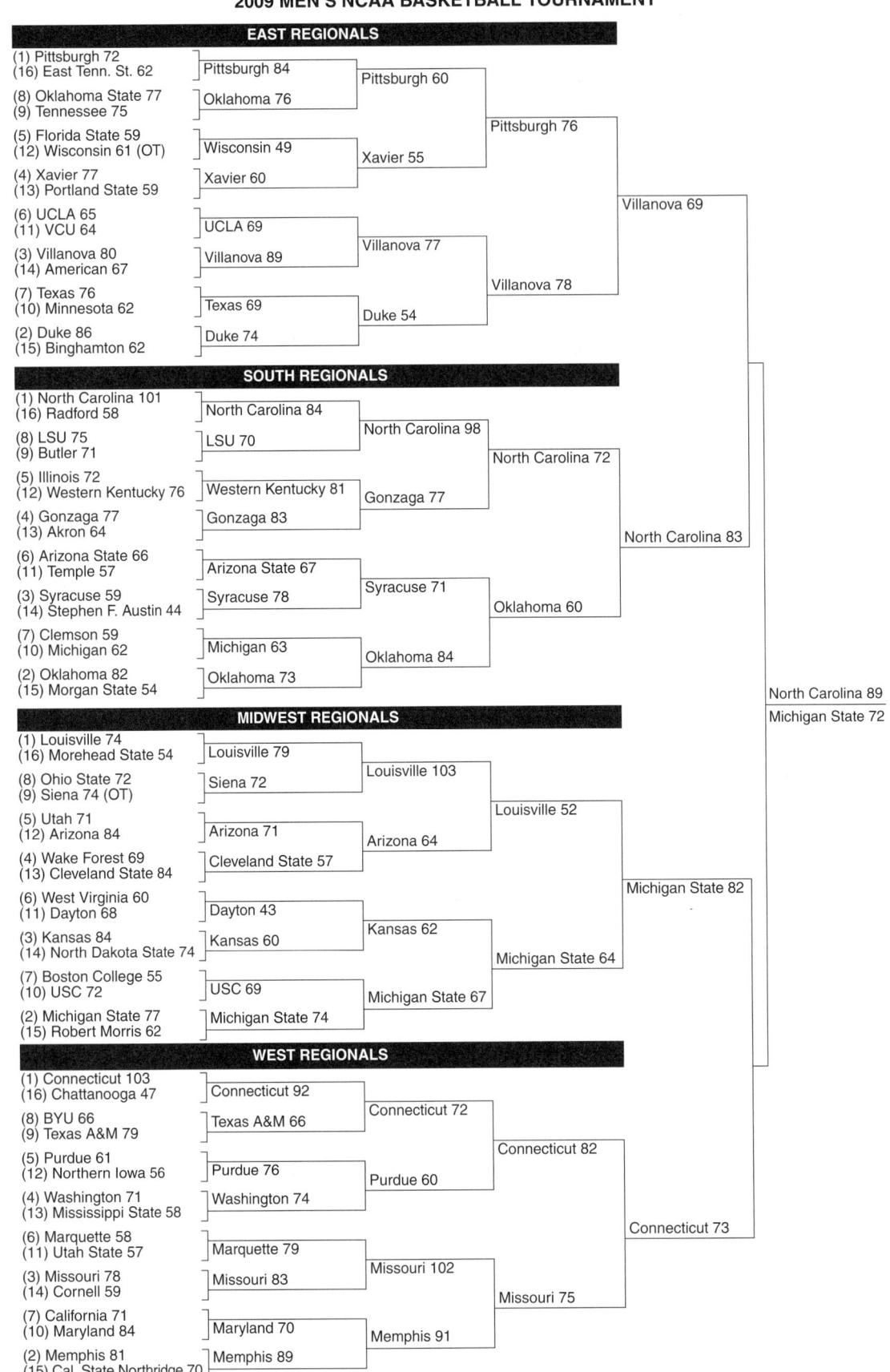

EAST REGIONALS

(1) Pittsburgh 72
(16) East Tenn. St. 62   Pittsburgh 84
                                                Pittsburgh 60
(8) Oklahoma State 77
(9) Tennessee 75   Oklahoma 76
                                                                Pittsburgh 76
(5) Florida State 59
(12) Wisconsin 61 (OT)   Wisconsin 49
                                                Xavier 55
(4) Xavier 77
(13) Portland State 59   Xavier 60
                                                                                Villanova 69
(6) UCLA 65
(11) VCU 64   UCLA 69
                                                Villanova 77
(3) Villanova 80
(14) American 67   Villanova 89
                                                                Villanova 78
(7) Texas 76
(10) Minnesota 62   Texas 69
                                                Duke 54
(2) Duke 86
(15) Binghamton 62   Duke 74

SOUTH REGIONALS

(1) North Carolina 101
(16) Radford 58   North Carolina 84
                                                North Carolina 98
(8) LSU 75
(9) Butler 71   LSU 70
                                                                North Carolina 72
(5) Illinois 72
(12) Western Kentucky 76   Western Kentucky 81
                                                Gonzaga 77
(4) Gonzaga 77
(13) Akron 64   Gonzaga 83
                                                                                North Carolina 83
(6) Arizona State 66
(11) Temple 57   Arizona State 67
                                                Syracuse 71
(3) Syracuse 59
(14) Stephen F. Austin 44   Syracuse 78
                                                                Oklahoma 60
(7) Clemson 59
(10) Michigan 62   Michigan 63
                                                Oklahoma 84
(2) Oklahoma 82
(15) Morgan State 54   Oklahoma 73

North Carolina 89
Michigan State 72

MIDWEST REGIONALS

(1) Louisville 74
(16) Morehead State 54   Louisville 79
                                                Louisville 103
(8) Ohio State 72
(9) Siena 74 (OT)   Siena 72
                                                                Louisville 52
(5) Utah 71
(12) Arizona 84   Arizona 71
                                                Arizona 64
(4) Wake Forest 69
(13) Cleveland State 84   Cleveland State 57
                                                                                Michigan State 82
(6) West Virginia 60
(11) Dayton 68   Dayton 43
                                                Kansas 62
(3) Kansas 84
(14) North Dakota State 74   Kansas 60
                                                                Michigan State 64
(7) Boston College 55
(10) USC 72   USC 69
                                                Michigan State 67
(2) Michigan State 77
(15) Robert Morris 62   Michigan State 74

WEST REGIONALS

(1) Connecticut 103
(16) Chattanooga 47   Connecticut 92
                                                Connecticut 72
(8) BYU 66
(9) Texas A&M 79   Texas A&M 66
                                                                Connecticut 82
(5) Purdue 61
(12) Northern Iowa 56   Purdue 76
                                                Purdue 60
(4) Washington 71
(13) Mississippi State 58   Washington 74
                                                                                Connecticut 73
(6) Marquette 58
(11) Utah State 57   Marquette 79
                                                Missouri 102
(3) Missouri 78
(14) Cornell 59   Missouri 83
                                                                Missouri 75
(7) California 71
(10) Maryland 84   Maryland 70
                                                Memphis 91
(2) Memphis 81
(15) Cal. State Northridge 70 Memphis 89

Men's Basketball Final Division I Conference Standings, 2008-09
(*conference tournament champion)

America East

	Conf. W	L	All W	L
Vermont	13	3	24	9
Binghamton*	13	3	23	9
Boston Univ.	11	5	17	13
Stony Brook	8	8	16	14
New Hampshire	8	8	14	16
UMBC	7	9	15	17
Albany	6	10	15	16
Maine	4	12	9	21
Hartford	2	14	7	26

Atlantic Coast

	Conf. W	L	All W	L
North Carolina	13	3	34	4
Duke*	11	5	30	7
Wake Forest	11	5	24	7
Florida State	10	6	25	10
Clemson	9	7	23	9
Boston Coll.	9	7	22	12
Maryland	7	9	21	14
Miami (FL)	7	9	19	13
Virginia Tech	7	9	19	15
NC State	6	10	16	14
Virginia	4	12	10	18
Georgia Tech	2	14	12	19

Atlantic Sun[1]

	Conf. W	L	All W	L
Jacksonville	15	5	18	14
E. Tennessee St.*	14	6	23	11
Belmont	14	6	20	13
Lipscomb	12	8	17	14
Mercer	11	9	17	15
Campbell	11	9	14	16
Stetson	9	11	13	17
SC Upstate	8	12	9	21
Florida Gulf Coast	7	13	11	20
North Florida	6	14	8	22
Kennesaw St.	3	17	7	22

Atlantic 10

	Conf. W	L	All W	L
Xavier	12	4	27	8
Dayton	11	5	27	8
Rhode Island	11	5	23	11
Temple*	11	5	22	12
Duquesne	9	7	21	13
La Salle	9	7	18	13
Richmond	9	7	20	16
St. Joseph's	9	7	17	15
Saint Louis	8	8	18	14
Massachusetts	7	9	12	18
St. Bonaventure	6	10	15	15
Charlotte	5	11	11	20
George Washington	4	12	10	18
Fordham	1	15	3	25

Big East

	Conf. W	L	All W	L
Louisville*	16	2	31	6
Pittsburgh	15	3	31	5
Connecticut	15	3	31	5
Villanova	13	5	30	8
Marquette	12	6	25	10
Syracuse	11	7	28	10
West Virginia	10	8	23	12
Providence	10	8	19	14
Notre Dame	8	10	21	15
Cincinnati	8	10	18	14
Seton Hall	7	11	17	15
Georgetown	7	11	16	15
St. John's	6	12	16	18
South Florida	4	14	9	22
Rutgers	2	16	11	21
DePaul	0	18	9	24

Big Sky

	Conf. W	L	All W	L
Weber State	15	1	21	10
Portland State*	11	5	23	10
Montana	11	5	17	12
Idaho State	9	7	13	19
Northern Colorado	8	8	14	18
Montana State	6	10	14	17
Eastern Washington	6	10	12	18
Northern Arizona	5	11	8	19
Sacramento St.	1	15	2	27

Big South

	Conf. W	L	All W	L
Radford*	15	3	21	12
VMI	13	5	24	8
Liberty	12	6	23	12
NC Asheville	10	8	15	16
Gardner-Webb	9	9	13	17
Presbyterian	9	9	12	17
Winthrop	9	9	11	19
Coastal Carolina	5	13	11	20
Charleston State	4	14	9	20
High Point	4	14	9	21

Big 10

	Conf. W	L	All W	L
Michigan State	15	3	31	7
Purdue*	11	7	27	10
Illinois	11	7	24	10
Penn State	10	8	27	11
Ohio State	10	8	22	11
Wisconsin	10	8	20	13
Minnesota	9	9	22	11
Michigan	9	9	21	14
Northwestern	8	10	17	14
Iowa	5	13	15	17
Indiana	1	17	6	25

Big 12

	Conf. W	L	All W	L
Kansas	14	2	27	8
Oklahoma	13	3	30	6
Missouri*	12	4	31	7
Texas A&M	9	7	24	10
Oklahoma State	9	7	23	12
Texas	9	7	23	12
Kansas State	9	7	22	12
Nebraska	8	8	18	13
Baylor	5	11	24	15
Iowa State	4	12	15	17
Texas Tech	3	13	14	19
Colorado	1	15	9	22

Big West[1]

	Conf. W	L	All W	L
CSU Northridge*	11	5	17	14
Pacific	10	6	21	13
Long Beach State	10	6	15	15
UC Riverside	8	8	17	13
UC Santa Barbara	8	8	16	15
UC Irvine	8	8	12	19
CSU Fullerton	7	9	15	17
UC Davis	7	9	13	19
Cal. Poly	3	13	7	21

Colonial Athletic Association

	Conf. W	L	All W	L
VCU*	14	4	24	10
George Mason	13	5	22	11
Old Dominion	12	6	25	10
Northeastern	12	6	19	13
Hofstra	11	7	21	11
Drexel	10	8	15	14
James Madison	9	9	21	15
Georgia State	8	10	12	20
Delaware	6	12	13	19
Towson	5	13	12	22
William & Mary	5	13	10	20
NC Wilmington	3	15	7	25

Conference USA

	Conf. W	L	All W	L
Memphis*	16	0	33	4
Tulsa	12	4	25	11
UAB	11	5	22	12
Houston	10	6	21	12
UTEP	10	6	23	14
Central Florida	7	9	17	14
Marshall	7	9	15	17
Tulane	7	9	14	17
East Carolina	5	11	13	17
Southern Miss.	4	12	15	17
Rice	4	12	10	22
SMU	3	13	9	21

Horizon League[1]

	Conf. W	L	All W	L
Butler	15	3	26	6
WI-Green Bay	13	5	22	11
Cleveland State*	12	6	26	11
Wright State	12	6	20	13
WI-Milwaukee	11	7	17	14
Illinois-Chicago	7	11	16	15
Youngstown State	7	11	11	19
Loyola Chicago	6	12	14	18
Valparaiso	5	13	9	22
Detroit	2	16	7	23

Ivy League[2]

	Conf. W	L	All W	L
Cornell	11	3	21	10
Princeton	8	6	13	14
Yale	8	6	13	15
Columbia	7	7	12	16
Dartmouth	7	7	9	19
Harvard	6	8	14	14
Pennsylvania	6	8	10	18
Brown	3	11	9	19

Metro Atlantic Athletic

	Conf. W	L	All W	L
Siena*	16	2	27	8
Niagara	14	4	26	9
Rider	12	6	19	13
Manhattan	9	9	16	14
Fairfield	9	9	17	15
St. Peter's	8	10	11	19
Iona	7	11	12	19
Loyola (MD)	7	11	12	20
Canisius	4	14	11	20
Marist	4	14	10	23

Mid-American
East Division

	Conf. W	L	All W	L
Buffalo	11	5	21	12
Bowling Green	11	5	19	14
Akron*	10	6	23	13
Miami (OH)	10	6	17	13
Kent State	10	6	19	15
Ohio	7	9	15	17

West Division

	Conf. W	L	All W	L
Ball State	7	9	14	17
Central Michigan	7	9	12	19
Western Michigan	7	9	10	21
Eastern Michigan	6	10	8	24
Northern Illinois	5	11	10	20
Toledo	5	11	7	25

Mid-Eastern Athletic

	Conf. W	L	All W	L
Morgan State*	13	3	23	12
South Carolina St.	10	6	17	14
Bethune-Cookman	9	7	17	16
NC A&T	9	7	16	16
Norfolk State	9	7	13	18
Coppin State	9	7	13	19
Hampton	8	8	16	16
Florida A&M	6	10	10	21
Howard	6	10	8	23
Delaware State	6	10	8	24
MD Eastern Shore	3	13	7	23

Missouri Valley

	Conf. W	L	All W	L
Creighton	14	4	27	8
Northern Iowa*	14	4	23	11
Illinois State	11	7	24	10
Bradley	10	8	21	15
Evansville	8	10	17	14
Wichita State	8	10	17	17
Southern Illinois	8	10	13	18
Drake	7	11	17	16
Indiana State	7	11	11	21
Missouri State	3	15	11	20

Mountain West

	Conf. W	L	All W	L
BYU	12	4	25	8
Utah*	12	4	24	10
New Mexico	12	4	22	12
San Diego State	11	5	26	10
UNLV	9	7	21	11
Wyoming	7	9	19	14
TCU	5	11	14	17
Colorado State	4	12	9	22
Air Force	0	16	10	21

Northeast

	Conf. W	L	All W	L
Robert Morris*	15	3	24	11
Mount St. Mary's	12	6	19	14
Sacred Heart	12	6	17	14
Long Island	12	6	16	14
Quinnipiac	10	8	15	16
Wagner	8	10	16	14
Central Conn. State	8	10	13	17
St. Francis (NY)	7	11	10	20
Monmouth	6	12	8	23
Fairleigh Dickinson	6	12	7	23
St. Francis (PA)	3	15	6	23

	Conf. W	L	All W	L
Ohio Valley				
Tennessee-Martin	14	4	22	10
Murray State	13	5	19	12
Austin Peay*	13	5	19	14
Morehead State......	12	6	20	16
Eastern Kentucky.....	10	8	18	13
Tennessee State	9	9	12	18
Eastern Illinois	8	10	12	18
Tennessee Tech	6	12	12	18
Jacksonville State	5	13	11	17
SE Missouri State	0	18	3	27
Pacific-10				
Washington	14	4	26	9
UCLA..............	13	5	26	9
Arizona State........	11	7	25	10
California	11	7	22	11
USC*	9	9	22	13
Arizona.............	9	9	21	14
Washington State	8	10	17	16
Oregon State	7	11	18	18
Stanford............	6	12	20	14
Oregon.............	2	16	8	23
Patriot				
American*	13	1	24	8
Holy Cross	11	3	18	14
Navy...............	8	6	19	11
Army	6	8	11	19
Lehigh	5	9	15	14
Colgate	5	9	10	20
Lafayette	4	10	8	22
Bucknell............	4	10	7	23
Southeastern				
East Division				
South Carolina......	10	6	21	10
Tennessee..........	10	6	21	13
Florida	9	7	25	11
Vanderbilt..........	8	8	19	12
Kentucky	8	8	22	14
Georgia	3	13	12	20
West Division				
LSU	13	3	27	8
Auburn	10	6	24	12
Mississippi State*....	9	7	23	13
Alabama...........	7	9	18	14
Mississippi	7	9	16	15
Arkansas	2	14	14	16

	Conf. W	L	All W	L
Southern				
North Division				
Western Carolina	11	9	16	15
Chattanooga*.......	11	9	18	17
Samford	9	11	16	16
Appalachian State ...	9	11	13	18
Elon	7	13	11	20
NC Greensboro	4	16	5	25
South Division				
Davidson...........	18	2	27	8
Charleston	15	5	27	9
Citadel	15	5	20	13
Wofford............	12	8	16	14
Georgia Southern....	5	15	8	22
Furman............	4	16	6	24
Southland				
East Division				
Steven F. Austin*	13	3	24	8
Nicholls State	12	4	20	11
SE Louisiana	7	9	13	17
McNeese State......	5	11	11	18
Northwestern State..	3	13	11	20
Central Arkansas	3	13	10	19
West Division				
Sam Houston State...	12	4	18	12
TX A&M-Corp. Christi.	11	5	18	15
Texas-Arlington	9	7	16	14
UTSA	8	8	19	13
Texas State	7	9	14	16
Lamar	6	10	15	15
Southwestern Athletic				
Alabama State*	16	2	22	10
Jackson State.......	15	3	18	15
Prairie View A&M....	12	6	17	16
Arkansas-Pine Bluff ...	11	7	13	18
Southern...........	8	10	8	23
Texas Southern	7	11	7	25
Miss. Valley State.....	7	11	7	25
Alabama A&M	6	12	8	19
Grambling State	4	14	6	23
Alcorn State	4	14	6	25
Summit League[1,3]				
North Dakota State*...	16	2	26	7
Oral Roberts........	14	4	16	15
Oakland	13	5	23	13
IUPUI	9	9	16	14
IPFW	8	10	13	17
Southern Utah	8	10	11	20
South Dakota State ..	7	11	13	20
Western Illinois......	6	12	9	20
Centenary..........	6	12	8	23
Missouri-Kansas City .	3	15	7	24

	Conf. W	L	All W	L
Sun Belt				
East Division				
Western Kentucky* ..	15	3	25	9
Troy..............	14	4	19	13
South Alabama	10	8	20	13
Middle Tenn. State .	10	8	18	14
Florida International	7	11	13	20
Florida Atlantic	2	16	6	26
West Division				
Arkansas-Little Rock	15	3	23	8
North Texas........	11	7	20	12
Denver............	9	9	15	16
LA-Lafayette	7	11	10	20
New Orleans	6	12	11	19
LA-Monroe	6	12	10	20
Arkansas State	5	13	13	17
West Coast				
Gonzaga*	14	0	28	6
St. Mary's	10	4	28	7
Portland............	9	5	19	13
Santa Clara........	7	7	16	17
San Diego	6	8	16	16
Pepperdine	5	9	9	23
San Francisco.......	3	11	11	19
Loyola Marymount ...	2	12	3	28
Western Athletic				
Utah State*	14	2	30	5
Nevada	11	5	21	13
Boise State	9	7	19	13
New Mexico State ...	9	7	17	15
Idaho.............	9	7	17	16
Louisiana Tech	6	10	15	18
San Jose State	6	10	13	17
Hawaii	5	11	13	17
Fresno State	3	13	13	21
Independents[1,2]				
Utah Valley	—	—	17	11
Chicago State	—	—	19	13
Longwood..........	—	—	17	14
Savannah State	—	—	15	14
TX Pan American	—	—	10	17
CSU Bakersfield	—	—	8	21
Bryant	—	—	8	21
Winston-Salem	—	—	8	22
Houston Baptist.....	—	—	5	25
NC Central	—	—	4	27
NJIT	—	—	1	30

(1) Conference changes in 2008 included: Gardner-Webb and Presbyterian to Big South; Samford to Southern; Bryant and Houston Baptist competed as Div. I Independents. (2) Schools do not participate in a tournament. (3) The Mid-Continent Conference became the Summit League in June 2007.

All-Time Winningest Division I College Basketball Teams by Percentage
(through 2008-09 season)

Team	Yrs.	Won	Lost	Pct.	Team	Yrs.	Won	Lost	Pct.	Team	Yrs.	Won	Lost	Pct.
Kentucky	106	1,988	635	0.758	W. Kentucky...	90	1,602	780	0.673	Indiana	109	1,641	909	0.644
North Carolina	99	1,984	703	0.738	St. John's-NY..	102	1,686	868	0.660	Arkansas......	86	1,487	822	0.644
Kansas.......	111	1,970	793	0.713	Utah.........	101	1,637	858	0.656	Missouri State	97	1,498	833	0.643
UNLV	51	1,058	429	0.711	Louisville	95	1,587	831	0.656	Connecticut....	105	1,499	839	0.641
Duke	104	1,876	815	0.697	Illinois	104	1,609	853	0.654	Temple	113	1,711	960	0.641
UCLA........	90	1,672	726	0.697	Arizona	104	1,568	858	0.646	Villanova	89	1,505	850	0.639
Syracuse	108	1,753	806	0.685	Notre Dame...	104	1,651	908	0.645	Penn	109	1,657	949	0.636

National Invitation Tournament Champions

The National Invitation Tournament (NIT), first played in 1938, is the oldest U.S. basketball tournament. The first National Collegiate Athletic Association (NCAA) national championship tournament was played one year later. In Aug. 2005, the NCAA agreed to purchase the NIT from the five New York City-area colleges that had run the NIT.

Year	Champion	Year	Champion	Year	Champion	Year	Champion	Year	Champion
1938	Temple	1953	Seton Hall	1968	Dayton	1982	Bradley	1996	Nebraska
1939	Long Island Univ.	1954	Holy Cross	1969	Temple	1983	Fresno State	1997	Michigan
1940	Colorado	1955	Duquesne	1970	Marquette	1984	Michigan	1998	Minnesota
1941	Long Island Univ.	1956	Louisville	1971	North Carolina	1985	UCLA	1999	California
1942	West Virginia	1957	Bradley	1972	Maryland	1986	Ohio State	2000	Wake Forest
1943	St. John's	1958	Xavier (Ohio)	1973	Virginia Tech	1987	So. Mississippi	2001	Tulsa
1944	St. John's	1959	St. John's	1974	Purdue	1988	Connecticut	2002	Memphis
1945	DePaul	1960	Bradley	1975	Princeton	1989	St. John's	2003	St. John's
1946	Kentucky	1961	Providence	1976	Kentucky	1990	Vanderbilt	2004	Michigan
1947	Utah	1962	Dayton	1977	St. Bonaventure	1991	Stanford	2005	South Carolina
1948	St. Louis	1963	Providence	1978	Texas	1992	Virginia	2006	South Carolina
1949	San Francisco	1964	Bradley	1979	Indiana	1993	Minnesota	2007	West Virginia
1950	CCNY	1965	St. John's	1980	Virginia	1994	Villanova	2008	Ohio State
1951	Brigham Young	1966	Brigham Young	1981	Tulsa	1995	Virginia Tech	2009	Penn State
1952	La Salle	1967	Southern Illinois						

John R. Wooden Award

Awarded to the nation's outstanding men's college basketball player by the Los Angeles Athletic Club since 1977; awarded under the same name to women since 2004.

1977 Marques Johnson, UCLA	1991 Larry Johnson, UNLV	2004 (M) Jameer Nelson, St. Joseph's
1978 Phil Ford, North Carolina	1992 Christian Laettner, Duke	(W) Alana Beard, Duke
1979 Larry Bird, Indiana State	1993 Calbert Cheaney, Indiana	2005 (M) Andrew Bogut, Utah
1980 Darrell Griffith, Louisville	1994 Glenn Robinson, Purdue	(W) Seimone Augustus, LSU
1981 Danny Ainge, Brigham Young	1995 Ed O'Bannon, UCLA	2006 (M) J. J. Redick, Duke
1982 Ralph Sampson, Virginia	1996 Marcus Camby, Massachusetts	(W) Seimone Augustus, LSU
1983 Ralph Sampson, Virginia	1997 Tim Duncan, Wake Forest	2007 (M) Kevin Durant, Texas
1984 Michael Jordan, North Carolina	1998 Antawn Jamison, North Carolina	(W) Candace Parker, Tennessee
1985 Chris Mullin, St. John's	1999 Elton Brand, Duke	2008 (M) Tyler Hansbrough, N. Carolina
1986 Walter Berry, St. John's	2000 Kenyon Martin, Cincinnati	(W) Candace Parker, Tennessee
1987 David Robinson, Navy	2001 Shane Battier, Duke	2009 (M) Blake Griffin, Oklahoma
1988 Danny Manning, Kansas	2002 Jay Williams, Duke	(W) Maya Moore, Connecticut
1989 Sean Elliott, Arizona	2003 T. J. Ford, Texas	
1990 Lionel Simmons, La Salle		

Most Coaching Victories in the NCAA Basketball Tournament

(Through 2009 tournament. Coaches active in 2008-09 season in **bold**.)

Coach, school(s), first/last appearance	Wins	Tournaments	Championships
Mike Krzyzewski, Duke, 1984/2009	71	25	3
Dean Smith, North Carolina, 1967/1997	65	27	2
Roy Williams; Kansas, N. Carolina; 1990/2009	55	20	2
John Wooden, UCLA, 1950/1975	47	16	10
Lute Olson; Iowa, Arizona; 1979/2007	46	27	1
Bob Knight; Indiana, Texas Tech; 1973/2007	45	28	3
Jim Calhoun; Northeastern, Connecticut; 1981/2009	43	21	2
Denny Crum, Louisville, 1972/2000	42	23	2
Jim Boeheim, Syracuse, 1977/2009	42	26	1
Rick Pitino; Boston, Providence, Kentucky, Louisville; 1983/2009	38	15	1

2009 Women's NCAA Tournament: Undefeated UConn Silences Underdog Louisville

The Connecticut Huskies defeated the Louisville Cardinals, 76-54, to claim the Women's 2009 Division I basketball title, Apr. 7, 2009, in St. Louis, MO. The Final Four win capped off a record-setting season for the undefeated UConn, which won each of its 39 games by a double-digit margin—a feat never before accomplished in college basketball. Huskies Center Tina Charles, who had been benched in the tournament only a year before by UConn head coach Geno Auriemma, scored 25 points and snagged 19 rebounds to be named the Most Outstanding Player.

NCAA Division I Women's Basketball Champions

Year	Champion	Coach	Final opponent	Score	Most outstanding player	Site
1982	Louisiana Tech	Sonja Hogg	Cheyney	76-62	Janice Lawrence, La. Tech	Norfolk, VA
1983	USC	Linda Sharp	Louisiana Tech	69-67	Cheryl Miller, USC	Norfolk, VA
1984	USC	Linda Sharp	Tennessee	72-61	Cheryl Miller, USC	Los Angeles, CA
1985	Old Dominion	Marianne Stanley	Georgia	70-65	Tracy Claxton, Old Dominion	Austin, TX
1986	Texas	Jody Conradt	USC	97-81	Clarissa Davis, Texas	Lexington, KY
1987	Tennessee	Pat Summitt	Louisiana Tech	67-44	Tonya Edwards, Tennessee	Austin, TX
1988	Louisiana Tech	Leon Barmore	Auburn	56-54	Erica Westbrooks, La. Tech	Tacoma, WA
1989	Tennessee	Pat Summitt	Auburn	76-60	Bridgette Gordon, Tennessee	Tacoma, WA
1990	Stanford	Tara VanDerveer	Auburn	88-81	Jennifer Azzi, Stanford	Knoxville, TN
1991	Tennessee	Pat Summitt	Virginia	70-67 (OT)	Dawn Staley, Virginia	New Orleans, LA
1992	Stanford	Tara VanDerveer	W. Kentucky	78-62	Molly Goodenbour, Stanford	Los Angeles, CA
1993	Texas Tech	Marsha Sharp	Ohio St.	84-82	Sheryl Swoopes, Texas Tech	Atlanta, GA
1994	North Carolina	Sylvia Hatchell	Louisiana Tech	60-59	Charlotte Smith, North Carolina	Richmond, VA
1995	Connecticut	Geno Auriemma	Tennessee	70-64	Rebecca Lobo, Connecticut	Minneapolis, MN
1996	Tennessee	Pat Summitt	Georgia	83-65	Michelle Marciniak, Tennessee	Charlotte, NC
1997	Tennessee	Pat Summitt	Old Dominion	68-59	Chamique Holdsclaw, Tennessee	Cincinnati, OH
1998	Tennessee	Pat Summitt	Louisiana Tech	93-75	Chamique Holdsclaw, Tennessee	Kansas City, MO
1999	Purdue	Carolyn Peck	Duke	62-45	Ukari Figgs, Purdue	San Jose, CA
2000	Connecticut	Geno Auriemma	Tennessee	71-52	Shea Ralph, Connecticut	Philadelphia, PA
2001	Notre Dame	Muffet McGraw	Purdue	68-66	Ruth Riley, Notre Dame	St. Louis, MO
2002	Connecticut	Geno Auriemma	Oklahoma	82-70	Swin Cash, Connecticut	San Antonio, TX
2003	Connecticut	Geno Auriemma	Tennessee	73-68	Diana Taurasi, Connecticut	Atlanta, GA
2004	Connecticut	Geno Auriemma	Tennessee	70-61	Diana Taurasi, Connecticut	New Orleans, LA
2005	Baylor	Kim Mulkey-Robertson	Michigan State	84-62	Sophia Young, Baylor	Indianapolis, IN
2006	Maryland	Brenda Frese	Duke	78-75 (OT)	Laura Harper, Maryland	Boston, MA
2007	Tennessee	Pat Summitt	Rutgers	59-46	Candace Parker, Tennessee	Cleveland, OH
2008	Tennessee	Pat Summitt	Stanford	64-48	Candace Parker, Tennessee	Tampa Bay, FL
2009	Connecticut	Geno Auriemma	Louisville	76-54	Tina Charles, Connecticut	St. Louis, MO

Wade Trophy

Awarded by the National Assn. for Girls and Women in Sport for character, leadership, and player performance.

Year	Player, school	Year	Player, school	Year	Player, school
1978	Carol Blazejowski, Montclair St.	1989	Clarissa Davis, Texas	2000	Edwina Brown, Texas
1979	Nancy Lieberman, Old Dominion	1990	Jennifer Azzi, Stanford	2001	Jackie Stiles, SW Missouri St.
1980	Nancy Lieberman, Old Dominion	1991	Daedra Charles, Tennessee	2002	Sue Bird, Connecticut
1981	Lynette Woodard, Kansas	1992	Susan Robinson, Penn St.	2003	Diana Taurasi, Connecticut
1982	Pam Kelly, Louisiana Tech	1993	Karen Jennings, Nebraska	2004	Alana Beard, Duke
1983	LaTaunya Pollard, Long Beach St.	1994	Carol Ann Shudlick, Minnesota	2005	Seimone Augustus, LSU
1984	Janice Lawrence, Louisiana Tech	1995	Rebecca Lobo, Connecticut	2006	Seimone Augustus, LSU
1985	Cheryl Miller, USC	1996	Jennifer Rizzotti, Connecticut	2007	Candace Parker, Tennessee
1986	Kamie Ethridge, Texas	1997	DeLisha Milton, Florida	2008	Candice Wiggins, Stanford
1987	Shelly Pennefeather, Villanova	1998	Ticha Penicheiro, Old Dominion	2009	Maya Moore, Connecticut
1988	Teresa Weatherspoon, Louisiana Tech	1999	Stephanie White-McCarty, Purdue		

2009 WOMEN'S NCAA BASKETBALL TOURNAMENT

TRENTON REGIONAL

(1) Connecticut 104
(16) Vermont 65
　Connecticut 87
(8) Florida 70
(9) Temple 57
　Florida 59
　　Connecticut 77

(5) Virginia 68
(12) Marist 61
　Virginia 73
(4) California 70
(13) Fresno State 47
　California 99
　　California 53
　　　Connecticut 83

(6) Arizona State 58
(11) Georgia 47
　Arizona State 63
(3) Florida State 83
(14) NC A&T 71
　Florida State 58
　　Arizona State 84

(7) Notre Dame 71
(10) Minnesota 79
　Minnesota 42
(2) Texas A&M 80
(15) Evansville 45
　Texas A&M 73
　　Texas A&M 69
　　　Arizona State 64

Connecticut 83

BERKELEY REGIONAL

(1) Duke 83
(16) Austin Peay 42
　Duke 49
(8) Middle Tenn. State 59
(9) Michigan State 60
　Michigan State 63
　　Michigan State 68

(5) Tennessee 55
(12) Ball State 71
　Ball State 57
(4) Iowa State 85
(13) East Tenn. State 53
　Iowa State 71
　　Iowa State 69
　　　Iowa State 53

(6) Texas 63
(11) Mississippi State 71
　Mississippi State 58
(3) Ohio State 77
(14) Sacred Heart 63
　Ohio State 64
　　Ohio State 66

(7) DePaul 70
(10) San Diego State 76
　San Diego State 49
(2) Stanford 74
(15) UC Santa Barbara 39
　Stanford 77
　　Stanford 84
　　　Stanford 74

Stanford 64

RALEIGH REGIONAL

(1) Maryland 82
(16) Dartmouth 53
　Maryland 71
(8) Villanova 30
(9) Utah 60
　Utah 56
　　Maryland 78

(5) Kansas State 68
(12) Drexel 44
　Kansas St. 61
(4) Vanderbilt 73
(13) Western Carolina 44
　Vanderbilt 74
　　Vanderbilt 74
　　　Maryland 60

(6) LSU 69
(11) Green Bay 59
　LSU 52
(3) Louisville 62
(14) Liberty 42
　Louisville 62
　　Louisville 56

(7) South Dakota State 90
(10) TCU 55
　South Dakota State 58
(2) Baylor 87 (OT)
(15) UTSA 82
　Baylor 60
　　Baylor 39
　　　Louisville 77

Louisville 61

Connecticut 83

OKLAHOMA CITY REGIONAL

(1) Oklahoma 76
(16) Prairie View 47
　Oklahoma 69
(8) Iowa 62
(9) Georgia Tech 76
　Georgia Tech 50
　　Oklahoma 70

(5) Xavier 59
(12) Gonzaga 75
　Gonzaga 60
(4) Pittsburgh 64
(13) Montana 35
　Pittsburgh 65
　　Pittsburgh 59
　　　Oklahoma 74

(6) Purdue 65
(11) Charlotte 52
　Purdue 85
(3) North Carolina 85
(14) Central Florida 80
　North Carolina 70
　　Purdue 67

(7) Rutgers 56
(10) VCU 49
　Rutgers 80
(2) Auburn 85
(15) Lehigh 49
　Auburn 52
　　Rutgers 61
　　　Purdue 68

Oklahoma 59

Connecticut 76

Louisville 54

COLLEGE FOOTBALL

Gators Beat Sooners to Claim BCS Championship

The Univ. of Florida Gators, ranked no. 2 in the BCS Poll at the end of the regular season, defeated top-ranked Oklahoma State, 24-14, to win their second BCS championship in three years Jan. 9, 2009, in Miami, FL. The Gators, coached by Urban Meyer, finished the season with 13 wins and 1 loss. Heisman Trophy-winner Tim Tebow, who threw a 4-yard touchdown pass and overcame a career-high 2 interceptions, was named the game's most outstanding player; Tebow finished the game 18-for-30 with 209 yards. Calls were renewed for a change to the BCS system, as three other teams—including an undefeated Utah—laid claim to share of the national title, based on regular season records and other bowl game results.

National College Football Champions, 1936-2008

The official champion, as determined by the BCS National Championship game (BCS No. 1 vs. BCS No. 2), is listed starting 2006. For years preceding 2006, the unofficial champion, as selected by the AP poll of writers and USA Today/ESPN (until 1991, UPI; 1991-1996 USA Today/CNN) poll of coaches, is listed. Where the polls disagreed, both teams are listed (AP winner first). The AP poll started in 1936; the UPI poll in 1950.

1936 Minnesota	1951 Tennessee	1966 Notre Dame	1980 Georgia	1994 Nebraska
1937 Pittsburgh	1952 Michigan St.	1967 USC	1981 Clemson	1995 Nebraska
1938 Texas Christian	1953 Maryland	1968 Ohio St.	1982 Penn St.	1996 Florida
1939 Texas A&M	1954 Ohio St./UCLA	1969 Texas	1983 Miami (FL)	1997 Michigan/Nebraska
1940 Minnesota	1955 Oklahoma	1970 Nebraska/Texas	1984 Brigham Young	1998 Tennessee
1941 Minnesota	1956 Oklahoma	1971 Nebraska	1985 Oklahoma	1999 Florida St.
1942 Ohio St.	1957 Auburn, Ohio St.	1972 USC	1986 Penn St.	2000 Oklahoma
1943 Notre Dame	1958 Louisiana St.	1973 Notre Dame/	1987 Miami (FL)	2001 Miami (FL)
1944 Army	1959 Syracuse	Alabama	1988 Notre Dame	2002 Ohio State
1945 Army	1960 Minnesota	1974 Oklahoma/USC	1989 Miami (FL)	2003 LSU/USC
1946 Notre Dame	1961 Alabama	1975 Oklahoma	1990 Colorado/GA Tech	2004 USC
1947 Notre Dame	1962 USC	1976 Pittsburgh	1991 Miami (FL)/	2005 Texas
1948 Michigan	1963 Texas	1977 Notre Dame	Washington	2006 Florida
1949 Notre Dame	1964 Alabama	1978 Alabama/USC	1992 Alabama	2007 LSU
1950 Oklahoma	1965 Alabama/Mich. St.	1979 Alabama	1993 Florida St.	2008 Florida

2008 Final Standings

Bowl Championship Series		Associated Press Poll		USA Today/ESPN Coaches' Poll	
Rank, team	Rank, team	Rank, team	Rank, team	Rank, team	Rank, team
1. Oklahoma	14. Georgia Tech	1. Florida	14. Mississippi	1. Florida	14. Virginia Tech
2. Florida	15. Georgia	2. Utah	15. Virginia Tech	2. USC	15. Mississippi
3. Texas	16. Brigham Young	3. USC	16. Oklahoma St.	3. Texas	16. Missouri
4. Alabama	17. Oregon	4. Texas	17. Cincinnati	4. Utah	17. Cincinnati
5. USC	18. Michigan State	5. Oklahoma	18. Oregon State	5. Oklahoma	18. Oklahoma St.
6. Utah	19. Virginia Tech	6. Alabama	19. Missouri	6. Alabama	19. Oregon State
7. Texas Tech	20. Pittsburgh	7. TCU	20. Iowa	7. TCU	20. Iowa
8. Penn State	21. Missouri	8. Penn State	21. Florida State	8. Penn State	21. Brigham Young
9. Boise State	22. Ball State	9. Ohio State	22. Georgia Tech	9. Oregon	22. Georgia Tech
10. Ohio State	23. Northwestern	10. Oregon	23. West Virginia	10. Georgia	23. Florida State
11. TCU	24. Boston College	11. Boise State	24. Michigan State	11. Ohio State	24. Michigan State
12. Cincinnati	25. Mississippi	12. Texas Tech	25. Brigham Young	12. Texas Tech	25. California
13. Oklahoma St.		13. Georgia		13. Boise State	

Note: BCS Poll is as of Dec. 7, 2008. AP and Coaches' Polls are as of Jan. 9, 2009, after bowl games. The American Football Coaches Assn. prohibits coaches from voting for schools on major NCAA probation.

Annual Results of Major Bowl Games

(Dates indicate year the game was played; bowl games are generally played in late December or early January.)

Rose Bowl, Pasadena, CA

1902	(Jan.) Michigan 49, Stanford 0	1948	Michigan 49, USC 0	1979	USC 17, Michigan 10
1916	Washington St. 14, Brown 0	1949	Northwestern 20, California 14	1980	USC 17, Ohio St. 16
1917	Oregon 14, Pennsylvania 0	1950	Ohio St. 17, California 14	1981	Michigan 23, Washington 6
1918-19	Service teams	1951	Michigan 14, California 6	1982	Washington 28, Iowa 0
1920	Harvard 7, Oregon 6	1952	Illinois 40, Stanford 7	1983	UCLA 24, Michigan 14
1921	California 28, Ohio St. 0	1953	USC 7, Wisconsin 0	1984	UCLA 45, Illinois 9
1922	Wash. & Jeff. 0, California 0	1954	Mich. St. 28, UCLA 20	1985	USC 20, Ohio St. 17
1923	USC 14, Penn St. 3	1955	Ohio St. 20, USC 7	1986	UCLA 45, Iowa 28
1924	Navy 14, Washington 14	1956	Mich. St. 17, UCLA 14	1987	Arizona St. 22, Michigan 15
1925	Notre Dame 27, Stanford 10	1957	Iowa 35, Oregon St. 19	1988	Mich. St. 20, USC 17
1926	Alabama 20, Washington 19	1958	Ohio St. 10, Oregon 7	1989	Michigan 22, USC 14
1927	Alabama 7, Stanford 7	1959	Iowa 38, California 12	1990	USC 17, Michigan 10
1928	Stanford 7, Pittsburgh 6	1960	Washington 44, Wisconsin 8	1991	Washington 46, Iowa 34
1929	Georgia Tech 8, California 7	1961	Washington 17, Minnesota 7	1992	Washington 34, Michigan 14
1930	USC 47, Pittsburgh 14	1962	Minnesota 21, UCLA 3	1993	Michigan 38, Washington 31
1931	Alabama 24, Wash. St. 0	1963	USC 42, Wisconsin 37	1994	Wisconsin 21, UCLA 16
1932	USC 21, Tulane 12	1964	Illinois 17, Washington 7	1995	Penn St. 38, Oregon 20
1933	USC 35, Pittsburgh 0	1965	Michigan 34, Oregon St. 7	1996	USC 41, Northwestern 32
1934	Columbia 7, Stanford 0	1966	UCLA 14, Mich. St. 12	1997	Ohio St. 20, Arizona St. 17
1935	Alabama 29, Stanford 13	1967	Purdue 14, USC 13	1998	Michigan 21, Wash. St. 16
1936	Stanford 7, SMU 0	1968	USC 14, Indiana 3	1999	Wisconsin 38, UCLA 31
1937	Pittsburgh 21, Washington 0	1969	Ohio St. 27, USC 16	2000	Wisconsin 17, Stanford 9
1938	California 13, Alabama 0	1970	USC 10, Michigan 3	2001	Washington 34, Purdue 24
1939	USC 7, Duke 3	1971	Stanford 27, Ohio St. 17	2002	Miami (FL) 37, Nebraska 14
1940	USC 14, Tennessee 0	1972	Stanford 13, Michigan 12	2003	Oklahoma 34, Washington St. 14
1941	Stanford 21, Nebraska 13	1973	USC 42, Ohio St. 17	2004	USC 28, Michigan 14
1942*	Oregon St. 20, Duke 16	1974	Ohio St. 42, USC 21	2005	Texas 38, Michigan 37
1943	Georgia 9, UCLA 0	1975	USC 18, Ohio St. 17	2006	Texas 41, USC 38
1944	USC 29, Washington 0	1976	UCLA 23, Ohio St. 10	2007	USC 32, Michigan 18
1945	USC 25, Tennessee 0	1977	USC 14, Michigan 6	2008	USC 49, Illinois 17
1946	Alabama 34, USC 14	1978	Washington 27, Michigan 20	2009	USC 38, Penn State 24
1947	Illinois 45, UCLA 14				

*Played in Durham, NC.

Orange Bowl, Miami, FL

1935 (Jan.) Bucknell 26, Miami (FL) 0	1960 Georgia 14, Missouri 0	1985 Washington 28, Oklahoma 17
1936 Catholic U. 20, Mississippi 19	1961 Missouri 21, Navy 14	1986 Oklahoma 25, Penn St. 10
1937 Duquesne 13, Mississippi St. 12	1962 LSU 25, Colorado 7	1987 Oklahoma 42, Arkansas 8
1938 Auburn 6, Michigan St. 0	1963 Alabama 17, Oklahoma 0	1988 Miami (FL) 20, Oklahoma 14
1939 Tennessee 17, Oklahoma 0	1964 Nebraska 13, Auburn 7	1989 Miami (FL) 23, Nebraska 3
1940 Georgia Tech 21, Missouri 7	1965 Texas 21, Alabama 17	1990 Notre Dame 21, Colorado 6
1941 Mississippi St. 14, Georgetown 7	1966 Alabama 39, Nebraska 28	1991 Colorado 10, Notre Dame 9
1942 Georgia 40, TCU 26	1967 Florida 27, Georgia Tech 12	1992 Miami (FL) 22, Nebraska 0
1943 Alabama 37, Boston Coll. 21	1968 Oklahoma 26, Tennessee 24	1993 Florida St. 27, Nebraska 14
1944 LSU 19, Texas A&M 14	1969 Penn St. 15, Kansas 14	1994 Florida St. 18, Nebraska 16
1945 Tulsa 26, Georgia Tech 12	1970 Penn St. 10, Missouri 3	1995 Nebraska 24, Miami (FL) 17
1946 Miami (FL) 13, Holy Cross 6	1971 Nebraska 17, LSU 12	1996 Florida St. 31, Notre Dame 26
1947 Rice 8, Tennessee 0	1972 Nebraska 38, Alabama 6	1996 (Dec.) Nebraska 41,
1948 Georgia Tech 20, Kansas 14	1973 Nebraska 40, Notre Dame 6	Virginia Tech 21
1949 Texas 41, Georgia 28	1974 Penn St. 16, LSU 9	1998 (Jan.) Nebraska 42, Tennessee 17
1950 Santa Clara 21, Kentucky 13	1975 Notre Dame 13, Alabama 11	1999 Florida 31, Syracuse 10
1951 Clemson 15, Miami (FL) 14	1976 Oklahoma 14, Michigan 6	2000 Michigan 35, Alabama 34 (OT)
1952 Georgia Tech 17, Baylor 14	1977 Ohio St. 27, Colorado 10	2001 Oklahoma 13, Florida St. 2
1953 Alabama 61, Syracuse 6	1978 Arkansas 31, Oklahoma 6	2002 Florida 56, Maryland 23
1954 Oklahoma 7, Maryland 0	1979 Oklahoma 31, Nebraska 24	2003 USC 38, Iowa 17
1955 Duke 34, Nebraska 7	1980 Oklahoma 24, Florida St. 7	2004 Miami 16, Florida State 14
1956 Oklahoma 20, Maryland 6	1981 Oklahoma 18, Florida St. 17	2005 USC 55, Oklahoma 19
1957 Colorado 27, Clemson 21	1982 Clemson 22, Nebraska 15	2006 Penn St. 26, Florida St. 23 (3 OT)
1958 Oklahoma 48, Duke 21	1983 Nebraska 21, LSU 20	2007 Louisville 24, Wake Forest 13
1959 Oklahoma 21, Syracuse 6	1984 Miami (FL) 31, Nebraska 30	2008 Kansas 24, Virginia Tech 21
		2009 Virginia Tech 20, Cincinnati 7

Sugar Bowl, New Orleans, LA

1935 (Jan.) Tulane 20, Temple 14	1960 Mississippi 21, LSU 0	1985 Nebraska 28, LSU 10
1936 TCU 3, LSU 2	1961 Mississippi 14, Rice 6	1986 Tennessee 35, Miami (FL) 7
1937 Santa Clara 21, LSU 14	1962 Alabama 10, Arkansas 3	1987 Nebraska 30, LSU 15
1938 Santa Clara 6, LSU 0	1963 Mississippi 17, Arkansas 13	1988 Syracuse 16, Auburn 16
1939 TCU 15, Carnegie Tech 7	1964 Alabama 12, Mississippi 7	1989 Florida St. 13, Auburn 7
1940 Texas A&M 14, Tulane 13	1965 LSU 13, Syracuse 10	1990 Miami (FL) 33, Alabama 25
1941 Boston Col. 19, Tennessee 13	1966 Missouri 20, Florida 18	1991 Tennessee 23, Virginia 22
1942 Fordham 2, Missouri 0	1967 Alabama 34, Nebraska 7	1992 Notre Dame 39, Florida 28
1943 Tennessee 14, Tulsa 7	1968 LSU 20, Wyoming 13	1993 Alabama 34, Miami (FL) 13
1944 Georgia Tech 20, Tulsa 18	1969 Arkansas 16, Georgia 2	1994 Florida 41, West Virginia 7
1945 Duke 29, Alabama 26	1970 Mississippi 27, Arkansas 22	1995 Florida St. 23, Florida 17
1946 Oklahoma A&M 33, St. Mary's 13	1971 Tennessee 34, Air Force 13	1995 (Dec.) Virginia Tech 28, Texas 10
1947 Georgia 20, N. Carolina 10	1972 Oklahoma 40, Auburn 22	1997 (Jan.) Florida 52, Florida St. 20
1948 Texas 27, Alabama 7	1972 (Dec.) Oklahoma 14, Penn St. 0	1998 Florida St. 31, Ohio St. 14
1949 Oklahoma 14, N. Carolina 6	1973 Notre Dame 24, Alabama 23	1999 Ohio St. 24, Texas A&M 14
1950 Oklahoma 35, LSU 0	1974 Nebraska 13, Florida 10	2000 Florida St. 46, Virginia Tech 29
1951 Kentucky 13, Oklahoma 7	1975 Alabama 13, Penn St. 6	2001 Miami (FL) 37, Florida 20
1952 Maryland 28, Tennessee 13	1977 (Jan.) Pittsburgh 27, Georgia 3	2002 LSU 47, Illinois 34
1953 Georgia Tech 24, Mississippi 7	1978 Alabama 35, Ohio St. 6	2003 Georgia 26, Florida St. 13
1954 Georgia Tech 42, West Virginia 19	1979 Alabama 14, Penn St. 7	2004 LSU 21, Oklahoma 14
1955 Navy 21, Mississippi 0	1980 Alabama 24, Arkansas 9	2005 Auburn 16, Virginia Tech 13
1956 Georgia Tech 7, Pittsburgh 0	1981 Georgia 17, Notre Dame 10	2006 West Virginia 38, Georgia 35*
1957 Baylor 13, Tennessee 7	1982 Pittsburgh 24, Georgia 20	2007 LSU 41, Notre Dame 14
1958 Mississippi 39, Texas 7	1983 Penn St. 27, Georgia 23	2008 Georgia 41, Hawaii 10
1959 LSU 7, Clemson 0	1984 Auburn 9, Michigan 7	2009 Utah 31, Alabama 17

*Played in Atlanta, GA.

Chick-fil-A Bowl, Atlanta, GA

(Known as the Peach Bowl, 1968-1997; Chick-fil-A Peach Bowl, 1998-2005.)

1968 (Dec.) LSU 31, Florida St. 27	1982 Iowa 28, Tennessee 22	1996 LSU 10, Clemson 7
1969 W. Virginia 14, S. Carolina 3	1983 Florida St. 28, N. Carolina 3	1998 (Jan.) Auburn 21, Clemson 17
1970 Arizona St. 48, N. Carolina 26	1984 Virginia 27, Purdue 22	1998 (Dec.) Georgia 35, Virginia 33
1971 Mississippi 41, Georgia Tech 18	1985 Army 31, Illinois 29	1999 Mississippi St. 27, Clemson 7
1972 N. Carolina St. 49, W. Virginia 13	1986 Va. Tech 25, N. Carolina St. 24	2000 LSU 28, Georgia Tech 14
1973 Georgia 17, Maryland 16	1988 (Jan.) Tennessee 28, Indiana 22	2001 North Carolina 16, Auburn 10
1974 Vanderbilt 6, Texas Tech 6	1988 (Dec.) N. Carolina St. 28, Iowa 23	2002 Maryland 30, Tennessee 3
1975 W. Virginia 13, N. Carolina St. 10	1989 Syracuse 19, Georgia 18	2003 Clemson 27, Tennessee 14
1976 Kentucky 21, N. Carolina 0	1990 Auburn 27, Indiana 23	2004 Miami (FL) 27, Florida 10
1977 N. Carolina St. 24, Iowa St. 14	1992 (Jan.) E. Carolina 37, NC St. 34	2005 LSU 40, Miami (FL) 3
1978 Purdue 41, Georgia Tech. 21	1993 N. Carolina 21, Mississippi St. 17	2006 Georgia 31, Virginia Tech 24
1979 Baylor 24, Clemson 18	1993 (Dec.) Clemson 14, Kentucky 13	2007 Auburn 23, Clemson 20 (OT)
1981 (Jan.) Miami (FL) 20, Virginia Tech 10	1995 (Jan.) N. Carolina St. 28, Miss. St. 24	2008 LSU 38, Georgia Tech 3
1981 (Dec.) W. Virginia 26, Florida 6	1995 (Dec.) Virginia 34, Georgia 27	

Cotton Bowl, Dallas, TX

1937 (Jan.) TCU 16, Marquette 6	1956 Mississippi 14, TCU 13	1975 Penn St. 41, Baylor 20
1938 Rice 28, Colorado 14	1957 TCU 28, Syracuse 27	1976 Arkansas 31, Georgia 10
1939 St. Mary's 20, Texas Tech 13	1958 Navy 20, Rice 7	1977 Houston 30, Maryland 21
1940 Clemson 6, Boston Coll. 3	1959 TCU 0, Air Force 0	1978 Notre Dame 38, Texas 10
1941 Texas A&M 13, Fordham 12	1960 Syracuse 23, Texas 14	1979 Notre Dame 35, Houston 34
1942 Alabama 29, Texas A&M 21	1961 Duke 7, Arkansas 6	1980 Houston 17, Nebraska 14
1943 Texas 14, Georgia Tech 7	1962 Texas 12, Mississippi 7	1981 Alabama 30, Baylor 2
1944 Randolph Field 7, Texas 7	1963 LSU 13, Texas 0	1982 Texas 14, Alabama 12
1945 Oklahoma A&M 34, TCU 0	1964 Texas 28, Navy 6	1983 SMU 7, Pittsburgh 3
1946 Texas 40, Missouri 27	1965 Arkansas 10, Nebraska 7	1984 Georgia 10, Texas 9
1947 Arkansas 0, LSU 0	1966 LSU 14, Arkansas 7	1985 Boston Coll. 45, Houston 28
1948 SMU 13, Penn St. 13	1966 (Dec.) Georgia 24, SMU 9	1986 Texas A&M 36, Auburn 16
1949 SMU 21, Oregon 13	1968 (Jan.) Texas A&M 20, Alabama 16	1987 Ohio St. 28, Texas A&M 12
1950 Rice 27, North Carolina 13	1969 Texas 36, Tennessee 13	1988 Texas A&M 35, Notre Dame 10
1951 Tennessee 20, Texas 14	1970 Texas 21, Notre Dame 17	1989 UCLA 17, Arkansas 3
1952 Kentucky 20, TCU 7	1971 Notre Dame 24, Texas 11	1990 Tennessee 31, Arkansas 27
1953 Texas 16, Tennessee 0	1972 Penn St. 30, Texas 6	1991 Miami (FL) 46, Texas 3
1954 Rice 28, Alabama 6	1973 Texas 17, Alabama 13	1992 Florida St. 10, Texas A&M 2
1955 Georgia Tech 14, Arkansas 6	1974 Nebraska 19, Texas 3	1993 Notre Dame 28, Texas A&M 3

1994 Notre Dame 24, Texas A&M 21
1995 USC. 55, Texas Tech 14
1996 Colorado 38, Oregon 6
1997 Brigham Young 19, Kansas St. 15
1998 UCLA 29, Texas A&M 23
1999 Texas 38, Mississippi St. 11

2000 Arkansas 27, Texas 6
2001 Kansas St. 35, Tennessee 21
2002 Oklahoma 10, Arkansas 3
2003 Texas 35, LSU 20
2004 Mississippi 31, Oklahoma St. 28

2005 Tennessee 38, Texas A&M 7
2006 Alabama 13, Texas Tech 10
2007 Auburn 17, Nebraska 14
2008 Missouri 38, Arkansas 7
2009 Mississippi 47, Texas Tech 34

Fiesta Bowl, Glendale, AZ*

1971 (Dec.) Arizona St. 45, Florida St. 38
1972 Arizona St. 49, Missouri 35
1973 Arizona St. 28, Pittsburgh 7
1974 Okla. St. 16, Brigham Young 6
1975 Arizona St. 17, Nebraska 14
1976 Oklahoma 41, Wyoming 7
1977 Penn St. 42, Arizona St. 30
1978 UCLA 10, Arkansas 10
1979 Pittsburgh 16, Arizona 10
1980 Penn St. 31, Ohio St. 19
1982 (Jan.) Penn St. 26, USC 10
1983 Arizona St. 32, Oklahoma 21
1984 Ohio St. 28, Pittsburgh 23
*Played in Tempe, AZ, 1971-2006.

1985 UCLA 39, Miami (FL) 37
1986 Michigan 27, Nebraska 23
1987 Penn St. 14, Miami (FL) 10
1988 Florida St. 31, Nebraska 28
1989 Notre Dame 34, W. Virginia 21
1990 Florida St. 41, Nebraska 17
1991 Louisville 34, Alabama 7
1992 Penn St. 42, Tennessee 17
1993 Syracuse 26, Colorado 22
1994 Arizona 29, Miami (FL) 0
1995 Colorado 41, Notre Dame 24
1996 Nebraska 62, Florida 24
1997 Penn St. 38, Texas 15

1997 (Dec.) Kansas St. 35, Syracuse 18
1999 (Jan.) Tennessee 23, Florida St. 16
2000 Nebraska 31, Tennessee 21
2001 Oregon St. 41, Notre Dame 9
2002 Oregon 38, Colorado 16
2003 Ohio St. 31, Miami 24 (2 OT)
2004 Ohio St. 35, Kansas St. 28
2005 Utah 35, Pittsburgh 7
2006 Ohio St. 34, Notre Dame 20
2007 Boise St. 43, Oklahoma 42 (OT)
2008 West Virginia 48, Oklahoma 28
2009 Texas 24, Ohio State 21

Gator Bowl, Jacksonville, FL

1946 (Jan.) Wake Forest 26, S. Carolina 14
1947 Oklahoma 34, N. Carolina St. 13
1948 Maryland 20, Georgia 20
1949 Clemson 24, Missouri 23
1950 Maryland 20, Missouri 7
1951 Wyoming 20, Washington & Lee 7
1952 Miami (FL) 14, Clemson 0
1953 Florida 14, Tulsa 13
1954 Texas Tech 35, Auburn 13
1954 (Dec.) Auburn 33, Baylor 13
1955 Vanderbilt 25, Auburn 13
1956 Georgia Tech 21, Pittsburgh 14
1957 Tennessee 3, Texas A&M 0
1958 Mississippi 7, Florida 3
1960 (Jan.) Arkansas 14, Georgia Tech 7
1960 (Dec.) Florida 13, Baylor 12
1961 Penn St. 30, Georgia Tech 15
1962 Florida 17, Penn St. 7
1963 N. Carolina 35, Air Force 0
1965 (Jan.) Florida St. 36, Okla. 19
1965 (Dec.) GA Tech 31, Texas Tech 21
1966 Tennessee 18, Syracuse 12

1967 Penn St. 17, Florida St. 17
1968 Missouri 35, Alabama 10
1969 Florida 14, Tennessee 13
1971 (Jan.) Auburn 35, Mississippi 28
1971 (Dec.) Georgia 7, N. Carolina 3
1972 Auburn 24, Colorado 3
1973 Texas Tech 28, Tennessee 19
1974 Auburn 27, Texas 3
1975 Maryland 13, Florida 0
1976 Notre Dame 20, Penn St. 9
1977 Pittsburgh 34, Clemson 3
1978 Clemson 17, Ohio St. 15
1979 N. Carolina 17, Michigan 15
1980 Pittsburgh 37, S. Carolina 9
1981 N. Carolina 31, Arkansas 27
1982 Florida St. 31, West Virginia 12
1983 Florida 14, Iowa 6
1984 Oklahoma St. 21, S. Carolina 14
1985 Florida St. 34, Oklahoma St. 23
1986 Clemson 27, Stanford 21
1987 LSU 30, S. Carolina 13

1989 (Jan.) Georgia 34, Michigan St. 27
1989 (Dec.) Clemson 27, W. Virginia 7
1991 (Jan.) Michigan 35, Mississippi 3
1991 (Dec.) Oklahoma 48, Virginia 14
1992 Florida 27, N. Carolina St. 10
1993 Alabama 24, N. Carolina 10
1994 Tennessee 45, Virginia Tech 23
1996 (Jan.) Syracuse 41, Clemson 0
1997 N. Carolina 20, W. Virginia 13
1998 N. Carolina 42, Virginia Tech 3
1999 Georgia Tech 35, Notre Dame 28
2000 Miami (FL) 28, Georgia Tech 13
2001 Virginia Tech 41, Clemson 20
2002 Florida St. 30, Virginia Tech 17
2003 N. Carolina St. 28, Notre Dame 6
2004 Maryland 41, West Virginia 7
2005 Florida St. 30, West Virginia 18
2006 Virginia Tech 35, Louisville 24
2007 West Virginia 38, Georgia Tech 35
2008 Texas Tech 31, VIrginia 28
2009 Nebraska 26, Clemson 21

Liberty Bowl, Memphis, TN

1976 Alabama 36, UCLA 6
1977 Nebraska 21, N. Carolina 17
1978 Missouri 20, LSU 15
1979 Penn St. 9, Tulane 6
1980 Purdue 28, Missouri 25
1981 Ohio St. 31, Navy 28
1982 Alabama 21, Illinois 15
1983 Notre Dame 19, Boston Coll. 18
1984 Auburn 21, Arkansas 15
1985 Baylor 21, LSU 7
1986 Tennessee 21, Minnesota 14
1987 Georgia 20, Arkansas 17
1988 Indiana 34, S. Carolina 10
1989 Mississippi 42, Air Force 29
1990 Air Force 23, Ohio St. 11
1991 Air Force 38, Mississippi St. 15
1992 Mississippi 13, Air Force 0

1993 Louisville 18, Michigan St. 7
1994 Illinois 30, East Carolina 0
1995 East Carolina 19, Stanford 13
1996 Syracuse 30, Houston 17
1997 So. Mississippi 41, Pittsburgh 7
1998 Tulane 41, Brigham Young 27
1999 So. Mississippi 23, Colorado St. 17
2000 Colorado St. 22, Louisville 17
2001 Louisville 28, BYU 10
2002 TCU 17, Colorado St. 3
2003 Utah 17, So. Mississippi 0
2004 Louisville 44, Boise St. 40
2005 Tulsa 31, Fresno St. 24
2006 South Carolina 44, Houston 36
2007 Mississippi State 10, UCF 3
2009 Kentucky 25, East Carolina 19

Sun Bowl, El Paso, TX

1936 (Jan.) Hardin-Simmons 14,
       New Mexico St. 14
1937 Hardin-Simmons 34, Texas Mines 6
1938 West Virginia 7, Texas Tech 6
1939 Utah 26, New Mexico 0
1940 Catholic U. 0, Arizona St. 0
1941 Western Reserve 26, Arizona St. 13
1942 Tulsa 6, Texas Tech 0
1943 2d Air Force 13, Hardin-Simmons 7
1944 Southwestern (TX) 7, New Mexico 0
1945 Southwestern (TX) 35,
       Univ. of Mexico 0
1946 New Mexico 34, Denver 24
1947 Cincinnati 18, Virginia Tech 6
1948 Miami (OH) 13, Texas Tech 12
1949 West Virginia 21, Texas Mines 12
1950 Texas Western 33, Georgetown 20
1951 West Texas St. 14, Cincinnati 13
1952 Texas Tech 25, Pacific (CA) 14
1953 Pacific (CA) 26, S. Mississippi 7
1954 Texas Western 37, S. Miss. 14
1955 Texas Western 47, Florida St. 20
1956 Wyoming 21, Texas Tech 14
1957 Geo. Washington 13, TX Western 0
1958 Louisville 34, Drake 20
1958 (Dec.) Wyoming 14, Hardin-Simmons 6

1959 New Mexico St. 28, N. Texas St. 8
1960 New Mexico St. 20, Utah St. 13
1961 Villanova 17, Wichita 9
1962 West Texas St. 15, Ohio U. 14
1963 Oregon 21, SMU 14
1964 Georgia 7, Texas Tech 0
1965 Texas Western 13, TCU 12
1966 Wyoming 28, Florida St. 20
1967 UTEP 14, Mississippi 7
1968 Auburn 34, Arizona 10
1969 Nebraska 45, Georgia 6
1970 Georgia Tech. 17, Texas Tech 9
1971 LSU 33, Iowa St. 15
1972 North Carolina 32, Texas Tech 28
1973 Missouri 34, Auburn 17
1974 Mississippi St. 26, North Carolina 24
1975 Pittsburgh 33, Kansas 19
1977 (Jan.) Texas A&M 37, Florida 14
1977 (Dec.) Stanford 24, LSU 14
1978 Texas 42, Maryland 0
1979 Washington 14, Texas 7
1980 Nebraska 31, Mississippi St. 17
1981 Oklahoma 40, Houston 14
1982 North Carolina 26, Texas 10
1983 Alabama 28, SMU 7

1984 Maryland 28, Tennessee 27
1985 Georgia 13, Arizona 13
1986 Alabama 28, Washington 6
1987 Oklahoma St. 35, West Virginia 33
1988 Alabama 29, Army 28
1989 Pittsburgh 31, Texas A&M 28
1990 Michigan St. 17, USC 16
1991 UCLA 6, Illinois 3
1992 Baylor 20, Arizona 15
1993 Oklahoma 41, Texas Tech 10
1994 Texas 35, North Carolina 31
1995 Iowa 38, Washington 18
1996 Stanford 38, Michigan St. 0
1997 Arizona St. 17, Iowa 7
1998 TCU 28, USC 19
1999 Oregon 24, Minnesota 20
2000 Wisconsin 21, UCLA 20
2001 Washington St. 33, Purdue 27
2002 Purdue 34, Washington 24
2003 Minnesota 31, Oregon 30
2004 Arizona St. 27, Purdue 23
2005 UCLA 50, Northwestern 39
2006 Oregon St. 39, Missouri 38
2007 Oregon 56, South Florida 21
2008 Oregon State 3, Pittsburgh 0

Other Bowl Results, Late 2008-Early 2009

Alamo Bowl, San Antonio, TX: Missouri 30, Northwestern 23

Armed Forces (fmr. Fort Worth) Bowl, Ft. Worth, TX: Houston 34, Air Force 28

Capital One Bowl, Orlando, FL: Georgia 24, Michigan State 12

Champs Sports Bowl, Orlando, FL: Florida State 42, Wisconsin 13

Meineke Car Care Bowl, Charlotte, NC: West Virginia 31, North Carolina 30

EagleBank Bowl, Washington, DC: Wake Forest 29, Navy 19

Emerald Bowl, San Francisco, CA: California 24, Miami 17

GMAC Bowl, Mobile, AL: Tulsa 45, Ball State 13

Hawaii Bowl, Honolulu, HI: Notre Dame 49, Hawaii 21

Holiday Bowl, San Diego, CA: Oregon 42, Oklahoma State 31

Humanitarian Bowl, Boise, ID: Maryland 42, Nevada 35

Independence Bowl, Shreveport, LA: Louisiana Tech 17, Northern Illinois 10

Insight Bowl, Tempe, AZ: Kansas 42, Minnesota 21

International Bowl, Toronto, Ontario: Connecticut 38, Buffalo 20

Las Vegas Bowl: Arizona 31, BYU 21

Motor City Bowl, Detroit, MI: Florida Atlantic 24, Central Michigan 21

Music City Bowl, Nashville, TN: Vanderbilt 16, Boston College 14

New Mexico Bowl, Albuquerque, NM: Colorado State 40, Fresno State 35

New Orleans Bowl: Southern Miss 30, Troy 27 (OT)

Outback Bowl, Tampa, FL: Iowa 31, South Carolina 10

PapaJohns.com Bowl, Birmingham, AL: Rutgers 29, NC State 23

Poinsettia Bowl, San Diego, CA: TCU 17, Boise State 16

St. Petersburg Bowl: South Florida 41, Memphis 14

Texas (fmr. Houston) Bowl, Houston, TX: Rice 38, Western Michigan 14

All-Time NCAA Division I-A (FBS) Statistical Leaders

(At end of 2008 season. Prior to 2002, postseason games were not included in NCAA final football statistics or records. Beginning with the 2002 season, all postseason games were included. Career rushing yards per game rankings do not include active players.)

Career Rushing Yards

Player, team	Yrs.	Carries	Yds.	Avg.
Ron Dayne, Wisconsin	1996-99	1,115	6,397	5.74
Ricky Williams, Texas	1995-98	1,011	6,279	6.21
Tony Dorsett, Pittsburgh	1973-76	1,074	6,082	5.66
DeAngelo Williams, Memphis	2002-05	969	6,026	6.22
Charles White, USC	1976-79	1,023	5,598	5.47

Career Rushing Yards/Game (min. 2,500 yds.)

Player, team	Yrs.	Carries	Yds.	Avg./game
Ed Marinaro, Cornell	1969-71	918	4,715	174.6
O. J. Simpson, USC	1967-68	621	3,214	164.4
Herschel Walker, Georgia	1980-82	994	5,259	159.4
Garrett Wolfe, N. Illinois	2004-06	807	5,164	156.5
LeShon Johnson, N. Illinois	1992-93	592	3,314	150.6

Career Passing Yards

Player, team	Yrs.	Comp./att.	Yds.
Timmy Chang, Hawaii	2000-04	1,388/2,436	17,072
Graham Harrell, Texas Tech	2005-08	1,403/2,010	15,793
Ty Detmer, BYU	1988-91	958/1,530	15,031
Colt Brennan, Hawaii	2005-07	1,115/1,584	14,193
Philip Rivers, North Carolina	2000-03	1,147/1,710	13,484

Career Receiving Yards

Player, team	Yrs.	Rec.	Yds.	Avg.
Trevor Insley, Nevada	1996-99	298	5,005	16.8
Marcus Harris, Wyoming	1993-96	259	4,518	17.4
Rashaun Woods, Oklahoma St.	2000-03	293	4,412	15.1
Ryan Yarborough, Wyoming	1990-93	229	4,357	19.0
Troy Edwards, Louisiana Tech	1996-98	280	4,352	15.5

All-Time Team Won-Lost Records

School	Years	Won	Lost	Tied	Total	Pct.	School	Years	Won	Lost	Tied	Total	Pct.
Michigan	129	872	295	36	1,203	0.740	LSU	115	700	383	47	1,130	0.640
Notre Dame	120	831	284	42	1,157	0.736	Miami-FL	82	544	310	19	873	0.634
Texas	116	832	317	33	1,182	0.718	Auburn	116	681	395	47	1,123	0.627
Oklahoma[1]	114	791	297	53	1,141	0.716	Florida	102	641	373	40	1,054	0.627
Ohio St.	119	808	307	53	1,168	0.714	Miami-OH	120	649	379	44	1,072	0.626
Alabama	114	799	316	43	1,158	0.709	South Fla. (2000)	12	87	52	0	139	0.626
USC	116	766	303	54	1,123	0.706	Arizona St.	96	545	334	24	903	0.617
Nebraska	119	817	337	40	1,194	0.701	Washington	119	650	398	50	1,098	0.615
Boise St. (1996)	41	339	144	2	485	0.701	Central Mich.	108	558	353	36	947	0.608
Tennessee	112	775	327	53	1,155	0.694	Colorado	119	663	426	36	1,125	0.605
Penn St.	122	800	349	41	1,190	0.689	Virginia Tech	115	657	425	46	1,128	0.603
Florida St.	62	459	221	17	697	0.671	Texas A&M	114	659	433	48	1,140	0.599
Georgia	115	723	384	54	1,161	0.646	W. Kentucky (2009)	89	511	337	30	878	0.599

Note: As of end of 2008 season. Includes records as senior college only. Bowl and playoff games are included, and each tie game is computed as half won and half lost. Teams listed with years in parentheses indicates reclassification to Division I-A (FBS). The year in parentheses is the first year of Division I-A (FBS) membership. Tiebreaker rule began with 1996 season. (1) Includes 2005 season, which Oklahoma was ordered to vacate after "failure to monitor" player employment. Oklahoma won an appeal of the penalty in Feb. 2008.

Heisman Trophy Winners

Awarded annually to the nation's outstanding college football player by the Downtown Athletic Club.

1935 Jay Berwanger, Chicago, HB	1960 Joe Bellino, Navy, HB	1985 Bo Jackson, Auburn, RB
1936 Larry Kelley, Yale, E	1961 Ernest Davis, Syracuse, HB	1986 Vinny Testaverde, Miami, QB
1937 Clinton Frank, Yale, HB	1962 Terry Baker, Oregon St., QB	1987 Tim Brown, Notre Dame, WR
1938 David O'Brien, Texas Christian, QB	1963 Roger Staubach, Navy, QB	1988 Barry Sanders, Oklahoma St., RB
1939 Nile Kinnick, Iowa, HB	1964 John Huarte, Notre Dame, QB	1989 Andre Ware, Houston, QB
1940 Tom Harmon, Michigan, HB	1965 Mike Garrett, USC, HB	1990 Ty Detmer, BYU, QB
1941 Bruce Smith, Minnesota, HB	1966 Steve Spurrier, Florida, QB	1991 Desmond Howard, Michigan, WR
1942 Frank Sinkwich, Georgia, HB	1967 Gary Beban, UCLA, QB	1992 Gino Torretta, Miami, QB
1943 Angelo Bertelli, Notre Dame, QB	1968 O. J. Simpson, USC, RB	1993 Charlie Ward, Florida St., QB
1944 Leslie Horvath, Ohio St., QB	1969 Steve Owens, Oklahoma, RB	1994 Rashaan Salaam, Colorado, RB
1945 Felix Blanchard, Army, FB	1970 Jim Plunkett, Stanford, QB	1995 Eddie George, Ohio St., RB
1946 Glenn Davis, Army, HB	1971 Pat Sullivan, Auburn, QB	1996 Danny Wuerffel, Florida, QB
1947 John Lujack, Notre Dame, QB	1972 Johnny Rodgers, Nebraska, RB-WR	1997 Charles Woodson, Michigan, CB
1948 Doak Walker, SMU, HB	1973 John Cappelletti, Penn St., RB	1998 Ricky Williams, Texas, RB
1949 Leon Hart, Notre Dame, E	1974 Archie Griffin, Ohio St., RB	1999 Ron Dayne, Wisconsin, RB
1950 Vic Janowicz, Ohio St., HB	1975 Archie Griffin, Ohio St., RB	2000 Chris Weinke, Florida St., QB
1951 Richard Kazmaier, Princeton, HB	1976 Tony Dorsett, Pittsburgh, RB	2001 Eric Crouch, Nebraska, QB
1952 Billy Vessels, Oklahoma, HB	1977 Earl Campbell, Texas, RB	2002 Carson Palmer, USC, QB
1953 John Lattner, Notre Dame, HB	1978 Billy Sims, Oklahoma, RB	2003 Jason White, Oklahoma, QB
1954 Alan Ameche, Wisconsin, FB	1979 Charles White, USC, RB	2004 Matt Leinart, USC, QB
1955 Howard Cassady, Ohio St., HB	1980 George Rogers, S. Carolina, RB	2005 Reggie Bush, USC, RB
1956 Paul Hornung, Notre Dame, QB	1981 Marcus Allen, USC, RB	2006 Troy Smith, Ohio State, QB
1957 John Crow, Texas A&M, HB	1982 Herschel Walker, Georgia, RB	2007 Tim Tebow, Florida, QB
1958 Pete Dawkins, Army, HB	1983 Mike Rozier, Nebraska, RB	2008 Sam Bradford, Oklahoma, QB
1959 Billy Cannon, LSU, HB	1984 Doug Flutie, Boston College, QB	

All-Time Division I-A (FBS) Coaching Victories

Joe Paterno 383	Hayden Fry 232	Jim Sweeney 200	**Joe Glenn** 188
Bobby Bowden 382	**Jim Tressel** 218	**Chris Ault** 198	Dennis Franchione 187
Paul "Bear" Bryant 323	**Frank Beamer** 217	Dana X. Bible 198	John Heisman 186
Glenn "Pop" Warner 319	Jess Neely 207	Dan McGugin 197	Johnny Majors 185
Amos Alonzo Stagg 314	Warren Woodson 203	Fielding Yost 196	Darrell Royal 184
LaVell Edwards 257	Don Nehlen 202	Howard Jones 194	**Dick Tomey** 181
Tom Osborne 255	Eddie Anderson 201	John Cooper 192	Gil Dobie 180
Lou Holtz 249	**Mack Brown** 201	John Vaught 190	Jackie Sherrill. 180
Woody Hayes 238	Vince Dooley 201	George Welsh 189	Carl Snavely 180
Bo Schembechler 234			

Note: Coaches active in 2008 shown in bold. Total victories through Jan. 9, 2009, including bowl games. John Gagliardi of St. John's Univ. (MN) (Div. III) holds the record for most college football victories, with 453.

College Football Coach of the Year

The Division I-A Coach of the Year has been selected by the American Football Coaches Assn. since 1935 and selected by the Football Writers Assn. of America since 1957. When polls disagree, both winners are indicated.

1935	Lynn Waldorf, Northwestern	1965	Tommy Prothro, UCLA (AFCA);	1987	Dick MacPherson, Syracuse
1936	Dick Harlow, Harvard		Duffy Daugherty, Mich. St. (FWAA)	1988	Don Nehlen, W. Virginia (AFCA);
1937	Edward Mylin, Lafayette	1966	Tom Cahill, Army		Lou Holtz, Notre Dame (FWAA)
1938	Bill Kern, Carnegie Tech	1967	John Pont, Indiana	1989	Bill McCartney, Colorado
1939	Eddie Anderson, Iowa	1968	Joe Paterno, Penn St. (AFCA);	1990	Bobby Ross, Georgia Tech
1940	Clark Shaughnessy, Stanford		Woody Hayes, Ohio St. (FWAA)	1991	Don James, Washington
1941	Frank Leahy, Notre Dame	1969	Bo Schembechler, Michigan	1992	Gene Stallings, Alabama
1942	Bill Alexander, Georgia Tech	1970	Charles McClendon, LSU, & Darrell	1993	Barry Alvarez, Wisconsin (AFCA);
1943	Amos Alonzo Stagg, Pacific		Royal, Texas (AFCA);		Terry Bowden, Auburn (FWAA)
1944	Carroll Widdoes, Ohio St.		Alex Agase, Northwestern (FWAA)	1994	Tom Osborne, Nebraska (AFCA);
1945	Bo McMillin, Indiana	1971	Paul "Bear" Bryant, Alabama (AFCA);		Rich Brooks, Oregon (FWAA)
1946	Earl "Red" Blaik, Army		Bob Devaney, Nebraska (FWAA)	1995	Gary Barnett, Northwestern
1947	Fritz Crisler, Michigan	1972	John McKay, USC	1996	Bruce Snyder, Arizona St.
1948	Bennie Oosterbaan, Michigan	1973	Paul "Bear" Bryant, Alabama (AFCA);	1997	Mike Price, Washington St.
1949	Bud Wilkinson, Oklahoma		Johnny Majors, Pittsburgh (FWAA)	1998	Phillip Fulmer, Tennessee
1950	Charlie Caldwell, Princeton	1974	Grant Teaff, Baylor	1999	Frank Beamer, Virginia Tech
1951	Chuck Taylor, Stanford	1975	Frank Kush, Arizona St. (AFCA);	2000	Bob Stoops, Oklahoma
1952	Biggie Munn, Michigan St.		Woody Hayes, Ohio St. (FWAA)	2001	Larry Coker, Miami (FL), & Ralph
1953	Jim Tatum, Maryland	1976	Johnny Majors, Pittsburgh		Friedgen, Maryland (AFCA); Ralph
1954	Henry "Red" Sanders, UCLA	1977	Don James, Washington (AFCA);		Friedgen, Maryland (FWAA)
1955	Duffy Daugherty, Michigan St.		Lou Holtz, Arkansas (FWAA)	2002	Jim Tressel, Ohio St.
1956	Bowden Wyatt, Tennessee	1978	Joe Paterno, Penn St.	2003	Pete Carroll, USC (AFCA); Nick
1957	Woody Hayes, Ohio St.	1979	Earle Bruce, Ohio St.		Saban, LSU (FWAA)
1958	Paul Dietzel, LSU	1980	Vince Dooley, Georgia	2004	Tommy Tuberville, Auburn (AFCA);
1959	Ben Schwartzwalder, Syracuse	1981	Danny Ford, Clemson		Urban Meyer, Utah (FWAA)
1960	Murray Warmath, Minnesota	1982	Joe Paterno, Penn St.	2005	Joe Paterno, Penn State (AFCA);
1961	Paul "Bear" Bryant, Ala. (AFCA);	1983	Ken Hatfield, Air Force (AFCA);		Charlie Weis, Notre Dame (FWAA)
	Darrell Royal, Texas (FWAA)		Howard Schnellenberger,	2006	Jim Grobe, Wake Forest (AFCA);
1962	John McKay, USC		Miami (FL) (FWAA)		Greg Schiano, Rutgers (FWAA)
1963	Darrell Royal, Texas	1984	LaVell Edwards, Brigham Young	2007	Mark Mangino, Kansas
1964	Ara Parseghian, Notre Dame, &	1985	Fisher De Berry, Air Force	2008	Kyle Whittingham, Utah (AFCA);
	Frank Broyles, Arkansas (AFCA);	1986	Joe Paterno, Penn St.		Nick Saban, Alabama (FWAA)
	Ara Parseghian (FWAA)				

NCAA Div. I-A (FBS) Football Conference Champions (1980-2008)

Atlantic Coast
1980 North Carolina
1981 Clemson
1982 Clemson
1983 Maryland
1984 Maryland
1985 Maryland
1986 Clemson
1987 Clemson
1988 Clemson
1989 Virginia, Duke
1990 Georgia Tech
1991 Clemson
1992 Florida St.
1993 Florida St.
1994 Florida St.
1995 Virginia, Florida St.
1996 Florida St.
1997 Florida St.
1998 Florida St., Georgia Tech
1999 Florida St.
2000 Florida St.
2001 Maryland
2002 Florida St.
2003 Florida St.
2004 Virginia Tech
2005 Florida St.
2006 Wake Forest
2007 Virginia Tech
2008 Virginia Tech

Big 12
1996 Texas
1997 Nebraska
1998 Texas A&M
1999 Nebraska
2000 Oklahoma
2001 Colorado
2002 Oklahoma
2003 Kansas St.
2004 Oklahoma
2005 Texas
2006 Oklahoma
2007 Oklahoma
2008 Oklahoma

Big East
1991 Miami (FL), Syracuse
1992 Miami (FL)
1993 West Virginia
1994 Miami (FL)
1995 Virginia Tech, Miami (FL)
1996 Virginia Tech, Miami (FL), Syracuse
1997 Syracuse
1998 Syracuse
1999 Virginia Tech
2000 Miami (FL)
2001 Miami (FL)
2002 Miami (FL)
2003 Miami (FL)
2004 Pittsburgh, W. Virginia, Boston, Syracuse
2005 West Virginia
2006 Louisville
2007 West Virginia
2008 Cincinnati

Big Ten
1980 Michigan
1981 Iowa, Ohio St.
1982 Michigan
1983 Illinois
1984 Ohio St.
1985 Iowa
1986 Michigan, Ohio St.
1987 Michigan St.
1988 Michigan
1989 Michigan
1990 Iowa, Ill., Mich., Mich. St.
1991 Michigan
1992 Michigan
1993 Ohio St., Wisconsin
1994 Penn St.
1995 Northwestern
1996 Ohio St., Northwestern
1997 Michigan
1998 Ohio St., Wisconsin, Michigan
1999 Wisconsin
2000 Michigan, Northwestern, Purdue
2001 Illinois
2002 Iowa, Ohio St.
2003 Michigan
2004 Iowa, Michigan
2005 Penn St., Ohio St.
2006 Ohio St.
2007 Ohio St.
2008 Penn St., Ohio St.

Big West
1980 Long Beach St.
1981 San Jose St.
1982 Fresno St.
1983 Cal St.-Fullerton
1984 Cal St.-Fullerton
1985 Fresno St.
1986 San Jose St.
1987 San Jose St.
1988 Fresno St.
1989 Fresno St.
1990 San Jose St.
1991 San Jose St., Fresno St.
1992 Nevada
1993 SW Louisiana, Utah St.
1994 Nevada, SW Louisiana, UNLV
1995 Nevada
1996 Nevada, Utah St.
1997 Nevada, Utah St.
1998 Idaho
1999 Boise St.
2000 Boise St.

Conference USA
1996 So. Mississippi, Houston
1997 So. Mississippi
1998 Tulane
1999 So. Mississippi
2000 Louisville
2001 Louisville
2002 Cincinnati, TCU
2003 So. Mississippi
2004 Louisville

2005 Tulsa
2006 Houston
2007 Central Florida
2008 East Carolina

Mid-American Athletic
1980 Central Michigan
1981 Toledo
1982 Bowling Green
1983 Northern Illinois
1984 Toledo
1985 Bowling Green
1986 Miami (OH)
1987 E. Michigan
1988 W. Michigan
1989 Ball St.
1990 Central Michigan
1991 Bowling Green
1992 Bowling Green
1993 Ball St.
1994 Central Michigan
1995 Toledo
1996 Ball St.
1997 Marshall
1998 Marshall
1999 Marshall
2000 Marshall
2001 Toledo
2002 Marshall
2003 Miami (OH)
2004 Toledo
2005 Akron
2006 Central Michigan
2007 Central Michigan
2008 Buffalo

Mountain West
1999 BYU, Colorado St., Utah
2000 Colorado St.
2001 BYU
2002 Colorado St.
2003 Utah
2004 Utah
2005 TCU
2006 BYU, TCU
2007 BYU
2008 Utah

Pacific Ten
1980 Washington
1981 Washington
1982 UCLA
1983 UCLA
1984 USC
1985 UCLA
1986 Arizona St.
1987 UCLA, USC
1988 USC
1989 USC
1990 Washington
1991 Washington
1992 Washington, Stanford
1993 UCLA, Arizona, USC
1994 Oregon
1995 USC, Washington
1996 Arizona St.
1997 Washington St., UCLA
1998 UCLA
1999 Stanford
2000 Washington, Oregon St., Oregon
2001 Oregon
2002 USC, Washington St.
2003 USC
2004 USC
2005 USC
2006 California, USC
2007 USC, Arizona State
2008 USC

Southeastern
1980 Georgia
1981 Georgia, Alabama
1982 Georgia
1983 Auburn
1984 Florida (title vacated)
1985 Tennessee
1986 LSU
1987 Auburn
1988 Auburn, LSU
1989 Ala., Tenn., Auburn
1990 Tennessee
1991 Florida
1992 Alabama
1993 Florida
1994 Florida
1995 Florida
1996 Florida
1997 Tennessee
1998 Tennessee
1999 Alabama
2000 Florida
2001 LSU
2002 Georgia
2003 LSU
2004 Auburn
2005 Georgia
2006 Florida
2007 LSU
2008 Florida

Sun Belt
2001 Middle Tenn. St., North Texas
2002 North Texas
2003 North Texas
2004 North Texas
2005 Arkansas St., LA-Lafayette, LA-Monroe
2006 Middle Tenn. St., Troy
2007 Florida Atlantic, Troy
2008 Troy

Western Athletic
1980 Brigham Young (BYU)
1981 Brigham Young
1982 Brigham Young
1983 Brigham Young
1984 Brigham Young
1985 BYU, Air Force
1986 San Diego St.
1987 Wyoming
1988 Wyoming
1989 Brigham Young
1990 Brigham Young
1991 Brigham Young
1992 Hawaii, BYU, Fresno St.
1993 Wyoming, Fresno St., BYU
1994 Colorado St.
1995 Colorado St., Air Force, Utah, BYU
1996 Brigham Young
1997 Colorado St.
1998 Air Force
1999 Fresno St., Hawaii, TCU
2000 Texas Christian, UTEP
2001 Louisiana Tech
2002 Boise State
2003 Boise State
2004 Boise State
2005 Boise State, Nevada
2006 Boise State
2007 Hawaii
2008 Boise State

NCAA Div. I-AA (FCS) Football Conference Champions (1990-2008)

Atlantic 10
1990 Massachusetts
1991 Delaware, Villanova
1992 Delaware
1993 Boston U.
1994 New Hampshire
1995 Delaware
1996 William & Mary
1997 Villanova
1998 Richmond
1999 J. Madison, Mass.
2000 Delaware, Richmond
2001 Hofstra, Maine, Villanova, Will. & Mary
2002 Maine, Northeastern
2003 Delaware, Mass.
2004 Delaware, J. Madison, New Hampshire, William & Mary
2005 New Hampshire, Richmond
2006 Massachusetts

Big Sky
1990 Nevada
1991 Nevada
1992 Idaho, Eastern Wash.
1993 Montana
1994 Boise St.
1995 Montana
1996 Montana
1997 Eastern Wash.
1998 Montana
1999 Montana
2000 Montana
2001 Montana
2002 Idaho St., Montana, Montana St.
2003 Montana St., Montana, No. Arizona
2004 Montana, Eastern Wash.
2005 Eastern Wash., Montana, Montana St.
2006 Montana
2007 Montana
2008 Montana, Weber St.

Big South
2002 Gardner-Webb
2003 Gardner-Webb
2004 Coastal Carolina
2005 Coastal Carolina, Charleston Southern
2006 Coastal Carolina
2007 Liberty
2008 Liberty

Colonial Athletic Association
2007 Massachusetts, Richmond
2008 James Madison

Gateway
1990 Northern Iowa
1991 Northern Iowa
1992 Northern Iowa
1993 Northern Iowa
1994 Northern Iowa
1995 N. Iowa, Eastern Ill.
1996 Northern Iowa
1997 Western Illinois
1998 Western Illinois
1999 Illinois St.
2000 Western Illinois
2001 Northern Iowa
2002 W. Illinois, W. Kentucky
2003 N. Iowa, S. Illinois
2004 S. Illinois
2005 N. Iowa, S. Illinois, Youngstown St.
2006 Youngstown St.
2007 N. Iowa

Great West
2004 Cal. Poly
2005 Cal. Poly, UC Davis
2006 North Dakota St.
2007 South Dakota St.
2008 Cal. Poly

Ivy League
1990 Cornell, Dartmouth
1991 Dartmouth
1992 Dartmouth, Princeton
1993 Penn
1994 Penn
1995 Princeton
1996 Dartmouth
1997 Harvard
1998 Penn
1999 Brown, Yale
2000 Penn
2001 Harvard
2002 Pennsylvania
2003 Pennsylvania
2004 Harvard
2005 Brown
2006 Yale, Princeton
2007 Harvard
2008 Harvard, Brown

Metro Atlantic
1993 Iona
1994 Marist, St. John's (NY)
1995 Duquesne
1996 Duquesne
1997 Georgetown
1998 Fairfield, Georgetown
1999 Duquesne
2000 Duquesne
2001 Duquesne
2002 Duquesne
2003 Duquesne
2004 Duquesne
2005 Duquesne
2006 Duquesne, Marist
2007 Iona, Duquesne, Marist

Mid-Eastern Athletic
1990 Florida A&M
1991 North Carolina A&T
1992 North Carolina A&T
1993 Howard
1994 South Carolina St.
1995 Florida A&M
1996 Florida A&M
1997 Hampton
1998 Florida A&M, Hampton
1999 North Carolina A&T
2000 Florida A&M
2001 Florida A&M
2002 Bethune-Cookman
2003 North Carolina A&T
2004 Hampton, South Carolina St.
2005 Hampton
2006 Hampton
2007 Delaware St.
2008 South Carolina St.

Missouri Valley
2008 N. Iowa, S. Illinois

Northeast
1996 R. Morris, Monmouth
1997 Robert Morris
1998 R. Morris, Monmouth
1999 Robert Morris
2000 Robert Morris
2001 Sacred Heart
2002 Albany (NY)
2003 Albany, Monmouth
2004 Central Conn. St., Monmouth
2005 Central Conn. St., Stony Brook
2006 Monmouth (NJ)
2007 Albany
2008 Albany

Ohio Valley
1990 E. Kentucky., Middle Tenn.
1991 Eastern Kentucky
1992 Middle Tennessee
1993 Eastern Kentucky
1994 Eastern Kentucky
1995 Murray St.
1996 Murray St.
1997 Eastern Kentucky
1998 Tennessee St.
1999 Tennessee St.
2000 Western Kentucky
2001 Eastern Illinois
2002 E. Illinois, Murray St.
2003 Jacksonville St.
2004 Jacksonville St.
2005 Eastern Illinois
2006 E. Illinois, Tenn.-Martin
2007 Eastern Kentucky
2008 Eastern Kentucky

Patriot
1990 Holy Cross
1991 Holy Cross
1992 Lafayette
1993 Lehigh
1994 Lafayette
1995 Lehigh
1996 Bucknell
1997 Colgate
1998 Lehigh
1999 Colgate, Lehigh
2000 Lehigh
2001 Lehigh
2002 Colgate, Fordham
2003 Colgate
2004 Lafayette, Lehigh
2005 Colgate, Lafayette
2006 Lafayette, Lehigh
2007 Fordham
2008 Colgate

Pioneer
1993 Dayton
1994 Dayton, Butler
1995 Drake
1996 Dayton
1997 Dayton
1998 Drake
1999 Dayton
2000 Dayton, Drake, Valparaiso
2001 Dayton
2002 Dayton
2003 Valparaiso
2004 Drake
2005 San Diego
2006 San Diego
2007 Dayton
2008 Jacksonville

Southern
1990 Furman
1991 Appalachian St.
1992 Citadel
1993 Georgia Southern
1994 Marshall
1995 Appalachian St.
1996 Marshall
1997 Georgia Southern
1998 Georgia Southern
1999 Appalachian St., GA Southern, Furman
2000 Georgia Southern
2001 Georgia Southern
2002 Georgia Southern
2003 Wofford
2004 Furman, GA Southern
2005 Appalachian St.
2006 Appalachian St.
2007 Appalachian St., Wofford
2008 Appalachian St.

Southland
1990 La.-Monroe
1991 McNeese St.
1992 La.-Monroe
1993 McNeese St.
1994 North Texas
1995 McNeese St.
1996 Troy St.
1997 McNeese St., Northwestern St.
1998 Northwestern St.
1999 Troy St., S. F. Austin
2000 Troy St.
2001 Sam Houston St., McNeese St.
2002 McNeese St.
2003 McNeese St.
2004 Northwestern St., Sam Houston St.
2005 Texas St., Nicholls St.
2006 McNeese St.
2007 McNeese St.
2008 Texas State

Southwestern Athletic
1990 Jackson St.
1991 Alabama St.
1992 Alcorn St.
1993 Southern
1994 Grambling St., Alcorn St.
1995 Jackson St.
1996 Jackson St.
1997 Southern
1998 Southern
1999 Southern
2000 Grambling St.
2001 Grambling St.
2002 Grambling St.
2003 Southern
2004 Alabama St.
2005 Grambling St.
2006 Alabama A&M
2007 Jackson St.
2008 Grambling St.

Selected NCAA Division I Teams

(Conferences and coaches listed are as of Sept. 2009.)

Team	Nickname	Team colors	Conference	Basketball coach	Football coach
Air Force	Falcons	Blue & silver	Mountain West	Jeff Reynolds	Troy Calhoun
Akron	Zips	Blue & gold	Mid-American	Keith Dambrot	J. D. Brookhart
Alabama	Crimson Tide	Crimson & white	Southeastern	Anthony Grant	Nick Saban
Appalachian State*	Mountaineers	Black & gold	Southern	Buzz Peterson	Jerry Moore
Arizona	Wildcats	Cardinal & navy	Pacific Ten	Sean Miller	Mike Stoops
Arizona State	Sun Devils	Maroon & gold	Pacific Ten	Herb Sendek	Dennis Erickson
Arkansas	Razorbacks	Cardinal & white	Southeastern	John Pelphrey	Bobby Petrino
Arkansas State	Red Wolves	Scarlet & black	Sun Belt	John Brady	Steve Roberts
Army	Black Knights	Black, gold, gray	Independent	Jim Crews	Rich Ellerson
Auburn	Tigers	Burnt orange & navy	Southeastern	Jeff Lebo	Gene Chizik
Ball State	Cardinals	Cardinal & white	Mid-American	Billy Taylor	Stan Parrish
Baylor	Bears	Green & gold	Big Twelve	Scott Drew	Art Briles
Boise State	Broncos	Blue & orange	Western Athletic	Greg Graham	Chris Petersen
Boston College	Eagles	Maroon & gold	Atlantic Coast	Al Skinner	Frank Spaziani
Bowling Green	Falcons	Orange & brown	Mid-American	Louis Orr	Dave Clawson
Brigham Young (BYU)	Cougars	Dark blue & white	Mountain West	Dave Rose	Bronco Mendenhall
Brown*	Bears	Brown, cardinal, white	Ivy League	Jesse Agel	Phil Estes
California	Golden Bears	Blue & gold	Pacific Ten	Mike Montgomery	Jeff Tedford
Central Michigan	Chippewas	Maroon & gold	Mid-American	Ernie Zeigler	Butch Jones
Cincinnati	Bearcats	Red & black	Big East	Mick Cronin	Brian Kelly
Citadel*	Bulldogs	Blue & white	Southern	Ed Conroy	Kevin Higgins
Clemson	Tigers	Burnt orange & purple	Atlantic Coast	Oliver Purnell	Dabo Swinney
Colgate*	Raiders	Maroon, gray, & white	Patriot League	Emmett Davis	Dick Biddle
Colorado	Buffaloes	Silver, gold, & black	Big Twelve	Jeff Bzdelik	Dan Hawkins
Colorado State	Rams	Green & gold	Mountain West	Tim Miles	Steve Fairchild
Columbia*	Lions	Columbia blue & white	Ivy League	Joe Jones	Norries Wilson
Connecticut	Huskies	Blue & white	Big East	Jim Calhoun	Randy Edsall
Cornell*	Big Red	Carnelian & white	Ivy League	Steve Donahue	Jim Knowles
Dartmouth*	Big Green	Dartmouth green & white	Ivy League	Terry Dunn	Buddy Teevens
Delaware*	Fightin' Blue Hens	Blue & gold	Colonial Athletic	Monté Ross	K. C. Keeler
Delaware State*	Hornets	Red & blue	Mid-Eastern Athletic	Greg Jackson	Al Lavan
Duke	Blue Devils	Royal blue & white	Atlantic Coast	Mike Krzyzewski	David Cutcliffe
East Carolina	Pirates	Purple & gold	Conference USA	Mack McCarthy	Skip Holtz
Eastern Illinois*	Panthers	Blue & gray	Ohio Valley	Mike Miller	Bob Spoo
Eastern Kentucky*	Colonels	Maroon & white	Ohio Valley	Jeff Neubauer	Dean Hood
Eastern Michigan	Eagles	Dark green & white	Mid-American	Charles E. Ramsey	Ron English
Eastern Washington*	Eagles	Red & white	Big Sky	Kirk Earlywine	Beau Baldwin
Florida	Gators	Orange & blue	Southeastern	Billy Donovan	Urban Meyer
Florida A&M*	Rattlers	Orange & green	Mid-Eastern Athletic	Eugene Harris	Joe Taylor
Florida State	Seminoles	Garnet & gold	Atlantic Coast	Leonard Hamilton	Bobby Bowden
Fresno State	Bulldogs	Red & blue	Western Athletic	Steve Cleveland	Pat Hill
Furman*	Paladins	Purple & white	Southern	Jeff Jackson	Bobby Lamb
Georgia	Bulldogs	Red & black	Southeastern	Mark Fox	Mark Richt
Georgia Southern*	Eagles	Blue & white	Southern	Charlton Young	Chris Hatcher
Georgia Tech	Yellow Jackets	Old gold & white	Atlantic Coast	Paul Hewitt	Paul Johnson
Grambling State*	Tigers	Black & gold	Southwestern Athletic	Rick Duckett	Rod Broadway
Harvard*	Crimson	Crimson & white	Ivy League	Tommy Amaker	Tim Murphy
Hawaii	Warriors	Green, black, white, silver	Western Athletic	Bob Nash	Greg McMackin
Holy Cross*	Crusaders	Royal purple	Patriot League	Sean Kearney	Tom Gilmore
Houston	Cougars	Scarlet & white	Conference USA	Tom Penders	Kevin Sumlin
Howard*	Bison	Blue, red & white	Mid-Eastern Athletic	Gil Jackson	Carey Bailey
Idaho	Vandals	Silver & gold	Western Athletic	Don Verlin	Robb Akey
Idaho State*	Bengals	Orange & black	Big Sky	Joe O'Brien	John Zamberlin
Illinois	Fighting Illini	Orange & blue	Big Ten	Bruce Weber	Ron Zook
Illinois State*	Redbirds	Red & white	Missouri Valley	Tim Jankovich	Brock Spack
Indiana	Hoosiers	Cream & crimson	Big Ten	Tom Crean	Bill Lynch
Indiana State*	Sycamores	Blue & white	Missouri Valley	Kevin McKenna	Trent Miles
Iowa	Hawkeyes	Old gold & black	Big Ten	Todd Lickliter	Kirk Ferentz
Iowa State	Cyclones	Cardinal & gold	Big Twelve	Greg McDermott	Paul Rhoads
Jackson State	Tigers	Blue & white	Southwestern Athletic	Tevester Anderson	Rick Comegy
James Madison*	Dukes	Purple & gold	Colonial Athletic	Matt Brady	Mickey Matthews
Kansas	Jayhawks	Crimson & blue	Big Twelve	Bill Self	Mark Mangino
Kansas State	Wildcats	Royal purple	Big Twelve	Frank Martin	Bill Snyder
Kent State	Golden Flashes	Navy blue & gold	Mid-American	Geno Ford	Doug Martin
Kentucky	Wildcats	Blue & white	Southeastern	John Calipari	Rich Brooks
Lafayette*	Leopards	Maroon & white	Patriot League	Fran O'Hanlon	Frank Tavani
Lehigh*	Mountain Hawks	Brown & white	Patriot League	Brett Reed	Andy Coen
Liberty*	Flames	Red, white, & blue	Big South	Dale Layer	Danny Rocco
Louisiana State (LSU)	Fighting Tigers	Purple & gold	Southeastern	Trent Johnson	Les Miles
Louisiana Tech	Bulldogs	Red & blue	Western Athletic	Kerry Rupp	Derek Dooley
Louisiana-Lafayette	Ragin' Cajuns	Vermilion & white	Sun Belt	Robert Lee	Rickey Bustle
Louisiana-Monroe	Warhawks	Maroon & gold	Sun Belt	Orlando Early	Charlie Weatherbie
Louisville	Cardinals	Red, black, & white	Big East	Rick Pitino	Steve Kragthorpe
Maine*	Black Bears	Blue & white	Colonial Athletic	Ted Woodward	Jack Cosgrove
Marshall	Thundering Herd	Kelly green & white	Conference USA	Donnie Jones	Mark Snyder
Maryland	Terrapins	Red, white, black, gold	Atlantic Coast	Gary Williams	Ralph Friedgen
Massachusetts*	Minutemen	Maroon & white	Colonial Athletic	Derek Kellogg	Kevin Morris
McNeese State*	Cowboys	Blue & gold	Southland	Dave Simmons	Matt Viator
Memphis	Tigers	Blue & gray	Conference USA	Josh Pastner	Tommy West
Miami (Florida)	Hurricanes	Orange, green, & white	Atlantic Coast	Frank Haith	Randy Shannon
Miami (Ohio)	RedHawks	Red & white	Mid-American	Charlie Coles	Mike Haywood
Michigan	Wolverines	Maize & blue	Big Ten	John Beilein	Rich Rodriguez
Michigan State	Spartans	Green & white	Big Ten	Tom Izzo	Mark Dantonio
Mid. Tennessee State	Blue Raiders	Royal blue & white	Sun Belt	Kermit Davis	Rick Stockstill
Minnesota	Golden Gophers	Maroon & gold	Big Ten	Tubby Smith	Tim Brewster
Mississippi	Rebels	Cardinal red & navy blue	Southeastern	Andy Kennedy	Houston Nutt
Mississippi State	Bulldogs	Maroon & white	Southeastern	Rick Stansbury	Dan Mullen
Mississippi Valley St.*	Delta Devils	Forest green & white	Southwestern Athletic	Sean Woods	Willie Totten

Team	Nickname	Team colors	Conference	Basketball coach	Football coach
Missouri	Tigers	Old gold & black	Big Twelve	Mike Anderson	Gary Pinkel
Montana*	Grizzlies	Copper, silver, & gold	Big Sky	Wayne Tinkle	Bobby Hauck
Montana State*	Bobcats	Blue & gold	Big Sky	Brad Huse	Rob Ash
Morehead State*	Eagles	Blue & gold	Pioneer	Donnie Tyndall	Matt Ballard
Morgan State*	Bears	Blue & orange	Mid-Eastern Athletic	Todd Bozeman	Donald Hill-Eley
Murray State*	Racers	Navy blue & gold	Ohio Valley	Billy Kennedy	Matt Griffin
Navy	Midshipmen	Navy blue & gold	Independent	Billy Lange	Ken Niumatalolo
Nebraska	Cornhuskers	Scarlet & cream	Big Twelve	Doc Sadler	Bo Pelini
Nev.-Las Vegas (UNLV)	Rebels	Scarlet & gray	Mountain West	Lon Kruger	Mike Sanford
Nevada	Wolf Pack	Cobalt blue & silver	Western Athletic	David Carter	Chris Ault
New Hampshire*	Wildcats	Blue & white	Colonial Athletic	Bill Herrion	Sean McDonnell
New Mexico	Lobos	Cherry & silver	Mountain West	Steve Alford	Mike Locksley
New Mexico State	Aggies	Crimson & white	Western Athletic	Marvin Menzies	DeWayne Walker
Nicholls State*	Colonels	Red & gray	Southland	J. P. Piper	Jay Thomas
North Carolina	Tar Heels	Carolina blue & white	Atlantic Coast	Roy Williams	Butch Davis
North Carolina State	Wolfpack	Red & white	Atlantic Coast	Sidney Lowe	Tom O'Brien
North Texas	Mean Green	Green & white	Sun Belt	Johnny Jones	Todd Dodge
Northeastern*	Huskies	Red & black	Colonial Athletic	Bill Coen	Rocky Hager
Northern Arizona*	Lumberjacks	Blue, gold, & sage	Big Sky	Mike Adras	Jerome Souers
Northern Illinois	Huskies	Cardinal & black	Mid-American	Ricardo Patton	Jerry Kill
Northern Iowa*	Panthers	Purple & gold	Missouri Valley	Ben Jacobson	Mark Farley
Northwestern	Wildcats	Purple & white	Big Ten	Bill Carmody	Pat Fitzgerald
Northwestern State*	Demons	Purple, white, & orange	Southland	Mike McConathy	Bradley Dale Peveto
Notre Dame	Fighting Irish	Gold & blue	Independent	Mike Brey	Charlie Weis
Ohio	Bobcats	Hunter green & white	Mid-American	John Groce	Frank Solich
Ohio State	Buckeyes	Scarlet & gray	Big Ten	Thad Matta	Jim Tressel
Oklahoma	Sooners	Crimson & cream	Big Twelve	Jeff Capel	Bob Stoops
Oklahoma State	Cowboys	Orange & black	Big Twelve	Travis Ford	Mike Gundy
Oregon	Ducks	Green & yellow	Pacific Ten	Ernie Kent	Chip Kelly
Oregon State	Beavers	Orange & black	Pacific Ten	Craig Robinson	Mike Riley
Penn State	Nittany Lions	Blue & white	Big Ten	Ed DeChellis	Joe Paterno
Pennsylvania*	Quakers	Red & blue	Ivy League	Glen Miller	Al Bagnoli
Pittsburgh	Panthers	Blue & gold	Big East	Jamie Dixon	Dave Wannstedt
Princeton*	Tigers	Orange & black	Ivy League	Sydney Johnson	Roger Hughes
Purdue	Boilermakers	Old gold & black	Big Ten	Matt Painter	Danny Hope
Rhode Island*	Rams	Keaney blue, dark blue, white	Colonial Athletic	Jim Baron	Joe Trainer
Rice	Owls	Blue & gray	Conference USA	Ben Braun	David Bailiff
Richmond*	Spiders	Red & blue	Colonial Athletic	Chris Mooney	Mike London
Rutgers	Scarlet Knights	Scarlet	Big East	Fred Hill	Greg Schiano
Sam Houston State*	Bearkats	Orange & white	Southland	Bob Marlin	Todd Whitten
Samford*	Bulldogs	Red & blue	Southern	Jimmy Tillette	Pat Sullivan
San Diego State	Aztecs	Scarlet & black	Mountain West	Steve Fisher	Brady Hoke
San Jose State	Spartans	Gold & blue	Western Athletic	George Nessman	Dick Tomey
SE Missouri State*	Redhawks	Red & black	Ohio Valley	Dickey Nutt	Tony Samuel
South Carolina	Gamecocks	Garnet & black	Southeastern	Darrin Horn	Steve Spurrier
South Carolina State*	Bulldogs	Garnet & blue	Mid-Eastern Athletic	Tim Carter	Oliver Pough
South Florida	Bulls	Green & gold	Big East	Stan Heath	Jim Leavitt
Southern California (USC)	Trojans	Cardinal & gold	Pacific Ten	Kevin O'Neill	Pete Carroll
Southern Illinois*	Salukis	Maroon & white	Missouri Valley	Chris Lowery	Dale Lennon
Southern Methodist (SMU)	Mustangs	Crimson & blue	Conference USA	Matt Doherty	June Jones
Southern Mississippi	Golden Eagles	Black & gold	Conference USA	Larry Eustachy	Larry Fedora
Stanford	Cardinal	Red & white	Pacific Ten	Johnny Dawkins	Jim Harbaugh
Stephen F. Austin*	Lumberjacks	Purple, white, & red	Southland	Danny Kaspar	J. C. Harper
Syracuse	Orange	Orange	Big East	Jim Boeheim	Doug Marrone
Temple	Owls	Cherry & white	Mid-American	Fran Dunphy	Al Golden
Tennessee	Volunteers	Orange & white	Southeastern	Bruce Pearl	Lane Kiffin
Tennessee State*	Tigers	Royal blue & white	Ohio Valley	John Cooper	James Webster
Tennessee Tech*	Golden Eagles	Purple & gold	Ohio Valley	Mike Sutton	Watson Brown
Tennessee-Martin*	Skyhawks	Orange, white, & blue	Ohio Valley	Jason James	Jason Simpson
Texas	Longhorns	Burnt orange & white	Big Twelve	Rick Barnes	Mack Brown
Texas A&M	Aggies	Maroon & white	Big Twelve	Mark Turgeon	Mike Sherman
Texas Christian (TCU)	Horned Frogs	Purple & white	Mountain West	Jim Christian	Gary Patterson
Texas Southern*	Tigers	Maroon & gray	Southwestern Athletic	Tony Harvey	Johnnie Cole
Texas State*	Bobcats	Maroon & gold	Southland	Doug Davalos	Brad Wright
Texas Tech	Red Raiders	Scarlet & black	Big Twelve	Pat Knight	Mike Leach
Toledo	Rockets	Midnight blue & gold	Mid-American	Gene Cross	Tim Beckman
Troy	Trojans	Cardinal, black, & silver	Sun Belt	Don Maestri	Larry Blakeney
Tulane	Green Wave	Olive green & sky blue	Conference USA	Dave Dickerson	Bob Toledo
Tulsa	Golden Hurricane	Blue, gold, & crimson	Conference USA	Doug Wojcik	Todd Graham
UCLA	Bruins	Blue & gold	Pacific Ten	Ben Howland	Rick Neuheisel
Utah	Utes	Crimson & white	Mountain West	Jim Boylen	Kyle Whittingham
Utah State	Aggies	Navy blue & white	Western Athletic	Stew Morrill	Gary Andersen
UTEP (Texas-El Paso)	Miners	Orange, blue, white, silver	Conference USA	Tony Barbee	Mike Price
Vanderbilt	Commodores	Black & gold	Southeastern	Kevin Stallings	Bobby Johnson
Villanova*	Wildcats	Blue & white	Colonial Athletic	Jay Wright	Andy Talley
Virginia	Cavaliers	Orange & navy blue	Atlantic Coast	Tony Bennett	Al Groh
Virginia Tech	Hokies	Burnt orange & maroon	Atlantic Coast	Seth Greenberg	Frank Beamer
Wake Forest	Demon Deacons	Old gold & black	Atlantic Coast	Dino Gaudio	Jim Grobe
Washington	Huskies	Purple & gold	Pacific Ten	Lorenzo Romar	Steve Sarkisian
Washington State	Cougars	Crimson & gray	Pacific Ten	Ken Bone	Paul Wulff
Weber State*	Wildcats	Royal purple & white	Big Sky	Randy Rahe	Ron McBride
West Virginia	Mountaineers	Old gold & blue	Big East	Bob Huggins	Bill Stewart
Western Carolina*	Catamounts	Purple & gold	Southern	Larry Hunter	Dennis Wagner
Western Illinois*	Leathernecks	Purple & gold	Missouri Valley	Jim Molinari	Don Patterson
Western Kentucky*	Hilltoppers	Red & white	Sun Belt	Ken McDonald	David Elson
Western Michigan	Broncos	Brown & gold	Mid-American	Steve Hawkins	Bill Cubit
William & Mary*	Tribe	Green, gold, & silver	Colonial Athletic	Tony Shaver	Jimmye Laycock
Wisconsin	Badgers	Cardinal & white	Big Ten	Bo Ryan	Bret Bielema
Wyoming	Cowboys	Brown & gold	Mountain West	Heath Schroyer	Dave Christensen
Yale*	Bulldogs, Elis	Yale blue & white	Ivy League	James Jones	Tom Williams
Youngstown State*	Penguins	Red & white	Missouri Valley	Jerry Slocum	Jon Heacock

*Football Championship Subdivision (FCS) team (formerly known as I-AA) as of the end of the 2008 regular season.

COLLEGE BASEBALL/SOFTBALL

NCAA Men's Baseball Division I Champions, 1947-2009

Year	Champion	Year	Champion	Year	Champion	Year	Champion	Year	Champion
1947	California	1959	Oklahoma St.	1972	USC	1985	Miami (FL)	1998	USC
1948	Southern California	1960	Minnesota	1973	USC	1986	Arizona	1999	Miami (FL)
1949	Texas	1961	USC	1974	USC	1987	Stanford	2000	LSU
1950	Texas	1962	Michigan	1975	Texas	1988	Stanford	2001	Miami (FL)
1951	Oklahoma	1963	USC	1976	Arizona	1989	Wichita St.	2002	Texas
1952	Holy Cross	1964	Minnesota	1977	Arizona St.	1990	Georgia	2003	Rice
1953	Michigan	1965	Arizona St.	1978	USC	1991	LSU	2004	Cal. St.-Fullerton
1954	Missouri	1966	Ohio St.	1979	Cal. St.-Fullerton	1992	Pepperdine	2005	Texas
1955	Wake Forest	1967	Arizona St.	1980	Arizona	1993	LSU	2006	Oregon St.
1956	Minnesota	1968	USC	1981	Arizona St.	1994	Oklahoma	2007	Oregon St.
1957	California	1969	Arizona St.	1982	Miami (FL)	1995	Cal. St.-Fullerton	2008	Fresno St.
1958	USC	1970	USC	1983	Texas	1996	LSU	2009	LSU
		1971	USC	1984	Cal. St.-Fullerton	1997	LSU		

NCAA Women's Softball Division I Champions, 1982-2009

Year	Champion	Year	Champion	Year	Champion	Year	Champion	Year	Champion
1982	UCLA	1988	UCLA	1994	Arizona	2000	Oklahoma	2005	Michigan
1983	Texas A&M	1989	UCLA	1995	UCLA	2001	Arizona	2006	Arizona
1984	UCLA	1990	UCLA	1996	Arizona	2002	California	2007	Arizona
1985	UCLA	1991	Arizona	1997	Arizona	2003	UCLA	2008	Arizona St.
1986	Cal St. Fullerton	1992	UCLA	1998	Fresno St.	2004	UCLA	2009	Washington
1987	Texas A&M	1993	Arizona	1999	UCLA				

COLLEGE HOCKEY

NCAA Hockey Champions, 1948-2009

Year	Champion	Year	Champion	Year	Champion	Year	Champion	Year	Champion
1948	Michigan	1961	Denver	1974	Minnesota	1986	Michigan State	1998	Michigan
1949	Boston College	1962	Michigan Tech	1975	Michigan Tech	1987	North Dakota	1999	Maine
1950	Colorado College	1963	North Dakota	1976	Minnesota	1988	Lake Superior St.	2000	North Dakota
1951	Michigan	1964	Michigan	1977	Wisconsin	1989	Harvard	2001	Boston College
1952	Michigan	1965	Michigan Tech	1978	Boston Univ.	1990	Wisconsin	2002	Minnesota
1953	Michigan	1966	Michigan State	1979	Minnesota	1991	N. Michigan	2003	Minnesota
1954	Rensselaer	1967	Cornell	1980	North Dakota	1992	Lake Superior St.	2004	Denver
1955	Michigan	1968	Denver	1981	Wisconsin	1993	Maine	2005	Denver
1956	Michigan	1969	Denver	1982	North Dakota	1994	Lake Superior St.	2006	Wisconsin
1957	Colorado College	1970	Cornell	1983	Wisconsin	1995	Boston Univ.	2007	Michigan State
1958	Denver	1971	Boston Univ.	1984	Bowling Green	1996	Michigan	2008	Boston College
1959	North Dakota	1972	Boston Univ.	1985	Rensselaer	1997	North Dakota	2009	Boston Univ.
1960	Denver	1973	Wisconsin						

NCAA Women's Hockey National Collegiate Champions, 2001-09

Year	Champion	Year	Champion	Year	Champion	Year	Champion	Year	Champion
2001	Minn.-Duluth	2003	Minn.-Duluth	2005	Minnesota	2007	Wisconsin	2009	Wisconsin
2002	Minn.-Duluth	2004	Minnesota	2006	Wisconsin	2008	Minn.-Duluth		

COLLEGE LACROSSE

NCAA Division I Lacrosse Champions, 1982-2009

Year	Men	Women	Year	Men	Women	Year	Men	Women
1982	North Carolina	Massachusetts	1992	Princeton	Maryland	2001	Princeton	Maryland
1983	Syracuse	Delaware	1993	Syracuse	Virginia	2002	Syracuse	Princeton
1984	Johns Hopkins	Temple	1994	Princeton	Princeton	2003	Virginia	Princeton
1985	Johns Hopkins	New Hampshire	1995	Syracuse	Maryland	2004	Syracuse	Virginia
1986	North Carolina	Maryland	1996	Princeton	Maryland	2005	Johns Hopkins	Northwestern
1987	Johns Hopkins	Penn St.	1997	Princeton	Maryland	2006	Virginia	Northwestern
1988	Syracuse	Temple	1998	Princeton	Maryland	2007	Johns Hopkins	Northwestern
1989	Syracuse	Penn St.	1999	Virginia	Maryland	2008	Syracuse	Northwestern
1990	Vacated	Harvard	2000	Syracuse	Maryland	2009	Syracuse	Northwestern
1991	North Carolina	Virginia						

COLLEGE SOCCER

NCAA Soccer Champions, 1982-2008

Year[1]	Men	Women	Year[1]	Men	Women	Year[1]	Men	Women
1982	Indiana	North Carolina	1991	Virginia	North Carolina	2000	Connecticut	North Carolina
1983	Indiana	North Carolina	1992	Virginia	North Carolina	2001	North Carolina	Santa Clara
1984	Clemson	North Carolina	1993	Virginia	North Carolina	2002	UCLA	Portland
1985	UCLA	George Mason	1994	Virginia	North Carolina	2003	Indiana	North Carolina
1986	Duke	North Carolina	1995	Wisconsin	Notre Dame	2004	Indiana	Notre Dame
1987	Clemson	North Carolina	1996	St. John's (NY)	North Carolina	2005	Maryland	Portland
1988	Indiana	North Carolina	1997	UCLA	North Carolina	2006	UC Santa Barbara	North Carolina
1989	Santa Clara/ Virginia (tie)	North Carolina	1998	Indiana	Florida	2007	Wake Forest	USC
1990	UCLA	North Carolina	1999	Indiana	North Carolina	2008	Maryland	North Carolina

(1) NCAA Championships began in 1959 for men, in 1982 for women.

COLLEGE WRESTLING

NCAA Division I Wrestling Champions, 1964-2009

Year	Champion	Year	Champion	Year	Champion	Year	Champion	Year	Champion
1964	Oklahoma State	1974	Oklahoma	1983	Iowa	1992	Iowa	2001	Minnesota
1965	Iowa State	1975	Iowa	1984	Iowa	1993	Iowa	2002	Minnesota
1966	Oklahoma State	1976	Iowa	1985	Iowa	1994	Oklahoma State	2003	Oklahoma State
1967	Michigan State	1977	Iowa State	1986	Iowa	1995	Iowa	2004	Oklahoma State
1968	Oklahoma State	1978	Iowa	1987	Iowa State	1996	Iowa	2005	Oklahoma State
1969	Iowa State	1979	Iowa	1988	Arizona State	1997	Iowa	2006	Oklahoma State
1970	Iowa State	1980	Iowa	1989	Oklahoma State	1998	Iowa	2007	Minnesota
1971	Oklahoma State	1981	Iowa	1990	Oklahoma State	1999	Iowa	2008	Iowa
1972	Iowa State	1982	Iowa	1991	Iowa	2000	Iowa	2009	Iowa
1973	Iowa State								

NATIONAL FOOTBALL LEAGUE
NFL 2008-09: Steelers Claim Record-Breaking Super Bowl Victory

The Pittsburgh Steelers became the first NFL franchise to capture six Super Bowl titles when they defeated the Arizona Cardinals, 27-23, in a thrilling Super Bowl XLIII. The Steelers marched into the postseason with the league's best defense, allowing just 223 points while holding opponents to 10 points or less eight times during the year. The Arizona Cardinals became the first team to reach the Super Bowl with nine wins or fewer in a regular (non-strike) season since the 1979 Los Angeles Rams. New Orleans Saints' QB Drew Brees threw for 5,069 yards, the second-highest single-season total in NFL history, but Cardinals' signal-caller Kurt Warner was the top-rated passer in the NFC. Warner's favorite target was wide receiver Larry Fitzgerald, who led the NFC for the second year in a row in receptions (96) and receiving yards (1,431). Second-year running back Adrian Peterson of the Minnesota Vikings rushed for a league-leading 1,760 rushing yards.

After notching an NFL-record 589 points in 2007, the New England Patriots suffered a severe blow in their first game of the 2008 season when QB Tom Brady injured his left knee and was lost for the rest of the year. Matt Cassel stepped in to lead the Pats to 11 victories, but the team missed the playoffs for the first time since 2002. Record-setting QB Brett Favre had announced his retirement after the 2007 season, but changed his mind and returned to the league with the New York Jets in 2008. Favre led the team to eight wins in its first 11 games, but the Jets faltered late and missed the playoffs. Thomas Jones led the Jets and the AFC in 2008 with 1,312 rushing yards. The Houston Texans' Andre Johnson topped the NFL with 115 receptions and led the AFC with 1,575 receiving yards.

The league reached beyond the borders and played two games outside of the United States in 2008. New Orleans defeated the San Diego Chargers, 37-32, on Oct. 26, 2008, at Wembley Stadium in London, England. The Buffalo Bills played a "home game" at Rogers Centre in Toronto, Canada, on Dec. 7, 2008, and were beaten by the Miami Dolphins, 16-3.

Final 2008 Standings

American Football Conference

East Division

	W	L	T	Pct	Pts	Opp	Div
Miami	11	5	0	.688	345	317	4-2
New England	11	5	0	.688	410	309	4-2
NY Jets	9	7	0	.563	405	356	4-2
Buffalo	7	9	0	.438	336	342	0-6

North Division

	W	L	T	Pct	Pts	Opp	Div
Pittsburgh	12	4	0	.750	347	223	6-0
*Baltimore.	11	5	0	.688	385	244	4-2
Cincinnati	4	11	1	.281	204	364	1-5
Cleveland	4	12	0	.250	232	350	1-5

South Division

	W	L	T	Pct	Pts	Opp	Div
Tennessee	13	3	0	.813	375	234	4-2
*Indianapolis.	12	4	0	.750	377	298	4-2
Houston	8	8	0	.500	366	394	2-4
Jacksonville	5	11	0	.313	302	367	2-4

West Division

	W	L	T	Pct	Pts	Opp	Div
San Diego	8	8	0	.500	439	347	5-1
Denver	8	8	0	.500	370	448	3-3
Oakland	5	11	0	.313	263	388	2-4
Kansas City	2	14	0	.125	291	440	2-4

*Wild card team.

National Football Conference

East Division

	W	L	T	Pct	Pts	Opp	Div
NY Giants	12	4	0	.750	427	294	4-2
*Philadelphia	9	6	1	.594	416	289	2-4
Dallas	9	7	0	.563	362	365	3-3
Washington	8	8	0	.500	265	296	3-3

North Division

	W	L	T	Pct	Pts	Opp	Div
Minnesota	10	6	0	.625	379	333	4-2
Chicago	9	7	0	.563	375	350	4-2
Green Bay	6	10	0	.375	419	380	4-2
Detroit	0	16	0	.000	268	517	0-6

South Division

	W	L	T	Pct	Pts	Opp	Div
Carolina.	12	4	0	.750	414	329	4-2
*Atlanta	11	5	0	.688	391	325	3-3
Tampa Bay.	9	7	0	.563	361	323	3-3
New Orleans	8	8	0	.500	463	393	2-4

West Division

	W	L	T	Pct	Pts	Opp	Div
Arizona	9	7	0	.563	427	426	6-0
San Francisco	7	9	0	.438	339	381	3-3
Seattle.	4	12	0	.250	294	392	3-3
St. Louis	2	14	0	.125	232	465	0-6

Note: Miami finished ahead of New England based on better conference record (8-4 to Patriots' 7-5); Baltimore was second Wild Card ahead of New England based on better conference record (8-4 to Patriots' 7-5); San Diego finished ahead of Denver based on better division record (5-1 to Broncos' 3-3).

AFC Playoffs—San Diego 23, Indianapolis 17 (OT); Baltimore 27, Miami 9; Baltimore 13, Tennessee 10; Pittsburgh 35, San Diego 24; Pittsburgh 23, Baltimore 14.

NFC Playoffs—Arizona 30, Atlanta 24; Philadelphia 26, Minnesota 14; Arizona 33, Carolina 13; Philadelphia 23, NY Giants 11; Arizona 32, Philadelphia 25.

2008 NFL Individual Leaders: American Football Conference

PASSING

	Att	Comp	Pct Comp	Yards	Yds/Att	Long	TD	Pct TD	Int	Rating
Philip Rivers, San Diego.	478	312	65.3%	4,009	8.39	67	34	7.1%	11	105.5
Chad Pennington, Miami	476	321	67.4	3,653	7.67	80T	19	4.0	7	97.4
Peyton Manning, Indianapolis	555	371	66.8	4,002	7.21	75	27	4.9	12	95.0
Matt Schaub, Houston	380	251	66.1	3,043	8.01	65	15	3.9	10	92.7
Matt Cassel, New England.	516	327	63.4	3,693	7.16	76T	21	4.1	11	89.4
Jay Cutler, Denver	616	384	62.3	4,526	7.35	93T	25	4.1	18	86.0
Trent Edwards, Buffalo	374	245	65.5	2,699	7.22	65	11	2.9	10	85.4
David Garrard, Jacksonville	535	335	62.6	3,620	6.77	41	15	2.8	13	81.7
Brett Favre, NY Jets.	522	343	65.7	3,472	6.65	56T	22	4.2	22	81.0
Joe Flacco, Baltimore.	428	257	60.0	2,971	6.94	70T	14	3.3	12	80.3
Kerry Collins, Tennessee	415	242	58.3	2,676	6.45	56T	12	2.9	7	80.2

RUSHING YARDS

	Yds	Att	Avg	Long	TD
Thomas Jones, NY Jets	1,312	290	4.5	59T	13
Steve Slaton, Houston	1,282	268	4.8	71T	9
Chris Johnson, Tennessee	1,228	251	4.9	66T	9
LaDainian Tomlinson, San Diego	1,110	292	3.8	45	11
Marshawn Lynch, Buffalo	1,036	250	4.1	50	8
Jamal Lewis, Cleveland	1,002	279	3.6	29	4
Ronnie Brown, Miami.	916	214	4.3	62T	10
Le'Ron McClain, Baltimore.	902	232	3.9	82T	10
Larry Johnson, Kansas City	874	193	4.5	65	5
Justin Fargas, Oakland.	853	218	3.9	42	1

RECEPTIONS

	Rec	Yds	Avg	Long	TD
Andre Johnson, Houston.	115	1,575	13.7	65	8
Wes Welker, New England	111	1,165	10.5	64	3
Brandon Marshall, Denver.	104	1,265	12.2	47	6
Tony Gonzalez, Kansas City (TE)	96	1,058	11.0	35	10
T.J. Houshmandzadeh, Cincinnati	92	904	9.8	46	4
Eddie Royal, Denver	91	980	10.8	93T	5
Dwayne Bowe, Kansas City.	86	1,022	11.9	36	7
Reggie Wayne, Indianapolis	82	1,145	14.0	65T	6
Hines Ward, Pittsburgh	81	1,043	12.9	49	7
Derrick Mason, Baltimore	80	1,037	13.0	54	5

SCORING—KICKERS

	PAT	FG	Long	Pts
Stephen Gostkowski, New England	40/40	36/40	50	148
Rob Bironas, Tennessee	40/40	29/33	51	127
Nate Kaeding, San Diego	46/46	27/32	57	127
Kris Brown, Houston	37/37	29/33	53	124
Rian Lindell, Buffalo	34/34	30/38	53	124

SCORING—NON-KICKERS

	TD	Rush	Rec	2-PT	Pts
Thomas Jones, NY Jets (RB)	15	13	2	0	90
LenDale White, Tennessee (RB)	15	15	0	0	90
Maurice Jones-Drew, Jacksonville (RB)	14	12	2	0	84
LaDainian Tomlinson, San Diego (RB)	12	11	1	0	72
Le'Ron McClain, Baltimore (RB)	11	10	1	0	66
Randy Moss, New England (WR)	11	0	11	0	66

INTERCEPTIONS

	No.	Yds	Avg	Long	TD
Ed Reed, Baltimore	9	264	29.3	107T	2
Michael Griffin, Tennessee	7	172	24.6	83T	1
Troy Polamalu, Pittsburgh	7	59	8.4	23	0
Brandon McDonald, Cleveland	5	146	29.2	98	1
Cortland Finnegan, Tennessee	5	100	20.0	99T	1
André Goodman, Miami	5	53	10.6	55	0
Darrelle Revis, NY Jets	5	38	7.6	32T	1

KICKOFF RETURNS

	No.	Yds	Avg	Long	TD
Ellis Hobbs, New England	45	1,281	28.5	95T	1
Leodis McKelvin, Buffalo	52	1,468	28.2	98T	1
Chris Carr, Tennessee	35	984	28.1	52	0
Eddie Royal, Denver	23	600	26.1	90	0
Darren Sproles, San Diego	53	1,376	26.0	103T	1
Leon Washington, NY Jets	48	1,231	25.6	94	1

PUNTING

	No.	Yds	Long	Avg
Shane Lechler, Oakland	90	4,391	70	48.8
Brett Kern, Denver	46	2,150	64	46.7
Mike Scifres, San Diego	51	2,332	67	45.7
Dave Zastudil, Cleveland	75	3,410	65	45.5
Sam Koch, Baltimore	84	3,777	74	45.0

PUNT RETURNS

	No.	Yds	Avg	LG	TD
Roscoe Parrish, Buffalo	21	322	15.3	63T	1
Johnnie Lee Higgins, Oakland	44	570	13.0	93T	3
Jacoby Jones, Houston	32	386	12.1	73T	2
Jim Leonhard, Baltimore	20	232	11.6	46	0
Darren Sproles, San Diego	22	249	11.3	43	0

SACKS: Joey Porter, Miami, 17.5; James Harrison, Pittsburgh, 16; Mario Williams, Houston, 12; Robert Mathis, Indianapolis, 11.5; LaMarr Woodley, Pittsburgh, 11.5; Dwight Freeney, Indianapolis, 10.5; Albert Haynesworth, Tennessee, 8.5; Shaun Ellis, NY Jets, 8; Richard Seymour, New England, 8; Terrell Suggs, Baltimore, 8; Shaun Phillips, San Diego, 7.5; Jacob Ford, Tennessee, 7; Calvin Pace, NY Jets, 7.

2008 NFL Individual Leaders: National Football Conference

PASSING

	Att	Comp	Pct Comp	Yds	Yds/Att	Long	TD	Pct TD	Int	Rating
Kurt Warner, Arizona	598	401	67.1%	4,583	7.66	79T	30	5.0%	14	96.9
Drew Brees, New Orleans	635	413	65.0	5,069	7.98	84T	34	5.4	17	96.2
Aaron Rodgers, Green Bay	536	341	63.6	4,038	7.53	71T	28	5.2	13	93.8
Tony Romo, Dallas	450	276	61.3	3,448	7.66	75T	26	5.8	14	91.4
Jeff Garcia, Tampa Bay	376	244	64.9	2,712	7.21	71T	12	3.2	6	90.2
Matt Ryan, Atlanta	434	265	61.1	3,440	7.93	70T	16	3.7	11	87.7
Shaun Hill, San Francisco	288	181	62.8	2,046	7.10	48T	13	4.5	8	87.5
Seneca Wallace, Seattle	242	141	58.3	1,532	6.33	90T	11	4.5	3	87.0
Eli Manning, NY Giants	479	289	60.3	3,238	6.76	48	21	4.4	10	86.4
Donovan McNabb, Philadelphia	571	345	60.4	3,916	6.86	90T	23	4.0	11	86.4

RUSHING YARDS

	Yds	Att	Avg	Long	TD
Adrian Peterson, Minnesota	1,760	363	4.8	67T	10
Michael Turner, Atlanta	1,699	376	4.5	70	17
DeAngelo Williams, Carolina	1,515	273	5.5	69T	18
Clinton Portis, Washington	1,487	342	4.3	131	9
Matt Forté, Chicago	1,238	316	3.9	50T	8
Ryan Grant, Green Bay	1,203	312	3.9	57	4
Brandon Jacobs, NY Giants	1,089	219	5.0	44	15
Steven Jackson, St. Louis	1,042	253	4.1	56T	7
Frank Gore, San Francisco	1,036	240	4.3	41T	6
Derrick Ward, NY Giants	1,025	182	5.6	51	2

RECEPTIONS

	Rec	Yds	Avg	Long	TD
Larry Fitzgerald, Arizona	96	1,431	14.9	78T	12
Anquan Boldin, Arizona	89	1,038	11.7	70T	11
Roddy White, Atlanta	88	1,382	15.7	70T	7
Antonio Bryant, Tampa Bay	83	1,248	15.0	71T	7
Chris Cooley, Washington	83	849	10.2	28	1
Jason Witten, Dallas	81	952	11.8	42	4
Greg Jennings, Green Bay	80	1,292	16.2	63	9
Santana Moss, Washington	79	1,044	13.2	67T	6
Lance Moore, New Orleans	79	928	11.7	70T	10
Steve Smith, Carolina	78	1,421	18.2	65T	6
Calvin Johnson, Detroit	78	1,331	17.1	96T	12

SCORING—KICKERS

	PAT	FG	Long	Pts
David Akers, Philadelphia	45/45	33/40	51	144
John Carney, NY Giants	38/38	35/38	51	143
Matt Bryant, Tampa Bay	35/36	32/38	49	131
John Kasay, Carolina	46/46	28/31	50	130
Jason Elam, Atlanta	42/42	29/31	50	129

SCORING—NON-KICKERS

	TD	Rush	Rec	2 Pt	Pts
DeAngelo Williams, Carolina (RB)	20	18	2	1	122
Michael Turner, Atlanta (RB)	17	17	0	0	102
Brandon Jacobs, NY Giants (RB)	15	15	0	0	90
Brian Westbrook, Philadelphia (RB)	14	9	5	0	84
Calvin Johnson, Detroit (WR)	12	0	12	1	74
Larry Fitzgerald, Arizona (WR)	12	0	12	0	72
Matt Forté, Chicago (RB)	12	8	4	0	72
Pierre Thomas, New Orleans (RB)	12	9	3	0	72

INTERCEPTIONS

	No.	Yds	Avg	Long	TD
Nick Collins, Green Bay	7	295	42.1	62T	3
Charles Woodson, Green Bay	7	169	24.1	62T	2
Oshiomogho Atogwe, St. Louis	5	91	18.2	43	0
Jason David, New Orleans	5	83	16.6	42	0
Tramon Williams, Green Bay	5	78	15.6	39	0
DeAngelo Hall, Oakland-Washington	5	37	7.4	21	0
D. Rodgers-Cromartie, Arizona	4	157	39.3	99T	1
Kevin Payne, Chicago	4	147	36.8	50	0
Josh Wilson, Seattle	4	135	33.8	75T	1
Ronde Barber, Tampa Bay	4	69	17.3	65T	1
Asante Samuel, Philadelphia	4	64	16.0	50T	1
Aqib Talib, Tampa Bay	4	32	8.0	19	0
Terence Newman, Dallas	4	2	0.5	2	0

KICKOFF RETURNS

	No.	Yds	Avg	Long	TD
Danieal Manning, Chicago	36	1,070	29.7	83T	1
Clifton Smith, Tampa Bay	36	992	27.6	97T	1
Allen Rossum, San Francisco	47	1,259	26.8	104T	1
Jerious Norwood, Atlanta	51	1,311	25.7	92	0
J. J. Arrington, Arizona	36	923	25.6	93T	1
Rock Cartwright, Washington	51	1,307	25.6	87	0

PUNTING

	No.	Yds	Long	Avg
Donnie Jones, St. Louis	82	4,100	68	50.0
Andy Lee, San Francisco	66	3,155	82	47.8
Chris Kluwe, Minnesota	73	3,473	62	47.6
Jon Ryan, Seattle	78	3,557	63	45.6
Josh Bidwell, Tampa Bay	77	3,426	64	44.5

PUNT RETURNS

	No.	Yds	Avg	Long	TD
Clifton Smith, Tampa Bay	23	324	14.1	70T	1
Reggie Bush, New Orleans	20	270	13.5	71T	3
Mark Jones, Carolina	39	443	11.4	55	0
Will Blackmon, Green Bay	36	398	11.1	76T	2
Domenik Hixon, NY Giants	24	242	10.1	50	0

SACKS: DeMarcus Ware, Dallas, 20; John Abraham, Atlanta, 16.5; Jared Allen, Minnesota, 14.5; Julius Peppers, Carolina, 14.5; Justin Tuck, NY Giants, 12; Darren Howard, Philadelphia, 10; Aaron Kampman, Green Bay, 9.5; Trent Cole, Philadelphia, 9; Kevin Williams, Minnesota, 8.5; Greg Ellis, Dallas, 8; Parys Haralson, San Francisco, 8; Bradie James, Dallas, 8; Mathias Kiwanuka, NY Giants, 8; Jay Ratliff, Dallas, 7.5.

Super Bowl XLIII: Pittsburgh 27, Arizona 23

The Pittsburgh Steelers defeated the Arizona Cardinals, 27-23, in Super Bowl XLIII on Feb. 1, 2009, at Raymond James Stadium in Tampa, FL. For the second straight year, the Super Bowl was decided by a touchdown pass in the last moments of the game. The Cardinals scored 16 unanswered points in the 4th quarter to take a 23-20 lead with less than three minutes remaining. Steelers' QB Ben Roethlisberger then led the team on a 78-yard drive, capped by a stunning 6-yard TD reception by WR Santonio Holmes, who stretched to catch the ball while deftly dragging his feet inbounds in the back right corner of the end zone. Holmes caught nine passes for 131 yards and was voted Super Bowl MVP. The Steelers won their NFL-record 6th Super Bowl title, while Arizona, which had recorded just two winning seasons since 1985, was making its first Super Bowl appearance. Cardinals QB Kurt Warner passed for 377 yards in a losing effort—the second-highest passing yards total in Super Bowl history and just shy of his own record 414 yards against Tennessee in Super Bowl XXXIV. The Steelers' record-breaking Super Bowl win included a 100-yard interception return by James Harrison, the longest scoring play in Super Bowl history. Pittsburgh's Mike Tomlin also became the youngest head coach to win a Super Bowl, at age 36. Cardinals WR Larry Fitzgerald caught a pair of TD passes in Super Bowl XLIII, and set NFL records for receptions (30), yards (546), and receiving touchdowns (7) in a single postseason.

Quarters

Team	1	2	3	4	Total
Pittsburgh	3	14	3	7	27
Arizona	0	7	0	16	23

Scoring

Pittsburgh: Jeff Reed, 18-yd field goal
Pittsburgh: Gary Russell, 1-yd run (Jeff Reed PAT)
Arizona: Ben Patrick, 1-yd pass from Kurt Warner (Neil Rackers PAT)
Pittsburgh: James Harrison, 100-yd interception return (Reed PAT)
Pittsburgh: Jeff Reed, 21-yd field goal
Arizona: Larry Fitzgerald, 1-yd pass from Kurt Warner (Rackers PAT)
Arizona: Safety, penalty on Justin Hartwig enforced in end zone
Arizona: Larry Fitzgerald, 64-yd pass from Kurt Warner (Rackers PAT)
Pittsburgh: Santonio Holmes, 6-yd pass from Ben Roethlisberger (Reed PAT)

Individual statistics

Rushing: Pittsburgh—Parker 19-53; Moore 1-6; Roethlisberger 3-2; Russell 2-minus-3, 1 TD. Arizona—James 9-33; Arrington 1-0; Hightower 1-0; Warner 1-0.
Passing: Pittsburgh—Ben Roethlisberger 21-30, 256 yds, 1 TD, 1 Int. Arizona—Kurt Warner 31-43, 377 yds, 3 TD, 1 Int.

Receiving: Pittsburgh—Holmes 9-131, 1 TD; Miller 5-57; Ward 2-43; Washington 1-11; Davis 1-6; Spaeth 1-6; Moore 1-4; Parker 1-minus-2. Arizona—Fitzgerald 7-127, 2 TD; Boldin 8-84; Breaston 6-71; Arrington 2-35; James 4-28; Urban 1-18; Hightower 2-13; Patrick 1-1, 1 TD.

Team statistics	Steelers	Cardinals
1st downs	20	23
Total net yards	292	407
Rushes-yards	25-58	12-33
Passing yards, net	234	374
Punt returns-yards	2-5	2-34
Kickoff returns-yards	4-80	5-91
Interception return-yards	1-100	1-1
Field goals made-attempts	2-2	0-0
Att.-comp.-int.	30-21-1	43-31-1
Sacked-yards lost	3-22	2-3
Punts-average	3-46.3	5-36.0
Fumbles-lost	0-0	2-1
Penalties-yards	7-56	11-106
Time of possession	33:01	26:59

Attendance: 70,774   **Game length:** 3:38

Super Bowl Results, 1967-2009

	Year	Winner	Loser	Winning coach	Site
I	1967	*Green Bay Packers, 35	Kansas City Chiefs, 10	Vince Lombardi	Memorial Coliseum, Los Angeles, CA
II	1968	Green Bay Packers, 33	*Oakland Raiders, 14	Vince Lombardi	Orange Bowl, Miami, FL
III	1969	*New York Jets, 16	Baltimore Colts, 7	Weeb Ewbank	Orange Bowl, Miami, FL
IV	1970	Kansas City Chiefs, 23	*Minnesota Vikings, 7	Hank Stram	Tulane Stadium, New Orleans, LA
V	1971	Baltimore Colts, 16	*Dallas Cowboys, 13	Don McCafferty	Orange Bowl, Miami, FL
VI	1972	Dallas Cowboys, 24	*Miami Dolphins, 3	Tom Landry	Tulane Stadium, New Orleans, LA
VII	1973	*Miami Dolphins, 14	Washington Redskins, 7	Don Shula	Memorial Coliseum, Los Angeles, CA
VIII	1974	*Miami Dolphins, 24	Minnesota Vikings, 7	Don Shula	Rice Stadium, Houston, TX
IX	1975	*Pittsburgh Steelers, 16	Minnesota Vikings, 6	Chuck Noll	Tulane Stadium, New Orleans, LA
X	1976	Pittsburgh Steelers, 21	*Dallas Cowboys, 17	Chuck Noll	Orange Bowl, Miami, FL
XI	1977	*Oakland Raiders, 32	Minnesota Vikings, 14	John Madden	Rose Bowl, Pasadena, CA
XII	1978	*Dallas Cowboys, 27	Denver Broncos, 10	Tom Landry	Superdome, New Orleans, LA
XIII	1979	Pittsburgh Steelers, 35	*Dallas Cowboys, 31	Chuck Noll	Orange Bowl, Miami, FL
XIV	1980	Pittsburgh Steelers, 31	*Los Angeles Rams, 19	Chuck Noll	Rose Bowl, Pasadena, CA
XV	1981	Oakland Raiders, 27	*Philadelphia Eagles, 10	Tom Flores	Superdome, New Orleans, LA
XVI	1982	*San Francisco 49ers, 26	Cincinnati Bengals, 21	Bill Walsh	Silverdome, Pontiac, MI
XVII	1983	Washington Redskins, 27	*Miami Dolphins, 17	Joe Gibbs	Rose Bowl, Pasadena, CA
XVIII	1984	*Los Angeles Raiders, 38	Washington Redskins, 9	Tom Flores	Tampa Stadium, FL
XIX	1985	*San Francisco 49ers, 38	Miami Dolphins, 16	Bill Walsh	Stanford Stadium, Stanford, CA
XX	1986	*Chicago Bears, 46	New England Patriots, 10	Mike Ditka	Superdome, New Orleans, LA
XXI	1987	New York Giants, 39	*Denver Broncos, 20	Bill Parcells	Rose Bowl, Pasadena, CA
XXII	1988	*Washington Redskins, 42	Denver Broncos, 10	Joe Gibbs	Jack Murphy Stadium, San Diego, CA
XXIII	1989	*San Francisco 49ers, 20	Cincinnati Bengals, 16	Bill Walsh	Joe Robbie Stadium, Miami, FL
XXIV	1990	San Francisco 49ers, 55	*Denver Broncos, 10	George Seifert	Superdome, New Orleans, LA
XXV	1991	New York Giants, 20	*Buffalo Bills, 19	Bill Parcells	Tampa Stadium, FL
XXVI	1992	*Washington Redskins, 37	Buffalo Bills, 24	Joe Gibbs	Metrodome, Minneapolis, MN
XXVII	1993	Dallas Cowboys, 52	*Buffalo Bills, 17	Jimmy Johnson	Rose Bowl, Pasadena, CA
XXVIII	1994	*Dallas Cowboys, 30	Buffalo Bills, 13	Jimmy Johnson	Georgia Dome, Atlanta, GA
XXIX	1995	*San Francisco 49ers, 49	San Diego Chargers, 26	George Seifert	Joe Robbie Stadium, Miami, FL
XXX	1996	*Dallas Cowboys, 27	Pittsburgh Steelers, 17	Barry Switzer	Sun Devil Stadium, Tempe, AZ
XXXI	1997	Green Bay Packers, 35	*New England Patriots, 21	Mike Holmgren	Superdome, New Orleans, LA
XXXII	1998	Denver Broncos, 31	*Green Bay Packers, 24	Mike Shanahan	Qualcomm Stadium, San Diego, CA
XXXIII	1999	Denver Broncos, 34	*Atlanta Falcons, 19	Mike Shanahan	Pro Player Stadium, Miami, FL
XXXIV	2000	*St. Louis Rams, 23	Tennessee Titans, 16	Dick Vermeil	Georgia Dome, Atlanta, GA
XXXV	2001	Baltimore Ravens, 34	*New York Giants, 7	Brian Billick	Raymond James Stadium, Tampa, FL
XXXVI	2002	New England Patriots, 20	*St. Louis Rams, 17	Bill Belichick	Superdome, New Orleans, LA

Year	Winner	Loser	Winning coach	Site
XXXVII	2003	*Tampa Bay Buccaneers, 48	Oakland Raiders, 21	Jon Gruden	Qualcomm Stadium, San Diego, CA
XXXVIII	2004	New England Patriots, 32	*Carolina Panthers, 29	Bill Belichick	Reliant Stadium, Houston, TX
XXXIX	2005	New England Patriots, 24	*Philadelphia Eagles, 21	Bill Belichick	Alltel Stadium, Jacksonville, FL
XL	2006	Pittsburgh Steelers, 21	*Seattle Seahawks, 10	Bill Cowher	Ford Field, Detroit, MI
XLI	2007	Indianapolis Colts, 29	*Chicago Bears, 17	Tony Dungy	Dolphin Stadium, Miami, FL
XLII	2008	*New York Giants, 17	New England Patriots, 14	Tom Coughlin	Univ. of Phoenix Stadium, Glendale, AZ
XLIII	2009	Pittsburgh Steelers, 27	*Arizona Cardinals, 23	Mike Tomlin	Raymond James Stadium, Tampa, FL

*Team that won the coin toss. All teams that won the toss elected to receive.

Future Super Bowl Sites

No.	Site	Date	No.	Site	Date
XLIV	Dolphin Stadium, Miami, FL	Feb. 7, 2010	XLVI	Lucas Oil Stadium, Indianapolis, IN	Feb. 2012
XLV	New Dallas Cowboys Stadium, Arlington, TX	Feb. 2011	XLVII	Louisiana Superdome, New Orleans, LA	Feb. 2013

Super Bowl Single-Game Statistical Leaders

Passing Yards

	Year	Att/Comp	Yds	TDs
Kurt Warner, Rams	2000	45/24	414	2
Kurt Warner, Cardinals	2009	43/31	377	3
Kurt Warner, Rams	2002	44/28	365	1
Donovon McNabb, Eagles	2005	51/30	357	3
Joe Montana, 49ers	1989	36/23	357	2

Passing Touchdowns

	Year	Att/Comp	Yds	TDs
Steve Young, 49ers	1995	36/24	325	6
Joe Montana, 49ers	1990	29/22	297	5
Troy Aikman, Cowboys	1993	30/22	273	4
Doug Williams, Redskins	1988	29/18	340	4
Terry Bradshaw, Steelers	1979	30/17	318	4

Receiving Yards

	Year	Recept.	Yds	TDs
Jerry Rice, 49ers	1989	11	215	1
Ricky Sanders, Redskins	1988	9	193	2
Isaac Bruce, Rams	2000	6	162	1

Scoring

	Year	Points	
Terrell Davis, Broncos	1998	18	3 TDs
Jerry Rice, 49ers	1995	18	3 TDs
Ricky Watters, 49ers	1995	18	3 TDs
Jerry Rice, 49ers	1990	18	3 TDs
Roger Craig, 49ers	1985	18	3 TDs
Don Chandler, Packers	1968	15	4 FG, 3 PATs

Rushing Yards

	Year	Attempts	Yds	TDs
Timmy Smith, Redskins	1988	22	204	2
Marcus Allen, Raiders	1984	20	191	2
John Riggins, Redskins	1983	38	166	1

Super Bowl MVPs

Year	MVP	Year	MVP	Year	MVP
1967	Bart Starr, Green Bay	1982	Joe Montana, San Francisco	1996	Larry Brown, Dallas
1968	Bart Starr, Green Bay	1983	John Riggins, Washington	1997	Desmond Howard, Green Bay
1969	Joe Namath, NY Jets	1984	Marcus Allen, L.A. Raiders	1998	Terrell Davis, Denver
1970	Len Dawson, Kansas City	1985	Joe Montana, San Francisco	1999	John Elway, Denver
1971	Chuck Howley, Dallas	1986	Richard Dent, Chicago	2000	Kurt Warner, St. Louis
1972	Roger Staubach, Dallas	1987	Phil Simms, NY Giants	2001	Ray Lewis, Baltimore
1973	Jake Scott, Miami	1988	Doug Williams, Washington	2002	Tom Brady, New England
1974	Larry Csonka, Miami	1989	Jerry Rice, San Francisco	2003	Dexter Jackson, Tampa Bay
1975	Franco Harris, Pittsburgh	1990	Joe Montana, San Francisco	2004	Tom Brady, New England
1976	Lynn Swann, Pittsburgh	1991	Ottis Anderson, NY Giants	2005	Deion Branch, New England
1977	Fred Biletnikoff, Oakland	1992	Mark Rypien, Washington	2006	Hines Ward, Pittsburgh
1978	Randy White, Harvey Martin, Dallas	1993	Troy Aikman, Dallas	2007	Peyton Manning, Indianapolis
1979	Terry Bradshaw, Pittsburgh	1994	Emmitt Smith, Dallas	2008	Eli Manning, NY Giants
1980	Terry Bradshaw, Pittsburgh	1995	Steve Young, San Francisco	2009	Santonio Holmes, Pittsburgh
1981	Jim Plunkett, Oakland				

First-Round Selections in the 2009 NFL Draft

Team	Player	Pos	College
1. Detroit	Matthew Stafford	QB	Georgia
2. St. Louis	Jason Smith	T	Baylor
3. Kansas City	Tyson Jackson	DE	LSU
4. Seattle	Aaron Curry	LB	Wake Forest
5. NY Jets[1]	Mark Sanchez	QB	USC
6. Cincinnati	Andre Smith	T	Alabama
Oakland	Darrius		
7.	Heyward-Bey	WR	Maryland
8. Jacksonville	Eugene Monroe	T	Virginia
9. Green Bay	B. J. Raji	DT	Boston College
10. San Francisco	Michael Crabtree	WR	Texas Tech
11. Buffalo	Aaron Maybin	DE	Penn St.
12. Denver	Knowshon Moreno	RB	Georgia
13. Washington	Brian Orakpo	DE	Texas
14. New Orleans	Malcolm Jenkins	CB	Ohio St.
15. Houston	Brian Cushing	LB	USC
16. San Diego	Larry English	LB	Northern Ill.
17. Tampa Bay[2]	Josh Freeman	QB	Kansas St.
18. Denver[3]	Robert Ayers	LB	Tennessee
19. Philadelphia[4]	Jeremy Maclin	WR	Missouri
20. Detroit[5]	Brandon Pettigrew	TE	Oklahoma St.
21. Cleveland[6]	Alex Mack	C	California
22. Minnesota	Percy Harvin	WR	Florida
23. Baltimore[7]	Michael Oher	T	Mississippi
24. Atlanta	Peria Jerry	DT	Mississippi
25. Miami	Vontae Davis	CB	Illinois
26. Green Bay[8]	Clay Matthews	LB	USC
27. Indianapolis	Donald Brown	RB	Connecticut
28. Buffalo[9]	Eric Wood	C	Louisville
29. NY Giants	Hakeem Nicks	WR	North Carolina
30. Tennessee	Kenny Britt	WR	Rutgers
31. Arizona	Chris Wells	RB	Ohio St.
32. Pittsburgh	Evander Hood	DT	Missouri

(1) From Cleveland. (2) From NY Jets through Cleveland. (3) From Chicago. (4) From Tampa Bay through Cleveland. (5) From Dallas. (6) From Philadelphia. (7) From New England. (8) From Baltimore through New England. (9) From Carolina through Philadelphia.

Number One NFL Draft Choices, 1936-2009

Year	Team	Player, pos., college	Year	Team	Player, pos., college
1936	Philadelphia	Jay Berwanger, HB, Chicago	1973	Houston	John Matuszak, DE, Tampa
1937	Philadelphia	Sam Francis, FB, Nebraska	1974	Dallas	Ed "Too Tall" Jones, DE, Tenn. St.
1938	Cleveland Rams	Corbett Davis, FB, Indiana	1975	Atlanta	Steve Bartkowski, QB, Cal.
1939	Chicago Cards	Ki Aldrich, C, TCU	1976	Tampa Bay	Lee Roy Selmon, DE, Oklahoma
1940	Chicago Cards	George Cafego, HB, Tennessee	1977	Tampa Bay	Ricky Bell, RB, USC
1941	Chicago Bears	Tom Harmon, HB, Michigan	1978	Houston	Earl Campbell, RB, Texas
1942	Pittsburgh	Bill Dudley, HB, Virginia	1979	Buffalo	Tom Cousineau, LB, Ohio St.
1943	Detroit	Frank Sinkwich, HB, Georgia	1980	Detroit	Billy Sims, RB, Oklahoma
1944	Boston Yanks	Angelo Bertelli, QB, Notre Dame	1981	New Orleans	George Rogers, RB, S. Carolina
1945	Chicago Cards	Charley Trippi, HB, Georgia	1982	New England	Kenneth Sims, DT, Texas
1946	Boston Yanks	Frank Dancewicz, QB, Notre Dame	1983	Baltimore Colts	John Elway, QB, Stanford
1947	Chicago Bears	Bob Fenimore, HB, Okla. A&M	1984	New England	Irving Fryar, WR, Nebraska
1948	Washington	Harry Gilmer, QB, Alabama	1985	Buffalo	Bruce Smith, DE, Va.Tech
1949	Philadelphia	Chuck Bednarik, C, Penn	1986	Tampa Bay	Bo Jackson, RB, Auburn
1950	Detroit	Leon Hart, E, Notre Dame	1987	Tampa Bay	Vinny Testaverde, QB, Miami (FL)
1951	NY Giants	Kyle Rote, HB, SMU	1988	Atlanta	Aundray Bruce, LB, Auburn
1952	L.A. Rams	Bill Wade, QB, Vanderbilt	1989	Dallas	Troy Aikman, QB, UCLA
1953	San Francisco	Harry Babcock, E, Georgia	1990	Indianapolis	Jeff George, QB, Illinois
1954	Cleveland	Bobby Garrett, QB, Stanford	1991	Dallas	Russell Maryland, DL, Miami (FL)
1955	Baltimore Colts	George Shaw, QB, Oregon	1992	Indianapolis	Steve Emtman, DL, Washington
1956	Pittsburgh	Gary Glick, DB, Col. A&M	1993	New England	Drew Bledsoe, QB, Washington St.
1957	Green Bay	Paul Hornung, QB, Notre Dame	1994	Cincinnati	Dan Wilkinson, DT, Ohio St.
1958	Chicago Cards	King Hill, QB, Rice	1995	Cincinnati	Ki-Jana Carter, RB, Penn State
1959	Green Bay	Randy Duncan, QB, Iowa	1996	NY Jets	Keyshawn Johnson, WR, USC
1960	L.A. Rams	Billy Cannon, HB, LSU	1997	St. Louis	Orlando Pace, T, Ohio St.
1961	Minnesota	Tommy Mason, HB, Tulane	1998	Indianapolis	Peyton Manning, QB, Tennessee
1962	Washington	Ernie Davis, HB, Syracuse	1999	Cleveland	Tim Couch, QB, Kentucky
1963	L.A. Rams	Terry Baker, QB, Oregon St.	2000	Cleveland	Courtney Brown, DE, Penn State
1964	San Francisco	Dave Parks, E, Texas Tech	2001	Atlanta	Michael Vick, QB, Virginia Tech
1965	NY Giants	Tucker Frederickson, HB, Auburn	2002	Houston	David Carr, QB, Fresno St.
1966	Atlanta	Tommy Nobis, LB, Texas	2003	Cincinnati	Carson Palmer, QB, USC
1967	Baltimore Colts	Bubba Smith, DT, Michigan St.	2004	San Diego	Eli Manning, QB, Mississippi
1968	Minnesota	Ron Yary, T, USC	2005	San Francisco	Alex D. Smith, QB, Utah
1969	Buffalo	O. J. Simpson, RB, USC	2006	Houston	Mario Williams, DE, NC State
1970	Pittsburgh	Terry Bradshaw, QB, La.Tech	2007	Oakland	JaMarcus Russell, QB, LSU
1971	New England	Jim Plunkett, QB, Stanford	2008	Miami	Jake Long, OT, Michigan
1972	Buffalo	Walt Patulski, DE, Notre Dame	2009	Detroit	Matthew Stafford, QB, Georgia

American Football League Champions 1960-69

Year	Eastern (W-L-T)	Western (W-L-T)	Championship
1960	Houston Oilers (10-4-0)	Los Angeles Chargers (10-4-0)	Houston 24, Los Angeles 16
1961	Houston Oilers (10-3-1)	San Diego Chargers (12-2-0)	Houston 10, San Diego 3
1962	Houston Oilers (11-3-0)	Dallas Texans (11-3-0)	Dallas 20, Houston 17 (2 overtimes)
1963	Boston Patriots (7-6-1)[1]	San Diego Chargers (11-3-0)	San Diego 51, Boston 10
1964	Buffalo Bills (12-2-0)	San Diego Chargers (8-5-1)	Buffalo 20, San Diego 7
1965	Buffalo Bills (10-3-1)	San Diego Chargers (9-2-3)	Buffalo 23, San Diego 0
1966	Buffalo Bills (9-4-1)	Kansas City Chiefs (11-2-1)	Kansas City 31, Buffalo 7
1967	Houston Oilers (9-4-1)	Oakland Raiders (13-1-0)	Oakland 40, Houston 7
1968	New York Jets (11-3-0)	Oakland Raiders (12-2-0)[2]	New York 27, Oakland 23
1969	New York Jets (10-4-0)	Oakland Raiders (12-1-1)	Kansas City 17, Oakland 7[3]

(1) Defeated Buffalo Bills in divisional playoff. (2) Defeated Kansas City Chiefs in divisional playoff. (3) Kansas City Chiefs defeated NY Jets and Oakland Raiders defeated Houston Oilers in divisional playoffs.

National Football League Champions 1933-69

Year	East (W-L-T)	West (W-L-T)	Championship
1933	New York Giants (11-3-0)	Chicago Bears (10-2-1)	Chicago Bears 23, New York 21
1934	New York Giants (8-5-0)	Chicago Bears (13-0-0)	New York 30, Chicago Bears 13
1935	New York Giants (9-3-0)	Detroit Lions (7-3-2)	Detroit 26, New York 7
1936	Boston Redskins (7-5-0)	Green Bay Packers (10-1-1)	Green Bay 21, Boston 6
1937	Washington Redskins (8-3-0)	Chicago Bears (9-1-1)	Washington 28, Chicago Bears 21
1938	New York Giants (8-2-1)	Green Bay Packers (8-3-0)	New York 23, Green Bay 17
1939	New York Giants (9-1-1)	Green Bay Packers (9-2-0)	Green Bay 27, New York 0
1940	Washington Redskins (9-2-0)	Chicago Bears (8-3-0)	Chicago Bears 73, Washington 0
1941	New York Giants (8-3-0)	Chicago Bears (10-1-1)[1]	Chicago Bears 37, New York 9
1942	Washington Redskins (10-1-1)	Chicago Bears (11-0-0)	Washington 14, Chicago Bears 6
1943	Washington Redskins (6-3-1)	Chicago Bears (8-1-1)	Chicago Bears, 41, Washington 21
1944	New York Giants (8-1-1)	Green Bay Packers (8-2-0)	Green Bay 14, New York 7
1945	Washington Redskins (8-2-0)	Cleveland Rams (9-1-0)	Cleveland 15, Washington 14
1946	New York Giants (7-3-1)	Chicago Bears (8-2-1)	Chicago Bears 24, New York 14
1947	Philadelphia Eagles (8-4-0)[1]	Chicago Cardinals (9-3-0)	Chicago Cardinals 28, Philadelphia 21
1948	Philadelphia Eagles (9-2-1)	Chicago Cardinals (11-1-0)	Philadelphia 7, Chicago Cardinals 0
1949	Philadelphia Eagles (11-1-0)	Los Angeles Rams (8-2-2)	Philadelphia 14, Los Angeles 0
1950	Cleveland Browns (10-2-0)[1]	Los Angeles Rams (9-3-0)[1]	Cleveland 30, Los Angeles 28
1951	Cleveland Browns (11-1-0)	Los Angeles Rams (8-4-0)	Los Angeles 24, Cleveland 17
1952	Cleveland Browns (8-4-0)	Detroit Lions (9-3-0)[1]	Detroit 17, Cleveland 7
1953	Cleveland Browns (11-1-0)	Detroit Lions (10-2-0)	Detroit 17, Cleveland 16
1954	Cleveland Browns (9-3-0)	Detroit Lions (9-2-1)	Cleveland 56, Detroit 10
1955	Cleveland Browns (9-2-1)	Los Angeles Rams (8-3-1)	Cleveland 38, Los Angeles 14
1956	New York Giants (8-3-1)	Chicago Bears (9-2-1)	New York 47, Chicago Bears 7
1957	Cleveland Browns (9-2-1)	Detroit Lions (8-4-0)[1]	Detroit 59, Cleveland 14
1958	New York Giants (9-3-0)[1]	Baltimore Colts (9-3-0)	Baltimore 23, New York 17[2]

Year	East (W-L-T)	West (W-L-T)	Championship
1959	New York Giants (10-2-0)	Baltimore Colts (9-3-0)	Baltimore 31, New York 16
1960	Philadelphia Eagles (10-2-0)	Green Bay Packers (8-4-0)	Philadelphia 17, Green Bay 13
1961	New York Giants (10-3-1)	Green Bay Packers (11-3-0)	Green Bay 37, New York 0
1962	New York Giants (12-2-0)	Green Bay Packers (13-1-0)	Green Bay 16, New York 7
1963	New York Giants (11-3-0)	Chicago Bears (11-1-2)	Chicago 14, New York 10
1964	Cleveland Browns (10-3-1)	Baltimore Colts (12-2-0)	Cleveland 27, Baltimore 0
1965	Cleveland Browns (11-3-0)	Green Bay Packers (10-3-1)[1]	Green Bay 23, Cleveland 12
1966	Dallas Cowboys (10-3-1)	Green Bay Packers (12-2-0)	Green Bay 34, Dallas 27
1967	Dallas Cowboys (9-5-0)	Green Bay Packers (9-4-1)	Green Bay 21, Dallas 17
1968	Cleveland Browns (10-4-0)	Baltimore Colts (13-1-0)	Baltimore 34, Cleveland 0
1969	Cleveland Browns (10-3-1)	Minnesota Vikings (12-2-0)	Minnesota 27, Cleveland 7

(1) Won divisional playoff. (2) Won at 8:15 of sudden death overtime period.

NFL Divisional Champions and Wild Cards 1970-1995

The American Football League and National Football League officially merged in 1966. At the beginning of the 1970 season, the two leagues became the AFC and NFC conferences in the new NFL. Regular-season records are in parentheses.

AMERICAN FOOTBALL CONFERENCE

Year	Eastern	Central	Western	Wild card
1970	Baltimore Colts (11-2-1)	Cincinnati Bengals (8-6-0)	Oakland Raiders (8-4-2)	Miami Dolphins (10-4-0)
1971	Miami Dolphins (10-3-1)	Cleveland Browns (9-5-0)	Kansas City Chiefs (10-3-1)	Baltimore Colts (10-4-0)
1972	Miami Dolphins (14-0-0)	Pittsburgh Steelers (11-3-0)	Oakland Raiders (10-3-1)	Cleveland Browns (10-4-0)
1973	Miami Dolphins (12-2-0)	Cincinnati Bengals (10-4-0)	Oakland Raiders (9-4-1)	Cincinnati Bengals (10-4-0)
1974	Miami Dolphins (11-3-0)	Pittsburgh Steelers (10-3-1)	Oakland Raiders (12-2-0)	Buffalo Bills (9-5-0)
1975	Baltimore Colts (10-4-0)	Pittsburgh Steelers (12-2-0)	Oakland Raiders (11-3-0)	Cincinnati Bengals (11-3-0)
1976	Baltimore Colts (11-3-0)	Pittsburgh Steelers (10-4-0)	Oakland Raiders (13-1-0)	New England Patriots (11-3-0)
1977	Baltimore Colts (10-4-0)	Pittsburgh Steelers (9-5-0)	Denver Broncos (12-2-0)	Oakland Raiders (11-3-0)
1978	New England Patriots (11-5-0)	Pittsburgh Steelers (14-2-0)	Denver Broncos (10-6-0)	Houston Oilers (10-6-0) Miami Dolphins (11-5-0)
1979	Miami Dolphins (10-6-0)	Pittsburgh Steelers (12-4-0)	San Diego Chargers (12-4-0)	Houston Oilers (11-5-0) Denver Broncos (10-6-0)
1980	Buffalo Bills (11-5-0)	Cleveland Browns (11-5-0)	San Diego Chargers (11-5-0)	Houston Oilers (11-5-0) Oakland Raiders (11-5-0)
1981	Miami Dolphins (11-4-1)	Cincinnati Bengals (12-4-0)	San Diego Chargers (10-6-0)	Buffalo Bills (10-6-0) NY Jets (10-5-1)
1982	Strike abbreviated season. See note.			
1983	Miami Dolphins (12-4-0)	Pittsburgh Steelers (10-6-0)	L.A. Raiders (12-4-0)	Denver Broncos (9-7-0) Seattle Seahawks (9-7-0)
1984	Miami Dolphins (14-2-0)	Pittsburgh Steelers (9-7-0)	Denver Broncos (13-3-0)	L.A. Raiders (11-5-0) Seattle Seahawks (12-4-0)
1985	Miami Dolphins (12-4-0)	Cleveland Browns (8-8-0)	L.A. Raiders (12-4-0)	New England Patriots (11-5-0) NY Jets (11-5-0)
1986	New England Patriots (11-5-0)	Cleveland Browns (12-4-0)	Denver Broncos (11-5-0)	Kansas City Chiefs (10-6-0) NY Jets (10-6-0)
1987	Indianapolis Colts (9-6-0)	Cleveland Browns (10-5-0)	Buffalo Bills (12-4-0)	Houston Oilers (9-6-0) Seattle Seahawks (9-6-0)
1988	Buffalo Bills (12-4-0)	Cincinnati Bengals (12-4-0)	Seattle Seahawks (9-7-0)	Cleveland Browns (10-6-0) Houston Oilers (10-6-0)
1989	Buffalo Bills (9-7-0)	Cleveland Browns (9-6-1)	Denver Broncos (11-5-0)	Houston Oilers (9-7-0) Pittsburgh Steelers (9-7-0)
1990	Buffalo Bills (13-3-0)	Cincinnati Bengals (9-7-0)	L.A. Raiders (12-4-0)	Houston Oilers (9-7-0) Kansas City Chiefs (11-5-0) Miami Dolphins (12-4-0)
1991	Buffalo Bills (13-3-0)	Houston Oilers (11-5-0)	Denver Broncos (12-4-0)	Kansas City Chiefs (11-5-0) Miami Dolphins (12-4-0) NY Jets (8-8-0)
1992	Miami Dolphins (11-5-0)	Pittsburgh Steelers (11-5-0)	San Diego Chargers (11-5-0)	Buffalo Bills (11-5-0) Houston Oilers (10-6-0) Kansas City Chiefs (10-6-0)
1993	Buffalo Bills (12-4-0)	Houston Oilers (12-4-0)	Kansas City Chiefs (11-5-0)	Denver Broncos (9-7-0) L.A. Raiders (10-6-0) Pittsburgh Steelers (9-7-0)
1994	Miami Dolphins (10-6-0)	Pittsburgh Steelers (12-4-0)	San Diego Chargers (11-5-0)	Cleveland Browns (11-5-0) Kansas City Chiefs (9-7-0) New England Patriots (10-6-0)
1995	Buffalo Bills (10-6-0)	Pittsburgh Steelers (11-5-0)	Kansas City Chiefs (13-3-0)	Miami Dolphins (9-7-0) Indianapolis Colts (9-7-0) San Diego Chargers (9-7-0)

NATIONAL FOOTBALL CONFERENCE

Year	Eastern	Central	Western	Wild card
1970	Dallas Cowboys (10-4-0)	Minnesota Vikings (12-2-0)	San Francisco 49ers (10-3-1)	Detroit Lions (10-4-0)
1971	Dallas Cowboys (11-3-0)	Minnesota Vikings (11-3-0)	San Francisco 49ers (9-5-0)	Washington Redskins (9-4-1)
1972	Washington Redskins (11-3-0)	Green Bay Packers (10-4-0)	San Francisco 49ers (8-5-1)	Dallas Cowboys (10-4-0)
1973	Dallas Cowboys (10-4-0)	Minnesota Vikings (12-2-0)	L.A. Rams (12-2-0)	Washington Redskins (10-4-0)
1974	St. Louis Cardinals (10-4-0)	Minnesota Vikings (10-4-0)	L.A. Rams (10-4-0)	Washington Redskins (10-4-0)
1975	St. Louis Cardinals (11-3-0)	Minnesota Vikings (12-2-0)	L.A. Rams (12-2-0)	Dallas Cowboys (10-4-0)
1976	Dallas Cowboys (11-3-0)	Minnesota Vikings (11-2-1)	L.A. Rams (10-3-1)	Washington Redskins (10-4-0)
1977	Dallas Cowboys (12-2-0)	Minnesota Vikings (9-5-0)	L.A. Rams (10-4-0)	Chicago Bears (9-5-0)
1978	Dallas Cowboys (12-4-0)	Minnesota Vikings (8-7-1)	L.A. Rams (12-4-0)	Atlanta Falcons (9-7-0) Philadelphia Eagles (9-7-0)
1979	Dallas Cowboys (11-5-0)	Tampa Bay Buccaneers (10-6-0)	L.A. Rams (9-7-0)	Chicago Bears (10-6-0) Philadelphia Eagles (11-5-0)

NATIONAL FOOTBALL CONFERENCE

Year	Eastern	Central	Western	Wild card
1980	Philadelphia Eagles (12-4-0)	Minnesota Vikings (9-7-0)	Atlanta Falcons (12-4-0)	Dallas Cowboys (12-4-0) L.A. Rams (11-5-0)
1981	Dallas Cowboys (12-4-0)	Tampa Bay Buccaneers (9-7-0)	San Francisco 49ers (13-3-0)	NY Giants (9-7-0) Philadelphia Eagles (10-6-0)
1982	Strike abbreviated season. See note.			
1983	Washington Redskins (14-2-0)	Detroit Lions (9-7-0)	San Francisco 49ers (10-6-0)	Dallas Cowboys (12-4-0) L.A. Rams (9-7-0)
1984	Washington Redskins (11-5-0)	Chicago Bears (10-6-0)	San Francisco 49ers (15-1-0)	L.A. Rams (10-6-0) NY Giants (9-7-0)
1985	Dallas Cowboys (10-6-0)	Chicago Bears (15-1-0)	L.A. Rams (11-5-0)	NY Giants (10-6-0) San Francisco 49ers (10-6-0)
1986	NY Giants (14-2-0)	Chicago Bears (14-2-0)	San Francisco 49ers (10-5-1)	L.A. Rams (10-6-0) Washington Redskins (12-4-0)
1987	Washington Redskins (11-4-0)	Chicago Bears (11-4-0)	San Francisco 49ers (13-2-0)	Minnesota Vikings (8-7-0) New Orleans Saints (12-3-0)
1988	Philadelphia Eagles (10-6-0)	Chicago Bears (12-4-0)	San Francisco 49ers (10-6-0)	L.A. Rams (10-6-0) Minnesota Vikings (11-5-0)
1989	NY Giants (12-4-0)	Minnesota Vikings (10-6-0)	San Francisco 49ers (14-2-0)	L.A. Rams (11-5-0) Philadelphia Eagles (11-5-0)
1990	NY Giants (13-3-0)	Chicago Bears (11-5-0)	San Francisco 49ers (14-2-0)	New Orleans Saints (8-8-0) Philadelphia Eagles (10-6-0) Washington Redskins (10-6-0)
1991	Washington Redskins (14-2-0)	Detroit Lions (12-4-0)	New Orleans Saints (11-5-0)	Atlanta Falcons (10-6-0) Chicago Bears (11-5-0) Dallas Cowboys (11-5-0)
1992	Dallas Cowboys (13-3-0)	Minnesota Vikings (11-5-0)	San Francisco 49ers (14-2-0)	New Orleans Saints (12-4-0) Philadelphia Eagles (11-5-0) Washington Redskins (9-7-0)
1993	Dallas Cowboys (12-4-0)	Detroit Lions (10-6-0)	San Francisco 49ers (10-6-0)	Green Bay Packers (9-7-0) Minnesota Vikings (9-7-0) NY Giants (11-5-0)
1994	Dallas Cowboys (12-4-0)	Minnesota Vikings (10-6-0)	San Francisco 49ers (13-3-0)	Chicago Bears (9-7-0) Detroit Lions (9-7-0) Green Bay Packers (9-7-0)
1995	Dallas Cowboys (12-4-0)	Green Bay Packers (11-5-0)	San Francisco 49ers (11-5-0)	Philadelphia Eagles (10-6-0) Detroit Lions (10-6-0) Atlanta Falcons (9-7-0)

Note: A strike shortened the 1982 season from 16 to 9 games. The top 8 teams in each conference played in a tournament to determine the conference champion. AFC—Miami Dolphins, New England Patriots, L.A. Raiders, Cleveland Browns, NY Jets, Cincinnati Bengals, San Diego Chargers, Pittsburgh Steelers. NFC—Washington Redskins, Detroit Lions, Green Bay Packers, St. Louis Cardinals, Dallas Cowboys, Tampa Bay Buccaneers, Minnesota Vikings, Atlanta Falcons.

NFL Playoff Results, 1996-2008

Year	Conference	Division	Winner (W-L-T)	Playoffs[1]	Year
1996	American	Eastern	New England Patriots (11-5-0)	Jacksonville* 30, Denver 27	1996
		Central	Pittsburgh Steelers (10-6-0)	New England 28, Pittsburgh 3	
		Western	Denver Broncos (13-3-0)	New England 20, Jacksonville* 6	
	National	Eastern	Dallas Cowboys (10-6-0)	Green Bay 35, San Francisco* 14	
		Central	Green Bay Packers (13-3-0)	Carolina 26, Dallas 17	
		Western	Carolina Panthers (12-4-0)	Green Bay 30, Carolina 13	
1997	American	Eastern	New England Patriots (10-6-0)	Pittsburgh 7, New England 6	1997
		Central	Pittsburgh Steelers (11-5-0)	Denver* 14, Kansas City 10	
		Western	Kansas City Chiefs (13-3-0)	Denver* 24, Pittsburgh 21	
	National	Eastern	New York Giants (10-5-1)	San Francisco 38, Minnesota* 22	
		Central	Green Bay Packers (13-3-0)	Green Bay 21, Tampa Bay* 7	
		Western	San Francisco 49ers (13-3-0)	Green Bay 23, San Francisco 10	
1998	American	Eastern	NY Jets (12-4-0)	Denver 38, Miami* 3	1998
		Central	Jacksonville Jaguars (11-5-0)	NY Jets 34, Jacksonville 24	
		Western	Denver Broncos (14-2-0)	Denver 23, NY Jets 10	
	National	Eastern	Dallas Cowboys (10-6-0)	Atlanta 20, San Francisco* 18	
		Central	Minnesota Vikings (15-1-0)	Minnesota 41, Arizona* 21	
		Western	Atlanta Falcons (14-2-0)	Atlanta 30, Minnesota 27 (OT)	
1999	American	Eastern	Indianapolis Colts (13-3-0)	Jacksonville 62, Miami* 7	1999
		Central	Jacksonville Jaguars (14-2-0)	Tennessee* 19, Indianapolis 16	
		Western	Seattle Seahawks (9-7-0)	Tennessee* 33, Jacksonville 14	
	National	Eastern	Washington Redskins (10-6-0)	Tampa Bay 14, Washington 13	
		Central	Tampa Bay Buccaneers (11-5-0)	St. Louis 49, Minnesota* 37	
		Western	St. Louis Rams (13-3-0)	St. Louis 11, Tampa Bay 6	
2000	American	Eastern	Miami Dolphins (11-5-0)	Oakland 27, Miami 0	2000
		Central	Tennessee Titans (13-3-0)	Baltimore* 24, Tennessee 10	
		Western	Oakland Raiders (12-4-0)	Baltimore* 16, Oakland 3	
	National	Eastern	NY Giants (12-4-0)	Minnesota 34, New Orleans 16	
		Central	Minnesota Vikings (11-5-0)	NY Giants 20, Philadelphia* 10	
		Western	New Orleans Saints (10-6-0)	NY Giants 41, Minnesota 0	
2001	American	Eastern	New England Patriots (11-5-0)	New England 16, Oakland 13	2001
		Central	Pittsburgh Steelers (13-3-0)	Pittsburgh 27, Baltimore 10	
		Western	Oakland Raiders (10-6-0)	New England 24, Pittsburgh 17	
	National	Eastern	Philadelphia Eagles (11-5-0)	Philadelphia 33, Chicago 19	
		Central	Chicago Bears (13-3-0)	St. Louis 45, Green Bay* 17	
		Western	St. Louis Rams (14-2-0)	St. Louis 29, Philadelphia 24	

Year	Conference	Division	Winner (W-L-T)	Playoffs[1]	Year
2002	American	East	NY Jets (9-7-0)		2002
		North	Pittsburgh Steelers (10-5-1)	Oakland 30, NY Jets 10	
		South	Tennessee Titans (11-5-0)	Tennessee 34, Pittsburgh 31	
		West	Oakland Raiders (11-5-0)	Oakland 41, Tennessee 24	
	National	East	Philadelphia Eagles (12-4-0)		
		North	Green Bay Packers (12-4-0)	Philadelphia 20, Atlanta* 6	
		South	Tampa Bay Buccaneers (12-4-0)	Tampa Bay 31, San Francisco 6	
		West	San Francisco 49ers (10-6-0)	Tampa Bay 27, Philadelphia 10	
2003	American	East	New England Patriots (14-2-0)		2003
		North	Baltimore Ravens (10-6-0)	Indianapolis 38, Kansas City 31	
		South	Indianapolis Colts (12-4-0)	New England 17, Tennessee* 14	
		West	Kansas City Chiefs (13-3-0)	New England 24, Indianapolis 14	
	National	East	Philadelphia Eagles (12-4-0)		
		North	Green Bay Packers (10-6-0)	Carolina 29, St. Louis 23	
		South	Carolina Panthers (11-5-0)	Philadelphia 20, Green Bay 17	
		West	St. Louis Rams (12-4-0)	Carolina 14, Philadelphia 3	
2004	American	East	New England Patriots (14-2-0)		2004
		North	Pittsburgh Steelers (15-1-0)	Pittsburgh 20, NY Jets 17* (OT)	
		South	Indianapolis Colts (12-4-0)	New England 20, Indianapolis 3	
		West	San Diego Chargers (12-4-0)	New England 41, Pittsburgh 27	
	National	East	Philadelphia Eagles (13-3-0)		
		North	Green Bay Packers (10-6-0)	Atlanta 47, St. Louis* 17	
		South	Atlanta Falcons (11-5-0)	Philadelphia 27, Minnesota* 14	
		West	Seattle Seahawks (9-7-0)	Philadelphia 27, Atlanta 10	
2005	American	East	New England Patriots (10-6-0)		2005
		North	Cincinnati Bengals (11-5-0)	Denver 27, New England 13	
		South	Indianapolis Colts (14-2-0)	Pittsburgh* 21, Indianapolis 18	
		West	Denver Broncos (13-3-0)	Pittsburgh* 34, Denver 17	
	National	East	NY Giants (11-5-0)		
		North	Chicago Bears (11-5-0)	Seattle 20, Washington* 10	
		South	Tampa Bay Buccaneers (11-5-0)	Carolina* 29, Chicago 21	
		West	Seattle Seahawks (13-3-0)	Seattle 34, Carolina* 14	
2006	American	East	New England Patriots (12-4-0)		2006
		North	Baltimore Ravens (13-3-0)	Indianapolis 15, Baltimore 6	
		South	Indianapolis Colts (12-4-0)	New England 24, San Diego 21	
		West	San Diego Chargers (14-2-0)	Indianapolis 38, New England 34	
	National	East	Philadelphia Eagles (10-6-0)		
		North	Chicago Bears (13-3-0)	New Orleans 27, Philadelphia 24	
		South	New Orleans Saints (10-6-0)	Chicago 27, Seattle 24 (OT)	
		West	Seattle Seahawks (9-7-0)	Chicago 39, New Orleans 14	
2007	American	East	New England Patriots (16-0-0)		2006
		North	Pittsburgh Steelers (10-6-0)	New England 31, Jacksonville* 20	
		South	Indianapolis Colts (13-3-0)	San Diego 28, Indianapolis 24	
		West	San Diego Chargers (11-5-0)	New England 21, San Diego 12	
	National	East	Dallas Cowboys (13-3-0)		
		North	Green Bay Packers (13-3-0)	Green Bay 42, Seattle 20	
		South	Tampa Bay Buccaneers (9-7-0)	NY Giants* 21, Dallas 17	
		West	Seattle Seahawks (10-6-0)	NY Giants 22, Green Bay 20	
2008	American	East	Miami Dolphins (11-5-0)		2008
		North	Pittsburgh Steelers (12-4-0)	Baltimore* 13, Tennessee 10	
		South	Tennessee Titans (13-3-0)	Pittsburgh 35, San Diego 24	
		West	San Diego Chargers (8-8-0)	Pittsburgh 23, Baltimore* 14	
	National	East	NY Giants (12-4-0)		
		North	Minnesota Vikings (10-6-0)	Arizona 33, Carolina 13	
		South	Carolina Panthers (12-4-0)	Philadelphia* 23, NY Giants 11	
		West	Arizona Cardinals (9-7-0)	Arizona 32, Philadelphia* 25	

*Wild card team. (1) Only the final two conference playoff rounds are shown.

American Football Conference Leaders
(American Football League, 1960-69)

Passing (based on QB rating points)						Receptions			
Player, team	Att	Com	YG	TD	Year	Player, team	Rec	YG	TD
Jack Kemp, L.A. Chargers	406	211	3,018	20	1960	Lionel Taylor, Denver	92	1,235	12
George Blanda, Houston	362	187	3,330	36	1961	Lionel Taylor, Denver	100	1,176	4
Len Dawson, Dallas Texans	310	189	2,759	29	1962	Lionel Taylor, Denver	77	908	4
Tobin Rote, San Diego	286	170	2,510	20	1963	Lionel Taylor, Denver	78	1,101	10
Len Dawson, Kansas City	354	199	2,879	30	1964	Charley Hennigan, Houston	101	1,546	8
John Hadl, San Diego	348	174	2,798	20	1965	Lionel Taylor, Denver	85	1,131	6
Len Dawson, Kansas City	284	159	2,527	26	1966	Lance Alworth, San Diego	73	1,383	13
Daryle Lamonica, Oakland	425	220	3,228	30	1967	George Sauer, NY Jets	75	1,189	6
Len Dawson, Kansas City	224	131	2,109	17	1968	Lance Alworth, San Diego	68	1,312	10
Greg Cook, Cincinnati	197	106	1,854	15	1969	Lance Alworth, San Diego	64	1,003	4
Daryle Lamonica, Oakland	356	179	2,516	22	1970	Marlin Briscoe, Buffalo	57	1,036	8
Bob Griese, Miami	263	145	2,089	19	1971	Fred Biletnikoff, Oakland	61	929	9
Earl Morrall, Miami	150	83	1,360	11	1972	Fred Biletnikoff, Oakland	58	802	7
Ken Stabler, Oakland	260	163	1,997	14	1973	Fred Willis, Houston	57	371	1
Ken Anderson, Cincinnati	328	213	2,667	18	1974	Lydell Mitchell, Baltimore Colts	72	544	2
Ken Anderson, Cincinnati	377	228	3,169	21	1975	Reggie Rucker, Cleveland	60	770	3
						Lydell Mitchell, Baltimore Colts	60	554	4
Ken Stabler, Oakland	291	194	2,737	27	1976	MacArthur Lane, Kansas City	66	686	1
Bob Griese, Miami	307	180	2,252	22	1977	Lydell Mitchell, Baltimore Colts	71	620	4
Terry Bradshaw, Pittsburgh	368	207	2,915	28	1978	Steve Largent, Seattle	71	1,168	8
Dan Fouts, San Diego	530	332	4,082	24	1979	Joe Washington, Baltimore Colts	82	750	3
Brian Sipe, Cleveland	554	337	4,132	30	1980	Kellen Winslow, San Diego	89	1,290	9
Ken Anderson, Cincinnati	479	300	3,754	29	1981	Kellen Winslow, San Diego	88	1,075	10

Passing (based on QB rating points)

Player, team	Att	Com	YG	TD	Year
Ken Anderson, Cincinnati	309	218	2,495	12	1982
Dan Marino, Miami	296	173	2,210	20	1983
Dan Marino, Miami	564	362	5,084	48	1984
Ken O'Brien, NY Jets	488	297	3,888	25	1985
Dan Marino, Miami	623	378	4,746	44	1986
Bernie Kosar, Cleveland	389	241	3,033	22	1987
Boomer Esiason, Cincinnati	388	223	3,572	28	1988
Boomer Esiason, Cincinnati	455	258	3,525	28	1989
Jim Kelly, Buffalo	346	219	2,829	24	1990
Jim Kelly, Buffalo	474	304	3,844	33	1991
Warren Moon, Houston	346	224	2,521	18	1992
John Elway, Denver	551	348	4,030	25	1993
Dan Marino, Miami	615	385	4,453	30	1994
Jim Harbaugh, Indianapolis	314	200	2,575	17	1995
John Elway, Denver	466	287	3,328	26	1996
Mark Brunell, Jacksonville	435	264	3,281	18	1997
Vinny Testaverde, NY Jets	421	259	3,256	29	1998
Peyton Manning, Indianapolis	533	331	4,135	26	1999
Brian Griese, Denver	336	216	2,688	19	2000
Rich Gannon, Oakland	549	361	3,828	27	2001
Chad Pennington, NY Jets	399	275	3,120	22	2002
Steve McNair, Tennessee	400	250	3,215	24	2003
Peyton Manning, Indianapolis	497	336	4,557	49	2004
Peyton Manning, Indianapolis	453	305	3,747	28	2005
Peyton Manning, Indianapolis	557	362	4,397	31	2006
Tom Brady, New England	578	398	4,806	50	2007
Philip Rivers, San Diego	478	312	4,009	34	2008

Receptions

Year	Player, team	Rec	YG	TD
1982	Kellen Winslow, San Diego	54	721	6
1983	Todd Christensen, L.A. Raiders	92	1,247	12
1984	Ozzie Newsome, Cleveland	89	1,001	5
1985	Lionel James, San Diego	86	1,027	6
1986	Todd Christensen, L.A. Raiders	95	1,153	8
1987	Al Toon, NY Jets	68	976	5
1988	Al Toon, NY Jets	93	1,067	5
1989	Andre Reed, Buffalo	88	1,312	9
1990	Haywood Jeffires, Houston	74	1,048	8
	Drew Hill, Houston	74	1,019	5
1991	Haywood Jeffires, Houston	100	1,181	7
1992	Haywood Jeffires, Houston	90	913	9
1993	Reggie Langhorne, Indianapolis	85	1,038	3
1994	Ben Coates, New England	96	1,174	7
1995	Carl Pickens, Cincinnati	99	1,234	17
1996	Carl Pickens, Cincinnati	100	1,180	12
1997	Tim Brown, Oakland	104	1,408	5
1998	O. J. McDuffie, Miami	90	1,050	7
1999	Jimmy Smith, Jacksonville	116	1,636	6
2000	Marvin Harrison, Indianapolis	102	1,413	14
2001	Rod Smith, Denver	113	1,343	11
2002	Marvin Harrison, Indianapolis	143	1,722	11
2003	LaDainian Tomlinson, San Diego	100	725	4
2004	Tony Gonzalez, Kansas City	102	1,258	7
2005	Chad Johnson, Cincinnati	97	1,432	9
2006	Andre Johnson, Houston	103	1,147	5
2007	Wes Welker, New England	112	1,175	8
2008	Andre Johnson, Houston	115	1,575	8

Scoring

Player, team	TD	PAT	FG	Pts	Year
Gene Mingo, Denver	6	33	18	123	1960
Gino Cappelletti, Boston	8	48	17	147	1961
Gene Mingo, Denver	4	32	27	137	1962
Gino Cappelletti, Boston	2	35	22	113	1963
Gino Cappelletti, Boston	7	36	25	155	1964
Gino Cappelletti, Boston	9	27	17	132	1965
Gino Cappelletti, Boston	6	35	16	119	1966
George Blanda, Oakland	0	56	20	116	1967
Jim Turner, NY Jets	0	43	34	145	1968
Jim Turner, NY Jets	0	33	32	129	1969
Jan Stenerud, Kansas City	0	26	30	116	1970
Garo Yepremian, Miami	0	33	28	117	1971
Bobby Howfield, NY Jets	0	40	27	121	1972
Roy Gerela, Pittsburgh	0	36	29	123	1973
Roy Gerela, Pittsburgh	0	33	20	93	1974
O. J. Simpson, Buffalo	23	0	0	138	1975
Toni Linhart, Baltimore Colts	0	49	20	109	1976
Errol Mann, Oakland	0	39	20	99	1977
Pat Leahy, NY Jets	0	41	22	107	1978
John Smith, New England	0	46	23	115	1979
John Smith, New England	0	51	26	129	1980
Jim Breech, Cincinnati	0	49	22	115	1981
Nick Lowery, Kansas City	0	37	26	115	
Marcus Allen, L.A. Raiders	14	0	0	84	1982
Gary Anderson, Pittsburgh	0	38	27	119	1983
Gary Anderson, Pittsburgh	0	45	24	117	1984
Gary Anderson, Pittsburgh	0	40	33	139	1985
Tony Franklin, New England	0	44	32	140	1986
Jim Breech, Cincinnati	0	25	24	97	1987
Scott Norwood, Buffalo	0	33	32	129	1988
David Treadwell, Denver	0	39	27	120	1989
Nick Lowery, Kansas City	0	37	34	139	1990
Pete Stoyanovich, Miami	0	28	31	121	1991
Pete Stoyanovich, Miami	0	34	30	124	1992
Jeff Jaeger, L.A. Raiders	0	27	35	132	1993
John Carney, San Diego	0	33	34	135	1994
Norm Johnson, Pittsburgh	0	39	34	141	1995
Cary Blanchard, Indianapolis	0	27	36	135	1996
Mike Hollis, Jacksonville	0	41	31	134	1997
Steve Christie, Buffalo	0	41	33	140	1998
Mike Vanderjagt, Indianapolis	0	43	34	145	1999
Matt Stover, Baltimore	0	30	35	135	2000
Mike Vanderjagt, Indianapolis	0	41	28	125	2001
Priest Holmes, Kansas City	24	0	0	144	2002
Priest Holmes, Kansas City	27	0	0	162	2003
Adam Vinatieri, New England	0	48	31	141	2004
Shayne Graham, Cincinnati	0	47	28	131	2005
LaDainian Tomlinson, San Diego	31	0	0	186	2006
Randy Moss, New England	23	0	0	138	2007
Stephen Gostkowski, New England	0	40	36	148	2008

Rushing

Year	Player, team	Yds	Att	TD
1960	Abner Haynes, Dallas Texans	875	156	9
1961	Billy Cannon, Houston	948	200	6
1962	Cookie Gilchrist, Buffalo	1,096	214	13
1963	Clem Daniels, Oakland	1,099	215	3
1964	Cookie Gilchrist, Buffalo	981	230	6
1965	Paul Lowe, San Diego	1,121	222	7
1966	Jim Nance, Boston	1,458	299	11
1967	Jim Nance, Boston	1,216	269	7
1968	Paul Robinson, Cincinnati	1,023	238	8
1969	Dickie Post, San Diego	873	182	6
1970	Floyd Little, Denver	901	209	3
1971	Floyd Little, Denver	1,133	284	6
1972	O. J. Simpson, Buffalo	1,251	292	6
1973	O. J. Simpson, Buffalo	2,003	332	12
1974	Otis Armstrong, Denver	1,407	263	9
1975	O. J. Simpson, Buffalo	1,817	329	16
1976	O. J. Simpson, Buffalo	1,503	290	8
1977	Mark van Eeghen, Oakland	1,273	324	7
1978	Earl Campbell, Houston	1,450	302	13
1979	Earl Campbell, Houston	1,697	368	19
1980	Earl Campbell, Houston	1,934	373	13
1981	Earl Campbell, Houston	1,376	361	10
1982	Freeman McNeil, NY Jets	786	151	6
1983	Curt Warner, Seattle	1,449	335	13
1984	Earnest Jackson, San Diego	1,179	296	8
1985	Marcus Allen, L.A. Raiders	1,759	380	11
1986	Curt Warner, Seattle	1,481	319	13
1987	Eric Dickerson, L.A. Rams-Ind.	1,288*	283	6
1988	Eric Dickerson, Indianapolis	1,659	388	14
1989	Christian Okoye, Kansas City	1,480	370	12
1990	Thurman Thomas, Buffalo	1,297	271	11
1991	Thurman Thomas, Buffalo	1,407	288	7
1992	Barry Foster, Pittsburgh	1,690	390	11
1993	Thurman Thomas, Buffalo	1,315	355	6
1994	Chris Warren, Seattle	1,545	333	9
1995	Curtis Martin, New England	1,487	368	14
1996	Terrell Davis, Denver	1,538	345	13
1997	Terrell Davis, Denver	1,750	369	15
1998	Terrell Davis, Denver	2,008	392	21
1999	Edgerrin James, Indianapolis	1,553	369	13
2000	Edgerrin James, Indianapolis	1,709	387	13
2001	Priest Holmes, Kansas City	1,555	327	8
2002	Ricky Williams, Miami	1,853	383	16
2003	Jamal Lewis, Baltimore	2,066	387	14
2004	Curtis Martin, NY Jets	1,697	371	12
2005	Larry Johnson, Kansas City	1,750	336	20
2006	LaDainian Tomlinson, San Diego	1,815	348	28
2007	LaDainian Tomlinson, San Diego	1,474	315	15
2008	Thomas Jones, NY Jets	1,312	290	13

*Includes 277 yards after being traded to NFC; 1,011 yards led AFC.

National Football Conference Leaders

(National Football League, 1960-69)

Passing (based on QB rating points) / Receptions

Player, team	Att	Com	YG	TD	Year	Player, team	Rec	YG	TD
Milt Plum, Cleveland	250	151	2,297	21	1960	Raymond Berry, Baltimore Colts	74	1,298	10
Milt Plum, Cleveland	302	177	2,416	18	1961	Jim Phillips, L.A. Rams	78	1,092	5
Bart Starr, Green Bay	285	178	2,438	12	1962	Bobby Mitchell, Washington	72	1,384	11
Y. A. Tittle, NY Giants	367	221	3,145	36	1963	Bobby Joe Conrad, St. Louis Cardinals	73	967	10
Bart Starr, Green Bay	272	163	2,144	15	1964	Johnny Morris, Chicago	93	1,200	10
Rudy Bukich, Chicago	312	176	2,641	20	1965	Dave Parks, San Francisco	80	1,344	12
Bart Starr, Green Bay	251	156	2,257	14	1966	Charley Taylor, Washington	72	1,119	12
Sonny Jurgensen, Washington	508	288	3,747	31	1967	Charley Taylor, Washington	70	990	9
Earl Morrall, Baltimore Colts	317	182	2,909	26	1968	Clifton McNeil, San Francisco	71	994	7
Sonny Jurgensen, Washington	442	274	3,102	22	1969	Dan Abramowicz, New Orleans	73	1,015	7
John Brodie, San Francisco	378	223	2,941	24	1970	Dick Gordon, Chicago	71	1,026	13
Roger Staubach, Dallas	211	126	1,882	15	1971	Bob Tucker, NY Giants	59	791	4
Norm Snead, NY Giants	325	196	2,307	17	1972	Harold Jackson, Philadelphia	62	1,048	4
Roger Staubach, Dallas	286	179	2,428	23	1973	Harold Carmichael, Philadelphia	67	1,116	9
Sonny Jurgensen, Washington	167	107	1,185	11	1974	Charles Young, Philadelphia	63	696	3
Fran Tarkenton, Minnesota	425	273	2,994	25	1975	Chuck Foreman, Minnesota	73	691	9
James Harris, L.A. Rams	158	91	1,460	8	1976	Drew Pearson, Dallas	58	806	6
Roger Staubach, Dallas	361	210	2,620	18	1977	Ahmad Rashad, Minnesota	51	681	2
Roger Staubach, Dallas	413	231	3,190	25	1978	Rickey Young, Minnesota	88	704	5
Roger Staubach, Dallas	461	267	3,586	27	1979	Ahmad Rashad, Minnesota	80	1,156	9
Ron Jaworski, Philadelphia	451	257	3,529	27	1980	Earl Cooper, San Francisco	83	567	4
Joe Montana, San Francisco	488	311	3,565	19	1981	Dwight Clark, San Francisco	85	1,105	4
Joe Thiesmann, Washington	252	161	2,033	13	1982	Dwight Clark, San Francisco	60	913	5
Steve Bartkowski, Atlanta	432	274	3,167	22	1983	Roy Green, St. Louis Cardinals	78	1,227	14
						Charlie Brown, Washington	78	1,225	8
						Earnest Gray, NY Giants	78	1,139	5
Joe Montana, San Francisco	432	279	3,630	28	1984	Art Monk, Washington	106	1,372	7
Joe Montana, San Francisco	494	303	3,653	27	1985	Roger Craig, San Francisco	92	1,016	6
Tommy Kramer, Minnesota	372	208	3,000	24	1986	Jerry Rice, San Francisco	86	1,570	15
Joe Montana, San Francisco	398	266	3,054	31	1987	J. T. Smith, St. Louis Cardinals	91	1,117	8
Wade Wilson, Minnesota	332	204	2,746	15	1988	Henry Ellard, L.A. Rams	86	1,414	10
Joe Montana, San Francisco	386	271	3,521	26	1989	Sterling Sharpe, Green Bay	90	1,423	12
Phil Simms, NY Giants	311	184	2,284	15	1990	Jerry Rice, San Francisco	100	1,502	13
Steve Young, San Francisco	279	180	2,517	17	1991	Michael Irvin, Dallas	93	1,523	8
Steve Young, San Francisco	402	268	3,465	25	1992	Sterling Sharpe, Green Bay	108	1,461	13
Steve Young, San Francisco	462	314	4,023	29	1993	Sterling Sharpe, Green Bay	112	1,274	11
Steve Young, San Francisco	461	324	3,969	35	1994	Cris Carter, Minnesota	122	1,256	7
Brett Favre, Green Bay	570	359	4,413	38	1995	Herman Moore, Detroit	123	1,686	14
Steve Young, San Francisco	316	214	2,410	14	1996	Jerry Rice, San Francisco	108	1,254	8
Steve Young, San Francisco	356	241	3,029	19	1997	Herman Moore, Detroit	104	1,293	8
Randall Cunningham, Minnesota	425	259	3,704	34	1998	Frank Sanders, Arizona	89	1,145	3
Kurt Warner, St. Louis	499	325	4,353	41	1999	Muhsin Muhammad, Carolina	96	1,253	8
Trent Green, St. Louis	240	145	2,063	16	2000	Muhsin Muhammad, Carolina	102	1,183	6
Kurt Warner, St. Louis	546	375	4,830	36	2001	Keyshawn Johnson, Tampa Bay	106	1,266	1
Brad Johnson, Tampa Bay	451	281	3,049	22	2002	Randy Moss, Minnesota	106	1,347	7
Daunte Culpepper, Minnesota	454	295	3,479	25	2003	Torry Holt, St. Louis	117	1,696	12
Daunte Culpepper, Minnesota	548	379	4,717	39	2004	Joe Horn, New Orleans	94	1,399	11
						Torry Holt, St. Louis	94	1,372	10
Matt Hasselbeck, Seattle	449	294	3,459	24	2005	Steve Smith, Carolina	103	1,563	12
						Larry Fitzgerald, Arizona	103	1,409	10
Drew Brees, New Orleans	554	356	4,418	26	2006	Mike Furrey, Detroit	98	1,086	6
Tony Romo, Dallas	520	335	4,211	36	2007	Larry Fitzgerald, Arizona	100	1,409	10
Kurt Warner, Arizona	598	401	4,583	30	2008	Larry Fitzgerald, Arizona	96	1,431	12

Scoring / Rushing

Player, team	TD	PAT	FG	Pts	Year	Player, team	Yds	Att	TD
Paul Hornung, Green Bay	15	41	15	176	1960	Jim Brown, Cleveland	1,257	215	9
Paul Hornung, Green Bay	10	41	15	146	1961	Jim Brown, Cleveland	1,408	305	8
Jim Taylor, Green Bay	19	0	0	114	1962	Jim Taylor, Green Bay	1,474	272	19
Don Chandler, NY Giants	0	52	18	106	1963	Jim Brown, Cleveland	1,863	291	12
Lenny Moore, Baltimore Colts	20	0	0	120	1964	Jim Brown, Cleveland	1,446	280	7
Gale Sayers, Chicago	22	0	0	132	1965	Jim Brown, Cleveland	1,544	289	17
Bruce Gossett, L.A. Rams	0	29	28	113	1966	Gale Sayers, Chicago	1,231	229	8
Jim Bakken, St. Louis Cardinals	0	36	27	117	1967	Leroy Kelly, Cleveland	1,205	235	11
Leroy Kelly, Cleveland	20	0	0	120	1968	Leroy Kelly, Cleveland	1,239	248	16
Fred Cox, Minnesota	0	43	26	121	1969	Gale Sayers, Chicago	1,032	236	8
Fred Cox, Minnesota	0	35	30	125	1970	Larry Brown, Washington	1,125	237	5
Curt Knight, Washington	0	27	29	114	1971	John Brockington, Green Bay	1,105	216	4
Chester Marcol, Green Bay	0	29	33	128	1972	Larry Brown, Washington	1,216	285	8
David Ray, L.A. Rams	0	40	30	130	1973	John Brockington, Green Bay	1,144	265	3
Chester Marcol, Green Bay	0	19	25	94	1974	Lawrence McCutcheon, L.A. Rams	1,109	236	3

Scoring Player, team	TD	PAT	FG	Pts	Year	Rushing Player, team	Yds	Att	TD
Chuck Foreman, Minnesota	22	0	0	132	1975	Jim Otis, St. Louis Cardinals	1,076	269	5
Mark Moseley, Washington	0	31	22	97	1976	Walter Payton, Chicago	1,390	311	13
Walter Payton, Chicago	16	0	0	96	1977	Walter Payton, Chicago	1,852	339	14
Frank Corral, L.A. Rams	0	31	29	118	1978	Walter Payton, Chicago	1,395	333	11
Mark Moseley, Washington	0	39	25	114	1979	Walter Payton, Chicago	1,610	369	14
Ed Murray, Detroit	0	35	27	116	1980	Walter Payton, Chicago	1,460	317	6
Ed Murray, Detroit	0	46	25	121	1981	George Rogers, New Orleans	1,674	378	13
Rafael Septien, Dallas	0	40	27	121					
Wendell Tyler, L.A. Rams	13	0	0	78	1982	Tony Dorsett, Dallas	745	177	5
Mark Moseley, Washington	0	62	33	161	1983	Eric Dickerson, L.A. Rams	1,808	390	18
Ray Wersching, San Francisco	0	56	25	131	1984	Eric Dickerson, L.A. Rams	2,105	379	14
Kevin Butler, Chicago	0	51	31	144	1985	Gerald Riggs, Atlanta	1,719	397	10
Kevin Butler, Chicago	0	36	28	120	1986	Eric Dickerson, L.A. Rams	1,821	404	11
Jerry Rice, San Francisco	23	0	0	138	1987	Charles White, L.A. Rams	1,374	324	11
Mike Cofer, San Francisco	0	40	27	121	1988	Herschel Walker, Dallas	1,514	361	5
Mike Cofer, San Francisco	0	49	29	136	1989	Barry Sanders, Detroit	1,470	280	14
Chip Lohmiller, Washington	0	41	30	131	1990	Barry Sanders, Detroit	1,304	255	13
Chip Lohmiller, Washington	0	56	31	149	1991	Emmitt Smith, Dallas	1,563	365	12
Morten Andersen, New Orleans	0	33	29	120	1992	Emmitt Smith, Dallas	1,713	373	18
Chip Lohmiller, Washington	0	30	30	120					
Jason Hanson, Detroit	0	28	34	130	1993	Emmitt Smith, Dallas	1,486	283	9
Fuad Reveiz, Minnesota	0	30	34	132	1994	Barry Sanders, Detroit	1,883	331	7
Emmitt Smith, Dallas	22	0	0	132					
Emmitt Smith, Dallas	25	0	0	150	1995	Emmitt Smith, Dallas	1,773	377	25
John Kasay, Carolina	0	34	37	145	1996	Barry Sanders, Detroit	1,553	307	11
Richie Cunningham, Dallas	0	24	34	126	1997	Barry Sanders, Detroit	2,053	335	11
Gary Anderson, Minnesota	0	59	35	164	1998	Jamal Anderson, Atlanta	1,846	410	14
Jeff Wilkins, St. Louis	0	64	20	124	1999	Stephen Davis, Washington	1,405	290	17
Marshall Faulk, St. Louis	26	0	0	156	2000	Robert Smith, Minnesota	1,521	295	7
Marshall Faulk, St. Louis	21	0	0	128	2001	Stephen Davis, Washington	1,432	356	5
Jay Feely, Atlanta	0	42	32	138	2002	Deuce McAllister, New Orleans	1,388	325	13
Jeff Wilkins, St. Louis	0	46	39	163	2003	Ahman Green, Green Bay	1,883	355	15
David Akers, Philadelphia	0	41	27	122	2004	Shaun Alexander, Seattle	1,696	353	16
Shaun Alexander, Seattle	28	0	0	168	2005	Shaun Alexander, Seattle	1,880	370	27
Robbie Gould, Chicago	0	47	32	143	2006	Frank Gore, San Francisco	1,695	312	8
Mason Crosby, Green Bay	0	48	31	141	2007	Adrian Peterson, Minnesota	1,341	238	12
David Akers, Philadelphia	0	45	33	144	2008	Adrian Peterson, Minnesota	1,760	363	10

NFL MVP, Defensive Player of the Year, and Rookie of the Year

The Most Valuable Player and Defensive Player of the Year are two of many awards given out annually by the Associated Press. Rookie of the Year is one of many awards given out annually by *The Sporting News*. Many other organizations give out annual awards honoring the NFL's best players.

Year	Most Valuable Player	Defensive Player of the Year	Rookie of the Year
1957	Jim Brown, Cleveland	—	—
1958	Gino Marchetti, Baltimore Colts	—	—
1959	Charley Conerly, NY Giants	—	—
1960	(tie) Norm Van Brocklin, Philadelphia; Joe Schmidt, Detroit	—	—
1961	Paul Hornung, Green Bay	—	—
1962	Jim Taylor, Green Bay	—	—
1963	Y. A. Tittle, NY Giants	—	—
1964	John Unitas, Baltimore Colts	—	Charley Taylor, Washington
1965	Jim Brown, Cleveland	—	Gale Sayers, Chicago
1966	Bart Starr, Green Bay	Larry Wilson, St. Louis	Tommy Nobis, Atlanta
1967	John Unitas, Baltimore Colts	Deacon Jones, Los Angeles	Mel Farr, Detroit
1968	Earl Morrall, Baltimore Colts	Deacon Jones, Los Angeles	Earl McCullouch, Detroit
1969	Roman Gabriel, L.A. Rams	Dick Butkus, Chicago	Calvin Hill, Dallas
1970	John Brodie, San Francisco	Dick Butkus, Chicago	NFC: Bruce Taylor, San Francisco AFC: Dennis Shaw, Buffalo
1971	Alan Page, Minnesota	Carl Eller, Minnesota	NFC: John Brockington, Green Bay AFC: Jim Plunkett, New England
1972	Larry Brown, Washington	Joe Greene, Pittsburgh	NFC: Chester Marcol, Green Bay AFC: Franco Harris, Pittsburgh
1973	O. J. Simpson, Buffalo	Alan Page, Minnesota	NFC: Chuck Foreman, Minnesota AFC: Boobie Clark, Cincinnati
1974	Ken Stabler, Oakland	Joe Greene, Pittsburgh	NFC: Wilbur Jackson, San Francisco AFC: Don Woods, San Diego
1975	Fran Tarkenton, Minnesota	Curley Culp, Houston	NFC: Steve Bartkowski, Atlanta AFC: Robert Brazile, Houston
1976	Bert Jones, Baltimore	Jerry Sherk, Cleveland	NFC: Sammy White, Minnesota AFC: Mike Haynes, New England
1977	Walter Payton, Chicago	Harvey Martin, Dallas	NFC: Tony Dorsett, Dallas AFC: A. J. Duhe, Miami
1978	Terry Bradshaw, Pittsburgh	Randy Gradishar, Denver	NFC: Al Baker, Detroit AFC: Earl Campbell, Houston

Year	Most Valuable Player	Defensive Player of the Year	Rookie of the Year
1979	Earl Campbell, Houston	Lee Roy Selmon, Tampa Bay	NFC: Ottis Anderson, St. Louis AFC: Jerry Butler, Buffalo
1980	Brian Sipe, Cleveland	Lester Hayes, Oakland	Billy Sims, Detroit
1981	Ken Anderson, Cincinnati	Joe Klecko, NY Jets	George Rogers, New Orleans
1982	Mark Moseley, Washington	Mark Gastineau, NY Jets	Marcus Allen, L.A. Raiders
1983	Joe Theismann, Washington	Jack Lambert, Pittsburgh	Dan Marino, Miami
1984	Dan Marino, Miami	Mike Haynes, L.A. Raiders	Louis Lipps, Pittsburgh
1985	Marcus Allen, L.A. Raiders	(tie) Howie Long, L.A. Raiders; Andre Tippett, New England	Eddie Brown, Cincinnati
1986	Lawrence Taylor, NY Giants	Lawrence Taylor, NY Giants	Rueben Mayes, New Orleans
1987	John Elway, Denver	Reggie White, Philadelphia	Robert Awalt, St. Louis
1988	Boomer Esiason, Cincinnati	Mike Singletary, Chicago	Keith Jackson, Philadelphia
1989	Joe Montana, San Francisco	Tim Harris, Green Bay	Barry Sanders, Detroit
1990	Joe Montana, San Francisco	Bruce Smith, Buffalo	Richmond Webb, Miami
1991	Thurman Thomas, Buffalo	Pat Swilling, New Orleans	Mike Croel, Denver
1992	Steve Young, San Francisco	Junior Seau, San Diego	Santana Dotson, Tampa Bay
1993	Emmitt Smith, Dallas	Bruce Smith, Buffalo	Jerome Bettis, L.A. Rams
1994	Steve Young, San Francisco	Deion Sanders, San Francisco	Marshall Faulk, Indianapolis
1995	Brett Favre, Green Bay	Bryce Paup, Buffalo	Curtis Martin, New England
1996	Brett Favre, Green Bay	Bruce Smith, Buffalo	Eddie George, Houston
1997	(tie) Brett Favre, Green Bay; Barry Sanders, Detroit	Dana Stubblefield, San Francisco	Warrick Dunn, Tampa Bay
1998	Terrell Davis, Denver	Reggie White, Green Bay	Randy Moss, Minnesota
1999	Kurt Warner, St. Louis	Warren Sapp, Tampa Bay	Edgerrin James, Indianapolis
2000	Marshall Faulk, St. Louis	Ray Lewis, Baltimore	Brian Urlacher, Chicago
2001	Kurt Warner, St. Louis	Michael Strahan, NY Giants	Kendrell Bell, Pittsburgh
2002	Rich Gannon, Oakland	Derrick Brooks, Tampa Bay	Clinton Portis, Denver
2003	(tie) Peyton Manning, Indianapolis; Steve McNair, Tennessee	Ray Lewis, Baltimore	Anquan Boldin, Arizona
2004	Peyton Manning, Indianapolis	Ed Reed, Baltimore	Ben Roethlisberger, Pittsburgh
2005	Shaun Alexander, Seattle	Brian Urlacher, Chicago	Carnell "Cadillac" Williams, Tampa Bay
2006	LaDainian Tomlinson, San Diego	Jason Taylor, Miami	Vince Young, Tennessee
2007	Tom Brady, New England	Bob Sanders, Indianapolis	Adrian Peterson, Minnesota
2008	Peyton Manning, Indianapolis	James Harrison, Pittsburgh	Matt Ryan, Atlanta

The Sporting News 2008 NFL All-Pro Team

Offense: Quarterback: Drew Brees, New Orleans. Running Back: Adrian Peterson, Minnesota; Michael Turner, Atlanta. Wide Receiver: Andre Johnson, Houston; Larry Fitzgerald, Arizona. Tight End: Tony Gonzalez, Kansas City. Tackle: Michael Roos, Tennessee; Jordan Gross, Carolina. Guard: Steve Hutchinson, Minnesota; Chris Snee, NY Giants. Center: Shaun O'Hara, NY Giants.

Defense: Linebacker: DeMarcus Ware, Dallas; James Harrison, Pittsburgh; Joey Porter, Miami. Defensive End: Julius Peppers, Carolina; Mario Williams, Houston. Defensive Tackle: Albert Haynesworth, Tennessee; Kris Jenkins, NY Jets. Cornerback: Nnamdi Asomugha, Oakland; Cortland Finnegan, Tennessee. Safety: Ed Reed, Baltimore; Troy Polamalu, Pittsburgh.

Special Teams: Kicker: Stephen Gostkowski, New England. Punter: Shane Lechler, Oakland. Kick Returner: Leodis McKelvin, Buffalo. Punt Returner: Reggie Bush, New Orleans.

All-Time Professional (NFL and AFL) Football Records

(at the end of the 2008 season; *active in 2008; (a) includes AFL statistics; **represents 2-point conversions scored)

Leading Lifetime Scorers

Player	Yrs.	TD	PAT	FG	Total
Morten Andersen	25	0	849	565	2,544
Gary Anderson	23	0	820	538	2,434
George Blanda (a)	26	9	943	335	2,002
John Carney*	21	0	575	460	1,955
Matt Stover*	18	0	558	462	1,944
Jason Elam*	16	0	643	424	1,915
Jason Hanson*	17	0	529	406	1,747
Norm Johnson	18	0	638	366	1,736
Nick Lowery	18	0	562	383	1,711
Jan Stenerud (a)	19	0	580	373	1,699
John Kasay*	17	0	476	386	1,634
Eddie Murray	19	0	538	352	1,594
Al Del Greco	17	0	543	347	1,584
Adam Vinatieri*	13	0	497**	331	1,492
Steve Christie	15	0	468	336	1,476
Pat Leahy	18	0	558	304	1,470
Jim Turner (a)	16	1	521	304	1,439
Matt Bahr	17	0	522	300	1,422
Jeff Wilkins	14	0	495	307	1,416
Mark Moseley	16	0	482	300	1,382

Leading Lifetime Touchdown Scorers

Player	Yrs.	Rush	Rec	Ret	TD
Jerry Rice	20	10	197	1	208
Emmitt Smith	15	164	11	0	175
Marcus Allen	16	123	21	1	145
Terrell Owens*	13	2	139	0	141
LaDainian Tomlinson* . .	8	126	15	0	141
Marshall Faulk	12	100	36	0	136
Randy Moss*	11	0	135	1	136
Cris Carter	16	0	130	1	131
Marvin Harrison*	13	0	128	0	128
Jim Brown	9	106	20	0	126
Walter Payton	13	110	15	0	125
John Riggins	14	104	12	0	116
Lenny Moore	12	63	48	2	113
Shaun Alexander*	9	100	12	0	112
Barry Sanders	10	99	10	0	109
Tim Brown	17	1	100	4	105
Don Hutson	11	3	99	3	105
Steve Largent	14	1	100	0	101
Franco Harris	13	91	9	0	100
Curtis Martin	11	90	10	0	100

Most Points, Season: 186, LaDainian Tomlinson, San Diego Chargers, 2006 (31 TDs).
Most Points, Game: 40, Ernie Nevers, Chicago Cardinals vs. Chicago Bears, Nov. 28, 1929 (6 TDs, 4 PATs).
Most Touchdowns, Season: 31, LaDainian Tomlinson, San Diego Chargers, 2006.
Most Touchdowns, Game: 6, Ernie Nevers, Chicago Cardinals vs. Chicago Bears, Nov. 28, 1929 (6 rushing); Dub Jones, Cleveland Browns vs. Chicago Bears, Nov. 25, 1951 (4 rushing, 2 pass receptions); Gale Sayers, Chicago Bears vs. San Francisco 49ers, Dec. 12, 1965 (4 rushing, 1 pass reception, 1 punt return).
Most Points After TD, Season: 74, Stephen Gostkowski, New England Patriots, 2007.
Most Consecutive Points After TD: 389, Matt Stover, Cleveland Browns-Baltimore Ravens, 1996-2008.
Most Field Goals, Season: 40, Neil Rackers, Arizona Cardinals, 2005.
Most Field Goals, Game: 8, Rob Bironas, Tennessee Titans vs. Houston Texans, Oct. 21, 2007.
Most Field Goals, Career: 565, Morten Andersen, New Orleans Saints-Atlanta Falcons-NY Giants-Kansas City Chiefs- Minnesota Vikings, 1982-2007.
Longest Field Goal: 63 yards, Tom Dempsey, New Orleans Saints vs. Detroit Lions, Nov. 8, 1970; Jason Elam, Denver Broncos vs. Jacksonville Jaguars, Oct. 25, 1998.

Defensive Records

Most Interceptions, Career: 81, Paul Krause, Washington Redskins-Minnesota Vikings, 1964-79.
Most Interceptions, Season: 14, Dick "Night Train" Lane, L.A. Rams, 1952.
Most Touchdowns, Career: 12, Rod Woodson, Pittsburgh Steelers-San Francisco 49ers-Baltimore Ravens-Oakland Raiders, 1987-2003.
Most Touchdowns, Season: 4, Ken Houston, Houston Oilers, 1971; Jim Kearney, Kansas City Chiefs, 1972; Eric Allen, Philadelphia Eagles, 1993.
Most Sacks, Career (since 1982): 200, Bruce Smith, Buffalo Bills-Washington Redskins, 1985-2003.
Most Sacks, Season (since 1982): 22.5, Michael Strahan, NY Giants, 2001.

Leading Lifetime Rushers
(ranked by rushing yards)

Player	Yrs.	Att	Yards	Avg	Long	TD	Player	Yrs.	Att	Yards	Avg	Long	TD
Emmitt Smith	15	4,409	18,355	4.2	75	164	Edgerrin James*	10	2,982	12,121	4.1	72	80
Walter Payton	13	3,838	16,726	4.4	76	110	Franco Harris	12	2,949	12,120	4.1	75	91
Barry Sanders	10	3,062	15,269	5.0	85	99	Thurman Thomas	13	2,877	12,074	4.2	80	65
Curtis Martin	11	3,518	14,101	4.0	70	90	LaDainian Tomlinson*	8	2,657	11,760	4.4	85	126
Jerome Bettis	13	3,479	13,662	3.9	71	91	John Riggins	14	2,916	11,352	3.9	66	104
Eric Dickerson	11	2,996	13,259	4.4	85	90	Fred Taylor*	11	2,428	11,271	4.6	80	62
Tony Dorsett	12	2,936	12,739	4.3	99	77	Corey Dillon	10	2,618	11,241	4.3	96	82
Jim Brown	9	2,359	12,312	5.2	80	106	O. J. Simpson	11	2,404	11,236	4.7	94	61
Marshall Faulk	12	2,836	12,279	4.3	71	100	Warrick Dunn	12	2,669	10,967	4.1	90	49
Marcus Allen	16	3,022	12,243	4.1	61	123	Ricky Watters	10	2,622	10,643	4.1	57	78

*Active in 2008. (a) Includes AFL statistics.

Most Yards Gained, Season: 2,105, Eric Dickerson, L.A. Rams, 1984.
Most Yards Gained, Game: 296, Adrian Peterson, Minnesota Vikings vs. San Diego Chargers, Nov. 4, 2007.
Most Touchdowns Rushing, Career: 164, Emmitt Smith, Dallas Cowboys-Arizona Cardinals, 1990-2004.
Most Touchdowns Rushing, Season: 28, LaDainian Tomlinson, San Diego Chargers, 2006.
Most Touchdowns Rushing, Game: 6, Ernie Nevers, Chicago Cardinals vs. Chicago Bears, Nov. 28, 1929.
Most Rushing Attempts, Game: 45, Jamie Morris, Washington Redskins vs. Cincinnati Bengals, Dec. 17, 1988 (OT).
Longest Run From Scrimmage: 99 yards, Tony Dorsett, Dallas Cowboys vs. Minnesota Vikings, Jan. 3, 1983 (TD).

Leading Lifetime Receivers
(ranked by number of receptions)

Player	Yrs.	Att	Yards	Avg	Long	TD	Player	Yrs.	Att	Yards	Avg	Long	TD
Jerry Rice	20	1,549	22,895	14.8	96	197	Torry Holt*	10	869	12,660	14.6	85	74
Marvin Harrison*	13	1,102	14,580	13.2	80	128	Jimmy Smith	12	862	12,287	14.3	75	67
Cris Carter	16	1,101	13,899	12.6	80	130	Irving Fryar	17	851	12,785	15.0	80	84
Tim Brown	17	1,094	14,934	13.7	80	100	Rod Smith	12	849	11,389	13.4	85	68
Isaac Bruce*	15	1,003	14,944	14.9	80	91	Randy Moss*	11	843	13,201	15.7	82	135
Terrell Owens*	13	951	14,122	14.8	91	139	Larry Centers	14	827	6,797	8.2	54	28
Andre Reed	16	951	13,198	13.9	83	87	Steve Largent	14	819	13,089	16.0	74	100
Art Monk	16	940	12,721	13.5	79	68	Shannon Sharpe	14	815	10,060	12.3	82	62
Tony Gonzalez*	12	916	10,940	11.9	73	76	Henry Ellard	16	814	13,777	16.9	81	65
Keenan McCardell	16	883	11,373	12.9	76	63	Keyshawn Johnson	11	814	10,571	13.0	76	64

*Active in 2008. (a) Includes AFL statistics.

Most Yards Gained, Career: 22,895, Jerry Rice, San Francisco 49ers-Oakland Raiders-Seattle Seahawks, 1985-2004.
Most Yards Gained, Season: 1,848, Jerry Rice, San Francisco 49ers, 1995.
Most Yards Gained, Game: 336, Willie "Flipper" Anderson, L.A. Rams vs. New Orleans Saints, Nov. 26, 1989 (OT).
Most Pass Receptions, Season: 143, Marvin Harrison, Indianapolis Colts, 2002.
Most Pass Receptions, Game: 20, Terrell Owens, San Francisco 49ers vs. Chicago Bears, Dec. 17, 2000 (283 yards).
Most Touchdown Receptions, Career: 197, Jerry Rice, San Francisco 49ers-Oakland Raiders-Seattle Seahawks, 1985-2004.
Most Touchdown Receptions, Season: 23, Randy Moss, New England Patriots, 2007.
Most Touchdown Receptions, Game: 5, Bob Shaw, Chicago Cardinals vs. Baltimore Colts, Oct. 2, 1950; Kellen Winslow, San Diego Chargers vs. Oakland Raiders, Nov. 22, 1981; Jerry Rice, San Francisco 49ers vs. Atlanta Falcons, Oct. 14, 1990.

Leading Lifetime Passers
(minimum 1,500 attempts; ranked by quarterback rating points)

Player	Yrs.	Att	Comp	Yards	TD	Int	Pts[1]	Player	Yrs.	Att	Comp	Yards	TD	Int	Pts[1]
Steve Young	15	4,149	2,667	33,124	232	107	96.8	Jeff Garcia*	10	3,676	2,264	25,537	161	83	87.5
Peyton Manning*	11	5,960	3,839	45,628	333	165	94.7	Dan Marino	17	8,358	4,967	61,361	420	252	86.4
Kurt Warner*	11	3,557	2,327	28,591	182	114	93.8	Trent Green*	11	3,740	2,266	28,475	162	114	86.0
Tom Brady*	9	3,653	2,301	26,446	197	86	92.9	Donovan McNabb*	10	4,303	2,534	29,320	194	90	85.9
Joe Montana	15	5,391	3,409	40,551	273	139	92.3	Marc Bulger*	7	2,924	1,829	21,345	117	87	85.6
Chad Pennington*	9	2,395	1,580	17,391	101	62	90.6	Brett Favre*	18	9,280	5,720	65,127	464	310	85.4
B. Roethlisberger*	5	1,905	1,189	14,974	101	69	89.4	Jake Delhomme*	8	2,434	1,452	17,877	115	76	85.1
Drew Brees*	8	3,650	2,334	26,258	168	99	89.4	Rich Gannon	16	4,206	2,533	28,743	180	104	84.7
Daunte Culpepper*	10	3,042	1,927	23,208	146	100	89.0	Matt Hasselbeck*	10	3,347	2,013	23,549	147	94	84.5
Carson Palmer*		2,165	1,380	15,630	107	67	88.9	Jim Kelly	11	4,779	2,874	35,467	237	175	84.4

(1) Rating points based on performances in the following categories: Percentage of completions, percentage of touchdown passes, percentage of interceptions, and average gain per pass attempt.

Most Yards Gained, Career: 65,127, Brett Favre, Atlanta Falcons-Green Bay Packers-NY Jets, 1991-2008.
Most Yards Gained, Season: 5,084, Dan Marino, Miami Dolphins, 1984.
Most Yards Gained, Game: 554, Norm Van Brocklin, L.A. Rams vs. NY Yanks, Sept. 28, 1951 (27 completions in 41 attempts).
Most Touchdowns Passing, Career: 464, Brett Favre, Atlanta Falcons-Green Bay Packers-NY Jets, 1991-2008.
Most Touchdowns Passing, Season: 50, Tom Brady, New England Patriots, 2007.
Most Touchdowns Passing, Game: 7, Sid Luckman, Chicago Bears vs. NY Giants, Nov. 14, 1943; Adrian Burk, Philadelphia Eagles vs. Washington Redskins, Oct. 17, 1954; George Blanda, Houston Oilers vs. NY Titans, Nov. 19, 1961; Y. A. Tittle, NY Giants vs. Washington Redskins, Oct. 28, 1962; Joe Kapp, Minnesota Vikings vs. Baltimore Colts, Sept. 28, 1969.
Most Passes Completed, Career: 5,720, Brett Favre, Atlanta Falcons-Green Bay Packers-NY Jets, 1991-2008.
Most Passes Completed, Season: 440, Drew Brees, New Orleans Saints, 2007.
Most Passes Completed, Game: 45, Drew Bledsoe, New England Patriots vs. Minnesota Vikings, Nov. 13, 1994 (OT).

All-Time NFL Coaching Victories

(at end of 2008 season; ranked by overall career wins; *active in 2008)

			Regular Season				Overall			
Coach	Team	Yrs.	W	L	T	Pct.	W	L	T	Pct.
Don Shula	Colts, Dolphins	33	328	156	6	.677	347	173	6	.666
George Halas	Bears	40	318	148	31	.682	324	151	31	.682
Tom Landry	Cowboys	29	250	162	6	.607	270	178	6	.603
Earl "Curly" Lambeau	Packers, Cardinals, Redskins	33	226	132	22	.631	229	134	22	.631
Chuck Noll	Steelers	23	193	148	1	.566	209	156	1	.572
Marty Schottenheimer	Browns, Chiefs, Redskins, Chargers	21	200	126	1	.613	205	139	1	.596
Dan Reeves	Broncos, Giants, Falcons	23	190	165	2	.535	201	174	2	.536
Chuck Knox	Rams, Bills, Seahawks	22	186	147	1	.558	193	158	1	.550
Bill Parcells	Giants, Patriots, Jets, Cowboys	19	172	130	1	.569	183	138	1	.570
Mike Holmgren*	Packers, Seahawks	17	161	111	0	.592	174	122	0	.588
Joe Gibbs	Redskins	21	154	94	0	.621	171	101	0	.629
Paul Brown	Browns, Bengals	21	166	100	6	.624	170	108	6	.612
Bud Grant	Vikings	18	158	96	5	.621	168	108	5	.608
Bill Cowher	Steelers	15	149	90	1	.623	161	99	1	.619
Mike Shanahan*	Raiders, Broncos	16	146	98	0	.598	154	103	0	.599
Marv Levy	Chiefs, Bills	17	143	112	0	.561	154	120	0	.562
Bill Belichick*	Browns, Patriots	14	138	86	0	.616	153	90	0	.630
Steve Owen	Giants	23	151	100	17	.602	153	108	17	.586
Tony Dungy*	Buccaneers, Colts	13	139	69	0	.668	148	79	0	.652
Hank Stram	Chiefs, Saints	17	131	97	10	.574	136	100	10	.576

NFL Stadiums[1]

Team: stadium, location, surface (year built)	Capacity
Bears: Soldier Field[2], Chicago, IL, G (1924)	61,500
Bengals: Paul Brown Stadium, Cincinnati, OH, A (2000)	65,515
Bills: Ralph Wilson Stadium, Orchard Park, NY, A (1973)	73,967
Broncos: Invesco Field at Mile High, Denver, CO, G (2001)	76,125
Browns: Cleveland Browns Stadium, Cleveland, OH, G (1999)	73,300
Buccaneers: Raymond James Stadium, Tampa, FL, G (1998)	65,908
Cardinals: University of Phoenix Stadium, Glendale, AZ, G (2006)	65,000
Chargers: Qualcomm Stadium[3], San Diego, CA, G (1967)	70,000
Chiefs: Arrowhead Stad., Kansas City, MO, G (1972)	79,451
Colts: Lucas Oil Stad.[4], Indianapolis, IN, A (1983)	63,000
Cowboys: Cowboys Stad.[5], Arlington, TX, A (2009)	80,000
Dolphins: Dolphin Stadium[6], Miami Gardens, FL, G (2009)	75,192
Eagles: Lincoln Financial Field, Philadelphia, PA, G (2003)	67,594
Falcons: Georgia Dome, Atlanta, GA, A (1992)	71,228
49ers: Monster Park[7], San Francisco, CA, G (1960)	69,732
Giants: Giants Stadium, E. Rutherford, NJ, A (1976)	80,242
Jaguars: Jacksonville Municipal Stadium[8], Jacksonville, FL, G (1946)	67,164
Jets: Giants Stadium, E. Rutherford, NJ, A (1976)	80,242
Lions: Ford Field, Detroit, MI, A (2002)	64,500
Packers: Lambeau Field[9], Green Bay, WI, G (1957)	72,928
Panthers: Bank of America Stadium[10], Charlotte, NC, G (1996)	73,504
Patriots: Gillette Stadium, Foxboro, MA, A (2002)	68,756
Raiders: McAfee Coliseum[11], Oakland, CA, G (1966)	63,132
Rams: Edward Jones Dome[12], St. Louis, MO, A (1995)	66,000
Ravens: M & T Bank Stadium[13], Baltimore, MD, A (1998)	70,008
Redskins: FedEx Field[14], Landover, MD, G (1997)	91,704
Saints: Louisiana Superdome, New Orleans, A (1975)	68,000
Seahawks: Qwest Field[15], Seattle, WA, A (2002)	67,000
Steelers: Heinz Field, Pittsburgh, PA, A (2001)	64,050
Texans: Reliant Stadium, Houston, TX, G (2002)	71,054
Titans: The Coliseum[16], Nashville, TN, G (1999)	69,143
Vikings: Hubert H. Humphrey Metrodome, Minneapolis, MN, A (1982)	64,121

G = Grass. A = Artificial turf. (1) As of the start of the 2007 season. (2) Renovation in 2002 replaced interior of stadium. (3) Formerly San Diego Stadium (1967-80); San Diego Jack Murphy Stadium (1981-97). (4) Formerly the Hoosier Dome (1983-94); RCA Dome (1983-2008). (5) Formerly Texas Stadium (1971-2008). (6) Formerly Joe Robbie Stadium (1987-96); Pro Player Stadium (1996-2005). (7) Formerly Candlestick Park (1960-94); 3Com Park at Candlestick Point (1995-2004). (8) Formerly ALLTEL Stadium (1997-2007); Jacksonville Municipal Stadium (1946-97). (9) Formerly City Stadium (1957-65). Renovation completed in 2003, added 11,625 seats. (10) Formerly Ericsson Stadium (1996-2003). (11) Formerly Oakland/Alameda County Coliseum until 1998; Network Associates Coliseum until 2005. (12) Formerly Trans World Dome (1995-2001); full name: Edward Jones Dome at America's Center. (13) Formerly PSINet Stadium (1998-2002); Ravens Stadium (2002-03). (14) Formerly Jack Kent Cooke Stadium (1997-99). (15) Formerly Seahawks Stadium (2002-04). (16) Formerly Adelphia Col. (1999-2002).

National Football League Franchise Origins
(Founding year, league; home stadium location; subsequent history.)

Arizona Cardinals: 1920, American Professional Football Association (APFA)[1]. Chicago, 1920-59; St. Louis, 1960-87; Tempe, AZ, 1988-2005; Glendale, AZ, 2006-present.

Atlanta Falcons: 1966, NFL. Atlanta, 1966-present.

Baltimore Ravens: 1996, NFL. Baltimore, 1996-present.

Buffalo Bills: 1960, American Football League (AFL)[2]. Buffalo, 1960-72; Orchard Park, NY, 1973-present.

Carolina Panthers: 1995, NFL. Clemson, SC, 1995; Charlotte, NC, 1996-present.

Chicago Bears: 1920, APFA. Decatur, IL, 1920; Chicago, 1921-present.

Cincinnati Bengals: 1968, AFL. Cincinnati, 1968-present.

Cleveland Browns: 1946, All-America Football Conference (AAFC)[3]. Cleveland, 1946-95; 1999-present.

Dallas Cowboys: 1960, NFL. Dallas, 1960-70; Irving, TX, 1971-present.

Denver Broncos: 1960, AFL. Denver, 1960-present.

Detroit Lions: 1930, NFL. Portsmouth, OH, 1930-33; Detroit, 1934-74; Pontiac, MI, 1975-2001; Detroit, 2002-present.

Green Bay Packers: 1921, APFA. Green Bay, WI, 1921-present.

Houston Texans: 2002, NFL. Houston, 2002-present.

Indianapolis Colts: 1953, NFL. Baltimore, 1953-83; Indianapolis, 1984-present.

Jacksonville Jaguars: 1995, NFL. Jacksonville, FL, 1995-present.

Kansas City Chiefs: 1960, AFL. Dallas, 1960-62; Kansas City, MO, 1963-present.

Miami Dolphins: 1966, AFL. Miami, 1966-2002; Miami Gardens, FL, 2003-present.

Minnesota Vikings: 1961, NFL. Bloomington, MN, 1961-81; Minneapolis, 1982-present.

New England Patriots: 1960, AFL. Boston, 1960-70; Foxboro, MA, 1971-present.

New Orleans Saints: 1967, NFL. New Orleans, 1967-2004; Baton Rouge and San Antonio, 2005; New Orleans, 2006-present.

New York Giants: 1925, NFL. New York, 1925-73, 1975; New Haven, CT, 1973-74; E. Rutherford, NJ, 1976-present.

New York Jets: 1960, AFL. New York, 1960-83; E. Rutherford, NJ, 1984-present.

Oakland Raiders: 1960, AFL. San Francisco, 1960-61; Oakland, CA, 1962-81; Los Angeles, 1982-94; Oakland, CA, 1995-present.

Philadelphia Eagles: 1933, NFL. Philadelphia, 1933-present.

Pittsburgh Steelers: 1933, NFL. Pittsburgh, 1933-present.

St. Louis Rams: 1937, NFL. Cleveland, 1936-45; Los Angeles, 1946-79; Anaheim, 1980-94; St. Louis, 1995-present.

San Diego Chargers: 1960, AFL. Los Angeles, 1960; San Diego, 1961-present.

Seattle Seahawks: 1976, NFL. Seattle, 1976-present.

San Francisco 49ers: 1946, AAFC. San Francisco, 1946-present.

Tampa Bay Buccaneers: 1976, NFL. Tampa, 1976-present.

Tennessee Titans: 1960, AFL. Houston, 1969-96; Memphis, 1997; Nashville, 1998-present.

Washington Redskins: 1932, NFL. Boston, 1932-36; Washington, DC, 1937-96; Landover, MD, 1997-present.

(1) The American Professional Football Association (APFA) was formed in 1920 to standardize the rules of professional football. In 1922, the name was changed to the National Football League. (2) The most successful of 4 separate leagues called the "American Football League" (1926; 1936-37; 1940-41; 1960-69). Congress approved an NFL/AFL merger in 1966. Baltimore, Cleveland, and Pittsburgh agreed to join the 10 incoming AFL teams to form the American Football Conference. The NFL began play in 1970 with 26 teams. (3) The All-America Football Conference, 1946-49. In 1950, 3 of its teams joined the NFL (Baltimore, Cleveland, and San Francisco). The Baltimore franchise failed, but the NFL awarded the city a second one, also called the Colts, in 1953.

Pro Football Hall of Fame, Canton, Ohio
(Asterisks indicate 2009 inductees.)

Herb Adderley	Bill Dudley	Charlie Joiner	Bobby Mitchell	Jackie Smith
Troy Aikman	Glen "Turk" Edwards	David "Deacon" Jones	Ron Mix	John Stallworth
George Allen	Carl Eller	Stan Jones	Art Monk	Bart Starr
Marcus Allen	John Elway	Henry Jordan	Joe Montana	Roger Staubach
Lance Alworth	Weeb Ewbank	Sonny Jurgensen	Warren Moon	Ernie Stautner
Doug Atkins	Tom Fears	Jim Kelly	Lenny Moore	Jan Stenerud
Morris "Red" Badgro	Jim Finks	Leroy Kelly	Marion Motley	Dwight Stephenson
Lem Barney	Ray Flaherty	Walt Kiesling	Mike Munchak	Hank Stram
Cliff Battles	Len Ford	Frank "Bruiser" Kinard	Anthony Munoz	Ken Strong
Sammy Baugh	Dr. Daniel Fortmann	Paul Krause	George Musso	Joe Stydahar
Chuck Bednarik	Dan Fouts	Earl "Curly" Lambeau	Bronko Nagurski	Lynn Swann
Bert Bell	Benny Friedman	Jack Lambert	Joe Namath	Fran Tarkenton
Bobby Bell	Frank Gatski	Tom Landry	Earle "Greasy" Neale	Charley Taylor
Raymond Berry	Bill George	Dick "Night Train" Lane	Ernie Nevers	Jim Taylor
Elvin Bethea	Joe Gibbs	Jim Langer	Ozzie Newsome	Lawrence "LT" Taylor
Charles Bidwill	Frank Gifford	Willie Lanier	Ray Nitschke	Emmitt Thomas
Fred Biletnikoff	Sid Gillman	Steve Largent	Chuck Noll	*Derrick Thomas
George Blanda	Otto Graham	Yale Lary	Leo Nomellini	Thurman Thomas
Mel Blount	Red Grange	Dante Lavelli	Merlin Olsen	Jim Thorpe
Terry Bradshaw	Bud Grant	Bobby Layne	Jim Otto	Andre Tippett
Bob Brown	Darrell Green	Alphonse "Tuffy"	Steve Owen	Y. A. Tittle
Jim Brown	Joe Greene	Leemans	Alan Page	George Trafton
Paul Brown	Forrest Gregg	Marv Levy	Clarence "Ace" Parker	Charley Trippi
Roosevelt Brown	Bob Griese	Bob Lilly	Jim Parker	Emlen Tunnell
Willie Brown	Lou Groza	Larry Little	Walter Payton	Clyde "Bulldog" Turner
Buck Buchanan	Joe Guyon	James Lofton	Joe Perry	Johnny Unitas
Nick Buoniconti	George Halas	Vince Lombardi	Pete Pihos	Gene Upshaw
Dick Butkus	Jack Ham	Howie Long	Fritz Pollard	Norm Van Brocklin
Earl Campbell	Dan Hampton	Ronnie Lott	Hugh "Shorty" Ray	Steve Van Buren
Tony Canadeo	John Hannah	Sid Luckman	Dan Reeves	Doak Walker
Joe Carr	Franco Harris	Roy "Link" Lyman	Mel Renfro	Bill Walsh
Harry Carson	Mike Haynes	Tom Mack	John Riggins	Paul Warfield
Dave Casper	*Bob Hayes	John Mackey	Jim Ringo	Bob Waterfield
Guy Chamberlin	Ed Healey	John Madden	Andy Robustelli	Mike Webster
Jack Christiansen	Mel Hein	Tim Mara	Art Rooney	Arnie Weinmeister
Earl "Dutch" Clark	Ted Hendricks	Wellington Mara	Dan Rooney	Roger Wehrli
George Connor	Wilbur "Pete" Henry	Gino Marchetti	Pete Rozelle	Randy White
Jim Conzelman	Arnold Herber	Dan Marino	Bob St. Clair	Reggie White
Lou Creekmur	Bill Hewitt	George Preston	Barry Sanders	Dave Wilcox
Larry Csonka	Gene Hickerson	Marshall	Charlie Sanders	Bill Willis
Al Davis	Clarke Hinkle	Bruce Mathews	Gale Sayers	Larry Wilson
Willie Davis	Elroy "Crazylegs" Hirsch	Ollie Matson	Joe Schmidt	*Ralph Wilson Jr.
Len Dawson	Paul Hornung	Don Maynard	Tex Schramm	Kellen Winslow
Fred Dean	Ken Houston	George McAfee	Lee Roy Selmon	Alex Wojciechowicz
Joe DeLamielleure	Cal Hubbard	Mike McCormack	Billy Shaw	Willie Wood
Eric Dickerson	Sam Huff	*Randall McDaniel	Art Shell	*Rod Woodson
Dan Dierdorf	Lamar Hunt	Tommy McDonald	Don Shula	Rayfield Wright
Mike Ditka	Don Hutson	Hugh McElhenny	O. J. Simpson	Ron Yary
Art Donovan	Michael Irvin	Johnny "Blood" McNally	Mike Singletary	Steve Young
Tony Dorsett	Jimmy Johnson	Mike Michalske	Jackie Slater	Jack Youngblood
John "Paddy" Driscoll	John Henry Johnson	Wayne Millner	*Bruce Smith	Gary Zimmerman

BASEBALL

World Series 2009

Yankees Beat Defending Champion Phillies, 4 Games to 2

The New York Yankees returned to Major League Baseball's pinnacle for the first time in nearly a decade by beating the defending champion Philadelphia Phillies in six games. Designated hitter Hideki Matsui tied a World Series single-game record with six RBI in the Game 6 clincher at the new Yankee Stadium on Nov. 4, 2009. Matsui was voted World Series MVP after hitting .615 (8-for-13) with three home runs and eight RBI to lead the Yankees to their 27th world championship and first World Series victory since beating the New York Mets in 2000.

Andy Pettitte allowed just three runs over 5 2/3 innings in Game 6 to earn his second win of the series. The Yankees were the first team to use only three starting pitchers in a three-round postseason, relying on A. J. Burnett, Pettitte, and CC Sabathia.

Veteran shortstop Derek Jeter added three hits and two runs in the deciding game, and batted .407 in the series. Jeter has 50 career World Series hits, which ranks fifth on the all-time list. Jeter, Pettitte, and veteran teammates Mariano Rivera and Jorge Posada are all five-time World Series winners during their Yankee careers.

The Yankees pulled out a series victory despite an outstanding effort from Phillies second baseman Chase Utley, who tied Reggie Jackson's single World Series record with 5 home runs. Phillies lefthander Cliff Lee shut down the Yankees with a complete-game, 6-1 victory at Yankee Stadium in the opener. Lee was 4-0 in five postseason starts.

Game 1

October 28, 2009, at Yankee Stadium

	1	2	3	4	5	6	7	8	9	R	H	E
Philadelphia	0	0	1	0	0	1	0	2	2	6	9	1
NY Yankees	0	0	0	0	0	0	0	0	1	1	6	0

Winning Pitcher: Cliff Lee
Losing Pitcher: CC Sabathia
Attendance: 50,207

Game 1 of the World Series was a pitching duel between two former Cleveland teammates. Philadelphia lefthander Cliff Lee outdueled New York's CC Sabathia in the first-ever World Series game at the new Yankee Stadium. A pair of solo home runs by Chase Utley gave Lee all the offensive support he would need for the 6-1 win.

Lee, acquired from Cleveland in late July, allowed just six hits, struck out 10, and did not walk a batter, as he went the distance to record his third win of the postseason. He allowed an unearned run in the ninth inning and lowered his 2009 playoff ERA to a microscopic 0.54.

Sabathia, the MVP of the AL Championship Series, allowed just four hits and struck out six in seven innings in a losing effort. In the third inning, Sabathia gave up a two-out home run to Utley, who connected again with a towering shot to right field in the sixth. The Phillies second baseman set a major-league record by reaching base in his 26th consecutive postseason game, breaking the mark held by former Baltimore Orioles first baseman Boog Powell.

The Phillies scored a pair of insurance runs in the eighth on a two-run single by Raúl Ibáñez. They added two more in the ninth on a run-scoring single by Shane Victorino and an RBI double by Ryan Howard, his second double of the game. The Phillies six-run output in Game 1 exceeded the five total runs they scored when the Yankees swept them in four games in the 1950 World Series—the first and only other time the franchises had met in the postseason.

Shortstop Derek Jeter had three of the six hits for the Yankees, who lost their fourth straight World Series game dating back to 2003. Jeter also scored New York's lone run, snapping the team's streak of 16 consecutive scoreless innings in World Series play.

Game 2

October 29, 2009, at Yankee Stadium

	1	2	3	4	5	6	7	8	9	R	H	E
Philadelphia	0	1	0	0	0	0	0	0	0	1	6	0
NY Yankees	0	0	0	1	0	1	0	1	0	X	3	8	0

Winning Pitcher: A. J. Burnett
Losing Pitcher: Pedro Martínez
Save: Mariano Rivera (1)
Attendance: 50,181

A. J. Burnett pitched seven strong innings and future Hall of Famer Mariano Rivera came in to shut the door as the Yankees evened the series at one game apiece. Burnett allowed just four hits and struck out nine for his first career postseason win. Rivera entered the game in the eighth inning and held the Phils scoreless over the final two innings for his World Series-record tenth career save.

Burnett's performance overshadowed a solid effort in a losing cause by Phillies starter Pedro Martínez. The veteran righthander pitched into the seventh inning and allowed three runs and six hits while striking out eight. Martínez, who like Game 1 winner Cliff Lee had joined the Phillies in midseason, had pitched in six previous playoff games against the Yankees as a member of the Boston Red Sox. He brought a 6-2 career postseason record into the game, but fell to 1-3 in four playoff decisions against New York.

The Phillies took a 1-0 lead in the second inning on a single by Matt Stairs that scored Raúl Ibáñez, who had doubled. Yankee bats were silent until the fourth when Mark Teixeira delivered a solo home run to tie the game at 1-1. Hideki Matsui gave the Yanks their first lead of the series with a solo homer in the sixth. They added another run in the seventh on a pinch-hit RBI single by catcher Jorge Posada.

Each team's biggest slugger struggled in Game 2. Philadelphia first baseman Ryan Howard, the MVP of the NL Championship Series, received a "golden sombrero" by striking out in each of his four at-bats, giving him a total of six strikeouts in the first two games. Yankees third baseman Alex Rodriguez, who entered the World Series with a .438 playoff batting average in 2009, went 0-for-4 with three strikeouts for the second straight game.

Game 3

October 31, 2009, at Citizens Bank Park

	1	2	3	4	5	6	7	8	9	R	H	E
NY Yankees	0	0	0	2	3	1	1	1	0	8	8	1
Philadelphia	0	3	0	0	0	1	0	0	1	5	6	0

Winning Pitcher: Andy Pettitte
Losing Pitcher: Cole Hamels
Attendance: 46,061

Alex Rodriguez made his first World Series hit memorable. His two-run fourth-inning homer began a Yankee comeback that culminated in an 8-5 victory over the Phillies in Game 3 at Citizens Bank Park. Veteran lefthander Andy Pet-titte allowed four runs and struck out seven in six innings for the win, which gave New York a 2-1 series lead.

The Phillies struck first in a game that was delayed 80 minutes by rain. Jayson Werth led off the second inning with a home run, his first of two. Later in the inning, Jimmy Rollins added a bases-loaded walk and Shane Victorino hit an RBI sacrifice fly to give the Phils a 3-0 lead.

Phillies starter Cole Hamels was cruising until he walked Mark Teixeira with one out in the fourth inning. Rodriguez followed with a long drive to right field that was originally ruled a double. Yankees manager Joe Girardi asked the umpires to check the replay, which showed that the ball hit off the lens of a TV camera perched on the wall. After a short review, the umpires awarded Rodriguez a home run. It was the first video-reviewed home run in World Series history and it cut the Phillies' lead to 3-2.

An RBI single by Pettitte in the fifth inning tied the score at 3-3. He became the first Yankee pitcher to record a World Series RBI since Jim Bouton in Game 6 of the 1964 series. Johnny Damon put New York ahead with a two-run double off Hamels, who suffered the loss after allowing five runs in less than five innings of work.

Nick Swisher and Hideki Matsui clubbed solo home runs, Jorge Posada added a run-scoring single, and a quartet of relievers combined to preserve the Yankees' second straight win.

Game 4

November 1, 2009, at Citizens Bank Park

	1	2	3	4	5	6	7	8	9	R	H	E
NY Yankees	2	0	0	0	2	0	0	0	3	7	9	1
Philadelphia	1	0	0	1	0	0	1	1	0	4	8	1

Winning Pitcher: Joba Chamberlain
Losing Pitcher: Brad Lidge
Save: Mariano Rivera (2)
Attendance: 46,145

The New York Yankees had an answer for each of the Phillies' comeback attempts in Game 4. New York's last rally, a three-run outburst in the ninth inning, put the nail in a 7-4 victory.

Johnny Damon had three hits for the Yankees and scored the go-ahead run in the ninth inning to break a 4-4 tie. Phillies reliever Brad Lidge got two quick outs in the inning, but Damon delivered a single and then stole second and third on the same play. Mark Teixeira was then hit by a pitch, and Alex Rodriguez lined a double to left to score Damon. Jorge Posada followed with a two-run single that allowed Teixeira and Rodriguez to score.

Philadelphia had twice battled back to tie the game after the Yankees took a two-run lead. New York got on the board with a pair of runs in the first inning off of starter Joe Blanton. Derek Jeter scored on Teixeira's groundout, and Damon, who had doubled, scored on Posada's sacrifice fly. The Phillies got a run back in the bottom of the first on an RBI double by Chase Utley and tied the game at 2-2 in the fourth on a run-scoring single by Pedro Feliz.

New York took a 4-2 lead in the fifth inning when Jeter and Damon delivered RBI singles, but Chase Utley cut into the lead with a solo home run off CC Sabathia in the seventh inning. Feliz hit a solo homer off reliever Joba Chamberlain to tie the score at 4-4 in the bottom of the eighth.

Sabathia, who started on only three days' rest, gave up three runs in 6 2/3 innings. He left the game in the seventh after the home run by Utley—the third homer he had allowed to the Phillies second baseman in two World Series starts. Mariano Rivera pitched a perfect ninth inning for his second save of the series.

Game 5

November 2, 2009, at Citizens Bank Park

	1	2	3	4	5	6	7	8	9	R	H	E
NY Yankees	1	0	0	0	1	0	0	3	1	6	10	0
Philadelphia	3	0	3	0	0	0	2	0	X	8	9	0

Winning Pitcher: Cliff Lee
Losing Pitcher: A. J. Burnett
Save: Ryan Madson (1)
Attendance: 46,178

Chase Utley again feasted on Yankees pitching to lead the Phillies to an 8-6 victory in Game 5. The win cut the Yankees' lead down to three games to two. Utley smacked a three-run homer in the first inning to give Philadelphia a 3-1 lead and then added a solo shot in the seventh. Utley's five homers in the series tied him with Reggie Jackson in 1977 for the most home runs in a single World Series.

The Phillies added three runs in the bottom of the third off Yankees starter A. J. Burnett, who allowed six runs and four walks in just two-plus innings. Jayson Werth and Raúl Ibáñez had RBI singles in the inning, and Carlos Ruíz added a run-scoring fielder's choice groundout.

Cliff Lee earned his second win of the series and fourth of the postseason. Lee was not as effective as in his complete-game effort in Game 1, though he pitched into the eighth inning. The lefthander was charged with five runs on seven hits. Ibáñez followed Utley's seventh-inning home run with a solo blast of his own, but the Yankees chipped away at the Phils' 8-2 lead with three runs in the eighth. Alex Rodriguez keyed the rally with a two-run double and later scored on a sacrifice fly by Robinson Cano.

Ryan Madson earned a hard-fought save by inducing a double-play ground ball from Derek Jeter to thwart a potential rally in the ninth. The double play scored Jorge Posada, who had led off the inning with a double. After Johnny Damon singled, Madson struck out Mark Teixeira to end the threat and send the series back to the Bronx for Game 6.

Game 6

November 4, 2009, at Yankee Stadium

	1	2	3	4	5	6	7	8	9	R	H	E
Philadelphia	0	0	1	0	0	2	0	0	0	3	6	0
NY Yankees	0	2	2	0	3	0	0	0	X	7	8	0

Winning Pitcher: Andy Pettitte
Losing Pitcher: Pedro Martínez
Attendance: 50,315

Baseball is considered one of the ultimate team sports, but it was a one-man show that clinched the 2009 World Series for the New York Yankees. Hideki Matsui tied a World Series single-game record with six RBI as the Yankees dethroned the defending champion Philadelphia Phillies with a 7-3 win at Yankee Stadium. The victory gave New York its first World Series championship since 2000.

Matsui jumped on Phillies starter Pedro Martínez in the second inning with a two-run homer deep into the right-field stands. The Yankees designated hitter added a two-run single with the bases loaded in the third and capped his record-tying night with a two-run double in the fifth. His six RBI in Game 6 equaled the mark set by the Yankees' Bobby Richardson in Game 3 of the 1960 World Series.

Matsui did not start any of the three games in Philadelphia because the designated hitter position was not used. Yet he earned the World Series Most Valuable Player Award after collecting eight hits in 13 at bats, with three home runs and eight RBI.

Yankees starter Andy Pettitte pitched 5 2/3 innings, allowing three runs on four hits for his fourth win of the 2009 playoffs and record 18th career postseason victory. New York shortstop Derek Jeter had three hits and scored two runs in Game 6. Mariano Rivera did not record a save in the game but got the final five outs in his World Series-record 24th career pitching appearance.

MLB 2009: Ichiro Sets Hits Record; Buehrle Perfect; Phillies Return to World Series

Major League Baseball saw several milestones reached during the 2009 regular season. Seattle Mariners outfielder Ichiro Suzuki became the first player to record nine consecutive 200-hit seasons. Chicago White Sox left-hander Mark Buehrle pitched a perfect game July 23, 2009, besting the Tampa Bay Rays at U.S. Cellular Field in Chicago; he became the 18th player in Major League history, and the first since Randy Johnson (2004), to throw a perfect game. The 45-year-old Johnson earned his 300th career victory on June 4 in the San Francisco Giants' 5-1 win over the Washington Nationals.

For the second year in a row, the American League Central Division champion was decided in a one-game tiebreaker. The Minnesota Twins, who had won 17 of their last 21 games and erased a 3-game deficit with 4 games left, beat the Detroit Tigers in 12-innings Oct. 6 at the Metrodome in Minneapolis, MN. The New York Yankees opened their new stadium and led the majors with 103 victories, 244 home runs, and a $206 million payroll; they advanced to the ALCS with a 3-game sweep of the Minnesota Twins in the ALDS. The Los Angeles Angels of Anaheim won their third straight AL West title, and advanced to the ALCS with a 3-game sweep of the wild-card-winning Boston Red Sox in the AL Division Series.

New York Yankee Andy Pettitte earned his Major League-record-setting 16th postseason win in the Yankees' 5-2 victory over the Los Angeles Angels of Anaheim in Game 6 of their American League Championship Series on Oct. 25, 2009. The Yankees won their 40th AL pennant and reached the World Series for the first time since 2003. CC Sabathia, who had won 19 regular-season games, had added a pair of victories over the Angels in the ALCS for MVP honors.

Manager Joe Torre led the Dodgers to the best National League record (95-67) and the team's second straight NL West title, despite missing a top star for a portion of the season. Outfielder Manny Ramirez was suspended for 50 games in May for violating Major League Baseball's drug policy. The Dodgers beat the NL Central-champion Cardinals in 3 games in their NL Division Series.

Philadelphia notched a 93-69 record en route to its third straight NL East crown, then earned a second consecutive trip to the World Series with a five-game victory over the Los Angeles Dodgers in the National League Championship Series. Phillies first baseman Ryan Howard was named MVP of the NLCS with 2 home runs and 8 RBI as the Phillies eliminated the Dodgers for the second year in a row. In NLCS play, Phillies left-hander Cliff Lee, who had been acquired from the Cleveland Indians mid-season, struck out 10 in a pivotal, 11-0 victory over the Dodgers in Game 3. Lee had allowed just 2 earned runs in 2 starts in the Phillies NL Division Series win over Colorado. The Rockies, who had a 74-42 record under new manager Jim Tracy, won the NL Wild Card playoff slot; Colorado had fired manager Clint Hurdle in May after an 18-28 start to the season.

National League Final Standings, 2009

Eastern Division

	W	L	Pct.	GB	Home	Road	vs. East	vs. Central	vs. West	vs. AL
Philadelphia	93	69	.574	—	45-36	48-33	44-28	23-16	20-13	6-12
Florida.............	87	75	.537	6	43-38	44-37	42-30	18-21	17-16	10-8
Atlanta............	86	76	.531	7	40-41	46-35	41-31	20-20	18-17	7-8
NY Mets	70	92	.432	23	41-40	29-52	28-44	23-17	14-21	5-10
Washington.........	59	103	.364	34	33-48	26-55	25-47	16-27	11-18	7-11

Central Division

	W	L	Pct.	GB	Home	Road	vs. East	vs. Central	vs. West	vs. AL
St. Louis	91	71	.562	—	46-35	45-36	17-16	46-34	19-15	9-6
Chicago Cubs	83	78	.516	7.5	46-34	37-44	15-17	47-32	15-20	6-9
Milwaukee..........	80	82	.494	11	40-41	40-41	19-15	42-37	14-20	5-10
Cincinnati	78	84	.481	13	40-41	38-43	16-19	46-34	10-22	6-9
Houston............	74	88	.457	17	44-37	30-51	16-17	31-47	21-15	6-9
Pittsburgh	62	99	.385	28.5	40-41	22-58	18-16	24-52	12-24	8-7

Western Division

	W	L	Pct.	GB	Home	Road	vs. East	vs. Central	vs. West	vs. AL
L.A. Dodgers........	95	67	.586	—	50-31	45-36	18-13	22-19	46-26	9-9
Colorado*	92	70	.568	3	51-30	41-40	17-16	31-11	33-39	11-4
San Francisco.......	88	74	.543	7	52-29	36-45	19-16	22-18	38-34	9-6
San Diego..........	75	87	.463	20	42-39	33-48	16-16	21-22	33-39	5-10
Arizona	70	92	.432	25	36-45	34-47	15-19	20-21	30-42	5-10

*Wild Card team.

American League Final Standings, 2009

Eastern Division

	W	L	Pct.	GB	Home	Road	vs. East	vs. Central	vs. West	vs. NL
NY Yankees	103	59	.636	—	57-24	46-35	45-27	25-9	23-15	10-8
Boston*............	95	67	.586	8	56-25	39-42	45-27	26-12	13-21	11-7
Tampa Bay	84	78	.519	19	52-29	32-49	40-32	19-20	12-21	13-5
Toronto............	75	87	.463	28	44-37	31-50	26-46	23-15	19-15	7-11
Baltimore...........	64	98	.395	39	39-42	25-56	24-48	17-20	12-23	11-7

*Wild Card team.

Central Division

	W	L	Pct.	GB	Home	Road	vs. East	vs. Central	vs. West	vs. NL
Minnesota**.........	87	76	.534	—	49-33	38-43	10-22	46-27	19-21	12-6
Detroit.............	86	77	.528	1	51-30	35-47	15-21	39-34	22-14	10-8
Chicago White Sox ...	79	83	.488	7.5	43-38	36-45	18-21	34-38	15-18	12-6
Cleveland	65	97	.401	21.5	35-46	30-51	19-21	30-42	11-21	5-13
Kansas City.........	65	97	.401	21.5	33-48	32-49	14-25	32-40	11-22	8-10

**Defeated Detroit in a one-game playoff for the Central Division title, which is reflected in the final standings.

Western Division

	W	L	Pct.	GB	Home	Road	vs. East	vs. Central	vs. West	vs. NL
L.A. Angels	97	65	.599	—	49-32	48-33	26-17	27-17	30-27	14-4
Texas	87	75	.537	10	48-33	39-42	27-20	21-19	30-27	9-9
Seattle.............	85	77	.525	12	48-33	37-44	21-19	22-25	31-26	11-7
Oakland............	75	87	.463	22	40-41	35-46	21-23	26-17	23-34	5-13

National League Statistics, 2009

(Individual statistics: Batting—at least 150 at-bats; Pitching—at least 70 innings or 10 saves; *changed teams within NL during season; entry includes statistics for more than 1 team; #changed teams to or from AL during season; entry includes only NL stats.)

TEAM BATTING

Team	BA	AB	R	H	HR	RBI
Los Angeles Dodgers	.270	5592	780	1511	145	739
New York Mets	.270	5453	671	1472	95	631
Florida Marlins	.268	5572	772	1493	159	727
Atlanta Braves	.263	5539	735	1459	149	700
Milwaukee Brewers	.263	5510	785	1447	182	757
St. Louis Cardinals	.263	5465	730	1436	160	694
Colorado Rockies	.261	5398	804	1408	190	760
Houston Astros	.260	5436	643	1415	142	616
Philadelphia Phillies	.258	5578	820	1439	224	788
Washington Nationals	.258	5493	710	1416	156	685
San Francisco Giants	.257	5493	657	1411	122	612
Chicago Cubs	.255	5486	707	1398	161	678
Arizona Diamondbacks	.253	5565	720	1408	173	686
Pittsburgh Pirates	.252	5417	636	1364	125	612
Cincinnati Reds	.247	5462	673	1349	158	637
San Diego Padres	.242	5425	638	1315	141	605

TEAM PITCHING

Team	ERA	IP	H	SO	BB	SV
Los Angeles Dodgers	3.41	1473.1	1265	1272	584	44
San Francisco Giants	3.55	1446.0	1268	1302	584	41
Atlanta Braves	3.57	1462.2	1399	1232	530	38
St. Louis Cardinals	3.66	1440.2	1407	1049	460	43
Chicago Cubs	3.84	1445.1	1329	1272	586	40
Philadelphia Phillies	4.16	1455.2	1479	1153	489	44
Cincinnati Reds	4.18	1458.1	1420	1069	577	41
Colorado Rockies	4.22	1438.1	1427	1154	528	45
Florida Marlins	4.29	1446.1	1425	1248	601	45
San Diego Padres	4.37	1450.2	1422	1187	603	45
Arizona Diamondbacks	4.42	1447.2	1470	1158	525	36
New York Mets	4.45	1426.0	1452	1031	616	39
Houston Astros	4.54	1430.0	1521	1144	546	39
Pittsburgh Pirates	4.59	1418.1	1491	919	563	28
Milwaukee Brewers	4.83	1435.0	1498	1104	607	44
Washington Nationals	5.00	1424.1	1533	911	629	33

Arizona Diamondbacks

BATTERS	AVG	AB	R	H	HR	RBI	SO	SB
Justin Upton	.300	526	84	158	26	86	137	20
Miguel Montero	.294	425	61	125	16	59	78	1
Gerardo Parra	.290	455	59	132	5	60	89	5
Ryan Roberts	.279	305	41	85	7	25	55	7
Stephen Drew	.261	533	71	139	12	65	87	5
Mark Reynolds	.260	578	98	150	44	102	223	24
Augie Ojeda	.246	264	38	65	1	16	28	3
Chad Tracy	.237	257	29	61	8	39	38	1
Eric Byrnes	.226	239	26	54	8	31	30	9
Chris Young	.212	433	54	92	15	42	133	11
Chris Snyder	.200	165	20	33	6	22	47	0

PITCHERS	ERA	W	L	IP	H	BB	SO	SV
Dan Haren	3.14	14	10	229.1	192	38	223	0
Chad Qualls	3.63	2	2	52.0	53	7	45	24
Juan Gutierrez	4.06	4	3	71.0	67	30	66	9
Doug Davis	4.12	9	14	203.1	203	103	146	0
Max Scherzer	4.12	9	11	170.1	166	63	174	0
Yusmeiro Petit	5.82	3	10	89.2	102	34	74	0
Billy Buckner	6.40	4	6	77.1	94	29	64	0

Manager: Bob Melvin; A. J. Hinch

Atlanta Braves

BATTERS	AVG	AB	R	H	HR	RBI	SO	SB
Matt Diaz	.313	371	56	116	13	58	90	12
Martin Prado	.307	450	64	138	11	49	59	1
Omar Infante	.305	203	24	62	2	27	28	2
Yunel Escobar	.299	528	89	158	14	76	62	5
Casey Kotchman#	.282	298	28	84	6	41	28	0
Brian McCann	.281	488	63	137	21	94	83	4
Adam LaRoche*#	.278	536	76	149	24	80	140	2
Ryan Church*	.273	359	46	98	4	40	58	6
Garret Anderson	.268	496	52	133	13	61	73	1
Chipper Jones	.264	488	80	129	18	71	89	4
Nate McLouth*	.256	507	86	130	20	70	99	19
Kelly Johnson	.224	303	47	68	8	29	54	7
Jordan Schafer	.204	167	18	34	2	8	63	2

PITCHERS	ERA	W	L	IP	H	BB	SO	SV
Mike Gonzalez	2.42	5	4	74.1	56	33	90	10
Jair Jurrjens	2.60	14	10	215.0	186	75	152	0
Peter Moylan	2.84	6	2	73.0	65	35	61	0
Javier Vazquez	2.87	15	10	219.1	181	44	238	0
Tommy Hanson	2.89	11	4	127.2	105	46	116	0
Rafael Soriano	2.97	1	6	75.2	53	27	102	27
Kenshin Kawakami	3.86	7	12	156.1	153	57	105	1
Derek Lowe	4.67	15	10	194.2	232	63	111	0

Manager: Bobby Cox

Chicago Cubs

BATTERS	AVG	AB	R	H	HR	RBI	SO	SB
Aramis Ramirez	.317	306	46	97	15	65	43	2
Derrek Lee	.306	532	91	163	35	111	109	1
Jeff Baker*	.288	226	27	65	4	24	53	1
Ryan Theriot	.284	602	81	171	7	54	93	21
Jake Fox	.259	216	23	56	11	44	47	0
Kosuke Fukudome	.259	499	79	129	11	54	112	6
Milton Bradley	.257	393	61	101	12	40	95	2
Reed Johnson	.255	165	23	42	4	22	27	2
Alfonso Soriano	.241	477	64	115	20	55	118	9
Micah Hoffpauir	.239	234	28	56	10	35	46	1
Koyie Hill	.237	253	26	60	2	24	78	0
Mike Fontenot	.236	377	38	89	9	43	83	4
Geovany Soto	.218	331	27	72	11	47	77	1
Aaron Miles	.185	157	17	29	0	5	21	3

PITCHERS	ERA	W	L	IP	H	BB	SO	SV
Randy Wells	3.05	12	10	165.1	165	46	104	0
Ted Lilly	3.10	12	9	177.0	151	36	151	0
John Grabow*	3.36	3	0	72.1	62	40	57	0
Carlos Marmol	3.41	2	4	74.0	43	65	93	15
Ryan Dempster	3.65	11	9	200.0	196	65	172	0
Carlos Zambrano	3.77	9	7	169.1	155	78	152	0
Rich Harden	4.09	9	9	141.0	122	67	171	0
Aaron Heilman	4.11	4	4	72.1	68	34	65	1
Sean Marshall	4.32	3	7	85.1	91	32	68	0
Kevin Gregg	4.72	5	6	68.2	60	30	71	23

Manager: Lou Piniella

Cincinnati Reds

BATTERS	AVG	AB	R	H	HR	RBI	SO	SB
Joey Votto	.322	469	82	151	25	84	106	4
Brandon Phillips	.276	584	78	161	20	98	75	25
Chris Dickerson	.275	255	31	70	2	15	66	11
Jonny Gomes	.267	281	39	75	20	51	85	3
Drew Stubbs	.267	180	27	48	8	17	49	10
Ryan Hanigan	.263	251	22	66	3	11	31	0
Ramon Hernandez	.258	287	25	74	5	37	34	1
Jerry Hairston Jr.#	.254	307	47	78	8	27	46	7
Willy Taveras	.240	404	56	97	1	15	58	25
Laynce Nix	.239	309	42	74	15	46	81	0
Jay Bruce	.223	345	47	77	22	58	75	3
Adam Rosales	.213	230	23	49	4	19	46	1
Paul Janish	.211	256	36	54	1	16	40	2
Alex Gonzalez#	.210	243	16	51	3	26	36	0

PITCHERS	ERA	W	L	IP	H	BB	SO	SV
Francisco Cordero	2.16	2	6	66.2	58	30	58	39
Nick Masset	2.37	5	1	76.0	54	24	70	0
Bronson Arroyo	3.84	15	13	220.1	214	65	127	0
Aaron Harang	4.21	6	14	162.1	186	43	142	0
Johnny Cueto	4.41	11	11	171.1	172	61	132	0
Homer Bailey	4.53	8	5	113.1	115	52	86	0
Kip Wells*	5.33	2	5	72.2	60	40	43	2
Micah Owings	5.34	7	12	119.2	126	64	68	1

Manager: Dusty Baker

Colorado Rockies

BATTERS	AVG	AB	R	H	HR	RBI	SO	SB
Todd Helton	.325	544	79	177	15	86	73	0
Troy Tulowitzki	.297	543	101	161	32	92	112	20
Seth Smith	.293	335	61	98	15	55	67	4
Yorvit Torrealba	.291	213	27	62	2	31	42	1
Brad Hawpe	.285	501	82	143	23	86	145	1
Carlos Gonzalez	.284	278	53	79	13	29	70	16
Dexter Fowler	.266	433	73	115	4	34	116	27
Clint Barmes	.245	550	69	135	23	76	121	12
Ryan Spilborghs	.241	352	55	85	8	48	79	9
Chris Iannetta	.228	289	41	66	16	52	75	0
Ian Stewart	.228	425	74	97	25	70	138	7
Garrett Atkins	.226	354	37	80	9	48	58	0

PITCHERS	ERA	W	L	IP	H	BB	SO	SV
Huston Street	3.06	4	1	61.2	43	13	70	35
Ubaldo Jimenez	3.47	15	12	218.0	183	85	198	0
Jason Marquis	4.04	15	13	216.0	218	80	115	0
Aaron Cook	4.16	11	6	158.0	175	47	78	0
Jason Hammel	4.33	10	8	176.2	203	42	133	0
Jorge De La Rosa	4.38	16	9	185.0	172	83	193	0

Manager: Clint Hurdle; Jim Tracy

Florida Marlins

BATTERS	AVG	AB	R	H	HR	RBI	SO	SB
Hanley Ramirez	.342	576	101	197	24	106	101	27
Chris Coghlan	.321	504	84	162	9	47	77	8
Nick Johnson*	.291	457	71	133	8	62	84	2
Jorge Cantu	.289	585	67	169	16	100	81	3
Ronny Paulino	.272	239	24	65	8	27	48	1
Wes Helms	.271	214	18	58	3	33	54	1
John Baker	.271	373	59	101	9	50	89	0
Cody Ross	.270	559	73	151	24	90	122	5
Ross Gload	.261	230	33	60	6	30	30	0
Jeremy Hermida	.259	429	48	111	13	47	101	5
Emilio Bonifacio	.252	461	72	116	1	27	95	21
Cameron Maybin	.250	176	30	44	4	13	51	1
Dan Uggla	.243	564	84	137	31	90	150	2

PITCHERS	ERA	W	L	IP	H	BB	SO	SV
Josh Johnson	3.23	15	5	209.0	184	58	191	0
Burke Badenhop	3.75	7	4	72.0	71	24	57	0
Anibal Sanchez	3.87	4	8	86.0	84	46	71	0
Leo Nunez	4.06	4	6	68.2	59	27	60	26
Sean West	4.79	8	6	103.1	115	44	70	0
Andrew Miller	4.84	3	5	80.0	85	43	59	0
Ricky Nolasco	5.06	13	9	185.0	188	44	195	0
Chris Volstad	5.21	9	13	159.0	169	59	107	0
Matt Lindstrom	5.89	2	1	47.1	54	24	39	15

Manager: Fredi Gonzalez

Houston Astros

BATTERS	AVG	AB	R	H	HR	RBI	SO	SB
Miguel Tejada	.313	635	83	199	14	86	48	5
Carlos Lee	.300	610	65	183	26	102	51	5
Michael Bourn	.285	606	97	173	3	35	140	61
Hunter Pence	.282	585	76	165	25	72	109	14
Lance Berkman	.274	460	73	126	25	80	98	7
Jeff Keppinger	.256	305	35	78	7	29	33	0
Ivan Rodriguez#	.251	327	41	82	8	34	74	0
Kazuo Matsui	.250	476	56	119	9	46	85	19
Geoff Blum	.247	381	34	94	10	49	61	0
Humberto Quintero	.236	157	11	37	4	14	41	0
Chris Coste*	.224	205	15	46	2	18	55	0

PITCHERS	ERA	W	L	IP	H	BB	SO	SV
LaTroy Hawkins	2.13	1	4	63.1	60	16	45	11
Jose Valverde	2.33	4	2	54.0	40	21	56	25
Wandy Rodriguez	3.02	14	12	205.2	192	63	193	0
Jeff Fulchino	3.40	6	4	82.0	70	27	71	0
Roy Oswalt	4.12	8	6	181.1	183	44	138	0
Mike Hampton	5.30	7	10	112.0	128	46	74	0
Brian Moehler	5.47	8	12	154.2	187	51	91	0
Russ Ortiz	5.57	3	6	85.2	95	48	65	0
Felipe Paulino	6.27	3	11	97.2	126	37	93	0

Manager: Cecil Cooper; Dave Clark

Los Angeles Dodgers

BATTERS	AVG	AB	R	H	HR	RBI	SO	SB
Juan Pierre	.308	380	57	117	0	31	27	30
Matt Kemp	.297	606	97	180	26	101	139	34
Manny Ramirez	.290	352	62	102	19	63	81	0
Orlando Hudson	.283	551	74	156	9	62	99	8
James Loney	.281	576	73	162	13	90	68	7
Casey Blake	.280	485	84	136	18	79	116	3
Ronnie Belliard*	.277	264	39	73	10	39	56	3
Andre Ethier	.272	596	92	162	31	106	116	6
Rafael Furcal	.269	613	92	165	9	47	89	12
Russell Martin	.250	505	63	126	7	53	80	11
Mark Loretta	.232	181	19	42	0	25	21	1

PITCHERS	ERA	W	L	IP	H	BB	SO	SV
Ronald Belisario	2.04	4	3	70.2	52	29	64	0
Jonathan Broxton	2.61	7	2	76.0	44	29	114	36
Ramon Troncoso	2.72	5	4	82.2	83	34	55	6
Clayton Kershaw	2.79	8	8	171.0	119	91	185	0
Randy Wolf	3.23	11	7	214.1	178	58	160	0
Jeff Weaver	3.65	6	4	79.0	87	33	64	0
Hiroki Kuroda	3.76	8	7	117.1	110	24	87	0
Jon Garland*	4.01	11	13	204.0	225	61	109	0
Chad Billingsley	4.03	12	11	196.1	173	86	179	0

Manager: Joe Torre

Milwaukee Brewers

BATTERS	AVG	AB	R	H	HR	RBI	SO	SB
Ryan Braun	.320	635	113	203	32	114	121	20
Felipe Lopez*	.310	604	88	187	9	57	100	6
Casey McGehee	.301	355	58	107	16	66	67	0
Prince Fielder	.299	591	103	177	46	141	138	2
Craig Counsell	.285	404	61	115	4	39	54	3
Corey Hart	.260	419	64	109	12	48	92	11
Mike Cameron	.250	544	78	136	24	70	156	7
Jason Kendall	.241	452	48	109	2	43	58	7
Jody Gerut*	.230	274	40	63	9	35	43	6
J. J. Hardy	.229	414	53	95	11	47	85	0
Bill Hall#	.201	214	22	43	6	24	72	1

PITCHERS	ERA	W	L	IP	H	BB	SO	SV
Trevor Hoffman	1.83	3	2	54.0	35	14	48	37
Todd Coffey	2.90	4	4	83.2	76	21	65	2
Yovani Gallardo	3.73	13	12	185.2	150	94	204	0
Braden Looper	5.22	14	7	194.2	226	64	100	0
Jeff Suppan	5.29	7	12	161.2	200	74	80	0
Carlos Villanueva	5.34	4	10	96.0	102	35	83	3
Manny Parra	6.36	11	11	140.0	179	77	116	0
Dave Bush	6.38	5	9	114.1	131	37	89	0

Manager: Ken Macha

New York Mets

BATTERS	AVG	AB	R	H	HR	RBI	SO	SB
Carlos Beltran	.325	308	50	100	10	48	43	11
David Wright	.307	535	88	164	10	72	140	27
Angel Pagan	.306	343	54	105	6	32	56	14
Luis Castillo	.302	486	77	147	1	40	58	20
Fernando Tatis	.282	340	42	96	8	48	54	4
Jeff Francoeur*	.280	593	72	166	15	76	92	6
Gary Sheffield	.276	268	44	74	10	43	46	2
Daniel Murphy	.266	508	60	135	12	63	69	4
Omir Santos	.260	281	28	73	7	40	44	0
Anderson Hernandez*	.251	366	39	92	3	37	63	7
Alex Cora	.251	271	31	68	1	18	28	8
Jeremy Reed	.242	161	9	39	0	9	36	0
Brian Schneider	.218	170	11	37	3	24	21	0

PITCHERS	ERA	W	L	IP	H	BB	SO	SV
Johan Santana	3.13	13	9	166.2	156	46	146	0
Francisco Rodriguez	3.71	3	6	68.0	51	38	73	35
Brian Stokes	3.97	2	4	70.1	72	38	45	0
Nelson Figueroa	4.09	3	8	70.1	80	24	59	0
John Maine	4.43	7	6	81.1	67	38	55	0
Mike Pelfrey	5.03	10	12	184.1	213	66	107	0
Tim Redding	5.10	3	6	120.0	122	50	76	0
Bobby Parnell	5.30	4	8	88.1	101	46	74	1

Manager: Jerry Manuel

Philadelphia Phillies

BATTERS	AVG	AB	R	H	HR	RBI	SO	SB
Shane Victorino.....	.292	620	102	181	10	62	71	25
Chase Utley	.282	571	112	161	31	93	110	23
Ryan Howard	.279	616	105	172	45	141	186	8
Raul Ibanez........	.272	500	93	136	34	93	119	4
Jayson Werth	.268	571	98	153	36	99	156	20
Pedro Feliz	.266	580	62	154	12	82	68	0
Carlos Ruiz	.255	322	32	82	9	43	39	3
Jimmy Rollins	.250	672	100	168	21	77	70	31
Greg Dobbs........	.247	154	15	38	5	20	29	1

PITCHERS	ERA	W	L	IP	H	BB	SO	SV
J. A. Happ........	2.93	12	4	166.0	149	56	119	0
Ryan Madson	3.26	5	5	77.1	73	22	78	10
Cliff Lee#.........	3.39	7	4	79.2	80	10	74	0
Joe Blanton........	4.05	12	8	195.1	198	59	163	0
Cole Hamels	4.32	10	11	193.2	206	43	168	0
Chan Ho Park	4.43	3	3	83.1	84	33	73	0
Brett Myers	4.84	4	3	70.2	74	23	50	0
Jamie Moyer	4.94	12	10	162	177	43	94	0
Brad Lidge........	7.21	0	8	58.2	72	34	61	31
Manager: Charlie Manuel								

Pittsburgh Pirates

BATTERS	AVG	AB	R	H	HR	RBI	SO	SB
Garrett Jones	.293	314	45	92	21	44	76	10
Andrew McCutchen..	.286	433	74	124	12	54	83	22
Lastings Milledge*...	.279	244	21	68	4	21	47	7
Jack Wilson#.......	.267	266	26	71	4	31	31	2
Delwyn Young	.266	354	40	94	7	43	90	2
Ronny Cedeno#	.258	155	17	40	5	21	29	2
Andy LaRoche	.258	524	64	135	12	64	84	3
Jason Jaramillo	.252	206	20	52	3	26	33	1
Ryan Doumit	.250	280	31	70	10	38	49	4
Brandon Moss......	.236	385	47	91	7	41	84	1
Ramon Vazquez	.230	204	17	47	1	16	47	1
Steve Pearce.......	.206	165	19	34	4	16	43	1

PITCHERS	ERA	W	L	IP	H	BB	SO	SV
Ross Ohlendorf.....	3.92	11	10	176.2	165	53	109	0
Zach Duke.........	4.06	11	16	213.0	231	49	106	0
Paul Maholm.......	4.44	8	9	194.2	221	60	119	0
Charlie Morton	4.55	5	9	97.0	102	40	62	0
Ian Snell#	5.36	2	8	80.2	87	44	52	0
Jeff Karstens	5.42	4	6	108.0	115	45	52	0
Kevin Hart*	5.44	4	9	81.0	97	44	52	0
Matt Capps	5.80	4	8	54.1	73	17	46	27
Manager: John Russell								

St. Louis Cardinals

BATTERS	AVG	AB	R	H	HR	RBI	SO	SB
Matt Holliday#......	.353	235	42	83	13	55	43	2
Albert Pujols	.327	568	124	186	47	135	64	16
Skip Schumaker	.303	532	85	161	4	35	69	2
Yadier Molina	.293	481	45	141	6	54	39	9
Brendan Ryan	.292	390	55	114	3	37	56	14
Ryan Ludwick	.265	486	63	129	22	97	106	4
Colby Rasmus	.251	474	72	119	16	52	95	3
Rick Ankiel	.231	372	50	86	11	38	99	4
Mark DeRosa#	.228	237	31	54	10	28	58	2
Chris Duncan	.227	260	25	59	5	32	67	0
Joe Thurston.......	.225	267	27	60	1	25	56	4
Khalil Greene	.200	170	21	34	6	24	35	2

PITCHERS	ERA	W	L	IP	H	BB	SO	SV
Ryan Franklin	1.92	4	3	61.0	49	24	44	38
Chris Carpenter	2.24	17	4	192.2	156	38	144	0
Adam Wainwright ...	2.63	19	8	233.0	216	66	212	0
Joel Pineiro	3.49	15	12	214.0	218	27	105	0
Kyle Lohse	4.74	6	10	117.2	125	36	77	0
Brad Thompson	4.84	2	6	80.0	85	23	34	0
Todd Wellemeyer ...	5.89	7	10	122.1	160	57	78	0
Manager: Tony La Russa								

San Diego Padres

BATTERS	AVG	AB	R	H	HR	RBI	SO	SB
Scott Hairston#	.299	197	26	59	10	29	45	8
Adrian Gonzalez ...	.277	552	90	153	40	99	109	1
Tony Gwynn.......	.270	393	59	106	2	21	65	11
Chase Headley	.262	543	62	142	12	64	133	10
David Eckstein.....	.260	503	64	131	2	51	46	3
Will Venable......	.256	293	38	75	12	38	89	6
Kevin Kouzmanoff ..	.255	529	50	135	18	88	106	1
Everth Cabrera	.255	377	59	96	2	31	88	25
Nick Hundley	.238	256	23	61	8	30	76	5
Henry Blanco......	.235	204	21	48	6	16	50	0
Edgar Gonzalez....	.216	153	16	33	4	18	36	1
Luis Rodriguez.....	.202	208	18	42	2	16	23	1
Brian Giles	.191	225	18	43	2	23	31	1

PITCHERS	ERA	W	L	IP	H	BB	SO	SV
Heath Bell	2.71	6	4	69.2	54	24	79	42
Luke Gregerson....	3.24	2	4	75.0	62	31	93	1
Tim Stauffer.......	3.58	4	7	73.0	71	34	53	0
Kevin Correia......	3.91	12	11	198.0	194	64	142	0
Edward Mujica.....	3.94	3	5	93.2	101	19	76	2
Jake Peavy#.......	3.97	6	6	81.2	69	28	92	0
Chad Gaudin#	5.13	4	10	105.1	105	56	105	0
Chris Young	5.21	4	6	76.0	70	40	50	0
Josh Geer	5.96	1	7	102.2	116	23	54	0
Manager: Bud Black								

San Francisco Giants

BATTERS	AVG	AB	R	H	HR	RBI	SO	SB
Pablo Sandoval	.330	572	79	189	25	90	83	5
Freddy Sanchez* ...	.293	457	56	134	7	41	76	5
Juan Uribe	.289	398	50	115	16	55	82	3
Andres Torres	.270	152	30	41	6	23	45	6
Nate Schierholtz ...	.267	285	33	76	5	29	58	3
Eugenio Velez	.267	285	40	76	5	31	55	11
Bengie Molina	.265	491	52	130	20	80	68	0
Randy Winn	.262	538	65	141	2	51	93	16
Travis Ishikawa....	.261	326	49	85	9	39	89	2
Aaron Rowand.....	.261	499	61	130	15	64	125	4
Fred Lewis	.258	295	49	76	4	20	84	8
Edgar Renteria.....	.250	460	50	115	5	48	69	7
Emmanuel Burriss ..	.238	202	18	48	0	13	34	11

PITCHERS	ERA	W	L	IP	H	BB	SO	SV
Tim Lincecum	2.48	15	7	225.1	168	68	261	0
Brian Wilson.......	2.74	5	6	72.1	60	27	83	38
Matt Cain.........	2.89	14	8	217.2	184	73	171	0
Barry Zito........	4.03	10	13	192.0	179	81	154	0
Jonathan Sanchez..	4.24	8	12	163.1	135	88	177	0
Randy Johnson	4.88	8	6	96.0	97	31	86	0
Manager: Bruce Bochy								

Washington Nationals

BATTERS	AVG	AB	R	H	HR	RBI	SO	SB
Nyjer Morgan*	.307	469	74	144	3	39	74	42
Ryan Zimmerman ..	.292	610	110	178	33	106	119	2
Cristian Guzman ...	.284	531	74	151	6	52	75	4
Adam Dunn	.267	546	81	146	38	105	177	0
Alberto Gonzalez...	.265	291	30	77	1	33	27	1
Josh Willingham.....	.260	427	70	111	24	61	104	4
Wil Nieves........	.259	224	20	58	1	26	45	1
Elijah Dukes.......	.250	364	38	91	8	58	74	3
Willie Harris	.235	323	47	76	7	27	62	11
Josh Bard........	.230	274	20	63	6	31	50	0
Austin Kearns......	.195	174	20	34	3	17	51	1

PITCHERS	ERA	W	L	IP	H	BB	SO	SV
Mike MacDougal# ..	3.60	1	1	50.0	45	31	31	20
John Lannan	3.88	9	13	206.1	210	68	89	0
J. D. Martin........	4.44	5	4	77.0	85	24	37	0
Jordan Zimmermann	4.63	3	5	91.1	95	29	92	0
Ross Detwiler......	5.00	1	6	75.2	87	33	43	0
Craig Stammen	5.11	4	7	105.2	112	24	48	0
Shairon Martis	5.25	5	3	85.2	83	39	34	0
Livan Hernandez* ..	5.44	9	12	183.2	220	67	102	0
Garrett Mock	5.62	3	10	91.1	114	44	72	0
Manager: Manny Acta; Jim Riggleman								

American League Team Statistics, 2009

(Individual statistics: Batting—at least 150 at-bats; Pitching—at least 70 innings or 10 saves; *changed teams within AL during season; entry includes statistics for more than 1 team; #changed teams to or from NL during season; entry includes only AL stats.)

TEAM BATTING

Team	BA	AB	R	H	HR	RBI
Los Angeles Angels . . .	.285	5622	883	1604	173	841
New York Yankees	.283	5660	915	1604	244	881
Minnesota Twins.	.274	5608	817	1539	172	770
Boston Red Sox	.270	5543	872	1495	212	822
Baltimore Orioles	.268	5618	741	1508	160	708
Toronto Blue Jays.	.266	5696	798	1516	209	766
Cleveland Indians.	.264	5568	773	1468	161	730
Tampa Bay Rays	.263	5462	803	1434	199	765
Oakland Athletics	.262	5584	759	1464	135	723
Detroit Tigers	.260	5540	743	1443	183	718
Texas Rangers	.260	5526	784	1436	224	748
Kansas City Royals . . .	.259	5532	686	1432	144	657
Chicago White Sox. . . .	.258	5463	724	1410	184	695
Seattle Mariners.	.258	5543	640	1430	160	613

TEAM PITCHING

Team	ERA	IP	H	SO	BB	SV
Seattle Mariners	3.87	1452.2	1359	1043	534	49
Chicago White Sox . . .	4.14	1439.2	1438	1119	507	36
Oakland Athletics	4.26	1447.1	1486	1124	523	38
New York Yankees	4.26	1450.0	1386	1260	574	51
Detroit Tigers.	4.29	1447.0	1449	1102	594	42
Tampa Bay Rays	4.33	1427.1	1421	1125	515	41
Boston Red Sox.	4.35	1436.2	1494	1230	530	41
Texas Rangers.	4.38	1434.2	1432	1016	531	45
Los Angeles Angels. . .	4.45	1445.0	1513	1062	523	51
Toronto Blue Jays	4.47	1451.0	1509	1181	551	25
Minnesota Twins	4.50	1453.0	1542	1052	466	48
Kansas City Royals . . .	4.83	1426.0	1486	1153	600	34
Cleveland Indians	5.06	1434.0	1570	986	598	25
Baltimore Orioles	5.15	1429.0	1633	933	546	31

Baltimore Orioles

BATTERS	AVG	AB	R	H	HR	RBI	SO	SB
Nick Markakis	.293	642	94	188	18	101	98	6
Matt Wieters	.288	354	35	102	9	43	86	0
Brian Roberts	.283	632	110	179	16	79	112	30
Nolan Reimold.	.279	358	49	100	15	45	77	8
Adam Jones	.277	473	83	131	19	70	93	10
Ty Wigginton	.273	410	44	112	11	41	57	1
Felix Pie.	.266	252	38	67	9	29	58	1
Melvin Mora.	.260	450	44	117	8	48	60	3
Luke Scott	.258	449	61	116	25	77	104	0
Cesar Izturis	.256	387	34	99	2	30	38	12
Robert Andino	.222	198	31	44	2	10	47	3

PITCHERS	ERA	W	L	IP	H	BB	SO	SV
George Sherrill	2.40	0	1	41.1	34	13	39	20
Brad Bergesen	3.43	7	5	123.1	126	32	65	0
Danys Baez.	4.02	4	6	71.2	59	22	40	0
Jim Johnson	4.11	4	6	70.0	73	23	49	10
Mark Hendrickson . . .	4.37	6	5	105.0	116	33	61	1
Brian Bass.	4.90	5	3	86.1	106	44	54	0
Jeremy Guthrie	5.04	10	17	200.0	224	60	110	0
David Hernandez	5.42	4	10	101.1	118	46	68	0
Jason Berken	6.54	6	12	119.2	164	44	66	0

Manager: David Trembley

Boston Red Sox

BATTERS	AVG	AB	R	H	HR	RBI	SO	SB
Kevin Youkilis.	.305	491	99	150	27	94	125	7
Victor Martinez*	.303	588	88	178	23	108	74	1
Jacoby Ellsbury	.301	624	94	188	8	60	74	70
Dustin Pedroia.	.296	626	115	185	15	72	45	20
Mike Lowell	.290	445	54	129	17	75	61	2
J. D. Drew	.279	452	84	126	24	68	109	2
Jason Bay	.267	531	103	142	36	119	162	13
Rocco Baldelli	.253	150	23	38	7	23	37	1
David Ortiz	.238	541	77	129	28	99	134	0
Brian Anderson*	.243	202	32	49	4	18	54	3
Nick Green	.236	276	35	65	6	35	69	1
Jason Varitek.	.209	364	41	76	14	51	90	0

PITCHERS	ERA	W	L	IP	H	BB	SO	SV
Jonathan Papelbon . .	1.85	1	1	68.0	54	24	76	38
Jon Lester	3.41	15	8	203.1	186	64	225	0
Josh Beckett	3.86	17	6	212.1	198	55	199	0
Clay Buchholz	4.21	7	4	92.0	91	36	68	0
Tim Wakefield	4.58	11	5	129.2	137	50	72	0
Brad Penny#	5.61	7	8	131.2	160	42	89	0

Manager: Terry Francona

Chicago White Sox

BATTERS	AVG	AB	R	H	HR	RBI	SO	SB
Scott Podsednik. . . .	.304	537	75	163	7	48	74	30
A. J. Pierzynski	.300	504	57	151	13	49	52	1
Mark Kotsay*	.278	187	16	52	4	23	21	3
Alexei Ramirez.	.277	542	71	150	15	68	66	14
Paul Konerko	.277	546	75	151	28	88	89	1
Gordon Beckham . . .	.270	378	58	102	14	63	65	7
Chris Getz	.261	375	49	98	2	31	54	25
Jermaine Dye.	.250	503	78	126	27	81	108	0
Jim Thome#	.249	345	55	86	23	74	116	0
Alex Rios*	.247	582	63	144	17	71	107	24
Carlos Quentin.	.236	351	47	83	21	56	52	3
Jayson Nix	.224	255	36	57	12	32	64	10
Josh Fields.	.222	239	29	53	7	30	76	2

PITCHERS	ERA	W	L	IP	H	BB	SO	SV
Matt Thornton	2.74	6	3	72.1	58	20	87	4
Bobby Jenks	3.71	3	4	53.1	52	16	49	29
D. J. Carrasco	3.76	5	1	93.1	103	29	62	0
John Danks	3.77	13	11	200.1	184	73	149	0
Mark Buehrle	3.84	13	10	213.1	222	45	105	0
Gavin Floyd	4.06	11	11	193.0	178	59	163	0
Clayton Richard# . . .	4.65	4	3	89.0	94	37	66	0
Jose Contreras#. . . .	5.42	5	13	114.2	121	45	89	0

Manager: Ozzie Guillen

Cleveland Indians

BATTERS	AVG	AB	R	H	HR	RBI	SO	SB
Asdrubal Cabrera. . .	.308	523	81	161	6	68	89	17
Shin-Soo Choo.	.300	583	87	175	20	86	151	21
Ryan Garko#	.285	239	29	68	11	39	40	0
Jamey Carroll.	.276	315	53	87	2	26	63	4
Travis Hafner	.272	338	46	92	16	49	67	0
Mark DeRosa#.	.270	278	47	75	13	50	63	1
Jhonny Peralta	.254	582	57	148	11	83	134	0
Matt LaPorta	.254	181	29	46	7	21	37	2
Ben Francisco#	.250	308	48	77	10	33	59	13
Luis Valbuena.	.250	368	52	92	10	31	83	2
Grady Sizemore	.248	436	73	108	18	64	92	13
Trevor Crowe	.235	183	22	43	1	17	39	6
Andy Marte	.232	155	20	36	6	25	30	0
Kelly Shoppach	.214	271	33	58	12	40	98	0

PITCHERS	ERA	W	L	IP	H	BB	SO	SV
Cliff Lee#	3.14	7	9	152.0	165	33	107	0
Kerry Wood	4.25	3	3	55.0	48	28	63	20
Aaron Laffey.	4.44	7	9	121.2	140	57	59	1
Justin Masterson* . . .	4.52	4	10	129.1	128	60	119	0
Jeremy Sowers	5.25	6	11	123.1	134	52	51	0
David Huff	5.61	11	8	128.1	159	41	65	0
Tomo Ohka.	5.96	1	5	71.0	77	19	31	0
Fausto Carmona . . .	6.32	5	12	125.1	151	70	79	0

Manager: Eric Wedge

Detroit Tigers

BATTERS	AVG	AB	R	H	HR	RBI	SO	SB
Miguel Cabrera	.324	611	96	198	34	103	107	6
Magglio Ordonez. . . .	.310	465	54	144	9	50	65	3
Ryan Raburn.	.291	261	44	76	16	45	60	5
Placido Polanco	.285	618	82	176	10	72	46	7
Ramon Santiago	.267	262	29	70	7	35	57	1
Marcus Thames	.252	258	33	65	13	36	72	0
Curtis Granderson . .	.249	631	91	157	30	71	141	20
Carlos Guillen	.242	277	36	67	11	41	56	1
Aubrey Huff*	.241	536	59	129	15	85	87	0
Clete Thomas	.240	275	46	66	7	39	77	3
Adam Everett	.238	345	43	82	3	44	61	5
Brandon Inge	.230	562	71	129	27	84	170	2
Gerald Laird	.225	413	49	93	4	33	68	5

PITCHERS	ERA	W	L	IP	H	BB	SO	SV
Brandon Lyon	2.86	6	5	78.2	56	31	57	3
Justin Verlander	3.45	19	9	240.0	219	63	269	0
Edwin Jackson	3.62	13	9	214.0	200	70	161	0
Jarrod Washburn* . . .	3.78	9	9	176.0	160	49	100	0
Rick Porcello	3.96	14	9	170.2	176	52	89	0
Zach Miner	4.29	7	5	92.1	101	45	62	1
Fernando Rodney . . .	4.40	2	5	75.2	70	41	61	37
Armando Galarraga .	5.64	6	10	143.2	158	67	95	0

Manager: Jim Leyland

Kansas City Royals

BATTERS	AVG	AB	R	H	HR	RBI	SO	SB
Billy Butler.	.301	608	78	183	21	93	103	1
Alberto Callaspo	.300	576	79	173	11	73	51	2
David DeJesus	.281	558	74	157	13	71	87	4
Brayan Pena	.273	165	17	45	6	18	18	0
Mark Teahen.	.271	524	69	142	12	50	123	8
Willie Bloomquist. . . .	.265	434	52	115	4	29	73	25
Miguel Olivo	.249	390	51	97	23	65	126	5
John Buck	.247	186	16	46	8	36	55	1
Yuniesky Betancourt*	.245	470	40	115	6	49	44	3
Mitch Maier	.243	341	42	83	3	31	76	9
Jose Guillen	.242	281	30	68	9	40	50	1
Josh Anderson*.	.240	283	42	68	1	24	43	25
Alex Gordon	.232	164	28	38	6	22	43	5
Mike Jacobs	.228	434	46	99	19	61	132	0
Coco Crisp	.228	180	30	41	3	14	23	13

PITCHERS	ERA	W	L	IP	H	BB	SO	SV
Zack Greinke.	2.16	16	8	229.1	195	51	242	0
Joakim Soria.	2.21	3	2	53.0	44	16	69	30
Robinson Tejeda	3.54	4	2	73.2	43	50	87	0
Jamey Wright	4.33	3	5	79.0	73	44	60	0
Brian Bannister	4.73	7	12	154.0	161	50	98	0
Gil Meche	5.09	6	10	129.0	144	58	95	0
Kyle Davies.	5.27	8	9	123.0	122	66	86	0
Luke Hochevar	6.55	7	13	143.0	167	46	106	0

Manager: Trey Hillman

Los Angeles Angels of Anaheim

BATTERS	AVG	AB	R	H	HR	RBI	SO	SB
Erick Aybar	.312	504	70	157	5	58	54	14
Kendry Morales.	.306	566	86	173	34	108	117	3
Maicer Izturis.	.300	387	74	116	8	65	41	13
Torii Hunter	.299	451	74	135	22	90	92	18
Chone Figgins.	.298	615	114	183	5	54	114	42
Vladimir Guerrero . . .	.295	383	59	113	15	50	56	2
Bobby Abreu	.293	563	96	165	15	103	113	30
Howie Kendrick	.291	374	61	109	10	61	71	11
Juan Rivera.	.287	529	72	152	25	88	57	0
Mike Napoli	.272	382	60	104	20	56	103	3
Gary Matthews Jr.. . .	.250	316	44	79	4	50	74	4
Jeff Mathis.	.211	237	26	50	5	28	73	2

PITCHERS	ERA	W	L	IP	H	BB	SO	SV
Darren Oliver	2.71	5	1	73.0	61	22	65	0
Jered Weaver.	3.75	16	8	211	196	66	174	0
John Lackey.	3.83	11	8	176.1	177	47	139	0
Brian Fuentes	3.93	1	5	55.0	53	24	46	48
Matt Palmer	3.93	11	2	121.1	105	55	69	0
Joe Saunders.	4.60	16	7	186.0	202	64	101	0
Scott Kazmir*.	4.89	10	9	147.1	149	60	117	0
Ervin Santana	5.03	8	8	139.2	159	47	107	0

Manager: Mike Scioscia

Minnesota Twins

BATTERS	AVG	AB	R	H	HR	RBI	SO	SB
Joe Mauer	.365	523	94	191	28	96	63	4
Denard Span	.311	578	97	180	8	68	89	23
Jason Kubel	.300	514	73	154	28	103	106	1
Orlando Cabrera*. . .	.284	656	83	186	9	77	71	13
Delmon Young	.284	395	50	112	12	60	92	2
Michael Cuddyer . . .	.276	588	93	162	32	94	118	6
Justin Morneau	.274	508	85	139	30	100	86	0
Brendan Harris.	.261	414	44	108	6	37	78	0
Matt Tolbert	.232	198	28	46	2	19	37	6
Carlos Gomez	.229	315	51	72	3	28	72	14
Nick Punto	.228	359	56	82	1	38	70	16
Joe Crede	.225	333	42	75	15	48	56	0
Alexi Casilla	.202	228	25	46	0	17	36	11

PITCHERS	ERA	W	L	IP	H	BB	SO	SV
Joe Nathan	2.10	2	2	68.2	42	22	89	47
Matt Guerrier	2.36	5	1	76.1	58	16	47	1
Brian Duensing	3.64	5	2	84.0	84	31	53	0
Nick Blackburn.	4.03	11	11	205.2	240	41	98	0
Scott Baker	4.37	15	9	200.0	190	48	162	0
Carl Pavano	4.64	5	4	73.2	85	16	59	0
Kevin Slowey	4.86	10	3	90.2	113	15	75	0
Carl Pavano*	5.10	14	12	199.1	235	39	147	0
Francisco Liriano . . .	5.80	5	13	136.2	147	65	122	0
Glen Perkins	5.89	6	7	96.1	120	23	45	0

Manager: Ron Gardenhire

New York Yankees

BATTERS	AVG	AB	R	H	HR	RBI	SO	SB
Derek Jeter	.334	634	107	212	18	66	90	30
Robinson Cano	.320	637	103	204	25	85	63	5
Mark Teixeira	.292	609	103	178	39	122	114	2
Alex Rodriguez	.286	444	78	127	30	100	97	14
Jorge Posada.	.285	383	55	109	22	81	101	1
Johnny Damon.	.282	550	107	155	24	82	98	12
Melky Cabrera	.274	485	66	133	13	68	59	10
Hideki Matsui	.274	456	62	125	28	90	75	0
Brett Gardner.	.270	248	48	67	3	23	40	26
Nick Swisher	.249	498	84	124	29	82	126	0

PITCHERS	ERA	W	L	IP	H	BB	SO	SV
Mariano Rivera	1.76	3	3	66.1	48	12	72	44
Phil Hughes	3.03	8	3	86.0	68	28	96	3
CC Sabathia	3.37	19	8	230.0	197	67	197	0
Alfredo Aceves.	3.54	10	1	84.0	69	16	69	1
A.J. Burnett	4.04	13	9	207.0	193	97	195	0
Andy Pettitte.	4.16	14	8	194.2	193	76	148	0
Joba Chamberlain . .	4.75	9	6	157.1	167	76	133	0

Manager: Joe Girardi

Oakland Athletics

BATTERS	AVG	AB	R	H	HR	RBI	SO	SB
Rajai Davis	.305	390	65	119	3	48	70	41
Ryan Sweeney	.293	484	68	142	6	53	67	6
Adam Kennedy	.289	529	65	153	11	63	86	20
Matt Holliday#	.286	346	52	99	11	54	58	12
Nomar Garciaparra . .	.281	160	17	45	3	16	28	2
Cliff Pennington	.279	208	27	58	4	21	46	7
Kurt Suzuki	.274	570	74	156	15	88	59	8
Daric Barton	.269	160	31	43	3	24	25	0
Mark Ellis	.263	377	52	99	10	61	54	10
Jack Cust	.240	513	88	123	25	70	185	4
Scott Hairston#	.236	233	24	55	7	35	38	3
Bobby Crosby	.223	238	35	53	6	29	44	2
Jason Giambi#	.193	269	39	52	11	40	72	0

PITCHERS	ERA	W	L	IP	H	BB	SO	SV
Andrew Bailey	1.84	6	3	83.1	49	24	91	26
Michael Wuertz	2.63	6	1	78.2	52	23	102	4
Brad Ziegler	3.07	2	4	73.1	82	28	54	7
Dallas Braden	3.89	8	9	136.2	144	42	81	0
Brett Anderson	4.06	11	11	175.1	180	45	150	0
Trevor Cahill	4.63	10	13	178.2	185	72	90	0
Vin Mazzaro	5.32	4	9	91.1	120	39	59	0
Gio Gonzalez	5.75	6	7	98.2	113	56	109	0

Manager: Bob Geren

Seattle Mariners

BATTERS	AVG	AB	R	H	HR	RBI	SO	SB
Ichiro Suzuki	.352	639	88	225	11	46	71	26
Franklin Gutierrez . . .	.283	565	85	160	18	70	122	16
Mike Sweeney	.281	242	25	68	8	34	31	0
Endy Chavez	.273	161	17	44	2	13	22	9
Jose Lopez	.272	613	69	167	25	96	69	3
Adrian Beltre	.265	449	54	119	8	44	74	13
Russell Branyan	.251	431	64	108	31	76	149	2
Kenji Johjima	.247	239	24	59	9	22	28	2
Ken Griffey Jr.	.214	387	44	83	19	57	80	0
Jack Hannahan*	.213	267	27	57	4	19	71	1
Rob Johnson	.213	258	21	55	2	27	60	1
Wladimir Balentien# . .	.213	155	18	33	4	13	43	1
Ronny Cedeno#	.167	186	15	31	5	17	50	3

PITCHERS	ERA	W	L	IP	H	BB	SO	SV
Felix Hernandez	2.49	19	5	238.2	200	71	217	0
David Aardsma	2.52	3	6	71.1	49	34	80	38
Erik Bedard	2.82	5	3	83.0	65	34	90	0
Mark Lowe	3.26	2	7	80.0	71	29	69	3
Ryan Rowland-Smith	3.74	5	4	96.1	87	27	52	0
Miguel Batista	4.04	7	4	71.1	79	39	52	1
Jason Vargas	4.91	3	6	91.2	98	24	54	0
Chris Jakubauskas . .	5.32	6	7	93.0	91	27	47	0
Garrett Olson	5.60	3	5	80.1	79	34	47	0

Manager: Don Wakamatsu

Tampa Bay Rays

BATTERS	AVG	AB	R	H	HR	RBI	SO	SB
Jason Bartlett	.320	500	90	160	14	66	89	30
Carl Crawford	.305	606	96	185	15	68	99	60
Ben Zobrist	.297	501	91	149	27	91	104	17
Akinori Iwamura	.290	231	28	67	1	22	44	9
Evan Longoria	.281	584	100	164	33	113	140	9
Gregg Zaun*	.260	262	34	68	8	27	48	0
Willy Aybar	.253	296	38	75	12	41	54	1
B. J. Upton	.241	560	79	135	11	55	152	42
Gabe Kapler	.239	205	26	49	8	32	39	5
Carlos Pena	.227	471	91	107	39	100	163	3
Gabe Gross	.227	282	31	64	6	36	79	6
Pat Burrell	.221	412	45	91	14	64	119	2
Dioner Navarro	.218	376	38	82	8	32	51	5

PITCHERS	ERA	W	L	IP	H	BB	SO	SV
J. P. Howell	2.84	7	5	66.2	47	33	79	17
Lance Cormier	3.26	3	3	77.1	75	25	36	2
Jeff Niemann	3.94	13	6	180.2	185	59	125	0
Matt Garza	3.95	8	12	203.0	177	79	189	0
James Shields	4.14	11	12	219.2	239	52	167	0
David Price	4.42	10	7	128.1	119	54	102	0
Andy Sonnanstine . .	6.77	6	9	99.2	131	34	60	0

Manager: Joe Maddon

Texas Rangers

BATTERS	AVG	AB	R	H	HR	RBI	SO	SB
Michael Young	.322	541	76	174	22	68	90	8
Julio Borbon	.312	157	30	49	4	20	28	19
Marlon Byrd	.283	547	66	155	20	89	98	8
David Murphy	.269	432	61	116	17	57	106	9
Josh Hamilton	.268	336	43	90	10	54	79	8
Elvis Andrus	.267	480	72	128	6	40	77	33
Omar Vizquel	.266	177	17	47	1	14	27	4
Nelson Cruz	.260	462	75	120	33	76	118	20
Ian Kinsler	.253	566	101	143	31	86	77	31
Chris Davis	.238	391	48	93	21	59	150	0
Hank Blalock	.234	462	62	108	25	66	108	2
Jarrod Saltalamacchia . .	.233	283	34	66	9	34	97	0
Taylor Teagarden . . .	.217	198	26	43	6	24	76	0
Andruw Jones	.214	281	43	60	17	43	72	5

PITCHERS	ERA	W	L	IP	H	BB	SO	SV
C. J. Wilson	2.81	5	6	73.2	66	32	84	14
Kevin Millwood	3.67	13	10	198.2	195	71	123	0
Frank Francisco	3.83	2	3	49.1	40	15	57	25
Scott Feldman	4.08	17	8	189.2	178	65	113	0
Tommy Hunter	4.10	9	6	112.0	113	33	64	0
Brandon McCarthy . .	4.62	7	4	97.1	96	36	65	0
Vicente Padilla#	4.92	8	6	108.0	120	42	59	0
Derek Holland	6.12	8	13	138.1	160	47	107	0

Manager: Ron Washington

Toronto Blue Jays

BATTERS	AVG	AB	R	H	HR	RBI	SO	SB
Scott Rolen#	.320	338	52	108	8	43	42	4
Adam Lind	.305	587	93	179	35	114	110	1
Aaron Hill	.286	682	103	195	36	108	98	6
Marco Scutaro	.282	574	100	162	12	60	75	14
Lyle Overbay	.265	423	57	112	16	64	95	0
Vernon Wells	.260	630	84	164	15	66	86	17
John McDonald	.258	151	18	39	4	13	18	0
Raul Chavez	.258	159	10	41	2	15	23	1
Travis Snider	.241	241	34	58	9	29	78	1
Edwin Encarnacion# . .	.240	154	25	37	8	23	29	1
Jose Bautista	.235	336	54	79	13	40	85	4
Rod Barajas	.226	429	43	97	19	71	76	1
Kevin Millar	.223	251	29	56	7	29	49	0

PITCHERS	ERA	W	L	IP	H	BB	SO	SV
Jason Frasor	2.50	7	3	57.2	43	16	56	11
Roy Halladay	2.79	17	10	239.0	234	35	208	0
Shawn Camp	3.50	2	6	79.2	73	29	58	1
Ricky Romero	4.30	13	9	178	192	79	141	0
Brandon League . . .	4.58	3	6	74.2	72	21	76	0
Brett Cecil	5.30	7	4	93.1	116	38	69	0
Brian Tallet	5.32	7	9	160.2	169	72	120	0
Scott Richmond	5.52	8	11	138.2	147	59	117	0

Manager: Cito Gaston

Major League Leaders in 2009

American League

Batting: Joe Mauer, Minnesota, .365; Ichiro Suzuki, Seattle, .352; Derek Jeter, NY Yankees, .334; Miguel Cabrera, Detroit, .324; Michael Young, Texas, .322.

Runs: Dustin Pedroia, Boston, 115; Chone Figgins, L.A. Angels, 114; Brian Roberts, Baltimore, 110; Johnny Damon, NY Yankees, 107; Derek Jeter, NY Yankees, 107.

Runs Batted In: Mark Teixeira, NY Yankees, 122; Jason Bay, Boston, 119; Adam Lind, Toronto, 114; Evan Longoria, Tampa Bay, 113; Aaron Hill, Toronto, 108; Victor Martinez, Cle.-Bos., 108; Kendry Morales, L.A. Angels, 108.

Hits: Ichiro Suzuki, Seattle, 225; Derek Jeter, NY Yankees, 212; Robinson Cano, NY Yankees, 204; Miguel Cabrera, Detroit, 198; Aaron Hill, Toronto, 195.

Doubles: Brian Roberts, Baltimore, 56; Billy Butler, Kansas City, 51; Robinson Cano, NY Yankees, 48; Dustin Pedroia, Boston, 48; Adam Lind, Toronto, 46.

Triples: Jacoby Ellsbury, Boston, 10; Denard Span, Minnesota, 10; Erick Aybar, L.A. Angels, 9; David DeJesus, Kansas City, 9; Elvis Andrus, Texas, 8; Willie Bloomquist, Kansas City, 8; Alberto Callaspo, Kansas City, 8; Carl Crawford, Tampa Bay, 8; Curtis Granderson, Detroit, 8.

Home Runs: Carlos Pena, Tampa Bay, 39; Mark Teixeira, NY Yankees, 39; Jason Bay, Boston, 36; Aaron Hill, Toronto, 36; Adam Lind, Toronto, 35.

Stolen Bases: Jacoby Ellsbury, Boston, 70; Carl Crawford, Tampa Bay, 60; Chone Figgins, L.A. Angels, 42; B.J. Upton, Tampa Bay, 42; Rajai Davis, Oakland, 41.

Pitching Wins: Felix Hernandez, Seattle, 19-5; CC Sabathia, NY Yankees, 19-8; Justin Verlander, Detroit, 19-9; Josh Beckett, Boston, 17-6; Scott Feldman, Texas, 17-8; Roy Halladay, Toronto, 17-10.

Earned Run Average: Zack Greinke, Kansas City, 2.16; Felix Hernandez, Seattle, 2.49; Roy Halladay, Toronto, 2.79; CC Sabathia, NY Yankees, 3.37; Jon Lester, Boston, 3.41.

Strikeouts: Justin Verlander, Detroit, 269; Zack Greinke, Kansas City, 242; Jon Lester, Boston, 225; Felix Hernandez, Seattle, 217; Roy Halladay, Toronto, 208.

Saves: Brian Fuentes, L.A. Angels, 48; Joe Nathan, Minnesota, 47; Mariano Rivera, NY Yankees, 44; David Aardsma, Seattle, 38; Jonathan Papelbon, Boston, 38.

National League

Batting: Hanley Ramirez, Florida, .342; Pablo Sandoval, San Francisco, .330; Albert Pujols, St. Louis, .327; Todd Helton, Colorado, .325; Joey Votto, Cincinnati, .322.

Runs: Albert Pujols, St. Louis, 124; Ryan Braun, Milwaukee, 113; Chase Utley, Philadelphia, 112; Ryan Zimmerman, Washington, 110; Ryan Howard, Philadelphia, 105.

Runs Batted In: Prince Fielder, Milwaukee, 141; Ryan Howard, Philadelphia, 141; Albert Pujols, St. Louis, 135; Ryan Braun, Milwaukee, 114; Derrek Lee, Chicago Cubs, 111.

Hits: Ryan Braun, Milwaukee, 203; Miguel Tejada, Houston, 199; Hanley Ramirez, Florida, 197; Pablo Sandoval, San Francisco, 189; Felipe Lopez, Ariz.-Milwaukee, 187.

Doubles: Miguel Tejada, Houston, 46; Albert Pujols, St. Louis, 45; Pablo Sandoval, San Francisco, 44; Jimmy Rollins, Philadelphia, 43; Jorge Cantu, Florida, 42; Andre Ethier, L.A. Dodgers, 42; Brad Hawpe, Colorado, 42; Hanley Ramirez, Florida, 42.

Triples: Shane Victorino, Philadelphia, 13; Michael Bourn, Houston, 12; Stephen Drew, Arizona, 12; Angel Pagan, NY Mets, 11; Dexter Fowler, Colorado, 10.

Home Runs: Albert Pujols, St. Louis, 47; Prince Fielder, Milwaukee, 46; Ryan Howard, Philadelphia, 45; Mark Reynolds, Arizona, 44; Adrian Gonzalez, San Diego, 40.

Stolen Bases: Michael Bourn, Houston, 61; Nyjer Morgan, Pitt.-Wash., 42; Matt Kemp, L.A. Dodgers, 34; Jimmy Rollins, Philadelphia, 31; Juan Pierre, L.A. Dodgers, 30.

Pitching Wins: Adam Wainwright, St. Louis, 19-8; Chris Carpenter, St. Louis, 17-4; Jorge De La Rosa, Colorado, 16-9; Bronson Arroyo, Cincinnati, 15-13; Ubaldo Jimenez, Colorado, 15-12; Josh Johnson, Florida, 15-5; Tim Lincecum, San Francisco, 15-7; Derek Lowe, Atlanta, 15-10; Jason Marquis, Colorado, 15-13; Joel Pineiro, St. Louis, 15-12; Javier Vazquez, Atlanta, 15-10.

Earned Run Average: Chris Carpenter, St. Louis, 2.24; Tim Lincecum, San Francisco, 2.48; Jair Jurrjens, Atlanta, 2.60; Adam Wainwright, St. Louis, 2.63; Clayton Kershaw, L.A. Dodgers, 2.79.

Strikeouts: Tim Lincecum, San Francisco, 261; Javier Vazquez, Atlanta, 238; Dan Haren, Arizona, 223; Adam Wainwright, St. Louis, 212; Yovani Gallardo, Milwaukee, 204.

Saves: Heath Bell, San Diego, 42; Francisco Cordero, Cincinnati, 39; Brian Wilson, San Francisco, 38; Ryan Franklin, St. Louis, 38; Trevor Hoffman, Milwaukee, 37.

All-Time Major League Single-Season Leaders

Source: www.mlb.com; *player active in 2009 season; records for "modern" era beginning 1901

Home Runs

Barry Bonds (2001)	73
Mark McGwire (1998)	70
Sammy Sosa (1998)	66
Mark McGwire (1999)	65
Sammy Sosa (2001)	64

Runs

Babe Ruth (1921)	177
Lou Gehrig (1936)	167
Lou Gehrig (1931)	163
Babe Ruth (1928)	163
Chuck Klein (1930)	158
Babe Ruth (1920, 1927)	158

Hits

Ichiro Suzuki* (2004)	262
George Sisler (1920)	257
Bill Terry (1930)	254
Lefty O'Doul (1929)	254
Al Simmons (1925)	253

Runs Batted In

Hack Wilson (1930)	191
Lou Gehrig (1931)	184
Hank Greenberg (1937)	183
Jimmie Foxx (1938)	175
Lou Gehrig (1927)	175

Batting Average

Rogers Hornsby (1924)	.424
Nap Lajoie (1901)	.422
George Sisler (1922)	.420
Ty Cobb (1911)	.420
Ty Cobb (1912)	.410

Stolen Bases

Rickey Henderson (1982)	130
Lou Brock (1974)	118
Vince Coleman (1985)	110
Vince Coleman (1987)	109
Rickey Henderson (1983)	108

Walks (Batter)

Barry Bonds (2004)	232
Barry Bonds (2002)	198
Barry Bonds (2001)	177
Babe Ruth (1923)	170
Mark McGwire (1998)	162
Ted Williams (1947, 1949)	162

Strikeouts (Batter)

Mark Reynolds* (2009)	223
Mark Reynolds* (2008)	204
Ryan Howard* (2007, 2008)	199
Jack Cust* (2008)	197
Adam Dunn* (2004)	195

Earned Run Average

Dutch Leonard (1914)	1.00
Mordecai Brown (1906)	1.04
Bob Gibson (1968)	1.12
Walter Johnson (1913)	1.14
Christy Mathewson (1909)	1.14

Wins

Jack Chesbro (1904)	41
Ed Walsh (1908)	40
Christy Mathewson (1908)	37
Walter Johnson (1913)	36
Joe McGinnity (1904)	35

Strikeouts

Nolan Ryan (1973)	383
Sandy Koufax (1965)	382
Randy Johnson* (2001)	372
Nolan Ryan (1974)	367
Randy Johnson* (1999)	364

Saves

Francisco Rodriguez* (2008)	62
Bobby Thigpen (1990)	57
Eric Gagne (2003)	55
John Smoltz* (2002)	55
Mariano Rivera* (2004)	53
Trevor Hoffman* (1998)	53
Randy Myers (1993)	53

All-Time Major League Leaders

Source: www.mlb.com; *player active in 2009 season

Games		At Bats		Runs Batted In		Runs	
Pete Rose	3,562	Pete Rose	14,053	Hank Aaron	2,297	Rickey Henderson	2,295
Carl Yastrzemski	3,308	Hank Aaron	12,364	Babe Ruth	2,213	Ty Cobb	2,245
Hank Aaron	3,298	Carl Yastrzemski	11,988	Cap Anson	2,076	Barry Bonds	2,227
Rickey Henderson	3,081	Cal Ripken Jr.	11,551	Barry Bonds	1,996	Hank Aaron	2,174
Ty Cobb	3,033	Ty Cobb	11,429	Lou Gehrig	1,995	Babe Ruth	2,174
Eddie Murray	3,026	Eddie Murray	11,336	Ty Cobb	1,961	Pete Rose	2,165
Stan Musial	3,026	Robin Yount	11,008	Stan Musial	1,951	Willie Mays	2,062
Cal Ripken Jr.	3,001	Dave Winfield	11,003	Jimmie Foxx	1,922	Cap Anson	1,996
Willie Mays	2,992	Stan Musial	10,972	Eddie Murray	1,917	Stan Musial	1,949
Barry Bonds	2,986	Rickey Henderson	10,961	Willie Mays	1,903	Lou Gehrig	1,888

Stolen Bases		Triples		Batting Average		Walks	
Rickey Henderson	1,406	Sam Crawford	309	Ty Cobb	.367	Barry Bonds	2,558
Lou Brock	938	Ty Cobb	297	Rogers Hornsby	.358	Rickey Henderson	2,190
Billy Hamilton	912	Honus Wagner	252	Joe Jackson	.356	Babe Ruth	2,062
Ty Cobb	892	Jake Beckley	243	Dan Brouthers	.349	Ted Williams	2,021
Tim Raines	808	Roger Connor	233	Lefty O'Doul	.349	Joe Morgan	1,865
Vince Coleman	752	Tris Speaker	222	Pete Browning	.349	Carl Yastrzemski	1,845
Eddie Collins	744	Fred Clarke	220	Dave Orr	.346	Mickey Mantle	1,733
Max Carey	738	Dan Brouthers	205	Ed Delahanty	.346	Mel Ott	1,708
Honus Wagner	722	Joe Kelley	194	Willie Keeler	.345	Frank Thomas	1,667
Joe Morgan	689	Paul Waner	190	Tris Speaker	.345	Jim Thome*	1,619

Strikeouts		Saves		Shutouts		Losses	
Nolan Ryan	5,714	Trevor Hoffman*	591	Walter Johnson	110	Cy Young	315
Randy Johnson*	4,875	Mariano Rivera*	526	Pete Alexander	90	Pud Galvin	302
Roger Clemens	4,672	Lee Smith	478	Christy Mathewson	79	Nolan Ryan	292
Steve Carlton	4,136	John Franco	424	Cy Young	76	Walter Johnson	279
Bert Blyleven	3,701	Dennis Eckersley	390	Eddie Plank	69	Phil Niekro	274
Tom Seaver	3,640	Billy Wagner*	385	Warren Spahn	63	Gaylord Perry	265
Don Sutton	3,574	Jeff Reardon	367	Nolan Ryan	61	Jack Powell	256
Gaylord Perry	3,534	Troy Percival*	358	Tom Seaver	61	Don Sutton	256
Walter Johnson	3,508	Randy Myers	347	Bert Blyleven	60	Eppa Rixey	251
Greg Maddux	3,371	Rollie Fingers	341	Don Sutton	58	Bert Blyleven	250

All-Time Home Run Leaders

Source: www.mlb.com; *player active in 2009 season

Barry Bonds	762	Manny Ramirez*	546	Willie Stargell	475	Jason Giambi*	409
Hank Aaron	755	Mickey Mantle	536	Carlos Delgado*	473	Vladimir Guerrero*	407
Babe Ruth	714	Jimmie Foxx	534	Dave Winfield	465	Duke Snider	407
Willie Mays	660	Willie McCovey	521	Jose Canseco	462	Andres Galarraga	399
Ken Griffey Jr.*	630	Frank Thomas	521	Carl Yastrzemski	452	Al Kaline	399
Sammy Sosa	609	Ted Williams	521	Jeff Bagwell	449	Dale Murphy	398
Frank Robinson	586	Ernie Banks	512	Dave Kingman	442	Joe Carter	396
Mark McGwire	583	Ed Mathews	512	Andre Dawson	438	Graig Nettles	390
Alex Rodriguez*	583	Mel Ott	511	Juan Gonzalez	434	Johnny Bench	389
Harmon Killebrew	573	Gary Sheffield	509	Cal Ripken Jr.	431	Andruw Jones*	388
Rafael Palmeiro	569	Eddie Murray	504	Mike Piazza	427	Dwight Evans	385
Jim Thome*	564	Lou Gehrig	493	Chipper Jones*	426	Harold Baines	384
Reggie Jackson	563	Fred McGriff	493	Billy Williams	426	Larry Walker	383
Mike Schmidt	548	Stan Musial	475	Darrell Evans	414		

Players With 3,000 Major League Hits

Source: www.mlb.com

Pete Rose	4,256	Cap Anson	3,418	George Brett	3,154	Rod Carew	3,053
Ty Cobb	4,191	Paul Molitor	3,319	Paul Waner	3,152	Lou Brock	3,023
Hank Aaron	3,771	Eddie Collins	3,314	Robin Yount	3,142	Rafael Palmeiro	3,020
Stan Musial	3,630	Willie Mays	3,283	Tony Gwynn	3,141	Wade Boggs	3,010
Tris Speaker	3,515	Eddie Murray	3,255	Dave Winfield	3,110	Al Kaline	3,007
Honus Wagner	3,430	Nap Lajoie	3,252	Craig Biggio	3,060	Roberto Clemente	3,000
Carl Yastrzemski	3,419	Cal Ripken Jr.	3,184	Rickey Henderson	3,055		

50 Home Run Club

Only Mark McGwire and Barry Bonds have ever hit 70 or more home runs in a season. Five players—including Babe Ruth and Roger Maris—have hit 60 or more, a feat Sammy Sosa accomplished for the third time in 2001. Those 5 are at the pinnacle of a select group of players to have hit 50 or more homers in a season. The following list shows each time a player achieved this mark.

HR	Player, team	Year	HR	Player, team	Year
73	Barry Bonds, San Francisco Giants	2001	54	Ralph Kiner, Pittsburgh Pirates	1949
70	Mark McGwire, St. Louis Cardinals	1998	54	Mickey Mantle, NY Yankees	1961
66	Sammy Sosa, Chicago Cubs	1998	54	Alex Rodriguez, NY Yankees	2007
65	Mark McGwire, St. Louis Cardinals	1999	52	Mickey Mantle, NY Yankees	1956
64	Sammy Sosa, Chicago Cubs	2001	52	Willie Mays, San Francisco Giants	1965
63	Sammy Sosa, Chicago Cubs	1999	52	George Foster, Cincinnati Reds	1977
61	Roger Maris, NY Yankees	1961	52	Mark McGwire, Oakland A's	1996
60	Babe Ruth, NY Yankees	1927	52	Alex Rodriguez, Texas Rangers	2001
59	Babe Ruth, NY Yankees	1921	52	Jim Thome, Cleveland Indians	2002
58	Jimmie Foxx, Philadelphia Athletics	1932	51	Andruw Jones, Atlanta Braves	2005
58	Hank Greenberg, Detroit Tigers	1938	51	Ralph Kiner, Pittsburgh Pirates	1947
58	Ryan Howard, Philadelphia Phillies	2006	51	Johnny Mize, NY Giants	1947
58	Mark McGwire, Oakland A's/St. Louis Cardinals	1997	51	Willie Mays, NY Giants	1955
57	Luis Gonzalez, Arizona Diamondbacks	2001	51	Cecil Fielder, Detroit Tigers	1990
57	Alex Rodriguez, Texas Rangers	2002	50	Jimmie Foxx, Boston Red Sox	1938
56	Hack Wilson, Chicago Cubs	1930	50	Albert Belle, Cleveland Indians	1995
56	Ken Griffey Jr., Seattle Mariners	1997	50	Brady Anderson, Baltimore Orioles	1996
56	Ken Griffey Jr., Seattle Mariners	1998	50	Greg Vaughn, San Diego Padres	1998
54	David Ortiz, Boston Red Sox	2006	50	Sammy Sosa, Chicago Cubs	2000
54	Babe Ruth, NY Yankees	1920	50	Prince Fielder, Milwaukee Brewers	2007
54	Babe Ruth, NY Yankees	1928			

Pitchers With 300 Major League Wins

Source: www.mlb.com; *player active in 2009 season

Cy Young	511	Kid Nichols	360	Eddie Plank	326	Charley Radbourn	310
Walter Johnson	417	Greg Maddux	355	Nolan Ryan	324	Mickey Welch	309
Grover Alexander	373	Roger Clemens	354	Don Sutton	324	Tom Glavine*	305
Christy Mathewson	373	Tim Keefe	342	Phil Niekro	318	Randy Johnson*	303
Warren Spahn	363	Steve Carlton	329	Gaylord Perry	314	Lefty Grove	300
Pud Galvin	361	John Clarkson	327	Tom Seaver	311	Early Wynn	300

Official Major League Perfect Games Since 1900

Date	Pitcher	Teams	Date	Pitcher	Teams
5/5/1904	Cy Young	Boston 3 vs. Phil. 0 (AL)	9/30/1984	Mike Witt	Calif. 1 vs. Texas 0 (AL)
10/2/1908	Addie Joss	Clev. 1 vs. Chicago 0 (AL)	9/16/1988	Tom Browning	Cincinnati 1 vs. L.A. 0 (NL)
4/30/1922	Charlie Robertson	Chicago 2 vs. Detroit 0 (AL)	7/28/1991	Dennis Martinez	Montreal 2 vs. L.A. 0 (NL)
10/8/1956	Don Larsen	NY (AL) 2 vs. Brooklyn 0*	7/28/1994	Kenny Rogers	Texas 4 vs. California 0 (AL)
6/21/1964	Jim Bunning	Phil. 6 at NY 0 (NL)	5/17/1998	David Wells	NY 4 vs. Minn. 0 (AL)
9/9/1965	Sandy Koufax	L.A. 1 vs. Chicago 0 (NL)	7/18/1999	David Cone	NY 6 vs. Montreal 0 (AL)
5/8/1968	Catfish Hunter	Oakland 4 vs. Minn. 0 (AL)	5/18/2004	Randy Johnson	Ariz. 2 vs. Atlanta 0 (NL)
5/15/1981	Len Barker	Clev. 3 vs. Toronto 0 (AL)	7/23/2009	Mark Buehrle	Chicago 5 vs. Tampa Bay 0 (AL)

*World Series game

Most Career Major League No-Hitters

No.	Pitcher
7	Nolan Ryan
4	Sandy Koufax
3	Larry Corcoran, Bob Feller, Cy Young
2	Jim Bunning, Steve Busby, Carl Erskine, Bob Forsch, Pud Galvin, Ken Holtzman, Randy Johnson, Addie Joss, Dutch Leonard, Jim Maloney, Christy Mathewson, Hideo Nomo, Allie Reynolds, Frank Smith, Warren Spahn, Bill Stoneman, Virgil Trucks, Johnny Vander Meer, Ed Walsh, Don Wilson

Home Run Leaders, by Season

*All-time single-season record for league.

	National League			American League	
Year	Player, team	HR	Year	Player, team	HR
1901	Sam Crawford, Cincinnati	16	1901	Napoleon Lajoie, Philadelphia	13
1902	Thomas Leach, Pittsburgh	6	1902	Socks Seybold, Philadelphia	16
1903	James Sheckard, Brooklyn	9	1903	Buck Freeman, Boston	13
1904	Harry Lumley, Brooklyn	9	1904	Harry Davis, Philadelphia	10
1905	Fred Odwell, Cincinnati	9	1905	Harry Davis, Philadelphia	8
1906	Timothy Jordan, Brooklyn	12	1906	Harry Davis, Philadelphia	12
1907	David Brain, Boston	10	1907	Harry Davis, Philadelphia	8
1908	Timothy Jordan, Brooklyn	12	1908	Sam Crawford, Detroit	7
1909	Red Murray, New York	7	1909	Ty Cobb, Detroit	9
1910	Fred Beck, Boston; Frank Schulte, Chicago	10	1910	Jake Stahl, Boston	10
1911	Frank Schulte, Chicago	21	1911	J. Franklin Baker, Philadelphia	11
1912	Henry Zimmerman, Chicago	14	1912	J. Franklin Baker, Philadelphia; Tris Speaker, Boston	10
1913	Gavvy Cravath, Philadelphia	19	1913	J. Franklin Baker, Philadelphia	13
1914	Gavvy Cravath, Philadelphia	19	1914	J. Franklin Baker, Philadelphia	9
1915	Gavvy Cravath, Philadelphia	24	1915	Robert Roth, Chicago-Cleveland	7
1916	Dave Robertson, NY; Fred (Cy) Williams, Chi.	12	1916	Wally Pipp, New York	12
1917	Dave Robertson, NY; Gavvy Cravath, Phi.	12	1917	Wally Pipp, New York	9
1918	Gavvy Cravath, Philadelphia	8	1918	Babe Ruth, Boston; Tilly Walker, Philadelphia	11
1919	Gavvy Cravath, Philadelphia	12	1919	Babe Ruth, Boston	29
1920	Cy Williams, Philadelphia	15	1920	Babe Ruth, New York	54
1921	George Kelly, New York	23	1921	Babe Ruth, New York	59
1922	Rogers Hornsby, St. Louis	42	1922	Ken Williams, St. Louis	39
1923	Cy Williams, Philadelphia	41	1923	Babe Ruth, New York	41

National League			American League		
Year	Player, team	HR	Year	Player, team	HR
1924	Jacques Fournier, Brooklyn	27	1924	Babe Ruth, New York	46
1925	Rogers Hornsby, St. Louis	39	1925	Bob Meusel, New York	33
1926	Hack Wilson, Chicago	21	1926	Babe Ruth, New York	47
1927	Hack Wilson, Chicago; Cy Williams, Philadelphia	30	1927	Babe Ruth, New York	60
1928	Hack Wilson, Chicago; Jim Bottomley, St. Louis	31	1928	Babe Ruth, New York	54
1929	Chuck Klein, Philadelphia	43	1929	Babe Ruth, New York	46
1930	Hack Wilson, Chicago	56	1930	Babe Ruth, New York	49
1931	Chuck Klein, Philadelphia	31	1931	Babe Ruth, Lou Gehrig, New York	46
1932	Chuck Klein, Philadelphia; Mel Ott, New York	38	1932	Jimmie Foxx, Philadelphia	58
1933	Chuck Klein, Philadelphia	28	1933	Jimmie Foxx, Philadelphia	48
1934	Rip Collins, St. Louis; Mel Ott, New York	35	1934	Lou Gehrig, New York	49
1935	Walter Berger, Boston	34	1935	Jimmie Foxx, Philadelphia; Hank Greenberg, Detroit	36
1936	Mel Ott, New York	33	1936	Lou Gehrig, New York	49
1937	Mel Ott, New York; Joe Medwick, St. Louis	31	1937	Joe DiMaggio, New York	46
1938	Mel Ott, New York	36	1938	Hank Greenberg, Detroit	58
1939	John Mize, St. Louis	28	1939	Jimmie Foxx, Boston	35
1940	John Mize, St. Louis	43	1940	Hank Greenberg, Detroit	41
1941	Dolph Camilli, Brooklyn	34	1941	Ted Williams, Boston	37
1942	Mel Ott, New York	30	1942	Ted Williams, Boston	36
1943	Bill Nicholson, Chicago	29	1943	Rudy York, Detroit	34
1944	Bill Nicholson, Chicago	33	1944	Nick Etten, New York	22
1945	Tommy Holmes, Boston	28	1945	Vern Stephens, St. Louis	24
1946	Ralph Kiner, Pittsburgh	23	1946	Hank Greenberg, Detroit	44
1947	Ralph Kiner, Pittsburgh; John Mize, New York	51	1947	Ted Williams, Boston	32
1948	Ralph Kiner, Pittsburgh; John Mize, New York	40	1948	Joe DiMaggio, New York	39
1949	Ralph Kiner, Pittsburgh	54	1949	Ted Williams, Boston	43
1950	Ralph Kiner, Pittsburgh	47	1950	Al Rosen, Cleveland	37
1951	Ralph Kiner, Pittsburgh	42	1951	Gus Zernial, Chicago-Philadelphia	33
1952	Ralph Kiner, Pittsburgh; Hank Sauer, Chicago	37	1952	Larry Doby, Cleveland	32
1953	Ed Mathews, Milwaukee	47	1953	Al Rosen, Cleveland	43
1954	Ted Kluszewski, Cincinnati	49	1954	Larry Doby, Cleveland	32
1955	Willie Mays, New York	51	1955	Mickey Mantle, New York	37
1956	Duke Snider, Brooklyn	43	1956	Mickey Mantle, New York	52
1957	Hank Aaron, Milwaukee	44	1957	Roy Sievers, Washington	42
1958	Ernie Banks, Chicago	47	1958	Mickey Mantle, New York	42
1959	Ed Mathews, Milwaukee	46	1959	Rocky Colavito, Cleve.; Harmon Killebrew, Wash.	42
1960	Ernie Banks, Chicago	41	1960	Mickey Mantle, New York	40
1961	Orlando Cepeda, San Francisco	46	1961	Roger Maris, New York	61*
1962	Willie Mays, San Francisco	49	1962	Harmon Killebrew, Minnesota	48
1963	Hank Aaron, Milwaukee; Willie McCovey, S.F.	44	1963	Harmon Killebrew, Minnesota	45
1964	Willie Mays, San Francisco	47	1964	Harmon Killebrew, Minnesota	49
1965	Willie Mays, San Francisco	52	1965	Tony Conigliaro, Boston	32
1966	Hank Aaron, Atlanta	44	1966	Frank Robinson, Baltimore	49
1967	Hank Aaron, Atlanta	39	1967	Carl Yastrzemski, Boston; Harmon Killebrew, Minn.	44
1968	Willie McCovey, San Francisco	36	1968	Frank Howard, Washington	44
1969	Willie McCovey, San Francisco	45	1969	Harmon Killebrew, Minnesota	49
1970	Johnny Bench, Cincinnati	45	1970	Frank Howard, Washington	44
1971	Willie Stargell, Pittsburgh	48	1971	Bill Melton, Chicago	33
1972	Johnny Bench, Cincinnati	40	1972	Dick Allen, Chicago	37
1973	Willie Stargell, Pittsburgh	44	1973	Reggie Jackson, Oakland	32
1974	Mike Schmidt, Philadelphia	36	1974	Dick Allen, Chicago	32
1975	Mike Schmidt, Philadelphia	38	1975	George Scott, Milwaukee; Reggie Jackson, Oakland	36
1976	Mike Schmidt, Philadelphia	38	1976	Graig Nettles, New York	32
1977	George Foster, Cincinnati	52	1977	Jim Rice, Boston	39
1978	George Foster, Cincinnati	40	1978	Jim Rice, Boston	46
1979	Dave Kingman, Chicago	48	1979	Gorman Thomas, Milwaukee	45
1980	Mike Schmidt, Philadelphia	48	1980	Reggie Jackson, New York; Ben Oglivie, Milwaukee	41
1981	Mike Schmidt, Philadelphia	31	1981	Bobby Grich, California; Tony Armas, Oakland; Dwight Evans, Boston; Eddie Murray, Baltimore	22
1982	Dave Kingman, New York	37	1982	Gorman Thomas, Milwaukee; Reggie Jackson, Cal.	39
1983	Mike Schmidt, Philadelphia	40	1983	Jim Rice, Boston	39
1984	Mike Schmidt, Philadelphia; Dale Murphy, Atlanta	36	1984	Tony Armas, Boston	43
1985	Dale Murphy, Atlanta	37	1985	Darrell Evans, Detroit	40
1986	Mike Schmidt, Philadelphia	37	1986	Jesse Barfield, Toronto	40
1987	Andre Dawson, Chicago	49	1987	Mark McGwire, Oakland	49
1988	Darryl Strawberry, New York	39	1988	Jose Canseco, Oakland	42
1989	Kevin Mitchell, San Francisco	47	1989	Fred McGriff, Toronto	36
1990	Ryne Sandberg, Chicago	40	1990	Cecil Fielder, Detroit	51
1991	Howard Johnson, New York	38	1991	Cecil Fielder, Detroit; Jose Canseco, Oakland	44
1992	Fred McGriff, San Diego	35	1992	Juan Gonzalez, Texas	43
1993	Barry Bonds, San Francisco	46	1993	Juan Gonzalez, Texas	46
1994	Matt Williams, San Francisco	43	1994	Ken Griffey Jr., Seattle	40
1995	Dante Bichette, Colorado	40	1995	Albert Belle, Cleveland	50
1996	Andres Galarraga, Colorado	47	1996	Mark McGwire, Oakland	52
1997[1]	Larry Walker, Colorado	49	1997[1]	Ken Griffey Jr., Seattle	56
1998	Mark McGwire, St. Louis	70	1998	Ken Griffey Jr., Seattle	56
1999	Mark McGwire, St. Louis	65	1999	Ken Griffey Jr., Seattle	48
2000	Sammy Sosa, Chicago	50	2000	Troy Glaus, Anaheim	47
2001	Barry Bonds, San Francisco	73*	2001	Alex Rodriguez, Texas	52
2002	Sammy Sosa, Chicago	49	2002	Alex Rodriguez, Texas	57
2003	Jim Thome, Philadelphia	47	2003	Alex Rodriguez, Texas	47
2004	Adrian Beltre, Los Angeles	48	2004	Manny Ramirez, Boston	43
2005	Andruw Jones, Atlanta	51	2005	Alex Rodriguez, New York	48
2006	Ryan Howard, Philadelphia	58	2006	David Ortiz, Boston	54
2007	Prince Fielder, Milwaukee	50	2007	Alex Rodriguez, New York	54
2008	Ryan Howard, Philadelphia	48	2008	Miguel Cabrera, Detroit	37
2009	Albert Pujols, St. Louis	47	2009	Carlos Pena, Tampa Bay	39

(1) In 1997, Mark McGwire hit 58 home runs; 34 with the Oakland Athletics (AL) and 24 with the St. Louis Cardinals (NL).

Runs Batted In Leaders, by Season

*All-time single-season record for league since beginning of "modern" era in 1901.

	National League			American League	
Year	**Player, team**	**RBI**	**Year**	**Player, team**	**RBI**
1907	Sherwood Magee, Philadelphia	85	1907	Ty Cobb, Detroit	116
1908	Honus Wagner, Pittsburgh	109	1908	Ty Cobb, Detroit	108
1909	Honus Wagner, Pittsburgh	100	1909	Ty Cobb, Detroit	107
1910	Sherwood Magee, Philadelphia	123	1910	Sam Crawford, Detroit	120
1911	Frank Schulte, Chicago	121	1911	Ty Cobb, Detroit .	144
1912	Henry Zimmerman, Chicago	103	1912	J. Franklin Baker, Philadelphia	133
1913	Gavvy Cravath, Philadelphia	128	1913	J. Franklin Baker, Philadelphia	126
1914	Sherwood Magee, Philadelphia	103	1914	Sam Crawford, Detroit	104
1915	Gavvy Cravath, Philadelphia	115	1915	Sam Crawford, Detroit; Robert Veach, Detroit	112
1916	Henry Zimmerman, Chicago-NewYork	83	1916	Del Pratt, St. Louis	103
1917	Henry Zimmerman, New York	102	1917	Robert Veach, Detroit	103
1918	Sherwood Magee, Philadelphia	76	1918	Robert Veach, Detroit	78
1919	Hi Myers, Boston.	73	1919	Babe Ruth, Boston	114
1920	George Kelly, NY; Rogers Hornsby, St. Louis	94	1920	Babe Ruth, New York	137
1921	Rogers Hornsby, St. Louis	126	1921	Babe Ruth, New York	171
1922	Rogers Hornsby, St. Louis	152	1922	Ken Williams, St. Louis	155
1923	Emil Meusel, New York	125	1923	Babe Ruth, New York	131
1924	George Kelly, New York	136	1924	Goose Goslin, Washington	129
1925	Rogers Hornsby, St. Louis	143	1925	Bob Meusel, New York	138
1926	Jim Bottomley, St. Louis	120	1926	Babe Ruth, New York	145
1927	Paul Waner, Pittsburgh	131	1927	Lou Gehrig, New York	175
1928	Jim Bottomley, St. Louis	136	1928	Babe Ruth, New York; Lou Gehrig, New York	142
1929	Hack Wilson, Chicago	159	1929	Al Simmons, Philadelphia	157
1930	Hack Wilson, Chicago	191*	1930	Lou Gehrig, New York	174
1931	Chuck Klein, Philadelphia	121	1931	Lou Gehrig, New York	184*
1932	Don Hurst, Philadelphia	143	1932	Jimmie Foxx, Philadelphia	169
1933	Chuck Klein, Philadelphia	120	1933	Jimmie Foxx, Philadelphia	163
1934	Mel Ott, New York	135	1934	Lou Gehrig, New York	165
1935	Walter Berger, Boston	130	1935	Hank Greenberg, Detroit	170
1936	Joe Medwick, St. Louis	138	1936	Hal Trosky, Cleveland	162
1937	Joe Medwick, St. Louis	154	1937	Hank Greenberg, Detroit	183
1938	Joe Medwick, St. Louis	122	1938	Jimmie Foxx, Boston	175
1939	Frank McCormick, Cincinnati	128	1939	Ted Williams, Boston	145
1940	John Mize, St. Louis	137	1940	Hank Greenberg, Detroit	150
1941	Adolph Camilli, Brooklyn	120	1941	Joe DiMaggio, New York	125
1942	John Mize, New York	110	1942	Ted Williams, Boston	137
1943	Bill Nicholson, Chicago	128	1943	Rudy York, Detroit	118
1944	Bill Nicholson, Chicago	122	1944	Vern Stephens, St. Louis	109
1945	Dixie Walker, Brooklyn	124	1945	Nick Etten, New York	111
1946	Enos Slaughter, St. Louis	130	1946	Hank Greenberg, Detroit	127
1947	John Mize, New York	138	1947	Ted Williams, Boston	114
1948	Stan Musial, St. Louis	131	1948	Joe DiMaggio, New York	155
1949	Ralph Kiner, Pittsburgh	127	1949	Ted Williams, Boston; Vern Stephens, Boston	159
1950	Del Ennis, Philadelphia	126	1950	Walt Dropo, Boston; Vern Stephens, Boston	144
1951	Monte Irvin, New York	121	1951	Gus Zernial, Chicago-Philadelphia	129
1952	Hank Sauer, Chicago	121	1952	Al Rosen, Cleveland	105
1953	Roy Campanella, Brooklyn	142	1953	Al Rosen, Cleveland	145
1954	Ted Kluszewski, Cincinnati	141	1954	Larry Doby, Cleveland	126
1955	Duke Snider, Brooklyn	136	1955	Ray Boone, Detroit; Jackie Jensen, Boston	116
1956	Stan Musial, St. Louis	109	1956	Mickey Mantle, New York	130
1957	Hank Aaron, Milwaukee	132	1957	Roy Sievers, Washington	114
1958	Ernie Banks, Chicago	129	1958	Jackie Jensen, Boston	122
1959	Ernie Banks, Chicago	143	1959	Jackie Jensen, Boston	112
1960	Hank Aaron, Milwaukee	126	1960	Roger Maris, New York	112
1961	Orlando Cepeda, San Francisco	142	1961	Roger Maris, New York	142
1962	Tommy Davis, Los Angeles	153	1962	Harmon Killebrew, Minnesota	126
1963	Hank Aaron, Milwaukee	130	1963	Dick Stuart, Boston	118
1964	Ken Boyer, St. Louis	119	1964	Brooks Robinson, Baltimore	118
1965	Deron Johnson, Cincinnati	130	1965	Rocky Colavito, Cleveland	108
1966	Hank Aaron, Atlanta	127	1966	Frank Robinson, Baltimore	122
1967	Orlando Cepeda, St. Louis	111	1967	Carl Yastrzemski, Boston	121
1968	Willie McCovey, San Francisco	105	1968	Ken Harrelson, Boston	109
1969	Willie McCovey, San Francisco	126	1969	Harmon Killebrew, Minnesota	140
1970	Johnny Bench, Cincinnati	148	1970	Frank Howard, Washington	126
1971	Joe Torre, St. Louis	137	1971	Harmon Killebrew, Minnesota	119
1972	Johnny Bench, Cincinnati	125	1972	Dick Allen, Chicago	113
1973	Willie Stargell, Pittsburgh	119	1973	Reggie Jackson, Oakland	117
1974	Johnny Bench, Cincinnati	129	1974	Jeff Burroughs, Texas	118
1975	Greg Luzinski, Philadelphia	120	1975	George Scott, Milwaukee	109
1976	George Foster, Cincinnati	121	1976	Lee May, Baltimore	109
1977	George Foster, Cincinnati	149	1977	Larry Hisle, Minnesota	119
1978	George Foster, Cincinnati	120	1978	Jim Rice, Boston	139
1979	Dave Winfield, San Diego	118	1979	Don Baylor, California	139
1980	Mike Schmidt, Philadelphia	121	1980	Cecil Cooper, Milwaukee	122
1981	Mike Schmidt, Philadelphia	91	1981	Eddie Murray, Baltimore	78
1982	Dale Murphy, Atlanta; Al Oliver, Montreal	109	1982	Hal McRae, Kansas City	133
1983	Dale Murphy, Atlanta	121	1983	Cecil Cooper, Milwaukee; Jim Rice, Boston	126
1984	Gary Carter, Montreal; Mike Schmidt, Phil.	106	1984	Tony Armas, Boston	123
1985	Dave Parker, Cincinnati	125	1985	Don Mattingly, New York	145
1986	Mike Schmidt, Philadelphia	119	1986	Joe Carter, Cleveland	121
1987	Andre Dawson, Chicago	137	1987	George Bell, Toronto	134
1988	Will Clark, San Francisco	109	1988	Jose Canseco, Oakland	124
1989	Kevin Mitchell, San Francisco	125	1989	Ruben Sierra, Texas	119
1990	Matt Williams, San Francisco	122	1990	Cecil Fielder, Detroit	132

National League

Year	Player, team	RBI
1991	Howard Johnson, New York	117
1992	Darren Daulton, Philadelphia	109
1993	Barry Bonds, San Francisco	123
1994	Jeff Bagwell, Houston	116
1995	Dante Bichette, Colorado	128
1996	Andres Galarraga, Colorado	150
1997	Andres Galarraga, Colorado	140
1998	Sammy Sosa, Chicago	158
1999	Mark McGwire, St. Louis	147
2000	Todd Helton, Colorado	147
2001	Sammy Sosa, Chicago	160
2002	Lance Berkman, Houston	128
2003	Preston Wilson, Colorado	141
2004	Vinny Castilla, Colorado	131
2005	Andruw Jones, Atlanta	128
2006	Ryan Howard, Philadelphia	149
2007	Matt Holliday, Colorado	137
2008	Ryan Howard, Philadelphia	146
2009	Prince Fielder, Milwaukee	141

American League

Year	Player, team	RBI
1991	Cecil Fielder, Detroit	133
1992	Cecil Fielder, Detroit	124
1993	Albert Belle, Cleveland	129
1994	Kirby Puckett, Minnesota	112
1995	Albert Belle, Cleveland; Mo Vaughn, Boston	126
1996	Albert Belle, Cleveland	148
1997	Ken Griffey Jr., Seattle	147
1998	Juan Gonzalez, Texas	157
1999	Manny Ramirez, Cleveland	165
2000	Edgar Martinez, Seattle	145
2001	Bret Boone, Seattle	141
2002	Alex Rodriguez, Texas	142
2003	Carlos Delgado, Toronto	145
2004	Miguel Tejada, Baltimore	150
2005	David Ortiz, Boston	148
2006	David Ortiz, Boston	137
2007	Alex Rodriguez, New York	156
2008	Josh Hamilton, Texas	130
2009	Mark Teixeira, New York	122

Batting Champions, by Season

*All-time single-season record for league since the beginning of the "modern" era in 1901.

National League

Year	Player	Team	Avg.
1901	Jesse C. Burkett	St. Louis	.382
1902	Clarence Beaumont	Pittsburgh	.357
1903	Honus Wagner	Pittsburgh	.355
1904	Honus Wagner	Pittsburgh	.349
1905	James Seymour	Cincinnati	.377
1906	Honus Wagner	Pittsburgh	.339
1907	Honus Wagner	Pittsburgh	.350
1908	Honus Wagner	Pittsburgh	.354
1909	Honus Wagner	Pittsburgh	.339
1910	Sherwood Magee	Philadelphia	.331
1911	Honus Wagner	Pittsburgh	.334
1912	Henry Zimmerman	Chicago	.372
1913	Jacob Daubert	Brooklyn	.350
1914	Jacob Daubert	Brooklyn	.329
1915	Larry Doyle	New York	.320
1916	Hal Chase	Cincinnati	.339
1917	Edd Roush	Cincinnati	.341
1918	Zach Wheat	Brooklyn	.335
1919	Edd Roush	Cincinnati	.321
1920	Rogers Hornsby	St. Louis	.370
1921	Rogers Hornsby	St. Louis	.397
1922	Rogers Hornsby	St. Louis	.401
1923	Rogers Hornsby	St. Louis	.384
1924	Rogers Hornsby	St. Louis	.424*
1925	Rogers Hornsby	St. Louis	.403
1926	Eugene Hargrave	Cincinnati	.353
1927	Paul Waner	Pittsburgh	.380
1928	Rogers Hornsby	Boston	.387
1929	Lefty O'Doul	Philadelphia	.398
1930	Bill Terry	New York	.401
1931	Chick Hafey	St. Louis	.349
1932	Lefty O'Doul	Brooklyn	.368
1933	Chuck Klein	Philadelphia	.368
1934	Paul Waner	Pittsburgh	.362
1935	Arky Vaughan	Pittsburgh	.385
1936	Paul Waner	Pittsburgh	.373
1937	Joe Medwick	St. Louis	.374
1938	Ernie Lombardi	Cincinnati	.342
1939	John Mize	St. Louis	.349
1940	Debs Garms	Pittsburgh	.355
1941	Pete Reiser	Brooklyn	.343
1942	Ernie Lombardi	Boston	.330
1943	Stan Musial	St. Louis	.357
1944	Dixie Walker	Brooklyn	.357
1945	Phil Cavarretta	Chicago	.355
1946	Stan Musial	St. Louis	.365
1947	Harry Walker	St. Louis-Phil.	.363
1948	Stan Musial	St. Louis	.376
1949	Jackie Robinson	Brooklyn	.342
1950	Stan Musial	St. Louis	.346
1951	Stan Musial	St. Louis	.355
1952	Stan Musial	St. Louis	.336
1953	Carl Furillo	Brooklyn	.344
1954	Willie Mays	New York	.345
1955	Richie Ashburn	Philadelphia	.338
1956	Hank Aaron	Milwaukee	.328
1957	Stan Musial	St. Louis	.351
1958	Richie Ashburn	Philadelphia	.350
1959	Hank Aaron	Milwaukee	.355
1960	Dick Groat	Pittsburgh	.325
1961	Roberto Clemente	Pittsburgh	.351
1962	Tommy Davis	Los Angeles	.346

American League

Year	Player	Team	Avg.
1901	Napoleon Lajoie	Philadelphia	.426*
1902	Ed Delahanty	Washington	.376
1903	Napoleon Lajoie	Cleveland	.355
1904	Napoleon Lajoie	Cleveland	.381
1905	Elmer Flick	Cleveland	.306
1906	George Stone	St. Louis	.358
1907	Ty Cobb	Detroit	.350
1908	Ty Cobb	Detroit	.324
1909	Ty Cobb	Detroit	.377
1910[1]	Ty Cobb	Detroit	.385
1911	Ty Cobb	Detroit	.420
1912	Ty Cobb	Detroit	.410
1913	Ty Cobb	Detroit	.390
1914	Ty Cobb	Detroit	.368
1915	Ty Cobb	Detroit	.369
1916	Tris Speaker	Cleveland	.386
1917	Ty Cobb	Detroit	.383
1918	Ty Cobb	Detroit	.382
1919	Ty Cobb	Detroit	.384
1920	George Sisler	St. Louis	.407
1921	Harry Heilmann	Detroit	.394
1922	George Sisler	St. Louis	.420
1923	Harry Heilmann	Detroit	.403
1924	Babe Ruth	New York	.378
1925	Harry Heilmann	Detroit	.393
1926	Henry Manush	Detroit	.378
1927	Harry Heilmann	Detroit	.398
1928	Goose Goslin	Washington	.379
1929	Lew Fonseca	Cleveland	.369
1930	Al Simmons	Philadelphia	.381
1931	Al Simmons	Philadelphia	.390
1932	Dale Alexander	Detroit-Boston	.367
1933	Jimmie Foxx	Philadelphia	.356
1934	Lou Gehrig	New York	.363
1935	Buddy Myer	Washington	.349
1936	Luke Appling	Chicago	.388
1937	Charlie Gehringer	Detroit	.371
1938	Jimmie Foxx	Boston	.349
1939	Joe DiMaggio	New York	.381
1940	Joe DiMaggio	New York	.352
1941	Ted Williams	Boston	.406
1942	Ted Williams	Boston	.356
1943	Luke Appling	Chicago	.328
1944	Lou Boudreau	Cleveland	.327
1945	George Stirnweiss	New York	.309
1946	Mickey Vernon	Washington	.353
1947	Ted Williams	Boston	.343
1948	Ted Williams	Boston	.369
1949	George Kell	Detroit	.343
1950	Billy Goodman	Boston	.354
1951	Ferris Fain	Philadelphia	.344
1952	Ferris Fain	Philadelphia	.327
1953	Mickey Vernon	Washington	.337
1954	Roberto Avila	Cleveland	.341
1955	Al Kaline	Detroit	.340
1956	Mickey Mantle	New York	.353
1957	Ted Williams	Boston	.388
1958	Ted Williams	Boston	.328
1959	Harvey Kuenn	Detroit	.353
1960	Pete Runnels	Boston	.320
1961	Norm Cash	Detroit	.361
1962	Pete Runnels	Boston	.326

Year	Player	Team	Avg.		Year	Player	Team	Avg.
1963	Tommy Davis	Los Angeles	.326		1963	Carl Yastrzemski	Boston	.321
1964	Roberto Clemente	Pittsburgh	.339		1964	Tony Oliva	Minnesota	.323
1965	Roberto Clemente	Pittsburgh	.329		1965	Tony Oliva	Minnesota	.321
1966	Matty Alou	Pittsburgh	.342		1966	Frank Robinson	Baltimore	.316
1967	Roberto Clemente	Pittsburgh	.357		1967	Carl Yastrzemski	Boston	.326
1968	Pete Rose	Cincinnati	.335		1968	Carl Yastrzemski	Boston	.301
1969	Pete Rose	Cincinnati	.348		1969	Rod Carew	Minnesota	.332
1970	Rico Carty	Atlanta	.366		1970	Alex Johnson	California	.329
1971	Joe Torre	St. Louis	.363		1971	Tony Oliva	Minnesota	.337
1972	Billy Williams	Chicago	.333		1972	Rod Carew	Minnesota	.318
1973	Pete Rose	Cincinnati	.338		1973	Rod Carew	Minnesota	.350
1974	Ralph Garr	Atlanta	.353		1974	Rod Carew	Minnesota	.364
1975	Bill Madlock	Chicago	.354		1975	Rod Carew	Minnesota	.359
1976	Bill Madlock	Chicago	.339		1976	George Brett	Kansas City	.333
1977	Dave Parker	Pittsburgh	.338		1977	Rod Carew	Minnesota	.388
1978	Dave Parker	Pittsburgh	.334		1978	Rod Carew	Minnesota	.333
1979	Keith Hernandez	St. Louis	.344		1979	Fred Lynn	Boston	.333
1980	Bill Buckner	Chicago	.324		1980	George Brett	Kansas City	.390
1981	Bill Madlock	Pittsburgh	.341		1981	Carney Lansford	Boston	.336
1982	Al Oliver	Montreal	.331		1982	Willie Wilson	Kansas City	.332
1983	Bill Madlock	Pittsburgh	.323		1983	Wade Boggs	Boston	.361
1984	Tony Gwynn	San Diego	.351		1984	Don Mattingly	New York	.343
1985	Willie McGee	St. Louis	.353		1985	Wade Boggs	Boston	.368
1986	Tim Raines	Montreal	.334		1986	Wade Boggs	Boston	.357
1987	Tony Gwynn	San Diego	.370		1987	Wade Boggs	Boston	.363
1988	Tony Gwynn	San Diego	.313		1988	Wade Boggs	Boston	.366
1989	Tony Gwynn	San Diego	.336		1989	Kirby Puckett	Minnesota	.339
1990	Willie McGee	St. Louis	.335		1990	George Brett	Kansas City	.329
1991	Terry Pendleton	Atlanta	.319		1991	Julio Franco	Texas	.341
1992	Gary Sheffield	San Diego	.330		1992	Edgar Martinez	Seattle	.343
1993	Andres Galarraga	Colorado	.370		1993	John Olerud	Toronto	.363
1994	Tony Gwynn	San Diego	.394		1994	Paul O'Neill	New York	.359
1995	Tony Gwynn	San Diego	.368		1995	Edgar Martinez	Seattle	.356
1996	Tony Gwynn	San Diego	.353		1996	Alex Rodriguez	Seattle	.358
1997	Tony Gwynn	San Diego	.372		1997	Frank Thomas	Chicago	.347
1998	Larry Walker	Colorado	.363		1998	Bernie Williams	New York	.339
1999	Larry Walker	Colorado	.379		1999	Nomar Garciaparra	Boston	.357
2000	Todd Helton	Colorado	.372		2000	Nomar Garciaparra	Boston	.372
2001	Larry Walker	Colorado	.350		2001	Ichiro Suzuki	Seattle	.350
2002	Barry Bonds	San Francisco	.370		2002	Manny Ramirez	Boston	.349
2003	Albert Pujols	St. Louis	.359		2003	Bill Mueller	Boston	.326
2004	Barry Bonds	San Francisco	.362		2004	Ichiro Suzuki	Seattle	.372
2005	Derrek Lee	Chicago	.335		2005	Michael Young	Texas	.331
2006	Freddy Sanchez	Pittsburgh	.344		2006	Joe Mauer	Minnesota	.347
2007	Matt Holliday	Colorado	.340		2007	Magglio Ordonez	Detroit	.363
2008	Chipper Jones	Atlanta	.364		2008	Joe Mauer	Minnesota	.328
2009	Hanley Ramirez	Florida	.342		2009	Joe Mauer	Minnesota	.365

(1) Some baseball researchers have concluded that Ty Cobb actually hit .382 in 1910 while Napoleon Lajoie, Cleveland, hit .383.

Earned Run Average Leaders, by Season

Year	Pitcher, team	G	IP	ERA		Year	Pitcher, team	G	IP	ERA
1977	John Candelaria, Pittsburgh	33	231	2.34		1977	Frank Tanana, California	31	241	2.54
1978	Craig Swan, New York	29	207	2.43		1978	Ron Guidry, New York	35	274	1.74
1979	J. R. Richard, Houston	38	292	2.71		1979	Ron Guidry, New York	33	236	2.78
1980	Don Sutton, Los Angeles	32	212	2.21		1980	Rudy May, New York	41	175	2.47
1981	Nolan Ryan, Houston	21	149	1.69		1981	Steve McCatty, Oakland	22	186	2.32
1982	Steve Rogers, Montreal	35	277	2.40		1982	Rick Sutcliffe, Cleveland	34	216	2.96
1983	Atlee Hammaker, San Francisco	23	172	2.25		1983	Rick Honeycutt, Texas	25	174	2.42
1984	Alejandro Pena, Los Angeles	28	199	2.48		1984	Mike Boddicker, Baltimore	34	261	2.79
1985	Dwight Gooden, New York	35	276	1.53		1985	Dave Stieb, Toronto	36	265	2.48
1986	Mike Scott, Houston	37	275	2.22		1986	Roger Clemens, Boston	33	254	2.48
1987	Nolan Ryan, Houston	34	211	2.76		1987	Jimmy Key, Toronto	36	261	2.76
1988	Joe Magrane, St. Louis	24	165	2.18		1988	Allan Anderson, Minnesota	30	202	2.45
1989	Scott Garrelts, San Francisco	30	193	2.28		1989	Bret Saberhagen, Kansas City	36	262	2.16
1990	Danny Darwin, Houston	48	162	2.21		1990	Roger Clemens, Boston	31	228	1.93
1991	Dennis Martinez, Montreal	31	222	2.39		1991	Roger Clemens, Boston	35	271	2.62
1992	Bill Swift, San Francisco	30	164	2.08		1992	Roger Clemens, Boston	32	246	2.41
1993	Greg Maddux, Atlanta	36	267	2.36		1993	Kevin Appier, Kansas City	34	238	2.56
1994	Greg Maddux, Atlanta	25	202	1.56		1994	Steve Ontiveros, Oakland	27	115	2.65
1995	Greg Maddux, Atlanta	28	209	1.63		1995	Randy Johnson, Seattle	30	214	2.48
1996	Kevin Brown, Florida	32	233	1.89		1996	Juan Guzman, Toronto	27	187	2.93
1997	Pedro Martinez, Montrea	31	241	1.90		1997	Roger Clemens, Toronto	34	264	2.05
1998	Greg Maddux, Atlanta	34	251	2.22		1998	Roger Clemens, Toronto	33	234	2.65
1999	Randy Johnson, Arizona	35	271	2.48		1999	Pedro Martinez, Boston	31	213	2.07
2000	Kevin K. Brown, Los Angeles	33	230	2.58		2000	Pedro Martinez, Boston	29	217	1.74
2001	Randy Johnson, Arizona	35	249	2.49		2001	Freddy Garcia, Seattle	34	238	3.05
2002	Randy Johnson, Arizona	35	260	2.32		2002	Pedro Martinez, Boston	30	199	2.26
2003	Jason Schmidt, San Francisco	29	207	2.34		2003	Pedro Martinez, Boston	29	186	2.22
2004	Jake Peavy, San Diego	27	166.1	2.27		2004	Johan Santana, Minnesota	34	228	2.61
2005	Roger Clemens, Houston	32	211.1	1.87		2005	Kevin Millwood, Cleveland	30	192	2.86
2006	Roy Oswalt, Houston	33	220.2	2.98		2006	Johan Santana, Minnesota	34	233.2	2.77
2007	Jake Peavy, San Diego	34	223.1	2.54		2007	John Lackey, Los Angeles	33	224.0	3.01
2008	Johan Santana, New York	34	234.1	2.53		2008	Cliff Lee, Cleveland	31	223.1	2.54
2009	Chris Carpenter, St. Louis	28	192.2	2.24		2009	Zack Greinke, Kansas City	33	229.1	2.16

Note: ERA is computed by multiplying earned runs allowed by 9, then dividing by innings pitched.

Strikeout Leaders, by Season

*All-time single-season record for league.

Year	National League Pitcher, team	SO	Year	American League Pitcher, team	SO
1901	Noodles Hahn, Cincinnati	239	1901	Cy Young, Boston	158
1902	Vic Willis, Boston	225	1902	Rube Waddell, Philadelphia	210
1903	Christy Mathewson, New York	267	1903	Rube Waddell, Philadelphia	302
1904	Christy Mathewson, New York	212	1904	Rube Waddell, Philadelphia	349
1905	Christy Mathewson, New York	206	1905	Rube Waddell, Philadelphia	287
1906	Fred Beebe, Chicago-St. Louis	171	1906	Rube Waddell, Philadelphia	196
1907	Christy Mathewson, New York	178	1907	Rube Waddell, Philadelphia	232
1908	Christy Mathewson, New York	259	1908	Ed Walsh, Chicago	269
1909	Orval Overall, Chicago	205	1909	Frank Smith, Chicago	177
1910	Earl Moore, Philadelphia	185	1910	Walter Johnson, Washington	313
1911	Rube Marquard, New York	237	1911	Ed Walsh, Chicago	255
1912	Grover Alexander, Philadelphia	195	1912	Walter Johnson, Washington	303
1913	Tom Seaton, Philadelphia	168	1913	Walter Johnson, Washington	243
1914	Grover Alexander, Philadelphia	214	1914	Walter Johnson, Washington	225
1915	Grover Alexander, Philadelphia	241	1915	Walter Johnson, Washington	203
1916	Grover Alexander, Philadelphia	167	1916	Walter Johnson, Washington	228
1917	Grover Alexander, Philadelphia	201	1917	Walter Johnson, Washington	188
1918	Hippo Vaughn, Chicago	148	1918	Walter Johnson, Washington	162
1919	Hippo Vaughn, Chicago	141	1919	Walter Johnson, Washington	147
1920	Grover Alexander, Chicago	173	1920	Stan Coveleski, Cleveland	133
1921	Burleigh Grimes, Brooklyn	136	1921	Walter Johnson, Washington	143
1922	Dazzy Vance, Brooklyn	134	1922	Urban Shocker, St. Louis	149
1923	Dazzy Vance, Brooklyn	197	1923	Walter Johnson, Washington	130
1924	Dazzy Vance, Brooklyn	262	1924	Walter Johnson, Washington	158
1925	Dazzy Vance, Brooklyn	221	1925	Lefty Grove, Philadelphia	116
1926	Dazzy Vance, Brooklyn	140	1926	Lefty Grove, Philadelphia	194
1927	Dazzy Vance, Brooklyn	184	1927	Lefty Grove, Philadelphia	174
1928	Dazzy Vance, Brooklyn	200	1928	Lefty Grove, Philadelphia	183
1929	Pat Malone, Chicago	166	1929	Lefty Grove, Philadelphia	170
1930	Bill Hallahan, St. Louis	177	1930	Lefty Grove, Philadelphia	209
1931	Bill Hallahan, St. Louis	159	1931	Lefty Grove, Philadelphia	175
1932	Dizzy Dean, St. Louis	191	1932	Red Ruffing, New York	190
1933	Dizzy Dean, St. Louis	199	1933	Lefty Gomez, New York	163
1934	Dizzy Dean, St. Louis	195	1934	Lefty Gomez, New York	158
1935	Dizzy Dean, St. Louis	190	1935	Tommy Bridges, Detroit	163
1936	Van Lingle Mungo, Brooklyn	238	1936	Tommy Bridges, Detroit	175
1937	Carl Hubbell, New York	159	1937	Lefty Gomez, New York	194
1938	Clay Bryant, Chicago	135	1938	Bob Feller, Cleveland	240
1939	Claude Passeau, Philadelphia-Chicago	137	1939	Bob Feller, Cleveland	246
	Bucky Walters, Cincinnati	137			
1940	Kirby Higbe, Philadelphia	137	1940	Bob Feller, Cleveland	261
1941	John Vander Meer, Cincinnati	202	1941	Bob Feller, Cleveland	260
1942	John Vander Meer, Cincinnati	186	1942	Tex Hughson, Boston	113
				Bobo Newsom, Washington	113
1943	John Vander Meer, Cincinnati	174	1943	Allie Reynolds, Cleveland	151
1944	Bill Voiselle, New York	161	1944	Hal Newhouser, Detroit	187
1945	Preacher Roe, Pittsburgh	148	1945	Hal Newhouser, Detroit	212
1946	Johnny Schmitz, Cincinnati	135	1946	Bob Feller, Cleveland	348
1947	Ewell Blackwell, Cincinnati	193	1947	Bob Feller, Cleveland	196
1948	Harry Brecheen, St. Louis	149	1948	Bob Feller, Cleveland	164
1949	Warren Spahn, Boston	151	1949	Virgil Trucks, Detroit	153
1950	Warren Spahn, Boston	191	1950	Bob Lemon, Cleveland	170
1951	Warren Spahn, Boston	164	1951	Vic Raschi, New York	164
	Don Newcombe, Brooklyn	164			
1952	Warren Spahn, Boston	183	1952	Allie Reynolds, New York	160
1953	Robin Roberts, Philadelphia	198	1953	Billy Pierce, Chicago	186
1954	Robin Roberts, Philadelphia	185	1954	Bob Turley, Baltimore	185
1955	Sam Jones, Chicago	198	1955	Herb Score, Cleveland	245
1956	Sam Jones, Chicago	176	1956	Herb Score, Cleveland	263
1957	Jack Sanford, Philadelphia	188	1957	Early Wynn, Cleveland	184
1958	Sam Jones, St. Louis	225	1958	Early Wynn, Chicago	179
1959	Don Drysdale, Los Angeles	242	1959	Jim Bunning, Detroit	201
1960	Don Drysdale, Los Angeles	246	1960	Jim Bunning, Detroit	201
1961	Sandy Koufax, Los Angeles	269	1961	Camilo Pacual, Minnesota	221
1962	Don Drysdale, Los Angeles	232	1962	Camilo Pacual, Minnesota	206
1963	Sandy Koufax, Los Angeles	306	1963	Camilo Pacual, Minnesota	202
1964	Bob Veale, Pittsburgh	250	1964	Al Downing, New York	217
1965	Sandy Koufax, Los Angeles	382*	1965	Sam McDowell, Cleveland	325
1966	Sandy Koufax, Los Angeles	317	1966	Sam McDowell, Cleveland	225
1967	Jim Bunning, Philadelphia	253	1967	Jim Lonborg, Boston	246
1968	Bob Gibson, St. Louis	268	1968	Sam McDowell, Cleveland	283
1969	Ferguson Jenkins, Chicago	273	1969	Sam McDowell, Cleveland	279
1970	Tom Seaver, New York	283	1970	Sam McDowell, Cleveland	304
1971	Tom Seaver, New York	289	1971	Mickey Lolich, Detroit	308
1972	Steve Carlton, Philadelphia	310	1972	Nolan Ryan, California	329
1973	Tom Seaver, New York	251	1973	Nolan Ryan, California	383*
1974	Steve Carlton, Philadelphia	240	1974	Nolan Ryan, California	367
1975	Tom Seaver, New York	243	1975	Frank Tanana, California	269
1976	Tom Seaver, New York	235	1976	Nolan Ryan, California	327
1977	Phil Niekro, Atlanta	262	1977	Nolan Ryan, California	341
1978	J. R. Richard, Houston	303	1978	Nolan Ryan, California	260
1979	J. R. Richard, Houston	313	1979	Nolan Ryan, California	223
1980	Steve Carlton, Philadelphia	286	1980	Len Barker, Cleveland	187
1981	Fernando Valenzuela, Los Angeles	180	1981	Len Barker, Cleveland	127
1982	Steve Carlton, Philadelphia	286	1982	Floyd Bannister, Seattle	209

National League			American League		
Year	**Pitcher, team**	**SO**	**Year**	**Pitcher, team**	**SO**
1983	Steve Carlton, Philadelphia	275	1983	Jack Morris, Detroit	232
1984	Dwight Gooden, New York	276	1984	Mark Langston, Seattle	204
1985	Dwight Gooden, New York	268	1985	Bert Blyleven, Cleveland-Minnesota	206
1986	Mike Scott, Houston	306	1986	Mark Langston, Seattle	245
1987	Nolan Ryan, Houston	270	1987	Mark Langston, Seattle	262
1988	Nolan Ryan, Houston	228	1988	Roger Clemens, Boston	291
1989	Jose DeLeon, St. Louis	201	1989	Nolan Ryan, Texas	301
1990	David Cone, New York	233	1990	Nolan Ryan, Texas	232
1991	David Cone, New York	241	1991	Roger Clemens, Boston	241
1992	John Smoltz, Atlanta	215	1992	Randy Johnson, Seattle	241
1993	Jose Rijo, Cincinnati	227	1993	Randy Johnson, Seattle	308
1994	Andy Benes, San Diego	189	1994	Randy Johnson, Seattle	204
1995	Hideo Nomo, Los Angeles	236	1995	Randy Johnson, Seattle	294
1996	John Smoltz, Atlanta	276	1996	Roger Clemens, Boston	257
1997	Curt Schilling, Philadelphia	319	1997	Roger Clemens, Toronto	292
1998	Curt Schilling, Philadelphia	300	1998	Roger Clemens, Toronto	271
1999	Randy Johnson, Arizona	364	1999	Pedro Martinez, Boston	313
2000	Randy Johnson, Arizona	347	2000	Pedro Martinez, Boston	284
2001	Randy Johnson, Arizona	372	2001	Hideo Nomo, Boston	220
2002	Randy Johnson, Arizona	334	2002	Pedro Martinez, Boston	239
2003	Kerry Wood, Chicago	266	2003	Esteban Loaiza, Chicago	207
2004	Randy Johnson, Arizona	290	2004	Johan Santana, Minnesota	265
2005	Jake Peavy, San Diego	216	2005	Johan Santana, Minnesota	238
2006	Aaron Harang, Cincinnati	216	2006	Johan Santana, Minnesota	245
2007	Jake Peavy, San Diego	240	2007	Scott Kazmir, Tampa Bay	239
2008	Tim Lincecum, San Francisco	265	2008	A. J. Burnett, Toronto	231
2009	Tim Lincecum, San Francisco	261	2009	Justin Verlander, Detroit	269

Victory Leaders by Season

*All-time single-season record for league in the "modern" era beginning in 1901.

National League			American League		
Year	**Pitcher, team**	**Wins**	**Year**	**Pitcher, team**	**Wins**
1901	Bill Donavan, Brooklyn	25	1901	Cy Young, Boston	33
1902	Jack Chesbro, Pittsburgh	28	1902	Cy Young, Boston	32
1903	Joe McGinnity, New York	31	1903	Cy Young, Boston	28
1904	Joe McGinnity, New York	35	1904	Jack Chesbro, New York	41*
1905	Christy Mathewson, New York	31	1905	Rube Waddell, Philadelphia	27
1906	Joe McGinnity, New York	27	1906	Al Orth, New York	27
1907	Christy Mathewson, New York	24	1907	Doc White, Chicago	27
1908	Christy Mathewson, New York	37*	1908	Ed Walsh, Chicago	40
1909	Mordecai Brown, Chicago	27	1909	George Mullin, Detroit	29
1910	Christy Mathewson, New York	27	1910	Jack Coombs, Philadelphia	31
1911	Grover Alexander, Chicago	28	1911	Jack Coombs, Philadelphia	28
1912	Rube Marquard, New York	26	1912	Joe Wood, Boston	34
1913	Tom Seaton, Philadelphia	27	1913	Walter Johnson, Washington	36
1914	Grover Alexander, Philadelphia	27	1914	Walter Johnson, Washington	28
1915	Grover Alexander, Philadelphia	31	1915	Walter Johnson, Washington	27
1916	Grover Alexander, Philadelphia	33	1916	Walter Johnson, Washington	25
1917	Grover Alexander, Philadelphia	30	1917	Eddie Cicotte, Chicago	28
1918	Hippo Vaughn, Chicago	22	1918	Walter Johnson, Washington	23
1919	Jesse Barnes, New York	25	1919	Eddie Cicotte, Chicago	29
1920	Grover Alexander, Philadelphia	27	1920	Jim Bagby, Cleveland	31
1921	Burleigh Grimes, Brooklyn	22	1921	Urban Shocker, St. Louis	27
1922	Eppa Rixey, Cincinnati	25	1922	Eddie Rommel, Philadelphia	27
1923	Dolf Luque, Cincinnati	27	1923	George Uhle, Cleveland	26
1924	Dazzy Vance, Brooklyn	28	1924	Walter Johnson, Washington	23
1925	Dazzy Vance, Brooklyn	22	1925	Eddie Rommel, Philadelphia	21
1926	Flint Rhem, St. Louis	20	1926	George Uhle, Cleveland	27
1927	Charlie Root, Chicago	26	1927	Ted Lyons, Chicago	22
1928	Burleigh Grimes, Pittsburgh	25	1928	George Pipgras, New York	24
1929	Pat Malone, Chicago	22	1929	George Earnshaw, Philadelphia	24
1930	Pat Malone, Chicago	20	1930	Lefty Grove, Philadelphia	28
1931	Heine Meine, Pittsburgh	19	1931	Lefty Grove, Philadelphia	31
1932	Lon Warneke, Chicago	22	1932	Alvin Crowder, Washington	26
1933	Carl Hubbell, New York	23	1933	Lefty Grove, Philadelphia	24
1934	Dizzy Dean, St. Louis	30	1934	Lefty Gomez, New York	26
1935	Dizzy Dean, St. Louis	28	1935	Wes Ferrell, Boston	25
1936	Carl Hubbell, New York	26	1936	Tommy Bridges, Detroit	23
1937	Carl Hubbell, New York	22	1937	Lefty Gomez, New York	21
1938	Bill Lee, Chicago	22	1938	Red Ruffing, New York	21
1939	Bucky Walters, Cincinnati	27	1939	Bob Feller, Cleveland	24
1940	Bucky Walters, Cincinnati	22	1940	Bob Feller, Cleveland	27
1941	Whit Wyatt, Brooklyn	22	1941	Bob Feller, Cleveland	25
1942	Mort Cooper, St. Louis	22	1942	Tex Hughson, Boston	22
1943	Rip Sewell, Pittsburgh	21	1943	Dizzy Trout, Detroit	20
1944	Bucky Walters, Cincinnati	23	1944	Hal Newhouser, Detroit	29
1945	Red Barrett, Boston-St. Louis	23	1945	Hal Newhouser, Detroit	25
1946	Howie Pollet, St. Louis	21	1946	Hal Newhouser, Detroit	26
1947	Ewell Blackwell, Cincinnati	22	1947	Bob Feller, Cleveland	20
1948	Johnny Sain, Boston	24	1948	Hal Newhouser, Detroit	21
1949	Warren Spahn, Boston	21	1949	Mel Parnell, Boston	25
1950	Warren Spahn, Boston	21	1950	Bob Lemon, Cleveland	23
1951	Sal Maglie, New York	23	1951	Bob Feller, Cleveland	22
1952	Robin Roberts, Philadelphia	28	1952	Bobby Shantz, Philadelphia	24
1953	Warren Spahn, Milwaukee	23	1953	Bob Porterfield, Washington	22
1954	Robin Roberts, Philadelphia	23	1954	Early Wynn, Cleveland	23
1955	Robin Roberts, Philadelphia	23	1955	Frank Sullivan, Boston	18
1956	Don Newcombe, Brooklyn	27	1956	Frank Lary, Detroit	21
1957	Warren Spahn, Milwaukee	21	1957	Billy Pierce, Chicago	20

National League			American League		
Year	Pitcher, team	Wins	Year	Pitcher, team	Wins
1958	Warren Spahn, Milwaukee	22	1958	Bob Turley, New York	21
1959	Warren Spahn, Milwaukee	21	1959	Early Wynn, Chicago	22
1960	Warren Spahn, Milwaukee	21	1960	Jim Perry, Cleveland	18
1961	Warren Spahn, Milwaukee	21	1961	Whitey Ford, New York	25
1962	Don Drysdale, Los Angeles	25	1962	Ralph Terry, New York	23
1963	Juan Marichal, San Francisco	25	1963	Whitey Ford, New York	24
1964	Larry Jackson, Chicago	24	1964	Gary Peters, Chicago	20
1965	Sandy Koufax, Los Angeles	26	1965	Mudcat (Jim) Grant, Minnesota	21
1966	Sandy Koufax, Los Angeles	27	1966	Jim Kaat, Minnesota	25
1967	Mike McCormick, San Francisco	22	1967	Earl Wilson, Detroit; Jim Lonborg, Boston	22
1968	Juan Marichal, San Francisco	26	1968	Denny McLain, Detroit	31
1969	Tom Seaver, New York	25	1969	Denny McLain, Detroit	24
1970	Gaylord Perry, San Francisco	23	1970	Jim Perry, Minnesota	24
1971	Fergie Jenkins, Chicago	24	1971	Mickey Lolich, Detroit	25
1972	Steve Carlton, Philadelphia	27	1972	Wilbur Wood, Chicago	24
1973	Ron Bryant, San Francisco	24	1973	Wilbur Wood, Chicago	24
1974	Phil Niekro, Atlanta	20	1974	Fergie Jenkins, Texas	25
1975	Tom Seaver, New York	22	1975	Jim Palmer, Baltimore	23
1976	Randy Jones, San Diego	22	1976	Jim Palmer, Baltimore	22
1977	Steve Carlton, Philadelphia	23	1977	Jim Palmer, Baltimore	20
1978	Gaylord Perry, San Diego	21	1978	Ron Guidry, New York	25
1979	Phil Niekro, Atlanta	21	1979	Mike Flanagan, Baltimore	23
1980	Steve Carlton, Philadelphia	24	1980	Steve Stone, Baltimore	25
1981	Tom Seaver, Cincinnati	14	1981	Pete Vuckovich, Milwaukee	14
1982	Steve Carlton, Philadelphia	23	1982	La Marr Hoyt, Chicago	19
1983	John Denny, Philadelphia	19	1983	La Marr Hoyt, Chicago	24
1984	Joaquin Andujar, St. Louis	20	1984	Mike Boddicker, Baltimore	20
1985	Dwight Gooden, New York	24	1985	Ron Guidry, New York	22
1986	Fernando Valenzuela, Los Angeles	21	1986	Roger Clemens, Boston	24
1987	Rick Sutcliffe, Chicago	18	1987	Dave Stewart, Oakland; Roger Clemens, Boston	20
1988	Danny Jackson, Cincinnati	23	1988	Frank Viola, Minnesota	24
1989	Mike Scott, Houston	20	1989	Bret Saberhagen, Kansas City	23
1990	Doug Drabek, Pittsburgh	22	1990	Bob Welch, Oakland	27
1991	John Smiley, Pittsburgh	20	1991	Bill Gullickson, Detroit	20
1992	Greg Maddux, Chicago	20	1992	Jack Morris, Toronto	21
1993	Tom Glavine, Atlanta	22	1993	Jack McDowell, Chicago	22
1994	Greg Maddux, Atlanta	16	1994	Jimmy Key, New York	17
1995	Greg Maddux, Atlanta	19	1995	Mike Mussina, Baltimore	19
1996	John Smoltz, Atlanta	24	1996	Andy Pettitte, New York	21
1997	Denny Neagle, Atlanta	20	1997	Roger Clemens, Toronto	21
1998	Tom Glavine, Atlanta	20	1998	Rick Helling, Texas; Roger Clemens, Toronto	20
1999	Mike Hampton, Houston	22	1999	Pedro Martinez, Boston	23
2000	Tom Glavine, Atlanta	21	2000	David Wells, Toronto	20
2001	Matt Morris, St. Louis; Curt Schilling, Arizona	22	2001	Mark Mulder, Oakland	21
2002	Randy Johnson, Arizona	24	2002	Barry Zito, Oakland	23
2003	Russ Ortiz, Atlanta	21	2003	Roy Halladay, Toronto	22
2004	Roy Oswalt, Houston	20	2004	Curt Schilling, Boston	21
2005	Dontrelle Willis, Florida	22	2005	Bartolo Colon, Los Angeles	21
2006	Aaron Harang, Cincinnati; Derek Lowe, Los Angeles; Brad Penny, Los Angeles; John Smoltz, Atlanta; Brandon Webb, Arizona; Carlos Zambrano, Chicago	16	2006	Johan Santana, Minnesota; Chien-Ming Wang, New York	19
2007	Jake Peavy, San Diego	19	2007	Josh Beckett, Boston	20
2008	Brandon Webb, Arizona	22	2008	Cliff Lee, Cleveland	22
2009	Adam Wainwright, St. Louis	19	2009	Felix Hernandez, Seattle; CC Sabathia, New York; Justin Verlander, Detroit	19

Cy Young Award Winners

Year	Pitcher, team	Year	Pitcher, team	Year	Pitcher, team
1956	Don Newcombe, Dodgers	1977	(NL) Steve Carlton, Phillies	1993	(NL) Greg Maddux, Braves
1957	Warren Spahn, Braves		(AL) Sparky Lyle, Yankees		(AL) Jack McDowell, White Sox
1958	Bob Turley, Yankees	1978	(NL) Gaylord Perry, Padres	1994	(NL) Greg Maddux, Braves
1959	Early Wynn, White Sox		(AL) Ron Guidry, Yankees		(AL) David Cone, Royals
1960	Vernon Law, Pirates	1979	(NL) Bruce Sutter, Cubs	1995	(NL) Greg Maddux, Braves
1961	Whitey Ford, Yankees		(AL) Mike Flanagan, Orioles		(AL) Randy Johnson, Mariners
1962	Don Drysdale, Dodgers	1980	(NL) Steve Carlton, Phillies	1996	(NL) John Smoltz, Braves
1963	Sandy Koufax, Dodgers		(AL) Steve Stone, Orioles		(AL) Pat Hentgen, Blue Jays
1964	Dean Chance, Angels	1981	(NL) Fernando Valenzuela, Dodgers	1997	(NL) Pedro Martinez, Expos
1965	Sandy Koufax, Dodgers		(AL) Rollie Fingers, Brewers		(AL) Roger Clemens, Blue Jays
1966	Sandy Koufax, Dodgers	1982	(NL) Steve Carlton, Phillies	1998	(NL) Tom Glavine, Braves
1967	(NL) Mike McCormick, Giants		(AL) Pete Vuckovich, Brewers		(AL) Roger Clemens, Blue Jays
	(AL) Jim Lonborg, Red Sox	1983	(NL) John Denny, Phillies	1999	(NL) Randy Johnson, Diamondbacks
1968	(NL) Bob Gibson, Cardinals		(AL) LaMarr Hoyt, White Sox		(AL) Pedro Martinez, Red Sox
	(AL) Dennis McLain, Tigers	1984	(NL) Rick Sutcliffe, Cubs	2000	(NL) Randy Johnson, Diamondbacks
1969	(NL) Tom Seaver, Mets		(AL) Willie Hernandez, Tigers		(AL) Pedro Martinez, Red Sox
	(AL) (tie) Dennis McLain, Tigers	1985	(NL) Dwight Gooden, Mets	2001	(NL) Randy Johnson, Diamondbacks
	Mike Cuellar, Orioles		(AL) Bret Saberhagen, Royals		(AL) Roger Clemens, Yankees
1970	(NL) Bob Gibson, Cardinals	1986	(NL) Mike Scott, Astros	2002	(NL) Randy Johnson, Diamondbacks
	(AL) Jim Perry, Twins		(AL) Roger Clemens, Red Sox		(AL) Barry Zito, Athletics
1971	(NL) Ferguson Jenkins, Cubs	1987	(NL) Steve Bedrosian, Phillies	2003	(NL) Eric Gagne, Dodgers
	(AL) Vida Blue, Athletics		(AL) Roger Clemens, Red Sox		(AL) Roy Halladay, Blue Jays
1972	(NL) Steve Carlton, Phillies	1988	(NL) Orel Hershiser, Dodgers	2004	(NL) Roger Clemens, Astros
	(AL) Gaylord Perry, Indians		(AL) Frank Viola, Twins		(AL) Johan Santana, Twins
1973	(NL) Tom Seaver, Mets	1989	(NL) Mark Davis, Padres	2005	(NL) Chris Carpenter, Cardinals
	(AL) Jim Palmer, Orioles		(AL) Bret Saberhagan, Royals		(AL) Bartolo Colon, Angels
1974	(NL) Mike Marshall, Dodgers	1990	(NL) Doug Drabek, Pirates	2006	(NL) Brandon Webb, Diamondbacks
	(AL) Jim "Catfish" Hunter, Athletics		(AL) Bob Welch, Athletics		(AL) Johan Santana, Twins
1975	(NL) Tom Seaver, Mets	1991	(NL) Tom Glavine, Braves	2007	(NL) Jake Peavy, Padres
	(AL) Jim Palmer, Orioles		(AL) Roger Clemens, Red Sox		(AL) CC Sabathia, Indians
1976	(NL) Randy Jones, Padres	1992	(NL) Greg Maddux, Cubs	2008	(NL) Tim Lincecum, Giants
	(AL) Jim Palmer, Orioles		(AL) Dennis Eckersley, Athletics		(AL) Cliff Lee, Indians

Most Valuable Players

As selected by the Baseball Writers' Assoc. of America. Prior to 1931, MVP honors were named by various sources.

National League

Year	Player, team	Year	Player, team	Year	Player, team
1931	Frank Frisch, St. Louis	1957	Hank Aaron, Milwaukee	1983	Dale Murphy, Atlanta
1932	Chuck Klein, Philadelphia	1958	Ernie Banks, Chicago	1984	Ryne Sandberg, Chicago
1933	Carl Hubbell, New York	1959	Ernie Banks, Chicago	1985	Willie McGee, St. Louis
1934	Dizzy Dean, St. Louis	1960	Dick Groat, Pittsburgh	1986	Mike Schmidt, Philadelphia
1935	Gabby Hartnett, Chicago	1961	Frank Robinson, Cincinnati	1987	Andre Dawson, Chicago
1936	Carl Hubbell, NY	1962	Maury Wills, L.A.	1988	Kirk Gibson, L.A.
1937	Joe Medwick, St. Louis	1963	Sandy Koufax, L.A.	1989	Kevin Mitchell, San Francisco
1938	Ernie Lombardi, Cincinnati	1964	Ken Boyer, St. Louis	1990	Barry Bonds, Pittsburgh
1939	Bucky Walters, Cincinnati	1965	Willie Mays, San Francisco	1991	Terry Pendleton, Atlanta
1940	Frank McCormick, Cincinnati	1966	Roberto Clemente, Pittsburgh	1992	Barry Bonds, Pittsburgh
1941	Dolph Camilli, Brooklyn	1967	Orlando Cepeda, St. Louis	1993	Barry Bonds, San Francisco
1942	Mort Cooper, St. Louis	1968	Bob Gibson, St. Louis	1994	Jeff Bagwell, Houston
1943	Stan Musial, St. Louis	1969	Willie McCovey, San Francisco	1995	Barry Larkin, Cincinnati
1944	Martin Marion, St. Louis	1970	Johnny Bench, Cincinnati	1996	Ken Caminiti, San Diego
1945	Phil Cavarretta, Chicago	1971	Joe Torre, St. Louis	1997	Larry Walker, Colorado
1946	Stan Musial, St. Louis	1972	Johnny Bench, Cincinnati	1998	Sammy Sosa, Chicago
1947	Bob Elliott, Boston	1973	Pete Rose, Cincinnati	1999	Chipper Jones, Atlanta
1948	Stan Musial, St. Louis	1974	Steve Garvey, L.A.	2000	Jeff Kent, San Francisco
1949	Jackie Robinson, Brooklyn	1975	Joe Morgan, Cincinnati	2001	Barry Bonds, San Francisco
1950	Jim Konstanty, Philadelphia	1976	Joe Morgan, Cincinnati	2002	Barry Bonds, San Francisco
1951	Roy Campanella, Brooklyn	1977	George Foster, Cincinnati	2003	Barry Bonds, San Francisco
1952	Hank Sauer, Chicago	1978	(Tie) Dave Parker, Pittsburgh	2004	Barry Bonds, San Francisco
1953	Roy Campanella, Brooklyn		Keith Hernandez, St. Louis	2005	Albert Pujols, St. Louis
1954	Willie Mays, NY	1980	Mike Schmidt, Philadelphia	2006	Ryan Howard, Philadelphia
1955	Roy Campanella, Brooklyn	1981	Mike Schmidt, Philadelphia	2007	Jimmy Rollins, Philadelphia
1956	Don Newcombe, Brooklyn	1982	Dale Murphy, Atlanta	2008	Albert Pujols, St. Louis

American League

Year	Player, team	Year	Player, team	Year	Player, team
1931	Lefty Grove, Philadelphia	1957	Mickey Mantle, NY	1983	Cal Ripken Jr., Baltimore
1932	Jimmie Foxx, Philadelphia	1958	Jackie Jensen, Boston	1984	Willie Hernandez, Detroit
1933	Jimmie Foxx, Philadelphia	1959	Nellie Fox, Chicago	1985	Don Mattingly, NY
1934	Mickey Cochrane, Detroit	1960	Roger Maris, NY	1986	Roger Clemens, Boston
1935	Hank Greenberg, Detroit	1961	Roger Maris, NY	1987	George Bell, Toronto
1936	Lou Gehrig, NY	1962	Mickey Mantle, NY	1988	Jose Canseco, Oakland
1937	Charley Gehringer, Detroit	1963	Elston Howard, NY	1989	Robin Yount, Milwaukee
1938	Jimmie Foxx, Boston	1964	Brooks Robinson, Baltimore	1990	Rickey Henderson, Oakland
1939	Joe DiMaggio, NY	1965	Zoilo Versalles, Minnesota	1991	Cal Ripken Jr., Baltimore
1940	Hank Greenberg, Detroit	1966	Frank Robinson, Baltimore	1992	Dennis Eckersley, Oakland
1941	Joe DiMaggio, NY	1967	Carl Yastrzemski, Boston	1993	Frank Thomas, Chicago
1942	Joe Gordon, NY	1968	Denny McLain, Detroit	1994	Frank Thomas, Chicago
1943	Spurgeon Chandler, NY	1969	Harmon Killebrew, Minnesota	1995	Mo Vaughn, Boston
1944	Hal Newhouser, Detroit	1970	John "Boog" Powell, Baltimore	1996	Juan Gonzalez, Texas
1945	Hal Newhouser, Detroit	1971	Vida Blue, Oakland	1997	Ken Griffey Jr., Seattle
1946	Ted Williams, Boston	1972	Dick Allen, Chicago	1998	Juan Gonzalez, Texas
1947	Joe DiMaggio, NY	1973	Reggie Jackson, Oakland	1999	Ivan Rodriguez, Texas
1948	Lou Boudreau, Cleveland	1974	Jeff Burroughs, Texas	2000	Jason Giambi, Oakland
1949	Ted Williams, Boston	1975	Fred Lynn, Boston	2001	Ichiro Suzuki, Seattle
1950	Phil Rizzuto, NY	1976	Thurman Munson, NY	2002	Miguel Tejada, Oakland
1951	Yogi Berra, NY	1977	Rod Carew, Minnesota	2003	Alex Rodriguez, Texas
1952	Bobby Shantz, Philadelphia	1978	Jim Rice, Boston	2004	Vladimir Guerrero, L.A.
1953	Al Rosen, Cleveland	1979	Don Baylor, California	2005	Alex Rodriguez, New York
1954	Yogi Berra, NY	1980	George Brett, Kansas City	2006	Justin Morneau, Minnesota
1955	Yogi Berra, NY	1981	Rollie Fingers, Milwaukee	2007	Alex Rodriguez, New York
1956	Mickey Mantle, NY	1982	Robin Yount, Milwaukee	2008	Dustin Pedroia, Boston

Rookies of the Year

(as selected by the Baseball Writers' Assoc. of America)

1947—Combined selection—Jackie Robinson, Brooklyn, 1B; 1948—Combined selection—Alvin Dark, Boston, NL, SS.

National League

Year	Player, team	Year	Player, team	Year	Player, team
1949	Don Newcombe, Brooklyn, P	1970	Carl Morton, Montreal, P	1989	Jerome Walton, Chicago, OF
1950	Sam Jethroe, Boston, OF	1971	Earl Williams, Atlanta, C	1990	Dave Justice, Atlanta, 1B
1951	Willie Mays, NY, OF	1972	Jon Matlack, NY, P	1991	Jeff Bagwell, Houston, 1B
1952	Joe Black, Brooklyn, P	1973	Gary Matthews, S.F., OF	1992	Eric Karros, L.A., 1B
1953	Jim Gilliam, Brooklyn, 2B	1974	Bake McBride, St. Louis, OF	1993	Mike Piazza, L.A., C
1954	Wally Moon, St. Louis, OF	1975	John Montefusco, S.F., P	1994	Raul Mondesi, L.A., OF
1955	Bill Virdon, St. Louis, OF	1976	Butch Metzger, San Diego, P	1995	Hideo Nomo, L.A., P
1956	Frank Robinson, Cincinnati, OF	(tie)	Pat Zachry, Cincinnati, P	1996	Todd Hollandsworth, L.A., OF
1957	Jack Sanford, Philadelphia, P	1977	Andre Dawson, Montreal, OF	1997	Scott Rolen, Philadelphia, 3B
1958	Orlando Cepeda, S.F., 1B	1978	Bob Horner, Atlanta, 3B	1998	Kerry Wood, Chicago, P
1959	Willie McCovey, S.F., 1B	1979	Rick Sutcliffe, L.A., P	1999	Scott Williamson, Cincinnati, P
1960	Frank Howard, L.A., OF	1980	Steve Howe, L.A., P	2000	Rafael Furcal, Atlanta, SS
1961	Billy Williams, Chicago, OF	1981	Fernando Valenzuela, L.A., P	2001	Albert Pujols, St. Louis, OF
1962	Ken Hubbs, Chicago, 2B	1982	Steve Sax, L.A., 2B	2002	Jason Jennings, Colorado, P
1963	Pete Rose, Cincinnati, 2B	1983	Darryl Strawberry, NY, OF	2003	Dontrelle Willis, Florida, P
1964	Richie Allen, Philadelphia, 3B	1984	Dwight Gooden, NY, P	2004	Jason Bay, Pittsburgh, OF
1965	Jim Lefebvre, L.A., 2B	1985	Vince Coleman, St. Louis, OF	2005	Ryan Howard, Philadelphia, 1B
1966	Tommy Helms, Cincinnati, 2B	1986	Todd Worrell, St. Louis, P	2006	Hanley Ramirez, Florida, SS
1967	Tom Seaver, NY, P	1987	Benito Santiago, San Diego, C	2007	Ryan Braun, Milwaukee, OF
1968	Johnny Bench, Cincinnati, C	1988	Chris Sabo, Cincinnati, 3B	2008	Geovany Soto, Chicago, C
1969	Ted Sizemore, L.A., 2B				

American League

Year	Player, team
1949	Roy Sievers, St. Louis, OF
1950	Walt Dropo, Boston, 1B
1951	Gil McDougald, NY, 3B
1952	Harry Byrd, Philadelphia, P
1953	Harvey Kuenn, Detroit, SS
1954	Bob Grim, NY, P
1955	Herb Score, Cleveland, P
1956	Luis Aparicio, Chicago, SS
1957	Tony Kubek, NY, IF-OF
1958	Albie Pearson, Washington, OF
1959	Bob Allison, Washington, OF
1960	Ron Hansen, Baltimore, SS
1961	Don Schwall, Boston, P
1962	Tom Tresh, NY,IF-OF
1963	Gary Peters, Chicago, P
1964	Tony Oliva, Minnesota, OF
1965	Curt Blefary, Baltimore, OF
1966	Tommie Agee, Chicago, OF
1967	Rod Carew, Minnesota, 2B
1968	Stan Bahnsen, NY, P
1969	Lou Piniella, Kansas City, OF
1970	Thurman Munson, NY, C
1971	Chris Chambliss, Cleveland, 1B
1972	Carlton Fisk, Boston, C
1973	Al Bumbry, Baltimore, OF
1974	Mike Hargrove, Texas, 1B
1975	Fred Lynn, Boston, OF
1976	Mark Fidrych, Detroit, P
1977	Eddie Murray, Baltimore, DH
1978	Lou Whitaker, Detroit, 2B
1979	John Castino, Minnesota, 3B
(tie)	Alfredo Griffin, Toronto, SS
1980	Joe Charboneau, Cleveland, OF
1981	Dave Righetti, NY, P
1982	Cal Ripken, Jr., Baltimore, SS
1983	Ron Kittle, Chicago, OF
1984	Alvin Davis, Seattle, 1B
1985	Ozzie Guillen, Chicago, SS
1986	Jose Canseco, Oakland, OF
1987	Mark McGwire, Oakland, 1B
1988	Walt Weiss, Oakland, SS
1989	Gregg Olson, Baltimore, P
1990	Sandy Alomar, Jr., Cleveland, C
1991	Chuck Knoblauch, Minnesota, 2B
1992	Pat Listach, Milwaukee, SS
1993	Tim Salmon, California, OF
1994	Bob Hamelin, Kansas City, DH
1995	Marty Cordova, Minnesota, OF
1996	Derek Jeter, NY, SS
1997	Nomar Garciaparra, Boston, SS
1998	Ben Grieve, Oakland, OF
1999	Carlos Beltran, Kansas City, OF
2000	Kazuhiro Sasaki, Seattle, P
2001	Ichiro Suzuki, Seattle, OF
2002	Eric Hinske, Toronto, 3B
2003	Angel Berroa, Kansas City, SS
2004	Bobby Crosby, Oakland, SS
2005	Huston Street, Oakland, P
2006	Justin Verlander, Detroit, P
2007	Dustin Pedroia, Boston, 2B
2008	Evan Longoria, Tampa Bay, 3B

Major League Pennant Winners, 1901-75

	National League						American League			
Year	Winner	Won	Lost	Pct	Manager	Year	Winner	Won	Lost	Pct	Manager
1901	Pittsburgh	90	49	.647	Clarke	1901	Chicago	83	53	.610	Griffith
1902	Pittsburgh	103	36	.741	Clarke	1902	Philadelphia	83	53	.610	Mack
1903	Pittsburgh	91	49	.650	Clarke	1903	Boston	91	47	.659	Collins
1904	New York	106	47	.693	McGraw	1904	Boston	95	59	.617	Collins
1905	New York	105	48	.686	McGraw	1905	Philadelphia	92	56	.622	Mack
1906	Chicago	116	36	.763	Chance	1906	Chicago	93	58	.616	Jones
1907	Chicago	107	45	.704	Chance	1907	Detroit	92	58	.613	Jennings
1908	Chicago	99	55	.643	Chance	1908	Detroit	90	63	.588	Jennings
1909	Pittsburgh	110	42	.724	Clarke	1909	Detroit	98	54	.645	Jennings
1910	Chicago	104	50	.675	Chance	1910	Philadelphia	102	48	.680	Mack
1911	New York	99	54	.647	McGraw	1911	Philadelphia	101	50	.669	Mack
1912	New York	103	48	.682	McGraw	1912	Boston	105	47	.691	Stahl
1913	New York	101	51	.664	McGraw	1913	Philadelphia	96	57	.627	Mack
1914	Boston	94	59	.614	Stallings	1914	Philadelphia	99	53	.651	Mack
1915	Philadelphia	90	62	.592	Moran	1915	Boston	101	50	.669	Carrigan
1916	Brooklyn	94	60	.610	Robinson	1916	Boston	91	63	.591	Carrigan
1917	New York	98	56	.636	McGraw	1917	Chicago	100	54	.649	Rowland
1918	Chicago	84	45	.651	Mitchell	1918	Boston	75	51	.595	Barrow
1919	Cincinnati	96	44	.686	Moran	1919	Chicago	88	52	.629	Gleason
1920	Brooklyn	93	60	.604	Robinson	1920	Cleveland	98	56	.636	Speaker
1921	New York	94	56	.614	McGraw	1921	New York	98	55	.641	Huggins
1922	New York	93	61	.604	McGraw	1922	New York	94	60	.610	Huggins
1923	New York	95	58	.621	McGraw	1923	New York	98	54	.645	Huggins
1924	New York	93	60	.608	McGraw	1924	Washington	92	62	.597	Harris
1925	Pittsburgh	95	58	.621	McKechnie	1925	Washington	96	55	.636	Harris
1926	St. Louis	89	65	.578	Hornsby	1926	New York	91	63	.591	Huggins
1927	Pittsburgh	94	60	.610	Bush	1927	New York	110	44	.714	Huggins
1928	St. Louis	95	59	.617	McKechnie	1928	New York	101	53	.656	Huggins
1929	Chicago	98	54	.645	McCarthy	1929	Philadelphia	104	46	.693	Mack
1930	St. Louis	92	62	.597	Street	1930	Philadelphia	102	52	.662	Mack
1931	St. Louis	101	53	.656	Street	1931	Philadelphia	107	45	.704	Mack
1932	Chicago	90	64	.584	Grimm	1932	New York	107	47	.695	McCarthy
1933	New York	91	61	.599	Terry	1933	Washington	99	53	.651	Cronin
1934	St. Louis	95	58	.621	Frisch	1934	Detroit	101	53	.656	Cochrane
1935	Chicago	100	54	.649	Grimm	1935	Detroit	93	58	.616	Cochrane
1936	New York	91	62	.597	Terry	1936	New York	102	51	.667	McCarthy
1937	New York	95	57	.625	Terry	1937	New York	102	52	.662	McCarthy
1938	Chicago	89	63	.586	Hartnett	1938	New York	99	53	.651	McCarthy
1939	Cincinnati	97	57	.630	McKechnie	1939	New York	106	45	.702	McCarthy
1940	Cincinnati	100	53	.654	McKechnie	1940	Detroit	90	64	.584	Baker
1941	Brooklyn	100	54	.649	Durocher	1941	New York	101	53	.656	McCarthy
1942	St. Louis	106	48	.688	Southworth	1942	New York	103	51	.669	McCarthy
1943	St. Louis	105	49	.682	Southworth	1943	New York	98	56	.636	McCarthy
1944	St. Louis	105	49	.682	Southworth	1944	St. Louis	89	65	.578	Sewell
1945	Chicago	98	56	.636	Grimm	1945	Detroit	88	65	.575	O'Neill
1946	St. Louis	98	58	.628	Dyer	1946	Boston	104	50	.675	Cronin
1947	Brooklyn	94	60	.610	Shotton	1947	New York	97	57	.630	Harris
1948	Boston	91	62	.595	Southworth	1948	Cleveland	97	58	.626	Boudreau
1949	Brooklyn	97	57	.630	Shotton	1949	New York	97	57	.630	Stengel
1950	Philadelphia	91	63	.591	Sawyer	1950	New York	98	56	.636	Stengel
1951	New York	98	59	.624	Durocher	1951	New York	98	56	.636	Stengel
1952	Brooklyn	96	57	.627	Dressen	1952	New York	95	59	.617	Stengel
1953	Brooklyn	105	49	.682	Dressen	1953	New York	99	52	.656	Stengel
1954	New York	97	57	.630	Durocher	1954	Cleveland	111	43	.721	Lopez
1955	Brooklyn	98	55	.641	Alston	1955	New York	96	58	.623	Stengel
1956	Brooklyn	93	61	.604	Alston	1956	New York	97	57	.630	Stengel
1957	Milwaukee	95	59	.617	Haney	1957	New York	98	56	.636	Stengel
1958	Milwaukee	92	62	.597	Haney	1958	New York	92	62	.597	Stengel
1959	Los Angeles	88	68	.564	Alston	1959	Chicago	94	60	.610	Lopez
1960	Pittsburgh	95	59	.617	Murtaugh	1960	New York	97	57	.630	Stengel
1961	Cincinnati	93	61	.604	Hutchinson	1961	New York	109	53	.673	Houk

National League

Year	Winner	Won	Lost	Pct	Manager
1962	San Francisco	103	62	.624	Dark
1963	Los Angeles	99	63	.611	Alston
1964	St. Louis	93	69	.574	Keane
1965	Los Angeles	97	65	.599	Alston
1966	Los Angeles	95	67	.586	Alston
1967	St. Louis	101	60	.627	Schoendienst
1968	St. Louis	97	65	.599	Schoendienst
1969	NY Mets	100	62	.617	Hodges
1970	Cincinnati	102	60	.630	Anderson
1971	Pittsburgh	97	65	.599	Murtaugh
1972	Cincinnati	95	59	.617	Anderson
1973	NY Mets	82	79	.509	Berra
1974	Los Angeles	102	60	.630	Alston
1975	Cincinnati	108	54	.667	Anderson

American League

Year	Winner	Won	Lost	Pct	Manager
1962	New York	96	66	.593	Houk
1963	New York	104	57	.646	Houk
1964	New York	99	63	.611	Berra
1965	Minnesota	102	60	.630	Mele
1966	Baltimore	97	63	.606	Bauer
1967	Boston	92	70	.568	Williams
1968	Detroit	103	59	.636	Smith
1969	Baltimore	109	53	.673	Weaver
1970	Baltimore	108	54	.667	Weaver
1971	Baltimore	101	57	.639	Weaver
1972	Oakland	93	62	.600	Williams
1973	Oakland	94	68	.580	Williams
1974	Oakland	90	72	.556	Dark
1975	Boston	95	65	.594	Johnson

Major League Pennant Winners, 1976-2009

National League

Year	East Winner	W	L	Pct	Manager	West Winner	W	L	Pct	Manager	Pennant winner
1976	Philadelphia	101	61	.623	Ozark	Cincinnati	102	60	.630	Anderson	Cincinnati
1977	Philadelphia	101	61	.623	Ozark	Los Angeles	98	64	.605	Lasorda	Los Angeles
1978	Philadelphia	90	72	.556	Ozark	Los Angeles	95	67	.586	Lasorda	Los Angeles
1979	Pittsburgh	98	64	.605	Tanner	Cincinnati	90	71	.559	McNamara	Pittsburgh
1980	Philadelphia	91	71	.562	Green	Houston	93	70	.571	Virdon	Philadelphia
1981(a)	Philadelphia	34	21	.618	Green	Los Angeles	36	21	.632	Lasorda	(c)
1981(b)	Montreal	30	23	.566	Williams, Fanning	Houston	33	20	.623	Virdon	Los Angeles
1982	St. Louis	92	70	.568	Herzog	Atlanta	89	73	.549	Torre	St. Louis
1983	Philadelphia	90	72	.556	Corrales, Owens	Los Angeles	91	71	.562	Lasorda	Philadelphia
1984	Chicago	96	65	.596	Frey	San Diego	92	70	.568	Williams	San Diego
1985	St. Louis	101	61	.623	Herzog	Los Angeles	95	67	.586	Lasorda	St. Louis
1986	NY Mets	108	54	.667	Johnson	Houston	96	66	.593	Lanier	New York
1987	St. Louis	95	67	.586	Herzog	San Francisco	90	72	.556	Craig	St. Louis
1988	NY Mets	100	60	.625	Johnson	Los Angeles	94	67	.584	Lasorda	Los Angeles
1989	Chicago	93	69	.571	Zimmer	San Francisco	92	70	.568	Craig	San Francisco
1990	Pittsburgh	95	67	.586	Leyland	Cincinnati	91	71	.562	Piniella	Cincinnati
1991	Pittsburgh	98	64	.605	Leyland	Atlanta	94	68	.580	Cox	Atlanta
1992	Pittsburgh	96	66	.593	Leyland	Atlanta	98	64	.605	Cox	Atlanta
1993	Philadelphia	97	65	.599	Fregosi	Atlanta	104	58	.642	Cox	Philadelphia

Year	Division	Winner	W	L	Pct	Manager	Playoffs	Pennant winner
1994(d)	East	Montreal	74	40	.649	Alou	—	—
	Central	Cincinnati	66	48	.579	Johnson		
	West	Los Angeles	58	56	.509	Lasorda		
1995	East	Atlanta	90	54	.625	Cox	Atlanta 3, Colorado* 1	Atlanta
	Central	Cincinnati	85	59	.590	Johnson	Cincinnati 3, Los Angeles 0	
	West	Los Angeles	78	66	.542	Lasorda	Atlanta 4, Cincinnati 0	
1996	East	Atlanta	96	66	.593	Cox	Atlanta 3, Los Angeles* 0	Atlanta
	Central	St. Louis	88	74	.543	La Russa	St. Louis 3, San Diego 0	
	West	San Diego	91	71	.562	Bochy	Atlanta 4, St. Louis 3	
1997	East	Atlanta	101	61	.623	Cox	Atlanta 3, Houston 0	Florida*(e)
	Central	Houston	84	78	.519	Dierker	Florida* 3, San Francisco 0	
	West	San Francisco	90	72	.556	Baker	Florida* 4, Atlanta 2	
1998	East	Atlanta	106	56	.654	Cox	Atlanta 3, Chicago* 0	San Diego
	Central	Houston	102	60	.630	Dierker	San Diego 3, Houston 1	
	West	San Diego	98	64	.605	Bochy	San Diego 4, Atlanta 2	
1999	East	Atlanta	103	59	.636	Cox	Atlanta 3, Houston 1	Atlanta
	Central	Houston	97	65	.599	Dierker	New York* 3, Arizona 1	
	West	Arizona	100	62	.617	Showalter	Atlanta 4, New York 2	
2000	East	Atlanta	95	67	.586	Cox	St. Louis 3, Atlanta 0	New York*(f)
	Central	St. Louis	95	67	.586	La Russa	New York* 3, San Francisco 1	
	West	San Francisco	97	65	.599	Baker	New York* 4, St. Louis 1	
2001	East	Atlanta	88	74	.543	Cox	Atlanta 3, Houston 0	Arizona
	Central	Houston	93	69	.574	Dierker	Arizona 3, St. Louis* 2	
	West	Arizona	92	70	.568	Brenly	Arizona 4, Atlanta 1	
2002	East	Atlanta	101	59	.631	Cox	St. Louis 3, Arizona 0	San Francisco*(g)
	Central	St. Louis	97	65	.599	La Russa	San Francisco* 3, Atlanta 2	
	West	Arizona	98	64	.605	Brenly	San Francisco 4, St. Louis 1	
2003	East	Atlanta	101	61	.623	Cox	Chicago 3, Atlanta 2	Florida*(i)
	Central	Chicago	88	74	.543	Baker	Florida* 3, San Francisco 2	
	West	San Francisco	100	61	.621	Alou	Florida* 4, Chicago 3	
2004	East	Atlanta	96	66	.593	Cox	Houston* 3, Atlanta 2	St. Louis
	Central	St. Louis	105	57	.648	La Russa	St. Louis 3, Dodgers 1	
	West	Los Angeles	93	69	.594	Tracy	St. Louis 4, Houston 3	
2005	East	Atlanta	90	72	.556	Cox	St. Louis 3, San Diego 0	Houston*(j)
	Central	St. Louis	100	62	.617	La Russa	Houston* 3, Atlanta 1	
	West	San Diego	82	80	.506	Bochy	Houston* 4, St. Louis 2	
2006	East	NY Mets	97	65	.599	Randolph	NY Mets 3, Los Angeles* 0	St. Louis
	Central	St. Louis	83	78	.516	La Russa	St. Louis 3, San Diego 1	
	West	San Diego	88	74	.543	Bochy	St. Louis 4, New York 3	
2007	East	Philadelphia	89	73	.549	Manuel	Colorado* 3, Philadelphia 0	Colorado*(m)
	Central	Chicago	85	77	.525	Piniella	Arizona 3, Chicago 0	
	West	Arizona	90	72	.556	Melvin	Colorado 4, Arizona 0	
2008	East	Philadelphia	92	70	.568	Manuel	Philadelphia 3, Milwaukee* 1	Philadelphia
	Central	Chicago	97	64	.602	Piniella	Los Angeles 3, Chicago 0	
	West	Los Angeles	84	78	.519	Torre	Philadelphia 4, Los Angeles 1	
2009	East	Philadelphia	93	69	.574	Manuel	Philadelphia 3, Colorado* 1	Philadelphia
	Central	St. Louis	91	71	.562	La Russa	Los Angeles 3, St. Louis 0	
	West	Los Angeles	95	67	.586	Torre	Philadelphia 4, Los Angeles 1	

American League

Year	East Winner	W	L	Pct	Manager	West Winner	W	L	Pct	Manager	Pennant Winner
1976	New York	97	62	.610	Martin	Kansas City	90	72	.556	Herzog	New York
1977	New York	100	62	.617	Martin	Kansas City	102	60	.630	Herzog	New York
1978	New York	100	63	.613	Martin, Lemon	Kansas City	92	70	.568	Herzog	New York
1979	Baltimore	102	57	.642	Weaver	California	88	74	.543	Fregosi	Baltimore
1980	New York	103	59	.636	Howser	Kansas City	97	65	.599	Frey	Kansas City
1981(a)	New York	34	22	.607	Michael	Oakland	37	23	.617	Martin	(c)
1981(b)	Milwaukee	31	22	.585	Rodgers	Kansas City	30	23	.566	Frey, Howser	New York
1982	Milwaukee	95	67	.586	Rodgers, Kuenn	California	93	69	.574	Mauch	Milwaukee
1983	Baltimore	98	64	.605	Altobelli	Chicago	99	63	.611	La Russa	Baltimore
1984	Detroit	104	58	.642	Anderson	Kansas City	84	78	.519	Howser	Detroit
1985	Toronto	99	62	.615	Cox	Kansas City	91	71	.562	Howser	Kansas City
1986	Boston	95	66	.590	McNamara	California	92	70	.568	Mauch	Boston
1987	Detroit	98	64	.605	Anderson	Minnesota	85	77	.525	Kelly	Minnesota
1988	Boston	89	73	.549	McNamara, Morgan	Oakland	104	58	.642	La Russa	Oakland
1989	Toronto	89	73	.549	Williams, Gaston	Oakland	99	63	.611	La Russa	Oakland
1990	Boston	88	74	.543	Morgan	Oakland	103	59	.636	La Russa	Oakland
1991	Toronto	91	71	.562	Gaston	Minnesota	95	67	.586	Kelly	Minnesota
1992	Toronto	96	66	.593	Gaston	Oakland	96	66	.593	La Russa	Toronto
1993	Toronto	95	67	.586	Gaston	Chicago	94	68	.580	Lamont	Toronto

Year	Division	Winner	W	L	Pct	Manager	Playoffs	Pennant Winner
1994(d)	East	New York	70	43	.619	Showalter	—	—
	Central	Chicago	67	46	.593	Lamont		
	West	Texas	52	62	.456	Kennedy		
1995	East	Boston	86	58	.597	Kennedy	Cleveland 3, Boston 0	Cleveland
	Central	Cleveland	100	44	.694	Hargrove	Seattle 3, New York* 2	
	West	Seattle	79	66	.545	Piniella	Cleveland 4, Seattle 2	
1996	East	New York	92	70	.568	Torre	Baltimore* 3, Cleveland 1	New York
	Central	Cleveland	99	62	.615	Hargrove	New York 3, Texas 1	
	West	Texas	90	72	.556	Oates	New York 4, Baltimore* 1	
1997	East	Baltimore	98	64	.605	Johnson	Baltimore 3, Seattle 1	Cleveland
	Central	Cleveland	86	75	.534	Hargrove	Cleveland 3, New York* 2	
	West	Seattle	90	72	.556	Piniella	Cleveland 4, Baltimore 2	
1998	East	New York	114	48	.704	Torre	New York 3, Texas 0	New York
	Central	Cleveland	89	73	.549	Hargrove	Cleveland 3, Boston* 1	
	West	Texas	88	74	.543	Oates	New York 4, Cleveland 2	
1999	East	New York	98	64	.605	Torre	New York 3, Texas 0	New York
	Central	Cleveland	97	65	.599	Hargrove	Boston* 3, Cleveland 2	
	West	Texas	95	67	.586	Oates	New York 4, Boston* 1	
2000	East	New York	87	74	.540	Torre	New York 3, Oakland 2	New York
	Central	Chicago	95	67	.586	Manuel	Seattle* 3, Chicago 0	
	West	Oakland	91	70	.565	Howe	New York 4, Seattle* 2	
2001	East	New York	95	65	.594	Torre	Seattle 3, Cleveland 2	New York
	Central	Cleveland	91	71	.562	Manuel	New York 3, Oakland 2	
	West	Seattle	116	46	.716	Piniella	New York 4, Seattle* 1	
2002	East	New York	103	58	.640	Torre	Anaheim* 3, New York 1	Anaheim*(h)
	Central	Minnesota	94	67	.584	Gardenhire	Minnesota 3, Oakland 2	
	West	Oakland	103	59	.636	Howe	Anaheim* 4, Minnesota 1	
2003	East	New York	101	61	.623	Torre	New York 3, Minnesota 1	New York
	Central	Minnesota	90	72	.556	Gardenhire	Boston* 3, Oakland 2	
	West	Oakland	96	66	.593	Macha	New York 4, Boston* 3	
2004	East	New York	101	61	.623	Torre	New York 3, Minnesota 1	Boston*(k)
	Central	Minnesota	92	70	.568	Gardenhire	Boston* 3, Anaheim 0	
	West	Anaheim	92	70	.568	Scioscia	Boston* 4, New York 3	
2005	East	New York	95	67	.586	Torre	Chicago 3, Boston* 0	Chicago
	Central	Chicago	99	63	.611	Guillen	Los Angeles 3, New York 2	
	West	Los Angeles	95	67	.586	Scioscia	Chicago 4, Los Angeles 1	
2006	East	New York	97	65	.599	Torre	Oakland 3, Minnesota 0	Detroit*(l)
	Central	Minnesota	96	66	.593	Gardenhire	Detroit* 3, New York 1	
	West	Oakland	93	69	.574	Macha	Detroit* 4, Oakland 0	
2007	East	Boston	96	66	.593	Francona	Boston 3, Los Angeles 0	Boston
	Central	Cleveland	96	66	.593	Wedge	Cleveland 3, New York* 1	
	West	Los Angeles	94	68	.580	Scioscia	Boston 4, Cleveland 3	
2008	East	Tampa Bay	97	65	.599	Maddon	Tampa Bay 3, Chicago 1	Tampa Bay
	Central	Chicago	89	74	.546	Guillen	Boston* 3, Los Angeles 1	
	West	Los Angeles	101	61	.623	Scioscia	Tampa Bay 4, Boston 3	
2009	East	New York	103	59	.636	Girardi	New York 3, Minnesota 0	New York
	Central	Minnesota	87	76	.534	Gardenhire	Los Angeles 3, Boston 0	
	West	Los Angeles	97	65	.599	Scioscia	New York 4, Los Angeles* 2	

*Wild card team. (a) First half. (b) Second half. (c) Montreal, L.A., NY Yankees, and Oakland won the divisional playoffs. (d) In Aug. 1994, a players' strike began that caused the cancellation of the remainder of the season, the playoffs, and the World Series. Teams listed as division "winners" for 1994 were leading their divisions at the time of the strike. (e) Florida manager: Jim Leyland. (f) New York manager Bobby Valentine. (g) San Francisco manager: Dusty Baker. (h) Anaheim manager: Mike Scioscia. (i) Florida manager: Jack McKeon. (j) Houston manager: Phil Garner. (k) Boston manager: Terry Francona. (l) Detroit manager: Jim Leyland. (m) Colorado manager: Clint Hurdle.

Rawlings Gold Glove Awards: 2008 and All-Time Leaders

American League

Mike Mussina, New York, P
Joe Mauer, Minneapolis, C
Carlos Pena, Tampa Bay, 1B
Dustin Pedroia, Boston, 2B
Adrian Beltre, Seattle, 3B

Michael Young, Texas, SS
Torii Hunter, Los Angeles, OF
Grady Sizemore, Cleveland, OF
Ichiro Suzuki, Seattle, OF
Greg Maddux, Los Angeles, P

National League

Yadier Molina, St. Louis, C
Adrian Gonzalez, San Diego, 1B
Brandon Phillips, Cincinnati, 2B
David Wright, New York, 3B

Jimmy Rollins, Philadelphia, SS
Carlos Beltran, New York, OF
Nate McLouth, Pittsburgh, OF
Shane Victorino, Philadelphia, OF

The following are the players at each position who have won the most Gold Gloves since the award was instituted in 1957.

Pitcher:	Greg Maddux 18	**Second base:**	Roberto Alomar 10	**Shortstop:**	Ozzie Smith 13
	Jim Kaat 16		Ryne Sandberg 9		Omar Vizquel 11
Catcher:	Ivan Rodriguez 13		Bill Mazeroski 8	**Outfield:**	Roberto Clemente . . .12
	Johnny Bench 10		Frank White 8		Willie Mays 12
First base:	Keith Hernandez 11	**Third base:**	Brooks Robinson 16		Al Kaline 10
	Don Mattingly 9		Mike Schmidt 10		Ken Griffey Jr. 10

World Series Results, 1903-2009

1903 Boston AL 5, Pittsburgh NL 3	1939 New York AL 4, Cincinnati NL 0	1975 Cincinnati NL 4, Boston AL 3
1904 No series	1940 Cincinnati NL 4, Detroit AL 3	1976 Cincinnati NL 4, New York AL 0
1905 New York NL 4, Philadelphia AL 1	1941 New York AL 4, Brooklyn NL 1	1977 New York AL 4, Los Angeles NL 2
1906 Chicago AL 4, Chicago NL 2	1942 St. Louis NL 4, New York AL 1	1978 New York AL 4, Los Angeles NL 2
1907 Chicago NL 4, Detroit AL 0, 1 tie	1943 New York AL 4, St. Louis NL 1	1979 Pittsburgh NL 4, Baltimore AL 3
1908 Chicago NL 4, Detroit AL 1	1944 St. Louis NL 4, St. Louis AL 2	1980 Philadelphia NL 4, Kansas City AL 2
1909 Pittsburgh NL 4, Detroit AL 3	1945 Detroit AL 4, Chicago NL 3	1981 Los Angeles AL 4, New York AL 2
1910 Philadelphia AL 4, Chicago NL 1	1946 St. Louis NL 4, Boston AL 3	1982 St. Louis NL 4, Milwaukee AL 3
1911 Philadelphia AL 4, New York NL 2	1947 New York AL 4, Brooklyn NL 3	1983 Baltimore AL 4, Philadelphia NL 1
1912 Boston AL 4, New York NL 3, 1 tie	1948 Cleveland AL 4, Boston NL 2	1984 Detroit AL 4, San Diego NL 1
1913 Philadelphia AL 4, New York NL 1	1949 New York AL 4, Brooklyn NL 1	1985 Kansas City AL 4, St. Louis NL 3
1914 Boston NL 4, Philadelphia AL 0	1950 New York AL 4, Philadelphia NL 0	1986 New York NL 4, Boston AL 3
1915 Boston AL 4, Philadelphia NL 1	1951 New York AL 4, New York NL 2	1987 Minnesota AL 4, St. Louis NL 3
1916 Boston AL 4, Brooklyn NL 1	1952 New York AL 4, Brooklyn NL 3	1988 Los Angeles NL 4, Oakland AL 1
1917 Chicago AL 4, New York NL 2	1953 New York AL 4, Brooklyn NL 2	1989 Oakland AL 4, San Francisco NL 0
1918 Boston AL 4, Chicago NL 2	1954 New York NL 4, Cleveland AL 0	1990 Cincinnati NL 4, Oakland AL 0
1919 Cincinnati NL 5, Chicago AL 3	1955 Brooklyn NL 4, New York AL 3	1991 Minnesota AL 4, Atlanta NL 3
1920 Cleveland AL 5, Brooklyn NL 2	1956 New York AL 4, Brooklyn NL 3	1992 Toronto AL 4, Atlanta NL 2
1921 New York NL 5, New York AL 3	1957 Milwaukee NL 4, New York AL 3	1993 Toronto AL 4, Philadelphia NL 2
1922 New York NL 4, New York AL 0, 1 tie	1958 New York AL 4, Milwaukee NL 3	1994 No series
1923 New York AL 4, New York NL 2	1959 Los Angeles NL 4, Chicago AL 2	1995 Atlanta NL 4, Cleveland AL 2
1924 Washington AL 4, New York NL 3	1960 Pittsburgh NL 4, New York AL 3	1996 New York AL 4, Atlanta NL 2
1925 Pittsburgh NL 4, Washington AL 3	1961 New York AL 4, Cincinnati NL 1	1997 Florida NL 4, Cleveland AL 3
1926 St. Louis NL 4, New York AL 3	1962 New York AL 4, San Francisco NL 3	1998 New York AL 4, San Diego NL 0
1927 New York AL 4, Pittsburgh NL 0	1963 Los Angeles NL 4, New York AL 0	1999 New York AL 4, Atlanta NL 0
1928 New York AL 4, St. Louis NL 0	1964 St. Louis NL 4, New York AL 3	2000 New York AL 4, New York NL 1
1929 Philadelphia AL 4, Chicago NL 1	1965 Los Angeles NL 4, Minnesota AL 3	2001 Arizona NL 4, New York AL 3
1930 Philadelphia AL 4, St. Louis NL 2	1966 Baltimore AL 4, Los Angeles NL 0	2002 Anaheim AL 4, San Francisco NL 3
1931 St. Louis NL 4, Philadelphia AL 3	1967 St. Louis NL 4, Boston AL 3	2003 Florida NL 4, New York AL 2
1932 New York AL 4, Chicago NL 0	1968 Detroit AL 4, St. Louis NL 3	2004 Boston AL 4, St. Louis NL 0
1933 New York NL 4, Washington AL 1	1969 New York NL 4, Baltimore AL 1	2005 Chicago AL 4, Houston NL 0
1934 St. Louis NL 4, Detroit AL 3	1970 Baltimore AL 4, Cincinnati NL 1	2006 St. Louis NL 4, Detroit AL 1
1935 Detroit AL 4, Chicago NL 2	1971 Pittsburgh NL 4, Baltimore AL 3	2007 Boston AL 4, Colorado NL 0
1936 New York AL 4, New York NL 2	1972 Oakland AL 4, Cincinnati NL 3	2008 Philadelphia NL 4, Tampa Bay AL 1
1937 New York AL 4, New York NL 1	1973 Oakland AL 4, New York NL 3	2009 New York AL 4, Philadelphia NL 2
1938 New York AL 4, Chicago NL 0	1974 Oakland AL 4, Los Angeles NL 1	

World Series Most Valuable Player

Year	Player, position, team	Year	Player, position, team	Year	Player, position, team
1955	Johnny Podres, P, Brooklyn	1975	Pete Rose, 3B, Cincinnati	1992	Pat Borders, C, Toronto
1956	Don Larsen, P, New York, AL	1976	Johnny Bench, C, Cincinnati	1993	Paul Molitor, DH, Toronto
1957	Lew Burdette, P, Milwaukee, NL	1977	Reggie Jackson, OF, NY, AL	1994	No series
1958	Bob Turley, P, New York, AL	1978	Bucky Dent, SS, NY, AL	1995	Tom Glavine, P, Atlanta
1959	Larry Sherry, P, L.A.	1979	Willie Stargell, 1B, Pittsburgh	1996	John Wetteland, P, NY, AL
1960[1]	Bobby Richardson, 2B, NY, AL	1980	Mike Schmidt, 3B, Philadelphia	1997	Livan Hernandez, P, Florida
1961	Whitey Ford, P, NY, AL	1981	Ron Cey, 3B, Los Angeles	1998	Scott Brosius, 3B, NY, AL
1962	Ralph Terry, P, NY, AL		Pedro Guerrero, OF, Los Angeles	1999	Mariano Rivera, P, NY, AL
1963	Sandy Koufax, P, Los Angeles, NL		Steve Yeager, C, L.A.	2000	Derek Jeter, SS, NY, AL
1964	Bob Gibson, P, St. Louis	1982	Darrell Porter, C, St. Louis	2001	Curt Schilling, P, Arizona
1965	Sandy Koufax, P, Los Angeles, NL	1983	Rick Dempsey, C, Baltimore		Randy Johnson, P, Arizona
1966	Frank Robinson, OF, Baltimore	1984	Alan Trammell, SS, Detroit	2002	Troy Glaus, 3B, Anaheim
1967	Bob Gibson, P, St. Louis	1985	Bret Saberhagen, P, Kansas City	2003	Josh Beckett, P, Florida
1968	Mickey Lolich, P, Detroit	1986	Ray Knight, 3B, NY, NL	2004	Manny Ramirez, OF, Boston
1969	Donn Clendenon, 1B, NY, NL	1987	Frank Viola, P, Minnesota	2005	Jermaine Dye, OF, Chicago
1970	Brooks Robinson, 3B, Baltimore	1988	Orel Hershiser, P, Los Angeles	2006	David Eckstein, SS, St. Louis
1971	Roberto Clemente, OF, Pittsburgh	1989	Dave Stewart, P, Oakland	2007	Mike Lowell, 3B, Boston
1972	Gene Tenace, C, Oakland	1990	Jose Rijo, P, Cincinnati	2008	Cole Hamels, P, Philadelphia
1973	Reggie Jackson, OF, Oakland	1991	Jack Morris, P, Minnesota	2009	Hideki Matsui, DH, New York
1974	Rollie Fingers, P, Oakland				

(1) Bobby Richardson won the MVP although Pittsburgh beat New York.

World Series Won-Lost Records, by Franchise[1]

Team	Wins	Losses	Team	Wins	Losses
New York Yankees	27	13	Toronto Blue Jays	2	0
St. Louis Cardinals	10	7	New York Mets	2	2
Philadelphia/Kansas City/Oakland A's	9	5	Cleveland Indians	2	3
Boston Red Sox	7	4	Philadelphia Phillies	2	5
Brooklyn/Los Angeles Dodgers	6	12	Chicago Cubs	2	8
Pittsburgh Pirates	5	2	L.A./California/Anaheim/L.A. Angels	1	0
Cincinnati Reds	5	4	Arizona Diamondbacks	1	0
New York/San Francisco Giants	5	12	Kansas City Royals	1	1
Detroit Tigers	4	6	Seattle Pilots/Milwaukee Brewers	0	1
Chicago White Sox	3	2	San Diego Padres	0	2
Washington Senators/Minnesota Twins	3	3	Houston Astros	0	1
St. Louis Browns/Baltimore Orioles	3	4	Colorado Rockies	0	1
Boston/Milwaukee/Atlanta Braves	3	6	Tampa Bay Rays	0	1
Florida Marlins	2	0			

(1) Through 2009. Figures represent overall series wins, not individual games.

All-Time World Series Career Leaders
(through 2009)
Batting Leaders

Batter (min. 50 PA)	Hits	AB	Avg.	Batter (min. 50 PA)	Hits	AB	Avg.
1. Pepper Martin	23	55	.418	6. Thurman Munson	25	67	.373
Paul Molitor	23	55	.418	7. George Brett	19	51	.373
3. Hal McRae	18	45	.400	8. Hank Aaron	20	55	.364
4. Lou Brock	34	87	.391	9. Home Run Baker	33	91	.363
5. Marquis Grissom	30	77	.390	10. Roberto Clemente	21	58	.362

Games Played
Yogi Berra	75
Mickey Mantle	65
Elston Howard	54
Hank Bauer	53
Gil McDougald	53
Phil Rizzuto	52
Joe DiMaggio	51
Frankie Frisch	50
Pee Wee Reese	44
Roger Maris	41
Babe Ruth	41

Hits
Yogi Berra	71
Mickey Mantle	59
Frankie Frisch	58
Joe DiMaggio	54
Derek Jeter	50
Hank Bauer	46
Pee Wee Reese	46
Gil McDougald	45
Phil Rizzuto	45
Lou Gehrig	43

Runs
Mickey Mantle	42
Yogi Berra	41
Babe Ruth	37
Derek Jeter	32
Lou Gehrig	30
Joe DiMaggio	27
Roger Maris	26
Elston Howard	25
Gil McDougald	23
Jackie Robinson	22

Runs Batted In
Mickey Mantle	40
Yogi Berra	39
Lou Gehrig	35
Babe Ruth	33
Joe DiMaggio	30
Bill Skowron	29
Duke Snider	26
Hank Bauer	24
Bill Dickey	24
Reggie Jackson	24
Gil McDougald	24

Home Runs
Mickey Mantle	18
Babe Ruth	15
Yogi Berra	12
Duke Snider	11
Lou Gehrig	10
Reggie Jackson	10
Joe DiMaggio	8
Frank Robinson	8
Bill Skowron	8
Hank Bauer	7
Goose Goslin	7
Gil McDougald	7
Chase Utley	7

Stolen Bases
Lou Brock	14
Eddie Collins	14
Frank Chance	10
Dave Lopes	10
Phil Rizzuto	10
Frankie Frisch	9
Kenny Lofton	9
Honus Wagner	9
Johnny Evers	8
Roberto Alomar	7
Rickey Henderson	7
Pepper Martin	7
Joe Morgan	7
Joe Tinker	7

Pitching Leaders

Games Pitched
Mariano Rivera	24
Whitey Ford	20
Mike Stanton	20
Rollie Fingers	16
Jeff Nelson	16
Allie Reynolds	15
Bob Turley	15
Clay Carroll	14
Clem Labine	13
Mark Wohlers	13
Waite Hoyt	12
Catfish Hunter	12
Art Nehf	12

Wins
Whitey Ford	10
Bob Gibson	7
Allie Reynolds	7
Red Ruffing	7
Chief Bender	6
Lefty Gomez	6
Waite Hoyt	6
Three Finger Brown	5
Jack Coombs	5
Catfish Hunter	5
Christy Mathewson	5
Herb Pennock	5
Andy Pettitte	5
Vic Raschi	5

Strikeouts
Whitey Ford	94
Bob Gibson	92
Allie Reynolds	62
Sandy Koufax	61
Red Ruffing	61
Chief Bender	59
George Earnshaw	56
Andy Pettitte	56
John Smoltz	52
Roger Clemens	49
Waite Hoyt	49
Christy Mathewson	48
Bob Turley	46

Saves
Mariano Rivera	11
Rollie Fingers	6
Johnny Murphy	4
Robb Nen	4
Allie Reynolds	4
John Wetteland	4
Roy Face	3
Firpo Marberry	3
Will McEnaney	3
Tug McGraw	3
Jonathan Papelbon	3
Herb Pennock	3
Troy Percival	3
Kent Tekulve	3
Todd Worrell	3

All-Star Baseball Games, 1933-2009

Year	Winner, score	Host team	Year	Winner, score	Host team	Year	Winner, score	Host team
1933*	American, 4-2	Chicago (AL)	1959*	American, 5-3	Los Angeles (NL)	1983	American, 13-3	Chicago (AL)
1934*	American, 9-7	New York (NL)	1960*	National, 5-3	Kansas City	1984	National, 3-1	San Francisco
1935*	American, 4-1	Cleveland	1960*	National, 6-0	New York (AL)	1985	National, 6-1	Minnesota
1936*	National, 4-3	Boston (NL)	1961*	National, 5-4³	San Francisco	1986	American, 3-2	Houston
1937*	American, 8-3	Washington	1961*	Called–rain, 1-1	Boston	1987	National, 2-0⁵	Oakland
1938*	National, 4-1	Cincinnati	1962*	National, 3-1³	Washington	1988	American, 2-1	Cincinnati
1939*	American, 3-1	New York (AL)	1962*	American, 9-4	Chicago (NL)	1989	American, 5-3	California
1940*	National, 4-0	St. Louis (NL)	1963*	National, 5-3	Cleveland	1990	American, 2-0	Chicago (NL)
1941*	American, 7-5	Detroit	1964*	National, 7-4	New York (NL)	1991	American, 4-2	Toronto
1942	American, 3-1	New York (NL)	1965*	National, 6-5	Minnesota	1992	American, 13-6	San Diego
1943	American, 5-3	Philadelphia (AL)	1966*	National, 2-1³	St. Louis	1993	American, 9-3	Baltimore
1944	National, 7-1	Pittsburgh	1967*	National, 2-1⁴	California	1994	National, 8-7³	Pittsburgh
1945	Not played		1968	National, 1-0	Houston	1995	National, 3-2	Texas
1946*	American, 12-0	Boston (AL)	1969*	National, 9-3	Washington	1996	National, 6-0	Philadelphia
1947*	American, 2-1	Chicago (NL)	1970	National, 5-4²	Cincinnati	1997	American, 3-1	Cleveland
1948*	American, 5-2	St. Louis (AL)	1971	American, 6-4	Detroit	1998	American, 13-8	Colorado
1949*	American, 11-7	Brooklyn	1972	National, 4-3³	Atlanta	1999	American, 4-1	Boston
1950*	National, 4-3¹	Chicago (AL)	1973	National, 7-1	Kansas City	2000	American, 6-3	Atlanta
1951*	National, 8-3	Detroit	1974	National, 7-2	Pittsburgh	2001	American, 4-1	Seattle
1952*	National, 3-2	Philadelphia (NL)	1975	National, 6-3	Milwaukee	2002	Tie, 7-7⁶	Milwaukee
1953*	National, 5-1	Cincinnati	1976	National, 7-1	Philadelphia	2003	American, 7-6⁷	Chicago (AL)
1954*	American, 11-9	Cleveland	1977	National, 7-5	New York (AL)	2004	American, 9-4	Houston
1955*	National, 6-5²	Milwaukee	1978	National, 7-3	San Diego	2005	American, 7-5	Detroit
1956*	National, 7-3	Washington	1979	National, 7-6	Seattle	2006	American, 3-2	Pittsburgh
1957*	American, 6-5	St. Louis	1980	National, 4-2	Los Angeles (NL)	2007	American, 5-4	San Francisco
1958*	American, 4-3	Baltimore	1981	National, 5-4	Cleveland	2008	American, 4-3⁸	New York (AL)
1959*	National, 5-4	Pittsburgh	1982	National, 4-1	Montreal	2009	American, 4-3	St. Louis

*Day game. (1) 14 innings. (2) 12 innings. (3) 10 innings. (4) 15 innings. (5) 13 innings. (6) Commissioner's decision, game called in the 11th inning when both teams ran out of pitchers. (7) Under rule change beginning in 2003, league winning All-Star games earned World Series home-field advantage. (8) 15 innings.

Baseball Stadiums[1]

NATIONAL LEAGUE

Team	Stadium (year opened)	Surface	Home run distances (ft.) LF	Center	RF	Seating capacity
Arizona Diamondbacks	Chase Field (1998)	Grass	330	407	334	48,652
Atlanta Braves	Turner Field (1997)	Grass	335	400	330	49,743
Chicago Cubs	Wrigley Field (1914)	Grass	355	400	353	41,160
Cincinnati Reds	Great American Ball Park (2003)	Grass	328	404	325	42,319
Colorado Rockies	Coors Field (1995)	Grass	347	415	350	50,449
Florida Marlins	Dolphin Stadium (1987)	Grass	330	434	345	38,560
Houston Astros	Minute Maid Park (2000)	Grass	315	435	326	40,976
Los Angeles Dodgers	Dodger Stadium (1962)	Grass	330	395	330	56,000
Milwaukee Brewers	Miller Park (2001)	Grass	344	400	345	41,900
New York Mets	Citi Field (2009)	Grass	335	408	330	42,000
Philadelphia Phillies	Citizens Bank Park (2004)	Grass	330	401	329	43,647
Pittsburgh Pirates	PNC Park (2001)	Grass	325	399	320	38,362
St. Louis Cardinals	Busch Stadium (2006)	Grass	336	400	335	43,975
San Diego Padres	PETCO Park (2004)	Grass	336	396	322	42,911
San Francisco Giants	AT&T Park (2000)	Grass	339	399	309	41,584
Washington Nationals	Nationals Park (2008)	Grass	336	404	335	41,888

AMERICAN LEAGUE

Team	Stadium (year opened)	Surface	LF	Center	RF	Seating capacity
Baltimore Orioles	Oriole Park at Camden Yards (1992)	Grass	333	400	318	48,190
Boston Red Sox	Fenway Park (1912)	Grass	310	420	302	36,945[2]
Chicago White Sox	U.S. Cellular Field (1991)	Grass	330	400	335	40,615
Cleveland Indians	Progressive Field (1994)	Grass	325	405	325	45,199
Detroit Tigers	Comerica Park (2000)	Grass	345	420	330	41,255
Kansas City Royals	Kauffman Stadium (1973)	Grass	330	410	330	38,177
Los Angeles Angels	Angel Stadium of Anaheim (1966)	Grass	333	404	333	42,257
Minnesota Twins	Hubert H. Humphrey Metrodome (1982)	FieldTurf	343	408	327	46,632
New York Yankees	New Yankee Stadium (2009)	Grass	318	408	314	52,325
Oakland A's	Oakland-Alameda County Coliseum (1968)	Grass	330	400	330	35,067
Seattle Mariners	Safeco Field (1999)	Grass	331	405	326	47,878
Tampa Bay Rays	Tropicana Field (1990)	FieldTurf	315	404	322	36,048
Texas Rangers	Rangers Ballpark in Arlington (1994)	Grass	332	400	325	49,170
Toronto Blue Jays	Rogers Centre (1989)	Turf	328	400	328	49,539

(1) As of 2009 season. (2) Daytime capacity; 37,373 for night games.

Major League Franchise Shifts and Additions

1953: Boston Braves (NL) became Milwaukee Braves.
1954: St. Louis Browns (AL) became Baltimore Orioles.
1955: Philadelphia Athletics (AL) became Kansas City Athletics.
1958: New York Giants (NL) became San Francisco Giants.
1958: Brooklyn Dodgers (NL) became L.A. Dodgers.
1961: Washington Senators (AL) became Minnesota Twins.
1961: L.A. Angels (renamed California Angels in 1965 and Anaheim Angels in 1997) enfranchised by the American League.
1961: Washington Senators enfranchised by the American League (a new team, replacing the former Washington club, whose franchise was moved to Minneapolis-St. Paul).
1962: Houston Colt .45's (renamed the Houston Astros in 1965) enfranchised by the National League.
1962: New York Mets enfranchised by the National League.
1966: Milwaukee Braves (NL) became Atlanta Braves.
1968: Kansas City Athletics (AL) became Oakland Athletics.

1969: Kansas City Royals and Seattle Pilots enfranchised by the American League; Montreal Expos and San Diego Padres enfranchised by the National League.
1970: Seattle Pilots became Milwaukee Brewers.
1971: Washington Senators became Texas Rangers (Dallas-Fort Worth area).
1977: Toronto Blue Jays and Seattle Mariners enfranchised by the American League.
1993: Colorado Rockies (Denver) and Florida Marlins (Miami) enfranchised by the National League.
1998: Tampa Bay Devil Rays began play in the American League; Arizona Diamondbacks (Phoenix) began play in the National League (both teams enfranchised in 1995). Milwaukee Brewers moved from the AL to the NL.
2005: Montreal Expos (NL) became Washington Nationals; Anaheim Angels became Los Angeles Angels of Anaheim.

Little League World Series, 1947-2009

The Little League World Series is played annually in Williamsport, PA.

Year	Winning team; losing team	Score	Year	Winning team; losing team	Score
1947	Williamsport, PA; Lock Haven, PA	16-7	1979	Taiwan; Campbell, CA	2-1
1948	Lock Haven, PA; St. Petersburg, FL	6-5	1980	Taiwan; Tampa, FL	4-3
1949	Hammonton, NJ; Pensacola, FL	5-0	1981	Taiwan; Tampa, FL	4-2
1950	Houston, TX; Bridgeport, CT	2-1	1982	Kirkland, WA; Taiwan	6-0
1951	Stamford, CT; Austin, TX	3-0	1983	Marietta, GA; Dominican Republic	3-1
1952	Norwalk, CT; Monongahela, PA	4-3	1984	South Korea; Altamonte Springs, FL	6-2
1953	Birmingham, AL; Schenectady, NY	1-0	1985	South Korea; Mexico	7-1
1954	Schenectady, NY; Colton, CA	7-5	1986	Taiwan; Tucson, AZ	12-0
1955	Morrisville, PA; Merchantville, NJ	4-3	1987	Chinese Taipei; Irvine, CA	21-1
1956	Roswell, NM; Delaware, NJ	3-1	1988	Chinese Taipei; Pearl City, HI	10-0
1957	Mexico; La Mesa, CA	4-0	1989	Trumbull, CT; Chinese Taipei	5-2
1958	Mexico; Kankakee, IL	10-1	1990	Chinese Taipei; Shippensburg, PA	9-0
1959	Hamtramck, MI; Auburn, CA	12-0	1991	Chinese Taipei; Danville, CA	11-0
1960	Levittown, PA; Ft. Worth, TX	5-0	1992	Long Beach, CA; Philippines*	6-0
1961	El Cajon, CA; El Campo, TX	4-2	1993	Long Beach, CA; Panama	3-2
1962	San Jose, CA; Kankakee, IL	3-0	1994	Venezuela; Northridge, CA	4-3
1963	Granada Hills, CA; Stratford, CT	2-1	1995	Taiwan; Spring, TX	17-3
1964	Staten Island, NY; Mexico	4-0	1996	Taiwan; Cranston, RI	13-3
1965	Windsor Locks, CT; Ontario, Canada	3-1	1997	Mexico; Mission Viejo, CA	5-4
1966	Houston, TX; W. New York, NJ	8-2	1998	Toms River, NJ; Japan	12-9
1967	Tokyo, Japan; Chicago, IL	4-1	1999	Japan; Phenix City, AL	5-0
1968	Osaka, Japan; Richmond, VA	1-0	2000	Venezuela; Bellaire, TX	3-2
1969	Taiwan; Santa Clara, CA	5-0	2001	Japan; Apopka, FL	2-1
1970	Wayne, NJ; Campbell, CA	2-0	2002	Louisville, KY; Japan	1-0
1971	Taiwan; Gary, IN	12-3	2003	Japan; East Boynton Beach, FL	10-1
1972	Taiwan; Hammond, IN	6-0	2004	Curacao; Conejo Valley of Thousand Oaks, CA	5-2
1973	Taiwan; Tucson, AZ	12-0	2005	Ewa Beach, HI; Curaçao, Neth. Antilles	7-6
1974	Taiwan; Red Bluff, CA	12-1	2006	Columbus, GA; Japan	2-1
1975	Lakewood, NJ; Tampa, FL	4-3	2007	Macon, GA; Japan	3-2
1976	Tokyo, Japan; Campbell, CA	10-3	2008	Waipahu, HI; Mexico	12-3
1977	Taiwan; El Cajon, CA	7-2	2009	Chula Vista, CA; Taiwan	6-3
1978	Taiwan; Danville, CA	11-1			

*Philippines won 15-4, but was disqualified for using ineligible players. Long Beach was awarded title by forfeit 6-0 (1 run per inning).

Manager of the Year

1983	(NL) Tommy Lasorda, L.A.
	(AL) Tony La Russa, Chicago
1984	(NL) Jim Frey, Chicago
	(AL) Sparky Anderson, Detroit
1985	(NL) Whitey Herzog, St. Louis
	(AL) Bobby Cox, Toronto
1986	(NL) Hal Lanier, Houston
	(AL) John McNamara, Boston
1987	(NL) Buck Rodgers, Montreal
	(AL) Sparky Anderson, Detroit
1988	(NL) Tommy Lasorda, L.A.
	(AL) Tony La Russa, Oakland
1989	(NL) Don Zimmer, Chicago
	(AL) Frank Robinson, Baltimore
1990	(NL) Jim Leyland, Pittsburgh
	(AL) Jeff Torborg, Chicago
1991	(NL) Bobby Cox, Atlanta
	(AL) Tom Kelly, Minnesota
1992	(NL) Jim Leyland, Pittsburgh
	(AL) Tony La Russa, Oakland
1993	(NL) Dusty Baker, San Francisco
	(AL) Gene Lamont, Chicago
1994	(NL) Felipe Alou, Montreal
	(AL) Buck Showalter, NY
1995	(NL) Don Baylor, Colorado
	(AL) Lou Piniella, Seattle
1996	(NL) Bruce Bochy, San Diego
	(AL) (Tie) Joe Torre, NY,
	Johnny Oates, Texas
1997	(NL) Dusty Baker, San Francisco
	(AL) Davey Johnson, Baltimore
1998	(NL) Larry Dierker, Houston
	(AL) Joe Torre, NY
1999	(NL) Jack McKeon, Cincinnati
	(AL) Jimy Williams, Boston
2000	(NL) Dusty Baker, San Francisco
	(AL) Jerry Manuel, Chicago
2001	(NL) Larry Bowa, Philadelphia
	(AL) Lou Piniella, Seattle
2002	(NL) Tony La Russa, St. Louis
	(AL) Mike Scioscia, Anaheim
2003	(NL) Jack McKeon, Florida
	(AL) Tony Pena, Kansas City
2004	(NL) Bobby Cox, Atlanta
	(AL) Buck Showalter, Texas
2005	(NL) Bobby Cox, Atlanta
	(AL) Ozzie Guillen, Chicago
2006	(NL) Joe Girardi, Florida
	(AL) Jim Leyland, Detroit
2007	(NL) Bob Melvin, Arizona
	(AL) Eric Wedge, Cleveland
2008	(NL) Lou Piniella, Chicago
	(AL) Joe Maddon, Tampa Bay

National Baseball Hall of Fame and Museum, Cooperstown, NY[1]

#Aaron, Hank "The Hammer"
Alexander, Grover Cleveland "Old Pete"
Alston, Walt
Anderson, George "Sparky"
Anson, Cap
Aparicio, Luis
Appling, Luke
Ashburn, Richie
Averill, Earl
Baker, Frank "Home Run"
Bancroft, Dave
#Banks, Ernie
Barlick, Al
Barrow, Edward G.
Beckley, Jake
Bell, James "Cool Papa"
#Bench, Johnny
Bender, Charles "Chief"
Berra, Lawrence "Yogi"
#Boggs, Wade
Bottomley, Jim
Boudreau, Lou
Bresnahan, Roger
#Brett, George
#Brock, Lou
Brouthers, Dan
Brown, Mordecai "Three Finger"
Brown, Ray
Brown, Willard
Bulkeley, Morgan C.
Bunning, Jim
Burkett, Jesse C.
Campanella, Roy
#Carew, Rod
Carey, Max
#Carlton, Steve
Carter, Gary
Cartwright, Alexander
Cepeda, Orlando
Chadwick, Henry
Chance, Frank
Chandler, Albert "Happy"
Charleston, Oscar
Chesbro, John
Chylak, Nestor
Clarke, Fred
Clarkson, John
#Clemente, Roberto
Cobb, Ty[2]
Cochrane, Mickey
Collins, Eddie
Collins, James
Combs, Earle
Comiskey, Charles A.
Conlan, John "Jocko"
Connolly, Thomas H.

Connor, Roger
Cooper, Andy
Coveleski, Stan
Crawford, Sam
Cronin, Joe
Cummings, W. A. "Candy"
Cuyler, Hazen "Kiki"
Dandridge, Ray
Davis, George "Gorgeous"
Day, Leon
Dean, Jay Hanna "Dizzy"
Delahanty, Ed
Dickey, Bill
Dihigo, Martín
DiMaggio, Joe
#Doby, Larry
Doerr, Bobby
Dreyfuss, Barney
Drysdale, Don
Duffy, Hugh
Durocher, Leo
#Eckersly, Dennis
Evans, Billy
Evers, John
Ewing, Buck
Faber, Urban "Red"
#Feller, Bob
Ferrell, Rick
Fingers, Rollie
Fisk, Carlton
Flick, Elmer H.
Ford, Whitey
Foster, Andrew "Rube"
Foster, Bill
Fox, Nellie
Foxx, Jimmie
Frick, Ford
Frisch, Frank
Galvin, James "Pud"
#Gehrig, Lou
Gehringer, Charles
#Gibson, Bob
Gibson, Josh
Giles, Warren
Gomez, Lefty
*Gordon, Joe
Goslin, Leon "Goose"
Gossage, Rich
Grant, Frank
Greenberg, Hank
Griffith, Clark
Grimes, Burleigh
Grove, Lefty
#Gwynn, Tony
Hafey, Charles "Chick"
Haines, Jesee
Hamilton, Bill
Hanlon, Ned
Harridge, Will

Harris, Bucky
Hartnett, Gabby
Heilmann, Harry
#*Henderson, Rickey
Herman, Billy
Hill, Pete
Hooper, Harry
Hornsby, Rogers
Hoyt, Waite
Hubbard, Cal
Hubbell, Carl
Huggins, Miller
Hulbert, William
Hunter, James "Catfish"
Irvin, Monte
#Jackson, Reggie
Jackson, Travis
Jenkins, Ferguson
Jennings, Hugh
Johnson, Byron "Ban"
Johnson, William "Judy"
Johnson, Walter[2]
Joss, Addie
#Kaline, Al
Keefe, Timothy
Keeler, William
Kell, George
Kelley, Joe
Kelly, George
Kelly, King
Killebrew, Harmon
Kiner, Ralph
Klein, Chuck
Klem, Bill
#Koufax, Sandy
*Kubek, Tony
Kuhn, Bowie
Lajoie, Napoleon
Landis, Kenesaw M.
Lasorda, Tom
Lazzeri, Tony
Lemon, Bob
Leonard, Buck
Lindstrom, Fred
Lloyd, Pop
Lombardi, Ernie
Lopez, Al
Lyons, Ted
Mack, Connie
Mackey, James "Biz"
MacPhail, Larry
MacPhail, Lee
Manley, Effa
#Mantle, Mickey
Manush, Henry
Maranville, Walter "Rabbit"
Marichal, Juan
Marquard, Rube
Mathews, Eddie

Mathewson, Christy[2]
#Mays, Willie
Mazeroski, Bill
McCarthy, Joe
McCarthy, Thomas
#McCovey, Willie
McGinnity, Joe
McGowan, Bill
McGraw, John
McKechnie, Bill
McPhee, John "Bid"
Medwick, Joe
Mendez, Jose
Mize, Johnny
#Molitor, Paul
#Morgan, Joe
#Murray, Eddie
#Musial, Stan
Newhouser, Hal
Nichols, Kid
Niekro, Phil
O'Malley, Walter
O'Rourke, James
Ott, Mel
Paige, Satchel
#Palmer, Jim
Pennock, Herb
Perez, Tony
Perry, Gaylord
*Peters, Nick
Plank, Ed
Pompez, Alex
Posey, Cum(berland)
#Puckett, Kirby
Radbourn, Charlie
Reese, Pee Wee
*Rice, Jim
Rice, Sam
Rickey, Branch
#Ripken, Cal, Jr.
Rixey, Eppa
Rizzuto, Phil "Scooter"
Roberts, Robin
#Robinson, Brooks
#Robinson, Frank
#Robinson, Jackie
Robinson, Wilbert
Rogan, Joe "Bullet"
Roush, Edd
Ruffing, Red
Rusie, Amos
#Ruth, Babe[2]
#Ryan, Nolan
Sandberg, Ryne
Santop, Louis
Schalk, Ray
#Schmidt, Mike
Schoendienst, Red
#Seaver, Tom
Selee, Frank
Sewell, Joe

Simmons, Al
Sisler, George
Slaughter, Enos
Smith, Hilton
#Smith, Ozzie
Snider, Duke
Southworth, Billy
#Spahn, Warren
Spalding, Albert
Speaker, Tris
#Stargell, Willie
Stearnes, Norman "Turkey"
Stengel, Casey
Sutter, Bruce
Suttles, George "Mule"
Sutton, Don
Taylor, Ben
Terry, Bill
Thompson, Sam
Tinker, Joe
Torriente, Cristobal
Traynor, Harold J. "Pie"
Vance, Arthur "Dazzy"
Vaughan, Joseph "Arky"
Veeck, Bill
Waddell, Rube
Wagner, Honus[2]
Wallace, Roderick "Bobby"
Walsh, Ed
Waner, Lloyd
Waner, Paul
Ward, John
Weaver, Earl
Weiss, George
Welch, Mickey
Wells, Willie
Wheat, Zach
White, Sol
Wilhelm, Hoyt
Wilkinson, J. L.
Williams, Billy
Williams, Joe "Smokey Joe"
Williams, Dick
#Williams, Ted
Willis, Vic
Wilson, Hack
Wilson, Jud
#Winfield, Dave
Wright, George
Wright, Harry
Wynn, Early
#Yastrzemski, Carl
Yawkey, Tom
Young, Cy
Youngs, Ross
#Yount, Robin

Note: Four players, Babe Ruth (1936), Lou Gehrig (1939), Joe DiMaggio (1955), and Roberto Clemente (1973), were inducted less than 5 years after retirement or, in Clemente's case, death. *2009 inductee. (1) Player must generally be retired for five complete seasons before being eligible for induction. (2) Players inducted in 1936 (the year the Hall of Fame began). #Players chosen in first year of Hall of Fame eligibility or under special circumstances earlier.

NATIONAL BASKETBALL ASSOCIATION

Bryant Carries L.A. Lakers to 2009 NBA Title; James Wins League MVP

The Los Angeles Lakers, led by star guard Kobe Bryant, returned to the NBA Finals for the sixth time in the last 10 years and defeated the Orlando Magic, four games to one, to earn the franchise's 15th NBA Championship. Bryant scored 30 points in the Lakers' decisive 99-86 win in Game 5 of the Finals as he earned his fourth championship ring and the club's first since 2002. Head coach Phil Jackson won his 10th NBA title, which moved him past Boston Celtics coaching legend Red Auerbach for the most titles in league history. Bryant earned NBA Finals MVP by averaging 32.4 points, 7.4 assists, and 5.6 rebounds.

The Orlando Magic won the Eastern Conference title by enduring a tough, seven-game series in the conference semifinals against the Boston Celtics, winning the series' final two games against the defending NBA champions. The Magic then vanquished the Cleveland Cavaliers in the Eastern Conference finals to advance to the league championship for the first time since 1995. All-Star center Dwight Howard scored 40 points to lead the Magic to a 103-90 victory over the Cavs in the deciding Game 6.

Cleveland had been unbeatable (literally) as it advanced to the conference finals by sweeping its first two playoff series against Detroit and Atlanta. Forward LeBron James averaged nearly 33 points per game in the first two series victories, but could not overcome the Magic despite 38.5 average points per game in the conference finals. James did earn league MVP honors during the season as he led the Cavs to a league-best 66-16 record. James averaged 28.4 points, 7.6 rebounds, and 7.2 assists during the year. Cleveland head coach Mike Brown earned Coach of the Year honors as the Cavaliers set a franchise record for victories and lost just two home games at Quicken Loans Arena during the regular season. Chicago Bulls guard Derrick Rose won the NBA Rookie of the Year award (averaging 16.8 points, 6.3 assists per game) as he helped the Bulls reach the postseason.

Shortly after the 2008-09 season, the Cavaliers made a splashy move when they acquired star center Shaquille O'Neal from the Phoenix Suns. O'Neal had teamed up with Bryant to win three straight NBA titles for the Lakers in 2000-02. A 15-time NBA All-Star who is currently fifth on the NBA all-time points list, O'Neal also led the Miami Heat to a league championship in 2006.

Final Standings, 2008-09 Season

(Playoff seeding in parentheses.)

Eastern Conference

Atlantic Division	W	L	Pct	GB
Boston Celtics (2)	62	20	.756	0
Philadelphia 76ers (6)	41	41	.500	21
New Jersey Nets	34	48	.415	28
Toronto Raptors	33	49	.402	29
New York Knicks	32	50	.390	30

Central Division	W	L	Pct	GB
Cleveland Cavaliers (1)	66	16	.805	0
Chicago Bulls (7)	41	41	.500	25
Detroit Pistons (8)	39	43	.476	27
Indiana Pacers	36	46	.439	30
Milwaukee Bucks	34	48	.415	32

Southeast Division	W	L	Pct	GB
Orlando Magic (3)	59	23	.720	0
Atlanta Hawks (4)	47	35	.573	12
Miami Heat (5)	43	39	.524	16
Charlotte Bobcats	35	47	.427	24
Washington Wizards	19	63	.232	40

Western Conference

Northwest Division	W	L	Pct	GB
Denver Nuggets (2)	54	28	.659	0
Portland Trail Blazers (4)	54	28	.659	0
Utah Jazz (8)	48	34	.585	6
Minnesota Timberwolves	24	58	.293	30
Oklahoma City Thunder	23	59	.280	31

Pacific Division	W	L	Pct	GB
Los Angeles Lakers (1)	65	17	.793	0
Phoenix Suns	46	36	.561	19
Golden State Warriors	29	53	.354	36
Los Angeles Clippers	19	63	.232	46
Sacramento Kings	17	65	.207	48

Southwest Division	W	L	Pct	GB
San Antonio Spurs (3)	54	28	.659	0
Houston Rockets (5)	53	29	.646	1
Dallas Mavericks (6)	50	32	.610	4
New Orleans Hornets (7)	49	33	.598	5
Memphis Grizzlies	24	58	.293	30

2008-09 NBA Regular Season Individual Highs

Minutes, game: 60, Jamal Crawford, Golden State v. Sacramento, Jan. 14

Points, game: 61, Kobe Bryant, L.A. Lakers v. New York, Feb. 2

Field goals, game: 22, Tony Parker, San Antonio v. Minnesota, Nov. 5

Field goal attempts, game: 39, Dwyane Wade, Miami v. Utah, Mar. 14

3-pointers, game: 11, J.R. Smith, Denver v. Sacramento, Apr. 13

3-pt. attempts, game: 18, J.R. Smith, Denver v. Sacramento, Apr. 13

Free throws, game: 24, Kevin Durant, Oklahoma City v. L.A. Clippers, Jan. 23

Free throw attempts, game: 26, Kevin Durant, Oklahoma City v. L.A. Clippers, Jan. 23; Kevin Martin, Sacramento v. Golden State, Apr. 1

Rebounds, game: 27, Marcus Camby, L.A. Clippers v. Chicago, Dec. 17

Assists, game: 22, Chris Duhon, New York v. Golden State, Nov. 29

Steals, game: 10, Brandon Roy, Portland v. Washington, Jan. 24

Blocks, game: 10, Dwight Howard, Orlando v. Oklahoma City, Nov. 12

Minutes played, season: 3,269, Andre Iguodala, Philadelphia

Off. rebounds, season: 336, Dwight Howard, Orlando

Def. rebounds, season: 757, Dwight Howard, Orlando

Personal fouls, season: 314, Jason Thompson, Sacramento

2009 NBA Playoff Results

Eastern Conference
Orlando defeated Philadelphia, 4 games to 2
Cleveland defeated Detroit, 4 games to 0
Boston defeated Chicago, 4 games to 3
Atlanta defeated Miami, 4 games to 3
Cleveland defeated Atlanta, 4 games to 0
Orlando defeated Boston, 4 games to 3
Orlando defeated Cleveland, 4 games to 2

Western Conference
Dallas defeated San Antonio, 4 games to 1
Denver defeated New Orleans, 4 games to 1
Houston defeated Portland, 4 games to 2
L.A. Lakers defeated Utah, 4 games to 1
Denver defeated Dallas, 4 games to 1
L.A. Lakers defeated Houston, 4 games to 3
L.A. Lakers defeated Denver, 4 games to 2

Championship
L.A. Lakers defeated Orlando, 4 games to 1 (100-75, 101-96, 104-108, 99-91, 99-86)

NBA Finals Composite Box Scores, 2009

L.A. Lakers	FG M-A	FT M-A	Reb O-T	Ast	Avg	Orlando Magic	FG M-A	FT M-A	Reb O-T	Ast	Avg
Kobe Bryant	58-135	37-44	3-28	37	32.4	Hedo Turkoglu	30-61	23-31	1-23	19	18.0
Pau Gasol	36-60	21-27	10-46	11	18.6	Rashard Lewis	30-74	11-13	9-38	20	17.4
Lamar Odom	26-48	11-16	10-39	4	13.4	Dwight Howard	21-43	35-58	18-76	11	15.4
Trevor Ariza	20-56	5-10	9-30	8	11.0	Rafer Alston	21-57	8-10	1-11	15	10.6
Derek Fisher	21-42	6-6	3-15	9	11.0	Mickael Pietrus	19-40	11-14	2-10	2	10.6
Andrew Bynum	12-33	6-9	10-21	3	6.0	Courtney Lee	12-32	3-4	2-7	1	5.8
Luke Walton	8-10	3-6	3-10	5	3.8	J.J. Redick	8-20	1-1	1-2	8	5.5
Jordan Farmar	7-19	2-2	2-6	2	3.4	Jameer Nelson	8-23	2-4	1-7	14	3.8
Josh Powell	2-4	0-0	2-4	1	2.5	Marcin Gortat	7-15	2-4	2-13	0	3.2
Shannon Brown	0-2	0-0	1-1	0	0.0	Tony Battie	5-11	0-0	1-4	2	2.0
Didier Ilunga-Mbenga	0-1	0-0	0-1	0	0.0						
Sasha Vujacic	0-6	0-0	0-2	2	0.0						

NBA Finals MVP, 1969-2009

1969	Jerry West, L.A. Lakers	1982	Magic Johnson, L.A. Lakers	1996	Michael Jordan, Chicago
1970	Willis Reed, New York	1983	Moses Malone, Philadelphia	1997	Michael Jordan, Chicago
1971	Lew Alcindor (Kareem Abdul-Jabbar), Milwaukee	1984	Larry Bird, Boston	1998	Michael Jordan, Chicago
		1985	Kareem Abdul-Jabbar, L.A. Lakers	1999	Tim Duncan, San Antonio
1972	Wilt Chamberlain, L.A. Lakers	1986	Larry Bird, Boston	2000	Shaquille O'Neal, L.A. Lakers
1973	Willis Reed, New York	1987	Magic Johnson, L.A. Lakers	2001	Shaquille O'Neal, L.A. Lakers
1974	John Havlicek, Boston	1988	James Worthy, L.A. Lakers	2002	Shaquille O'Neal, L.A. Lakers
1975	Rick Barry, Golden State	1989	Joe Dumars, Detroit	2003	Tim Duncan, San Antonio
1976	JoJo White, Boston	1990	Isiah Thomas, Detroit	2004	Chauncey Billups, Detroit
1977	Bill Walton, Portland	1991	Michael Jordan, Chicago	2005	Tim Duncan, San Antonio
1978	Wes Unseld, Washington	1992	Michael Jordan, Chicago	2006	Dwyane Wade, Miami
1979	Dennis Johnson, Seattle	1993	Michael Jordan, Chicago	2007	Tony Parker, San Antonio
1980	Magic Johnson, L.A. Lakers	1994	Hakeem Olajuwon, Houston	2008	Paul Pierce, Boston Celtics
1981	Cedric Maxwell, Boston	1995	Hakeem Olajuwon, Houston	2009	Kobe Bryant, L.A. Lakers

NBA Finals All-Time Statistical Leaders

(At the end of the 2009 NBA Finals. *Player active in 2008-09 season. Minimum 10 games.)

Scoring average leader	G	FG	FT	Pts	Avg	Scoring average leader	G	FG	FT	Pts	Avg
Rick Barry	10	138	87	363	36.3	Elgin Baylor	44	442	277	1,161	26.4
Michael Jordan	35	438	258	1,176	33.6	Julius Erving	22	216	128	561	25.5
Jerry West	55	612	455	1,679	30.5	Joe Fulks	11	84	104	272	24.7
*Shaquille O'Neal	30	340	185	865	28.8	*Kobe Bryant	30	267	170	737	24.6
Bob Pettit	25	241	227	709	28.4	Clyde Drexler	15	126	108	367	24.5
Hakeem Olajuwon	17	187	91	467	27.5						

Games played		Rebounds		Assists	
Bill Russell	70	Bill Russell	1,718	Magic Johnson	584
Sam Jones	64	Wilt Chamberlain	862	Bob Cousy	400
Kareem Abdul-Jabbar	56	Elgin Baylor	593	Bill Russell	315
Jerry West	55	Kareem Abdul-Jabbar	507	Jerry West	306
Tom Heinsohn	52	Tom Heinsohn	473	Dennis Johnson	228

NBA Scoring Leaders, 1947-2009

Year	Scoring champion	Pts	Avg	Year	Scoring champion	Pts	Avg
1947	Joe Fulks, Philadelphia	1,389	23.2	1979	George Gervin, San Antonio	2,365	29.6
1948	Max Zaslofsky, Chicago	1,007	21.0	1980	George Gervin, San Antonio	2,585	33.1
1949	George Mikan, Minneapolis	1,698	28.3	1981	Adrian Dantley, Utah	2,452	30.7
1950	George Mikan, Minneapolis	1,865	27.4	1982	George Gervin, San Antonio	2,551	32.3
1951	George Mikan, Minneapolis	1,932	28.4	1983	Alex English, Denver	2,326	28.4
1952	Paul Arizin, Philadelphia	1,674	25.4	1984	Adrian Dantley, Utah	2,418	30.6
1953	Neil Johnston, Philadelphia	1,564	22.3	1985	Bernard King, New York	1,809	32.9
1954	Neil Johnston, Philadelphia	1,759	24.4	1986	Dominique Wilkins, Atlanta	2,366	30.3
1955	Neil Johnston, Philadelphia	1,631	22.7	1987	Michael Jordan, Chicago	3,041	37.1
1956	Bob Pettit, St. Louis	1,849	25.7	1988	Michael Jordan, Chicago	2,868	35.0
1957	Paul Arizin, Philadelphia	1,817	25.6	1989	Michael Jordan, Chicago	2,633	32.5
1958	George Yardley, Detroit	2,001	27.8	1990	Michael Jordan, Chicago	2,753	33.6
1959	Bob Pettit, St. Louis	2,105	29.2	1991	Michael Jordan, Chicago	2,580	31.5
1960	Wilt Chamberlain, Philadelphia	2,707	37.9	1992	Michael Jordan, Chicago	2,404	30.1
1961	Wilt Chamberlain, Philadelphia	3,033	38.4	1993	Michael Jordan, Chicago	2,541	32.6
1962	Wilt Chamberlain, Philadelphia	4,029	50.4	1994	David Robinson, San Antonio	2,383	29.8
1963	Wilt Chamberlain, San Francisco	3,586	44.8	1995	Shaquille O'Neal, Orlando	2,315	29.3
1964	Wilt Chamberlain, San Francisco	2,948	36.5	1996	Michael Jordan, Chicago	2,465	30.4
1965	Wilt Chamberlain, San Francisco, Phil.	2,534	34.7	1997	Michael Jordan, Chicago	2,431	29.6
1966	Wilt Chamberlain, Philadelphia	2,649	33.5	1998	Michael Jordan, Chicago	2,357	28.7
1967	Rick Barry, San Francisco	2,775	35.6	1999	Allen Iverson, Philadelphia	1,284	26.8
1968	Dave Bing, Detroit	2,142	27.1	2000	Shaquille O'Neal, L.A. Lakers	2,344	29.7
1969	Elvin Hayes, San Diego	2,327	28.4	2001	Allen Iverson, Philadelphia	2,207	31.1
1970	Jerry West, L.A. Lakers	2,309	31.2	2002	Allen Iverson, Philadelphia	1,883	31.4
1971	Lew Alcindor (Abdul-Jabbar), Milwaukee	2,596	31.7	2003	Tracy McGrady, Orlando	2,407	32.1
1972	Kareem Abdul-Jabbar, Milwaukee	2,822	34.8	2004	Tracy McGrady, Orlando	1,878	28.0
1973	Nate Archibald, Kansas City-Omaha	2,719	34.0	2005	Allen Iverson, Philadelphia	2,302	30.7
1974	Bob McAdoo, Buffalo	2,261	30.6	2006	Kobe Bryant, L.A. Lakers	2,832	35.4
1975	Bob McAdoo, Buffalo	2,831	34.5	2007	Kobe Bryant, L.A. Lakers	2,430	31.6
1976	Bob McAdoo, Buffalo	2,427	31.1	2008	LeBron James, Cleveland	2,250	30.0
1977	Pete Maravich, New Orleans	2,273	31.1	2009	Dwyane Wade, Miami	2,386	30.2
1978	George Gervin, San Antonio	2,232	27.2				

NBA Most Valuable Player, 1956-2009

1956	Bob Pettit, St. Louis	1961	Bill Russell, Boston	1966	Wilt Chamberlain, Philadelphia
1957	Bob Cousy, Boston	1962	Bill Russell, Boston	1967	Wilt Chamberlain, Philadelphia
1958	Bill Russell, Boston	1963	Bill Russell, Boston	1968	Wilt Chamberlain, Philadelphia
1959	Bob Pettit, St. Louis	1964	Oscar Robertson, Cincinnati	1969	Wes Unseld, Baltimore
1960	Wilt Chamberlain, Philadelphia	1965	Bill Russell, Boston	1970	Willis Reed, New York

1971	Lew Alcindor (Abdul-Jabbar), Milw.	1984	Larry Bird, Boston	1997	Karl Malone, Utah
1972	Kareem Abdul-Jabbar, Milwaukee	1985	Larry Bird, Boston	1998	Michael Jordan, Chicago
1973	Dave Cowens, Boston	1986	Larry Bird, Boston	1999	Karl Malone, Utah
1974	Kareem Abdul-Jabbar, Milwaukee	1987	Magic Johnson, L.A. Lakers	2000	Shaquille O'Neal, L.A. Lakers
1975	Bob McAdoo, Buffalo	1988	Michael Jordan, Chicago	2001	Allen Iverson, Philadelphia
1976	Kareem Abdul-Jabbar, L.A. Lakers	1989	Magic Johnson, L.A. Lakers	2002	Tim Duncan, San Antonio
1977	Kareem Abdul-Jabbar, L.A. Lakers	1990	Magic Johnson, L.A. Lakers	2003	Tim Duncan, San Antonio
1978	Bill Walton, Portland	1991	Michael Jordan, Chicago	2004	Kevin Garnett, Minnesota
1979	Moses Malone, Houston	1992	Michael Jordan, Chicago	2005	Steve Nash, Phoenix
1980	Kareem Abdul-Jabbar, L.A. Lakers	1993	Charles Barkley, Phoenix	2006	Steve Nash, Phoenix
1981	Julius Erving, Philadelphia	1994	Hakeem Olajuwon, Houston	2007	Dirk Nowitzki, Dallas
1982	Moses Malone, Houston	1995	David Robinson, San Antonio	2008	Kobe Bryant, L.A. Lakers
1983	Moses Malone, Philadelphia	1996	Michael Jordan, Chicago	2009	LeBron James, Cleveland

NBA Champions, 1947-2009

	Regular season		Playoffs		
Year	Eastern Conference	Western Conference	Champion	Coach	Runner-up
1947	Washington Capitols	Chicago Stags	Philadelphia	Ed Gottlieb	Chicago
1948	Philadelphia Warriors	St. Louis Bombers	Baltimore	Buddy Jeannette	Philadelphia
1949	Washington Capitols	Rochester	Minneapolis	John Kundla	Washington
1950	Syracuse	Minneapolis	Minneapolis	John Kundla	Syracuse
1951	Philadelphia Warriors	Minneapolis	Rochester	Lester Harrison	New York
1952	Syracuse	Rochester	Minneapolis	John Kundla	New York
1953	New York	Minneapolis	Minneapolis	John Kundla	New York
1954	New York	Minneapolis	Minneapolis	John Kundla	Syracuse
1955	Syracuse	Ft. Wayne	Syracuse	Al Cervi	Ft. Wayne
1956	Philadelphia Warriors	Ft. Wayne	Philadelphia	George Senesky	Ft. Wayne
1957	Boston	St. Louis	Boston	Red Auerbach	St. Louis
1958	Boston	St. Louis	St. Louis	Alex Hannum	Boston
1959	Boston	St. Louis	Boston	Red Auerbach	Minneapolis
1960	Boston	St. Louis	Boston	Red Auerbach	St. Louis
1961	Boston	St. Louis	Boston	Red Auerbach	St. Louis
1962	Boston	L.A. Lakers	Boston	Red Auerbach	L.A. Lakers
1963	Boston	L.A. Lakers	Boston	Red Auerbach	L.A. Lakers
1964	Boston	San Francisco	Boston	Red Auerbach	San Francisco
1965	Boston	L.A. Lakers	Boston	Red Auerbach	L.A. Lakers
1966	Philadelphia	L.A. Lakers	Boston	Red Auerbach	L.A. Lakers
1967	Philadelphia	San Francisco	Philadelphia	Alex Hannum	San Francisco
1968	Philadelphia	St. Louis	Boston	Bill Russell	L.A. Lakers
1969	Baltimore	L.A. Lakers	Boston	Bill Russell	L.A. Lakers
1970	New York	Atlanta	New York	Red Holzman	L.A. Lakers

Year	Atlantic	Central	Midwest	Pacific	Champion	Coach	Runner-up
1971	New York	Baltimore	Milwaukee	L.A. Lakers	Milwaukee	Larry Costello	Baltimore
1972	Boston	Baltimore	Milwaukee	L.A. Lakers	L.A. Lakers	Bill Sharman	New York
1973	Boston	Baltimore	Milwaukee	L.A. Lakers	New York	Red Holzman	L.A. Lakers
1974	Boston	Capital	Milwaukee	L.A. Lakers	Boston	Tom Heinsohn	Milwaukee
1975	Boston	Washington	Chicago	Golden State	Golden State	Al Attles	Washington
1976	Boston	Cleveland	Milwaukee	Golden State	Boston	Tom Heinsohn	Phoenix
1977	Philadelphia	Houston	Denver	L.A. Lakers	Portland	Jack Ramsay	Philadelphia
1978	Philadelphia	San Antonio	Denver	Portland	Washington	Dick Motta	Seattle
1979	Washington	San Antonio	Kansas City	Seattle	Seattle	Len Wilkens	Washington
1980	Boston	Atlanta	Milwaukee	L.A. Lakers	L.A. Lakers	Paul Westhead	Philadelphia
1981	Boston	Milwaukee	San Antonio	Phoenix	Boston	Bill Fitch	Houston
1982	Boston	Milwaukee	San Antonio	L.A. Lakers	L.A. Lakers	Pat Riley	Philadelphia
1983	Philadelphia	Milwaukee	San Antonio	L.A. Lakers	Philadelphia	Billy Cunningham	L.A. Lakers
1984	Boston	Milwaukee	Utah	L.A. Lakers	Boston	K.C. Jones	L.A. Lakers
1985	Boston	Milwaukee	Denver	L.A. Lakers	L.A. Lakers	Pat Riley	Boston
1986	Boston	Milwaukee	Houston	L.A. Lakers	Boston	K.C. Jones	Houston
1987	Boston	Atlanta	Dallas	L.A. Lakers	L.A. Lakers	Pat Riley	Boston
1988	Boston	Detroit	Denver	L.A. Lakers	L.A. Lakers	Pat Riley	Detroit
1989	New York	Detroit	Utah	L.A. Lakers	Detroit	Chuck Daly	L.A. Lakers
1990	Philadelphia	Detroit	San Antonio	L.A. Lakers	Detroit	Chuck Daly	Portland
1991	Boston	Chicago	San Antonio	Portland	Chicago	Phil Jackson	L.A. Lakers
1992	Boston	Chicago	Utah	Portland	Chicago	Phil Jackson	Portland
1993	New York	Chicago	Houston	Phoenix	Chicago	Phil Jackson	Phoenix
1994	New York	Atlanta	Houston	Seattle	Houston	Rudy Tomjanovich	New York
1995	Orlando	Indiana	San Antonio	Phoenix	Houston	Rudy Tomjanovich	Orlando
1996	Orlando	Chicago	San Antonio	Seattle	Chicago	Phil Jackson	Seattle
1997	Miami	Chicago	Utah	Seattle	Chicago	Phil Jackson	Utah
1998	Miami	Chicago	Utah	L.A. Lakers	Chicago	Phil Jackson	Utah
1999	Miami	Indiana	San Antonio	Portland	San Antonio	Gregg Popovich	New York
2000	Miami	Indiana	Utah	L.A. Lakers	L.A. Lakers	Phil Jackson	Indiana
2001	Philadelphia	Milwaukee	San Antonio	L.A. Lakers	L.A. Lakers	Phil Jackson	Philadelphia
2002	New Jersey	Detroit	San Antonio	Sacramento	L.A. Lakers	Phil Jackson	New Jersey
2003	New Jersey	Detroit	San Antonio	Sacramento	San Antonio	Gregg Popovich	New Jersey
2004	New Jersey	Indiana	Minnesota	L.A. Lakers	Detroit	Larry Brown	L.A. Lakers

Year	Atlantic	Central	Southeast	Northwest	Pacific	Southwest	Champion	Coach	Runner-up
2005	Boston	Detroit	Miami	Seattle	Phoenix	San Antonio	San Antonio	Gregg Popovich	Detroit
2006	New Jersey	Detroit	Miami	Denver	Phoenix	San Antonio	Miami	Pat Riley	Dallas
2007	Toronto	Detroit	Miami	Utah	Phoenix	Dallas	San Antonio	Gregg Popovich	Cleveland
2008	Boston	Detroit	Orlando	Utah	L.A. Lakers	New Orleans	Boston	Glenn "Doc" Rivers	L.A. Lakers
2009	Boston	Cleveland	Orlando	Denver	L.A. Lakers	San Antonio	L.A. Lakers	Phil Jackson	Orlando

All-NBA and All-Defensive Teams, 2008-09

	All-NBA Team			All-Defensive Team	
First Team	Second Team	Position	First Team	Second Team
LeBron James, Cleveland	Tim Duncan, San Antonio	Forward	LeBron James, Cleveland	Shane Battier, Houston
Dirk Nowitzki, Dallas	Paul Pierce, Boston	Forward	Kevin Garnett, Boston	Ron Artest, Houston
Dwight Howard, Orlando	Yao Ming, Houston	Center	Dwight Howard, Orlando	Tim Duncan, San Antonio
Kobe Bryant, L.A. Lakers	Brandon Roy, Portland	Guard	Kobe Bryant, L.A. Lakers	Dwyane Wade, Miami
Dwyane Wade, Miami	Chris Paul, New Orleans	Guard	Chris Paul, New Orleans	Rajon Rondo, Boston

NBA Coach of the Year, 1963-2009

Year	Coach	Year	Coach	Year	Coach
1963	Harry Gallatin, St. Louis	1979	Cotton Fitzsimmons, Kansas City	1995	Del Harris, L.A. Lakers
1964	Alex Hannum, San Francisco	1980	Bill Fitch, Boston	1996	Phil Jackson, Chicago
1965	Red Auerbach, Boston	1981	Jack McKinney, Indiana	1997	Pat Riley, Miami
1966	Dolph Schayes, Philadelphia	1982	Gene Shue, Washington	1998	Larry Bird, Indiana
1967	Johnny Kerr, Chicago	1983	Don Nelson, Milwaukee	1999	Mike Dunleavy, Portland
1968	Richie Guerin, St. Louis	1984	Frank Layden, Utah	2000	Glenn "Doc" Rivers, Orlando
1969	Gene Shue, Baltimore	1985	Don Nelson, Milwaukee	2001	Larry Brown, Philadelphia
1970	Red Holzman, New York	1986	Mike Fratello, Atlanta	2002	Rick Carlisle, Detroit
1971	Dick Motta, Chicago	1987	Mike Schuler, Portland	2003	Gregg Popovich, San Antonio
1972	Bill Sharman, L.A. Lakers	1988	Doug Moe, Denver	2004	Hubie Brown, Memphis
1973	Tom Heinsohn, Boston	1989	Cotton Fitzsimmons, Phoenix	2005	Mike D'Antoni, Phoenix
1974	Ray Scott, Detroit	1990	Pat Riley, L.A. Lakers	2006	Avery Johnson, Dallas
1975	Phil Johnson, Kansas City-Omaha	1991	Don Chaney, Houston	2007	Sam Mitchell, Toronto
1976	Bill Fitch, Cleveland	1992	Don Nelson, Golden State	2008	Byron Scott, New Orleans
1977	Tom Nissalke, Houston	1993	Pat Riley, New York	2009	Mike Brown, Cleveland
1978	Hubie Brown, Atlanta	1994	Lenny Wilkens, Atlanta		

NBA Statistical Leaders, 2008-09

Scoring Average
(Minimum 70 games or 1,400 pts)

	G	FG	FT	Pts	Avg
Dwyane Wade, Miami	79	854	590	2,386	30.2
LeBron James, Cleveland	81	789	594	2,304	28.4
Kobe Bryant, L.A. Lakers	82	800	483	2,201	26.8
Dirk Nowitzki, Dallas	81	774	485	2,094	25.9
Danny Granger, Indiana	67	571	404	1,728	25.8
Kevin Durant, Oklahoma	74	661	452	1,871	25.3
Chris Paul, New Orleans	78	631	455	1,781	22.8
Carmelo Anthony, Denver	66	535	371	1,504	22.8
Chris Bosh, Toronto	77	615	504	1,746	22.7
Brandon Roy, Portland	78	633	416	1,765	22.6

Rebounds per Game
(Minimum 70 games or 800 rebounds)

	G	Off	Def	Tot	Avg
Dwight Howard, Orlando	79	336	757	1,093	13.8
Troy Murphy, Indiana	73	146	715	861	11.8
David Lee, New York	81	256	695	951	11.7
Tim Duncan, San Antonio	75	201	599	800	10.7
Emeka Okafor, Charlotte	82	275	552	827	10.1
Chris Bosh, Toronto	77	215	556	771	10.0
Yao Ming, Houston	77	204	557	761	9.9
Pau Gasol, L.A. Lakers	81	262	518	780	9.6
Kevin Love, Minnesota	81	274	460	734	9.1
Antawn Jamison, Washington	81	196	525	721	8.9

3-Point Field Goal Percentage
(Minimum 55 3-point field goals made)

	3-FGM	3-FGA	Pct
Anthony Morrow, Golden State	86	184	.467
Jameer Nelson, Orlando	82	181	.453
Troy Murphy, Indiana	161	358	.450
Kelenna Azubuike, Golden State	94	210	.448
Bobby Simmons, New Jersey	117	262	.447
Mehmet Okur, Utah	90	202	.446
Eddie House, Boston	151	340	.444
Matt Bonner, San Antonio	118	268	.440
D. J. Augustin, Charlotte	108	246	.439
Steve Nash, Phoenix	108	246	.439

Assists per Game
(Minimum 70 games or 400 assists)

	G	Ast	Avg
Chris Paul, New Orleans	78	861	11.0
Deron Williams, Utah	68	725	10.7
Steve Nash, Phoenix	74	717	9.7
Jose Calderon, Toronto	68	607	8.9
Jason Kidd, Dallas	81	702	8.7
Rajon Rondo, Boston	80	659	8.2
Baron Davis, L.A. Clippers	65	501	7.7
Dwyane Wade, Miami	79	589	7.5
LeBron James, Cleveland	81	587	7.2
Chris Duhon, New York	79	566	7.2

Field Goal Percentage
(Minimum 300 field goals made)

	FGM	FGA	Pct
Shaquille O'Neal, Phoenix	512	841	.609
Nene Hilario, Denver	428	709	.604
Andris Biedrins, Golden State	308	533	.578
Dwight Howard, Orlando	560	979	.572
Pau Gasol, L.A. Lakers	592	1,045	.567
Emeka Okafor, Charlotte	433	772	.561
David Lee, New York	522	951	.549
Yao Ming, Houston	566	1,032	.548
Amar'e Stoudemire, Phoenix	404	749	.539
Paul Millsap, Utah	400	749	.534

Steals per Game
(Minimum 70 games or 125 steals)

	G	Stl	Avg
Chris Paul, New Orleans	78	216	2.8
Dwyane Wade, Miami	79	173	2.2
Jason Kidd, Dallas	81	160	2.0
Mario Chalmers, Miami	82	160	2.0
Rajon Rondo, Boston	80	149	1.9
Gerald Wallace, Charlotte	71	121	1.7
Ronnie Brewer, Utah	81	138	1.7
LeBron James, Cleveland	81	137	1.7
Trevor Ariza, L.A. Lakers	82	137	1.7
Andre Iguodala, Philadelphia	82	131	1.6

Free Throw Percentage
(Minimum 125 free throws made)

	FTM	FTA	Pct
Jose Calderon, Toronto	151	154	.981
Ray Allen, Boston	237	249	.952
Steve Nash, Phoenix	196	210	.933
Chauncey Billups, Detroit-Denver	418	458	.913
Mo Williams, Cleveland	208	228	.912
D. J. Augustin, Charlotte	208	233	.893
Dirk Nowitzki, Dallas	485	545	.890
David West, New Orleans	367	415	.884
Manu Ginobili, San Antonio	168	190	.884
Leandro Barbosa, Phoenix	171	194	.881

Blocked Shots per Game
(Minimum 70 games or 100 blocked shots)

	G	Blk	Avg
Dwight Howard, Orlando	79	231	2.9
Chris Andersen, Denver	71	175	2.5
Marcus Camby, L.A. Clippers	62	132	2.1
Ronny Turiaf, Golden State	79	168	2.1
Jermaine O'Neal, Toronto-Miami	68	136	2.0
Kendrick Perkins, Boston	76	150	2.0
Yao Ming, Houston	77	150	1.9
Tyrus Thomas, Chicago	79	151	1.9
Brook Lopez, New Jersey	82	151	1.8
Samuel Dalembert, Philadelphia	82	146	1.8

NBA Defensive Player of the Year, 1983-2009

1983	Sidney Moncrief, Milwaukee	1993	Hakeem Olajuwon, Houston	2002	Ben Wallace, Detroit
1984	Sidney Moncrief, Milwaukee	1994	Hakeem Olajuwon, Houston	2003	Ben Wallace, Detroit
1985	Mark Eaton, Utah	1995	Dikembe Mutombo, Denver	2004	Ron Artest, Indiana
1986	Alvin Robertson, San Antonio	1996	Gary Payton, Seattle	2005	Ben Wallace, Detroit
1987	Michael Cooper, L.A. Lakers	1997	Dikembe Mutombo, Atlanta	2006	Ben Wallace, Detroit
1988	Michael Jordan, Chicago	1998	Dikembe Mutombo, Atlanta	2007	Marcus Camby, Denver
1989	Mark Eaton, Utah	1999	Alonzo Mourning, Miami	2008	Kevin Garnett, Boston
1990	Dennis Rodman, Detroit	2000	Alonzo Mourning, Miami	2009	Dwight Howard, Orlando
1991	Dennis Rodman, Detroit	2001	Dikembe Mutombo, Philadelphia-		
1992	David Robinson, San Antonio		Atlanta		

NBA Rookie of the Year, 1953-2009

1953 Don Meineke, Ft. Wayne	1972 Sidney Wicks, Portland	1992 Larry Johnson, Charlotte
1954 Ray Felix, Baltimore	1973 Bob McAdoo, Buffalo	1993 Shaquille O'Neal, Orlando
1955 Bob Pettit, Milwaukee	1974 Ernie DiGregorio, Buffalo	1994 Chris Webber, Golden State
1956 Maurice Stokes, Rochester	1975 Keith Wilkes, Golden State	1995 Grant Hill, Detroit;
1957 Tom Heinsohn, Boston	1976 Alvan Adams, Phoenix	Jason Kidd, Dallas (tie)
1958 Woody Sauldsberry, Philadelphia	1977 Adrian Dantley, Buffalo	1996 Damon Stoudamire, Toronto
1959 Elgin Baylor, Minneapolis	1978 Walter Davis, Phoenix	1997 Allen Iverson, Philadelphia
1960 Wilt Chamberlain, Philadelphia	1979 Phil Ford, Kansas City	1998 Tim Duncan, San Antonio
1961 Oscar Robertson, Cincinnati	1980 Larry Bird, Boston	1999 Vince Carter, Toronto
1962 Walt Bellamy, Chicago	1981 Darrell Griffith, Utah	2000 Elton Brand, Chicago;
1963 Terry Dischinger, Chicago	1982 Buck Williams, New Jersey	Steve Francis, Houston (tie)
1964 Jerry Lucas, Cincinnati	1983 Terry Cummings, San Diego	2001 Mike Miller, Orlando
1965 Willis Reed, New York	1984 Ralph Sampson, Houston	2002 Pau Gasol, Memphis
1966 Rick Barry, San Francisco	1985 Michael Jordan, Chicago	2003 Amar'e Stoudemire, Phoenix
1967 Dave Bing, Detroit	1986 Patrick Ewing, New York	2004 LeBron James, Cleveland
1968 Earl Monroe, Baltimore	1987 Chuck Person, Indiana	2005 Emeka Okafor, Charlotte
1969 Wes Unseld, Baltimore	1988 Mark Jackson, New York	2006 Chris Paul, New Or./Okla. City
1970 Lew Alcindor (Abdul-Jabbar), Milw.	1989 Mitch Richmond, Golden State	2007 Brandon Roy, Portland
1971 Dave Cowens, Boston;	1990 David Robinson, San Antonio	2008 Kevin Durant, Seattle
Geoff Petrie, Portland (tie)	1991 Derrick Coleman, New Jersey	2009 Derrick Rose, Chicago

NBA Sixth Man Award, 1983-2009

1983 Bobby Jones, Philadelphia	1992 Detlef Schrempf, Indiana	2001 Aaron McKie, Philadelphia
1984 Kevin McHale, Boston	1993 Clifford Robinson, Portland	2002 Corliss Williamson, Detroit
1985 Kevin McHale, Boston	1994 Dell Curry, Charlotte	2003 Bobby Jackson, Sacramento
1986 Bill Walton, Boston	1995 Anthony Mason, New York	2004 Antawn Jamison, Dallas
1987 Ricky Pierce, Milwaukee	1996 Toni Kukoc, Chicago	2005 Ben Gordon, Chicago
1988 Roy Tarpley, Dallas	1997 John Starks, New York	2006 Mike Miller, Memphis
1989 Eddie Johnson, Phoenix	1998 Danny Manning, Phoenix	2007 Leandro Barbosa, Phoenix
1990 Ricky Pierce, Milwaukee	1999 Darrell Armstrong, Orlando	2008 Manu Ginobili, San Antonio
1991 Detlef Schrempf, Indiana	2000 Rodney Rogers, Phoenix	2009 Jason Terry, Dallas

2009 NBA Player Draft, First-Round Picks
(Held June 25, 2009)

Team	Player, position, college/team
1. L.A. Clippers	Blake Griffin, Forward, Oklahoma
2. Memphis	Hasheem Thabeet, Center, Connecticut
3. Oklahoma City	James Harden, Guard, Arizona State
4. Sacramento	Tyreke Evans, Guard, Memphis
5. Minnesota[1]	Ricky Rubio, Guard, DKV Joventut (Spain)
6. Minnesota	Jonny Flynn, Guard, Syracuse
7. Golden State	Stephen Curry, Guard, Davidson
8. New York	Jordan Hill, Forward, Arizona
9. Toronto	DeMar DeRozan, Guard/Forward, USC
10. Milwaukee	Brandon Jennings, Guard, Lottomatica Virtus Roma (Italy)
11. New Jersey	Terrence Williams, Guard/Forward, Louisville
12. Charlotte	Gerald Henderson, Guard, Duke
13. Indiana	Tyler Hansbrough, Forward, North Carolina
14. Phoenix	Earl Clark, Forward, Louisville
15. Detroit	Austin Daye, Forward, Gonzaga
16. Chicago	James Johnson, Forward, Wake Forest

Team	Player, position, college/team
17. Philadelphia	Jrue Holiday, Guard, UCLA
18. Minnesota[2]	Ty Lawson, Guard, North Carolina
19. Atlanta	Jeff Teague, Guard, Wake Forest
20. Utah	Eric Maynor, Guard, Virginia Commonwealth
21. New Orleans	Darren Collison, Guard, UCLA
22. Portland[3]	Victor Claver, Forward, Pamesa Valencia (Spain)
23. Sacramento[4]	Omri Casspi, Forward, Maccabi Tel Aviv (Israel)
24. Dallas[5]	B. J. Mullens, Center, Ohio State
25. Oklahoma City[6]	Rodrigue Beaubois, Guard, Cholet (France)
26. Chicago[7]	Taj Gibson, Forward, USC
27. Memphis[8]	DeMarre Carroll, Forward, Missouri
28. Minnesota[9]	Wayne Ellington, Guard, North Carolina
29. L.A. Lakers[10]	Toney Douglas, Guard, Florida State
30. Cleveland	Christian Eyenga, Guard/Forward, DKV Joventut (Spain)

(1) Rights traded from Washington. (2) Rights traded from Miami; rights to Lawson traded to Denver for future considerations. (3) Rights traded from Dallas. (4) Rights traded from Portland; traded to Okla. City for rights to Beaubois. (6) Rights traded from San Antonio; traded to Dallas for rights to Mullens. (7) Rights traded from Denver through Okla. City. (8) Rights traded from Orlando. (9) Rights traded from Boston. (10) Rights traded to New York. (11) Rights traded to Sacramento via Houston. (12) Rights traded to Seattle.

Number-One First-Round NBA Draft Picks, 1966-2009

Year	Team	Player, college/team
1966	New York	Cazzie Russell, Michigan
1967	Detroit	Jimmy Walker, Providence
1968	San Diego	Elvin Hayes, Houston
1969	Milwaukee	Lew Alcindor (Kareem Abdul-Jabbar), UCLA
1970	Detroit	Bob Lanier, St. Bonaventure
1971	Cleveland	Austin Carr, Notre Dame
1972	Portland	LaRue Martin, Loyola-Chicago
1973	Philadelphia	Doug Collins, Illinois State
1974	Portland	Bill Walton, UCLA
1975	Atlanta	David Thompson[1], N.C. State
1976	Houston	John Lucas, Maryland
1977	Milwaukee	Kent Benson, Indiana
1978	Portland	Mychal Thompson, Minnesota
1979	L.A. Lakers	Earvin "Magic" Johnson, Michigan State
1980	Golden State	Joe Barry Carroll, Purdue
1981	Dallas	Mark Aguirre, DePaul
1982	L.A. Lakers	James Worthy, North Carolina
1983	Houston	Ralph Sampson, Virginia
1984	Houston	Hakeem Olajuwon, Houston
1985	New York	Patrick Ewing, Georgetown
1986	Cleveland	Brad Daugherty, North Carolina
1987	San Antonio	David Robinson, Navy
1988	L.A. Clippers	Danny Manning, Kansas
1989	Sacramento	Pervis Ellison, Louisville
1990	New Jersey	Derrick Coleman, Syracuse
1991	Charlotte	Larry Johnson, UNLV
1992	Orlando	Shaquille O'Neal, LSU
1993	Orlando	Chris Webber[2], Michigan
1994	Milwaukee	Glenn Robinson, Purdue
1995	Golden State	Joe Smith, Maryland
1996	Philadelphia	Allen Iverson, Georgetown
1997	San Antonio	Tim Duncan, Wake Forest
1998	L.A. Clippers	Michael Olowokandi, Pacific
1999	Chicago	Elton Brand, Duke
2000	New Jersey	Kenyon Martin, Cincinnati
2001	Washington	Kwame Brown, Glynn Academy (HS)
2002	Houston	Yao Ming, Shanghai Sharks (China)
2003	Cleveland	LeBron James, St. Vincent-St. Mary (HS)
2004	Orlando	Dwight Howard, Southwest Atlanta Christian Academy (HS)
2005	Milwaukee	Andrew Bogut, Utah
2006	Toronto	Andrea Bargnani, Benneton Treviso (Italy)
2007	Portland	Greg Oden, Ohio State
2008	Chicago	Derrick Rose, Memphis
2009	L.A. Clippers	Blake Griffin, Oklahoma

(1) Signed with Denver of the ABA. (2) Traded to Golden State for rights to Anfernee Hardaway and three future first-round draft choices.

All-Time NBA Statistical Leaders

(At the end of the 2008-09 season. *Player active in 2008-09 season.)

Scoring Average
(Minimum 400 games or 10,000 points)

	G	Pts	Avg
Michael Jordan	1,072	32,292	30.1
Wilt Chamberlain	1,045	31,419	30.1
*LeBron James	472	12,993	27.5
Elgin Baylor	846	23,149	27.4
*Allen Iverson	886	23,983	27.1
Jerry West	932	25,192	27.0
Bob Pettit	792	20,880	26.4
George Gervin	791	20,708	26.2
Oscar Robertson	1,040	26,710	25.7
*Kobe Bryant	948	23,820	25.1

Field Goal Percentage
(Minimum 2,000 field goals made)

	FGA	FGM	Pct
Artis Gilmore	9,570	5,732	.599
*Shaquille O'Neal	18,793	10,934	.582
Mark West	4,356	2,528	.580
Steve Johnson	4,965	2,841	.572
Darryl Dawkins	6,079	3,477	.572
James Donaldson	5,442	3,105	.571
*Dwight Howard	4,384	2,489	.568
Bo Outlaw	3,534	2,005	.567
Jeff Ruland	3,734	2,105	.564
Kareem Abdul-Jabbar	28,307	15,837	.559

Free Throw Percentage
(Minimum 1,200 free throws made)

	FTA	FTM	Pct
Mark Price	2,362	2,135	.904
*Steve Nash	2,628	2,366	.900
Rick Barry	4,243	3,818	.900
*Peja Stojakovic	2,368	2,118	.894
*Ray Allen	4,068	3,632	.893
Calvin Murphy	3,864	3,445	.892
*Chauncey Billups	3,943	3,506	.889
Scott Skiles	1,741	1,548	.889
Reggie Miller	7,026	6,237	.888
Larry Bird	4,471	3,960	.886

3-Point Field Goal Percentage
(Minimum 250 3-point field goals made)

	3-FGA	3-FGM	Pct
Steve Kerr	1,599	726	.454
*Jason Kapono	848	385	.454
Hubert Davis	1,651	728	.441
Drazen Petrovic	583	255	.437
*Steve Nash	3,148	1,360	.432
Tim Legler	603	260	.431
B. J. Armstrong	1,026	436	.425
Wesley Person	2,754	1,150	.418
*Anthony Parker	848	352	.415
*Ben Gordon	1,856	770	.415

Minutes Played

Kareem Abdul-Jabbar	57,446
Karl Malone	54,852
Elvin Hayes	50,000
Wilt Chamberlain	47,859
John Stockton	47,764
Reggie Miller	47,619
Gary Payton	47,117
John Havlicek	46,471
Robert Parish	45,704
Moses Malone	45,071

Field Goals Attempted

Kareem Abdul-Jabbar	28,307
Karl Malone	26,210
Michael Jordan	24,537
Elvin Hayes	24,272
John Havlicek	23,930
Wilt Chamberlain	23,497
Dominique Wilkins	21,589
Alex English	21,036
Hakeem Olajuwon	20,991
Elgin Baylor	20,171

Points

Kareem Abdul-Jabbar	38,387
Karl Malone	36,928
Michael Jordan	32,292
Wilt Chamberlain	31,419
*Shaquille O'Neal	27,619
Moses Malone	27,409
Elvin Hayes	27,313
Hakeem Olajuwon	26,946
Oscar Robertson	26,710
Dominique Wilkins	26,668

Games Played

Robert Parish	1,611
Kareem Abdul-Jabbar	1,560
John Stockton	1,504
Karl Malone	1,476
Kevin Willis	1,424
Reggie Miller	1,389
Clifford Robinson	1,380
Gary Payton	1,335
Moses Malone	1,329
Buck Williams	1,307

Field Goals Made

Kareem Abdul-Jabbar	15,837
Karl Malone	13,528
Wilt Chamberlain	12,681
Michael Jordan	12,192
Elvin Hayes	10,976
*Shaquille O'Neal	10,934
Hakeem Olajuwon	10,749
Alex English	10,659
John Havlicek	10,513
Dominique Wilkins	9,963

Rebounds

Wilt Chamberlain	23,924
Bill Russell	21,620
Kareem Abdul-Jabbar	17,440
Elvin Hayes	16,279
Moses Malone	16,212
Karl Malone	14,968
Robert Parish	14,715
Nate Thurmond	14,464
Walt Bellamy	14,241
Wes Unseld	13,769

Personal Fouls

Kareem Abdul-Jabbar	4,657
Karl Malone	4,578
Robert Parish	4,443
Charles Oakley	4,421
Hakeem Olajuwon	4,383
Buck Williams	4,267
Elvin Hayes	4,193
Clifford Robinson	4,176
Kevin Willis	4,172
Otis Thorpe	4,146

3-Point Field Goals Attempted

Reggie Miller	6,486
*Ray Allen	5,777
*Jason Kidd	4,348
Tim Hardaway	4,345
Nick Van Exel	4,278
Dale Ellis	4,266
Antoine Walker	4,264
Eddie Jones	4,147
Vernon Maxwell	3,931
*Peja Stojakovic	3,904

Assists

John Stockton	15,806
Mark Jackson	10,334
*Jason Kidd	10,199
Magic Johnson	10,141
Oscar Robertson	9,887
Isiah Thomas	9,061
Gary Payton	8,966
Rod Strickland	7,987
*Steve Nash	7,505
Maurice Cheeks	7,392

Blocks

Hakeem Olajuwon	3,830
*Dikembe Mutombo	3,289
Kareem Abdul-Jabbar	3,189
Mark Eaton	3,064
David Robinson	2,954
Patrick Ewing	2,894
*Shaquille O'Neal	2,628
Tree Rollins	2,542
Robert Parish	2,361
Alonzo Mourning	2,356

3-Point Field Goals Made

Reggie Miller	2,560
*Ray Allen	2,299
Dale Ellis	1,719
*Peja Stojakovic	1,571
Glen Rice	1,559
Eddie Jones	1,546
Tim Hardaway	1,542
Nick Van Exel	1,528
*Jason Kidd	1,486
*Chauncey Billups	1,432

Steals

John Stockton	3,265
Michael Jordan	2,514
Gary Payton	2,445
Maurice Cheeks	2,310
Scottie Pippen	2,307
Clyde Drexler	2,207
*Jason Kidd	2,198
Hakeem Olajuwon	2,162
Alvin Robertson	2,112
Karl Malone	2,085

All-Time NBA Regular Season Coaching Victories

(At the end of the 2008-09 season, ranked by wins. *Active through 2008-09 season.)

Coach	W-L	Pct	Coach	W-L	Pct	Coach	W-L	Pct
Lenny Wilkens	1,332-1,155	.536	Red Auerbach	938-479	.662	John MacLeod	707-657	.518
*Don Nelson	1,309-1,007	.565	Dick Motta	935-1,017	.479	Red Holzman	696-603	.536
Pat Riley	1,210-694	.636	*George Karl	933-642	.592	*Gregg Popovich	686-330	.675
*Jerry Sloan	1,137-751	.602	Jack Ramsay	864-783	.525	Mike Fratello	667-548	.549
*Larry Brown	1,045-847	.552	*Rick Adelman	860-537	.616	Chuck Daly	638-437	.593
*Phil Jackson	1,041-435	.705	Cotton Fitzsimmons	832-775	.518	Doug Moe	628-529	.543
Bill Fitch	944-1,106	.460	Gene Shue	784-861	.477	*Mike Dunleavy	592-688	.463

Naismith Memorial Basketball Hall of Fame, Springfield, MA

(*2009 inductee. **Enshrined as both a player and coach.)

Players
Abdul-Jabbar, Kareem
Archibald, Nate
Arizin, Paul
Barkley, Charles
Barlow, Thomas
Barry, Rick
Baylor, Elgin
Beckman, John
Bellamy, Walt
Belov, Sergei
Bing, Dave
Bird, Larry
Blazejowski, Carol
Borgmann, Bennie
Bradley, Bill
Brennan, Joseph
Cervi, Al
Chamberlain, Wilt
Cooper, Charles
Cosic, Kresimir
Cousy, Bob
Cowens, Dave
Crawford, Joan
Cunningham, Billy
Curry, Denise
Dalipagic, Drazen
Dantley, Adrian
Davies, Bob
DeBernardi, Forrest
DeBusschere, Dave
Dehnert, Henry "Dutch"
Donovan, Anne
Drexler, Clyde
Dumars, Joe
Endacott, Paul
English, Alex
Erving, Julius
Ewing, Patrick
Foster, Bud
Frazier, Walt
Friedman, Max
Fulks, Joe
Gale, Lauren
Gallatin, Harry
Gates, William "Pop"
Gervin, George
Gola, Tom
Goodrich, Gail
Greer, Hal
Gruenig, Robert "Ace"

Hagan, Cliff
Hanson, Victor
Harris-Stewart, Lusia
Havlicek, John
Hawkins, Cornelius "Connie"
Hayes, Elvin
Haynes, Marques
Heinsohn, Tom
Holman, Nat
Houbregs, Bob
Howell, Bailey
Hyatt, Chuck
Issel, Dan
Jeannette, Harry "Buddy"
Johnson, Earvin "Magic"
Johnson, William
Johnston, Neil
Jones, K.C.
Jones, Sam
*Jordan, Michael
Krause, Ed "Moose"
Kurland, Bob
Lanier, Bob
Lapchick, Joe
Lieberman, Nancy
Lovellette, Clyde
Lucas, Jerry
Luisetti, Angelo "Hank"
Macauley, Ed
Malone, Moses
Maravich, Pete
Marcari, Hortencia
Martin, Slater
McAdoo, Bob
McCracken, Branch
McCracken, Jack
McDermott, Bobby
McGuire, Dick
McHale, Kevin
Meneghin, Dino
Meyers, Ann
Mikan, George
Mikkelsen, Vern
Miller, Cheryl
Monroe, Earl
Murphy, Calvin
Murphy, Charles "Stretch"
Olajuwon, Hakeem
Page, Harlan "Pat"
Parish, Robert

Petrovic, Drazen
Pettit, Bob
Phillip, Andy
Pollard, Jim
Ramsey, Frank
Reed, Willis
Risen, Arnie
Robertson, Oscar
*Robinson, David
Roosma, John
Russell, Bill
Russell, John "Honey"
Schayes, Adolph
Schmidt, Ernest
Schommer, John
Sedran, Barney
Semjonova, Uljana
**Sharman, Bill
*Stockton, John
Steinmetz, Christian
Stokes, Maurice
Thomas, Isiah
Thompson, Cat
Thompson, David
Thurmond, Nate
Twyman, Jack
Unseld, Wes
Vandivier, Robert "Fuzzy"
Wachter, Edward
Walton, Bill
Wanzer, Bobby
West, Jerry
White, Nera
**Wilkens, Lenny
Wilkins, Dominique
Woodard, Lynette
**Wooden, John
Worthy, James
Yardley, George

Coaches
Allen, Forrest C. "Phog"
Anderson, Harold
Auerbach, Arnold "Red"
Auriemma, Geno
Barmore, Leon
Barry, Justin "Sam"
Blood, Ernest
Boeheim, Jim
Brown, Hubert "Hubie"

Brown, Larry
Calhoun, Jim
Cann, Howard
Carlson, Clifford
Carnesecca, Lou
Carnevale, Ben
Carril, Pete
Case, Everett
Chancellor, Van
Chaney, John
Conradt, Jody
Crum, Denzil "Denny"
Daly, Chuck
Dean, Everett
Diaz-Miguel, Antonio
Diddle, Edgar
Drake, Bruce
Ferrandiz, Pedro
Gaines, Clarence
Gamba, Sandro
Gardner, James "Jack"
Gill, Amory "Slats"
Gomelsky, Aleksandr
Gunter, Sue
Hannum, Alex
Harshman, Marv
Haskins, Don
Hickey, Edgar
Hobson, Howard
Holzman, William "Red"
Iba, Hank
Jackson, Phil
Julian, Alvin
Keaney, Frank
Keogan, George
Knight, Bob
Krzyzewski, Mike
Kundla, John
Lambert, Ward
Litwack, Harry
Loeffler, Kenneth
Lonborg, Dutch
McCutchan, Arad
McGuire, Al
McGuire, Frank
McLendon, John
Meanwell, Dr. Walter
Meyer, Ray
Miller, Ralph
Moore, Billie

Newell, Pete
Nikolic, Aleksandar
Novosel, Mirko
Olson, Robert "Lute"
Ramsay, John "Jack"
Riley, Pat
Rubini, Cesare
Rupp, Adolph
Rush, Cathy
Sachs, Leonard
**Sharman, Bill
Shelton, Everett
*Sloan, Jerry
Smith, Dean
*Stringer, C. Vivian
Summitt, Pat
Taylor, Fred
Thompson, John
Wade, Margaret
Watts, Stan
**Wilkens, Lenny
Williams, Roy
**Wooden, John
Woolpert, Phil
Wootten, Morgan
Yow, Kay

Teams
Buffalo Germans
First Team
Harlem Globetrotters
New York Renaissance
Original Celtics
Texas Western

Referees
Enright, James
Hepbron, George
Hoyt, George
Kennedy, Matthew
Leith, Lloyd
Mihalik, Zigmund "Red"
Nucatola, John
Quigley, Ernest
Rudolph, Marvin "Mendy"
Shirley, J. Dallas
Strom, Earl
Tobey, David
Walsh, David

Contributors
Abbott, Senda Berenson
Bee, Clair
Biasone, Danny
Brown, Walter
Bunn, John
Colangelo, Jerry
Davidson, Bill
Douglas, Bob
Duer, Al
Embry, Wayne
Fagan, Cliff
Fisher, Harry
Fleisher, Larry
Gavitt, David
Gottlieb, Edward
Gulick, Dr. Luther
Harrison, Lester
Hearn, Francis "Chick"
Hepp, Dr. Ferenc
Hickox, Edward
Hinkle, Tony
Irish, Edward "Ned"
Jones, R. William
Kennedy, Walter
Lemon, Meadowlark
Liston, Emil
Lloyd, Earl
Mokray, Bill
Morgan, Ralph
Morgenweck, Frank
Naismith, Dr. James
Newton, C. M.
O'Brien, John
O'Brien, Larry
Olsen, Harold
Podoloff, Maurice
Porter, Henry V.
Reid, William
Ripley, Elmer
St. John, Lynn
Saperstein, Abe
Schabinger, Arthur
Stagg, Alonzo
Stankovic, Boris
Steitz, Edward
Taylor, Chuck
Teague, Bertha
Tower, Oswald
Trester, Arthur
Wells, Clifford
Wilke, Lou
Zollner, Fred

NBA Home Courts[1]

Team	Name (built)	Capacity	Team	Name (built)	Capacity
Atlanta	Philips Arena (1999)	18,729	Milwaukee	Bradley Center (1988)	18,717
Boston	TD Garden[2] (1995)	18,624	Minnesota	Target Center (1990)	19,356
Charlotte	Time Warner Cable Arena (2005)	19,077	New Jersey	IZOD Center[4] (1981)	18,974
Chicago	United Center (1994)	20,917	New Orleans[5]	New Orleans Arena (1999)	17,188
Cleveland	Quicken Loans Arena (1994)	20,562	New York	Madison Square Garden (IV) (1968)	19,763
Dallas	American Airlines Center (2001)	19,200	Oklahoma City	Ford Center[6] (2002)	18,203
Denver	Pepsi Center (1999)	19,155	Orlando	Amway Arena[7] (1989)	17,451
Detroit	The Palace of Auburn Hills (1988)	22,076	Philadelphia	Wachovia Center[8] (1996)	20,318
Golden State	ORACLE Arena[3] (1966)	19,596	Phoenix	US Airways Center[9] (1992)	18,422
Houston	Toyota Center (2003)	18,043	Portland	Rose Garden (1995)	19,980
Indiana	Conseco Fieldhouse (1999)	18,165	Sacramento	ARCO Arena (1988)	17,317
L.A. Clippers	STAPLES Center (1999)	19,060	San Antonio	AT&T Center[10] (2002)	18,797
L.A. Lakers	STAPLES Center (1999)	18,997	Toronto	Air Canada Centre (1999)	19,800
Memphis	FedExForum (2004)	18,119	Utah	EnergySolutions Arena[11] (1991)	19,911
Miami	AmericanAirlines Arena (1999)	19,600	Washington	Verizon Center[12] (1997)	20,173

(1) At the end of the 2008-09 season. (2) Fleet Center, 1995-2005. (3) Oakland Coliseum Arena, 1966-96; Arena in Oakland, 1997-2006. (4) Brendan Byrne/Meadowlands Arena, 1981-96; Continental Airlines Arena, 1996-2007. (5) Because of damage to New Orleans Arena due to Hurricane Katrina, the Hornets played 35 games in the Ford Center (built 2002; capacity 19,599) in Oklahoma City, OK, 3 games in New Orleans Arena, and 3 games at other locations during the 2005-06 season. In 2006-07, the Hornets played 35 games at the Ford Center and 6 games in New Orleans Arena. The Hornets played 2007-08 home games in New Orleans Arena. (6) The Seattle SuperSonics relocated to Oklahoma City prior to the 2008-09 season. (7) CoreStates Center, 1996-98; First Union Center, 1998-2003. (8) America West Arena, 1992-2006. (9) SBC Center, 2002-06. (10) Seattle Center Coliseum, 1962-94; renovated, expanded, and renamed in 1995. The SuperSonics moved to Oklahoma City as the Thunder after the 2007-08 season and were expected to play home games at the Ford Center. (11) Delta Center, 1991-2006. (12) MCI Center, 1997-2006.

WOMEN'S PROFESSIONAL BASKETBALL

Phoenix Mercury Defeat Indiana Fever for WNBA Title

The Phoenix Mercury won their second WNBA title in three years, taking the last two games of the best-of-five championship series against the Indiana Fever. Diana Taurasi led the Mercury with 26 points in the deciding Game 5, a 94-86 victory Oct. 9, 2009, at US Airways Center in Phoenix. Taurasi was named the WNBA Finals' Most Valuable Player, averaging 20.4 points per game. She had earned the league's regular season MVP award with an identical scoring average.

WNBA 2009 Final Standings

x-clinched playoff berth; y-clinched top seed

Eastern Conference	W	L	Pct	GB	Western Conference	W	L	Pct	GB
y-Indiana Fever	22	12	.647	0	y-Phoenix Mercury	23	11	.676	0
x-Atlanta Dream	18	16	.529	4	x-Seattle Storm	20	14	.588	3
x-Detroit Shock	18	16	.529	4	x-Los Angeles Sparks	18	16	.529	5
x-Washington Mystics	16	18	.471	6	x-San Antonio Silver Stars	15	19	.441	8
Chicago Sky	16	18	.471	6	Minnesota Lynx	14	20	.412	9
Connecticut Sun	16	18	.471	6	Sacramento Monarchs	12	22	.353	11
New York Liberty	13	21	.382	9					

2009 WNBA Playoffs

(Playoff seeding in parentheses; conference winner automatically gets top seed)

Eastern Conference
(1) Indiana defeated (4) Washington, 2 games to 0
(3) Detroit defeated (2) Atlanta, 2 games to 0
(1) Indiana defeated (3) Detroit, 2 games to 1

Western Conference
(1) Phoenix defeated (4) San Antonio, 2 games to 1
(3) Los Angeles defeated (2) Seattle, 2 games to 1
(1) Phoenix defeated (3) Los Angeles, 2 games to 1

2009 WNBA Championship

Phoenix defeated Indiana, 3 games to 2 (120-116 (OT), 84-93, 85-86, 90-77, 94-86) in the best-of-five series.

2009 All-WNBA Teams

First team	Position	Second team	Position
Diana Taurasi, Phoenix	Forward	Candace Parker, Los Angeles	Guard/Forward
Tamika Catchings, Indiana	Forward	Sophia Young, San Antonio	Forward
Lauren Jackson, Seattle	Forward/Center	Lisa Leslie, Los Angeles	Center
Becky Hammon, San Antonio	Guard	Katie Douglas, Indiana	Guard
Cappie Pondexter, Phoenix	Guard	Deanna Nolan, Detroit	Guard

WNBA Statistical Leaders and Awards in 2009

Minutes played: 1,194, Lindsey Harding, Washington
Total points: 648, Cappie Pondexter, Phoenix
Points per game: 20.4, Diana Taurasi, Phoenix
Highest field goal pct.: .599, Sylvia Fowles, Chicago
Highest 3-pt. field goal pct.: .452, Tangela Smith, Phoenix
Highest free throw pct.: .979, Nicole Powell, Sacramento
Total rebounds: 309, Erika de Souza, Atlanta
Rebounds per game: 9.8, Candace Parker, Los Angeles

Total assists: 179, Sue Bird, Seattle
Assists per game: 5.77, Sue Bird, Seattle
Total steals: 99, Tamika Catchings, Indiana
Steals per game: 2.91, Tamika Catchings, Indiana
Total blocked shots: 57, Tangela Smith, Phoenix
Coach of the year: Marynell Meadors, Atlanta
Defensive player of year: Tamika Catchings, Indiana
Most improved player: Crystal Langhorne, Washington

WNBA Champions, 1997-2009

Year	Regular Season Eastern Conference	Western Conference	Champion	Playoffs Coach	Opponent
1997	Houston Comets	Phoenix Mercury	Houston	Van Chancellor	New York
1998	Cleveland Rockers	Houston Comets	Houston	Van Chancellor	Phoenix
1999	New York Liberty	Houston Comets	Houston	Van Chancellor	New York
2000	New York Liberty	Los Angeles Sparks	Houston	Van Chancellor	New York
2001	Cleveland Rockers	Los Angeles Sparks	Los Angeles	Michael Cooper	Charlotte
2002	New York Liberty	Los Angeles Sparks	Los Angeles	Michael Cooper	New York
2003	Detroit Shock	Los Angeles Sparks	Detroit	Bill Laimbeer	Los Angeles
2004	Connecticut Sun	Los Angeles Sparks	Seattle	Ann Donovan	Connecticut
2005	Connecticut Sun	Sacramento Monarchs	Sacramento	John Whisenant	Connecticut
2006	Connecticut Sun	Sacramento Monarchs	Detroit	Bill Laimbeer	Sacramento
2007	Detroit Shock	Phoenix Mercury	Phoenix	Paul Westhead	Detroit
2008	Detroit Shock	San Antonio Silver Stars	Detroit	Bill Laimbeer	San Antonio
2009	Indiana Fever	Phoenix Mercury	Phoenix	Corey Gaines	Indiana

WNBA Scoring Leaders, 1997-2009

(average points per game; 10 games minimum)

Year	Leader, team	Pts	Avg	Year	Leader, team	Pts	Avg	Year	Leader, team	Pts	Avg
1997	Cynthia Cooper, Houston	621	22.2	2002	Chamique Holdsclaw, Washington	397	19.9	2006	Diana Taurasi, Phoenix	860	25.3
1998	Cynthia Cooper, Houston	680	22.7					2007	Lauren Jackson, Seattle	739	23.8
1999	Cynthia Cooper, Houston	686	22.1	2003	Lauren Jackson, Seattle	698	21.2	2008	Diana Taurasi, Phoenix	820	24.1
2000	Sheryl Swoopes, Houston	643	20.7	2004	Lauren Jackson, Seattle	634	20.5	2009	Diana Taurasi, Phoenix	631	20.4
2001	Katie Smith, Minnesota	739	23.1	2005	Sheryl Swoopes, Houston	614	18.6				

WNBA Finals MVP

Year	Player
1997	Cynthia Cooper, Houston
1998	Cynthia Cooper, Houston
1999	Yolanda Griffith, Sacramento
2000	Sheryl Swoopes, Houston
2001	Lisa Leslie, Los Angeles
2002	Sheryl Swoopes, Houston
2003	Lauren Jackson, Seattle
2004	Lisa Leslie, Los Angeles
2005	Sheryl Swoopes, Houston
2006	Deanna Nolan, Detroit
2007	Cappie Pondexter, Phoenix
2008	Katie Smith, Detroit
2009	Diana Taurasi, Phoenix

WNBA Most Valuable Player

Year	Player
1997	Cynthia Cooper, Houston
1998	Cynthia Cooper, Houston
1999	Cynthia Cooper, Houston
2000	Cynthia Cooper, Houston
2001	Lisa Leslie, Los Angeles
2002	Lisa Leslie, Los Angeles
2003	Ruth Riley, Detroit
2004	Betty Lennox, Seattle
2005	Yolanda Griffith, Sacramento
2006	Lisa Leslie, Los Angeles
2007	Lauren Jackson, Seattle
2008	Candace Parker, Los Angeles
2009	Diana Taurasi, Phoenix

WNBA Rookie of the Year

Year	Player
1997	No award
1998	Tracy Reid, Charlotte
1999	Chamique Holdsclaw, Washington
2000	Betty Lennox, Minnesota
2001	Jackie Stiles, Portland
2002	Tamika Catchings, Indiana
2003	Cheryl Ford, Detroit
2004	Diana Taurasi, Phoenix
2005	Temeka Johnson, Washington
2006	Seimone Augustus, Minnesota
2007	Armintie Price, Chicago
2008	Candace Parker, Los Angeles
2009	Angel McCoughtry, Atlanta

NATIONAL HOCKEY LEAGUE
Redemptive Stanley Cup Final; Record Attendance in 2008-09

In a classic rematch, the Pittsburgh Penguins beat the defending champion Detroit Red Wings in seven games to avenge their 2008 Finals loss to the Red Wings and capture their third Stanley Cup in franchise history. The Penguins defeated the Red Wings in Detroit, 2-1, on June 12, 2009, and were just the third team in NHL history to win Game 7 on the road in the Stanley Cup Final. The Penguins also became only the second team to win the Cup after losing the first two games of the Finals on the road.

The Penguins were well-served by their young guns throughout the postseason. Center Evgeni Malkin won the Conn Smythe Trophy as the playoffs' most valuable player. The 22-year-old Malkin recorded 8 points in the Stanley Cup Finals and totaled 36 points (14 goals, 22 assists) in 24 postseason games. The Penguins' 21-year-old center Sidney Crosby was the youngest captain in NHL history to hoist the Stanley Cup.

In regular season play, the NHL enjoyed record attendance for the fourth consecutive season (21,475,223) and began the season on Oct. 4-5 with a pair of overseas match-ups. NHL Premiere-Stockholm 2008, a two-game series in Stockholm, Sweden, featured the Penguins and Ottawa Senators, while the New York Rangers and Tampa Bay Lightning met at NHL Premiere-Prague 2008 in the Czech Republic.

The Red Wings and Chicago Blackhawks met in the league's second outdoor Winter Classic on New Year's Day at Wrigley Field, home of Major League Baseball's Chicago Cubs, which was outfitted with a portable rink. A crowd of 40,818 braved the 32-degree weather as Detroit won, 6-4.

Final NHL Standings 2008-09

(Playoff seeding in parentheses; division winners automatically seeded 1, 2, or 3; teams tied at the end of regulation time are each awarded 1 point, an additional point is awarded to the overtime winner.)

Eastern Conference

Atlantic Division	W	L	OTL	GF	GA	PTS
New Jersey Devils (3)	51	27	4	244	209	106
Pittsburgh Penguins (4)	45	28	9	264	239	99
Philadelphia Flyers (5)	44	27	11	264	238	99
New York Rangers (7)	43	30	9	210	218	95
New York Islanders	26	47	9	201	279	61

Northeast Division	W	L	OTL	GF	GA	PTS
Boston Bruins (1)	53	19	10	274	196	116
Montréal Canadiens (8)	41	30	11	249	247	93
Buffalo Sabres	41	32	9	250	234	91
Ottawa Senators	36	35	11	217	237	83
Toronto Maple Leafs	34	35	13	250	293	81

Southeast Division	W	L	OTL	GF	GA	PTS
Washington Capitals (2)	50	24	8	272	245	108
Carolina Hurricanes (6)	45	30	7	239	226	97
Florida Panthers	41	30	11	234	231	93
Atlanta Thrashers	35	41	6	257	280	76
Tampa Bay Lightning	24	40	18	210	279	66

Western Conference

Central Division	W	L	OTL	GF	GA	PTS
Detroit Red Wings (2)	51	21	10	295	244	112
Chicago Blackhawks (4)	46	24	12	264	216	104
St. Louis Blues (6)	41	31	10	233	233	92
Columbus Blue Jackets (7)	41	31	10	226	230	92
Nashville Predators	40	34	8	213	233	88

Northwest Division	W	L	OTL	GF	GA	PTS
Vancouver Canucks (3)	45	27	10	246	220	100
Calgary Flames (5)	46	30	6	254	248	98
Minnesota Wild	40	33	9	219	200	89
Edmonton Oilers	38	35	9	234	248	85
Colorado Avalanche	32	45	5	199	257	69

Pacific Division	W	L	OTL	GF	GA	PTS
San Jose Sharks (1)	53	18	11	257	204	117
Anaheim Ducks (8)	42	33	7	245	238	91
Dallas Stars	36	35	11	230	257	83
Phoenix Coyotes	36	39	7	208	252	79
Los Angeles Kings	34	37	11	207	234	79

2009 Stanley Cup Playoff Results

Eastern Conference
Boston defeated Montréal, 4-0
Washington defeated NY Rangers, 4-3
Carolina defeated New Jersey, 4-3
Pittsburgh defeated Philadelphia, 4-2
Carolina defeated Boston, 4-3
Pittsburgh defeated Washington, 4-3
Pittsburgh defeated Carolina, 4-0

Western Conference
Anaheim defeated San Jose, 4-2
Detroit defeated Columbus, 4-0
Vancouver defeated St. Louis, 4-0
Chicago defeated Calgary, 4-2
Detroit defeated Anaheim, 4-3
Chicago defeated Vancouver, 4-2
Detroit defeated Chicago, 4-1

Finals
Pittsburgh defeated Detroit (1-3, 1-3, 4-2, 4-2, 0-5, 2-1, 2-1), 4-3

Stanley Cup Champions, 1927-2009

Year	Champion	Coach	Final opponent	Year	Champion	Coach	Final opponent
1927	Ottawa	Dave Gill	Boston	1952	Detroit	Tommy Ivan	Montréal
1928	NY Rangers	Lester Patrick	Montréal Maroons	1953	Montréal	Dick Irvin	Boston
				1954	Detroit	Tommy Ivan	Montréal
1929	Boston	Cy Denneny	NY Rangers	1955	Detroit	Jimmy Skinner	Montréal
1930	Montréal	Cecil Hart	Boston	1956	Montréal	Toe Blake	Detroit
1931	Montréal	Cecil Hart	Chicago	1957	Montréal	Toe Blake	Boston
1932	Toronto	Dick Irvin	NY Rangers	1958	Montréal	Toe Blake	Boston
1933	NY Rangers	Lester Patrick	Toronto	1959	Montréal	Toe Blake	Toronto
1934	Chicago	Tommy Gorman	Detroit	1960	Montréal	Toe Blake	Toronto
1935	Montréal Maroons	Tommy Gorman	Toronto	1961	Chicago	Rudy Pilous	Detroit
1936	Detroit	Jack Adams	Toronto	1962	Toronto	Punch Imlach	Chicago
1937	Detroit	Jack Adams	NY Rangers	1963	Toronto	Punch Imlach	Detroit
1938	Chicago	Bill Stewart	Toronto	1964	Toronto	Punch Imlach	Detroit
1939	Boston	Art Ross	Toronto	1965	Montréal	Toe Blake	Chicago
1940	NY Rangers	Frank Boucher	Toronto	1966	Montréal	Toe Blake	Detroit
1941	Boston	Cooney Weiland	Detroit	1967	Toronto	Punch Imlach	Montréal
1942	Toronto	Hap Day	Detroit	1968	Montréal	Toe Blake	St. Louis
1943	Detroit	Jack Adams	Boston	1969	Montréal	Claude Ruel	St. Louis
1944	Montréal	Dick Irvin	Chicago	1970	Boston	Harry Sinden	St. Louis
1945	Toronto	Hap Day	Detroit	1971	Montréal	Al MacNeil	Chicago
1946	Montréal	Dick Irvin	Boston	1972	Boston	Tom Johnson	NY Rangers
1947	Toronto	Hap Day	Montréal	1973	Montréal	Scotty Bowman	Chicago
1948	Toronto	Hap Day	Detroit	1974	Philadelphia	Fred Shero	Boston
1949	Toronto	Hap Day	Detroit	1975	Philadelphia	Fred Shero	Buffalo
1950	Detroit	Tommy Ivan	NY Rangers	1976	Montréal	Scotty Bowman	Philadelphia
1951	Toronto	Joe Primeau	Montréal	1977	Montréal	Scotty Bowman	Boston

Year	Champion	Coach	Final opponent	Year	Champion	Coach	Final opponent
1978	Montréal	Scotty Bowman	Boston	1994	NY Rangers	Mike Keenan	Vancouver
1979	Montréal	Scotty Bowman	NY Rangers	1995	New Jersey	Jacques Lemaire	Detroit
1980	NY Islanders	Al Arbour	Philadelphia	1996	Colorado	Marc Crawford	Florida
1981	NY Islanders	Al Arbour	Minnesota	1997	Detroit	Scotty Bowman	Philadelphia
1982	NY Islanders	Al Arbour	Vancouver	1998	Detroit	Scotty Bowman	Washington
1983	NY Islanders	Al Arbour	Edmonton	1999	Dallas	Ken Hitchcock	Buffalo
1984	Edmonton	Glen Sather	NY Islanders	2000	New Jersey	Larry Robinson	Dallas
1985	Edmonton	Glen Sather	Philadelphia	2001	Colorado	Bob Hartley	New Jersey
1986	Montréal	Jean Perron	Calgary	2002	Detroit	Scotty Bowman	Carolina
1987	Edmonton	Glen Sather	Philadelphia	2003	New Jersey	Pat Burns	Anaheim
1988	Edmonton	Glen Sather	Boston	2004	Tampa Bay	John Tortorella	Calgary
1989	Calgary	Terry Crisp	Montréal	2005	No competition		
1990	Edmonton	John Muckler	Boston	2006	Carolina	Peter Laviolette	Edmonton
1991	Pittsburgh	Bob Johnson	Minnesota	2007	Anaheim	Randy Carlyle	Ottawa
1992	Pittsburgh	Scotty Bowman	Chicago	2008	Detroit	Mike Babcock	Pittsburgh
1993	Montréal	Jacques Demers	Los Angeles	2009	Pittsburgh	Dan Bylsma	Detroit

Most NHL Goals in a Season

Player	Team	Season	Goals	Player	Team	Season	Goals
Wayne Gretzky	Edmonton	1981-82	92	Jari Kurri	Edmonton	1984-85	71
Wayne Gretzky	Edmonton	1983-84	87	Mario Lemieux	Pittsburgh	1987-88	70
Brett Hull	St. Louis	1990-91	86	Bernie Nicholls	Los Angeles	1988-89	70
Mario Lemieux	Pittsburgh	1988-89	85	Brett Hull	St. Louis	1991-92	70
Phil Esposito	Boston	1970-71	76	Mike Bossy	NY Islanders	1978-79	69
Teemu Selanne	Winnipeg	1992-93	76	Mario Lemieux	Pittsburgh	1992-93	69
Alexander Mogilny	Buffalo	1992-93	76	Mario Lemieux	Pittsburgh	1995-96	69
Wayne Gretzky	Edmonton	1984-85	73	Phil Esposito	Boston	1973-74	68
Brett Hull	St. Louis	1989-90	72	Mike Bossy	NY Islanders	1980-81	68
Wayne Gretzky	Edmonton	1982-83	71	Jari Kurri	Edmonton	1985-86	68

All-Time Regular Season Leading Scorers

Player	Goals	Assists	Points	Player	Goals	Assists	Points	Player	Goals	Assists	Points
Wayne Gretzky	894	1,963	2,857	Joe Sakic	625	1,016	1,641	Bryan Trottier	524	901	1,425
Mark Messier	694	1,193	1,887	Jaromir Jagr	646	953	1,599	Adam Oates	341	1,079	1,420
Gordie Howe	801	1,049	1,850	Phil Esposito	717	873	1,590	Doug Gilmour	450	964	1,414
Ron Francis	549	1,249	1,798	Ray Bourque	410	1,169	1,579	Dale Hawerchuk	518	891	1,409
Marcel Dionne	731	1,040	1,771	Paul Coffey	396	1,135	1,531	Jari Kurri	601	797	1,398
Steve Yzerman	692	1,063	1,755	Stan Mikita	541	926	1,467	Luc Robitaille	668	726	1,394
Mario Lemieux	690	1,033	1,723	Mark Recchi	545	897	1,442				

Note: Through end of 2008-09 season.

Hart Memorial Trophy (MVP)

1927	Herb Gardiner, Montréal	1955	Ted Kennedy, Toronto	1982	Wayne Gretzky, Edmonton
1928	Howie Morenz, Montréal	1956	Jean Beliveau, Montréal	1983	Wayne Gretzky, Edmonton

1927 Herb Gardiner, Montréal — 1955 Ted Kennedy, Toronto — 1982 Wayne Gretzky, Edmonton
1928 Howie Morenz, Montréal — 1956 Jean Beliveau, Montréal — 1983 Wayne Gretzky, Edmonton
1929 Roy Worters, NY Americans — 1957 Gordie Howe, Detroit — 1984 Wayne Gretzky, Edmonton
1930 Nels Stewart, Montréal Maroons — 1958 Gordie Howe, Detroit — 1985 Wayne Gretzky, Edmonton
1931 Howie Morenz, Montréal — 1959 Andy Bathgate, NY Rangers — 1986 Wayne Gretzky, Edmonton
1932 Howie Morenz, Montréal — 1960 Gordie Howe, Detroit — 1987 Wayne Gretzky, Edmonton
1933 Eddie Shore, Boston — 1961 Bernie Geoffrion, Montréal — 1988 Mario Lemieux, Pittsburgh
1934 Aurel Joliat, Montréal — 1962 Jacques Plante, Montréal — 1989 Wayne Gretzky, Los Angeles
1935 Eddie Shore, Boston — 1963 Gordie Howe, Detroit — 1990 Mark Messier, Edmonton
1936 Eddie Shore, Boston — 1964 Jean Beliveau, Montréal — 1991 Brett Hull, St. Louis
1937 Babe Siebert, Montréal — 1965 Bobby Hull, Chicago — 1992 Mark Messier, NY Rangers
1938 Eddie Shore, Boston — 1966 Bobby Hull, Chicago — 1993 Mario Lemieux, Pittsburgh
1939 Toe Blake, Montréal — 1967 Stan Mikita, Chicago — 1994 Sergei Fedorov, Detroit
1940 Ebbie Goodfellow, Detroit — 1968 Stan Mikita, Chicago — 1995 Eric Lindros, Philadelphia
1941 Bill Cowley, Boston — 1969 Phil Esposito, Boston — 1996 Mario Lemieux, Pittsburgh
1942 Tom Anderson, Brooklyn Americans — 1970 Bobby Orr, Boston — 1997 Dominik Hasek, Buffalo
1943 Bill Cowley, Boston — 1971 Bobby Orr, Boston — 1998 Dominik Hasek, Buffalo
1944 Babe Pratt, Toronto — 1972 Bobby Orr, Boston — 1999 Jaromir Jagr, Pittsburgh
1945 Elmer Lach, Montréal — 1973 Bobby Clarke, Philadelphia — 2000 Chris Pronger, St. Louis
1946 Max Bentley, Chicago — 1974 Phil Esposito, Boston — 2001 Joe Sakic, Colorado
1947 Maurice Richard, Montréal — 1975 Bobby Clarke, Philadelphia — 2002 Jose Theodore, Montréal
1948 Buddy O'Connor, NY Rangers — 1976 Bobby Clarke, Philadelphia — 2003 Peter Forsberg, Colorado
1949 Sid Abel, Detroit — 1977 Guy Lafleur, Montréal — 2004 Martin St. Louis, Tampa Bay
1950 Chuck Rayner, NY Rangers — 1978 Guy Lafleur, Montréal — 2006 Joe Thornton, San Jose
1951 Milt Schmidt, Boston — 1979 Bryan Trottier, NY Islanders — 2007 Sidney Crosby, Pittsburgh
1952 Gordie Howe, Detroit — 1980 Wayne Gretzky, Edmonton — 2008 Alexander Ovechkin, Washington
1953 Gordie Howe, Detroit — 1981 Wayne Gretzky, Edmonton — 2009 Alexander Ovechkin, Washington
1954 Al Rollins, Chicago

Conn Smythe Trophy (MVP in Playoffs)

1965 Jean Beliveau, Montréal — 1976 Reg Leach, Philadelphia — 1987 Ron Hextall, Philadelphia
1966 Roger Crozier, Detroit — 1977 Guy Lafleur, Montréal — 1988 Wayne Gretzky, Edmonton
1967 Dave Keon, Toronto — 1978 Larry Robinson, Montréal — 1989 Al MacInnis, Calgary
1968 Glenn Hall, St. Louis — 1979 Bob Gainey, Montréal — 1990 Bill Ranford, Edmonton
1969 Serge Savard, Montréal — 1980 Bryan Trottier, NY Islanders — 1991 Mario Lemieux, Pittsburgh
1970 Bobby Orr, Boston — 1981 Butch Goring, NY Islanders — 1992 Mario Lemieux, Pittsburgh
1971 Ken Dryden, Montréal — 1982 Mike Bossy, NY Islanders — 1993 Patrick Roy, Montréal
1972 Bobby Orr, Boston — 1983 Billy Smith, NY Islanders — 1994 Brian Leetch, NY Rangers
1973 Yvan Cournoyer, Montréal — 1984 Mark Messier, Edmonton — 1995 Claude Lemieux, New Jersey
1974 Bernie Parent, Philadelphia — 1985 Wayne Gretzky, Edmonton — 1996 Joe Sakic, Colorado
1975 Bernie Parent, Philadelphia — 1986 Patrick Roy, Montréal — 1997 Mike Vernon, Detroit

1998	Steve Yzerman, Detroit	2002	Nicklas Lidstrom, Detroit	2007	Scott Niedermayer, Anaheim
1999	Joe Nieuwendyk, Dallas	2003	Jean-Sebastien Giguere, Anaheim	2008	Henrik Zetterberg, Detroit
2000	Scott Stevens, New Jersey	2004	Brad Richards, Tampa Bay	2009	Evgeni Malkin, Pittsburgh
2001	Patrick Roy, Colorado	2006	Cam Ward, Carolina		

Calder Memorial Trophy (Rookie of the Year)

1933	Carl Voss, Detroit	1959	Ralph Backstrom, Montréal	1984	Tom Barrasso, Buffalo
1934	Russ Blinco, Montréal Maroons	1960	Bill Hay, Chicago	1985	Mario Lemieux, Pittsburgh
1935	Dave Schriner, NY Americans	1961	Dave Keon, Toronto	1986	Gary Suter, Calgary
1936	Mike Karakas, Chicago	1962	Bobby Rousseau, Montréal	1987	Luc Robitaille, Los Angeles
1937	Syl Apps, Toronto	1963	Kent Douglas, Toronto	1988	Joe Nieuwendyk, Calgary
1938	Cully Dahlstrom, Chicago	1964	Jacques Laperriere, Montréal	1989	Brian Leetch, NY Rangers
1939	Frank Brimsek, Boston	1965	Roger Crozier, Detroit	1990	Sergei Makarov, Calgary
1940	Kilby MacDonald, NY Rangers	1966	Brit Selby, Toronto	1991	Ed Belfour, Chicago
1941	John Quilty, Montréal	1967	Bobby Orr, Boston	1992	Pavel Bure, Vancouver
1942	Grant Warwick, NY Rangers	1968	Derek Sanderson, Boston	1993	Teemu Selanne, Winnipeg
1943	Gaye Stewart, Toronto	1969	Danny Grant, Minnesota	1994	Martin Brodeur, New Jersey
1944	Gus Bodnar, Toronto	1970	Tony Esposito, Chicago	1995	Peter Forsberg, Quebec
1945	Frank McCool, Toronto	1971	Gilbert Perreault, Buffalo	1996	Daniel Alfredsson, Ottawa
1946	Edgar Laprade, NY Rangers	1972	Ken Dryden, Montréal	1997	Bryan Berard, NY Islanders
1947	Howie Meeker, Toronto	1973	Steve Vickers, NY Rangers	1998	Sergei Samsonov, Boston
1948	Jim McFadden, Detroit	1974	Denis Potvin, NY Islanders	1999	Chris Drury, Colorado
1949	Pentti Lund, NY Rangers	1975	Eric Vail, Atlanta	2000	Scott Gomez, New Jersey
1950	Jack Gelineau, Boston	1976	Bryan Trottier, NY Islanders	2001	Evgeni Nabokov, San Jose
1951	Terry Sawchuk, Detroit	1977	Willi Plett, Atlanta	2002	Dany Heatley, Atlanta
1952	Bernie Geoffrion, Montréal	1978	Mike Bossy, NY Islanders	2003	Barret Jackman, St. Louis
1953	Gump Worsley, NY Rangers	1979	Bobby Smith, Minnesota	2004	Andrew Raycroft, Boston
1954	Camille Henry, NY Rangers	1980	Ray Bourque, Boston	2006	Alexander Ovechkin, Washington
1955	Ed Litzenberger, Chicago	1981	Peter Stastny, Quebec	2007	Evgeni Malkin, Pittsburgh
1956	Glenn Hall, Detroit	1982	Dale Hawerchuk, Winnipeg	2008	Patrick Kane, Chicago
1957	Larry Regan, Boston	1983	Steve Larmer, Chicago	2009	Steve Mason, Columbus
1958	Frank Mahovlich, Toronto				

Lady Byng Memorial Trophy (Most Gentlemanly Player)

1925	Frank Nighbor, Ottawa	1953	Red Kelly, Detroit	1981	Rick Kehoe, Pittsburgh
1926	Frank Nighbor, Ottawa	1954	Red Kelly, Detroit	1982	Rick Middleton, Boston
1927	Billy Burch, NY Americans	1955	Sid Smith, Toronto	1983	Mike Bossy, NY Islanders
1928	Frank Boucher, NY Rangers	1956	Earl Reibel, Detroit	1984	Mike Bossy, NY Islanders
1929	Frank Boucher, NY Rangers	1957	Andy Hebenton, NY Rangers	1985	Jari Kurri, Edmonton
1930	Frank Boucher, NY Rangers	1958	Camille Henry, NY Rangers	1986	Mike Bossy, NY Islanders
1931	Frank Boucher, NY Rangers	1959	Alex Delvecchio, Detroit	1987	Joe Mullen, Calgary
1932	Joe Primeau, Toronto	1960	Don McKenney, Boston	1988	Mats Naslund, Montréal
1933	Frank Boucher, NY Rangers	1961	Red Kelly, Toronto	1989	Joe Mullen, Calgary
1934	Frank Boucher, NY Rangers	1962	Dave Keon, Toronto	1990	Brett Hull, St. Louis
1935	Frank Boucher, NY Rangers	1963	Dave Keon, Toronto	1991	Wayne Gretzky, Los Angeles
1936	Doc Romnes, Chicago	1964	Ken Wharram, Chicago	1992	Wayne Gretzky, Los Angeles
1937	Marty Barry, Detroit	1965	Bobby Hull, Chicago	1993	Pierre Turgeon, NY Islanders
1938	Gordie Drillon, Toronto	1966	Alex Delvecchio, Detroit	1994	Wayne Gretzky, Los Angeles
1939	Clint Smith, NY Rangers	1967	Stan Mikita, Chicago	1995	Ron Francis, Pittsburgh
1940	Bobby Bauer, Boston	1968	Stan Mikita, Chicago	1996	Paul Kariya, Anaheim
1941	Bobby Bauer, Boston	1969	Alex Delvecchio, Detroit	1997	Paul Kariya, Anaheim
1942	Syl Apps, Toronto	1970	Phil Goyette, St. Louis	1998	Ron Francis, Pittsburgh
1943	Max Bentley, Chicago	1971	John Bucyk, Boston	1999	Wayne Gretzky, NY Rangers
1944	Clint Smith, Chicago	1972	Jean Ratelle, NY Rangers	2000	Pavol Demitra, St. Louis
1945	Bill Mosienko, Chicago	1973	Gil Perreault, Buffalo	2001	Joe Sakic, Colorado
1946	Toe Blake, Montréal	1974	John Bucyk, Boston	2002	Ron Francis, Carolina
1947	Bobby Bauer, Boston	1975	Marcel Dionne, Detroit	2003	Alexander Mogilny, Toronto
1948	Buddy O'Connor, NY Rangers	1976	Jean Ratelle, NYR.-Boston	2004	Brad Richards, Tampa Bay
1949	Bill Quackenbush, Detroit	1977	Marcel Dionne, Los Angeles	2006	Pavel Datsyuk, Detroit
1950	Edgar Laprade, NY Rangers	1978	Butch Goring, Los Angeles	2007	Pavel Datsyuk, Detroit
1951	Red Kelly, Detroit	1979	Bob MacMillan, Atlanta	2008	Pavel Datsyuk, Detroit
1952	Sid Smith, Toronto	1980	Wayne Gretzky, Edmonton	2009	Pavel Datsyuk, Detroit

James Norris Memorial Trophy (Outstanding Defenseman)

1954	Red Kelly, Detroit	1973	Bobby Orr, Boston	1991	Ray Bourque, Boston
1955	Doug Harvey, Montréal	1974	Bobby Orr, Boston	1992	Brian Leetch, NY Rangers
1956	Doug Harvey, Montréal	1975	Bobby Orr, Boston	1993	Chris Chelios, Chicago
1957	Doug Harvey, Montréal	1976	Denis Potvin, NY Islanders	1994	Ray Bourque, Boston
1958	Doug Harvey, Montréal	1977	Larry Robinson, Montréal	1995	Paul Coffey, Detroit
1959	Tom Johnson, Montréal	1978	Denis Potvin, NY Islanders	1996	Chris Chelios, Chicago
1960	Doug Harvey, Montréal	1979	Denis Potvin, NY Islanders	1997	Brian Leetch, NY Rangers
1961	Doug Harvey, Montréal	1980	Larry Robinson, Montréal	1998	Rob Blake, Los Angeles
1962	Doug Harvey, NY Rangers	1981	Randy Carlyle, Pittsburgh	1999	Al MacInnis, St. Louis
1963	Pierre Pilote, Chicago	1982	Doug Wilson, Chicago	2000	Chris Pronger, St. Louis
1964	Pierre Pilote, Chicago	1983	Rod Langway, Washington	2001	Nicklas Lidstrom, Detroit
1965	Pierre Pilote, Chicago	1984	Rod Langway, Washington	2002	Nicklas Lidstrom, Detroit
1966	Jacques Laperriere, Montréal	1985	Paul Coffey, Edmonton	2003	Nicklas Lidstrom, Detroit
1967	Harry Howell, NY Rangers	1986	Paul Coffey, Edmonton	2004	Scott Niedermayer, New Jersey
1968	Bobby Orr, Boston	1987	Ray Bourque, Boston	2006	Nicklas Lidstrom, Detroit
1969	Bobby Orr, Boston	1988	Ray Bourque, Boston	2007	Nicklas Lidstrom, Detroit
1970	Bobby Orr, Boston	1989	Chris Chelios, Montréal	2008	Nicklas Lidstrom, Detroit
1971	Bobby Orr, Boston	1990	Ray Bourque, Boston	2009	Zdeno Chara, Boston
1972	Bobby Orr, Boston				

Art Ross Trophy (Leading Points Scorer)

Trophy first awarded in 1948. Prior years list NHL scoring leader.

1927 Bill Cook, NY Rangers	1955 Bernie Geoffrion, Montréal	1982 Wayne Gretzky, Edmonton
1928 Howie Morenz, Montréal	1956 Jean Beliveau, Montréal	1983 Wayne Gretzky, Edmonton
1929 Ace Bailey, Toronto	1957 Gordie Howe, Detroit	1984 Wayne Gretzky, Edmonton
1930 Cooney Weiland, Boston	1958 Dickie Moore, Montréal	1985 Wayne Gretzky, Edmonton
1931 Howie Morenz, Montréal	1959 Dickie Moore, Montréal	1986 Wayne Gretzky, Edmonton
1932 Harvey Jackson, Toronto	1960 Bobby Hull, Chicago	1987 Wayne Gretzky, Edmonton
1933 Bill Cook, NY Rangers	1961 Bernie Geoffrion, Montréal	1988 Mario Lemieux, Pittsburgh
1934 Charlie Conacher, Toronto	1962 Bobby Hull, Chicago	1989 Mario Lemieux, Pittsburgh
1935 Charlie Conacher, Toronto	1963 Gordie Howe, Detroit	1990 Wayne Gretzky, Los Angeles
1936 Dave Schriner, NY Americans	1964 Stan Mikita, Chicago	1991 Wayne Gretzky, Los Angeles
1937 Dave Schriner, NY Americans	1965 Stan Mikita, Chicago	1992 Mario Lemieux, Pittsburgh
1938 Gordie Drillon, Toronto	1966 Bobby Hull, Chicago	1993 Mario Lemieux, Pittsburgh
1939 Toe Blake, Montréal	1967 Stan Mikita, Chicago	1994 Wayne Gretzky, Los Angeles
1940 Milt Schmidt, Boston	1968 Stan Mikita, Chicago	1995 Jaromir Jagr, Pittsburgh
1941 Bill Cowley, Boston	1969 Phil Esposito, Boston	1996 Mario Lemieux, Pittsburgh
1942 Bryan Hextall, NY Rangers	1970 Bobby Orr, Boston	1997 Mario Lemieux, Pittsburgh
1943 Doug Bentley, Chicago	1971 Phil Esposito, Boston	1998 Jaromir Jagr, Pittsburgh
1944 Herbie Cain, Boston	1972 Phil Esposito, Boston	1999 Jaromir Jagr, Pittsburgh
1945 Elmer Lach, Montréal	1973 Phil Esposito, Boston	2000 Jaromir Jagr, Pittsburgh
1946 Max Bentley, Chicago	1974 Phil Esposito, Boston	2001 Jaromir Jagr, Pittsburgh
1947 Max Bentley, Chicago	1975 Bobby Orr, Boston	2002 Jarome Iginla, Calgary
1948 Elmer Lach, Montréal	1976 Guy Lafleur, Montréal	2003 Peter Forsberg, Colorado
1949 Roy Conacher, Chicago	1977 Guy Lafleur, Montréal	2004 Martin St. Louis, Tampa Bay
1950 Ted Lindsay, Detroit	1978 Guy Lafleur, Montréal	2006 Joe Thornton, San Jose
1951 Gordie Howe, Detroit	1979 Bryan Trottier, NY Islanders	2007 Sidney Crosby, Pittsburgh
1952 Gordie Howe, Detroit	1980 Marcel Dionne, Los Angeles	2008 Alexander Ovechkin, Washington
1953 Gordie Howe, Detroit	1981 Wayne Gretzky, Edmonton	2009 Evgeni Malkin, Pittsburgh
1954 Gordie Howe, Detroit		

Vezina Trophy (Outstanding Goalie)*

1927 George Hainsworth, Montréal	1956 Jacques Plante, Montréal	1982 Bill Smith, NY Islanders
1928 George Hainsworth, Montréal	1957 Jacques Plante, Montréal	1983 Pete Peeters, Boston
1929 George Hainsworth, Montréal	1958 Jacques Plante, Montréal	1984 Tom Barrasso, Buffalo
1930 Tiny Thompson, Boston	1959 Jacques Plante, Montréal	1985 Pelle Lindbergh, Philadelphia
1931 Roy Worters, NY Americans	1960 Jacques Plante, Montréal	1986 John Vanbiesbrouck,
1932 Charlie Gardiner, Chicago	1961 Johnny Bower, Toronto	NY Rangers
1933 Tiny Thompson, Boston	1962 Jacques Plante, Montréal	1987 Ron Hextall, Philadelphia
1934 Charlie Gardiner, Chicago	1963 Glenn Hall, Chicago	1988 Grant Fuhr, Edmonton
1935 Lorne Chabot, Chicago	1964 Charlie Hodge, Montréal	1989 Patrick Roy, Montréal
1936 Tiny Thompson, Boston	1965 Sawchuk, Bower, Toronto	1990 Patrick Roy, Montréal
1937 Normie Smith, Detroit	1966 Worsley, Hodge, Montréal	1991 Ed Belfour, Chicago
1938 Tiny Thompson, Boston	1967 Hall, DeJordy, Chicago	1992 Patrick Roy, Montréal
1939 Frank Brimsek, Boston	1968 Worsley, Vachon, Montréal	1993 Ed Belfour, Chicago
1940 Dave Kerr, NY Rangers	1969 Hall, Plante, St. Louis	1994 Dominik Hasek, Buffalo
1941 Turk Broda, Toronto	1970 Tony Esposito, Chicago	1995 Dominik Hasek, Buffalo
1942 Frank Brimsek, Boston	1971 Giacomin, Villemure,	1996 Jim Carey, Washington
1943 Johnny Mowers, Detroit	NY Rangers	1997 Dominik Hasek, Buffalo
1944 Bill Durnan, Montréal	1972 Esposito, Smith, Chicago	1998 Dominik Hasek, Buffalo
1945 Bill Durnan, Montréal	1973 Ken Dryden, Montréal	1999 Dominik Hasek, Buffalo
1946 Bill Durnan, Montréal	1974 Bernie Parent, Philadelphia;	2000 Olaf Kolzig, Washington
1947 Bill Durnan, Montréal	Tony Esposito, Chicago	2001 Dominik Hasek, Buffalo
1948 Turk Broda, Toronto	1975 Bernie Parent, Philadelphia	2002 Jose Theodore, Montréal
1949 Bill Durnan, Montréal	1976 Ken Dryden, Montréal	2003 Martin Brodeur, New Jersey
1950 Bill Durnan, Montréal	1977 Dryden, Larocque, Montréal	2004 Martin Brodeur, New Jersey
1951 Al Rollins, Montréal	1978 Dryden, Larocque, Montréal	2006 Miikka Kiprusoff, Calgary
1952 Terry Sawchuk, Detroit	1979 Dryden, Larocque, Montréal	2007 Martin Brodeur, New Jersey
1953 Terry Sawchuk, Detroit	1980 Sauve, Edwards, Buffalo	2008 Martin Brodeur, New Jersey
1954 Harry Lumley, Toronto	1981 Sevigny, Larocque, Herron,	2009 Tim Thomas, Boston
1955 Terry Sawchuk, Detroit	Montréal	

*Before 1982, awarded to the goalie or goalies who played a minimum of 25 games for the team that allowed the fewest goals; since 1982, awarded to the outstanding goalie, as determined by a vote of NHL general managers.

NHL Home Ice[1]

Team	Name (built)	Capacity	Team	Name (built)	Capacity
Anaheim	Honda Center[2] (1993)	17,174	Montréal	Le Centre Bell[9] (1996)	21,273
Atlanta	Philips Arena (1999)	18,750	Nashville	Sommet Center[10] (1997)	17,113
Boston	TD Banknorth Garden[3] (1995)	17,565	New Jersey	Prudential Center (2007)	17,625
Buffalo	HSBC Arena[4] (1996)	18,690	NY Islanders	Nassau Veterans Mem. Col. (1972)	16,234
Calgary	Pengrowth Saddledome[5] (1983)	19,289	NY Rangers	Madison Square Garden (1968)	18,200
Carolina	RBC Center[6] (1999)	18,176	Ottawa	Scotiabank Place[11] (1996)	19,153
Chicago	United Center (1994)	20,500	Philadelphia	Wachovia Center[12] (1996)	19,537
Colorado	Pepsi Center (1999)	18,007	Phoenix	Jobing.com Arena[13] (2003)	17,125
Columbus	Nationwide Arena (2000)	18,500	Pittsburgh	Mellon Arena[14] (1961)	16,940
Dallas	American Airlines Center (2001)	18,532	St. Louis	Scottrade Center[15] (1994)	19,150
Detroit	Joe Louis Arena (1979)	20,058	San Jose	HP Pavilion[16] (1993)	17,483
Edmonton	Rexall Place[7] (1974)	16,839	Tampa Bay	St. Pete Times Forum[17] (1996)	19,758
Florida	BankAtlantic Center[8] (1998)	19,250	Toronto	Air Canada Centre (1999)	18,200
Los Angeles	Staples Center (1999)	18,118	Vancouver	General Motors Place (1995)	18,630
Minnesota	Xcel Energy Arena (2000)	18,064	Washington	Verizon Center[18] (1997)	18,277

(1) At the end of the 2008-09 season. (2) The Arrowhead Pond of Anaheim, 1993-2006. (3) FleetCenter 1995-2005. (4) Marine Midland Arena, 1996-99. (5) Olympic Saddledome, 1983-96; Canadian Airlines Saddledome, 1996-2000. (6) Raleigh Entertainment & Sports Arena, 1999-2002. (7) Northlands Col., 1974-79; Edmonton Col., 1979-98; Skyreach Centre, 1998-2003. (8) National Car Rental Center, 1998-2002; Office Depot Center, 2002-05. (9) Le Centre Molson, 1996-2002. (10) Nashville Arena, 1997-99; Gaylord Entertainment Center, 1999-2007. (11) Corel Centre, 1996-2006. (12) CoreStates Center, 1996-98; First Union Center, 1998-2003. (13) Glendale Arena, 2003-06. (14) Civic Arena, 1961-99. (15) Kiel Center, 1994-2000; Savvis Center, 2000-06. (16) San Jose Arena, 1993-2001; Compaq Center, 2001-02. (17) Ice Palace, 1996-2002. (18) MCI Center, 1997-2006.

Hockey Hall of Fame, Toronto, Ontario
(Asterisks denote 2008 inductees.)

PLAYERS

Abel, Sid
Adams, Jack
Anderson, Glenn
Apps, Syl
Armstrong, George
Bailey, Ace
Bain, Dan
Baker, Hobey
Barber, Bill
Barry, Marty
Bathgate, Andy
Bauer, Bobby
Beliveau, Jean
Benedict, Clint
Bentley, Doug
Bentley, Max
Blake, Hector "Toe"
Boivin, Leo
Boon, Dickie
Bossy, Mike
Bouchard, Butch
Boucher, Frank
Boucher, George
Bourque, Ray
Bower, Johnny
Bowie, Dubbie
Brimsek, Frank
Broadbent, Harry L. "Punch"
Broda, Turk
Bucyk, John
Burch, Billy
Cameron, Harry
Cheevers, Gerry
Clancy, King
Clapper, Aubrey "Dit"
Clarke, Bobby
Cleghorn, Sprague
Coffey, Paul
Colville, Neil
Conacher, Charlie
Conacher, Lionel
Conacher, Roy
Connell, Alex
Cook, Bill
Cook, Frederick "Bun"
Coulter, Art
Cournoyer, Yvan
Cowley, Bill
Crawford, Rusty
Darragh, Jack
Davidson, Scotty
Day, Clarence "Hap"
Delvecchio, Alex
Denneny, Cy
Dionne, Marcel
Drillon, Gordie
Drinkwater, Graham
Dryden, Ken
Duff, Terrance "Dick"
Dumart, Woody
Dunderdale, Tommy
Durnan, Bill
Dutton, Red
Dye, Babe
Esposito, Phil
Esposito, Tony
Farrel, Arthur
Federko, Bernie
Fetisov, Viacheslav
Flaman, Fernie
Foyston, Frank
Francis, Ron

Fredrickson, Frank
Fuhr, Grant
Gadsby, Bill
Gainey, Bob
Gardiner, Chuck
Gardiner, Herb
Gardiner, Jimmy
Gartner, Mike
Geoffrion, Bernie
Gerard, Eddie
Giacomin, Eddie
Gilbert, Rod
Gillies, Clark
Gilmour, Billy
Goheen, Frank "Moose"
Goodfellow, Ebbie
Goulet, Michel
Grant, Mike
Green, Wilfred "Shorty"
Gretzky, Wayne
Griffis, Si
Hainsworth, George
Hall, Glenn
Hall, Joe
Harvey, Doug
Hawerchuk, Dale
Hay, George
Hern, Riley
Hextall, Bryan
Holmes, Hap
Hooper, Tom
Horner, Red
Horton, Tim
Howe, Gordie
Howe, Syd
Howell, Harry
Hull, Bobby
*Hull, Brett
Hutton, Bouse
Hyland, Harry
Irvin, Dick
Jackson, Busher
Johnson, Ching
Johnson, Ernie
Johnson, Tom
Joliat, Aurel
Keats, Duke
Kelly, Red
Kennedy, Ted
Keon, Dave
Kharlamov, Valeri
Kurri, Jari
Lach, Elmer
Lafleur, Guy
LaFontaine, Pat
Lalonde, Newsy
Langway, Rod
Laperriere, Jacques
Lapointe, Guy
Laprade, Edgar
Larionov, Igor
Laviolette, Jack
LeSueur, Percy
*Leetch, Brian
Lehman, Hughie
Lemaire, Jacques
Lemieux, Mario
Lewis, Herbie
Lindsay, Ted
Lumley, Harry
MacInnis, Al
MacKay, Mickey
Mahovlich, Frank
Malone, Joe

Mantha, Sylvio
Marshall, Jack
Maxwell, Fred
McDonald, Lanny
McGee, Frank
McGimsie, Billy
McNamara, George
Messier, Mark
Mikita, Stan
Moore, Dickie
Moran, Paddy
Morenz, Howie
Mosienko, Bill
Mullen, Joe
Murphy, Larry
Neely, Cam
Nighbor, Frank
Noble, Reg
O'Connor, Buddy
Oliver, Harry
Olmstead, Bert
Orr, Bobby
Parent, Bernie
Park, Brad
Patrick, Lester
Patrick, Lynn
Perreault, Gilbert
Phillips, Tom
Pilote, Pierre
Pitre, Didier
Plante, Jacques
Potvin, Denis
Pratt, Babe
Primeau, Joe
Pronovost, Marcel
Pulford, Bob
Pulford, Harvey
Quackenbush, Bill
Rankin, Frank
Ratelle, Jean
Rayner, Chuck
Reardon, Kenny
Richard, Henri
Richard, Maurice
Richardson, George
Roberts, Gordie
Robinson, Larry
*Robitaille, Luc
Ross, Art
Roy, Patrick
Russel, Blair
Russell, Ernie
Ruttan, Jack
Salming, Börje
Savard, Denis
Savard, Serge
Sawchuk, Terry
Scanlan, Fred
Schmidt, Milt
Schriner, Sweeney
Seibert, Earl
Seibert, Oliver
Shore, Eddie
Shutt, Steve
Siebert, Babe
Simpson, Joe
Sittler, Darryl
Smith, Alf
Smith, Billy
Smith, Clint
Smith, Hooley
Smith, Tommy
Stanley, Allan
Stanley, Barney

Stastny, Peter
Stevens, Ronald Scott
Stewart, Jack
Stewart, Nels
Stuart, Bruce
Stuart, Hod
Taylor, Frederick "Cyclone"
Thompson, Cecil "Tiny"
Tretiak, Vladislav
Trihey, Harry
Trottier, Bryan
Ullman, Norm
Vezina, Georges
Walker, Jack
Walsh, Marty
Watson, Harry "Moose"
Watson, Harry Percival
Weiland, Cooney
Westwick, Harry
Whitcroft, Fred
Wilson, Gordon Allan "Phat"
Worsley, Gump
Worters, Roy
*Yzerman, Steve

BUILDERS

Adams, Charles
Adams, Weston
Ahearn, John "Bunny"
Ahearn, Frank
Allan, Sir Montagu
Allen, Keith
Arbour, Al
Ballard, Harold
Bauer, Father David
Bickell, J. P.
Bowman, Scotty
Brooks, Herbert
Brown, George
Brown, Walter
Buckland, Frank
Bush, Walter, Jr.
Butterfield, Jack
Calder, Frank
Campbell, Angus
Campbell, Clarence
Cattarinich, Joseph
Chynoweth, Ed
Costello, Murray
Dandurand, Leo
Dilio, Frank
Dudley, George
Dunn, James
Fletcher, Cliff
Francis, Emile
Gibson, Jack
Gorman, Tommy
Gregory, Jim
Griffiths, Frank
Hanley, Bill
Hay, Charles
Hendy, Jim
Hewitt, Foster
Hewitt, William
Hotchkiss, Harley
Hume, Fred
Ilitch, Mike
Imlach, Punch
Ivan, Tommy
Jennings, William
Johnson, Bob
Juckes, Gordon
Kilpatrick, John

Kilrea, Brian
Knox, Seymour
*Lamoriello, Lou
Leader, Al
LeBel, Robert
Lockhart, Thomas
Loicq, Paul
Mariucci, John
Mathers, Frank
McLaughlin, Frederic
Milford, Jake
Molson, Sen. Hartland
Morrison, Ian "Scotty"
Murray, Athol "Père"
Neilson, Roger
Nelson, Francis
Norris, Bruce
Norris, James
Norris, James, Sr.
Northey, William
O'Brien, J. Ambrose
O'Neill, Brian Francis
Page, Frederick
Patrick, Craig
Patrick, Frank
Pickard, Allan
Pilous, Rudy
Poile, Bud
Pollock, Sam
Raymond, Sen. Donat
Robertson, John Ross
Robinson, Claude
Ross, Phillip
Sabetzki, Gunther
Sather, Glen
Selke, Frank
Sinden, Harry
Smith, Frank
Smythe, Conn
Snider, Ed
Stanley, Lord (of Preston)
Sutherland, Capt. James T.
Tarasov, Anatoli
Torrey, Bill
Turner, Lloyd
Tutt, William
Voss, Carl
Waghorne, Fred
Wirtz, Arthur
Wirtz, Bill
Ziegler, John A., Jr.

REFEREES AND LINESMEN

Armstrong, Neil
Ashley, John
Chadwick, Bill
D'Amico, John
Elliott, Chaucer
Hayes, George
Hewiston, Bobby
Ion, Mickey
Pavelich, Matt
Rodden, Mike
Scapinello, Ray
Smeaton, Cooper
Storey, Red
Udvari, Frank
Van Hellemond, Andy

SOCCER

Major League Soccer

The Columbus Crew won the Major League Soccer (MLS) Championship with a 3-1 win against the New York Red Bulls at The Home Depot Center in Carson, CA, on Nov. 23, 2008. Guillermo Barros Schelotto set an MLS Cup record with three assists in the game to earn the MLS Cup Most Valuable Player Award. Schelotto won league MVP honors during the 2008 season, joining Tony Meola (2000) and Carlos Ruiz (2002) as the only players in league history to earn dual MVP honors in the same season. Columbus Head Coach Sigi Schmid also was voted the 2008 MLS Coach of the Year as he led the Crew to a league-best 17-7-6 regular season record.

Major League Soccer continued its efforts to expand the league, culminating in two more new clubs. Commissioner Don Garber announced in Mar. 2009, that new franchises in Vancouver and Portland, OR, will join the MLS in 2011. The Seattle Sounders FC began play in 2009 as the 15th MLS team, and Philadelphia will be added as the league's 16th club in 2010.

Major League Soccer (MLS) Cup Champions, 1996-2008

Year	Winner	Final opponent	Score	Site	MVP
1996	D.C. United	Los Angeles Galaxy	3-2 (OT)	Foxboro, MA	Marco Etcheverry
1997	D.C. United	Colorado Rapids	2-1	Washington, DC	Jaime Moreno
1998	Chicago Fire	D.C. United	2-0	Pasadena, CA	Peter Nowak
1999	D.C. United	Los Angeles Galaxy	2-0	Foxboro, MA	Ben Olsen
2000	Kansas City Wizards	Chicago Fire	1-0	Washington, DC	Tony Meola
2001	San Jose Earthquakes	Los Angeles Galaxy	2-1 (OT)	Columbus, OH	Dwayne De Rosario
2002	Los Angeles Galaxy	New England Revolution	1-0 (OT)	Foxboro, MA	Carlos Ruiz
2003	San Jose Earthquakes	Chicago Fire	4-2	Carson, CA	Landon Donovan
2004	D.C. United	Kansas City Wizards	3-2	Carson, CA	Alecko Eskandarian
2005	Los Angeles Galaxy	New England Revolution	1-0 (OT)	Frisco, TX	Guillermo Ramirez
2006	Los Angeles Galaxy	New England Revolution	1-1 (4-3)*	Frisco, TX	Brian Ching
2007	Houston Dynamo	New England Revolution	2-1	Washington, DC	Dwayne De Rosario
2008	Columbus Crew	New York Red Bulls	3-1	Carson, CA	Guillermo Barros Schelotto

*Match decided in penalty kicks (shootout score in parentheses).

Major League Soccer Final Standings, 2008

(Does not include playoff games.)

Eastern Division	GP	W	L	T	PTS	GF	GA	GD	Western Division	GP	W	L	T	PTS	GF	GA	GD
Columbus	30	17	7	6	57	50	36	14	Houston	30	13	5	12	51	45	32	13
Chicago	30	13	10	7	46	44	33	11	Chivas USA	30	12	11	7	43	40	41	−1
New England	30	12	11	7	43	40	43	−3	Real Salt Lake	30	10	10	10	40	40	39	1
Kansas City	30	11	10	9	42	37	39	−2	Colorado	30	11	14	5	38	44	45	−1
New York	30	10	11	9	39	42	48	−6	FC Dallas	30	8	10	12	36	45	41	4
D.C. United	30	11	15	4	37	43	51	−8	Los Angeles	30	8	13	9	33	55	62	−7
Toronto FC	30	9	13	8	35	34	43	−9	San Jose	30	8	13	9	33	32	38	−6

Major League Soccer Scoring Leaders, 2008

Player	Club	GP	Goals	Player	Club	GP	Goals
Landon Donovan	Los Angeles	25	20	Luciano Emilio	D.C.	27	11
Kenny Cooper	Dallas	30	18	Jaime Moreno	D.C.	25	10
Edson Buddle	Los Angeles	27	15	Chad Barrett	Chicago/Toronto	29	9
Juan Pablo Angel	New York	23	14	Alejandro Moreno	Columbus	27	9
Brian Ching	Houston	25	13	Chris Rolfe	Chicago	26	9
Conor Casey	Colorado	21	11				

Women's Professional Soccer Kicks Off

The inaugural Women's Professional Soccer (WPS) season began on Mar. 29, 2009. Seven WPS teams began play, based in the San Francisco Bay Area (FC Gold Pride), Boston, Chicago, Los Angeles, New Jersey/New York (Sky Blue FC), St. Louis, and Washington, DC. Heather O'Reilly scored the lone goal in the first WPS Championship Game to lead Sky Blue FC to a 1-0 victory over the Los Angeles Sol on Aug. 22, 2009, at The Home Depot Center in Carson, CA. The league's eighth and ninth franchises, Philadelphia and Atlanta, were scheduled to begin play in 2010.

Women's Professional Soccer Final Standings, 2009

(Does not include playoff games.)

Team	W	L	T	PTS	GF	GA	GD	Team	W	L	T	PTS	GF	GA	GD
Los Angeles Sol	12	3	5	41	27	10	17	Boston Breakers	7	9	4	25	18	20	−2
Saint Louis Athletica	10	6	4	34	19	15	4	Chicago Red Stars	5	10	5	20	18	25	−7
Washington Freedom	8	7	5	29	32	32	0	FC Gold Pride	4	10	6	18	17	28	−11
Sky Blue FC	7	8	5	26	19	20	−1								

Women's Professional Soccer Championship

Year	Winner	Final opponent	Score	Site	MVP
2009	Sky Blue FC	Los Angeles Sol	1-0	Carson, CA	Marta

European Championships, 1960-2008

The final rounds of the 2008 UEFA European Championships were jointly hosted by Austria and Switzerland and opened June 7, 2008, in Basel, Switzerland, with the final match at Ernst Happle Stadium in Vienna, Austria, on June 29, 2008.

Year	Winner	Final opponent	Score	Site
1960	USSR	Yugoslavia	2-1 (extra time)	France
1964	Spain	USSR	2-1	Spain
1968	Italy	Yugoslavia	2-0	Italy
1972	W. Germany	USSR	3-0	Belgium
1976	Czechoslovakia	W. Germany	2-2 (Czech. won 5-3 on pens.)	Yugoslavia
1980	W. Germany	Belgium	2-1	Italy
1984	France	Spain	2-0	France
1988	Netherlands	USSR	2-0	W. Germany
1992	Denmark	Germany	2-0	Sweden
1996	Germany	Czech Rep.	2-1 (extra time)	England
2000	France	Italy	2-1 (extra time)	Belgium/Neth.
2004	Greece	Portugal	1-0	Portugal
2008	Spain	Germany	1-0	Austria

UEFA Championship League Winners, 1956-2009

Year	Winner	Final opponent	Score	Year	Winner	Final opponent	Score
1956	Real Madrid	Reims	4-3	1983	Hamburg	Juventus	1-0
1957	Real Madrid	Fiorentina	2-0	1984	Liverpool	Roma	1-1 (4-2)*
1958	Real Madrid	AC Milan	3-2#	1985	Juventus	Liverpool	1-0
1959	Real Madrid	Reims	2-0	1986	Steaua	Barcelona	0-0 (2-0)*
1960	Real Madrid	Eintracht	7-3	1987	Porto	Bayern Munich	2-1
1961	Benfica	Barcelona	3-2	1988	PSV	Benfica	0-0 (6-5)*
1962	Benfica	Real Madrid	5-3	1989	AC Milan	Steaua	4-0
1963	AC Milan	Benfica	2-1	1990	AC Milan	Benfica	1-0
1964	Inter Milan	Real Madrid	3-1	1991	Crvena zvezda	Marseille	0-0 (5-3)*
1965	Inter Milan	Benfica	1-0	1992	Barcelona	Sampdoria	1-0#
1966	Real Madrid	Partizan	2-1	1993	Marseille	AC Milan	1-0
1967	Celtic	Inter Milan	2-1	1994	AC Milan	Barcelona	4-0
1968	Man. United	Benfica	4-1#	1995	Ajax	AC Milan	1-0
1969	AC Milan	Ajax	4-1	1996	Juventus	Ajax	1-1 (4-2)*
1970	Feyenoord	Celtic	2-1#	1997	Dortmund	Juventus	3-1
1971	Ajax	Panathinaikos	2-0	1998	Real Madrid	Juventus	1-0
1972	Ajax	Inter Milan	2-0	1999	Man. United	Bayern Munich	2-1
1973	Ajax	Juventus	1-0	2000	Real Madrid	Valencia	3-0
1974	Bayern Munich	Atlético	5-1[1]	2001	Bayern Munich	Valencia	1-1 (5-4)*
1975	Bayern Munich	Leeds	2-0	2002	Real Madrid	Leverkusen	2-1
1976	Bayern Munich	St-Etienne	1-0	2003	AC Milan	Juventus	0-0 (3-2)*
1977	Liverpool	Mönchen-gladbach	3-1	2004	Porto	Monaco	3-0
1978	Liverpool	Club Brugge	1-0	2005	Liverpool	AC Milan	3-3 (3-2)*
1979	Notts Forest	Malmö	1-0	2006	Barcelona	Arsenal	2-1
1980	Notts Forest	Hamburg	1-0	2007	AC Milan	Liverpool	2-1
1981	Liverpool	Real Madrid	1-0	2008	Manchester United	Chelsea	1-1 (6-5)*
1982	Villa	Bayern Munich	1-0	2009	Barcelona	Manchester United	2-0

*Match decided in penalty kicks (shootout score in parentheses). (#) Match decided in extra time. (1) Aggregate score. First game 1-1; second, 4-0.

Germany Defeats Brazil for 2007 Women's World Cup Title

Germany successfully defended its Women's World Cup title Sept. 30, 2007, defeating Brazil 2-0 at Hongkou Stadium in Shanghai, China. Germany set several records along the way, outscoring its opponents 21-0. With the help of stellar performances by goalkeeper Nadine Angerer, Germany became the first team in World Cup history to completely shut out its opponents in tournament play. Led by coach Silvia Neid, the team was also the first women's soccer team in history to successfully defend its title at the World Cup. Brazilian superstar midfielder Marta scored 7 goals during the tournament and, despite her team's defeat, won both the Golden Ball, which is given to the tournament's best player, and the Golden Shoe, which is given to its top scorer.

The no. 1-ranked U.S. team had suffered a disappointing end to its 51-game undefeated streak, as they lost 4-0 to Brazil in the semifinals Sept. 27, 2007, in Hangzhou, China. U.S. coach Greg Ryan made the widely-criticized decision to start the more experienced 36-year-old Briana Scurry in place of goalkeeper Hope Solo, and U.S. midfielder Leslie Osborne headed a goal in on her own team. The U.S. was able to come back to win the match against Norway, 4-1, for third place Sept. 30.

Women's World Cup, 1991-2007

Year	Winner	Final opponent	Score	Site	Third place
1991	U.S.	Norway	2-1	China	Germany
1995	Norway	Germany	2-0	Sweden	U.S.
1999	U.S.	China	0-0*	Pasadena, CA	Brazil
2003	Germany	Sweden	2-1 (OT)	Carson, CA	U.S.
2007	Germany	Brazil	2-0	China	U.S.

*U.S. 5-4, penalty kicks

FIFA Confederations Cup South Africa, 2009

The United States men's soccer team created much excitement at the Confederations Cup tournament in South Africa in June 2009. In one of the greatest upset victories in U.S. men's soccer history, Jozy Altidore and Clint Dempsey each scored to support a solid effort in goal by Tim Howard as the United States beat Spain, 2-0, in the semifinals of the tournament at Bloemfontein, South Africa. Spain entered the match as the world's top-ranked team, boasting 15 consecutive victories and a 35-match unbeaten streak. The United States eventually lost to Brazil, 3-2, in the tournament final, the country's first-ever appearance in a FIFA tournament championship match. Dempsey and Landon Donovan scored to give the U.S. a 2-0 halftime lead, but Brazil responded with three unanswered second-half goals for its second straight Confederations Cup victory and third overall.

FIFA Confederations Cup Winners, 1997-2009

Year	Winner	Final opponent	Score	Third place	Fourth place	Site
1997	Brazil	Australia	6-0	Czech Republic	Uruguay	Saudi Arabia
1999	Mexico	Brazil	4-3	USA	Saudi Arabia	Mexico
2001	France	Japan	1-0	Australia	Brazil	Korea/Japan
2003	France	Cameroon	1-0	Turkey	Colombia	France
2005	Brazil	Argentina	4-1	Germany	Mexico	Germany
2009	Brazil	USA	3-2	Spain	South Africa	South Africa

Italy Wins 2006 FIFA World Cup

Italy defeated France, 5-3 on penalty kicks July 9, after a 1-1 draw continued through 30 minutes of extra time, to win the final match of the 2006 World Cup in Berlin, Germany. The tournament set records for the total number of yellow cards (345) and red cards (28) issued by referees, including France midfielder Zinedine Zidane's red card, received for head-butting Italy's Marco Materazzi in the chest in the final. Italy, coached by Marcello Lippi and captained by defender Fabio Cannavaro, won its fourth World Cup. Zidane nevertheless received the Golden Ball award as the tournament's best player. German striker Miroslav Klose, who scored 5 goals during the tournament—including the 80th-minute goal that tied Germany's quarterfinal match, enabling the home team to win in penalty kicks—was awarded the Golden Boot as the tournament's top scorer.

Final Round Results, 2006

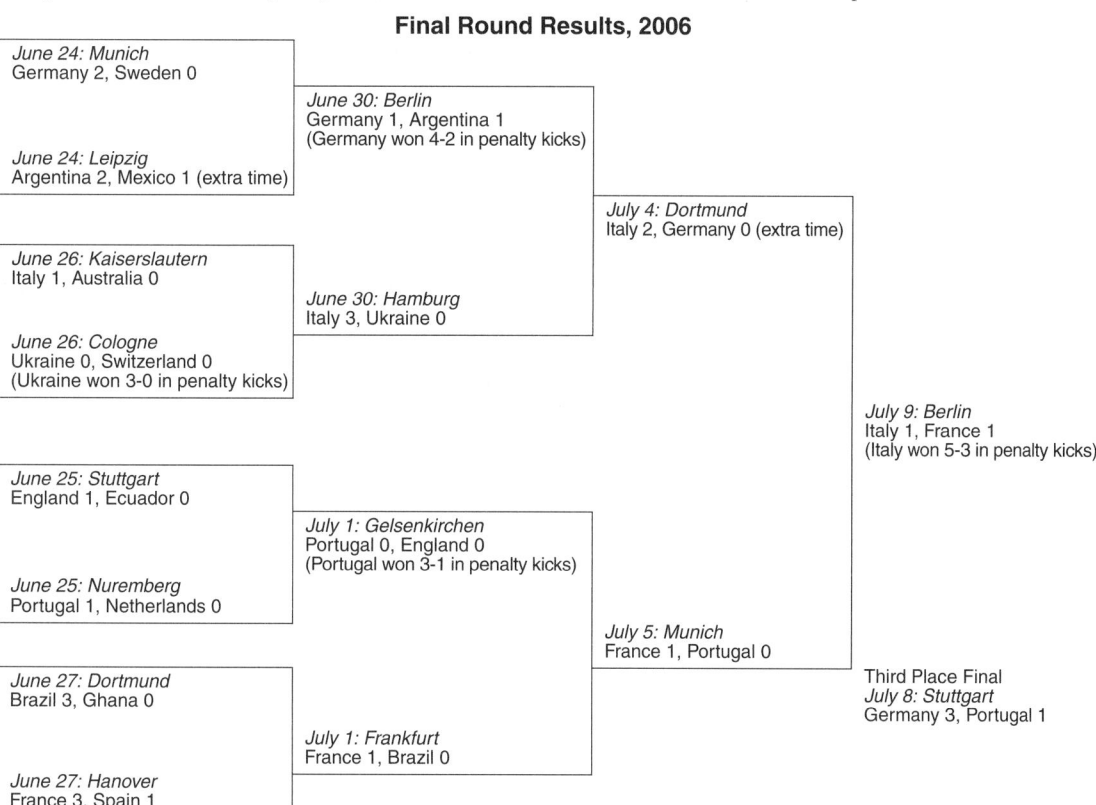

June 24: Munich
Germany 2, Sweden 0

June 24: Leipzig
Argentina 2, Mexico 1 (extra time)

June 30: Berlin
Germany 1, Argentina 1
(Germany won 4-2 in penalty kicks)

June 26: Kaiserslautern
Italy 1, Australia 0

June 26: Cologne
Ukraine 0, Switzerland 0
(Ukraine won 3-0 in penalty kicks)

June 30: Hamburg
Italy 3, Ukraine 0

July 4: Dortmund
Italy 2, Germany 0 (extra time)

June 25: Stuttgart
England 1, Ecuador 0

June 25: Nuremberg
Portugal 1, Netherlands 0

July 1: Gelsenkirchen
Portugal 0, England 0
(Portugal won 3-1 in penalty kicks)

June 27: Dortmund
Brazil 3, Ghana 0

June 27: Hanover
France 3, Spain 1

July 1: Frankfurt
France 1, Brazil 0

July 5: Munich
France 1, Portugal 0

July 9: Berlin
Italy 1, France 1
(Italy won 5-3 in penalty kicks)

Third Place Final
July 8: Stuttgart
Germany 3, Portugal 1

Men's World Cup, 1930-2006

Year	Winner	Final opponent	Score	Site	Year	Winner	Final opponent	Score	Site
1930	Uruguay	Argentina	4-2	Uruguay	1974	W. Germany	Netherlands	2-1	W. Germany
1934	Italy	Czechoslovakia	2-1*	Italy	1978	Argentina	Netherlands	3-1*	Argentina
1938	Italy	Hungary	4-2	France	1982	Italy	W. Germany	3-1	Spain
1950	Uruguay	Brazil	2-1	Brazil	1986	Argentina	W. Germany	3-2	Mexico
1954	W. Germany	Hungary	3-2	Switzerland	1990	W. Germany	Argentina	1-0	Italy
1958	Brazil	Sweden	5-2	Sweden	1994	Brazil	Italy	0-0[1]	U.S.
1962	Brazil	Czechoslovakia	3-1	Chile	1998	France	Brazil	3-0	France
1966	England	W. Germany	4-2*	England	2002	Brazil	Germany	2-0	Japan/S. Korea
1970	Brazil	Italy	4-1	Mexico	2006	Italy	France	1-1[2]	Germany

*Extra time. (1) Brazil won 3-2 on penalty kicks. (2) Italy won 5-3 on penalty kicks.

GOLF
Men's All-Time Major Professional Championship Leaders
(Through the 2009 season; *active PGA player in 2009; (a) = amateur.)

Player	Masters	U.S. Open	British Open	PGA	Total
Jack Nicklaus	1963, '65-'66, '72, '75, '86	1962, '67, '72, '80	1966, '70, '78	1963, '71, '73, '75, '80	18
Tiger Woods*	1997, 2001-02, '05	2000, '02, '08	2000, '05-'06	1999, 2000, '06-'07	14
Walter Hagen	—	1914, '19	1922, '24, '28-'29	1921, '24-'27	11
Ben Hogan	1951, '53	1948, '50-'51, '53	1953	1946, '48	9
Gary Player	1961, '74, '78	1965	1959, '68, '74	1962, '72	9
Tom Watson	1977, '81	1982	1975, '77, '80, '82-'83	—	8
Bobby Jones (a)	—	1923, '26, '29-'30	1926-27, '30	—	7
Arnold Palmer	1958, '60, '62, '64	1960	1961-62	—	7
Gene Sarazen	1935	1922, '32	1932	1922-23, '33	7
Sam Snead	1949, '52, '54	—	1946	1942, '49, '51	7
Harry Vardon	—	1900	1896, '98-99, 1903, '11, '14	—	7
Nick Faldo	1989-90, '96	—	1987, '90, '92	—	6
Lee Trevino	—	1968, '71	1971-72	1974, '84	6

Professional Golfers' Association Leading Money Winners, 1946-2008

Year	Player	Earnings	Year	Player	Earnings	Year	Player	Earnings
1946	Ben Hogan	$42,556	1967	Jack Nicklaus	$188,988	1988	Curtis Strange	$1,147,644
1947	Jimmy Demaret	27,936	1968	Billy Casper	205,168	1989	Tom Kite	1,395,278
1948	Ben Hogan	36,812	1969	Frank Beard	175,223	1990	Greg Norman	1,165,477
1949	Sam Snead	31,593	1970	Lee Trevino	157,037	1991	Corey Pavin	979,430
1950	Sam Snead	35,758	1971	Jack Nicklaus	244,490	1992	Fred Couples	1,344,188
1951	Lloyd Mangrum	26,088	1972	Jack Nicklaus	320,542	1993	Nick Price	1,478,557
1952	Julius Boros	37,032	1973	Jack Nicklaus	308,362	1994	Nick Price	1,499,927
1953	Lew Worsham	34,002	1974	Johnny Miller	353,201	1995	Greg Norman	1,654,959
1954	Bob Toski	65,819	1975	Jack Nicklaus	323,149	1996	Tom Lehman	1,780,159
1955	Julius Boros	65,121	1976	Jack Nicklaus	266,438	1997	Tiger Woods	2,066,833
1956	Ted Kroll	72,835	1977	Tom Watson	310,653	1998	David Duval	2,591,031
1957	Dick Mayer	65,835	1978	Tom Watson	362,429	1999	Tiger Woods	6,616,585
1958	Arnold Palmer	42,407	1979	Tom Watson	462,636	2000	Tiger Woods	9,188,321
1959	Art Wall Jr.	53,167	1980	Tom Watson	530,808	2001	Tiger Woods	5,687,777
1960	Arnold Palmer	75,262	1981	Tom Kite	375,699	2002	Tiger Woods	6,912,625
1961	Gary Player	64,540	1982	Craig Stadler	446,462	2003	Vijay Singh	7,573,907
1962	Arnold Palmer	81,448	1983	Hal Sutton	426,668	2004	Vijay Singh	10,905,166
1963	Arnold Palmer	128,230	1984	Tom Watson	476,260	2005	Tiger Woods	10,628,024
1964	Jack Nicklaus	113,284	1985	Curtis Strange	542,321	2006	Tiger Woods	9,941,563
1965	Jack Nicklaus	140,752	1986	Greg Norman	653,296	2007	Tiger Woods	10,867,052
1966	Billy Casper	121,944	1987	Curtis Strange	925,941	2008	Vijay Singh	6,601,094

Masters Golf Tournament Winners, 1934-2009

Year	Winner	Year	Winner	Year	Winner	Year	Winner	Year	Winner
1934	Horton Smith	1952	Sam Snead	1967	Gay Brewer Jr.	1982	Craig Stadler	1996	Nick Faldo
1935	Gene Sarazen	1953	Ben Hogan	1968	Bob Goalby	1983	Seve Ballesteros	1997	Tiger Woods
1936	Horton Smith	1954	Sam Snead	1969	George Archer	1984	Ben Crenshaw	1998	Mark O'Meara
1937	Byron Nelson	1955	Cary Middlecoff	1970	Billy Casper	1985	Bernhard Langer	1999	Jose Maria
1938	Henry Picard	1956	Jack Burke	1971	Charles Coody	1986	Jack Nicklaus		Olazabal
1939	Ralph Guldahl	1957	Doug Ford	1972	Jack Nicklaus	1987	Larry Mize	2000	Vijay Singh
1940	Jimmy Demaret	1958	Arnold Palmer	1973	Tommy Aaron	1988	Sandy Lyle	2001	Tiger Woods
1941	Craig Wood	1959	Art Wall Jr.	1974	Gary Player	1989	Nick Faldo	2002	Tiger Woods
1942	Byron Nelson	1960	Arnold Palmer	1975	Jack Nicklaus	1990	Nick Faldo	2003	Mike Weir
1943-45	Not played	1961	Gary Player	1976	Ray Floyd	1991	Ian Woosnam	2004	Phil Mickelson
1946	Herman Keiser	1962	Arnold Palmer	1977	Tom Watson	1992	Fred Couples	2005	Tiger Woods
1947	Jimmy Demaret	1963	Jack Nicklaus	1978	Gary Player	1993	Bernhard Langer	2006	Phil Mickelson
1948	Claude Harmon	1964	Arnold Palmer	1979	Fuzzy Zoeller	1994	Jose Maria	2007	Zach Johnson
1949	Sam Snead	1965	Jack Nicklaus	1980	Seve Ballesteros		Olazabal	2008	Trevor Immelman
1950	Jimmy Demaret	1966	Jack Nicklaus	1981	Tom Watson	1995	Ben Crenshaw	2009	Angel Cabrera
1951	Ben Hogan								

United States Open Winners, 1934-2009
(First contested in 1895.)

Year	Winner	Year	Winner	Year	Winner	Year	Winner	Year	Winner
1934	Olin Dutra	1952	Julius Boros	1967	Jack Nicklaus	1982	Tom Watson	1996	Steve Jones
1935	Sam Parks Jr.	1953	Ben Hogan	1968	Lee Trevino	1983	Larry Nelson	1997	Ernie Els
1936	Tony Manero	1954	Ed Furgol	1969	Orville Moody	1984	Fuzzy Zoeller	1998	Lee Janzen
1937	Ralph Guldahl	1955	Jack Fleck	1970	Tony Jacklin	1985	Andy North	1999	Payne Stewart
1938	Ralph Guldahl	1956	Cary Middlecoff	1971	Lee Trevino	1986	Ray Floyd	2000	Tiger Woods
1939	Byron Nelson	1957	Dick Mayer	1972	Jack Nicklaus	1987	Scott Simpson	2001	Retief Goosen
1940	Lawson Little	1958	Tommy Bolt	1973	Johnny Miller	1988	Curtis Strange	2002	Tiger Woods
1941	Craig Wood	1959	Billy Casper	1974	Hale Irwin	1989	Curtis Strange	2003	Jim Furyk
1943-45	Not played	1960	Arnold Palmer	1975	Lou Graham	1990	Hale Irwin	2004	Retief Goosen
1946	Lloyd Mangrum	1961	Gene Littler	1976	Jerry Pate	1991	Payne Stewart	2005	Michael Campbell
1947	L. Worsham	1962	Jack Nicklaus	1977	Hubert Green	1992	Tom Kite	2006	Geoff Ogilvy
1948	Ben Hogan	1963	Julius Boros	1978	Andy North	1993	Lee Janzen	2007	Angel Cabrera
1949	Cary Middlecoff	1964	Ken Venturi	1979	Hale Irwin	1994	Ernie Els	2008	Tiger Woods
1950	Ben Hogan	1965	Gary Player	1980	Jack Nicklaus	1995	Corey Pavin	2009	Lucas Glover
1951	Ben Hogan	1966	Billy Casper	1981	David Graham				

British Open Winners, 1934-2009
(First contested in 1860.)

Year	Winner	Year	Winner	Year	Winner	Year	Winner	Year	Winner
1934	Henry Cotton	1954	Peter Thomson	1968	Gary Player	1982	Tom Watson	1996	Tom Lehman
1935	Alf Perry	1955	Peter Thomson	1969	Tony Jacklin	1983	Tom Watson	1997	Justin Leonard
1936	Alf Padgham	1956	Peter Thomson	1970	Jack Nicklaus	1984	Seve Ballesteros	1998	Mark O'Meara
1937	T. H. Cotton	1957	Bobby Locke	1971	Lee Trevino	1985	Sandy Lyle	1999	Paul Lawrie
1938	R. A. Whitcombe	1958	Peter Thomson	1972	Lee Trevino	1986	Greg Norman	2000	Tiger Woods
1939	Richard Burton	1959	Gary Player	1973	Tom Weiskopf	1987	Nick Faldo	2001	David Duval
1940-45	Not played	1960	Kel Nagle	1974	Gary Player	1988	Seve Ballesteros	2002	Ernie Els
1946	Sam Snead	1961	Arnold Palmer	1975	Tom Watson	1989	Mark Calcavecchia	2003	Ben Curtis
1947	Fred Daly	1962	Arnold Palmer	1976	Johnny Miller	1990	Nick Faldo	2004	Todd Hamilton
1948	Henry Cotton	1963	Bob Charles	1977	Tom Watson	1991	Ian Baker-Finch	2005	Tiger Woods
1949	Bobby Locke	1964	Tony Lema	1978	Jack Nicklaus	1992	Nick Faldo	2006	Tiger Woods
1950	Bobby Locke	1965	Peter Thomson	1979	Seve Ballesteros	1993	Greg Norman	2007	Padraig Harrington
1951	Max Faulkner	1966	Jack Nicklaus	1980	Tom Watson	1994	Nick Price	2008	Padraig Harrington
1952	Bobby Locke	1967	Roberto de Vicenzo	1981	Bill Rogers	1995	John Daly	2009	Stewart Cink
1953	Ben Hogan								

PGA Championship Winners, 1934-2009
(First contested in 1916.)

Year	Winner	Year	Winner	Year	Winner	Year	Winner	Year	Winner
1934	Paul Runyan	1950	Chandler Harper	1965	Dave Marr	1980	Jack Nicklaus	1995	Steve Elkington
1935	Johnny Revolta	1951	Sam Snead	1966	Al Geiberger	1981	Larry Nelson	1996	Mark Brooks
1936	Denny Shute	1952	James Turnesa	1967	Don January	1982	Ray Floyd	1997	Davis Love III
1937	Denny Shute	1953	Walter Burkemo	1968	Julius Boros	1983	Hal Sutton	1998	Vijay Singh
1938	Paul Runyan	1954	Melvin Harbert	1969	Ray Floyd	1984	Lee Trevino	1999	Tiger Woods
1939	Henry Picard	1955	Doug Ford	1970	Dave Stockton	1985	Hubert Green	2000	Tiger Woods
1940	Byron Nelson	1956	Jack Burke	1971	Jack Nicklaus	1986	Bob Tway	2001	David Toms
1941	Victor Ghezzi	1957	Lionel Hebert	1972	Gary Player	1987	Larry Nelson	2002	Rich Beem
1942	Sam Snead	1958	Dow Finsterwald	1973	Jack Nicklaus	1988	Jeff Sluman	2003	Shaun Micheel
1943	Not played	1959	Bob Rosburg	1974	Lee Trevino	1989	Payne Stewart	2004	Vijay Singh
1944	Bob Hamilton	1960	Jay Hebert	1975	Jack Nicklaus	1990	Wayne Grady	2005	Phil Mickelson
1945	Byron Nelson	1961	Jerry Barber	1976	Dave Stockton	1991	John Daly	2006	Tiger Woods
1946	Ben Hogan	1962	Gary Player	1977	Lanny Wadkins	1992	Nick Price	2007	Tiger Woods
1947	Jim Ferrier	1963	Jack Nicklaus	1978	John Mahaffey	1993	Paul Azinger	2008	Padraig Harrington
1948	Ben Hogan	1964	Bob Nichols	1979	David Graham	1994	Nick Price	2009	Y.E. Yang
1949	Sam Snead								

FedExCup, 2007-09

The FedExCup, a season-long, $10 mil competition with points awarded by finishing rank in each tournament, divides the PGA Tour into a regular season lasting 33 weeks, combined with a 4-week-long playoff that ends with The Tour Championship at East Lake Golf Club in Atlanta, Georgia.

Tiger Woods, who missed the first two months of the 2009 season following knee surgery, won his second FedExCup on Sept. 27, 2009, with a 2nd-place finish in Atlanta; Phil Mickelson placed first at The Tour Championship event.

The inaugural FedExCup had been clinched by Tiger Woods on Sept. 16, 2007. Vijay Singh won the 2nd FedExCup Sept. 28, 2008.

Women's All-Time Major Professional Championship Leaders
(Through the 2009 season; *active in 2009 LPGA season.)

Player	Nabisco[1]	LPGA	U.S. Women's Open	du Maurier/ British Open[2]	Titleholders[3]	Western Open[4]	Total
Patty Berg	—	—	1946	—	1937-39, '48, '53, '55, '57	1941, '43, '48, '51, '55, '57-'58	15
Mickey Wright	—	1958, '60-'61, '63	1958-59, '61, '64	—	1961-62	1962-63, '66	13
Louise Suggs	—	1957	1949, '52	—	1946, '54, '56, '59	1946-47, '49, '53	11
Babe Zaharias	—	—	1948, '50, '54	—	1947, '50, '52	1940, '44-'45, '50	10
Annika Sorenstam	2001-02, '05	2003-05	1995-96, 2006	2003	—	—	10
Betsy Rawls	—	1959, '69	1951, '53, '57, '60	—	—	1952, '59	8
Juli Inkster*	1984, '89	1999, 2000	1999, 2002	1984	—	—	7
Karrie Webb*	2000, '06	2001	2000-01	1999, 2002	—	—	7
Pat Bradley	1986	1986	1981	1980, '85-'86	—	—	6
Betsy King	1987, '90, '97	1992	1989-90	—	—	—	6
Patty Sheehan	1996	1983-84, '93	1992, '94	—	—	—	6
Kathy Whitworth	—	1967, '71, '75	—	—	1965-66	1967	6

(1) Nabisco Championship, formerly Nabisco Dinah Shore (1982-99), designated major in 1983. (2) In 2001, the British Open replaced the du Maurier Classic as the LPGA's 4th major. (3) Titleholders Championship was a major from 1930 to 1972. (4) Western Open was a major from 1937 to 1967.

Ladies Professional Golf Association Leading Money Winners, 1954-2008

Year	Player	Earnings	Year	Player	Earnings	Year	Player	Earnings
1954	Patty Berg	$16,011	1973	Kathy Whitworth	$82,854	1991	Pat Bradley	$763,118
1955	Patty Berg	16,492	1974	JoAnne Carner	87,094	1992	Dottie Mochrie	693,335
1956	Marlene Hagge	20,235	1975	Sandra Palmer	94,805	1993	Betsy King	595,992
1957	Patty Berg	16,272	1976	Judy Rankin	150,734	1994	Laura Davies	687,201
1958	Beverly Hanson	12,629	1977	Judy Rankin	122,890	1995	Annika Sorenstam	666,533
1959	Betsy Rawls	26,774	1978	Nancy Lopez	189,813	1996	Karrie Webb	1,002,000
1960	Louise Suggs	16,892	1979	Nancy Lopez	215,987	1997	Annika Sorenstam	1,236,789
1961	Mickey Wright	22,236	1980	Beth Daniel	231,000	1998	Annika Sorenstam	1,092,748
1962	Mickey Wright	21,641	1981	Beth Daniel	206,977	1999	Karrie Webb	1,591,959
1963	Mickey Wright	31,269	1982	JoAnne Carner	310,399	2000	Karrie Webb	1,876,853
1964	Mickey Wright	29,800	1983	JoAnne Carner	291,404	2001	Annika Sorenstam	2,105,868
1965	Kathy Whitworth	28,658	1984	Betsy King	266,771	2002	Annika Sorenstam	2,863,904
1966	Kathy Whitworth	33,517	1985	Nancy Lopez	416,472	2003	Annika Sorenstam	2,029,506
1967	Kathy Whitworth	32,937	1986	Pat Bradley	492,021	2004	Annika Sorenstam	2,544,707
1968	Kathy Whitworth	48,379	1987	Ayako Okamoto	466,034	2005	Annika Sorenstam	2,588,240
1969	Carol Mann	49,152	1988	Sherri Turner	347,255	2006	Lorena Ochoa	2,592,872
1970	Kathy Whitworth	30,235	1989	Betsy King	654,132	2007	Lorena Ochoa	4,364,994
1971	Kathy Whitworth	41,181	1990	Beth Daniel	863,578	2008	Lorena Ochoa	2,763,193
1972	Kathy Whitworth	65,063						

Kraft Nabisco Championship Winners, 1983-2009[1]

Year	Winner	Year	Winner	Year	Winner	Year	Winner	Year	Winner
1983	Amy Alcott	1989	Juli Inkster	1995	Nanci Bowen	2001	Annika Sorenstam	2005	Annika Sorenstam
1984	Juli Inkster	1990	Betsy King	1996	Patty Sheehan	2002	Annika Sorenstam	2006	Karrie Webb
1985	Alice Miller	1991	Amy Alcott	1997	Betsy King	2003	Patricia Meunier-	2007	Morgan Pressel
1986	Pat Bradley	1992	Dottie Pepper	1998	Pat Hurst		Lebouc	2008	Lorena Ochoa
1987	Betsy King	1993	Helen Alfredsson	1999	Dottie Pepper	2004	Grace Park	2009	Brittany Lincicome
1988	Amy Alcott	1994	Donna Andrews	2000	Karrie Webb				

(1) Formerly the Colgate Dinah Shore (1972-81), the Nabisco Dinah Shore (1982-99), the Nabisco Championship (2000-01). Designated as a major championship in 1983.

LPGA Championship Winners, 1955-2009

Year	Winner	Year	Winner	Year	Winner	Year	Winner	Year	Winner
1955	Beverly Hanson	1966	Gloria Ehret	1977	Chako Higuchi	1988	Sherri Turner	1999	Juli Inkster
1956	Marlene Hagge	1967	Kathy Whitworth	1978	Nancy Lopez	1989	Nancy Lopez	2000	Juli Inkster
1957	Louise Suggs	1968	Sandra Post	1979	Donna Caponi	1990	Beth Daniel	2001	Karrie Webb
1958	Mickey Wright	1969	Betsy Rawls	1980	Sally Little	1991	Meg Mallon	2002	Se Ri Pak
1959	Betsy Rawls	1970	Shirley Englehorn	1981	Donna Caponi	1992	Betsy King	2003	Annika Sorenstam
1960	Mickey Wright	1971	Kathy Whitworth	1982	Jan Stephenson	1993	Patty Sheehan	2004	Annika Sorenstam
1961	Mickey Wright	1972	Kathy Ahern	1983	Patty Sheehan	1994	Laura Davies	2005	Annika Sorenstam
1962	Judy Kimball	1973	Mary Mills	1984	Patty Sheehan	1995	Kelly Robbins	2006	Se Ri Pak
1963	Mickey Wright	1974	Sandra Haynie	1985	Nancy Lopez	1996	Laura Davies	2007	Suzann Pettersen
1964	Mary Mills	1975	Kathy Whitworth	1986	Pat Bradley	1997	Chris Johnson	2008	Yani Tseng
1965	Sandra Haynie	1976	Betty Burfeindt	1987	Jane Geddes	1998	Se Ri Pak	2009	Anna Nordqvist

U.S. Women's Open Winners, 1946-2009

Year	Winner	Year	Winner	Year	Winner	Year	Winner	Year	Winner
1946	Patty Berg	1960	Betsy Rawls	1972	Susie Maxwell	1984	Hollis Stacy	1997	Alison Nicholas
1947	Betty Jameson	1961	Mickey Wright		Berning	1985	Kathy Baker	1998	Se Ri Pak
1948	Babe Zaharias	1962	Murle Lindstrom	1973	Susie Maxwell	1986	Jane Geddes	1999	Juli Inkster
1949	Louise Suggs	1963	Mary Mills		Berning	1987	Laura Davies	2000	Karrie Webb
1950	Babe Zaharias	1964	Mickey Wright	1974	Sandra Haynie	1988	Liselotte Neumann	2001	Karrie Webb
1951	Betsy Rawls	1965	Carol Mann	1975	Sandra Palmer	1989	Betsy King	2002	Juli Inkster
1952	Louise Suggs	1966	Sandra Spuzich	1976	JoAnne Carner	1990	Betsy King	2003	Hilary Lunke
1953	Betsy Rawls	1967	Catherine Lacoste	1977	Hollis Stacy	1991	Meg Mallon	2004	Meg Mallon
1954	Babe Zaharias		(amateur)	1978	Hollis Stacy	1992	Patty Sheehan	2005	Birdie Kim
1955	Fay Crocker	1968	Susie Maxwell	1979	Jerilyn Britz	1993	Lauri Merten	2006	Annika Sorenstam
1956	Kathy Cornelius		Berning	1980	Amy Alcott	1994	Patty Sheehan	2007	Cristie Kerr
1957	Betsy Rawls	1969	Donna Caponi	1981	Pat Bradley	1995	Annika Sorenstam	2008	Inbee Park
1958	Mickey Wright	1970	Donna Caponi	1982	Janet Alex	1996	Annika Sorenstam	2009	Eun-Hee Ji
1959	Mickey Wright	1971	JoAnne Carner	1983	Jan Stephenson				

Women's British Open Winners, 1979-2009[1]

Year	Winner	Year	Winner	Year	Winner	Year	Winner	Year	Winner
1979	Amy Alcott	1986	Pat Bradley	1992	Sherri Steinhauer	1998	Brandie Burton	2004	Karen Stupples
1980	Pat Bradley	1987	Jody Rosenthal	1993	Brandie Burton	1999	Karrie Webb	2005	Jeong Jang
1981	Jan Stephenson	1988	Sally Little	1994	Martha Nause	2000	Meg Mallon	2006	Sherri Steinhauer
1982	Sandra Haynie	1989	Tammie Green	1995	Jenny Lidback	2001	Se Ri Pak	2007	Lorena Ochoa
1983	Hollis Stacy	1990	Cathy Johnston	1996	Laura Davies	2002	Karrie Webb	2008	Ji-Yai Shin
1984	Juli Inkster	1991	Nancy Scranton	1997	Colleen Walker	2003	Annika Sorenstam	2009	Catriona Matthew
1985	Pat Bradley								

(1) First held as the Ladies' British Open in 1976; became the LPGA's 4th major championship in 2001, replacing the du Maurier Classic. Winners listed 1979-2000 are for the du Maurier Classic (Peter Jackson Classic, 1979-82).

International Golf

Ryder Cup

Began as a biennial team competition between pro golfers from the U.S. and Great Britain. The British team was expanded in 1973 to include players from Ireland and in 1979 from the rest of Europe. The Ryder Cup moved to even years after being postponed following the terrorist attacks of Sept. 11, 2001. The U.S. beat Europe for the 2008 Ryder Cup at Valhalla Golf Club in Louisville, KY, Sept. 21, for its largest margin of victory at the Ryder Cup since 1981. The 2010 Ryder Cup was scheduled to be held Oct. 1-3, at the Celtic Manor Resort in Newport, South Wales, UK.

Year	Winner	Year	Winner	Year	Winner	Year	Winner
1927	U.S., 9½-2½	1953	U.S., 6½-5½	1973	U.S., 19-13	1991	U.S., 14½-13½
1929	Britain-Ireland, 7-5	1955	U.S., 8-4	1975	U.S., 21-11	1993	U.S., 15-13
1931	U.S., 9-3	1957	Britain-Ireland, 7½-4½	1977	U.S., 12½-7½	1995	Europe, 14½-13½
1933	Britain, 6½-5½	1959	U.S., 8½-3½	1979	U.S., 17-11	1997	Europe, 14½-13½
1935	U.S., 9-3	1961	U.S., 14½-9½	1981	U.S., 18½-9½	1999	U.S., 14½-13½
1937	U.S., 8-4	1963	U.S., 23-9	1983	U.S., 14½-13½	2002	Europe, 15½-12½
1939-45	Not played	1965	U.S., 19½-12½	1985	Europe, 16½-11½	2004	Europe, 18½-9½
1947	U.S., 11-1	1967	U.S., 23½-8½	1987	Europe, 15-13	2006	Europe, 18½-9½
1949	U.S., 7-5	1969	Draw, 16-16	1989	Draw, 14-14	2008	U.S., 16½-11½
1951	U.S., 9½-2½	1971	U.S., 18½-13½				

Solheim Cup

Began in 1990 as a biennial team competition between pro women golfers from Europe and the U.S. Competition moved to odd years in 2003 to alternate with the Ryder Cup, which had been postponed and moved to even years after the Sept. 2001 terrorist attacks. The U.S. won its third straight Solheim Cup in Aug. 2009, defeating Europe, 16-12, at Rich Harvest Farms in Sugar Grove, IL. Team USA and Europe were tied, 8-8, heading into the final on Aug. 23, 2009, but the U.S. won 8 of 12 final-round matches. The next Solheim Cup was scheduled to be played at Killeen Castle in Ireland, Sept. 23-25, 2011.

Year	Winner	Year	Winner	Year	Winner	Year	Winner
1990	U.S., 11½-4½	1996	U.S., 17-11	2002	U.S., 15½-12½	2007	U.S., 16-12
1992	Europe, 11½-6½	1998	U.S., 16-12	2003	Europe, 17½-12½	2009	U.S., 16-12
1994	U.S., 13-7	2000	Europe, 14½-11½	2005	U.S., 15½-12½		

TENNIS
Australian Open Singles Champions, 1969-2009
(First contested 1905 for men, 1922 for women. Became an Open Championship in 1969.)
*2 tournaments held in 1977 (Jan. & Dec.). **In 1986 tournament moved to Jan. 1987; no championship in 1986.

	Men's Singles			Women's Singles	
Year	Champion	Final opponent	Year	Champion	Final opponent
1969	Rod Laver	Andres Gimeno	1969	Margaret Smith Court	Billie Jean King
1970	Arthur Ashe	Dick Crealy	1970	Margaret Smith Court	Kerry Melville Reid
1971	Ken Rosewall	Arthur Ashe	1971	Margaret Smith Court	Evonne Goolagong
1972	Ken Rosewall	Mal Anderson	1972	Virginia Wade	Evonne Goolagong
1973	John Newcombe	Onny Parun	1973	Margaret Smith Court	Evonne Goolagong
1974	Jimmy Connors	Phil Dent	1974	Evonne Goolagong	Chris Evert
1975	John Newcombe	Jimmy Connors	1975	Evonne Goolagong	Martina Navratilova
1976	Mark Edmondson	John Newcombe	1976	Evonne Goolagong Cawley	Renata Tomanova
1977*	Roscoe Tanner	Guillermo Vilas	1977*	Kerry Reid	Dianne Balestrat
	Vitas Gerulaitis	John Lloyd		Evonne Goolagong Cawley	Helen Gourlay
1978	Guillermo Vilas	John Marks	1978	Chris O'Neill	Betsy Nagelsen
1979	Guillermo Vilas	John Sadri	1979	Barbara Jordan	Sharon Walsh
1980	Brian Teacher	Kim Warwick	1980	Hana Mandlikova	Wendy Turnbull
1981	Johan Kriek	Steve Denton	1981	Martina Navratilova	Chris Evert Lloyd
1982	Johan Kriek	Steve Denton	1982	Chris Evert Lloyd	Martina Navratilova
1983	Mats Wilander	Ivan Lendl	1983	Martina Navratilova	Kathy Jordan
1984	Mats Wilander	Kevin Curren	1984	Chris Evert Lloyd	Helena Sukova
1985**	Stefan Edberg	Mats Wilander	1985**	Martina Navratilova	Chris Evert Lloyd
1987	Stefan Edberg	Pat Cash	1987	Hana Mandlikova	Martina Navratilova
1988	Mats Wilander	Pat Cash	1988	Steffi Graf	Chris Evert
1989	Ivan Lendl	Miloslav Mecir	1989	Steffi Graf	Helena Sukova
1990	Ivan Lendl	Stefan Edberg	1990	Steffi Graf	Mary Joe Fernandez
1991	Boris Becker	Ivan Lendl	1991	Monica Seles	Jana Novotna
1992	Jim Courier	Stefan Edberg	1992	Monica Seles	Mary Joe Fernandez
1993	Jim Courier	Stefan Edberg	1993	Monica Seles	Steffi Graf
1994	Pete Sampras	Todd Martin	1994	Steffi Graf	Arantxa Sánchez Vicario
1995	Andre Agassi	Pete Sampras	1995	Mary Pierce	Arantxa Sánchez Vicario
1996	Boris Becker	Michael Chang	1996	Monica Seles	Anke Huber
1997	Pete Sampras	Carlos Moya	1997	Martina Hingis	Mary Pierce
1998	Petr Korda	Marcelo Rios	1998	Martina Hingis	Conchita Martínez
1999	Yevgeny Kafelnikov	Thomas Enqvist	1999	Martina Hingis	Amelie Mauresmo
2000	Andre Agassi	Yevgeny Kafelnikov	2000	Lindsay Davenport	Martina Hingis
2001	Andre Agassi	Arnaud Clement	2001	Jennifer Capriati	Martina Hingis
2002	Thomas Johansson	Marat Safin	2002	Jennifer Capriati	Martina Hingis
2003	Andre Agassi	Rainer Schuettler	2003	Serena Williams	Venus Williams
2004	Roger Federer	Marat Safin	2004	Justine Henin	Kim Clijsters
2005	Marat Safin	Lleyton Hewitt	2005	Serena Williams	Lindsay Davenport
2006	Roger Federer	Marcos Baghdatis	2006	Amelie Mauresmo	Justine Henin
2007	Roger Federer	Fernando Gonzalez	2007	Serena Williams	Maria Sharapova
2008	Novak Djokovic	Jo-Wilfried Tsonga	2008	Maria Sharapova	Ana Ivanovic
2009	Rafael Nadal	Roger Federer	2009	Serena Williams	Dinara Safina

French Open (Roland Garros) Singles Champions, 1968-2009
(First contested 1891 for men, 1897 for women. Became an Open Championship in 1968.)

	Men's Singles			Women's Singles	
Year	Champion	Final opponent	Year	Champion	Final opponent
1968	Ken Rosewall	Rod Laver	1968	Nancy Richey	Ann Jones
1969	Rod Laver	Ken Rosewall	1969	Margaret Smith Court	Ann Jones
1970	Jan Kodes	Zeljko Franulovic	1970	Margaret Smith Court	Helga Niessen
1971	Jan Kodes	Ilie Nastase	1971	Evonne Goolagong	Helen Gourlay
1972	Andres Gimeno	Patrick Proisy	1972	Billie Jean King	Evonne Goolagong
1973	Ilie Nastase	Nikki Pilic	1973	Margaret Smith Court	Chris Evert
1974	Bjorn Borg	Manuel Orantes	1974	Chris Evert	Olga Morozova
1975	Bjorn Borg	Guillermo Vilas	1975	Chris Evert	Martina Navratilova
1976	Adriano Panatta	Harold Solomon	1976	Sue Barker	Renata Tomanova
1977	Guillermo Vilas	Brian Gottfried	1977	Mima Jausovec	Florenza Mihai
1978	Bjorn Borg	Guillermo Vilas	1978	Virginia Ruzici	Mima Jausovec
1979	Bjorn Borg	Victor Pecci	1979	Chris Evert Lloyd	Wendy Turnbull
1980	Bjorn Borg	Vitas Gerulaitis	1980	Chris Evert Lloyd	Virginia Ruzici
1981	Bjorn Borg	Ivan Lendl	1981	Hana Mandlikova	Sylvia Hanika
1982	Mats Wilander	Guillermo Vilas	1982	Martina Navratilova	Andrea Jaeger
1983	Yannick Noah	Mats Wilander	1983	Chris Evert Lloyd	Mima Jausovec
1984	Ivan Lendl	John McEnroe	1984	Martina Navratilova	Chris Evert Lloyd
1985	Mats Wilander	Ivan Lendl	1985	Chris Evert Lloyd	Martina Navratilova
1986	Ivan Lendl	Mikael Pernfors	1986	Chris Evert Lloyd	Martina Navratilova
1987	Ivan Lendl	Mats Wilander	1987	Steffi Graf	Martina Navratilova
1988	Mats Wilander	Henri Leconte	1988	Steffi Graf	Natalia Zvereva
1989	Michael Chang	Stefan Edberg	1989	Arantxa Sánchez Vicario	Steffi Graf
1990	Andres Gomez	Andre Agassi	1990	Monica Seles	Steffi Graf
1991	Jim Courier	Andre Agassi	1991	Monica Seles	Arantxa Sánchez Vicario
1992	Jim Courier	Petr Korda	1992	Monica Seles	Steffi Graf
1993	Sergi Bruguera	Jim Courier	1993	Steffi Graf	Mary Joe Fernandez
1994	Sergi Bruguera	Alberto Berasategui	1994	Arantxa Sánchez Vicario	Mary Pierce
1995	Thomas Muster	Michael Chang	1995	Steffi Graf	Arantxa Sánchez Vicario
1996	Yevgeny Kafelnikov	Michael Stich	1996	Steffi Graf	Arantxa Sánchez Vicario
1997	Gustavo Kuerten	Sergei Bruguera	1997	Iva Majoli	Martina Hingis
1998	Carlos Moya	Alex Corretja	1998	Arantxa Sánchez Vicario	Monica Seles
1999	Andre Agassi	Andrei Medvedev	1999	Steffi Graf	Martina Hingis
2000	Gustavo Kuerten	Magnus Norman	2000	Mary Pierce	Conchita Martinez
2001	Gustavo Kuerten	Alex Corretja	2001	Jennifer Capriati	Kim Clijsters
2002	Albert Costa	Juan Carlos Ferrero	2002	Serena Williams	Venus Williams
2003	Juan Carlos Ferrero	Martin Verkerk	2003	Justine Henin	Kim Clijsters
2004	Gaston Gaudio	Guillermo Coria	2004	Anastasia Myskina	Elena Dementieva
2005	Rafael Nadal	Mariano Puerta	2005	Justine Henin	Mary Pierce
2006	Rafael Nadal	Roger Federer	2006	Justine Henin	Svetlana Kuznetsova
2007	Rafael Nadal	Roger Federer	2007	Justine Henin	Ana Ivanovic
2008	Rafael Nadal	Roger Federer	2008	Ana Ivanovic	Dinara Safina
2009	Roger Federer	Robin Soderling	2009	Svetlana Kuznetsova	Dinara Safina

All-England Champions, Wimbledon, 1925-2009

(First contested 1877 for men, 1884 for women. Became an Open Championship in 1968. Not held 1940-45.)

Men's Singles

Year	Champion	Final opponent
1925	Rene Lacoste	Jean Borotra
1926	Jean Borotra	Howard Kinsey
1927	Henri Cochet	Jean Borotra
1928	Rene Lacoste	Henri Cochet
1929	Henri Cochet	Jean Borotra
1930	Bill Tilden	Wilmer Allison
1931	Sidney B. Wood	Francis X. Shields
1932	Ellsworth Vines	Henry Austin
1933	Jack Crawford	Ellsworth Vines
1934	Fred Perry	Jack Crawford
1935	Fred Perry	Gottfried von Cramm
1936	Fred Perry	Gottfried von Cramm
1937	Donald Budge	Gottfried von Cramm
1938	Donald Budge	Henry Austin
1939	Bobby Riggs	Elwood Cooke
1946	Yvon Petra	Geoff E. Brown
1947	Jack Kramer	Tom P. Brown
1948	Bob Falkenburg	John Bromwich
1949	Ted Schroeder	Jaroslav Drobny
1950	Budge Patty	Frank Sedgman
1951	Dick Savitt	Ken McGregor
1952	Frank Sedgman	Jaroslav Drobny
1953	Vic Seixas	Kurt Nielsen
1954	Jaroslav Drobny	Ken Rosewall
1955	Tony Trabert	Kurt Nielsen
1956	Lew Hoad	Ken Rosewall
1957	Lew Hoad	Ashley Cooper
1958	Ashley Cooper	Neale Fraser
1959	Alex Olmedo	Rod Laver
1960	Neale Fraser	Rod Laver
1961	Rod Laver	Chuck McKinley
1962	Rod Laver	Martin Mulligan
1963	Chuck McKinley	Fred Stolle
1964	Roy Emerson	Fred Stolle
1965	Roy Emerson	Fred Stolle
1966	Manuel Santana	Dennis Ralston
1967	John Newcombe	Wilhelm Bungert
1968	Rod Laver	Tony Roche
1969	Rod Laver	John Newcombe
1970	John Newcombe	Ken Rosewall
1971	John Newcombe	Stan Smith
1972	Stan Smith	Ilie Nastase
1973	Jan Kodes	Alex Metreveli
1974	Jimmy Connors	Ken Rosewall
1975	Arthur Ashe	Jimmy Connors
1976	Bjorn Borg	Ilie Nastase
1977	Bjorn Borg	Jimmy Connors
1978	Bjorn Borg	Jimmy Connors
1979	Bjorn Borg	Roscoe Tanner
1980	Bjorn Borg	John McEnroe
1981	John McEnroe	Bjorn Borg
1982	Jimmy Connors	John McEnroe
1983	John McEnroe	Chris Lewis
1984	John McEnroe	Jimmy Connors
1985	Boris Becker	Kevin Curren
1986	Boris Becker	Ivan Lendl
1987	Pat Cash	Ivan Lendl
1988	Stefan Edberg	Boris Becker
1989	Boris Becker	Stefan Edberg
1990	Stefan Edberg	Boris Becker
1991	Michael Stich	Boris Becker
1992	Andre Agassi	Goran Ivanisevic
1993	Pete Sampras	Jim Courier
1994	Pete Sampras	Goran Ivanisevic
1995	Pete Sampras	Boris Becker
1996	Richard Krajicek	MaliVai Washington
1997	Pete Sampras	Cedric Pioline
1998	Pete Sampras	Goran Ivanisevic
1999	Pete Sampras	Andre Agassi
2000	Pete Sampras	Patrick Rafter
2001	Goran Ivanisevic	Patrick Rafter
2002	Lleyton Hewitt	David Nalbandian
2003	Roger Federer	Mark Philippoussis
2004	Roger Federer	Andy Roddick
2005	Roger Federer	Andy Roddick
2006	Roger Federer	Rafael Nadal
2007	Roger Federer	Rafael Nadal
2008	Rafael Nadal	Roger Federer
2009	Roger Federer	Andy Roddick

Women's Singles

Year	Champion	Final opponent
1925	Suzanne Lenglen	Joan Fry
1926	Kathleen McKane Godfree	Lili de Alvarez
1927	Helen Wills	Lili de Alvarez
1928	Helen Wills	Lili de Alvarez
1929	Helen Wills	Helen Jacobs
1930	Helen Wills Moody	Elizabeth Ryan
1931	Cilly Aussem	Hilde Kranwinkel
1932	Helen Wills Moody	Helen Jacobs
1933	Helen Wills Moody	Dorothy Round
1934	Dorothy Round	Helen Jacobs
1935	Helen Wills Moody	Helen Jacobs
1936	Helen Jacobs	Hilde Kranwinkel Sperling
1937	Dorothy Round	Jadwiga Jedrzejowska
1938	Helen Wills Moody	Helen Jacobs
1939	Alice Marble	Kay Stammers
1946	Pauline Betz	Louise Brough
1947	Margaret Osborne	Doris Hart
1948	Louise Brough	Doris Hart
1949	Louise Brough	Margaret Osborne duPont
1950	Louise Brough	Margaret Osborne duPont
1951	Doris Hart	Shirley Fry
1952	Maureen Connolly	Louise Brough
1953	Maureen Connolly	Doris Hart
1954	Maureen Connolly	Louise Brough
1955	Louise Brough	Beverly Fleitz
1956	Shirley Fry	Angela Buxton
1957	Althea Gibson	Darlene Hard
1958	Althea Gibson	Angela Mortimer
1959	Maria Bueno	Darlene Hard
1960	Maria Bueno	Sandra Reynolds
1961	Angela Mortimer	Christine Truman
1962	Karen Hantze-Susman	Vera Sukova
1963	Margaret Smith	Billie Jean Moffitt
1964	Maria Bueno	Margaret Smith
1965	Margaret Smith	Maria Bueno
1966	Billie Jean King	Maria Bueno
1967	Billie Jean King	Ann Haydon Jones
1968	Billie Jean King	Judy Tegart
1969	Ann Haydon-Jones	Billie Jean King
1970	Margaret Smith Court	Billie Jean King
1971	Evonne Goolagong	Margaret Smith Court
1972	Billie Jean King	Evonne Goolagong
1973	Billie Jean King	Chris Evert
1974	Chris Evert	Olga Morozova
1975	Billie Jean King	Evonne Goolagong Cawley
1976	Chris Evert	Evonne Goolagong Cawley
1977	Virginia Wade	Betty Stove
1978	Martina Navratilova	Chris Evert
1979	Martina Navratilova	Chris Evert Lloyd
1980	Evonne Goolagong	Chris Evert Lloyd
1981	Chris Evert Lloyd	Hana Mandlikova
1982	Martina Navratilova	Chris Evert Lloyd
1983	Martina Navratilova	Andrea Jaeger
1984	Martina Navratilova	Chris Evert Lloyd
1985	Martina Navratilova	Chris Evert Lloyd
1986	Martina Navratilova	Hana Mandlikova
1987	Martina Navratilova	Steffi Graf
1988	Steffi Graf	Martina Navratilova
1989	Steffi Graf	Martina Navratilova
1990	Martina Navratilova	Zina Garrison
1991	Steffi Graf	Gabriela Sabatini
1992	Steffi Graf	Monica Seles
1993	Steffi Graf	Jana Novotna
1994	Conchita Martinez	Martina Navratilova
1995	Steffi Graf	Arantxa Sánchez Vicario
1996	Steffi Graf	Arantxa Sánchez Vicario
1997	Martina Hingis	Jana Novotna
1998	Jana Novotna	Nathalie Tauziat
1999	Lindsay Davenport	Steffi Graf
2000	Venus Williams	Lindsay Davenport
2001	Venus Williams	Justine Henin
2002	Serena Williams	Venus Williams
2003	Serena Williams	Venus Williams
2004	Maria Sharapova	Serena Williams
2005	Venus Williams	Lindsay Davenport
2006	Amelie Mauresmo	Justine Henin
2007	Venus Williams	Marion Bartoli
2008	Venus Williams	Serena Williams
2009	Serena Williams	Venus Williams

U.S. Open Champions, 1925-2009

(Became an Open Championship in 1970.)

Men's Singles (First contested 1881.)			Women's Singles (First contested 1887.)		
Year	Champion	Final opponent	Year	Champion	Final opponent
1925	Bill Tilden	William Johnston	1925	Helen Willis	Kathleen McKane
1926	Rene Lacoste	Jean Borotra	1926	Molla B. Mallory	Elizabeth Ryan
1927	Rene Lacoste	Bill Tilden	1927	Helen Wills	Betty Nuthall
1928	Henri Cochet	Francis Hunter	1928	Helen Wills	Helen Jacobs
1929	Bill Tilden	Francis Hunter	1929	Helen Wills	M. Watson
1930	John Doeg	Francis Shields	1930	Betty Nuthall	L. A. Harper
1931	H. Ellsworth Vines	George Lott	1931	Helen Wills Moody	E. B. Whittingstall
1932	H. Ellsworth Vines	Henri Cochet	1932	Helen Jacobs	Carolin A. Babcock
1933	Fred Perry	John Crawford	1933	Helen Jacobs	Helen Wills Moody
1934	Fred Perry	Wilmer Allison	1934	Helen Jacobs	Sarah H. Palfrey
1935	Wilmer Allison	Sidney Wood	1935	Helen Jacobs	Sarah Palfrey Fabyan
1936	Fred Perry	Don Budge	1936	Alice Marble	Helen Jacobs
1937	Don Budge	Baron G. von Cramm	1937	Anita Lizana	Jadwiga Jedrzejowska
1938	Don Budge	C. Gene Mako	1938	Alice Marble	Nancye Wynne
1939	Robert Riggs	S. Welby Van Horn	1939	Alice Marble	Helen Jacobs
1940	Don McNeill	Robert Riggs	1940	Alice Marble	Helen Jacobs
1941	Robert Riggs	F. L. Kovacs	1941	Sarah Palfrey Cooke	Pauline Betz
1942	F. R. Schroeder Jr.	Frank Parker	1942	Pauline Betz	Louise Brough
1943	Joseph Hunt	Jack Kramer	1943	Pauline Betz	Louise Brough
1944	Frank Parker	William Talbert	1944	Pauline Betz	Margaret Osborne
1945	Frank Parker	William Talbert	1945	Sarah Palfrey Cooke	Pauline Betz
1946	Jack Kramer	Thomas Brown Jr.	1946	Pauline Betz	Doris Hart
1947	Jack Kramer	Frank Parker	1947	Louise Brough	Margaret Osborne
1948	Pancho Gonzales	Eric Sturgess	1948	Margaret Osborne duPont	Louise Brough
1949	Pancho Gonzales	F. R. Schroeder Jr.	1949	Margaret Osborne duPont	Doris Hart
1950	Arthur Larsen	Herbert Flam	1950	Margaret Osborne duPont	Doris Hart
1951	Frank Sedgman	E. Victor Seixas Jr.	1951	Maureen Connolly	Shirley Fry
1952	Frank Sedgman	Gardnar Mulloy	1952	Maureen Connolly	Doris Hart
1953	Tony Trabert	E. Victor Seixas Jr.	1953	Maureen Connolly	Doris Hart
1954	E. Victor Seixas Jr.	Rex Hartwig	1954	Doris Hart	Louise Brough
1955	Tony Trabert	Ken Rosewall	1955	Doris Hart	Patricia Ward
1956	Ken Rosewall	Lewis Hoad	1956	Shirley Fry	Althea Gibson
1957	Malcolm Anderson	Ashley Cooper	1957	Althea Gibson	Louise Brough
1958	Ashley Cooper	Malcolm Anderson	1958	Althea Gibson	Darlene Hard
1959	Neale A. Fraser	Alejandro Olmedo	1959	Maria Bueno	Christine Truman
1960	Neale A. Fraser	Rod Laver	1960	Darlene Hard	Maria Bueno
1961	Roy Emerson	Rod Laver	1961	Darlene Hard	Ann Haydon
1962	Rod Laver	Roy Emerson	1962	Margaret Smith	Darlene Hard
1963	Rafael Osuna	F. A. Froehling 3rd	1963	Maria Bueno	Margaret Smith
1964	Roy Emerson	Fred Stolle	1964	Maria Bueno	Carole Graebner
1965	Manuel Santana	Cliff Drysdale	1965	Margaret Smith	Billie Jean Moffitt
1966	Fred Stolle	John Newcombe	1966	Maria Bueno	Nancy Richey
1967	John Newcombe	Clark Graebner	1967	Billie Jean King	Ann Haydon Jones
1968	Arthur Ashe	Tom Okker	1968	Virginia Wade	Billie Jean King
1969	Rod Laver	Tony Roche	1969	Margaret Smith Court	Nancy Richey
1970	Ken Rosewall	Tony Roche	1970	Margaret Smith Court	Rosemary Casals
1971	Stan Smith	Jan Kodes	1971	Billie Jean King	Rosemary Casals
1972	Ilie Nastase	Arthur Ashe	1972	Billie Jean King	Kerry Melville
1973	John Newcombe	Jan Kodes	1973	Margaret Smith Court	Evonne Goolagong
1974	Jimmy Connors	Ken Rosewall	1974	Billie Jean King	Evonne Goolagong
1975	Manuel Orantes	Jimmy Connors	1975	Chris Evert	Evonne Goolagong Cawley
1976	Jimmy Connors	Bjorn Borg	1976	Chris Evert	Evonne Goolagong Cawley
1977	Guillermo Vilas	Jimmy Connors	1977	Chris Evert	Wendy Turnbull
1978	Jimmy Connors	Bjorn Borg	1978	Chris Evert	Pam Shriver
1979	John McEnroe	Vitas Gerulaitis	1979	Tracy Austin	Chris Evert Lloyd
1980	John McEnroe	Bjorn Borg	1980	Chris Evert Lloyd	Hana Mandlikova
1981	John McEnroe	Bjorn Borg	1981	Tracy Austin	Martina Navratilova
1982	Jimmy Connors	Ivan Lendl	1982	Chris Evert Lloyd	Hana Mandlikova
1983	Jimmy Connors	Ivan Lendl	1983	Martina Navratilova	Chris Evert Lloyd
1984	John McEnroe	Ivan Lendl	1984	Martina Navratilova	Chris Evert Lloyd
1985	Ivan Lendl	John McEnroe	1985	Hana Mandlikova	Martina Navratilova
1986	Ivan Lendl	Miloslav Mecir	1986	Martina Navratilova	Helena Sukova
1987	Ivan Lendl	Mats Wilander	1987	Martina Navratilova	Steffi Graf
1988	Mats Wilander	Ivan Lendl	1988	Steffi Graf	Gabriela Sabatini
1989	Boris Becker	Ivan Lendl	1989	Steffi Graf	Martina Navratilova
1990	Pete Sampras	Andre Agassi	1990	Gabriela Sabatini	Steffi Graf
1991	Stefan Edberg	Jim Courier	1991	Monica Seles	Martina Navratilova
1992	Stefan Edberg	Pete Sampras	1992	Monica Seles	Arantxa Sánchez Vicario
1993	Pete Sampras	Cedric Pioline	1993	Steffi Graf	Helena Sukova
1994	Andre Agassi	Michael Stich	1994	Arantxa Sánchez Vicario	Steffi Graf
1995	Pete Sampras	Andre Agassi	1995	Steffi Graf	Monica Seles
1996	Pete Sampras	Michael Chang	1996	Steffi Graf	Monica Seles
1997	Patrick Rafter	Greg Rusedski	1997	Martina Hingis	Venus Williams
1998	Patrick Rafter	Mark Philippoussis	1998	Lindsay Davenport	Martina Hingis
1999	Andre Agassi	Todd Martin	1999	Serena Williams	Martina Hingis
2000	Marat Safin	Pete Sampras	2000	Venus Williams	Lindsay Davenport
2001	Lleyton Hewitt	Pete Sampras	2001	Venus Williams	Serena Williams
2002	Pete Sampras	Andre Agassi	2002	Serena Williams	Venus Williams
2003	Andy Roddick	Juan Carlos Ferrero	2003	Justine Henin	Kim Clijsters
2004	Roger Federer	Lleyton Hewitt	2004	Svetlana Kuznetsova	Elena Dementieva
2005	Roger Federer	Andre Agassi	2005	Kim Clijsters	Mary Pierce
2006	Roger Federer	Andy Roddick	2006	Maria Sharapova	Justine Henin
2007	Roger Federer	Novak Djokovic	2007	Justine Henin	Svetlana Kuznetsova
2008	Roger Federer	Andy Murray	2008	Serena Williams	Jelena Jankovic
2009	Juan Martin del Potro	Roger Federer	2009	Kim Clijsters	Caroline Wozniacki

Davis Cup, 1900-2008

Year	Result	Year	Result	Year	Result
1900	U.S. 3, British Isles 0	1937	U.S. 4, Great Britain 1	1976	Italy 4, Chile 1
1901	Not held	1938	U.S. 3, Australia 2	1977	Australia 3, Italy 1
1902	U.S. 3, British Isles 2	1939	Australia 3, U.S. 2	1978	U.S. 4, Great Britain 1
1903	British Isles 4, U.S. 1	1940-45	Not held	1979	U.S. 5, Italy 0
1904	British Isles 5, Belgium 0	1946	U.S. 5, Australia 0	1980	Czechoslovakia 4, Italy 1
1905	British Isles 5, U.S. 0	1947	U.S. 4, Australia 1	1981	U.S. 3, Argentina 1
1906	British Isles 5, U.S. 0	1948	U.S. 5, Australia 0	1982	U.S. 4, France, 1
1907	Australia 3, British Isles 2	1949	U.S. 4, Australia 1	1983	Australia 3, Sweden 2
1908	Australasia 3, U.S. 2	1950	Australia 4, U.S. 1	1984	Sweden 4, U.S. 1
1909	Australasia 5, U.S. 0	1951	Australia 3, U.S. 2	1985	Sweden 3, W. Germany 2
1910	Not held	1952	Australia 4, U.S. 1	1986	Australia 3, Sweden 2
1911	Australasia 5, U.S. 0	1953	Australia 3, U.S. 2	1987	Sweden 5, India 0
1912	British Isles 3, Australasia 2	1954	U.S. 3, Australia 2	1988	W. Germany 4, Sweden 1
1913	U.S. 3, British Isles 2	1955	Australia 5, U.S. 0	1989	W. Germany 3, Sweden 2
1914	Australasia 3, U.S. 2	1956	Australia 5, U.S. 0	1990	U.S. 3, Australia 2
1915-18	Not held	1957	Australia 3, U.S. 2	1991	France 3, U.S. 1
1919	Australasia 4, British Isles 1	1958	U.S. 3, Australia 2	1992	U.S. 3, Switzerland 1
1920	U.S. 5, Australasia 0	1959	Australia 3, U.S. 2	1993	Germany 4, Australia 1
1921	U.S. 5, Japan 0	1960	Australia 4, Italy 1	1994	Sweden 4, Russia 1
1922	U.S. 4, Australasia 1	1961	Australia 5, Italy 0	1995	U.S. 3, Russia 2
1923	U.S. 4, Australasia 1	1962	Australia 5, Mexico 0	1996	France 3, Sweden 2
1924	U.S. 5, Australasia 0	1963	U.S. 3, Australia 2	1997	Sweden 5, U.S. 0
1925	U.S. 5, France 0	1964	Australia 3, U.S. 2	1998	Sweden 4, Italy 1
1926	U.S. 4, France 1	1965	Australia 4, Spain 1	1999	Australia 3, France 2
1927	France 3, U.S. 2	1966	Australia 4, India 1	2000	Spain 3, Australia 1
1928	France 4, U.S. 1	1967	Australia 4, Spain 1	2001	France 3, Australia 2
1929	France 3, U.S. 2	1968	U.S. 4, Australia	2002	Russia 3, France 2
1930	France 4, U.S. 1	1969	U.S. 5, Romania 0	2003	Australia 3, Spain 1
1931	France 3, Great Britain 2	1970	U.S. 5, W. Germany 0	2004	Spain 3, U.S. 2
1932	France 3, U.S. 2	1971	U.S. 3, Romania 2	2005	Croatia 3, Slovakia 2
1933	Great Britain 3, France 2	1972*	U.S. 3, Romania 2	2006	Russia 3, Argentina 2
1934	Great Britain 4, U.S. 1	1973	Australia 5, U.S. 0	2007	U.S. 4, Russia 1
1935	Great Britain 5, U.S. 0	1974	South Africa (default by India)	2008	Spain 3, Argentina 1
1936	Great Britain 3, Australia 2	1975	Sweden 3, Czechoslovakia 2		

*The challenge round format, which guaranteed the previous year's winner a spot in the finals at home, was eliminated in 1972.

All-Time Grand Slam Singles Titles Leaders

Men	Australian Open	French Open[2]	Wimbledon	U.S. Open	Total
Roger Federer[1]	2004, '06-'07	2009	2003-07, '09	2004-08	15
Pete Sampras	1994, '97	—	1993-95, 1997-2000	1990, '93, '95-'96, 2002	14
Roy Emerson	1961, '63-'67	1963, '67	1964-65	1961, '64	12
Bjorn Borg	—	1974-75, 1978-81	1976-80	—	11
Rod Laver	1960, '62, '69	1962, '69	1961-62, '68-'69	1962, '69	11
Bill Tilden	—	—	1920-21, '30	1920-25, '29	10
Andre Agassi	1995, 2000, '01, '03	1999	1992	1994, '99	8
Jimmy Connors	1974	—	1974, '82	1974, '76, '78, '82-'83	8
Ivan Lendl	1989-90	1984, '86-'87	—	1985-87	8
Fred Perry	1934	1935	1934-36	1933-34, '36	8
Ken Rosewall	1953, '55, '71-'72	1953, '68	—	1956, '70	8
Women					
Margaret Smith Court	1960-66, '69-'71, '73	1962, '64, '69-'70, '73	1963, '65, '70	1962, '65, '69-'70, '73	24
Steffi Graf	1988-90, '94	1987-88, '93, '95-'96, '99	1988-89, '91-'93, '95-'96	1988-89, '93, '95-'96	22
Helen Wills Moody	—	1928-30, '32	1927-30, '32-'33, '35, '38	1923-25, '27-'29, '31	19
Chris Evert	1982, '84	1974-75, '79-'80, '83, '85-'86	1974, '76, '81	1975-78, '80, '82	18
Martina Navratilova	1981, '83, '85	1982, '84	1978-79, '82-'87, '90	1983-84, '86-'87	18
Billie Jean King	1968	1972	1966-68, '72-'73, '75	1967, '71-'72, '74	12
Suzanne Lenglen	—	1920-23, '25-'26	1919-23, '25	—	12
Serena Williams[1]	2003, '05, '07, '09	2002	1999, 2002, '09	2002-03, '08	11
Maureen Connolly	1953	1953-54	1952-54	1951-53	9
Monica Seles	1991-93, '96	1990-92	—	1991-92	9

(1) Active player in 2009. (2) Prior to 1925, French Open entry was limited to members of French clubs.

RIFLE AND PISTOL CHAMPIONSHIPS

Source: National Rifle Association

NRA Bianchi Cup National Action Pistol Championships, 2009

Action Pistol: Bruce Piatt, Montvale, NJ, 1920-181X
Woman Action Pistol: Julie Golob, Glasgow, MT, 1907-138-X
Junior Action Pistol: Jordan Dick, Hutchinson, KS, 1909-160X

National Outdoor Rifle and Pistol Championships, 2009

Pistol: SSG James Henderson, U.S. Army, Columbus, GA, 2646-141X
Civilian Pistol: Brian H. Zins, Centreville, VA, 2637-131X
Woman Pistol: Judy Tant, East Lansing, MI, 2566-72X
Smallbore Rifle Prone: SPC Joseph A. Hein, U.S. Army, Ft. Benning, GA, 4790-354X
Civilian Smallbore Rifle Prone: Richard Fowke, Great Britain, 4790-355X
Woman Smallbore Rifle Prone: Reya Kempley, Carson City, NV, 4789-374X
Smallbore Rifle NRA 3-Position: SPC Joseph A. Hein, U.S. Army, Ft. Benning, GA, 2363-146X

Civilian Smallbore Rifle NRA 3-Position: Tarl Kempley, Carson City, NV, 2376-142X
Woman Smallbore Rifle NRA 3-Position: Reya Kempley, Carson City, NV, 2363-146X
High Power Rifle: Norman G. Houle, Warwick, RI, 2387-124X
Civilian High Power Rifle: Norman G. Houle, Warwick, RI, 2387-124X
Woman High Power Rifle: SPC Sherri Gallagher, U.S. Army, Phenix City, AL, 2382-148X
High Power Rifle Long Range: SPC Sherri Gallagher, U.S. Army, Phenix City, AL, 1245-62X
Woman High Power Rifle Long Range: SPC Sherri Gallagher, U.S. Army, Phenix City, AL, 1245-62X

National Indoor Rifle and Pistol Championships, 2009

Smallbore Rifle 4-Position: Michael Aberhard, Monticello, WI, 797-64X
Woman Smallbore Rifle 4-Position: Kaitlen Pennell, Antelope, CA, 795-64X
Smallbore Rifle NRA 3-Position: Michelle Bohren, Taylor, MI, 1180-74X
Woman Smallbore Rifle NRA 3-Position: Michelle Bohren, Taylor, MI, 1180-74X
Intl. Smallbore Rifle: Abigail Fong, New York, NY, 1182-85X
Woman Intl. Smallbore Rifle: Abigail Fong, New York, NY, 1182-85X
Air Rifle: Patrick Sartz, Fairbanks, AK, 795-64X

Woman Air Rifle: Taylor Beard, Parker, CO, 589
Conventional Pistol: Robert Park, Mitchell, AL, 891-42X
Woman Conventional Pistol: Kathy Chatterton, Glen Rock, NJ, 859-29X
International Free Pistol: John Zurek, Chandler, AZ, 559
Woman Intl. Free Pistol: Lindsay Daniels, Salt Lake City, UT, 477
Intl. Standard Pistol: John Bickar, Menlo Park, CA, 578
Woman Intl. Standard Pistol: Kathy Chatterton, Glen Rock, NJ, 538
Air Pistol: Jay Williams, Vancouver, WA, 574
Woman Air Pistol: Brenda Martin Shinn, Riverside, CA, 565

AUTO RACING
Indianapolis 500 Winners, 1911-2009
(At Indianapolis Motor Speedway in Indianapolis, IN.)

Year	Winner, car[1]	MPH[2]	Year	Winner, car[1]	MPH[2]
1911	Ray Harroun, Marmon	74.602	1963	Parnelli Jones, Watson-Offy	143.137
1912	Joe Dawson, National	78.719	1964	A. J. Foyt Jr., Watson-Offy	147.350
1913	Jules Goux, Peugeot	75.933	1965	Jim Clark, Lotus-Ford	150.686
1914	Rene Thomas, Delage	82.474	1966	Graham Hill, Lola-Ford	144.317
1915	Ralph DePalma, Mercedes	89.840	1967	A. J. Foyt Jr., Coyote-Ford	151.207
1916	Dario Resta, Peugeot	84.001	1968	Bobby Unser, Eagle-Offy	152.882
1917-18	Not held		1969	Mario Andretti, Hawk-Ford	156.867
1919	Howdy Wilcox, Peugeot	88.050	1970	Al Unser, P.J. Colt-Ford	155.749
1920	Gaston Chevrolet, Frontenac	88.618	1971	Al Unser, P.J. Colt-Ford	157.735
1921	Tommy Milton, Frontenac	89.621	1972	Mark Donohue, McLaren-Offy	162.962
1922	Jimmy Murphy, Duesenberg-Miller	94.484	1973	Gordon Johncock, Eagle-Offy	159.036
1923	Tommy Milton, Miller	90.954	1974	Johnny Rutherford, McLaren-Offy	158.589
1924	L. L. Corum-Joe Boyer, Duesenberg	98.234	1975	Bobby Unser, Eagle-Offy	149.213
1925	Peter DePaolo, Duesenberg	101.127	1976	Johnny Rutherford, McLaren-Offy	148.725
1926	Frank Lockhart, Miller	95.904	1977	A. J. Foyt Jr., Coyote-Foyt	161.331
1927	George Souders, Duesenberg	97.545	1978	Al Unser, Lola-Cosworth	161.363
1928	Louie Meyer, Miller	99.482	1979	Rick Mears, Penske-Cosworth	158.899
1929	Ray Keech, Miller	97.585	1980	Johnny Rutherford, Chaparral-Cosworth	142.862
1930	Billy Arnold, Summers-Miller	100.448	1981	Bobby Unser, Penske-Cosworth	139.084
1931	Louis Schneider, Stevens-Miller	96.629	1982	Gordon Johncock, Wildcat-Cosworth	162.029
1932	Fred Frame, Wetteroth-Miller	104.144	1983	Tom Sneva, March-Cosworth	162.117
1933	Louie Meyer, Miller	104.162	1984	Rick Mears, March-Cosworth	163.612
1934	Bill Cummings, Miller	104.863	1985	Danny Sullivan, March-Cosworth	152.982
1935	Kelly Petillo, Wetteroth-Offy	106.240	1986	Bobby Rahal, March-Cosworth	170.722
1936	Louie Meyer, Stevens-Miller	109.069	1987	Al Unser, March-Cosworth	162.175
1937	Wilbur Shaw, Shaw-Offy	113.580	1988	Rick Mears, Penske-Chevy Indy V8	144.809
1938	Floyd Roberts, Wetteroth-Miller	117.200	1989	Emerson Fittipaldi, Penske-Chevy Indy V8	167.581
1939	Wilbur Shaw, Maserati	115.035	1990	Arie Luyendyk, Lola-Chevy Indy V8	185.981*
1940	Wilbur Shaw, Maserati	114.277	1991	Rick Mears, Penske-Chevy Indy V8	176.457
1941	Floyd Davis-Mauri Rose, Wetteroth-Offy	115.117	1992	Al Unser Jr., Galmer-Chevy Indy V8A	134.477
1942-45	Not held		1993	Emerson Fittipaldi, Penske-Chevy Indy V8C	157.207
1946	George Robson, Adams-Sparks	114.820	1994	Al Unser Jr., Penske-Mercedes Benz	160.872
1947	Mauri Rose, Deidt-Offy	116.338	1995	Jacques Villeneuve, Reynard-Ford Cosworth XB	153.616
1948	Mauri Rose, Deidt-Offy	119.814	1996	Buddy Lazier, Reynard-Ford Cosworth	147.956
1949	Bill Holland, Deidt-Offy	121.327	1997	Arie Luyendyk, G Force-Aurora	145.827
1950	Johnnie Parsons, Kurtis-Offy	124.002	1998	Eddie Cheever, Dallara-Aurora	145.155
1951	Lee Wallard, Kurtis-Offy	126.244	1999	Kenny Brack, Dallara-Aurora	153.176
1952	Troy Ruttman, Kuzma-Offy	128.922	2000	Juan Montoya, G Force-Aurora	167.607
1953	Bill Vukovich, KK500A-Offy	128.740	2001	Helio Castroneves, Reynard-Honda	131.294
1954	Bill Vukovich, KK500A-Offy	130.840	2002	Helio Castroneves, Reynard-Honda	166.499
1955	Bob Sweikert, KK500C-Offy	128.213	2003	Gil de Ferran, G Force-Toyota	156.291
1956	Pat Flaherty, Watson-Offy	128.490	2004	Buddy Rice, G Force-Honda	138.518
1957	Sam Hanks, Salih-Offy	135.601	2005	Dan Wheldon, Dallara-Honda	157.603
1958	Jimmy Bryan, Salih-Offy	133.791	2006	Sam Hornish Jr., Dallara-Honda	157.085
1959	Rodger Ward, Watson-Offy	135.857	2007	Dario Franchitti, Dallara-Honda	151.774
1960	Jim Rathmann, Watson-Offy	138.767	2008	Scott Dixon, Dallara-Honda	143.567
1961	A. J. Foyt Jr., Trevis-Offy	139.130	2009	Helio Castroneves, Dallara-Honda	150.318
1962	Rodger Ward, Watson-Offy	140.293			

(1) Chassis-engine. (2) Average speed. *Race record. **Note:** The race was less than 500 mi in the following years: 1916 (300 mi), 1926 (400 mi), 1950 (345 mi), 1973 (332.5 mi), 1975 (435 mi), 1976 (255 mi), 2004 (450 mi), 2007 (415 mi).

Champ Car World Series Vanderbilt Cup Winners, 1959-2007

(U.S. Auto Club Champions, 1959-78; Championship Auto Racing Teams [CART] Champions, 1979-2003; Champ Car World Series Champion, 2004-07. Vanderbilt Cup became the series championship trophy in 2000. Merged with Indy Racing League, 2008.)

Year	Driver	Year	Driver	Year	Driver	Year	Driver	Year	Driver
1959	Roger Ward	1969	Mario Andretti	1979	Rick Mears	1989	Emerson Fittipaldi	1999	Juan Montoya
1960	A. J. Foyt	1970	Al Unser	1980	Johnny Rutherford	1990	Al Unser Jr.	2000	Gil de Ferran
1961	A. J. Foyt	1971	Joe Leonard	1981	Rick Mears	1991	Michael Andretti	2001	Gil de Ferran
1962	Rodger Ward	1972	Joe Leonard	1982	Rick Mears	1992	Bobby Rahal	2002	Cristiano da Matta
1963	A. J. Foyt	1973	Roger McCluskey	1983	Al Unser	1993	Nigel Mansell	2003	Paul Tracy
1964	A. J. Foyt	1974	Bobby Unser	1984	Mario Andretti	1994	Al Unser Jr.	2004	Sébastien Bourdais
1965	Mario Andretti	1975	A. J. Foyt	1985	Al Unser	1995	Jacques Villeneuve	2005	Sébastien Bourdais
1966	Mario Andretti	1976	Gordon Johncock	1986	Bobby Rahal	1996	Jimmy Vasser	2006	Sébastien Bourdais
1967	A. J. Foyt	1977	Tom Sneva	1987	Bobby Rahal	1997	Alex Zanardi	2007	Sébastien Bourdais
1968	Bobby Unser	1978	Tom Sneva	1988	Danny Sullivan	1998	Alex Zanardi		

Indy Racing League (IRL) Winners, 1996-2008

(The Indy Racing League was begun in 1994 by a break-away group of CART drivers; its first championship was awarded in 1996. Merged with Champ Car Series, 2008.)

Year	Driver	Year	Driver	Year	Driver	Year	Driver	Year	Driver
1996	Scott Sharp,	1998	Kenny Brack	2001	Sam Hornish Jr.	2004	Tony Kanaan	2007	Dario Franchitti
	Buzz Calkins (tie)	1999	Greg Ray	2002	Sam Hornish Jr.	2005	Dan Wheldon	2008	Scott Dixon
1997	Tony Stewart	2000	Buddy Lazier	2003	Scott Dixon	2006	Sam Hornish Jr.		

NASCAR Racing
Sprint Cup Champions, 1949-2008
(Strictly Stock, 1949; Grand National, 1950-70; Winston Cup 1971-2003)

Year	Driver	Year	Driver	Year	Driver	Year	Driver	Year	Driver
1949	Red Byron	1961	Ned Jarrett	1973	Benny Parsons	1985	Darrell Waltrip	1997	Jeff Gordon
1950	Bill Rexford	1962	Joe Weatherly	1974	Richard Petty	1986	Dale Earnhardt	1998	Jeff Gordon
1951	Herb Thomas	1963	Joe Weatherly	1975	Richard Petty	1987	Dale Earnhardt	1999	Dale Jarrett
1952	Tim Flock	1964	Richard Petty	1976	Cale Yarborough	1988	Bill Elliott	2000	Bobby Labonte
1953	Herb Thomas	1965	Ned Jarrett	1977	Cale Yarborough	1989	Rusty Wallace	2001	Jeff Gordon
1954	Lee Petty	1966	David Pearson	1978	Cale Yarborough	1990	Dale Earnhardt	2002	Tony Stewart
1955	Tim Flock	1967	Richard Petty	1979	Richard Petty	1991	Dale Earnhardt	2003	Matt Kenseth
1956	Buck Baker	1968	David Pearson	1980	Dale Earnhardt	1992	Alan Kulwicki	2004	Kurt Busch
1957	Buck Baker	1969	David Pearson	1981	Darrell Waltrip	1993	Dale Earnhardt	2005	Tony Stewart
1958	Lee Petty	1970	Bobby Isaac	1982	Darrell Waltrip	1994	Dale Earnhardt	2006	Jimmie Johnson
1959	Lee Petty	1971	Richard Petty	1983	Bobby Allison	1995	Jeff Gordon	2007	Jimmie Johnson
1960	Rex White	1972	Richard Petty	1984	Terry Labonte	1996	Terry Labonte	2008	Jimmie Johnson

NASCAR Rookie of the Year, 1958-2008

Year	Driver	Year	Driver	Year	Driver	Year	Driver	Year	Driver
1958	Shorty Rollins	1969	Dick Brooks	1979	Dale Earnhardt	1989	Dick Trickle	1999	Tony Stewart
1959	Richard Petty	1970	Bill Dennis	1980	Jody Riley	1990	Rob Moroso	2000	Matt Kenseth
1960	David Pearson	1971	Walter Ballard	1981	Ron Bouchard	1991	Bobby Hamilton	2001	Kevin Harvick
1961	Woodie Wilson	1972	Larry Smith	1982	Geoff Bodine	1992	Jimmy Hensley	2002	Ryan Newman
1962	Tom Cox	1973	Lennie Pond	1983	Sterling Marlin	1993	Jeff Gordon	2003	Jamie McMurray
1963	Billy Wade	1974	Earl Ross	1984	Rusty Wallace	1994	Jeff Burton	2004	Kasey Kahne
1964	Doug Cooper	1975	Bruce Hill	1985	Ken Schrader	1995	Ricky Craven	2005	Kyle Busch
1965	Sam McQuagg	1976	Skip Manning	1986	Alan Kulwicki	1996	Johnny Benson	2006	Denny Hamlin
1966	James Hylton	1977	Ricky Rudd	1987	Davey Allison	1997	Mike Skinner	2007	Juan Montoya
1967	Donnie Allison	1978	Ronnie Thomas	1988	Ken Bouchard	1998	Kenny Irwin	2008	Regan Smith
1968	Pete Hamilton								

Daytona 500 Winners, 1959-2009
(At Daytona International Speedway in Daytona Beach, FL.)

Year	Driver, car	Avg. mph	Year	Driver, car	Avg. mph	Year	Driver, car	Avg. mph
1959	Lee Petty, Oldsmobile	135.521	1976	David Pearson, Mercury	152.181	1993	Dale Jarrett, Chevrolet	154.972
1960	Junior Johnson, Chevrolet	124.740	1977	Cale Yarborough, Chevrolet	153.218	1994	Sterling Marlin, Chevrolet	156.931
1961	Marvin Panch, Pontiac	149.601	1978	Bobby Allison, Ford	159.730	1995	Sterling Marlin, Chevrolet	141.710
1962	Fireball Roberts, Pontiac	152.529	1979	Richard Petty, Oldsmobile	143.977	1996	Dale Jarrett, Ford	154.308
1963	Tiny Lund, Ford	151.566	1980	Buddy Baker, Oldsmobile	177.602	1997	Jeff Gordon, Chevrolet	148.295
1964	Richard Petty, Plymouth	154.334	1981	Richard Petty, Buick	169.651	1998	Dale Earnhardt, Chevrolet	172.712
1965	Fred Lorenzen, Ford (a)	141.539	1982	Bobby Allison, Buick	153.991	1999	Jeff Gordon, Chevrolet	161.551
1966	Richard Petty, Plymouth (b)	160.627	1983	Cale Yarborough, Pontiac	155.979	2000	Dale Jarrett, Ford	155.669
1967	Mario Andretti, Ford	146.926	1984	Cale Yarborough, Chevrolet	150.994	2001	Michael Waltrip, Chevrolet	161.783
1968	Cale Yarborough, Mercury	143.251	1985	Bill Elliott, Ford	172.265	2002	Ward Burton, Dodge	142.971
1969	LeeRoy Yarbrough, Ford	160.875	1986	Geoff Bodine, Chevrolet	148.124	2003	Michael Waltrip, Chevrolet (d)	133.870
1970	Pete Hamilton, Plymouth	149.601	1987	Bill Elliott, Ford	176.263	2004	Dale Earnhardt Jr., Chevrolet	156.345
1971	Richard Petty, Plymouth	144.456	1988	Bobby Allison, Buick	137.531	2005	Jeff Gordon, Chevrolet	135.173
1972	A. J. Foyt, Mercury	161.550	1989	Darrell Waltrip, Chevrolet	148.466	2006	Jimmie Johnson, Chevrolet	142.667
1973	Richard Petty, Dodge	157.205	1990	Derrike Cope, Chevrolet	165.761	2007	Kevin Harvick, Chevrolet	149.335
1974	Richard Petty, Dodge (c)	140.894	1991	Ernie Irvan, Chevrolet	148.148	2008	Ryan Newman, Dodge	152.672
1975	Benny Parsons, Chevrolet	153.649	1992	Davey Allison, Ford	160.256	2009	Matt Kenseth, Ford	132.816

(a) 322.5 mi. (b) 495 mi. (c) 450 mi. (d) 272.5 mi.

Coca-Cola 600 Winners, 1960-2009
(At Lowe's Motor Speedway in Concord, NC. Known as World 600, 1960-85. * = rain-shortened)

Year	Driver, car	Avg. mph	Year	Driver, car	Avg. mph	Year	Driver, car	Avg. mph
1960	Joe Lee Johnson, Chevrolet	107.735	1977	Richard Petty, Dodge	137.676	1994	Jeff Gordon, Chevrolet	139.445
1961	David Pearson, Pontiac	111.633	1978	Darrell Waltrip, Chevrolet	138.355	1995	Bobby Labonte, Chevrolet	151.952
1962	Nelson Stacy, Ford	125.552	1979	Darrell Waltrip, Chevrolet	136.674	1996	Dale Jarrett, Ford	147.581
1963	Fred Lorenzen, Ford	132.418	1980	Benny Parsons, Chevrolet	119.265	1997	Jeff Gordon, Chevrolet*	136.745
1964	Jim Paschal, Plymouth	125.772	1981	Bobby Allison, Buick	129.326	1998	Jeff Gordon, Chevrolet	136.424
1965	Fred Lorenzen, Ford	121.772	1982	Neil Bonnett, Ford	130.058	1999	Jeff Burton, Ford	151.367
1966	Marvin Panch, Plymouth	135.042	1983	Neil Bonnett, Chevrolet	140.707	2000	Matt Kenseth, Ford	142.640
1967	Jim Paschal, Plymouth	135.832	1984	Bobby Allison, Buick	129.233	2001	Jeff Burton, Ford	138.107
1968	Buddy Baker, Dodge*	104.207	1985	Darrell Waltrip, Chevrolet	141.807	2002	Mark Martin, Ford	137.729
1969	LeeRoy Yarborough, Mercury	134.361	1986	Dale Earnhardt, Chevrolet	140.406	2003	Jimmie Johnson, Chevrolet*	126.198
1970	Donnie Allison, Ford	129.680	1987	Kyle Petty, Ford	131.483	2004	Jimmie Johnson, Chevrolet	142.763
1971	Bobby Allison, Mercury	140.422	1988	Darrell Waltrip, Chevrolet	124.460	2005	Jimmie Johnson, Chevrolet	114.698
1972	Buddy Baker, Dodge	142.255	1989	Darrell Waltrip, Chevrolet	144.077	2006	Kasey Kahne, Dodge	128.840
1973	Buddy Baker, Dodge	134.890	1990	Rusty Wallace, Pontiac	137.650	2007	Casey Mears, Chevrolet	130.222
1974	David Pearson, Mercury	135.720	1991	Davey Allison, Ford	138.951	2008	Kasey Kahne, Dodge	135.722
1975	Richard Petty, Dodge	145.327	1992	Dale Earnhardt, Chevrolet	132.980	2009	David Reutimann, Toyota	120.899
1976	David Pearson, Mercury	137.352	1993	Dale Earnhardt, Chevrolet	145.504			

Allstate 400 at the Brickyard Winners, 1994-2009
(At Indianapolis Motor Speedway in Indianapolis, IN)

Year	Driver, car	Avg. mph	Year	Driver, car	Avg. mph	Year	Driver, car	Avg. mph
1994	Jeff Gordon, Chevrolet	131.977	2000	Bobby Labonte, Pontiac	155.912	2005	Tony Stewart, Chevrolet	118.782
1995	Dale Earnhardt, Chevrolet	155.206	2001	Jeff Gordon, Chevrolet	130.790	2006	Jimmie Johnson, Chevrolet	137.180
1996	Dale Jarrett, Ford	139.508	2002	Bill Elliott, Dodge	125.033	2007	Tony Stewart, Chevrolet	117.379
1997	Ricky Rudd, Ford	130.814	2003	Kevin Harvick, Chevrolet	134.554	2008	Jimmie Johnson, Chevrolet	115.117
1998	Jeff Gordon, Chevrolet	126.772	2004	Jeff Gordon, Chevrolet	115.037	2009	Jimmie Johnson, Chevrolet	145.882
1999	Dale Jarrett, Ford	148.194						

Sharpie 500 Winners, 1961-2009

(At Bristol Motor Speedway in Bristol, TN. Known as the Volunteer 500, 1961-75, '78-79; Volunteer 400, 1976-77; Busch 500, 1980-90; Bud 500, 1991-93; Goody's 500, 1994-99; goracing.com 500, 2000. * = rain-shortened)

Year	Driver, car	Avg. mph	Year	Driver, car	Avg. mph	Year	Driver, car	Avg. mph
1961	Jack Smith, Pontiac	68.37	1978	Cale Yarborough, Oldsmobile	88.628	1994	Rusty Wallace, Ford	91.363
1962	Bobby Johns, Pontiac	73.32	1979	Darrell Waltrip, Chevrolet	91.493	1995	Terry Labonte, Chevrolet	81.979
1963	Fred Lorenzen, Ford	74.844	1980	Cale Yarborough, Chevrolet	86.973	1996	Rusty Wallace, Ford	91.267
1964	Fred Lorenzen, Ford	78.044	1981	Darrell Waltrip, Buick	84.723	1997	Dale Jarrett, Ford	80.013
1965	Ned Jarrett, Ford	61.826	1982	Darrell Waltrip, Buick	94.318	1998	Mark Martin, Ford	86.949
1966	Paul Goldsmith, Plymouth	77.963	1983	Darrell Waltrip, Chevrolet*	89.43	1999	Dale Earnhardt, Chevrolet	91.276
1967	Richard Petty, Plymouth	78.705	1984	Terry Labonte, Chevrolet	85.365	2000	Rusty Wallace, Ford	85.394
1968	David Pearson, Ford	76.31	1985	Dale Earnhardt, Chevrolet	81.388	2001	Tony Stewart, Pontiac	85.106
1969	David Pearson, Ford	79.737	1986	Darrell Waltrip, Chevrolet	86.934	2002	Jeff Gordon, Chevrolet	77.097
1970	Bobby Allison, Dodge	84.88	1987	Dale Earnhardt, Chevrolet	90.373	2003	Kurt Busch, Ford	77.421
1971	Charlie Glotzbach, Chevrolet	101.074	1988	Dale Earnhardt, Chevrolet	78.775	2004	Dale Earnhardt Jr., Chevrolet	88.538
1972	Bobby Allison, Chevrolet	92.735	1989	Darrell Waltrip, Chevrolet	85.554	2005	Matt Kenseth, Ford	84.678
1973	Benny Parsons, Chevrolet	91.342	1990	Ernie Irvan, Chevrolet	91.782	2006	Matt Kenseth, Ford	90.025
1974	Cale Yarborough, Chevrolet	75.43	1991	Alan Kulwicki, Ford	82.028	2007	Carl Edwards, Ford	89.006
1975	Richard Petty, Dodge	97.016	1992	Darrell Waltrip, Chevrolet	91.198	2008	Carl Edwards, Ford	91.581
1976	Cale Yarborough, Chevrolet	99.175	1993	Mark Martin, Ford	88.172	2009	Kyle Busch, Toyota	84.820
1977	Cale Yarborough, Chevrolet	79.726						

NASCAR Sprint All-Star Race, 1985-2009

(at Lowe's Motor Speedway in Concord, NC. Known as The Winston, 1985-2003; The Winston Select, 1995-96.)

Year	Driver, car	Year	Driver, car	Year	Driver, car
1985	Darrell Waltrip, Chevrolet	1994	Geoffrey Bodine, Ford	2002	Ryan Newman, Ford
1986	Bill Elliott, Ford	1995	Jeff Gordon, Chevrolet	2003	Jimmie Johnson, Chevrolet
1987	Dale Earnhardt, Chevrolet	1996	Michael Waltrip, Chevrolet	2004	Matt Kenseth, Ford
1988	Terry Labonte, Chevrolet	1997	Jeff Gordon, Chevrolet	2005	Mark Martin, Ford
1989	Rusty Wallace, Ford	1998	Mark Martin, Ford	2006	Jimmie Johnson, Chevrolet
1990	Dale Earnhardt, Chevrolet	1999	Terry Labonte, Chevrolet	2007	Kevin Harvick, Chevrolet
1991	Davey Allison, Ford	2000	Dale Earnhardt Jr., Chevrolet	2008	Kasey Kahne, Dodge
1992	Davey Allison, Ford	2001	Jeff Gordon, Chevrolet	2009	Tony Stewart, Chevrolet
1993	Dale Earnhardt, Chevrolet				

Formula One Racing
World Grand Prix Champions, 1950-2008

Year	Driver, country	Year	Driver, country	Year	Driver, country
1950	Nino Farini, Italy	1970	Jochen Rindt, Austria	1990	Ayrton Senna, Brazil
1951	Juan Manuel Fangio, Argentina	1971	Jackie Stewart, Scotland	1991	Ayrton Senna, Brazil
1952	Alberto Ascari, Italy	1972	Emerson Fittipaldi, Brazil	1992	Nigel Mansell, Britain
1953	Alberto Ascari, Italy	1973	Jackie Stewart, Scotland	1993	Alain Prost, France
1954	Juan Manuel Fangio, Argentina	1974	Emerson Fittipaldi, Brazil	1994	Michael Schumacher, Germany
1955	Juan Manuel Fangio, Argentina	1975	Niki Lauda, Austria	1995	Michael Schumacher, Germany
1956	Juan Manuel Fangio, Argentina	1976	James Hunt, England	1996	Damon Hill, England
1957	Juan Manuel Fangio, Argentina	1977	Niki Lauda, Austria	1997	Jacques Villeneuve, Canada
1958	Mike Hawthorne, England	1978	Mario Andretti, United States	1998	Mika Hakkinen, Finland
1959	Jack Brabham, Australia	1979	Jody Scheckter, South Africa	1999	Mika Hakkinen, Finland
1960	Jack Brabham, Australia	1980	Alan Jones, Australia	2000	Michael Schumacher, Germany
1961	Phil Hill, United States	1981	Nelson Piquet, Brazil	2001	Michael Schumacher, Germany
1962	Graham Hill, England	1982	Keke Rosberg, Finland	2002	Michael Schumacher, Germany
1963	Jim Clark, Scotland	1983	Nelson Piquet, Brazil	2003	Michael Schumacher, Germany
1964	John Surtees, England	1984	Niki Lauda, Austria	2004	Michael Schumacher, Germany
1965	Jim Clark, Scotland	1985	Alain Prost, France	2005	Fernando Alonso, Spain
1966	Jack Brabham, Australia	1986	Alain Prost, France	2006	Fernando Alonso, Spain
1967	Denis Hulme, New Zealand	1987	Nelson Piquet, Brazil	2007	Kimi Raikkonen, Finland
1968	Graham Hill, England	1988	Ayrton Senna, Brazil	2008	Lewis Hamilton, England
1969	Jackie Stewart, Scotland	1989	Alain Prost, France		

24 Hours of Le Mans Race, 2009

Spain's Marc Gene, Australia's David Brabham, and Austria's Alexander Wurz teamed up to win the 77th 24 Hours of Le Mans endurance race on June 14, 2009, in a diesel-powered Peugeot #9. The team completed 382 laps in 24 hours, one lap more than the 2nd-place Peugeot #8 car driven by France's Sébastien Bourdais, Franck Montagny, and Stéphane Sarrazin. Defending champions Tom Kristensen, Rinaldo Capello, and Allan McNish finished third in Audi's #1 car, six laps behind, after experiencing a pair of mechanical problems in the 21st hour of the race. Audi teams had won the previous five races and eight of the last 10. Racing is a family affair for David Brabham, whose father, Jack, is a former three-time Formula One champion while his brother, Geoff, also won Le Mans with Peugeot in 1993.

Notable One-Mile Land Speed Records

Andy Green, a Royal Air Force pilot, broke the sound barrier and set the world's first supersonic speed record on land, Oct. 15, 1997, in Black Rock Desert, NV. Green, driving a car built by Richard Noble, had 2 runs at an average speed of 763.035 mph, as calculated under the rules of the Fédération Internationale de l'Automobile (FIA). This record and speed exceeded the speed of sound, calculated at 751.251 mph for that place and time.

Date	Driver	Car	MPH	Date	Driver	Car	MPH
1/26/1906	Marriott	Stanley (Steam)	127.659	11/19/37	Eyston	Thunderbolt 1	311.42
3/16/10	Oldfield	Benz	131.724	9/16/38	Eyston	Thunderbolt 1	357.5
4/23/11	Burman	Benz	141.732	8/23/39	Cobb	Railton	368.9
2/12/19	DePalma	Packard	149.875	9/16/47	Cobb	Railton-Mobil	394.2
4/27/20	Milton	Dusenberg	155.046	8/05/63	Breedlove	Spirit of America	407.45
4/28/26	Parry-Thomas	Thomas Special	170.624	10/27/64	Arfons	Green Monster	536.71
3/29/27	Seagrave	Sunbeam	203.790	11/15/65	Breedlove	Spirit of America	600.601
4/22/28	Keech	White Triplex	207.552	10/23/70	Gabelich	Blue Flame	622.407
3/11/29	Seagrave	Irving-Napier	231.446	10/09/79	Barrett	Budweiser Rocket	638.637*
2/05/31	Campbell	Napier-Campbell	246.086	10/04/83	Noble	Thrust 2	633.468
2/24/32	Campbell	Napier-Campbell	253.96	9/25/97	Green	Thrust SSC	714.144
2/22/33	Campbell	Napier-Campbell	272.109	10/15/97	Green	Thrust SSC	763.035
9/03/35	Campbell	Bluebird Special	301.13				

*Not recognized as official by sanctioning bodies.

BOXING

There are many boxing governing bodies, including the World Boxing Assn. (WBA; known as the National Boxing Assn. [NBA] until 1962), World Boxing Council (WBC), International Boxing Fed. (IBF), World Boxing Org., U.S. Boxing Assn., N. American Boxing Fed., and European Boxing Union. All have their own champions and divisions.

Champions by Classes*

Class (weight limit)	WBA	WBC	IBF
Heavyweight	Nikolai Valuev, Russia	Vitali Klitschko, Ukraine	Wladimir Klitschko, Ukraine
Cruiserweight (200 lb)	Guillermo Jones, Panama	Giacobbe Fragomeni, Italy	Tomasz Adamek, Poland
Light Heavyweight (175 lb)	Gabriel Campillo, Spain	Jean Pascal, Haiti/Canada	Tavoris Cloud, U.S.
Super Middleweight (168 lb)	Mikkel Kessler, Denmark[s]	Carl Froch, England	Lucian Bute, Romania/Canada
Middleweight (160 lb)	Felix Sturm, Germany	Kelly Pavlik, U.S. / Sebastian Zbik, Germany[i]	Sebastian Sylvester, Germany
Super Welterweight/ Jr. Middleweight (154 lb)	Daniel Santos, Puerto Rico / Nobuhiro Ishida, Japan[i]	Sergio Martinez, Argentina	Cory Spinks, U.S.
Welterweight (147 lb)	Shane Mosley, U.S.[s] / Vyacheslav Senchenko, Ukraine[r]	Andre Berto, U.S.	Isaac Hlatshwayo, South Africa
Super Lightweight/ Jr. Welterweight (140 lb)	Amir Khan, England / Marcos Maidana, Argentina[i]	Devon Alexander, U.S.	Juan Urango, Colombia
Lightweight (135 lb)	Paulus Moses, Namibia / Juan Manuel Marquez, Mexico[s] / Miguel Acosta, Venezuela[i]	Edwin Valero, Venezuela	Vacant
Super Featherweight/ Jr. Lightweight (130 lb)	Jorge Linares, Venezuela	Humberto Soto, Mexico	Robert Guerrero, U.S.
Featherweight (126 lb)	Chris John, Indonesia / Yuriorkis Gamboa, Cuba[r]	Elio Rojas, Dominican Republic	Cristobal Cruz, Mexico
Super Bantamweight/ Jr. Featherweight (122 lb)	Poonsawat Kratingdaenggym, Thai. / Celestino Caballero, Panama[s]	Toshiaki Nishioka, Japan	Celestino Caballero, Panama
Bantamweight (118 lb)	Anselmo Moreno, Panama / Nehomar Cermeño, Venezuela[i]	Hozumi Hasegawa, Japan	Joseph Agbeko, Ghana
Super Flyweight/ Jr. Bantamweight (115 lb)	Nobuo Nashiro, Japan / Vic Darchinyan, Armenia/Australia[s] / Nonito Donaire, Philippines[i]	Vic Darchinyan, Armenia/Australia / Tomas Rojas, Mexico[i]	Simphiwe Nongqayi, South Africa
Flyweight (112 lb)	Denkaosan Kaowichit, Thailand	Daisuke Naito, Japan / Pongsaklek Wonjongkam, Thailand[i]	Vacant
Light/Jr. Flyweight (108 lb)	Giovanni Segura, Mexico / Juan Carlos Reveco, Argentina[i] / Brahim Asloum, France[1]	Edgar Sosa, Mexico	Brian Viloria, U.S.
Minimumweight/ Mini Flyweight (105 lb)	Roman Gonzalez, Nicaragua	Oleydong Sithsamerchai, Thailand / Juan Palacios, Nicaragua[i]	Raul Garcia, Mexico

*As of Sept. 26, 2009. **Note:** (i) Interim champion. (s) Super champion. (w) World champion. (1) "Champion in recess."

Ring Champions by Years

International Boxing Hall of Fame inductees in *italics*.
(*abandoned the title or was stripped of it; IBF champions listed only for heavyweight division)

Heavyweights

1882-92	*John L. Sullivan*[1]	1978	Leon Spinks (WBC*/WBA)[5];	1994	Michael Moorer (WBA/IBF)
1892-97	*James J. Corbett*[2]		*Ken Norton* (WBC)	1994-95	Oliver McCall (WBC);
1897-99	*Bob Fitzsimmons*	1978-83	*Larry Holmes* (WBC)[6]		George Foreman (WBA*/IBF*)
1899-1905	*James J. Jeffries*[*,3]	1979-80	John Tate (WBA)	1995	Frans Botha* (IBF)
1905-06	Marvin Hart	1980-82	Mike Weaver (WBA)	1995-96	Bruce Seldon (WBA);
1906-08	*Tommy Burns*	1982-83	Michael Dokes (WBA)		Frank Bruno (WBC)
1908-15	*Jack Johnson*	1983-84	Gerrie Coetzee (WBA)	1996	Mike Tyson (WBC*/WBA)
1915-19	*Jess Willard*	1983-85	Larry Holmes (IBF)[6]	1996-97	Michael Moorer (IBF)
1919-26	*Jack Dempsey*	1984	Tim Witherspoon (WBC)	1996-99	Evander Holyfield (WBA/IBF)
1926-28	*Gene Tunney**	1984-85	Greg Page (WBA)	1997-2001	*Lennox Lewis* (WBC)
1928-30	Vacant	1984-86	Pinklon Thomas (WBC)	1999-2001	*Lennox Lewis* (WBA*/WBC/IBF)
1930-32	*Max Schmeling*	1985-86	Tony Tubbs (WBA)	2000-01	Evander Holyfield (WBA)
1932-33	*Jack Sharkey*	1985-87	*Michael Spinks** (IBF)	2001-03	John Ruiz (WBA)
1933-34	Primo Carnera	1986	Tim Witherspoon (WBA);	2001	Hasim Rahman (WBC/IBF)
1934-35	*Max Baer*		Trevor Berbick (WBC)	2001-02	*Lennox Lewis* (IBF*)
1935-37	*James J. Braddock*	1986-87	Mike Tyson (WBC);	2001-04	*Lennox Lewis* (WBC)
1937-49	*Joe Louis**		James "Bonecrusher" Smith	2002-06	Chris Byrd (IBF)
1949-51	*Ezzard Charles*		(WBA)	2003	Roy Jones Jr. (WBA*)
1951-52	*Joe Walcott*	1987	Tony Tucker (IBF)	2004-05	John Ruiz (WBA)[7];
1952-56	*Rocky Marciano**	1987-90	Mike Tyson (WBC/WBA/IBF)		Vitali Klitschko (WBC*)
1956-59	*Floyd Patterson*	1990	"Buster" Douglas	2005-06	Hasim Rahman (WBC)
1959-60	*Ingemar Johansson*		(WBA/WBC/IBF)	2005-07	Nicolay Valuev (WBA)
1960-62	*Floyd Patterson*	1990-92	Evander Holyfield	2006-08	Oleg Maskaev (WBC)
1962-64	*Sonny Liston*		(WBA/WBC/IBF)	2006-	Wladimir Klitschko (IBF)
1964-67	*Cassius Clay (Muhammad Ali)*[4]	1992-93	Riddick Bowe	2007-08	Ruslan Chagaev (WBA)
1970-73	*Joe Frazier*		(WBA/IBF/WBC*)	2008	Samuel Peter (WBC)
1973-74	*George Foreman*	1992-94	*Lennox Lewis* (WBC)	2008-	Nikolai Valuev (WBA)
1974-78	*Muhammad Ali*	1993-94	Evander Holyfield (WBA/IBF)	2009	Vitali Klitschko (WBC)
1978-79	*Muhammad Ali** (WBA)				

(1) London Prize Ring (bare knuckle champion). (2) First Marquis of Queensberry champion. (3) Jeffries vacated title (1905), designated Marvin Hart and Jack Root as logical contenders. Hart defeated Root in 12 rounds (1905); in turn was defeated by Tommy Burns (1906), who claimed the title. Jack Johnson def. Burns (1908) and was recognized as champ. Johnson won the title by defeating Jeffries in the latter's attempted comeback (1910). (4) Title declared vacant by the WBA and others in 1967 after Ali refused military induction for religious reasons during the Vietnam War. Joe Frazier recognized as champ by six states, Mexico, and S. America. Jimmy Ellis declared champ by the WBA. Frazier KOd Ellis, Feb. 16, 1970. (5) After Spinks defeated Ali, the WBC recognized Ken Norton as champ. Ali defeated Spinks in 1978 rematch for WBA title, retired in 1979. (6) Holmes relinquished WBC title in Dec. 1983 to fight as champ of the new IBF. (7) James Toney defeated Ruiz Apr. 30, 2005, to claim the title, but it was rescinded when Toney tested positive for steroids.

Light Heavyweights

Year	Champion	Year	Champion	Year	Champion
1903	Jack Root, George Gardner	1968-74	Bob Foster*	1990-91	Dennis Andries (WBC)
1903-05	Bob Fitzsimmons	1974-77	John Conteh (WBC)	1991-94	Jeff Harding (WBC)
1905-12	Philadelphia Jack O'Brien*	1974-78	Victor Galindez (WBA)	1991-92	Thomas Hearns (WBA)
1912-16	Jack Dillon	1977-78	Miguel Cuello (WBC)	1992	Iran Barkley* (WBA)
1916-20	Battling Levinsky	1978	Mate Parlov (WBC)	1992-97	Virgil Hill (WBA)
1920-22	George Carpentier	1978-79	Mike Rossman (WBA);	1994-95	Mike McCallum (WBC)
1922-23	Battling Siki		Marvin Johnson (WBC)	1995-96	Fabrice Tiozzo* (WBC)
1923-25	Mike McTigue	1979-81	Matthew Saad Muhammad	1996-97	Roy Jones Jr. (WBC)
1925-26	Paul Berlenbach		(WBC)	1997	Montell Griffin (WBC);
1926-27	Jack Delaney*	1979-80	Marvin Johnson (WBA)		Roy Jones Jr. (WBC);
1927-29	Tommy Loughran*	1980-81	Eddie Mustafa Muhammad		Darius Michalczewski* (WBA)
1930-34	Maxie Rosenbloom		(WBA)	1997-98	Lou Del Valle (WBA)
1934-35	Bob Olin	1981-83	Michael Spinks (WBA);	1998-2003	Roy Jones Jr. (WBA*, WBC*)
1935-39	John Henry Lewis*		Dwight Muhammed-Qawi	2003	Mehdi Sahnoune (WBA);
1939	Melio Bettina		Braxton (WBC)		Antonio Tarver (WBC)
1939-41	Billy Conn*	1983-85	Michael Spinks*	2003-04	Roy Jones Jr. (WBA/WBC*)
1941	Anton Christoforidis	1985-86	J. B. Williamson (WBC)	2004	Antonio Tarver (WBC)
	(won NBA title)	1986-87	Marvin Johnson (WBA);	2004-06	Fabrice Tiozzo (WBA)
1941-48	Gus Lesnevich, Freddie Mills		Dennis Andries (WBC)	2005-07	Tomasz Adamek (WBC)
1948-50	Freddie Mills	1987	Leslie Stewart (WBA)	2006-07	Silvio Branco (WBA)
1950-52	Joey Maxim	1987-91	Virgil Hill (WBA)	2007-08	Chad Dawson (WBC);
1952-62	Archie Moore	1987	Thomas Hearns* (WBC)		Stipe Drews (WBA)
1962-63	Harold Johnson	1987-88	Don Lalonde (WBC)	2008	Hugo Hernan Garay (WBA);
1963-65	Willie Pastrano	1988	Sugar Ray Leonard* (WBC)		Adrian Diaconu (WBC)
1965-66	Jose Torres	1989	Dennis Andries (WBC)	2009	Gabriel Campillo (WBA);
1966-68	Dick Tiger	1989-90	Jeff Harding (WBC)		Jean Pascal (WBC)

Middleweights

Year	Champion	Year	Champion	Year	Champion
1884-91	Jack "Nonpareil" Dempsey	1957	Gene Fullmer; Ray Robinson	1987-88	Thomas Hearns (WBC)
1891-97	Bob Fitzsimmons*	1957-58	Carmen Basilio	1988-89	Iran Barkley (WBC)
1897-1907	Tommy Ryan*	1958	Ray Robinson	1989-90	Roberto Duran* (WBC)
1907-08	Stanley Ketchel; Billy Papke	1959	Gene Fullmer (NBA);	1989-91	Mike McCallum (WBA)
1908-10	Stanley Ketchel		Ray Robinson (NY)	1990-93	Julian Jackson (WBC)
1911-13	Vacant	1960	Gene Fullmer (NBA);	1992-93	Reggie Johnson (WBA)
1913	Frank Klaus; George Chip		Paul Pender (NY and MA)	1993-95	Gerald McClellan* (WBC)
1914-17	Al McCoy	1961	Gene Fullmer (NBA);	1993-94	John David Jackson (WBA)
1917-20	Mike O'Dowd		Terry Downes (NY, MA, Europe)	1994-97	Jorge Castro (WBA)
1920-23	Johnny Wilson	1962	Gene Fullmer;	1995	Julian Jackson (WBC)
1923-26	Harry Greb		Dick Tiger (NBA);	1995-96	Quincy Taylor (WBC);
1926-31	Theodore "Tiger" Flowers;		Paul Pender (NY and MA)*		Shinji Takehara (WBA)
	Mickey Walker	1963	Dick Tiger (universal)	1996-98	Keith Holmes (WBC)
1931-32	William "Gorilla" Jones (NBA)	1963-65	Joey Giardello	1996-97	William Joppy (WBA)
1932-37	Marcel Thil	1965-66	Dick Tiger	1997	Julio Cesar Green (WBA)
1938	Al Hostak (NBA);	1966-67	Emile Griffith	1998-2001	William Joppy (WBA)
	Solly Krieger (NBA)	1967	Nino Benvenuti	1998-99	Hassine Cherifi (WBC)
1939-40	Al Hostak (NBA)	1967-68	Emile Griffith	1999-2001	Keith Holmes (WBC)
1941-47	Tony Zale	1968-70	Nino Benvenuti	2001	Felix Trinidad (WBA)
1947-48	Rocky Graziano	1970-77	Carlos Monzon*	2001-05	Bernard Hopkins (WBC, WBA)
1948	Tony Zale; Marcel Cerdan	1977-78	Rodrigo Valdez	2005-06	Jermain Taylor (WBA)
1949-51	Jake LaMotta	1978-79	Hugo Corro	2005-07	Jermain Taylor (WBC)
1951	Ray Robinson;	1979-80	Vito Antuofermo	2006-07	Javier Castillejo (WBA)[1]
	Randy Turpin;	1980	Alan Minter	2007-08	Felix Sturm (WBA);
	Ray Robinson*	1980-87	Marvin Hagler		Kelly Pavlik (WBC)
1953-55	Carl "Bobo" Olson	1987	Sugar Ray Leonard* (WBC)	2009	Sebastian Zbik
1955-57	Ray Robinson	1987-89	Sumbu Kalambay (WBA)		

(1) Castillejo lost title to Mariano Carrera Dec. 2, 2006, but regained it Feb. 23, 2007, after Carrera tested positive for steroids.

Welterweights

Year	Champion	Year	Champion	Year	Champion
1892-94	"Mysterious" Billy Smith	1938-40	Henry Armstrong	1976-80	Jose "Pepino" Cuevas (WBA)
1894-96	Tommy Ryan	1940-41	Fritzie Zivic	1979	Wilfred Benitez (WBC)
1896	Kid McCoy*	1941-46	Fred Cochrane	1979-80	Sugar Ray Leonard (WBC)
1900	Rube Ferns; Matty Matthews	1946	Marty Servo*	1980	Roberto Duran (WBC)
1901	Rube Ferns	1946-51	Ray Robinson*[1]	1980-81	Thomas Hearns (WBA)
1901-04	Joe Walcott	1951	Johnny Bratton (NBA)	1980-82	Sugar Ray Leonard*
1904-06	Dixie Kid; Joe Walcott;	1951-54	Kid Gavilan	1983-85	Donald Curry (WBA);
	William "Honey" Mellody	1954-55	Johnny Saxton		Milton McCrory (WBC)
1907-11	Mike Sullivan	1955	Tony De Marco	1985-86	Donald Curry
1911-15	Vacant	1955-56	Carmen Basilio	1986-87	Lloyd Honeyghan (WBC)
1915-19	Ted Lewis	1956	Johnny Saxton	1987	Mark Breland (WBA)
1919-22	Jack Britton	1956-57	Carmen Basilio*	1987-88	Marlon Starling (WBA);
1922-26	Mickey Walker	1958	Virgil Akins		Jorge Vaca (WBC)
1926	Pete Latzo	1958-60	Don Jordan	1988-89	Tomas Molinares (WBA);
1927-29	Joe Dundee	1960-61	Benny Paret		Lloyd Honeyghan (WBC)
1929	Jackie Fields	1961	Emile Griffith	1989-90	Marlon Starling (WBC);
1930	Jack Thompson;	1961-62	Benny Paret		Mark Breland (WBA)
	Tommy Freeman	1962-63	Emile Griffith	1990-91	Maurice Blocker (WBC);
1931	Tommy Freeman;	1963	Luis Rodriguez		Aaron Davis (WBA)
	Jack Thompson;	1963-66	Emile Griffith*	1991	Simon Brown (WBC)
	Lou Brouillard	1966-69	Curtis Cokes	1991-92	Meldrick Taylor (WBA)
1932	Jackie Fields	1969-70	Jose Napoles	1991-93	Buddy McGirt (WBC)
1933	Young Corbett;	1970-71	Billy Backus	1992-94	Crisanto Espana (WBA)
	Jimmy McLarnin	1971-75	Jose Napoles	1993-97	Pernell Whitaker (WBC)
1934	Barney Ross;	1975-76	John Stracey (WBC);	1994-98	Ike Quartey (WBA*)
	Jimmy McLarnin		Angel Espada (WBA)	1997-99	Oscar De La Hoya (WBC*)
1935-38	Barney Ross	1976-79	Carlos Palomino (WBC)	1998	James Page (WBA*)

1999-00	Felix Trinidad (WBC*)	2003	Ricardo Mayorga	2006-08	Floyd Mayweather Jr. (WBC);
2000	Oscar De La Hoya (WBC*)		(WBA, WBC)		Miguel Cotto (WBA)
2000-02	Shane Mosley (WBC)	2003-05	Cory Spinks (WBA, WBC)	2008	Antonio Margarito (WBA);
2001-02	Andrew Lewis (WBA)	2005-06	Zab Judah (WBA, WBC)		Andre Berto (WBC)
2002	Ricardo Mayorga (WBA)	2006	Ricky Hatton (WBA);	2009	Shane Mosley (WBA)
2002-03	Vernon Forrest (WBC)		Carlos Baldomir (WBC)		

(1) Robinson gained the title by defeating Tommy Bell in an elimination agreed to by the New York Commission and the National Boxing Association. Both claimed Robinson waived his title when he won the middleweight crown from LaMotta in 1951.

Lightweights

1896-99	Kid Lavigne	1965	Ismael Laguna	1990	Juan Nazario (WBA)
1899-02	Frank Erne	1965-68	Carlos Ortiz	1990-92	Pernell Whitaker*
1902-08	Joe Gans	1968-69	Teo Cruz	1992	Joey Gamache (WBA)
1908-10	Oscar "Battling" Nelson	1969-70	Mando Ramos	1992-96	Miguel Angel Gonzalez* (WBC)
1910-12	Ad Wolgast	1970	Ismael Laguna	1992-93	Tony Lopez (WBA)
1912-14	Willie Ritchie	1970-72	Ken Buchanan (WBA)	1993	Dingaan Thobela (WBA)
1914-17	Freddie Welsh	1971-72	Pedro Carrasco (WBC)	1993-98	Orzubek Nazarov (WBA)
1917-25	Benny Leonard*	1972-79	Roberto Duran* (WBA)	1996-97	Jean-Baptiste Mendy (WBC)
1925	Jimmy Goodrich;	1972	Mando Ramos (WBC);	1997-98	Steve Johnston (WBC)
	Rocky Kansas		Chango Carmona (WBC)	1998-99	Jean-Baptiste Mendy (WBA);
1926-30	Sammy Mandell	1972-74	Rodolfo Gonzalez (WBC)		Cesar Bazan (WBC)
1930	Al Singer; Tony Canzoneri	1974-76	Ishimatsu Suzuki (WBC)	1999	Julian Lorcy (WBA);
1930-33	Tony Canzoneri	1976-78	Esteban De Jesus (WBC)		Stefano Zoff (WBA)
1933-35	Barney Ross*	1979-81	Jim Watt (WBC)	1999-2000	Gilberto Serrano (WBA);
1935-36	Tony Canzoneri	1979-80	Ernesto Espana (WBA)		Steve Johnston (WBC)
1936-38	Lou Ambers	1980-81	Hilmer Kenty (WBA)	2000-01	Takanori Hatakeyama (WBA)
1938	Henry Armstrong	1981	Sean O'Grady (WBA);	2000-02	Jose Luis Castillo (WBC)
1939	Lou Ambers		Claude Noel (WBA)	2001	Julien Lorcy (WBA)
1940	Lew Jenkins	1981-83	Alexis Arguello* (WBC)	2001-02	Raul Balbi (WBA)
1941-43	Sammy Angott	1981-82	Arturo Frias (WBA)	2002-03	Leonard Dorin (WBA)
1944	S. Angott (NBA);	1982-84	Ray Mancini (WBA)	2002-04	Floyd Mayweather (WBC)
	J. Zurita (NBA)	1983-84	Edwin Rosario (WBC)	2004	Lakva Sim (WBA)
1945-51	Ike Williams (NBA; later	1984-86	Livingstone Bramble (WBA)	2004-05	Jose Luis Castillo (WBC)
	universal)	1984-85	Jose Luis Ramirez (WBC)	2004-08	Juan Diaz (WBA)
1951-52	James Carter	1985-86	Hector "Macho" Camacho	2005-06	Diego Corrales (WBC)
1952	Lauro Salas; James Carter		(WBC)	2006	Joel Casamayor (WBC)
1953-54	James Carter	1986-87	Edwin Rosario (WBA)	2006-08	David Diaz (WBC)
1954	Paddy De Marco;	1987-88	Julio Cesar Chavez (WBA);	2008	Nate Campbell (WBA);
	James Carter		Jose Luis Ramirez (WBC)		Manny Pacquiao (WBC)
1955	James Carter; Bud Smith	1988-89	Julio Cesar Chavez (WBA,	2009	Edwin Valero (WBC);
1956	Bud Smith; Joe Brown		WBC)		Paulus Moses (WBA)
1956-62	Joe Brown	1989-90	Edwin Rosario (WBA);		
1962-65	Carlos Ortiz		Pernell Whitaker (WBC)		

Featherweights

1892-1900	George Dixon (disputed)	1968-71	Shozo Saijyo (WBA)	1991-93	Park Yung Kyun (WBA);
1900-01	Terry McGovern;	1969-70	Johnny Famechon (WBC)		Paul Hodkinson (WBC)
	Young Corbett*	1970	Vicente Salvidar (WBC)	1993	Goyo Vargas (WBC)
1901-12	Abe Attell	1970-72	Kuniaki Shibata (WBC)	1993-95	Kevin Kelley (WBC)
1912-23	Johnny Kilbane	1971-72	Antonio Gomez (WBA)	1993-96	Eloy Rojas (WBA)
1923	Eugene Criqui; Johnny Dundee	1972	Clemente Sanchez* (WBC)	1995	Alejandro Gonzalez (WBC)
1923-25	Johnny Dundee*	1972-74	Ernesto Marcel* (WBA)	1995-96	Manuel Medina (WBC)
1925-27	Kid Kaplan*	1972-73	Jose Legra (WBC)	1995-99	Luisito Espinosa (WBC)
1927-28	Benny Bass; Tony Canzoneri	1973-74	Eder Jofre* (WBC)	1996-97	Wilfredo Vasquez* (WBA)
1928-29	Andre Routis	1974	Ruben Olivares (WBA)	1998	Freddie Norwood (WBA)
1929-32	Battling Battalino*	1974-75	Bobby Chacon (WBC)	1998-99	Antonio Ceremeno (WBA)
1932-34	Tommy Paul (NBA)	1974-76	Alexis Arguello* (WBA)	1999	Cesar Soto (WBC);
1933-36	Freddie Miller	1975	Ruben Olivares (WBC)		Naseem Hamed* (WBC);
1936-37	Petey Sarron	1975-76	David Kotey (WBC)		Freddie Norwood (WBA)
1937-38	Henry Armstrong*	1976-80	Danny Lopez (WBC)	2000-01	Guty Espadas (WBC)
1938-40	Joey Archibald	1977	Rafael Ortega (WBA)	2000-03	Derrick Gainer (WBA)
1940-41	Harry Jeffra	1977-78	Cecilio Lastra (WBA)	2001-04	Erik Morales (WBC)[1]
1942-48	Willie Pep	1978-85	Eusebio Pedroza (WBA)	2003-06	Juan Manuel Marquez (WBA)
1948-49	Sandy Saddler	1980-82	Salvador Sanchez (WBC)	2004-06	In-Jin Chi (WBC)
1949-50	Willie Pep	1982-84	Juan LaPorte (WBC)	2006-08	Chris John (WBA)
1950-57	Sandy Saddler*	1984	Wilfredo Gomez (WBC)	2006	Takashi Koshimoto (WBC)
1957-59	Hogan "Kid" Bassey	1984-88	Azumah Nelson (WBC)	2006	Rodolfo Lopez (WBC)
1959-63	Davey Moore	1985-86	Barry McGuigan (WBA)	2006-07	In-Jin Chi (WBC)
1963-64	Ultiminio "Sugar" Ramos	1986-87	Steve Cruz (WBA)	2007-08	Jorge Linares (WBC)
1964-67	Vicente Saldivar*	1987-91	Antonio Esparragoza (WBA)	2008	Oscar Larios (WBC)
1968	Paul Rojas (WBA)	1988-90	Jeff Fenech* (WBC)	2009	Elio Rojas (WBC)
1968-69	Jose Legra (WBC)	1990-91	Marcos Villasana (WBC)		

(a) Marco Antonio Barrera won unan. decision over Morales, June 22, 2002, but refused WBC title. Morales regained WBC title with unan. decision over Paulie Ayala, Nov. 16, 2002. Morales moved up to Junior Lightweight div. in 2004.

International Boxing Hall of Fame 2009 Inductees

Source: International Boxing Hall of Fame, 1 Hall of Fame Dr., Canastota, NY 13032. www.ibhof.com

Modern	Orlando Canizales, 50-5-1 (37 KOs)	Lennox Lewis, 41-2-1 (32 KOs)	Brian Mitchell, 45-1-3 (21 KOs)
Old-Timer	William "Gorilla" Jones, 101-24-13 (52 KOs)	"Mysterious" Billy Smith, 30-24-26 (9 ND; 22 KOs)	Billy Soose, 34-6-1 (13 KOs)
Pioneer	Tom Hyer		
Non-participant	Billy Gibson, manager	Abe J. Greene, commissioner	Akihiko Honda, promoter
	Bob Goodman, publicist/matchmaker/promoter		
Observer	Hugh McIlvanney, journalist	Larry Merchant, broadcaster	Paul Gallico, journalist

Title-Changing Heavyweight Championship Bouts, 1889-2009

1889: July 8, John L. Sullivan def. Jake Kilrain, 75, Richburg, MS.

1892: Sept. 7, James J. Corbett def. John L. Sullivan, 21, New Orleans.

1897: Mar. 17, Bob Fitzsimmons def. James J. Corbett, 14, Carson City, NV.

1899: June 9, James J. Jeffries def. Bob Fitzsimmons, 11, Coney Island, NY. (Jeffries retired as champion in 1905.)

1905: July 3, Marvin Hart KOd Jack Root, 12, Reno, NV. (Jeffries refereed, gave title to Hart. Jack O'Brien also claimed the title.)

1906: Feb. 23, Tommy Burns def. Marvin Hart, 20, Los Angeles.

1908: Dec. 26, Jack Johnson KOd Tommy Burns, 14, Sydney, Australia. (Police halted contest.)

1915: Apr. 5, Jess Willard KOd Jack Johnson, 26, Havana, Cuba.

1919: July 4, Jack Dempsey KOd Jess Willard, Toledo. (Willard failed to answer bell for 4th round.)

1926: Sept. 23, Gene Tunney def. Jack Dempsey, 10, Philadelphia. (Tunney retired as champion in 1928.)

1930: June 12, Max Schmeling def. Jack Sharkey, 4, New York City. (Resulted in the election of a successor to Tunney.)

1932: June 21, Jack Sharkey def. Max Schmeling, 15, NYC.

1933: June 29, Primo Carnera KOd Jack Sharkey, 6, NYC.

1934: June 14, Max Baer KOd Primo Carnera, 11, NYC.

1935: June 13, James J. Braddock def. Max Baer, 15, NYC.

1937: June 22, Joe Louis KOd James J. Braddock, 8, Chicago. (Louis retired as champion in 1949.)

1949: June 22, Ezzard Charles def. Joe Walcott, 15, Chicago; NBA recognition only.

1951: July 18, Joe Walcott KOd Ezzard Charles, 7, Pittsburgh.

1952: Sept. 23, Rocky Marciano KOd Joe Walcott, 13, Philadelphia. (Marciano retired as champion in 1956.)

1956: Nov. 30, Floyd Patterson KOd Archie Moore, 5, Chicago.

1959: June 26, Ingemar Johansson KOd Floyd Patterson, 3, NYC.

1960: June 20, Floyd Patterson KOd Ingemar Johansson, 5, NYC.

1962: Sept. 25, Sonny Liston KOd Floyd Patterson, 1, Chicago.

1964: Feb. 25, Cassius Clay (Muhammad Ali) KOd Sonny Liston, 7, Miami Beach, FL. (In 1967, Ali was stripped of his title by the WBA and others for refusing military service.)

1970: Feb. 16, Joe Frazier KOd Jimmy Ellis, 5, NYC. (Frazier def. Ali in 15 rounds, Mar. 8, 1971, in NYC.)

1973: Jan. 22, George Foreman KOd Joe Frazier, 2, Jamaica.

1974: Oct. 30, Muhammad Ali KOd George Foreman, 8, Kinshasa, Zaire.

1978: Feb. 15, Leon Spinks def. Muhammad Ali, 15, Las Vegas. (WBC recognized Ken Norton as champion after Spinks refused to fight him before his rematch with Ali.); June 9, (WBC) Larry Holmes def. Ken Norton, 15, Las Vegas; Sept. 15, (WBA) Muhammad Ali def. Leon Spinks, 15, New Orleans. (Ali retired as champion in 1979.)

1979: Oct. 20, (WBA) John Tate def. Gerrie Coetzee, 15, Pretoria, South Africa.

1980: Mar. 31, (WBA) Mike Weaver KOd John Tate, 15, Knoxville, TN.

1982: Dec. 10, (WBA) Michael Dokes KOd Mike Weaver, 1, Las Vegas.

1983: Sept. 23, (WBA) Gerrie Coetzee KOd Michael Dokes, 10, Richfield, OH; in Dec., Larry Holmes relinquished the WBC title and was named champion of the newly formed IBF.

1984: Mar. 9, (WBC) Tim Witherspoon def. Greg Page, 12, Las Vegas; Aug. 31, (WBC) Pinklon Thomas def. Tim Witherspoon, 12, Las Vegas; Dec. 2, (WBA) Greg Page KOd Gerrie Coetzee, 8, Sun City, Bophuthatswana, South Africa.

1985: Apr. 29, (WBA) Tony Tubbs def. Greg Page, 15, Buffalo, NY; Sept. 21, (IBF) Michael Spinks def. Larry Holmes, 15, Las Vegas. (Spinks relinquished title in Feb. 1987.)

1986: Jan. 17, (WBA) Tim Witherspoon def. Tony Tubbs, 15, Atlanta, GA; Mar. 23, (WBC) Trevor Berbick def. Pinklon Thomas, 12, Miami; Nov. 22, (WBC) Mike Tyson KOd Trevor Berbick, 2, Las Vegas; Dec. 12, (WBA) James "Bonecrusher" Smith KOd Tim Witherspoon, 1, NYC.

1987: Mar. 7, (WBA, WBC) Mike Tyson def. James "Bonecrusher" Smith, 12, Las Vegas; May 30, (IBF) Tony Tucker KOd James "Buster" Douglas, 10, Las Vegas; Aug. 1, (WBA, WBC, IBF) Mike Tyson def. Tony Tucker, 12, Las Vegas. (Tyson became undisputed champion.)

1990: Feb. 11, (WBA, WBC, IBF) James "Buster" Douglas KOd Mike Tyson, 10, Tokyo; Oct. 25, (WBA, WBC, IBF) Evander Holyfield KOd James "Buster" Douglas, 3, Las Vegas.

1992: Nov. 13, (WBA, WBC, IBF) Riddick Bowe def. Evander Holyfield, 12, Las Vegas. (Lennox Lewis was later named WBC champion when Bowe refused to fight him.)

1993: Nov. 6, (WBA, IBF) Evander Holyfield def. Riddick Bowe, 12, Las Vegas.

1994: Apr. 22, (WBA, IBF) Michael Moorer def. Evander Holyfield, 12, Las Vegas; Sept. 24, (WBC) Oliver McCall KOd Lennox Lewis, 2, London; Nov. 5, (WBA, IBF) George Foreman KOd Michael Moorer, 10, Las Vegas. (In Mar. 1995, Foreman was stripped of the WBA title; he relinquished the IBF title in June.)

1995: Sept. 2, (WBC) Frank Bruno def. Oliver McCall, 12, London; Dec. 9, (IBF) Frans Botha def. Axel Schulz, 12, Las Vegas. (Botha was subsequently stripped of title.)

1996: Mar. 16, (WBC) Mike Tyson KOd Frank Bruno, 3, Las Vegas; June 22, (IBF) Michael Moorer def. Axel Schulz, 12, Dortmund, Germany; Sept. 7, (WBA, WBC) Mike Tyson KOd Bruce Seldon, 1, Las Vegas. (Tyson was subsequently stripped of WBC title.); Nov. 9, (WBA) Evander Holyfield KOd Mike Tyson, 11, Las Vegas.

1997: Feb. 7, (WBC) Lennox Lewis KOd Oliver McCall, 5, Las Vegas; Nov. 8, (IBF) Evander Holyfield def. Michael Moorer, 8, Las Vegas.

1999: Nov. 13, (WBA, WBC, IBF) Lennox Lewis def. Evander Holyfield, 12, Las Vegas. (Lewis became undisputed champion. In April 2000, Lewis was stripped of his WBA title.)

2000: Aug. 12, (WBA) Evander Holyfield def. John Ruiz, 12, Las Vegas.

2001: Mar. 3, (WBA) John Ruiz def. Evander Holyfield, 12, Las Vegas; Apr. 21, (WBC, IBF) Hasim Rahman KOd Lennox Lewis, 5, Brakpan, South Africa; Nov. 17, (WBC, IBF) Lennox Lewis KOd Hasim Rahman, 4, Las Vegas.

2002: Dec. 14, (IBF) Chris Byrd def. Evander Holyfield, 12, Atlantic City, NJ.

2003: Mar. 1, (WBA) Roy Jones Jr. def. John Ruiz, 12, Las Vegas.

2004: Feb. 20, (WBA) Ruiz gained title when Roy Jones Jr. relinquished it; Apr. 24, (WBC) Vitali Klitschko TKOd Corrie Sanders, 8, Los Angeles, to win title vacated when champ Lennox Lewis retired in Feb.

2005: Apr. 30, (WBA) James Toney def. John Ruiz, 12, NYC (Toney tested positive for steroids; title returned to Ruiz); Nov. 9, (WBC) Hasim Rahman gained title when Vitali Klitschko retired; Dec. 17, (WBA) Nikolai Valuev def. John Ruiz, 12, Berlin, Germany.

2006: Aug. 12, (WBC) Oleg Maskaev TKOd Hasim Rahman, 12, Las Vegas.; Apr. 22, (IBF) Wladimir Klitschko TKOd Chris Byrd, 7, Mannheim, Germany.

2007: Apr. 14, (WBA) Ruslan Chagaev def. Nicolay Valuev, 12, Stuttgart, Germany.

2008: Mar. 8, (WBC) Samuel Peter TKOd Oleg Maskaev, 6, Cancun, Mexico; Aug. 30, (WBA) Nikolai Valuev def. John Ruiz, 12, Berlin, Germany; Oct. 11, (WBC) Vitali Klitschko TKOd Samuel Peter, 8, Berlin, Germany; Dec. 13, (IBF) Wladimir Klitschko TKOd Hasim Rahman, 7, Mannheim, Germany; Dec. 20, (WBA) Nikolai Valuev def. Evander Holyfield, Zurich, Switzerland.

2009: Mar. 21, (WBC) Vitali Klitschko TKOd Juan Carlos Gomez, 9, Stuttgart, Germany; June 20, (IBF) Wladimir Klitschko TKOd Ruslan Chagaev, 10, Gelsenkirchen, Germany.

Other International Hall of Famers

Modern		Old-Timer		
Fred Apostoli	Beau Jack	Alberto "Baby" Arizmendi	Harry Harris	Kid Norfolk
Jackie "Kid" Berg	Nicolino Locche	Jimmy Barry	Pete Herman	Billy Petrolle
Jimmy Bivins	Duilio Loi	Panama Al Brown	Peter Jackson	Tom Sharkey
Charley Burley	Richardo Lopez	Kid Chocolate	Joe Jeanette	Jimmy Slattery
Miguel Canto	Bob Montgomery	Joe Choynski	Fidel LaBarba	Freddie Steele
Michael Carbajal	Terry Norris	Johnny Coulon	Sam Langford	William "Young" Stribling
Antonio Cervantes	Manuel Ortiz	Les Darcy	Benny Lynch	Charles "Bud" Taylor
Jeff Chandler	Laszlo Papp	Jim Driscoll	Joe Lynch	Lew Tendler
Gabriel "Flash" Elorde	Pascual Perez	Sixto Escobar	Jack McAuliffe	Pancho Villa
Khaosai Galaxy	Aaron Pryor	Frankie Genaro	Patrick "Packey"	Jimmy Wilde
Humberto Gonzalez	Albert "Chalky"	Mike Gibbons	McFarland	Kid Williams
Billy Graham	Wright	Tommy Gibbons	Sam McVey	Harry Wills
Masahiko "Fighting"	Daniel Zaragoza	George Godfrey	Charley Mitchell	Midget Wolgast
Harada	Carlos Zarate	Young Griffo	Pedro Montanez	Teddy Yarosz
			Owen Moran	

THOROUGHBRED RACING

Triple Crown Winners

Since 1920, colts have carried 126 lb in Triple Crown events; fillies, 121 lb.

(Kentucky Derby, Preakness, and Belmont Stakes)

Year	Horse	Jockey	Trainer	Year	Horse	Jockey	Trainer
1919	Sir Barton	J. Loftus	H. G. Bedwell	1946	Assault	W. Mehrtens	M. Hirsch
1930	Gallant Fox	E. Sande	J. Fitzsimmons	1948	Citation	E. Arcaro	H. A. Jones
1935	Omaha	W. Sanders	J. Fitzsimmons	1973	Secretariat	R. Turcotte	L. Laurin
1937	War Admiral	C. Kurtsinger	G. Conway	1977	Seattle Slew	J. Cruguet	W. H. Turner Jr.
1941	Whirlaway	E. Arcaro	B. A. Jones	1978	Affirmed	S. Cauthen	L. S. Barrera
1943	Count Fleet	J. Longden	G. D. Cameron				

Kentucky Derby

Churchill Downs, Louisville, KY; inaug. 1875; distance 1-1/4 mi; 1-1/2 mi until 1896. 3-year-olds.
Best time: 1:59 2/5, by Secretariat, 1973; 2009 time: 2:02 3/5.

Year	Winner	Jockey	Year	Winner	Jockey	Year	Winner	Jockey
1875	Aristides	O. Lewis	1920	Paul Jones	T. Rice	1965	Lucky Debonair	W. Shoemaker
1876	Vagrant	R. Swim	1921	Behave Yourself	C. Thompson	1966	Kauai King	D. Brumfield
1877	Baden Baden	W. Walker	1922	Morvich	A. Johnson	1967	Proud Clarion	R. Ussery
1878	Day Star	Carter	1923	Zev	E. Sande	1968	Dancer's Image#	R. Ussery
1879	Lord Murphy	C. Schauer	1924	Black Gold	J. D. Mooney	1969	Majestic Prince	W. Hartack
1880	Fonso	G. Lewis	1925	Flying Ebony	E. Sande	1970	Dust Commander	M. Manganello
1881	Hindoo	J. McLaughlin	1926	Bubbling Over	A. Johnson	1971	Canonero II	G. Avila
1882	Apollo	B. Hurd	1927	Whiskery	L. McAtee	1972	Riva Ridge	R. Turcotte
1883	Leonatus	W. Donohue	1928	Reigh Count	C. Lang	1973	Secretariat	R. Turcotte
1884	Buchanan	I. Murphy	1929	Clyde Van Dusen	L. McAtee	1974	Cannonade	A. Cordero
1885	Joe Cotton	E. Henderson	1930	Gallant Fox	E. Sande	1975	Foolish Pleasure	J. Vasquez
1886	Ben Ali	P. Duffy	1931	Twenty Grand	C. Kurtsinger	1976	Bold Forbes	A. Cordero
1887	Montrose	I. Lewis	1932	Burgoo King	E. James	1977	Seattle Slew	J. Cruguet
1888	Macbeth II	G. Covington	1933	Brokers Tip	D. Meade	1978	Affirmed	S. Cauthen
1889	Spokane	T. Kiley	1934	Cavalcade	M. Garner	1979	Spectacular Bid	R. Franklin
1890	Riley	I. Murphy	1935	Omaha	W. Saunders	1980	Genuine Risk*	J. Vasquez
1891	Kingman	I. Murphy	1936	Bold Venture	I. Hanford	1981	Pleasant Colony	J. Velasquez
1892	Azra	A. Clayton	1937	War Admiral	C. Kurtsinger	1982	Gato del Sol	E. Delahoussaye
1893	Lookout	E. Kunze	1938	Lawrin	E. Arcaro	1983	Sunny's Halo	E. Delahoussaye
1894	Chant	F. Goodale	1939	Johnstown	J. Stout	1984	Swale	L. Pincay
1895	Halma	J. Perkins	1940	Gallahadion	C. Bierman	1985	Spend a Buck	A. Cordero
1896	Ben Brush	W. Simms	1941	Whirlaway	E. Arcaro	1986	Ferdinand	W. Shoemaker
1897	Typhoon II	F. Garner	1942	Shut Out	W. D. Wright	1987	Alysheba	C. McCarron
1898	Plaudit	W. Simms	1943	Count Fleet	J. Longden	1988	Winning Colors*	G. Stevens
1899	Manuel	F. Taral	1944	Pensive	C. McCreary	1989	Sunday Silence	P. Valenzuela
1900	Lieut. Gibson	J. Boland	1945	Hoop, Jr.	E. Arcaro	1990	Unbridled	C. Perret
1901	His Eminence	J. Winkfield	1946	Assault	W. Mehrtens	1991	Strike the Gold	C. Antley
1902	Alan-a-Dale	J. Winkfield	1947	Jet Pilot	E. Guerin	1992	Lil E. Tee	P. Day
1903	Judge Himes	H. Booker	1948	Citation	E. Arcaro	1993	Sea Hero	J. Bailey
1904	Elwood	F. Prior	1949	Ponder	S. Brooks	1994	Go for Gin	C. McCarron
1905	Agile	J. Martin	1950	Middleground	W. Boland	1995	Thunder Gulch	G. Stevens
1906	Sir Huon	R. Troxler	1951	Count Turf	C. McCreary	1996	Grindstone	J. Bailey
1907	Pink Star	A. Minder	1952	Hill Gail	E. Arcaro	1997	Silver Charm	G. Stevens
1908	Stone Street	A. Pickens	1953	Dark Star	H. Moreno	1998	Real Quiet	K. Desormeaux
1909	Wintergreen	V. Powers	1954	Determine	R. York	1999	Charismatic	C. Antley
1910	Donau	F. Herbert	1955	Swaps	W. Shoemaker	2000	Fusaichi Pegasus	K. Desormeaux
1911	Meridian	G. Archibald	1956	Needles	D. Erb	2001	Monarchos	J. Chavez
1912	Worth	C. H. Shilling	1957	Iron Liege	W. Hartack	2002	War Emblem	V. Espinoza
1913	Donerail	R. Goose	1958	Tim Tam	I. Valenzuela	2003	Funny Cide	J. Santos
1914	Old Rosebud	J. McCabe	1959	Tomy Lee	W. Shoemaker	2004	Smarty Jones	S. Elliot
1915	Regret*	J. Notter	1960	Venetian Way	W. Hartack	2005	Giacomo	M. Smith
1916	George Smith	J. Loftus	1961	Carry Back	J. Sellers	2006	Barbaro	E. Prado
1917	Omar Khayyam	C. Borel	1962	Decidedly	W. Hartack	2007	Street Sense	C. Borel
1918	Exterminator	W. Knapp	1963	Chateaugay	B. Baeza	2008	Big Brown	K. Desormeaux
1919	Sir Barton	J. Loftus	1964	Northern Dancer	W. Hartack	2009	Mine That Bird	C. Borel

*Regret, Genuine Risk, and Winning Colors are the only fillies to have won the Derby. #Dancer's Image was disqualified from purse money after tests disclosed that he had run with a pain-killing drug, phenylbutazone, in his system. All wagers were paid on Dancer's Image. Forward Pass was awarded first place money. Only two jockeys have won the Kentucky Derby five times: Eddie Arcaro, 1938, 1941, 1945, 1948, and 1952; and Bill Hartack, 1957, 1960, 1962, 1964, and 1969. It was won four times by Willie Shoemaker, 1955, 1959, 1965, and 1986; and three times by each of 4 jockeys: Isaac Murphy, 1884, 1890, and 1891; Earle Sande, 1923, 1925, and 1930; Angel Cordero, 1974, 1976, and 1985; Gary Stevens, 1988, 1995, and 1997; and Kent Desormeaux, 1998, 2000, and 2008.

Fastest Winning Times for the Kentucky Derby

(Kentucky Derby times measured in fifths of a second according to tradition.)

Time	Horse	Jockey	Year	Time	Horse	Jockey	Year
1m. 59 2/5 s.	Secretariat	Ron Turcotte	1973	2m. 1 1/5 s.	Thunder Gulch	Gary Stevens	1995
1m. 59 4/5 s.	Monarchos	Jorge Chavez	2001		Affirmed	Steve Cauthen	1978
2m.	Northern Dancer	Bill Hartack	1964		Lucky Debonair	Bill Shoemaker	1965
2m. 1/5 s.	Spend a Buck	Angel Cordero Jr.	1985	2m. 1 2/5 s.	Whirlaway	Eddie Arcaro	1941
2m. 2/5 s.	Decidedly	Bill Hartack	1962		Barbaro	Edgar Prado	2006
2m. 3/5 s.	Proud Clarion	Robert Ussery	1967	2m. 1 3/5 s.	Bold Forbes	Angel Cordero Jr.	1976
2m. 1 s.	Funny Cide	Jose Santos	2003		Hill Gail	Eddie Arcaro	1952
	War Emblem	Victor Espinoza	2002		Middleground	William Boland	1950
	Fusaichi Pegasus	Kent Desormeaux	2000				
	Grindstone	Jerry Bailey	1996				

Preakness Stakes

Pimlico Race Course, Baltimore, MD; inaug. 1873; distance 1-3/16 mi. 3-year-olds.
Best time: 1:53 2/5, by Tank's Prospect (1985), Louis Quatorze (1996), and Curlin (2007); 2009 time: 1:55.08.

Year	Winner	Jockey	Year	Winner	Jockey	Year	Winner	Jockey
1873	Survivor	G. Barbee	1920	Man o' War	C. Kummer	1965	Tom Rolfe	R. Turcotte
1874	Culpepper	M. Donohue	1921	Broomspun	F. Coltiletti	1966	Kauai King	D. Brumfield
1875	Tom Ochiltree	L. Hughes	1922	Pillory	L. Morris	1967	Damascus	W. Shoemaker
1876	Shirley	G. Barbee	1923	Vigil	B. Marinelli	1968	Forward Pass	I. Valenzuela
1877	Cloverbrook	C. Holloway	1924	Nellie Morse	J. Merimee	1969	Majestic Prince	W. Hartack
1878	Duke of Magenta	C. Holloway	1925	Coventry	C. Kummer	1970	Personality	E. Belmonte
1879	Harold	L. Hughes	1926	Display	J. Malben	1971	Canonero II	G. Avila
1880	Grenada	L. Hughes	1927	Bostonian	A. Abel	1972	Bee Bee Bee	E. Nelson
1881	Saunterer	W. Costello	1928	Victorian	R. Workman	1973	Secretariat	R. Turcotte
1882	Vanguard	W. Costello	1929	Dr. Freeland	L. Schaefer	1974	Little Current	M. Rivera
1883	Jacobus	G. Barbee	1930	Gallant Fox	E. Sande	1975	Master Derby	D. McHargue
1884	Knight of Ellerslie	S. H. Fisher	1931	Mate	G. Ellis	1976	Elocutionist	J. Lively
1885	Tecumseh	J. McLaughlin	1932	Burgoo King	E. James	1977	Seattle Slew	J. Cruguet
1886	The Bard	S. H. Fisher	1933	Head Play	C. Kurtsinger	1978	Affirmed	S. Cauthen
1887	Dunboyne	W. Donohue	1934	High Quest	R. Jones	1979	Spectacular Bid	R. Franklin
1888	Refund	F. Littlefield	1935	Omaha	W. Saunders	1980	Codex	A. Cordero
1889	Buddhist	G. Anderson	1936	Bold Venture	G. Woolf	1981	Pleasant Colony	J. Velasquez
1890	Montague	W. Martin	1937	War Admiral	C. Kurtsinger	1982	Aloma's Ruler	J. Kaenel
1894	Assignee	F. Taral	1938	Dauber	M. Peters	1983	Deputed	
1895	Belmar	F. Taral	1939	Challedon	G. Seabo		Testamony	D. Miller
1896	Margrave	H. Griffin	1940	Bimelech	F. A. Smith	1984	Gate Dancer	A. Cordero
1897	Paul Kauvar	C. Thorpe	1941	Whirlaway	E. Arcaro	1985	Tank's Prospect	P. Day
1898	Sly Fox	W. Simms	1942	Alsab	B. James	1986	Snow Chief	A. Solis
1899	Half Time	R. Clawson	1943	Count Fleet	J. Longden	1987	Alysheba	C. McCarron
1900	Hindus	H. Spencer	1944	Pensive	C. McCreary	1988	Risen Star	E. Delahoussaye
1901	The Parader	F. Landry	1945	Polynesian	W. D. Wright	1989	Sunday Silence	P. Valenzuela
1902	Old England	L. Jackson	1946	Assault	W. Mehrtens	1990	Summer Squall	P. Day
1903	Flocarline	W. Gannon	1947	Faultless	D. Dodson	1991	Hansel	J. Bailey
1904	Bryn Mawr	E. Hildebrand	1948	Citation	E. Arcaro	1992	Pine Bluff	C. McCarron
1905	Cairngorm	W. Davis	1949	Capot	T. Atkinson	1993	Prairie Bayou	M. Smith
1906	Whimsical	W. Miller	1950	Hill Prince	E. Arcaro	1994	Tabasco Cat	P. Day
1907	Don Enrique	G. Mountain	1951	Bold	E. Arcaro	1995	Timber Country	P. Day
1908	Royal Tourist	E. Dugan	1952	Blue Man	C. McCreary	1996	Louis Quatorze	P. Day
1909	Effendi	W. Doyle	1953	Native Dancer	E. Guerin	1997	Silver Charm	G. Stevens
1910	Layminster	R. Estep	1954	Hasty Road	J. Adams	1998	Real Quiet	K. Desormeaux
1911	Watervale	E. Dugan	1955	Nashua	E. Arcaro	1999	Charismatic	C. Antley
1912	Colonel Holloway	C. Turner	1956	Fabius	W. Hartack	2000	Red Bullet	J. Bailey
1913	Buskin	J. Butwell	1957	Bold Ruler	E. Arcaro	2001	Point Given	G. Stevens
1914	Holiday	A. Schuttinger	1958	Tim Tam	I. Valenzuela	2002	War Emblem	V. Espinoza
1915	Rhine Maiden	D. Hoffman	1959	Royal Orbit	W. Harmatz	2003	Funny Cide	J. Santos
1916	Damrosch	L. McAtee	1960	Bally Ache	R. Ussery	2004	Smarty Jones	S. Elliot
1917	Kalitan	E. Haynes	1961	Carry Back	J. Sellers	2005	Afleet Alex	J. Rose
1918*	War Cloud	J. Loftus	1962	Greek Money	J. L. Rotz	2006	Bernardini	J. Castellano
	Jack Hare Jr.	C. Peak	1963	Candy Spots	W. Shoemaker	2007	Curlin	R. Albarado
1919	Sir Barton	J. Loftus	1964	Northern Dancer	W. Hartack	2008	Big Brown	K. Desormeaux
						2009	Rachel Alexandra	C. Borel

*Horses ran in 2 divisions.

Belmont Stakes

Belmont Park, Elmont, NY; inaug. 1867; distance 1-1/2 mi. 3-year-olds. Best time: 2:24, Secretariat, 1973; 2009 time: 2:27.54.

Year	Winner	Jockey	Year	Winner	Jockey	Year	Winner	Jockey
1867	Ruthless	J. Gilpatrick	1902	Masterman	J. Bullman	1939	Johnstown	J. Stout
1868	General Duke	R. Swim	1903	Africander	J. Bullman	1940	Bimelech	F. A. Smith
1869	Fenian	C. Miller	1904	Delhi	G. Odom	1941	Whirlaway	E. Arcaro
1870	Kingfisher	W. Dick	1905	Tanya	E. Hildebrand	1942	Shut Out	E. Arcaro
1871	Harry Bassett	W. Miller	1906	Burgomaster	L. Lyne	1943	Count Fleet	J. Longden
1872	Joe Daniels	J. Rowe	1907	Peter Pan	G. Mountain	1944	Bounding Home	G. L. Smith
1873	Springbok	J. Rowe	1908	Colin	J. Notter	1945	Pavot	E. Arcaro
1874	Saxon	G. Barbee	1909	Joe Madden	E. Dugan	1946	Assault	W. Mehrtens
1875	Calvin	R. Swim	1910	Sweep	J. Butwell	1947	Phalanx	R. Donoso
1876	Algerine	W. Donohue	1913	Prince Eugene	R. Troxler	1948	Citation	E. Arcaro
1877	Cloverbrook	C. Holloway	1914	Luke McLuke	M. Buxton	1949	Capot	T. Atkinson
1878	Duke of Magenta	L. Hughes	1915	The Finn	G. Byrne	1950	Middleground	W. Boland
1879	Spendthrift	S. Evans	1916	Friar Rock	E. Haynes	1951	Counterpoint	D. Gorman
1880	Grenada	L. Hughes	1917	Hourless	J. Butwell	1952	One Count	E. Arcaro
1881	Saunterer	T. Costello	1918	Johren	F. Robinson	1953	Native Dancer	E. Guerin
1882	Forester	J. McLaughlin	1919	Sir Barton	J. Loftus	1954	High Gun	E. Guerin
1883	George Kinney	J. McLaughlin	1920	Man o' War	C. Kummer	1955	Nashua	E. Arcaro
1884	Panique	J. McLaughlin	1921	Grey Lag	E. Sande	1956	Needles	D. Erb
1885	Tyrant	P. Duffy	1922	Pillory	C. H. Miller	1957	Gallant Man	W. Shoemaker
1886	Inspector	B. J. McLaughlin	1923	Zev	E. Sande	1958	Cavan	P. Anderson
1887	Hanover	J. McLaughlin	1924	Mad Play	E. Sande	1959	Sword Dancer	W. Shoemaker
1888	Sir Dixon	J. McLaughlin	1925	American Flag	A. Johnson	1960	Celtic Ash	W. Hartack
1889	Eric	W. Hayward	1926	Crusader	A. Johnson	1961	Sherluck	B. Baeza
1890	Burlington	S. Barnes	1927	Chance Shot	E. Sande	1962	Jaipur	W. Shoemaker
1891	Foxford	E. Garrison	1928	Vito	C. Kummer	1963	Chateaugay	B. Baeza
1892	Patron	W. Hayward	1929	Blue Larkspur	M. Garner	1964	Quadrangle	M. Ycaza
1893	Comanche	W. Simms	1930	Gallant Fox	E. Sande	1965	Hail to All	J. Sellers
1894	Henry of Navarre	W. Simms	1931	Twenty Grand	C. Kurtsinger	1966	Amberoid	W. Boland
1895	Belmar	F. Taral	1932	Faireno	T. Malley	1967	Damascus	W. Shoemaker
1896	Hastings	H. Griffin	1933	Hurryoff	M. Garner	1968	Stage Door Johnny	H. Gustines
1897	Scottish Chieftain	J. Scherrer	1934	Peace Chance	W. D. Wright	1969	Arts and Letters	B. Baeza
1898	Bowling Brook	F. Littlefield	1935	Omaha	W. Saunders	1970	High Echelon	J. L. Rotz
1899	Jean Bereaud	R. R. Clawson	1936	Granville	J. Stout	1971	Pass Catcher	W. Blum
1900	Ildrim	N. Turner	1937	War Admiral	C. Kurtsinger	1972	Riva Ridge	R. Turcotte
1901	Commando	H. Spencer	1938	Pasteurized	J. Stout	1973	Secretariat	R. Turcotte

Year	Winner	Jockey	Year	Winner	Jockey	Year	Winner	Jockey
1974	Little Current	M. Rivera	1987	Bet Twice	C. Perret	1998	Victory Gallop	G. Stevens
1975	Avatar	W. Shoemaker	1988	Risen Star	E. Delahoussaye	1999	Lemon Drop Kid	J. Santos
1976	Bold Forbes	A. Cordero	1989	Easy Goer	P. Day	2000	Commendable	P. Day
1977	Seattle Slew	J. Cruguet	1990	Go and Go	M. Kinane	2001	Point Given	G. Stevens
1978	Affirmed	S. Cauthen	1991	Hansel	J. Bailey	2002	Sarava	E. Prado
1979	Coastal	R. Hernandez	1992	A.P. Indy	E. Delahoussaye	2003	Empire Maker	J. Bailey
1980	Temperence Hill	E. Maple	1993	Colonial Affair	J. Krone	2004	Birdstone	E. Prado
1981	Summing	G. Martens	1994	Tabasco Cat	P. Day	2005	Afleet Alex	J. Rose
1982	Conquistador Cielo	L. Pincay	1995	Thunder Gulch	G. Stevens	2006	Jazil	F. Jara
1983	Caveat	L. Pincay	1996	Editor's Note	R. Douglas	2007	Rags to Riches	J. Velazquez
1984	Swale	L. Pincay	1997	Touch Gold	C. McCarron	2008	Da' Tara	A. Garcia
1985	Creme Fraiche	E. Maple				2009	Summer Bird	K. Desormeaux
1986	Danzig Connection	C. McCarron						

Annual Leading Jockey — Money Won[1]

(as of Dec. 31, 2008)

Year	Jockey	Earnings	Year	Jockey	Earnings	Year	Jockey	Earnings
1957	Bill Hartack	$3,060,501	1975	Braulio Baeza	$3,695,198	1992	Kent Desormeaux	$14,193,006
1958	Willie Shoemaker	2,961,693	1976	Angel Cordero Jr.	4,709,500	1993	Mike Smith	14,024,815
1959	Willie Shoemaker	2,843,133	1977	Steve Cauthen	6,151,750	1994	Mike Smith	15,979,820
1960	Willie Shoemaker	2,123,961	1978	Darrel McHargue	6,029,885	1995	Jerry Bailey	16,311,876
1961	Willie Shoemaker	2,690,819	1979	Laffit Pincay Jr.	8,193,535	1996	Jerry Bailey	19,465,376
1962	Willie Shoemaker	2,916,844	1980	Chris McCarron	7,663,300	1997	Jerry Bailey	18,320,743
1963	Willie Shoemaker	2,526,925	1981	Chris McCarron	8,397,604	1998	Gary Stevens	19,622,855
1964	Willie Shoemaker	2,649,553	1982	Angel Cordero Jr.	9,483,590	1999	Pat Day	18,092,845
1965	Braulio Baeza	2,582,702	1983	Angel Cordero Jr.	10,116,697	2000	Pat Day	17,479,838
1966	Braulio Baeza	2,951,022	1984	Chris McCarron	12,045,813	2001	Jerry Bailey	22,597,720
1967	Braulio Baeza	3,088,888	1985	Laffit Pincay Jr.	13,353,299	2002	Jerry Bailey	22,871,814
1968	Braulio Baeza	2,835,108	1986	Jose Santos	11,329,297	2003	Jerry Bailey	22,829,570
1969	Jorge Velasquez	2,542,315	1987	Jose Santos	12,375,433	2004	John R. Velazquez	22,248,661
1970	Laffit Pincay Jr.	2,626,526	1988	Jose Santos	14,877,298	2005	John R. Velazquez	20,770,272
1971	Laffit Pincay Jr.	3,784,377	1989	Jose Santos	13,838,389	2006	Edgar Prado	19,604,413
1972	Laffit Pincay Jr.	3,225,827	1990	Gary Stevens	13,881,198	2007	Garrett K. Gomez	23,740,421
1973	Laffit Pincay Jr.	4,093,492	1991	Chris McCarron	14,441,083	2008	Garrett K. Gomez	23,344,351
1974	Laffit Pincay Jr.	4,251,060						

(1) Total earnings for all horses that jockey raced in year listed; does not reflect jockey's earnings.

Breeders' Cup World Thoroughbred Championships

The Breeders' Cup was inaugurated in 1984 and through 2006 consisted of seven races at one track on one day to determine thoroughbred racing's champion contenders. In 2007, it expanded to two days, and three new races debuted: the Filly and Mare Sprint, won in 2007 by Maryfield (jockey: E. Trujillo) and in 2008 by Ventura (G. Gomez); the Juvenile Turf, won in 2007 by Nownownow (J. Leparoux) and 2008 by Donativum (F. Dettori); and the Dirt Mile, won in 2007 by Corinthian (K. Desormeaux) and 2008 by Albertus Maximus (G. Gomez). In 2008, a "Ladies' Day" for fillies and four more races debuted: Turf Sprint, won by Desert Code (R. Migliore); Marathon, won by Muhannak (P. Smullen); Juvenile Fillies Turf, won by Maram (J. Lezcano). The Ladies' Classic replaced the race formerly known as Distaff. The Breeders' Cup has been held at the following locations:

1984 Hollywood Park, CA	1990 Belmont Park, NY	1996 Woodbine Racetrack, ON	2002 Arlington Park, IL
1985 Aqueduct Racetrack, NY	1991 Churchill Downs, KY	1997 Hollywood Park, CA	2003 Santa Anita Park, CA
1986 Santa Anita Park, CA	1992 Gulfstream Park, FL	1998 Churchill Downs, KY	2004 Lone Star Park, TX
1987 Hollywood Park, CA	1993 Santa Anita Park, CA	1999 Gulfstream Park, FL	2005 Belmont Park, NY
1988 Churchill Downs, KY	1994 Churchill Downs, KY	2000 Churchill Downs, KY	2006 Churchill Downs, KY
1989 Gulfstream Park, FL	1995 Belmont Park, NY	2001 Belmont Park, NY	2007 Monmouth Park, NJ
			2008 Santa Anita Park, CA

Classic

Distance: 1-1/4 mi.

Year	Horse	Jockey	Year	Horse	Jockey	Year	Horse	Jockey
1984	Wild Again	P. Day	1993	Arcangues	J. Bailey	2001	Tiznow	C. McCarron
1985	Proud Truth	J. Velasquez	1994	Concern	J. Bailey	2002	Volponi	P. Johnson
1986	Skywalker	L. Pincay Jr.	1995	Cigar	J. Bailey	2003	Pleasantly Perfect	A. Solis
1987	Ferdinand	W. Shoemaker	1996	Alphabet Soup	C. McCarron	2004	Ghostzapper	J. Castellano
1988	Alysheba	C. McCarron	1997	Skip Away	M. Smith	2005	Saint Liam	J. Bailey
1989	Sunday Silence	C. McCarron	1998	Awesome Again	P. Day	2006	Invasor	F. Jara
1990	Unbridled	P. Day	1999	Cat Thief	P. Day	2007	Curlin	R. Albarado
1991	Black Tie Affair	J. Bailey	2000	Tiznow	C. McCarron	2008	Raven's Pass	F. Dettori
1992	A.P. Indy	E. Delahoussaye						

Juvenile

Distances: 1 mi 1984-85, 1987; 1-1/16 mi 1986 and since 1988.

Year	Horse	Jockey	Year	Horse	Jockey	Year	Horse	Jockey
1984	Chief's Crown	D. MacBeth	1992	Gilded Time	C. McCarron	2000	Macho Uno	J. Bailey
1985	Tasso	L. Pincay Jr.	1993	Brocco	G. Stevens	2001	Johannesburg	M. Kinane
1986	Capote	L. Pincay Jr.	1994	Timber Country	P. Day	2002	Vindication	M. Smith
1987	Success Express	J. Santos	1995	Unbridled's Song	M. Smith	2003	Action This Day	D. Flores
1988	Is It True	L. Pincay Jr.	1996	Boston Harbor	J. Bailey	2004	Wilko	F. Dettori
1989	Rhythm	C. Perret	1997	Favorite Trick	P. Day	2005	Stevie Wonderboy	G. Gomez
1990	Fly So Free	J. Santos	1998	Answer Lively	J. Bailey	2006	Street Sense	C. Borel
1991	Arazi	P. Valenzuela	1999	Anees	G. Stevens	2007	War Pass	C. Velasquez
						2008	Midshipman	G. Gomez

Juvenile Fillies

Distances: 1 mi 1984-85, 1987; 1-1/16 mi 1986 and since 1988. Outstandingly won the 1984 race by disqualification.

Year	Horse	Jockey	Year	Horse	Jockey	Year	Horse	Jockey
1984	Outstandingly	W. Guerra	1993	Phone Chatter	L. Pincay Jr.	2001	Tempera	D. Flores
1985	Twilight Ridge	J. Velasquez	1994	Flanders	P. Day	2002	Storm Flag Flying	J. Velazquez
1986	Brave Raj	P. Valenzuela	1995	My Flag	J. Bailey	2003	Halfbridled	J. Krone
1987	Epitome	P. Day	1996	Storm Song	C. Perret	2004	Sweet Catomine	C. Nakatani
1988	Open Mind	A. Cordero Jr.	1997	Countess Diana	S. Sellers	2005	Folklore	E. Prado
1989	Go for Wand	R. Romero	1998	Silverbulletday	G. Stevens	2006	Dreaming of Anna	R. Douglas
1990	Meadow Star	J. Santos	1999	Cash Run	J. Bailey	2007	Indian Blessing	G. Gomez
1991	Pleasant Stage	E. Delahoussaye	2000	Caressing	J. Velazquez	2008	Stardom Bound	M. Smith
1992	Eliza	P. Valenzuela						

Sprint
Distance: 6 furlongs.

Year	Horse	Jockey	Year	Horse	Jockey	Year	Horse	Jockey
1984	Eillo	C. Perret	1993	Cardmania	E. Delahoussaye	2001	Squirtle Squirt	J. Bailey
1985	Precisionist	C. McCarron	1994	Cherokee Run	M. Smith	2002	Orientate	J. Bailey
1986	Smile	J. Vasquez	1995	Desert Stormer	K. Desormeaux	2003	Cajun Beat	C. Velasquez
1987	Very Subtle	P. Valenzuela	1996	Lit De Justice	C. Nakatani	2004	Speightstown	J. Velazquez
1988	Gulch	A. Cordero Jr.	1997	Elmhurst	C. Nakatani	2005	Silver Train	E. Prado
1989	Dancing Spree	A. Cordero Jr.	1998	Reraise	C. Nakatani	2006	Thor's Echo	C. Nakatani
1990	Safely Kept	C. Perret	1999	Artax	J. Chaves	2007	Midnight Lute	G. Gomez
1991	Sheikh Albadou	P. Eddery	2000	Kona Gold	A. Solis	2008	Midnight Lute	G. Gomez
1992	Thirty Slews	E. Delahoussaye						

Mile

Year	Horse	Jockey	Year	Horse	Jockey	Year	Horse	Jockey
1984	Royal Heroine	F. Toro	1993	Lure	M. Smith	2001	Val Royal	J. Valdivia Jr.
1985	Cozzene	W. Guerra	1994	Barathea	L. Dettori	2002	Domedriver	T. Thulliez
1986	Last Tycoon	Y. St.-Martin	1995	Ridgewood Pearl	J. Murtagh	2003	Six Perfections	J. Jacques
1987	Miesque	F. Head	1996	Da Hoss	G. Stevens	2004	Singletary	D. Flores
1988	Miesque	F. Head	1997	Spinning World	C. Asmussen	2005	Artie Schiller	G. Gomez
1989	Steinlen	J. Santos	1998	Da Hoss	J. Velazquez	2006	Miesque's Approval	E. Castro
1990	Royal Academy	L. Piggott	1999	Silic	C. Nakatani	2007	Kip Deville	C. Velasquez
1991	Opening Verse	P. Valenzuela	2000	War Chant	G. Stevens	2008	Goldikova	O. Peslier
1992	Lure	M. Smith						

Filly and Mare Turf
Distances: 1-3/8 mi 1999-2000, 2004, 2006-07; 1-1/4 mi 2001-03, 2005.

Year	Horse	Jockey	Year	Horse	Jockey	Year	Horse	Jockey
1999	Soaring Softly	J. Bailey	2003	Islington	K. Fallon	2006	Ouija Board (GB)	F. Dettori
2000	Perfect Sting	J. Bailey	2004	Ouija Board	K. Fallon	2007	Lahudood	A. Garcia
2001	Banks Hill	O. Peslier	2005	Intercontinental	R. Bejarano	2008	Forever Together	J. Leparoux
2002	Starine	J. Velazquez						

Ladies' Classic
Distances: 1-1/4 mi 1984-87; 1-1/8 mi since 1988. Race known as Distaff, 1984-2007.

Year	Horse	Jockey	Year	Horse	Jockey	Year	Horse	Jockey
1984	Princess Rooney	E. Delahoussaye	1993	Hollywood Wildcat	E. Delahoussaye	2001	Unbridled Elaine	P. Day
1985	Life's Magic	A. Cordero Jr.	1994	One Dreamer	G. Stevens	2002	Azeri	M. Smith
1986	Lady's Secret	P. Day	1995	Inside Information	M. Smith	2003	Adoration	P. Valenzuela
1987	Sacahuista	R. Romero	1996	Jewel Princess	C. Nakatani	2004	Ashado	J. Velazquez
1988	Personal Ensign	R. Romero	1997	Ajina	M. Smith	2005	Pleasant Home	C. Velasquez
1989	Bayakoa	L. Pincay Jr.	1998	Escena	G. Stevens	2006	Round Pond	E. Prado
1990	Bayakoa	L. Pincay Jr.	1999	Beautiful Pleasure	J. Chaves	2007	Ginger Punch	R. Bejarano
1991	Dance Smartly	P. Day	2000	Spain	V. Espinoza	2008	Zenyatta	M. Smith
1992	Paseana	C. McCarron						

Turf
Distance: 1-1/2 mi.

Year	Horse	Jockey	Year	Horse	Jockey	Year	Horse	Jockey
1984	Lashkari	Y. St.-Martin	1992	Fraise	P. Valenzuela	2001	Fantastic Light	L. Dettori
1985	Pebbles	P. Eddery	1993	Kotashaan	K. Desormeaux	2002	High Chaparral	M. Kinane
1986	Manila	J. Santos	1994	Tikkanen	M. Smith	2003	(tie) High Chaparral	M. Kinane
1987	Theatrical	P. Day	1995	Northern Spur	C. McCarron		Johar	A. Solis
1988	Great Communicator	R. Sibille	1996	Pilsudski	W. Swinburn	2004	Better Talk Now	R. Dominguez
1989	Prized	E. Delahoussaye	1997	Chief Bearhart	J. Santos	2005	Shirocco	C. Soumillon
1990	In The Wings	G. Stevens	1998	Buck's Boy	S. Sellers	2006	Red Rocks	F. Dettori
1991	Miss Alleged	E. Legrix	1999	Daylami	L. Dettori	2007	English Channel	J. Velasquez
			2000	Kalanisi	J. Murtagh	2008	Conduit	R. Moore

Eclipse Awards
The Eclipse Awards, honoring the Horse of the Year and other champions of the sport, began in 1971 and are sponsored by the *Daily Racing Form*, the National Thoroughbred Racing Association, and the National Turf Writers Assn. Prior to 1971, the *DRF* (1936-70) and the NTRA (1950-70) issued separate selections for Horse of the Year.

Eclipse Awards for 2008
Horse of the Year: Curlin
2-year-old male: Midshipman
2-year-old female: Stardom Bound
3-year-old male: Big Brown
3-year-old female: Proud Spell
Older male (4-year-old+): Curlin

Older female (4-year-old+): Zenyatta
Male sprinter: Benny the Bull
Female sprinter: Indian Blessing
Male turf horse: Conduit
Female turf horse: Forever Together
Steeplechase horse: Good Night Shirt

Trainer: Steve Asmussen
Jockey: Garrett Gomez
Apprentice jockey: Pascacio Lopez
Breeder: Adena Springs
Owner: Stronach Stable

Horse of the Year, 1936-2008

1936 Granville	1948 Citation	1958 Round Table	1969 Arts and Letters
1937 War Admiral	1949 Capot	1959 Sword Dancer	1970 Fort Marcy (DRF)
1938 Seabiscuit	1950 Hill Prince	1960 Kelso	Personality (TRA)
1939 Challedon	1951 Counterpoint	1961 Kelso	1971 Ack Ack
1940 Challedon	1952 One Count (DRF)	1962 Kelso	1972 Secretariat
1941 Whirlaway	Native Dancer (TRA)	1963 Kelso	1973 Secretariat
1942 Whirlaway	1953 Tom Fool	1964 Kelso	1974 Forego
1943 Count Fleet	1954 Native Dancer	1965 Roman Brother (DRF)	1975 Forego
1944 Twilight Tear	1955 Nashua	Moccasin (TRA)	1976 Forego
1945 Busher	1956 Swaps	1966 Buckpasser	1977 Seattle Slew
1946 Assault	1957 Bold Ruler (DRF)	1967 Damascus	1978 Affirmed
1947 Armed	Dedicate (TRA)	1968 Dr. Fager	1979 Affirmed

1980 Spectacular Bid	1988 Alysheba	1995 Cigar	2002 Azeri
1981 John Henry	1989 Sunday Silence	1996 Cigar	2003 Mineshaft
1982 Conquistador Cielo	1990 Criminal Type	1997 Favorite Trick	2004 Ghostzapper
1983 All Along	1991 Black Tie Affair	1998 Skip Away	2005 Saint Liam
1984 John Henry	1992 A.P. Indy	1999 Charismatic	2006 Invasor
1985 Spend A Buck	1993 Kotashaan	2000 Tiznow	2007 Curlin
1986 Lady's Secret	1994 Holy Bull	2001 Point Given	2008 Curlin
1987 Ferdinand			

HARNESS RACING
Harness Horse of the Year
(Chosen by the U.S. Trotting Assn. and the U.S. Harness Writers Assn.)

1947 Victory Song	1963 Speedy Scot	1979 Niatross	1994 Cam's Card Shark
1948 Rodney	1964 Bret Hanover	1980 Niatross	1995 CR Kay Suzie
1949 Good Time	1965 Bret Hanover	1981 Fan Hanover	1996 Continental Victory
1950 Proximity	1966 Bret Hanover	1982 Cam Fella	1997 Malabar Man
1951 Pronto Don	1967 Nevele Pride	1983 Cam Fella	1998 Moni Maker
1952 Good Time	1968 Nevele Pride	1984 Fancy Crown	1999 Moni Maker
1953 Hi Lo's Forbes	1969 Nevele Pride	1985 Nihilator	2000 Gallo Blue Chip
1954 Stenographer	1970 Fresh Yankee	1986 Forrest Skipper	2001 Bunny Lake
1955 Scott Frost	1971 Albatross	1987 Mack Lobell	2002 Real Desire
1956 Scott Frost	1972 Albatross	1988 Mack Lobell	2003 No Pan Intended
1957 Torpid	1973 Sir Dalrae	1989 Matt's Scooter	2004 Rainbow Blue
1958 Emily's Pride	1974 Delmonica Hanover	1990 Beach Towel	2005 Rocknroll Hanover
1959 Bye Bye Byrd	1975 Savoir	1991 Precious Bunny	2006 Glidemaster
1960 Adios Butler	1976 Keystone Ore	1992 Artsplace	2007 Donato Hanover
1961 Adios Butler	1977 Green Speed	1993 Staying Together	2008 Somebeachsomewhere
1962 Su Mac Lad	1978 Abercrombie		

The Hambletonian (3-year-old trotters), 1965-2009

Year	Winner	Driver	Year	Winner	Driver
1965	Egyptian Candor	Del Cameron	1988	Armbro Goal	John Campbell
1966	Kerry Way	Frank Ervin	1989	Park Avenue Joe	Ron Waples
1967	Speedy Streak	Del Cameron	1990	Harmonious	John Campbell
1968	Nevele Pride	Stanley Dancer	1991	Giant Victory	Jack Moiseyev
1969	Lindy's Pride	Howard Beissinger	1992	Alf Palema	Mickey McNicholl
1970	Timothy T.	John Simpson Sr.	1993	American Winner	Ron Pierce
1971	Speedy Crown	Howard Beissinger	1994	Victory Dream	Michel Lachance
1972	Super Bowl	Stanley Dancer	1995	Tagliabue	John Campbell
1973	Flirth	Ralph Baldwin	1996	Continental Victory	Michel Lachance
1974	Christopher T	Bill Haughton	1997	Malabar Man	Malvern Burroughs
1975	Bonefish	Stanley Dancer	1998	Muscles Yankee	John Campbell
1976	Steve Lobell	Bill Haughton	1999	Self Possessed	Mike Lachance
1977	Green Speed	Bill Haughton	2000	Yankee Paco	Trevor Ritchie
1978	Speedy Somolli	Howard Beissinger	2001	Scarlet Knight	Stefan Melander
1979	Legend Hanover	George Sholty	2002	Chip Chip Hooray	Eric Ledford
1980	Burgomeister	Bill Haughton	2003	Amigo Hall	Mike Lachance
1981	Shiaway St. Pat	Ray Remmen	2004	Windsong's Legacy	Trond Smedshammer
1982	Speed Bowl	Tommy Haughton	2005	Vivid Photo	Roger Hammer
1983	Duenna	Stanley Dancer	2006	Glidemaster	John Campbell
1984	Historic Freight	Ben Webster	2007	Donato Hanover	Ron Pierce
1985	Prakas	Bill O'Donnell	2008	Deweycheatumnhowe	Ray Schnittker
1986	Nuclear Kosmos	Ulf Thoresen	2009	Muscle Hill	Brian Sears
1987	Mack Lobell	John Campbell			

BOWLING
Professional Bowlers Association
PBA Tournament of Champions, 1965-2009[1]

Year	Winner	Year	Winner	Year	Winner	Year	Winner
1965	Billy Hardwick	1977	Mike Berlin	1987	Pete Weber	1998	Bryan Goebel
1966	Wayne Zahn	1978	Earl Anthony	1988	Mark Williams	1999	Jason Couch
1967	Jim Stefanich	1979	George Pappas	1989	Del Ballard Jr.	2000	Jason Couch
1968	Dave Davis	1980	Wayne Webb	1990	Dave Ferraro	2002	Jason Couch
1969	Jim Godman	1981	Steve Cook	1991	David Ozio	2003	Patrick Healey Jr.
1970	Don Johnson	1982	Mike Durbin	1992	Marc McDowell	2005	Steve Jaros
1971	Johnny Petraglia	1983	Joe Berardi	1993	George Branham III	2006	Chris Barnes
1972	Mike Durbin	1984	Mike Durbin	1994	Norm Duke	2007	Tommy Jones
1973	Jim Godman	1985	Mark Williams	1996	Dave D'Entremont	2008	Michael Haugen Jr.
1974	Earl Anthony	1986	Marshall Holman	1997	John Gant	2009	Patrick Allen
1975	Dave Davis						
1976	Marshall Holman						

(1) No tournament held in 2001; the tournament now takes place in Apr. at the end of the PBA season (previously held in Dec.).

PBA Hall of Fame — Performance

Bill Allen	Don Carter	Billy Hardwick	George Pappas	Brian Voss
Glenn Allison	Pat Colwell	Marshall Hollman	Johnny Petraglia	Wayne Webb
Earl Anthony	Steve Cook	Tommy Hudson	Dick Ritger	Dick Weber
Mike Aulby	Dave Davis	Dave Husted	Mark Roth	Pete Weber
Joe Berardi	Gary Dickinson	Don Johnson	Carmen Salvino	Billy Welu
Ray Bluth	Mike Durbin	Joe Joseph	Ernie Schlegel	Mark Williams
Parker Bohn III	Buzz Fazio	Larry Laub	Harry Smith	Walter Ray Williams Jr.
Roy Buckley	Dave Ferraro	Amleto Monacelli	Dave Soutar	Wayne Zahn
Nelson Burton Jr.	Jim Godman	David Ozio	Jim Stefanich	

PBA Leading Money Winners

Total winnings are from PBA, American Bowling Congress (ABC) Masters, and Bowling Proprietors' Assn. of America (BPAA) all-star tournaments only. In 2001, the PBA began an Oct.-Apr. season schedule. After 2000, year shown is year the season ended.

Year	Bowler	Amount	Year	Bowler	Amount	Year	Bowler	Amount
1962	Don Carter	$49,972	1978	Mark Roth	$134,500	1994	Norm Duke	$273,753
1963	Dick Weber	46,333	1979	Mark Roth	124,517	1995	Mike Aulby	219,792
1964	Bob Strampe	33,592	1980	Wayne Webb	116,700	1996	Walter Ray Williams Jr.	241,330
1965	Dick Weber	47,674	1981	Earl Anthony	164,735	1997	Walter Ray Williams Jr.	240,544
1966	Wayne Zahn	54,720	1982	Earl Anthony	134,760	1998	Walter Ray Williams Jr.	238,225
1967	Dave Davis	54,165	1983	Earl Anthony	135,605	1999	Parker Bohn III	240,912
1968	Jim Stefanich	67,377	1984	Mark Roth	158,712	2000	Norm Duke	143,325
1969	Billy Hardwick	64,160	1985	Mike Aulby	201,200	2002	Parker Bohn III	245,200
1970	Mike McGrath	52,049	1986	Walter Ray Williams Jr.	145,550	2003	Walter Ray Williams Jr.	419,700
1971	Johnny Petraglia	85,065	1987	Pete Weber	175,491	2004	Mika Koivuniemi	238,590
1972	Don Johnson	56,648	1988	Brian Voss	225,485	2005	Patrick Allen	350,740
1973	Don McCune	69,000	1989	Mike Aulby	298,237	2006	Tommy Jones	301,700
1974	Earl Anthony	99,585	1990	Amleto Monacelli	204,775	2007	Doug Kent	200,530
1975	Earl Anthony	107,585	1991	David Ozio	225,585	2008	Norm Duke	176,855
1976	Earl Anthony	110,833	1992	Marc McDowell	174,215	2009	Norm Duke	199,130
1977	Mark Roth	105,583	1993	Walter Ray Williams Jr.	296,370			

Leading PBA Averages by Year

Year	Bowler	Average	Year	Bowler	Average	Year	Bowler	Average
1962	Don Carter	212.84	1979	Mark Roth	221.66	1994	Norm Duke	222.83
1963	Billy Hardwick	210.34	1980	Earl Anthony	218.53	1995	Mike Aulby	225.49
1964	Ray Bluth	210.51	1981	Mark Roth	216.69	1996	Walter Ray Williams Jr.	225.37
1965	Dick Weber	211.89	1982	Marshall Holman	212.84	1997	Walter Ray Williams Jr.	222.00
1966	Wayne Zahn	208.66	1983	Earl Anthony	216.64	1998	Walter Ray Williams Jr.	226.13
1967	Wayne Zahn	212.34	1984	Marshall Holman	213.91	1999	Parker Bohn III	228.04
1968	Jim Stefanich	211.89	1985	Mark Baker	213.71	2000	Chris Barnes	220.93
1969	Bill Hardwick	212.95	1986	John Gant	214.37	2002	Parker Bohn III	221.54
1970	Nelson Burton Jr.	214.90	1987	Marshall Holman	216.80	2003	Walter Ray Williams Jr.	224.94
1971	Don Johnson	213.97	1988	Mark Roth	218.03	2004	Mika Koivuniemi	222.73
1972	Don Johnson	215.29	1989	Pete Weber	215.43	2005	Walter Ray Williams Jr.	227.07
1973	Earl Anthony	215.79	1990	Amleto Monacelli	218.15	2006	Norm Duke	224.29
1974	Earl Anthony	219.39	1991	Norm Duke	218.20	2007	Norm Duke	228.47
1975	Earl Anthony	219.06	1992	Dave Ferraro	219.70	2008	Walter Ray Williams Jr.	228.34
1976	Mark Roth	215.97	1993	Walter Ray Williams Jr.	222.98	2009	Wes Malott	222.98
1977	Mark Roth	218.17						
1978	Mark Roth	219.83						

United States Bowling Congress

Formed Jan. 1, 2005, from a merger of the American Bowling Congress (ABC), Women's International Bowling Congress, the Young American Bowling Alliance, and USA Bowling. Before 2006, certified games and champions are for ABC only.

Most Certified 300 Games — Men

Note: As of Oct. 30, 2009.

Jim Hosier, Wayne, NJ.	109	Dean Wolf, Reading, PA	91	Robert Heuser, Elmira, NY	74
John Delp III, West Lawn, PA	102	Ron Krippelcz, St. Louis, MO	88	Eric Roddy, New Orleans, LA	74
Gordon Childers, Benton, AR.	100	Jack Kurent, Luzerne, PA	87	Warren Tam Wasson, Garland, TX.	74
Fero Williams, Miamisburg, OH	99	Jeff Carter, Springfield, IL	86	Shannon Buchan, Waterloo, IA.	73
Chris Hayward, Toledo, OH	95	Jeff Ripic, Endicott, NY	86	Dale Strike, Saginaw, MI.	73
Frank Massengale Jr., Hixon, TN.	93	Jim Tomek Jr., Camp Hill, PA	86	John Chacko Jr., Larksville, PA	72
Stephen Aiello, New Halledon, NJ.	91	Jerry Kessler, Dayton, OH.	81	Ricky Fuller, Springfield, OH.	72
Joe Jimenez, Saginaw, MI	91	David Bingham, Brainard, NY	80	Jay Bradshaw, O'Fallon, IL.	70

USBC Masters Tournament Champions

Year	Winner, hometown	Year	Winner, hometown	Year	Winner, hometown
1980	Neil Burton, St. Louis, MO	1990	Chris Warren, Dallas, TX	2001	Parker Bohn III, Jackson, NJ
1981	Randy Lightfoot, St. Charles, MO	1991	Doug Kent, Canandaigua, NY	2002	Brett Wolfe, Reno, NV
1982	Joe Berardi, Brooklyn, NY	1992	Ken Johnson, N. Richmond Hills, TX	2003	Bryon Smith, Roseburg, OR
1983	Mike Lastowski, Havre de Grace, MD	1993	Norm Duke, Oklahoma City, OK	2004	Walter Ray Williams Jr., FL (Jan.); Danny Wiseman, MD (Oct.)
1984	Earl Anthony, Dublin, CA	1994	Steve Fehr, Cincinnati, OH		
1985	Steve Wunderlich, St. Louis, MO	1995	Mike Aulby, Indianapolis, IN	2005	Mike Scroggins, Amarillo, TX
1986	Mark Fahy, Chicago, IL	1996	Ernie Schlegel, Vancouver, WA	2006	Doug Kent, Newark, NY
1987	Rick Steelsmith, Wichita, KS	1997	Jason Queen, Decatur, IL	2007	Sean Rash, Wichita, KS
1988	Del Ballard Jr., Richardson, TX	1998	Mike Aulby, Indianapolis, IN	2008	No tournament
1989	Mike Aulby, Indianapolis, IN	1999	Brian Boghosian, Middletown, CT	2009	John Nolen, Waterford, MI
		2000	Mika Koivuniemi, Finland		

Open Champions, 2009

Regular Singles: Bryan Young, Everett, WA
Regular Doubles: John Socha, Oak Creek, WI, and Dennis Rakauskas, Apopka, FL
Regular All-Events: Jay Futrell, Derby, KS
Regular Team: Team Tilt, Lawrence, KS
Team All-Events: Fox Bowl 2, Wheaton, IL

Classified Singles: Jack Wilson, Centreville, MD
Classified Doubles: Bill Calhoon and Jacqueline Snyder, Cooksville, IL
Classified All-Events: Daniel Dabkowski, Columbia, SC
Classified Team: Cardinal Lanes, Hoisington, KS

USBC Queens and Women's Champions, 2009

Note: Formerly WIBC Queens.

Queens Tournament: Liz Johnson, Cheektowaga, NY
Classic Singles: Michelle Feldman, Auburn, NY
Classic Doubles: Clara Guererro, Austin, TX, and Jenifer Larson, Tupper Lake, NY
Classic All-Events: Robin Romeo, Newhall, CA
Classic Team: Together Once Again, Keller, TX

Div. 1 Singles: Linda Freeland, Dade City, FL
Div. 1 Doubles: Marilyn Brown, Bellingham, WA, and Janice Eisenhut, Ferndale, WA
Div. 1 All-Events: Sheryl Ishihara, Anchorage, AK
Div. 1 Team: It's a Little Thang, Bronx, NY

Most Certified 300 Games — Women
Note: As of Oct. 30, 2009.

Altramese Webb, Detroit, MI 42	Shannon Duplantis, New Orleans, LA. 29	Jodi Woessner, Oregon, OH 23
Tish Johnson, Colorado Springs, CO . 42	Aleta Sill, Dearborn, MI 28	Cheryl Daniels, Detroit, MI 22
Jodi Musto, Schenectady, NY 37	Anne Marie Duggan, Edmond, OK . . . 27	Jackie Mitskavich, DuBois, PA 22
Marianne DiRupo, Succasunna, NJ. . . 33	Alicia Kellow, Louisville, KY 25	Mandy Wilson, Dayton, OH 22
Tammy Jones, Decatur, IL. 33	Teri Haefke, Austintown, OH. 24	Carolyn Dorin-Ballard, North Richland
Debbie McMullen, Denver, CO 31	Jeanne Naccarato, Tacoma, WA 24	Hills, TX 21
Dede Davidson, Woodland Hills, CA. . 30	Vicki Fischel, Wheat Ridge, CO 23	Jodi Hughes, Piedmont, SC 21
Leanne Hulsenberg, Roseville, CA . . . 30	Kim Terrell-Kearney, Grand Prairie, TX 23	Liz Johnson, Cheektowaga, NY 21
Jeanette Adams, Antelope, CA 29		

CHESS
World Chess Champions
Sources: U.S. Chess Federation; International Chess Federation (FIDE)
Official world champions since the title was first used, as of Oct. 30, 2009.

1886-94	Wilhelm Steinitz, Austria	1972-75	Bobby Fischer, U.S. (b)
1894-1921	Emanuel Lasker, Germany	1975-85	Anatoly Karpov, USSR
1921-27	Jose R. Capablanca, Cuba	1985-2000	Garry Kasparov, USSR/Russia (c)
1927-35	Alexander Alekhine, France	1993-99	Anatoly Karpov, Russia (FIDE)
1935-37	Max Euwe, Netherlands	1999-2000	Alexander Khalifman, Russia (FIDE)
1937-46	Alexander Alekhine, France (a)	2000-02	Viswanathan Anand, India (FIDE)
1948-57	Mikhail Botvinnik, USSR	2000-06	Vladimir Kramnik, Russia (classical) (d,e)
1957-58	Vassily Smyslov, USSR	2002-04	Ruslan Ponomariov, Ukraine (FIDE)
1958-59	Mikhail Botvinnik, USSR	2004-05	Rustam Kasimdzhanov, Uzbekistan (FIDE)
1960-61	Mikhail Tal, USSR	2005-06	Veselin Topalov, Bulgaria (FIDE)
1961-63	Mikhail Botvinnik, USSR	2006-07	Vladimir Kramnik, Russia (e)
1963-69	Tigran Petrosian, USSR	2007-	Viswanathan Anand, India
1969-72	Boris Spassky, USSR		

(a) After Alekhine died in 1946, the title was vacant until 1948, when Botvinnik won the 1st world championship event sanctioned by FIDE. (b) Defaulted championship after refusing to accept FIDE rules for a championship match, Apr. 1975. (c) Kasparov broke with FIDE, Feb. 26, 1993. FIDE stripped Kasparov of his FIDE title Mar. 23. Kasparov then defeated Nigel Short of Great Britain in a world championship match played Sept.-Oct. 1993 under the auspices of a new organization the two had founded, the Professional Chess Association (PCA). FIDE held a replacement championship match between Anatoly Karpov (Russia) and Jan Timman (Netherlands), which Karpov won in Nov. 1993. The PCA folded in 1995, but Kasparov was still considered the "classical" world champion. (d) In Nov. 2000, Vladimir Kramnik (Russia) defeated Garry Kasparov (Russia) for the classical world championship title in London. (e) Vladimir Kramnik, the classical world champion since 2000, and Veselin Topalov, FIDE champion since 2005, met at the world chess championship match in Elista, Russia, to compete for a unified championship, which Kramnik won Oct. 13, 2006.
Further information: www.fide.com

FIGURE SKATING
U.S. and World Individual Champions, 1952-2009

U.S. Champions			World Champions	
Men	**Women**	**YEAR**	**Men**	**Women**
Dick Button	Tenley Albright	1952	Dick Button, U.S.	Jacqueline du Bief, France
Hayes Jenkins	Tenley Albright	1953	Hayes Jenkins, U.S.	Tenley Albright, U.S.
Hayes Jenkins	Tenley Albright	1954	Hayes Jenkins, U.S.	Gundi Busch, W. Germany
Hayes Jenkins	Tenley Albright	1955	Hayes Jenkins, U.S.	Tenley Albright, U.S.
Hayes Jenkins	Tenley Albright	1956	Hayes Jenkins, U.S.	Carol Heiss, U.S.
Dave Jenkins	Carol Heiss	1957	Dave Jenkins, U.S.	Carol Heiss, U.S.
Dave Jenkins	Carol Heiss	1958	Dave Jenkins, U.S.	Carol Heiss, U.S.
Dave Jenkins	Carol Heiss	1959	Dave Jenkins, U.S.	Carol Heiss, U.S.
Dave Jenkins	Carol Heiss	1960	Alain Giletti, France	Carol Heiss, U.S.
Bradley Lord	Laurence Owen	1961	None	None
Monty Hoyt	Barbara Roles Pursley	1962	Don Jackson, Canada	Sjoukje Dijkstra, Netherlands
Tommy Litz	Lorraine Hanlon	1963	Don McPherson, Canada	Sjoukje Dijkstra, Netherlands
Scott Allen	Peggy Fleming	1964	Manfred Schnelldorfer, W. Germany	Sjoukje Dijkstra, Netherlands
Gary Visconti	Peggy Fleming	1965	Alain Calmat, France	Petra Burka, Canada
Scott Allen	Peggy Fleming	1966	Emmerich Danzer, Austria	Peggy Fleming, U.S.
Gary Visconti	Peggy Fleming	1967	Emmerich Danzer, Austria	Peggy Fleming, U.S.
Tim Wood	Peggy Fleming	1968	Emmerich Danzer, Austria	Peggy Fleming, U.S.
Tim Wood	Janet Lynn	1969	Tim Wood, U.S.	Gabriele Seyfert, E. Germany
Tim Wood	Janet Lynn	1970	Tim Wood, U.S.	Gabriele Seyfert, E. Germany
John Misha Petkevich	Janet Lynn	1971	Ondrej Nepela, Czechoslovakia	Beatrix Schuba, Austria
Ken Shelley	Janet Lynn	1972	Ondrej Nepela, Czechoslovakia	Beatrix Schuba, Austria
Gordon McKellen Jr.	Janet Lynn	1973	Ondrej Nepela, Czechoslovakia	Karen Magnussen, Canada
Gordon McKellen Jr.	Dorothy Hamill	1974	Jan Hoffmann, E. Germany	Christine Errath, E. Germany
Gordon McKellen Jr.	Dorothy Hamill	1975	Sergei Volkov, USSR	Dianne de Leeuw, Neth.-U.S.
Terry Kubicka	Dorothy Hamill	1976	John Curry, Gr. Britain	Dorothy Hamill, U.S.
Charles Tickner	Linda Fratianne	1977	Vladimir Kovalev, USSR	Linda Fratianne, U.S.
Charles Tickner	Linda Fratianne	1978	Charles Tickner, U.S.	Anett Poetzsch, E. Germany
Charles Tickner	Linda Fratianne	1979	Vladimir Kovalev, USSR	Linda Fratianne, U.S.
Charles Tickner	Linda Fratianne	1980	Jan Hoffmann, E. Germany	Anett Poetzsch, E. Germany
Scott Hamilton	Elaine Zayak	1981	Scott Hamilton, U.S.	Denise Biellmann, Switzerland
Scott Hamilton	Rosalynn Sumners	1982	Scott Hamilton, U.S.	Elaine Zayak, U.S.
Scott Hamilton	Rosalynn Sumners	1983	Scott Hamilton, U.S.	Rosalynn Sumners, U.S.
Scott Hamilton	Rosalynn Sumners	1984	Scott Hamilton, U.S.	Katarina Witt, E. Germany
Brian Boitano	Tiffany Chin	1985	Aleksandr Fadeev, USSR	Katarina Witt, E. Germany
Brian Boitano	Debi Thomas	1986	Brian Boitano, U.S.	Debi Thomas, U.S.
Brian Boitano	Jill Trenary	1987	Brian Orser, Canada	Katarina Witt, E. Germany
Brian Boitano	Debi Thomas	1988	Brian Boitano, U.S.	Katarina Witt, E. Germany
Christopher Bowman	Jill Trenary	1989	Kurt Browning, Canada	Midori Ito, Japan
Todd Eldredge	Jill Trenary	1990	Kurt Browning, Canada	Jill Trenary, U.S.

	U.S. Champions		YEAR		World Champions	
Men	**Women**			**Men**		**Women**
Todd Eldredge	Tonya Harding		1991	Kurt Browning, Canada		Kristi Yamaguchi, U.S.
Christopher Bowman	Kristi Yamaguchi		1992	Viktor Petrenko, Ukraine		Kristi Yamaguchi, U.S.
Scott Davis	Nancy Kerrigan		1993	Kurt Browning, Canada		Oksana Baiul, Ukraine
Scott Davis	Vacant[1]		1994	Elvis Stojko, Canada		Yuka Sato, Japan
Todd Eldredge	Nicole Bobek		1995	Elvis Stojko, Canada		Chen Lu, China
Rudy Galindo	Michelle Kwan		1996	Todd Eldredge, U.S.		Michelle Kwan, U.S.
Todd Eldredge	Tara Lipinski		1997	Elvis Stojko, Canada		Tara Lipinski, U.S.
Todd Eldredge	Michelle Kwan		1998	Alexei Yagudin, Russia		Michelle Kwan, U.S.
Michael Weiss	Michelle Kwan		1999	Alexei Yagudin, Russia		Maria Butyrskaya, Russia
Michael Weiss	Michelle Kwan		2000	Alexei Yagudin, Russia		Michelle Kwan, U.S.
Timothy Goebel	Michelle Kwan		2001	Yevgeny Plushenko, Russia		Michelle Kwan, U.S.
Todd Eldredge	Michelle Kwan		2002	Alexei Yagudin, Russia		Irina Slutskaya, Russia
Michael Weiss	Michelle Kwan		2003	Yevgeny Plushenko, Russia		Michelle Kwan, U.S.
Johnny Weir	Michelle Kwan		2004	Yevgeny Plushenko, Russia		Shizuka Arakawa, Japan
Johnny Weir	Michelle Kwan		2005	Stephane Lambiel, Switzerland		Irina Slutskaya, Russia
Johnny Weir	Sasha Cohen		2006	Stephane Lambiel, Switzerland		Kimmie Meissner, U.S.
Evan Lysacek	Kimmie Meissner		2007	Brian Joubert, France		Miki Ando, Japan
Evan Lysacek	Mirai Nagasu		2008	Jeffrey Buttle, Canada		Mao Asada, Japan
Jeremy Abbott	Alissa Czisny		2009	Evan Lysacek, U.S.		Yu-Na Kim, South Korea

(1) Tonya Harding was stripped of title.

SKIING
World Cup Alpine Champions, 1967-2009

Year	Men's champion, country	Year	Men's champion, country	Year	Women's champion, country
1967	Jean Claude Killy, France	1997	Luc Alphand, France	1981	Marie-Theres Nadig, Switzerland
1968	Jean Claude Killy, France	1998	Hermann Maier, Austria	1982	Erika Hess, Switzerland
1969	Karl Schranz, Austria	1999	Lasse Kjus, Norway	1983	Tamara McKinney, U.S.
1970	Karl Schranz, Austria	2000	Hermann Maier, Austria	1984	Erika Hess, Switzerland
1971	Gustavo Thoeni, Italy	2001	Hermann Maier, Austria	1985	Michela Figini, Switzerland
1972	Gustavo Thoeni, Italy	2002	Stephan Eberharter, Austria	1986	Maria Walliser, Switzerland
1973	Gustavo Thoeni, Italy	2003	Stephan Eberharter, Austria	1987	Maria Walliser, Switzerland
1974	Piero Gros, Italy	2004	Hermann Maier, Austria	1988	Michela Figini, Switzerland
1975	Gustavo Thoeni, Italy	2005	Bode Miller, U.S.	1989	Vreni Schneider, Switzerland
1976	Ingemar Stenmark, Sweden	2006	Benjamin Raich, Austria	1990	Petra Kronberger, Austria
1977	Ingemar Stenmark, Sweden	2007	Aksel Lund Svindal, Norway	1991	Petra Kronberger, Austria
1978	Ingemar Stenmark, Sweden	2008	Bode Miller, U.S.	1992	Petra Kronberger, Austria
1979	Peter Luescher, Switzerland	2009	Aksel Lund Svindal, Norway	1993	Anita Wachter, Austria
1980	Andreas Wenzel, Liechtenstein			1994	Vreni Schneider, Switzerland
1981	Phil Mahre, U.S.	**Year**	**Women's champion, country**	1995	Vreni Schneider, Switzerland
1982	Phil Mahre, U.S.	1967	Nancy Greene, Canada	1996	Katja Seizinger, Germany
1983	Phil Mahre, U.S.	1968	Nancy Greene, Canada	1997	Pernilla Wiberg, Sweden
1984	Pirmin Zurbriggen, Switzerland	1969	Gertrud Gabl, Austria	1998	Katja Seizinger, Germany
1985	Marc Girardelli, Luxembourg	1970	Michele Jacot, France	1999	Alexandra Meissnitzer, Austria
1986	Marc Girardelli, Luxembourg	1971	Annemarie Proell, Austria	2000	Renate Goetschl, Austria
1987	Pirmin Zurbriggen, Switzerland	1972	Annemarie Proell, Austria	2001	Janica Kostelic, Croatia
1988	Pirmin Zurbriggen, Switzerland	1973	Annemarie Proell, Austria	2002	Michaela Dorfmeister, Austria
1989	Marc Girardelli, Luxembourg	1974	Annemarie Proell, Austria	2003	Janica Kostelic, Croatia
1990	Pirmin Zurbriggen, Switzerland	1975	Annemarie Proell, Austria	2004	Anja Paerson, Sweden
1991	Marc Girardelli, Luxembourg	1976	Rose Mittermaier, W. Germany	2005	Anja Paerson, Sweden
1992	Paul Accola, Switzerland	1977	Lise-Marie Morerod, Switzerland	2006	Janica Kostelic, Croatia
1993	Marc Girardelli, Luxembourg	1978	Hanni Wenzel, Liechtenstein	2007	Nicole Hosp, Austria
1994	Kjetil Andre Aamodt, Norway	1979	Annemarie Proell Moser, Austria	2008	Lindsey Vonn, U.S.
1995	Alberto Tomba, Italy	1980	Hanni Wenzel, Liechtenstein	2009	Lindsey Vonn, U.S.
1996	Lasse Kjus, Norway				

CYCLING
2009 Tour de France

Alberto Contador of Spain won the 96th Tour de France, cycling's premier race July 26, 2009. Contador's win was his second in three years, and the fourth straight Tour victory for a Spaniard. The race also marked the return to the Tour de France of seven-time winner Lance Armstrong of the U.S., who had retired after his 2005 victory. Armstrong finished third in the 2,150-mile race, behind Contador and second-place finisher Andy Schleck of Luxembourg.

The doping scandals that had dominated headlines during the past three years were overshadowed by the rivalry between Contador and Armstrong, both members of the Astana team. Prior to the race, Astana manager Johan Bruyneel had awarded Contador the symbolic jersey of team leader. The pecking order within the Kazakh-sponsored team was closely watched throughout the race. The day after the teammates shared the Tour podium, Contador called his relationship with Armstrong "zero."

Tour de France Winners, 1980-2009

Year	Winner, nationality	Year	Winner, nationality	Year	Winner, nationality
1980	Zoop Zoetemelk, Netherlands	1990	Greg LeMond, U.S.	2000	Lance Armstrong, U.S.
1981	Bernard Hinault, France	1991	Miguel Indurain, Spain	2001	Lance Armstrong, U.S.
1982	Bernard Hinault, France	1992	Miguel Indurain, Spain	2002	Lance Armstrong, U.S.
1983	Laurent Fignon, France	1993	Miguel Indurain, Spain	2003	Lance Armstrong, U.S.
1984	Laurent Fignon, France	1994	Miguel Indurain, Spain	2004	Lance Armstrong, U.S.
1985	Bernard Hinault, France	1995	Miguel Indurain, Spain	2005	Lance Armstrong, U.S.
1986	Greg LeMond, U.S.	1996	Bjarne Riis, Denmark	2006	Óscar Pereiro, Spain*
1987	Stephen Roche, Ireland	1997	Jan Ullrich, Germany	2007	Alberto Contador, Spain
1988	Pedro Delgado, Spain	1998	Marco Pantani, Italy	2008	Carlos Sastre, Spain
1989	Greg LeMond, U.S.	1999	Lance Armstrong, U.S.	2009	Alberto Contador, Spain

*Floyd Landis, U.S., was stripped of the title, Sept. 20, 2007, for doping. Landis lost a final appeal of the ruling June 30, 2008.

SWIMMING
World Swimming Records

Long course (50 m), as of Oct. 2009. Records marked with an asterisk (*) were pending.

Men's Records
Freestyle

Distance	Time	Holder	Nationality	Location	Date
50 meters	0:20.94	Frédérick Bousquet	France	Montpellier, France	Apr. 26, 2009
100 meters	0:46.91*	Cesar Cielo Filho	Brazil	Rome, Italy	July 30, 2009
200 meters	1:42.00*	Paul Biedermann	Germany	Rome, Italy	July 28, 2009
400 meters	3:40.07*	Paul Biedermann	Germany	Rome, Italy	July 26, 2009
800 meters	7:32.12*	Lin Zhang	China	Rome, Italy	July 29, 2009
1,500 meters	14:34.56	Grant Hackett	Australia	Fukuoka, Japan	July 29, 2001

Backstroke

Distance	Time	Holder	Nationality	Location	Date
50 meters	0:24.04*	Liam Tancock	UK	Rome, Italy	Aug. 2, 2009
100 meters	0:52.38*	Aschwin Wildeboer	Spain	Pescara, Italy	July 1, 2009
200 meters	1:51.92*	Aaron Peirsol	U.S.	Rome, Italy	July 31, 2009

Breaststroke

Distance	Time	Holder	Nationality	Location	Date
50 meters	0:26.67*	Cameron van der Burgh	South Africa	Rome, Italy	July 29, 2009
100 meters	0:58.58*	Brenton Rickard	Australia	Rome, Italy	July 27, 2009
200 meters	2:07.31*	Christian Sprenger	Australia	Rome, Italy	July 30, 2009

Butterfly

Distance	Time	Holder	Nationality	Location	Date
50 meters	0:22.43	Rafael Muñoz	Spain	Malaga, Spain	May 4, 2009
100 meters	0:49.82*	Michael Phelps	U.S.	Rome, Italy	Aug. 1, 2009
200 meters	1:52.03	Michael Phelps	U.S.	Beijing, China	Aug. 13, 2008

Individual medley

Distance	Time	Holder	Nationality	Location	Date
200 meters	1:54.10*	Ryan Lochte	U.S.	Rome, Italy	July 30, 2009
400 meters	4:03.84	Michael Phelps	U.S.	Beijing, China	Aug. 10, 2008

Freestyle relay

Distance	Time	Holder	Nationality	Location	Date
400 mtrs. (4×100)	3:08.24	Phelps, Weber-Gale, Jones, Lezak	U.S.	Beijing, China	Aug. 11, 2008
800 mtrs. (4×200)	6:58.55*	Phelps, Berens, Walters, Lochte	U.S.	Rome, Italy	July 31, 2009

Medley relay

Distance	Time	Holder	Nationality	Location	Date
400 mtrs. (4×100)	3:27.28*	Peirsol, Shanteau, Phelps, Walters	U.S.	Rome, Italy	Aug. 2, 2009

Women's Records
Freestyle

Distance	Time	Holder	Nationality	Location	Date
50 meters	0:23.73*	Britta Steffen	Germany	Rome, Italy	Aug. 2, 2009
100 meters	0:52.07*	Britta Steffen	Germany	Rome, Italy	July 31, 2009
200 meters	1:52.98*	Federica Pellegrini	Italy	Rome, Italy	July 29, 2009
400 meters	3:59.15*	Federica Pellegrini	Italy	Rome, Italy	July 26, 2009
800 meters	8:14.10	Rebecca Adlington	UK	Beijing, China	Aug. 16, 2008
1,500 meters	15:42.54	Kate Zeigler	U.S.	Mission Viejo, CA	June 17, 2007

Backstroke

Distance	Time	Holder	Nationality	Location	Date
50 meters	0:27.06*	Jing Zhao	China	Rome, Italy	July 30, 2009
100 meters	0:58.12*	Gemma Spofforth	UK	Rome, Italy	July 28, 2009
200 meters	2:04.81*	Kirsty Coventry	Zimbabwe	Rome, Italy	Aug. 1, 2009

Breaststroke

Distance	Time	Holder	Nationality	Location	Date
50 meters	0:30.09*	Yuliya Efimova	Russia	Rome, Italy	Aug. 2, 2009
100 meters	1:04.84*	Rebecca Soni	U.S.	Rome, Italy	July 27, 2009
200 meters	2:20.12*	Annamay Pierse	U.S.	Rome, Italy	July 30, 2009

Butterfly

Distance	Time	Holder	Nationality	Location	Date
50 meters	0:25.07*	Therese Alshammar	Sweden	Rome, Italy	July 31, 2009
100 meters	0:56.06*	Sarah Sjostrom	Sweden	Rome, Italy	July 27, 2009
200 meters	2:03.41*	Jessica Schipper	Australia	Rome, Italy	July 30, 2009

Individual medley

Distance	Time	Holder	Nationality	Location	Date
200 meters	2:06.15*	Ariana Kukors	U.S.	Rome, Italy	July 27, 2009
400 meters	4:29.45	Stephanie Rice	Australia	Beijing, China	Aug. 10, 2008

Freestyle relay

Distance	Time	Holder	Nationality	Location	Date
400 mtrs. (4×100)	3:31.72*	Dekker, Kromowidjojo, Heemskerk, Veldhuis	Netherlands	Rome, Italy	July 26, 2009
800 mtrs. (4×200)	7:42.08*	Yang, Zhu, Liu, Pang	China	Rome, Italy	July 30, 2009

Medley relay

Distance	Time	Holder	Nationality	Location	Date
400 mtrs. (4×100)	3:52.19*	Zhao, Chen, Jiao, Li	China	Rome, Italy	Aug. 1, 2009

DOGS
2009 Iditarod Trail Sled Dog Race

Lance Mackey won the 37th annual Iditarod Trail Sled Dog Race from Anchorage to Nome, Alaska, Mar. 18, 2009, capturing the $69,000 prize. Mackey, who finished the 1,131-mile southern course to Nome in 9 days, 21 hours, 38 minutes, and 46 seconds, won the race for the third consecutive year. The 2010 race was scheduled to begin Mar. 6 in Anchorage and follow the 1,112-mile course along the northern Iditarod route.

Westminster Kennel Club Best-In-Show, 1989-2009

Year	Best-In-show	Breed	Owner(s)
1989	Ch. Royal Tudor's Wild As The Wind	Doberman	Sue and Art Kemp; Richard and Carolyn Vida; Beth Wilhite
1990	Ch. Wendessa Crown Prince	Pekingese	Ed Jenner
1991	Ch. Whisperwind on a Carousel	Poodle	Joan and Frederick Hartsock
1992	Ch. Registry's Lonesome Dove	Fox Terrier	Marion and Sam Lawrence
1993	Ch. Salilyn's Condor	English Springer Spaniel	Donna and Roger Herzig
1994	Ch. Chidley Willum	Norwich Terrier	Ruth Cooper and Patricia Lussier
1995	Ch. Gaelforce Post Script	Scottish Terrier	Dr. Vandra Huber and Dr. Joe Kinnarney
1996	Ch. Clussexx Country Sunrise	Clumber Spaniel	Judith and Richard Zaleski
1997	Ch. Parsifal Di Casa Netzer	Standard Schnauzer	Rita Holloway and Gabrio Del Torre
1998	Ch. Fairewood Frolic	Norwich Terrier	Sandina Kennels
1999	Ch. Loteki Supernatural Being	Papillon	John Oulton
2000	Ch. Salilyn 'N Erin's Shameless	English Springer Spaniel	Carl Blain, Fran Sunseri, and Julia Gasow
2001	Ch. Special Times Just Right	Bichon Frise	Cecilia Ruggles, E. McDonald, and F. Werneck
2002	Ch. Surrey Spice Girl	Poodle (Miniature)	Ron L. and Barbara Scott
2003	Ch. Torum's Scarf Michael	Kerry Blue Terrier	Marilu Hanson
2004	Ch. Darbydale's All Rise Pouchcove	Newfoundland	Peggy Helming and Carol A. Bernard Bergmann
2005	Ch. Kan-Point's VJK Autumn Roses	German Shorthaired Pointer	Linda & Richard Stark; Carol Cronk; Valerie Nunes-Atkinson
2006	Ch. Rocky Top's Sundance Kid	Bull Terrier (colored)	Barbara Bishop, W. F. Poole, N. Shepherd, and R. P. Poole
2007	Ch. Felicity's Diamond Jim	English Springer Spaniel	Teresa and Allen Patton; Ruth Dehmel; D. Hadsall
2008	Ch. K-Run's Park Me In First	Beagle (15 in.)	Caroline Dowell, Eddie Dziuk, Jon Woodring, Kathy Weichert
2009	Ch. Clussexx Three D Grinchy Glee	Sussex Spaniel	Cecilia Ruggles, Beth Dowd, and Scott Sommer

MARATHONS
World Marathon Majors

Five of the world's leading marathons (Berlin, Boston, Chicago, London, and New York) agreed Jan. 23, 2006, to form a series called the World Marathon Majors. Marathon runners will be awarded points relative to their finish in each race in the series, and in Olympic and other world championship marathons. The male and female runners with the most points at the end of each two-year cycle will win $500,000. The 2008-09 World Marathon Majors series winners were Samuel Wanjiru, Ethiopia, and Irina Mikitenko, Germany.

Boston Marathon Winners, 1972-2009
All times in hour:minute:second format. *Course records.

Men's winner, country	Time	Year	Women's winner, country	Time
Olavi Suomalainen, Finland	2:15:39	1972	Nina Kuscsik, U.S.	3:10:26
Jon Anderson, U.S.	2:16:03	1973	Jacqueline Hansen, U.S.	3:05:59
Neil Cusack, Ireland	2:13:39	1974	Michiko Gorman, U.S.	2:47:11
Bill Rodgers, U.S.	2:09:55	1975	Liane Winter, West Germany	2:42:24
Jack Fultz, U.S.	2:20:19	1976	Kim Merritt, U.S.	2:47:10
Jerome Drayton, Canada	2:14:46	1977	Michiko Gorman, U.S.	2:48:33
Bill Rodgers, U.S.	2:10:13	1978	Gayle S. Barron, U.S.	2:44:52
Bill Rodgers, U.S.	2:09:27	1979	Joan Benoit, U.S.	2:35:15
Bill Rodgers, U.S.	2:12:11	1980	Jacqueline Gareau, Canada	2:34:28
Toshihiko Seko, Japan	2:09:26	1981	Allison Roe, N. Zealand	2:26:46
Alberto Salazar, U.S.	2:08:52	1982	Charlotte Teske, West Germany	2:29:33
Greg Meyer, U.S.	2:09:00	1983	Joan Benoit, U.S.	2:22:43
Geoff Smith, Great Britain	2:10:34	1984	Lorraine Moller, New Zealand	2:29:28
Geoff Smith, Great Britain	2:14:05	1985	Lisa Larsen Weidenbach, U.S.	2:34:06
Robert de Castella, Australia	2:07:51	1986	Ingrid Kristiansen, Norway	2:24:55
Toshihiko Seko, Japan	2:11:50	1987	Rosa Mota, Portugal	2:25:21
Ibrahim Hussein, Kenya	2:08:43	1988	Rosa Mota, Portugal	2:24:30
Abebe Mekonnen, Ethiopia	2:09:06	1989	Ingrid Kristiansen, Norway	2:24:33
Gelindo Bordin, Italy	2:08:19	1990	Rosa Mota, Portugal	2:25:24
Ibrahim Hussein, Kenya	2:11:06	1991	Wanda Panfil, Poland	2:24:18
Ibrahim Hussein, Kenya	2:08:14	1992	Olga Markova, Russia	2:23:43
Cosmas Ndeti, Kenya	2:09:33	1993	Olga Markova, Russia	2:25:27
Cosmas Ndeti, Kenya	2:07:15	1994	Uta Pippig, Germany	2:21:45
Cosmas Ndeti, Kenya	2:09:22	1995	Uta Pippig, Germany	2:25:11
Moses Tanui, Kenya	2:09:15	1996	Uta Pippig, Germany	2:27:12
Lameck Aguta, Kenya	2:10:34	1997	Fatuma Roba, Ethiopia	2:26:23
Moses Tanui, Kenya	2:07:34	1998	Fatuma Roba, Ethiopia	2:23:21
Joseh Chebet, Kenya	2:09:52	1999	Fatuma Roba, Ethiopia	2:23:25
Elijah Lagat, Kenya	2:09:47	2000	Catherine Ndereba, Kenya	2:26:11
Lee Bong-ju, S. Korea	2:09:43	2001	Catherine Ndereba, Kenya	2:23:53
Rodgers Rop, Kenya	2:09:02	2002	Margaret Okayo, Kenya	2:20:43*
Robert K. Cheruiyot, Kenya	2:10:11	2003	Svetlana Zakharova, Russia	2:25:20
Timothy Cherigat, Kenya	2:10:37	2004	Catherine Ndereba, Kenya	2:24:27
Hailu Negussie, Ethiopia	2:11:45	2005	Catherine Ndereba, Kenya	2:25:13
Robert Cheruiyot, Kenya	2:07:14*	2006	Rita Jeptoo, Kenya	2:23:38
Robert Cheruiyot, Kenya	2:14:13	2007	Lidiya Grigoryeva, Russia	2:29:18
Robert Cheruiyot, Kenya	2:07:46	2008	Dire Tune, Ethiopia	2:25:25
Deriba Merga, Ethiopia	2:08:42	2009	Salina Kosgei, Kenya	2:32:16

Boston Marathon Winners, 1897-1971

The first Boston Marathon was held in 1897. Women were officially accepted into the race in 1972.

Year	Winner, state/country	Time	Year	Winner, state/country	Time
1897	John J. McDermott, New York	2:55:10	1935	John A. Kelley, Massachusetts	2:32:07
1898	Ronald J. MacDonald, Canada	2:42:00	1936	Ellison M. Brown, Rhode Island	2:33:40
1899	Lawrence Brignolia, Massachusetts	2:54:38	1937	Walter Young, Canada	2:33:20
1900	John Caffery, Canada	2:39:44	1938	Leslie S. Pawson, Rhode Island	2:35:34
1901	John Caffery, Canada	2:29:23	1939	Ellison M. Brown, Rhode Island	2:28:51
1902	Sammy Mellor, New York	2:43:12	1940	Gerard Cote, Canada	2:28:28
1903	John Lorden , Massachusetts	2:41:29	1941	Leslie S. Pawson, Rhode Island	2:30:38
1904	Michael Spring, New York	2:38:04	1942	Joe Smith, Massachusetts	2:26:51
1905	Frederick Lorz, New York	2:38:25	1943	Gerard Cote, Canada	2:28:25
1906	Tim Ford, Massachusetts	2:45:45	1944	Gerard Cote, Canada	2:31:50
1907	Thomas Longboat, Canada	2:24:24	1945	John A. Kelley, Massachusetts	2:30:40
1908	Thomas Morrissey, New York	2:25:43	1946	Stylianos Kyriakides, Greece	2:29:27
1909	Henri Renaud, New Hampshire	2:53:36	1947	Yun Bok Suh, Korea	2:25:39
1910	Fred Cameron, Canada	2:28:52	1948	Gerard Cote, Canada	2:31:02
1911	Clarence DeMar, Massachusetts	2:21:39	1949	Karl Leandersson, Sweden	2:31:50
1912	Michael Ryan, New York	2:21:18	1950	Kee Yong Ham, Korea	2:32:39
1913	Fritz Carlson, Minnesota	2:25:14	1951	Shigeki Tanaka, Japan	2:27:45
1914	James Duffy, Canada	2:25:14	1952	Doroteo Flores, Guatemala	2:31:53
1915	Edouard Fabre, Canada	2:31:41	1953	Keizo Yamada, Japan	2:18:51
1916	Arthur Roth, Massachusetts	2:27:16	1954	Veikko Karvonen, Finland	2:20:39
1917	Bill Kennedy, New York	2:28:37	1955	Hideo Hamamura, Japan	2:18:22
1918	Military Relay, Camp Devens	2:29:53	1956	Antti Viskari, Finland	2:14:14
1919	Carl Linder, Massachusetts	2:29:13	1957	John J. Kelley, Connecticut	2:20:05
1920	Peter Trivoulides, New York	2:29:31	1958	Franjo Mihalic, Yugoslavia	2:25:54
1921	Frank Zuna, New York	2:18:57	1959	Eino Oksanen, Finland	2:22:42
1922	Clarence DeMar, Massachusetts	2:18:10	1960	Paavo Kotila, Finland	2:20:54
1923	Clarence DeMar, Massachusetts	2:23:47	1961	Eino Oksanen, Finland	2:23:39
1924	Clarence DeMar, Massachusetts	2:29:40	1962	Eino Oksanen, Finland	2:23:48
1925	Charles Mellor, Illinois	2:33:00	1963	Aurele Vandendriessche, Belgium	2:18:58
1926	John C. Miles, Canada	2:25:40	1964	Aurele Vandendriessche, Belgium	2:19:59
1927	Clarence DeMar, Massachusetts	2:40:22	1965	Morio Shigematsu, Japan	2:16:33
1928	Clarence DeMar, Massachusetts	2:37:07	1966	Kenji Kemihara, Japan	2:17:11
1929	John C. Miles, Canada	2:33:08	1967	David McKenzie, New Zealand	2:15:45
1930	Clarence DeMar, Massachusetts	2:34:48	1968	Amby Burfoot, Connecticut	2:22:17
1931	James P. Henigan, Massachusetts	2:46:45	1969	Yoshiaki Unetani, Japan	2:13:49
1932	Paul DeBruyn, Germany	2:33:36	1970	Ron Hill, Great Britain	2:10:30
1933	Leslie S. Pawson, Rhode Island	2:31:01	1971	Alvaro Mejia, Colombia	2:18:45
1934	Dave Komonen, Canada	2:32:53			

New York City Marathon Winners, 1970-2009

All time in hour:minute:second format; *Course records.

Men's winner, country	Time	Year	Women's winner, country	Time
Gary Muhrcke, U.S.	2:31:38	1970	No finisher	—
Norman Higgins, U.S.	2:22:54	1971	Beth Bonner, U.S.	2:55:22
Sheldon Karlin, U.S.	2:27:52	1972	Nina Kuscsik, U.S.	3:08:41
Tom Fleming, U.S.	2:19:25	1973	Nina Kuscsik, U.S.	2:57:07
Norbert Sander, U.S.	2:26:30	1974	Katherine Switzer, U.S.	3:07:29
Tom Fleming, U.S.	2:19:27	1975	Kim Merritt, U.S.	2:46:14
Bill Rodgers, U.S.	2:10:10	1976	Miki Gorman, U.S.	2:39:11
Bill Rodgers, U.S.	2:11:28	1977	Miki Gorman, U.S.	2:43:10
Bill Rodgers, U.S.	2:12:12	1978	Grete Waitz, Norway	2:32:30
Bill Rodgers, U.S.	2:11:42	1979	Grete Waitz, Norway	2:27:33
Alberto Salazar, U.S.	2:09:41	1980	Grete Waitz, Norway	2:25:42
Alberto Salazar, U.S.	2:08:13	1981	Allison Roe, New Zealand	2:25:29
Alberto Salazar, U.S.	2:09:29	1982	Grete Waitz, Norway	2:27:14
Rod Dixon, New Zealand	2:08:59	1983	Grete Waitz, Norway	2:27:00
Orlando Pizzolato, Italy	2:14:53	1984	Grete Waitz, Norway	2:29:30
Orlando Pizzolato, Italy	2:11:34	1985	Grete Waitz, Norway	2:28:34
Gianni Poli, Italy	2:11:06	1986	Grete Waitz, Norway	2:28:06
Ibrahim Hussein, Kenya	2:11:01	1987	Priscilla Welch, England	2:30:17
Steve Jones, Great Britain	2:08:20	1988	Grete Waitz, Norway	2:28:07
Juma Ikangaa, Tanzania	2:08:01	1989	Ingrid Kristiansen, Norway	2:25:30
Douglas Wakiihuri, Kenya	2:12:39	1990	Wanda Panfil, Poland	2:30:45
Salvador Garcia, Mexico	2:09:28	1991	Liz McColgan, Great Britain	2:27:32
Willie Mtolo, South Africa	2:09:29	1992	Lisa Ondieki, Australia	2:24:40
Andres Espinosa, Mexico	2:10:04	1993	Uta Pippig, Germany	2:26:24
German Silva, Mexico	2:11:21	1994	Tegla Loroupe, Kenya	2:27:37
German Silva, Mexico	2:11:00	1995	Tegla Loroupe, Kenya	2:28:06
Giacomo Leone, Italy	2:09:54	1996	Anuta Catuna, Romania	2:28:43
John Kagwe, Kenya	2:08:12	1997	F. Rochat-Moser, Switzerland	2:28:43
John Kagwe, Kenya	2:08:45	1998	Franca Fiacconi, Italy	2:25:17
Joseph Chebet, Kenya	2:09:14	1999	Adriana Fernandez, Mexico	2:25:06
Abdelkhader El Mouaziz, Morocco	2:10:09	2000	Ludmila Petrova, Russia	2:25:45
Tesfaye Jifar, Ethiopia	2:07:43*	2001	Margaret Okayo, Kenya	2:24:21
Rodgers Rop, Kenya	2:08:07	2002	Joyce Chepchumba, Kenya	2:25:56
Martin Lel, Kenya	2:10:30	2003	Margaret Okayo, Kenya	2:22:31*
Hendrik Ramaala, South Africa	2:09:28	2004	Paula Radcliffe, England	2:23:10
Paul Tergat, Kenya	2:09:30	2005	Jelena Prokopcuka, Latvia	2:24:41
Marilson Gomes dos Santos, Brazil	2:09:58	2006	Jelena Prokopcuka, Latvia	2:25:05
Martin Lel, Kenya	2:09:04	2007	Paula Radcliffe, England	2:23:09
Marilson Gomes dos Santos, Brazil	2:08:43	2008	Paula Radcliffe, England	2:23:56
Meb Keflezighi, U.S.	2:09:15	2009	Derartu Tulu, Ethiopia	2:28:52

Other Marathon Results in 2009

Paris Marathon: Apr. 5. Men: Vincent Kipruto, Kenya, 2:05:47. Women: Atsede Bayisa, Ethiopia, 2:24:42.
Rotterdam Marathon: Apr. 5. Men: Ducan Kibet, Kenya, 2:04:27. Women: Nailya Yulamanova, Russia, 2:26:30.
London Marathon: Apr. 26. Men: Samuel Wanjiru, Kenya, 2:05:10. Women: Irina Mikitenko, Germany, 2:22:11.

Los Angeles Marathon: May 25. Men: Wesley Korir, Kenya, 2:08:24. Women: Tatiana Petrova, Russia, 2:25:59.
Berlin Marathon: Sept. 20. Men: Haile Gebrselassie, Ethiopia, 2:06:08. Women: Atsede Habtamu Besuye, Ethiopia, 2:24:47.
Chicago Marathon: Oct. 11. Men: Samuel Wanjiru, Kenya, 2:05:41. Women: Liliya Shobukhova, Russia, 2:25:56.

Ironman Triathlon World Championships, 1978-2009

The Ironman Triathlon World Championships—a 2.4-mile ocean swim, 112-mile bike ride, and 26.2-mile run—are held annually at Kailua-Kona, Hawaii.

(All times in hour:minute:second format. *Course records.)

Men's winner, country	Time	Year	Women's winner, country	Time
Gordon Haller, U.S.	11:46:58	1978	No finisher	—
Tom Warren, U.S.	11:15:56	1979	Lyn Lemaire, U.S.	12:55:00
Dave Scott, U.S.	9:24:33	1980	Robin Beck, U.S.	11:21:24
John Howard, U.S.	9:38:29	1981	Linda Sweeney, U.S.	12:00:32
Dave Scott, U.S.	9:08:23	1982	Julie Leach, U.S.	10:54:08
Dave Scott, U.S.	9:05:57	1983	Sylviane Puntous, Canada	10:43:36
Dave Scott, U.S	8:54:20	1984	Sylvanie Puntous, Canada	10:25:13
Scott Tinley, U.S.	8:50:54	1985	Joanne Ernst, U.S.	10:25:22
Dave Scott, U.S.	8:28:37	1986	Paula Newby-Fraser, Zimbabwe	9:49:14
Dave Scott, U.S.	8:34:13	1987	Erin Baker, New Zealand	9:35:25
Scott Molina, U.S.	8:31:00	1988	Paula Newby-Fraser, Zimbabwe	9:01:01
Mark Allen, U.S.	8:09:15	1989	Paula Newby-Fraser, Zimbabwe	9:00:56
Mark Allen, U.S.	8:28:17	1990	Erin Baker, New Zealand	9:13:42
Mark Allen, U.S.	8:18:32	1991	Paula Newby-Fraser, Zimbabwe	9:07:52
Mark Allen, U.S.	8:09:08	1992	Paula Newby-Fraser, Zimbabwe	8:55:28*
Mark Allen, U.S.	8:07:45	1993	Paula Newby-Fraser, Zimbabwe	8:58:23
Greg Welch, Australia	8:20:27	1994	Paula Newby-Fraser, Zimbabwe	9:20:14
Mark Allen, U.S.	8:20:34	1995	Karen Smyers, U.S.	9:16:46
Luc Van Lierde, Belgium	8:04:08*	1996	Paula Newby-Fraser, Zimbabwe	9:06:49
Thomas Hellriegel, Germany	8:33:01	1997	Heather Fuhr, Canada	9:31:43
Peter Reid, Canada	8:24:20	1998	Natascha Badmann, Switzerland	9:24:16
Luc Van Lierde, Belgium	8:17:17	1999	Lori Bowden, U.S.	9:13:02
Peter Reid, Canada	8:21:01	2000	Natascha Badmann, Switzerland	9:26:16
Timothy Deboom, U.S.	8:31:18	2001	Natascha Badmann, Switzerland	9:28:37
Timothy Deboom, U.S.	8:29:56	2002	Natascha Badmann, Switzerland	9:07:54
Peter Reid, Canada	8:22:35	2003	Lori Bowden, Canada	9:11:55
Normann Stadler, Germany	8:33:29	2004	Natascha Badmann, Switzerland[1]	9:50:04
Faris al-Sultan, Germany	8:14:17	2005	Natascha Badmann, Switzerland	9:09:30
Normann Stadler, Germany	8:11:56	2006	Michellie Jones, U.S.	9:18:31
Chris McCormack, Australia	8:15:34	2007	Chrissie Wellington, UK	9:08:45
Craig Alexander, Australia	8:17:45	2008	Chrissie Wellington, UK	9:06:23
Craig Alexander, Australia	8:20:21	2009	Chrissie Wellington, UK	8:54:02

(1) First-place finisher Nina Kraft (Germany) admitted to using performance-enhancing drugs and was disqualified, Nov. 15, 2004.

SULLIVAN AWARD
James E. Sullivan Memorial Trophy Winners

The James E. Sullivan Memorial Trophy, named after the former president of the Amateur Athletic Union (AAU) and inaugurated in 1930, is awarded annually by the AAU to the athlete who "by his or her performance, example and influence as an amateur, has done the most during the year to advance the cause of sportsmanship."

Year	Winner	Sport	Year	Winner	Sport	Year	Winner	Sport
1930	Bobby Jones	Golf	1960	Rafer Johnson	Track	1987	Jim Abbott	Baseball
1931	Barney Berlinger	Track	1961	Wilma Rudolph Ward	Track	1988	Florence Griffith Joyner	Track
1932	Jim Bausch	Track	1962	James Beatty	Track	1989	Janet Evans	Swimming
1933	Glenn Cunningham	Track	1963	John Pennel	Track	1990	John Smith	Wrestling
1934	Bill Bonthron	Track	1964	Don Schollander	Swimming	1991	Mike Powell	Track
1935	Lawson Little	Golf	1965	Bill Bradley	Basketball	1992	Bonnie Blair	Speed skating
1936	Glenn Morris	Track	1966	Jim Ryun	Track	1993	Charlie Ward	Football, basketball
1937	Don Budge	Tennis	1967	Randy Matson	Track	1994	Dan Jansen	Speed skating
1938	Don Lash	Track	1968	Debbie Meyer	Swimming	1995	Bruce Baumgartner	Wrestling
1939	Joe Burk	Rowing	1969	Bill Toomey	Track	1996	Michael Johnson	Track
1940	Greg Rice	Track	1970	John Kinsella	Swimming	1997	Peyton Manning	Football
1941	Leslie MacMitchell	Track	1971	Mark Spitz	Swimming	1998	Chamique Holdsclaw	Basketball
1942	Cornelius Warmerdam	Track	1972	Frank Shorter	Track	1999	Coco Miller and Kelly Miller	Basketball
1943	Gilbert Dodds	Track	1973	Bill Walton	Basketball	2000	Rulon Gardner	Wrestling
1944	Ann Curtis	Swimming	1974	Rick Wohlhutter	Track	2001	Michelle Kwan	Figure skating
1945	Doc Blanchard	Football	1975	Tim Shaw	Swimming	2002	Sarah Hughes	Figure skating
1946	Arnold Tucker	Football	1976	Bruce Jenner	Track	2003	Michael Phelps	Swimming
1947	John Kelly Jr.	Rowing	1977	John Naber	Swimming	2004	Paul Hamm	Gymnastics
1948	Robert Mathias	Track	1978	Tracy Caulkins	Swimming	2005	J. J. Redick	Basketball
1949	Dick Button	Skating	1979	Kurt Thomas	Gymnastics	2006	Jessica Long	Swimming (paralympics)
1950	Fred Wilt	Track	1980	Eric Heiden	Speed skating	2007	Tim Tebow	Football
1951	Rev. Robert Richards	Track	1981	Carl Lewis	Track	2008	Shawn Johnson	Gymnastics
1952	Horace Ashenfelter	Track	1982	Mary Decker	Track			
1953	Dr. Sammy Lee	Diving	1983	Edwin Moses	Track			
1954	Mal Whitfield	Track	1984	Greg Louganis	Diving			
1955	Harrison Dillard	Track	1985	Joan Benoit Samuelson	Marathon			
1956	Patricia McCormick	Diving	1986	Jackie Joyner-Kersee	Track			
1957	Bobby Joe Morrow	Track						
1958	Glenn Davis	Track						
1959	Parry O'Brien	Track						

YACHTING
The America's Cup

In the 32nd America's Cup, the Swiss boat *Alinghi* defended its title against *Emirates Team New Zealand*, 5-2, in a best-of-nine series held in the Mediterranean Sea off the coast of Valencia, Spain, in June-July 2007. Owned by Swiss businessman Ernesto Bertarelli, who also served as the yacht's strategist, *Alinghi* was skippered by New Zealander Brad Butterworth. Russell Coutts, who had skippered the *Alinghi* to victory in 2003, reportedly had been fired after clashing with Bertarelli in 2004. Unlike the last three Cups, which had been swept handily, the 2007 event had the two teams struggling for an edge up through the 4th race. The *Alinghi* won the 7th and final race by just 1 second—the closest margin of victory in the history of the America's Cup.

Competition for the America's Cup grew out of the first contest to establish a world yachting championship, one of the carnival features of the London Exposition of 1851. The race covered a 60-mile course around the Isle of Wight. The prize was a cup worth about $500, donated by the Royal Yacht Squadron of England, known as the "America's Cup" because it was first won by the U.S. yacht *America*. It was held by American yachts until 1983.

Winners of the America's Cup, 1851-2007

1851 America
1870 Magic defeated Cambria, England (1-0)
1871 Columbia (first three races) and Sappho (last two races) defeated Livonia, England (4-1)
1876 Madeline defeated Countess of Dufferin, Canada (2-0)
1881 Mischief defeated Atalanta, Canada (2-0)
1885 Puritan defeated Genesta, England (2-0)
1886 Mayflower defeated Galatea, England (2-0)
1887 Volunteer defeated Thistle, Scotland (2-0)
1893 Vigilant defeated Valkyrie II, England (3-0)
1895 Defender defeated Valkyrie III, England (3-0)
1899 Columbia defeated Shamrock, England (3-0)
1901 Columbia defeated Shamrock II, England (3-0)
1903 Reliance defeated Shamrock III, England (3-0)
1920 Resolute defeated Shamrock IV, England (3-2)
1930 Enterprise defeated Shamrock V, England (4-0)
1934 Rainbow defeated Endeavour, England (4-2)
1937 Ranger defeated Endeavour II, England (4-0)

1958 Columbia defeated Sceptre, England (4-0)
1962 Weatherly defeated Gretel, Australia (4-1)
1964 Constellation defeated Sovereign, England (4-0)
1967 Intrepid defeated Dame Pattie, Australia (4-0)
1970 Intrepid defeated Gretel II, Australia (4-1)
1974 Courageous defeated Southern Cross, Australia (4-0)
1977 Courageous defeated Australia, Australia (4-0)
1980 Freedom defeated Australia, Australia (4-1)
1983 Australia II, Australia, defeated Liberty (4-3)
1987 Stars & Stripes defeated Kookaburra III, Australia (4-0)
1988 Stars & Stripes defeated New Zealand, New Zealand (2-0)
1992 America³ (cubed) defeated Il Moro di Venezia, Italy (4-1)
1995 Black Magic 1, New Zealand, defeated Young America (5-0)
2000 New Zealand, NZ, defeated Luna Rossa, Italy (5-0)
2003 Alinghi, Switzerland, defeated Team New Zealand, NZ (5-0)
2007 Alinghi, Switzerland, defeated Emirates Team New Zealand, NZ (5-2)

POWER BOATING
American Power Boat Association Gold Cup Champions, 1970-2009

Year	Boat	Driver	Year	Boat	Driver
1970	Miss Budweiser	Dean Chenoweth	1990	Miss Budweiser	Tom D'Eath
1971	Miss Madison	Jim McCormick	1991	Winston Eagle	Mark Tate
1972	Atlas Van Lines	Bill Muncey	1992	Miss Budweiser	Chip Hanauer
1973	Miss Budweiser	Dean Chenoweth	1993	Miss Budweiser	Chip Hanauer
1974	Pay'N Pak	George Henley	1994	Smokin' Joe's	Mark Tate
1975	Pay'N Pak	George Henley	1995	Miss Budweiser	Chip Hanauer
1976	Miss U.S.	Tom D'Eath	1996	Pico American Dream	Dave Villwock
1977	Atlas Van Lines	Bill Muncey	1997	Miss Budweiser	Dave Villwock
1978	Atlas Van Lines	Bill Muncey	1998	Miss Budweiser	Dave Villwock
1979	Atlas Van Lines	Bill Muncey	1999	Miss PICO	Chip Hanauer
1980	Miss Budweiser	Dean Chenoweth	2000	Miss Budweiser	Dave Villwock
1981	Miss Budweiser	Dean Chenoweth	2001	Miss Tubby's Subs	Mike Hanson
1982	Atlas Van Lines	Chip Hanauer	2002	Miss Budweiser	Dave Villwock
1983	Atlas Van Lines	Chip Hanauer	2003	Miss Fox Hills	Mitch Evans
1984	Atlas Van Lines	Chip Hanauer	2004	Miss Detroit Yacht Club	Nate Brown
1985	Miller American	Chip Hanauer	2005	Miss Al Deeby Dodge	Terry Troxell
1986	Miller American	Chip Hanauer	2006	Miss Beacon Plumbing	Jean Theoret
1987	Miller American	Chip Hanauer	2007	Miss Elam Plus	Dave Villwock
1988	Circus Circus	Chip Hanauer	2008	Race not held (wind)	
1989	Miss Budweiser	Tom D'Eath	2009	Miss Elam Plus	Dave Villwock

RODEO
Pro Rodeo Cowboy Association All-Around Champions, 1977-2008

Year	Winner, hometown	Earnings	Year	Winner, hometown	Earnings
1977	Tom Ferguson, Miami, OK	$76,730	1993	Ty Murray, Stephenville, TX	$297,896
1978	Tom Ferguson, Miami, OK	103,734	1994	Ty Murray, Stephenville, TX	246,170
1979	Tom Ferguson, Miami, OK	96,272	1995	Joe Beaver, Huntsville, TX	141,753
1980	Paul Tierney, Rapid City, SD	105,568	1996	Joe Beaver, Huntsville, TX	166,103
1981	Jimmie Cooper, Monument, NM	105,862	1997	Dan Mortensen, Manhattan, MT	184,559
1982	Chris Lybbert, Coyote, CA	123,709	1998	Ty Murray, Stephenville, TX	264,673
1983	Roy Cooper, Durant, OK	153,391	1999	Fred Whitfield, Hockley, TX	217,819
1984	Dee Pickett, Caldwell, ID	122,618	2000	Joe Beaver, Huntsville, TX	225,396
1985	Lewis Feild, Elk Ridge, UT	130,347	2001	Cody Ohl, Stephensville, TX	296,419
1986	Lewis Feild, Elk Ridge, UT	166,042	2002	Trevor Brazile, Anson, TX	273,997
1987	Lewis Feild, Elk Ridge, UT	144,335	2003	Trevor Brazile, Anson, TX	294,839
1988	Dave Appleton, Arlington, TX	121,546	2004	Trevor Brazile, Decatur, TX	253,170
1989	Ty Murray, Odessa, TX	134,806	2005	Ryan Jarrett, Summerville, GA	263,665
1990	Ty Murray, Stephenville, TX	213,772	2006	Trevor Brazile, Decatur, TX	329,924
1991	Ty Murray, Stephenville, TX	244,230	2007	Trevor Brazile, Decatur, TX	425,115
1992	Ty Murray, Stephenville, TX	225,992	2008	Trevor Brazile, Decatur, TX	419,868

GENERAL INDEX

Note: Page numbers in **boldface** indicate key reference. Page numbers in *italics* indicate photo or illustration captions.

SPORTS QUICK REFERENCE INDEX

For complete index, see pages 979-1007.

POULTNEY HIGH SCHOOL LIBRARY
154 E. Main Street
Poultney, VT 05764